DIRECTORY OF OBSOLETE SECURITIES

2019 EDITION

*Companion
to the
Library Reference Service
@
www.fiinet.com*

Phone: (800) 367-3441
www.fiinet.com

Copyright 2019
FINANCIAL INFORMATION, INC.

All rights reserved. No part of this book may be reproduced in whole or in part, nor stored in a retrieval system, or transferred in any form by an electronic, mechanical, photocopying, recording means or otherwise, without prior written permission of FINANCIAL INFORMATION, INC.

CUSIP® description and numerical identification data (Copyright© 1969 thru 2019 inclusive, American Bankers Association) are used with permission. All rights reserved. CUSIP® is a registered trademark of the American Bankers Association. The information in this publication has been obtained from sources believed to be reliable but its accuracy and completeness is not guaranteed. Neither the Publisher nor the American Bankers Association (or its assignees or licensees) shall be liable for errors in or omissions from this publication, or mistakes by humans or machines.

ISBN 978-1-882363-81-0

PREFACE

This directory contains a brief profile of banks and companies whose original identities have been lost as a result of one or more of the following actions:

- CHANGE IN NAME
- MERGER
- ACQUISITION
- DISSOLUTION
- REORGANIZATION
- BANKRUPTCY
- CHARTER CANCELLATION

The statement "Additional Information in Active" refers to the Annual Guide to Stocks©. Any name change to, or exchange of stock for a stock which is not listed in the Directory of Obsolete Securities would be found in the Annual Guide to Stocks©, unless referring to privately held companies which are not listed in the guides.

Company names use CUSIP abbreviations, where applicable, in order to be consistent with practices of the securities industry. CUSIP Abbreviations Table begins on following page *iv*.

The listing for each company indicates the manner in which the company's identity or securities became obsolete; each listing also includes the new name of the company (if any) and the year in which the action occurred. Every successor company's listing should also be checked because exchange ratios are listed only once for each company.

Whenever possible to further complete each company's history, an indication has been made as to whether its stock has any remaining value, or any stockholders' equity still exists.

Material for this directory has been compiled from data originally published in the Financial Daily Card Service© and the Annual Guide to Stocks© during the years 1926 thru 2018.

Securities of companies whose charter of incorporation has been cancelled are not necessarily worthless. Each state has an office of Secretary of State responsible for the incorporation status of companies (for Canadian provinces they are usually referred to as Province Ministry). A list of telephone numbers of government offices for each state and Canadian province is provided on page *ii*.. While every effort has been made by Financial Information Inc. to determine the final outcome of these companies, sometimes calling the Secretary of State is the last resort for companies with too few assets to properly wind up their affairs after their business fails. A determination of worthlessness cannot be documented for securities formerly issued by a company that later had their corporate charter cancelled.

The editors of the Directory of Obsolete Securities recommend that security holders confirm company charter cancellations through the appropriate Secretary of State, *before writing off securities of such companies*. A company's corporate charter may be cancelled, then reinstated at a future date.

Charter cancellations are included in the Directory of Obsolete Securities, for the sole purpose of identifying companies that we can no longer contact and whose securities are no longer transferable. It is assumed that these companies went out of business. A small percentage, roughly one out of a thousand, of these companies will reinstate their corporate charter by submitting past due taxes, fees and annual reports to the state where they were last incorporated. However, the longer the time period between the charter cancellation and the present day, the less likely it is that the company has reinstated its charter.

Due care and caution have been used in the preparation of the Directory of Obsolete Securities. The information contained in this Directory has been obtained from sources believed to be both accurate and reliable, but because of the possibility of human and mechanical error, its accuracy and completeness cannot and is not guaranteed.

FINANCIAL INFORMATION, INC.

SECRETARY OF STATE PHONE LIST

ALABAMA (334) 242-5324
www.sos.state.al.us
ALASKA (907) 465-2550
www.gov.state.ak.us
ALBERTA Letter only
    Since 1998 research provided by
    private sector call (780) 427-7013
ARIZONA (602) 542-3026
www.azcc.gov
ARKANSAS (501) 682-3409
www.sosweb.state.ar.us
BRITISH COLUMBIA Letter only
    Ministry of Finance & Corporate Registry
    940 Blanshard St
    Victoria, BC, Canada V8W 3E6
    (250) 387-5101
    P.O. Box 9431
    Station Prov. Govt.
    Victoria, BC, Canada
    V8W 9V3
    Fee: $10
CANADA FEDERAL (613) 941-9042
CALIFORNIA Letter only
    Office of the Secretary of State
    Division of Corporations
    1500 11th Street
    Sacramento, CA 95814
    Fee: $4
COLORADO (303) 894-2200
www.sos.state.co.us
DELAWARE
www.delecorp.delaware.gov Fee: $10
D.C. (202) 442-4400
FLORIDA (850) 245-6000
www.sunbiz.org
GEORGIA (404) 656-2817
www.sos.state.ga.us
HAWAII (808) 586-2744
IDAHO (208) 334-2301
www.sos.idaho.gov
ILLINOIS (217) 785-3000
www.ilsos.net
INDIANA (317) 232-6531
www.in.gov
IOWA (515) 281-5204
www.sos.state.ia.us
KANSAS (785) 296-4564
www.kssos.org
KENTUCKY (502) 564-3490
www.sos.state.ky.us
LOUISIANA (225) 925-4704
www.sec.state.la.us
MAINE (207) 624-7736
www.state.me.us

MANITOBA Letter only
    Corporations Branch,
    Woodsworth Building, Rm 1010
    405 Broadway
    Winnipeg, Manitoba, Canada R3C 3L6
    (204) 945-2500
    Fee: $5
MARYLAND (410) 767-1330
www.sos.state.md.us
MASSACHUSETTS (617) 727-9640
www.state.ma.us
MICHIGAN (517) 322-1144
www.michigan.gov
MINNESOTA (651) 296-2803
www.state.mn.us
MISSISSIPPI (601) 359-1633
www.sos.state.ms.us
MISSOURI (573) 751-4153
www.sos.state.mo.us
MONTANA (406) 444-3665
www.state.mt.us
NEBRASKA (402) 471-4079
www.sos.state.ne.us
NEVADA (775) 684-5708
www.sos.state.nv.us
NEW BRUNSWICK (506) 453-2703
www.snb.ca
NEW HAMPSHIRE (603) 271-3246
www.sos.state.nh.us
NEW JERSEY Letter only
www.sos.state.nj.us
    Office of the Department of State
    CIC Section
    CN 451
    Trenton, NJ 08625
    Fee: $5
NEW MEXICO (505) 827-3600
    (800) 477-3632
www.sos.state.nm.us
NEW YORK (900) 835-2677 Fee: $4
www.dos.state.ny.us
NEWFOUNDLAND (709) 729-3317
NORTH CAROLINA (919) 807-2225
    (888) 246-7630
www.secstate.state.nc.us
NORTH DAKOTA (701) 328-2900
www.state.nd.us/sec
NOVA SCOTIA (800) 225-8227
OKLAHOMA (900) 555-2424
www.sos.state.ok.us
OHIO (614) 466-3910
www.state.oh.us

SECRETARY OF STATE PHONE LIST

ONTARIO   Letter only
    Companies Branch,
    Ministry of Consumer & Corporate Relations
    393 University Ave, Ste 200
    Toronto, Ontario, Canada M5G 2M2
    (416) 314-8880
    Fee: $12

OREGON   (503) 986-2200
  www.sos.state.or.us

PENNSYVANIA   (717) 787-1057
  www.dos.state.pa.us

PRINCE EDWARD ISLD (902) 368-4550
  www.gov.pe.ca

QUEBEC   (418) 644-4545
  www.registreenterprises.gouv.ca

RHODE ISLAND   (401) 222-3040
  www.sos.ri.gov

SASKATCHEWAN   Letter only
    Corporations Branch
    1301 1st Ave
    Regina, Saskatchewan, Canada S4R 8H2
    (306) 787-2962
    Fee: $10

SOUTH CAROLINA   (803) 734-2158
  www.scsos.com

SOUTH DAKOTA   (605) 773-3537
  www.sos.sd.gov

TENNESSEE   (615) 741-2286
  www.tn.gov

TEXAS   (512) 475-2755
  www.sos.state.tx.us

UTAH   (801) 530-4849
  www.corporations.utah.gov

VERMONT   (802) 828-2386
  www.sec.state.vt.us

VIRGINIA   (804) 371-9733
  www.scc.virginia.gov

WASHINGTON   (360) 725-0377
  www.sos.wa.gov

WEST VIRGINIA   (304) 558-8000
  www.apps.sos.wv.gov

WISCONSIN   (608) 261-9555
  www.wdfi.org

WYOMING   (307) 777-7311
  www.soswy.state.wy.us

YUKON   (867) 667-5442 Fee: $5
    307 Black St. 1st Fl
    Whitehorse, Yukon, Canada Y1A 2N1

TABLE OF CUSIP ABBREVIATIONS

ACC–Accident
ACCEP–Acceptance
ADJ–Adjustment–Adjusted
ADMIN–Administration
ADR–American Depository–Receipts
AGRIC–Agricultural
AGY–Agency
AIRL–Airline
ALA–Alabama
ALTA–Alberta
ALUM–Aluminum
AMAL–Amalgamated
AMER–America
AMERN–American
AMORT–Amortization
&–And
ANTIC–Anticipation
APT–Apartment
ARIZ–Arizona
ARK–Arkansas
ARPT–Airport
ASNTD–Assented
ASSD–Associated
ASSMT–Assessment
ASSN–Association
ASSOC–Associates
ASSUR–Assured
ASSURN–Assurance
ATT–Attached
AUD–Auditorium
AUTH–Authority
AUTHZ–Authorized
AVE–Avenue
AWY–Airway
B C–British Columbia
BD–Bond
BD MTG–Bond and Mortgage
BEN–Beneficial
BEN INT–Beneficial Interest
BENEV–Benevolent
BK–Bank
BK & TR–Bank & Trust
BKG–Banking
BLDG–Building
BLDR–Builder
BLVD–Boulevard
BORO–Borough
BR–Bearer
BRD–Board
BRD ED–Board of Education
BRD PUB INSTRN–Board of Public Instruction
BRD REGT–Board of Regents
BRDG–Bridge
BRH–Branch
BRIT–British
BRITN–Britain
BROS–Brothers
BUR–Bureau

C Z–Canal Zone
CALIF–California
CALL–Callable
CAP–Capital
CAS–Casualty
CDA–Canada
CDN–Canadian
CEM–Cement
CENT–Central
CENT HIGH SCH DIST–Central High School District
CENT SCH DIST–Central School District
CENTY–Century
CHEM–Chemical
CIG TAX–Cigarette Tax
CITY HSG AUTH–City Housing Authority
CL–Class
CMNTY–Community
CMNTY CONS HIGH SCH DIST–Community Consolidated High School District
CMNTY CONS SCH DIST–Community Consolidated School District
CMNTY HIGH SCH DIST–Community High School District
CMNTY SCH DIST–Community School District
CMNTY UNIT HIGH SCH DIST–Community Unit High School District
CMNTY UNIT SCH DIST–Community Unit School District
CNTY–County
CO–Company
COLL–Collateral
COLL TR–Collateral Trust
COLO–Colorado
COM–Common
COML–Commercial
COMM–Commerce
COMMN–Commission
COMMR–Commerce
COMWLTH–Commonwealth
CONN–Connecticut
CONS–Consolidated
CONS HIGH SCH DIST–Consolidated High School District
CONS SCH DIST–Consolidated School District
CONSLDTN–Consolidation
CONSTR–Construction
CONSV–Conservation
CONTL–Continental
CONV–Convertible
COOP–Cooperative

CORP–Corporation
CPN–Coupon
CR–Credit
CSWY–Causeway
CT HSE–Court House
CTF–Certificate
CTF BEN INT–Certificate of Beneficial Interest
CTF DEP–Certificate of Deposit
CTF INDBT–Certificate of Indebtedness
CTL–Control
CTR–Center
CTRY–Country
CTZN–Citizen
CUM–Cumulative
D C–District of Columbia
DEB–Debenture
DEFD–Deferred
DEL–Delaware
DEP–Deposit
DEPT–Department
DEV–Development
DISC–Discount
DISP–Disposal
DIST–District
DISTR–Distribution
DISTRG–Distributing
DISTRS–Distributors
DIV–Division
DIVID–Dividend
DLR or $–Dollar
DORM–Dormitory
DRAIN–Drainage
DTD–Dated
EASTN–Eastern
ED–Education
EDL–Educational
ELEC–Electric
ELECTR–Electronic
ELEM–Elementary
ELEM SCH DIST–Elementary School District
ELIM–Elimination
ENG–England
ENGR–Engineering
ENTMT–Entertainment
EQUIP–Equipment
EQUIP TR–Equipment Trust
ETC–Et Cetera
EXHIB–Exhibition
EXMP–Exempted
EXMP VLG SCH DIST–Exempted Village School District
EXP–Expire–Expires
EXPL–Exploration
EXPT–Export
EXPWY–Expressway
EXTD–Extended

EXTL–External
EXTN–Extension
FAC–Facility
FD–Fund
FDG–Funding
FDRY–Foundry
FED–Federal
FEDN–Federation
FEDT–Federated
FGHT–Freight
FGN–Foreign
FID–Fidelity
FIN–Finance
FING–Financing
FINL–Financial
FLA–Florida
FMR–Farmer
FNDTN–Foundation
FR–Fractional
FST PRESV–Forest Preserve
FT–Fort
GA–Georgia
GAS & ELEC–Gas & Electric
GEN–General
GNT–Grant
GOVT–Government
GD–Guaranteed
GTEE–Guarantee
GTR–Greater
GTY–Guaranty
GYM–Gymnasium
HBR–Harbor
HIGH SCH DIST–High School District
HLDG–Holding
HOSP–Hospital
HSG–Housing
HSG AUTH–Housing Authority
HWY–Highway
ILL–Illinois
ILLUM–Illuminating
IMPT–Improvement
INC–Incorporate–Incorporated
INCIN–Incinerator
INCL–Inclusive
IND–Indiana
IND–Industry
INDBT–Indebtedness
INDENT–Indenture
INDL–Industrial
INDPT–Independent
INDPT HIGH SCH DIST–Independent High School District
INDPT SCH DIST–Independent School District
INDTY–Indemnity
INS–Insurance
INSD–Insured
INST–Institute

iv

INSTL–Institutional
INSTN–Institution
INSTR–Instrument
INSTRN–Instruction
INT–Interest
INTER–Intermediate
INTL–International
INTST–Interstate
INV–Investor
INVT–Investment
IRR–Irrigation
IS–Island–Islands
JCT–Junction
JR–Junior
JT–Joint
KANS–Kansas
KY–Kentucky
LA–Louisiana
LAB–Laboratory
LD–Land
LD GNT–Land Grant
LD TR CTF–Land Trust Certificate
LIBR–Library
LIQ–Liquidation
LMBR–Lumber
LN–Loan
LN NT–Loan Note
LOC–Local
LOC HIGH SCH DIST–Local High School District
LOC SCH DIST–Local School District
LT–Light
LTD–Limited
LTD VTG STK–Limited Voting Stock
LTD VTG TR–Limited Voting Trust
LTG–Lighting
MACH–Machine
MACHY–Machinery
MAN–Manitoba
MASS–Massachusetts
MAT–Maturity
MATL–Material
MD–Maryland
ME–Maine
MED–Medical
MEM–Memorial
MET–Metropolitan
MFG–Manufacturing
MFR–Manufacturer
MGMT–Management
MICH–Michigan
MINN–Minnesota
MISS–Mississippi
MKT–Market
MLG–Milling
MLS–Mills
MNG–Mining
MO–Missouri
MONT–Montana
MT–Mount
MTG–Mortgage
MTN–Mountain
MTR–Motor

MUN–Municipal
MUT–Mutual
N B–New Brunswick
N C–North Carolina
N D–North Dakota
N H–New Hampshire
N J–New Jersey
N MEX–New Mexico
N S–Nova Scotia
N Y–New York
NAT–Natural
NATL–National
NAV–Navigation
NEB–Nebraska
NETH–Netherlands
NEV–Nevada
NEW HSG AUTH–New Housing Authority
NFLD–Newfoundland
NO–Number
NO PAR–No Par Value
NON CUM–Non-Cumulative
NON CUM PFD–Non-Cumulative Preferred
NON VTG–Non Voting
NORTH EASTN–North Eastern
NORTH WESTN–North Western
NORTHEASTN–Northeastern
NORTHN–Northern
NORTHWESTN–Northwestern
NT–Note
OBLIG–Obligation
OKLA–Oklahoma
ONT–Ontario
OPER–Operating
OPT–Option
OPTL–Optional
ORD–Ordinary
ORE–Oregon
ORIG–Original
P R–Puerto Rico
PA–Pennsylvania
PAC–Pacific
PAR–Par Value
PART–Participating
PARTN–Participation
PAV–Paving
PAY–Payable
%–Percent
PERM–Permanent
PERP–Perpetual
PERS–Personal
PETE–Petroleum
PFD–Preferred
PK–Park
PKG–Parking
PKWY–Parkway
PL–Place
PLG–Pledge
PLGD–Playground
PLT–Plant
PMT–Payment
POL–Policy
PPTY–Property
PR–Prior
PR LIEN–Prior Lien

PREF–Preference
PRELIM–Preliminary
PRELIM LN NT–Preliminary Loan Note
PREM–Premium
PRIM–Primary
PRIN–Principal
PRIV–Privilege
PROD–Product
PRODTN–Production
PROJ–Project
PROM–Promissory
PROT–Protective
PROTN–Protection
PROV–Province
PRTG–Printing
PT–Part
PUB–Public
PUB HIGH SCH DIST–Public High School District
PUB HSG AUTH–Public Housing Authority
PUB SCH DIST–Public School District
PUBG–Publishing
PUBN–Publication
PUR–Purchase
PURP–Purpose
PWR–Power
QUE–Quebec
R I–Rhode Island
RCPT–Receipt
RD–Road
REC–Recreation
RECON–Reconstruction
RED–Redeemable
REDEV–Redevelopment
REF–Refunding
REFNG–Refining
REFRIG–Refrigeration
REG–Registered
REGL–Regional
REGL HIGH SCH DIST–Regional High School District
REGL SCH DIST–Regional School District
REGR–Regular
REGT–Regents
REINS–Reinsurance
RENT–Rental
REORG–Reorganized
REORG HIGH SCH DIST–Reorganized High School District
REORG SCH DIST–Reorganized School District
REORGN–Reorganization
REP–Republic
REPST–Represent
REPSTD–Represented
REPSTG–Representing
RES–Resources
RESH–Research
RESV–Reserve
REV–Revenue
RIV–River
RLTY–Realty

RR–Railroad
RT–Right
RT–Route
RTY–Royalty
RUBR–Rubber
RY–Railway
S C–South Carolina
S D–South Dakota
SAN–Sanitary
SANTN–Sanitation
SASK–Saskatchewan
SCH–School
SCH DIST–School District
SEC–Security
SECD–Secured
SECT–Section
SER–Series
SEW–Sewage, Sewerage
SF–Sinking Fund
SH–Share
SMLT–Smelting
SOC–Society
SOUTH EASTN–South Eastern
SOUTH WESTN–South Western
SOUTHEASTN–Southeastern
SOUTHN–Southern
SOUTHWESTN–Southwestern
SPL–Special
SPL SCH DIST–Special School District
SR–Senior
SS–Steamship–Steamships
ST–Saint
ST–State
STA–Station
STAD–Stadium
STAT–Statutory
STD–Standard
STK–Stock
STKYD–Stockyard
STL–Steel
STPD–Stamped
STR–Street
SUB–Subordinated
SUB DEB–Subordinated Debenture
SUBDIV–Subdivision
SUBN–Suburban
SUBS–Subscription
SUBT–Substitute
SURP–Surplus
SVC–Service
SVG–Savings
SWITZ–Switzerland
SWR–Sewer
SYND–Syndicate
SYS–System–Systems
TEL–Telephone
TELEG–Telegraph
TEMP–Temporary
TENN–Tennessee
TER–Terrace
TERM–Terminal
TERR–Territory
TEX–Texas
THORO–Thoroughfare

THRU–Through
TOB–Tobacco
TPK–Turnpike
TR–Trust
TRAN–Transit
TRANS–Transport
TRANSN–Transportation
TRCNTNTL–Transcontinental
TREAS–Treasury
TREASR–Treasurer
TUIT–Tuition
TUNL–Tunnel
TWP–Township
TWY–Thruway
TWY–Tollway
U A R–United Arab Republic
U K–United Kingdom
U S–United States
U S A–United States of America
UN–Union
UN FREE HIGH SCH DIST– Union Free High School District
UN FREE SCH DIST–Union Free School District
UN HIGH SCH DIST–Union High School District
UN SCH DIST–Union School District
UNDER INDENT–Under Indenture
UNI–Unified
UNI HIGH SCH DST–Unified High School District
UNI SCH DST–Unified School District
UNIV–University
UNVL–Universal
UTD–United
UTIL–Utility
V I–Virgin Islands
VA–Virginia
VAR–Various
VEH–Vehicle
VET–Veteran
VIC–Vicinity
VLG–Village
VOL–Voluntary
VT–Vermont
VTG–Voting
VTG TR CTF–Voting Trust Certificates
VY–Valley
W VA–West Virginia
WASH–Washington
WESTN–Western
WHSE–Warehouse
WHSL–Wholesale
WIS–Wisconsin
WK–Work
WT–Warrants
WTR–Water
WTRWKS–Waterworks
WW–With Warrants
WYO–Wyoming
YD–Yard
YR–Year

When the plural is desired, add "s" to the above abbreviations.

E.G., STATE–ST

STATES–STS

AGENCY–AGY

AGENCIES–AGYS

ABBREVIATIONS FOR FOREIGN CURRENCY

Country	Currency	Abbreviations
Australia	dollar	**AUD**
Austria	euro	**EUR**
Belgium	euro	**EUR**
Canada	dollar	**CAD**
Denmark	krone	**DKK**
Finland	euro	**EUR**
France	euro	**EUR**
Germany	euro	**EUR**
Italy	euro	**EUR**
Mexico	peso	**MXN**
Netherlands	euro	**EUR**
Norway	krone	**NOK**
South Africa	rand	**ZAR**
Sweden	krone	**SEK**
Switzerland	franc	**CHF**
United Kingdom	pound	**GBP**

All other currencies will not be abbreviated.

FINANCIAL INFORMATION, INC.

A. K. F., INC. (GA)
Administratively dissolved 05/16/2008

A & A INTL INDS INC (BC)
Recapitalized 08/05/1997
Recapitalized from A & A Foods Ltd. to A & A International Industries Inc. 08/05/1997
Each share Common no par exchanged for (0.02) share Common no par
Cease trade order effective 05/01/2000

A & C UTD AGRICULTURE DEVELOPING INC (NV)
Name changed to Velt International Group Inc. 09/13/2017

A & E CAP FDG CORP (CANADA)
Each share Common no par exchanged for (0.5) Single Share no par and (0.5) Multiple Share no par 07/21/1997
Recapitalized as E & E Capital Funding Inc. 10/18/2005
Each Multiple Share no par exchanged for (0.05) share Common no par
Each Single Share no par exchanged for (0.05) share Common no par
E & E Capital Funding Inc. merged into GC-Global Capital Corp. 01/09/2006 which name changed to Fountain Asset Corp. 09/02/2015

A & E PLASTIK PAK INC (DE)
Reincorporated 06/12/1973
Common no par split (3) for (1) by issuance of (2) additional shares 05/30/1969
Common no par changed to $1 par 08/24/1970
State of incorporation changed from (CA) to (DE) 06/12/1973 Reacquired 06/22/1978
Each share Common $1 par exchanged for $10 cash

A & F, INC. (MA)
Acquired by Apollo Industries, Inc. (ME) 06/29/1962
Each share Common $1 par exchanged for (2.5) shares Common $5 par
(See Apollo Industries, Inc.)

A & J VENTURE CAPITAL GROUP INC (NV)
Common $0.001 par changed to $0.0001 par 02/19/2010
Recapitalized as ReliaBrand Inc. 02/24/2011
Each share Common $0.0001 par exchanged for (0.01) share Common $0.0001 par

A & K PETROLEUM CO. (DE)
Name changed to Kerlyn Oil Co. 04/12/1937
Kerlyn Oil Co. recapitalized as Kerr-McGee Oil Industries, Inc. 02/23/1946 which name changed to Kerr-McGee Corp. 11/01/1965
(See Kerr-McGee Corp.)

A & M FOOD SVCS INC (NV)
Acquired by PepsiCo, Inc. (DE) 07/09/1986
Each share Common 1¢ par exchanged for (0.44) share Capital Stock $1.66666666 par
PepsiCo, Inc. (DE) reincorporated in North Carolina 12/04/1986

A & M INSTRUMENT, INC. (NY)
Name changed to LRL Corp. 03/15/1963
(See LRL Corp.)

A & S MOTOR CO. (IL)
Proclaimed dissolved for failure to pay taxes and file reports 04/09/1929

A & W BRANDS INC (DE)
Common 1¢ par split (3) for (2) by issuance of (0.5) additional share 02/16/1993
Merged into Lincoln Acquisition, Inc. 10/13/1993
Each share Common 1¢ par exchanged for $24.50 cash

A & W CO. (AR)
Acquired by Sierra Trading Corp. 11/19/1968
Each share Common 50¢ par exchanged for (1.56) shares Capital Stock 50¢ par
(See Sierra Trading Corp.)

A A A STAMP COIN BULLION INC (BC)
Cease trade order 04/27/1999

A A IMPORTING INC (DE)
Merged into Guild Hall, Inc. 08/31/1983
Details not available

A A R T COMMUNICATIONS CORP (CO)
Charter revoked for failure to file reports and pay fees 10/14/1971

A.B. SEE ELEVATOR CO. (NJ)
Acquired by Westinghouse Electric & Manufacturing Co. 00/00/1937
Details not available

A B A INDS INC (FL)
Common 10¢ par split (5) for (4) by issuance of (0.25) additional share 01/30/1981
Common 10¢ par split (5) for (4) by issuance of (0.25) additional share 01/29/1982
Stock Dividend - 100% 04/20/1980
Merged into General Defense Corp. 01/12/1983
Each share Common 10¢ par exchanged for $13.25 cash

A.B.C. BREWING CORP.
Acquired by Terre Haute Brewing Co., Inc. 00/00/1937
Details not available

A.B.C. TRUST SHARES
Series D Trust Agreement terminated and liquidated 00/00/1935
Series E Trust Agreement terminated 00/00/1934
Details not available

A B C ASSOC INC (IL)
Proclaimed dissolved for failure to pay taxes and file reports 11/16/1973

A B C CORP (NV)
Name changed to Comoro Exploration Ltd. 11/02/1970
Comoro Exploration Ltd. recapitalized as AWR-America West Resources, Inc. 12/10/1993 which name changed to Integrated Information International Group Co. Ltd. 10/08/1999 which name changed to Intervest Group. Ltd. 04/21/2001
(See Intervest Group. Ltd.)

A B C ENERGY LTD (BC)
Recapitalized as St. Clair Resources Ltd. 06/01/1983
Each share Common no par exchanged for (0.33333333) share Common no par
(See St. Clair Resources Ltd.)

A B G INDS INC (DE)
Charter cancelled and declared inoperative and void for non-payment of taxes 03/01/1976

A B HLDG GROUP INC (NY)
Name changed to AG-Bag International Ltd. (NY) 10/12/1990
AG-Bag International Ltd. (NY) reincorporated in Delaware 01/00/1995 which name changed to AB Holding Group, Inc. 01/24/2005
(See AB Holding Group, Inc.)

A B S RESOURCES LTD. (BC)
Reincorporated under the laws of Canada as A B S Technology Ltd. 05/12/1989
A B S Technology Ltd. name changed to Darius Technology Ltd. 05/28/1991
(See Darius Technology Ltd.)

A B S TECHNOLOGY LTD (CANADA)
Name changed to Darius Technology Ltd. 05/28/1991
(See Darius Technology Ltd.)

A-B STOVES, INC. (MI)
Acquired by Detroit-Michigan Stove Co. on a (0.5) for (1) basis 00/00/1945
Detroit-Michigan Stove Co. merged into Welbilt Corp. 05/17/1955
(See Welbilt Corp.)

A B WATLEY GROUP INC (DE)
SEC revoked common stock registration 07/08/2015

A BUCK OR TWO STORES CORP (ON)
Name changed to Denninghouse Inc. 04/03/1995
(See Denninghouse Inc.)

A C & C SYS CORP (UT)
Reorganized under the laws of Oklahoma as Environmental Remediation Services, Inc. 12/15/1989
Each share Common $0.001 par exchanged for (0.025) share Common 4¢ par
(See Environmental Remediation Services, Inc.)

A C E INDUSTRIES, INC. (DE)
Name changed to Spectrum Resources, Inc. 01/23/1969
Spectrum Resources, Inc. name changed to Transmarine Resources, Inc. 06/03/1970
(See Transmarine Resources, Inc.)

A C GLOBAL CAP CORP (AB)
Reincorporated 10/10/2002
Place of incorporation changed from (BC) to (AB) 10/10/2002
Merged into Arsenal Energy Inc. (Old) 11/14/2002
Each share Common no par exchanged for (0.8) share Common no par
Arsenal Energy Inc. (Old) merged into Arsenal Energy Inc. (New) 05/29/2003 which merged into Prairie Provident Resources Inc. 09/16/2016

A C L N LTD (CYPRUS)
Each share Ordinary CYP 0.01 par split (5) for (4) by issuance of (0.25) additional share payable 09/18/2000 to holders of record 09/01/2000
SEC revoked Ordinary share registration 09/27/2004

A C MOORE ARTS & CRAFTS INC (PA)
Common no par split (2) for (1) by issuance of (1) additional share payable 07/31/2002 to holders of record 07/15/2002 Ex date - 08/01/2002
Acquired by Nicole Crafts L.L.C. 11/18/2011
Each share Common no par exchanged for $1.60 cash

A C SIMMONDS & SONS INC (NV)
SEC revoked common stock registration 10/06/2017

A C T HLDGS INC (DE)
Name changed to Advanced Cell Technology, Inc. 06/23/2005
Advanced Cell Technology, Inc. name changed to Ocata Therapeutics, Inc. 11/14/2014
(See Ocata Therapeutics, Inc.)

A C T INDL CORP (BC)
Name changed to Rhona Online.com Inc. 07/06/2000
Rhona.com Online Inc. recapitalized as Winchester Minerals & Gold Exploration Ltd. 04/16/2004

A C TELECONNECT CORP (NY)
Reincorporated under the laws of Delaware as ACC Corp. 01/15/1987
ACC Corp. merged into Teleport Communications Group Inc. 04/22/1998 which merged into AT&T Corp. 07/24/1998 which merged into AT&T Inc. 11/18/2005

A CAP COS GROUP INC (NV)
Charter revoked for failure to file reports and pay fees 02/01/1989

A CO INC (CA)
Common no par changed to 10¢ par 01/31/1973
Majority shares acquired by Sterndent Corp. through purchase offer 08/21/1974
Public interest eliminated

A CONSULTING TEAM INC (NY)
Each share old Common 1¢ par. exchanged for (0.25) share new Common 1¢ par 01/07/2004
Name changed to Helios & Matheson North America Inc. (NY) 01/30/2007
Helios & Matheson North America Inc. (NY) reincorporated in Delaware 11/20/2009 which recapitalized as Helios & Matheson Information Technology Inc. 06/27/2011 which name changed to Helios & Matheson Analytics Inc. 05/06/2013

A D A M INC (GA)
Merged into Ebix, Inc. 02/08/2011
Each share Common 1¢ par exchanged for (0,3122) share Common 10¢ par

A D A M SOFTWARE INC (GA)
Name changed to Adam.com, Inc. 10/20/1999
Adam.com, Inc. name changed to A.D.A.M., Inc. 07/31/2001 which merged into Ebix, Inc. 02/08/2011

A D C MEDICAL INSTRUMENTS CORP. (NY)
Merged into Miogab Real Estate Co. 07/07/1987
Each share Common 1¢ par exchanged for $4 cash

A D DATA SYS INC (NY)
Merged into Techtran Industries, Inc. 05/10/1977
Each share Common 50¢ par exchanged for (14) shares Common 1¢ par
Techtran Industries, Inc. merged into Photographic Sciences Corp. 11/10/1986 which name changed to PSC Inc. 05/28/1992
(See PSC Inc.)

A.D.F. CO.
Liquidation completed
Each share Capital Stock $5 par stamped to indicate initial distribution of $8 cash 00/00/1946
Each share Stamped Capital Stock $5 par stamped to indicate second distribution of $5 cash 00/00/1947
Each share Stamped Capital Stock $5 par stamped to indicate third distribution of $1 cash 00/00/1948
Each share Stamped Capital Stock $5 par exchanged for fourth and final distribution of $1.70 cash 12/00/1950

A.E.G. ENTERPRISES (CA)
Charter suspended for failure to pay taxes 04/02/1962

A E G AG (GERMANY)
Name changed 06/28/1985
Name changed from AEG-Telefunken to AEG AG 06/28/1985
Acquired by Daimler-Benz A.G. 10/24/1996
Each ADR for Ordinary DM50 par exchanged for $76.94 cash

A E VENTURES LTD (AB)
Cease trade order effective 11/23/2001

A.F. LIQUIDATING CORP. (MO)
Liquidation completed
Each share Common $1 par exchanged for initial distribution of (0.05581) share International Telephone & Telegraph Corp. (MD) 4% Conv. Preferred Ser. E $100 par and (0.20064) share Capital Stock no par 08/31/1964
International Telephone & Telegraph Corp. (MD) reincorporated in Delaware 01/31/1968
Note: Details on subsequent distributions, if any, are not available

A F M HLDG INC (NY)
Adjudicated bankrupt 09/09/1974
Stockholders' equity unlikely

A FEM MED CORP (NV)
Name changed to Quantrx Biomedical Corp. 12/23/2005

A G AUTOMOTIVE WHSES INC (DE)
Charter forfeited for failure to maintain a registered agent 08/26/1995

A G BARR PLC (SCOTLAND)
ADR agreement terminated 05/21/2018
No ADR's remain outstanding

A G C MGMT ENTERPRISES INC (NV)
Charter revoked for failure to file reports and pay fees 03/31/2006

A G F MGMT LTD (ON)
Name changed 07/31/1976
Class B Preference no par split (3) for (1) by issuance of (2) additional shares 08/13/1969
Under the merger name changed from A.G.F. Management Ltd. to A.G.F. Management Ltd.-La Societe de Gestion A.G.F. Ltee. 07/31/1976
Class B Preference no par split (4) for (1) by issuance of (3) additional shares 07/02/1986
Name changed to AGF Management Ltd. 12/23/1994

A G FOODS INC (MD)
Class A Common no par reclassified as Common no par 04/01/1966
Common no par split (3) for (2) by issuance of (0.5) additional share 04/21/1966
Common no par split (3) for (2) by issuance of (0.5) additional share 04/28/1967
Common no par split (2) for (1) by issuance of (1) additional share 05/01/1968
Name changed to Gino's, Inc. 04/03/1969
(See Gino's, Inc.)

A.G.I., INC. (FL)
Proclaimed dissolved for failure to file reports and pay fees 06/28/1971

A G M DRUG CO. (AL)
Merged into Reid-Provident Laboratories Inc. 06/06/1971
Each share Class A $10 par exchanged for (1) share Common $1 par
Reid-Provident Laboratories Inc. name changed to Reid-Rowell, Inc. 12/04/1985
(See Reid-Rowell, Inc.)

A G MEDIA GROUP INC (DE)
Recapitalized as Heart Health, Inc. (DE) 11/01/2007
Each share Common $0.001 par exchanged for (0.01) share Common $0.001 par
Heart Health, Inc. (DE) reincorporated in Nevada as Blue Gold Beverages, Inc. 06/15/2010 which recapitalized as Dragon Polymers Inc. 04/27/2012 which name changed to Hitec Corp. 11/04/2015 which recapitalized as Lead Innovation Corp. 03/27/2018

A-G-N MANUFACTURING INC. (GA)
Company filed for bankruptcy 00/00/1973
Stockholders' equity unlikely

A G VOLNEY CTR INC (DE)
Recapitalized as Buddha Steel, Inc. 06/11/2010
Each share Common $0.001 par exchanged for (0.00537634) share Common $0.001 par

A H BELO CORP (DE)
Reincorporated under the laws of Texas 06/29/2018

A H C P MICH INC (MI)
Name changed to Founders Financial Corp. (MI) 10/01/1970
(See Founders Financial Corp. (MI))

A I C INTL INC (DE)
Name changed 04/02/1986
Name changed from AIC Photo, Inc. to AIC International, Inc. 04/02/1986
Merged into Maxwell Electronics, Ltd. 00/00/1999
Details not available

A I M COS INC (DE)
Filed petition in bankruptcy under Chapter XI 06/09/1971
No stockholders' equity

A I N LEASING CORP (NY)
Each share old Common 1¢ par exchanged for (0.060024) share new Common 1¢ par 08/30/1995
Recapitalized as Metropolitan Asset Management Corp. 09/27/1996
Each share new Common 1¢ par exchanged for (0.1) share Common 1¢ par
Metropolitan Asset Management Corp. name changed to Diamond Laser International, Ltd. (NY) 12/04/1996 which reorganized in Nevada as Access TradeOne.Com, Inc. 06/11/1999
(See Access TradeOne.Com, Inc.)

A I S INC (DE)
Name changed to Troll's Seafood Ltd. 06/02/1989
Troll's Seafood Ltd. name changed to Valdor Ltd. 05/00/1998 which name changed to Pear Technologies, Inc. 06/12/1998 which recapitalized as Sanswire Technologies Inc. 05/20/2002 which name changed to Wireless Holdings Group, Inc. 03/30/2005 which recapitalized as Vega Promotional Systems, Inc. (DE) 12/26/2006 which reorganized in Wyoming as Vega Biofuels, Inc. 07/29/2010

A I SOFTWARE INC (BC)
Name changed to Network Gaming International Corp. 07/02/1996
Network Gaming International Corp. recapitalized as Network Exploration Ltd. 06/22/2004 which name changed to Ynvisible Interactive Inc. 01/12/2018

A I T S INC (MA)
Plan of reorganization under Chapter 11 Federal Bankruptcy proceedings confirmed 02/12/1985
No stockholders' equity

A J INDS INC (DE)
Reincorporated 04/30/1968
State of incorporation changed from (WV) to (DE) and Capital Stock $2 par reclassified as Common Stock $2 par 04/30/1968
Merged into Rokkor Industries, Inc. 04/07/1977
Each share Common $2 par exchanged for $5 cash

A K ELEC CORP (NY)
Name changed to Infosite Advertising Systems, Inc. 12/17/1985
(See Infosite Advertising Systems, Inc.)

A L C FINANCE, INC. (IN)
5% Preferred 1950 Ser. called for redemption 03/30/1964
Acquired by State Loan & Finance Corp. 03/31/1964
Details not available

A L D INC (DE)
Each share old Common $1 par exchanged for (0.00333333) share new Common $1 par 11/27/1995
Note: In effect holders received $0.05 cash per share and public interest was eliminated

A L I TECHNOLOGIES INC (BC)
Acquired by McKesson Corp. 09/12/2002
Each share Common no par exchanged for $43.50 cash

A L PHARMA INC (DE)
Name changed 10/03/1994
Class A Common 20¢ par split (3) for (2) by issuance of (0.5) additional share 08/02/1985
Class A Common 20¢ par split (3) for (2) by issuance of (0.5) additional share 07/09/1986
Class A Common 20¢ par split (3) for (2) by issuance of (0.5) additional share 04/29/1991
Name changed from A.L. Laboratories, Inc. to A.L. Pharma Inc. 10/03/1994
Name changed to Alpharma Inc. 09/18/1995
(See Alpharma Inc.)

A LITTLE REMINDER INC (WY)
Administratively dissolved 06/25/2001

A M B I INC (NY)
Name changed to Nutrition 21 Inc. 03/09/2001
(See Nutrition 21 Inc.)

A M CAP CORP (DE)
Completely liquidated and dissolved 08/28/1974
Details not available

A.M.D.G. PUBLISHING CO., INC. (NY)
Proclaimed dissolved for failure to file reports and pay fees 12/15/1970

A M E INC (CA)
Merged into A.M.E. Acquisition Co. 09/20/1989
Each share Common no par exchanged for $12.50 cash

A M I, INC. (DE)
Reorganized 01/02/1952
Reorganized from (MI) to under the laws of Delaware 01/02/1952
Each share 6% Preferred $20 par exchanged for (4) shares Common no par
Common no par changed to $3 par 05/04/1955
Merged into Automatic Canteen Co., of America 03/27/1959
Each share Common $3 par exchanged for (0.525) share Common $2.50 par and $0.118125 cash
Automatic Canteen Co. of America name changed to Canteen Corp. 02/16/1966 which merged into International Telephone & Telegraph Corp. (DE) 04/25/1969 which name changed to ITT Corp. 12/31/1983 which reorganized in Indiana as ITT Industries, Inc. 12/19/1995 which name changed to ITT Corp. 07/01/2006

A M P EXPLS & MNG LTD (BC)
Recapitalized as Silverstone Resources Ltd. 05/27/1991
Each share Common no par exchanged for (0.33333333) share Common no par
Silverstone Resources Ltd. recapitalized as Sorel Ventures Ltd. 10/19/2001

A M R CORPORATE GROUP LTD (BC)
Recapitalized as Consolidated A.M.R. Corporate Ltd. 12/03/1998
Each share Common no par exchanged for (0.25) share Common no par
Consolidated A.M.R. Corporate Ltd. recapitalized as Consolidated A.M.R. Development Corp. 10/17/2000 which recapitalized as West Hawk Development Corp. 01/09/2002

A NOVO BROADBAND INC (DE)
SEC revoked common stock registration 03/11/2008

A-NY & B-NY REALIZING CORP.
Dissolved 00/00/1949
No stockholders' equity

A.O.I. MINERALS CORP. (NV)
Name changed to Century Medical, Inc. 12/02/1968
(See Century Medical, Inc.)

A O K ENTERPRISES LTD (NY)
Each share old Common 10¢ par exchanged for (0.2) share new Common 10¢ par 01/15/1986
Reorganized under the laws of Nevada as Environmental Protective Industries Inc. 11/30/1987
Each share new Common 10¢ par exchanged for (1) share Common $0.001 par
(See Environmental Protective Industries Inc.)

A 1 KOTZIN CO (CA)
Stock Dividend - 100% 08/18/1975
Name changed to Tobias Kotzin Co. 09/22/1975
(See Tobias Kotzin Co.)

A-1 RES LTD (BC)
Name changed to Transtech Industries Ltd. 07/22/1988
Transtech Industries Ltd. name changed to Canadian Transtech Industries Ltd. 08/18/1988
(See Canadian Transtech Industries Ltd.)

A 1 STL & IRON FDRY LTD (BC)
Merged into Ardiem Industrial Corp. 01/02/1976
Each share Class A Preferred no par exchanged for (10) shares Class A no par
Each share Class B no par exchanged for (10) shares Class A no par
(See Ardiem Industrial Corp.)

A P S INC (DE)
Common $1 par split (2) for (1) by issuance of (1) additional share 07/01/1971
Common $1 par split (2) for (1) by issuance of (1) additional share 03/29/1976
Merged into Gulf & Western Industries, Inc. 03/26/1981
Each share Common $1 par exchanged for $13.50 cash

A.P.W. PAPER CO., INC. (NY)
Name changed to A.P.W. Products Co., Inc. 00/00/1944
A.P.W. Products Co., Inc. name changed to Allied-Albany Paper Corp. 01/16/1957
(See Allied-Albany Paper Corp.)

A.P.W. PRODUCTS CO., INC. (NY)
Name changed to Allied-Albany Paper Corp. 01/16/1957
(See Allied-Albany Paper Corp.)

A PEA IN THE POD INC (TX)
Merged into Mothers Work, Inc. 04/05/1995
Each share Common 1¢ par exchanged for $5.50 cash

A PLUS COMMUNICATIONS INC (TN)
Name changed to A+ Network, Inc. 10/24/1995
A+ Network, Inc. merged into Metrocall, Inc. 11/15/1996
(See Metrocall, Inc.)

A PLUS NETWORK INC (TN)
Merged into Metrocall, Inc. 11/15/1996
Each share Common 1¢ par

exchanged for (1.17877) shares Common 1¢ par and (1) Variable Common Stock Purchase Right
(See Metrocall, Inc.)

A PWR AGRO AGRICULTURE DEV INC (NV)
Name changed to Sino Agro Food Inc. 12/04/2007

A POWER ENERGY GENERATION SYS LTD (BRITISH VIRGIN ISLANDS)
SEC revoked common stock registration 04/24/2013

A R C INDS INC (TX)
Name changed to Appalachian Resources Co. 09/08/1971
(See Appalachian Resources Co.)

A R C RESINS INTL CORP (BC)
Merged into Tembec Inc. 12/28/2000
Each share Common no par exchanged for $0.40 cash

A R C TOYS INC (NY)
Dissolved by proclamation 03/29/2000

A R E WIND CORP (NV)
Each share Common $0.001 par received initial distribution from liquidation of assets of $15.64 cash payable 12/12/2008 to holders of record 12/11/2008
Name changed to Cascade Wind Corp. 12/17/2008
Cascade Wind Corp. name changed to XZERES Wind Corp. 05/17/2010 which name changed to XZERES Corp. 05/17/2011
(See XZERES Corp.)

A R I INC (WA)
Reincorporated under the laws of Delaware as Advanced Recording Instruments, Inc. 08/18/1987
Advanced Recording Instruments, Inc. recapitalized as Immunis Corp. 02/28/1997 which recapitalized as Star8 Corp. 09/28/2010

A R I LTD (AUSTRALIA)
Name changed to Gwalia Resources International Ltd. 07/14/1988
(See Gwalia Resources International Ltd.)

A R T INTL INC (ON)
Each share 12% Conv. Preference Class 1 Ser. A no par exchanged for (0.5837142) share Common no par 07/17/2000
Each share 12% Conv. Preference Class 2 Ser. A no par exchanged for (0.711214) share Common no par 07/17/2000
Common no par split (3) for (1) by issuance of (2) additional shares payable 08/15/2000 to holders of record 08/02/2000 Ex date - 08/16/2000
Recapitalized as ART International Corp. 06/16/2003
Each share Common no par exchanged for (0.1) share Common no par
ART International Corp. name changed to Diamant Art Corp. 11/26/2004
(See Diamant Art Corp.)

A R V CORP (AB)
Delisted from Canadian Venture Stock Exchange 05/15/2001

A-REAL CORP. (CO)
Charter revoked for failure to file reports and pay fees 01/26/1965

A S C CORP. (IN)
Name changed to Allison Coupon Co., Inc. 01/02/1963
(See Allison Coupon Co., Inc.)

A.S.D. LIQUIDATING CORP. (DE)
Liquidation completed
Each share Common 10¢ par exchanged for initial distribution of (0.05) share Capital Alliance Corp.

Common $1 par and $1 cash 06/24/1966
(See Capital Alliance Corp.)
Each share Common 10¢ par received second and final distribution of $0.155 cash 09/20/1967

A/S DAMPSKIBSSELSKABET TORM (DENMARK)
Sponsored ADR's for Common split (2) for (1) by issuance of (1) additional ADR payable 05/10/2004 to holders of record 05/06/2004
Sponsored ADR's for Common split (2) for (1) by issuance of (1) additional ADR payable 05/31/2007 to holders of record 05/23/2007 Ex date - 06/01/2007
Name changed to Torm A.S. 05/28/2009

A S M INDS INC (DE)
Adjudicated bankrupt 03/28/1974
Stockholders' equity unlikely

A S P I INC (DE)
Proclaimed inoperative and void for failure to file reports and pay taxes 04/15/1972

A.S.R. PRODUCTS CORP. (VA)
Acquired by Morris (Philip), Inc. 05/03/1960
Each share Capital Stock $5 par exchanged for (0.23076923) share Common $5 par
Morris (Philip), Inc. reorganized as Morris (Philip) Companies Inc. 07/01/1985 which name changed to Altria Group, Inc. 01/27/2003

A S V INC (MN)
Common 1¢ par split (3) for (2) by issuance of (0.5) additional share payable 01/17/1997 to holders of record 01/06/1997
Common 1¢ par split (3) for (2) by issuance of (0.5) additional share payable 05/14/1998 to holders of record 05/04/1998
Common 1¢ par split (2) for (1) by issuance of (1) additional share payable 08/24/2005 to holders of record 08/10/2005 Ex date - 08/25/2005
Merged into Terex Corp. 03/03/2008
Each share Common 1¢ par exchanged for $18 cash

A 77 CAP INC (QC)
Name changed to Amadeus International Inc. 01/19/2005

A T & E CORP (DE)
Reincorporated 06/29/1993
State of incorporation changed from (UT) to (DE) and Common 10¢ par changed to 1¢ par 06/29/1983
Charter cancelled and declared inoperative and void for non-payment of taxes 03/01/1996

A T & T CDA INC OLD (CANADA)
Class A Deposit Receipts no par split (2) for (1) by issuance of (1) additional Receipt payable 10/28/1999 to holders of record 10/22/1999
Class B Deposit Receipts no par split (2) for (1) by issuance of (1) additional Receipt payable 10/28/1999 to holders of record 10/22/1999
Class A Deposit Receipts no par called for redemption at $51.21 on 10/08/2002
Class B Deposit Receipts no par called for redemption at $51.21 on 10/08/2002
Class B Common no par split (2) for (1) by issuance of (1) additional share payable 10/28/1999 to holders of record 10/22/1999
Plan of Arrangement under Companies' Creditors Arrangement Act effective 04/01/2003
No stockholders' equity

A T F, INC. (NJ)
Name changed to Daystrom, Inc. 01/31/1951
(See Daystrom, Inc.)

A T H FD INC (BC)
Struck off register and declared dissolved for failure to file returns 11/12/1993

A T I INC (DE)
Charter cancelled and declared inoperative and void for non-payment of taxes 04/15/1972

A T O INC (OH)
Name changed to Figgie International Inc. (OH) 06/01/1981
Figgie International Inc. (OH) reorganized in Delaware as Figgie International Holdings Inc. 07/18/1983 which name changed to Figgie International Inc. 12/31/1986 which name changed to Scott Technologies, Inc. 05/20/1998 which merged into Tyco International Ltd. (Bermuda) 05/03/2001 which reincorporated in Switzerland 03/17/2009 which merged into Johnson Controls International PLC 09/06/2016

AT&T CORP (NY)
Each share old Common $1 par received distribution of (0.324084) share Lucent Technologies Inc. Common no par payable 09/30/1996 to holders of record 09/17/1996 Ex date - 10/01/1996
Each share old Common $1 par received distribution of (0.0625) share NCR Corp. (New) Common 1¢ par payable 12/31/1996 to holders of record 12/13/1996 Ex date - 01/02/1997
Old Common $1 par split (3) for (2) by issuance of (0.5) additional share payable 04/15/1999 to holders of record 03/31/1999 Ex date - 04/16/1999
Common Liberty Media Group Class A $1 par split (2) for (1) by issuance of (1) additional share payable 06/11/1999 to holders of record 05/28/1999 Ex date - 06/14/1999
Common Liberty Media Group Class B $1 par split (2) for (1) by issuance of (1) additional share payable 06/11/1999 to holders of record 05/28/1999 Ex date - 06/14/1999
Issue Information - 360,000,000 shares of AT&T WIRELESS GROUP COM offered at $29.50 per share on 04/26/2000
Each share AT&T Wireless Group Common exchanged for (1) share AT&T Wireless Services Inc. Common $1 par 07/09/2001
Each share Common Liberty Media Group Class A $1 par exchanged for (1) share Liberty Media Corp. (New) Common Ser. A $1 par 08/09/2001
Each share Common Liberty Media Group Class B $1 par exchanged for (1) share Liberty Media Corp. (New) Common Ser. B $1 par 08/09/2001
Each share old Common $1 par received distribution of (0.3218) share AT&T Wireless Services Inc. Common $1 par payable 07/09/2001 to holders of record 06/22/2001 Ex date - 07/09/2001
Each share old Common $1 par received distribution of (0.3235) share Comcast Corp. (New) Class A Common 1¢ par 11/18/2002 to holders of record 11/15/2002
Each share old Common $1 par exchanged exchanged for (0.2) share new Common $1 par 11/18/2002
Merged into AT&T Inc. 11/18/2005
Each share new Common $1 par exchanged for (0.77942) share Common $1 par

A T U PRODUCTIONS INC (NY)
Name changed to Computerology, Inc. 11/01/1968
Computerology, Inc. name changed to W.S.C. Group, Inc. 02/04/1971
(See W.S.C. Group, Inc.)

A-3 HLDGS INC (TN)
Name changed to Sullivan Broadcast Holdings, Inc. 01/04/1996
(See Sullivan Broadcast Holdings, Inc.)

A TIME TO GROW INC (TX)
Recapitalized as American Enterprise Development Corp. 09/26/2003
Each share Common $0.0001 par exchanged for (0.33333333) share Common $0.0001 par
(See American Enterprise Development Corp.)

A TRYSTING PL INC (FL)
Completely liquidated 01/30/1970
Each share Common 10¢ par exchanged for first and final distribution of (1) share Castlewood International Corp. Common 10¢ par and (1) share Wildside Corp. Common 1¢ par
(See each company's listing)

A U M CORP (DE)
Charter revoked and declared inoperative and void for non-payment of taxes 04/15/1970

A V C CORP (DE)
Participation Certificates (which are in bearer form only) stamped to indicate initial distribution of $3 cash per share 06/19/1967
Each Participation Certificate exchanged for second and final distribution of $1.54 cash 03/21/1969
Common $25 par changed to $1 par 11/29/1963
Common $1 par split (4) for (1) by issuance of (3) additional shares 06/30/1967
Common $1 par changed to $0.66666666 par and (0.5) additional share issued 09/30/1975
Stock Dividend - 10% 01/24/1975
Merged into Raybestos-Manhattan, Inc. (CT) 04/30/1981
Each share Common $0.66666666 par exchanged for (0.4) share Common $12.50 par
Raybestos-Manhattan, Inc. (CT) name changed to Raymark Corp. 06/28/1982 which reorganized in Delaware as Raytech Corp. 10/15/1986
(See Raytech Corp.)

A V ELECTRS INC (CA)
Common no par changed to 10¢ par and (2) additional shares issued 10/07/1968
Adjudicated bankrupt 06/30/1972
No stockholders' equity

A V I INDS INC (DE)
Charter cancelled and declared inoperative and void for non-payment of taxes 03/01/1976

A&B GEOSCIENCE CORP (BRITISH WEST INDIES)
Reincorporated 04/11/1995
Place of incorporation changed from (BC) to (British West Indies) 04/11/1995
Name changed to Arawak Energy Corp. (British West Indies) 06/18/2003
Arawak Energy Corp. (British West Indies) reincorporated in Channel Islands as Arawak Energy Ltd. 06/03/2008
(See Arawak Energy Ltd.)

AA OIL CORP. (MT)
Merged into Cardinal Petroleum Co. 06/00/1970
Each share Capital Stock 5¢ par exchanged for $0.07 cash

AAA BEST CAR RENT INC (NV)
Reorganized as Stevia Nutra Corp. 03/05/2012
Each share Common $0.001 par exchanged for (15) shares Common $0.001 par

AAA ENERGY INC (NV)
Common $0.001 par split (6) for (1) by issuance of (5) additional shares payable 08/15/2006 to holders of record 08/15/2006
Recapitalized as FIGO Ventures, Inc. 12/17/2013
Each share Common $0.001 par exchanged for (0.04) share Common $0.001 par
FIGO Ventures, Inc. recapitalized as Precious Investments, Inc. 08/100/2015

AAA ENTERPRISES INC (GA)
Each share Common 20¢ par exchanged for (4) shares Common 10¢ par 04/17/1969
Adjudicated bankrupt 02/04/1971
Company's attorney's opinion is there is no stockholders' equity

AAA MFG INC (NV)
Recapitalized as Gulf West Property, Inc. (NV) 03/10/2005
Each share Common $0.0001 par exchanged for (0.02) share Common $0.0001 par
Gulf West Property, Inc. (NV) reincorporated in Colorado as Titan Global Entertainment, Inc. 11/10/2005 which recapitalized as Sunset Island Group, Inc. 05/30/2008

AAA MINERALS INC (NV)
Name changed to AAA Energy, Inc. 08/15/2006
AAA Energy, Inc. recapitalized as FIGO Ventures, Inc. 12/17/2013 which recapitalized as Precious Investments, Inc. 08/10/2015

AAA PUB ADJUSTING GROUP INC (FL)
Each share old Common $0.0001 par exchanged for (15) shares new Common $0.0001 par 03/18/2011
Each share new Common $0.0001 par exchanged again for (0.05) share new Common $0.0001 par 01/13/2012
Name changed to Emperial Americas, Inc. 04/02/2012

AAA TRAILER SALES INC (CO)
Stock Dividend - 10% 10/15/1962
Merged into AAA Trailer Supply 05/30/1995
Each share Common 25¢ par exchanged for $4 cash

AABBAX INTL FINL CORP (BC)
Delisted from Vancouver Stock Exchange 11/17/1995

AABCO INDS INC (DE)
Name changed to ASM Industries, Inc. and Common 50¢ par changed to 1¢ par 07/05/1972
(See ASM Industries Inc.)

AABCO VENTURES INC (BC)
Name changed 09/02/1987
Name changed from Aabco Oil & Gas Inc. to Aabco Ventures Inc. 09/02/1987
Struck off register and declared dissolved for failure to file reports 05/08/1998

AABRO MNG & OILS LTD (AB)
Struck off register for failure to file annual returns 03/15/1974

AAC ACOUSTIC TECHNOLOGIES HLDGS INC (CAYMAN ISLANDS)
Name changed to AAC Technologies Holdings Inc. 07/18/2011

AACE ENVIRONMENTAL SVCS INC (AB)
Recapitalized as Enviro FX Inc. 02/01/1997
Each share Common no par exchanged for for (0.47619847) share Common no par
Enviro FX Inc. recapitalized as Niaski Environmental Inc. 12/31/1998 which recapitalized as Rimron Resources Inc. 11/22/2002 which recapitalized as Caribou Resources Corp. 01/22/2004 which merged into JED Oil Inc. 07/31/2007
(See JED Oil Inc.)

AACRONN CHEMOPLASTICS CO., INC. (PA)
Name changed to General Industrial Container Corp. 05/07/1962
(See General Industrial Container Corp.)

AADAN CORP (CO)
Proclaimed dissolved for failure to file reports and pay fees 01/01/1980

AADCO AUTOMOTIVE INC (AB)
Name changed 02/18/2002
Name changed from AADCO Industries.com Inc. to AADCO Automotive Inc. 02/18/2002
Recapitalized as Royce Resources Corp. (AB) 01/02/2008
Each share Common no par exchanged for (0.2) share Common no par
Royce Resources Corp. (AB) reincorporated in British Columbia 05/11/2011 which name changed to Lithium X Energy Corp. 11/30/2015
(See Lithium X Energy Corp.)

AAER INC (CANADA)
Plan of arrangement under Companies' Creditors Arrangement Act effective 08/11/2010
Each share Common no par received $0.0000001 cash
Note: Certificates were not required to be surrendered and are without value
No distributions of $10 or less will be made

AAFP INC (NY)
Dissolved by proclamation 12/23/1992

AAI CORP (MD)
Merged into United Industrial Corp. 03/07/1977
Each share Common $1 par exchanged for $10 cash

AAI INDS INC (ON)
Name changed to Bridgebank Capital Inc. 04/27/1990
Bridgebank Capital Inc. recapitalized as Aquarius Coatings Inc. 09/28/1992 which recapitalized as Aquarius Surgical Technologies Inc. 02/24/2017

AAIPHARMA INC (DE)
Common $0.001 par split (3) for (2) by issuance of (0.5) additional share payable 03/10/2003 to holders of record 02/19/2003 Ex date - 03/11/2003
Plan of reorganization under Chapter 11 Federal Bankruptcy Code effective 03/06/2006
No stockholders' equity

AALENIAN RES LTD (BC)
Recapitalized as Silverado Mines Ltd. 08/03/1977
Each share Capital Stock no par exchanged for (0.33333333) share Capital Stock no par
Silverado Mines Ltd. recapitalized as Silverado Gold Mines Ltd. 05/23/1997
(See Silverado Gold Mines Ltd.)

AAMES FINL CORP (DE)
Old Common $0.001 par split (4) for (3) by issuance of (0.33333333) additional share 05/03/1993
Old Common $0.001 par split (3) for (2) by issuance of (0.5) additional share payable 05/17/1996 to holders of record 05/06/1996
Old Common $0.001 par split (3) for (2) by issuance of (0.5) additional share payable 02/21/1997 to holders of record 02/10/1997 Ex date - 02/24/1997
Each share old Conv. Preferred Ser. C $0.001 par exchanged for (0.2) share new Conv. Preferred Ser. C $0.001 par 04/14/2000
Each share old Common $0.001 par exchanged for (0.2) share new Common $0.001 par 04/14/2000
Merged into Aames Investment Corp. 11/05/2004
Each share new Conv. Preferred Ser. C $0.001 par exchanged for (0.16118539) share Common 1¢ par and $1.37007583 cash
Each share Conv. Preferred Ser. D exchanged for (0.16118539) share Common 1¢ par and $1.37007583 cash
Each share new Common $0.001 par exchanged for (0.14016121) share Common 1¢ par and $1.19137029 cash
Aames Investment Corp. merged into Accredited Home Lenders Holding Co. 10/02/2006
(See Accredited Home Lenders Holding Co.)

AAMES INVT CORP (MD)
Merged into Accredited Home Lenders Holding Co. 10/02/2006
Each share Common 1¢ par exchanged for (0.0936) share Common 1¢ par
(See Accredited Home Lenders Holding Co.)

AAMINEX GOLD CORP (NV)
Reincorporated 01/29/1981
State of incorporation changed from (TN) to (NV) 01/29/1981
Common 20¢ par changed to 1¢ par 02/01/1983
Name changed from Aaminex Gold Corp. to Aaminex Capital Corp. 12/23/1986
Charter revoked for failure to file reports and pay fees 02/01/2010

AAMPRO GROUP INC (NV)
Old Common $0.001 par split (3) for (1) by issuance of (2) additional shares payable 08/08/2003 to holders of record 07/31/2003 Ex date - 08/11/2003
Each share old Common $0.001 par received distribution of (0.002000023) share SK Realty Ventures, Inc. Restricted Common $0.0001 par payable 03/31/2004 to holders of record 11/15/2003
Each share old Common $0.001 par exchanged for (0.00333333) share new Common $0.001 par 06/15/2007
SEC revoked common stock registration 11/09/2011

AAN VENTURES INC (BC)
Recapitalized as Parana Copper Corp. 08/28/2017
Each share Common no par exchanged for (0.66666666) share Common no par
Parana Copper Corp. name changed to Redfund Capital Corp. 08/14/2018

AAO AQUACULTURE INTL CORP (BC)
Struck off register and declared dissolved for failure to file returns 12/03/1993

AAPC LTD (AUSTRALIA)
ADR agreement terminated 12/19/1997
Each Sponsored ADR for Ordinary exchanged for (20) shares Ordinary

AARD RI INTL INC (AB)
Name changed to 7 Crowns Corp. 07/18/1991
(See 7 Crowns Corp.)

AARDEN-BRYN ENTERPRISES INC (FL)
Name changed to Corbetts Clear Cool Water, Inc. 09/04/1998
Corbetts Clear Cool Water, Inc. name changed to Corbetts Cool Clear Water, Inc. 09/01/1998 which name changed to Canadian Cool Clear Water, Inc. 10/27/1998 which name changed to Canadian Cool Clear Wtaa, Inc. 02/05/1999 which name changed to WTAA International, Inc. 10/27/1999 which name changed to Gravitas International, Inc. (FL) 12/06/2001 which reorganized in Nevada as Formcap Corp. 10/12/2007

AARDMORE HLDGS INC (AB)
Name changed to Enercan Group Inc. 08/24/1984
(See Enercan Group Inc.)

AARDVARK, INC. (OK)
Charter suspended for failure to pay taxes 01/29/1971

AARN EXPLORATION & DEVELOPMENT CO. LTD. (BC)
Name changed to Century Interplex Corp. Ltd. 09/14/1971
Each share Capital Stock 50¢ par exchanged for (1) share Capital Stock 50¢ par
(See Century Interplex Corp. Ltd.)

AARO BROADBAND WIRELESS COMMUNICATIONS INC (NV)
SEC revoked common stock registration 04/17/2008
Stockholders' equity unlikely

AARO FILMS INC. (MN)
Recapitalized as LaBelle Air Transportation Co. 04/17/1972
Each share Common 20¢ par exchanged for (2) shares Common $0.025 par
(See LaBelle Air Transportation Co.)

AARON BROS ART MARTS INC (DE)
Merged into ABAM Investors L.P. 04/06/1988
Each share Common 1¢ par exchanged for $13 cash

AARON BROS CORP (CA)
Merged into Chromalloy American Corp. (DE) 10/03/1977
Each share Common 10¢ par exchanged for (0.16667) share $5 Conv. Preferred 1¢ par
Chromalloy American Corp. (DE) merged into Sun Chemical Corp. 12/23/1986 which name changed to Sequa Corp. 05/08/1987
(See Sequa Corp.)

AARON INDS INC (NV)
Name changed to Winner Industries Inc. 04/17/1973
Winner Industries Inc. name changed to Kiva Corp. 10/28/1981
(See Kiva Corp.)

AARON MINES LTD (BC)
Name changed 12/05/1986
Name changed from Aaron Mining Ltd. to Aaron Mines Ltd. 12/05/1986
Struck off register and declared dissolved for failure to file returns 10/02/1992

AARON OIL CORP (AB)
Name changed to Altmark Energy Inc. 07/11/1995
Altmark Energy Inc. merged into Purcell Energy Ltd. (New) 03/07/1997
(See Purcell Energy Ltd. (New))

AARON RENTS INC (GA)
Common $1 par split (3) for (2) by issuance of (0.5) additional share 05/31/1983
Each share Common $1 par reclassified as (1) share Class A Common 50¢ par and (1) share Non-Vtg. Class B Common 50¢ par 10/30/1992

Non-Vtg. Class B Common 50¢ par reclassified as Non-Vtg. Common 50¢ par 05/07/1996
Class A Common 50¢ par split (2) for (1) by issuance of (1) additional share payable 06/03/1996 to holders of record 05/20/1996
Non-Vtg. Common 50¢ par split (2) for (1) by issuance of (1) additional share payable 06/03/1996 to holders of record 05/20/1996
Class A Common 50¢ par split (3) for (2) by issuance of (0.5) additional share payable 08/15/2003 to holders of record 08/01/2003 Ex date - 08/18/2003
Non-Vtg. Common 50¢ par split (3) for (2) by issuance of (0.5) additional share payable 08/15/2003 to holders of record 08/01/2003 Ex date - 08/18/2003
Class A Common 50¢ par split (3) for (2) by issuance of (0.5) additional share payable 08/16/2004 to holders of record 08/02/2004 Ex date - 08/17/2004
Non-Vtg. Common 50¢ par split (3) for (2) by issuance of (0.5) additional share payable 08/16/2004 to holders of record 08/02/2004 Ex date - 08/17/2004
Name changed to Aaron's, Inc. 04/17/2009

AARONSON BROS STORES CORP (TX)
70¢ Conv. Preferred $2.50 par called for redemption 06/20/1967
Each share Common $2.50 par exchanged for (4) shares Common $1 par 09/08/1967
Class A Common $1 par reclassified as Common $1 par 10/01/1974
Acquired by Volume Merchandise, Inc. 09/24/1984
Each share Common $1 par exchanged for $2 cash

AAROW ENVIRONMENTAL GROUP INC (NV)
Name changed to Aaro Broadband Wireless Communications, Inc. 09/25/2000
(See Aaro Broadband Wireless Communications, Inc.)

AARP GROWTH TR (MA)
Trust terminated 12/31/2001
Details not available

AARP INCOME TR (MA)
High Quality Bond Fund reclassified as High Quality Short Term Bond Fund 02/01/1998
Name changed to Scudder Income Trust 07/17/2000
Scudder Income Trust name changed to DWS Income Trust 12/29/2005

AARP TAX FREE INCOME TR (MA)
Name changed 07/31/1991
Name changed from AARP Insured Tax Free Income Funds to AARP Tax Free Income Trust 07/31/1991
Trust terminated 12/31/2001
Details not available

AASCHE TRANSN SVCS INC (DE)
Name changed to Asche Transportation Services, Inc. 05/19/1999
(See Asche Transportation Services, Inc.)

AASTRA TECHNOLOGIES LTD (CANADA)
Recapitalized 05/01/1997
Recapitalized from Aastra Technologies Inc. to Aastra Technologies Ltd. 05/01/1997
Each share Common no par exchanged for (0.16666666) share Common no par
Merged into Mitel Networks Corp. 02/04/2014
Each share Common no par exchanged for (3.6) shares Common no par and USD$6.52 cash

Note: Unexchanged certificates will be cancelled and become without value 02/04/2020

AASTROM BIOSCIENCES INC (MI)
Each share old Common no par exchanged for (0.125) share new Common no par 02/18/2010
Each share new Common no par exchanged again for (0.05) share new Common no par 10/16/2013
Name changed to Vericel Corp. 11/25/2014

AATRA RES LTD (BC)
Struck off register and declared dissolved for failure to file returns 08/25/1995

AAV COS (OH)
Name changed to Tranzonic Companies 12/13/1983
(See Tranzonic Companies)

AAV LTD (AUSTRALIA)
Name changed to Staging Connections Group Ltd. 01/10/2007
(See Staging Connections Group Ltd.)

AAVDEX CORP (ON)
Name changed to Richmond Minerals Inc. 11/17/2005

AAVID THERMAL TECHNOLOGIES INC (DE)
Merged into Willis Stein & Partners 02/01/2000
Each share Common 1¢ par exchanged for $25.50 cash

AAXIS LTD (BERMUDA)
Acquired by BHI Corp. 03/31/1998
Each share Common no par exchanged for (1) share Ordinary 1¢ par
BHI Corp. name changed to Carlisle Holdings Ltd. 06/02/1999 which name changed to BB Holdings Ltd. 08/18/2005
(See BB Holdings Ltd.)

AAZ CORP (NV)
Reorganized as North American Natural Resources 04/13/1995
Each share Common $0.002 par exchanged for (32.867708) shares Common $0.002 par
North American Natural Resources recapitalized as PinkMonkey.com, Inc. 06/22/1998
(See PinkMonkey.com, Inc.)

AB FORTIA (SWEDEN)
Name changed to Pharmacia AB 06/01/1983
Pharmacia AB merged into Pharmacia & Upjohn Inc. 11/02/1995 which merged into Pharmacia Corp. 03/31/2000 which merged into Pfizer Inc. 04/16/2003

AB HLDG GROUP INC (DE)
Completely liquidated
Each share Common 1¢ par received first and final distribution of $0.171 cash payable 12/16/2005 to holders of record 12/15/2005

AB LIETUVOS TELEKOMAS (LITHUANIA)
Name changed to TEO LT, AB 05/05/2006
(See TEO LT, AB)

ABAC RES LTD (BC)
Recapitalized as Quality Learning Systems (International) Inc. 12/29/1992
Each share Common no par exchanged for (0.2) share Common no par
Quality Learning Systems (International) Inc. name changed to Carta Resources Ltd. 05/27/1996 which name changed to Earthramp.com Communications Inc. (BC) 12/24/1999 which reincorporated in Alberta 00/00/2001 which name changed to Champlain Resources Inc. 09/18/2007 which recapitalized as Beacon Resources Inc. 04/20/2012

ABACA RES INDS INC (BC)
Name changed 02/08/1974
Name changed from Abaca Mining Ltd. to Abaca Resource Industries Inc. 02/08/1974
Recapitalized as Corpac Minerals Ltd. 08/17/1978
Each share Common no par exchanged for (0.25) share Common no par
(See Corpac Minerals Ltd.)

ABACA RESOURCES LTD. (BC)
Name changed to Reba Resources Ltd. 01/19/1984
(See Reba Resources Ltd.)

ABACAN RESOURCE CORP OLD (AB)
Merged into Abacan Resource Corp. (New) 02/10/1995
Each share Common no par exchanged for (1) share Common no par
(See Abacan Resource Corp. (New))

ABACAN RES CORP NEW (AB)
Filed a petition under Bankruptcy and Insolvency Act 03/02/2000
Stockholders' equity unlikely

ABACON DEVELOPMENTS LTD. (ON)
Charter cancelled for failure to pay taxes and file returns 11/16/1967

ABACUS CITIES LTD (AB)
Common no par split (5) for (1) by issuance of (4) additional shares 07/22/1976
Discharged from receivership 06/25/1996
No stockholders' equity

ABACUS DIRECT CORP (DE)
Merged into DoubleClick Inc. 11/23/1999
Each share Common $0.001 par exchanged for (1.05) shares Common $0.001 par
(See DoubleClick Inc.)

ABACUS FD INC (DE)
Name changed 03/31/1964
Name changed from Abacus Fund (MA) to Abacus Fund, Inc. (DE) 03/31/1964
Common $1 par changed to $0.33333333 par and (2) additional shares issued 03/31/1966
Merged into Paine, Webber, Jackson & Curtis Inc. 04/03/1972
Each share Common $0.33333333 par exchanged for (0.5) share $1.30 Conv. Preferred Ser. A $20 par and (0.5) share Common $1 par
Paine, Webber, Jackson & Curtis Inc. reorganized as Paine Webber Inc. 02/01/1974 which name changed to Paine Webber Group Inc. 05/21/1984 which merged into UBS AG 11/03/2000
(See UBS AG)

ABACUS GOLD MINES LTD. (ON)
Name changed to Signet Petroleums Ltd. 00/00/1952
Signet Petroleums Ltd. acquired by Consolidated Peak Oils Ltd. 00/00/1953 which was acquired by Western Allenbee Oil & Gas Co. Ltd. 06/20/1960 which name changed to Convoy Capital Corp. 04/28/1989 which recapitalized as Hariston Corp. 09/25/1992 which recapitalized as Midland Holland Inc. (Canada) 02/10/1999 which reincorporated in Yukon 03/11/1999 which name changed to Mercury Partners & Co. Inc. 02/22/2000 which name changed to Black Mountain Capital Corp. 05/02/2005 which recapitalized as Grand Peak Capital Corp. (YT) 11/20/2007 which reincorporated in British Columbia 04/27/2010

ABACUS MINERALS CORP (BC)
Recapitalized as Abacus Mining & Exploration Corp. 04/23/2001
Each share Common no par exchanged for (0.1) share Common no par

ABACUS MINES & REALTY LTD. (ON)
Recapitalized as Abacon Developments Ltd. 03/21/1963
Each share Common no par exchanged for (0.1) share Common no par
(See Abacon Developments Ltd.)

ABACUS MINES LTD. (ON)
Name changed to Abacus Mines & Realty Ltd. 00/00/1962
Abacus Mines & Realty Ltd. recapitalized as Abacon Developments Ltd. 03/21/1963
(See Abacon Developments Ltd.)

ABACUS SOFTWARE GROUP INC (AB)
Name changed 07/04/1996
Name changed from Abacus Accounting Systems Inc. to Abacus Software Group Inc. 07/04/1996
Discharged from receivership 00/00/2002
No stockholders' equity

ABADDON RES INC (BC)
Recapitalized as Consolidated Abaddon Resources Inc. 01/31/2001
Each share Common no par exchanged for (0.1) share Common no par
Consolidated Abaddon Resources Inc. name changed to Aben Resources Ltd. 01/13/2011

ABADEX MINES LTD. (QC)
Declared dissolved for failure to file reports and pay fees 06/01/1974

ABALARD GOLD MINES LTD. (ON)
Charter cancelled and proclaimed dissolved for failure to pay taxes and file returns 11/08/1977

ABALONE RES INC (BC)
Name changed to AAO Aquaculture International Corp. 08/05/1988
(See AAO Aquaculture International Corp.)

ABANA MINES, LTD.
Acquired by Mining Corp. of Canada, Ltd. 00/00/1933
Details not available

ABARON CORP (NY)
Dissolved by proclamation 12/24/1991

ABASAND OILS LTD. (CANADA)
Each share Part. Preferred exchanged for (2) shares old Common no par 03/23/1938
Each share Common exchanged for (0.2) share old Common no par 03/23/1938
Each share old Common no par exchanged for (0.1) share new Common no par 05/07/1954
Acquired by Canadian Industrial Gas & Oil Ltd. 08/30/1966
Each share new Common no par exchanged for (0.25) share Common no par
Canadian Industrial Gas & Oil Ltd. merged into Norcen Energy Resources Ltd. (AB) 10/28/1975 which reincorporated in Canada 04/15/1977 which merged into Union Pacific Resources Group Inc. 04/17/1998 which merged into Anadarko Petroleum Corp. 07/14/2000

ABASKA MINING CO. LTD. (SK)
Reincorporated 00/00/1957
Place of incorporation changed from (ON) to (SK) 00/00/1957
Merged into Continental Consolidated Mines & Oils Co. Ltd. 10/04/1957
Each share Common no par

exchanged for (0.1) share Common no par
(See Continental Consolidated Mines & Oils Co. Ltd.)

ABASKA URANIUM MINES LTD. (ON)
Name changed to Abaska Mining Co. Ltd. (ON) 00/00/1956
Abaska Mining Co. Ltd. (ON) reincorporated in Saskatchewan 00/00/1957 which merged into Continental Consolidated Mines & Oils Co. Ltd. 10/04/1957
(See Continental Consolidated Mines & Oils Co. Ltd.)

ABATERRA ENERGY LTD (BC)
Reincorporated under the laws of Alberta as Simba Oils Ltd. 03/09/1989
Simba Oils Ltd. merged into Petromines Ltd. 12/01/1989
(See Petromines Ltd.)

ABATIX CORP (DE)
Name changed 05/29/1999
Name changed from Abatix Environmental Corp. to Abatix Corp. 05/29/1999
Each share old Common $0.001 par exchanged for (0.000025) share new Common $0.001 par 10/05/2012
Note: In effect holders received $14.75 cash per share and public interest was eliminated

ABATON RES LTD (BC)
Merged into Advanced Gravis Computer Technology Ltd. 04/30/1987
Each share Common no par exchanged for (1) share Common no par
(See Advanced Gravis Computer Technology Ltd.)

ABATRONIX INC (DE)
Charter cancelled and declared inoperative and void for non-payment of taxes 03/01/1975

ABATTIS BIOLOGIX CORP (BC)
Recapitalized as Abattis Bioceuticals Corp. 09/11/2012
Each share Common no par exchanged for (0.2) share Common no par

ABAXIS INC (CA)
Acquired by Zoetis Inc. 07/31/2018
Each share Common no par exchanged for $83 cash

ABAZIAS INC (DE)
Each share old Common $0.001 par exchanged for (0.025) share new Common $0.001 par 09/11/2006
Acquired by OmniReliant Holdings, Inc. 08/27/2009
Each share new Common $0.001 par exchanged for (4.1067) shares Conv. Preferred Ser. E $0.00001 par

ABB AB (SWEDEN)
Stock Dividend - 900% payable 12/22/1998 to holders of record 12/17/1998
ADR agreement terminated 08/07/2000
Each Sponsored ADR for Ordinary exchanged for $13.87248987 cash

ABB AG (SWITZERLAND)
ADR agreement terminated 12/17/1999
Each Sponsored ADR for Ordinary exchanged for $188.59316 cash

ABB SPL FIN CORP
Money Market Preferred Ser. A called for redemption at $1,000,000 on 11/09/2001
Money Market Preferred Ser. B called for redemption at $1,000,000 on 11/19/2001

ABBA MEDIX GROUP INC (CANADA)
Recapitalized as Canada House Wellness Group Inc. 11/09/2016
Each share Common no par exchanged for (0.66666666) share Common no par

ABBA MINES LTD.
Acquired by Casakirk Gold Mines Ltd. on a (1) for (10) basis 00/00/1936
(See Casakirk Gold Mines Ltd.)

ABBASTAR HLDGS LTD (BC)
Name changed to Abbastar Uranium Corp. 05/31/2009
Abbastar Uranium Corp. name changed to Abbastar Resources Corp. 07/28/2009 which reorganized as Glenmark Capital Corp. 07/29/2013 which recapitalized as Aldever Resources Inc. 08/05/2015

ABBASTAR RES CORP (BC)
Name changed 07/28/2009
Name changed from Abbastar Uranium Corp. to Abbastar Resources Corp. 07/28/2009
Each share old Common no par exchanged for (0.25) new Common no par 08/10/2011
Each share new Common no par exchanged again for (0.16666666) new Common no par 12/27/2012
Reorganized as Glenmark Capital Corp. 07/29/2013
Each share Common no par exchanged for (4) shares Common no par
Glenmark Capital Corp. recapitalized as Aldever Resources Inc. 08/05/2015

ABBEVILLE CAP CORP (SC)
Merged into Community Capital Corp. 03/04/2004
Each share Common $5 par exchanged for (1.0689) shares Common $1 par

ABBEVILLE GOLD MINES LTD. (QC)
Dissolved 00/00/1943
No stockholders' equity

ABBEY EXPL INC (CANADA)
Involuntarily dissolved for failure to file annual returns 05/06/2004

ABBEY GARTH APARTMENTS, INC. (IL)
Reverted to private company 12/11/1969
Each share Capital Stock no par exchanged for $278 cash

ABBEY GLEN PPTY CORP (ON)
Common no par reclassified as Class A Special no par 11/05/1976
Acquired by Genstar Ltd. 03/01/1977
Each share Class A Special no par exchanged for $6.75 cash

ABBEY GROUP INC (NY)
Each share old Common 1¢ par exchanged for (0.2) share new Common 1¢ par 03/06/1995
Reincorporated under the laws of Delaware as Power Phone, Inc. 06/16/1995
Power Phone, Inc. name changed to TMC Agroworld Corp. 08/09/1996 which name changed to Dominican Cigar Corp. 08/22/1997 which name changed to DCGR International Holdings, Inc. 06/01/1998 which recapitalized as American Way Home Based Business Systems, Inc. 04/12/2004 which name changed to American Way Business Development Corp. (DE) 09/30/2004 which reincorporated in Florida as Harvard Learning Centers, Inc. 10/30/2006 which name changed to Americas Learning Centers, Inc. 09/25/2007 which recapitalized as Hackett's Stores, Inc. 01/26/2009 which recapitalized as WiseBuys, Inc. 06/17/2010 which name changed to Empire Pizza Holdings, Inc. 04/20/2011 which recapitalized as Vestiage, Inc. 03/22/2013

ABBEY HEALTHCARE GROUP INC (DE)
Merged into Apria Healthcare Group Inc. 06/28/1995
Each share Common $0.001 par exchanged for (1.4) shares Common $0.001 par
(See Apria Healthcare Group Inc.)

ABBEY LAND & IMPROVEMENT CO.
Acquired by Cypress Abbey Co. 00/00/1934
Details not available

ABBEY LEE SPORTSWEAR INC (NY)
Out of business 08/00/1974
No stockholders' equity

ABBEY MED SUPPLY CORP (NY)
Name changed to Abbey Group Inc. (NY) 05/27/1983
Abbey Group Inc. (NY) reincorporated in Delaware as Power Phone, Inc. 06/16/1995 which name changed to TMC Agroworld Corp. 08/09/1996 which name changed to Dominican Cigar Corp. 08/22/1997 which name changed to DCGR International Holdings, Inc. 06/01/1998 which recapitalized as American Way Home Based Business Systems, Inc. 04/12/2004 which name changed to American Way Business Development Corp. (DE) 09/30/2004 which reincorporated in Florida as Harvard Learning Centers, Inc. 10/30/2006 which name changed to Americas Learning Centers, Inc. 09/25/2007 which recapitalized as Hackett's Stores, Inc. 01/26/2009 which recapitalized as WiseBuys, Inc. 06/17/2010 which name changed to Empire Pizza Holdings, Inc. 04/20/2011 which recapitalized as Vestiage, Inc. 03/22/2013

ABBEY NATL PLC (UNITED KINGDOM)
Sponsored ADR's for Ser. A called for redemption at $25.70 plus $0.0875 accrued dividends on 07/22/2003
7% Subordinate Capital Securities called for redemption at $25 on 04/29/2004
7.25% Perpetual Subordinate Capital Securities called for redemption at $25 on 06/15/2004
Merged into Banco Santander Central Hispano S.A. 11/12/2004
Each Sponsored ADR for Ordinary exchanged for (2) ADR's for Ordinary and $1.1334 cash
ADR's for Ser. B Dollar Preference called for redemption at $25.92 plus $0.46094 accrued dividends on 11/09/2006
Banco Santander Central Hispano S.A. name changed to Banco Santander, S.A. 08/24/2007

ABBEY RENTS (CA)
Name changed to 600 Normandie Co. 06/15/1967
600 Normandie Co. liquidated for Consolidated Foods Corp. 06/27/1967 which name changed to Sara Lee Corp. 04/02/1985 which recapitalized as Hillshire Brands Co. 06/29/2012
(See Hillshire Brands Co.)

ABBEY WOODS DEVS LTD (BC)
Acquired by Westbank Holdings Ltd. 08/17/2000
Each share Common no par exchanged for $0.67 cash

ABBICAN MINES LTD. (ON)
Charter cancelled and proclaimed dissolved for failure to pay taxes and file returns 09/28/1964

ABBOT ENERGY CORP (BC)
Reincorporated under the laws of Delaware as Dale Energy Corp. 09/03/1992
(See Dale Energy Corp.)

ABBOTSFORD ST BK (ABBOTSFORD, WI)
Name changed to AbbyBank (Abbotsford, WI) 11/17/2003

ABBOTT APTS. LIQUIDATION TRUST
Liquidation completed 00/00/1940
Details not available

ABBOTT INDS INC (DE)
Completely liquidated 05/30/1973
Each share Common $1 par exchanged for first and final distribution of $4 cash

ABBOTT LABS (IL)
4% Preferred $100 par called for redemption 03/05/1962
Common Stock Purchase Rights declared for Common stockholders of record 09/23/1988 were redeemed at $0.0025 per right 08/15/1992 for holders of record 07/15/1992
(Additional Information in Active)

ABBOTT MINES INC.
Name changed to California Quicksilver Mines, Inc. 00/00/1951
California Quicksilver Mines, Inc. acquired by COG Minerals Corp. 08/07/1958
(See COG Minerals Corp.)

ABBOTT MINES LTD (NV)
Common $0.00001 par split (5) for (2) by issuance of (1.5) additional shares payable 05/10/2002 to holders of record 05/09/2002
Ex date - 05/13/2002
Name changed to WARP Technology Holdings, Inc. 09/03/2002
WARP Technology Holdings, Inc. name changed to Halo Technology Holdings, Inc. 04/03/2006
(See Halo Technology Holdings, Inc.)

ABBOTTS DAIRIES INC. (MD)
Each share old Common no par exchanged for (5) shares new Common no par 00/00/1930
New Common no par split (2) for (1) by issuance of (1) additional share 05/13/1960
Merged into Fairmont Foods Co. 11/29/1960
Each share Common no par or VTC's for Common no par exchanged for (0.1) share 5% Jr. Preferred $50 par and (0.8) share Common $1 par
Fairmont Foods Co. merged into American Financial Corp. 07/24/1980
(See American Financial Corp.)

ABBY INVT CORP (BC)
Recapitalized 02/07/1984
Recapitalized from Abby Energy Corp. to Abby Investment Corp. 02/07/1984
Each share Common no par exchanged for (0.5) share Class A Common no par and (0.5) share Class B Common no par
Recapitalized as Eagle Industries Ltd. 04/06/1988
Each share Class A Common no par exchanged for (0.2) share Class A Common no par
Each share Class B Common no par exchanged for (0.2) share Class B Common no par
Eagle Industries Ltd. name changed to Innovative Waste Technologies Inc. 06/08/1992 which recapitalized as International Tire & Manufacturing Corp. 06/08/1995 which recapitalized as Intirmac Industrial Corp. 12/05/1997 which name changed to Sniper Enterprises Inc. 12/07/1998 which name changed to TransAmerican Energy Inc. 08/16/2005 which recapitalized as American Biofuels Inc. 09/12/2018

ABBY VENDING MFG. CORP. (NY)
Proclaimed dissolved and charter

forfeited for failure to file reports and pay taxes 12/15/1966

ABC AIR FREIGHT CO., INC. (NY)
Completely liquidated 06/30/1967
Each share Common 10¢ par exchanged for first and final distribution of (1) share ABC Freight Forwarding Corp. Common 10¢ par
(See ABC Freight Forwarding Corp.)

ABC BANCORP (GA)
Common no par split (4) for (3) by issuance of (0.33333333) additional share 07/31/1995
Common no par split (5) for (4) by issuance of (0.25) additional share payable 04/30/1997 to holders of record 04/15/1997
Common no par split (6) for (5) by issuance of (0.2) additional share payable 12/31/1999 to holders of record 12/15/1999
Common no par split (6) for (5) by issuance of (0.2) additional share payable 03/31/2005 to holders of record 3/15/2005 Ex date - 03/11/2005
Name changed to Ameris Bancorp 12/01/2005

ABC BANCORP CAP TR I (DE)
9% Guaranteed Trust Preferred Securities called for redemption at $10 on 09/30/2006

ABC CELLOPHANE CORP (NY)
Completely liquidated 12/26/1967
Each share Class A 10¢ par or Class B 10¢ par exchanged for first and final distribution of (0.0329) share Instrument Systems Corp. (NY) Common 25¢ par
Instrument Systems Corp. (NY) reincorporated in Delaware 04/15/1971 which name changed to Griffon Corp. 03/03/1995

ABC CONSOLIDATED CORP. (DE)
Completely liquidated 12/04/1967
Each share Common $1 par exchanged for first and final distribution of (0.4) share Ogden Corp. $1.875 Conv. Preferred $1 par and (0.33333333) share Common 50¢ par
Ogden Corp. name changed to Covanta Energy Corp. 03/14/2001
(See Covanta Energy Corp.)

ABC DISPENSING TECHNOLOGIES INC (FL)
Each share old Common 1¢ par exchanged for (0.001) share new Common 1¢ par 09/21/2005
Recapitalized as Ka Wang Holding, Inc. 03/21/2007
Each share new Common 1¢ par exchanged for (0.04545454) share Common 1¢ par

ABC DISSOLUTION CORP. (CA)
Liquidation completed
Each share Capital Stock no par exchanged for initial distribution of $2 cash 07/10/1967
Each share Capital Stock no par received second distribution of $0.20 cash 05/12/1969
Each share Capital Stock no par received third and final distribution of $0.09092 cash 02/20/1970

ABC FDG INC (NV)
Name changed to Cross Canyon Energy Corp. 05/05/2009
(See Cross Canyon Energy Corp.)

ABC FGHT FORWARDING CORP (NY)
Merged into 201 Eleventh Avenue Corp. 02/11/1975
Each share Common 10¢ par received $1 cash
Note: Certificates were not required to be surrendered and are without value

ABC GREAT STS INC (DE)
Merged into ABC Theatre Holdings, Inc. 03/12/1974
Each share Common $25 par exchanged for $120 cash

ABC HOMECARE SPECIALISTS INC (NV)
Reorganized as Global Wireless & Digital, Inc. 05/05/1997
Each share Common $0.001 par exchanged for (8) shares Common $0.001 par
Global Wireless & Digital, Inc. name changed to AmerElite Solutions, Inc. 05/18/2005 which reorganized as RegalWorks Media, Inc. 08/26/2013

ABC INDS INC (NY)
Merged into SFN Companies, Inc. 06/29/1983
Each share Capital Stock 10¢ par exchanged for $12.98 cash

ABC INVT CO (DE)
Voluntarily dissolved 09/09/1992
Details not available

ABC MNG VENTURES INC (BC)
Name changed to Dundee Mines Ltd. 10/12/2007
Dundee Mines Ltd. name changed to Duncastle Gold Corp. 05/28/2008 which name changed to Group Ten Metals Inc. 02/26/2015

ABC-NACO INC (DE)
Assets sold for the benefit of creditors 01/11/2002
No stockholders' equity

ABC OREGON FINANCIAL GROUP, INC. (OR)
Involuntarily dissolved 08/31/1990

ABC RAIL PRODS CORP (DE)
Name changed to ABC-NACO Inc. 02/19/1999
(See ABC-NACO Inc.)

ABC RLTY CO (NC)
Name changed to China Education Alliance, Inc. 11/23/2004

ABC TECHNOLOGIES INC (BC)
Delisted from Vancouver Stock Exchange 11/04/1993

ABC VENDING CORP. (DE)
Common $1 par split (2) for (1) by issuance of (1) additional share 06/02/1961
Name changed to ABC Consolidated Corp. 05/01/1964
ABC Consolidated Corp. acquired by Ogden Corp. 12/04/1967 which name changed to Covanta Energy Corp. 03/14/2001
(See Covanta Energy Corp.)

ABCANA CAP INC (BC)
Name changed to Casa Minerals Inc. 12/07/2017

ABCANN GLOBAL CORP (CANADA)
Name changed to VIVO Cannabis Inc. 08/07/2018

ABCI HLDGS INC (DE)
Reorganized under the laws of Nevada as Metaphor Corp. 01/06/2005
Each share Common $0.16666666 par exchanged for (0.005) share Common $0.0001 par
Metaphor Corp. name changed to China Media Networks International, Inc. 08/25/2005 which name changed to Medical Solutions Mgmt, Inc 08/04/2006
(See Medical Solutions Management Inc.)

ABCO, INC. (CA)
Merged into Nationwide Safety Centers 10/31/1961
Each share Common $1 par exchanged for (0.66666666) share Class A 50¢ par
(See Nationwide Safety Centers)

ABCO, INC. (UT)
Name changed to Club Aquarius, Inc. 09/01/1989
(See Club Aquarius, Inc.)

ABCO ICE CREAM INC (DE)
Charter cancelled and declared inoperative and void for non-payment of taxes 03/01/1992

ABCO MINES LTD. (BC)
Charter revoked for failure to file reports and pay fees 00/00/1944

ABCO MNG LTD (BC)
Name changed to Aselo Industries Ltd. and Common 50¢ par changed to no par 02/00/1971
Aselo Industries Ltd. recapitalized as Fairmont Gas & Oil Corp. 10/15/1979 which recapitalized as Cater Energy, Inc. 05/23/1984 which recapitalized as Houston Metals Corp. 10/27/1986 which recapitalized as Pacific Houston Resources, Inc. 03/30/1989
(See Pacific Houston Resources, Inc.)

ABCOURT METALS INC (QC)
Name changed to Les Mines d'Argent Abcourt Inc. 03/18/1980
Les Mines d'Argent Abcourt Inc. name changed to Abcourt Mines Inc.-Mines Abcourt Inc. 04/23/1985

ABCOURT MINES INC (QC)
Each share 1st Conv. Preferred 1985 Ser. no par received distribution of (2) shares Class B no par 02/23/1995
Each share 1st Conv. Preferred 1985 Ser. no par automatically became (4) shares shares Class B no par 02/23/1995
(Additional Information in Active)

ABDA INTL HLDGS CORP (BC)
Struck off register and declared dissolved for failure to file returns 02/25/1994

ABDO GOEMBEL & MCGUIRE INC (MN)
Name changed to SaveAll Healthcare Services, Inc. 10/08/1993
SaveAll Healthcare Services, Inc. recapitalized as Clinical Aesthetics Centre, Inc. (MN) 03/13/1997 which reincorporated in Nevada as Tricom Technology Group, Inc. 07/30/1998 which name changed to Omninet Media.com Inc. 02/18/2000 which name changed to Omninet Media Corp. 06/01/2001 which name changed to Aquagold International, Inc. 03/28/2008

ABE RES INC (CANADA)
Each share old Common no par exchanged for (0.5) share new Common no par 05/12/2017
Name changed to Vision Lithium Inc. 03/27/2018

ABEK INC (CO)
Proclaimed dissolved for failure to pay taxes and file annual reports 01/01/1991

ABEL BLACK LTD (ON)
Name changed to Black Photo Corp. Ltd. 07/21/1971
(See Black Photo Corp. Ltd.)

ABEL INDUSTRIES, INC. (MN)
Assets sold for the benefit of creditors 00/00/1971
No stockholders' equity

ABELA VENTURE GROUP INC (DE)
Name changed to Condor International Inc. 07/07/1986 which name changed back to Abela Venture Group Inc. 01/28/1989
Charter cancelled and declared inoperative and void for non-payment of taxes 03/01/1999

ABELL (A.S.) CO. (MD)
Merged into Times Mirror Co. 10/27/1986

Each VTC for Capital Stock $10 par exchanged for $5,741.18 cash

ABELLA RES LTD (BC)
Capital Stock 50¢ par changed to no par 08/25/1976
Struck off register and declared dissolved for failure to file returns 02/14/1986

ABENAKIS MINES LTD. (ON)
Charter cancelled for failure to pay taxes and file returns 05/00/1958

ABENDROTH BROTHERS
Out of existence 00/00/1934
No stockholders' equity

ABENGOA SA (SPAIN)
Each Sponsored ADR for Class B received distribution of (0.71096) Sponsored ADR for Class B payable 05/09/2014 to holders of record 04/08/2014 Ex date - 04/09/2014
ADR agreement terminated 05/12/2016
Each Sponsored ADR for Class B exchanged for $1.000823 cash
(Additional Information in Active)

ABENGOA YIELD PLC (ENGLAND & WALES)
Name changed to Atlantica Yield PLC 06/03/2016

ABENTEUER RES CORP (BC)
Reincorporated 12/31/2010
Place of incorporation changed from (AB) to (BC) 12/31/2010
Name changed to Volt Energy Corp. 05/01/2017

ABER DIAMOND CORP (CANADA)
Name changed to Harry Winston Diamond Corp. 11/19/2007
Harry Winston Diamond Corp. name changed to Dominion Diamond Corp. 03/27/2013
(See Dominion Diamond Corp.)

ABER RES LTD NEW (BC)
Reincorporated under the laws of Canada as Aber Diamond Corp. 08/18/2000
Aber Diamond Corp. name changed to Harry Winston Diamond Corp. 11/19/2007 which name changed to Dominion Diamond Corp. 03/27/2013
(See Dominion Diamond Corp.)

ABER RES LTD OLD (BC)
Merged into Aber Resources Ltd. (BC) (New) 04/19/1994
Each share Common no par exchanged for (1) share Common no par
Aber Resources Ltd. (BC) (New) reincorporated in Canada as Aber Diamond Corp. 08/18/2000 which name changed to Harry Winston Diamond Corp. 11/19/2007 which name changed to Dominion Diamond Corp. 03/27/2013
(See Dominion Diamond Corp.)

ABERCOM GROUP LTD (SOUTH AFRICA)
ADR agreement terminated 09/08/2009
Details not available

ABERCORN GROWTH FUND (BC)
Name changed to International Energy Fund 10/01/1971

ABERCROMBIE & FITCH CO (NY)
Company filed petition under Chapter 11 Federal Bankruptcy Code 11/08/1976
Details not available

ABERCROMBIE INC (NV)
Name changed to Spectre Motor Cars Inc. 06/01/1995
Spectre Motor Cars Inc. recapitalized as Spectre Industries Inc. 11/19/1997 which name changed to Sensor System Solutions, Inc. 12/08/2004 which recapitalized as

Victor Mining Industry Group Inc. 04/15/2014

ABERDEEN ASIA-PACIFIC INCOME FD INC (MD)
Auction Market Preferred Ser. B called for redemption at $25,000 on 04/22/2008
Auction Market Preferred Ser. E called for redemption at $25,000 on 04/22/2008
Auction Market Preferred Ser. G called for redemption at $25,000 on 04/23/2008
Auction Market Preferred Ser. H called for redemption at $25,000 on 04/24/2008
Auction Market Preferred Ser. I called for redemption at $25,000 on 04/25/2008
Auction Market Preferred Ser. F called for redemption at $25,000 on 04/28/2008
Auction Market Preferred Ser. C called for redemption at $25,000 on 04/29/2008
Auction Market Preferred Ser. D called for redemption at $25,000 on 05/06/2008
Auction Market Preferred Ser. A called for redemption at $25,000 on 05/13/2008
(Additional Information in Active)

ABERDEEN ASSET MGMT PLC (UNITED KINGDOM)
ADR agreement terminated 08/29/2017
Each ADR for Ordinary exchanged for $8.28335 cash

ABERDEEN CHILE FD INC (MD)
Name changed to Aberdeen Emerging Markets Equity Income Fund, Inc. 04/30/2018

ABERDEEN EMERGING MKTS SMALLER CO OPPORTUNITIES FD INC (MD)
Name changed 11/04/2010
Name changed 03/21/2013
Name changed from Aberdeen Emerging Markets Telecommunications Fund, Inc. to Aberdeen Emerging Markets Telecommunications & Infrastructure Fund, Inc. 11/04/2010
Name changed from Aberdeen Emerging Markets Telecommunications & Infrastructure Fund, Inc. to Aberdeen Emerging Markets Smaller Company Opportunities Fund, Inc. 03/21/2013
Under plan of reorganization each share Common $0.001 par automatically became (1.6215) shares Aberdeen Emerging Markets Equity Income Fund, Inc. Common $0.001 par 04/30/2018

ABERDEEN FD (NJ)
Merged into Steadman Investment Fund, Inc. (New) 01/25/1973
Each Trust Share 25¢ par exchanged for (1.2299) shares Common 25¢ par
Steadman Investment Fund, Inc. name changed to Ameritor Investment Fund 09/23/1998
(See Ameritor Investment Fund)

ABERDEEN G7 TR (ON)
Trust terminated 12/31/2017
Each Trust Unit received $6.859719 cash

ABERDEEN GLOBAL INCOME FUND INC (MD)
Name changed 07/01/2002
Name changed from Aberdeen Commonwealth Income Fund, Inc. to Aberdeen Global Income Fund, Inc. 07/01/2002
Auction Market Preferred Ser. W-7 called for redemption at $25,000 on 03/13/2008
(Additional Information in Active)

ABERDEEN GTR CHINA FD INC (MD)
Under plan of reorganization each share Common $0.001 par automatically became (1.3383) shares Aberdeen Emerging Markets Equity Income Fund, Inc. Common $0.001 par 04/30/2018

ABERDEEN INDONESIA FD INC (MD)
Under plan of reorganization each share Common $0.001 par automatically became (0.7824) share Aberdeen Emerging Markets Equity Income Fund, Inc. Common $0.001 par 04/30/2018

ABERDEEN INTL INC (YUKON)
Reincorporated under the laws of Ontario 07/04/2006

ABERDEEN ISRAEL FD INC (MD)
Under plan of reorganization each share Common $0.001 par automatically became (2.0631) shares Aberdeen Emerging Markets Equity Income Fund, Inc. Common $0.001 par 04/30/2018

ABERDEEN LATIN AMER EQUITY FD INC (MD)
Under plan of reorganization each share Common $0.001 par automatically became (2.9187) shares Aberdeen Emerging Markets Equity Income Fund, Inc. Common $0.001 par 04/30/2018

ABERDEEN MFG CORP (NY)
Common $1 par split (4) for (3) by issuance of (0.33333333) additional share 06/16/1969
Stock Dividend - 10% 09/21/1973
Name changed to AMC Investors, Inc. 11/30/1979
(See AMC Investors, Inc.)

ABERDEEN MINERALS LTD. (BC)
Struck off register and declared dissolved for failure to file returns 10/09/1987

ABERDEEN MINERALS LTD (AB)
Recapitalized as Black Gold Resources (1973) Ltd. 11/22/1973
Each share Common no par exchanged for (0.33333333) share Common no par
Black Gold Resources (1973) Ltd. name changed to Black Gold Oil & Gas Ltd. 08/29/1980 which merged into Intensity Resources Ltd. 09/17/1990 which merged into Renata Resources Inc. 04/25/1997 which merged into Rio Alto Exploration Ltd. 06/21/2000 which merged into Canadian Natural Resources Ltd. 07/01/2002

ABERDEEN MNG CO (NV)
Name changed 12/10/2003
Name and state of incorporation changed from Aberdeen Idaho Mining Co. (ID) to Aberdeen Mining Co. (NV) and Common 10¢ par changed to $0.001 par 12/10/2003
Name changed to MotivNation, Inc. 05/06/2004

ABERDEEN OILS LTD. (AB)
Completely liquidated 05/01/1959
Each share Capital Stock no par exchanged for first and final distribution of $0.01 cash

ABERDEEN PETE CORP (DE)
Capital Stock $1 par reclassified as Class A $1 par 00/00/1953
Merged into Adobe Royalty Inc. 05/05/1976
Each share Class A $1 par exchanged for $5.25 cash

ABERDEEN SCOTS TR (ON)
Trust terminated 05/29/2009
Each Trust Unit received $23.58 cash

ABERDEEN SINGAPORE FD INC (MD)
Under plan of reorganization each share Common $0.001 par automatically became (1.4958) shares Aberdeen Emerging Markets Equity Income Fund, Inc. Common $0.001 par 04/30/2018

ABERDENE MINES LTD (NV)
Common $0.00001 par split (6) for (1) by issuance of (5) additional shares payable 11/22/2002 to holders of record 11/18/2002 Ex date - 11/25/2002
Common $0.00001 par split (2.3) for (1) by issuance of (1.3) additional shares payable 01/06/2004 to holders of record 01/05/2004 Ex date - 01/07/2004
Common $0.00001 par split (2) for (1) by issuance of (1) additional share payable 06/16/2004 to holders of record 06/14/2004 Ex date - 06/17/2004
Name changed to Canyon Copper Corp. (NV) 08/11/2006
Canyon Copper Corp. (NV) reorganized in British Columbia 05/31/2013

ABERFORD RES LTD (CANADA)
Reincorporated 07/05/1982
Place of incorporation changed from (AB) to (Canada) 07/05/1982
Merged into Encor Energy Corp. Inc. 03/17/1987
Each share Common no par exchanged for (0.725) share Common no par and (0.3) share Abermin Corp. Common no par
(See each company's listing)

ABERFOYLE CO (PA)
Completely liquidated 12/18/1970
Each share Common $12.50 par exchanged for first and final distribution of (2.5) shares Rolfite Co. Common 10¢ par
(See Rolfite Co.)

ABERFOYLE MANUFACTURING CO. (PA)
Each share Common $100 par exchanged for (4) shares Common $25 par 00/00/1948
Name changed to Aberfoyle Co. and Common $25 par changed to $12.50 par 01/25/1966
Aberfoyle Co. completely liquidated for Rolfite Co. 12/18/1970
(See Rolfite Co.)

ABERLE INDS INC (PA)
Common 1¢ par split (2) for (1) by issuance of (1) additional share 07/21/1969
Former officer advised that company is out of business as of 00/00/1974
Details not available

ABERMIN CORP (CANADA)
Filed assignment in bankruptcy under Canada Federal Bankruptcy Statute 03/22/1990
No stockholders' equity

ABETA MNG LTD (QC)
Reincorporated under the laws of Ontario as Ateba Mines Inc. and Capital Stock $1 par reclassified as Common no par 08/30/1978
Ateba Mines Inc. recapitalized as Ateba Technology & Environmental Inc. 03/08/2001 which recapitalized as Ateba Resources Inc. 10/16/2008

ABEX CORP (DE)
Common no par split (2) for (1) by issuance of (1) additional share 05/20/1966
Merged into Illinois Central Industries, Inc. 12/26/1968
Each share Common no par exchanged for (0.72) share $3.50 Conv. 2nd Preferred Ser. 1 no par
Illinois Central Industries, Inc. name changed to IC Industries, Inc. 05/21/1975
(See IC Industries, Inc.)

ABEX INC (DE)
Under plan of merger each share Common 1¢ par exchanged for (0.25) share Mafco Consolidated Group Inc. Common 1¢ par, (1) share Power Control Technologies Inc. Common 1¢ par and (1) MVR Inc. Value Support Right expiring 06/15/1998 on 06/15/1995
(See each company's listing)

ABEX LTD (NV)
Each share old Common 1¢ par exchanged for (0.1) share new Common 1¢ par 10/03/1983
Reorganized under the laws of the West Indies as Gold Trust & Reinsurance Corp. 10/20/1992
Each share new Common 1¢ par exchanged for (0.01) share Common 1¢ par

ABEX LTD NEW (NV)
Name changed to Phoenix Summus Corp. (NV) 09/08/1993
Phoenix Summus Corp. (NV) reincorporated in New Jersey 01/00/1999 which name changed to I-Transaction.net, Inc. 11/11/1999 which name changed to Global Alliance Networks Inc. 10/11/2005
(See Global Alliance Networks Inc.)

ABEX MINES LTD (ON)
Merged into Highland-Crow Resources Ltd. 09/25/1978
Each share Common $1 par exchanged for (0.02) share Capital Stock no par
Highland-Crow Resources Ltd. merged into Noramco Mining Corp. 01/01/1988 which name changed to Quest Capital Corp. 01/03/1995 which name changed to Quest Oil & Gas Inc. 11/15/1996 which merged into EnerMark Income Fund 04/18/1997 which merged into Enerplus Resources Fund 06/22/2001 which reorganized as Enerplus Resources Corp. 01/03/2011

ABF ENERGY CORP (DE)
Each share old Common $0.00005 par exchanged for (0.008) share new Common $0.00005 par 05/24/2000
Name changed to Crown Jewel Resources Corp. 06/09/2000
(See Crown Jewel Resources Corp.)

ABGENIX INC (DE)
Common $0.0001 par split (2) for (1) by issuance of (1) additional share payable 04/06/2000 to holders of record 03/16/2000
Common $0.0001 par split (2) for (1) by issuance of (1) additional share payable 07/07/2000 to holders of record 06/19/2000
Merged into Amgen Inc. 04/01/2006
Each share Common $0.0001 par exchanged for $22.50 cash

ABI AMERN BUSINESSPHONES INC (DE)
Merged into Pacific Telesis Group 10/31/1988
Each share Common 1¢ par exchanged for (0.3557) share Common 10¢ par
Pacific Telesis Group merged into SBC Communications, Inc. 04/01/1997 which name changed to AT&T Inc. 11/18/2005

ABI CAP CORP (AB)
Name changed to Automated Benefits Corp. 04/09/2002
Automated Benefits Corp. name changed to Symbility Solutions Inc. 09/24/2012

ABI CAP TR (DE)
8.5% Guaranteed Trust Preferred Securities called for redemption at $10 plus $0.051944 accrued dividends on 04/22/2004

ABIDONNE OILS LTD. (AB)
Merged into Ulster Petroleums Ltd. 01/12/1970
Each share Common no par

exchanged for (0.66666666) share Capital Stock no par
Ulster Petroleums Ltd. merged into Anderson Exploration Ltd. 05/23/2000
(See Anderson Exploration Ltd.)

ABIGAIL ADAMS NATL BANCORP INC (DE)
Common $10 par changed to 1¢ par and (2) additional shares issued payable 07/02/1996 to holders of record 05/31/1996
Common 1¢ par split (5) for (4) by issuance of (0.25) additional share payable 12/31/1998 to holders of record 12/10/1998
Common 1¢ par split (5) for (4) by issuance of (0.25) additional share payable 12/31/2001 to holders of record 12/15/2001 Ex date - 12/12/2001
Stock Dividends - 10% payable 12/31/2002 to holders of record 12/27/2002 Ex date - 12/24/2002; 10% payable 01/14/2005 to holders of record 01/03/2005 Ex date - 12/30/2004
Merged into Premier Financial Bancorp, Inc. 10/01/2009
Each share Common 1¢ par exchanged for (0.4461) share Common no par

ABINGDON EXPL LTD (AB)
Acquired by Drilcorp Energy Ltd. 12/11/2002
Each share Common no par exchanged for (0.4) share Common no par
Drilcorp Energy Ltd. merged into Twin Butte Energy Ltd. 06/02/2006

ABINGTON BANCORP CAP TR (DE)
8.25% Trust Preferred Securities called for redemption at $10 on 12/31/2004

ABINGTON BANCORP INC (DE)
Reorganized back as Abington Savings Bank (Abington, MA) (New) 12/29/1992
Each share Common 10¢ par automatically became (1) share Common 10¢ par
Abington Savings Bank (Abington, MA) (New) reorganized as Abington Bancorp, Inc. (New) 01/31/1997
(See Abington Bancorp, Inc. (New))

ABINGTON BANCORP INC (PA)
Merged into Susquehanna Bancshares, Inc. 10/03/2011
Each share Common 1¢ par exchanged for (1.32) shares Common $2 par
Susquehanna Bancshares, Inc. merged into BB&T Corp. 08/01/2015

ABINGTON BANCORP INC NEW (MA)
Common 10¢ par split (2) for (1) by issuance of (1) additional share payable 12/12/1997 to holders of record 11/14/1997
Merged into Seacoast Financial Services Corp. 04/29/2004
Each share Common 10¢ par exchanged for $34 cash

ABINGTON CMNTY BANCORP INC (PA)
Reorganized as Abington Bancorp, Inc. 06/28/2007
Each share Common 1¢ par exchanged for (1.6) shares Common 1¢ par
Abington Bancorp, Inc. merged into Susquehanna Bancshares, Inc. 10/03/2011 which merged into BB&T Corp. 08/01/2015

ABINGTON SVGS BK (ABINGTON, MA)
Ctfs. dated prior to 02/01/1988
Under plan of reorganization each share Common 10¢ par automatically became (1) share Abington Bancorp, Inc. (Old) Common 10¢ par 02/01/1988
Abington Bancorp, Inc. (Old) reorganized as Abington Savings Bank (New) (Abington, MA) 12/29/1992 which reorgannized as Abington Bancorp, Inc. (New) 01/31/1997
(See Abington Bancorp, Inc. (New))

ABINGTON SVGS BK NEW (ABINGTON, MA)
Under plan of reorganization each share Common 10¢ par automatically became (1) share Abington Bancorp, Inc. (New) Common 10¢ par 01/31/1997
(See Abington Bancorp, Inc. (New))

ABINGTON VENTURES INC (BC)
Recapitalized as Abington Resources Ltd. 10/06/2009
Each share Common no par exchanged for (0.16666666) share Common no par

ABINO CO., INC. (NY)
Liquidation completed
Each share Common $5 par stamped to indicate initial distribution of $8 cash 10/02/1967
Each share Stamped Common $5 par stamped to indicate second distribution of $4 cash 02/06/1968
Each share Stamped Common $5 par stamped to indicate third distribution of $0.80 cash 04/24/1968
Each share Stamped Common $5 par exchanged for fourth and final distribution of $0.955 cash 12/31/1968

ABINO GOLD MINES LTD (ON)
Capital Stock $1 par changed to no par 03/19/1976
Merged into Goldquest Exploration Inc. 08/09/1982
Each share Capital Stock no par exchanged for (0.07727975) share Common no par
Goldquest Exploration Inc. merged into Goldcorp Inc. (New) 03/31/1994

ABITCA CORP. LTD. (CANADA)
Adjudicated bankrupt 02/06/1963
No stockholders' equity

ABITCA LUMBER & TIMBER CORP. LTD. (CANADA)
Name changed to Abitca Corp. Ltd. 11/30/1959
(See Abitca Corp. Ltd.)

ABITIBI ASBESTOS MNG LTD (QC)
Common $1 par changed to no par 06/19/1980
Name changed to Imco Resources Ltd. 12/16/1985
Imco Resources Ltd. recapitalized as Meridian Peak Resources Corp. (QC) 07/18/1995 which reincorporated in Canada 05/12/1997 which reorganized as Meridian Peak Resources Corp. (New) (Canada) 06/23/1999 which reincorporated in Yukon 10/04/1999 which name changed to Arcata Resources Corp. 09/26/2001 which recapitalized as Goldrush Resources Ltd. (YT) 05/14/2003 which reincorporated in British Columbia 08/10/2006 which merged into First Mining Finance Corp. 01/11/2016 which name changed to First Mining Gold Corp. 01/11/2018

ABITIBI-CONSOLIDATED INC (CANADA)
Merged into AbitibiBowater Inc. 10/29/2007
Each share Common no par exchanged for (0.06261) share Common $1 par
(See AbitibiBowater Inc.)

ABITIBI COPPER MINES LTD (ON)
Recapitalized as Abitibi Resources Ltd.-Les Ressources Abitibi Ltee. 04/08/1983
Each share Capital Stock $1 par exchanged for (0.33333333) share Common no par
Abitibi Resources Ltd.-Les Ressources Abitibi Ltee. merged into Consolidated Abitibi Resources Ltd. 05/31/1989 which merged into Aur Resources Inc. 11/22/1999 which was acquired by Teck Cominco Ltd. 09/28/2007 which name changed to Teck Resources Ltd. 04/27/2009

ABITIBI METAL MINES LTD (QC)
Recapitalized as Concorde Exploration Ltd. 09/22/1989
Each share Capital Stock $1 par exchanged for (0.06666666) share Capital Stock $1 par
(See Concorde Exploration Ltd.)

ABITIBI MILLS OF CANADA LTD. (CANADA)
Name changed to Abitca Lumber & Timber Corp. Ltd. 00/00/1954
Abitca Lumber & Timber Corp. Ltd. name changed to Abitca Corp. Ltd. 11/30/1959
(See Abitca Corp. Ltd.)

ABITIBI POWER & PAPER CO. LTD. (CANADA)
Each share 7% Preferred $100 par exchanged for (5) shares Prior Preferred $20 par 00/00/1946
Each share 6% Preferred $100 par exchanged for (4) shares Preferred $20 par and (2) shares Common no par 00/00/1946
Each share Common no par exchanged for (0.5) share new Common no par 00/00/1946
Each share old Common no par exchanged for (3) shares new Common no par 00/00/1951
New Common no par split (4) for (1) by issuance of (3) additional shares 12/16/1963
4.5% Preferred $25 par called for redemption 12/31/1964
Name changed to Abitibi Paper Co. Ltd. 12/01/1965
Abitibi Paper Co. Ltd. name changed to Abitibi-Price Inc. 10/15/1979 which name changed to Abitibi-Consolidated Inc. 05/30/1997 which merged into AbitibiBowater Inc. 10/29/2007

ABITIBI PRICE INC (CANADA)
Name changed 10/15/1979
Name changed from Abitibi Paper Co. Ltd. to Abitibi-Price Inc. 10/15/1979
$2.17 Conv. Preferred Ser. E no par called for redemption 12/01/1984
Common no par split (3) for (1) by issuance of (2) additional shares 05/06/1985
10% Preferred Ser B no par called for redemption 06/16/1985
7.5% Preferred Ser. A no par called for redemption 07/24/1989
$0.94 Ser. F Preferred no par called for redemption 03/31/1997
Common Stock Purchase Rights declared for Common stockholders of record 09/12/1994 were redeemed at $0.00001 per right 05/30/1997 for holders of record 05/29/1979
Name changed to Abitibi-Consolidated Inc. 05/30/1997
Abitibi-Consolidated Inc. merged into AbitibiBowater Inc. 10/29/2007
(See AbitibiBowater Inc.)

ABITIBI RES LTD (ON)
Merged into Consolidated Abitibi Resources Ltd. 05/31/1989
Each share Common no par exchanged for (0.17270262) share Common no par
Consolidated Abitibi Resources Ltd. merged into Aur Resources Inc. 11/22/1999 which was acquired by Teck Cominco Ltd. 09/28/2007 which name changed to Teck Resources Ltd. 04/27/2009

ABITIBI VENTURES LTD. (QC)
Charter annulled for failure to file annual reports 09/03/1976

ABITIBIBOWATER CDA INC (CANADA)
Chapter 11 bankruptcy proceedings of AbitibiBowater Inc. effective 12/09/2010
No stockholders' equity

ABITIBIBOWATER INC (DE)
Plan of reorganization under Chapter 11 Federal Bankruptcy proceedings effective 12/09/2010
No stockholders' equity
Name changed to Resolute Forest Products Inc. 05/24/2012

ABKCO INDS INC (DE)
Stock Dividends - 10% 10/23/1970; 10% 02/15/1973
Merged out of existence 04/01/1987
Details not available

ABL CDA INC (CANADA)
Name changed to AldeaVision Inc. 07/07/2000
(See AldeaVision Inc.)

ABL LIQUIDATING CO. (PA)
Liquidation completed
Each share Common 5¢ par exchanged for initial distribution of (0.58) share INA Corp. Common $1 par 06/16/1970
Each share Common 5¢ par received second distribution of (0.04) share INA Corp. Common $1 par 10/24/1971
Each share Common 5¢ par received third distribution of (0.02) share INA Corp. Common $1 par 08/20/1973
Each share Common 5¢ par received fourth distribution of (0.010455) share INA Corp. Common $1 par 12/20/1974
Each share Common 5¢ par received fifth and final distribution of $0.10 cash 05/29/1976
INA Corp. merged into Cigna Corp. 04/01/1982

ABLE ASSOC FD (DE)
Merged into Evergreen Total Return Fund, Inc. 10/28/1982
Each share Common $1 par exchanged for (1.234) share Common 10¢ par
Evergreen Total Return Fund, Inc. name changed to Evergreen Total Return Fund (MD) 07/31/1986 which reincorporated in Delaware as Evergreen Income & Growth Fund 02/06/1997

ABLE EXPLS LTD (BC)
Reorganized as Arrowhead Resources Ltd. 07/03/1979
Each share Common 50¢ par exchanged for (1) share Common no par
Arrowhead Resources Ltd. recapitalized as Double Arrow Oil & Gas Ltd. 08/23/1995 which name changed to Arrowhead Minerals Corp. 12/02/1996 which recapitalized as Gemini Energy Corp. 10/25/1999 which merged into Bucking Horse Energy Inc. 03/03/2008

ABLE LABS INC (DE)
Each share old Common 1¢ par exchanged for (0.06666666) share new Common 1¢ par 06/03/2002
Plan of reorganization under Chapter 11 Federal Bankruptcy Code effective 08/09/2006
No stockholders' equity

ABLE LAND & MINERALS LTD. (ON)
Acquired by Canaveral International Corp. 05/01/1963
Each share Capital Stock $1 par exchanged for (0.05) share Common 50¢ par
Canaveral International Corp.

ABLE TELCOM HLDG CORP (FL)
Reincorporated 00/00/1991
State of incorporation changed from (CO) to (FL) 00/00/1991
Each share Common no par exchanged for (0.02) share Common $0.001 par 06/11/1991
Merged into Bracknell Corp. 12/22/2000
Each share Common $0.001 par exchanged for (0.6) share Common $0.001 par
(See Bracknell Corp.)

ABLEAUCTIONS COM INC (FL)
Each share old Common $0.001 par exchanged for (0.25) share new Common $0.001 par on 09/07/1999
Each share new Common $0.001 par exchanged again for (0.08333333) share new Common $0.001 par on 01/15/2010
Recapitalized as SinoCoking Coal & Coke Chemical Industries, Inc. 02/05/2010
Each share new Common $0.001 par exchanged for (0.05) share Common $0.001 par
Note: Holders will receive future distributions from Able (U.S.) Liquidating Trust
SinoCoking Coal & Coke Chemical Industries, Inc. name changed to Hongli Clean Energy Technologies Corp. 07/28/2015

ABLEST INC (DE)
Merged into Koosharem Corp. 06/08/2007
Each share Common 5¢ par exchanged for $11 cash

ABLEVEST HLDGS LTD (AB)
Name changed to PTR Resources Ltd. 12/01/1997
PTR Resources Ltd. merged into Westlinks Resources Ltd. 06/30/1998 which name changed to Enterra Energy Corp. 12/18/2001 which recapitalized as Enterra Energy Trust 11/25/2003 which reorganized as Equal Energy Ltd. 06/03/2010
(See Equal Energy Ltd.)

ABLYNX NV (BELGIUM)
Acquired by Sanofi 06/22/2018
Each Sponsored ADR for Ordinary exchanged for $53.872645 cash

ABM COMPUTER SYS (CA)
Name changed to Franklin Telecommunications Corp. (CA) 02/27/1987
Franklin Telecommunications Corp. (CA) reorganized in Nevada as Franklin Wireless Corp. 01/22/2008

ABM GOLD CORP (BC)
Reorganized as NorthWest Gold Corp. 06/01/1990
Each share Class A Common no par exchanged for (1) share Class A Subordinate no par
NorthWest Gold Corp. merged into Northgate Exploration Ltd. (ON) 06/08/1993 which reincorporated in British Columbia 07/01/2001 which name changed to Northgate Minerals Corp. 05/20/2004 which merged into AuRico Gold Inc. 10/26/2011

ABN AMRO CAP FDG TR I (DE)
7.50% Guaranteed Trust Preferred Securities called for redemption at $25 on 09/30/2003

ABN AMRO CAP FDG TR II (DE)
7.125% Guaranteed Trust Preferred Securities called for redemption at $25 on 04/01/2004

ABN AMRO CAP FDG TR V (DE)
Name changed to RBS Capital Funding Trust V 09/28/2009
(See RBS Capital Funding Trust V)

ABN AMRO CAP FDG TR VI (DE)
Name changed to RBS Capital Funding Trust VI 09/28/2009
(See RBS Capital Funding Trust VI)

ABN AMRO CAP FDG TR VII (DE)
Name changed to RBS Capital Funding Trust VII 09/28/2009
(See RBS Capital Funding Trust VII)

ABN AMRO HLDG N V (NETHERLANDS)
Sponsored ADR's for Ordinary split (3) for (1) by issuance of (2) additional ADR's payable 05/16/1997 to holders of record 05/12/1997
Acquired by RFS Holdings B.V. 09/22/2008
Each Sponsored ADR for Ordinary exchanged for $50.4089 cash

ABN AMRO NORTH AMER CAP FDG TR I (DE)
144A Fixed/Floating Rate Trust Preferred Securities called for redemption at $1,000 plus $1.637569 accrued dividends on 08/01/2013

ABN AMRO NORTH AMER CAP FDG TR II (DE)
144A Trust Preferred Securities called for redemption at $1,000 plus $1.660313 accrued dividends on 08/01/2013

ABN AMRO NORTH AMER HLDG CAP FDG LLC X (DE)
Floating Rate Preferred called for redemption at $100 plus $1.852 accrued dividends on 04/03/2013

ABN AMRO NORTH AMER HLDG CAP FDG LLC XI (DE)
Floating Rate Preferred called for redemption at $100 plus $0.674 accrued dividends on 04/03/2013

ABN AMRO NORTH AMER INC (IL)
144A Adjustable Rate Preferred Ser. B called for redemption at $1,000 on 09/19/2000
144A Preferred Ser. C called for redemption at $1,000 on 09/19/2000
144A Adjustable Fixed Rate Preferred Ser. F called for redemption at $1,000 on 12/15/2001
Adjustable Fixed Rate Preferred Ser. II called for redemption at $50 on 12/15/2001
Adjustable Fixed Rate Preferred Ser. JJ called for redemption at $50 on 12/15/2001
144 A Adjustable Fixed Rate Preferred Ser. G called for redemption at $1,000 on 12/15/2003
144A Preferred Ser. A called for redemption at $1,000 on 06/30/2004
144A 7.15% Ser. D Preferred called for redemption at $25 on 10/31/2005
144A Fixed Adjustable Rate Preferred Ser. E called for redemption at $25 on 10/31/2005
144A 6.59% Ser. H Preferred called for redemption at $1,000 on 03/15/2007
6.46% Ser. L Preferred called for redemption at $1,000 on 06/15/2007

ABN AMRO PFD CAP TR I (DE)
144A Exchangeable Perpetual Preferred Class A called for redemption at $1,000 on 10/31/2007
144A Exchangeable Perpetual Preferred Class B called for redemption at $1,000 on 10/31/2007
144A Exchangeable Perpetual Preferred Class C called for redemption at $1,000 on 10/31/2007

ABO RESOURCE CORP (BC)
Name changed 05/22/1986
Name changed from Abo Oil Corp. to Abo Resource Corp. 05/22/1986
Name changed to Puma Minerals Corp. 06/23/1995
Puma Minerals Corp. recapitalized as Consolidated Puma Minerals Corp. 07/22/1999 which merged into Sage Gold Inc. 08/07/2009

ABODE MTG HLDGS CORP (BC)
Recapitalized as Ayubowan Capital Ltd. 08/19/2013
Each share Common no par exchanged for (0.01) share Common no par
Ayubowan Capital Ltd. name changed to Discovery Metals Corp. 06/13/2017

ABOITIZ EQUITY VENTURES INC (PHILIPPINES)
Stock Dividend - 30% payable 10/14/1996 to holders of record 08/30/1996
GDR agreement terminated 00/00/1998
Details not available
(Additional Information in Active)

ABOT MNG CO (ID)
Common 10¢ par changed to $0.0001 par 04/11/2011
Recapitalized as ABT Mining Co. Inc. 05/19/2015
Each share Common $0.0001 par exchanged for (0.00043478) share Common $0.0001 par
ABT Mining Co. Inc. name changed to ABT Holdings, Inc. 09/01/2015 which name changed to Scoobeez Global Inc. 03/29/2017

ABOUND GOLD MINES LTD. (ON)
Charter cancelled for failure to pay taxes and file returns 00/00/1955

ABOUT COM INC (DE)
Merged into Primedia Inc. 02/28/2001
Each share Common $0.001 par exchanged for (2.3409) shares Common 1¢ par
(See Primedia Inc.)

ABOVENET COMMUNICATIONS INC (DE)
Common $0.001 par split (2) for (1) by issuance of (1) additional share payable 05/07/1999 to holders of record 04/14/1999
Merged into Metromedia Fiber Network, Inc. 09/08/1999
Each share Common $0.001 par exchanged for (1.175) shares Class A Common 1¢ par
(See Metromedia Fiber Network, Inc.)

ABOVENET INC (DE)
Stock Dividend - 100% payable 09/03/2009 to holders of record 08/20/2009 Ex date - 09/04/2009
Acquired by Zayo Group L.L.C. 07/02/2012
Each share Common 1¢ par exchanged for $84 cash

ABOVO INTERNATIONAL CORP. (UT)
Proclaimed dissolved for failure to file annual reports 03/01/1987

ABP EQUITIES INC (CO)
Declared defunct and inoperative for failure to pay taxes and file annual reports 03/01/1992

ABQ CORP (DE)
Dissolved 05/15/1991
No stockholders' equity

ABR INFORMATION SVCS INC (FL)
Common 1¢ par split (3) for (2) by issuance of (0.5) additional share 07/13/1995
Common 1¢ par split (3) for (2) by issuance of (0.5) additional share payable 02/19/1996 to holders of record 01/29/1996
Common 1¢ par split (2) for (1) by issuance of (1) additional share payable 02/19/1997 to holders of record 02/03/1997
Merged into Ceridian Corp. 07/22/1999
Each share Common 1¢ par exchanged for $25.50 cash

ABRAHAM & STRAUS, INC.
Acquired by Federated Department Stores, Inc. 00/00/1949
Each share Common no par exchanged for (3.25) shares Common $5 par
Federated Department Stores, Inc. name changed to Macy's, Inc. 06/01/2007

ABRAHAM LINCOLN FED SVGS BK (DRESHER, PA)
Placed in conservatorship 09/19/1991
Stockholders' equity unlikely

ABRAHAM LINCOLN INS CO (IL)
Merged into Commonwealth Industries Corp. (IL) 05/06/1971
Each share Common $1 par exchanged for (3) shares Class A Common no par
Commonwealth Industries Corp. (IL) reincorporated in Delaware 04/20/1981
(See Commonwealth Industries Corp.)

ABRAMS INDS INC (GA)
Name changed 01/17/1972
Reincorporated 09/13/1984
Name changed from Abrams A R Inc. to Abrams Industries Inc. 01/17/1972
Each share Common $1 par exchanged for (1) share Common $1 par
State of incorporation changed from (DE) to (GA) 09/13/1984
Common $1 par split (3) for (2) by issuance of (0.5) additional share 01/04/1985
Common $1 par split (5) for (4) by issuance of (0.25) additional share 09/30/1988
Common $1 par split (4) for (3) by issuance of (0.33333333) additional share 06/30/1999
Stock Dividends - 30% 04/25/1973; 30% 03/31/1976; 10% 07/28/1982; 10% 09/22/1983; 10% 06/26/1984; 10% payable 10/11/2005 to holders of record 09/27/2005 Ex date - 09/23/2005
Name changed to Servidyne, Inc. 07/17/2006
(See Servidyne, Inc.)

ABRASIVE & METAL PRODUCTS CO. (MI)
Name changed to Wakefield Corp. 04/28/1961
Wakefield Corp. name changed to 729 Meldrum Corp. 02/24/1966
(See 729 Meldrum Corp.)

ABRASIVE CO.
Acquired by Simonds Saw & Steel Co. 00/00/1927
Details not available

ABRASIVE PRODS INC (MA)
7% Preferred $100 par called for redemption 08/01/1962
100% acquired through purchase offer by Michigan General Corp. as of 05/14/1969
Public interest eliminated

ABRAXAS ENERGY PARTNERS L P (DE)
Merged into Abraxas Petroleum Corp. 10/05/2009
Each Common Unit exchanged for (4.25) shares Common 1¢ par

ABRAXIS BIOSCIENCE INC NEW
Merged into Celgene Corp. 10/15/2010
Each share Common $0.001 par exchanged for (0.2617) share Common 1¢ par, (1) Contingent Value Right and $58 cash
Note: Each Contingent Value Right received distribution of $6.932592 cash payable 10/07/2013 to holders of record 10/04/2013 Ex date - 10/08/2013

ABRAXIS BIOSCIENCE INC OLD (DE)
Each share Common $0.001 par received distribution of (0.25) share Abraxis BioScience, Inc. (New) Common $0.001 par payable 11/13/2007 to holders of record 11/13/2007
Name changed to APP Pharmaceuticals, Inc. 11/13/2007
(See APP Pharmaceuticals, Inc.)

ABREMOR METAL MINES LTD. (ON)
Charter cancelled for failure to pay taxes and file returns 00/00/1955

ABS GROUP INC (DE)
Recapitalized as African American Medical Network, Inc. 07/21/2004
Each share Common $0.0001 par exchanged for (0.01) share Common $0.0001 par
African American Medical Network, Inc. name changed to AFMN, Inc. 01/18/2005 which recapitalized as Motion Picture Group, Inc. 02/23/2006

ABS INDS INC (DE)
Reincorporated 08/17/1979
State of incorporation changed from (OH) to (DE) 08/17/1979
Old Common no par split (3) for (1) by issuance of (2) additional shares 04/14/1989
Old Common no par split (2) for (1) by issuance of (1) additional share 06/11/1993
Each share old Common no par exchanged for (1) share new Common no par to reflect a (1) for (500) reverse split followed by a (500) for (1) foward split 12/07/2007
Note: In effect holders of (499) of fewer pre-split shares received $0.33 cash per share and public interest was eliminated

ABSA GROUP LTD (SOUTH AFRICA)
ADR agreement terminated 02/14/2005
Each Sponsored Reg. S ADR for Ordinary exchanged for $25.502 cash
Each 144A Sponsored ADR for Ordinary exchanged for $25.502 cash
Each old Sponsored ADR for Ordinary exchanged for (0.68) new Sponsored ADR for Ordinary and $8.152576 cash 08/17/2005
Name changed to Barclays Africa Group Ltd. 08/23/2013
Barclays Africa Group Ltd. name changed to Absa Group Ltd. 07/16/2018

ABSAM MINES LTD (QC)
Charter annulled for failure to file annual reports 08/17/1974

ABSARAKA URANIUM, INC. (UT)
Name changed to Sunny Hill Mines Inc. 10/30/1969
Sunny Hill Mines Inc. name changed to Bagley Corp. 07/31/1981
(See Bagley Corp.)

ABSOL CO (TX)
Name changed to Group Nine Financial Corp. 06/16/1988
(See Group Nine Financial Corp.)

ABSOLUT RES CORP (YT)
Reincorporated 03/14/2003
Each share old Common no par exchanged for (0.1) share new Common no par 02/16/2001
Each share new Common no par received distribution of (1.81) shares Tanqueray Resources Ltd. Common no par payable 05/01/2001 to holders of record 12/22/2000
Each share new Common no par received distribution of (0.4) share Stansbury Holdings Corp. Common 25¢ par payable 02/14/2002 to holders of record 12/22/2000
Place of incorporation changed from (AB) to (YT) 03/14/2003
Merged into Aquiline Resources Inc. 04/01/2008
Each share Common no par exchanged for (0.111111111) share Common no par
Aquiline Resources Inc. acquired by Pan American Silver Corp. 01/22/2010

ABSOLUTE ENTMT INC (NJ)
Filed plan of liquidation under Chapter 7 Federal Bankruptcy Code 03/27/1996
Stockholders' equity unlikely

ABSOLUTE GLASS PROTN INC (NV)
Each share old Common $0.001 par exchanged for (0.005) share new Common $0.001 par 06/20/2005
Name changed to Jagged Peak, Inc. 07/18/2005
(See Jagged Peak, Inc.)

ABSOLUTE LIFE SOLUTIONS INC (NV)
Name changed to Infinity Augmented Reality, Inc. 03/07/2013
(See Infinity Augmented Reality, Inc.)

ABSOLUTE WASTE SVCS INC (FL)
Recapitalized as Absolute Potential, Inc. 11/03/2006
Each share Common $0.0001 par exchanged for (0.01) share Common $0.0001 par

ABSOLUTEFUTURE COM INC (NV)
Charter permanently revoked 09/30/2003

ABSOLUTESKY INC (NV)
SEC revoked common stock registration 05/24/2010

ABSORPTIVE TECHNOLOGY INC (BC)
Recapitalized as International Absorbents Inc. 12/18/1990
Each share Common no par exchanged for (0.2) share Common no par
(See International Absorbents Inc.)

ABSS CORP (DE)
Reorganized under the laws of Nevada as NT Holding Corp. 08/04/2004
Each share Common 1¢ par exchanged for (0.25) share Common $0.001 par
NT Holding Corp. recapitalized as HST Global, Inc. 07/07/2008

ABSTRACT & TITLE GUARANTY CO. (MI)
Dissolved 10/01/1960
Details not available

ABSTRACT & TITLE INSURANCE CORP. (NY)
Merged into Title Guarantee Co. 03/07/1960
Details not available

ABSTRACT GTY CO (IA)
Acquired by Clear Title Acquisition Co. 03/30/2012
Each share Common exchanged for $774.47 cash

ABSTRACT TITLE & MORTGAGE CORP.
Name changed to Abstract & Title Insurance Corp. 00/00/1951
Abstract & Title Insurance Corp. merged into Title Guarantee Co. 03/07/1960
(See Title Guarantee Co.)

ABT BLDG PRODS CORP (DE)
Merged into Louisiana-Pacific Corp. 02/25/1999
Each share Common 1¢ par exchanged for $15 cash

ABT GLOBAL PHARMACEUTICAL CORP (CA)
Name changed to Pharmaprint Inc. 11/04/1996
(See Pharmaprint Inc.)

ABT GROWTH & INCOME TR (MA)
Acquired by Evergreen Value Fund 06/30/1995
Details not available

ABT HLDGS INC (ID)
Name changed to Scoobeez Global Inc. 03/29/2017

ABT INVT SER INC
Merged into Evergreen Trust 06/30/1995
Details not available

ABT MNG CO INC (ID)
Name changed to ABT Holdings, Inc. 09/01/2015
ABT Holdings, Inc. name changed to Scoobeez Global Inc. 03/29/2017

ABT MONEY MKT SER INC (MD)
Trust terminated 02/24/1994
Details not available

ABT SOUTHN MASTER TR (MA)
Acquired by Evergreen Municipal Trust 06/30/1995
Details not available

ABT UTIL INCOME FD (MD)
Stock Dividends - 20% 02/14/1986; 20% 09/14/1989
Acquired by Evergreen Utility Fund 06/30/1995
Details not available

ABTO INC (DE)
Voluntarily dissolved 09/30/1975
No stockholders' equity

ABTRONICS, INC. (CA)
Charter suspended for failure to file reports and pay fees 05/01/1975

ABTS INC (SC)
Merged into MNC Financial, Inc. 11/30/1989
Each share Common $1 par exchanged for (0.4) share Common $2.50 par
MNC Financial, Inc. merged into NationsBank Corp. 10/01/1993 which reincorporated in Delaware as BankAmerica Corp. (Old) 09/25/1998 which merged into BankAmerica Corp. (New) 09/30/1998 which name changed to Bank of America Corp. 04/28/1999

ABUCK GOLD MINES LTD. (ON)
Charter cancelled for failure to pay taxes and file returns 00/00/1955

ABUY GOLD MINES LTD. (ON)
Charter cancelled and proclaimed dissolved for failure to pay taxes and file returns 03/10/1958

ABV GOLD INC (NV)
Recapitalized as PharmaCom BioVet Inc. 09/10/2008
Each share Common $0.001 par exchanged for (0.06666666) share Common $0.001 par

ABVIVA INC (NV)
Each share old Common $0.0001 par exchanged for (0.05) share new Common $0.0001 par 09/12/2008
SEC revoked common stock registration 12/15/2011

ABX HLDGS INC (DE)
Name changed 12/31/2007
Name changed from ABX Air, Inc. to ABX Holdings, Inc. 12/31/2007
Name changed to Air Transport Services Group, Inc. 05/16/2008

ABX RES INC (AB)
Recapitalized as Expedition Energy Inc. 09/23/2003
Each share Common no par exchanged for (0.2) share Common no par
(See Expedition Energy Inc.)

AC & S CORP (PA)
Stock Dividends - 200% 04/15/1970; 100% 05/03/1971; 40% 09/01/1971
Name changed to Irex Corp. 05/12/1983
(See Irex Corp.)

AC ENERGY INC (AB)
Delisted from NEX 06/25/2004

AC ENERGY INC (NV)
SEC revoked common stock registration 03/05/2009

AC ORGANIZATION LTD (NY)
Dissolved by proclamation 06/23/1993

ACA CAP HLDGS INC (DE)
Recapitalized as Manifold Capital Corp. 08/05/2009
Each share Common 10¢ par exchanged for (0.00001) share Common 10¢ par
Note: Holders of (99,999) or fewer pre-split shares received $0.165 cash per share

ACA JOE, INC. (CA)
Name changed 11/26/1986
Name changed from ACA Joe to ACA Joe, Inc. 11/26/1986
Reorganized under Chapter 11 Federal Bankruptcy Code 06/19/1989
Each share old Common 10¢ par exchanged for (0.05) share new Common 10¢ par
Charter cancelled for failure to file reports and pay taxes 08/02/1993

ACA JOE EASTN LTD (NY)
Merged into ACA Joe, Inc. 01/16/1987
Each share Common 1¢ par exchanged for (1.2) shares Common 10¢ par
(See ACA Joe, Inc.)

ACA JOE INTERCON INC (DE)
Merged into Aca Joe, Inc. 01/15/1987
Each share Common 1¢ par exchanged for (0.95) share Common 10¢ par
(See ACA Joe, Inc.)

ACABIT EXPL INC (QC)
Name changed to Western Pacific Mining Exploration Inc. 10/17/1996
Western Pacific Mining Exploration Inc. recapitalized as Sierra Minerals Inc. 12/05/2002 which recapitalized as Goldgroup Mining Inc. 05/07/2010

ACACIA AUTOMOTIVE INC (TX)
Name changed to Acacia Diversified Holdings, Inc. 10/18/2012

ACACIA CAP CORP CDA (YT)
Dissolved and struck off register 03/01/2006

ACACIA GOLD MINING CO. (CO)
Charter revoked for failure to file reports and pay fees 10/20/1964

ACACIA MINERAL DEV LTD (BC)
Recapitalized as AMD Resources Corp. 09/25/1989
Each share Common $1 par exchanged for (0.2) share Common no par
AMD Resources Corp. name changed to Halo Gaming Corp. 04/24/1992
(See Halo Gaming Corp.)

ACACIA RESH CORP (CA)
Common no par split (2) for (1) by issuance of (1) additional share payable 06/12/1998 to holders of record 05/29/1998
Reincorporated under the laws of Delaware 12/28/1999

ACADAMAX VENTURES INC (BC)
Reincorporated under the laws of Bermuda as XMP Mining Ltd. 12/10/1997
XMP Mining Ltd. (Bermuda) reorganized in British Columbia as Nu XMP Ventures Ltd. 06/05/2003 which name changed to New Pacific Metals Corp. (Old) 11/04/2004 which name changed to New Pacific Holdings Corp. 07/04/2016 which name changed to New Pacific Metals Corp. (New) 07/24/2017

ACADEMIC COMPUTER SYS INC (NJ)
Name changed to Worlds, Inc. 12/02/1997
Worlds, Inc. name changed to Worlds.com Inc. (NJ) 12/15/1999 which reincorporated in Delaware as Worlds Inc. 02/14/2011

ACADEMIC DEV CORP (NY)
Dissolved by proclamation 12/20/1977

ACADEMIC INDEX INC (DE)
Name changed to Summers Industries, Inc. 04/28/1972
(See Summers Industries, Inc.)

ACADEMIC INDS INC (DE)
Charter cancelled and declared inoperative and void for non-payment of taxes 03/01/2003

ACADEMIC PRESS INC (NY)
Acquired by Harcourt, Brace & World Inc. 11/14/1969
Each share Common $1 par exchanged for (0.45) share Common $1 par
Harcourt, Brace & World, Inc. name changed to Harcourt Brace Jovanovich, Inc. 06/02/1970 which merged into General Cinema Corp. 11/25/1991 which name changed to Harcourt General, Inc. 03/15/1993
(See Harcourt General, Inc.)

ACADEMIC SYS & MGMT CORP (DE)
Adjudicated bankrupt 07/27/1971
Charter subsequently cancelled and declared inoperative and void for non-payment of taxes 04/15/1972

ACADEMY CAP CORP (ON)
Name changed to Baymount Inc. 01/18/2006

ACADEMY COMPUTING CORP (OK)
Common 50¢ par changed to 1¢ par 03/15/1984
Name changed to Ametech, Inc. 01/09/1991
(See Ametech, Inc.)

ACADEMY EXPLS LTD (ON)
Delisted from Canadian Dealer Network 03/23/1992

ACADEMY INS & FINL SVCS INC (NV)
Name changed to Guardian Insurance & Financial Services Inc. 01/02/1996
Guardian Insurance & Financial Services Inc. name changed to Genesis Insurance & Financial Services, Inc. 06/07/1996
(See Genesis Insurance & Financial Services, Inc.)

ACADEMY INS GROUP INC (DE)
Reincorporated 06/17/1988
Conv. Preferred 10¢ par called for redemption on 03/31/1981
Common 10¢ par split (2) for (1) by issuance of (1) additional share 10/31/1983
State of incorporation changed from (PA) to (DE) 06/17/1988
Merged into Academy Mergerco, Inc. 03/25/1991
Each share Common 10¢ par exchanged for $1.325 cash

ACADEMY LIFE INSURANCE CO. (CO)
Acquired by Security Life & Accident Co. 12/31/1963
Each share Common 30¢ par exchanged for (0.05555555) share Series A Common $4 par
Security Life & Accident Co. name changed to Security Life of Denver Insurance Co. 05/29/1981
(See Security Life of Denver Insurance Co.)

ACADEMY RES INC (NV)
Common $0.001 par split (5) for (1) by issuance of (4) additional shares payable 05/29/2000 to holders of record 05/05/2000
Recapitalized as Law Enforcement Associates Corp. 12/28/2001
Each share Common $0.001 par exchanged for (0.33333333) share Common $0.001 par
(See Law Enforcement Associates Corp.)

ACADEMY RES LTD (BC)
Recapitalized as Acadamax Ventures Inc. (BC) 12/02/1994
Each share Common no par exchanged for (0.25) share Common no par
Acadamax Ventures Inc. (BC) reincorporated in Bermuda as XMP Mining Ltd. 12/10/1997 which reorganized in British Columbia as Nu XMP Ventures Ltd. 06/05/2003 which name changed to New Pacific Metals Corp. (Old) 11/04/2004 which name changed to New Pacific Holdings Corp. 07/04/2016 which name changed to New Pacific Metals Corp. (New) 07/24/2017

ACADEMY VENTURES INC (BC)
Name changed to First Bauxite Corp. and (1) additional share issued 12/05/2008

ACADIA APARTMENTS LTD. (QC)
Liquidated 00/00/1951
Details not available

ACADIA ATLANTIC SUGAR REFINERIES LTD (ON)
Each share old Class A no par exchanged for (1) share new Class A no par and (1) share Common no par 00/00/1951
Common no par split (3) for (1) by issuance of (2) additional shares 05/24/1961
Name changed to Atlantic Sugar Refineries Co. Ltd. 05/03/1962
Atlantic Sugar Refineries Co. Ltd. merged into Jannock Corp. Ltd. 07/04/1973 which reorganized as Jannock Ltd. 07/05/1977
(See Jannock Ltd.)

ACADIA GROUP INC (CO)
SEC revoked common stock registration 03/11/2008

ACADIA INC (NY)
Each share Common 10¢ par exchanged for (0.001) share Common $100 par 10/19/1979
Note: In effect holders received $3 cash per share and public interest was eliminated

ACADIA METALS, LTD. (CANADA)
Charter cancelled for failure to file annual reports 10/15/1932

ACADIA MINERALS CORP (CANADA)
Reincorporated 04/21/1987
Recapitalized 06/20/1996
Place of incorporation changed from (NS) to (Canada) 04/21/1987
Recapitalized from Acadia Mineral Ventures Ltd. to Acadia Minerals Corp. 06/20/1996
Each share Common no par exchanged for (0.1) share Common no par
Merged into Lydia Diamond Exploration of Canada Ltd. 05/16/2001
Each share Common no par exchanged for (1) share Common no par

ACADIA NATL HEALTH SYS INC (CO)
Name changed to Acadia Group, Inc. 11/19/1999
(See Acadia Group, Inc.)

ACADIA PETE CORP (CO)
Merged into Kee Exploration, Inc. 12/06/1983
Each share Common no par exchanged for (0.08333333) share Common $0.001 par
Kee Exploration, Inc. merged into Wichita River Oil Corp. (VA) (New) 11/04/1987 which reincorporated in Delaware 03/30/1990
(See Wichita River Oil Corp. (DE))

ACADIA RES CORP (BC)
Each share old Common no par exchanged for (0.33333333) share new Common no par 07/22/2013
Reincorporated under the laws of Jersey as Horizon Petroleum PLC 10/08/2013
Horizon Petroleum PLC (Jersey) reincorporated in Alberta as Horizon Petroleum Ltd. 04/05/2016

ACADIA RES INC (NV)
Reorganized as Sunovia Energy Technologies, Inc. 12/18/2007
Each share Common $0.001 par exchanged for (4.5) shares Common $0.001 par
Sunovia Energy Technologies, Inc. name changed to Evolucia Inc. 08/16/2012
(See Evolucia Inc.)

ACADIA SUGAR REFINING CO., LTD. (NS)
Property sold and company liquidated 00/00/1939
Details not available

ACADIA SUGAR REFINING CO. LTD. (ON)
Name changed to Acadia-Atlantic Sugar Refineries, Ltd. 06/00/1945
Acadia-Atlantic Sugar Refineries, Ltd. name changed to Atlantic Sugar Refineries Co. Ltd. 05/03/1962 which merged into Jannock Corp. Ltd. 07/04/1973 which reorganized as Jannock Ltd. 07/05/1977
(See Jannock Ltd.)

ACADIA URANIUM MINES LTD (ON)
Charter cancelled and proclaimed dissolved for failure to pay taxes and file returns 03/16/1976

ACADIAN GOLD CORP (CANADA)
Name changed to Acadian Mining Corp. 06/28/2007
(See Acadian Mining Corp.)

ACADIAN MINING & SMELTING CORP. (QC)
Voluntarily dissolved 03/28/1963
Details not available

ACADIAN MNG CORP (CANADA)
Each share old Common no par exchanged for (0.1) share new Common no par 11/17/2010
Acquired by LionGold Corp. Ltd. 10/11/2013
Each share new Common no par exchanged for $0.12 cash

ACADIAN TIMBER INCOME FD (ON)
Reincorporated under the laws of Canada as Acadian Timber Corp. and Units no par reclassified as Common no par 01/05/2010

ACADIANA BANCSHARES INC (LA)
Closed by the State Banking Department 04/20/1990
Stockholders' equity unlikely

ACADIANA BANCSHARES INC NEW (LA)
Merged into Iberiabank Corp. 02/28/2003
Each share Common 1¢ par exchanged for (0.7919) share Common $1 par and $7.88 cash

ACAMBIS PLC (UNITED KINGDOM)
Sponsored ADR's for Ordinary split (5) for (1) by issuance of (4) additional ADR's payable 02/23/2004 to holders of record 02/20/2004 Ex date - 02/24/2004
ADR agreement terminated 02/14/2007
Each Sponsored ADR for Ordinary exchanged for $4.97252 cash

ACANA CAP CORP (BC)
Each share old Common no par exchanged for (0.1) share new Common no par 05/14/2012
Name changed to Mag One Products Inc. 05/28/2015

ACANA MINES LTD. (QC)
Charter annulled for failure to file reports 09/02/1978

ACANO EXPLS LTD (BC)
Recapitalized as Onaca Explorations Ltd. 07/30/1976
Each share Common no par exchanged for (0.2) share Common no par
Onaca Explorations Ltd. name changed to Osec Petroleum Corp. 00/00/1977 which recapitalized as ProAm Exploration Corp. 12/06/1993

ACANTHUS REAL ESTATE CORP (CANADA)
Merged into Cadim Inc. 10/11/2000
Each share Common no par exchanged for $9.40 cash

ACAP CORP (DE)
Each share old Common 10¢ par exchanged for (0.003) share new Common 10¢ par 04/26/1993
Each share new Common 10¢ par exchanged again for (0.5) share new Common 10¢ par 05/14/2003
Note: In effect holders of fewer than (2) shares received $485 cash per share
Merged into UTG, Inc. 11/14/2011
Each share new Common 10¢ par exchanged for (233) shares Common no par

ACAPLOMO MNG & DEV LTD (BC)
Name changed to Phillips Equity Corp. 06/15/1979
Phillips Equity Corp. recapitalized as Corvette Petroleum Corp. 08/24/1979 which recapitalized as Armor Development Corp. 05/17/1985
(See Armor Development Corp.)

ACAPULCO RESTAURANTS (CA)
Merged into Restaurant Associates Industries, Inc. 02/04/1986
Each share Common 10¢ par exchanged for (1) share 50¢ Conv. Preferred $1 par
(See Restaurant Associates Industries, Inc.)

ACAPULCO Y LOS ARCOS RESTAURANTES (CA)
Stock Dividend - 25% 01/05/1981
Name changed to Acapulco Restaurants 03/26/1984
Acapulco Restaurants merged into Restaurant Associates Industries, Inc. 02/04/1986
(See Restaurant Associates Industries, Inc.)

ACARA ROUYN MINES LTD. (ON)
Charter cancelled for failure to pay taxes and file returns 09/17/1962

ACC CONSUMER FIN CORP (DE)
Merged into Household International, Inc. 10/21/1997
Each share Common $0.001 par exchanged for (0.160821) share Common $1 par and $3.50 cash

ACC CORP (DE)
Common $0.015 par split (3) for (2) by issuance of (0.5) additional share 02/04/1993
Common $0.015 par split (3) for (2) by issuance of (0.5) additional share payable 08/08/1996 to holders of record 07/03/1996
Merged into Teleport Communications Group Inc. 04/22/1998
Each share Common $0.015 par exchanged for (0.90909) share Class A Common 1¢ par
Teleport Communications Group Inc. merged into AT&T Corp. 07/24/1998 which merged into AT&T Inc. 11/18/2005

ACC TELENTERPRISES LTD (ON)
Merged into ACC Acquisition Corp. 01/02/1997
Each share Common no par exchanged for $21.50 cash

ACCEL ENERGY GROUP INC (DE)
Recapitalized as Power-Save Energy Corp. 01/09/2006
Each share Common $0.001 par exchanged for (0.00333333) share Common $0.001 par
Power-Save Energy Corp. name changed to Disability Access Corp. (DE) 11/01/2006 which reorganized in Nevada 11/30/2006
(See Disability Access Corp. (NV))

ACCEL FINL GROUP LTD (AB)
Merged into T&W Financial Services Co. 04/12/1999
Each share Common no par exchanged for $2.50 cash

ACCEL INTL CORP (DE)
Reincorporated 08/11/1978
Name changed 06/25/1987
Common no par split (3) for (2) by issuance of (0.5) additional share 02/10/1978
Common no par changed to 10¢ par 06/00/1978
State of incorporation changed from (OH) to (DE) 08/11/1978
Name changed from Acceleration Corp. to Accel International Corp. 06/25/1987
Recapitalized as SN United Enterprises, Inc. 05/09/2006
Each share Common 10¢ par exchanged for (0.01) share Common 10¢ par
SN United Enterprises, Inc. name changed to Itzyourmall, Inc. 06/08/2006

ACCELERATED BLDG CONCEPTS CORP (DE)
Recapitalized as WhereverTV Broadcasting Corp. 09/12/2012
Each share Common 1¢ par exchanged for (0.01) share Common 1¢ par

ACCELERATED LEARNING LANGUAGES INC (DE)
Recapitalized as Integrated Enterprises Inc. 06/20/2001
Each share Common $0.001 par exchanged for (0.1) share Common $0.001 par
Integrated Enterprises Inc. recapitalized as SeaLife Corp. (DE) 12/20/2002 which reincorporated in Nevada 10/06/2016

ACCELERATED NETWORKS INC (DE)
Name changed to Occam Networks, Inc. 05/15/2002
Occam Networks, Inc. merged into Calix, Inc. 02/22/2011

ACCELERATOR CAP CORP (BC)
Name changed to Oceanside Capital Corp. (BC) 05/14/2009
Oceanside Capital Corp. (BC) reorganized in Ontario as Gaming Nation Inc. 06/15/2015
(See Gaming Nation Inc.)

ACCELERATORS INC (TX)
Common 25¢ par changed to no par and (2) additional shares issued 08/20/1971
Acquired by Veeco Instruments, Inc. 12/18/1979
Each share Common no par exchanged for $1.0625 cash

ACCELERITAS CORP (NV)
Name changed to Hollywall Entertainment Inc. 12/24/2013

ACCELERIZE NEW MEDIA INC (DE)
Name changed to Accelerize Inc. 10/14/2014

ACCELEWARE CORP (AB)
Name changed to Acceleware Ltd. 05/03/2011

ACCELGRAPHICS INC (DE)
Merged into Evans & Sutherland Computer Corp. 06/26/1998
Each share Common $0.001 par exchanged for either $5.75 value of Common 20¢ par, $5.75 cash, or Common 20¢ par and cash equal to a total of $5.75 payable in 52% stock and 48% cash

ACCELIO CORP (CANADA)
Merged into Adobe Systems Inc. 04/15/2002
Each share Common no par exchanged for (0.072573) share Common $0.0001 par
Adobe Systems Inc. name changed to Adobe Inc. 10/09/2018

ACCELRATE PWR SYS INC (BC)
Each share old Common no par exchanged for (0.2) share new Common no par 12/01/2008
Each share new Common no par exchanged again for (0.33333333) share new Common no par 01/08/2010
Name changed to Goldstrike Resources Ltd. 06/21/2011

ACCELR8 TECHNOLOGY CORP (CO)
Each share old Common no par exchanged for (0.25) share new Common $0.001 par 11/19/1996
Reincorporated under the laws of Delaware as Accelerate Diagnostics, Inc. and Common no par changed to $0.001 par 12/26/2012

ACCELRYS INC (DE)
Acquired by Dassault Systemes S.A. 04/29/2014
Each share Common $0.0001 par exchanged for $12.50 cash

ACCEND CAP CORP (BC)
Name changed to M2 Cobalt Corp. 11/29/2017

ACCEND MEDIA (NV)
Common $0.001 par split (5) for (1) by issuance of (4) additional shares payable 05/07/2012 to holders of record 05/04/2012 Ex date - 05/08/2012
Name changed to Cloud Star Corp. 05/24/2012
Cloud Star Corp. name changed to Cloud Security Corp. 06/03/2013 which name changed to US-China Biomedical Technology, Inc. 02/09/2018

ACCENT COLOR SCIENCES INC (CT)
Chapter 7 bankruptcy proceedings terminated 03/19/2010
No stockholders' equity

ACCENT RES LTD (BC)
Recapitalized as Midas Resources Ltd. 03/10/1975
Each share Capital Stock 50¢ par exchanged for (0.33333333) share Capital Stock no par
Midas Resources Ltd. recapitalized as Continental Silver Corp. 03/14/1977 which merged into Arizona Silver Corp. 08/01/1985 which recapitalized as ASC Industries Ltd. 06/06/1995 which name changed to Acero-Martin Exploration Inc. 11/24/2004 which name changed to AM Gold Inc. 06/08/2010
(See AM Gold Inc.)

ACCENT SOFTWARE INTL LTD (ISRAEL)
Ordinary Stock NIS 0.01 par split (3) for (2) by issuance of (0.5) additional share payable 06/06/1996 to holders of record 06/03/1996
Name changed to LanguageWare.net (Company) Ltd. 10/18/1999
(See LanguageWare.net (Company) Ltd.)

ACCENTIA BIOPHARMACEUTICALS INC (FL)
SEC revoked common stock registration 01/15/2016

ACCENTURE LTD (BERMUDA)
Reincorporated under the laws of Ireland as Accenture PLC and Class A Common USD$0.0000225 par reclassified as Class A Ordinary USD$0.0000225 par 09/01/2009

ACCEPTANCE CORP. OF FLORIDA (FL)
Each share Common no par exchanged for (0.05) share Common $20 par 00/00/1945
Stock Dividends - 300% 02/15/1958; 50% 10/15/1963
Merged into United States Finance Co., Inc. 02/01/1965
Each share 6% Preferred $10 par exchanged for $10 cash
Each share Common $20 par exchanged for $30.25 cash

ACCEPTANCE INS COS INC (DE)
Chapter 11 bankruptcy proceedings converted to Chapter 7 on 09/07/2010
Stockholders' equity unlikely

ACCEPTANCE INS HLDGS INC (NE)
Acquired by Stoneridge Resources, Inc. 04/12/1990
Each share Common 1¢ par exchanged for $22.55 cash

ACCERIS COMMUNICATIONS INC (FL)
Name changed to C2 Global Technologies Inc. 08/15/2005
C2 Global Technologies Inc. name changed to Counsel RB Capital Inc. 02/04/2011 which changed name to Heritage Global Inc. 08/29/2013

ACCESMED INC (DE)
Name changed to Kinti Mining, Ltd. 05/27/2008
Kinti Mining, Ltd. name changed to Swift International, Inc. 05/27/2011

ACCESS ANYTIME BANCORP INC (DE)
Stock Dividend - 2% payable 12/01/1997 to holders of record 10/31/1997
Merged into First State Bancorporation 01/03/2006
Each share Common 1¢ par exchanged for (0.791) share Common no par
(See First State Bancorporation)

ACCESS ATM NETWORK INC (CANADA)
Merged into Ancom ATM International Inc. 01/18/1988
Each share Common no par exchanged for (0.33333333) share Common no par and (0.33333333) Common Stock Purchase Warrant expiring 12/31/1992
(See Ancom ATM International Inc.)

ACCESS BANKING NETWORK INC. (CANADA)
Recapitalized as Access ATM Network Inc. 05/24/1985
Each share Common no par exchanged for (0.1) share Common no par
Access ATM Network Inc. merged into Ancom ATM International Inc. 01/18/1988
(See Ancom ATM International Inc.)

ACCESS BEVERAGE INC (NV)
Each shares old Common $0.001 par exchanged for (0.00333333) share new Common $0.001 par 06/15/2009
Name changed to Unity Auto Parts Inc. 09/22/2009
Unity Auto Parts Inc. name changed to Unity Management Group, Inc. 01/08/2010 which name changed to Petrotech Oil & Gas, Inc. 03/26/2013

ACCESS BEYOND INC (DE)
Name changed to Hayes Corp. 12/31/1997
(See Hayes Corp.)

ACCESS CAP INC (DE)
Name changed to Dreamcar Holdings, Inc. 06/14/1989
(See Dreamcar Holdings, Inc.)

ACCESS GROUP INC (NV)
Name changed to Zipnet, Inc. 12/31/1998

ACCESS HEALTH ALTERNATIVES INC (FL)
Plan of reorganization under Chapter 11 Federal Bankruptcy Code effective 10/03/2002
Each share old Common $0.001 par exchanged for (0.01) share new Common $0.001 par
Name changed to IPMC Holdings Corp. (FL) 01/07/2003
IPMC Holdings Corp. (FL) reincorporated in Nevada as Coil Tubing Technology, Inc. 12/22/2005

ACCESS HEALTH INC (DE)
Name changed 03/29/1995
Name changed from Access Health Marketing, Inc. to Access Health Inc. 03/29/1995
Common $0.001 par split (3) for (2) by issuance of (0.5) additional share payable 02/02/1996 to holders of record 02/15/1996
Merged into HBO & Co. 12/10/1998
Each share Common $0.001 par exchanged for (1.45) shares Common 5¢ par
HBO & Co. merged into McKesson HBOC Inc. 01/12/1999 which name changed to McKesson Corp. 07/30/2001

ACCESS HEALTHMAX HLDGS INC (FL)
Recapitalized as Access Health Alternatives, Inc. 03/15/1999
Each share Common $0.001 par exchanged for (0.1) share Common $0.001 par
Access Health Alternatives, Inc. name changed to IPMC Holdings Corp. (FL) 01/07/2003 which reincorporated in Nevada as Coil Tubing Technology, Inc. 12/22/2005

ACCESS HEALTHNET INC (DE)
Each share old Common $0.001 par exchanged for (0.16666666) share new Common $0.001 par 04/01/1992
Each share new Common $0.001 par exchanged again for (0.4) share new Common $0.001 par 07/05/1993
Charter forfeited for failure to maintain a registered agent 04/14/1996

ACCESS INTEGRATED TECHNOLOGIES INC (DE)
Name changed to Cinedigm Digital Cinema Corp. 10/05/2009
Cinedigm Digital Cinema Corp. name changed to Cinedigm Corp. 10/09/2013

ACCESS MED CORP (NV)
Name changed to Shoreline Software Solutions Inc. 05/25/1994
Shoreline Software Solutions Inc. name changed to American Home Alliance Industries Ltd. 05/23/1995 which recapitalized as Alliance Industries 09/18/1996
(See Alliance Industries)

ACCESS MIDSTREAM PARTNERS L P (DE)
Common Units split (1.06152) for (1) by issuance of (0.06152) additional Unit payable 02/02/2015 to holders of record 01/30/2015 Ex date - 02/02/2015
Under plan of merger name changed to Williams Partners L.P. (New) 02/02/2015
Williams Partners L.P. (New) merged

ACC-ACC

ACCESS (continued)
into Williams Companies, Inc. 08/10/2018

ACCESS NETWORK CORP (NV)
Reorganized as EUPA International Corp. 10/16/2001
Each share Common $0.001 par exchanged for (19.94017946) shares Common $0.001 par
(See EUPA International Corp.)

ACCESS ONE COMMUNICATIONS CORP (NJ)
Merged into TALK.com Inc. 08/10/2000
Each share Common $0.001 par exchanged for (0.5142852) share Common 1¢ par
Note: Each share Common $0.001 par received an additional distribution of approximately (0.0571428) share from escrow 08/09/2001
Talk.com Inc. name changed to Talk America Holdings Inc. 04/10/2001
(See Talk America Holdings Inc.)

ACCESS PHARMACEUTICALS INC (DE)
Each share Common 4¢ par exchanged for (0.05) share old Common 1¢ par 06/18/1998
Each share old Common 1¢ par exchanged for (0.2) share new Common 1¢ par 06/05/2006
Recapitalized as PlasmaTech Biopharmaceuticals, Inc. 10/24/2014
Each share new Common 1¢ par exchanged for (0.02) share Common 1¢ par
PlasmaTech Biopharmaceuticals, Inc. name changed to Abeona Therapeutics Inc. 06/22/2015

ACCESS PLANS INC (OK)
Acquired by Affinity Insurance Services, Inc. 05/31/2012
Each share Common $0.001 par exchanged for $3.28 cash

ACCESS PLANS USA INC (OK)
Acquired by Alliance HealthCard, Inc. (GA) 04/01/2009
Each share Common 1¢ par exchanged for (0.33548529) share Common $0.001 par
Alliance HealthCard, Inc. (GA) reincorporated in Oklahoma as Access Plans, Inc. 01/19/2010
(See Access Plans, Inc.)

ACCESS PWR INC (FL)
Name changed to Access-Power, Inc. 09/06/2018

ACCESS RES LTD (BC)
Struck off register and declared dissolved for failure to file returns 08/22/1986

ACCESS SOLUTIONS INTL INC (DE)
Liquidation completed
Each share Common 1¢ par received initial distribution of $0.28 cash payable 12/27/2002 to holders of record 12/13/2002 Ex date - 12/30/2002
Each share Common 1¢ par received second distribution of $0.14 cash payable 12/10/2003 to holders of record 11/28/2003 Ex date - 12/11/2003
Each share Common 1¢ par received third and final distribution of $0.04 cash payable 11/30/2004 to holders of record 08/26/2004
Note: Certificates were not required to be surrendered and are without value

ACCESS TECHNOLOGIES INC (BC)
Struck off register and declared dissolved for failure to file returns 04/24/1992

ACCESS TO MONEY INC (DE)
Acquired by Cardtronics USA, Inc. 11/01/2011
Each share Common $0.001 par exchanged for $0.285 cash

ACCESS TRADEONE COM INC (NV)
SEC revoked common stock registration 01/28/2008

ACCESS WEST CAP CORP (BC)
Name changed to Journey Unlimited Omni Brand Corp. 06/20/2002
Journey Unlimited Omni Brand Corp. name changed to Journey Resources Corp. 11/29/2005 which recapitalized as Musgrove Minerals Corp. 12/17/2010 which recapitalized as RewardStream Solutions Inc. 08/04/2016

ACCESS WORLDWIDE COMMUNICATIONS INC (DE)
Company terminated common stock registration and is no longer public as of 09/08/2008

ACCESSIBLE SOFTWARE INC (NJ)
Merged into International Business Machines Corp. 02/11/2000
Each share Common no par exchanged for $7.10 cash

ACCESSITY CORP (NY)
Each share old Common $0.015 par exchanged for (0.2) share new Common $0.015 par 01/07/2004
Reincorporated under the laws of Delaware as Pacific Ethanol, Inc. 03/24/2005

ACCESSKEY IP INC (NV)
SEC revoked common stock registration 05/14/2013

ACCESSO CORP (WA)
Each share 6% Preferred $10 par exchanged for (1) share new Common no par 01/05/1965
Each share old Common no par exchanged for (0.16666666) share new Common no par 01/05/1965
Out of business 09/08/1967
No stockholders' equity

ACCESSPOINT CORP (NV)
SEC revoked common stock registration 12/07/2011

ACCESSTEL INC (UT)
Each share old Common $0.001 par exchanged for (0.01122359) share new Common $0.001 par 12/12/2003
Each share new Common $0.001 par exchanged again for (0.01) share new Common $0.001 par to reflect a (1) for (10,000) reverse split followed by a (100) for (1) forward split 08/24/2004
SEC revoked common stock registration 03/30/2011

ACCIDENT PREVENTION PLUS INC (NV)
Each share old Common $0.001 par exchanged for (0.1) share new Common $0.001 par 11/26/2001
Each share new Common $0.001 par exchanged again for (1.2) shares new Common $0.001 par 04/10/2002
Name changed to Transportation Safety Technology, Inc. 12/20/2004
Each share Common $0.001 par exchanged for (1) share Common $0.001 par
Transportation Safety Technology, Inc. recapitalized as Inca Designs, Inc. 03/26/2007

ACCIDENTAL MINING & MILLING CO. (CO)
Charter revoked for failure to file reports and pay fees 09/16/1913

ACCIONA S A (SPAIN)
ADR agreement terminated 08/06/2018
No ADR's remain outstanding

ACCLAIM ENERGY TR (AB)
Each old Trust Unit exchanged for (0.4) new Trust Unit 06/05/2003
Acquired by Canetic Resources Trust 01/05/2006
Each new Trust Unit exchanged for (0.8333) Trust Unit, (0.8333) share TriStar Oil & Gas Ltd. Common no par and (0.0175) Common Stock Purchase Warrant expiring 02/06/2006
(See each company's listing)
Note: Holders of (993) or fewer shares received cash in lieu of TriStar Oil & Gas Ltd. Stock and Warrants

ACCLAIM ENTMT INC (DE)
Each share Common no par exchanged for (0.5) share Common 2¢ par 07/25/1989
Common 2¢ par split (3) for (2) by issuance of (0.5) additional share 08/23/1993
Filed plan of liquidation under Chapter 7 Federal Bankruptcy Code 09/01/2004
Stockholders' equity unlikely

ACCO WORLD CORP (DE)
Common 5¢ par split (3) for (2) by issuance of (0.5) additional share 10/23/1984
Common 5¢ par split (3) for (2) by issuance of (0.5) additional share 06/01/1987
Merged into American Brands, Inc. 08/20/1987
Each share Common 5¢ par exchanged for $29 cash

ACCOM INC (DE)
Ceased operations 09/00/2005
No stockholders' equity

ACCOR CAP CORP (DE)
Auction Rate Preferred called for redemption at $500,000 on 02/11/2000

ACCOR S A (FRANCE)
ADR agreement terminated 08/31/2005
Each old Sponsored ADR for Ordinary exchanged for $32.83319 cash (Additional Information in Active)

ACCORD ADVANCED TECHNOLOGIES INC (NV)
Common $0.0001 par split (3) for (1) by issuance of (2) additional shares payable 10/02/1998 to holders of record 09/25/1998
Recapitalized as Central Utilities Production Corp. 07/30/2001
Each share Common $0.0001 par exchanged for (0.5) share Common $0.0001 par
(See Central Utilities Production Corp.)

ACCORD CAP CORP (AB)
Recapitalized as Consolidated Accord Capital Corp. 12/17/1991
Each share Common no par exchanged for (0.2) share Common no par
Consolidated Accord Capital Corp. merged into Peak Energy Services Ltd. (Old) 06/14/1996 which reorganized as Peak Energy Services Trust 05/01/2004 which reorganized as Peak Energy Services Ltd. (New) 01/06/2011
(See Peak Energy Services Ltd. (New))

ACCORD CONS MINERALS CORP
Merged into Kelcord International Inc. 10/28/1997
Each share Common exchanged for (1) share Common $0.0001 par
(See Kelcord International Inc.)

ACCORD GROUP INC (DE)
Each share old Common exchanged for (0.01) share new Common 12/19/1997
Name changed to Thermotek International Inc. 10/27/1998
Thermotek International Inc. name changed to Eagle Worldwide Marketing, Inc. (DE) 02/25/2003 which reincorporated in Washington 04/27/2005 which recapitalized as IPhone2, Inc. 07/18/2005
(See IPhone2, Inc.)

ACCORD NETWORKS LTD (ISRAEL)
Merged into Polycom, Inc. 02/28/2001
Each share Ordinary NIS 0.01 par exchanged for (0.0365) share Common $0.0005 par
(See Polycom, Inc.)

ACCORD RES INC (ON)
Recapitalized as International Accord Inc. 03/01/1995
Each share Common no par exchanged for (0.2) share Common no par
(See International Accord Inc.)

ACCORD VENTURES INC (NV)
Name changed to Virtual World of Sports Inc. 05/24/2000
(See Virtual World of Sports Inc.)

ACCORDIA GOLF CO LTD (JAPAN)
Basis changed from (1:0.01) to (1:1) 10/01/2013
ADR agreement terminated 07/24/2017
Each Sponsored ADR for Common exchanged for $10.946101 cash

ACCOUNTABILITIES INC (DE)
Each share old Common $0.0001 par exchanged for (0.2) share new Common $0.0001 par 04/03/2006
Name changed to Corporate Resource Services, Inc. 04/21/2010

ACCOUNTING CORP. OF AMERICA (DE)
Name changed to Var-Aca, Inc. 09/17/1987
(See Var-Aca, Inc.)

ACCRA EXPLS LTD (ON)
Capital Stock $1 par changed to no par 04/16/1971
Merged into Xtra Developments Inc. 05/25/1972
Each share Capital Stock no par exchanged for (0.125) share Capital Stock no par
Xtra Developments Inc. merged into Sumtra Diversified Inc. 08/30/1978

ACCREDITED HOME LENDERS HLDG CO (DE)
Merged into LSF5 Accredited Merger Co., Inc. 10/12/2007
Each share Common $0.001 exchanged for $11.75 cash

ACCREDITED HOSP & LIFE INS CO (MO)
Capital Stock $2.50 par changed to $3.75 par 08/22/1969
Capital Stock $3.75 par changed to $1.25 par and (2) additional shares issued 12/30/1969
Became private 00/00/1976
Details not available

ACCREDITED MEMBERS HLDG CORP (CO)
Name changed to Hangover Joe's Holding Corp. 08/01/2012

ACCREDITED MTG LN REIT TR (MD)
In process of liquidation
Each share 9.75% Perpetual Preferred Ser. A $1 par received initial distribution of $5 cash payable 02/22/2013 to holders of record 02/06/2013
Each share 9.75% Perpetual Preferred Ser. A $1 par received second distribution of $1.25 cash payable 11/14/2014 to holders of record 11/03/2014 Ex date - 11/17/2014
Each share 9.75% Perpetual Preferred Ser. A $1 par received third and final distribution of $1.96 cash payable 10/28/2016 to holders of record 10/14/2016

ACCREDO HEALTH INC (DE)
Common 1¢ par split (3) for (2) by issuance of (0.5) additional share

payable 02/21/2000 to holders of record 02/11/2000
Common 1¢ par split (3) for (2) by issuance of (0.5) additional share payable 02/23/2001 to holders of record 02/09/2001 Ex date - 02/26/2001
Common 1¢ par split (3) for (2) by issuance of (0.5) additional share payable 12/02/2002 to holders of record 11/15/2002
Common 1¢ par split (3) for (2) by issuance of (0.5) additional share payable 12/02/2002 to holders of record 11/15/2002 Ex date - 12/03/2002
Merged into Medco Health Solutions, Inc. 08/18/2005
Each share Common 1¢ par exchanged for (0.49107) share Common 1¢ par and $22 cash
Medco Health Solutions, Inc. merged into Express Scripts Holding Co. 04/02/2012

ACCRETE ENERGY INC (AB)
Merged into Pengrowth Energy Trust 09/30/2008
Each share Common no par exchanged for (0.276624) Trust Unit, (0.25) share Argosy Energy Inc. Common no par and (0.125) Common Stock Purchase Warrant expiring 11/14/2008
(See each company's listing)

ACCRETIVE FLOW-THROUGH 2005 LTD PARTNERSHIP (BC)
Completely liquidated
Each Unit received first and final distribution of $1.5195 cash payable 06/30/2008 to holders of record 06/27/2008

ACCRETIVE HEALTH INC (DE)
Name changed to R1 RCM Inc. 02/01/2017

ACCRUE SOFTWARE INC (DE)
Chapter 11 Bankruptcy proceedings converted to Chapter 7 on 09/29/2003
Stockholders' equity unlikely

ACCSYS GLOBAL NETWORK INC (NV)
Name changed to Classic Golf Corp. 01/30/1998
Classic Golf Corp. recapitalized as Indexonly Technologies Inc. 09/14/1999 which name changed to Nutrifeeds Technologies Inc. 05/05/2003 which name changed to Advanced Solutions & Technologies, Inc. 01/16/2004
(See Advanced Solutions & Technologies, Inc.)

ACCU FORE INC (DE)
Reincorporated under the laws of Nevada as Equishare Development Corp. 06/01/1990
Equishare Development Corp. recapitalized as Southland Financial Inc. 05/02/1995 which name changed to StarBridge Global Inc. 11/20/2000 which recapitalized as China Mulans Nano Technology Corp., Ltd. 01/29/2007

ACCU TEST SYS INC (DE)
Reorganized under Chapter 11 Federal Bankruptcy Code as Pacific Eastern Corp. 04/23/1986
Each share Common 1¢ par exchanged for (0.2) share Common 1¢ par
(See Pacific Eastern Corp.)

ACCUFACTS PRE-EMPLOYMENT SCREENING INC (FL)
Merged into First Advantage Corp. 06/07/2006
Each share Common $0.001 par exchanged for $0.75 cash

ACCUGRAPH CORP (CANADA)
Each share Common no par exchanged for (0.4) share Class A Common no par 04/12/1986
Merged into Architel Systems Corp. 06/16/1998
Each share Class A Common no par exchanged for (0.0833) share Common no par
Architel Systems Corp. merged into Nortel Networks Corp. (New) 07/03/2000
(See Nortel Networks Corp. (New))

ACCUHEALTH INC (NY)
Chapter 11 bankruptcy proceedings converted to Chapter 7 on 04/29/2002
Stockholders' equity unlikely

ACCUIMAGE DIAGNOSTICS CORP (NV)
Merged into Merge Technologies Inc. 01/28/2005
Each share Class A Common $0.001 par exchanged for $0.121 cash

ACCUMED INTL INC (CA)
Each share old Common 1¢ par exchanged for (0.16666666) share new Common 1¢ par 05/21/1998
Acquired by Molecular Diagnostics, Inc. 09/17/2001
Each share new Common 1¢ par exchanged for (0.6552) share Common no par
Molecular Diagnostics, Inc. name changed to CytoCore, Inc. 08/17/2006 which name changed to Medite Cancer Diagnostics, Inc. 12/11/2014

ACCUMULATION FUND OF AMERICA, INC.
Out of business 00/00/1941
No stockholders' equity

ACCUMULATIVE ROYALTIES CORP. (DE)
Name changed to James Petroleum Corp. 00/00/1941
(See James Petroleum Corp.)

ACCUPOLL HLDG CORP (NV)
Common $0.001 par split (4) for (1) by issuance of (3) additional shares payable 07/29/2002 to holders of record 07/18/2002 Ex date - 07/30/2002
Recapitalized as Rudy Nutrition 02/08/2008
Each share Common $0.001 par exchanged for (0.00011111) share Common $0.001 par
(See Rudy Nutrition)

ACCURA RES INC (BC)
Name changed to CT & T Telecommunications Inc. 07/20/1994
CT & T Telecommunications Inc. recapitalized as Global CT & T Telecommunications Inc. 02/12/1998
(See Global CT & T Telecommunications Inc.)

ACCURACY INC. (MA)
Adjudicated bankrupt 06/12/1964
No stockholders' equity

ACCURAND CORP. (MN)
Declared insolvent 09/00/1968
Stockholders' equity unlikely

ACCURATE AIR ENGR INC (CA)
Merged into Ellanbee Enterprises, Inc. 06/21/1977
Each share Common no par exchanged for $3 cash

ACCURATE BUSINESS SYS INC (DE)
Charter cancelled and declared inoperative and void for non-payment of taxes 06/27/1989

ACCURATE CALCULATOR CORP (DE)
Reincorporated 11/17/1971
State of incorporation changed from (NY) to (DE) 11/17/1971
Charter cancelled and declared inoperative and void for non-payment of taxes 03/01/1975

ACCURATE ELECTRS INC (DE)
Name changed to Dagger Industries Corp. 03/29/1974
(See Dagger Industries Corp.)

ACCURATE SPECIALTIES CO., INC. (NY)
Name changed to Lodi Liquidating Corp. 06/11/1962
(See Lodi Liquidating Corp.)

ACCURAY CORP (DE)
Merged into Combustion Engineering, Inc. 03/27/1987
Each share Common $1 par exchanged for $45 cash

ACCUREXA INC (DE)
Reincorporated under the laws of Marshall Islands as Medisun Precision Medicine Ltd. 06/30/2017

ACCURIDE CORP NEW (DE)
Each share old Common 1¢ par exchanged for (0.1) share new Common 1¢ par 11/19/2010
Acquired by Armor Parent Corp. 11/18/2016
Each share Common 1¢ par exchanged for $2.58 cash

ACCURIDE CORP OLD (DE)
Reorganized as Accuride Corp. (New) 02/26/2010
Each share Common 1¢ par exchanged for approximately (0.04209915) share Common 1¢ par and (0.46432889) Common Stock Purchase Warrant expiring 02/26/2012
(See Accuride Corp. (New))

ACCUSHARES COMMODITIES TR I (DE)
Each old AccuShares Spot CBOE VIX Down Share no par automatically became (0.1) new AccuShares Spot CBOE VIX Down Share no par 09/25/2015
Each old AccuShares Spot CBOE VIX Up Share no par automatically became (0.1) new AccuShares Spot CBOE VIX Up Share no par 09/25/2015
Each old AccuShares Spot CBOE VIX Down Share no par received distribution of (1) old AccuShares Spot CBOE VIX Up Share no par payable 10/22/2015 to holders of record 10/20/2015
Each old AccuShares Spot CBOE VIX Up Share no par received distribution of (1) old AccuShares Spot CBOE VIX Down Share no par payable 10/22/2015 to holders of record 10/20/2015
Each old AccuShares Spot CBOE VIX Down Share no par automatically became (0.1) new AccuShares Spot CBOE VIX Down Share no par 10/23/2015
Each old AccuShares Spot CBOE VIX Up Share no par automatically became (0.1) new AccuShares Spot CBOE VIX Up Share no par 10/23/2015
Under plan of reorganization each new AccuShares Spot CBOE VIX Down Share and new AccuShares Spot CBOE VIX Up Share no par automatically became (0.33333333) AccuShares Trust I AccuShares Spot CBOE VIX Down Share no par or AccuShares Spot CBOE VIX Up Share no par respectively 06/23/2016
(See AccuShares Trust I)

ACCUSHARES TR I (DE)
Each old AccuShares Spot CBOE VIX Down Share no par automatically became (0.33333333) new AccuShares Spot CBOE VIX Down Share no par 08/15/2016
Each old AccuShares Spot CBOE VIX Up Share no par automatically became (0.33333333) new AccuShares Spot CBOE VIX Up Share no par 08/15/2016 Trust terminated 09/09/2016
Each AccuShares S&P GSCI Crude Oil Excess Return Down Share no par received $23.563833 cash
Each AccuShares S&P GSCI Crude Oil Excess Return Up Share no par received $24.838613 cash
Each new AccuShares Spot CBOE VIX Down Share no par received $4.678979 cash
Each new AccuShares Spot CBOE VIX Up Share no par received $4.302119 cash

ACCUSTAFF INC (FL)
Common 1¢ par split (2) for (1) by issuance of (1) additional share 11/27/1995
Common 1¢ par split (3) for (1) by issuance of (2) additional shares payable 03/27/1996 to holders of record 03/20/1996
Name changed to Modis Professional Services, Inc. 10/01/1998
Modis Professional Services, Inc. name changed to MPS Group, Inc. 01/01/2002
(See MPS Group, Inc.)

ACD SYS INTL INC (BC)
Reincorporated 02/21/2006
Place of incorporation changed from (AB) to (BC) 02/21/2006
Merged into 0770303 B.C. Ltd. 03/22/2007
Each share Common no par exchanged for $0.575 cash

ACDS SYSTEME GRAPHIQUE INC (CANADA)
Struck off register and declared dissolved for failure to file returns 05/06/2004

ACE CAP TR I (DE)
8.875% Trust Originated Preferred Securities called for redemption at $25 on 12/22/2005

ACE CASH EXPRESS INC (TX)
Common 1¢ par split (3) for (2) by issuance of (0.5) additional share payable 11/30/1996 to holders of record 11/15/1996
Common 1¢ par split (3) for (2) by issuance of (0.5) additional share payable 12/15/1997 to holders of record 11/30/1997
Merged into JLL Partners Fund V, L.P. 10/05/2006
Each share Common 1¢ par exchanged for $30 cash

ACE COMM CORP (MD)
Merged into Ariston Global Holding LLC 09/22/2008
Each share Common 1¢ par exchanged for $0.545 cash

ACE CONSULTING MGMT INC (DE)
Name changed to Safco Investment Holding Corp. 12/04/2014
Safco Investment Holding Corp. recapitalized as Boly Group Holdings Corp. 01/24/2017 which name changed to US VR Global.com Inc. 02/07/2018

ACE DEVS LTD (BC)
Recapitalized as ASP123.com Systems, Inc. 08/11/1999
Each share Common no par exchanged for (0.25) share Common no par

ACE INDS INC (NY)
Charter cancelled and proclaimed dissolved for failure to pay taxes 09/24/1980

ACE LTD (CAYMAN ISLANDS)
Ordinary $0.125 par changed to $0.041666667 par and (2) additional shares issued payable 03/02/1998 to holders of record 02/17/1998 Ex date - 03/03/1998
Each Income Pride received (1.8991) shares Ordinary $0.041666667 par 05/16/2003

Redeemable Preferred Ser. A called for redemption at $50 on 06/16/2003 7.8% Preference Ser. C called for redemption at $25 on 06/13/2008 Reincorporated under the laws of Switzerland and Ordinary $0.041666667 par changed to Common CHF 33.74 par 07/17/2008

ACE LTD (SWITZERLAND)
Under plan of merger name changed to Chubb Ltd. 01/15/2016

ACE MARKETING & PROMOTIONS INC (NY)
Name changed to Mobiquity Technologies, Inc. 09/19/2013

ACE MNG LTD (BC)
Merged into Avino Mines & Resources Ltd. 08/25/1969
Each share Capital Stock 50¢ par exchanged for (0.5) share Common no par
Avino Mines & Resources Ltd. recapitalized as International Avino Mines Ltd. 05/12/1995 which name changed to Avino Silver & Gold Mines Ltd. 08/29/1997

ACE PUBG CORP (NY)
Name changed to Charter Communications, Inc. 06/26/1970
(See Charter Communications, Inc.)

ACE SEC LAMINATES CORP (ON)
Ceased operations 02/29/2008
No stockholders' equity

ACE TROPHIES CORP (NY)
Name changed to Wright Energy Corp. 01/10/1980
(See Wright Energy Corp.)

ACE YELLOWKNIFE MINES LTD. (ON)
Charter cancelled for failure to pay taxes and file returns 11/03/1966

ACELLUS COMMUNICATIONS INC (NV)
Recapitalized as Worldwide Internet Inc. 05/08/2009
Each share Common $0.001 par exchanged for (0.001) share Common $0.001 par
Worldwide Internet Inc. name changed to Worldwide Diversified Holdings, Inc. 01/05/2015

ACENETX INC (ON)
Delisted from Toronto Venture Stock Exchange 11/14/2002

ACEPHARM INC (AB)
Delisted from Alberta Stock Exchange 02/07/1997

ACER CAP CORP (AB)
Delisted from Canadian Venture Stock Exchange 05/31/2001

ACER COMMUNICATIONS & MULTIMEDIA INC (TAIWAN)
Reg. S Sponsored GDR's for Common split (2) for (1) by issuance of (1) additional GDR payable 09/11/2000 to holders of record 09/08/2000 Ex date - 09/12/2000
144A Sponsored GDR's for Common split (5) for (4) by issuance of (0.25) additional GDR payable 08/08/2001 to holders of record 06/13/2001 Ex date - 06/13/2001
Stock Dividends - 20% payable 09/29/2000 to holders of record 06/26/2000; 25% payable 08/08/2001 to holders of record 06/13/2001
Name changed to Benq Corp. 01/02/2002
Benq Corp. recapitalized as Qisda Corp. 10/15/2007

ACER INC (TAIWAN)
Each Sponsored Reg. S Temporary GDR for Common exchanged for (1) Sponsored Reg. S GDR for Common 10/22/1997
Sponsored 144A GDR's for Common split (5) for (4) by issuance of (0.25) additional GDR payable 09/15/2000 to holders of record 07/28/2000 Ex date - 07/31/2000
Sponsored Reg. S GDR's for Common split (5) for (4) by issuance of (0.25) additional GDR payable 09/15/2000 to holders of record 07/28/2000 Ex date - 07/31/2000
Stock Dividends - 40% payable 08/22/1996 to holders of record 06/19/1996; 25% payable 09/18/1997 to holders of record 07/03/1997; 25% payable 09/10/1998 to holders of record 07/03/1998; 20% payable 09/20/1999 to holders of record 07/20/1999; 10.12% payable 09/11/2001 to holders of record 08/02/2001
Merged into Acer Inc. (New) 03/27/2002
Each share Common exchanged for (0.4) Sponsored Reg. S GDR for Common
Each Sponsored 144A GDR for Common exchanged for (0.4) Sponsored 144A GDR for Common

ACER PERIPHERALS INC (TAIWAN)
Name changed to Acer Communications & Multimedia Inc. 09/05/2000
Acer Communications & Multimedia Inc. name changed to Benq Corp. 01/02/2002 which recapitalized as Qisda Corp. 10/15/2007

ACER THERAPEUTICS INC (TX)
Reincorporated under the laws of Delaware and Common 1¢ par changed to $0.0001 par 05/15/2018

ACERALIA CORPORACION SIDERURGICA S A (SPAIN)
ADR agreement terminated 12/06/2001
Details not available

ACERGY S A (LUXEMBOURG)
Name changed to Subsea 7 S.A. 01/10/2011

ACERO-MARTIN EXPL INC (BC)
Each share old Common no par exchanged for (0.25) share new Common no par 10/07/2009
Name changed to AM Gold Inc. 06/08/2010
(See AM Gold Inc.)

ACESITA S A (BRAZIL)
Name changed 05/12/1999
Each old Sponsored ADR for Preferred exchanged for (0.36) new Sponsored ADR for Preferred 02/17/1998
Each old Sponsored ADR for Ordinary exchanged for (0.36) new ADR for Ordinary 02/17/1998
Stock Dividend - 5% payable 04/12/1996 to holders of record 04/03/1996
Name changed from Acesita - Cia Acos Especiais Itabira to Acesita S.A. 05/12/1999
Basis changed from (1:5,000) to (1:0.5) 11/19/2004
ADR agreement terminated 12/27/2006
Each new Sponsored ADR for Preferred exchanged for $26.99599 cash
Each new Sponsored ADR for Ordinary exchanged for $26.98188 cash

ACETEX CORP (AB)
Merged into Celanese Corp. 07/20/2005
Each share Common no par exchanged for $9 cash

ACETO CHEM CO (NY)
Common 1¢ par split (6) for (5) by issuance of (0.2) additional share 06/10/1977
Common 1¢ par split (4) for (3) by issuance of (0.33333333) additional share 12/30/1982
Common 1¢ par split (3) for (2) by issuance of (0.5) additional share 02/08/1985
Stock Dividends - 50% 02/29/1975; 13% 05/02/1980
Name changed to Aceto Corp. 11/21/1985

ACETOL PRODUCTS, INC.
Dissolved and liquidated 00/00/1935
Details not available

ACEWAY CORP (NV)
Name changed to SweeGen, Inc. 01/12/2015

ACF-BRILL MOTORS CO. (DE)
Merged into ACF-Wrigley Stores, Inc. 12/30/1955
Each share Common $2.50 par exchanged for (1) share Common $1 par
ACF-Wrigley Stores, Inc. name changed to Allied Supermarkets, Inc. (DE) 11/10/1961 which reincorporated in Michigan 08/18/1982 which name changed to Vons Companies, Inc. 07/22/1987 which merged into Safeway Inc. 04/08/1997
(See Safeway Inc.)

ACF INDS INC (NJ)
Common $25 par changed to no par and (1) additional share issued 09/24/1963
Each share 7% Preferred $100 par exchanged for $4 cash and (2) shares 5% Preferred $50 par 00/00/1954
5% Preferred $50 par called for redemption 01/18/1957
Common no par split (2) for (1) by issuance of (1) additional share 09/20/1965
Common no par split (3) for (2) by issuance of (0.5) additional share 06/22/1976
Merged into a private company 06/29/1984
Each share Common no par exchanged for $54.50 cash

ACF WRIGLEY STORES INC (DE)
Name changed to Allied Supermarkets, Inc. (DE) 11/10/1961
Allied Supermarkets, Inc. (DE) reincorporated in Michigan 08/18/1982 which name changed to Vons Companies, Inc. 07/22/1987 which merged into Safeway Inc. 04/08/1997
(See Safeway Inc.)

ACFAW COM INC (CANADA)
Recapitalized as St-Georges Platinum & Base Metals Ltd. 05/04/2010
Each share Class A Common no par exchanged for (0.5) share Common no par
St-Georges Platinum & Base Metals Ltd. name changed to St-Georges Eco-Mining Corp. 12/22/2017

ACHATES RES LTD (BC)
Reorganized under the laws of Canada as Greenhope Resources Inc. 03/31/1995
Each share Common no par exchanged for (0.2) share Common no par
Greenhope Resources Inc. name changed to Head4 Solutions Inc. 06/29/2000 which recapitalized as Saratoga Electronic Solutions Inc. 01/25/2005 which name changed to Abba Medix Group Inc. 05/14/2015 which recapitalized as Canada House Wellness Group Inc. 11/09/2016

ACHERON INC (NV)
Each share old Common $0.001 par exchanged for (0.4) share new Common $0.001 par 02/04/2008
Name changed to SJ Electronics, Inc. 05/15/2008
(See SJ Electronics, Inc.)

ACHERON MINES LTD (BC)
Recapitalized as Pan Acheron Resources Ltd. 07/30/1976
Each share Common 50¢ par exchanged for (0.25) share Common no par
Pan Acheron Resources Ltd. merged into Acheron Resources Ltd. 10/01/1982 which recapitalized as Abaddon Resources Inc. 09/12/1994 which recapitalized as Consolidated Abaddon Resources Inc. 01/31/2001 which name changed to Aben Resources Ltd. 01/13/2011

ACHERON RES LTD (BC)
Recapitalized as Abaddon Resources Inc. 09/12/1994
Each share Common no par exchanged for (0.11111111) share Common no par
Abaddon Resources Inc. recapitalized as Consolidated Abaddon Resources Inc. 01/31/2001 which name changed to Aben Resources Ltd. 01/13/2011

ACHIEVA DEV CORP (BC)
Recapitalized as Angus Ventures Corp. 07/09/2008
Each share Common no par exchanged for (0.25) share Common no par
Angus Ventures Corp. name changed to Encanto Potash Corp. 07/15/2009

ACHIEVEMENT INC (DE)
Charter cancelled and declared inoperative and void for non-payment of taxes 04/15/1973

ACHIEVEMENT TEC HLDGS INC (DE)
Name changed to Clickable Enterprises, Inc. 01/06/2004
(See Clickable Enterprises, Inc.)

ACHIEVERS MAGAZINE INC (NV)
Common $0.001 par split (8) for (5) by issuance of (0.6) additional share payable 01/21/2008 to holders of record 01/21/2008 Ex date - 01/22/2008
Name changed to China Carbon Graphite Group, Inc. 02/06/2008

ACHIEVERS TRAINING GROUP INC (CANADA)
Recapitalized 11/06/1992
Recapitalized from Achievers Media Corp. to Achievers Training Group Inc. 11/06/1992
Each share Common no par exchanged for (0.2) share Common no par
Reincorporated under the laws of British Columbia as Rockwealth International Resource Corp. 06/21/1993
Rockwealth International Resource Corp. name changed to Strathmore Resources Ltd. 08/07/1996 which recapitalized as Strathmore Minerals Corp. 09/18/2000 which merged into Energy Fuels Inc. 08/30/2013

ACHIEVOR RECOVERY LTD (NV)
Reorganized as Rapid Recovery Health Services, Inc. 03/02/2005
Each share Common $0.001 par exchanged for (7) shares Common $0.001 par
Rapid Recovery Health Services, Inc. recapitalized as Tennalta Petroleum Corp. 02/02/2007 which recapitalized as GRIT International Groups Inc. 07/10/2007 which recapitalized as GRIT International Inc. 12/23/2008

ACHILLES RES LTD (BC)
Merged into Aegis Resources Ltd. 08/01/1990
Each share Common no par exchanged for (0.22222222) share Common no par
Aegis Resources Ltd. recapitalized as New Aegis Resources Ltd. 03/17/1993 which was acquired by Norcan Resources Ltd. 08/19/1994

which recapitalized as Odyssey Exploration Inc. 06/07/2000 which recapitalized as Consolidated Odyssey Exploration Inc. 12/08/2000 which reorganized as Odyssey Petroleum Corp. 08/25/2005 which recapitalized as Petrichor Energy Inc. 03/03/2011

ACI ASSET MGMT INC (NV)
Recapitalized as Interactive Business Development, Inc. (Old) 04/27/2005
Each share Common $0.001 par exchanged for (0.5) share Common $0.001 par
Interactive Business Development, Inc. Inc. (Old) name changed to Baby Bee Bright Corp. (Old) 07/27/2005 which name changed to Lab Holdings, Inc. 05/02/2006 which name changed to Mountain Top Properties, Inc. 12/13/2006

ACI HLDGS INC (DE)
Acquired by AMR Corp. 04/30/1987
Each share Common no par exchanged for $15 cash
Under plan of dissolution each share $1.20 Conv. Exchangeable Preferred $1 par exchanged for $10.30 cash 07/15/1987
Public interest eliminated

ACI INC (DE)
Assets assigned for the benefit of creditors 00/00/1974
No stockholders' equity

ACI TELECENTRICS INC (MN)
Name changed to Jaguar Mining Enterprises, Inc. 07/31/2009
Jaguar Mining Enterprises, Inc. recapitalized as Green Street Capital Corp. 07/16/2010

ACIER LEROUX INC (QC)
Common no par reclassified as Multiple Class A no par 07/07/1993
Acquired by Russel Metals Inc. 07/28/2003
Each share Class A Multiple no par exchanged for either (1.2353) shares Common no par, (0.33333333) share Common no par and $4.60 cash or $6.30 cash
Each share Class B Subordinate no par exchanged for either (1.2353) shares Common no par, (0.33333333) share Common no par and $4.60 cash or $6.30 cash

ACIES CORP (NV)
SEC revoked common stock registration 01/21/2014

ACINO HLDG AG (SWITZERLAND)
ADR agreement terminated 07/09/2015
No ADR's remain outstanding

ACKERLEY GROUP INC (DE)
Name changed 10/02/1996
Common 1¢ par split (2) for (1) by issuance of (1) additional share payable 10/15/1996 to holders of record 10/04/1996 Ex date - 10/16/1996
Name changed from Ackerley Communications Inc. to Ackerley Group Inc. 10/02/1996
Stock Dividend - In Conv. Class B Common to holders of Common - 100% 07/29/1987
Merged into Clear Channel Communications, Inc. 06/14/2002
Each share Conv. Class B Common 1¢ par exchanged for (0.35) share Common 10¢ par
Each share Common 1¢ par exchanged for (0.35) share Common 10¢ par
(See Clear Channel Communications, Inc.)

ACKERMAN GOLD MINES LTD. (ON)
Charter cancelled and proclaimed dissolved for failure to pay taxes and file returns 03/00/1958

ACKLANDS LTD (CANADA)
Reincorporated 11/30/1996
6% 1st Preference $25 par called for redemption 02/28/1973
Conv. 2nd Preference $5 par reclassified as Conv. 3rd Preference $5 par which was converted into Common no par share for share as of 02/28/1973
6% Conv. 2nd Preference Ser. A $16 par called for redemption 03/23/1984
Place of incorporation changed from (MB) to (Canada) 11/30/1996
Name changed to Acktion Corp. 07/18/1997
Acktion Corp. name changed to Morguard Corp. 06/13/2002

ACKTION CORP (CANADA)
Name changed to Morguard Corp. 06/13/2002

ACL INTL LTD (AB)
Name changed to Bow Energy Ltd. 02/15/2017
Bow Energy Ltd. merged into Petrolia Energy Corp. 03/07/2018

ACL LABS INTL INC (NY)
Charter cancelled and proclaimed dissolved for failure to pay taxes 03/25/1981

ACL SEMICONDUCTORS INC (DE)
Common $0.001 par split (6) for (5) by issuance of (0.2) additional share payable 05/28/2012 to holders of record 05/14/2012 Ex date - 05/11/2012
Name changed to USmart Mobile Device Inc. 04/17/2013
USmart Mobile Device Inc. name changed to Eagle Mountain Corp. 05/06/2015

ACLARA BIOSCIENCES INC (DE)
Merged into ViroLogic, Inc. 12/10/2004
Each share Common $0.001 par exchanged for (1.7) shares Common $0.001 par and (1.7) Contingent Value Rights
ViroLogic, Inc. name changed to Monogram Biosciences, Inc. 09/07/2005
(See Monogram Biosciences, Inc.)

ACLOR INTL INC (DE)
SEC revoked common stock registration 06/11/2014

ACM CORP (NV)
Charter revoked 04/30/2014

ACM GOVT SECS FD INC (MD)
Merged into ACM Government Income Fund, Inc. 12/19/2000
Each share Common 1¢ par exchanged for (0.99168) share Common 1¢ par
ACM Government Income Fund, Inc. name changed to ACM Income Fund, Inc. 08/31/2001 which name changed to AllianceBernstein Income Fund, Inc. 01/26/2007

ACM GOVT SPECTRUM FD INC (MD)
Merged into ACM Government Income Fund, Inc. 12/19/2000
Each share Common 1¢ par exchanged for (0.80262) share Common 1¢ par
ACM Government Income Fund, Inc. name changed to ACM Income Fund, Inc. 08/31/2001 which name changed to AllianceBernstein Income Fund, Inc. 01/26/2007

ACM INCOME FD INC (MD)
Name changed 08/31/2001
Name changed from ACM Government Income Fund, Inc. to ACM Income Fund, Inc. 08/31/2001
Under plan of merger name changed to AllianceBernstein Income Fund, Inc. 01/26/2007

ACM MANAGED DLR INCOME FD (MD)
Acquired by AllianceBernstein Global High Income Fund, Inc. 09/25/2009
Each share Common 1¢ par exchanged for (0.5826) share Common 1¢ par

ACM MANAGED INCOME FD INC (MD)
Remarketed Preferred Ser. A called for redemption at $100,000 on 12/14/2006
Completely liquidated
Each share Common 1¢ par received first and final distribution of $3.88 cash payable 08/29/2007 to holders of record 08/20/2007
Note: Certificates were not required to be surrendered and are without value

ACM MANAGED MULTI-MKT TR INC (MD)
Reorganized as Alliance Multi-Market Strategy Trust, Inc. 05/05/1995
Each share Common 1¢ par exchanged for Class A $0.001 par on a net asset basis
Alliance Multi-Market Strategy Trust, Inc. name changed to AllianceBernstein Multi-Market Strategy Trust, Inc. 03/31/2003
(See AllianceBernstein Multi-Market Strategy Trust, Inc.)

ACM MUN SECS INCOME FD INC (MD)
Merged into AllianceBernstein National Municipal Income Fund, Inc. 05/18/2007
Each share Common 1¢ par exchanged for (0.7297) share Common $0.001 par

ACM OPPORTUNITY FD INC (MD)
Name changed 12/15/2006
Name changed from ACM Government Opportunity Fund, Inc. to ACM Opportunity Fund, Inc. 12/15/2006
Merged into AllianceBernstein Income Fund, Inc. 01/26/2007
Each share Common 1¢ par exchanged for (0.98347757) share Common 1¢ par

ACMATIC INDS INC (DE)
Name changed to National Medical Products, Inc. 12/30/1970
(See National Medical Products, Inc.)

ACME ALUMINUM ALLOYS, INC. (OH)
Name changed to Acme Precision Products, Inc. (OH) 09/17/1956
Acme Precision Products, Inc. (OH) reorganized in Delaware 09/30/1969
(See Acme Precision Products, Inc. (DE))

ACME ARTIFICIAL SILK CO.
Acquired by Acme Rayon Corp. 00/00/1926
Details not available

ACME AUDIT CO. (OH)
Voluntarily dissolved 02/14/1925
Details not available

ACME BAG & SALVAGE CO., INC.
Liquidated 00/00/1936
Details not available

ACME BRICK CO. (TX)
Name changed to First Worth Corp. 09/06/1968
First Worth Corp. recapitalized as Justin Industries Inc. 10/13/1972
(See Justin Industries, Inc.)

ACME CAP CORP (AB)
Recapitalized as Pivot Technology Solutions, Inc. 04/01/2013
Each share Common no par exchanged for (0.125) share Common no par

ACME CEMENT CORP.
Acquired by North American Cement Corp. 00/00/1926
Details not available

ACME CLEVELAND CORP (OH)
Common $1 par split (2) for (1) by issuance of (1) additional share 11/18/1968
Merged into WEC Acquisition Corp. 07/10/1996
Each share Common $1 par exchanged for $30 cash

ACME COMMUNICATIONS INC (DE)
Each share Common 1¢ par received distribution of (0.05297) share LIN TV Corp. Class A Common 1¢ par payable 12/29/2011 to holders of record 12/23/2011
Each share Common 1¢ par received distribution of (0.018695) share LIN TV Corp. Class A Common 1¢ par and $0.22 cash payable 04/10/2012 to holders of record 04/04/2012 Ex date - 04/11/2012
Completely liquidated
Each share Common 1¢ par received first and final distribution of $0.0432 cash payable 12/30/2016 to holders of record 12/26/2016 Ex date - 01/03/2017

ACME CORP. (CT)
Name changed to Acme United Corp. 07/02/1971

ACME DIE CASTING CO.
Merged into Michigan Die Casting Co. 00/00/1937
Details not available

ACME EAGLE CORP. (DE)
Merged into Allied Products Corp. (MI) 04/05/1965
Each share Common $1 par exchanged for (0.8) share Common $5 par
Allied Products Corp. (MI) reincorporated in Delaware 01/31/1968
(See Allied Products Corp. (DE))

ACME ELEC CORP (NY)
5% Preferred $10 par called for redemption 06/01/1977
Common $1 par split (2) for (1) by issuance of (1) additional share 03/21/1977
Common $1 par split (2) for (1) by issuance of (1) additional share 03/26/1979
Stock Dividends - 100% 12/18/1967; 10% 03/27/1978; 10% 03/19/1984
Merged into Key Components LLC 11/21/2000
Each share Common $1 par exchanged for $9 cash

ACME ELECTRIC & MANUFACTURING CO.
Recapitalized as Acme Electric Corp. 00/00/1946
Each share Preferred $100 par exchanged for (1) share 5% Preferred $100 par
Each share Class A or B Common no par exchanged for (16) shares Common $1 par
(See Acme Electric Corp.)

ACME ENTMT INC (NV)
Name changed to INQB8 Corp. 10/17/2005
INQB8 Corp. name changed to Aventura Resorts, Inc. 11/25/2005 which recapitalized as Borneo Resource Investments Ltd. 08/05/2011

ACME FINANCE CO. (PA)
Charter revoked for failure to file reports and pay fees 04/30/1962

ACME FUND, INC. (NY)
Merged into Burnham Fund 04/12/1973
Each share Capital Stock 1¢ par exchanged for (0.365) share Common $1 par
Burnham Fund merged into Drexel Burnham Fund 06/16/1975

ACME GAS & OIL LTD (ON)
Charter cancelled for failure to pay taxes and file returns 02/14/1978

ACME GEN CORP (CA)
Common no par split (3) for (2) by issuance of (0.5) additional share 07/28/1972
Common no par split (4) for (3) by issuance of (0.33333333) additional share 07/15/1983
Acquired by an investor group 06/14/1985
Each share Common no par exchanged for $16 cash

ACME GLOVE & APPAREL, LTD. (CANADA)
Recapitalized 00/00/1936
Each share 1st Preferred $50 par exchanged for (0.5) share Preferred $100 par and (0.2) additional share in settlement of dividend arrears
Each share 2nd Preferred $50 par exchanged for (0.25) share Preferred $100 par and (1.5) shares Common no par
Each share Class B Common no par exchanged for (1) share Common no par
Common no par exchanged (2) for (1) 00/00/1946 Bankrupt 00/00/1954
No stockholders' equity

ACME GLOVE WORKS, LTD. (CANADA)
Name changed to Acme Glove & Apparel Ltd. 02/01/1953
(See Acme Glove & Apparel Ltd.)

ACME HAMILTON MFG CORP (NJ)
Each share Common 10¢ par exchanged for (0.2) share Common 50¢ par 05/28/1965
Adjudicated bankrupt 10/15/1979
Stockholders' equity unlikely

ACME INDS INC (DE)
Stock Dividends - 10% 11/15/1950; 10% 12/15/1952; 10% 12/15/1953
Completely liquidated 06/03/1971
Each share Common $1 par exchanged for first and final distribution of (0.23) share City Investing Co. (DE) $2 Conv. Preference Ser. B $1 par
(See City Investing Co. (DE))

ACME INTL CORP (NV)
Each share Common 10¢ par exchanged for (0.2) share Common 50¢ par 03/29/1972
Name changed to Financial Business Computers, Inc. and Common 50¢ par changed to 1¢ par 05/17/1984
Financial Business Computers, Inc. name changed to Prudential Resources Inc. 05/18/1988 which name changed back to Acme International Corp. 08/13/1991 which name changed to Beckett Industries Inc. 10/05/1994 which name changed to International Supercell Ltd. 05/11/1995 which name changed to Bargaincity.com, Inc. 03/25/1999
(See Bargaincity.com, Inc.)

ACME INVESTMENTS LTD. (AB)
Name changed to Compass Investments of Alberta Ltd. 05/15/1975
(See Compass Investments of Alberta Ltd.)

ACME KNITTING MACHINE & NEEDLE CO. (NH)
Sold and liquidated 00/00/1954
Details not available

ACME MATTRESS CO., INC.
Bankrupt 00/00/1950
Details not available

ACME METALS INC (DE)
Plan of reorganization under Chapter 11 Federal Bankruptcy Code effective 11/25/2002
No stockholders' equity

ACME MINES & MILL, INC.
Reorganized as Acme Mining Co. 00/00/1931
Details not available

ACME MNG CO (CA)
Reincorporated under the laws of Nevada as Acme International Corp. 01/11/1972
Acme International Corp. name changed to Financial Business Computers, Inc. 05/17/1984 which name changed to Prudential Resources Inc. 05/08/1988 which name changed back to Acme International Corp. 08/13/1991 which name changed to Beckett Industries Inc. 10/05/1994 which name changed to International Supercell Ltd. 05/11/1995 which name changed to Bargaincity.com, Inc. 03/25/1999
(See Bargaincity.com, Inc.)

ACME MISSILES & CONSTR CORP (DE)
Charter cancelled and declared inoperative and void for non-payment of taxes 04/15/1971

ACME MKTS INC (DE)
Name changed to American Stores Co. (Old) 12/29/1973
American Stores Co. (Old) merged into American Stores Co. (New) 07/26/1979 which merged into Albertson's, Inc. 06/23/1999 which merged into Supervalu Inc. 06/02/2006

ACME MOLYBDENITE MINING CO. LTD. (QC)
Assets liquidated for benefit of creditors 09/11/1958
No stockholders' equity

ACME OIL CORP (DE)
Recapitalized as Variant Corp. (DE) 02/20/1970
Each share Common $1 par exchanged for (2) shares Common 25¢ par
Variant Corp. (DE) reincorporated in Kansas 12/24/1974
(See Variant Corp.)

ACME PACKET INC (DE)
Acquired by Oracle Corp. 03/28/2013
Each share Common $0.001 par exchanged for $29.25 cash

ACME PACKING CO. (MI)
Property sold 00/00/1927
Details not available

ACME PETROLEUM CORP. (OK)
Charter cancelled for failure to pay taxes 07/09/1965

ACME PRECISION PRODS INC (DE)
Reorganized 09/30/1969
Reorganized from under the laws of (OH) to (DE) 09/30/1969
Each share $1.10 Conv. Preferred $17.50 par exchanged for (4) shares Common $1 par
Each share Common $1 par exchanged for (1) share Common $1 par
Charter forfeited for failure to maintain registered agent 02/25/1991

ACME RAYON CO.
Out of business 00/00/1941
No stockholders' equity

ACME RAYON CORP.
Acquired by Acme Rayon Co. 00/00/1937
Details not available

ACME RES INC (BC)
Name changed to Affinity Metals Corp. 03/01/2017

ACME ROAD MACHINERY CO.
Adjudicated bankrupt 05/00/1937
No stockholders' equity

ACME SHEAR CO (CT)
Name changed to Acme Corp. 04/30/1971
Acme Corp. name changed to Acme United Corp. 07/02/1971

ACME SPORTS & ENTMT INC (NV)
Recapitalized as Casa Havana, Inc. 06/17/2008
Each share Common $0.001 par exchanged for (0.1) share Common $0.001 par
Casa Havana, Inc. name changed to Design Marketing Concepts, Inc. 12/09/2009
(See Design Marketing Concepts, Inc.)

ACME STL CO (DE)
Name changed to Acme Metals Inc. 05/26/1992
(See Acme Metals Inc.)

ACME STL CO (IL)
Each share Common $25 par exchanged for (3) shares Common $10 par 04/17/1945
$5.75 Preferred $100 par called for redemption 02/28/1964
Merged into Interlake Steel Corp. (NY) 12/22/1964
Each share $6.50 Preferred $100 par exchanged for (1) share $6.50 Preferred $100 par
Each share Common $10 par exchanged for (0.7) share Common $1 par
Interlake Steel Corp. (NY) reincorporated in Delaware as Interlake, Inc. 05/15/1970 which reorganized as Interlake Corp. 05/29/1986
Stock Dividend - 100% 06/15/1949
(See Interlake Corp.)

ACME UNITED LIFE INSURANCE CO. (GA)
Merged into American Heritage Life Insurance Co. 10/31/1960
Each share Common $10 par exchanged for (0.8) share Common $1 par
American Heritage Life Insurance Co. reorganized as American Heritage Life Investment Corp. 12/31/1968 which merged into Allstate Corp. 10/31/1999

ACME UNITED LIFE INSURANCE CO. (IL)
Merged into Bankers United Life Assurance Co. 02/09/1967
Each share Common $1 par exchanged for (1) share Common $1 par
(See Bankers United Life Assurance Co.)

ACME URANIUM MINES, INC. (DE)
Recapitalized as United American Industries Inc. 09/24/1968
Each share Common 1¢ par exchanged for (0.05) share Common 20¢ par
(See United American Industries Inc.)

ACME VISIBLE RECORDS INC (DE)
Common $1 par changed to 50¢ par and (0.5) additional share issued 03/09/1966
Merged into American Brands, Inc. (NJ) 10/01/1970
Each share Common 50¢ par exchanged for $47.50 cash

ACME WIRE CO. (CT)
Each share Common $20 par exchanged for (2) shares Common $10 par 00/00/1939
Stock Dividend - 50% 04/24/1951
Merged into Acme Eagle Corp. share for share 05/08/1964
Acme Eagle Corp. merged into Allied Products Corp. (MI) 04/05/1965 which reincorporated in Delaware 01/31/1968
(See Allied Products Corp. (DE))

ACNIELSEN CORP (DE)
Merged into VNU N.V. 02/16/2001
Each share Common 1¢ par exchanged for $36.75 cash

ACOI INC (NV)
Name changed to Hallmark Financial Services Inc. 01/06/1994

ACOJE MNG INC (PHILIPPINES)
Stock Dividends - 50% 08/04/1960; 25% 12/29/1961
Each share Common 10 Centavos par exchanged for (10) shares Common 1 Centavo par 07/15/1974
Delisted from Philippine Stock Exchange 07/17/1998

ACOLA CORP (DE)
Each share old Common $0.0001 par exchanged for (0.025) share new Common $0.0001 par 03/11/2004
Name changed to Teda Travel Group Inc. 04/21/2004
Teda Travel Group Inc. name changed to Network CN, Inc. 08/15/2006

ACOLOGY INC (FL)
Name changed to Medtainer, Inc. 10/05/2018

ACOMA URANIUM & OIL CORP. (DE)
Dissolved 05/18/1966
No stockholders' equity

ACONDA MINES LTD. (ON)
Inactive since the late 1930's Has no assets; made no distributions

ACONIC MNG CORP (QC)
Each VTC for Capital Stock $1 par exchanged for (1) share Capital Stock $1 par 01/18/1962
Declared dissolved for failure to file reports or pay fees 06/01/1974

ACORDIA INC (DE)
Merged into Anthem Insurance Companies, Inc. 07/15/1997
Each share Common $1 par exchanged for $40 cash

ACORDIA PORCUPINE GOLD MINES LTD.
Succeeded by Delcore Porcupine Mines Ltd. on a (1) for (2) basis 00/00/1944
(See Delcore Porcupine Mines Ltd.)

ACORN FACTOR INC (DE)
Name changed to Acorn Energy, Inc. 01/01/2008

ACORN HLDG CORP (DE)
Each share old Common 1¢ par exchanged for (0.4) share new Common 1¢ par 04/19/1999
Name changed to Valentec Systems, Inc. 04/17/2006
(See Valentec Systems, Inc.)

ACORN INCOME CORP (AB)
Completely liquidated
Each share Class A no par received first and final distribution of $0.316 cash payable 07/18/2014 to holders of record 07/14/2014

ACORN INDUSTRIES, INC. (NY)
Adjudicated bankrupt 10/00/1960
Stockholders' equity unlikely

ACORN INVT TR (MA)
Reincorporated 01/01/1981
Reorganized 07/01/1992
State of incorporation changed from (DE) to (MD) 01/01/1981
Reorganized from Acorn Fund, Inc. (MD) to Acorn Investment Trust (MA) 07/01/1992
Acorn Fund $1 par split (5) for (1) by issuance of (4) additional shares 12/16/1993
Name changed to Liberty Acorn Trust 09/29/2000
Liberty Acorn Trust name changed to Columbia Acorn Trust 10/13/2003

ACORN MINERALS LTD. (ON)
Name changed to Spearhead Explorations Ltd. 11/00/1952
(See Spearhead Explorations Ltd.)

ACORN PETROLEUM CORP. (DE)
No longer in existence having

become inoperative and void for non-payment of taxes 03/18/1925

ACORN PRODS INC (DE)
Each share old Common $0.001 par exchanged for (0.1) share new Common $0.001 par 11/21/2002
Merged into Oaktree Capital Management LLC 05/05/2003
Each share new Common $0.001 par exchanged for $3.50 cash

ACORN RES LTD (BC)
Recapitalized as Consolidated Acorn Resources Ltd. 07/23/1990
Each share Common no par exchanged for (0.2) share Common no par
(See Consolidated Acorn Resources Ltd.)

ACORN SECS LTD (AUSTRALIA)
Recapitalized as Indonesian Diamond Ltd. 06/13/1990
Each ADR for Ordinary exchanged for (0.1) ADR for Ordinary
(See Indonesian Diamond Ltd.)

ACORN VENTURE CAP CORP (DE)
Name changed to Acorn Holding Corp. 11/06/1997
Acorn Holding Corp. name changed to Valentec Systems, Inc. 04/17/2006
(See Valentec Systems, Inc.)

ACOUSTIC CHEM CORP (NY)
Each share Common 1¢ par exchanged for (0.1) share Common 10¢ par 11/16/1967
Name changed to A.C. Organization Ltd. 05/15/1970
(See A.C. Organization Ltd.)

ACOUSTICA ASSOC INC (NY)
Charter cancelled and proclaimed dissolved for failure to pay taxes 03/25/1981

ACOUSTICON SYS CORP (DE)
Out of business 09/00/1977
Details not available

ACP ACE VENTURE CORP (YT)
Name changed to Cantronic Systems Inc. (YT) 03/01/2005
Cantronic Systems Inc. (YT) merged into Cantronic Systems Inc. (BC) 11/30/2006
(See Cantronic Systems Inc.)

ACQUA GROUP INC (DE)
Each share Common $0.001 par exchanged for (0.5) share Common $0.002 par 05/07/1993
Charter cancelled and declared inoperative and void for non-payment of taxes 03/01/1997

ACQUALIN RES LTD (BC)
Name changed to Cobra Enterprises Ltd. 10/22/1985
Cobra Enterprises Ltd. recapitalized as MVS Modular Vehicle Systems Ltd. 08/22/1994 which recapitalized as Cobra Pacific Systems Inc. 03/28/1996 which name changed to Marathon Foods Inc. 02/16/1998

ACQUERRE CORP. (MN)
Name changed to Raster Devices Corp. 06/16/1989
Raster Devices Corp. name changed to Lasermaster Technologies, Inc. 06/22/1990 which name changed to Virtualfund.com, Inc. 04/01/1998 which recapitalized as ASFG, Inc. 08/11/2004

ACQUEST CORP (NV)
Charter permanently revoked 02/28/2000

ACQUEST ENTERPRISES LTD (BC)
Struck off register and declared dissolved for failure to file returns 09/27/1991

ACQUICOR TECHNOLOGY INC (DE)
Name changed to Jazz Technologies, Inc. 02/21/2007
Jazz Technologies, Inc. merged into Tower Semiconductor Ltd. 09/17/2008

ACQUIRE LTD (UT)
Reincorporated under the laws of Delaware and Common $0.005 par changed to 1¢ par 05/15/1981

ACQUISICORP CAP LTD (BC)
Struck off register and declared dissolved for failure to file returns 01/22/1993

ACQUISITION CAPABILITY INC (DE)
Each share old Common $0.0001 par exchanged for (0.125) share new Common $0.001 par 01/02/1991
Name changed to Actrade International, Ltd. 10/14/1992
Actrade International, Ltd. name changed to Actrade Financial Technologies, Ltd. 08/21/2000
(See Actrade Financial Technologies Ltd.)

ACQUISITION INC (NV)
Name changed to Nightwing Group, Inc. 10/23/1987
Nightwing Group, Inc. name changed to Nightwing Entertainment Group, Inc. 12/25/1995 which name changed to Entertainment Arts Inc. 03/13/2000

ACQUISITION INDS INC (CO)
Administratively dissolved 05/02/1995

ACQUISITION MEDIA, INC. (NV)
Name changed to Actionview International, Inc. 08/20/2003
Actionview International, Inc. recapitalized as AVEW Holdings, Inc. 07/31/2015

ACQUISITION NEWSLETTER INC (DE)
Merged into National Modular Housing Components Inc. 06/28/1971
Each share Common 1¢ par exchanged for (1) share Common 1¢ par
(See National Modular Housing Components Inc.)

ACQUISITOR MINES LTD (CANADA)
Reincorporated 01/29/1987
Place of incorporation changed from (BC) to (Canada) 01/29/1987
Involuntarily dissolved for failure to file annual returns 05/02/2002

ACQUITRON INC (MN)
Name changed to Beltron Computer Corp. 07/29/1987
(See Beltron Computer Corp.)

ACQUITY GROUP LTD (CAYMAN ISLANDS)
Acquired by Accenture Holdings B.V. 07/08/2013
Each Sponsored ADS for Ordinary exchanged for $12.95 cash

ACQUIVENTURE INC (UT)
Name changed to IIBA Holdings, Inc. 06/24/1988
(See IIBA Holdings, Inc.)

ACR GROUP INC (TX)
Merged into Watsco, Inc. 08/10/2007
Each share Common 1¢ par exchanged for $6.75 cash

ACRES GAMING INC (NV)
Merged into International Game Technology 10/27/2003
Each share Common 1¢ par exchanged for $11.50 cash

ACRES LTD (AB)
Reincorporated 04/24/1975
Place of incorporation changed from (ON) to (AB) 04/24/1975
Acquired by Traders Group Ltd. 09/10/1975
Each share 7.2% Preference Ser. A $50 par exchanged for (1) share 7.5% Preferred $50 par
Each share Common no par exchanged for (0.6) shares Class A Common no par and $5 cash
(See Traders Group Ltd.)

ACREX VENTURES LTD (BC)
Recapitalized as Alba Minerals Ltd. 07/10/2014
Each share Common no par exchanged for (0.2) share Common no par

ACRITE INDS INC (NY)
Common 10¢ par split (2) for (1) by issuance of (1) additional share 01/20/1970
Adjudicated bankrupt 12/31/1974
No stockholders' equity

ACRO CHEM PRODS CORP (NJ)
In process of liquidation
Each share Common $1 par exchanged for initial distribution of $2 cash 12/30/1980
Each share Common $1 par received second distribution of $1.4133 cash 07/15/1981
Note: Details on subsequent distributions, if any, are not available

ACRO ELECTRONIC PRODUCTS CO. (PA)
Merged into Castle Group, Inc. (DE) 10/01/1971
Each share Class A Common $1 par exchanged for (1) share Common 1¢ par
(See Castle Group, Inc. (DE))

ACRO ENERGY CORP (CA)
Chapter 11 Federal Bankruptcy Code converted to Chapter 7 on 09/27/1989
Stockholders' equity unlikely

ACRO ENERGY TECHNOLOGIES CORP (BC)
Acquired by Lonestar Renewable Technologies Corp. 04/11/2012
Each share Common no par exchanged for $0.04 cash

ACRO INC (NV)
Old Common $0.001 par split (2) for (1) by issuance of (1) additional share payable 11/02/2006 to holders of record 10/30/2006 Ex date - 11/03/2006
Each share old Common $0.001 par exchanged for (0.1) share new Common $0.001 par 01/13/2012
Recapitalized as TransAtlantic Capital Inc. 08/08/2014
Each share new Common $0.001 par exchanged for (0.00666666) share Common $0.001 par

ACRO MANUFACTURING CO. (OH)
Acquired by Robertshaw-Fulton Controls Co. 01/10/1957
Each share Common 25¢ par exchanged for (1) share Common $1 par
Robertshaw-Fulton Controls Co. name changed to Robertshaw Controls Co. 04/10/1963
(See Robertshaw Controls Co.)

ACROBE AUTOMATION TECHNOLOGY INC (FL)
Involuntarily dissolved for failure to file reports and pay fees 11/04/1988

ACROBOO INC (NV)
Name changed to Ezy Cloud Holding Inc. 03/09/2016

ACRODYNE COMMUNICATIONS INC (DE)
Name changed 06/09/1995
Name changed from Acrodyne Holdings, Inc. to Acrodyne Communications, Inc. 06/09/1995
Assets sold for the benefit of creditors and voluntarily dissolved 02/17/2010
No stockholders' equity

ACROFUND LTD (CANADA)
Name changed to Bullock Growth Fund Ltd. 04/00/1985
(See Bullock Growth Fund Ltd.)

ACROLL PETES LTD (AB)
Recapitalized 12/30/1977
Recapitalized from Acroll Oil & Gas Ltd. to Acroll Petroleums Ltd. 12/30/1977
Each share Common no par exchanged for (0.25) share Common no par
Merged into Trans-Canada Resources Ltd. (New) 11/01/1982
Each share Common no par exchanged for (0.43478260) share Class A Common no par
Trans-Canada Resources Ltd. (New) recapitalized as Consolidated Trans-Canada Resources Ltd. 09/22/1988 which merged into Ranchmen's Resources Ltd. 09/30/1989 which merged into Crestar Energy Inc. 10/11/1995 which was acquired by Gulf Canada Resources Ltd. 11/13/2000
(See Gulf Canada Resources Ltd.)

ACRON GENOMICS INC (NV)
SEC revoked common stock registration 04/23/2014

ACROPOLIS PRECIOUS METALS INC (NV)
Name changed to China Prosperous Clean Energy Corp. 10/14/2008

ACROSS AMER FINL SVCS INC (CO)
Name changed to Omni Bio Pharmaceutical, Inc. 07/21/2009

ACROSS AMER REAL ESTATE CORP (CO)
Name changed 07/27/2005
Name changed from Across America Real Estate Development Corp. to Across America Real Estate Corp. 07/27/2005
Recapitalized as Capterra Financial Group, Inc. (CO) 07/21/2008
Each share Common $0.001 par exchanged for (0.5) share Common $0.001 par
Capterra Financial Group, Inc. (CO) reincorporated in Delaware as NexCore Healthcare Capital Corp. 04/14/2011
(See NexCore Healthcare Capital Corp.)

ACROSS AMER REAL ESTATE EXCHANGE INC (CO)
Name changed to Accredited Members Holding Corp. 05/27/2010
Accredited Members Holding Corp. name changed to Hangover Joe's Holding Corp. 08/01/2012

ACROSS CANADA TRUST SHARES, SERIES 10
Trust terminated 00/00/1936
Details not available

ACROSS DATA SYS INC (NY)
Name changed to Level 8 Systems, Inc. (NY) 10/04/1996
Level 8 Systems, Inc. (NY) reincorporated in Delaware 06/23/1999 which recapitalized as Cicero, Inc. 01/16/2007

ACROTECH INC (NV)
Charter revoked for failure to file reports and pay fees 02/01/1990

ACRYLIC OPTICS CORP (DE)
Stock Dividend - 100% 08/15/1977
Name changed to D.O.C. Optics Corp. 06/30/1981
(See D.O.C. Optics Corp.)

ACRYVIN CORP. OF AMERICA (DE)
Stock Dividend - 10% 09/07/1955
No longer in existence having become inoperative and void for non-payment of taxes 04/01/1958

ACS ENTERPRISES INC (PA)
Common 5¢ par split (3) for (1) by issuance of (2) additional shares 10/29/1993
Each share Common 1¢ par exchanged for (0.2) share Common 5¢ par 12/01/1992

ACS-ACT

Merged into CAI Wireless Systems, Inc. 09/29/1995
Each share Common 5¢ par exchanged for (1.65) shares Common no par and $3.50 cash
CAI Wireless Systems, Inc. merged into MCI Worldcom, Inc. 08/31/1999 which name changed to WorldCom Inc. (New) 05/01/2000
(See WorldCom Inc. (New))

ACS FREEZERS INCOME TR (ON)
Name changed to Atlas Cold Storage Income Trust 06/25/2001
(See Atlas Cold Storage Income Trust)

ACS HLDGS INC (NV)
Each share old Common $0.001 par exchanged for (0.025) share new Common $0.001 par 08/25/2004
Recapitalized as Kairos Holdings Inc. 05/27/2005
Each share new Common $0.001 par exchanged for (0.0008) share Common $0.001 par
Kairos Holdings Inc. name changed to VitalTrust Business Development Corp. 02/27/2007 which name changed to Renew Energy Resources, Inc. 05/27/2008
(See Renew Energy Resources, Inc.)

ACS INDS INC (RI)
Each share Common 10¢ par exchanged for (0.001) share Common $100 par 05/18/1990
Note: Holders of (999) or fewer pre-split shares received an undetermined amount of cash and public interest was eliminated

ACS INVS INC (TX)
Merged into Mercantile National Bank (Dallas, TX) 12/01/1975
Each share Common 10¢ par exchanged for $2 cash

ACS MEDIA INCOME FD (ON)
Fund terminated 11/24/2006
Each Unit no par received $9.40 cash

ACS MOTION CONTROL LTD (ISRAEL)
Acquired by KZAI Systems Ltd. 12/21/2016
Each share Ordinary ILS 0.01 par exchanged for $3.50 cash

ACS SYS INC (DE)
Filed a petition under Chapter 7 Federal Bankrupcy Code 02/18/1988
No stockholders' equity

ACS-TECH80 LTD (ISRAEL)
Name changed 03/05/2001
Name changed from A.C.S. Electronics Ltd. to ACS-Tech80 Ltd. 03/05/2001
Name changed to ACS Motion Control Ltd. 04/03/2006
(See ACS Motion Control Ltd.)

ACSI-BIOREX INC (CANADA)
Voluntarily dissolved 10/18/1993
Details not available

ACSI GROUP LTD (CANADA)
Reorganized as ACSI-BIOREX Inc. 01/01/1989
Details not available

ACSYS INC (GA)
Merged into Tiberia B.V. 07/06/2000
Each share Common no par exchanged for $5 cash

ACT AURORA CTL TECHNOLOGIES CORP (BC)
Name changed to Aurora Solar Technologies Inc. 05/28/2015

ACT INTL INC (NV)
SEC revoked common stock registration 05/09/2008

ACT MFG INC (DE)
Plan of reorganization under Chapter 11 Federal Bankruptcy Code effective 08/25/2003
No stockholders' equity

ACT NETWORKS INC (DE)
Merged into Clarent Corp. 08/10/2000
Each share Common 1¢ par exchanged for (0.4198) share Common $0.001 par
(See Clarent Corp.)

ACT TELECONFERENCING INC (CO)
Acquired by Premiere Global Services, Inc. 09/10/2013
Each share Conv. Preferred Ser. A no par exchanged for $286.5438 cash
Each share Conv. Preferred Ser. A no par received an additional distribution of $29.62795500 cash from escrow 01/13/2016
No Common stockholders' equity

ACTAVA GROUP INC (DE)
Under plan of merger name changed to Metromedia International Group, Inc. 11/01/1995
(See Metromedia International Group, Inc.)

ACTAVIS INC (NV)
Reorganized under the laws of Ireland as Actavis PLC 10/01/2013
Each share Common $0.0033 par exchanged for (1) share Ordinary USD$0.0001 par
Actavis PLC name changed to Allergan PLC 06/15/2015

ACTAVIS PLC (IRELAND)
Name changed to Allergan PLC 06/15/2015

ACTEL CORP (CA)
Acquired by Microsemi Corp. 11/02/2010
Each share Common $0.001 par exchanged for $20.88 cash

ACTELION LTD (SWITZERLAND)
Each ADR for Ordinary received distribution of $3.92827 cash payable 07/17/2017 to holders of record 07/10/2017 Ex date - 07/06/2017
ADR agreement terminated 12/08/2017
Each ADR for Ordinary issued by Bank of New York exchanged for $69.95 cash

ACTEON GOLD MINES LTD. (BC)
Charter revoked for failure to file reports and pay fees 04/11/1957

ACTERNA CORP (DE)
Plan of reorganization under Chapter 11 Federal Bankruptcy Code effective 10/14/2003
No stockholders' equity

ACTFIT COM INC (ON)
Name changed to Telum International Corp. 12/05/2001
(See Telum International Corp.)

ACTIDEV INC (QC)
Name changed to Alimentation Couche-Tard Inc. 12/15/1994

ACTIGA CORP (NV)
Name changed to Avisio, Inc. 08/20/2009
Avisio, Inc. recapitalized as Deal A Day Group Corp. 11/03/2011

ACTING SCOUT INC (NV)
Name changed to Goldtown Investments Corp. 09/20/2007
Goldtown Investments Corp. name changed to Global Health Ventures Inc. 10/24/2008 which recapitalized as Kedem Pharmaceuticals Inc. 11/07/2011
(See Kedem Pharmaceuticals Inc.)

ACTION ASSOC INC (DE)
Name changed to SRSI Capital Group Inc. 10/09/1987
SRSI Capital Group Inc. name changed to Sector Associates, Ltd. 01/17/1989 which recapitalized as Viragen (Europe) Ltd. 01/08/1996 which name changed to Viragen International, Inc. 03/27/2002
(See Verigen International, Inc.)

ACTION AUTO RENT INC (DE)
Common 1¢ par split (3) for (2) by issuance of (0.5) additional share 09/15/1988
Liquidating Plan of Reorganization under Chapter 11 Federal Bankruptcy Code effective 06/28/1994
No stockholders' equity

ACTION AUTO STORES INC (MI)
Plan of reorganization under Chapter 11 Federal Bankruptcy proceedings confirmed 11/05/1992
No stockholders' equity

ACTION CARD EXPRESS INC (MN)
Name changed to O-Jay Inc. 09/11/1990
O-Jay Inc. name changed to Omni International Trading, Inc. 04/13/1993
(See Omni International Trading, Inc.)

ACTION COMMUNICATIONS INC (CO)
Administratively dissolved 08/01/2001.

ACTION COVERS INC (UT)
Proclaimed dissolved for failure to file reports 05/01/1991

ACTION DISCOUNT DOLLARS CORP. (DE)
Adjudicated bankrupt 10/17/1963
No stockholders' equity

ACTION DYNAMICS INC (CO)
Each share old Common $0.0001 par exchanged for (0.01) share new Common $0.0001 par 10/29/1990
Charter suspended for failure to maintain a resident agent 12/21/1991

ACTION ENERGY CORP (NV)
Name changed to SMC Recordings Inc. 09/03/2009
SMC Recordings Inc. recapitalized as SMC Entertainment, Inc. 05/06/2011

ACTION ENERGY INC (AB)
Discharged from receivership 10/19/2010
No stockholders' equity

ACTION ENTERPRISES CORP (DE)
Name changed to General Enterprises Corp. 06/06/1973
(See General Enterprises Corp.)

ACTION FASHIONS LTD (CO)
Reincorporated under the laws of Nevada as Mexus Gold US 11/05/2009

ACTION INDUSTRIES INC. (MO)
Charter forfeited for failure to file reports 01/01/1979

ACTION INDS INC (NV)
Reincorporated 03/05/2008
State of incorporation changed from (GA) to (NV) 03/05/2008
Recapitalized as Longhai Steel Inc. 07/16/2010
Each share Common $0.001 par exchanged for (0.008) share Common $0.001 par

ACTION INDS INC (PA)
Common 10¢ par split (5) for (4) by issuance of (0.25) additional share 04/15/1970
Common 10¢ par split (3) for (2) by issuance of (0.5) additional share 05/31/1972
Common 10¢ par split (3) for (1) by issuance of (2) additional shares 07/21/1983
Recapitalized as SkyFrames Communications, Inc. 01/09/2007
Each share Common 10¢ par exchanged for (0.005) share Common 10¢ par
SkyFrames Communications, Inc. name changed to Princeton Holdings, Inc. 06/13/2007 which name changed to Axiom Management, Inc. 07/24/2007
(See Axiom Management, Inc.)

ACTION MINERALS INC (BC)
Recapitalized as Aroway Minerals Inc. 02/05/2009
Each share Common no par exchanged for (0.025) share Common no par
Aroway Minerals Inc. name changed to Aroway Energy Inc. 02/04/2011
(See Aroway Energy Inc.)

ACTION PACKETS INC (FL)
Common $0.001 par changed to $0.000025 par and (39) additional shares issued 11/07/1986
Recapitalized as Action Products International, Inc. (FL) 06/01/1988
Each share Common $0.000025 par exchanged for (0.025) share Common $0.001 par
Action Products International, Inc. (FL) reincorporated in Nevada as COREwafer Industries, Inc. 05/25/2012 which recapitalized as Aluf Holdings, Inc. 08/31/2015

ACTION PERFORMANCE COS INC (AZ)
Common 1¢ par split (2) for (1) by issuance of (1) additional share payable 05/28/1996 to holders of record 05/03/1996
Merged into Motorsports Authentics, Inc. 12/09/2005
Each share Common 1¢ par exchanged for $13 cash

ACTION PRODS INC (CO)
Each share Common $0.0001 par exchanged for (0.01) share Common 1¢ par 08/25/1989
Merged into Action Products, Inc. (AZ) 08/25/1989
Details not available

ACTION PRODS INTL INC (FL)
Each share Common $0.001 par received distribution of (1) Common Stock Purchase Warrant expiring 06/09/2006 payable 06/30/2003 to holders of record 06/12/2003
Each share Common $0.001 par received distribution of (1) Common Stock Purchase Warrant expiring 01/06/2006 payable 01/24/2005 to holders of record 01/07/2005
Each share Common $0.001 par received distribution of (1) Common Stock Purchase Warrant expiring 01/31/2008 payable 07/20/2006 to holders of record 07/18/2006
Stock Dividend - 5% payable 11/11/2011 to holders of record 10/22/2011 Ex date - 10/19/2011
Reincorporated under the laws of Nevada as COREwafer Industries, Inc. 05/25/2012
COREwafer Industries, Inc. recapitalized as Aluf Holdings, Inc. 08/31/2015

ACTION RES LTD (BC)
Merged into Interaction Resources Ltd. (BC) 12/22/1982
Each share Common no par exchanged for (0.25) share Common no par
Interaction Resources Ltd. (BC) reincorporated in Alberta 04/28/1994 which recapitalized as Ketch Energy Ltd. 06/16/2000 which merged into Acclaim Energy Trust 10/01/2002
(See Acclaim Energy Trust)

ACTION SVGS BK S L A (SOMERS POINT, NJ)
Placed in receivership and assets subsequently sold 10/25/1991
No stockholders' equity

ACTION SPORTS INTL (WY)
Recapitalized 01/15/1999
Recapitalized from Action Sports Ltd. to Action Sports International, Inc. 01/15/1999
Each share Common no par exchanged for (0.03333333) share Common no par

Recapitalized as United Sports International, Inc. 07/09/1999
Each share Common no par exchanged for (0.03333333) share Common no par
United Sports International, Inc. recapitalized as Tour Design International, Inc. 04/12/2000 which name changed to Carolina Co. At Pinehurst Inc. 10/31/2001
(See Carolina Co. At Pinehurst Inc.)

ACTION STAFFING INC (NY)
Stock Dividend - 100% 04/24/1989
Dissolved by proclamation 09/27/1995

ACTION STKS INC (NV)
Recapitalized as Specialized Home Medical Services, Inc. 07/03/2003
Each share Common $0.001 par exchanged for (0.5) share Common $0.001 par
Specialized Home Medical Services, Inc. name changed to IGSM Group, Inc. 11/23/2007 which recapitalized as Continental Rail Corp. 08/09/2013 which recapitalized as MediXall Group, Inc. 11/22/2016

ACTION TECHNOLOGY INC (UT)
Recapitalized as Atlantic Turnkey Corp. (UT) 12/07/1992
Each share Common $0.001 par exchanged for (0.05) share Common $0.001 par
Atlantic Turnkey Corp. (UT) reorganized in Nevada as NuVoci, Inc. 01/28/2005 which reorganized as Cyberhand Technologies International, Inc. 05/13/2005 which name changed to ChromoCure, Inc. 07/09/2009

ACTION TRADERS INC (ON)
Name changed to ATI Corp. 06/21/1988
ATI Corp. name changed to Prairie Capital Inc. (ON) 06/30/1999 which reorganized in Canada as Continental (CBOC) Corp. 08/30/2002 which name changed to Stonington Capital Corp. 06/22/2004 which merged into Pyxis Capital Inc. 02/27/2006
(See Pyxis Capital Inc.)

ACTIONPOINT INC (DE)
Name changed to Captiva Software Corp. 08/01/2002
(See Captiva Software Corp.)

ACTIONS SEMICONDUCTOR CO LTD (CAYMAN ISLANDS)
Acquired by Supernova Investment Ltd. 12/16/2016
Each ADR for Ordinary exchanged for $2.15 cash

ACTIONVIEW INTL INC (NV)
Each share old Common $0.001 par exchanged for (0.0025) share new Common $0.001 par 04/03/2009
Recapitalized as AVEW Holdings, Inc. 07/31/2015
Each share new Common $0.001 par exchanged for (0.00333333) share Common $0.001 par

ACTIONWEAR INC (CO)
Charter suspended for failure to file annual reports 09/28/1981

ACTIS GLOBAL VENTURES INC (NV)
SEC revoked common stock registration 12/15/2011

ACTIVCARD CORP (DE)
Name changed to ActivIdentity Corp. 02/27/2006
(See ActivIdentity Corp.)

ACTIVCARD S A (FRANCE)
94.8% acquired by Activcard Corp. through voluntary exchange offer of (1) share Common $0.001 par for each Sponsored ADR for Common which expired 02/03/2003
Note: An additional 4.6% was acquired through a follow-on exchange offer of (0.95) share Common for each ADR which expired 07/17/2003
Public interest eliminated
Activcard Corp. name changed to ActivIdentity Corp. 02/27/2006

ACTIVE APPAREL GROUP INC (DE)
Name changed to Everlast Worldwide Inc. 10/24/2000
(See Everlast Worldwide Inc.)

ACTIVE ASSETS & ASSOC INC (BC)
Recapitalized as Focus Ventures Ltd. (BC) 05/16/2002
Each share Common no par exchanged for (0.1) share Common no par
Focus Ventures Ltd. (BC) reorganized in Yukon as CROPS Inc. 04/23/2018

ACTIVE BIOTECH AB (SWEDEN)
ADR agreement terminated 05/21/2018
No ADR's remain outstanding

ACTIVE BUYERS NETWORK INC (MN)
Recapitalized as Syneco Systems, Inc. 10/31/1985
Each share Common no par exchanged for (0.2) share Common 1¢ par
(See Syneco Systems, Inc.)

ACTIVE CAP INC (DE)
Charter cancelled and declared inoperative and void for non-payment of taxes 03/01/1994

ACTIVE CTL TECHNOLOGY INC (ON)
Each share old Common no par exchanged for (1) share new Common no par to reflect a (1) for (100) reverse split by a (100) for (1) forward split 08/20/2007
Note: Holders of (99) or fewer pre-split shares received $0.227 cash per share
Each share new Common no par exchanged again for (0.05) share new Common no par 08/18/2011
Each share new Common no par exchanged again for (1) share new Common no par to reflect a (1) for (100) reverse split followed by a (100) for (1) forward split 08/12/2013
Note: Holders of (99) or fewer pre-split shares received $0.04 cash per share
Acquired by 2421987 Ontario Ltd. 08/07/2014
Each share new Common no par exchanged for $0.03 cash
Note: Unexchanged certificates were cancelled and became without value 08/07/2015

ACTIVE GOLD CORP (NV)
Each share old Common $0.001 par exchanged for (0.1) share new Common $0.001 par 03/12/1997
Voluntarily dissolved 10/16/2015
Details not available

ACTIVE GROWTH CAP INC (CANADA)
Reorganized 07/22/2013
Reorganized from under the laws of (ON) to (Canada) 07/22/2013
Each share Common no par exchanged for (0.2) share Common no par
Name changed to Quantum Numbers Corp. 12/06/2016

ACTIVE IQ TECHNOLOGIES INC (MN)
Name changed to Wits Basin Precious Minerals Inc. 07/10/2003

ACTIVE LINK COMMUNICATIONS INC (CO)
Filed a petition under Chapter 7 Federal Bankruptcy Code 09/15/2003
No stockholders' equity

ACTIVE NETWORK INC (DE)
Acquired by Athlaction Holdings, LLC 11/15/2013
Each share Common $0.001 par exchanged for $14.50 cash

ACTIVE PWR INC (DE)
Each share old Common $0.001 par exchanged for (0.2) share new Common $0.001 par 12/24/2012
Name changed to P10 Industries, Inc. 11/30/2016
P10 Industries, Inc. name changed to P10 Holdings, Inc. 12/05/2017

ACTIVE SOFTWARE INC (DE)
Merged into webMethods, Inc. 08/16/2000
Each share Common $0.001 par exchanged for (0.527) share Common 1¢ par
(See webMethods, Inc.)

ACTIVE VOICE CORP (WA)
Common no par split (2) for (1) by issuance of (1) additional share payable 03/22/2000 to holders of record 03/08/2000
Merged into Cisco Systems, Inc. 02/14/2001
Each share Common no par exchanged for (0.5796) share Common no par

ACTIVE WEIGHTING FDS ETF TR (DE)
Trust terminated 04/24/2018
Each share Democratic Policies Fund no par received $21.326636 cash
Each share Republican Policies Fund no par received $22.494039 cash
(Additional Information in Active)

ACTIVE WITH ME INC (NV)
Common $0.001 par split (3.25) for (1) by issuance of (2.25) additional shares payable 09/19/2016 to holders of record 08/16/2016 Ex date - 09/20/2016
Name changed to Rasna Therapeutics, Inc. 09/27/2016

ACTIVECORE TECHNOLOGIES INC (NV)
SEC revoked common stock registration 03/01/2011

ACTIVENERGY INCOME FD (AB)
Under plan of reorganization each Trust Unit automatically became (1) share Middlefield Mutual Funds Ltd. ACTIVEnergy Income Fund Ser. F 06/05/2017
Note: U.S. holders were redeemed for cash

ACTIVEWORLDS CORP (DE)
Name changed 06/27/2001
Each share old Common $0.001 par exchanged for (0.66666666) share new Common $0.001 par 04/10/2000
Name changed from Activeworlds.com, Inc. to Activeworlds Corp. 06/27/2001
Name changed to Kingold Jewelry Inc. 02/18/2010

ACTIVIDENTITY CORP (DE)
Acquired by ASSA ABLOY Inc. 12/16/2010
Each share Common $0.001 par exchanged for $3.25 cash

ACTIVISION INC NEW (DE)
Reincorporated 12/15/1992
Name changed to Mediagenic 08/17/1988 which recapitalized back to Activision, Inc. (CA) 08/03/1992
State of incorporation changed from (CA) to (DE) 12/15/1992
Each share Common no par exchanged for (0.33333333) share Common $0.00001 par 10/20/1993
Common $0.00001 par split (3) for (2) by issuance of (0.5) additional share payable 11/20/2001 to holders of record 11/06/2001 Ex date - 11/21/2001
Common $0.00001 par split (3) for (2) by issuance of (0.5) additional share payable 06/06/2003 to holders of record 05/16/2003 Ex date - 06/09/2003
Common $0.00001 par split (3) for (2) by issuance of (0.5) additional share payable 03/15/2004 to holders of record 02/23/2004 Ex date - 03/16/2004
Common $0.00001 par split (4) for (3) by issuance of (0.33333333) additional share payable 03/22/2005 to holders of record 03/07/2005 Ex date - 03/23/2005
Common $0.00001 par split (4) for (3) by issuance of (0.33333333) additional share payable 10/24/2005 to holders of record 10/10/2005 Ex date - 10/25/2005
Name changed to Activision Blizzard, Inc. 07/09/2008

ACTMEDIA INC (DE)
Common 1¢ par split (3) for (2) by issuance of (0.5) additional share 05/22/1985
Common 1¢ par split (3) for (2) by issuance of (0.5) additional share 03/16/1987
Merged into Heritage Media Corp. (IA) 07/19/1989
Each share Common 1¢ par exchanged for (3.1795) shares Class A Common 1¢ par
Heritage Media Corp. (IA) reincorporated in Delaware 07/15/1996 which merged into News Corp., Ltd. 08/20/1997 which reorganized as News Corp. (Old) 11/03/2004 which name changed to Twenty-First Century Fox, Inc. 07/01/2013

ACTOMA RES LTD (BC)
Struck off register and declared dissolved for failure to file returns 03/05/1993

ACTON CORP (DE)
Common $0.06666666 par split (5) for (4) by issuance of (0.25) additional share 12/15/1980
Each share Common $0.06666666 par exchanged for (0.2) share Common $0.33333333 par 06/25/1987
Stock Dividends - 10% 12/01/1978; 10% 12/01/1979; 10% 08/01/1983
Name changed to Sunstates Corp. (New) 01/03/1994
(See Sunstates Corp. (New))

ACTON LIMESTONE QUARRIES LTD. (ON)
Merged into Industrial Minerals of Canada Ltd. 11/30/1967
Each share Common no par exchanged for (0.01) share Capital Stock no par
Industrial Minerals of Canada Ltd. merged into Indusmin Ltd. 11/06/1968
(See Indusmin Ltd.)

ACTRADE FINL TECHNOLOGIES LTD (DE)
Plan of reorganization under Chapter 11 Federal Bankruptcy Code effective 01/08/2004
Holders may receive an undetermined amount of cash

ACTRADE INTL LTD (DE)
Name changed to Actrade Financial Technologies Ltd. 08/21/2000
(See Actrade Financial Technologies Ltd.)

ACTRON ELECTRS INC (UT)
Recapitalized as Actron Inc. 03/01/1990
Each share Common $0.001 par exchanged for (0.2) share Common $0.001 par
(See Actron Inc.)

ACTRON INC (UT)
Voluntarily dissolved 01/03/2008
Details not available

ACT360 SOLUTIONS LTD (BC)
Recapitalized as Kona Bay Technologies Inc. 06/03/2016
Each share Common no par exchanged for (0.1) share Common no par

ACTUATE CORP (DE)
Name changed 05/24/1999
Name changed from Actuate Software Corp. to Actuate Corp. 05/24/1999
Common $0.001 par split (2) for (1) by issuance of (1) additional share payable 12/02/1999 to holders of record 11/24/1999
Common $0.001 par split (2) for (1) by issuance of (1) additional share payable 08/14/2000 to holders of record 08/07/2000 Ex date - 08/15/2000
Acquired by Open Text Corp. 01/16/2015
Each share Common $0.001 par exchanged for $6.60 cash

ACTUS MINERALS CORP (BC)
Recapitalized as Arak Resources Ltd. 09/26/2014
Each share Common no par exchanged for (0.2) share Common no par
Arak Resources Ltd. reorganized as Cobalt 27 Capital Corp. 04/10/2017

ACTV INC (DE)
Merged into OpenTV Corp. 07/01/2003
Each share Common 10¢ par exchanged for (0.73333) share Class A Ordinary no par
(See OpenTV Corp.)

ACU-TECH CORP. (NJ)
Assets assigned for the benefit of creditors 12/31/1976
No stockholders' equity

ACUBID COM INC (DE)
Name changed to Asia Web Holdings, Inc. 06/01/2000
Asia Web Holdings, Inc. name changed to Case Financial, Inc. 05/22/2002
(See Case Financial, Inc.)

ACUITY ALL CAP & INCOME TR (ON)
Merged into Acuity Growth & Income Trust 12/28/2007
Each Trust Unit no par automatically became (0.901164) Trust Unit no par
Acuity Growth & Income Trust merged into Acuity Growth & Income Fund 07/08/2011

ACUITY DIVERSIFIED TOTAL RETURN TR (ON)
Merged into Acuity Growth & Income Trust 12/28/2007
Each Unit no par received (0.689882) Trust Unit no par
Acuity Growth & Income Trust merged into Acuity Growth & Income Fund 07/08/2011

ACUITY FOCUSED TOTAL RETURN TR (ON)
Merged into Acuity Growth & Income Fund 07/08/2011
Each Trust Unit exchanged for Class A Units on a net asset basis

ACUITY GROWTH & INCOME TR (ON)
Merged into Acuity Growth & Income Fund 07/08/2011
Each Trust Unit automatically became Class A Units on a net asset basis

ACUITY IMAGING INC (DE)
Merged into Robotic Vision Systems, Inc. 09/20/1995
Each share Common 5¢ par exchanged for (0.581138) share Common 1¢ par
(See Robotic Vision Systems, Inc.)

ACUITY INTL INC (NV)
Involuntarily dissolved 12/29/2011

ACUITY MULTI-CAP TOTAL RETURN TR (ON)
Merged into Acuity Growth & Income Trust 12/28/2007
Each Trust Unit no par received (0.686986) Trust Unit no par
Acuity Growth & Income Trust merged into Acuity Growth & Income Fund 07/08/2011

ACUITY SMALL CAP CORP (ON)
Merged into Acuity Canadian Small Cap Fund 07/08/2011
Each share Class A no par exchanged for Class A Units on a net asset basis

ACUMA INTL INC (AB)
Bankruptcy trustee discharged 09/00/2003
No stockholders' equity

ACUMEDSPA HLDGS INC (NV)
Recapitalized as Organic Plant Health, Inc. 02/02/2011
Each share Common $0.001 par exchanged for (0.02) share Common $0.001 par

ACUMEN TECHNOLOGIES INC (AB)
Name changed to Polyair Tires Inc. 03/06/1989
Polyair Tires Inc. recapitalized as Bartizan Capital Corp. 06/12/1998
(See Bartizan Capital Corp.)

ACUMEN TRADING INC (DE)
Charter forfeited for failure to maintain a registered agent 12/24/1978

ACUNET CORP (DE)
Recapitalized as Corsaire Snowboard Inc. 03/20/1995
Each share Common $0.001 par exchanged for (0.01) share Common $0.001 par
Corsaire Snowboard Inc. name changed to Corsaire Inc. 07/21/1997 which name changed to Net Command Tech, Inc. (DE) 05/12/1999 which reincorporated in Florida 02/01/2000
(See Net Command Tech, Inc.)

ACUNETX INC (NV)
SEC revoked common stock registration 12/09/2013

ACUSHNET CO (MA)
Merged into American Brands, Inc. (NJ) 06/04/1976
Each share Common $1 par exchanged for (1) share $1.70 Conv. Preferred no par or $21.50 cash
Note: Option to receive cash expired 06/18/1976
(See American Brands, Inc. (NJ))

ACUSHNET PROCESS CO. (MA)
Each share Common no par exchanged for (20) shares Common $2 par 00/00/1951
Common $2 par changed to $1 par and (5) additional shares issued 06/10/1966
Name changed to Acushnet Co. 06/03/1968
(See Acushnet Co.)

ACUSON (DE)
Common $0.0001 par split (3) for (2) by issuance of (0.5) additional share 08/31/1990
Merged into Siemens AG 11/08/2000
Each share Common $0.0001 par exchanged for $23 cash

ACUSTAR CORP (DE)
Reported out of business 00/00/1991
Details not available

ACUVISION SYS INC (BC)
Recapitalized as International AcuVision Systems Inc. (BC) 08/27/1991
Each share Common no par exchanged for (0.2) share Common no par
International AcuVision Systems Inc. (BC) reincorporated in Delaware 09/15/1993 which recapitalized as AcuBid.Com, Inc. 03/18/1999 which name changed to Asia Web Holdings, Inc. 06/01/2000 which name changed to Case Financial, Inc. 05/22/2002
(See Case Financial, Inc.)

ACX TECHNOLOGIES INC (CO)
Common 1¢ par split (2) for (1) by issuance of (1) additional share 09/18/1995
Each share Common 1¢ par received distribution of (0.25) share CoorsTek, Inc. Common 1¢ par payable 12/31/1999 to holders of record 12/17/1999 Ex date - 01/03/2000
Name changed to Graphic Packaging International Corp. 05/12/2000
Graphic Packaging International Corp. merged into Graphic Packaging Corp. (New) 08/08/2003 which name changed to Graphic Packaging Holding Co. 03/10/2008

ACXIOM HLDGS CORP (DE)
Reorganized 09/21/2018
Common 10¢ par split (2) for (1) by issuance of (1) additional share 11/30/1992
Common 10¢ par split (2) for (1) by issuance of (1) additional share 01/10/1995
Common 10¢ par split (2) for (1) by issuance of (1) additional share payable 11/11/1996 to holders of record 10/25/1996 Ex date - 11/12/1996
Under plan of reorganization each share Acxiom Corp. Common 10¢ par automatically became (1) share Acxiom Holdings, Inc. Common 10¢ par 09/21/2018
Name changed to LiveRamp Holdings, Inc. 10/02/2018

AD-A-CAB AMER LTD (CO)
Name changed to Questex Group, Ltd. (New) 09/01/1994
Questex Group, Ltd. (New) recapitalized as Garcis USA, Inc. 12/28/1994
(See Garcis USA, Inc.)

AD ART ELECTRONIC SIGN CORP (NV)
SEC revoked common stock registration 10/24/2008

AD ASTRA MINERALS LTD. (CANADA)
Recapitalized as Consolidated Ad Astra Minerals Ltd. 08/13/1965
Each share Capital Stock no par exchanged for (0.1) share Capital Stock no par
(See Consolidated Ad Astra Minerals Ltd.)

AD CARE INC (NV)
Each share old Common $0.001 par exchanged for (0.1) share new Common $0.001 par 05/03/1989
Name changed to Care Visions Corp. 01/08/1990
(See Care Visions Corp.)

AD COM MKTG INC (BC)
Cease trade order effective 04/28/1989

AD DOME INTL LTD (BC)
Delisted from Vancouver Stock Exchange 03/01/1989

AD MAR RESH INC (NY)
Merged into ARC Merger Corp. 07/28/1978
Each share Common 10¢ par exchanged for $4.25 cash

AD OPT TECHNOLOGIES INC (CANADA)
Acquired by Kronos Inc. 11/18/2004
Each share Common no par exchanged for $6.25 cash

AD PRESS LTD (DE)
Name changed to M.L.J.W. Corp. 02/28/1984
(See M.L.J.W. Corp.)

AD SHOW NETWORK INC (NV)
Name changed to Atlantic Syndication Network, Inc. 08/17/1995
Atlantic Syndication Network, Inc. name changed to Zealous Trading Group, Inc. 10/05/2007 which name changed to Adult Entertainment Capital, Inc. 08/25/2008 which name changed to Zealous, Inc. 03/05/2009 which name changed to CoreStream Energy Inc. 09/03/2010
(See CoreStream Energy Inc.)

AD SYS COMMUNICATIONS INC (NV)
Common $0.001 par split (8) for (1) by issuance of (7) additional shares payable 04/09/2010 to holders of record 04/09/2010
Common $0.001 par split (6) for (1) by issuance of (5) additional shares payable 07/19/2010 to holders of record 07/19/2010 Ex date 07/20/2010
Company terminated common stock registration and is no longer public as of 11/01/2012

AD SYS INC (UT)
Reorganized as Asyst Corp. 12/19/2000
Each share Common $0.001 par exchanged for (0.01) share Common $0.001 par to reflect a (1) for (500) reverse split followed by a (5) for (1) forward split
Note: Holders of (499) shares or fewer pre-split shares received $1 cash per share
Asyst Corp. name changed to Amazon Biotech, Inc. 03/10/2004

AD VENTURE PARTNERS INC (DE)
Under plan of merger name changed to 180 Connect Inc. (DE) 08/24/2007
(See 180 Connect Inc. (DE))

ADA-ES INC (CO)
Reincorporated under the laws of Delaware as Advanced Emissions Solutions, Inc. and Common no par changed to $0.001 par 07/01/2013

ADA EXPLORATIONS LTD. (ON)
Merged into Drope Lake Explorations Ltd. 02/10/1967
Each share Capital Stock $1 par exchanged for (0.25) share Common no par
Drope Lake Explorations Ltd. name changed to Drope Lake Metals & Holdings Ltd. 12/22/1970
(See Drope Lake Metals & Holdings Ltd.)

ADA FINL SVC CORP (NJ)
Stock Dividend - 20% 05/17/1971
Merged into Ross (W.M.) & Co., Inc. 02/01/1991
Each share Common 10¢ par exchanged for $1.75 cash

ADA RES INC (DE)
Name changed to Adams Resources & Energy, Inc. 05/14/1979

ADAC LABS (CA)
Common no par split (2) for (1) by issuance of (1) additional share 11/19/1982
Each share old Common no par exchanged for (0.33333333) share new Common no par 03/15/1993
Merged into Koninklijke Philips Electronics N.V. 12/18/2000
Each share new Common no par exchanged for $18.50 cash

ADACORP INC (DE)
Reincorporated 01/06/1987
Each share old Common no par exchanged for (0.33333333) share new Common no par 07/30/1980
State of incorporation changed from (CA) to (DE) and new Common no par changed to 10¢ par 01/06/1987
Charter cancelled and declared inoperative and void for non-payment of taxes 03/01/1993

FINANCIAL INFORMATION, INC. ADA-ADA

ADAGE INC (PA)
Reincorporated 05/31/1991
Common $1 par split (3) for (1) by issuance of (2) additional shares 12/06/1968
Each share Special Class Common $1 par exchanged for (1) share Common $1 par 01/02/1974
Common $1 par changed to 10¢ par 06/27/1978
Common 10¢ par split (3) for (2) by issuance of (0.5) additional share 02/27/1981
Common 10¢ par split (2) for (1) by issuance of (1) additional share 09/15/1983
State of incorporation changed from (MA) to (PA) 05/31/1991
Each share Common 10¢ par exchanged for (0.16666666) share Common 60¢ par 06/14/1991
Reincorporated under the laws of Nevada as RELM Wireless Corp. 01/30/1998
RELM Wireless Corp. name changed to BK Technologies, Inc. 06/05/2018

ADAGIO INVTS INC (BC)
Each share old Common no par exchanged for (0.33333333) share new Common no par 04/30/1992
Dissolved 09/08/1995
No stockholders' equity

ADAIR INTL OIL & GAS INC (TX)
Name changed to EnDevCo, Inc. 10/09/2003
(See EnDevCo, Inc.)

ADAK ENERGY CORP (UT)
Recapitalized as Post Data Services Corp. 09/22/1983
Each share Common $0.001 par exchanged for (0.33333333) share Common $0.003 par
(See Post Data Services Corp.)

ADAL GROUP INC (DE)
Common $0.0001 par split (7) for (1) by issuance of (6) additional shares payable 10/13/2005 to holders of record 10/06/2005 Ex date - 10/14/2005
SEC revoked common stock registration 04/20/2011

ADALGO CAP CORP (FL)
Proclaimed dissolved for failure to file reports and pay fees 10/13/1989

ADALTIS INC (CANADA)
Discharged from bankruptcy 05/13/2011
No stockholders' equity

ADAM COM INC (GA)
Name changed to A.D.A.M., Inc. 07/31/2001
A.D.A.M., Inc. merged into Ebix, Inc. 02/08/2011

ADAM CONSOLIDATED INDUSTRIES, INC. (NY)
Name changed to Vanderbilt Tire & Rubber Corp. 11/20/1959
Vanderbilt Tire & Rubber Corp. name changed to VTR, Inc. 01/03/1962
(See VTR, Inc.)

ADAM HAT STORES, INC. (NY)
Name changed to Adam Consolidated Industries, Inc. 06/01/1956
Adam Consolidated Industries, Inc. name changed to Vanderbilt Tire & Rubber Corp. 11/20/1959 which name changed to VTR, Inc. 01/03/1962
(See VTR, Inc.)

ADAM TECHNOLOGIES INC (AB)
Reorganized under the laws of Ontario as Nucontex Corp. 01/11/2001
Each share Class A no par exchanged for (0.5) share Class A no par
(See Nucontex Corp.)

ADAM ZACHARY INC (CO)
Name changed to Securities USA, Inc. 07/20/1988
Securities USA, Inc. recapitalized as Securities PR, Inc. 04/28/1989

ADAMAS RES CORP (BC)
Recapitalized as Britannica Resources Corp. 08/27/2002
Each share Common no par exchanged for (0.10526315) share Common no par
Britannica Resources Corp. name changed to Trinity Valley Energy Corp. 10/08/2013 which recapitalized as Smooth Rock Ventures Corp. 11/15/2017

ADAMAS RES INC (AB)
Name changed to Zeacan Products Ltd. 03/20/1989
Zeacan Products Ltd. recapitalized as Canadian Zeolite Ltd. 07/26/1993 which name changed to Canadian Mining Co. Ltd. 01/08/1997 which name changed to Zeo-Tech Enviro Corp. 05/19/2000 which name changed to Canadian Mining Co. Inc. (AB) 02/08/2007 which reincorporated in British Columbia as Canadian Zeolite Corp. 02/08/2016 which name changed to International Zeolite Corp. 03/06/2018

ADAMS AIR EXPRESS, INC. (DE)
Charter cancelled and declared inoperative and void for non-payment of taxes 04/01/1932

ADAMS (C.F.) CO.
Property sold 00/00/1934
Details not available

ADAMS CNTY NATL BK (GETTYSBURG, PA)
Under plan of reorganization each share Common $5 par automatically became (1) share ACNB Corp. Common $5 par 07/01/1983

ADAMS DANA SILVERSTEIN INC (NY)
Name changed to Gaynor & Co., Inc. 05/28/1970
(See Gaynor & Co., Inc.)

ADAMS DRUG INC (DE)
Merged into Pantry Pride, Inc. (New) 11/19/1984
Each share Common 10¢ par exchanged for $24.39 cash

ADAMS ENGINEERING CO., INC. (FL)
Adjudicated bankrupt 04/27/1965
No stockholders' equity

ADAMS ENGINEERING CO. (OH)
Completely liquidated 06/13/1969
Each share Common $1 par exchanged for first and final distribution of (0.224283) share Warner & Swasey Co. Common $1 par
Warner & Swasey Co. merged into Bendix Corp. 03/31/1980 which merged into Allied Corp. 01/31/1983 which merged into Allied-Signal Inc. 09/19/1985 which name changed to AlliedSignal Inc. 04/26/1993 which name changed to Honeywell International Inc. 12/01/1999

ADAMS EXPL LTD (BC)
Struck off register and declared dissolved for failure to file returns 11/04/1994

ADAMS EXPRESS CO (MD)
Reincorporated 05/28/1976
Each share Common $100 par exchanged for (10) shares Common no par 00/00/1929
Common no par changed to $1 par 00/00/1944
Common $1 par split (2) for (1) by issuance of (1) additional share 04/05/1968
Stock Dividend - 100% 10/18/1955
State of incorporation changed from (NY) to (MD) 05/28/1976
Common $1 par split (3) for (2) by issuance of (0.5) additional share payable 10/19/2000 to holders of record 09/28/2000 Ex date - 10/20/2000
Common $1 par changed to $0.001 par 11/08/2006
Name changed to Adams Diversified Equity Fund, Inc. 03/31/2015

ADAMS GOLF INC (DE)
Each share old Common $0.001 par exchanged for (0.25) share new Common $0.001 par 02/19/2008
Acquired by Taylor Made Golf Co., Inc. 06/01/2012
Each share new Common $0.001 par exchanged for $10.80 cash

ADAMS HARD FACING CO (OK)
6% Conv. Preferred $100 par called for redemption 03/01/1969
Stock Dividend - 25% 06/12/1975
Merged into AHF Holding Corp. 10/09/1984
Each share Class A Common 50¢ par exchanged for $5.375 cash
Each share Class B Common 50¢ par exchanged for $5.375 cash

ADAMS INTL METALS CORP (CA)
Company went out of business 00/00/1990
No stockholders' equity

ADAMS JOHN LIFE CORP (CA)
Company terminated registration of common stock and is no longer public as of 03/26/1998
Details not available

ADAMS (J.D.) MANUFACTURING CO. (IN)
Acquired by State Street Investment Corp. 10/15/1958
Each share Common no par exchanged for (0.94626) share Common $10 par
State Street Investment Corp. name changed to State Street Investment Trust 05/01/1989 which name changed to State Street Master Investment Trust 12/14/1989 which name changed to State Street Research Master Investment Trust 05/25/1995
(See State Street Research Master Investment Trust)

ADAMS MILLIS CORP (NC)
Common no par split (3) for (1) by issuance of (2) additional shares 04/08/1960
Common no par split (2) for (1) by issuance of (1) additional share 05/01/1968
Common no par split (2) for (1) by issuance of (1) additional share 12/16/1986
Acquired by Sara Lee Corp. 10/25/1988
Each share Common no par exchanged for (0.3636) share Common $1.33333333 par
Sara Lee Corp. recapitalized as Hillshire Brands Co. 06/29/2012
(See Hillshire Brands Co.)

ADAMS OIL & GAS CO.
Liquidation approved 11/23/1943
Distribution of (0.25) share Common $25 par of Standard Oil Co. (OH) paid 02/24/1944
Cash liquidation completed 10/25/1944

ADAMS OIL CO. (CA)
Dissolved 00/00/1952
Details not available

ADAMS-PHILLIPS, INC. (CA)
Dissolved 03/01/1958
Details not available

ADAMS R P INC (NY)
Completely liquidated
Each share Common $1 par received first and final distribution of $6 cash payable 12/20/2006 to holders of record 12/04/2006 Ex date - 12/22/2006
Note: Certificates were not required to be surrendered and are without value

ADAMS RESPIRATORY THERAPEUTICS INC (DE)
Merged into Reckitt Benckiser Group PLC 01/30/2008
Each share Common 1¢ par exchanged for $60 cash

ADAMS ROYALTY CO.
Name changed to Adams Oil & Gas Co. 00/00/1937
(See Adams Oil & Gas Co.)

ADAMS-RUSSELL ELECTRONICS CO., INC. (DE)
Reincorporated under the laws of Massachusetts as Adams-Russell, Inc. 03/27/1989
(See Adams-Russell, Inc.)

ADAMS RUSSELL INC (MA)
Each share Common $1 par exchanged for (4) shares Common 50¢ par to effect a (2) for (1) split and 100% stock dividend 10/24/1967
Common 50¢ par split (3) for (2) by issuance of (0.5) additional share 11/22/1982
Stock Dividends - 40% 10/16/1979; 50% 10/15/1980
Acquired by Cablevision Systems Corp. 01/04/1988
Each share Common 50¢ par exchanged for $43.075 cash

ADAMS RUSSELL INC (MA)
Merged into M/A-Com, Inc. 10/01/1990
Each share Common 1¢ par exchanged for $15.50 cash

ADAMS SILVER RES INC (BC)
Name changed to Adams Exploration Ltd. 05/14/1986
(See Adams Exploration Ltd.)

ADAMSON BROS HLDGS CORP (DE)
Name changed to Red Mountain Pharmaceuticals, Inc. 06/07/2005
Red Mountain Pharmaceuticals, Inc. name changed to Zalemark Holding Co., Inc. 12/24/2008

ADAMSON MACHINE CO.
Acquired by United Engineering & Foundry Co. 01/01/1945
Details not available

ADAMUS RESOURCES LTD (AUSTRALIA)
Merged into Endeavour Mining Corp. 12/05/2011
Each share Common no par exchanged for (0.285) share Ordinary USD $0.01 par
Note: U.S. residents and other ineligible holders received CAD $0.7377718 cash per share

ADANAC GOLD MINES, LTD. (ON)
Name changed to Adanac Quebec Gold Mines, Ltd. 00/00/1936
(See Adanac Quebec Gold Mines, Ltd.)

ADANAC MNG & EXPL LTD (BC)
Merged into Bell Molybdenum Mines Inc. 04/12/1995
Each share Common 50¢ par exchanged for (1) share Common no par
Bell Molybdenum Mines Inc. name changed to Bell Earth Sciences Inc. 08/08/1997
(See Bell Earth Sciences Inc.)

ADANAC MOLY CORP (BC)
Name changed 11/04/2004
Name changed from Adanac Gold Corp. to Adanac Moly Corp. 11/04/2004
Name changed to Adanac Molybdenum Corp. 11/06/2006
(See Adanac Molybdenum Corp.)

ADANAC MOLYBDENUM CORP (BC)
Each share old Common no par exchanged for (0.00666666) share new Common no par 03/03/2011
Acquired by Whitebox Advisors LLC 12/16/2015
Each share new Common no par exchanged for $0.1837 cash
Note: Unexchanged certificates will be cancelled and become without value 12/16/2021

ADANAC QUEBEC GOLD MINES LTD. (ON)
Charter cancelled and proclaimed dissolved for failure to pay taxes and file returns 12/03/1962

ADAPTEC INC (DE)
Reincorporated 03/12/1998
Common $0.001 par split (2) for (1) by issuance of (1) additional share 04/03/1992
Common $0.001 par split (2) for (1) by issuance of (1) additional share 01/28/1994
Common $0.001 par split (2) for (1) by issuance of (1) additional share payable 11/15/1996 to holders of record 11/01/1996 Ex date - 11/18/1996
State of incorporation changed from (CA) to (DE) 03/12/1998
Each share Common $0.001 par received distribution of (0.1646) share Roxio, Inc. Common $0.001 par payable 05/11/2001 to holders of record 04/30/2001
Name changed to ADPT Corp. 06/22/2010
ADPT Corp. recapitalized as Steel Excel Inc. 10/05/2011 which merged into Steel Partners Holdings L.P. 02/15/2017

ADAPTIVE BROADBAND CORP (DE)
Common 10¢ par split (2) for (1) by issuance of (1) additional share payable 03/30/2000 to holders of record 03/23/2000
In process of liquidation
Each share Common 10¢ par received initial distribution of $0.08 cash payable 12/12/2008 to holders of record 10/17/2008 Ex date - 12/15/2008
SEC revoked common stock registration 04/30/2010
Note: Name changed to AB Liquidating Corp. 10/30/2001

ADAPTIVE MARKETING SOLUTIONS INC (BC)
Recapitalized as Permission Marketing Solutions Inc. 01/18/2002
Each share Common no par exchanged for (0.5) share Common no par
Permission Marketing Solutions Inc. name changed to Pacific Asia China Energy Inc. 01/04/2006
(See Pacific Asia China Energy Inc.)

ADAPTIVE PERFORMANCE INC (DE)
Name changed to Great Cities Media, Inc. 11/17/2005
(See Great Cities Media, Inc.)

ADAPTIVE SOLUTIONS INC (OR)
Each share old Common no par exchanged for (0.2) share new Common no par 04/22/1998
Filed a petition under Chapter 7 Federal Bankruptcy Code 10/29/1998
No stockholders' equity

ADAPTIVE TECHNOLOGIES CDA INC (BC)
Struck off register and declared dissolved for failure to file returns 09/27/1991

ADAPTIVE TECHNOLOGIES INC (WA)
Name changed to Atlantic Pacific International Inc. (WA) 07/16/1997
Atlantic Pacific International Inc. (WA) reincorporated in Nevada as API Dental, Inc. 07/30/1999
(See API Dental, Inc.)

ADAR RES LTD (BC)
Name changed to Northern Engineered Gold Resources Ltd. 09/10/1982
Northern Engineered Gold Resources Ltd. name changed to Petrocel Industries Inc. 08/29/1983
(See Petrocel Industries Inc.)

ADARNA ENERGY CORP (DE)
SEC revoked common stock registration 12/23/2014

ADASTRA MINERALS INC (YT)
Merged into First Quantum Minerals Ltd. 08/11/2006
Each share Common no par exchanged for (0.0581) share Common no par and $0.4339 cash

ADASTRAL RES LTD (BC)
Name changed to Diagem International Resource Corp. (BC) 07/09/1996
Diagem International Resource Corp. (BC) reincorporated in Canada as Diagem Inc. 11/18/2004
(See Diagem Inc.)

ADATOM COM INC (DE)
Reincorporated under the laws of Ontario as First Canadian American Holding Corp. 09/19/2002
First Canadian American Holding Corp. (ON) reincorporated in Wyoming 12/05/2004 which name changed to Blackout Media Corp. 01/09/2006

ADB INTL GROUP INC (DE)
Reincorporated 08/04/2014
State of incorporation changed from (NJ) to (DE) 08/04/2014
Each share Common $0.0001 par exchanged for (0.01) share Common $0.00001 par
Name changed to E- Qure Corp. 10/09/2014

ADB SYS INTL INC (ON)
Name changed to ADB Systems International Ltd. 11/01/2002
ADB Systems International Ltd. name changed to Northcore Technologies Inc. 07/18/2006

ADB SYS INTL LTD (ON)
Name changed to Northcore Technologies Inc. 07/18/2006

ADC TELECOMMUNICATIONS INC (MN)
Old Common 20¢ par split (3) for (2) by issuance of (0.5) additional share 04/25/1986
Old Common 20¢ par split (3) for (2) by issuance of (0.5) additional share 10/27/1987
Old Common 20¢ par split (2) for (1) by issuance of (1) additional share 06/28/1993
Old Common 20¢ par split (2) for (1) by issuance of (1) additional share 02/28/1995
Old Common 20¢ par split (2) for (1) by issuance of (1) additional share payable 10/31/1996 to holders of record 10/15/1996
Old Common 20¢ par split (2) for (1) by issuance of (1) additional share payable 02/15/2000 to holders of record 01/25/2000
Old Common 20¢ par split (2) for (1) by issuance of (1) additional share payable 07/17/2000 to holders of record 06/26/2000
Each share old Common 20¢ par exchanged for (0.14285714) share new Common 20¢ par 05/10/2005
Acquired by Tyco Electronics Ltd. 12/09/2010
Each share new Common 20¢ par exchanged for $12.75 cash

ADCARE HEALTH SYS INC (GA)
Reincorporated 12/13/2013
Each share old Common no par exchanged for (0.4) share new Common no par 01/03/2006
Stock Dividends - 5% payable 10/15/2010 to holders of record 09/30/2010 Ex date - 09/28/2010; 5% payable 10/14/2011 to holders of record 09/30/2011 Ex date - 09/28/2011; 5% payable 10/22/2012 to holders of record 10/08/2012 Ex date - 10/03/2012
State of incorporation changed from (OH) to (GA) 12/13/2013
Name changed to Regional Health Properties, Inc. 10/02/2017

ADCO TECHNOLOGIES INC (DE)
Merged into ACC Acquisition Corp. 10/08/1996
Each share Common 1¢ par exchanged for $10.25 cash

ADCOM METALS INC (GA)
Merged into Leggett & Platt, Inc. 05/31/1978
Each share Common 10¢ par exchanged for $5.05 cash

ADCOM SYS INC (NV)
Name changed to Aurtex, Inc. 12/04/1992
Aurtex, Inc. recapitalized as Sector Communications Inc. 06/17/1996 which name changed to Options Talent Group 01/11/2002 which name changed to Trans Continental Entertainment Group Inc. 01/16/2003
(See Trans Continental Entertainment Group Inc.)

ADCOR ELECTRS INC (GA)
Proclaimed dissolved for failure to file annual reports 08/06/1996

ADCORE CAP INC (BC)
Name changed to Wind River Energy Corp. 08/13/2010

ADDA RES LTD (BC)
Name changed 01/18/1996
Name changed from Adda Minerals Co., Ltd. to Adda Resources Ltd. 01/18/1996
Delisted from Toronto Venture Stock Exchange 06/05/2002

ADDAX PETE CORP (CANADA)
Acquired by Sinopec International Petroleum Exploration & Production Corp. 10/05/2009
Each share Common no par exchanged for $52.80 cash
Each share 144A Common no par exchanged for $52.80 cash

ADDED CAP CORP (AB)
Reincorporated under the laws of Ontario as Lakeside Steel Inc. 10/30/2008
(See Lakeside Steel Inc.)

ADDENDA CAP INC (QC)
Merged into Co-operators Group Ltd. 04/22/2008
Each share Common no par exchanged for $26.50 cash

ADDINGTON MINES LTD. (ON)
Charter cancelled and proclaimed dissolved for failure to pay taxes and file returns 12/00/1969

ADDINGTON RES INC (DE)
Common no par split (2) for (1) by issuance of (1) additional share 05/25/1989
Merged into Republic Industries Inc. 12/20/1996
Each share Common no par exchanged for (0.9) share Common no par
Republic Industries Inc. name changed to AutoNation, Inc. 04/06/1999

ADDISON BANCSHARES, INC. (DE)
Acquired by Affiliated Banc Group, Inc. 11/13/1985
Details not available

ADDISON-DAVIS DIAGNOSTICS INC (DE)
Each share old Common $0.001 par exchanged for (0.00571428) share new Common $0.001 par 04/18/2006
Chapter 11 bankruptcy proceedings dismissed 12/02/2008
Stockholders' equity unlikely

ADDISON INDS INC (DE)
Reorganized under the laws of Nevada as Bonanza Land Holdings, Inc. 05/16/2006
Each share new Common $0.001 par exchanged for (0.01) share Common $0.001 par
Bonanza Land Holdings, Inc. name changed to VLinx Technology, Inc. 11/08/2011 which name changed to Vision Plasma Systems, Inc. 04/03/2012

ADDISON WESLEY PUBG INC (MA)
Class A Common no par and Class B Common no par split (4) for (1) by issuance of (3) additional shares respectively 03/15/1961
Class A Common no par and Class B Common no par split (2) for (1) by issuance of (1) additional share respectively 12/15/1964
Class A Common no par and Class B Common no par split (3) for (1) by issuance of (2) additional shares respectively 03/01/1966
Each share old Class A Common no par exchanged for (0.33333333) share new Class A Common no par and (0.66666666) share Class B Common no par 12/05/1986
Merged into AWP Acquisition Inc. 03/31/1988
Each share new Class A Common no par exchanged for $105 cash
Each share Class B Common no par exchanged for $105 cash

ADDITIVE TECHNOLOGY CORP (MA)
Proclaimed dissolved for failure to file reports and pay fees 12/31/1990

ADDRESSOGRAPH INTERNATIONAL CORP. (DE)
Name changed to Addressograph-Multigraph Corp. 05/05/1931
Addressograph-Multigraph Corp. name changed to AM International, Inc. (Old) 01/02/1979 which reorganized as AM International, Inc. (New) 10/13/1993 which recapitalized as Multigraphics, Inc. 05/28/1997
(See Multigraphics, Inc.)

ADDRESSOGRAPH MULTIGRAPH CORP (DE)
Common no par changed to $10 par 00/00/1933
Common $10 par changed to $5 par and (2) additional shares issued 09/16/1958
Common $5 par changed to $2.50 par and (1) additional share issued 05/13/1960
Name changed to AM International, Inc. (Old) 01/02/1979
AM International, Inc. (Old) reorganized as AM International, Inc. (New) 10/13/1993 which recapitalized as Multigraphics, Inc. 05/28/1997
(See Multigraphics, Inc.)

ADDRESSOGRAPH SECURITIES CO. (DE)
Name changed to Addressograph International Corp. 00/00/1929
Addressograph International Corp. name changed to Addressograph-Multigraph Corp. 05/05/1931 which name changed to AM International, Inc. (Old) 01/02/1979 which reorganized as AM International, Inc. (New)

10/13/1993 which recapitalized as Multigraphics, Inc. 05/28/1997
(See Multigraphics, Inc.)

ADDSCO INDS INC (AL)
Acquired by Atlantic Marine Holding Co. at $40 per share through purchase offer which expired 12/22/1992
Public interest eliminated

ADDVANTAGE MEDIA GROUP INC (OK)
Each share old Common 1¢ par exchanged for (0.25) share new Common 1¢ par 10/09/1998
Name changed to ADDvantage Technologies Group, Inc. 12/30/1999

ADDWEST MINERALS INTL LTD (BC)
Delisted from Toronto Venture Stock Exchange 03/10/2003

ADE CORP (MA)
Merged into KLA-Tencor Corp. 10/11/2006
Each share Common 1¢ par exchanged for $32.50 cash

ADECCO SA (SWITZERLAND)
Sponsored ADR's for Ordinary split (5) for (1) by issuance of (4) additional ADR's payable 05/16/2001 to holders of record 05/11/2001 Ex date - 05/17/2001
ADR agreement terminated 06/04/2007
Each Sponsored ADR for Ordinary exchanged for $13.005554 cash
Name changed to Adecco Group AG 06/03/2016

ADECKA FACTORS INC (AB)
Struck off register for failure to file annual returns 03/01/1989

ADELAIDE HLDGS INC (NV)
Name changed to Tasty Fries, Inc. 09/28/1993
(See Tasty Fries, Inc.)

ADELAIDE MINING LTD. (ON)
Charter cancelled and proclaimed dissolved for failure to pay taxed and file returns 11/28/1973

ADELE MALARTIC MINES LTD. (ON)
Charter cancelled and proclaimed dissolved for failure to pay taxes and file returns 05/26/1958

ADELEMONT GOLD MINES LTD (ON)
Charter cancelled and proclaimed dissolved for failure to pay taxes and file returns 12/07/1977

ADELINE LAKE GOLD MINES LTD. (CANADA)
Acquired by Horne Fault Mines Ltd. 00/00/1944
Each share Common exchanged for (0.14285714) share Common 1¢ par Horne Fault Mines Ltd. recapitalized as Horne Fault Mines Ltd.-Les Mines de la Faille Horne Ltee. 07/21/1976
Horne Fault Mines Ltd.-Les Mines Horne de la Faille Horne Ltee. liquidated for Spider Resources Inc. 10/22/1992
(See Spider Resources Inc.)

ADELPHI ELECTRONICS, INC. (NY)
Acquired by Milo Electronics Corp. 11/01/1967
Each share Common 10¢ par exchanged for (0.076923) share Common $1 par
(See Milo Electronics Corp.)

ADELPHIA BUSINESS SOLUTIONS INC (DE)
Stock Dividends - in Preferred to holders of Preferred 3.21875% payable 07/15/2000 to holders of record 07/01/2000; 3.21875% payable 10/16/2000 to holders of record 10/01/2000 Ex date - 09/27/2000; 3.21875% payable 01/15/2001 to holders of record 01/01/2001 Ex date - 12/27/2000; 3.21875% payable 04/16/2001 to holders of record 04/01/2001 Ex date - 03/28/2001; 3.21875% payable 07/17/2001 to holders of record 07/01/2001 Ex date - 06/27/2001; 3.21875% payable 10/17/2001 to holders of record 10/01/2001 Ex date - 10/02/2001
Plan of reorganization under Chapter 11 Federal Bankruptcy Code effective 04/07/2004
No stockholders' equity

ADELPHIA COMMUNICATIONS CORP (DE)
Each share Class A Common 1¢ par received distribution of (0.49809619) share Adelphia Business Solutions Inc. Class A Common 1¢ par payable 01/11/2002 to holders of record 01/08/2002 Ex date - 01/04/2002
Plan of reorganization under Chapter 11 Federal Bankruptcy Code effective 02/13/2007
Each share 13% Ser. B Exchangeable Preferred exchanged for (100) Adelphia Contingent Value Vehicle ACC-6B Units
Each share 5.5% Conv. Preferred Ser. D Preferred exchanged for (200) Adelphia Contingent Value Vehicle ACC-6D Units
Each share 7.5% Mandatory Conv. Preferred Ser. E exchanged for (25.67708) Adelphia Contingent Value Vehicle ACC-6E/F Units
Each share 7.5% Conv. Preferred Ser. F exchanged for (25.28125) Adelphia Contingent Value Vehicle ACC-6E/F Units
Each share Class A Common 1¢ par exchanged for (1) Adelphia Contingent Value Vehicle ACC-7 Unit
No stockholders' equity for holders of 13% 144A Exchangeable Preferred Ser. A
Note: Unexchanged certificates were cancelled and became without value 02/13/2008
Adelphia Contingent Value Vehicle name changed to Adelphia Recovery Trust 03/30/2007

ADELPHIA RECOVERY TR (DE)
Name changed 03/30/2007
Name changed from Adelphia Contingent Value Vehicle to Adelphia Recovery Trust 03/30/2007
Completely liquidated
Each CVV Ser. RF Int. received initial distribution of $0.9347826 cash payable payable 12/21/2010 to holders of record 12/13/2010
Each CVV Ser. RF Int. received second and final distribution of $0.06521739 cash payable 03/01/2012 to holders of record 02/23/2012
CVV Ser. ACC-4, CVV Ser. ACC-5, CVV Ser. ACC-6B, CVV Ser. ACC-6B1, CVV Ser. ACC-6D, CVV Ser. ACC-6D1, CVV Ser. ACC-6E/F, CVV Ser. ACC-6E/F1, CVV Ser. ACC-7, CVV Ser. ACC-7A and CVV Ser. ESL were cancelled and became without value 09/23/2015
Note: The CVV Interests are units in a trust pursuing certain claims against third party lenders, accountants and other parties
(Additional Information in Active)

ADELT DESIGN INC
Recapitalized as CLS Holdings USA, Inc. 12/10/2014
Each share Common $0.0001 par exchanged for (0.625) share Common $0.0001 par

ADEN ENTERPRISES INC (CA)
Each share old Common no par exchanged for (0.03846153) share new Common no par 10/26/1992
SEC revoked common stock registration 01/28/2008

ADEN SOLUTIONS INC (NV)
Common $0.00001 par split (2) for (1) by issuance of (1) additional share payable 08/28/2009 to holders of record 08/27/2009 Ex date - 08/31/2009
Common $0.00001 par split (7) for (1) by issuance of (6) additional shares payable 09/14/2010 to holders of record 08/31/2010 Ex date - 09/15/2010
SEC revoked common stock registration 03/21/2014

ADENT CAP CORP (BC)
Each share old Common no par exchanged for (0.33333333) share new Common no par 06/16/2017
Reorganized under the laws of Canada as Khiron Life Sciences Corp. 05/24/2018
Each share new Common no par exchanged for (0.125) share Common no par

ADEONA PHARMACEUTICALS INC (NV)
Reincorporated 10/16/2009
State of incorporation changed from (DE) to (NV) 10/16/2009
Name changed to Synthetic Biologics, Inc. 02/16/2012

ADEPT TECHNOLOGY INC (DE)
Reincorporated 11/04/2005
Each share old Common no par exchanged for (0.2) share new Common no par 02/25/2005
State of incorporation changed from (CA) to (DE) and and new Common no par changed to $0.001 par 11/04/2005
Acquired by OMRON Corp. 10/23/2015
Each share Common $0.001 par exchanged for $13 cash

ADEPTRON TECHNOLOGIES CORP (ON)
Reincorporated 11/22/2011
Place of incorporation changed from (AB) to (ON) 11/22/2011
Recapitalized as Artaflex Inc. 03/27/2012
Each share Common no par exchanged for (0.04) share Common no par
(See Artaflex Inc.)

ADEPTUS HEALTH INC (DE)
Plan of reorganization under Chapter 11 Federal Bankruptcy proceedings effective 10/02/2017
Holders may be entitled to receive a pro rata amount of a future distribution

ADERA FINL LTD (BC)
Recapitalized as Pacific Adera Financial Corp. 08/24/1987
Each share Common no par exchanged for (0.5) share Common no par
(See Pacific Adera Financial Corp.)

ADERA MNG LTD (BC)
Common $1 par changed to no par 04/03/1970
Recapitalized as Western Adera Ltd. (BC) 08/14/1972
Each share Common no par exchanged for (0.25) share Common no par
Western Adera Ltd. (BC) reincorporated in Colorado 10/17/1975 which name changed to Aerolift, Inc. 03/07/1984
(See Aerolift, Inc.)

ADESA CORP (IN)
Merged into Minnesota Power & Light Co. 07/01/1995
Each share Common no par exchanged for $17 cash

ADESA INC (DE)
Merged into KAR Holdings, Inc. 04/20/2007
Each share Common 1¢ par exchanged for $27.85 cash

ADESSO CORP (AB)
Name changed to Ryan Energy Technologies Inc. 04/04/1994
(See Ryan Energy Technologies Inc.)

ADEX MEDIA INC (DE)
Company terminated common stock registration and is no longer public as of 04/15/2010

ADEX MNG CORP (ON)
Recapitalized as Adex Mining Inc. 07/15/1996
Each share Common no par exchanged for (0.2) share Common no par

ADEZA BIOMEDICAL CORP (DE)
Merged into Cytyc Corp. 04/02/2007
Each share Common $0.001 par exchanged for $24 cash

ADFLEX SOLUTIONS INC (DE)
Merged into Innovex, Inc. 09/13/1999
Each share Common 1¢ par exchanged for $3.80 cash

ADFORCE INC (DE)
Merged into CMGI, Inc. 01/11/2000
Each share Common $0.001 par exchanged for (0.524) share Common 1¢ par
CMGI, Inc. name changed to ModusLink Global Solutions, Inc. 09/30/2008

ADG LIQUIDATING CORP. (NY)
Liquidation completed
Each share Common 10¢ par exchanged for initial distribution of $7.75 cash 01/06/1964
Each share Common 10¢ par received second and final distribution of $0.029577 cash 07/29/1966

ADHEREX TECHNOLOGIES INC (BC)
Reincorporated 08/30/2011
Each share old Common no par received distribution of (1) share Cadherin Biomedical Inc. Class A Preferred no par payable 11/28/2002 to holders of record 11/14/2002
Each share old Common no par exchanged for (0.2) share new Common no par 08/02/2005
Place of incorporation changed from (Canada) to (BC) 08/30/2011
Each share new Common no par exchanged for (0.05555555) share Common no par
Recapitalized as Fennec Pharmaceuticals Inc. 09/05/2014
Each share Common no par exchanged for (0.33333333) share Common no par

ADHESIVE PRODUCTS CO.
Acquired by American-Marietta Co. 00/00/1946
Details not available

ADI CORP (TAIWAN)
Each old 144A GDR for Common exchanged for (0.553) new 144A GDR for Common 01/03/2002
Stock Dividends - 15% payable 10/09/1996 to holders of record 07/11/1996; 15% payable 09/22/1997 to holders of record 07/09/1997; 12% payable 09/18/1998 to holders of record 07/24/1998; 5% payable 11/08/1999 to holders of record 08/24/1999
GDR agreement terminated 09/18/2002
No GDR holders' equity

ADI ELECTRS INC (NY)
Charter dissolved by proclamation 09/25/1991

ADI TECHNOLOGIES INC (BC)
Company ceased operations 08/21/2002

No stockholders' equity

ADIA S A (SWITZERLAND)
Name changed to Adecco S.A. 09/06/1996
(See Adecco S.A.)

ADIA SVCS INC (CA)
Merged into Adia S.A. 01/09/1995
Each share Common 25¢ par exchanged for (1) Sponsored ADR for Bearer and $16.42 cash
Adia S.A. name changed to Adecco S.A. 09/06/1996
(See Adecco S.A.)

ADIAN GOLD MINES LTD. (ON)
Completely liquidated 04/19/1949
Each share Common no par received first and final distribution of $0.012 cash

ADIDAS AG (GERMANY)
Name changed 06/06/2006
Name changed from adidas-Salomon AG to adidas AG 06/06/2006
144A Sponsored ADR's for Ordinary split (4) for (1) by issuance of (3) additional ADR's payable 06/12/2006 to holders of record 06/08/2006 Ex date - 06/13/2006
ADR agreement terminated 02/01/2010
Each 144A Sponsored ADR for Ordinary exchanged for $32.003944 cash
(Additional Information in Active)

ADIENCE INC (DE)
Company terminated registration of common stock and is no longer public as of 01/31/1995
Details not available

ADIKANN GOLDFIELDS LTD (BC)
Recapitalized as Harben Industries Ltd. 05/03/1999
Each share Common no par exchanged for (0.05) share Common no par
Harben Industries Ltd. name changed to Merit Industries Inc. 07/19/2000 which recapitalized as Ialta Industries Ltd. 07/02/2002
(See Ialta Industries Ltd.)

ADINA INC (DE)
Each share Common $0.001 par exchanged for (0.03333333) share Common $0.00002 par 09/24/1997
Common $0.00002 par split (10) for (1) by issuance of (9) additional shares payable 09/10/1998 to holders of record 09/10/1998
Name changed to Eventures Group Inc. 08/25/1999
Eventures Group Inc. name changed to Novo Networks Inc. 12/12/2000 which recapitalized as Berliner Communications, Inc. 09/19/2005 which name changed to UniTek Global Services, Inc. 07/06/2010
(See UniTek Global Services, Inc.)

ADIRA ENERGY LTD (CANADA)
Each share old Common no par exchanged for (0.33333333) share new Common no par 08/13/2013
Each share new Common no par exchanged again for (0.2) share new Common no par 10/01/2014
Name changed to Empower Clinics Inc. 04/30/2018

ADIRONDACK FINL SVCS BANCORP INC (DE)
Merged into CNB Bancorp Inc. 02/01/1999
Each share Common $25 par exchanged for $21.92 cash

ADIRONDACK INDS INC (NY)
Merged into Rowan Industries, Inc. 10/15/1968
Each share Common $1 par exchanged for (0.5714) share Common $2.50 par
Rowan Industries, Inc. name changed to De Tomaso Industries, Inc. 11/02/1973 which name changed to Trident Rowan Group Inc. 08/22/1996 which name changed to Comtech Group Inc. 08/02/2004 which name changed to Cogo Group, Inc. (MD) 05/13/2008 which reincorporated in Cayman Islands 08/03/2011 which name changed to Viewtran Group, Inc. 11/26/2013

ADIRONDACK INVESTORS, INC.
Dissolved 00/00/1931
Details not available

ADIRONDACK POWER & LIGHT CO.
Acquired by New York Power & Light Corp. 00/00/1927
Details not available

ADIRONDACK PURE SPRINGS MT WTR INC (NY)
Reincorporated under the laws of Delaware as Continental Beverage & Nutrition, Inc. and Common 1¢ par changed to $0.0001 par 01/13/2004
(See Continental Beverage & Nutrition, Inc.)

ADITYA BIRLA NUVO (INDIA)
GDR agreement terminated 12/08/2015
Each 144A GDR for Ordinary exchanged for $16.429341 cash

ADJUSTABLE RATE MBS TR (ON)
Merged into Claymore Global Monthly Advantaged Dividend ETF 07/03/2009
Each Unit no par received (1.6015) Advisor Class Units

ADKINS-PHELPS CO. (AR)
Completely liquidated 10/16/1967
Each share Common $1 par exchanged for first and final distribution of (0.47619) share Air Products & Chemicals, Inc. Common $1 par

ADLER BUILT INDS INC (FL)
Proclaimed dissolved for failure to file reports and pay fees 12/16/1981

ADLER ELECTRONICS, INC. (NY)
Liquidation completed
Each share Common 10¢ par received initial distribution of (0.17) share Litton Industries, Inc. Common $1 par 11/12/1963
Each share Common 10¢ par exchanged for second and final distribution of (0.0262) share Litton Industries, Inc. Common $1 par 02/10/1965
(See Litton Industries, Inc.)

ADLEY CORP (CT)
Merged into Yellow Freight System, Inc. 06/30/1977
Each share Common $2 par exchanged for $6.25 cash

ADM INDS INC (IN)
Name changed to Shelter Components, Inc. 12/31/1984
Shelter Components, Inc. merged into Shelter Components Corp. 02/05/1988
(See Shelter Components Corp.)

ADMAC INC (DE)
Merged into Flow Systems, Inc. 02/23/1989
Each share Common 1¢ par exchanged for (0.46082949) share Common 1¢ par
Flow Systems, Inc. name changed to Flow International Corp. (DE) 03/08/1989 which reincorporated in Washington 10/01/1998

ADMAR GROUP INC (FL)
Each share old Common $0.001 par exchanged for (0.2) share new Common $0.001 par 07/12/1991
Merged into Principal Health Care, Inc. 03/06/1996
Each share new Common $0.001 par exchanged for $2.25 cash

ADMAX RES INC (NV)
Each share old Common $0.00001 par exchanged for (10) shares new Common $0.00001 par 01/29/2007
Name changed to China YouTV Corp. 03/05/2007
China YouTV Corp. recapitalized as Microelectronics Technology Co. 10/06/2009

ADMAX TECHNOLOGY INC (DE)
Name changed to Aamaxan Transport Group, Inc. 08/28/1998

ADMINISTAFF INC (DE)
Common 1¢ par split (2) for (1) by issuance of (1) additional share payable 10/16/2000 to holders of record 09/25/2000 Ex date - 10/17/2000
Name changed to Insperity, Inc. 03/09/2011

ADMINISTERED FUND, INC. (DE)
Under plan of merger name changed to Axe-Houghton Fund, Inc. 10/31/1940
Axe-Houghton Fund, Inc. name changed to Axe-Houghton Fund A, Inc. (DE) (New) 02/23/1951 which reincorporated in Maryland 00/00/1973 which name changed to Axe-Houghton Income Fund, Inc. Income Fund 09/24/1976 which reorganized as Axe-Houghton Funds, Inc. 10/31/1990
(See Axe-Houghton Funds, Inc.)

ADMINISTERED FUND SECOND, INC. (DE)
Name changed to Administered Fund, Inc. 01/26/1940
Administered Fund, Inc. name changed to Axe-Houghton Fund, Inc. 10/31/1940 which name changed to Axe-Houghton Fund A, Inc. (DE) (New) 02/23/1951 which reincorporated in Maryland 00/00/1973 which name changed to Axe-Houghton Income Fund, Inc. 09/24/1976 which reorganized as Axe-Houghton Funds, Inc. Income Fund 10/31/1990
(See Axe-Houghton Funds, Inc.)

ADMINISTRADORA DE FONDOS DE PENSIONES PROVIDA S A (CHILE)
ADR agreement terminated 09/18/2014
Each Sponsored ADR for Common exchanged for $50.197372 cash

ADMINISTRATION & TR CO (MONTREAL, QC)
Capital Stock $25 par changed to $5 par and (4) additional shares issued 02/01/1962
Merged into General Trust of Canada (Montreal, QC) 01/07/1971
Each share Capital Stock $5 par exchanged for (1.333333) shares Common $5 par
General Trust of Canada (Montreal, QC) acquired by General Trustco of Canada Inc. 06/03/1986 which name changed to Genecan Financial Corp. 01/14/1994
(See Genecan Financial Corp.)

ADMINISTRATIVE & RESEARCH CORP. (NY)
Liquidated 00/00/1944
Details not available

ADMINISTRATIVE SYS INC (NY)
Charter cancelled and proclaimed dissolved for failure to pay taxes 04/15/1973

ADMIRAL BAY RES INC (ON)
Reincorporated 03/10/2004
Place of incorporation changed from (BC) to (ON) 03/10/2004
Reincorporated under the laws of British Columbia 03/10/2006

ADMIRAL BENBOW INN, INC. (TN)
Merged into Morrison Inc. (FL) 03/11/1968
Each share Common Capital Stock no par exchanged for (0.33333333) share Common $5 par
Morrison Inc. (FL) reincorporated in Delaware 10/01/1987 which name changed to Morrison Restaurants Inc. 10/01/1992 which merged into Piccadilly Cafeterias, Inc. 07/31/1998
(See Piccadilly Cafeterias, Inc.)

ADMIRAL BOAT CO. (CA)
Recapalized as Admiral United Industries, Inc. 10/17/1962
Each share Common $1 par exchanged for (0.25) share Common no par
Admiral United Industries, Inc. name changed to Emeryville Marina Enterprises 12/28/1972
(See Emeryville Marina Enterprises)

ADMIRAL CONS MNG CO (WA)
Recapitalized as IBC / Integrated Business Computers Inc. 10/10/1997
Each share Common 10¢ par exchanged for (0.06666666) share Common 10¢ par
(See IBC / Integrated Business Computers Inc.)

ADMIRAL CORP (DE)
Each share Capital Stock no par exchanged for (100) shares Capital Stock $3 par 00/00/1941
Each share Capital Stock $3 par exchanged for (4) shares Capital Stock $1 par 00/00/1943
Capital Stock $1 par split (2) for (1) by issuance of (1) additional share 07/01/1966
Capital Stock $1 par reclassified as Common $1 par 05/04/1967
Stock Dividends - 11-11111111% 12/31/1948; 100% 12/07/1949; 20% 10/19/1953
Merged into Rockwell International Corp. 04/09/1974
Each share Common $1 par exchanged for (0.5) share Common $1 par
Rockwell International Corp. merged into Boeing Co. 12/06/1996

ADMIRAL FIN CORP (DE)
Acquired by General Acceptance Corp. (New) 06/13/1958
Each share 60¢ Preferred $5 par exchanged for (1) share 60¢ Preference no par
Each share Common 10¢ par exchanged for approximately (0.1041) share Common $1 par
General Acceptance Corp. (New) name changed to GAC Corp. (PA) 07/01/1968 which reincorporated in Delaware 12/20/1973
(See GAC Corp. (DE))

ADMIRAL FINL CORP (FL)
Proclaimed dissolved for failure to file reports and pay fees 11/09/1990

ADMIRAL HOMES INC (PA)
Stock Dividend - 10% 12/01/1956
Placed in bankruptcy 02/23/1968
No stockholders' equity

ADMIRAL HOSPS INC (UT)
Charter suspended for failure to maintain a registered agent 12/31/1975

ADMIRAL INDUSTRIES, INC. (DE)
Charter cancelled and declared inoperative and void for non-payment of taxes 04/15/1972

ADMIRAL INTL ENTERPRISES CORP (DE)
Merged into Admiral Corp. 12/20/1973
Each share Common $1 par exchanged for $20 cash

ADMIRAL MINES LTD (BC)
Recapitalized as Camino Resources Ltd. 09/17/1986
Each share Common no par exchanged for (0.5) share Common no par
Camino Resources Ltd. recapitalized as Advanced Projects Ltd.

03/08/1991 which recapitalized as Skye Resources Inc. 05/23/2001 which was acquired by HudBay Minerals Inc. 08/26/2008

ADMIRAL OILS LTD. (CANADA)
Recapitalized as Canadian Admiral Oils Ltd. 00/00/1952
Each share Common no par exchanged for (0.33333333) share Common no par
Canadian Admiral Oils Ltd. acquired by Canadian Homestead Oils Ltd. 11/22/1957 which merged into Inter-City Gas Corp. 04/14/1980 which reorganized as Inter-City Products Corp. (MB) 04/18/1990 which reincorporated in Canada 06/05/1992 which name changed to International Comfort Products Corp. 07/09/1997
(See International Comfort Products Corp Corp.)

ADMIRAL PHOTO CORP. (DE)
Adjudicated bankrupt 11/06/1963
No stockholders' equity

ADMIRAL PLASTICS CORP. (NY)
Name changed to APL Corp. 12/02/1963
(See APL Corp.)

ADMIRAL SANTN INC (ON)
Name changed to Admiral Inc. 03/23/1998

ADMIRAL ST BK (TULSA, OK)
Stock Dividend - 100% 05/10/1980
Name changed to Century Bank (Tulsa, OK) and Capital Stock $10 par reclassified as Common $10 par 06/01/1981

ADMIRAL TRANSN GROUP INC (FL)
Proclaimed dissolved for failure to file reports and pay fees 10/13/1989

ADMIRAL UTD INDS INC (CA)
Name changed to Emeryville Marina Enterprises 12/28/1972
Each share Common no par exchanged for (1) share Common no par

ADMIRAL YELLOWKNIFE MINES LTD. (ON)
Charter cancelled and proclaimed dissolved for failure to pay taxes and file returns 11/07/1978

ADMIRALTY ALASKA GOLD MNG CO (AK)
Charter cancelled for failure to file reports and pay taxes 00/00/1978

ADMIRALTY BANCORP INC (DE)
Stock Dividends - 12.91% payable 01/30/2000 to holders of record 12/31/1999; 5% payable 11/16/2001 to holders of record 11/09/2001
Ex date - 11/07/2001
Merged into Royal Bank of Canada (Montreal, QC) 01/30/2003
Each share Class B Common no par exchanged for $26 cash

ADMIRALTY FD (DE)
Merged into Oppenheimer A.I.M. Fund, Inc. 12/07/1976
Each share Growth Series Stock $1 par exchanged for (0.3736854) share Capital Stock $1 par
Each share Income Series Stock $1 par exchanged for (0.3931176) share Capital Stock $1 par
Each share Insurance Series Stock $1 par exchanged for (0.8245874) share Capital Stock $1 par
Oppenheimer A.I.M. Fund, Inc. name changed to Oppenheimer Global Fund 02/01/1987

ADMIRALTY HLDG CO (CO)
SEC revoked common stock registration 03/25/2011

ADMIRALTY RES NL (AUSTRALIA)
Each old Sponsored ADR for Common exchanged for (0.2) new Sponsored ADR for Common 12/15/2010
ADR agreement terminated 10/02/2017
Each new Sponsored ADR for Common exchanged for $0.388197 cash

ADMOR MEMORY CORP (NV)
Recapitalized as Atlas Resources, Inc. 12/24/2003
Each share Common $0.001 par exchanged for (0.05) share Common $0.001 par
Atlas Resources, Inc. recapitalized as Globaltech Holdings, Inc. 08/01/2007

ADNARON COPPER LTD (QC)
Charter annulled for failure to file reports or pay fees 02/03/1973

ADNEW SILVER-COBALT MINES LTD. (ON)
Charter cancelled and proclaimed dissolved for failure to pay taxes and file returns 05/00/1960

ADNOR MINES LTD. (QC)
Dissolved 06/18/1977
Details not available

ADOBE BLDG CTRS INC (DE)
Merged into Imperial Industries, Inc. 09/29/1978
Each share Class A Common 1¢ par exchanged for (1) share Common 10¢ par
(See Imperial Industries, Inc.)

ADOBE BRICK & SUPPLY CO. (DE)
Ctfs. dated prior to 07/12/1972
Through voluntary exchange offer over 99% acquired by Stylon Corp. 00/00/1969
Public interest eliminated

ADOBE BRICK & SUPPLY CO. (DE)
Ctfs. dated after 07/12/1972
Name changed to Adobe Building Centers, Inc. 05/07/1973
Adobe Building Centers, Inc. merged into Imperial Industries, Inc. 09/29/1978
(See Imperial Industries, Inc.)

ADOBE CORP (DE)
Each share Class A 10¢ par exchanged for (0.95) share Common 30¢ par 04/17/1972
Merged into Adobe Oil & Gas Corp. 10/26/1977
Each share Common 30¢ par exchanged for $10.50 cash

ADOBE INVESTMENT CORP. (TX)
Each share Common $5 par exchanged for (5) shares Common $1 par 10/14/1968
Through voluntary exchange offer of (1.66666666) shares Adobe Corp. Common 30¢ par for each share Common $1 par 100% was acquired as of 09/10/1970
Public interest eliminated
(See Adobe Corp.)

ADOBE OIL & GAS CORP (DE)
Common 30¢ par split (5) for (4) by issuance of (0.25) additional share 05/30/1980
Common 30¢ par split (3) for (2) by issuance of (0.5) additional share 01/23/1981
Merged into Adobe Resources Corp. 10/31/1985
Each share Common 30¢ par exchanged for (0.4) share 12% Preferred $20 par, (0.36) share 9.2% Conv. Preferred $20 par, (0.3) share Common 1¢ par and (1) share AOI Coal Co. Common 30¢ par
Note: Distribution of Adobe Resources Corp. shares was made against (0.76) share and shares of AOI Coal Co. against (0.24) share Adobe Oil & Gas Corp. respectively
Adobe Resources Corp. merged into Santa Fe Energy Resources, Inc. 05/19/1992 which name changed to Santa Fe Snyder Corp. 05/05/1999 which merged into Devon Energy Corp. (New) 08/29/2000

ADOBE RES CORP (DE)
Merged into Santa Fe Energy Resources, Inc. 05/19/1992
Each share 9.2% Preferred $20 par exchanged for (0.5065) share 7% Conv. Preferred 1¢ par and (0.5974) share Common 1¢ par
Each share 12% Preferred $20 par exchanged for (0.5959) share 7% Conv. Preferred 1¢ par and (0.7029) share Common 1¢ par
Each share Common 1¢ par exchanged for (0.6) share Common 1¢ par
Santa Fe Energy Resources, Inc. name changed to Santa Fe Snyder Corp 05/05/1999 which merged into Devon Energy Corp. (New) 08/29/2000

ADOBE RES LTD (AB)
Merged into BriAlto Energy Corp. 12/31/1997
Each share Common no par exchanged for (0.2) Class A Common no par
BriAlto Energy Corp. name changed to Highland Energy Inc. 09/09/1999 which merged into Interaction Resources Ltd. 05/30/2000 which recapitalized as Ketch Energy Ltd. 06/16/2000 which merged into Acclaim Energy Trust 10/01/2002
(See Acclaim Energy Trust)

ADOBE SYS INC (DE)
Reincorporated 05/30/1997
Common no par split (2) for (1) by issuance of (1) additional share 03/11/1987
Common no par split (2) for (1) by issuance of (1) additional share 11/22/1988
Common no par split (2) for (1) by issuance of (1) additional share 08/10/1993
State of incorporation changed from (CA) to (DE) and Common no par changed to $0.0001 par 05/30/1997
Each share Common $0.0001 par received distribution of (0.01) share Netscape Communications Corp. Common $0.0001 par payable 08/27/1997 to holders of record 07/31/1997
Each share Common $0.0001 par received distribution of (0.0033333) share Siebel Systems, Inc. Common $0.001 par payable 12/01/1997 to holders of record 10/31/1997
Common $0.0001 par split (2) for (1) by issuance of (1) additional share payable 10/26/1999 to holders of record 10/04/1999
Common $0.0001 par split (2) for (1) by issuance of (1) additional share payable 10/24/2000 to holders of record 10/02/2000 Ex date - 10/25/2000
Common $0.0001 par split (2) for (1) by issuance of (1) additional share payable 05/23/2005 to holders of record 05/02/2005 Ex date - 05/24/2005
Name changed to Adobe Inc. 10/09/2018

ADOBE VENTURES INC (BC)
Each share old Common no par exchanged for (0.27777777) share new Common no par 02/21/2003
Name changed to Coalcorp Mining Inc. 10/27/2005
Coalcorp Mining Inc. name changed to Melior Resources Inc. 09/29/2011

ADOLA MNG CORP (BC)
Cease trade order effective 07/28/1989
Stockholders' equity unlikely

ADOLOR CORP (DE)
Acquired by Cubist Pharmaceuticals, Inc. 12/12/2011
Each share Common $0.0001 par exchanged for (1) Contingent Value Right and $4.25 cash

ADONIS MINES LTD (BC)
Recapitalized as Global Energy Corp. 02/25/1977
Each share Capital Stock $1 par exchanged for (0.2) share Capital Stock no par
Global Energy Corp. recapitalized as United Global Petroleum Inc. 09/13/1985
(See United Global Petroleum Inc.)

ADONOS RES INC (BC)
Merged into ADEX Mining Corp. 01/07/1993
Each share Common no par exchanged for (4.3333333) shares Common no par
ADEX Mining Corp. recapitalized as Adex Mining Inc. 07/15/1996

ADOODLE INC (DE)
Name changed to Olfactory Biosciences Corp. 04/20/2010

ADORE RES LTD (BC)
Name changed to Krieger Data International Corp. 10/14/1986
Krieger Data International Corp. name changed to Promark Software Inc. 11/17/1987 which name changed to clipclop.com Enterprises Inc. 08/30/1999 which recapitalized as Worldwide Technologies Inc. 09/10/2001
(See Worldwide Technologies Inc.)

ADPADS INC (CO)
SEC revoked common stock registration 02/13/2008

ADPT CORP (DE)
Recapitalized as Steel Excel Inc. 10/05/2011
Each share Common $0.001 par exchanged for (0.002) share Common $0.001 par
Note: Holders of (499) or fewer pre-split shares received $2.55345 cash per share
Steel Excel Inc. merged into Steel Partners Holdings L.P. 02/15/2017

ADR CAP CORP (BC)
Name changed to Delta Gold Corp. 02/19/2013
Delta Gold Corp. recapitalized as Mission Gold Ltd. 07/09/2015

ADR EXPLORATIONS LTD (ON)
Reorganized as cs-live.com inc. 08/30/2000
Each share Common no par exchanged for (1) share Common no par and (1) Common Stock Purchase Warrant expiring 03/08/2002 cs-live.com inc. name changed to Intelligent Web Technologies Inc. 09/18/2001
(See Intelligent Web Technologies Inc.)

ADR GLOBAL ENTERPRISES LTD (BC)
Name changed to Sonic Environmental Solutions Inc. 12/17/2002
Sonic Environmental Solutions Inc. name changed to Sonic Technology Solutions Inc. 06/27/2004 which name changed to Sonoro Energy Ltd. (BC) 07/07/2010 which reincorporated in Alberta 08/07/2013

ADRENALIN INTERACTIVE INC (DE)
Each share Common 1¢ par exchanged for (0.33333333) share Common 3¢ par 12/29/1998
Name changed to McGlen Internet Group, Inc. 12/03/1999
McGlen Internet Group, Inc. recapitalized as Northgate Innovations, Inc. 03/20/2002 which name changed to Digital Lifestyles Group, Inc. 06/25/2004 which name changed to TN-K Energy Group Inc. 10/29/2009

ADRENALINA (NV)
Each share old Common $0.001 par exchanged for (0.05) share new Common $0.001 par 11/09/2010
Name changed to ID Perfumes, Inc. 02/07/2013

ADRENALINE NATION MEDIA NETWORKS INC (TN)
Recapitalized 09/06/2007
Each share Common $0.001 par exchanged for (0.0001) share new Common $0.001 par 01/29/2007
Recapitalized from Adrenaline Nation Entertainment, Inc. to Adrenaline Nation Media Networks, Inc. 09/06/2007
Each share new Common $0.001 par exchanged for (0.01) share Common $0.001 par
Name changed to Greenstar Lighting, Inc. 10/12/2009

ADRIAN CO. (MI)
Name changed to Adrian Gas & Fuel Co. 00/00/1951
Adrian Gas & Fuel Co. name changed to Citizens Gas Fuel Co. (New) 00/00/1951 which was acquired by MCN Corp. 07/31/1990 which name changed to MCN Energy Group Inc. 04/28/1997

ADRIAN GAS & FUEL CO. (MI)
Name changed to Citizens Gas Fuel Co. (New) 00/00/1951
Citizens Gas Fuel Co. (New) acquired by MCN Corp. 07/31/1990 which name changed MCN Energy Group Inc. 04/28/1997

ADRIAN RES LTD (BC)
Name changed to Petaquilla Minerals Ltd. 10/12/2004
Each share Common no par exchanged for (1) share Common no par

ADRIAN STATE BANK (ADRIAN, MI)
Stock Dividends - 10% 03/01/1974; 25% 04/21/1978; 10% 04/02/1979; 15% 04/01/1980
Under plan of reorganization each share Common $10 par automatically became (1) share ASB Bankcorp, Inc. Common $10 par 10/01/1986
ASB Bankcorp, Inc. merged into Mid Am, Inc. 03/01/1995 which merged into Sky Financial Group, Inc. 10/02/1998 which merged into Huntington Bancshares Inc. 07/02/2007

ADRIAN STL CO NEW (MI)
4% Sr. Preferred called for redemption at $500 plus $3.33 accrued dividends on 09/30/2016

ADRIAN STL CO OLD (MI)
Stock Dividends - 10% 09/15/1978; 10% 09/14/1979
Reorganized as Adrian Steel Co. (New) 08/01/2011
Each share Common $1 par exchanged for (1) share 4% Sr. Preferred and (1) Non-Transferable Common Stock Purchase Warrant
(See Adrian Steel Co. (New))

ADRIANA RES INC (CANADA)
Under plan of merger name changed to Sprott Resource Holdings Inc. 02/13/2017

ADRIANA VENTURES INC (CANADA)
Name changed to Adriana Resources Inc. 08/08/2005
Adriana Resources Inc. name changed to Sprott Resource Holdings Inc. 02/13/2017

ADRIATIC HLDGS LTD (NV)
Name changed to Heartland Oil & Gas Corp. 11/05/2002
(See Heartland Oil & Gas Corp.)

ADRIATIC RES CORP (BC)
Recapitalized as AIC International Resources Corp. 11/26/1987
Each share Common no par exchanged for (0.2) share Common no par
(See AIC International Resources Corp.)

ADRIEN ARPEL INC (NY)
Each share 14.5% Preferred $25 par received distribution of (5.43102) share Common 1¢ par payable 01/08/1999 to holders of record 11/06/1998
Assets sold for the benefit of creditors 00/00/1999
No stockholders' equity

ADROIT RES INC (BC)
Recapitalized as iMetal Resources Inc. 11/09/2015
Each share Common no par exchanged for (0.1) share Common no par

ADS INC (CANADA)
Name changed 07/31/1996
Name changed from ADS associes ltee to ADS Inc. and (1) additional share issued 07/31/1996
Merged into 7097697 Canada Inc. 02/23/2009
Each share Common no par exchanged for $0.90 cash

ADS MEDIA GROUP INC (UT)
Each share old Common $0.001 par exchanged for (0.2) share new Common $0.001 par 01/22/2007
SEC revoked common stock registration 11/16/2011

ADS SYSTEMS LTD (NV)
Recapitalized as Remington Ventures, Inc. 11/18/2004
Each share Common $0.001 par exchanged for (0.001) share Common $0.001 par
(See Remington Ventures, Inc.)

ADSERO CORP (DE)
Each share old Common $0.001 par exchanged for (0.02) share new Common $0.001 par 12/06/2007
Name changed to Quantum Telecom Inc. 05/27/2008

ADSON INDS INC (NY)
Name changed to Gaynor Industries, Inc. 01/24/1969
Gaynor Industries, Inc. name changed to Gaynor-Stafford Industries, Inc. 11/20/1970
(See Gaynor-Stafford Industries, Inc.)

ADSONLY GROUP INC (CA)
Name changed to ResourceNet Communications, Inc. 04/15/1997
(See ResourceNet Communications, Inc.)

ADSTAR COM INC (DE)
Name changed to AdStar, Inc. 07/16/2001

ADSURE INC (CANADA)
Name changed to iForum Financial Network Inc. 12/11/2000

ADT CORP (DE)
Acquired by Prime Security Services Borrower, LLC 05/02/2016
Each share Common 1¢ par exchanged for $42 cash

ADT FIN INC (CANADA)
Each Non-Vtg. Exchangeable Share Ser. A no par exchanged for (1) share ADT Ltd. U.S. Common 10¢ par 06/30/1995
ADT Ltd. merged into Tyco International Ltd. (Bermuda) 07/02/1997 which reincorporated in Switzerland 03/17/2009 which merged into Johnson Controls International PLC 09/06/2016

ADT INC (NJ)
Each share Common $1 par received distribution of (0.2) share Aritech Corp. Common $2 par 07/01/1986
Merged into Hawley Group Ltd. 10/09/1987

Each share Common $1 par exchanged for $52 cash

ADT JOHN B CO (MD)
Name changed to Columbia Precision Corp. 01/18/1971
(See Columbia Precision Corp.)

ADT LTD (BERMUDA)
Each share U.S. Common 1¢ par exchanged for (0.1) share U.S. Common 10¢ par 06/17/1991
Each ADR for U.S. Common 10¢ par exchanged for (1) share U.S. Common 10¢ par 02/28/1992
Merged into Tyco International Ltd. (Bermuda) 07/02/1997
Each share U.S. Common 10¢ par exchanged for (0.48133) share Common 20¢ par
Tyco International Ltd. (Bermuda) reincorporated in Switzerland 03/17/2009 which merged into Johnson Controls International PLC 09/06/2016

ADTEC INC (DE)
Charter cancelled and declared inoperative and void for non-payment of taxes 03/01/1993

ADTOMIZE INC (NV)
Each share old Common $0.0001 par exchanged for (80) shares new Common $0.0001 par 09/08/2010
Name changed to Potash America, Inc. 03/07/2011

ADULIS MINERALS CORP (AB)
Recapitalized as Adulis Resources Inc. 05/01/2001
Each share Common no par exchanged for (0.25) share Common no par
Adulis Resources Inc. name changed to Solana Resources Ltd. 10/18/2005 which merged into Gran Tierra Energy Inc. (NV) 11/17/2008 which reincorporated in Delaware 10/31/2016

ADULIS RES INC (AB)
Name changed to Solana Resources Ltd. 10/18/2005
Solana Resources Ltd. merged into Gran Tierra Energy Inc. (NV) 11/17/2008 which reincorporated in Delaware 10/31/2016

ADULT ENTMT CAP INC (NV)
Name changed to Zealous, Inc. 03/05/2009
Zealous, Inc. name changed to CoreStream Energy Inc. 09/03/2010
(See CoreStream Energy Inc.)

ADUROMED INDS INC (DE)
Name changed to MedClean Technologies, Inc. 01/26/2009
(See MedClean Technologies, Inc.)

ADV FD INC (DE)
Name changed to WPG Fund, Inc. (DE) 04/16/1985
WPG Fund, Inc. (DE) reincorporated in Massachusetts 04/29/1988 which name changed to WPG Growth & Income Fund 12/29/1989 which name changed to WPG Large Cap Growth Fund 10/18/2000

ADVA INTL INC (DE)
SEC revoked common stock registration 03/11/2008

ADVACARE INC (DE)
Merged into Medaphis Corp. 11/30/1994
Each share Common 1¢ par exchanged for (0.0673) share Common 1¢ par
Medaphis Corp. name changed to Per-Se Technologies, Inc. 08/16/1999
(See Per-Se Technologies, Inc.)

ADVANCE ALUMINUM CASTINGS CORP. (IL)
Stock Dividend - 10% 03/17/1945
Under plan of partial liquidation each share Common $5 par received $10 cash per share and cancellation of (0.8) of each share 12/12/1958
Under plan of merger name changed to Advance Ross Electronics Corp. and each share Common $5 par exchanged for (10) shares Common 50¢ par 07/29/1959
Advance Ross Electronics Corp. acquired by Byllesby (H.M.) & Co. 05/16/1963 which name changed to Advance Ross Corp. (Old) 04/23/1964 which reorganized as Advance Ross Corp. (New) 06/17/1993 which merged into CUC International Inc. 01/10/1996 which name changed to Cendant Corp. 12/17/1997 which reorganized as Avis Budget Group, Inc. 09/01/2006

ADVANCE AMER CASH ADVANCE CTRS INC (DE)
Merged into Grupo Elektra S.A. de C.V. 04/23/2012
Each share Common 1¢ par exchanged for $10.50 cash

ADVANCE BAG & PAPER CO., INC.
Merged into Southern Advance Bag & Paper Co., Inc. 00/00/1939
Details not available

ADVANCE BANCORP INC (DE)
Merged into Charter One Financial, Inc. 06/06/2003
Each share Common $1 par exchanged for (32.16) shares Common 1¢ par
(See Charter One Financial, Inc.)

ADVANCE CIRCUITS INC (MN)
Common 10¢ par split (3) for (1) by issuance of (2) additional shares 06/25/1981
Common 10¢ par split (5) for (4) by issuance of (0.25) additional share 01/19/1990
Common 10¢ par split (5) for (4) by issuance of (0.25) additional share 07/02/1992
Stock Dividend - 200% 04/25/1980
Merged into Johnson Matthery PLC 10/06/1995
Each share Common 10¢ par exchanged for $22.50 cash

ADVANCE COMPUTER UTILS CORP (DE)
Name changed to Computer Utilities Corp. 01/18/1969
(See Computer Utilities Corp.)

ADVANCE CONTAINER CORP (CA)
Common $3.50 par changed to $1.75 par and (1) additional share issued 08/23/1972
Adjudicated bankrupt 01/08/1976
Stockholders' equity unlikely

ADVANCE DATA CORP (PA)
Name changed to Motek Corp. 02/09/1971
Each share Common 1¢ par exchanged for (1) share Common 1¢ par

ADVANCE DISPLAY TECHNOLOGIES INC (CO)
Each share old Common $0.001 par exchanged for (0.2) share new Common $0.001 par 11/26/1990
Each share new Common $0.001 par exchanged again for (0.1) share new Common $0.001 par 05/05/1993
Each share new Common $0.001 par exchanged again for (0.00066666) share new Common $0.001 par 09/24/2010
Note: In effect holders received $0.02 cash per share and public interest was eliminated
No holder will receive less than $1

ADVANCE ENGR CO (MN)
Acquired by Cornelius Co. 04/25/1969
Each share Class A $1 par exchanged for (0.7857) share Common 20¢ par
Each share Common 50¢ par

exchanged for (0.33333333) share Common 20¢ par
(See Cornelius Co.)

ADVANCE EXPLORATION CO. (DE)
Name changed to Advance Petroleum Co. 00/00/1956
Advance Petroleum Co. assets sold to Reiter-Foster Oil Corp. 09/23/1957 which merged into Baruch-Foster Corp. 01/11/1960
(See Baruch-Foster Corp.)

ADVANCE FINL BANCORP (DE)
Merged into Parkvale Financial Corp. 12/31/2004
Each share Common 10¢ par exchanged for $26 cash

ADVANCE GROWTH CAP CORP (IL)
Liquidation completed
Each share Common $1 par received initial distribution of $2.50 cash 10/28/1982
Each share Common $1 par received second distribution of $0.92 cash 01/31/1983
Each share Common $1 par received third distribution of $3.38 cash 10/28/1983
Each share Common $1 par received fourth distribution of $2 cash 10/16/1985
Each share Common $1 par received fifth distribution of $0.35 cash 06/10/1986
Each share Common $1 par received sixth distribution of $2 cash 10/13/1987
Each share Common $1 par exchanged for seventh and final distribution of $0.346789 cash 06/15/1989

ADVANCE INDUSTRIES, INC. (MA)
Acquired by Wilson Brothers 01/22/1964
Each share Common exchanged for (6.25) shares Common
Wilson Brothers name changed to Wilson Brothers USA, Inc. 08/20/1997
(See Wilson Brothers USA, Inc.)

ADVANCE INDUSTRIES LTD. (DE)
Charter cancelled and declared inoperative and void for non-payment of taxes 04/15/1973

ADVANCE INVS CORP (DE)
Reincorporated 08/30/1976
State of incorporation changed from (MD) to (DE) 08/30/1976
Merged into Windsor Fund, Inc. (MD) 12/27/1978
Each share Common 10¢ par exchanged for (1.13026) shares Capital Stock $1 par
Windsor Fund, Inc. (MD) which reincorporated in Pennsylvania 01/02/1985 which reincorporated in Maryland as Windsor Funds, Inc. 12/30/1985 which name changed to Vanguard/Windsor Funds, Inc. (MD) 04/30/1993 which reincorporated in Delaware as Vanguard Windsor Funds 05/29/1998

ADVANCE METAL PRODS INC (FL)
Proclaimed dissolved for failure to file reports and pay fees 09/03/1976

ADVANCE MTG CORP (MI)
Common $1 par split (1.333) for (1) by issuance of (0.333) additional share 08/25/1969
Merged into FNCB-Advance Corp. 07/31/1970
Each share Common $1 par exchanged for $29.50 cash

ADVANCE MULTIMEDIA CORP (AB)
Name changed to DiscoverWare Inc. 04/22/1996
(See DiscoverWare Inc.)

ADVANCE MURGOR EXPLS LTD (ON)
Recapitalized as Murgor Resources Inc.-Les Ressources Murgor Inc. (ON) 07/23/1985
Each share Common no par exchanged for (0.5) share Common no par
Murgor Resources Inc.-Les Ressources Murgor Inc. (ON) reincorporated in Canada 09/22/1989 which merged into Alexandria Minerals Corp. 03/12/2015

ADVANCE NANOTECH INC (DE)
Reincorporated 06/19/2006
State of incorporation changed from (CO) to (DE) and Common no par changed to $0.001 par 06/19/2006
SEC revoked common stock registration 03/22/2013

ADVANCE OIL CO., LTD. (CANADA)
Each share Capital Stock $1 par exchanged for (3.33333333) shares Capital Stock no par 00/00/1929
Completely liquidated 01/01/1964
Each share Capital Stock no par exchanged for first and final distribution of $0.035 cash

ADVANCE PARADIGM INC (DE)
Common 1¢ par split (2) for (1) by issuance of (1) additional share payable 11/30/1999 to holders of record 11/11/1999
Name changed to AdvancePCS and Common 1¢ par reclassified as Class A Common 1¢ par 01/11/2001
AdvancePCS merged into Caremark Rx, Inc. 03/24/2004 which merged into CVS/Caremark Corp. 03/22/2007 which name changed to CVS Caremark Corp. 05/10/2007

ADVANCE PETROLEUM CO. (DE)
Merged into Reiter-Foster Oil Corp. 09/23/1957
Each share Common 10¢ par exchanged for (0.653846) share Common 50¢ par
Reiter-Foster Oil Corp. merged into Baruch-Foster Corp. 01/11/1960
(See Baruch-Foster Corp.)

ADVANCE PUBLISHING CORP. (MA)
Charter revoked for failure to file reports and pay fees 12/13/1961

ADVANCE RED LAKE GOLD MINES LTD (ON)
Recapitalized as Titan Empire Inc. 12/08/1989
Each share Common $1 par exchanged for (0.2) share Class A Subordinate no par and (1) share Class B Multiple no par
Titan Empire Inc. recapitalized as AWG American-WestJava Gold Corp. (ON) 11/02/1994 which reincorporated in British Columbia 01/04/1995 which reorganized in Ontario as AWG American-WestJava Gold Inc. 11/13/1995 which recapitalized as Kalimantan Gold Corp. (ON) 05/03/1996 which reincorporated in Bermuda as Kalimantan Gold Corp. Ltd. 12/19/1997 which name changed to Asiamet Resources Ltd. 07/27/2015
(See Asiamet Resources Ltd.)

ADVANCE ROSS CORP (DE)
Under plan of reorganization each share 5% Preferred $25 par and Common 10¢ par automatically became (1) share Advance Ross Corp. (New) 5% Preferred $25 par and Common 1¢ par respectively 06/17/1993
Advance Ross Corp. (New) merged into CUC International Inc. 01/10/1996 which name changed to Cendant Corp. 12/17/1997 which reorganized as Avis Budget Group, Inc. 09/01/2006

ADVANCE ROSS CORP NEW (DE)
Common 1¢ par split (2) for (1) by issuance of (1) additional share 02/04/1994
Common 1¢ par split (2) for (1) by issuance of (1) additional share 09/08/1995
Merged into CUC International Inc. 01/10/1996
Each share 5% Preferred $25 par exchanged for (0.8245) share Common 1¢ par
Each share Common 1¢ par exchanged for (0.83333333) share Common 1¢ par
CUC International Inc. name changed to Cendant Corp. 12/17/1997 which reorganized as Avis Budget Group, Inc. 09/01/2006

ADVANCE ROSS ELECTRONICS CORP. (IL)
Common 50¢ par changed to 25¢ par and (1) additional share issued 11/25/1960
Acquired by Byllesby (H.M.) & Co. on a share for share basis 05/16/1963
Byllesby (H.M.) & Co. name changed to Advance Ross Corp. (Old) 04/23/1964 which reorganized as Advance Ross Corp. (New) 06/17/1993 which merged into CUC International Inc. 01/10/1996 which name changed to Cendant Corp. 12/17/1997 which reorganized as Avis Budget Group, Inc. 09/01/2006

ADVANCE RUMELY CO.
Recapitalized as Advance Rumely Corp. 00/00/1930
Details not available

ADVANCE RUMELY CORP.
Dissolved 00/00/1935
Details not available

ADVANCE SPORTS MEDICINE CORP (AB)
Recapitalized as Indo Pacific Resources Ltd. 06/29/1995
Each share Common no par exchanged for (0.2) share Common no par
(See Indo Pacific Resources Ltd.)

ADVANCE TAX REPRESENTATION INC (NV)
Merged into Show Offs Disposable Products Corp. 10/10/1986
Details not available

ADVANCE TECHNOLOGIES INC (NV)
Each share old Common $0.001 par exchanged for (0.02857142) share new Common $0.001 par 02/25/1999
Recapitalized as China SXAN Biotech, Inc. 09/10/2007
Each share new Common $0.001 par exchanged for (0.01960784) share Common $0.001 par
China SXAN Biotech, Inc. recapitalized as China Organic Fertilizer, Inc. 04/21/2010
(See China Organic Fertilizer, Inc.)

ADVANCE TIRE SYS INC (BC)
Recapitalized as ATS Wheel Inc. 11/17/1993
Each share Common no par exchanged for (0.2) share Common no par
ATS Wheel Inc. name changed to JSS Resources, Inc. 07/20/1998 which name changed to WSI Interactive Corp. 07/26/1999 which recapitalized as iaNett International Systems Ltd. 05/07/2001 which name changed to Data Fortress Systems Group Ltd. 09/03/2002

ADVANCED ACCELERATOR APPLICATIONS S A (FRANCE)
ADS agreement terminated 02/25/2018
Each Sponsored ADS for Ordinary exchanged for $81.95 cash

ADVANCED ACQUISITIONS INC (CO)
Name changed to Ocean Corp. 07/23/1989

ADVANCED AERO WING SYS CORP (BC)
Struck off register and declared dissolved for failure to file returns 10/27/1989

ADVANCED AERODYNAMICS & STRUCTURES INC (DE)
Name changed to Mooney Aerospace Group, Ltd. 07/23/2002
(See Mooney Aerospace Group, Ltd.)

ADVANCED ANALOGIC TECHNOLOGIES INC (DE)
Acquired by Skyworks Solutions, Inc. 01/10/2012
Each share Common $0.001 par exchanged for $5.80 cash

ADVANCED APPEARANCE AMER INC (NV)
Recapitalized as ATR Industries Inc. 01/06/1998
Each share Common $0.001 par exchanged for (0.005) share Common $0.001 par
ATR Industries Inc. name changed to Beautymerchant.com Inc. 09/17/1999 which name changed to National Beauty Corp. 03/30/2001 which recapitalized as Hairmax International, Inc. 08/01/2003 which name changed to China Digital Media Corp. 03/31/2005
(See China Digital Media Corp.)

ADVANCED BATTERY TECHNOLOGIES INC (DE)
SEC revoked common stock registration 12/31/2015

ADVANCED BIO / CHEM INC (NV)
Name changed to Industrial Enterprises of America, Inc. 12/09/2004
(See Industrial Enterprises of America, Inc.)

ADVANCED BIOLOGICAL SYS INC (DE)
Each share old Common $0.001 par exchanged for (0.33333333) share new Common $0.001 par 08/25/1992
Each share new Common $0.001 par exchanged for (0.03333333) share Common $0.0001 par 08/14/1996
Name changed to ABS Group, Inc. 10/11/1996
ABS Group, Inc. recapitalized as African American Medical Network, Inc. 07/21/2004 which name changed to AFMN, Inc. 01/18/2005 which recapitalized as Motion Picture Group, Inc. 02/23/2006

ADVANCED BIOPHOTONICS INC (DE)
Ceased operations 01/25/2008
Stockholders' equity unlikely

ADVANCED BIOTHERAPY INC (DE)
Reincorporated 09/01/2000
Reincorporated from Advanced Biotherapy Concepts, Inc. (NV) to under the laws of Delaware as Advanced Biotherapy, Inc. 09/01/2000
Merged into Lime Energy Co. 03/04/2009
Each share Common $0.001 par exchanged for (0.002124) share Common $0.0001 par

ADVANCED BODYMETRICS CORP (DE)
Reorganized under the laws of Nevada as ICM Telecommunications, Inc. 01/24/2002
Each share Common $0.001 par exchanged for (0.05) share Common $0.001 par
ICM Telecommunications, Inc. recapitalized as eHolding Technologies, Inc. 05/26/2006 which recapitalized as Pine Ridge Holdings, Inc. 03/10/2008 which name changed to Mike the Pike

Productions, Inc. (NV) 08/05/2009 which reorganized in Wyoming 03/03/2011

ADVANCED BUSINESS SCIENCES INC (DE)
Name changed to iSecureTrac Corp. 06/19/2001
iSecureTrac Corp. name changed to Technology Monitoring Solutions, Inc. 04/09/2014
(See Technology Monitoring Solutions, Inc.)

ADVANCED CANNABIS SOLUTIONS INC (CO)
Name changed to General Cannabis Corp. 06/25/2015

ADVANCED CELL TECHNOLOGY INC (DE)
Each share old Common $0.001 par exchanged for (0.01) share new Common $0.001 par 08/28/2014
Name changed to Ocata Therapeutics, Inc. 11/14/2014
(See Ocata Therapeutics, Inc.)

ADVANCED CELLULAR INC (NV)
Each share old Common $0.0001 par exchanged for (5) shares new Common $0.0001 par 02/20/2013
Name changed to Makism 3D Corp. 10/28/2013

ADVANCED CELLULAR TECHNOLOGY INC (CA)
Recapitalized as Auto Underwriters of America, Inc. 03/20/2004
Each share Common no par exchanged for (0.01) share Common no par
(See Auto Underwriters of America, Inc.)

ADVANCED CHEM TECHNOLOGY (CA)
Merged into Plant Industries, Inc. (DE) 08/28/1981
Each share Common no par exchanged for (0.392) share Common 50¢ par and $2.25 cash
(See Plant Industries, Inc. (DE))

ADVANCED CLEAN TECHNOLOGIES INC (NV)
Name changed to Act Clean Technologies, Inc. 12/09/2009

ADVANCED CLOUD STORAGE INC (NV)
Reorganized as Montalvo Spirits, Inc. 02/01/2013
Each share Common $0.001 par exchanged for (31.4552) shares Common $0.001 par

ADVANCED COATING TECHNOLOGIES INC (NV)
Name changed to VitroSeal Inc. 01/19/1999
VitroSeal Inc. name changed to VitriSeal Inc. 02/18/1999 which name changed to Liquitek Enterprises Inc. 07/31/2000
(See Liquitek Enterprises Inc.)

ADVANCED COMMUNICATION SYS INC (DE)
Merged into Titan Corp. 02/25/2000
Each share Common 1¢ par exchanged for (0.56774194) share Common 1¢ par
(See Titan Corp.)

ADVANCED COMMUNICATIONS GROUP INC (DE)
Name changed to WorldPages.com, Inc. 02/24/2000
(See WorldPages.com, Inc.)

ADVANCED COMMUNICATIONS TECHNOLOGIES INC (FL)
Each share Common no par received distribution of (0.00165291) share Herborium Group, Inc. Common $0.001 par payable 12/14/2006 to holders of record 08/11/2006
Name changed to Encompass Group Affiliates, Inc. 05/20/2008
(See Encompass Group Affiliates, Inc.)

ADVANCED COMPUTER TECHNIQUES CORP (NY)
$0.37 Preferred $3.70 par called for redemption 06/30/1986
Acquired by PRT Group Inc. 01/31/1998
Details not available

ADVANCED CONTENT SVCS INC (NV)
Recapitalized as New Wave Holdings, Inc. 12/08/2014
Each share Common $0.001 par exchanged for (0.005) share Common $0.001 par
New Wave Holdings, Inc. name changed to PAO Group, Inc. 06/29/2017

ADVANCED DEFENSE TECHNOLOGIES INC (FL)
Recapitalized as Star Jets International, Inc. 02/12/2018
Each share Common $0.001 par exchanged for (0.01) share Common - $0.001 par

ADVANCED DEFINITION SYS INC (NV)
Each share Common $0.0001 par received distribution of (1) share Advanced Definition International Restricted Common payable 09/01/2004 to holders of record 07/01/2004
Recapitalized as Mobile Wireless Security, Inc. 11/24/2004
Each share Common $0.0001 par exchanged for (0.001) share Common $0.0001 par
Mobile Wireless Security, Inc. name changed to Hightowers Petroleum Holdings Ltd. 06/13/2006 which name changed to International Oil & Gas Holdings Corp. 07/19/2006 which name changed to Inscor, Inc. 05/26/2011 which recapitalized as Oicintra, Inc. 01/14/2016

ADVANCED DEPOSITION TECHNOLOGIES INC (DE)
Chapter 11 bankruptcy proceedings converted to Chapter 7 on 04/22/2002
Stockholders' equity unlikely

ADVANCED DETECTORS INC (DE)
Company terminated registration of common stock and is no longer public as of 03/17/1997
Details not available

ADVANCED DEVELOPMENT LABORATORIES INC. (DE)
Name changed to CDM, Inc. 11/16/1965
CDM, Inc. acquired by Sanders Associates, Inc. (DE) 12/21/1965
(See Sanders Associates, Inc. (DE))

ADVANCED DIAGNOSTIC VENTURES INC (NV)
Recapitalized as X Mark Corp. 04/24/1986
Each share Common $0.001 par exchanged for (0.33333333) share Common $0.001 par
(See X Mark Corp.)

ADVANCED DIGITAL INFORMATION CORP (WA)
Common no par split (2) for (1) by issuance of (1) additional share payable 08/11/1999 to holders of record 07/30/1999 Ex date - 08/12/1999
Common no par split (2) for (1) by issuance of (1) additional share payable 03/13/2000 to holders of record 03/01/2000
Merged into Quantum Corp. 08/22/2006
Each share Common no par exchanged for $12.25 cash

ADVANCED DIGITAL SYS INC (DE)
Adjudicated bankrupt 10/16/1975
Stockholders' equity unlikely

ADVANCED DRILLING SYS INC (TX)
Dissolved 04/30/1986
No stockholders' equity

ADVANCED ECOLOGY SYS CORP (BC)
Recapitalized as Consolidated Advanced Ecology Corp. 01/09/1990
Each share Common no par exchanged for (0.33333333) share Common no par
(See Consolidated Advanced Ecology Corp.)

ADVANCED ELECTR SUPPORT PRODS INC (FL)
Name changed to AESP, Inc. 08/13/2002
(See AESP, Inc.)

ADVANCED ELECTRS CORP (NY)
Adjudicated bankrupt 07/25/1966
No stockholders' equity

ADVANCED ENCRYPTION TECHNOLOGY AMER INC (NV)
Each share old Common $0.001 par exchanged for (0.1) share new Common $0.001 par 02/24/1999
Charter permanently revoked for failure to file reports and pay fees 07/03/2000

ADVANCED ENERGY CONCEPTS INC (ME)
Each share Common 1¢ par exchanged for (0.33333333) share Common $0.001 par 06/28/1983
Charter suspended for failure to file annual reports 09/03/1991

ADVANCED ENERGY CORP (FL)
Proclaimed dissolved for failure to file reports and pay fees 11/14/1986

ADVANCED ENERGY RES INC (DE)
Plan of reorganization under Chapter 11 bankruptcy proceedings confirmed 07/27/1990
No stockholders' equity

ADVANCED ENVIRONMENTAL PETE PRODUCERS INC (FL)
Name changed to Oncolix, Inc. 11/29/2017

ADVANCED ENVIRONMENTAL RECYCLING TECHNOLOGIES INC (DE)
Acquired by Oldcastle Architectural, Inc. 05/01/2017
Each share Class A Common 1¢ par exchanged for $0.135936 cash

ADVANCED ENVIRONMENTAL SOLUTIONS INC (DE)
Common $0.001 par split (2) for (1) by issuance of (1) additional share payable 05/09/1997 to holders of record 04/28/1997
Name changed to Viva Holdings, Inc. 07/01/1998
Viva Holdings, Inc. name changed to Chemicorp International, Inc. 12/23/1998

ADVANCED ENVIRONMENTAL SYS INC (NY)
Merged into AES Acquisition Corp. 02/01/1998
Each share Common $0.0001 par exchanged for $0.0059 cash

ADVANCED EXPLORATIONS INC (ON)
Filed Notice of Intention to Make a Proposal under the Bankrupcy & Insolvency Act 07/10/2015
Stockholders' equity unlikely

ADVANCED FIBER TECHNOLOGIES AFT INCOME FD (QC)
Acquired by Aikawa Iron Works Co. Ltd. 03/29/2006
Each Unit received $3 cash

ADVANCED FIBRE COMMUNICATIONS INC (DE)
Common 1¢ par split (2) for (1) by issuance of (1) additional share payable 09/22/1997 to holders of record 09/08/1997
Acquired by Tellabs, Inc. 11/30/2004
Each share Common 1¢ par exchanged for (0.504) share Common 1¢ par and $12 cash
(See Tellabs, Inc.)

ADVANCED FINL INC (DE)
Each share old Common $0.001 par exchanged for (0.1) share new Common $0.001 par 12/30/1991
Plan of reorganization under Chapter 11 Federal Bankruptcy Code effective 02/12/1999
Each share Preferred Ser. A exchanged for (0.05269) share new Common $0.001 par
Each share 10.50% Preferred Ser. B exchanged for (0.05269) share new Common $0.001 par
Each share new Common $0.001 par exchanged again for (0.05269) share new Common $0.001 par
Recapitalized as Advanced Energy Recovery, Inc. 08/20/2004
Each share new Common $0.001 par exchanged for (0.33333333) share Common $0.001 par 08/20/2004

ADVANCED FUEL SYS INC (WA)
Name changed to AirSensors, Inc. (WA) 07/08/1983
AirSensors, Inc. (WA) reincorporated in Delaware 12/11/1985 which name changed to IMPCO Technologies, Inc. 09/15/1997 which recapitalized as Fuel Systems Solutions, Inc. 08/25/2006 which merged into Westport Fuel Systems Inc. 06/08/2016

ADVANCED GAMING TECHNOLOGY INC (WY)
Each share old Common $0.005 par exchanged for (0.25) share new Common $0.005 par 07/07/1998
Each share new Common $0.005 par exchanged again for approximately (0.01515151) share new Common $0.005 par 08/19/1999
Each share new Common $0.005 par exchanged for (0.01) share new Common $0.005 par 06/25/2003
Name changed to Mediaworx, Inc. 07/17/2003
(See Mediaworx, Inc.)

ADVANCED GENETIC SCIENCES INC (DE)
Merged into DNA Plant Technology Corp. 11/22/1988
Each share Common 1¢ par exchanged for (0.5) share Common 1¢ par
DNA Plant Technology Corp. merged into DNAP Holding Corp. 09/26/1996 which name changed to Bionova Holding Corp. 04/29/1999
(See Bionova Holding Corp.)

ADVANCED GLOBAL INDS CORP (NV)
Name changed to Synova Healthcare Group, Inc. 02/10/2005
(See Synova Healthcare Group, Inc.)

ADVANCED GRAVIS COMPUTER TECHNOLOGY LTD (BC)
Merged into Pyramid Acquisition Corp. 01/23/1997
Each share Common no par exchanged for $0.50 cash

ADVANCED GROWING SYS INC (NV)
SEC revoked common stock registration 04/13/2012

ADVANCED GROWTH SYS INC (BC)
Struck off register and declared dissolved for failure to file returns 05/28/1993

ADVANCED HEALTH CORP (DE)
Name changed to AHT Corp. 02/01/1999
(See AHT Corp.)

ADVANCED HEALTHCARE TECHNOLOGIES INC (NV)
Recapitalized as Global Resource Corp. 09/14/2004
Each share Common $0.001 par exchanged for (0.01) share Common $0.001 par
(See Global Resource Corp.)

ADVANCED ID CORP (NV)
Reincorporated 05/26/2006
State of incorporation changed from (SD) to (NV) 05/26/2006
SEC revoked common stock registration 03/05/2013

ADVANCED IMAGE TECHNOLOGY INC (DE)
Charter forfeited for failure to maintain a registered agent 02/25/1991

ADVANCED INDL MINERALS INC (DE)
Merged into AIM Group, Inc. 03/31/1995
Each share Common no par exchanged for (0.426825) share Common 1¢ par
AIM Group, Inc. name changed to Cereus Technology Partners, Inc. 12/06/1999 which merged into Verso Technologies, Inc. 10/02/2000

ADVANCED INFO SVC LTD (THAILAND)
Name changed to Advanced Information Service PLC 11/13/1992

ADVANCED INSTL MGMT SOFTWARE INC (NY)
Dissolved by proclamation 12/24/2002

ADVANCED INTEGRATED MGMT SVCS INC (UT)
Reorganized as AIMSI Technologies, Inc. 11/17/2004
Each share Common no par exchanged for (5) shares Common no par
(See AIMSI Technologies, Inc.)

ADVANCED INTERACTIVE INC NEW (NV)
SEC revoked common stock registration 05/09/2008

ADVANCED INTERVENTIONAL SYS INC (CA)
Merged into Spectranetics Corp. 06/10/1994
Each share Common no par exchanged for (0.80282) share Common $0.001 par
(See Spectranetics Corp.)

ADVANCED KNOWLEDGE INC (DE)
Name changed to Sporting Magic Inc. 06/09/2000
Sporting Magic Inc. name changed to Next, Inc. 12/27/2002

ADVANCED LASER PRODS INC (DE)
Each share old Common $0.001 par exchanged for (0.02) share new Common $0.001 par 04/20/1998
Recapitalized as Digs Inc. 10/16/1998
Each share new Common $0.001 par exchanged for (0.05) share Common $0.001 par
Digs Inc. name changed to iVideoNow, Inc. (DE) 06/15/2000 which reorganized in Florida as 99 Cent Stuff, Inc. 09/15/2003
(See 99 Cent Stuff, Inc.)

ADVANCED LOGIC RESH INC (DE)
Merged into Gateway 2000, Inc. 07/23/1997
Each share Common 1¢ par exchanged for $15.50 cash

ADVANCED LOGIC SYS INC (CA)
Chapter 11 Federal Bankruptcy code converted to Chapter 7 on 05/19/1989
Stockholders' equity unlikely

ADVANCED LTG TECHNOLOGIES INC (OH)
Plan of reorganization under Chapter 11 Federal Bankruptcy proceedings effective 12/10/2003
Each Share of Bene. Int. received initial distribution of approximately $0.53 cash 12/10/2003
Each share Common $0.001 par automatically became (1) ADLT Class 7 Liquidating Trust Share of Bene. Int. 01/06/2004

ADVANCED LUMITECH INC (NV)
Name changed to Brightec, Inc. 11/13/2006

ADVANCED MACH VISION CORP (CA)
Merged into Key Technology, Inc. 07/13/2000
Each share Class A Common no par exchanged for (0.1) share Conv. Preferred Ser. B 1¢ par, (0.025) Common Stock Purchase Warrant expiring 01/01/2005 and $1 cash
(See Key Technology, Inc.)

ADVANCED MAGNETICS INC (DE)
Common 1¢ par split (3) for (2) by issuance of (0.5) additional share 09/25/1991
Name changed to AMAG Pharmaceuticals, Inc. 07/25/2007

ADVANCED MAMMOGRAPHY SYS INC (DE)
Merged into Caprius, Inc. 11/10/1997
Each share Common 1¢ par exchanged for (0.4) share Common 1¢ par
(See Caprius, Inc.)

ADVANCED MFG SYS INC (DE)
Charter forfeited for failure to maintain a registered agent 11/21/1992

ADVANCED MARKETING SVCS INC (DE)
Common $0.001 par split (3) for (2) by issuance of (0.5) additional share payable 02/15/1999 to holders of record 02/01/1999
Common $0.001 par split (3) for (2) by issuance of (0.5) additional share payable 01/17/2000 to holders of record 01/03/2000
Common $0.001 par split (3) for (2) by issuance of (0.5) additional share payable 05/11/2001 to holders of record 04/27/2001 Ex date - 05/14/2001
Plan of reorganization under Chapter 11 Federal Bankruptcy Code effective 12/04/2007
No stockholders' equity

ADVANCED MARKETING TECHNOLOGY CORP (NY)
Dissolved by proclamation 12/29/1993

ADVANCED MATL RES LTD (CANADA)
Reincorporated 08/08/1994
Place of incorporation changed from (AB) to (Canada) 08/08/1994
Each share old Common no par exchanged for (0.2) share new Common no par 12/18/1996
Name changed to AMR Technologies Inc. 06/10/1998
AMR Technologies Inc. name changed to Neo Material Technologies, Inc. 04/28/2006 which merged into Molycorp, Inc. (New) 06/14/2012
(See Molycorp, Inc. (New))

ADVANCED MATLS GROUP INC (NV)
Chapter 11 bankruptcy proceedings dismissed 12/11/2009
No stockholders' equity

ADVANCED MED DYNAMICS INC (DE)
Each share Common $0.0001 par exchanged for (0.1) share Common $0.001 par 06/16/1989
Name changed to Advanced Financial, Inc. 05/07/1991
Advanced Financial, Inc. recapitalized as Advanced Energy Recovery, Inc. 08/20/2004

ADVANCED MED IMAGING CORP (NY)
Name changed to Epic Health Group, Inc. 12/01/1987
(See Epic Health Group, Inc.)

ADVANCED MED INC (DE)
Name changed 09/07/1990
Name changed from Advanced Medical Technologies, Inc. to Advanced Medical Inc. 09/07/1990
10% Preferred 1¢ par called for redemption 12/16/1996
Name changed to ALARIS Medical, Inc. 05/30/1997
ALARIS Medical, Inc. name changed to ALARIS Medical Systems, Inc. 06/30/2003
(See ALARIS Medical Systems, Inc.)

ADVANCED MED INST INC (NV)
SEC revoked common stock registration 01/18/2013

ADVANCED MED ISOTOPE CORP (DE)
Each share old Common $0.001 par exchanged for (0.01) share new Common $0.001 par 10/11/2016
Name changed to Vivos Inc. 01/02/2018

ADVANCED MED OPTICS INC (DE)
Acquired by Abbott Laboratories 02/26/2009
Each share Common 1¢ par exchanged for $22 cash

ADVANCED MED PRODS INC (DE)
Each share Common $0.0001 par exchanged for (0.01) share Common 1¢ par 09/13/1989
Reorganized under Chapter 11 Federal Bankruptcy Code as ADVA International Inc. 03/13/2000
Each share new Common 1¢ par exchanged for (0.1) share Common 1¢ par
(See ADVA International Inc.)

ADVANCED MED SCIENCES INC (DE)
Charter cancelled and declared inoperative and void for non-payment of taxes 03/01/1976

ADVANCED MED SCIENCES INC (VA)
Reorganized under the laws of Nevada as America's Shopping Mall, Inc. 07/14/1999
Each share Common $0.005 par exchanged for (0.03333333) share Common $0.001 par
America's Shopping Mall, Inc. name changed to Eagle Ventures International, Inc. 11/26/2007
(See Eagle Ventures International, Inc.)

ADVANCED MED TECHNOLOGIES INC (NV)
Each share old Common $0.001 par exchanged for (0.04) share new Common $0.001 par 03/26/2002
Name changed to Gold Entertainment Group, Inc. (NV) 04/05/2002
Gold Entertainment Group, Inc. (NV) reincorporated in Florida 08/28/2007
(See Gold Entertainment Group, Inc.)

ADVANCED MEDIA INC (DE)
Each share old Common $0.0001 par exchanged for (0.1) share new Common $0.0001 par 06/23/1997
Name changed to Advanced Media Training, Inc. 08/10/2004
Advanced Media Training, Inc. name changed to Dematco, Inc. 02/07/2007
(See Dematco, Inc.)

ADVANCED MEDIA TRAINING INC (DE)
Common $0.0001 par split (6) for (1) by issuance of (5) additional shares payable 02/10/2006 to holders of record 02/03/2006 Ex date - 02/13/2006
Name changed to Dematco, Inc. 02/07/2007
(See Dematco, Inc.)

ADVANCED MEMORY SYS INC (DE)
Under plan of merger name changed to Intersil, Inc. (New) 11/09/1976
(See Intersil, Inc. (New))

ADVANCED MESSAGING SOLUTIONS INC (NV)
Name changed to XcelMobility Inc. 03/29/2011

ADVANCED MICRO DEVICES INC (DE)
Conv. Exchangeable Depositary Preferred 10¢ par called for redemption 03/13/1995
Conv. Exchangeable Preferred 10¢ par called for redemption 03/13/1995
Preferred Stock Purchase Rights declared for Common stockholders of record 02/20/1990 were redeemed at $0.01 per right 05/25/1995 for holders of record 05/03/1995
(Additional Information in Active)

ADVANCED MINERAL TECHNOLOGIES INC (NV)
Each share old Common $0.001 par exchanged for (0.33333333) share new Common $0.001 par 11/16/2010
SEC revoked common stock registration 02/07/2012

ADVANCED MODULAR SYS INC (DE)
Charter cancelled and declared inoperative and void for non-payment of taxes 04/15/1972

ADVANCED MODULAR TECHNOLOGY INC (DE)
Charter cancelled and declared inoperative and void for non-payment of taxes 04/15/1972

ADVANCED MONITORING SYS INC
SEC revoked common stock registration 06/23/2009

ADVANCED NEUROMODULATION SYS INC (TX)
Common 1¢ par split (3) for (2) by issuance of (0.5) additional share payable 07/11/2003 to holders of record 06/20/2003 Ex date - 07/14/2003
Merged into St. Jude Medical, Inc. 11/29/2005
Each share Common 1¢ par exchanged for $61.25 cash

ADVANCED NMR SYS INC (DE)
Merged into Caprius, Inc. 11/10/1997
Each share Common 1¢ par exchanged for (0.1) share Common 1¢ par
(See Caprius, Inc.)

ADVANCED NUTRACEUTICALS INC (TX)
Each share old Common 1¢ par exchanged for (0.25) share new Common 1¢ par 06/01/2001
Recapitalized as Bactolac Pharmaceutical, Inc. 09/11/2006
Each share new Common 1¢ par exchanged for (0.002) share Common 1¢ par
Note: Holders of (499) or fewer pre-split shares will receive $4 cash per share

ADVANCED OCULAR SYS LTD (AUSTRALIA)
ADR agreement terminated 12/03/2012
Each Sponsored ADR for Ordinary exchanged for (10) shares Ordinary
Note: Unexchanged ADR's will be sold and the proceeds, if any, held for claim after 04/03/2013

ADVANCED OIL TOOLS, INC. (DE)
No longer in existence having become inoperative and void for non-payment of taxes 04/01/1966

ADVANCED OPTICS ELECTRONICS INC (NV)
SEC revoked common stock registration 07/25/2011

ADVANCED ORBITAL SVCS INC (DE)
Name changed to Sea Star Group Inc. 12/18/2006

ADVANCED ORTHOPEDIC TECHNOLOGIES INC (NV)
Each share old Common $0.001 par exchanged for (0.33333333) share new Common $0.001 par 12/10/1992
Merged into AOT Acquisition Corp. 12/05/1996
Each share new Common $0.001 par exchanged for $3.05241807 cash

ADVANCED PACKAGING INC (DE)
Charter cancelled and declared inoperative and void for non-payment of taxes 04/15/1972

ADVANCED PATENT TECHNOLOGY INC (NV)
Name changed to Gaming & Technology, Inc. 03/24/1983
Gaming & Technology, Inc. name changed to United Gaming, Inc. 12/05/1988 which name changed to Alliance Gaming Corp. 12/19/1994 which name changed to Bally Technologies, Inc. 03/08/2006
(See Bally Technologies, Inc.)

ADVANCED PHOTONIX INC (DE)
Merged into Luna Innovations Inc. 05/08/2015
Each share Class A Common $0.001 par exchanged for (0.31782) share Common $0.001 par

ADVANCED PLT PHARMACEUTICALS INC (DE)
Each share Common $0.0001 par exchanged for (0.14285714) share Common $0.0007 par 11/15/1994
Stock Dividend - 100% payable 11/25/1996 to holders of record 11/15/1996
Name changed to World Health Energy Holdings, Inc. 06/09/2010

ADVANCED POLYMER SYS INC (DE)
Name changed to A.P. Pharma, Inc. 05/14/2001
A.P. Pharma, Inc. recapitalized as Heron Therapeutics, Inc. 01/13/2014

ADVANCED PWR TECHNOLOGY INC (DE)
Merged into Microsemi Corp. 04/28/2006
Each share Common 1¢ par exchanged for (0.435) share Common 20¢ par and $2 cash
(See Microsemi Corp.)

ADVANCED PRECISION TECHNOLOGY INC (NV)
Each share old Common $0.001 par exchanged for (0.25) share new Common $0.001 par 06/17/1994
Name changed to Exact Identification Corp. 03/24/2002
Exact Indentification Corp. recapitalized as Powin Corp. 07/08/2008 which name changed to Powin Energy Corp. 02/10/2017

ADVANCED PRIM MINERALS CORP (CANADA)
Reincorporated 07/18/2012
Each share old Common no par exchanged for (0.14285714) share new Common no par 12/18/2009
Place of incorporation changed from (ON) to (Canada) 07/18/2012
Recapitalized as Morien Resources Corp. 11/09/2012
Each share new Common no par exchanged for (0.12738853) share Common no par

ADVANCED PROCESS TECHNOLOGIES INC (ID)
Name changed to Integrated Pharmaceuticals, Inc. 12/12/2000
(See Integrated Pharmaceuticals, Inc.)

ADVANCED PRODS & TECHNOLOGIES INC (WA)
Charter cancelled and proclaimed dissolved for failure to pay fees 01/30/1992

ADVANCED PRODS GROUP INC (DE)
Name changed to Cloudtech Sensors, Inc. 06/25/2007
(See Cloudtech Sensors, Inc.)

ADVANCED PRODTNS INC (DE)
Charter cancelled and declared inoperative and void for non-payment of taxes 04/15/1972

ADVANCED PROFESSIONAL SALES INC (NY)
Reincorporated under the laws of Delaware as Omnicorp Ltd. 03/11/1987
(See Omnicorp Ltd.)

ADVANCED PROJS LTD (BC)
Recapitalized as Skye Resources Inc. 05/23/2001
Each share Common no par exchanged for (0.2) share Common no par
Skye Resources Inc. acquired by HudBay Minerals Inc. 08/26/2008

ADVANCED PROMOTION TECHNOLOGIES INC (DE)
Reorganized as Xinetix Inc. 01/18/1998
Each share Preferred Ser. A 1¢ par exchanged for (2.5) shares Common 1¢ par and (0.7) Common Stock Purchase Warrant expiring 00/00/2002
Each share Preferred Ser. B 1¢ par exchanged for (2.5) shares Common 1¢ par and (0.7) Common Stock Purchase Warrant expiring 00/00/2002
Each share Common 1¢ par exchanged for (2.5) shares Common 1¢ par and (0.7) Common Stock Purchase Warrant expiring 00/00/2002

ADVANCED PULTRUSION TECHNOLOGIES INC (ON)
Delisted from Alberta Stock Exchange 02/21/1997

ADVANCED RADIO TELECOM CORP (DE)
Plan of reorganization under Chapter 11 Federal Bankruptcy code effective 12/20/2001
No stockholders' equity

ADVANCED RECLAMATION INC (DE)
Charter cancelled and declared void for failure to pay franchise taxes 03/01/1996

ADVANCED RECORDING INSTRS INC (DE)
Recapitalized as Immunis Corp. 02/28/1997
Each share Common 1¢ par exchanged for (0.02288329) share Common 1¢ par
Immunis Corp. recapitalized as Star8 Corp. 09/28/2010

ADVANCED RECRUITMENT TECHNOLOGIES INC (ON)
Name changed to Canadian States Gas Ltd. 12/19/1994
Canadian States Gas Ltd. name changed to Canadian States Resources Inc. 10/26/1995 which name changed to High North Resources Inc. 07/07/1997 which recapitalized as HNR Ventures Inc. 06/30/2000 which recapitalized as RMM Ventures Inc. (ON) 06/06/2006 which reorganized in Alberta as PowerComm Inc. 12/31/2006 which name changed to PetroCorp Group Inc. 12/23/2009

ADVANCED RECYCLING SCIENCES INC (NV)
SEC revoked common stock registration 01/29/2008

ADVANCED REFRACTIVE TECHNOLOGIES INC (DE)
Charter cancelled and declared inoperative and void for non-payment of taxes 03/01/2007

ADVANCED REFRIG TECHNOLOGIES INC (CA)
Name changed to Joystar, Inc. 05/26/2004
Joystar, Inc. name changed to Travelstar, Inc. 06/27/2007
(See Travelstar, Inc.)

ADVANCED REHAB TECHNOLOGY CORP (NV)
Each share old Common $0.001 par exchanged for (0.03333333) share new Common $0.001 par 09/17/1999
New Common $0.001 par split (3) for (1) by issuance of (2) additional shares payable 11/17/2000 to holders of record 11/09/2000 Ex date - 11/20/2000
Name changed to Siberian Energy Group Inc. 12/03/2003

ADVANCED REMOTE COMMUNICATION SOLUTIONS INC (CA)
Assets sold for the benefit of creditors 08/18/2003
No stockholders' equity

ADVANCED RESEARCH ASSOCIATES, INC. (MD)
Charter forfeited for failure to file reports and pay taxes 11/29/1966

ADVANCED SCIENTIFIC INSTRUMENTS, INC. (MN)
Liquidation completed 07/15/1963
Each share Common 10¢ par exchanged for first and final distribution of $0.19 cash

ADVANCED SEMICONDUCTOR ENGR INC (TAIWAN)
Stock Dividends - 80% payable 07/23/1996 to holders of record 05/17/1996; 38% payable 07/17/1997 to holders of record 05/19/1997; 72% payable 06/17/1998 to holders of record 04/20/1998; 10.7% payable 09/17/1999 to holders of record 07/14/1999; 31.5% payable 10/25/2000 to holders of record 08/07/2000
Each 144A GDR for Common 1999 converted into (1) 144A GDR for Common 09/25/2000
Each 144A GDR for Common converted into (1) Sponsored ADR for Common 09/25/2000
GDR agreement terminated 03/30/2001
Each GDR for Common exchanged for (0.1) Sponsored ADR for Common
Note: Unexchanged GDR's will be sold and proceeds, if any, held for claim after 10/01/2001
Stock Dividends - 31.5% payable 10/25/2000 to holders of record 08/07/2000; 17% payable 09/17/2001 to holders of record 07/19/2001; 10% payable 10/22/2003 to holders of record 08/26/2003 Ex date - 08/22/2003; 5.74% payable 10/19/2004 to holders of record 08/27/2004; 9.98166% payable 11/04/2005 to holders of record 09/09/2005 Ex date - 09/07/2005; 14.79322% payable 09/27/2007 to holders of record 08/22/2007 Ex date - 08/20/2007; 2.89292% payable 09/26/2008 to holders of record 08/15/2008 Ex date - 08/13/2008; 9.9904% payable 09/10/2010 to 08/13/2008; 9.9904% payable 09/10/2010 to holders of record 07/29/2010 Ex date - 07/27/2010; 11.48977% payable 09/23/2011 to holders of record 08/16/2011 Ex date - 08/12/2011; 13.9882% payable 10/05/2012 to holders of record 08/22/2012 Ex date - 08/20/2012
ADR agreement terminated 04/30/2018
Each Sponsored ADR for Common exchanged for (1.25) ASE Industrial Holding Co., Ltd. Sponsored ADR's for Common
ASE Industrial Holding Co., Ltd. name changed to ASE Technology Holding Co., Ltd. 06/22/2018

ADVANCED SEMICONDUCTOR MATLS INTL NV (NETHERLANDS)
Common DFl0.03 par split (3) for (1) by issuance of (2) additional shares payable 03/15/1996 to holders of record 03/01/1996
Name changed to ASM International N.V. 12/03/1996

ADVANCED SENSING SYS INC (AB)
Recapitalized as IROC Systems Corp. (AB) 12/20/2000
Each share Common no par exchanged for (0.5) share Common no par
IROC Systems Corp. (AB) merged into IROC Systems Corp. (Canada) 02/28/2003 which name changed to IROC Energy Services Corp. 05/22/2007 which merged into Western Energy Services Corp. 04/22/2013

ADVANCED SENSOR INDS INC (DE)
Name changed to Fonix Corp. 05/13/1994
(See Fonix Corp.)

ADVANCED SOLUTIONS & TECHNOLOGIES INC (NV)
SEC revoked common stock registration 04/18/2005

ADVANCED STRUCTURES INC (NM)
Charter revoked for failure to file reports and pay fees 01/25/2001

ADVANCED SURGICAL INC (DE)
Merged into Urohealth Systems, Inc. 12/29/1995
Each share Common 1¢ par exchanged for (0.2893) share Class A Common no par
Urohealth Systems, Inc. name changed to Imagyn Medical Technologies, Inc. 09/29/1997
(See Imagyn Medical Technologies, Inc.)

ADVANCED SUSPENSION TECHNOLOGIES INC (NV)
Reorganized as Dalton International Resources Inc. 12/27/1996
Each share Common $0.001 par exchanged for (3) shares Common $0.001 par
Dalton International Resources Inc. name changed to E-Commerce Group Inc. 08/20/1999 which recapitalized as Yizhong Bioengineering (USA), Inc. 06/12/2006 which name changed to Tianxin Mining (USA), Inc. 07/12/2007
(See Tianxin Mining (USA), Inc.)

ADVANCED SWITCHING COMMUNICATIONS INC (DE)
Liquidation completed
Each share Common $0.0025 par received initial distribution of $1.32 cash payable 12/16/2002 to holders of record 12/02/2002 Ex date - 12/17/2002
Each share Common $0.0025 par received second distribution of $0.09 cash payable 06/02/2003 to holders of record 05/19/2003 Ex date - 06/03/2003
Assets transferred to Advanced Switching Communications

FINANCIAL INFORMATION, INC.

ADV-ADV

Liquidating Trust and Common $0.0025 par reclassified as Shares of Bene. Int. $0.0025 par 05/24/2003
Each Share of Bene. Int. $0.0025 par received third and final distribution of $0.0325 cash payable 12/05/2005 to holders of record 05/19/2003
Note: Certificates were not required to be surrendered and are without value

ADVANCED SYS INC (DE)
Ctfs. dated after 10/04/1976
Common 10¢ par split (3) for (2) by issuance of (0.5) additional share 07/11/1983
Merged into National Education Corp. 12/29/1987
Each share Common 10¢ par exchanged for (1.625) shares Common 1¢ par $3.50 Conv. Preferred Ser. A 50¢ par called for redemption 02/03/1988
National Education Corp. merged into Harcourt General, Inc. 06/10/1997
(See Harcourt General, Inc.)

ADVANCED SYS INTL INC (NV)
Each share Common $0.001 par received distribution of (1) share Advanced Systems Enterprises Restricted Common payable 03/16/2007 to holders of record 02/28/2007
SEC revoked common stock registration 01/28/2008

ADVANCED SYSTEMS, INC. (DE)
Reincorporated 08/23/1973
Ctfs. dated prior to 10/04/1976
Stock Dividend - 50% 06/14/1971
State of incorporation changed from (IL) to (DE) 08/23/1973
Merged into URS Delaware, Inc. 10/04/1976
Each share Common 10¢ par exchanged for $3.50 cash

ADVANCED TECHNETIX INC (NV)
Name changed to AccessKey IP, Inc. 03/26/2007
(See AccessKey IP, Inc.)

ADVANCED TECHNICAL PRODS INC (DE)
Merged into General Dynamics Corp. 06/14/2002
Each share Common 1¢ par exchanged for $33.50 cash

ADVANCED TECHNOLOGIES, INC. (UT)
Name changed to Snack Factory, Inc. 10/26/1984
Snack Factory, Inc. name changed to MaidRite Industries Inc. 03/28/1985 which name changed to Delta Rental Systems Inc. 12/15/1987
(See Delta Rental Systems Inc.)

ADVANCED TECHNOLOGIES GROUP INC (DE)
Name changed to Cra-Z Products, Inc. 09/11/1998
Cra-Z Products, Inc. recapitalized as Advanced Products Group Inc. 05/15/1999 which name changed to Cloudtech Sensors, Inc. 06/25/2007

ADVANCED TECHNOLOGIES INC. (NV)
Charter dissolved 05/20/1996

ADVANCED TECHNOLOGY ACQUISITION CORP (DE)
Completely liquidated 07/07/2009
Each Unit exchanged for first and final distribution of $8.12212682 cash
Each share Common $0.0001 par exchanged for first and final distribution of $8.12212682 cash

ADVANCED TECHNOLOGY GROUP INTL INC (DE)
Name changed back to Mathematical Applications Group, Inc. 08/05/1975
(See Mathematical Applications Group, Inc.)

ADVANCED TECHNOLOGY INDS INC (DE)
Name changed to Brilliant Technologies Corp. 05/01/2006

ADVANCED TECHNOLOGY LABS INC (WA)
Reincorporated 05/11/1995
State of incorporation changed from (DE) to (WA) 05/11/1995
Name changed to ATL Ultrasound, Inc. 07/01/1997
(See ATL Ultrasound, Inc.)

ADVANCED TECHNOLOGY MATLS INC (DE)
Under plan of reorganization each share Common 1¢ par automatically became (1) share ATMI, Inc. Common 1¢ par 10/10/1997
(See ATMI, Inc.)

ADVANCED TECHNOLOGY SYS INC (FL)
Merged into Handy & Harman 01/29/1975
Each share Common 1¢ par exchanged for (0.0843) share Common $1 par
(See Handy & Harman)

ADVANCED TELECOMMUNICATIONS CORP (DE)
Merged into LDDS Communications Inc. (DE) 12/04/1992
Each share Common 2¢ par exchanged for (0.83) share Class A Common 1¢ par
LDDS Communications Inc. (DE) merged into Resurgens Communications Group, Inc. 09/15/1993 which name changed to LDDS Communications, Inc. (GA) 09/15/1993 which name changed to WorldCom, Inc. 05/26/1995 which name changed to MCI WorldCom, Inc. 09/14/1998 which name changed to WorldCom Inc. (New) 05/01/2000
(See WorldCom Inc. (New))

ADVANCED THERAPEUTIC SYSTEMS LTD (BERMUDA)
Acquired by Elan Corp., PLC 10/30/1996
Each share Common 1¢ par exchanged for $36 cash

ADVANCED 3-D ULTRASOUND SVCS INC (FL)
Each share old Common $0.0001 par exchanged for (0.0025) share new Common $0.0001 par 12/29/2003
Name changed to World Energy Solutions, Inc. 11/18/2005
World Energy Solutions, Inc. name changed to EClips Energy Technologies, Inc. (FL) 03/26/2009 which reincorporated in Delaware as EClips Media Technologies, Inc. 05/13/2010 which name changed to Silver Horn Mining Ltd. (DE) 04/27/2011 which reorganized in Nevada as Great West Resources, Inc. 04/21/2014 which name changed to Orbital Tracking Corp. 02/20/2015

ADVANCED TISSUE SCIENCES INC (DE)
Class A Common 1¢ par reclassified as Common 1¢ par 06/04/1992
Under plan of reorganization each share Common 1¢ par automatically became (1) ATS Liquidating Trust Non-Transferable Share of Bene Int. 03/31/2003
Liquidation completed
Each Share of Bene. Int. received initial distribution of $0.065 cash payable 05/30/2003 to holders of record 03/31/2003
Each Share of Bene. Int. received second distribution of $0.03 cash payable 06/15/2004 to holders of record 03/31/2003 Ex date - 06/16/2004
Each Share of Bene. Int. received third distribution of $0.05 cash payable 06/15/2005 to holders of record 03/31/2005 Ex date - 06/17/2005
Each Share of Bene. Int. received fourth distribution of $0.028 cash payable 06/21/2006 to holders of record 03/31/2006 Ex date - 06/22/2006
Each Share of Bene. Int. received fifth distribution of $0.07 cash payable 02/01/2007 to holders of record 12/26/2006 Ex date - 02/05/2007
Each Share of Bene. Int. received sixth and final distribution of $0.014 cash payable 03/06/2009 to holders of record 02/27/2009 Ex date - 03/30/2009

ADVANCED TOB PRODS INC (TX)
Acquired by IVAX Corp. 09/23/2003
Each share Common 1¢ par exchanged for (0.02852313) share Common 10¢ par
(See IVAX Corp.)

ADVANCED VENTURES CORP (DE)
Each share old Common $0.0001 par exchanged for (15) shares new Common $0.0001 par 03/07/2012
Name changed to Gold Union Inc. 01/07/2014
Gold Union Inc. name changed to Noble Vici Group, Inc. 03/26/2018

ADVANCED VIDEO ROBOTICS CORP (NV)
Charter revoked for failure to file reports and pay fees 01/01/1990

ADVANCED VIRAL RESH CORP (DE)
SEC revoked common stock registration 04/24/2012

ADVANCED VISION SYS CORP (AB)
Reorganized under the laws of British Columbia as Windamere Ventures Ltd. 08/27/2010
Each share Common no par exchanged for (0.25) share Common no par
Windamere Ventures Ltd. (BC) reincorporated in Ontario as Antofagasta Gold Inc. 02/12/2013 which name changed to Arena Minerals Inc. 12/06/2013

ADVANCED VISUAL SYS INC (NV)
Name changed to Visual Management Sciences, Inc. 05/27/2016
(See Visual Management Sciences, Inc.)

ADVANCED VOICE TECHNOLOGIES INC (DE)
Recapitalized as Gaming Transactions Inc. 10/05/2004
Each share Common $0.0001 par exchanged for (0.01) share Common $0.0001 par

ADVANCED WIRELESS COMMUNICATIONS INC (NV)
Name changed to CoConnect, Inc. 02/04/2005
Each share Common $0.001 par exchanged for (1) share Common $0.001 par
CoConnect, Inc. name changed to Mastermind, Inc. 06/22/2018

ADVANCED WIRELESS SYS INC (AL)
Reorganized under the laws of Nevada as Advanced Wireless Communications, Inc. 10/22/2004
Each share Common 1¢ par exchanged for (0.1) share Common 1¢ par
Advanced Wireless Communications, Inc. name changed to CoConnect, Inc. 02/04/2005 which changed to Mastermind, Inc. 06/22/2018

ADVANCED WOUND TECHNOLOGIES MIDATLANTIC INC (NV)
Recapitalized as American CryoStem Corp. (Old) 02/03/2009
Each share Common $0.001 par exchanged for (0.005) share Common $0.001 par
American Cryostem Corp. (Old) name changed to ACS Global, Inc. 06/15/2011

ADVANCEPCS (DE)
Class A Common 1¢ par split (2) for (1) by issuance of (1) additional share payable 11/02/2001 to holders of record 10/23/2001 Ex date - 11/05/2001
Merged into Caremark Rx, Inc. 03/24/2004
Each share Class A Common 1¢ par exchanged for (1.935) shares Common $0.001 par and $7.01 cash
Caremark Rx, Inc. merged into CVS/Caremark Corp. 03/22/2007 which name changed to CVS Caremark Corp. 05/10/2007

ADVANCEPIERRE FOODS HLDGS INC (DE)
Acquired by Tyson Foods, Inc. 06/07/2017
Each share Common 1¢ par exchanged for $40.25 cash

ADVANCIERS GROUP INC (DE)
Charter cancelled and declared inoperative and void for non-payment of taxes 03/01/1992

ADVANCIS PHARMACEUTICAL CORP (DE)
Name changed to MiddleBrook Pharmaceuticals, Inc. 06/29/2007
(See MiddleBrook Pharmaceuticals, Inc.)

ADVANCO INDS INC (NY)
Charter cancelled and proclaimed dissolved for failure to pay taxes and file reports 12/15/1975

ADVANT CORP (NV)
Charter revoked for failure to file reports and pay fees 04/01/1984

ADVANTA CORP (DE)
Common 1¢ par reclassified as Class A Common 1¢ par 04/24/1992
Each share Class A Common 1¢ par received distribution of (1) share Non-Vtg. Class B Common 1¢ par 05/06/1992
Class A Common 1¢ par split (3) for (2) by issuance of (0.5) additional share 10/15/1993
Non-Vtg. Class B Common 1¢ par split (3) for (2) by issuance of (0.5) additional share 10/15/1993
Each Conv. Stock Appreciation Income Linked Security Depositary Share Class B exchanged for (1) share Class B Common 1¢ par 09/15/1999
Class A Common 1¢ par split (3) for (2) by issuance of (0.5) additional share payable 06/15/2007 to holders of record 05/25/2007 Ex date - 06/18/2007
Non-Vtg. Class B Common 1¢ par split (3) for (2) by issuance of (0.5) additional share payable 06/15/2007 to holders of record 05/25/2007 Ex date - 06/18/2007
Plan of reorganization under Chapter 11 Federal Bankruptcy proceedings effective 02/28/2011
No stockholders' equity

ADVANTAGE BANCORP (WI)
Common 1¢ par split (5) for (4) by issuance of (0.25) additional share payable 02/23/1996 to holders of record 02/05/1996
Merged into Marshall & Ilsley Corp. (Old) 04/01/1998
Each share Common 1¢ par exchanged for (1.2) shares Common $1 par
(See Marshall & Ilsley Corp. (Old))

ADVANTAGE BK (BRANCHBURG, NJ)
Stock Dividends - 5% payable

03/31/2000 to holders of record 03/15/2000; 5% payable 02/28/2001 to holders of record 02/15/2001; 6% payable 02/28/2002 to holders of record 02/15/2002; 7% payable 02/28/2003 to holders of record 02/14/2003 Ex date - 02/12/2003; 7% payable 02/27/2004 to holders of record 02/13/2004 Ex date - 02/11/2004
Merged into Sun Bancorp, Inc. 01/19/2006
Each share Common $5 par exchanged for (0.87) share Common $1 par
Sun Bancorp, Inc. merged into OceanFirst Financial Corp. 01/31/2018

ADVANTAGE CAP CORP (AB)
Name changed to Acepharm Inc. 09/29/1992
(See Acepharm Inc.)

ADVANTAGE CAP DEV CORP (NV)
Each share Common $0.001 par received distribution of (16.48) shares Global IT Holdings, Inc. Restricted Common $0.001 par payable 02/24/2006 to holders of record 02/20/2006
Note: Holders of (999) or fewer shares received cash
SEC revoked common stock registration 04/13/2012

ADVANTAGE COS INC (DE)
Merged into Thorn Americas Inc. 01/02/1996
Each share Common 1¢ par exchanged for $18.50 cash

ADVANTAGE COS INC (TN)
Each share Common 10¢ par exchanged for (0.1) share Common $1 par 05/01/1987
Merged into LDDS Communications, Inc. (DE) 08/11/1989
Each share Common $1 par exchanged for (0.25641025) share Class A Common 1¢ par
LDDS Communications, Inc. (DE) merged into Resurgens Communications Group, Inc. 09/15/1993 which name changed to LDDS Communications, Inc. (GA) 09/15/1993 which name changed to WorldCom, Inc. 05/26/1995 which name changed to MCI WorldCom, Inc. 9/14/98 which name changed to WorldCom Inc. (New) 05/01/2000
(See WorldCom Inc. (New))

ADVANTAGE ENERGY INCOME FD (AB)
Reorganized as Advantage Oil & Gas Ltd. 07/09/2009
Each Trust Unit no par exchanged for (1) share Common no par
Note: Unexchanged certificates were cancelled and became without value 07/09/2014

ADVANTAGE GROWTH FD (MA)
Name changed to Northstar Advantage Growth Fund and Shares of Bene. Int. no par reclassified as Ser. T no par 09/02/1995
Northstar Advantage Growth Fund name changed to Northstar Growth Fund 08/12/1996 which name changed to Pilgrim Growth Opportunities Fund 11/01/1999 which name changed to ING Growth Opportunities Fund 03/01/2002

ADVANTAGE HEALTH CORP (DE)
Merged into HealthSouth Corp. 03/15/1996
Each share Common 1¢ par exchanged for (1.3768) shares Common 1¢ par
HealthSouth Corp. name changed to Encompass Health Corp. 01/02/2018

ADVANTAGE LEARNING SYS INC (WI)
Common 1¢ par split (2) for (1) by issuance of (1) additional share payable 02/26/1999 to holders of record 02/11/1999
Name changed to Renaissance Learning Inc. 04/20/2001
(See Renaissance Learning, Inc.)

ADVANTAGE LIFE PRODS INC (DE)
Name changed 10/10/1989
Reincorporated 08/22/1994
Name changed from Advantage Entertainment, Inc. to Advantage Life Products, Inc. 10/10/1989
State of incorporation changed from (CO) to (DE) 08/22/1994
Each share old Common $0.008 par exchanged for (0.33333333) share new Common $0.008 par 10/20/1994
Each share new Common $0.008 par exchanged for (0.05) share old Common no par 08/01/1995
Each share old Common no par exchanged for (0.05) share new Common no par 06/24/1996
Each share new Common no par exchanged for (0.03333333) share old Common 16¢ par 10/27/1997
Each share old Common 16¢ par exchanged for (0.03703703) share new Common 16¢ par 08/30/1999
SEC revoked common stock registration 03/18/2011

ADVANTAGE LINK INC (CANADA)
Involuntarily dissolved for failure to file annual returns 11/02/2005

ADVANTAGE MARKETING SYS INC (OK)
Each share old Common $0.0001 par exchanged for (0.125) share new Common $0.0001 par 10/29/1996
Name changed to AMS Health Sciences, Inc. 09/10/2004
AMS Health Sciences, Inc. recapitalized as SA Recovery Corp. 11/20/2008 which name changed to Truli Media Group, Inc. (OK) 08/21/2012 which reorganized in Delaware 03/17/2015

ADVANTAGE OPPORTUNITY CORP (NV)
Common $0.0001 par split (300) for (1) by issuance of (299) additional shares payable 04/04/2005 to holders of record 03/10/2005 Ex date - 04/05/2005
Name changed to Kachina Gold Corp. 04/04/2005
Kachina Gold Corp. recapitalized as Osage Energy Corp. (NV) 05/15/2006 which reincorporated in Delaware as Osage Exploration & Development, Inc. 07/17/2007

ADVANTAGE PLANNING INC (NY)
Charter cancelled and proclaimed dissolved for failure to pay taxes 12/27/2000

ADVANTAGE SPL FD (MA)
Name changed to Northstar Advantage Special Fund and Shares of Bene. Int. no par reclassified as Class T no par 09/02/1995
Northstar Advantage Special Fund name changed to Northstar Special Fund 08/12/1996 which name changed to Pilgrim SmallCap Opportunities Fund 11/01/1999 which name changed to ING SmallCap Opportunities Fund 03/01/2002

ADVANTAGE TECHNOLOGIES INC (NV)
Recapitalized as Expo Holdings Inc. 05/30/2006
Each share Common $0.001 par exchanged for (0.004) share Common $0.001 par

ADVANTAGE TR (MA)
Name changed to Liberty Advantage Trust 09/29/1989
Liberty Advantage Trust reorganized as Liberty Financial Trust 08/03/1992
(See Liberty Financial Trust)

ADVANTAGE WALLSYSTEMS INC (AB)
Acquired by PFB Corp. 05/02/2003
Each share Common no par exchanged for (0.02) share Common no par

ADVANTAGED PFD SH TR (ON)
Trust terminated 05/31/2016
Each Unit received $19.61651592 cash

ADVANTEXCEL COM COMMUNICATIONS CORP (ON)
Delisted from Toronto Venture Stock Exchange 06/05/2002

ADVANTICA RESTAURANT GROUP INC (DE)
Name changed to Denny's Corp. 07/11/2002

ADVANTISTICS INC (DE)
Name changed to Auto-Swab Corp. 05/16/1991

ADVANTUS MONEY MKT FD INC (MN)
Merged into Ivy Funds, Inc. 12/08/2003
Each share Common 1¢ par exchanged for Shares of Bene. Int. no par on a net asset basis

ADVANTUS MTG SECS FD INC (MN)
Merged into Ivy Funds, Inc. 12/08/2003
Details not available

ADVATEX ASSOC INC (DE)
Recapitalized as Color Imaging, Inc. (DE) 07/07/2000
Each share Common 1¢ par exchanged for (0.16453403) share Common 1¢ par
Color Imaging, Inc. (DE) reincorporated in Georgia 08/31/2010

ADVAXIS INC (CO)
Reincorporated under the laws of Delaware 06/20/2006

ADVEN INC (WY)
Reincorporated 12/16/2003
Each share old Common $0.0001 par exchanged for (0.04) share new Common $0.0001 par 12/28/1990
Each share new Common $0.0001 par exchanged again for (0.25) share new Common $0.0001 par 12/29/1993
Each share new Common $0.0001 par exchanged again for (0.1) share new Common $0.0001 par 06/03/2003
State of incorporation changed from (WA) to (WY) 12/16/2003
Name changed to West Africa Gold, Inc. 01/21/2004
West Africa Gold, Inc. name changed to Great West Gold, Inc. 10/29/2004 which name changed to Fortress Financial Group, Inc. 10/08/2007
(See Fortress Financial Group, Inc.)

ADVENT / CLAYMORE ENHANCED GROWTH & INCOME FD (DE)
Merged into Advent Claymore Convertible Securities & Income Fund 08/27/2018
Each Common Share of Bene. Int. $0.001 par exchanged for (0.49513764) Common Share of Bene. Int. $0.001 par

ADVENT CLAYMORE CONV SECS & INCOME FD (DE)
Auction Market Preferred Ser. W7 $0.001 par called for redemption at $25,000 on 06/13/2013
Auction Market Preferred Ser. W-28 $0.001 par called for redemption at $25,000 on 06/13/2013
Auction Market Preferred Ser. TH-28 $0.001 par called for redemption at $25,000 on 06/14/2013
Auction Market Preferred Ser. F7 $0.001 par called for redemption at $25,000 on 06/17/2013
Auction Market Preferred Ser. M7 $0.001 par called for redemption at $25,000 on 06/18/2013
Auction Market Preferred Ser. TH28 $0.001 par called for redemption at $25,000 on 06/26/2013
(Additional Information in Active)

ADVENT CLAYMORE CONV SECS & INCOME FD II (DE)
Name changed 02/28/2012
Name changed from Advent /Claymore Global Convertible Securities & Income Fund to Advent Claymore Convertible Securities & Fund II 02/28/2012
144A Auction Market Preferred Ser. T7 $0.001 par called for redemption at $25,000 on 06/19/2013
144A Auction Market Preferred Ser. W7 $0.001 par called for redemption at $25,000 on 06/20/2013
Merged into Advent Claymore Convertible Securities & Income Fund 08/27/2018
Each Common Share of Bene. Int. $0.001 par exchanged for (0.3630276) Common Share of Bene. Int. $0.001 par

ADVENT COMMUNICATIONS CORP (BC)
Recapitalized as Advent Wireless Inc. 08/19/2003
Each share Common no par exchanged for (0.33333333) share Common no par
Advent Wireless Inc. name changed to Advent-AWI Holdings Inc. 03/23/2017

ADVENT CORP (MA)
Chapter 11 bankruptcy proceedings converted to Chapter 7 on 04/27/1982
No stockholders' equity

ADVENT DEVS INC (BC)
Struck off register and declared dissolved for failure to file returns 03/27/1981

ADVENT ENERGY CAP INC (AB)
Merged into Zaio Corp. 02/23/2004
Each share Common no par exchanged for (0.45) share Common no par
Zaio Corp. name changed to Clarocity Corp. 10/17/2016

ADVENT SOFTWARE INC (DE)
Common 1¢ par split (3) for (2) by issuance of (0.5) additional share payable 08/16/1999 to holders of record 07/30/1999
Common 1¢ par split (2) for (1) by issuance of (1) additional share payable 03/13/2000 to holders of record 02/28/2000
Common 1¢ par split (2) for (1) by issuance of (1) additional share payable 01/18/2011 to holders of record 01/03/2011 Ex date - 01/19/2011
Acquired by SS&C Technologies Holdings, Inc. 07/08/2015
Each share Common 1¢ par exchanged for $44.25 cash

ADVENT TECHNOLOGIES INC (FL)
Each share old Common $0.0005 par exchanged for (0.33333333) share new Common $0.0005 par 11/16/1993
Recapitalized as Newreach Communications Inc. 09/26/1996
Each share new Common $0.0005 par exchanged for (0.01) share Common $0.0005 par
Newreach Communications Inc. name changed to Henley Group, Inc. (FL) 04/02/1997 which name changed to CIS.com, Inc. 05/27/1999 which name changed to InterAmerican Resources, Inc. 08/13/2001 which

name changed to Allixon Corp. 06/04/2004 which recapitalized as Simcoe Mining Resources Corp. 01/16/2008

ADVENT WIRELESS INC (BC)
Name changed to Advent-AWI Holdings Inc. 03/23/2017

ADVENTO INC (NV)
Reorganized as Joymain International Development Group Inc. 04/10/2013
Each share Common $0.001 par exchanged for (300) shares Common $0.001 par

ADVENTRX PHARMACEUTICALS INC (DE)
Each share old Common $0.001 par exchanged for (0.04) share new Common $0.001 par 04/26/2010
Name changed to Mast Therapeutics, Inc. 03/11/2013
Mast Therapeutics, Inc. recapitalized as Savara Inc. 04/28/2017

ADVENTURE CAP CORP (AB)
Name changed to HealthCare Capital Corp. 10/21/1994
HealthCare Capital Corp. recapitalized as Sonus Corp. 02/09/1998
(See Sonus Corp.)

ADVENTURE ELECTRS INC (CANADA)
Discharged from receivership 06/00/2002
No stockholders' equity

ADVENTURE ENERGY INC (FL)
Name changed to US Natural Gas Corp. 04/14/2010
US Natural Gas Corp. name changed to Sylios Corp. 06/20/2014

ADVENTURE GOLD INC (CANADA)
Merged into Probe Metals Inc. 06/13/2016
Each share Common no par exchanged for (0.39) share Common no par
Note: Unexchanged certificates will be cancelled and become without value 06/13/2022

ADVENTURE LDS AMER INC (IA)
Common $3 par changed to no par 11/00/1976
Merged into Iowa Entertainment Corp. 10/29/1985
Each share Common no par exchanged for $3.50 cash

ADVENTURE MINERALS INC (NV)
Common $0.001 par split (5) for (1) by issuance of (4) additional shares payable 05/22/2000 to holders of record 05/22/2000 Ex date - 05/23/2000
Name changed to Planet Earth Recycling Inc. 11/06/2000
(See Planet Earth Recycling Inc.)

ADVENTURE VEHICLE DYNAMICS INC (BC)
Struck off register and declared dissolved for failure to file returns 05/13/1994

ADVENTURX COM INC (AB)
Name changed to Nettron.Com, Inc. 09/28/1999
Nettron.Com, Inc. recapitalized as Valcent Products Inc. 05/03/2005 which name changed to Alterrus Systems Inc. 06/12/2012

ADVERGUIDE PUBLISHING, INC. (TX)
Charter cancelled for failure to pay taxes 05/08/1972

ADVERTAIN ON-LINE INC (NV)
Recapitalized as RetinaPharma International Inc. 06/18/2001
Each share Common $0.001 par exchanged for (0.05) share Common $0.001 par
RetinaPharma International Inc. name changed to Xtra-Gold Resources

Corp. (NV) 12/19/2003 which reincorporated in British Virgin Islands 12/24/2012

ADVERTECH CORP (FL)
Certificates never issued; spun off by Technological Industries Corp. 09/30/1970 but prior to distribution Advertech Corp. merged into Coastland Enterprises, Inc. share for share and holders of Technological Industries Corp. received Coastland Enterprises, Inc. Common 5¢ par on 10/16/1970
(See Coastland Enterprises, Inc.)

ADVERTISER PUBG CO (HI)
Dissolved 11/30/1978
Details not available

ADVERTISING PARTNERS INC (NY)
Each share old Common $0.00001 par exchanged for (0.04) share new Common $0.00001 par 12/01/1989
Administratively dissolved 09/28/1994

ADVERTISING UNLIMITED INC (MN)
Stock Dividend - 15% 07/30/1976
Merged into Polk (R.L.) & Co. 10/30/1987
Each share Common 10¢ par exchanged for $56 cash

ADVEST GROUP INC (DE)
Common $1 par split (3) for (2) by issuance of (0.5) additional share 01/03/1983
Common $1 par split (3) for (2) by issuance of (0.5) additional share 09/14/1983
Stock Dividends - 10% 01/04/1982; 10% 06/20/1986; 10% 06/16/1987
Merged into MONY Group Inc. 01/31/2001
Each share Common $1 par exchanged for (0.8696) share Common 1¢ par
(See MONY Group Inc.)

ADVFN PLC (ENGLAND & WALES)
Basis changed from (1:100) to (1:4) 09/04/2014
ADR agreement terminated 08/04/2017
Each Sponsored ADR for Ordinary exchanged for $2.114244 cash

ADVISORS CAP TECHNOLOGY CORP (NY)
Each share Common $0.0001 par exchanged for (0.1) share Common $0.001 par 08/22/1988
Recapitalized as Enviro-Green Tech., Inc. 08/08/1994
Each share Common $0.001 par exchanged for (0.0666) share Common $0.001 par
(See Enviro-Green Tech., Inc.)

ADVISORS CASH RESV INC (MD)
Name changed 09/00/1985
Name changed from Advisors Cash Reserve Fund, Inc. to Advisors Cash Reserves, Inc. 09/00/1985
Name changed to G.T. Money Market Series, Inc. 10/00/1987
(See G.T. Money Market Series, Inc.)

ADVISORS FD L P (DE)
Merged into Smith Barney Fundamental Value Fund Inc. (WA) 12/16/1994
Each Class A Limited Partnership Unit exchanged for (3.2428) Class A Shares $0.001 par
Each Class B Limited Partnership Unit exchanged for (3.204) Class B Shares $0.001 par
Smith Barney Fundamental Value Fund Inc. (WA) reincorporated in Maryland 05/24/1995 which name changed to Legg Mason Partners Fundamental Value Fund, Inc. 05/01/2006
(See Legg Mason Partners Fundamental Value Fund, Inc.)

ADVISORS INNER CIRCLE FD (MA)
WHG Balanced Fund Institutional Class no par reclassified as Westwood Balanced Fund Institutional Class no par 03/01/2012
Completely liquidated 12/20/2012
Each share Westwood Balanced Fund Institutional Class no par received net asset value
(Additional Information in Active)

ADVISORSHARES TR (DE)
Trust terminated 08/15/2012
Each share Dent Tactical ETF received $17.77 cash
Trust terminated 06/21/2013
Each share Rockledge SectorSAM ETF received $23.69162 cash
Global Alpha & Beta ETF reclassified as EquityPro ETF 12/02/2013
Cambria Global Tactical ETF reclassified as Morgan Creek Global Tactical ETF 07/28/2014
Trust terminated 01/16/2015
Each share Accuvest Global Opportunities ETF received $23.88287 cash
Each share Athena International Bear ETF received $19.74997 cash
Trust terminated 01/30/2015
Each share Gartman Gold/British Pound ETF received $12.99301 cash
Each share International Gold ETF received $13.76412 cash
Trust terminated 08/14/2015
Each share Accuvest Global Long Short ETF received $19.34253 cash
Trust terminated 10/09/2015
Each share Pring Turner Business Cycle ETF received $24.08207 cash
Trust terminated 10/28/2016
Each share EquityPro ETF received $27.65314 cash
Trust terminated 10/31/2016
Each share YieldPro ETF received $23.44997 cash
Trust terminated 04/07/2017
Each share Athena High Dividend ETF received $18.1866 cash
Trust terminated 05/19/2017
Each share Global Echo ETF received $64.9221 cash
Each share Morgan Creek Global Tactical ETF received $24.381 cash
Trust terminated 06/30/2017
Each share Market Adaptive Unconstrained Income ETF received $24.53634 cash
Each share QAM Equity Hedge ETF received $28.99394 cash
Trust terminated 10/20/2017
Each share Gartman Gold/Euro ETF received $11.75 cash
Each share Gartman Gold/Yen ETF received $11.70 cash
Trust terminated 04/06/2018
Each share Meidell Tactical Advantage ETF received $33.08413 cash
Trust terminated 10/08/2018
Each share KIM Korea Equity ETF received $26.53 cash
(Additional Information in Active)

ADVISORY BRD CO (DE)
Common 1¢ par split (2) for (1) by issuance of (1) additional share payable 06/18/2012 to holders of record 05/31/2012 Ex date - 06/19/2012
Acquired by UnitedHealth Group Inc. 11/17/2017
Each share Common 1¢ par exchanged for $53.81 cash

ADVITECH INC (CANADA)
Each share old Common no par exchanged for (0.125) share new Common no par 11/26/2009
Recapitalized as Botaneco Corp. 10/14/2011
Each share new Common no par exchanged for (0.25) share Common no par
Botaneco Corp. name changed to Natunola AgriTech Inc. 07/09/2013
(See Natunola AgriTech Inc.)

ADVO INC (DE)
Name changed 01/23/1992
Name changed from ADVO-System, Inc. to ADVO, Inc. 01/23/1992
Common 1¢ par split (5) for (4) by issuance of (0.25) additional share 03/05/1993
Common 1¢ par split (3) for (2) by issuance of (0.5) additional share payable 11/07/2003 to holders of record 10/24/2003
Merged into Valassis Communications, Inc. 03/02/2007
Each share Common 1¢ par exchanged for $33 cash

ADVOCAT INC (DE)
Name changed to Diversicare Healthcare Services Inc. 03/18/2013

ADVOCATE MINES LTD (ON)
Assets expropriated by Executive Council for the Province of Newfoundland 09/03/1982
No stockholders' equity

ADWALL CAP CORP (WY)
Reincorporated 08/06/1998
Place of incorporation changed from (AB) to (WY) 08/06/1998
Administratively dissolved 06/10/2003

ADWOOD CORP. (MI)
Liquidated 00/00/1953
Details not available

ADZONE RESH INC (DE)
SEC revoked common stock registration 04/04/2013

AE & CI LTD (SOUTH AFRICA)
ADR agreement terminated 09/11/2017
No ADR's remain outstanding

AE BIOFUELS (NV)
Name changed to Aemetis, Inc. 11/15/2011

AEC HLDGS CORP (NV)
Each share old Common $0.001 par exchanged for (0.01) share new Common $0.001 par 08/14/2007
Charter revoked for failure to file reports and pay taxes 04/30/2010

AEC INC (DE)
Common $1 par split (3) for (2) by issuance of (0.5) additional share 03/30/1984
Merged into Sterling Inc. 05/27/1988
Each share Common $1 par exchanged for $15 cash

AEC PIPELINES L P (AB)
Each Instalment Receipt no par exchanged for (1) Class A Unit of Limited Partnership Int. no par 03/31/1998
Merged into Alberta Energy Co. Ltd. 09/22/2000
Each Class A Unit of Limited Partnership Int. exchanged for (0.1552) share Common no par
Alberta Energy Co. Ltd. merged into EnCana Corp. 01/03/2003

AECO CORP (NV)
Recapitalized as Universal Services Alliance Inc. 09/17/1984
Each share Common 10¢ par exchanged for (0.01) share Common 10¢ par
(See Universal Services Alliance Inc.)

AECOM TECHNOLOGY CORP (DE)
Name changed to AECOM 01/06/2015

AEGEA INC (CO)
Recapitalized as FutureLand, Corp. 05/01/2015
Each share Common no par exchanged for (0.0025) share Common no par

AEGEAN CORP (UT)
Proclaimed dissolved for failure to pay taxes 09/30/1979

AEGEAN EARTH & MARINE CORP (CAYMAN ISLANDS)
Recapitalized as Hellenic Solutions Corp. 06/18/2010
Each share Ordinary $0.00064 par exchanged for (0.18511662) share Ordinary $0.00345728 par

AEGEAN GOLD INC (YT)
Recapitalized as Aegean International Gold Inc. 12/09/1999
Each share Common no par exchanged for (0.5) share Common no par
Aegean International Gold Inc. recapitalized as MinRes Resources Inc. 10/20/2003 which name changed to Geoinformatics Exploration Inc. 02/11/2005 which recapitalized as Kiska Metals Corp. 08/05/2009 which merged into AuRico Metals Inc. 03/14/2017
(See AuRico Metals Inc.)

AEGEAN INTL GOLD INC (YT)
Recapitalized as MinRes Resources Inc. 10/20/2003
Each share Common no par exchanged for (0.1) share Common no par
MinRes Resources Inc. name changed to Geoinformatics Exploration Inc. 02/11/2005 which recapitalized as Kiska Metals Corp. 08/05/2009 which merged into AuRico Metals Inc. 03/14/2017
(See AuRico Metals Inc.)

AEGEAN METALS GROUP INC (BC)
Merged into Mariana Resources Ltd. 01/20/2015
Each share Common no par exchanged for (1.902) shares Ordinary £0.0001 par
Mariana Resources Ltd. merged into Sandstorm Gold Ltd. 07/06/2017

AEGEAN RES CORP (BC)
Recapitalized as Realsearch International Systems Corp. 07/09/1985
Each share Capital Stock no par exchanged for (0.4) share Common no par
Realsearch International Systems Corp. name changed to Allmed International Investments Corp. 04/11/1989 which name changed to Ecoprogress Canada Holdings Inc. 02/07/1997 which recapitalized as Consolidated Ecoprogress Technology Inc. 05/06/1998

AEGERION PHARMACEUTICALS INC (DE)
Merged into Novelion Therapeutics Inc. 12/01/2016
Each share Common no par exchanged for (1.0256) shares Common no par

AEGIS ASSMTS INC (DE)
SEC revoked common stock registration 07/06/2012

AEGIS COMMUNICATIONS GROUP INC (DE)
Merged into World Focus 11/03/2006
Each share Common 1¢ par exchanged for $0.05 cash

AEGIS CONSUMER FDG GROUP INC (DE)
SEC revoked common stock registration 04/22/2009

AEGIS CORP (DE)
Merged into Minstar, Inc. 11/13/1984
Each (90.9) shares exchanged for $500 principal amount of Variable Rate Subord. Exchangeable Debentures due 11/12/1994
Note: Holdings of (90.8) shares or fewer exchanged for $5.50 cash per share

AEGIS ENERGY LTD (AB)
Name changed 07/18/1998
Name changed from Aegis Development Corp. to AEGIS Energy Ltd. 07/18/1998
Merged into Surge Petroleum Inc. 07/07/2000
Each share Common no par exchanged for (0.3030303) share Common no par
Surge Petroleum Inc. merged into Innova Exploration Ltd. 04/16/2004
(See Innova Exploration Ltd.)

AEGIS INDS INC (DE)
Reincorporated 07/00/1990
State of incorporation changed from (TX) to (DE) 07/00/1990
Charter cancelled and declared inoperative and void for non-payment of taxes 03/01/1992

AEGIS INDS INC (NV)
Name changed to Fortified Holdings Corp. 06/19/2007
(See Fortified Holdings Corp.)

AEGIS RLTY INC (MD)
Merged into Doubleday Station LLC 03/26/2003
Each share Common 1¢ par exchanged for $11.664 cash

AEGIS RES LTD (BC)
Ctfs. dated prior to 06/13/1986
Name changed to Louisiana Mining Corp. 06/13/1986
(See Louisiana Mining Corp.)

AEGIS RES LTD (BC)
Ctfs. dated after 08/01/1990
Recapitalized as New Aegis Resources Ltd. 03/17/1993
Each share Common no par exchanged for (0.14285714) share Common no par
New Aegis Resources Ltd. acquired by Norcan Resources Ltd. 08/19/1994 which recapitalized as Odyssey Exploration Inc. 06/07/2000 which recapitalized as Consolidated Odyssey Exploration Inc. 12/08/2000 which reorganized as Odyssey Petroleum Corp. 08/25/2005 which recapitalized as Petrichor Energy Inc. 03/03/2011

AEGON N V (NETHERLANDS)
6.875% Perpetual Capital Securities called for redemption at $25 on 03/15/2014
(Additional Information in Active)

AEI ENVIRONMENTAL INC (CO)
Company terminated common stock registration and is no longer public as of 05/02/2002

AEI REAL ESTATE FD LTD PARTNERSHIP (MN)
Limited Partnership 85-A liquidated and legally dissolved 09/30/2003
Details not available
Liquidation completed
Each Unit of Ltd. Partnership Int. 86-A received initial distribution of $114.55 cash 00/00/2003
Each Unit of Ltd. Partnership Int. 86-A received second and final distribution of $167.24 cash 09/30/2004
Liquidation completed
Each Unit of Ltd. Partnership Int. XVI received initial distribution of $195.92 cash 00/00/2003
Each Unit of Ltd. Partnership Int. XVI received second and final distribution of $124.54 cash 09/30/2004
Limited Partnership 85-B completely liquidated 06/30/2005
Details not available
Completely liquidated
Each Unit of Ltd. Partnership Int. XV received first and final distribution of $156.84 cash payable 01/05/2007 to holders of record 12/31/2006

AEICOR INC (DE)
Each share 6% Preferred Ser. A no par exchanged for (60) shares Common 40¢ par 12/17/1982
Each share 6% Preferred Ser. B no par exchanged for (13.966) shares Common 40¢ par 12/17/1982
Name changed to Doskocil Companies Inc. 09/30/1983
Doskocil Companies Inc. name changed to Foodbrands America Inc. 05/15/1995 which merged into IBP, Inc. 05/07/1997 which merged into Tyson Foods, Inc. 09/28/2001

AEL INDS INC (PA)
Class A Common $1 par split (3) for (2) by issuance of (0.5) additional share 08/24/1984
Class B Common $1 par split (3) for (2) by issuance of (0.5) additional share 08/24/1984
Class A Common $1 par split (3) for (2) by issuance of (0.5) additional share 08/08/1985
Class B Common $1 par split (3) for (2) by issuance of (0.5) additional share 08/08/1985
Merged into Tracor Inc. (New) 02/22/1996
Each share Class A Common $1 par exchanged for $24.25 cash
Each share Class B Common $1 par exchanged for $24.25 cash
(See Tracor Inc. (New))

AELUS WING INC (NJ)
Charter declared void for non-payment of taxes 04/06/1995

AENA S A (SPAIN)
Name changed to Aena SME, S.A. 11/03/2017

AENEID EQUITIES INC (DE)
Name changed to New York Magazine Co., Inc. 05/04/1973
(See New York Magazine Co., Inc.)

AEOLIAN SKINNER ORGAN CO (MA)
4% Preferred called for redemption 00/00/1966
Each share Common $1 par exchanged for (1) share Common 25¢ par 02/04/1969
Proclaimed dissolved for failure to file reports and pay fees 12/31/1990

AEOLIAN-WEBER PIANO & PIANOLA CO.
Name changed to International Holding Corp. of Garwood 00/00/1932
(See International Holding Corp. of Garwood)

AEON HLDGS INC (DE)
Name changed to BCM Energy Partners, Inc. 04/13/2011

AEON VENTURES INC (BC)
Recapitalized as Statesman Resources Ltd. 06/28/2004
Each share Common no par exchanged for (0.33333333) share Common no par

AEP INDS INC (DE)
Common 1¢ par split (3) for (2) by issuance of (0.5) additional share 12/07/1989
Common 1¢ par split (3) for (2) by issuance of (0.5) additional share 01/11/1994
Acquired by Berry Plastics Group, Inc. 01/20/2017
Each share Common 1¢ par exchanged for $110 cash

AEP TEX CENT CO (TX)
4% Preferred $100 par called for redemption at $105.75 plus $0.3333 accrued dividends on 12/01/2011
4.2% Preferred $100 par called for redemption at $103.75 plus $0.35 accrued dividends on 12/01/2011

AEP TEX NORTH CO (TX)
4.4% Preferred $100 par called for redemption at $107 plus $0.73333 accrued dividends on 12/01/2011

AEQUITRON MED INC (MN)
Common 10¢ par split (3) for (2) by issuance of (0.5) additional share 10/25/1983
Merged into Nellcor Puritan Bennett Inc. 12/05/1996
Each share Common 10¢ par exchanged for (0.467) share Common $0.001 par
(See Nellcor Puritan Bennett Inc.)

AER ENERGY RES INC (GA)
Each share old Common no par exchanged for (0.01) share new Common no par 07/08/2010
Reincorporated under the laws of Nevada and Common no par changed to $0.001 par 06/27/2011

AER LINGUS GROUP PLC (IRELAND)
ADR agreement terminated 01/29/2016
Each ADR for Ordinary exchanged for $27.25 cash

AER NICKEL CORP. LTD. (ON)
Charter cancelled for failure to pay taxes and file returns 05/06/1980

AER VENTURES INC (NV)
Reincorporated under the laws of Delaware as Telanetix, Inc. and Common $0.001 par changed to $0.0001 par 03/23/2006
(See Telanetix, Inc.)

AERCO CORP.
Acquired by Adel Precision Products Corp. 00/00/1947
Details not available

AERCO CORP (NJ)
Recapitalized 01/08/1966
Each share 5% Preferred $100 par exchanged for (2) shares old Common no par
Each share Class B Common no par exchanged for (10) shares old Common no par
Each share Class A Common no par exchanged for (1) share old Common no par
Each share old Common no par exchanged for (4) shares new Common no par 03/15/1967
Acquired by Aerco International Corp. 01/01/1975
Details not available

AERIAL ACQUISITIONS INC (DE)
Name changed to Ultra Shield Products International Inc. 12/08/1993

AERIAL ASSAULT INC (DE)
Name changed to PTI Holding Inc. 09/09/1994
(See PTI Holding Inc.)

AERIAL COMMUNICATIONS INC (DE)
Merged into Voicestream Wireless Corp. 05/05/2000
Each share Common $1 par exchanged for either (0.455) share Common no par, $18 cash, or a combination thereof
Note: Option to receive stock and cash or cash only expired 06/09/2000
Voicestream Wireless Corp. merged into Deutsche Telekom AG 05/31/2001

AERIAL EXPLORATION SYNDICATE
Property acquired by Akaitcho Yellowknife Gold Mines Ltd. 00/00/1945
Details not available

AERIUS (NV)
Name changed to Aerius International, Inc. 10/31/2007

AERO ALARM CO.
Bankrupt 00/00/1931
Stockholders' equity unlikely

AERO CHATILLON CORP (NY)
Merged into Macrodyne-Chatillon Corp. 04/01/1969
Each share Common 10¢ par exchanged for (0.4) share Conv.

Preferred Ser. A $1 par and (0.6) share Common 10¢ par Macrodyne-Chatillon Corp. merged into Macrodyne Industries, Inc. 01/01/1974
(See Macrodyne Industries, Inc.)

AERO CORP. OF CALIFORNIA
Acquired by Western Air Express Corp. 00/00/1930
Details not available

AERO-CRAFTS CORP.
Name changed to Technical Crafts Corp. 08/00/1946
(See Technical Crafts Corp.)

AERO ENERGY LTD (BC)
Placed in receivership 07/26/1983
No stockholders' equity

AERO ENGINES OF CANADA LTD.
Dissolved 00/00/1938
Details not available

AERO FLEX CORP (CA)
Out of business 02/07/1967
No stockholders' equity

AERO FLOW DYNAMICS INC (NY)
Merged into United Telecommunications, Inc. 01/04/1983
Each share Common $1 par exchanged for $60 cash

AERO GEO ASTRO CORP. (VA)
Recapitalized as Keltec Industries, Inc. 11/02/1964
Each share Common 20¢ par exchanged for (0.5) share Capital Stock 40¢ par
Keltec Industries, Inc. acquired by Aiken Industries, Inc. 08/15/1967
(See Aiken Industries, Inc.)

AERO INDEMNITY CO.
Liquidated 00/00/1932
Details not available

AERO INDS INC (DE)
Name changed to Allied Aero Industries, Inc. 04/22/1964
(See Allied Aero Industries, Inc.)

AERO INDUSTRIES TECHNICAL INSTITUTE, INC.
Name changed to Aero-Crafts Corp. 00/00/1940
Aero-Crafts Corp. name changed to Technical Crafts Corp. 08/00/1946
(See Technical Crafts Corp.)

AERO INSURANCE CO.
Liquidated 00/00/1932
Details not available

AERO MARINE ENGINE INC (NV)
Each share old Common $0.001 par exchanged for (0.01) share new Common $0.001 par 08/09/2004
Name changed to Axial Vector Engine Corp. 06/09/2005
Axial Vector Engine Corp. recapitalized as AVEC Corp. 03/07/2011
(See AVEC Corp.)

AERO MECHANISM INC (CA)
Placed in bankruptcy 03/06/1972
No stockholders' equity

AERO MINING CORP. (QC)
Acquired by Chess Mining Corp. share for share 08/11/1958
(See Chess Mining Corp.)

AERO NAUTICAL APPLIANCE CO. (CA)
Charter suspended for failure to file reports and pay fees 03/00/1939

AERO PERFORMANCE PRODS INC (NV)
SEC revoked common stock registration 12/07/2011

AERO RES INC (CA)
Charter cancelled for failure to file reports and pay taxes 06/01/1979

AERO SERVICE CORP. (DE)
Each share Common $25 par exchanged for (75) shares Common $1 par 03/16/1954
Stock Dividend - 10% 04/07/1958
Name changed to ASC Inc. 12/21/1961
ASC Inc. acquired by Litton Industries, Inc. 01/12/1962
(See Litton Industries, Inc.)

AERO SVCS INTL INC (LA)
Name changed to b-Fast Corp. 10/01/1999
(See b-Fast Corp.)

AERO SUPPLY MANUFACTURING CO., INC. (NY)
Each share old Class B Common no par exchanged for (3) shares new Common no par 00/00/1929
Class A Common no par changed to $1 par 00/00/1939 and called for redemption 07/01/1946
Class B Common no par changed to $1 par 00/00/1939
Class B Common $1 par reclassified as Common $1 par 00/00/1946
Name changed to Aero-Flow Dynamics, Inc. 05/04/1961
(See Aero-Flow Dynamics, Inc.)

AERO SYS ENGR INC (MN)
Common 20¢ par split (3) for (2) by issuance of (0.5) additional share payable 03/06/1998 to holders of record 02/02/1998
Stock Dividend - 15% payable 03/31/1999 to holders of record 03/10/1999
Merged into Tonka Bay Equity Partners LLC 01/03/2006
Each share Common 20¢ par exchanged for $6.401 cash
Each share Common 20¢ par received an initial distribution of $0.16042765 cash from escrow 02/06/2006
Each share Common 20¢ par received a second and final distribution of $0.47870926 cash from escrow 07/12/2007

AERO SYS INC (FL)
Common 10¢ par changed to 2¢ par and (4) additional shares issued 11/30/1967
Common 2¢ par split (5) for (4) by issuance of (0.25) additional share 05/03/1982
Stock Dividend - 25% 01/15/1981
Proclaimed dissolved for failure to file reports and pay fees 08/25/1995

AERO TECH INC (DE)
Name changed to Artko Corp. 03/24/1971
(See Artko Corp.)

AERO TRAILS CORP (NV)
Name changed to Techni-Culture, Inc. 01/15/1971
Each share Common 40¢ par exchanged for (1) share Common 40¢ par

AERO UNDERWRITERS CORP.
Liquidation completed 00/00/1936
Details not available

AEROBIC CREATIONS INC (DE)
Recapitalized as Summit Global Logistics, Inc. 03/12/2007
Each share Common $0.001 par exchanged for (0.08907766) share Common $0.001 par
(See Summit Global Logistics, Inc.)

AEROBIC CREATIONS INC (NV)
Reorganized under the laws of Delaware 08/21/2006
Each share Common $0.001 par exchanged for (0.2) share Common $0.001 par
Aerobic Creations, Inc. (DE) recapitalized as Summit Global Logistics, Inc. 03/12/2007
(See Summit Global Logistics, Inc.)

AEROBIC LIFE INDS INC (NV)
Each share old Common $0.001 par exchanged for (0.06666666) share new Common $0.001 par 08/26/1994
Name changed to Diagnostics International Inc. 11/17/1995

AEROBIC LIFE PRODS INC (MT)
Name changed to Diversified Environmental Resources, Inc. 11/21/1989
Diversified Environmental Resources, Inc. recapitalized as Trade The Planet Corp. (MT) 05/01/2001 which reincorporated in Nevada as Human Science Systems Inc. 04/04/2005 which recapitalized as Nutralogix Laboratories, Inc. 11/14/2005 which reorganized as Matrix Denture Systems International, Inc. 10/09/2007

AEROCEANIC CORP (DE)
Reincorporated 05/15/1970
Under plan of merger state of incorporation changed from (CA) to (DE) and each share Common $1 par exchanged for (1) share Common 10¢ par 05/15/1970
Merged into Evans Industries, Inc. 05/07/1975
Each share Common 10¢ par exchanged for (0.298) share Common 10¢ par
(See Evans Industries, Inc.)

AEROCON INC (NY)
Merged into Alphanumeric, Inc. 01/28/1972
Each share Common 1¢ par exchanged for (0.1) share Common $0.33333333 par
(See Alphanumeric, Inc.)

AERODEX INC (DE)
Adjudicated bankrupt 09/09/1976
No stockholders' equity

AERODYNAMIC RECYCLING TECHNOLOGY CORP (NV)
Charter revoked for failure to file reports and pay fees 05/31/2008

AERODYNE MACHY CORP (MN)
Under plan of reorganization each share Common 2¢ par automatically became (1) share General Resource Corp. Common 2¢ par 12/09/1970

AERODYNE PRODS CORP (DE)
Name changed to Industrial Technologies Inc. 02/03/1994
(See Industrial Technologies, Inc.)

AEROFLEX HLDG CORP (DE)
Acquired by Cobham PLC 09/12/2014
Each share Common 1¢ par exchanged for $10.50 cash

AEROFLEX INC (DE)
Common 10¢ par split (5) for (4) by issuance of (0.25) additional share payable 07/07/2000 to holders of record 06/26/2000
Common 10¢ par split (2) for (1) by issuance of (1) additional share payable 11/22/2000 to holders of record 11/16/2000 Ex date - 11/24/2000
Merged into AX Holding Corp. 08/15/2007
Each share Common 10¢ par exchanged for $14.50 cash

AEROFLEX LABS INC (DE)
Common $1 par changed to 10¢ par 03/02/1976
Stock Dividends - 10% 05/15/1979; 20% 11/30/1979; 10% 10/24/1980; 25% 03/13/1981; 50% 06/01/1981; 10% 12/15/1982; 25% 06/18/1983; 10% 11/27/1984
Under plan of reorganization each share Common 10¢ par automatically became (1) share ARX, Inc. Common 10¢ par 10/28/1985
ARX, Inc. name changed to AeroFlex Inc. 11/10/1994
(See AeroFlex Inc.)

AEROFLOT RUSSIAN AIRLS JSC (RUSSIA)
Name changed to PJSC Aeroflot Russian Airlines 10/21/2015

AEROFLOT RUSSIAN INTL AIRLS (RUSSIA)
Sponsored 144A GDR's for Ordinary split (20) for (1) by issuance of (19) additional GDR's payable 01/06/2014 to holders of record 01/03/2014 Ex date - 01/07/2014
Sponsored Reg. S GDR's for Ordinary split (20) for (1) by issuance of (19) additional GDR's payable 01/06/2014 to holders of record 01/03/2014
Basis changed from (1:100) to (1:5) 01/07/2014
Name changed to PJSC Aeroflot Russian Airlines 10/21/2015

AEROGEN INC (DE)
Each share old Common $0.001 par exchanged for (0.2) share new Common $0.001 par 10/31/2003
Merged into Nektar Therapeutics 10/20/2005
Each share new Common $0.001 par exchanged for $0.75 cash

AEROGROUP INC (UT)
SEC revoked common stock registration 03/14/2008

AEROJET GEN CORP (OH)
Common $10 par changed to $1 par and (9) additional shares issued 03/27/1958
3% Preferred $1,000 par called for redemption 10/01/1963
Merged into General Tire & Rubber Co. 11/10/1972
Each share Common $1 par exchanged for (1.312) shares Common 30¢ par
General Tire & Rubber Co. name changed to GenCorp Inc. (OH) 03/30/1984 which reincorporated in Delaware 04/14/2014 which name changed to Aerojet Rocketdyne Holdings, Inc. 04/27/2015

AEROLIFT INC (CO)
Charter suspended for failure to maintain a resident agent 09/30/1989

AEROLOGICAL RESH INC (DE)
Adjudicated bankrupt 03/03/1971
Stockholders' equity unlikely

AEROMARINE ELECTRS INC (CA)
Charter cancelled for failure to file reports and pay taxes 03/02/1992

AEROMAT, INC. (MN)
Name changed to Favco, Inc. 12/21/1970
(See Favco, Inc.)

AEROMECHANICAL SVCS LTD (CANADA)
Name changed to FLYHT Aerospace Solutions Ltd. 05/17/2012

AEROMETALS INC (DE)
Charter forfeited for failure to maintain a registered agent 01/05/1996

AERONAUTICAL CORP. OF AMERICA (OH)
Name changed to Aeronca Aircraft Corp. 05/13/1941
Aeronca Aircraft Corp. name changed to Aeronca Manufacturing Corp. 06/01/1950 which name changed to Aeronca, Inc. 05/17/1966
(See Aeronca, Inc.)

AERONAUTICAL ELECTRONICS, INC. (NC)
Name changed to Aerotron, Inc. (NC) 05/05/1966
Aerotron, Inc. (NC) reincorporated in Delaware 10/29/1971
(See Aerotron, Inc. (DE))

AERONAUTICAL INDUSTRIES, INC.
Acquired by National Aviation Corp. 00/00/1930

AER-AET

Details not available

AERONAUTICAL PRODUCTS, INC. (MI)
Merged into McQuay, Inc. 12/23/1947
Each share Common $1 par exchanged for (0.16666666) share Common $1 par and (0.16666666) share 5% Preferred $20 par
McQuay, Inc. name changed to McQuay-Perfex Inc. 06/23/1971 which name changed back to McQuay, Inc. 05/31/1983
(See McQuay, Inc.)

AERONAUTICAL RESH & DEV CORP (MA)
Proclaimed dissolved for failure to file reports and pay fees 10/04/1972

AERONAUTICAL SECURITIES, INC.
Assets acquired by Bullock Fund, Ltd. 03/00/1951
Each share Common $1 par exchanged for (0.3352) share Capital Stock $1 par
Bullock Fund, Ltd. name changed to Bullock Growth Shares, Inc. 04/08/1985 which merged into Chemical Fund, Inc. 03/13/1987 which name changed to Alliance Fund, Inc. 04/01/1987 which name changed to Alliance Mid-Capital Growth Fund Inc. 02/01/2002 which name changed to AllianceBernstein Mid-Capital Growth Fund, Inc. 03/31/2003

AERONCA AIRCRAFT CORP. (OH)
Name changed to Aeronca Manufacturing Corp. 06/01/1950
Aeronca Manufacturing Corp. name changed to Aeronca, Inc. 05/17/1966
(See Aeronca, Inc.)

AERONCA INC (OH)
5.5% Prior Preferred $20 par called for redemption 03/20/1968
55¢ Preferred $10 par called for redemption 03/20/1968
$6 Prior Preferred $100 par called for redemption 10/01/1986
$6 Conv. Preference Ser. A no par called for redemption 10/01/1986
Acquired by Fleet Aerospace Corp. 09/17/1986
Each share Common $1 par exchanged for $6 cash

AERONCA MANUFACTURING CORP. (OH)
Reorganized 04/05/1955
Each share 5.5% Prior Preferred $100 par exchanged for (26) shares 5.5% Prior Preferred $20 par, (5) shares Common $1 par and $8.875 cash
Each share $0.55 Preferred $1 par exchanged for (1.4) shares $0.55 Preferred $10 par and $0.40 cash
Name changed to Aeronca, Inc. 05/17/1966
(See Aeronca, Inc.)

AERONIX INC (NJ)
Each share Common $1 par exchanged for (0.25) share Class A Common 10¢ par 05/06/1974
Stock Dividend - 25% 03/10/1976
Charter declared void for non-payment of taxes 11/17/1983

AEROPLAN INCOME FD (ON)
Merged into Groupe Aeroplan Inc. 06/27/2008
Each Unit no par exchanged for (1) share Common no par
Groupe Aeroplan Inc. name changed to Aimia Inc. 05/09/2012

AEROPOSTALE INC (DE)
Common 1¢ par split (3) for (2) by issuance of (0.5) additional share payable 04/26/2004 to holders of record 04/12/2004 Ex date - 04/27/2004
Common 1¢ par split (3) for (2) by issuance of (0.5) additional share payable 08/21/2007 to holders of record 08/06/2007 Ex date - 08/22/2007
Common 1¢ par split (3) for (2) by issuance of (0.5) additional share payable 03/04/2010 to holders of record 02/24/2010 Ex date - 03/05/2010
Name changed to ARO Liquidation, Inc. 08/16/2017
(See ARO Liquidation, Inc.)

AEROQUEST INTL LTD (ON)
Acquired by Geotech Ltd. 05/14/2012
Each share Common no par exchanged for $0.15 cash
Note: Unexchanged certificates were cancelled and became without value 05/14/2018

AEROQUIP CORP. (MI)
Completely liquidated 09/30/1968
Each share Common $1 par exchanged for first and final distribution of (0.8) share Libbey-Owens-Ford Co. $4.75 Conv. Preferred Ser. A no par
Libbey-Owens-Ford Co. name changed to Trinova Corp. 08/01/1986
(See Trinova Corp.)

AEROQUIP-VICKERS INC (OH)
Merged into Eaton Corp. 04/09/1999
Each share Common $5 par exchanged for $58 cash

AEROSOL CORP. OF AMERICA (DE)
Dissolved 06/06/1967
Preferred no par retired
No stockholders' equity for Class A, B or C Common no par

AEROSOL CORP. OF AMERICA (MA)
Acquired by Shulton, Inc. 11/17/1961
Each (6.5) shares Common no par exchanged for (1) share Class A Common 50¢ par or Class B Common 50¢ par
Shulton, Inc. merged into American Cyanamid Co. 04/15/1971
(See American Cyanamid Co.)

AEROSOL TECHNIQUES INC (NY)
Common 10¢ par changed to 8¢ par and (0.25) additional share issued 02/16/1965
Name changed to ATI, Inc. (NY) 03/05/1975
ATI, Inc. (NY) name changed to ATI Pharmaceuticals Inc. 12/29/1987 which name changed to Armstrong Pharmaceuticals Inc. 05/15/1991 which merged into Medeva PLC 01/14/1993 which merged into Celltech Group plc 01/26/2000
(See Celltech Group plc)

AEROSONIC CORP (DE)
Each share Common 10¢ par exchanged for (0.25) share Common 40¢ par 08/06/1971
Common 40¢ par split (2) for (1) by issuance of (1) additional share 06/05/1978
Common 40¢ par split (2) for (1) by issuance of (1) additional share 03/31/1980
Acquired by TransDigm Group Inc. 06/10/2013
Each share Common 40¢ par exchanged for $7.75 cash

AEROSONIC CORP (FL)
Merged into Instrument Technology Corp. 01/12/1970
Each share Common 10¢ par exchanged for (1.877) shares Common 10¢ par
Instrument Technology Corp. name changed to Aerosonic Corp. (DE) 09/21/1970

AEROSPACE TECHNOLOGY CORP (DE)
Reincorporated 07/31/1970
State of incorporation changed from (NJ) to (DE) 07/31/1970
Name changed to Automated Technology Corp. 08/09/1971
(See Automated Technology Corp.)

AEROSYSTEMS TECHNOLOGY CORP (NJ)
Merged into Technology General Corp. 09/02/1987
Each share Common 10¢ par exchanged for (4) shares Common 10¢ par

AEROTELESIS INC (DE)
Each share old Common $0.00008 par exchanged for (1.02) shares new Common $0.00008 par 06/16/2004
SEC revoked common stock registration 12/15/2011

AEROTEST LABORATORIES INC. (NY)
Name changed to United Aerotest Laboratories, Inc. 06/26/1964
United Aerotest Laboratories, Inc. acquired by Ogden Corp. 12/13/1966 which name changed to Covanta Energy Corp. 03/14/2001
(See Covanta Energy Corp.)

AEROTRON INC (DE)
Reincorporated 10/29/1971
State of incorporation changed from (NC) to (DE) 10/29/1971
Merged into Siemens A.G. 01/15/1980
Each share Common $1 par exchanged for $8 cash

AEROVIAS DE MEXICO S A DE C V (MEXICO)
Merged into Cintra S.A. 06/28/1996
Details not available

AEROVIAS SUD AMERICANA INC (FL)
Adjudicated bankrupt 05/21/1969
Stockholders' equity unlikely

AEROVOX CORP (MA)
Stock Dividend - 100% 10/18/1950
Merged into AVX Ceramics Corp. 06/04/1973
Each share Common $1 par exchanged for (0.9) share Common $1 par
AVX Ceramics Corp. merged into AVX Corp. 08/22/1973 which was acquired by Kyocera Corp. 01/18/1990

AEROVOX INC (DE)
Plan of reorganization under Chapter 11 Federal Bankruptcy Code effective 10/14/2003
No stockholders' equity

AEROX CORP. (UT)
Name changed to Dixon Oil Co. 09/09/1981

AES CHINA GENERATING CO. LTD. (BERMUDA)
Merged into AES Corp. 05/08/1997
Each share Class A Common 1¢ par exchanged for (0.29) share Common 1¢ par

AES TECHNOLOGY SYS INC (DE)
Common 1¢ par split (2) for (1) by issuance of (1) additional share 02/20/1979
Filed a petition under Chapter 7 Federal Bankruptcy Code 06/27/1988
No stockholders' equity

AES TIETE S A (BRAZIL)
Sponsored ADR's for Preferred split (12) for (1) by issuance of (11) additional ADR's payable 04/04/2008 to holders of record 04/01/2008 Ex date - 04/07/2008
Sponsored ADR's for Ordinary split (12) for (1) by issuance of (11) additional ADR's payable 04/04/2008 to holders of record 04/01/2008 Ex date - 04/07/2008
Basis changed from (1:3,000) to (1:1) 04/04/2008

ADR agreement terminated 02/12/2016
Each Sponsored ADR's for Preferred exchanged for $2.876336 cash
Each Sponsored ADR for Ordinary exchanged for $2.876336 cash

AES TR I (DE)
Each $2.6875 Conv. Trust Security Ser. A exchanged for (2.7624) shares AES Corp. Common 1¢ par 06/14/2000

AES TR III (DE)
3.375% Trust Conv. Preferred Security called for redemption at $50 plus $0.647 accrued dividends on 06/23/2017

AESOP INC (DE)
Name changed to Ocutec Holdings Inc. 05/05/1989
(See Ocutec Holdings Inc.)

AESP INC (FL)
Merged into Stein & Briskin 07/03/2007
Each share Common $0.001 par exchanged for $0.05 cash

AET INC (DE)
Charter cancelled and declared inoperative and void for non-payment of taxes 03/01/1993

AETERNA LABORATORIES INC (CANADA)
Subordinate no par split (2) for (1) by issuance of (1) additional share payable 08/13/1996 to holders of record 08/08/1996 Ex date - 08/06/1996
Reorganized as AEterna Zentaris Inc. 05/26/2004
Each share Subordinate no par exchanged for (1) share Common no par

AETHER HLDGS INC (DE)
Name changed to NexCen Brands, Inc. 11/01/2006
(See NexCen Brands, Inc.)

AETHER SYSTEMS INC (DE)
Reorganized as Aether Holding, Inc. 07/13/2005
Each share Common 1¢ par exchanged for (1) share Common 1¢ par
Aether Holding, Inc. name changed to NexCen Brands, Inc. 11/01/2006
(See NexCen Brands, Inc.)

AETNA BALL & ROLLER BEARING CO. (IL)
Common $1 par changed to $5 par 00/00/1949
Stock Dividend - 100% 11/03/1944
Merged into Parkersburg-Aetna Corp. 01/29/1954
Each share Common $5 par exchanged for (1) share Common $1 par
Parkersburg-Aetna Corp. name changed to Paco, Inc. (WV) 09/27/1963
(See Paco, Inc.)

AETNA BALL BEARING MANUFACTURING CO. (IL)
Name changed to Aetna Ball & Roller Bearing Co. 00/00/1944
Aetna Ball & Roller Bearing Co. merged into Parkersburg-Aetna Corp. 01/29/1954 which name changed to Paco, Inc. (WV) 09/27/1963
(See Paco, Inc.)

AETNA BANCORP INC (IL)
Merged into River Forest Bancorp, Inc. 09/30/1991
Each share Common $5 par exchanged for $3.44 cash

AETNA BK (CHICAGO, IL)
Under plan of reorganization each share Common $5 par automatically became (1) share Aetna Bancorp Inc. Common $5 par 10/01/1980
(See Aetna Bancorp Inc.)

AETNA CASUALTY & SURETY CO. (CT)
Each share Capital Stock $100 par exchanged for (10) shares Capital Stock $10 par 00/00/1929
Capital Stock $10 par changed to $5 par and (1) additional share issued plus a 25% stock dividend paid 03/01/1960
Capital Stock $5 par changed to $3.50 par and (0.42857142) additional share issued plus a 40% stock dividend paid 03/25/1962
Stock Dividends - 100% 03/01/1945; 50% 11/15/1955
Acquired by Aetna Life Insurance Co. 12/29/1964
Each share Capital Stock $3.50 par exchanged for (1.9) shares Common $3.50 par
Aetna Life Insurance Co. name changed to Aetna Life & Casualty Co. 12/27/1967 which name changed to Aetna, Inc. (CT) 07/19/1996 which merged into ING Groep N.V. 12/13/2000

AETNA CORP. (CA)
Name changed to Capital Reserve Corp. and each share Capital Stock $2 par exchanged for (1) share Capital Stock no par 12/20/1961
Capital Reserve Corp. name changed to Capital Energy Corp. 12/14/1977 which name changed to Life Chemistry Inc. 11/28/1983
(See Life Chemistry Inc.)

AETNA DEV CORP (DC)
Recapitalized as Israel International Corp. 06/22/1972
Each share Common 5¢ par exchanged for (0.33333333) share Common 5¢ par
(See Israel International Corp.)

AETNA FD INC (MD)
Merged into Aetna Variable Fund, Inc. 12/31/1977
Each share Common $1 par exchanged for (0.64) share Common $1 par

AETNA FIN CO (MO)
Name changed to A.F. Liquidating Corp. 08/31/1964
(See A.F. Liquidating Corp.)

AETNA GOLDALE INVTS LTD (BC)
Reorganized as Goldale Investments Ltd. (BC) 06/30/1977
Each share Capital Stock 50¢ par exchanged for (0.16) share Class A no par and (0.04) share Class B no par
Goldale Investments Ltd. (BC) reincorporated in Ontario 10/12/1977 which name changed to Viner (E.A.) Holdings Ltd. 11/14/1986 which name changed to Fahnestock Viner Holdings Inc. 06/28/1988 which name changed to Oppenheimer Holdings Inc. (ON) 09/02/2003 which reincorporated in Canada 05/11/2005 which reincorporated in Delaware 05/11/2009

AETNA INC (CT)
6.25% Preferred Class C 1¢ par called for redemption at (0.8197) share Common on 07/19/1999
Merged into ING Groep N.V. 12/13/2000
Each share Common 1¢ par exchanged for $35.332247 cash
Each share Common 1¢ par received distribution of (1) share Aetna, Inc. (PA) Common 1¢ par payable 12/14/2000 to holders of record 12/13/2000

AETNA INCOME SHS INC (MD)
Reorganized as ING VP Bond Portfolio 03/25/2002
Details not available

AETNA INSURANCE CO. (CT)
Each share Capital Stock $100 par exchanged for (10) shares Capital Stock $10 par 00/00/1930
Merged into Connecticut General Insurance Corp. 12/19/1967
Each share Capital Stock $10 par exchanged for (2.25) shares Common $2.50 par
Connecticut General Insurance Corp. reorganized as Connecticut General Corp. 07/01/1981 which merged Cigna Corp. 04/01/1982

AETNA INVESTMENT CORP. LTD. (BC)
Name changed to Aetna-Goldale Investments Ltd. 08/02/1972
Aetna-Goldale Investments Ltd. reorganized as Goldale Investments Ltd. (BC) 06/30/1977 which reincorporated in Ontario 10/12/1977 which name changed to Viner (E.A.) Holdings Ltd. 11/14/1986 which name changed to Fahnestock Viner Holdings Inc. 06/28/1988 which name changed to Oppenheimer Holdings Inc. (ON) 09/02/2003 which reincorporated in Canada 05/11/2005 which reincorporated in Delaware 05/11/2009

AETNA LIFE & CAS CO (CT)
Common $3.50 par changed to $1.75 par and (1) additional share issued 05/15/1974
Common $1.75 par changed to no par and (0.5) additional share issued 06/01/1979
$2 Conv. Preferred no par called for redemption 05/31/1985
Floating Rate Preferred Ser. A no par called for redemption 08/03/1987
Single Point Adjustable Rate Class C Non-Vtg. Preferred Ser. A no par called for redemption 04/27/1989
Single Point Adjustable Rate Class C Non-Vtg. Preferred Ser. B no par called for redemption 05/04/1989
Name changed to Aetna, Inc. (CT) 07/19/1996
Aetna, Inc. (CT) merged into ING Groep N.V. 12/13/2000

AETNA LIFE INSURANCE CO. (CT)
Each share Capital Stock $100 par exchanged for (10) shares Capital Stock $10 par 00/00/1929
Capital Stock $10 par changed to $5 par and (1) additional share issued plus a 33.33333333% stock dividend paid 11/16/1959
Capital Stock $5 par changed to $2.50 par and (1) additional share issued plus a 25% stock dividend paid 12/10/1964
Stock Dividends - 33.33333333% 03/01/1950; 50% 03/02/1953
Name changed to Aetna Life & Casualty Co. and Capital Stock $2.50 par changed to $3.50 par 12/27/1967
Aetna Life & Casualty Co. name changed to Aetna, Inc. (CT) 07/19/1996 which merged into ING Groep N.V. 12/13/2000

AETNA LIFE INS CO CDA (ON)
Adjustable Rate Preferred Ser. 1 $25 par called for redemption 09/30/1993

AETNA MAINTENANCE CO. (CA)
Name changed to Haydon Switch & Instrument, Inc. (CA) 03/31/1965
Haydon Switch & Instrument, Inc. (CA) merged into Haydon Switch & Instrument, Inc. (DE) 11/29/1968
(See Haydon Switch & Instrument, Inc. (DE))

AETNA MILLS
Recapitalized as Shirreffs Worsted Co. 10/11/1937
Each share 6% Preferred $100 par exchanged for (1) share Prior Preference $35 par and (8) shares new Common no par
Each share old Common no par exchanged for (1) share new Common no par
(See Shirreffs Worsted Co.)

AETNA MINES LTD. (ON)
Completely liquidated 06/16/1959
Each share Capital Stock $1 par received first and final distribution of (1) share Norstar Lake Mines Ltd. Common $1 par

AETNA MORTGAGE CORP.
Liquidated 00/00/1929
Details not available

AETNA OIL CO.
Acquired by Ashland Oil & Refining Co. 01/16/1950
Each share Preferred $100 par exchanged for (1) share $5 Preferred no par
Each share Common $10 par exchanged for (0.542) share $1.20 Preferred no par and (0.4792) share $5 Preferred no par
(See Ashland Oil & Refining Co.)

AETNA REAL ESTATE ASSOC L P (DE)
Partnership terminated 03/28/2003
Each share Depositary Unit received first and final distribution of $0.034 cash 01/08/2004

AETNA RUBBER CO.
Liquidation completed 12/00/1948
Details not available

AETNA SER FD INC (MD)
Name changed to ING Series Fund, Inc. 03/01/2002

AETNA SER FD INC (MD)
Name changed to ING Series Fund, Inc. 03/01/2002

AETNA ST BK (CHICAGO, IL)
Common $12.50 par changed to $5 par and (1.5) additional shares issued 02/23/1968
Stock Dividends - 20% 03/23/1971; 14.2% 04/16/1974; 12.5% 04/16/1976
Name changed to Aetna Bank (Chicago, IL) 03/14/1977
Aetna Bank (Chicago, IL) reorganized as Aetna Bancorp Inc. 10/01/1980
(See Aetna Bancorp Inc.)

AETNA-STANDARD ENGINEERING CO. (OH)
Common no par changed to $1 par 00/00/1938
Each share 7% Preferred $100 par exchanged for (1.4) shares 5% Preferred $100 par 00/00/1940
Common $1 par exchanged (2) for (1) 00/00/1946
Stock Dividends - 10% 07/20/1956; 10% 08/23/1957
Liquidation completed
Each share Common $1 par exchanged for initial distribution of $25 cash plus a Receipt 03/20/1959
Each Receipt received second distribution of $5 cash 05/15/1959
Each Receipt received third distribution of $1.50 cash 01/15/1960
Each Receipt received fourth distribution of $0.25 cash 02/19/1960
Each Receipt received fifth distribution of $0.50 cash 07/09/1961
Each Receipt exchanged for sixth and final distribution of $0.37 cash 12/20/1962

AETRIUM INC (MN)
Old Common $0.001 par split (3) for (2) by issuance of (0.5) additional share 08/25/1995
Each share old Common $0.001 par exchanged for (0.1) share new Common 0.001 par 10/11/2013
Name changed to ATRM Holdings, Inc. 12/12/2014

AEW REAL ESTATE INCOME FD (MA)
Completely liquidated
Each Auction Market Preferred Share Ser. M received first and final distribution of $25,000 cash payable 04/13/2007 to holders of record 04/09/2007
Each share Common $0.00001 par received first and final distribution of $24.1973 cash payable 04/13/2007 to holders of record 04/09/2007

AEX MINERALS CORP (BC)
Name changed to Canadian Natural Resources Ltd. (BC) 12/16/1975
Canadian Natural Resources Ltd. (BC) reincorporated in Alberta 01/06/1982

AF BK (WEST JEFFERSON, NC)
Under plan of reorganization each share Common 1¢ par automatically became (1) share AF Bankshares, Inc. Common 1¢ par 06/16/1998
AF Bankshares, Inc. name changed to AF Financial Group, Inc. 11/04/2002 which name changed to LifeStore Financial Group 12/22/2009 which name changed to LifeStore Financial Group, Inc. 06/01/2018

AF FINL GROUP INC (NC)
Name changed 11/04/2002
Name changed from AF Bankshares, Inc. to AF Financial Group, Inc. 11/04/2002
Name changed to LifeStore Financial Group 12/22/2009
LifeStore Financial Group name changed to LifeStore Financial Group, Inc. 06/01/2018

AFA FDS INC (MD)
Name changed to Hancock (John) Technology Series, Inc. 12/20/1991
(See Hancock (John) Technology Series, Inc.)

AFA MUSIC GROUP LTD (FL)
Reincorporated 01/17/2008
Reincorporated from AFA Music Group Ltd. (DE) to under the laws of Florida as AFA Music Group, Inc. 01/17/2008
Each share old Common $0.00001 par exchanged for (0.00002) share new Common $0.00001 par 07/30/2008
Name changed to 3D Eye Solutions, Inc. 09/16/2008

AFC BLDG TECHNOLOGIES INC (NV)
Common $0.001 par split (8) for (1) by issuance of (7) additional shares payable 01/14/2014 to holders of record 01/14/2014
Name changed to First Colombia Development Corp. 04/26/2018

AFC CABLE SYS INC (DE)
Common 1¢ par split (5) for (4) by issuance of (0.25) additional share payable 10/20/1997 to holders of record 10/06/1997
Merged into Tyco International Ltd. (Bermuda) 11/22/1999
Each share Common 1¢ par exchanged for (1) share Common 20¢ par
Tyco International Ltd. (Bermuda) reincorporated in Switzerland 03/17/2009 which merged into Johnson Controls International PLC 09/06/2016

AFC ENERGY CORP (BC)
Struck off register and declared dissolved for failure to file returns 05/06/1988

AFC ENTERPRISES INC (MN)
Name changed to Popeyes Louisiana Kitchen, Inc. 01/21/2014
(See Popeyes Louisiana Kitchen, Inc.)

AFC-AFF

AFC FINL CORP (DE)
Each share old Common 10¢ par exchanged for (0.2) share new Common 10¢ par 12/19/1984
Charter cancelled and declared inoperative and void for non-payment of taxes 03/01/1999

AFC-LOW INCOME HOUSING CREDIT PARTNERS-I INVESTMENT IN AFFORDABLE HOUSING, A CALIFORNIA LIMITED PARTNERSHIP (CA)
SEC revoked limited partnership interest registration 07/02/2009
Stockholders' equity unlikely

AFCA INC (DE)
Recapitalized as Teckla, Inc. 11/18/1970
Each share Common 1¢ par exchanged for (0.33333333) share Common 3¢ par
(See Teckla, Inc.)

AFCAN MNG CORP (QC)
Merged into Eldorado Gold Corp. (New) 09/13/2005
Each share Common no par exchanged for (0.15384615) share Common no par

AFCOA (CA)
Common 10¢ par split (1.4) for (1) by issuance of (0.4) additional share 11/17/1970
Adjudicated bankrupt 09/07/1973
Stockholders' equity unlikely

AFD CAP GROUP INC (DE)
Each share Common $0.0001 par exchanged for (0.2) share Common $0.0005 par 07/06/1990
Name changed to International Framing & Arts Ltd. 10/16/1991
International Framing & Arts Ltd. recapitalized as J.A. Industries Inc. 11/02/1992 which recapitalized as Electronic Manufacturing Services Group Inc. 07/30/1996

AFD CAP GROUP INC (NV)
Name changed to Aquasol Technologies Inc. (NV) 06/24/1998
Aquasol Technologies Inc. (NV) recapitalized as Ilink Telecom Inc. 02/16/1999 which name changed to 9278 Communications Inc. (NV) 12/29/1999 which reincorporated in Delaware 04/24/2000
(See 9278 Communications Inc.)

AFEXA LIFE SCIENCES INC (AB)
Acquired by Valeant Pharmaceuticals International, Inc. 12/12/2011
Each share Common no par exchanged for $0.85 cash

AFF AUTOMATED FAST FOODS LTD (BC)
Name changed to Brier Resources Corp. 07/31/1998
Brier Resources Corp. name changed to Ashlar Financial Services Corp. 08/02/2000
(See Ashlar Financial Services Corp.)

AFF CAP CORP (DE)
11% Fixed Rate Preferred $1 par called for redemption 09/30/1988
Public interest eliminated

AFFERRO MNG INC (BC)
Acquired by International Mining & Infrastucture Corp. 12/19/2013
Each share Common no par exchanged for £0.40 principal amount of 8% Conv. Unsecured Notes due 12/31/2015 and £0.80 cash

AFFIANCE INC NEW (NV)
Reorganized as SMI Financial Group Inc. 11/14/2000
Each share Common $0.0001 par exchanged for (30) shares Common $0.0001 par
SMI Financial Group Inc. name changed to AmeraMex International Inc. 05/30/2001

AFFIANCE INC OLD (NV)
Recapitalized as N2Awareness.Com 04/29/1999
Each share Common $0.001 par exchanged for (0.1) share Common $0.0001 par
N2Awareness.Com Inc. name changed to Affiance, Inc. (New) 05/17/1999 which reorganized as SMI Financial Group Inc. 11/14/2000 which name changed to AmeraMex International Inc. 05/30/2001

AFFILIATED ADJUSTERS INC (FL)
Name changed to dot com Entertainment Group, Inc. (FL) 02/02/1999
dot com Entertainment Group, Inc. (FL) reincorporated in Ontario as Parlay Entertainment Inc. 12/16/2004 which recapitalized as Oramericas Corp. (ON) 12/10/2012 which reincorporated in British Columbia 02/21/2014 which name changed to Backstageplay Inc. 02/09/2016

AFFILIATED AUDIO-VISUAL NETWORK, INC. (NY)
Charter revoked for failure to file reports and pay fees 12/16/1962

AFFILIATED BANC CORP (MA)
Involuntarily dissolved 08/31/1998

AFFILIATED BANC GROUP, INC. (IL)
Acquired by Comerica, Inc. 00/00/1987
Details not available

AFFILIATED BK CORP (WI)
Merged into Marshall & Ilsley Corp. (Old) 12/31/1980
Each share Common $5 par exchanged for (1.3) shares Common $2.50 par
(See Marshall & Ilsley Corp. (Old))

AFFILIATED BK CORP WYO (WY)
Name changed to Wyoming National Bancorp 06/28/1988
(See Wyoming National Bancorp)

AFFILIATED BANKSHARES COLO INC (CO)
Common $5 par split (2) for (1) by issuance of (1) additional share 07/22/1981
Common $5 par split (3) for (2) by issuance of (0.5) additional share 11/21/1983
Merged into Banc One Corp. 11/02/1992
Each share 9% Conv. Preferred Ser. A $50 par exchanged for (3.025242) shares Common no par
Each share Common $5 par exchanged for (0.726) share Common no par
Banc One Corp. merged into Bank One Corp. 10/02/1998 which merged into J.P. Morgan Chase & Co. 12/31/2000 which name changed to JPMorgan Chase & Co. 07/20/2004

AFFILIATED CAP CORP (TX)
Merged into ACC Aquisition Corp. 07/29/1983
Each share Common 50¢ par exchanged for $22.50 cash

AFFILIATED CAP CORP (UT)
Each share old Common $0.001 par exchanged for (0.25) share new Common $0.001 par 08/09/1985
Proclaimed dissolved for failure to pay taxes 04/01/1987

AFFILIATED CMNTY BANCORP INC (MA)
Common 10¢ par split (5) for (4) by issuance of (0.25) additional share payable 05/30/1997 to holders of record 05/15/1997
Merged into UST Corp. 08/07/1998
Each share Common 10¢ par exchanged for (1.41) shares Common $0.625 par
(See UST Corp.)

AFFILIATED COMPUTER SVCS INC (DE)
Class A Common 1¢ par split (2) for (1) by issuance of (1) additional share payable 11/22/1996 to holders of record 11/11/1996
Class A Common 1¢ par split (2) for (1) by issuance of (1) additional share payable 02/22/2002 to holders of record 02/15/2002 Ex date - 02/25/2002
Merged into Xerox Corp. 02/08/2010
Each share Class A Common 1¢ par exchanged for (4.935) shares Common $1 par and $18.60 cash

AFFILIATED COMPUTER SYS INC (TX)
Under plan of reorganization each share Common 10¢ par automatically became (1) share ACS Investors, Inc. Common 10¢ par 07/01/1972
(See ACS Investors, Inc.)

AFFILIATED FD INC (MD)
Reincorporated 11/26/1975
Each share Capital Stock 25¢ par exchanged for (0.2) share Common $1.25 par 09/21/1936
Common $1.25 par reclassified as Capital Stock $1.25 par 01/10/1952
State of incorporation changed from (DE) to (MD) 11/26/1975
Name changed to Lord Abbett Affiliated Fund, Inc. 03/01/1996

AFFILIATED FOOD STORES INC (TX)
Liquidating plan of reorganization under Chapter 11 Federal Bankruptcy proceedings confirmed 01/27/1994
No stockholders' equity

AFFILIATED GAS EQUIPMENT, INC. (DE)
Merged into Carrier Corp. 02/28/1955
Each share old $3 Preferred $50 par exchanged for (1) share new $3 Preferred $50 par
Each share Common $1 par exchanged for (0.1) share 4.5% Preferred $50 par and (0.18181818) share Common $10 par
Carrier Corp. acquired by United Technologies Corp. 07/06/1979

AFFILIATED GENERAL AGENCY, INC. (OK)
Liquidation completed
Each share Capital Stock 10¢ par exchanged for initial distribution of $3 cash 10/12/1973
Each share Capital Stock 10¢ par received second and final distribution of $0.785786 cash 06/05/1974

AFFILIATED HOSP PRODS INC (DE)
Merged into Splint, Inc. 03/29/1985
Each share Common $1 par exchanged for $36 cash

AFFILIATED INVESTORS, INC.
Name changed to Affiliated Trading Corp. 00/00/1936
(See Affiliated Trading Corp.)

AFFILIATED INVESTORS FUND, INC. (DE)
Name changed to Affiliated Fund, Inc. (DE) 05/14/1934
Affiliated Fund, Inc. (DE) reincorporated in Maryland 11/26/1975 which name changed to Lord Abbett Affiliated Fund, Inc. 03/01/1996

AFFILIATED INVTS INC (MS)
Charter suspended for failure to file reports and pay taxes 03/24/1982

AFFILIATED LITHIUM MINES LTD. (ON)
Charter surrendered 08/31/1966
No stockholders' equity

AFFILIATED MANAGERS GROUP INC (DE)
Each Income Preferred Redeemable Increased Dividend Equity Security received (0.4461) share Common 1¢ par 11/17/2004
(Additional Information in Active)

AFFILIATED NATL INC (NY)
Name changed to Global Environmental Corp. 06/20/1989
Global Environmental Corp. name changed to Danzer Corp. 10/06/1999 which reincorporated in Delaware as Obsidian Enterprises, Inc. 10/17/2001
(See Obsidian Enterprises, Inc.)

AFFILIATED NETWORKS INC (FL)
Common 1¢ par split (3) for (1) by issuance of (2) additional shares payable 03/25/1999 to holders of record 03/24/1999
Name changed to Marex.com, Inc. 11/22/1999
Marex.com, Inc. name changed to Marex, Inc. 05/29/2001
(See Marex, Inc.)

AFFILIATED PRODUCTS, INC.
Acquired by American Home Products Corp. 04/15/1936
Each share Capital Stock no par exchanged for (0.2) share Capital Stock $1 par
American Home Products Corp. name changed to Wyeth 03/11/2002 which was acquired by Pfizer Inc. 10/15/2009

AFFILIATED PUBNS INC NEW (MA)
Merged into New York Times Co. 10/01/1993
Each share Ser. A Common 1¢ par exchanged for (0.6) share Class A Common 10¢ par
Each share Ser. B Common 1¢ par exchanged for (0.6) share Class A Common 10¢ par

AFFILIATED PUBNS INC OLD (MA)
Common 1¢ par split (3) for (2) by issuance of (0.5) additional share 02/07/1983
Common 1¢ par split (3) for (2) by issuance of (0.5) additional share 01/25/1985
Common 1¢ par split (3) for (2) by issuance of (0.5) additional share 01/24/1986
Common 1¢ par split (2) for (1) by issuance of (1) additional share 01/23/1987
Common 1¢ par reclassified as Common Ser. A 1¢ par 06/30/1988
Each share Common Ser. A 1¢ par received distribution of (1) share Conv. Common Ser. B 1¢ par 06/30/1988
Stock Dividend - 50% 02/14/1980
Merged into McCaw Cellular Communications, Inc. 05/31/1989
Each share Common Ser. A 1¢ par exchanged for (0.84017405) share Class A Common 1¢ par
Each share Conv. Common Ser. B 1¢ par exchanged for (0.84017405) share Class A Common 1¢ par
McCaw Cellular Communications, Inc. merged into AT&T Corp. 09/19/1994 which merged into AT&T Inc. 11/18/2005

AFFILIATED TRADING CORP.
Dissolved 00/00/1940
Details not available

AFFILIATED VENTURES INC (DE)
Recapitalized as Covasorb Bionic Surfaces, Inc. 11/18/1987
Each share Common $0.00001 par exchanged for (0.1) share Common $0.0001 par
(See Covasorb Bionic Surfaces, Inc.)

AFFINITEK CORP (AB)
Name changed to MediaNet Communications Corp. and Common no par reclassified as Non-Voting Class B no par 12/23/1999

AFFINITY BANCORP INC (PA)
Merged into First Priority Financial Corp. 02/28/2013
Each share Common $1 par exchanged for (0.9813) share Common $1 par
First Priority Financial Corp. merged into Mid Penn Bancorp, Inc. 08/01/2018

AFFINITY BIOTECH INC (DE)
Name changed to IBAH, Inc. 04/27/1994
IBAH, Inc. merged into Omnicare, Inc. 06/29/1998
(See Omnicare, Inc.)

AFFINITY ENTMT INC (DE)
Name changed 07/03/1996
Name changed from Affinity Teleproductions, Inc. to Affinity Entertainment Inc. 07/03/1996
Each share old Common 1¢ par exchanged for (0.1) share new Common 1¢ par 09/19/1997
Name changed to Tour CFG Inc. 11/04/1997
(See Tour CFG Inc.)

AFFINITY INTL MARKETING INC (FL)
Name changed to Global Security & Intelligence Group Inc. 01/03/2003
(See Global Security & Intelligence Group Inc.)

AFFINITY INTL TRAVEL SYS INC (NV)
SEC revoked common stock registration 05/24/2005

AFFINITY MEDIAWORKS CORP (NV)
Old Common $0.00001 par split (20) for (1) by issuance of (19) additional shares payable 01/30/2009 to holders of record 01/30/2009
Each share old Common $0.00001 par exchanged for (0.00129032) share new Common $0.00001 par 02/21/2014
Reorganized under the laws of Maryland as American Housing Income Trust, Inc. 06/10/2015
Each share new Common $0.00001 par exchanged for (0.001) share Common 1¢ par
American Housing Income Trust, Inc. (MD) reincorporated in Wyoming as Corix Bioscience, Inc. 08/02/2017

AFFINITY TECHNOLOGY GROUP INC (DE)
Chapter 11 bankruptcy proceedings dismissed 05/18/2009
No stockholders' equity

AFFIRM CAP INC (AB)
Completely liquidated
Each share Common no par received first and final distribution of (0.18117) Canadian Equipment Rental Fund L.P. Unit of Ltd. Partnership Int. payable 06/23/2005 to holders of record 06/21/2005
Canadian Equipment Rental Fund L.P. reorganized as CERF Inc. 10/03/2011
CERF Inc. name changed to Canadian Equipment Rentals Corp. 06/27/2016 which name changed to Zedcor Energy Inc. 06/30/2017

AFFIRMATIVE INS HLDGS INC (DE)
Chapter 11 bankruptcy proceedings converted to Chapter 7 on 03/10/2016
Stockholders' equity unlikely

AFFITECH A S (DENMARK)
ADR agreement terminated 08/15/2013
No ADR's remain outstanding

AFFORD A HOME IND CORP (AB)
Recapitalized as Rawlins Industries Inc. 08/17/1988
Each share Common no par exchanged for (0.2) share Common no par
Rawlins Industries Inc. name changed to Vertimac Development Inc. 06/12/1989 which name changed to Copper States Resources Inc. 12/15/1995 which recapitalized as American Coppermine Resources Ltd. 08/26/1996 which recapitalized as Carleton Resources Corp. 02/04/1997
(See Carleton Resources Corp.)

AFFORDABLE HOMES AMER INC (NV)
Name changed to World Homes Inc. 10/16/2000
World Homes Inc. name changed to Composite Industries of America, Inc. 08/23/2001 which recapitalized as Composite Holdings, Inc. 05/08/2002 which name changed to Gold Rock Holdings, Inc. 01/07/2005

AFFORDABLE RESIDENTIAL CMNTYS INC (MD)
Name changed to Hilltop Holdings Inc. 07/31/2007

AFFORDABLE TELECOMMUNICATIONS TECHNOLOGY CORP (TX)
Each share old Common 1¢ par exchanged for (0.02) share new Common 1¢ par 07/19/2002
Each share new Common 1¢ par exchanged again for (0.0025) share new Common 1¢ par 12/10/2002
Name changed to Buzz Technologies, Inc. 03/21/2006

AFFYMAX N V (NETHERLANDS)
99% acquired by Glaxo Venture Ltd. at $30 per share through purchase offer which expired 05/15/1996
Public interest eliminated

AFFYMETRIX INC (DE)
Reincorporated 09/29/1998
State of incorporation changed from (CA) to (DE) and Common no par changed to 1¢ 09/29/1998
Common 1¢ par split (2) for (1) by issuance of (1) additional share payable 08/21/2000 to holders of record 08/10/2000
Acquired by Thermo Fisher Scientific Inc. 03/31/2016
Each share Common 1¢ par exchanged for $14 cash

AFG ENTERPRISES USA INC (NV)
Name changed 08/24/2005
Name changed from AFG Enterprises, Inc. to AFG Enterprises USA, Inc. 08/24/2005
Each share old Common $0.001 par exchanged for (0.02) share new Common $0.001 par 03/09/2006
Reincorporated under the laws of Delaware as FP Technology, Inc. 07/06/2006
FP Technology, Inc. name changed to Firepond, Inc. 07/12/2007
(See Firepond, Inc.)

AFG INDS INC (DE)
Common $1 par split (3) for (2) by issuance of (0.5) additional share 06/01/1983
Common $1 par split (3) for (2) by issuance of (0.5) additional share 04/11/1986
Common $1 par split (3) for (2) by issuance of (0.5) additional share 05/14/1987
Merged into Clarity Holdings Corp. 07/08/1988
Each share Common $1 par exchanged for $33 cash

AFG INVT TR (DE)
Liquidating Trust formed 12/31/2002
Liquidating Trust formed 12/31/2004
AFG Investment Trust A assets transferred to AFG Investment Trust A Liquidating Trust 12/31/2002
AFG Investment Trust B assets transferred to AFG Investment Trust B Liquidating Trust 12/31/2002
Completely liquidated
Each Trust A Class A Share of Bene. Int. received first and final distribution of approximately $4.65 cash 12/16/2003
Each Trust B Class A Share of Bene. Int. received first and final distribution of approximately $4.37 cash 12/16/2003
AFG Investment Trust C assets transferred to AFG Investment Trust C Liquidating Trust 12/31/2004
AFG Investment Trust D assets transferred to AFG Investment Trust D Liquidating Trust 12/31/2004
Completely liquidated
Each Trust D Class A Share of Bene. Int. received initial distribution of approximately $1.89 cash payable 12/30/2005 to holders of record 12/30/2005
Each Trust C Class A Share of Bene. Int. received initial distribution of $0.94 cash payable 10/13/2006 to holders of record 09/29/2006
Each Trust C Class A Share of Bene. Int. received second and final distribution of $1.18 cash payable 12/19/2006 to holders of record 12/06/2006
Each Trust D Class A Share of Bene. Int. received second and final distribution of approximately $0.91 cash payable 12/06/2006 to holders of record 12/06/2006

AFGL INTL INC (NV)
Reincorporated under the laws of Delaware as Headway Corporate Resources, Inc. 11/14/1996
(See Headway Corporate Resources, Inc.)

AFI CORP (DE)
Chapter 11 Bankruptcy proceedings dismissed 06/22/1982
No stockholders' equity

AFITEX FINL SVCS INC (ON)
Delisted from Canadian Dealer Network 10/13/2000

A5 LABORATORIES INC (NV)
Name changed to Hydrogen Future Corp. 12/27/2013

AFL CAP VENTURES INC (YT)
Reincorporated under the laws of Canada as Grey Horse Capital Corp. 01/18/2005
Grey Horse Capital Corp. name changed to Grey Horse Corp. 06/25/2007 which name changed to Equity Financial Holdings Inc. 12/21/2010
(See Equity Financial Holdings Inc.)

AFLAC INC (GA)
Variable/Fixed Rate Preferred Ser. 1980 $12.75 par called for redemption 00/00/1985
(Additional Information in Active)

AFLEASE GOLD & URANIUM RES LTD (SOUTH AFRICA)
Merged into sxr Uranium One Inc. 12/27/2005
Each ADR for Ordinary ZAR 0.1 par exchanged for (1.8) shares Common no par
sxr Uranium One Inc. name changed to Uranium One Inc. 06/18/2007
(See Uranium One Inc.)

AFLEASE GOLD LTD (SOUTH AFRICA)
Merged into Gold One International Ltd. 05/25/2009
Each Sponsored ADR for Ordinary exchanged for (1) ADR for Ordinary
(See Gold One International Ltd.)

AFM HOSPITALITY CORP (CANADA)
Reincorporated 09/18/2003
Place of incorporation changed from (ON) to (Canada) 09/18/2003
Discharged from receivership 05/31/2010
Stockholders' equity unlikely

AFMIN HLDGS LTD (SOUTH AFRICA)
ADR agreement terminated 00/00/1999
No ADR holders' equity

AFMN INC (DE)
Recapitalized as Motion Picture Group, Inc. 02/23/2006
Each share Common $0.0001 par exchanged for (0.05) share Common $0.0001 par

AFN INC (UT)
Each share old Common $0.001 par exchanged for (0.18181818) share new Common $0.001 par 01/04/1991
Charter expired 07/11/2001

AFO INTL INC (NV)
Name changed to Human Unitec International, Inc. 12/15/2008

AFORTRESS INCOME FD INC (DE)
Voluntarily dissolved 09/16/1974
Details not available

A4S SEC INC (CO)
Name changed to Security With Advanced Technology, Inc. 10/09/2006
Security With Advanced Technology, Inc. recapitalized as PepperBall Technologies, Inc. 09/29/2008
(See PepperBall Technologies, Inc.)

AFRAM INC (FL)
Adjudicated bankrupt 01/21/1971
Stockholders' equity unlikely

AFRASIA MINERAL FIELDS INC (BC)
Recapitalized as Westbay Ventures Inc. 01/24/2017
Each share Common no par exchanged for (0.25) share Common no par
Westbay Ventures Inc. name changed to Cryptanite Blockchain Technologies Corp. 03/12/2018

AFREN PLC (UNITED KINGDOM)
ADR agreement terminated 09/21/2015
ADR holders' equity unlikely

AFRICA DIAMOND HLDGS LTD (AB)
Reincorporated under the laws of Bermuda as Sierra Leone Diamond Co. Ltd. 01/06/2004
Sierra Leone Diamond Co. Ltd. name changed to African Minerals Ltd. 08/15/2007

AFRICA HYDROCARBONS INC (AB)
Reincorporated 04/25/2013
Place of incorporation changed from (BC) to (AB) 04/25/2013
Each share old Common no par exchanged for (0.05) share new Common no par 06/30/2017
Name changed to Blockchaink2 Corp. 05/30/2018

AFRICA ISRAEL INVTS LTD (ISRAEL)
ADR agreement terminated 06/03/2014
Each Sponsored ADR for Ordinary exchanged for $0.398101 cash

AFRICA U S A INC (DE)
Adjudicated bankrupt 12/16/1971
Stockholders' equity unlikely

AFRICA WEST MINERALS CORP (BC)
Recapitalized as Advance Gold Corp. 05/03/2010
Each share Common no par exchanged for (0.5) share Common no par

AFRICAN AMERN MED NETWORK INC (DE)
Name changed to AFMN, Inc. 01/18/2005
AFMN, Inc. recapitalized as Motion Picture Group, Inc. 02/23/2006

AFRICAN AURA MINING INC (BC)
Reorganized as Afferro Mining Inc. 04/13/2011
Each share Common no par exchanged for (1) share Common no par and (1) share Aureus Mining Inc. Common no par
(See each company's listing)
Note: Unexchanged certificates were cancelled and became without value 04/13/2017

AFRICAN AURA RESOURCES LTD (BRITISH VIRGIN ISLANDS)
Merged into African Aura Mining Inc. 10/14/2009
Each Registered Share exchanged for (0.19625) share Common no par
(See African Aura Mining Inc.)

AFRICAN BK INVTS LTD (SOUTH AFRICA)
ADR agreement terminated 04/07/2016
Each Sponsored ADR for Ordinary exchanged for $0.20864 cash

AFRICAN BARRICK GOLD PLC (UNITED KINGDOM)
Name changed to Acacia Mining PLC 12/22/2014

AFRICAN COPPER CORP (NV)
SEC revoked common stock registration 02/16/2016

AFRICAN DIAMOND CO INC (NV)
SEC revoked common stock registration 08/31/2009

AFRICAN GEM RES LTD (SOUTH AFRICA)
ADR agreement terminated 04/20/2009
No ADR's remain outstanding

AFRICAN GEMSTONES LTD (BC)
Cease trade order effective 01/07/2003

AFRICAN METALS CORP (YT)
Reincorporated under the laws of British Columbia 01/04/2005

AFRICAN QUEEN MINES LTD (BC)
Recapitalized as Desert Mountain Energy Corp. 04/10/2018
Each share Common no par exchanged for (0.25) share Common no par

AFRICAN RES INC (NV)
Name changed to Viking Exploration Inc. 04/06/1999
Viking Exploration Inc. recapitalized as Sierra Gold Corp. (New) 08/11/2006

AFRICAN SELECTION MNG CORP (YT)
Reincorporated 04/23/1998
Place of incorporation changed from (ON) to (YT) 04/23/1998
Struck off register for failure to file annual returns 09/03/2008

AFRICANA MNG LTD (QC)
Name changed to Panacan Resources Ltd. 09/10/1971
Panacan Resources Ltd. merged into Panacan Minerals & Oils Ltd.-Societe des Mineraux et des Petroles Panacan Ltee. 04/08/1974 which was acquired by Sackville Oils & Minerals Ltd. 05/05/1975 which merged into Seagull Resources Ltd. 01/03/1978
(See Seagull Resources Ltd.)

AFRICO RES LTD (CANADA)
Acquired by Camrose Resources Ltd. 07/11/2016
Each share Common no par exchanged for $1 cash
Note: Unexchanged certificates will be cancelled and become without value 07/11/2022

AFRIKANDER LEASE LTD (SOUTH AFRICA)
Recapitalized as Aflease Gold & Uranium Resources Ltd. 02/07/2005
Each Sponsored ADR for Ordinary ZAR 0.1 par exchanged for (0.1) ADR for Ordinary ZAR 0.1 par
Aflease Gold & Uranium Resources Ltd. merged into sxr Uranium One Inc. 12/27/2005 which name changed to Uranium One Inc. 06/18/2007
(See Uranium One Inc.)

AFRIORE LTD (BRITISH VIRGIN ISLANDS)
Reincorporated 07/30/1997
Reincorporated 07/31/2001
Reincorporated 05/19/2005
Place of incorporation changed from (Canada) to (NB) 07/30/1997
Place of incorporation changed from (NB) to (Barbados) 07/31/2001
Place of incorporation changed from (Barbados) to (British Virgin Islands) 05/19/2005
Acquired by Lonmin PLC 02/19/2007
Each share Common no par exchanged for CDN$8.75 cash

AFROMEDIA MARKETING INC (NY)
Name changed to Abaron Corp. 07/01/1971
(See Abaron Corp.)

AFS ENERGY INC (AB)
Recapitalized as Flagship Energy Inc. 05/24/2005
Each share Common no par exchanged for (0.06668831) share Class A no par and (0.01500487) share Class B no par
Flagship Energy Inc. recapitalized as Insignia Energy Ltd. 08/08/2008
(See Insignia Energy Ltd.)

AFS FINL CORP (MN)
Name changed to American Federal Corp. 10/01/1997
(See American Federal Corp.)

AFSA DATA CORP (CA)
Merged into First Chicago Corp. 08/01/1973
Each share Common 10¢ par exchanged for (0.069) share Common $10 par
First Chicago Corp. merged into First Chicago NBD Corp. 12/01/1995 which merged into Bank One Corp. 10/02/1998 which merged into J.P. Morgan Chase & Co. 07/01/2004 which name changed to JPMorgan Chase & Co. 07/20/2004

AFSALA BANCORP INC (DE)
Merged into Ambanc Holding Co., Inc. 11/16/1998
Each share Common 10¢ par exchanged for (1.07) shares Common 1¢ par
(See Ambanc Holding Co., Inc.)

AFTER SIX INC (PA)
Merged into After Six Holdings, Inc. 09/19/1984
Each share Common 50¢ par exchanged for $15 cash

AFTERMARKET ENTERPRISES INC (NV)
Name changed to AllDigital Holdings, Inc. 09/09/2011

AFTERMARKET TECHNOLOGY CORP (DE)
Name changed to ATC Technology Corp. 06/03/2008
(See ATC Technology Corp.)

AFTERSOFT GROUP INC (DE)
Name changed to MAM Software Group, Inc. 05/27/2010

AFTON FOOD GROUP LTD (ON)
Each share old Common no par exchanged for (0.1) share new Common no par 08/02/1999
Assets sold for the benefit of creditors 09/30/2006
No stockholders' equity

AFTON MINES LTD. (ON)
Charter cancelled for failure to pay taxes and file returns 00/00/1957

AFTON MINES LTD (CANADA)
Reincorporated 03/09/1981
Place of incorporation changed from (BC) to (Canada) 03/09/1981
Merged into Teck Corp. 08/14/1981
Each share Capital Stock no par exchanged for (1) share Conv. Preferred Ser. C no par or $55 cash
Teck Corp. name changed to Teck Cominco Ltd. 09/12/2001 which name changed to Teck Resources Ltd. 04/27/2009

AFUTURE FD INC (DE)
Name changed to Centurion Growth Fund Inc. 12/21/1992
(See Centurion Growth Fund Inc.)

AFV SOLUTIONS INC (NV)
Recapitalized as Pure Transit Technologies, Inc. 06/18/2008
Each share Common $0.001 par exchanged for (0.1) share Common $0.001 par

AG ARMENO MINES & MINERALS INC (BC)
Recapitalized as Golden Nugget Exploration, Inc. 04/27/2000
Each share Common no par exchanged for (0.06666666) share Common no par
Golden Nugget Exploration, Inc. recapitalized as Lucky 1 Enterprises Inc. 05/02/2002 which recapitalized as Bronx Ventures Inc. 01/24/2005 which reorganized as ZAB Resources Inc. 03/19/2007 which recapitalized as Kokomo Enterprises Inc. 04/15/2009 which recapitalized as High 5 Ventures Inc. 08/29/2012 which recapitalized as 37 Capital Inc. 07/07/2014

AG ASSOCS INC (CA)
Merged into Steag Electronic Systems GmbH 03/02/1999
Each share Common no par exchanged for $5.50 cash

AG-BAG INTL LTD (DE)
Reincorporated 01/00/1995
State of incorporation changed from (NY) to (DE) 01/00/1995
Name changed to AB Holding Group, Inc. 01/24/2005

AG-CHEM EQUIP INC (MN)
Common 10¢ par changed to 1¢ par and (9) additional shares issued 03/08/1995
Common 1¢ par split (4) for (1) by issuance of (3) additional shares 06/30/1995
Merged into AGCO Corp. 04/17/2001
Each share Common 1¢ par exchanged for (1.2317) shares Common 1¢ par and $15.398 cash

AG GROWTH INCOME FD (ON)
Reincorporated under the laws of Canada as Ag Growth International Inc. and Trust Units no par reclassified as Common no par 06/08/2009

AG GROWTH INDS INC (AB)
Acquired by 628554 Saskatchewan Ltd. 05/23/2000
Each share Common no par exchanged for $1.25 cash

AG HLDGS INC (WA)
Recapitalized as Bahui USA, Inc. 12/03/1997
Each share Common $0.0001 par exchanged for (0.002) share Common $0.0001 par
Bahui USA, Inc. name changed back to A G Holdings, Inc. 04/06/1998
Name changed to Wasatch Interactive Learning Corp. 01/20/2000
Wasatch Interactive Learning Corp. merged into Plato Learning, Inc. 04/05/2001
(See Plato Learning, Inc.)

AG MET INC (DE)
Name changed to Refinemet International Co. 09/18/1980
(See Refinemet International Co.)

AG SVCS AMER INC (IA)
Common no par split (2) for (1) by issuance of (1) additional share 07/29/1994
Acquired by Rabobank Nederland 12/31/2003
Each share Common no par exchanged for $8.50 cash

AGA AB (SWEDEN)
Acquired by Linde Gas AG 02/01/2001
Each Sponsored ADR for Ordinary SEK 5 par exchanged for approximately $15 cash

AGA MED HLDGS INC (DE)
Merged into St. Jude Medical, Inc. 11/18/2010
Each share Common 1¢ par exchanged for (0.27) share Common 10¢ par and $10.40 cash
St. Jude Medical, Inc. merged into Abbott Laboratories 01/04/2017

AGA RES INC (NV)
Each share old Common $0.00001 par exchanged for (10) shares new Common $0.00001 par 06/08/2006
Name changed to Greater China Media & Entertainment Corp. 08/21/2006

AGAMENTICUS MOUNTAIN INC (ME)
Charter suspended for non-payment of taxes 01/01/1975

AGAMI GOLD MINES LTD. (ON)
Charter cancelled for failure to pay taxes and file returns 08/06/1957

AGAPE FILMS, INC. (CA)
Charter suspended for failure to file reports and pay taxes 08/01/1974

AGARD ELECTRS CORP (NY)
Merged into La Pointe Industries, Inc. 04/14/1977
Each share Common 10¢ par exchanged for (0.1247396) share Common $1 par
La Pointe Industries, Inc. name changed to Titan International Inc. (CT) 03/29/1996 which reorganized in Utah as Enrol Corp. 07/18/1997 which name changed to E-Power International Inc. 01/22/2001 which recapitalized as Integrated Services Group Inc. 01/29/2003
(See Integrated Services Group Inc.)

AGARWAL RES LTD (BC)
Recapitalized as Consolidated Agarwal Resources Ltd. 10/01/1997
Each share Common no par exchanged for (0.33333333) share Common no par
(See Consolidated Agarwal Resources Ltd.)

AGASSIZ MINES LTD (MB)
Recapitalized as Royal Agassiz Mines Ltd. 10/29/1969
Each share Capital Stock no par exchanged for (0.33333333) share Capital Stock no par
Royal Agassiz Mines Ltd. recapitalized as Agassiz Resources Ltd. 12/14/1977
(See Agassiz Resources Ltd.)

AGASSIZ RES LTD (MB)
Assets sold for the benefit of creditors 05/17/1993
No stockholders' equity

AGATE BAY RES LTD (BC)
Recapitalized as Geodex Minerals Ltd. (BC) 04/14/1998
Each share Common no par exchanged for (0.25) share Common no par
Geodex Minerals Ltd. (BC) reincorporated in Ontario as Intercontinental Gold & Metals Ltd. 11/06/2017

AGATE TECHNOLOGIES INC (DE)
Recapitalized as PowerHouse

Technologies Group, Inc. 04/30/2003
Each share Common $0.0001 par exchanged for (0.00819672) share Common $0.0001 par PowerHouse Technologies Group, Inc. name changed to Migo Software, Inc. 08/14/2006
(See Migo Software, Inc.)

AGAU MINES INC (DE)
Reorganized under the laws of Montana as United States Antimony Corp. 09/05/1973
Each share Common 1¢ par exchanged for (1) share Common 1¢ par

AGAVE SILVER CORP (BC)
Name changed to First Energy Metals Ltd. 12/20/2016

AGC AMERS GOLD CORP (BC)
Reincorporated under the laws of Yukon as Timebeat.com Enterprises Inc. 10/04/1999
Timebeat.com Enterprises Inc. (YT) reincorporated in Nevada 10/16/2001 which name changed to New Morning Corp. 09/30/2004 which name changed to Window Rock Capital Holdings, Inc. 10/28/2005
(See Window Rock Capital Holdings, Inc.)

AGC INDS INC (DE)
Each share Common $1 par exchanged for (0.2) share Common 25¢ par 12/17/1975
Under plan of merger each share Common 25¢ par exchanged for $1.25 cash 09/30/1976

AGCO CORP (DE)
Each share $16.25 Conv. Depositary Exchangeable Preferred exchanged for $25 principal amount of 6.5% Conv. Subordinated Debentures due 06/01/2008 on 06/01/1995
(Additional Information in Active)

AGCO INDUSTRIES, INC. (CO)
Declared defunct and inoperative for failure to pay taxes and file annual reports 09/30/1983

AGE HIGH INCOME FD INC (DE)
Name changed 12/01/1980
Reincorporated 10/01/1996
Name changed from Age Fund Inc. to Age High Income Fund, Inc. 12/01/1980
Common 1¢ par reclassified as Class I no par 05/15/1995
State of incorporation changed from (CO) to (DE) 10/01/1996
Class I no par reclassified as Age Fund Class I no par 01/01/1999
Name changed to Franklin High Income Trust, Class I no par and Class II no par reclassified as Class A no par or Class C no par respectively 10/01/2006

AGE RESH INC (DE)
Each share old Common $0.001 par exchanged for (0.02857142) share new Common $0.001 par 06/15/2004
Name changed to SalesTactix, Inc. 08/02/2004
SalesTactix, Inc. name changed to Strativation, Inc. 10/14/2005 which name changed to CNS Response, Inc. 03/09/2007 which name changed to MYnd Analytics, Inc. 01/12/2016

AGEMARK CORP (NV)
In process of liquidation
Each share Common $0.001 par received initial distribution of $2 cash 05/31/2004
Note: Details on subsequent distributions, if any, are not available

AGEN LTD (AUSTRALIA)
Acquired by Biotech Capital Ltd. 06/24/1998
Each Sponsored ADR for Ordinary exchanged for approximately $0.73 cash

AGENA MNG LTD (ON)
Charter cancelled for failure to pay taxes and file returns 09/20/1972

AGENCY COM LTD (DE)
Merged into Seneca Investments LLC 11/01/2001
Each share Common $0.001 par exchanged for $3.35 cash

AGENCY LITHOGRAPH CO. (OR)
Name changed to Graphic Arts Center, Inc. 08/11/1972
(See Graphic Arts Center, Inc.)

AGENCY RENT A CAR INC (DE)
Common 5¢ par split (3) for (2) by issuance of (0.5) additional share 08/14/1985
Common 5¢ par split (2) for (1) by issuance of (1) additional share 07/07/1986
Name changed to National Auto Credit Inc. (Old) 08/15/1994
National Auto Credit Inc. (Old) reorganized as National Auto Credit Inc. (New) 12/28/1995 which name changed to iDNA, Inc. 03/08/2006
(See iDNA, Inc.)

AGENIX LTD (AUSTRALIA)
Each old Sponsored ADR for Ordinary exchanged for (0.04) new Sponsored ADR for Ordinary 11/26/2012
Basis changed from (1:50) to (1:10) 01/04/2017
ADR agreement terminated 04/04/2017
Each new Sponsored ADR for Ordinary exchanged for $0.155 cash

AGENT 155 MEDIA GROUP INC (DE)
Recapitalized as Cavico Corp. 05/12/2006
Each share Common $0.001 par exchanged for (0.00333333) share Common $0.001 par
(See Cavico Corp.)

AGENTS EQUITY CORP (WA)
Recapitalized as United Securities Financial Corp. 05/15/1971
Each share Common 10¢ par exchanged for (2) shares Common 10¢ par
(See United Securities Financial Corp.)

AGENTS FINL GROUP INC (OH)
Charter declared void for non-payment of taxes 12/22/1998

AGERE SYS INC (DE)
Each share Class A Common 1¢ par exchanged for (0.1) share Common 1¢ par 05/27/2005
Each share Class B Common 1¢ par exchanged for (0.1) share Common 1¢ par 05/27/2005
Merged into LSI Logic Corp. 04/02/2007
Each share Common 1¢ par exchanged for (2.16) shares Common 1¢ par
LSI Logic Corp. name changed to LSI Corp. 04/06/2007
(See LSI Corp.)

AGES HEALTH SVCS INC (MA)
Name changed to AHSI Inc. 04/15/1997
(See AHSI Inc.)

AGF AMERN GROWTH FD LTD (CANADA)
Under plan of reorganization each Mutual Fund Share no par automatically became (1) share AGF International Group Ltd. American Growth Class Ser. A no par 10/01/1994

AGF CDN BD FD (ON)
Under plan of merger each Mutual Fund Ser. automatically became (0.4598842) AGF Group of Funds Fixed Income Plus Fund Mutual Fund Ser. 05/20/2016

AGF LTD PARTNERSHIP (ON)
Merged into AGF Master Ltd. Partnership 01/23/1998
Each Unit of Ltd. Partnership Int.-1991 exchanged for (3.27) Units of Ltd. Partnership
Each Unit of Ltd. Partnership Int.-1992 exchanged for (2.49) Units of Ltd. Partnership
(See AGF Master Ltd. Partnership)

AGF LTD PARTNERSHIP 1994 (ON)
Merged into AGF Master Ltd. Partnership 01/23/1998
Each Unit of Ltd. Partnership Int. exchanged for (0.71) Unit of Ltd. Partnership
(See AGF Master Ltd. Partnership)

AGF LTD PARTNERSHIP 1995 (ON)
Merged into AGF Master Ltd. Partnership 01/23/1998
Each Unit of Ltd. Partnership exchanged for (1.04) Units of Ltd. Partnership
(See AGF Master Ltd. Partnership)

AGF MASTER LTD PARTNERSHIP (ON)
Merged 01/23/1998
Merged from AGF Ltd. Partnership 1993 to AGF Master Ltd. Partnership 01/23/1998
Each Unit of Ltd. Partnership exchanged for (3.12) Units of Ltd. Partnership
Completely liquidated 11/05/2012
Each Unit of Ltd. Partnership received first and final distribution of $0.02 cash

AGFA-ANSCO CORP. (DE)
Reincorporated 04/15/1939
State of incorporation changed from (NY) to (DE) 04/15/1939
Merged into General Aniline & Film Corp. 12/29/1939
Each share Common $1 par exchanged for (0.33333333) share Class A Common no par
General Aniline & Film Corp. name changed to GAF Corp. 04/24/1968
(See GAF Corp.)

AGFEED INDS INC (NV)
Plan of reorganization under Chapter 11 Federal Bankruptcy proceedings effective 11/10/2014
Holders will receive an undetermined amount of cash

AGGERS PRODUCTION CO. (DE)
Charter cancelled for non-payment of taxes 01/23/1924

AGGIE OIL CO (OK)
Charter suspended for failure to pay taxes 02/13/1984

AGGREGATE INC (NV)
Recapitalized as Gold Coast Resources, Inc. 12/22/2003
Each share Common $0.001 par exchanged for (0.33333333) share Common $0.001 par

AGGREGATES, INC. (OH)
Liquidation completed
Each share Common no par exchanged for initial distribution of $1 cash 10/21/1963
Each share Common no par received second distribution of $24 cash 01/20/1964
Each share Common no par received third distribution of $1.40 cash 08/29/1966
Each share Common no par received fourth and final distribution of $0.12132 cash 12/16/1966

AGGRESSIVE GROWTH SHS INC (MD)
Name changed to Bullock Aggressive Growth Shares, Inc. 01/00/1985
Bullock Aggressive Growth Shares, Inc. reorganized as Surveyor Fund, Inc. 03/13/1987 which name changed to Alliance Global Capital Fund, Inc. 09/17/1990 which name changed to AllianceBernstein Global Small Capital Fund, Inc. 03/31/2003
(See AllianceBernstein Global Small Capital Fund, Inc.)

AGGRESSIVE MNG LTD (ON)
Recapitalized as Sound Capital Inc. 08/15/1988
Each share Common $1 par exchanged for (0.1) share Common no par
Sound Capital Inc. merged into Luminart Inc. 04/30/1994
(See Luminart Inc.)

AGGRITE (1962) INC. (QC)
Adjudicated bankrupt 04/01/1968
No stockholders' equity

AGIC CONV & INCOME FD (MA)
Name changed to AllianzGI Convertible & Income Fund 01/28/2013

AGIC CONV & INCOME FD II (MA)
Name changed to AllianzGI Convertible & Income Fund II 01/28/2013

AGIC EQUITY & CONV INCOME FD (MA)
Name changed to AllianzGI Equity & Convertible Income Fund 01/28/2013

AGIC GLOBAL EQUITY & CONV INCOME FD (MA)
Name changed to AllianzGI Global Equity & Convertible Income Fund 01/28/2013
AllianzGI Global Equity & Convertible Income Fund merged into AllianzGI Equity & Convertible Income Fund 01/24/2014

AGIC INTL & PREM STRATEGY FD (MA)
Name changed to AllianzGI International & Premium Strategy Fund 01/28/2013
(See AllianzGI International & Premium Strategy Fund)

AGILE PPTY HLDGS LTD (CAYMAN ISLANDS)
Name changed to Agile Group Holdings Ltd. 08/02/2016

AGILE SOFTWARE CORP (DE)
Common $0.001 par split (2) for (1) by issuance of (1) additional share payable 03/16/2000 to holders of record 03/03/2000
Merged into Oracle Corp. 07/16/2007
Each share Common $0.001 par exchanged for $8.10 cash

AGILITY CAP INC (TX)
SEC revoked preferred and common stock registration 05/22/2009

AGINCOURT EXPLS INC (BC)
Name changed to AGX Resources Corp. (BC) 11/29/1995
AGX Resources Corp. (BC) reincorporated in Yukon 05/22/1996 which recapitalized as Consolidated AGX Resources Corp. (YT) 11/26/1999 which reincorporated in British Columbia 07/09/2007 which name changed to Petro Rubiales Energy Corp. 07/17/2007 which name changed to Pacific Rubiales Energy Corp. 01/23/2008 which name changed to Pacific Exploration & Production Corp. 08/18/2015

AGINCOURT VENTURES LTD (NV)
Recapitalized as Grand Resort International Ltd. 12/27/1991
Each share Common $0.001 par exchanged for (0.002) share Common $0.001 par
(See Grand Resort International Ltd.)

AGIO RES CORP (BC)
Struck off register and declared

dissolved for failure to file returns 12/18/1992

AGISS CORP (DE)
Charter cancelled and declared inoperative and void for non-payment of franchise taxes 03/01/2001

AGL CAP TR II (DE)
8% Trust Preferred Securities called for redemption at $25 on 05/21/2006

AGL RES INC (GA)
Acquired by Southern Co. 07/01/2016
Each share Common $5 par exchanged for $66 cash

AGM CAP CORP (BC)
Reincorporated under the laws of Yukon as Dueling Grounds Thoroughbred Racing Corp. 09/22/1993
Dueling Grounds Thoroughbred Racing Corp. reincorporated in Delaware as Dueling Grounds Entertainment Corp. 12/20/1995
(See Dueling Grounds Entertainment Corp.)

AGM INDS INC (DE)
Common $1 par split (4) for (3) by issuance of (0.33333333) additional share 09/15/1965
Common $1 par split (4) for (3) by issuance of (0.33333333) additional share 12/20/1968
Acquired by 3900 Corp. 04/01/1985
Each share Common $1 par exchanged for $30 cash

AGNC INVT CORP (DE)
8% Preferred Ser. A 1¢ par called for redemption at $25 plus $0.333 accrued dividends on 09/15/2017
(Additional Information in Active)

AGNEW SURPASS SHOE STORES LTD (CANADA)
Common no par exchanged (4) for (1) 00/00/1947
5.5% Preferred $10 par called for redemption 02/27/1959
Through purchase offer 100% acquired by Genesco Inc. as of 10/00/1974
Public interest eliminated

AGNICO EAGLE MINES LTD (ON)
Name changed to Agnico Eagle Mines Ltd. 04/30/2013

AGNICO MINES LTD (ON)
Merged into Agnico-Eagle Mines Ltd. 06/01/1972
Each share Capital Stock $1 par exchanged for (1) share Common no par
Agnico-Eagle Mines Ltd. name changed to Agnico Eagle Mines Ltd. 04/30/2013

AGOIL INC (TX)
Recapitalized as Aegis Industries Inc. (TX) 07/20/1989
Each share Common 1¢ par exchanged for (0.2) share Common 1¢ par
Aegis Industries Inc. (TX) reincorporated in Delaware 07/00/1990
(See Aegis Industries Inc.)

AGORA INDS INC (DE)
Liquidation completed
Each share Common 20¢ par exchanged for initial distribution of (0.25) share Cramer Electronics, Inc. Common $1 par and (0.5) share 21st Century Electronics, Inc. Common 10¢ par 07/26/1971
Each share Common 20¢ par received second distribution of $0.06 cash 12/23/1971
Each share Common 20¢ par received third and final distribution of $0.05 cash 07/13/1973
(See each company's listing)

AGORA SA (POLAND)
GDR agreement terminated 01/19/2010
GDR holders may receive cash proceeds from the sale of underlying shares

AGOURON PHARMACEUTICALS INC (CA)
Common no par split (2) for (1) by issuance of (1) additional share payable 08/26/1997 to holders of record 08/15/1997
Merged into Warner-Lambert Co. 05/17/1999
Each share Common no par exchanged for (0.8934) share Common $1 par
Warner-Lambert Co. merged into Pfizer Inc. 06/19/2000

AGP & CO INC (NJ)
Each share old Common no par exchanged for (0.33333333) share new Common no par 10/09/1992
Completely liquidated
Each share new Common no par received first and final distribution of $0.045 cash payable 05/09/2003 to holders of record 04/18/2003
Ex date - 05/14/2003
Note: Certificates were not required to be surrendered and are without value

AGRA EMPREENDIMENTOS IMOBILIARIOS SA (BRAZIL)
Merged into Agre Empreendimentos Imobiliarios S.A. 02/11/2010
Each Sponsored 144A ADR for Ordinary exchanged for $5.463958 cash
Each Sponsored Reg. S ADR for Ordinary exchanged for $5.463958 cash

AGRA INC (CANADA)
Reincorporated 01/05/1977
Name changed 01/09/1997
Common no par reclassified as Conv. Class A Common no par 04/08/1976
Place of incorporation changed from (SK) to (Canada) 01/05/1977
Each share Conv. Class A Common no par exchanged for (1) share new Class A Common no par 06/27/1983
Each share Conv. Class B Common no par exchanged for (1) share Conv. Class B Non-Vtg. no par 06/27/1983
New Class A Common no par split (2) for (1) by issuance of (1) additional share 03/14/1988
Conv. Class B Non-Vtg. no par split (2) for (1) by issuance of (1) additional share 03/14/1988
Each share new Class A Common no par exchanged for (1.05) shares Common no par 10/23/1996
Each share Conv. Class B Non-Vtg. no par exchanged for (1) share Common no par 10/23/1996
Name changed from AGRA Industries Ltd. to AGRA Inc. 01/09/1997
Merged into AMEC PLC 04/20/2000
Each share Common no par exchanged for $16 cash

AGRA TECH INC (NV)
SEC revoked common stock registration 12/07/2004

AGRA VEGETABLE OIL PRODS LTD (SK)
Name changed to AGRA Industries Ltd. (SK) 08/10/1970
Agra Industries Ltd. (SK) reincorporated in Canada 01/05/1977 which name changed to AGRA Inc. 01/09/1997
(See AGRA Inc.)

AGRATEC INDUSTRIES LTD. (AB)
Name changed to Foremost International Industries Ltd. 09/20/1971
Foremost International Industries Ltd. recapitalized as Canadian Foremost Ltd. 05/06/1976 which name changed to Foremost Industries Inc. 06/01/1994
(See Foremost Industries Inc.)

AGRESOURCE GROUP INC (MN)
Name changed to Electronic Industries Holding, Inc. 09/01/1987
(See Electronic Industries Holding, Inc.)

AGRI BIO-SCIENCES INC (DE)
SEC revoked common stock registration 04/17/2008

AGRI ENERGY INC (MN)
Statutorily dissolved 12/31/1992

AGRI ENERGY LTD (AUSTRALIA)
ADR agreement terminated 09/17/2008
No ADR's remain outstanding

AGRI-FOODS INTL INC (NV)
Recapitalized as ATWEC Technologies, Inc. 10/10/2003
Each share Common $0.001 par exchanged for (0.00125) share Common $0.001 par

AGRI-NUTRITION GROUP LTD (DE)
Name changed to Virbac Corp. 03/05/1999
(See Virbac Corp.)

AGRI-QUEST MNG INC (DE)
Each share Class B Common 1¢ par exchanged for (1) share Class A Common 1¢ par 12/31/1992
Reorganized under the laws of Nevada as New Century Media, Ltd. 09/01/1994
Each share Class A Common 1¢ par exchanged for (0.01) share Class A Common $0.001 par
New Century Media, Ltd. name changed to LBU, Inc. 03/24/1995
(See LBU, Inc.)

AGRI QUIP MFG INC (MN)
Adjudicated bankrupt 06/09/1976
Stockholders' equity unlikely

AGRI SEAL INC (OR)
Name changed to Mega Gold, Inc. 11/06/1986
Mega Gold, Inc. recapitalized as Gold Dome Mining Co. 07/11/1988 which name changed to American Development Corp. 04/17/1991
(See American Development Corp.)

AGRI SUL INC (TX)
Name changed to Texas American Resources Inc. 01/24/1980
Texas American Resources Inc. name changed to Tari Co. 12/20/1994
(See Tari Co.)

AGRI-TEK CORP. (MN)
Charter cancelled for failure to file reports and pay fees 06/09/1970

AGRI WORLD TRADE DEV CORP (UT)
Common $0.001 par split (4) for (1) by issuance of (3) additional shares 05/22/1987
Recapitalized as Industrial Ecosystems, Inc. 03/07/1994
Each share Common $0.001 par exchanged for (0.0005) share Common $0.001 par
(See Industrial Ecosystems, Inc.)

AGRIA CORP (CAYMAN ISLANDS)
ADR agreement terminated 01/02/2018
Each Sponsored ADR for Ordinary exchanged for (2) shares Ordinary
Note: Unexchanged ADR's will be sold and the proceeds, if any, held for claim after 05/07/2018

AGRIBIOTECH INC (CO)
Merged into FiberChem, Inc. (DE) 11/21/1979
Each (6) shares Common no par exchanged for (1) Unit consisting of (5) shares new Common $0.0001 par, (1) Class A Common Stock Purchase Warrant expiring 09/15/1991, (1) Class B Common Stock Purchase Warrant expiring 09/15/1992 and (1) Class C Common Stock Purchase Warrant expiring 09/15/1993
FiberChem, Inc. (DE) name changed to DecisionLink, Inc. 12/05/2000
(See DecisionLink, Inc.)

AGRIBIOTECH INC (NV)
Plan of reorganization under Chapter 11 Federal Bankruptcy Code effective 04/23/2001
No stockholders' equity

AGRIBRANDS INTL INC (MO)
Merged into Cargill Inc. 04/30/2001
Each share Common 1¢ par exchanged for $54.50 cash

AGRIC DEV CORP (DE)
Name changed to Wil Wright's Ice Cream, Inc. 04/15/1983
(See Wil Wright's Ice Cream, Inc.)

AGRICEUTICALS TECHNOLOGIES INC (NV)
Name changed to PlayandWin, Inc. 07/13/1999
PlayandWin, Inc. name changed to D'Angelo Brands Inc. 11/19/2001

AGRICHEM CORP. (FL)
Merged into Agrichem Corp. (MA) 11/01/1966
Each share Common $10 par exchanged for (1) share Common $1 par
(See Agrichem Corp. (MA))

AGRICHEM CORP. (MA)
Proclaimed dissolved for failure to file reports and pay taxes 12/29/1982

AGRICOLA MINES LTD. (BC)
Struck off register and declared dissolved for failure to file returns 12/09/1974

AGRICO GLOBAL CORP (DE)
Recapitalized as StrategaBiz, Inc. 12/16/2014
Each share Common $0.0001 par exchanged for (0.03333333) share Common $0.0001 par
Note: Holders of (29) or fewer shares received $0.10 cash per share
StrategaBiz, Inc. name changed to CryptoSign, Inc. 07/06/2015 which name changed to NABUfit Global, Inc. 12/10/2015 which name changed to NewBridge Global Ventures, Inc. 12/12/2017

AGRICULTURAL & INDL DEV INC (KS)
Liquidation completed
Each share Common 10¢ par exchanged for initial distribution of $1.625 cash 10/01/1980
Each share Common 10¢ par received second distribution of $0.25 cash 03/02/1981
Each share Common 10¢ par received third distribution of $0.15 cash 03/12/1984
Each share Common 10¢ par received fourth and final distribution of $0.085 cash 12/27/1991

AGRICULTURAL BK OF GREECE S A (GREECE)
ADR agreement terminated 07/11/2011
No ADR's remain outstanding

AGRICULTURAL EQUIPMENT CORP. (CO)
Each share Preferred $1 par or Common no par exchanged for (2) shares Common 10¢ par 01/31/1957
Recapitalized as Thermodynamics, Inc. 10/10/1960
Each share Common 10¢ par exchanged for (0.33333333) share Common 30¢ par
(See Thermodynamics, Inc.)

AGRICULTURAL INVESTMENT CO.
Liquidated 00/00/1942
Details not available

AGRICULTURAL LIFE INSURANCE CO.
Taken over by Michigan Insurance Dept. 00/00/1938
Stockholders' equity unlikely

AGRICULTURAL MFG CORP (MN)
Name changed to Dahlman, Inc. 01/15/1974
Dahlman, Inc. merged into NFD Inc. 10/31/1978
(See NFD Inc.)

AGRICULTURAL MARKETING ASSOCIATION (NM)
Charter revoked for failure to pay franchise tax 10/03/1960

AGRICULTURAL MINERALS CO L P (DE)
Name changed to Terra Nitrogen Co., L.P. 10/20/1994
(See Terra Nitrogen Co., L.P.)

AGRICULTURAL NATIONAL BANK (PITTSFIELD, MA)
Each share Capital Stock $100 par exchanged for (4) shares Capital Stock $25 par 01/23/1956
Under plan of merger name changed to First Agricultural National Bank of Berkshire County (Pittsfield, MA) 04/04/1962
First Agricultural National Bank of Berkshire County (Pittsfield, MA) name changed to First Agricultural Bank (Pittsfield, MA) 01/24/1977 which name changed to Multibank West (Pittsfield, MA) 07/01/1991
(See Multibank West (Pittsfield, MA))

AGRICULTURAL RESEARCH (CO)
Recapitalized as Agricultural Research Development, Inc. 05/11/1960
Each share Common 10¢ par exchanged for (2) shares Common 5¢ par
Agricultural Research Development, Inc. name changed to American Hog Co. 05/01/1962
(See American Hog Co.)

AGRICULTURAL RESEARCH DEVELOPMENT, INC. (CO)
Name changed to American Hog Co. 05/01/1962
(See American Hog Co.)

AGRIDYNE TECHNOLOGIES INC (DE)
Merged into Biosys Inc. 03/15/1996
Each share Common 6¢ par exchanged for (0.28664) share new Common $0.001 par
(See Biosys Inc.)

AGRIFUTURE INC (DE)
Proclaimed dissolved 12/29/1995

AGRIMARINE HOLDINGS INC (BC)
Each share old Common no par exchanged for (0.06666666) share new Common no par 05/27/2013
Acquired by Dundee Agricultural Corp. 05/22/2015
Each share Common no par exchanged for $0.03 cash
Note: Unexchanged certificates will be cancelled and become without value 05/22/2021

AGRIPOST INC (FL)
Out of business 06/00/1992
Stockholders' equity unlikely

AGRITECH & ENERGY CORP (NJ)
Merged into Grayhound Electronics, Inc. 08/03/1987
Each share Common no par exchanged for (0.1) share Common $0.001 par
(See Grayhound Electronics, Inc.)

AGRITEK BIO INGREDIENTS CORP (BC)
Name changed to Innovium Capital Corp. 12/15/1999
Innovium Capital Corp. name changed to Innovium Media Properties Corp. 09/24/2007

AGRITHERM CORP (NV)
Each share old Common 1¢ par exchanged for (0.1) share new Common 1¢ par 09/15/1995
Recapitalized as Infotex Holdings Ltd. 12/30/1997
Each share new Common 1¢ par exchanged for (0.0005) share Common 1¢ par
(See Infortex Holdings Ltd.)

AGRITOPE INC (DE)
Merged into Exelixis, Inc. 12/08/2000
Each share Preferred Ser. A exchanged for (0.35) share Common $0.001 par
Each share Common 1¢ par exchanged for (0.35) share Common $0.001 par

AGRIUM INC (CANADA)
Common no par split (3) for (1) by issuance of (2) additional shares payable 01/05/1996 to holders of record 12/29/1995 Ex date - 12/27/1995
8% Canadian Originated Preferred Securities called for redemption at USD$25 on 02/14/2005
Merged into Nutrien Ltd. 01/02/2018
Each share Common no par exchanged for (2.23) shares Common no par
Note: Unexchanged certificates will be cancelled and become without value 01/01/2021

AGRIVEST AMERS INC (DE)
Recapitalized as NXChain Inc. 01/06/2016
Each share Common $0.001 par exchanged for (0.02963243) share Common $0.001 par

AGRO INTL HLDGS INC (BC)
Name changed to HOST International Holdings Inc. 06/01/2004
(See HOST International Holdings Inc.)

AGRO PAC INDS LTD (CANADA)
Reincorporated 05/21/2002
Place of incorporation changed from (BC) to (Canada) 05/21/2002
Recapitalized as Adriana Ventures Inc. 07/16/2004
Each share Common no par exchanged for (0.1) share Common no par
Adriana Ventures Inc. name changed to Adriana Resources Inc. 08/08/2005 which name changed to Sprott Resource Holdings Inc. 02/13/2017

AGROCAN CORP (DE)
Name changed to Greensmart Corp. 06/03/2003

AGROLIFE CORP (DE)
Charter cancelled and declared inoperative and void for non-payment of taxes 03/01/1991

AGRONIX INC (FL)
Common $0.001 par split (2) for (1) by issuance of (1) additional share payable 01/09/2002 to holders of record 01/09/2002
Recapitalized as China Yingxia International, Inc. 07/21/2006
Each share Common $0.001 par exchanged for (0.04016064) share Common $0.001 par
(See China Yingxia International, Inc.)

AGROTECH GREENHOUSES INC (BC)
Recapitalized as Archer Petroleum Corp. 04/30/2010
Each share Common no par exchanged for (0.33333333) share Common no par
Archer Petroleum Corp. name changed to Atlas Engineered Products Ltd. 11/09/2017

AGROW INDS INC (DE)
Chapter 7 bankruptcy proceedings confirmed 12/01/1988

Stockholders' equity unlikely

AGS COMPUTERS INC (NY)
Common 10¢ par split (3) for (1) by issuance of (2) additional shares 10/01/1981
Common 10¢ par split (2) for (1) by issuance of (1) additional share 05/29/1987
Stock Dividend - 100% 01/15/1980
Acquired by NYNEX Corp. 10/06/1988
Each share Common 10¢ par exchanged for $21 cash

AGS ENERGY 2005-1 LTD PARTNERSHIP (ON)
Under plan of merger each Unit of Ltd. Partnership automatically became (0.7535) share AGS Lawrence Resource Fund Ltd. Class A Ser. 1 no par 05/14/2007
AGS Lawrence Resource Fund Ltd. name changed to CGS Resource Fund Ltd. 02/10/2010

AGS LAWRENCE RESOURCE FUND LTD. (ON)
Name changed to CGS Resource Fund Ltd. and Class A Ser. 1 no par reclassified as Class A no par 02/10/2010

AGT BIOSCIENCES LTD (AUSTRALIA)
Name changed to ChemGenex Pharmaceuticals Ltd. 07/07/2004
(See ChemGenex Pharmaceuticals Ltd.)

AGT DATA SYS LTD (CANADA)
Acquired by Multiple Access Ltd. 00/00/1979
Each share Common no par exchanged for (0.2857142) share Common no par
(See Multiple Access Ltd.)

AGTECH INCOME FD (ON)
Name changed to Alliance Grain Traders Income Fund 12/07/2007
Alliance Grain Traders Income Fund reorganized as Alliance Grain Traders Inc. 09/15/2009 which name changed to AGT Food & Ingredients Inc. 10/03/2014

AGTSPORTS INC (CO)
Reorganized under the laws of Nevada as HealthRenu Medical, Inc. 09/19/2003
Each share Common $0.001 par exchanged for (0.00117647) share Common $0.001 par
(See HealthRenu Medical, Inc.)

AGU ENTMT CORP (DE)
Reincorporated 10/21/2004
State of incorporation changed from (CO) to (DE) and Common no par changed to $0.0001 par 10/21/2004
Name changed to Tube Media Corp. 03/07/2006
(See Tube Media Corp.)

AGUA PURA WATER CO.
Dissolved 00/00/1930
Details not available

AGUILA AMERICAN RESOURCES LTD (BAHAMAS)
Reincorporated 01/14/2008
Place of incorporation changed from Bahamas to British Columbia 01/14/2008
Name changed to Aguila American Gold Ltd. 05/26/2011

AGUIRRE CO (MA)
Common $5 par changed to $2 par and (1) additional share issued 12/09/1968
In process of liquidation
Each share Common $2 par exchanged for initial distribution of $1.016 cash 01/22/1979
Each share Common $2 par received second distribution of (1) share Aguirre Corp. of Puerto Rico

Common $2 par and $8.024 cash 01/29/1979
Each share Common $2 par received third distribution of $1.40 cash 08/01/1979
Each share Common $2 par received fourth distribution of $1 cash 02/01/1980
Each share Common $2 par received fifth distribution of $1 cash 11/01/1980
Each share Common $2 par received sixth distribution of $2 cash 12/01/1981
Note: Details on subsequent distributions, if any, are not available

AGUIRRE CORP P R (PR)
Ceased operations 00/00/1980
Details not available

AGX RES CORP (YT)
Reincorporated 05/22/1996
Place of incorporation changed from (BC) to (YT) 05/22/1996
Recapitalized as Consolidated AGX Resources Corp. (YT) 11/26/1999
Each share Common no par exchanged for (0.25) share Common no par
Consolidated AGX Resources Corp. (YT) reincorporated in British Columbia 07/09/2007 which name changed to Petro Rubiales Energy Corp. 07/17/2007 which name changed to Pacific Rubiales Energy Corp. 01/23/2008 which name changed to Pacific Exploration & Production Corp. 08/18/2015

AHA AUTOMOTIVE TECHNOLOGIES CORP (ON)
Retractable Class A Special Shares no par called for redemption 11/00/1984
Placed in receivership and assets liquidated 03/00/1990
No stockholders' equity

AHCHUK FURNISHINGS INC (NV)
Name changed to China Datacom Corp. 05/05/2005
China Datacom Corp. name changed to Digital Paint International Holding Co. Ltd. 02/15/2008 which recapitalized as Direct Coating, Inc. 07/06/2009
(See Direct Coating, Inc.)

AHED CORP (ON)
Name changed 08/30/1978
Name changed from Ahed Music Corp. Ltd. to Ahed Corp. 08/30/1978
Name changed to ECO Corp. 07/30/1987
ECO Corp. recapitalized as American Eco Corp. 11/15/1993
(See American Eco Corp.)

AHI HEALTHCARE SYS INC (DE)
Merged into FPA Medical Management, Inc. 03/17/1997
Each share Common 1¢ par exchanged for (0.391) share Common no par
(See FPA Medical Management, Inc.)

AHL FING
Trust Originated Preferred Securities called for redemption at $50 on 08/16/2002

AHL GROUP LTD (ON)
Acquired by Ivaco Inc. 08/27/1985
Each share Class X no par exchanged for (0.24) share $2.40 Preferred Ser. E no par and (0.3024) share Class A Subordinate no par
Each share Conv. Class Y no par exchanged for (0.24) share $2.40 Preferred Ser. E no par and (0.3024) share Class A Subordinate no par
(See Ivaco Inc.)

AHL SVCS INC (GA)
Merged into CGW Southeast Partners IV, L.P. 08/21/2003
Each share Common 1¢ par exchanged for $1.50 cash

AHLSTROM MANUFACTURING CORP. (NY)
Name changed 03/08/1991
Name changed from Ahlstrom Kamyr Corp. to Ahlstrom Manufacturing Corp. 03/08/1991
Voluntarily dissolved 04/01/1994
Details not available

AHM VENTURES INC (UT)
Proclaimed dissolved for failure to pay taxes 06/01/1990

AHMANSON H F & CO (DE)
Reincorporated 05/22/1985
State of incorporation changed from (CA) to (DE) and Common no par changed to 1¢ par 05/22/1985
Common 1¢ par split (3) for (1) by issuance of (2) additional shares 06/10/1986
9.6% Depositary Preferred Ser. B called for redemption 09/03/1996
8.4% Depositary Preferred Ser. C called for redemption at $25 on 03/02/1998
6% Depositary Preferred Ser. DS called for redemption at $51.50 on 09/01/1998
Merged into Washington Mutual, Inc. 10/01/1998
Each share Common $1 par exchanged for (1.68) shares Common no par
(See Washington Mutual, Inc.)

AHOLD N V (NETHERLANDS)
Each ADR for Ordinary Bearer exchanged for (2) ADR's for Ordinary Bearer 12/31/1985
Stock Dividend - 10% 08/14/1987
Reorganized as Koninklijke Ahold N.V. 10/11/1989
Each ADR for Ordinary Bearer exchanged for (1) Sponsored ADR for Common
Koninklijke Ahold N.V. name changed to Koninklijke Ahold Delhaize N.V. 07/25/2016

AHPC HLDGS INC (MD)
Charter forfeited 10/02/2009

AHRENS-FOX FIRE ENGINE CO.
Dissolved 00/00/1940
Details not available

AHSC HLDGS CORP (DE)
Name changed to Alco Health Distribution Corp. 02/14/1992
Alco Health Distribution Corp. name changed to AmeriSource Distribution Corp. 07/15/1994 which name changed to AmeriSource Health Corp. 03/30/1995 which merged into AmerisourceBergen Corp. 08/29/2001

AHSI INC (MA)
Involuntarily dissolved 05/31/2007

AHT CORP (AB)
Each share Special Preferred no par exchanged for (0.6410257) share Common no par 03/11/2011
Reincorporated under the laws of Canada as Simsmart Inc. 07/03/2001
(See Simsmart Inc.)

AHT CORP (DE)
Assets sold for the benefit of creditors 11/22/2000
No stockholders' equity

AHUMADA LEAD CO.
Dissolved 00/00/1933
Details not available

AI SOFTWARE INC (NV)
Each share old Common $0.00001 par exchanged for (14) shares new Common $0.00001 par 04/07/2003
Name changed to Pluristem Life Systems, Inc. 06/30/2003
Pluristem Life Systems, Inc. recapitalized as Pluristem Therapeutics Inc. 11/26/2007

AIA INDS INC (DE)
Plan of reorganization under Chapter 11 Federal Bankruptcy proceedings confirmed 11/03/1988
Stockholders' equity unlikely

AIC CORP (DE)
Each share Common $1 par exchanged for (0.2) share Capital Stock $1 par 03/01/1965
Capital Stock $1 par reclassified as Common $1 par 12/16/1966
Name changed to Crutcher Resources Corp. 12/31/1968
(See Crutcher Resources Corp.)

AIC DIVERSIFIED CANADA FUND (AB)
Name changed to Manulife Diversified Canada Fund 08/23/2010
Manulife Diversified Canada Fund merged into Manulife Canadian Focused Fund 11/04/2011

AIC DIVERSIFIED CDA SPLIT CORP (ON)
Reorganized as AIC Diversified Canada Fund 06/30/2009
Each Preferred Share no par automatically became (0.745601) Mutual Fund Unit
Each Capital Share no par automatically became (0.560658) Mutual Fund Unit
AIC Diversified Canada Fund name changed to Manulife Diversified Canada Fund 08/23/2010 which merged into Manulife Canadian Fund 11/04/2011

AIC GLOBAL FINL SPLIT CORP (ON)
Preferred Shares no par called for redemption at $10 plus $0.08798 accrued dividends on 05/31/2011
Class A Shares no par called for redemption at $0.0643 on 05/31/2011

AIC INTL RES CORP (BC)
Company believed out of business 01/00/2001
Details not available

AICI CAP TR (DE)
Acceptance Insurance Companies Inc., Guarantor of Trust, Chapter 11 bankruptcy proceeding converted to Chapter 7 on 09/07/2010
Stockholders' equity unlikely

AICORP INC (DE)
Name changed to Trinzic Corp. 10/01/1992
Trinzic Corp. merged into PLATINUM Technology, Inc. 08/25/1995 which name changed to Platinum Technology International Inc. 01/04/1999 which merged into Computer Associates International, Inc. 06/29/1999 which name changed to CA, Inc. 02/01/2006

AID AUTO STORES INC NEW (CO)
Reincorporated 12/15/2003
State of incorporation changed from (DE) to (CO) 12/15/2003
Recapitalized as Inca Enterprises Corp. 01/22/2004
Each share Common $0.001 par exchanged for (0.00125) share Common $0.001 par
Inca Enterprises Corp. name changed to Velocity International Corp. (CO) 05/10/2004 which reincorporated in Nevada as Deep Blue, Inc. 03/13/2006 which recapitalized as Bell Rose Capital, Inc. 03/05/2014

AID AUTO STORES INC OLD (DE)
Recapitalized 11/29/1972
Recapitalized from Aid Stores, Inc. to Aid Auto Stores, Inc. (Old) 11/29/1972
Each share Common 1¢ par exchanged for (0.25) share Common 1¢ par
Stock Dividends - 10% 02/15/1976; 10% 06/15/1980; 10% 05/24/1981; 10% 07/16/1982; 10% 06/24/1983; 10% 07/26/1984
Merged into Export Agencies International Corp. 06/03/1985
Each share Common 1¢ par exchanged for $5.25 cash

AID CORP (IA)
Name changed to Allied Group, Inc. 05/14/1987
(See Allied Group, Inc.)

AID INC (CO)
Declared defunct and inoperative for failure to pay taxes and file reports 10/19/1974

AID INC (CO)
Merged into INA Corp. 06/16/1978
Each share Class A Common 5¢ par exchanged for (0.54) share Common $1 par and $0.351 cash
INA Corp. merged into Cigna Corp. 04/01/1982

AID INVESTMENT & DISCOUNT, INC. (OH)
Acquired by General Acceptance Corp. (New) 12/01/1964
Each share 5.5% Preferred Ser. A or 5.5% Preferred Ser. B $25 par exchanged for (2.5) shares 60¢ Preference no par and $0.23 cash
Each share Common $1 par exchanged for (0.0851064) share $2.50 Conv. Preference no par
General Acceptance Corp. (New) name changed to GAC Corp. (PA) 07/01/1968 which reincorporated in Delaware 12/20/1973
(See GAC Corp. (DE))

AID INVT FD INC (MD)
Completely liquidated 06/25/1975
Each share Capital Stock $1 par exchanged for first and final distribution of $4.034 cash

AIDA INDS INC (FL)
Name changed to Shopping Sherlock, Inc. 03/24/1999
Shopping Sherlock, Inc. name changed to ASPi Europe, Inc. (FL) 05/12/2000 which reincorporated in Delaware 12/19/2000 which name changed to Sharps Elimination Technologies Inc. 05/06/2002 which name changed to Armagh Group Inc. 09/17/2002 which recapitalized as SmartVideo Technologies, Inc. 01/06/2003 which name changed to uVuMobile, Inc. 06/04/2007
(See uVumobile, Inc.)

AIDA MINERALS CORP (BC)
Name changed to BLOK Technologies Inc. 02/02/2018

AIDCO CORP (DE)
Name changed to Fedonics, Inc. 04/28/1969
(See Fedonics, Inc.)

AIDS INTL DIVERSIFIED SVCS INC (DE)
Charter cancelled and declared inoperative and void for non-payment of taxes 03/01/1991

AIFS INC (DE)
Acquired by Marina Holdings Corp. 08/31/1990
Each share Common 10¢ par exchanged for $6.50 cash

AIG SUNAMERICA GLOBAL FING III
144A Auction Market Securities called for redemption at $1,000 on 12/13/2005

AIG SUNAMERICA GLOBAL FING XII
144A Auction Market Equity Securities called for redemption at $1,000 plus $0.90333 accrued dividends on 05/30/2007

AIGNER HLDGS LTD (BC)
Struck off register and declared dissolved for failure to file returns 01/21/1994

AIGUEBELLE GOLDFIELDS LTD. (ON)
Charter cancelled for failure to pay taxes and file returns 01/10/1968

AIGUEBELLE RES INC (QC)
Merged into Cambior Inc. 02/16/1987
Each share Common no par exchanged for $1.158 cash

AIKEN CNTY NATL BK (AIKEN, SC)
Merged into Carolina First Corp. 04/10/1995
Each share Common $5 par exchanged for (1.125) shares Common $1 par
Carolina First Corp. name changed to South Financial Group, Inc. 04/24/2000 which merged into Toronto-Dominion Bank (Toronto, ON) 09/30/2010

AIKEN INDS INC (DE)
Merged into Norlin Industries Inc. 12/30/1977
Each share Common $1 par exchanged for $6.20 cash

AIKEN RED LAKE GOLD MINES LTD. (ON)
Merged into Aiken-Russet Red Lake Mines Ltd. 12/01/1965
Each share Capital Stock $1 par exchanged for (0.5) share Common no par
Aiken-Russet Red Lake Mines Ltd. merged into Canhorn Mining Corp. 01/09/1986 which merged into Canhorn Chemical Corp. 04/26/1995 which merged into Nayarit Gold Inc. 05/02/2005 which merged into Capital Gold Corp. 08/02/2010 which merged into Gammon Gold Inc. (QC) 04/08/2011 which reincorporated in Ontario as AuRico Gold Inc. 06/14/2011 which merged into Alamos Gold Inc. (New) 07/06/2015

AIKEN RUSSET RED LAKE MINES LTD (ON)
Merged into Canhorn Mining Corp. 01/09/1986
Each share Common no par exchanged for (0.0273224) share Common no par
Canhorn Mining Corp. merged into Canhorn Chemical Corp. 04/26/1995 which merged into Nayarit Gold Inc. 05/02/2005 which merged into Capital Gold Corp. 08/02/2010 which merged into Gammon Gold Inc. (QC) 04/08/2011 which reincorporated in Ontario as AuRico Gold Inc. 06/14/2011 which merged into Alamos Gold Inc. (New) 07/06/2015

AIL ABSORBENT INDS LTD (BC)
Struck off register and declared dissolved for failure to file returns 02/28/1992

AIL TECHNOLOGIES INC. (DE)
Merged into EDO Corp. 05/01/2000
Each share Common exchanged for (1.3296) shares Common $1 par
(See EDO Corp.)

AILEEN INC (NY)
Common $1 par split (2) for (1) by issuance of (1) additional share 06/05/1969
Common $1 par split (2) for (1) by issuance of (1) additional share 07/09/1971
Chapter 11 bankruptcy proceedings terminated 03/20/2006
No stockholders' equity

AILERON VENTURES LTD (AB)
Reincorporated under the laws of Canada as Integrated Energy Storage Corp. 12/02/2016

AIM ADVISOR FDS (DE)
Reincorporated 09/11/2000
Name and state of incorporation changed from AIM Advisor Funds,

Inc. (MD) to AIM Advisor Funds (DE) 09/11/2000
Flex Fund Class A, B and C merged into AIM Funds Group 09/10/2001
Details not available
International Value Fund Class A, B and C reclassified as International Core Equity Fund Class A, B or C respectively 07/01/2002
International Core Equity Fund Class A, B and C merged into INVESCO International Funds, Inc. 10/27/2003
Details not available
Real Estate Fund Class A, B and C merged into AIM Investment Securities Funds 10/29/2003
Details not available

AIM EXPLORATIONS LTD (BC)
Each share old Common no par exchanged for (0.5) share new Common no par 03/13/2017
Name changed to DMG Blockchain Solutions Inc. 02/13/2018

AIM FLOATING RATE FD (DE)
Merged into AIM Counselor Series Trust 04/13/2006
Details not available

AIM GOVT FDS INC (MD)
Merged into Short-Term Investments Co. 10/03/1990
Details not available

AIM HEALTH GROUP INC (ON)
Acquired by 2291094 Ontario Inc. 09/01/2011
Each share Common no par exchanged for $0.25 cash
Note: Unexchanged certificates were cancelled and became without value 09/01/2017

AIM INVT FDS (DE)
Latin American Growth Fund Class A, B, and C reclassified as Developing Markets Fund Class A, B, or C respectively 09/07/2001
Global Consumer Products & Services Fund Class A, B, and C merged into AIM Series Trust 09/10/2001
Details not available
Global Telecommunications & Technology Fund Class A, B, and C reclassified as Global Science & Technology Fund Class A, B, or C respectively 07/01/2002
Under plan of merger each share Strategic Income Fund Class A, B and C automatically became (1) share AIM Investment Securities Funds Inc. Income Fund Class A, B, or C respectively 06/23/2003
Global Financial Services Fund Class A, B, and C merged into AIM Sector Funds 11/03/2003
Details not available
Global Resources Fund Class A, B, and C merged into AIM Sector Funds 11/03/2003
Details not available
Global Science & Technology Fund Class A, B, and C merged into AIM Sector Funds 11/03/2003
Details not available
(Additional Information in Active)

AIM INVT FDS INVESCO INVT FDS (DE)
Under plan of merger each share Invesco Commodities Strategy Fund Class A automatically became (1.41041041) shares Balanced-Risk Commodity Strategy Fund Class A 06/11/2012
Under plan of merger each share Invesco Commodities Strategy Fund Class B automatically became (1.40950455) shares Balanced-Risk Commodity Strategy Fund Class B 06/11/2012
Under plan of merger each share Invesco Commodities Strategy Fund Class C automatically became (1.41093117) shares Balanced-Risk Commodity Strategy Fund Class C 06/11/2012
Under plan of merger each share Invesco Commodities Strategy Fund Class R automatically became (1.40781563) shares Balanced-Risk Commodity Strategy Fund Class R 06/11/2012
Under plan of merger each share Invesco Commodities Strategy Fund Class Y automatically became (1.40656064) shares Balanced-Risk Commodity Strategy Fund Class Y 06/11/2012
Under plan of merger each share Invesco Commodities Strategy Fund Institutional Class automatically became (1.4119403) shares Balanced-Risk Commodity Strategy Fund Institutional Class 06/11/2012
(Additional Information in Active)

AIM INVT SECS FDS INVESCO INVT SECS FDS (DE)
Merged into AIM Investment Securities Funds, Inc. 07/15/2013
Each share Invesco High Yield Securities Fund Class A exchanged for (4.0456621) shares Invesco High Yield Fund Class A
Each share Invesco High Yield Securities Fund Class B exchanged for (4.00228311) shares Invesco High Yield Fund Class B
Each share Invesco High Yield Securities Fund Class C exchanged for (4.02745995) shares Invesco High Yield Fund Class C
Each share Invesco High Yield Securities Fund Class Y exchanged for (4.01822323) shares Invesco High Yield Fund Class Y
(Additional Information in Active)

AIM MED TECHNOLOGIES INC (AB)
Recapitalized as PLM Group Ltd. 06/12/1995
Each share Common no par exchanged for (0.5) share Common no par
(See PLM Group Ltd.)

AIM SAFETY INC (BC)
Name changed to AimGlobal Technologies Co., Inc. 01/29/1999
(See AimGlobal Technologies Co., Inc.)

AIM SELECT REAL ESTATE INCOME FD (DE)
Auction Rate Preferred Ser. M called for redemption at $25,000 on 10/24/2006
Auction Rate Preferred Ser. F called for redemption at $25,000 on 10/30/2006
Auction Rate Preferred Ser. W called for redemption at $25,000 on 11/02/2006
Auction Rate Preferred Ser. R called for redemption at $25,000 on 11/10/2006
Merged into AIM Counselor Series Trust 03/12/2007
Details not available

AIM SER TR (DE)
Merged into AIM Growth Series 11/04/2003
Details not available

AIM SMART CORP (DE)
Reincorporated 08/13/2007
Common no par split (2) for (1) by issuance of (1) additional share payable 10/15/1997 to holders of record 10/08/1997
State of incorporation changed from (CO) to (DE) and Common no par changed to $0.001 par 08/13/2007
Each share old Common $0.001 par exchanged for (0.00133333) share new Common $0.001 par 10/19/2007
Name changed to American Tony Pharmaceuticals, Inc. 09/24/2008
American Tony Pharmaceuticals, Inc. name changed to Tongli Pharmaceuticals (USA), Inc. 10/30/2008

AIM SPL OPPORTUNITIES FDS (DE)
Large Cap Opportunities Fund Class A, B and C reclassified as Opportunities III Fund Class A, B or C respectively 07/01/2002
Mid Cap Opportunities Fund Class A, B, and C reclassified as Opportunities II Fund Class A, B, or C respectively 07/01/2002
Small Cap Opportunities Fund Class A, B, and C reclassified as Opportunities I Fund Class A, B, or C respectively 07/01/2002
Merged into AIM Funds Group 04/19/2007
Details not available

AIM TELS INC (NJ)
Charter revoked for failure to file annual reports 08/31/1994

AIM TREASURERS SER FDS INC (MD)
Reincorporated under the laws of Delaware as AIM Treasurer's Series Trust 11/25/2003

AIM1 VENTURES INC (ON)
Recapitalized as James E. Wagner Cultivation Corp. 06/11/2018
Each share Common no par exchanged for (0.20629071) share Common no par

AIM2 VENTURES INC (ON)
Reorganized as Canopy Rivers Inc. 09/20/2018
Each share Common no par exchanged for (0.03764351) Subordinate Share

AIMCO, INC. (NV)
Recapitalized as Colt Technology, Inc. 03/31/1983
Each share Common 50¢ par exchanged for (0.5) share Common $1 par

AIMCO CLO SER 2001-A
3C7 144A Preference called for redemption at $1 on 07/12/2005

AIMCO INDS LTD (ON)
Through voluntary exchange offer International Telephone & Telegraph Corp. acquired 98% as of 10/22/1971
Public interest eliminated

AIMEX INTL CORP (NV)
Name changed to Auto Stack International 12/15/1997
Auto Stack International name changed to BTC Financial Services 04/30/1999 which name changed to First Equity Holding Corp. 09/19/2000 which recapitalized as Chilmark Entertainment Group, Inc. 06/23/2003 which recapitalized as Integrated Bio Energy Resources, Inc. 03/13/2007 which name changed to Onslow Holdings, Inc. 01/30/2014

AIMEXCO INC (CO)
Name changed to Barrett Resources Corp. (CO) 01/25/1984
Barrett Resources Corp. (CO) reincorporated in Delaware 07/22/1987 which merged into Williams Companies, Inc. 08/02/2001

AIMGLOBAL TECHNOLOGIES INC (BC)
Placed in receivership 10/03/2002
Stockholders' equity unlikely

AIMS BIOTECH CORP (BC)
Struck off register and declared dissolved for failure to file returns 03/28/1991

AIMS WORLDWIDE INC (NV)
SEC revoked common stock registration 09/18/2013

AIMSI TECHNOLOGIES INC (UT)
SEC revoked common stock registration 03/31/2008

AINSBROOKE CORP. (NY)
Merged into Genesco Inc. 11/01/1965
Each share Capital Stock $1 par exchanged for (0.1941747) share Common $1 par

AINSLEY CORP (TX)
Name changed to Automated Compliance & Training Inc. (TX) 04/29/1993
Automated Compliance & Training Inc. (TX) reincorporated in Utah as Chequemate International Inc. 08/30/1996 which name changed to C-3D Digital, Inc. 01/08/2002
(See C-3D Digital, Inc.)

AINSLIE CORP (MA)
Stock Dividend - 40% 02/15/1962
Completely liquidated
Each share Common $1 par received first and final distribution of $4.36 cash payable 03/29/2016 to holders of record 02/22/2016

AINSWORTH BASE METALS LTD. (BC)
Recapitalized as New Ainsworth Base Metals Ltd. 00/00/1957
Each share Capital Stock 50¢ par exchanged for (0.33333333) share Capital Stock no par
New Ainsworth Base Metals Ltd. recapitalized as Angus River Mines Ltd. 01/27/1969 which was acquired by Abco Mining Ltd. 07/23/1969 which name changed to Aselo Industries Ltd. 02/00/1971 which recapitalized as Fairmont Gas & Oil Corp. 10/15/1979 which recapitalized as Cater Energy, Inc. 05/23/1984 which recapitalized as Houston Metals Corp. 10/27/1986 which recapitalized as Pacific Houston Resources, Inc. 03/30/1989
(See Pacific Houston Resources, Inc.)

AINSWORTH LMBR LTD (BC)
Reorganized from British Columbia to under the laws of Canada 07/29/2008
Each share Common no par exchanged for (0.2731) share Common no par, (0.5936) Common Stock Purchase Warrant expiring 00/00/2010 and (1) Net Litigation Proceeds Right CUSIP® changed from (C01023 20 6) 04/15/2013
Merged into Norbord Inc. 04/02/2015
Each share Common no par exchanged for (0.1321) share Common no par
Note: Unexchanged certificates will be cancelled and become without value 04/02/2021

AINSWORTH MANUFACTURING CORP. (MI)
Each share Common $10 par exchanged for (3) shares Common $5 par 12/07/1936
Acquired by Harsco Corp. 10/31/1957
Each share Common $5 par exchanged for (0.2575) share Common $2.50 par

AINSWORTH RES LTD (BC)
Struck off register 04/04/1985

AINTREE RES INC (BC)
Each share old Common no par exchanged for (0.25) share new Common no par 07/07/2016
Name changed to Viva Gold Corp. 01/08/2018

AINTREE RES LTD (BC)
Name changed to ICCI Integrated Credit & Commerce Inc. 04/27/1994
(See ICCI Integrated Credit & Commerce Inc.)

AIOI INS CO LTD (JAPAN)
Merged into MS&AD Insurance Group Holdings, Inc. 04/01/2010
Each Unsponsored ADR for Common

AIR-AIR

exchanged for (1.51998599) ADR's for Common

AIR & SPACE UNDERWRITERS, INC. (IN)
Charter revoked for failure to file reports 03/10/1969

AIR & WTR TECHNOLOGIES CORP (DE)
Name changed to Aqua Alliance, Inc. 10/13/1998
(See Aqua Alliance, Inc.)

AIR ACADEMY NATL BANCORP (CO)
Preferred 1¢ par called for redemption 07/00/1996
Merged into Air Academy Acquisition Corp. 03/19/1997
Each share Common 1¢ par exchanged for $30 cash

AIR ACADEMY NATL BK (COLORADO SPRINGS, CO)
Common Capital Stock $1 par changed to $2 par 03/22/1977
Reorganized as Air Academy National Bancorp 07/01/1991
Each share Common Capital Stock $2 par exchanged for (1) share Preferred 1¢ par and (1) share Common 1¢ par
(See Air Academy National Bancorp)

AIR AMERICA, INC. (DE)
Incorporated 04/30/1948
No longer in existence having become inoperative and void for non-payment of taxes 04/01/1956

AIR ASSOCIATES, INC. (NJ)
Reincorporated 10/01/1940
State of incorporation changed from (NY) to (NJ) 10/01/1940
Name changed to Electronic Communications, Inc. 04/30/1957
(See Electronic Communications, Inc.)

AIR BALANCE INC (PA)
Name changed to ABL Liquidating Co. 06/16/1970
(See ABL Liquidating Co.)

AIR-BORNE CARGO LINES, INC. (NY)
Bankrupt 00/00/1948
Details not available

AIR BROOK ARPT EXPRESS INC (DE)
Name changed to SportsQuest, Inc. 09/20/2007

AIR CALIF (CA)
Merged into Westgate-California Corp. 10/12/1977
Each share Common $1 par exchanged for (1) Non-transferable Common Equivalent Ctf. or $15 cash
(See Westgate-California Corp.)

AIR CDA INC (CANADA)
Plan of Arrangement under Companies' Creditors Arrangement Act effective 09/30/2004
Each share Common no par and Non-Vtg. Class A no par received distribution of (0.00008407) share ACE Aviation Holdings Inc. Class B Share no par
Note: U.S. citizens will receive (0.00008407) share Class A Variable shares no par
Note: Certificates were not required to be exchanged and are without value (Additional Information in Active)

AIR CARGO EQUIP CORP (DE)
Common $1 par split (3) for (2) by issuance of (0.5) additional share 05/23/1980
Common $1 par split (3) for (2) by issuance of (0.5) additional share 12/01/1985
Common $1 par split (3) for (2) by issuance of (0.5) additional share 09/12/1986
Merged into Ace Acquisition Corp. 03/08/1989

Each share Common $1 par exchanged for $8.50 cash

AIR CARGO TRANSPORT CORP.
Adjudicated bankrupt 06/30/1948
No stockholders' equity

AIR CHAPARRAL INC (NV)
Filed a petition under Chapter 11 Federal Bankruptcy Code 02/01/1983
Became completely non-operational
No stockholders' equity

AIR CHARTER EXPRESS INC (NV)
SEC revoked common stock registration 01/03/2006

AIR CONTROL PRODUCTS, INC. (FL)
Common $1 par changed to 50¢ par and (1) additional share issued 05/15/1959
Name changed to Keller Industries, Inc. 01/04/1965
(See Keller Industries, Inc.)

AIR CRAFT MARINE ENGINEERING CORP. (CA)
Charter revoked for failure to file reports and pay fees 01/02/1963

AIR-CURE TECHNOLOGIES INC (DE)
Name changed 08/01/1995
Name changed from Air-Cure Environmental, Inc. to Air-Cure Technologies, Inc. 08/01/1995
Name changed to Iteq Inc. 03/10/1997
(See Iteq Inc.)

AIR DEFENSE ELECTRS INC (NV)
Name changed to Zephyr International, Inc. 06/25/1990

AIR DEVICES CORP.
Name changed to Connecticut Telephone & Electric Corp. 04/00/1940
Connecticut Telephone & Electric Corp. acquired by Great American Industries, Inc. 12/31/1942
(See Great American Industries, Inc.)

AIR DISPATCH INC.
Liquidation completed
Each share Common exchanged for initial distribution of (6.3485) shares 4% Conv. Preferred Ser. B $50 par and (5.2904) shares Common $1 par of Novo Industrial Corp. 12/14/1966
Each share Common received second and final distribution of (0.63492) share Novo Industrial Corp. Common $1 par 06/00/1967
Novo Industrial Corp. name changed to Novo Corp. 05/05/1969
(See Novo Corp.)

AIR DYNAMICS CORP. (WA)
Merged into International-United Corp. 04/01/1970
Each share Common $1 par exchanged for (1) share Common 10¢ par
(See International-United Corp.)

AIR ENERGY INC (NV)
Name changed to Powerhouse International Corp. 12/24/1997
Powerhouse International Corp. name changed to iLive, Inc. 10/21/1999
(See iLive, Inc.)

AIR EPICUREAN INC (NV)
Recapitalized as Ikon Ventures Inc. 05/06/1997
Each share Common $0.001 par exchanged for (0.1) share Common $0.001 par
Ikon Ventures Inc. name changed to Sutton Trading Solutions Inc. 10/31/2001 which recapitalized as Global Diversified Acquisition Corp. 04/24/2003 which name changed to Mailkey Corp. 04/13/2004 which name changed to IElement Corp. 08/25/2005
(See IElement Corp.)

AIR EXPRESS INTERNATIONAL AGENCY, INC. (NY)
Name changed to Air Express International Corp. (NY) 00/00/1953
Air Express International Corp. (NY) acquired by Wings & Wheels Express, Inc. 09/12/1967 which reincorporated in Illinois as Air Express International Corp. 10/18/1972 which reincorporated in Delaware 12/31/1981
(See Air Express International Corp.)

AIR EXPRESS INTERNATIONAL CORP. (NY)
Acquired by Wings & Wheels Express, Inc. 09/12/1967
Each share 6% Conv. Preferred $100 par exchanged for (1.192) shares $6 Conv. Preferred $1 par
Each share Common 50¢ par exchanged for (0.6) share Common 1¢ par
Wings & Wheels Express, Inc. name changed to Air Express International Corp. (IL) 10/18/1972 which reincorporated in Delaware 12/31/1981
(See Air Express International Corp.)

AIR EXPRESS INTL CORP (DE)
Reincorporated 12/31/1981
Class B 1¢ par reclassified as Common 1¢ par 01/01/1978
$6 Conv. Preferred $1 par called for redemption 10/06/1980
State of incorporation changed from (IL) to (DE) 12/31/1981
Common 1¢ par split (3) for (2) by issuance of (0.5) additional share 08/15/1991
Common 1¢ par split (3) for (2) by issuance of (0.5) additional share 07/31/1992
Common 1¢ par split (3) for (2) by issuance of (0.5) additional share 12/21/1994
Common 1¢ par split (3) for (2) by issuance of (0.5) additional share payable 07/25/1997 to holders of record 07/11/1997
Merged into Deutsche Post AG 02/15/2000
Each share Common 1¢ par exchanged for $33 cash

AIR FLA SYS INC (DE)
$2.40 Conv. Preferred Ser. B 50¢ par called for redemption 06/29/1981
Name changed to Jet Florida System, Inc. 08/15/1985
(See Jet Florida System, Inc.)

AIR FORWARDERS INC (DE)
Plan of arrangement confirmed and assets subsequently sold 01/17/1980
No stockholders' equity

AIR FRANCE (FRANCE)
Name changed to Air France-KLM 09/15/2004

AIR INDS CORP (CA)
Merged into AIC Investment Co. 12/31/1973
Each share Common no par exchanged for $2.50 cash

AIR INDS GROUP INC (DE)
Each share old Common $0.001 par exchanged for (0.0025) share new Common $0.001 par 10/14/2010
Reincorporated under the laws of Nevada 09/03/2013

AIR INVESTORS, INC. (DE)
Name changed to Century Investors, Inc. 03/00/1949
Century Investors, Inc. merged into American Manufacturing Co., Inc. 12/20/1960 which assets were transferred to American Manufacturing Co., Inc. Liquidating Trust 05/20/1980
(See American Manufacturing Co., Inc. Liquidating Trust)

AIR KING CORP (IL)
Class A $2 par reclassified as Common $2 par 08/09/1973
Adjudicated bankrupt 06/02/1975
Stockholders' equity unlikely

AIR L A INC (DE)
Each share Common $0.001 par exchanged for (0.1) share Common 10¢ par 05/02/1994
SEC revoked common stock registration 06/23/2009

AIR MARSHALL CORP. (DE)
No longer in existence having become inoperative and void for non-payment of taxes 04/01/1955

AIR METAL INDUSTRIES, INC. (FL)
Proclaimed dissolved and charter cancelled for non-payment of taxes 06/30/1967

AIR METHODS CORP (DE)
Each share Common 1¢ par exchanged for (0.16666666) share Common 6¢ par 04/07/1992
Common 6¢ par split (3) for (1) by issuance of (2) additional shares payable 12/28/2012 to holders of record 12/14/2012 Ex date - 12/31/2012
Acquired by ASP AMC Holdings, Inc. 04/21/2017
Each share Common 6¢ par exchanged for $43 cash

AIR MICH INC (MI)
Common $5 par changed to $1 par 06/22/1971
Name changed to Professional Health Systems, Inc. and Common $1 par changed to 1¢ par 05/01/1976
Professional Health Systems, Inc. name changed to International Dasa Corp. 12/11/1981 which name changed to Johnson International Corp. 06/18/1984
(See Johnson International Corp.)

AIR MIDWEST INC (KS)
Stock Dividend - 100% 12/22/1982
Merged into Mesa Airlines, Inc. (NM) 07/12/1991
Each share Common $1 par exchanged for (0.45) share Common no par and $3 cash
Mesa Airlines, Inc. (NM) reincorporated in Nevada as Mesa Air Group, Inc. 09/27/1996
(See Mesa Air Group, Inc.)

AIR NIAGARA EXPRESS INC (CANADA)
Involuntarily dissolved for failure to file annual returns 12/23/2002

AIR ONE INC (DE)
Plan of reorganization under Chapter 11 Federal Bankruptcy proceedings confirmed 12/01/1986
No stockholders' equity

AIR PACKAGING TECHNOLOGIES INC (DE)
Each share old Common no par exchanged for (0.1) share new Common no par 01/04/2000
SEC revoked common stock registration 12/28/2005

AIR POLLUTION CTL CORP (DE)
Charter cancelled and proclaimed inoperative and void for non-payment of taxes 03/01/1978

AIR POLLUTION INDS INC (DE)
Merged into Neptune International Corp. 04/14/1977
Each share Common 5¢ par exchanged for $1.50 cash

AIR PRODS & CHEMS INC (DE)
$4.75 Conv. Preferred $1 par called for redemption 05/28/1971
$4.75 Conv. Preferred Ser. B $1 par called for redemption 05/28/1971
(Additional Information in Active)

AIR PRODUCTS, INC. (MI)
Merged into Air Products &

Chemicals, Inc. 07/13/1961
Each share Common $1 par exchanged for (1) share Common $1 par

AIR-Q WI-FI CORP (DE)
Name changed to AirRover Wi-Fi Corp. 06/04/2004
AirRover Wi-Fi Corp. name changed to Diamond I, Inc. 01/28/2005 which recapitalized as ubroadcast, inc. 02/09/2009 which name changed to Santeon Group Inc. 06/11/2010

AIR REDUCTION INC (NY)
Each share Common no par exchanged for (3) shares Common no par 00/00/1928
Each share Common no par exchanged for (3) shares Common no par 00/00/1936
4.50% Preferred 1951 Ser. called for redemption 12/05/1960
Common no par changed to $1 par and (1) additional share issued 05/16/1967
Name changed to Airco, Inc. (NY) 10/01/1971
Airco, Inc. (NY) reincorporated in Delaware 08/03/1977
(See Airco, Inc. (DE))

AIR RES CORP (CO)
Reincorporated under the laws of Virginia as Spurlock Industries, Inc. and Common $0.001 par changed to no par 07/15/1996
(See Spurlock Industries, Inc.)

AIR SENSORS INC (DE)
Reincorporated 12/11/1985
State of incorporation changed from (WA) to (DE) and Common 30¢ par changed to $0.001 par 12/11/1985
Each share old Common $0.001 par exchanged for (0.16666666) share new Common $0.001 par 02/22/1993
Name changed to IMPCO Technologies, Inc. 09/15/1997
IMPCO Technologies, Inc. recapitalized as Fuel Systems Solutions, Inc. 08/25/2006 which merged into Westport Fuel Systems Inc. 06/08/2016

AIR-SPACE DEVICES, INC. (DE)
Name changed to A.S.D. Liquidating Corp. 06/17/1966
(See A.S.D. Liquidating Corp.)

AIR SPRINGS INC (NY)
Each share Common 10¢ par exchanged for (5) shares Common 2¢ par 03/23/1955
Assets sold for benefit of creditors 07/23/1973
No stockholders' equity

AIR SURVEY CORP. (MD)
Merged into Lockwood, Kessler & Bartlett, Inc. (NY) 06/28/1968
Each share Class A Common $5 par or Class B Common $5 par exchanged for (0.33333333) share Class A 25¢ par
Lockwood, Kessler & Bartlett, Inc. (NY) reincorporated in Delaware as Viatech Inc. 07/30/1971 which name changed to Continental Can Co., Inc. 10/21/1992 which merged into Suiza Foods Corp. 05/29/1998 which name changed to Dean Foods Co. (New) 12/21/2001

AIR SYS PLUS INC (ON)
Name changed to Sales Initiatives International Inc. 06/01/1993
Sales Initiatives International Inc. name changed to Greenlight Communications Inc. 06/14/1994
(See Greenlight Communications Inc.)

AIR TEMP NORTH AMER INC (FL)
Acquired by Air Temp Holdings, Inc. 09/15/2015
Each share Common $0.0001 par exchanged for $0.035 cash

AIR TEST TECHNOLOGY INC (DE)
Name changed to Visual Frontier, Inc. 04/04/2003
(See Visual Frontier, Inc.)

AIR TO WTR CO (WY)
Name changed to New Horizon Group, Inc. 10/15/2008
(See New Horizon Group, Inc.)

AIR TRANS GROUP HLDGS INC (NV)
Common $0.001 par split (10) for (1) by issuance of (9) additional shares payable 03/09/2009 to holders of record 02/27/2009 Ex date - 03/10/2009
Recapitalized as Pharmagreen Biotech Inc. 07/02/2018
Each share Common $0.001 par exchanged for (0.005) share Common $0.001 par

AIR TRANSN HLDG INC (DE)
Each share Common 5¢ par exchanged for (0.2) share Common 25¢ par 05/16/1994
Name changed to Air T, Inc. 09/30/1999

AIR-WAY ELECTRIC APPLIANCE CORP. (DE)
Recapitalized 04/00/1942
Each share 7% 1st Preferred $100 par exchanged for (20) shares Common $3 par
Each share Common no par exchanged for (0.06) share Common $3 par
Name changed to Air-Way Industries, Inc. 03/23/1955
Air-Way Industries, Inc. name changed to Lamb Industries, Inc. 12/31/1958 which name changed to Lamb Communications, Inc. 08/28/1967
(See Lamb Communications, Inc.)

AIR-WAY INDUSTRIES, INC. (DE)
Stock Dividend - 100% 10/14/1955
Name changed to Lamb Industries, Inc. 12/31/1958
Lamb Industries, Inc. name changed to Lamb Communications, Inc. 08/28/1967
(See Lamb Communications, Inc.)

AIR WEST INC (DE)
Name changed to AW Liquidating Co. 04/01/1970
(See AW Liquidating Co.)

AIR WIS INC (WI)
Common no par changed to $1 par 06/30/2007
Common $1 par split (2) for (1) by issuance of (1) additional share 01/31/1979
Common $1 par changed to 25¢ par and (1) additional share issued 04/24/1980
Common 25¢ par split (3) for (2) by issuance of (0.5) additional share 05/01/1981
Stock Dividends - 10% 06/30/1977; 100% 06/30/1978
Under plan of reorganization each share Common 25¢ par automatically became (1) share Air Wis Services, Inc. Common 10¢ par 07/22/1983
Air Wis Services, Inc. merged into UAL Corp. 01/27/1992
(See UAL Corp.)

AIR WIS SVCS INC (WI)
Stock Dividends - 10% 04/23/1984; 10% 10/10/1988; 10% 06/16/1989
Merged into UAL Corp. 01/27/1992
Each share Common 10¢ par exchanged for either (0.0606) share Common $5 par or $9 cash
Note: Option to elect to receive cash expired 02/18/1992
(See UAL Corp.)

AIR WTR INTL CORP (NV)
SEC revoked common stock registration 05/22/2009

AIR X INDS INC (NY)
Ceased doing business and shares became worthless 00/00/1965

AIRBEE WIRELESS INC (DE)
SEC revoked common stock registration 03/08/2012

AIRBOMB COM INC (DE)
Reincorporated 05/09/2000
Name and place of incorporation changed from Airbomb.com Marketing Ltd. (BC) to Airbomb.com, Inc. (DE) and Common no par changed to $0.001 par 05/09/2000
Name changed to RT Petroleum Inc. 05/18/2005
(See RT Petroleum Inc.)

AIRBORNE DATA MARKETING LTD (BC)
Recapitalized as International Airborne Systems Corp. 09/11/1987
Each share Common no par exchanged for (0.5) share Common no par
International Airborne Systems Corp. name changed to Gateway Waste Systems Inc. 06/10/1994 which name changed to Gateway Technologies Corp. 12/04/1995 which recapitalized as Trevali Resources Corp. 07/06/2006 which name changed to Trevali Mining Corp. 04/07/2011

AIRBORNE FGHT CORP (DE)
Merged 10/17/1968
Common $5 par changed to $1 par and (4) additional shares issued 07/23/1963
Each share Common $1 par exchanged for (2) shares Common 50¢ par 06/15/1965
Merged from Airborne Freight Corp. (CA) to Airborne Freight Corp. (DE) 10/17/1968
Each share Common 50¢ par exchanged for (1.329) shares Common $1 par
Common $1 par split (3) for (2) by issuance of (0.5) additional share 06/03/1976
Common $1 par split (2) for (1) by issuance of (1) additional share 05/30/1990
Common $1 par split (2) for (1) by issuance of (1) additional share payable 02/13/1998 to holders of record 02/09/1998 Ex date - 02/17/1998
Under plan of reorganization each share Common $1 par automatically became (1) share Airborne, Inc. Common $1 par 12/26/2000
Airborne, Inc. merged into ABX Air, Inc. 08/15/2003 which name changed to ABX Holdings, Inc. 12/31/2007 which name changed to Air Transport Services Group, Inc. 05/16/2008

AIRBORNE FLOWER & FREIGHT TRAFFIC, INC. (CA)
Name changed to Airborne Freight Corp. (CA) 04/12/1956
Airborne Freight Corp. (CA) merged into Airborne Freight Corp. (DE) 10/17/1968 which reorganized as Airborne, Inc. 12/26/2000 which merged into ABX Air, Inc. 08/15/2003

AIRBORNE INC (DE)
Merged into ABX Air, Inc. 08/15/2003
Each share Common $1 par exchanged for (1) share Common 1¢ par and $21.25 cash

AIRBORNE INSTRUMENTS LABORATORY, INC. (DE)
Acquired by Cutler-Hammer, Inc. 05/29/1958
Each share Capital Stock exchanged for (1) share Common $10 par
(See Cutler-Hammer, Inc.)

AIRBORNE RECORDS INC (DE)
Recapitalized as Golden Ore Inc. 03/24/1995
Each share Common $0.0001 par exchanged for (0.001) share Common $0.0001 par
Golden Ore Inc. recapitalized as Cybersensor International, Inc. 06/29/2004 which recapitalized as Angel Telecom Corp. 06/06/2007

AIRBORNE SEC & PROT SVCS INC (FL)
Ctfs. dated prior to 09/30/2009
Name changed to Harbor Brewing Co., Inc. and Common $0.001 par changed to $0.0001 par 09/30/2009
Harbor Brewing Co., Inc. name changed to CTGX Mining, Inc. 02/28/2013

AIRBOSS LTD (AUSTRALIA)
Each old Sponsored ADR for Ordinary no par exchanged for (0.05) new Sponsored ADR for Ordinary no par 12/24/1993
ADR agreement terminated 12/23/1997
Each new Sponsored ADR for Ordinary no par exchanged for $0.507 cash

AIRBUS GROUP (NETHERLANDS)
Name changed to Airbus S.E. 04/19/2017

AIRCAL INC (DE)
Reincorporated 03/14/1985
State of incorporation changed from (CA) to (DE) 03/14/1985
Under plan of reorganization each share $1.20 Conv. Exchangeable Preferred $1 par and Common no par automatically became (1) share ACI Holdings Inc. $1.20 Conv. Exchangeable Preferred $1 par and (1) share Common no par respectively 07/15/1986
(See ACI Holdings Inc.)

AIRCAPITOL MANUFACTURERS, INC. (KS)
Charter revoked for failure to file reports and pay fees 09/01/1965

AIRCO INC (DE)
Reincorporated 08/03/1977
State of incorporation changed from (NY) to (DE) 08/03/1977
Merged into BOC Financial Corp. 05/09/1978
Each share Common $1 par exchanged for $50 cash

AIRCOA HOSPITALITY SVCS INC (DE)
Merged into AHS Acquisition Co. 06/17/1991
Each share Common 1¢ par exchanged for $0.55 cash

AIRCOA HOTEL PARTNERS L P (DE)
Merged into Regal-Hotel Management, Inc. 09/29/1997
Each Class A Depositary Unit exchanged for $3.10 cash

AIRCOMB TECHNOLOGY CORP (DE)
Charter cancelled and declared inoperative and void for non-payment of taxes 04/15/1972

AIRCOOLED MOTORS CORP.
Acquired by Republic Aviation Corp. 00/00/1945
Details not available

AIRCRAFT & ARPT SVCS INC (MI)
Acquired by Howell International, Inc. 09/01/1967
Each share Common $1 par exchanged for $5.25 cash

AIRCRAFT & DIESEL EQUIPMENT CORP. (DE)
Bankrupt 00/00/1949
Details not available

AIRCRAFT ACCEP CORP (OH)
Common no par split (3.1) for (1) by

issuance of (2.1) additional shares 06/30/1969
Charter cancelled for failure to pay taxes 08/15/1977

AIRCRAFT ACCESSORIES CORP.
54¢ Preferred called for redemption 07/30/1943
Name changed to Aireon Manufacturing Corp. 12/00/1944
(See Aireon Manufacturing Corp.)

AIRCRAFT ARMAMENTS, INC. (MD)
Name changed to AAI Corp. 06/06/1966
(See AAI Corp.)

AIRCRAFT DEVELOPMENT CORP.
Name changed to Detroit Aircraft Corp. 00/00/1929
(See Detroit Aircraft Corp.)

AIRCRAFT DYNAMICS INTERNATIONAL CORP. (DE)
No longer in existence having become inoperative and void for non-payment of taxes 04/01/1961

AIRCRAFT INCOME PARTNERS L.P. (DE)
Partnership terminated 11/14/2002
Details not available

AIRCRAFT INSTR & DEV INC (KS)
Charter forfeited for failure to file annual reports 07/15/1991

AIRCRAFT MAINTENANCE INTERNATIONAL, INC.
Bankrupt 00/00/1951
Details not available

AIRCRAFT MECHANICS INC (CO)
Name changed to AMI Industries, Inc. 10/15/1975
(See AMI Industries, Inc.)

AIRCRAFT PLYWOOD CO. (WA)
Merged into United States Plywood Corp. 05/06/1937
Details not available

AIRCRAFT PRECISION PRODUCTS, INC.
Each share Common $5 par exchanged for (5) shares Common $1 par 03/00/1940
Acquired by United Aircraft Products, Inc. 08/05/1940
Each share Common $1 par exchanged for (0.33333333) share Common $1 par
(See United Aircraft Products, Inc.)

AIRCRAFT PROTECTIVE PRODUCTS CORP. (DE)
No longer in existence having become inoperative and void for non-payment of taxes 04/01/1945

AIRCRAFT RADIO CORP. (NJ)
Merged into Cessna Aircraft Co. 02/03/1959
Each share Common $1 par exchanged for (0.66666666) share Common $1 par
(See Cessna Aircraft Co.)

AIRCRAFT SERVICE CORP.
Placed in receivership 00/00/1951
Details not available

AIRCRAFT SHARES, INC.
Dissolved 00/00/1931
Details not available

AIRDECK CORP. (LA)
Charter revoked for failure to file annual reports 05/13/1982

AIRE-O-DYNE FILTER CORP. (NY)
Merged into Environmental Filtration Corp. 07/12/1971
Each share Common 5¢ par exchanged for (0.33333333) share Common 5¢ par
(See Environmental Filtration Corp.)

AIRE WRAP SYS INTL INC (UT)
Recapitalized as Homestyle Harmony Inc. 09/16/1996
Each share Common $0.001 par exchanged for (0.1) share Common $0.001 par

Homestyle Harmony Inc. name changed to Catalyst Communications Inc. 12/31/1996 which name changed to DNAPrint Genomics, Inc. 07/07/2000
(See DNAPrint Genomics, Inc.)

AIREDALE FINL CORP (BC)
Completely liquidated 01/23/2004
Each share Common no par exchanged for (0.5) Jet Gold Corp. Unit consisting of (1) share Common no par and (0.5) Common Stock Purchase Warrant expiring 01/23/2005

AIREMAQUE EXPLORERS LTD. (ON)
Charter cancelled 08/00/1972

AIREON MANUFACTURING CORP. (CA)
Reorganized 05/29/1948
No stockholders' equity

AIRESURF NETWORKS HLDGS INC (ON)
Each share Class A Common no par exchanged for (1) share Common no par 11/09/2006
Merged into IsoEnergy Ltd. 10/19/2016
Each share Common no par exchanged for (0.020833) share Common no par

AIRFLEETS, INC. (DE)
Merged into Atlas Corp. 05/31/1956
Each share Common $1 par exchanged for (2.4) shares Common $1 par
(See Atlas Corp.)

AIRGAS INC (DE)
Common 1¢ par split (2) for (1) by issuance of (1) additional share 11/25/1992
Common 1¢ par split (2) for (1) by issuance of (1) additional share 11/24/1993
Common 1¢ par split (2) for (1) by issuance of (1) additional share payable 04/15/1996 to holders of record 04/01/1996
Acquired by Air Liquide 05/23/2016
Each share Common 1¢ par exchanged for $143 cash

AIRGATE PCS INC (DE)
Each share old Common 1¢ par exchanged for (0.2) share new Common 1¢ par 02/17/2004
Merged into Alamosa Holdings, Inc. 04/01/2005
Each share new Common 1¢ par exchanged for (2.012079) shares Common 1¢ par and $10.94671 cash
(See Alamosa Holdings, Inc.)

AIRGEN CORP (AB)
Discharged from receivership 08/01/2000
No stockholders' equity

AIRGUIDE INC (OK)
Name changed to Amerex Group, Inc. 03/01/2007
(See Amerex Group, Inc.)

AIRKEM, INC. (NY)
Name changed to Airwick Industries, Inc. 01/02/1968
(See Airwick Industries, Inc.)

AIRLEASE LTD (CA)
Liquidation completed
Each Depositary Unit received initial distribution of $0.88 cash payable 08/06/2004 to holders of record 07/22/2004 Ex date - 08/09/2004
Each Depositary Unit received second and final distribution of $0.085 cash payable 10/15/2004 to holders of record 09/30/2004 Ex date - 10/18/2004
Note: Certificates were not required to be surrendered and are without value

AIRLIFT INTL INC (FL)
Plan of reorganization under Chapter 11 Federal Bankruptcy proceedings confirmed 01/26/1989
No stockholders' equity

AIRLINE BK (HOUSTON, TX)
Acquired by Texas Commerce Bancshares, Inc. 11/20/1972
Each share Capital Stock $5 par exchanged for (0.7143) share Common $4 par
Texas Commerce Bancshares, Inc. acquired by Chemical New York Corp. 05/01/1987 which name changed to Chemical Banking Corp. 04/29/1988 which name changed to Chase Manhattan Corp. (New) 03/31/1996 which name changed to J.P. Morgan Chase & Co. 12/31/2000 which name changed to JPMorgan Chase & Co. 07/20/2004

AIRLINE FOODS CORP. (DE)
Name changed to Old Judge Foods Corp. 10/00/1953
Old Judge Foods Corp. merged into Williams (R.C.) & Co., Inc. 12/09/1957
(See Williams (R.C.) & Co., Inc.)

AIRLINE NATL BK (HOUSTON, TX)
Name changed to Airline Bank (Houston, TX) and Capital Stock $10 par changed to $5 par 08/21/1969
Airline Bank (Houston, TX) acquired by Texas Commerce Bancshares, Inc. 11/20/1972 which was acquired by Chemical New York Corp. 05/01/1987 which name changed to Chemical Banking Corp. 04/29/1988 which name changed to Chase Manhattan Corp. (New) 03/31/1996 which name changed to J.P. Morgan Chase & Co. 12/31/2000 which changed to JPMorgan Chase & Co. 07/20/2004

AIRLINE SOFTWARE INC (NV)
Recapitalized as Mining Corp. 11/03/1992
Each share Common $0.001 par exchanged for (0.2) share Common $0.005 par
Mining Corp. name changed to Latin American Resources, Inc. 10/14/1993

AIRLINE TRAINING INTL LTD (AB)
Filed notice of intention under Bankruptcy and Insolvency Act 06/30/2003
Stockholders' equity unlikely

AIRLINE VIRGIN ISLANDS INC (TX)
Reincorporated 09/00/1993
Name and place of incorporation changed from Airline of the Virgin Islands, Ltd. (Virgin Islands) to Airline of the Virgin Islands, Inc. (TX) 09/00/1993
Recapitalized as Colorado Casino Resorts, Inc. 03/01/1994
Each share Common $0.001 par exchanged for (0.5) share Common $0.001 par
(See Colorado Casino Resorts, Inc.)

AIRMAC CORP (MN)
Merged into Apache Corp. 03/03/1969
Each share Common $1 par exchanged for (0.222222) share Common $1.25 par

AIRMOTIVE MACHINING & ENGINEERING CORP. (MN)
Name changed to Airmac Corp. 02/15/1967
Airmac Corp. merged into Apache Corp. 03/03/1969

AIRNADO INC (NY)
Charter cancelled and proclaimed dissolved for failure to pay taxes 10/28/2009

AIRNET COMMUNICATIONS CORP (DE)
Each share old Common $0.001 par exchanged for (0.1) share new Common $0.001 par 12/09/2004
Plan of reorganization under Chapter 11 Federal Bankruptcy proceedings effective 10/13/2006
No stockholders' equity

AIRNET SYS INC (OH)
Merged into AirNet Holdings, Inc. 06/10/2008
Each share Common 1¢ par exchanged for $2.81 cash

AIRNET WIRELESS INC (DE)
Name changed to AIT Wireless, Inc. 12/30/2003
AIT Wireless, Inc. name changed to Petroleum Communication Holdings, Inc. 12/22/2005

AIRNORTH MINES LTD (ON)
Voluntarily dissolved 11/02/1976
No stockholders' equity

AIROLITE CO (OH)
Stock Dividends - 100% 03/01/1956; 100% 03/01/1961; 100% 03/01/1966; 100% 09/15/1980
Acquired by Greenheck Fan Corp. 00/00/2004
Details not available

AIRONET WIRELESS COMMUNICATION INC (DE)
Merged into Cisco Systems, Inc. 03/15/2000
Each share Common 1¢ par exchanged for (0.637) share Common no par

AIRPARTS & TOOL CORP. (MI)
Acquired by Ex-Cell-O Aircraft & Tool Co. 00/00/1930
Details not available

AIRPAX ELECTRS INC (MD)
Class A $1 par and Class B $1 par reclassified as Common $1 par 04/07/1960
Stock Dividend - 10% 06/15/1972
Merged into North American Philips Corp. 05/14/1976
Each share Common $1 par exchanged for (0.444444) share Common $5 par
(See North American Philips Corp.)

AIRPLANE & MARINE DIRECTION FINDER, INC. (DE)
Reorganized as Airplane & Marine Direction Finder Corp. 08/00/1937
Each share Preferred exchanged for (10) shares Common $1 par
Each share Common exchanged for (0.58383333) share Common $1 par
Airplane & Marine Direction Finder Corp. name changed to Airplane & Marine Instruments, Inc. 00/00/1942 which merged into Dumont-Airplane & Marine Instruments, Inc. 04/06/1953
(See Dumont-Airplane & Marine Instruments, Inc.)

AIRPLANE & MARINE DIRECTION FINDER CORP. (DE)
Name changed to Airplane & Marine Instruments, Inc. 00/00/1942
Airplane & Marine Instruments, Inc. merged into Dumont-Airplane & Marine Instruments, Inc. 04/06/1953
(See Dumont-Airplane & Marine Instruments, Inc.)

AIRPLANE & MARINE INSTRUMENTS, INC. (NY)
Stock Dividend - 50% 12/01/1943
Merged into Dumont-Airplane & Marine Instruments, Inc. 04/06/1953
Each share Capital Stock $1 par exchanged for (1) share Common $1 par
(See Dumont-Airplane & Marine Instruments, Inc.)

AIRPLANE MANUFACTURING & SUPPLY CORP. (CA)
Name changed to Pacific Airmotive Corp. 03/24/1945
Pacific Airmotive Corp. acquired by Purex Corp., Ltd. 09/15/1967 which name changed to Purex Corp. (CA) 11/05/1973 which reincorporated in

Delaware as Purex Industries, Inc. 10/31/1978
(See Purex Industries, Inc.)

AIRPORT PARKING CO. OF AMERICA (DE)
Class A Common no par split (2) for (1) by issuance of (1) additional share 06/30/1961
Stock Dividend - 25% 12/29/1961
Acquired by ITT Consumer Services Corp. 11/14/1966
Each share Class A Common no par exchanged for (0.285) share Conv. Preferred Ser. A $1 par
Each share Class B Common no par exchanged for (0.285) share 2nd Preferred Ser. B $1 par
(See ITT Consumer Services Corp.)

AIRPORT SVCS INC (DE)
Name changed to Electric Car Co. of America, Inc. 02/20/1980
(See Electric Car Co. of America, Inc.)

AIRPORT SYS INTL INC (KS)
Name changed to Elecsys Corp. 11/01/2000
(See Elecsys Corp.)

AIRPRO INDS INC (BC)
Recapitalized as Camelot Industries Inc. 05/08/1995
Each share Common no par exchanged for (0.21276595) share Common no par
Camelot Industries Inc. merged into DC Diagnosticare, Inc. 07/15/1996
(See DC Diagnosticare, Inc.)

AIRPROTEK INTL INC (NV)
Each share old Common $0.001 par exchanged for (0.33333333) share new Common $0.001 par 10/17/2006
Reorganized under the laws of Wyoming as Rafarma Pharmaceuticals, Inc. 11/20/2012
Each share new Common $0.001 par exchanged for (0.1) share Common $0.001 par

AIRROVER WI-FI CORP (DE)
Common $0.001 par split (4) for (1) by issuance of (3) additional shares payable 09/08/2004 to holders of record 09/07/2004 Ex date - 09/09/2004
Name changed to Diamond I, Inc. 01/28/2005
Diamond I, Inc. recapitalized as ubroadcast, inc. 02/09/2009 which name changed to Santeon Group Inc. 06/11/2010

AIRSCOOTER CORP (NV)
Recapitalized as Tatyana Designs, Inc. 08/13/2012
Each share Common $0.001 par exchanged for (0.06666666) share Common $0.001 par

AIRSHIP INDS LTD (ENGLAND)
Placed in receivership 09/00/1990
ADR holders' equity unlikely

AIRSHIP INTL LTD (NY)
Each share 8% Conv. Class A Preferred 1¢ par exchanged for (3) shares Common 1¢ par 06/10/1998
Name changed to Entertainment International, Ltd. 10/06/1998
Entertainment International, Ltd. name changed to Clean Systems Technology Group, Ltd. 12/27/2001
(See Clean Systems Technology Group, Ltd.)

AIRSPAN NETWORKS INC (WA)
Each share old Common $0.0003 par exchanged for (0.06666666) share new Common $0.0003 par 09/18/2009
Reorganized under the laws of Delaware 08/19/2010
Each share new Common $0.0003 par exchanged for (0.05) share Common $0.0003 par

AIRSPRAY NV (NETHERLANDS)
Acquired by Rexam PLC 05/23/2007
Each Sponsored ADR for Ordinary exchanged for $36.30287 cash

AIRSTAR TECHNOLOGIES INC (NV)
SEC revoked common stock registration 03/14/2007

AIRSTOCKS, INC.
Liquidation completed 00/00/1930
Details not available

AIRSTREAM, INC. (DE)
Completely liquidated 12/01/1967
Each share Common $1 par exchanged for first and final distribution of (0.458333) share Beatrice Foods Co. Common no par
Beatrice Foods Co. name changed to Beatrice Companies, Inc. 06/05/1984
(See Beatrice Companies, Inc.)

AIRTECH INTL GROUP INC (WY)
Each share Common 1¢ par exchanged for (0.2) share Common 5¢ par 11/09/1998
Each share Common 5¢ par received distribution of (0.1) share Humitech Inc. Common $0.001 par payable 11/15/2001 to holders of record 10/31/2001
SEC revoked common stock registration 03/11/2008

AIRTECHNOLOGY CORP. (DE)
Name changed to Columbia Scientific Corp. and Common no par changed to 1¢ par 12/31/1968
(See Columbia Scientific Corp.)

AIRTEK DYNAMICS, INC. (CA)
Name changed to Ketria, Inc. (CA) 07/24/1967
Ketria, Inc. (CA) reincorporated in Florida 06/25/1969 which name changed to United Resources, Inc. 12/08/1969
(See United Resources, Inc.)

AIRTH MINING CO. LTD. (AB)
Charter cancelled 03/31/1977

AIRTIMEDSL (NV)
Common $0.001 par split (5) for (2) by issuance of (1.5) additional shares payable 04/03/2009 to holders of record 04/01/2009 Ex date - 04/06/2009
Name changed to Clear-Lite Holdings, Inc. 07/06/2009
(See Clear-Lite Holdings, Inc.)

AIRTOUCH COMMUNICATIONS INC (DE)
Reincorporated 12/21/1994
Reincorporated from AirTouch Communications (CA) to AirTouch Communications, Inc. (DE) 12/12/1994
Merged into Vodafone Airtouch PLC 06/30/1999
Each share 6% Conv. Preferred Class B 1¢ par exchanged for (0.403) Sponsored ADR 5p par and $7.25 cash
Each share Common 1¢ par exchanged for (0.5) Sponsored ADR 5p par and $9 cash
4.25% Conv. Preferred Class C called for redemption 09/27/1999
Vodafone Airtouch PLC name changed to Vodafone Group PLC (New) 06/28/2000

AIRTRAN CORP (MN)
Common 1¢ par split (2) for (1) by issuance of (1) additional share 05/06/1992
Name changed to Mesaba Holdings, Inc. 08/29/1995
Mesaba Holdings, Inc. name changed to MAIR Holdings Inc. 08/25/2003

AIRTRAN HLDGS INC (DE)
Merged into Southwest Airlines Co. 05/02/2011
Each share Common $0.001 par exchanged for (0.321) share Common $1 par and $3.75 cash

AIRTRONICS INTL CORP FLA (FL)
Each share old Common 10¢ par exchanged for (0.1) share new Common 10¢ par 05/24/1966
Dissolved for failure to file annual reports 02/13/1989

AIRVANA INC (DE)
Acquired by 72 Mobile Holdings, LLC 04/09/2010
Each share Common $0.001 par exchanged for $7.65 cash

AIRWARE LABS CORP (DE)
Name changed to Item 9 Labs Corp. 04/27/2018

AIRWAVE COMMUNICATIONS CORP AMER (DE)
Charter cancelled and declared inoperative and void for non-payment of taxes 03/01/1987

AIRWAYS CORP (DE)
Merged into AirTran Holdings Inc. 11/18/1997
Each share Common 1¢ par exchanged for (1) share Common 1¢ par
AirTran Holdings Inc. merged into Southwest Airlines Co. 05/02/2011

AIRWAYS ENTERPRISES INC (DE)
Charter cancelled and declared inoperative and void for non-payment of taxes 03/01/1976

AIRWICK INDS INC (NY)
Class A Common 10¢ par and Class B Common 10¢ par changed to 5¢ par and (1) additional share issued respectively 05/15/1968
Class A Common 5¢ par and Class B Common 5¢ par split (3) for (2) by issuance of (0.5) additional share respectively 05/15/1972
Class A Common 5¢ par and Class B Common 5¢ par reclassified as Common 5¢ par 02/05/1973
Common 5¢ par split (2) for (1) by issuance of (1) additional share 02/15/1973
Merged into Ciba-Geigy Corp. 09/05/1974
Each share Common 5¢ par exchanged for $12.50 cash

AIRWORK CORP (DE)
Completely liquidated 06/20/1968
Each share Common $1 par exchanged for first and final distribution of (0.3) share Purex Corp., Ltd. Common $1 par
Purex Corp., Ltd. name changed to Purex Corp. (CA) 11/05/1973 which reincorporated in Delaware as Purex Industries, Inc. 10/31/1978
(See Purex Industries, Inc.)

AIRWORKS MEDIA INC (AB)
Name changed 06/28/1996
Name changed from Airworks Media Services Ltd. to AirWorks Media Inc. 06/28/1996
Cease trade order effective 06/24/1999

AISI RESH CORP (BC)
Struck off register and declared dissolved for failure to file returns 01/15/1993

AISYSTEMS INC (NV)
SEC revoked common stock registration 10/27/2014

AIT ADVANCED INFORMATION TECHNOLOGY CORP (CANADA)
Acquired by 3M Canada Co. 07/19/2002
Each share Common no par exchanged for $2.88 cash

AIT WIRELESS INC (DE)
Name changed to Petroleum Communication Holdings, Inc. 12/22/2005

AITCHISON CAP CORP (BC)
Name changed to TransGlobe Internet & Telecom Co., Ltd. 06/19/2002
(See Transglobe Internet & Telecom Co., Ltd.)

AITEC CAP CORP (AB)
Recapitalized as Infiniti Resources International Ltd. 03/24/2000
Each share Common no par exchanged for (0.33333333) share Common no par
Infiniti Resources International Ltd. acquired by Welton Energy Corp. (New) 08/04/2005 which merged into Churchill Energy Inc. 02/13/2009 which merged into Zargon Energy Trust 09/23/2009 which reorganized as Zargon Oil & Gas Ltd. (New) 01/07/2011

AITEC DEV CORP (BC)
Name changed to Frozya Industries Inc. 10/13/1988
Frozya Industries Inc. name changed to Canex Resources Corp. 08/31/1994
(See Canex Resources Corp.)

AIXTRON SE (GERMANY)
Name changed 12/22/2010
Name changed from Aixtron AG to Aixtron S.E. 12/22/2010
ADR agreement terminated 02/16/2017
Each Sponsored ADR for Ordinary exchanged for $6.620274 cash

AJ GREENTECH HLDGS LTD (NV)
Each share old Common $0.001 par exchanged for (0.00066666) share new Common $0.001 par 06/30/2015
Name changed to Sino United Worldwide Consolidated Ltd. 07/17/2017

AJ PERRON GOLD CORP (ON)
Struck off register and declared dissolved for failure to file reports 03/27/2000

AJA MERCHANT BKG CORP (MN)
Name changed to Image-Photo Systems Inc. 12/09/1998
Image-Photo Systems Inc. name changed to e-bidd.com, Inc. 09/08/1999 which name changed to xraymedia.com, Inc. 06/28/2000 which name changed to Xraymedia, Inc. 12/04/2003 which recapitalized as T.W. Christian, Inc. 08/14/2007
(See T.W. Christian, Inc.)

AJAX, INC.
Liquidated 00/00/1943
Details not available

AJAX FIRE INSURANCE CO. (NJ)
Acquired by Sussex Fire Insurance Co. 00/00/1931
Details not available

AJAX MAGNETHERMIC CORP (OH)
Stock Dividend - 10% 05/25/1964
Merged into Guthrie Delaware, Inc. 09/30/1975
Each share Common no par exchanged for $50 cash

AJAX MERCURY MINES LTD (BC)
Name changed to Ajax Resources Ltd. 07/21/1971
Each share Common no par exchanged for (1) share Common no par
Ajax Resources Ltd. name changed to Pan-Ajax Resources Ltd. 07/09/1973 which recapitalized as Aleta Resource Industries Ltd. 10/10/1974 which name changed to Mandarin Capital Corp. 09/12/1984 which reorganized as H.I.S.A. Investments Ltd. 12/29/1989
(See H.I.S.A. Investments Ltd.)

AJAX MINERALS LTD (ON)
Capital Stock $1 par changed to no par 07/20/1972

AJA-AKR

AJAX OIL & GAS CO., LTD.
Charter cancelled for failure to pay taxes and file returns 02/14/1978
Liquidation completed 08/13/1946
Each share Common no par received first and final distribution of $2.2395 cash

AJAX OIL CO.
Placed in receivership and assets sold 04/03/1926
No stockholders equity

AJAX PETROLEUMS LTD. (ON)
Capital Stock no par changed to 50¢ par 00/00/1952
Recapitalized as Canadian Industrial Gas Ltd. 06/02/1960
Each share Capital Stock 50¢ par exchanged for (0.2) share Capital Stock $2.50 par
Canadian Industrial Gas Ltd. merged into Canadian Industrial Gas & Oil Ltd. 05/31/1965 which merged into Norcen Energy Resources Ltd. (ALTA) 10/28/1975 which reincorporated in Canada 04/15/1977 which merged into Union Pacific Resources Group Inc. 04/17/1998 which merged into Anadarko Petroleum Corp. 07/14/2000

AJAX REINS LTD (DE)
Recapitalized as Nathaniel Energy Corp. (Old) 12/11/1998
Each share Common $0.001 par exchanged for (0.1) share Common $0.001 par
Nathaniel Energy Corp. (Old) reorganized as Nathaniel Energy Corp. (New) 12/00/1998 which name changed to Vista International Technologies, Inc. 12/20/2007

AJAX RES CORP (NV)
Name changed to U.S. Water Co., Inc. 04/25/1977
U.S. Water Co., Inc. name changed to Ajax Resources, Inc. 07/02/1979 which name changed to Min-Tex Energy, Corp. 07/30/1981
(See Min-Tex Energy, Corp.)

AJAX RES INC (NV)
Common $2.50 par changed to 1¢ par 12/31/1979
Common 1¢ par changed to $0.001 par 03/25/1981
Name changed to Min-Tex Energy, Corp. 07/30/1981
(See Min-Tex Energy, Corp.)

AJAX RES LTD (BC)
Ctfs. dated prior to 07/09/1973
Name changed to Pan-Ajax Resources Ltd. 07/09/1973
Pan-Ajax Resources Ltd. recapitalized as Aleta Resource Industries Ltd. 10/10/1974 which name changed to Mandarin Capital Corp. 09/12/1984 which reorganized as H.I.S.A. Investments Ltd. 12/29/1989
(See H.I.S.A. Investments Ltd.)

AJAX RES LTD (BC)
Ctfs. dated after 08/05/1980
Struck off register and declared dissolved for failure to file returns 10/22/1993

AJAX RUBBER CO., INC.
Out of business 00/00/1935
Details not available

AJAX TUNGSTEN & MOLYBDENITE MINES LTD.
Acquired by Buckhorn Mines Ltd. share for share 00/00/1942
(See Buckhorn Mines Ltd.)

AJAX TUNGSTEN CORP. (NV)
Recapitalized as Ajax Resources Corp. 12/01/1967
Each share Common 25¢ par exchanged for (0.1) share Common $2.50 par
Ajax Resources Corp. name changed to U.S. Water Co., Inc. 04/25/1977 which name changed to Ajax Resources, Inc. 07/02/1979 which name changed to Min-Tex, Energy, Corp. 07/30/1981
(See Min-Tex Energy, Corp.)

AJAX URANIUM CORP. (WY)
Charter revoked for failure to file reports and pay fees 03/21/1962

AJAY ENTERPRISES CORP (WI)
Completely liquidated 01/12/1972
Each share Common 10¢ par exchanged for first and final distribution of (0.34) share Fuqua Industries, Inc. Common $1 par
Fuqua Industries, Inc. name changed to Actava Group Inc. 07/21/1993 which name changed to Metromedia International Group, Inc. 11/01/1995
(See Metromedia International Group, Inc.)

AJAY RES INC (BC)
Delisted from Vancouver Stock Exchange 11/06/1987

AJAY SPORTS INC (DE)
Each share old Common 1¢ par exchanged for (0.16666666) share new Common 1¢ par 08/14/1998
Chapter 11 bankruptcy proceedings converted to Chapter 7 on 10/18/2007
Stockholders' equity unlikely

AJL PEPS TR (NY)
Each Premium Exchangeable Participating Share no par exchanged for an undetermined amount of Amway Japan Ltd. Common no par or Sponsored ADR's for Common no par 02/15/1999
(See Amway Japan Ltd.)

AJP ENTERPRISES INC (WA)
Name changed to Hartz Restaurants, Inc. (WA) 07/05/1989
Hartz Restaurants, Inc. (WA) reincorporated in Delaware 04/13/1989 which name changed to Hartz Restaurants International Inc. 02/16/1996

AJS BANCORP INC (USA)
Reorganized under the laws of Maryland 10/10/2013
Each share Common 1¢ par exchanged for (1.146) shares Common 1¢ par

AK STL HLDG CORP (DE)
7% Appreciation Income Linked Securities Conv. Preferred 1¢ par called for redemption 10/16/1997
$3.625 Conv. Preferred Ser. B called for redemption at $50.3625 on 09/30/2002
(Additional Information in Active)

AKA VENTURES INC (BC)
Name changed to Phoenix Copper Corp. 09/07/2012
Phoenix Copper Corp. recapitalized as Phoenix Metals Corp. 12/04/2013 which name changed to Envirotek Remediation Inc. 04/27/2018

AKADEMIA ENTERPRISES INC (AB)
Struck off register for failure to file annual returns 11/01/1997

AKAI ELEC LTD (JAPAN)
ADR agreement terminated 00/00/1995
Details not available

AKAI HLDGS LTD (HONG KONG)
ADR agreement terminated 03/20/2003
Each Sponsored ADR for Ordinary exchanged for $0.0011 cash

AKAICHO YELLOWKNIFE GOLD MINES LTD. (ON)
Name changed to Akaitcho Yellowknife Gold Mines Ltd. 05/04/1945
Akaitcho Yellowknife Gold Mines Ltd. merged into Royal Oak Mines Inc. 07/23/1991 which recapitalized as Royal Oak Ventures Inc. 02/14/2000
(See Royal Oak Ventures Inc.)

AKAITCHO YELLOWKNIFE GOLD MINES LTD (ON)
Capital Stock $1 par reclassified as Common no par 07/29/1983
Merged into Royal Oak Mines Inc. 07/23/1991
Each share Common no par exchanged for (0.6) share Common no par
Royal Oak Mines Inc. recapitalized as Royal Oak Ventures Inc. 02/14/2000
(See Royal Oak Ventures Inc.)

AKASH VENTURES INC (BC)
Recapitalized as International Akash Ventures Inc. 12/08/1999
Each share Common no par exchanged for (0.33333333) share Common no par
International Akash Ventures Inc. name changed to Healthscreen Solutions Inc. 01/18/2001
(See Healthscreen Solutions Inc.)

AKBAR GOLD MINES, LTD. (ON)
Charter reported cancelled 00/00/1951

AKEENA SOLAR INC (DE)
Recapitalized as Westinghouse Solar, Inc. 04/14/2011
Each share Common $0.001 par exchanged for (0.25) share Common $0.001 par
Westinghouse Solar, Inc. name changed to Andalay Solar, Inc. 09/27/2013

AKELA PHARMA INC (CANADA)
Each share old Common no par exchanged for (0.14285714) share new Common no par 10/10/2007
Assets foreclosed upon and operations ceased 03/09/2013
No stockholders' equity

AKER KVAERNER A S A (NORWAY)
Name changed to Kvaerner A.S.A. (New) 04/14/2004
(See Kvaerner A.S.A. (New))

AKER SOLUTIONS ASA (NORWAY)
Name changed to Akastor A.S.A. 09/29/2014

AKER YDS ASA (NORWAY)
Name changed to STX Europe ASA 11/18/2008
(See STX Europe ASA)

AKERS MED TECHNOLOGY LTD (CANADA)
Recapitalized as Digital Fusion Multimedia Corp. 10/26/1994
Each share Common no par exchanged for (0.2) share Common no par
(See Digital Fusion Multimedia Corp.)

AKESIS PHARMACEUTICALS INC (NV)
Filed a petition under Chapter 7 Federal Bankruptcy Code 01/30/2009
No stockholders' equity

AKF FOODS INC (DE)
Plan of liquidation under Chapter 11 Federal Bankruptcy proceedings confirmed 09/19/1985
No stockholders' equity

AKID CORP (CO)
Reincorporated under the laws of Nevada as Mazal Plant Pharmaceuticals, Inc. 11/21/2005
(See Mazal Plant Pharmaceuticals, Inc.)

AKIKO GOLD RES LTD (BC)
Reincorporated under the laws of Yukon as Prospex Mining Inc. 07/30/1997
Prospex Mining Inc. merged into Semafo Inc. 06/30/1999

AKIKO LORI GOLD RES LTD (BC)
Merged into Akiko Gold Resources Ltd. (BC) 11/09/1992
Each share Common no par exchanged for (1) share Common no par
Akiko Gold Resources Ltd. (BC) reincorporated in Yukon as Prospex Mining Inc. 07/30/1997 which merged into Semafo Inc. 06/30/1999

AKIRA CORP (FL)
Proclaimed dissolved for failure to file reports and pay fees 10/01/2004

AKIYAMA FINL CORP (CO)
Name changed to United States Exploration Inc. 06/07/1990
(See United States Exploration Inc.)

AKOUSTIS TECHNOLOGIES INC (NV)
Reincorporated under the laws of Delaware 12/16/2016

AKRIKHIN JSC (RUSSIA)
Name changed 11/27/2015
Name changed from Akrikhin Pharmaceuticals OAO to Akrikhin JSC 11/27/2015
GDR agreement terminated 05/07/2018
Each 144A GDR for Preference exchanged for (0.01) share Preference
Each 144A GDR for Ordinary exchanged for (0.01) share Ordinary
Each Reg. S GDR for Preference exchanged for (0.01) share Preference
Each Reg. S GDR for Ordinary exchanged for (0.01) share Ordinary
Note: Unexchanged GDR's will be sold and the proceeds, if any, held for claim after 05/10/2018

AKROKERI-ASHANTI GOLD MINES INC (CANADA)
Ceased operations 05/14/2004
No stockholders' equity

AKRON, CANTON & YOUNGSTOWN RAILWAY CO. (OH)
Reorganized as Akron, Canton & Youngstown Railroad Co. 1/27/44
Each share Capital Stock $100 par exchanged for (1) Class B conditional warrant
(See Akron, Canton & Youngstown Railroad Co.)

AKRON BRASS MANUFACTURING CO. INC. (OH)
Each share Common no par exchanged for (2) shares Common 50¢ par 00/00/1940
Stock Dividends - 10% 12/20/1957; 100% 01/05/1959; 50% 01/10/1962
Merged into Premier Industrial Corp. 05/21/1962
Each share Common 50¢ par exchanged for (0.76923076) share Common $1 par
Premier Industrial Corp. merged into Farnell Electronics PLC 04/11/1996 which name changed to Premier Farnell PLC 04/11/1996
(See Premier Farnell PLC)

AKRON CANTON & YOUNGSTOWN RR CO (OH)
Each share Common $100 par exchanged for (5) shares Common no par 00/00/1954
Acquired by Norfolk & Western Railway Co. 10/16/1964
Each share Common no par exchanged for $53.164 cash

AKRON-DIME BANK (AKRON, OH)
Stock Dividend - 50% 06/21/1965
Name changed to Akron National Bank & Trust Co. (Akron, OH) and Capital Stock $10 par changed to Common $10 par 12/01/1966
(See Akron National Bank (Akron, OH))

AKRON GUARANTEED MTGE. CO.
Liquidation completed 00/00/1944
Details not available

AKRON NATL BK & TR CO (AKRON, OH)
Stock Dividend - 10% 03/26/1969
Name changed to Akron National Bank (Akron, OH) 02/01/1977
(See Akron National Bank (Akron, OH))

AKRON NATIONAL BANK (AKRON, OH)
Through voluntary exchange offer BancOhio Corp. held 99.73% as of 01/00/1977
Public interest eliminated

AKRON PURE MILK CO.
Acquired by National Dairy Products Corp. 00/00/1929
Details not available

AKRON RUBBER RECLAIMING CO.
Acquired by Midwest Rubber Reclaiming Co. 00/00/1937
Details not available

AKRON STANDARD MOLD CO. (OH)
Merged into Eagle-Picher Co. 07/13/1964
Each share Common $8 par exchanged for (1) share $1.40 Conv. Preference Ser. A no par
Eagle-Picher Co. name changed to Eagle-Picher Industries, Inc. 04/01/1966
(See Eagle-Picher Industries, Inc.)

AKRON STEAM HEATING CO.
Merged into Ohio Edison Co. 07/05/1930
Details not available

AKSARBEN, INC. (UT)
Name changed to Northern Sun Holdings, Inc. 02/04/1983
(See Northern Sun Holdings, Inc.)

AKSYS LTD (DE)
Preferred Stock Purchase Rights declared for Common stockholders of record 11/08/1996 were redeemed at $0.01 per right 06/06/2006 for holders of record 05/23/2006
Authorized an assignment for the benefit of creditors 03/28/2007
No stockholders' equity

AKTECH INC (NV)
Each share old Common $0.001 par exchanged for (0.05) share new Common $0.001 par 08/14/1991
Name changed to Oilex International Investments, Inc. 01/23/1992
Oilex International Investments, Inc. name changed to Oilex, Inc. 07/08/1996
(See Oilex, Inc.)

AKZO N V (NETHERLANDS)
Each old ADR for American Shares exchanged for (1) new Unsponsored ADR for American Shares 08/06/1985
Each new Unsponsored ADR for American Shares exchanged for (2) Sponsored ADR's for American Shares 02/06/1989
Basis changed from (1:1) to (1:0.5) 02/06/1989
Name changed to AKZO Nobel N.V. 02/25/1994

AKZONA INC (DE)
Merged into Akzo N.V. 09/13/1982
Each share Common $1.25 par exchanged for $16.25 cash

AL-AHRAM BEVERAGE CO S A E (EGYPT)
144A GDR's for Ordinary split (2) for (1) by issuance of (1) additional GDR payable 11/18/1999 to holders of record 11/17/1999
ADR agreement terminated 02/07/2003
Each 144A GDR for Ordinary exchanged for $13.92 cash
Each Reg. S GDR for Ordinary exchanged for $13.92 cash

AL EZZ STL REBARS S A E (EGYPT)
Name changed to Ezz Steel Co. JSC 03/23/2011

AL-FASSI ALI CONSORTIUM INC (VA)
Recapitalized as Consolidated American Industries, Inc. (VA) 10/05/1983
Each share Common $0.0001 par exchanged for (0.2) share Common $0.005 par
(See Consolidated American Industries, Inc.)

AL INTL INC (DE)
Name changed to Youngevity International, Inc. 07/23/2013

AL-KEM MINES, INC. (NV)
Charter revoked for failure to file reports and pay fees 03/06/1961

AL NOOR HOSPS GROUP PLC (UNITED KINGDOM)
Name changed to Mediclinic International PLC 04/01/2016

AL-ZAR LTD (FL)
Completely liquidated
Each Unit of Ltd. Partnership received first and final distribution of $64 cash payable 06/17/2002 to holders of record 06/06/2002 Ex date - 07/24/2002
Note: Certificates were not required to be surrendered and are without value

ALA MOANA HAWAII PTTYS (HI)
Liquidation completed
Each Depositary Receipt received initial distribution of $1.50 cash 02/13/1986
Each Depositary Receipt received second and final distribution of $0.53 cash 05/11/1988
Note: Certificates were not required to be surrendered and are without value

ALABAMA & NORTHWESTERN R. R.
Operations discontinued 00/00/1934
Details not available

ALABAMA & VICKSBURG RY (MS)
Merged into Illinois Central Railroad Co. 05/29/1959
Each share Capital Stock $100 par exchanged for (3.032) shares Common no par
Illinois Central Railroad Co. merged into Illinois Central Industries, Inc. 08/10/1972 which name changed to IC Industries, Inc. 05/21/1975 which name changed to Whitman Corp. (Old) 12/01/1988 which name changed to Whitman Corp. (New) 11/30/2000 which name changed to PepsiAmericas, Inc. (DE) 01/24/2001 which merged into PepsiCo, Inc. 02/26/2010

ALABAMA & WESTERN FLORIDA RAILROAD CO.
Road abandoned 00/00/1939
Details not available

ALABAMA AIRCRAFT INDS INC (DE)
Chapter 11 bankruptcy proceedings converted to Chapter 7 on 11/03/2011
Stockholders' equity unlikely

ALABAMA ASPHALTIC LIMESTONE CO. (AL)
Liquidation completed
Each share Capital Stock no par exchanged for initial distribution of (0.142857) share Southern Industries Corp. Common no par, $4.5396 principal amount of 7% Income Debentures due 11/01/1982 and $2.15 cash 07/17/1967
Each share Capital Stock no par received second and final distribution of $0.73 cash 12/19/1967
Southern Industries Corp. merged into Dravo Corp. 06/01/1979
(See Dravo Corp.)

ALABAMA BANCORPORATION (DE)
Stock Dividend - 25% 09/08/1978
Name changed to AmSouth Bancorporation 04/20/1981
AmSouth Bancorporation merged into Regions Financial Corp. 11/04/2006

ALABAMA BY PRODS CORP (DE)
Each share 6% Preferred no par exchanged for (1) share $4 Prior Preferred $100 par and (3) shares old Class B Common no par 00/00/1949
Each share Common no par exchanged for (1) share old Common Class A Common no 00/00/1949
$4 Prior Preferred $100 par called for redemption 01/01/1964
Each share old Class A Common no par exchanged for (10) shares new Class A Common no par 04/22/1970
Each share old Class B Common no par exchanged for (10) shares new Class B Common no par 04/22/1970
Merged into Drummond Holding Corp. 08/13/1985
Each share new Class A Common no par exchanged for $75.60 cash
Each share new Class B Common no par exchanged for $75.60 cash

ALABAMA-CALIFORNIA GOLD MINES CO. (WA)
Merged into International Oil & Metals 02/28/1956
Each share Common 10¢ par exchanged for (0.1) share Common $1 par
International Oil & Metals liquidated for Perfect Photo, Inc. 03/24/1965 which was acquired by United Whelan Corp. 06/30/1966 which name changed to Perfect Film & Chemical Corp. 05/31/1967 which name changed to Cadence Industries Corp. 10/22/1970
(See Cadence Industries Corp.)

ALABAMA CASH CREDIT CORP.
Merged into Franklin Plan Corp. 00/00/1932
Details not available

ALABAMA DRY DOCK & SHIPBUILDING CO (AL)
Each share Common $100 par exchanged for (3) shares Common no par and (1) share Preferred $100 par 00/00/1931
Each share old Common no par exchanged for (4) shares new Common no par 00/00/1936
Common no par split (3) for (1) by issuance of (2) additional shares 11/23/1977
7% 1st Preferred $100 par called for redemption 08/31/1977
Stock Dividends - 10% 06/27/1941; 10% 06/30/1948; 50% 01/03/1951; 10% 01/30/1958; 10% 08/15/1974; 10% 08/22/1975; 20% 01/14/1977; 10% 08/16/1977
Name changed to Addsco Industries, Inc. 01/01/1983
(See Addsco Industries, Inc.)

ALABAMA FED SVGS & LN ASSN BIRMINGHAM (AL)
Common 1¢ par split (3) for (2) by issuance of (0.5) additional share 06/05/1987
Common 1¢ par split (3) for (2) by issuance of (0.5) additional share 06/06/1988
Name changed to Secor Bank, Federal Savings Bank (Birmingham, AL) 09/12/1988
Secor Bank, Federal Savings Bank (Birmingham, AL) merged into First Alabama Bancshares, Inc. 12/31/1993 which name changed to Regions Financial Corp. (Old)
05/02/1994 which merged into Regions Financial Corp. (New) 07/01/2004

ALABAMA FINL GROUP INC (DE)
Common $10 par changed to $5 par and (1) additional share issued 03/02/1973
Name changed to Southern Bancorporation 04/17/1974
Southern Bancorporation name changed to Southern Bancorporation of Alabama 04/21/1975 which name changed to SouthTrust Corp. 09/18/1981 which merged into Wachovia Corp. (Ctfs. dated after 09/01/2001) 11/01/2004 which merged into Wells Fargo & Co. (New) 12/31/2008

ALABAMA FUEL & IRON CO. (AL)
Each share Capital Stock $100 par exchanged for (5) shares Capital Stock $20 par 00/00/1936
Capital Stock $20 par changed to $10 par and a liquidating dividend of $10 per share paid 00/00/1951
Liquidation completed 00/00/1953
Details not available

ALABAMA GAS CORP (AL)
$3.50 Prior Preferred $50 par called for redemption 12/30/1958
$5.50 Preferred Ser. A $100 par called for redemption 09/01/1965
Common $2 par changed to $1 par and (1) additional share issued 02/08/1968
Name changed to Alagasco Inc. 01/18/1979
Alagasco Inc. name changed to Energen Corp. 10/01/1985

ALABAMA GRAPHITE CORP (BC)
Merged into Westwater Resources, Inc. 04/23/2018
Each share Common no par exchanged for (0.08) share Common $0.001 par
Note: Unexchnaged certificates will be cancelled and become without value 04/23/2021

ALABAMA GREAT SOUTHN RR CO (AL)
Merged into Southern Railway Co. 01/31/1969
Each share Preferred $50 par or Ordinary $50 par exchanged for (2.85) shares Common no par
Southern Railway Co. merged into Norfolk Southern Corp. 06/01/1982

ALABAMA MILLS, INC. (DE)
Common $1 par changed to $5 par and (1) additional share issued 03/29/1956
Acquired by Dan River Mills, Inc. 08/10/1956
Each share Common $5 par exchanged for (0.5) share Common $5 par
Dan River Mills, Inc. name changed to Dan River Inc. 07/01/1970
(See Dan River Inc.)

ALABAMA MILLS CO.
Reorganized as Alabama Mills, Inc. 00/00/1933
Details not available

ALABAMA NATL BANCORPORATION (AL)
Reincorporated under the laws of Delaware 04/07/1994
Alabama National BanCorporation (DE) merged into Royal Bank of Canada (Montreal, QC) 02/22/2008

ALABAMA NATL BANCORPORATION (DE)
Merged into Royal Bank of Canada (Montreal, QC 02/22/2008
Each share Common $1 par exchanged for (1.6) shares Common no par

ALABAMA NATL BK (MONTGOMERY, AL)
Capital Stock $10 par changed to $5 par 01/11/1963
Stock Dividends - 33.33333333% 01/00/1952; 25% 01/00/1955; 20% 10/14/1957; 16.66666666% 10/09/1959; 14.28% 01/11/1963; 25% 01/18/1966; 20% 01/19/1971
Merged into Alabama Bancorporation 09/28/1973
Each share Capital Stock $5 par exchanged for (2) shares Common $1 par
Alabama Bancorporation name changed to AmSouth Bancorporation 04/20/1981 which merged into Regions Financial Corp. 11/04/2006

ALABAMA NATL LIFE INS CO (AL)
Placed in receivership 03/28/1970
Receiver advised no stockholders' equity and to take tax loss for 00/00/1970

ALABAMA OXYGEN INC (DE)
Merged into Tennessee Natural Gas Lines, Inc. 12/28/1977
Each share Common 10¢ par exchanged for $6.25 cash
Note: An additional payment of $0.2044565 cash per share was made 09/08/1980

ALABAMA PWR CAP TR I (DE)
7.375% Trust Preferred Securities called for redemption at $25 on 10/31/2002

ALABAMA PWR CAP TR II (DE)
7.6% Trust Originated Preferred Securities called for redemption at $25 on 10/31/2002

ALABAMA PWR CAP TR III (DE)
Guaranted Capital Auction Preferred Securities called for redemption at $50,000 on 11/29/2002

ALABAMA PWR CO (AL)
$5 Preferred no par called for redemption 05/18/1946
$6 Preferred no par called for redemption 05/18/1946
$7 Preferred no par called for redemption 05/18/1946
15.68% Class A Preferred $1 par called for redemption 02/03/1986
11% Preferred $100 par called for redemption 06/07/1991
Adjustable Rate Class A Preferred 1983 Ser. $1 par called for redemption 04/01/1992
9.24% Preferred $100 par called for redemption 04/01/1992
9.44% Preferred $100 par called for redemption 04/01/1992
9% Preferred $100 par called for redemption 09/02/1992
8.72% Depositary Preferred called for redemption 02/26/1993
8.28% Preferred $100 par called for redemption 09/20/1993
8.04% Preferred $100 par called for redemption 11/29/1993
8.16% Preferred $100 par called for redemption 12/06/1993
Adjustable Rate Class A Preferred 1988 Ser. $1 par called for redemption 12/23/1993
7.6% Class A Preferred $1 par called for redemption 02/18/1997
5.96% Preferred $100 par called for redemption at $103.37 on 06/03/1997
6.88% Preferred $100 par called for redemption at $103.37 on 06/03/1997
7.6% Class A 2nd Preferred $100 par called for redemption at $25 on 07/02/1997
6.8% Class A Preferred $100 par called for redemption at $25 on 10/01/1998
6.4% Class A Preferred $100 par called for redemption at $25 on 11/02/1998
Adjustable Rate Preferred Class A Ser. 1993 $100 par called for redemption at $25 on 01/04/1999
Class A Auction Preferred Ser. 1993 called for redemption at $100,000 on 11/06/2002
Class A Unit Auction Preferred Ser. 1998 called for redemption at $100,000 on 11/13/2002
Money Market Preferred Class A called for redemption at $100,000 on 01/01/2008
5.2% Preferred Class A $1 par called for redemption at $25 plus $0.1589 accrued dividends on 05/15/2015
5.3% Class A Preferred $1 par called for redemption at $25 plus $0.1619 accrued dividends on 05/15/2015
5.625% Preference $1 par called for redemption at $25 plus $0.1719 accrued dividends on 05/15/2015
5.83% Class A Preferred $1 par called for redemption at $25 plus $0.040486 accrued dividends on 10/11/2017
6.45% Non-Cum. Preference $1 par called for redemption at $25 plus $0.044792 accrued dividends on 10/11/2017
6.5% Non-Cum. Preference $1 par called for redemption at $25 plus $0.045139 accrued dividends on 10/11/2017
(Additional Information in Active)

ALABAMA STEEL & SHIPBUILDING CO.
Dissolved 00/00/1932
Details not available

ALABAMA TENN NAT GAS CO (AL)
Reincorporated 01/01/1967
Common $1 par split (2) for (1) by issuance of (1) additional share 09/10/1965
Stock Dividends - 100% 05/15/1952; 25% 12/28/1955; 20% 03/09/1959; 25% 06/04/1962
State of incorporation changed from (DE) to (AL) 01/01/1967
Common $1 par split (5) for (2) by issuance of (0.2) additional share 06/02/1980
Under plan of reorganization each share Common $1 par automatically became (1) share AlaTenn Resources, Inc. Common $1 par 10/01/1982
AlaTenn Resources, Inc. name changed to Atrion Corp. (AL) 05/07/1996 which reincorporated in Delaware 02/25/1997

ALABASTINE CO. LTD.
Reorganized as Canada Gypsum & Alabastine, Ltd. 00/00/1927
Details not available

ALADDIN-CHIBOUGAMAU MINES LTD. (ON)
Charter cancelled and proclaimed dissolved for failure to pay taxes and file returns 01/04/1960

ALADDIN GOLD MINING CO., LTD. (NV)
Charter revoked for failure to file reports and pay fees 03/04/1940

ALADDIN-GROUNDHOG MINES LTD. (ON)
Name changed to Aladdin-Chibougamau Mines Ltd. 00/00/1956
(See Aladdin-Chibougamau Mines Ltd.)

ALADDIN INTL INC (NV)
Reincorporated 12/30/2014
Common 5¢ par split (3) for (1) by issuance of (2) additional shares 06/20/1983
Common 5¢ par split (4) for (1) by issuance of (3) additional shares payable 02/15/2000 to holders of record 02/03/2000
Common 5¢ par changed to no par 08/06/2013
State of incorporation changed from (MN) to (NV) and Common no par changed to $0.001 par 12/30/2014
Name changed to Moregain Pictures Inc. 09/18/2018

ALADDIN KNOWLEDGE SYSTEMS LTD (ISRAEL)
Ordinary NIS 0.01 par split (3) for (2) by issuance of (0.5) additional share 09/15/1995
Merged into Magic Lamp Corp. 03/24/2009
Each share Ordinary NIS 0.01 par exchanged for $11.50 cash

ALADDIN OIL CORP (CO)
SEC revoked common stock registration 02/06/2007

ALADDIN RES CORP (BC)
Name changed to Gold Point Exploration Ltd. 01/27/2004
Gold Point Exploration Ltd. name changed to Gold Point Energy Corp. 06/22/2005 which merged into San Leon Energy PLC 05/28/2009

ALADDIN SYS HLDGS INC (NV)
Name changed to Monterey Bay Tech, Inc. 11/11/2004
Monterey Bay Tech, Inc. name changed to SecureLogic Corp. 05/20/2005
(See SecureLogic Corp.)

ALADDIN TRADING & CO (UT)
Each share old Common $0.001 par exchanged for (0.04) share new Common $0.001 par 09/22/2006
Each share new Common $0.001 par exchanged again for (0.01) share new Common $0.001 par 05/30/2008
Each share new Common $0.001 par exchanged again for (0.001) share new Common $0.001 par 10/31/2008
Reincorporated under the laws of Florida as Caribbean Casino & Gaming Corp. 05/15/2009
Caribbean Casino & Gaming Corp. recapitalized as Caribbean International Holdings, Inc. 01/17/2013 which name changed to BioStem Technologies, Inc. 12/09/2014

ALADDIN URANIUM CORP. (UT)
Merged into Elaterite Basin Uranium Co. 07/15/1954
Each share Capital Stock $10 par exchanged for (0.1) share Capital Stock $2.50 par
Elaterite Basin Uranium Co. merged into Sun Tide Co. 11/15/1957 which name changed to Maxa Corp. 04/13/1974
(See Maxa Corp.)

ALADIN INTL INC (ON)
Name changed 10/17/1986
Name changed from Aladin Minerals Ltd. to Aladin International Inc. 10/17/1986
Delisted from Alberta Stock Exchange 09/05/1990

ALADIN OIL & REFINING CO. (WA)
Stricken from the records for failure to pay fees 07/01/1924

ALAFIRST BANCSHARES INC (DE)
Common 1¢ par split (3) for (2) by issuance of (0.5) additional share 06/12/1992
Name changed to Bancfirst Corp. 03/01/1993
Bancfirst Corp. name changed to BNF Bancorp, Inc. 03/02/1994 which was acquired by Union Planters Corp. 09/01/1994 which merged into Regions Financial Corp. (New) 07/01/2004

ALAGASCO INC (AL)
Common $1 par split (2) for (1) by issuance of (1) additional share 09/04/1984
Name changed to Energen Corp. 10/01/1985

ALAKON METALS LTD (BC)
Recapitalized as Gold Valley Resources Ltd. 03/13/1974
Each share Capital Stock no par exchanged for (0.2) share Capital Stock no par
Gold Valley Resources Ltd. recapitalized as NCA Minerals Corp. 06/06/1977
(See NCA Minerals Corp.)

ALAMAC MINES LTD. (QC)
Charter surrendered 03/18/1963
No stockholders' equity

ALAMANCE NATL BK (GRAHAM, NC)
Stock Dividend - 20% payable 02/16/2001 to holders of record 02/02/2001
Reorganized as United Financial, Inc. 10/01/2002
Each share Common exchanged for (1) share Common $1 par
United Financial, Inc. merged into FNB Corp. 11/04/2005 name changed to FNB United Corp. 04/28/2006 which name changed to CommunityOne Bancorp 07/01/2013 which merged into Capital Bank Financial Corp. 10/26/2016

ALAMAND CORP (DE)
Name changed to Moraga Corp. 12/26/1978
(See Moraga Corp.)

ALAMAR BIOSCIENCES INC (CA)
Name changed to AccuMed International Inc. 12/29/1995
AccuMed International Inc. acquired by Molecular Diagnostics, Inc. 09/17/2001 which name changed to CytoCore, Inc. 08/17/2006 which name changed to Medite Cancer Diagnostics, Inc. 12/11/2014

ALAMAR INDUSTRIES LTD. (ON)
Reorganized as Ascot Energy Corporation of Canada Ltd. 07/00/1978
Each share Common no par exchanged for (6) shares Common no par
Ascot Energy Corporation of Canada Ltd. name changed to Crosscut Explorations Inc. 10/29/1981 which recapitalized as Renaissance Industrial Corp. 12/19/1984 which name changed to D.A.S. Electronics Industries, Inc. 01/29/1988 which recapitalized as Pace Corp. 09/30/1993
(See Pace Corp.)

ALAMAR MINES LTD. (ON)
Recapitalized as Alamar Industries Ltd. 09/15/1977
Each share Capital Stock $1 par exchanged for (0.03333333) share Common no par
Alamar Industries Ltd. reorganized as Ascot Energy Corporation of Canada Ltd. 07/00/1978 which name changed to Crosscut Explorations Inc. 10/29/1981 which recapitalized as Renaissance Industrial Corp. 12/19/1984 which name changed to D.A.S. Electronics Industries, Inc. 01/29/1988 which recapitalized as Pace Corp. 09/30/1993
(See Pace Corp.)

ALAMCO INC (DE)
Common $1 par changed to 1¢ par 11/15/1988
Each share Common 1¢ par exchanged for (0.1) share Common 10¢ par 12/18/1989
Preferred Stock Purchase Rights declared for Common stockholders of record 12/12/1994 were redeemed at $0.01 per right 08/07/1997 for holders of record 08/07/1997

Merged into Columbia Gas System, Inc. 08/07/1997
Each share Common 10¢ par exchanged for $15.75 cash

ALAMEDA BANCORPORATION INC (DE)
Common Capital Stock $10 par split (2) for (1) by issuance of (1) additional share 07/02/1979
Common Capital Stock $10 par changed to $5 par and (1) additional share issued 09/23/1980
Common Capital Stock $5 par changed to $2.50 par and (1) additional share issued 04/16/1986
Stock Dividend - 50% 04/06/1972
Name changed to Northern California Community Bancorporation, Inc. 06/01/1990
Northern California Community Bancorporation, Inc. merged into California Bancshares Inc. 07/01/1991 which merged into U.S. Bancorp (OR) 06/06/1996 which merged into U.S. Bancorp 08/01/1997

ALAMEDA 1ST CORP (CA)
Reincorporated under the laws of Delaware as Alameda Bancorporation, Inc. 11/17/1971
Alameda Bancorporation, Inc. name changed to Northern California Community Bancorporation, Inc. 06/01/1990 which merged into California Bancshares Inc. 07/01/1991 which merged into U.S. Bancorp (OR) 06/06/1996 which merged into U.S. Bancorp 08/01/1997

ALAMEDA 1ST NATL BK (ALAMEDA, CA)
99.65% held by Alameda Bancorporation, Inc. and bank directors as of 04/04/1975
Public interest eliminated

ALAMEDA MINES LTD. (ON)
Charter reported cancelled 00/00/1952

ALAMEDA SHOPPING CTR INC (CO)
Each share 6% Preferred $100 par exchanged for (1) share 7% Preferred $100 par 01/31/1958
Each share Common no par exchanged for (5) shares Common $2.50 par 01/31/1958
Adjudicated bankrupt 12/29/1965
No stockholders' equity

ALAMEDA SUGAR CO.
Merged into Sutter Buttes Land Co. 00/00/1934
Details not available

ALAMITO CO (AZ)
Merged into Osceola Energy Inc. 06/04/1986
Each share Common no par exchanged for $165 cash

ALAMO BANCSHARES INC (DE)
Merged into Federated Texas Bancorporation, Inc. 05/01/1973
Each share Common $5 par exchanged for (1.288) shares Common $5 par
Federated Texas Bancorporation, Inc. merged into Federated Capital Corp. 01/29/1974 which merged into Mercantile Texas Corp. 12/30/1976 which name changed to MCorp 10/11/1984
(See MCorp)

ALAMO CORP (TX)
Stock Dividends - 2.75% payable 02/28/2001 to holders of record 12/31/2000 Ex date - 03/15/2001; 3% payable 02/28/2002 to holders of record 12/31/2001 Ex date - 03/14/2002; 3.25% payable 02/28/2003 to holders of record 12/31/2002 Ex date - 03/28/2003; 3.75% payable 02/28/2004 to holders of record 12/31/2003
Ex date - 03/18/2004; 4% payable 02/28/2005 to holders of record 12/31/2004 Ex date - 03/29/2005
Acquired by Cullen Frost Bankers, Inc. 02/28/2006
Each share Common exchanged for $99.09 cash

ALAMO DEVS LTD (BC)
Name changed to United Beverages Ltd. 01/04/1988
(See United Beverages Ltd.)

ALAMO IRON WKS (TX)
Common $100 par changed to $5 par and (19) additional shares issued 07/20/1951
Stock Dividend - 10% 07/25/1951
Chapter 11 bankruptcy proceedings converted to Chapter 7 on 06/30/2010
No stockholders' equity

ALAMO LIFE INS CO (TX)
Merged into First Continental Life & Accident Insurance Co. 05/31/1972
Each share Common no par exchanged for (0.0345) share Common $1 par
First Continental Life & Accident Insurance Co. merged into First Continental Life Group, Inc. 12/31/1972
(See First Continental Life Group, Inc.)

ALAMO MORTGAGE CORP. (TX)
Charter forfeited for failure to pay taxes 04/18/1962

ALAMO NATL BK (SAN ANTONIO, TX)
Each share Capital Stock $100 par exchanged for (5) shares Capital Stock $20 par 00/00/1946
Each share Capital Stock $20 par exchanged for (2) shares Capital Stock $10 par 01/08/1963
Capital Stock $10 par changed to $5 par and a 25% stock dividend paid 02/01/1966
Stock Dividends - 40% 12/27/1941; 20% 06/07/1948; 16.66666666% 04/26/1951; 20% 11/19/1956; 12.5% 11/06/1959
Under plan of reorganization each share Capital Stock $5 par automatically became (1) share Alamo Bancshares, Inc. (DE) Common $5 par 01/05/1972
Alamo Bancshares, Inc. merged into Federated Texas Bancorporation, Inc. 05/01/1973 which merged into Federated Capital Corp. 01/29/1974 which merged into Mercantile Texas Corp. 12/30/1976 which name changed to MCorp 10/11/1984
(See MCorp)

ALAMO SVGS ASSN TEX (TX)
Name changed 06/11/1979
Name changed from Alamo Savings Association to Alamo Savings Association of Texas 06/11/1979
Stock Dividends - 100% 03/31/1983; 50% 06/30/1983
Placed in receivership 06/28/1989
No stockholders' equity

ALAMO SILVER LEAD MINING CO., LTD. (ON)
Charter cancelled for failure to pay taxes and file returns 00/00/1951

ALAMOGORDO FINL CORP (USA)
Reorganized under the laws of Maryland as Bancorp 34, Inc. 10/12/2016
Each share Common 10¢ par exchanged for (2.0473) shares Common 1¢ par

ALAMOS GOLD INC OLD (BC)
Merged into Alamos Gold Inc. (New) 07/06/2015
Each share Common no par exchanged for (1) share Class A Common no par, (0.4397) share AuRico Metals Inc. Common no par and USD$0.0001 cash
(See each company's listing)
Note: Unexchanged certificates will be cancelled and become without value 07/06/2021

ALAMOS MINERALS LTD (BC)
Merged into Alamos Gold Inc. (Old) 02/20/2003
Each share Common no par exchanged for (0.5) share Common no par
Alamos Gold Inc. (Old) merged into Alamos Gold Inc. (New) 07/06/2015

ALAMOS MINES LTD. (BC)
Struck off register and declared dissolved for failure to file returns 07/17/1969

ALAMOSA HLDGS INC (DE)
Merged into Sprint Nextel Corp. 02/01/2006
Each share Conv. Preferred Ser. B exchanged for $1,378.69 cash
Each share Common 1¢ par exchanged for $18.75 cash

ALAMOSA PCS HLDGS INC (DE)
Name changed to Alamosa Holdings, Inc. 02/14/2001
(See Alamosa Holdings, Inc.)

ALAN ACCEPTANCE CORP (OH)
Charter cancelled for failure to pay taxes 04/01/2009

ALAN R J & CO (DE)
Name changed to Winners Circle Management, Inc. 10/24/1988
(See Winners Circle Management, Inc.)

ALAN-RANDAL CO., INC. (CA)
Merged into Rocky Mountain Airways, Inc. 05/11/1972
Each share Class A Common $1 par exchanged for (0.16666666) share Common 1¢ par
Rocky Mountain Airways, Inc. merged into Rocky Mountain Aviation, Inc. 08/24/1984
(See Rocky Mountain Aviation, Inc.)

ALAN WOOD STL CO (PA)
Recapitalized 00/00/1948
Each share 7% Preferred $100 par exchanged for (1) share 5% Preferred $100 par, (4) shares Common $10 par and $10 cash
Each share Common no par exchanged for (1) share Common $10 par
Common $10 par changed to $5 par 10/22/1965
Name changed to Vesper Corp. 09/11/1979
(See Vesper Corp.)

ALANA MINES LTD. (ON)
Charter cancelled for failure to pay taxes and file returns 06/09/1958

ALANCO ENVIRONMENTAL CORP (AZ)
Recapitalized 07/09/1992
Recapitalized from Alanco Ltd. to Alanco Resources Corp. 07/03/1990
Each share Common no par exchanged for (0.25) share Common no par
Recapitalized from Alanco Resources Corp. to Alanco Environmental Resources Corp. 07/09/1992
Each share Common no par exchanged for (0.2) share new Common no par
Each share new Common no par exchanged again for (0.1428571) share new Common no par 05/13/1998
Name changed to Alanco Technologies, Inc. 11/12/1999

ALANDA ENERGY CORP (BC)
Struck off register and declared dissolved for failure to file returns 05/10/1985

ALANGE ENERGY CORP (BC)
Recapitalized as PetroMagdalena Energy Corp. 07/19/2011
Each share Common no par exchanged for (0.14285714) share Common no par
(See PetroMagdalena Energy Corp.)

ALANTEC CORP (DE)
Merged into Fore Systems, Inc. 02/23/1996
Each share Common $0.001 par exchanged for (1) share Common 1¢ par
(See Fore Systems, Inc.)

ALANTHUS CORP (DE)
Merged into Altank Corp. 08/14/1978
Each share Common $1 par exchanged for $6.50 cash

ALANTRA VENTURE CORP (BC)
Delisted from NEX 06/25/2004

ALARION BK (OCALA, FL)
Under plan of reorganization each share Common 1¢ par automatically became (1) share Alarion Financial Services, Inc. Common 1¢ par 11/16/2005
Alarion Financial Services, Inc. merged into Heritage Financial Group, Inc. 09/30/2014 which merged into Renasant Corp. 06/30/2015

ALARION FINL SVCS INC (FL)
Merged into Heritage Financial Group, Inc. 09/30/2014
Each share Common 1¢ par exchanged for (0.44) share Common 1¢ par
Heritage Financial Group, Inc. merged into Renasant Corp. 06/30/2015

ALARIS MED SYS INC (DE)
Name changed 06/30/2003
Name changed from ALARIS Medical, Inc. to ALARIS Medical Systems, Inc. 06/30/2003
Merged into Cardinal Health, Inc. 07/07/2004
Each share Common 1¢ par exchanged for $22.35 cash

ALARKO CARRIER SANAYI VE TICARET A S (TURKEY)
ADR agreement terminated 11/21/2002
No ADR holders' equity

ALARM DEVICE MANUFACTURING CO., INC. (NY)
Stock Dividends - 25% 02/24/1961; 20% 05/22/1962
Name changed to ADG Liquidating Corp. 08/30/1963
(See ADG Liquidating Corp.)

ALARM PRODS INTL INC (NY)
Common 10¢ par split (2) for (1) by issuance of (1) additional share 07/21/1972
Stock Dividend - 10% 03/27/1970
Recapitalized as API Enterprises, Inc. 08/29/1985
Each share Common 10¢ par exchanged for (3) shares Common 10¢ par
API Enterprises, Inc. recapitalized as Ceco Environmental Corp. (NY) 09/28/1992 which reincorporated in Delaware 01/11/2002

ALARMFORCE INDS INC (CANADA)
Acquired by BCE Inc. 01/08/2018
Each share Common no par exchanged for $16 cash
Note: Unexchanged certificates will be cancelled and become without value 01/08/2024

ALARMGUARD HLDGS INC (DE)
Merged into Tyco International Ltd. 02/22/1999
Each share Common $0.0001 par exchanged for $9.25 cash

ALARMING DEVICES INC (NV)
Reincorporated under the laws of

ALA-ALA

Delaware as StationDigital Corp. 08/08/2014
(See StationDigital Corp.)

ALAS AVIATION CORP (DE)
Name changed to Energie Holdings, Inc. 02/13/2014
Energie Holdings, Inc. name changed to ExeLED Holdings Inc. 12/30/2015

ALAS INTL HLDGS INC (NV)
Name changed 07/11/2011
Name changed from Alas Defense Systems, Inc. to ALAS International Holdings, Inc. 07/11/2011
Each share Common $0.001 par received distribution of (0.00566572) share IMAG Group, Inc. Common $0.001 par payable 08/13/2013 to holders of record 08/12/2013
Name changed to PV Enterprises International, Inc. 08/19/2013
PV Enterprises International, Inc. recapitalized as Drone Services USA, Inc. 04/29/2015

ALASCO GOLD & OIL CORP (CO)
Reorganized as Talkeetna Gold Exploration Ltd. 08/15/1975
Each share Common 5¢ par exchanged for (0.33333333) share Common $0.001 par
Talkeetna Gold Exploration Ltd. recapitalized as Founders Equity Corp. 01/08/1986
(See Founders Equity Corp.)

ALASKA AIRLS INC (AK)
$2.77 Conv. Preferred $1 par called for redemption 12/09/1982
Under plan of reorganization each share Common $1 par automatically became (1) share Alaska Air Group, Inc. (DE) Common $1 par 05/23/1985

ALASKA APOLLO RES INC (BC)
Recapitalized 10/14/1992
Recapitalized from Alaska Apollo Gold Mines Ltd. to Alaska Apollo Resources Inc. 10/14/1992
Each share Common no par exchanged for (0.06666666) share Common no par
Recapitalized as Daugherty Resources, Inc. 06/29/1998
Each share Common no par exchanged for (0.2) share Common no par
Daugherty Resources, Inc. name changed to NGAS Resources Inc. 07/05/2004 which merged into Magnum Hunter Resources Corp. 04/13/2011
(See Magnum Hunter Resources Corp.)

ALASKA BANCORPORATION (AK)
Out of business 00/00/1989
No stockholders' equity

ALASKA BANCSHARES INC (AK)
Each share old Preferred no par exchanged for (0.06) share new Preferred no par 05/28/1971
Each share old Common 5¢ par exchanged for (0.06) share new Common 5¢ par 05/28/1971
Acquired by Alaska Bancorporation 02/07/1979
Each share new Preferred no par exchanged for (22.96) shares Common 1¢ par
Each share new Common 5¢ par exchanged for (0.87) share Common 1¢ par
Note: Holders entitled to receive fewer than (100) shares of Alaska Bancorporation received $5.75 cash per share
(See Alaska Bancorporation)

ALASKA BK COMM (ANCHORAGE, AK)
Capital Stock $10 par changed to $2 par and (4) additional shares issued 03/15/1977
Stock Dividends - 10% 01/30/1981; 10% 01/29/1982

Name changed to First Interstate Bank of Alaska (Anchorage, AK) 10/06/1983
First Interstate Bank of Alaska (Anchorage, AK) reorganized as First Interstate Corp. of Alaska 08/01/1985
(See First Interstate Corp. of Alaska)

ALASKA BRITISH COLUMBIA METALS CO (WA)
Charter revoked for failure to file reports and pay fees 07/01/1928

ALASKA COASTAL AIRLINES, INC. (AK)
5.5% Preferred $1 par called for redemption 05/31/1967
Merged into Alaska Airlines, Inc. (AK) 04/01/1968
Each share Common $1 par exchanged for (0.5185) share Common $1 par
Alaska Airlines, Inc. (AK) reorganized in Delaware as Alaska Air Group, Inc. 05/23/1985

ALASKA COASTAL-ELLIS AIRLINES (AK)
Name changed to Alaska Coastal Airlines, Inc. 05/16/1966
Alaska Coastal Airlines, Inc. merged into Alaska Airlines, Inc. (AK) 04/01/1968 which reorganized in Delaware as Alaska Air Group, Inc. 05/23/1985

ALASKA CONS OIL INC (DE)
No longer in existence having become inoperative and void for non-payment of taxes 04/01/1963

ALASKA CONTL BANCORP (AK)
Went out of business 08/03/1988
No stockholders' equity

ALASKA CONTINENTAL BANK (ANCHORAGE, AK)
Reorganized as Alaska Continental Bancorp 10/12/1984
Each share Common $1 par exchanged for (2.5) shares Common $1 par
(See Alaska Continental Bancorp)

ALASKA DIVERSIFIED RES INC (AK)
Name changed to Microfast Software Corp. 07/01/1983

ALASKA-ENDICOTT MINING & MILLING CO. (WA)
Dissolved for non payment of fees 07/01/1929

ALASKA FIBERGLASS MFG HLDG INC (UT)
Involuntarily dissolved 12/01/1993

ALASKA FREIGHTWAYS INC (NV)
Reincorporated under the laws of Delaware as Hythiam, Inc. 09/29/2003
Hythiam, Inc. name changed to Catasys, Inc. 03/17/2011

ALASKA GLACIER ICE WTR INC (CO)
Administratively dissolved 02/01/2000

ALASKA GOLD CO (DE)
Merged into Mueller Industries, Inc. 03/14/1996
Each share Common 10¢ par exchanged for $0.25 cash

ALASKA GOLD CORP (NV)
SEC revoked common stock registration 09/30/2014

ALASKA GOLD MINES (ME)
Properties sold to Alaska Mining & Power Co. 00/00/1932
(See Alaska Mining & Power Co.)

ALASKA GOLD MINING & EXPLORATION CO. (AZ)
Charter expired for failure to file reports and pay fees 08/08/1929

ALASKA HOME RAILWAY (WA)
Dissolved for non-payment of fees 07/01/1923

ALASKA HOTEL PPTYS INC (AK)
Name changed to Alaska Diversified Resources, Inc. 09/10/1980
Alaska Diversified Resources, Inc. name changed to Microfast Software Corp. 07/01/1983

ALASKA INTERNATIONAL AIR, INC. (AK)
Name changed to Alaska International Industries, Inc. 05/14/1974
(See Alaska International Industries, Inc.)

ALASKA INTL CORP (NV)
Recapitalized as C/W Industries Group, Inc. 03/29/1978
Each share Common 3¢ par exchanged for (1) share Common 1¢ par
(See C/W Industries Group, Inc.)

ALASKA INTL INDS INC (AK)
Stock Dividend - 10% 02/01/1978
Merged into Bergt Corp. 09/17/1979
Each share Common 10¢ par exchanged for $11.50 cash

ALASKA INTST CO (AK)
Common $1 par split (2) for (1) by issuance of (1) additional share 06/20/1980
Reincorporated under the laws of Delaware as Enstar Corp. 06/04/1982
(See Enstar Corp. (DE))

ALASKA JUNEAU GOLD MINING CO. (WV)
Capital Stock $10 par changed to $2 par 03/18/1957
Name changed to A.J. Industries, Inc. (WV) 06/25/1959
A.J. Industries, Inc. (WV) reincorporated in Delaware 04/30/1968
(See A.J. Industries, Inc. (DE))

ALASKA KENAI OILS LTD (BC)
Recapitalized as Kenai Oils Ltd. 03/01/1976
Each share Capital Stock no par exchanged for (0.1) share Capital Stock no par

ALASKA MEXICAN GOLD MINING CO.
Completely liquidated 02/07/1938
Each share Capital Stock received (0.22727272) share Treadwell Yukon Corp. Ltd. Capital Stock
(See Treadwell Yukon Corp. Ltd.)

ALASKA MINES & MINERALS INC (AK)
Proclaimed dissolved for failure to file reports and pay fees 10/07/1974

ALASKA MINING & POWER CO.
Assets sold to Alaska Juneau Gold Mining Co. 00/00/1934. Liquidation approved and (2.5) shares Alaska Juneau Gold Mining Co. Capital Stock $10 par distributed 01/15/1935; (0.65) additional share distributed 10/00/1940
Cash liquidation completed 11/00/1941
Alaska Juneau Gold Mining Co. name changed to A.J. Industries, Inc. (WV) 06/25/1959 which reincorporated in Delaware 04/30/1968
(See A.J. Industries, Inc. (DE))

ALASKA MUT BANCORPORATION (AK)
Stock Dividends - 10% 03/09/1984; 10% 12/30/1985
Merged into Alliance Bancorporation 12/29/1987
Each share Common $5 par exchanged for (0.12) share Common $5 par
(See Alliance Bancorporation)

ALASKA MUT BK (ANCHORAGE, AK)
Reorganized as Alaska Mutual Bancorporation 12/28/1983
Each share Common $10 par exchanged for (2) shares Common $5 par
Alaska Mutual Bancorporation merged into Alliance Bancorporation 12/29/1987
(See Alliance Bancorporation)

ALASKA NATL BK OF THE NORTH (FAIRBANKS, AK)
Stock Dividend - 10% 04/09/1984
Declared insolvent and FDIC appointed receiver 10/22/1987
Stockholders' equity unlikely

ALASKA NICKEL CO., INC. (AK)
Dissolved for failure to file reports and pay fees 10/24/1969

ALASKA-NORTH AMERICA INVESTMENT CO. (MD)
Acquired by Shares in American Industry, Inc. 05/18/1962
Each share Common 25¢ par exchanged for (0.337) share Common $1 par
Shares in American Industry, Inc. name changed to Steadman's Shares in American Industry, Inc. 05/19/1966 which name changed to Steadman American Industry Fund, Inc. 10/19/1967 which name changed to Ameritor Industry Fund 09/23/1998
(See Ameritor Industry Fund)

ALASKA NORTHWEST PPTYS INC (AK)
Each share old Common $1 par exchanged for (0.1) share new Common $1 par 06/17/1987
Merged 03/12/1997
Details not available

ALASKA OIL & GAS DEVELOPMENT CO., INC. (AK)
Charter revoked for failure to file reports and pay fees 01/03/1966

ALASKA OIL & GAS LTD (DE)
Name changed to Transworld Oil & Gas, Ltd. 07/29/2005
Transworld Oil & Gas, Ltd. recapitalized as Caribbean Exploration Ventures Inc. 01/16/2007 which name changed to Siguiri Basin Mining, Inc. (DE) 03/28/2007 which reorganized in Nevada as Anything Brands Online Inc. 01/17/2008 which name changed to MyFreightWorld Technologies, Inc. 05/13/2010

ALASKA PAC BANCORPORATION (AK)
Stock Dividends - 10% 02/12/1983; 10% 02/22/1984
Acquired by Key Banks, Inc. 07/01/1985
Each share Common no par exchanged for $27 cash

ALASKA PAC BANCSHARES INC (AK)
Merged into Northrim BanCorp, Inc. 04/01/2014
Each share Common 1¢ par exchanged for (0.5553) share Common $1 par and $3.32 cash

ALASKA PACIFIC BANK (ANCHORAGE, AK)
Merged into Alaska Pacific Bancorporation 07/11/1979
Each share Common $10 par exchanged for (2.75) shares Common no par
(See Alaska Pacific Bancorporation)

ALASKA-PACIFIC CONSOLIDATED MINING CO. (WA)
Completely liquidated 12/15/1977
Each share Common 1¢ par received first and final distribution of $0.041452783 cash
Note: Certificates were not required to be surrendered and are now valueless

ALASKA PACIFIC SALMON CO. (NV)
Name changed to Alpac Corp. 04/18/1957
(See Alpac Corp.)

ALASKA PACIFIC SALMON CORP. (NV)
Reorganized as Alaska Pacific Salmon Co. 00/00/1933
Details not available

ALASKA PACKERS ASSOCIATION (CA)
Merged into California Packing Corp. 05/15/1967
Each share Capital Stock $100 par exchanged for (14) shares Capital Stock $2.50 par
California Packing Corp. name changed to Del Monte Corp. 06/28/1967
(See Del Monte Corp.)

ALASKA PETE & MNG INC (AK)
Common no par changed to 10¢ par 06/10/1974
Completely liquidated 11/06/1975
Each share Common 10¢ par exchanged for first and final distribution of (1) Non-Transferable Ctf. of Overriding Royalty Interest
Note: No new certificates were actually issued. Each stockholder's interest was recorded in the counties in which the oil and gas leases are located. Possibility of any stockholders' equity may not be determined for several years

ALASKA PETROLEUM, INC. (DE)
No longer in existence having become inoperative and void for non-payment of taxes 04/01/1962

ALASKA PIPELINE CO. (AK)
Through voluntary exchange offer 100% acquired by Alaska Interstate Co. as of 12/00/1966
Public interest eliminated

ALASKA-PITTSBURGH GOLD MINING CO. (DE)
No longer in existence having become inoperative and void for non-payment of taxes 03/17/1920

ALASKA PRECIOUS METALS LTD (CO)
Each share old Common $0.0001 par exchanged for (0.03333333) share new Common $0.0001 par 04/14/1989
Reincorporated under the laws of California as U-Corp Inc. 01/01/1993

ALASKA REFRIGERATOR CORP.
Dissolved 00/00/1934
Details not available

ALASKA SALMON CO.
Name changed to Bristol Bay Packing Co. 00/00/1944
(See Bristol Bay Packing Co.)

ALASKA ST BK (ANCHORAGE, AK)
Each share Common $10 par exchanged for (2) shares Common $5 par 12/16/1970
Stock Dividends - 10% 11/20/1968; 100% 10/01/1975
Declared insolvent and closed 02/03/1991
Stockholders' equity unlikely

ALASKA TELEPHONE & TELEGRAPH CO. (NY)
Liquidation completed
Each share Capital Stock $5 par stamped to indicate initial distribution of $4 cash 12/08/1958
Each share Stamped Capital Stock $5 par stamped to indicate second distribution of $4.50 cash 01/12/1959
Each share Stamped Capital Stock $5 par exchanged for third and final distribution of $1.235 cash 12/01/1962

ALASKA TELEPHONE CORP. (AK)
Reorganized 09/30/1955

No stockholders' equity

ALASKA TREADWELL GOLD MINING CO.
Completely liquidated 02/07/1938
Each share Capital Stock received (2) shares Treadwell Yukon Corp. Ltd. Capital Stock
(See Treadwell Yukon Corp. Ltd.)

ALASKA UNITED GOLD MINING CO.
Liquidation completed 01/24/1938
Details not available

ALASKA WRANGELL MLS INC (WA)
Common $5 par changed to $2 par 05/28/1962
Liquidation completed
Each share Common $2 par exchanged for initial distribution of $4.50 cash 06/01/1973
Each share Common $2 par received second distribution of $5.25 cash 01/10/1974
Each share Common $2 par received third and final distribution of $0.25 cash 03/25/1974

ALASKA YUKON PIPELINES LTD (CANADA)
Involuntarily dissolved for failure to file annual returns 12/16/1980

ALASKA YUKON REFINERS & DISTRS LTD (AB)
Each share 6% Preferred $25 par exchanged for (20) shares Common no par and (10) Stock Purchase Warrants 01/08/1965
Struck off register for failure to file annual returns 11/15/1978

ALASKAGOLD MINES LTD (BC)
Delisted from Toronto Venture Stock Exchange 06/20/2003

ALASKON RES LTD (BC)
Recapitalized as El Bravo Gold Mining Ltd. (BC) 06/07/1993
Each share Common no par exchanged for (0.2) share Common no par
El Bravo Gold Mining Ltd. (BC) reincorporated in Bermuda 07/03/1995 which name changed to El Bravo Resources International Ltd. 11/07/1997 which recapitalized as Tri-X International Ltd. 09/18/2000
(See Tri-X International Ltd.)

ALATENN RES INC (AL)
Common $1 par split (2) for (1) by issuance of (1) additional share 06/03/1983
Common $1 par changed to 10¢ par 05/15/1986
Name changed to Atrion Corp. (AL) 05/07/1996
Atrion Corp. (AL) reincorporated in Delaware 02/25/1997

ALAVA VENTURES INC (AB)
Cease trade order effective 11/08/2002
Stockholders' equity unlikely

ALAWAS GOLD CORP (BC)
Merged into Kaaba Resources Inc. 04/13/1989
Each share Common no par exchanged for (1) share Common no par
Kaaba Resources Inc. recapitalized as International Kaaba Gold Corp. 04/17/1990
(See International Kaaba Gold Corp.)

ALAZZIO ENTMT CORP (NV)
Name changed to America Resources Exploration Inc. 04/29/2015
America Resources Exploration Inc. recapitalized as PetroGas Co. 03/07/2016

ALBA EXPLORATIONS LTD. (ON)
Recapitalized as Accra Explorations Ltd. 12/21/1962
Each share Capital Stock $1 par exchanged for (0.25) share Capital Stock $1 par

Accra Explorations Ltd. merged into Xtra Developments Inc. 05/25/1972 which merged into Sumtra Diversified Inc. 08/30/1978

ALBA GOLD MINES LTD. (ON)
Charter revoked for failure to file reports and pay fees 00/00/1949

ALBA MINERAL EXPL INC (DE)
Name changed to Bergio International, Inc. 11/09/2009

ALBA PETE CORP (ON)
Merged into Alberta Oil & Gas Ltd. 12/31/1990
Each share Class A Common no par exchanged for (0.46511627) share Common no par
Alberta Oil & Gas Ltd. recapitalized as Alberta Oil & Gas Petroleum Corp. 11/19/1997 which recapitalized as Edge Energy Inc. 04/14/1998 which merged into Ventus Energy Ltd. 08/11/2000 which name changed to Navigo Energy Inc. 05/24/2002
(See Navigo Energy Inc.)

ALBA WALDENSIAN INC (DE)
Name changed 01/01/1962
Name changed from Alba Hosiery Mills Inc. to Alba-Waldensian, Inc. 01/01/1962
Common $5 par changed to $2.50 par and (1) additional share issued 04/28/1969
Common $2.50 par split (3) for (2) by issuance of (0.5) additional share payable 11/16/1998 to holders of record 11/06/1998 Ex date - 11/17/1998
Common $2.50 par split (4) for (3) by issuance of (0.33333333) additional share payable 06/04/1999 to holders of record 05/25/1999 Ex date - 06/07/1999
Merged into Tefron Ltd. 12/13/1999
Each share Common $2.50 par exchanged for $18.50 cash

ALBAN EXPLS LTD (BC)
Recapitalized as Pacific Amber Resources Ltd. (BC) 05/19/1994
Each share Common no par exchanged for (0.2) share Common no par
Pacific Amber Resources Ltd. (BC) reincorporated in Alberta 07/25/2002 which recapitalized as Grand Banks Energy Corp. 05/14/2003
(See Grand Banks Energy Corp.)

ALBANK FINL CORP (DE)
Common 1¢ par split (6) for (5) by issuance of (0.2) additional share payable 04/01/1996 to holders of record 03/15/1996
Merged into Charter One Financial, Inc. 11/30/1998
Each share Common 1¢ par exchanged for (2.268) shares Common 1¢ par
(See Charter One Financial, Inc.)

ALBANY & SUSQUEHANNA RAILROAD CO. (NY)
Acquired by Delaware & Hudson Co. 07/02/1945
Each share Capital Stock $100 par exchanged for (1) share Delaware & Hudson Co. Capital Stock $100 par and $150 principal amount of Albany & Susquehanna Railroad Co. 4.5% Bonds due 07/01/1975
Delaware & Hudson Co. name changed to Champlain National Corp. 07/01/1964 which merged into International Industries, Inc. (DE) 03/27/1969 which merged into IHOP Corp. 09/17/1976
(See IHOP Corp.)

ALBANY BK & TR CO N A (CHICAGO, IL)
Merged into Albank Corp. 12/01/2006
Each share Common $12.50 par exchanged for $410 cash

Note: Holders of (8,436) or more shares retained their interests

ALBANY CONSOLIDATED MINES LTD.
Merged into Gencona Mines Ltd. on a (1) for (5.173) basis 00/00/1944
Gencona Mines Ltd. recapitalized as Kelly Lake Nickel Mines Ltd. 09/16/1968 which name changed to Albany Oil & Gas Ltd. (MAN) 03/22/1971 which reincorporated in Alberta 11/10/1980 which name changed to Albany Corp. 05/17/1988 which merged into LifeSpace Environmental Walls Inc. 08/17/1993 which merged into SMED International Inc. 07/01/1996
(See SMED International Inc.)

ALBANY CORP (AB)
Merged into LifeSpace Environmental Walls Inc. 08/17/1993
Each share Common no par exchanged for (0.021) share Common no par
LifeSpace Environmental Walls Inc. merged into SMED International Inc. 07/01/1996
(See SMED International Inc.)

ALBANY FELT CO (NY)
Name changed to Albany International Corp. 07/30/1969
(See Albany International Corp.)

ALBANY FROZEN FOODS INC (OR)
Merged into Spring Mills, Inc. 02/28/1974
Each share Common no par exchanged for $0.775 cash

ALBANY INDS (GA)
Adjudicated bankrupt 04/26/1971
No stockholders' equity

ALBANY INTL CORP (NY)
Capital Stock $2.50 par changed to $1.25 par and (1) additional share issued 04/26/1972
Capital Stock $1.25 par split (5) for (4) by issuance of (0.25) additional share 10/01/1979
Merged into A.I.C. Investors Corp. 08/04/1983
Each share Capital Stock $1.25 par exchanged for $40 cash

ALBANY MOLECULAR RESH INC (DE)
Common 1¢ par split (2) for (1) by issuance of (1) additional share payable 08/24/2000 to holders of record 08/08/2000 Ex date - 08/25/2000
Acquired by Carlyle Group L.P. 08/31/2017
Each share Common 1¢ par exchanged for $21.75 cash

ALBANY OIL & GAS INC (CO)
Administratively dissolved 02/01/2001

ALBANY OIL & GAS LTD (AB)
Reincorporated 11/10/1980
Place of incorporation changed from (MB) to (AB) 11/10/1980
Name changed to Albany Corp. 05/17/1988
Albany Corp. merged into LifeSpace Environmental Walls Inc. 08/17/1993 which merged into SMED International Inc. 07/01/1996
(See SMED International Inc.)

ALBANY PACKING CO., INC. (NY)
Merged into Tobin Packing Co., Inc. 11/28/1942
Details not available

ALBANY PERFORATED WRAPPING PAPER CO. (NY)
Name changed to A.P.W. Paper Co., Inc. 00/00/1930
A.P.W. Paper Co., Inc. name changed to A.P.W. Products Co., Inc. 00/00/1944 which name changed to Allied-Albany Paper Corp. 01/16/1957
(See Allied-Albany Paper Corp.)

ALBANY RES LTD (BC)
Recapitalized as International Albany Resources Inc. (BC) 04/07/1995
Each share Common no par exchanged for (0.14285714) share Common no par
International Albany Resources Inc. (BC) reincorporated in Bahamas as Brazilian Goldfields Ltd. 03/21/1997 which recapitalized as Brazilian International Goldfields Ltd. 11/27/1998 which recapitalized as Aguila American Resources Ltd. (Bahamas) 03/08/2002 which reincorporated in British Columbia 01/14/2008 which name changed to Aguila American Gold Ltd. 05/26/2011

ALBANY RIVER GOLD MINES LTD.
Acquired by Pickle Crow Gold Mines Ltd. on a (0.1) for (1) basis 12/00/1945
(See Pickle Crow Gold Mines Ltd.)

ALBANY RIVER MINES LTD.
Acquired by Albany River Gold Mines Ltd. on a (0.4) for (1) basis 07/15/1938
Albany River Gold Mines Ltd. acquired by Pickle Crow Gold Mines Ltd. 12/00/1945
(See Pickle Crow Gold Mines Ltd.)

ALBARA CORP (CO)
Each share old Common no par exchanged for (0.33333333) share new Common no par 09/23/1991
Recapitalized as Leapfrog Smart Products, Inc. 02/23/2000
Each share new Common no par exchanged for (0.14285714) share Common no par
Leapfrog Smart Products, Inc. name changed to Red Alert Group, Inc. 07/15/2003

ALBARMONT 1985 INC (QC)
Recapitalized 07/19/1985
Recapitalized from Albarmont Mines Corp. to Albarmont (1985) Inc. 07/19/1985
Each share Common no par exchanged for (3) shares Common no par
Company believed out of business 00/00/1990
Details not available

ALBATROS GOLD MINES LTD (QC)
Charter cancelled 08/17/1985

ALBATROSS STEEL FURNITURE CO. LTD.
Property foreclosed 00/00/1937
Details not available

ALBEDENA OILS LTD (AB)
Name changed to Nitracell Canada Ltd. 09/20/1968
Nitracell Canada Ltd. recapitalized as Magnum Resources Ltd. 01/09/1975
(See Magnum Resources Ltd.)

ALBEE HOMES INC (OH)
Common no par split (2) for (1) by issuance of (1) additional share 11/10/1961
Plan of Arrangement under Chapter XI Federal Bankruptcy Act confirmed 10/09/1979
No stockholders' equity

ALBEMARLE FIRST BK (CHARLOTTESVILLE, VA)
Merged into Premier Community Bankshares, Inc. 07/01/2006
Each share Common $4 par exchanged for (0.75077) share Common $1 par
Premier Community Bankshares, Inc. merged into United Bankshares, Inc. 07/16/2007

ALBEMARLE PAPER MANUFACTURING CO. (VA)
Each share Common $100 par exchanged for (10) shares Common $10 par 00/00/1947
Recapitalized 00/00/1953
Each share Class B $10 par exchanged for (0.2) share Class A Common $5 par and (1.8) shares Class B Common $5 par
Each share Common $10 par exchanged for (1) share Class A Common $5 par and (1) share Class B Common $5 par
Recapitalized 07/02/1956
Each (20) shares 6% 1st Preferred $100 par exchanged for (21) shares 6% Preferred A $100 par
Stock Dividends - 100% 01/03/1956; 25% 01/22/1960
Under plan of acquisition name changed to Ethyl Corp. 11/30/1962
Ethyl Corp. reorganized as NewMarket Corp. 06/18/2004

ALBERCALIF PETROLEUMS LTD. (ON)
Charter cancelled and declared dissolved for default in filing reports 11/27/1961

ALBERCAN OIL CORP. (DE)
Merged into Canada Southern Oils Ltd. and 02/24/1954
Each (2.444) shares Capital Stock 1¢ par exchanged for (1) Voting Trust Certificate
(See Canada Southern Oils Ltd.)

ALBERENE STONE CORP. OF VIRGINIA (VA)
Merged into Georgia Marble Co. 04/11/1959
Each share Capital Stock $5 par exchanged for (0.8333333) share Common $10 par
Georgia Marble Co. merged into Walter (Jim) Corp. 02/21/1969
(See Walter (Jim) Corp.)

ALBERFIELD OIL & GAS LTD. (ON)
Charter revoked for failure to file reports and pay fees 00/00/1959

ALBERMONT PETROLEUMS LTD. (ON)
Merged into Western Decalta Petroleum 03/23/1956
Each share Common no par exchanged for (0.5) share Common no par 03/23/1956
(See Western Decalta Petroleum Ltd.)

ALBERNI GOLD MINING CO. LTD.
Dissolved 00/00/1948
Details not available

ALBERNI MINES LTD (BC)
Struck off register 02/02/1983

ALBERO CORP (NV)
Name changed to Vitaxel Group Ltd. and Common $0.001 par changed to $0.000001 par 01/19/2016

ALBERS SUPER MARKETS, INC. (OH)
Merged into Colonial Stores, Inc. on a (1.25) for (1) basis 06/18/1955
(See Colonial Stores, Inc.)

ALBERT BREWING CO.
Declared insolvent 00/00/1939
Details not available

ALBERT FISHER GROUP PLC (UNITED KINGDOM)
Stock Dividends - 33.33333333% 12/05/1986; 50% 05/20/1987; 50% 01/26/1988
ADR agreement terminated 07/31/2003
No ADR holders' equity

ALBERTA-CANADA OILS, INC. (DE)
Name changed to Dakota-Montana Oil Leaseholds, Inc. 00/00/1953
(See Dakota-Montana Oil Leaseholds, Inc.)

ALBERTA CLIPPER ENERGY INC (AB)
Acquired by NAL Oil & Gas Trust 06/01/2009
Each share Common no par exchanged for (0.078875) Trust Unit no par
NAL Oil & Gas Trust reorganized as NAL Energy Corp. 01/06/2011 which merged into Pengrowth Energy Corp. 06/05/2012

ALBERTA CONSOLIDATED GAS UTILITIES LTD. (CANADA)
Name changed to Great Northern Gas Utilities Ltd. 05/20/1954
Great Northern Gas Utilities Ltd. name changed to Great Northern Capital Co. Ltd. 05/08/1962
(See Great Northern Capital Co. Ltd.)

ALBERTA COPPER & RES LTD (BC)
Recapitalized as Alberta Petroleum & Resources Ltd. 05/23/1972
Each share Common 50¢ par exchanged for (0.33333333) share Common no par
(See Alberta Petroleum & Resources Ltd.)

ALBERTA DIAMONDFIELDS INC (AB)
Recapitalized as Delray Ventures Inc. (AB) 08/21/2002
Each share Common no par exchanged for (0.25) share Common no par
Delray Ventures Inc. (AB) reincorporated in British Columbia as Clydesdale Resources Inc. 08/08/2008

ALBERTA DISTILLERS LTD (AB)
Voting Trust Agreement terminated 05/25/1964
Each VTC for Capital Stock $1 par exchanged for (1) share Capital Stock $1 par
Acquired by National Distillers & Chemical Corp. 11/16/1964
Each share Capital Stock $1 par exchanged for $4 cash

ALBERTA EASTN GAS LTD (AB)
Merged into Ocelot Industries Ltd. 08/04/1978
Each share Capital Stock no par exchanged for $22 cash

ALBERTA ENERGY LTD (AB)
15% 1st Preferred Ser. A $25 par called for redemption 12/01/1986
11.25% Conv. 2nd Preferred Ser. 1 $25 par called for redemption 07/01/1987
7.75% Deferred 2nd Preferred Ser. 2 $25 par called for redemption 09/12/1994
Common no par split (3) for (1) by issuance of (2) additional shares 05/07/1980
Merged into EnCana Corp. 01/03/2003
Each share Common no par exchanged for (1.472) shares Common no par
Preferred not affected except for change of name

ALBERTA FOCUSED INCOME & GROWTH FD (AB)
Merged into ACTIVEnergy Income Fund 10/26/2007
Each Unit received (0.78214715) Trust Unit
ACTIVEnergy Income Fund reorganized as Middlefield Mutual Funds Ltd. 06/05/2017

ALBERTA GAS TRUNK LINE LTD (AB)
5.75% Preferred Ser. B $100 par called for redemption 07/16/1965
6.25% Preferred Ser. A $100 par called for redemption 07/16/1965
Class A Common $5 par changed to $1.25 par and (3) additional shares issued 09/30/1972
Name changed to Nova, An Alberta Corp. 08/06/1980
Nova, An Alberta Corp. name changed to Nova Corp. of Alberta 09/01/1987 which name changed to Nova Gas Transmission Ltd. 05/11/1994
(See Nova Gas Transmission Ltd.)

ALBERTA GIANT OIL CO. LTD. (AB)
Struck off register for failure to file annual returns 11/30/1972

ALBERTA HOTEL DEV CORP (AB)
Became private 12/31/1993
Details not available

ALBERTA HOTELS & RESORTS INC (AB)
Recapitalized as Canadian Destination Properties Inc. 06/05/2002
Each share Common no par exchanged for (0.2) share Common no par
(See Canadian Destination Properties Inc.)

ALBERTA NAT GAS LTD (CANADA)
Name changed from Alberta Natural Gas Ltd. to Alberta Natural Gas Co. Ltd. 07/08/1971
Capital Stock $10 par changed to no par 05/14/1979
Capital Stock no par split (5) for (1) by issuance of (4) additional shares 06/02/1980
Capital Stock no par split (3) for (1) by issuance of (2) additional shares 06/04/1984
Merged into TransCanada PipeLines Ltd. 03/12/1996
Each share Capital Stock no par exchanged for either (1.3588) shares Common no par or $26.25 cash
Note: Option to receive stock expired 04/02/1996
TransCanada PipeLines Ltd. reorganized as TransCanada Corp. 05/15/2003

ALBERTA OIL & GAS PETE CORP (AB)
Recapitalized 11/19/1997
Recapitalized from Alberta Oil & Gas Ltd. to Alberta Oil & Gas Petroleum Corp. 11/19/1997
Each share Common no par exchanged for (0.1) share Common no par
Recapitalized as Edge Energy Inc. 04/14/1998
Each share Common no par exchanged for (0.33333333) share Common no par
Edge Energy Inc. merged into Ventus Energy Ltd. 08/11/2000 which name changed to Navigo Energy Inc. 05/24/2002
(See Navigo Energy Inc.)

ALBERTA OIL LEASEHOLDS LTD.
Merged into West Plains Oil Resources Ltd. 00/00/1952
Each share Common no par exchanged for (0.33333333) share Common no par 00/00/1952
(See West Plains Oil Resources Ltd.)

ALBERTA OILSANDS INC (AB)
Under plan of merger name changed to Marquee Energy Ltd. (New) 12/08/2016

ALBERTA PAC LEASING CORP (AB)
Name changed to Envirodyne International Inc. 07/18/1989
Envirodyne International Inc. recapitalized as Envirodyne Industries Inc. 03/07/1991 which recapitalized as Telesis Industrial Group Inc. 08/07/1992 which name changed to Merendon Canada Inc. 10/09/1998 which recapitalized as Richfield Explorations Inc. 03/08/2000
(See Richfield Explorations Inc.)

ALBERTA PACIFIC CONSOLIDATED OILS LTD. (AB)
Capital Stock $1 par changed to no par 03/07/1955
Merged into Canadian Industrial Gas & Oil Ltd. 03/08/1965
Each share Capital Stock no par exchanged (0.07299270) share Capital Stock $2.50 par

Canadian Industrial Gas & Oil Ltd. merged into Norcen Energy Resources Ltd. (AB) 10/28/1975 which reincorporated in Canada 04/15/1977 which merged into Union Pacific Resources Group Inc. 04/17/1998 which merged into Anadarko Petroleum Corp. 07/14/2000

ALBERTA PACIFIC GRAIN CO., LTD.
Assets liquidated for benefit of creditors 00/00/1943
No stockholders' equity

ALBERTA PETE & RES LTD (BC)
Acquired by Plains Investment Ltd. 04/14/1976
Each share Common 50¢ par exchanged for $1.25 cash

ALBERTA RESOURCE CAP CORP (AB)
Struck off register for failure to file annual returns 02/01/1999

ALBERTA REV PPTY CORP (AB)
Merged into Plaser Light Corp. 07/17/1991
Each share Common no par exchanged for (0.0421) share Common no par
(See Plaser Light Corp.)

ALBERTA STAR DEV CORP (AB)
Each share old Common no par exchanged for (0.2) share new Common no par 03/11/2010
Name changed to Elysee Development Corp. 07/15/2015

ALBERTA STAR MINING CORP (AB)
Recapitalized as Alberta Star Development Corp. 09/20/2001
Each share Common no par exchanged for (0.2) share Common no par
Alberta Star Development Corp. name changed to Elysee Development Corp. 07/15/2015

ALBERTA SURFACE SYS LTD (AB)
Recapitalized as MSI Energy Services Inc. 07/14/1999
Each share Common no par exchanged for (0.1) share Common no par
(See MSI Energy Services Inc.)

ALBERTA WTRS INTL INC (AB)
Recapitalized as Loma Petroleum Resources Ltd. 03/06/1995
Each share Common no par exchanged for (0.25) share Common no par
Loma Petroleum Resources Ltd. recapitalized as Loma Oil & Gas Ltd. 11/21/1997

ALBERTECH INDS LTD (AB)
Struck off register for failure to file annual returns 05/01/1994

ALBERTO-CULVER CO NEW (DE)
Acquired by Unilever N.V. 05/10/2011
Each share Common 1¢ par exchanged for $37.50 cash

ALBERTO CULVER CO OLD (DE)
Common no par split (2) for (1) by issuance of (1) additional share 04/05/1963
Common no par split (3) for (2) by issuance of (0.5) additional share 03/06/1964
Common no par split (3) for (2) by issuance of (0.5) additional share 11/10/1969
Common no par split (3) for (2) by issuance of (0.5) additional share 02/20/1985
Common no par split (3) for (2) by issuance of (0.5) additional share 02/20/1986
Common no par reclassified as Conv. Class B Common 22¢ par 04/16/1986
Each share Conv. Class B Common 22¢ par received distribution of (0.33333333) share Class A Common 22¢ par 04/28/1986
Class A Common 22¢ par split (2) for (1) by issuance of (1) additional share 02/20/1990
Conv. Class B Common 22¢ par split (2) for (1) by issuance of (1) additional share 02/20/1990
Class A Common 22¢ par split (2) for (1) by issuance of (1) additional share payable 02/20/1997 to holders of record 02/03/1997 Ex date - 02/21/1997
Conv. Class B Common 22¢ par split (2) for (1) by issuance of (1) additional share payable 02/20/1997 to holders of record 02/03/1997 Ex date - 02/21/1997
Class A Common 22¢ par reclassified as Conv. Class B Common 22¢ par 11/06/2003
Conv. Class B Common 22¢ par reclassified as Common 22¢ par 01/23/2004
Common no par split (3) for (2) by issuance of (0.5) additional share payable 02/20/2004 to holders of record 02/02/2004 Ex date - 02/23/2004
Reorganized as Alberto-Culver Co. (New) 11/16/2006
Each share Common 22¢ par exchanged for (1) share Common 1¢ par, (1) share Sally Beauty Holdings, Inc. Common 1¢ par and $25 cash
(See each company's listing)

ALBERTON CORP. (OH)
Liquidation completed 00/00/1952
Details not available

ALBERTS INC (DE)
Stock Dividend - 50% 04/02/1973
Name changed to Valor Investment Fund Inc. (DE) 07/12/1978
Valor Investment Fund Inc. (DE) reincorporated in Michigan 10/08/1979
(See Valor Investment Fund Inc.)

ALBERTSONS INC (DE)
Reincorporated 08/01/1969
6% Preferred $100 par called for redemption 11/01/1963
Class A Common $1 par and Class B Common $1 par reclassified as Common $1 par 05/18/1964
Common $1 par split (3) for (1) by issuance of (2) additional shares 11/01/1965
State of incorporation changed from (NV) to (DE) 08/01/1969
Common $1 par split (2) for (1) by issuance of (1) additional share 03/25/1980
Common $1 par split (2) for (1) by issuance of (1) additional share 06/27/1983
Common $1 par split (2) for (1) by issuance of (1) additional share 10/02/1987
Common $1 par split (2) for (1) by issuance of (1) additional share 06/26/1990
Common $1 par split (2) for (1) by issuance of (1) additional share 10/04/1993
Stock Dividend - 10% 06/01/1973
Merged into Supervalu Inc. 06/02/2006
Each share Common $1 par exchanged for (0.182) share Common $1 par and $20.35 cash
Each 7.25% Corporate Unit exchanged for (0.15952) share Supervalu Inc. Common $1 par and $17.83596 cash 05/16/2007
(See Supervalu Inc.)

ALBERTVILLE BANCSHARES, INC. (AL)
Acquired by First Alabama Bancshares, Inc. 00/00/1987
Details not available

ALBETA MINES LTD. (BC)
Liquidated 03/00/1978
Details not available

ALBION AVIATION INC (DE)
Common $0.001 par split (3) for (2) by issuance of (0.5) additional share payable 12/12/2002 to holders of record 12/05/2002 Ex date - 12/13/2002
Name changed to Aradyme Corp. (DE) 01/05/2003
Aradyme Corp. (DE) reincorporated in Utah 12/29/2006
(See Aradyme Corp.)

ALBION BANC CORP (DE)
Merged into Niagara Bancorp, Inc. 03/24/2000
Each share Common 1¢ par exchanged for $15.75 cash

ALBION INTL RES INC (DE)
Merged into Eglinton Exploration PLC 12/29/1989
Each share Common 1¢ par exchanged for (0.1) share Ordinary Stock 10p par

ALBION MALLEABLE IRON CO. (MI)
Under plan of merger each share Common $10 par exchanged for (10) shares Common $1 par 02/01/1960
Common $1 par split (5) for (4) by issuance of (0.25) additional share 11/28/1966
Merged into Hayes-Albion Corp. (MI) 08/14/1967
Each share Common $1 par exchanged for (0.544) share Common $5 par
Hayes-Albion Corp. (MI) reincorporated in Delaware 12/11/1968 which reincorporated back in Michigan 12/31/1979
(See Hayes-Albion Corp. (MI))

ALBION PERSHING GOLD MINES LTD. (ON)
Name changed to Endeavor Mining Corp. Ltd. 00/00/1954
Endeavor Mining Corp. Ltd. merged into Mining Endeavor Co. Ltd. 03/28/1956
(See Mining Endeavor Co. Ltd.)

ALBION PETE LTD (AB)
Reorganized under the laws of British Columbia as First Mining Finance Corp. 04/06/2015
Each share Common no par exchanged for (0.25) share Common no par
First Mining Finance Corp. name changed to First Mining Gold Corp. 01/11/2018

ALBRIGHT BOAT & MARINE CO. (NC)
Name changed to Albright Industries, Inc. 03/28/1961
(See Albright Industries, Inc.)

ALBRIGHT INDUSTRIES, INC. (NC)
Adjudicated bankrupt 07/02/1962
No stockholders' equity

ALBRO INDS CORP (NV)
Stock Dividends - 10% 08/31/1973; 10% 02/15/1974
Name changed to Energy Resources of America, Inc. and Common $1 par changed to 50¢ par 07/28/1977

ALBUQUERQUE ASSOCIATED OIL CO. (NM)
Merged into Atlas Corp. 05/31/1956
Each share Common $1 par exchanged for (1) share Common $1 par
(See Atlas Corp.)

ALBUQUERQUE NATL BK (ALBUQUERQUE, NM)
Name changed to Albuquerque National Trust & Savings Bank (Albuquerque, NM) 10/08/1928 which name changed back to Albuquerque National Bank (Albuquerque, NM) 12/31/1948
Capital Stock $100 par changed to $20 par and (4) additional shares issued plus a 40% stock dividend paid 01/29/1958
Capital Stock $20 par changed to $5 par and (3) additional shares issued plus a 25% stock dividend paid 02/21/1967
Stock Dividends - 20% 12/22/1950; 20% 02/09/1960; 20% 01/26/1962; 66.66666666% 04/01/1970
99.9% acquired by First New Mexico Bankshare Corp. through exchange offer which expired 11/15/1968
Public interest eliminated

ALBUQUERQUE NATIONAL TRUST & SAVINGS BANK (ALBUQUERQUE, NM)
Stock Dividends - 100% 09/21/1945; 66.66666666% 12/31/1948
Name changed to Albuquerque National Bank (Albuquerque, NM) 12/31/1948
(See Albuquerque National Bank (Albuquerque, NM))

ALBUQUERQUE NATURAL GAS CO.
Reorganized as New Mexico Gas Co. 08/14/1936
Each share Preferred exchanged for (10) shares Common
Each share Common exchanged for (1) share Common
New Mexico Gas Co. merged into Southern Union Gas Co. (DE) (New) 11/24/1942 which name changed to Southern Union Co. (Old) 05/07/1976
(See Southern Union Co. (Old))

ALBUQUERQUE WESTN SOLAR INDS INC (NM)
Each share old Common 1¢ par exchanged for (4) shares new Common 1¢ par 06/10/1977
Name changed to Technology International Ltd. and new Common 1¢ par changed to no par 12/12/1985
(See Technology International Ltd.)

ALBURY RES LTD (AB)
Voluntarily dissolved 11/03/2009
Stockholders' equity unlikely

ALC COMMUNICATIONS CORP (DE)
Each share old Common 1¢ par exchanged for (0.2) share new Common 1¢ par 09/03/1991
$1.60 Preferred $20 par called for redemption 12/31/1993
Merged into Frontier Corp. 08/17/1995
Each share new Common 1¢ par exchanged for (2) shares Common $1 par
Frontier Corp. merged into Global Crossing Ltd. 09/28/1999
(See Global Crossing Ltd.)

ALCA INDUSTRIES CORP. (DE)
5% Preferred Ser. A $5 par called for redemption 06/07/1966
5% Preferred Ser. B $5 par called for redemption 06/16/1967
Public interest eliminated

ALCAN INC (CANADA)
Name changed 07/24/1987
Name changed 03/01/2001
$1.70 Preferred $40 par called for redemption 04/15/1980
Common no par split (2) for (1) by issuance of (1) additional share 04/18/1980
Common no par split (3) for (2) by issuance of (0.5) additional share 06/01/1987
Under plan of merger name changed from Alcan Aluminium Ltd. (Old) to Alcan Aluminium Ltd. (New) 07/24/1987
$2 1st Preference no par called for redemption 12/01/1987
$2.1875 Retractable Preference Ser.

ALC-ALC

B no par called for redemption 09/01/1988
$2.3125 Retractable Preference Ser. A no par called for redemption 09/01/1988
Adjustable Rate Preference Ser. F no par called for redemption 06/30/1992
Floating Rate U.S. Dollar Preference Ser. D no par called for redemption 06/01/1998
Common no par split (3) for (2) by issuance of (0.5) additional share 06/09/1989
Name changed from Alcan Aluminium Ltd. (New) to Alcan Inc. 03/01/2001
Each share Common no par received distribution of (0.2) share Novelis Inc. Common no par payable 01/18/2005 to holders of record 01/11/2005 Ex date - 01/19/2005
Floating Rate Preference Ser. C no par called for redemption at $25 on 09/03/2007
Preference Ser. E no par called for redemption at $25 on 09/03/2007
Merged into Rio Tinto PLC 11/15/2007
Each share Common no par exchanged for $101 cash

ALCAN YELLOWKNIFE GOLD MINES LTD. (ON)
Charter cancelled for failure to pay taxes and file returns 09/00/1957

ALCANTA INTERNATIONAL EDUCATION LTD. (CAYMAN ISLANDS)
Name changed to Access International Education Ltd. 01/17/2001

ALCANTARA BRANDS CORP (NV)
Common $0.001 par split (10) for (1) by issuance of (9) additional shares payable 05/18/2009 to holders of record 05/11/2009 Ex date - 05/19/2009
Recapitalized as Bollente Companies Inc. 10/22/2010
Each share Common $0.001 par exchanged for (0.02) share Common $0.001 par
Bollente Companies Inc. name changed to Trutankless, Inc. 07/02/2018

ALCAR INSTRS INC (NJ)
Adjudicated bankrupt 06/26/1968
Operations ceased and assets sold for benefit of creditors
No stockholders' equity

ALCARD CHEMICALS GROUP INC (DE)
Name changed to Alcar Chemicals Group, Inc. 04/03/2006

ALCATEL CDA INC (CANADA)
Each Exchangeable Share no par exchanged for (1) Alcatel S.A. Sponsored ADR for Class A 07/29/2005
(Additional Information in Active)

ALCATEL LUCENT (FRANCE)
Name changed 08/31/1998
Name changed 11/30/2006
Name changed from Alcatel Alsthom to Alcatel 08/31/1998
Basis changed from (1:0.2) to (1:1) 05/22/2000
Under plan of merger name changed from Alcatel to Alcatel-Lucent 11/30/2006
ADR agreement terminated 02/24/2016
Each Sponsored ADR for Ordinary exchanged for $2.676512 cash

ALCATEL NETWORKS CORP (CANADA)
Name changed to Alcatel Canada Inc. 09/29/2000
(See Alcatel Canada Inc.)

ALCATEL OPTRONICS (FRANCE)
Each Sponsored ADR for Class O exchanged for (1) Alcatel Sponsored ADR for Class A 04/17/2003
Alcatel name changed to Alcatel-Lucent 11/30/2006
(See Alcatel-Lucent)

ALCAZAR HOTEL, INC. (OH)
Liquidation completed
Each share Common no par exchanged for initial distribution of $50 cash 10/01/1948
Each share Common no par received second distribution of $5 cash 03/21/1950
Each share Common no par received third distribution of $13.25 cash 07/02/1951
Each share Common no par received fourth and final distribution of $1.40 cash 10/12/1954

ALCHEMIA LTD (AUSTRALIA)
ADR agreement terminated 07/03/2017
No ADR's remain outstanding

ALCHEMY CREATIVE INC (FL)
Administratively dissolved 09/26/2008

ALCHEMY ENTERPRISES LTD (NV)
Each share Common $0.001 par exchanged for (17.6471) shares Common $0.001 par 03/01/2006
Name changed to Ecotality, Inc. 11/27/2006
(See Ecotality, Inc.)

ALCHEMY EQUITIES LTD (CO)
Name changed to Heritage Mines Ltd. 12/14/1995
Heritage Mines Ltd. name changed to Southern Cosmetics, Inc. 07/20/2005 which name changed to Revenge Designs, Inc. 12/18/2007 which name changed to Cartel Blue, Inc. 09/18/2015

ALCHEMY HLDGS INC (FL)
SEC revoked common stock registration 04/17/2008

ALCHEMY VENTURES LTD (BC)
Reincorporated under the laws of Canada as i-minerals inc. 01/22/2004
i-minerals inc. name changed to I-Minerals Inc. 12/15/2011

ALCHIB DEV LTD (ON)
Merged into Kalrock Developments Ltd. 10/23/1978
Each share Capital Stock no par exchanged for (0.33333333) share Capital Stock no par
Kalrock Developments Ltd. merged into Kalrock Resources Ltd. 08/08/1990 which merged into Cercal Minerals Corp. 07/09/1993
(See Cercal Minerals Corp.)

ALCIDE CORP (DE)
Each share old Common 1¢ par exchanged for (0.1) share new Common 1¢ par 10/09/1992
Each share $2.625 Conv. Preferred Ser. 1 1¢ par exchanged for (1) share Preferred Ser. 2 1¢ par and (0.2) share new Common 1¢ par 09/30/1994
Preferred Ser. 2 1¢ par called for redemption at $2.625 on 07/29/2004
Acquired by Ecolab Inc. 07/30/2004
Each share new Common 1¢ par exchanged for (0.6744) share Common $1 par

ALCIDE PORCUPINE MINES LTD. (ON)
Charter cancelled for failure to pay taxes and file returns 10/28/1957

ALCINA DEV CORP (BC)
Struck off register and declared dissolved for failure to file returns 09/25/1987

ALCLARE RES INC (BC)
Name changed to Chesapeake Computer Systems Inc. 01/21/1987
(See Chesapeake Computer Systems Inc.)

ALCO ADVANCED TECHNOLOGIES INC (NV)
Each share old Common $0.001 par exchanged for (0.02) share new Common $0.001 par 07/22/2010
Recapitalized as Southern ITS International, Inc. 04/11/2012
Each share new Common $0.001 par exchanged for (0.00333333) share Common $0.001 par

ALCO CHEMICAL CORP. (OH)
Each share Common 1¢ par exchanged for (0.16666666) share Common no par 08/23/1963
Name changed to Alco Standard Corp. 01/17/1966
Alco Standard Corp. name changed to IKON Office Solutions, Inc. 01/24/1997
(See IKON Office Solutions, Inc.)

ALCO CORP (UT)
Each share Common 10¢ par exchanged for (0.2) share Common 1¢ par 05/28/1970
Proclaimed dissolved for failure to pay taxes 12/31/1975

ALCO ENERGY CORP (NV)
Name changed to A & J Venture Capital Group, Inc. 08/21/2009
A & J Venture Capital Group, Inc. recapitalized as ReliaBrand Inc. 02/24/2011

ALCO HEALTH DISTR CORP (DE)
Name changed to AmeriSource Distribution Corp. 07/15/1994
AmeriSource Distribution Corp. name changed to AmeriSource Health Corp. 03/30/1995 which merged into AmerisourceBergen Corp. 08/29/2001

ALCO HEALTH SVCS CORP (DE)
Merged into AHSC Holdings Corp. 10/31/1989
Each share Common 1¢ par exchanged for $3.10 principal amount of 18.5% Subordinated Debentures due 10/31/2004

ALCO INDS INC (AZ)
Charter revoked for non-payment of taxes 11/12/1969

ALCO INTL GROUP INC (DE)
Each share old Common $0.001 par exchanged for (0.25) share new Common $0.001 par 12/06/1991
New Common $0.001 par split (2) for (1) by issuance of (1) additional share 03/02/1992
Name changed to Incomed Corp. 08/05/1993
Incomed Corp. recapitalized as International Ally Group, Inc. 03/14/2007 which recapitalized as Green Shores Inc. 07/27/2009 which name changed to Pacific Shore Holdings, Inc. 10/12/2010

ALCO OIL & CHEMICAL CORP. (OH)
$6 Preferred called for redemption 07/31/1959
Name changed to Alco Chemical Corp. 01/16/1962
Alco Chemical Corp. name changed to Alco Standard Corp. 01/17/1966 which name changed to IKON Office Solutions, Inc. 01/24/1997
(See IKON Office Solutions, Inc.)

ALCO OIL & GAS CORP (IL)
Merged into Ladd Petroleum Corp. 07/11/1969
Each share Common $0.03333333 par exchanged for (0.5) share Common 10¢ par and (0.1) 1972 Ser. Common Stock Purchase Warrant
Ladd Petroleum Corp. merged into Utah International Inc. 11/30/1973 which merged into General Electric Co. 12/20/1976

ALCO PRODUCTS, INC. (NY)
7% Preferred called for redemption 08/08/1958
Name changed to Citadel Industries, Inc. (NY) 12/31/1964
Citadel Industries, Inc. (NY) reincorporated in Delaware 08/17/1966
(See Citadel Industries, Inc. (DE))

ALCO STD CORP (OH)
Common no par split (2) for (1) by issuance of (1) additional share 09/30/1968
$1 Conv. Preferred no par called for redemption 12/31/1971
Common no par split (2) for (1) by issuance of (1) additional share 05/15/1981
Common no par split (2) for (1) by issuance of (1) additional share 06/26/1987
Preferred Ser. 10 conversion privilege expired 02/27/1991
Common no par split (2) for (1) by issuance of (1) additional share 11/09/1995
Depositary Preferred Ser. AA called for redemption 02/09/1996
Conv. Preferred Ser. AA no par called for redemption 02/09/1996
Each share Common no par received distribution of (0.5) share Unisource Worldwide, Inc. Common no par payable 12/31/1996 to holders of record 12/13/1996 Ex date - 01/02/1997
Name changed to IKON Office Solutions, Inc. 01/24/1997
(See IKON Office Solutions, Inc.)

ALCO URANIUM CORP (UT)
Recapitalized as Alco Corp. 07/18/1969
Each share Capital Stock 1¢ par exchanged for (0.025) share Common 10¢ par
(See Alco Corp.)

ALCOA INC (PA)
Old Common $1 par split (2) for (1) by issuance of (1) additional share payable 02/25/1999 to holders of record 02/08/1999 Ex date - 02/26/1999
Old Common $1 par split (2) for (1) by issuance of (1) additional share payable 06/09/2000 to holders of record 05/26/2000
Each share old Common $1 par exchanged for (0.33333333) share new Common $1 par 10/06/2016
Each share new Common $1 par received distribution of (0.33333333) share Alcoa Corp. Common 1¢ par payable 11/01/2016 to holders of record 10/20/2016 Ex date - 11/01/2016
Name changed to Arconic Inc. (PA) 11/01/2016
Arconic Inc. (PA) reincorporated in Delaware 12/31/2017

ALCOA INTL HLDGS CO (DE)
Each share Variable Term Preferred Ser. A $100 par exchanged for (1) share Variable Term Exchangeable Preferred Ser. A $100 par 11/01/1988
Each share Variable Term Preferred Ser. B $100 par exchanged for (1) share Variable Term Exchangeable Preferred Ser. B $100 par 11/01/1988
Each share Variable Term Preferred Ser. C $100 par exchanged for (1) share Variable Term Exchangeable Preferred Ser. C $100 par 11/01/1988
Each share Variable Term Exchangeable Preferred Ser. A $100 par exchanged for (1) share Star Exchangeable Preferred Ser. A $100 par 04/15/1991
Each share Variable Term Exchangeable Preferred Ser. C $100 par exchanged for (1) share Star Exchangeable Preferred Ser. A $100 par 04/15/1991

Variable Term Exchangeable Preferred Ser. B $100 par called for redemption 04/05/1995
Star Exchangable Preferred Ser. A $100 par called for redemption 04/26/1995
Public interest eliminated

ALCOBRA LTD (ISRAEL)
Recapitalized as Arcturus Therapeutics Ltd. 11/16/2017
Each share Ordinary ILS 0.01 par exchanged for (0.14285714) share Ordinary ILS 0.01 par

ALCOGAS INC (CO)
Charter suspended for failure to file annual reports 09/30/1983

ALCOHOL SENSORS INTL LTD (DE)
Chapter 11 bankruptcy case terminated 06/08/2001
No stockholders' equity

ALCOLAC CHEM CORP (MD)
Common 20¢ par and Class B Common 20¢ par changed to 10¢ par and (1) additional share issued respectively 11/13/1964
Name changed to Alcolac, Inc. 10/13/1970
(See Alcolac, Inc.)

ALCOLAC INC (MD)
Each share Class B Common 10¢ par exchanged for (1) share Common 10¢ par 01/04/1974
Acquired by Tunnel Holdings Ltd. 04/09/1981
Each share Common 10¢ par exchanged for $17 cash

ALCON DATA CORP (MD)
Name changed to F.A. Corp. 07/01/1980
(See F.A. Corp.)

ALCON INC (SWITZERLAND)
Merged into Novartis AG 04/08/2011
Each share Common CHF 0.20 par exchanged for (2.9228) Sponsored ADR's for Ordinary and $8.20 cash

ALCON LABS INC (TX)
Common 50¢ par changed to 25¢ par and (1) additional share issued 06/16/1969
Common 25¢ par changed to no par and (1) additional share issued 09/22/1972
Stock Dividend - 50% 07/16/1971
Merged into Delaware Bay Co. 05/31/1978
Each share Common no par exchanged for $42 cash

ALCONA MINES LTD. (ON)
Charter cancelled 05/16/1975

ALCOR ENERGY & RECYCLING SYS INC (NJ)
Each share old Common no par exchanged for (0.05) share new Common no par 12/21/1994
Recapitalized as Compost America Holding Inc. (NJ) 02/09/1995
Each share new Common no par exchanged for (0.05) share Common no par
Compost America Holding Inc. (NJ) reorganized in Delaware as Phoenix Waste Services Co., Inc. 09/29/2000
(See Phoenix Waste Services Co., Inc.)

ALCOR FINL CORP (AB)
Merged into Renoir Water Inc. 12/31/1991
Each share Common no par exchanged for (2) shares Common no par
Renoir Water Inc. name changed to Frank's Corp. 08/20/1996 which recapitalized as True North Water Corp. (AB) 02/23/1999 which reincorporated in Canada 12/12/2003 which name changed to Watertowne International Inc. 03/19/2004 which recapitalized as Sightus Inc. 03/15/2006

(See Sightus Inc.)

ALCOR MINERALS LTD (AB)
Recapitalized as Consolidated Alcor Resources Ltd. 04/16/1974
Each share Common no par exchanged for (0.2) share Common no par
(See Consolidated Alcor Resources Ltd.)

ALCOR RES LTD (BC)
Common no par split (4) for (1) by issuance of (3) additional shares payable 08/21/2007 to holders of record 08/16/2007 Ex date - 08/14/2007
Name changed to Balto Resources Ltd. 06/16/2008

ALCORN FOOD PRODS INC (DE)
Name changed to Freedom Synthetic Oil Co., Inc. 01/24/1980
(See Freedom Synthetic Oil Co., Inc.)

ALCOURT MINES LTD. (ON)
Charter cancelled for failure to pay taxes and file returns 11/29/1972

ALCUM MNG LTD (BC)
Name changed to Code Petroleum Ltd. 06/26/1981
(See Code Petroleum Ltd.)

ALCYLITE PLASTICS & CHEMICAL CORP. (CA)
Adjudicated bankrupt 01/00/1963
No stockholders' equity

ALCYONE RES LTD (AUSTRALIA)
ADR agreement terminated 02/02/2017
No ADR holders' equity

ALD SVCS INC (NV)
Common $0.001 par split (1.6184211) for (1) by issuance of (0.6184211) additional share payable 02/15/2002 to holders of record 02/04/2002 Ex date - 02/19/2002
Name changed to MicroIslet, Inc. 05/09/2002
(See MicroIslet, Inc.)

ALDA INDS CORP (BC)
Recapitalized as Crux Industries Inc. 07/14/1999
Each share Common no par exchanged for (0.16666666) share Common no par
Crux Industries Inc. name changed to Mont Blanc Resources Inc. 11/18/2005 which name changed to Sonora Gold & Silver Corp. 07/17/2008

ALDA MINES LTD. (BC)
Dissolved 03/18/1977
Details not available

ALDA PHARMACEUTICALS CORP (BC)
Each share old Common no par exchanged for (0.1) share new Common no par 03/08/2012
Name changed to Nuva Pharmaceuticals Inc. 07/26/2013
Nuva Pharmaceuticals Inc. name changed to Vanc Pharmaceuticals Inc. 08/07/2014

ALDABRA ACQUISITION CORP (DE)
Merged into Great Lakes Dredge & Dock Corp. 12/27/2006
Each share Common $0.0001 par exchanged for (1) share Common $0.0001 par

ALDABRA 2 ACQUISITION CORP (DE)
Name changed to Boise Inc. 02/22/2008
(See Boise Inc.)

ALDAGE MINES LTD. (ON)
Merged into Alchib Developments Ltd. 07/10/1969
Each share Capital Stock no par exchanged for (0.09) share Capital Stock no par
Alchib Developments Ltd. merged into Kalrock Developments Ltd.

10/23/1978 which merged into Kalrock Resources Ltd. 08/08/1990 which merged into Cercal Minerals Corp. 07/09/1993
(See Cercal Minerals Corp.)

ALDAR GROUP INC (NV)
Name changed to NanoTech Entertainment, Inc. 06/11/2009

ALDEA VISION INC (CANADA)
Each share old Common no par exchanged for (0.1) share new Common no par 07/07/2006
Plan of arrangement effective 10/04/2006
Each share new Common no par exchanged for (1) share AldeaVision Solutions Inc. Common no par and (0.0118737) share VSG Seismic Canada Inc. Common no par
(See each company's listing)

ALDEAVISION SOLUTIONS INC (CANADA)
Plan of Arrangement under Companies' Creditors Arrangement Act effective 01/14/2008
No stockholders' equity

ALDEBARAN DRILLING INC (CO)
Each share Common 1¢ par exchanged for (0.05) share Common 5¢ par 03/29/1985
Charter suspended for failure to maintain a resident agent and file annual reports 09/30/1988

ALDEN CARE ENTERPRISES INC (DE)
In process of liquidation
Each share Common 10¢ par exchanged for initial distribution of $0.45 cash 04/17/1978
Each share Common 10¢ par received second distribution of $0.15 cash 02/10/1981
Each share Common 10¢ par received third distribution of $0.40 cash 08/31/1981
Each share Common 10¢ par received fourth distribution of $0.08 cash 02/19/1982
Each share Common 10¢ par received fifth distribution of $0.20 cash 08/15/1982
Each share Common 10¢ par received sixth distribution of $0.10 cash 02/15/1983
Note: Details on subsequent distributions, if any, are not available

ALDEN ELECTRS INC (MA)
Name changed 06/13/1983
Name changed from Alden Electronic & Impulse Recording Equipment Co. to Alden Electronics, Inc. 06/13/1983
Voluntarily dissolved 04/30/1999
Details not available

ALDEN INN, INC. (DE)
Completely liquidated 05/04/1945
Each share Capital Stock Trust Ctf. no par exchanged for first and final distribution of $27.67 cash

ALDEN PRESS CO (DE)
Merged into APC Merger Corp. 03/02/1993
Each share Common 1¢ par exchanged for $15 cash

ALDEN SELF TRAN SYS CORP (MA)
Common $1 par split (4) for (1) by issuance of (3) additional shares 10/26/1970
Involuntarily dissolved 01/10/1979

ALDENS INC (IL)
4.25% Dividend Rate Preferred $100 par increased to 4.5% on 05/23/1961
Common $5 par split (2) for (1) by issuance of (1) additional share 01/01/1962
Stock Dividends - 50% 05/07/1954; 10% 08/12/1955
Merged into Gamble-Skogmo, Inc. 12/31/1964
Each share Conv. 2nd Preference no

par exchanged for (42.37) shares $1.60 Conv. Preferred $5 par and (6.35) shares Common $5 par
Each share Common $5 par exchanged for (1) share $1.60 Conv. Preferred $5 par
4.5% Preferred $100 par called for redemption 10/15/1965
Gamble-Skogmo, Inc. merged into Wickes Companies, Inc. 01/26/1985 which name changed to Collins & Aikman Group Inc. 07/17/1992
(See Collins & Aikman Group Inc.)

ALDER CREEK MINING CORP. (MN)
Charter revoked for failure to file reports and pay fees 01/13/1962

ALDER RES LTD (ON)
Reincorporated 03/25/2013
Place of incorporation changed from (BC) to (ON) 03/25/2013
Merged into Rosita Mining Corp. 07/28/2015
Each share Common no par exchanged for (0.181) share Common no par
Note: Unexchanged certificates will be cancelled and become without value 07/28/2021

ALDERMAC COPPER CORP., LTD. (CANADA)
Assets liquidated for benefit of creditors 00/00/1946
No stockholders' equity

ALDERMAC MINES, LTD.
Acquired by Aldermac Copper Corp., Ltd. 07/00/1936
Each share Common no par exchanged for (0.25) share Common no par 07/00/1936
(See Aldermac Copper Corp., Ltd.)

ALDERON RESOURCE CORP (BC)
Each share old Common no par exchanged for (0.5) share new Common no par 03/04/2010
Name changed to Alderon Iron Ore Corp. 10/05/2011

ALDEROX INC (CO)
Chapter 7 bankruptcy proceedings terminated 07/07/2011
No stockholders' equity

ALDERSHOT RES LTD (AB)
Merged into Eagle Lake Explorations Ltd. 08/12/1988
Each share Common no par exchanged for (1) share Common no par
Eagle Lake Explorations Ltd. recapitalized as Canalta Minerals Ltd. 12/16/1991 which name changed to New Energy West Corp. 11/14/1994 which was acquired by Gastar Exploration Ltd. (AB) 11/20/2001 which reincorporated in Delaware as Gastar Exploration, Inc. (Old) 11/15/2013 which reorganized as Gastar Exploration, Inc. (New) 02/03/2014

ALDERSON RESH INDS INC (DE)
Reorganized as Stebar National Corp. (DE) 06/20/1973
Each share Conv. Preferred Ser. A 1¢ par exchanged for (2) shares Common 1¢ par
Each share Class A Common 1¢ par reclassified as (1) share Common 1¢ par
Stebar National Corp. (DE) reincorporated in Oklahoma as Tetra International Corp. 03/07/1983
(See Tetra International Corp.)

ALDERSON RESH LABS INC (NY)
Merged into Alderson Research Industries, Inc. 12/30/1968
Each share Common 10¢ par exchanged for (1) share Class A Common 1¢ par
Alderson Research Industries, Inc. reorganized as Stebar National Corp. (DE) 06/20/1973 which

reincorporated in Oklahoma as Tetra International Corp. 03/07/1983
(See Tetra International Corp.)

ALDERWOODS GROUP INC (DE)
Merged into Service Corporation International 11/28/2006
Each share Common 1¢ par exchanged for $20 cash

ALDILA INC (DE)
Old Common 1¢ par split (2) for (1) by issuance of (1) additional share 03/15/1994
Each share old Common 1¢ par exchanged for (0.33333333) share new Common 1¢ par 06/04/2002
Acquired by Mitsubishi Rayon America, Inc. 04/01/2013
Each share new Common 1¢ par exchanged for $4 cash

ALDON INDS INC (PA)
Assets sold for benefit of creditors 10/20/1988
No stockholders' equity

ALDONA RES LTD (QC)
Name changed 06/09/1994
Name changed from Aldona Mines Ltd. to Aldona Resources Ltd. 06/09/1994
Merged into TCF Energy Inc. 07/10/1995
Each share Common no par exchanged for (0.1) share Common no par
TCF Energy Inc. merged into TriGas Exploration Inc. 07/01/1996
(See TriGas Exploration Inc.)

ALDRICH CHEM INC (DE)
Reincorporated 05/01/1971
State of incorporation changed from (WI) to (DE) 05/01/1971
Merged into Sigma-Aldrich Corp. 07/31/1975
Each share Common $1 par exchanged for (2) shares Common $1 par
(See Sigma-Aldrich Corp.)

ALDRIDGE MINERALS INC (BC)
Reincorporated under the laws of Canada 05/28/2013

ALDRIDGE RES LTD (BC)
Recapitalized as Aldridge Minerals Inc. (BC) 04/22/2004
Each share Common no par exchanged for (0.25) share Common no par
Aldridge Minerals Inc. (BC) reincorporated in Canada 05/28/2013

ALDRIN RESOURCE CORP (BC)
Each share old Common no par exchanged for (0.16666666) share new Common no par 12/04/2014
Name changed to Power Metals Corp. 12/02/2016

ALDSWORTH APARTMENTS, INC.
Liquidated 00/00/1940
Details not available

ALDUS CORP (WA)
Acquired by Adobe Systems Inc. (CA) 09/01/1994
Each share Common 1¢ par exchanged for (1) share Common no par
Adobe Systems Inc. (CA) reincorporated in Delaware 05/30/1997

ALDVAN MINES LTD. (ON)
Charter revoked for failure to file reports and pay taxes 00/00/1970

ALEC BRADLEY CIGAR CORP (FL)
Name changed to Online Vacation Center Holdings Corp. 03/17/2006

ALEDO OIL & GAS CO (UT)
Name changed to Spindletop Oil & Gas Co. (UT) 01/24/1983
Spindletop Oil & Gas Co. (UT) merged into into Spindletop Oil & Gas Co. (TX) 07/13/1990

ALEEYAH CAP CORP (BC)
Name changed to Kesselrun Resources Ltd. 07/25/2012

ALEGRIA CAP INC (AB)
Name changed to Pilot Energy Ltd. 06/08/2004
Pilot Energy Ltd. merged into Crescent Point Energy Trust 01/16/2008 which reorganized as Crescent Point Energy Corp. 07/07/2009

ALEGRO HEALTH CORP (CANADA)
Name changed to Centric Health Corp. 09/01/2009

ALEMCO ASSOCIATES, INC. (MA)
Dissolved 00/00/1941
Details not available

ALEMITE DIE CASTING & MANUFACTURING CO.
Acquired by Electric Auto-Lite Co. 00/00/1935
Details not available

ALENT PLC (ENGLAND & WALES)
Each old ADR for Ordinary exchanged for (0.95652173) new ADR for Ordinary 09/29/2014
ADR agreement terminated 12/28/2015
Each new ADR for Ordinary exchanged for $15.100635 cash

ALENTUS CORP (NV)
Common $0.001 par split (5) for (2) by issuance of (1.5) additional shares payable 04/04/2008 to holders of record 03/26/2008 Ex date - 04/07/2008
Recapitalized as Areti Web Innovations, Inc. 07/05/2012
Each share Common $0.001 par exchanged for (0.02) share Common $0.001 par

ALERE INC (DE)
98.5% of Conv. Perpetual Preferred Ser. B $0.001 par acquired at $402 per share through purchase offer which expired 10/03/2017
Non tendered shares are convertible at $294.29 cash per share
Acquired by Abbott Laboratories 10/03/2017
Each share Common $0.001 par exchanged for $51 cash

ALERIS INTL INC (DE)
Acquired by Aurora Acquisition Holdings, Inc. 12/19/2006
Each share Common 10¢ par exchanged for $52.50 cash

ALERITAS CAP CORP (DE)
SEC revoked common stock registration 08/28/2009

ALERT CARE CORP (ON)
Merged into Alert Holdings Corp. 11/16/1999
Each share Non-Vtg. Class A no par exchanged for $1.10 cash
Each share Common no par exchanged for $1.10 cash

ALERT CENTRE INC (DE)
Merged into ADT Acquisition Corp. 02/15/1996
Each share Common 1¢ par exchanged for $9.25 cash

ALERT PRODS INC (UT)
Proclaimed dissolved for failure to file annual report 01/01/1996

ALESCO FINL INC (MD)
Recapitalized as Cohen & Co. Inc. (Old) 12/16/2009
Each share Common $0.001 par exchanged for (0.1) share Common $0.001 par
Cohen & Co. Inc. (Old) name changed to Institutional Financial Markets, Inc. 01/24/2011 which reorganized as Cohen & Co. Inc. (New) 09/05/2017

ALET INC (NY)
Charter cancelled and proclaimed dissolved for failure to pay taxes 09/24/1997

ALETA RES INDS LTD (BC)
Name changed to Mandarin Capital Corp. 09/12/1984
Mandarin Capital Corp. reorganized as H.I.S.A. Investments Ltd. 12/29/1989
(See H.I.S.A. Investments Ltd.)

ALEX BROWN FINL GROUP (CA)
Acquired by First Interstate Bank of California (Los Angeles, CA) 09/01/1989
Each share Common no par exchanged for $16.27 cash

ALEX BROWN INC (MD)
Common 10¢ par split (3) for (2) by issuance of (0.5) additional share 05/29/1987
Common 10¢ par split (3) for (2) by issuance of (0.5) additional share payable 01/15/1997 to holders of record 12/30/1996 Ex date - 01/16/1997
Merged into Bankers Trust New York Corp. 09/01/1997
Each share Common 10¢ par exchanged for (0.83) share Common $1 par
Bankers Trust New York Corp. name changed to Bankers Trust Corp. 04/23/1998
(See Bankers Trust Corp.)

ALEXA VENTURES INC (BC)
Name changed to Eiger Technology, Inc. (BC) 11/26/1999
Eiger Technology, Inc. (BC) reincorporated in Ontario 11/00/2000 which recapitalized as GameCorp Ltd. 06/24/2008 which name changed to DealNet Capital Corp. 09/13/2012

ALEXANDER & ALEXANDER INC (MD)
Common no par split (2) for (1) by issuance of (1) additional share 05/11/1971
Under plan of reorganization each share Common no par automatically became (1) share Alexander & Alexander Services Inc. Common $1 par 05/26/1973
(See Alexander & Alexander Services Inc.)

ALEXANDER & ALEXANDER SVCS INC (MD)
Stock Dividend - 100% 09/29/1978
Merged into Aon Corp. 02/21/1997
Each share Common $1 par exchanged for $17.50 cash $3.625 144A Conv. Preferred Ser. A $1 par called for redemption 03/22/1997
Public interest eliminated

ALEXANDER & BALDWIN, LTD. (HI)
Capital Stock $100 par changed to $20 par 00/00/1944
Stock Dividend - 50% 05/01/1957
Capital Stock $20 par changed to no par and (3) additional shares issued 06/16/1961
Under plan of merger name changed to Alexander & Baldwin, Inc. (Old) and Capital Stock no par reclassified as Common no par 01/01/1962
Alexander & Baldwin, Inc. (Old) name changed to Alexander & Baldwin Holdings, Inc. 06/06/2012 which name changed to Matson, Inc. 06/29/2012

ALEXANDER & BALDWIN HLDGS INC (HI)
Each share Common no par received distribution of (1) share Alexander & Baldwin, Inc. (New) Common no par payable 06/29/2012 to holders of record 06/18/2012 Ex date - 07/02/2012
Name changed to Matson, Inc. 06/29/2012

ALEXANDER & BALDWIN INC OLD (HI)
Common no par split (3) for (1) by issuance of (2) additional shares 10/15/1968
Common no par split (2) for (1) by issuance of (1) additional share 03/09/1984
Common no par split (3) for (2) by issuance of (0.5) additional share 06/05/1986
Common no par split (2) for (1) by issuance of (1) additional share 06/02/1988
Name changed to Alexander & Baldwin Holdings, Inc. 06/06/2012

ALEXANDER ENERGY CORP (OK)
Each share Common 1¢ par exchanged for (0.33333333) share Common 3¢ par 06/14/1991
Merged into National Energy Group, Inc. 08/30/1996
Each share Common 3¢ par exchanged for (1.7) shares Common 1¢ par
(See National Energy Group, Inc.)

ALEXANDER ENERGY LTD (AB)
Recapitalized as Spartan Energy Corp. 02/28/2014
Each share Common no par exchanged for (0.25) share Common no par
Spartan Energy Corp. merged into Vermilion Energy Inc. 05/31/2018

ALEXANDER FILM CO. (DE)
Each share old Common $1 par exchanged for (6) shares new Common $1 par 02/28/1957
Dissolved 03/22/1966
No stockholders' equity

ALEXANDER HAMILTON INST INC (DE)
In process of liquidation
Each share Common $1 par received initial distribution of $49.12 cash payable 04/05/2013 to holders of record 03/15/2013
Note: Details on additional distribution(s), if any, are not available

ALEXANDER HAMILTON INSTITUTE (NJ)
Merged into Alexander Hamilton Institute, Inc. 12/16/1939
Details not available

ALEXANDER INDUSTRIES, INC.
Out of business 00/00/1935
Details not available

ALEXANDER INTL LTD (DE)
SEC revoked common stock registration 06/23/2009

ALEXANDER MARK INVT USA INC (CO)
Reorganized as Wincroft, Inc. (CO) 05/18/1998
Each share Common no par exchanged for (100) shares Common no par
Wincroft, Inc. (CO) reorganized in Nevada 02/12/2008 which name changed to Apollo Solar Energy, Inc. 11/03/2008

ALEXANDER MINING PLC (ENGLAND & WALES)
Ordinary 10p par changed to 0.1p par 06/14/2012
Delisted from Toronto Venture Stock Exchange 01/10/2013

ALEXANDER NATL GROUP INC (IN)
Name changed to ANG, Inc. 02/02/1981
(See ANG, Inc.)

ALEXANDER NATIONAL INSURANCE GROUP, INC. (IN)
Common $1 par changed to 25¢ par and (3) additional shares issued 05/27/1965
Name changed to Alexander National Group, Inc. 00/00/1968

Alexander National Group, Inc. name changed to ANG, Inc. 02/02/1981
(See ANG, Inc.)

ALEXANDER NUBIA INTL INC (CANADA)
Each share old Common no par exchanged for (0.2) share new Common no par 03/16/2015
Reincorporated under the laws of British Columbia as Aton Resources Inc. 06/27/2016

ALEXANDER RED LAKE MINES LTD (ON)
Recapitalized as Senlac Resources Inc. 12/28/1976
Each share Capital Stock $1 par exchanged for (0.1) share Common no par
Senlac Resources Inc. merged into Heenan Senlac Resources Ltd. 08/07/1986 which merged into Mining & Allied Supplies (Canada) Ltd. 08/25/1992 which name changed to Bearing Power (Canada) Ltd. 03/28/1994
(See Bearing Power (Canada) Ltd.)

ALEXANDER RES INTL INC (AB)
Recapitalized 01/10/1996
Name changed 10/29/1998
Recapitalized from Alexander News Corp. to Alexander News International Inc. 01/10/1996
Each share Common no par exchanged for (0.2) share Common no par
Name changed from Alexander News International Inc. to Alexander Resources International Inc. 10/29/1998
Name changed to African Sky Communications Inc. 09/27/1999

ALEXANDER TOUCHE INSURANCE INC (BERMUDA)
Acquired by Merchant Private Ltd. 09/29/1995
Each share Common no par exchanged for $3.50 cash

ALEXANDER'S SECURITIES CORP. (NY)
Name changed to Retail Realty Inc. 07/10/1958
Retail Realty Inc. merged into Alexander's, Inc. 01/23/1969

ALEXANDERS DEPT STORES INC (NY)
Common $1 par and Non-Vtg. Common $1 par changed to 10¢ par 02/25/1958
Merged into Alexander's, Inc. 01/23/1969
Each share Common 10¢ par or Non-Vtg. Common 10¢ par exchanged for (5.57813) shares Common $1 par

ALEXANDRIA APTS. (ON)
Dissolved 00/00/1947
Details not available

ALEXANDRIA MGMT CORP (VA)
Merged into Potomac Partners 01/20/1998
Each share Common $1 par exchanged for $95 cash

ALEXANDRIA NATIONAL BANK (ALEXANDRIA, VA)
Capital Stock $10 par split (3) for (2) by issuance of (0.5) additional share 01/09/1951
Each share Capital Stock $100 par exchanged for (14) shares Capital Stock $10 par to effect a (10) for (1) split and a 40% stock dividend 02/19/1960
Stock Dividend - 10% 02/05/1970
Name changed to Alexandria National Bank of Northern Virginia (Alexandria, VA) 11/15/1973
Alexandria National Bank of Northern Virginia (Alexandria, VA) merged into First American Bank of Virginia (McLean, VA) 03/31/1978
(See First American Bank of Virginia (McLean, VA))

ALEXANDRIA NATL BK NORTHN VA (ALEXANDRIA, VA)
Stock Dividend - 10% 03/01/1977
Merged into First American Bank of Virginia (McLean, VA) 03/31/1978
Each share Capital Stock $10 par exchanged for (2.3) shares Common $10 par
(See First American Bank of Virginia (McLean, VA))

ALEXANDRIA REAL ESTATE EQUITIES INC (MD)
9.5% Preferred Ser. A 1¢ par called for redemption at $25 plus $0.540972 accrued dividends on 07/07/2004
9.1% Preferred Ser. B 1¢ par called for redemption at $25 plus $0.410763 accrued dividends on 03/20/2007
8.375% Preferred Ser. C 1¢ par called for redemption at $25 plus $0.523438 accrued dividends on 04/13/2012
6.45% Preferred Ser. E 1¢ par called for redemption at $25 on 04/14/2017
(Additional Information in Active)

ALEXANDRINE HOTEL CO. (MI)
Completely liquidated 11/02/1965
Each share Common $1 par exchanged for first and final distribution of $2.09 cash

ALEXCO RESOURCE CORP (YT)
Reincorporated under the laws of British Columbia 12/28/2007

ALEXIS MINERALS CORP (ON)
Reincorporated 01/26/2004
Place of incorporation changed from (BC) to (ON) 01/26/2004
Recapitalized as QMX Gold Corp. 07/05/2012
Each share Common no par exchanged for (0.05) share Common no par

ALEXIS NIHON FIN INC (QC)
7.4% Retractable Preferred Ser. 1 no par called for redemption 04/24/1991
Public interest eliminated

ALEXIS NIHON REAL ESTATE INVT TR (QC)
Merged into Homburg Invest Inc. 05/24/2007
Each Unit exchanged for $18.60 cash

ALEXIS RES LTD (BC)
Recapitalized as Alexis Minerals Corp. (BC) 05/22/2003
Each share Common no par exchanged for (0.33333333) share Common no par
Alexis Minerals Corp. (BC) reincorporated in Ontario 01/26/2004 which recapitalized as QMX Gold Corp. 07/05/2012

ALEXZA PHARMACEUTICALS INC (DE)
Each share old Common $0.0001 par exchanged for (0.1) share new Common $0.0001 par 06/13/2012
Merged into Ferrer Pharma Inc. 06/21/2016
Each share new Common $0.0001 par exchanged for (1) Contingent Value Right and $0.90 cash

ALF INDS INC (DE)
Charter cancelled and declared inoperative and void for non-payment of taxes 03/01/1976

ALFA CORP (DE)
Common $1 par split (2) for (1) by issuance of (1) additional share 06/01/1987
Common $1 par split (2) for (1) by issuance of (1) additional share 06/01/1993
Common $1 par split (2) for (1) by issuance of (1) additional share payable 06/17/2002 to holders of record 06/03/2002 Ex date - 06/18/2002
Merged into Alfa Mutual Insurance Co. 04/15/2008
Each share Common $1 par exchanged for $22 cash

ALFA INDS INC (CO)
Recapitalized as Environmental Recovery Systems Inc. 05/01/1992
Each share Common $0.001 par exchanged for (0.0666) share Common $0.001 par
Environmental Recovery Systems Inc. recapitalized as Recycling Industries Inc. 06/27/1995
(See Recycling Industries Inc.)

ALFA INTL CORP (NJ)
Each share old Common 1¢ par exchanged for (0.04) share new Common 1¢ par 08/04/1995
Reincorporated under the laws of Delaware as Alfa International Holdings Corp. 10/10/2005
Alfa International Holdings Corp. name changed to Omagine, Inc. 06/22/2007

ALFA INTL HLDGS CORP (DE)
Name changed to Omagine, Inc. 06/22/2007

ALFA LEISURE INC (TX)
Merged into Alfa Leisure Acquisition Corp. 09/30/1999
Each share Common no par exchanged for $2.75 cash

ALFA RES INC (CO)
Recapitalized as Capco Energy, Inc. 11/19/1999
Each share Common $0.001 par exchanged for (0.01) share Common $0.001 par
(See Capco Energy, Inc.)

ALFA S A DE C V (MEXICO)
ADR agreement terminated 01/09/2009
Details not available

ALFA UTIL SVCS INC (DE)
Voluntarily dissolved 03/28/2003
No stockholders' equity

ALFAB INC (CO)
Each share old Common $0.0001 par exchanged for (0.02272727) share new Common $0.0001 par 05/04/1989
Name changed to Fantastic Foods International, Inc. 10/10/1991
Fantastic Foods International, Inc. recapitalized as DCI Telecommunications, Inc. 01/11/1995
(See DCI Telecommunications, Inc.)

ALFACELL CORP (DE)
Name changed to Tamir Biotechnology, Inc. 07/02/2010
(See Tamir Biotechnology, Inc.)

ALFALFA-640 TRUST (CA)
In process of liquidation 00/00/1973
Details not available

ALFIN INC (NY)
Name changed 12/08/1986
Common 1¢ par split (2) for (1) by issuance of (1) additional share 02/19/1986
Name changed from Alfin Fragrances, Inc. to Alfin, Inc. 12/08/1986
Name changed to Adrien Arpel Inc. 07/27/1998
(See Adrien Arpel Inc.)

ALFORD REFRIGERATED WHSES INC (TX)
Plan of reorganization under Chapter 11 Federal Bankruptcy Code effective 12/16/2002
No stockholders' equity

ALGAE FARM USA INC (NV)
Each share old Common $0.000001 par exchanged for (1.1) shares new Common $0.000001 par 06/30/2011
Recapitalized as Diversified Energy Holdings, Inc. 07/18/2013
Each share new Common $0.000001 par exchanged for (0.01) share Common $0.000001 par

ALGAE INTL GROUP INC (NV)
Reincorporated under the laws of Wyoming as North American Cannabis Holdings, Inc. 06/10/2015

ALGAE TEC LTD (AUSTRALIA)
Name changed to Affinity Energy & Health Ltd. 08/29/2018

ALGAM CORP. (NY)
Merged into Yonkers Raceway, Inc. share for share 08/00/1954
(See Yonkers Raceway, Inc.)

ALGEMENE BK NEDERLAND N V (NETHERLANDS)
Merged into Amro Bank 01/31/1992
Each ADR for Ordinary no par exchanged for $19.83 cash

ALGEMENE KUNSTZIJDE UNIE N V (NETHERLANDS)
Stock Dividend - 10% 06/16/1965
Name changed to AKZO N.V. 11/04/1969
AKZO N.V. name changed to AKZO Nobel N.V. 02/25/1994

ALGENE BIOTECHNOLOGIES INC (QC)
Name changed to SignalGene Inc. and Class B Subordinated no par reclassified as Common no par 06/09/1999
SignalGene Inc. recapitalized as SignalEnergy Inc. 03/11/2004 which reorganized as Fortress Energy Inc. 02/20/2007 which name changed to Alvopetro Inc. 03/11/2013 which name changed to Fortaleza Energy Inc. 11/19/2013

ALGER GOLD MINES LTD. (ON)
Recapitalized as New Alger Mines Ltd. 12/00/1948
Each share Common no par exchanged for (0.33333333) share Common no par
(See New Alger Mines Ltd.)

ALGERAN INC (CA)
Common 1¢ par split (5) for (4) by issuance of (0.25) additional share 05/08/1980
Under plan of reorganization name changed to Athanor Group, Inc. 09/02/1986
(See Athanor Group, Inc.)

ALGETA ASA (NORWAY)
ADR agreement terminated 04/01/2014
Each ADR for Ordinary exchanged for $30.237046 cash

ALGIERS BANCORP INC (LA)
Acquired by SNB, Inc. 05/30/2003
Each share Common 1¢ par exchanged for $15.71839 cash

ALGO RES LTD (BC)
Struck off register and declared dissolved for failure to file returns 10/01/1993

ALGODON WINES & LUXURY DEV GROUP INC (DE)
Name changed to Algodon Group, Inc. 10/03/2018

ALGODYNE ETHANOL ENERGY CORP (NV)
Common $0.001 par split (8) for (1) by issuance of (7) additional shares payable 11/06/2006 to holders of record 11/06/2006
Recapitalized as Easylink Solutions, Corp. 12/05/2008
Each share Common $0.001 par exchanged for (0.005) share Common $0.001 par

ALGOLD MINES, LTD.
Reorganized as Amherst Gold Mines, Ltd. 11/00/1938

Each share Capital Stock exchanged for (0.5) share Capital Stock
(See Amherst Gold Mines, Ltd.)

ALGOM URANIUM MINES LTD. (ON)
Merged into Rio Algom Mines Ltd. 06/30/1960
Each share Common $1 par exchanged for (1.65) shares Capital Stock no par
Rio Algom Mines Ltd. name changed to Rio Algom Ltd. 04/30/1975
(See Rio Algom Ltd.)

ALGOMA CENT & HUDSON BAY RY (CANADA)
6% Conv. Preferred $50 par called for redemption 04/15/1963
Common $10 par changed to $2 par and (4) additional shares issued 12/10/1964
Name changed to Algoma Central Railway 06/30/1965
Algoma Central Railway name changed to Algoma Central Corp. 04/26/1990

ALGOMA CENT RY (CANADA)
Name changed to Algoma Central Corp. 04/26/1990

ALGOMA CONSOLIDATED CORP. LTD.
Liquidated 00/00/1939
Details not available

ALGOMA COPPER MINES LTD. (ON)
Name changed to Bi-Ore Mines Ltd. 07/11/1944
Bi-Ore Mines Ltd. acquired by Consolidated Bi-Ore Mines Ltd. 06/08/1956
(See Consolidated Bi-Ore Mines Ltd.)

ALGOMA FIN CORP (ON)
Due to partial redemption each share old 5.50% Preferred $25 par exchanged for (1) share new 5.50% Preferred $25 par representing balance 10/31/1992
Due to partial redemption each share new 5.50% Preferred $25 par exchanged for (1) share old Non-Vtg. 5.50% Preferred $25 par representing balance 04/30/1993
Due to partial redemption each share old Non-Vtg. 5.50% Preferred $25 par exchanged for (1) share new Non-Vtg. 5.50% Preferred $25 par representing balance 04/30/1994
Due to partial redemption each share new Non-Vtg. 5.50% Preferred $25 par exchanged for (1) share 5.50% Preferred 1995 Ser. $25 par representing balance 04/30/1995
Merged into Algoma Steel Inc. 07/12/1995
Each share 5.50% Preferred 1995 Ser. $25 par exchanged for either (2.75) shares Common no par, $24 cash or (0.6875) share Common no par, (1) Contingent Value Right and $18.1875 cash
Note: Option to receive stock, or cash only expired 08/09/1995
(See Algoma Steel Inc.)

ALGOMA STEEL CO.
Insolvent 00/00/1932
Details not available

ALGOMA STEEL CORP. LTD. (ON)
Common no par exchanged (4) for (1) 00/00/1936
Common no par exchanged (4) for (1) 00/00/1949
Common no par exchanged (4) for (1) 07/02/1957
Name changed to Algoma Steel Corp., Ltd. (The) 10/15/1960
Algoma Steel Corp., Ltd. (The) reorganized as Algoma Steel Inc. 06/01/1992
(See Algoma Steel Inc.)

ALGOMA STL INC (ON)
Plan of Arrangement under the Creditors Arrangement Act effective 01/29/2002
No old Common stockholders' equity
Acquired by Essar Global Ltd. 06/20/2007
Each share new Common no par exchanged for $56 cash

ALGOMA STL LTD (ON)
Common no par split (2) for (1) by issuance of (1) additional share 05/17/1966
Merged into Dofasco Inc. 10/15/1988
For Canadian Residents: Each share $2 Conv. Class B Preference Ser. 1 no par exchanged for (0.91) share Common no par
Each share Common no par exchanged for (0.92) share Common no par
For Non-Canadian Residents: Each share $2 Conv. Class B Preference Ser. 1 no par exchanged for $26.25 cash
Each share Common no par exchanged for $26.50 cash
(See Dofasco Inc.)
Reorganized as Algoma Steel Inc. 06/01/1992
Each share 8% Preference Ser. A $25 par exchanged for (1.08620391) shares Common no par
Each share 9.75% Preference Ser. B $25 par exchanged for (1.11073146) shares Common no par
(See Algoma Steel Inc.)

ALGOMA SUMMIT GOLD MINES, LTD.
Reorganized as Magino Gold Mines, Ltd. 00/00/1939
Each share Capital Stock exchanged for (0.25) share new Capital Stock $1 par
(See Magino Gold Mines, Ltd.)

ALGONKIAN URANIUM CORP. LTD. (ON)
Charter surrendered 11/05/1956
Details not available

ALGONQUIN BLDG CRS LTD (ON)
6.5% Preference $20 par reclassified as Class A Part. Preference 5¢ par 03/07/1969
Name changed to Algonquin Mercantile Corp. 01/21/1977
Algonquin Mercantile Corp. name changed to Automodular Corp. 06/05/2001 which merged into HLS Therapeutics Inc. 03/14/2018

ALGONQUIN CORP (MD)
Charter annulled for failure to file reports 01/28/1975

ALGONQUIN MERCANTILE CORP (ON)
Non-Vtg. Class A Participating Preference no par reclassified as Common no par 07/10/1987
Common no par split (5) for (1) by issuance of (4) additional shares 07/13/1987
Each share Common no par received distribution of (1.25) shares Dominion Citrus Ltd. Common no par payable 01/15/2001 to holders of record 01/02/2001 Ex date - 12/28/2000
Name changed to Automodular Corp. 06/05/2001
Automodular Corp. merged into HLS Therapeutics Inc. 03/14/2018

ALGONQUIN MINERALS INC (BC)
Recapitalized as Asean Holdings Inc. 06/02/1992
Each share Common no par exchanged for (0.33333333) share Common no par
(See Asean Holdings Inc.)

ALGONQUIN OIL & GAS LTD (AB)
Recapitalized as PetroShale Inc. 03/19/2012
Each share Common no par exchanged for (0.1) share Common no par

ALGONQUIN PETE CORP (AB)
Recapitalized as Algonquin Oil & Gas Ltd. 04/10/2000
Each share Common no par exchanged for (0.25) share Common no par
Algonquin Oil & Gas Ltd. recapitalized as PetroShale Inc. 03/19/2012

ALGONQUIN PWR INCOME FD (ON)
Merged into Algonquin Power & Utilities Corp. 10/27/2009
Each Trust Unit exchanged for (1) share Common no par

ALGONQUIN PRINTING CO.
Dissolved 00/00/1941
Details not available

ALGOOD GOLD MINES LTD. (ON)
Acquired by Don Cameron Exploration Co. Ltd. 00/00/1959
Each share Capital Stock no par exchanged for (0.1) share Capital Stock no par
Don Cameron Exploration Co. Ltd. merged into Milestone Exploration Ltd. 07/23/1968 which merged into Jubilee Gold Inc. 01/01/2010 which merged into Jubilee Gold Exploration Ltd. 01/25/2013

ALGOREX CORP (DE)
Name changed 12/02/1975
Name changed from Algorex Data Corp. to Algorex Corp. 12/02/1975
Charter cancelled and declared inoperative and void for non-payment of taxes 03/01/1994

ALGORHYTHM TECHNOLOGIES CORP (NV)
Name changed to Quikbiz Internet Group, Inc. 07/07/1998
(See Quikbiz Internet Group, Inc.)

ALGORITHM MEDIA INC (BC)
Recapitalized as Avere Energy Inc. 12/18/2009
Each share Common no par exchanged for (0.5) share Common no par
Avere Energy Inc. name changed to East West Petroleum Corp. 08/10/2010

ALGOS PHARMACEUTICAL CORP (DE)
Merged into Endo Pharmaceuticals Holdings Inc. 07/17/2000
Each share Common 1¢ par exchanged for (1) share Common 1¢ par and (1) Common Stock Purchase Warrant expiring 12/31/2002
Endo Pharmaceuticals Holdings Inc. name changed to Endo Health Solutions Inc. 05/23/2012 which merged into Endo International PLC 03/03/2014

ALGREY DRUG CO. INC. (NY)
Charter revoked for failure to file reports and pay fees 12/15/1941

ALGRO URANIUM MINES LTD. (ON)
Charter cancelled and proclaimed dissolved for failure to pay taxes and file returns 09/23/1963

ALHAMBRA ATLANTA GOLD MINES & PPTYS INC (DE)
Reincorporated 01/03/1978
State of incorporation changed from (UT) to (DE) 01/03/1978
Name changed to Alhambra Mines, Inc. 02/13/1981
Alhambra Mines, Inc. recapitalized as American Eagle Resources, Inc. (DE) 08/31/1989 which reincorporated in British Columbia 02/06/2008 which merged into Lion One Metals Ltd. 01/31/2011

ALHAMBRA MINES INC (DE)
Recapitalized as American Eagle Resources, Inc. (DE) 08/31/1989
Each share Common 1¢ par exchanged for (0.01) share Common 1¢ par
American Eagle Resources, Inc. (DE) reincorporated in British Columbia 02/06/2008 which merged into Lion One Metals Ltd. 01/31/2011

ALHOM, INC. (KY)
Name changed to Cardinal Extrusions, Inc. 09/10/1974
Cardinal Extrusions, Inc. name changed to Cardinal Aluminum Co. 09/30/1981

ALIANT COMMUNICATIONS CO (DE)
5% Preferred $100 par called for redemption at $105 on 05/15/1998
(Additional Information in Active)

ALIANT COMMUNICATIONS INC (NE)
Merged into Alltel Corp. 07/02/1999
Each share Common $25 par exchanged for (0.67) share Common $1 par
(See Alltel Corp.)

ALIANT INC (CANADA)
Reorganized under the laws of Ontario as Bell Aliant Regional Communications Income Fund 07/10/2006
Each share Common no par exchanged for (1) Unit
Note: Holders of (25) shares or fewer and Non-qualified U.S. holders received a pro rata distribution of cash from the sale of Units
Bell Aliant Regional Communications Income Fund (ON) reorganized in Canada as Bell Aliant Inc. 01/04/2011 which merged into BCE Inc. 10/31/2014

ALIAS RESH INC (ON)
Merged into Silicon Graphics, Inc. 06/15/1995
Each share Common no par exchanged for (0.9) share Common $0.001 par
(See Silicon Graphics Inc.)

ALIBABA COM LTD (CAYMAN ISLANDS)
ADR agreement terminated 02/16/2012
Each ADR for Common exchanged for $8.649799 cash

ALIBABA INNOVATIONS CORP (BC)
Name changed to 4D Virtual Space Ltd. 06/26/2015
4D Virtual Space Ltd. name changed to Supreme Metals Corp. 12/28/2016

ALICE ARM MNG LTD (BC)
Recapitalized as New Congress Resources Ltd. 01/20/1976
Each share Capital Stock 50¢ par exchanged for (0.2) share Capital Stock no par
New Congress Resources Ltd. recapitalized as Levon Resources Ltd. (Old) 01/12/1983
(See Levon Resources Ltd. (Old))

ALICE BANCSHARES INC (TX)
Merged into ABI Merger Co. 09/15/1995
Each share Common $2 par exchanged for $52.64 cash

ALICE LAKE MINES LTD (BC)
Recapitalized as Consolidated Alice Lake Mines Ltd. 10/29/1993
Each share Common $1 par exchanged for (0.22222222) share Common no par
Consolidated Alice Lake Mines Ltd. name changed to International Sales Information Systems Inc. 06/01/1994 which name changed to Versatile Mobile Systems (Canada) Inc. (BC) 09/18/2000 which reincorporated in Yukon 02/23/2004 which reincorporated in British Columbia as Versatile Systems Inc. 11/16/2005

ALICE NATL BK (ALICE, TX)
Name changed 00/00/1957
Name changed from Alice Bank &

Trust Co. (Alice, TX) to Alice National Bank (Alice, TX) 00/00/1957
Under plan of reorganization each share Common $2 par automatically became (1) share Alice Bancshares Inc. Common $2 par 08/31/1984
(See Alice Bancshares Inc.)

ALICE SILVER LEAD MNG CO (ID)
Completely liquidated 11/02/1970
Each share Capital Stock 10¢ par exchanged for first and final distribution of (1.463) shares Alice Consolidated Mines, Inc. Common 10¢ par

ALICO LD DEV CO (FL)
Name changed to Alico, Inc. 01/14/1974

ALIENZOO INC (NV)
Charter revoked for failure to file reports and pay fees 08/01/2003

ALIGN-RITE INTL INC (CA)
Merged into Photronics, Inc. 06/08/2000
Each share Common 1¢ par exchanged for (0.85) share Common 1¢ par

ALIGNVEST ACQUISITION CORP (ON)
Units separated 08/04/2015
Reorganized under the laws of British Columbia as Trilogy International Partners Inc. 02/09/2017
Each Class A Restricted Share exchanged for (1) share Common no par

ALIHP INC (DE)
Name changed to Communication Resources, Inc. 01/26/1987

ALINA INTL INDS LTD (BC)
Name changed 01/26/1972
Name changed from Alina Mines & Oils Ltd. to Alina International Industries Ltd. 01/26/1972
Capital Stock 50¢ par changed to no par 11/22/1974
Recapitalized as Addwest Minerals International Ltd. 05/30/1997
Each share Common no par exchanged for (0.1) share Common no par
(See Addwest Minerals International Ltd.)

ALINGHI MINERALS INC (BC)
Name changed to Dorex Minerals Inc. 04/05/2006
Dorex Minerals Inc. name changed to Cipher Resources Inc. 09/18/2017

ALISON AYERS, INC. (NY)
Dissolved by proclamation 01/25/2012

ALISON INTL INC (DE)
Charter cancelled and declared inoperative and void for non-payment of taxes 04/15/1972

ALISON MTG INVT TR (CA)
Name changed to First Newport Realty Investors 04/26/1977
First Newport Realty Investors name changed to First Newport Corp. 10/31/1979 which was acquired by Coldwell, Banker & Co. 09/15/1981 which merged into Sears, Roebuck & Co. 12/31/1981 which merged into Sears Holdings Corp. 03/24/2005

ALITA RESOURCES LTD (BC)
Name changed to Nexus Gold Corp. 08/12/2014

ALITALIA-LINEE AEREE ITALIANE S P A (ITALY)
Administrator authorized sale of assets 11/20/2008
ADR holders' equity unlikely

ALIVE INTL INC (ON)
Name changed to Simberi Gold Corp. 04/14/2004
Simberi Gold Corp. name changed to Simberi Mining Corp. 08/10/2006 which recapitalized as Greenock Resources Inc. 09/29/2009 which name changed to BeWhere Holdings Inc. 02/03/2016

ALIX OF MIAMI, INC. (FL)
Acquired by Logan (Jonathan), Inc. 10/01/1965
Each share Class A Common 25¢ par exchanged for (0.06666666) share Common 50¢ par
(See Logan (Jonathan), Inc.)

ALIX RES CORP (BC)
Each share old Common no par exchanged for (0.06666666) share new Common no par 08/06/2010
Each share new Common no par exchanged again for (0.1) share new Common no par 12/17/2014
Each share new Common no par exchanged again for (0.25) share new Common no par 11/21/2017
Name changed to Infinite Lithium Corp. 12/06/2017

ALJO MINES LTD (ON)
Charter cancelled and declared dissolved for failure to pay taxes and file returns 12/07/1977

ALKAN CORP (NJ)
Recapitalized as Imaging Diagnostic Systems, Inc. (NJ) 04/24/1994
Each share Common no par exchanged for (0.01) share Common no par
Imaging Diagnostic Systems, Inc. (NJ) reincorporated in Florida 07/01/1995
(See Imaging Diagnostic Systems, Inc.)

ALKENORE-BUFFALO GOLD MINES LTD. (ON)
Charter cancelled 00/00/1957

ALKERMES INC (PA)
Common 1¢ par split (2) for (1) by issuance of (1) additional share payable 05/12/2000 to holders of record 04/28/2000 Ex date - 05/15/2000
$3.25 Conv. Exchangeable Preferred called for redemption at $52.275 plus $0.0712 accrued dividends on 03/08/2001
Conv. Exchangeable Preferred 144A called for redemption at $52.275 plus $0.0712 accrued dividends on 03/08/2001
Merged into Alkermes PLC 09/16/2011
Each share Common 1¢ par exchanged for (1) share Ordinary USD $0.01 par

ALKEY INDS LTD (BC)
Name changed to American Volcano Minerals Corp. 10/24/1983
American Volcano Minerals Corp. name changed to Genco Industries Inc. 02/24/1987 which recapitalized as Consolidated Genco Industries Inc. 05/08/1990
(See Consolidated Genco Industries Inc.)

ALKON INDS INC (DE)
Adjudicated bankrupt 10/14/1975
Stockholders' equity unlikely

ALL AMER CASTING INTL INC (NV)
Name changed to VOIP MDU.COM 02/25/2004
VOIP MDU.COM name changed to VoIP-PAL.com Inc. 09/21/2006

ALL AMERICA GENERAL CORP.
Dissolved 00/00/1934
Details not available

ALL-AMERICA LATINA LOGISTICA S A (BRAZIL)
144A GDR basis changed from (1:2) to (1:10) 03/11/2005
144A GDR's for Common split (10) for (1) by issuance of (9) additional GDR's payable 09/12/2006 to holders of record 09/11/2006
144A GDR's for Common split (10) for (1) by issuance of (9) additional GDR's payable 09/12/2006 to holders of record 09/11/2006
144A GDR Units for Preferred split (10) for (1) by issuance of (9) additional Units payable 09/12/2006 to holders of record 09/11/2006
Reg. S GDR Units for Ordinary split (10) for (1) by issuance of (9) additional Units payable 09/12/2006 to holders of record 09/11/2006
Reg. S GDR for Preferred reclassified as Reg. S GDR for Common 10/27/2010
GDR agreement terminated 10/27/2010
Details not available
Each 144A GDR Unit for Common exchanged for $1.404795 cash 04/24/2015
Each Sponsored Reg. S Unit for Common exchanged for $1.404795 cash 04/24/2015

ALL AMER TERM TR INC (MD)
Trust terminated 12/30/2002
Each share Common $0.001 par received first and final distribution of $12.1973 cash

ALL AMERICA UTILITY SECURITIES CORP.
Liquidation completed 00/00/1934
Details not available

ALL AMERICAN AIRWAYS, INC. (DE)
Name changed to Allegheny Airlines, Inc. 01/02/1953
Allegheny Airlines, Inc. name changed to U S Air, Inc. 10/29/1979 which reorganized as USAir Group, Inc. 02/01/1983 which name changed to US Airways Group, Inc. 02/21/1997
(See US Airways Group, Inc.)

ALL AMERN ASSURN CO (NC)
Reincorporated 04/28/1972
Under plan of merger state of incorporation changed from (LA) to (NC) and each share Common $1 par exchanged for (0.468603) share Common $1 par 04/28/1972
Merged into I.C.H. Corp. 11/19/1982
Each share Common $1 par exchanged for (0.5441) share Common $1 par
I.C.H. Corp. name changed to Southwestern Life Corp. (New) 06/15/1994 which name changed to I.C.H. Corp. (New) 10/10/1995
(See I.C.H. Corp. (New))

ALL AMERICAN AVIATION, INC. (DE)
Name changed to All American Airways, Inc. 09/20/1948
All American Airways, Inc. name changed to Allegheny Airlines, Inc. 01/02/1953 which name changed to U S Air, Inc. 10/29/1979 which reorganized as USAir Group, Inc. 02/01/1983 which name changed to US Airways Group, Inc. 02/21/1997
(See US Airways Group, Inc.)

ALL AMERICAN BANK (CHICAGO, IL)
Capital Stock $10 par changed to $6 par 05/12/1976
100% acquired by First Colonial Bankshares Corp. as of 09/02/1985
Public interest eliminated

ALL AMERN BEVERAGES INC (DE)
Name changed to American Pepsi-Cola Bottlers, Inc. 01/12/1972
American Pepsi-Cola Bottlers, Inc. merged into General Cinema Corp. 03/30/1973 which name changed to Harcourt General, Inc. 03/15/1993
(See Harcourt General, Inc.)

ALL AMERICAN BROKERS, INC. (NJ)
Charter revoked for non-payment of taxes 00/00/1925

ALL AMERN BURGER INC (DE)
Reincorporated 07/27/1983
State of incorporation changed from (CA) to (DE) and each share Capital Stock 10¢ par exchanged for (1) share Common 1¢ par 07/27/1983
Name changed to All American Group, Inc. 07/30/1987
All American Group, Inc. name changed to Bexy Communications, Inc. 11/30/1993 which recapitalized as Cheniere Energy, Inc. 07/03/1996

ALL AMERICAN BUS LINES, INC. (DE)
Name changed to American Buslines, Inc. 04/10/1946
(See American Buslines, Inc.)

ALL AMERICAN CASUALTY CO. (IL)
Name changed to All American Life & Casualty Co. 02/01/1956
All American Life & Casualty Co. acquired by All American Life & Financial Corp. 03/18/1968 which was acquired by USLIFE Corp. 02/25/1974 which merged into American General Corp. 06/17/1997 which merged into American International Group, Inc. 08/29/2001

ALL AMERN COFFEE & BEVERAGE INC (NV)
SEC revoked common stock registration 11/17/2009

ALL AMERN COMMUNICATIONS INC (DE)
Each share old Common $0.0001 par exchanged for (0.25) share new Common $0.0001 par 03/20/1992
Merged into Pearson PLC 11/07/1997
Each share new Common $0.0001 par exchanged for $25.50 cash
Each share Class B Common $0.0001 par exchanged for $25.50 cash

ALL AMERN CONSULTANT AIRCRAFT INC (TX)
Name changed to MarketCentral.Net Corp. 02/03/1999
MarketCentral.Net Corp. recapitalized as Trezac Corp. 09/16/2002 which name changed to Trezac International Corp. 02/26/2003 which recapitalized as Millagro International Corp. 01/20/2004 which name changed to Telatinos Inc. 11/08/2004 which name changed to Netco Investments, Inc. (TX) 11/04/2005
(See Netco Investments, Inc.)

ALL AMERN ENERGY CORP (NV)
Name changed to Core Lithium Corp. 04/11/2018

ALL AMERN ENERGY HLDG INC (NV)
Each share old Common $0.001 par exchanged for (0.33333333) share new Common $0.001 par 02/04/2014
Recapitalized as All American Energy Corp. 11/14/2017
Each share new Common $0.001 par exchanged for (0.0090909) share Common $0.001 par
All American Energy Corp. name changed to Core Lithium Corp. 04/11/2018

ALL AMERN ENGR CO (DE)
Name changed to All American Industries, Inc. 06/11/1970
All American Industries, Inc. merged into International Controls Corp. 05/07/1982
(See International Controls Corp.)

ALL AMERN FD INC (MD)
Capital Stock 25¢ par split (4) for (1) by issuance of (3) additional shares 08/20/1965
Merged into American Birthright Trust 11/01/1976
Each share Capital Stock 25¢ par received (0.04) Share of Bene. Int. $1 par
Note: Certificates were not required to

ALL-ALL   FINANCIAL INFORMATION, INC.

be surrendered and are without value
American Birthright Trust name changed to ABT Growth & Income Trust 12/01/1984
(See ABT Growth & Income Trust)

ALL AMERN FOOD GROUP INC (NJ)
Each share old Common no par exchanged for (0.1) share new Common no par 03/05/1998
Chapter 11 bankruptcy proceedings converted to Chapter 7 on 11/30/1998
Stockholders' equity unlikely

ALL AMERN FROZEN YOGURT CO (OR)
Each share old Common $0.001 par exchanged for (0.00008) share new Common $0.001 par 04/09/1998
Note: In effect holders received an undetermined amount of cash and public interest was eliminated

ALL AMERN GOURMET CO (DE)
Common 10¢ par split (2) for (1) by issuance of (1) additional share 04/18/1986
Merged into Kraft, Inc. 08/17/1987
Each share Common 10¢ par exchanged for $18 cash

ALL AMERICAN GROUP, INC. (DE)
Name changed to Bexy Communications, Inc. 11/30/1993
Bexy Communications, Inc. recapitalized as Cheniere Energy, Inc. 07/03/1996

ALL AMERN GROUP INC (IN)
Acquired by All American Group Holdings, L.L.C. 03/25/2011
Each share Common no par exchanged for (1) Specialty Vehicles Liquidating Trust Unit and $0.20 cash

ALL AMERICAN INDUSTRIES, INC. (DE)
Ctfs. dated prior to 11/12/1947
Common 25¢ par changed to $1 par 07/00/1947
Name changed to American Steel & Pump Corp. 11/12/1947
(See American Steel & Pump Corp.)

ALL AMERN INDS INC (DE)
Ctfs. dated after 06/10/1970
Merged into International Controls Corp. 05/07/1982
Each share Common 10¢ par exchanged for (0.75) share Common 10¢ par
(See International Controls Corp.)

ALL AMERN LIFE & CAS CO (IL)
Acquired by All American Life & Financial Corp. 03/18/1968
Each share Common $1 par exchanged for (1) share Common $1 par
(See All American Life & Financial Corp.)

ALL AMERN LIFE & FINL CORP (DE)
Stock Dividend - 25% 03/23/1970
Acquired by USLIFE Corp. 02/25/1974
Each share Common $1 par exchanged for (0.55) share Common $1 par and (0.1) share O'Hare International Bank (N.A.) (Chicago, IL) Common $5 par
(See each company's listing)

ALL AMERICAN MARBLE CO. (NM)
Name changed to Ultra Marbles, Inc. 02/19/1963

ALL AMERICAN PRODUCTS CO.
Dissolved 00/00/1944
Details not available

ALL AMERN RLTY INC (PA)
Plan of liquidation under Chapter 11 Federal Bankruptcy proceedings confirmed 11/26/1986
No stockholders' equity

ALL AMERN SEMICONDUCTOR INC (DE)
Each share old Common 1¢ par exchanged for (0.2) share new Common 1¢ par 06/02/1999
Stock Dividend - 25% 03/13/1989
Plan of reorganization under Chapter 11 Federal Bankruptcy proceedings effective 04/22/2009
Each share new Common 1¢ par received inital distribution of $5.68 cash payable 05/19/2016 to holders of record 04/22/2009

ALL AMERN TELEVISION INC (DE)
Name changed to All American Communications Inc. 02/25/1991
(See All American Communications Inc.)

ALL ASIA LICENSING INC (NV)
Old Common $0.001 par split (40) for (1) by issuance of (39) additional shares payable 12/06/2007 to holders of record 12/06/2007
Each share old Common $0.001 par exchanged for (0.001) share new Common $0.001 par 01/07/2014
Name changed to Recruits, Inc. 03/06/2014
Recruits, Inc. name changed to FlexWeek, Inc. 12/16/2015 which name changed to Holy Grail Co. 03/24/2017

ALL CAN HLDGS LTD (BC)
Class A Common no par reclassified as Class B Common no par 01/02/1974
Discharged from receivership 00/00/1981
No stockholders' equity

ALL CDA BOWLING LTD (ON)
Merged into Charlo Holdings Ltd. 06/01/1978
Each share Common no par exchanged for $2.50 cash

ALL CANADIAN COMMON STOCK TRUSTEE SHARES SERIES A (CANADA)
Trust terminated 11/01/1940
Each Share Ser. A exchanged for $10.7036 cash

ALL-CANADIAN RESOURCES CORP. (CANADA)
Dissolved for non-compliance 10/17/2008

ALL CDN VENTURE FD LTD (CANADA)
Name changed to Cundill Value Fund Ltd. 12/20/1977
(See Cundill Value Fund Ltd.)

ALL-COMM MEDIA CORP (NV)
Name changed to Marketing Services Group, Inc. 07/01/1997
Marketing Services Group, Inc. name changed to MKTG Services, Inc. 03/26/2002 which name changed to Media Services Group, Inc. 12/26/2003 which name changed to MSGI Security Solutions, Inc. 02/09/2005
(See MSGI Security Solutions, Inc.)

ALL COMMUNICATIONS CORP (NJ)
Merged into Wire One Technologies, Inc. 05/18/2000
Each share Common no par exchanged for (1.65) shares Common no par
Wire One Technologies, Inc. name changed to Glowpoint, Inc. 09/24/2003

ALL FOR A DOLLAR INC (DE)
Recapitalized as Think Again, Inc. 08/13/2004
Each share Common 1¢ par exchanged for (0.001) share Common 1¢ par
Think Again, Inc. name changed to Caribbean Developments, Inc. 11/12/2004 which recapitalized as VShield Software Corp. 01/30/2007

ALL FUELS & ENERGY CO (DE)
Common 1¢ par split (3) for (2) by issuance of (0.5) additional share payable 05/21/2007 to holders of record 05/14/2007 Ex date - 05/22/2007
Recapitalized as All Energy Corp. 01/17/2012
Each share Common 1¢ par exchanged for (0.02) share Common 1¢ par

ALL IN WEST CAP CORP (CANADA)
Assets sold for the benefit of creditors 08/16/2017
No stockholders' equity

ALL LINE INC (NV)
Charter revoked for failure to file reports and pay fees 06/30/2008

ALL METAL PRODUCTS CORP. (DE)
Common $2 par reclassified as Class A Common $2 par 00/00/1946
Class A Common $2 par and Class B Common $2 par reclassified as Common $2 par 00/00/1949
Adjudicated bankrupt 00/00/1957
No stockholders' equity

ALL NATIONS DEPOSIT BANK (PITTSBURGH, PA)
Bank dissolved 00/00/1931
No stockholders' equity

ALL NIPPON AWYS LTD (JAPAN)
Name changed to ANA Holdings Inc. 04/01/2013

ALL NORTH RES LTD (BC)
Recapitalized as International All-North Resources Ltd. 07/10/1996
Each share Common no par exchanged for (0.2) share Common no par
International All-North Resources Ltd. recapitalized as Kaieteur Resource Corp. 04/14/1999 which name changed to Samba Gold Inc. 03/21/2005 which recapitalized as Caerus Resource Corp. 02/26/2009 which name changed to Angel Gold Corp. 10/04/2012

ALL-PENN OIL & GAS CO. (PA)
Liquidation completed 12/20/1956
Details not available

ALL-PRO PRODS INC (DE)
Charter cancelled and declared inoperative and void for non-payment of taxes 03/01/1996

ALL-PRO SPORTS MARKETING INC (FL)
Name changed to Mutual Exchange International, Inc. (FL) 06/12/1998
Mutual Exchange International, Inc. (FL) reorganized in Delaware as Avenue Exchange Corp. 07/16/2008 which name changed to Eyes on the Go, Inc. 06/27/2011

ALL-PRODUCT DISTR CORP (FL)
Name changed to Phage Therapeutics International, Inc. 09/08/1998
Phage Therapeutics International, Inc. recapitalized as S S G I, Inc. 02/22/2008 which recapitalized as Vicapsys Life Sciences, Inc. 11/02/2017

ALL-Q-TELL CORP (NV)
Charter revoked 10/31/2014

ALL QUOTES DATA LTD (BC)
Name changed to AmCan Minerals Ltd. 03/08/1995
(See AmCan Minerals Ltd.)

ALL-QUOTES INC (DE)
Each share Common $0.00001 par exchanged for (0.01) share Common 1¢ par 05/28/1992
Name changed to SunRiver Corp. 01/06/1995
SunRiver Corp. name changed to Boundless Corp. 05/27/1997
(See Boundless Corp.)

ALL SEASONS GLOBAL FD INC (MD)
Name changed to Royce Global Trust, Inc. 11/01/1996
Royce Global Trust, Inc. name changed to Royce Focus Trust, Inc. 05/10/1999 which name changed to Sprott Focus Trust, Inc. 03/09/2015

ALL SEASONS RESORTS INC (WA)
Common 10¢ par split (3) for (2) by issuance of (0.5) additional share 08/20/1984
Plan of reorganization under Chapter 11 Federal Bankruptcy proceedings effective 11/01/1993
No stockholders' equity

ALL SOFT GELS INC (NV)
Name changed to Brain Scientific, Inc. 09/19/2018

ALL STAR INS CORP (WI)
Common $1 par changed to 50¢ par 06/05/1961
Common 50¢ par changed to $1 par 03/05/1962
Common $1 par changed to 75¢ par 04/05/1965
Each share Common 75¢ par exchanged for (0.162074) share Common $5 par 05/02/1968
Each share Common $5 par exchanged for (0.005) share Common $1,000 par 04/13/1971
Public interest eliminated

ALL STAR TITLE INSURANCE, INC. (WI)
Common $1 par changed to $1.50 par 09/16/1966
Name changed to Capitol Land Title Insurance, Inc. 01/18/1967
(See Capitol Land Title Insurance, Inc.)

ALL STAR WORLD WIDE, INC. (DE)
Under plan of merger name changed to Camera Corp. of America 01/12/1965
(See Camera Corp. of America)

ALL-STATE AUTO RENTAL CORP. (NY)
Name changed to Sandgate Corp. (NY) 11/02/1967
Sandgate Corp. (NY) reincorporated in Delaware 06/27/1969
(See Sandgate Corp.)

ALL ST CR CORP (NY)
Adjudicated bankrupt 01/31/1969
No stockholders' equity

ALL ST METAL STAMPING INC (NY)
Merged into Radak Holding Corp. 12/28/1979
Each share Common 1¢ par exchanged for $1 cash

ALL ST MICROFILM INC (DE)
Name changed to ECR All State Ltd. 12/18/1985
(See ECR All State Ltd.)

ALL ST PPTYS L P (DE)
Reorganized 09/20/1984
Capital Stock $1 par changed to 10¢ par 04/05/1971
Reorganized from All-State Properties, Inc. to All-State Properties L.P. 09/20/1984
Each share Capital Stock 10¢ par exchanged for (1) All-State Properties L.P. Unit of Ltd. Partnership
Under plan of partial liquidation each Unit of Ltd. Partnership received distribution of $0.05 cash payable 02/06/2007 to holders of record 01/23/2007 Ex date - 02/12/2007
Reincorporated under the laws of Nevada as All State Properties Holdings, Inc. and Units of Ltd. Partnership reclassified as Common $0.0001 par 01/09/2009

ALL STATES FREIGHT, INC. (RI)
Reincorporated 02/28/1962
State of incorporation changed from (OH) to (RI) 02/28/1962
6% Preferred $100 par called for redemption 01/31/1964
Merged into Pacific Intermountain Express Co. (RI) 05/31/1966
Each share Common $1 par exchanged for (1) share Common $2 par
Pacific Intermountain Express Co. acquired by International Utilities Corp. 11/30/1971

ALL STATES LIFE INSURANCE CO. (TX)
Name changed to Professional & Business Men's Insurance Co. 02/21/1961
Professional & Business Men's Insurance Co. acquired by Kentucky Central Life Insurance Co. 08/28/1963
(See Kentucky Central Life Insurance Co.)

ALL STS LIFE INS CO (AL)
Capital Stock $10 par changed to $5 par 00/00/1933
Capital Stock $5 par changed to $1 par 00/00/1951
Ceased operations 12/31/1973
No stockholders' equity

ALL TECH INDS INC (FL)
Stock Dividends - 10% 11/15/1965; 10% 11/30/1966; 100% 03/10/1967
Name changed to Clabir Corp. (FL) 04/21/1976
Clabir Corp. (FL) reincorporated in Delaware 07/01/1977 which merged into Empire of Carolina, Inc. 12/29/1989
(See Empire of Carolina, Inc.)

ALL THINGS INC (NV)
Each share Common $0.0001 par exchanged for (0.1) share Common $0.001 par 08/10/1984
Name changed to New Environmental Technologies Inc. 10/11/1984
New Environmental Technologies Inc. name changed to Victory Capital Holdings Corp. 04/28/2003 which name changed to Victory Energy Corp. 05/11/2006 which name changed to Victory Oilfield Tech, Inc. 05/31/2018

ALL-TIME HIGH, INC. (UT)
Name changed to New Century Technologies Corp. (UT) 07/00/1993
New Century Technologies Corp. (UT) name changed to Cybernet Internet Services International, Inc. (UT) 05/22/1997 which reincorporated in Delaware 09/18/1998
(See Cybernet Internet Services International, Inc. (DE))

ALL WESTN ENTERPRISES INC (UT)
Reorganized under the laws of Nevada as Fibertrek, Inc. 03/07/2007
Each share Common $0.001 par exchanged for (0.02) share Common $0.001 par
Note: Holders of between (10) and (499) shares received (10) shares
Holders of (9) or fewer shares were not affected by the reverse split
Each share Common $0.0001 par received distribution of (1) share Westernteck, Ltd. Restricted Common payable 03/16/2007 to holders of record 02/28/2007
Fibertrek, Inc. name changed to Asset Capital Group, Inc. 08/01/2007 which name changed to Solutions Group, Inc. 12/15/2008

ALL WRAPPED UP INC (NV)
Reorganized as China West International Inc. 03/25/1997
Each share Common $0.001 par exchanged for (4) shares Common $0.001 par

China West International Inc. name changed to Intergold Corp. 08/27/1997 which name changed to Lexington Resources, Inc. 11/20/2003
(See Lexington Resources, Inc.)

ALLACART INC (DE)
Name changed to IBS Computer Corp. 06/23/1989
(See IBS Computer Corp.)

ALLAIRE CMNTY BK (SEA GIRT, NJ)
Merged into Central Jersey Bancorp (Ctfs. dtd. after 01/01/2005) 01/01/2005
Each share Common $3.33333 par exchanged for (1) share Common 1¢ par
(See Central Jersey Bancorp (Ctfs. dtd. after 01/01/2005))

ALLAIRE CORP (DE)
Common 1¢ par split (2) for (1) by issuance of (1) additional share payable 03/14/2000 to holders of record 02/15/2000
Merged into Macromedia Inc. 03/21/2001
Each share Common 1¢ par exchanged for (0.2) share Common $0.001 par and $3 cash
Macromedia Inc. merged into Adobe Systems Inc. 12/03/2005 which name changed to Adobe Inc. 10/09/2018

ALLAIRE STATE BANK (MANASQUAN, NJ)
Capital Stock $5 par changed to $2.50 par and (1) additional share issued 10/30/1974
Merged into National Community Bank of New Jersey (Rutherford, NJ) 12/31/1981
Each (1.85) shares Capital Stock $2.50 par exchanged for (1) share Common $6.25 par
National Community Bank of New Jersey (Rutherford, NJ) reorganized as National Community Banks, Inc. 02/28/1989 which merged into Bank of New York Co., Inc. 08/11/1993 which merged into Bank of New York Mellon Corp. 07/01/2007

ALLAN RES INC (BC)
Name changed to Fortress Financial Corp. 02/08/1996
Fortress Financial Corp. merged into Berwick Retirement Communities Ltd. 04/02/2001
(See Berwick Retirement Communities Ltd.)

ALLANA POTASH CORP (ON)
Acquired by Israel Chemicals Ltd. 06/24/2015
Each share Common no par exchanged for $0.50 cash
Note: Unexchanged certificates will be cancelled and become without value 06/24/2021

ALLANA RES INC (ON)
Name changed to Allana Potash Corp. 01/22/2010
(See Allana Potash Corp.)

ALLANCO IOLITE MONITOR CORP (BC)
Recapitalized as AIM Safety Co., Inc. 01/09/1989
Each share Common no par exchanged for (0.2) share Common no par
AIM Safety Co., Inc. name changed to AimGlobal Technologies Co., Inc. 01/29/1999
(See AimGlobal Technologies Co., Inc.)

ALLARAE HEALTHCARE INC (DE)
Recapitalized as MP2 Technologies, Inc. 09/12/2008
Each share Common $0.001 par exchanged for (0.01) share Common $0.001 par

MP2 Technologies, Inc. recapitalized as The Kiley Group, Inc. 11/03/2009

ALLARCO DEVS LTD (AB)
7% Conv. 1st Preference Ser. A $25 par called for redemption 08/14/1980
Merged into Carma Developers Ltd. 01/02/1981
Each share Common no par exchanged for $141 cash

ALLARD RIVER MINES LTD. (ON)
Charter cancelled for failure to pay taxes and file returns 04/01/1969

ALLASTICS, INC. (GA)
Merged into Bethlehem Steel Corp. 05/28/1971
Each share Common $1 par exchanged for (0.129899) share Common $8 par
(See Bethlehem Steel Corp.)

ALLATOONA FED SVGS BK (ACWORTH, GA)
Merged into Premier Lending Corp. 04/28/1995
Each share Common no par exchanged for $15.60 cash

ALLBANC SPLIT CORP (ON)
Class A Capital Shares no par split (4) for (1) by issuance of (3) additional shares payable 03/10/2008 to holders of record 03/07/2008 Ex date - 03/05/2008
Preferred Shares no par called for redemption at $25 on 03/10/2003
Capital Shares no par called for redemption at $47.12 on 03/10/2003
Class A Preferred no par called for redemption at $60.80 on 03/10/2008
Class B Preferred no par called for redemption at $26.27 on 03/08/2013
Class A Preferred Ser. 1 no par called for redemption at $31.64 on 03/09/2018
Class A Capital Shares no par called for redemption at $75.7558 on 03/09/2018

ALLBANC SPLIT CORP II (ON)
Preferred Shares no par called for redemption at $25 on 02/28/2011
Class B Preferred Ser. 1 no par called for redemption at $21.80 on 02/28/2016
(Additional Information in Active)

ALLCITY INS CO (NY)
Common $5 par changed to $1 par and (1) additional share issued 11/01/1965
Stock Dividends - 10% 12/01/1966; 20% 12/21/1967; 10% 12/20/1968; 25% 12/20/1974
Merged into Leucadia National Corp. 11/12/2003
Each share Common $1 par exchanged for $2.75 cash

ALLCOM INC (TX)
Name changed to M/A/R/C Inc. 08/27/1984
(See M/A/R/C Inc.)

ALLCOP MINES LTD (ON)
Charter cancelled for failure to pay taxes and file returns 10/24/1973

ALLCOPIERS CORP (FL)
Name changed to Saguaro Holdings Corp. 05/15/2002

ALLCORP UTD INC (ON)
Class C no par called for redemption 07/15/1997
Recapitalized as Ntex Inc. 11/07/1997
Each share Class A Common no par exchanged for (0.05555555) share Common no par
Each share Common no par exchanged for (0.05555555) share Common no par
(See Ntex Inc.)

ALLE PROCESSING CORP (NY)
Merged into WWSH Corp. 02/15/2001
Each share Common 1¢ par exchanged for $3.20 cash

ALLEANZA ASSICURAZIONI SPA (ITALY)
ADR agreement terminated 09/03/2010
No ADR's remain outstanding

ALLECO INC (MD)
Merged into Lapides Corp. 10/18/1988
Each share Common $1 par exchanged for $10 cash

ALLEGHANY CORP (DE)
Each share 5.75% Mandatorily Conv. Preferred $1 par exchanged for (1.0139) shares Common $1 par 06/15/2009
(Additional Information in Active)

ALLEGHANY CORP (MD)
Common no par changed to $1 par 00/00/1942
$2.50 Prior Preferred no par called for redemption 10/01/1953
5.5% Preferred Ser. A $100 par called for redemption 10/30/1959
$4 Prior Preferred no par called for redemption 03/31/1960
6% Conv. Preferred $10 par called for redemption 05/04/1970 Completely liquidated 12/31/1986
Each share Preferred Ser. A $1 par exchanged for first and final distribution of $28.631 cash
Each share Common $1 par exchanged for first and final distribution of (1) share Alleghany Corp. (DE) Common $1 par and $43.05 cash

ALLEGHANY PHARMACAL CORP (NY)
Acquired by AP Acquisition Corp. 07/02/2010
Each share Common 1¢ par exchanged for $0.93874 cash

ALLEGHENY & WESTN ENERGY CORP (WV)
Reincorporated 06/00/1984
State of incorporation changed from (DE) to (WV) 06/00/1984
Acquired by Energy Corp. of America 06/23/1995
Each share Common 1¢ par exchanged for $12 cash

ALLEGHENY AIRLS INC (DE)
Name changed to U S Air, Inc. 10/29/1979
U S Air, Inc. reorganized as USAir Group, Inc. 02/01/1983 which name changed to US Airways Group, Inc. 02/21/1997
(See US Airways Group, Inc.)

ALLEGHENY-ARROW OIL CO.
Liquidated 00/00/1947
Details not available

ALLEGHENY BANKSHARES CORP. (WV)
Acquired by Horizon Bancorp, Inc. 04/01/1993
Each share Common $10 par exchanged for (1.2566) shares Common $1 par
Horizon Bancorp, Inc. merged into City Holding Co. 12/31/1998

ALLEGHENY BEVERAGE CORP (MD)
Each share Conv. Preferred Ser. B $1 par exchanged for (2) shares Common $1 par 02/20/1980
Conv. Preferred Ser. C $1 par called for redemption 05/27/1983
Common $1 par split (3) for (2) by issuance of (0.5) additional share 01/15/1984
Stock Dividend - 10% 04/02/1973
Name changed to Alleco Inc. 10/22/1987
(See Alleco Inc.)

ALLEGHENY COAL CO. (WV)
Charter revoked for failure to file reports and pay fees 06/24/1939

ALL-ALL

ALLEGHENY ENERGY INC (MD)
Merged into FirstEnergy Corp. 02/25/2011
Each share Common $1.25 par exchanged for (0.667) share Common 10¢ par

ALLEGHENY ENTERPRISES LTD (AB)
Name changed to Allegheny Mines Corp. 03/04/1991
(See Allegheny Mines Corp.)

ALLEGHENY GAS CORP.
Reorganized as Cumberland Gas Corp. 00/00/1934
No stockholders' equity

ALLEGHENY INTL INC (PA)
$3 Conv. Preferred $1 par called for redemption 05/18/1981
Reorganized under the laws of Delaware as Sunbeam-Oster Co., Inc. 09/28/1990
Each (100) shares $2.19 Preferred no par exchanged for (79.2) Common Stock Purchase Warrants expiring 09/28/1995
Each (100) shares $11.25 Conv. Preferred no par exchanged for (153.9) Common Stock Purchase Warrants expiring 09/28/1995
Each (100) shares Common $0.66666666 par exchanged for (7.9) Common Stock Purchase Warrants expiring 09/28/1995 or $16.40 cash
Note: Option to receive Warrants in lieu of cash expired 11/12/1990

ALLEGHENY LD & MINERAL CO (DE)
Name changed to Alamco, Inc. 06/03/1983
(See Alamco, Inc.)

ALLEGHENY LUDLUM CORP (PA)
Common 10¢ par split (3) for (2) by issuance of (0.5) additional share 07/02/1990
Common 10¢ par split (2) for (1) by issuance of (1) additional share 07/01/1993
Merged into Allegheny Teledyne Inc. 08/15/1996
Each share Common 10¢ par exchanged for (1) share Common 10¢ par
Allegheny Teledyne Inc. recapitalized as Allegheny Technologies Inc. 11/29/1999

ALLEGHENY LUDLUM INDUSTRIES, INC. (PA)
Common $1 par changed to $0.66666666 par and (0.5) additional share issued 01/10/1977
Name changed to Allegheny International Inc. 04/29/1981
(See Allegheny International Inc.)

ALLEGHENY LUDLUM STL CORP (PA)
Common no par changed to $1 par 00/00/1953
Common $1 par split (2) for (1) by issuance of (1) additional share 02/03/1956
Each share $2.70 Preferred no par exchanged for (1) share $3 Conv. Preferred $1 par 08/01/1969
Name changed to Allegheny Ludlum Industries, Inc. 04/24/1970
Allegheny Ludlum Industries, Inc. name changed to Allegheny International Inc. 04/29/1981
(See Allegheny International Inc.)

ALLEGHENY MINES CORP (AB)
Delisted from Alberta Stock Exchange 07/20/1999

ALLEGHENY MNG & EXPL LTD (ON)
Charter cancelled for failure to pay taxes and file returns 03/07/1973

ALLEGHENY NATURAL GAS & OIL CORP. (DE)
No longer in existence having become inoperative and void for non-payment of taxes 04/01/1958

ALLEGHENY PEPSI COLA BOTTLING CO (DE)
Common 50¢ par changed to 25¢ par and (1) additional share issued 04/01/1969
Stock Dividend - 50% 05/10/1968
Acquired by Allegheny Beverage Corp. 03/20/1970
Each share Common 25¢ par exchanged for (1) share Conv. Preferred Ser. C $1 par
(See Allegheny Beverage Corp.)

ALLEGHENY PWR SYS INC (MD)
Common $5 par changed to $2.50 par and (1) additional share issued 06/03/1964
Common $2.50 par changed to $1.25 par and (1) additional share issued 11/18/1993
Name changed to Allegheny Energy, Inc. 09/16/1997
Allegheny Energy, Inc. merged into FirstEnergy Corp. 02/25/2011

ALLEGHENY STEEL CO. (PA)
Under plan of merger name changed to Allegheny Ludlum Steel Corp. 08/16/1938
Allegheny Ludlum Steel Corp. name changed to Allegheny Ludlum Industries, Inc. 04/24/1970 which name changed to Allegheny International Inc. 04/29/1981
(See Allegheny International Inc.)

ALLEGHENY TELEDYNE INC (DE)
Each share Common 10¢ par received distribution of (0.14285714) share Teledyne Technologies, Inc. Common 1¢ par payable 11/29/1999 to holders of record 11/22/1999
Each share Common 10¢ par received distribution of (0.05) share Water Pik Technologies, Inc. Common 1¢ par payable 11/29/1999 to holders of record 11/22/1999
Recapitalized as Allegheny Technologies Inc. 11/29/1999
Each share Common 10¢ par exchanged for (0.5) share Common 10¢ par

ALLEGHENY TRACTION CO.
Merged into Pittsburgh Railways Co. 09/30/1950
Each share Common $50 par exchanged for (4.2) shares Common no par and $5 cash
Pittsburgh Railways Co. name changed to Pittway Corp. (PA) 11/28/1967 which merged into Pittway Corp. (DE) 12/28/1989
(See Pittway Corp. (DE))

ALLEGHENY VY BANCORP INC (PA)
Stock Dividends - 0.263% payable 06/22/2012 to holders of record 06/08/2012 Ex date - 06/06/2012; 0.269% payable 09/20/2012 to holders of record 09/04/2012 Ex date - 08/30/2012; 0.2729% payable 12/14/2012 to holders of record 11/30/2012 Ex date - 11/28/2012; 0.2623% payable 03/18/2013 to holders of record 03/06/2013; 0.25% payable 06/18/2013 to holders of record 06/06/2013 Ex date - 06/04/2013; 0.2607% payable 09/20/2013 to holders of record 09/06/2013 Ex date - 09/04/2013; 0.2658% payable 12/16/2013 to holders of record 12/04/2013 Ex date - 12/02/2013; 0.2722% payable 03/20/2014 to holders of record 03/10/2014 Ex date - 03/06/2014; 0.2653% payable 06/16/2014 to holders of record 06/06/2014 Ex date - 06/04/2014; 0.2764% payable 09/22/2014 to holders of record 09/10/2014 Ex date - 09/08/2014; 0.2605% payable 12/15/2014 to holders of record 12/03/2014; 0.2615% payable 03/20/2015 to holders of record 03/10/2015 Ex date - 03/06/2015; 0.2603% payable 06/17/2015 to holders of record 06/10/2015 Ex date - 06/08/2015; 0.2815% payable 09/21/2015 to holders of record 09/10/2015 Ex date - 09/08/2015; 0.273% payable 12/15/2015 to holders of record 12/03/2015 Ex date - 12/01/2015; 0.2697% payable 03/21/2016 to holders of record 03/10/2016 Ex date - 03/08/2016; 0.2721% payable 06/21/2016 to holders of record 06/10/2016 Ex date - 06/08/2016; 0.2634% payable 09/21/2016 to holders of record 09/09/2016 Ex date - 09/07/2016; 0.2271% payable 12/15/2016 to holders of record 12/02/2016 Ex date - 11/30/2016; 0.2041% payable 03/24/2017 to holders of record 03/10/2017 Ex date - 03/08/2017
Merged into Standard AVB Financial Corp. 04/10/2017
Each share Common $1 par exchanged for (2.083) shares Common 1¢ par

ALLEGHENY VALLEY BK (PITTSBURGH, PA)
Reorganized as Allegheny Valley Bancorp, Inc. 10/01/1987
Each share Common $50 par exchanged for (50) shares Common $1 par
Allegheny Valley Bancorp, Inc. merged into Standard AVB Financial Corp. 04/10/2017

ALLEGHENY VENTURA CORP (NV)
Name changed to Ventura International, Inc. 01/11/1968
(See Ventura International, Inc.)

ALLEGIANCE BANC CORP (DE)
Common $1 par split (6) for (5) by issuance of (0.2) additional share 06/30/1994
Merged into F & M National Corp. 10/01/1996
Each share Common $1 par exchanged for (0.7984) share Common $2 par
F & M National Corp. merged into BB&T Corp. 08/09/2001

ALLEGIANCE BK NORTH AMER (BALA CYNWYD, PA)
Bank closed and FDIC appointed receiver 11/19/2010
Stockholders' equity unlikely

ALLEGIANCE CORP (DE)
Common $1 par split (2) for (1) by issuance of (1) additional share payable 08/25/1998 to holders of record 08/10/1998 Ex date - 08/26/1998
Merged into Cardinal Health, Inc. 02/03/1999
Each share Common $1 par exchanged for (0.6225) share Common no par

ALLEGIANCE EQUITY CORP (ON)
Name changed to Canadian Bioceutical Corp. 12/16/2014
Canadian Bioceutical Corp. name changed to MPX Bioceutical Corp. 11/06/2017

ALLEGIANCE TELECOM INC (DE)
Common 1¢ par split (3) for (2) by issuance of (0.5) additional share payable 02/28/2000 to holders of record 02/18/2000
Plan of reorganization under Chapter 11 Federal Bankruptcy Code effective 06/23/2004
No stockholders' equity

ALLEGIANT BANCORP INC (MO)
Common 1¢ par split (5) for (4) by issuance of (0.25) additional share payable 01/21/1998 to holders of record 01/07/1998
Stock Dividends - 10% payable 01/16/1996 to holders of record 01/02/1996; 10% payable 01/15/1997 to holders of record 01/02/1997
Merged into National City Corp. 04/09/2004
Each share Common 1¢ par exchanged for $27.25 cash

ALLEGIANT CAP TR I (DE)
9.875% Guaranteed Trust Preferred Securities called for redemption at $10 on 09/21/2004

ALLEGIANT CAP TR II (DE)
9% Trust Preferred Securities called for redemption at $25 plus $0.5625 accrued dividends on 10/02/2006

ALLEGIANT PHYSICIAN SVCS INC (DE)
Plan of reorganization under Chapter 11 Federal Bankruptcy Code effective 01/19/2000
Each share Common Stock $0.001 par exchanged for $0.10 cash
Note: Cash distribution made 08/00/2004

ALLEGIANT TECHNOLOGIES INC (WA)
Recapitalized as Shampan Lamport Holdings Ltd. 07/21/1998
Each share Common no par exchanged for (0.25) share Common no par
Shampan Lamport Holdings Ltd. name changed to takeoutmusic.com Holdings Corp. 02/10/2000
(See takeoutmusic.com Holdings Corp.)

ALLEGIS CORP (DE)
Name changed to UAL Corp. 05/27/1988
(See UAL Corp.)

ALLEGRI TECH INC (NJ)
Common 50¢ par changed to 1¢ par 12/15/1972
Assets assigned for benefit of creditors 11/17/1975
No stockholders' equity

ALLEGRO BIODIESEL CORP (DE)
In process of liquidation 12/01/2010
Stockholders' equity unlikely

ALLEGRO GROUP INC (DE)
Name changed to Brandt Inc. 03/13/2008

ALLEGRO NEW MEDIA INC (DE)
Name changed to Software Publishing Corporation Holdings, Inc. 06/16/1997
Software Publishing Corporation Holdings, Inc. name changed to Vizacom Inc. 07/15/1999
(See Vizacom Inc.)

ALLEGRO PPTY INC (BC)
Name changed to Valdor Fiber Optics Inc. 07/05/2000
Valdor Fiber Optics Inc. recapitalized as Valdor Technology International Inc. 07/21/2008

ALLELIX BIOPHARMACEUTICALS INC (CANADA)
Merged into NPS Pharmaceuticals Inc. 12/23/1999
Each share Common no par held by Canadian residents exchanged for either (0.3238) share NPS Allelix Inc. Non-Vtg. Exchangeable share no par, or (0.3238) share NPS Pharmaceuticals Inc. Common no par
(See NPS Allelix Inc.)
Each share Common no par held by non-Canadian residents exchanged for (0.3238) share NPS Pharmaceuticals Inc. Common no par
Note: Non-electing Canadian residents received NPS Pharmaceuticals Inc.

ALLEMANNIA FIRE INSURANCE CO. OF PITTSBURGH (PA)
Common $50 par changed to $10 par 00/00/1930
Merged into United States Fire Insurance Co. 05/31/1951
Each share Common $10 par exchanged for (1) share Capital Stock $3 par
(See United States Fire Insurance Co.)

ALLEN AIRCRAFT RADIO INC (DE)
Name changed to AAR Corp. 10/30/1969

ALLEN BILL ENTERPRISES INC (NC)
Adjudicated bankrupt 08/20/1976
Stockholders' equity unlikely

ALLEN (R.C.) BUSINESS MACHINES, INC. (MI)
Name changed to Allen (R.C.), Inc. (MI) 05/07/1968
Allen (R.C.), Inc. (MI) reincorporated in Delaware 04/28/1972
(See Allen (R.C.), Inc. (DE))

ALLEN (A.) CO.
Dissolution approved 00/00/1941
Details not available

ALLEN COUNTY BANK & TRUST CO. (LEO, IN)
Name changed 04/11/1980
Name changed from Allen County State Bank (Leo, IN) to Allen County Bank & Trust Co. (Leo, IN) 04/11/1980
Stock Dividend - 10% 04/30/1980
Bank failed 11/23/1985
No stockholders' equity

ALLEN DENTAL MED DEV CORP (NY)
Merged into ADC Merging Corp. 12/19/1990
Each share Common 10¢ par exchanged for $6.80 cash

ALLEN ELEC & EQUIP CO (DE)
Reincorporated 05/01/1969
Common $10 par changed to $1 par 00/00/1936
State of incorporation changed from (MI) to (DE) 05/01/1969
Name changed to Allen Group Inc. 05/05/1972
Allen Group Inc. name changed to Allen Telecom Inc. 02/28/1997 which merged into Andrew Corp. 07/15/2003 which merged into CommScope, Inc. 12/27/2007
(See CommScope, Inc.)

ALLEN ELECTR INDS INC (DE)
Charter cancelled and declared inoperative and void for non-payment of taxes 04/15/1971

ALLEN ENERGY CO (DE)
Charter cancelled and declared void for failure to pay franchise taxes 03/01/1995

ALLEN GROUP INC (DE)
Common $1 par split (5) for (4) by issuance of (0.25) additional share 04/04/1979
Common $1 par split (5) for (4) by issuance of (0.25) additional share 01/17/1986
$1.75 Conv. Exchangeable Preferred Ser. A no par called for redemption 07/16/1993
Common $1 par split (2) for (1) by issuance of (1) additional share 10/18/1993
Stock Dividend - 10% 01/17/1992
Name changed to Allen Telecom Inc. 02/28/1997
Allen Telecom Inc. merged into Andrew Corp. 07/15/2003 which merged into CommScope, Inc. 12/27/2007
(See CommScope, Inc.)

ALLEN INDS INC (DE)
Each share Common no par exchanged for (3) shares Common $1 par 00/00/1935
Stock Dividends - 100% 10/14/1947; 10% 09/15/1955; 10% 12/23/1957; 25% 09/15/1959; 10% 01/06/1964; 10% 12/30/1966
Merged into Dayco Corp. (DE) 02/28/1969
Each share Common $1 par exchanged for $45 principal amount of 6% Conv. Subord. Debentures due 01/01/1994

ALLEN LEON B FD INC (NY)
Name changed to First Investors Trend Fund, Inc. 05/08/1974
First Investors Trend Fund, Inc. name changed to First Investors Option Fund, Inc. 02/03/1979 which merged into First Investors High Yield Fund, Inc. 11/01/1988
(See First Investors High Yield Fund, Inc.)

ALLEN-MORRISON INC (VA)
Name changed 12/21/1961
Name changed from Allen-Morrison Sign Co., Inc. to Allen-Morrison, Inc. 12/21/1961
Charter forfeited for failure to maintain a registered agent 07/01/1997

ALLEN OIL CO (NJ)
Each share Common 10¢ par exchanged for (0.02857142) share Common $3.50 par 12/20/1974
Merged into Allen International 12/29/1975
Each share Common $3.50 par exchanged for $140 cash

ALLEN ORGAN CO (PA)
Class A Common $1 par split (2) for (1) by issuance of (1) additional share 03/29/1985
Class B Common $1 par split (2) for (1) by issuance of (1) additional share 03/29/1985
Stock Dividends - 10% 03/15/1966; 10% 03/15/1967; 10% 03/23/1984
Merged into Sycamore Networks, Inc. 09/06/2006
Each share Class A Common $1 par exchanged for $48.82679 cash
Note: Each share Class A Common $1 par received initial distribution of $7.2024509 cash from escrow 03/06/2008
Each share Class A Common $1 par received second distribution of $7.443148 cash from escrow 09/15/2009
Each share Class A Common $1 par received third distribution of $3.4267033 cash from escrow 09/15/2010
Each share Class B Common $1 par exchanged for $48.82679 cash
Note: Each share Class B Common $1 par received initial distribution of $7.2024509 cash from escrow 03/06/2008
Each share Class B Common $1 par received second distribution of $7.443148 cash from escrow 09/15/2009
Each share Class B Common $1 par received third distribution of $3.4267033 cash from escrow 09/15/2010

ALLEN R C INC (DE)
Reincorporated 04/28/1972
State of incorporation changed from (MI) to (DE) 04/28/1972
Merged into United Industrial Syndicate Inc. 06/15/1977
Each share Common 1¢ par exchanged for $2 cash

ALLEN-SQUIRE CO. (MA)
Charter revoked for failure to file reports and pay fees 05/14/1958

ALLEN TELECOM INC (DE)
Merged into Andrew Corp. 07/15/2003
Each share Conv. Preferred Ser. D exchanged for (1) share 7.75% Conv. Preferred Ser. A no par
Each share Common $1 par exchanged for (1.775) shares Common 1¢ par
Andrew Corp. merged into CommScope, Inc. 12/27/2007
(See CommScope, Inc.)

ALLEN VANGUARD CORP (ON)
Plan of arrangement under Companies' Creditors Arrangement Act effective 12/18/2009
No stockholders' equity

ALLENBEE PETROLEUMS LTD. (CANADA)
Merged into Consolidated Allenbee Oil & Gas Co. Ltd. 00/00/1952
Each (5) shares Capital Stock no par exchanged for (3) shares Common $1 par
Consolidated Allenbee Oil & Gas Co. Ltd. recapitalized as Western Allenbee Oil & Gas Co. Ltd. 04/06/1960 which name changed to Convoy Capital Corp. 04/28/1989 which recapitalized as Hariston Corp. 09/25/1992 which recapitalized as Midland Holland Inc. (Canada) 02/10/1999 which reincorporated in Yukon 03/11/1999 which name changed to Mercury Partners & Co. Inc. 02/22/2000 which name changed to Black Mountain Capital Corp. 05/02/2005 which recapitalized as Grand Peak Capital Corp. (YT) 11/20/2007 which reincorporated in British Columbia 04/27/2010

ALLENDALE CORP.
Dissolved 00/00/1938
Details not available

ALLENTOWN RAILROAD CO.
Merged into Reading Co. share for share 12/31/1945
Reading Co. merged into Reading Entertainment Inc. (DE) 10/15/1996 which reincorporated in Nevada 12/29/1999 which merged into Reading International, Inc. 12/31/2001

ALLERAYDE SAB INC (FL)
Name changed to Stragenics, Inc. 04/28/2014

ALLERCARE INC (MN)
Charter declared inoperative and void for failure to file reports 09/25/1998

ALLERGAN INC (DE)
Each share Common 1¢ par received distribution of (0.05) share Allergan Specialty Therapeutics, Inc. Common 1¢ par payable 03/10/1998 to holders of record 02/17/1998 Ex date - 03/11/1998
Common 1¢ par split (2) for (1) by issuance of (1) additional share payable 12/09/1999 to holders of record 11/18/1999 Ex date - 12/10/1999
Each share Common 1¢ par received distribution of (0.22222222) share Advanced Medical Optics, Inc. Common 1¢ par payable 07/01/2002 to holders of record 06/14/2002 Ex date - 07/01/2002
Common 1¢ par split (2) for (1) by issuance of (1) additional share payable 06/22/2007 to holders of record 6/11/2007 Ex date - 06/25/2007
Merged into Actavis PLC 03/17/2015
Each share Common 1¢ par exchanged for (0.3683) share Ordinary USD$0.0001 par and $129.22 cash

ALLERGAN LIGAND RETINOID THERAPEUTICS INC (DE)
Acquired by Ligand Pharmaceuticals Inc. 11/21/1997
Each share Common $1 par exchanged for approximately (0.97) share Common $0.001 par and $7.69 cash

ALLERGAN PHARMACEUTICALS INC (DE)
Reincorporated 04/14/1977
Stock Dividend - 50% 03/14/1973
State of incorporation changed from (CA) to (DE) 04/14/1977
Common no par split (3) for (2) by issuance of (0.5) additional share 09/01/1978
Merged into SmithKline Corp. 04/11/1980
Each share Common no par exchanged for (1.1) shares Common 25¢ par
SmithKline Corp. name changed to SmithKline Beckman Corp. 03/04/1982 which merged into SmithKline Beecham p.l.c. 07/26/1989 which merged into GlaxoSmithKline PLC 12/27/2000

ALLERGAN PLC (IRELAND)
Each share 5.5% Conv. Preferred Ser. A USD $0.0001 par automatically became (3.533) shares Ordinary USD $0.0001 par 03/01/2018
(Additional Information in Active)

ALLERGAN SPECIALTY THERAPEUTICS INC (DE)
Acquired by Allergan, Inc. 04/20/2001
Each share Common $1 par exchanged for $21.70 cash

ALLERGY IMMUNO TECHNOLOGIES INC (DE)
Name changed to BP International, Inc. 07/25/2003
(See BP International, Inc.)

ALLERGY RESH GROUP INC (FL)
Merged into Longhorn Acquisition Corp. 09/12/2008
Each share Common $0.001 par exchanged for $1.33 cash

ALLERION INC (NJ)
Plan of reorganization under Chapter 11 Federal Bankruptcy proceedings confirmed 06/04/1996
No stockholders' equity

ALLERTECH INC (CO)
Recapitalized as Centerscope Inc. 05/18/1990
Each share Common $0.0001 par exchanged for (0.01) share Common $0.0001 par
Centerscope Inc. recapitalized as CWE Inc. 09/23/1991
(See CWE Inc.)

ALLERTON NEW YORK CORP. (NY)
Liquidation completed 08/11/1961
Details not available

ALLERTON PROPERTIES CORP.
Dissolved 11/00/1944
No stockholders' equity

ALLERTON RES INC (DE)
Charter cancelled and declared inoperative and void for non-payment of taxes 03/01/1982

ALLES & FISHER, INC. (MA)
Common no par changed to $1 par 00/00/1942
Name changed to A & F, Inc. 07/00/1961
A & F, Inc. acquired by Apollo Industries, Inc. (ME) 06/29/1962
(See Apollo Industries, Inc.)

ALLETE (MN)
Name changed to Allete, Inc. 05/07/2001

ALLETE CAP I (DE)
8.05% Guaranteed Quarterly Income Preferred Securities called for redemption at $25 on 12/18/2003

ALLEZOE MED HLDGS INC (DE)
Reorganized under the laws of Florida as Novation Holdings, Inc. 11/07/2012
Each share Common $0.001 par

exchanged for (0.06666666) share Common $0.001 par

ALLGEMEINE ELEKTRICITAETS-GESELLSCHAFT (GERMANY)
Name changed to AEG-Telefunken 01/01/1967
AEG-Telefunken name changed to AEG AG 06/28/1985
(See AEG AG)

ALLGREEN PPTYS LTD (SINGAPORE)
ADR agreement terminated 11/10/2006
No ADR's remain outstanding
ADR agreement terminated 09/10/2012
No ADR's remain outstanding

ALLIANCE & LEICESTER PLC (ENGLAND)
ADR agreement terminated 08/18/2016
No ADR's remain outstanding

ALLIANCE ACQUISITIONS INC (CO) .
Recapitalized as Sterling Alliance Group Ltd. 11/30/1994
Each share Common $0.0001 par exchanged for (0.1) share Common $0.0001 par

ALLIANCE ALL-MARKET ADVANTAGE FD INC (MD)
Acquired by AllianceBernstein Large Cap Growth Fund, Inc. 02/01/2008
Each share Common 1¢ par received (0.5697287) share Class A Common

ALLIANCE ATLANTIS COMMUNICATIONS INC (ON)
Each share Class C no par exchanged for (20) shares Class B no par 09/21/2001
Merged into CanWest Global Communications Corp. 08/16/2007
Each share Class A Common no par exchanged for $53 cash
Each share Non-Vtg. Class B Common no par exchanged for $53 cash

ALLIANCE BALANCED SHS (MD)
Name changed to AllianceBernstein Balanced Shares, Inc. 03/31/2003

ALLIANCE BANCORP (DE)
Common 1¢ par split (3) for (2) by issuance of (0.5) additional share payable 09/26/1997 to holders of record 09/12/1997
Merged into Charter One Financial, Inc. 07/02/2001
Each share Common 1¢ par exchanged for (0.72) share Common 1¢ par and $5.25 cash
(See Charter One Financial, Inc.)

ALLIANCE BANCORP INC PA (PA)
Merged into WSFS Financial Corp. 10/09/2015
Each share Common 1¢ par exchanged for $22 cash

ALLIANCE BANCORP INC PA (USA)
Reorganized under the laws of Pennsylvania 01/18/2011
Each share Common 1¢ par exchanged for (0.82) share Common 1¢ par

ALLIANCE BANCORP NEW ENG INC (DE)
Common 1¢ par split (3) for (2) by issuance of (0.5) additional share payable 05/26/1998 to holders of record 05/12/1998 Ex date - 05/27/1998
Stock Dividend - 10% payable 05/26/2002 to holders of record 05/12/2002
Merged into NewAlliance Bancshares, Inc. 04/02/2004
Each share Common 1¢ par exchanged for (2.501) shares Common 1¢ par
NewAlliance Bancshares, Inc. merged into First Niagara Financial Group, Inc. (New) 04/15/2011 which merged into KeyCorp (New) 08/01/2016

ALLIANCE BANCORPORATION (AK)
Voluntarily dissolved 04/26/1990
Details not available

ALLIANCE BANCSHARES CALIF (CA)
Chapter 7 bankruptcy proceedings terminated 03/01/2017
Stockholders' equity unlikely

ALLIANCE BK & TR CO (GASTONIA, NC)
Reorganized as AB&T Financial Corp. 09/03/2008
Each share Common $5 par exchanged for (1) share Common $1 par

ALLIANCE BK (CULVER CITY, CA)
Common no par split (2) for (1) by issuance of (1) additional share 10/13/1981
Under plan of reorganization each share Common no par automatically became (1) share Alliance Bancshares California Common no par 12/01/2001
(See Alliance Bancshares California)

ALLIANCE BK CORP (VA)
Common $4 par split (3) for (2) by issuance of (0.5) additional share payable 10/26/2001 to holders of record 10/05/2001 Ex date - 10/29/2001
Under plan of reorganization each share Common $4 par automatically became (1) share Alliance Bankshares Corp. Common $4 par 08/16/2002
Alliance Bankshares Corp. merged into WashingtonFirst Bankshares, Inc. 12/21/2012 which merged into Sandy Spring Bancorp, Inc. 01/01/2018

ALLIANCE BANKSHARES CORP (VA)
Common $4 par split (3) for (2) by issuance of (0.5) additional share payable 09/29/2003 to holders of record 09/17/2003 Ex date - 09/30/2003
Stock Dividend - 15% payable 06/30/2006 to holders of record 06/09/2006 Ex date - 06/07/2006
Merged into WashingtonFirst Bankshares, Inc. 12/21/2012
Each share Common $4 par exchanged for (0.4435) share Common $5 par
WashingtonFirst Bankshares, Inc. merged into Sandy Spring Bancorp, Inc. 01/01/2018

ALLIANCE BD FD (MD)
Name changed 03/29/1985
Name and state of incorporation changed from Alliance Bond Fund, Inc. (DE) to Alliance Bond Fund (MA) and Common 10¢ par reclassified as High Grade Portfolio Common $0.001 par 03/29/1985
Reorganized under the laws of Maryland as Alliance Bond Fund, Inc. 12/07/1987
Each share High Grade Portfolio Common $0.001 par exchanged for (9.02092) shares Monthly Income Portfolio Common $0.001 par 03/00/1989
Alliance Bond Fund, Inc. name changed to AllianceBernstein Bond Fund, Inc. 03/31/2003

ALLIANCE BLDG LTD (ON)
7% Conv. Preferred Ser. A $10 par called for redemption 05/14/1973
Under plan of merger each share Common no par exchanged for $5.25 cash 09/29/1978

ALLIANCE BOOTS PLC (UNITED KINGDOM)
Acquired by AB Acquisitions Ltd. 07/20/2007
Each ADR for Ordinary exchanged for $22.88718 cash

ALLIANCE BROADCASTING GROUP INC (DE)
Each share old Common 1¢ par exchanged for (0.18518518) share new Common 1¢ par 05/05/1997
Recapitalized as Emission Controls Corp. 02/15/2002
Each share new Common 1¢ par exchanged for (0.00333333) share Common 1¢ par

ALLIANCE CAP MGMT HLDG L P (DE)
Name changed to AllianceBernstein Holding L.P. 02/24/2006

ALLIANCE CAP MGMT L P (DE)
Units of Ltd. Partnership Int. split (2) for (1) by issuance of (1) additional Unit 03/15/1993
Units of Ltd. Partnership Int. split (2) for (1) by issuance of (1) additional Unit payable 04/02/1998 to holders of record 03/11/1998 Ex date - 04/03/1998
Name changed to Alliance Capital Management Holding L.P. 09/22/1999
Alliance Capital Management Holding L.P. name changed to AllianceBernstein Holding L.P. 02/24/2006

ALLIANCE CASUALTY CO.
Acquired by Indemnity Insurance Co. of North America 00/00/1933
Details not available

ALLIANCE COMMUNICATIONS CORP (CANADA)
Each share Common no par exchanged for (0.5) share Class A Common no par and (0.5) share Non-Vtg. Class B Common no par 05/23/1995
Under plan of merger name changed to Alliance Atlantis Communications Inc. 09/21/1998
(See Alliance Atlantis Communications Inc.)

ALLIANCE COMMUNICATIONS GROUP INC (NJ)
Charter declared void for non-payment of taxes 06/26/1990

ALLIANCE CONSUMER INTL INC (CA)
Each share old Common no par exchanged for (0.02) share new Common no par 03/12/2001
Name changed to NutraStar Inc. 12/14/2001
NutraStar Inc. name changed to NutraCea 08/12/2003 which name changed to RiceBran Technologies 10/26/2012

ALLIANCE CONV FD (MA)
Merged into Alliance Growth & Income Fund, Inc. 05/10/1991
Each Share of Bene. Int. 1¢ par exchanged for (1) share Capital Stock 25¢ par
Alliance Growth & Income Fund, Inc. name changed to AllianceBernstein Growth & Income Fund, Inc. 03/31/2003

ALLIANCE CORPORATE CASH RESVS INC (MD)
Completely liquidated 03/08/1988
Each share Common $0.001 par received net asset value

ALLIANCE COUNTERPOINT FD (MA)
Acquired by Alliance Premier Growth Fund, Inc. 00/00/1996
Details not available

ALLIANCE CREDIT CORP. (QC)
Class A $3 par changed to no par 11/06/1964
Ordinary $1 par changed to no par 11/06/1964 Adjudicated bankrupt 02/14/1968
No stockholders' equity

ALLIANCE DISCIPLINED VALUE FD INC (DE)
Name changed to AllianceBernstein Disciplined Value Fund, Inc. 02/28/2001
AllianceBernstein Disciplined Value Fund, Inc. name changed to AllianceBernstein Focused Growth & Income Fund, Inc. 12/15/2004

ALLIANCE DISTRS HLDG INC (DE)
Name changed to Alliance Media Holdings Inc. 06/26/2015

ALLIANCE DIVID SHS INC (MD)
Name changed to Alliance Growth & Income Fund, Inc. 10/17/1989
Alliance Growth & Income Fund, Inc. name changed to AllianceBernstein Growth & Income Fund, Inc. 03/31/2003

ALLIANCE DROP FORGING CO. (OH)
Acquired by Huron Forge Machine Co. 07/01/1981
Details not available

ALLIANCE ENERGY INC (AB)
Acquired by APF Energy Trust 04/17/2001
Each share Common no par exchanged for either (0.201) Trust Unit no par or (0.00204) Trust Unit and $1.999495 cash
Note: Option to receive stock only expired 06/15/2001
(See APF Energy Trust)

ALLIANCE ENTERPRISES INC (DE)
Name changed to Bio-Sys Ltd. (DE) 04/11/1994
Bio-Sys Ltd. (DE) reorganized in Nevada as Equity Systems Ltd. 05/05/1995 which recapitalized as North American Graphics Ltd. 11/25/1996 which name changed to Environmental Technology Systems Inc. 08/18/1997 which recapitalized as Tombao Antiques & Art Group 04/05/2012

ALLIANCE ENTMT CORP (DE)
Plan of reorganization under Chapter 11 Federal Bankruptcy Code effective 08/20/1998
No stockholders' equity

ALLIANCE ENVIRONMENTAL TECHNOLOGIES, INC. (DE)
SEC revoked common stock registration 03/01/2008

ALLIANCE EXPLORATIONS LTD (CANADA)
Reincorporated under the laws of Nevada as Rox Resources Ltd. and Common no par changed to $0.001 par 07/23/2004

ALLIANCE FD INC (MD)
Name changed to Alliance Mid-Cap Growth Fund Inc. 02/01/2002
Alliance Mid-Cap Growth Fund Inc. name changed to AllianceBernstein Mid-Cap Growth Fund, Inc. 03/31/2003

ALLIANCE FIBER OPTIC PRODS INC (DE)
Each share old Common $0.001 par exchanged for (0.2) share new Common $0.001 par 08/27/2010
New Common $0.001 par split (2) for (1) by issuance of (1) additional share payable 09/16/2013 to holders of record 08/30/2013 Ex date - 09/17/2013
Acquired by Corning Inc. 06/06/2016
Each share new Common $0.001 par exchanged for $18.50 cash

ALLIANCE FINANCE CORP. (DE)
Charter forfeited for failure to maintain a registered agent 10/01/1958

ALLIANCE FINL CORP (MI)
Stock Dividends - 25% 01/31/1985; 25% 01/15/1986
Merged into Comerica, Inc. 12/07/1989

Each share Common $10 par exchanged for $48.28 cash

ALLIANCE FINL CORP (NY)
Stock Dividend - 5% payable 07/10/2000 to holders of record 07/03/2000
Merged into NBT Bancorp Inc. 03/08/2013
Each share Common $1 par exchanged for (2.1779) shares Common 1¢ par

ALLIANCE FING GROUP INC (ON)
Recapitalized as Stream Ventures Inc. 11/30/2010
Each share Common no par exchanged for (0.33333333) share Common no par
Stream Ventures Inc. recapitalized as Beleave Inc. 12/31/2015

ALLIANCE FST PRODS INC (CANADA)
Merged into Bowater Inc. 09/24/2001
Each share Common no par exchanged for (0.166) share Common no par and $13 cash
Bowater Inc. merged into AbitibiBowater Inc. 10/29/2007
(See AbitibiBowater Inc.)

ALLIANCE GAMING CORP (NV)
15% Sr. Pay-In-Kind Special Preferred Ser. B 10¢ par called for redemption at $100 on 09/08/1997
Each share old Common 10¢ par exchanged for (0.28571428) share new Common 10¢ par 02/01/1999
New Common 10¢ par split (2) for (1) by issuance of (1) additional share payable 08/20/2001 to holders of record 07/31/2001 Ex date - 08/21/2001
New Common 10¢ par split (2) for (1) by issuance of (1) additional share payable 04/05/2002 to holders of record 04/03/2002 Ex date - 04/08/2002
Stock Dividend - In Non-Vtg. Jr. Special Stock to holders of Non-Vtg. Jr. Special Stock 2.875% payable 01/02/1998 to holders of record 12/26/1997
Name changed to Bally Technologies, Inc. 03/08/2006
(See Bally Technologies, Inc.)
11.5% Non-Vtg. Jr. Special Stock Ser. E 10¢ par called for redemption at $100 on 04/30/2013

ALLIANCE GLOBAL ENVIRONMENT FD (MD)
Name changed 10/03/1997
Name changed from Alliance Global Environment Fund, Inc. to Alliance Global Environment Fund 10/03/1997
Each share Common 1¢ par exchanged for (1) share Class A 1¢ par Completely liquidated 07/14/2000
Each share Class A exchanged for first and final distribution of $6.84 cash
Each share Class B exchanged for first and final distribution of $6.71 cash
Each share Class C exchanged for first and final distribution of $6.68 cash
Each share Advisor Class exchanged for first and final distribution of $6.92 cash

ALLIANCE GLOBAL FD (MA)
Merged into Alliance Quasar Fund, Inc. 04/27/1989
Details not available

ALLIANCE GRAIN TRADERS INC (ON)
Name changed to AGT Food & Ingredients Inc. 10/03/2014

ALLIANCE GRAIN TRADERS INCOME FD (ON)
Reorganized as Alliance Grain Traders Inc. 09/15/2009

Each Unit no par exchanged for (1) share Common no par
Alliance Grain Traders Inc. name changed to AGT Food & Ingredients Inc. 10/03/2014

ALLIANCE GTR CHINA 97 FD INC (MD)
Name changed to AllianceBernstein Greater China 97 Fund, Inc. 03/31/2003

ALLIANCE GROWTH & INCOME FD INC (MD)
Name changed to AllianceBernstein Growth & Income Fund, Inc. 03/31/2003

ALLIANCE GROWTH FD INC (NJ)
Name changed to Cumberland Growth Fund, Inc. 02/12/1980
(See Cumberland Growth Fund, Inc.)

ALLIANCE HEALTH ENTERPRISE INC (NV)
Name changed to Alliance Technologies, Inc. 02/15/1997
Alliance Technologies, Inc. name changed to Stereoscape.Com, Inc. 02/04/1999 which name changed to Marx Toys & Entertainment Corp. 03/21/2003 which recapitalized as Toyshare, Inc. 07/03/2007 which name changed to Capital Financial Global, Inc. 05/27/2011

ALLIANCE HEALTHCARD INC (GA)
Common $0.001 split (3) for (1) by issuance of (2) additional shares payable 11/28/2000 to holders of record 11/01/2000 Ex date - 12/13/2000
Reincorporated under the laws of Oklahoma as Access Plans, Inc. 01/19/2010
(See Access Plans, Inc.)

ALLIANCE HEALTHCARE SVCS INC (DE)
Name changed 02/17/2009
Plan of reorganization effective 12/18/1997
Each share old Common 1¢ par exchanged for $11 cash
Note: Option to retain shares expired 12/17/1998
Merged into Kohlberg Kravis Roberts & Co. L.P. 11/02/1999
Each share old Common 1¢ par exchanged for $55.96881237 cash
Issue Information - 9,375,000 shares COM offered at $13 per share on 07/26/2001
Name changed from Alliance Imaging, Inc. (New) to Alliance HealthCare Services, Inc. 02/17/2009
Each share old Common 1¢ par exchanged for (0.2) share new Common 1¢ par 12/27/2012
Acquired by Tahoe Investment Group Co., Ltd. 08/21/2017
Each share new Common 1¢ par exchanged for $13.25 cash

ALLIANCE HLDGS GP L P (DE)
Merged into Alliance Resource Partners, L.P. 06/01/2018
Each Common Unit exchanged for approximately (1.47818116) Common Units

ALLIANCE IMAGING INC OLD (DE)
Merged into Casper Acquisition Corp. 11/15/1988
Each share Common 1¢ par exchanged for $9.75 cash

ALLIANCE INCOME BLDR FD INC (MD)
Merged into Alliance Balanced Shares, Inc. 11/13/1998
Each share Class A Common $0.001 par exchanged for (1.690295939) shares Class A Common $1 par
Each share Class B Common $0.001 par exchanged for (1.709310590) shares Class B Common $1 par
Each share Class C Common $0.001

par exchanged for (1.703756201) shares Class C Common $1 par
Alliance Balanced Shares, Inc. name changed to AllianceBernstein Balanced Shares, Inc. 03/31/2003

ALLIANCE INDS (NV)
Charter revoked for failure to file reports and pay fees 02/01/1998

ALLIANCE INSD CALIF TAX EXEMPT SHS INC (MD)
Under plan of reorganization each share Common $1 par automatically became (1) share Alliance Tax-Free Income Fund California Portfolio 1¢ par 11/16/1987
Alliance Tax-Free Income Fund name changed to Alliance Municipal Income Fund, Inc. 09/27/1988 which name changed to AllianceBernstein Municipal Income Fund, Inc. 03/31/2003

ALLIANCE INSTL FDS INC (MA)
Name changed to AllianceBernstein Institutional Funds, Inc. 03/31/2003

ALLIANCE INSURANCE CO.
Acquired by Insurance Co. of North America share for share 06/01/1928
Insurance Co. of North America acquired by INA Corp. 05/29/1968 which merged into Cigna Corp. 04/01/1982

ALLIANCE INS CO (AL)
Found bankrupt and insolvent and placed in receivership 12/14/1971
No stockholders' equity

ALLIANCE INTL FD INC (MA)
Reincorporated 11/01/1985
State of incorporation changed from (MD) to (MA) 11/01/1985
Merged into AllianceBernstein International Value Fund 08/23/2002
Each share Class A 1¢ par automatically became (1) share Class A 1¢ par on a net asset basis
Each share Class B 1¢ par automatically became (1) share Class B 1¢ par on a net asset basis
Each share Class C 1¢ par automatically became (1) share Class C 1¢ par on a net asset basis

ALLIANCE INVESTMENT CORP.
Liquidation completed 12/01/1943
Each share 6% Preferred Ser. A received $102.25 cash
Each share Common received $3.95 cash

ALLIANCE LIFE INSURANCE CO.
Acquired by Republic National Life Insurance Co. 07/00/1949
Details not available

ALLIANCE MANUFACTURING CO. (OH)
Each share Common $1 par exchanged for (3) shares Common $0.33333333 par 00/00/1949
Liquidation completed 08/31/1954
Details not available

ALLIANCE MED INDS INC (DE)
Ceased operations 05/00/1976
No stockholders' equity

ALLIANCE MEDIA GROUP HLDGS INC (NV)
Name changed to Alliance Bioenergy Plus, Inc. 12/05/2014

ALLIANCE MEDICAL INNS, INC. (DE)
Name changed to Alliance Medical Industries, Inc. 06/03/1971
(See Alliance Medical Industries, Inc.)

ALLIANCE MID-CAP GROWTH FD INC (MD)
Name changed to AllianceBernstein Mid-Cap Growth Fund, Inc. 03/31/2003

ALLIANCE MINING & SECURITIES LTD. (CANADA)
Company inactive since 00/00/1937
Charter dissolved 12/15/1980

ALLIANCE MTG SECS INCOME FD INC (MD)
Merged into Alliance Bond Fund, Inc. (MD) 12/15/2000
Each share Class A 1¢ par automatically became (1) share U.S. Government Portfolio Class A $0.001 par on a net asset basis
Alliance Bond Fund, Inc. name changed to AllianceBernstein Bond Fund, Inc. 03/31/2003

ALLIANCE MULTI MKT INCOME & GROWTH TR INC (MD)
Name changed to Alliance Income Builder Fund, Inc. and Common $0.001 reclassified as Class C $0.001 par on 03/29/1994
Alliance Income Builder Fund, Inc. merged into Alliance Balanced Shares, Inc. 11/13/1998 which name changed to AllianceBernstein Balanced Shares, Inc. 03/31/2003

ALLIANCE MUN INCOME FD INC (MD)
Name changed to AllianceBernstein Municipal Income Fund, Inc. 03/31/2003

ALLIANCE MUN INCOME FD II (MA)
Name changed to AllianceBernstein Municipal Income Fund II 03/31/2003

ALLIANCE NATL BK (DALTON, GA)
Acquired by Community & Southern Holdings, Inc. 08/20/2014
Each share Common no par exchanged for $13.60 cash

ALLIANCE NATL INC (NV)
Name changed to Vantas Inc. 07/23/1999
(See Vantas Inc.)

ALLIANCE NATL MUN INCOME FD (MD)
Under plan of merger name changed to AllianceBernstein National Municipal Income Fund, Inc. 05/18/2007

ALLIANCE NETWORK COMMUNICATIONS HLDGS INC (DE)
Name changed to BioCube, Inc. 01/05/2011

ALLIANCE NEW YORK MUN INCOME FD (MD)
Auction Preferred Ser. M called for redemption at $25,000 on 08/25/2015
Auction Preferred Ser. T called for redemption at $25,000 on 08/25/2015
Completely liquidated
Each share Common $0.001 par received first and final distribution of $14.38 cash payable 09/21/2015 to holders of record 08/10/2015

ALLIANCE NORTHWEST INDS INC (NV)
Chapter 7 bankruptcy proceedings terminated 05/26/1999
No stockholders' equity

ALLIANCE OIL DEV AUSTRALIA N L (AUSTRALIA)
Each share Common A50¢ par exchanged for (0.5) share Common A20¢ par 06/28/1977
Merged into Santos Ltd. 06/11/1985
Details not available

ALLIANCE OILS LTD. (CANADA)
Struck off register and declared dissolved for failure to file returns 10/05/1982

ALLIANCE ONE INTL INC (VA)
Each share old Common no par exchanged for (0.1) share new Common no par 06/29/2015
Name changed to Pyxus International, Inc. 09/12/2018

ALL-ALL

ALLIANCE PAC GOLD CORP (YT)
Recapitalized as International Alliance Resources, Inc. 09/24/1998
Each share Common no par exchanged for (0.06666666) share Common no par
International Alliance Resources, Inc. name changed to Bluenose Gold Corp. 07/25/2012

ALLIANCE PETE CORP (NV)
Name changed to Malaysia Pro-Guardians Security Management Corp. 01/14/2013
Malaysia Pro-Guardians Security Management Corp. recapitalized as Shenzhen-ZhongRong Morgan Investment Holding Group Co., Ltd. 06/21/2017

ALLIANCE PHARMACEUTICAL CORP (NY)
Each share old Common 1¢ par exchanged for (0.2) share new Common 1¢ par 10/18/2001
SEC revoked common stock registration 10/18/2013

ALLIANCE PORTFOLIOS (MD)
Merged into Alliance Balanced Shares, Inc. 02/01/1999
Each share Strategic Balanced Fund Class A exchanged for (1.28966425) shares Class A Common $0.001 par
Each share Strategic Balanced Fund Class B exchanged for (1.07817811) shares Class B Common $0.001 par
Each share Strategic Balanced Fund Class C exchanged for (1.07525423) shares Class C Common $0.001 par
Alliance Balanced Shares, Inc. name changed to AllianceBernstein Balanced Shares, Inc. 03/31/2003

ALLIANCE REALTY CO. (NY)
Liquidation completed 01/19/1956
Details not available

ALLIANCE RES LTD (BC)
Recapitalized as Acrex Ventures Ltd. 10/19/1993
Each share Common no par exchanged for (0.2) share Common no par
Acrex Ventures Ltd. recapitalized as Alba Minerals Ltd. 07/10/2014

ALLIANCE RES PLC (UNITED KINGDOM)
Each share old Ordinary Stock 10p par exchanged for (0.025) share new Ordinary Stock 10p par 04/30/1997
Merged into AROC Inc. 12/08/1999
Each share new Ordinary 10p par exchanged for (1) share Common 1¢ par
(See AROC Inc.)

ALLIANCE SVGS & LN ASSN (HOUSTON, TX)
Placed in receivership 05/13/1988
No stockholders' equity

ALLIANCE SEMICONDUCTOR CORP (DE)
Common 1¢ par split (3) for (2) by issuance of (0.5) additional share 01/06/1995
Common 1¢ par split (3) for (2) by issuance of (0.5) additional share 07/31/1995
In process of liquidation
Each share Common 1¢ par received initial distribution of $3.75 cash payable 07/17/2007 to holders of record 07/06/2007 Ex date - 07/18/2007
Each share Common 1¢ par received second distribution of $0.25 cash payable 04/08/2008 to holders of record 03/31/2008 Ex date - 03/27/2008
Each share Common 1¢ par received third distribution of $0.10 cash payable 05/20/2008 to holders of record 05/12/2008 Ex date - 05/08/2008
Each share Common 1¢ par received fourth distribution of $0.25 cash payable 07/01/2008 to holders of record 06/24/2008 Ex date - 07/02/2008
Each share Common 1¢ par received fifth distribution of $0.05 cash payable 09/26/2008 to holders of record 09/19/2008 Ex date - 09/23/2008
Each share Common 1¢ par received sixth distribution of $0.02 cash payable 10/17/2008 to holders of record 10/10/2008 Ex date - 10/15/2008
Each share Common 1¢ par received seventh distribution of $0.02 cash payable 01/30/2009 to holders of record 01/26/2009 Ex date - 01/26/2009
Each share Common 1¢ par received eighth distribution of $0.03 cash payable 09/07/2010 to holders of record 08/31/2010 Ex date - 09/10/2010
Name changed to Alimco Financial Corp. 01/18/2017

ALLIANCE SHORT-TERM MULTI-MKT TR INC (MD)
Merged into Alliance Multi-Market Strategy Trust, Inc. 11/13/1998
Each share Class A Common 1¢ par exchanged for (1.119515885) shares Class A Common $0.001 par
Each share Class B Common 1¢ par exchanged for (1.117647059) shares Class B Common $0.001 par
Each share Class C Common 1¢ par exchanged for (1.119335347) shares Class C Common $0.001 par
Alliance Multi-Market Strategy Trust, Inc. name changed to AllianceBernstein Multi-Market Strategy Trust, Inc. 03/31/2003
(See AllianceBernstein Multi-Market Strategy Trust, Inc.)

ALLIANCE SPLIT INCOME TRUST (ON)
Preferred Securities no par called for redemption at $10 plus $0.050820 accrued dividends on 08/01/2008
Merged into Premier Value Income Trust 08/01/2008
Each Capital Unit no par received (1.58155481) Trust Units no par
Premier Value Income Trust merged into Sentry Canadian Income Fund 02/04/2011

ALLIANCE TAX EXEMPT RESVS (MD)
Reincorporated under the laws of Massachusetts as Alliance Municipal Trust 11/01/1991
Alliance Municipal Trust name changed to AllianceBernstein Municipal Trust 10/28/2003
(See AllianceBernstein Municipal Trust)

ALLIANCE TAX FREE INCOME FD INC (MA)
Name changed to Alliance Municipal Income Fund, Inc., High Bracket Tax Free Portfolio 1¢ par and High Income Tax Free Portfolio 1¢ par reclassified as Insured National Portfolio Class A $0.001 par or National Portfolio Class A $0.001 par respectively 09/27/1988
Alliance Municipal Income Fund, Inc. name changed to AllianceBernstein Municipal Income Fund, Inc. 03/31/2003

ALLIANCE TAX FREE SHS INC (MD)
Merged into Alliance Tax-Free Income Fund 07/10/1987
Each share Common $1 par exchanged for High Bracket Tax Free Portfolio 1¢ par on a net asset basis
Alliance Tax-Free Income Fund name changed to Alliance Municipal Income Fund, Inc. 09/27/1988 which name changed to AllianceBernstein Municipal Income Fund, Inc. 03/31/2003

ALLIANCE TECHNOLOGIES INC (NV)
Name changed to Stereoscape.Com, Inc. 02/04/1999
Stereoscape.Com, Inc. name changed to Marx Toys & Entertainment Corp. 03/21/2003 which recapitalized as Toyshare, Inc. 07/03/2007 which name changed to Capital Financial Global, Inc. 05/27/2011

ALLIANCE TOWERS INC (FL)
Reincorporated under the laws of Delaware as Enclaves Group, Inc. 07/29/2005
(See Enclaves Group, Inc.)

ALLIANCE TRANSCRIPTION SVCS INC (NV)
Charter revoked for failure to file reports and pay fees 05/30/2009

ALLIANCE TROPHY CLUB INC (DE)
Name changed to Gamesboro.com Inc. 06/08/2000
Gamesboro.com Inc. name changed to PLP Holdings Inc. 06/18/2002 which name changed to Tonogold Resources, Inc. 09/13/2004

ALLIANCE URANIUM MINES LTD. (ON)
Charter cancelled and proclaimed dissolved for failure to pay taxes and file returns 06/01/1959

ALLIANCE UTIL INCOME FD INC (MD)
Name changed to AllianceBernstein Utility Income Fund, Inc. 02/28/2001

ALLIANCE VARIABLE PRODS SER FD INC (MD)
Name changed to AllianceBernstein Variable Products Series Fund, Inc. 05/01/2003

ALLIANCE WELL SVC INC (NV)
Recapitalized as Alliance Northwest Industries, Inc. 07/30/1993
Each share Common 1¢ par exchanged for (0.04) share Common 1¢ par
(See Alliance Northwest Industries, Inc.)

ALLIANCE WORLD DLR GOVT FD II INC (MD)
Name changed to AllianceBernstein Global High Income Fund, Inc. 01/26/2007

ALLIANCE WORLD DLR GOVT FD INC (MD)
Merged into AllianceBernstein Global High Income Fund, Inc. 04/13/2007
Each share Common 1¢ par exchanged for (0.9764) share Common 1¢ par

ALLIANCE WORLD INCOME TR INC (MD)
Merged into Alliance Multi-Market Strategy Trust, Inc. 10/16/1998
Each share Common $0.001 par exchanged for (1.238403614) shares Class A Common $0.001 par
Alliance Multi-Market Strategy Trust, Inc. name changed to AllianceBernstein Multi-Market Strategy Trust, Inc. 03/31/2003
(See AllianceBernstein Multi-Market Strategy Trust, Inc.)

ALLIANCEBERNSTEIN ALL-ASIA INVT FD INC (MD)
Name changed 03/31/2003
Name changed from Alliance All-Asia Investment Fund, Inc. to AllianceBernstein All-Asia Investment Fund, Inc. 03/31/2003
Merged into AllianceBernstein International Research Growth Fund, Inc. 06/24/2005
Each share Class A exchanged for (0.660569106) share Class A
Each share Class B exchanged for (0.6433942) share Class B
Each share Class C exchanged for (0.644849785) share Class C
Each share Advisor Class exchanged for (0.661354582) share Advisor Class

ALLIANCEBERNSTEIN CAP RESVS (MA)
Reincorporated 04/07/2003
Name and state of incorporation changed from Alliance Capital Reserves, Inc. (MD) to AllianceBernstein Capital Reserves (MA) 04/07/2003
Completely liquidated 06/24/2005
Details not available

ALLIANCEBERNSTEIN DISCIPLINED GROWTH FD INC (MD)
Name changed 03/31/2003
Name changed from Alliance Disciplined Growth Fund, Inc. to AllianceBernstein Disciplined Growth Fund, Inc. 03/31/2003
Completely liquidated 06/19/2004
Details not available

ALLIANCEBERNSTEIN DISCIPLINED VALUE FD INC (MD)
Name changed to AllianceBernstein Focused Growth & Income Fund, Inc. 12/15/2004

ALLIANCEBERNSTEIN DYNAMIC GROWTH FD INC (MD)
Name changed 03/31/2003
Name changed from Alliance Dynamic Growth Fund, Inc. to AllianceBernstein Dynamic Growth Fund, Inc. 03/31/2003
Completely liquidated 06/30/2004
Details not available

ALLIANCEBERNSTEIN EMERGING MKT DEBT FD (MD)
Name changed 03/31/2003
Name changed from Alliance Emerging Market Debt Fund, Inc. to AllianceBernstein Emerging Market Debt Fund, Inc. 03/31/2003
Name changed to AllianceBernstein High Income Fund, Inc. 01/28/2008

ALLIANCEBERNSTEIN GLOBAL GOVT INCOME TR (MD)
Name changed 03/31/2003
Name changed 02/01/2006
Name changed from Alliance Americas Government Income Trust, Inc. to AllianceBernstein Americas Government Income Trust, Inc. 03/31/2003
Name changed from AllianceBernstein Americas Government Income Trust, Inc. to AllianceBernstein Global Government Income Trust, Inc. 02/01/2006
Name changed to AllianceBernstein Global Bond Fund, Inc. 11/05/2007

ALLIANCEBERNSTEIN GLOBAL GROWTH TRENDS FD INC (MD)
Name changed 03/31/2003
Name changed from Alliance Global Growth Trends Fund, Inc. to AllianceBernstein Global Growth Trends Fund, Inc. 03/31/2003
Name changed to AllianceBernstein Global Research Growth Fund, Inc. 12/15/2003

ALLIANCEBERNSTEIN GLOBAL SMALL CAP FD (MD)
Name changed 03/31/2003
Name changed from Alliance Global Small Capital Fund, Inc. to AllianceBernstein Global Small Cap Fund 03/31/2003
Completely liquidated 03/01/2005
Each share Class A $1 par received net asset value
Each share Class B $1 par received net asset value
Each share Class C $1 par received net asset value

Each share Advisor Class $1 par received net asset value

ALLIANCEBERNSTEIN GLOBAL STRATEGIC INCOME TR (MD)
Name changed 03/31/2003
Name changed from Alliance Global Strategic Income Trust to AllianceBernstein Global Strategic Income Trust, Inc. 03/31/2003
Name changed to AllianceBernstein Diversified Yield Fund, Inc. 11/05/2007

ALLIANCEBERNSTEIN GOVT RESVS INC (MA)
Reincorporated 11/01/1984
Name changed 04/07/2003
Name change and state of incorporation changed from Alliance Government Reserves, Inc. (MD) to Alliance Government Reserves (MA) 11/01/1984
Name changed from Alliance Government Reserves to AllianceBernstein Government Reserves 04/07/2003
Completely liquidated 06/24/2005
Details not available

ALLIANCEBERNSTEIN HEALTH CARE FD INC (MD)
Name changed 03/31/2003
Name changed from Alliance Health Care Fund, Inc. to AllianceBernstein Health Care Fund, Inc. 03/31/2003
Name changed to AllianceBernstein Global Health Care Fund, Inc. 12/15/2004

ALLIANCEBERNSTEIN HIGH YIELD FUND INC (MD)
Name changed 03/31/2003
Name changed from Alliance High Yield Fund, Inc. to AllianceBernstein High Yield Fund, Inc. 03/31/2003
Under plan of merger each share Class A, Class B, Class C or Advisor Class automatically became (1) share AllianceBernstein Emerging Market Debt Fund, Inc. Class A, Class B, Class C or Advisor Class respectively 01/25/2008
AllianceBernstein Emerging Market Debt Fund, Inc. name changed to AllianceBernstein High Income Fund, Inc. 01/28/2008

ALLIANCEBERNSTEIN INSTL RESVS INC (MD)
Name changed 08/27/2003
Name changed from Alliance Institutional Reserves, Inc. to AllianceBernstein Institutional Reserves, Inc. 08/27/2003
Name changed to AllianceBernstein Fixed-Income Shares, Inc. 02/24/2006

ALLIANCEBERNSTEIN INTL PREMIER GROWTH FD INC (MD)
Name changed 03/31/2003
Name changed from Alliance International Premier Growth Fund, Inc. to AllianceBernstein International Premier Growth Fund, Inc. 03/31/2003
Name changed to AllianceBernstein International Research Growth Fund, Inc. 05/13/2005

ALLIANCEBERNSTEIN MULTI MKT STRATEGY TR INC (MD)
Name changed 03/31/2003
Name changed from Alliance Multi-Market Strategy Trust, Inc. to AllianceBernstein Multi-Market Strategy Trust, Inc. 03/31/2003
Completely liquidated 08/04/2006
Details not available

ALLIANCEBERNSTEIN MUN TR (MA)
Name changed 10/28/2003
Name changed from Alliance Municipal Trust to AllianceBernstein Municipal Trust 10/28/2003
Completely liquidated 06/24/2005
Details not available

ALLIANCEBERNSTEIN NEW EUROPE FD INC (MD)
Name changed 03/31/2003
Name changed from Alliance New Europe Fund, Inc. to AllianceBernstein New Europe Fund, Inc. 03/31/2003
Merged into AllianceBernstein International Research Growth Fund, Inc. 07/08/2005
Each share Class A 1¢ par exchanged for (1.657921292) shares Class A
Each share Class B exchanged for (1.545842217) shares Class B
Each share Class C exchanged for (1.552238806) shares Class C
Each share Advisor Class exchanged for (1.646884273) shares Advisor Class

ALLIANCEBERNSTEIN PREMIER GROWTH FD INC (MD)
Name changed 03/31/2003
Name changed from Alliance Premier Growth Fund, Inc. to AllianceBernstein Premier Growth Fund, Inc. 03/31/2003
Name changed to AllianceBernstein Large Cap Growth Fund, Inc. 12/15/2004

ALLIANCEBERNSTEIN REAL ESTATE INVT FD INC INC
Name changed 02/28/2001
Name changed from Alliance Real Estate Investment Fund, Inc. to AllianceBernstein Real Estate Investment Fund Inc. 02/28/2001
Name changed to AllianceBernstein Global Real Estate Investment Fund, Inc. 03/01/2007

ALLIANCEBERNSTEIN SELECT INV SER (MD)
Name changed 03/31/2003
Name changed from Alliance Select Investor Series, Inc. to AllianceBernstein Select Investor Series, Inc. 03/31/2003
Completely liquidated 07/31/2003
Each share Small Cap Growth Portfolio Class A, Small Cap Growth Portfolio Class B, and Small Cap Growth Portfolio Class C received net asset value
Completely liquidated 03/01/2005
Each share Biotechnology Portfolio Class A, Biotechnology Portfolio Class B, and Biotechnology Portfolio Class C received net asset value
Each share Premier Portfolio Class A, Premier Portfolio Class B, and Premier Technology Portfolio Class C received net asset value
Each share Technology Portfolio Class A, Technology Portfolio Class B, and Technology Portfolio Class C received net asset value

ALLIANCEBERNSTEIN SMALL CAP GROWTH FD INC (MD)
Name changed 03/31/2003
Name changed 11/01/2003
Name changed from Alliance Quasar Fund, Inc. to AllianceBernstein Quasar Fund, Inc. 03/31/2003
Name changed from AllianceBernstein Quasar Fund, Inc. to AllianceBernstein Small Cap Growth Fund, Inc. 11/01/2003
Name changed to AllianceBernstein Cap Fund, Inc. 09/08/2004

ALLIANCEBERNSTEIN TECHNOLOGY FD INC (MD)
Name changed 03/31/2003
Name changed from Alliance Technology Fund, Inc. to AllianceBernstein Technology Fund, Inc. 03/31/2003
Name changed to AllianceBernstein Global Technology Fund, Inc. 12/15/2004

ALLIANCEBERNSTEIN WORLDWIDE PRIVATIZATION FD (MD)
Name changed 03/31/2003
Name changed from Alliance Worldwide Privatization Fund, Inc. to AllianceBernstein Worldwide Privatization Fund, Inc. 03/31/2003
Name changed to AllianceBernstein International Growth Fund, Inc. 05/16/2005

ALLIANCEPHARMA INC (QC)
Name changed to KDA Group Inc. 02/01/2017

ALLIANCEWARE, INC. (OH)
Each share Common $1 par exchanged for (2) shares Common 50¢ par 05/22/1947
$2.50 Preferred $50 par called for redemption 12/20/1950
Merged into American Metal Products Co. (MI) 05/20/1956
Each share Common 50¢ par exchanged for (1.16666666) share Common $2 par
American Metal Products Co. (MI) acquired by Lear Siegler, Inc. 11/15/1966
(See Lear Siegler, Inc.)

ALLIANT COMPUTER SYS CORP (DE)
Filed a petition under Chapter 11 Federal Bankruptcy Code 05/26/1992
Company has subsequently been liquidated and there is no stockholders' equity

ALLIANT DIAGNOSTICS INC (DE)
Each share old Common 1¢ par exchanged for (0.1) share new Common 1¢ par 03/05/2007
Name changed to Navicus, Inc. 03/05/2008
Navicus, Inc. name changed to Super Nova Resources, Inc. 11/13/2008

ALLIANT TECHSYSTEMS INC (DE)
Common 1¢ par split (3) for (2) by issuance of (0.5) additional share payable 11/27/2000 to holders of record 11/10/2000 Ex date - 11/28/2000
Common 1¢ par split (3) for (2) by issuance of (0.5) additional share payable 09/07/2001 to holders of record 08/17/2001 Ex date - 09/10/2001
Common 1¢ par split (3) for (2) by issuance of (0.5) additional share payable 06/10/2002 to holders of record 05/17/2002 Ex date - 06/11/2002
Each share Common 1¢ par received distribution of (2) shares Vista Outdoor Inc. Common 1¢ par payable 02/09/2015 to holders of record 02/02/2015
Under plan of merger name changed to Orbital ATK, Inc. 02/09/2015
(See Orbital ATK, Inc.)

ALLIANZ AG (GERMANY)
Name changed to Allianz SE 10/13/2006

ALLIANZGI GLOBAL EQUITY & CONV INCOME FD (MA)
Merged into AllianzGI Equity & Convertible Income Fund 01/24/2014
Each share Common $0.00001 par exchanged for (0.76991984) share Common $0.00001 par

ALLIANZGI INTL & PREM STRATEGY FD (MA)
Completely liquidated 10/28/2013
Each Common Share of Bene. Int. $0.00001 par received $11.03068 cash

ALLIBABA ENERGY RES LTD (BC)
Name changed to Talon Energy Corp. 05/02/1983
Talon Energy Corp. name changed to Talon Resources Ltd. 05/31/1984

ALLICAN RES INC (CANADA)
Dissolved for non-compliance 03/12/2007

ALLICO CORP (DE)
Charter cancelled and declared inoperative and void for non-payment of taxes 03/01/1994

ALLIE ANNIE LAURIE GOLD MINES, INC.
Lease terminated 00/00/1939
Details not available

ALLIED AERO INDS INC (DE)
Charter cancelled and declared inoperative and void for non-payment of taxes 03/01/1974

ALLIED-ALBANY PAPER CORP. (NY)
Liquidation completed 05/11/1959
Details not available

ALLIED AMERICAN INDUSTRIES, INC.
Acquired by Guardian Investors Corp. 00/00/1930
Details not available

ALLIED ARTISTS ENTMT GROUP INC (NV)
Recapitalized as International Synergy Holding Co. Ltd. 07/10/2001
Each share Common no par exchanged for (0.125) share Common no par
International Synergy Holding Co. Ltd. name changed to Along Mobile Technologies, Inc. 12/27/2005
(See Along Mobile Technologies, Inc.)

ALLIED ARTISTS ENTMT INC. (UT)
Proclaimed dissolved for failure to pay taxes 01/01/1994

ALLIED ARTISTS INDS INC (DE)
Charter cancelled and declared inoperative and void for non-payment of taxes 06/17/1993

ALLIED ARTISTS PICTURES CORP (DE)
5.5% Conv. Preferred $10 par called for redemption 01/20/1976
Merged into Allied Artists Industries, Inc. 01/20/1976
Each share Common $1 par exchanged for (2) shares Common 10¢ par
(See Allied Artists Industries, Inc.)

ALLIED ATLAS CORP.
Dissolved 00/00/1934
Details not available

ALLIED BANCSHARES INC (DE)
Reincorporated 04/22/1987
Common $1 par split (4) for (3) by issuance of (1/3) additional share 12/31/1979
Common $1 par split (3) for (2) by issuance of (0.5) additional share 12/12/1980
Common $1 par split (3) for (2) by issuance of (0.5) additional share 11/16/1981
Common $1 par split (5) for (4) by issuance of (0.25) additional share 12/31/1982
Common $1 par split (5) for (4) by issuance of (0.25) additional share 12/31/1983
Stock Dividend - 20% 05/15/1978
State of incorporation changed from (TX) to (DE) 04/22/1987
Merged into First Interstate Bancorp 01/29/1988
Each share Common $1 par exchanged for (0.1) share Adjustable Rate Preferred Ser. B no par and (1) share Class A Common 1¢ par
Note: In addition each share Common $1 par received distribution of (1) share National Asset Bank (Houston, TX) Common 1¢ par 02/22/1988
First Interstate Bancorp merged into Wells Fargo & Co. (Old) 04/01/1996

which merged into Wells Fargo & Co. (New) 11/02/1998

ALLIED BK CAP INC (NC)
Common $1 par split (2) for (1) by issuance of (1) additional share 12/02/1994
Merged into First Citizens BancShares, Inc. 02/14/1996
Each share Common $1 par exchanged for $25.25 cash

ALLIED BANKERS LIFE INS CO (TX)
Stock Dividends - 10% 04/15/1965; 10% 10/20/1971; 20% 11/21/1973
Placed in permanent receivership 05/10/1990
No stockholders' equity

ALLIED BKS INC (FL)
Merged into Holiday Bank (Holiday, FL) 04/02/1986
Each share Common $1 par exchanged for (3) shares Common $100 par
Holiday Bank (Holiday, FL) name changed to Florida State Bank (Holiday, FL) 02/21/1989
(See Florida State Bank (Holiday, FL))

ALLIED BANKSHARES INC (GA)
Common $1 par split (5) for (4) by issuance of (0.25) additional share 08/29/1988
Common $1 par split (5) for (4) by issuance of (0.25) additional share 12/01/1993
Common $1 par split (5) for (4) by issuance of (0.25) additional share 12/01/1994
Common $1 par split (5) for (4) by issuance of (0.25) additional share 12/01/1994
Stock Dividends - 10% 05/18/1992; 10% 11/30/1992; 10% 06/01/1993; 10% payable 03/01/1996 to holders of record 02/09/1996
Merged into Regions Financial Corp. (Old) 01/31/1997
Each share Common $1 par exchanged for (0.226) share Common $0.625 par
Regions Financial Corp. (Old) merged into Regions Financial Corp. (New) 07/01/2004

ALLIED BIOTECHNOLOGY INTL INC (NV)
Recapitalized as Dragon Energy Group Ltd. 04/10/1998
Each share Common $0.001 par exchanged for (0.06666666) share Common $0.001 par
Dragon Energy Group Ltd. recapitalized as Seven Angels Ventures, Inc. 03/05/2004 which name changed to Twister Networks, Inc. 03/25/2004 which recapitalized as Reynaldos Mexican Food Co., Inc. 03/04/2005

ALLIED BLDRS CORP (CA)
Adjudicated bankrupt 02/28/1975
No stockholders' equity

ALLIED BREWERIES LTD (ENGLAND)
Name changed to Allied-Lyons PLC 11/30/1981
Allied-Lyons PLC name changed to Allied Domecq PLC 09/19/1994 which merged into Pernod Ricard S.A. 07/26/2005
(See Pernod Ricard S.A.)

ALLIED CAP ADVISERS INC (MD)
Merged into Allied Capital Corp. (New) 12/31/1997
Each share Common $0.001 par exchanged for (0.31) share Common $0.0001 par
Allied Capital Corp. (New) merged into Ares Capital Corp. 04/01/2010

ALLIED CAP COML CORP (MD)
Merged into Allied Capital Corp. (New) 12/31/1997
Each share Common $0.0001 par exchanged for (1.6) shares Common $0.0001 par
Allied Capital Corp. (New) merged into Ares Capital Corp. 04/01/2010

ALLIED CAP CORP II (MD)
Reincorporated 06/18/1991
State of incorporation changed from (DC) to (MD) 06/18/1991
Merged into Allied Capital Corp. (New) 12/31/1997
Each share Common $1 par exchanged for (1.4) shares Common $0.0001 par
Allied Capital Corp. (New) merged into Ares Capital Corp. 04/01/2010

ALLIED CAP CORP NEW (MD)
Merged into Ares Capital Corp. 04/01/2010
Each share Common $0.0001 par exchanged for (0.325) share Common $0.001 par

ALLIED CAP CORP OLD (MD)
Reincorporated 05/10/1991
Common $1 par split (5) for (4) by issuance of (0.25) additional share 06/17/1983
Common $1 par split (3) for (2) by issuance of (0.5) additional share 02/28/1986
Common $1 par split (5) for (4) by issuance of (0.25) additional share 01/30/1987
Stock Dividends - 100% 09/29/1971; 100% 11/21/1972; 25% 10/14/1988
Place of incorporation changed from (DC) to (MD) 05/10/1991
Each share Common $1 par received distribution of (0.54545454) share Allied Capital Lending Corp. Common $0.0001 par 01/06/1995
Merged into Allied Capital Corp. (New) 12/31/1997
Each share Common $1 par exchanged for (1.07) shares Common $0.0001 par
Allied Capital Corp. (New) merged into Ares Capital Corp. 04/01/2010

ALLIED CAP LENDING CORP (MD)
Under plan of merger name changed to Allied Capital Corp. (New) 12/31/1997
Allied Capital Corp. (New) merged into Ares Capital Corp. 04/01/2010

ALLIED CARSON CORP (NY)
Charter cancelled and proclaimed dissolved for failure to pay taxes 01/10/1979

ALLIED CELLULAR SYS LTD (BC)
Delisted from Vancouver Stock Exchange 05/04/1993

ALLIED CHEM & DYE CORP (NY)
Common no par changed to $18 par 04/23/1956
Stock Dividend - 300% 09/01/1950
Name changed to Allied Chemical Corp. 04/29/1958
Allied Chemical Corp. name changed to Allied Corp. 04/27/1981 which merged into Allied-Signal Inc. 09/19/1985 which name changed to AlliedSignal Inc. 04/26/1993 which name changed to Honeywell International Inc. 12/01/1999

ALLIED CHEMICAL CORP. (NY)
Common $18 par changed to $9 par and (1) additional share issued 01/22/1960
Name changed to Allied Corp. and Common $9 par changed to $1 par 04/27/1981
Allied Corp. merged into Allied-Signal Inc. 09/19/1985 which name changed to AlliedSignal Inc. 04/26/1993 which name changed to Honeywell International Inc. 12/01/1999

ALLIED CLINICAL LABS INC (DE)
Merged into N Acquisition Corp. 06/23/1994
Each share Common $1 par exchanged for $21.50 cash

ALLIED COLLOIDS GROUP PLC (UNITED KINGDOM)
ADR agreement terminated 05/10/1998
Each Sponsored ADR for Ordinary 10p par exchanged for $8.20 cash

ALLIED COLORADO ENTERPRISES CO. (CO)
Charter revoked for failure to file reports and pay fees 10/11/1963

ALLIED CONS ENERGY INC (AB)
Recapitalized as Allied Oil & Gas Corp. 04/19/1999
Each share Common no par exchanged for (0.2) share Common no par
(See Allied Oil & Gas Corp.)

ALLIED CTL INC (NY)
Reorganized 00/00/1948
Each share 55¢ Preferred $8 par exchanged for (1) share 7% Preferred $4 par
Old Common had no equity
7% Preferred $4 par called for redemption 08/15/1958
Common $1 par changed to 50¢ and (1) additional share issued 04/21/1960
Merged into Gould Inc. 06/04/1974
Each share Common 50¢ par exchanged for (0.55) share Common $4 par
(See Gould Inc.)

ALLIED CORP (NY)
Common $1 par split (3) for (2) by issuance of (0.5) additional share 05/29/1984
Merged into Allied-Signal Inc. 09/19/1985
Each share Adjustable Rate Preferred Ser. F no par exchanged for (1) share Adjustable Rate Preferred Ser. F no par
Each share $6.74 Conv. Preferred Ser. C no par exchanged for (1) share $6.74 Conv. Preferred Ser. C no par
Each share $12 Conv. Preferred Ser. D no par exchanged for (1) share $12 Conv. Preferred Ser. D no par
Each share Common $1 par exchanged for (1) share Common $1 par
Allied-Signal Inc. name changed to AlliedSignal Inc. 04/26/1993 which name changed to Honeywell International Inc. 12/01/1999

ALLIED CREDIT CORP.
Dissolved 00/00/1941
Details not available

ALLIED DEFENSE GROUP INC (DE)
Liquidation completed
Each share Common 10¢ par exchanged for initial distribution of $5.11 cash 12/23/2013
Each share Common 10¢ par received second and final distribution of $0.10 cash payable 12/29/2014 to holders of record 12/23/2013

ALLIED DEVICES CORP (NV)
Plan of reorganization under Chapter 11 Federal Bankruptcy Code effective 09/23/2003
Each share Common $0.001 par exchanged for (0.03333333) share Deep Well Oil & Gas, Inc. Common $0.001 par

ALLIED DIGITAL TECHNOLOGIES CORP (DE)
Merged into Analog Acquisition Corp. 09/24/1998
Each share Common 1¢ par exchanged for $5 cash

ALLIED DISCOUNT CO. INC. (NY)
Name changed to Allied-Carson Corp. 02/09/1966
(See Allied-Carson Corp.)

ALLIED DOMECQ PLC (UNITED KINGDOM)
Each old Sponsored ADR for Ordinary exchanged for (0.25) new Sponsored ADR for Ordinary 07/15/2002
Basis changed from (1:1) to (1:4) 07/15/2002
Merged into Pernod Ricard S.A. 07/26/2005
Each new Sponsored ADR for Ordinary exchanged for (0.2528) Sponsored ADR for Ordinary and $38.69718 cash
(See Pernod Ricard S.A.)

ALLIED DRUG PRODS CO (DE)
Charter cancelled and declared inoperative and void for non-payment of taxes 05/19/1970

ALLIED EGRY BUSINESS SYS INC (OH)
5.5% Preferred $100 par called for redemption 03/18/1984
Public interest eliminated

ALLIED ELECTRIC PRODUCTS, INC. (NJ)
Adjudicated bankrupt 08/17/1955
No stockholders' equity

ALLIED EMPIRE, INC. (CA)
Name changed to Riverside Financial Corp. 06/06/1963
Riverside Financial Corp. name changed to Quanta Industries, Inc. 10/01/1983
(See Quanta Industries, Inc.)

ALLIED ENERGY CORP (UT)
Each share Common $0.005 par exchanged for (0.1) share Common 5¢ par 12/15/1982
Charter expired 06/29/2007

ALLIED ENERGY GROUP INC (FL)
Name changed to Allied Energy, Inc. 04/22/2010

ALLIED ENERGY INC (NV)
Common $0.001 par split (5) for (1) by issuance of (4) additional shares payable 06/03/2004 to holders of record 06/01/2004 Ex date - 06/04/2004
Name changed to FloodSmart, Inc. 09/29/2005
FloodSmart, Inc. name changed to Axis Energy Corp. 08/01/2006

ALLIED ENTERTAINMENT CORP. OF AMERICA, INC. (DE)
Merged into Jay Boy Music Corp. 03/26/1968
Each share Common 5¢ par exchanged for (0.5) share Common 1¢ par
(See Jay Boy Music Corp.)

ALLIED ENVIRONMENTAL SVCS CORP (BC)
Name changed to Philip Environmental Services Corp. 08/22/1991
Philip Environmental Services Corp. recapitalized as Devco Enterprises Inc. 05/17/1993 which recapitalized as SBI Skin Biology Inc. (BC) 11/03/1995 which reincorporated in Yukon 08/22/1996 which reorganized in British Columbia as Realm Energy International Corp. 10/26/2009 which merged into San Leon Energy PLC 11/10/2011

ALLIED EQUITIES CORP (NV)
Name changed to Precision Technologies 09/23/1983
(See Precision Technologies)

ALLIED EQUITIES LTD (AB)
Delisted from Alberta Stock Exchange 02/07/1994

ALLIED EXECUTIVE INDUSTRIES, INC. (CO)
Each share Capital Stock $0.001 par exchanged for (0.2) share Capital Stock $0.005 par 06/14/1971

Name changed to Pacific Resource Group, Inc. 04/15/1980

ALLIED FARM EQUIP INC (IL)
Proclaimed dissolved for failure to pay taxes and file reports 01/02/1991

ALLIED FIN CO (TX)
Stock Dividends - 50% 03/10/1956; 20% 02/25/1960; 20% 03/18/1966
Merged into Republic Financial Services, Inc. 12/28/1972
Each share Common $5 par exchanged for (3) shares Common $5 par
Details not available for 6% Preferred 1958 Ser. $100 par
(See Republic Financial Services, Inc.)

ALLIED FOODS INC (DE)
Merged into Fabro, Inc. 10/15/1982
Each share Common 40¢ par exchanged for $4.40 cash

ALLIED GAS CO. (IL)
Each share Common $10 par exchanged for (5) shares Common $5 par 02/11/1955
Common $5 par split (3) for (2) by issuance of (0.5) additional share 12/02/1957
Stock Dividend - 50% 03/01/1961
Acquired by Northern Illinois Gas Co. 12/31/1962
Each share Common $5 par exchanged for (0.25) share 5% Conv. Preferred $100 par
Northern Illinois Gas Co. reorganized as Nicor Inc. 04/30/1976 which merged into AGL Resources Inc. 12/09/2011

ALLIED GEN INC (FL)
Incorporated 04/28/1969
Name changed to A.G.I., Inc. 06/18/1969
(See A.G.I., Inc.)

ALLIED GENERAL, INC. (FL)
Incorporated 01/26/1968
Proclaimed dissolved for failure to file reports and pay fees 12/11/1976

ALLIED GENERAL CORP. (NY)
Dissolved 10/24/1935
Details not available

ALLIED GOLD LTD. (AUSTRALIA)
Reorganized under the laws of England & Wales as Allied Gold Mining PLC 06/30/2011
Each share Ordinary exchanged for (0.16666666) share Ordinary 10p par
(See Allied Gold Mining PLC)

ALLIED GOLD MINING PLC (ENGLAND & WALES)
Merged into St. Barbara Ltd. 09/07/2012
Each share Ordinary 10p par exchanged for (0.8) share Ordinary and AUD$1.025 cash
Note: Unexchanged certificates were cancelled and became without value 09/07/2018

ALLIED GRAPHIC ARTS, INC. (NY)
Stock Dividend - 33.33333333% 10/23/1964 Completely liquidated 07/18/1966
Each share Common $1 par exchanged for first and final distribution of $7.875 cash

ALLIED GROUP INC (IA)
Common no par split (3) for (2) by issuance of (0.5) additional share 06/30/1993
Common no par split (3) for (2) by issuance of (0.5) additional share payable 11/29/1996 to holders of record 11/15/1996
Common no par split (3) for (2) by issuance of (0.5) additional share payable 11/28/1997 to holders of record 11/14/1997 Ex date - 12/01/1997

Merged into Nationwide Mutual Insurance Co. 11/12/1998
Each share Common no par exchanged for $48.25 cash

ALLIED HEALTHCARE INTL INC (NY)
Each share Preferred Ser. A 1¢ par exchanged for (1) share Common 1¢ par 07/00/2004
Acquired by Saga Group Ltd. 10/20/2011
Each share Common 1¢ par exchanged for $3.90 cash

ALLIED HLDGS INC (GA)
Plan of reorganization under Chapter 11 Federal Bankruptcy Code effective 05/29/2007
No stockholders' equity

ALLIED HOTEL PPTYS INC (CANADA)
Reincorporated under the laws of British Columbia 06/22/2009

ALLIED INTERNATIONAL INVESTING CORP. (DE)
Each share Part. Preference no par exchanged for (2) shares $3 Preferred no par and (2) shares Common no par 00/00/1929
Each share $3 Preferred no par exchanged for (3.8645) shares Capital Stock $1 par 00/00/1947
Each share Common no par exchanged for (0.0544) share Capital Stock $1 par 00/00/1947
Each share Capital Stock $1 par exchanged for (1) share new Capital Stock $1 par 02/29/1956
Name changed to Dorsey Corp. 03/26/1959
Dorsey Corp. name changed to Constar International Inc. 05/01/1987
(See Constar International Inc.)

ALLIED INVESTORS, INC.
Dissolved 00/00/1930
Details not available

ALLIED INVS SYND LTD (BAHAMAS)
Name changed to A.I.S. Resources Ltd. 09/16/1971

ALLIED IRISH BKS P L C (IRELAND)
Sponsored ADR's for Preference called for redemption at $25 on 06/04/1998
Old Sponsored ADR's for Ordinary split (3) for (1) by issuance of (2) additional ADR's payable 05/14/1999 to holders of record 05/13/1999 Ex date - 05/17/1999
Each old Sponsored ADR for Ordinary exchanged for (0.2) new Sponsored ADR for Ordinary 02/23/2011
ADR basis changed from (1:2) to (1:10) 02/23/2011
ADR agreement terminated 10/10/2011
Each new Sponsored ADR for Ordinary exchanged for $1.220093 cash

ALLIED IRON & SULPHUR MINES LTD. (ON)
Charter revoked for failure to file reports and pay fees 11/05/1956

ALLIED KID CO (MA)
Common $5 par split (2) for (1) by issuance of (1) additional share 04/08/1959
Stock Dividends - 10% 02/15/1944; 10% 05/15/1945
Merged into Cudahy Co. 11/29/1968
Each share Common $5 par exchanged for (1) share $1.25 Conv. Preferred Ser. A $2.50 par and (0.692) share Common $5 par
Cudahy Co. merged into General Host Corp. 02/24/1972
(See General Host Corp.)

ALLIED LABORATORIES, INC. (DE)
Common no par split (2) for (1) by issuance of (1) additional share 05/01/1956
Stock Dividend - 10% 12/30/1957

Acquired by Dow Chemical Co. 12/30/1960
Each share Common no par exchanged for (0.66666666) share Common $5 par
Dow Chemical Co. merged into DowDuPont Inc. 09/01/2017

ALLIED LEISURE INDS INC (FL)
Name changed to Centuri Inc. 08/19/1980
(See Centuri Inc.)

ALLIED LIFE FINL CORP (IA)
Merged into Nationwide Mutual Insurance Co. 11/12/1998
Each share Common no par exchanged for $30 cash

ALLIED LIFE INS CO (AL)
Common $3 par changed to $1 par 03/29/1968
Name changed to Allied Life Insurance Co. of America 04/08/1969
Allied Life Insurance Co. of America recapitalized as American Allied Life Insurance Co. (AL) 12/29/1971 which reincorporated in Iowa as Statesman Life Insurance Co. 10/04/1976
(See Statesman Life Insurance Co.)

ALLIED LIFE INS CO AMER (AL)
Recapitalized as American Allied Life Insurance Co. (AL) 12/29/1971
Each share Common $1 par exchanged for (0.5) share Common $1 par
American Allied Life Insurance Co. (AL) reincorporated in Iowa as Statesman Life Insurance Co. 10/04/1976
(See Statesman Life Insurance Co.)

ALLIED LYONS PLC (ENGLAND)
Each Unsponsored ADR for Ordinary 25p par exchanged for (1) Sponsored ADR for Ordinary 25p par 01/02/1987
Name changed to Allied Domecq PLC 09/19/1994
Allied Domecq PLC merged into Pernod Ricard S.A. 07/26/2005
(See Pernod Ricard S.A.)

ALLIED MAINTENANCE CORP (NY)
Capital Stock $3.75 par changed to $3 par and (0.25) additional share issued 12/20/1961
Capital Stock $3 par changed to $1.50 par and (1) additional share issued 05/31/1968
Capital Stock $1.50 par reclassified as Common $1.20 par and (0.25) additional share issued 09/30/1970
Merged into Ogden Corp. 09/15/1982
Each share Common $1.20 par exchanged for (1.75) shares Common 50¢ par
Ogden Corp. name changed to Covanta Energy Corp. 03/14/2001
(See Covanta Energy Corp.)

ALLIED MGMT & SYS CORP (DE)
Charter cancelled and declared inoperative and void for non-payment of taxes 03/01/1974

ALLIED MANAGEMENT CORP. (DE)
Charter cancelled and declared inoperative and void for non-payment of taxes 03/01/1984

ALLIED MATRIX CORP (NV)
Charter permanently revoked for failure to file reports and pay fees 08/31/2003

ALLIED MNG CORP (QC)
Merged into United Asbestos Inc. 06/29/1973
Each share Common no par exchanged for (1) share Common no par
United Asbestos Inc. merged into Campbell Resources Inc. (New) 06/08/1983
(See Campbell Resources Inc. (New))

ALLIED MISSION OIL INC (DE)
Plan of Arrangement under Chapter XI confirmed 12/07/1965
Attorney opined stock is worthless

ALLIED MLS INC (IN)
Common no par changed to $3 par and (2) additional shares issued 10/07/1968
Stock Dividend - 10% 07/13/1970
Merged into Continental Grain Co. 04/08/1974
Each share Common $3 par exchanged for $26 cash

ALLIED MTG & DEV INC (TN)
Name changed to Alodex Corp. 04/18/1969
(See Alodex Corp.)

ALLIED MOTOR INDUSTRIES, INC.
Dissolved 00/00/1934
No stockholders' equity

ALLIED NEV GOLD CORP (DE)
Plan of reorganization under Chapter 11 Federal Bankruptcy proceedings effective 10/22/2015
Each share Common no par exchanged for initial distribution of (0.05742988) Hycroft Mining Corp. Common Stock Purchase Warrant expiring 10/12/2022
Each share Common no par received second and final distribution of (0.04342849) Common Stock Purchase Warrant expiring 10/12/2022 payable 12/16/2015 to holders of record 10/22/2015

ALLIED NORTHN CAP CORP (ON)
Name changed to Shoal Point Energy Ltd. 11/09/2010

ALLIED NORTHN RES LTD (ON)
Name changed to Allied Northern Capital Corp. 01/08/2009
Allied Northern Capital Corp. name changed to Shoal Point Energy Ltd. 11/09/2010

ALLIED NUCLEAR CORP (WY)
Completely liquidated 08/01/1979
Each share Common 20¢ par exchanged for first and final distribution of (1) share New Allied Development Corp. Common no par
New Allied Development Corp. recapitalized as Consolidated Biofuels Inc. 08/01/2005

ALLIED NURSING CARE INC (DE)
Merged into HealthCor, Inc. 12/31/1989
Each share Common 1¢ par exchanged for $0.02 cash

ALLIED OIL & GAS CORP (AB)
Acquired by City of Medicine Hat (AB, Canada) 01/28/2002
Each share Common no par exchanged for $2.65 cash

ALLIED OIL & MINERALS CO (UT)
Name changed to Community Equities Corp. 11/23/1970
Community Equities Corp. name changed to Atlantica, Inc. 03/26/1996

ALLIED OIL CORP. (DE)
No longer in existence having become inoperative and void for non-payment of taxes 03/16/1927

ALLIED OIL PRODUCERS LTD.
Merged into Canadian Atlantic Oil Co., Ltd. 10/00/1951
Each share Common exchanged for (0.16666666) share Common $2 par
Canadian Atlantic Oil Co., Ltd. acquired by Pacific Petroleums Ltd. 12/25/1958
(See Pacific Petroleums Ltd.)

ALLIED PAC PPTYS & HOTELS LTD (BC)
Merged into Allied Holdings Ltd. 03/31/2008
Each share Common no par exchanged for $0.125 cash

Note: Unexchanged certificates were cancelled and became without value 03/31/2011

ALLIED PACKERS, INC.
Acquired by Hygrade Food Products Corp. 00/00/1929
Details not available

ALLIED PAPER CORP. (IL)
Common $20 par changed to $8 par and (1.5) additional shares issued 05/16/1957
Common $8 par changed to $1 par 06/01/1964
Completely liquidated 12/31/1967
Each share Common $1 par exchanged for first and final distribution of (0.42) share SCM Corp. Common $5 par
(See SCM Corp.)

ALLIED PERSONNEL CORP (DE)
Name changed to Allied Management Corp. 04/10/1975
(See Allied Management Corp.)

ALLIED PETE INC (AB)
Recapitalized as Allied Consolidated Energy Inc. 10/20/1998
Each share Common no par exchanged for (0.5) share Common no par
Allied Consolidated Energy Inc. recapitalized as Allied Oil & Gas Corp. 04/19/1999
(See Allied Oil & Gas Corp.)

ALLIED PETRO PRODS INC (FL)
Name changed 11/10/1959
Name changed from Allied Petro-Chemicals to Allied Petro-Products, Inc. and Class A Common 10¢ par and Class B Common 10¢ par reclassified as Common 10¢ par 11/10/1959
Adjudicated bankrupt 09/09/1968
No stockholders' equity

ALLIED PETROLEUM OF CANADA LTD. (ON)
Charter cancelled for failure to pay taxes and file returns 05/00/1965

ALLIED PITCH ORE MINES LTD (ON)
Charter cancelled for failure to pay taxes and file returns 05/24/1972

ALLIED POWER & LIGHT CORP.
Acquired by Commonwealth & Southern Corp. 00/00/1930
Details not available

ALLIED PPTYS (CA)
Assets transferred 03/31/1977
4-1/2% Conv. Preferred $50 par called for redemption 06/22/1974
Liquidation completed
Each share Common no par stamped to indicate initial distribution of $51.306204 cash 11/15/1976
Each share Stamped Common no par stamped to indicate second distribution of $18.472303 cash 02/15/1977
Each share Stamped Common no par stamped to indicate third distribution of $11.975642 cash 03/29/1977
Assets transferred to Allied Properties Liquidating Trust 03/31/1977
Each share Stamped Common no par stamped to indicate fourth distribution of $10 cash 12/02/1977
Each share Stamped Common no par stamped to indicate fifth distribution of $7 cash 05/16/1979
Each share Stamped Common no par stamped to indicate sixth distribution of $4 cash 03/17/1981
Each share Stamped Common no par stamped to indicate seventh distribution of $1.50 cash 02/04/1983
Each share Stamped Common no par received eighth and final distribution of $1.265485 cash 06/22/1984

ALLIED PRODS CORP (DE)
Reincorporated 12/31/1937
Reincorporated 01/31/1968
State of incorporation changed from (IL) to (MI) 12/31/1937
Each share Common $10 par exchanged for (2) shares Common $5 par 00/00/1946
Stock Dividend - 100% 06/29/1956
State of incorporation changed from (MI) to (DE) 01/31/1968
$3 Conv. Preferred Ser. A no par called for redemption 07/31/1986
Common Stock Purchase Rights declared for Common stockholders of record 02/15/1991 were redeemed at $0.01 per right 08/10/1999 for holders of record 07/30/1999
Common $5 par split (3) for (2) by issuance of (0.5) additional share 08/18/1980
Common $5 par changed to 1¢ par 00/00/1990
Common 1¢ par split (3) for (2) by issuance of (0.5) additional share 09/05/1997 to holders of record 08/15/1997 Ex date - 09/08/1997
Plan of reorganization under Chapter 11 Federal Bankruptcy Code effective 08/14/2003
No stockholders' equity

ALLIED PRODUCTS OF FLORIDA, INC. (FL)
Proclaimed dissolved for non-payment of taxes 06/28/1965

ALLIED PUBLISHERS INC (OR)
Ceased operations and stock became valueless 00/00/1970

ALLIED RADIO CORP. (IL)
Name changed to ARC Liquidating Corp. 10/27/1967
(See ARC Liquidating Corp.)

ALLIED REFRIGERATION INDUSTRIES, INC.
Name changed to Allied American Industries, Inc. 00/00/1929
Allied American Industries, Inc. acquired by Guardian Investors Corp. 00/00/1930
(See Guardian Investors Corp.)

ALLIED RESH CORP (DE)
Name changed 05/24/1988
Common 25¢ par changed to 10¢ par 04/21/1965
Name changed from Allied Research Associates, Inc. to Allied Research Corp. 05/24/1988
Name changed to Allied Defense Group, Inc. 01/02/2003
(See Allied Defense Group, Inc.)

ALLIED RESOURCES FUND, INC. (MN)
Name changed to Apache Fund, Inc. 00/00/1959
Apache Fund, Inc. name changed to Viking Growth Fund, Inc. 12/01/1963 which merged into Industries Trend Fund Inc. 09/29/1975 which merged into Pilot Fund, Inc. 05/01/1981 which name changed to Transamerica Technology Fund 06/23/1989 which name changed to Transamerica Capital Appreciation Fund 04/19/1991 which merged into Hancock (John) Capital Growth Fund 12/22/1994
(See Hancock (John) Capital Growth Fund)

ALLIED RES INC (WV)
Reincorporated under the laws of Nevada 04/05/2002

ALLIED RISER COMMUNICATIONS CORP (DE)
Merged into Cogent Communications Group, Inc. 02/05/2002
Each share Common $0.0001 par exchanged for (0.0321679) share Common $0.0001 par
Cogent Communications Group, Inc. name changed to Cogent Communications Holdings, Inc. 05/16/2014

ALLIED ROXANA MINERALS LTD (AB)
Merged into Cavalier Energy Inc. (ON) 03/01/1974
Each share Common 10¢ par exchanged for (0.282485) share Common no par
Cavalier Energy Inc. (ON) reincorporated in Alberta as Cavalier Energy Ltd. 02/07/1978
(See Cavalier Energy Ltd.)

ALLIED SCALE CORP. (NY)
Name changed to InAmerica Corp. (NY) 11/21/1986
InAmerica Corp. (NY) reincorporated in Oklahoma 08/31/1988

ALLIED SEC INC (PA)
Merged into AS Acquisition Corp. 03/15/1990
Each share Common 5¢ par exchanged for $62 cash

ALLIED SECURITY INSURANCE CO. (SC)
Stock Dividends - 25% 04/15/1960; 20% 08/18/1961; 10% 05/10/1962
Merged into United Family Life Insurance 12/31/1963
Each share Common $1 par exchanged for (1.5) shares Common $1 par
United Family Life Insurance Co. reorganized as Interfinancial Inc. 07/01/1969
(See Interfinancial Inc.)

ALLIED SILVER LEAD CO (ID)
Reorganized under the laws of Delaware as Planet Resources Inc. 01/16/1996
Each share Common 2¢ par exchanged for (0.2) share Common 2¢ par
Planet Resources Inc. name changed to Internet Law Library, Inc. 07/15/1999 which name changed to ITIS Inc. 10/24/2001 which reorganized in Nevada as ITIS Holdings Inc. 09/18/2002
(See ITIS Holdings Inc.)

ALLIED SMALL BUSINESS INVESTMENT CORP. (DC)
Name changed to Allied Capital Corp. (Old) (DC) and Common $8 par changed to $1 par 08/31/1961
Allied Capital Corp. (Old) (DC) reincorporated in Maryland 05/10/1991 which merged into Allied Capital Corp. (New) 12/31/1997 which merged into Ares Capital Corp. 04/01/2010

ALLIED STORES CORP NEW (DE)
Merged into Federated Department Stores, Inc. 02/04/1992
Details not available

ALLIED STORES CORP OLD (DE)
Common no par split (5) for (2) by issuance of (1.5) additional shares 07/15/1966
Common no par split (2) for (1) by issuance of (1) additional share 04/01/1977
4% Preferred $100 par called for redemption 04/30/1984
Common no par split (2) for (1) by issuance of (1) additional share 04/01/1986
Merged into Campeau Corp. 12/31/1986
Each share Common no par exchanged for $69 cash

ALLIED STRATEGIES INC (BC)
Recapitalized as Sleeman Breweries Ltd. 05/30/1996
Each share Common no par exchanged for (0.2) share Common no par
(See Sleeman Breweries Ltd.)

ALLIED SUPERMARKETS INC (MI)
Reincorporated 08/18/1982
Common $1 par changed to 10¢ par 09/18/1981
State of incorporation changed from (DE) to (MI) 08/18/1982
Name changed to Vons Companies, Inc. 07/22/1987
Vons Companies, Inc. merged into Safeway Inc. 04/08/1997
(See Safeway Inc.)

ALLIED TECHNOLOGIES GROUP INC (NV)
Common $0.001 par split (100) for (1) by issuance of (99) additional shares payable 01/02/2013 to holders of record 12/31/2012
Ex date - 01/03/2013
Name changed to Trio Resources, Inc. 01/09/2013

ALLIED TECHNOLOGY INC (OH)
Merged into TSC, Inc. 01/04/1982
Each share Common no par exchanged for (0.1) share Common no par
Note: Unexchanged certificates were cancelled and became without value 07/01/1983

ALLIED TEL CO (AR)
Each share Class A Common $5 par exchanged for (2.6) shares Class A Common $2.50 par to effect a (2) for (1) split and a 30% stock dividend 12/31/1965
Each share Class B Common $5 par exchanged for (2.6) shares Class B Common $2.50 par to effect a (2) for (1) split and a 30% stock dividend 12/31/1965
Each share Class A Common $2.50 par exchanged for (1.5625) shares Class A Common $2 par to effect a (5) for (4) split and a 25% stock dividend 12/31/1967
6% Preferred $25 par called for redemption 06/30/1968
Each share Class A Common $2 par exchanged for (10) shares Class A Common 20¢ par 12/15/1969
Class B Common $2 par reclassified as Common $2 par 12/15/1969
Each share Class A Common 20¢ par exchanged for (0.114285) share Common $2 par 08/11/1972
5.5% Preferred $25 par called for redemption 08/15/1983
Stock Dividends - Class A & B Common - 25% 12/31/1966; 25% 12/31/1968
Stock Dividends - Common - 33.33333333% 12/18/1972; 10% 05/29/1981
Merged into Alltel Corp. (OH) 10/25/1983
Each share Common $2 par exchanged for (1) share Common $1 par
Alltel Corp. (OH) reincorporated in Delaware 05/15/1990
(See Alltel Corp.)

ALLIED TELEMEDIA LTD. (ON)
Charter cancelled and proclaimed dissolved for failure to pay taxes and file returns 03/16/1976

ALLIED TELEPHONE UTILITIES CO.
Dissolved 00/00/1937
Details not available

ALLIED TELESIS HLDGS K K (JAPAN)
ADR agreement terminated 06/30/2009
Each Sponsored ADR for Common exchanged for $3.20767 cash

ALLIED TELEVISION FILM CORP. (CA)
Name changed to Allied Empire, Inc. 07/27/1961
Allied Empire, Inc. name changed to Riverside Financial Corp. 06/06/1963 which name changed to Quanta Industries, Inc. 10/01/1983

(See Quanta Industries, Inc.)

ALLIED THERMAL CORP (CT)
Common $25 par changed to $12.50 par and (1) additional share issued 05/15/1967
Common $12.50 par changed to $6.25 par and (1) additional share issued 07/01/1976
Stock Dividends - 100% 08/17/1955; 50% 10/31/1969
Merged into Interpace Corp. 02/03/1978
Each share Common $6.25 par exchanged for $30 cash

ALLIED TOWERS MERCHANTS LTD. (ON)
Acquired by Oshawa Wholesale Ltd. 11/00/1971
Each share 6% Preferred exchanged for (0.3) share Class A no par
Each (17) Voting Trust Certificates exchanged for (1) share Class A no par
Each (13) shares Common exchanged for (1) share Class A no par
Oshawa Wholesale Ltd. name changed to Oshawa Group Ltd. 08/13/1971 which was acquired by Sobeys Canada Inc. 01/25/1999 which name changed to Sobeys Inc. 06/01/1999
(See Sobeys Inc.)

ALLIED URANIUM MINES, INC. (DE)
No longer in existence having become inoperative and void for non-payment of taxes 04/01/1958

ALLIED VAN LINES INC (DE)
Under plan of merger each share Class B no par exchanged for $10 cash 03/22/1982

ALLIED VENTURE PPTYS LTD (AB)
Reorganized as Buckingham International Holdings Ltd. 03/22/1979
Each share Common no par exchanged for (1) share Common no par
(See Buckingham International Holdings Ltd.)

ALLIED VENTURES HLDGS CORP (NV)
Name changed to Longwen Group Corp. 01/26/2017

ALLIED WASTE INDS INC (DE)
Each share Common $0.001 par exchanged for (0.1) share Common 1¢ par 12/28/1990
Each share old Common 1¢ par exchanged for (0.5) share new Common 1¢ par 06/22/1992
Each share 6.25% Conv. Mandatory Sr. Preferred Ser. C 10¢ par received (4.9358) shares new Common 1¢ par 04/01/2006
Each share 6.25% Conv. Mandatory Sr. Preferred Ser. D 10¢ par received (25.3165) shares new Common 1¢ par 03/01/2008
Merged into Republic Services, Inc. 12/05/2008
Each share Common 1¢ par exchanged for (0.45) share Common 1¢ par

ALLIED WESTERN OIL CORP. (DE)
No longer in existence having become inoperative and void for non-payment of taxes 10/01/1953

ALLIED WORLD ASSURANCE COMPANY HOLDINGS AG (SWITZERLAND)
Merged into Fairfax Financial Holdings Ltd. 08/28/2017
Each share Common CHF 4.10 par exchanged for (0.057937) Subordinate Share no par and USD$23 cash

ALLIED WORLD ASSURANCE COMPANY HOLDINGS LTD (BERMUDA)
Reorganized under the laws of Switzerland as Allied World Assurance Co. Holdings, AG 12/01/2010
Each share Common 3¢ par exchanged for (1) Registered Share CHF 15 par
(See Allied World Assurance Co. Holdings, AG)

ALLIED ZURICH PLC (ENGLAND)
Merged into Zurich Financial Services 10/24/2000
Each Sponsored ADR for Ordinary 25p par exchanged for (2.1464) Sponsored ADR's for Ordinary
Zurich Financial Services name changed to Zurich Insurance Group Ltd. 04/09/2012

ALLIEDSIGNAL INC (DE)
Name changed 04/26/1993
8.25% Conv. Preferred Ser. AA no par called for redemption 12/16/1985
Adjustable Rate Preferred Ser. F no par called for redemption 02/03/1986
$6.74 Conv. Preferred Ser. C no par called for redemption 08/15/1986
$12 Conv. Preferred Ser. D no par called for redemption 10/28/1986
$86.25 Preferred Ser. G no par called for redemption 02/27/1987
$91.25 Preferred Ser. A no par called for redemption 02/27/1987
Name changed from Allied-Signal Inc. to AlliedSignal Inc. 04/26/1993
Preferred Stock Purchase Rights declared for Common stockholders of record 06/09/1986 were redeemed at $0.05 per 03/10/1994 for holders of record 02/18/1994
Common $1 par split (2) for (1) by issuance of (1) additional share 03/14/1994
Common $1 par split (2) for (1) by issuance of (1) additional share payable 09/15/1997 to holders of record 08/21/1997 Ex date - 09/16/1997
Under plan of merger name changed to Honeywell International Inc. 12/01/1999

ALLIGATOR CO. (DE)
Common no par split (2) for (1) by issuance of (1) additional share 03/04/1952
Name changed to Bingham Liquidating Co. 06/25/1965
(See Bingham Liquidating Co.)

ALLIN COMMUNICATIONS CORP (DE)
Name changed to Allin Corp. 01/13/1999

ALLING & CORY CO (NY)
Merged into Union Camp Corp. 08/02/1996
Each share Common $2.50 par exchanged for (2.301) share Common $1 par
Union Camp Corp. merged into International Paper Co. 04/30/1999

ALLION HEALTHCARE INC (DE)
Acquired by Brickell Bay Acquisition Corp. 01/13/2010
Each share Common $0.001 par exchanged for $6.60 cash
Note: An additional initial distribution of approximately $0.18 cash per share was paid from escrow 05/17/2011

ALLIQUA INC (FL)
Each share old Common $0.001 par exchanged for (0.02285714) share new Common $0.001 par 11/19/2013
Reincorporated under the laws of Delaware as Alliqua BioMedical, Inc. 06/06/2014

ALLIS-CHALMERS ENERGY INC (DE)
Name changed 01/01/2005
Common $10 par changed to $1 par 06/28/1974
Reorganized under Chapter 11 Federal Bankruptcy Code 12/02/1988
Each share $5.875 Conv. Preferred Ser. C no par exchanged for (0.919625) share Common 1¢ par
Each share Common $1 par exchanged for (0.122039) share Common 1¢ par
Note: Unexchanged certificates were cancelled became without value 12/02/1989
Each share Common 1¢ par exchanged for (0.06) share Common 15¢ par 07/08/1992
Each share Common 15¢ par exchanged for (0.2) share Common 1¢ par 06/14/2004
Name changed from Allis-Chalmers Corp. to Allis-Chalmers Energy, Inc. 01/01/2005
Merged into Seawell Ltd. 02/23/2011
Each share Common 1¢ par exchanged for $4.25 cash

ALLIS-CHALMERS MANUFACTURING CO. (DE)
Each share Common $100 par exchanged for (4) shares Common no par 00/00/1929
Common no par changed to $20 par 00/00/1953
Common $20 par changed to $10 par and (1) additional share issued 06/15/1956
4.08% Conv. Preferred $100 par called for redemption 03/10/1966
4.2% Conv. Preferred $100 par called for redemption 01/18/1968
Name changed to Allis-Chalmers Corp. 05/28/1971
Allis-Chalmers Corp. name changed to Allis-Chalmers Energy, Inc. 01/01/2005
(See Allis-Chalmers Energy, Inc.)

ALLIS LOUIS CO (WI)
Stock Dividend - 100% 05/06/1965
4.8% Conv. Preferred $25 par called for redemption 12/15/1966
Completely liquidated 02/16/1967
Each share Common $10 par exchanged for first and final distribution of (0.49) share Litton Industries, Inc. Conv. Preference Part. Ser. $2.50 par
(See Litton Industries, Inc.)

ALLISON CPN INC (IN)
5% Preferred 1940 Ser. $100 par called for redemption 08/31/1964
5% Preferred 1949 Ser. $100 par called for redemption 08/31/1964

ALLISON INDUSTRIES, INC. (NY)
Completely liquidated 12/15/1965
Each share Common 5¢ par exchanged for first and final distribution of (1) share Halco Industries, Inc. Common 25¢ par

ALLISON INDS LTD (MT)
Involuntarily dissolved for failure to file annual report 12/02/1987

ALLISON PASS MNG LTD (BC)
Struck off register and declared dissolved for failure to file returns 09/23/1974

ALLISON STL MFG CO (AZ)
Each share Common $5 par exchanged for (2.5) shares Common $2 par 04/07/1966
75¢ Conv. Preferred $10 par called for redemption 01/01/1967
Stock Dividend - 10% 12/10/1956
Merged into Marathon Manufacturing Co. 08/11/1972
Each share Common $2 par exchanged for (0.29108) share Common $1 par
Marathon Manufacturing Co. merged into Penn Central Corp. 12/18/1979 which name changed to American Premier Underwriters, Inc. 03/25/1994 which merged into American Premier Group, Inc. 04/03/1995 which name changed to American Financial Group, Inc. 06/09/1995 which merged into American Financial Group, Inc. (Holding Co.) merged 12/02/1997

ALLISONS PL INC (CA)
Reorganized under Chapter 11 Federal Bankruptcy Code as Value Trading Industries, Inc. 03/30/1991
Each share Common 1¢ par exchanged for (1) share Common 1¢ par and (1) Common Stock Purchase Warrant expiring 04/30/1996
(See Value Trading Industries, Inc.)

ALLISTER CORP (PA)
Each share old Common no par exchanged for (0.00040518) share new Common no par 11/10/1984
Note: In effect holders received $0.945 cash per share and public interest was eliminated

ALLITH-PROUTY CO.
Bankrupt 00/00/1935
Details not available

ALLIXON CORP (FL)
Recapitalized as Simcoe Mining Resources Corp. 01/16/2008
Each share Common $0.0005 par exchanged for (0.06666666) share Common $0.0005 par

ALLMAN TECHNOLOGIES INC (CANADA)
Name changed to Avaranta Resources Ltd. (Canada) 04/27/2009
Avaranta Resources Ltd. (Canada) reincorporated in British Columbia as Evrim Resources Corp. 01/25/2011

ALLMARINE CONSULTANTS CORP (NV)
Each share old Common $0.001 par exchanged for (0.1) share new Common $0.001 par 03/23/2007
Name changed to BAXL Holdings, Inc. 10/05/2007
(See BAXL Holdings, Inc.)

ALLMED INTL INVTS CORP (BC)
Name changed to Ecoprogress Canada Holdings Inc. 02/07/1997
Ecoprogress Canada Holdings Inc. recapitalized as Consolidated Ecoprogress Technology Inc. 05/06/1998

ALLMERICA FINL CORP (DE)
Name changed to Hanover Insurance Group, Inc. 12/01/2005

ALLMERICA PPTY & CAS COS INC (DE)
Common $1 par split (3) for (1) by issuance of (2) additional shares 01/14/1994
Merged into Allmerica Financial Corp. 07/16/1997
Each share Common $1 par exchanged for either (0.85714) share Common 1¢ par, $33 cash, or (0.4) share Common 1¢ par and $17.60 cash
Note: Option to receive stock or cash only expired 08/13/1997
Allmerica Financial Corp. name changed to Hanover Insurance Group, Inc. 12/01/2005

ALLMERICA SECS TR (MA)
Liquidation completed
Each Share of Bene. Int. $1 par exchanged for initial distribution of $9.92 cash 05/12/2006
Each Share of Bene. Int. $1 par received second and final distribution of $0.02 cash payable 12/28/2007 to holders of record 05/12/2006

ALL-ALL

ALLMETAL MINES LTD. (ON)
Charter cancelled for failure to pay taxes and file returns 00/00/1953

ALLMINE INC. (NV)
Recapitalized as Ad Art Electronic Sign Corp. 10/22/1996
Each share Common 5¢ par exchanged (0.016666666) share Common $0.001 par
(See Ad Art Electronic Sign Corp.)

ALLMON CHARLES TR INC (MD)
Name changed to Liberty All-Star Growth Fund, Inc. 11/07/1995

ALLNATION LIFE INS CO PA (PA)
Charter withdrawn 01/07/1993

ALLNET COMMUNICATION SVCS INC (IL)
Merged into ALC Communications Corp. 12/19/1985
Each share Common no par exchanged for (0.0557) share Class A Preferred $20 par, (0.2) share Common 1¢ par and $0.444 cash
ALC Communicatons Corp. merged into Frontier Corp. 08/17/1995 which merged into Global Crossing Ltd. 09/28/1999
(See Global Crossing Ltd.)

ALLNETSERVICE COM CORP (FL)
Recapitalized as Allcopiers Corp. 08/01/2001
Each share Common $0.0001 par exchanged for (0.06666666) share Common $0.0001 par
Allcopiers Corp. name changed to Saguaro Holdings Corp. 05/15/2002

ALLOGRAPH CORP (DE)
Charter cancelled and declared inoperative and void for non-payment of taxes 04/15/1972

ALLON THERAPEUTICS INC (CANADA)
Combined Units separated 10/18/2011
Assets acquired by Paladin Labs Inc. 07/16/2013
No stockholders' equity

ALLORA MINERALS INC (NV)
Name changed to EPOD Solar Inc. 08/12/2009
EPOD Solar Inc. name changed to Hybrid Coating Technologies Inc. 09/07/2011

ALLOS THERAPEUTICS INC (DE)
Acquired by Spectrum Pharmaceuticals, Inc. 09/05/2012
Each share Common $0.001 par exchanged for $1.82 cash

ALLOU HEALTHCARE INC (DE)
Name changed 09/26/2002
Name changed from Allou Health & Beauty Care, Inc. to Allou Healthcare, Inc. 09/26/2002
Chapter 11 bankruptcy proceedings converted to Chapter 7 on 09/16/2003
Stockholders' equity unlikely

ALLOY CAP CORP (AB)
Recapitalized as Mkango Resources Ltd. 01/06/2011
Each share Common no par exchanged for (0.4) share Common no par

ALLOY COMPUTER PRODS INC (MA)
Plan of reorganization under Chapter 11 Federal Bankruptcy proceedings effective 05/20/1993
No stockholders' equity

ALLOY INC (DE)
Name changed 07/26/2001
Name changed from Alloy Online, Inc. to Alloy, Inc. 07/26/2001
Each share old Common 1¢ par received distribution of (0.5) share dELiA*s, Inc. (New) Common $0.001 par payable 12/19/2005 to holders of record 12/07/2005 Ex date - 12/20/2005
Each share old Common 1¢ par exchanged for (0.25) share new Common 1¢ par 02/01/2006
Acquired by Alloy Media Holdings, L.L.C. 11/09/2010
Each share new Common 1¢ par exchanged for $9.80 cash

ALLOY METAL PRODS INC (IA)
Filed a petition under Chapter 7 Federal Bankruptcy Code 00/00/1990
No stockholders' equity

ALLOY STEEL SPRING & AXLE CO.
Dissolved 00/00/1934
Details not available

ALLOYCORP MNG INC (BC)
Each share old Common no par exchanged for (0.1) share new Common no par 04/27/2016
Acquired by Resource Capital Fund IV L.P. 08/09/2016
Each share new Common no par exchanged for $0.05 cash
Note: Unexchanged certificates will be cancelled and become without value 08/09/2022

ALLOYS & CHEMICALS CORP. (OH)
Completely liquidated 10/26/1964
Each share Common $1 par exchanged for first and final distribution of $15 cash

ALLOYS UNLIMITED INC (NY)
Common 10¢ par split (3) for (1) by issuance of (2) additional shares 01/10/1967
Merged into Plessey Co. PLC 07/16/1970
Each share Common 10¢ par exchanged for (6.5) ADR's for Dollar Shares 10s par
(See Plessey Co. PLC)

ALLRED URANIUM CORP.
Merged into Midwest Consolidated Uranium Corp. 06/10/1955
Each share Common exchanged for (0.03333333) share Common
Midwest Consolidated Uranium Corp. merged into COG Minerals Corp. 05/01/1956
(See COG Minerals Corp.)

ALLRICH ENERGY GROUP INC (AB)
Name changed to AltaRex Corp. 08/02/1996
(See AltaRex Corp.)

ALLRIGHT AUTO PKS INC (DE)
Class B, Ser. 1, $1 par reclassified as Common $1 par 07/01/1965
Class B, Ser. 2, $1 par reclassified as Common $1 par 07/01/1966
Common $1 par changed to 75¢ par and (0.333) additional share issued 05/12/1972
Common 75¢ par split (3) for (2) by issuance of (0.5) additional share 09/04/1981
Stock Dividends - 10% 11/16/1964; 10% 09/02/1977; 10% 08/31/1978; 10% 08/24/1979; 10% 08/25/1980
Merged into Deanlake Investments Ltd. 07/30/1982
Each share Common 75¢ par exchanged for $27.12 cash

ALLSCOPE RES INTL INC (UT)
Proclaimed dissolved for failure to pay taxes 01/01/1989

ALLSCRIPTS INC (DE)
Merged into Allscripts Healthcare Solutions, Inc. 01/08/2001
Each share Common 1¢ par exchanged for (1) share Common 1¢ par
Allscripts Healthcare Solutions, Inc. name changed to Allscripts-Misys Healthcare Solutions, Inc. 10/10/2008 which name changed back to Allscripts Healthcare Solutions, Inc. 08/23/2010

ALLSCRIPTS-MISYS HEALTHCARE SOLUTIONS INC (DE)
Name changed 10/10/2008
Name changed from Allscripts Healthcare Solutions, Inc. to Allscripts-Misys Healthcare Solutions, Inc. 10/10/2008
Under plan of merger name changed back to Allscripts Healthcare Solutions, Inc. 08/24/2010

ALLSEASONS BLDG PRODS INC (AB)
Name changed to Gemini Corp. 09/27/1999

ALLSERVICE LIFE INSURANCE CO. (CO)
Merged into Western Empire Life Insurance Co. 09/24/1963
Each share Common 20¢ par exchanged for (0.071428) share Common $1.35 par
Western Empire Life Insurance Co. merged into Bankers Union Life Insurance Co. 03/12/1973 which merged into I.C.H. Corp. 10/14/1982 which name changed to Southwestern Life Corp. (New) 06/15/1994 which name changed to I.C.H. Corp. (New) 10/10/1995
(See I.C.H. Corp. (New))

ALLSTAR INNS INC (DE)
Liquidation completed
Each share Common 1¢ par received initial distribution of $28 cash payable 05/22/1997 to holders of record 05/08/1997
Each share Common 1¢ par received second and final distribution of $3.04 cash payable 01/19/1999 to holders of record 12/28/1999
Note: Certificates were not required to be surrendered and are without value

ALLSTAR INNS L P (DE)
Recapitalized as Allstar Inns, Inc. 11/25/1993
Each Depositary Unit exchanged for (0.06666666) share Common 1¢ par
(See Allstar Inns, Inc.)

ALLSTAR MANUFACTURING CO. (TN)
Completely liquidated 05/15/1965
No stockholders' equity

ALLSTAR RESTAURANTS (NV)
Name changed to China Pharmaceuticals Inc. 03/30/2010

ALLSTAR SYS INC (DE)
Name changed to I-Sector Corp. 07/12/2000
I-Sector Inc. name changed to INX Inc. 01/03/2006
(See INX Inc.)

ALLSTAR VIDEO INC (WY)
Charter revoked for failure to pay taxes 03/11/1993

ALLSTATE ACCEP CORP (CA)
Acquired by New World Industries, Inc. 06/30/1972
Each share Common $1 par exchanged for (1) share Common 20¢ par
(See New World Industries, Inc.)

ALLSTATE ACCEP CORP (DE)
Reorganized as Mineral Acceptance Corp. (DE) 12/31/1996
Each share Common 1¢ par exchanged for (5) shares Common 1¢ par
Mineral Acceptance Corp. (DE) reincorporated in New Jersey 01/01/1997

ALLSTATE BOWLING CENTERS, INC. (NY)
Name changed to ABC Industries, Inc. 04/04/1963
(See ABC Industries, Inc.)

ALLSTATE CORP (DE)
Preferred Stock Purchase Rights declared for Common stockholders of record 02/26/1999 were redeemed at $0.01 per right 01/02/2004 for holders of record 11/28/2003
6.75% Depositary Preferred Ser. C called for redemption at $25 on 10/15/2018
(Additional Information in Active)

ALLSTATE ENTERPRISES STK FD INC (MD)
Merged into Morgan (W.L.) Growth Fund, Inc. 04/27/1979
Each share Common $1 par exchanged for (1.096659) shares Common 10¢ par
Morgan (W.L.) Growth Fund, Inc. name changed to Vanguard/Morgan Growth Fund, Inc. (MD) 05/07/1990 which reorganized in Delaware as Vanguard Morgan Growth Fund 06/30/1998

ALLSTATE FINL CORP (VA)
Reincorporated 11/30/2000
State of incorporation changed from (VA) to (DE) 11/30/2000
Name changed to Harbourton Financial Corp. 05/01/2001
Harbourton Financial Financial Corp. recapitalized as Harbourton Capital Group, Inc. 04/15/2005

ALLSTATE FINL GLOBAL FDG LLC (DE)
144A Auction Market Equity Securities called for redemption at $1,000 on 07/12/2011

ALLSTATE FING I (DE)
7.95% Guaranteed Quarterly Income Preferred Securities Ser. AA called for redemption at $25 on 12/07/2001

ALLSTATE INDUSTRIES CORP. (NV)
Name changed to Creative Classics International 12/18/1989
(See Creative Classics International)

ALLSTATE INDS INC (CA)
Charter suspended for failure to file reports and pay fees 06/09/1972

ALLSTATE INVT CORP (DE)
Charter cancelled and declared inoperative and void for non-payment of taxes 04/15/1975

ALLSTATE LAWN PRODS INC (MN)
Name changed to Haberco, Inc. 01/29/1980
(See Haberco, Inc.)

ALLSTATE MUN INCOME OPPORTUNITIES TR (MA)
Name changed to Municipal Income Opportunities Trust 03/01/1993
Municipal Income Opportunities Trust name changed to Morgan Stanley Dean Witter 12/21/1998 which name changed to Morgan Stanley Trusts 12/20/2001
(See Morgan Stanley Trusts)

ALLSTATE MUN INCOME OPPORTUNITIES TR II (MA)
Name changed to Municipal Income Opportunities Trust II 03/01/1993
Municipal Income Opportunities Trust II name changed to Morgan Stanley Dean Witter 12/21/1998 which name changed to Morgan Stanley Trusts 12/20/2001 which name changed to Morgan Stanley Funds 12/16/2002

ALLSTATE MUN INCOME OPPORTUNITES TR III (MA)
Name changed to Municipal Income Opportunities Trust III 03/01/1993
Municipal Income Opportunities Trust III name changed to Morgan Stanley Dean Witter 12/21/1998 which name changed to Morgan Stanley Trusts 12/20/2001 which name changed to Morgan Stanley Funds 12/16/2002

ALLSTATE MUN INCOME TR (MA)
Name changed to Municipal Income Trust 03/01/1993
Municipal Income Trust name changed to Morgan Stanley Dean

Witter 12/21/1998 which name changed to Morgan Stanley Trusts 12/20/2001
(See Morgan Stanley Trusts)

ALLSTATE MUN INCOME TR II (MA)
Name changed to Municipal Income Trust II 03/01/1993
Municipal Income Trust II name changed to Morgan Stanley Dean Witter 12/21/1998 which name changed to Morgan Stanley Trusts 12/20/2001
(See Morgan Stanley Trusts)

ALLSTATE MUN INCOME TR III (MA)
Name changed to Municipal Income Trust III 03/01/1993
Municipal Income Trust III name changed to Morgan Stanley Dean Witter 12/21/1998 which name changed to Morgan Stanley Trusts 12/20/2001
(See Morgan Stanley Trusts)

ALLSTATE MUN PREM INCOME TR (MA)
Name changed to Municipal Premium Income Trust 03/01/1993
Municipal Premium Income Trust name changed to Morgan Stanley Dean Witter 12/21/1998 which name changed to Morgan Stanley Trusts 12/20/2001
(See Morgan Stanley Trusts)

ALLSTATE PRIME INCOME TR (MA)
Name changed to Prime Income Trust 03/01/1993
Prime Income Trust name changed to Morgan Stanley Dean Witter Prime Income Trust 06/22/1998 which name changed to Morgan Stanley Prime Income Trust 06/18/2001

ALLSTATE TELECOM INC (UT)
Reincorporated under the laws of Nevada as Mach One Corp. 07/20/1994
Mach One Corp. name changed to Capsalus Corp. 10/20/2010 which recapitalized as ForU Holdings, Inc. 07/03/2014

ALLSTREAM INC (CANADA)
Acquired by Manitoba Telecom Services Inc. 06/04/2004
Each share Class A no par exchanged for (1.0909) shares Class B Non-Vtg. Exchangeable Preference no par and $23 cash
Each share Class B Limited Vtg. no par exchanged for (1.0909) shares Class B Non-Vtg. Exchangeable Preference no par and $23 cash
Manitoba Telecom Services Inc. merged into BCE Inc. 03/20/2017

ALLTAPES INC (DE)
Merged into Pickwick International, Inc. 11/01/1972
Each share Common 25¢ par exchanged for (0.045869) share Common 25¢ par
Pickwick International, Inc. (NY) reincorporated in Delaware 10/27/1975
(See Pickwick International, Inc. (DE))

ALLTEL CORP (DE)
Reincorporated 05/15/1990
4% Preferred Ser. G $25 par converted into Common $1 par 03/00/1986
Common $1 par split (3) for (2) by issuance of (0.5) additional share 05/29/1987
Common $1 par split (3) for (2) by issuance of (0.5) additional share 07/14/1989
State of incorporation changed from (OH) to (DE) 05/15/1990
9% Preferred Ser. B no par called for redemption 06/15/1992
Common $1 par split (2) for (1) by issuance of (1) additional share 07/09/1993
5% Preferred Ser. A $25 par called for redemption at $25 on 12/15/1999

5% Preferred Ser. C $25 par called for redemption at $25 on 12/15/1999
5.5% Preferred Ser. F $25 par called for redemption at $25 on 12/15/1999
5.5% Preferred Ser. I $25 par called for redemption at $25 on 12/15/1999
6% Preferred Ser. E $25 par called for redemption at $25 on 12/15/1999
6% Preferred Ser. H $25 par called for redemption at $25 on 12/15/1999
6% Preferred Ser. J $25 par called for redemption at $25 on 12/15/1999
Each Corporate Unit received (0.88576312) share Common $1 par 05/17/2005
Each share Common $1 par received distribution of (1.0339267) shares Windstream Corp. Common $0.0001 par payable 07/17/2006 to holders of record 07/12/2006 Ex date - 07/18/2006
Acquired by GS Capital Partners VI Fund, L.P. 11/16/2007
Each share $2.06 Preferred Ser. C Conv. no par exchanged for $523.22 cash
Each share $2.25 Preferred Ser. D Conv. no par exchanged for $481.37 cash
Each share Common $1 par exchanged for $71.50 cash

ALLTRISTA CORP (DE)
Reincorporated 12/19/2001
State of incorporation changed from (IN) to (DE) and Common no par changed to 1¢ par 12/19/2001
Name changed to Jarden Corp. 06/03/2002
Jarden Corp. merged into Newell Brands Inc. 04/18/2016

ALLURA FASHIONS INC (DE)
Name changed to Aristocrat Apparel, Inc. 06/01/1973
(See Aristocrat Apparel, Inc.)

ALLURE COSMETICS LTD (DE)
SEC revoked common stock registration 08/05/2009

ALLURE INDS CORP (BC)
Recapitalized as Allied Environmental Services Corp. 08/29/1990
Each share Common no par exchanged for (0.25) share Common no par
Allied Environmental Services Corp. name changed to Philip Environmental Services Corp. 08/22/1991 which recapitalized as Devco Enterprises Inc. 05/17/1993 which recapitalized as SBI Skin Biology Inc. (BC) 11/03/1995 which reincorporated in Yukon 08/22/1996 which reorganized in British Columbia as Realm Energy International Corp. 10/26/2009 which merged into San Leon Energy PLC 11/10/2011

ALLURE RESOURCE CORP. (BC)
Name changed to Allure Industries Corp. 08/08/1987
Allure Industries Corp. recapitalized as Allied Environmental Services Corp. 08/29/1990 which name changed to Philip Environmental Services Corp. 08/22/1991 which recapitalized as Devco Enterprises Inc. 05/17/1993 which recapitalized as SBI Skin Biology Inc. (BC) 11/03/1995 which reincorporated in Yukon 08/22/1996 which reorganized in British Columbia as Realm Energy International Corp. 10/26/2009 which merged into San Leon Energy PLC 11/10/2011

ALLURISTICS INC (DE)
Name changed to Donnebrooke Corp. 10/01/1989
Donnebrooke Corp. name changed to Virtual Academics.com Inc. 01/04/2000 which name changed to Cenuco, Inc. 12/16/2002 which name changed to Ascendia Brands, Inc. 05/12/2006

(See Ascendia Brands, Inc.)

ALLVAC METALS CO. (NC)
Acquired by Vanadium-Alloys Steel Co. 02/03/1965
Each share Common exchanged for (0.173) share Capital Stock $5 par
Vanadium-Alloys Steel Co. name changed to Vasco Metals Corp. 06/08/1965 which was acquired by Teledyne, Inc. 06/30/1966 which merged into Allegheny Teledyne, Inc. 08/15/1996 which name changed to Allegheny Technologies Inc. 11/29/1999

ALLVEND INDS INC (DE)
Reincorporated 11/08/1985
Common 10¢ par split (3) for (1) by issuance of (2) additional shares 06/30/1971
State of incorporation changed from (NY) to (DE) 11/08/1985
Name changed to Kingsoil Co., Ltd. and Common 10¢ par changed to $0.001 par 07/01/1988

ALLWASTE INC (DE)
Common 1¢ par split (2) for (1) by issuance of (1) additional share 12/01/1989
Merged into Philip Services Corp. (ON) 07/31/1997
Each share Common 1¢ par exchanged for (0.611) share Common no par
Philip Services Corp. (ON) reorganized in Delaware as Philip Services Corporation 04/07/2000
(See Philip Services Corporation)

ALLWEST INDS LTD (BC)
Struck off register and declared dissolved for failure to file returns 10/04/1985

ALLWEST SYS INTL INC (NV)
Each share old Common $0.001 par exchanged for (0.06666666) share new Common $0.001 par 03/01/2000
Name changed to Lyon Capital Venture Corp. 09/10/2004
Lyon Capital Venture Corp. name changed to UTEC, Inc. 03/21/2007 which name changed to Tiger Oil & Energy, Inc. 09/23/2010

ALLY & GARGANO INC (DE)
Acquired by Marketing Corp. of America 08/28/1986
Each share Common $1 par exchanged for $12 cash

ALLY FINL INC (DE)
7% 144A Perpetual Preferred Ser. G 1¢ par called for redemption at $1,000 plus $5.64 accrued dividends on 12/14/2015
Fixed/Floating Rate Perpetual Preferred Ser. A 1¢ par called for redemption at $25 on 05/16/2016 (Additional Information in Active)

ALLY MEDIA GROUP INC (NV)
Each share old Common $0.002 par exchanged for (0.001) share new Common $0.002 par 04/14/1999
Reorganized as Success Financial Services Group, Inc. 01/31/2001
Each share Common $0.002 par exchanged for (3) shares Common $0.002 par 01/31/2001
Success Financial Services Group, Inc. name changed to Consolidated American Industries Corp. 03/01/2005

ALLY PHARMA US INC (FL)
Recapitalized as TPT Global Tech, Inc. 12/02/2014
Each share Common $0.001 par exchanged for (0.1) share Common $0.001 par

ALLYN & BACON INC (DE)
Common $1 par changed to 50¢ par and (1) additional share issued 09/01/1960
Acquired by Esquire, Inc. 07/02/1981

Each share Common 50¢ par exchanged for $10 principal amount of 10% Subord. Promissory Notes due 07/02/1991 and $2.15 cash

ALLYN RES INC (BC)
Reincorporated 00/00/2004
Place of incorporation changed from (AB) to (BC) 00/00/2004
Recapitalized as Troy Energy Corp. (BC) 01/14/2008
Each share Common no par exchanged for (0.2) share Common no par
Troy Energy Corp. (BC) reincorporated in Alberta 02/24/2011

ALMA INDS INC (AB)
Recapitalized as Dynamax Petrochemical Corp. 09/01/1989
Each share Common no par exchanged for (0.33333333) share Common no par
Dynamax Petrochemical Corp. recapitalized as Wildrose Ventures Inc. 12/18/1992
(See Wildrose Ventures Inc.)

ALMA INTL INC (FL)
Reincorporated under the laws of Delaware as Dynasty Energy Resources, Inc. 12/31/2007
Dynasty Energy Resources, Inc. recapitalized as Fifth Season International, Inc. 10/28/2010

ALMA LINCOLN MINING CO. (CO)
Charter revoked for failure to file reports and pay fees 09/23/1957

ALMA OIL & GAS LTD (AB)
Merged into Hornet Energy Ltd. 12/31/1999
Each share Class A no par exchanged for (0.1613) share Common no par
(See Hornet Energy Ltd.)

ALMA RES LTD (BC)
Name changed to Remstar Resources Ltd. 05/15/2008
Remstar Resources Ltd. name changed to Avarone Metals Inc. 02/03/2014

ALMA SYNDICATE, INC. (CO)
Each share Common no par exchanged for (3) shares Common $1 par 00/00/1939
Charter revoked for failure to file reports and pay fees 10/10/1941

ALMA TRAILER CO. (MI)
Completely liquidated 10/05/1962
Each share Class B $1 par exchanged for first and final distribution of $2.42735 cash

ALMADARO MINERALS CORP (NV)
Name changed to TapSlide, Inc. 03/24/2008

ALMADEN RES CORP (BC)
Acquired by Almaden Minerals Ltd. 02/11/2002
Each share Common no par exchanged for (0.77) share Common no par

ALMADEN-SANTA CLARA VINEYARDS (CA)
Name changed to Almaden Vineyards, Inc. 12/16/1964
Almaden Vineyards, Inc. name changed to Paicines Properties Co. 06/15/1967
(See Paicines Properties Co.)

ALMADEN VINEYARDS INC (CA)
Name changed to Paicines Properties Co. 06/15/1967
(See Paicines Properties Co.)

ALMADEN VINEYARDS INC (DE)
Merged into National Distillers & Chemical Corp. 06/30/1977
Each share Common 10¢ par exchanged for $12.25 cash

ALMADEX MINERALS LTD OLD (BC)
Plan of arrangement effective 05/25/2018

Each share Common no par exchanged for (1) share Azucar Minerals Ltd. Common no par and (1) share Almadex Minerals Ltd. (New) Common no par

ALMAH INC (NV)
Common $0.001 par split (11) for (1) by issuance of (10) additional shares payable 05/24/2013 to holders of record 05/24/2013 Ex date - 05/28/2013
Name changed to Arch Therapeutics, Inc. 06/05/2013

ALMAHURST ENERGY CORP (BC)
Name changed to Canadian Entech Research Corp. 01/17/1984
Canadian Entech Research Corp. recapitalized as Canadian Entech Resources Inc. 03/31/1995 which name changed to H20 Entertainment Corp. 07/15/1996 which recapitalized as Consolidated H2O Entertainment Corp. 07/14/2005 which name changed to Tri-River Ventures Inc. 07/30/2007

ALMAR RAINWEAR CORP. (GA)
Acquired by B.V.D. Co., Inc. 06/17/1966
Each share Common $1 par exchanged for (0.18833) share Common $1 par
B.V.D. Co., Inc. acquired by Glen Alden Corp. (DE) 05/19/1967 which merged into Rapid-American Corp. (DE) 11/06/1972
(See Rapid-American Corp. (DE))

ALMAR SHIELDS CORP (PA)
Merged into Uni-Shield International Corp. 09/20/1972
Each share Common 10¢ par exchanged for (1) share Common $0.26666666 par
(See Uni-Shield International Corp.)

ALMAR STORES CO.
Succeeded by Almar Stores Corp. 00/00/1931
Details not available

ALMAR SUPPLY CO., INC. (PA)
Recapitalized as Almar-Shields Corp. 04/06/1971
Each share Common 1¢ par exchanged for (0.1) share Common 10¢ par
Almar-Shields Corp. merged into Uni-Shield International Corp. 09/20/1972
(See Uni-Shield International Corp.)

ALMARCO INDS LTD (AB)
Struck off register for failure to file annual returns 03/13/1999

ALMARK CAP LTD (ON)
Reorganized under the laws of Canada as Bioniche Inc. 01/31/1992
Each share Common no par exchanged for (0.25) share Common no par
Bioniche Inc. name changed to Bioniche Life Sciences Inc. 09/14/1999 which name changed to Telesta Therapeutics Inc. 12/01/2014 which merged into ProMetic Life Sciences Inc. 11/01/2016

ALMAZ SPACE CORP (NV)
Name changed to Ready When You Are Funwear, Inc. 04/14/1992
Ready When You Are Funwear, Inc. recapitalized as Rhombic Corp. 02/17/1995 which recapitalized as Silverado Financial Inc. 04/29/2003 which name changed to MediaTechnics Corp. 05/23/2008

ALMENDRAL S A (CHILE)
ADR agreement terminated 01/30/2003
Each Sponsored 144A ADR for Ordinary exchanged for $0.65206 cash
Each Sponsored Reg. S ADR for Ordinary exchanged for $0.65206 cash

ALMINE RES LTD (BC)
Struck off register and declared dissolved for failure to file returns 08/18/1989

ALMINEX LTD (CANADA)
Merged into Canadian Superior Oil Ltd. 08/31/1978
Each share Capital Stock no par exchanged for (0.76923076) share Common $1 par and $7 cash
Canadian Superior Oil Co. merged into Superior Oil Co. (NV) 01/24/1980
(See Superior Oil Co. (NV))

ALMINSTER OILS LTD. (ON)
Merged into Continental Consolidated Mines & Oils Co. Ltd. 10/04/1957
Each share Common exchanged for (0.1) share Common
(See Continental Consolidated Mines & Oils Co. Ltd.)

ALMO CAP CORP (BC)
Name changed to Blackrock Gold Corp. 07/27/2016

ALMO INDUSTRIAL ELECTRONICS, INC. (PA)
Stock Dividend - 10% 04/01/1967
Merged into Sterling Electronics Corp. 07/18/1968
Each share Class A $1 par exchanged for (0.2) share Common 50¢ par
(See Sterling Electronics Corp.)

ALMONT CAP CORP (AB)
Reincorporated under the laws of Canada as Biophage Pharma Inc. 11/30/2001

ALMONTY INDS INC (BC)
Reincorporated under the laws of Canada 03/27/2012

ALMORE EXPLS LTD (ON)
Merged into Tri-Bridge Consolidated Gold Mines Ltd. 10/13/1973
Each share Capital Stock $1 par exchanged for (0.1) share Common no par
Tri-Bridge Consolidated Gold Mines Ltd. merged into Lobo Gold & Resources Inc. 07/06/1983 which recapitalized as Lobo Capital Inc. 06/11/1992 which name changed to Q & A Communications Inc. 03/01/1993 which recapitalized as Q & A Capital Inc. 11/05/1997 which recapitalized as Leader Capital Corp. 08/17/1998
(See Leader Capital Corp.)

ALMOST CTRY PRODUCTIONS INC (NV)
Name changed to XVariant, Inc. 08/29/2001
XVariant, Inc. name changed to Easy Groups, Ltd. 12/08/2006 which name changed to China Bionanometer Industries Corp. 07/24/2007
(See China Bionanometer Industries Corp.)

ALMOST FAMILY INC (DE)
Common 10¢ par split (2) for (1) by issuance of (1) additional share payable 01/12/2007 to holders of record 01/05/2007 Ex date - 01/16/2007
Merged into LHC Group, Inc. 04/01/2018
Each share Common 10¢ par exchanged for (0.915) share Common 1¢ par

ALMS & DOEPKE CO (OH)
Common $100 par changed to $10 par 00/00/1935
Common $10 par changed to no par 00/00/1937
Voluntarily dissolved 12/26/1985
Details not available

ALMS HOTEL CORP. (OH)
Reorganized 00/00/1935
Reorganized as Alms Hotel Co. to Alms Hotel Corp. 00/00/1935
Each share Preferred exchanged for (1) share Preferred $100 par and (0.2) share Common $1 par
Each share Common exchanged for (0.6) share Common $1 par
Merged into Sheraton Louisiana Corp. 04/30/1956
Each share Preferred $100 par exchanged for (21) shares Common $1 par
Each share Class A or B Common $1 par exchanged for (1) share Common $1 par
(See Sheraton Louisiana Corp.)

ALMUR COSMETICS INC (UT)
Recapitalized as Multi-Media Industries Corp. 06/19/1995
Each share Common $0.001 par exchanged for (0.05) share Common $0.001 par
Multi-Media Industries Corp. recapitalized as Worldnet Resources Group Inc. 02/14/2000 which recapitalized as Asset Equity Group, Inc. 12/12/2001
(See Asset Equity Group, Inc.)

ALMY STORES INC (DE)
Acquired by Federal Street Investors Inc. 07/16/1984
Each share Common $1 par exchanged for $15 cash

ALN RES CORP (OK)
Recapitalized as American Natural Energy Corp. (Ctfs. dtd. prior to 07/19/1994) 12/01/1992
Each share Common no par exchanged for (0.1) share Common no par
American Natural Energy Corp. (Ctfs. dtd. prior to 07/19/1994) acquired by Alexander Energy Corp. 07/19/1994 which merged into National Energy Group, Inc. 08/30/1996
(See National Energy Group, Inc.)

ALNAN INC (NV)
Completely liquidated 01/19/1983
Each share Common $1 par exchanged for first and final distribution of $7.14 cash

ALO SCHERER HEALTHCARE INC (DE)
Name changed to Scherer Healthcare, Inc. 08/14/1987
(See Scherer Healthcare, Inc.)

ALOAK CORP (AB)
Name changed to Okalla Corp. 06/27/2006
Okalla Corp. recapitalized as SportsClick Inc. 07/10/2008

ALODEX CORP (TN)
Charter revoked for non-payment of taxes 01/21/1980

ALOE (A.S.) CO. (MO)
Each share Common $20 par exchanged for (4) shares Common $5 par 04/00/1946
Merged into Brunswick-Balke-Collender Co. on a (0.95) for (1) basis 06/30/1959
Brunswick-Balke-Collender Co. name changed to Brunswick Corp. 04/18/1960

ALOE CREME LABS INC (FL)
Reorganized under the laws of Delaware as Alo-Scherer Healthcare, Inc. 02/17/1982
Each share Common $1 par exchanged for (0.25) share Common 1¢ par
Alo-Scherer Healthcare, Inc. name changed to Scherer Healthcare, Inc. 08/14/1987
(See Scherer Healtcare, Inc.)

ALOE VERA NATUREL, INC. (MN)
Name changed to Longhorn Energy Services, Inc. 05/20/1983

Longhorn Energy Services, Inc. recapitalized as Equisure, Inc. 05/10/1996
(See Equisure, Inc.)

ALOETTE COSMETICS INC (PA)
Merged into ACI Acquisition 06/23/1998
Each share Common no par exchanged for $5.25 cash

ALOHA AIRLS INC (HI)
Each share 6% Non-Cum. Conv. Preferred 25¢ par exchanged for (0.2) share 6% Non-Cum. Conv. Preferred $1.25 par 03/08/1973
Each share Common 25¢ par exchanged for (0.2) share Common $1.25 par 03/08/1973
Stock Dividend - 10% 02/29/1984
Under plan of reorganization each share 6% Non-Cum. Conv. Preferred $1.25 par and Common $1.25 par automatically became (1) share Aloha, Inc. 6% Non-Cum. Conv. Preferred $1.25 par and Common $1.25 par respectively 03/30/1984
(See Aloha, Inc.)

ALOHA INC (HI)
Merged into AQ Corp. 03/30/1987
Each share 6% Conv. Non-Cum. Preferred $1.25 par exchanged for $28.50 cash
Each share Common $1.25 par exchanged for $28.50 cash

ALON, INC. (KS)
Merged into Mooney Corp. 10/01/1967
Each share Common $1 par exchanged for (0.01) share Common $1 par
(See Mooney Corp.)

ALON BLUE SQUARE ISRAEL LTD (ISRAEL)
Name changed 05/06/2013
Name changed from Alon Holdings Blue Square - Israel Ltd. to Alon Blue Square Israel Ltd. 05/06/2013
Each old Sponsored ADR for Ordinary exchanged for (0.1) new Sponsored ADR for Ordinary 12/14/2015
Basis changed from (1:1) to (1:10) 12/14/2015
ADR agreement terminated 09/23/2016
Each new Sponsored ADR for Ordinary exchanged for $0.874581 cash

ALON USA ENERGY INC (DE)
Merged into Delek US Holdings, Inc. (New) 07/01/2017
Each share Common 1¢ par exchanged for (0.504) share Common 1¢ par

ALON USA PARTNERS LP (DE)
Merged into Delek US Holdings, Inc. (New) 02/07/2018
Each Common Unit exchanged for (0.49) share Common 1¢ par

ALONA URANIUM MINES LTD. (ON)
Charter cancelled for failure to pay taxes and file returns 12/07/1959

ALONG MOBILE TECHNOLOGIES INC (NV)
SEC revoked common stock registration 03/13/2013

ALOPEX GOLD INC (CANADA)
Name changed to AEX Gold Inc. 06/08/2018

ALOTTAFUN INC (DE)
Name changed to Upside Development, Inc. 03/05/2001
Upside Development, Inc. recapitalized as AmoroCorp, Inc. 05/25/2006
(See AmoroCorp, Inc.)

ALOTTAFUN INC (DE)
Each share old Common 1¢ par exchanged for (0.5) share new Common 1¢ par 08/25/1997

Reincorporated under the laws of Delaware 08/06/1998
Alottafun Inc. (DE) name changed to Upside Development, Inc. 03/05/2001 which recapitalized as AmoroCorp, Inc. 05/25/2006
(See AmoroCorp, Inc.)

ALOUETTE MINES LTD. (QC)
Declared dissolved for failure to file reports or pay fees 11/11/1972

ALOUETTES 1974 CAP INC (ON)
Reincorporated 12/31/2001
Place of incorporation changed from (AB) to (ON) 12/31/2001
Name changed to Caxton Group Inc. 02/06/2002
Caxton Group Inc. name changed to Pareto Corp. 07/23/2002
(See Pareto Corp.)

ALPA CORP (UT)
Charter revoked for failure to file reports and pay fees 05/01/1990

ALPA INDS LTD (ON)
Merged into Reed Paper Ltd. 03/24/1975
Each share Common no par exchanged for $12 cash

ALPAC CORP (NV)
Merged into New Alpac Corp. 04/30/1979
Each share Common no par exchanged for $146.34 cash

ALPACA INC (NV)
Name changed to Integral Health, Inc. 10/24/1997

ALPARGATAS S A I C (ARGENTINA)
ADR agreement terminated 11/15/1999
No ADR holders equity

ALPENA BANCSHARES INC (MI)
Reorganized under the laws of Maryland as First Federal Northern Michigan Bancorp, Inc. 04/01/2005
Each share Common $1 par exchanged for (1.8477) shares Common 1¢ par First Federal Northern Michigan Bancorp, Inc. merged into Mackinac Financial Corp. 05/18/2018

ALPENA SVGS BK (ALPENA, MI)
Each share Capital Stock $10 par exchanged for (2.5) shares Capital Stock $5 par to effect a (2) for (1) split and a 25% stock dividend paid 05/20/1971
Stock Dividends - 33.33333333% 01/24/1968; 10% 04/21/1978
Merged into First of America Bank Corp. 12/31/1985
For holdings of (100) shares or fewer each share Capital Stock $5 par exchanged for $37 cash
For holdings of (101) shares or more each share Capital Stock $5 par exchanged for (0.8) share Common $10 par and $5 cash
First of America Bank Corp. merged into National City Corp. 03/31/1998 which was acquired by PNC Financial Services Group, Inc. 12/31/2008

ALPETRO RES LTD (AB)
Acquired by Big Coulee Resources Ltd. 12/05/2011
Each share Common no par exchanged for $0.39 cash

ALPEX COMPUTER CORP (DE)
Reincorporated 12/11/1970
State of incorporation changed from (NY) to (DE) 12/11/1970
Charter cancelled and declared inoperative and void for non-payment of taxes 03/01/1986

ALPEX CORP. (DE)
Recapitalized as Alumacraft Marine Products Corp. 10/23/1968
Each share Common 40¢ par exchanged for (0.5) share Common 40¢ par

Alumacraft Marine Products Corp. name changed to Timpte, Inc. 10/01/1970 which name changed to Timpte Industries, Inc. 10/21/1970
(See Timpte Industries, Inc.)

ALPHA ARACON RADIO ELECTRONICS LTD. (ON)
Assets sold for benefit of creditors 06/00/1966
No stockholders' equity

ALPHA BK & TR (ALPHARETTA, GA)
Placed in receivership 10/24/2008
Stockholders' equity unlikely

ALPHA BK A E (GREECE)
Old 144A Sponsored GDR's for Common split (3) for (2) by issuance of (0.5) additional GDR payable 06/09/2000 to holders of record 06/01/2000
Old Reg. S Sponsored GDR's for Common split (3) for (2) by issuance of (0.5) additional GDR payable 06/09/2000 to holders of record 06/01/2000
Each old 144A Sponsored GDR for Common exchanged for (0.02) new 144A Sponsored GDR for Common 12/07/2015
Stock Dividends - In GDR's to holders of GDR's 20% payable 05/28/2004 to holders of record 05/14/2004; 20% payable 05/27/2005 to holders of record 05/20/2005; 40% payable 05/30/2006 to holders of record 05/18/2006; In ADR's to holders of ADR's 40% payable 05/30/2006 to holders of record 05/18/2006
Ex date - 05/31/2006
Each old Reg. S Sponsored GDR for Common exchanged for (0.02) new Reg. S Sponsored GDR for Common 12/07/2015
GDR agreement terminated 05/03/2017
Each new 144A Sponsored GDR for Common exchanged for $0.523897 cash
Each new Reg. S Sponsored GDR for Common exchanged for $0.523897 cash
(Additional Information in Active)

ALPHA BASICS INC (DE)
Reincorporated 04/12/1984
State of incorporation changed from (UT) to (DE) 04/12/1984
Each share old Common $0.001 par exchanged for (0.05) share new Common $0.001 par 06/02/1986
Charter cancelled and declared inoperative and void for non-payment of taxes 03/01/1987

ALPHA BETA FOOD MARKETS, INC. (CA)
Each share Common $10 par exchanged for (2.5) shares Common $1 par 00/00/1956
Under plan of merger each share 5% Preferred A $10 par exchanged for (2.5) shares 6% Preferred $25 par 05/27/1959 which was subsequently called for redemption 11/25/1960
Merged into American Stores Co. (Old) 01/16/1961
Each share Common $1 par exchanged for (0.277778) share Common $1 par
American Stores Co. (Old) name changed to Acme Markets, Inc. 06/28/1962 which name changed back to American Stores Co. (Old) 12/29/1973 which merged into American Stores Co. (New) 07/26/1979 which merged into Albertson's, Inc. 06/23/1999 which merged into Supervalu Inc. 06/02/2006

ALPHA BETA HLDGS LTD (CO)
Each share old Common no par exchanged for (0.1) share new Common no par 10/29/1998
Name changed to MDU

Communications International, Inc. (CO) 12/02/1998
MDU Communications International, Inc. (CO) reincorporated in Delaware 04/20/1999
(See MDU Communications International, Inc.)

ALPHA BETA TECHNOLOGY INC (MA)
Assets sold for the benefit of creditors 01/28/1999
No stockholders' equity

ALPHA BYTES INC (CO)
Each share Common $0.0001 par received distribution of (0.03412969) share of TRB Systems International Inc. Common payable 10/13/1997 to holders of record 04/18/1997
Name changed to H-Net.com, Inc. 12/15/1999
H-Net.com, Inc. name changed to H-Net.Net Inc. 08/01/2000

ALPHA CAP CORP (CO)
Name changed to Time-Tell International Corp. 06/18/1987
(See Time-Tell International Corp.)

ALPHA CAP CORP (NY)
Charter cancelled and proclaimed dissolved for failure to pay taxes 09/26/1979

ALPHA CELL TECHNOLOGIES INC (NV)
Charter permanently revoked 02/01/2001

ALPHA COMMUNICATIONS CORP (ON)
Name changed to Lingo Media Inc. 09/01/2000
Lingo Media Inc. recapitalized as Lingo Media Corp. 10/16/2007

ALPHA CONS INC (MN)
Name changed to Mar-Mac, Inc. 04/01/1974

ALPHA CR BK A E (GREECE)
Sponsored ADR's for Ordinary split (4) for (3) by issuance of (0.33333333) additional ADR payable 08/08/1996 to holders of record 04/04/1996
Sponsored ADR's for Ordinary split (2) for (1) by issuance of (1) additional ADR payable 04/28/1999 to holders of record 04/07/1999
Name changed to Alpha Bank A.E. 06/01/2000

ALPHA DIAMOND CORP (NV)
Each share old Common $0.00001 par exchanged for (0.05) share new Common $0.00001 par 09/16/1997
Name changed to African Resources, Inc. 07/09/1998
African Resources, Inc. name changed to Viking Exploration Inc. 04/06/1999
(See Viking Exploration Inc.)

ALPHA DISTRIBUTING, INC. (MN)
Merged into Cardinal Wholesale, Inc. 04/03/1979
Each share Common 10¢ par exchanged for $1.40 principal amount of 10% 5-year Debentures due 06/04/1984 or $1.15 cash
Note: Option to receive Debentures expired 06/04/1979

ALPHA ELECTRONICS, INC. (MN)
Name changed to Alpha Distributing, Inc. 04/06/1970
(See Alpha Distributing, Inc.)

ALPHA ENERGY & GOLD (UT)
Each share old Common 1¢ par exchanged for (0.03846153) share new Common 1¢ par 04/10/1993
Reorganized under the laws of the District of Columbia as Century Industries Inc. 04/30/1993
Each share new Common 1¢ par exchanged for (0.5) share Common 1¢ par

Century Industries Inc. (DC) reorganized in Nevada 02/16/2000
(See Century Industries Inc. (NV))

ALPHA ENTERPRISES, INC. (NV)
Each share Common $1 par exchanged for (10) shares Common 10¢ par 01/12/1971 (Holders were not requested to surrender certificates until 02/08/1971)
Charter revoked for failure to file reports and pay fees 03/07/1977

ALPHA EXPL INC (BC)
Merged into ALX Uranium Corp. 09/25/2015
Each share Common no par exchanged for (0.5) share Common no par
Note: Unexchanged certificates will be cancelled and become without value 09/25/2021

ALPHA FD INC (GA)
Common $1 par changed to $0.33333333 par and (2) additional shares issued 04/21/1986
Reorganized under the laws of Maryland as Enterprise Group of Funds, Inc. and Common $0.33333333 par reclassified as Growth Portfolio $0.001 par 09/14/1987
(See Enterprise Group of Funds, Inc.)

ALPHA GENERATION INC (TX)
Name changed to Ouranos Resources Inc. 01/07/2005
(See Ouranos Resources Inc.)

ALPHA GOLD CORP (BC)
Recapitalized as ALQ Gold Corp. 08/20/2013
Each share Common no par exchanged for (0.1) share Common no par

ALPHA HLDG INC (DE)
Name changed to Sea Sun Capital Corp. 11/19/2004
(See Sea Sun Capital Corp.)

ALPHA HOSPITALITY CORP (DE)
Each share old Common 1¢ par exchanged for (0.1) share new Common 1¢ par 06/27/2001
Name changed to Empire Resorts, Inc. 05/21/2003

ALPHA INCOME FD INC (MD)
Merged into Fidelity Corporate Bond Fund, Inc. 04/14/1983
Each share Common $1 par exchanged for (0.82377) share Capital Stock $1 par
Fidelity Corporate Bond Fund, Inc. name changed to Fidelity Flexible Bond Fund 10/25/1985 which name changed to Fidelity Fixed Income Trust 04/15/1992

ALPHA INDS INC (DE)
Common $1 par changed to 50¢ par and (1) additional share issued 04/24/1967
Common 50¢ par changed to 25¢ par and (1) additional share issued 11/15/1967
Common 25¢ par split (3) for (2) by issuance of (0.5) additional share 03/03/1980
Common 25¢ par split (2) for (1) by issuance of (1) additional share 12/13/1982
Common 25¢ par split (3) for (2) by issuance of (0.5) additional share payable 02/18/1999 to holders of record 02/08/1999
Common 25¢ par split (2) for (1) by issuance of (1) additional share payable 04/19/2000 to holders of record 03/29/2000
Name changed to Skyworks Solutions, Inc. 06/26/2002

ALPHA INDS INC (MT)
Proclaimed dissolved 12/01/1988

ALPHA INNOTECH CORP (DE)
Acquired by Cell Biosciences, Inc. 10/28/2009
Each share Common 1¢ par exchanged for $1.50 cash

ALPHA INVS FD INC (MD)
Name changed to Alpha Income Fund, Inc. 01/31/1976
Alpha Income Fund, Inc. merged into Fidelity Corporate Bond Fund, Inc. 04/14/1983 which name changed to Fidelity Flexible Bond Fund 10/25/1985 which name changed to Fidelity Fixed Income Trust 04/15/1992

ALPHA-LARDER MINES LTD. (ON)
Charter cancelled for failure to pay taxes and file returns 00/00/1957

ALPHA LUJO INC (NY)
Recapitalized as IBITX Software Inc. 01/22/2018
Each share Common $0.001 par exchanged for (0.005) share Common $0.001 par

ALPHA MED INC (MA)
Merged into Croesus Industries, Inc. 02/05/1973
Each share Common 1¢ par exchanged for (0.16666666) share Common 1¢ par
(See Croesus Industries, Inc.)

ALPHA MICROSYSTEMS (CA)
Reincorporated under the laws of Delaware as NQL Inc. 09/01/2000
(See NQL Inc.)

ALPHA MINERALS INC (AB)
Merged into Fission Uranium Corp. 12/06/2013
Each share Common no par exchanged for (5.725) shares Common no par, (0.5) share Alpha Exploration Inc. Common no par and $0.0001 cash
(See each company's listing)
Note: Unexchanged certificates will be cancelled and become without value 12/06/2019

ALPHA MOTORSPORT INC (NV)
Each share old Common $0.001 par exchanged for (10) shares new Common $0.001 par 04/27/2006
Recapitalized as Healthcare Providers Direct, Inc. 02/02/2007
Each share new Common $0.001 par exchanged for (0.5) share Common $0.001 par
(See Healthcare Providers Direct, Inc.)

ALPHA NAT RES INC (DE)
Plan of reorganization under Chapter 11 Federal Bankruptcy proceedings effective 07/26/2016
No stockholders' equity

ALPHA NUTRA INC (NV)
Reorganized 02/08/2005
Reorganized from Alpha Nutraceuticals Inc. to Alpha Nutra, Inc. 02/08/2005
Each share Common $0.001 par exchanged for (0.02222222) share Common $0.001 par
Name changed to China Broadband, Inc. 05/16/2007
China Broadband, Inc. name changed to YOU On Demand Holdings, Inc. 04/05/2011 which name changed to Wecast Network, Inc. 11/14/2016 which name changed to Seven Stars Cloud Group, Inc. 07/17/2017

ALPHA OMEGA CAP CORP (DE)
Name changed to Tradux Corp. 08/09/1989
(See Tradux Corp.)

ALPHA OMEGA CAP INC (CO)
Declared defunct and inoperative for failure to pay taxes and file annual reports 05/01/1997

ALPHA OMEGA ENGR CORP (CO)
Name changed to Marathon Medical Equipment Corp. 09/17/1982
(See Marathon Medical Equipment Corp.)

ALPHA OMEGA INDS INC (BC)
Name changed 09/18/1985
Name changed from Alpha-Omega Resources Corp. to Alpha-Omega Industries Inc. 09/18/1985
Struck off register and declared dissolved for failure to file returns 08/09/1991

ALPHA 1 BIOMEDICALS INC (DE)
Name changed to RegeneRx Biopharmaceuticals, Inc. 12/16/2000

ALPHA ONE CORP (ON)
Recapitalized as Solvista Gold Corp. 05/16/2011
Each share Common no par exchanged for (0.470588) share Common no par
Solvista Gold Corp. name changed to Rockcliff Copper Corp. 10/21/2015 which name changed to Rockcliff Metals Corp. 11/02/2017

ALPHA ONLINE PWR CORP (DE)
Common $0.0001 par split (4) for (1) by issuance of (3) additional shares payable 08/08/2001 to holders of record 10/01/2000 Ex date - 08/24/2001
Charter cancelled and declared inoperative and void for non-payment of taxes 03/01/2003

ALPHA PEAK LEISURE INC OLD (BC)
Under plan of reorganization each share Common no par automatically became (1) share Alpha Peak Leisure Inc. (New) Common no par 06/23/2015

ALPHA PETE EXPL CORP (NY)
Dissolved by proclamation 03/25/1992

ALPHA PORTLAND CEMENT CO. (NJ)
Each share Common $100 par exchanged for (3) shares Common no par 00/00/1926
Common no par changed to $10 par and (2) additional shares issued 04/26/1955
Name changed to Alpha Portland Industries, Inc. 05/05/1972
Alpha Portland Industries, Inc. name changed to Slattery Group Inc. 05/03/1985
(See Slattery Group Inc.)

ALPHA PORTLAND INDS INC (NJ)
Name changed to Slattery Group Inc. 05/03/1985
(See Slattery Group Inc.)

ALPHA RES INC (DE)
Name changed to National Technologies, Inc. 12/31/1987
(See National Technologies, Inc.)

ALPHA SEC GROUP CORP (DE)
Completely liquidated 08/20/2009
Each Unit exchanged for first and final distribution of $10.00047 cash
Each share Common $0.0001 par exchanged for first and final distribution of $10.00047 cash

ALPHA SENSORS LTD (AUSTRALIA)
Name changed to Alpha Technologies Corp. Ltd. 01/09/2003
(See Alpha Technologies Corp. Ltd.)

ALPHA SOLARCO INC (CO)
Each share old Common no par exchanged for (0.01) share new Common no par 11/17/1995
Recapitalized as Fiber Application Systems Technology Ltd. (CO) 02/14/2003
Each share new Common no par exchanged for (0.001) share Common no par
Fiber Application Systems Technology Ltd. (CO) reorganized in Florida as Innovative Food Holdings, Inc. 03/10/2004

ALPHA SPACECOM INC (NV)
Reorganized 06/30/2005
Reorganized from under the laws of (CO) to (NV) 06/30/2005
Each share Common $0.001 par exchanged for (0.1) share Common $0.001 par
Name changed to Beicang Iron & Steel, Inc. 10/31/2006
(See Beicang Iron & Steel, Inc.)

ALPHA TAX EXEMPT BD FD INC (GA)
Merged into Fidelity Municipal Bond Fund, Inc. (MD) 04/14/1983
Each share Common $1 par exchanged for (0.94366) share Capital Stock 1¢ par
Fidelity Municipal Bond Fund, Inc. (MD) reorganized in Massachusetts as Fidelity Municipal Bond Fund 08/01/1984

ALPHA TECHNOLOGIES CORP LTD (AUSTRALIA)
ADR agreement terminated 05/22/2012
No ADR's remain outstanding

ALPHA TECHNOLOGIES GROUP INC (DE)
Company terminated registration of common stock and is no longer public as of 04/11/2008

ALPHA VENTURES INC (AB)
Reincorporated under the laws of Ontario as Alpha Communications Corp. 06/29/1998
Alpha Communications Corp. name changed to Lingo Media Inc. 09/01/2000 which recapitalized as Lingo Media Corp. 10/16/2007

ALPHA VIRTUAL INC (DE)
Each share old Common $0.001 par exchanged for (0.2) share new Common $0.001 par 10/31/2002
Each share new Common $0.001 par exchanged again for (0.14285714) share new Common $0.001 par 04/16/2003
Name changed to Veridicom International, Inc. 02/23/2004
(See Veridicom International, Inc.)

ALPHA WIRELESS BROADBAND INC (NV)
Recapitalized as Seamless Wi-Fi, Inc. 06/03/2005
Each share Common 1¢ par exchanged for (0.001) share Common $0.001 par
Seamless Wi-Fi, Inc. name changed to Seamless Corp. (NV) 08/21/2008 which reincorporated in Florida as GDT TEK, Inc. 11/25/2009
(See GDT TEK, Inc.)

ALPHA YELLOWKNIFE GOLD MINES LTD. (ON)
Charter cancelled for failure to pay taxes and file returns 01/29/1952

ALPHACOM CORP (DE)
Old Common $0.0001 par changed to $0.001 par and (3) additional shares issued 03/30/2001
Each share old Common $0.001 par exchanged for (0.04) share new Common $0.001 par 03/07/2003
Name changed to TVE Corp. 03/24/2003
TVE Corp. name changed to Echo Resources, Inc. 08/13/2004 which name changed to Fortress Exploration, Inc. (DE) 09/30/2009 which reincorporated in Nevada 06/04/2010 which name changed to Greenworld Development, Inc. 08/20/2010

ALPHAGENICS INST LTD (DE)
Recapitalized as Official Systems, Inc. 01/30/1986
Each share Common 1¢ par exchanged for (0.33333333) share Common 1¢ par
Official Systems, Inc. recapitalized as Air L.A., Inc. 06/21/1990
(See Air L.A., Inc.)

ALPHALA CORP (NV)
Common $0.001 par split (30) for (1) by issuance of (29) additional shares payable 05/01/2014 to holders of record 04/25/2014
Ex date - 05/02/2014
Name changed to FV Pharma International Corp. 08/06/2014

ALPHAMIN RES CORP (BC)
Reincorporated under the laws of Mauritius 09/30/2014

ALPHANET SOLUTIONS INC (NJ)
Merged into Ciber, Inc. 06/25/2003
Each share Common 1¢ par exchanged for $4.05 cash

ALPHANET TELECOM INC (ON)
Discharged from receivership 07/04/2005
No stockholders' equity

ALPHANUMERIC INC (DE)
Common 10¢ par split (4) for (1) by issuance of (3) additional shares 05/17/1967
Common 10¢ par changed to $0.03333333 par and (2) additional shares issued 05/23/1968
Charter cancelled and declared inoperative and void for non-payment of taxes 03/01/1990

ALPHAPOINT TECHNOLOGY INC (DE)
Name changed to LevelBlox, Inc. 10/19/2018

ALPHAREL INC (CA)
Recapitalized as Altris Software, Inc. 10/25/1996
Each share Common no par exchanged for (0.5) share Common no par
Altris Software, Inc. name changed to Spescom Software Inc. 02/20/2004 which name changed to Enterprise Informatics, Inc. 05/16/2007

ALPHARMA INC (DE)
Acquired by King Pharmaceuticals, Inc. 12/30/2008
Each share Class A Common 20¢ par exchanged for $37 cash

ALPHARX INC (BRITISH VIRGIN ISLANDS)
Name changed to UMeWorld Ltd. 04/15/2013

ALPHARX INC (DE)
Each share old Common $0.0001 par exchanged for (0.2) share new Common $0.0001 par 03/21/2002
Each share new Common $0.0001 par exchanged again for (0.2) share new Common $0.0001 par 05/29/2012
Reincorporated under the laws of British Virgin Islands and new Common $0.0001 par changed to no par 03/20/2013
AlphaRx, Inc. (British Virgin Islands) name changed to UMeWorld Ltd. 04/15/2013

ALPHASMART INC (DE)
Merged into Renaissance Learning, Inc. 06/27/2005
Each share Common $0.0001 par exchanged for (0.1877) share Common 1¢ par
(See Renaissance Learning, Inc.)

ALPHASTAR INSURANCE GROUP LTD (BERMUDA)
Chapter 11 bankruptcy petition converted to Chapter 7 on 06/02/2005
Stockholders' equity unlikely

ALPHATRADE COM (NV)
Each share old Common $0.001 par

exchanged for (0.02) share new
Common $0.001 par 01/14/2002
Stock Dividend - 10% payable
07/31/2007 to holders of record
07/27/2007 Ex date - 07/25/2007
Plan of reorganization under Chapter
11 Federal Bankruptcy proceedings
effective 03/15/2013
No stockholders' equity

ALPHATYPE CORP (DE)
Merged into Berthold (H.) AG
04/02/1981
Each share Common $1 par
exchanged for $15 cash

ALPHEUS TECHNOLOGY INC (NJ)
Charter declared void for
non-payment of taxes 01/31/1994

ALPICO, INC. (DE)
Liquidation completed 05/13/1958
Details not available

ALPINE AIR EXPRESS INC (DE)
Each share old Common $0.001 par
exchanged for (3) shares new
Common $0.001 par 01/26/2006
Each share new Common $0.001 par
exchanged again for (1) share new
Common $0.001 par to reflect a (1)
for (2,000) reverse split followed by
a (2,000) for (1) forward split
12/30/2011
Note: Holders of (1,999) or fewer
pre-split shares received $0.16482
cash per share
Acquired by KEB Enterprises
06/23/2014
Each share new Common $0.001 par
exchanged for $0.9728 cash

ALPINE DISCOVERIES INC (CO)
Name changed to Premar Emerald
Co., Inc. 12/16/1987

ALPINE EXPL CORP (BC)
Reincorporated under the laws of
Yukon as Shiega Resources Corp.
11/14/1997
Shiega Resources Corp. recapitalized
as African Metals Corp. (YT)
01/17/2000 which reincorporated in
British Columbia 01/04/2005

ALPINE GAMING INC (CO)
Reincorporated under the laws of
Delaware as Century Casinos, Inc.
05/25/1994

ALPINE GLOBAL DYNAMIC DIVID FD (DE)
Each old Common Share of Bene. Int.
no par exchanged for (0.5) share
new Common Share of Bene. Int. no
par 01/21/2014
Name changed to Aberdeen Global
Dynamic Dividend Fund 05/07/2018

ALPINE GLOBAL PREMIER PPTYS FD (DE)
Name changed to Aberdeen Global
Premier Properties Fund 05/07/2018

ALPINE GOLD & SILVER MINES LTD. (ON)
Charter revoked for failure to file
reports and pay taxes 00/00/1968

ALPINE GROUP INC (DE)
Name changed 10/15/1980
Name changed 11/27/1984
Reincorporated 02/06/1987
Name changed from Alpine
Geophysical Associates, Inc. to
Alpine Geophysical Corp.
10/15/1980
Name changed from Alpine
Geophysical Corp. to Alpine Group,
Inc. (NJ) 11/27/1984
State of incorporation changed from
(NJ) to (DE) 02/06/1987
Each share old Common 10¢ par
exchanged for (1) share new
Common 10¢ par to reflect a (1) for
(100) reverse split followed by a
(100) for (1) forward split 12/29/2004
Note: Holders of (99) shares or fewer
pre-split shares received $2.06 cash
per share

Preferred Ser. A 10¢ par called for
redemption at $380 on 09/30/2012
Liquidation completed
Each share new Common 10¢ par
received initial distribution of $0.25
cash payable 04/30/2014 to holders
of record 04/25/2014 Ex date -
04/24/2014
Each share new Common 10¢ par
received second distribution of $0.40
cash payable 10/15/2014 to holders
of record 10/09/2014 Ex date -
10/16/2014
Each share new Common 10¢ par
received third distribution of $0.18
cash payable 07/15/2016 to holders
of record 07/05/2016 Ex date -
07/26/2016
Each share new Common 10¢ par
received fourth and final distribution
of $0.025 cash payable 09/28/2018
to holders of record 09/14/2018

ALPINE GROUP INC (NJ)
Reincorporated under the laws of
Delaware 02/06/1987
(Additional Information in Active)

ALPINE INDS INC (DE)
Charter cancelled and declared
inoperative and void for
non-payment of taxes 03/01/1986

ALPINE INTL CORP (DE)
Reincorporated 09/28/1994
State of incorporation changed from
(CA) to (DE) 09/28/1994
Recapitalized as Heng Fai China
Industries, Inc. 11/10/1994
Each share Common 5¢ par
exchanged for (0.025) share
Common 1¢ par
Heng Fai China Industries, Inc. name
changed to Powersoft Technologies
Inc. (DE) 04/03/1998 which
reorganized in Colorado as Asia
Supernet Corp. 12/22/1999
(See Asia Supernet Corp.)

ALPINE LACE BRANDS INC (DE)
Merged into Land O'Lakes, Inc.
12/05/1997
Each share Common 1¢ par
exchanged for $9.125 cash

ALPINE MEADOWS TAHOE INC (DE)
Reincorporated 08/27/1994
State of incorporation changed from
(CA) to (DE) 08/27/1994
Acquired by Powdr Merger Corp.
05/17/1994
Each share Common 25¢ par
exchanged for $10.67 cash

ALPINE MINING & MILLING CO.
Out of business 00/00/1939
Details not available

ALPINE MINING CO. (DE)
Charter cancelled and declared
inoperative and void for
non-payment of taxes 04/01/1941

ALPINE MNG CO. (NV)
Charter revoked for failure to file
reports and pay taxes 05/31/2010

ALPINE OIL SVCS CORP (AB)
Merged into Weatherford Oil
Services, Inc. 08/10/2000
Each share Common no par
exchanged for (0.039)
Exchangeable Share Ser. 1 no par
Weatherford Oil Services, Inc.
exchanged for Weatherford
International Inc. (New) (DE)
04/20/2001 which reincorporated in
Bermuda 06/26/2002 which
reincorporated in Switzerland
02/25/2009 which reincorporated in
Ireland as Weatherford International
PLC 06/18/2014

ALPINE RES CORP (NV)
Name changed to American Uranium
Corp. and (49) additional shares
issued 04/10/2007
(See American Uranium Corp.)

ALPINE SVGS BK (HIGHLAND, IL)
Merged into First Collinsville Bancorp
09/30/1999
Each share Common exchanged for
$8.80 cash

ALPINE SILVER, INC. (ID)
Charter forfeited for failure to file
reports 11/30/1975

ALPINE SILVER LTD. (BC)
Recapitalized as High Level
Resources Ltd. 12/13/1984
Each share Common no par
exchanged for (0.25) share Common
no par
High Level Resources Ltd.
recapitalized as Colorfax
International Inc. 11/23/1990
(See Colorfax International Inc.)

ALPINE SUBSURFACE ELECTRS INC (AB)
Name changed to Alpine Oil Services
Corp. 03/01/1994
Alpine Oil Services Corp. merged into
Weatherford Oil Services, Inc.
08/10/2000 which was exchanged
for Weatherford International Inc.
(New) (DE) 04/20/2001 which
reincorporated in Bermuda
06/26/2002 which reincorporated in
Switzerland 02/25/2009 which
reincorporated in Ireland as
Weatherford International PLC
06/18/2014

ALPINE TLI GROUP INC (NV)
Recapitalized as SOHM, Inc.
09/11/2008
Each share Common $0.001 par
exchanged for (0.02) share Common
$0.0001 par

ALPINE TOTAL DYNAMIC DIVID FD (DE)
Each old Common Share of Bene. Int.
no par exchanged for (0.5) new
Common Share of Bene. Int. no par
01/21/2014
Name changed to Aberdeen Total
Dynamic Dividend Fund 05/07/2018

ALPINE URANIUM CORP. (UT)
Recapitalized as Interstate
Resources, Inc. 09/16/1959
Each share Common 3¢ par
exchanged for (0.05) share Common
no par
(See Interstate Resources, Inc.)

ALPNET INC (UT)
Merged into SDL PLC 02/04/2002
Each share Common no par exchanged
for $0.21 cash

ALPS ETF TR (DE)
Trust terminated 12/28/2011
Each share Jefferies TR/J CRB
Global Agriculture Equity Index Fund
received $42.279619 cash
Each share Jefferies TR/J CRB
Global Industrial Metals Equity Index
Fund received $31.115017 cash
Trust terminated 04/27/2012
Each share Jefferies TR/J CRB
Wildcatters Equity ETF received
$39.40 cash
Jefferies TR/J CRB Global
Commodity Equity Index Fund
reclassified as Global Commodity
Equity ETF 04/03/2014
Trust terminated 08/28/2014
Each share GS Momentum Builder
Asia ex-Japan Equities & US
Treasuries Index ETF received
$23.9601 cash
Each share GS Momentum Builder
Growth Growth Markets Equities &
US Treasuries Index ETF received
$22.2435 cash
Each share GS Momentum Builder
Multi-Asset Index ETF received
$27.6721 cash
Each share GS Risk-Adjusted Return
US Large Cap Index ETF received
$34.8329 cash
Trust terminated 11/21/2014
Each share VelocityShares Emerging

Asia DR ETF received $59.89 cash
Each share VelocityShares Emerging
Markets DR ETF received $48.64
cash
Each share VelocityShares Russia
Select DR ETF received $35.89
cash
VelocityShares Tail Risk Hedged
Large Cap ETF reclassified as
Janus Velocity Tail Risk Hedged
Large Cap ETF 01/23/2015
VelocityShares Volatility Hedged
Large Cap ETF reclassified as
Janus Velocity Volatility Hedged
Large Cap ETF 01/23/2015
Trust terminated 03/28/2016
Each share Global Commodity Equity
Index ETF received $32.0694 cash
Each share Sector Leaders ETF
received $24.5792 cash
Each share Sector Low Volatility ETF
received $27.0417 cash
Each share STOXX Europe 600 ETF
received $23.1263 cash
Trust terminated 06/27/2016
Each share Enhanced Put Write
Strategy ETF received $25.1842
cash
Under plan of reorganization each
share Janus Velocity Tail Risk
Hedged Large Cap ETF and Janus
Velocity Volatility Hedged Large Cap
ETF automatically became (1) share
Janus Detroit Street Trust Janus
Velocity Tail Risk Hedged Large Cap
ETF Cap ETF $0.001 par or Janus
Velocity Volatility Hedged Large Cap
ETF $0.001 par respectively
07/18/2016
Trust terminated 06/26/2017
Each share U.S. Equity High Volatility
Put Write Index Fund received
$19.9718 cash
(Additional Information in Active)

ALPS INDS LTD (INDIA)
Reg. S Sponsored GDR's for Equity
Shares Rs. 10 par split (2) for (1) by
issuance of (1) additional GDR
payable 10/20/2006 to holders of
record 09/22/2006
GDR agreement terminated
04/22/2014
No GDR's remain outstanding

ALQUIN MINES LTD. (BC)
Name changed to Alquin Pacific Ltd.
08/06/1969
(See Alquin Pacific Ltd.)

ALQUIN PAC LTD (BC)
Struck off register and declared
dissolved for failure to file returns
10/15/1974

ALRAC CORP (DE)
Charter cancelled and declared
inoperative and void for
non-payment of taxes 03/01/1981

ALRENCO INC (IN)
Reincorporated under the laws of
Delaware as Home Choice Holdings,
Inc. and Common no par changed to
1¢ par 06/23/1998
Home Choice Holdings, Inc. merged
into Rent-Way, Inc. 12/10/1998
(See Rent-Way, Inc.)

ALROM CORP (NY)
Reincorporated under the laws of
Delaware as American United
Global Inc. 12/23/1991
American United Global Inc. name
changed to Solar Thin Films, Inc.
07/10/2006

ALRON CHEM INC (UT)
Name changed to Great American
Lumber Co., Inc. 12/15/1986
(See Great American Lumber Co., Inc.)

ALROY INDS INC (DE)
Recapitalized as NTN
Communications, Inc. 03/13/1985
Each share Common $0.001 par
exchanged for (0.25) share Common
$0.005 par
NTN Communications, Inc. name

changed to NTN Buzztime, Inc. 01/01/2006

ALROY KIRKLAND MINES LTD. (ON)
Charter revoked for failure to file reports and pay fees 04/18/1960

ALS FORMAL WEAR INC (NV)
Merged into Al's Inc. 05/31/1991
Each share Common 1¢ par exchanged for $0.27 cash

ALS PLT CARE INC (NV)
Recapitalized as Nutri Pharmaceuticals Research Inc. 12/15/2003
Each share Common $0.001 par exchanged for (0.3125) share Common $0.001 par

ALSAB MINES LTD (QC)
Charter annullled for failure to file annual reports 02/15/1975

ALSCO INC (DE)
Each share Common $1 par exchanged for (0.1) share Class A Common $1 par 06/27/1963
Acquired by Harvard Industries, Inc. 11/21/1969
Each share Class A Common $1 par exchanged for (0.2) share $2 Conv. Preferred Ser. A $10 par
(See Harvard Industries, Inc.)

ALSCOPE CONS LTD (AB)
Recapitalized as Almarco Industries Ltd. 08/03/1976
Each share Common no par exchanged for (0.1) share Common no par
(See Almarco Industries Ltd.)

ALSCOPE EXPLORATIONS LTD. (AB)
Each share Common no par exchanged for (0.14285714) share new Common no par 02/28/1961
Name changed to Alscope Consolidated Ltd. 06/20/1961
Alscope Consolidated Ltd. recapitalized as Almarco Industries Ltd. 08/03/1976
(See Almarco Industries Ltd.)

ALSET ENERGY CORP (BC)
Name changed to Alset Minerals Corp. 05/04/2017
Alset Minerals Corp. name changed to OrganiMax Nutrient Corp. 08/28/2018

ALSET MINERALS CORP (BC)
Each share old Common no par exchanged for (0.33333333) share new Common no par 02/28/2018
Name changed to OrganiMax Nutrient Corp. 08/28/2018

ALSIDE INC (OH)
Merged into United States Steel Corp. 06/02/1969
Each share Common no par exchanged for $18.50 cash

ALSIUS CORP (DE)
Liquidation completed
Each share Common $0.0001 par received initial distribution of $0.30 cash payable 07/08/2009 to holders of record 05/05/2009 Ex date - 07/09/2009
Assets transferred to ALUS Liquidating Corp. 05/26/2009
Each share Common $0.0001 par received second and final distribution of $0.06 cash payable 05/07/2010 to holders of record 05/05/2009

ALSOF MINES LTD. (ON)
Charter cancelled 08/00/1972

ALSON INDS INC (FL)
Name changed to Industrial Services of America, Inc. 12/27/1984

ALSON MFG INC (FL)
Name changed to Alson Industries, Inc. 07/31/1970
Alson Industries, Inc. name changed to Industrial Services of America, Inc. 12/27/1984

ALSTER ENERGY LTD (BC)
Name changed to New Alster Energy Ltd. 10/21/1983
New Alster Energy Ltd. recapitalized as Anacondo Explorations Inc. 03/26/1990 which name changed to O-Tech Ventures Corp. 09/16/1992 which recapitalized as Bright Star Ventures Ltd. 06/26/1996
(See Bright Star Ventures Ltd.)

ALSTOM (FRANCE)
ADR agreement terminated 11/26/2004
Each Sponsored ADR for Ordinary exchanged for $0.744 cash
(Additional Information in Active)

ALSTON ENERGY INC (AB)
Placed in receivership 05/09/2014
Stockholders' equity unlikely

ALSTON VENTURES INC (BC)
Reincorporated under the laws of Alberta as Alston Energy Inc. 12/29/2011
(See Alston Energy Inc.)

ALT DON GAMUT INC (NY)
Name changed 10/31/1972
Name changed from Alt (Don) & Associates, Inc. to Alt (Don)/Gamut, Inc. 10/31/1972
Name changed to Gamut Agency Inc. 01/15/1975
Gamut Agency Inc. name changed to Northwood Corp. 03/16/1985 which name changed to Allied Scale Corp. 02/16/1986 which name changed to InAmerica Corp. (NY) 11/21/1986 which reincorporated in Oklahoma 08/31/1988

ALTA CHAMPION MINING CO.
Name changed to Alta United Mines Co. 00/00/1932
Alta United Mines Co. name changed to Mansfield Investments Inc. 09/09/2004 which name changed to Sea Alive Wellness Inc. 05/13/2005

ALTA CONSOLIDATED MINING CO.
Acquired by Alta United Mines Co. 00/00/1932
Details not available

ALTA ENERGY CORP (DE)
Reorganized 01/29/1993
Each (0.4621) share Conv. Preferred Ser. 1 $1 par exchanged for (1) share new Common 1¢ par 09/18/1989
Each share old Common 1¢ par exchanged for (0.05) share new Common 1¢ par 09/18/1989
Under plan of reorganization state of incorporation changed from (TX) to (DE) 01/29/1993
Each share new Common 1¢ par exchanged for (0.66666666) share Common 1¢ par
Merged into Devon Energy Corp. (DE) 05/18/1994
For holdings of (334) shares or more each share Common 1¢ par exchanged for (0.3) share Common 10¢ par and $0.35 cash
For holdings of (333) shares or fewer each share Common 1¢ par exchanged for $7.14 cash
Note: All holdings received the right to a contingent payment based upon future earnings
Devon Energy Corp. (DE) reincorporated in Oklahoma 06/07/1995 which merged into Devon Energy Corp. (New) (DE) 08/17/1999

ALTA EXPLS INC (BC)
Recapitalized as Akash Ventures Inc. 03/15/1994
Each share Common no par exchanged for (0.2) share Common no par
Akash Ventures Inc. recapitalized as International Akash Ventures Inc. 12/08/1999 which name changed to Healthscreen Solutions Inc. 01/18/2001
(See Healthscreen Solutions Inc.)

ALTA GENETICS INC (CANADA)
Acquired by Houdstermaatschappij Wilg B.V. 08/01/2000
Each share Common no par exchanged for $4 cash

ALTA GOLD CO (NV)
SEC revoked common stock registration 05/08/2008

ALTA GOLD CORP (UT)
Merged into Active Gold Corp. 08/30/1988
Details not available

ALTA HEALTH STRATEGIES INC (DE)
Merged into First Financial Management Corp. 04/01/1992
Each share Common 1¢ par exchanged for (0.4702) share Common 10¢ par
First Financial Management Corp. merged into First Data Corp. (Old) 10/27/1995
(See First Data Corp. (Old))

ALTA-HELENA MINING & MILLING CO. (UT)
Name changed to April Industries, Inc. (UT) 11/10/1969
April Industries, Inc. (UT) reorganized in Delaware 12/07/1971
(See April Industries, Inc. (DE))

ALTA INDS CORP (DE)
Common $10 par changed to $5 par and (1) additional share issued 07/13/1970
Common $5 par split (2) for (1) by issuance of (1) additional share 12/04/1970
Common $5 par changed to $2.50 par and (1) additional share issued 06/30/1971
Under plan of liquidation each share Common $2.50 par received distribution of $0.725 cash 06/28/1977
Stock Dividend - 54.83% 06/28/1977
Reorganized as Alta Industries Ltd. 09/13/1979
Each share Common $2.50 par exchanged for (1.167) Units of Ltd. Partnership or $12 cash
Note: Holdings of more than (2,000) shares received combination of Units and cash

ALTA-KOR INC (AB)
Discharged from receivership 06/00/2003
No stockholders' equity

ALTA LAKES CORP (UT)
Involuntarily dissolved 10/01/1992

ALTA LOMA OIL CO (UT)
Merged into Energy Resources Corp. 06/29/1979
Each share Capital Stock 10¢ par exchanged for $0.24 cash

ALTA MERGER MINES CO.
Acquired by Alta United Mines Co. 00/00/1932
Details not available

ALTA MICHIGAN MINES CO.
Acquired by Alta United Mines Co. 00/00/1932
Details not available

ALTA MINES LTD. (QC)
Name changed to Carbec Mines Ltd. 05/12/1959
Carbec Mines Ltd. merged into Triton Explorations Ltd. 12/15/1969
(See Trition Explorations Ltd.)

ALTA MIRA ENERGY CORP (AB)
Recapitalized as Miralta Energy Corp. 08/09/1988
Each share Common no par exchanged for (0.25) share Common no par
Miralta Energy Corp. merged into CanEuro Resources Ltd. 07/09/1990 which merged into Attock Oil Corp. 02/04/1991 which recapitalized as Attock Energy Corp. 08/02/1995
(See Attock Energy Corp.)

ALTA PAC CAP CORP (AB)
Common no par split (5) for (2) by issuance of (1.5) additional shares payable 10/28/1997 to holders of record 10/27/1997
Recapitalized as Conquistador Resources Ltd. 12/14/1999
Each share Common no par exchanged for (0.2) share Common no par
Conquistador Resources Ltd. recapitalized as Bandera Gold Ltd. 03/28/2001 which name changed to Jaeger Resources Corp. 07/09/2018

ALTA PAC MINERALS INC (DE)
Name changed to Arturion Entertainment Inc. 08/29/2002
Arturion Entertainment Inc. name changed to POW! Entertainment, Inc. 06/10/2004

ALTA PETE LTD (AB)
Merged into CanEuro Resources Ltd. 04/04/1989
Each share Common no par exchanged for (0.8) share Class A Common no par
CanEuro Resources Ltd. merged into Attock Oil Corp. 02/04/1991 which recapitalized as Attock Energy Corp. 08/02/1995
(See Attock Energy Corp.)

ALTA TERRA VENTURES CORP (AB)
Delisted from Toronto Venture Stock Exchange 06/20/2003

ALTA TUNNEL & TRANSPORTATION CO. (UT)
Name changed to Altamina Mining Corp. 00/00/1946
Altamina Mining Corp. name changed to Altamina, Inc. 07/09/1971 which merged into Sportsman Camping Centers of America, Inc. 07/25/1972 which name changed to Sportco 12/02/1976 which name changed to Pan American Investments, Inc. 12/24/1979 which name changed to Oxtec Medical Industries, Inc. 11/18/1983 which Industries, Inc. 11/18/1983 which Industries, Inc. 05/12/1986
(See Federal Medical Industries, Inc.)

ALTA UTD MINES (UT)
Name changed to Mansfield Investments Inc. 09/09/2004
Each share Common $1 par exchanged for (1) share Common $1 par
Mansfield Investments Inc. name changed to Sea Alive Wellness Inc. 05/13/2005

ALTA VENTURES INC (BC)
Name changed to International Bio Waste Systems Inc. 03/05/1992
International Bio Waste Systems Inc. recapitalized as Bioflow Environmental Technologies Inc. 04/22/1994 which recapitalized as Strategic Merchant Bancorp Inc. 05/15/1997 which name changed to Strategic Nevada Resources Corp. 08/03/2006 which name changed to SNS Silver Corp. 02/26/2007 which name changed to SNS Precious Metals Inc. 05/17/2010 which recapitalized as Gold Finder Explorations Ltd. 10/08/2010 which recapitalized as Venzee Technologies Inc. 01/05/2018

ALTA VISTA VENTURES LTD (BC)
Each share old Common no par exchanged for (0.5) share new Common no par 05/09/2014
Name changed to Global UAV Technologies Ltd. 05/17/2017

ALTACANADA ENERGY CORP (AB)
Recapitalized as Montana Exploration Corp. 02/28/2011
Each share Common no par exchanged for (0.1) share Common no par

ALTACHEM PHARMA LTD (AB)
Name changed to Quest PharmaTech Inc. 10/06/2005

ALTADYNE INC (NV)
Name changed to Stem Cell International, Inc. 10/14/2005
Stem Cell International, Inc. name changed to Stem Cell Therapy International, Inc. 10/18/2005 which name changed to AmStem Corp. 02/23/2010

ALTAGAS INCOME TR (CANADA)
Each Trust Unit no par received distribution of (0.07163) share AltaGas Utility Group Inc. Common no par payable 11/17/2005 to holders of record 11/14/2005 Ex date - 11/09/2005
Each Trust Unit no par received distribution of (0.01) share AltaGas Utility Group Inc. Common no par payable 09/17/2007 to holders of record 08/27/2007 Ex date - 08/23/2007
Plan of Arrangement effective 07/06/2010
Each Trust Unit no par exchanged for (1) share AltaGas Ltd. Common no par

ALTAGAS SVCS INC (CANADA)
Reorganized as AltaGas Income Trust 05/01/2004
Each share Common no par exchanged for (1) Trust Unit no par AltaGas Income Trust reorganized as AltaGas Ltd. 07/06/2010

ALTAGAS UTIL GROUP INC (CANADA)
Acquired by AltaGas Income Trust 10/14/2009
Each share Common no par exchanged for $10.50 cash

ALTAGEM RES INC (AB)
Cease trade order effective 11/08/2002

ALTAI INC (TX)
Common no par split (5) for (4) by issuance of (0.25) additional share 07/20/1994
Merged into PLATINUM Technology, Inc. 08/25/1995
Each share Common no par exchanged for (0.448) share Common $0.001 par
Note: An additional distribution of (0.021079) share for each share exchanged was made 08/23/1997
PLATINUM Technology, Inc. name changed to Platinum Technology International Inc. 01/04/1999 which merged into Computer Associates International, Inc. 06/29/1999 which name changed to CA, Inc. 02/01/2006

ALTAIR CORP (PR)
Liquidation completed
Each share Common $1 par received initial distribution of $12 cash 11/12/1982
Each share Common $1 par received second distribution of $4.50 cash 07/15/1983
Each share Common $1 par received third distribution of $3 cash 07/31/1984
Each share Common $1 par received fourth distribution of $1 cash 07/23/1986
Each share Common $1 par received fifth and final distribution of $2 cash 12/22/1986
Note: Certificates were not required to be surrendered and are without value

ALTAIR GOLD INC (BC)
Each share old Common no par exchanged for (0.06666666) share new Common no par 07/16/2015
Name changed to Altair Resources Inc. 06/03/2016

ALTAIR INTL INC (CANADA)
Name changed 11/06/1996
Reincorporated 07/02/2002
Name changed from Altair International Gold Inc. to Altair International Inc. (ON) 11/06/1996
Place of incorporation changed from (ON) to (Canada) 07/02/2002
Name changed to Altair Nanotechnologies Inc. (Canada) 07/17/2002
Altair Nanotechnologies Inc. (Canada) reincorporated in Delaware 05/15/2012

ALTAIR LABS INC (NJ)
Charter declared void for non-payment of taxes 04/14/1975

ALTAIR MINING CORP. LTD. (BC)
Recapitalized as Consolidated Altair Developments Ltd. 05/18/1972
Each share Capital Stock 50¢ par exchanged for (0.25) share Capital Stock no par
Consolidated Altair Developments Ltd. recapitalized as Super Scoop Ice-Cream Corp. 09/13/1976 which name changed to Trojan Energy Corp. 01/07/1983 which recapitalized as International Trojan Development Corp. 04/18/1985 which recapitalized as Trojan Ventures Inc. (BC) 06/20/1991 which reorganized in Cayman Islands as Alcanta International Education Ltd. 03/26/1999 which name changed to Access International Education Ltd. 01/17/2001

ALTAIR NANOTECHNOLOGIES INC (CANADA)
Each share old Common no par exchanged for (0.25) share new Common no par 11/16/2010
Reincorporated under the laws of Delaware and Common no par changed to $0.001 par 05/15/2012

ALTAIR VENTURES INC (BC)
Each share old Common no par exchanged for (0.33333333) share new Common no par 01/20/2012
Name changed to Altair Gold Inc. 09/11/2012
Altair Gold Inc. name changed to Altair Resources Inc. 06/03/2016

ALTAMIL CORP (DE)
Reincorporated 08/13/1963
State of incorporation changed from (CA) to (DE) 08/13/1963
Merged into Great Lakes Corp. 01/03/1984
Each share Common 50¢ par exchanged for $22.50 cash

ALTAMINA INC (UT)
Name changed 07/09/1971
Each share Common $5 par exchanged for (20) shares Common no par 11/05/1970
Name changed from Altimina Mining Corp. to Altamina, Inc. 07/09/1971
Merged into Sportsman Camping Centers of America, Inc. 07/25/1972
Each share Common no par exchanged for (1) share Common no par
Sportsman Camping Centers of America, Inc. name changed to Sportco 12/02/1976 which name changed to Pan American Investments, Inc. 12/24/1979 which name changed to Oxtec Medical Industries, Inc. 11/18/1983 which recapitalized as Federal Medical Industries, Inc. 05/12/1986
(See Federal Medical Industries, Inc.)

ALTAMONT MINES LTD. (QC)
Charter annulled for failure to file annual reports 10/28/1978

ALTANA AKTIENGESELLSCHAFT (GERMANY)
ADR agreement terminated 07/15/2009
Each Sponsored ADR for Ordinary no par exchanged for $20.466675 cash

ALTAPACIFIC BK (SANTA ROSA, CA)
Stock Dividend - 5% payable 02/26/2010 to holders of record 02/12/2010 Ex date - 02/10/2010
Under plan of reorganization each share Common no par automatically became (1) share AltaPacific Bancorp Common no par 11/19/2010

ALTAQUEST ENERGY CORP (AB)
Name changed to Chain Energy Corp. 06/27/2000
Chain Energy Corp. was acquired by Argonauts Group Ltd. 03/31/2002 which name changed to Cequel Energy Inc. 06/07/2002
(See Cequel Energy Inc.)

ALTAR GOLD & RES LTD (BC)
Name changed to Northern Dancer Resources Ltd. 12/15/1989
(See Northern Dancer Resources Ltd.)

ALTARA INTL CORP (NV)
Name changed to Zygon Corp. 08/20/1995
Zygon Corp. name changed to Essential Resources Inc. 01/17/1996
(See Essential Resources Inc.)

ALTAREX CORP (AB)
Each share old Common no par exchanged for (0.25) share new Common no par 12/10/1996
Each share new Common no par exchanged again for (0.25) share new Common no par 11/27/2000
Plan of arrangement effective 02/03/2004
Each share new Common no par exchanged for (0.1) share Twin Butte Energy Ltd. Common no par and (1) share AltaRex Medical Corp. Common no par
Note: Holders of between (151) and (1,000) shares received (1) share AltaRex Medical Corp. and $0.05 cash per share
Holders of (150) or fewer shares received $0.55 cash per share
(See each company's listing)

ALTAREX MED CORP (AB)
Acquired by ViRexx Medical Corp. 01/21/2005
Each share Common no par exchanged for (0.2) share Restricted Common no par and (0.3) share Common no par
(See ViRexx Medical Corp.)

ALTARICH ENERGY INC (AB)
Name changed to Millennium Communications Inc. 09/26/1996
Millennium Communications Inc. recapitalized as Strategy Web Communications Inc. 03/31/2000

ALTAVISTA MINES INC (CANADA)
Recapitalized as Jitec Inc. 07/13/2000
Each share Common no par exchanged for (0.25) share Common no par
Jitec Inc. name changed to Advantage Link Inc. 06/19/2001
(See Advantage Link Inc.)

ALTEC COMPANIES, INC. (DE)
Acquired by Ling Temco Vought, Inc. through share for share exchange offer 00/00/1960
Public interest eliminated

ALTEC CORP (DE)
Plan of reorganization under Chapter 11 Federal Bankruptcy proceedings confirmed 05/21/1987
Each share Conv. Preferred Ser. B $1 par exchanged for $0.29 cash
No Common stockholders' equity

ALTEC ENTERPRISES LTD (NV)
Name changed to Agri-Foods International, Inc. 02/14/1998
Agri-Foods International, Inc. recapitalized as ATWEC Technologies, Inc. 10/10/2003
(See ATWEC Technologies, Inc.)

ALTEC SERVICE CORP. (DE)
Name changed to Altec Companies, Inc. 06/08/1956
Altec Companies, Inc. was acquired by Ling Temco Vought, Inc. 00/00/1960
(See Ling Temco Vought, Inc.)

ALTECH CAP CORP (CO)
Common $0.001 par changed to $0.0001 par 05/05/1987
Name changed to Auto Club of America Corp. 01/25/1988
Auto Club of America Corp. name changed to Auto Club Marketing Corp. 04/01/2002 which reorganized as Evolution Solar Corp. 05/23/2008

ALTECH RESOURCE SVCS LTD (AB)
Acquired by Canadian Fracmaster Ltd. 03/30/1990
Each share Common no par exchanged for $0.485 cash

ALTEON INC (DE)
Recapitalized as Synvista Therapeutics, Inc. 07/25/2007
Each share Common 1¢ par exchanged for (0.02) share Common 1¢ par
(See Synvista Therapeutics, Inc.)

ALTEON WEBSYSTEMS INC (DE)
Merged into Nortel Networks Corp. (New) 10/05/2000
Each share Common $0.001 par exchanged for (1.83148) shares Common no par
(See Nortel Networks Corp. (New))

ALTER NRG CORP (AB)
Each share old Common no par exchanged for (0.25) share new Common no par 06/30/2014
Acquired by Sunshine Kaidi New Energy Group Co., Ltd. 09/01/2015
Each share new Common no par exchanged for $5 cash

ALTER SALES INC (FL)
Each share old Common $0.0001 par exchanged for (0.25) share new Common $0.0001 par 12/12/1991
Each share new Common $0.0001 par exchanged for (0.05) share Common $0.0002 par 03/20/1995
Name changed to ICIS Management Group, Inc. 10/13/1995
(See ICIS Management Group, Inc.)

ALTERA CORP (CA)
Common no par split (2) for (1) by issuance of (1) additional share 05/31/1995
Common no par split (2) for (1) by issuance of (1) additional share payable 01/06/1997 to holders of record 12/18/1996
Common no par split (2) for (1) by issuance of (1) additional share payable 05/19/1999 to holders of record 05/04/1999
Common no par split (2) for (1) by issuance of (1) additional share payable 08/10/2000 to holders of record 07/26/2000
Acquired by Intel Corp. 12/28/2015
Each share Common no par exchanged for $54 cash

ALTERA HLDGS CORP (DE)
Reorganized under the laws of Nevada as Nurovysn Biotech Corp. 01/18/2006
Each share Common $0.001 par

exchanged for (3.030303) shares
Common $0.001 par
(See Nurovysn Biotech Corp.)

ALTERA RES INC (BC)
Recapitalized as Ad Com Marketing
Inc. 06/27/1986
Each share Common no par
exchanged for (0.33333333) share
Common no par
(See Ad Com Marketing Inc.)

ALTERIO RES LTD (AB)
Merged into Paragon Petroleum Corp.
01/01/1991
Each share Common no par
exchanged for (0.04545454) share
Common no par
(See Paragon Petroleum Corp.)

ALTERNACARE CORP (DE)
Merged into Medical Care
International, Inc. 03/16/1988
Each share Common 5¢ par
exchanged for (0.85) share Common
1¢ par
Medical Care International, Inc.
merged into Medical Care America,
Inc. 09/09/1992 which merged into
Columbia/HCA Healthcare Corp.
09/16/1994 which name changed to
HCA - The Healthcare Co.
05/25/2000 which name changed to
HCA Inc. (Ctfs. dated after
06/29/2001) 06/29/2001
(See HCA Inc. (Ctfs. dated after
06/29/2001))

ALTERNAFUELS INC (FL)
SEC revoked common stock
registration 07/01/2011

ALTERNATE ENERGY CORP (NV)
Recapitalized as Treaty Energy Corp.
01/27/2009
Each share Common $0.001 par
exchanged for (0.12449218) share
Common $0.001 par

ALTERNATE ENERGY SYS INC (NV)
Name changed to Shiloh Resources,
Inc. 07/30/1979
(See Shiloh Resources, Inc.)

ALTERNATE MARKETING NETWORKS INC (DE)
Name changed 06/01/1998
Reincorporated 08/01/2002
Stock Dividend - 10% payable
07/21/2000 to holders of record
06/30/2000
Name changed from Alternate Postal
Delivery, Inc. to Alternate Marketing
Networks, Inc. 06/01/1998
State of incorporation changed from
(MI) to (DE) and Common no par
changed to 1¢ par 08/01/2002
Name changed to USSPI Media, Inc.
06/28/2012
(See USSPI Media, Inc.)

ALTERNATIVE ASSET MGMT ACQUISITION CORP. (DE)
Under plan of reorganization each
share Common $0.0001 par
automatically became (2) shares
Great American Group, Inc.
Common $0.0001 par 07/31/2009
Great American Group, Inc. name
changed to B. Riley Financial, Inc.
11/07/2014

ALTERNATIVE CONSTR TECHNOLOGIES INC (FL)
Name changed 01/15/2008
Name changed from Alternative
Construction Co., Inc. to Alternative
Construction Technologies, Inc.
01/15/2008
SEC revoked common stock
registration 01/11/2011

ALTERNATIVE DISTRS CORP (DE)
Charter cancelled and declared
inoperative and void for
non-payment of taxes 03/01/1995

ALTERNATIVE EARTH RES INC (BC)
Each share old Common no par
exchanged for (0.5) share new
Common no par 08/05/2016
Recapitalized as Black Sea Copper &
Gold Corp. 09/28/2016
Each share new Common no par
exchanged for (0.80645161) share
Common no par

ALTERNATIVE ENERGY & ENVIRONMENTAL SOLUTIONS INC (NV)
Common $0.0001 par split (3) for (1)
by issuance of (2) additional shares
payable 08/21/2012 to holders of
record 05/23/2012 Ex date -
08/22/2012
Name changed to Point of Care
Nano-Technology, Inc. 04/07/2015

ALTERNATIVE ENERGY MEDIA INC (NV)
Name changed to Mirage Capital
Corp. 09/20/2012
(See Mirage Capital Corp.)

ALTERNATIVE ENERGY RES INC (UT)
Each share old Common 1¢ par
exchanged for (0.05) share new
Common 1¢ par 10/08/1997
Name changed to Trafalgar
Resources, Inc. and new Common
1¢ par reclassified as Class A
Common 1¢ par 07/17/2006

ALTERNATIVE ENERGY SOURCES INC (DE)
Old Common $0.0001 par split (4) for
(1) by issuance of (3) additional
shares payable 05/27/2005 to
holders of record 05/17/2005
Ex date - 06/10/2005
Each share old Common $0.0001 par
exchanged for (0.46875) share new
Common $0.0001 par 07/08/2005
New Common $0.0001 par split (5)
for (2) by issuance of (1.5)
additional shares payable
05/22/2006 to holders of record
05/22/2006 Ex date - 05/23/2006
SEC revoked common stock
registration 08/01/2012

ALTERNATIVE ENERGY TECHNOLOGY CTR INC (DE)
Recapitalized as Alternative Energy
Technology Inc. 08/04/2008
Each share Common $0.001 par
exchanged for (0.02) share Common
$0.001 par

ALTERNATIVE ENTMT INC (DE)
Name changed to BoysToys.com, Inc.
01/04/1999
BoysToys.com, Inc. recapitalized as
Environmental Credits, Ltd. (DE)
10/23/2008 which reincorporated in
Nevada as GlyEco, Inc. 11/23/2011

ALTERNATIVE ENTMT INC (NV)
Reincorporated under the laws of
Delaware and Common $0.001 par
changed to 1¢ par 04/21/1997
Alternative Entertainment Inc. (DE)
name changed to BoysToys.com,
Inc. 01/04/1999 which recapitalized
as Environmental Credits, Ltd. (DE)
10/23/2008 which reincorporated in
Nevada as GlyEco, Inc. 11/23/2011

ALTERNATIVE ETHANOL TECHNOLOGIES INC (DE)
Name changed to Clean Tech
Biofuels, Inc. 11/14/2007

ALTERNATIVE FUEL SYS INC (AB)
Plan of arrangement effective
06/30/2004
Each share Common no par
exchanged for (0.02) share
Alternative Fuel Systems (2004) Inc.
Common no par and (0.102) share
AFS Energy Inc. Common no par
Note: Unexchanged certificates were
cancelled and became without value
06/30/2010
(See each company's listing)

ALTERNATIVE FUEL SYS 2004 INC (AB)
Acquired by Fuel Systems Solutions,
Inc. 06/01/2011
Each share Common no par
exchanged for $0.50 cash

ALTERNATIVE FUELS AMER INC (DE)
Name changed to Kaya Holdings, Inc.
04/07/2015

ALTERNATIVE HEALTH CARE SYS INC (DE)
Charter cancelled and declared
inoperative and void for
non-payment of taxes 03/01/1990

ALTERNATIVE LIVING SVCS INC (DE)
Name changed to Alterra Healthcare
Corp. 05/19/1999
(See Alterra Healthcare Corp.)

ALTERNATIVE NRG INC (NV)
Common $0.001 par split (19) for (1)
by issuance of (18) additional
shares payable 07/06/2007 to
holders of record 07/05/2007
Ex date - 07/09/2007
Charter revoked for failure to file
reports and pay fees 02/27/2009

ALTERNATIVE RES CORP (DE)
Common 1¢ par split (2) for (1) by
issuance of (1) additional share
05/22/1995
Merged into Pomeroy IT Solutions,
Inc. 07/22/2004
Each share Common 1¢ par
exchanged for $0.70 cash
(See Pomeroy IT Solutions, Inc.)

ALTERNATIVE TECHNOLOGY RES INC (DE)
Name changed to National
Healthcare Exchange Services, Inc.
02/09/2004
(See National Healthcare Exchange
Services, Inc.)

ALTERO TECHNOLOGIES INC (BC)
Struck off register and declared
dissolved for failure to file returns
06/10/1994

ALTERRA CAP HLDGS LTD (BERMUDA)
Merged into Markel Corp. 05/01/2013
Each share Common $1 par
exchanged for (0.04315) share
Common no par and $10 cash

ALTERRA HEALTHCARE CORP (DE)
Plan of reorganization under Chapter
11 Federal Bankruptcy Code
effective 12/04/2003
No stockholders' equity

ALTERRA PWR CORP (BC)
Each share old Common no par
exchanged for (0.1) share new
Common no par 09/09/2016
Merged into Innergex Renewable
Energy Inc. 02/07/2018
Each share new Common no par
exchanged for approximately
(0.34608) share Common no par
and $3.1175 cash
Note: Unexchanged certificates will
be cancelled and become without
value 02/07/2024

ALTERRA RES INC (ON)
Delisted from Canadian Dealer
Network 10/13/2000

ALTERRUS SYS INC (AB)
Made an assignment under
Bankruptcy & Insolvency Act
01/21/2014
Stockholders' equity unlikely

ALTES BREWING CO. (MI)
Stock Dividend - 15% 03/01/1951
Name changed to National Brewing
Co. of Michigan 01/28/1955
National Brewing Co. of Michigan
merged into National Brewing Co.
(MD) 05/01/1967 which name
changed to O-W Fund, Inc.
10/31/1975 which merged into New
York Venture Fund, Inc. 12/14/1988
(See New York Venture Fund, Inc.)

ALTEVA (NY)
Acquired by MBS Holdings, Inc.
12/21/2015
Each share Common 1¢ par
exchanged for $4.70 cash

ALTEX OIL CORP (UT)
Reincorporated under the laws of
Delaware as Altex Industries Inc.
10/30/1985

ALTEX OILS LTD. (AB)
Recapitalized as New Superior Oils of
Canada Ltd. 10/10/1958
Each share Capital Stock no par
exchanged for (0.13333333) share
Capital Stock $1 par
New Superior Oils of Canada Ltd.
acquired by Canadian Petrofina Ltd.
06/29/1960 which name changed to
Petrofina Canada Ltd. 08/01/1968
which name changed to Petrofina
Canada Inc. 09/26/1979 which name
changed to Petro-Canada
Enterprises Inc./Entreprises
Petro-Canada Inc. 11/16/1981
(See Petro-Canada Enterprises
Inc./Entreprises Petro-Canada Inc.)

ALTEX RES LTD (AB)
Merged into ATCOR Resources Ltd.
01/04/1993
Each share Common no par
exchanged for (0.4040404) share
Non-Vtg. Class A no par
(See ATCOR Resources Ltd.)

ALTHOUSE INC (DE)
Recapitalized as Brakes Express, Inc.
07/31/1998
Each share Common 1¢ par
exchanged for (0.33333333) share
Common 1¢ par

ALTHOUSE PLACERS INC (OR)
Reorganized under the laws of
Delaware as Althouse, Inc.
09/20/1995
Each share Common 1¢ par
exchanged for (0.02) share Common
1¢ par
Althouse, Inc. recapitalized as Brakes
Express, Inc. 07/31/1998

ALTICE N V (NETHERLANDS)
Name changed to Altice Europe N.V.
07/12/2018

ALTICE S A (LUXEMBOURG)
ADR agreement terminated
09/21/2015
Each ADR for Common exchanged
for $29.199749 cash

ALTIMO GROUP CORP (NV)
Name changed to Success
Entertainment Group International
Inc. 08/22/2014

ALTIPLANO MINERALS LTD (BC)
Name changed to Altiplano Minerals
Inc. 06/06/2018

ALTIRIS INC (DE)
Acquired by Symantec Corp.
04/06/2007
Each share Common $0.0001 par
exchanged for $33 cash

ALTISOURCE RESIDENTIAL CORP (MD)
Class B Common 1¢ par reclassified
as Common 1¢ par 04/05/2013
Name changed to Front Yard
Residential Corp. 02/21/2018

ALTITUDE ORGANIC CORP (NV)
Name changed to Tranzbyte Corp.
02/22/2012
Tranzbyte Corp. name changed to
American Green, Inc. 07/01/2014

ALTITUDE VENTURE CAP CORP (CANADA)
Name changed to D-BOX
Technologies Inc. 12/27/2000

ALTIUS CORP (CA)
Common 50¢ changed to 25¢ par and

(1) additional share issued 08/17/1979
Stock Dividend - 10% 04/28/1978
Name changed to Staruni Corp. and Common 25¢ par changed to no par 12/30/1996
Staruni Corp. recapitalized as Elephant Talk Communications, Inc. (CA) 01/22/2002 which reincorporated in Delaware 09/26/2011 which name changed to Pareteum Corp. 11/03/2016

ALTIVA FINL CORP (DE)
Assets sold for the benefit of creditors 10/31/2000
Stockholders' equity unlikely

ALTMAN (B.) & CO. (NY)
Filed a petition under Chapter 11 Federal Bankruptcy Code 08/09/1989
Details not available

ALTMARK ENERGY INC (AB)
Merged into Purcell Energy Ltd. (New) 03/07/1997
Each share Common no par exchanged for (0.6) share Common no par
(See Purcell Energy Ltd. (New))

ALTO CASINO CORP (NV)
Charter revoked for failure to file reports and pay fees 09/30/2009

ALTO COMMUNICATIONS INC (CA)
Ceased operations 10/30/1975
Company has no assets

ALTO DEVELOPMENT CO.
Name changed to American Silver Corp. 00/00/1946
(See American Silver Corp.)

ALTO EXPL LTD (BC)
Name changed to General Western Industries Ltd. 12/19/1985
General Western Industries Ltd. recapitalized as Consolidated General Western Industries Ltd. 10/23/1986 which recapitalized as Danco Industries Ltd. 12/02/1991
(See Danco Industries Ltd.)

ALTO GROUP HLDGS INC (NV)
Common $0.00001 par split (8) for (1) by issuance of (7) additional shares payable 12/18/2009 to holders of record 12/08/2009 Ex date - 12/21/2009
SEC revoked common stock registration 12/22/2014

ALTO MINERALS INC (BC)
Name changed 04/07/1997
Name changed from Alto Industries Inc. to Alto Minerals Inc. 04/07/1997
Recapitalized as Alto Ventures Ltd. 04/19/2002
Each share Common no par exchanged for (0.28571428) share Common no par

ALTO PALERMO S A (ARGENTINA)
Name changed to IRSA Propiedades Comerciales S.A. 02/13/2015

ALTOMAC URANIUM MINES LTD. (ON)
Charter cancelled and proclaimed dissolved for failure to pay taxes and file returns 09/21/1959

ALTON BOX BRD CO (DE)
Common $5 par changed to $10 par and (4) additional shares issued 07/01/1950
Common $10 par changed to $5 par and (1) additional share issued 05/03/1974
Name changed to Alton Packaging Corp. 03/25/1981
(See Alton Packaging Corp.)

ALTON CORP (ON)
Merged into Interquest Resources Corp. 06/11/1985
Each share Common no par exchanged for (1) share Common no par
Interquest Resources Corp. name changed to Interquest Technologies Inc. 10/23/1992 which recapitalized as Interquest Inc. 09/30/1995
(See Interquest Inc.)

ALTON GROUP INC (CA)
Each share old Common no par exchanged for (0.125) share new Common no par 03/30/1992
Name changed to Source Scientific, Inc. 02/03/1995
(See Source Scientific, Inc.)

ALTON OILS LTD. (DE)
Acquired by Triad Oil Co. Ltd. 02/24/1952
Each share Capital Stock $1 par exchanged for (12) shares Capital Stock no par
Triad Oil Co. Ltd. name changed to BP Oil & Gas Ltd. 07/02/1970 which merged into BP Canada Ltd. (ON) 10/18/1972 which name changed to BP Canada Ltd.-BP Canada Ltee. 04/27/1973 which reincorporated in Canada as BP Canada Inc. 07/06/1979
(See BP Canada Inc.)

ALTON PACKAGING CORP (DE)
Merged into Jefferson Smurfit Group Ltd. 10/09/1981
Each share Common $5 par exchanged for $27.50 cash

ALTON-ST. LOUIS BRIDGE CO.
Property and assets sold at foreclosure 00/00/1934
Stockholders' equity unlikely

ALTON VENTURES INC (NV)
Reorganized as Arkanova Energy Corp. 11/01/2006
Each share Common $0.001 par exchanged for (2) shares Common $0.001 par

ALTOONA & LOGAN VALLEY ELECTRIC RAILWAY CO. (PA)
Stock Dividend - 300% 11/01/1946
Assets acquired by General Public Utilities Corp. (NY) on a (1.6) for (1) basis 10/01/1961
General Public Utilities Corp. (NY) reincorporated in Pennsylvania 07/01/1969
General Public Utilities Corp. (PA) name changed to GPU, Inc. 08/01/1996
(See GPU, Inc.)

ALTOONA CENTRAL BANK & TRUST CO. (ALTOONA, PA)
Merged into Mid-State Bank & Trust Co. (Altoona, PA) 12/31/1965
Each share Capital Stock $10 par exchanged for (1.3) shares Capital Stock $10 par
Mid-State Bank & Trust Co. (Altoona, PA) reorganized as Mid-State Bancorp Inc. 01/12/1982 which merged into Keystone Financial, Inc. 12/31/1984 which merged into M&T Bank Corp. 10/06/2000

ALTORO GOLD CORP (BC)
Merged into Solitario Resources Corp. 10/18/2000
Each share Common no par exchanged for (0.33333333) share Common no par
Solitario Resources Corp. name changed to Solitario Exploration & Royalty Corp. 06/17/2008 which name changed to Solitario Zinc Corp. 07/18/2017

ALTOS COMPUTER SYS (CA)
Merged into AAC Acquisition Corp. 09/07/1990
Each share Common no par exchanged for $8.35 cash
Each share Conv. Ser. B Common no par exchanged for $8.35 cash

ALTOS HORNOS DE MEXICO S A (MEXICO)
Placed in bankruptcy 05/00/1999
Details not available

ALTOVIDA INC (NV)
Charter revoked 08/01/2016

ALTRA HLDGS INC (DE)
Name changed to Altra Industrial Motion Corp. 12/05/2013

ALTRA VENTURES INC (BC)
Recapitalized as Odin Mining & Exploration Ltd. 01/23/1996
Each share Common no par exchanged for (0.66666666) share Common no par
Odin Mining & Exploration Ltd. name changed to Lumina Gold Corp. 11/01/2016

ALTRACK LTD (AUSTRALIA)
Name changed to AirBoss Ltd. 07/03/1992
(See AirBoss Ltd.)

ALTREX INC (NV)
Common $0.001 par split (10) for (1) by issuance of (9) additional shares payable 08/17/2000 to holders of record 08/14/2000 Ex date - 08/18/2000
Name changed to iCall Systems, Inc. 01/22/2001 iCall Systems, Inc. name changed to inCall Systems, Inc. 02/01/2002

ALTRIMEGA HEALTH CORP (NV)
Each share old Common $0.001 par exchanged for (4) shares new Common $0.001 par 03/19/2001
Name changed to Creative Holdings & Marketing Corp. 08/28/2002
Creative Holdings & Marketing Corp. name changed to American Racing Capital, Inc. 10/07/2005

ALTRIS SOFTWARE INC (CA)
Name changed to Spescom Software Inc. 02/20/2004
Spescom Software Inc. name changed to Enterprise Informatics, Inc. 05/16/2007

ALTRON INC (MA)
Common 5¢ par split (3) for (2) by issuance of (0.5) additional share 09/03/1993
Common 5¢ par split (3) for (2) by issuance of (0.5) additional share 02/10/1995
Common 5¢ par split (3) for (2) by issuance of (0.5) additional share payable 05/10/1996 to holders of record 04/18/1996
Merged into Sanmina Corp. 11/30/1998
Each share Common 5¢ par exchanged for (0.4545) share Common 1¢ par
Sanmina Corp. name changed to Sanmina-SCI Corp. 12/10/2001 which name changed back to Sanmina Corp. 11/15/2012

ALTURA GOLD MINES LTD. (ON)
Charter cancelled and proclaimed dissolved for failure to pay taxes and file returns 09/23/1963

ALTURA MINING CO. (ID)
Merged into Yreka United, Inc. (ID) 06/07/1957
Each share Common exchanged for (0.33333333) share Common 50¢ par
Yreka United, Inc. (ID) reorganized in Nevada as Southern Home Medical Equipment, Inc. 10/23/2006 which name changed to Southern Home Medical, Inc. 07/27/2012

ALTUS BK-A FED SVGS BK (MOBILE, AL)
Taken over by RTC 05/17/1991
No stockholders' equity

ALTUS EXPLORATIONS INC (NV)
Old Common $0.001 par split (8) for (1) by issuance of (7) additional shares payable 12/05/2003 to holders of record 11/05/2003 Ex date - 12/08/2003
Old Common $0.001 par split (4) for (1) by issuance of (3) additional shares payable 02/23/2004 to holders of record 02/02/2004 Ex date - 02/24/2004
Each share old Common $0.001 par exchanged for (0.05) share new Common $0.001 par 05/22/2007
Name changed by Canadian Tactical Training Academy Inc. 11/29/2010
Canadian Tactical Training Academy Inc. recapitalized as Earth Life Sciences Inc. 06/02/2014

ALTUS GROUP INCOME FD (ON)
Under plan of reorganization each Unit no par automatically became (1) share Altus Group Ltd. Common no par 01/04/2011

ALTUS HEALTHCARE INC (NV)
Old Common $0.001 par split (5) for (1) by issuance of (4) additional shares payable 04/13/2006 to holders of record 04/13/2006 Ex date - 04/17/2006
Each share old Common $0.001 par exchanged for (0.1) share new Common $0.001 par 04/20/2007
Name changed to DAL International Ltd. 06/14/2007
(See DAL International Ltd.)

ALTUS PHARMACEUTICALS INC (DE)
Filed a petition under Chapter 7 Federal Bankruptcy Code 11/11/2009
No stockholders' equity

ALUBEC INDS INC (CANADA)
Merged into HoloPak Technologies, Inc. 03/17/1993
Each share Common no par exchanged for (0.0554) share Common 1¢ par, (0.0497) Non-transferable Contingent Warrant and $1.30 cash
HoloPak Technologies, Inc. merged into Foilmark, Inc. 04/23/1999
(See Foilmark, Inc.)

ALUMACRAFT MARINE PRODS CORP (DE)
Name changed to Timpte, Inc. 10/01/1970
Timpte, Inc. name changed to Timpte Industries, Inc. 10/21/1970
(See Timpte Industries, Inc.)

ALUMATRON INTERNATIONAL, INC. (FL)
Charter cancelled for non-payment of taxes 06/30/1967

ALUMAX INC (DE)
$4 Conv. Preferred Ser. A $1 par called for redemption 12/18/1996
Preferred Stock Purchase Rights declared for Common stockholders of record 02/22/1996 were redeemed at $0.01 per right 03/30/1998 for holders of record 03/18/1998
Merged into Aluminum Co. of America 07/31/1998
Each share Common 1¢ par exchanged for (0.6975) share Common $1 par
Aluminum Co. of America name changed to Alcoa Inc. 01/01/1999 which name changed to Arconic Inc. (PA) 11/01/2016 which reincorporated in Delaware 12/31/2017

ALUMET CORP (DE)
Merged into Templet Industries, Inc. 01/31/1973
Each share Common 25¢ par exchanged for (1) share Class A Common 25¢ par

ALUMINA FERRITE CORP AMER (CA)
Name changed to AFCOA 10/20/1970
(See AFCOA)

ALUMINIUM LTD. (CANADA)
Shares no par exchanged (5) for (1) 00/00/1948

ALU-AM

Shares no par exchanged (2) for (1) 00/00/1952
Shares no par split (3) for (1) by issuance of (2) additional shares 05/18/1957
Shares no par reclassified as Common no par 08/09/1963
Name changed to Alcan Aluminium Ltd. (Old) 04/29/1966
Alcan Aluminium Ltd. (Old) merged into Alcan Aluminium Ltd. (New) 07/24/1987 which name changed to Alcan Inc. 03/01/2001
(See Alcan Inc.)

ALUMINUM & CHEM CORP (DE)
Each share Common 10¢ par exchanged for (0.33333333) share Common 30¢ par 05/15/1957
Completely liquidated 12/14/1981
Each share Common 30¢ par exchanged for first and final distribution of $0.21 cash

ALUMINUM CO. OF CANADA LTD. (CANADA)
5% Preferred $100 par called for redemption 06/05/1946
5.75% 2nd Preferred $100 par called for redemption 12/15/1955
Name changed to Aluminum Co. of Canada Ltd.-Alumimum du Canada Ltee. 08/10/1965
Aluminum Co. of Canada Ltd.-Aluminum du Canada Ltd. merged into Alcan Aluminum Ltd. (New) 07/24/1987 which name changed to Alcan Inc. 03/01/2001
(See Alcan Inc.)

ALUMINUM CO AMER (PA)
Each share old Common no par exchanged for (3) shares new Common no par 11/16/1943
Each share new Common no par exchanged for (2) shares Common $1 par 04/17/1953
Common $1 par split (2) for (1) by issuance of (1) additional share 06/10/1955
Common $1 par split (3) for (2) by issuance of (0.5) additional share 02/01/1974
Common $1 par split (2) for (1) by issuance of (1) additional share 02/20/1981
Preferred Stock Purchase Rights declared for Common stockholders of record 03/17/1986 were redeemed at $0.05 per right 08/25/1990 for holders of record 08/03/1990
Common $1 par split (2) for (1) by issuance of (1) additional share 02/25/1995
Name changed to Alcoa Inc. 01/01/1999
Alcoa Inc. name changed to Arconic Inc. (PA) 11/01/2016 which reincorporated in Delaware 12/31/2017

ALUMINUM CO CDA LTD (CANADA)
4.5% 2nd S.F. Preferred $50 par called for redemption 05/31/1980
4% 1st S.F. Preferred $25 par called for redemption 06/01/1980
$2 3rd Preferred $25 par reclassified as $2 1st Preferred no par 06/30/1980
Under plan of merger name changed to Alcan Aluminum Ltd. (New) 07/24/1987
Alcan Aluminum Ltd. (New) name changed to Alcan Inc. 03/01/2001
(See Alcan Inc.)

ALUMINUM GOODS MANUFACTURING CO. (NJ)
Each share Common $100 par exchanged for (10) shares Common no par 00/00/1928
Common no par changed to $10 par 04/18/1957
Name changed to Mirro Aluminum Co. 12/31/1957

Mirro Aluminum Co. name changed to Mirro Corp. 05/01/1979
(See Mirro Corp.)

ALUMINUM HOME PRODUCTS CORP. (KY)
Name changed to Alhom, Inc. 00/00/1959
Alhom, Inc. name changed to Cardinal Extrusions, Inc. 09/10/1974 which name changed to Cardinal Aluminum Co. 09/30/1981

ALUMINUM INDUSTRIES, INC. (OH)
Each share Common no par exchanged for (0.01) share Common $100 par 08/07/1959
Stock Dividend - 100% 12/15/1947
Completely liquidated 03/19/1964
Each share Common $100 par exchanged for first and final distribution of $1,000 cash

ALUMINUM INDUSTRIES INC. (MO)
Dissolved 06/15/1968
No stockholders' equity

ALUMINUM INSULATING INC (FL)
Name changed to Perfecto Mfg. Co., Inc. 09/26/1973
Perfecto Mfg. Co., Inc. merged into Dade Engineering Corp. 04/22/1977

ALUMINUM MANUFACTURES, INC.
Merged into Aluminum Co. of America 11/16/1943
Each share Preferred exchanged for (1) share 6% Preferred $100 par
Each share Common exchanged for (1.25) shares new Common no par
Aluminum Co. of America name changed to Alcoa Inc. 01/01/1999 which name changed to Arconic Inc. (PA) 11/01/2016 which reincorporated in Delaware 12/31/2017

ALUMINUM SPECIALTY CO (WI)
Common $10 par changed to $5 par and (0.5) additional share issued 03/14/1962
$1.20 Conv. Preferred Ser. A $20 par called for redemption 05/31/1962
$1.20 Conv. Preferred Ser. C no par called for redemption 05/31/1962
Common $5 par changed to $1 par and (0.5) additional share issued 11/20/1968
Acquired by Kraftco Corp. 02/12/1974
Each share Common $1 par exchanged for $11.75 cash

ALUMINUM TOP SHINGLE CORP. (OR)
Out of business 06/22/1960
No stockholders' equity

ALUNITE CORP. OF UTAH (UT)
Charter revoked for failure to file reports and pay fees 03/31/1959

ALUNITE MINING & PRODUCTS CO., LTD. (BC)
Struck off register and declared dissolved for failure to file reports 10/14/1927

ALVARADA INC (NV)
Recapitalized as IGG International, Inc. 03/03/1995
Each share Common $0.001 par exchanged for (0.01279754) share Common 1¢ par
IGG International, Inc. name changed to Safescience, Inc. 01/21/1998 which name changed to GlycoGenesys, Inc. 11/07/2001
(See GlycoGenesys, Inc.)

ALVAUTON ENTMT CORP (CANADA)
Voluntarily dissolved 07/28/1997
Details not available

ALVEAR TECHNOLOGIES INC (AB)
Recapitalized as Nortech Geomatics International Inc. 04/20/1998
Each share Common no par exchanged for (0.5) share Common no par
(See Nortech Geomatics International Inc.)

ALVERON ENERGY CORP (DE)
Name changed to Safebrain Systems, Inc. 07/26/2012

ALVIJA MINES LTD (BC)
Recapitalized as Paulson Mines Ltd. 10/14/1976
Each share Common 50¢ par exchanged for (0.25) share Common no par
Paulson Mines Ltd. recapitalized as Samson Energy Corp. 12/31/1979 which merged into Kala Exploration Ltd. 09/10/1982 which recapitalized as Kala Feedlots Ltd. 01/06/1987 which name changed to Kala Canada Ltd. 03/27/1989
(See Kala Canada Ltd.)

ALVIN CONSULTING INC (WA)
Name changed to Realty Technologies, Inc. 07/09/1999
Realty Technologies, Inc. name changed to eCourierCorps Inc. 05/16/2000 which name changed to Azul Studios International Inc. 09/15/2004 which name changed to Modern City Entertainment, Inc. 04/27/2007
(See Modern City Entertainment, Inc.)

ALVIN HOTEL CO (DE)
Charter cancelled and declared inoperative and void for non-payment of taxes 03/01/1977

ALVOPETRO INC (AB)
Name changed to Fortaleza Energy Inc. 11/19/2013

ALWIN MNG LTD (BC)
Recapitalized as Advent Developments Inc. 11/20/1973
Each share Common no par exchanged for (0.2) share Common no par
(See Advent Developments Inc.)

ALWYN PORCUPINE MINES LTD. (ON)
Charter cancelled and proclaimed dissolved for failure to pay taxes and file returns 11/08/1977

ALYA INTL INC (DE)
Recapitalized as WW Energy, Inc. 06/30/2004
Each share Common $0.0001 par exchanged for (0.0025) share Common $0.0001 par

ALYA VENTURES LTD (BC)
Name changed to Snipp Interactive Inc. 03/06/2012

ALYATTES ENTERPRISES INC (ON)
Recapitalized 06/28/1999
Recapitalized from Alyattes Resources Inc. to Alyattes Enterprises Inc. 06/28/1999
Each share Common no par exchanged for (0.5) share Common no par
Recapitalized as Wedge Energy International Inc. (ON) 02/01/2007
Each share Common no par exchanged for (0.75) share Common no par
Wedge Energy International Inc. (ON) reorganized in British Columbia as Undur Tolgoi Minerals Inc. 11/14/2011 which reincorporated in British Virgin Islands as Khot Infrastructure Holdings, Ltd. 01/15/2014 which name changed to Blockhain Holdings Ltd. 10/12/2018

ALYDAAR SOFTWARE CORP (NC)
Reincorporated 02/24/1994
State of incorporation changed from (UT) to (NC) 02/24/1994
Name changed to Information Architects Corp. 06/30/1999

ALYN CORP (DE)
Filed a petition under Chapter 7 Federal Bankruptcy proceedings 07/31/2000
Stockholders' equity unlikely

ALYNX CO (NV)
Reorganized under the laws of Florida as MiMedx Group, Inc. 04/02/2008
Each share Common $0.001 par exchanged for (0.3234758) share Common $0.001 par

ALYSIS TECHNOLOGIES INC (DE)
Merged into Pitney Bowes Inc. 05/03/2001
Each share Common 1¢ par exchanged for $1.39 cash

ALYSON HLDGS LTD (AB)
Name changed to Continental Waste Conversion Inc. 07/12/1993
Continental Waste Conversion Inc. name changed to EnviroPower Industries Inc. 10/09/1997
(See EnviroPower Industries Inc.)

ALYST ACQUISITION CORP (DE)
Reorganized under the laws of British Virgin Islands as China Networks International Holdings, Ltd. 06/26/2009
Each share Common $0.0001 par exchanged for (1) share Ordinary $0.0001 par

ALYX MED INSTRS INC (DE)
Charter dissolved 01/02/1990

ALZA CORP (DE)
Reincorporated 05/04/1987
Common no par changed to $1 par 07/25/1969
Common $1 par reclassified as Class A Common $1 par 01/27/1978
Class A Common $1 par changed to no par 00/00/1978
Class A Common no par split (2) for (1) by issuance of (1) additional share 07/08/1986
State of incorporation changed from (CA) to (DE) and Class A Common no par changed to 1¢ par 05/04/1987
Class A Common 1¢ par split (2) for (1) by issuance of (1) additional share 12/18/1991
Class A Common 1¢ par reclassified as Common 1¢ par 04/30/1993
Each share Common 1¢ par received distribution of (0.5) share Crescendo Pharmaceutical Corp. Class A Common 1¢ par payable 09/30/1997 to holders of record 09/18/1997
Common 1¢ par split (2) for (1) by issuance of (1) additional share payable 11/15/2000 to holders of record 11/01/2000 Ex date - 11/16/2000
Merged into Johnson & Johnson 06/22/2001
Each share Common 1¢ par exchanged for (0.98) share Common $1 par

AM CABLE TV INDS INC (DE)
Common 10¢ par split (3) for (2) by issuance of (0.5) additional share 05/15/1981
Name changed to AM Communications, Inc. 11/18/1986
(See AM Communications, Inc.)

AM-CH INC (DE)
Completely liquidated 09/23/2005
Each share Ser. A Preferred 1¢ par exchanged for $0.005 cash
Each share Common 1¢ par exchanged for $0.03 cash

AM COMMUNICATIONS INC (DE)
Chapter 11 bankruptcy proceedings converted to Chapter 7 on 03/23/2004
Stockholders' equity unlikely

AM DIAGNOSTICS INC (IN)
Charter dissolved by proclamation 01/31/1994

AM GOLD INC (BC)
Each share old Common no par exchanged for (0.1) share new Common no par 02/06/2014
Each share new Common no par

exchanged again for (0.2) share new
Common no par 01/19/2016
Acquired by 1079170 B.C. Ltd.
08/29/2016
Each share new Common no par
exchanged for $0.17 cash
Note: Unexchanged certificates will
be cancelled and become without
value 08/29/2022

AM INTL INC (DE)
Plan of reorganization under Chapter
11 bankruptcy proceedings
confirmed 09/11/1984
Each share Common $2.50 par
exchanged for initial distribution of
(0.91776) share Common no par
10/30/1984
Common no par changed to 1¢ par
02/28/1985
Each share Common 1¢ par received
second distribution of (0.33828)
share Common 1¢ par 09/00/1985
Each share Common 1¢ par received
third distribution of (0.07970) share
Common 1¢ par 01/00/1986
Each share Common 1¢ par received
fourth distribution of (0.05209) share
Common 1¢ par 06/00/1986
Reorganized as AM International, Inc.
(New) 10/13/1993
Each share $2 Conv. Exchangeable
Preferred 1¢ par exchanged for
(0.04100683) share Common 1¢ par
and (0.32073203) Common Stock
Purchase Warrant expiring
10/15/1996
Each share new Common 1¢ par
exchanged for (0.00148955) share
Common 1¢ par
Note: Unexchanged certificates were
cancelled and became without value
10/13/1995
AM International, Inc. (New)
recapitalized as Multigraphics, Inc.
05/28/1997

AM INTL INC NEW (DE)
Recapitalized as Multigraphics, Inc.
05/28/1997
Each share Common 1¢ par
exchanged for (0.4) share Common
$0.025 par
(See Multigraphics, Inc.)

AM OIL RES & TECHNOLOGY INC (NV)
Name changed to Medical Care
Technologies Inc. 11/20/2009

AM-PAC INTL INC (NV)
SEC revoked common stock
registration 07/18/2001

AM TECHNOLOGIES LTD (AB)
Reorganized under the laws of
Canada as Moncoa Corp.
07/12/2002
Each share Common no par
exchanged for (0.25) share Common
no par
Moncoa Corp. recapitalized as
Monument Mining Ltd. 07/09/2007

AM TEL INC (UT)
Involuntarily dissolved 06/01/1989

AM/TEX OIL & GAS INC (NV)
Name changed to Critical Point
Resources, Inc. 04/21/2008
Critical Point Resources, Inc.
reorganized as Renewable Energy
Solution Systems, Inc. 02/24/2012

AMA MONEY FD INC (MD)
Voluntarily dissolved 01/22/1991
Details not available

AMAC INC (DE)
Recapitalized as Auto Data Network
Inc. 10/16/2001
Each share Common $0.001 par
exchanged for (0.04) share Common
$0.001 par
(See Auto Data Network Inc.)

AMACAN RES CORP (UT)
Recapitalized as Spire International
Inc. 04/18/1996
Each share Common 25¢ par
exchanged for (0.14285714) share
Common 25¢ par
Spire International Inc. name changed
to Sento Technical Innovations Corp.
09/10/1996 which name changed to
Sento Corp. 08/11/1998
(See Sento Corp.)

AMACORP INDL LEASING CO (CA)
Recapitalized as Franklin Industries,
Inc. 04/07/1971
Each share 7% Conv. Non-Cum.
Preferred $10 par exchanged for
(0.33333333) share 7% Conv.
Non-Cum Preferred $10 par
Each share Common no par
exchanged for (0.33333333) share
Capital Stock 5¢ par
(See Franklin Industries, Inc.)

AMADA LTD (JAPAN)
Name changed to Amada Holdings
Co., Ltd. 04/01/2015

AMADAC INDS INC (DE)
Name changed to Miller Shoe
Industries, Inc. 01/28/1984
Miller Shoe Industries, Inc.
recapitalized as Apparel America
Inc. 01/11/1989
(See Apparel America Inc.)

AMADEUS ENERGY LTD (AUSTRALIA)
Name changed to Lonestar
Resources Ltd. 02/04/2013
(See Lonestar Resources Ltd.)

AMADEUS HLDGS INC (DE)
Recapitalized as National Equities
Holdings Inc. 01/20/1993
Each share Common $0.025 par
exchanged for (0.06666666) share
Common $0.025 par
National Equities Holdings Inc. name
changed to Skye Petroleum, Inc.
04/05/2010

AMADEUS INTL INC (QC)
Each share old Common no par
exchanged for (0.05) share new
Common no par 03/14/2007
Ceased operations 07/09/2008
Stockholders' equity unlikely

AMADEUS IT HLDG S A (SPAIN)
Name changed to Amadeus IT Group,
S.A. 08/16/2016

AMADEUS OIL N L (AUSTRALIA)
Name changed to Amadeus Energy
Ltd. 01/29/2002
Amadeus Energy Ltd. name changed
to Lonestar Resources Ltd.
02/04/2013
(See Lonestar Resources Ltd.)

AMADOR HIGHLAND VALLEY COPPERS LTD. (BC)
Name changed to Highmont
Resources Ltd. 09/25/1961
Highmont Resources Ltd. acquired by
Torwest Resources (1962) Ltd.
02/08/1962 which merged into
Highmont Mining Corp. 07/04/1977
which merged into Teck Corp.
09/28/1979 which name changed to
Teck Cominco Ltd. 09/12/2001
which name changed to Teck
Resources Ltd. 04/27/2009

AMADOR RES LTD (BC)
Merged into Artesian Petroleum Corp.
03/31/1981
Each share Common no par
exchanged for (0.66666666) share
Common no par
(See Artesian Petroleum Corp.)

AMADOR UTD GOLD MINES INC (CA)
Charter suspended for failure to pay
taxes 02/02/1998

AMADOR VY SVGS & LOAN ASSN (CA)
Failed 09/11/1993
No stockholders' equity

AMADYNE INC (WA)
Proclaimed dissolved for
non-payment of license fees
07/01/1973

AMAIZE BEVERAGE CORP (NV)
Name changed to Curative
Biosciences, Inc. 03/14/2018

AMALFI CAP CORP (AB)
Reorganized under the laws of
Ontario as Royal Coal Corp.
08/24/2010
Each share Common no par
exchanged for (0.5) share Common
no par

AMALGAMATED AUTOMOTIVE INDS INC (PA)
Common 1¢ par changed to $0.005
par and (1) additional share issued
07/10/1975
Common $0.005 par changed to
$0.0025 par and (1) additional share
issued 04/26/1976
Plan of reorganization under Chapter
11 Federal Bankruptcy Code
effective 08/01/1996
Each share Common $0.0025 par
exchanged for $0.01 cash

AMALGAMATED BKS SOUTH AFRICA LTD (SOUTH AFRICA)
Name changed to ABSA Group Ltd.
09/26/1997
ABSA Group Ltd. name changed to
Barclays Africa Group Ltd.
08/23/2013 which name changed to
Absa Group Ltd. 07/16/2018

AMALGAMATED BEAU BELLE MINES LTD (ON)
Dissolved 03/01/1982
Details not available

AMALGAMATED BONANZA PETE LTD (AB)
Each share Capital Stock no par
received distribution of (1) share
Bonanza Oil & Gas Ltd. Common no
par payable 01/12/1979
Merged into Gulf Canada Ltd., Gulf
Canada Western Ltd. and Royalite
Co., Inc. 12/07/1979
Each share Capital Stock no par
exchanged for either (0.35460992)
share Gulf Canada Ltd. Common no
par or $30 cash
Note: Option to receive Common
Stock expired 01/11/1980
Gulf Canada Ltd. acquired by Gulf
Canada Corp. 02/10/1986 which
reorganized as Gulf Canada
Resources Ltd. 07/01/1987
(See Gulf Canada Resources Ltd.)

AMALGAMATED CANGOLD INC (ON)
Merged into Central Asia Goldfields
Corp. 01/08/1996
Each share 7% Conv. Retractable
Conv. Preferred Ser. A no par
exchanged for (1) share 7% Conv.
Retractable Conv. Preferred Ser. A
no par
Each share Common no par
exchanged for (1) share Common
no par
(See Central Asia Goldfields Corp.)

AMALGAMATED CHIBOUGAMAU GOLD MINES LTD. (QC)
Dissolved 12/23/1972
Details not available

AMALGAMATED ENTMT INC (DE)
Each shares old Common 1¢ par
exchanged for (0.03333333) share
new Common 1¢ par 04/06/1999
New Common 1¢ par split (5) for (2)
by issuance of (1.5) additional
shares 09/13/1999
Name changed to MegaMedia
Networks, Inc. 11/15/1999
(See MegaMedia Networks, Inc.)

AMALGAMATED EXPLORATIONS INC (CO)
Each share old Common $0.0001 par
exchanged for (0.1) share new
Common $0.0001 par 01/25/1996
SEC revoked common stock
registration 04/06/2010

AMALGAMATED GEN RES LTD (BC)
Struck off register and declared
dissolved for failure to file returns
08/26/1983

AMALGAMATED GOLD & SILVER INC (FL)
Recapitalized as Rainforest
Resources Inc. 03/15/2016
Each share Common no par
exchanged for (0.00071428) share
Common no par

AMALGAMATED GOLD FIELDS CORP. LTD. (CANADA)
Charter surrendered 09/16/1958
No distributions to stockholders

AMALGAMATED INCOME LTD PARTNERSHIP (BC)
Each old Unit of Ltd. Partnership Int.
exchanged for (0.1) new Unit of Ltd.
Partnership Int. 12/01/2005
Completely liquidated
Each new Unit of Ltd. Partnership Int.
received initial distribution of $1.75
cash payable 05/14/2010 to holders
of record 04/30/2010
Each new Unit of Ltd. Partnership Int.
received second and final
distribution of $1.46 cash payable
08/31/2010 to holders of record
08/30/2010

AMALGAMATED KIRKLAND MINES LTD. (ON)
Merged into Mayfield Explorations &
Developments Ltd. 06/21/1971
Each share Capital Stock $1 par
exchanged for (1) share Capital
Stock $1 par
Mayfield Explorations &
Developments Ltd. merged into
Microsolve Computer Capital Inc.
02/11/1998 which name changed to
Homebank Technologies Inc.
12/20/2000 which name changed to
Selient Inc. 06/15/2005
(See Selient Inc.)

AMALGAMATED KNEE LAKE MINES LTD. (MB)
Charter cancelled and declared
dissolved for failure to file returns
03/31/1976

AMALGAMATED LARDER MINES LTD (ON)
Capital Stock $1 par changed to no
par 08/10/1973
Recapitalized as Larder Resources
Inc. 09/08/1980
Each share Capital Stock no par
exchanged for (0.5) share Capital
Stock no par
Larder Resources Inc. merged into
International Larder Minerals Inc.
05/01/1986 which merged into
Explorers Alliance Corp. 10/13/2000
(See Explorers Alliance Corp.)

AMALGAMATED LAUNDRIES, INC.
Property sold 00/00/1932
Details not available

AMALGAMATED LEATHER COS INC (DE)
Recapitalized 00/00/1933
Preferred $100 par changed to $50
par
Common no par changed to $1 par
Recapitalized 00/00/1936
Each share Preferred $50 par
exchanged for (1) share 6% Conv.
Preferred $50 par and (5) shares
new Common $1 par
Each share old Common $1 par
exchanged for (0.4) share new
Common $1 par
6% Conv. Preferred $50 par called for
redemption 01/21/1963
Each share new Common $1 par
exchanged for (0.25) share Common
$4 par 05/28/1964
Charter cancelled and declared
inoperative and void for
non-payment of taxes 03/01/1974

AMALGAMATED METAL CORP (ENGLAND)
ADR agreement terminated 02/15/1983
Details not available

AMALGAMATED MNG DEV CORP (QC)
Acquired by Amalgamated Mining Western Ltd. 12/20/1984
Each share Capital Stock $1 par exchanged for (1) share Common no par
Note: Unexchanged certificates were cancelled and holders received distribution of new shares 01/24/1985
Amalgamated Mining Western Ltd. recapitalized as Westall Resources Ltd. 07/12/1994
(See Westall Resources Ltd.)

AMALGAMATED MNG WESTN LTD (BC)
Recapitalized as Westall Resources Ltd. 07/12/1994
Each share Common no par exchanged for (0.33333333) share Common no par
(See Westall Resources Ltd.)

AMALGAMATED OIL CO. (1950) LTD. (BC)
Out of business 03/31/1964
No stockholders' equity

AMALGAMATED OILS LTD. (AB)
Liquidation completed 10/15/1958
Each share Common received final distribution of $0.06666666 cash per share
Note: Previous distribution payments totalling $0.50 cash per share made from 01/00/1944 to 05/00/1955

AMALGAMATED PPTYS LTD (CANADA)
Merged into Greenland Properties Ltd. 09/11/1979
Each share Common no par exchanged for $1.54 cash

AMALGAMATED PROPERTIES, INC. (DE)
Voluntarily dissolved 06/20/1910
Details not available

AMALGAMATED RARE EARTH MINES LTD (ON)
Common $1 par changed to no par 10/10/1973
Recapitalized as Rare Earth Resources Ltd. 10/15/1979
Each share Common no par exchanged for (0.2) share Common no par
Rare Earth Resources Ltd. name changed to Golden Earth Resources Inc. 05/22/1984 which merged into Health & Environment Technologies Inc. 05/03/1989
(See Health & Environment Technologies Inc.)

AMALGAMATED RES LTD (BC)
Capital Stock 50¢ par changed to no par 06/14/1972
Recapitalized as Great Bear Mining Ltd. 06/19/1974
Each share Capital Stock no par exchanged for (0.2) share Capital Stock no par
Great Bear Mining Ltd. recapitalized as Aries Resources Inc. (BC) 05/26/1977 which reincorporated in Yukon as Total Global Ventures Inc. 05/19/1999 which recapitalized as JNB Developments Co. Ltd. 10/03/2001 which name changed to Cooper Minerals Inc. (YT) 07/14/2004 which reincorporated in British Columbia as United Coal Holdings 05/28/2012

AMALGAMATED SILK CORP.
Bankrupt 00/00/1930
Details not available

AMALGAMATED SILVERS & GOLD MINES, CO., INC. (NV)
Charter revoked for failure to file reports and pay fees 03/01/1926

AMALGAMATED STL MLS BERHAD (MALAYSIA)
Name changed to Amsteel Corp. Berhad 12/16/1994
(See Amsteel Corp. Berhad)

AMALGAMATED SUGAR CO (UT)
Each share Preferred $100 par exchanged for (20) shares 5% 1st Preferred $10 par and (20) shares Common $1 par 00/00/1936
Each share old Common no par exchanged for (0.75) share 5% 1st Preferred $10 par and (1) share Common $1 par 00/00/1936
Common $1 par changed to no par and (2) additional shares issued 02/10/1961
5% 1st Preferred $10 par called for redemption 11/01/1967
Common no par split (10) for (1) by issuance of (9) additional shares 05/14/1984
Merged into Valhi, Inc. 03/10/1987
Each share Common no par exchanged for (14) shares Common 1¢ par

AMALGAMATED TECHNOLOGIES INC (DE)
Name changed to ProLink Holdings Corp. 01/26/2006
(See ProLink Holdings Corp.)

AMALGAMATED TEXTILES LTD (DE)
Under plan of merger name changed to Photometric Corp. and Common $1 par changed to 10¢ par 06/13/1963

AMALGAMATED TR & SVGS BK (CHICAGO, IL)
Name changed to Amalgamated Bank of Chicago (Chicago, IL) 12/16/1991

AMALIE MINING CO. (SD)
Charter cancelled for failure to file annual reports 07/01/1970

AMALTA OILS & MINERALS LTD (AB)
Recapitalized 07/05/1966
Recapitalized from Amalta Oils Ltd. to Amalta Oils & Minerals Ltd. 07/05/1966
Each share Capital Stock no par exchanged for (0.2) share Capital Stock no par
Name changed to Paracorp Ltd. 11/20/1981
(See Paracorp Ltd.)

AMANA COPPER LTD (BC)
Name changed to International Wastewater Systems Inc. 10/28/2015
International Wastewater Systems Inc. recapitalized as Sharc International Systems Inc. 09/11/2017

AMANA REFRIGERATION, INC. (IA)
Acquired by Raytheon Co. 03/01/1965
Each share Common $6.25 par exchanged for (0.56) share Common $5 par

AMANASU ENERGY CORP (NV)
Name changed to Amanasu Environment Corp. 11/13/2002

AMANDA CO (UT)
Each share old Common 1¢ par exchanged for (0.1) share new Common 1¢ par 02/08/2002
Charter expired 12/26/2002

AMANDA MINES LTD. (MB)
Name changed to Explorers Alliance Ltd. 07/09/1956
(See Explorers Alliance Ltd.)

AMANDA RES LTD (BC)
Struck off register and declared dissolved for failure to file returns 03/05/1993

AMANTA RES LTD (WY)
Reincorporated under the laws of British Columbia 08/31/2004

AMAR VENTURES INC (CANADA)
Reincorporated 02/23/1995
Place of incorporation changed from (BC) to (Canada) 02/23/1995
Involuntarily dissolved for failure to file annual returns 03/03/2003

AMARA MNG PLC (ENGLAND & WALES)
Delisted from Toronto Stock Exchange 10/25/2013
In order to trade holders must convert to UK main register

AMARADO RES LTD (CANADA)
Reincorporated 05/25/1995
Place of incorporation changed from (BC) to (Canada) 05/25/1995
Reorganized as AfriOre Ltd. (Canada) 08/29/1995
Each share Common no par exchanged for (0.4) share Common no par
AfriOre Ltd. (Canada) reincorporated in New Brunswick 07/30/1997 which reincorporated in Barbados 07/31/2001 which reincorporated in British Virgin Islands 05/19/2005
(See AfriOre Ltd.)

AMARANTUS BIOSCIENCE INC (DE)
Name changed to Amarantus BioScience Holdings, Inc. 04/18/2013

AMARANTUS BIOSCIENCES INC (DE)
Common $0.001 par split (25) for (1) by issuance of (24) additional shares payable 06/13/2011 to holders of record 06/06/2011
Ex date - 06/14/2011
Name changed to Amarantus BioScience, Inc. 12/28/2012
Amarantus BioScience, Inc. name changed to Amarantus BioScience Holdings, Inc. 04/18/2013

AMARCO RES CORP (DE)
Reincorporated 05/20/1980
State of incorporation changed from (CO) to (DE) 05/20/1980
Each share Common 1¢ par exchanged for (0.2) share Common 1¢ par
Name changed to Bestway Rental, Inc. 03/28/1988
Bestway Rental, Inc. reorganized as Bestway Inc. 06/07/1995
(See Bestway Inc.)

AMAREX INC (DE)
Reincorporated 08/04/1970
State of incorporation changed from (TX) to (DE) 08/04/1970
Common $1 par changed to no par 10/14/1980
Common no par split (2) for (1) by issuance of (1) additional share 12/15/1980
Stock Dividend - 100% 02/15/1980
Plan of reorganization under Chapter 11 Federal Bankruptcy proceedings confirmed 09/12/1985
No stockholders' equity

AMARILLO ENTERPRISES INC (ON)
Recapitalized as Cromwell Resources Ltd. 08/15/1988
Each share Common no par exchanged for (0.25) share Common no par

AMARILLO MESQUITE GRILL INC (KS)
Chapter 11 bankruptcy proceedings converted to Chapter 7 on 09/20/2004
Stockholders' equity unlikely

AMARIUM TECHNOLOGIES INC (NV)
Recapitalized as Calissio Resources Group, Inc. 10/06/2014
Each share Common $0.001 par exchanged for (0.005) share Common $0.001 par

AMARK EXPLS LTD (BC)
Name changed to O.E.X. Electromagnetic Inc. 03/13/1987
(See O.E.X. Electromagnetic Inc.)

AMARLITE CORP. (DE)
Acquired by Anaconda Co. 07/09/1963
Each share Common $1 par exchanged for (0.32) share Capital Stock $50 par
Anaconda Co. merged into Atlantic Richfield Co. (PA) 01/13/1977 which reincorporated in Delaware 05/07/1985 which merged into BP Amoco PLC 04/18/2000 which name changed to BP PLC 05/01/2001

AMAROK ENERGY INC (AB)
Recapitalized as Powder Mountain Energy Ltd. 06/20/2014
Each share Common no par exchanged for (0.2) share Common no par
Powder Mountain Energy Ltd. merged into Canamax Energy Ltd. 08/04/2015
(See Canamax Energy Ltd.)

AMAROK RES INC (NV)
Common $0.001 par split (60) for (1) by issuance of (59) additional shares payable 02/22/2010 to holders of record 02/11/2010
Ex date - 02/23/2010
Recapitalized as 3DX Industries Inc. 11/22/2013
Each share Common $0.001 par exchanged for (0.02) share Common $0.001 par

AMASYS CORP (DE)
Recapitalized as StemGen, Inc. 02/05/2013
Each share Common 1¢ par exchanged for (0.0125) share Common 1¢ par

AMATEUR GOLFERS ASSN AMER INC (DE)
Company went private 00/00/1987
Details not available

AMATI COMMUNICATIONS CORP (DE)
Merged into Texas Instruments Inc. 03/02/1998
Each share Common 20¢ par exchanged for $20 cash

AMATO EXPL LTD (BC)
Name changed to Aurora Royalties Inc. 02/16/2018

AMAX ATHABASCA URANIUM MINES LTD. (ON)
Merged into Pardee Amalgamated Mines Ltd. 12/31/1954
Each share Common exchanged for (0.2) share Common $1 par
Pardee Amalgamated Mines Ltd. liquidated for Rio Algom Mines Ltd. 11/09/1961 which name changed to Rio Algom Ltd. 04/30/1975
(See Rio Algom Ltd.)

AMAX FINL CORP (DE)
Name changed to University Group, Inc. 07/01/1975
University Group, Inc. merged into Southmark Corp. 02/08/1984
(See Southmark Corp.)

AMAX GOLD INC (DE)
Common 1¢ par split (3) for (2) by issuance of (0.5) additional share 07/15/1988
Merged into Kinross Gold Corp. 06/01/1998
Each share Common 1¢ par exchanged for (0.8004) share Common no par
Name changed to Kinam Gold, Inc. (DE) 09/18/1998
(See each company's listing)

AMAX INC (NY)
Common $1 par split (3) for (2) by issuance of (0.5) additional share 06/15/1979
Conv. Preferred Ser. A $1 par called for redemption 09/01/1979
Preferred Ser. E $1 par called for redemption 06/01/1986
Common Stock Purchase Rights declared for Common stockholders of record 06/24/1988 were redeemed at $0.05 per right 12/02/1991 for holders of record 11/12/1991
$3 Conv. Preferred Ser. B $1 par called for redemption 09/01/1993
Merged into Cyprus Amax Minerals Co. 11/15/1993
Each share 144A Conv. Preferred Ser. A $1 par exchanged for (0.66666666) share Cyprus Amax Minerals Co. $4 Conv. Preferred Ser. A $1 par and (0.33333333) share Alumax Inc. $4 Conv. Preferred Ser. A $1 par
Each share Common $1 par exchanged for (0.5) share Common no par
Cyprus Amax Minerals Co. merged into Phelps Dodge Corp. 12/02/1999 which merged into Freeport-McMoRan Copper & Gold Inc. 03/19/2007 which name changed to Freeport-McMoRan Inc. 07/14/2014

AMAYA GAMING GROUP INC (QC)
Name changed to Amaya Inc. (QC) 12/04/2014
Amaya Inc. (QC) reincorporated in Ontario as Stars Group Inc. 08/01/2017

AMAYA INC (QC)
Reincorporated under the laws of Ontario as Stars Group Inc. 08/01/2017

AMAZING TECHNOLOGIES CORP (NV)
Name changed to Mvive Inc. 08/24/2007
(See Mvive Inc.)

AMAZON GOLDSANDS LTD (NV)
Name changed to First Colombia Gold Corp. 11/29/2010

AMAZON MNG HLDG PLC (ENGLAND & WALES)
Name changed to Verde Potash PLC 04/26/2011
Verde Potash PLC name changed to Verde Agritech PLC 07/28/2016

AMAZON NAT TREASURES COM INC (NV)
Charter permanently revoked 12/31/2004

AMAZON NAT TREASURES INC (NV)
Reincorporated 08/18/1997
State of incorporation changed from (UT) to (NV) 08/18/1997
Recapitalized as Amazon Natural Treasures.com, Inc. 02/06/2001
Each share Common $0.001 par exchanged for (0.09090909) share Common $0.001 par
(See Amazon Natural Treasures.com, Inc.)

AMAZON OIL & ENERGY CORP (NV)
Name changed to AEC Holdings, Corp. 02/20/2007
(See AEC Holdings, Corp.)

AMAZON OIL CO., INC. (DE)
Dissolved 01/09/1922
Details not available

AMAZON PETE CORP (BC)
Recapitalized as Brigadier Resources Ltd. 02/24/1992
Each share Common no par exchanged for (0.28571428) share Common no par
Brigadier Resources Ltd. recapitalized as Parametric Ventures Inc. 04/04/1994 which recapitalized as Centura Resources Inc. 11/12/1999 which recapitalized as Polar Resources Corp. 02/14/2005

AMAZON TECHNOLOGIES INC (CO)
Charter suspended for failure to file annual reports 09/30/1986

AMAZONICA CORP (NV)
Common $0.001 par split (175) for (1) by issuance of (174) additional shares payable 05/24/2013 to holders of record 05/08/2013 Ex date - 05/28/2013
Common $0.001 par changed to $0.0001 par 10/13/2014
Recapitalized as Xfuels Inc. 01/29/2016
Each share Common $0.0001 par exchanged for (0.002) share Common $0.0001 par

AMB PPTY CORP (MD)
8.5% Preferred Ser. A 1¢ par called for redemption at $25 plus $0.0826 accrued dividends on 07/28/2003
Merged into Prologis, Inc. 06/03/2011
Each share 6.5% Preferred Ser. L 1¢ par exchanged for (1) share 6.5% Preferred Ser. L 1¢ par
Each share 6.75% Preferred Ser. M 1¢ par exchanged for (1) share 6.75% Preferred Ser. M 1¢ par
Each share 6.85% Preferred Ser. P 1¢ par exchanged for (1) share 6.85% Preferred Ser. P 1¢ par
Each share 7% Preferred Ser. O 1¢ par exchanged for (1) share 7% Preferred Ser. O 1¢ par
Each share Common 1¢ par exchanged for (1) share Common 1¢ par

AMBAC FINL GROUP INC (DE)
Name changed 07/11/1997
Name changed from AMBAC Inc. to Ambac Financial Group, Inc. 07/11/1997
Old Common 1¢ par split (2) for (1) by issuance of (1) additional share payable 09/10/1997 to holders of record 08/29/1997 Ex date - 09/11/1997
Old Common 1¢ par split (3) for (2) by issuance of (0.5) additional share payable 12/12/2000 to holders of record 11/27/2000 Ex date - 12/13/2000
Each Corporate Unit automatically became $50 principal amount of 9.5% Sr. Notes due 02/15/2021 on 12/02/2010
Plan of reorganization under Chapter 11 Federal Bankruptcy proceedings effective 05/01/2013
No old Common stockholders' equity (Additional Information in Active)

AMBAC INDS INC (NY)
Common $2 par split (2) for (1) by issuance of (1) additional share 01/30/1969
Merged into United Technologies Corp. 07/14/1978
Each share Common $2 par exchanged for (1) share $3.875 Conv. Preferred $1 par

AMBANC CORP (IN)
Stock Dividends - 5% payable 12/02/1996 to holders of record 11/20/1996; 5% payable 12/08/1997 to holders of record 11/26/1997
Merged into Union Planters Corp. 08/31/1998
Each share Common $10 par exchanged for (0.4841) share Common $5 par
Union Planters Corp. merged into Regions Financial Corp. (New) 07/01/2004

AMBANC HLDG INC (DE)
Merged into Hudson River Bancorp, Inc. 03/08/2002
Each share Common 1¢ par exchanged for $21.50 cash

AMBAR INC (DE)
Merged into AI Acquisitions Corp. 08/09/1996
Each share Common 1¢ par exchanged for $18 cash

AMBASSADOR AIRLS INC (NV)
Name changed to General International Film Corp. 03/01/1971
(See General International Film Corp.)

AMBASSADOR APTS INC (MD)
Merged into Apartment Investment & Management Co. 05/08/1998
Each share Common 1¢ par exchanged for (0.553) share Common 1¢ par

AMBASSADOR BK COMWLTH (ALLLENTOWN, PA)
Merged into Fulton Financial Corp. 09/11/1998
Each share Common $4 par exchanged for (1.4) shares Common $2.50 par

AMBASSADOR BUILDING CORP.
Capital Stock sold 00/00/1948
Holders of VTC'S received $7 per share

AMBASSADOR DEV CORP CDA LTD (BC)
Merged into Ambassador Industries Ltd. (Old) 06/01/1978
Each share Common no par exchanged for (0.25) share Common no par
(See Ambassador Industries Ltd. (Old))

AMBASSADOR EAST, INC. (DE)
Merged into Hotel Sherman, Inc. 00/00/1960
Details not available

AMBASSADOR EYEWEAR GROUP INC (DE)
Recapitalized as Interage, Ltd. 05/10/2004
Each share Common 1¢ par exchanged for (0.1) share Common 1¢ par

AMBASSADOR FDS (MD)
Reorganized as Munder Funds Trust 06/23/1995
Details not available

AMBASSADOR FINL GROUP INC (FL)
Proclaimed dissolved for failure to file reports and pay fees 10/11/1991

AMBASSADOR GOLD MINES, LTD.
Bankrupt 00/00/1940
Details not available

AMBASSADOR GROUP INC (DE)
Common 10¢ par split (5) for (2) by issuance of (2.5) additional shares 08/01/1977
Stock Dividends - 10% 07/03/1975; 10% 07/15/1976; 20% 08/01/1978; 50% 07/15/1980
Charter cancelled and declared inoperative and void for non-payment of taxes 03/01/1990

AMBASSADOR HOTEL CO. OF LOS ANGELES (CA)
Through voluntary purchase offer majority of shares acquired by Schine Enterprises, Inc. 11/00/1972
Public interest eliminated

AMBASSADOR HOTEL OF NEW YORK, INC. (DE)
6% 2nd Preferred $50 par called for redemption 03/11/1958
Liquidation completed
Each share Common $1 par exchanged for initial distribution of $15 cash 03/11/1958
Each share Common $1 par received second distribution of $2 cash 05/28/1958
Each share Common $1 par received third distribution of $2 cash 09/28/1958
Each share Common $1 par received fourth distribution of $0.80 cash 03/28/1962
Each share Common $1 par received fifth and final distribution of $0.09 cash 01/21/1964

AMBASSADOR INDS LTD NEW (BC)
Company went private 12/31/2002
Each share Common no par exchanged for $2.10 cash

AMBASSADOR INDS LTD OLD (BC)
Each share old Common no par exchanged for (4) shares new Common no par 12/21/1989
Plan of arrangement effective 04/24/1997
Each share new Common no par exchanged for (4) shares Barrier Mining Corp. Common no par and (1) share Ambassador Industries Ltd. (New) Common no par
(See each company's listing)

AMBASSADOR INVT CORP (MO)
Attorney advised company is defunct and without assets 11/15/1982
No stockholders' equity

AMBASSADOR MINES CORP. (WA)
Merged into Sunny Peak Mining Co. 00/00/1954
Each share Common 10¢ par exchanged for (0.25) share Capital Stock 20¢ par
(See Sunny Peak Mining Co.)

AMBASSADOR MINES LTD (BC)
Recapitalized as Petrowest Resources Ltd. 06/18/1973
Each share Capital Stock 50¢ par exchanged for (0.2) share Capital Stock no par
(See Petrowest Resources Ltd.)

AMBASSADOR MINING DEVELOPMENTS LTD. (ON)
Recapitalized as New Ambassador Developments Ltd. 06/18/1973
Each share Common exchanged for (0.1) share Common
(See New Ambassador Developments Ltd.)

AMBASSADOR OIL CORP. (DE)
Liquidation completed
Each share Common $1 par stamped to indicate initial distribution of $5.50 cash 08/16/1965
Each share Stamped Common $1 par exchanged for second distribution of $0.65 cash 06/14/1966
Each share Stamped Common $1 par received third and final distribution of $0.06 cash 12/26/1967

AMBER ENERGY INC (AB)
Common no par split (2) for (1) by issuance of (1) additional share payable 05/03/1996 to holders of record 04/30/1996 Ex date - 04/26/1996
Common no par split (2) for (1) by issuance of (1) additional share payable 05/30/1997 to holders of record 05/26/1997 Ex date - 05/22/1997
Merged into Alberta Energy Co. Ltd. 11/13/1998
Each share Common no par exchanged for either (0.225) share Common no par, $7.50 cash, or a combination thereof
Note: Option to receive either stock or combination of stock and cash expired 01/12/1999
Alberta Energy Co. Ltd. merged into EnCana Corp. 01/03/2003

AMBER ENTERPRISES INC (CO)
Name changed to 1st American Business Development Group, Inc. (CO) 08/31/1988
1st American Business Development Group, Inc. (CO) reorganized in Delaware as 21st Century Rehabilitation, Inc. 01/26/1993

AMBER GROUP INC (NV)
Name changed to Natural Health Farm Holdings Inc. 03/17/2017

AMBER MINING & EXPLORATION CO. LTD. (ON)
Charter cancelled for failure to pay taxes and file returns 08/20/1953

AMBER OIL CO. (OH)
Voluntarily dissolved 12/20/1940
Details not available

AMBER RES CO COLORADO (DE)
Name changed 06/00/2003
Each share Common $0.003125 par exchanged for (0.05) share Common $0.0625 par 09/18/1989
Name changed from Amber Resources Co. to Amber Resources Company of Colorado 06/00/2003
Plan of reorganization under Chapter 11 Federal Bankruptcy proceedings effective 08/31/2012
No stockholders' equity

AMBER RES LTD (BC)
Name changed to Banner Resources Ltd. 01/29/1980
Banner Resources Ltd. recapitalized as Angus Resources Ltd. 03/05/1984 which recapitalized as Canadian Angus Resources Ltd. (BC) 12/31/1987 which reincorporated in Alberta 08/29/1988 which merged into Abacan Resource Corp. (New) 02/10/1995
(See Abacan Resource Corp. (New))

AMBERGATE EXPLS INC (BC)
Merged into Kenrich Mining Corp. (New) 08/15/1994
Each share Common no par exchanged for (1) share Common no par
Kenrich Mining Corp. (New) recapitalized as Kenrich-Eskay Mining Corp. 11/19/2001 which name changed to Eskay Mining Corp. (BC) 11/03/2009 which reincorporated in Ontario 11/02/2010

AMBERGRIS CAYE INC (NV)
Charter revoked for failure to file reports and pay fees 11/01/2000

AMBERGRIS CONSOLIDATED MINING CO.
Out of existence 00/00/1939
Details not available

AMBERHILL MINING EXPLORATIONS LTD. (BC)
Name changed to Amberhill Petroleums Ltd. 10/25/1982
(See Amberhill Petroleums Ltd.)

AMBERHILL PETES LTD (BC)
Struck off register and declared dissolved for failure to file returns 09/29/1989

AMBERLEY INDUSTRIES LTD. (ON)
Dissolved 05/27/1968
Details not available

AMBERQUEST RES LTD (CANADA)
Reincorporated 12/09/1988
Place of incorporation changed from (BC) to (Canada) 12/09/1988
Involuntarily dissolved for failure to file annual returns 07/12/2004

AMBERS STORES INC (TX)
Chapter 7 bankruptcy proceedings terminated 11/20/2002
No stockholders' equity

AMBIENT CORP (DE)
Each share old Common $0.001 par exchanged for (0.01) share new Common $0.001 par 07/20/2011
Name changed to AMBT Liquidating Corp. 11/13/2014

AMBIENT TECHNOLOGY CORP (CO)
Charter suspended for failure to file annual reports 03/05/1984

AMBINA CORP (OH)
Assets sold for benefit of creditors 06/13/1977

No stockholders' equity

AMBIT BIOSCIENCES CORP (DE)
Merged into Daiichi Sankyo Co., Ltd. 11/12/2014
Each share Common $0.001 par exchanged for (1) Non-Transferrable Contingent Value Right and $15 cash

AMBIT MICROSYSTEMS CORP (TAIWAN)
Stock Dividends - In Reg. S Sponsored GDR's for Common to holders of Reg. S Sponsored GDR's for Common 27% payable 08/15/2002 to holders of record 07/11/2002 Ex date - 07/09/2002; 10% payable 09/05/2003 to holders of record 07/30/2003; in 144A Sponsored GDR's for Common to holders of 144A Sponsored GDR's for Common 10% payable 09/05/2003 to holders of record 07/30/2003
Merged into Hon Hai Precision Industry Ltd. 04/01/2004
Each 144A Sponsored GDR for Common exchanged for (0.672) 144A GDR for Common
Each Reg. S Sponsored GDR for Common exchanged for (0.672) Reg. S GDR for Common
Note: Holders who did not exchange their GDR's prior to 07/01/2004 will receive cash

AMBLE GREEN VENTURES INC (BC)
Recapitalized as Western Logic Technologies Inc. 06/23/1993
Each share Common no par exchanged for (0.5) share Common no par
Western Logic Technologies Inc. name changed to Western Logic Resources Inc. 09/18/1996
(See Western Logic Resources Inc.)

AMBLE RES LTD (BC)
Acquired by Valar Resources Ltd. 10/00/1986
Each share Common no par exchanged for (0.33333333) share Common no par
(See Valar Resources Ltd.)

AMBLIN RES INC (AB)
Recapitalized as Amblin Technologies Inc. 01/15/2002
Each share Common no par exchanged for (0.2) share Common no par
(See Amblin Technologies Inc.)

AMBLIN TECHNOLOGIES INC (AB)
Delisted from Toronto Venture Stock Exchange 06/20/2003

AMBRA OIL & GAS CO (UT)
Charter expired 05/23/2002

AMBRA OIL INC. (UT)
Merged into Ambra Oil & Gas Co. 08/31/1979
Each share Capital Stock 1¢ par exchanged for (1) share Common 10¢ par
(See Ambra Oil & Gas Co.)

AMBRA RES GROUP INC (UT)
Recapitalized 10/15/1996
Recapitalized from Ambra Royalty, Inc. to Ambra Resources Group Inc. 10/15/1996
Each share old Common $0.001 par exchanged for (0.1) share new Common $0.001 par
Recapitalized as Apex Resources Group Inc. 03/27/2003
Each share new Common $0.001 par exchanged for (0.05) share $0.001 par
(See Apex Resources Group Inc.)

AMBREX MNG CORP (ON)
Reorganized under the laws of Alberta as Karmin Exploration Inc. 09/15/1999
Each share Common no par exchanged for (0.33333333) share Common no par

AMBRIT INC (DE)
12.125% Conv. Exchangeable Preferred $1 par called for redemption 09/25/1987
Merged into Empire of Carolina, Inc. 12/29/1989
Each share Common 10¢ par exchanged for (0.3) share Common 10¢ par
(See Empire of Carolina, Inc.)

AMBRO MINING CORP. (DE)
No longer in existence having become inoperative and void for non-payment of taxes 03/17/1926

AMBROOK INDUSTRIES, INC. (DE)
Merged into Ambrook Industries, Inc. 06/01/1956
Each share Common 25¢ par exchanged for (0.66666666) share Common 25¢ par
Ambrook Industries, Inc. (RI) merged into Barker Bros. Corp. (RI) 03/14/1958 which name changed to Larchfield Corp. 10/05/1960
(See Larchfield Corp.)

AMBROOK INDUSTRIES, INC. (RI)
Merged into Barker Bros. Corp. (RI) 03/14/1958
Each share Common 25¢ par exchanged for (2) shares Common $1 par
Barker Bros. Corp. (RI) name changed to Larchfield Corp. 10/05/1960
(See Larchfield Corp.)

AMBROSIA MINERALS, INC. (NV)
Charter revoked for failure to file reports and pay fees 03/06/1961

AMBULATORY MED CARE INC (OH)
Reverted to a private company 09/27/1993
Each share Common no par exchanged for $5.50 cash

AMBUSH MEDIA INC (FL)
Name changed to Azia Corp. 03/19/2010
Azia Corp. name changed to Axxess Unlimited Inc. 03/20/2013 which name changed to Encompass Compliance Corp. 06/22/2015

AMC AMERICAN MUSIC CORP INC (DE)
Recapitalized as Mercantile Gold Co. (DE) 10/05/2004
Each share Common $0.001 par exchanged for (0.05) share Common $0.001 par
Mercantile Gold Co. (DE) reincorporated in Wyoming 09/23/2005 which recapitalized as Anglo Andean Mining Co. 02/07/2006 which name changed to MGM Mineral Resources Inc. 04/28/2006 which recapitalized as Brownstone Resources, Inc. 10/05/2007 which recapitalized as Pomsta Group, Inc. 10/12/2010 which name changed to Oidon Co., Ltd. 12/31/2010

AMC ENTMT INC (DE)
Common $1 par changed to $0.66666666 par and (0.5) additional share issued 10/24/1985
$1.75 Conv. Preferred $0.66666666 par called for redemption at $25.75 on 04/14/1998
Acquired by Marquee Holdings Inc. 12/23/2004
Each share Common $0.66666666 par exchanged for $19.50 cash

AMC FINL INC (DE)
In process of liquidation
Each share Common 1¢ par received initial distribution of $3.80 cash payable 10/18/2000 to holders of record 10/02/2000
Each share Common 1¢ par received second distribution of $3.35 cash payable 03/30/2001 to holders of record 03/16/2001
Each share Common 1¢ par received third distribution of $2 cash payable 11/05/2002 to holders of record 10/25/2002
Each share Common 1¢ par received fourth distribution of $1 cash payable 09/29/2003 to holders of record 09/18/2003 Ex date - 09/30/2003
Name changed to AMC Financial Holdings, Inc. 04/13/2004

AMC INVS INC (NY)
Proclaimed dissolved 11/24/1992

AMCA INTL LTD (CANADA)
8.84% Retractable Preferred Ser. 1 no par called for redemption 03/30/1990
Recapitalized as United Dominion Industries Ltd. 06/04/1990
Each share Common no par exchanged for (0.2) share Common no par
Preferreds were not affected except for change of name
United Dominion Industries Ltd. acquired by SPX Corp. 05/24/2001

AMCA MINES, LTD.
Bankrupt and assets sold 00/00/1938
Details not available

AMCA RES LTD (BC)
Name changed 12/04/1980
Name changed from Amca Industries Ltd. to Amca Resources Ltd. 12/04/1980
Struck off register and declared dissolved for failure to file returns 07/16/1993

AMCAN CYPHERMASTER LTD (BC)
Merged into Aura Systems, Inc. 04/15/1988
Each share Common no par exchanged for (1) share Common $0.005 par
(See Aura Systems, Inc.)

AMCAN INDS CORP (ON)
Assets sold for benefit of creditors 09/15/1982
No stockholders' equity

AMCAN INS SVCS INC (AB)
Discharged from receivership 00/00/1994
No stockholders' equity

AMCAN MINERALS LTD (BC)
Delisted from NEX 04/20/2004

AMCAP CORP (NV)
Name changed to ASB Capital Corp. 11/18/1985
(See ASB Capital Corp.)

AMCAP INVESTMENTS, INC. (IL)
Charter revoked for failure to file reports and pay fees 11/16/1964

AMCARE CTRS INC (NY)
Charter cancelled and proclaimed dissolved for failure to pay taxes and file reports 12/16/1974

AMCAST INDL CORP (OH)
Common no par split (2) for (1) by issuance of (1) additional share 02/10/1984
Plan of reorganization under Chapter 11 Federal Bankruptcy Code effective 08/03/2005
No stockholders' equity

AMCHEM PRODS INC (PA)
Merged into Union Carbide Co. (Old) 04/27/1977
Each share Common 1¢ par exchanged for (0.1667) share Common $1 par
Union Carbide Co. (Old) reorganized as Union Carbide Co. (New) 07/01/1989 which merged into Dow Chemical Co. 02/06/2001 which merged into DowDuPont Inc. 09/01/2017

AMCI INTL INC (UT)
Each share old Common $0.001 par exchanged for (5.435034) shares

new Common $0.001 par 10/27/1999
Name changed to Shopss.com, Inc. 12/28/1999
Shopss.com, Inc. name changed to AccessTel, Inc. 02/15/2001
(See AccessTel, Inc.)

AMCO ENERGY CORP (UT)
Name changed to Amcole Energy Corp. 07/12/1978
(See Amcole Energy Corp.)

AMCO INDL HLDGS LTD (ON)
Capital Stock no par reclassified as Conv. Class A Common no par 07/23/1984
Recapitalized as International Amco Corp. (ON) 11/04/1985
Each share Conv. Class A Common no par exchanged for (0.2) share Conv. Class A Common no par
Each share Conv. Class B Common no par exchanged for (0.2) share Conv. Class B Common no par
International Amco Corp. (ON) reorganized in England & Wales as Amco Corp. PLC 11/10/1989 which name changed to Billington Holdings Plc 03/31/2009

AMCO INDS INC (DE)
Reincorporated 06/27/1969
State of incorporation changed from (IL) to (DE) 06/27/1969
Merged into Toyota Motor Sales, U.S.A., Inc. 12/02/1975
Each share Common $1 par exchanged for $4.6021 cash

AMCO PLC (ENGLAND & WALES)
Name changed to Billington Holdings PLC 03/31/2009

AMCO RES INC (NV)
Name changed to Amco Building Corp. 03/31/1988

AMCO TRANS HLDGS INC (DE)
Recapitalized as Business Development Solutions, Inc. 02/28/2006
Each share Common $0.00001 par exchanged for (0.2) share Common $0.00001 par
(See Business Development Solutions, Inc.)

AMCOL INTL CORP (DE)
Common 1¢ par split (3) for (2) by issuance of (0.5) additional share payable 12/01/1997 to holders of record 11/17/1997
Under plan of partial liquidation each share Common 1¢ par received distribution of $14 cash payable 06/30/2000 to holders of record 06/16/2000
Acquired by Minerals Technologies Inc. 05/09/2014
Each share Common 1¢ par exchanged for $45.75 cash

AMCOLE ENERGY CORP (UT)
Each share Common no par exchanged for (0.06666666) share new Common no par 05/16/1983
Plan of reorganization under Chapter 11 Federal Bankruptcy proceedings effective 01/09/1990
No stockholders' equity

AMCOMP INC NEW (DE)
Merged into Employers Holdings, Inc. 10/31/2008
Each share Common 1¢ par exchanged for $12.15 cash

AMCOMP INC OLD (DE)
Merged into Datapoint Services, Inc. 01/17/1977
Each share Common 10¢ par exchanged for $1.81 cash

AMCON INDS INC (OH)
100% acquired by Garsite Products, Inc. through exchange offer which expired 03/31/1981
Public interest eliminated

AMCON INTL INC (TN)
Ceased operations 05/01/1977
No stockholders' equity

AMCOR CAP CORP (DE)
Each share old Common $0.002 par exchanged for (0.5) share new Common $0.002 par 02/24/1997
Name changed to USA Biomass Corp. 08/31/1998
(See USA Biomass Corp.)

AMCOR INC (UT)
Common 50¢ par split (2) for (1) by issuance of (1) additional share 11/16/1970
Merged into Diversified Earth Sciences, Inc. 12/27/1972
Each share Common 50¢ par exchanged for (0.225) share Common 80¢ par
(See Diversified Earth Sciences, Inc.)

AMCORD INC (DE)
6.25% Class A Preferred $100 par called for redemption 01/01/1977
Ser. A Preferred no par called for redemption 12/01/1977
Merged into Gifford-Hill & Co. Inc. 12/07/1979
Each share Common $5 par exchanged for $34 cash
$1.25 Preferred $25 par called for redemption 12/31/1979
Public interest eliminated

AMCORE FINL INC (NV)
Common $1 par changed to 50¢ par and (1) additional share issued 06/04/1986
Common 50¢ par changed to 33¢ par and (0.5) additional share issued 12/13/1993
Common 33¢ par changed to 22¢ par and (0.5) additional share issued payable 09/17/1997 to holders of record 09/05/1997
Stock Dividend - 10% 05/28/1992
Plan of liquidation under Chapter 11 Federal Bankruptcy proceedings effective 06/22/2011
No stockholders' equity

AMCORP INDS INC (BC)
Name changed to Molycor Gold Corp. 05/17/1996
Molycor Gold Corp. name changed to Nevada Clean Magnesium Inc. 04/17/2012

AMCOURT SYS INC (FL)
Proclaimed dissolved for failure to file reports and pay fees 12/11/1976

AMCV CAP TR I (DE)
Plan of reorganization under Chapter 11 Federal Bankruptcy Code effective 10/01/2003
Each share 7% Trust Conv. Preferred Security 1¢ par exchanged for an undetermined amount of cash

AMD RES CORP (BC)
Name changed to Halo Gaming Corp. 04/24/1992
(See Halo Gaming Corp.)

AMDAHL CORP (DE)
Common 5¢ par split (2) for (1) by issuance of (1) additional share 05/04/1978
Common 5¢ par split (2) for (1) by issuance of (1) additional share 06/13/1983
Common 5¢ par split (2) for (1) by issuance of (1) additional share 09/02/1988
Merged into Fujitsu Ltd. 09/18/1997
Each share Common 5¢ par exchanged for $12.40 cash

AMDC GROUP INC (CO)
Administratively dissolved 08/02/1997

AMDEK CORP (MA)
Voluntarily dissolved 01/27/1988
Details not available

AMDISCO CORP (MD)
Under plan of reorganization each share Common $1 par exchanged for $29.60 cash 10/03/1983

AMDIV COM INC (NV)
SEC revoked common stock registration 03/14/2007

AMDL INC (DE)
Each share old Common $0.001 par exchanged for (0.05) share new Common $0.001 par 09/28/1998
Each share new Common $0.001 par exchanged again for (0.1) share new Common $0.001 par 04/01/1999
Each share new Common $0.001 par exchanged again for (0.2) share new Common $0.001 par 09/28/2006
Name changed to Radient Pharmaceuticals Corp. 09/22/2009
(See Radient Pharmaceuticals Corp.)

AMDOCS AUTOMATIC COM EXCHANGE SEC TR (NY)
Each 6.75% Trust Automatic Common Exchange Security exchanged for (1) share Amdocs Ltd. Common 1¢ par 09/11/2002

AMDURA CORP (DE)
Reorganized under Chapter 11 Federal Bankruptcy Code 10/23/1991
Each Depositary Preferred exchanged for (0.08935751) share new Common $1 par
Each share $4.75 Conv. Preferred Ser. A $100 par exchanged for (0.31416902) share new Common $1 par
Each share $4.75 Conv. Preferred Ser. B (0.34048348) share new Common $1 par
Each share 5% Conv. Preferred Ser. C $100 par exchanged for (0.35714285) share new Common $1 par
Each share old Common $1 par exchanged for (0.0522875) share new Common $1 par
Merged into ADU Acquisition Inc. 04/24/1995
Each share new Common $1 par exchanged for $2.30 cash

AME - HIS, INC. (NY)
Charter cancelled and proclaimed dissolved for failure to pay taxes 03/28/2001

AME LTD (ON)
Merged into Kassner Investment Corp. Ltd. 10/01/1993
Each share Common no par exchanged for $2.85 cash

AME RESOURCE CAP CORP (BC)
Common no par reclassified as Class A Common no par 05/20/1999
Recapitalized as Western Pacific Trust Co. 09/03/1999
Each share Class A Common no par exchanged for (0.25) share Common no par

AMEC FOSTER WHEELER PLC (ENGLAND & WALES)
Name changed 11/13/2014
Each Unsponsored ADR for Ordinary exchanged for (1) Sponsored ADR for Ordinary 10/02/2014
Sponsored ADR's for Ordinary split (3) for (1) by issuance of (2) additional ADR's payable 10/20/2014 to holders of record 10/17/2014 Ex date - 10/21/2014
Name changed from Amec PLC to Amer Foster Wheeler PLC 11/13/2014
Acquired by John Wood Group PLC 11/03/2017
Each Sponsored ADR for Ordinary exchanged for $7.016199 cash

AMECHE-GINO FOODS, INC. (MD)
Name changed to A-G Foods, Inc. 05/03/1962
A-G Foods, Inc. name changed to Gino's Inc. 04/03/1969
(See Gino's, Inc.)

AMECO ELECTRONIC CORP. (NY)
Charter revoked for failure to file reports and pay fees 12/15/1967

AMECO INC (AZ)
Charter revoked for failure to file reports and pay fees 05/10/1980

AMECS INC (NV)
Common $0.00001 par split (7) for (1) by issuance of (6) additional shares payable 01/04/2008 to holders of record 01/02/2008 Ex date - 01/07/2008
Name changed to 4C Controls, Inc. 02/26/2008

AMEDCO, INC. (DE)
Certificates dated prior to 05/15/1962
Recapitalized as Gulf States Industries, Inc. 05/15/1962
Each share Capital Stock 1¢ par exchanged for (0.25) share Capital Stock 10¢ par
(See Gulf States Industries, Inc.)

AMEDCO INC (DE)
Certificates dated after 12/27/1972
Common $1 par split (3) for (2) by issuance of (0.5) additional share 12/30/1982
Common $1 par split (2) for (1) by issuance of (1) additional share 08/01/1983
Acquired by Service Corp. International 09/26/1986
Each share Common $1 par exchanged for (0.42553191) share Common $1 par

AMEDIA NETWORKS INC (DE)
Common $0.001 par split (10) for (1) by issuance of (9) additional shares payable 08/29/2007 to holders of record 08/24/2007 Ex date - 08/30/2007
Ceased operations 02/12/2008
Stockholders' equity unlikely

AMEE INC (WY)
Name changed to Aquaplan, Inc. 12/01/1998
Aquaplan, Inc. name changed to Oxford Funding Corp. 05/18/2007 which recapitalized as Emerging Healthcare Solutions, Inc. 08/12/2009

AMEGY BANCORPORATION INC (TX)
Merged into Zions Bancorporation 12/03/2005
Each share Common $1 par exchanged for (0.3136) share Common no par
Zions Bancorporation merged into Zions Bancorporation, N.A (Salt Lake City, UT) 10/01/2018

AMELCO CORP (CA)
Company terminated registration of common stock and is no longer public as of 12/30/1997
Details not available

AMELOT HLDGS INC (WY)
Recapitalized as HLK Biotech Holding Group, Inc. 02/23/2018
Each share Common $0.0001 par exchanged for (0.001) share Common $0.0001 par

AMENITY, INC. (UT)
Name changed to Elkin, Weiss & Companies, Inc. 07/21/1986
(See Elkin, Weiss & Companies, Inc.)

AMER GROUP PLC (FINLAND)
Name changed 09/01/1997
Name changed from Amer Group Ltd. to Amer Group PLC 09/01/1997
ADR's for Ordinary FIM20 par split (3) for (1) by issuance of (2) additional ADR's payable 12/21/2004 to holders of record 12/16/2004 Ex date - 12/22/2004
Name changed to Amer Sports Corp. 04/29/2005

AMER ITAL GOURMET INC (CA)
Name changed to F & M Importing, Inc. 05/17/1985
F & M Importing, Inc. recapitalized as MarCor Development Co., Inc. (CA) 11/03/1986 which reincorporated in Nevada 08/31/1988 which name changed to MarCor Resorts, Inc. 07/13/1989 which name changed to Rio Hotel & Casino Inc. 03/02/1992 which merged into Harrah's Entertainment, Inc. 01/01/1999
(See Harrah's Entertainment, Inc.)

AMER-TEX ENERGY, INC. (NV)
Merged into Lincoln Petroleum Resources Corp. 12/28/2001
Details not available

AMERA INDS INC (BC)
Recapitalized as International Amera Industries Corp. 02/10/1995
Each share Common no par exchanged for (0.125) share Common no par
International Amera Industries Corp. recapitalized as IMA Resource Corp. 02/21/1996 which recapitalized as IMA Exploration Inc. 07/07/1998 which recapitalized as Kobex Minerals Inc. 09/30/2009 which name changed to Kobex Capital Corp. 08/29/2014 which name changed to Itasca Capital Ltd. 06/23/2016

AMERA RES CORP (BC)
Recapitalized as Panthera Exploration Inc. 12/23/2008
Each share Common no par exchanged for (0.1) share Common no par
Panthera Exploration Inc. name changed to Iron South Mining Corp. 02/28/2012 which name changed to Argentina Lithium & Energy Corp. 09/21/2016

AMERAC ENERGY CORP (DE)
Each share $4 Sr. Preferred $1 par exchanged for (9) shares Common 5¢ par 07/12/1996
Each share old Common 5¢ par exchanged for (0.06666666) share new Common 5¢ par 11/21/1996
Merged into Southern Mineral Corp. 01/28/1998
Each share new Common 5¢ par exchanged for (0.850918) share Common 1¢ par
(See Southern Mineral Corp.)

AMERACE CORP (DE)
$3.50 Preferred $50 par called for redemption 07/08/1959
Common $12.50 par split (3) for (1) by issuance of (2) additional shares 07/07/1961
Under plan of merger name changed to Amerace Esna Corp. and Common $12.50 par changed to $5 par 08/30/1968
Amerace Esna Corp. name changed back to Amerace Corp. 04/27/1973
4.5% Preferred $100 par called for redemption 03/31/1962
$2.60 Conv. Preferred Ser. A $10 par called for redemption 10/29/1984
Acquired by RaceCo, Inc. 10/30/1984
Each share Common $5 par exchanged for $47.50 cash

AMERACE ESNA CORP (DE)
Name changed to Amerace Corp. 04/27/1973
(See Amerace Corp.)

AMERACOL TECHNOLOGY, INC. (NV)
Name changed to Chiropractic 21 International, Inc. 05/31/1983
Chiropractic 21 International, Inc. name changed to visionGATEWAY, Inc. 03/10/2004
(See visionGATEWAY, Inc.)

AMERACRUDE RES INC (BC)
Name changed to Camino Energy Corp. 11/27/1981
(See Camino Energy Corp.)

AMERADA CORP. (DE)
Name changed to Amerada Petroleum Corp. 12/24/1941
Amerada Petroleum Corp. merged into Amerada Hess Corp. 06/20/1969 which name changed to Hess Corp. 05/03/2006

AMERADA HESS CORP (DE)
$3.50 Conv. Preferred $1 par called for redemption 09/17/1987
Common $1 par split (2) for (1) by issuance of (1) additional share 08/28/1980
Name changed to Hess Corp. 05/03/2006

AMERADA PETE CORP (DE)
Common no par split (2) for (1) by issuance of (1) additional share 05/27/1946
Common no par split (2) for (1) by issuance of (1) additional share 06/01/1951
Common no par split (2) for (1) by issuance of (1) additional share 05/24/1955
Common no par split (2) for (1) by issuance of (1) additional share 05/29/1963
Common no par changed to $1 par 05/07/1968
Merged into Amerada Hess Corp. 06/20/1969
Each share Common $1 par exchanged for (1) share $3.50 Conv. Preferred $1 par
Amerada Hess Corp. name changed to Hess Corp. 05/03/2006

AMERALIA INC (UT)
Each share Common $0.001 par exchanged for (0.025) share Common 1¢ par 01/19/1993
Name changed to Natural Resources USA Corp. 12/07/2010
(See Natural Resources USA Corp.)

AMERAND INC (OK)
Common $1 par changed to 5¢ par 12/18/1968
Charter suspended for failure to pay taxes 02/25/1972

AMERANIUM MINES LTD (ON)
Capital Stock $1 par changed to no par 03/26/1971
Recapitalized as Jamestown Explorations Inc. 08/21/1972
Each share Capital Stock no par exchanged for (0.125) share Capital Stock no par
Jamestown Explorations Inc. recapitalized as Jamestown Resources Inc. 10/15/1981
(See Jamestown Resources Inc.)

AMERASIA KHAN ENTERPRISES LTD (NV)
Name changed to Zagg, Inc. (NV) 03/13/2007
Zagg, Inc. (NV) reincorporated in Delaware 06/27/2016

AMERATECH SYS CORP (BC)
Delisted from Canadian Venture Stock Exchange 05/31/2000

AMERCO (NV)
8.50% Preferred Ser. A no par called for redemption at $25 on 06/01/2011
(Additional Information in Active)

AMERCO INC (CA)
Merged into Royal Industries, Inc. (DE) 06/02/1969
Each share Common $1 par exchanged for (0.31888) share Common $1 par
(See Royal Industries, Inc. (DE))

AMERCOEUR ENERGY CDN LTD (ON)
Cease trade order effective 08/18/1988
Stockholders' equity unlikely

AMERCON CORP. (DE)
Completely liquidated 03/27/1967
Each share Capital Stock no par exchanged for first and final distribution of (0.5) share General Precision Equipment Corp. $1.60 Conv. Preference no par and (0.666666) share Common $1 par General Precision Equipment Corp. merged into Singer Co. (NJ) 07/11/1968 which reincorporated in Delaware 00/00/1988 which name changed to Bicoastal Corp. 10/16/1989
(See Bicoastal Corp.)

AMERDYNE CORP (NV)
Name changed to Pantheon 09/21/1969
Pantheon name changed to Medical Dispensing Systems, Inc. Northeast 07/20/1983
(See Medical Dispensing Systems, Inc. Northeast)

AMERDYNE INDS INC (FL)
Name changed to Leisure Capital Corp. of America and Common $0.005 par changed to $0.0001 par 06/27/1985
(See Leisure Capital Corp. of America)

AMERECEN INDS (NV)
Name changed to Amrec Industries Inc. 02/23/1973
(See Amrec Industries, Inc.)

AMERECO (NV)
SEC revoked common stock registration 11/01/2010

AMERECO ENVIRONMENTAL SVCS INC (MO)
Plan of reorganization under Chapter 11 Federal Bankruptcy Code effective 11/05/1991
No stockholders' equity

AMERECO INC (UT)
Involuntarily dissolved 04/26/1999

AMEREL MINING CO. LTD. (ON)
Merged into Twentieth Century Explorations Ltd. (QC) 09/12/1969
Each share Capital Stock $1 par exchanged for (0.05) share Capital Stock no par
Twentieth Century Explorations Ltd. (QC) reincorporated in Ontario as Twentieth Century Explorations Inc. 03/01/1975 which recapitalized as Minefinders Corp. Ltd. 04/26/1979 which merged into Pan American Silver Corp. 04/02/2012

AMERELITE SOLUTIONS INC (NV)
Each share Common $0.000125 par exchanged for (0.1) share Common $0.00125 par 12/07/2006
Reorganized as RegalWorks Media, Inc. 08/26/2013
Each share Common $0.00125 par exchanged for (0.04) share Common $0.001 par

AMEREN CORP (MO)
Each Adjustable Rate Equity Security Unit received (0.5364) share Common 1¢ par 05/16/2005
(Additional Information in Active)

AMEREX DEV CORP (BC)
Struck off register and declared dissolved for failure to file returns 08/22/1986

AMEREX GROUP INC (OK)
Assets assigned to creditors 08/24/2009
Stockholders' equity unlikely

AMEREX HOLDING CORP.
Dissolved 12/04/1950
Each share Capital Stock $10 par exchanged for (3) shares American Express Co. Capital Stock $10 par

AMERFORD INTL CORP (NY)
Common 10¢ par split (2) for (1) by issuance of (1) additional share 01/31/1979
Common 10¢ par split (2) for (1) by issuance of (1) additional share 02/06/1981
Stock Dividend - 50% 11/16/1981
Acquired by Thyssen Inc. 09/12/1989
Each share Common 10¢ par exchanged for $4.72 cash

AMERGENCE GROUP INC (NV)
Each share old Common $0.001 par exchanged for (0.001) share new Common $0.001 par 06/25/2007
Name changed to Altitude Organic Corp. 05/16/2011
Altitude Organic Corp. name changed to Tranzbyte Corp. 02/22/2012 which name changed to American Green, Inc. 07/01/2014

AMERI-CAN AGRI CO (BC)
Name changed to Acana Capital Corp. 02/08/2016

AMERI-CAN RY SYS INC (NH)
Name changed to ARS Networks, Inc. 04/10/2000
ARS Networks, Inc. recapitalized as Green Mountain Capital Inc. (NH) 09/24/2004 which reincorporated in Nevada 07/12/2005 which name changed to IT Group Holdings, Inc. 02/26/2007

AMERI-DREAM ENTMT INC (CA)
Name changed to Soleil Film & Television, Inc. 11/07/2003
Soleil Film & Television, Inc. reorganized as Soleil Film, Inc. 07/13/2004 which name changed to Imperia Entertainment, Inc. (CA) 08/04/2005 which reincorporated in Nevada 08/28/2006 which recapitalized as Viratech Corp. 10/11/2011

AMERI-FIRST FINL GROUP INC (DE)
Reincorporated 03/22/2000
Reincorporated under the laws of Delaware 03/22/2000
Each share Common $0.001 par exchanged for (0.04) share old Common $0.00001 par 01/23/2001
Each share old Common $0.00001 par exchanged for (0.000002) share new Common $0.00001 par 05/30/2007
Reincorporated under the laws of Nevada as Eight Dragons Co. and Common $0.00001 par changed to $0.0001 par 12/07/2007
Eight Dragons Co. name changed to Rokk3r Inc. 06/18/2018

AMERIANA BANCORP (IN)
Common $1 par split (3) for (2) by issuance of (0.5) additional share 01/07/1994
Common $1 par split (4) for (3) by issuance of (0.33333333) additional share payable 04/05/1996 to holders of record 03/15/1996
Stock Dividend - 10% payable 01/04/1999 to holders of record 12/18/1998
Merged into First Merchants Corp. 12/31/2015
Each share Common $1 par exchanged for (0.9037) share Common no par

AMERIANA SVGS BK F S B (NEW CASTLE, IN)
Under plan of reorganization each share Common $1 par automatically became (1) share Ameriana Bancorp Common $1 par 03/19/1990
Ameriana Bancorp merged into First Merchants Corp. 12/31/2015

AMERIBANC INC (MO)
Common $10 par changed to $5 par and (1) additional share issued 11/26/1975
Merged into Mercantile Bancorporation, Inc. 05/01/1992
Each share Common $5 par exchanged for $26 cash

AMERIBANC INVS GROUP (MD)
6% Conv. Preferred $21 par called for redemption 03/31/1995
Merged into First Union Corp. 04/01/1995
Each Share of Bene. Int. $1 par exchanged for $3 cash

AMERIBANK BANCSHARES INC (FL)
Merged into Wachovia Corp. (New) (Ctfs. dated between 05/20/1991 and 09/01/2001) 04/01/1998
Each share Common $5 par exchanged for (3.5019) share Common $5 par
Wachovia Corp. (New) (Ctfs. dated between 05/20/1991 and 09/01/2001) merged into Wachovia Corp. (Ctfs. dated after 09/01/2001) 09/01/2001 which merged into Wells Fargo & Co. (New) 12/31/2008

AMERIC MINES LTD (QC)
Recapitalized as Novamin Inc. 12/31/1985
Each share Capital Stock $1 par exchanged for (0.125) share Common no par
Novamin Inc. merged into Breakwater Resources Ltd. (BC) 05/18/1988 which reincorporated in Canada 05/11/1992
(See Breakwater Resources Ltd.)

AMERIC RES CORP (BC)
Reincorporated under the laws of Canada as Rolland Virtual Business Systems Ltd. 04/27/2001
Rolland Virtual Business Systems Ltd. name changed to Rolland Energy Inc. 02/16/2007 which recapitalized as Gale Force Petroleum Inc. 06/04/2008 which merged into Montana Exploration Corp. 09/22/2015

AMERICA & ISRAEL GROWTH FUND, INC. (MD)
Merged into Israel American Diversified Fund, Inc. 07/29/1968
Each share Capital Stock 10¢ par exchanged for (1.107) shares Common 20¢ par
(See Israel American Diversified Fund, Inc.)

AMERICA ASIA CORP (NV)
Each share old Common $0.001 par exchanged for (0.02) share new Common $0.001 par 12/20/2004
Reincorporated under the laws of Washington as America Asia Energy Corp. 11/08/2005
America Asia Energy Corp. name changed to Renegade Energy Corp. 09/14/2006 which recapitalized as Carson Development Corp. 10/20/2008
(See Carson Development Corp.)

AMERICA ASIA ENERGY CORP (WA)
Each share old Common $0.001 par exchanged for (0.005) share new Common $0.001 par 12/12/2005
Name changed to Renegade Energy Corp. 09/14/2006
Renegade Energy Corp. recapitalized as Carson Development Corp. 10/20/2008
(See Carson Development Corp.)

AMERICA ASIA PETE CORP (NV)
Old Common $0.001 par split (10) for (1) by issuance of (9) additional shares payable 08/28/2006 to holders of record 08/25/2006 Ex date - 08/29/2006
Each share old Common $0.001 par exchanged for (0.025) share new Common $0.001 par 04/27/2007
Voluntarily dissolved 03/21/2008
Details not available

AMERICA CALIF BK (SAN FRANCISCO, CA)
Acquired by FNB Bancorp 09/04/2015
Each share Common $5 par exchanged for $10.60 cash

AMERICA CAP CORP (FL)
Name changed 05/30/1996
Stock Dividend - in $3.75 Ser. A Preferred to holders of $3.75 Ser. A Preferred 30% 03/23/1990
Name changed from American Capital Corp. to America Capital Corp. 05/30/1996
Plan of reorganization under Chapter 11 Federal Bankruptcy Code effective 02/27/2009
No stockholders' equity

AMERICA CORP. (DE)
Reorganized 12/31/1963
Reorganized from America Corp. (OH) to America Corp. (DE) 12/31/1963
Each share $4 Preferred $10 par exchanged for $60 of 4% Sub. Debs. Ser. A due 00/00/1978, (5) Common Stock Purchase Warrants and $2 cash
Each share $6 Preferred $10 par exchanged for $60 of 4% Sub. Debs. Ser. B due 00/00/1978, (10) Common Stock Purchase Warrants and $3 cash
Common $1 par exchanged share for share
America Corp. (DE) name changed to Pathe Industries, Inc. (DE) 11/20/1964
(See Pathe Industries, Inc. (DE))

AMERICA FIRST APT INV L P (DE)
Merged into America First Apartment Investors, Inc. 01/01/2003
Each Ctf. of Bene. Int. exchanged for (1) share Common 1¢ par
(See America First Apartment Investors, Inc.)

AMERICA FIRST APT INVS INC (MD)
Merged into Sentinel Real Estate Corp. 09/18/2007
Each share Common 1¢ par exchanged for $25.30 cash

AMERICA FIRST FINL FD 1987-A LTD PARTNERSHIP (DE)
Merged into Bay View Capital Corp. 01/02/1998
Each Beneficial Unit Certificate exchanged for (1.137915) shares Common 1¢ par
Note: Each Beneficial Unit Certificate received distribution of $11.3553 cash 03/25/1998
Bay View Capital Corp. name changed to Great Lakes Bancorp, Inc. (New) 05/01/2006 which merged into First Niagara Financial Group, Inc. (New) 02/15/2008 which merged into KeyCorp (New) 08/01/2016

AMERICA FIRST MTG INVTS INC (MD)
Name changed to MFA Mortgage Investments, Inc. 08/13/2002
MFA Mortgage Investments, Inc. name changed to MFA Financial, Inc. 01/01/2009

AMERICA FIRST PART PFD EQUITY MTG FD LTD PARTNERSHIP (DE)
Merged into America First Mortgage Investments, Inc. 04/09/1998
Each Exchangeable Unit exchanged for (1) share Common 1¢ par
America First Mortgage Investments, Inc. name changed to MFA Mortgage Investments, Inc. 08/13/2002 which name changed to MFA Financial, Inc. 01/01/2009

AMERICA FIRST PREP FD 2 LTD PARTNERSHIP (DE)
Merged into America First Mortgage Investments, Inc. 04/09/1998
Each Bene. Unit Ctf. exchanged for (1.26) shares Common 1¢ par
America First Mortgage Investments, Inc. name changed to MFA Mortgage Investments, Inc. 08/13/2002 which name changed to MFA Financial, Inc. 01/01/2009

AMERICA FIRST PREP FD 2 PENSION SER LTD PARTNERSHIP (DE)
Merged into America First Mortgage Investments, Inc. 04/09/1998
Each Unit of Ltd. Partnership exchanged for (1) share Common 1¢ par
America First Mortgage Investments, Inc. name changed to MFA Mortgage Investments, Inc. 08/13/2002 which name changed to MFA Financial, Inc. 01/01/2009

AMERICA FIRST REAL ESTATE INVT PARTNERS L P (DE)
Merged into America First Apartment Investors, Inc. 06/03/2004
Each Unit of Ltd. Partnership Int. exchanged for (0.791) share Common 1¢ par and $0.39 cash
(See America First Apartment Investors, Inc.)

AMERICA FIRST REIT INC (DE)
Merged into Mid-America Apartment Communities, Inc. 06/29/1995
Each share Common 1¢ par exchanged for (0.88082696) share Common 1¢ par

AMERICA FIRST TAX EXEMPT INVS L P (DE)
Name changed to America First Multifamily Investors, L.P. 11/12/2013

AMERICA FIRST TAX EXEMPT MTG FD (DE)
Merged into America First Tax Exempt Investors, L.P. 02/01/1999
Each Beneficial Unit Certificate exchanged for (1) Beneficial Unit Certificate
America First Tax Exempt Investors, L.P. name changed to America First Multifamily Investors, L.P. 11/12/2013

AMERICA FIRST TAX EXEMPT MTG FD 2 (DE)
Name changed to America First Apartment Investors L.P. 08/20/1996
America First Apartment Investors L.P. merged into America First Apartment Investors, Inc. 01/01/2003
(See America First Apartment Investors, Inc.)

AMER HOME FOOD PRODS INC (NY)
Name changed to Artisanal Brands, Inc. 11/04/2010

AMERICA MINERAL FIELDS INC (YUKON)
Name changed to Adastra Minerals Inc. 05/12/2004
Adastra Minerals Inc. merged into First Quantum Minerals Ltd. 08/11/2006

AMERICA MOVIL S A DE C V (MEXICO)
Sponsored ADR's for Ser. A Shares split (3) for (1) by issuance of (2) additional ADR's payable 07/20/2005 to holders of record 07/18/2005 Ex date - 07/21/2005
Sponsored ADR's for Ser. L Shares split (3) for (1) by issuance of (2) additional ADR's payable 07/20/2005 to holders of record 07/18/2005 Ex date - 07/21/2005
Name changed to America Movil, S.A.B. de C.V. 12/13/2006

AMERICA ONLINE INC (CO)
Name changed to Morlex, Inc. (New) (CO) 06/02/1988
Morlex, Inc. (New) (CO) reincorporated in Delaware as Superfly Advertising, Inc. 11/20/2008
(See Superfly Advertising, Inc.)

AMERICA ONLINE INC (DE)
Common 1¢ par split (2) for (1) by issuance of (1) additional share 11/24/1994
Common 1¢ par split (2) for (1) by issuance of (1) additional share 04/27/1995
Common 1¢ par split (2) for (1) by issuance of (1) additional share 11/28/1995
Common 1¢ par split (2) for (1) by issuance of (1) additional share payable 03/16/1998 to holders of record 02/23/1998 Ex date - 03/17/1998
Common 1¢ par split (2) for (1) by issuance of (1) additional share payable 11/17/1998 to holders of record 11/03/1998 Ex date - 11/18/1998
Common 1¢ par split (2) for (1) by issuance of (1) additional share payable 02/22/1999 to holders of record 02/08/1999 Ex date - 02/23/1999
Common 1¢ par split (2) for (1) by issuance of (1) additional share payable 11/22/1999 to holders of record 11/08/1999 Ex date - 11/23/1999
Merged into AOL Time Warner Inc. 01/11/2001
Each share Common 1¢ par exchanged for (1) share Common 1¢ par
AOL Time Warner Inc. name changed to Time Warner Inc. (New) 10/16/2003 which merged into AT&T Inc. 06/15/2018

AMERICA ONLINE LATIN AMER INC (DE)
Plan of reorganization under Chapter 11 Federal Bankruptcy Code effective 06/30/2006
No stockholders' equity

AMERICA POP INC (DE)
Name changed to Amerihost Properties, Inc. 09/11/1987
Amerihost Properties, Inc. name changed to Arlington Hospitality, Inc. 05/24/2001
(See Arlington Hospitality, Inc.)

AMERICA RES EXPL INC (NV)
Common $0.001 par split (15) for (1) by issuance of (14) additional shares payable 04/29/2015 to holders of record 04/29/2015
Recapitalized as PetroGas Co. 03/07/2016
Each share Common $0.001 par exchanged for (0.01) share Common $0.001 par

AMERICA SVC GROUP INC (DE)
Common 1¢ par split (3) for (2) by issuance of (0.5) additional share payable 10/29/2004 to holders of record 10/08/2004 Ex date - 11/01/2004
Acquired by Valitas Health Services, Inc. 06/03/2011
Each share Common 1¢ par exchanged for $26 cash

AMERICA SOUTHWEST CORP (DE)
Name changed to U.S. Energy Search, Inc. 11/04/1977
U.S. Energy Search, Inc. name changed to Espero Energy Corp. 05/15/1989
(See Espero Energy Corp.)

AMERICA TELECOM S A DE C V (MEXICO)
Merged into America Movil, S.A.B. de C.V. 01/22/2007
Each Sponsored ADR for Ordinary exchanged for (0.407128) Sponsored ADR for Ser. L

AMERICA TIME EAST MEDIA GROUP INC (NV)
Each share old Common $0.001 par exchanged for (0.1) share Common $0.001 par 09/20/2001
Name changed to Starwin Media Holdings Inc. 07/18/2005

AMERICA WEST AIRLS INC (DE)
Plan of reorganization under Chapter

11 Federal Bankruptcy Code effective 08/25/1994
Each share Common 25¢ par exchanged for (0.1) share Class B Common 1¢ par and (0.28) Class B Common Stock Purchase Warrant expiring 08/25/1999
Under plan of reorganization each share Class B Common 1¢ par automatically became (1) share America West Holdings Corp. Class B Common 1¢ par 12/31/1996
America West Holdings Corp. merged into US Airways Group, Inc. (Ctfs. dated after 09/27/2005) 09/27/2005 which merged into American Airlines Group Inc. 12/09/2013

AMERICA WEST CAP CORP (BC)
Name changed to AME Resource Capital Corp. 03/07/1997
AME Resource Capital Corp. recapitalized as Western Pacific Trust Co. 09/03/1999

AMERICA WEST HLDG CORP (DE)
Ctfs. dated after 09/27/2005
Merged into US Airways Group, Inc. 09/27/2005
Each share Class B Common 1¢ par exchanged for (0.4125) share Common 1¢ par
US Airways Group, Inc. merged into American Airlines Group Inc. 12/09/2013

AMERICABILIA COM INC (FL)
Reincorporated under the laws of Nevada as Crystalix Group International Inc. 12/06/2002
Crystalix Group International Inc. recapitalized as Seaena, Inc. 03/31/2006
(See Seaena, Inc.)

AMERICAID INC (PA)
Name changed to American Leisure Services, Inc. 11/27/1972

AMERICAN & CONTINENTAL CORP. (DE)
Merged into American General Corp. 11/23/1935
Each share Class A and/or Common no par exchanged for (0.3) share $2 Ser. Preferred $1 par
American General Corp. merged into Equity Corp. 10/17/1950 which name changed to Wheelabrator-Frye Inc. 11/04/1971 which merged into Signal Companies, Inc. 02/01/1983 which merged into Allied-Signal Inc. 09/19/1985 which name changed to AlliedSignal Inc. 04/26/1993 which name changed to Honeywell International Inc. 12/01/1999

AMERICAN & DOMINION CORP.
Bankrupt 00/00/1933
Details not available

AMERICAN & EFIRD MILLS, INC. (NC)
Stock Dividends - Class A & B Common - 10% 05/01/1957; 50% 02/01/1966; 33.33333333% 04/01/1967
Merged into Ruddick Corp. 10/28/1968
Each share 4% Conv. Preferred Ser. C $100 par or 4% Conv. Preferred Ser. D $100 par exchanged for (1) share 56¢ Conv. Preference $5 par
Each share Class A Common $1 par or Class B Common $1 par exchanged for (1) share 56¢ Conv. Preference $5 par and (1) share Common $1 par
Ruddick Corp. name changed to Harris Teeter Supermarkets, Inc. (New) 04/02/2012
(See Harris Teeter Supermarkets, Inc. (New))

AMERICAN & FGN PWR INC (ME)
Reorganized 02/29/1952
Each share $7 Preferred no par exchanged for (4.0021) shares new Common no par and $90 principal amount of 4.80% Debentures due 01/01/1987
Each share $7 2nd Preferred Ser. A no par exchanged for (0.85) share new Common no par
Each share $6 Preferred no par exchanged for (3.2032) shares new Common no par and $80 principal amount of 4.80% Debentures due 01/01/1987
Each share old Common no par exchanged for (0.02) share new Common no par
Note: Unexchanged certificates were cancelled and became without value 03/01/1958
Merged into Electric Bond & Share Co. 12/31/1967
Each share new Common no par exchanged for (0.6) share Common $5 par
Electric Bond & Share Co. name changed to Esbasco Industries Inc. 05/09/1968 which merged into Boise Cascade Corp. 08/31/1969 which name changed to OfficeMax Inc. 11/01/2004

AMERICAN & FOREIGN PRODUCTIONS, INC. (DE)
No longer in existence having become inoperative and void for non-payment of taxes 04/01/1955

AMERICAN & FOREIGN SHARE CORP.
Out of business 00/00/1932
Details not available

AMERICAN & GENERAL SECURITIES CORP. (MD)
Merged into American General Corp. 11/23/1935
Each share $3 Preferred no par exchanged for (1) share $3 Ser. Preferred $1 par
Each share Class A Common $1 par exchanged for (1.2) shares Common 10¢ par
Each share Class B Common 10¢ par exchanged for (0.05) share Common 10¢ par
American General Corp. merged into Equity Corp. 10/17/1950 which name changed to Wheelabrator-Frye Inc. 11/04/1971 which merged into Signal Companies, Inc. 02/01/1983 which merged into Allied-Signal Inc. 09/19/1985 which name changed to AlliedSignal Inc. 04/26/1993 which name changed to Honeywell International Inc. 12/01/1999

AMERICAN & OVERSEAS CORP. (FL)
Name changed to First Research Corp. 09/09/1968
(See First Research Corp.)

AMERICAN & SCOTTISH INVESTMENT CO. (DE)
Charter cancelled and declared inoperative and void for non-payment of taxes 04/01/1934

AMERICAN & SOUTHN CORP (FL)
Charter revoked for failure to file reports and pay fees 06/07/1966

AMERICAN ABSORBENTS NAT PRODS INC (UT)
Each share old Common $0.001 par exchanged for (0.47619047) share new Common $0.001 par 06/21/2001
Reincorporated under the laws of Delaware as Earful of Books, Inc. 08/24/2001
(See Earful of Books, Inc.)

AMERICAN ACCESS TECHNOLOGIES INC (FL)
Recapitalized as American Electric Technologies, Inc. 05/16/2007
Each share Common $0.001 par exchanged for (0.2) share Common $0.001 par

AMERICAN ACCUMULATIVE TRUST SHARES
Trust liquidated 00/00/1936
Details not available

AMERICAN ACOUSTICS, INC. (DE)
Adjudicated bankrupt 04/29/1948
No stockholders' equity

AMERICAN ACQUISITION CORP (NJ)
Name changed to Savin Electronics Inc. and Common $0.004 par changed to $0.0001 par 03/18/1996
Savin Electronics Inc. name changed to Hidenet Secure Architectures, Inc. 07/12/1999 which recapitalized as Bio Nitrogen Corp. 11/08/2011 which name changed to BioNitrogen Holdings Corp. 10/15/2013

AMERICAN ACQUISITIONS INC (CO)
Name changed to Natural Alternatives, Inc. 09/05/1986
Natural Alternatives, Inc. name changed to Natural Alternatives International, Inc. (CO) 04/22/1988 which reincorporated in Delaware 12/08/1989

AMERICAN ACUPUNCTURE MED INSTRS INC (FL)
Charter cancelled for non-payment of taxes 09/03/1976

AMERICAN ADDICTION CTRS INC (NV)
Merged into AAC Holdings, Inc. 11/10/2014
Each share Common $0.001 par exchanged for (1.571119) shares Common $0.001 par

AMERICAN ADJUSTABLE RATE TERM TR INC - 1995 (MN)
Trust liquidated 04/17/1995
Each share Common 1¢ par exchanged for final and final distribution of $9.76922 cash

AMERICAN ADJUSTABLE RATE TERM TR INC-1998 (MN)
Merged into Piper Funds Inc. II 09/05/1995
Each share Common 1¢ par exchanged for (1.0889375) shares Adjustable Rate Mortgage Securities Fund
Piper Funds Inc. II merged into First American Investment Funds Inc. 07/31/1998

AMERICAN ADVENTURE INC (DE)
Reorganized 03/27/1987
Stock Dividend - 10% 07/12/1985
Reorganized from under the laws of (WA) to (DE) 03/27/1987
Each share Common no par exchanged for (0.1) share Common no par
Charter cancelled and declared inoperative and void for non-payment of taxes 03/01/2000

AMERICAN AERO LIQUIDS CORP (DE)
Charter cancelled and declared inoperative and void for non-payment of taxes 04/15/1972

AMERICAN AFFILIATES INC (IN)
Acquired by 1st Source Corp. 10/01/1983
Details not available

AMERICAN AGGREGATES CORP (OH)
Common $100 par changed to old Common no par 00/00/1928
Each share 7% Cum. Preferred $100 par exchanged for (1) share 7% Non-Cum. Preferred $100 par and (1) share old Common no par 00/00/1933
Each share 7% Non-Cum. Preferred $100 par exchanged for (1) share 5% Preferred $100 par 00/00/1940
Each share old Common no par exchanged for (3) shares Common $5 par 10/03/1955
5% Preferred $100 par called for redemption 07/01/1963
Common $5 par changed to new Common no par and (1) additional share issued 04/08/1968
Common no par split (2) for (1) by issuance of (1) additional share 09/22/1978
Common no par split (2) for (1) by issuance of (1) additional share 08/16/1985
Common no par split (2) for (1) by issuance of (1) additional share 12/05/1986
Stock Dividend - 10% 01/29/1954
Merged into ARC America Corp. 05/01/1987
Each share Common no par exchanged for $30.625 cash

AMERICAN AGRI FUELS CORP (MO)
Charter forfeited for failure to file reports 01/01/1986

AMERICAN AGRI-TECHNOLOGY CORP (CANADA)
Involuntarily dissolved for failure to file annual returns 06/10/2004

AMERICAN AGRICULTURAL CHEMICAL CO. (CT)
Reorganized under the laws of Delaware 01/02/1931
Each share 6% Preferred exchanged for (1) share Common no par
Each share old Common exchanged for (0.1) share new Common no par
American Agricultural Chemical Co. (DE) merged into Continental Oil Co. (DE) 10/21/1963 which name changed to Conoco Inc. 07/02/1979 which was acquired by Du Pont (E.I.) De Nemours & Co. 09/30/1981

AMERICAN AGRICULTURAL CHEMICAL CO. (DE)
Common no par exchanged (3) for (1) 00/00/1938
Common no par split (3) for (1) by the issuance of (2) additional shares 05/08/1959
Merged into Continental Oil Co. (DE) 10/21/1963
Each share Common no par exchanged for (1) share $2 Conv. Preferred no par
Continental Oil Co. (DE) name changed to Conoco Inc. 07/02/1979 which was acquired by Du Pont (E.I.) De Nemours & Co. 09/30/1981

AMERICAN AGRONOMICS CATTLE CORP. (FL)
Name changed to Kaplan Industries, Inc. 08/03/1981
Kaplan Industries, Inc. name changed to Grand Lux, Inc. 11/06/2003 which recapitalized as World Hockey Association Corp. 09/23/2005

AMERICAN AGRONOMICS CORP (FL)
Common 10¢ par changed to $0.06666666 par and (0.5) additional share issued 01/31/1969
Common $0.06666666 par split (2) for (1) by issuance of (1) additional share 09/30/1979
Common $0.06666666 par split (3) for (2) by issuance of (0.5) additional share 02/29/1980
Common $0.06666666 par changed to 5¢ par 04/18/1980
Common 5¢ par split (2) for (1) by issuance of (1) additional share 08/15/1980
Common 5¢ par split (2) for (1) by issuance of (1) additional share 07/15/1981
Stock Dividends - 50% 02/24/1970; 10% 08/18/1978
Reorganized as Orange-Co, Inc. 04/29/1987
Each share Common 5¢ par exchanged for (0.1) share Common 50¢ par
(See Orange-Co. Inc.)

AMERICAN AGY FINL CORP (GA)
Merged into Vereinigte Haftpflicht Versicherung 12/27/1979
Each share Common $1 par exchanged for $2.2033351 cash

AMERICAN AGY LIFE INS CO (GA)
Under plan of reorganization each share Common $1 par automatically became (1) share American Agency Financial Corp. Common $1 par 08/11/1969
(See American Agency Financial Corp.)

AMERICAN AIR FILTER INC (DE)
Class A, B & C Common no par changed to $1 par 00/00/1939
Each share Class A, B & C Common $1 par exchanged for (2) shares Common $1 par 00/00/1946
5% Preference called for redemption 01/05/1959
Common $1 par split (2) for (1) by issuance of (1) additional share 03/12/1959
7% Preferred called for redemption 07/05/1959
Common $1 par split (2) for (1) by issuance of (1) additional share 10/17/1966
Common $1 par split (2) for (1) by issuance of (1) additional share 04/10/1972
Merged into Allis-Chalmers Corp. 10/02/1978
Each share Common $1 par exchanged for $34 cash

AMERICAN AIRCARRIERS SUPPORT INC (DE)
Petition under Chapter 11 bankruptcy proceedings dismissed 03/01/2003
Stockholders' equity unlikely

AMERICAN AIRCRAFT, INC. (CO)
Charter revoked for failure to file reports and pay fees 10/17/1967

AMERICAN AIRCRAFT CORP (OR)
Each share Common $0.001 par exchanged for (0.25) share Common $0.004 par 01/19/1988
Each share Common $0.004 par exchanged for (0.2) share Common 2¢ par 12/14/1992
Reincorporated under the laws of Nevada as Hunter Aircraft Corp. 09/27/1996
Hunter Aircraft Corp. recapitalized as Prepaid Depot Inc. 08/18/2001 which recapitalized as Reed Holdings Corp. 07/30/2002 which name changed to Ostara Corp., Inc. 03/12/2004 which name changed to Rheologics Technologies, Inc. 10/18/2005 which name changed to KKS Venture Management, Inc. 07/24/2007 which recapitalized as Codima, Inc. 06/09/2008
(See Codima, Inc.)

AMERICAN AIRLS GROUP INC (DE)
Each share Mandatory Conv. Preferred Ser. A 1¢ par (approximately 26.6% of total holdings) automatically became (0.989906) share Common 1¢ par 01/09/2014
Each share Mandatory Conv. Preferred Ser. A 1¢ par (approximately 39.73% of total holdings) exchanged for (0.60271906) share Mandatory Conv. Preferred Ser. A 1¢ par and (0.30676287) share Common 1¢ par 02/10/2014
Each share Mandatory Conv. Preferred Ser. A 1¢ par (approximately 4.15% of total holdings) exchanged for (0.29517468) share Mandatory Conv. Preferred Ser. A 1¢ par and (0.52934866) share Common 1¢ par 03/10/2014
Each share Mandatory Conv. Preferred Ser. A 1¢ par (remaining balance of total holdings) exchanged for (0.7548805) share Common 1¢ par 04/09/2014
(Additional Information in Active)

AMERICAN AIRLS INC (DE)
Each share Common $10 par exchanged for (2) shares Common $5 par 00/00/1944
Each share Common $5 par exchanged for (5) shares Common $1 par 00/00/1946
3.5% Preferred $100 par called for redemption 06/01/1967
Common $1 par split (2) for (1) by issuance of (1) additional share 06/30/1967
Each Depositary Receipt (issued per merger of Trans Caribbean Airways, Inc.) exchanged for (0.029) share Common $1 par 05/31/1974
Under plan of reorganization each share $2.1875 Preferred no par and Common $1 par automatically became (1) share AMR Corp. $2.1875 Preferred no par and Common $1 par respectively 10/01/1982
(See AMR Corp.)

AMERICAN AQUATECH INTL INC (BC)
Struck off register and declared dissolved for failure to file returns 10/09/1992

AMERICAN ARCH CO., INC. (NY)
Liquidation completed
Each share Capital Stock no par received initial distribution of $8 cash 07/22/1950
Each share Capital Stock no par received second distribution of $4 cash 12/15/1950
Each share Capital Stock no par received third distribution of $5 cash 06/15/1951
Each share Capital Stock no par received fourth and final distribution of $0.46 cash 05/15/1953
Note: Certificates were not required to be surrendered and are without value

AMERICAN ARCH CO. (DE)
Liquidation completed
Each share Capital Stock no par received initial distribution of (1) share American Arch Co., Inc. Capital Stock no par and $32.50 cash 01/14/1950
Each share Capital Stock no par received second distribution of $6 cash 12/15/1950
Each share Capital Stock no par received third distribution of $1 cash 06/15/1951
Each share Capital Stock no par received fourth and final distribution of $0.12 cash 05/15/1953
Note: Certificates were not required to be surrendered and are without value

AMERICAN ARCHITECTURAL PRODS INC (DE)
Plan of reorganization under Chapter 11 Federal Bankruptcy Code effective 08/04/2003
No stockholders' equity

AMERICAN ARLINGTON BK (JACKSONVILLE, FL)
99.97% held by American Banks of Florida, Inc. through exchange offer which expired 06/30/1974
Public interest eliminated

AMERICAN ARMS INC (UT)
Name changed to American Industries Inc. 03/29/1988
American Industries Inc. name changed to Dolce Ventures Inc. 05/21/2002 which recapitalized as Sino Gas International Holdings, Inc. 11/17/2006
(See Sino Gas International Holdings, Inc.)

AMERICAN ART METALS CO. (DE)
6% Preferred $100 par called for redemption 01/22/1959
Class A Common and Common $1 par split (2) for (1) by issuance of (1) additional share 12/15/1961
Name changed to Amarlite Corp. and Class A Common $1 par reclassified as Common $1 par 03/07/1962
Amarlite Corp. acquired by Anaconda Co. 07/09/1963 which merged into Atlantic Richfield Co. (PA) 01/13/1977 which reincorporated in Delaware 05/07/1985 which merged into BP Amoco PLC 04/18/2000 which name changed to BP PLC 05/01/2001

AMERICAN ARTISTS ENTMT CORP (MO)
Name changed 02/05/1999
Name changed from American Artists Film Corp./Setab Alpha Inc. to American Artists Entertainment Corp. 02/05/1999
Charter dissolved 03/24/2000

AMERICAN ARTS & CRAFTS INC (TX)
Name changed to Salem National Corp. 06/03/1976
(See Salem National Corp.)

AMERICAN ASBESTOS URANIUM CORP. LTD. (QC)
Charter annulled for failure to file reports 11/20/1976

AMERICAN ASPHALT ROOF CORP. (MO)
Merged into Ruberoid Co. on a share for share basis 09/30/1952
Ruberoid Co. merged into General Aniline & Film Corp. 05/26/1967 which name changed to GAF Corp. 04/24/1968
(See GAF Corp.)

AMERICAN ASSET DEV INC (NV)
SEC revoked common stock regsitration 01/17/2014

AMERICAN ASSET MGMT CORP (NJ)
Each share old Common no par exchanged for (0.2) share new Common no par 02/21/1995
Stock Dividend - 41.25% 04/22/1994
SEC revoked common stock registration 03/30/2011

AMERICAN ASSET YIELD FD (MA)
Out of business 00/00/1985
Details not available

AMERICAN ASSETS, INC. (LA)
Liquidation completed
Each share Common $1 par exchanged for initial distribution of $24 cash 01/21/1982
Each share Common $1 par received second and final distribution of $0.35 cash 08/16/1983

AMERICAN ASSETS INC (CO)
Name changed to Elana, Inc. 09/16/1987

AMERICAN ASSOC GROUP INC (NV)
Recapitalized as Clean Hydrogen Producers, Ltd. 06/11/2007
Each share Common $0.0001 par exchanged for (0.16666666) share Common $0.0001 par
Clean Hydrogen Producers, Ltd. name changed to Golden Developing Solutions, Inc. 09/27/2017

AMERICAN ASSOCIATED INDUSTRIES, INC. (DE)
Charter cancelled and declared inoperative and void for non-payment of taxes 04/15/1972

AMERICAN ASSOCIATION OLD LINE LIFE INSURANCE CO. (TN)
Each share old Common $1 par exchanged for (0.5) share new Common $1 par 12/21/1966
Merged into American Pyramid Companies Inc. 12/10/1969

Each share new Common $1 par exchanged for (1.25) shares Common no par
American Pyramid Companies Inc. merged into American Consolidated Corp. 02/28/1977 which merged into I.C.H. Corp. 04/18/1985 which name changed to Southwestern Life Corp. (New) 06/15/1994 which name changed to I.C.H. Corp. (New) 10/10/1995
(See I.C.H. Corp. (New))

AMERICAN ASSURN UNDERWRITERS GROUP INC (FL)
Each share Common $0.00001 par exchanged for (0.2) share Common $0.00005 par 09/25/1987
Proclaimed dissolved for failure to file reports and pay fees 10/13/1989

AMERICAN ATLANTIC CO (PA)
Acquired by Weeks Marine, Inc. 07/25/2011
Each share Common $2.50 par exchanged for $47.796 cash

AMERICAN ATLAS RES CORP (DE)
SEC revoked common stock registration 11/01/2010

AMERICAN ATM CORP (FL)
Old Common $0.001 par split (5) for (4) by issuance of (0.25) additional share payable 01/05/1998 to holders of record 12/22/1997
Each share old Common $0.001 par exchanged for (0.02) share new Common $0.001 par 01/25/2000
Name changed to American Wireless Web Corp. 04/07/2000
(See American Wireless Web Corp.)

AMERICAN AURUM INC (NV)
Reincorporated 05/04/1995
Each share old Common 5¢ par exchanged for (0.002) share new Common 5¢ par 05/04/1995
State of incorporation changed from (UT) to (NV) 06/07/1995
Name changed to AWG, Ltd. 12/18/1995
(See AWG, Ltd.)

AMERICAN AUSTIN CAR CO., INC.
Liquidated 00/00/1935
Details not available

AMERICAN AUTO STORES, INC. (MO)
Acquired by Goodyear Tire & Rubber Co. on a (0.22946) for (1) basis 03/29/1963

AMERICAN AUTOMATIC VENDING CORP (OH)
Name changed to AAV Companies 06/27/1972
AAV Companies name changed to Tranzonic Companies 12/13/1983
(See Tranzonic Companies)

AMERICAN AUTOMATION TRAINING CTRS INC (DE)
Name changed to Coleman American Companies, Inc. 10/11/1971
(See Coleman American Companies, Inc.)

AMERICAN AUTOMOBILE LEASING CORP (TX)
Charter cancelled and dissolved by Court Order 06/20/1969
No stockholders' equity

AMERICAN B&T CORP. (DE)
Stock Dividends - 20% 03/30/1971; 20% 12/20/1971; 10% 12/21/1972; 10% 12/30/1974
Adjudicated bankrupt 05/15/1979
Stockholders' equity unlikely

AMERICAN BAKERIES CO. (FL)
$2 Conv. Class A no par called for redemption 03/27/1944
Class B no par changed to Capital Stock no par and (1) additional share issued 04/24/1944
Capital Stock no par split (2) for (1) by issuance of (1) additional share 06/04/1946

Merged into American Bakeries Co. (DE) 06/15/1953
Each share Capital Stock no par exchanged for (0.1) share 4.5% Preferred $100 par and (1) share Common no par
(See American Bakeries Co. (DE))

AMERICAN BAKERIES CO (DE)
4.5% Preferred $100 par called for redemption 06/15/1959
5% Conv. Preferred $100 par called for redemption 01/27/1986
Stock Dividend - 10% 12/31/1981
$1.80 Prior Preferred $25 par called for redemption 12/12/1986
Merged into BCA Corp. 12/15/1986
Each share Common no par exchanged for $44 cash

AMERICAN BAKERIES CORP. (FL)
Name changed to American Bakeries Co. (FL) 00/00/1938
American Bakeries Co. (FL) merged into American Bakeries Co. (DE) 06/15/1953
(See American Bakeries Co. (DE))

AMERICAN BALANCED FD INC (MD)
Reincorporated under the laws of Delaware as American Balanced Fund and Common $1 par reclassified as Class A 03/01/2010

AMERICAN BANCORP (NJ)
Stock Dividends - 10% 01/15/1975; 10% 01/15/1976
Liquidation completed
Each share Common $2 par received initial distribution of $7.09 cash 01/03/1977
Each share Common $2 par exchanged for second distribution of $0.72 cash 05/29/1980
Each share Common $2 par received third and final distribution of $0.095 cash 04/05/1981

AMERICAN BANCORP INC (CT)
Stock Dividend - 10% 03/31/1986
Merged into Constitution Bancorp of New England, Inc. 05/31/1988
Each share Common $5 par exchanged for (1.5) shares Common $1 par
Constitution Bancorp of New England, Inc. name changed to Lafayette American Bancorp, Inc. 05/21/1991 which reorganized as Lafayette American Bank & Trust Co. (Hamden, CT) 02/23/1994 which merged into HUBCO, Inc. 07/01/1996 which name changed to Hudson United Bancorp 04/21/1999 which merged into TD Banknorth Inc. 01/31/2006
(See TD Banknorth Inc.)

AMERICAN BANCORP INC (LA)
Reverted to private company 09/29/2004
Each share Common $5 par exchanged for $140.24 cash

AMERICAN BANCORP INC (PA)
Merged into Meridian Bancorp, Inc. 06/30/1983
Each share Capital Stock $5 par exchanged for (0.5) share Common $5 par
Meridian Bancorp, Inc. merged into CoreStates Financial Corp 04/09/1996 which merged into First Union Corp. 04/28/1998 which name changed to Wachovia Corp. (Ctfs. dated after 09/01/2001) 09/01/2001 which merged into Wells Fargo & Co. (New) 12/31/2008

AMERICAN BANCORP NEV (NV)
Common 10¢ par split (4) for (3) by issuance of (0.33333333) additional share 04/11/1995
Stock Dividends - 15% 04/10/1990; 15% 04/09/1991; 10% 04/07/1992; 15% 04/19/1993; 15% 04/12/1994; 15% payable 04/09/1996 to holders of record 04/02/1996

Merged into First Security Corp. 06/30/1997
Each share Common 10¢ par exchanged for (0.9054) share Common $1.25 par
First Security Corp. merged into Wells Fargo & Co. (New) 10/26/2000

AMERICAN BANCORP NJ INC (NJ)
Acquired by Investors Bancorp, Inc. (Old) 05/31/2009
Each share Common 10¢ par exchanged for (0.9218) share Common 1¢ par
Investors Bancorp, Inc. (Old) reorganized as Investors Bancorp, Inc. (New) 05/07/2014

AMERICAN BANCORPORATION (OH)
7% Conv. Preferred Ser. A $100 par called for redemption 05/00/1976
Common no par split (5) for (2) by issuance of (1.5) additional shares 04/24/1968
Each share old Common no par exchanged for (0.2) share new Common no par 06/01/1981
Each share new Common no par exchanged again for (0.1) share new Common no par 12/15/1988
New Common no par split (2) for (1) by issuance of (1) additional share 03/16/1994
New Common no par split (2) for (1) by issuance of (1) additional share payable 10/23/1997 to holders of record 10/08/1997
Stock Dividends - 10% 01/10/1969; 10% 02/20/1973
Merged into WesBanco, Inc. 03/01/2002
Each share new Common no par exchanged for (1.1) shares Common $2.0833 par

AMERICAN BANCORPORATION INC ST PAUL MINN (DE)
Merged into Firstar Corp. 07/12/1996
Each share Common no par exchanged for (4.146) shares Common $1.25 par and $40.164 cash
Firstar Corp. merged into Firstar Corp. (New) 11/20/1998 which merged into U.S. Bancorp (DE) 02/27/2001

AMERICAN BANCSERVICE CORP (FL)
Name changed to Diagonal Data Corp. 12/05/1984
(See Diagonal Data Corp.)

AMERICAN BANCSHARES (NC)
Acquired by First Union Corp. 05/31/1994
Each share Common $1 par exchanged for (0.211) share Common $3.33333333 par
First Union Corp. name changed to Wachovia Corp. (Ctfs. dated after 09/01/2001) 09/01/2001 which merged into Wells Fargo & Co. (New) 12/31/2008

AMERICAN BANCSHARES HOUMA INC (LA)
Merged into Regions Financial Corp. (Old) 09/12/1996
Each share Common $3 par exchanged for (1.66) shares Common $0.625 par
Regions Financial Corp. (Old) merged into Regions Financial Corp. (New) 07/01/2004

AMERICAN BANCSHARES INC (FL)
Merged into Gold Banc Corp., Inc. 03/20/2000
Each share Common $1.175 par exchanged for (1.6527) shares Common $1 par
Gold Banc Corp., Inc. merged into Marshall & Ilsley Corp. (Old) 04/01/2006
(See Marshall & Ilsley Corp. (Old))

AMERICAN BANCSHARES INC (FL)
Name changed to Great American Banks, Inc. 06/25/1980
(See Great American Banks, Inc.)

AMERICAN BANK & TRUST CO. (SOUTH BEND, IN)
Name changed to American National Bank & Trust Co. (South Bend, IN) 09/09/1968
(See American National Bank & Trust Co. (South Bend, IN))

AMERICAN BK & TR CO (BATON ROUGE, LA)
Stock Dividends - 50% 12/15/1954; 10% 12/15/1955; 10% 12/16/1957; 10% 12/15/1958; 10% 12/16/1960; 10% 01/02/1965
Reorganized as Great American Corp. 01/17/1970
Each share Capital Stock $10 par exchanged for (1) share Common $10 par
(See Great American Corp.)

AMERICAN BK & TR CO (CA)
Charter suspended for failure to file reports and pay fees 1/3/95

AMERICAN BK & TR CO (DALLAS, TX)
Stock Dividends - 14.28571428% 02/13/1962; 20% 08/20/1964
Merged into First International Bancshares, Inc. 08/02/1973
Each share Capital Stock $10 par exchanged for (1.9) shares Common $5 par
First International Bancshares, Inc. name changed to InterFirst Corp. 12/31/1981 which merged into First RepublicBank Corp. 06/06/1987
(See First RepublicBank Corp.)

AMERICAN BK & TR CO (LAFAYETTE, LA)
Stock Dividends - 50% 11/30/1979; 33.33333333% 11/29/1980
Under plan of reorganization each share Common $10 par automatically became (4) shares Acadiana Bancshares, Inc. Common $2.50 par 07/01/1981
(See Acadiana Bancshares Inc.)

AMERICAN BK & TR CO (LANSING, MI)
Common $20 par changed to $10 par and (1) additional share issued 03/03/1964
Stock Dividends - 10% 02/01/1944; 25% 01/23/1953; 10% 02/17/1961; 10% 01/21/1967; 10% 06/02/1969; 10% 02/16/1971; 10% 05/30/1972
Reorganized as American Bankcorp, Inc. 10/01/1973
Each share Common $10 par exchanged for (1) share Common $10 par
American Bankcorp, Inc. merged into First American Bank Corp. 02/13/1978 which name changed to First of America Bank Corp. 01/14/1983 which merged into National City Corp. 03/31/1998 which was acquired by PNC Financial Services Group, Inc. 12/31/2008

AMERICAN BK & TR CO (MARION, IN)
Acquired by Summcorp 02/28/1986
Each share Capital Stock $10 par exchanged for $9.50 cash

AMERICAN BK & TR CO (MONROE, NC)
Merged into United Carolina Bancshares Corp. 07/31/1970
Each share Capital Stock $5 par exchanged for (1.2) shares Common $5 par
United Carolina Bancshares merged into BB&T Corp. 07/01/1997

AMERICAN BK & TR CO (NEW YORK, NY)
Class A Common $10 par reclassified as Common $10 par 03/29/1968
Stock Dividends - 20% 03/31/1969; 20% 02/26/1970
Under plan of reorganization each share Common $10 par automatically became (1) share American B&T Corp. Common $10 par 05/01/1970
(See American B&T Corp.)

AMERICAN BK & TR CO (ORANGEBURG, SC)
Each share Common $10 par exchanged for (3) shares Common $5 par to effect a (2) for (1) split and a 50% stock dividend 02/27/1970
Common $5 par changed to $2.50 par and (1) additional share issued 03/15/1972
Reorganized as American Bank Trust Shares, Inc. 12/30/1972
Each share Common $2.50 par exchanged for (1) share Common $2.50 par
American Bank Trust Shares, Inc. name changed to ABTS, Inc. 07/02/1981 which merged into MNC Financial, Inc. 11/30/1989 which merged into NationsBank Corp. 10/01/1993 which reincorporated in Delaware as BankAmerica Corp. (Old) 09/25/1998 which merged into BankAmerica Corp. (New) 09/30/1998 which name changed to Bank of America Corp. 04/28/1999

AMERICAN BK & TR CO (SHREVEPORT, LA)
Declared insolvent and taken over by the FDIC 01/11/1991
Stockholders' equity unlikely

AMERICAN BK & TR CO PA (READING, PA)
Stock Dividends - 100% 11/16/1970; 10% 05/12/1975; 10% 05/26/1978; 10% 02/15/1979; 10% 05/09/1980; 10% 07/01/1981
Under plan of reorganization each share Capital Stock $5 par automatically became (1) share American Bancorp, Inc. Capital Stock $5 par 09/02/1981
American Bancorp, Inc. merged into Meridian Bancorp, Inc. 06/30/1983 which merged into CoreStates Financial Corp 04/09/1996 which merged into First Union Corp. 04/28/1998 which name changed to Wachovia Corp. (Ctfs. dated after 09/01/2001) 09/01/2001 which merged into Wells Fargo & Co. (New) 12/31/2008

AMERICAN BK & TR INC (BOWLING GREEN, KY)
Merged into Ambanc Holding Co. 04/17/2001
Each share Common $2 par exchanged for (1) share Common $2 par

AMERICAN BK (ALLENTOWN, PA)
Reorganized as American Bank Inc. 01/02/2002
Each share Common $2.50 par exchanged for (1) share Common 10¢ par

AMERICAN BK (ATLANTA, GA)
Name changed to Peoples American Bank (Atlanta, GA) 10/02/1968
Peoples American Bank (Atlanta, GA) name changed to First Georgia Bank (Atlanta, GA) 03/31/1972 which was acquired by First Georgia Bancshares, Inc. 08/01/1973 which merged into First Railroad & Banking Co. of Georgia 06/26/1986 which was acquired by First Union Corp. 11/01/1986 which name changed to Wachovia Corp. (Ctfs. dated after 09/01/2001) 09/01/2001 which merged into Wells Fargo &

AMERICAN BK (BRADENTON, FL)
Under plan of reorganization each share Common $1.175 par automatically became (1) share American Bancshares, Inc. Common $1.175 par 02/05/1996
American Bancshares, Inc. merged into Gold Banc Corp., Inc. 03/20/2000 which merged into Marshall & Ilsley Corp. (Old) 04/01/2006
(See Marshall & Ilsley Corp. (Old))

AMERICAN BK COMM (ALBUQUERQUE, NM)
Capital Stock $10 par changed to $6 par 12/29/1964
Through voluntary purchase and exchange offers Bank Securities, Inc. held 100% as of 12/31/1972
Public interest eliminated

AMERICAN BK COMM (EL PASO, TX)
Reorganized as American Southwest Bancshares, Inc. 12/17/1982
Each share Common $5 par exchanged for (1) share Common $5 par
(See American Southwest Bancshares, Inc.)

AMERICAN BK CONN (WATERBURY, CT)
Capital Stock $1 par split (2) for (1) by issuance of (1) additional share 05/23/1986
Capital Stock $1 par split (2) for (1) by issuance of (1) additional share payable 04/24/1998 to holders of record 04/10/1998 Ex date - 04/27/1998
Stock Dividend - 100% 10/19/1984
Merged into American Financial Holdings, Inc. 01/18/2002
Each share Common $1 par exchanged for $30 cash

AMERICAN BK HLDGS INC (DE)
Each share old Common $0.001 par exchanged for (0.0005) share new Common $0.001 par 03/02/2007
Note: Holders of (1,999) or fewer pre-split shares received $12.50 cash per share
Merged into Congressional Bancshares Inc. 02/19/2016
Each share new Common $0.001 par exchanged for (2,375) shares Common
Note: Congressional Bancshares Inc. is privately held

AMERICAN BK MD (SILVER SPRING, MD)
Under plan of merger name changed to First American Bank of Maryland (Silver Spring, MD) 12/31/1978
(See First American Bank of Maryland (Silver Spring, MD))

AMERICAN BK NT CO (NY)
Common $10 par changed to $5 par and (1) additional share issued 05/16/1962
Acquired by International Banknote Co., Inc. 02/07/1973
Each share 6% Preferred $50 par exchanged for $50 cash
Each share Common $5 par exchanged for $22 cash

AMERICAN BK NT HOLOGRAPHICS INC NEW (DE)
Merged into JDS Uniphase Corp. 02/13/2008
Each share Common 1¢ par exchanged for (0.4479) share Common $0.001 par and $1 cash
JDS Uniphase Corp. name changed to Viavi Solutions Inc. 08/04/2015

AMERICAN BK NT HOLOGRAPHICS INC OLD (DE)
Plan of reorganization under Chapter 11 Federal Bankruptcy Code effective 10/01/2002
Each share Common 1¢ par received an undetermined amount of American Banknote Corp. new Common 1¢ par and Common Stock Purchase Warrants Ser. 1 and Ser. 2 which expired 10/01/2007
(See American Banknote Corp.)

AMERICAN BANK OF COMMERCE (AKRON, OH)
Name changed to Centran Bank (Akron, OH) 07/01/1974
(See Centran Bank (Akron, OH))

AMERICAN BANK OF HOLLYWOOD (HOLLYWOOD, FL)
Under plan of reorganization each share Common $10 par automatically became (1) share Ameribank Bancshares, Inc. Common $5 par 08/31/1983
Ameribank Bancshares, Inc. merged into Wachovia Corp. (New) (Ctfs. dated between 05/20/1991 and 09/01/2001) 04/01/1998 which merged into Wachovia Corp. (Ctfs. dated after 09/01/2001) 09/01/2001 which merged into Wells Fargo & Co. (New) 12/31/2008

AMERICAN BANK STATIONERY CO. (MD)
Merged into Mosler Safe Co. 04/01/1966
Each share Common $1.25 par exchanged for (2) shares Common $1 par
(See Mosler Safe Co.)

AMERICAN BANK STOCKS TRUST SHARES
Trust terminated 05/01/1945
Details not available

AMERICAN BK THREE RIVERS (THREE RIVERS, MI)
Merged into American National Holding Co. 01/29/1973
Each share Common $10 par exchanged for (1) share Common $10 par
American National Holding Co. merged into Old Kent Financial Corp. 07/31/1986 which merged into Fifth Third Bancorp 04/02/2001

AMERICAN BANK TRUST SHARES, INC. (SC)
Common $2.50 par changed to $1 par 00/00/1981
Name changed to ABTS, Inc. 07/02/1981
ABTS, Inc. merged into MNC Financial, Inc. 11/30/1989 which merged into NationsBank Corp. 10/01/1993 which reincorporated in Delaware as BankAmerica Corp. (Old) 09/25/1998 which merged into BankAmerica Corp. (New) 09/30/1998 which name changed to Bank of America Corp. 04/28/1999

AMERICAN BANKCORP INC (MI)
Stock Dividend - 50% 05/30/1974
Merged into First American Bank Corp. 02/13/1978
Each share Common $10 par exchanged for (1.485) shares Common $10 par
First American Bank Corp. name changed to First of America Bank Corp. 01/14/1983 which merged into National City Corp. 03/31/1998 which was acquired by PNC Financial Services Group, Inc. 12/31/2008

AMERICAN BANKERS INS CO FLA (FL)
Each share Class A Common $10 par or Class B Common $10 par exchanged for (8) shares Class A Common $2.50 par or Class B Common $2.50 par to effect a (4) for (1) split and 100% stock dividend 09/07/1955
8% Preferred $10 par called for redemption 12/07/1961
Each share Class B Common $2.50 par exchanged for (0.909091) share Class A Common $2.50 par 05/28/1967
Class A Common $2.50 par reclassified as Common $2.50 par 11/28/1967
Common $2.50 par changed to $1 par and (1.5) additional shares issued 12/18/1972
Stock Dividends - Paid on Class A & B Common in Class A Common - 50% 12/11/1959; 25% 12/16/1960; 20% 12/27/1961; 25% 12/20/1963; 20% 12/22/1964; 20% 12/22/1965; 10% 12/21/1966
Common - 10% 12/22/1967; 20% 12/20/1968; 15% 12/23/1969; 15% 12/22/1970; 15% 12/21/1971; 20% 12/14/1973
Reorganized as American Bankers Insurance Group, Inc. 12/02/1980
Each share Common $1 par exchanged for (1.03) shares Common $1 par
(See American Bankers Insurance Group, Inc.)

AMERICAN BANKERS INS GROUP INC (FL)
Common $1 par split (2) for (1) by issuance of (1) additional share payable 09/12/1997 to holders of record 08/29/1997 Ex date - 09/15/1997
Merged into Fortis NL 08/18/1999
Each share $3.125 Conv. Preferred Ser. B $1 par exchanged for $109.857 cash
Each share Common $1 par exchanged for $55 cash

AMERICAN BANKERS INVESTMENT CO.
Dissolved 00/00/1930
Details not available

AMERICAN BANKERS LIFE ASSURN CO FLA (FL)
Each share Class A Common $10 par or Class B Common $10 par exchanged for (10) shares Class A Common $1 par or Class B Common $1 par respectively 05/15/1956
Class A Common $1 par and Class B Common $1 par reclassified as Common $1 par 09/17/1958
Stock Dividends - 10% 06/01/1962; 10% 05/01/1963; 10% 05/29/1964; 10% 05/28/1965; 10% 05/27/1966; 10% 05/27/1967; 10% 05/24/1968; 10% 05/16/1969; 10% 05/29/1970; 10% 05/28/1971; 10% 05/29/1972; 15% 05/28/1973; 15% 05/30/1974; 15% 05/23/1975; 15% 05/21/1976; 10% 05/25/1979; 20% 05/30/1980
Reorganized as American Bankers Insurance Group, Inc. 12/02/1980
Each share Common $1 par exchanged for (1.315) shares Common $1 par
(See American Bankers Insurance Group, Inc.)

AMERICAN BANKNOTE CORP (DE)
Plan of reorganization under Chapter 11 Federal Bankruptcy Code effective 10/01/2002
Each old Preferred Ser. B received (0.02121342) share new Common 1¢ par, (0.00721293) Common Stock Purchase Warrant Ser. 1 expiring 10/1/2007, and (0.00721252) Common Stock Purchase Warrant Ser. 2 expiring 10/01/2007
Each old Common 1¢ par received (0.02121349) share new Common 1¢ par, (0.00721272) Common Stock Purchase Warrant Ser. 1 expiring 10/01/2007, and (0.00721272) Common Stock Purchase Warrant Ser. 2 expiring 10/01/2007

Note: Certificates not required to be surrendered and are without value
Plan of reorganization under Chapter 11 Federal Bankruptcy Code effective 04/15/2005
Each share new Common 1¢ par held by holders of (500,000) or more exchanged for (0.023115) share new Common and $0.3564 cash
Each share new Common 1¢ par held by holders of (499,999) shares or fewer exchanged for $0.63183 cash
Note: Unexchanged certificates were cancelled and became without value 04/15/2006
The reorganized company is now private

AMERICAN BKS FLA INC (FL)
Merged into SouthTrust Corp. 06/19/1998
Each share Class A Common $1 par exchanged for (3.23574794) shares Common $2.50 par
Each share Class B Common $1 par exchanged for (3.23574794) shares Common $2.50 par
Note: An additional final distribution of (0.1941885) share Common $2.50 par per share was made 12/21/1998
Southtrust Corp. merged into Wachovia Corp. (Ctfs. dated after 09/01/2001) 11/01/2004 which merged into Wells Fargo & Co. (New) 12/31/2008

AMERICAN BANKSHARES CORP. (WI)
Capital Stock $20 par changed to $10 par and (1) additional share issued 05/04/1966
Capital Stock $10 par changed to $5 par and (1) additional share issued 05/04/1970 Declared insolvent 10/21/1975
No stockholders' equity

AMERICAN BANKSHARES INC (GA)
Name changed to Riverside Bancshares Inc. 08/19/1998
Riverside Bancshares Inc. merged into Synovus Financial Corp. 03/24/2006

AMERICAN BANTAM CAR CO. (PA)
Common no par changed to $1 par 06/24/1945
Common $1 par reclassified as Class A $1 par 07/06/1948
Reorganized 01/17/1955
Each share Class A $1 par exchanged for (1) share Common $1 par
Class B no par had no equity
Under plan of merger name changed to Pressed Metals of America, Inc. (PA) and
Common $1 par changed to 10¢ par 05/15/1956
Pressed Metals of America, Inc. (PA) recapitalized as Klion (H.L.) Inc. (PA) 10/17/1960 which reincorporated in New York 10/31/1963 which was acquired by Korvette (E.J.), Inc. 08/23/1965 which merged into Spartans Industries, Inc. (NY) 09/25/1966 which merged into Arlen Realty & Development Corp. 02/26/1971 which name changed to Arlen Corp. 10/16/1985
(See Arlen Corp.)

AMERICAN BARGE LINE CO. (DE)
Merged into American Commercial Barge Line Co. 08/01/1957
Each share Common exchanged for (1.6116) shares Common $3 par
American Commercial Barge Line Co. name changed to American Commercial Lines Inc. 04/30/1964 which merged into Texas Gas Transmission Corp. 05/15/1968
(See Texas Gas Transmission Corp.)

AMERICAN BARRICK RES CORP (ON)
Common no par split (2) for (1) by issuance of (1) additional share 07/15/1987
$0.114 Conv. 1st Preferred Ser. A no par called for redemption 11/30/1987
Common no par split (2) for (1) by issuance of (1) additional share 12/29/1989
Common no par split (2) for (1) by issuance of (1) additional share 03/01/1993
Name changed to Barrick Gold Corp. 01/18/1995

AMERICAN BASIC-BUSINESS SHARES CORP.
Merged into Administrative & Research Corp. 00/00/1932
Details not available

AMERICAN BEACH BLVD BK (JACKSONVILLE, FL)
Merged into American Banks of Florida, Inc. 00/00/1974
Each share Common exchanged for (2.5491) shares Class A Common $1 par and (0.0025491) share Class B Common $1 par
American Banks of Florida, Inc. merged into SouthTrust Corp. 06/19/1998 which merged into Wachovia Corp. (Ctfs. dated after 09/01/2001) 11/01/2004 which merged into Wells Fargo & Co. (New) 12/31/2008

AMERICAN BEAUTY HOMES, INC. (DE)
No longer in existence having become inoperative and void for non-payment of taxes 04/01/1958

AMERICAN BEEF PACKERS INC (DE)
Reincorporated 12/30/1969
State of incorporation changed from (IA) to (DE) 12/30/1969
Name changed to Sudbury Holdings, Inc. and Common $1 par changed to 1¢ par 08/18/1983
Sudbury Holdings, Inc. reorganized as Sudbury, Inc. 05/27/1987
(See Sudbury, Inc.)

AMERICAN BEET SUGAR CO. (NJ)
Name changed to American Crystal Sugar Co. 07/26/1934
(See American Crystal Sugar Co.)

AMERICAN BEMBERG CORP.
Merged into Beaunit Mills, Inc. 08/10/1949
Each share Common no par exchanged for (1) share $1.25 Preferred no par
4.5% Class A Preferred $100 par called for redemption 10/14/1949
Class B Preferred $100 par called for redemption 10/14/1949
Beaunit Mills, Inc. name changed to Beaunit Corp. 06/29/1962 which merged into El Paso Natural Gas Co. 10/11/1967 which reorganized as El Paso Co. 06/13/1974 which merged into Burlington Northern Inc. 12/13/1983
(See Burlington Northern Inc.)

AMERICAN BENEFITS GROUP INC (FL)
Common no par split (3) for (1) by issuance of (2) additional shares payable 02/27/1998 to holders of record 11/11/1997
Name changed to Prom Resources, Inc. 10/19/2006

AMERICAN BENZOL CORP. (DE)
No longer in existence having become inoperative and void for non-payment of taxes 04/01/1931

AMERICAN BERYL CORP. (CO)
Merged into Beryllium International, Inc. 10/17/1961
Each share Common 1¢ par exchanged for (0.1) share Common 1¢ par
Beryllium International, Inc. merged into U.S. Beryllium, Inc. 01/25/1969
(See U.S. Beryllium, Inc.)

AMERICAN BEVERAGE CORP. (DE)
Common no par changed to $5 par 01/00/1933
Common $5 par changed to $1 par 11/00/1933
4% Conv. Preferred $5 par called for redemption 11/30/1965
Prior Preferred $1 par called for redemption 11/30/1965
Merged into Holiday General Corp. 03/22/1968
Each share Common $1 par exchanged for $16 cash

AMERICAN BEVERAGE CORP (NY)
Assets transferred to American Beverage Trust 09/28/1982
(See American Beverage Trust)

AMERICAN BEVERAGE TRUST (NY)
Liquidation completed
Each share Common 50¢ par received initial distribution of $1 cash 11/05/1982
Each share Common 50¢ par received second distribution of $1 cash 08/09/1983
Each share Common 50¢ par received third and final distribution of $1.27877 cash 02/12/1986
Note: Certificates were not required to be surrendered and are without value

AMERICAN BILTRITE INC (DE)
Name changed 05/03/1973
Stock Dividend - 50% 12/22/1964
Name changed from American Biltrite Rubber Co., Inc. to American Biltrite Inc. 05/03/1973
$0.80 2nd Preferred no par called for redemption 06/15/1979
6.5% 1st Preferred $100 par called for redemption 06/15/1979
(Additional Information in Active)

AMERICAN BINGO & GAMING CORP (DE)
Name changed to Littlefield Corp. 06/14/2000

AMERICAN BIO-DENTAL CORP (DE)
Name changed to BioLok International Inc. 08/07/1996
(See BioLok International Inc.)

AMERICAN BIOCHEMICALS CO., INC. (OH)
Charter cancelled for failure to pay taxes 10/30/1968

AMERICAN BIOCULTURE INC (NY)
Capital Stock 10¢ par changed to 2¢ par and (2) additional shares issued 04/24/1969
Adjudicated bankrupt 08/11/1977
Stockholders' equity unlikely

AMERICAN BIODIESEL FUELS CORP (NV)
Name changed to Planet Resource Recovery, Inc. 03/09/2007

AMERICAN BIODYNAMICS INC (BC)
Reincorporated under the laws of Florida as Biodynamics International, Inc. and Common no par changed to 1¢ par 06/01/1992
Biodynamics International, Inc. name changed to Tutogen Medical, Inc. 04/15/1998 which merged into RTI Biologics, Inc. 02/27/2008 which name changed to RTI Surgical, Inc. 07/18/2013

AMERICAN BIODYNE INC (DE)
Merged into Medco Containment Services, Inc. 12/18/1992
Each share Common 1¢ par exchanged for (0.723) share Common 1¢ par
(See Medco Containment Services, Inc.)

AMERICAN BIOGENETIC SCIENCES INC (DE)
Class A Common $0.0001 par reclassified as Common $0.0001 par 11/29/2005
Each share old Common $0.0001 par exchanged for (0.005) share new Common $0.0001 par 05/04/2010
Name changed to USA Equities Corp. 08/24/2015

AMERICAN BIOMATERIALS CORP (VA)
Charter cancelled and proclaimed dissolved for failure to file reports 09/01/1989

AMERICAN BIOMED INC (DE)
Chapter 7 Federal Bankruptcy proceedings terminated 12/14/2004
Stockholders' equity unlikely

AMERICAN BIOMEDICAL CORP (TX)
Liquidation completed
Each share Common no par exchanged for initial distribution of (0.08432) share Revlon, Inc. Common $1 par 05/31/1978
Each share Common no par received second distribution of (0.00011) share Revlon, Inc. Common $1 par 10/15/1978
Each share Common no par received third and final distribution of (0.00937) share Revlon, Inc. Common $1 par 06/15/1979
(See Revlon, Inc.)

AMERICAN BIONETICS INC (CA)
Chapter 11 Federal Bankruptcy proceedings converted to Chapter 7 on 05/24/1991
No stockholders' equity

AMERICAN BIRTHRIGHT TR (MA)
Stock Dividends - 18% 11/29/1979; 20% 11/28/1980
Name changed to ABT Growth & Income Trust 12/01/1984
(See ABT Growth & Income Trust)

AMERICAN BKG CORP (FL)
Merged into Citizens Banking Corp. 06/01/2004
Each share Common 50¢ par exchanged for $48.25 cash

AMERICAN BLDG CTL INC (DE)
Name changed to MDI, Inc. 09/24/2004
(See MDI, Inc.)

AMERICAN BLDG MAINTENANCE INDS (DE)
Reincorporated 05/01/1985
Common no par split (3) for (2) by issuance of (0.5) additional share 07/25/1968
Common no par split (3) for (2) by issuance of (0.5) additional share 03/31/1971
Common no par split (3) for (2) by issuance of (0.5) additional share 02/03/1983
State of incorporation changed from (CA) to (DE) 05/01/1985
Name changed to ABM Industries Inc. 03/16/1994

AMERICAN BLDGS CO (DE)
Ctfs. dated prior to 12/30/1977
Stock Dividend - 10% 06/15/1977
Name changed to ABC Investment Co. 12/30/1977
(See ABC Investment Co.)

AMERICAN BLDGS CO (DE)
Ctfs. dated after 04/27/1994
Merged into Onex Corp. 05/12/1999
Each share Common 1¢ par exchanged for $36 cash

AMERICAN BLOOD PROTN SYS INC (NV)
Name changed to Energex Corp. 03/23/1987

AMERICAN BLOODPRESSURE CTRS INC (NY)
Petition under Chapter 7 Federal Bankruptcy Code filed 11/26/1985

No stockholders' equity

AMERICAN BLOWER CORP.
Acquired by American Radiator Co. 00/00/1928
Details not available

AMERICAN BOARDING CO (DE)
Name changed to Microlin Bio, Inc. 01/14/2016

AMERICAN BOARDSPORTS (NV)
Common $0.0001 par split (3) for (2) by issuance of (0.5) additional share payable 07/26/1999 to holders of record 07/25/1999
Name changed to Sierra Pacific Gypsum Corp. 11/00/1999
Sierra Pacific Gypsum Corp. name changed to Sanitec Holdings USA 06/16/2000 which recapitalized as Co-Media Inc. 11/25/2000 which reorganized as Jarvis Group Inc. 01/18/2002 which name changed to Cash 4 Homes 247 on 05/21/2003 which name changed to Vegas Equity International Corp. 02/01/2006
(See Vegas Equity International Corp.)

AMERICAN BOAT BLDG CORP (RI)
Charter revoked for failure to file reports and pay fees 12/31/1966

AMERICAN BODY ARMOR & EQUIP INC (FL)
Each share Common 1¢ par exchanged for (0.33333333) share Common 3¢ par 09/21/1993
Reincorporated under the laws of Delaware as Armor Holdings, Inc. 08/21/1996
(See Armor Holdings, Inc.)

AMERICAN BONANZA GOLD CORP (BC)
Merged into Kerr Mines Inc. 07/07/2014
Each share Common no par exchanged for (0.53) share Common no par
Note: Unexchanged certificates were cancelled and became without value 07/07/2016

AMERICAN BONANZA GOLD MNG CORP (BC)
Merged into American Bonanza Gold Corp. 03/31/2005
Each share Class A Common no par exchanged for (0.25) share Common no par
American Bonanza Gold Corp. merged into Kerr Mines Inc. 07/07/2014

AMERICAN BONANZA RES CORP (NV)
Name changed to Clenergen Corp. 03/23/2009

AMERICAN BOND & MORTGAGE CO. (IL)
Bankrupt 00/00/1931
Details not available

AMERICAN BOND & SHARE CORP. OF DELAWARE
Bankrupt 00/00/1935
Details not available

AMERICAN BOND & TRUST CO. OF DELAWARE
Bankrupt 00/00/1935
Details not available

AMERICAN BOOK CO. (NY)
Each share Capital Stock $100 par exchanged for (2) shares Capital Stock $50 par 00/00/1952
Capital Stock $50 par changed to $20 par and (1.5) additional shares issued 05/11/1959
Capital Stock $20 par changed to $5 par and (3) additional shares issued 02/10/1966
Stock Dividends - 10% 08/02/1954; 10% 01/11/1957
Acquired by Litton Industries, Inc. 03/31/1967

Each share Capital Stock $5 par (value set at $51.695825) exchanged for like value of Litton Industries, Inc. Convertible Participating Preference $2.50 par (value set at $102.775) or Common $1 par (value set at $99.875)
Note: Option to receive Common expired after 03/21/1967
(See Litton Industries, Inc.)

AMERICAN BOOK STRATFORD PRESS INC (NY)
Stock Dividend - 10% 06/30/1967
Each share old Common $1 par exchanged for (0.00166666) share new Common $1 par 00/00/1985
Reacquired 00/00/1988
Each share new Common $1 par exchanged for $240 cash

AMERICAN BOSCH ARMA CORP. (NY)
5% Preferred Ser. A $100 par called for redemption 10/01/1962
5% Preferred Ser. B $100 par called for redemption 10/01/1962
Name changed to Ambac Industries, Inc. 04/30/1968
Ambac Industries, Inc. merged into United Technologies Corp. 07/14/1978

AMERICAN BOSCH CORP. (NY)
Each share Capital Stock $1 par exchanged for (1) share Class A $1 par 06/02/1948
Each share Class A $1 par exchanged for (1) share Common $2 par 03/18/1949
Stock Dividend - 20% 01/15/1951
Name changed to American Bosch Arma Corp. 07/21/1954
American Bosch Arma Corp. name changed to Ambac Industries, Inc. 04/30/1968 which merged into United Technologies Corp. 07/14/1978

AMERICAN BOSCH MAGNETO CORP. (NY)
Name changed to United American Bosch Corp. 12/18/1930
United American Bosch Corp. name changed to American Bosch Corp. 09/27/1938 which name changed to American Bosch Arma Corp. 07/21/1954 which name changed to Ambac Industries, Inc. 04/30/1968 which merged into United Technologies Corp. 07/14/1978

AMERICAN BOWLA-BOWLA CORP. (NJ)
Name changed to Diversifax Corp. 10/27/1961
(See Diversifax Corp.)

AMERICAN BOWLING ENTERPRISES INC (NY)
Name changed to Reltron Corp. and Common $1 par changed to 1¢ par 03/21/1972
Reltron Corp. name changed to Voit Corp. 03/26/1985
(See Voit Corp.)

AMERICAN BOWLING REALTY CORP. (NY)
Charter cancelled and proclaimed dissolved for failure to pay taxes 07/17/1970

AMERICAN BOX BOARD CO. (MI)
Common no par changed to $1 par 00/00/1936
Stock Dividend - 50% 11/15/1954
Merged into Packaging Corp. of America 07/31/1959
Each share Common $1 par exchanged for (1.25) shares Common $5 par
Packaging Corp. of America was acquired by Tennessee Gas Transmission Co. 06/08/1965 which name changed to Tenneco Inc. 04/11/1966 which merged into El Paso Natural Gas Co. 12/12/1996

which reorganized as El Paso Energy Corp. 08/01/1998 which name changed to El Paso Corp. 02/05/2001

AMERICAN BRAKE SHOE & FOUNDRY CO. (DE)
Name changed to American Brake Shoe Co. 04/27/1943
American Brake Shoe Co. name changed to Abex Corp. 05/05/1966 which merged into Illinois Central Industries, Inc. 12/26/1968 which name changed to IC Industries, Inc. 05/21/1975
(See IC Industries, Inc.)

AMERICAN BRAKE SHOE CO (DE)
74% Preferred called for redemption 06/30/1958
Stock Dividend - 10% 01/10/1951
Name changed to Abex Corp. 05/05/1966
Abex Corp. merged into Illinois Central Industries, Inc. 12/26/1968 which name changed to IC Industries, Inc. 05/21/1975
(See IC Industries, Inc.)

AMERICAN BRAKEBLOK CORP.
Merged into American Brake Shoe & Foundry Co. 00/00/1937
Details not available

AMERICAN BRANDS CORP (NV)
Name changed to ABC Corp. 09/01/1970
ABC Corp. name changed to Comoro Exploration Ltd. 11/02/1970 which recapitalized as AWR-America West Resources, Inc. 12/10/1993 which name changed to Integrated Information International Group Co. Ltd. 10/08/1999 which name changed to Intervest Group, Ltd. 04/21/2001
(See Intervest Group, Ltd.)

AMERICAN BRANDS INC (DE)
Reincorporated 01/01/1986
$6 Conv. Preferred no par called for redemption 10/30/1979
Common $6.25 par changed to $3.125 par and (1) additional share issued 05/22/1981
$1.70 Conv. Preferred no par called for redemption 10/09/1985
State of incorporation changed from (NJ) to (DE) 01/01/1986
Common $3.125 par split (2) for (1) by issuance of (1) additional share 09/30/1986
Common $3.125 par split (2) for (1) by issuance of (1) additional share 10/25/1990
$2.75 Preferred no par called for redemption 08/17/1992
Each share Common $3.125 par received distribution of (1) Gallaher Group PLC Sponsored ADR for Ordinary 10p par payable 05/30/1997 to holders of record 05/30/1997 Ex date - 06/02/1997
Name changed to Fortune Brands, Inc. 05/30/1997
Fortune Brands, Inc. name changed to Beam Inc. 10/04/2011

AMERICAN BREWING CO. OF ROCHESTER (NY)
Each share Common $100 par exchanged for (10) shares Common $10 par 00/00/1937 Liquidation completed 12/28/1954
Details not available

AMERICAN BREWING CO INC (WA)
Name changed to New Age Beverages Corp. 08/05/2016

AMERICAN BRIT ENTERPRISES INC (UT)
Reorganized under the laws of Delaware as Reserve Energy & Capital Corp. 10/29/1990
Each share Common $0.001 par exchanged for (0.33333333) share Common $0.001 par

(See Reserve Energy & Capital Corp.)

AMERICAN BRITISH & CONTINENTAL CORP.
Merged into Equity Corp. 00/00/1935
Details not available

AMERICAN BROADCASTING CO.
Bankrupt 00/00/1929
Details not available

AMERICAN BROADCASTING CO., INC. (DE)
Merged into American Broadcasting-Paramount Theatres, Inc. 02/09/1953
Each share Common $1 par exchanged for (0.36) share 5% Preferred $20 par and (15/38) share Common $1 par
American Broadcasting-Paramount Theatres, Inc. name changed to American Broadcasting Companies, Inc. 07/02/1965
(See American Broadcasting Companies, Inc.)

AMERICAN BROADCASTING COS INC (NY)
Common $1 par split (3) for (2) by issuance of (0.5) additional share 12/30/1969
Common $1 par split (2) for (1) by issuance of (1) additional share 03/20/1973
Common $1 par split (3) for (2) by issuance of (0.5) additional share 10/10/1978
Merged into Capital Cities/ABC, Inc. 01/03/1986
Each share Common $1 par exchanged for (0.1) Common Stock Purchase Warrant expiring 07/29/1988 and $118 cash

AMERICAN BROADCASTING-PARAMOUNT THEATRES, INC. (NY)
5% Preferred $20 par called for redemption 10/20/1961
Name changed to American Broadcasting Companies, Inc. 07/02/1965
(See American Broadcasting Companies, Inc.)

AMERICAN BROADCASTING SYS INC (DE)
Charter cancelled and declared inoperative and void for non-payment of taxes 03/01/1996

AMERICAN BROWN BOVERI ELECTRIC CORP. (NY)
Name changed to New York Shipbuilding Corp. 07/22/1931
(See New York Shipbuilding Corp.)

AMERICAN BUDGETEL INC (BC)
Recapitalized as ISO Ventures Inc. 01/26/1989
Each share Common no par exchanged for (0.2) share Common no par
ISO Ventures Inc. recapitalized as Steadfast Ventures Inc. 06/29/1993
(See Steadfast Ventures Inc.)

AMERICAN BUILDING CORP. (DE)
Charter cancelled and declared inoperative and void for non-payment of taxes 01/00/1951

AMERICAN BULLION MINERALS LTD (BC)
Acquired by Imperial Metals Corp. 06/13/2011
Each share Common no par exchanged for $2 cash
Note: Unexchanged certificates were cancelled and became without value 06/13/2014

AMERICAN BUSINESS & COML LIFE INS CO (TX)
Merged into Western Resources Corp. 04/12/1973
Each share Common $2 par

exchanged for (0.65) share Common $1 par
Western Resources Corp. name changed to Western Resources Life Insurance Co. 01/08/1980 which merged into Tidelands Capital Corp. 06/06/1980 which merged into Western Preferred Corp. 03/06/1981
(See Western Preferred Corp.)

AMERICAN BUSINESS & MERCANTILE INS GROUP INC (DE)
Merged into Old Republic International Corp. 02/03/1998
Each share Class A Common 1¢ par exchanged for $60 cash

AMERICAN BUSINESS ALLIANCE INC (UT)
Involuntarily dissolved 03/01/1989

AMERICAN BUSINESS COMPUTERS CORP (FL)
Name changed to ABC Dispensing Technologies, Inc. 05/01/1996
ABC Dispensing Technologies, Inc. recapitalized as Ka Wang Holding, Inc. 03/21/2007

AMERICAN BUSINESS CREDIT CORP. (DE)
Merged into Crown Finance Co., Inc. 09/28/1950
Each share Class A Common $1 par exchanged for (0.125) share Class A Common $1 par
Each (2.66666666) shares Class B Common $1 par exchanged for (1) share Class A Common $1 par
(See Crown Finance Co., Inc.)

AMERICAN BUSINESS FINL SVCS INC (DE)
Stock Dividends - 5% payable 09/27/1999 to holders of record 09/03/1999; 10% payable 11/05/2001 to holders of record 10/22/2001 Ex date - 10/18/2001; 10% payable 09/13/2002 to holders of record 09/03/2002 Ex date - 08/29/2002; 5% payable 01/08/2004 to holders of record 12/26/2003 Ex date - 12/23/2003; 10% payable 06/08/2004 to holders of record 05/25/2004
Chapter 11 bankruptcy proceedings converted to Chapter 7 on 05/17/2005
Stockholders' equity unlikely

AMERICAN BUSINESS HLDGS INC (DE)
Name changed to SOKO Fitness & Spa Group, Inc. 06/06/2008
(See SOKO Fitness & Spa Group, Inc.)

AMERICAN BUSINESS INFORMATION INC (DE)
Common $0.0025 par split (3) for (2) by issuance of (0.5) additional share 08/14/1995
Common $0.0025 par reclassified as Class B Common $0.0025 par 10/03/1997
Each share Class B Common $0.0025 par received distribution of (1) share Class A Common $0.0025 par payable 10/09/1997 to holders of record 10/03/1997
Name changed to infoUSA Inc. 07/31/1998
infoUSA Inc. name changed to infoGroup Inc. 06/04/2008
(See infoGroup Inc.)

AMERICAN BUSINESS MERGERS INC (TX)
Each share Common $0.0001 par exchanged for (0.03030303) share Common $0.0033 par 08/07/1989
Name changed to Baker Videoactive Corp. 09/29/1989

AMERICAN BUSINESS PRODS INC (DE)
Common $2 par split (3) for (2) by

issuance of (0.5) additional share 06/15/1971
Common $2 par split (5) for (4) by issuance of (0.25) additional share 11/15/1972
Common $2 par split (3) for (2) by issuance of (0.5) additional share 06/13/1975
Common $2 par split (3) for (2) by issuance of (0.5) additional share 12/15/1983
Reincorporated under the laws of Georgia 04/30/1986
(See American Business Products, Inc. (GA))

AMERICAN BUSINESS PRODS INC (GA)
Common $2 par split (5) for (4) by issuance of (0.25) additional share 06/29/1989
Common $2 par split (3) for (2) by issuance of (0.5) additional share 12/16/1991
Common $2 par split (3) for (2) by issuance of (0.5) additional share 06/15/1995
Merged into Mail-Well, Inc. 02/22/2000
Each share Common $2 par exchanged for $20 cash

AMERICAN BUSINESS SHS INC (DE)
Capital Stock $1 par changed to 50¢ par 00/00/1933
Each share Capital Stock 50¢ par exchanged for (0.2) share Capital Stock $1 par 00/00/1938
Name changed to Lord Abbett Income Fund, Inc. (DE) 11/17/1975
Lord Abbett Income Fund, Inc. (DE) reincorporated in Maryland 07/09/1975 which name changed to Lord Abbett U.S. Government Securities Fund, Inc. 09/23/1985
(See Lord Abbett U.S. Government Securities Fund, Inc.)

AMERICAN BUSINESS SYS INC (PA)
Completely liquidated 03/21/1969
Each share Common no par exchanged for first and final distribution of (0.0879) share Control Data Corp. (DE) Common $5 par
Control Data Corp. (DE) name changed to Ceridian Corp. (Old) 06/03/1992
(See Ceridian Corp. (Old))

AMERICAN BUSINESSMEN'S LIFE INSURANCE CO. OF KENTUCKY (KY)
Merged into Western Pioneer Life Insurance Co. 11/16/1972
Each share Common $1 par exchanged for (0.257069) share Common $1 par
Western Pioneer Life Insurance Co. merged into I.C.H. Corp. 04/18/1985 which name changed to Southwestern Life Corp. (New) 06/15/1994 which name changed to I.C.H. Corp. (New) 10/10/1995
(See I.C.H. Corp. (New))

AMERICAN BUSINESSPHONES INC (NJ)
Reincorporated under the laws of Delaware as ABI American Businessphones, Inc. and Common no par changed to 1¢ par 04/24/1987
ABI American Businessphones, Inc. merged into Pacific Telesis Group 10/31/1988 which merged into SBC Communications, Inc. 04/01/1997 which name changed to AT&T Inc. 11/18/2005

AMERICAN BUSING CORP (NV)
Name changed to Giant Motorsports, Inc. 04/05/2004

AMERICAN BUSLINES, INC. (DE)
Recapitalized 06/22/1951
Each share Preferred no par exchanged for (1) share 5%

Preferred $100 par and (2) shares Common $1 par
Each share Common no par exchanged for (1) share Common $1 par
Reorganized 09/22/1958
No Preferred or Common stockholders' equity

AMERICAN BUYERS CREDIT CO. (AZ)
Name changed to American Contract Mortgage Exchange 5/6/64
(See American Contract Mortgage Exchange)

AMERICAN BUYERS LIFE INSURANCE CO. (AZ)
Reorganized as American Estate Life Insurance Co. 04/16/1964
Each dollar amount of Trust Fund Dividend Ctf. exchanged for (0.32556) share Common $1 par
Each share Common $1 par exchanged for (32.556) shares Common $1 par
(See American Estates Life Insurance Co.)

AMERICAN BUYERS LIFE INSURANCE CO. (UT)
Name changed to American Investors Assurance Co. 6/1/65
(See American Investors Assurance Co.)

AMERICAN CABLE & RADIO CORP. (DE)
Merged into International Telephone & Telegraph Corp. (MD) 11/01/1961
Each share Common $1 par exchanged for (0.04) share 4% Conv. Preferred Ser. B $100 par and (0.14285714) share Common no par
International Telephone & Telegraph Corp. (MD) reincorporated in Delaware 01/31/1968 which name changed to ITT Corp. 12/31/1983 which reorganized in Indiana as ITT Industries, Inc. 12/19/1995 which name changed to ITT Corp. 07/01/2006

AMERICAN CABLE CO., INC. (DE)
Merged into American Chain Co., Inc. 00/00/1934
Details not available

AMERICAN CABLE TV INVESTORS 3 (CA)
Completely liquidated 04/06/1998
Details not available

AMERICAN CABLE TV INVESTORS 4, LTD. (CO)
Liquidation completed
Each Unit of Ltd. Partnership received initial distribution of $675 cash payable 01/00/1996 to holders of record 12/01/1995
Each Unit of Ltd. Partnership received second and final distribution of $61.72 cash payable 05/11/2000 to holders of record 03/01/2000

AMERICAN CABLE TV INVESTORS 5, LTD. (CO)
Liquidation completed
Each Unit of Ltd. Partnership received initial distribution of $165 cash 01/00/1996
Each Unit of Ltd. Partnership received second distribution of $370 cash 00/00/1997
Each Unit of Ltd. Partnership received third distribution of $203 cash 00/00/2000
Each Unit of Ltd. Partnership received fourth and final distribution of an undetermined amount of cash 00/00/2005

AMERICAN CABLESYSTEMS CORP (DE)
Merged into Continental Cablevision, Inc. 02/29/1988
Each share Class A Common $1 par exchanged for $46.50 cash

AMERICAN CABLEVISION LEASING CORP (DE)
Proclaimed inoperative and void for non-payment of taxes 04/15/1971

AMERICAN CADUCEUS INDS INC (DE)
Common 10¢ par changed to 1¢ par 04/11/1968
Merged out of existence 04/29/1991
Details not available

AMERICAN CAN CDA INC (ON)
Name changed to Onex Packaging Inc. 01/15/1987
(See Onex Packaging Inc.)

AMERICAN CAN CO (NJ)
7% Preferred $100 par changed to $25 par and (3) additional shares issued 00/00/1952
Common $25 par changed to $12.50 par and (3) additional shares issued 00/00/1952
Each share 7% Preferred $25 par exchanged for (1) share $2.80 Preferred no par plus $0.1342 cash, $21.6342 cash only or a combination of $2.80 Preferred $25 par and cash 04/29/1980
Note: Option to receive Preferred expired 06/16/1980
Common $12.50 par changed to $1 par 05/22/1984
$2.80 Preferred no par called for redemption 01/06/1986
Common $1 par split (2) for (1) by issuance of (1) additional share 03/12/1987
Name changed to Primerica Corp. (NJ) 04/28/1987
Primerica Corp. (NJ) acquired by Primerica Corp. (DE) 12/15/1988 which name changed to Travelers Inc. 12/31/1993 which name changed to Travelers Group Inc. 04/26/1995 which name changed to Citigroup Inc. 10/08/1998

AMERICAN CANADIAN OIL CO. (WA)
Charter revoked for failure to file reports and pay fees 07/01/1923

AMERICAN CANADIAN PROPERTIES CORP.
Dissolved 00/00/1944
Details not available

AMERICAN CDN SYS INC (BC)
Name changed to Maxcard Systems International Inc. 04/03/1991
(See Maxcard Systems International Inc.)

AMERICAN-CANADIAN URANIUM CO., LTD. (DE)
Name changed to Athabasca Uranium Mines Ltd. 00/00/1953
Athabasca Uranium Mines Ltd. liquidated for Pippin Mining & Uranium Corp. Ltd. 08/18/1958
(See Pippin Mining & Uranium Corp. Ltd.)

AMERICAN CANDY CO. (IL)
Merged into Raymond-Commerce Corp. 12/31/1954
Each share Common $10 par exchanged for (1) share 50¢ Preferred $1 par
(See Raymond-Commerce Corp.)

AMERICAN CAP & RESH CORP (DE)
Name changed to ICF International Inc. 03/01/1991
ICF International Inc. name changed to ICF Kaiser International, Inc. 06/26/1993 which recapitalized as Kaiser Group International, Inc. 12/27/1999 which reorganized as Kaiser Group Holdings, Inc. 12/18/2000

AMERICAN CAP AGY CORP (DE)
Name changed to AGNC Investment Corp. 10/03/2016

AMERICAN CAP ALLIANCE INC (NV)
Recapitalized as American Petroleum Group, Inc. 11/01/2004

Each share Common $0.001 par exchanged for (0.05) share Common $0.001 par
American Petroleum Group, Inc. name changed to High Velocity Alternative Energy Corp. 09/14/2007 which name changed to Reflectkote, Inc. 07/31/2009

AMERICAN CAP BD FD INC (MD)
Name changed to Van Kampen American Capital Bond Fund, Inc. (MD) 12/29/1995
Van Kampen American Capital Bond Fund, Inc. (MD) reincorporated in Delaware 10/31/1996 which name changed to Van Kampen Bond Fund 08/28/1998 which name changed to Invesco Van Kampen Bond Fund 06/01/2010 which name changed to Invesco Bond Fund 12/03/2012

AMERICAN CAP CONV SECS INC (MD)
Name changed to Van Kampen American Capital Convertible Securities, Inc. (MD) 12/29/1995
Van Kampen American Capital Convertible Securities, Inc. (MD) reincorporated in Delaware 10/29/1996 which name changed to Van Kampen Convertible Securities Inc. 08/28/1998 which reorganized as Van Kampen American Capital Harbor Fund 08/15/2000

AMERICAN CAP CORPORATE BD FD INC (MD)
Common $1 par reclassified as Class A 1¢ par 09/28/1992
Reincorporated under the laws of Delaware as Van Kampen American Capital Corporate Bond Fund 08/05/1995
Van Kampen American Capital Corporate Bond Fund name changed to Van Kampen Corporate Bond Fund 07/14/1998

AMERICAN CAP EMERGING GROWTH FD INC (MD)
Reorganized under the laws of Delaware as Van Kampen American Capital Emerging Growth Fund 08/03/1995
Details not available

AMERICAN CAP ENTERPRISE FD INC (MD)
Common $1 par reclassified as Class A 1¢ par 12/20/1991
Reincorporated under the laws of Delaware as Van Kampen American Capital Enterprise Fund 08/03/1995
Van Kampen American Capital Enterprise Fund name changed to Van Kampen Enterprise Fund 08/31/1998

AMERICAN CAP EQUITY INCOME FD INC (DE)
Common $1 par reclassified as Class A $1 par 05/01/1992
Merged into Van Kampen American Capital Equity Income Fund 08/18/1995
Details not available

AMERICAN CAP GROWTH & INCOME FD INC (MD)
Reincorporated 07/06/1993
State of incorporation changed from (NY) to (MD) 07/06/1993
Common $1 par reclassified as Class A 1¢ par 08/02/1993
Reincorporated under the laws of Delaware as Van Kampen American Capital Growth & Income Fund 07/31/1995
Van Kampen American Capital Growth & Income Fund name changed to Van Kampen Growth & Income Fund 07/14/1998

AMERICAN CAP GROWTH FD INC (MD)
Merged into American Capital Enterprise Fund, Inc. 06/29/1990

Details not available

AMERICAN CAP HBR FD INC (MD)
Reincorporated under the laws of Delaware as Van Kampen American Capital Harbor Fund and Common 1¢ par reclassified as Class A 1¢ par 08/19/1995
Van Kampen American Capital Harbor Fund name changed to Van Kampen Harbor Fund 07/14/1998

AMERICAN CAP HIGH YIELD INVTS INC (MD)
Merged into Van Kampen American Capital High Income Corporate Bond Fund 08/05/1995
Details not available

AMERICAN CAP HLDGS (NV)
Each share old Common $0.001 par exchanged for (0.1) share new Common $0.001 par 12/27/2002
Name changed to Symphony Investments, Inc. 05/09/2003
Symphony Investments, Inc. name changed to International Pharmacy Outlets Inc. 09/29/2003 which name changed to Bionic Products, Inc. 12/11/2006 which recapitalized as Texas Oil & Minerals Inc. 02/01/2012

AMERICAN CAP HLDGS INC (DE)
Charter cancelled and declared void for failure to pay franchise taxes 03/01/1999

AMERICAN CAP INCOME TR (MA)
Name changed to Van Kampen American Capital Income Trust 12/29/1995
Van Kampen American Capital Income Trust name changed to Van Kampen Income Trust 08/28/1998
(See Van Kampen Income Trust)

AMERICAN CAP LTD (DE)
Each share Common 1¢ par received distribution of (0.332) share Common 1¢ par payable 08/07/2009 to holders of record 06/22/2009 Ex date - 06/18/2009
Merged into Ares Capital Corp. 01/03/2017
Each share Common 1¢ par exchanged for (0.483) share Common $0.001 par and $10.13 cash

AMERICAN CAP MGMT & RESH INC (DE)
Acquired by Primerica Corp. 10/29/1990
Each share Common 10¢ par exchanged for (0.32) share Common 1¢ par
Primerica Corp. name changed to Travelers Inc. 12/31/1993 which name changed to Travelers Group Inc. 04/16/1995 which name changed to Citigroup Inc. 10/08/1998

AMERICAN CAP MTG INVT CORP (MD)
Name changed to MTGE Investment Corp. 10/03/2016
MTGE Investment Corp. merged into Annaly Capital Management, Inc. 09/07/2018

AMERICAN CAP PARTNERS LTD INC (NV)
SEC revoked common stock registration 11/08/2011

AMERICAN CAP SR FLOATING LTD (MD)
Liquidation completed
Each share Common 1¢ par received initial distribution of $8.80 cash payable 08/27/2018 to holders of record 08/16/2018 Ex date - 08/28/2018
Each share Common 1¢ par received second and final distribution of $3.69 cash payable 09/18/2018 to holders of record 09/11/2018 Ex date - 09/19/2018

AMERICAN CAP STRATEGIES LTD (DE)
Name changed to American Capital, Ltd. 07/08/2008
American Capital, Ltd. merged into Ares Capital Corp. 01/03/2017

AMERICAN CAP VENTURE FD INC (MD)
Name changed to American Capital Emerging Growth Fund, Inc. 07/24/1990
(See American Capital Emerging Growth Fund, Inc.)

AMERICAN CAPACITY GROUP INC (DE)
Merged into ACGI Acquisition Corp. 08/31/1989
Each share Common $1 par exchanged for $18 cash

AMERICAN CAPITAL CORP.
Merged into Pacific-American Investors, Inc. (DE) 08/27/1943
Each share old Prior Preferred exchanged for (1) share new Prior Preferred $100 par
Each share old Preferred exchanged for (1.25) shares new Preferred $5 par and (7.5) shares Common 10¢ par
Each share Class A Common exchanged for (1) share Common 10¢ par
Each share Class B Common exchanged for (0.1) share Common 10¢ par
Pacific-American Investors, Inc. (DE) merged into American Mutual Fund, Inc. (DE) 02/01/1956 which reincorporated in Maryland 09/20/1983 which reincorporated in Delaware as American Mutual Fund 01/01/2011

AMERICAN CAPITAL LIFE INSURANCE CO. (DC)
Class A Common $1.66 par changed to $1.18 par 11/23/1965
Class A Common $1.18 par changed to $1.05 par 09/26/1966
Class A Common $1.05 par changed to $1 par 12/29/1967
Each share Class A Common $1 par exchanged for (1) share Common $0.685 par 07/26/1970
Each share Class B Common 20¢ par exchanged for (0.2) share Common $0.685 par 07/26/1970
Over 96% owned by N.C. Mutual as of 07/16/1980
Public interest eliminated

AMERICAN CAPITOL INS CO (TX)
Stock Dividend - 50% 04/14/1967
Under plan of reorganization each share Capital Stock no par automatically became (1) share Acap Corp. (DE) Common 10¢ par 10/31/1985
Acap Corp. merged into UTG, Inc. 11/14/2011

AMERICAN CAR & FOUNDRY CO. (NJ)
Common no par changed to $25 par and 10% stock dividend distributed 09/25/1952
Stock Dividend - 10% 08/15/1953
Name changed to ACF Industries, Inc. 06/01/1954
(See ACF Industries, Inc.)

AMERICAN CAR & FOUNDRY MOTORS CO.
Merged into ACF-Brill Motors Co. 08/01/1944
Each share 7% Preferred exchanged for (7) shares Common $2.50 par
Each share Common exchanged for a warrant to purchase (1) share Common $2.50 par
ACF-Brill Motors Co. merged into ACF-Wrigley Stores, Inc. 12/30/1955 which name changed to Allied Supermarkets, Inc. (DE) 11/10/1961 which reincorporated in Michigan 08/18/1982 which name changed to Vons Companies, Inc. 07/22/1987 which merged into Safeway Inc. 04/08/1997
(See Safeway Inc.)

AMERICAN CARE CTRS INC (OR)
Name changed to American Pacific Business Ventures, Inc. 09/10/1979
(See American Pacific Business Ventures, Inc.)

AMERICAN CAREER CTRS INC (NV)
Each share old Common $0.0001 par exchanged for (0.08333333) share new Common $0.0001 par 03/25/2002
Name changed to American Water Star, Inc. 05/10/2002
American Water Star, Inc. recapitalized Prime Star Group, Inc. 09/12/2008
(See Prime Star Group, Inc.)

AMERICAN-CARIBBEAN OIL CO. (DE)
Merged into Elgin Gas & Oil Co 06/30/1959
Each share Common 10¢ par exchanged for (0.16) share Common 10¢ par
(See Elgin Gas & Oil Co.)

AMERICAN CARIBBEAN OIL CORP. (DE)
Name changed to Florida Land Co. 05/08/1959
Florida Land Co. name changed to Florida-Patsand Corp. 11/04/1959
(See Florida-Patsand Corp.)

AMERICAN CARRIERS INC (DE)
Common no par split (2) for (1) by issuance of (1) additional share 02/10/1984
Name changed to Anuhco Inc. 07/11/1991
Anuhco Inc. reorganized as TransFinancial Holdings, Inc. 07/01/1997
(See TransFinancial Holdings, Inc.)

AMERICAN CASCADE ENERGY INC (TX)
Each share old Common $0.0001 par exchanged for (0.25) share new Common $0.0001 par 04/19/1993
Chapter 7 bankruptcy proceedings terminated 07/11/2003
Stockholders' equity unlikely

AMERICAN CASH CREDIT CORP.
Merged into Franklin Plan Corp. 00/00/1931
Details not available

AMERICAN CASINO ENTERPRISES INC NEW (NV)
Name changed to American Vantage Companies 04/11/1997
(See American Vantage Companies)

AMERICAN CASINO ENTERPRISES INC OLD (NV)
Each share old Common 1¢ par exchanged for (0.66666666) share new Common 1¢ par 09/22/1982
Name changed to American Enterprises, Inc. 03/15/1985
American Enterprises, Inc. name changed to American Casino Enterprises, Inc. (New) 11/19/1993 which name changed to American Vantage Companies 04/11/1997
(See American Vantage Companies)

AMERICAN CASINOS INTL INC (NV)
Each share old Common $0.001 par exchanged for (0.02) share new Common $0.001 par 11/17/1997
Name changed to Enterprise Solutions, Inc. 03/15/1999
Enterprise Solutions, Inc. name changed to Enterprises Solutions Inc. 09/01/1999
(See Enterprises Solutions Inc.)

AMERICAN CATALINA CAP INC (CO)
Charter suspended for failure to file annual reports 09/30/1989

AMERICAN CDI CORP (DE)
Merged into PolyMedica Industries, Inc. 09/15/1992
Each share Common $0.001 par exchanged for (0.46424) share Common 1¢ par
PolyMedica Industries, Inc. name changed to PolyMedica Corp. 09/19/1997
(See PolyMedica Corp.)

AMERICAN CELLULAR NETWORK CORP (NJ)
Common 1¢ par changed to $0.0067 par and (0.5) additional share issued 09/25/1987
Acquired by Comcast Corp. (Old) 06/27/1988
Each share Common 1¢ par exchanged for $25 cash

AMERICAN CELLULAR TEL CORP (FL)
Acquired by Mobile Communications Corp. of America 06/30/1986
Each share Class A Common 1¢ par exchanged for $7.25 cash

AMERICAN CELLULOSE & CHEMICAL MANUFACTURING CO., LTD. (DE)
Name changed to Celanese Corp. of America 04/28/1927
Celanese Corp. of America name changed to Celanese Corp. 04/13/1966
(See Celanese Corp.)

AMERICAN CEM CORP (DE)
Name changed to Amcord, Inc. 05/02/1973
(See Amcord, Inc.)

AMERICAN CENTENNIAL LIFE INSURANCE CO. (MD)
98% owned by Tidewater Group Inc. as of 12/00/1978
Public interest eliminated

AMERICAN CENTRAL LIFE INSURANCE CO.
Merged into American United Life Insurance Co. 09/00/1936
Details not available

AMERICAN CENTRAL MANUFACTURING CORP.
Acquired by Aviation Corp. 11/30/1946
Each share Common $1 par exchanged for (2.125) share Common $3 par
Aviation Corp. name changed to Avco Manufacturing Corp. 03/25/1947 which name changed to Avco Corp. 04/10/1959
(See Avco Corp.)

AMERICAN CENTRALITY GROUP INC (NV)
Name changed 03/05/2007
Name changed from American Centrality Investments, Inc. to American Centrality Group, Inc. 03/05/2007
SEC revoked common stock registration 04/23/2015

AMERICAN CENTRIFUGAL CORP. (DE)
Apparently out of business 00/00/1941
Charter revoked and proclaimed inoperative and void for non-payment of taxes 06/01/1942

AMERICAN CENTURY MORTGAGE INVESTORS (MA)
Name changed to American Century Trust (MA) 10/03/1980
American Century Trust (MA) reorganized in Delaware as American Century Corp. 11/18/1982 which recapitalized as Tescorp Inc. 07/11/1990
(See Tescorp Inc.)

AMERICAN CENTURY TRUST (MA)
Reorganized under the laws of

Delaware as American Century Corp. 11/18/1982
Each Share of Bene. Int. no par exchanged for (1) share Common $1 par
American Century Corp. (DE) recapitalized as Tescorp Inc. 07/11/1990
(See Tescorp Inc.)

AMERICAN CENTY CORP (DE)
Common $1 par split (3) for (2) by issuance of (0.5) additional share 08/26/1983
Reorganized under Chapter 11 Federal Bankruptcy Code as Tescorp Inc. 07/11/1990
Each share Common $1 par received distribution of (0.253) Common Stock Purchase Warrant expiring 07/12/1993
Note: Certificates were not required to be exchanged and are without value

AMERICAN CERAMIC PRODS INC (CA)
Adjudicated bankrupt 12/28/1967
No stockholders' equity

AMERICAN CEREAL FOOD CORP.
Property sold 00/00/1940
Details not available

AMERICAN CHAIN & CABLE INC (NY)
Common no par changed to $1 par and (1) additional share issued 02/10/1965
Merged into Newco Industrial Corp. 05/04/1976
Each share Common $1 par exchanged for $29 cash

AMERICAN CHAIN CO., INC. (NY)
7% Preferred called for redemption 11/02/1936
Name changed to American Chain & Cable Co., Inc. 12/29/1936
(See American Chain & Cable Co., Inc.)

AMERICAN CHAMPION ENTMT INC (DE)
Each share old Common $0.0001 par exchanged for (0.25) share new Common $0.0001 par 01/04/2000
Name changed to Pacific Systems Control Technology, Inc. 08/08/2001
(See Pacific Systems Control Technology, Inc.)

AMERICAN CHATILLON CORP.
Merged into Tubize Chatillon Corp. 00/00/1930
Details not available

AMERICAN CHECKMASTER SYS INC (DE)
Charter revoked and proclaimed inoperative and void for non-payment of taxes 04/15/1971

AMERICAN CHIBOUGAMAU MINES LTD (QC)
Charter annulled for failure to file annual reports 10/00/1974

AMERICAN CHICLE CO. (NJ)
Common no par split (2) for (1) by issuance of (1) additional share 12/23/1958
Stock Dividends - 200% 07/30/1947; 10% 02/21/1956
Merged into Warner-Lambert Pharmaceutical Co. 10/02/1962
Each share of Common no par exchanged for (2.7) shares Common $1 par and (0.12) share $4 Conv. Preferred $100 par
Warner-Lambert Pharmaceutical Co. name changed to Warner-Lambert Co. 11/13/1970 which merged into Pfizer Inc. 06/19/2000

AMERICAN CHLOROPHYLL, INC.
Merged into Strong, Cobb & Co., Inc. 04/28/1952
Each share Common $1 par exchanged for (1.33333333) share Common $1 par

Strong, Cobb & Co., Inc. merged into merged into Strong Cobb Arner Inc. 06/08/1959
(See Strong Cobb Arner Inc.)

AMERICAN CHROME CO. (NV)
Merged into Goldfield Corp. (WY) 03/15/1963
Each share Capital Stock $1 par exchanged for (2.25) shares Capital Stock $1 par
Goldfield Corp. (WY) reincorporated in Delaware 08/30/1968

AMERICAN CHROMIUM LTD (AB)
Each share Common no par exchanged for (0.5) share Conv. Class A Common no par and (0.5) share Non-Vtg. Class B Common no par 01/13/1981
Merged into Rhonda Mining Corp. 01/31/1992
Each share Conv. Class A Common no par exchanged for (0.1) share Common no par
Each share Non-Vtg. Class B Common no par exchanged for (0.1) share Common no par
Rhonda Mining Corp. name changed to Rhonda Corp. 06/26/2000
(See Rhonda Corp.)

AMERICAN CIGAR CO. (NJ)
Name changed to American Cigarette & Cigar Co. 00/00/1936
American Cigarette & Cigar Co. merged into American Tobacco Co. 12/31/1953 which name changed to American Brands, Inc. (NJ) 07/01/1969 which reincorporated in Delaware 01/01/1986 which name changed Fortune Brands, Inc. 05/30/1997 which name changed to Beam Inc. 10/04/2011
(See Beam Inc.)

AMERICAN CIGARETTE & CIGAR CO. (NJ)
Merged into American Tobacco Co. 12/31/1953
Each share Preferred $100 par exchanged for (1.1) shares 6% Preferred $100 par
Each share Common $70 par exchanged for (8) shares Common $25 par
American Tobacco Co. name changed to American Brands, Inc. (NJ) 07/01/1969 which reincorporated in Delaware 01/01/1986 which name changed to Fortune Brands, Inc. 05/30/1997 which name changed to Beam Inc. 10/04/2011
(See Beam Inc.)

AMERICAN CINEMASTORES INC (DE)
Common $0.001 par split (2) for (1) by issuance of (1) additional share 08/15/1994
Name changed to Apparel Technologies Inc. 11/10/1997
(See Apparel Technologies Inc.)

AMERICAN CIRRUS ENGINES, INC.
Liquidated 00/00/1930
Details not available

AMERICAN CITADEL INC (WA)
Name changed to Country Maid Foods Inc. 04/30/1994
Country Maid Foods Inc. recapitalized as Country Maid Financial, Inc. 10/09/1998
(See Country Maid Financial, Inc.)

AMERICAN CITIES POWER & LIGHT CORP.
$3 Conv. Class A Preferred called for redemption 10/01/1946 Liquidation completed 06/22/1951
Details not available

AMERICAN CITY BANCORP INC
Each share old Common exchanged for (1) share new Common to reflect a (1) for (250) reverse split followed by a (250) for (1) forward split 04/27/2000

Note: In effect holders received $120 cash per share and public interest was eliminated

AMERICAN CITY BK (LOS ANGELES, CA)
Capital Stock $20 par changed to $15 par and (0.33333333) additional share issued 12/29/1967
Capital Stock $15 par changed to $5 par and (2) additional shares issued 08/19/1971
Capital Stock $5 par changed to $2.50 par and (1) additional share issued 10/10/1979
Declared insolvent and bank closed by California Superintendent of banking 02/25/1983
Stockholders' equity unlikely

AMERICAN CITY BUSINESS JOURNALS INC (DE)
Each share $1.50 Conv. Exchangeable Preferred 1¢ par exchanged for $25 principal amount of 6% Conv. Subordinated Debentures due 12/31/2011 on 01/04/1993
Common 1¢ par split (2) for (1) by issuance of (1) additional share 04/29/1994
Merged into Advance Publications, Inc. 10/18/1995
Each share Common 1¢ par exchanged for $28 cash

AMERICAN CLADMETALS CO. (PA)
Under plan of merger name changed to Salem-Brosius, Inc. 05/12/1953
Salem-Brosius, Inc. name changed to Salem Corp. 06/01/1970
(See Salem Corp.)

AMERICAN CLAIMS EVALUATION INC (NY)
Common 1¢ par split (2) for (1) by issuance of (1) additional share 08/14/1990
Common 1¢ par split (2) for (1) by issuance of (1) additional share 11/12/1991
Name changed to American Learning Corp. 03/18/2010
(See American Learning Corp.)

AMERICAN CLASSIC VOYAGES CO (DE)
Plan of liquidation under Chapter 11 Federal Bankruptcy Code effective 10/01/2003
No stockholders' equity

AMERICAN CLIPPER CORP (CA)
Liquidation completed
Each share Common no par received initial distribution of $1.84 cash 05/19/1982
Each share Common no par received second and final distribution of $0.505525 cash 07/29/1985
Note: Certificates were not required to be surrendered and are without value

AMERICAN CO.
Liquidation completed 00/00/1949
Details not available

AMERICAN COACH & BODY CO.
Liquidation completed 00/00/1951
Details not available

AMERICAN COAL CORP NEW (NV)
Name changed to Kevcorp Services, Inc. 06/22/2004
Kevcorp Services, Inc. recapitalized as Center For Wound Healing, Inc. 02/15/2006
(See Center For Wound Healing, Inc.)

AMERICAN COAL CORP OLD (NV)
Recapitalized as US Jet, Inc. 08/25/1998
Each share Common $0.001 par exchanged for (0.01) share Common $0.001 par
US Jet, Inc. recapitalized as American Coal Corp. (New) 10/29/1999 which name changed to Kevcorp Services, Inc. 06/22/2004 which recapitalized

as Center For Wound Healing, Inc. 02/15/2006
(See Center For Wound Healing, Inc.)

AMERICAN COATING MILLS, INC.
Acquired by Owens-Illinois Glass Co. 00/00/1947
Each share Common no par exchanged for (0.33333333) share Common $12.50 par
Owens-Illinois Glass Co. name changed to Owens-Illinois, Inc. 04/28/1965
(See Owens-Illinois, Inc.)

AMERICAN COILS CO.
Acquired by Brunner Manufacturing Co. 00/00/1948
Details not available

AMERICAN COIN & STAMP VENTURES INC (DE)
Recapitalized as Colony International Inc. 01/27/1997
Each share Common $0.0001 par exchanged for (0.05018568) share Common $0.0001 par
Colony International Inc. name changed to Mobile Pet Systems, Inc. 01/12/1999 which name changed to Molecular Imaging Corp. 05/01/2003
(See Molecular Imaging Corp.)

AMERICAN COIN MERCHANDISING INC (DE)
Merged into ACMI Holdings, Inc. 02/11/2002
Each share Common 1¢ par exchanged for $8.50 cash

AMERICAN COIN MERCHANDISING TR I (DE)
Ascending Rate Trust Preferred Securities called for redemption at $10 on 08/05/2004

AMERICAN COLD LITE TECHNOLOGIES INC (NV)
Name changed to Southern Land & Exploration, Inc. 12/21/1989
Southern Land & Exploration, Inc. name changed to Investment & Consulting International, Inc. (Old) 06/22/1991 which name changed to Currentsea 07/02/1991 which name changed back to Investment & Consulting International, Inc. (New) 06/02/1993 which recapitalized as KleenAir Systems, Inc. 04/11/1995 which recapitalized as Migami, Inc. 03/02/2006

AMERICAN COLLEGE LECTURE BUR INC (NY)
Acquired by Growth Canadian, Inc. 08/21/1972
Each share Common 1¢ par exchanged for (1) share Common 1¢ par
Growth Canadian, Inc. name changed to Growth Energy Inc. 05/20/1975 which name changed to Dalco Liquids, Inc. 01/10/1980 which name changed to International Drilling & Energy Corp. 11/10/1980
(See Drilling & Energy Corp.)

AMERICAN COLLOID CO (DE)
Common $1 par split (2) for (1) by issuance of (1) additional share 06/18/1987
Common $1 par split (2) for (1) by issuance of (1) additional share 06/24/1988
Common $1 par split (3) for (2) by issuance of (0.5) additional share 01/04/1993
Common $1 par changed to 1¢ par 05/10/1993
Common 1¢ par split (2) for (1) by issuance of (1) additional share 06/23/1993
Name changed to Amcol International Corp. 06/01/1995
(See Amcol International Corp.)

AMERICAN COLONIAL CORP.
Merged into Connecticut Investment Management Corp. 00/00/1931

Details not available

AMERICAN COLONY INSURANCE CO.
Merged into North Star Insurance Co. 12/00/1934
Details not available

AMERICAN COLORTYPE CO. (NJ)
Each share Common $100 par exchanged for (5) shares Common no par 00/00/1927
Common no par changed to $10 par 00/00/1932
Merged into Rapid-American Corp. (OH) 12/31/1957
Each share Common $10 par exchanged for $40 principal amount 7% S.F. Subord. Debentures due 11/15/1967

AMERICAN COMBINING CORP (NY)
Merged into ACC Purchasing Corp. 09/08/1988
Each share Common 1¢ par exchanged for $0.034 cash

AMERICAN COMMERCE NATIONAL BANK (ANAHEIM, CA)
Closed by the Comptroller of the Currency and FDIC named receiver 04/30/1993
Stockholders' equity unlikely

AMERICAN COML AGY INC (NC)
Each share old Common $1 par exchanged for (0.1) share new Common $1 par 12/03/1963
Completely liquidated 01/10/1969
Each share new Common $1 par exchanged for first and final distribution of (1.43) shares NCNB Corp. Common $5 par
NCNB Corp. name changed to NationsBank Corp. (NC) 12/31/1991 which reincorporated in Delaware 09/25/1998

AMERICAN COMMERCIAL ALCOHOL CORP.
Each share Common $20 par exchanged for (1) share American Distilling Co. Common $20 par 00/00/1942
American Distilling Co. name changed to Amdisco Corp. 11/14/1980
(See Amdisco Corp.)

AMERICAN COMMERCIAL BANK (CHARLOTTE, NC)
Merged into North Carolina National Bank (Charlotte, NC) 06/30/1960
Each share Capital Stock $10 par exchanged for (2.42) shares Common $5 par
North Carolina National Bank (Charlotte, NC) reorganized as NCNB Corp. 11/04/1968 which name changed to NationsBank Corp. 12/31/1991 which reincorporated in Delaware as BankAmerica Corp. (Old) 09/25/1998 which merged into BankAmerica Corp. (New) 09/30/1998 which name changed to Bank of America Corp. 04/28/1999

AMERICAN COML BK (SPOKANE, WA)
Stock Dividends - 10% 05/31/1977; 10% 04/28/1978; 10% 05/31/1979
In process of liquidation
Each share Capital Stock $10 par received initial distribution of $54.55 cash 03/24/1980
Each share Capital Stock $10 par received second distribution of $3.15 cash 02/02/1981
Note: Details on subsequent distributions, if any, are not available

AMERICAN COMMERCIAL BANK (VENTURA, CA)
Under plan of reorganization each share Common $15 par automatically became (1) share Americorp $1 par 05/02/1988
(See Americorp)

AMERICAN COMMERCIAL BARGE LINE CO. (DE)
Name changed to American Commercial Lines Inc. 04/30/1964
American Commercial Lines Inc. merged into Texas Gas Transmission Corp. 05/15/1968
(See Texas Gas Transmission Corp.)

AMERICAN COML LINES INC (DE)
Stock Dividend - 20% 05/13/1965
Merged into Texas Gas Transmission Corp. 05/15/1968
Each share Common $3 par exchanged for (1.65) shares $1.50 Conv. Preference $5 par
(See Texas Gas Transmission Corp.)
Old Common 1¢ par split (4) for (1) by issuance of (3) additional shares payable 08/15/2005 to holders of record 08/01/2005 Ex date - 08/16/2005
Old Common 1¢ par split (2) for (1) by issuance of (1) additional share payable 02/20/2007 to holders of record 02/06/2007 Ex date - 02/21/2007
Each share old Common 1¢ par exchanged for (0.25) share new Common 1¢ par 05/26/2009
Acquired by Finn Holding Corp. 12/21/2010
Each share new Common 1¢ par exchanged for $33 cash

AMERICAN COML SVGS BK INC (NC)
Under plan of reorganization each share Common $1 par automatically became (1) share American Bancshares Common $1 par 09/14/1992
American Bancshares acquired by First Union Corp. 05/31/1994 which name changed to Wachovia Corp. (Ctfs. dated after 09/01/2001) 09/01/2001 which merged into Wells Fargo & Co. (New) 12/31/2008

AMERICAN COMWLTH FINL CORP (DE)
Merged into I.C.H. Corp. 10/26/1982
Each share Common $1 par exchanged for (0.4317) share Common $1 par
I.C.H. Corp. name changed to Southwestern Life Corp. (New) 06/15/1994 which name changed to I.C.H. Corp. (New) 10/10/1995
(See I.C.H. Corp. (New))

AMERICAN COMMONWEALTHS POWER CORP. (DE)
Assets and securities sold to Commonwealths Distribution, Inc. 00/00/1934
No stockholders' equity

AMERICAN COMMUNICATIONS & TELEVISION INC (DE)
Reincorporated 09/18/1987
State of incorporation changed from (FL) to (DE) 09/18/1987
Each share old Common $0.001 par exchanged for (0.025) share new Common $0.0001 par 08/06/1991
Charter cancelled and declared inoperative and void for non-payment of taxes 03/01/1993

AMERICAN COMMUNICATIONS ENTERPRISES INC (NV)
Common $0.001 par split (4) for (1) by issuance of (3) additional shares payable 11/16/2000 to holders of record 11/06/2000 Ex date - 11/17/2000
Name changed to NeoGenomics, Inc. 01/14/2002

AMERICAN COMMUNICATIONS INDS INC (DE)
Plan of reorganization under Chapter 11 confirmed 12/07/1982
No stockholders' equity

AMERICAN COMMUNICATIONS SVCS INC (DE)
Reincorporated 09/29/1994
State of incorporation changed from (CO) to (DE) 09/29/1994
Name changed to e.spire Communications Inc. 04/15/1998
(See e.spire Communications Inc.)

AMERICAN CMNTY BANCORP INC (IN)
Stock Dividends - 5% payable 06/09/2006 to holders of record 05/25/2006 Ex date - 05/23/2006; 5% payable 06/08/2007 to holders of record 05/24/2007 Ex date - 05/22/2007; 5% payable 06/06/2008 to holders of record 05/22/2008 Ex date - 05/20/2008; 5% payable 06/11/2009 to holders of record 05/28/2009 Ex date - 05/26/2009; 5% payable 06/14/2010 to holders of record 05/27/2010 Ex date - 05/25/2010
Merged into German American Bancorp, Inc. 01/03/2011
Each share Common no par exchanged for (0.725) share Common no par

AMERICAN CMNTY BANCSHARES INC (NC)
Common $5 par split (3) for (2) by issuance of (0.5) additional share payable 02/21/2006 to holders of record 02/07/2006 Ex date - 02/22/2006
Stock Dividend - 10% payable 01/31/2002 to holders of record 01/16/2002 Ex date - 01/14/2002
Merged into Yadkin Valley Financial Corp. 04/17/2009
Each share Common $5 par exchanged for either (0.8517) share Common $1 par or (0.63) share Common $1 par and $3.0875 cash
Note: Option to receive stock and cash expired 05/15/2009
Yadkin Valley Financial Corp. recapitalized as Yadkin Financial Corp. 05/28/2013 which merged into F.N.B. Corp. 03/11/2017

AMERICAN CMNTY BK (MONROE, NC)
Stock Dividend - 20% payable 12/17/1999 to holders of record 12/03/1999
Under plan of reorganization each share Common $5 par automatically became (1) share American Community Bancshares Inc. Common $5 par 04/28/2000
American Community Bancshares Inc. merged into Yadkin Valley Financial Corp. 04/17/2009 which recapitalized as Yadkin Financial Corp. 05/28/2013 which merged into F.N.B. Corp. 03/11/2017

AMERICAN CMNTY DEV GROUP INC (DE)
Name changed to Wialan Technologies, Inc. 01/22/2014

AMERICAN CMNTY DEV GROUP INC (FL)
Proclaimed dissolved for failure to file reports and pay fees 08/25/1995

AMERICAN CMNTY DEV INC (CO)
Recapitalized as UMF Group Inc. 02/23/2017
Each share Common no par exchanged for (0.002) share Common no par

AMERICAN CMNTY NEWSPAPERS INC (DE)
Chapter 11 bankruptcy proceedings dismissed 10/06/2009
No stockholders' equity

AMERICAN CMNTY PPTYS TR (MD)
Acquired by FCP Fund I, L.P. 12/30/2009
Each share Common 1¢ par exchanged for $7.75 cash

AMERICAN CMNTY SVCS INC (ID)
Charter forfeited for failure to file reports 12/02/1991

AMERICAN COMPLEX CARE INC (NY)
Each share old Common $0.001 par exchanged for (0.2) share new Common $0.001 par 10/26/1992
Assets sold for the benefit of creditors 04/00/1995
No stockholders' equity

AMERICAN COMPONENT INDS (UT)
Proclaimed dissolved for failure to pay taxes 03/31/1985

AMERICAN COMPOSITE TRUST SHARES
Trust terminated 00/00/1935
Details not available

AMERICAN COMPUTER LEASING CORP (OH)
Name changed to American Financial Leasing & Services Co. 04/29/1971
American Financial Leasing & Services Co. merged into American Financial Corp. 12/26/1974
(See American Financial Corp.)

AMERICAN COMPUTER SVC INC (DE)
Charter cancelled and declared inoperative and void for non-payment of taxes 03/01/1974

AMERICAN COMPUTERLIFE CORP (OH)
Proclaimed dissolved 05/22/1992

AMERICAN COMSTOCK EXPLS LTD (BC)
Recapitalized as International Comstock Exploration Ltd. 01/09/1998
Each share Common no par exchanged for (0.2) share Common no par
International Comstock Exploration Ltd. recapitalized as Secureview Systems Inc. 09/27/2001 which name changed to Global Immune Technologies Inc. (BC) 05/03/2005 which reincorporated in Wyoming 05/12/2006

AMERICAN CONCRETE & STEEL PIPE CO.
Name changed to American Pipe & Construction Co. (DE) 00/00/1942
American Pipe & Construction Co. (DE) reorganized in California 12/01/1961 which name changed to Ameron, Inc. (CA) which reincorporated in Delaware 03/25/1986 which name changed to Ameron International Corp. 04/16/1996
(See Ameron International Corp.)

AMERICAN CONFECTIONERY CORP (UT)
Plan of reorganization under Chapter 11 Federal Bankruptcy proceedings effective 07/03/1992
No stockholders' equity

AMERICAN CONS CORP (DE)
Merged into I.C.H. Corp. 04/18/1985
Each share Common no par exchanged for (0.67) share Common $1 par
I.C.H. Corp name changed to Southwestern Life Corp. (New) 06/15/1994 which name changed to I.C.H. Corp. (New) 10/10/1995
(See I.C.H. Corp. (New))

AMERICAN CONS GROWTH CORP (DE)
Name changed 05/31/1991
Name changed from American Consolidated Gold Corp. to American Consolidated Growth Corp. 05/31/1991
Each share old Common 10¢ par exchanged for (0.1) share new Common 10¢ par 05/05/1993

SEC revoked common stock registration 11/01/2010

AMERICAN CONS LABORATORIES INC (FL)
Reorganized under the laws of Delaware as Strategic Global Investments, Inc. 06/01/2010
Each share Common 5¢ par exchanged for (0.001) share Common 5¢ par

AMERICAN CONS MGMT GROUP INC (UT)
SEC revoked common stock registration 03/25/2011

AMERICAN CONS MINERALS CORP (BC)
Each share old Common no par exchanged for (0.1) share new Common no par 09/12/2013
Merged into Starcore International Mines Ltd. 12/03/2014
Each share new Common no par exchanged for (0.33333333) share Common no par
Note: Unexchanged certificates will be cancelled and become without value 12/03/2020

AMERICAN CONS MNG CO (UT)
Each share Common $0.001 par exchanged for (0.1) share Common 1¢ par 07/28/1986
Recapitalized as American Consolidated Management Group, Inc. 07/01/2002
Each share Common 1¢ par exchanged for (0.01) share Common 1¢ par
(See American Consolidated Management Group, Inc.)

AMERICAN CONSOLIDATED MINES (UT)
Name changed to American Resources, Inc. (UT) 08/04/1970

AMERICAN CONSTITUTION FIRE ASSURANCE CO.
Merged into American Home Fire Assurance Co. 00/00/1932
Details not available

AMERICAN CONSTR CO (NV)
Name changed to General Steel Holdings, Inc. 03/07/2005

AMERICAN CONSULTING INC (DE)
Merged into FKB Group PLC 10/31/1988
Each share Common 1¢ par exchanged for $5.50 cash

AMERICAN CONSUMER CORP. (CO)
Charter suspended for failure to maintain a resident agent 08/06/1985

AMERICAN CONSUMER INDS INC (NJ)
Each share 6% Preferred $100 par exchanged for (6) shares Common no par 07/01/1964
Merged into Trans Canada Freezers Corp. 06/11/1979
Each share Common no par exchanged for $26 cash

AMERICAN CONSUMER PRODS INC (OH)
Common 10¢ par split (5) for (4) by issuance of (0.25) additional share 06/07/1988
96.02% acquired by Vista 2000 Inc. through voluntary cash purchase offer which expired 09/28/1995
Public interest eliminated

AMERICAN CONSUMERS INC (GA)
Each share old Common 10¢ par exchanged for (1) share new Common 10¢ par to reflect a (1) for (400) reverse split followed by a (400) for (1) forward split 04/11/2011
Note: Holders of (399) or fewer pre-split shares received $1 cash per share
Chapter 11 bankruptcy proceedings dismissed 11/17/2017

No stockholders' equity

AMERICAN CONTL CORP (OH)
Reincorporated 05/21/1974
Name changed 06/21/1978
State of incorporation changed from (DE) to (OH) 05/21/1974
Name changed from American Continental Homes, Inc. to American Continental Corp. 06/21/1978
Each share old Common $1 par exchanged for (0.00666666) share new Common $1 par 09/29/1978
New Common $1 par changed to 1¢ par and (399) additional shares issued 08/26/1983
Common 1¢ par split (3) for (2) by issuance of (0.5) additional share 05/08/1987
Liquidating plan of reorganization under Chapter 11 Federal Bankruptcy Code effective 02/08/1991
No stockholders' equity

AMERICAN CONTL INDS INC (DE)
Adjudicated bankrupt 04/03/1969
Stockholders' equity unlikely

AMERICAN CONTL LD INVT CORP (AZ)
Name changed 06/22/1981
Name changed from American Continental Life Insurance Co. to American Continental Land Investment Corp. 06/22/1981
Administratively dissolved 01/10/1996

AMERICAN CONTRACT MTG EXCHANGE (AZ)
Charter revoked for failure to file reports and pay fees 12/26/1973

AMERICAN CONTROLLED INDS INC. (OH)
Assets transferred 12/15/1986
Liquidation completed
Each share Common no par exchanged for initial distribution of (0.088095) share Central Bancorporation, Inc. Common $5 par, (0.176426) share Cincinnati Bell Inc. (Old) Common $1 par, (0.059943) share Fifth Third Bancorp Common no par, (0.651556) share Vulcan Corp. Common no par and $30.20 cash 12/15/1986
Note: Holders entitled to fewer than (10) shares of stock received additional cash in lieu of shares
Assets transferred to American Controlled Industries, Inc. Liquidating Trust and Common no par reclassified as Shares of Bene. Int. no par 12/15/1986
Each Share of Bene. Int. no par received second distribution of $20.50 cash 07/22/1987
Each Share of Bene. Int. no par received third distribution of $4.35 cash 08/27/1987
Each Share of Bene. Int. no par received fourth distribution of $4.80 cash 06/06/1990
Each Share of Bene. Int. no par received fifth and final distribution of $0.12 cash 12/05/1990
(See American Controlled Industries, Inc. Liquidating Trust)

AMERICAN CONTROLLED OILFIELDS, INC. (MD)
Out of business 00/00/1931
Details not available

AMERICAN COPPER & URANIUM CORP. (NV)
Charter revoked for failure to file reports and pay fees 03/05/1960

AMERICAN COPPER CO. (AZ)
Charter expired by time limitation 09/28/1926

AMERICAN COPPER CO (CA)
Out of business 00/00/1990
Stockholders' equity undetermined

AMERICAN COPPER CORP (BC)
Under plan of merger name changed to American Consolidated Minerals Corp. 01/30/2009
American Consolidated Minerals Corp. merged into Starcore International Mines Ltd. 12/03/2014

AMERICAN COPPER CORP (NV)
Name changed to Black River Petroleum Corp. 11/04/2013
Black River Petroleum Corp. name changed to Viva Entertainment Group, Inc. 08/02/2016

AMERICAN COPPER CORP (YT)
Name changed to E-Phoria Online Systems Inc. 07/29/1999
(See E-Phoria Online Systems Inc.)

AMERICAN COPPERMINE RES LTD (AB)
Recapitalized as Carleton Resources Corp. 02/04/1997
Each share Common no par exchanged for (0.3125) share Common no par
(See Carleton Resources Corp.)

AMERICAN CORE-TWINE CO.
Name changed to American Twine & Fabric Corp. 00/00/1943
(See American Twine & Fabric Corp.)

AMERICAN CORP. (DE)
Name changed to American Western Resources, Inc. 08/05/1977
American Western Resources, Inc. merged into Ro-Mac Gold, Ltd. 05/17/1978 which name changed to Phoenix Associates Land Syndicate 10/24/1996
(See Phoenix Associates Land Syndicate)

AMERICAN CORPORATE INVS INC (DE)
Each share old Common $0.0001 par exchanged for (0.01) share new Common $0.0001 par 06/10/1996
Name changed to Ramoil Management, Ltd. (DE) 01/26/2000
Ramoil Management, Ltd. (DE) reincorporated in Wyoming 01/25/2011 which name changed to Advantis Corp. 11/24/2015

AMERICAN CORPORATE TR (NY)
Trust terminated 07/24/1996
Details not available

AMERICAN COSMETICS LABORATORIES, INC. (TX)
Charter forfeited for failure to pay taxes 11/20/1989

AMERICAN COTTON SUPPLY CORP.
Liquidation completed 08/10/1951
Details not available

AMERICAN COUNTRY LIFE INSURANCE CO. (IN)
Common $2 par changed to no par 05/30/1972
Name changed to Lumbermens Life Insurance Co. 11/20/1975
(See Lumbermens Life Insurance Co.)

AMERICAN CR CARD TEL CO (DE)
Name changed to Card*Tel, Inc. 09/28/1987
(See Card*Tel, Inc.)

AMERICAN CR CORP (NC)
Ctfs. dated after 06/30/1976
Merged into Barclay Bank International Ltd. 05/23/1979
Each share Common $1 par exchanged for $50 cash

AMERICAN CRAFT BREWING INTERNATIONAL LTD (BERMUDA)
Assets assigned for the benefit of creditors 06/01/1998
Stockholders' equity unlikely

AMERICAN CRANK, INC. (UT)
Involuntarily dissolved 12/01/1989

AMERICAN CRAYON CO. (OH)
Each share Common $100 par exchanged for (5) shares Common no par 00/00/1935
Merged into Dixon (Joseph) Crucible Co. 01/30/1957
Each share Common $100 par exchanged for (0.76) share Common $100 par
(See Dixon (Joseph) Crucible Co.)

AMERICAN CREDIT CORP. (NC)
Certificates dated prior to 07/01/1970
Merged into Wachovia Corp. 07/01/1970
Each share 5% Preferred Ser. 1954, $25 par, 5% Preferred Ser. 1955, $25 par, 5.25% Preferred Ser. 1964, $25 par, 5.125% Preferred Ser. 1963, $25 par, 5.5% Preferred Ser. 1955, $25 par, 6% Preferred Ser. 1957, $25 par, 6.25% Preferred Ser. 1958, $25 par, 6.375% Preferred Ser. 1959, $25 par and 6.875% Preferred Ser. 1968, $25 par exchanged for (0.5) share $2.20 Conv. Preferred Ser. A $5 par
Each share Common $1 par exchanged for (0.5) share $2.20 Conv. Preferred Ser. A $5 par
(See Wachovia Corp.)

AMERICAN CREDIT OPTICAL INC. (NV)
Each share Common $0.003 par exchanged for (0.1) share Common 3¢ par 05/18/1989
Name changed to ACOI, Inc. 05/20/1991
ACOI, Inc. name changed to Hallmark Financial Services Inc. 01/06/1994

AMERICAN CRUISE LINES INC (DE)
Stock Dividend - 10% 12/17/1986
Chapter 11 Federal Bankruptcy Code converted to Chapter 7 on 12/20/1988
No stockholders' equity

AMERICAN CRYOGENICS, INC. (GA)
Common 50¢ par split (2) for (1) by issuance of (1) additional share 12/29/1961
Acquired by Standard Oil Co. (NJ) 04/09/1964
Each share Common 50¢ par exchanged for (0.212766) share Capital Stock $7 par
Standard Oil Co. (NJ) name changed to Exxon Corp. 11/01/1972 which name changed to Exxon Mobil Corp. 11/30/1999

AMERICAN CRYOSTEM CORP OLD (NV)
Name changed to ACS Global, Inc. 06/15/2011

AMERICAN CRYSTAL SUGAR CO (NJ)
Common no par changed to $10 par 00/00/1935
Common $10 par changed to $5 par and (2) additional shares issued 07/09/1964
Acquired by Crystal Growers Corp. 02/21/1973
Each share 4.5% Prior Preferred $100 par exchanged for $105 cash
Each share Common $5 par exchanged for $39.039 cash

AMERICAN CTRY HLDGS INC (DE)
Each share old Common 60¢ par exchanged for (0.25) share new Common 60¢ par 05/09/2000
Merged into Kingsway Financial Services 04/08/2002
Each share new Common 60¢ par exchanged for $2.10 cash

AMERICAN CUSTOM COMPONENTS INC (NV)
SEC revoked common stock registration 12/22/2008

AMERICAN CYANAMID CO (ME)
Class A Common $20 par and Class B Common $20 par changed to no par 00/00/1929
Class A Common no par and Class B

Common no par changed to $10 par 00/00/1932
Class A Common $10 par and Class B Common $10 par changed to Common $10 par 00/00/1944
5% Preference $10 par called for redemption 07/30/1947
3.5% Conv. Preferred Ser. A $100 par called for redemption 04/15/1953
3.5% Conv. Preferred Ser. B $100 par called for redemption 05/04/1956
3.75% Conv. Preferred Ser. C $100 par called for redemption 03/29/1957
3.5% Conv. Preferred Ser. D $100 par called for redemption 09/30/1963
Common $10 par changed to $5 par and (1) additional share issued 05/06/1966
Common $5 par split (2) for (1) by issuance of (1) additional share 06/12/1987
Stock Dividends - 100% 07/16/1952; 100% 07/12/1957
Preferred Stock Purchase Rights declared for Common stockholders of record 03/25/1986 were redeemed at $0.02 per right 12/30/1994 for holders of record 09/26/1994
Acquired by American Home Products Corp. 12/30/1994
Each share Common $5 par exchanged for $101 cash

AMERICAN CYTOGENETICS INC (DE)
Name changed 09/30/1982
Stock Dividend - 100% 01/30/1981
Name changed from American Cytology Services Corp. to American Cytogenetics, Inc. 09/30/1982
Charter forfeited for failure to maintain a registered agent 02/25/1998

AMERICAN DAIRIES, INC. (DE)
Out of business 00/00/1932
Details not available

AMERICAN DAIRY INC (UT)
Name changed to Feihe International, Inc. 11/08/2010
(See Feihe International, Inc.)

AMERICAN DAIRY PRODUCTS CORP. (NY)
Charter cancelled and proclaimed dissolved for failure to pay taxes and file reports 12/16/1957

AMERICAN DALECO TECHNOLOGIES INC (BC)
Reorganized under the laws of California as International Daleco Technologies Corp. 10/20/1987
Each share Common no par exchanged for (0.33333333) share Common no par
International Daleco Technologies Corp. recapitalized as International Daleco Corp. 06/21/1990

AMERICAN DATA MACHINES, INC. (DE)
Adjudicated bankrupt 09/29/1963
No stockholders' equity

AMERICAN DATA SVCS INC (NJ)
Each share old Common 1¢ par exchanged for (0.5) new Common 1¢ par 04/05/1973
Charter declared void for non-payment of taxes 03/01/1977

AMERICAN DATA SVCS INC (OR)
99.5% acquired by Orbanco, Inc. through exchange offer which expired 07/08/1971
Public interest eliminated

AMERICAN DE FOREST WIRELESS TELEGRAPH CO. (ME)
Charter suspended for non-payment of franchise taxes 00/00/1909

AMERICAN DEFENDER LIFE INS CO (NC)
99.95% held by ERC Corp. as of 12/07/1976
Public interest eliminated

AMERICAN DEFENSE LINE, INC. (NY)
Charter revoked for failure to file reports and pay fees 12/15/1966

AMERICAN DENTAL HEALTH ASSURANCE CO., INC. (IN)
Public offering per prospectus dated 11/01/1969 was terminated 10/14/1970
Each share Common $2 par purchased under the offer was recalled and exchanged for $4.468 cash

AMERICAN DENTAL PARTNERS INC (DE)
Common 1¢ par split (3) for (2) by issuance of (0.5) additional share payable 10/14/2005 to holders of record 09/20/2005 Ex date - 10/17/2005
Acquired by JLL Crown Holdings, LLC 02/09/2012
Each share Common 1¢ par exchanged for $19 cash

AMERICAN DENTAL PRODS CORP (MT)
Proclaimed dissolved for failure to file annual reports 12/02/1994

AMERICAN DENTAL TECHNOLOGIES INC (DE)
Name changed 06/01/1993
Name changed from American Dental Laser, Inc. to American Dental Technologies, Inc. 06/01/1993
Each share Common 1¢ par exchanged for (0.25) share Common 4¢ par 03/17/1997
Name changed to American Medical Technologies, Inc. 06/20/2000
(See American Medical Technologies, Inc.)

AMERICAN DEPARTMENT STORES CORP. (DE)
Reorganized as Brager-Eisenberg, Inc. 00/00/1937
Each share 7% Preferred exchanged for (0.25) share Capital Stock $1 par and $10 principal amount of 5% Notes
No stockholders' equity for Second Preferred and Common
(See Brager-Eisenberg, Inc.)

AMERICAN DEPT STORES INC (FL)
Merged into Southwest Florida Enterprises, Inc. 05/01/1969
Each share Common 10¢ par exchanged for (0.6) share Common 10¢ par
(See Southwest Florida Enterprises, Inc.)

AMERICAN DESIGN CORP (DE)
Recapitalized as ResortShips International, Inc. 11/13/2006
Each share Common $0.001 par exchanged for (0.03333333) share Common $0.001 par
ResortShips International, Inc. recapitalized as American Design Inc. 03/26/2007

AMERICAN DESIGN INC (DE)
Reincorporated under the laws of Nevada as Ventana Biotech Inc. 11/20/2008
(See Ventana Biotech Inc.)

AMERICAN DEVELOPMENT CORP. (OR)
Involuntarily dissolved for failure to file reports and pay fees 05/25/1995

AMERICAN DG ENERGY INC (DE)
Each share Common $0.001 par received distribution of (0.1) share EuroSite Power Inc. Common $0.001 payable 08/15/2013 to holders of record 07/25/2013 Ex date - 07/23/2013
Merged into Tecogen Inc. 05/19/2017
Each share Common $0.001 par exchanged for (0.092) share Common $0.001 par

AMERICAN DIAGNOSTICS CORP (CA)
Merged into Hoffman-LaRoche Inc. 06/27/1984
Each share Common no par exchanged for $5.44 cash
Each share Common no par received an initial additional distribution of $0.22 cash 08/00/1985
Each share Common no par received a second and final additional distribution of $0.07 cash 10/20/1986

AMERICAN DIAMOND CORP (NV)
Recapitalized as All American Coffee & Beverage, Inc. 03/21/2006
Each share Common $0.001 par exchanged for (0.004) share Common $0.001 par
(See All American Coffee & Beverage, Inc.)

AMERICAN DIAMOND MINING CORP. (DE)
Proclaimed inoperative and void for non-payment of taxes 02/01/1955

AMERN DIGITAL COMMUNICATION INC (WY)
Common $0.0001 par split (2) for (1) by issuance of (1) additional share 12/21/1993
Name changed to TrackPower, Inc. (WY) 09/20/1999
TrackPower, Inc. (WY) reorganized in Nevada as Gate to Wire Solutions, Inc. 09/26/2008
(See Gate to Wire Solutions, Inc.)

AMERICAN DIGITAL INDS LTD (BC)
Struck off register and declared dissolved for failure to file returns 06/21/1991

AMERICAN DIMENSIONS CORP. (NY)
Charter cancelled and proclaimed dissolved for failure to pay taxes and file reports 12/15/1967

AMERICAN DISC CO (GA)
Merged into American Credit Corp. 12/31/1964
Each share 5% Preferred $50 par exchanged for (2) shares 5% Preferred $25 par
Each share Common no par exchanged for (2.25) shares Common $1 par
American Credit Corp. merged into Wachovia Corp. 07/01/1970
(See Wachovia Corp.)

AMERICAN DISCOUNT CO. OF GEORGIA (GA)
Merged into American Discount Co. 10/02/1961
5% Preferred $50 par exchanged for (1) share 5% Preferred $50 par
Each share Common no par exchanged for (2.59) shares Common no par
American Discount Co. merged into American Credit Corp. 12/03/1964 which merged into Wachovia Corp. 07/01/1970
(See Wachovia Corp.)

AMERICAN DISP SVCS INC (DE)
Merged into Allied Waste Industries, Inc. 10/15/1998
Each share Common 1¢ par exchanged for (1.65) shares new Common 1¢ par
Allied Waste Industries, Inc. merged into Republic Services, Inc. 12/05/2008

AMERICAN DIST TELEG CO (NJ)
Common no par changed to $1 par and (1.649296) additional shares issued 01/29/1968
Common $1 par split (3) for (1) by issuance of (2) additional shares 05/28/1968
Common $1 par split (2) for (1) by issuance of (1) additional share 05/24/1983
Stock Dividend - 500% 02/16/1950

Name changed to ADT, Inc. 05/13/1986
(See ADT, Inc.)

AMERICAN DISTILLING CO (MD)
5% Preferred called for redemption 12/20/1943
Common $20 par split (2) for (1) by issuance of (1) additional share 04/11/1956
Common $20 par changed to $10 par and (1) additional share issued 09/19/1960
Common $10 par split (3) for (2) by issuance of (0.5) additional share 04/30/1969
Common $10 par changed to $1 par 06/25/1969
Stock Dividends - 10% 05/29/1959; 10% 11/29/1963
Name changed to Amdisco Corp. 11/14/1980
(See Amdisco Corp.)

AMERICAN DIVERSIFIED, INC. (CO)
Merged into National Insurance Co. of America 10/06/1966
Each share Common $1 par exchanged for (0.25) share Class A Common $1 par
(See National Insurance Co. of America)

AMERICAN DIVERSIFIED CORP (NV)
Recapitalized as Natural Pharmaceutical International Inc. 06/18/1990
Each share Common 10¢ par exchanged for (0.2) share Common no par

AMERICAN DIVERSIFIED GROUP INC (NV)
Reincorporated under the laws of Delaware as GlobeTel Communications Corp. and Common $0.001 par changed to $0.00001 par 07/24/2002
GlobeTel Communications Corp. name changed to Sanswire Corp. 09/24/2008 which name changed to World Surveillance Group Inc. 04/27/2011

AMERICAN DIVERSIFIED HLDGS INC (NV)
Name changed to Amdiv.Com Inc. 12/03/1998
(See Amdiv.Com Inc.)

AMERICAN DIVERSIFIED HLDG CORP INC (OH)
Completely liquidated 00/00/1981
No stockholders' equity

AMERICAN DIVERSIFIED INDS CORP (DE)
Name changed to Brewer Alcohol Fuels Corp. 08/29/1980
Brewer Alcohol Fuels Corp. recapitalized as National Gas & Power Co., Inc. 11/21/1983
(See National Gas & Power Co., Inc.)

AMERICAN DIVERSIFIED INVS FD INC (MD)
Acquired by Selected American Shares, Inc. 01/20/1975
Each share Common $1 par exchanged for (1.132) shares Common $1.25 par

AMERICAN DIVERSIFIED MUTUAL SECURITIES CO. (DE)
Name changed to American Diversified Securities, Inc. 09/29/1959
(See American Diversified Securities, Inc.)

AMERICAN DIVERSIFIED SECURITIES, INC. (DE)
Each share Common $1 par exchanged for (0.2) share new Common $1 par plus a stock dividend of (2.4) shares Class A 33¢ par 08/01/1960
Charter cancelled for non-payment of taxes 04/01/1963

AMERICAN DREAM ENTMT INC (MN)
Company believed out of business 00/00/2006
Details not available

AMERICAN DREDGING CO (PA)
Each share Common $100 par exchanged for (4) shares Common $12.50 par 00/00/1953
Common $12.50 par changed to $2.50 par and (3) additional shares issued 04/15/1964
Stock Dividend - 100% 06/26/1986
Name changed to American Atlantic Co. 02/26/1993
(See American Atlantic Co.)

AMERICAN DRUG CO (DE)
Name changed to Five Star Products, Inc. 08/10/1999
(See Five Star Products, Inc.)

AMERICAN DRUG SCREENS INC (OK)
Name changed to MBF USA, Inc. (OK) 05/24/1993
MBF USA, Inc. (OK) reorganized in Maryland 12/18/1995 which name changed to WRP Corp. 06/23/1998 which name changed to AHPC Holdings, Inc. 05/14/2004

AMERICAN DRUGGISTS INS CO (OH)
Capital Stock $25 par changed to $5 par and (4) additional shares issued 04/01/1964
Stock Dividend - 33-1/3% 04/01/1958
Merged into Armco Inc. 05/08/1980
Each share Capital Stock $5 par exchanged for (3.43) shares Common $5 par
Armco Inc. merged into AK Steel Holding Corp. 09/30/1999

AMERICAN DRUGGISTS SYNDICATE (NY)
Merged into Vadsco Sales Corp. 00/00/1929
Details not available

AMERICAN DRYER CORP. (PA)
Name changed to Utronics Corp. 03/28/1962
Utronics Corp. acquired by Defiance Industries, Inc. 07/10/1963 which merged into El-Tronics, Inc. 10/03/1969 which name changed to ELT, Inc. 01/04/1974 which name changed to Dutch Boy, Inc. 02/23/1977 which name changed to Artra Group Inc. 12/31/1980 which merged into Entrade Inc. 09/23/1999
(See Entrade Inc.)

AMERICAN DRYICE CORP.
Dissolved 00/00/1934
Details not available

AMERICAN DUAL VEST FD INC (DE)
Income Preferred Shares $13.80 par called for redemption 06/29/1979
Name changed to ADV Fund Inc. 07/02/1979
ADV Fund Inc. name changed to WPG Fund, Inc. (DE) 04/16/1985 which reincorporated in Massachusetts 04/29/1988 which name changed to WPG Growth & Income Fund 12/29/1989 which name changed to WPG Large Cap Growth Fund 10/18/2000

AMERICAN DUCHESS OIL & METALS CORP (NV)
Merged into International Land & Development Corp. 05/03/1965
Each share Common 5¢ par exchanged for (0.05) share Capital Stock $1 par
International Land & Development Corp. name changed to International Chemical Development Corp. 10/25/1968 which recapitalized as Columbia Autocar, Inc. 04/15/1980 which name changed to American Peat Co. 04/22/1982 which name changed to American National Hydrocarbon, Inc. 11/15/1982

(See American National Hydrocarbon, Inc.)

AMERICAN DUCHESS URANIUM & OIL CO. (NV)
Name changed to American Duchess Oil & Metals Corp. 07/01/1957
American Duchess Oil & Metals Corp. merged into International Land & Development Corp. 05/03/1965 which name changed to International Chemical Development Corp. 10/25/1968 which recapitalized as Columbia Autocar, Inc. 04/15/1980 which name changed to American Peat Co. 04/22/1982 which name changed to American National Hydrocarbon, Inc. 11/15/1982
(See American National Hydrocarbon, Inc.)

AMERICAN DURALITE CORP (DE)
Reincorporated 04/29/1967
State of incorporation changed from (NY) to (DE) and Common 10¢ par reclassified as Class A Common 10¢ par 04/29/1967
Each share Class A Common 10¢ par exchanged for (0.33333333) share Class A Common 15¢ par 11/18/1968
Adjudicated bankrupt 07/02/1969
No stockholders' equity

AMERICAN DYNAMICS CORP. (MA)
Completely liquidated 09/25/1968
Each share Common no par received first and final distribution of $0.25 cash
Note: Certificates were not required to be surrendered and are without value

AMERICAN DYNAMICS CORP (NV)
Plan of reorganization under Chapter 11 Federal Bankruptcy proceedings effective 01/09/1990
No stockholders' equity

AMERICAN EAGLE AIRCRAFT CORP. OF DELAWARE (DE)
Merged into American Eagle-Lincoln Aircraft Corp. 05/14/1931
Details not available

AMERICAN EAGLE CORP. (CA)
Merged into Acme Eagle Corp. 05/08/1964
Each share Common $1 par exchanged for (0.66666666) share Common $1 par
Acme Eagle Corp. merged into Allied Products Corp. (MI) 04/05/1965 which reincorporated in Delaware 01/31/1968
(See Allied Products Corp. (DE))

AMERICAN EAGLE ENERGY CORP (NV)
Each share old Common $0.001 par exchanged for (0.25) share new Common $0.001 par 03/19/2014
Plan of reorganization under Chapter 11 Federal Bankruptcy proceedings effective 12/05/2016
No stockholders' equity

AMERICAN EAGLE ENERGY INC (NV)
Old Common $0.001 par split (2) for (1) by issuance of (1) additional share payable 10/26/2009 to holders of record 10/26/2009
Each share old Common $0.001 par exchanged for (0.66666666) share new Common $0.001 par 01/24/2011
Merged into Eternal Energy Corp. 12/20/2011
Each share new Common $0.001 par exchanged for (3.641) shares Common $0.001 par
Eternal Energy Corp. recapitalized as American Eagle Energy Corp. 12/20/2011
(See American Eagle Energy Corp.)

AMERICAN EAGLE FD INC (MD)
Name changed to U.S. Eagle Fund, Inc. 01/22/1990
(See U.S. Eagle Fund, Inc.)

AMERICAN EAGLE GROUP INC (DE)
Recapitalized as Pacific Ventures Group, Inc. 11/08/2012
Each share Common 1¢ par exchanged for (0.02) share Common $0.001 par
Note: No holder will receive fewer than (100) post-split shares

AMERICAN EAGLE INDS INC (WY)
Administratively dissolved for failure to pay taxes 05/31/2006

AMERICAN EAGLE INTERNATIONAL, INC. (DE)
Each share old Common 1¢ par exchanged for (0.06666666) share new Common 1¢ par 10/01/1961
Name changed to American Modular Manufacturing Corp. 12/08/1961
American Modular Manufacturing Corp. name changed to Chemola Corp. 03/05/1969
(See Chemola Corp.)

AMERICAN EAGLE-LINCOLN AIRCRAFT CORP. (DE)
No longer in existence having become inoperative and void for non-payment of taxes 04/01/1934

AMERICAN EAGLE MFG CO (NV)
Each share old Common $0.001 par exchanged for (0.1) share new Common $0.001 par 09/03/2004
Name changed to No Borders, Inc. 10/27/2004

AMERICAN EAGLE OUTFITTERS INC OLD (DE)
Reincorporated 11/02/1998
Common no par split (3) for (2) by issuance of (0.5) additional share 01/05/1998 to holders of record 12/19/1997
Common no par split (3) for (2) by issuance of (0.5) additional share payable 05/08/1998 to holders of record 04/24/1998
State of incorporation changed from (OH) to (DE) 11/02/1998
Under plan of reorganization each share Common no par automatically became (1) share American Eagle Outfitters, Inc. (New) Common no par 04/07/1999

AMERICAN EAGLE PETES LTD (CANADA)
Reincorporated 10/20/1982
Reincorporated 09/17/1992
Place of incorporation changed from (SK) to (AB) 10/20/1982
Place of incorporation changed from (AB) to (Canada) 09/17/1992
Merged into CS Resources Ltd./Les Ressources CS Ltee. 08/01/1993
Each share Common no par exchanged for (0.02) share Common no par, (0.016) Common Stock Purchase Warrant expiring 07/31/1996 and $0.125 cash
(See CS Resources Ltd./Les Ressources CS Ltee.)

AMERICAN EAGLE RES INC (BC)
Reincorporated 02/06/2008
Place of incorporation changed from (DE) to (BC) 02/06/2008
Merged into Lion One Metals Ltd. 01/31/2011
Each share Common 1¢ par exchanged for (1) share Common no par

AMERICAN EAGLE URANIUM INC. (DE)
Name changed to American Eagle International Inc. 07/29/1958
American Eagle International Inc. name changed to American Modular Manufacturing Corp. 12/08/1961 which name changed to Chemola Corp. 03/05/1969

(See Chemola Corp.)

AMERICAN ECO CORP (ON)
Chapter 11 bankruptcy proceedings converted to Chapter 7 on 06/28/2002
Stockholders' equity unlikely

AMERICAN ECOLOGY CORP (DE)
Reincorporated 05/12/1987
State of incorporation changed from (CA) to (DE) and Common no par changed to 1¢ par 05/12/1987
Old Common no par split (3) for (2) by issuance of (0.5) additional share 07/15/1992
Each share old Common 1¢ par exchanged for (1) share new Common 1¢ par to reflect a (1) for (100) reverse split followed by a (100) for (1) forward split 07/02/2001
Note: Holders of (99) or fewer pre-split shares received $2.43 cash per share
Name changed to US Ecology, Inc. 02/22/2010

AMERICAN ED CORP (NV)
Reincorporated 01/01/2004
State of incorporation changed from (CO) to (NV) 01/01/2004
Each share old Common $0.025 par exchanged for (0.05) share new Common $0.025 par to reflect a (1) for (2,000) reverse split followed by a (100) for (1) forward split 09/07/2006
Note: Holders of (1,999) shares or fewer pre-split shares received $0.55 cash per share
Acquired by K12 Inc. 12/03/2010
Each share new Common $0.025 par exchanged for $20.38716398 cash
Note: An additional initial distribution of $0.13160025 cash per share was paid from escrow 03/18/2011
An additional second distribution of $2.6219424 cash per share was paid from escrow 12/21/2011

AMERICAN EDL COMPUTER INC (DE)
Common 1¢ par split (3) for (1) by issuance of (2) additional shares 09/05/1984
Merged into CMS Advertising, Inc. 03/10/1989
Each share Common 1¢ par exchanged for (0.10621348) share Common 1¢ par and (0.09469696) Common Stock Purchase Warrant expiring 03/10/1994
CMS Advertising, Inc. name changed to Unico, Inc. 09/29/1989 which recapitalized as ABSS Corp. (DE) 04/25/2002 which reorganized in Nevada as NT Holding Corp. 08/04/2004

AMERICAN EDL PRODS INC (CO)
Each share Common 1¢ par exchanged for (0.2) share Common 5¢ par 04/22/1997
Merged into Nasco International, Inc. 06/22/2001
Each share Common 5¢ par exchanged for $10 cash

AMERICAN EDL TELEVISION NETWORK INC (CA)
Charter suspended for failure to file reports and pay fees 12/01/1983

AMERICAN EDUCATIONAL LIFE INSURANCE CO. (TN)
Declared insolvent 01/13/1967
No stockholders' equity

AMERICAN EDUCATORS FINL CORP (DE)
Recapitalized as Asia Ventures Corp. 08/03/2007
Each share Common $0.0001 par exchanged for (0.005) share Common $0.0001 par
(See Asia Ventures Corp.)

AMERICAN ELEC AUTOMOBILE INC (DE)
Each share old Common $0.0001 par exchanged for (0.33333333) share new Common $0.0001 par 04/05/2000
Name changed to American Entertainment & Animation Corp. 07/16/2002
American Entertainment & Animation Corp. name changed to Silver Dragon Resources Inc. 03/01/2005

AMERICAN ELEC PWR INC (NY)
Each Equity Unit received (1.2225) shares Common $6.50 par 08/16/2005
(Additional Information in Active)

AMERICAN ELECTR COMPONENTS INC (IN)
Merged into Echlin Inc. 12/28/1995
Each share Common no par exchanged for (0.366) share Common $1 par
Echlin Inc. merged into Dana Corp. 07/09/1998
(See Dana Corp.)

AMERICAN ELECTR LABS INC (PA)
Each share Class A Common $10 par exchanged for (5) shares Class A Common $2 par 10/01/1959
Each share Class B Common $10 par exchanged for (5) shares Class B Common $2 par 10/01/1959
Preferred $10 par called for redemption 04/30/1960
Class A Common $2 par and Class B Common $2 par changed to $1 par and (1) additional share issued respectively 03/26/1962
Class A Common $1 par and Class B Common $1 par split (5) for (4) by issuance of (0.25) additional share respectively 11/20/1965
Class A Common $1 par and Class B Common $1 par split (6) for (5) by issuance of (0.2) additional share respectively 10/21/1966
Class A Common $1 par and Class B Common $1 par split (3) for (2) by issuance of (0.5) additional share respectively 11/17/1967
Class A Common $1 par and Class B Common $1 par split (2) for (1) by issuance of (1) additional share respectively 11/22/1968
Stock Dividends - In Class A and B Common Stock - 10% 02/24/1961; 10% 12/27/1963; 10% 11/13/1964
Name changed to AEL Industries, Inc. 10/01/1976
(See AEL Industries, Inc.)

AMERICAN ELECTRIC CORP.
Name changed to Belding Hall Electric Corp. 00/00/1927
(See Belding Hall Electric Corp.)

AMERICAN ELECTRIC POWER CO.
Acquired by American Electric Power Corp. 00/00/1927
Details not available

AMERICAN ELECTRIC POWER CORP.
Reorganized as Penn Western Gas & Electric Co. 00/00/1935
Details not available

AMERICAN ELECTRIC SECURITIES CORP. (DE)
Preferred $20 par changed to $5 par 05/00/1932
Each share Preferred $5 par exchanged for (5) shares Preferred $1 par 10/00/1932
Common no par changed to $1 par 00/00/1937
Acquired by Lehman Corp. (DE) 03/30/1964
Each share Preferred $1 par exchanged for (0.34441) share Capital Stock $1 par
Each share Common $1 par exchanged for (0.68206) share Capital stock $1 par

Lehman Corp. (DE) reincorporated in Maryland 04/30/1977 which name changed to Salomon Brothers Fund Inc. 05/01/1990 which name changed to Legg Mason Partners Equity Fund, Inc. 11/20/2006 which name changed to Legg Mason Partners Equity Trust 04/16/2007

AMERICAN ELECTROMEDICS CORP (DE)
Common 10¢ par split (3) for (1) by issuance of (2) additional shares 01/07/1985
Each share old Common 10¢ par exchanged for (0.2) share new Common 10¢ par 11/08/1996
Name changed to Equidyne Corp. 01/05/2000
Equidyne Corp. name changed to Cathay Merchant Group, Inc. 10/06/2004 which name changed to Mansfelder Metals Ltd. 02/21/2008

AMERICAN ELECTRONICS CO. (MN)
Name changed to American Monarch Corp. 12/00/1961
American Monarch Corp. acquired by Minneapolis Scientific Controls Corp. 06/15/1965
(See Minneapolis Scientific Controls Corp.)

AMERICAN ELECTRS INC (CA)
Each share old Common $1 par exchanged for (0.2) share new Common $1 par 05/25/1967
Name changed to American Pacesetter 06/03/1970
(See American Pacesetter)

AMERICAN EMERGICENTER INC (CA)
Merged into U.S. Medical Enterprises, Inc. 12/12/1985
Each share Common 1¢ par exchanged for (0.5142564) share Common 10¢ par
Note: An additional stock distribution may be made subject to fulfillment of earnings projections
U.S. Medical Enterprises, Inc. merged into InterCare, Inc. 01/07/1987
(See Intercare, Inc.)

AMERICAN EMPIRE LIFE CORP. (LA)
Charter revoked 05/13/1982

AMERICAN EMPIRE LIFE INSURANCE CO. (TX)
Merged into Great Plains Life Insurance Co. on a (1/3) for (1) basis 04/03/1963
Great Plains Life Insurance Co. acquired by American Educational Life Insurance Co. 10/31/1964
(See American Educational Life Insurance Co.)

AMERICAN ENCAUSTIC TILING CO., INC. (NY)
Approximately 99.8% acquired by National Gypsum Co. (Old) through exchange offer which expired 03/13/1959
National Gypsum Co. purchased outstanding shares for cash until 00/00/1986
Public interest eliminated

AMERICAN ENCAUSTIC TILING CO., LTD.
Reorganized as American Encaustic Tiling Co., Inc. 00/00/1936
Each share Common exchanged for (0.1) share Common $1 par
(See American Encaustic Tiling Co., Inc.)

AMERICAN ENERGY & TECHNOLOGY INC (DE)
Each share old Common 1¢ par exchanged for (0.01333333) share new Common 1¢ par 02/19/1985
Recapitalized as Breccia International Minerals Inc. 02/21/1997
Each share new Common 1¢ par exchanged for (0.05) share Common 1¢ par

Breccia International Minerals Inc. name changed to Nano World Projects Corp. 03/01/2000
(See Nano World Projects Corp.)

AMERICAN ENERGY CORP (BC)
Recapitalized as Nickling Resources Inc. 06/05/1984
Each share Common no par exchanged for (0.2) share Common no par
Nickling Resources Inc. recapitalized as Florin Resources Inc. 05/09/1989 which merged into Crimsonstar Mining Corp. 06/19/1991 which recapitalized as Mountain View Ventures Inc. 05/21/1993 which recapitalized as Blackrun Ventures Inc. 04/08/1997 which recapitalized as Blackrun Minerals Inc. 06/10/1999 which name changed to Diversified Industries Ltd. 03/29/2000
(See Diversified Industries Ltd.)

AMERICAN ENERGY FIELDS INC (DE)
Common $0.0001 par split (12.2) for (1) by issuance of (11.2) additional shares payable 01/22/2010 to holders of record 01/15/2010 Ex date - 01/25/2010
Name changed to Continental Resources Group, Inc. 07/28/2011
Continental Resources Group, Inc. merged into Pershing Gold Corp. 03/04/2013

AMERICAN ENERGY GROUP LTD (NV)
Plan of reorganization under Chapter 11 Federal Bankruptcy Code effective 09/03/2003
No old Common stockholders' equity
(Additional Information in Active)

AMERICAN ENERGY PARTNERS INC. (UT)
Involuntarily dissolved 04/01/1988

AMERICAN ENERGY PRODUCTION INC (DE)
Name changed 07/16/2002
Name changed from American Energy Partners, Inc. to American Energy Production Inc. 07/16/2002
Each share old Common $0.0001 par exchanged for (0.04) share new Common $0.0001 par 09/14/2007
Stock Dividend - 20% payable 09/13/2002 to holders of record 08/16/2002 Ex date - 08/14/2002
SEC revoked common stock registration 10/17/2013

AMERICAN ENERGY SVCS INC (TX)
Each share old Common $0.001 par exchanged for (0.1) share new Common $0.001 par 01/02/1996
SEC revoked common stock registration 08/04/2010

AMERICAN ENGRAVING, INC. (OK)
Charter suspended for failure to file reports and pay fees 01/29/1971

AMERICAN ENKA CORP (DE)
Common no par changed to $5 par 08/10/1955
Common $5 par changed to $2.50 par and (1) additional share issued 04/09/1963
Common $2.50 par changed to $1.25 par and (1) additional share issued 04/09/1965
Common $1.25 par split (3) for (2) by issuance of (0.5) additional share 04/11/1969
Stock Dividend - 200% 11/30/1951
Under plan of merger name changed to Akzona Inc. 09/30/1970
(See Akzona Inc.)

AMERICAN ENTERPRISE COM CORP (FL)
Each share old Common no par exchanged for (0.25) share new Common no par 03/24/2000

Name changed to Nanobac Pharmaceuticals, Inc. 06/17/2003
(See Nanobac Pharmaceuticals, Inc.)

AMERICAN ENTERPRISE DEV CORP (TX)
SEC revoked common stock registration 11/16/2011

AMERICAN ENTERPRISES FD INC (NY)
Name changed to Intercontinental Securities, Ltd. and Common $1 par changed to 10¢ par 12/05/1974
Intercontinental Securities, Ltd. name changed to Golconda Investors Ltd. (NY) 03/12/1975 which reorganized in Maryland as Bull & Bear Gold Investors Ltd. 10/26/1987 which name changed to Midas Investments Ltd. 06/30/1999 which merged into Midas Fund, Inc. (MD) 11/16/2001 which reorganized in Delaware as Midas Series Trust 10/12/2012

AMERICAN ENTERPRISES INC. (OH)
Voluntarily dissolved 06/21/1976
No stockholders' equity

AMERICAN ENTERPRISES INC (NV)
Each share old Common 1¢ par exchanged for (0.2) share new Common 1¢ par 04/01/1986
Name changed to American Casino Enterprises, Inc. (New) 11/19/1993
American Casino Enterprises, Inc. (New) name changed to American Vantage Companies 04/11/1997
(See American Vantage Companies)

AMERICAN ENTMT & ANIMATION CORP (DE)
Name changed to Silver Dragon Resources Inc. 03/01/2005

AMERICAN ENTMT VENTURE CORP (NV)
Recapitalized as American Capital Holding Corp. 12/11/1990
Each share Common $0.001 par exchanged for (0.5) share Common $0.001 par

AMERICAN ENTREPENEURIAL FDG CORP (DE)
Name changed to Franchise Management International Inc. 12/22/1997
Franchise Management International Inc. recapitalized as Flight Management International, Inc. 10/01/2007 which recapitalized as Native American Energy Group, Inc. 11/05/2009

AMERICAN ENVIRONMENTAL CORP (NV)
Name changed to Carnegie Cooke & Co. 09/22/2000
Carnegie Cooke & Co. name changed to TrackBets International Inc. 01/25/2008
(See TrackBets International Inc.)

AMERICAN ENVIRONMENTAL CTL CORP (DE)
Charter cancelled and declared inoperative and void for non-payment of taxes 04/15/1972

AMERICAN ENVIRONMENTAL ENTERPRISES CORP (AB)
Struck off register for failure to file annual returns 03/01/1992

AMERICAN ENVIRONMENTAL SCIENCES LTD (NV)
Common 10¢ par changed to 5¢ par 07/21/1970
Completely liquidated 06/04/1976
Each share Common 5¢ par exchanged for first and final distribution of $0.0304 cash

AMERICAN EQUINE PRODS INC (DE)
Chapter 11 bankruptcy proceedings terminated 11/24/1997
No stockholders' equity

AMERICAN EQUITABLE ASSURANCE CO.
Merged into American Equitable Assurance Co. of New York 00/00/1930
Details not available

AMERICAN EQUITABLE ASSURANCE CO. OF NEW YORK (NY)
Each share Common $5 par exchanged for (0.4) share Capital Stock $5 par 00/00/1932
Recapitalized 12/31/1960
Each share Capital Stock $5 par exchanged for (2.1) shares Capital Stock $2.50 par
Merged into Reliance Insurance Co. 06/30/1965
Each share Capital Stock $2.50 par exchanged for (0.79) share Common $5 par
(See Reliance Insurance Co.)

AMERICAN EQUITIES CO.
Merged into International Utilities Corp. 00/00/1937
Each share Capital Stock exchanged for (0.1) share $3.50 Prior Preferred no par and (0.5) share Class B $1 par
International Utilities Corp. name changed to IU International Corp. 04/27/1973
(See IU International Corp.)

AMERICAN EQUITIES CORP. (NV)
Dissolved 04/00/1962
No stockholders' equity

AMERICAN EQUITIES FINL CORP (DE)
Charter cancelled and declared inoperative and void for non-payment of taxes 03/01/1989

AMERICAN EQUITY BANCORP INC (WI)
Merged into Anchor BanCorp Wisconsin Inc. 06/30/1995
Each share Common 1¢ par exchanged for (0.976) share Common 10¢ par
(See Anchor BanCorp Wisconsin Inc.)

AMERICAN EQUITY CAP TR I (DE)
8% Accredited Investors Conv. Trust Preferred Securities called for redemption at $30 plus $0.066666 accrued dividends on 07/10/2012

AMERICAN EQUITY CORP (TN)
Out of business 00/00/1990
No stockholders' equity

AMERICAN EQUITY FD INC (DE)
Name changed to American Option & Equity Fund, Inc. 11/06/1978
(See American Option & Equity Fund, Inc.)

AMERICAN EQUITY INVT TR (IA)
Liquidation completed
Each Share of Bene. Int. $1 par exchanged for initial distribution of $23.50 cash 09/14/1984
Each Share of Bene. Int. $1 par received second and final distribution of $0.685 cash 11/30/1984

AMERICAN EQUITY LIFE INSURANCE CO. (SC)
Merged into Loyal American Life Insurance Co. 06/01/1964
Each share Common $1 par exchanged for (0.75) share Common 50¢ par
(See Loyal American Life Insurance Co.)

AMERICAN EQUITY TR INC (MD)
Charter forfeited for failure to file annual reports 10/06/1998

AMERICAN ESTATE LIFE INS CO (AZ)
Each share Common 12¢ par exchanged for (0.00125) share Common $96 par 03/05/1982
Note: In effect holders received $0.30 cash per share and public interest was eliminated

AMERICAN ETHANOL INTL CORP (CANADA)
Name changed to American Agri-Technology Corp. 08/19/1996
(See American Agri-Technology Corp.)

AMERICAN EUROPEAN SECS INC (PANAMA)
Name changed to AMEROSEC (Investment), Inc. 01/09/1984

AMERICAN EUROPEAN SECURITIES CO. (DE)
$4.50 Preferred Ser. B called for redemption 06/30/1947
Completely liquidated 05/31/1972
Each share Common no par exchanged for first and final distribution of (1) share American European Securities, Inc. Common 1¢ par
American European Securities, Inc. name changed to AMEROSEC (Investment), Inc. 01/09/1984

AMERICAN EXCELSIOR CORP. (DE)
Name changed to Chicago Holding Corp. 11/14/1967
(See Chicago Holding Corp.)

AMERICAN EXCHANGE BANCORP INC (OK)
Ceased operations 08/20/1987
Stockholders' equity unlikely

AMERICAN EXCHANGE SECURITIES CORP.
Dissolved 00/00/1931
Details not available

AMERICAN EXPL CO (DE)
Common 5¢ par split (5) for (4) by issuance of (0.25) additional share 01/09/1984
Each share old Common 5¢ par exchanged for (0.1) share new Common 5¢ par 06/13/1995
Merged into Louis Dreyfus Natural Gas Corp. 10/14/1997
Each $2.25 Depositary Preferred Ser. C exchanged for (1) $2.25 Depositary Preferred
Each share $2.25 Conv. Preferred Ser. C $1 par exchanged for (1) share $2.25 Conv. Preferred 1¢ par
Each share new Common 5¢ par exchanged for (0.72) share Common 1¢ par and $3 cash
Louis Dreyfus Natural Corp. merged into Dominion Resources, Inc. (New) 11/01/2001 which name changed to Dominion Energy, Inc. 05/11/2017

AMERICAN EXPL CORP (AB)
Name changed to Asia Minerals Corp. (AB) 08/25/1993
Asia Minerals Corp. (AB) reincorporated in British Columbia 06/07/1994 which name changed to American Bonanza Gold Mining Corp. 10/16/2000 which merged into American Bonanza Gold Corp. 03/31/2005 which merged into Kerr Mines Inc. 07/07/2014

AMERICAN EXPL CORP (NV)
Stock Dividend - 50% payable 04/14/2009 to holders of record 03/26/2009 Ex date - 04/15/2009
Recapitalized as Spotlight Innovation Inc. 12/19/2013
Each share Common $0.001 par exchanged for (0.002) share Common $0.001 par

AMERICAN EXPORT AIRLINES, INC.
Name changed to American Overseas Airlines, Inc. 00/00/1945
(See American Overseas Airlines, Inc.)

AMERICAN EXPORT ISBRANDTSEN CO., INC. (DE)
Stock Dividend - 10% 02/09/1967
Merged into American Export Industries, Inc. 10/17/1967
Each share 6% 1st Preferred $100 par exchanged for (1) share $6 Preferred Ser. A no par
Each share Common 40¢ par exchanged for (1) share Common 40¢ par
American Export Industries, Inc. name changed to Aeicor, Inc. 03/31/1978 which name changed to Doskocil Companies Inc. 09/30/1983 which name changed to Foodbrands America Inc. 05/15/1995 which merged into IBP, Inc. 05/07/1997 which merged into Tyson Foods, Inc. 09/28/2001

AMERICAN EXPRESS CAP FD INC (DE)
Name changed to Capital Fund of America, Inc. 07/25/1975
Capital Fund of America, Inc. merged into New Perspective Fund, Inc. (MD) 11/03/1978 which reincorporated in Delaware as New Perspective Fund 12/01/2012

AMERICAN EXPRESS CO (NY)
$1.50 Conv. Preferred $1.66666666 par called for redemption 12/31/1973
$2.30 Conv. Preferred $1.66666666 par called for redemption 12/31/1973
Money Market Preferred Ser. B $1.66666666 par called for redemption 12/04/1991
Money Market Preferred Ser. D $1.66666666 par called for redemption 12/26/1991
Money Market Preferred Ser. C $1.66666666 par called for redemption 01/08/1992
Money Market Preferred Ser. A $1.66666666 par called for redemption 01/15/1992
(Additional Information in Active)

AMERICAN EXPRESS CO CAP TR I (DE)
7% Quarterly Income Preferred Securities I called for redemption at $25 on 07/16/2003

AMERICAN EXPRESS FDS (MA)
Completely liquidated 00/00/1994
Details not available

AMERICAN EXPRESS GOVT SECS FD INC (MD)
Name changed to American Fund of Government Securities, Inc. 07/25/1975

AMERICAN EXPRESS INCOME FD INC (DE)
Name changed to American Income Investments, Inc. 07/25/1975
American Income Investments, Inc. merged into Income Fund of America, Inc. (DE) 07/31/1976 which reincorporated in Maryland 09/22/1983 which reorganized in Delaware as Income Fund of America 10/01/2010

AMERICAN EXPRESS INVT FD INC (DE)
Name changed to American Balanced Fund, Inc. (MD) 07/25/1975
American Balanced Fund, Inc. (MD) reincorporated in Delaware as American Balanced Fund 03/01/2010

AMERICAN EXPRESS SPL FD INC (DE)
Name changed to American Special Fund, Inc. 07/25/1975
American Special Fund, Inc. merged into Growth Fund of America, Inc. (DE) 08/31/1976 which reincorporated in Maryland 09/22/1983 which reorganized in Delaware 05/01/2013

AMERICAN EXPRESS STK FD INC (DE)
Name changed to Stock Fund of America, Inc. 07/25/1975
Stock Fund of America, Inc. merged into Investment Co. of America 06/25/1976

AMERICAN EXPT INDS INC (DE)
Name changed to Aeicor, Inc. 03/31/1978
Aeicor, Inc. name changed to Doskocil Companies Inc. 09/30/1983 which name changed to Foodbrands America Inc. 05/15/1995 which merged into IBP, Inc. 05/07/1997 which merged into Tyson Foods, Inc. 09/28/2001

AMERICAN EXPT ISBRANDTSEN LINES INC (NY)
Stock Dividend - 10% 06/15/1964
Name changed back to American Export Lines, Inc. 07/18/1972
(See American Export Lines, Inc.)

AMERICAN EXPT LINES INC (NY)
Each share Common $1 par exchanged for (2.5) shares Common 40¢ par 00/00/1946
Name changed to American Export Isbrandtsen Lines, Inc. 04/20/1964 which name changed back to American Export Lines, Inc. 07/18/1972
Merged into Farrell Lines Inc. 03/28/1978
Each share Common 40¢ par exchanged for $25.50 cash

AMERICAN FACSIMILE CORP (DE)
Name changed to A S P I, Inc. and Common 10¢ par changed to 1¢ par 05/22/1970
(See A S P I, Inc.)

AMERICAN FACTORS LTD. (HI)
Each share Capital Stock $100 par exchanged for (5) shares Capital Stock $20 par and a stock dividend of (3.66666666) shares paid 00/00/1927
Capital Stock $20 par changed to $10 par and (1) additional share issued 06/01/1960
Capital Stock $10 par split (3) fo. (2) by issuance of (0.5) additional share 10/14/1963
Name changed to Amfac, Inc. 04/30/1966
(See Amfac, Inc.)

AMERICAN FAMILY CORP (GA)
Common 10¢ par split (5) for (4) by issuance of (0.25) additional share 10/15/1976
Common 10¢ par split (3) for (2) by issuance of (0.5) additional share 06/03/1985
Common 10¢ par split (4) for (3) by issuance of (0.33333333) additional share 03/01/1986
Common 10¢ par split (2) for (1) by issuance of (1) additional share 02/02/1987
Stock Dividends - 10% 03/15/1978; 10% 09/01/1979; 20% 12/13/1983; 10% 12/01/1984
Name changed to AFLAC Inc. 01/01/1992

AMERICAN FAMILY LIFE ASSURN CO COLUMBUS (GA)
Common 50¢ par changed to $1 par 11/25/1968
Stock Dividends - 10% 3/31/1966; 15% 06/01/1967; 15% 05/15/1968; 40% 01/31/1969; 20% 02/16/1970; 10% 05/30/1971; 20% 07/20/1972
Reorganized as American Family Corp. 08/21/1973
Each share Common $1 par exchanged for (2) shares Common 10¢ par
American Family Corp. name changed to AFLAC Inc. 01/01/1992

AMERICAN FAMILY LIFE INSURANCE CO. (GA)
Common $1 par changed to 50¢ par and (1) additional share issued 06/01/1962
Name changed to American Family

Life Assurance Co. of Columbus 11/02/1964
American Family Life Assurance Co. of Columbus reorganized as American Family Corp. 08/21/1973 which name changed to AFLAC Inc. 01/01/1992

AMERICAN FAMILY PIZZA INC (FL)
Company reported out of business 00/00/1988
Details not available

AMERICAN FAMILY REC CTRS INC (DE)
Charter cancelled and declared inoperative and void for non-payment of taxes 10/31/1974

AMERICAN FAMILY RESTAURANTS INC (GA)
Name changed to Denamerica Corp. 03/29/1996
Denamerica Corp. name changed to Phoenix Restaurant Group, Inc. 07/06/1999 which name changed to Hiru Corp. 11/18/2008

AMERICAN FAMILY SEC GROUP (KY)
Merged into American Family Security Insurance Co. 09/13/1976
Each share Capital Stock no par exchanged for (0.11111111) share Common $1 par and (2) shares Non-Voting Class A Common $1 par
American Family Security Insurance Co. merged into Kentucky Central Life Insurance Co. 01/01/1983
(See Kentucky Central Life Insurance Co.)

AMERICAN FAMILY SEC INS CO (KY)
Merged into Kentucky Central Life Insurance Co. 01/01/1983
Each share Common $1 par exchanged for (0.16666666) share Class A Common $1 par
Each share Non-Vtg. Class A Common $1 par exchanged for (0.16666666) share Class A Common $1 par
(See Kentucky Central Life Insurance Co.)

AMERICAN FARMLAND CO (MD)
Merged into Farmland Partners Inc. 02/02/2017
Each share Common 1¢ par exchanged for (0.7417) share Common 1¢ par

AMERICAN FDG CORP (CA)
Merged into Zenith Funding Corp. 05/13/1971
Each share Common $1 par exchanged for (0.55) share Common 1¢ par and (1) Common Stock Purchase Warrant
Zenith Funding Corp. name changed to Zenith American Corp. 05/30/1973
(See Zenith American Corp.)

AMERICAN FED BK FSB (GREENVILLE, SC)
Merged into CCB Financial Corp. 07/31/1997
Each share Common $1 par exchanged for (0.445) share Common $5 par
CCB Financial Corp. merged into National Commerce Bancorporation 07/05/2000 which name changed to National Commerce Financial Corp. 04/25/2001 which merged into SunTrust Banks, Inc. 10/01/2004

AMERICAN FED CORP (MN)
Company became private through market repurchases 00/00/1991
Public interest eliminated

AMERICAN FEDERAL LEASING & FINANCE CO., INC. (ID)
Reincorporated under the laws of Delaware as Cemetery Services International, Inc. and Common 25¢ par changed to 1¢ par 12/17/1969
Cemetery Services International, Inc. name changed to Morlan International Inc. 05/01/1974 which merged into Service Corp. International 11/06/1987

AMERICAN FED SVGS & LN ASSN COLO DENVER (USA)
Common 1¢ par split (3) for (2) by issuance of (0.5) additional share 03/22/1983
Common 1¢ par split (4) for (3) by issuance of (0.33333333) additional share 03/22/1984
Reincorporated under the laws of Delaware as AmFed Financial Corp. 03/25/1988
(See AmFed Financial Corp.)

AMERICAN FED SVGS & LN ASSN SULLIVAN (MO)
Acquired by Mid-Missouri Holding Co., Inc. 06/30/1997
Each share Common $1 par exchanged for (0.206494) share Common $10 par and $14.7415 cash

AMERICAN FED SVGS BK (ROCKVILLE, MD)
Stock Dividends - 5% payable 02/15/2000 to holders of record 02/01/2000; 5% payable 02/28/2001 to holders of record 02/15/2001 Ex date - 02/13/2001; 5% payable 03/25/2002 to holders of record 03/15/2002 Ex date - 03/13/2002
Under plan of reorganization each share Common $1 par automatically became (1) share American Bank Holdings, Inc. Common $0.001 par 03/21/2003
(See American Bank Holdings, Inc.)

AMERICAN FED SVGS BK DUVAL CNTY (JACKSONVILLE, FL)
Name changed to FloridaBank, A Federal Savings Bank (Jacksonville, FL) 01/09/1992
FloridaBank, A Federal Savings Bank (Jacksonville, FL) merged into AmSouth Bancorporation 02/10/1994 which merged into Regions Financial Corp. (New) 11/04/2006

AMERICAN FELT CO. (MA)
Common $100 par changed to $5 par 03/00/1928
Each share Common $5 par exchanged for (3) shares Common no par 04/00/1928
Each share Common no par exchanged for (3) shares Common $10 par 00/00/1952
Through voluntary exchange offer by Ruberoid Co. over 99% acquired by 10/31/1966
Preferred $100 par called for redemption 04/01/1968
Public interest eliminated

AMERICAN FIBER OPTICS CORP (CA)
Charter cancelled for failure to file reports and pay taxes 09/01/1989

AMERICAN FIBRE CORP (BC)
Merged into Heritage American Resource Corp. 07/25/1994
Each share Common no par exchanged for (0.125) share Common no par
Heritage American Resource Corp. recapitalized as Heritage Explorations Ltd. 09/17/2001 which merged into St Andrew Goldfields Ltd. 08/22/2005 which merged into Kirkland Lake Gold Inc. 01/29/2016 which merged into Kirkland Lake Gold Ltd. 12/06/2016

AMERICAN FID FINL SVCS INC (NV)
Name changed to Trinity Capital Partners, Inc. 11/10/2006

AMERICAN FID FIRE INS CO (NY)
Common $5 par changed to $30 par 05/04/1962
Placed in liquidation by Court Order 03/26/1986
No stockholders' equity

AMERICAN FID INVTS (OH)
Merged into Leader Development Corp. 01/04/1983
Each Share of Bene. Int. no par exchanged for (1) share Common no par
Leader Development Corp. name changed to Clinton Gas Systems Inc. 12/31/1987
(See Clinton Gas Systems Inc.)

AMERICAN FID LIFE INS CO (FL)
Stock Dividends - 10% 06/14/1960; 10% 06/27/1967; 10% 10/05/1970; 10% 10/15/1971; 10% 04/25/1972; 10% 07/24/1973
Reincorporated under the laws of Delaware as AMFI Corp. and Common $1 par reclassified as Class A Common $1 par 07/30/1982
(See AMFI Corp.)

AMERICAN FIDELITY & CASUALTY CO., INC. (VA)
Each share 7% Preferred Class A $25 par exchanged for (2.5) shares Common $5 par 00/00/1937
Each share Class B Common $1 par exchanged for (8.125) shares Common $5 par 00/00/1937
Liquidation completed
Each share Common $5 par received initial distribution of $4.75 cash 12/31/1963
Each share Common $5 par received second distribution of $2.50 cash 04/20/1964
Each share Common $5 par exchanged for third distribution of $37.06 cash 08/28/1964
Each share Common $5 par received fourth distribution of (0.5236) share Fidelity Bankers Life Insurance Co. Common $1 par 09/22/1964
Each share Common $5 par received fifth and final distribution of $0.2068 cash 12/28/1965
Fidelity Bankers Life Insurance Co. name changed to Fidelity Corp. 12/31/1967 which name changed to Drum Financial Corp. 08/01/1979 which was acquired by St. Regis Paper Co. 09/11/1981 which name changed to St. Regis Corp. 04/28/1983 which merged into Champion International Corp. 11/20/1984 which merged into International Paper Corp. 06/20/2000

AMERICAN FILM TECHNOLOGIES INC (DE)
Each share Common $0.001 par exchanged for (0.5) share Common $0.002 par 03/16/1990
Ceased operations 03/00/2001
Stockholders' equity unlikely

AMERICAN FILTRONA CORP (VA)
Common $1 par split (2) for (1) by issuance of (1) additional share 08/25/1986
Merged into Brunzl PLC 09/23/1997
Each share Common $1 par exchanged for $46.52 cash

AMERICAN FIN SYS INC (DE)
Each share Class A Common $1 par automatically became (1) share Common $1 par 05/03/1971
Each share Class B Common $1 par exchanged for (1.25) shares Common $1 par 05/03/1971
Merged into Security Pacific Corp. 12/15/1978
Each share 6% Preferred $25 par exchanged for $25.25 cash
Each share Common $1 par exchanged for (0.3215) share Common $10 par
Security Pacific Corp. merged into BankAmerica Corp. (Old) 04/22/1992 which merged into BankAmerica Corp. (New) 09/30/1998 which name changed to Bank of America Corp. 04/28/1999

AMERICAN FINL CAP TR I (DE)
9.125% Trust Originated Preferred Securities called for redemption at $25 plus $0.32 accrued dividends on 03/05/2004

AMERICAN FINL CORP (OH)
Common no par split (4) for (3) by issuance of (0.33333333) additional share 03/10/1966
Common no par split (4) for (3) by issuance of (0.33333333) additional share 10/01/1967
Common no par split (2) for (1) by issuance of (1) additional share 07/15/1968
Common no par split (3) for (2) by issuance of (0.5) additional share 03/16/1970
Common no par split (2) for (1) by issuance of (1) additional share 06/15/1972
$1.80 Preferred Ser. C $1 par called for redemption 09/20/1978
Each share $3.15 Preferred Ser. G $1 par exchanged for (3) shares $1.05 Preferred Ser. G $1 par 12/10/1979
Common no par split (3) for (2) by issuance of (0.5) additional share 07/03/1980
Under plan of merger each share Common no par exchanged for (1) share $3.95 Preferred Ser. H $1.50 par
Note: Above ratio applies to holdings of (100) shares or more. Holdings of (99) shares or fewer received $28 cash per share
$3.95 Preferred Ser. H $1.50 par called for redemption 07/31/1989
$1 Preferred Ser. D $10.50 par called for redemption 00/00/1992
$2.66 Preferred Ser. I 1¢ par called for redemption 00/00/1994
Preferred Ser. E $1 par called for redemption 12/03/1995
Each share $1.80 Preferred Ser. F $1 par exchanged for either (0.9912) share $2 Preferred Ser. J $1 par or $24.78 cash 12/02/1997
Each share $1.05 Preferred Ser. G $1 par exchanged for either (0.42) share $2 Preferred Ser. J $1 par or $10.50 cash 12/02/1997
Each share $2 Preferred Ser. J $1 par exchanged for (1.1434) shares American Financial Group, Inc. (Holding Co.) Common no par 11/20/2003

AMERICAN FINL ENTERPRISES INC (CT)
Merged into American Financial Group, Inc. 12/02/1997
Each share Common $1 par exchanged for (1) share Common no par

AMERICAN FINL GROUP INC (OH)
Reorganized as a holding company under the same name and Common $1 par changed to no par 12/02/1997

AMERICAN FINL HLDGS INC (DE)
Common $0.0001 par split (3) for (1) by issuance of (2) additional shares payable 08/12/2005 to holders of record 08/11/2005 Ex date - 08/15/2005
Recapitalized as Tactical Solution Partners, Inc. 01/19/2006
Each share Common $0.0001 par exchanged for (0.33333333) Common $0.0001 par
Tactical Solution Partners, Inc. name changed to Brekford International Corp. 05/13/2008 which name changed to Brekford Corp. 07/21/2010 which name changed to Brekford Traffic Safety, Inc. 06/08/2017 which merged into Novume Solutions, Inc. 08/28/2017

AMERICAN FINL HLDGS INC (DE)
Merged into Banknorth Group, Inc. (ME) 02/14/2003
Each share Common 1¢ par exchanged for either (1.22) shares Common 1¢ par or (0.5017433) share Common 1¢ par and $18.83952 cash
Note: Option to receive cash and stock expired 02/18/2003
Banknorth Group, Inc. (ME) merged into TD Banknorth Inc. 03/01/2005
(See TD Banknorth Inc.)

AMERICAN FINL HLDGS INC (FL)
Each share Common 1¢ par exchanged for (0.1) share Common 10¢ par 11/16/1982
Proclaimed dissolved for failure to file reports and pay fees 11/04/1988

AMERICAN FINL HLDG INC (DE)
Reorganized 10/12/1992
Reorganized from (CO) to under the laws of Delaware 10/12/1992
Each share Common $0.001 par exchanged for (0.05) share Common 1¢ par
Each share old Common 1¢ par exchanged for (0.04672897) share new Common 1¢ par 05/30/2001
Name changed to Isolagen, Inc. 11/13/2001
(See Isolagen, Inc.)

AMERICAN FINL LEASING & SVCS CO (OH)
Common no par split (3) for (2) by issuance of (0.5) additional share 10/01/1971
Merged into American Financial Corp. 12/26/1974
Each share Common no par exchanged for $6 cash

AMERICAN FINL RLTY TR (MD)
Merged into Gramercy Capital Corp. 04/01/2008
Each share Common $0.001 par exchanged for (0.12096) share Common $0.001 par and $5.50 cash
Gramercy Capital Corp. name changed to Gramercy Property Trust Inc. 04/15/2013 which merged into Gramercy Property Trust 12/17/2015
(See Gramercy Property Trust)

AMERICAN FINL SEMINARS INC (FL)
Name changed to Environmental Oil Technologies, Inc. 10/26/1998
Environmental Oil Technologies, Inc. name changed to American Industrial Minerals Group, Inc. 01/14/1999 which name changed to Networthusa.com Inc. 04/06/1999 which name changed to EBUX Inc. 10/06/2000 which name changed to Petapeer Holdings Inc. 05/05/2001 which name changed to Studio Bromont Inc. 02/14/2002 which name changed to United American Corp. 03/01/2004

AMERICAN FIRE & CAS CO (FL)
Each share Common $10 par exchanged for (2) shares Common $5 par 00/00/1954
Each share Common $5 par exchanged for (2) shares Common $2.50 par 03/24/1964
Merged into Ohio Casualty Insurance Co. 08/27/1969
Each share Common $2.50 par exchanged for (0.476191) share Capital Stock 50¢ par
Ohio Casualty Insurance Co. reorganized as Ohio Casualty Corp. 01/01/1970
(See Ohio Casualty Corp.)

AMERICAN FIRE & MARINE INSURANCE CO.
Merged into American Indemnity Co. (TX) 00/00/1931
Each (10) shares Capital Stock exchanged for (6.5) shares Capital Stock $10 par
(See American Indemnity Co. (TX))

AMERICAN FIRE PUMP CO (MI)
Plan of reorganization under Chapter 11 Bankruptcy proceedings confirmed 07/15/1985
No stockholders' equity

AMERICAN FIRE RETARDANT CORP (NV)
Each share old Common $0.001 par exchanged for (0.1) share new Common $0.001 par 09/12/2002
Each share new Common $0.001 par exchanged again for (0.005) share new Common $0.001 par 06/27/2003
Each share new Common $0.001 par exchanged again for (0.004) share new Common $0.001 par 03/22/2004
Each share new Common $0.001 par exchanged again for (0.004) share new Common $0.001 par 09/01/2004
Each share new Common $0.001 par exchanged again for (0.0005) share new Common $0.001 par 11/01/2004
Reorganized under the laws of Florida as Global Materials & Services, Inc. 01/06/2005
Each share Common $0.001 par exchanged for (0.0005) share Common no par
(See Global Materials & Services, Inc.)

AMERICAN FIRST CORP (OK)
Common $1 par split (2) for (1) by issuance of (1) additional share 12/30/1982
Common $1 par changed to 1¢ par 05/11/1989
Petition filed under Chapter 7 Federal Bankruptcy Code 10/30/1990
No stockholders' equity

AMERICAN 1ST CORP (TX)
Common $10 par changed to $2 par and (4) additional shares issued 02/20/1970
Merged into Federated Texas Bancorporation, Inc. 05/01/1973
Each share Common $2 par exchanged for (1) share Common $5 par
Federated Texas Bancorporation, Inc. merged into Federated Capital Corp. 01/29/1974 which merged into Mercantile Texas Corp. 12/30/1976 which name changed to MCorp 10/11/1984
(See MCorp)

AMERICAN-FIRST HOLDING CO. (OK)
Merged into First Oklahoma Bancorporation, Inc. 11/16/1970
Holders had option to exchange each share Common $1 par for (1.5) shares 50¢ Preferred $5 par or (1.5) shares Common $5 par
Option to receive Common $5 par expired 12/17/1970
(See First Oklahoma Bancorporation, Inc.)

AMERICAN-FIRST TITLE & TRUST CO. (OKLAHOMA CITY, OK)
Each share Common $25 par exchanged for (2.6) shares Common $10 par to effect a (2.5) for (1) split and a 4% stock dividend 02/01/1962
Under plan of reorganization each share Common $10 par automatically became (1) share American-First Holding Co. Common $1 par 03/26/1970
American-First Holding Co. merged into First Oklahoma Bancorporation, Inc. 11/16/1970
(See First Oklahoma Bancorporation, Inc.)

AMERICAN FLAG CO. (NY)
Dissolved 00/00/1956
Details not available

AMERICAN FLAT-LITE CO. (OH)
Involuntarily dissolved 06/02/1931

AMERICAN FLETCHER CORP (IN)
Common $10 par changed to $5 par and (2) additional shares issued 05/20/1971
Common $5 par split (2) for (1) by issuance of (1) additional share 05/10/1985
Merged into Banc One Corp. (DE) 01/26/1987
Each share Common $5 par exchanged for (2.1505) shares Common no par
Banc One Corp. (DE) reincorporated in Ohio 05/01/1989 which merged into Bank One Corp. 10/02/1998 which merged into J.P. Morgan Chase & Co. 12/31/2000 which name changed to JPMorgan Chase & Co. 07/20/2004

AMERICAN FLETCHER MTG INVS (MA)
Name changed to U.S. Shelter 12/23/1981
U.S. Shelter merged into U.S. Shelter Corp. (DE) 05/31/1984
(See U.S. Shelter Corp. (DE))

AMERICAN FLETCHER NATL BK & TR CO (INDIANAPOLIS, IN)
Stock Dividends - 10.325% 02/15/1962; 15% 02/17/1966
Under plan of reorganization each share Common Capital Stock $10 par automatically became (1) share American Fletcher Corp. Common $10 par 12/31/1968
American Fletcher Corp. merged into Banc One Corp. (DE) 01/26/1987 which reincorporated in Ohio 05/01/1989 which merged into Bank One Corp. 10/02/1998 which merged into J.P. Morgan Chase & Co. 12/31/2000 which name changed to JPMorgan Chase & Co. 07/20/2004

AMERICAN FLINTLOCK CO (NV)
Name changed to Page Active Holdings Inc. 05/1819/99
Page Active Holdings Inc. name changed to TriVantage Group, Inc. 08/07/2001 which recapitalized as Proteo Inc. 01/28/2002

AMERICAN FLUORITE CORP (BC)
Name changed to AFC Energy Corp. 03/26/1983
(See AFC Energy Corp.)

AMERICAN FNDTN LIFE INS CO (AR)
Each share Class A Common no par exchanged for (0.2) share Capital Stock $1 par 12/18/1963
Merged into McWane Co. 01/19/1979
Each share Capital Stock $1 par exchanged for $13 cash

AMERICAN FOOD HLDGS INC (FL)
Each share old Common $0.001 par exchanged for (0.05) share new Common $0.001 par 08/28/2007
Each share new Common $0.001 par exchanged again for (0.01) share new Common $0.001 par 03/26/2008
Name changed to Plateau Mineral Development, Inc. 09/15/2008

AMERICAN FOOD MACHY CORP (TN)
Charter revoked for non-payment of taxes 04/30/1976

AMERICAN FOODS INC (FL)
Stock Dividend - 10% 07/15/1964
Merged into A.M. Foods, Inc. 05/31/1977
Each share Common 10¢ par exchanged for $6 cash

AMERICAN FOODWORKS INC (NY)
Dissolved by proclamation 12/24/1991

AMERICAN FOREIGN INVESTING CORP.
Name changed to Bowling Green Fund, Inc. 00/00/1947
Bowling Green Fund, Inc. name changed to Winfield Growth Industries Fund, Inc. 12/30/1957 which name changed to Winfield Growth Fund, Inc. 09/21/1966 which name changed to Research Equity Fund, Inc. (DE) 01/26/1973 which reincorporated in Maryland 09/09/1973 which reincorporated in California as Franklin Equity Fund 10/10/1984

AMERICAN FOREST PRODS CORP (DE)
Each share Capital Stock $10 par exchanged for (4) shares Capital Stock $2.50 par 03/31/1955
Capital Stock $2.50 par reclassified as Common $2.50 par 09/19/1966
Common $2.50 par changed to no par and (1) additional share issued 08/18/1969
Merged into Bendix Corp. 10/30/1970
Each share Common no par exchanged for (0.7578) share $3 Conv. Preferred Ser. A no par
(See Bendix Corp.)

AMERICAN FOREST PRODUCTS CO.
Name changed to American Excelsior Corp. 00/00/1929
American Excelsior Corp. name changed to Chicago Holding Corp. 11/14/1967
(See Chicago Holding Corp.)

AMERICAN FORGE & MACHINE CO.
Bankrupt 00/00/1931
Details not available

AMERICAN FORGING & SOCKET CO (MI)
Each share Common no par exchanged for (10) shares Common $1 par 00/00/1936
Completely liquidated 12/28/1966
Each share Common $1 par exchanged for first and final distribution of $12.85 cash

AMERICAN FORK & HOE CO.
Name changed to True Temper Corp. 00/00/1949
True Temper Corp. merged into Allegheny Ludlum Steel Corp. 07/31/1967 which name changed to Allegheny Ludlum Industries, Inc. 04/24/1970 which name changed to Allegheny International Inc. 04/29/1981
(See Allegheny International Inc.)

AMERICAN FORK CONSOLIDATED MINES (UT)
Name changed to American Consolidated Mines 00/00/1956
American Consolidated Mines name changed to American Resources, Inc. (UT) 08/04/1970

AMERICAN FOUNDATION/PIONEER WESTERN LIFE INSURANCE CO. (AR)
Name changed to American Foundation Life Insurance Co. 07/03/1963
(See American Foundation Life Insurance Co.)

AMERICAN FOUNDERS CORP. (MD)
Common no par changed to $1 par 04/11/1933
Merged into American General Corp. 11/23/1935
Each share 7% Ser. A and/or 7% Ser. B 1st Preferred $50 par exchanged for (1.2) shares $2 Ser. Preferred $1 par and (0.2) share Common 10¢ par
Each share 6% Ser. D 1st Preferred $50 par exchanged for (1.2) shares $2 Ser. Preferred $1 par
Each share Common $1 par

exchanged for (0.08) share Common 10¢ par
American General Corp. merged into Equity Corp. 10/17/1950 which name changed to Wheelabrator-Frye Inc. 11/04/1971 which merged into Signal Companies, Inc. 02/01/1983 which merged into Allied-Signal Inc. 09/19/1985 which name changed to AlliedSignal Inc. 04/26/1993 which name changed to Honeywell International Inc. 12/01/1999

AMERICAN FOUNDERS LIFE INSURANCE CO. OF DENVER (CO)
Name changed to Falcon National Life Insurance Co. 02/01/1961
Falcon National Life Insurance Co. merged into Denver National Life Insurance Co. 02/15/1963 which name changed to Denver National Financial, Inc. 05/20/1965 which was acquired by National Western Life Insurance Co. 08/14/1967

AMERICAN FOUNDERS LIFE INS CO (TX)
Stock Dividends - 25% 11/20/1964; 20% 03/10/1969; 10% 03/15/1971; 10% 03/03/1972; 20% 04/16/1973
Merged into Anderson, Clayton & Co. 08/31/1977
Each share Common $1 par exchanged for (0.902175) share Common $1 par or $18.50 cash
Note: Option to receive cash expired 09/20/1977
(See Anderson, Clayton & Co.)

AMERICAN FOUNDERS TRUST (MA)
Acquired by American Founders Corp. 10/01/1928
Each share 1st Preferred exchanged for (1) share 1st Preferred
Each share 2nd Preferred exchanged for (1) share 2nd Preferred
Each share Common exchanged for (2) shares Common no par
American Founders Corp. merged into American General Corp. 11/23/1935 which merged into Equity Corp. 10/17/1950 which name changed to Wheelabrator-Frye Inc. 11/04/1971 which merged into Signal Companies, Inc. 02/01/1983 which merged into Allied-Signal Inc. 09/19/1985 which name changed to AlliedSignal Inc. 04/26/1993 which name changed to Honeywell International Inc. 12/01/1999

AMERICAN-FRANCE JET, LTD. (DE)
No longer in existence having become inoperative and void for non-payment of taxes 04/01/1963

AMERICAN FRANCHISE GROUP INC (DE)
Each share Common 1¢ par exchanged for (0.25) share Common 4¢ par 05/12/1992
Name changed to BCT International, Inc. 07/31/1992
(See BCT International, Inc.)

AMERICAN FRANCHISE NETWORK CORP (NY)
Under plan of reorganization each share Common 1¢ par automatically became (1) share of Canusa Holdings Ltd. (DE) 06/25/1970
Canusa Holdings, Ltd. (DE) name changed to Anusound Inc. 02/13/1973
(See Anusound Inc.)

AMERICAN FREIGHTWAYS CORP (AR)
Common 1¢ par split (2) for (1) by issuance of (1) additional share 05/27/1993
Merged into FedEx Corp. 02/12/2001
Each share Common 1¢ par exchanged for (0.6639) share Common 10¢ par

AMERICAN FRONTIER CORP. (TN)
Merged into American Frontier Life Insurance Co. 08/04/1962

Each share Class A Common $1 par exchanged for (3.72) shares Common $1 par
Each share Class B Common $1 par exchanged for (2) shares Common $1 par
American Frontier Life Insurance Co. merged into Lincoln American Life Insurance Co. 09/01/1964 which reorganized as Lincoln American Corp. (TN) 04/01/1969 which merged into Lincoln American Corp. (NY) 05/01/1972 which merged into American General Corp. 09/01/1980 which merged into American International Group, Inc. 08/29/2001

AMERICAN FRONTIER EXPL INC (DE)
Each share Common $0.001 par exchanged for (0.02754820) share Common $0.0363 par 12/15/1983
Acquired by ABEG Hydrocarbons Inc. 06/30/1986
Each share Common $0.0363 par exchanged for $0.90 cash

AMERICAN FRONTIER LIFE INSURANCE CO. (TN)
Merged into Lincoln American Life Insurance Co. 09/01/1964
Each share Common $1 par exchanged for (0.66666666) share Common $1 par
Lincoln American Life Insurance Co. reorganized as Lincoln American Corp. (TN) 04/01/1969 which merged into Lincoln American Corp. (NY) 05/01/1972 which merged into American General Corp. 09/01/1980 which merged into American International Group, Inc. 08/29/2001

AMERICAN FRONTIER MINING & REFINING CO. LTD. (ON)
Charter cancelled and proclaimed dissolved for failure to pay taxes and file returns 01/14/1963

AMERICAN FROZEN FOOD LOCKERS, INC.
Bankrupt 00/00/1948
Details not available

AMERICAN FRUCTOSE CORP (DE)
Each share Common 10¢ par exchanged for (0.5) share Class A Common 10¢ par and (0.5) share Class B Common 10¢ par 10/18/1984
Merged into American Maize-Products Co. 02/26/1993
Each share Class A Common 10¢ par exchanged for (1) share Class A Common 80¢ par
Each share Class B Common 10¢ par exchanged for (1) share Class A Common 80¢ par
(See American Maize-Products Co.)

AMERICAN FRUIT GROWERS, INC. (DE)
Each share Preferred $100 par exchanged for (1) share Preferred $50 par and (5) shares Common no par 00/00/1935
Recapitalized 00/00/1942
Each share Preferred $50 par exchanged for (4) shares Common $1 par
Each share Common no par exchanged for (0.33333333) share Common $1 par
Merged into American National Foods, Inc. 00/00/1954
Each share Common $1 par exchanged for $11 principal amount of 4.5% Debentures

AMERICAN FUEL & POWER CO.
Bankrupt 00/00/1936
Details not available

AMERICAN FUEL & PWR CORP (FL)
Involuntarily dissolved 10/13/1989

AMERICAN FUEL OIL & TRANSPORTATION CO., INC. (DE)
No longer in existence having become inoperative and void for non-payment of taxes 03/17/1926

AMERICAN FUEL TECHNOLOGIES INC (DE)
Filed a petition under Chapter 7 Federal Bankruptcy Code 07/30/1987
No stockholders' equity

AMERICAN FUEL TRANSIT CORP (WA)
Charter cancelled and proclaimed dissolved for failure to pay fees 02/09/1990

AMERICAN FUNERAL HOMES INC (IA)
Merged into IFS Industries, Inc. 03/31/1978
Each share Common $1 par exchanged for $1.85 cash

AMERICAN FUNERAL SVC CORP (DE)
Merged into Service Corp. International 12/22/1992
Each share Common 5¢ par exchanged for $15.01 cash

AMERICAN FURNITURE INC (VA)
Common no par changed to $1 par 00/00/1937
Stock Dividends - 100% 06/00/1946; 50% 07/01/1947; 100% 01/19/1951
Merged into Ladd Furniture, Inc. 10/31/1986
Each share Common $1 par exchanged for $16 cash

AMERICAN FURNITURE MART BUILDING CO., INC. (DE)
Name changed to American Furniture Mart Corp. 05/01/1956
American Furniture Mart Corp. name changed to American Mart Corp. 04/05/1974
(See American Mart Corp.)

AMERICAN FURNITURE MART BUILDING CORP.
Reorganized as American Furniture Mart Building Co., Inc. 00/00/1935
Details not available

AMERICAN FURNITURE MART CORP (DE)
Common $1 par changed to $10 par 09/19/1958
Common $10 par changed to $20 par 12/20/1960
Common $20 par changed to $25 par 12/17/1963
Common $25 par changed to $30 par 12/19/1970
Name changed to American Mart Corp. 04/05/1974
(See American Mart Corp.)

AMERICAN FURNITURE WHSL INC (NV)
Name changed to Newriders, Inc. 07/02/1996
Newriders, Inc. merged into EasyRiders, Inc. 09/23/1998
(See EasyRiders, Inc.)

AMERICAN GAMING & ENTMT LTD (DE)
Recapitalized as Wow Entertainment, Inc. 10/13/2000
Each share Common 1¢ par exchanged for (0.16666666) share Common 1¢ par
Wow Entertainment, Inc. name changed to Fortune Diversified Industries, Inc. (DE) 08/16/2001 which reorganized in Indiana 06/02/2005 which name changed to Fortune Industries, Inc. 04/17/2006
(See Fortune Industries, Inc.)

AMERICAN GARDEN PRODS INC (DE)
Merged into Amfac, Inc. 03/28/1980
Each share Common 20¢ par exchanged for (0.94715) share Common no par
(See Amfac, Inc.)

AMERICAN GAS & ELECTRIC CO. (NY)
Common no par changed to $10 par 00/00/1940
Each share Common $10 par exchanged for (2) shares Common $5 par 00/00/1953
Common $5 par changed to $10 par and (0.5) additional share issued 06/15/1956
Name changed to American Electric Power Co., Inc. 05/12/1958

AMERICAN GAS & POWER CO. (DE)
Reorganized 00/00/1935
Each share 1st Preferred no par exchanged for (2) shares Common $1 par, a warrant expiring 08/01/1953 to suscribe to (1) additional share Common and a warrant to subscribe to $100 principal amount of 10-Yr. Secured Notes
Each share Preference no par exchanged for (0.475) share Common $1 par and a warrant to subscribe to $100 principal amount of 10-Yr. Secured Notes
Each share Common no par exchanged for (0.1) share Common $1 par and a warrant to subscribe to $10 principal amount of 10-Yr. Secured Notes
Reorganized as Minneapolis Gas Co. 07/30/1948
Each share Common $1 par exchanged for (1) share Common $1 par
Minneapolis Gas Co. name changed to Minnesota Gas Co. 05/10/1974
(See Minnesota Gas Co.)

AMERICAN GAS ACCUMULATOR CO.
Merged into Elastic Stop Nut Corp. of America 00/00/1952
Each share Common $4 par exchanged for (1) share Common $1 par
Elastic Stop Nut Corp. of America merged into Amerace Esna Corp. 08/30/1968 which name changed to Amerace Corp. 04/27/1973
(See Amerace Corp.)

AMERICAN GAS CO. (IA)
Merged into American Gas Co. of Wisconsin, Inc. 02/10/1968
Each share Common $1 par exchanged for (0.1288) share Common $4 par
American Gas Co. of Wisconsin, Inc. merged into AGC Industries, Inc. 04/01/1970
(See AGC Industries, Inc.)

AMERICAN GAS CO WIS INC (WI)
Merged into AGC Industries, Inc. 04/01/1970
Each share Common $4 par exchanged for (1) share Common $1 par
(See AGC Industries, Inc.)

AMERICAN GAS INDEX FD INC (MD)
Name changed to FBR American Gas Index Fund Inc. 04/30/2002
(See FBR American Gas Index Fund Inc.)

AMERICAN GAS-TOOL CO. (SD)
Charter expired by time limitation 02/11/1935

AMERICAN GASOHOL REFINERS INC (KS)
Name changed to High Plains Corp. 08/04/1983
(See High Plains Corp.)

AMERICAN GASOLINE CORP. (DE)
No longer in existence having become inoperative and void for non-payment of taxes 04/01/1931

AMERICAN GATEWAY FINL CORP (VA)
Merged into Business First Bancshares, Inc. 03/31/2015

Each share Common $10 par exchanged for (11.88) shares Common $1 par and $10 cash

AMERICAN GEM CORP (ON)
Name changed to Digital Gem Corp. 10/27/1999
Digital Gem Corp. name changed to Northern Financial Corp. 10/03/2000 which recapitalized as Added Capital Inc. 07/23/2014

AMERICAN GEN BD FD INC (MD)
Name changed to American Capital Bond Fund, Inc. 09/12/1983
American Capital Bond Fund, Inc. name changed to Van Kampen American Capital Bond Fund, Inc. (MD) 12/29/1995 which reincorporated in Delaware 10/31/1996 which name changed to Van Kampen Bond Fund 08/28/1998 which name changed to Invesco Van Kampen Bond Fund 06/01/2010 which name changed to Invesco Bond Fund 12/03/2012

AMERICAN GEN CAP BD FD INC (MD)
Name changed to American Capital Corporate Bond Fund, Inc. (MD) 09/09/1983
American Capital Corporate Bond Fund, Inc. (MD) reincorporated in Delaware as Van Kampen American Capital Corporate Bond Fund 08/05/1995 which name changed to Van Kampen Corporate Bond Fund 07/14/1998

AMERICAN GEN CAP LLC (DE)
8.45% Monthly Income Preferred Securities Ser. A called for redemption at $25 on 07/31/2001
8.125% Monthly Income Preferred Securities Ser. B called for redemption at $25 on 07/31/2001

AMERICAN GEN COMSTOCK FD INC (MD)
Name changed to American Capital Comstock Fund, Inc. 09/12/1983

AMERICAN GEN CONV SECS INC (MD)
Name changed to American Capital Convertible Securities, Inc. (MD) 09/12/1983
American Capital Convertible Securities, Inc. (MD) name changed to Van Kampen Captial Convertible Securities, Inc. (MD) 12/29/1995 which reincorporated in Delaware 10/29/1996 which name changed to Van Kampen Convertible Securities Inc. 08/28/1998 which reorganized as Van Kampen American Capital Harbor Fund 08/15/2000

AMERICAN GEN CORP (TX)
90¢ Conv. Preferred 1975 Ser. $1.50 par called for redemption 03/01/1981
Common $1.50 par changed to 50¢ par and (2) additional shares issued 05/16/1983
$3.25 Conv. Jr. Preferred 1980 Ser. $1.50 par called for redemption 09/03/1985
Adjustable Rate Conv. Preferred Ser. B $1.50 par called for redemption 11/05/1985
$2.64 Conv. Preferred $1.50 par called for redemption 05/16/1986
Adjustable Rate Preferred Ser. A $1.50 par called for redemption 11/04/1987
Common 50¢ par split (2) for (1) by issuance of (1) additional share 03/01/1993
7% Conv. Preferred 50¢ par called for redemption at (0.8264) share Common on 03/01/2000
Common 50¢ par split (2) for (1) by issuance of (1) additional share payable 03/01/2001 to holders of record 02/08/2001 Ex date - 03/02/2001
Merged into American International Group, Inc. 08/29/2001
Each share Common 50¢ par exchanged for (0.579) share Common $2.50 par

AMERICAN GEN ENTERPRISE FD INC (MD)
Name changed to American Capital Enterprise Fund, Inc. (MD) 09/09/1983
American Capital Enterprise Fund, Inc. (MD) reincorporated in Delaware as Van Kampen American Capital Enterprise Fund 08/03/1995 which name changed to Van Kampen Enterprise Fund 08/31/1998

AMERICAN GEN FIN CORP (IN)
Auction Market Preferred Ser. A no par called for redemption 06/06/1990
Auction Market Preferred Ser. B no par called for redemption 06/20/1990
Public interest eliminated

AMERICAN GEN GROWTH FD INC (MD)
Name changed to American Capital Growth Fund, Inc. 09/09/1983
(See American Capital Growth Fund, Inc.)

AMERICAN GEN HBR FD (MD)
Name changed to American Capital Harbor Fund, Inc. (MD) 09/12/1983
American Capital Harbor Fund, Inc. (MD) reincorporated in Delaware as Van Kampen American Capital Harbor Fund 08/19/1995 which name changed to Van Kampen Harbor Fund 07/14/1998

AMERICAN GEN HIGH YIELD INVTS INC (TX)
Reincorporated under the laws of Maryland as American Capital High Yield Investments, Inc. 09/09/1983
(See American Capital High Yield Investments, Inc.)

AMERICAN GEN HOSPITALITY CORP (MD)
Merged into MeriStar Hospitality Corp. 08/03/1998
Each share Common 1¢ par exchanged for (0.8475) share Common 1¢ par
(See MeriStar Hospitality Corp.)

AMERICAN GEN INDS (CA)
Name changed to Pagers Plus 11/18/1987
Pagers Plus name changed to PagePrompt USA 03/09/1994
(See PagePrompt USA)

AMERICAN GEN INS CO (TX)
Each share Capital Stock $100 par exchanged for (10) shares Capital Stock $10 par 00/00/1929
Capital Stock $10 par changed to no par and (3) additional shares issued 03/09/1956
Capital Stock no par changed to $2.50 par 08/07/1957
Capital Stock $2.50 par changed to $1.50 par and (2/3) additional share issued 05/10/1960
Capital Stock $1.50 par reclassified as Common $1.50 par 06/26/1964
$1.80 Conv. Preferred $1.50 par called for redemption 09/01/1979
Stock Dividends - 25% 12/31/1936; 33.33333333% 12/31/1943; 20% 03/12/1949; 33.33333333% 12/31/1952; 12.5% 04/02/1963; 20% 05/12/1964; 200% 03/24/1967
Under plan of reorganization each share 90¢ Conv. Preferred 1975 Ser. $1.50 par and Common $1.50 par automatically became (1) share American General Corp. 90¢ Conv. Preferred 1975 Ser. $1.50 par and Common $1.50 par respectively 07/01/1980
American General Corp. merged into American International Group, Inc. 08/29/2001

AMERICAN GEN MUN BD FD INC (TX)
Name changed to American Capital Municipal Bond Fund, Inc. 09/09/1983

AMERICAN GEN PACE FD INC (MD)
Stock Dividend - 100% 01/22/1983
Name changed to American Capital Pace Fund, Inc. 09/09/1983

AMERICAN GEN RESV FD INC (MD)
Name changed to American Capital Reserve Fund, Inc. 09/09/1983

AMERICAN GEN SHS INC (MD)
Merged into American General Enterprise Fund, Inc. 08/31/1979
Each share Capital Growth Fund 1¢ par exchanged for (0.6667217918) share Capital Stock $1 par
Each share Income Fund 1¢ par exchanged for (0.8427943185) share Capital Stock $1 par
American General Enterprise Fund, Inc. name changed to American Capital Enterprise Fund, Inc. (MD) 09/09/1983 which reincorporated in Delaware as Van Kampen American Capital Enterprise Fund 08/03/1995 which name changed to Van Kampen Enterprise Fund 08/31/1998

AMERICAN GEN TOTAL RETURN FD INC (MD)
Merged into Fund of America, Inc. (NY) 12/31/1979
Each share Common $1 par exchanged for (0.963646) share Capital Stock $1 par
Fund of America, Inc. (NY) name changed to American Capital Growth & Income Fund, Inc. (NY) 07/23/1990 which reincorporated in Delaware as Van Kampen American Capital Growth & Income Fund 07/31/1995 which name changed to Van Kampen Growth & Income Fund 07/14/1998

AMERICAN GEN VENTURE FD INC (MD)
Name changed to American Capital Venture Fund, Inc. 09/09/1983
American Capital Venture Fund, Inc. name changed to American Capital Emerging Growth Fund, Inc. 07/24/1990
(See American Capital Emerging Growth Fund, Inc.)

AMERICAN GEN VENTURES INC (NV)
Each share old Common $0.001 par exchanged for (0.02) share new Common $0.001 par 08/14/1995
Recapitalized as Nucleus, Inc. (NV) 12/09/1998
Each share new Common $0.001 par exchanged for (0.1) share Common $0.001 par
Nucleus, Inc. (NV) reorganized in Delaware as eNucleus, Inc. 07/14/2000 which recapitalized as EC Development, Inc. 08/10/2010
(See EC Development, Inc.)

AMERICAN GEN CAP I (DE)
7.875% Trust Originated Preferred Securities called for redemption at $25 on 09/08/2004

AMERICAN GEN CAP III (DE)
8.5% Trust Preferred Securities called for redemption at $25 on 12/07/2005

AMERICAN GENERAL CORP. (DE)
Merged into Equity Corp. 10/17/1950
Each share $3 Preferred $1 par exchanged for (1) share $2 Preferred $1 par, (1) share Class A 10¢ par and (2) shares Common 10¢ par
Each share $2.50 Preferred $1 par exchanged for (1) share $2 Preferred $1 par, (0.5) share Class A 10¢ par and (1) share Common 10¢ par
Each share $2 Preferred $1 par exchanged for (1) share $2 Preferred $1 par
Each share Common 10¢ par exchanged for (1.2) shares Common 10¢ par
Equity Corp. name changed to Wheelabrator-Frye Inc. 11/04/1971 which merged into Signal Companies, Inc. 02/01/1983 which merged into Allied-Signal Inc. 09/19/1985 which name changed to AlliedSignal Inc. 04/26/1993 which name changed to Honeywell International Inc. 12/01/1999

AMERICAN GENERAL OIL & GAS CO. (DE)
Completely liquidated 12/08/1969
Each share Common 1¢ par exchanged for first and final distribution of (0.05) share Gil Development Corp. Common 1¢ par
(See Gil Development Corp.)

AMERICAN GENETICS INTL INC (CO)
Filed a petition under Chapter 7 Federal Bankruptcy Code 08/12/1985
No stockholders' equity

AMERICAN GEOLOGICAL ENTERPRISES INC (UT)
Reincorporated under the laws of Delaware as Emtec, Inc. 01/16/2001

AMERICAN GEOTHERMAL ENERGY, INC. (UT)
Name changed to American Geological Enterprises, Inc. (UT) 12/24/1975
American Geological Enterprises, Inc. (UT) reincorporated in Delaware as Emtec, Inc. 01/16/2001

AMERICAN GILSONITE CO (OK)
Each share Common no par received distribution of (1) Bonanza Royalties LLC Restricted Unit payable 08/07/2006 to holders of record 07/24/2006
Merged into American Gilsonite Corp. 03/14/2008
Each share Common no par exchanged for $1.18641395 cash
Each share Common no par received an initial additional distribution of $0.03374947 cash from escrow 10/23/2008
Each share Common no par received a second additional distribution of $0.00116672 cash from escrow 04/27/2009
Each share Common no par received a third additional distribution of $0.08548328 cash from escrow 12/07/2010
Each share Common no par received a fourth and final additional distribution of $0.00519314 cash from escrow 01/07/2011

AMERICAN GIRL FASHIONS INC (MA)
Adjudicated bankrupt 06/27/1975
No stockholders' equity

AMERICAN GIRL RES INC (BC)
Recapitalized as T.K.O. Resources Inc. 04/01/1991
Each share Common no par exchanged for (0.4) share Common no par
T.K.O. Resources Inc. name changed to Canadian Imperial Venture Corp. 06/02/1999

AMERICAN GLUE CO.
Name changed to Eastern Equities Corp. 00/00/1930
(See Eastern Equities Corp.)

AMERICAN GOLD CAP CORP (CAYMAN ISLANDS)
Merged into Chesapeake Gold Corp. 02/23/2007
Each share Common no par exchanged for (0.29) share Common no par, (0.029) share Class A Ser. 1 no par, and Common Stock Purchase Warrant expiring 02/23/2012
Note: Unexchanged certificates were cancelled and became without value 02/23/2013

AMERICAN GOLD DEPOSITORY CORP (NY)
Dissolved by proclamation 12/23/1992

AMERICAN GOLD GROUP INC (NV)
Name changed to American Group, Inc. 08/26/1992
American Group, Inc. name changed to Global Science Corp. 12/25/1993 which name changed to Sochrys.Com Inc. 08/25/1999 which name changed to Validian Corp. 02/06/2003

AMERICAN GOLD MINERALS CORP (CO)
Merged into Altex Oil Corp. (UT) 09/28/1984
Each share Common no par exchanged for (1/6) share Common no par
Altex Oil Corp. (UT) reorganized in Delaware as Altex Industries Inc. 10/30/1985

AMERICAN GOLD RESOURCES CORP (IL)
Involuntarily dissolved 03/12/2010

AMERICAN GOLDFIELDS INC (NV)
Recapitalized as Goldfields International Inc. 06/07/2012
Each share Common $0.001 par exchanged for (0.01) share Common $0.001 par

AMERICAN GOLDRUSH CORP (CANADA)
Name changed to Rush Metals Corp. 11/02/2009
Rush Metals Corp. recapitalized as Rush Exploration Inc. 12/13/2011
(See Rush Exploration Inc.)

AMERICAN GOVT INCOME PORTFOLIO INC (MN)
Reorganized into First American Investment Funds, Inc. 08/28/1998
Each share Common 1¢ par exchanged for Fixed Income Fund Class A $0.0001 par shares at $6.994 net asset value

AMERICAN GOVT TERM TR INC (MN)
Completely liquidated 12/21/1995
Each share Common 1¢ par exchanged for first and final distribution of $8.91887 cash

AMERICAN GREAT LAKES CORP (NV)
Recapitalized as Unique Transportation Solutions, Inc. 12/02/2009
Each share Common $0.001 par exchanged for (0.00111111) share Common $0.001 par
(See Unique Transportation Solutions, Inc.)

AMERICAN-GRECIAN OIL CO., INC. (MD)
Charter forfeited for failure to file annual reports 10/30/1959

AMERICAN GREEN GROUP INC (NV)
Each share old Common $0.001 par exchanged for (0.05) share new Common $0.001 par 08/21/2008
New Common $0.001 par split (5) for (1) by issuance of (4) additional shares payable 08/04/2009 to holders of record 07/31/2009
Ex date - 08/05/2009
Charter revoked for failure to file reports and pay taxes 05/31/2011

AMERICAN GREETING PUBLISHERS, INC. (OH)
Name changed to American Greetings Corp. and Capital Stock no par changed to Common $1 par 00/00/1951

AMERICAN GREETINGS CORP (OH)
Each share Common $1 par exchanged for (0.6) share Class A Common $1 par and (0.4) share Class B Common $1 par 11/07/1955
Class A Common $1 par and Class B Common $1 par split (2) for (1) by issuance of (1) additional share respectively 09/10/1960
Class A Common $1 par and Class B Common $1 par split (3) for (2) by issuance of (0.5) additional share respectively 03/11/1968
Class A Common $1 par and Class B Common $1 par split (3) for (2) by issuance of (0.5) additional share respectively 03/10/1971
Class A Common $1 par and Class B Common $1 par split (3) for (2) by issuance of (0.5) additional share respectively 03/10/1972
Class A Common $1 par and Class B Common $1 par split (3) for (2) by issuance of (0.5) additional share respectively 03/12/1973
Class A Common $1 par and Class B Common $1 par split (2) for (1) by issuance of (1) additional share respectively 02/07/1983
Class A Common $1 par and Class B Common $1 par split (2) for (1) by issuance of (1) additional share respectively 09/10/1993
Acquired by Century Intermediate Holding Co. 08/09/2013
Each share Class A Common $1 par exchanged for $19 cash
Each share Class B Common $1 par exchanged for $19 cash

AMERICAN GROUP INC (NV)
Name changed to Global Science Corp. 12/25/1993
Global Science Corp. name changed to Sochrys.Com Inc. 08/25/1999 which name changed to Validian Corp. 02/06/2003

AMERICAN GROUP INC (NV)
Each share old Common $0.001 par exchanged for (0.1) share new Common $0.001 par 11/00/1998
Each share new Common $0.001 par exchanged again for (0.01) share new Common $0.001 par 12/28/1998
Each share new Common $0.001 par exchanged again for (0.05) share new Common $0.001 par 09/29/2000
SEC revoked common stock registration 11/14/2005

AMERICAN GROWTH FD LTD (CANADA)
Common $1 par and Deferred $1 par changed to 50¢ par and (1) additional share issued respectively 04/29/1959
Common 50¢ par and Deferred 50¢ par changed to 20¢ par and (1.5) additional shares issued respectively 08/27/1965
Common 20¢ par reclassified as Mutual Fund Shares 20¢ par 03/25/1966
Name changed to AGF American Growth Fund Ltd. 11/22/1989

AMERICAN GTY CORP (OR)
Name changed to American Guaranty Financial Corp. 12/04/1970
American Guaranty Financial Corp. name changed to Encore Group Inc. 07/18/1990
(See Encore Group Inc.)

AMERICAN GTY CORP (RI)
Stock Dividend - 100% 05/15/1969
Merged into American Guaranty Corp. (New) 09/30/1980
Each share 30¢ Preferred $1 par exchanged for (0.1) share new Common $1 par and $0.50 cash
Each share old Common $1 par exchanged for (0.01) share new Common $1 par
Each share new Common $1 par exchanged for (1/13954) share Common $1 par 04/05/1982
Note: In effect holders received $18 cash per share and public interest was eliminated

AMERICAN GTY FINL CORP (OR)
Stock Dividends - 10% 05/01/1974; 10% 05/05/1975; 10% 05/14/1976; 10% 04/27/1977; 10% 04/28/1978; 10% 05/09/1979; 10% 05/07/1980; 10% 05/13/1981; 10% 05/19/1982
Name changed to Encore Group Inc. 07/18/1990
(See Encore Group Inc.)

AMERICAN GTY LIFE INS CO (OR)
Common $2.50 par changed to $2 par and (0.25) additional share issued 03/02/1963
Common $2 par changed to $1 par and (1) additional share issued plus a 25% stock dividend paid 03/20/1964
Reorganized as American Guaranty Corp. (OR) 07/01/1969
Each share Common $1 par exchanged for (1) share Common no par
American Guaranty Corp. (OR) name changed to American Guaranty Financial Corp. 12/04/1970 which name changed to Encore Group Inc. 07/18/1990
(See Encore Group Inc.)

AMERICAN GTY LIFE INS CO (TX)
Found insolvent by the Court 00/00/1978
No stockholders' equity

AMERICAN GUARANTY CO. (DE)
No longer in existence having become inoperative and void for non-payment of taxes 04/01/1953

AMERICAN GUARANTY CORP.
Acquired by United Guaranty Corp. 00/00/1930
Details not available

AMERICAN GUARANTY LIFE, HEALTH & ACCIDENT INSURANCE CO. (TX)
Name changed to American Guaranty Life Insurance Co. (TX) 04/06/1961
(See American Guaranty Life Insurance Co.)

AMERICAN GUARANTY UNDERWRITERS INC. (TX)
Voluntarily dissolved 04/16/1958
Details not available

AMERICAN GUARDIAN LIFE INSURANCE CO. (UT)
Name changed to American Protectors Insurance Co. 06/20/1964
(See American Protectors Insurance Co.)

AMERICAN GYPSUM CO. (NM)
6% Preferred $3 par called for redemption 10/01/1965
Acquired by Susquehanna Corp. 12/13/1965
Each share Common $1 par exchanged for (0.5263157) share Capital Stock $1 par
(See Susquehanna Corp.)

AMERICAN GYPSUM CO. (OH)
Acquired by Celotex Corp. 00/00/1939
Each share Preferred exchanged for (3.5) shares Common no par
Each share Common exchanged for (2.5) shares Common no par
Celotex Corp. merged into Walter (Jim) Corp. 08/31/1964
(See Walter (Jim) Corp.)

AMERICAN HAIR & FELT CO. (DE)
Recapitalized 00/00/1935
Each share 8% 1st Preferred $100 par exchanged for (1.1) shares 6% Preferred $100 par
Each share 8% 2nd Preferred $100 par exchanged for (1) share $6 Preferred no par, (5) shares Common no par and $5 cash
Recapitalized 00/00/1946
Common no par changed to $5 par
Name changed to Ozite Corp. 06/29/1962
Ozite Corp. merged into Brunswick Corp. 08/16/1974

AMERICAN HARD RUBBER CO. (NY)
Common $100 par changed to $50 par 00/00/1933
Each share 8% Preferred $100 par exchanged for (1) share $7 Preferred $100 par and (1) share Common $25 par 00/00/1942
Each share Common $50 par exchanged for (1) share Common $25 par 00/00/1942
Each share $7 Preferred $100 par exchanged for (2) shares 7% Preferred $50 par 00/00/1952
Each share Common $25 par exchanged for (2) shares Common $12.50 par 00/00/1952
Merged into Amerace Corp. 05/29/1957
Each share 7% Preferred $50 par exchanged for (1) share $3.50 Preferred $50 par
Each share Common $12.50 par exchanged for (1) share Common $12.50 par
Amerace Corp. name changed to Amerace Esna Corp. 08/30/1968 which name changed back to Amerace Corp. 04/23/1973
(See Amerace Corp.)

AMERICAN HARDWARE CORP. (CT)
Common $25 par changed to $12.50 par and (1) additional share issued 12/28/1955
Stock Dividends - 15% 12/23/1958; 10% 07/26/1963
Merged into Emhart Corp. (CT) 06/30/1964
Each share Common $12.50 par exchanged for (1) share Common $12.50 par
Emhart Corp. (CT) reincorporated in Virginia 05/04/1976
(See Emhart Corp. (VA))

AMERICAN HAWAII VENTURES INC (HI)
Involuntarily dissolved for failure to file annual reports 10/25/1995

AMERICAN HEALTH COS INC (DE)
Stock Dividend - 10% 09/15/1987
Merged into CDI Holdings, Inc. 10/14/1988
Each share Common 1¢ par exchanged for $22.50 cash

AMERICAN HEALTH CREDIT PLAN OF OREGON (OR)
Name changed to Health Accounting Service, Inc. 02/23/1965
Health Accounting Service, Inc. name changed to First Pacific Corp. 01/23/1974
(See First Pacific Corp.)

AMERICAN HEALTH FOODS, INC. (DE)
Under plan of merger name changed to American Health Industries, Inc. 09/25/1973
American Health Industries, Inc. recapitalized as American Cytology Services Corp. 07/21/1975 which name changed to American Cytogenetics, Inc. 09/30/1982
(See American Cytogenetics, Inc.)

AMERICAN HEALTH INDS INC (DE)
Recapitalized as American Cytology Services Corp. 07/21/1975
Each share 9% Preferred $10 par automatically became (1) share 9% Preferred $10 par
Each share Common 1¢ par exchanged for (0.25) share Common 1¢ par
American Cytology Services Corp. name changed to American Cytogenetics, Inc. 09/30/1982
(See American Cytogenetics, Inc.)

AMERICAN HEALTH PPTYS INC (DE)
Merged into Health Care Property Investors, Inc. 11/04/1999
Each share 8.6% Depositary Preferred Ser. B automatically became (1) share 8.6% Depositary Preferred Ser. C
Each share 8.7% Preferred Ser. B $1 par automatically became (1) share 8.7% Preferred Ser. B $1 par
Each share Common 1¢ par exchanged for (0.78) share Common $1 par
Health Care Property Investors, Inc. name changed to HCP, Inc. 09/07/2007

AMERICAN HEALTH PRODS INC (WA)
Each share old Common $0.00001 par exchanged for (0.01) share new Common $0.00001 par 00/00/1996
Note: In effect holders received an undetermined amount of cash and public interest was eliminated

AMERICAN HEALTH PROFILES, INC. (TN)
Voluntarily dissolved 01/08/1985
No stockholders' equity

AMERICAN HEALTH PROVIDERS CORP (ID)
Name changed to Bitterroot Mining Co. 11/11/1999
Bitterroot Mining Co. recapitalized as Advanced Process Technologies Inc. 09/20/2000 which name changed to Integrated Pharmaceuticals, Inc. 12/12/2000
(See Integrated Pharmaceuticals, Inc.)

AMERICAN HEALTH SVCS CORP (DE)
Merged into InSight Health Services Corp. 06/26/1996
Each share Common 3¢ par exchanged for (0.1) share Common $0.001 par
(See InSight Health Services Corp.)

AMERICAN HEALTH SVCS INC (MA)
Name changed to Ages Health Services Inc. 04/18/1994
Ages Health Services Inc. name changed to AHSI Inc. 04/15/1997
(See AHSI Inc.)

AMERICAN HEALTH SVCS INC (VA)
Acquired by INA Corp. 10/20/1980
Each share Common 50¢ par exchanged for $19.70 cash

AMERICAN HEALTH SYS INC (NV)
Each share old Common $0.001 par exchanged for (0.1) share new Common $0.001 par 08/01/2000
Charter permanently revoked 09/30/1999

AMERICAN HEALTHCARE MGMT INC (DE)
Reincorporated 02/29/1984
State of incorporation changed from (TX) to (DE) 02/29/1984
Common 10¢ par reclassified as Class A Common 10¢ par 10/17/1984
Reorganized under Chapter 11 Federal Bankruptcy Code 12/29/1989
Each share Class A Common 10¢ par exchanged for (0.1) share Common 1¢ par

Merged into OrNda HealthCorp 04/19/1994
Each share Common 1¢ par exchanged for (0.6) share Common 1¢ par
OrNda HealthCorp merged into Tenet Healthcare Corp. 01/30/1997

AMERICAN HEALTHCARE PROVIDERS INC (DE)
Charter cancelled and declared inoperative and void for non-payment of taxes 03/01/2001

AMERICAN HEALTHCHOICE INC (NY)
Each share old Common $0.001 par exchanged for (1) share new Common $0.001 par 09/09/2000
SEC revoked common stock registration 06/20/2010

AMERICAN HEALTHWAYS INC (DE)
Name changed 01/25/2000
Name changed from American Healthcorp, Inc. to American Healthways, Inc. 01/25/2000
Common $0.001 par split (3) for (2) by issuance of (0.5) additional share 11/12/1993
Each share Common $0.001 par received distribution of (0.092165) share Class A Common no par and (0.593817) share Class B Common no par of AmSurg Corp. payable 12/03/1997 to holders of record 11/25/1997
Common $0.001 par split (3) for (2) by issuance of (0.5) additional share payable 11/23/2001 to holders of record 11/09/2001 Ex date - 11/26/2001
Common $0.001 par split (2) for (1) by issuance of (1) additional share payable 12/19/2003 to holders of record 12/05/2003 Ex date - 12/22/2003
Name changed to Healthways, Inc. 02/01/2006
Healthways, Inc. name changed to Tivity Health, Inc. 01/11/2017

AMERICAN HEART & LUNG TECHNOLOGIES, INC. (DE)
Charter cancelled for failure to pay taxes and maintain registered agent 11/30/1992

AMERICAN HELIOTHERMAL CORP (CO)
Each share Common 1¢ par exchanged for (0.2) share Common $0.001 par 02/23/1984
Charter suspended for failure to file annual reports 09/30/1987

AMERICAN HELIUM & MNG CORP (NV)
Each share Common 10¢ par exchanged for (0.1) share Common $1 par 06/13/1972
Name changed to "999" 10/30/1980
"999" reincorporated in Delaware as 999 Inc. 05/01/1991

AMERICAN HERITAGE FD INC (NY)
Completely liquidated 12/04/2008
Each share Common 10¢ par received net asset value

AMERICAN HERITAGE INVESTMENT CORP. (IN)
Charter revoked for failure to file reports and pay fees 03/03/1969

AMERICAN HERITAGE LIFE INS CO (FL)
Reorganized as American Heritage Life Investment Corp. 12/31/1968
Each share Common $1 par exchanged for (1) share Common $1 par
American Heritage Life Investment Corp. merged into Allstate Corp. 10/31/1999

AMERICAN HERITAGE LIFE INVT CORP (FL)
Common $1 par split (3) for (2) by issuance of (0.5) additional share 05/22/1987
Common $1 par split (4) for (3) by issuance of (1/3) additional share 02/26/1990
Common $1 par split (4) for (3) by issuance of (1/3) additional share 02/28/1992
Common $1 par split (3) for (2) by issuance of (0.5) additional share 05/20/1993
Common $1 par split (2) for (1) by issuance of (1) additional share payable 03/04/1998 to holders of record 02/18/1998 Ex date - 03/05/1998
Merged into Allstate Corp. 10/31/1999
Each share Common $1 par exchanged for (1.34973) shares Common 1¢ par

AMERICAN HERITAGE PUBG CO (NY)
Merged into McGraw-Hill, Inc. 10/20/1969
Each share Common 25¢ par exchanged for (0.55) share Common $1 par
Each share Class B 25¢ par exchanged for (0.55) share Common $1 par
McGraw-Hill, Inc. name changed to McGraw-Hill Companies, Inc. 04/28/1995 which name changed to McGraw Hill Financial, Inc. 05/02/2013 which name changed to S&P Global Inc. 04/28/2016

AMERICAN HIDE & LEATHER CO. (NJ)
Common $100 par changed to no par 00/00/1927
Recapitalized 00/00/1935
Each share Preferred $100 par exchanged for (1) share 6% Preferred $50 par and (4) shares Common $1 par
Common no par changed to $1 par
Name changed to General American Industries, Inc. 11/30/1956
General American Industries, Inc. name changed to Tandy Corp. (NJ) 11/14/1960 which reincorporated in Delaware 02/27/1968 which name changed to RadioShack Corp. 05/18/2000 which name changed to RS Legacy Corp. 09/23/2015
(See RS Legacy Corp.)

AMERICAN HIGHLAND MNG CORP (BC)
Name changed to Cryocon Containers Inc. 02/26/1992
Cryocon Containers Inc. recapitalized as Cryocon-Pacific Containers Inc. 06/17/1993 which recapitalized as Alda Industries Corp. 05/06/1996 which recapitalized as Crux Industries Inc. 07/14/1999 which name changed to Mont Blanc Resources Inc. 11/18/2005 which name changed to Sonora Gold & Silver Corp. 07/17/2008

AMERICAN HLDGS INC (CO)
Name changed to Gemini Marketing, Inc. 03/13/1990
Gemini Marketing, Inc. recapitalized as Gemini Shareware Inc. 11/21/1990
(See Gemini Shareware Inc.)

AMERICAN HLDGS INC (DE)
SEC revoked common stock registration 07/23/2009

AMERICAN HLDGS INC N J (DE)
Name changed to Pure World Inc. 09/27/1995
(See Pure World Inc.)

AMERICAN HOG CO (CO)
Went private 00/00/1973
Details not available

AMERICAN HOIST & DERRICK CO (DE)
Each share old Capital Stock $1 par exchanged for (2.5) shares new Capital Stock $1 par 00/00/1950
Under plan of merger new Capital Stock $1 par reclassified as Common $1 par 09/27/1967
Common $1 par split (2) for (1) by issuance of (1) additional share 04/09/1968
Name changed to Amdura Corp. 02/13/1989
(See Amdura Corp.)

AMERICAN HOLDING CORP.
Liquidated 00/00/1940
Details not available

AMERICAN HLDG INVTS INC (NV)
SEC revoked common stock registration 08/12/2010

AMERICAN HOME ALLIANCE CORP (DE)
Name changed to Ember Therapeutics, Inc. 02/24/2016

AMERICAN HOME ALLIANCE INDS LTD (NV)
Reorganized as Alliance Industries 09/18/1996
Each share Common $0.001 par exchanged for (2) shares Common $0.001 par
(See Alliance Industries)

AMERICAN HOME ASSURN CO (NY)
Merged into American International Group Corp. 08/01/1969
Details not available

AMERICAN HOME CAP CORP (NV)
Charter revoked for failure to file reports and pay fees 07/31/2010

AMERICAN HOME FIRE ASSURANCE CO. (NY)
Each share Capital Stock $20 par exchanged for (0.97309) share Capital Stock $10 par 00/00/1932
Name changed to American Home Assurance Co. 00/00/1954
(See American Home Assurance Co.)

AMERICAN HOME FURNISHERS CORP.
Out of business 00/00/1933
Details not available

AMERICAN HOME INDS CORP (CA)
Common 10¢ par split (3) for (2) by issuance of (0.5) additional share 05/27/1971
Common 10¢ par changed to no par 07/19/1983
Plan of reorganization under Chapter 11 Federal Bankruptcy proceedings confirmed 11/03/1983
4% Conv. Preferred 10¢ par cancelled
Charter suspended by order of the franchise tax board 03/00/2000

AMERICAN HOME INVT CO (IA)
Charter cancelled for failure to file annual reports 12/01/1983

AMERICAN HOME MTG HLDGS INC (DE)
Under plan of merger each share Common 1¢ par automatically became (1) share American Home Mortgage Investment Corp. Common 1¢ par 12/03/2003
(See American Home Mortgage Investment Corp.)

AMERICAN HOME MTG INVT CORP (MD)
Plan of reorganization under Chapter 11 Federal Bankruptcy proceedings effective 11/30/2010
No stockholders' equity

AMERICAN HOME PARTNERS INC (DE)
Company went private through cash purchase offer which expired 10/16/2002
Holders received approximately $1 cash per share

AMERICAN HOME PATIENT CTRS INC (DE)
Name changed to Wessex Corp. 05/27/1986
Wessex Corp. name changed to Diversicare Corp. of America 05/01/1989
(See Diversicare Corp. of America)

AMERICAN HOME PRODS CORP (DE)
Capital Stock no par changed to $1 par 00/00/1933
Capital Stock $1 par split (2) for (1) by issuance of (1) additional share 11/25/1957
Capital Stock $1 par split (3) for (1) by issuance of (2) additional shares 10/06/1961
Capital Stock $1 par reclassified as Common $1 par 09/30/1965
Common $1 par split (2) for (1) by issuance of (1) additional share 05/10/1967
Common $1 par changed to $0.33333333 par and (2) additional shares issued 05/11/1973
Common $0.33333333 par split (2) for (1) by issuance of (1) additional share 05/01/1990
Common $0.33333333 par split (2) for (1) by issuance of (1) additional share payable 05/06/1996 to holders of record 04/24/1996 Ex date - 05/07/1996
Common $0.33333333 par split (2) for (1) by issuance of (1) additional share payable 05/05/1998 to holders of record 04/24/1998 Ex date - 05/06/1998
Stock Dividend - 200% 11/01/1946
Name changed to Wyeth 03/11/2002
Wyeth acquired by Pfizer Inc. 10/15/2009

AMERICAN HOME SAVINGS & LOAN ASSOCIATION (MO)
Acquired by First Banks, Inc. 12/01/1993
Each share Common $1 par exchanged for $1.50 cash

AMERICAN HOME SEC LIFE INS CO (NM)
Each share Class A Common 20¢ par and Class A-1 Common 20¢ par exchanged for (0.2) share Class A Common 50¢ par and Class A-1 Common 50¢ par respectively 05/18/1970
Merged into S.N.L. Financial Corp. 04/16/1982
Each share Class A Common 50¢ par exchanged for (1) share Preferred $1 par
Each share Class A-1 Common 50¢ par exchanged for (1) share Preferred $1 par
S.N.L. Financial Corp. name changed to Security National Financial Corp. 12/27/1990

AMERICAN HOME SHIELD CORP (DE)
Each share Common 1¢ par exchanged for (0.25) Common 4¢ par 08/15/1983
Merged into ServiceMaster Limited Partnership 10/27/1989
Each share Common 4¢ par exchanged for $9.50 cash
Note: An additional payment of $0.245 cash per share was made 09/25/1992

AMERICAN HOMEOWNERS INS CO (DC)
Capital Stock $1 par changed to 50¢ par 08/01/1965
Capital Stock 50¢ par changed to 30¢ par 02/03/1966
Capital Stock 30¢ par changed to 50¢ par 10/29/1977
Completely liquidated 12/01/1982
Each share Capital Stock 50¢ par received first and final distribution of $1.53 cash

Note: Certificates were not required to be surrendered and are without value

AMERICAN HOMEPATIENT INC (NV)
Reincorporated 06/30/2010
Common 1¢ par split (3) for (2) by issuance of (0.5) additional share payable 07/12/1996 to holders of record 06/28/1996
State of incorporation changed from (DE) to (NV) 06/30/2010
Acquired by Highland Capital Management, L.P. 10/12/2010
Each share Common 1¢ par exchanged for $0.67 cash

AMERICAN HOMES 4 RENT (MD)
Each 5% Participating Preferred Share of Bene. Int. Ser. A 1¢ par automatically became (1.3106) Class A Common Shares of Bene. Int. 1¢ par 10/03/2017
Each 5% Participating Preferred Share of Bene. Int. Ser. B 1¢ par automatically became (1.3106) Class A Common Shares of Bene. Int. 1¢ par 10/03/2017
Each 5.5% Participating Preferred Share of Bene. Int. Ser. C 1¢ par automatically became (1.42747736) Class A Common Shares of Bene. Int. 1¢ par 04/05/2018
(Additional Information in Active)

AMERICAN HOMESTAR CORP OLD (TX)
Common 5¢ par split (5) for (4) by issuance of (0.25) additional share payable 01/18/1996 to holders of record 01/05/1996
Common 5¢ par split (5) for (4) by issuance of (0.25) additional share payable 02/07/1997 to holders of record 01/24/1997
Common 5¢ par split (3) for (2) by issuance of (0.5) additional share payable 10/31/1997 to holders of record 10/17/1997
Plan of reorganization under Chapter 11 Federal Bankruptcy Code effective 10/03/2001
No stockholders' equity

AMERICAN HOPPI-COPTERS, INC. (MD)
Name changed to Helicopter Corp. of America 00/00/1958
(See Helicopter Corp. of America)

AMERICAN HORSE RACING STABLES, INC. (NV)
Charter revoked for failure to file reports and pay fees 03/07/1960

AMERICAN HOSP & LIFE INS CO (TX)
Name changed to American Security Life Insurance Co. (TX) 06/01/1972
(See American Security Life Insurance Co. (TX))

AMERICAN HOSP RES INC (UT)
Stock Dividend - 5% payable 07/31/2003 to holders of record 07/15/2003 Ex date - 07/11/2003
Name changed to HAPS USA, Inc. 05/12/2005
HAPS USA, Inc. name changed to PGMI, Inc. 03/16/2006
(See PGMI, Inc.)

AMERICAN HOSP SUPPLY CORP (IL)
Each share Common no par exchanged for (2) shares Common $4 par 00/00/1951
Common $4 par changed to $2 par and (2) additional shares issued 05/08/1959
Common $2 par changed to no par and (2) additional shares issued 05/19/1961
Common no par split (3) for (1) by issuance of (2) additional shares 06/15/1968
Common no par split (3) for (2) by issuance of (0.5) additional share 07/26/1982

Merged into Baxter Travenol Laboratories, Inc. 11/25/1985
Each share Common no par exchanged for (0.2) share Adjustable Rate Preferred no par, (0.32) share Conv. Exchangeable Preferred no par and (1.83) shares Common $1 par
Baxter Travenol Laboratories, Inc. name changed to Baxter International Inc. 05/18/1988

AMERICAN HOST (UT)
Proclaimed dissolved for failure to pay taxes 11/09/1974

AMERICAN HOST CORP. (TX)
Charter forfeited for failure to pay taxes 03/10/1975

AMERICAN HOTELS CORP (DE)
Each (10) shares 8% Preferred $100 par exchanged for (5) shares new 8% Preferred $100 par and (5) shares new 4% Preferred $100 par 00/00/1936
Voluntarily dissolved 12/06/1973
Details not available

AMERICAN HSG INCOME TR (MD)
Reincorporated under the laws of Wyoming as Corix Bioscience, Inc. 08/02/2017

AMERICAN HSG PARTNERS (CA)
Terminated registration of Limited Partnership and is no longer public as of 09/14/2000
Details not available

AMERICAN HSG SYS CORP (OH)
Name changed to Ambina Corp. 07/09/1974
(See Ambina Corp.)

AMERICAN HYDROCARBON CORP (DE)
Charter cancelled and declared inoperative and void for non-payment of taxes 03/01/1987

AMERICAN I.G. CHEMICAL CORP. (DE)
Name changed to General Aniline & Film Corp. 10/31/1939
General Aniline & Film Corp. name changed to GAF Corp. 04/24/1968
(See GAF Corp.)

AMERICAN ICE CO. (NJ)
Each share Common $100 par exchanged for (4) shares Common no par 00/00/1927
Name changed to American Consumer Industries, Inc. 09/22/1961
(See American Consumer Industries, Inc.)

AMERICAN IDC CORP (FL)
Name changed to Smart SMS Corp. 11/18/2005

AMERICAN ILLINOIS LIFE INSURANCE CO. (IL)
Merged into Inland Life Insurance Co. 06/30/1964
Each share Common 25¢ par exchanged for (0.35) share Common 50¢ par
Inland Life Insurance Co. reorganized as Inland National Corp. 07/23/1969 which was acquired by Zenith National Corp. 06/08/1973 which merged into First Continental Life Group, Inc. 10/28/1979
(See First Continental Life Group, Inc.)

AMERICAN IMAGE MTR INC (ID)
Each share Common 10¢ par exchanged for (4.7) shares Common 10¢ par 09/23/1996
Administratively dissolved 08/10/2007

AMERICAN IMAGING INC (FL)
Name changed to Seascape Entertainment, Inc. 06/12/2000

AMERICAN IMPORTING & EXPORTING CO. (ME)
Charter suspended for failure to file annual reports 00/00/1917

AMERICAN INCOME FD INC (VA)
Name changed to Nuveen Multi-Market Income Fund, Inc. (VA) 09/08/2014
Nuveen Multi-Market Income Fund, Inc. (VA) reincorporated in Massachusetts as Nuveen Multi-Market Income Fund 11/19/2014

AMERICAN INCOME HLDG INC (DE)
Merged into TMK Acquisition Corp. 11/10/1994
Each share Common 1¢ par exchanged for $35 cash

AMERICAN INCOME INVTS INC (DE)
Merged into Income Fund of America, Inc. (DE) 07/31/1976
Each share Capital Stock $1 par exchanged for (0.582163) share Capital Stock $1 par
Income Fund of America, Inc. (DE) reincorporated in Maryland 09/22/1983 which reorganized in Delaware as Income Fund of America 10/01/2010

AMERICAN INCOME LIFE INS CO (IN)
Stock Dividends - 10% 07/12/1963; 10% 06/10/1965; 10% 03/25/1966; 10% 03/24/1967; 27% 03/29/1968; 10% 06/25/1969; 10% 06/18/1971; 10% 03/24/1972; 25% 03/29/1974; 100% 04/16/1979; 100% 06/20/1980; 100% 04/20/1983
Acquired by Golder, Thoma & Cressey 05/01/1989
Each share Common $1 par exchanged for $19 cash

AMERICAN INCOME PPTYS L P (DE)
Completely liquidated 12/21/1988
Each Unit of Ltd. Partnership Int. received first and final distribution of (0.9) share of Dial Reit Inc. Common 1¢ par
Note: Certificates were not required to be surrendered and are now valueless
Dial Reit Inc. name changed to Mid-America Realty Investments, Inc. 04/28/1994 which merged into Bradley Real Estate, Inc. 08/06/1998
(See Bradley Real Estate, Inc.)

AMERICAN INCOME TR (ON)
Merged into Income Financial Trust 06/19/2006
Each Trust Unit received (0.493092) Trust Unit

AMERICAN INDEMNITY CO. (MD)
Completely liquidated 01/00/1962
Details not available

AMERICAN INDEPENDENCE CORP (DE)
Each share old Common 1¢ par exchanged for (0.33333333) share new Common 1¢ par 02/13/2003
Acquired by Independence Holding Co. (New) 08/31/2016
Each share new Common 1¢ par exchanged for $24.74 cash

AMERICAN INDEPENDENCE INVESTMENT CO. (CO)
Merged into General Life of Missouri Investment Co. 04/20/1966
Each share Common $1 par exchanged for (1) share Class A Common 20¢ par
General Life of Missouri Investment Co. merged into Guaranty Corp. 01/17/1974

AMERICAN INDEPENDENT REINSURANCE CO. (FL)
Merged into American Fire & Casualty Co. on a (1) for (3.1) basis 04/08/1964
American Fire & Casualty Co. merged into Ohio Casualty Insurance Co.

08/27/1969 which reorganized as Ohio Casualty Corp. 01/01/1970
(See Ohio Casualty Corp.)

AMERICAN INDIAN NATIONAL BANK (WASHINGTON, DC)
Acquired by Metropolitan Bancshares, Inc. 03/31/1988
Each share Capital Stock $5 par exchanged for $16.39 cash

AMERICAN INDIAN OIL & GAS CO. (OK)
Liquidation completed
Each share Capital Stock $1 par exchanged for initial distribution of $2.65 cash 06/20/1961
Each share Capital Stock $1 par received second and final distribution of $0.5164 cash 02/19/1965
Note: Unexchanged certificates were cancelled and became without value 06/20/1964

AMERICAN INDPT BK N A (GARDENIA, CA)
Merged into First Coastal Bank (El Segundo, CA) 03/08/1999
Each share Common $5 par exchanged for $7 cash

AMERICAN INDPT NETWORK INC (DE)
Each share old Common no par exchanged for (0.2) share new Common no par 11/03/1998
Name changed to Hispanic Television Network Inc. 12/22/1999
(See Hispanic Television Network Inc.)

AMERICAN INDTY CO (TX)
Common $10 par changed to $3.33333333 par and (2) additional shares issued 10/27/1972
Through voluntary exchange offer 99.9% acquired by American Indemnity Financial Corp. as of 04/07/1977
Public interest eliminated

AMERICAN INDTY FINL CORP (DE)
Stock Dividends - 25% 02/24/1977; 10% 03/02/1981; 10% 03/02/1982
Merged into United Fire & Casualty Co. 08/10/1999
Each share Common $3.33333333 par exchanged for $14.3553 cash
Note: An additional distribution of approximately $0.014 cash from escrow was made 06/04/2004 to holders of record 08/10/1999

AMERICAN INDUSTRIAL LIFE INSURANCE CO. (PA)
Merged into Chesapeake Life Insurance Co. 10/31/1966
Each share Common $10 par exchanged (2) shares Class A $1 par and (10) shares Class B $1 par
Chesapeake Life Insurance Co. (MD) recapitalized in Oklahoma 09/27/1993
(See Chesapeake Life Insurance Co.)

AMERICAN INDL LN ASSN INC (VA)
Name changed to Approved Financial Corp. 07/19/1996
(See Approved Financial Corp.)

AMERICAN INDL MINERALS GROUP INC (FL)
Name changed to Networthusa.com, Inc. 05/20/1999
Networthusa.com, Inc. name changed to EBUX Inc. 10/06/2000 which name changed to Petapeer Holdings Inc. 05/05/2001 which name changed to Studio Bromont Inc. 02/14/2002 which name changed to United American Corp. 03/01/2004

AMERICAN INDL PPTYS REIT (TX)
Each old Share of Bene. Int. 10¢ par exchanged for (0.2) new Share of Bene. Int. 10¢ par 10/15/1997
Merged into Developers Diversified Realty Corp. 05/14/2001

Each new Share of Bene. Int. 10¢ par exchanged for $12.89 cash
Note: An additional distribution of approximately $0.05 cash per share was made 04/00/2004

AMERICAN INDUSTRIES, INC. (NV)
Completely liquidated 11/16/1966
Each share Common $1 par exchanged for first and final distribution of (1.5) shares Empire Petroleum Co. Common $1 par
Empire Petroleum Co. name changed to Empire International, Inc. 07/15/1980
(See Empire International, Inc.)

AMERICAN INDS INC (UT)
Each share old Common $0.001 par exchanged for (0.1) share new Common $0.001 par 10/12/1990
Name changed to Dolce Ventures Inc. 05/21/2002
Dolce Ventures Inc. recapitalized as Sino Gas International Holdings, Inc. 11/17/2006
(See Sino Gas International Holdings, Inc.)

AMERICAN INDUSTRIES LIFE INSURANCE CO. (AZ)
Merged into Investors United Life Insurance Co. 10/20/1967
Details not available

AMERICAN INDS LTD (NV)
SEC revoked common stock registration 09/01/2010

AMERICAN INFLATABLES INC (DE)
Name changed to American Sports Development Group, Inc. 06/18/2002
(See American Sports Development Group, Inc.)

AMERICAN INFORMATION TECHNOLOGIES CORP (DE)
Common $1 par split (3) for (2) by issuance of (0.5) additional share 01/23/1987
Common $1 par split (2) for (1) by issuance of (1) additional share 01/23/1989
Name changed to Ameritech Corp. 04/26/1991
Ameritech Corp. merged into SBC Communications Inc. 10/08/1999 which name changed to AT&T Inc. 11/18/2005

AMERICAN INSTL DEVELOPERS INC (DE)
Class A Common 5¢ par split (2) for (1) by issuance of (1) additional share 05/14/1969
Name changed to AID, Inc. (DE) 05/15/1970
AID, Inc. (DE) merged into INA Corp. 06/16/1978 which merged into Cigna Corp. 04/01/1982

AMERICAN INSULATOR CORP (DE)
Each share 8% 2nd Preferred $50 par exchanged for (2) shares Prior Preferred $10 par 00/00/1938
Each share Common no par exchanged for (0.5) share Common $1 par 00/00/1938
$1.50 Prior Preferred $10 par called for redemption 12/15/1955
Liquidation completed
Each share Common $1 par received initial distribution of $15 cash 07/01/1982
Each share Common $1 par received second distribution of $10 cash 02/01/1983
Each share Common $1 par received third distribution of $2.75 cash 04/11/1983
Each share Common $1 par received fourth and final distribution of $0.55 cash 11/15/1984
Note: Certificates were not required to be surrendered and are without value

AMERICAN INSULOCK INC (BC)
Name changed to Lexicon Building Systems Ltd. 04/27/2011

AMERICAN INS & INDL FD INC (MD)
Name changed to Midamerica High Growth Fund, Inc. 05/09/1983
(See Midamerica High Growth Fund, Inc.)

AMERICAN INS CO (NJ)
Capital Stock $5 par changed to $2.50 par 00/00/1932
Stock Dividend - 20% 10/26/1956
Merged into Firemen's Fund Insurance Co. 06/22/1972
Each share Capital Stock $2.50 par exchanged for $40 cash

AMERICAN INSURANCE FOUNDERS INC. (DC)
Charter revoked for failure to file reports and pay fees 09/09/1963

AMERICAN INS GROUP INC (DE)
Name changed to Pace American Group, Inc. 03/31/1993
(See Pace American Group, Inc.)

AMERICAN INS INVS STK FD INC (MD)
Name changed to American Insurance & Industrial Fund, Inc. 03/12/1971
American Insurance & Industrial Fund, Inc. name changed to Midamerica High Growth Fund, Inc. 05/09/1983
(See Midamerica High Growth Fund, Inc.)

AMERICAN INSURANCE MANAGEMENT CORP. (OH)
Merged into Koehler Management Corp. 06/29/1970
Each share Common $1 par exchanged for (3.59) shares Common no par
(See Koehler Management Corp.)

AMERICAN INSURANSTOCKS CORP.
Dissolved 00/00/1940
Details not available

AMERICAN INSD MTG INVS (CA)
Completely liquidated 02/24/2004
Each Depositary Unit of Limited Partnership exchanged for $1.60 cash

AMERICAN INSD MTG-INVS L P SER 85 (CA)
Completely liquidated 08/08/2005
Each Depositary Unit exchanged for first and final distribution of $1.32 cash

AMERICAN INSD MTG INVS L P SER 86 (CA)
Completely liquidated 02/13/2004
Each Depositary Unit of Ltd. Partnership Int. exchanged for first and final distribution of $1.28 cash

AMERICAN INSD MTG INVS L P SER 88 (CA)
Completely liquidated 02/13/2004
Each Depositary Unit of Ltd. Partnership Int. exchanged for first and final distribution of $1.555 cash

AMERICAN INSURORS DEVELOPMENT CO. (MS)
Merged into Certified Credit Corp. 02/05/1962
Each share Capital Stock $1 par exchanged for (0.33333333) share Class A Common $2 par
(See Certified Credit Corp.)

AMERICAN INTEGRITY CORP (PA)
Common 1¢ par split (3) for (2) by issuance of (0.5) additional share 04/15/1971
Plan of reorganization under Chapter 7 Federal Bankruptcy proceedings effective 01/29/2001
No stockholders' equity

AMERICAN INTERACTIVE MEDIA INC (DE)
Reincorporated 01/12/1998
State of incorporation changed from (NV) to (DE) 01/12/1998
Charter cancelled and declared inoperative and void for non-payment of taxes 03/01/2002

AMERICAN-INTERNATIONAL ALUMINUM CORP. (FL)
Reincorporated under the laws of Delaware as A.I.M. Companies, Inc. 09/06/1968
(See A.I.M. Companies, Inc.)

AMERICAN INTL ASSETS INC (UT)
Charter expired 07/15/2003

AMERICAN INTL BK (LOS ANGELES, CA)
Common $6.25 par changed to $2 par 11/20/1984
Merged into East West Bancorp, Inc. 01/14/2000
Each share Common $2 par exchanged for $0.25989925 cash

AMERICAN INTERNATIONAL BOWLING CORP. (DE)
Adjudicated bankrupt 11/18/1964
No stockholders' equity

AMERICAN INTERNATIONAL CORP. (NY)
Each share old Common no par exchanged for (2) shares new Common no par 00/00/1929
New Common no par changed to $1 par 02/23/1955
Stock Dividend - 100% 10/18/1955
Merged into Adams Express Co. (NY) 01/01/1969
Each share Common $1 par exchanged for (1.121) shares Common $1 par
Adams Express Co. (NY) reincorporated in Maryland 05/28/1976 which name changed to Adams Diversified Equity Fund, Inc. 03/31/2015

AMERICAN INTL CORP (NV)
Recapitalized as American Diversified Corp. (NV) 01/10/1985
Each share Common 10¢ par exchanged for (0.2) share Common 10¢ par
American Diversified Corp. (NV) recapitalized as Natural Pharmaceutical International Inc. 06/18/1990

AMERICAN INTL DEV CORP (DE)
Incorporated 12/27/1960
Name changed to Cenvill Communities, Inc. 05/19/1972
Cenvill Communities, Inc. reorganized as Cenvill Investors, Inc. 07/31/1981 which name changed to CV Reit, Inc. 05/10/1990 which merged into Kramont Realty Trust 06/16/2000
(See Kramont Realty Trust)

AMERICAN INTERNATIONAL DEVELOPMENT CORP. (DE)
Incorporated 09/19/1945
Dissolved 09/19/1952
Details not available

AMERICAN INTERNATIONAL ENTERPRISES, INC. (DE)
Common 10¢ par changed to $5 par 08/00/1967
Name changed to American International Group, Inc. 11/13/1968

AMERICAN INTL FDG CORP (OH)
Charter cancelled for non-payment of taxes 10/30/1980

AMERICAN INTL FOOD CORP (FL)
Recapitalized as Travoo, Inc. 06/25/2009
Each share Common $0.001 par exchanged for (0.05) share Common $0.001 par
Travoo, Inc. recapitalized as Yingtui Holdings Ltd. 04/05/2013

AMERICAN INTL GROUP INC (DE)
$2 Conv. Preferred Ser. A $5 par called for redemption 02/11/1975
Each share Exchangeable Money Market Preferred Ser. T-1 $5 par exchanged for (1) share Exchangeable Money Market Preferred Ser. M-1 $5 par 06/02/1986
Each share Exchangeable Money Market Preferred Ser. T-2 $5 par exchanged for (1) share Exchangeable Money Market Preferred Ser. M-2 $5 par 06/02/1986
$5.85 Conv. Preferred Ser. B $5 par called for redemption 10/01/1986
Money Market Exchangeable Preferred Ser. M-2 $5 par called for redemption 03/05/1993
Money Market Exchangeable Preferred Ser. M-1 $5 par called for redemption 04/02/1993
Each Corporate Unit automatically became (0.04156) share new Common $2.50 par 08/01/2011
(Additional Information in Active)

AMERICAN INTL HEALTH SVCS INC (MA)
Common 1¢ par split (3) for (2) by issuance of (0.5) additional share 07/15/1981
Stock Dividend - 100% 03/16/1981
Recapitalized as PHC, Inc. 04/21/1993
Each share Common 1¢ par exchanged for (0.05) share Class A Common 1¢ par
PHC, Inc. merged into Acadia Healthcare Co., Inc. 11/01/2011

AMERICAN INTERNATIONAL INSURANCE CO. (NY)
Acquired by Continental Insurance Co. 09/01/1970
Each share Capital Stock $10 par exchanged for $55 cash

AMERICAN INTL MED SUPPLY CO (UT)
Each share old Common $0.001 par exchanged for (0.0125) share new Common $0.001 par 02/28/1994
Name changed to Quick Tent, Inc. 04/14/1994
Quick Tent, Inc. recapitalized as FiltaKleen Inc. 04/01/2003 which recapitalized as IPTV Corp. 10/31/2006

AMERICAN INTERNATIONAL MINERALS CORP. (DE)
Recapitalized as Seaboard American Corp. 01/25/1962
Each share Capital Stock 10¢ par exchanged for (0.1) share Capital Stock 1¢ par
(See Seaboard American Corp.)

AMERICAN INTL PETE CORP (NV)
Each share Common 4¢ par exchanged for (0.5) share old Common 8¢ par 05/15/1984
Each share old Common 8¢ par exchanged for (0.1) share new Common 8¢ par 10/28/1993
SEC revoked common stock registration 12/19/2006

AMERICAN INTL PICTURES INC (DE)
Reincorporated 08/27/1976
Common 20¢ par split (5) for (4) by issuance of (0.25) additional share 03/26/1976
Stock Dividend - 100% 04/30/1975
State of incorporation changed from (CA) to (DE) 08/27/1976
Merged into Filmways, Inc. 07/12/1979
Each share Common 20¢ par exchanged for $12.50 principal amount of 10% Subord. Debentures due 03/01/1999

AMERICAN INTL REINS INC (PANAMA)
Common no par split (2) for (1) by issuance of (1) additional share 08/01/1972
Stock Dividends - 25% 07/10/1974; 25% 06/15/1977
Merged into American International Group, Inc. 09/20/1978
Each share Common no par exchanged for (1.1) shares Common $2.50 par

AMERICAN INTERNATIONAL RESOURCES CO. (DE)
Name changed to Uniquad Resource Co. 05/03/1984
(See Uniquad Resources Co.)

AMERICAN INTERNATIONAL SAVINGS & LOAN ASSOCIATION, INC. (MD)
Charter revoked for failure to file reports and pay fees 12/02/1964

AMERICAN INTST BK (NEWPORT BEACH, CA)
Closed by the California Superintendent of Banks and the FDIC was appointed receiver 06/12/1992
Stockholders equity unlikely

AMERICAN INTST INS CORP WIS (WI)
Each share Common $2 par exchanged for (0.002) share Common $250 par 09/23/1974
Note: In effect holders received $1.15 cash per share and public interest was eliminated

AMERICAN INVESTMENT & INCOME FUND, INC. (DE)
Name changed to American Investment Fund, Inc. 04/18/1960
(See American Investment Fund, Inc.)

AMERICAN INVT CAP CORP (AB)
Recapitalized as Westland Investment Corp. 06/13/1991
Each share Common no par exchanged for (0.5) share Common no par
Westland Investment Corp. (AB) reincorporated in Yukon 11/27/1996 which name changed to Sepik Gold Corp. 08/15/1997
(See Sepik Gold Corp.)

AMERICAN INVESTMENT CO. OF ILLINOIS (DE)
Common no par changed to $1 par 00/00/1940
Common $1 par split (2) for (1) by issuance of (1) additional share 12/01/1955
Stock Dividend - 25% 11/22/1950
Name changed to American Investment Co. 11/30/1963
(See American Investment Co.)

AMERICAN INVESTMENT CO. OF SOUTH BEND, INC. (IN)
Recapitalized as American Affiliates, Inc. 03/31/1972
Each share Common no par exchanged for (0.4) share Common no par
(See American Affiliates, Inc.)

AMERICAN INVT CO (DE)
5.25% Prior Preferred $100 par called for redemption 08/12/1978
Acquired by Leucadia National Corp. 12/03/1980
Each share 5.50% Preference Ser. B exchanged for $13 cash
Each share 5.50% Preference exchanged for $13 cash
Each share Common $1 par exchanged for $13 cash

AMERICAN INVESTMENT CORP.
Liquidated 00/00/1930
Details not available

AMERICAN INVT COUNSELING FD INC (CA)
Capital Stock $1 par changed to 20¢ par and (4) additional shares issued 04/10/1968
Acquired by Pegasus Fund, Inc. 12/31/1972
Each share Capital Stock 20¢ par exchanged for (1.4) shares Capital Stock $1 par
Pegasus Fund, Inc. name changed to Vanderbilt Growth Fund, Inc. 07/01/1975 which merged into St. Paul Capital Fund, Inc. 06/14/1977 which name changed to AMEV Capital Fund, Inc. 05/01/1985 which reorganized as Fortis Equity Portfolios Inc. 02/22/1992
(See Fortis Equity Portfolios Inc.)

AMERICAN INVESTMENT FUND, INC. (DE)
Liquidation completed 09/04/1963
Details not available

AMERICAN INVT PPTYS CORP (FL)
Name changed to One Family Investment, Inc. 11/20/1998
(See One Family Investment, Inc.)

AMERICAN INVESTMENT SECURITIES CO.
Liquidated 00/00/1944
Details not available

AMERICAN INVESTMENT TRUST SHARES
Liquidated 00/00/1935
Details not available

AMERICAN INVESTMENTS LTD. (OK)
Charter cancelled for failure to pay taxes 03/08/1974

AMERICAN INVESTORS, INC.
Dissolved 00/00/1935
Details not available

AMERICAN INVESTORS ASSURANCE CO. (UT)
Each share Common $10 par exchanged for (2) shares Common $5 par 06/04/1965
Each share Common $5 par exchanged for (5) shares Common $1 par 05/06/1969
Plan of Rehabilitation approved 04/20/1973
No stockholders' equity

AMERICAN INVESTORS CORP. (TN)
Reorganized under the laws of Delaware as AIC Corp. 12/31/1964
Each share Common $1 par exchanged for (1) share Common $1 par
AIC Corp. name changed to Crutcher Resources Corp. 12/31/1968
(See Crutcher Resources Corp.)

AMERICAN INVESTORS FUND, INC. (NY)
Capital Stock 1¢ par split (4) for (1) by issuance of (3) additional shares 08/01/1968
Name changed to American Investors Growth Fund, Inc. (NY) 09/19/1986
American Investors Growth Fund, Inc. (NY) reincorporated in Maryland 10/05/1989
(See American Investors Growth Fund, Inc. (MD))

AMERICAN INVS GROWTH FD INC (MD)
Reincorporated 10/05/1989
State of incorporation changed from (NY) to (MD) and Capital Stock 1¢ par changed to $0.001 par 10/05/1989
Merged into Ivy Fund 01/28/1993
Details not available

AMERICAN INVS INCOME FD INC (CT)
Merged out of existence 11/01/1989
Details not available

AMERICAN INVESTORS LIFE INSURANCE CO. (TX)
Merged into American Investors Corp. 07/03/1959
Each share Common no par exchanged for (1) share Common $1 par
American Investors Corp. reincorporated in Delaware as AIC Corp. 12/31/1964 which name changed to Crutcher Resources Corp. 12/31/1968
(See Crutcher Resources Corp.)

AMERICAN INVS LIFE INS INC (KS)
Common $1 par split (5) for (4) by issuance of (0.25) additional share 02/16/1970
Stock Dividends - 25% 06/20/1968; 25% 07/15/1969; 25% 02/22/1971; 10% 06/01/1972; 25% 04/10/1986
Under plan of reorganization each share Common $1 par received distribution of (1) share AmVestors Financial Corp. Common no par 08/27/1986
Note: Certificates were not required to be surrendered and are without value
AmVestors Financial Corp. merged into AmerUs Life Holdings, Inc. 12/19/1997 which name changed to Amerus Group Co. 09/20/2000
(See Amerus Group Co.)

AMERICAN INVS MONEY FD INC (MD)
Common 1¢ par changed to $0.001 par 07/31/1989
Merged into Ivy Fund 01/28/1993
Details not available

AMERICAN INVESTORS SYNDICATE, INC. (LA)
Name changed to Louisiana Investment Shares, Inc. 8/15/60

AMERICAN IR TECHNOLOGIES INC (NV)
Name changed to American Product Corp. 12/14/2002
American Product Corp. recapitalized as American Capital Partners Ltd., Inc. 03/01/2004
(See American Capital Partners Ltd., Inc.)

AMERICAN IRON & MACHINE WORKS CO. (DE)
Acquired by American Machine & Foundry Co. 02/09/1955
Each share Common $1 par exchanged for (0.4423) share Common $7 par
American Machine & Foundry Co. name changed to AMF Inc. 04/30/1970
(See AMF Inc.)

AMERICAN IRONING MACHINE CO.
Merged into Barlow & Seelig Manufacturing Co. 00/00/1947
Each share Capital Stock exchanged for (0.8) share Common $1 par
Barlow & Seelig Manufacturing Co. name changed to Speed Queen Corp 00/00/1949 which was acquired by McGraw Electric Co. 09/30/1956 which name changed to McGraw-Edison Co. 01/02/1957
(See McGraw-Edison Co.)

AMERICAN-ISRAEL PAUL EHRLICH MEDICAL INSTITUTE, INC. (DE)
No longer in existence having become inoperative and void for non-payment of taxes 01/00/1960

AMERICAN ISRAEL PHOSPHATE INC (DE)
Name changed to Ultramar Minerals Corp. 11/13/1969
(See Ultramar Minerals Corp.)

AMERICAN ISRAELI PAPER MLS LTD (ISRAEL)
Ordinary I£1 par and Ordinary I£1 par (New York Register) split (5) for (4) by issuance of (0.25) additional share 02/27/1969
Basis changed from (1:8) to (1:10) 01/11/1985
Each share Ordinary I£1 par exchanged for (1.4) shares Ordinary IS10 par 11/26/1980
Each share Ordinary I£1 par (New York Register) exchanged for (1.4)

shares Ordinary IS10 par (New York Register) 11/26/1980
Each ADR for Ordinary I£1 par exchanged for (1.4) shares Ordinary IS10 par (New York Register) 11/26/1980
Each share Ordinary IS10 par exchanged for (1.4) shares Ordinary IS1 par 09/19/1981
Each share Ordinary IS10 par (New York Register) exchanged for (1.4) shares Ordinary IS1 par (New York Register) 09/19/1981
Stock Dividend - Ordinary - 60% 07/05/1965
Basis changed from (1:5) to (1:8) 07/05/1965
Stock Dividends - Ordinary, Ordinary (New York Register) and ADR's for Ordinary - 10% 07/15/1974; 15% 07/15/1975; 15% 04/29/1976; 25% 10/30/1978; 50% 10/25/1979
Name changed to Hadera Paper Ltd. 07/08/2008

AMERICAN ISTEG STEEL CORP. (NY)
Name changed to Webrib Steel Corp. 00/00/1947
Webrib Steel Corp. name changed to Hico Corp. of America 05/00/1957
(See Hico Corp. of America)

AMERICAN ITALIAN PASTA CO (DE)
Acquired by Ralcorp Holdings, Inc. (New) 07/27/2010
Each share Class A Common $0.001 par exchanged for $53 cash

AMERICAN JET HLDGS INC (CO)
Recapitalized as OTS Holdings Inc. 12/03/1990
Each share Common no par exchanged for (0.01) share Common no par
OTS Holdings Inc. name changed to Thin Film Battery Inc. 04/18/2000 which name changed to Global Acquisition, Inc. 04/17/2001 which name changed to Oak Ridge Micro-Energy, Inc. 02/21/2002 which name changed to Oak Ridge Energy Technologies, Inc. 08/28/2013 which name changed to Oakridge Global Energy Solutions, Inc. 11/07/2014

AMERICAN JEWELRY CORP (NV)
Reincorporated 01/31/2002
Each share old Common $0.001 par exchanged for (0.00333333) share new Common $0.001 par 05/02/2001
State of incorporation changed from (DE) to (NV) 01/31/2002
Each share Common $0.001 par exchanged for (0.00014285) share Common 1¢ par 06/17/2002
Name changed to MSM Jewelry Corp. 06/24/2002
MSM Jewelry Corp. name changed to GEMZ Corp. 10/27/2003

AMERICAN JIANYE GREENTECH HLDGS LTD (NV)
Common $0.001 par split (7.89) for (1) by issuance of (6.89) additional shares payable 03/02/2010 to holders of record 01/04/2010
Ex date - 03/03/2010
Name changed to AJ Greentech Holdings Ltd. 03/13/2014
AJ Greentech Holdings Ltd. name changed to Sino United Worldwide Consolidated Ltd. 07/17/2017

AMERICAN KEFIR CORP (NY)
Reincorporated under the laws of Delaware as Brighton Information Systems Corp. 06/21/1990
Brighton Information Systems Corp. name changed to Greater China Corp. 11/14/1995
(See Greater China Corp.)

AMERICAN KIOSK CORP (DE)
SEC revoked common stock registration 05/23/2008

AMERICAN KITCHEN FOODS INC (DE)
Name changed to AKF Foods, Inc. 04/05/1979
(See AKF Foods, Inc.)

AMERICAN KOSHER PROVISIONS INC (NY)
Chapter XI Bankruptcy proceedings closed 07/26/1968
No stockholders' equity

AMERICAN-LA FRANCE & FOAMITE CORP.
Reorganized as American-La France-Foamite Corp. 00/00/1936
Each share Preferred $100 par exchanged for (1) share new Common $10 par and a Common Stock Purchase Warrant
Each share old Common received (0.1) Common Stock Purchase Warrant
American-La France-Foamite Corp. merged into Sterling Precision Instrument Corp. 06/09/1955 which merged into Sterling Precision Corp. 01/03/1956 which name changed to Steego Corp. 08/23/1979
(See Steego Corp.)

AMERICAN LA FRANCE FIRE ENGINE CO., INC.
Name changed to American-La France & Foamite Corp. 00/00/1927
American-La France & Foamite Corp. reorganized as American-La France-Foamite Corp. 00/00/1936 which merged into Sterling Precision Instrument Corp. 06/09/1955 which merged into Sterling Precision Corp. 01/03/1956 which name changed to Steego Corp. 08/23/1979
(See Steego Corp.)

AMERICAN-LA FRANCE-FOAMITE CORP. (NY)
Stock Dividend - 20% 12/17/1948
Merged into Sterling Precision Instrument Corp. 06/09/1955
Each share Common $10 par exchanged for (6) shares Common 10¢ par
Sterling Precision Instrument Corp. merged into Sterling Precision Corp. 01/03/1956 which name changed to Steego Corp. 08/23/1979
(See Steego Corp.)

AMERICAN LABORATORIES, INC. (CA)
Name changed to American Medical Enterprises, Inc. 01/26/1965
American Medical Enterprises, Inc. name changed to American Medical International, Inc. (CA) 01/28/1972 which reincorporated in Delaware 08/31/1976 which merged into American Medical Holdings, Inc. 04/12/1990 which merged into National Enterprises, Inc. 02/28/1995 which name changed to Tenet Healthcare Corp. 06/23/1995

AMERICAN LACE MANUFACTURING CO.
Liquidation completed 00/00/1945
Details not available

AMERICAN LAFRANCE INC (DE)
Merged into A-T-O Inc. 06/06/1975
Each share Common 10¢ par exchanged for (1.75) shares Conv. Preference 3rd Ser. $1 par
A-T-O Inc. name changed to Figgie International Inc. (OH) 06/01/1981 which reorganized in Delaware as Figgie International Holdings Inc. 07/18/1983 which name changed to Figgie International Inc. 12/31/1986
(See Figgie International Inc. (DE))

AMERICAN LAND CORP. (OH)
Completely liquidated 12/31/1979
Each share Common no par received first and final distribution of $4.03 cash
Note: Certificates were not required to exchange and are without value

AMERICAN LAUNDRY MACHY INC (OH)
Each (4) shares Capital Stock $25 par exchanged for (5) shares Capital Stock $20 par 00/00/1927
Acquired by McGraw-Edison 09/01/1960
Each share Capital Stock $20 par exchanged for (1.2) shares Common $1 par
(See McGraw-Edison Co.)

AMERICAN LD CO (DE)
Common $1 par changed to 10¢ par 04/05/1960
Common 10¢ par changed to 1¢ par 12/13/1972
Each share Common 1¢ par exchanged for (0.2) share Common 5¢ par 07/20/1978
Charter cancelled and declared inoperative and void for non-payment of taxes 03/14/1984

AMERICAN LD CRUISERS INC (FL)
Name changed to Cruise America, Inc. 05/18/1988
Cruise America, Inc. merged into Budget Group, Inc. 01/28/1998
(See Budget Group, Inc.)

AMERICAN LD EQUITY INC (DE)
Each share Common 10¢ par exchanged for (0.005) share Common $100 par 08/09/1976
Note: In effect holders received $300 cash per share and public interest was eliminated

AMERICAN LD LEASE INC (DE)
Merged into GCP REIT II 03/16/2009
Each share Common 1¢ par exchanged for $14.20 cash
Each share old 7.75% Preferred Ser. A 1¢ par exchanged for (1) share new 7.75% Preferred Ser. A 1¢ par to reflect a (1) for (4) reverse split followed by a (4) for (1) forward split 12/31/2010
Note: Holders of (3) or fewer pre-split shares will receive $27.42 cash per share
Each share new 7.75% Preferred Ser. A 1¢ par exchanged again for (1) share new 7.75% Preferred Ser. A 1¢ par to reflect a (1) for (12) reverse split followed by a (12) for (1) forward split 03/21/2012 03/21/2012
Note: Holders of (11) or fewer pre-split shares will receive $27.42 cash per share
Each share new 7.75% Preferred Ser. A 1¢ par exchanged again for (1) share new 7.75% Preferred Ser. A 1¢ par to reflect a (1) for (4) reverse split followed by a (4) for (1) forward split 01/07/2013
Note: Holders of (3) or fewer pre-split shares will receive $27.42 cash per share
New 7.75% Preferred Ser. A 1¢ par called for redemption at $25 plus $0.14 accrued dividends on 12/26/2014
Public interest eliminated

AMERICAN LEAD PENCIL CO.
Name changed to Venus Pen & Pencil Corp. 00/00/1956
Venus Pen & Pencil Corp. name changed to Venus Esterbrook Corp. 11/29/1967 which name changed to Domac Enterprises Inc. (NY) 10/05/1973 which reincorporated in Delaware 10/01/1975
(See Domac Enterprises Inc.)

AMERICAN LEADERS FD INC (MD)
Capital Stock $1 par changed to 20¢ par and (4) additional shares issued 11/13/1970
Common 20¢ par reclassified as Class A 20¢ par 04/21/1993
Name changed to Federated American Leaders Fund, Inc. and Fortress Shares 20¢ par reclassified as Class F 20¢ par 03/31/1996
Federated American Leaders Fund, Inc. reorganized as Federated Equity Funds 09/18/2009

AMERICAN LEAGUE BASEBALL CO. OF ST. LOUIS (MO)
Name changed to Baltimore Baseball Club, Inc. 00/00/1953
Baltimore Baseball Club, Inc. name changed to Bird Fund, Inc. 11/27/1979
(See Bird Fund, Inc.)

AMERICAN LEAGUE PROFESSIONAL FOOTBALL TEAM OF BOSTON, INC. (MA)
Name changed to Boston Patriots Football Club, Inc. 07/01/1968
Boston Patriots Football Club, Inc. name changed to New England Patriots Football Clubs, Inc. 04/01/1971
(See New England Patriots Football Club, Inc.)

AMERICAN LEARNING CORP (DE)
Merged into JW Acquisition Corp. 09/28/1992
Each share Common 1¢ par exchanged for $0.50 cash

AMERICAN LEARNING CORP (NY)
Acquired by G Acquisition, Inc. 01/02/2014
Each share Common 1¢ par exchanged for $0.20 cash

AMERICAN LEDUC PETES LTD (AB)
Acquired by Veteran Resources Inc. 10/17/2003
Each share Common no par exchanged for $0.23 cash

AMERICAN LEISURE CORP. (KY)
Voluntarily dissolved 03/02/1981
Details not available

AMERICAN LEISURE CORP (DE)
Common no par reclassified as Class B Common 1¢ par 01/17/1984
Merged into American Midland Corp. 07/06/1984
Each share Class A Common 1¢ par exchanged for (1) share Common 1¢ par
Each share Class B Common 1¢ par exchanged for (1) share Common 1¢ par and (1) Common Stock Purchase Warrant expiring 12/31/1985
(See American Midland Corp.)

AMERICAN LEISURE CORP (NJ)
Under plan of merger each share Common no par automatically became (1) share American Leisure Corp. (DE) Common no par 11/24/1982
American Leisure Corp. (DE) merged into American Midland Corp. 07/06/1984
(See American Midland Corp.)

AMERICAN LEISURE ENTMT INC (DE)
Recapitalized as National Restaurant Group, Inc. 10/14/1994
Each share Common $0.001 par exchanged for (0.1) share Common 10¢ par
National Restaurant Group, Inc. name changed to Galconda Corp. (New) 08/02/1996 which recapitalized as Jax International Inc. 12/03/1996
(See Jax International Inc.)

AMERICAN LENDING & ACQUISITION GROUP INC (FL)
Recapitalized as Exosphere Aircraft Co., Inc. 06/19/2006
Each share Common $0.001 par exchanged for (0.001) share Common $0.001 par
Exosphere Aircraft Co., Inc. name changed to Business Continuity Solutions Inc. 07/14/2011 which name changed to Tall Trees LED

Co. 08/05/2016 which recapitalized as Light Engine Design Corp. 12/21/2016

AMERICAN LEVERAGE FD INC (CO)
Name changed to Data National Corp. 03/23/1987
(See Data National Corp.)

AMERICAN LIBERTY FINL CORP (LA)
Merged into Citizens, Inc. 09/14/1995
Each share 8% Preferred $24.875 par exchanged for (2.926) shares Class A Common no par
Each share Common $0.125 par exchanged for (1.1) shares Class A Common no par

AMERICAN LIBERTY INVESTMENT CORP. (OH)
Completely liquidated 04/28/1967
Each share Common $1 par exchanged for first and final distribution of (1) share Liberty American Life Insurance Co. Common $1 par
Liberty American Life Insurance Co. merged into Coastal States Life Insurance Co. 12/31/1969 which reorganized as Coastal States Corp. 10/05/1972

AMERICAN LIBERTY LIFE INSURANCE CO. (AL)
Through purchase offer all but (1,200) shares reacquired 00/00/1980
Public interest eliminated

AMERICAN LIBERTY LIFE INSURANCE CO. (MS)
Merged into Consolidated American Life Insurance Co. (MS) 12/31/1964
Each share Class A or B par exchanged for (0.43) share Common $1 par
(See Consolidated American Life Insurance Co. (MS))

AMERICAN LIBERTY PETE CORP (NV)
Recapitalized as Avant Diagnostics, Inc. 03/02/2015
Each share Common $0.00001 par exchanged for (0.05882352) share Common $0.00001 par

AMERICAN LIFE & ACC INS CO KY (KY)
Capital Stock $1 par changed to $10 par 03/17/1959
Capital Stock $10 par changed to $20 par 05/25/1966
Capital Stock $20 par changed to $40 par 04/13/1984
Each share Capital Stock $40 par exchanged for (1/9) share Non-Vtg. Class A $4 par and (1) share Class B $4 par 11/15/1991
Under plan of reorganization each share Non-Vtg. Class A Common $4 par and Class B Common $4 par automatically became (1) share Hardscuffle, Inc. Non-Vtg. Class A Common $4 par and Class B Common $4 par respectively 12/31/1999

AMERICAN LIFE COS INC (DE)
Name changed to Statesman Group, Inc. 07/31/1969
(See Statesman Group, Inc.)

AMERICAN LIFE HLDG CO (DE)
$2.16 Preferred 1¢ par called for redemption at $26.52 on 09/30/1997
Public interest eliminated

AMERICAN LIFE INSURANCE CO. (AL)
Each share Common $5 par exchanged for (5) shares Common $1 par 05/01/1956
Stock Dividends - 100% 07/15/1959; 25% 06/01/1962
Under plan of merger name changed to American-Amicable Life Insurance Co. 03/01/1965
(See American-Amicable Life Insurance Co.)

AMERICAN LIFE INS CO MICH (MI)
Acquired by American Presidents Life Insurance Co. 04/16/1969
Each share Common $1 par exchanged for (0.5) share Common $1 par
American Presidents Life Insurance Co. acquired by Hamilton International Corp. 12/31/1969
(See Hamilton International Corp.)

AMERICAN LIFE INVESTORS, INC. (IL)
Name changed to Reliv' International, Inc. (IL) 02/17/1992
Reliv' International, Inc. (IL) reincorporated in Delaware 04/10/2000

AMERICAN LIFE UNDERWRITERS INC (TX)
Charter forfeited for failure to pay taxes 05/08/1972

AMERICAN LIGHT & TRACTION CO. (NJ)
Name changed to American Natural Gas Co. (NJ) and Common $25 par changed to no par 00/00/1949
American Natural Gas Co. (NJ) reincorporated in Delaware 04/30/1964 which reincorporated in Michigan 06/30/1978 which name changed to American Natural Resources Co. (MI) 05/10/1976 which reincorporated in Delaware 06/30/1983
(See American Natural Resources Co. (DE))

AMERICAN LIGHTWAVE CORP (BC)
Delisted from Vancouver Stock Exchange 01/10/1990

AMERICAN LIMA CORP. (NY)
Reorganized as Brooklyn Poly Industries, Inc. 11/10/1969
Each share Common 1¢ par exchanged for (1) share Common 10¢ par
(See Brooklyn Poly Industries, Inc.)

AMERICAN LINEN CO.
Out of business 00/00/1932
Details not available

AMERICAN LINES CO.
Dissolved 00/00/1941
Details not available

AMERICAN LINSEED CO.
Merged into Gold Dust Corp. 00/00/1928
Details not available

AMERICAN LIQUID TR (MA)
Name changed to Keystone Liquid Trust 04/29/1978
Keystone Liquid Trust merged into Evergreen Money Market Trust 07/31/1997

AMERICAN LIST CORP (DE)
Common 1¢ par split (3) for (1) by issuance of (2) additional shares 09/26/1983
Common 1¢ par split (3) for (2) by issuance of (0.5) additional share 06/23/1986
Common 1¢ par split (3) for (2) by issuance of (0.5) additional share 08/06/1993
Stock Dividend - 10% 05/09/1994
Merged into Snyder Communications Inc. 07/11/1997
Each share Common 1¢ par exchanged for (1.14) shares SNC Common $0.001 par
Snyder Communications Inc. merged into Havas Advertising S.A. 09/26/2000 which name changed to Havas S.A. 05/24/2002
(See Havas S.A.)

AMERICAN LITHIUM CO. LTD. (QC)
Declared dissolved for failure to file reports or pay fees 08/26/1972

AMERICAN LITHOGRAPHIC CO.
Name changed to Holding Corp. of American Lithographic Co., Inc. 00/00/1927
Holding Corp. of American Lithographic Co., Inc. name changed to Publication Corp. 00/00/1929 which merged into Crowell Collier & Macmillan, Inc. 05/31/1968 which name changed to Macmillan, Inc. 01/01/1973
(See Macmillan, Inc.)

AMERICAN LN & FIN CO (OH)
Assets sold under Court confirmed reorganization 10/31/1972
No stockholders' equity

AMERICAN LOAN CO. (IN)
Name changed to A L C Finance, Inc. 12/31/1960
A L C Finance, Inc. acquired by State Loan & Finance Corp. 03/31/1964 which name changed to American Finance System Inc. 05/01/1968 which merged into Security Pacific Corp. 12/15/1978 which merged into BankAmerica Corp. (Old) 04/22/1992 which merged into BankAmerica Corp. (New) 09/30/1998 which name changed to Bank of America Corp. 04/28/1999

AMERICAN LOCKER INC (DE)
Recapitalized 00/00/1941
Class A no par changed to $5 par
Class B no par changed to $1 par
Recapitalized 00/00/1947
Each share Class A $5 par exchanged for (5) shares Class A $1 par
Each share Class B $1 par exchanged for (5) shares Class B 20¢ par
Completely liquidated 12/20/1968
Each share Class A $1 par exchanged for first and final distribution of $7.50 cash
Each share Class B 20¢ par exchanged for first and final distribution of $5.50 cash

AMERICAN LOCOMOTIVE CO. (NY)
Common no par changed to $1 par 00/00/1945
Name changed to Alco Products, Inc. 04/20/1955
Alco Products, Inc. name changed to Citadel Industries, Inc. (NY) 12/31/1964 which reincorporated in Delaware 08/17/1966
(See Citadel Industries, Inc. (DE))

AMERICAN LONDON & EMPIRE CORP.
Acquired by Standard Investing Corp. 00/00/1930
Details not available

AMERICAN LONGEVITY INST INC (DE)
Charter cancelled and declared inoperative and void for non-payment of taxes 03/01/1994

AMERICAN LORAIN CORP (NV)
Reincorporated 11/09/2009
State of incorporation changed from (DE) to (NV) 11/09/2009
Recapitalized as Planet Green Holdings Corp. 10/01/2018
Each share Common $0.001 par exchanged for (0.04) share Common $0.001 par

AMERICAN LUMBER & TREATING CO. (DE)
Acquired by Koppers Co. Inc. and liquidated 06/30/1954
Details not available

AMERICAN M.A.R.C. INC. (PA)
Common $1 par changed to no par 11/19/1956
Common no par changed to 50¢ par 01/25/1957
Merged into Pike Corp. of America 04/15/1966
Each share Common 50¢ par exchanged for (0.2) share $1 Conv. Preferred no par

Pike Corp. of America merged into Fluor Corp. Ltd. 01/02/1969 which name changed to Fluor Corp. (CA) 05/22/1969 which reincorporated in Delaware 07/14/1978 which name changed to Massey Energy Co. 11/30/2000 which merged into Alpha Natural Resources, Inc. 06/01/2011
(See Alpha Natural Resources, Inc.)

AMERICAN MACH & FDRY CO (NJ)
Each share Common $100 par exchanged for (3) share old Common no par 00/00/1926
Each share old Common no par exchanged for (2) shares new Common no par 00/00/1930
New Common no par changed to $7 par 00/00/1953
Common $7 par changed to $3.50 par and (1) additional share issued 11/09/1959
Common $3.50 par changed to $1.75 par and (1) additional share issued 05/15/1961
5% Preferred $100 par called for redemption 07/15/1966
5% Preferred 1954 Series $100 par called for redemption 07/15/1966
Name changed to AMF Inc. 04/30/1970
(See AMF Inc.)

AMERICAN MACHINE & METALS, INC. (DE)
Capital Stock no par split (2) for (1) by issuance of (1) additional share 04/15/1959
Name changed to AMETEK, Inc. (Old) 11/30/1961
AMETEK, Inc. (Old) merged into Culligan Water Technologies, Inc. 07/31/1997

AMERICAN MACHINERY CORP. (FL)
Each share Common 20¢ par exchanged for (0.04) share Common $3 par 07/07/1958
Acquired by Wallace & Tiernan Inc. 07/11/1961
Each share Common $3 par exchanged for (0.25) share Common 50¢ par
Wallace & Tiernan Inc. merged into Pennwalt Corp. 03/31/1969
(See Pennwalt Corp.)

AMERICAN MAGNETICS CORP (CA)
Name changed to Damon Group Inc. 04/05/1990
(See Damon Group Inc.)

AMERICAN MAID PRODS CORP (OR)
Completely liquidated 08/00/1982
No stockholders' equity

AMERICAN MAIL LINE LTD (DE)
Reincorporated 00/00/1947
State of incorporation changed from (NV) to (DE) 00/00/1947
Each share old Common no par exchanged for (4) shares new Common no par 00/00/1951
Stock Dividends - 10% 12/27/1951; 10% 12/31/1952; 10% 12/31/1953
Merged into American President Lines Ltd. 08/18/1971
Details not available

AMERICAN MAIZE PRODS CO (ME)
Each share Common $100 par exchanged for (10) shares Common no par 00/00/1929
Common no par split (3) for (1) by issuance of (2) additional shares 07/16/1962
Common no par split (2) for (1) by issuance of (1) additional share 07/20/1966
Common no par reclassified as Class A Common $1 par 07/10/1969
Each share Class A Common $1 par received distribution of (0.5) share Class B Common $1 par 07/31/1969
Class A Common $1 par and Class B Common $1 par changed to 80¢ par and (0.25) additional share issued respectively 02/12/1976

Stock Dividend - 10% 12/23/1980
Merged into Eridania Beghin-Say S.A. 11/06/1995
Each share Class A Common 80¢ par exchanged for $40 cash
Each share Class B Common 80¢ par exchanged for $40 cash

AMERICAN MALTING CO. (MI)
Charter voided for failure to file reports and pay fees 08/31/1944

AMERICAN MGMT ED CORP (NY)
Name changed to Four Corners Financial Corp. 04/12/1988
(See Four Corners Financial Corp.)

AMERICAN MGMT SYS INC (DE)
Common 1¢ par split (2) for (1) by issuance of (1) additional share 06/09/1986
Common 1¢ par split (2) for (1) by issuance of (1) additional share 06/10/1987
Common 1¢ par split (3) for (2) by issuance of (0.5) additional share 06/19/1992
Common 1¢ par split (3) for (2) by issuance of (0.5) additional share 10/28/1994
Common 1¢ par split (3) for (2) by issuance of (0.5) additional share 08/28/1995
Common 1¢ par split (3) for (2) by issuance of (0.5) additional share payable 01/05/1996 to holders of record 12/15/1995
Merged into Groupe CGI Inc. 05/03/2004
Each share Common 1¢ par exchanged for $19.40 cash

AMERICAN MANGANESE STEEL CO.
Merged into American Brake Shoe & Foundry Co. 00/00/1937
Details not available

AMERICAN MANOR CORP (CANADA)
Recapitalized as American Manor Enterprises Inc. 08/10/2000
Each share Common no par exchanged for (0.5) share Common no par
American Manor Enterprises Inc. name changed to Overland Realty Ltd. 10/25/2006
(See Overland Realty Ltd.)

AMERICAN MANOR ENTERPRISES INC (CANADA)
Name changed to Overland Realty Ltd. 10/25/2006
(See Overland Realty Ltd.)

AMERICAN MANUFACTURING CO., INC. LIQUIDATING TRUST (DE)
Liquidation completed
Each share Common $6.25 par received fourth distribution of $0.06 cash 02/28/1981
Each share Common $6.25 par received fifth distribution of $1.19 cash 02/25/1982
Each share Common $6.25 par received sixth distribution of $0.60 cash 02/18/1983
Each share Common $6.25 par received seventh and final distribution of $0.93576 cash 05/19/1983

AMERICAN MANUFACTURING CO. (MA)
Common $100 par changed to $25 par and (3) additional shares distributed 00/00/1945
Reincorporated under the laws of Delaware as American Manufacturing Co., Inc. 04/01/1957
American Manufacturing Co., Inc. (DE) assets transferred to American Manufacturing Co., Inc. Liquidating Trust 05/20/1980
(See American Manufacturing Co., Inc. Liquidating Trust)

AMERICAN MFG INC (DE)
Common $25 par changed to $12.50 par and (1) additional share issued 12/21/1959
Common $12.50 par changed to $6.25 par and (1) additional share issued 12/28/1964
Common $6.25 par split (2) for (1) by issuance of (1) additional share 05/22/1978
In process of liquidation
Each share Common $6.25 par received initial distribution of $0.50 cash 10/29/1979
Each share Common $6.25 par received second distribution of $62 cash 01/21/1980
Each share Common $6.25 par exchanged for third distribution of (0.25) share Safety Railway Service Corp. Common $5 par and $14.48 cash 05/15/1980
Assets transferred to American Manufacturing Co., Inc. Liquidating Trust 05/20/1980
(See American Manufacturing Co., Inc. Liquidating Trust)

AMERICAN MARACAIBO CO. (DE)
Capital Stock no par changed to $1 par 00/00/1931
Name changed to Felmont Petroleum Corp. 05/21/1958
Felmont Petroleum Corp. name changed to Felmont Oil Corp. 06/30/1965 which merged into HomeStake Mining Co. 06/19/1984 which merged into Barrick Gold Corp. 12/14/2001

AMERICAN-MARIETTA CO. (IL)
Each share Class A Common no par exchanged for (5) shares Common $2 par 12/00/1947
Each share Class B Common no par exchanged for (5) shares Class B Common $2 par 12/00/1947
Common $2 par and Class B Common $2 par split (2) for (1) respectively by issuance of (1) additional share 02/21/1955
Common $2 par and Class B Common $2 par split (5) for (4) respectively by issuance of (0.25) additional share 07/16/1956
Common $2 par and Class B Common $2 par split (3) for (2) respectively by issuance of (0.5) additional share 10/15/1957
Common $2 par and Class B Common $2 par split (5) for (4) respectively by issuance of (0.25) additional share 08/01/1959
Stock Dividend - 100% 02/28/1952
Merged into Martin Marietta Corp. (Old) on a share for share basis 10/10/1961
Martin Marietta Corp. (Old) merged into Martin Marietta Corp. (New) 04/02/1993

AMERICAN MARINAS, INC. (NY)
Assets liquidated for benefit of creditors 00/00/1964
No stockholders' equity

AMERICAN MARINE BK (BANBRIDGE ISLAND, WA)
Under plan of reorganization each share Common $10 par automatically became (1) share AMB Financial Services Corp. Common no par 09/05/1997

AMERICAN MARINE LTD (NV)
Charter revoked for failure to file reports and pay fees 03/07/1977

AMERICAN MART CORP (DE)
Company went private 00/00/1987
Details not available

AMERICAN MASON SAFETY TREAD CO (MA)
Name changed to AMST, Inc. 11/18/1968
(See AMST, Inc.)

AMERICAN MATLS & TECHNOLOGIES CORP (DE)
Merged into Cytec Industries Inc. 10/09/1998
Each share Common 1¢ par exchanged for (0.3098) share Common 1¢ par
(See Cytec Industries Inc.)

AMERICAN MAXIFACT SYS INC (NV)
Name changed to First American Co. 06/25/1990

AMERICAN MAYFLOWER LIFE INS CO N Y (NY)
Common $2.50 par changed to $1.50 par 06/21/1967
Acquired by First Colony Life Insurance Co. 05/08/1975
Each share Common $1.50 par exchanged for $6.20 cash

AMERICAN MED AFFILIATES INC (PA)
Reincorporated 01/01/1972
State of incorporation changed from (DE) to (PA) 01/01/1972
Stock Dividends - 10% 11/01/1977; 10% 12/29/1978; 10% 12/31/1979; 10% 01/30/1981
Liquidation completed
Each share $0.60 Preferred Ser. A 10¢ par exchanged for first and final distribution of $7.21 cash 01/06/1983
Each share Common 10¢ par exchanged for initial distribution of $17.81 principal amount of Unicare Services Inc. 12% Limited Liability Bonds due 05/31/1994 on 05/09/1983
Note: Holdings of fewer than (57) shares received $17.81 cash per share
Each share Common 10¢ par received second and final distribution of $4.09 cash 05/20/1983

AMERICAN MED ALERT CORP (NY)
Acquired by Tunstall Healthcare Group Ltd. 12/22/2011
Each share Common 1¢ par exchanged for $8.55 cash and (1) Contingent Payment Right

AMERICAN MED ASSN TAX EXEMPT INCOME FD INC (MD)
Merged into Nuveen Municipal Bond Fund, Inc. 09/18/1980
Each share Common $1 par exchanged for (0.964366) share Common 10¢ par
(See Nuveen Municipal Bond Fund, Inc.)

AMERICAN MED BLDGS INC (DE)
Name changed 04/11/1975
Common 10¢ par split (2) for (1) by issuance of (1) additional share 06/09/1972
Common 10¢ par split (5) for (4) by issuance of (0.25) additional share 09/14/1973
Name changed from American Medical Building Guild, Inc. to American Medical Buildings, Inc. 04/11/1975
Common 10¢ par split (5) for (4) by issuance of (0.25) additional share 04/04/1983
Common 10¢ par split (3) for (2) by issuance of (0.5) additional share 07/19/1983
Conv. Preferred Ser. A $1 par called for redemption 05/19/1987
Stock Dividends - 25% 08/31/1978; 25% 05/15/1979
Plan of reorganization under Chapter 11 Federal Bankruptcy proceedings confirmed 04/22/1991
No stockholders' equity

AMERICAN MED CORP (DE)
Name changed to Texas Energy & Manufacturing Co. 08/17/1979
Texas Energy & Manufacturing Co. name changed to Southern Retail Marketing Corp. 05/23/1986
(See Southern Retail Marketing Corp.)

AMERICAN MED ELECTRS INC (MN)
Common no par split (5) for (4) by issuance of (0.25) additional share 06/20/1988
Common no par split (5) for (4) by issuance of (0.25) additional share 05/10/1991
Merged into Orthofix International N.V. (Curacao) 08/21/1995
Each share Common no par exchanged for (0.447486) share Common 10¢ par and $2.284372 cash
Note: Each share Common held by eligible record holders received additional distribution of approximately $0.07 cash 06/28/1999
Each share Common held by eligible record holders received final distribution of $0.66401 cash 08/31/2004
Orthofix International N.V. (Curacao) reorganized in Delaware as Orthofix Medical Inc. 08/01/2018

AMERICAN MED FINL CORP (NC)
Chapter 11 Federal Bankruptcy Code converted to Chapter 7 on 01/15/1986
Stockholders' equity unlikely

AMERICAN MED HLDGS INC (DE)
Merged into National Medical Enterprises, Inc. 02/28/1995
Each share Common 1¢ par exchanged for (0.42) share Common $0.075 par and $19 cash
National Medical Enterprises, Inc. name changed to Tenet Healthcare Corp. 06/23/1995

AMERICAN MED INTL INC (DE)
Reincorporated 8/31/76
State of incorporation changed from (CA) to (DE) and Common no par changed to $1 par 08/31/1976
Common $1 par split (5) for (4) by issuance of (0.25) additional share 10/31/1979
Common $1 par split (3) for (2) by issuance of (0.5) additional share 11/12/1980
Common $1 par split (3) for (2) by issuance of (0.5) additional share 11/02/1981
Common $1 par split (4) for (3) by issuance of (1/3) additional share 02/02/1983
Stock Dividend - 10% 08/15/1978
Merged into American Medical Holdings, Inc. 04/12/1990
Each share Common $1 par exchanged for (1) share Common 1¢ par

AMERICAN MED PWR INC (DE)
Charter forfeited for failure to maintain a registered agent 07/28/1984

AMERICAN MED PRODS CORP (NJ)
Stock Dividend - 100% 06/15/1981
Acquired by Delmed, Inc. 06/25/1982
Each share Common no par exchanged for (0.66666666) share Common 10¢ par
Delmed, Inc. recapitalized as Fresenius USA, Inc. 12/30/1991 which merged into Fresenius Medical Care AG 09/30/1996 which name changed to Fresenius Medical Care AG & Co. KGaA 02/10/2006

AMERICAN MED RESPONSE INC (DE)
Merged into Laidlaw Inc. 02/24/1997
Each share Common 1¢ par exchanged for $40 cash

AMERICAN MED SEC GROUP INC (WI)
Acquired by PacifiCare Health Systems, Inc. (New) 12/13/2004

Each share Common no par exchanged for $32.75 cash

AMERICAN MED SVCS INC (WI)
Common 10¢ par split (3) for (2) by issuance of (0.5) additional share 06/15/1981
Common 10¢ par split (3) for (2) by issuance of (0.5) additional share 05/16/1983
Common 10¢ par split (5) for (4) by issuance of (0.25) additional share 08/21/1985
Stock Dividends - 10% 06/16/1980; 10% 05/25/1984
Acquired by Transworld Corp. 11/20/1986
Each share Common 10¢ par exchanged for $21.35 cash

AMERICAN MED SYS (CA)
Name changed to International Hospital Supply Corp. 03/10/1972
(See International Hospital Supply Corp.)

AMERICAN MED SYS HLDGS INC (DE)
Common 1¢ par split (2) for (1) by issuance of (1) additional share payable 03/21/2005 to holders of record 03/14/2005
Acquired by Endo Pharmaceuticals Holdings Inc. 06/17/2011
Each share Common 1¢ par exchanged for $30 cash

AMERICAN MED TECHNOLOGIES INC (DE)
Incorporated 11/06/1987
Name changed to Tidel Technologies, Inc. 08/04/1997
Tidel Technologies, Inc. name changed to Secure Alliance Holdings Corp. 06/19/2007 which recapitalized as aVinci Media Corp. 06/09/2008
(See aVinci Media Corp.)

AMERICAN MED TECHNOLOGIES INC (DE)
Incorporated 11/21/1989
Ceased operations 04/09/2009
Stockholders' equity unlikely

AMERICAN MED TECHNOLOGY INC (DE)
Charter cancelled and declared inoperative and void for non-payment of taxes 03/01/1992

AMERICAN MEDCARE CORP (DE)
Merged into InfoCure Corp. 07/10/1997
Each share Common no par exchanged for (0.05966) share Common $0.001 par
InfoCure Corp. name changed to VitalWorks, Inc. 08/06/2001 which name changed to AMICAS, Inc. 01/03/2005
(See AMICAS, Inc.)

AMERICAN MEDCENTERS INC (MN)
Merged into Partners National Health Plans 12/22/1986
Each share Common $0.001 par exchanged for $8.50 cash

AMERICAN MEDI DENT INC (CA)
Chapter 11 Federal Bankruptcy Code converted to Chapter 7 on 06/29/1987
Stockholders' equity unlikely

AMERICAN MEDIA INC (DE)
Merged into EMP Acquisition Corp. 05/07/1999
Each share Class A Common 1¢ par exchanged for $7 cash

AMERICAN MEDICAL ENTERPRISES, INC. (CA)
Common no par split (3) for (2) by issuance of (0.5) additional share 08/19/1968
Common no par split (2) for (1) by issuance of (1) additional share 02/28/1969
Stock Dividend - 10% 02/10/1965
Name changed to American Medical International, Inc. (CA) 01/28/1972
American Medical International, Inc. (CA) reincorporated in Delaware 08/31/1976 which merged into American Medical Holdings, Inc. 04/12/1990 which merged into National Medical Enterprises, Inc. 02/28/1995 which name changed to Tenet Healthcare Corp. 06/23/1995

AMERICAN MEDICAL LIFE ASSOCIATES, INC.
Liquidation completed 00/00/1941
Details not available

AMERICAN MEDICINAL SPIRITS CO.
Dissolved 00/00/1936
Details not available

AMERICAN MEDICORP INC (DE)
Common 1¢ par split (2) for (1) by issuance of (1) additional share 03/03/1969
Common 1¢ par split (2) for (1) by issuance of (1) additional share 07/22/1969
Merged into Humana Inc. 09/27/1978
Each share Common 1¢ par exchanged for $26.375 principal amount of 11.70% Sinking Fund Subord. Debentures due 06/30/1998

AMERICAN MEDSERVE CORP (DE)
Merged into Omnicare, Inc. 09/12/1997
Each share Common 1¢ par exchanged for $18 cash

AMERICAN MERCHANT DATA SVC INC (OK)
Reincorporated 01/31/2008
State of incorporation changed from (FL) to (OK) 01/31/2008
Reorganized under the laws of Delaware as Desert Gateway, Inc. 06/24/2009
Each share Common $0.0001 par exchanged for (0.01) share Common $0.0001 par
Desert Gateway, Inc. name changed to Retrophin, Inc. 02/21/2013

AMERICAN MERCHANT MARINE INSURANCE CO.
Merged into American Colony Insurance Co. 03/00/1934
Details not available

AMERICAN MERCURY INSURANCE CO. (DC)
Completely liquidated 10/07/1966
Each share Common $1 par exchanged for first and final distribution of (0.5) share Maine Insurance Co. Common $1 par
(See Maine Insurance Co.)

AMERICAN MERGER CTL INC (CO)
Common $0.001 par split (3) for (1) by issuance of (2) additional shares 01/13/1989
Each share old Common $0.001 par exchanged for (0.06666666) share new Common $0.001 par 04/02/1990
Name changed to Ultratech Knowledge Systems, Inc. 04/26/1990
Ultratech Knowledge Systems, Inc. name changed to AGTsports Inc. (CO) 06/13/1993 which reorganized in Nevada as HealthRenu Medical, Inc. 09/19/2003
(See HealthRenu Medical, Inc.)

AMERICAN MET ENTERPRISES LTD (ON)
Name changed to AME Ltd. 09/25/1972
(See AME Ltd.)

AMERICAN METAL CAP CO.
Acquired by Anchor Cap Corp. 00/00/1929
Details not available

AMERICAN METAL CLIMAX INC (NY)
4.5% Preferred called for redemption 12/01/1961
4.25% Conv. Preferred $100 par called for redemption 09/01/1969
Common $1 par split (3) for (2) by issuance of (0.5) additional share 09/18/1969
Name changed to Amax Inc. 07/01/1974
Amax Inc. merged into Cyprus Amax Minerals Co. 11/15/1993 which merged into Phelps Dodge Corp. 12/02/1999 which merged into Freeport-McMoRan Copper & Gold Inc. 03/19/2007 which name changed to Freeport-McMoRan Inc. 07/14/2014

AMERICAN METAL CO. LTD. (NY)
Common no par split (2) for (1) by issuance of (1) additional share 05/09/1952
Common no par split (2) for (1) by issuance of (1) additional share 05/18/1956
Under plan of merger name changed to American Metal Climax, Inc. and Common no par changed to $1 par 12/31/1957
American Metal Climax, Inc. name changed to Amax Inc. 07/01/1974 which merged into Cyprus Amax Minerals Co. 11/15/1993 which merged into Phelps Dodge Corp. 12/02/1999 which merged into Freeport-McMoRan Copper & Gold Inc. 03/19/2007 which name changed to Freeport-McMoRan Inc. 07/14/2014

AMERICAN METAL FINISHING CO. (MI)
Name changed to American Metal Hardware Co. 07/00/1955
(See American Metal Hardware Co.)

AMERICAN METAL HARDWARE CO (MI)
Dissolved 02/16/1968
No stockholders' equity

AMERICAN METAL PRODUCTS CO. (MI)
5.5% Preferred $20 par called for redemption 03/31/1959
Stock Dividend - 100% 10/25/1948
Completely liquidated 11/15/1966
Each share Common $2 par exchanged for first and final distribution of (0.5) share Lear Siegler, Inc. $4.50 Conv. Preferred no par
(See Lear Siegler, Inc.)

AMERICAN METAL PRODUCTS CO. (WI)
Name changed to Ampco Metal, Inc. 00/00/1930
Ampco Metal, Inc. merged into Ampco-Pittsburgh Corp. 12/31/1970

AMERICAN METALLIC CHEMICALS CORP. (DE)
No longer in existence having become inoperative and void for non-payment of taxes 04/01/1955

AMERICAN METALS SVC INC (FL)
Reincorporated under the laws of Delaware as Golf Rounds.com, Inc. 07/30/1999
Golf Rounds.com, Inc. recapitalized as Fuse Medical, Inc. 05/30/2014

AMERICAN METER CO., INC. (DE)
Each share old Capital Stock no par exchanged for (2) shares new Capital Stock no par 00/00/1930
New Capital Stock no par split (2) for (1) by issuance of (1) additional share 05/15/1962
Stock Dividends - 25% 03/10/1948; 100% 05/15/1950; 10% 05/18/1956
Under plan of merger name changed to Amercon Corp. 03/17/1966
Amercon Corp. acquired by General Precision Equipment Corp. 03/27/1967 which merged into Singer Co. (NJ) 07/11/1968 which reincorporated in Delaware 00/00/1988 which name changed to Bicoastal Corp. 10/16/1989
(See Bicoastal Corp.)

AMERICAN METHYL CORP (UT)
Recapitalized as National Surety Corp. (UT) 02/14/1989
Each share Common $0.001 par exchanged for (0.02) share Common $0.001 par
National Surety Corp. (UT) reincorporated in Nevada 04/30/1989 which name changed to Stratum International Holdings, Inc. 07/02/1990

AMERICAN METRIX CORP (DE)
Charter cancelled and declared inoperative and void for non-payment of taxes 03/01/1975

AMERICAN METROPOLITAN INVESTMENT CO. (DE)
Liquidation completed
Each share Class A Common $1 par or Class B Common $1 par received initial distribution of $10 cash 02/12/1969
Each share Class A Common $1 par or Class B Common $1 par received second and final distribution of $0.453 cash 08/14/1970

AMERICAN-MEXICO MINING & DEVELOPING CO. (SD)
Charter expired by time limitation 12/12/1922

AMERICAN MICRO DEVICES INC (MN)
Statutorily dissolved 10/04/1991

AMERICAN MICRO MEDIA INC (NY)
Name changed to American Bio Medica Corp. 09/04/1992

AMERICAN MICRO-SYSTEMS, INC. (CA)
Name changed to American Microsystems, Inc. 04/25/1974
American Microsystems, Inc. acquired by Gould Inc. 02/17/1982
(See Gould Inc.)

AMERICAN MICROLINK INC (BC)
Recapitalized as International Union Resources Inc. 02/28/1986
Each share Common no par exchanged for (0.33333333) share Common no par
International Union Resources Inc. reorganized as Tropical Submarine Safaris Ltd. 01/08/1987 which recapitalized as International Submarine Safaris (Canada) Ltd. 08/02/1989
(See International Submarine Safaris (Canada) Ltd.)

AMERICAN MICROSYSTEMS INC (CA)
Acquired by Gould Inc. 02/17/1982
Each share Common $1 par exchanged for (1.78) shares Common $4 par
(See Gould Inc.)

AMERICAN MIDLAND CORP (NY)
Each share old Common 1¢ par exchanged for (0.1) share new Common 1¢ par 01/08/1988
SEC revoked common stock registration 06/10/2010

AMERICAN MILL SUPPLY CO.
Out of business 00/00/1941
Details not available

AMERICAN MILLENNIUM INC (DE)
Reincorporated 04/19/2004
State of incorporation changed from (NM) to (DE) 04/19/2004
SEC revoked common stock registration 06/10/2010

AMERICAN MILLING CO. OF PEORIA, ILLINOIS
Merged into Allied Mills, Inc. 00/00/1929
Details not available

AME-AME FINANCIAL INFORMATION, INC.

AMERICAN MINE OWNERS CASUALTY CORP.
Merged into Commonwealth Casualty Co. 05/00/1931
Details not available

AMERICAN MINERAL GROUP INC (NV)
Each share old Common $0.001 par exchanged for (0.008) share new Common $0.001 par 04/24/2013
Name changed to Telco Cuba Inc. 07/21/2015

AMERICAN MINERAL RESOURCES DEVELOPMENT CO. (NV)
Charter revoked for failure to file reports and pay fees 03/02/1970

AMERICAN MINERALS & RESEARCH CORP. (NV)
Name changed to Intercontinental Products Corp. 05/11/1983

AMERICAN MINES & MINERALS LTD (QC)
Charter annulled for failure to file annual reports 02/16/1974

AMERICAN MNG & DEV CO (NV)
Capital Stock $1 par changed to 50¢ par 08/23/1967
Capital Stock 50¢ par changed to 10¢ par 02/02/1971
Recapitalized as American International Corp. (NV) 06/01/1972
Each share Capital Stock 10¢ par exchanged for (0.1) share Capital Stock 10¢ par
American International Corp. (NV) recapitalized as American Diversified Corp. (NV) 01/10/1985 which recapitalized as Natural Pharmaceutical International Inc. 06/18/1990

AMERICAN MINING & OIL CO. (NM)
Name changed back to American Uranium Corp. 08/27/1968

AMERICAN MINING CO. (NV)
Charter revoked for failure to file reports and pay fees 03/06/1967

AMERICAN MNG CO (UT)
Merged into Toledo Mining Co. 09/16/1968
Each share Capital Stock $10 par exchanged for (2.5) shares Common 10¢ par
Toledo Mining Co. name changed to Toledo Technology, Inc. 03/26/1984 which recapitalized as HIPP International Inc. 08/31/1994 which name changed to Assembly & Manufacturing Systems Corp. 04/12/1995 which recapitalized as American Ship Inc. 09/05/1997 which name changed to Petshealth, Inc. 05/20/1998
(See Petshealth, Inc.)

AMERICAN MNG CORP (NV)
Name changed to Cannabics Pharmaceuticals Inc. 06/20/2014

AMERICAN MKT SUPPORT NETWORK INC (NV)
Name changed to Arizona Aircraft Spares, Inc. 09/25/2003
Arizona Aircraft Spares, Inc. name changed to Cell Wireless Corp. 01/07/2005
(See Cell Wireless Corp.)

AMERICAN MLG CORP (DE)
Name changed to American Corp. 02/26/1971
American Corp. name changed to American Western Resources, Inc. 08/05/1977 which merged into Ro-Mac Gold, Ltd. 05/17/1978 which name changed to Phoenix Associates Land Syndicate 10/24/1996
(See Phoenix Associates Land Syndicate)

AMERICAN MOBILE CMNTYS INC (CO)
Name changed to Marco Foods, Inc. 07/22/1986
(See Marco Foods, Inc.)

AMERICAN MOBILE PWR CORP (DE)
Charter cancelled and declared inoperative and void for non-payment of taxes 03/01/1986

AMERICAN MOBILE SATELLITE CORP (DE)
Name changed to Motient Corp. 04/21/2000
Motient Corp. name changed to TerreStar Corp. 08/16/2007
(See TerreStar Corp.)

AMERICAN MOBILE SYS INC (DE)
Reincorporated 01/30/1987
Each share old Common 1¢ par exchanged for (0.5) share new Common 1¢ par 01/21/1986
State of incorporation changed from (NJ) to (DE) 01/30/1987
Each share old Common 1¢ par exchanged for (0.33333333) share new Common 1¢ par 11/30/1990
Merged into Nextel Communications, Inc. 07/31/1995
Each share new Common 1¢ par exchanged for (0.62) share Class A Common $0.001 par
Nextel Communications, Inc. merged into Sprint Nextel Corp. 08/12/2005 which merged into Sprint Corp. (DE) 07/10/2013

AMERICAN MODULAR CORP. (DE)
No longer in existence having become inoperative and void for non-payment of taxes 04/01/1962

AMERICAN MODULAR MANUFACTURING CORP. (DE)
Each share old Common 1¢ par exchanged for (0.2) share new Common 1¢ par 07/01/1966
Name changed to Chemola Corp. 03/05/1969
Chemola Corp. merged into Hi-Port Industries, Inc. 04/29/1974
(See Hi-Port Industries, Inc.)

AMERICAN MOLASSES CO. (NY)
Each share Common no par exchanged for (1.5) shares Common $1 par 00/00/1946
Name changed to Sucrest Corp. 10/20/1961
Sucrest Corp. name changed to Ingredient Technology Corp. (NY) 02/15/1977 which reincorporated in Delaware 06/30/1978
(See Ingredient Technology Corp. (DE))

AMERICAN MOLD GUARD INC (CA)
Ceased operations 04/07/2008
Stockholders' equity unlikely

AMERICAN MOLDED FIBERGLASS CO. (NJ)
Each share Common 10¢ par exchanged for (0.25) share Common 40¢ par 01/29/1961
Adjudicated bankrupt 07/14/1964
No stockholders' equity

AMERICAN MOLLERIZING CORP. (NV)
Name changed to Amerdyne Corp. 01/06/1969
Amerdyne Corp. name changed to Pantheon 09/21/1969 which name changed to Medical Dispensing Systems, Inc. Northeast 07/20/1983
(See Medical Dispensing Systems, Inc. Northeast)

AMERICAN MONARCH CORP. (MN)
Completely liquidated 06/18/1965
Each share Common 10¢ par exchanged for first and final distribution of (0.25) share Minneapolis Scientific Controls Corp. Common 50¢ par
(See Minneapolis Scientific Controls Corp.)

AMERICAN MONEY INSTRS INC (MD)
Acquired by Merrill Lynch Ready Assets Trust 11/01/1977
Each share Capital Stock $1 par exchanged for (10) Shares of Bene. Int. 10¢ par
Merrill Lynch Ready Assets Trust name changed to Ready Assets Prime Money Fund 05/04/2009

AMERICAN MONITOR CORP (IN)
Common no par split (2) for (1) by issuance of (1) additional share 03/04/1981
Common no par split (2) for (1) by issuance of (1) additional share 05/24/1982
Reorganized under Chapter 11 Federal Bankruptcy Code as AM Diagnostics, Inc. 09/17/1990
Each share Common no par exchanged for (0.48) share Common no par and (1) Common Stock Purchase Warrant which expired 09/17/1993
(See AM Diagnostics, Inc.)

AMERICAN MONORAIL CO. (OH)
Common no par split (15) for (1) by issuance of (14) additional shares 00/00/1946
Common no par split (2) for (1) by issuance of (1) additional share payable 00/00/1948
Common no par split (3) for (1) by issuance of (2) additional shares payable 00/00/1951
Common no par changed to $1 par 12/24/1956
$1.20 Conv. Preferred 1956 Ser. called for redemption 04/30/1964
Merged into American Monorail Co. (New) 02/10/1965
Each share Common $1 par received $10.50 cash
Note: Certificates were not required to be surrendered and are without value

AMERICAN MORTGAGE & INVESTMENT CO. (OK)
Through voluntary exchange offer First National Bank & Trust Co. (Oklahoma City, OK) held all but (10) shares as of 04/15/1968
Public interest eliminated

AMERICAN MTG ACCEP CO (MA)
Plan of reorganization under Chapter 11 Federal Bankruptcy proceedings effective 10/15/2010
No stockholders' equity

AMERICAN MTG CO INC (TX)
Name changed to National Scientific Corp. 05/16/1996
National Scientific Corp. recapitalized as Cipherloc Corp. 03/23/2015

AMERICAN MTG INS CO (NC)
Stock Dividend - 66.2275% 12/31/1968
Common $2.50 par changed to $1 par and (1.5) additional shares issued 04/30/1968
Under plan of reorganization name changed to AMIC Corp. 08/01/1970
(See AMIC Corp.)

AMERICAN MTG INVS TR (MA)
Name changed to American Mortgage Acceptance Co. 04/26/1999
(See American Mortgage Acceptance Co.)

AMERICAN MOTOR BODY CORP.
Name changed to Hale & Kilburn Corp. 00/00/1927
(See Hale & Kilburn Corp.)

AMERICAN MOTORCYCLE CORP (ID)
SEC revoked common stock registration 05/30/2008

AMERICAN MOTORISTS INS CO (IL)
Each share Capital Stock $30 par exchanged for (6) shares Capital Stock $5 par 00/00/1947
Under plan of merger each share Capital Stock $5 par exchanged for (2) shares Capital Stock $3 par 00/00/1953
Stock Dividends - 13.33333333% 12/28/1955; 12.5% 12/22/1959
Acquired by Kemperco, Inc. 05/31/1968
Each share Capital Stock $3 par exchanged for (1) share Common $5 par
Kemperco, Inc. name changed to Kemper Corp. (Old) 01/15/1974
(See Kemper Corp. (Old))

AMERICAN MOULDING CORP. (DE)
Dissolved 11/06/1961
Details not available

AMERICAN MTR INNS INC (VA)
Each share Common 20¢ par exchanged for (0.5) share Common 40¢ par 07/22/1968
Common 40¢ par changed to 20¢ par and (1) additional share issued 12/26/1980
Common 20¢ par changed to 10¢ par and (1) additional share issued 05/18/1984
Merged into Prime Motor Inns, Inc. 01/03/1985
Each share Common 10¢ par exchanged for $21.50 cash

AMERICAN MTRS CORP (MD)
Capital Stock $5 par changed to $1.66666666 par and (2) additional shares issued 03/01/1960
Capital Stock $1.66666666 par reclassified as Common $1.66666666 par 04/27/1983
Common $1.66666666 par changed to 1¢ par 09/08/1986
Merged into Chrysler Corp. 08/05/1987
Each share $2.375 Conv. Preferred 1¢ par exchanged for (1) share $2.375 Conv. Preferred 1¢ par or (0.9683) share Common $1 par and $1.04 cash
Note: Option to receive combination of Common stock and cash expired 10/05/1987
Each share Common 1¢ par exchanged for (0.1162) share Common $1 par
Chrysler Corp. merged into DaimlerChrysler AG 11/12/1998 which name changed to Daimler AG 10/19/2007

AMERICAN MULTI LERT CORP (PA)
Adjudicated bankrupt 07/00/1976
Stockholders' equity unlikely

AMERICAN MULTIGRAPH CO. (OH)
Merged into Addressograph International Corp. 12/00/1930
Details not available

AMERICAN MULTIMEDIA INC (NY)
Merged into Clay Colour, Ltd. 05/23/1975
Each share Common 1¢ par exchanged for $0.60 cash

AMERICAN MULTIPLEXER CORP (NC)
Common no par split (3) for (2) by issuance of (0.5) additional share payable 05/07/2004 to holders of record 04/23/2004 Ex date - 05/10/2004
Recapitalized as eFotoXpress, Inc. 10/01/2005
Each share Common no par exchanged for (0.33333333) share Common no par
(See eFotoXpress, Inc.)

AMERICAN MUN INCOME PORTFOLIO INC (MN)
Remarketed Preferred Ser. T called for redemption at $25,000 on 05/07/2014
Remarketed Preferred Ser. TH called for redemption at $25,000 on 05/09/2014
Merged into Nuveen Investment

Quality Municipal Fund, Inc. 10/06/2014
Each 144A Variable Rate MuniFund Term Preferred Share Ser. 2017 1¢ par exchanged for (1) 144A Variable Rate MuniFund Term Preferred Share Ser. 2017 1¢ par
Each Common Share of Bene. Int. 1¢ par exchanged for (0.97287208) Common Share of Bene. Int. 1¢ par

AMERICAN MUN TERM TR INC (MN)
Remarketed Preferred called for redemption at $25 on 10/12/2000
Trust terminated 4/15/2001
Each share Common 1¢ par exchanged for $9.3351 cash

AMERICAN MUN TERM TR INC II (MN)
Remarketed Preferred called for redemption at $25,000 on 11/20/2001
Trust terminated 04/10/2002
Each share Common 1¢ par exchanged for $10.3426 cash

AMERICAN MUN TERM TR INC III (MN)
Remarketed Preferred called for redemption at $25,000 on 12/20/2002
Completely liquidated 04/07/2003
Each share Common 1¢ par exchanged for first and final distribution of $10.66 cash

AMERICAN MUSEUM HISTORICAL DOCUMENTS CHARTERED (NV)
Name changed to Gallery of History, Inc. 05/29/1990
(See Gallery of History, Inc.)

AMERICAN MUSIC STORES INC (DE)
Reincorporated 12/01/1969
State of incorporation changed from (MI) to (DE) 12/01/1969
Liquidation completed
Each share Common $1 par stamped to indicate initial distribution of $10.95 cash 12/23/1977
Each share Stamped Common $1 par exchanged for second and final distribution of $0.91 cash 11/30/1979

AMERICAN MUT FD INC (MD)
Reincorporated 09/20/1983
Common $1 par split (2) for (1) by issuance of (1) additional share 02/10/1955
State of incorporation changed from (DE) to (MD) 09/20/1983
Common $1 par changed to $0.001 par 11/16/1999
Common $0.001 par reclassified as Class A $0.001 par 03/15/2000
Reincorporated under the laws of Delaware as American Mutual Fund 01/01/2011

AMERICAN MUTUAL BUILDING & LOAN CO. (UT)
Name changed to American Savings & Loan Association (UT) 02/14/1940
(See American Savings & Loan Association (UT))

AMERICAN NAT ENERGY CORP (OK)
Certificates dated after 02/12/2002
Common 1¢ par changed to $0.001 par 06/23/2005
Each share old Common $0.001 par exchanged for (0.1) share new Common $0.001 par 10/27/2010
Plan of reorganization under Chapter 11 Federal Bankruptcy proceedings effective 05/05/2016
No stockholders' equity

AMERICAN NAT ENERGY CORP (OK)
Certificates dated prior to 07/19/1994
Acquired by Alexander Energy Corp. 07/19/1994
Each share Common no par exchanged for (1.62) shares Common 3¢ par

Alexander Energy Corp. merged into National Energy Group, Inc. 08/30/1996
(See National Energy Group, Inc.)

AMERICAN NAT FOODS MARKETING INC (OR)
Each share old Common $0.001 par exchanged for (0.005) share new Common $0.001 par 06/17/1996
Each share new Common $0.001 par exchanged again for (0.01) share new Common $0.001 par 06/10/1997
Reincorporated under the laws of Nevada as Aquatic Cellulose International Corp. 12/03/1997
Aquatic Cellulose International Corp. name changed to Valor Energy Corp. 06/02/2008
(See Valor Energy Corp.)

AMERICAN NAT RES CO (DE)
Reincorporated 06/30/1983
State of incorporation changed from (MI) to (DE) 06/30/1983
Common $1 par split (3) for (2) by issuance of (0.5) additional share 05/01/1984
Merged into Coastal Corp. 05/14/1985
Each share Common $1 par exchanged for $65 cash

AMERICAN NATL BANCORP INC (DE)
Merged into Crestar Financial Corp. 11/13/1997
Each share Common 1¢ par exchanged for (0.426) share Common $5 par
Crestar Financial Corp. merged into SunTrust Banks, Inc. 12/31/1998

AMERICAN NATIONAL BANK & TRUST (MONTCLAIR, NJ)
Reorganized as Princeton American Bancorp 01/01/1972
Each share Common $4 par exchanged for (1) share Common $4 par
Princeton American Bancorp name changed to Horizon Bancorp 12/31/1973
(See Horizon Bancorp)

AMERICAN NATIONAL BANK & TRUST CO. (RAPID CITY, SD)
Merged 08/31/1962
Merged from American National Bank (Rapid City, SD) to American National Bank & Trust Co. (Rapid City, SD) 08/31/1962
Each share Capital Stock $25 par exchanged for (0.8625) share Capital Stock $25 par
Capital Stock $25 par changed to $10 par and (1.5) additional shares issued 00/00/1964
Stock Dividend - 19.6579% 12/28/1962
Merged into First Bank System, Inc. 01/04/1968
Each share Capital Stock $10 par exchanged for (1.2722) shares Common $5 par
First Bank System, Inc. name changed to U.S. Bancorp 08/01/1997

AMERICAN NATIONAL BANK & TRUST CO. OF MICHIGAN (KALAMAZOO, MI)
Stock Dividends - 20% 10/21/1966; 10% 02/15/1968
Reorganized under the laws of Delaware as American National Holding Co. 02/01/1972
Each share Common $10 par exchanged for (1) share Common $10 par
American National Holding Co. merged into Old Kent Financial Corp. 07/31/1986 which merged into Fifth Third Bancorp 04/02/2001

AMERICAN NATL BK & TR CO (BOWLING GREEN, KY)
Stock Dividends - 100% 02/15/1973; 10% 06/30/1978; 105% 04/15/1981
Merged into First Kentucky National Corp. 02/11/1985
Each share Common $5 par exchanged for $43 cash

AMERICAN NATL BK & TR CO (CHATTANOOGA, TN)
Each share Capital Stock $100 par exchanged for (5) shares Capital Stock $20 par 00/00/1949
Capital Stock $20 par changed to $10 par and (1) additional share issued plus a 14.28571429% stock dividend paid 09/15/1963
Stock Dividends - 33.33333333% 00/00/1950; 25% 10/22/1954; 20% 05/15/1959, 16.66666666% 09/12/1961
Reorganized as American National Corp. (TN) 01/01/1973
Each share Capital Stock $10 par exchanged for (1) share Common $10 par
American National Corp. (TN) name changed to Ancorp Bancshares, Inc. 12/28/1973 which merged into Third National Corp. 12/31/1982 which merged into SunTrust Banks, Inc. 12/29/1986

AMERICAN NATL BK & TR CO (CHICAGO, IL)
Capital Stock $100 par changed to $10 par and (9) additional shares issued 08/20/1963
Stock Dividends - 50% 12/22/1943; 25% 12/27/1946; 33.33333333% 10/25/1950; 25% 08/20/1954; 10% 12/28/1956; 25% 09/16/1959; 33.33333333% 11/15/1961; 25% 07/06/1965; 20% 10/13/1967
Reorganized under the laws of Delaware as Anbatco Inc. 03/31/1969
Each share Capital Stock $10 par exchanged for (1.33333) shares Common $1 par
Anbatco Inc. name changed to American National Corp. 11/14/1969
(See American National Corp.)

AMERICAN NATL BK & TR CO (DANVILLE, VA)
Capital Stock $100 par changed to $10 par and (9) additional shares issued 01/28/1929
Stock Dividends - 100% 01/22/1957; 25% 03/15/1966; 33.33333333% 04/17/1972; 100% 05/20/1975; 50% 06/27/1983
Reorganized as American National Bankshares Inc. 09/01/1984
Each share Capital Stock $10 par exchanged for (2) shares Common $1 par

AMERICAN NATL BK & TR CO (FORT LAUDERDALE, FL)
100% acquired by First Bancshares of Florida, Inc. through exchange offer which expired 05/30/1974
Public interest eliminated

AMERICAN NATL BK & TR CO (KALAMAZOO, MI)
Each share Common $100 par exchanged for (5) shares Common $25 par to effect a (4) for (1) split and a 25% stock dividend 00/00/1950
Common $25 par changed to $10 par and (1.5) additional shares issued 07/12/1963
Stock Dividends - 20% 08/19/1940; 25% 11/18/1954; 20% 11/05/1959; 20% 12/20/1965; 10% 02/15/1968
Name changed to American National Bank & Trust Co. of Michigan (Kalamazoo, MI) 10/18/1966
American National Bank & Trust Co. of Michigan (Kalamazoo, MI) reorganized in Delaware as American National Holding Co.

02/01/1972 which merged into Old Kent Financial Corp. 07/31/1986 which merged into Fifth Third Bancorp 04/02/2001

AMERICAN NATL BK & TR CO (MOBILE, AL)
Each share Capital Stock $25 par exchanged for (2.5) shares Capital Stock $10 par plus a 20% stock dividend paid 00/00/1953
Stock Dividend - 23% 10/29/1956
Merged into Alabama Bancorporation 09/28/1972
Each share Capital Stock $10 par exchanged for (1.4) shares Common $1 par
Alabama Bancorporation name changed to AmSouth Bancorporation 04/20/1981 which merged into Regions Financial Corp. 11/04/2006

AMERICAN NATL BK & TR CO (ROCKFORD, IL)
Stock Dividends - 11.1% 01/18/1961; 100% 03/02/1970
Under plan of reorganization each share Capital Stock $40 par automatically became (1) share Americorp Financial Inc. Common $1 par 06/30/1983
Americorp Financial Inc. name changed to AMCORE Financial, Inc. 11/26/1985
(See AMCORE Financial, Inc.)

AMERICAN NATL BK & TR CO (SHAWNEE, OK)
Stock Dividends - 50% 01/31/1961; 33.33333333% 01/00/1964
Acquired by Arvest Bank Group 09/00/1998
Details not available

AMERICAN NATL BK & TR CO (SOUTH BEND, IN)
Stock Dividends - 10% 02/02/1970; 10% 02/10/1978
Merged into Valley Bank & Trust Co. (Mishawaka, IN) 10/01/1983
Each share Capital Stock $10 par exchanged for $42 cash

AMERICAN NATL BK & TR CO (ST. PAUL, MN)
97.2% acquired by American Bancorporation, Inc. through exchange offer which expired 03/00/1978
Public interest eliminated

AMERICAN NATL BK & TR CO (WAUKEGAN, IL)
Acquired by Grand National Bank (Wauconda, IL) 02/20/1996
Details not available

AMERICAN NATL BK & TR CO ST PETERSBURG FLA (ST PETERSBURG, FL)
99.8% acquired by Southeast Banking Corp. through exchange offer as of 09/30/1973
Public interest eliminated

AMERICAN NATIONAL BANK (AMARILLO, TX)
Stock Dividends - 20% 11/16/1951; 12% 04/20/1953
Merged into Fort Worth National Corp. 01/30/1973
Each share Capital Stock $100 par exchanged for (0.595238) share Common $5 par
Fort Worth National Corp. name changed to Texas American Bancshares Inc. 04/26/1974
(See Texas American Bancshares Inc.)

AMERICAN NATL BK (APPLETON, WI)
Under plan of reorganization each share Common $25 par automatically became (1) share American National Bancorp, Inc. Common no par 10/27/1998

AMERICAN NATL BK (AUSTIN, TX)
Each share Capital Stock $100 par

exchanged for (8.333333) shares Capital Stock $20 par to effect a (5) for (1) split and 66.66666666% stock dividend 01/18/1950
Stock Dividends - 50% 01/20/1954; 33.33333333% 02/10/1961
Under plan of reorganization each share Capital Stock $20 par automatically became (1) share American First Corp. Common $10 par 06/02/1969
American First Corp. merged into Federated Texas Bancorporation, Inc. 05/01/1973 which merged into Federated Capital Corp. 01/29/1974 which merged into Mercantile Texas Corp. 12/30/1976 which name changed to MCorp 10/11/1984
(See MCorp)

AMERICAN NATL BK (BAKERSFIELD, CA)
Common $7.50 par changed to $3.75 par and (1) additional share issued 03/26/1973
Common $3.75 par changed to $4 par 03/29/1974
Stock Dividend - 10% 12/27/1979
Reorganized as Central Pacific Corp. 09/15/1981
Each share Common $4 par exchanged for (1) share Common no par
Central Pacific Corp. acquired by Wells Fargo & Co. (Old) 03/31/1990 which merged into Wells Fargo & Co. (New) 11/02/1998

AMERICAN NATL BK (BEAUMONT, TX)
Each share Capital Stock $100 par exchanged for (5) shares Capital Stock $20 par 00/00/1947
Capital Stock $20 par changed to $10 par and (1) additional share issued plus a 20% stock dividend paid 06/09/1965
Stock Dividends - 50% 10/22/1947; 20% 02/15/1957
Merged into Texas Commerce Bancshares, Inc. 10/12/1972
Each share Capital Stock $10 par exchanged for (1) share $1.80 Conv. Preferred $10 par
(See Texas Commerce Bancshares, Inc.)

AMERICAN NATIONAL BANK (BEAVER DAM, WI)
Capital Stock $100 par changed to $20 par and (4) additional shares issued 11/25/1969
Reorganized as Ambanc Financial Services, Inc. 12/20/1984
Each share Capital Stock $20 par exchanged for (1) share Common $20 par

AMERICAN NATIONAL BANK (BIRMINGHAM, AL)
Name changed to National Bank of Commerce (Birmingham, AL) 05/27/1968
National Bank of Commerce (Birmingham, AL) reorganized as National Commerce Corp. 12/26/1979 which merged into Alabama National BanCorporation (DE) 01/03/1996 which merged into Royal Bank of Canada (Montreal, QC) 02/22/2008

AMERICAN NATL BK (BRUNSWICK, GA)
Reorganized as ANB Bankshares, Inc. 11/19/1984
Each share Common $10 par exchanged for (1) share Common $10 par
ANB Bankshares, Inc. acquired by Barnett Banks, Inc. 01/16/1989 which merged into NationsBank Corp. 01/09/1998 which reincorporated in Delaware as BankAmerica Corp. (Old) 09/25/1998 which merged into BankAmerica Corp. (New)

09/30/1998 which name changed to Bank of America Corp. 04/28/1999

AMERICAN NATIONAL BANK (CLEARWATER, FL)
Name changed to Landmark Bank of Clearwater, N.A. (Clearwater, FL) 10/01/1974
(See Landmark Bank of Clearwater, N.A. (Clearwater, FL))

AMERICAN NATL BK (GADSDEN, AL)
Each share Capital Stock $12.50 par exchanged for (5) shares Capital Stock $2.50 par 02/10/1970
Stock Dividend - 100% 01/18/1965
Merged into AmSouth Bancorporation 03/16/1984
Each share Capital Stock $2.50 par exchanged for $18 cash

AMERICAN NATL BK (GONZALES, TX)
Under plan of reorganization each share Common $1.50 par automatically became (1) share ANB Bancshares, Inc. Common $1.50 par 5/9/97

AMERICAN NATL BK (GREEN BAY, WI)
99% acquired by Citizens Bancorporation through purchase offer which expired 04/01/1976
Public interest eliminated

AMERICAN NATL BK (HAMDEN, CT)
Common $10 par changed to $5 par and (1) additional share issued 04/10/1974
Under plan of reorganization each share Common $5 par automatically became (1) share American Bancorp, Inc. (CT) Common $5 par 08/30/1985
American Bancorp, Inc. (CT) merged into Constitution Bancorp of New England, Inc. 05/31/1988 which name changed to Lafayette American Bancorp, Inc. 05/21/1991 which reorganized as Lafayette American Bank & Trust Co. (Hamden, CT) 02/23/1994 which merged into HUBCO, Inc. 07/01/1996 which merged into Hudson United Bancorp 04/21/1999 which merged into TD Banknorth Inc. 01/31/2006
(See TD Banknorth Inc.)

AMERICAN NATL BK (HUNTSVILLE, AL)
Merged into Alabama Bancorporation 09/28/1973
Each share Capital Stock $5 par exchanged for (1.1) shares Common $1 par
Alabama Bancorporation name changed to AmSouth Bancorporation 04/20/1981 which merged into Regions Financial Corp. 11/04/2006

AMERICAN NATIONAL BANK (INDIANAPOLIS, IN)
Stock Dividend - 33.33333333% 06/07/1944
Merged into American Fletcher National Bank & Trust Co. (Indianapolis, IN) 01/01/1955
Each share Common $10 par exchanged for (1) share Common Capital Stock $10 par
American Fletcher National Bank & Trust Co. (Indianapolis, IN) reorganized as American Fletcher Corp. 12/31/1968 which merged into Banc One Corp. (DE) 01/26/1987 which reincorporated in Ohio 05/01/1989 which merged into Bank One Corp. 10/02/1998 which merged into J.P. Morgan Chase & Co. 12/31/2000 which name changed to JPMorgan Chase & Co. 07/20/2004

AMERICAN NATL BK (JACKSONVILLE, FL)
Capital Stock $100 par changed to

$10 par and split (10) for (1) 00/00/1960
Through voluntary exchange offer 99.9% acquired by American Banks of Florida, Inc. as of 06/30/1974
Public interest eliminated

AMERICAN NATIONAL BANK (KALAMAZOO, MI)
Stock Dividend - 20% 08/19/1940
Name changed to American National Bank & Trust Co. (Kalamazoo, MI) 02/02/1953
American National Bank & Trust Co. (Kalamazoo, MI) name changed to American National Bank & Trust Co. of Michigan (Kalamazoo, MI) 10/18/1966 which reorganized in Delaware as American National Holding Co. 02/01/1972 which merged into Old Kent Financial Corp. 07/31/1986 which merged into Fifth Third Bancorp 04/02/2001

AMERICAN NATL BK (OMAHA, NE)
Stock Dividends - 25% 02/14/1977; 33.33333333% 02/16/1979
Reorganized as American National Corp. (NE) 09/30/1980
Each share Capital Stock $2.50 par exchanged for (1.5) shares Common $1 par
(See American National Corp. (NE))

AMERICAN NATL BK (PARMA, OH)
Common $10 par changed to $5 par and (1) additional share issued 03/19/1973
Under plan of reorganization each share Common $5 par held by holders of (999) shares or fewer exchanged for $2.20 cash 12/31/1996
Public interest eliminated

AMERICAN NATL BK (PORTSMOUTH, VA)
Each share Common $10 par exchanged for (3.5) shares Common $5 par 12/31/1966
Through voluntary exchange offer 100% acquired by Fidelity American Bankshares, Inc. as of 11/07/1969
Public interest eliminated

AMERICAN NATIONAL BANK (SAN BERNARDINO, CA)
Each share Capital Stock $100 par exchanged for (20) shares Capital Stock $5 par 06/14/1961
Stock Dividend - 16.66666666% 12/27/1956
Acquired by Bank of California, N.A. (San Francisco, CA) 06/26/1964
Each share Capital Stock $5 par exchanged for (1.381578) shares Common Capital Stock $10 par
Bank of California, N.A. (San Francisco, CA) reorganized as BanCal Tri-State Corp. 05/01/1972
(See BanCal Tri-State Corp.)

AMERICAN NATIONAL BANK (SHAWNEE, OK)
Each share Capital Stock $100 par exchanged for (20) shares Capital Stock $10 par to effect a (10) for (1) split and a 100% stock dividend 06/30/1954
Stock Dividends - 25% 12/00/1937; 100% 06/30/1949
Name changed to American National Bank & Trust Co. (Shawnee, OK) 08/01/1958
(See American National Bank & Trust Co. (Shawnee, OK))

AMERICAN NATIONAL BANK (SILVER SPRING, MD)
Stock Dividend - 75% 02/11/1963
Name changed to American National Bank of Maryland (Silver Spring, MD) 05/17/1963
American National Bank of Maryland (Silver Spring, MD) reorganized as American Bank of Maryland (Silver Spring, MD) 04/01/1977 which name changed to First American Bank of

Maryland (Silver Spring, MD) 12/31/1978
(See First American Bank of Maryland (Silver Spring, MD))

AMERICAN NATL BK (SOUTH CHICAGO HEIGHTS, IL)
Bank closed 12/31/2005
Details not available

AMERICAN NATIONAL BANK (ST. JOSEPH, MO)
Each share Capital Stock exchanged for (10.66666666) shares Capital Stock $10 par 12/06/1963
Reorganized as Ameribanc, Inc. 03/10/1971
Each share Capital Stock $10 par exchanged for (1) share Common $10 par
(See Ameribanc, Inc.)

AMERICAN NATIONAL BANK (ST. PAUL, MN)
Stock Dividends - 66.66666666% 02/07/1952; 20% 02/03/1960
Name changed to American National Bank & Trust Co. (St. Paul, MN) 06/01/1965
(See American National Bank & Trust Co. (St. Paul, MN))

AMERICAN NATL BK (ST LOUIS, MO)
Stock Dividends - 25% 05/21/1947; 10% 07/19/1956; 100% 01/18/1965; 50% 11/04/1969
Merged into CharterCorp 03/07/1983
Each share Capital Stock $20 par exchanged for (1.75) shares Common $6.25 par
CharterCorp merged into Boatmen's Bancshares, Inc. 01/28/1985 which merged into NationsBank Corp. (NC) 01/07/1997 which reincorporated in Delaware as BankAmerica Corp. (Old) 9/25/1998 which merged into BankAmerica Corp. (New) 09/30/1998 which name changed to Bank of America Corp. 04/28/1999

AMERICAN NATL BK (VINCENNES, IN)
Capital Stock $50 par changed to $10 par and (4) additional shares issued 02/15/1967
Stock Dividends - 20% 01/17/1955; 100% 03/11/1980
Under plan of reorganization each share Capital Stock $10 par automatically became (1) share AMBANC Corp. Common $10 par 10/01/1982
AMBANC Corp. merged into Union Planters Corp. 08/31/1998 which merged into Regions Financial Corp. (New) 07/01/2004

AMERICAN NATL BK (WICHITA FALLS, TX)
Recapitalized as Ameribancshares, Inc. 05/01/1997
Each share Common $2.50 par exchanged for (0.33333333) share Common $2.50 par

AMERICAN NATL BK MD (SILVER SPRING, MD)
Capital Stock $10 par changed to $5 par and (1) additional share issued plus a 10% stock dividend paid 02/10/1966
Stock Dividends - 10% 02/10/1965; 10% 02/10/1967
Reorganized as American Bank of Maryland (Silver Spring, MD) 04/01/1977
Each share Capital Stock $5 par exchanged for (1) share Common $10 par
American Bank of Maryland (Silver Spring, MD) name changed to First American Bank of Maryland (Silver Spring, MD) 12/31/1978
(See First American Bank of Maryland (Silver Spring, MD))

AMERICAN NATIONAL BANK OF EVANSTON (EVANSTON, IL)
Name changed to First Chicago Bank of Evanston, N.A. (Evanston, IL) 04/10/1989
(See First Chicago Bank of Evanston, N.A. (Evanston, IL))

AMERICAN NATIONAL BANK OF NEW YORK (FLEISCHMANNS, NY)
Bank closed 01/24/1992
No stockholders' equity

AMERICAN NATL BD FD INC (TX)
Reincorporated under the laws of Maryland as Triflex Fund, Inc. 11/20/1987
Triflex Fund, Inc. name changed to SM&R Balanced Fund, Inc. 07/09/2010
(See SM&R Balanced Fund, Inc.)

AMERICAN NATIONAL BUILDING CO. (OK)
Completely liquidated 07/01/1975
Each share Common $1 par received first and final distribution of (2) shares American National Bank (Midwest City, OK) Capital Stock $5 par
Notes: Certificates were not required to be surrendered and are without value
Above ratio includes a (2) for (1) split issued to holders of American National Bank (Midwest City, OK) 06/30/1975

AMERICAN NATL CAN GROUP INC (DE)
Merged into Rexam PLC 07/25/2000
Each share Common 1¢ par exchanged for $18 cash

AMERICAN NATIONAL CO.
Out of business 00/00/1941
Details not available

AMERICAN NATL CORP (DE)
Stock Dividend - 25% 06/10/1971
Completely liquidated 07/31/1973
Each share Common $1 par received first and final distribution of $50 cash
Note: Certificates were not required to be surrendered and are without value

AMERICAN NATL CORP (NE)
Merged into American Commerce Bancshares, Inc. 07/13/1986
Each share Common $1 par exchanged for $6 cash

AMERICAN NATL CORP (TN)
Name changed to Ancorp Bancshares, Inc. and Common $10 par changed to $3.50 par 12/28/1973
Ancorp Bancshares, Inc. merged into Third National Corp. 12/31/1982 which merged into SunTrust Banks, Inc. 12/29/1986

AMERICAN NATL ENTERPRISES INC (UT)
Stock Dividend - Common received 50% in 5% Non-Cum. Pfd. Ser. A 04/24/1972
Merged into Peregrine Entertainment Ltd. 11/28/1986
Each (5.25) shares 5% Non-Cum. Preferred Ser. A no par exchanged for (1) share new Common no par
Each (6.75) shares Common no par exchanged for (1) share new Common no par
(See Peregrine Entertainment Ltd.)

AMERICAN NATIONAL FINANCE CORP. (DE)
Each share Preferred no par exchanged for (0.2) share Preferred $100 par 00/00/1946
Each share Common no par exchanged for (1) share new Common no par
Stock Dividends - 100% 06/15/1948; 10% 04/01/1952 Liquidation completed 11/01/1957

Details not available

AMERICAN NATL FINL CORP (DE)
Under plan of reorganization each share Common $1 par automatically became (1) share American National Insurance Co. Common $1 par 11/08/1979

AMERICAN NATL FINL INC (CA)
Common no par split (5) for (4) by issuance of (0.25) additional share payable 07/18/2002 to holders of record 07/08/2002 Ex date - 07/19/2002
Stock Dividend - 10% payable 06/21/2001 to holders of record 06/07/2001 Ex date - 06/05/2001
Name changed to ANFI, Inc. 12/12/2002
ANFI, Inc. merged into Fidelity National Financial, Inc. 03/26/2003 which merged into Fidelity National Information Services, Inc. 11/09/2006

AMERICAN NATL FIRE INS CO (NY)
Acquired by Great American Insurance Co. 07/00/1964
Each share Capital Stock $5 par exchanged for $46.48 cash

AMERICAN NATL GROWTH FD INC (MD)
Name changed to SM&R Growth Fund, Inc. and Common $1 par reclassified as Class A 1¢ par 01/01/1999
(See SM&R Growth Fund, Inc.)

AMERICAN NATL HLDG CO (DE)
Common $10 par split (5) for (4) by issuance of (0.25) additional share 02/11/1972
Common $10 par changed to $5 par and (1) additional share issued 03/15/1973
Merged into Old Kent Financial Corp. 07/31/1986
Each share Common $5 par exchanged for (1.1364) shares Common $1 par
Old Kent Financial Corp. merged into Fifth Third Bancorp 04/02/2001

AMERICAN NATL HYDROCARBON INC (NV)
Charter revoked for failure to file reports and pay fees 06/01/1989

AMERICAN NATL INCOME FD INC (MD)
Reincorporated 08/23/1989
State of incorporation changed from (TX) to (MD) 08/23/1989
Name changed to SM&R Equity Income Fund, Inc. and Common $1 par reclassified as Class A 1¢ par 01/01/1999
SM&R Equity Income Fund, Inc. merged into California Investment Trust 07/09/2010

AMERICAN NATL INS CO (TX)
Each share Common $100 par exchanged for (10) shares Common $10 par 00/00/1946
Each share Common $10 par exchanged for (15) shares Common $1 par 05/15/1956
Stock Dividends - 150% 03/00/1946; 100% 03/09/1948; 100% 03/10/1955; 50% 05/11/1956; 10% 07/01/1958
Under plan of reorganization each share Common $1 par automatically became (1) share American National Financial Corp. (DE) Common $1 par 12/31/1971
American National Financial Corp. reorganized as American National Insurance Co. 11/08/1979

AMERICAN NATL MONEY MKT FD INC (TX)
Fund terminated 04/19/1993
Details not available

AMERICAN NATL PETE CO (DE)
Each share old Common 1¢ par exchanged for (0.25) share new Common 1¢ par 09/24/1985
Merged into Patrick Petroleum Co. 07/29/1993
Each share new Common 1¢ par exchanged for (1.23) shares Common 20¢ par and $3.40 cash
Patrick Petroleum Co. merged into Goodrich Petroleum Corp. 08/15/1995
(See Goodrich Petroleum Corp.)

AMERICAN NATL PETE CO (TX)
Reincorporated under the laws of Delaware and Common no par changed to 1¢ par 03/13/1985
American National Petroleum Co. (DE) merged into Patrick Petroleum Co. 07/29/1993 which merged into Goodrich Petroleum Corp. 08/15/1995
(See Goodrich Petroleum Corp.)

AMERICAN NATL RLTY CORP (DE)
Charter cancelled and declared inoperative and void for non-payment of taxes 03/01/1980

AMERICAN NATL SVGS BK F S B (BALTIMORE, MD)
Merged into American National Bancorp, Inc. 10/31/1995
Each share Common 1¢ par exchanged for (1.94) shares Common 1¢ par
American National Bancorp, Inc. merged into Crestar Financial Corp. 11/13/1997 which merged into SunTrust Banks, Inc. 12/31/1998

AMERICAN NATURAL GAS CO. (DE)
Reincorporated 06/30/1975
State of incorporation changed from (DE) to (MI) and Common $10 par changed to $1 par 06/30/1975
Name changed to American Natural Resources Co. (MI) 05/10/1976
American Natural Resources Co. (MI) reincorporated in Delaware 06/30/1983
(See American Natural Resources Co. (DE))

AMERICAN NATURAL GAS CO. (NJ)
Common no par changed to $25 par 04/27/1955
6% Preferred $25 par called for redemption 02/09/1960
Common $25 par changed to $10 par and (1.5) additional shares issued 06/01/1961
Stock Dividend - 10% 06/10/1959
Reincorporated under the laws of Delaware 04/30/1964
American Natural Gas Co. (DE) reincorporated in Michigan 06/30/1975 which name changed to American Natural Resources Co. (MI) 05/10/1976 which reincorporated in Delaware 06/30/1983
(See American Natural Resources Co. (DE))

AMERICAN NATURAL GAS CORP.
Bankrupt 00/00/1932
Stockholders' equity unlikely

AMERICAN NEPHELINE LTD. (ON)
Capital Stock no par changed to 50¢ par 00/00/1953
Recapitalized as Industrial Minerals of Canada Ltd. 05/01/1961
Each share Capital Stock 50¢ par exchanged for (0.1) share Capital Stock no par
Industrial Minerals of Canada Ltd. merged into Indusmin Ltd. 11/06/1968
(See Indusmin Ltd.)

AMERICAN NETWORK GROUP INC (DE)
Each share old Common 1¢ par exchanged for (0.1) share new Common 1¢ par 07/17/1992
Merged into Paxson Communications Corp. 11/04/1994
Each share new Common 1¢ par exchanged for (0.26787388) share Common $0.001 par
Paxson Communications Corp. name changed to ION Media Networks, Inc. 06/30/2006
(See ION Media Networks, Inc.)

AMERICAN NETWORK INC (OR)
Acquired by ITT Corp. 05/25/1988
Each share Common no par exchanged for $0.25 cash

AMERICAN NEV GOLD CORP (BC)
Recapitalized as Northern Canadian Minerals Inc. 08/06/2004
Each share Common no par exchanged for (0.2) share Common no par
Northern Canadian Minerals Inc. name changed to Northern Canadian Uranium Inc. 04/09/2007 which merged into Bayswater Uranium Corp. (New) 12/21/2007 which recapitalized as Green Thumb Industries Inc. 06/13/2018

AMERICAN NEWS CO., INC.
Name changed to American News New York Corp. 00/00/1934
American News New York Corp. merged into American News Co. 00/00/1937 which name changed to Ancorp National Services, Inc. 04/30/1969
(See Ancorp National Services, Inc.)

AMERICAN NEWS CO (DE)
Capital Stock no par split (2) for (1) by issuance of (1) additional share 04/15/1960
Stock Dividend - 100% 03/23/1946
Name changed to Ancorp National Services, Inc. 04/30/1969
(See Ancorp National Services, Inc.)

AMERICAN NEWS NEW YORK CORP.
Merged into American News Co. 00/00/1937
Each share old Capital Stock no par exchanged for (2) shares new Capital Stock no par
American News Co. name changed to Ancorp National Services, Inc. 04/30/1969
(See Ancorp National Services, Inc.)

AMERICAN NORTEL COMMUNICATIONS INC (WY)
Reincorporated 02/09/1993
Place of incorporation changed from (BC) to (WY) 02/09/1993
Reincorporated under the laws of Nevada 08/03/2007

AMERICAN NORTHLAND OIL CO (CA)
Each old share Capital Stock $2 par exchanged for (0.1) new share Capital Stock $2 par 06/05/1974
Charter suspended for failure to file reports and pay fees 03/01/1988

AMERICAN NUCLEAR CORP (CO)
Out of business 00/00/1994
No stockholders' equity

AMERICAN NUCLEONICS CORP (CA)
Merged into Eaton Corp. 12/22/1986
Each share Capital Stock $0.03333333 par exchanged for $3.03 cash

AMERICAN NUMISMATIC INVTS INC (OH)
Charter revoked for failure to file reports and pay fees 05/10/1968

AMERICAN NURSERY PRODS INC (DE)
Plan of reorganization under Chapter 11 Federal Bankruptcy Code effective 02/22/1994
No stockholders' equity

AMERICAN NUT INC (GA)
Name changed to Consolidated American Companies, Inc. 11/14/1969

AMERICAN OAK LEATHER CO. (OH)
Completely liquidated 00/00/1952
Details not available

AMERICAN OAKWOOD ENERGY LTD (AB)
Name changed to American Ore Ltd. 11/06/1986
American Ore Ltd. recapitalized as American Exploration Corp. 04/14/1992 which name changed to Asia Minerals Corp. (AB) 08/25/1993 which reincorporated in British Columbia 06/07/1994 which name changed to American Bonanza Gold Mining Corp. 10/16/2000 which merged into American Bonanza Gold Corp. 03/31/2005 which merged into Kerr Mines Inc. 07/07/2014

AMERICAN OIL & GAS CORP (DE)
Merged into K N Energy, Inc. 07/13/1994
Each share Common 4¢ par exchanged for (0.47) share Common $5 par
K N Energy, Inc. name changed to Kinder Morgan, Inc. (KS) 10/07/1999
(See Kinder Morgan, Inc. (KS))

AMERICAN OIL & GAS CORP (TX)
Reincorporated under the laws of Delaware 07/23/1986
American Oil & Gas Corp. (DE) merged into K N Energy, Inc. 07/13/1994 which name changed to Kinder Morgan, Inc. (KS) 10/07/2000
(See Kinder Morgan, Inc. (KS))

AMERICAN OIL & GAS INC NEW (NV)
Merged into Hess Corp. 12/17/2010
Each share Common $0.001 par exchanged for (0.1373) share Common $1 par

AMERICAN OIL & MINERALS INC (NV)
Charter revoked for failure to file reports and pay fees 02/01/1987

AMERICAN OIL & REFINING CO.
Liquidated 00/00/1944
Details not available

AMERICAN OIL & REFINING CO., INC (LA)
Charter revoked for failure to file annual reports 01/10/1986

AMERICAN OIL SHALE CORP (UT)
Name changed to American Geothermal Energy, Inc. 02/14/1975
American Geothermal Energy, Inc. name changed to American Geological Enterprises, Inc. (UT) 12/24/1975 which reincorporated in Delaware as Emtec, Inc. 01/16/2001

AMERICAN OILFIELD DIVERS INC (LA)
Name changed to Ceanic Corp. 05/15/1998
(See Ceanic Corp.)

AMERICAN ONCOLOGY RES INC (DE)
Common 1¢ par split (2) for (1) by issuance of (1) additional share payable 06/10/1996 to holders of record 05/31/1996
Under plan of merger name changed to U.S. Oncology, Inc. 06/15/1999
(See U.S. Oncology, Inc.)

AMERICAN OPT & EQUITY FD INC (DE)
Completely liquidated 12/27/1978
Each share Common $1 par exchanged for first and final distribution of $4.56 cash

AMERICAN OPTICAL CO. (MA)
Common no par changed to $1 par 03/31/1955
Common $1 par split (2) for (1) by issuance of (1) additional share 09/30/1964
Stock Dividends - 25% 03/14/1952; 10% 01/03/1966
Completely liquidated 04/24/1967
Each share Common $1 par exchanged for first and final distribution of (2.1) shares Warner-Lambert Pharmaceutical Co. Common $1 par
Warner-Lambert Pharmaceutical Co. name changed to Warner-Lambert Co. 11/13/1970 which merged into Pfizer Inc. 06/19/2000

AMERICAN ORDNANCE CORP.
Dissolved 00/00/1947
No stockholders' equity

AMERICAN ORE LTD (AB)
Recapitalized as American Exploration Corp. 04/14/1992
Each share Common no par exchanged for (0.2) share Common no par
American Exploration Corp. name changed to Asia Minerals Corp. (AB) 08/25/1993 which reincorporated in British Columbia 06/07/1994 which name changed to American Bonanza Gold Mining Corp. 10/16/2000 which merged into American Bonanza Gold Corp. 03/31/2005 which merged into Kerr Mines Inc. 07/07/2014

AMERICAN ORIENTAL CO.
Liquidated 00/00/1930
Details not available

AMERICAN OSTRICH CORP (UT)
Each share old Common no par exchanged for (0.00003125) share new Common no par 03/31/1999
Note: No holder received fewer than (100) post split shares
Reincorporated under the laws of Delaware as CallNOW.com, Inc. and Common no par changed to $0.001 par 04/06/1999
(See CallNOW.com, Inc.)

AMERICAN OVERSEAS AIRLINES, INC.
Liquidation completed 00/00/1951
Details not available

AMERICAN PAC BK (AUMSVILLE, OR)
Each share Common no par exchanged for (0.1) share Class A Common no par 11/29/1990
Each share Class A Common no par exchanged for (0.25) share Class B Common no par 05/19/1997
Stock Dividend - 10% payable 12/29/2000 to holders of record 12/22/2000 Ex date - 12/20/2000
Merged into Riverview Bancorp. Inc. 04/22/2005
Each share Class B Common no par exchanged for (0.563) share Common 1¢ par

AMERICAN PAC BUSINESS VENTURES INC (OR)
Common no par split (3) for (1) by issuance of (2) additional shares 04/01/1983
Acquired by Summit Health Ltd. 02/08/1985
Each share Common no par exchanged for $8 cash

AMERICAN PAC CORP (DE)
Acquired by H.I.G. Capital, LLC 02/27/2014
Each share Common 10¢ par exchanged for $46.50 cash

AMERICAN PAC FD INC (HI)
Name changed to Professional Portfolio Fund Inc. 07/30/1970
Professional Portfolio Fund Inc. acquired by Pegasus Fund, Inc. 05/11/1973 which name changed to Vanderbilt Growth Fund, Inc. 07/01/1975 which merged into St. Paul Capital Fund, Inc. 06/14/1977 which name changed to AMEV Capital Fund, Inc. 05/01/1985 which reorganized as Fortis Equity Portfolios Inc. 02/22/1992
(See Fortis Equity Portfolios Inc.)

AMERICAN PAC FINL SVCS (NV)
Recapitalized as FilmWorld, Inc. 07/19/1999
Each share Common $0.001 par exchanged for (0.1) share Common $0.001 par
FilmWorld, Inc. name changed to SulphCo, Inc. 04/11/2001
(See SulphCo, Inc.)

AMERICAN PAC GROUP INC (HI)
Completely liquidated 03/03/1972
Each share Common $1 par exchanged for first and final distribution of (0.377358) share Hawaii Corp. Common no par
(See Hawaii Corp.)

AMERICAN PAC INTL INC (NV)
Merged into Worldwide Energy Corp. 10/09/1984
Each share Common 1¢ par exchanged for (0.25) share Common 20¢ par
Worldwide Energy Corp. merged into Triton Energy Corp. (TX) 11/18/1986 which reincorporated in Delaware 05/12/1995 which merged into Triton Energy Ltd. 03/25/1996
(See Triton Energy Ltd.)

AMERICAN PAC LIFE INS CO CALIF (CA)
Capital Stock 40¢ par changed to 80¢ par 11/25/1970
Each (27,160.4) shares old Capital Stock 80¢ par exchanged for (1) share new Capital Stock 80¢ par 12/00/1975
Note: In effect holders received $2.74 cash per share and public interest was eliminated

AMERICAN PAC MINERALS LTD (BC)
Cease trade order effective 01/23/1997
Stockholders' equity unlikely

AMERICAN PAC MNG INC (CANADA)
Reincorporated 11/14/1988
Place of incorporation changed from (BC) to (Canada) 11/14/1988
Merged into Breakwater Resources Ltd. (BC) 03/15/1990
Each share Common no par exchanged for (3) shares Common no par
Breakwater Resources Ltd. (BC) reincorporated in Canada 05/11/1992
(See Breakwater Resources Ltd.)

AMERICAN PAC MINT INC (NV)
Each share old Common 1¢ par exchanged for (0.16666666) share new Common 1¢ par 08/24/1988
Name changed to Dallas Gold & Silver Exchange Inc. 06/18/1992
Dallas Gold & Silver Exchange Inc. name changed to DGSE Companies, Inc. 06/27/2001

AMERICAN PAC RIM COMM GROUP (CA)
Each share old Common $0.001 par exchanged for (0.001) share new Common $0.001 par 10/31/2011
Reincorporated under the laws of Florida as American Pacific Rim Commerce Corp. 11/21/2012

AMERICAN PAC ST BK (SHERMAN OAKS, CA)
Stock Dividends - 10% 01/02/1995; 5% payable 01/02/1998 to holders of record 12/10/1997; 5% payable 01/04/1999 to holders of record 12/11/1998
Acquired by City National Corp. 08/27/1999
Each share Common no par exchanged for $15.65 cash

AMERICAN PAC ST BK (SUN VALLEY, CA)
Under plan of reorganization each share Common $6 par automatically became (1) share APSB Bancorp Common no par 11/19/1982
APSB Bancorp name changed to American Pacific State Bank (Sherman Oaks, CA) 12/27/1990
(See American Pacific State Bank (Sherman Oaks, CA))

AMERICAN PACEMAKER CORP (MA)
Through exchange offer approximately 97% acquired by Intermedics, Inc. as of 08/11/1982
Public interest eliminated
Note: Non-tendered shares were cancelled and became without value 08/11/1987

AMERICAN PACESETTER (CA)
Common $1 par changed to 10¢ par 06/11/1970
Conv. Preference $10 par called for redemption 12/28/1976
6% Conv. Preferred Ser. A $10 par called for redemption 12/28/1976
6% Conv. Preferred Ser. B $10 par called for redemption 12/28/1976
Each share old Common 10¢ par exchanged for (0.5) share new Common 10¢ par 08/22/1980
Note: To holdings of (199) shares or fewer election to receive stock expired 09/29/1980 after which they received $2.39 cash per share
Plan of reorganization under Chapter 11 Federal Bankruptcy Code effective 03/11/1993
No stockholders' equity

AMERICAN PACIFIC EXPLORATION LTD. (BC)
Struck off register and declared dissolved for failure to file returns 05/15/1969

AMERICAN PACIFIC MINES, INC. (NV)
Recapitalized as National Laser Systems, Inc. 06/09/1987
Each share Common 1¢ par exchanged for (2) shares Common $0.002 par
National Laser Systems, Inc. name changed to End Rust USA, Inc. 06/14/1988 which recapitalized as Wray-Tech Instruments Inc. 03/25/1991

AMERICAN PACIFIC PETROLEUM, INC. (UT)
Charter revoked for failure to file reports and pay fees 03/31/1961

AMERICAN PACKING CO. (WA)
Charter cancelled and proclaimed dissolved for failure to pay fees 07/01/1967

AMERICAN PACKING CO (MO)
Completely liquidated 01/01/1976
Details not available

AMERICAN PAD & PAPER CO (MA)
Common $20 par changed to $10 par and (1) additional share issued 07/30/1971
Common $10 par changed to $6.66666666 par and (0.5) additional share issued 07/15/1972
Common $6.66666666 par changed to $3.33333333 par and (1) additional share issued 06/21/1977
Common $3.33333333 par changed to $1.66666666 par and (1) additional share issued 03/31/1983
Stock Dividend - 100% 03/20/1968
Name changed to Ampad Corp. 06/22/1983
(See Ampad Corp.)

AMERICAN PAD & PAPER CO NEW (DE)
Chapter 11 bankruptcy proceedings converted to Chapter 7 on 12/21/2001
Stockholders' equity unlikely

AMERICAN PAGING INC (DE)
Merged into Telephone & Data Systems, Inc. 03/20/1998

Each share Common $1 par exchanged for $2.50 cash

AMERICAN PAIN & STRESS INC (NV)
Chapter 11 Federal Bankruptcy Code converted to Chapter 7 on 05/12/1989
Stockholders' equity unlikely

AMERICAN PALLET LEASING INC (DE)
SEC revoked common stock registration 06/23/2010

AMERICAN PAPER GOODS CO. (NJ)
Each share Common $100 par exchanged for (4) shares Common $25 par 00/00/1931
Acquired by Continental Can Co., Inc. 00/00/1954
Each share Common $25 par exchanged for (0.881) share Common $20 par
Continental Can Co., Inc. name changed to Continental Group, Inc. 04/27/1976
(See Continental Group, Inc.)

AMERICAN PARAMOUNT GOLD CORP (NV)
Old Common $0.001 par split (2) for (1) by issuance of (1) additional share payable 04/12/2010 to holders of record 04/12/2010
Each share old Common $0.001 par exchanged for (0.025) share new Common $0.001 par 01/26/2012
Name changed to Indigenous Roots Corp. 02/09/2018

AMERICAN PARTICIPATIONS, INC.
Liquidated 00/00/1951
Details not available

AMERICAN PASSAGE MKTG CORP (WA)
Name changed to Seattle Filmworks, Inc. 02/22/1989
Seattle Filmworks, Inc. name changed to PhotoWorks Inc. 02/01/2000
(See PhotoWorks Inc.)

AMERICAN PATENTS UNLIMITED INC (FL)
Involuntarily dissolved 11/04/1988

AMERICAN PATRIOT CORP (NV)
Charter revoked for failure to file reports and pay taxes 07/30/2010

AMERICAN PATRIOT FDG INC (NV)
SEC revoked common stock registration 06/20/2010

AMERICAN PATTERN & FOUNDRY CO. (MI)
Liquidation completed
Each share Capital Stock $1 par exchanged for initial distribution of $2.50 cash 02/05/1970
Each share Capital Stock $1 par received second and final distribution of $0.3937 cash 06/30/1971

AMERICAN PAULIN SYSTEM, INC.
Acquired by General Instrument Corp. (NJ) 00/00/1929
Details not available

AMERICAN PEAT CO (NV)
Name changed to American National Hydrocarbon, Inc. 11/15/1982
(See American National Hydrocarbon, Inc.)

AMERICAN PENN LIFE INSURANCE CO. (PA)
Merged into First National Life Insurance (AZ) 06/30/1963
Each share Capital Stock $10 par exchanged for (3.5) share Common $4 par
First National Life Insurance Co. (AZ) merged into First National Life Insurance Co. (AL) 12/31/1967 which reorganized as First National Corp. (NV) 12/31/1969 which recapitalized as Seal Fleet, Inc. 08/09/1979 which reorganized as Seal Holdings Corp. 06/30/1997 which name changed to Le@p Technology, Inc. 07/06/2000

AMERICAN PEPSI COLA BOTTLERS INC (DE)
Merged into General Cinema Corp. 03/30/1973
Each share Common $1 par exchanged for (0.5) share Common $1 par
General Cinema Corp. name changed to Harcourt General, Inc. 03/15/1993
(See Harcourt General, Inc.)

AMERICAN PERS BLOOD SVGS BK INC (UT)
Name changed to Convergent Companies, Inc. 05/13/1991
Convergent Companies, Inc. name changed to Zerotree Technologies, Inc. 01/17/2001 which recapitalized as Global Equity Fund, Inc. 03/20/2006
(See Global Equity Fund, Inc.)

AMERICAN PERSPECTIVE BK (SAN LUIS OBISPO, CA)
Acquired by PacWest Bancorp 08/01/2012
Each share Common no par exchanged for $13 cash

AMERICAN PET CO (DE)
Adjudicated bankrupt 12/06/1977
Stockholders' equity unlikely

AMERICAN PETE GROUP INC (NV)
Name changed to High Velocity Alternative Energy Corp. 09/14/2007
High Velocity Alternative Energy Corp. name changed to Reflectkote, Inc. 07/31/2009

AMERICAN PETROCHEMICAL CORP. (MN)
Completely liquidated 11/21/1967
Each share Common 50¢ par exchanged for first and final distribution of (0.142757) share Whittaker Corp. (CA) Common $1 par
Whittaker Corp. (CA) reincorporated in Delaware 06/16/1986
(See Whittaker Corp. (DE))

AMERICAN PETROFINA INC (DE)
Name changed to Fina, Inc. 04/18/1991
(See Fina, Inc.)

AMERICAN PFD LIFE INS CO (AL)
Name changed to American Tidelands Life Insurance Co. 12/29/1972
American Tidelands Life Insurance Co. merged into Tidelands Capital Corp. 05/03/1977 which merged into Western Preferred Corp. 03/06/1981
(See Western Preferred Corp.)

AMERICAN PHARMACEUTICAL PARTNERS INC (DE)
Common $0.001 par split (3) for (2) by issuance of (0.5) additional share payable 09/02/2003 to holders of record 08/18/2003 Ex date - 09/03/2003
Name changed to Abraxis BioScience, Inc. (Old) 04/19/2006
Abraxis BioScience, Inc. (Old) name changed to APP Pharmaceuticals, Inc. 11/13/2007
(See APP Pharmaceuticals, Inc.)

AMERICAN PHENIX CORP.
Liquidated 00/00/1933
Details not available

AMERICAN PHENOLIC CORP. (IL)
Name changed to Amphenol Electronics Corp. 04/17/1956
Amphenol Electronics Corp. merged into Amphenol-Borg Electronics Corp. 01/01/1959 which name changed to Amphenol Corp. (Old) 05/11/1965 which merged into Bunker Ramo Corp. (New) 06/03/1968 which merged into Allied Corp. 07/31/1981 which merged into Allied-Signal Inc. 09/19/1985 which name changed to AlliedSignal Inc. 04/26/1993 which name changed to Honeywell International Inc. 12/01/1999

AMERICAN PHOENIX CORP. (DE)
Completely liquidated 08/18/1964
Each share Unsubordinated Class A $1 par exchanged for first and final distribution of (0.66666666) share Drew Properties Corp. Class A $1 par
Each share Subordinated Class A $1 par exchanged for first and final distribution of (0.5) share Drew Properties Corp. Class A $1 par
Drew Properties Corp. name changed to Drew National Corp. 01/30/1968 which into Pratt Hotel Corp. 05/31/1985 which name changed to Greate Bay Casino Corp. 12/31/1996
(See Greate Bay Casino Corp.)

AMERICAN PHOENIX GROUP INC (DE)
Name changed to TAL Wireless Networks, Inc. 05/22/1997
(See TAL Wireless Networks, Inc.)

AMERICAN PHOENIX GROUP INC (NV)
Merged into American Phoenix Group Inc. (DE) 09/26/1996
Each share Common 1¢ par exchanged for (0.4225) share Common $0.001 par
American Phoenix Group Inc. (DE) name changed to TAL Wireless Networks, Inc. 05/22/1997
(See TAL Wireless Networks, Inc.)

AMERICAN PHOTOCOPY EQUIP CO (DE)
Reincorporated 05/15/1969
Common $1 par changed to no par and (2) additional shares issued 05/06/1959
Common no par split (3) for (1) by issuance of (2) additional shares 04/28/1961
State of incorporation changed from (IL) to (DE) and Common no par changed to 50¢ par 05/15/1969
Name changed to Apeco Corp. 04/13/1971
Apeco Corp. recapitalized as Lori Corp. 08/29/1985 which name changed to COMFORCE Corp. 12/01/1995
(See COMFORCE Corp.)

AMERICAN PHYSICIAN PARTNERS INC (DE)
Name changed to Radiologix, Inc. 09/24/1999
Radiologix, Inc. merged into Primedex Health Systems, Inc. 11/15/2006 which recapitalized as RadNet, Inc. (NY) 11/28/2006 which reincorporated in Delaware 09/03/2008

AMERICAN PHYSICIANS CAP INC (MI)
Common no par split (3) for (2) by issuance of (0.5) additional share payable 11/01/2006 to holders of record 10/11/2006 Ex date - 11/02/2006
Common no par split (4) for (3) by issuance of (0.33333333) additional share payable 07/31/2009 to holders of record 07/10/2009 Ex date - 08/03/2009
Acquired by The Doctors Co. 10/22/2010
Each share Common no par exchanged for $41.50 cash

AMERICAN PHYSICIANS SVC GROUP INC (TX)
Acquired by ProAssurance Corp. 12/01/2010
Each share Common 10¢ par exchanged for $32.50 cash

AMERICAN PIONEER CORP (FL)
Common $2 par changed to $1 par 06/26/1981
Stock Dividend - 10% 05/24/1974
Merged into First Fidelity Savings & Loan Association 11/01/1982
Each share Common $1 par exchanged for (1) share Common $1 par
First Fidelity Savings & Loan Association name changed to American Pioneer Savings Bank (Orlando, FL) 07/01/1985 which reorganized as American Pioneer Inc. 10/03/1988
(See American Pioneer Inc.)

AMERICAN PIONEER INC (FL)
Assets sold 05/00/1990
No stockholders' equity

AMERICAN PIONEER LIFE INS CO (FL)
Reorganized as American Pioneer Corp. 12/31/1970
Each share Common $2 par exchanged for (1) share Common $2 par
American Pioneer Corp. merged into First Fidelity Savings & Loan Association 11/01/1982 which name changed to American Pioneer Savings Bank (Orlando, FL) 07/01/1985 which reorganized as American Pioneer Inc. 10/03/1988
(See American Pioneer Inc.)

AMERICAN PIONEER SVGS BK (ORLANDO, FL)
Reorganized as American Pioneer Inc. 10/03/1988
Each share Conv. Preferred $10 par exchanged for (1) share Conv. Preferred $10 par
Each share Conv. Preferred Class B Ser. 2 $1 par exchanged for (1) share Conv. Preferred Class B Ser. 2 $1 par
Each share Common $1 par exchanged for (1) share Common $1 par
(See American Pioneer Inc.)

AMERICAN PIPE & CONSTR CO (CA)
Reorganized 12/01/1961
Each share Common no par exchanged for (2.25) shares Common $1 par 00/00/1953
Stock Dividends - 10% 01/14/1957; 10% 01/10/1958; 40% 01/15/1960
Reorganized from (DE) to under the laws of (CA) 12/01/1961
Each share Common $1 par exchanged for (2) shares Common $5 par
Name changed to Ameron, Inc. (CA) 01/06/1970
Ameron, Inc. (CA) reincorporated in Delaware 03/25/1986 which name changed to Ameron International Corp. 04/16/1996
(See Ameron International Corp.)

AMERICAN PIPE & CONSTRUCTION CO. (PA)
Dissolved 00/00/1938
Details not available

AMERICAN PIPELINE & EXPL CO (DE)
Charter cancelled and declared inoperative and void for non-payment of taxes 03/01/1986

AMERICAN PIZZA INC (NV)
Each share old Common $0.001 par exchanged for (0.05) share new Common $0.001 par 03/14/1990
Charter revoked for failure to file reports and pay fees 01/01/2005

AMERICAN PLAN CORP. (NY)
Stock Dividends - 10% 01/03/1972; 10% 09/15/1972; 10% 04/05/1973
Dissolved by proclamation 06/23/1993

AMERICAN PLAN LIFE INS CO (MT)
Involuntarily dissolved 12/03/1990
Stockholders' equity unlikely

AME-AME   FINANCIAL INFORMATION, INC.

AMERICAN PLANNED CMNTYS INC (DE)
Merged into Cenjerprop Corp. 10/30/1979
Each share Common 10¢ par exchanged for $1 cash

AMERICAN PLASTICS & CHEMS INC (DE)
Common 5¢ par changed to 1¢ par 04/00/1992
SEC revoked common stock registration 11/18/2005

AMERICAN PLATE GLASS CORP.
Property sold 00/00/1932
Details not available

AMERICAN PLATINUM INC (BC)
Struck off register and declared dissolved for failure to file returns 09/03/1993

AMERICAN PLEASURE INC (NY)
Name changed to Great American Backrub Store Inc. (NY) 12/08/1994
Great American Backrub Store Inc. (NY) reorganized in Delaware as International Diversified Industries Inc. 08/03/1998
(See International Diversified Industries Inc.)

AMERICAN PNEUMATIC SERVICE CO. (DE)
Name changed to Lamson Corp. of Delaware (DE) 04/07/1941
Lamson Corp. of Delaware (DE) reorganized in New York as Lamson Corp. 03/26/1962 which merged into Diebold, Inc. 07/16/1965

AMERICAN POLICYHOLDERS INS CO (MA)
Capital Stock $30 par changed to $20 par 00/00/1936
Capital Stock $20 par changed to $10 par 00/00/1952
Capital Stock $10 par changed to $15 par 11/07/1975
100% owned by A M Inc. as of 02/14/1983
Public interest eliminated

AMERICAN POLLUTN PREVENTION INC (DE)
Name changed to International Broadcasting Corp. 05/02/1978
(See International Broadcasting Corp.)

AMERICAN POLYMERS INC (NJ)
Out of business 10/25/1983
No stockholders' equity

AMERICAN PORTABLE TELECOM INC (DE)
Name changed to Aerial Communications Inc. 11/25/1996
Aerial Communications Inc. merged into Voicestream Wireless Corp. 05/05/2000 which merged into Deutsche Telekom AG 05/31/2001

AMERICAN POST TENSION INC (DE)
Name changed to Crown City Pictures, Inc. 10/07/2011
Crown City Pictures, Inc. recapitalized as World Poker Fund Holdings, Inc. 01/06/2015

AMERICAN POSTAL CORP (OH)
Each share old Common no par exchanged for (0.25) share new Common no par 06/30/1970
Charter cancelled for non-payment of taxes 04/15/1977

AMERICAN POTASH & CHEMICAL CORP. (DE)
Class A no par split (5) for (2) by issuance of (1.5) additional shares 05/08/1956
Class B no par reclassified as Common no par and (1.5) additional shares issued 05/08/1956
Class A no par reclassified as Common no par 05/01/1958
$4 Preferred Ser. A no par called for redemption 12/22/1967
$5 Special Preferred no par called for redemption 12/22/1967
Stock Dividend - 10% 01/07/1955
Merged into Kerr-McGee Corp. 12/29/1967
Each share Common no par exchanged for (0.125) share $4.50 Conv. Preferred Ser. A no par and (0.306) share Common $1 par
(See Kerr-McGee Corp.)

AMERICAN POTASH CORP (BC)
Each share old Common no par exchanged for (0.2) share new Common no par 01/25/2016
Name changed to New Tech Lithium Corp. 01/22/2018

AMERICAN POWDER CO.
Acquired by American Cyanamid Co. 00/00/1929
Details not available

AMERICAN POWER & LIGHT CO. (ME)
$5 Preferred Ser. A no par exchanged for $5 Preferred no par 00/00/1932
Each share $6 Preferred no par exchanged for (1.242) shares of Florida Power & Light Co. Common, (0.304) share of Minnesota Power & Light Co. Common, (1.255) shares of Montana Power Co. Common, (2.231) shares of Texas Utilities Co. Common, (1.188) shares of American Power & Light Co. Capital Stock no par and $0.75 cash 00/00/1950
Each share $5 Preferred no par exchanged for (1.045) shares of Florida Power & Light Co. Common, (0.256) share of Minnesota Power & Light Co. Common, (1.057) shares of Montana Power Co. Common, (1.878) shares of Texas Utilities Co. Common, (1) share of American Power & Light Co. Capital Stock no par and $0.625 cash 00/00/1950
Each share Common no par exchanged for (0.147) share of Florida Power & Light Co. Common, (0.036) share of Minnesota Power & Light Co. Common, (0.148) share of Montana Power Co. Common, (0.263) share of Texax Utilities Co. Common and (0.14) share of American Power & Light Co. Capital Stock no par 00/00/1950
Liquidation completed
Each share Capital Stock no par received initial distribution of (0.023) share Portland Gas & Coke Co. Common no par and $0.95 cash 09/02/1953
Each share Capital Stock no par received second distribution of $1.44 cash 10/31/1955
Each share Capital Stock no par received third and final distribution of $0.95171 cash 10/23/1958
Note: Certificates were not required to be surrendered and are without value

AMERICAN PWR & WASTE MGMT INC (BC)
Recapitalized as Columbia Fuels Inc. 11/15/1994
Each share Common no par exchanged for (0.2) share Common no par
(See Columbia Fuels Inc.)

AMERICAN PWR CONVERSION CORP (MA)
Common 1¢ par split (5) for (4) by issuance of (0.25) additional share 06/01/1989
Common 1¢ par split (3) for (1) by issuance of (2) additional shares 09/28/1990
Common 1¢ par split (2) for (1) by issuance of (1) additional share 12/06/1991
Common 1¢ par split (2) for (1) by issuance of (1) additional share 12/17/1992
Common 1¢ par split (2) for (1) by issuance of (1) additional share 09/24/1993
Stock Dividend - 100% payable 05/28/1999 to holders of record 05/07/1999
Merged into Schneider Electric S.A. 02/14/2007
Each share Common 1¢ par exchanged for $31 cash

AMERICAN PWR CORP (NV)
SEC revoked common stock registration 02/02/2016

AMERICAN PWR TECH INC (NV)
Recapitalized as Black Art Beverage, Inc. 06/01/2009
Each share Common $0.001 par exchanged for (0.01) share Common $0.001 par
Black Art Beverage, Inc. recapitalized as VoxPop Worldwide, Inc. 12/15/2010 which name changed to Renovate Neighborhoods, Inc. 01/06/2014

AMERICAN PRECIOUS METALS INC (DE)
Name changed to American International Ventures, Inc. 02/06/2001

AMERICAN PRECISION INDS INC (DE)
Reincorporated 12/09/1986
Common $0.55555555 par changed to $1 par 04/26/1968
Common $1 par changed to $0.66666666 par and (0.5) additional share issued 10/06/1981
Common $0.66666666 par split (3) for (2) by issuance of (0.5) additional share 08/15/1984
Common $0.66666666 par split (3) for (2) by issuance of (0.5) additional share 06/20/1986
State of incorporation changed from (NY) to (DE) 12/09/1986
Stock Dividends - 20% 08/15/1978; 20% 06/10/1983; 10% 06/20/1985
Merged into Danaher Corp. 04/03/2000
Each share Common $0.66666666 par exchanged for $19.25 cash

AMERICAN PREFERRED CORP. (OK)
Completely liquidated 08/12/1965
Each share Common $1 par exchanged for first and final distribution of (0.05657) share Kennesaw Life & Accident Insurance Co. Common $1.25 par
Kennesaw Life & Accident Insurance Co. merged into Lykes-Youngstown Financial Corp. 11/14/1969 which name changed to LifeSurance Corp. 05/10/1971 which merged into Regan Holding Corp. 10/31/1991
(See Regan Holding Corp.)

AMERICAN PREMIER GROUP INC (OH)
Name changed to American Financial Group, Inc. 06/09/1995
American Financial Group, Inc. reorganized as a holding company under the same name 12/02/1997

AMERICAN PREMIER INSURANCE CO. (MN)
Stock Dividend - 25% 12/30/1960
Acquired by Northwestern National Insurance Co. 04/08/1963
Details not available

AMERICAN PREMIER UNDERWRITERS INC (PA)
Under plan of merger each share Common $1 par automatically became (1) share American Premier Group, Inc. Common $1 par 04/03/1995
American Premier Group, Inc. name changed to American Financial Group, Inc. 06/09/1995 which reorganized as a holding company under the same name 12/02/1997

AMERICAN PREMIERE FINL CORP (UT)
Involuntarily dissolved 11/01/1989

AMERICAN PRESIDENT COS LTD (DE)
Common 1¢ par split (3) for (2) by issuance of (0.5) additional share 05/30/1985
$3.50 Conv. Exchangeable Preferred Ser. B 1¢ par called for redemption 09/27/1989
Common 1¢ par split (2) for (1) by issuance of (1) additional share 01/28/1994
Name changed to APL Ltd. 06/01/1996
(See APL Ltd.)

AMERICAN PRESIDENT LINES LTD (DE)
5% Preferred $100 par called for redemption 09/15/1978
Merged into Natomas Co. 06/28/1979
Each share Class A no par exchanged for (5.42185) shares Common $1 par
Each share Class B $1 par exchanged for (1.08437) share Common $1 par
Natomas Co. merged into Diamond Shamrock Corp. 08/31/1983 which name changed to Maxus Energy Corp. 04/30/1987
(See Maxus Energy Corp.)

AMERICAN PRESIDENTS LIFE INS CO (MI)
Acquired by Hamilton International Corp. 12/31/1969
Each share Common $1 par exchanged for (0.25) share 4% Conv. Preferred $20 par
(See Hamilton International Corp.)

AMERICAN PRINCIPLE BK (SAN LUIS OBISPO, CA)
Name changed to American Perspective Bank (San Luis Obispo, CA) 07/19/2010
(See American Perspective Bank (San Luis Obispo, CA))

AMERICAN PRINTING CO.
Liquidated 00/00/1936
Details not available

AMERICAN PROCESS EQUIP CORP (NV)
Common Capital Stock $1 par changed to 50¢ par and (1) additional share issued 07/21/1969
Charter revoked for failure to file reports and pay fees 03/03/1975

AMERICAN PROD CORP (NV)
Recapitalized as American Capital Partners Ltd., Inc. 03/01/2004
Each share Common $0.001 par exchanged for (0.00166666) share Common $0.001 par
(See American Capital Partners Ltd., Inc.)

AMERICAN PRODUCTS CO.
Liquidated 00/00/1947
Details not available

AMERICAN PROFESSIONAL HLDG INC (UT)
Merged into Unison Healthcare Corp. 10/31/1996
Each share Common $0.001 par exchanged for (0.051) share Common $0.001 par
(See Unison Healthcare Corp.)

AMERICAN PROFESSIONAL SPORTS PRODS INC (UT)
Reorganized as Dyna Graphics International, Inc. 03/27/1975
Each share Class A Common 10¢ par exchanged for (1) share Common 1¢ par
(See Dyna Graphics International, Inc.)

AMERICAN PROGRAM BUR INC (MA)
Each share old Common 1¢ par

exchanged for (0.1) share new
Common 1¢ par 06/04/1987
Stock Dividend - 200% 11/16/1970
Merged into New American Program
Bureau, Inc. 02/13/1997
Each share new Common 1¢ par
exchanged for $0.01 cash

AMERICAN PPTY GROUP INC (DE)
Charter cancelled and declared
inoperative and void for
non-payment of taxes 03/01/1988

AMERICAN PROPERTY INVESTORS (CA)
Each Ser. V Unit exchanged for
(17.65) American Real Estate
Partners, L.P. Depositary Units
00/00/1987
Each Ser. VI Unit exchanged for
(20.05) American Real Estate
Partners, L.P. Depositary Units
00/00/1987
Each Ser. VIII Unit exchanged for
(14.85) American Real Estate
Partners, L.P. Depositary Units
00/00/1987
Each Ser. IX Unit exchanged for
(16.1) American Real Estate
Partners, L.P. Depositary Units
00/00/1987
Each Ser. X Unit exchanged for
(18.25) American Real Estate
Partners, L.P. Depositary Units
00/00/1987
Each Ser. XI Unit exchanged for
(22.7) American Real Estate
Partners, L.P. Units 00/00/1987
Each Ser. 82 Unit exchanged for
(19.1) American Real Estate
Partners, L.P. Depositary Units
00/00/1987
Each Ser. 83 Unit exchanged for
(18.1) American Real Estate
Partners, L.P. Depositary Units
00/00/1987

AMERICAN PROPERTY INVESTORS (CO)
Each Ser. II Unit exchanged for (55.5)
American Real Estate Partners, L.P.
Depositary Units 00/00/1987
Each Ser. III Unit exchanged for
(16.6) American Real Estate
Partners, L.P. Depositary Units
00/00/1987
Each Ser. IV Unit exchanged for
(16.1) American Real Estate
Partners, L.P. Depositary Units
00/00/1987
Each Ser. VII Unit exchanged for
(18.1) American Real Estate
Partners, L.P. Depositary Units
00/00/1987

AMERICAN PROPERTY INVESTORS I (DE)
Each Ser. I Unit exchanged for
(97.25) American Real Estate
Property, L.P. Depositary Units
00/00/1987

AMERICAN PROTECTORS INS CO. (UT)
Class A Common $10 par changed to
$2 par and (4) additional shares
issued 00/00/1965
Class A Common $2 par changed to
$1 par and (1) additional share
issued 00/00/1972
Liquidation completed 00/00/2001
No stockholders' equity

AMERICAN PROTN INDS INC (DE)
Each share Common 10¢ par
exchanged for (0.1) share Common
$1 par 06/21/1974
Merged into Corelo Services Corp.
02/17/1976
Each share Common $1 par
exchanged for $8.80 cash

AMERICAN PROVIDENT INVESTORS CORP. (DE)
Name changed to Servico, Inc.
04/22/1966
(See Servico, Inc.)

AMERICAN PUB ENERGY CO (TX)
Merged into AmQuest Corp.
09/15/1982
Each share Common 1¢ par
exchanged for (1) share Common
1¢ par
(See Amquest Corp.)

AMERICAN PUB HLDGS INC (MS)
Merged into American Fidelity Corp.
07/21/2000
Each share Common no par
exchanged for $16.64715 cash

AMERICAN PUB LIFE INS CO (MS)
Each share Class A Common $1 par
exchanged for (0.05) share Common
$20 par 07/10/1986
Stock Dividend - 10% 04/15/1966
Under plan of reorganization each
share Common $20 par
automatically became (1) share
American Public Holdings Inc.
Common no par 11/30/1996
(See American Public Holdings Inc.)

AMERICAN PUBG CO (DE)
Name changed to Hollinger
International Inc. 10/16/1995
Hollinger International Inc. name
changed to Sun-Times Media
Group, Inc. 07/14/2006
(See Sun-Times Media Group, Inc.)

AMERICAN PUBLIC LIFE INSURANCE CO. INC. (WI)
Each share Common 40¢ par
exchanged for (0.4) share Common
$1 par 7/15/65
Name changed to NN Investors Life
Insurance Co., Inc. 4/9/68
(See NN Investors Life Insurance Co., Inc.)

AMERICAN PUBLIC SERVICE CO.
Merged into Central & South West
Corp. in 1947
Each share 7% Preferred $100 par
exchanged for (9.1666) shares new
Common $5 par and $19.8916 in
cash
Each share Common $80 par
exchanged for (8) shares new
Common $5 par

AMERICAN PUBLIC UTILITIES CO.
Merged into Midland United Co.
00/00/1930
Details not available

AMERICAN PUBLIC WELFARE TRUST
Liquidated 00/00/1945
Details not available

AMERICAN PUDDLED IRON CO.
Dissolved 00/00/1939
Details not available

AMERICAN PULLEY CO. (PA)
Each share Capital Stock $50 par
exchanged for (4) shares Capital
Stock $12.50 par 00/00/1942
Merged into Van Norman Industries,
Inc. 04/30/1960
Each share Capital Stock $12.50 par
exchanged for (2) shares Common
$2.50 par
Van Norman Industries, Inc. merged
into Universal American Corp. (DE)
(Ctfs. dtd. prior to 01/12/1968)
01/31/1962 which merged into Gulf
& Western Industries, Inc. (DE)
01/12/1968
(See Gulf & Western Industries, Inc. (DE))

AMERICAN PULP EXCHANGE INC (FL)
Name changed to Penthouse
International, Inc. 11/18/2002
(See Penthouse International, Inc.)

AMERICAN PYRAMID COS INC (KY)
Merged into American Consolidated
Corp. 2/28/77
Each (3.925) shares 8% Non-Cum.
Conv. Preferred $5 par exchanged
for (1) share Common no par
Each (7.85) share Common no par
exchanged for (1) share Common
no par
American Consolidated Corp. merged
into I.C.H. Corp. 4/18/85 which
name changed to Southwestern Life
Corp. (New) 6/15/94 which name
changed to I.C.H. Corp. (New)
10/10/95
(See I.C.H. Corp. (New))

AMERICAN PYRAMID RES INC (BC)
Struck off register and declared
dissolved for failure to file returns
11/01/1991

AMERICAN QUANTUM CYCLES INC (FL)
Each share old Common $0.001 par
exchanged for (0.25) share new
Common $0.001 par 06/03/1999
Administratively dissolved for failure
to file annual reports 09/21/2001

AMERICAN QUASAR PETE CO (TX)
Common no par split (5) for (4) by
issuance of (0.25) additional share
02/07/1977
Common no par split (3) for (2) by
issuance of (0.5) additional share
07/03/1978
Common no par split (2) for (1) by
issuance of (1) additional share
12/01/1980
Reorganized under the laws of
Delaware as Wolverine Exploration
Co. 07/08/1987
Each share Common no par
exchanged for (0.005) share
Common 5¢ par
Wolverine Exploration Co. name
changed to Amerac Energy Corp.
03/17/1995 which merged into
Southern Mineral Corp. 01/28/1998
(See Southern Mineral Corp.)

AMERICAN RACEWAYS INC (DE)
Adjudicated bankrupt 01/10/1972
Stockholders' equity unlikely

AMERICAN RADIATOR & STANDARD SANITARY CORP. (DE)
Common no par changed to $5 par
04/24/1953
Name changed to American Standard
Inc. 06/01/1967
(See American Standard Inc.)

AMERICAN RADIATOR CO. (NJ)
Merged into American Radiator &
Standard Sanitary Corp. 03/26/1929
Details not available

AMERICAN RADIO & TELEVISION, INC. (AR)
Dissolved 08/01/1967
No stockholders' equity

AMERICAN RADIO EMPIRE INC (WY)
SEC revoked common stock
registration 10/28/2011

AMERICAN RADIO SYS CORP (DE)
Merged into American Tower Systems
Corp. 06/04/1998
Each share Class A Common 1¢ par
exchanged for (1) share Class A
Common 1¢ par and $44 cash
American Tower Systems Corp. name
changed to American Tower Corp.
(Old) 06/17/1998 which reorganized
as American Tower Corp. (New)
01/03/2012

AMERICAN RAILWAY EXPRESS CO.
Name changed to Railway & Express
Co. 03/00/1929
Railway & Express Co. merged into
Adams Express Co. (NY)
11/00/1929 which reincorporated in
Maryland 05/28/1976 which name
changed to Adams Diversified Equity
Fund, Inc. 03/31/2015

AMERICAN RAILWAY SUPPLY CO.
Dissolved in 1936
Details not available

AMERICAN RAILWAY TRUST SHARES
Liquidated in 1930
Details not available

AMERICAN RAILWAYS CO.
Acquired by American Railways Corp.
in 1933
Details not available

AMERICAN RAILWAYS CORP.
Liquidation completed in 1947
Details not available

AMERICAN RAND EXPANDED METALS CORP. (OK)
Name changed to Amerand, Inc.
5/30/68
(See Amerand, Inc.)

AMERICAN RAYON PRODUCTS CORP. (DE)
No longer in existence having
become inoperative and void for
non-payment of taxes 4/1/32

AMERICAN RE CAP
8.50% Guaranteed Quarterly Income
Preferred Securities called for
redemption at $25 on 2/21/2002

AMERICAN RE CORP (DE)
Acquired by a group of foreign
investors 11/25/1996
Each share Common 1¢ par
exchanged for $65 cash

AMERICAN RE INS CO (NY)
Each share Capital Stock $100 par
exchanged for (10) shares Capital
Stock $10 par 00/00/1928
Each share Capital Stock $10 par
exchanged for (2) shares Capital
Stock $5 par 00/00/1953
Capital Stock $5 par changed to $4
par and (0.25) additional share
issued 01/22/1969
Capital Stock $4 par changed to $3
par and (0.33333333) additional
share issued 02/26/1970
Capital Stock $3 par changed to
$1.50 par and (1) additional share
issued 05/09/1972
Stock Dividends - 100% 12/00/1945;
25% 01/26/1959; 10% 12/22/1961
Merged into Aetna Life & Casualty
Co. 08/07/1979
Each share Capital Stock $1.50 par
exchanged for $62 cash

AMERICAN REAL ESTATE INVT CORP (DE)
State of incorporation changed from
(DE) to (MD) 8/31/94
Name changed to Keystone Property
Trust 10/13/99
(See Keystone Property Trust)

AMERICAN REAL ESTATE INVESTMENTS (CA)
Charter suspended for failure to file
reports and pay fees 1/2/74

AMERICAN REAL ESTATE PARTNERS L P (DE)
Stock Dividends - In Preferred to
holders of Preferred 5% payable
03/31/2000 to holders of record
03/15/2000; 5% payable 04/02/2001
to holders of record 03/15/2001; 5%
payable 04/01/2002 to holders of
record 03/15/2002; 5% payable
03/31/2003 to holders of record
03/14/2003; 5% payable 03/31/2004
to holders of record 03/12/2004; 5%
payable 03/31/2005 to holders of
record 03/15/2005 Ex date -
03/11/2005; 5% payable 03/31/2006
to holders of record 03/15/2006
Ex date - 03/13/2006; 5% payable
03/30/2007 to holders of record
03/15/2007 Ex date - 03/13/2007
Name changed to Icahn Enterprises
L.P. 09/17/2007

AMERICAN REALTY & PETROLEUM CORP. (OK)
Name changed to AMREP Corp.
10/06/1967

AMERICAN RLTY CAP HEALTHCARE TR INC (MD)
Merged into Ventas, Inc. 01/16/2015
Each share Common 1¢ par

exchanged for (0.1688) share Common 25¢ par

AMERICAN RLTY CAP NEW YORK RECOVERY REIT INC (MD)
Name changed to New York REIT, Inc. 04/14/2014

AMERICAN RLTY CAP PPTYS INC (MD)
Name changed to VEREIT, Inc. 07/31/2015

AMERICAN RLTY CAP TR INC (MD)
Merged into Realty Income Corp. 01/22/2013
Each share Common 1¢ par exchanged for (0.2874) share Common $1 par and $0.35 cash

AMERICAN RLTY CAP TR III INC (MD)
Acquired by American Realty Capital Properties, Inc. 02/28/2013
Each share Common 1¢ par exchanged for (0.95) share Common 1¢ par
American Realty Capital Properties, Inc. name changed to VEREIT, Inc. 07/31/2015

AMERICAN RLTY CAP TR IV INC (MD)
Merged into American Realty Capital Properties, Inc. 01/03/2014
Each share Common 1¢ par exchanged for (0.5937) share 6.7% Preferred Ser. F 1¢ par, (0.519) share Common 1¢ par and $9 cash
American Realty Capital Properties, Inc. name changed to VEREIT, Inc. 07/31/2015

AMERICAN REALTY HOLDING CORP. (OH)
Merged into Franklin Capital Corp. (DE) 6/27/84
Each share Common $1 par exchanged for (1) share Common $1 par
(See Franklin Capital Corp. (DE))

AMERICAN RLTY MGMT SVCS CORP (GA)
Name changed to bib.net Corp. 06/15/1999
bib.net Corp. recapitalized as Obee's Franchise Systems, Inc. 10/29/2004
(See Obee's Franchise Systems, Inc.)

AMERICAN RLTY TR INC (GA)
Reorganized 06/24/1988
Reorganized from American Realty Trust (DC) to American Realty Trust, Inc. (GA) and Shares of Bene. Int. $1 par reclassified as Common $1 par 06/24/1988
Each share Common $1 par exchanged for (0.5) share Common $2 par 09/15/1989
Each share Common $2 par exchanged for (1/3) share Common 1¢ par 12/10/1990
Common 1¢ par split (2) for (1) by issuance of (1) additional share payable 01/12/1996 to holders of record 01/02/1996 Ex date - 01/16/1996
Preferred Stock Purchase Rights declared for Common stockholders of record 04/23/1990 were redeemed at $0.01 per 07/08/1996 for holders of record 06/21/1996
Common 1¢ par split (2) for (1) by issuance of (1) additional share payable 02/28/1997 to holders of record 02/17/1997 Ex date - 03/03/1997
Merged into American Realty Investors Inc. 08/02/2000
Each share Conv. Preferred Ser. F 1¢ par exchanged for (1) share Conv. Preferred Ser. A 1¢ par
Each share new Common 1¢ par exchanged for (0.91) share Common 1¢ par

AMERICAN REC CO HLDGS INC (DE)
Merged into Bell Sports Corp. 7/3/95
Each share Common 1¢ par exchanged for (0.689) share Common 1¢ par
(See Bell Sports Corp.)

AMERICAN REC CORP (DE)
Charter cancelled and declared inoperative and void for non-payment of taxes 4/15/72

AMERICAN REC CTRS INC (CA)
Capital Stock no par split (5) for (4) by issuance of (0.25) additional share 6/30/78
Capital Stock no par split (2) for (1) by issuance of (1) additional share 7/2/79
Capital Stock no par split (5) for (4) by issuance of (0.25) additional share 7/6/82
Capital Stock no par split (3) for (2) by issuance of (0.5) additional share 4/29/83
Capital Stock no par split (5) for (4) by issuance of (0.25) additional share 7/31/85
Capital Stock no par split (5) for (4) by issuance of (0.25) additional share 7/31/86
Stock Dividend - 10% 7/30/84
Merged into AMF Bowling Centers, Inc. 4/24/97
Each share Common no par exchanged for $8.50 cash

AMERICAN REC GROUP INC (DE)
Common $1 par split (2) for (1) by issuance of (1) additional share 6/19/72
Name changed to Exarg Corp. 12/9/75
(See Exarg Corp.)

AMERICAN REC SVCS INC (DE)
Charter revoked and declared inoperative and void for non-payment of taxes 03/01/1975

AMERICAN RECREATIONAL ENTERPRISES INC (NV)
Name changed to Bidville, Inc. 12/11/2003
Bidville, Inc. name changed to PrimEdge, Inc. 08/17/2006
(See PrimEdge, Inc.)

AMERICAN RECREATIONAL PPTYS INC (NM)
Charter revoked 01/22/2001

AMERICAN REENFORCED PAPER CO.
Name changed to American Sisalkraft Corp. in 1954

AMERICAN REGITEL CORP (DE)
Acquired by General Instrument Corp. (Incorporated 06/12/1967) 04/11/1974
Each share Common 10¢ par exchanged for (0.217) share Common $1 par
(See General Instrument Corp. (Incorporated 06/12/1967))

AMERICAN RELIANCE GROUP INC (NJ)
Name changed to ARI Holdings, Inc. 7/1/93
(See ARI Holdings, Inc.)

AMERICAN RENAISSANCE ASSOCIATES INC. (NY)
Charter revoked for failure to file reports and pay fees 12/15/43

AMERICAN RENT ALL INC (LA)
Charter revoked for failure to file annual reports 11/19/1990

AMERICAN REP BANCORP (CA)
Stock Dividends - 10% 11/30/87; 10% 3/31/89
Name changed to Republic Bank (Torrance, CA) 9/9/92
(See Republic Bank (Torrance, CA))

AMERICAN REP CORP (DE)
Name changed to Rush Industries, Inc. 04/15/1970
Rush Industries, Inc. name changed to Post American Corp. 05/08/1973
(See Post American Corp.)

AMERICAN REPROGRAPHICS CO (DE)
Issue Information - 13,350,000 shares COM offered at $13 per share on 02/03/2005
Name changed to ARC Document Solutions, Inc. 01/02/2013

AMERICAN REPUBLIC BANCSHARES, INC. (NM)
Merged into Norwest Corp. 01/06/1995
Details not available

AMERICAN REPUBLIC LIFE INSURANCE CO. (MS)
Name changed to American Public Life Insurance Co. 06/29/1962
American Public Life Insurance Co. reorganized as American Public Holdings Inc. 11/30/1996
(See American Public Holdings Inc.)

AMERICAN REPUBLICS CORP. (DE)
Liquidation completed 05/31/1955
Details not available

AMERICAN RESERVE INSURANCE CO. (NY)
Merged into American Re-Insurance Co. 12/31/1955
Each share Capital Stock $10 par exchanged for $81.14 cash

AMERICAN RESH & DEV CORP (MA)
Common $1 par split (3) for (1) by issuance of (2) additional shares 3/7/60
Common $1 par split (4) for (1) by issuance of (3) additional shares 8/29/69
Merged into Textron Inc. 5/18/72
Each share Common $1 par exchanged for (0.3) share Common 25¢ par

AMERICAN RESIDENTIAL FDG INC (NV)
Name changed to CJT Financial, Inc. 08/28/2008
CJT Financial, Inc. name changed to Gold & Silver Mining of Nevada, Inc. 09/20/2013 which recapitalized as Rainmaker Worldwide Inc. 06/15/2017

AMERICAN RESIDENTIAL HLDG CORP (DE)
Merged into Chamres, Inc. 9/8/94
Each share Common 1¢ par exchanged for $28.25 cash

AMERICAN RESIDENTIAL INVT TR INC (MD)
Name changed to AmNet Mortgage, Inc. 05/05/2004
(See AmNet Mortgage, Inc.)

AMERICAN RESIDENTIAL PPTYS INC (MD)
Merged into American Homes 4 Rent 02/29/2016
Each share Common 1¢ par exchanged for (1.135) Class A Common Shares of Bene. Int. 1¢ par

AMERICAN RESIDENTIAL SVCS INC (DE)
Merged into ServiceMaster Co. 04/27/1999
Each share Common $0.001 par exchanged for $5.75 cash

AMERICAN RESOURCE CORP. LTD. (BERMUDA)
Acquired by International Pagurian Corp. Ltd. 00/00/1988
Each share Class A Preference $0.001 par exchanged for (1) share Common no par
International Pagurian Corp. Ltd. name changed to Canadian Express Ltd. (Old) 05/12/1988 which recapitalized as Consolidated Canadian Express Ltd. 12/24/1990 which name changed to Canadian Express Ltd. (New) 05/18/2001 which recapitalized as BNN Investments Ltd. 11/02/2001 which name changed to BAM Investments Corp. 07/05/2006 which name changed to Partners Value Fund Inc. 06/10/2013 name changed to Partners Value Investments Inc. 05/25/2015 which reorganized as Partners Value Investments L.P. 07/04/2016

AMERICAN RESOURCE CORP (AB)
Delisted from Canadian Venture Stock Exchange 05/31/2000

AMERICAN RESOURCE INC (NV)
Each share old Common 1¢ par exchanged for (0.05) share new Common 1¢ par 03/04/1992
Each share new Common 1¢ par exchanged again for (0.1) share new Common 1¢ par 12/17/1993
Merged into Rea Gold Corp. 06/26/1996
Each share new Common 1¢ par exchanged for (2.47) shares Common no par
(See Rea Gold Corp.)

AMERICAN RESOURCE LTD (BERMUDA)
Acquired by Canadian Express International Ltd. 02/13/2014
Each share Non-Vtg. Class A $0.001 par exchanged for USD$0.6134 cash

AMERICAN RESOURCE MGMT INC (DE)
Each share old Common $0.0001 par exchanged for (0.005) share new Common $0.0001 par 02/01/2007
Name changed to EffTec International, Inc. 09/21/2007

AMERICAN RESOURCES, INC. (NV)
Charter revoked for failure to file reports and pay fees 03/04/1968

AMERICAN RES & DEV CO (UT)
SEC revoked common stock registration 11/08/2011

AMERICAN RES DEL INC (DE)
Each share Common 3¢ par exchanged for (0.25) share Common $0.00001 par 06/10/1994
Name changed to American Resources Offshore, Inc. 10/29/1998
American Resources Offshore, Inc. merged into Blue Dolpin Energy Co. 02/20/2002

AMERICAN RES INC (TX)
Charter forfeited for failure to pay taxes 08/22/1985

AMERICAN RES LTD (UT)
Reincorporated under the laws of Delaware as Resources International, Ltd. 12/21/1982
(See Resources International, Ltd.)

AMERICAN RES MGMT CORP (UT)
Reincorporated 4/12/77
Capital Stock $1 par changed to 50¢ par 12/20/73
State of incorporation changed from (DE) to (UT) 4/12/77
Capital Stock 50¢ par split (2) for (1) by issuance of (1) additional share 12/8/78
Proclaimed dissolved for failure to pay taxes 9/30/86

AMERICAN RES OFFSHORE INC (DE)
Merged into Blue Dolphin Energy Co. 02/20/2002
Each share 8% Conv. Preferred $12 par exchanged for (0.0301) share Common 1¢ par
Each share Common $0.00001 par exchanged for (0.0362) share Common 1¢ par

AMERICAN RESTAURANT CONCEPTS INC (FL)
Each share old Class A Common 1¢ par exchanged for (0.14285714) share new Class A Common 1¢ par 11/04/2013
Reincorporated under the laws of Nevada as ARC Group Inc. 07/23/2014

AMERICAN RESTAURANT MGMT INC (UT)
Recapitalized as Global Web, Inc. 03/12/1999
Each share Common $0.001 par exchanged for (0.01) share Common $0.001 par

AMERICAN RESTAURANTS CORP (CA)
Name changed to Hudson's Grill of America, Inc. 06/14/1991
(See Hudson's Grill of America, Inc.)

AMERICAN RESV CORP (DE)
Common $2 par split (3) for (2) by issuance of (0.5) additional share 04/30/1970
Stock Dividends - 50% 03/31/1969; 100% 03/31/1972
Chapter XI converted to Chapter 7 Bankruptcy Act 11/17/1981
No stockholders' equity

AMERICAN RESV ENERGY CORP (AB)
Name changed to bcMetals Corp. 05/28/2003
(See bcMetals Corp.)

AMERICAN RESV MNG CORP (BC)
Recapitalized as AMI Resources Inc. 12/21/1994
Each share Common no par exchanged for (0.0625) share Common no par
AMI Resources Inc. name changed to Ashanti Sankofa Inc. 01/19/2017

AMERICAN RETIREMENT CORP (TN)
Merged into Brookdale Senior Living Inc. 07/25/2006
Each share Common 1¢ par exchanged for $33 cash

AMERICAN RETIREMENT VILLAS PPTYS L P (CA)
Units of Ltd. Partnership terminated 10/00/1995
Details not available
Merged into ARVP III Acquistion, L.P. 07/00/2004
Each Unit of Ltd. Partnership III exchanged for $400 cash
Merged into ARVP II Acquistion, L.P. 09/28/2004
Each Unit of Ltd. Partnership II exchanged for $400 cash

AMERICAN RICE INC (DE)
Merged into SOS Cuetara S.A. 12/31/2003
Each share Common 1¢ par exchanged for $7.43 cash
Note: $0.88 cash per share was withheld to cover tax liabliities
U.S citizens and residents who did not submit a FIRPTA Affidavit for Entities prior to 01/16/2004 will be required to apply to the IRS for a refund of any distribution(s)
Each share Common 1¢ par received initial distribution of approximately $0.0398 cash 12/04/2009

AMERICAN RICE INC (TX)
Each share old Common $1 par exchanged for (0.2) share new Common $1 par 09/08/1994
Plan of reorganization under Chapter 11 Federal Bankruptcy Code effective 10/01/1999
No stockholders' equity

AMERICAN RICE PRODUCTS CO. (DE)
No longer in existence having become inoperative and void for non-payment of taxes 04/01/1928

AMERICAN RIDING TOURS INC (NV)
Name changed to First Harvest Corp. 07/28/2016
First Harvest Corp. name changed to Arias Intel Corp. 12/01/2017

AMERICAN RISK MGMT GROUP INC (FL)
Each share old Common $0.001 par exchanged for (0.04) share new Common $0.001 par 07/13/2000
Name changed to Comprehensive Medical Diagnostics Group Inc. 07/21/2000
Comprehensive Medical Diagnostics Group Inc. recapitalized as My Vintage Baby, Inc. 06/01/2007
(See My Vintage Baby, Inc.)

AMERICAN RIV BK (SACRAMENTO, CA)
Common no par split (2) for (1) by issuance of (1) additional share 03/30/1990
Common no par split (6) for (5) by issuance of (0.2) additional share 03/29/1991
Under plan of reorganization each share Common no par automatically became (1) share American River Holdings Common no par 06/16/1995
American River Holdings name changed to American River Bankshares 06/02/2004

AMERICAN RIV HLDGS (CA)
Common no par split (3) for (2) by issuance of (0.5) additional share payable 10/31/2003 to holders of record 10/17/2003 Ex date - 11/03/2003
Stock Dividends - 5% payable 10/22/1997 to holders of record 10/08/1997; 5% payable 10/21/1998 to holders of record 10/07/1998; 5% payable 10/14/1999 to holders of record 09/29/1999; 5% payable 12/19/2000 to holders of record 12/04/2000 Ex date - 11/30/2000; 5% payable 10/19/2001 to holders of record 10/05/2001 Ex date - 10/03/2001; 5% payable 10/18/2002 to holders of record 10/04/2002
Name changed to American River Bankshares 06/02/2004

AMERICAN RIVS OIL CO (WY)
Each share Common 1¢ par received distribution of (0.25) share Bishop Capital Corp. Common 1¢ par payable 06/20/1997 to holders of record 11/18/1996
Merged into AROC Inc. 12/08/1999
Each share Common 1¢ par exchanged for (0.11) share Common 1¢ par
(See AROC Inc.)

AMERICAN ROAD MACHINERY CORP.
Assets liquidated for benefit of creditors 00/00/1932
No stockholders' equity

AMERICAN ROCK WOOL CORP. (IN)
Each share Common no par exchanged for (3) shares Common $5 par 00/00/1950
Assets sold to United States Gypsum Co. (IL) 07/01/1959 and initial liquidating distribution of (2017/8788) share Common $4 par for each share Common $5 par made 08/11/1959
Each share Common $5 par exchanged for second and final liquidating distribution of $0.129837 cash 10/24/1961
United States Gypsum Co. (IL) reorganized in Delaware 06/30/1966 which reorganized as USG Corp. 01/01/1985

AMERICAN ROLLING MILL CO.
Name changed to Armco Steel Corp. 00/00/1948
Armco Steel Corp. name changed to Armco Inc. 07/01/1978 which merged into AK Steel Holding Corp. 09/30/1999

AMERICAN ROYALTY TRUST
Completely liquidated 12/31/1979
Each Trust Certificate exchanged for first and final distribution of 14% of the face value

AMERICAN RTY TR (TX)
Trust terminated 12/22/1987
Each Ctf. of Bene. Int. no par exchanged for $8.56 cash

AMERICAN RUBR & PLASTICS CORP (IN)
Name changed to ARP Corp. 03/01/1976
(See ARP Corp.)

AMERICAN SAFETY CLOSURE CORP (NY)
Common 1¢ par split (2) for (1) by issuance of (1) additional share 08/29/1986
Each share Common 1¢ par exchanged for (0.33333333) share Common 3¢ par 01/23/1990
Each share Common 3¢ par exchanged for (0.1) share Common 30¢ par 08/31/1992
Merged into Seda Specialty Packaging Corp. 07/15/1996
Each share Common 30¢ par exchanged for (0.125) share Common no par
(See Seda Specialty Packaging Corp.)

AMERICAN SAFETY EQUIP CORP (NY)
Common 25¢ par split (3) for (1) by issuance of (2) additional shares 12/20/1962
Common 25¢ par split (2) for (1) by issuance of (1) additional share 04/28/1965
Merged into Marmon Group, Inc. 07/28/1978
Each share Common 25¢ par exchanged for $10.50 cash

AMERICAN SAFETY INS HLDS LTD (BERMUDA)
Name changed 06/20/2003
Name changed from American Safety Insurance Group, Ltd. to American Safety Insurance Holdings, Ltd. 06/20/2003
Acquired by Fairfax Holdings Ltd. 10/03/2013
Each share Common 1¢ par exchanged for CAD$30.25 cash

AMERICAN SAFETY RAZOR CO (DE)
Merged into RSA Holdings Corp. of Delaware 07/01/1999
Each share Common 1¢ par exchanged for $14.20 cash

AMERICAN SAFETY RAZOR CORP. (VA)
Capital Stock $100 par changed to no par 00/00/1926
Each share Capital Stock no par exchanged for (3) shares Capital Stock $18.50 par 00/00/1936
Each share Capital Stock $18.50 par exchanged for (3) shares Capital Stock $5 par 00/00/1946
Name changed to A.S.R. Products Corp. 07/01/1957
A.S.R. Products Corp. acquired by Morris (Philip), Inc. 05/03/1960 which reorganized as Morris (Philip) Companies Inc. 07/01/1985 which name changed to Altria Group, Inc. 01/27/2003

AMERICAN SAFETY TABLE CO., INC. (PA)
Common 10¢ par reclassified as Class A 10¢ par 02/18/1963
Stock Dividends - 50% 03/26/1965; 20% 03/29/1966
Completely liquidated 08/21/1967
Each share Class A 10¢ par exchanged for first and final distribution of (0.061896) share Teledyne, Inc. $3.50 Conv. Preferred $1 par
(See Teledyne, Inc.)

AMERICAN SAINT GOBAIN CORP (DE)
Name changed to ASG Industries, Inc. and Common $7.50 par changed to $1 par 08/04/1970
ASG Industries, Inc. name changed to AFG Industries, Inc. 10/22/1979
(See AFG Industries, Inc.)

AMERICAN SALAMANDRA CORP.
Dissolved 00/00/1934
Details not available

AMERICAN SALES BOOK CO. LTD.
Merged into Moore Corp. Ltd. 00/00/1928
Details not available

AMERICAN SALT CORP. (DE)
99.55% held by Cudahy Corp. as of 02/08/1972
Public interest eliminated

AMERICAN SASH-WEIGHT FOUNDRY CO. (IA)
Charter cancelled for failure to file annual reports 04/04/1927

AMERICAN SATELLITE & TELEVISION INC (FL)
Name changed to American Communications & Television, Inc. 03/04/1983
(See American Communications & Television, Inc.)

AMERICAN SVGS & LN ASSN (CA)
Placed in receivership 09/12/1988
No stockholders' equity

AMERICAN SVGS & LN ASSN (UT)
Perm. Reserve Guarantee Class A $1 par reclassified as Perm. Reserve Guarantee $0.33333333 par and (2) additional shares issued 11/27/1962
Placed in receivership 02/17/1989
No stockholders' equity

AMERICAN SVGS & LN ASSN FLA (FL)
Capital Stock $1.50 par reclassified as old Common $1.50 par 12/16/1976
Old Common $1.50 par changed to 50¢ par and (2) additional shares issued 01/16/1978
Old Common 50¢ par split (2) for (1) by issuance of (1) additional share 05/02/1983
Stock Dividend - 10% 11/15/1979
Acquired by Kinder-Care, Inc. 04/29/1988
Each share old Common 50¢ par exchanged for $17 cash
Under plan of reorganization name changed to American Savings of Florida, F.S.B. 05/14/1991
American Savings of Florida, F.S.B. acquired by First Union Corp. 07/01/1995 which name changed to Wachovia Corp. (Ctfs. dated after 09/01/2001) 09/01/2001 which merged into Wells Fargo & Co. (New) 12/31/2008

AMERICAN SVGS & LN ASSN HOUSTON (TX)
Permanent Reserve Fund Stock $1 par changed to no par 02/16/1970
Permanent Reserve Fund Stock no par split (2) for (1) by issuance of (1) additional share 03/16/1970
Merged into Penncorp Financial, Inc. 09/14/1979
Each share Permanent Reserve Fund Stock no par exchanged for $4.537 cash
Note: An additional payment of $0.992090 cash per share was made 09/23/1983

AMERICAN SVGS & LN ASSN WATERBURY (CT)
Name changed to American Bank of

Connecticut (Waterbury, CT) 09/01/1982
(See American Bank of Connecticut (Waterbury, CT))

AMERICAN SAVINGS BANK, F.S.B. (TACOMA, WA)
Stock Dividend - 15% 01/16/1987
Under plan of reorganization each share Common $1 par automatically became (1) share American Savings Financial Corp. Common $1 par 06/01/1987
American Savings Financial Corp. merged into BankAmerica Corp. (Old) 12/01/1989 which merged into BankAmerica Corp. (New) 09/30/1998 which name changed to Bank of America Corp. 04/28/1999

AMERICAN SVGS BK (NEW YORK, NY)
Name changed 12/29/1989
Name changed from American Savings Bank FSB (New York, NY) to American Savings Bank (New York, NY) 12/29/1989
Placed in receivership with FDIC 06/12/1992
No stockholders' equity

AMERICAN SVGS BK (SOUTH CHICAGO HEIGHTS, IL)
Stock Dividend - 66-2/3% 03/05/1971
Name changed to American National Bank (South Chicago Heights, IL) 01/02/1974
(See American National Bank (South Chicago Heights, IL))

AMERICAN SVGS BK (TAMAQUA, PA)
Acquired by Keystone Financial, Inc. 10/31/1994
Each share Common $1 par exchanged for $19.69 cash

AMERICAN SVGS FINL CORP (WA)
Merged into BankAmerica Corp. (Old) 12/01/1989
Each share Common $1 par exchanged for (1.0539) shares Common $1.5625 par
BankAmerica Corp. (Old) merged into BankAmerica Corp. (New) 09/30/1998 which name changed to Bank of America Corp. 04/28/1999

AMERICAN SVGS FLA FSB (FL)
$2.19 Conv. Preferred Ser. A 1¢ par called for redemption 12/30/1992
Each share old Common 50¢ par exchanged for (0.2) share new Common 50¢ par 04/27/1993
Acquired by First Union Corp. 07/01/1995
Each share new Common 50¢ par exchanged for (0.4626) share Common $3.33333333 par
First Union Corp. name changed to Wachovia Corp. (Ctfs. dated after 09/01/2001) 09/01/2001 which merged into Wells Fargo & Co. (New) 12/31/2008

AMERICAN SCANTIC LINE, INC. (DE)
Name changed to Moore-McCormack Lines, Inc. 09/16/1938
Moore-McCormack Lines, Inc. name changed to Moore & McCormack Co., Inc. 02/25/1965 which name changed to Moore McCormack Resources Inc. 02/08/1974
(See Moore McCormack Resources Inc.)

AMERICAN SCIENCE & ENGR INC (MA)
Common $0.66666666 par split (3) for (2) by issuance of (0.5) additional share 04/30/1973
Common $0.66666666 par split (7) for (4) by issuance of (0.75) additional share 07/15/1975
Common $0.66666666 par split (2) for (1) by issuance of (1) additional share 03/01/1976

Acquired by OSI Systems, Inc. 09/09/2016
Each share Common $0.66666666 par exchanged for $37 cash

AMERICAN SCIENTIFIC, INC. (DE)
Name changed to Scientific Industries, Inc. 05/16/1955

AMERICAN SCIENTIFIC CORP. (VA)
Common $1 par changed to 50¢ par 12/12/1962
Adjudicated bankrupt 11/28/1966
No stockholders' equity

AMERICAN SCIENTIFIC INDS INTL (UT)
Involuntarily dissolved 12/31/1985

AMERICAN SCREEN CO (DE)
Charter cancelled and declared inoperative and void for non-payment of taxes 03/01/1991

AMERICAN SCREW CO. (RI)
Common $100 par changed to $25 par 00/00/1933
Stock Dividend - 100% 03/28/1946
Assets sold to Noma Lites, Inc. on a (7) for (1) basis 04/04/1960
Noma Lites, Inc. name changed to Noma Corp. 07/24/1962 which was merged into Ward Foods, Inc. 05/22/1964
(See Ward Foods, Inc.)

AMERICAN SCRUBBING & EQUIPMENT CO.
Succeeded by Finnell System, Inc. 00/00/1928
Details not available

AMERICAN SEAL-KAP CORP. OF DELAWARE (DE)
Common no par changed to $2 par 00/00/1936
5% Preferred 2nd Ser. $100 par called for redemption 04/14/1964
5% Preferred 3rd Ser. $100 par called for redemption 04/14/1964
5% Preferred 4th Ser. $100 par called for redemption 04/14/1964
Name changed to AMK Corp. 05/20/1965
AMK Corp. merged into United Brands Co. 06/30/1970 which name changed to Chiquita Brands International, Inc. 03/20/1990
(See Chiquita Brands International, Inc.)

AMERICAN SEALANTS CO. (CT)
Stock Dividend - 100% 02/01/1963
Name changed to Loctite Corp. (CT) 07/16/1963
Loctite Corp. (CT) reincorporated in Delaware 05/13/1988
(See Loctite Corp.)

AMERICAN SEALCONE CO., INC.
Dissolved 00/00/1933
Details not available

AMERICAN SEALCONE CORP. (NY)
Each share Common $1 par exchanged for (0.1) share Common $5 par 00/00/1933
Each share Common $5 par exchanged for (0.1) share Common 10¢ par 00/00/1946
Dissolved by proclamation 06/23/1993

AMERICAN SEATING CO (DE)
Reincorporated 04/29/1966
Each share Common no par exchanged for (2) shares Common $10 par 00/00/1952
State of incorporation changed from (NJ) to (DE) 04/29/1966
Common $10 par changed to $5 par and (1) additional share issued 05/18/1966
Stock Dividends - 10% 12/14/1949; 20% 12/18/1950
Acquired by Fuqua Industries, Inc. 01/19/1983
Each share Common $5 par exchanged for (0.9135) share Common $1 par
Fuqua Industries, Inc. name changed

to Actava Group Inc. 07/21/1993 which name changed to Metromedia International Group, Inc. 11/01/1995
(See Metromedia International Group, Inc.)

AMERICAN SEC & TR CO (WASHINGTON, DC)
(Units issued only in Non-Separable Units of (1) share American Security & Trust Co. (Washington, DC) Capital Stock $3.33-1/3 par and (1) share American Security Corp. (Old) Common 66-2/3¢ par)
Each share Capital Stock $100 par exchanged for (10) shares Capital Stock $10 par 00/00/1948
Capital Stock $10 par changed to $3.33-1/3 par and (2) additional shares issued 01/29/1964
Stock Dividends - 10% 01/22/1954; 10% 01/18/1962; 10% 04/28/1972
Merged into American Security Corp. (New) 04/01/1976
Each Unit exchanged for (1) share Common $4 par
American Security Corp. (New) merged into Maryland National Corp. 03/16/1987 which name changed to MNC Financial, Inc. 04/29/1987 which merged into NationsBank Corp. 10/01/1993 which reincorporated in Delaware as BankAmerica Corp. (Old) 09/25/1998 which merged into BankAmerica Corp. (New) 09/30/1998 which name changed to Bank of America Corp. 04/28/1999

AMERICAN SEC BK (HONOLULU, HI)
Capital Stock $5 par changed to $10 par 05/03/1973
Name changed to First Interstate Bank of Hawaii (Honolulu, HI) 04/11/1983
First Interstate Bank of Hawaii (Honolulu, HI) reorganized as First Interstate of Hawaii Inc. 12/31/1985
(See First Interstate of Hawaii Inc.)

AMERICAN SEC CORP NEW (DC)
Common $4 par changed to $3 par and (1) additional share issued 05/15/1978
Common $3 par changed to $1.50 par and (1) additional share issued 05/24/1982
Common $1.50 par changed to $1 par and (0.5) additional share issued 05/25/1984
Merged into Maryland National Corp. 03/16/1987
Each share Common $1 par exchanged for (0.81) share Common $2.50 par
Maryland National Corp. name changed to MNC Financial, Inc. 04/29/1987 which merged into NationsBank Corp. 10/01/1993 which reincorporated in Delaware as BankAmerica Corp. (Old) 09/25/1998 which merged into BankAmerica Corp. (New) 09/30/1998 which name changed to Bank of America Corp. 04/28/1999 and American Security Corp. (Old)

AMERICAN SEC INVT CO (SC)
Preferred $100 par called for redemption 08/23/1968
Name changed to Brigadier Industries Corp. (SC) and Common $2 par changed to 50¢ par 03/05/1969
Brigadier Industries Corp. (SC) merged into Town & Country Mobile Homes, Inc. 09/02/1981 which name changed to Brigadier Industries Corp. (TX) 04/05/1982 which merged into U.S. Home Corp. (Old) 01/07/1983 which reorganized as U.S. Home Corp. (New) 06/21/1993 which merged into Lennar Corp. 05/02/2000

AMERICAN SEC LIFE INS CO (IL)
Each share Common 20¢ par

exchanged for (0.2) share Common $1 par 11/07/1966
Merged into Reserve Life Insurance Co. 12/31/1969
Details not available

AMERICAN SEC LIFE INS CO (TX)
Merged into American National Insurance Co. 06/29/1990
Each share Common $1 par exchanged for $16.116 cash

AMERICAN SECS INC (DE)
Name changed to Pan American Securities, Inc. 08/31/1998

AMERICAN SECURITY CORP. OLD (DC)
(Units issued in Non-Separable Units of (1) share American Security & Trust Co. (Washington, DC) Capital Stock $3.33-1/3 par and (1) share American Security Corp. (Old) Common 66-2/3¢ par)
Common $2 par changed to 66-2/3¢ par and (2) additional shares issued 01/29/1964
Stock Dividends - 10% 01/18/1962; 10% 04/28/1972
(See American Security & Trust Co. (Washington, DC))

AMERICAN SECURITY LIFE INSURANCE CO. (AL)
Merged into American Life Insurance Co. 00/00/1931
Details not available

AMERICAN SECURITY LIFE INSURANCE CO. (IN)
Merged into Wabash Life Insurance Co. on a (1) for (1.2857143) basis 10/30/1964
Wabash Life Insurance Co. name changed to Wabash International Corp. 12/28/1967
(See Wabash International Corp.)

AMERICAN SEEDING MACHINE CO.
Merged into Oliver Farm Equipment Co. 00/00/1929
Details not available

AMERICAN SELECT PORTFOLIO INC (MN)
Merged into Diversified Real Asset Income Fund 09/08/2014
Each share Common 1¢ par exchanged for (0.590315) Common Share of Bene. Int. 1¢ par
Diversified Real Asset Income Fund merged into Nuveen Real Asset Income & Growth Fund 09/11/2017

AMERICAN SELF SVC STORES INC (MO)
Stock Dividend - 20% 11/15/1968
Acquired by Volume Shoe Corp. 05/07/1971
Each share Common no par exchanged for $14 cash

AMERICAN SENSORS INC (ON)
Common no par split (2) for (1) by issuance of (1) additional share 01/04/1995
Company placed in receivership 09/15/1997
No stockholders' equity

AMERICAN SENTINEL LIFE INSURANCE CO. (SC)
Common $1 par reclassified as Class A 25¢ par 04/29/1971
Merged into American Foundation Life Insurance Co. 01/05/1981
Each share Class A 25¢ par exchanged for $5 cash
Each share Class B 25¢ par exchanged for $5 cash

AMERICAN SERVICE CO. (MD)
Common no par changed to $1 par 00/00/1941
Recapitalized 12/31/1959
Each share $3 Preferred no par exchanged for $100 principal amount of 4-1/2% Debentures due 10/01/1979

Merged into Southland Corp. (TX) 04/27/1966
Each share Class A no par or Common $1 par exchanged for (0.666667) share Common 1¢ par
Southland Corp. (TX) name changed to 7-Eleven Inc. 04/28/1999
(See 7-Eleven Inc.)

AMERICAN SVC CORP (DE)
Merged into Service Control Corp. 04/16/1987
Each share Common 10¢ par exchanged for $37 cash

AMERICAN SVC INDS INC (DE)
Charter cancelled and declared inoperative and void for non-payment of taxes 3/1/79

AMERICAN SERVICE LIFE INSURANCE CO. (OK)
Merged into Mid-America Life Insurance Co. on a (1.1) for (1) basis 12/27/1960
Mid-America Life Insurance Co. merged into National Empire Life Insurance Co. 01/01/1965 which merged into Empire Life Insurance Co. of America (AL) 06/30/1966
(See Empire Life Insurance Co. of America (AL))

AMERICAN SERVICE PUBLISHING CO., INC. (VA)
Charter revoked for failure to file reports and pay fees 6/1/67

AMERICAN SEWING MACHINE BUYERS COOPERATIVE (UT)
Proclaimed dissolved for failure to pay taxes 12/9/74

AMERICAN SHIP & COMMERCE CORP.
Assets sold in 1941
No stockholders' equity

AMERICAN SHIP BLDG CO (NJ)
Common $100 par changed to no par and $40 cash paid 00/00/1930
Common no par split (5) for (1) by issuance of (4) additional shares 11/01/1960
Common no par split (2) for (1) by issuance of (1) additional share 04/07/1966
Common no par changed to $1 par 09/26/1968
Common $1 par split (3) for (2) by issuance of (0.5) additional share 01/14/1977
5% Conv. Preferred Ser. A $1 par called for redemption 06/30/1980
Common $1 par split (3) for (2) by issuance of (0.5) additional share 11/20/1980
Stock Dividend - 20% 02/26/1978
Plan of reorganization under Chapter 11 Federal Bankruptcy proceedings effective 01/03/1996
Each share Common $1 par exchanged for pro rata share of $400,000 cash
Note: Holders also retained the right to receive a pro rata distribution of funds held in reserve bond account

AMERICAN SHIP INC (UT)
Name changed to Petshealth, Inc. (UT) 05/20/1998
(See Petshealth, Inc.)

AMERICAN SHOE MACHINERY & TOOL CO.
Acquired by Landis Machine Co. (MO) in 1944
Details not available

AMERICAN SHOPPING CENTERS, INC. (DE)
Recapitalized 02/29/1960
Each share Class A Common 10¢ par exchanged for (1.5) shares Preferred Ser. A $1 par and (1.1) shares Class A Common 1¢ par
Each share Class B Common 10¢ par exchanged for (0.005) share Class A Common 1¢ par

Name changed to United States Baking Co., Inc. 01/29/1965
United States Baking Co., Inc. name changed to Mareight Corp. 12/27/1967
(See Mareight Corp.)

AMERICAN SIDEWINDER OIL CORP (BC)
Recapitalized as Texas Sidewinder Oil Corp. 11/23/1992
Each share Common no par exchanged for (0.33333333) share Common no par
Texas Sidewinder Oil Corp. name changed to Archon Minerals Ltd. 05/29/1995

AMERICAN SILICA CORP.
Reorganized as American Silica Sand Co. in 1931
Details not available

AMERICAN SILICA SAND CO. (DE)
Reorganized as American Silica Sand Co. Inc. 6/25/53
No Common stockholders' equity

AMERICAN SILICA SAND CO (DE)
Merged into Ottawa Silica Co. 3/19/69
Each share Class A Common $1 par exchanged for $1.28 cash

AMERICAN SILVER CO.
Liquidated 00/00/1935
Details not available

AMERICAN SILVER CORP. (NV)
Bankrupt 00/00/1948
Details not available

AMERICAN SILVER GOLD URANIUM CORP (ID)
Name changed to Nuclear Silver Corp. and Common 10¢ par changed to 1¢ par 4/6/71
Nuclear Silver Corp. reincorporated in Delaware as Technimed Corp. 1/6/84
(See Technimed Corp.)

AMERICAN SKIING CO (DE)
Reincorporated 10/13/1999
State of incorporation changed from (ME) to (DE) 10/13/1999
Voluntarily dissolved 09/13/2007
No stockholders' equity

AMERICAN SMLT & REFNG CO (NJ)
Each share Common $100 par exchanged for (8) shares Common no par 00/00/1928
Common no par split (2) for (1) by issuance of (1) additional share 05/28/1964
Common no par split (2) for (1) by issuance of (1) additional share 03/14/1969
Stock Dividends - 20% 12/23/1947; 100% 11/30/1951; 33.333333% 08/08/1968
Name changed to Asarco Inc. 04/23/1975
(See Asarco Inc.)

AMERICAN SNACKS INC (DE)
Stock Dividend - 100% 6/28/68
Under plan of merger each share Common 10¢ par exchanged for $5 principal amount of Variable Rate Senior Subord. Debentures due 1999 or $5 cash 5/4/81

AMERICAN SNUFF CO. (NJ)
Each share Common $100 par exchanged for (4) shares Common $25 par in 1929
Common $25 par changed to $8-1/3 par and (2) additional shares issued 5/25/62
Name changed to Conwood Corp. (NJ) 7/1/66
Conwood Corp. (NJ) reorganized in Delaware 12/1/66
(See Conwood Corp.)

AMERICAN SODA CO. (AZ)
Charter expired 7/12/32

AMERICAN SOFTWARE TECHNOLOGY INC (FL)
Each share old Common $0.0001 par exchanged for (0.2) share new Common $0.0001 par 8/25/86
Proclaimed dissolved for failure to file reports and pay fees 11/16/87

AMERICAN SOLAR KING CORP (TX)
Common no par split (2) for (1) by issuance of (1) additional share 01/25/1983
Common no par split (3) for (2) by issuance of (0.5) additional share 06/20/1983
Name changed to Ask Corp. 11/23/1988
(See Ask Corp.)

AMERICAN SOLVENTS & CHEMICAL CORP.
Properties and assets transferred to Rossville Alcohol & Chemical Corp. under
Plan of Reorganization 00/00/1932
Details not available
(See Rossville Alcohol & Chemical Corp.)

AMERICAN SOUND CORP (MN)
Statutorily dissolved 10/07/1991

AMERICAN SOUTH AFRICAN INVT LTD (SOUTH AFRICA)
Common ZAR 2 par changed to ZAR 1 par and (1) additional share issued 05/27/1966
Name changed to ASA Ltd. (South Africa) and Common ZAR 1 par changed to ZAR 50 par 05/10/1973
ASA Ltd. (South Africa) reincorporated in Bermuda 11/19/2004 which name changed to ASA Gold & Precious Metals Ltd. 03/28/2011

AMERICAN SOUTHWEST BANCSHARES, INC. (TX)
Merged into Sunwest Financial Services, Inc. 01/12/1988
Each share Common $5 par exchanged for $38 cash

AMERICAN SOUTHWEST DISTR INC (DE)
Name changed to Petro America Corp. 06/12/2009

AMERICAN SOUTHWEST HLDGS INC (DE)
Company terminated common stock registration and is no longer public as of 12/13/2006

AMERICAN SOUTHWEST MTG INVTS CORP (MD)
Name changed to ASR Investments Corp. 06/23/1992
ASR Investments Corp. merged into United Dominion Realty Trust, Inc. (VA) 03/27/1998 which reincorporated in Maryland 06/11/2003 which name changed to UDR, Inc. 03/14/2007

AMERICAN SPECIALTY FOODS INC (DE)
Acquired by CAC Corp. 01/16/1989
Each share Common 1¢ par exchanged for $332 cash

AMERICAN SPECTRUM MARKETING CORP (CA)
Name changed to Castle View Equine Center, Inc. 06/17/1986
(See Castle View Equine Center, Inc.)

AMERICAN SPIRIT CORP (DE)
Charter cancelled and declared inoperative and void for non-payment of taxes 03/01/1991

AMERICAN SPL FD INC (DE)
Merged into Growth Fund of America, Inc. (DE) 08/31/1976
Each share Common $1 par exchanged for (1.292) shares Common 10¢ par
Growth Fund of America, Inc. (DE) reincorporated in Maryland

09/22/1983 which reorganized in Delaware 05/01/2013

AMERICAN SPORTS ADVISORS INC (NY)
Each share old Common 1¢ par exchanged for (0.1) share new Common 1¢ par 01/08/1990
Dissolved by proclamation 06/26/1996

AMERICAN SPORTS DEV GROUP INC (DE)
SEC revoked common stock registration 02/03/2010

AMERICAN SPORTS HISTORY INC (NV)
Each share old Common $0.001 par exchanged for (0.1) share new Common $0.001 par 05/16/1997
Company terminated common stock registration and is no longer public as of 05/22/2008

AMERICAN SPORTS MACH INC (FL)
Reincorporated under the laws of Delaware as Softquad Software Ltd. 04/11/2000
Softquad Software Ltd. merged into Corel Corp. 03/15/2002
(See Corel Corp.)

AMERICAN SPRING & MANUFACTURING CORP. (DE)
Name changed to American Spring of Holly, Inc. 00/00/1944
(See American Spring of Holly, Inc.)

AMERICAN SPRING OF HOLLY, INC. (DE)
Stock Dividend - 10% 12/30/1953
Liquidation completed 09/15/1961
Details not available

AMERICAN SR BENEFITS INC (MN)
Name changed to Orlando Supercard, Inc. 04/09/1997

AMERICAN ST BK (LUBBOCK, TX)
Merged into American State Financial Corp. 12/31/1978
Each share Capital Stock $100 par exchanged for (1) share Common $10 par
American State Financial Corp. merged into Prosperity Bancshares, Inc. 07/01/2012

AMERICAN ST BK (NEWPORT BEACH, CA)
Reorganized 12/26/1974
Location changed from Orange, CA to Newport Beach, CA 12/26/1974
Common $2.50 par changed to $1.25 par and (1) additional share issued 07/11/1978
Stock Dividends - 10% 06/16/1980; 10% 06/16/1981
Name changed to American Interstate Bank (Newport Beach, CA) 11/17/1984
(See American Interstate Bank (Newport Beach, CA))

AMERICAN ST BK (PORTLAND, OR)
Each share old Common exchanged for (0.004) share new Common 11/16/2000
Note: In effect holders received $36 cash per share and public interest was eliminated

AMERICAN STAMPING & ENAMELING CO.
Out of business 00/00/1930
Details not available

AMERICAN STAMPING CO. (OH)
Stock Dividend - 100% 12/22/1952
Merged into Alco Standard Corp. 04/30/1968
Each share Common $2 par exchanged for (1) share Common no par
Alco Standard Corp. name changed to IKON Office Solutions, Inc. 01/24/1997
(See IKON Office Solutions, Inc.)

AMERICAN STANDARD LIFE INSURANCE CO.
Merged into American Life Insurance Co. 00/00/1931
Details not available

AMERICAN STANDARD LIFE INSURANCE CO. (MO)
Merged into Appalachian National Life Insurance Co. 05/20/1967
Each share Capital Stock $1 par exchanged for (1) share Common $1 par
Appalachian National Life Insurance Co. reorganized as Anco Corp. 06/08/1970 which name changed to Appalachian National Corp. 05/02/1972
(See Appalachian National Corp.)

AMERICAN STANDARD MINES LTD. (BC)
Acquired by Consolidated Standard Mines Ltd. 12/30/1959
Each share Capital Stock $1 par exchanged for (0.33333333) share Capital Stock $1 par
Consolidated Standard Mines Ltd. recapitalized as Golden Standard Mines Ltd. 05/20/1975 which recapitalized as International Standard Resources Ltd. 02/27/1979 which recapitalized as First Standard Mining Ltd. 03/15/1988 which name changed to First Standard Ventures Ltd. 07/16/1993 which recapitalized as LRG Restaurant Group, Inc. 09/05/1995
(See LRG Restaurant Group, Inc.)

AMERICAN STATE BANK (MILWAUKEE, WI)
Stock Dividend - (1) for (7) 07/02/1956
Completely liquidated 03/20/1965
Each share Capital Stock $20 par exchanged for (1) share American Bankshares Corp. Common $20 par
(See American Bankshares Corp.)

AMERICAN STATE FINANCIAL CORP. (TX)
Merged into Prosperity Bancshares, Inc. 07/01/2012
Each share Common $10 par exchanged for either (3.411) shares Common $1 par or $71.42 cash

AMERICAN STATES OIL CO. (IL)
Each share Common 10¢ par exchanged for (0.05) share Common $2 par 06/30/1959
Involuntarily dissolved 11/12/1964

AMERICAN STATES PUBLIC SERVICE CO.
Reorganized as American States Utilities Corp. 00/00/1937
Details not available

AMERICAN STATES SECURITIES CORP.
Merged into American Commonwealths Power Corp. 00/00/1929
Details not available

AMERICAN STATES UTILITIES CORP.
Dissolved 00/00/1948
Details not available

AMERICAN STD BLDG SYS INC
Plan of reorganization under Chapter 11 Federal Bankruptcy Code effective 03/05/1997
No stockholders' equity

AMERICAN STD COS INC (DE)
Common 1¢ par split (3) for (1) by issuance of (2) additional shares payable 05/27/2004 to holders of record 05/18/2004 Ex date - 05/28/2004
Each share Common 1¢ par received distribution of (0.33333333) share WABCO Holdings Inc. Common 1¢ par payable 07/31/2007 to holders of record 07/19/2007 Ex date - 08/01/2007
Name changed to Trane Inc. 11/28/2007
Trane Inc. merged into Ingersoll-Rand Co. Ltd. (Bermuda) 06/05/2008 which reincorporated in Ireland as Ingersoll-Rand PLC 07/01/2009

AMERICAN STD ENERGY CORP (DE)
Plan of reorganization under Chapter 11 Federal Bankruptcy proceedings effective 09/26/2016
No stockholders' equity

AMERICAN STD ENERGY INC (NV)
Name changed to Sports Wheels, Inc. 04/17/2003
Sports Wheels, Inc. recapitalized as Automotive Specialty Concepts, Inc. 02/01/2005 which name changed to Drake Gold Resources, Inc. 02/13/2006 which name changed to Universal Apparel & Textile Co. 04/27/2015

AMERICAN STD INC (DE)
$4.75 Conv. Preference Ser. A no par called for redemption 04/03/1979
Common $5 par changed to $1 par 05/09/1979
Common $1 par split (2) for (1) by issuance of (1) additional share 12/23/1980
7% Preferred $100 par called for redemption 04/30/1988
Merged into ASI Holding Corp. 06/29/1988
Each share Common $1 par exchanged for $78 cash

AMERICAN STD LEASING CO (DE)
Charter cancelled and declared inoperative and void for non-payment of taxes 06/24/1991

AMERICAN STEEL & COPPER INDUSTRIES, INC.
Merged into Continental Copper & Steel Industries, Inc. 00/00/1948
Each share Preferred $100 par exchanged for (4) shares 5% Preferred $25 par
Each share Common 1¢ par exchanged for (0.04) share 5% Preferred $25 par and (0.579) share Common $2 par
Continental Copper & Steel Industries, Inc. name changed to CCX, Inc. 12/01/1982
(See CCX, Inc.)

AMERICAN STEEL FOUNDRIES (NJ)
Common no par changed to $1 par 01/26/1956
Common $1 par split (2) for (1) by issuance of (1) additional share 02/15/1960
Name changed to Amsted Industries Inc. (NJ) 01/25/1962
Amsted Industries Inc. (NJ) reincorporated in Delaware 01/31/1968
(See Amsted Industries Inc. (DE))

AMERICAN STEEL PRODUCTS CO.
Acquired by Globe American Corp. (IN) 00/00/1930
Details not available

AMERICAN STEINWINTER INC (UT)
Name changed to Lo Boy Inc. 07/01/1994
(See Lo Boy Inc.)

AMERICAN STELLAR ENERGY INC (NV)
Name changed to Tara Gold Resources Corp. 02/23/2006
(See Tara Gold Resources Corp.)

AMERICAN STEREOPHONIC CORP. (NY)
Merged into Allied Entertainment Corp. of America, Inc. 01/00/1963
Each share Common 1¢ par exchanged for (0.666666) share Common 5¢ par
Allied Entertainment Corp. of America, Inc. merged into Jay Boy Music Corp. 03/26/1968
(See Jay Boy Music Corp.)

AMERICAN STERILIZER CO (PA)
Common $10 par changed to $3.33333333 par and (2) additional shares issued 02/23/1960
Common $3.33333333 par changed to $1.66666666 par and (1) additional share issued 05/16/1968
Common $1.66666666 par changed to $0.83333333 par and (1) additional share issued 06/01/1973
Merged into AMSCO Holdings, Inc. 02/08/1985
Each share Common $0.83333333 par exchanged for $22.50 cash

AMERICAN STL & PUMP CORP (DE)
Common $1 par changed to 47¢ par and (1-6/47) additional shares issued 00/00/1950
Common 47¢ par split (3) for (1) by issuance of (2) additional shares 12/08/1969
Merged into Investment Advisors Corp. 12/31/1971
Each share Common 47¢ par exchanged for $8 cash

AMERICAN STL & WIRE CORP (DE)
Merged into Birmingham Steel Corp. 11/23/1993
Each share Common 20¢ par exchanged for (0.23436) share Common 1¢ par and $0.60946 cash
(See Birmingham Steel Corp.)

AMERICAN STONE INDS INC (DE)
Each share old Common $0.001 par exchanged for (0.1) share new Common $0.001 par 06/02/1997
Liquidation completed
Each share Common $0.001 par received initial distribution of $7 cash payable 12/21/2007 to holders of record 12/19/2007 Ex date - 02/01/2008
Name changed to ASI Liquidating Corp. 01/31/2008
(See ASI Liquidating Corp.)

AMERICAN STORES CO NEW (DE)
Common $1 par split (3) for (1) by issuance of (2) additional shares 07/29/1983
$5.51 Preferred $1 par called for redemption 11/12/1984
$6.80 Exchangeable Preferred Ser. B $1 par called for redemption 08/15/1988
$4.375 Conv. Exchangeable Preferred Ser. A $1 par called for redemption 10/13/1989
Common $1 par split (2) for (1) by issuance of (1) additional share 07/16/1991
Common $1 par split (2) for (1) by issuance of (1) additional share 04/21/1994
Common $1 par split (2) for (1) by issuance of (1) additional share payable 07/16/1997 to holders of record 07/01/1997 Ex date - 07/17/1997
Merged into Albertson's, Inc. 06/23/1999
Each share Common $1 par exchanged for (0.63) shares Common $1 par
Albertson's, Inc. merged into Supervalu Inc. 06/02/2006

AMERICAN STORES CO OLD (DE)
Common no par changed to $1 par 00/00/1953
Name changed to Acme Markets, Inc. 06/28/1962 which name changed back to American Stores Co. 12/29/1973
Common $1 par split (3) for (2) by issuance of (0.5) additional share 07/01/1975
Merged into American Stores Co. (New) 07/26/1979
Each share Common $1 par exchanged for (0.7) share $5.51 Preferred $1 par and (0.6925) share Common $1 par
American Stores Co. (New) merged into Albertson's Inc. 06/23/1999 which merged into Supervalu Inc. 06/02/2006

AMERICAN STOVE CO.
Name changed to Magic Chef, Inc. 00/00/1951
Magic Chef, Inc. name changed to Magic Chef-Food Giant Markets, Inc. 08/05/1957 which name changed to Food Giant Markets, Inc. 02/17/1958 which merged into Vornado, Inc. (DE) 09/29/1967 which reorganized as Vornado Realty Trust (MD) 05/06/1993

AMERICAN STRATEGIC INCOME PORTFOLIO INC (MN)
Merged into Diversified Real Asset Income Fund 09/08/2014
Each share Common 1¢ par exchanged for (0.57489) Common Share of Bene. Int. 1¢ par
Diversified Real Asset Income Fund merged into Nuveen Real Asset Income & Growth Fund 09/11/2017

AMERICAN STRATEGIC INCOME PORTFOLIO INC II (MN)
Merged into Diversified Real Asset Income Fund 09/08/2014
Each share Common 1¢ par exchanged for (0.493745) Common Share of Bene. Int. 1¢ par
Diversified Real Asset Income Fund merged into Nuveen Real Asset Income & Growth Fund 09/11/2017

AMERICAN STRATEGIC INCOME PORTFOLIO INC III (MN)
Merged into Diversified Real Asset Income Fund 09/08/2014
Each share Common 1¢ par exchanged for (0.408545) Common Share of Bene. Int. 1¢ par
Diversified Real Asset Income Fund merged into Nuveen Real Asset Income & Growth Fund 09/11/2017

AMERICAN STRATEGIC METALS INC (CO)
Common $0.001 par changed to $0.000166 par and (5) additional shares issued 04/17/1985
Filed a petition under Chapter 7 Federal Bankruptcy Code 02/00/1990
Stockholders' equity unlikely

AMERICAN STRATEGIC MINERALS CORP (NV)
Common $0.0001 par split (1.3626126) for (1) by issuance of (0.3626126) additional share payable 12/13/2011 to holders of record 12/13/2011
Name changed to Marathon Patent Group, Inc. 02/21/2013

AMERICAN STS FINL CORP (IN)
Merged into Safeco Corp. 10/01/1997
Each share Common no par exchanged for $47 cash

AMERICAN STS INS CO (IN)
Class A $10 par and Class B $10 par changed to $5 par 00/00/1945
Each share Class A $5 par exchanged for (5) shares Class A $1 par 11/01/1954
Each share Class B Common $5 par exchanged for (5) shares Class B $1 par 11/01/1954
Each share Class A $1 par exchanged for (1) share Common $1 par 08/23/1961
Each share Class B $1 par exchanged for (5) shares Common $1 par 08/23/1961
Stock Dividends - (Paid in Class A to holders of Class A & B) - 10% 07/16/1957; 10% 02/15/1958; 10% 02/20/1959; 10% 02/23/1960
Acquired by Lincoln National Corp. 11/16/1973
Each share Common $1 par exchanged for $225 cash
Preferred $10 par called for redemption 06/29/1992

Public interest eliminated

AMERICAN STS LEASING CORP (CA)
Name changed to Amstat Corp. 01/09/1984
(See Amstat Corp.)

AMERICAN STS LIFE INS CO (IN)
Common $1 par split (3) for (2) by issuance of (0.5) additional share 06/29/1979
Acquired by Lincoln National Corp. 01/03/1984
Each share Common $1 par exchanged for (43/56.75) share Common $1.25 par

AMERICAN STS WTR CO (CA)
4% Preferred $25 par called for redemption at $27 on 04/05/2002
4.25% Preferred $25 par called for redemption at $26.50 on 04/05/2002
5% Preferred $25 par called for redemption 04/05/2002
(Additional Information in Active)

AMERICAN STUDIOS INC (NC)
Common $0.001 par split (3) for (2) by issuance of (0.5) additional share 01/15/1993
Merged into PCA International, Inc. 02/28/1997
Each share Common $0.001 par exchanged for $2.50 cash

AMERICAN SUGAR CO (DE)
Reincorporated 12/31/1966
Common $12.50 par split (2) for (1) by issuance of (1) additional share 05/03/1963
State of incorporation changed from (NJ) to (DE) 12/31/1966
Name changed to Amstat Corp. 10/29/1970
(See Amstat Corp.)

AMERICAN SUGAR REFINING CO. (NJ)
7% Preferred $100 par and Common $100 par changed to $25 par respectively and (3) additional shares issued 05/13/1957
Merged into American Sugar Co. (NJ) 04/19/1963
Each share 7% Preferred $25 par exchanged for (1) share 5.44% Preferred $12.50 par and $25 principal amount of 5.3% Subord. Debentures due 04/02/1993
Each share Common $25 par exchanged for (1) share Common $12.50 par
American Sugar Co. (NJ) reincorporated in Delaware 12/31/1966 which name changed to Amstat Corp. 10/29/1970
(See Amstat Corp.)

AMERICAN SULPHUR CO. (DE)
No longer in existence having become inoperative and void for non-payment of taxes 04/01/1961

AMERICAN SUMATRA TOBACCO CORP. (DE)
Each share Common no par exchanged for (3) shares Common $5 par 00/00/1947
Merged into Tobacco Holdings, Inc. 11/18/1960
Each share Common $5 par exchanged for $17 cash

AMERICAN SUPERPOWER CORP.
Name changed to Webb & Knapp, Inc. 00/00/1952
(See Webb & Knapp, Inc.)

AMERICAN SURETY CO. OF NEW YORK (NY)
Each share Common $50 par exchanged for (2) shares Common $25 par 00/00/1929
Common $25 par changed to $6.25 par and (3) additional shares issued 05/01/1956
Merged into Transamerica Insurance Co. 12/31/1963

Each share Common $6.25 par exchanged for $25.74 cash

AMERICAN SURFACE TECHNOLOGIES INTL INC (FL)
Name changed to Global Environmental, Inc. 06/22/2006 which name changed back to American Surface Technologies International, Inc. 10/18/2007
Reorganized under the laws of Delaware as Ravenwood Bourne, Ltd. 10/30/2008
Each share Common $0.001 par exchanged for (0.01333333) share Common $0.001 par
Ravenwood Bourne, Ltd. name changed to PopBig, Inc. 11/07/2011 which name changed to EMAV Holdings, Inc. 01/03/2014

AMERICAN SURGERY CTRS CORP (UT)
Recapitalized as Daleigh Holdings Corp. 01/21/1997
Each share Common $0.00152 par exchanged for (0.1) share Common $0.00152 par
(See Daleigh Holdings Corp.)

AMERICAN SURGICAL HLDGS INC (DE)
Each share old Common $0.001 par exchanged for (0.5) share new Common $0.001 par 04/26/2007
Acquired by AH Holdings, Inc. 03/23/2011
Each share new Common $0.001 par exchanged for $2.91075501 cash

AMERICAN SURGICAL LASER INC (UT)
Reorganized under the laws of Delaware as Eclipse Imports, Inc. 07/17/1997
Each share Common $0.001 par exchanged for (0.005) share Common $0.001 par
Eclipse Imports, Inc. recapitalized as Neurochemical Research International, Inc. 03/22/1999 which name changed to Ultimate Sports Entertainment Inc. 04/12/1999

AMERICAN SWISS INTL CORP (DE)
Charter cancelled and declared inoperative and void for non-payment of taxes 03/01/1989

AMERICAN SYN FUELS INC (DE)
Name changed to American Fuel Technologies Inc. 10/21/1983
(See American Fuel Technologies Inc.)

AMERICAN SYS INC (CA)
Each share old Common $1 par exchanged for (0.066667) share Common $15 par 06/30/1997
Each share Common $15 par exchanged for (15) shares new Common $1 par 04/07/1969
Charter suspended for failure to file reports and pay fees 01/02/1980

AMERICAN TACKLE & EQUIPMENT CO. (PA)
$1.50 Preferred $30 par called for redemption 04/10/1958
Public interest eliminated

AMERICAN TALENT ASSOCIATES, INC. (NY)
Recapitalized as American Talent Inc. 08/14/1985
Each share Common $0.0001 par exchanged for (0.11111111) share Common $0.0009 par
(See American Talent Inc.)

AMERICAN TALENT INC (NY)
Proclaimed dissolved 03/24/1993

AMERICAN TECHNICAL CERAMICS CORP (DE)
Common 1¢ par split (2) for (1) by issuance of (1) additional share payable 05/15/2000 to holders of record 04/24/2000
Merged into AVX Corp. 09/25/2007

Each share Common 1¢ par exchanged for $24.75 cash

AMERICAN TECHNICAL INDS INC (NY)
Stock Dividends - 20% 12/20/1977; 10% 12/20/1978
Merged into Papercraft Corp. 03/13/1981
Each share Common $0.06666666 par exchanged for $12.50 cash
$1.28 Preferred $1 par called for redemption 03/23/1981
Public interest eliminated

AMERICAN TECHNICAL MACHINERY CORP. (NY)
Common 10¢ par changed to $0.06666666 par and (0.5) additional share issued 01/25/1967
Stock Dividends - 25% 09/29/1967; 10% 03/29/1968
Name changed to American Technical Industries, Inc. (NY) 05/02/1968
(See American Technical Industries, Inc. (NY))

AMERICAN TECHNICAL RESOURCES, INC. (DE)
Reincorporated 3/4/83
State of incorporation changed from (UT) to (DE) 3/4/83
Charter cancelled and declared inoperative and void for non-payment of taxes 8/1/86

AMERICAN TECHNOLOGIES GROUP INC (NV)
Each share old Common $0.001 par exchanged for (0.00333333) share new Common $0.001 par 12/05/2005
SEC revoked common stock registration 08/19/2013

AMERICAN TECHNOLOGY & INFORMATION INC (BC)
Struck off register and declared dissolved for failure to file returns 02/24/1989

AMERICAN TECHNOLOGY CORP (DE)
Reorganized 07/14/1992
Each share Common $0.001 par exchanged for (0.005) share Common 2¢ par 09/29/1982
Reorganized from (UT) to under the laws of Delaware 07/14/1992
Each share Common 2¢ par exchanged for (0.2) share Common $0.00001 par
Name changed to LRAD Corp. 03/25/2010

AMERICAN TECHNOLOGY EXPL CORP (NV)
Recapitalized as Olympic Environmental Ltd. 04/16/2002
Each share Common $0.001 par exchanged for (0.01) share Common $0.001 par
Olympic Environmental Ltd. merged into Neoteric Group Inc. 06/17/2002
(See Neoteric Group Inc.)

AMERICAN TEL & TELEG CO (NY)
Capital Stock $100 par changed to $33-1/3 par and (2) additional shares issued 6/1/59
Capital Stock 33-1/3 par changed to $16-2/3 par and (1) additional share issued 6/22/64
Capital Stock $16-2/3 par reclassified as Common $16-2/3 par 6/3/71
Common $16-2/3 par changed to $1 par 5/19/83
$4 Conv. Preferred $1 par called for redemption 9/30/83
$3.74 Preferred $1 par called for redemption 2/1/88
$3.64 Preferred $1 par called for redemption 5/1/88
Name changed to AT&T Corp. 4/20/94
AT&T Corp. merged into AT&T Inc. 11/18/2005

AMERICAN TEL ADVERTISING HLDGS INC (CO)
Administratively dissolved 8/1/2002

AMERICAN TEL PLUS DATA INC (DE)
Charter cancelled and declared inoperative and void for non-payment of taxes 03/01/1997

AMERICAN TELECASTING INC (DE)
Merged into Sprint Corp. 9/23/99
Each share Common 1¢ par exchanged for $6.50 cash

AMERICAN TELECOM CORP (NY)
Charter cancelled and proclaimed dissolved for failure to pay taxes 06/27/2001

AMERICAN TELECOMMUNICATION STANDARDS INTL INC (NV)
Name changed to PSA Inc. 04/01/1998
PSA Inc. name changed to Shearson American REIT, Inc. 10/16/2009

AMERICAN TELECOMMUNICATIONS CORP (BC)
Reorganized under the laws of Delaware as ATC, Inc. 12/13/1990
Each share Common no par exchanged for (0.33333333) share Common 1¢ par
ATC, Inc. name changed to ATC II, Inc. 07/27/1993
(See ATC II, Inc.)

AMERICAN TELECOMMUNICATIONS CORP (CA)
Stock Dividend - 50% 04/14/1972
Merged into General Dynamics Corp. 12/01/1978
Each share Common 10¢ par exchanged for (0.47) share $4.25 Conv. Preferred Ser. A $1 par
(See General Dynamics Corp.)

AMERICAN TELECOMMUNICATIONS TR (MA)
Name changed to SLH Telecommunications Trust 02/28/1990
SLH Telecommunications Trust name changed to Shearson Lehman Brothers Telecommunications Trust 03/06/1991
(See Shearson Lehman Brothers Telecommunications Trust)

AMERICAN TELEGRAPH & CABLE CO.
Liquidated 00/00/1931
Details not available

AMERICAN TELEGRAPHONIC CO. (DC)
Company went bankrupt in the 1920's
Litigation concluded 00/00/1936 with stockholders receiving no equity

AMERICAN TELEMAIL CORP. (NY)
Incorporated 03/29/1977
Charter cancelled and proclaimed dissolved for failure to pay taxes 03/25/1981

AMERICAN TELEMEDIA NETWORK INC (UT)
Name changed to ATNN, Inc. 12/22/1989
ATNN, Inc. recapitalized as EuroTelecom Communications, Inc. 08/11/1997 which recapitalized as BENE IO, Inc. 07/24/2006
(See BENE IO, Inc.)

AMERICAN TELESOURCE INTL INC (DE)
Each share Common $0.001 par received distribution of (0.05) share GlobalSCAPE, Inc. Common $0.001 par payable 09/12/2000 to holders of record 07/14/2000
Name changed to ATSI Communications, Inc. (DE) 03/29/2001
ATSI Communications, Inc. (DE) reorganized in Nevada 05/24/2004 which name changed to Digerati Technologies, Inc. 03/21/2011

AMERICAN TELESOURCE INTL INC (ON)
Reincorporated under the laws of Delaware as American TeleSource International Inc. and Common no par changed to $0.001 par 05/15/1998
American TeleSource International Inc. name changed to ATSI Communications, Inc. (DE) 03/29/2001 which reorganized in Nevada 05/24/2004 which name changed to Digerati Technologies, Inc. 03/21/2011

AMERICAN TELETRONICS INC (CO)
Recapitalized as Shine Holdings, Inc. 03/13/2006
Each share Common no par exchanged for (0.001) share Common no par
(See Shine Holdings, Inc.)

AMERICAN TELEVISION & COMMUNICATIONS CORP (DE)
Ctfs. dated prior to 11/14/1978
Merged into Time Inc. 11/14/1978
Each share Common 75¢ par exchanged for (1.55) shares $1.575 Conv. Preferred Ser. B $1 par
(See Time Inc.)

AMERICAN TELEVISION & COMMUNICATIONS CORP NEW (DE)
Ctfs. dated after 08/12/1986
Merged into Time Warner Inc. 06/29/1992
Each share Class A Common 1¢ par exchanged for $82.50 principal amount of Redeemable Reset Notes due 08/15/2002

AMERICAN TELEVISION & FILM CO (NV)
Name changed to Spotlight Homes, Inc. 4/6/2004

AMERICAN TELEVISION & FILM CO INC (TX)
Name changed to First Pet Life, Inc. 8/4/2005

AMERICAN TELEVISION & RADIO CO. (MN)
Recapitalized as ATR Electronics, Inc. 3/25/61
Each share Common 50¢ par exchanged for (2) shares Common 10¢ par

AMERICAN TELEVISION CORP. (NY)
Proclaimed dissolved for failure to pay taxes and file reports 12/16/68

AMERICAN TELNET CORP (UT)
Common 1¢ par split (5) for (1) by issuance of (4) additional shares 8/20/80
Proclaimed dissolved for failure to pay taxes 9/30/85

AMERICAN TEMPERATURE CTL INC (CO)
Name changed to Connectivity & Technologies, Inc. 12/10/1993
Connectivity & Technologies, Inc. recapitalized as Peacock Financial Corp. (CO) 02/27/1996 which reorganized in Nevada as Broadleaf Capital Partners, Inc. 03/22/2002 which recapitalized as EnergyTek Corp. 07/23/2014 which recapitalized as TimefireVR Inc. 11/22/2016

AMERICAN TERRA VEHS CORP (NV)
Each share old Common $0.001 par exchanged for (0.05) share new Common $0.001 par 06/27/2008
Name changed to Bayside Petroleum Co., Inc. 10/21/2008
Bayside Petroleum Co., Inc. recapitalized as Bayside Corp. 06/20/2011

AMERICAN TEXTILE CO., INC. (RI)
Acquired by Liberty Fabrics of New York, Inc. 5/28/62

Each share Common $10 par exchanged for $11 cash

AMERICAN TEXTILE WOOLEN CO.
Liquidated 00/00/1948
Details not available

AMERICAN THEATRES CORP. (MA)
Proclaimed dissolved for failure to file reports and pay fees 01/10/1979

AMERICAN THERMAL RES INC (NV)
Charter revoked for failure to file reports and pay fees 1/1/91

AMERICAN THERMOS BOTTLE CO. (OH)
Each share old Common no par exchanged for (3) shares new Common no par 11/23/46
4-1/4% Preferred $50 par called for redemption 8/2/48
New Common no par changed to $4 par in 1949
Name changed to American Thermos Products Co. 4/27/56
American Thermos Products Co. merged into King-Seeley Thermos Co. 12/9/60 which merged into Household Finance Corp. 9/30/68 which reorganized as Household International, Inc. 6/26/81

AMERICAN THERMOS PRODUCTS CO. (OH)
Merged into King-Seeley Thermos Co. on a (1.55) for (1) basis 12/9/60
King-Seeley Thermos Co. merged into Household Finance Corp. 9/30/68 which reorganized as Household International, Inc. 6/26/81

AMERICAN THORIUM INC (NV)
Recapitalized as Cementitious Materials, Inc. 10/21/2003
Each share Common $0.0001 par exchanged for (0.25) share Common $0.001 par
Cementitious Materials, Inc. name changed to NaturalNano, Inc. 12/02/2005 which name changed to Omni Shrimp, Inc. 05/03/2017

AMERICAN THROTTLE CO., INC. (NY)
Liquidation completed 09/01/1956
Details not available

AMERICAN TIDELANDS, INC. (DE)
Merged into Marine Drilling, Inc. on a (0.25) for (1) basis 08/24/1957
Marine Drilling, Inc. name changed to Great National Corp. 07/08/1964 which name changed to GNC Energy Corp. 08/05/1981
(See GNC Energy Corp.)

AMERICAN TIDELANDS LIFE INS CO (AL)
Merged into Tidelands Capital Corp. 5/3/77
Each share Common $1 par exchanged for (6.75) shares Common no par
Tidelands Capital Corp. merged into Western Preferred Corp. 3/6/81
(See Western Preferred Corp.)

AMERICAN TIGHT COOPERAGE, INC. (MI)
Charter voided for failure to file reports or pay fees 8/31/39

AMERICAN TIMBER HOLDING CO.
Liquidated in 1948
No Common stockholders' equity

AMERICAN TIME CORP.
Name changed to Specialty Converters, Inc. in 1950
Specialty Converters, Inc. name changed to Specialty Composites Corp. 5/16/73
(See Specialty Composites Corp.)

AMERICAN TIN CORP. (CA)
Name changed to Mining & Oil Shale Development Corp. 03/12/1968
Mining & Oil Shale Development Corp. merged into Consolidated General Corp. 04/28/1969 which name changed to Chisholm Resources Inc. (NV) 03/24/1998
(See Chisholm Resources Inc.)

AMERICAN TIN SMELTERIES, INC. (DE)
Charter repealed for failure to pay taxes 01/23/1924

AMERICAN TIRE CORP. (DE)
Charter cancelled for non-payment of taxes in 1923

AMERICAN TIRE CORP (NV)
Name changed to Ameritrye Corp. 12/12/2000

AMERICAN TITLE & GUARANTY CO.
Liquidated 00/00/1945
Details not available

AMERICAN TITLE & INSURANCE CO. (FL)
Stock Dividend - 11.11111111% 12/18/1958
Name changed to American Title Insurance Co. 03/31/1959
(See American Title Insurance Co.)

AMERICAN TITLE INS CO (FL)
Stock Dividend - 10% 04/12/1960
Through purchase offer 99% acquired by Continental Corp. as of 07/01/1967
Public interest eliminated

AMERICAN TOB CO (NJ)
Each share Common $50 par exchanged for (2) shares Common $25 par 00/00/1930
Each share Class B $50 par exchanged for (2) shares Class B $25 par 00/00/1930
Class B Common $25 par reclassified as Common $25 par 00/00/1948
Common $25 par changed to $12.50 par and (1) additional share issued 05/02/1960
Common $12.50 par changed to $6.25 par and (1) additional share issued 04/30/1962
Recapitalized 06/30/1965
Each share 6% Preferred $100 par exchanged for either $50 cash and $100 principal amount of 4.625% Subord. Debentures due 07/01/1990 or $150 cash
Note: Option to receive cash and debentures expired 07/30/1965
Name changed to American Brands, Inc. (NJ) 07/01/1969
American Brands, Inc. (NJ) reincorporated in Delaware 01/01/1986 which name changed to Fortune Brands, Inc. 05/30/1997 which name changed to Beam Inc. 10/04/2011
(See Beam Inc.)

AMERICAN TOLL BRIDGE CO. (DE)
Liquidation completed 00/00/1944
Details not available

AMERICAN TOLL BRIDGE CO. OF CALIFORNIA
Dissolved 00/00/1940
Details not available

AMERICAN TONERSERV CORP (DE)
Each share old Common $0.001 par exchanged for (0.01) share new Common $0.001 par 03/17/2006
Each share new Common $0.001 par exchanged again for (10) shares new Common $0.001 par 08/22/2006
Plan of reorganization under Chapter 11 Federal Bankruptcy proceedings confirmed 06/22/2012
Stockholders' equity unlikely

AMERICAN TONY PHARMACEUTICALS INC (DE)
Name changed to Tongli Pharmaceuticals (USA), Inc. 10/30/2008

AMERICAN TOWER CORP NEW (DE)
Each share 5.25% Mandatory Conv. Preferred Ser. A 1¢ par automatically became (0.9337) share Common 1¢ par 05/15/2017
Each share 5.5% Mandatory Conv. Depositary Preferred Ser. B automatically became (0.8742) share Common 1¢ par 02/15/2018
(Additional Information in Active)

AMERICAN TOWER CORP OLD (DE)
Name changed 06/17/1998
Name changed from American Tower Systems Corp. to American Tower Corp. (Old) 06/17/1998
Secondary Offering - 29,374,911 shares CL A offered at $23.50 per share on 07/01/1998
Additional Offering - 12,500,000 shares CL A offered at $41.25 per share on 06/22/2000
Reorganized as American Tower Corp. (New) 01/03/2012
Each share Class A Common 1¢ par exchanged for (1) share Common 1¢ par

AMERICAN TOXXIC CTL INC (DE)
Common 10¢ par changed to $0.001 par 07/01/1988
Name changed to United States Filter Corp. (New) 12/10/1990
(See United States Filter Corp. (New))

AMERICAN TOY VENDING INC (NV)
Charter revoked for failure to file reports and pay fees 04/01/2009

AMERICAN TOYS INC (DE)
Each share old Common 1¢ par exchanged for (0.25) share new Common 1¢ par 05/31/1996
Name changed to U.S. Wireless Corp. 10/21/1996
(See U.S. Wireless Corp.)

AMERICAN TRACK SYS INTL INC (DE)
Chapter 11 bankruptcy proceedings converted to Chapter 7 on 01/13/2000
Stockholders' equity unlikely

AMERICAN TRACTOR CORP. (NY)
Common 50¢ par changed to 25¢ par and (1) additional share issued 08/17/1955
Merged into Case (J.I.) Co. 01/10/1957
Each share Common 25¢ par exchanged for (1) share 6.5% 2nd Preferred $7 par par and (0.5) share Common $12.50 par
Case (J.I.) Co. acquired by Tenneco Inc. 08/04/1970 which merged into El Paso Natural Gas Co. 12/12/1996 which reorganized as El Paso Energy Corp. 08/01/1998 which name changed to El Paso Corp. 02/05/2001 which merged into Kinder Morgan, Inc. (New) 05/25/2012

AMERICAN TRADING & EXCHANGE CORP (WA)
Each share Common 10¢ par exchanged for (0.1) share Common no par 06/05/1987
Charter expired 06/30/2001

AMERICAN TRAINING SVCS INC (NJ)
Common 10¢ par split (3) for (2) by issuance of (0.5) additional share 01/24/1972
Common 10¢ par split (2) for (1) by issuance of (1) additional share 06/26/1972
Common 10¢ par changed to 1¢ par 03/28/1978
Name changed to Educom Corp. 06/29/1981
Educom Corp. name changed to CareerCom Corp. (NJ) 02/21/1985 which reincorporated in Pennsylvania 07/15/1987
(See CareerCom Corp. (PA))

AMERICAN TRANSIT CORP. (MO)
6% Conv. Preferred Ser. A $25 par called for redemption 12/21/1965
Merged into Chromalloy American Corp. (NY) 03/01/1966
Each share Common $1 par exchanged for (1) share Common 10¢ par
Chromalloy American Corp. (NY) reincorporated in Delaware 10/31/1968 which merged into Sun Chemical Corp. 12/23/1986 which name changed to Sequa Corp. 05/08/1987
(See Sequa Corp.)

AMERICAN TRANSN TELEVISION NETWORK INC (CANADA)
Involuntarily dissolved for failure to file annual returns 07/07/1997

AMERICAN TRAVELERS LIFE INSURANCE CO. (IN)
Merged into Midwestern United Life Insurance Co. 07/31/1961
Each share Common $1 par exchanged for (0.1) share Common $1 par
(See Midwestern United Life Insurance Co.)

AMERICAN TRAVELLERS CORP (PA)
Common 1¢ par split (2) for (1) by issuance of (1) additional share 05/10/1990
Common 1¢ par split (3) for (2) by issuance of (0.5) additional share payable 04/10/1996 to holders of record 03/20/1996
Merged into Conseco, Inc. 12/17/1996
Each share Common 1¢ par exchanged for (0.5836) share Common no par
(See Conseco, Inc.)

AMERICAN TRIPOLETE PRODUCTS CO. INC. (DE)
No longer in existence having become inoperative and void for non-payment of taxes 03/19/1924

AMERICAN TRUCK SVC CLUB INC (DE)
Recapitalized as American Service Industries, Inc. 02/22/1971
Each share Common 10¢ par exchanged for (4) shares Common 1¢ par
(See American Service Industries, Inc.)

AMERICAN TRUST & BANKING CO. (CHATTANOOGA, TN)
Stock Dividends - 20% 00/00/1939; 36.36% 11/00/1945
Name changed to American National Bank & Trust Co. (Chattanooga, TN) 10/01/1948
American National Bank & Trust Co. (Chattanooga, TN) reorganized as American National Corp. (TN) 01/01/1973 which name changed to Ancorp Bancshares, Inc. 12/28/1973 which merged into Third National Corp. 12/31/1982 which merged into SunTrust Banks, Inc. 12/29/1986

AMERICAN TRUST CO. (NEW YORK, NY)
Each share Common $25 par exchanged for (2.5) shares Common $10 par 00/00/1951
Name changed to American Bank & Trust Co. (New York, NY) 04/01/1966
American Bank & Trust Co. (New York, NY) reorganized as American B&T Corp. 05/01/1970
(See American B&T Corp.)

AMERICAN TRUST CO. (SAN FRANCISCO, CA)
Each share Common $100 par exchanged for (5) shares Common $20 par 03/05/1936
Common $20 par changed to $10 par and (1) additional share issued 02/11/1953
Stock Dividend - 10% 01/15/1960
Merged into Wells Fargo Bank American Trust Co. (San Francisco, CA) 03/25/1960
Each share Common $10 par exchanged for (1) share Capital Stock $10 par
Wells Fargo Bank American Trust Co. (San Francisco, CA) name changed to Wells Fargo Bank (San Francisco, CA) 01/31/1962 which name changed to Wells Fargo Bank N.A. (San Francisco, CA) 08/15/1968 which reorganized as Wells Fargo & Co. (CA) 02/28/1969 which reincorporated in Delaware 06/30/1987 which merged into Wells Fargo & Co. (New) 11/02/1998

AMERICAN TRUST CO. (SOUTH BEND, IN)
Capital Stock $10 par split (10) for (1) issuance of (9) additional shares 06/14/1955
Stock Dividend - 100% 10/21/1955
Name changed to American Bank & Trust Co. (South Bend, IN) 01/19/1962
American Bank & Trust Co. (South Bend, IN) name changed to American National Bank & Trust Co. (South Bend, IN) 09/09/1968
(See American National Bank & Trust Co. (South Bend, IN))

AMERICAN TR LIFE INS CO (TX)
Acquired by Empire Life Insurance Co. of America (AL) 02/10/1969
Each share Preferred $1 par exchanged for (1) share Class A Common $1 par
Each share Common no par exchanged for (0.122249) share Class A Common $1 par
(See Empire Life Insurance Co. of America (AL))

AMERICAN TRUSTEE INC (OK)
Stock Dividend - 50% 03/10/1982
Assets placed in receivership 08/00/1987
Stockholders' equity unlikely

AMERICAN TRUSTEE LIFE CORP (OK)
Reorganized as American Trustee Inc. 06/22/1981
Each share Common $1 par exchanged for (1) share Common $1 par
(See American Trustee Inc.)

AMERICAN TUBE & STAMPING CO.
Acquired by Stanley Works 00/00/1926
Details not available

AMERICAN TWINE & FABRIC CO (NH)
Liquidation completed
Each share Common no par received initial distribution of $10 cash 01/15/1969
Each share Common no par exchanged for second distribution of $3 cash 06/30/1969
Each share Common no par received third and final distribution of $2.3943 cash 03/00/1972

AMERICAN TWIST DRILL CO. (MI)
Acquired by Nelco Tool Co. Inc. 09/18/1959
Each share Common exchanged for $14 cash

AMERICAN TYPE FOUNDERS, INC. (NJ)
Name changed to A T F, Inc. 06/30/1946
A T F, Inc. name changed to Daystrom, Inc. 01/31/1951 which was acquired by Schlumberger, Ltd. 02/01/1962

AMERICAN TYPE FOUNDERS CO. (NJ)
Reorganized as American Type Founders, Inc. 05/15/1936
Each share Preferred exchanged for (2.25) shares Capital Stock $10 par
Each share Common $10 par exchanged for (0.5) share Capital Stock $10 par
American Type Founders, Inc. name changed to A T F, Inc. 06/30/1946 which name changed to Daystrom, Inc. 01/31/1951 which was acquired by Schlumberger, Ltd. 02/01/1962

AMERICAN UNDERWRITERS, INC. (IN)
Each share old Common no par exchanged for (0.5) share new Common no par 08/23/1971
Name changed to American Underwriters Group, Inc. 04/28/1981
(See American Underwriters Group, Inc.)

AMERICAN UNDERWRITERS CORP. (WA)
Merged into Sunset Life Insurance Co. of America 00/00/1960
Details not available

AMERICAN UNDERWRITERS GROUP INC (IN)
Stock Dividend - 10% 10/29/1984
Dissolved 10/23/1992
No stockholders' equity

AMERICAN UNIFORM CO.
Liquidated 00/00/1926
Details not available

AMERICAN UTD ENERGY CORP (UT)
Proclaimed dissolved for failure to pay taxes 12/31/1984

AMERICAN UNITED GLOBAL INC (DE)
Common 1¢ par split (1.9) for (1) by issuance of (0.9) additional share 12/31/1991
Each share old Common 1¢ par exchanged for (0.04) share new Common 1¢ par 12/17/2001
Name changed to Solar Thin Films, Inc. 07/10/2006

AMERICAN UTD GOLD CORP (NV)
Common $0.001 par split (7) for (1) by issuance of (6) additional shares payable 05/17/2007 to holders of record 05/14/2007 Ex date - 05/18/2007
SEC revoked common stock registration 03/21/2012

AMERICAN UTD INNS INC (OH)
Adjudicated bankrupt 09/24/1976
Stockholders' equity unlikely

AMERICAN UTD PRODS CORP (DE)
Charter cancelled and declared inoperative and void for non-payment of taxes 03/01/1979

AMERICAN UNITY INVTS INC (FL)
Common $0.001 par split (2) for (1) by issuance of (1) additional share payable 08/29/2006 to holders of record 08/21/2006 Ex date - 08/30/2006
Administratively dissolved 09/14/2007

AMERICAN UNIVEND CORP. (DE)
No longer in existence having become inoperative and void for non-payment of taxes 04/01/1964

AMERICAN UNVL INS CO (RI)
Stock Dividends - 20% 12/00/1952; 10% 12/01/1954; 16.66666666% 10/00/1955; 33.33333333% 06/25/1971
Through purchase offer 100% acquired by Chromalloy American Corp. as of 03/27/1978
Public interest eliminated

AMERICAN URANIUM (UT)
Charter revoked for failure to file reports and pay fees 09/29/1961

AMERICAN URANIUM CORP (NM)
Name changed to American Mining & Oil Co. 04/27/1959 which name changed back to American Uranium Corp. 08/27/1968
Charter cancelled 09/30/1978

AMERICAN URANIUM CORP (NV)
Each share old Common $0.00001 par exchanged for (0.02173913) share new Common $0.00001 par 10/20/2008
New Common $0.00001 par changed to $0.0001 par 07/17/2015
Recapitalized as Blue Star Global Inc. 08/03/2015
Each share Common $0.0001 par exchanged for (0.2) share Common $0.0001 par

AMERICAN URANIUM INC (FL)
Reincorporated 06/24/2000
State of incorporation changed from (NJ) to (FL) 06/24/2000
Name changed to Visual Bible International Inc. 08/10/2000
Visual Bible International Inc. recapitalized as Secure Luggage USA, Inc. 06/09/2008 which reorganized as Ambush Media, Inc. 09/16/2009 which name changed to Azia Corp. 03/19/2010 which name changed to Axxess Unlimited Inc. 03/20/2013 which name changed to Encompass Compliance Corp. 06/22/2015

AMERICAN URANIUM LTD. (BC)
Recapitalized as Sonic Drying Systems Ltd. 07/10/1972
Each share Capital Stock 50¢ par exchanged for (0.33333333) share Capital Stock no par
(See Sonic Drying Systems Ltd.)

AMERICAN URANIUM MNG INC (DE)
Name changed to F3 Technologies, Inc. 09/29/2008
F3 Technologies, Inc. name changed to Here to Serve Holding Corp. 11/05/2013

AMERICAN URBAN DEV CORP (FL)
Common 1¢ par split (2) for (1) by issuance of (1) additional share payable 07/02/1971
Stock Dividend - 10% 09/04/1970
Proclaimed dissolved for failure to file reports and pay fees 12/14/1982

AMERICAN URETHANE, INC. (CA)
Each share Common $1 par exchanged for (0.1) share Common no par 07/03/1963
Completely liquidated 09/23/1966
Each share Common no par exchanged for first and final distribution of $6.25 cash

AMERICAN UTIL SHS INC (MD)
Merged into Lord Abbett Income Fund, Inc. 07/31/1978
Each share Capital Stock $1 par exchanged for (4.534) shares Capital Stock $1 par
Lord Abbett Income Fund, Inc. name changed to Lord Abbett U.S. Government Securities Fund, Inc. 09/23/1985
(See Lord Abbett U.S. Government Securities Fund, Inc.)

AMERICAN UTILICRAFT CORP (DE)
Common $0.00001 par split (2) for (1) by issuance of (1) additional share payable 07/19/2004 to holders of record 06/28/2004
Each share Common $0.00001 par received (1) share of Utilicraft Aerospace Industries, Inc. Common $0.0001 par payable 10/05/2005 to holders of record 09/22/2005
Company terminated registration of common stock and is no longer public as of 03/31/2005
Details not available

AMERICAN UTILITIES & GENERAL CORP.
Reorganized as American & Dominion Corp. 00/00/1932
Details not available

AMERICAN UTILITIES CO.
Liquidated 00/00/1936
Details not available

AMERICAN UTILITIES SERVICE CORP.
Merged into Central Electric & Gas Co. 00/00/1946
Each share Common $20 par exchanged for (0.33333333) share Common $1 par
Central Electric & Gas Co. name changed to Western Power & Gas Co. 05/01/1961 which name changed to Western Power & Gas Co. Inc. 07/01/1965 which name changed to Central Telephone & Utilities Corp. 06/05/1968 which name changed to Centel Corp. 04/30/1982 which was acquired by Sprint Corp. (KS) 03/09/1993 which name changed to Sprint Nextel Corp. 08/12/2005 which merged into Sprint Corp. (DE) 07/10/2013

AMERICAN VACCINE CORP (DE)
Merged into North American Vaccine, Inc. 02/28/1990
Each share Common 1¢ par exchanged for (1) share Common no par
North American Vaccine, Inc. merged into Baxter International Inc. 06/26/2000

AMERICAN VALLEY BANK (EL CAJON, CA)
Reorganized as BSD Bancorp, Inc. (CA) 03/26/1982
Each share Common $5.75 par exchanged for (1) share Common no par
BSD Bancorp, Inc. (CA) reincorporated in Delaware 09/02/1987
(See BSD Bancorp, Inc.)

AMERICAN VANADIUM CORP (CANADA)
Recapitalized as Monitor Ventures Inc. 07/20/2017
Each share Common no par exchanged for (0.04) share Common no par

AMERICAN VANTAGE COS (NV)
Each share old Common 1¢ par exchanged for (0.33333333) share new Common 1¢ par 12/01/1999
SEC revoked common stock registration 07/31/2013

AMERICAN VARIETY INTL INC (DE)
Common 1¢ par split (4) for (1) by issuance of (3) additional shares 02/05/1973
Name changed to AVI Entertainment Group Inc. 06/04/1987

AMERICAN VARIETY STORES, INC. (FL)
Name changed to American Department Stores, Inc. 12/01/1965
American Department Stores, Inc. merged into Southwest Florida Enterprises, Inc. 05/01/1969
(See Southwest Florida Enterprises, Inc.)

AMERICAN VENTURES INC (BC)
Recapitalized as Asha Ventures Inc. 04/01/1992
Each share Common no par exchanged for (0.33333333) share Common no par
Asha Ventures Inc. name changed to Cost Miser Coupons (International) Inc. 09/28/1992 which recapitalized as Integrated Media Communications Inc. 02/24/1994 which recapitalized as IMC Ventures, Inc. (BC) 09/29/1998 which reincorporated in Yukon as Triumph Gold Corp. 03/29/2004 which reincorporated in British Columbia 08/26/2004 which recapitalized as Kenai Resources Ltd. 05/01/2007 which merged into Serabi Gold PLC 07/22/2013

AMERICAN VENTURES INC (CO)
Name changed to Park Group, Ltd. (CO) 02/27/1987
Park Group, Ltd. (CO) reincorporated in Delaware as Sonus Communication Holdings, Inc. 04/16/1999
(See Sonus Communication Holdings, Inc.)

AMERICAN VENTURES INC (DE)
Each share old Common $0.0001 par exchanged for (0.14285714) share new Common $0.0001 par 11/15/1989
Charter cancelled and declared inoperative and void for non-payment of taxes 06/24/1991

AMERICAN VERRE-MURAL, INC.
Completely liquidated 00/00/1952
Details not available

AMERICAN VETERINARY PRODS INC (NY)
Each share old Common $0.0001 par exchanged for (0.05) share new Common $0.002 par 04/06/1990
Each share new Common $0.002 par exchanged for (0.5) share Common $0.04 par 03/19/1992
Name changed to GEN/Rx, Inc. 03/10/1993
(See GEN/Rx, Inc.)

AMERICAN VIDEO CLEARING HOUSE INC (NV)
Charter revoked for failure to file reports and pay fees 09/01/1993

AMERICAN VIDEO IMAGING INC (DE)
Charter cancelled and declared inoperative and void for non-payment of taxes 06/24/1991

AMERICAN VIDEO TELECONFERENCING CORP (NY)
Reincorporated under the laws of Delaware and Common 1¢ par changed to $0.001 par 10/14/2008

AMERICAN VIDEONETICS CORP (CA)
Voluntarily dissolved 09/11/1984
No stockholders' equity

AMERICAN VISCOSE CORP. (DE)
Each share Common $100 par exchanged for (0.51) share Preferred $100 par and (3.5) shares Common $14 par 00/00/1941
Each share Common $14 par exchanged for (2) shares Common $25 par 00/00/1950
Stock Dividend - 25% 11/23/1955
Name changed to A.V.C. Corp. 08/06/1963
A.V.C. Corp. merged into Raybestos-Manhattan, Inc. (CT) 04/30/1981 which name changed to Raymark Corp. 06/28/1982 which reorganized in Delaware as Raytech Corp. 10/15/1986
(See Raytech Corp.)

AMERICAN VISION CTRS INC (NY)
Each share Common 1¢ par exchanged for (0.0005) share Common $20 par 06/28/1991
Merged into Amvis Inc. 10/16/1996
Each share Common $20 par exchanged for $75 cash

AMERICAN VISION FDS INC
Fund dissolved by agreement with SEC 03/18/1992
Details not available

AMERICAN VISUAL APPLIANCES INC (NV)
Merged into Optical Technologies Corp. 09/28/1999
Details not available

AMERICAN VITRIFIED PRODS CO (NJ)
Each share Preferred $100 par exchanged for (1) share Preferred no par and (3) shares Common no par 00/00/1933
Common $50 par changed to no par 00/00/1933
Common no par changed to $1 par 00/00/1943
Name changed to IU Industrials, Inc. 05/21/1970
(See IU Industrials, Inc.)

AMERICAN VOLCANO MINERALS CORP (BC)
Name changed to Genco Industries Inc. 02/24/1987
Genco Industries Inc. recapitalized as Consolidated Genco Industries Inc. 05/08/1990
(See Consolidated Genco Industries Inc.)

AMERICAN VOTING MACHINE CO. (ME)
Out of business 03/12/1915
Details not available

AMERICAN WAGERING INC (NV)
Acquired by William Hill PLC 06/27/2012
Each share Common 1¢ par exchanged for $0.90 cash

AMERICAN WASTE SVCS INC (OH)
Each share Class A Common no par received distribution of (0.125) share Avalon Holdings Inc. Class A Common 1¢ par payable 06/24/1998 to holders of record 06/17/1998
Merged into USA Waste Services, Inc. 06/18/1998
Each share Class A Common no par exchanged for $4 cash

AMERICAN WATER WORKS & ELECTRIC CO., INC. (DE)
Liquidation completed 01/15/1948
Each share $6 Ser. 1st Preferred exchanged for $100.25 cash and a certificate evidencing right to participate in further distributions if any 10/15/1947
Each share Common exchanged for (1) share West Penn Electric Co. Common no par 01/15/1948
West Penn Electric Co. name changed to Allegheny Power System, Inc. 11/10/1960 which name changed to Allegheny Energy, Inc. 09/16/1997 which merged into FirstEnergy Corp. 02/25/2011

AMERICAN WAY BUSINESS DEV CORP (DE)
Name changed 09/30/2004
Common 1¢ par split (100) for (1) by issuance of (99) additional shares payable 09/30/2004 to holders of record 09/27/2004 Ex date - 10/01/2004
Name changed from American Way Home Based Business Systems, Inc. to American Way Business Development Corp. 09/30/2004
Each share old Common 1¢ par exchanged for (0.00333333) share new Common 1¢ par 11/23/2004
Each share new Common 1¢ par exchanged again for (0.1) share new Common 1¢ par 01/21/2005
Each share new Common 1¢ par exchanged again for (0.0002) share new Common 1¢ par 09/12/2006
Reincorporated under the laws of Florida as Harvard Learning Centers, Inc. and Common 1¢ par changed to $0.0001 par 10/30/2006
Harvard Learning Centers, Inc. name changed to Americas Learning Centers, Inc. 09/25/2007 which recapitalized as Hackett's Stores, Inc. 01/26/2009 which recapitalized as WiseBuys, Inc. 06/17/2010 which name changed to Empire Pizza Holdings, Inc. 04/20/2011 which recapitalized as Vestiage, Inc. 03/22/2013

AMERICAN WAY INVS INC (IN)
Merged into Southern Securities Corp. 01/29/1971
Each share Common no par exchanged for (1) share Common $1 par
(See Southern Securities Corp.)

AMERICAN WELDING & MFG CO (OH)
Stock Dividends - 50% 01/31/1968; 100% 07/17/1981
Merged into Hoover Universal, Inc. 10/15/1982
Each share Common no par exchanged for $27.50 cash

AMERICAN WELL SERVICING CORP (NV)
Each share Common 1¢ par exchanged for (0.25) share Common 4¢ par 05/04/1982
Reorganized under the laws of Texas as American Oil & Gas Corp. 05/08/1984
Each share Common 4¢ par exchanged for (1) share Common 4¢ par
American Oil & Gas Corp. (TX) reincorporated in Delaware 07/23/1986 which merged into K N Energy, Inc. 07/13/1994 which name changed to Kinder Morgan, Inc. (KS) 10/07/1999
(See Kinder Morgan, Inc. (KS))

AMERICAN WELLHEAD SVCS INC (BC)
Recapitalized as Coronado Resources Inc. 05/13/1994
Each share Common no par exchanged for (0.5) share Common no par
Coronado Resources Inc. recapitalized as Habanero Resources Inc. 10/27/1997 which recapitalized as Sienna Resources Inc. 01/24/2014

AMERICAN WENSHEN STL GROUP INC (DE)
Each share Common $0.001 par received distribution of (0.4636) share HXT Holdings, Inc. Common $0.001 par payable 04/14/2009 to holders of record 03/31/2009
Ex date - 03/27/2009
SEC revoked common stock registration 08/12/2013

AMERICAN WEST BK NATL ASSN (ENCINO, CA)
Merged into Bank of Los Angeles (New) (Los Angeles, CA) 03/31/1997
Each share Common $5 par exchanged for (1) share Common no par
Bank of Los Angeles (New) (Los Angeles, CA) merged into Western Bancorp 10/26/1998 which merged into U.S. Bancorp 11/15/1999

AMERICAN WEST FINL INC (DE)
Charter cancelled and declared inoperative and void for non-payment of taxes 03/01/1987

AMERICAN WEST NURSING CTRS INC (DE)
Charter cancelled and declared inoperative and void for non-payment of taxes 03/01/1983

AMERICAN WESTERN RESOURCES, INC. (DE)
Merged into Ro-Mac Gold, Ltd. 05/17/1978
Each share Common 10¢ par exchanged for (1) share Common 1¢ par
Ro-Mac Gold, Ltd. name changed to Phoenix Associated Land Syndicate 10/24/1996
(See Phoenix Associated Land Syndicate)

AMERICAN WESTN CORP NEW (DE)
Acquired by Carlisle Plastics, Inc. 03/23/1990
Each share Common 10¢ par exchanged for $12.50 cash

AMERICAN WESTN CORP OLD (DE)
Stock Dividends - 10% 05/16/1980; 15% 05/15/1981; 15% 05/21/1982; 15% 11/19/1982; 15% 05/18/1983; 15% 11/14/1983
Under plan of reorganization each share Common 10¢ par automatically became (1) share American Western Corp. (New) Common 10¢ par 00/00/1983
(See American Western Corp. (New))

AMERICAN WESTN LIFE INS CO (UT)
Each share Common $2 par exchanged for (2) shares Common $1 par 08/15/1967
Merged into United American Life Insurance Co. (CO) 12/31/1977
Each share Common $1 par exchanged for (0.37243947) share Common $1 par
United American Life Insurance Co. (CO) merged into World Service Life Insurance Co. (CO) 07/31/1978 which merged into Western Preferred Corp. 02/21/1979
(See Western Preferred Corp.)

AMERICAN WESTWATER TECHNOLOGY GROUP LTD (BC)
Common no par split (5) for (1) by issuance of (4) additional shares 11/16/1987
Struck off register and declared dissolved for failure to file returns 11/11/1993

AMERICAN WHEEL & VEHICLE CO. (AZ)
Charter revoked for failure to file reports or pay fees 12/29/1931

AMERICAN WHITE CROSS INC (DE)
Plan of reorganization under Chapter 11 Federal Bankruptcy Code effective 09/22/1997
No stockholders' equity

AMERICAN WILD WOODLAND GINSENG CORP (CANADA)
Chapter 11 bankruptcy proceedings converted to Chapter 7 on 07/09/2004
No stockholders' equity

AMERICAN WIND TURBINE INC (DE)
Name changed to American Energy & Technology, Inc. 10/16/1981
American Energy & Technology, Inc. recapitalized as Breccia International Minerals Inc. 02/21/1997 which name changed to Nano World Projects Corp. 03/01/2000
(See Nano World Projects Corp.)

AMERICAN WINDOW GLASS CO. (PA)
Each share Preferred $100 par exchanged for (3) shares 5% Preferred $25 par and (3) shares Common $12.50 par 00/00/1941
Each share Class A $100 par exchanged for (0.8) share 5% Preferred $25 par and (1) share Common $12.50 par 00/00/1941
Each share Common no par exchanged for (0.25) share Common $12.50 par 00/00/1941
5% Preferred $25 par reclassified as 5% Class B Preferred $25 par 02/27/1956
Merged into American Saint Gobain Corp. 05/26/1958
Each share 5% Prior Preferred $25 par exchanged for (1) share 5% Preferred $25 par
Each share Common $12.50 par exchanged for (1) share Common $7.50 par
American Saint Gobain Corp. name changed to ASG Industries, Inc. 08/04/1970 which name changed to AFG Industries, Inc. 10/22/1979
(See AFG Industries, Inc.)

AMERICAN WINDOW GLASS MACHINE CO.
Merged into American Window Glass Co. 00/00/1929
Details not available

AMERICAN WINE CO.
Property sold and Company dissolved 00/00/1950
Details not available

AMERICAN WIRELESS SYS INC (DE)
Each share old Common 1¢ par exchanged for (0.33333333) share new Common 1¢ par 10/18/1994
Merged into Heartland Wireless Communications, Inc. 02/23/1996
Each share new Common 1¢ par exchanged for (0.22905) share Common $0.001 par
Note: An additional escrow distribution of (0.0033694) share Common $0.001 par per share was made 07/24/1996
An additional final distribution of (0.01804796) share Common $0.001 par per share was made 00/00/1997
(See Heartland Wireless Communications, Inc.)

AMERICAN WIRELESS WEB CORP (FL)
SEC revoked common stock registration 09/25/2008

AMERICAN WOLLASTONITE MNG CORP (BC)
Recapitalized as Previa Resources Ltd. 04/25/1997
Each share Common no par exchanged for (0.14925373) share Common no par
Previa Resources Ltd. recapitalized as Rose Marie Resources Ltd. 10/18/2006 which recapitalized as Cheetah Ventures Ltd. 07/17/2008 which name changed to Emperor Minerals Ltd. 10/21/2010 which name changed to Emperor Oil Ltd. 08/24/2012

AMERICAN WOMAN'S REALTY CO. INC.
Name changed to Hudson (Henry) Hotel Corp. 00/00/1946
(See Hudson (Henry) Hotel Corp.)

AMERICAN WOMAN'S REALTY CORP.
Reorganized as American Woman's Realty Co., Inc. 00/00/1937
Each share Preferred exchanged for (2) shares new Common no par
Each share old Common exchanged for (1) share new Common no par
American Woman's Realty Co., Inc. name changed to Hudson (Henry) Hotel Corp. 00/00/1946
(See Hudson (Henry) Hotel Corp.)

AMERICAN WOOLEN CO. (MA)
Common $100 par changed to no par 00/00/1932
Merged into Textron American, Inc. 02/24/1955
Each share $4 Prior Preference no par exchanged for $105 principal amount of 5% Debentures and 50¢ cash
Each share 7% Preferred $100 par exchanged for $120 principal amount of 5% Debentures and $0.29166666 cash
Each share Common no par exchanged for (2) shares Common 50¢ par
Textron American, Inc. name changed to Textron Inc. (RI) 05/15/1956 which reincorporated in Delaware 01/02/1968

AMERICAN WORLD TRAVEL CORP (DE)
Charter cancelled and declared inoperative and void for non-payment of taxes 03/01/1977

AMERICAN WRINGER CO., INC. (RI)
Each share Common no par exchanged for (3) shares Common $10 par 00/00/1934
Each share Common $10 par exchanged for (2.5) shares Common $4 par 04/30/1946
Merged into Ambrook Industries, Inc. (RI) 06/01/1956
Each share Common $4 par exchanged for (1.6) shares Common 25¢ par
Ambrook Industries, Inc. merged into Barker Bros. Corp. (RI) 03/14/1958 which name changed to Larchfield Corp. 10/05/1960
(See Larchfield Corp.)

AMERICAN WRITING PAPER CO., INC. (DE)
Reorganized as American Writing Paper Corp. 00/00/1937
Each share Preferred no par exchanged for (0.5) share Common no par
Each share Common $1 par exchanged for (0.05) share Common no par
American Writing Paper Corp. name changed to Holyoke Shares, Inc. 12/31/1962
(See Holyoke Shares, Inc.)

AMERICAN WRITING PAPER CO. (DE)
Reorganized as American Writing Paper Co., Inc. 00/00/1927
Details not available

AMERICAN WRITING PAPER CORP. (DE)
Common no par changed to $5 par 00/00/1941
Name changed to Holyoke Shares, Inc. 12/31/1962
(See Holyoke Shares, Inc.)

AMERICAN WTR RES INC (DE)
Charter cancelled and declared inoperative and void for non-payment of taxes 03/01/1992

AMERICAN WTR STAR INC (NV)
Recapitalized as Prime Star Group, Inc. 09/12/2008
Each share Common $0.0001 par exchanged for (0.01) share Common $0.001 par
Note: No holder will receive fewer than (100) shares
(See Prime Star Group, Inc.)

AMERICAN WTR WKS INC OLD (DE)
5.2% Preferred $25 par called for redemption 07/08/1963
6% Preferred $25 par called for redemption 07/08/1963
Common $5 par changed to $2.50 par and (1) additional share issued 01/19/1965
Common $2.50 par split (2) for (1) by issuance of (1) additional share 03/01/1985
Common $2.50 par changed to $1.25 par and (1) additional share issued 05/28/1987
4.1% Preferential Stock $35 par called for redemption 12/01/1987
5.5% Preferred 1961 Ser. $25 par called for redemption 09/01/1991
4.9% Preferred $25 par called for redemption 06/01/1993
Common $1.25 par split (2) for (1) by issuance of (1) additional share payable 07/25/1996 to holders of record 07/15/1996 Ex date - 07/26/1996
5% Preferred $25 par called for redemption at $25.25 on 03/01/2002
5% Preference $25 par called for redemption at $25 on 03/01/2002
Merged into RWE AG 01/10/2003
Each share Common $1.25 par exchanged for $46 cash

AMERICAN XTAL TECHNOLOGY INC (DE)
Name changed to AXT, Inc. 04/28/2000

AMERICAN YACHTING SYSTEMS, INC. (NY)
Name changed to Doric Distributors, Inc. 10/04/1967
(See Doric Distributors, Inc.)

AMERICAN YARN & PROCESSING CO.
Name changed to American & Efird Mills, Inc. 00/00/1952
American & Efird Mills, Inc. merged into Ruddick Corp. 10/28/1968 which name changed to Harris Teeter Supermarkets, Inc. (New) 04/02/2012
(See Harris Teeter Supermarkets, Inc. (New))

AMERICAN YELLOWKNIFE GOLD MINES LTD. (ON)
Name changed to American Yellowknife Mines Ltd. 00/00/1952
American Yellowknife Mines Ltd. recapitalized as Rayrock Mines Ltd. 00/00/1954 which name changed to Rayrock Resources Ltd. 07/21/1978 which merged into Rayrock Yellowknife Resources Inc. 02/03/1986 which name changed to Rayrock Resources Inc. 11/27/1998
(See Rayrock Resources Inc.)

AMERICAN YELLOWKNIFE MINES LTD. (ON)
Recapitalized as Rayrock Mines Ltd. 00/00/1954
Each share Capital Stock $1 par exchanged for (0.25) share Capital Stock $1 par
Rayrock Mines Ltd. name changed to Rayrock Resources Ltd. 07/21/1978 which merged into Rayrock Yellowknife Resources Inc. 02/03/1986 which name changed to Rayrock Resources Inc. 11/27/1998
(See Rayrock Resources Inc.)

AMERICAN YVETTE INC (DE)
Each share Preference no par exchanged for (6) shares new Common $1 par 08/01/1955
Common no par changed to old Common $1 par 00/00/1932
Each share old Common $1 par exchanged for (0.01) share Common $10 par 00/00/1942
Each share Common $10 par exchanged for (7) shares new Common $1 par 08/01/1955
Merged into MEI Regis Glemby Salon 12/27/1990
Details not available

AMERICAN ZINC, LEAD & SMELTING CO. (ME)
Common $25 par changed to no par 00/00/1930
Common no par changed to $1 par 00/00/1932
Stock Dividend - 25% 08/29/1955
Name changed to American Zinc Co. 12/02/1966
American Zinc Co. name changed to Azcon Corp. 11/16/1972
(See Azcon Corp.)

AMERICAN ZINC CO (ME)
Name changed to Azcon Corp. 11/16/1972
(See Azcon Corp.)

AMERICANA FURNITURE, INC.
Name changed to American Radio & Television, Inc. 00/00/1950
(See American Radio & Television, Inc.)

AMERICANA GOLD & DIAMOND HLDGS INC (DE)
Each share old Common $0.001 par exchanged for (0.1) share new Common $0.001 par 09/11/1998

Recapitalized as MineCore International, Inc. (DE) 06/29/2004
Each share new Common $0.001 par exchanged for (0.1) share Common $0.001 par
MineCore International, Inc. (DE) reincorporated in Nevada 04/09/2008
(See MineCore International, Inc.)

AMERICANA HOTELS & RLTY CORP (MD)
Completely liquidated
Each share Common $1 par received initial distribution of $8 cash 08/01/1989
Each share Common $1 par received second distribution of $3.50 cash 12/14/1990
Each share Common $1 par received third distribution of $0.75 cash 04/07/1992
Each share Common $1 par received fourth distribution of $0.50 cash 03/06/1995
Each share Common $1 par received fifth distribution of $2 cash payable 06/18/1996 to holders of record 06/11/1996
Each share Common $1 par received sixth and final distribution of $1.16 cash payable 06/24/1998 to holders of record 06/10/1998
Note: Certificates were not required to be surrendered and are without value

AMERICANA INVT CO (OH)
Class A no par reclassified as Common no par 02/14/1979
Merged into Monumental Corp. 11/05/1982
Each share Common no par exchanged for (0.25) share Common $3.50 par
Note: Option for holders of (99) shares or fewer to receive $4.94 cash per share in lieu of stock expired 12/10/1982
(See Monumental Corp.)

AMERICANA LIFE INSURANCE CO. (FL)
Each share Common $1 par exchanged for (0.5) share Class A Common $1 par 05/12/1967
Merged into Kennesaw Life & Accident Insurance Co. 01/02/1968
Each share Class A Common $1 par exchanged for (1.2) shares Common $1 par
Kennesaw Life & Accident Insurance Co. merged into Lykes-Youngstown Financial Corp. 11/14/1969 which name changed to LifeSurance Corp. 05/10/1971 which merged into Regan Holding Corp. 10/31/1991
(See Regan Holding Corp.)

AMERICANA MOTOR HOTELS, INC. (CO)
Charter revoked for failure to file reports and pay fees 10/19/1964

AMERICANA PROPERTIES, INC. (DE)
Incorporated 00/00/1950
Charter cancelled and declared inoperative and void for non-payment of taxes 04/01/1964

AMERICANA PUBG INC (CO)
Each share old Common $0.001 par exchanged for (0.025) share new Common $0.001 par 08/26/2004
Name changed to Americana Distribution, Inc. 01/09/2006

AMERICANADA LTD (DE)
Name changed to Knusaga Corp. 08/31/1977
(See Knusaga Corp.)

AMERICANADIAN MINING & EXPLORATION CO., LTD. (ON)
Charter cancelled and proclaimed dissolved for failure to pay taxes and file returns 08/09/1972

AMERICANINO CAP CORP (DE)
Charter cancelled and declared void for failure to pay franchise taxes 03/01/2003

AMERICANWEST BANCORPORATION (WA)
Stock Dividends - 10% payable 02/01/2002 to holders of record 01/18/2002 Ex date - 01/16/2002; 10% payable 02/14/2003 to holders of record 01/31/2003 Ex date - 01/30/2003; 10% payable 02/20/2004 to holders of record 02/09/2004 Ex date - 02/05/2004
Plan of reorganization under Chapter 11 Federal Bankruptcy proceedings effective 10/04/2013
No stockholders' equity

AMERICAR INC (FL)
Common 50¢ par split (2) for (1) by issuance of (1) additional share 10/15/1968
Merged into Westinghouse Electric Corp. 10/30/1970
Each share Common 50¢ par exchanged for (0.10164) share Common $6.25 par plus an Interim Ctf. representing right to receive an additional (0.8898) share subject to certain conditions
(See Westinghouse Electric Corp.)

AMERICARE CORP (OH)
Each share old Class A Common no par exchanged for (0.002) share new Class A Common no par 01/02/1983
New Class A Common no par split (400) for (1) by issuance of (399) additional shares 11/29/1983
New Class A Common no par split (2) for (1) by issuance of (1) additional share 09/14/1984
Plan of reorganization under Chapter 11 Federal Bankruptcy proceedings confirmed 04/20/1990
No stockholders' equity

AMERICARE GROWTH FD INC (DE)
Merged into Eaton & Howard Growth Fund, Inc. 02/05/1976
Each share Capital Stock $1 par exchanged for (0.812) share Capital Stock $1 par
Eaton & Howard Growth Fund, Inc. name changed to Eaton Vance Special Equities Fund, Inc. 09/24/1982 which name changed to Eaton Vance Special Investment Trust 07/21/1992

AMERICARE HEALTH CORP (DE)
Merged into AHC Acquisition Corp. 12/31/1986
Each share Common no par exchanged for $13 cash

AMERICARE HEALTH GROUP INC (DE)
Each share old Common $0.0002 par exchanged for (0.2) share new Common $0.0002 par 08/09/1993
Name changed to Zagreus Inc. 03/26/1999

AMERICARE HEALTH SCAN INC (FL)
SEC revoked common stock registration 06/02/2010

AMERICARE MIDWEST, INC. (OH)
Acquired by Care Enterprises 11/00/1990
Each share Common no par exchanged for $7.12 cash

AMERICAS ALL SEASON FD INC (MD)
Name changed to All Seasons Global Fund, Inc. 06/01/1995
All Seasons Global Fund, Inc. name changed to Royce Global Trust, Inc. 11/01/1996 which name changed to Royce Focus Trust, Inc. 05/10/1999 which name changed to Sprott Focus Trust, Inc. 03/09/2015

AMERICAS BEAUTIFUL CITIES (NV)
Charter revoked for failure to file reports and pay fees 03/03/1980

AMERICAS BULLION RTY CORP (BC)
Merged into Till Capital Ltd. 04/24/2014
Each share Common no par exchanged for (0.01) Restricted Share USD$0.001 par

AMERICAS COFFEE CUP INC (CO)
Reincorporated 03/01/1995
Each share Common $0.0001 par exchanged for (0.01) share Common 1¢ par 02/23/1990
Each share Common 1¢ par exchanged for (0.1) share Common 10¢ par 11/26/1993
State of incorporation changed from (DE) to (CO) 03/01/1995
Each share Common 10¢ par exchanged for (0.25) share Common 40¢ par 09/01/1995
Name changed to Midland Inc. 02/17/1997
(See Midland Inc.)

AMERICAS CORP (DE)
Adjudicated bankrupt 02/07/1975
Stockholders' equity unlikely

AMERICAS DIAMOND CORP (NV)
Common $0.001 par split (5) for (1) by issuance of (4) additional shares payable 10/15/2012 to holders of record 10/15/2012
Name changed to Midwest Oil & Gas Inc. 06/12/2014

AMERICAS DRIVING RANGES INC (NV)
Name changed to U.S. Natural Nutrients & Minerals, Inc. 11/10/2009
U.S. Natural Nutrients & Minerals, Inc. reorganized as U.S. Rare Earth Minerals, Inc. 05/02/2011

AMERICAS ENERGY CO (NV)
Chapter 11 bankruptcy proceedings converted to Chapter 7 on 02/28/2013
Stockholders' equity unlikely

AMERICAS FINEST WTRS INC (NV)
Each share old Common $0.001 par exchanged for (1/6) share new Common $0.001 par 11/18/1991
Each share new Common $0.001 par exchanged again for (0.02) share new Common $0.001 par 09/29/1998
Name changed to Jumpmusic.com Inc. 05/05/1999
Jumpmusic.com Inc. recapitalized as PureSpectrum, Inc. (NV) 06/12/2006 which merged into PureSpectrum, Inc. (DE) 11/04/2009

AMERICAS FIRST HOME STORE INC (AZ)
Reincorporated under the laws of Delaware as Buyer One Inc. and Common no par changed to $0.001 par 03/01/1987
(See Buyer One Inc.)

AMERICAS GAMING INTL INC (DE)
Charter cancelled and declared inoperative and void for non-payment of taxes 03/01/1998

AMERICAS GROWTH FD INC (MD)
Merged into JWGenesis Financial Corp. 12/18/1998
Each share Common 1¢ par exchanged for (0.431) share Common $0.001 par
(See JWGenesis Financial Corp.)

AMERICAS INCOME TR INC (MN)
Reorganized as First American Investment Funds, Inc. 07/31/1998
Each share Common 1¢ par exchanged for (0.9198034) Strategic Income Fund Retail Class A $0.0001 par

AMERICAS LEARNING CTRS INC (FL)
Each share old Common $0.0001 par exchanged for (0.001) share new Common $0.0001 par 03/22/2007
Recapitalized as Hackett's Stores, Inc. 01/26/2009
Each share Common $0.0001 par exchanged for (0.0001) share Common $0.0001 par
Hackett's Stores, Inc. recapitalized as WiseBuys, Inc. 06/17/2010 which name changed to Empire Pizza Holdings, Inc. 04/20/2011 which recapitalized as Vestiage, Inc. 03/22/2013

AMERICAS MNG CORP (UT)
Name changed to Carmina Technologies, Inc. 12/01/2000
Carmina Technologies, Inc. recapitalized as Advanced Integrated Management Services, Inc. 06/29/2004 which reorganized as AIMSI Technologies, Inc. 11/17/2004
(See AIMSI Technologies, Inc.)

AMERICAS PETROGAS INC (AB)
Name changed to GrowMax Resources Corp. 08/09/2016

AMERICAS PWR PARTNERS INC (CO)
Company terminated common stock registration and is no longer public as of 05/11/2005

AMERICAS PRODTNS INC (DE)
Charter cancelled and declared inoperative and void for non-payment of taxes 03/01/1984

AMERICAS PRODTNS INC (MA)
Reincorporated 01/10/1973
Recapitalized as America's Productions, Inc. (DE) 01/10/1973
Each share Common 1¢ par exchanged for (0.33333333) share Common 1¢ par
(See America's Productions, Inc.)

AMERICAS SHOPPING MALL INC (NV)
Each share old Common $0.001 par exchanged for (0.01) share new Common $0.001 par 11/13/2007
Note: Holders of between (100) and (9,999) shares received (100) shares
Holders of (99) or fewer shares were not affected
Name changed to Eagle Ventures International, Inc. 11/26/2007
(See Eagle Ventures International, Inc.)

AMERICAS SPORTS VOICE INC (NY)
Name changed to Milagro Holdings Inc. 04/20/2004
(See Milagro Holdings Inc.)

AMERICAS SR FINL SVCS INC (FL)
Name changed to Amstar Financial Services, Inc. 10/01/2003
Amstar Financial Services, Inc. recapitalized as Remodel Auction Inc. 08/10/2009 which name changed to North Carolina Natural Energy, Inc. 01/11/2012 which name changed to Appalachian Mountain Brewery, Inc. 01/08/2014

AMERICAS UTD BK (GLENDALE, CA)
Merged into Bank of Southern California, N.A. (San Diego, CA) 07/31/2018
Each share Common no par exchanged for (0.4746) share Common $5 par and $7 cash

AMERICASBANK CORP (MD)
Each share old Common 1¢ par exchanged for (0.25) share new Common 1¢ par 08/23/2005
Acquired by Capital Funding Bancorp, Inc. 08/25/2009
Each share Common 1¢ par exchanged for $0.102 cash

AMERICHIP INTL INC (NV)
Each share Common $0.001 par exchanged for (0.14285714) share Common $0.00001 par 08/13/2007
SEC revoked common stock registration 10/04/2011

AMERICLEAN INC (DE)
Each share old Common $0.0001 par exchanged for (0.25) share new Common $0.0001 par 01/14/1999
Recapitalized as Calypso Enterprises Inc. 10/12/2001
Each share new Common $0.0001 par exchanged for (0.01333333) share Common $0.0001 par
Calypso Enterprises Inc. name changed to Huron Ventures Inc. 06/18/2001 which name changed to Cano Petroleum, Inc. 06/01/2004
(See Cano Petroleum, Inc.)

AMERICOL PETROLEUM, INC. (CO)
Charter revoked for failure to file reports and pay fees 10/28/1959

AMERICOLD CORP (OR)
Merged into Vornado Realty Trust 10/31/1997
Each share Common 1¢ par exchanged for $20.70 cash

AMERICOM BUSINESS CTRS INC (FL)
Name changed 11/08/1991
Name changed from American International Corp. to Americom Business Centers Inc. 11/08/1991
Proclaimed dissolved for failure to file reports and pay fees 08/25/1995

AMERICOM NETWORKS INTL INC (DE)
Name changed 07/10/1998
Reincorporated 02/06/2008
Name changed from Americom Networks Corp. to Americom Networks International Inc. 07/10/1998
State of incorporation changed from (FL) to (DE) 02/06/2008
Recapitalized as Highland Ridge, Inc. 08/29/2008
Each share Common $0.001 par exchanged for (0.02) share Common $0.001 par
Highland Ridge, Inc. name changed to TEC Technology, Inc. (DE) 07/15/2010 which reincorporated in Nevada 06/30/2012

AMERICOM USA INC (DE)
Common no par reclassified as Class A no par 01/01/2000
Charter cancelled and declared inoperative and void for non-payment of franchise taxes 03/01/2002

AMERICOMM RES CORP (DE)
Name changed 07/26/1995
Name changed from Americomm Corp. to Americomm Resources Corp. 07/26/1995
Each share old Common $0.001 par exchanged for (0.33333333) share new Common $0.001 par 06/27/1996
Name changed to Empire Petroleum Corp. 08/15/2001

AMERICONNECT INC (DE)
Merged into Phoenix Network, Inc. 10/08/1996
Each share Common 1¢ par exchanged for (0.3605) share Common $0.001 par
Phoenix Network, Inc. merged into Qwest Communications International Inc. 03/30/1998 which merged into CenturyLink, Inc. 04/01/2011

AMERICORP (CA)
Common $1 par split (2) for (1) by issuance of (1) additional share payable 05/06/1999 to holders of record 04/15/1999
Merged into Mid-State Bancshares 09/28/2001

Each share Common $1 par exchanged for $28.75 cash

AMERICORP FINL INC (NV)
Name changed to AMCORE Financial, Inc. 11/26/1985
(See AMCORE Financial, Inc.)

AMERICORP INC (GA)
Merged into Bank Corporation of Georgia 03/27/1996
Each share Common 1¢ par exchanged for (0.084615) share Common $1 par
Bank Corporation of Georgia merged into Century South Banks, Inc. 12/16/1997 which merged into BB&T Corp. 06/07/2001

AMERICORP INTL INC (CO)
Recapitalized as Double Eagle Resources, Inc. 01/13/1989
Each share Common $0.001 par exchanged for (0.1) share Common $0.001 par
Double Eagle Resources, Inc. name changed to Biomed Science International Corp. 05/14/1993

AMERICREDIT CORP (TX)
Common 1¢ par split (2) for (1) by issuance of (1) additional share payable 09/30/1998 to holders of record 09/11/1998 Ex date - 10/01/1998
Acquired by General Motors Holdings LLC 10/01/2010
Each share Common 1¢ par exchanged for $24.50 cash

AMERICUS FDG CORP (CO)
Each share old Common no par exchanged for (0.005) share new Common no par 06/15/1990
Recapitalized as Neotherapeutics, Inc. (CO) 08/28/1996
Each share new Common no par exchanged for (0.4) share Common no par
Neotherapeutics, Inc. (CO) reincorporated in Delaware 06/17/1997 which name changed to Spectrum Pharmaceuticals Inc. 12/11/2002

AMERICUS MGMT CORP (DE)
Charter cancelled and declared inoperative and void for non-payment of taxes 03/01/1993

AMERIDATA TECHNOLOGIES INC (DE)
Merged into General Electric Capital Corp. 07/22/1996
Each share Common 1¢ par exchanged for $16 cash

AMERIDEX MINERALS CORP (BC)
Name changed to Rocher Deboule Minerals Corp. 09/15/2006
Rocher Deboule Minerals Corp. name changed to American Manganese Inc. 01/20/2010

AMERIFAX INC (DE)
Name changed to Americonnect Inc. 05/27/1994
Americonnect Inc. merged into Phoenix Network, Inc. 10/08/1996 which merged into Qwest Communications International Inc. 03/30/1998 which merged into CenturyLink, Inc. 04/01/2011

AMERIFED FINL CORP (DE)
Merged into NBD Bancorp, Inc. 01/09/1995
Each share Common 1¢ par exchanged for (1.597) shares Common $1 par
NBD Bancorp, Inc. name changed to First Chicago NBD Corp. 12/01/1995 which merged into Bank One Corp. 10/02/1998 which merged into J.P. Morgan Chase & Co. 12/31/2000 which name changed to JPMorgan Chase & Co. 07/20/2004

AMERIFIN CORP (DE)
$4.07 Conv. Preferred no par called for redemption 09/05/1984
In process of liquidation
Each share 4% Preferred $100 par exchanged for initial distribution of $102.33 cash 10/31/1984
Each share 5.5% Preferred $100 par exchanged for initial distribution of $105.46 cash 10/31/1984
Each share Common 25¢ par exchanged for initial distribution of approximately $36 cash 10/31/1984
Note: Details on subsequent distribution(s), if any, are not available

AMERIFIRST BANK FED SVGS BK (MIAMI, FL)
Name changed 03/01/1988
Name changed from AmeriFirst Federal Savings & Loan Association to AmeriFirst Bank, A Federal Savings Bank (Miami, FL) 03/01/1988
Closed and declared insolvent by Office of Thrift Supervision 03/15/1991
No stockholders' equity

AMERIFIRST BK N A (UNION SPRINGS, AL)
Reorganized under the laws of Delaware as USAL Bancorp, Inc. 09/01/1998
Each share Common $10 par exchanged for (5) shares Common $10 par

AMERIGO ENERGY INC (DE)
Name changed to Quest Solution, Inc. 06/10/2014

AMERIGOLD INC (OH)
Charter cancelled for failure to pay taxes 12/15/1993

AMERIGON INC (MI)
Reincorporated 05/20/2005
Each share old Class A Common no par exchanged for (0.2) share new Class A Common par 01/25/1999
New Class A Common no par reclassified as Common no par 05/24/2000
State of incorporation changed from (CA) to (MI) 05/20/2005
Name changed to Gentherm Inc. 09/07/2012

AMERIGROUP CORP (DE)
Common 1¢ par split (2) for (1) by issuance of (1) additional share payable 01/18/2005 to holders of record 12/31/2004 Ex date - 01/19/2005
Acquired by WellPoint, Inc. 12/24/2012
Each share Common 1¢ par exchanged for $92 cash

AMERIHEALTH INC (DE)
Merged into Champion Healthcare Corp. 12/06/1994
Each share Common 1¢ par exchanged for (0.17532847) share Common 1¢ par
Champion Healthcare Corp. merged into Paracelsus Healthcare Corp. 08/16/1996
(See Paracelsus Healthcare Corp.)

AMERIHEALTH INC (FL)
Reorganized under the laws of Delaware 12/19/1985
Each share Common $0.0001 par exchanged for (0.02) share Common 1¢ par
AmeriHealth, Inc. (DE) merged into Champion Healthcare Corp. 12/06/1994 which merged into Paracelsus Healthcare Corp. 08/16/1996
(See Paracelsus Healthcare Corp.)

AMERIHOST PPTYS INC (DE)
Each share Common $0.0001 par exchanged for (0.02) share Common $0.005 par 10/16/1989

Name changed to Arlington Hospitality, Inc. 05/24/2001
(See Arlington Hospitality, Inc.)

AMERIKING INC (DE)
Stock Dividends - in 3.25% Sr. Exchangeable Preferred to holders of 3.25% Sr. Exchangeable Preferred 3.205% payable 09/01/1999 to holders of record 08/20/1999; 3.25% payable 03/01/2000 to holders of record 02/18/2000; 3.25% payable 09/01/2000 to holders of record 08/21/2000 Ex date - 08/21/2000; 3.25% payable 03/01/2001 to holders of record 02/19/2001 Ex date - 02/14/2001; 3.25% payable 06/01/2001 to holders of record 05/21/2001 Ex date - 05/17/2001; 3.25% payable 09/01/2001 to holders of record 08/20/2001 Ex date - 08/16/2001; 3.25% payable 12/01/2001 to holders of record 11/20/2001; 3.25% payable 03/01/2002 to holders of record 02/20/2002 Ex date - 03/05/2002; 3.25% payable 06/01/2002 to holders of record 05/20/2002 Ex date - 06/04/2002; 3.25% payable 09/01/2002 to holders of record 08/20/2002 Ex date - 08/22/2002
Chapter 11 bankruptcy proceedings converted to Chapter 7 on 06/08/2004
No stockholders' equity

AMERILINK CORP (OH)
Merged into Tandy Corp. 07/30/1999
Each share Common no par exchanged for (0.4036) share Common $1 par
Tandy Corp. name changed to RadioShack Corp. 05/18/2000 which name changed to RS Legacy Corp. 09/23/2015
(See RS Legacy Corp.)

AMERILITHIUM CORP (NV)
Common $0.001 par split (8) for (1) by issuance of (7) additional shares payable 03/09/2010 to holders of record 03/09/2010
Name changed to Integrated Energy Solutions, Inc. 09/26/2014
Integrated Energy Solutions, Inc. name changed to Patten Energy Solutions Group, Inc. 05/03/2016

AMERIMARK CORP (DE)
Recapitalized as Amerishop Corp. 07/10/1992
Each share Common $0.00001 par exchanged for (0.1) share Common $0.00001 par
(See Amerishop Corp.)

AMERIMINE RES INC (FL)
Each share old Common $0.001 par exchanged for (0.001) share new Common $0.001 par 04/17/2006
Name changed to American Unity Investments, Inc. 08/09/2006
(See American Unity Investments, Inc.)

AMERIMMUNE PHARMACEUTICALS INC (CO)
Chapter 7 bankruptcy proceedings dismissed 10/03/2003
No stockholders' equity

AMERIN CORP (DE)
Merged into Radian Group Inc. 06/09/1999
Each share Common 1¢ par exchanged for (0.5333) share Common $0.001 par

AMERINET CORP (NV)
Charter permanently revoked 02/01/2004

AMERINET GROUP COM INC (DE)
Name changed to Fields Technologies Inc. (DE) 07/03/2001
Fields Technologies Inc. (DE)

reincorporated in Nevada as Park City Group, Inc. 08/08/2002

AMERINST INS GROUP INC (DE)
Reincorporated under the laws of Bermuda as AmerInst Insurance Group Ltd. 07/02/1999

AMERIPAGE INC (NV)
Company believed out of business 00/00/1996
Details not available

AMERIPATH INC (DE)
Merged into Welsh, Carson, Anderson & Stowe 03/27/2003
Each share Common 1¢ par exchanged for $21.25 cash

AMERIPLAS HLDGS LTD (CANADA)
Recapitalized as Downtown Industries Ltd. (Canada) 07/13/2010
Each share Common no par exchanged for (0.05) share Common no par
Downtown Industries Ltd. (Canada) reincorporated in British Columbia as Inform Resources Corp. 11/04/2010

AMERIPRINT INTL LTD (NV)
Name changed to True North Energy Corp. 03/30/2006

AMERIQUEST INC. (MT)
Name changed to Hair Analysis, Inc. 06/11/1982
Hair Analysis. Inc. recapitalized as OTC Stock Journal, Inc. 03/16/1983
(See OTC Stock Journal, Inc.)

AMERIQUEST TECHNOLOGIES INC (DE)
SEC revoked registration of securities 10/31/2005

AMERIS BANCORP (GA)
Fixed Rate Perpetual Preferred Ser. A called for redemption at $1,000 plus $9.25 accrued dividends on 03/24/2014
(Additional Information in Active)

AMERISCRIBE CORP (DE)
Merged into Pitney Bowes Inc. 10/29/1993
Each share Common 1¢ par exchanged for (0.3703) share Common $2 par

AMERISERV FINL CORP (DE)
Each share old Common 1¢ par exchanged for (0.08333333) share new Common 1¢ par 07/01/1994
Recapitalized as Namibian Copper Mines, Ltd. 07/14/1995
Each share new Common 1¢ par exchanged for (0.02) share Common $0.001 par
Namibian Copper Mines, Ltd. name changed to American Southwest Holdings Inc. 06/09/2000
(See American Southwest Holdings Inc.)

AMERISHOP CORP (DE)
Voluntarily dissolved 09/03/1997
Details not available

AMERISOURCE DISTRIBUTION CORP. (DE)
Name changed to AmeriSource Health Corp. 03/30/1995
AmeriSource Health Corp. merged into AmerisourceBergen Corp. 08/29/2001

AMERISOURCE HEALTH CORP (DE)
Class A Common 1¢ par split (2) for (1) by issuance of (1) additional share payable 03/24/1999 to holders of record 03/03/1999 Ex date - 03/25/1999
Under plan of merger each share Class A Common 1¢ par, Class B Common 1¢ par and Class C Common 1¢ par exchanged for (1) share AmerisourceBergen Corp. Common 1¢ par 08/29/2001

AMERISTAR CASINOS INC (NV)
Common 1¢ par split (2) for (1) by issuance of (1) additional share payable 06/20/2005 to holders of record 06/06/2005 Ex date - 06/21/2005
Acquired by Pinnacle Entertainment, Inc. 08/14/2013
Each share Common 1¢ par exchanged for $26.50 cash

AMERISTAR CORP (NV)
Merged into InTechnologies, Inc. 01/25/2000
Each share Common exchanged for (0.25) share Common $0.001 par
(See InTechnologies, Inc.)

AMERISTAR INTL HLDGS CORP (TN)
Administratively dissolved 08/20/1999

AMERISTAR RSP INCOME TR (ON)
Merged into Income Financial Trust 06/19/2006
Each Trust Unit automatically became (0.608722) Trust Unit

AMERISTOCK ETF TR (DE)
Completely liquidated 06/20/2008
Each Ameristock/Ryan 1 Year Treasury ETF Share of Bene. Int. $0.001 par received first and final distribution of $25.32734 cash
Each Ameristock/Ryan 2 Year Treasury ETF Share of Bene. Int. $0.001 par received first and final distribution of $25.56757 cash
Each Ameristock/Ryan 5 Year Treasury ETF Share of Bene. Int. $0.001 par received first and final distribution of $25.68296 cash
Each Ameristock/Ryan 10 Year Treasury ETF Share of Bene. Int. $0.001 par received first and final distribution of $25.81253 cash
Each Ameristock/Ryan 20 Year Treasury ETF Share of Bene. Int. $0.001 par received first and final distribution of $25.72965 cash

AMERITECH CORP (DE)
Common $1 par split (2) for (1) by issuance of (1) additional share 01/21/1994
Common $1 par split (2) for (1) by issuance of (1) additional share payable 01/26/1998 to holders of record 12/31/1997 Ex date - 01/27/1998
Merged into SBC Communications, Inc. 10/08/1999
Each share Common $1 par exchanged for (1.316) shares Common $1 par
SBC Communications, Inc. name changed to AT&T Inc. 11/18/2005

AMERITECH DENMARK FDG CORP
Stated Rate Auction Preferred Ser. C called for redemption at $100,000 on 11/7/2001
Stated Rate Auction Preferred Ser. D called for redemption at $100,000 on 11/14/2001
Stated Rate Auction Preferred Ser. A called for redemption at $100,000 on 12/5/2001
Stated Rate Auction Preferred Ser. B called for redemption at $100,000 on 12/12/2001

AMERITEL ENTERPRISES INC (OH)
Name changed to Americare Corp. 06/19/1978
(See Americare Corp.)

AMERITEL MGMT INC (WA)
Reincorporated 02/13/1992
Common no par split (2) for (1) by issuance of (1) additional share 01/18/1991
Place of incorporation changed from (BC) to (WA) 02/13/1992
Recapitalized as WCT Communications, Inc. 06/04/1992
Each share Common no par exchanged for (0.33333333) share Common no par
(See WCT Communications, Inc.)

AMERITEST CORP (DE)
Charter cancelled and declared inoperative and void for non-payment of 03/01/1989

AMERITEX INC (NV)
Charter revoked for failure to file reports and pay fees 01/01/1988

AMERITEX RES LTD (BC)
Struck off register and declared dissolved for failure to file returns 08/28/1992

AMERITOR IND FD (DC)
Completely liquidated 03/07/2001
Each share Common $1 par received first and final distribution of approximately $0.33 cash

AMERITOR INVT FD (DC)
Completely liquidated 07/24/2007
No stockholders' equity

AMERITOR SEC TR (DC)
Completely liquidated 12/27/2011
Each Class 1 Share of Bene. Int. no par received net asset value

AMERITRADE HLDG CORP NEW (DE)
Name changed to TD Ameritrade Holding Corp. 01/24/2006

AMERITRADE HLDG CORP OLD (DE)
Class A Common 1¢ par split (2) for (1) by issuance of (1) additional share payable 08/17/1998 to holders of record 08/07/1998
Class A Common 1¢ par split (2) for (1) by issuance of (1) additional share payable 02/22/1999 to holders of record 02/05/1999
Class A Common 1¢ par split (3) for (1) by issuance of (2) additional shares payable 07/02/1999 to holders of record 06/11/1999
Merged into Ameritrade Holding Corp. (New) 09/09/2002
Each share Class A Common 1¢ par exchanged for (1) share Common 1¢ par

AMERITRON CORP (UT)
Involuntarily dissolved 01/01/1992

AMERITRUST CORP (DE)
Common $6.66666666 par changed to $3.33333333 par and (1) additional share issued 05/03/1985
Common $3.33333333 par changed to $1.66666666 par and (1) additional share issued 06/02/1987
Merged into Society Corp. 03/16/1992
Each share Common $1.66666666 par exchanged for (0.65) share Common $1 par
Society Corp. merged into KeyCorp (New) 03/01/1994

AMERIVEST PPTYS INC (BC)
Struck off register and declared dissolved for failure to file returns 08/18/1989

AMERIVEST PPTYS INC (MD)
Liquidation completed
Each share Common $0.001 par received initial distribution of $3.50 cash payable 11/16/2006 to holders of record 11/10/2006 Ex date - 11/17/2006
Each share Common $0.001 par received second distribution of $1.75 cash payable 12/18/2006 to holders of record 12/11/2006
Each share Common $0.001 par received third distribution of $0.43 cash payable 03/14/2007 to holders of record 12/27/2006
Assets transferred to AMV Liquidating Trust (CO) and Common $0.001 par reclassified as Shares of Bene. Int. $0.001 par 12/27/2006
Each Share of Bene. Int. $0.001 par received fourth and final distribution of $0.065142 cash payable 12/21/2009 to holders of record 12/27/2006
Note: Certificates were not required to be surrendered and are without value

AMERIWEST ENERGY CORP (NV)
SEC revoked common stock registration 08/29/2012

AMERIWEST FINL CORP (DE)
Stock Dividend - 10% 07/10/1987
Name changed to ABQ Corp. 04/08/1988
(See ABQ Corp.)

AMERIWEST MINERALS CORP (NV)
Name changed to Ameriwest Petroleum Corp. 12/23/2010
Ameriwest Petroleum Corp. name changed to Falconridge Oil Technologies Corp. 07/02/2013

AMERIWEST PETE CORP (NV)
Common $0.001 par split (6) for (1) by issuance of (5) additional shares payable 12/23/2010 to holders of record 12/23/2010
Name changed to Falconridge Oil Technologies Corp. 07/02/2013

AMERIWOOD INDS INTL CORP (MI)
Common $5 par split (2) for (1) by issuance of (1) additional share 05/31/1993
Merged into Dorel Industries Inc. 05/05/1998
Each share Common $5 par exchanged for $9.625 cash

AMERIWORKS FINL SVCS INC (NJ)
Recapitalized as AmeriWorks, Inc. 01/29/2014
Each share Common no par exchanged for (0.01) share Common no par

AMERIX PRECIOUS METALS CORP (ON)
Each share old Common no par exchanged for (0.33333333) share new Common no par 05/02/2011
Recapitalized as Eagle Graphite Inc. 01/22/2015
Each share Common no par exchanged for (0.05) share Common no par

AMERLINE CORP. (IL)
Completely liquidated 03/22/1965
Each share Class A or B Common $1 par exchanged for (0.711346) share Revlon, Inc. Common $1 par
(See Revlon, Inc.)

AMERLING INDS INC (NY)
Charter cancelled and proclaimed dissolved for failure to pay taxes 03/25/1981

AMEROIL CORPORATION (CA)
Charter suspended by order of the franchise tax board 10/01/1937

AMEROIL ENERGY CORP (AB)
Reincorporated 08/00/1989
Place of incorporation changed from (BC) to (AB) 08/00/1989
Reincorporated under the laws of Oklahoma as ALN Resources Corp. 11/07/1990
ALN Resources Corp. recapitalized as American Natural Energy Corp. (Ctfs. dtd. prior to 07/19/1994) 12/01/1992 which was acquired by Alexander Energy Corp. 07/19/1994 which merged into National Energy Group, Inc. 08/30/1996
(See National Energy Group, Inc.)

AMERON INTL CORP (DE)
Reincorporated 03/25/1986
Name changed 04/16/1996
State of incorporation changed from (CA) to (DE) 03/25/1986
Common $5 par changed to $2.50 par and (1) additional share issued 04/07/1986
Name changed from Ameron, Inc. to Ameron International Corp. 04/16/1996
Common $2.50 par split (2) for (1) by issuance of (1) additional share payable 05/27/2003 to holders of

record 05/01/2003 Ex date - 05/28/2003
Acquired by National Oilwell Varco, Inc. 10/05/2011
Each share Common $2.50 par exchanged for $85 cash

AMEROSSI EC INC (WY)
Recapitalized as Nanotech Industries, Inc. 10/25/2007
Each share Common no par exchanged for (0.00001) share Common no par
(See Nanotech Industries, Inc.)

AMEROSSI ENERGY CORP (WY)
Reorganized 07/31/2007
Reorganized 07/31/2007
Each share old Common no par exchanged for (1) share new Common no par and (10,000) shares Restricted Common no par
Name changed to Nadir Energy & Mining Corp. 06/11/2008
(See Nadir Energy & Mining Corp.)

AMEROSSI INTL GROUP INC (WY)
Recapitalized as Bio-Med Technologies, Inc. 11/19/2007
Each share Common no par exchanged for (0.000002) share Common no par
(See Bio-Med Technologies, Inc.)

AMERPRO INDS INC (AB)
Reorganized under the laws of British Columbia as Amerpro Resources Inc. 03/06/2009
Each share Class A Common no par exchanged for (0.2) share Class A Common no par
Amerpro Resources Inc. name changed to Electric Metals Inc. 10/14/2009 which merged into Moimstone Corp. 09/12/2013 which name changed to Apivio Systems Inc. 05/23/2014
(See Apivio Systems Inc.)

AMERPRO RES INC (BC)
Name changed to Electric Metals Inc. 10/14/2009
Electric Metals Inc. merged into Moimstone Corp. 09/12/2013 which name changed to Apivio Systems Inc. 05/23/2014
(See Apivio Systems Inc.)

AMERPSYCH, INC. (FL)
Liquidation completed
Each share Capital Stock no par exchanged for initial distribution of $1.82 cash 05/08/1972
Each share Capital Stock no par received second and final distribution of $0.68 cash 07/02/1973

AMERSHAM PLC (UNITED KINGDOM)
Merged into General Electric Co. 04/08/2004
Each Sponsored ADR for Ordinary exchanged for (2.4165) shares Common 1¢ par

AMERSIN LIFE SCIENCES CORP (NV)
Recapitalized as Golden Tech Group, Ltd. 05/21/2007
Each share Common $0.001 par exchanged for (0.05) share Common $0.001 par
Golden Tech Group, Ltd. name changed to Mega Win Investments, Inc. 03/02/2018 which name changed to Invech Holdings, Inc. 08/07/2018

AMERTEK INC (ON)
Reincorporated 06/27/1989
Place of incorporation changed from (Canada) to (ON) 06/27/1989
Went out of business 00/00/1993
Stockholders' equity unlikely

AMERTRANZ WORLDWIDE HLDG CORP (DE)
Name changed to Target Logistics, Inc. 12/04/1998
(See Target Logistics, Inc.)

AMERUS GROUP CO (IA)
Each Adjustable Conversion Rate Equity Security Unit received (0.9237) share Common no par 07/27/2001
Each 6.25% Income Preferred Redeemable Increased Dividend Equity Security received (0.8497) share Common no par 08/16/2006
Non-Cumulative Perpetual Preferred Ser. A called for redemption at $26.03 plus $0.453125 accrued dividends on 09/13/2006
Merged into Aviva PLC 11/15/2006
Each share Common no par exchanged for $69 cash

AMERUS LIFE HLDGS INC / AMERUS CAP II
Under plan of merger name changed to Amerus Group Co. 09/20/2000
(See Amerus Group Co.)

AMERUS LIFE HLDGS INC (IA)
Name changed to Amerus Group Co. 09/20/2000
(See Amerus Group Co.)

AMES (O.) CO. (DE)
Name changed to McDonough Co. 07/01/1955
(See McDonough Co.)

AMES BALDWIN WYOMING CO.
Name changed to Ames (O.) Co. 00/00/1951
Ames (O.) Co. name changed to McDonough Co. 07/01/1955
(See McDonough Co.)

AMES BALDWIN WYOMING SHOVEL CO.
Name changed to Ames Baldwin Wyoming Co. 00/00/1931
Ames Baldwin Wyoming Co. name changed to Ames (O.) Co. 00/00/1951 which name changed to McDonough Co. 07/01/1955
(See McDonough Co.)

AMES DEPT STORES INC (DE)
Class A Common 50¢ par split (3) for (2) by issuance of (0.5) additional share 06/10/1968
Class A Common 50¢ par reclassified as Common 50¢ par 06/16/1969
Common 50¢ par split (5) for (4) by issuance of (0.25) additional share 04/12/1971
Common 50¢ par split (3) for (2) by issuance of (0.5) additional share 05/03/1972
Common 50¢ par split (5) for (4) by issuance of (0.25) additional share 06/16/1978
$1.50 Conv. Preferred no par called for redemption 09/12/1980
Common 50¢ par split (3) for (2) by issuance of (0.5) additional share 09/11/1981
Common 50¢ par split (3) for (2) by issuance of (0.5) additional share 09/09/1983
Common 50¢ par split (2) for (1) by issuance of (1) additional share 08/10/1984
$5.32 Conv. Preferred Ser. A no par called for redemption 05/22/1985
Common 50¢ par split (2) for (1) by issuance of (1) additional share 11/08/1985
Stock Dividends - 20% 10/10/1966; 10% 06/15/1979
Plan of reorganization under Chapter 11 Federal Bankruptcy Code effective 12/30/1992
No stockholders' equity
Plan of reorganization under Chapter 11 Federal Bankruptcy proceedings effective 11/19/2013
New Common 1¢ par stockholders' equity unlikely

AMES FINL CORP (DE)
Acquired by Brenton Banks, Inc. 10/01/1992
Each share Common 1¢ par exchanged for (1.358) shares Common $5 par
Brenton Banks, Inc. merged into Wells Fargo & Co. 12/01/2000

AMES IRON WORKS, INC. (NY)
Merged into Fitzgibbons Boiler Co. 01/10/1962
Each share Capital Stock $1 par exchanged for $4 cash

AMES MERCANTILE CO., INC. (CA)
Completely liquidated 10/31/1966
Each share Capital Stock $1 par exchanged for first and final distribution of (0.4) share Castle & Cooke, Inc. (Old) Common $10 par
Castle & Cooke, Inc. (Old) name changed to Dole Food Co., Inc. (HI) 07/30/1991 which reincorporated in Delaware 07/01/2001
(See Dole Food Co., Inc. (Old) (DE))

AMES W R CO (CA)
Each share Capital Stock $5 par exchanged for (5) shares Capital Stock $2 par 03/25/1957
Name changed to First Milpitas Corp. 03/15/1968
(See First Milpitas Corp.)

AMESBURY ELECTRIC LIGHT CO. (MA)
Merged into Merrimack-Essex Electric Co. on a (1.625) for (1) basis 07/30/1957
Merrimack-Essex-Electric Co. acquired by New England Electric System 06/30/1959
(See New England Electric System)

AMETAL MINING CORP. (QC)
Charter cancelled 10/00/1974

AMETECH INC (OK)
Filed petition under Chapter 11 Federal Bankruptcy Code effective 02/02/1998
Stockholders' equity unlikely

AMETEK INC OLD (DE)
Capital Stock no par and VTC's for Capital Stock no par split (2) for (1) by issuance of (1) additional share respectively 05/01/1964
Capital Stock no par reclassified as Common $1 par and VTC's for Capital Stock no par reclassified as VTC's for Common $1 par 04/01/1969
Common $1 par and VTC's for Common $1 par split (2) for (1) by issuance of (1) additional share respectively 05/01/1969
Voting Trust agreement terminated and each VTC for Common $1 par automatically became (1) share Common $1 par 00/00/1973
Common $1 par split (2) for (1) by issuance of (1) additional share 12/24/1979
Common $1 par split (2) for (1) by issuance of (1) additional share 07/15/1983
Common $1 par split (2) for (1) by issuance of (1) additional share 11/19/1987
Each share Common $1 par received distribution of (1) share AMETEK, Inc. (New) Common 1¢ par payable 08/07/1997 to holders of record 07/31/1997
Merged into Culligan Water Technologies, Inc. 07/31/1997
Each share Common $1 par exchanged for (0.105) share Common 1¢ par
Culligan Water Technologies, Inc. merged into United States Filter Corp. (New) 06/15/1998
(See United States Filter Corp. (New))

AMETEX CORP (NV)
Charter revoked for failure to file reports and pay fees 02/01/1984

AMETEX INC (WA)
Charter cancelled and proclaimed dissolved for failure to file reports 00/00/1986

AMETRINE CAP INC (DE)
Recapitalized as New Source Energy Group, Inc. 04/25/2011
Each share Common 1¢ par exchanged for (0.4699999) share Common 1¢ par
New Source Energy Group, Inc. name changed to Encompass Energy Services, Inc. 04/19/2012

AMEUROTECH CORP (FL)
Reincorporated 04/18/2007
State of incorporation changed from (NV) to (FL) 04/18/2007
Recapitalized as Scott Contracting Holdings, Inc. 07/11/2007
Each (198) shares Common $0.001 par exchanged for (1) share Common $0.001 par
Note: No holder will receive fewer than (100) shares
Scott Contracting Holdings, Inc. name changed to Liverpool Group, Inc. 04/29/2008

AMEV ADVANTAGE PORTFOLIOS INC (MN)
Name changed to Fortis Advantage Portfolios, Inc. 02/22/1992
(See Fortis Advantage Portfolios, Inc.)

AMEV ADVISERS, INC. (MN)
Name changed to Fortis Advisers, Inc. 02/22/1992
(See Fortis Advisers, Inc.)

AMEV CAP FD INC (MN)
Under plan of reorganization each share Common 1¢ par automatically became (1) share Fortis Equity Portfolios Inc. Capital Fund Common 1¢ par 02/22/1992
(See Fortis Equity Portfolios Inc.)

AMEV FIDUCIARY FD INC (MN)
Name changed to Fortis Fiduciary Fund Inc. 02/22/1992
Fortis Fiduciary Fund Inc. merged into Fortis Equity Portfolios Inc. 10/22/1998
(See Fortis Equity Portfolios Inc.)

AMEV GOVT MONEY FD INC (MN)
Fund terminated 03/14/1986
Each share Common 1¢ par received $1 cash

AMEV GROWTH FD INC (MN)
Name changed to Fortis Growth Fund, Inc. 02/22/1992
(See Fortis Growth Fund, Inc.)

AMEV MONEY FD INC (MN)
Name changed to Fortis Money Portfolios Inc. 02/22/1992
(See Fortis Money Portfolios Inc.)

AMEV N V (NETHERLANDS)
Name changed to Fortis Amev N.V. 06/09/1994
Fortis Amev N.V. name changed to Fortis NL 01/01/1999 which name changed to Ageas 05/14/2010

AMEV SECS INC (MN)
Name changed to Fortis Securities, Inc. (MN) 01/08/1993
Fortis Securities, Inc. (MN) reorganized in Maryland as Hartford Income Shares Fund, Inc. 07/16/2002 which merged into Rivus Bond Fund 10/22/2010 which name changed to Cutwater Select Income Fund 12/09/2011 which name changed to Insight Select Income Fund 12/29/2016

AMEV SER FDS INC (MN)
Money Management Portfolio reclassified as Money Market Portfolio 05/01/1990
Name changed to Fortis Series Fund, Inc. and Growth Stock Portfolio Capital Stock 1¢ par, Income Portfolio Capital Stock 1¢ par, Managed Portfolio Capital Stock 1¢ par, Money Market Portfolio Capital Stock 1¢ par and U.S. Government

Securities Portfolio Capital Stock 1¢ par reclassified as Growth Stock Series Common 1¢ par, Diversified Income Series Common 1¢ par, Asset Allocation Series Common 1¢ par, Money Market Series Common 1¢ par and U.S. Government Securities Series Common 1¢ par respectively 02/22/1992
(See Fortis Series Fund, Inc.)

AMEV SPL FD INC (MN)
Name changed to Special Portfolios, Inc. 08/31/1989
Special Portfolios, Inc. merged into Fortis Growth Fund, Inc. 03/01/1996
(See Fortis Growth Fund, Inc.)

AMEV TAX FREE FD INC (MN)
Name changed to Fortis Tax Free Portfolios Inc. 02/22/1992
(See Fortis Tax Free Portfolios Inc.)

AMEV U S GOVT SECS FD INC (MN)
Name changed to Fortis Income Portfolios, Inc. 02/22/1992
(See Fortis Income Portfolios, Inc.)

AMEV WORLDWIDE PORTFOLIOS INC (MN)
Name changed to Fortis Worldwide Portfolios, Inc. 02/22/1992
(See Fortis Worldwide Portfolios, Inc.)

AMEX ACQUISITIONS CORP (CO)
Recapitalized as Air Resources Corp. (CO) 08/17/1990
Each share Common $0.001 par exchanged for (0.01) share Common $0.001 par
Air Resources Corp. (CO) reincorporated in Virginia as Spurlock Industries, Inc. 07/15/1996
(See Spurlock Industries, Inc.)

AMEX CORP. (NJ)
Charter revoked for failure to file reports and pay fees 01/06/1995

AMEX SYS CORP (NV)
Capital Stock 50¢ par changed to 5¢ par 09/14/1979
Each share Common 5¢ par exchanged for (0.05) share Common $1 par 05/20/1994
Recapitalized as Millenium Holding Group Inc. 06/04/1999
Each share Common $1 par exchanged for (0.03178639) share Common $1 par
(See Millenium Holding Group Inc.)

AMEX VENTURES INC (BC)
Name changed to Global SortWeb.com Inc. and (3) additional shares issued 08/01/2001
Global SortWeb.com Inc. reorganized as Mantra Mining Inc. 06/12/2006 which name changed to TintinaGold Resources Inc. 09/28/2009 which name changed to Tintina Resources Inc. 05/26/2011 which name changed to Sandfire Resources America Inc. 02/02/2018

AMEXAN INC (NV)
Name changed to Nostalgia Motorcars, Inc. 06/01/1998
Nostalgia Motorcars, Inc. recapitalized as Elution Technologies Inc. 06/26/2002 which name changed to Tankless Systems Worldwide, Inc. 07/25/2003 which name changed to Skye International, Inc. 11/11/2005
(See Skye International, Inc.)

AMF BOWLING INC (DE)
Plan of reorganization under Chapter 11 Federal Bankruptcy Code effective 09/24/2002
No stockholders' equity

AMF BOWLING WORLDWIDE INC (DE)
Merged into Code Hennessy & Simmons LLC 02/27/2004
Each share Common 1¢ par exchanged for $25 cash

AMF CAP GROUP INC (NV)
Common $0.001 par split (3) for (1) by issuance of (2) additional shares payable 06/17/2009 to holders of record 06/05/2009 Ex date - 06/18/2009
Name changed to Blackrock Resources, Inc. 06/18/2009
Blackrock Resources, Inc. name changed to Artepharm Global Corp. 01/14/2010 which name changed to Sharprock Resources Inc. 07/20/2011 which recapitalized as Evergreen-Agra, Inc. (NV) 10/23/2013 which reincorporated in Delaware as Evergreen-Agra Global Investments, Inc. 11/01/2017

AMF CAP INC (NV)
Name changed to Pro Motors Group Corp. 10/29/2007
Pro Motors Group Corp. recapitalized as Hydrogen Hybrid Corp. 11/25/2008 which name changed to Get Real USA Inc. 01/12/2011

AMF INC (NJ)
Merged into Minstar Inc. 10/03/1985
Each share Common $1.75 par exchanged for $18.25 principal amount of 10% Sr. Subord. Debentures due 10/15/1995
3.90% Preferred $100 par called for redemption 11/18/1985

AMFAC INC (HI)
Capital Stock $10 par reclassified as Common no par and (0.4) additional share issued 12/06/1968
Common no par split (3) for (2) by issuance of (0.5) additional share 06/14/1971
$1.875 Conv. Exchangeable Preferred no par called for redemption 07/25/1988
$1 Conv. Preferred Ser. B no par called for redemption 09/16/1988
$2.50 Conv. Preferred no par called for redemption 09/16/1988
Acquired by JMB Realty Corp. 11/18/1988
Each share Common no par exchanged for $49.10 cash

AMFED FINL CORP (DE)
Bank placed in receivership 05/18/1990
Stockholders' equity unlikely

AMFED FINL INC (NV)
Stock Dividend - 10% 09/10/1993
Merged into Norwest Corp. 01/18/1996
Each share Common 10¢ par exchanged for (1.0251) shares Common $1.66666666 par
Norwest Corp. name changed to Wells Fargo & Co. (New) 11/02/1998

AMFESCO INDS INC (NY)
Stock Dividends - 100% 05/01/1980; 200% 07/15/1981; 10% 06/12/1983
Reorganized under the laws of Delaware as New American Shoe Co., Inc. 04/14/1988
Each share Common 10¢ par exchanged for (1) share Common 1¢ par
(See New American Shoe Co., Inc.)

AMFICO CORP. (DE)
Charter cancelled and declared inoperative and void for non-payment of taxes 03/01/1976

AMFIRST BANCORPORATION (WA)
Merged into Cascade Financial Corp. (DE) 08/01/1997
Each share Common $1 par exchanged for (2.412) shares Common 1¢ par
Cascade Financial Corp. (DE) reincorporated in Washington 05/12/2003
(See Cascade Financial Corp. (WA))

AMFIT CORP (WA)
Name changed to American Fuel Transit Corp. 04/21/1986

(See American Fuel Transit Corp.)

AMFLO PETE CORP (BC)
Acquired by American Fluorite Corp. 12/31/1980
Each share Common no par exchanged for (0.75) share Common no par
American Fluorite Corp. name changed to AFC Energy Corp. 03/26/1983
(See AFC Energy Corp.)

AMFM INC (DE)
$3 Conv. Exchangeable Preferred called for redemption at $52.40 on 08/24/1999
7% Conv. Preferred called for redemption at $52.45 on 01/19/2000
Merged into Clear Channel Communications, Inc. 08/30/2000
Each share Common 1¢ par exchanged for (0.94) share Common 10¢ par
(See Clear Channel Communications, Inc.)

AMFOOD INDS INC (IL)
Chapter 11 bankruptcy proceedings converted to Chapter 7 on 04/28/1988
Stockholders' equity unlikely

AMFRE GRANT INC (NY)
Name changed to Emons Industries, Inc. (NY) 06/15/1972
Emons Industries, Inc. (NY) reorganized in Delaware as Emons Holdings Inc. 12/31/1986 which name changed to Emons Transportation Group Inc. 12/01/1993
(See Emons Transportation Group Inc.)

AMG CAP TR I (DE)
Each 5.1% Conv. 144A Preferred Trust Security automatically became (1) 5.1% Conv. Preferred Trust Security 05/03/2012
5.1% Conv. Trust Preferred Securities called for redemption at $50 plus $0.576023 accrued dividends on 03/31/2014

AMG OIL LTD (CANADA)
Reincorporated 12/04/2008
Place of incorporation changed from (NV) to (Canada) 12/04/2008
Name changed to Adira Energy Ltd. 01/21/2010
Adira Energy Ltd. name changed to Empower Clinics Inc. 04/30/2018

AMGEN (CA)
Reincorporated under the laws of Delaware and Common no par changed to $0.0001 par 02/17/1987

AMGLO INDS INC (WI)
Merged into Amglobal Corp. 05/17/1989
Each share Common 1¢ par exchanged for (4) shares Common $0.001 par
(See Amglobal Corp.)

AMGLOBAL CORP (DE)
Charter cancelled and declared inoperative and void for non-payment of taxes 03/01/1990

AMHAWK RES CORP (BC)
Recapitalized as Consolidated Amhawk Enterprises Ltd. 05/27/1987
Each share Common no par exchanged for (0.25) share Common no par
(See Consolidated Amhawk Enterprises Ltd.)

AMHEALTH PHYSICAL CARE INC (DE)
Charter forfeited for failure to maintain a registered agent 02/25/1998

AMHERST ASSOC INC (DE)
Merged into HBO & Co. 02/28/1985
Each share Common 1¢ par

exchanged for (1.05) shares Common 5¢ par
HBO & Co. merged into McKesson HBOC Inc. 01/12/1999 which name changed to McKesson Corp. 07/30/2001

AMHERST COAL CO (WV)
Merged into Diamond Shamrock Corp. 08/04/1981
Each share Common no par exchanged for (333.588) shares Common no par
Diamond Shamrock Corp. name changed to Maxus Energy Corp. 04/30/1987
(See Maxus Energy Corp.)

AMHERST GOLD MINES LTD.
Out of business 00/00/1942
Details not available

AMHERST WATER CO.
Acquired by the Town of Amherst, MA 00/00/1941
Details not available

AMHN INC (NV)
Reincorporated 07/20/2010
State of incorporation changed from (UT) to (NV) and Common 10¢ par changed to $0.001 par 07/20/2010
Recapitalized as TherapeuticsMD, Inc. 10/03/2011
Each share Common $0.001 par exchanged for (0.01) share Common $0.001 par

AMI INDS INC (CO)
97% held by Ad/Ross Corp. as of 01/14/1977
Public interest eliminated

AMI INDS INC (NY)
Charter cancelled and proclaimed dissolved for failure to pay taxes 09/30/1981

AMI RES INC (BC)
Each share old Common no par exchanged for (0.2) share new Common no par 02/22/2013
Name changed to Ashanti Sankofa Inc. 01/19/2017

AMI SYS INC (TX)
Charter forfeited for failure to pay taxes 02/14/1995

AMIC CORP (NC)
Common $1 par changed to 75¢ par and (0.33333333) additional share issued 05/24/1976
Common 75¢ par changed to 50¢ par and (0.5) additional share issued 05/22/1978
Stock Dividend - 25% 08/31/1971
Merged into Merrill Lynch & Co., Inc. 02/14/1979
Each share Common 50¢ par exchanged for $26.75 cash

AMICA MATURE LIFESTYLES INC (CANADA)
Each share old Common no par exchanged for (0.33333333) share new Common no par 01/13/2003
Acquired by BayBridge Seniors Housing Inc. 12/22/2015
Each share new Common no par exchanged for $18.75 cash
Note: Unexchanged certificates will be cancelled and become without value 12/22/2021

AMICABLE LIFE INSURANCE CO. (TX)
Capital Stock $10 par changed to $5 par and (1) additional share issued 05/01/1964
Stock Dividends - 50% 03/11/1952; 33.33333333% 03/10/1953
Merged into American-Amicable Life Insurance Co. 03/01/1965
Each share Capital Stock $5 par exchanged for (4) shares Common $1 par
(See American-Amicable Life Insurance Co.)

AMICAN PETROLEUM & NATURAL GAS CORP. LTD. (SK)
Liquidation completed 00/00/1960
Details not available

AMICAS INC (DE)
Acquired by Merge Healthcare Inc. 04/28/2010
Each share Common $0.001 par exchanged for $6.05 cash

AMICHI GOLD MINES LTD. (ON)
Charter cancelled for failure to pay taxes and file returns 11/00/1958

AMICO PPTYS (WA)
Shares of Bene. Int. $1 par reclassified as Common Shares of Bene. Int. $1 par 03/04/1969
Recapitalized as United States Equity & Mortgage Trust 09/27/1971
Each share $6.60 Conv. Preference Shares of Bene. Int. Ser. A $100 par exchanged for (10) shares $0.66 Conv. Preference Shares of Bene. Int. Ser. A $1 par
Common Shares of Bene. Int. $1 par only affected by change of name
(See United States Equity & Mortgage Trust)

AMICON CORP (MA)
Common $0.33333333 par split (5) for (4) by issuance of (0.25) additional share 03/01/1979
Merged into Grace (W.R.) & Co. (CT) 03/10/1983
Each share Common $0.33333333 par exchanged for $23.63 cash
Note: An additional payment of $1.481749 cash per share was made 03/24/1984

AMICOR INC (DE)
Recapitalized as Keystone Camera Products Corp. 06/20/1984
Each share Common 2¢ par exchanged for (0.05) share Common 40¢ par
(See Keystone Camera Products Corp.)

AMICUS CAP CORP (BC)
Reorganized as Polo Biology Global Group Corp. 11/25/2008
Each share Common no par exchanged for (0.8667013) share Common no par
Polo Biology Global Group Corp. recapitalized as P&P Ventures Inc. 11/23/2012

AMIGA TELEPHONY CORP (DE)
Name changed to Streamscape Networks Inc. 03/03/2000
(See Streamscape Networks Inc.)

AMIGO MINES LTD (QC)
Charter annulled for failure to file annual reports 03/14/1987

AMIGO SILVER MINES LTD (BC)
Struck off register and declared dissolved for failure to file returns 10/02/1992

AMIGULA INC (CO)
SEC revoked common stock registration 08/28/2006

AMIL PARTICIPACOES SA (BRAZIL)
ADR agreement terminated 06/27/2013
Each ADR for Ordinary exchanged for $13.192018 cash

AMINEX CORP. (DE)
Name changed to Aminex Resources Corp. 12/10/74
(See Aminex Resources Corp.)

AMINEX RES CORP (DE)
Merged into Kaneb Services, Inc. 08/18/1981
Each share Common 1¢ par exchanged for $0.20 cash

AMINI OIL CO (UT)
Merged into Teal Petroleum Co. 10/18/1974
Each share Common 5¢ par exchanged for $8 cash

AMINT INVTS LTD (AB)
Struck off register for failure to file annual returns 10/01/1991

AMIR MINES LTD (BC)
Merged into Bema Gold Corp. (BC) 12/08/1988
Each share Common no par exchanged for (1) share Common no par
Bema Gold Corp. (BC) reincorporated in Canada 07/19/2002 which merged into Kinross Gold Corp. 02/27/2007

AMIR VENTURES CORP (BC)
Reorganized under the laws of Yukon as America Mineral Fields Inc. 08/08/1995
Each share Common no par exchanged for (1.5) shares Common no par
America Mineral Fields Inc. name changed to Adastra Minerals Inc. 05/12/2004 which merged into First Quantum Minerals Ltd. 08/11/2006

AMIS HLDGS INC (DE)
Merged into ON Semiconductor Corp. 03/17/2008
Each share Common 1¢ par exchanged for (1.15) shares Common 1¢ par

AMISH NATURALS INC (NV)
SEC revoked common stock registration 10/04/2011

AMISK INC (QC)
6.5% Conv. Preferred Ser. 1 called for redemption at $3 plus $0.034 accrued dividends on 12/05/2004
Completely liquidated
Each share Class A Multiple no par received first and final distribution of $0.84 cash payable 11/06/2007 to holders of record 10/31/2007
Each share Class B Subordinate no par received first and final distribution of $0.84 cash payable 11/06/2007 to holders of record 10/31/2007
Note: Certificates were not required to be surrendered and are without value

AMISTAR CORP (CA)
Company terminated common stock registration and is no longer public as of 03/28/2007

AMISYS MANAGED CARE SYS INC (DE)
Merged into HBO & Co. 06/13/1997
Each share Common $0.001 par exchanged for (0.35) share Common 5¢ par
HBO & Co. merged into McKesson HBOC Inc. 01/12/1999 which name changed to McKesson Corp. 07/30/2001

AMITELO COMMUNICATIONS INC (FL)
SEC revoked common stock registration 03/10/2005

AMITY BANCORP INC (CT)
Name changed to CBC Bancorp Inc. 06/15/1993
(See CBC Bancorp Inc.)

AMITY BANCSHARES INC (DE)
Merged into Advantage Bancorp, Inc. 12/17/1994
Each share Common 1¢ par exchanged for $36.25 cash

AMITY BK (WOODBRIDGE, CT)
Under plan of reorganization each share Common $2.50 par automatically became (1) share Amity Bancorp Inc. Common $2.50 par 02/25/1987
Amity Bancorp Inc. name changed to CBC Bancorp Inc. 06/15/1993
(See CBC Bancorp Inc.)

AMITY GOLD MINES, LTD.
Out of existence 00/00/1944
Details not available

AMJ CAMPBELL INC (ON)
Acquired by AMJ Management Acquisition Inc. 02/28/2003
Each share Common no par exchanged for $2.30 cash

AMK CORP (DE)
Common $2 par split (2) for (1) by issuance of (1) additional share 07/12/1968
Under plan of merger each share $3 Conv. Preferred no par, $3.20 Conv. Preference no par and Common $2 par automatically became (1) share United Brands Co. $3 Conv. Preferred no par, $3.20 Conv. Preference Ser. B no par and Common $1 par respectively 06/30/1970
United Brands Co. name changed to Chiquita Brands International, Inc. 03/20/1990
(See Chiquita Brands International, Inc.)

AML COMMUNICATIONS INC (DE)
Common 1¢ par split (3) for (2) by issuance of (0.5) additional share payable 06/28/1996 to holders of record 06/05/1996
Acquired by Microsemi Corp. 05/27/2011
Each share Common 1¢ par exchanged for $2.50 cash

AMLARTIC GOLD MINES LTD. (ON)
Charter cancelled for failure to pay taxes and file returns 11/00/1973

AMLI RESIDENTIAL PPTYS TR (MD)
Merged into Prime Property Fund, LLC 02/07/2006
Each Conv. Preferred Share of Bene. Int. Ser. B exchanged for $37.952667 cash
Each Conv. Preferred Share of Bene. Int. Ser. D exchanged for $34.23 cash
Each Share of Bene. Int. 1¢ par exchanged for $37.952667 cash

AMLIN PLC (UNITED KINGDOM)
ADR agreement terminated 02/26/2016
Each ADR for Ordinary exchanged for $38.496439 cash

AMM GOLD MINES LTD. (ON)
Charter cancelled for failure to pay taxes and file returns 03/10/1958

AMMANN (JACK) PHOTOGRAMMETRIC ENGINEERS, INC. (TX)
Merged into Geotechnics & Resources, Inc. 01/05/1962
Each share Common $1 par exchanged for (1.25) shares Class A Common 25¢ par and (1.25) shares Class B 25¢ par
(See Geotechnics & Resources, Inc.)

AMMEST GROUP INC (KS)
Name changed 06/05/1973
Name changed from Ammest Inc. to Ammest Group, Inc. 06/05/1973
Merged into Academy Insurance Group, Inc. 08/31/1978
Each share Common $1 par exchanged for (1) share Conv. Preferred 10¢ par
(See Academy Insurance Group, Inc.)

AMMEX GOLD MNG CORP (NV)
Recapitalized as Wind Works Power Corp. 06/11/2009
Each share Common $0.001 par exchanged for (0.1) share Common $0.001 par

AMMON CORP (UT)
Proclaimed dissolved for failure to pay taxes 09/30/1975

AMMONIA HOLD INC (UT)
Name changed to TS&B Holdings, Inc. 10/11/2001
TS&B Holdings, Inc. recapitalized as CALI Holdings Inc. 04/08/2005 which name changed to Sovereign

Exploration Associates International, Inc. 10/27/2005

AMMONITE ENERGY LTD (AB)
Merged into Novus Energy Inc. 12/11/2009
Each share Common no par exchanged for (0.825) share Common no par
Note: Unexchanged certificates were cancelled and became without value 12/11/2015
(See Novus Energy Inc.)

AMN CAP CORP (BC)
Recapitalized as Altan Rio Minerals Ltd. 01/12/2012
Each share Common no par exchanged for (0.600006) share Common no par

AMNET MTG INC (MD)
Merged into Wachovia Corp. (Ctfs. dated after 09/01/2001) 12/12/2005
Each share Common 1¢ par exchanged for $10.30 cash

AMNEX INC (NY)
Each share old Common $0.001 par exchanged for (0.1) share new Common $0.001 par 09/25/1992
Filed a petition under Chapter 11 Federal Bankruptcy Code 05/05/1999
No stockholders' equity

AMNIS ENERGY INC (FL)
Name changed to Homeland Security Group International, Inc. 10/10/2005
Homeland Security Group International, Inc. recapitalized as Domestic Energy Corp. 04/07/2008
(See Domestic Energy Corp.)

AMNIS SYS INC (DE)
Name changed to Corridor Communications Corp. 03/31/2004
(See Corridor Communications Corp.)

AMNUTRIA DAIRY INC (NV)
Name changed to Emerald Dairy Inc. 01/28/2008
(See Emerald Dairy Inc.)

AMOCO CORP (IN)
Common no par split (2) for (1) by issuance of (1) additional share 03/27/1989
Common no par split (2) for (1) by issuance of (1) additional share payable 04/28/1998 to holders of record 03/31/1998 Ex date - 04/29/1998
Merged into BP Amoco p.l.c. 12/31/1998
Each share Common no par exchanged for (0.66167) Sponsored ADR for Ordinary 25p par
BP Amoco p.l.c. name changed to BP PLC 05/01/2001

AMOIL RES INC (AB)
Recapitalized 01/23/1997
Recapitalized from Amoil Petroleums Inc. to Amoil Resources Inc. 01/23/1997
Each share Common no par exchanged for (0.33333333) share Common no par
Name changed to River Valley Energy Services Corp. 12/08/2000
River Valley Energy Services Corp. recapitalized as River Valley Energy Services Ltd. 11/28/2002 which reorganized as River Valley Income Fund 10/05/2004 which name changed to Eveready Income Fund 03/31/2005 which reorganized as Eveready Inc. 01/07/2009 which was acquired by Clean Harbors, Inc. 07/31/2009

AMOR EXPLORATION LTD.
Liquidated 00/00/1946
Details not available

AMORE MINERALS INC. (BC)
Name changed to Amore Resources Inc. 11/10/1980
Amore Resources Inc. recapitalized

as Freeway Resources Ltd. 07/31/1984 which recapitalized as GRD Industries Ltd. 05/10/1989
(See GRD Industries Ltd.)

AMORE RES INC (BC)
Recapitalized as Freeway Resources Ltd. 07/31/1984
Each share Capital Stock no par exchanged for (0.2) share Common no par
Freeway Resources Ltd. recapitalized as GRD Industries Ltd. 05/10/1989
(See GRD Industries Ltd.)

AMORE TV INC (NV)
Each share old Common $0.001 par exchanged for (0.01) share new Common $0.001 par 11/20/2006
Recapitalized as Rapid Fitness, Inc. 05/11/2007
Each share new Common $0.001 par exchanged for (0.01) share Common $0.001 par
Note: Holders of between (201) and (19,999) shares received (200) shares
Holders of (200) or fewer shares were not affected by the reverse split
Rapid Fitness, Inc. name changed to Tri-Star Holdings Inc. 08/27/2008 which recapitalized as Macada Holding, Inc. (NV) 08/20/2009 which reincorporated in Wyoming 02/22/2011 which recapitalized as KMA Holding, Inc. 03/17/2011
(See KMA Holding, Inc.)

AMORFIX LIFE SCIENCES LTD (CANADA)
Name changed to ProMIS Neurosciences Inc. 07/14/2015

AMOROCORP INC (DE)
SEC revoked common stock registration 07/06/2007

AMOS MINES LTD (QC)
Merged into Jonpol Explorations Ltd. 04/28/1982
Each share Common $1 par exchanged for (0.13333333) share Common no par
Jonpol Explorations Ltd. merged into Eastern Platinum Ltd. 04/26/2005

AMOSKEAG BK SHS INC (NH)
Common $1 par split (2) for (1) by issuance of (1) additional share 02/26/1986
Taken over by FDIC 10/10/1991
No stockholders' equity

AMOSKEAG CO. (NH)
Each share Common no par received distribution of (3) additional shares 00/00/1955
Completely liquidated 01/03/1966
Each share Preferred no par exchanged for first and final distribution of $100 principal amount of Amoskeag Co. (DE) 5% Debentures due 01/01/1976 or $100 cash
Each share Common no par exchanged for first and final distribution of (3) shares Amoskeag Co. (DE) Common no par
(See Amoskeag Co. (DE))

AMOSKEAG CO (DE)
Common no par split (2) for (1) by issuance of (1) additional share 12/18/1980
Common no par changed to $1 par 04/27/1987
Each share Common $1 par received distribution of (1) share Non-transferable Conv. Class B Common $1 par 05/07/1987
Merged into Fieldcrest Cannon, Inc. 12/01/1993
Each share Common $1 par exchanged for $40 cash
Each share Non-transferable Conv. Class B Common $1 par exchanged for $40 cash
Note: Unexchanged certificates were cancelled and became without value 06/01/1994

AMOSKEAG MANUFACTURING CO.
Liquidation completed 00/00/1941
Details not available

AMOSKEAG NATL BK & TR CO (MANCHESTER, NH)
Capital Stock $100 par changed to $5 par and (19) additional shares issued 08/01/1979
Merged into Amoskeag Bank Shares, Inc. 10/31/1984
Each share Capital Stock $5 par exchanged for (4.5) shares Common $1 par
(See Amoskeag Bank Shares, Inc.)

AMOUR FIBER CORE INC (NV)
Reorganized 05/24/2004
Reorganized from (WA) to under the laws of Nevada 05/24/2004
Each share Common no par exchanged for (1/6) share Common $0.001 par
Name changed to American Fiber Green Products, Inc. 06/18/2004

AMOY PPTYS LTD (HONG KONG)
Name changed to Hang Lung Properties Ltd. 01/10/2002

AMP HLDG INC (NV)
Name changed to Workhorse Group Inc. 04/16/2015

AMP INC (PA)
Reincorporated 04/21/1989
Common $1 par and Endorsed Shares of Common $1 par changed to no par and (2) additional shares issued respectively 06/02/1961
Common no par and Endorsed Shares of Common no par split (2) for (1) by issuance of (1) additional share respectively 06/05/1967
No Common no par (unendorsed) were outstanding as of 12/31/1972
Endorsed Shares of Common no par split (3) for (1) by issuance of (2) additional shares 06/08/1973
Endorsed Shares of Common no par split (3) for (1) by issuance of (2) additional shares 06/08/1984
State of incorporation changed from (NJ) to (PA) 04/21/1989
Common no par split (2) for (1) by issuance of (1) additional share 03/01/1995
Merged into Tyco International Ltd. (Bermuda) 04/01/1999
Each share Common no par exchanged for (0.7507) share Common 20¢ par
Tyco International Ltd. (Bermuda) reincorporated in Switzerland 03/17/2009 which merged into Johnson Controls International PLC 09/06/2016

AMP PRODUCTIONS LTD (NV)
Each share old Common $0.0001 par exchanged for (0.1) share new Common $0.0001 par 09/17/2010
Recapitalized as Computer Graphics International Inc. 06/07/2011
Each share new Common $0.0001 par exchanged for (0.45871559) share Common $0.0001 par

AMPAC NATL CORP (CO)
Recapitalized as IPT Corp. 07/20/1992
Each share Common 25¢ par exchanged for (0.05) share Common 25¢ par

AMPAC PETROLEUM RESOURCES INC. (BC)
Name changed to W.I. Wheels International Ltd. 10/16/1987
W.I. Wheels International Ltd. recapitalized as Annisquam Art Co., Ltd. 06/08/1990 which name changed to PHL Pinnacle Holdings Ltd. 07/18/1994 which recapitalized as Citrine Holdings Ltd. 01/09/1997

AMPACE CORP (DE)
Plan of reorganization under Chapter 11 Federal Bankruptcy proceedings effective 02/00/2000
No stockholders' equity

AMPAD CORP (MA)
Common $1.66666666 par changed to $0.83333333 par and (1) additional share issued 07/06/1983
Common $0.83333333 par changed to $0.55555555 par and (0.5) additional share issued 01/02/1985
Merged into Mead Corp. 01/13/1987
Each share Common $0.55555555 par exchanged for $22.50 cash

AMPAL AMERN ISRAEL CORP (NY)
Each share 4% Conv. Preferred $5 par exchanged for (5) shares Class A Common $1 par and $2.58 cash 07/31/2006
Each share 6.50% Conv. Preferred $5 par exchanged for (3) shares Class A Common $1 par and $4.09 cash 07/31/2006
(Additional Information in Active)

AMPAL-AMERICAN PALESTINE TRADING CORP. (NY)
Name changed to Ampal-American Israel Corp. 00/00/1954

AMPARO DEV CORP (BC)
Struck off register and declared dissolved for failure to file returns 02/02/1983

AMPARO MINING CO.
Liquidated 00/00/1940
Details not available

AMPCO METAL INC (WI)
Each share old Common no par exchanged for (6) shares new Common no par 00/00/1941
Recapitalized 00/00/1942
Each share Preferred $100 par exchanged for (10) shares 6% Preferred $10 par
New Common no par changed to $2.50 par
Common $2.50 par changed to $1 par and (0.25) additional share issued 05/13/1966
Common $1 par split (3) for (2) by issuance of (0.5) additional share 04/14/1967
Merged into Ampco-Pittsburgh Corp. 12/31/1970
Each share Common $1 par exchanged for (1.9) shares Common $1 par

AMPCO METAL PRODUCTS CO. (MO)
Charter cancelled for failure to file annual report 01/01/1926

AMPCO MFG. CO. (NJ)
Name changed to Amex Corp. 06/30/1962
(See Amex Corp.)

AMPCO TWIST DRILL CO.
Acquired by Greenfield Tap & Die Corp. 00/00/1948
Details not available

AMPEG INC (NY)
Merged into Unimusic, Inc. 12/04/1970
Each share Common 1¢ par exchanged for $1.25 cash

AMPERSAND MED CORP (DE)
Under plan of merger name changed to Molecular Diagnostics, Inc. 09/17/2001
Molecular Diagnostics, Inc. name changed to CytoCore, Inc. 08/17/2006 which name changed to Medite Cancer Therapeutics, Inc. 12/11/2014

AMPET CORP (OK)
Charter cancelled for failure to pay taxes 05/27/1966

AMPEX CORP (CA)
Common 50¢ par changed to $1 par and (1.5) additional shares issued 08/25/1958
Common $1 par split (3) for (1) by issuance of (2) additional shares 02/19/1960
Merged into Signal Companies, Inc. 01/15/1981
Each share Common $1 par exchanged for (1.275) shares Common $2 par
Signal Companies, Inc. merged into Allied-Signal Inc. 09/19/1985 which name changed to AlliedSignal Inc. 04/26/1993 which name changed to Honeywell International Inc. 12/01/1999

AMPEX CORP (DE)
Each share old Class A Common 1¢ par exchanged for (0.05) share new Class A Common 1¢ par 06/12/2003
Plan of reorganization under Chapter 11 Federal Bankruptcy Code effective 10/03/2008
No stockholders' equity

AMPHENOL-BORG ELECTRONICS CORP. (DE)
Name changed to Amphenol Corp. (Old) 05/11/1965
Amphenol Corp. (Old) merged into Bunker Ramo Corp. (New) 06/03/1968 which merged into Allied Corp. 07/31/1981 which merged into Allied-Signal Inc. 09/19/1985 which name changed to AlliedSignal Inc. 04/26/1993 which name changed to Honeywell International Inc. 12/01/1999

AMPHENOL CORP. (DE)
Ctfs. dtd. prior to 06/03/1968
Common $1 par split (2) for (1) by issuance of (1) additional share 05/16/1966
Merged into Bunker Ramo Corp. (New) 06/03/1968
Each share Common $1 par exchanged for (0.75) share $1.50 Conv. Preferred no par and (1) share Common no par
Bunker Ramo Corp. (New) merged into Allied Corp. 07/31/1981 which merged into Allied-Signal Inc. 09/19/1985 which name changed to AlliedSignal Inc. 04/26/1993 which name changed to Honeywell International Inc. 12/01/1999

AMPHENOL CORP OLD (DE)
Merged into Amphenol Corp. (New) 05/19/1997
Each share Class A Common $0.001 par exchanged for (1) share Class A Common $0.001 par or $26 cash

AMPHENOL ELECTRONICS CORP. (IL)
Merged into Amphenol-Borg Electronics Corp. 01/01/1959
Each share Common $1 par exchanged for (1) share Common $1 par
Amphenol-Borg Electronics Corp. name changed to Amphenol Corp. (Old) 05/11/1965 which merged into Bunker Ramo Corp. (New) 06/03/1968 which merged into Allied Corp. 07/31/1981 which merged into Allied-Signal Inc. 09/19/1985 which name changed to AlliedSignal Inc. 04/26/1993 which name changed to Honeywell International Inc. 12/01/1999

AMPHIBIOUS BOATS, INC. (TX)
Charter revoked for failure to file reports and pay fees 10/04/1962

AMPLE-TEE INC (NV)
Name changed to Airborne Wireless Network 06/28/2016

AMPLICA INC (CA)
Merged into Communications Satellite Corp. 01/15/1982
Each share Common $1 par exchanged for $13.50 cash

AMPLICON INC (CA)
Common 1¢ par split (2) for (1) by issuance of (1) additional share payable 10/17/1997 to holders of record 09/26/1997
Name changed to California First National Bancorp 05/24/2001

AMPLIDYNE INC (DE)
Name changed to Wi-Tron, Inc. 11/16/2005

AMPLIFY ETF TR (MA)
Trust terminated 04/30/2018
Each share YieldShares Oil Hedged MLP Income ETF 1¢ par received $9.7065 cash
(Additional Information in Active)

AMPLIFY SNACK BRANDS INC (DE)
Acquired by Hershey Co. 01/31/2018
Each share Common $0.0001 par exchanged for $12 cash

AMPLUS TECHNOLOGIES CORP (AB)
Name changed to Applied High Technology AHT Corp. 10/24/1995
Applied High Technology AHT Corp. reorganized as AHT Corp. (AB) 03/12/1999 which reincorporated in Canada as Simsmart Inc. 07/03/2001
(See Simsmart Inc.)

AMPOL EXPL LTD (AUSTRALIA)
ADR agreement terminated 11/21/1975
Each old ADR for Ordinary exchanged for (5) new ADR's for Ordinary
Reorganized as Ampolex Ltd. 06/05/1992
Each new ADR for Ordinary exchanged for (1) Sponsored ADR for Ordinary
(See Ampolex Ltd.)

AMPOL LTD (AUSTRALIA)
Acquired by Pioneer Concrete Services Ltd. 01/11/1989
Each share Ordinary exchanged for $3.67 cash
Each ADR for Ordinary exchanged for $3.144 cash

AMPOL PETROLEUM LTD. (AUSTRALIA)
Depositary agreement terminated 11/21/1975
Each old ADR for Ordinary exchanged for (5) shares Ordinary
Name changed to Ampol Ltd. 01/21/1982
(See Ampol Ltd.)

AMPOLEX LTD (AUSTRALIA)
Acquired by Mobil Exploration & Producing Australia Pty Ltd. 03/31/1997
Each Sponsored ADR for Ordinary exchanged for $3.6464 cash

AMPOR MARINE CORP (NY)
Charter cancelled and proclaimed dissolved for failure to pay taxes 12/15/1973

AMPOULES INC (OH)
Common no par split (4) for (1) by issuance of (3) additional shares 12/05/1961
Adjudicated bankrupt 03/17/1975
Stockholders' equity unlikely

AMPOWER TECHNOLOGIES INC (DE)
Name changed 11/29/1983
Name changed from Ampower Instrument Co., Inc. to Ampower Technologies, Inc. 11/29/1983
Charter cancelled and declared inoperative and void for non-payment of taxes 03/01/1988

AMPRO CORP.
Acquired by General Precision Equipment Corp. 00/00/1944
Details not available

AMPRO INTL GOLF TOUR INC (FL)
Recapitalized as Planet Entertainment Corp. 09/01/1996
Each share Common $0.001 par exchanged for (0.00333333) share Common $0.001 par
(See Planet Entertainment Corp.)

AMQUEST CORP (DE)
Plan of reorganization under Chapter 11 bankruptcy proceedings confirmed 08/19/1985
No stockholders' equity

AMQUEST INTL LTD (NV)
Charter revoked for failure to file reports and pay fees 12/01/1999

AMR CORP (DE)
$2.125 Conv. Preferred no par called for redemption 02/15/1985
$2.1875 Preferred no par called for redemption 07/01/1986
Depositary Shares Ser. A no par called for redemption 05/20/1996
$3 Conv. Preferred Ser. A no par called for redemption 05/20/1996
Common $1 par split (2) for (1) by issuance of (1) additional share payable 06/09/1998 to holders of record 05/26/1998 Ex date - 06/10/1998
Each share Common $1 par received distribution of (0.722652) share Sabre Holdings Corp. Class A Common 1¢ par payable 03/15/2000 to holders of record 03/01/2000
Plan of reorganization under Chapter 11 Federal Bankruptcy proceedings effective 12/09/2013
Each share Common $1 par exchanged for (0.0665) share American Airlines Group Inc. Common 1¢ par
Each share Common $1 par received an initial additional distribution of (0.1319) share Common 1¢ par payable 01/09/2014 to holders of record 12/09/2013
Each share Common $1 par received a second additional distribution of (0.175) share Common 1¢ par payable 02/10/2014 to holders of record 12/09/2013
Each share Common $1 par received a third additional distribution of (0.1842) share Common 1¢ par payable 03/10/2014 to holders of record 12/09/2013
Each share Common $1 par received a fourth additional distribution of (0.1864) share Common 1¢ par payable 04/10/2014 to holders of record 12/09/2013

AMR TECHNOLOGIES INC (CANADA)
Name changed to Neo Material Technologies, Inc. 04/28/2006
Neo Material Technologies, Inc. merged into Molycorp, Inc. (New) 06/14/2012
(See Molycorp, Inc. (New))

AMRA CORP. (NY)
Merged into American Bosch Corp. 03/18/1949
Each share Common exchanged for (0.8) share Class A $1 par
American Bosch Corp. name changed to American Bosch Arma Corp. 07/21/1954 which name changed to Ambac Industries, Inc. 04/30/1968 which merged into United Technologies Corp. 07/14/1978

AMRAD CORP.
Acquired by Magnavox Co., Ltd. 00/00/1930
Details not available

AMRAD CORP LTD (AUSTRALIA)
Name changed to Zenyth Therapeutics Ltd. 12/09/2005
(See Zenyth Therapeutics Ltd.)

AMRAD OIL & MINERALS CORP (NV)
Recapitalized as Mountain Corp. 12/19/1980
Each share Capital Stock 50¢ par exchanged for (0.1) share Capital Stock 5¢ par
(See Mountain Corp.)

AMRE INC (DE)
Common 1¢ par split (2) for (1) by issuance of (1) additional share 06/30/1987
Common 1¢ par split (3) for (2) by issuance of (0.5) additional share 10/20/1988
Plan of reorganization under Chapter 11 Federal Bankruptcy proceedings confirmed 08/27/1997
No stockholders' equity

AMREC INDS (NV)
Charter revoked for failure to file reports and pay fees 03/04/1975

AMRED, INC. (DE)
Charter cancelled and declared inoperative and void for non-payment of taxes 04/15/1971

AMREIT (MD)
Reincorporated 05/21/2009
Class B Common 1¢ par called for redemption at $10.18 on 12/20/2007
Place of incorporation changed from (TX) to (MD) 05/21/2009
Under plan of merger each share Class A Common 1¢ par automatically became (1) share AmREIT, Inc. (New) Common 1¢ par 11/24/2009
(See AmREIT, Inc. (New))

AMREIT INC NEW (MD)
Common 1¢ par reclassified as (0.5) share Class A Common 1¢ par 07/26/2012
Class A Common 1¢ par reclassified as Class B Common 1¢ par 04/25/2013
Class B Common 1¢ par reclassified as Common 1¢ par 04/26/2013
Acquired by Edens Investment Trust 02/18/2015
Each share Common 1¢ par exchanged for $26.55 cash

AMREIT INC OLD (MD)
Reincorporated under the laws of Texas as AmREIT 12/22/2002
AmREIT (TX) reincorporated in Maryland 05/21/2009 which merged into AmREIT, Inc. (New) 11/24/2009
(See AmREIT, Inc. (New))

AMRESCO CAP TR (TX)
Liquidation completed
Each Common Share of Bene. Int. 1¢ par received initial distribution of $0.30 cash payable 10/19/2000 to holders of record 10/06/2000
Each Common Share of Bene. Int. 1¢ par received second distribution of $0.35 cash payable 11/21/2000 to holders of record 11/09/2000
Each Common Share of Bene. Int. 1¢ par received third distribution of $0.35 cash payable 01/17/2001 to holders of record 12/31/2000
Each Common Share of Bene. Int. 1¢ par received fourth distribution of $2.60 cash payable 03/30/2001 to holders of record 03/19/2001
Each Common Share of Bene. Int. 1¢ par received fifth distribution of $7 cash payable 08/09/2001 to holders of record 07/30/2001
Each Common Share of Bene. Int. 1¢ par received sixth and final distribution of $1.545 cash payable 04/20/2002 to holders of record 04/18/2002
Note: Certificates were not required to be surrendered and are without value

AMRESCO INC (DE)
Each share old Common 5¢ par exchanged for (0.2) share new Common 5¢ par 08/28/2000
Plan of Liquidation under Chapter 11 Federal Bankruptcy Code effective 08/06/2002
No stockholders' equity

AMRION INC (CO)
Common $0.0011 par split (3) for (2) by issuance of (0.5) additional share 09/15/1993
Merged into Whole Foods Market, Inc. 09/11/1997
Each share Common $0.0011 par exchanged for (0.87) share Common no par
(See Whole Foods Market, Inc.)

AMS HEALTH SCIENCES INC (OK)
Recapitalized as SA Recovery Corp. 11/20/2008
Each share Common $0.0001 par exchanged for (0.00149253) share Common $0.0001 par
SA Recovery Corp. name changed to Truli Media Group, Inc. (OK) 08/21/2012 which reorganized in Delaware 03/17/2015

AMS HOMECARE INC (BC)
SEC revoked common stock registration 03/22/2013

AMS INC (DE)
Reincorporated under the laws of Oklahoma as Advantage Marketing Systems, Inc. 12/11/1995
Advantage Marketing Systems, Inc. name changed to AMS Health Sciences, Inc. 09/10/2004 which recapitalized as SA Recovery Corp. 11/20/2008 which name changed to Truli Media Group, Inc. (OK) 08/21/2012 which reorganized in Delaware 03/17/2015

AMS REALSTAR INC (CO)
Declared defunct and inoperative for failure to pay taxes and file annual reports 01/01/1991

AMSAP INTL INC (UT)
Charter revoked for failure to pay taxes 03/28/1998

AMSCAN HLDGS INC (DE)
Acquired by GS Capital Partners II, L.P. 12/19/1997
Each share Common 10¢ par exchanged for $16.50 cash

AMSCO INTL INC (DE)
Merged into STERIS Corp. 05/13/1996
Each share Common 1¢ par exchanged for (0.46) share Common no par
STERIS Corp. merged into STERIS PLC 11/03/2015

AMSERV HEALTHCARE INC (DE)
Name changed 08/04/1992
Name changed from Amserv, Inc. to Amserv Healthcare Inc. 08/04/1992
Merged into Star Multi Care Services, Inc. 08/23/1996
Each share Common 1¢ par exchanged for (0.409) share Common $0.001 par
(See Multi Care Services, Inc.)

AMSHAW PORCUPINE GOLD MINES LTD. (ON)
Charter cancelled and proclaimed dissolved for failure to pay taxes and file annual returns 09/30/1957

AMSNAX INC (DE)
Charter forfeited for failure to maintain a registered agent 12/31/1990

AMSOUTH BANCORPORATION (DE)
Common $1 par split (3) for (2) by issuance of (0.5) additional share 01/18/1984
Common $1 par split (3) for (2) by issuance of (0.5) additional share 01/15/1986
Common $1 par split (3) for (2) by issuance of (0.5) additional share 01/15/1992
Common $1 par split (3) for (2) by issuance of (0.5) additional share payable 04/30/1997 to holders of record 04/04/1997 Ex date - 05/01/1997

Common $1 par split (3) for (2) by issuance of (0.5) additional share payable 04/30/1998 for holders of record 04/03/1998 Ex date - 05/01/1998
Common $1 par split (3) for (2) by issuance of (0.5) additional share 05/24/1999 to holders of record 04/30/1999 Ex date - 05/25/1999
Merged into Regions Financial Corp. (New) 11/04/2006
Each share Common $1 par exchanged for (0.7974) share Common 1¢ par

AMST, INC. (MA)
Liquidation completed
Each share Capital Stock no par received initial distribution of $2 cash 04/01/1969
Each share Capital Stock no par received second distribution of $2 cash 11/28/1969
Each share Capital Stock no par received third distribution of $1 cash 11/02/1970
Each share Capital Stock no par received fourth distribution of $0.40 cash 07/23/1971
Each share Capital Stock no par received fifth and final distribution of $1 cash 12/15/1972
Note: Certificates were not required to be surrendered and are without value

AMSTAR AMERN PETE CORP (BC)
Name changed to Amstar Venture Corp. 06/11/1985
Amstar Venture Corp. recapitalized as Golden-Tonkin Resources Ltd. 02/23/1989
(See Golden-Tonkin Resources Ltd.)

AMSTAR CORP (DE)
Common $12.50 par changed to $1 par and (1) additional share issued 11/15/1976
$2.65 Conv. Jr. Preferred Ser. A no par called for redemption 12/14/1983
Merged into Amstar Holdings, Inc. 02/08/1984
Each share Common $1 par exchanged for $47 cash
5.44% Preferred $12.50 par called for redemption 07/02/1986
Public interest eliminated

AMSTAR FINL HLDGS INC (NV)
Recapitalized as China Du Kang Co. Ltd. 03/19/2008
Each share Common $0.001 par exchanged for (0.1) share Common $0.001 par

AMSTAR FINL SVCS INC (FL)
Recapitalized as Remodel Auction Inc. 08/10/2009
Each share Common $0.001 par exchanged for (0.05) share Common $0.001 par
Remodel Auction Inc. name changed to North Carolina Natural Energy, Inc. 01/11/2012 which name changed to Appalachian Mountain Brewery, Inc. 01/08/2014

AMSTAR VENTURE CORP (BC)
Recapitalized as Golden-Tonkin Resources Ltd. 02/23/1989
Each share Common no par exchanged for (0.2) share Common no par
(See Golden-Tonkin Resources Ltd.)

AMSTAT CORP (CA)
Charter suspended for failure to file reports and pay fees 06/16/1998

AMSTED INDS INC (DE)
Reincorporated 01/31/1968
State of incorporation changed from (NJ) to (DE) 01/31/1968
Common $1 par split (2) for (1) by issuance of (1) additional share 03/22/1976
Common $1 par split (2) for (1) by issuance of (1) additional share 06/08/1978
Acquired by an investment group 06/02/1986
Each share Common $1 par exchanged for $27 principal amount of Amsted Industries Inc. Subord. Discount Debentures Ser. B due 06/02/2006, (0.08) share 12% Preferred Ser. A no par and $33 cash
12% Preferred Ser. A no par called for redemption 08/31/1988
Public interest eliminated

AMSTEEL CORP BERHAD (MALAYSIA)
Each old Sponsored ADR for Ordinary exchanged for (0.2) new Sponsored ADR for Ordinary 05/23/2003
ADR agreement terminated 02/20/2009
Each new Sponsored ADR for Ordinary exchanged for (1) share Ordinary M$0.50 par
Note: Unexchanged ADR's will be sold and the proceeds, if any, held for claim after 02/20/2010

AMSTEM CORP (NV)
SEC revoked common stock registration 02/22/2012

AMSTERDAM CAP INC (NV)
Name changed to Care Concepts, Inc. (NV) 06/16/1989
Care Concepts, Inc. (NV) reorganized in Delaware 11/30/1992 which name changed to Care Concepts I, Inc. 10/24/2002 which name changed to Interactive Brand Development, Inc. 12/01/2004
(See Interactive Brand Development, Inc.)

AMSTERDAM ROTTERDAM BK N V (NETHERLANDS)
Merged into Algemene Bank Nederland N.V. 05/15/1990
Each ADR for Ordinary exchanged for $38.40 cash

AMSURG CORP (TN)
Class A Common no par reclassified as Common no par 07/13/2001
Class B Common no par reclassified as Common no par 07/13/2001
Common no par split (3) for (2) by issuance of (0.5) additional share payable 03/24/2004 to holders of record 03/08/2004 Ex date - 03/25/2004
Under plan of merger each share 5.25% Mandatory Conv. Preferred Ser. A-1 no par and Common no par automatically became (1) share Envision Healthcare Corp. (DE) 5.25% Mandatory Conv. Preferred Ser. A-1 1¢ par or (1) share Common 1¢ par respectively 12/02/2016
(See Envision Healthcare Corp.)

AMSWISS HLDGS LTD (CANADA)
Recapitalized as Lifequest International Inc. 04/09/1987
Each share Common no par exchanged for (0.06756756) share Common no par
Lifequest International Inc. recapitalized as Amswiss Pharmaceuticals Inc. 09/21/1988 which recapitalized as Amswiss Scientific Inc. 03/05/1990
(See Amswiss Scientific Inc.)

AMSWISS SCIENTIFIC INC (CANADA)
Recapitalized 03/05/1990
Recapitalized from Amswiss Pharmaceuticals Inc. to Amswiss Scientific Inc. 03/05/1990
Each share Common no par exchanged for (0.2) share Common no par
Dissolved for non-compliance 03/02/2010

AMT CORP (DE)
Name changed to 1225 Maple Corp. 08/10/1978
(See 1225 Maple Corp.)

AMT ENVIRONMENTAL PRODS INC (BC)
Reorganized under the laws of Nevada as Polymer Solutions, Inc. 02/27/1997
Each share Common no par exchanged for (0.33333333) share Common no par
(See Polymer Solutions, Inc.)

AMT FINE FOODS LTD (ON)
Recapitalized as Skor Food Group Inc. 06/27/2002
Each share Common no par exchanged for (0.1) share Common no par
(See Skor Food Group Inc.)

AMT GROUP INC (NV)
Each share old Common $0.001 par exchanged for (0.1) share new Common $0.001 par 07/10/2008
SEC revoked common stock registration 01/07/2011

AMT INTL MNG CORP (ON)
Company directors resigned 11/30/2006
Stockholders' equity unlikely

AMTEC INC (DE)
Name changed to Terremark Worldwide, Inc. 05/01/2000
(See Terremark Worldwide, Inc.)

AMTEC INDS INC (UT)
Name changed to Nature's Sunshine Products, Inc. 10/06/1982

AMTECH CORP (TX)
Common 1¢ par split (3) for (2) by issuance of (0.5) additional share 02/13/1992
Common 1¢ par split (5) for (4) by issuance of (0.25) additional share 06/25/1993
Name changed to CustomTracks Corp. 09/01/1998
CustomTracks Corp. name changed to Zixit Corp. 09/16/1999 which name changed to Zix Corp. 08/13/2002

AMTECH GROUP LTD (TX)
Charter forfeited for failure to pay taxes 06/20/1988

AMTECH RES INC (CO)
Reincorporated 12/15/2003
State of incorporation changed from (NV) to (CO) 12/15/2003
Recapitalized as Hat Trick Beverage, Inc. 12/10/2004
Each share Common 10¢ par exchanged for (0.1) share Common $0.001 par

AMTEK AUTO LTD (INDIA)
GDR agreement terminated 12/26/2017
No GDR's remain outstanding

AMTEL INC (RI)
Common 50¢ par split (3) for (2) by issuance of (0.5) additional share 03/25/1968
Merged into AMCA International Corp. 06/05/1978
Each share Common 50¢ par exchanged for $16.50 cash

AMTEL N V (RUSSIA)
Name changed 09/18/2009
Name changed from Amtel-Vredestein N.V. to Amtel N.V. 09/18/2009
ADR agreement terminated 03/03/2011
Company is in bankruptcy

AMTELECOM GROUP INC (ON)
Name changed to Century II Holdings Inc. 04/11/2003
(See Century II Holdings Inc.)

AMTELECOM INCOME FD (ON)
Merged into Bragg Communications Inc. 06/01/2007
Each Unit no par exchanged for $14.25 cash

AMTERRE DEV INC (DE)
Liquidation completed
Each share Common 1¢ par received initial distribution of $1 cash 12/26/1980
Each share Common 1¢ par received second distribution of $0.25 cash 03/12/1981
Under plan of liquidation each share Common 1¢ par exchanged for (1) Amterre Limited Partnership Non-Transferable Unit of Ltd. Partnership 03/09/1981
(See Amterre Limited Partnership)

AMTERRE LIMITED PARTNERSHIP (DE)
Liquidation completed
Each Non-Transferable Unit of Ltd. Partnership received initial distribution of $0.50 cash 06/29/1981
Each Non-Transferable Unit of Ltd. Partnership received second distribution of $0.50 cash 12/31/1981
Each Non-Transferable Unit of Ltd. Partnership received third distribution of $0.5075 cash 11/29/1984
Each Non-Transferable Unit of Ltd. Partnership received fourth distribution of $1 cash 11/14/1985
Each Non-Transferable Unit of Ltd. Partnership received fifth distribution of $0.36 cash 12/12/1985
Each Non-Transferable Unit of Ltd. Partnership received sixth and final distribution of $0.0425 cash 12/29/1986

AMTRAN INC (IN)
Name changed to ATA Holdings Corp. 5/13/2002
(See ATA Holdings Corp.)

AMTROL INC (RI)
Merged into Cypress Group 11/13/96
Each share Common 1¢ par exchanged for $28.25 cash

AMTRON INC (MN)
Statutorily dissolved 6/15/95

AMTRONICS ENTERPRISES LTD (BC)
SEC revoked common stock registration 06/22/2010

AMTRUST CAP CORP (DE)
Merged into Richmond Mutual Bancorporation, Inc. 7/1/2002
Each share Common 1¢ par exchanged for $10.50 cash

AMTRUST FINL GROUP INC (DE)
Merged into AFG Acquisition 08/07/2007
Each share Common $0.001 par exchanged for $8.24419 cash

AMULET GOLD MINES LTD. (CANADA)
Name changed to Amulet Mines Ltd. 00/00/1927
Amulet Mines Ltd. merged into Waite Amulet Mines Ltd. 00/00/1933 which was acquired by Noranda Mines Ltd. 05/11/1962 which name changed to Noranda Inc. 05/28/1984 which name changed to Falconbridge Ltd. (New) 2005 on 07/01/2005
(See Falconbridge Ltd. (New) 2005)

AMULET MINES LTD. (CANADA)
Merged into Waite Amulet Mines Ltd. 00/00/1933
Each share Capital Stock exchanged for (0.33333333) share Capital Stock
Waite Amulet Mines Ltd. acquired by Noranda Mines Ltd. 05/11/1962 which name changed to Noranda Inc. 05/28/1984 which name changed to Falconbridge Ltd. (New) 2005 on 07/01/2005
(See Falconbridge Ltd. (New) 2005)

AMULET RES CORP (BC)
Recapitalized as Golden Unicorn Mining Corp. 06/11/1990
Each share Common no par exchanged for (0.33333333) share Common no par
Golden Unicorn Mining Corp. recapitalized as Consolidated Golden Unicorn Mining Corp. 03/29/1995 which recapitalized as Kirkstone Ventures Ltd. 12/09/1999 which name changed to Balaton Power Inc. 07/24/2000
(See Balaton Power Inc.)

AMURANIUM CORP. (DE)
No longer in existance having become inoperative and void for non-payment of taxes 4/1/59

AMUREX OIL CO. (DE)
Class A Common $5 par changed to $1 par 12/04/1958
Acquired by Murphy Oil Co. Ltd. 01/04/1962
Each share Class A Common $1 par exchanged for (1) share Common $1 par
(See Murphy Oil Co. Ltd.)

AMUREX OIL DEVELOPMENT CO. (DE)
Name changed to Amurex Oil Co. 9/28/55
Amurex Oil Co. acquired by Murphy Oil Co. Ltd. 1/4/62
(See Murphy Oil Co. Ltd.)

AMUSEMENTS INTL LTD (AB)
Recapitalized as BlueGrouse Seismic Solutions Ltd. 07/14/2005
Each share Class A Common no par exchanged for (0.06666666) share Common no par
BlueGrouse Seismic Solutions Ltd. acquired by Divestco Inc. 05/03/2007

AMVESCAP INC (NS)
Name changed to INVESCO Inc. (NS) 05/29/2007
INVESCO Inc. (NS) reorganized in Bermuda as Invesco Ltd. 12/04/2007

AMVESCAP PLC (ENGLAND & WALES)
Sponsored ADR's for Ordinary split (2) for (1) by issuance of (1) additional ADR payable 04/24/1998 to holders of record 04/17/1998
Ex date - 04/27/1998
Sponsored ADR's for Ordinary split (5) for (2) by issuance of (1.5) additional ADR's payable 11/07/2000 to holders of record 11/06/2000
Ex date - 11/08/2000
Name changed to INVESCO PLC (New) (England & Wales) 05/23/2007
INVESCO PLC (New) (England & Wales) reorganized in Bermuda as Invesco Ltd. 12/04/2007

AMVESCO PLC (ENGLAND & WALES)
Name changed to AMVESCAP PLC 05/08/1997
AMVESCAP PLC name changed to INVESCO PLC (New) (England & Wales) 05/23/2007 which reorganized in Bermuda as Invesco Ltd. 12/04/2007

AMVESTORS FINL CORP (KS)
$2.125 Conv. Exchangeable Preferred Ser. A $1 par called for redemption 02/01/1988
Common no par split (5) for (4) by issuance of (0.25) additional share 06/19/1987
Common no par split (5) for (4) by issuance of (0.25) additional share 07/15/1988
Common no par split (5) for (4) by issuance of (0.25) additional share 05/01/1989
Each share old Common no par exchanged for (0.4) share new Common no par 06/11/1993
Preferred Stock Purchase Rights declared for Common stockholders of record 08/05/1988 were redeemed at $0.01 per right 08/08/1994 for holders of record 07/22/1994
Merged into AmerUs Life Holdings, Inc. 12/19/1997
Each share new Common no par exchanged for (0.6724) share Common no par
AmerUs Life Holdings, Inc. name changed Amerus Group Co. 09/20/2000
(See Amerus Group Co.)

AMWAY ASIA PAC LTD (BERMUDA)
Merged into Apple Hold Co., L.P. 04/27/2000
Each share Common 1¢ par exchanged for $18 cash

AMWAY JAPAN LTD (JAPAN)
ADR agreement terminated 10/03/2000
Each Sponsored ADR for Common exchanged for $4.407 cash

AMWEST ENVIRONMENTAL GROUP INC (NV)
SEC revoked common stock registration 06/23/2010

AMWEST IMAGING INC (NV)
Common $0.001 par split (26) for (1) by issuance of (25) additional shares payable 11/07/2011 to holders of record 10/31/2011
Ex date - 11/08/2011
Recapitalized as Intertech Solutions, Inc. 07/31/2013
Each share Common $0.001 par exchanged for (0.0005) share Common $0.001 par

AMWEST INS GROUP INC (DE)
Reincorporated 09/11/1987
Stock Dividend - 10% 02/15/1987
State of incorporation changed from (CA) to (DE) and Common no par changed to 1¢ par 09/11/1987
Chapter 11 bankruptcy proceedings converted to Chapter 7 on 04/02/2004
Stockholders' equity unlikely

AMX CORP NEW (TX)
Acquired by Duchossois Industries, Inc. 04/08/2005
Each share Common 1¢ par exchanged for $22.50 cash

AMX CORP OLD (TX)
Name changed to Panja Inc. 09/13/1999
Panja Inc. name changed to AMX Corp. (New) 08/23/2001
(See AMX Corp. (New)

AMX INTL INC (DE)
Charter cancelled and declared inoperative and void for non-payment of 03/01/1989

AMY YELLOWKNIFE MINES LTD. (ON)
Charter cancelled and proclaimed dissolved for failure to pay taxes and file returns 09/00/1962

AMYLIN PHARMACEUTICALS INC (DE)
Acquired by Bristol-Myers Squibb Co. 08/08/2012
Each share Common $0.001 par exchanged for $31 cash

AMZAC RES INC (NY)
Each share old Common $0.001 par exchanged for (0.125) share new Common $0.001 par 05/11/1998
Name changed to Royal Pictures Inc. 09/01/1998
Royal Pictures Inc. recapitalized as Iconfidential Inc. 06/05/2001 which recapitalized as Quality of Life Health Corp. 03/04/2003 which recapitalized as LifeHouse Retirement Properties, Inc. 07/14/2005

AN CON GENETICS INC (DE)
Each share Common $0.001 par exchanged for (0.06666666) share new Common $0.001 par 01/06/1994
Name changed to Bovie Medical Corp. 09/08/1998

ANA URANIUM MINES LTD. (ON)
Charter cancelled for failure to pay taxes and file returns 09/21/1959

ANABAC INDS INC (DE)
Charter cancelled and declared inoperative and void for non-payment of taxes 04/15/1972

ANABAR MINING & DEVELOPMENT CO. LTD. (ON)
Charter cancelled 11/00/1973

ANABIE GOLD MINES LTD. (ON)
Charter cancelled for failure to pay taxes and file returns 07/11/1955

ANAC HLDG CORP (DE)
Filed a petition under Chapter 11 Federal Bankruptcy Code 07/28/1988
Details not available

ANACOMP INC (OLD) (IN)
Reorganized under Chapter 11 Federal Bankruptcy Code as Anacomp Inc. (New) 12/31/2001
Each share Common 1¢ par exchanged for (0.0002769) share Class B Common 1¢ par and (194.12) Class B Common Stock Purchase Warrants expiring 12/10/2006

ANACOMP INC NEW (IN)
Reincorporated under the laws of Delaware and Class A and B Common 1¢ par reclassified as Common $0.000001 par 03/20/2013

ANACOMP INC OLD (IN)
Common $1 par split (3) for (2) by issuance of (0.5) additional share 12/22/1969
Common $1 par split (3) for (2) by issuance of (0.5) additional share 09/20/1978
Common $1 par split (5) for (4) by issuance of (0.25) additional share 03/28/1980
Common $1 par split (5) for (4) by issuance of (0.25) additional share 06/09/1981
Each share $0.75 Conv. Preferred Ser. A $1 par exchanged for (4) shares Common $1 par 02/17/1987
Common $1 par changed to 1¢ par 02/25/1987
Stock Dividends - 25% 04/15/1976; 10% 09/01/1977; 10% 04/11/1978; 20% 04/24/1979
Plan of reorganization under Chapter 11 Federal Bankruptcy Code effective 06/04/1996
Each $1,000 liquidation value of Conv. Exchangeable Adjustable Rate Preferred Ser. 1 1¢ par exchanged for (3.4801) Anacomp Inc. (New) Common Stock Purchase Warrants expiring 00/00/2001
Each share Common 1¢ par exchanged for (0.0008) Common Stock Purchase Warrant expiring 00/00/2001
Note: Unexchanged certificates were cancelled and became without value 06/04/1998

ANACON EXTENSION LTD. (QC)
Name changed to Anthonian Mining Corp. Ltd. 00/00/1952
(See Anthonian Mining Corp. Ltd.)

ANACON LEAD MINES, LTD. (ON)
Capital Stock no par changed to 20¢ par 00/00/1953
Recapitalized as Key Anacon Mines Ltd. 02/14/1964
Each share Capital Stock 20¢ par exchanged for (0.33333333) share Capital Stock 20¢ par
(See Key Anacon Mines Ltd.)

ANACONDA CO (MT)
Capital Stock $50 par changed to no par 05/22/1964
Capital Stock no par split (2) for (1) by issuance of (1) additional share 06/09/1967
Capital Stock no par reclassified as Common no par 05/21/1969
Merged into Atlantic Richfield Co. (PA) 01/13/1977
Each share Common no par exchanged for (0.5) share Common $5 par and $6 cash
Atlantic Richfield Co. (PA) reincorporated in Delaware 05/07/1985 which merged into BP Amoco PLC 04/18/2000 which name changed to BP PLC 05/01/2001

ANACONDA COPPER MINING CO. (MT)
Name changed to Anaconda Co. 06/18/1955
Anaconda Co. merged into Atlantic Richfield Co. (PA) 01/13/1977 which reincorporated in Delaware 05/07/1985 which merged into BP Amoco PLC 04/18/2000

ANACONDA GOLD CORP (ON)
Recapitalized as Anaconda Mining Inc. 04/18/2007
Each share Common no par exchanged for (0.5) share Common no par

ANACONDA LEAD & SILVER CO., INC. (NV)
Charter revoked for failure to file reports and pay fees 03/19/1964

ANACONDA MINING & MILLING CO. (SD)
Charter expired due to time limitation 02/27/1953

ANACONDA OIL CO., LTD. (CANADA)
Capital Stock $1 par changed to no par 00/00/1937
Recapitalized as Canadian Anaconda Oils Ltd. 00/00/1957
Each share Capital Stock no par exchanged for (0.25) share Capital Stock no par
Canadian Anaconda Oils Ltd. recapitalized as Anaconda Petroleum Ltd. 03/25/1957 which name changed to Zebedee Oil Ltd. 01/20/1971 which name changed to Osias Resources Canada Ltd. 04/19/1971 which recapitalized as Troy Gold Industries Ltd. (Canada) 06/12/1974 which reincorporated in Alberta 09/06/1978
(See Troy Gold Industries Ltd.)

ANACONDA PETE LTD (CANADA)
Name changed to Zebedee Oil Ltd. 01/20/1971
Zebedee Oil Ltd. name changed to Osias Resources Canada Ltd. 04/19/1971 which recapitalized as Troy Gold Industries Ltd. (Canada) 06/12/1974 which reincorporated in Alberta 09/06/1978
(See Troy Gold Industries Ltd.)

ANACONDA REAL ESTATE INVT TR (FL)
Ctfs. of Bene. Int. no par changed to $1 par 11/23/1971
Proclaimed dissolved for failure to file reports and pay fees 12/11/1976

ANACONDA URANIUM CORP (BC)
Reorganized under the laws of Ontario as Anaconda Gold Corp. 08/16/2002
Each share Common no par exchanged for (0.33333333) share Common no par
Anaconda Gold Corp. recapitalized as Anaconda Mining Inc. 04/18/2007

ANACONDA WIRE & CABLE CO. (DE)
Stock Dividend - 100% 12/23/1947
Acquired by Anaconda Co. 12/31/1963
Each share Capital Stock no par exchanged for (0.7) share Capital Stock $50 par
Anaconda Co. merged into Atlantic Richfield Co. (PA) 01/13/1977 which reincorporated in Delaware 05/07/1985 which merged into BP Amoco PLC 04/18/2000

ANACONDO EXPLS INC (BC)
Name changed to O-Tech Ventures Corp. 09/16/1992
O-Tech Ventures Corp. recapitalized as Bright Star Ventures Ltd. 06/26/1996
(See Bright Star Ventures Ltd.)

ANACOR PHARMACEUTICALS INC (DE)
Acquired by Pfizer Inc. 06/24/2016
Each share Common $0.001 par exchanged for $99.25 cash

ANADAC INC (VA)
Merged into Identix Inc. (CA) 10/23/1992
Each share Common 10¢ par exchanged for (3.946474) shares Common no par
Indentix Inc. (CA) reincorporated in Delaware 12/16/1998 which merged into L-1 Identify Solutions, Inc. 08/30/2006
(See L-1 Identity Solutions, Inc.)

ANADARKO PETE CORP (DE)
5.46% Depositary Preferred Ser. B called for redemption at $100 on 06/30/2008
Each 7.5% Tangible Equity Unit received (0.8921) Western Gas Equity Partners, L.P. Common Unit 06/07/2018
(Additional Information in Active)

ANADIGICS INC (DE)
Common 1¢ par split (3) for (2) by issuance of (0.5) additional share payable 02/20/1997 to holders of record 02/10/1997
Common 1¢ par split (3) for (2) by issuance of (0.5) additional share payable 02/29/2000 to holders of record 02/10/2000
Acquired by II-VI Inc. 03/15/2016
Each share Common 1¢ par exchanged for $0.85 cash

ANADIME CORP (AB)
Each share old Common no par exchanged for (0.2) share new Common no par 03/19/1999
Merged into Newalta Corp. (Old) 08/20/2001
Each share new Common no par exchanged for (0.16666666) share Common no par
Note: Holders of (599) or fewer shares received $0.56 cash per share
Newalta Corp. (Old) recapitalized as Newalta Income Fund 03/10/2003 which reorganized as Newalta Inc. 12/31/2008 which name changed to Newalta Corp. (New) 01/22/2010 which reorganized as Tervita Corp. 07/24/2018

ANADIS LTD (AUSTRALIA)
Name changed to Immuron Ltd. 12/05/2008

ANADITE INC (NV)
Reincorporated 12/21/1978
Common no par split (2) for (1) by issuance of (1) additional share 05/19/1967
Common no par split (5) for (4) by issuance of (0.25) additional share 03/15/1968
Stock Dividends - 10% 02/01/1962; 33.33333333% 06/14/1966; 33.33333333% 01/03/1967
State of incorporation changed from (CA) to (NV) and Common no par changed to 10¢ par 12/21/1978
3.5% Conv. Preferred $50 par called for redemption 10/30/1986
Merged into Industrial Equity (Pacific) Ltd. 12/31/1986
Each share Common 10¢ par exchanged for $7.75 cash

ANADYS PHARMACEUTICALS INC (DE)
Acquired by Hoffmann-La Roche Inc. 11/23/2011
Each share Common $0.001 par exchanged for $3.70 cash

ANAEROBIC ENERGY SYS INC (DE)
Name changed to Sun Coast Plastics, Inc. 04/19/1983
Sun Coast Plastics, Inc. name changed to Sun Coast Industries, Inc. 03/04/1994
(See Sun Coast Industries, Inc.)

ANAFUEL UNLIMITED (UT)
Name changed to American Methyl Corp. 07/02/1982
American Methyl Corp. recapitalized as National Surety Corp. (UT) 02/14/1989 which reincorporated in Nevada 04/30/1989 which name changed to Stratum International Holdings, Inc. 07/02/1990

ANAGRAM PLUS INC (DE)
Reincorporated under the laws of Florida as Playworld Interactive Holding Corp. 07/09/2013
Playworld Interactive Holding Corp. name changed to Smart Technologies Holding Corp. 01/16/2015 which name changed to EM Quantum Technologies Inc. 07/07/2016

ANAGRAPHIC CORP. (MN)
Dissolved 03/19/1967
No stockholders' equity

ANAHEIM NATIONAL BANK (ANAHEIM, CA)
Reorganized as California Bancorp, Inc. 06/30/1979
Each share Common $5 par exchanged for (1) share Common $5 par
(See California Bancorp, Inc.)

ANAHEIM UNION WATER CO. (CA)
Merged into Pacific Holding Corp. 07/14/1969
Each share Capital Stock $100 par exchanged for (46.5573) shares Common $1 par
(See Pacific Holding Corp.)

ANALEX CORP (DE)
Merged into QinetiQ North America Operations LLC 03/14/2007
Each share Common 2¢ par exchanged for $3.70 cash

ANALOG DEVICES INC (MA)
Preferred Stock Purchase Rights declared for holders of record 03/17/1998 were redeemed at $0.0005 per right 03/15/2006 for holders of record 02/24/2006
(Additional Information in Active)

ANALOGIC CORP (MA)
Each share Common 10¢ par exchanged for (2) shares Common 5¢ par 09/30/1977
Common 5¢ par split (2) for (1) by issuance of (1) additional share 06/24/1983
Stock Dividends - 100% 12/14/1978; 100% 09/26/1980
Acquired by ANLG Holding Co., Inc. 06/22/2018
Each share Common 5¢ par exchanged for $84 cash

ANALOGUE CONTROLS, INC. (NY)
Adjudicated bankrupt 11/00/1966
No stockholders' equity

ANALOGY INC (OR)
Merged into Avant! Corp. 03/22/2000
Each share Common no par exchanged for $2.474 cash

ANALYSIS & TECHNOLOGY INC (CT)
Common no par split (3) for (2) by issuance of (0.5) additional share payable 01/29/1998 to holders of record 01/02/1998
Merged into Anteon Corp. 06/23/1999
Each share Common no par exchanged for $26 cash

ANALYST ASSOCIATES, INC. (NY)
Dissolved 06/08/1965
Details not available

ANALYSTS INTL CORP (MN)
Old Common 10¢ par split (5) for (4) by issuance of (0.25) additional share 07/05/1983
Old Common 10¢ par split (3) for (2) by issuance of (0.5) additional share 08/16/1983
Old Common 10¢ par split (5) for (4) by issuance of (0.25) additional share 08/14/1989
Old Common 10¢ par split (3) for (2) by issuance of (0.5) additional share 09/30/1993
Old Common 10¢ par split (2) for (1) by issuance of (1) additional share payable 09/30/1996 to holders of record 09/09/1996
Old Common 10¢ par split (3) for (2) by issuance of (0.5) additional share payable 12/03/1997 to holders of record 11/19/1997
Each share old Common 10¢ par exchanged for (0.2) share new Common 10¢ par 03/01/2010
Stock Dividend - 25% 07/20/1987
Acquired by American CyberSystems, Inc. 10/11/2013
Each share new Common 10¢ par exchanged for $6.45 cash

ANALYTIC OPTIONED EQUITY FD INC (CA)
Common no par split (10) for (1) by issuance of (9) additional shares 06/30/1986
Acquired by PBHG Advisor Defensive Equity Fund 08/31/1998
Details not available

ANALYTICAL NURSING MGMT CORP (DE)
Name changed to AMEDISYS, Inc. 08/11/1995

ANALYTICAL SECURITY CORP.
Dissolved 00/00/1949
Details not available

ANALYTICAL SOFTWARE INC (WY)
Administratively dissolved 06/11/2002

ANALYTICAL SURVEYS INC (CO)
Each share old Common no par exchanged for (0.05) share new Common no par 10/09/1987
New Common no par split (3) for (2) by issuance of (0.5) additional share payable 07/01/1996 to holders of record 06/27/1996
Each share new Common no par exchanged again for (0.1) share new Common no par 10/02/2002
Recapitalized as Axion International Holdings, Inc. 08/04/2008
Each share Common no par exchanged for (0.25) share Common no par
(See Axion International Holdings, Inc.)

ANALYTICAL SYS INC (DE)
Charter cancelled and declared inoperative and void for non-payment of taxes 03/01/1981

ANALYTICAL SYS INC (NY)
Reorganized under the laws of Delaware 09/30/1972
Each share Common 1¢ par exchanged for (2) shares Common 1¢ par
(See Analytical Systems, Inc. (DE))

ANALYTIX INC (DE)
Name changed to Alyx Medical Instruments, Inc. 07/20/1987
(See Alyx Medical Instruments, Inc.)

ANAM SEMICONDUCTOR INC (KOREA)
Each 144A Unsponsored GDR for Ordinary exchanged for (0.7768197) 144A Sponsored GDR for Ordinary 06/17/1999
Assets acquired by Amkor Technology, Inc. 00/00/2000
Details not available

ANAMETRICS INC (NY)
Merged into Anamet Corp. 05/16/1979
Each share Common 5¢ par exchanged for $2.15 cash

ANANDA CAP CORP (AB)
Recapitalized as Colonial Coal International Corp. 10/12/2010
Each share Common no par exchanged for (0.5) share Common no par

ANANGEL-AMERN SHIPHOLDINGS LTD (CAYMAN ISLANDS)
Acquired by Superior Navigation Ltd. 07/12/2002
Each Sponsored ADR for Ordinary exchanged for $5 cash

ANARCHIST CHROME CO. LTD. (BC)
Charter revoked for failure to file reports and pay fees 09/19/1968

ANARCHIST MTN RES LTD (BC)
Name changed to Cent-Ram Development Corp. 09/16/1982
Cent-Ram Development Corp. name changed to I.S.L. Industries Ltd. 01/07/1983
(See I.S.L. Industries Ltd.)

ANAREN INC (NY)
Name changed 12/20/2002
Common 1¢ par split (3) for (2) by issuance of (0.5) additional share payable 06/09/2000 to holders of record 05/12/2000
Common 1¢ par split (2) for (1) by issuance of (1) additional share payable 11/27/2000 to holders of record 11/17/2000 Ex date - 11/28/2000
Stock Dividend - 100% 03/27/1981
Name changed from Anaren Microwave, Inc. to Anaren, Inc. 12/20/2002
Acquired by ANVC Holding Corp. 02/18/2014
Each share Common 1¢ par exchanged for $28 cash

ANASAZI ENERGY CORP (NV)
Name changed to Solar Quartz Technologies, Inc. 12/19/2016

ANATHON COMPUTER & EDUCATIONAL SYS INC (NY)
Merged into Perathon Inc. 10/01/1969
Each share Common 10¢ par exchanged for (1) share Common 10¢ par
Perathon Inc. name changed to Pope, Evans & Robbins Inc. 11/16/1971
(See Pope, Evans & Robbins Inc.)

ANATOLIA ENERGY CORP (AB)
Merged into Cub Energy Inc. 07/01/2013
Each share Common no par exchanged for (0.106) share Common no par

ANATOLIA MINERALS DEV LTD (YT)
Name changed to Alacer Gold Corp. 02/23/2011

ANB BANKSHARES INC (GA)
Common $10 par split (2) for (1) by issuance of (1) additional share 11/19/1986
Acquired by Barnett Banks, Inc. 01/16/1989
Each share Common $10 par exchanged for (1.33) shares Common $2 par

FINANCIAL INFORMATION, INC.   ANB-ANC

Barnett Banks, Inc. merged into NationsBank Corp. 01/09/1998 which reincorporated in Delaware as BankAmerica Corp. (Old) 09/25/1998 which merged into BankAmerica Corp. (New) 09/30/1998 which name changed to Bank of America Corp. 04/28/1999

ANB CORP (IN)
Common no par split (5) for (3) by issuance of (0.66666666) additional share 07/14/1989
Common no par split (2) for (1) by issuance of (1) additional share 12/31/1992
Common no par split (2) for (1) by issuance of (1) additional share 12/29/1995
Merged into Old National Bancorp 03/13/2000
Each share Common no par exchanged for (1.3125) shares Common no par

ANB FINL CORP (WA)
Merged into First Hawaiian, Inc. 08/30/1996
Each share Common $1 exchanged for (4.08) shares Common $5 par
First Hawaiian, Inc. name changed to BancWest Corp. (New) 11/01/1998
(See BancWest Corp. (New))

ANBATCO INC (DE)
Name changed to American National Corp. 11/14/1969
(See American National Corp.)

ANC RENT CORP (DE)
Plan of reorganization under Chapter 11 Federal Bankruptcy Code plan effective 02/03/2005
No stockholders' equity

ANCESTRY COM INC (DE)
Acquired by Global Generations International Inc. 12/31/2012
Each share Common $0.001 par exchanged for $32 cash

ANCHOR ALLOYS INC (NY)
Common 10¢ par split (3) for (1) by issuance of (2) addtional shares 08/31/1973
Dissolved by proclamation 09/24/1980

ANCHOR BANCORP INC (DE)
Merged into Dime Bancorp, Inc. (New) 01/13/1995
Each share Common 1¢ par exchanged for (1.77) shares Common 1¢ par
Dime Bancorp, Inc. (New) merged into Washington Mutual, Inc. 01/04/2002

ANCHOR BANCORP WIS INC (DE)
Merged into Old National Bancorp 05/01/2016
Each share Common 1¢ par exchanged for (1.91678779) shares Common no par and $22.31658695 cash

ANCHOR BANCORP WIS INC (WI)
Common 10¢ par split (5) for (4) by issuance of (0.25) additional share 10/27/1995
Common 10¢ par split (2) for (1) by issuance of (1) additional share payable 08/15/1997 to holders of record 08/01/1997
Common 10¢ par split (2) for (1) by issuance of (1) additional share payable 08/24/1998 to holders of record 08/10/1998
Plan of reorganization under Chapter 11 Federal Bankruptcy proceedings effective 09/27/2013
No stockholders' equity

ANCHOR CAP ACCUMULATION TR (MA)
Name changed to Progressive Capital Accumulation Trust 01/21/1999
(See Progressive Capital Accumulation Trust)

ANCHOR CAP CORP.
Name changed to Anchor Hocking Glass Corp. 12/31/1937
Anchor Hocking Glass Corp. name changed to Anchor Hocking Corp. 05/08/1969
(See Anchor Hocking Corp.)

ANCHOR CAP FD INC (MD)
Merged into Anchor Spectrum Fund, Inc. 12/31/1973
Each share Capital Stock $1 par exchanged for (0.9225) share Capital Stock $1 par
Anchor Spectrum Fund, Inc. merged into Growth Fund of America, Inc. (DE) 08/31/1978 which reincorporated in Maryland 09/22/1983 which reorganized in Delaware 05/01/2013

ANCHOR CORP (DE)
Class B Common 50¢ par changed to 25¢ par and (2) additional shares issued 11/22/1968
Merged into Washington National Corp. 08/22/1969
Each share Class B Common 25¢ par exchanged for (0.22) share $2.50 Conv. Preferred $5 par and (0.2) share Common $5 par
(See Washington National Corp.)

ANCHOR COUPLING INC (IL)
97% acquired by Amerace Corp. through purchase offer which expired 10/23/1975
Public interest eliminated

ANCHOR DAILY INCOME FD INC (MD)
Merged into Cash Management Trust of America 10/05/1978
Each share Capital Stock 1¢ par exchanged for (1) Share of Bene. Int. $1 par
(See Cash Management Trust of America)

ANCHOR FDG SVCS INC (DE)
Common $0.001 par changed to $0.0001 par 10/19/2009
Name changed to FlexShopper, Inc. 11/06/2013

ANCHOR FINL CORP (SC)
Common $6 par split (2) for (1) by issuance of (1) additional share 09/29/1995
Common $6 par split (3) for (2) by issuance of (0.5) additional share payable 09/26/1997 to holders of record 08/29/1997
Common $6 par changed to no par 04/30/1998
Merged into South Financial Group, Inc. 06/07/2000
Each share Common no par exchanged for (2.175) shares Common $1 par
South Financial Group, Inc. merged into Toronto-Dominion Bank (Toronto, ON) 09/30/2010

ANCHOR GAMING (NV)
Common 1¢ par split (2) for (1) by issuance of (1) additional share payable 11/15/2000 to holders of record 10/31/2000 Ex date - 11/16/2000
Merged into International Game Technology 12/30/2001
Each share Common 1¢ par exchanged for (1) share Common $0.000625 par
International Game Technology merged into International Game Technology PLC 04/07/2015

ANCHOR GLASS CONTAINER CORP NEW (DE)
Plan of reorganization under Chapter 11 Federal Bankruptcy Code effective 08/30/2002
Each share 10% Conv. Preferred Ser. A received distribution of approximately $0.01 cash per share
Note: Certificates were not required to be surrendered and are without value
No old Common stockholders' equity
Issue Information - 7,500,000 shares COM NEW offered at $16 per share on 09/24/2003
Plan of reorganization under Chapter 11 Federal Bankruptcy Code effective 05/03/2006
No new Common stockholders' equity

ANCHOR GLASS CONTAINER CORP OLD (DE)
Common 1¢ par split (2) for (1) by issuance of (1) additional share 03/24/1987
Merged into THR Corp. 05/02/1990
Each share Common 1¢ par exchanged for $21.25 cash
Reorganized as Anchor Glass Container Corp. (New) 02/05/2000
Each share Class A exchanged for (1) share Common 10¢ par
Each share Class C exchanged for (1) share Common 10¢ par
(See Anchor Glass Container Corp. (New))

ANCHOR GOLD CORP (BC)
Struck off register and declared dissolved for failure to file returns 04/30/1993

ANCHOR GROWTH CORP. (UT)
Recapitalized as Aura Systems, Inc. (UT) 03/02/1987
Each share Common 1¢ par exchanged for (0.3) share Common $0.005 par
Aura Systems, Inc. (UT) reincorporated in Delaware 03/27/1987

ANCHOR GROWTH FD INC (DE)
Merged into Amcap Fund, Inc. 08/31/1981
Each share Capital Stock $1 par exchanged for (1.603) shares Capital Stock $1 par

ANCHOR HOCKING CORP (DE)
Common $6.25 par changed to $3.25 par and (1) additional share issued 05/22/1969
Common $3.25 par changed to $1 par and (0.5) additional share issued 05/17/1979
$4 Preferred no par called for redemption 07/17/1985
Merged into Newell Co. 07/02/1987
Each share Common $1 par exchanged for (1) share $2.08 Conv. Preferred $1 par
(See Newell Co.)

ANCHOR HOCKING GLASS CORP (DE)
Common no par changed to $12.50 par 00/00/1940
Each share Common $12.50 par exchanged for (2) shares Common $6.25 par 00/00/1950
Common $6.25 par split (2) for (1) by issuance of (1) additional share 01/23/1959
Name changed to Anchor Hocking Corp. 05/08/1969
(See Anchor Hocking Corp.)

ANCHOR INCOME FD INC (DE)
Merged into Income Fund of America, Inc. (DE) 07/31/1978
Each share Capital Stock $1 par exchanged for (0.859202) share Capital Stock $1 par
Income Fund of America, Inc. (DE) reincorporated in Maryland 09/22/1983 which reorganized in Delaware as Income Fund of America 10/01/2010

ANCHOR INTL BD TR (MA)
Completely liquidated 11/19/2003
Each share Common no par and Class A no par received net asset value

ANCHOR INVT CORP (FL)
Acquired by Anchor Acquisition, Inc. 10/24/2001
Each share Class A Common 1¢ par exchanged for $82 cash
Each share Class B Common 1¢ par exchanged for $82 cash

ANCHOR LAMINA INC (ON)
Name changed 03/26/1991
Name changed from Anchor Machine & Manufacturing Ltd. to Anchor Lamina Inc. 03/26/1991
Merged into Harrowston Inc. 08/06/1997
Each share Common no par exchanged for $8 cash

ANCHOR LIFE INSURANCE CO.
Merged into Atlas Life Insurance Co. 00/00/1929
Details not available

ANCHOR MINES, INC. (ID)
Common $1 par changed to 25¢ par 00/00/1949
Recapitalized as Midwestern Oil & Gas Corp. and Common 25¢ par changed to 5¢ par 00/00/1956
Midwestern Oil & Gas Corp. was liquidated for Coast Exploration Co. 03/13/1964
(See Coast Exploration Co.)

ANCHOR MINES LTD. (MB)
Charter cancelled for failure to file annual reports 00/00/1970

ANCHOR MINES LTD (BC)
Recapitalized as Eltron Security Systems Corp. 12/09/1975
Each share Capital Stock 50¢ par exchanged for (0.2) share Capital Stock no par
Eltron Security Systems Corp. name changed to Eltron Energy Corp. 02/22/1982
(See Eltron Energy Corp.)

ANCHOR NATIONAL LIFE INSURANCE CO. (KY)
Acquired by American Pyramid Companies Inc. 03/31/1969
Each share Common $1.75 par exchanged for (2.5) shares Common no par
American Pyramid Companies Inc. merged into American Consolidated Corp. 02/28/1977 which merged into I.C.H. Corp. 04/18/1985 which name changed to Southwestern Life Corp. (New) 06/15/1994 which name changed to I.C.H. Corp. (New) 10/10/1995
(See I.C.H. Corp. (New))

ANCHOR PAC UNDERWRITERS INC (DE)
Recapitalized as CGrowth Capital, Inc. 02/23/2010
Each share Common 2¢ par exchanged for (0.005) share Common 2¢ par

ANCHOR PETE CORP (BC)
Recapitalized as Logo Resources Ltd. 05/30/1983
Each share Capital Stock no par exchanged for (0.2) share Common no par
(See Logo Resources Ltd.)

ANCHOR PETES LTD (ON)
Charter cancelled for failure to pay taxes and file returns 05/24/1972

ANCHOR POST FENCE CO.
Name changed to Anchor Post Products, Inc. 00/00/1946
Anchor Post Products, Inc. acquired by Sunshine Mining Co. (WA) 05/29/1969 which reincorporated in Delaware 03/12/1980 which name changed to Sunshine Mining & Refining Co. 06/20/1994
(See Sunshine Mining & Refining Co.)

ANCHOR POST IRON WORKS
Name changed to Anchor Post Fence Co. 00/00/1927

Anchor Post Fence Co. name changed to Anchor Post Products, Inc. 00/00/1946 which was acquired by Sunshine Mining Co. (WA) 05/29/1969 which reincorporated in Delaware 03/12/1980 which name changed to Sunshine Mining & Refining Co. 06/20/1994
(See Sunshine Mining & Refining Co.)

ANCHOR POST PRODS INC (NJ)
Acquired by Sunshine Mining Co. (WA) 05/29/1969
Each share Common $2 par exchanged for (1.4) shares Capital Stock 5¢ par
Sunshine Mining Co. (WA) reincorporated in Delaware 03/12/1980 which name changed to Sunshine Mining & Refining Co. 06/20/1994
(See Sunshine Mining & Refining Co.)

ANCHOR PRECISION CORP. (DE)
No longer in existence having become inoperative and void for non-payment of taxes 10/01/1958

ANCHOR RESV FD INC (DE)
Merged into Anchor Daily Income Fund, Inc. 12/31/1976
Each share Common $1 par exchanged for (10.006972) shares Capital Stock $1 par
Anchor Daily Income Fund, Inc. merged into Cash Management Trust of America 10/05/1978
(See Cash Management Trust of America)

ANCHOR SVGS & LN ASSN SOMERS PT (NJ)
Name changed to Action Savings Bank SLA (Somers Point, NJ) 02/01/1989
(See Action Savings Bank SLA (Somers Point, NJ))

ANCHOR SVGS ASSN (KS)
99.7% held by ISC Industries, Inc. through purchase offer which expired 10/15/1973
Public interest eliminated

ANCHOR SVGS BK (ST PETERSBURG, FL)
Merged into Pinellas Community Bank (St. Petersburg, FL) 12/15/1997
Each share Common exchanged for $4.50 cash

ANCHOR SVGS BK FSB (HEWLETT, NY)
Reorganized under the laws of Delaware as Anchor Bancorp, Inc. and Common $1 par changed to 1¢ par 03/29/1991
Anchor Bancorp, Inc. merged into Dime Bancorp, Inc. (New) 01/13/1995 which merged into Washington Mutual, Inc. 01/04/2002
(See Washington Mutual, Inc.)

ANCHOR SER TR (MA)
Completely liquidated 09/26/2011
Each share Money Market Portfolio received net asset value

ANCHOR SPECTRUM FD INC (MD)
Merged into Growth Fund of America, Inc. (DE) 08/31/1978
Each share Capital Stock $1 par exchanged for (0.583376) share Common 10¢ par
Growth Fund of America, Inc. (DE) reincorporated in Maryland 09/22/1983 which reorganized in Delaware 05/01/2013

ANCHOR STEEL & CONVEYOR CO. (MI)
Merged into Standard Alliance Industries, Inc. 07/24/1968
Each share Common $1 par exchanged for (0.1) share 5.25% Conv. Preferred Ser. A $100 par
(See Standard Alliance Industries, Inc.)

ANCHOR VENTURE FD INC (DE)
Capital Stock $1 par split (4) for (1) by issuance of (3) additional shares 07/11/1972
Merged into Anchor Spectrum Fund, Inc. 12/31/1973
Each share Capital Stock $1 par exchanged for (1.92) shares Capital Stock $1 par
Anchor Spectrum Fund, Inc. merged into Growth Fund of America, Inc. (DE) 08/31/1978 which reincorporated in Maryland 09/22/1983 which reorganized in Delaware 05/01/2013

ANCHORAGE CAROLINA CORP (DE)
Reincorporated 04/27/1972
State of incorporation changed from (SC) to (DE) 04/27/1972
Adjudicated bankrupt 03/13/1975
Stockholders' equity unlikely

ANCHORAGE GAS & OIL DEV INC (AK)
Dissolved 10/20/1970
No stockholders' equity

ANCHORAGE HOMES, INC.
Declared insolvent 00/00/1948
Stockholders' equity unlikely

ANCO CORP (TN)
Name changed to Appalachian National Corp. 05/02/1972
(See Appalachian National Corp.)

ANCO EXPLORATION LTD. (AB)
Acquired by T.C. Explorations Ltd. 06/01/1970
Each share Common no par exchanged for (3) shares Common no par
T.C. Explorations Ltd. recapitalized as Decca Resources Ltd. 10/20/1970 which name changed to Sceptre Resources Ltd. (BC) 12/27/1977 which reincorporated in Canada 10/31/1979 which merged into Canadian Natural Resources Ltd. 08/15/1996

ANCO EXPLORATIONS LTD. (ON)
Charter cancelled and declared dissolved for default in filing returns and paying fees 08/29/1960

ANCOM ATM INTL INC (ON)
Discharged from receivership 07/00/1993
No stockholders' equity

ANCONA GROUP LTD (DE)
Name changed to American Home Alliance Corp. 10/08/1993

ANCONA MNG CORP (NV)
Common $0.00001 par split (5) for (1) by issuance of (4) additional shares payable 11/22/2002 to holders of record 11/18/2002 Ex date - 11/25/2002
Common $0.00001 par split (3) for (2) by issuance of (0.5) additional share payable 10/27/2004 to holders of record 10/25/2004 Ex date - 10/28/2004
Name changed to VisualMED Clinical Solutions Corp. 11/30/2004

ANCOR COMMUNICATIONS INC (MN)
Merged into QLogic Corp. 08/02/2000
Each share Common 1¢ par exchanged for (0.5275) share Common $0.001 par
QLogic Corp. merged into Cavium, Inc. 08/16/2016 which merged into Marvell Technology Group Ltd. 07/06/2018

ANCOR RES INC (NV)
Name changed to Nu-Mex Uranium Corp. 06/06/2007
Nu-Mex Uranium Corp. name changed to Uranium International Corp. 03/11/2008 which name changed to Mercer Gold Corp. 06/09/2010 which name changed to Tresoro Mining Corp. 11/04/2011

(See Tresoro Mining Corp.)

ANCORP BANCSHARES INC (TN)
Common $3.50 par split (3) for (1) by issuance of (2) additional shares 01/15/1974
Merged into Third National Corp. 12/31/1982
Each share Common $3.50 par exchanged for (1.18) shares Common $10 par
Third National Corp. merged into SunTrust Banks, Inc. 12/29/1986

ANCORP NATL SVCS INC (DE)
Merged into Sodexho 02/21/1979
Each share Capital Stock no par exchanged for $0.60 cash

ANCR INC (CO)
Name changed to CEA Lab, Inc. (CO) 10/30/1987
CEA Lab, Inc. (CO) reincorporated in Kansas 10/16/1995 which name changed to Courtleigh Capital Inc. 09/29/1997 which reincorporated in Nevada as Stockup.Com Inc. 02/22/1999 which reorganized as Preference Technologies Inc. 02/23/2000
(See Preference Technologies Inc.)

ANDACOLLO MNG LTD (ON)
Charter cancelled for failure to pay taxes and file returns 03/16/1976

ANDAIN INC (NV)
SEC revoked common stock registration 01/14/2016

ANDAL CORP (NY)
Each share old Common $1 par exchanged for (0.05) share new Common $1 par 06/14/1993
Merged into Cafco Holding Corp. 11/19/1998
Each share new Common $1 par exchanged for $37 cash

ANDAR GOLD MINES LTD. (ON)
Charter cancelled for failure to pay taxes and file returns 09/17/1962

ANDATACO INC (MA)
Merged into nStor Technologies, Inc. 11/02/1999
Each share Class A Common 1¢ par exchanged for (0.155) share Common 5¢ par
(See nStor Technologies, Inc.)

ANDAUREX INDS INC (BC)
Name changed 02/13/1981
Name changed 12/02/1992
Name changed 08/31/1995
Name changed from Anderado Resources Inc. to Andaurex Resources Inc. 02/13/1981
Name changed from Andaurex Resources Inc. to Andaurex Capital Resources Inc. 12/02/1992
Name changed from Andaurex Capital Resources Inc. to Andaurex Industries Inc. 08/31/1995
Reorganized under the laws of Canada as San Anton Resource Corp. 12/06/2006
Each share Common no par exchanged for (1) share Common no par
San Anton Resource Corp. merged into Kings Minerals NL 09/29/2010 which name changed to Cerro Resources NL 12/10/2010
(See Cerro Resources NL)

ANDEAN AMERN GOLD CORP (BC)
Merged into Lupaka Gold Corp. 10/01/2012
Each share Common no par exchanged for (0.245) share Common no par
Note: Unexchanged certificates were cancelled and became without value 10/01/2018

ANDEAN AMERN MNG CORP (BC)
Reincorporated 08/22/2005
Place of incorporation changed from (NB) to (BC) 08/22/2005

Name changed to Andean American Gold Corp. 09/07/2010
Andean American Gold Corp. merged into Lupaka Gold Corp. 10/01/2012

ANDEAN DEV CORP (FL)
Each share old Common $0.0001 par exchanged for (0.03333333) share new Common $0.0001 par 08/01/2005
New Common $0.0001 par split (7.6) for (1) by issuance of (6.6) additional shares payable 11/08/2005 to holders of record 11/01/2005 Ex date - 11/09/2005
Name changed to Ever-Glory International Group, Inc. 12/12/2005

ANDEAN RES LTD (AUSTRALIA)
Merged into Goldcorp Inc. (New) 12/09/2010
Each share Ordinary exchanged for (0.14) share Common no par

ANDEAVOR (DE)
Merged into Marathon Petroleum Corp. 10/01/2018
Each share Common $0.16666666 par exchanged for (1.632884) shares Common 1¢ par and $19.30784 cash

ANDELE CAP CORP (BC)
Name changed to Network Media Group Inc. 01/03/2012

ANDERSEN GROUP INC (DE)
Name changed 07/11/1979
Reincorporated 06/28/1998
Name changed from Andersen Laboratories, Inc. to Andersen Group, Inc. 07/11/1979
State of incorporation changed from (CT) to (DE) 06/28/1998
Common no par split (3) for (2) by issuance of (0.5) additional share 06/29/1981
Common no par split (3) for (2) by issuance of (0.5) additional share 06/30/1983
Stock Dividend - 10% 07/15/1982
Name changed to Moscow CableCom Corp. 02/24/2004
(See Moscow CableCom Corp.)

ANDERSEN 2000 INC (DE)
Reorganized 09/30/1971
Each share Common $1 par exchanged for (4) shares Common 25¢ par 10/05/1971
Reorganized from Utah to under the laws of Delaware 09/30/1971
Each share Common 25¢ par exchanged for (0.33333333) share Capital Stock 25¢ par
Stock Dividends - 100% 10/02/1978; 100% 03/20/1981
Merged into Crown Andersen Inc. 01/31/1986
Each share Capital Stock 25¢ par exchanged for (0.45454545) share Common 10¢ par
(See Crown Andersen Inc.)

ANDERSON BKG CO (ANDERSON, IN)
Each share Capital Stock $100 par exchanged for (10) shares Capital Stock $10 par plus a 40% stock dividend paid 00/00/1943
Stock Dividends - 20% 00/00/1950; 50% 00/00/1955; 11.11111111% 12/15/1958; 20% 12/31/1963; 25% 01/14/1969; 20% 04/14/1974
Merged into Merchants National Corp. 12/19/1986
Each share Capital Stock $10 par exchanged for (3.1589) shares Common no par
Merchants National Corp. merged into National City Corp. 05/02/1992 which was acquired by PNC Financial Services Group, Inc. 12/31/2008

ANDERSON CLAYTON & CO (DE)
Common $1 par changed to $21.80 par 00/00/1945
Common $21.80 par changed to $1

par and (1) additional share issued 04/09/1973
Common $1 par split (2) for (1) by issuance of (1) additional share 01/17/1977
Stock Dividend - 100% 09/17/1951
Merged into Quaker Oats Co. 10/31/1986
Each share Common $1 par exchanged for $66 cash

ANDERSON CMNTY BK (ANDERSON, IN)
Merged into First Merchants Corp. 04/21/1999
Each share Common no par exchanged for (1.38) shares Common no par

ANDERSON COMPUTERS/TIDALWAVE CORP (FL)
Name changed to Tidalwave Holdings Inc. 08/21/2000
(See Tidalwave Holdings Inc.)

ANDERSON COOK INC (MI)
Reincorporated 01/01/1990
State of incorporation changed from (DE) to (MI) 01/01/1990
Merged into ACI Acquisition 08/26/1996
Each share Common $1 par exchanged for $25 cash

ANDERSON ELEC CORP (AL)
6% Preferred $8.50 par called for redemption 05/25/1964
Common $1 par and Class B Common $1 par changed to 50¢ par and (1) additional share issued respectively 08/01/1964
Each share Class B Common 50¢ par exchanged for (1) share Common 50¢ par 12/05/1966
Acquired by Square D Co. (MI) 04/29/1970
Each share Common 50¢ par exchanged for (0.875) share Common $1.66666666 par
Square D Co. (MI) reincorporated in Delaware 06/16/1989
(See Square D Co. (DE))

ANDERSON ENERGY INC (AB)
Each share old Common no par exchanged for (0.001) share new Common no par 06/20/2016
Note: Holders of (999) or fewer pre-split shares were cancelled and are without value
Name changed to InPlay Oil Corp. 11/10/2016

ANDERSON ENERGY LTD (AB)
Name changed to Anderson Energy Inc. 01/27/2015
Anderson Energy Inc. name changed to InPlay Oil Corp. 11/10/2016

ANDERSON EXPL LTD (CANADA)
Common no par split (2) for (1) by issuance of (1) additional share 08/05/1994
Merged into Devon Energy Corp. 10/16/2001
Each share Common no par exchanged for $40 cash

ANDERSON GREENWOOD & CO (TX)
Common no par split (3) for (2) by issuance of (0.5) additional share 02/17/1981
Stock Dividends - 10% 07/25/1974; 15% 07/25/1975; 10% 07/28/1977; 15% 06/29/1983; 15% 03/05/1986
Merged into Keystone International, Inc. 07/16/1986
Each share Common no par exchanged for (1.023) shares Common $1 par
Keystone International, Inc. merged into Tyco International Ltd. (Bermuda) 08/29/1997 which reincorporated in Switzerland 03/17/2009 which merged into Johnson Controls International PLC 09/06/2016

ANDERSON INDS INC (TX)
Merged into AI Holdings, Inc. 09/05/1986
Each share Common $1 par exchanged for $6 cash

ANDERSON INDS INC (UT)
Name changed to Environ Corp. and Common $0.0004 par changed to Common 1¢ par 12/14/1974
(See Environ Corp.)

ANDERSON JACOBSON INC (DE)
Reincorporated 04/01/1980
Common no par changed to 10¢ par 08/12/1976
State of incorporation changed from (CA) to (DE) 04/01/1980
Stock Dividend - 10% 03/30/1982
Merged into CXR Telcom Corp. 08/23/1988
Each share Common 10¢ par exchanged for (0.364) share Common $0.0033 par
CXR Telcom Corp. reorganized as CXR Corp. 11/01/1989 which name changed to Microtel International Inc. 03/07/1995 which name changed to EMRISE Corp. 09/15/2004

ANDERSON NEW ENGLAND CAPITAL CORP. (MA)
Name changed to Anec Capital Corp. 05/17/1968
Anec Capital Corp. acquired by Mahon Technology Group Inc. 07/10/1969
(See Mahon Technology Group Inc.)

ANDERSON-PRICHARD OIL CORP. (DE)
Common $10 par split (2) for (1) by issuance of (1) additional share 05/11/1956
Liquidation completed
Each share Common $10 par stamped to indicate initial distribution of $49 cash 04/03/1961
Each share Stamped Common $10 par exchanged for second and final distribution of $0.585 cash 12/17/1962

ANDERSON STOKES INC (DE)
Common 1¢ par split (3) for (1) by issuance of (2) additional shares 08/16/1971
Name changed to Asco, Ltd. 07/08/1975 which recapitalized back as Anderson-Stokes, Inc. 11/20/1984
Each share Common 1¢ par exchanged for (2) shares Common 5¢ par
Reorganized 11/20/1990
Each share Common 5¢ par received (0.01) share ASCO Liquidating Corp. Common $5 par
Note: In effect holders received $0.625 cash per share and public interest was eliminated
Certificates were not required to be surrendered and are without value
(See ASCO Liquidating Corp.)

ANDES COPPER MNG CO (DE)
Capital Stock no par changed to $20 par 00/00/1936
Capital Stock $20 par changed to $14 par and $6 cash distributed 00/00/1952
Completely liquidated 03/31/1977
Each share Capital Stock $14 par received first and final distribution of $6.66 cash
Each share Class B Capital Stock $35 par received first and final distribution of $6.66 cash
Note: Certificates were not required to be surrendered and are without value

ANDES ENERGIA PLC (ENGLAND & WALES)
Each old Sponsored ADR for Ordinary exchanged for (0.674) new Sponsored ADR for Ordinary 07/12/2012
ADR agreement terminated 02/28/2018
Each new Sponsored ADR for Ordinary exchanged for $13.204851 cash

ANDES PETROLEUM CORP.
Company declared inoperative and void 00/00/1933

ANDES RANGE & FURNACE CORP.
Out of business 00/00/1952
Details not available

ANDEX MINES LTD (BC)
Recapitalized as Consolidated Andex Resources Ltd. 04/30/1984
Each share Common no par exchanged for (0.25) share Common no par
(See Consolidated Andex Resources Ltd.)

ANDIAMO CORP (NV)
Reincorporated under the laws of Wyoming 10/12/2015

ANDINA ACQUISITION CORP (CAYMAN ISLANDS)
Units separated 11/25/2013
Name changed to Tecnoglass, Inc. 12/23/2013

ANDINA ACQUISITION CORP II (CAYMAN ISLANDS)
Units separated 06/16/2018
Merged into Lazydays Holdings, Inc. 03/16/2018
Each share Ordinary $0.0001 par exchanged exchanged for (1) share Common $0.0001 par

ANDINA DEV CORP (AB)
Recapitalized as Carmanah Technologies Corp. (AB) 07/06/2001
Each share Common no par exchanged for (0.66666666) share Common no par
Carmanah Technologies Corp. (AB) reincorporated in British Columbia 08/24/2010

ANDINA GROUP INC (NV)
SEC revoked common stock registration 11/10/2014

ANDINA MINERALS INC (AB)
Acquired by Hochschild Mining PLC 02/22/2013
Each share Common no par exchanged for $0.80 cash

ANDOR MNG INC (ON)
Recapitalized as Trident Gold Corp. (ON) 02/20/2013
Each share Common no par exchanged for (0.2199978) share Common no par
Trident Gold Corp. (ON) reorganized in British Columbia as Sebastiani Ventures Corp. 04/25/2017

ANDORRA CAP CORP (DE)
Recapitalized as Savenergy Holdings, Inc. 08/04/2010
Each share Common $0.001 par exchanged for (0.001) share Common $0.001 par

ANDOVER APARTMENTS, INC.
Liquidated 00/00/1940
Details not available

ANDOVER APPAREL GROUP INC (DE)
Name changed 06/03/1998
Common 10¢ par split (5) for (4) by issuance of (0.25) additional share 05/04/1992
Name changed from Andover Togs, Inc. to Andover Apparel Group, Inc. 06/03/1998
Stock Dividend - 10% 12/09/1991
SEC revoked common stock registration 08/28/2006

ANDOVER BANCORP INC (DE)
Common 10¢ par split (5) for (4) by issuance of (0.25) additional share payable 05/18/1998 to holders of record 05/04/1998
Merged into Banknorth Group, Inc. (ME) 10/31/2001
Each share Common 10¢ par exchanged for (2.27) shares Common 1¢ par
Banknorth Group, Inc. (ME) merged into TD Banknorth Inc. 03/01/2005
(See TD Banknorth Inc.)

ANDOVER BANK (ANDOVER, OH)
Reorganized as Andover Bancorp, Inc. 09/01/1984
Each share Capital Stock $12.50 par exchanged for (1) share Common no par

ANDOVER CTLS CORP (MA)
Merged into BICC plc 08/08/1989
Each share Common 1¢ par exchanged for $16 cash

ANDOVER EQUITIES CORP (FL)
Recapitalized as Rainbow Medical Inc. 04/30/1997
Each share Common $0.001 par exchanged for (0.0109589) share Common $0.001 par
(See Rainbow Medical Inc.)

ANDOVER INST BUSINESS INC (MA)
Adjudicated bankrupt 06/07/1973
No stockholders' equity

ANDOVER MED INC (DE)
Recapitalized as Hot Mama's Foods, Inc. 08/06/2013
Each share Common $0.001 par exchanged for (0.02564102) share Common $0.001 par

ANDOVER MINING & EXPLORATION LTD. (ON)
Recapitalized as Andover Resources Ltd. 05/31/1971
Each share Capital Stock 25¢ par exchanged for (0.2) share Capital Stock no par
Andover Resources Ltd. name changed to Andover Telecommunications Inc. 10/02/1986 which name changed to Kennecom Inc. 06/02/1989 which recapitalized as Deltona Industries Inc. 01/25/1995
(See Deltona Industries Inc.)

ANDOVER MNG CORP (BC)
Deemed bankrupt 02/12/2014
No stockholders' equity

ANDOVER NET INC (DE)
Merged into VA Linux Systems, Inc. 06/07/2000
Each share Common 1¢ par exchanged for (0.425) share Common $0.001 par
VA Linux Systems, Inc. name changed to VA Software Corp. 12/06/2001 which name changed to SourceForge, Inc. 05/24/2007 which name changed to Geeknet, Inc. 11/04/2009
(See Geeknet, Inc.)

ANDOVER RES LTD (ON)
Name changed to Andover Telecommunications Inc. 10/02/1986
Andover Telecommunications Inc. name changed to Kennecom Inc. 06/02/1989 which recapitalized as Deltona Industries Inc. 01/25/1995
(See Deltona Industries Inc.)

ANDOVER SVGS BK (ANDOVER, MA)
Under plan of reorganization each share Common 10¢ par automatically became (1) share Andover Bancorp, Inc. Common 10¢ par 11/02/1987
Andover Bancorp, Inc. merged into Banknorth Group, Inc. (ME) 10/31/2001 which merged into TD Banknorth Inc. 03/01/2005
(See TD Banknorth Inc.)

ANDOVER TELECOMMUNICATIONS INC (ON)
Name changed to Kennecom Inc. 06/02/1989

Kennecom Inc. recapitalized as Deltona Industries Inc. 01/05/1995
(See Deltona Industries Inc.)

ANDOVER VENTURES INC (BC)
Name changed to Andover Mining Corp. 01/06/2012
(See Andover Mining Corp.)

ANDOWAN MINES LTD. (ON)
Charter cancelled 03/31/1981

ANDRAPLEX CORP (CO)
Name changed to Yaak River Resources Inc. 01/29/1992
Yaak River Resources Inc. recapitalized as Lifeline Therapeutics, Inc. 10/05/2004 which name changed to LifeVantage Corp. (CO) 02/02/2007 which reincorporated in Delaware 03/09/2018

ANDREA RADIO CORP (NY)
Common $1 par changed to 50¢ par and (1) additional share issued 01/24/1969
Name changed to Andrea Electronics Corp. 08/21/1991

ANDREAE-COLE FUND LTD. (ON)
Name changed to Andreae Equity Investment Fund Ltd. 08/15/1963
Andreae Equity Investment Fund Ltd. name changed to Itco Investment Fund Ltd. 11/12/1975
(See Itco Investment Fund Ltd.)

ANDREAE EQUITY INVT FD LTD (ON)
Name changed to Itco Investment Fund Ltd. 11/12/1975
(See Itco Investment Fund Ltd.)

ANDRES WINES LTD (CANADA)
Name changed 10/23/1970
Name changed from Andres Wines (Canada) Ltd. to Andres Wines Ltd. 10/23/1970
Reorganized as Andres Wines Ltd.-Les Vins Andres Ltee. 10/30/1978
6% Preferred Ser. A $10 par reclassified as 6% Preference Ser. A no par
Each share Common no par exchanged for (1) share Non-Vtg. Class A no par and (1) share Conv. Vtg. Class B no par
6% Preference Ser. A no par called for redemption 12/29/1994
Non-Vtg. Class A no par split (2) for (1) by issuance of (1) additional share 09/16/1985
Conv. Vtg. Class B no par split (2) for (1) by issuance of (1) additional share 09/16/1985
Name changed to Andrew Peller Ltd. 10/27/2006

ANDRESMIN GOLD CORP (MT)
Each share old Common $0.001 par exchanged for (3) shares new Common $0.001 par 10/18/2004
SEC revoked common stock registration 03/24/2011

ANDREW CORP (DE)
Reincorporated 02/05/1987
Stock Dividend - 100% 11/16/1981
State of incorporation changed from (IL) to (DE) and Common $1 par changed to 1¢ par 02/05/1987
Each share 7.75% Conv. Ser. A Preferred no par exchanged for (11.526) shares Common 1¢ par 03/14/2005
Common 1¢ par split (2) for (1) by issuance of (1) additional share 03/03/1993
Common 1¢ par split (3) for (2) by issuance of (0.5) additional share 03/02/1994
Common 1¢ par split (3) for (2) by issuance of (0.5) additional share 03/08/1995
Common 1¢ par split (3) for (2) by issuance of (0.5) additional share payable 03/06/1996 to holders of record 02/21/1996
Common 1¢ par split (3) for (2) by issuance of (0.5) additional share payable 03/11/1997 to holders of record 02/25/1997
Merged into CommScope, Inc. 12/27/2007
Each share Common 1¢ par exchanged for (0.031543) share Common 1¢ par and $13.50 cash
(See CommScope, Inc.)

ANDREW WOLF CELLARS LTD (AB)
Merged into Celebration Cellars Ltd. 10/14/1999
Each share Common no par exchanged for (0.2) share Common no par
Celebration Cellars Ltd. name changed to WNS Inc. 07/03/2001 which name changed to WNS Emergent Inc. 05/01/2002 which name changed to CriticalControl Solutions Corp. 06/14/2004 which name changed to Critical Control Energy Services Corp. 07/03/2015

ANDREW YELLOWKNIFE MINES LTD. (ON)
Merged into Pardee Amalgamated Mines Ltd. 12/00/1954
Each share Common no par exchanged for (0.03333333) share Common $1 par
Pardee Amalgamated Mines Ltd. liquidated for Rio Algom Mines Ltd. 11/09/1961 which name changed to Rio Algom Ltd. 04/30/1975
(See Rio Algom Ltd.)

ANDREWS GROUP INC (CA)
Merged into MacAndrews & Forbes Holdings Inc. 06/04/1990
Each share Common 10¢ par exchanged for $7.25 principal amount of Andrews Group Inc. 10% Sr. Subordinated Debentures due 12/30/1999

ANDREWS (F.L.) INVESTMENT TRUST
Liquidated 00/00/1950
No stockholders' equity

ANDREWS LEAD CO., INC.
Acquired by American Smelting & Refining Co. 00/00/1940
Details not available

ANDRIA RES INC (BC)
Struck off register and declared dissolved for failure to file returns 09/24/1993

ANDRO URANIUM CORP. (NM)
Charter revoked for failure to file reports and pay fees 10/03/1960

ANDROCK INC (ON)
Name changed to Autrex Inc. 01/20/1986
Autrex Inc. merged into Basis 100 Inc. 10/29/1999
(See Basis 100 Inc.)

ANDROID CORP (UT)
Name changed to Appliance Parts Plus International, Inc. 02/16/1993
Appliance Parts Plus International, Inc. name changed to International Equity Resources, Inc. 10/25/1993 which name changed to International Protection Technologies, Inc. 07/27/1998 which name changed to HyperSecur Corp. 03/04/1999

ANDROMED INC (QC)
Name changed to Sonomed Inc. 05/23/2006
Sonomed Inc. reorganized as SND Energy Ltd. 06/29/2007 which recapitalized as Boyuan Construction Group, Inc. 02/24/2009

ANDROMEDA CAP CORP (NV)
Name changed to Home Capital Investment Corp. 12/16/1994
(See Home Capital Investment Corp.)

ANDROMEDA INC (UT)
Proclaimed dissolved for failure to pay taxes 01/01/1988

ANDROMEDA MEDIA CAP CORP LTD (ON)
Name changed to Tri-Media Integrated Marketing Technologies Inc. 05/27/2008

ANDROMEDA I INC (DE)
Recapitalized as Sin Jin Technology, Inc. 01/30/1996
Each share Common $0.001 par exchanged for (0.08) share Common $0.001 par
(See Sin Jin Technology, Inc.)

ANDROMEDA VENTURES INC (BC)
Struck off register and declared dissolved for failure to file returns 12/01/1992

ANDROMEDIA INC (CA)
Merged into Macromedia, Inc. 12/01/1999
Each share Preferred Ser. E no par exchanged for (0.2467) share Common $0.001 par
Each share Common no par exchanged for (0.2467) share Common $0.001 par
Macromedia Inc. merged into Adobe Systems Inc. 12/03/2005 which name changed to Adobe Inc. 10/09/2018

ANDRONE RES LTD (BC)
Merged into Pezgold Resource Corp. (New) 09/01/1988
Each share Common no par exchanged for (1) share Common no par
Pezgold Resource Corp. (New) recapitalized as Braiden Resources Ltd. 06/15/1990 which recapitalized as Pure Pioneer Ventures Ltd. 06/14/2002

ANDROPOLLIS INC (UT)
Each share old Common $0.001 par exchanged for (0.01666666) share new Common $0.001 par 03/26/1996
Reincorporated under the laws of Florida as Cyber-Centurian, Inc. 04/25/1996
(See Cyber-Centurian, Inc.)

ANDROS HOTELS & CASINOS INC (NV)
Each share old Common $0.001 par received distribution of (0.001) share Auto Auction.com Inc. Common $0.000001 par payable 08/16/1999 to holders of record 07/31/1999
Each share old Common $0.001 par received distribution of (0.001) share New Horizons Airways, Inc. Common $0.001 par payable 08/16/1999 to holders of record 07/31/1999
Each share old Common $0.001 par exchanged for (0.005) share new Common $0.001 par 04/28/2000
Recapitalized as American Associates Group, Inc. 08/09/2005
Each share new Common $0.001 par exchanged for (0.02) share Common $0.0001 par
Note: Holders of (99) or fewer shares not affected by reverse split
American Associates Group, Inc. recapitalized as Clean Hydrogen Producers, Ltd. 06/11/2007 which name changed to Golden Developing Solutions, Inc. 09/27/2017

ANDROS INC (CA)
Name changed 12/03/1990
Name changed from Andros Analyzers Inc. to Andros Inc. 12/03/1990
Merged into Andros Holdings Inc. 05/14/1996
Each share Common no par exchanged for $18 cash

ANDROS IS HOTEL & CASINO INC (NV)
Reorganized as Andros Hotels & Casinos, Inc. 05/31/1999
Each share Common $0.001 par exchanged for (10) shares Common $0.001 par
Andros Hotels & Casinos, Inc. recapitalized as American Associates Group, Inc. 08/9/2005 which recapitalized as Clean Hydrogen Producers, Ltd. 06/11/2007 which name changed to Golden Developing Solutions, Inc. 09/27/2017

ANDROS ISLE DEV CORP (NV)
Charter revoked 07/31/2009

ANDROSCOGGIN & KENNEBEC RAILWAY
Property sold 00/00/1941
No stockholders' equity

ANDROSCOGGIN ELECTRIC CO.
Merged into Central Maine Power Co. 00/00/1935
Details not available

ANDROSCOGGIN MILLS
Assets acquired by Bates Manufacturing Co. 00/00/1946
Details not available

ANDROSCOGGIN PULP CO.
Acquired by Gair (Robert) Co., Inc. 00/00/1935
Details not available

ANDRX CORP (DE)
Each share Cybear Group Common $0.001 par exchanged for (0.00964) share Andrx Group Common $0.001 par 05/17/2002
Merged into Watson Pharmaceuticals, Inc. 11/03/2006
Each share Andrx Group Common $0.001 par exchanged for $25 cash

ANDRX CORP (FL)
Common $0.001 par split (2) for (1) by issuance of (1) additional share payable 06/01/1999 to holders of record 05/17/1999
Common $0.001 par split (2) for (1) by issuance of (1) additional share payable 04/03/2000 to holders of record 03/15/2000
Merged into Andrx Corp. (DE) 09/07/2000
Each share Common $0.001 par exchanged for (1) share Andrx Group Common $0.001 par and (0.1489) share Cybear Group Common $0.001 par
(See each company's listing)

ANDY GARD CORP (PA)
Merged into Meridian Industries, Inc. 09/29/1971
Each share Common $1 par exchanged for (1) share Common 10¢ par
(See Meridian Industries, Inc.)

ANDY YELLOWKNIFE MINES LTD. (ON)
Charter cancelled for failure to pay taxes and file returns 00/00/1952

ANDYNE COMPUTING LTD (ON)
Merged into Hummingbird Communications Ltd. 12/22/1997
Each share Common no par exchanged for (0.18745) share Common no par
Hummingbird Communications Ltd. name changed to Hummingbird Ltd. 04/25/2000
(See Hummingbird Ltd.)

ANDYS INTL (NV)
Ceased operations 00/00/1973
Details not available

ANEC CAP CORP (MA)
Completely liquidated 07/10/1969
Each share Common $1 par exchanged for first and final distribution of (1) share Mahon

Technology Group Inc. Common $1 par
(See Mahon Technology Group Inc.)

ANECO REINS LTD (BERMUDA)
Name changed to Forum Re Group (Bermuda) Ltd. 08/09/1988
(See Forum Re Group (Bermuda) Ltd.)

ANEFCO INC (NY)
Dissolved by proclamation 06/23/1993

ANELEX CORP (NH)
Common $1 par split (3) for (1) by issuance of (2) additional shares 12/21/1961
Merged into Mohawk Data-Sciences Corp. 10/20/1967
Each share Common $1 par exchanged for (1/3) share Common 10¢ par
Mohawk Data Sciences Corp. name changed to Qantel Corp. 09/17/1987
(See Qantel Corp.)

ANELLUX SYS CORP (UT)
Charter suspended for failure to file reports 12/31/1974

ANEMOSTAT CORP. OF AMERICA (DE)
Class A or B Common exchanged for Common $2 par 00/00/1946
Merged into Dynamics Corp. of America 11/26/1963
Details not available

ANERGEN INC (CA)
Merged into Corixa Corp. 02/10/1999
Each share Common no par exchanged for (0.055919) share Common $0.001 par
(See Corixa Corp.)

ANERGY CAP INC (BC)
Reorganized under the laws of Canada as Kraken Sonar Inc. 02/24/2015
Each share Common no par exchanged for (0.44444444) share Common no par
Kraken Sonar Inc. name changed to Kraken Robotics Inc. 09/22/2017

ANESIVA INC (DE)
Chapter 7 bankruptcy proceedings terminated 06/10/2014
Stockholders' equity unlikely

ANESTA CORP (DE)
Merged into Cephalon, Inc. 10/11/2000
Each share Common $0.001 par exchanged for (0.4765) share Common 1¢ par
(See Cephalon, Inc.)

ANESTHESIA RESPIRATORY TECHNOLOGY INC (IN)
Name changed to Artec Inc. 09/18/1989
(See Artec Inc.)

ANETH CORP (UT)
Merged into Aneth United, Inc. 04/30/1969
Each share Common 50¢ par exchanged for (1) share Common 50¢ par
(See Aneth United, Inc.)

ANETH UTD INC (UT)
Charter suspended for failure to file annual reports 12/31/1974

ANEXCO RES LTD (BC)
Name changed to Kaneh Bosm Biotechnology Inc. 11/05/2014
Kaneh Bosm Biotechnology Inc. name changed to ICC International Cannabis Corp. (New) 09/20/2018

ANF TELECAST INC (AZ)
Recapitalized as Protec Industries, Inc. (AZ) 12/13/2002
Each share Common $0.001 par exchanged for (0.01) share Common $0.001 par
Protec Industries, Inc. (AZ) reincorporated in Washington 03/02/2004

ANFI INC (CA)
Merged into Fidelity National Financial, Inc. 03/26/2003
Each share Common no par exchanged for (0.454) share Common $0.0001 par
Fidelity National Financial, Inc. merged into Fidelity National Information Services, Inc. 11/09/2006

ANFIELD GOLD CORP (BC)
Merged into Equinox Gold Corp. 12/22/2017
Each share Common no par exchanged for (0.407) share Common no par
Note: Unexchanged certificates will be cancelled and become without value 12/22/2023

ANFIELD NICKEL CORP (BC)
Name changed to Anfield Gold Corp. 05/11/2016
Anfield Gold Corp. merged into Equinox Gold Corp. 12/22/2017 which merged into Equinox Gold Corp. 12/22/2017

ANFIELD RES INC (BC)
Recapitalized as Anfield Energy Inc. 12/27/2017
Each share Common no par exchanged for (0.1) share Common no par

ANFIELD VENTURES INC (BC)
Name changed to Anfield Nickel Corp. 08/18/2009
Anfield Nickel Corp. name changed to Anfield Gold Corp. 05/11/2016

ANG, INC. (IN)
Liquidation completed
Each share Conv. Preferred Ser. A $3 par exchanged for first and final distribution of $3.03 cash 03/31/1981
Each share Common 25¢ par exchanged for initial distribution of $4 cash 03/31/1981
Each share Common 25¢ par received second and final distribution of $2.68 cash 09/11/1981

ANGANG STL CO LTD (CHINA)
Name changed 11/09/2006
Name changed from Angang New Steel Co. Ltd. to Angang Steel Co. Ltd. 11/09/2006
ADR agreement terminated 04/03/2018
Each Sponsored ADR for H Shares exchanged for (40) H Shares
Note: Unexchanged ADR's will be sold and the proceeds, if any, held for claim after 04/08/2019

ANGEION CORP (MN)
Each share old Common 1¢ par exchanged for (0.1) share new Common 1¢ par 05/17/1999
Plan of reorganization under Chapter 11 Federal Bankruptcy Code effective 10/25/2002
Each share new Common 1¢ par received (0.05) share Common 10¢ par and (0.05) Common Stock Purchase Warrant expiring 10/31/2007
Note: Certificates were not required to be surrendered and are without value
Name changed to MGC Diagnostics Corp. 08/21/2012
(See MGC Diagnostics Corp.)

ANGEL ACQUISITION CORP (NV)
SEC revoked common stock registration 08/20/2014

ANGEL BIOVENTURES INC (AB)
Each share old Common no par exchanged for (0.1) share new Common no par 03/02/2015
Reorganized under the laws of British Columbia as AbraPlata Resource Corp. 03/28/2017

Each share new Common no par exchanged for (0.2) share Common no par

ANGELAUDIO COM INC (NV)
Name changed to Whatsupmusic.com Inc. 11/28/2000
Whatsupmusic.com Inc. name changed to New Millennium Development Group 05/14/2001 which name changed to Millennium National Events, Inc. 10/05/2004 which recapitalized as Extensions, Inc. 08/24/2007
(See Extensions, Inc.)

ANGELCITI ENTMT INC (NV)
Common $0.001 par split (6) for (1) by issuance of (5) additional shares payable 05/08/2003 to holders of record 05/07/2003 Ex date - 05/09/2003
Each share Common $0.001 par exchanged for (4) shares old Common $0.00025 par 10/15/2003
Each share old Common $0.00025 par exchanged for (0.01) share new Common $0.00025 par 08/27/2004
Each share new Common $0.00025 par received distribution of (1) share Midas Entertainment, Inc. Common $0.00001 par payable 09/24/2004 to holders of record 09/22/2004
Each share new Common $0.00025 par received distribution of (0.2) share Midas Entertainment, Inc. Common $0.00001 par payable 03/25/2005 to holders of record 03/23/2005
SEC revoked common stock registration 08/09/2012

ANGELES CORP (CA)
Reincorporated 12/15/1977
Each share Common 50¢ par exchanged for (0.02) share Common 10¢ par 09/28/1976
State of incorporation changed from (DE) to (CA) and Common 10¢ par changed to no par 12/15/1977
Each share old Common no par exchanged for (2) shares new Common no par to reflect a (1) for (15) reverse split followed by a (30) for (1) forward split 07/30/1979
Note: Holders of (14) or fewer pre-split shares received $33 cash per share
New Common no par split (2) for (1) by issuance of (1) additional share 11/07/1980
New Common no par split (2) for (1) by issuance of (1) additional share 12/11/1981
Each share new Common no par received distribution of (1) Non-Transferable Unit of Angeles Future Interest Partnership Ltd. 11/05/1982
New Common no par split (3) for (2) by issuance of (0.5) additional share 12/02/1983
12% Preferred $1.80 Ser. no par called for redemption 03/30/1984
Conv. Jr. Preferred no par called for redemption 02/28/1986
Stock Dividend - 50% 02/28/1983
Plan of reorganization under Chapter 11 Federal Bankruptcy Code confirmed 03/07/1995
No stockholders' equity

ANGELES CREST DEV INC (CA)
Adjudicated bankrupt 03/14/1977
Stockholders' equity unlikely

ANGELES FIN PARTNERS (CA)
Under plan of reorganization each Depositary Receipt automatically became (1) share Angeles Finance Trust Class A Shares of Bene. Int. $1 par 03/07/1989
Angeles Finance Trust liquidated for Angeles Corp. 03/02/1990

ANGELES FIN TR (CA)
Completely liquidated 03/02/1990
Each Class A Share of Bene. Int. $1

par exchanged for first and final distribution of (0.82) Angeles Corp. Unit consisting of $20 principal amount of 12.5% Subordinated Debentures due 04/15/2001 and (0.5) share new Common no par

ANGELES INCOME PPTYS LTD L P (CA)
Merged into AIMCO Properties, L.P. 01/23/2012
Each Unit of Ltd. Partnership Int. VI $1,000 par exchanged for either (11.65) Common Units or $268.04 cash
Note: Option to receive to Units expired 03/01/2012
Residents of California, Massachusetts and New York will receive cash
(Additional Information in Active)

ANGELES MTG INVT TR (CA)
Merged into Insignia Properties Trust 09/17/1998
Each Class A Share of Bene. Int. no par exchanged for (1.516) Common Shares of Bene. Int. no par
Insignia Properties Trust merged into Apartment Investment & Management Co. 02/26/1999

ANGELES MTG PARTNERS LTD (CA)
Under plan of reorganization name changed to Angeles Mortgage Investment Trust and Depositary Receipts reclassified as Class A Shares of Bene. Int. no par 01/01/1989
Note: Certificates reflecting the above were issued 03/00/1989
Note: All outstanding Depositary Receipts have been cancelled and are without value

ANGELES OPPORTUNITY PPTYS (CA)
Liquidation completed 03/30/2010
Details not available

ANGELES PART MTG TR (CA)
Name changed to Starwood Financial Trust (CA) 03/13/1998
Starwood Financial Trust (CA) merged into Starwood Financial Trust (MD) 06/18/1998 which name changed to Starwood Financial Inc. 11/04/1999 which name changed to iStar Financial Inc. 05/01/2000 which name changed to iStar Inc. 08/19/2015

ANGELES PARTNERS (CA)
In process of liquidation 08/06/1997
Unit of Ltd. Partnership Int. XVI equity unlikely
In process of liquidation 12/31/1998
Unit of Ltd. Partnership Int. XV equity unlikely
In process of liquidation 09/30/1999
Unit of Ltd. Partnership Int. VIII equity unlikely
In process of liquidation 11/30/2003
Unit of Ltd. Partnership Int. XIV details not available
Units of Ltd. Partnership Int. VII terminated registration 03/31/2004
Details not available
Units of Ltd. Partnership Int. IX terminated registration 11/07/2006
Details not available
Merged into AIMCO Properties, L.P. 01/23/2012
Each Unit of Ltd. Partnership Int. XII exchanged for either (21.01) Common Units or $483.14 cash
Note: Option to receive to Units expired 03/01/2012
Residents of California, Massachusetts and New York will receive cash
(Additional Information in Active)

ANGELICA CORP (MO)
Common $1 par split (2) for (1) by issuance of (1) additional share 01/06/1969
Common $1 par split (2) for (1) by

issuance of (1) additional share 10/31/1972
Common $1 par split (3) for (2) by issuance of (0.5) additional share 04/08/1983
Acquired by Clothesline Holdings, Inc. 08/04/2008
Each share Common $1 par exchanged for $22 cash

ANGELICA UNIFORM CO. (MO)
Stock Dividends - 50% 10/15/1965; 100% 08/16/1967
Name changed to Angelica Corp. 10/25/1967
(See Angelica Corp.)

ANGELL FOODS INC (NV)
Charter revoked for failure to file reports and pay fees 05/01/1992

ANGELL REAL ESTATE CO (DE)
Reorganized 01/01/1988
Reorganized from Angell Care Master Limited Partnership to Angell Real Estate Co., Inc. and Units of Ltd. Partnership reclassified as Common 1¢ par 01/01/1988
Name changed to Health Equity Properties, Inc. (DE) 02/12/1990
Health Equity Properties, Inc. (DE) reincorporated in North Carolina 06/03/1991 which merged into Omega Healthcare Investors, Inc. 09/30/1994

ANGELO & MAXIES INC (DE)
Name changed to AM-CH, Inc. 02/07/2005
(See AM-CH, Inc.)

ANGELS WITH DIRTY FACES
Units of Bene. Int. Ser. 1 called for redemption 12/10/1996

ANGELUS PETROLEUMS (1965) LTD. (ON)
Charter cancelled and proclaimed dissolved for failure to pay taxes and file returns 11/28/1978

ANGELUS PETROLEUMS LTD. (ON)
Recapitalized as Angelus Petroleums (1965) Ltd. 11/22/1966
Each share Capital Stock no par exchanged for (0.2) share Capital Stock no par
(See Angelus Petroleums (1965) Ltd.)

ANGELWEST CAP CORP (BC)
Name changed to Greenangel Energy Corp. 10/29/2009
Greenangel Energy Corp. name changed to TIMIA Capital Corp. 09/24/2015

ANGERMAN CO., INC. (NY)
Acquired by Diana Stores Corp. 00/00/1953
Each share Common $1 par exchanged for $8 cash

ANGHEL LABS INC (DE)
Acquired by Radiation Systems, Inc. 02/04/1993
Each share Common $0.001 par exchanged for $0.80 cash

ANGICOR LTD (MN)
Reorganized under Chapter 11 Federal Bankruptcy Code as AorTech, Inc. 02/15/1990
Each (21.4) shares Common no par exchanged for (1) share Common 1¢ par and (1) Common Stock Purchase Warrant expiring 03/31/1993
AorTech, Inc. name changed to Calendar Capital, Inc. 03/26/1993 which name changed to IQUniverse, Inc. 04/11/2001
(See IQUniverse, Inc.)

ANGIES LIST INC (DE)
Merged into ANGI Homeservices Inc. 10/02/2017
Each share Common $0.001 par exchanged for (1) share Class A Common $0.001 par

ANGIO MED CORP (DE)
Charter cancelled and declared inoperative and void for non-payment of taxes 03/01/1992

ANGIOMEDICS INC (MN)
Merged into Pfizer Inc. 03/13/1987
Each share Common 1¢ par exchanged for $13.25 cash

ANGIOTECH PHARMACEUTICALS INC (BC)
Common no par split (2) for (1) by issuance of (1) additional share payable 03/21/2003 to holders of record 03/17/2003 Ex date - 03/13/2003
Common no par split (2) for (1) by issuance of (1) additional share payable 02/10/2004 to holders of record 02/03/2004 Ex date - 01/30/2004
Plan of arrangement effective 05/12/2011
No stockholders' equity

ANGKASA MARKETING BERHAD (MALAYSIA)
Name changed to Silverstone Corporation Berhad 04/08/2003

ANGKOR MINERALS INC (NV)
Name changed to Hemisphere Gold Inc. 11/29/2006
(See Hemisphere Gold Inc.)

ANGLE ENERGY INC (AB)
Merged into Bellatrix Exploration Ltd. 12/16/2013
Each share Common no par exchanged for (0.3693) share Common no par and $0.847 cash

ANGLE RES LTD NEW (BC)
Name changed 01/01/1988
Under plan of merger name changed from Angle Resources Ltd. (Old) to Angle Resources Ltd. (New) and each share Common no par exchanged for (1) share Common no par 01/01/1988
Merged into Nexus Resource Corp. 05/05/1988
Each share Common no par exchanged for (0.89) share Common no par
Nexus Resource Corp. recapitalized as Pacific Gold Corp. (BC) 07/05/1990 which reincorporated in Alberta 05/12/1994 which reincorporated in Ontario 06/27/1995 which name changed to Worldtek (Canada) Ltd. 07/04/1996
(See Worldtek (Canada) Ltd.)

ANGLESEA ENTERPRISES INC (NV)
Name changed to Sports Field Holdings, Inc. 06/30/2014

ANGLETON BK COMM (ANGLETON, TX)
Capital Stock $10 par split (2) for (1) by issuance of (1) additional share 01/22/1979
Merged into Victoria Bankshares, Inc. 09/30/1982
Each share Capital Stock $10 par exchanged for (0.55) share Common $10 par
Victoria Bankshares, Inc. merged into Norwest Corp. 04/11/1996 which name changed to Wells Fargo & Co. (New) 11/02/1998

ANGLIN-NORCROSS, LTD.
Sold to Anglin-Norcross Corp., Ltd. 00/00/1931
Details not available

ANGLO ALPHA CEM LTD (SOUTH AFRICA)
ADR agreement terminated 05/24/1996
Each ADR for Ordinary exchanged for $16.71 cash

ANGLO ALUM CORP (BC)
Recapitalized as Navasota Resources Inc. 07/12/2013
Each share Common no par exchanged for (0.1) share Common no par

ANGLO AMERN COAL LTD (SOUTH AFRICA)
Stock Dividends - 2.2155% payable 01/16/1998 to holders of record 12/19/1997; 3.8513% payable 07/27/1998 to holders of record 06/11/1998
ADR agreement terminated 12/18/1998
Each ADR for Ordinary exchanged for approximately $49.90 cash

ANGLO AMERN CORP CDA LTD (CANADA)
Name changed to Minorco Canada Ltd. 08/28/1981
(See Minorco Canada Ltd.)

ANGLO AMERN CORP SOUTH AFRICA LTD (SOUTH AFRICA)
Each share Ordinary Reg. Rand-1 par exchanged for (10) shares Ordinary Reg. Rand-10 par 06/23/1969
Each ADR for Ordinary exchanged for (10) ADR's for Ordinary 06/23/1969
Reincorporated under the laws of United Kingdom as Anglo American PLC 05/24/1999

ANGLO AMERICAN EXPLORATION LTD. (AB)
Common no par changed to $4.75 par 00/00/1955
Common $4.75 par changed to $1 par 05/28/1962
Acquired by British American Oil Co. Ltd. 12/00/1962
Each share Common $1 par exchanged for (1) share Norcan Oils Ltd. Common and $6 cash
Norcan Oils Ltd. merged into Gridoil Freehold Leases Ltd. 02/18/1963 which merged into Canadian Gridoil Ltd. 02/18/1966 which merged into Ashland Oil Canada Ltd. 09/14/1970 which name changed to Kaiser Petroleum Ltd. 03/23/1979
(See Kaiser Petroleum Ltd.)

ANGLO AMERN GOLD INVT LTD (SOUTH AFRICA)
Each old ADR for Ordinary exchanged for (10) new ADR's for Ordinary 09/04/1984
Merged into Anglo American PLC 05/24/1999
Each new ADR for Ordinary exchanged for (0.1379) ADR for Ordinary

ANGLO AMERN INVT TR LTD (SOUTH AFRICA)
ADR's for Ordinary split (10) for (1) by issuance of (9) additional ADR's 08/31/1990
Stock Dividend - 1.40303% payable 01/09/1998 to holders of record 10/31/1997
Merged into Anglo American PLC 05/24/1999
Each ADR for Ordinary exchanged for approximately (0.58115) ADR for Ordinary

ANGLO-AMERICAN MINES LTD. (QC)
Charter cancelled 11/11/1978

ANGLO AMERICAN MINING CORP. LTD. (DE)
Capital Stock $2 par changed to $1 par 00/00/1936
Liquidated 00/00/1954
Details not available

ANGLO AMERICAN MOLYBDENITE MINING CORP. (QC)
Recapitalized as Cadillac Moly Mines Ltd. 09/06/1968
Each share Common $1 par exchanged for (0.2) share Common no par
(See Cadillac Moly Mines Ltd.)

ANGLO AMERN NICKEL MNG LTD (ON)
Charter cancelled for failure to pay taxes and file returns 05/18/1976

exchanged for (0.1) share Common no par

ANGLO-AMERICAN OIL CO. (TX)
Charter forfeited for failure to pay taxes 03/17/1950

ANGLO AMERICAN OILS LTD. (AB)
Name changed to Scenic Oils Ltd. 05/18/1962
(See Scenic Oils Ltd.)

ANGLO AMERN PLATINUM CORP LTD NEW (SOUTH AFRICA)
Name changed to Anglo Platinum Ltd. 05/30/2005
Anglo Platinum Ltd. name changed to Anglo American Platinum Ltd. 05/25/2011

ANGLO AMERN PLATINUM LTD (SOUTH AFRICA)
Stock Dividends - 2.5085% payable 05/09/1996 to holders of record 03/15/1996; 2.2183% payable 10/18/1996 to holders of record 08/23/1996; 1.3003% payable 04/24/1997 to holders of record 02/28/1997
ADR agreement terminated 10/27/1997
Each ADR for Ordinary exchanged for between $7.784 and $7.818 cash depending on the issuing depositary

ANGLO AMERN PPTYS INC (NY)
Charter cancelled and proclaimed dissolved for failure to pay taxes 09/29/1993

ANGLO AMERN RES INC (BC)
Struck off register and declared dissolved for failure to file returns 11/26/1993

ANGLO AMERICAN TIMBER CORP. (ON)
Charter revoked for failure to file reports and pay fees 05/27/1965

ANGLO-ANDEAN EXPLS INC (CANADA)
Reincorporated 05/20/1994
Place of incorporation changed from (BC) to (Canada) 05/20/1994
Involuntarily dissolved for failure to file annual returns 05/15/2006

ANGLO ANDEAN MNG CO (WY)
Name changed to MGM Mineral Resources Inc. 04/28/2006
Each share Common $0.001 par exchanged for (1) share Common no par
MGM Mineral Resources Inc. recapitalized as Brownstone Resources, Inc. 10/05/2007 which recapitalized as Pomsta Group, Inc. 10/12/2010 which name changed to Oidon Co., Ltd. 12/31/2010

ANGLO CALIFORNIA NATIONAL BANK (SAN FRANCISCO, CA)
Stock Dividend - 21.951% 04/08/1944
Merged into Crocker-Anglo National Bank (San Francisco, CA) 02/10/1956
Each share Common $20 par exchanged for (2) shares Common Capital Stock $10 par
Crocker-Anglo National Bank merged into Crocker-Citizens National Bank (San Francisco, CA) 11/01/1963 which reorganized in Delaware as Crocker National Corp. 04/21/1969
(See Crocker National Corp.)

ANGLO CANADIAN BOND & SHARE CORP. (QC)
Dissolved 02/19/1968
Details not available

ANGLO-CANADIAN CORP (BC)
Recapitalized as Jager Metal Corp. 01/20/2011
Each share Common no par exchanged for (0.25) share Common no par
Jager Metal Corp. name changed to Jagercor Energy Corp. 01/27/2014

ANGLO-CANADIAN DEVELOPMENT & HOLDING CO. LTD.
Name changed to Anglo-Canadian Oil Co. Ltd. 00/00/1938
Anglo-Canadian Oil Co. Ltd. acquired by Canadian Oil Companies Ltd. 11/03/1955
(See Canadian Oil Companies Ltd.)

ANGLO-CANADIAN MNG CORP (BC)
Name changed 08/29/2011
Name changed from Anglo-Canadian Uranium Corp. to Anglo-Canadian Mining Corp. 08/29/2011
Each share old Common no par exchanged for (0.1) share new Common no par 11/22/2016
Name changed to Canada One Mining Corp. 08/30/2017

ANGLO CDN MNG CORP (BC)
Delisted from Toronto Stock Exchange 01/25/1993

ANGLO-CANADIAN OIL CO. LTD. (AB)
Acquired by Canadian Oil Companies Ltd. 11/03/1955
Each share Capital Stock no par exchanged for (0.14285714) share Common no par and $2.75 cash
(See Canadian Oil Companies Ltd.)

ANGLO CDN OIL CORP (AB)
Merged into Tallgrass Energy Corp. 12/31/2012
Each share Common no par exchanged for (0.0690193) share Common no par
(See Tallgrass Energy Corp.)

ANGLO-CANADIAN PULP & PAPER LTD.
Acquired by Canada Power & Paper Corp. 00/00/1930
Details not available

ANGLO CDN PULP & PAPER MLS LTD (QC)
$2.80 Preferred $50 par called for redemption 11/23/1964
Capital Stock no par reclassified as Common no par 11/23/1964
Common no par split (4) for (1) by issuance of (3) additional shares 11/24/1964
4.5% Conv. Preferred $25 par called for redemption 01/31/1974
Acquired by Reed Paper Ltd.-Les Papiers Reed Ltee. 01/20/1975
Each share Common no par exchanged for (1) share $2 Conv. Preferred $25 par
(See Reed Paper Ltd.-Les Papiers Reed)

ANGLO CDN TEL CO (QC)
Acquired by General Telephone & Electronics Corp. 06/29/1965
Each share Class A $10 par exchanged for (2.5) shares Common $3.33333333 par
$2.65 Preferred $50 par called for redemption at $53 on 07/15/2000
$2.90 Preferred $50 par called for redemption at $53 on 07/15/2000
$3.15 Preferred $50 par called for redemption at $53 on 07/15/2000
4.5% Preferred $50 par called for redemption at $53 on 07/15/2000
Public interest eliminated

ANGLO-CHILEAN CONSOLIDATED NITRATE CORP. (DE)
Liquidated 00/00/1933
No stockholders' equity

ANGLO-CHILEAN NITRATE CORP.
Merged into Anglo-Lautaro Nitrate Corp. 00/00/1951
Each share Ordinary P50 par exchanged for (1) share Class A $2.40 par
Anglo-Lautaro Nitrate Corp. reorganized as Anglo-Lautaro Nitrate Co. Ltd. 07/08/1968 which name changed to Anglo Co. Ltd. 05/10/1972 which name changed to Anglo Energy Ltd. (Bahamas) 12/17/1980 which reorganized in Delaware as Anglo Energy, Inc. 07/14/1986 which name changed to Nabors Industries, Inc. (DE) 03/07/1989 which reincorporated in Bermuda as Nabors Industries Ltd. 06/24/2002

ANGLO CO. LTD. (BAHAMAS)
Conv. Class A, BSD $12 par changed to BSD $2.40 par 04/17/1973
Class B, BSD 15¢ par changed to BSD 5¢ par 04/17/1973
Conv. Class C, BSD $1.20 par changed to BSD 24¢ par 04/17/1973
Conv. Class A, BSD $2.40 par changed to BSD 48¢ par 03/28/1975
Class B, BSD 5¢ par changed to BSD 1¢ par 03/28/1975
Conv. Class C, BSD 24¢ par changed to BSD $0.048 par 03/28/1975
Name changed to Anglo Energy Ltd. (Bahamas) 12/17/1980
Anglo Energy Ltd. (Bahamas) reorganized in Delaware as Anglo Energy, Inc. 08/28/1986 which name changed to Nabors Industries, Inc. 03/07/1989 which reincorporated in Bermuda as Nabors Industries Ltd. 06/24/2002

ANGLO DOMINION GOLD EXPL LTD (ON)
Merged into QSR Ltd. 09/07/1993
Each share Common no par exchanged for (0.18) share Common no par
QSR Ltd. name changed to Coniagas Resources Ltd. 06/25/1999 which name changed to Lithium One Inc. 07/23/2009
(See Lithium One Inc.)

ANGLO ECUADORIAN OILFIELDS LTD (ENGLAND)
Stock Dividend - 100% 05/25/1965
ADR agreement terminated 04/22/1977
Each ADR for Ordinary exchanged for $1.258 cash

ANGLO ENERGY INC (DE)
Name changed to Nabors Industries, Inc. (DE) 03/07/1989
Nabors Industries, Inc. (DE) reincorporated in Bermuda as Nabors Industries Ltd. 06/24/2002

ANGLO ENERGY LTD (BAHAMAS)
Reorganized under the laws of Delaware as Anglo Energy, Inc. 08/28/1986
Each share Conv. Class A, BSD48¢ par exchanged for (0.306) share Common 10¢ par
Each (48) shares Class B, BSD1¢ par exchanged for (0.006375) share Common 10¢ par
Each (10) shares Conv. Class C, BSD$0.048 par exchanged for (0.0306) share Common 10¢ par
Note: Holders also received Common Stock Purchase Warrants
Anglo Energy, Inc. name changed to Nabors Industries, Inc. (DE) 03/07/1989 which reincorporated in Bermuda as Nabors Industries Ltd. 06/24/2002

ANGLO-HURONIAN LTD. (ON)
Merged into Kerr Addison Mines Ltd. 11/18/1963
Each share Capital Stock exchanged for (0.625) share Capital Stock no par
Kerr Addison Mines Ltd. merged into Noranda Inc. 04/11/1996 which name changed to Falconbridge Ltd. (New) 2005 on 07/01/2005
(See Falconbridge Ltd. (New) 2005)

ANGLO-IRANIAN OIL CO., LTD. (ENGLAND)
Stock Distribution - Ordinary Reg. 50% 06/20/1937; ADR's for Ordinary Reg. 50% 07/08/1937
Name changed to British Petroleum Co. Ltd. 00/00/1954
British Petroleum Co. Ltd. name changed to British Petroleum Co. PLC 01/04/1982 which merged into BP Amoco PLC 12/31/1998

ANGLO IRISH BK CORP PLC (IRELAND)
Sponsored ADR's for Ordinary split (2) for (1) by issuance of (1) additional ADR payable 05/04/2005 to holders of record 04/22/2005
Ex date - 05/05/2005
Sponsored ADR's for Ordinary split (10) for (1) by issuance of (9) additional ADR's payable 12/11/2006 to holders of record 12/08/2006
Ex date - 12/12/2006
Basis changed from (1:10) to (1:1) 12/11/2006
ADR agreement terminated 03/09/2010
No ADR holders' equity

ANGLO KENO DEVS LTD (ON)
Name changed to Lumsden Building Corp., Inc. (Old) 01/10/1978
Lumsden Building Corp., Inc. (Old) merged into Lumsden Building Corp., Inc. (New) 08/15/1978
(See Lumsden Building Corp., Inc. (New))

ANGLO-LAUTARO NITRATE CO. LTD. (BAHAMAS)
Name changed to Anglo Co. Ltd. and Conv. Class A, BSD $12 par changed to BSD $2.40 par, Class B, BSD 25¢ par changed to BSD BSD 5¢ par and Conv. Class C, BSD $1.20 par changed to BSD 24¢ par 05/10/1972
Anglo Co. Ltd. name changed to Anglo Energy Ltd. (Bahamas) 12/17/1980 which reorganized in Delaware as Anglo Energy, Inc. 07/14/1986 which name changed to Nabors Industries, Inc. 03/07/1989 which reincorporated in Bermuda as Nabors Industries Ltd. 06/24/2002

ANGLO-LAUTARO NITRATE CORP. (CHILE)
Class A $2.40 par changed to $12 par, Class B 5¢ par changed to 25¢ par and Class C 24¢ par changed to $1.20 par 01/22/1964
Reorganized under the laws of Bahamas as Anglo-Lautaro Nitrate Co. Ltd. 07/08/1968
Each share Class A $12 par exchanged for (1) share Conv. Class A, BSD $12 par
Each share Class B 25¢ par exchanged for (1) share Class B, BSD 25¢ par
Each share Class C $1.20 par exchanged for (1) share Conv. Class C, BSD $1.20 par
Anglo-Lautaro Nitrate Co. Ltd. name changed to Anglo Co. Ltd. 05/10/1972 which name changed to Anglo Energy Ltd. (Bahamas) 12/17/1980 which reorganized in Delaware as Anglo Energy, Inc. 07/14/1986 which name changed to Nabors Industries, Inc. (DE) 03/07/1989 reincorporated in Bermuda as Nabors Industries Ltd. 06/24/2002

ANGLO MINERALS LTD (AB)
Name changed to Anglo Potash Ltd. 02/29/2008
(See Anglo Potash Ltd.)

ANGLO MURMONT MINING CORP. LTD. (SK)
Struck off register for failure to file annual returns 09/00/1961

ANGLO-NATIONAL CORP.
Liquidation completed 00/00/1945
Details not available

ANGLO-NEWFOUNDLAND DEVELOPMENT CO., LTD. (NL)
Stock Dividend - 200% 12/22/1950
Name changed to Price (Nfld.) Pulp & Paper Ltd. 05/03/1965

ANGLO NORWEGIAN HOLDINGS LTD. (QC)
Recapitalized as Anglo-Scandinavian Investment Corp. of Canada 04/07/1955
Each share Common no par exchanged for (0.1) share Common no par
Anglo-Scandinavian Investment Corp. of Canada name changed to Hambro Corp. of Canada Ltd. 04/01/1971
(See Hambro Corp. of Canada Ltd.)

ANGLO OIL & EXPLORATION CO. (UT)
Charter revoked for failure to file reports and pay fees 03/31/1958

ANGLO PAC DEVS LTD (AB)
Name changed to Farm Energy Corp. 10/21/1991
Farm Energy Corp. name changed to High Energy Ventures Inc. 02/09/2001
(See High Energy Ventures Inc.)

ANGLO PAC EXPLS LTD (BC)
Struck off register and declared dissolved for failure to file returns 02/04/1983

ANGLO-PACIFIC OIL & GAS LTD. (BC)
Struck off register and declared dissolved for failure to file reports and pay fees 04/03/1969

ANGLO PERM CORPORATE HLDGS LTD (ON)
Each (25) shares Non-Cum. Part. Preferred no par exchanged for (2) shares Class A Special $1.50 par and (5) shares Class B Special 15¢ par 10/25/1974
Acquired by Imperial Life Assurance Co. of Canada 11/16/1984
Details not available

ANGLO-PERSIAN OIL CO., LTD. (ENGLAND)
Name changed to Anglo-Iranian Oil Co., Ltd. 00/00/1935
Anglo-Iranian Oil Co., Ltd. name changed to British Petroleum Co. Ltd. 00/00/1954 which name changed to British Petroleum Co. PLC 01/04/1982 which merged into BP Amoco PLC 12/31/1998

ANGLO PLATINUM LTD (SOUTH AFRICA)
ADR's for Ordinary split (6) for (1) by issuance of (5) additional ADR's payable 11/23/2010 to holders of record 11/16/2010 Ex date - 11/24/2010
Name changed to Anglo American Platinum Ltd. 05/25/2011

ANGLO PORCUPINE GOLD MINES LTD (ON)
Capital Stock $5 par reclassified as Common no par 10/31/1986
Merged into Control Advancements, Inc. 04/12/1996
Each share Common no par exchanged for (0.2) share Common no par
Control Advancements, Inc. name changed to Betacom Corp. Inc. 07/28/2000
(See Betacom Corp. Inc.)

ANGLO POTASH LTD (AB)
Acquired by BHP Billiton Ltd. 07/11/2008
Each share Common no par exchanged for $8.15 cash

ANGLO ROUYN MINES LTD (ON)
Merged into Canadian Memorial Services Ltd. 09/28/1973
Each share Capital Stock $1 par exchanged for (0.25) share Common no par
Canadian Memorial Services Ltd. name changed to Arbor Capital Resources Inc./Arbor Ressources Financieres Inc. 05/01/1975 which

name changed to Arbor Capital Corp. 05/15/1986 which name changed to Arbor Memorial Services Inc. 03/31/1994

ANGLO SCANDINAVIAN INVT CORP CDA (QC)
Each share Common no par exchanged for (10) shares Common $5 par 02/13/1959
Name changed to Hambro Corp. of Canada Ltd. 04/01/1971
(See Hambro Corp. of Canada Ltd.)

ANGLO SIERRA RES CORP (DE)
Recapitalized as Bullet Environmental Technologies, Inc. 03/15/1999
Each share Common $0.0001 par exchanged for (0.02) share Common $0.0001 par
Bullet Environmental Technologies, Inc. name changed to ComCam, Inc. 07/24/2002 which recapitalized as Monkey Rock Group, Inc. 05/05/2010

ANGLO SWISS INDS INC (BC)
Recapitalized 07/22/1992
Recapitalized from Anglo Swiss Mining Corp. to Anglo Swiss Industries Inc. 07/22/1992
Each share Common no par exchanged for (0.06666666) share Common no par
Name changed to Anglo Swiss Resources Inc. 11/28/1997
Anglo Swiss Resources Inc. recapitalized as Gungnir Resources Inc. 06/20/2014

ANGLO SWISS RES INC (BC)
Recapitalized as Gungnir Resources Inc. 06/20/2014
Each share Common no par exchanged for (0.2) share Common no par

ANGLO TRANSVAAL CONS INVT LTD (SOUTH AFRICA)
Name changed to Anglovaal Ltd. 11/20/1981
Anglovaal Ltd. name changed to Anglovaal Mining Ltd. 12/21/1998 which name changed to African Rainbow Minerals Ltd. 05/10/2004

ANGLO TRANSVAAL INDS LTD (SOUTH AFRICA)
ADR agreement terminated 06/19/2000
Each ADR for Ordinary exchanged for $1.85976 cash

ANGLO UTD DEV LTD (ON)
Merged into Anglo United plc 11/24/1986
Each share Capital Stock no par exchanged for $0.53 cash

ANGLO WESTERN OIL & GAS LTD. (BC)
Recapitalized as Anglo Western Petroleums Ltd. (Old) 07/26/1961
Each share Capital Stock 50¢ par exchanged for (0.1) share Capital Stock no par
Anglo Western Petroleums Ltd. (Old) name changed to Anglo Western Minerals Ltd. 04/01/1966 which recapitalized as Anglo Western Petroleums Ltd. (New) 07/29/1977
(See Anglo Western Petroleums Ltd. (New))

ANGLO WESTERN PETROLEUMS LTD. (OLD) (BC)
Name changed to Anglo Western Minerals Ltd. 04/01/1966
Anglo Western Minerals Ltd. recapitalized as Anglo Western Petroleums Ltd. (New) 07/29/1977
(See Anglo Western Petroleums Ltd. (New))

ANGLO WESTN PETES LTD NEW (BC)
Recapitalized 07/29/1977
Recapitalized from Anglo Western Minerals Ltd. to Anglo Western Petroleums Ltd. (New) 07/29/1977

Each share Common no par exchanged for (0.25) share Common no par
Struck off register and declared dissolved for failure to file returns 05/31/1991

ANGLOGOLD LTD (SOUTH AFRICA)
Each ADR for Ordinary exchanged for (0.2) Sponsored ADR for Ordinary 06/29/1998
ADR basis changed from (1:0.5) to (1:1) 12/26/2002
Under plan of merger name changed to AngloGold Ashanti Ltd. 04/26/2004

ANGLOTAJIK MINERALS INC (NV)
Name changed to Intercontinental Resources, Inc. 05/31/2006
Intercontinental Resources, Inc. name changed to China Valves Technology, Inc. 01/09/2008

ANGLOVAAL HLDGS LTD (SOUTH AFRICA)
ADR agreement terminated 05/28/1999
Each ADR for Ordinary exchanged for exchanged for $0.569 cash

ANGLOVAAL MINING LTD (SOUTH AFRICA)
Name changed 12/21/1998
Name changed from Anglovaal Ltd. to Anglovaal Mining Ltd. 12/21/1998
Stock Dividends - in Reg. S ADR's for Ordinary to holders of Reg. S ADR's for Ordinary 0.0147% payable 12/22/1999 to holders of record 11/12/1999; in ADR's for Ordinary to holders of ADR's for Ordinary 1.5786% payable 12/21/1999 to holders of record 11/12/1999; in Reg. S Sponsored ADR's for Ordinary to holders of Reg. S Sponsored ADR's for Ordinary 1.57861% payable 12/22/1999 to holders of record 11/12/1999; in 144A ADR's for Ordinary to holders of 144A ADR's for Ordinary 1.57861% payable 12/22/1999 to holders of record 11/12/1999
Name changed to African Rainbow Minerals Ltd. 05/10/2004

ANGOSS SOFTWARE CORP (ON)
Each share old Common no par exchanged for (0.199995) share new Common no par to reflect a (1) for (7,500) reverse split followed by a (1,500) for (1) forward split 01/21/2008
Note: Holders of (7,499) or fewer pre-split shares received approximately $0.18 cash per share
Acquired by Peterson Partners, Inc. 04/25/2013
Each share new Common no par exchanged for $0.525 cash
Note: Unexchanged certificates will be cancelled and become without value 04/25/2019

ANGOSTURA-WUPPERMANN CORP. (NY)
Completely liquidated 06/17/1968
Each share Common $1 par exchanged for first and final distribution of (1.5) shares Iroquois Industries, Inc. Common $1 par
Iroquois Industries, Inc. name changed to Iroquois Brands, Ltd. 06/01/1973
(See Iroquois Brands, Ltd.)

ANGSTROM MICROSYSTEMS CORP (NV)
SEC revoked common stock registration 04/18/2012

ANGSTROM TECHNOLOGIES CORP (NV)
Common $0.001 par split (2) for (1) by issuance of (1) additional share payable 02/19/2008 to holders of record 02/19/2008

Name changed to Angstrom Microsystems Corp. 05/02/2008
(See Angstrom Microsystems Corp.)

ANGSTROM TECHNOLOGIES INC (DE)
Company terminated common stock registration and is no longer public as of 01/29/2002

ANGSTRON HLDGS CORP (NV)
Name changed to HK Graphene Technology Corp. 07/31/2015

ANGUS ENERGY CORP (NV)
Charter revoked for failure to file reports and pay taxes 09/30/2010

ANGUS MINES LTD. (QC)
Liquidated 00/00/1951
No stockholders' equity

ANGUS MNG NAMIBIA LTD (ON)
Name changed to Angus Mining Inc. 07/16/2012

ANGUS PETROLEUMS LTD. (AB)
Struck off register for failure to file annual reports 01/15/1960

ANGUS RES INC (BC)
Name changed to Batero Gold Corp. 07/19/2010

ANGUS RES LTD (BC)
Recapitalized as Canadian Angus Resources Ltd. (BC) 12/31/1987
Each share Common no par exchanged for (0.5) share Common no par
Canadian Angus Resources Ltd. (BC) reincorporated in Alberta 08/29/1988 which merged into Abacan Resource Corp. (New) 02/10/1995
(See Abacan Resource Corp. (New))

ANGUS RIVER MINES LTD. (BC)
Acquired by Abco Mining Ltd. 07/23/1969
Each share Capital Stock exchanged for (1) share Common 50¢ par
Abco Mining Ltd. name changed to Aselo Industries Ltd. 02/00/1971 which recapitalized as Fairmont Gas & Oil Corp. 10/15/1979 which recapitalized as Cater Energy, Inc. 05/23/1984 which recapitalized as Houston Metals Corp. 10/27/1986 which recapitalized as Pacific Houston Resources, Inc. 03/30/1989
(See Pacific Houston Resources, Inc.)

ANGUS VENTURES CORP (BC)
Incorporated 01/10/1986
Name changed to Encanto Potash Corp. 07/15/2009

ANHANGUERA EDUCACIONAL PARTICIPACOES S A (BRAZIL)
Stock Dividend - 200% payable 05/16/2013 to holders of record 05/13/2013 Ex date - 05/17/2013
GDR agreement terminated 07/31/2014
Each Sponsored 144A GDR for Common exchanged for $17.12842 cash

ANHEUSER BUSCH COS INC (DE)
Common $1 par split (3) for (1) by issuance of (2) additional shares 06/14/1985
Common $1 par split (2) for (1) by issuance of (1) additional share 09/12/1986
$3.60 Conv. Preferred Ser. A $1 par called for redemption 11/02/1987
Each Ctf. for Common Trusted Shares $1 par exchanged for (1) share Common $1 par 09/29/1989
Each share Common $1 par received distribution of (0.04) share Earthgrains Co. Common $1 par payable 03/26/1996 to holders of record 03/19/1996
Common $1 par split (2) for (1) by issuance of (1) additional share payable 09/12/1996 to holders of record 08/15/1996 Ex date - 09/13/1996
Common $1 par split (2) for (1) by

issuance of (1) additional share payable 09/18/2000 to holders of record 08/17/2000 Ex date - 09/19/2000
Acquired by InBev N.V./S.A. 11/18/2008
Each share Common $1 par exchanged for $70 cash

ANHEUSER BUSCH INC (MO)
Each share Common $100 par exchanged for (5) shares Common $20 par 00/00/1938
Each share Common $20 par exchanged for (5) shares Common $4 par 00/00/1947
Each Ctf. for Common Trusteed Shares $4 par exchanged for (2) Ctfs. for Common Trusteed Shares $2 par 04/28/1965
Common $4 par changed to $2 par and (1) additional share issued 05/19/1965
Each Ctf. for Common Trusteed Shares $2 par exchanged for (2) Ctfs. for Common Trusteed Shares $1 par 04/24/1968
Common $2 par changed to $1 par and (1) additional share issued 05/20/1968
Common $1 par and Ctfs. for Common Trusteed Shares $1 par split (2) for (1) by issuance of (1) additional share respectively 05/20/1971
Stock Dividend - 10% 01/31/1966
Reorganized under the laws of Delaware as Anheuser-Busch Companies, Inc. 10/01/1979
Each share Common $1 par exchanged for (1) share Common $1 par
Each Ctf. for Common Trusteed Share $1 par exchanged for (1) Ctf. for Common Trusteed Share $1 par
(See Anheuser-Busch Companies, Inc.)

ANHUI TAIYANG POULTRY CO INC (DE)
SEC revoked common stock registration 10/17/2013

ANICOM INC (DE)
Common $0.001 par split (2) for (1) by issuance of (1) additional share payable 10/07/1996 to holders of record 10/01/1996
Plan of reorganization under Chapter 11 Federal Bankruptcy proceedings effective 09/25/2005
No stockholders' equity

ANIFORMS INC (NY)
Stock Dividend - 25% 09/30/1969
Merged into Comart Associates Inc. 05/15/1972
Each share Common 1¢ par exchanged for (0.5) share Common 1¢ par
Comart Associates Inc. name changed to CCI Holding Corp. 06/01/1985
(See CCI Holding Corp.)

ANIKA RESH INC (MA)
Name changed to Anika Therapeutics, Inc. 01/09/1997

ANIMAL CARE PLAN INC (NY)
Charter cancelled and proclaimed dissolved for failure to pay taxes and file reports 12/16/1974

ANIMAL CLONING SCIENCES INC (WA)
Each share old Common no par exchanged for (0.1) share new Common no par 03/09/2004
SEC revoked common stock registration 07/29/2011

ANIMAL FOUNDATION, INC. (NY)
Liquidation completed 09/11/1957
Details not available

ANIMAL GOLD CROSS PLAN INC (NY)
Charter cancelled and proclaimed

ANIMAL HEALTH INTL INC (DE)
Acquired by Lextron, Inc. 06/10/2011
Each share Common 1¢ par
exchanged for $4.25 cash

ANIMAL INSURANCE CO. OF AMERICA (NY)
Common $2 par changed to $2.50 par 11/26/1962
90¢ Non-Cum. Preferred $1 par called for redemption 08/16/1963
Name changed to American Mayflower Life Insurance Co. of New York 05/06/1964
(See American Mayflower Life Insurance Co. of New York)

ANIMAL TRAP CO. OF AMERICA (PA)
Each share Common $25 par exchanged for (3) shares Common no par 00/00/1928
Name changed to Woodstream Corp. and (3) additional shares issued 04/01/1966
(See Woodstream Corp.)

ANIMAS CORP (DE)
Merged into Johnson & Johnson 02/17/2006
Each share Common 1¢ par exchanged for $24.50 cash

ANIMAS RES LTD (BC)
Merged into GoGold Resources Inc. 04/23/2014
Each share Common no par exchanged for (0.0851) share Common no par and $0.07 cash

ANIMATED ELECTRS INC (OR)
Name changed to MSM Systems, Corp. 11/07/1983
(See MSM Systems, Corp.)

ANIMATED NEON CORP., LTD. (NV)
Charter revoked for failure to file reports and pay fees 03/04/1940

ANIMATRONIX ENTMT CORP (BC)
Name changed to Creative Entertainment Technologies Inc. 07/13/1995
(See Creative Entertainment Technologies Inc.)

ANIMED INC (NY)
Chapter 11 bankruptcy proceedings converted to Chapter 7 on 07/12/1990
Stockholders' equity unlikely

ANINA RES INC (BC)
Reincorporated under the laws of Wyoming as ImmuDyne, Inc. 09/28/1987
ImmuDyne, Inc. (WY) reincorporated in Delaware 06/30/1994 which name changed to Conversion Labs, Inc. 06/22/2018

ANITA LYNN COSMETICS INC (CA)
Charter suspended for failure to file reports and pay taxes 11/01/1974

ANITA RES INC (BC)
Recapitalized as Pluton Resource Corp. 07/09/1984
Each share Common no par exchanged for (0.4) share Common no par
Pluton Resource Corp. name changed to Pluton Industries Ltd. 07/03/1986 which recapitalized as Clarion Enviromental Technologies, Inc. 12/18/1992 which name changed to Clarion Resources Ltd. 12/05/1997
(See Clarion Resources Ltd.)

ANITE PLC (UNITED KINGDOM)
ADR agreement terminated 08/12/2016
No ADR's remain outstanding

ANITEC IMAGE TECHNOLOGY CORP (DE)
Common 10¢ par split (3) for (2) by issuance of (0.5) additional share 10/17/1986
Merged into International Paper Co. 12/17/1987
Each share Common 10¢ par exchanged for (0.5263) share Common $1 par

ANITECH ENTERPRISES INC (AB)
Reorganized under the laws of Canada as IPICO Inc. 03/30/2006
Each share Common no par exchanged for (0.00521907) share Common no par
Note: Holders of (19,159) shares or fewer will receive $1 cash per share
(See IPICO Inc.)

ANIXTER BROS INC (DE)
Common $1 par split (2) for (1) by issuance of (1) additional share 09/19/1980
Common $1 par split (2) for (1) by issuance of (1) additional share 07/31/1981
Common $1 par split (2) for (1) by issuance of (1) additional share 04/30/1986
Stock Dividend - 100% 10/10/1968
Merged into Itel Corp. 01/14/1987
Each share Common $1 par exchanged for $14 cash

ANKA RESH LTD (NY)
Dissolved by proclamation 03/26/1980

ANKEN CHEM & FILM CORP (NJ)
Name changed to Anken Industries 05/25/1970
(See Anken Industries)

ANKEN INDS (NJ)
Acquired by Rhone-Poulenc Inc. 10/11/1979
Each share Common 20¢ par exchanged for $21 cash

ANKENO MINES LTD. (ON)
Recapitalized as Bankeno Mines Ltd. (ON) 04/04/1955
Each share Capital Stock $1 par exchanged for (0.2) share Capital Stock $1 par
Bankeno Mines Ltd. (ON) reincorporated in Alberta 01/30/1979 which name changed to Bankeno Resources Ltd. 01/28/1987
(See Bankeno Resources Ltd.)

ANKER COAL GROUP INC (DE)
Acquired by ICG Inc. 11/18/2005
Details not available

ANKER-HOLTH MANUFACTURING CO.
Assets sold and company dissolved 00/00/1950
Details not available

ANLAGE INC (MN)
Name changed to Quartz, Inc. 09/10/1987
(See Quartz, Inc.)

ANM HLDGS CORP (NV)
Name changed to International Menu Solutions Corp. 07/15/1998
International Menu Solutions Corp. name changed to Dunwynn Resources, Inc. 11/05/2004 which recapitalized as Dunwynn Exploration, Inc. 06/24/2005
(See Dunwynn Exploration, Inc.)

ANN ARBOR BK (ANN ARBOR, MI)
Common $10 par changed to $20 par 00/00/1947
Common $20 par changed to $10 par and (1) additional share issued plus a 10% stock dividend paid 03/01/1967
Stock Dividends - 50% 02/04/1958; 10% 05/13/1963; 10% 02/10/1964; 10% 03/01/1965; 10% 03/01/1966
Reorganized as Mid-America Fidelity Corp. 02/14/1974
Each share Common $10 par exchanged for (1) share Common $10 par
Mid-America Fidelity Corp. merged into American Bankcorp, Inc. 04/30/1975 which merged into First American Bank Corp. 02/13/1978 which name changed to First of America Bank Corp. 01/14/1983 which merged into National City Corp. 03/31/1998 which was acquired by PNC Financial Services Group, Inc. 12/31/2008

ANN ARBOR BIO IMAGE SYS LTD (BC)
Name changed to Promethean Technologies Inc. 10/24/1986
(See Promethean Technologies Inc.)

ANN ARBOR LIFE INSURANCE CO.
Acquired by Liberty Life & Accident Insurance Co. 00/00/1952
Each share Common $5 par exchanged for (4) shares Class A $1 par and (1) share Class B $1 par
Liberty Life & Accident Insurance Co. merged into Independent Liberty Life Insurance Co. 03/30/1966
(See Independent Liberty Life Insurance Co.)

ANN ARBOR RR CO (MI)
Declared bankruptcy 10/16/1973
Stockholders' equity unlikely

ANN ARBOR TR CO (ANN ARBOR, MI)
Common $20 par changed to $10 par and (1) additional share issued 04/12/1979
Under plan of merger name changed to Citizens Trust (Ann Arbor, MI) 12/31/1983
Citizens Trust (Ann Arbor, MI) reorganized as Citizens Trust Bancorp, Inc. 07/01/1986 which merged into Trustcorp, Inc. 09/30/1987 which was acquired by Society Corp. 01/05/1990 which merged into KeyCorp (New) 03/01/1994

ANN INC (DE)
Merged into Ascena Retail Group, Inc. 08/21/2015
Each share Common $0.0068 par exchanged for (0.68) share Common 1¢ par and $37.34 cash

ANNABEL GOLD MINES INC (BC)
Name changed to Carissa Mining Corp. 03/02/1994
Carissa Mining Corp. recapitalized as Rockwell Ventures Inc. 10/27/1995 which name changed to Rockwell Diamonds Inc. 05/17/2007

ANNABELLE INC (QC)
Name changed to Waitsfield Capital Inc. 10/22/1999
(See Waitsfield Capital Inc.)

ANNALY CAP MGMT INC (MD)
Name changed 08/02/2006
Name changed from Annaly Mortgage Management, Inc. to Annaly Capital Management, Inc. 08/02/2006
Each share 6% Conv. Preferred Ser. B 1¢ par exchanged for (3.0614) shares Common 1¢ par 04/03/2012
7.625% Preferred Ser. E 1¢ par called for redemption at $25 on 02/08/2018
(Additional Information in Active)

ANNAMAQUE MINES LTD. (ON)
Recapitalized as Adelaide Mining Ltd. 03/25/1965
Each share Capital Stock $1 par exchanged for (0.16666666) share Capital Stock $1 par
(See Adelaide Mining Ltd.)

ANNANDALE CORP (CA)
Charter suspended for failure to file reports and pay fees 06/01/1992

ANNAPOLIS BANCORP INC (MD)
Name changed 05/17/2001
Name changed from Annapolis National Bancorp Inc. to Annapolis Bancorp, Inc. 05/17/2001
Common 1¢ par split (4) for (3) by issuance of (0.33333333) additional share payable 08/24/2001 to holders of record 08/03/2001 Ex date - 08/27/2001
Common 1¢ par split (4) for (3) by issuance of (0.33333333) additional share payable 12/03/2004 to holders of record 11/05/2004 Ex date - 12/06/2004
Merged into F.N.B. Corp. 04/06/2013
Each share Common 1¢ par exchanged for (1.143) shares Common 1¢ par and $0.15 cash

ANNAPOLIS BANCSHARES INC (MD)
Common $1 par split (6) for (5) by issuance of (0.2) additional share 12/04/1995
Merged into Sandy Spring Bancorp, Inc. 08/29/1996
Each share Common $1 par exchanged for (0.62585) share Common $1 par

ANNAPOLIS BKG & TR CO (ANNAPOLIS, MD)
Merged into Mercantile Bankshares Corp. 09/01/1970
Each share Common $10 par exchanged for (1) share $3 Conv. Class C Preferred no par
Mercantile Bankshares Corp. merged into PNC Financial Services Group, Inc. 03/02/2007

ANNAPOLIS CAP HLDGS INC (DE)
Name changed to Podium Venture Group, Inc. 08/30/2006
Podium Venture Group, Inc. name changed to Capital Oil & Gas, Inc. 08/07/2008 which recapitalized as Southcorp Capital, Inc. 01/28/2009

ANNAX VENTURES INC (BC)
Recapitalized as International Annax Ventures Inc. 09/28/1995
Each share Common no par exchanged for (0.33333333) share Common no par
International Annax Ventures Inc. merged into Herald Resources Ltd. 10/26/2002
(See Herald Resources Ltd.)

ANNEX EXPL CORP (BC)
Recapitalized as Redhawk Resources, Inc. 03/29/1994
Each share Common no par exchanged for (0.33333333) share Common no par
Redhawk Resources, Inc. merged into CopperBank Resources Corp. 09/04/2018

ANNIE CREEK MINING CO. (SD)
Charter expired by time limitation 09/09/1947

ANNIE LAKE MINES LTD (BC)
Recapitalized as Cheryl Resources Inc. 07/11/1984
Each share Common no par exchanged for (0.2) share Common no par
Cheryl Resources Inc. merged into Tymar Resources Inc. 10/31/1989 which recapitalized as Baja Gold, Inc. 01/25/1993 which merged into Viceroy Resource Corp. 05/30/1996 which merged into Quest Capital Corp. (BC) 06/30/2003 which reincorporated in Canada 05/27/2008 which name changed to Sprott Resource Lending Corp. 09/10/2010 which merged into Sprott Inc. 07/24/2013

ANNIES BOOK STOP INC (UT)
Proclaimed dissolved for failure to pay taxes 06/01/1989

ANNIES HOMEGROWN INC (DE)
Each share old Common $0.001 par exchanged for (0.0005) share new Common $0.001 par 03/29/2002
Acquired by Solera Capital, LLC 08/12/2002
Details not available

ANNIES INC (DE)
Acquired by General Mills, Inc. 10/21/2014
Each share Common $0.001 par exchanged for $46 cash

ANNIS MINES LTD (BC)
Struck off register and declared dissolved for failure to file returns 09/03/1974

ANNISQUAM ART LTD (BC)
Name changed to PHL Pinnacle Holdings Ltd. 07/18/1994.
PHL Pinnacle Holdings Ltd. recapitalized as Citrine Holdings Ltd. 01/09/1997

ANNISTON NATIONAL BANK (ANNISTON, AL)
Stock Dividend - 20% 01/24/1958
Merged into First Alabama Bancshares, Inc. 08/27/1982
Each share Capital Stock $50 par exchanged for $65 cash

ANNMAR MINING LTD. (BC)
Recapitalized as Abaca Mining Ltd. 07/27/1972
Each share Common no par exchanged for (0.1) share Common no par
Abaca Mining Ltd. name changed to Abaca Resource Industries Inc. 02/08/1974 which recapitalized as Corpac Minerals Ltd. 08/17/1978
(See Corpac Minerals Ltd.)

ANNOVA BUSINESS GROUP INC (BC)
Recapitalized 04/27/1995
Recapitalized from Annova International Holdings Corp. to Annova Business Group Inc. 04/27/1995
Each share Common no par exchanged for (0.25) share Common no par
Recapitalized as Capital Alliance Group Inc. 11/27/1998
Each share Common no par exchanged for (0.5) share Common no par
Capital Alliance Group Inc. name changed to CIBT Education Group Inc. 11/14/2007

ANNTAYLOR STORES CORP (DE)
Common $0.0068 par split (3) for (2) by issuance of (0.5) additional share payable 05/20/2002 to holders of record 05/02/2002 Ex date - 05/21/2002
Common $0.0068 par split (3) for (2) by issuance of (0.5) additional share payable 05/26/2004 to holders of record 05/11/2004 Ex date - 05/27/2004
Name changed to Ann Inc. 03/16/2011
Ann Inc. merged into Ascena Retail Group, Inc. 08/21/2015

ANNUITY & LIFE RE HOLDINGS LTD (BERMUDA)
Merged into Pope Investments II LLC 09/25/2009
Each share Common $1 par exchanged for $0.44580421 cash

ANNUITY AGENCY CO. (IL)
Completely liquidated 10/31/1967
Each share Common 20¢ par received first and final distribution of (0.394) share Columbia National Corp. Common no par
Note: Certificates were not required to be surrendered and are without value
(See Columbia National Corp.)

ANODYNE ENERGY CORP (DE)
Charter cancelled and declared inoperative and void for non-payment of taxes 03/01/1989

ANODYNE INC (NY)
Plan of arrangement under Chapter XI bankruptcy proceedings confirmed 05/24/1977
No stockholders' equity

ANOKI GOLD MINES LTD.
Acquired by Queenston Gold Mines Ltd. (ON) 00/00/1941
Each share Common exchanged for (0.08333333) share Common $1 par
Queenston Gold Mines Ltd. (ON) reincorporated in Alberta 00/00/1981 which reincorporated in Canada 04/23/1985 which merged into Queenston Mining Inc. 01/02/1990 which merged into Osisko Mining Corp. 01/02/2013
(See Osisko Mining Corp.)

ANONYMOUS DATA CORP (NV)
Recapitalized as ShareCom, Inc. 07/25/2001
Each share Common $0.001 par exchanged for (0.00310559) share Common $0.001 par
ShareCom, Inc. name changed to Primary Business Systems Inc. 03/28/2003 which recapitalized as PBS Holding, Inc. 10/03/2005

ANOORAQ RES CORP (BC)
Name changed to Atlatsa Resources Corp. 05/14/2012

ANORAK CAP CORP (AB)
Name changed to Total Energy Services Ltd. 12/03/1997
Total Energy Services Ltd. merged into Total Energy Services Trust 04/28/2005 which reorganized as Total Energy Services Inc. 05/20/2009

ANORMED INC (CANADA)
Merged into Genzyme Corp. 11/08/2006
Each share Common no par exchanged for USD$13.50 cash

ANOVA CAP CORP (TX)
Recapitalized as Trim-A-Lawn Corp. (TX) 05/18/1989
Each share Common no par exchanged for (0.5) share Common $0.0001 par
Trim-A-Lawn Corp. (TX) reincorporated in Nevada 02/20/2004 which recapitalized as Litfiber, Inc. 02/26/2004 which recapitalized as Grifco International, Inc. 11/19/2004
(See Grifco International, Inc.)

ANOVA VENTURES CORP (DE)
Name changed to Liberty Military Sales, Inc. 01/01/1988
(See Liberty Military Sales, Inc.)

ANPATH GROUP INC (DE)
Plan of reorganization under Chapter 11 Federal Bankruptcy proceedings effective 12/23/2010
Each share old Common $0.0001 par automatically became (0.02862656) share new Common $0.0001 par
Each share new Common $0.0001 par exchanged again for (0.5) share new Common $0.0001 par 03/18/2013
Each share new Common $0.0001 par exchanged again for (0.14285714) share new Common $0.0001 par 08/05/2015
Name changed to Q2Power Technologies, Inc. 12/11/2015
Q2Power Technologies, Inc. name changed to Q2Earth, Inc. 08/31/2017

ANR PIPELINE CO (DE)
$2.12 Preferred $1 par called for redemption 06/16/1994
$2.675 Preferred $1 par called for redemption 06/16/1994
Public interest eliminated

ANRET INC (DE)
Common $1 par changed to 20¢ par and (4) additional shares issued 01/25/1983
Name changed to Sunlite Inc. 12/13/1983
(See Sunlite Inc.)

ANSALDO SIGNAL N V (NETHERLANDS)
Acquired by Ansaldo Trasporti S.p.A. 05/08/2002
Each share Common NLG 0.01 par exchanged for $4.05 cash

ANSAMA CORP (DE)
Each share old Common 1¢ par exchanged for (0.1) share new Common 1¢ par 11/20/1998
Name changed to Nutrisystem.Com, Inc. 08/19/1999
Nutrisystem.Com name changed to Nutri/System, Inc. 09/25/2000 which name changed to NutriSystem, Inc. 05/13/2003

ANSAN PHARMACEUTICALS INC (DE)
Name changed 10/22/1996
Name changed from Ansan, Inc. to Ansan Pharmaceuticals, Inc. 10/22/96
Recapitalized as Discovery Laboratories, Inc. (New) 12/01/1997
Each share Common $0.001 par exchanged for (0.33333333) share Common $0.001 par
Discovery Laboratories, Inc. (New) name changed to Windtree Therapeutics, Inc. 04/19/2016

ANSBACHER CORP.
Merged into Ansbacher-Siegle Corp. 00/00/1929
Details not available

ANSBACHER-SIEGLE CORP. (NY)
Merged into Sun Chemical Corp. 00/00/1957
Details not available

ANSCHUTZ DRILLING CO., INC. (CO)
Recapitalized as Webb Resources, Inc. 10/17/1961
Each share Common $1 par exchanged for (1) share Common 10¢ par
Webb Resources, Inc. merged into Standard Oil Co. (OH) 12/11/1979
(See Standard Oil Co. (OH))

ANSCO PHOTO PRODUCTS, INC.
Merged into Agfa-Ansco Corp. (NY) 00/00/1928
Details not available

ANSCO RES B C LTD (BC)
Recapitalized as Sunstate Resources Ltd. 05/15/1989
Each share Common no par exchanged for (0.33333333) share Common no par
Sunstate Resources Ltd. recapitalized as International Sunstate Ventures Ltd. 12/06/1999 which recapitalized as Thelon Ventures Ltd. 05/23/2002 which recapitalized as Thelon Capital Ltd. 02/04/2010 which name changed to THC BioMed Intl Ltd. 04/29/2015 which name changed to Global Li-Ion Graphite Corp. 07/14/2017

ANSCOTT CHEM INDS INC (NJ)
Acquired by Liquidix, Inc. 04/09/2003
Details not available

ANSCOTT INDS INC (FL)
SEC revoked common stock registration 05/08/2008

ANSEL CAP CORP (AB)
Name changed to DeTech Corp. 03/04/1997
(See DeTech Corp.)

ANSEL LAKE MINES, LTD. (ON)
Charter revoked for failure to file reports and pay taxes 02/08/1950

ANSELL CAP CORP (BC)
Recapitalized as BriaCell Therapeutics, Inc. 12/03/2014
Each share Common no par exchanged for (0.3076923) share Common no par

ANSELL LAKE RES LTD (ON)
Recapitalized as Diversafile International Inc. 10/17/1996
Each share Common no par exchanged for (0.2) share Common no par
(See Diversafile International Inc.)

ANSELL LTD (AUSTRALIA)
ADR agreement terminated 06/05/2006
Each ADR for Ordinary exchanged for $26.349301 cash

ANSIL RES LTD (ON)
Recapitalized 01/08/1982
Recapitalized from Ansil Mines Ltd. to Ansil Resources Ltd. 01/08/1982
Each share Capital Stock no par exchanged for (0.2) share Common no par
Merged into Jubilee Gold Exploration Ltd. 01/25/2013
Each share Common no par exchanged for (0.551) share Common no par

ANSLEY GOLD MINES LTD. (ON)
Recapitalized as Consolidated Ansley Mines Ltd. 00/00/1949
Each share Capital Stock $1 par exchanged for (0.33333333) share Capital Stock $1 par
Consolidated Ansley Mines Ltd. reorganized as Ankeno Mines Ltd. 00/00/1951 which recapitalized as Bankeno Mines Ltd. (ON) 04/04/1955 which reincorporated in Alberta 01/30/1979 which name changed to Bankeno Resources Ltd. 01/28/1987
(See Bankeno Resources Ltd.)

ANSLEY RADIO CORP.
Bankrupt 00/00/1948
No stockholders' equity

ANSOFT CORP (DE)
Common 1¢ par split (2) for (1) by issuance of (1) additional share payable 05/09/2006 to holders of record 05/02/2006 Ex date - 05/10/2006
Merged into ANSYS, Inc. 07/31/2008
Each share Common 1¢ par exchanged for (0.431882) share Common 1¢ par and $16.25 cash

ANSON BANCORP INC (NC)
Merged into Uwharrie Capital Corp. 01/18/2000
Each share Common no par exchanged for $17.30 cash

ANSON BK & TR CO (WADESBORO, NC)
Merged into American Bank & Trust Co. (Monroe, NC) 7/1/69
Each share Common $5 par exchanged for (2) shares Capital Stock $5 par
American Bank & Trust Co. (Monroe, NC) merged into United Carolina Bancshares Corp. 7/31/70 which merged into BB&T Corp. 7/1/97

ANSON-CARTWRIGHT MINES LTD. (ON)
Charter cancelled 10/00/1977

ANSON PETROLEUMS LTD. (CANADA)
Merged into Bailey Selburn Oil & Gas Ltd. 00/00/1952
Each share Capital Stock no par exchanged for (0.1) share Class A $1 par
(See Bailey Selburn Oil & Gas Ltd.)

ANSONIA DERBY WTR CO (CT)
Common no par split (2) for (1) by issuance of (1) additional share 07/17/1993
Name changed to Birmingham Utilities, Inc. 07/19/1993
Birmingham Utilities, Inc. name changed to BIW Ltd. 07/01/2002
(See BIW Ltd.)

ANSONIA WIRE & CABLE CO (CT)
Stock Dividend - 200% 2/26/63
Placed in receivership 1/22/73
No stockholders' equity

ANSONIA WTR CO (CT)
Merged into Ansonia Derby Water Co. 01/01/1972
Each share Common $25 par exchanged for (4) shares Common no par
Ansonia Derby Water Co. name changed to Birmingham Utilities, Inc. 07/19/1993 which name changed to BIW Ltd. 07/01/2002
(See BIW Ltd.)

ANSTAT INC (DE)
Charter cancelled and declared inoperative and void for non-payment of taxes 3/1/85

ANSUE CAP CORP (BC)
Recapitalized as Caracara Silver Inc. 08/25/2011
Each share Common no par exchanged for (0.33333333) share Common no par

ANSUL CHEMICAL CO. (WI)
Each share restricted and non-restricted Common no par exchanged for (10) shares Common no par 00/00/1950
Each share Common no par exchanged for (4) shares Common $3 par 00/00/1954
Common $3 par changed to $1 par and (0.5) additional share issued 07/03/1961
Stock Dividend - 50% 07/31/1956
Name changed to Ansul Co. 01/25/1964
(See Ansul Co.)

ANSUL CO (WI)
Common $1 par split (3) for (2) by issuance of (0.5) additional share 04/05/1965
Common $1 par split (2) for (1) by issuance of (1) additional share 02/03/1966
Stock Dividend - 10% 11/23/1965
Merged into Wormald International Ltd. 02/12/1979
Each share Common $1 par exchanged for $28 cash

ANSWERS CORP (DE)
Acquired by AFCV Holdings, L.L.C. 04/15/2011
Each share Common $0.001 par exchanged for $10.50 cash

ANSWERTHINK INC (FL)
Name changed 06/20/2000
Name changed from Answerthink Consulting Group, Inc. to Answerthink, Inc. 06/20/2000
Name changed to Hackett Group, Inc. 01/01/2008

ANTA CORP. LIQUIDATING TRUST (DE)
Liquidation completed
Each Share of Bene. Int. $1 par received initial distribution of (1.1235) shares Bonray Drilling Corp. Common 10¢ par and $10 cash 04/25/1985
Each Share of Bene. Int. $1 par received second distribution of $2.40 cash 02/05/1986
Each Share of Bene. Int. $1 par received third and final distribution of $2.1845 cash 11/24/1989
Note: Certificates were not required to be surrendered and are without value
(See Anta Corp. for previous distributions)

ANTA CORP (DE)
Each share Common $1 par received initial distribution of (1) share Bonray Energy Corp. Common 50¢ par 05/04/1984
Each share Common $1 par received second distribution of $9 cash 06/11/1984
Assets transferred to ANTA Corp. Liquidating Trust and Common $1 par reclassified as Shares of Bene. Int. $1 par 04/18/1985
(See ANTA Corp. Liquidating Trust)

ANTAEUS ACQUISITIONS INC (DE)
Name changed to Sharp Wheel Corp. 01/10/1991

ANTAEUS RES CORP (DE)
Merged into DA Capo Co., Ltd. 05/31/1985
Details not available

ANTAGA INTL CORP (NV)
Old Common $0.001 par split (18) for (1) by issuance of (17) additional shares payable 10/01/2012 to holders of record 10/01/2012
Recapitalized as Mix 1 Life, Inc. 10/07/2013
Each share new Common $0.001 par exchanged for (0.33333333) share Common $0.001 par

ANTAM RES INTL LTD (YT)
Reorganized as International Antam Resources Ltd. 06/08/1999
Each share Common no par exchanged for (0.14285714) share Common no par
International Antam Resources Ltd. name changed to Goldsource Mines Inc. 01/23/2004

ANTAMENA CAP CORP (BC)
Recapitalized as Xtierra Inc. 09/03/2008
Each share Common no par exchanged for (0.5) share Common no par

ANTAMOK GOLDFIELDS MINING CO.
Merged into Atlas Consolidated Mining & Development Corp. 00/00/1953
Each share Common P0.10 par exchanged for (0.750) share Capital Stock P0.10 par

ANTARENNI INDS INC (NY)
Stock Dividend - 200% 05/24/1974
Adjudicated bankrupt 09/16/1975
Stockholders' equity unlikely

ANTARES CAP CORP (CO)
SEC revoked common stock registration 03/14/2007

ANTARES LTD. (LIBERIA)
Acquired by Trasa AG 10/30/1969
Each share Common 1¢ par exchanged for (1) share Bearer Common $1 par
Note: Holders received $0.25 cash per share for certificates surrendered after 02/13/1970

ANTARES MINERALS INC (AB)
Each share Common no par received distribution of (0.4505) share Regulus Resources Inc. Common no par payable 12/20/2010 to holders of record 12/20/2010
Merged into First Quantum Minerals Ltd. 12/20/2010
Each share Common no par exchanged for (0.07619) share Common no par
Note: Unexchanged certificates were cancelled and became without value 12/20/2016

ANTARES MNG & EXPL CORP (ON)
Name changed to Caussa Capital Corp. 09/03/1999
Caussa Capital Corp. recapitalized as Rainbow Gold Ltd. 01/20/2003 which recapitalized as Jaguar Mining Inc. 10/16/2003

ANTARES OIL CORP (CO)
Each share old Common 1¢ par exchanged for (0.33333333) share new Common 1¢ par 10/22/1980
Merged into Oxford Consolidated, Inc. 09/18/1985
Each share new Common 1¢ par exchanged for (0.0763710) share Common 10¢ par
(See Oxford Consolidated, Inc.)

ANTARES PHARMA INC (MN)
Reincorporated under the laws of Delaware 04/30/2005

ANTARES RES CORP (NY)
Each share old Common 10¢ par exchanged for (0.02) share new Common 10¢ par 12/19/1994
Each share new Common 10¢ par exchanged for (0.25) share old Common $0.001 par 06/01/1995
Old Common $0.001 par split (2) for (1) by issuance of (1) additional share 01/31/1996 to holders of record 01/05/1996
Each share old Common $0.001 par exchanged for (0.1) share new Common $0.001 par 12/26/1996
Chapter 11 bankruptcy proceedings terminated 09/16/2008
Stockholders' equity unlikely

ANTAREX METALS LTD (AB)
Recapitalized as International Antarex Metals Ltd. 08/22/2001
Each share Common no par exchanged for (0.2) share Common no par

ANTE CORP (MN)
Reorganized under the laws of Delaware as G-III Apparel Group Ltd. 11/01/1989
Each share Common 1¢ par exchanged for (1/3) share Common 1¢ par

ANTE CORP II (MN)
Name changed to Northgate Industries, Inc. 08/07/1990
Northgate Industries, Inc. name changed to Northgate Computer Corp. 09/27/1990
(See Northgate Computer Corp.)

ANTEC CORP (DE)
Under plan of merger name changed to ARRIS Group, Inc. (Old) 08/03/2001
ARRIS Group, Inc. (Old) reorganized as ARRIS Group, Inc. (New) 04/16/2013 which merged into ARRIS International PLC 01/05/2016

ANTE5 INC (DE)
Name changed to Black Ridge Oil & Gas, Inc. (DE) 04/05/2012
Black Ridge Oil & Gas, Inc. (DE) reincorporated in Nevada 12/10/2012

ANTE4 INC (DE)
Name changed to Voyager Oil & Gas, Inc. (DE) 05/25/2010
Voyager Oil & Gas, Inc. (DE) reincorporated in Montana 06/03/2011 which name changed to Emerald Oil, Inc. (MT) 09/04/2012 which reincorporated in Delaware 06/11/2014
(See Emerald Oil, Inc.)

ANTEK INTL INC (NV)
Recapitalized as Tika Corp. 10/31/2005
Each share Common 1¢ par exchanged for (0.05) share Common 1¢ par
Tika Corp. name changed to Paypad, Inc. 03/27/2006 which name changed to 3Pea International, Inc. 10/27/2006

ANTELOPE OIL & GAS CO. (WA)
Common 10¢ par changed to 25¢ par 05/16/1956
Name changed to Antelope Uranium Oil Co. 06/12/1956
Antelope Uranium Oil Co. merged into Western Resources, Inc. 04/25/1958
(See Western Resources, Inc.)

ANTELOPE RESOURCES INC. (ID)
Recapitalized as Jotan, Inc. (ID) 09/22/1994
Each share Common 1¢ par exchanged for (0.2) share Common 1¢ par
Jotan, Inc. (ID) reincorporated in Florida 05/14/1996
(See Jotan, Inc.)

ANTELOPE RESOURCES INC. (ON)
Proclaimed dissolved 11/21/1991
Details not available

ANTELOPE RES LTD (BC)
Merged into Antelope Resources Inc. (ON) 02/28/1989
Each share Common no par exchanged for (1) share Common no par
(See Antelope Resources Inc. (ON))

ANTELOPE URANIUM OIL CO. (WA)
Merged into Western Resources, Inc. 04/25/1958
Each share Common 25¢ par exchanged for (1) share Common 25¢ par
(See Western Resources, Inc.)

ANTELOPE VY BK (LANCASTER, CA)
Common no par split (3) for (2) by issuance of (0.5) additional share payable 06/07/1996 to holders of record 04/24/1996
Merged into Eldorado Bancshares, Inc. 01/22/1999
Each share Common no par exchanged for (3.625) shares Common 1¢ par
Eldorado Bancshares, Inc. merged into Zions Bancorporation 03/30/2001 which merged into Zions Bancorporation, N.A. (Salt Lake City, UT) 10/01/2018

ANTELOPE VY ENTERPRISES INC (CA)
Name changed to Alfalfa-640 Trust and Common 10¢ par reclassified as Ctfs. of Bene. Int. 10¢ par 12/31/1972
(See Alfalfa-640 Trust)

ANTELOPE VALLEY SAVINGS & LOAN ASSOCIATION (CA)
Merged into Homefed Bank, Federal Savings Bank (San Francisco, CA) 03/31/1990
Each share Common $10 par exchanged for $2.6636 cash

ANTENA 3 DE TELEVISION SA (SPAIN)
Name changed to Atresmedia Corporacion de Medios de Comunicacion, S.A. 01/13/2017

ANTENNA PRODS INC (TX)
Common $2 par split (2) for (1) by issuance of (1) additional share payable 02/12/1998 to holders of record 01/30/1998
Name changed to Phazar Corp. 03/12/2001
(See Phazar Corp.)

ANTENNA SYSTEMS, INC. (MA)
Adjudicated bankrupt 11/00/1964
No stockholders' equity

ANTENNA TV SA (GREECE)
ADR agreement terminated 09/23/2003
Each ADR for Capital Stock exchanged for $0.151617 cash

ANTENNAS AMER INC (UT)
Name changed to ARC Wireless Solutions, Inc. 10/11/2000
ARC Wireless Solutions, Inc. recapitalized as ARC Group Worldwide, Inc. 08/08/2012

ANTENNAS FOR COMMUNICATIONS INC (DE)
Merged into Microdyne Corp. 04/16/1980
Each share Common 10¢ par exchanged for (0.875) share Common 10¢ par
(See Microdyne Corp.)

ANTEON INTL CORP (DE)
Acquired by General Dynamics Corp. 06/08/2006
Each share Common 1¢ par exchanged for $55.50 cash

ANTERRA CORP (AB)
Merged into Anterra Energy Inc. 05/08/2007
Each share Common no par exchanged for (0.5714285) share Class A Common no par and (0.0132) share Class B Common no par

ANTEX BIOLOGICS INC (DE)
Each share old Common 1¢ par exchanged for (0.2) share new Common 1¢ par 07/20/2000
Plan of reorganization under Chapter 11 Federal Bankruptcy Code effective 02/27/2004
No stockholders' equity

ANTEX CORP (OH)
Name changed to Natmar, Inc. 07/05/1985
(See Natmar, Inc.)

ANTHEM ELECTRS INC (DE)
Reincorporated 06/03/1983
Common no par split (3) for (2) by issuance of (0.5) additional share 03/31/1983
State of incorporation changed from (CA) to (DE) and Common no par changed to $0.125 par 06/03/1983
Common $0.125 par split (2) for (1) by issuance of (1) additional share 01/20/1984
Common $0.125 par split (4) for (3) by issuance of (0.33333333) additional share 07/15/1987
Merged into Arrow Electronics Inc. 11/28/1994
Each share Common $0.125 par exchanged for (0.875) share Common $1 par

ANTHEM EQUITY CORP (UT)
Name changed to Anthem Resources, Ltd. 11/15/1988
(See Anthem Resources, Ltd.)

ANTHEM INC NEW (IN)
Each Corporate Unit automatically became (0.2406) share Common 1¢ par 05/01/2018
(Additional Information in Active)

ANTHEM INC OLD (IN)
Each 6% Equity Security Unit received (1.14) shares Common 1¢ par 11/15/2004
Under plan of merger name changed to WellPoint, Inc. 12/01/2004
WellPoint, Inc. name changed to Anthem, Inc. (New) 12/03/2014

ANTHEM INVT CORP (DE)
Recapitalized as Wysak Petroleum Inc. 04/24/2003
Each share Common 1¢ par exchanged for (0.01333333) share Common 1¢ par
Wysak Petroleum Inc. name changed to Wild Brush Energy Inc. 04/11/2006

ANTHEM PPTYS CORP (BC)
Name changed to Anthem Works Ltd. 07/31/2003
(See Anthem Works Ltd.)

ANTHEM RECORDING WEST INC (CA)
Common $0.001 par split (3) for (1) by issuance of (2) additional shares payable 05/01/2000 to holders of record 04/28/2000
Name changed to uDate.com, Inc. (CA) 05/30/2000
uDate.com, Inc. (CA) reincorporated in Delaware 03/29/2001 which merged into USA Interactive 04/07/2003 which name changed to InterActiveCorp 06/23/2003 which name changed to IAC/InterActiveCorp 07/14/2004

ANTHEM RES INC (BC)
Merged into Boss Power Corp. 07/23/2015
Each share Common no par exchanged for (0.75) share Common no par
Note: Unexchanged certificates will be cancelled and become without value 07/23/2021
Boss Power Corp. name changed to Eros Resources Corp. 07/29/2015

ANTHEM RES LTD (UT)
Proclaimed dissolved for failure to file annual reports 01/01/1992

ANTHEM UTD INC (BC)
Merged into JDL Gold Corp. 10/07/2016
Each share Common no par exchanged for (0.12) share Common no par
JDL Gold Corp. name changed to Trek Mining Inc. 03/31/2017 which name changed to Equinox Gold Corp. 12/22/2017

ANTHEM VENTURES CAP CORP (BC)
Name changed to West Kirkland Mining Inc. 06/08/2010

ANTHEM WKS LTD (BC)
Acquired by Anthem Acquisition Ltd. 05/31/2004
Each share Common no par exchanged for $14.50 cash

ANTHES-IMPERIAL CO. LTD. (CANADA)
Common no par reclassified as Class A Common no par 02/26/1960
Name changed to Anthes Imperial Ltd. 05/07/1962
Anthes Imperial Ltd. acquired by Molson Industries Ltd. 00/00/1968 which name changed to Molson Companies Ltd. 08/17/1973 which name changed to Molson Inc. 06/29/1999 which merged into Molson Coors Brewing Co. 02/09/2005

ANTHES IMPERIAL LTD (CANADA)
Class A Common no par and Class B Common no par split (4) for (1) by issuance of (3) additional shares respectively 05/22/1962
Class A Common no par and Class B Common no par split (2) for (1) by issuance of (1) additional share respectively 04/13/1965
Acquired by Molson Industries Ltd. 00/00/1968
Each share Class A Common no par exchanged for (1.7) Class A Conv. Common no par and $3 cash
Each share Class B Common no par exchanged for (1.7) Class C Conv. Common no par and $3 cash
5.25% Preferred Ser. C $100 par called for redemption 03/24/1980
5.5% Preferred Ser. B $100 par called for redemption 03/24/1980
Molson Industries Ltd. name changed to Molson Companies Ltd. 08/17/1973 which name changed to Molson Inc. 06/29/1999 which merged into Molson Coors Brewing Co. 02/09/2005

ANTHES INDS INC (BC)
Name changed to Patheon Inc. 05/12/1993
(See Patheon Inc.)

ANTHEX INDS LTD (ON)
Recapitalized 06/26/1975
Recapitalized from Anthex Industries Inc. to Anthex Industries Ltd. 06/26/1975
Each share Capital Stock $1 par exchanged for (0.33333333) share Capital Stock no par
Charter cancelled for failure to pay taxes and file returns 01/16/1984

ANTHIAN RESOURCE CORP (CANADA)
Reincorporated 06/19/1997
Place of incorporation changed from (BC) to (Canada) 06/19/1997
Recapitalized as Sudamet Ventures Inc. 08/18/2000
Each share Common no par exchanged for (0.1) share Common no par
Sudamet Ventures Inc. recapitalized as Avigo Resources Corp. 05/05/2005 which name changed to Carbon Friendly Solutions Inc. 08/08/2008 which name changed to MicroCoal Technologies Inc. 07/22/2013 which reorganized as Targeted Microwave Solutions Inc. 05/22/2015

ANTHONIAN MNG LTD (QC)
Charter annulled for failure to file annual reports 05/02/1982

ANTHONY & SYLVAN POOLS CORP (OH)
Acquired by Stuart D. Neidus 12/17/2004
Each share Common no par exchanged for $5.50 cash

ANTHONY BROS. FIBRE GLASS POOL CORP. (CA)
Name changed to Anthony Powercraft 09/14/1959
(See Anthony Powercraft)

ANTHONY C R CO NEW (OK)
Merged into Stage Stores, Inc. 06/26/1997
Each share Common 1¢ par exchanged for (0.3992) share Common 1¢ par
(See Stage Stores, Inc.)

ANTHONY GAS & OIL EXPLS LTD (ON)
Name changed to Anthex Industries Inc. 06/27/1973
Anthex Industries Inc. recapitalized as Anthex Industries Ltd. 06/26/1975
(See Anthex Industries Ltd.)

ANTHONY INDS INC (DE)
Common $1 par split (5) for (4) by issuance of (0.25) additional share 01/24/1979
Common $1 par split (5) for (4) by issuance of (0.25) additional share 07/16/1986
Common $1 par split (3) for (2) by issuance of (0.5) additional share 09/12/1988
Stock Dividend - 10% 12/30/1974
Name changed to K2 Inc. 05/31/1996
K2 Inc. merged into Jarden Corp. 08/08/2007

ANTHONY POOLS INC (DE)
Name changed to Anthony Industries, Inc. 10/31/1969
Anthony Industries, Inc. name changed to K2 Inc. 05/31/1996 which merged into Jarden Corp. 08/08/2007

ANTHONY POWERCRAFT (CA)
Completely liquidated 08/11/1964
Each share Preferred exchanged for first and final distribution of (0.05) share Anthony Pools, Inc. Common $1 par
No equity for Common stockholders
Anthony Pools, Inc. name changed to Anthony Industries, Inc. 10/31/1969 which name changed to K2 Inc. 05/31/1996 which merged into Jarden Corp. 08/08/2007

ANTHONY WAYNE BK (FORT WAYNE, IN)
Stock Dividends - 10% 05/30/1973; 20% 01/02/1978; 33.33333333% 01/02/1980; 20% 01/04/1982; 25% 01/03/1983; 33.33333333% 01/03/1984
Under plan of reorganization each share Common Capital Stock $10 par automatically became (1) share General Bancshares Corp. of Indiana Common Capital Stock $10 par 07/02/1984
General Bancshares Corp. of Indiana merged into SummCorp. 04/30/1987 which merged into NBD Bancorp, Inc. 07/01/1992 which name changed to First Chicago NBD Corp. 12/01/1995 which merged into Bank One Corp. 10/02/1998 which merged into J.P. Morgan Chase & Co. 12/31/2000 which name changed to JPMorgan Chase & Co. 07/20/2004

ANTHONY WAYNE BK (WAYNE, NJ)
Stock Dividend - 25% 01/02/1979
Merged into Broadway Bank & Trust Co. (Paterson, NJ) 09/30/1983
Each share Capital Stock $5 par exchanged for $10.85 cash

ANTHRACITE CAP INC (MD)
10% Conv. Preferred Ser. B $0.001 par called for redemption at $25.24 on 05/06/2004
Chapter 7 bankruptcy proceedings terminated 03/06/2015
No stockholders' equity

ANTI AGING MED GROUP CORP (DE)
Each share old Common $0.001 par exchanged for (0.004) share new Common $0.001 par 03/09/2007
Name changed to Innolife Pharma, Inc. 05/02/2007

ANTI-POLLUTION DEVICES INC (MN)
Out of business 09/17/1974
Company has no assets

ANTICLINE URANIUM, INC. (CA)
Charter revoked for failure to file reports and pay fees 12/01/1961

ANTICLINE URANIUM INC (NV)
Name changed to LipidViro Tech, Inc. 02/05/2004
LipidViro Tech, Inc. name changed to NAC Global Technologies, Inc. 07/18/2014

ANTICOSTI CORP.
Merged into Consolidated Paper Corp. Ltd. 00/00/1931
Details not available

ANTICUS INTL CORP (NV)
Each share old Common $0.001 par exchanged for (3) shares new Common $0.001 par 09/13/2004
New Common $0.001 par split (3) for (1) by issuance of (2) additional shares payable 11/22/2004 to holders of record 11/18/2004
Ex date - 11/23/2004
SEC revoked common stock registration 08/20/2015

ANTIETAM HOTEL CORP. (MD)
Liquidated 08/18/1960
Details not available

ANTIGENICS INC (DE)
Contingent Value Rights expired without value 07/06/2002
Name changed to Agenus Inc. 01/06/2011

ANTIGUA ENTERPRISES INC (YT)
Reincorporated 07/17/1998
Place of incorporation changed from (BC) to (YT) 07/17/1998
Acquired by Ashley NA, LLC 04/26/2010
Each share Common no par exchanged for USD$0.31 cash
Note: Unexchanged certificates were cancelled and became without value 04/26/2016

ANTILLES RES LTD (BC)
Recapitalized as Golden Palm Resources Ltd. (BC) 09/27/1996
Each share Common no par exchanged for (0.2) share Common no par
Golden Palm Resources Ltd. (BC) reincorporated in Yukon 12/06/1996
(See Golden Palm Resources Ltd.)

ANTILLIAN CORP.
Out of business 00/00/1950
Details not available

ANTIMONY GOLD MINING & SMELTING CORP. LTD. (ON)
Charter cancelled for failure to pay taxes and file returns 03/00/1958

ANTIOCH RES LTD (NV)
Recapitalized 03/01/1988
Recapitalized from Antioch Resources, Inc. to Antioch Resources Ltd. 03/01/1988
Each share Common 1¢ par exchanged for (0.1) share Common $0.001 par
Each share Class A Common 1¢ par exchanged for (0.1) share Common $0.001 par
Merged into Consolidated Nevada Goldfields Corp. 06/25/1991
Each share Common 1¢ par exchanged for (0.0556) share Common no par and $0.00334 cash
Consolidated Nevada Goldfields Corp. recapitalized as Real Del Monte Mining Corp. 05/14/1998
(See Real Del Monte Mining Corp.)

ANTIOQUIA GOLD INC (AB)
Reincorporated under the laws of British Columbia 03/24/2016

ANTIPODES GOLD LTD (BC)
Recapitalized as Chatham Rock Phosphate Ltd. 02/24/2017
Each share Common no par exchanged for (0.1) share Common no par

ANTISOMA PLC (UNITED KINGDOM)
ADR agreement terminated 05/21/2014
Each Sponsored ADR for Ordinary exchanged for $0.557303 cash

ANTIVIRALS INC (OR)
Name changed to AVI BioPharma, Inc. 09/22/1998
AVI BioPharma, Inc. recapitalized as Sarepta Therapeutics, Inc. (OR) 07/12/2012 which reincorporated in Delaware 06/10/2013

ANTLER CREEK ENERGY CORP (AB)
Name changed to Pinecrest Energy Inc. 07/29/2010
Pinecrest Energy Inc. reorganized as Virginia Hills Oil Corp. 04/17/2015
(See Virginia Hills Oil Corp.)

ANTLER GOLD MINES LTD. (ON)
Charter cancelled for failure to pay taxes and file returns 00/00/1949

ANTLER HILL OIL & GAS LTD (AB)
Name changed to Antler Hill Mining Ltd. 06/29/2017

ANTLER RES LTD (BC)
Merged into Winspear Resources Ltd. (New) 01/13/1997
Each share Common no par exchanged for (2.5) shares Common no par
Winspear Resources Ltd. (New) name changed to Winspear Diamonds, Inc. 06/13/2000
(See Winspear Diamonds, Inc.)

ANTLERS OIL, MINING & MILLING, INC. (UT)
Merged into American Mining & Development Co. 03/26/1959
Each share Common 25¢ par exchanged for (0.1) share Capital Stock 50¢ par
American Mining & Development Co. recapitalized as American International Corp. (NV) 06/01/1972 which recapitalized as American Diversified Corp. (NV) 01/10/1985 which recapitalized as Natural Pharmaceutical International Inc. 06/18/1990

ANTOFAGASTA GOLD INC (ON)
Name changed to Arena Minerals Inc. 12/06/2013

ANTOFAGASTA PLC (UNITED KINGDOM)
Name changed 12/17/1999
Name changed from Antofagasta Holdings PLC to Antofagasta PLC 12/17/1999
Sponsored ADR's for Ordinary split (5) for (1) by issuance of (4) additional ADR's payable 06/22/2006 to holders of record 06/16/2006 Ex date - 06/23/2006
ADR agreement terminated 07/22/2016
Each Sponsored ADR for Ordinary exchanged for $24.913882 cash

ANTOINE SILVER MINES LTD (BC)
Struck off register and declared dissolved for failure to file returns 10/00/1974

ANTOINETTE LAKE MINES LTD. (ON)
Charter cancelled 10/00/1974

ANTON DIST INC (MT)
Reorganized as Andresmin Gold Corp. 05/10/2004
Each share Common $0.001 par exchanged for (13) shares Common $0.001 par

ANTON-IMCO ELECTRONICS CORP. (DE)
Acquired by Lionel Corp. 10/14/1960
Each share Common $1 par exchanged for (1.33333333) share Common $2.50 par
(See Lionel Corp.)

ANTONE PETROLEUMS LTD. (ON)
Merged into American Leduc Petroleums Ltd. 06/08/1955
Each share Common exchanged for (0.33333333) share Common no par
American Leduc Petroleums Ltd. acquired by Veteran Resources Inc. 10/17/2003 which merged into Bear Ridge Resources Ltd. 01/19/2006

ANTONOVICH INC (DE)
Chapter 11 bankruptcy proceedings converted to Chapter 7 on 10/10/1991
No stockholders' equity

ANTONY RES INC (BC)
Name changed to Sidewinder Conversions International Inc. 01/03/1990
Sidewinder Conversions International Inc. recapitalized as Pacific Axis Ventures, Inc. (BC) 11/28/1995 which reorganized in Yukon as Petrolex Energy Corp. 02/03/1997
(See Petrolex Energy Corp.)

ANTOX INC (DE)
Name changed to Chemanox Inc. 01/24/1972
(See Chemanox Inc.)

ANTRA HLDGS GROUP INC (UT)
Recapitalized as Peku Manufacturing, Inc. 11/15/2005
Each share Common $0.001 par exchanged for (0.005) share Common $0.001 par
Peku Manufacturing, Inc. name changed to GHL Technologies, Inc. 03/03/2006 which recapitalized as NXGen Holdings, Inc. 09/07/2007 which name changed to Green Bridge Industries, Inc. 08/20/2009

ANTRIABIO INC (DE)
Each share old Common $0.001 par exchanged for (0.16666666) share new Common $0.001 par 05/01/2014
Name changed to Rezolute, Inc. 12/19/2017

ANTRIM RES LTD (BC)
Name changed to Kenridge Mineral Corp. 01/31/1984
Kenridge Mineral Corp. recapitalized as Pacific Kenridge Ventures Inc. 03/20/1987
(See Pacific Kenridge Ventures Inc.)

ANTS SOFTWARE INC (DE)
Name changed 04/05/2001
Common $0.0002 par split (2) for (1) by issuance of (1) additional share payable 01/14/2000 to holders of record 01/07/2000
Name changed from ANTs software.com to ANTs software, inc. 04/05/2001
SEC revoked common stock registration 02/22/2013

ANUBIS CORP (DE)
Recapitalized as CE Software Holdings Inc. 04/19/1990
Each share Common 1¢ par exchanged for (0.5) share Common 2¢ par
CE Software Holdings Inc. name changed to Lightning Rod Software, Inc. 05/02/2000
(See Lightning Rod Software, Inc.)

ANUBIS II CORP (DE)
Name changed to Casino America, Inc. 06/02/1992
Casino America, Inc. name changed to Isle of Capri Casinos, Inc. 10/01/1998
(See Isle of Capri Casinos, Inc.)

ANUHCO INC (DE)
Common no par changed to 1¢ par 06/01/1993
Reorganized as TransFinancial Holdings, Inc. 07/01/1997
Each share Common 1¢ par exchanged for (1) share Common 1¢ par to reflect a (1) for (100) reverse split followed by a (100) for (1) forward split
Note: Holders of (99) shares or fewer received $8.8875 cash per share
(See TransFinancial Holdings, Inc.)

ANUSOUND LTD (DE)
Voluntarily dissolved 02/13/1973
Details not available

ANUWON URANIUM MINES LTD (ON)
Charter cancelled for failure to pay taxes and file returns 03/16/1976

ANVEX INTL INC (NV)
Common $0.001 par split (12.98) for (1) by issuance of (11.98) additional shares payable 04/26/2012 to holders of record 04/26/2012 Ex date - 04/27/2012
Name changed to Health Revenue Assurance Holdings, Inc. 05/02/2012

ANVIL BRAND, INC. (NC)
Acquired by B.V.D. Co., Inc. 02/01/1966
Each share 5% Preferred $50 par exchanged for (2.1) shares Common $1 par
Each share Class A Common $5 par exchanged for (0.6424) share Common $1 par
B.V.D. Co., Inc. acquired by Glen Alden Corp. (DE) 05/19/1967 which merged into Rapid-American Corp. (DE) 11/06/1972
(See Rapid-American Corp. (DE))

ANVIL EQUIPMENT CO.
Under plan of merger each share Common $1 par exchanged for $11 cash 00/00/1980

ANVIL FST PRODS INC (NV)
Name changed to Easy Scripts Inc. 06/24/2009

ANVIL HLDGS INC (DE)
Stock Dividends - 3.25% payable 09/15/1999 to holders of record
09/01/1999; 3.25% payable 03/15/2000 to holders of record
03/01/2000; 3.25% payable 06/15/2000 to holders of record
06/01/2000; 3.25% payable 09/15/2000 to holders of record
09/01/2000; 3.25% payable 03/15/2001 to holders of record
03/01/2001; 3.25% payable 06/15/2001 to holders of record
06/01/2001; 3.25% payable 09/15/2001 to holders of record
09/01/2001; 3.25% payable 12/15/2001 to holders of record
12/01/2001; 3.25% payable 03/15/2002 to holders of record 03/01/2002
Plan of reorganization under Chapter 11 Federal Bankruptcy Code effective 02/05/2007
Each 144A 13% Sr. Exchangeable Preferred 1¢ par exchanged for approximately (0.064) share Common 1¢ par, (0.77) Common Stock Purchase Warrant, Class A expiring in 2012, and (0.788) Common Stock Purchase Warrant, Class B expiring 00/00/2012
Each Accredited Investors 13% Sr. Exchangeable Preferred 1¢ par exchanged for approximately (0.064) share Common 1¢ par, (0.77) Common Stock Purchase Warrant, Class A expiring in 2012, and (0.788) Common Stock Purchase Warrant, Class B expiring 00/00/2012
Each 13% Sr. Exchangeable Preferred Ser. B 1¢ par exchanged for approximately (0.064) share Common 1¢ par, (0.77) Common Stock Purchase Warrant, Class A expiring in 2012, and (0.788) Common Stock Purchase Warrant, Class B expiring 00/00/2012
Acquired by Gildan Activewear Inc. 05/08/2012
Each share Common 1¢ par exchanged for approximately $3.70 cash

ANVIL INV SVCS INC (NJ)
Charter revoked for failure to file reports and pay fees 06/30/1994

ANVIL MNG LTD (NT)
Acquired by Minmetals Resources Ltd. 02/22/2012
Each share Common no par exchanged for $8 cash

ANVIL PORCUPINE GOLD MINES LTD. (ON)
Name changed to Burrex Mines Ltd. 00/00/1954
Burrex Mines Ltd. recapitalized as Burrgold Mines Ltd. 12/00/1973
(See Burrgold Mines Ltd.)

ANVIL RANGE MNG CORP (CANADA)
Plan of Arrangement effective 05/00/2003
No stockholders' equity

ANVIL RES LTD (BC)
Recapitalized as Geocore Exploration Inc. 07/24/2003
Each share Common no par exchanged for (0.1) share Common no par
Geocore Exploration Inc. recapitalized as Emerick Resources Corp. 12/31/2007 which name changed to Medgold Resources Corp. 12/17/2012

ANW INC (DE)
Charter cancelled and declared inoperative and void for non-payment of taxes 03/01/2001

ANYDAY COM INC (DE)
Acquired by Palm, Inc. 06/28/2000
Each share Common exchanged for $14 cash

ANYMED SVC CORP (NY)
Dissolved by proclamation 03/25/1992

ANYOX RES INC (NV)
Name changed to Forefront Inc. 06/06/2000
(See Forefront Inc.)

ANYTHING BRANDS ONLINE INC (NV)
Name changed to MyFreightWorld Technologies, Inc. 05/13/2010

ANYTHING INTERNET CORP (CO)
Name changed to Inform Worldwide Holdings Inc. (CO) 11/14/2000
Inform Worldwide Holdings Inc. (CO) reincorporated in Florida 02/21/2005
(See Inform Worldwide Holdings Inc.)

ANYTHINGIT INC (DE)
Each share old Common 1¢ par exchanged for (0.33333333) share new Common 1¢ par 06/12/2012
Name changed to WeedHire International, Inc. 11/18/2014

ANYTHING2SHIP INC (DE)
Charter cancelled and declared inoperative and void for non-payment of taxes 03/01/2004

ANYTRANSLATION CORP (NV)
Name changed to Vibe Wireless Corp. 11/23/2015
Vibe Wireless Corp. name changed to Green Vision Biotechnology Corp. 10/24/2016

ANZ EXCHANGEABLE PFD TR (DE)
8% Trust Unit Exchangeable Preference shares called for redemption at $25 on 12/12/2003

ANZ EXCHANGEABLE PFD TR II (DE)
8.08% Trust Unit Exchangeable Preference shares called for redemption at $25 on 12/12/2003

ANZA CAP INC (NV)
Each share old Common $0.001 par exchanged for (0.05) share new Common $0.001 par 04/21/2003
Recapitalized as Renhuang Pharmaceutical, Inc. 08/11/2006
Each share new Common $0.001 par exchanged for (0.03333333) share Common $0.001 par
Renhuang Pharmaceutical, Inc. name changed to China Botanic Pharmaceutical Inc. 11/22/2010

ANZA INNOVATIONS INC (NV)
Each share old Common $0.001 par exchanged for (4) shares new Common $0.001 par 02/05/2004
Name changed to Gaofeng Gold Corp. 02/17/2004
Gaofeng Gold Corp. recapitalized as Sun Oil & Gas Corp. 01/03/2005 which recapitalized as China 3C Group 12/20/2005 which recapitalized as Yosen Group, Inc. 12/31/2012

ANZA PAC CORP (CA)
Completely liquidated 04/08/1976
Each share Capital Stock $1 par exchanged for first and final distribution of (1) Anza Shareholders' Liquidating Trust Unit of Bene. Int.
(See Anza Shareholders' Liquidating Trust)

ANZA SHAREHOLDERS LIQUIDATING TR (CA)
Liquidation completed
Each Unit of Bene. Int. received initial distribution of $0.85 cash 01/20/1978
Each Unit of Bene. Int. received second distribution of $1.25 cash 01/26/1979
Each Unit of Bene. Int. received third distribution of $1.25 cash 08/17/1979
Each Unit of Bene. Int. received fourth distribution of $2.15 cash 01/21/1980
Each Unit of Bene. Int. received fifth distribution of $3 cash 11/21/1980
Each Unit of Bene. Int. received sixth distribution of $2.50 cash 01/23/1981
Each Unit of Bene. Int. received seventh distribution of $3.75 cash 04/24/1981
Each Unit of Bene. Int. received eighth distribution of $2.75 cash 07/31/1981
Each Unit of Bene. Int. received ninth distribution of $1.25 cash 01/31/1982
Each Unit of Bene. Int. received tenth distribution of $1.25 cash 07/30/1982
Each Unit of Bene. Int. received eleventh distribution of $2.25 cash 01/28/1983
Each Unit of Bene. Int. received twelfth distribution of $3 cash 06/24/1983
Each Unit of Bene. Int. received thirteenth distribution of $2.15 cash 12/30/1983
Each Unit of Bene. Int. received fourteenth and final distribution of $0.86 cash 09/07/1984
Note: Certifcates were not required to be surrendered and are without value

ANZEX RES LTD (YT)
Recapitalized as Helena Resources Ltd. 12/23/2003
Each share Common no par exchanged for (0.125) share Common no par
Helena Resources Ltd. name changed to THEMAC Resources Group Ltd. 03/05/2007

AO INDS INC (DE)
Name changed to Aegis Corp. 06/01/1974
(See Aegis Corp.)

AO TATNEFT (RUSSIA)
Each Reg. S Sponsored ADR for Ordinary exchanged for (1) Sponsored ADR for Ordinary 03/25/1998
Each 144A Sponsored ADR for Ordinary exchanged for (1) Sponsored ADR for Ordinary 07/08/1999
Name changed to OAO Tatneft and Sponsored ADR's reclassified as GDR's for Ordinary 11/16/2006
OAO Tatneft name changed to Tatneft PJSC 12/08/2015

AO TORGOVY DOM GUM (RUSSIA)
ADR agreement terminated 12/11/2014
Each Sponsored ADR for Ordinary exchanged for $0.942122 cash

AOE VENTURES INC (CO)
Administratively dissolved 01/01/1993

AOI COAL CO (DE)
Charter cancelled for failure to pay taxes and maintain registered agent 02/14/1995

AOL INC (DE)
Acquired by Verizon Communications Inc. 06/23/2015
Each share Common 1¢ par exchanged for $50 cash

AOL TIME WARNER INC (DE)
Name changed to Time Warner Inc. (New) 10/16/2003
Time Warner Inc. (New) merged into AT&T Inc. 06/15/2018

AOM MINERALS LTD (NV)
Each share old Common $0.001 par exchanged for (5) shares new Common $0.001 par 11/02/2007
Name changed to Purio Inc. (NV) 12/07/2007
Purio Inc. (NV) reincorporated in Wyoming 08/14/2010 which name changed to BitFrontier Capital Holdings, Inc. 02/05/2018

AON CORP (DE)
Common $1 par split (2) for (1) by issuance of (1) additional share 05/26/1987
Common $1 par split (3) for (2) by issuance of (0.5) additional share 05/16/1994
Each share Conversion Preferred Ser. B $1 par exchanged for (1.5) shares Common $1 par 12/01/1994
6.25% Conv. Exchangeable Preferred $1 par called for redemption 11/01/1996
Common $1 par split (3) for (2) by issuance of (0.5) additional share payable 05/14/1997 to holders of record 05/01/1997 Ex date - 05/15/1997
8% Perpetual Preferred $1 par called for redemption at $25 on 11/03/1997
Common $1 par split (3) for (2) by issuance of (0.5) additional share payable 05/17/1999 to holders of record 05/04/1999
Reorganized under the laws of England & Wales as Aon PLC 04/02/2012
Each share Common $1 par exchanged for (1) share Class A Ordinary USD $0.01 par

AONE DENTAL INTL GROUP INC (UT)
SEC revoked common stock registration 07/12/2012

A1 INTERNET COM INC (NV)
Name changed to WorldTeq Group International, Inc. 10/19/2001
WorldTeq Group International, Inc. name changed to China Printing, Inc. 04/19/2005 which name changed to CYIOS Corp. 11/07/2005

A123 SYS INC (DE)
Plan of reorganization under Chapter 11 Federal Bankruptcy proceedings effective 06/28/2013
No stockholders' equity

AOREC CORP (NY)
Acquired by BAC Development Corp. (NY) 03/01/1969
Each share Common 1¢ par exchanged for (0.4) share Common 1¢ par
BAC Development Corp. (NY) reincorporated in Delaware 12/31/1970 which liquidated for First Reality Investment Corp. (DE) 06/19/1972 which name changed to Thor Corp. (DE) 06/08/1976 which name changed to Thor Energy Resources, Inc. 07/31/1981
(See Thor Energy Resources, Inc.)

AORTECH INC (MN)
Name changed to Calendar Capital, Inc. 03/26/1993
Calendar Capital, Inc. name changed to IQUniverse, Inc. 04/11/2001
(See IQUniverse, Inc.)

AOXIN TIANLI GROUP INC (BRITISH VIRGIN ISLANDS)
Each share Common $0.001 par exchanged for (0.25) share Common $0.004 par 09/09/2016
Name changed to Renmin Tianli Group, Inc. 11/13/2017

AP EVENT INC (NV)
Name changed to Leafbuyer Technologies, Inc. 04/28/2017

AP HENDERSON GROUP (NV)
SEC revoked common stock registration 05/21/2012

AP OFFICE EQUIP INC (CO)
Name changed to Ednet, Inc. (CO) 09/29/1995
Ednet, Inc. (CO) reorganized in Delaware as Entertainment Digital Network, Inc. 02/22/1999 which merged into Visual Data Corp. 08/03/2001 which name changed to Onstream Media Corp. 01/01/2005

AP PARTS CORP. (MI)
Merged into Dunhill International, Inc. 10/31/1967
Each share Class B Common $2.50 par exchanged for (1.74) shares Conv. Preferred $1 par
Each share Common $2.50 par exchanged for (1.74) shares Common $1 par
Dunhill International, Inc. name changed to Questor Corp. 12/01/1968
(See Questor Corp.)

AP PHARMA INC (DE)
Each share old Common 1¢ par exchanged for (0.25) share new Common 1¢ par 05/25/2007
Recapitalized as Heron Therapeutics, Inc. 01/13/2014
Each share Common 1¢ par exchanged for (0.05) share Common 1¢ par

AP SALES INC (CO)
Reincorporated under the laws of Florida as Quest Net Corp. and Common no par changed to $0.0001 par 07/13/1998
Quest Net Corp. recapitalized as Markland Technologies Inc. 06/21/2001
(See Markland Technologies Inc.)

APA ENTERPRISES INC (MN)
Name changed 08/25/2004
Common 1¢ par split (2) for (1) by issuance of (1) additional share 03/31/1989
Name changed from APA Optics, Inc. to APA Enterprises, Inc. 08/25/2004
Name changed to Clearfield, Inc. 01/02/2008

APAC CUSTOMER SVCS INC (IL)
Name changed 07/12/1999
Common 1¢ par split (2) for (1) by issuance of (1) additional share payable 05/15/1996 to holders of record 04/26/1996
Name changed from APAC TeleServices, Inc. to APAC Customer Services, Inc. 07/12/1999
Acquired by Blackhawk Acquisition Parent, L.L.C. 10/17/2011
Each share Common 1¢ par exchanged for $8.55 cash

APAC MINERALS INC (BC)
Name changed to Golden China Resources Corp. (BC) 03/15/2005
Golden China Resources Corp. (BC) reincorporated in Canada 07/01/2005 which merged into Sino Gold Mining Ltd. 12/19/2007

APAC RES INC (BC)
Recapitalized as XORTX Therapeutics Inc. 01/11/2018
Each share Common no par exchanged for (0.25) share Common no par

APAC TELECOMMUNICATIONS CORP (BC)
Delisted from Toronto Stock Venture Exchange 06/05/2002

APACHE CORP (DE)
6.5% Preferred $20 par called for redemption 01/01/1981
Each share 6.5% Depositary Preferred Ser. C converted into (0.9016) share Common $1.25 par 05/15/2002
5.68% Depositary Preferred Ser. B called for redemption at $100 plus $0.947 accrued dividends on 12/30/2009
6% Depositary Preferred Ser. D exchanged for (0.56946) share Common $0.625 par 08/01/2013
(Additional Information in Active)

APACHE DRILLING CO., INC. (AZ)
Merged into Arizona Helium Corp. 09/13/1968
Details not available

APACHE EXPL CORP (DE)
Name changed to Apexco, Inc. 06/04/1973
(See Apexco, Inc.)

APACHE FUND, INC. (MN)
Name changed to Viking Growth Fund, Inc. 12/01/1963
Viking Growth Fund, Inc. merged into Industries Trend Fund Inc. 09/29/1975 which merged into Pilot

Fund, Inc. 05/01/1981 which name changed to Transamerica Technology Fund 06/23/1989 which name changed to Transamerica Capital Appreciation Fund 04/19/1991 which merged into Hancock (John) Capital Growth Fund 12/22/1994
(See Hancock (John) Capital Growth Fund)

APACHE INVTS INC (CO)
Recapitalized as Dog World Inc. 09/30/1991
Each share Common no par exchanged for (0.05) share Common no par
Dog World Inc. name changed to Medical Management Systems Inc. (CO) 04/25/1995 which reincorporated in Delaware as Dominix, Inc. 07/26/2000 which recapitalized as 110 Media Group, Inc. 06/04/2004 which name changed to Web2 Corp. 07/31/2006 which recapitalized as Full Motion Beverage, Inc. 12/08/2008

APACHE MED SYS INC (DE)
Name changed to Aros Corp. 07/02/2001
Aros Corp. name changed to ReGen Biologics, Inc. 11/20/2002
(See ReGen Biologics, Inc.)

APACHE MINES CO.
Liquidated 00/00/1952
Details not available

APACHE MTR CORP (NV)
Each share old Common $0.001 par exchanged for (0.01333333) share new Common $0.001 par 06/07/2004
Each share new Common $0.001 par exchanged again for (2) shares new Common $0.001 par 10/14/2005
Name changed to Transnational Automotive Group, Inc. 01/12/2006
Transnational Automotive Group, Inc. name changed to Transnational Group, Inc. 07/24/2014

APACHE OIL CORP. (DE)
Common $2.50 par changed to Common $1.25 par and (1) additional share issued 04/15/1959
Name changed to Apache Corp. 04/14/1960

APACHE PETROLEUM CO (DE)
Reincorporated 05/08/1986
State of incorporation changed from (TX) to (DE) 05/08/1986
Through exchange offer limited partnership units acquired by Key Production Co., Inc. 09/26/1988
Public interest eliminated

APACHE PROPERTIES, INC. (DE)
Merged into Apache Corp. 12/15/1960
Each share Common $1 par exchanged for (0.5) share Common $1.25 par

APACHE RLTY CORP (MN)
Merged into Apache Corp. 04/02/1962
Each share 6.5% Conv. Preferred $20 par exchanged for (1) share 6.5% Conv. Preferred $20 par
Each share Common $1 par exchanged for (0.125) share Common $1.25 par

APACHE RES LTD (CO)
Each share old Common 10¢ par exchanged for (0.5) share new Common 10¢ par 05/20/1981
Recapitalized as Danzar Investment Group, Inc. 01/24/1986
Each share new Common no par exchanged for (0.1) share Common no par
Danzar Investment Group, Inc. recapitalized as Alexander Mark Investments (USA), Inc. 12/26/1996 which reorganized as Wincroft, Inc. (CO) 05/18/1998 which reorganized in Nevada 02/12/2008 which name changed to Apollo Solar Energy, Inc. 11/03/2008

APACHE SILVER & OIL INC (UT)
Recapitalized as Insurance Kingdome Agency, Inc. 02/14/1985
Each share Common 1¢ par exchanged for (0.1) share Common $0.001 par

APACHE URANIUM CORP. (UT)
Merged into International Oil & Metals Corp. 03/29/1956
Each share Common 1¢ par exchanged for (0.03333333) share Common $1 par
International Oil & Metals Corp. liquidated for Perfect Photo, Inc. 03/24/1965 which was acquired by United Whelan Corp. 06/30/1966 which name changed to Perfect Film & Chemical Corp. 05/31/1967 which name changed to Cadence Industries Corp. 10/22/1970
(See Cadence Industries Corp.)

APANI LABORATORIES INC (NV)
Name changed to Text 2 Win International 12/15/2004
Text 2 Win International name changed to Entertainment Factory, Inc. (NV) 09/20/2005 which reorganized in Delaware as Tri-Hub International, Ltd. 07/16/2008

APARTMENT INVT & MGMT CO (MD)
Each share Ser. E Preferred 1¢ par automatically became (1) share Class A Common 1¢ par 01/15/1999
Each share 8% Conv. Class K Preferred 1¢ par exchanged for (0.5944) share Class A Common 1¢ par plus $0.4167 accrued dividend 04/18/2002
9% Class C Preferred 1¢ par called for redemption at $25 plus $0.475 accrued dividend on 06/30/2003
9.50% Ser. H Preferred 1¢ par called for redemption at $25 on 08/18/2003
Conv. Class P Preferred 1¢ par called for redemption at $25 plus $0.0375 accrued dividend on 04/21/2004
8.75% Class D Preferred 1¢ par called for redemption at $25 plus $0.0425 accrued dividend on 01/21/2005
10.1% Class Q Preferred 1¢ par called for redemption at $25 plus $0.035 accrued dividends on 03/19/2006
10% Preferred Ser. R 1¢ par called for redemption at $25 plus $0.243 accrued dividends on 07/20/2006
9.375% Preferred Ser. G 1¢ par called for redemption at $25 plus $0.5469 accrued dividends on 10/07/2010
Class V Preferred 1¢ par called for redemption at $25 plus $0.3445 accrued dividends on 06/15/2012
7.875% Class Y Preferred 1¢ par called for redemption at $25 plus $0.338 accrued dividends on 06/15/2012
8% Preferred Ser. T 1¢ par called for redemption at $25 plus $0.3445 accrued dividends on 06/15/2012
7.75% Class U Preferred 1¢ par called for redemption at $25 plus $0.0646 accrued dividends on 07/26/2012
7% Class Z Preferred 1¢ par called for redemption at $25 plus $0.0729 accrued dividends on 07/29/2016
(Additional Information in Active)

APASCO S A DE C V (MEXICO)
ADR agreement terminated 01/12/2004
Each Sponsored ADR for Ser. A no par exchanged for $38.20 cash
Each Sponsored ADR for Ser. B no par exchanged for $38.20 cash

APC TELECOMMUNICATIONS INC (NV)
Name changed to Innofone, Inc. 03/30/1999
(See Innofone.com, Inc.)

APC VENTURES INC (WA)
Name changed to Yukon Gold Corp. (WA) 02/29/1996
Yukon Gold Corp. (WA) reincorporated in Yukon as Alliance Pacific Gold Corp. 06/12/1997 which recapitalized as International Alliance Resources, Inc. 09/24/1998 which name changed to Bluenose Gold Corp. 07/25/2012

APCO ARGENTINA INC (CAYMAN ISLANDS)
Ordinary 1¢ par split (4) for (1) by issuance of (3) additional shares payable 11/16/2007 to holders of record 10/17/2007 Ex date - 11/19/2007
Name changed to Apco Oil & Gas International Inc. 07/13/2009
(See Apco Oil & Gas International Inc.)

APCO ARGENTINA INC (DE)
Reorganized under the laws of the Cayman Islands 04/06/1979
Each share Common 1¢ par exchanged for (1) share Ordinary 1¢ par
Apco Argentina Inc. (Cayman Islands) name changed to Apco Oil & Gas International Inc. 07/13/2009
(See Apco Oil & Gas International Inc.)

APCO MANUFACTURING CO.
Merged into Apco-Mossberg Corp. 00/00/1927
Details not available

APCO-MOSSBERG CORP.
Reorganized as Apco-Mossberg Co. 00/00/1937
No stockholders' equity

APCO OIL & GAS INTL INC (CAYMAN ISLANDS)
Acquired by Pluspetrol Resources Corp. 01/29/2015
Each share Ordinary 1¢ par exchanged for $14.50 cash

APCO OIL CORP (DE)
Common $1 par split (5) for (2) by issuance of (1.5) additional shares 01/10/1961
In process of liquidation
Each share Common $1 par exchanged for initial distribution of $40 cash 06/12/1978
Each share Common $1 par received second distribution of (1) share Apco Argentina, Inc. (DE) Common 1¢ par and $5 cash 10/16/1978
(See Apco Argentina, Inc. (Cayman Islands) formerly (DE))
Each share Common $1 par received third distribution of $0.879 cash 01/31/1980
Each share Common $1 par received fourth distribution of $0.458 cash 01/23/1981
Each share Common $1 par received fifth distribution of (0.467) share Apco Argentina, Inc. (Cayman Islands) Ordinary Stock 1¢ par 04/20/1981
Each share Common $1 par received sixth distribution of $2.50 cash 09/30/1982
Each share Common $1 par received seventh distribution of $1.117 cash 01/31/1985
Note: Details on subsequent distributions, if any, are not available

APD ANTIQUITIES INC (NV)
Name changed to American Cordillera Mining Corp. 12/31/2012

APECO CORP (DE)
Common 50¢ par changed to 1¢ par 08/05/1982
Recapitalized as Lori Corp. 08/29/1985
Each share Common 1¢ par exchanged for (0.03333333) share Common 1¢ par
Lori Corp. name changed to COMFORCE Corp. 12/01/1995
(See COMFORCE Corp.)

APELLA RES INC (BC)
Name changed to PacificOre Mining Corp. 05/28/2012
PacificOre Mining Corp. name changed to Vanadiumcorp Resource Inc. 11/22/2013

APERIAN INC (DE)
Name changed to Fourthstage Technologies, Inc. 08/20/2001
(See Fourthstage Technologies, Inc.)

APERTUS TECHNOLOGIES INC (MN)
Name changed to Carleton Corp. 08/01/1998
(See Carleton Corp.)

APEX BIOVENTURES ACQUISITION CORP (DE)
Completely liquidated 06/03/2009
Each Unit exchanged for first and final distribution of $7.84808427 cash
Each share Common $0.0001 par exchanged for first and final distribution of $7.84808427 cash

APEX CAP CORP (AB)
Name changed to Traxion Energy Inc. 07/14/2005
Traxion Energy Inc. name changed to Anglo Canadian Oil Corp. 04/23/2010 which merged into Tallgrass Energy Corp. 12/31/2012
(See Tallgrass Energy Corp.)

APEX CONSOLIDATED RESOURCES LTD. (ON)
Recapitalized as Abacus Mines Ltd. 06/01/1959
Each share Common no par exchanged for (0.16666666) share Common no par
Abacus Mines Ltd. name changed to Abacus Mines & Realty Ltd. 00/00/1962 which recapitalized as Abacon Developments Ltd. 03/21/1963
(See Abacon Developments Ltd.)

APEX CORP (AB)
Acquired by Bentall Capital Ltd. Partnership 10/30/2001
Each share Class A Common no par exchanged for $2.60 cash

APEX DATA INC (DE)
Merged into SMART Modular Technologies, Inc. 07/28/1995
Each share Common $0.0001 par exchanged for (0.1) share Common no par
SMART Modular Technologies, Inc. merged into Solectron Corp. 12/01/1999 which merged into Flextronics International Ltd. 10/01/2007 which name changed to Flex Ltd. 09/28/2016

APEX ELECTRICAL MANUFACTURING CO. (OH)
Each share Common no par exchanged for (4) shares Common $1 par 00/00/1946
Merged into White Sewing Machine Corp. 10/01/1956
Each share Common $1 par exchanged for (0.3) share $3 Conv. Preferred $50 par
White Sewing Machine Corp. name changed to White Consolidated Industries, Inc. 05/15/1964
(See White Consolidated Industries, Inc.)

APEX ELECTRS INC (NJ)
90% privately held as of 09/20/1991
Public interest eliminated

APEX ENERGY CORP (BC)
Recapitalized as Nu-Apex Energy Corp. 03/03/1995
Each share Common no par

exchanged for (0.25) share Common no par
Nu-Apex Energy Corp. recapitalized as Digital Ventures Inc. 01/04/2000 which recapitalized as Castleworth Ventures Inc. 01/04/2002 which name changed to Pan-Nevada Gold Corp. 01/20/2006 which merged into Midway Gold Corp. 04/13/2007
(See Midway Gold Corp.)

APEX ENERGY INC (UT)
Proclaimed dissolved for failure to pay taxes 12/31/1983

APEX INC (WA)
Merged into Avocent Corp. 07/01/2000
Each share Common no par exchanged for (1.0905) shares Common $0.001 par
(See Avocent Corp.)

APEX LD CORP (AB)
Name changed to Apex Corp. 09/10/1999
(See Apex Corp.)

APEX MINERALS CORP (NV)
Each share Capital Stock 10¢ par exchanged for (0.15) share Capital Stock $1 par 04/14/1961
Recapitalized as Limotran Corp. 08/01/1972
Each share Capital Stock $1 par exchanged for (0.02) share Common $1 par

APEX MINING & INDUSTRIAL CO. (UT)
Merged into Conix Western, Inc. 12/27/1972
Each share Capital Stock 3¢ par exchanged for (0.05) share Capital Stock 50¢ par
(See Conix Western, Inc.)

APEX MTG CAP INC (MD)
Merged into American Home Mortgage Investment Corp. 12/03/2003
Each share Common 1¢ par exchanged for (0.25762) share Common 1¢ par
(See American Home Mortgage Investment Corp.)

APEX MUN FD INC (MD)
Name changed to BlackRock Apex Municipal Fund, Inc. 10/02/2006
BlackRock Apex Municipal Fund, Inc. merged into BlackRock MuniAssets Fund, Inc. 02/25/2011

APEX OIL CORP.
Assets sold to Lion Oil Refining Co. 00/00/1940
Details not available

APEX OILS & MINES LTD.
Acquired by Apex Consolidated Resources Ltd. 00/00/1946
Each share Capital Stock $1 par exchanged for (0.4) share Capital Stock no par
Apex Consolidated Resources Ltd. recapitalized as Abacus Mines Ltd. 06/01/1959 which name changed to Abacus Mines & Realty Ltd. 00/00/1962 which recapitalized as Abacon Developments Ltd. 03/21/1963
(See Abacon Developments Ltd.)

APEX PC SOLUTIONS INC (WA)
Common no par split (3) for (2) by issuance of (0.5) additional share payable 03/03/1999 to holders of record 02/10/1999
Name changed to Apex Inc. 07/01/1999
Apex Inc. merged into Avocent Corp. 07/01/2000
(See Avocent Corp.)

APEX PHARMACEUTICALS INC (CO)
Recapitalized as Biotech Industries Inc. 09/18/2000
Each share Common no par exchanged for (0.004) share Common no par
Biotech Industries Inc. recapitalized as ValuShip Ltd. (CO) 06/01/2001 which reincorporated in Bahamas 01/04/2002 which reorganized in Delaware as Vorsatech Ventures Inc. 03/03/2004 which name changed to Synutra International, Inc. 09/12/2005
(See Synutra International, Inc.)

APEX RESORTS CORP (BC)
Recapitalized as A.M.R. Corporate Group Ltd. 11/12/1996
Each share Common no par exchanged for (0.1) share Common no par
A.M.R. Corporate Group Ltd. recapitalized as Consolidated A.M.R. Corporate Ltd. 12/03/1998 which recapitalized as Consolidated A.M.R. Development Corp. 10/17/2000 which recapitalized as West Hawk Development Corp. 01/09/2002

APEX RES GROUP INC (UT)
SEC revoked common stock registration 11/03/2011

APEX SILVER MINES LTD (CAYMAN ISLANDS)
Plan of reorganization under Chapter 11 Federal Bankruptcy Code effective 03/24/2009
No stockholders' equity

APEX SMELTING CO. (IL)
Each share Common no par exchanged for (2) shares Common $10 par 00/00/1945
Stock Dividend - 100% 08/15/1950
Merged into American Metal Climax, Inc. 08/31/1962
Each share Common $10 par exchanged for (0.45) share 4.25% Conv. Preferred $100 par
(See American Metal Climax, Inc.)

APEX URANIUM, INC. (CO)
Charter revoked for failure to file reports and pay fees 09/23/1957

APEX URANIUM, INC. (NV)
Name changed to Apex Minerals Corp. 08/23/1956
Apex Minerals Corp. recapitalized as Limotran Corp. 08/01/1972

APEX WEALTH ENTERPRISES LTD (BRITISH VIRGIN ISLANDS)
Name changed to China Security & Surveillance Technology, Inc. (British Virgin Islands) 02/07/2006
China Security & Surveillance Technology, Inc. (British Virgin Islands) reincorporated in Delaware 11/24/2006
(See China Security & Surveillance Technology, Inc. (DE))

APEXCO INC (DE)
Stock Dividend - 10% 07/15/1976
Merged into Natomas Co. 01/03/1977
Each share Common $1 par exchanged for $31.50 cash

APEXTALK HLDGS INC (DE)
Each share old Common $0.001 par exchanged for (0.05) share new Common $0.001 par 11/12/2009
Company deregistered common stock registraton and is no longer public as of 09/30/2011

APEXX INVESTING GROUP (CA)
Merged into Apexx Investing Group II Inc. 03/31/1985
Each share Common 1¢ par exchanged for $0.31 cash

APF ELECTRS INC (NY)
Common 1¢ par split (2) for (1) by issuance of (1) additional share 07/15/1976
Out of business 00/00/1983
No stockholders' equity

APF ENERGY TR (AB)
Merged into StarPoint Energy Trust 06/21/2005
Each share exchanged for (0.63) Trust Unit no par and (0.16666666) share Rockyview Energy Inc. Common no par
(See each company's listing)

APHTON CORP (DE)
Reincorporated 01/29/1998
State of incorporation changed from (CA) to (DE) and Common no par changed to $0.001 par 01/29/1998
Plan of reorganization under Chapter 11 Federal Bankruptcy Code effective 04/09/2007
Stockholders' equity unlikely

API DENTAL INC (NV)
Charter revoked 10/31/2011

API ELECTRONICS GROUP CORP (DE)
Merged into API Nanotronics Corp. 11/07/2006
Each share Common no par exchanged for (10) shares Common $0.001 par
API Nanotronics Corp. name changed to API Technologies Corp. 10/27/2009
(See API Technologies Corp.)

API ELECTRONICS GROUP INC (ON)
Reorganized under the laws of Delaware as API Electronics Group Corp. 09/15/2004
Each share Common no par exchanged for (0.1) share Common no par
API Electronics Group Corp. merged into API Nanotronics Corp. 11/07/2006 which name changed to API Technologies Corp. 10/27/2009
(See API Technologies Corp.)

API ENTERPRISES INC (NY)
Recapitalized as Ceco Environmental Corp. (NY) 09/28/1992
Each share Common 1¢ par exchanged for (0.2) share Common 1¢ par
Ceco Environmental Corp. (NY) reincorporated in Delaware 01/11/2002

API INSTRS CO (OH)
Merged into LFE Corp. 04/03/1970
Each share Common $1 par exchanged for (0.3) share 50¢ Conv. Preferred Ser. A no par and (1) share Common $1 par
(See LFE Corp.)

API NANOTRONICS CORP (DE)
Old Common $0.001 par split (5) for (1) by issuance of (4) additional shares payable 11/19/2007 to holders of record 11/12/2007
Ex date - 11/20/2007
Each share old Common $0.001 par exchanged for (0.06666666) share new Common $0.001 par 09/22/2008
Name changed to API Technologies Corp. 10/27/2009
(See API Technologies Corp.)

API TECHNOLOGIES CORP. (DE)
Each share old Common $0.001 par exchanged for (0.25) share new Common $0.001 par 12/29/2010
Acquired by RFI Holding Co. 04/22/2016
Each share new Common $0.001 par exchanged for $2 cash

API TR (MA)
Merged into Todal, Inc. 03/18/1983
Each Share of Bene. Int. $1 par exchanged for $3 cash

APIC PETE CORP (CANADA)
Merged into Longreach Oil & Gas Ltd. 12/20/2012
Each share Common no par exchanged for (0.1857148) share Common no par
Note: Unexchanged certificates will be cancelled and become without value 12/20/2018
Longreach Oil & Gas Ltd. name changed to PetroMaroc Corp. PLC 07/14/2014

APIC PETE CORP (DE)
Reincorporated under the laws of Canada 06/08/2012
APIC Petroleum Corp. (Canada) merged into Longreach Oil & Gas Ltd. 12/20/2012 which name changed to PetroMaroc Corp. PLC 07/14/2014

APIGEE CORP (DE)
Acquired by Alphabet Inc. 11/10/2016
Each share Common $0.001 par exchanged for $17.40 cash

APIVA COM WEB CORP (BC)
Name changed to Apiva Ventures Ltd. 12/18/2001
Apiva Ventures Ltd. recapitalized as Mark One Global Industries, Inc. 08/13/2008
(See Mark One Global Industries, Inc.)

APIVA VENTURES LTD (BC)
Recapitalized as Mark One Global Industries, Inc. 08/13/2008
Each share Common no par exchanged for (0.001) share Common no par
(See Mark One Global Industries, Inc.)

APIVIO SYS INC (BC)
Acquired by Nuri Telecom Co. Ltd. 08/15/2017
Each share Common no par exchanged for $0.45 cash

APL CORP (NY)
Class B Conv. Preferred Ser. B $1 par called for redemption 04/01/1975
Common 10¢ par split (2) for (1) by issuance of (1) additional share 07/18/1975
$1.06 Class B Conv. Preferred Ser. C $1 par called for redemption 04/26/1976
Plan of reorganization under Chapter 11 Federal Bankruptcy proceedings confirmed 06/08/1995
No stockholders' equity

APL LTD (DE)
Merged into Neptune Orient Lines Ltd. 11/12/1997
Each share Common 1¢ par exchanged for $33.50 cash

APLOX CORP (NV)
Name changed to Mirador Inc. 07/25/2001
Mirador Inc. recapitalized as VWAY International 07/05/2004 which name changed to WorldWide Cannery & Distribution, Inc. 02/08/2006 which name changed to Global Diamond Exchange Inc. 09/22/2006

APM LTD (AUSTRALIA)
Recapitalized as Amcor Ltd. 01/22/1987
Each ADR for Ordinary exchanged for (1) ADR for Ordinary

APN NEWS & MEDIA LTD (AUSTRALIA)
ADR agreement terminated 06/16/2017
No ADR's remain outstanding

APO HEALTH INC (NV)
Common $0.0002 par split (10) for (1) by issuance of (9) additional shares payable 05/12/2006 to holders of record 05/10/2006
Under plan of merger name changed to Paivis, Corp. 05/19/2006
(See Paivis, Corp.)

APOG CORP.
Dissolved 00/00/1946
Details not available

APOGEE INC (DE)
Name changed to Integra, Inc. 07/17/1998
(See Integra, Inc.)

APOGEE MINERALS LTD (ON)
Reincorporated 01/21/2005
Place of incorporation changed from (BC) to (ON) 01/21/2005
Name changed to Apogee Silver Ltd. 03/28/2011
Apogee Silver Ltd. name changed to Apogee Opportunities Inc. 09/16/2016

APOGEE ROBOTICS INC (DE)
Reorganized 01/08/2008
Each share old Common no par exchanged for (0.1) share new Common no par 10/31/1986
Reorganized from (CO) to under the laws of Delaware 01/08/2008
Each share new Common no par exchanged for (0.02) share Common $0.001 par
Recapitalized as China Swine Genetics, Inc. 10/27/2009
Each share Common $0.001 par exchanged for (0.04166666) share Common $0.001 par
China Swine Genetics, Inc. name changed to Sen Yu International Holdings, Inc. 08/25/2010
(See Sen Yu International Holdings, Inc.)

APOGEE SILVER LTD (ON)
Each share old Common no par exchanged for (0.01538461) share new Common no par 06/12/2015
Name changed to Apogee Opportunities Inc. 09/16/2016

APOGEE TECHNOLOGY INC (DE)
Common 1¢ par split (2) for (1) by issuance of (1) additional share payable 12/11/2003 to holders of record 11/17/2003 Ex date - 12/12/2003
SEC revoked common stock registration 08/07/2012

APOGENT TECHNOLOGIES INC (WI)
Merged into Fisher Scientific International Inc. 08/02/2004
Each share Common 1¢ par exchanged for (0.56) share Common 1¢ par
Fisher Scientific International Inc. merged into Thermo Fisher Scientific Inc. 11/09/2006

APOKA CAP CORP (BC)
Name changed to Mala Noche Resources Corp. 10/31/2008
Mala Noche Resources Corp. recapitalized as Primero Mining Corp. 08/06/2010 which merged into First Majestic Silver Corp. 05/11/2018

APOLLO ACQUISITIONS FLA II INC (FL)
Recapitalized as Prism Group Inc. 03/23/1992
Each share Common $0.0001 par exchanged for (0.01) share Common 1¢ par
(See Prism Group Inc.)

APOLLO ACQUISITIONS INC (FL)
Name changed to Americom International Corp. 04/28/1989
Americom International Corp. name changed to Americom Business Centers Inc. 11/08/1991
(See Americom Business Centers Inc.)

APOLLO CAP GROUP INC (FL)
SEC revoked common stock registration 09/18/2013

APOLLO COML REAL ESTATE FIN INC (MD)
8.625% Perpetual Preferred Ser. A 1¢ par called for redemption at $25 plus $0.1079 accrued dividends on 08/02/2017
(Additional Information in Active)

APOLLO COMPUTER INC (DE)
Common 2¢ par split (3) for (2) by issuance of (0.5) additional share 02/29/1984
Merged into Hewlett-Packard Co. (CA) 05/18/1989
Each share Common 2¢ par exchanged for $13.125 cash

APOLLO DEV INC (YT)
Reincorporated 09/27/1996
Place of incorporation changed from (BC) to (YT) 09/27/1996
Recapitalized as Sedna Geotech Inc. 01/10/1997
Each share Common no par exchanged for (0.5) share Common no par
(See Sedna Geotech Inc.)

APOLLO DOCUMENTATION SERVICES, INC. (NY)
Adjudicated bankrupt 03/29/1972
No stockholders' equity

APOLLO DRILLING INC (DE)
Common $0.001 par split (7) for (1) by issuance of (6) additional shares payable 10/18/2006 to holders of record 10/18/2006
Recapitalized as Southwest Resources, Inc. (DE) 10/05/2009
Each share Common $0.001 par exchanged for (0.0004) share Common $0.001 par
Southwest Resources, Inc. (DE) reorganized in Nevada as Puration, Inc. 02/29/2012

APOLLO ED GROUP INC (AZ)
Name changed 11/15/2013
Class A Common no par split (4) for (3) by issuance of (0.33333333) additional share 04/29/1995
Class A Common no par split (3) for (2) by issuance of (0.5) additional share 09/22/1995
Class A Common no par split (3) for (2) by issuance of (0.5) additional share payable 02/29/1996 to holders of record 02/16/1996
Class A Common no par split (3) for (2) by issuance of (0.5) additional share payable 05/31/1996 to holders of record 05/21/1996
Class A Common no par split (3) for (2) by issuance of (0.5) additional share payable 04/27/1998 to holders of record 04/13/1998
Class A Common no par split (3) for (2) by issuance of (0.5) additional share payable 02/05/2001 to holders of record 01/22/2001
University of Phoenix Online Common no par split (3) for (2) by issuance of (0.5) additional share payable 07/20/2001 to holders of record 07/10/2001 Ex date - 07/23/2001
Class A Common no par split (3) for (2) by issuance of (0.5) additional share payable 04/25/2002 to holders of record 04/15/2002 Ex date - 04/26/2002
University of Phoenix Online Common no par split (4) for (3) by issuance of (0.33333333) additional share payable 04/25/2002 to holders of record 04/15/2002 Ex date - 04/26/2002
Each share University of Phoenix Online Common no par exchanged for (1.11527) shares Class A Common no par 08/27/2004
Name changed from Apollo Group, Inc. to Apollo Education Group, Inc. 11/15/2013
Acquired by Apollo Global Management, LLC 02/01/2017
Each share Class A Common no par exchanged for $10 cash

APOLLO ENERGY INC (UT)
Involuntarily dissolved 12/31/1984

APOLLO ENTMT GROUP INC (FL)
Name changed to Apollo Capital Group, Inc. 03/30/2010

(See Apollo Capital Group, Inc.)

APOLLO EYE GROUP INC (DE)
Charter cancelled and declared inoperative and void for non-payment of taxes 03/01/1999

APOLLO FD INC (DE)
Name changed to Founders Special Fund, Inc. 10/20/1970
Founders Special Fund, Inc. reorganized as Founders Funds, Inc. 08/31/1987 which name changed to Dreyfus Founders Funds, Inc. 12/31/1999 which name changed to Dreyfus Discovery Fund 12/01/2008

APOLLO GAS INCOME FD (ON)
Each Installment Receipt plus final payment of $4 cash received (1) Unit prior to 05/07/1999
Completely liquidated 02/01/2001
Each Unit received first and final distribution of $1.74 cash

APOLLO GOLD CORP (YT)
Reincorporated 05/28/2003
Place of incorporation changed from (ON) to (YT) 05/28/2003
Recapitalized as Brigus Gold Corp. (YT) 06/25/2010
Each share Common no par exchanged for (0.25) share Common no par
Brigus Gold Corp. (YT) reincorporated in Canada 06/09/2011
(See Brigus Gold Corp.)

APOLLO GROUP LTD (AUSTRALIA)
Name changed to Global Petroleum Ltd. 09/13/2002
(See Global Petroleum Ltd.)

APOLLO HLDGS INC (DE)
Name changed to GTREX, Inc. 02/27/2004
GTREX, Inc. name changed to GTREX Capital, Inc. 03/07/2005 which recapitalized as Green Globe International, Inc. 03/10/2008

APOLLO INDS INC (ME)
Common $5 par changed to $1 par 07/01/1969
6% Preferred $100 par called for redemption 05/23/1984
Company went private 00/00/1987
Details not available

APOLLO INDS INC (UT)
Proclaimed dissolved for failure to file annual report 01/01/1994

APOLLO INTL DEL INC (DE)
SEC revoked common stock registration 07/22/2010

APOLLO LASERS INC (CA)
Merged into Allied Corp. 08/28/1981
Each share Common 10¢ par exchanged for (0.167) share Common $1 par
Allied Corp. merged into Allied-Signal Inc. 09/19/1985 which name changed to AlliedSignal Inc. 04/26/1993 which name changed to Honeywell International Inc. 12/01/1999

APOLLO MAGNETO CORP.
Dissolved 00/00/1948
Details not available

APOLLO MINERALS LTD. (BC)
Struck off register and declared dissolved for failure to file returns 12/06/1976

APOLLO OIL URANIUM CO. (CO)
Charter revoked for failure to file reports and pay fees 09/23/1957

APOLLO PORCUPINE MINES LTD. (ON)
Charter cancelled and proclaimed dissolved for failure to pay taxes and file returns 04/01/1965

APOLLO PRODUCTS CORP. (MN)
Completely liquidated 10/15/1975
No stockholders' equity

APOLLO RESIDENTIAL MTG INC (MD)
Under plan of merger each share 8% Perpetual Preferred Ser. A 1¢ par automatically became (1) Apollo Commercial Real Estate Finance, Inc. 8% Perpetual Preferred Ser. C 1¢ par 08/31/2016
Merged into Apollo Commercial Real Estate Finance, Inc. 08/31/2016
Each share Common 1¢ par exchanged for (0.417571) share Common 1¢ par and $6.86 cash

APOLLO RES INC (DE)
Recapitalized as FirstSouth Commercial Corp. 06/04/1990
Each share Common 1¢ par exchanged for (0.5) share Common 2¢ par
FirstSouth Commercial Corp. recapitalized as Lonestar Hospitality Corp. 07/20/1994 which recapitalized as Citadel Computer Systems Inc. 05/01/1996 which name changed to Citadel Technology Inc. 02/27/1998 which name changed to CT Holdings, Inc. 11/30/1999 which recapitalized as CT Holdings Enterprises, Inc. 02/28/2007 which recapitalized as Xcorporeal, Inc. 10/15/2007

APOLLO RES INTL INC (UT)
SEC revoked common stock registration 06/16/2011

APOLLO SVGS & LN ASSN (IL)
Placed in receivership 04/30/1968
No stockholders' equity

APOLLO SVGS & LOAN CO (OH)
Merged into Mid Am, Inc. 03/19/1993
Each share Common $1 par exchanged for (1.98) shares Common no par
Mid Am, Inc. merged into Sky Financial Group, Inc. 10/02/1998 which merged into Huntington Bancshares Inc. 07/02/2007

APOLLO STEEL CO.
Liquidated 00/00/1947
Details not available

APOLO ACQUISITION CORP (ON)
Recapitalized as CryptoGlobal Corp. 01/29/2018
Each share Common no par exchanged for (0.253936) share Common no par

APOLO GOLD & ENERGY INC (NV)
Name changed 05/31/2005
Name changed from Apolo Gold Inc. to Apolo Gold & Energy Inc. 05/31/2005
Each share old Common $0.001 par exchanged for (0.05) share new Common $0.001 par 11/29/2010
Name changed to Wincash Apolo Gold & Energy Inc. 07/07/2015
Wincash Apolo Gold & Energy Inc. name changed to Banny Cosmic International Holdings, Inc. 07/27/2018

APOQUINDO MINERALS INC (BC)
Name changed to AQM Copper Inc. 06/11/2010
(See AQM Copper Inc.)

APOTEC INVT CORP (MN)
Placed in receivership 04/30/1970
No stockholders' equity

APP APPLIED POLYMER PRODS INC (CANADA)
Liquidation completed 05/00/1992
No stockholders' equity

APP PHARMACEUTICALS INC (DE)
Merged into Fresenius SE 09/10/2008
Each share Common $0.001 par exchanged for (1) Fresenius Kabi Pharmaceuticals Holding, Inc. Contingent Value Right and and $23 cash

APPALACHES RES INC (QC)
Discharged from receivership 09/22/2016
No stockholders' equity

APPALACHIAN BANCSHARES INC (GA)
Common $5 par split (2) for (1) by issuance of (1) additional share payable 05/15/1998 to holders of record 05/01/1998
Common $5 par changed to 1¢ par and (1) additional share issued payable 05/15/2000 to holders of record 04/12/2000
Stock Dividend - 10% payable 07/01/2003 to holders of record 05/27/2003 Ex date - 05/22/2003
Principal asset placed in receivership 12/17/2010
Stockholders' equity unlikely

APPALACHIAN COAL & LUMBER CO. (WV)
Proclaimed dissolved for non-payment of taxes 02/12/1945

APPALACHIAN COMPUTER SVCS INC (KY)
Merged into First Financial Management Corp. 12/13/1988
Each share Common $1 par exchanged for (0.812299) share Common 10¢ par and $19.40 cash
First Financial Management Corp. merged into First Data Corp. (Old) 10/27/1995
(See First Data Corp. (Old))

APPALACHIAN CONDUIT CO. (VA)
Charter revoked for non-payment of fees 08/22/1913

APPALACHIAN CORP.
Liquidated 00/00/1937
Details not available

APPALACHIAN ELECTRIC POWER CO. (VA)
$6 Preferred called for redemption 01/20/1941
$7 Preferred called for redemption 01/20/1941
Name changed to Appalachian Power Co. (New) 04/27/1958
(See Appalachian Power Co. (New))

APPALACHIAN GAS CORP. (DE)
Reorganized as Commonwealth Gas Corp. 00/00/1933
Details not available

APPALACHIAN LIFE INS CO (WV)
Capital Stock $5 par changed to $4.30 par 04/04/1952
Capital Stock $4.30 par changed to $4.10 par 04/05/1956
Capital Stock $4.10 par changed to $1.23 par 05/06/1958
Capital Stock $1.23 par changed to $1 par 05/19/1961
Capital Stock $1 par changed to $0.33333333 par 07/01/1968
Capital Stock $0.33333333 par changed to 35¢ par 04/15/1970
Capital Stock 35¢ par changed to 56¢ par 06/13/1982
Each share Capital Stock 56¢ par exchanged for (0.5) share Capital Stock $1.12 par 04/19/1988
Each (118,700) shares old Capital Stock $1.12 par exchanged for (1) share new Capital Stock $1.12 par 10/26/2001
Note: In effect holders received $6.50 cash per share and public interest was eliminated

APPALACHIAN NATL CORP (TN)
Merged into Mutuelles Unies of America 01/22/1982
Each share Common $1 par exchanged for $2.70 cash

APPALACHIAN NATL LIFE INS CO (TN)
Reorganized as Anco Corp. 06/08/1970
Each share Common $1 par exchanged for (1) share Common $1 par
Anco Corp. name changed to Appalachian National Corp. 05/02/1972
(See Appalachian National Corp.)

APPALACHIAN OIL & GAS CO., INC. (PA)
Out of business 00/00/1963
No stockholders' equity

APPALACHIAN OIL & GAS INC (UT)
Each share old Common $0.001 par exchanged for (0.1) share new Common 1¢ par 11/10/1993
SEC revoked common stock registration 11/29/2007

APPALACHIAN POWER CO. OLD (VA)
Merged into Appalachian Electric Power Co. 00/00/1929
Details not available

APPALACHIAN PWR CO NEW (VA)
$3.75 Preferred no par called for redemption 11/01/1987
$3.80 Preferred no par called for redemption 11/01/1987
$4.18 Preferred no par called for redemption 12/01/1987
$2.65 Preferred no par called for redemption 05/01/1993
9% Preferred no par called for redemption 11/01/1993
8.12% Preferred $100 par called for redemption 11/21/1993
8.52% Preferred $100 par called for redemption 11/21/1993
7.4% Preferred $100 par called for redemption 11/01/1996
4.5% Sinking Fund Preferred $100 par called for redemption 11/30/1996
7.8% Preferred $100 par called for redemption 04/01/1997
6.85% Preferred $100 par called for redemption at $100 on 08/01/2000
5.9% Preferred called for redemption at $100 on 11/01/2004
5.92% Preferred called for redemption at $100 on 11/01/2004
4.5% Preferred no par called for redemption at $110 plus $0.375 accrued dividends on 12/01/2011

APPALACHIAN RES CO (TX)
Merged into Ruhrkohle-Stinnes Corp. 12/09/1974
Each share Common 50¢ par exchanged for $10 cash

APPALACHIAN RES CORP (DE)
Name changed to Arco Industries Inc. 07/02/1969
(See Arco Industries Inc.)

APPALACHIAN SAVINGS & LOAN ASSOCIATION, INC. (NC)
Merged into Scottish Savings & Loan Association, Inc. (New) 04/01/1981
Each share Common $5 par exchanged for (1.1656) shares Common $1 par
Scottish Savings & Loan Association, Inc. (New) merged into Southeastern Savings & Loan Co. 01/17/1984 which name changed to Southeastern Savings Bank, Inc. 07/13/1988
(See Southeastern Savings Bank, Inc.)

APPAREL AMER INC (DE)
Plan of reorganization under Chapter 11 Federal Bankruptcy proceedings confirmed 05/27/1999
No stockholders' equity

APPAREL RETAILERS INC (DE)
Through purchase offer 100% acquired by Volume Shoe Co. as of 11/01/1972
Public interest eliminated

APPAREL TECHNOLOGIES INC (DE)
Filed a petition under Chapter 7 Federal Bankruptcy Code 10/30/1998
Stockholders' equity unlikely

APPAREO SOFTWARE INC NEW (BC)
Merged 03/14/2001
Merged from Appareo Software Inc. (Old) to Appareo Software Inc. (New) 03/14/2001
Each share Common no par exchanged for (1) share Common no par
Name changed to Cellstop Systems Inc. 09/29/2004

APPCOIN INNOVATIONS INC (NV)
Name changed to ICOX Innovations Inc. 02/14/2018

APPELL OIL & GAS CORP. (DE)
Recapitalized as Appell Petroleum Corp. 09/17/1957
Each share Common 10¢ par exchanged for (0.16666666) share Common $1 par
(See Appell Petroleum Corp.)

APPELL PETE CORP (DE)
Charter cancelled and declared inoperative and void for non-payment of taxes 04/15/1968

APPIAN ENERGY CORP (BC)
Merged into Tiber Energy Corp. 02/19/1982
Each share Common no par exchanged for (0.125) share Common no par
(See Tiber Energy Corp.)

APPIAN RES LTD (BC)
Recapitalized as Sultan Minerals Inc. 05/04/1992
Each share Common no par exchanged for (0.25) share Common no par
Sultan Minerals Inc. recapitalized as Apex Resources Inc. 07/18/2016

APPIAN TECHNOLOGY INC (DE)
Reincorporated 10/29/1986
State of incorporation changed from (CA) to (DE) 10/29/1986
Charter cancelled and declared inoperative and void for non-payment of taxes 05/13/1994

APPIANT TECHNOLOGIES INC (DE)
Ceased operations 03/27/2003
Stockholders' equity unlikely

APPLAUSE CORP. (AB)
Company announced it had received a Notice of Intention to Enforce Security on loans by its lender and all officers had resigned as of 02/01/2002
Stockholders' equity unlikely

APPLAUSE NETWORKS INC (DE)
Recapitalized as Internet Broadcast Networks Inc. 06/10/1999
Each share Common 2¢ par exchanged for (1) share Common 2¢ par
Internet Broadcast Networks Inc. name changed to Mediacom Entertainment Inc. 08/10/2001
(See Mediacom Entertainment Inc.)

APPLE BANCORP INC (DE)
Preferred Stock Purchase Rights declared for Common stockholders of record 12/14/1989 were redeemed at $0.01 per right 10/09/1990 for holders of record 10/01/1990
Acquired by a private investor 05/01/1991
Each share Common $1 par exchanged for $38 cash

APPLE BK FOR SVGS (NEW YORK, NY)
Reorganized under the laws of Delaware as Apple Bancorp, Inc. 09/29/1989
Each share Common $1 par exchanged for (1) share Common $1 par
(See Apple Bancorp, Inc.)

APPLE CAP INC (BC)
Each share old Common no par exchanged for (0.16666666) share new Common no par 12/02/2015
Name changed to YDreams Global Interactive Technologies Inc. 07/22/2016

APPLE COMPUTER INC (CA)
Common no par split (2) for (1) by issuance of (1) additional share 06/15/1987
Common no par split (2) for (1) by issuance of (1) additional share payable 06/20/2000 to holders of record 05/19/2000
Common no par split (2) for (1) by issuance of (1) additional share payable 02/25/2005 to holders of record 02/18/2005 Ex date - 02/28/2005
Name changed to Apple Inc. 01/09/2007

APPLE CORP (ID)
Reincorporated under the laws of Nevada as Trans Energy Inc. and Common $0.005 par changed to $0.001 par 11/15/1993
(See Trans Energy Inc.)

APPLE HOMES CORP (DE)
Each share Common $0.001 par received distribution of (0.1) share Southern States Lenders Inc. Common $0.001 par payable 04/01/1999 to holders of record 03/01/1999
Name changed to Genfinity Corp. 10/03/2000
(See Genfinity Corp.)

APPLE HOSPITALITY FIVE INC (VA)
Merged into Inland American Real Estate Trust Inc. 10/05/2007
Each Unit exchanged for $14.05 cash

APPLE HOSPITALITY TWO INC (VA)
Merged into Lion ES Hotels, LP 05/23/2007
Each Unit received $11.20 cash

APPLE ORTHODONTIX INC (DE)
Plan of reorganization under Chapter 11 Federal Bankruptcy proceedings confirmed 05/25/2001
No stockholders' equity

APPLE REIT SIX INC (VA)
Merged into BRE Select Hotels Corp. 05/14/2013
Each share Common no par exchanged for (1) share 7% Preferred Ser. A and $9.20 cash

APPLE RESIDENTIAL INCOME TR INC (VA)
Merged into Cornerstone Realty Income Trust, Inc. 07/23/1999
Each share Common exchanged for (0.4) share Conv. Preferred Ser. A no par
(See Cornerstone Realty Income Trust, Inc.)

APPLE SOUTH FING I (DE)
Name changed to Avado Financing I 10/19/1998
(See Avado Financing I)

APPLE SOUTH INC (GA)
Common 1¢ par split (3) for (2) by issuance of (0.5) additional share 11/16/1992
Common 1¢ par split (3) for (2) by issuance of (0.5) additional share 02/09/1993
Common 1¢ par split (3) for (2) by issuance of (0.5) additional share 09/10/1993
Common 1¢ par split (3) for (2) by issuance of (0.5) additional share 06/17/1994
Name changed to Avado Brands Inc. 10/13/1998
(See Avado Brands Inc.)

APPLE SUITES INC (VA)
Merged into Apple Hospitality Two, Inc. 01/31/2003
Each share Common no par exchanged for (1) Unit consisting of

(1) share Preferred Ser. A and (1) share Common
(See Apple Hospitality Two, Inc.)

APPLE VY BK & TR CO (CHESHIRE, CT)
Acquired by New England Bancshares, Inc. 06/08/2009
Each share Common no par exchanged for (1) share Common 1¢ par
New England Bancshares, Inc. merged into United Financial Bancorp, Inc. (MD) 11/19/2012 which merged into United Financial Bancorp, Inc. (CT) 05/01/2014

APPLE VALLEY BUILDING & DEVELOPMENT CO. (CA)
Acquired by Reserve Oil & Gas Co. 04/29/1966
Each share Class A Common $10 par exchanged for (0.256) share 5.5% Conv. Preferred Ser. B $25 par and (5.136) shares Common $1 par
(See Reserve Oil & Gas Co.)

APPLE VENTURES INC (NV)
Recapitalized as Kelcord International Inc. 10/26/1997
Each share Common $0.0001 par exchanged for (0.1) share Common $0.0001 par
(See Kelcord International Inc.)

APPLE WEAR CO (NV)
Name changed to American Blood Protection Systems, Inc. 04/07/1986
American Blood Protection Systems, Inc. name changed to Energex Corp. 03/23/1987

APPLEBAUMS FOOD MKTS INC (MN)
Stock Dividend - 50% 04/25/1968
Acquired by National Tea Co. 07/27/1979
Each share Common $1 par exchanged for $15.25 cash

APPLEBEES INTL INC (DE)
Common 1¢ par split (2) for (1) by issuance of (1) additional share 06/25/1993
Common 1¢ par split (3) for (2) by issuance of (0.5) additional share 01/28/1994
Common 1¢ par split (3) for (2) by issuance of (0.5) additional share payable 06/12/2001 to holders of record 05/25/2001 Ex date - 06/13/2001
Common 1¢ par split (3) for (2) by issuance of (0.5) additional share payable 06/11/2002 to holders of record 05/24/2002 Ex date - 06/12/2002
Common 1¢ par split (3) for (2) by issuance of (0.5) additional share payable 06/15/2004 to holders of record 05/28/2004 Ex date - 06/16/2004
Merged into IHOP Corp. 11/29/2007
Each share Common 1¢ par exchanged for $25.50 cash

APPLEMAN ART GLASS WORKS (NJ)
Name changed to Electriglas Corp. 00/00/1952
(See Electriglas Corp.)

APPLERA CORP (DE)
Celera Genomics Group Common 1¢ par reclassified as Celera Group Common 1¢ par 12/01/2006
Each share Celera Group Common 1¢ par exchanged for (1) share Celera Corp. Common 1¢ par 07/01/2008
(See Celera Corp.)
Name changed to Applied Biosystems Inc. and Common Applied Biosystems Group 1¢ par reclassified as Common 1¢ par 07/01/2008
Applied Biosystems Inc. merged into Life Technologies Corp. 11/21/2008
(See Life Technologies Corp.)

APPLETON (D.)-CENTURY CO., INC.
Name changed to Appleton-Century-Crofts, Inc. 00/00/1947
(See Appleton-Century-Crofts, Inc.)

APPLETON-CENTURY-CROFTS, INC. (NY)
7% Preferred called for redemption 01/16/1961
Acquired by Meredith Publishing Co. 03/31/1962
Details not available

APPLETON CO.
Acquired by Stevens (J.P.) & Co., Inc. 00/00/1950
Each share Common no par exchanged for (0.75) share Capital Stock $15 par
(See Stevens (J.P.) & Co., Inc.)

APPLETON (D.) CO.
Merged into Appleton (D.)-Century Co. Inc. 00/00/1933
Details not available

APPLETON EXPL INC (BC)
Recapitalized as Cornerstone Metals Inc. 06/01/2012
Each share Common no par exchanged for (0.2) share Common no par
Cornerstone Metals Inc. name changed to First Vanadium Corp. 09/25/2018

APPLETON MANUFACTURING CO.
Out of business 00/00/1950
Details not available

APPLETREE ART PUBLISHERS INC (DE)
Charter forfeited for failure to maintain a registered agent 06/24/1999

APPLETREE INC (DE)
Each share old Common $0.001 par exchanged for (0.2) share new Common $0.001 par 10/28/1994
Chapter 11 bankruptcy proceedings dismissed 12/20/1999
Stockholders' equity unlikely

APPLEWOODS INC (DE)
Old Common $0.0001 par split (2) for (1) by issuance of (1) additional share payable 05/28/1996 to holders of record 05/23/1996
Each share old Common $0.0001 par exchanged for (0.125) share new Common $0.0001 par 02/06/1998
Company's sole asset placed in receivership 05/06/1999
Stockholders' equity unlikely

APPLEWOODS RESTAURANTS INC (NV)
Recapitalized as Securac Corp. 10/21/2004
Each share Common 1¢ par exchanged for (0.06666666) share Common 1¢ par

APPLIANCE PTS PLUS INTL INC (UT)
Name changed to International Equity Resources, Inc. 10/25/1993
International Equity Resources, Inc. name changed to International Protection Technologies, Inc. 07/27/1998 which name changed to HyperSecur Corp. 03/04/1999

APPLIANCE RECYCLING CTRS AMER INC (MN)
Each share old Common no par exchanged for (0.25) share new Common no par 02/21/1997
Reincorporated under the laws of Nevada and new Common no par changed to $0.001 par 03/12/2018

APPLICA INC (FL)
Preferred Stock Purchase Rights declared for Common stockholders of record 03/01/1995 were redeemed at $0.00001 per right 04/01/2003 for holders of record 03/24/2003
Merged into Harbinger Capital Partners Special Situations Fund, L.P. 01/23/2007
Each share Common 10¢ par exchanged for $8.25 cash

APPLICATION ENGR CORP (DE)
Reincorporated 03/13/1980
Stock Dividend - 10% 01/31/1979
State of incorporation changed from (IL) to (DE) 03/13/1980
Name changed to AEC Inc. 08/17/1982
(See AEC Inc.)

APPLICON INC (MA)
Acquired by Schlumberger Ltd. 01/12/1982
Each share Common 5¢ par exchanged for (0.66666666) share Common $1 par

APPLIED ALUM RESH CORP (LA)
Name changed to Toth Aluminum Corp. 08/20/1973
(See Toth Aluminum Corp.)

APPLIED ANALYTICAL INDS INC (DE)
Name changed to aaiPharma Inc. 11/30/2000
(See aaiPharma Inc.)

APPLIED ARTS CORP. (MI)
Common $1 par split (2) for (1) by issuance of (1) additional share 12/06/1963
Stock Dividend - 100% 11/20/1946
Acquired by AGM Industries, Inc. 12/31/1964
Each share Common $1 par exchanged for (1) share Common $1 par
(See AGM Industries, Inc.)

APPLIED BIOMEDICAL SCIENCES INC (DE)
Plan of reorganization under Chapter 11 Federal Bankruptcy proceedings confirmed 10/22/1990
No stockholders' equity

APPLIED BIOMETRICS INC (MN)
Each share Common 1¢ par received distribution of (0.0864827) share Cardia Inc. Common 1¢ par payable 02/11/1999 to holders of record 01/25/1999
Under plan of partial liquidation each share Common 1¢ par received distribution of $0.1285 cash payable 04/18/2006 to holders of record 01/03/2006 Ex date - 05/01/2006
Reincorporated under the laws of Nevada as Jade Mountain Corp. and Common 1¢ par changed to $0.0001 par 06/28/2007

APPLIED BIOSCIENCE INTL INC (DE)
Common 1¢ par split (2) for (1) by issuance of (1) additional share 01/11/1991
Common 1¢ par split (2) for (1) by issuance of (1) additional share 04/30/1992
Merged into Pharmaceutical Product Development, Inc. 09/26/1996
Each share Common 1¢ par exchanged for (0.4054) share Common 10¢ par
(See Pharmaceutical Product Development, Inc.)

APPLIED BIOSENSORS INC (NV)
Reorganized under the laws of Delaware as Ansama Corp. 08/25/1994
Each share Common $0.001 par exchanged for (0.01) share Common 1¢ par
Ansama Corp. name changed to Nutrisystems.com, Inc. 10/04/1999 which name changed to Nutri/System, Inc. 09/25/2000 which name changed to NutriSystem, Inc. 05/13/2003

APPLIED BIOSYSTEMS INC (CA)
Common no par split (2) for (1) by issuance of (1) additional share 03/20/1985
Merged into Perkin-Elmer Corp. 02/18/1993
Each share Common no par exchanged for (0.678) share Common $1 par
Perkin-Elmer Corp. name changed to PE Corp. 05/05/1999 which name changed to Applera Corp. 11/30/2000
(See Applera Corp.)

APPLIED BIOSYSTEMS INC (DE)
Merged into Life Technologies Corp. 11/21/2008
Each share Common 1¢ par exchanged for (0.4543) share Common 1¢ par and $18.149433 cash
(See Life Technologies Corp.)

APPLIED CAP FDG INC (CO)
Common no par split (2) for (1) by issuance of (1) additional share payable 2/22/99 to holders of record 2/22/99
Reincorporated under the laws of Delaware as On2.com, Inc. 6/15/99

APPLIED CARBON TECHNOLOGY INC (ON)
Name changed to Merchant Capital Group Inc. 07/17/2000
(See Merchant Capital Group)

APPLIED CELLULAR TECHNOLOGY INC (MO)
Name changed to Applied Digital Solutions, Inc. 07/01/1999
Applied Digital Solutions, Inc. name changed to Digital Angel Corp. (New) 06/20/2008 which recapitalized as VeriTeQ Corp. 10/22/2013

APPLIED CIRCUIT TECHNOLOGY INC (CA)
Name changed to Towne-Paulsen, Inc. 08/06/1987
(See Towne-Paulsen, Inc.)

APPLIED COATINGS TECHNOLOGY INC (UT)
Each share old Common $0.001 par exchanged for (0.0025) share new Common $0.001 par 06/17/1987
Involuntarily dissolved 07/01/1992

APPLIED COMMUNICATIONS INC (NE)
Merged into USWIS Acquisition Co. 07/24/1986
Each share Common 10¢ par exchanged for $27 cash

APPLIED COMPUTER SCIENCES INC (DE)
Charter cancelled and declared inoperative and void for non-payment of taxes 4/15/73

APPLIED COMPUTER TECHNOLOGY INC (CO)
Recapitalized as Amigula, Inc. 12/03/2003
Each share Common 1¢ par exchanged for (0.00125) share Common 1¢ par
(See Amigula, Inc.)

APPLIED CONCEPTS INC (DE)
Name changed to Citipostal Inc. 07/08/1983
(See Citipostal Inc.)

APPLIED CTL SYS INC (DE)
Charter cancelled and declared inoperative and void for non-payment of taxes 8/14/89

APPLIED DATA COMMUNICATIONS INC (DE)
Charter cancelled and declared inoperative and void for non-payment of taxes 3/1/91

APPLIED DATA INC (DE)
Name changed 09/01/1982
Name changed from Applied Data Processing, Inc. to Applied Data, Inc. 09/01/1982
Company dissolved 04/19/1996

Each share Common 10¢ par exchanged for $0.10 cash

APPLIED DATA RESH INC (NJ)
Common 25¢ par reclassified as Class B Common 25¢ par 5/19/81
Class B Common 25¢ par split (2) for (1) by issuance of (1) additional share 4/4/83
Class B Common 25¢ par reclassified as Common 25¢ par 5/17/85
Stock Dividend - 50% 3/28/68
Merged into American Information Technologies Corp. 1/15/86
Each share Common 25¢ par exchanged for $32 cash

APPLIED DEV HLDGS LTD (HONG KONG)
ADR agreement terminated 10/02/2017
Each Sponsored ADR for Common exchanged for $0.737569 cash

APPLIED DEVICES CORP (NY)
Each share Common 50¢ par exchanged for (0.25) share Common 1¢ par 8/30/74
Dissolved by proclamation 9/29/93

APPLIED DIGITAL ACCESS INC (CA)
Merged into Dynatech Corp. 11/09/1999
Each share Common no par exchanged for $5.37 cash

APPLIED DIGITAL DATA SYS INC (DE)
Merged into NCR Corp. 11/07/1980
Each share $1 Conv. Preferred $1 par exchanged for $27 cash
Each share Common 1¢ par exchanged for $12 cash

APPLIED DIGITAL SOLUTIONS INC (DE)
Reincorporated 04/20/2007
Each share Common $0.001 par exchanged for (0.1) share Common 1¢ par 04/05/2004
State of incorporation changed from (MO) to (DE) 04/20/2007
Name changed to Digital Angel Corp. (New) 06/20/2008
Digital Angel Corp. (New) recapitalized as VeriTeQ Corp. 10/22/2013

APPLIED DNA SCIENCES INC (NV)
Common $0.0001 par changed to 50¢ par 12/03/2003
Common 50¢ par changed to $0.001 par 02/14/2005
Reincorporated under the laws of Delaware 12/17/2008

APPLIED DNA SYS INC (DE)
Recapitalized as Nu-Tech Bio-Med Inc. 11/16/1994
Each share Common 1¢ par exchanged for (0.02857142) share Common 1¢ par
Nu-Tech Bio-Med Inc. recapitalized as United Diagnostic, Inc. 12/23/1998 which name changed to SPO Medical Inc. 04/21/2005 which recapitalized as SPO Global Inc. 10/07/2013

APPLIED DYNAMICS INC (MI)
Acquired by Reliance Electric Co. 12/30/1969
Each share Common $1 par exchanged for (0.667) share Common $2.50 par
(See Reliance Electric Co.)

APPLIED EARTH TECHNOLOGIES INC (CA)
Name changed to Diatect International Corp. 06/05/1998
(See Diatect International Corp.)

APPLIED ELECTRONICS CORP. OF N.J. (NJ)
Name changed to Taft Electrosystems, Inc. 09/16/1968
(See Taft Electrosystems, Inc.)

APPLIED ENERGY INC (BC)
Struck from the register and dissolved 07/21/1995

APPLIED EQUITIES INC (DE)
Each share old Common $0.001 par exchanged for (0.2) share new Common $0.001 par 09/09/1991
Name changed to Soma Technologies International Inc. 05/25/1993

APPLIED EXTRUSION TECHNOLOGIES INC (DE)
Plan of reorganization under Chapter 11 Federal Bankruptcy Code effective 03/08/2005
Each share Common 1¢ par received $0.156 cash
Note: Certificates were not required to be surrendered and are without value

APPLIED FILMS CORP (CO)
Merged into Applied Materials, Inc. 07/07/2006
Each share Common no par exchanged for $28.50 cash

APPLIED FLUIDICS INC (DE)
Name changed to AFI Corp. 01/22/1980
(See AFI Corp.)

APPLIED GAMING SOLUTIONS CDA INC (AB)
Recapitalized as Pacific Lottery Corp. 11/14/2002
Each share Common no par exchanged for (0.1) share Common no par

APPLIED GENETIC VENTURES INC (NV)
Each share old Common $0.001 par exchanged for (10) shares new Common $0.001 par 10/10/1985
Name changed to American General Ventures, Inc. 02/18/1993
American General Ventures, Inc. recapitalized as Nucleus, Inc. (NV) 12/09/1998 which reorganized in Delaware as eNucleus, Inc. 07/14/2000 which recapitalized as EC Development, Inc. 08/10/2010
(See EC Development, Inc.)

APPLIED GEODATA SYS INC (MA)
Name changed to Techven Association, Inc. 06/15/1970
Techven Association, Inc. name changed to Computer Devices, Inc. (MA) 05/25/1979 which reorganized in Maryland 06/30/1986
(See Computer Devices, Inc. (MD))

APPLIED GEOMETRICS INC (FL)
Name changed to #1 Sports Fan, Inc. 05/22/1989
(See #1 Sports Fan, Inc.)

APPLIED GRAPHICS TECHNOLOGIES INC (DE)
Each share old Common 1¢ par exchanged for (0.4) share new Common 1¢ par 12/05/2000
Merged into KAGT Holdings, Inc. 10/10/2003
Each share new Common 1¢ par exchanged for $0.85 cash

APPLIED HEALTH SVCS INC (DE)
Common $0.001 par split (2) for (1) by issuance of (1) additional share 07/20/1972
Under plan of merger each share Common $0.001 par automatically became (1) share Dento-Med Industries, Inc. Common 1¢ par 11/14/1980
Dento-Med Industries, Inc. name changed to Hydron Technologies Inc. 07/29/1993

APPLIED HIGH TECHNOLOGY AHT CORP (AB)
Recapitalized as AHT Corp. (AB) 03/12/1999
Each share old Common no par exchanged for (0.1) share Special Preferred no par and (0.1) share new Common no par
AHT Corp. (AB) reincorporated in Canada as Simsmart Inc. 07/03/2001
(See Simsmart Inc.)

APPLIED IMAGING CORP (DE)
Each share old Common $0.001 par exchanged for (0.25) share new Common $0.001 par 05/20/2005
Merged into Genetix Group PLC 11/24/2006
Each share new Common $0.001 par exchanged for $4.20 cash

APPLIED IMMUNE SCIENCES INC (DE)
Merged into Rhone Poulenc-Rorer Inc. 11/27/1995
Each share Common 1¢ par exchanged for $11.75 cash

APPLIED INDS INC (NY)
93.5% owned as of 04/25/1979
Public interest eliminated

APPLIED INDS INC (UT)
Recapitalized as Asbestec Industries, Inc. (UT) 01/13/1986
Each share Common no par exchanged for (0.2) share Common no par
Asbestec Industries, Inc. (UT) reorganized in Delaware as PDG Environmental, Inc. 12/17/1990

APPLIED INNOVATION INC (DE)
Common 1¢ par split (3) for (2) by issuance of (0.5) additional share 02/26/1993
Common 1¢ par split (2) for (1) by issuance of (1) additional share 03/02/1994
Common 1¢ par split (2) for (1) by issuance of (1) additional share 08/31/1995
Merged into KEG Holdings, Inc. 05/10/2007
Each share Common 1¢ par exchanged for $3.46 cash

APPLIED INTELLIGENCE GROUP INC (OK)
Name changed to viaLink Co. (OK) 10/16/1998
viaLink Co. (OK) reincorporated in Delaware 11/16/1999 which recapitalized as Prescient Applied Intelligence, Inc. 01/03/2005
(See Prescient Applied Intelligence, Inc.)

APPLIED INTELLIGENT SYS INC
Merged into Electro Scientific Industries, Inc. 12/01/1997
Each share Common exchanged for (0.3046) share Common no par

APPLIED INTL HLDGS LTD (HONG KONG)
Sponsored ADR's for Common split (20) for (1) by issuance of (19) additional ADR's 01/18/1994
Basis changed from (1:200) to (1:10) 01/18/1994
Name changed to Applied Development Holdings Ltd. 11/03/2006
(See Applied Development Holdings Ltd.)

APPLIED INVENTIONS MGMT INC (ON)
Recapitalized as Applied Inventions Management Corp. 08/29/2014
Each share Class A Subordinate exchanged for (0.33333333) share Class A Subordinate
Each share Class B Multiple exchanged for (0.33333333) share Class B Multiple

APPLIED LASER SYS (CA)
Name changed to ARC Capital 11/16/1995
ARC Capital name changed to Advanced Machine Vision Corp. 04/21/1997 which merged into Key Technology, Inc. 07/13/2000
(See Key Technology, Inc.)

APPLIED LOGIC CORP (NJ)
Each share Common 10¢ par exchanged for (0.2) share Common 50¢ par 12/29/1971
Adjudicated bankrupt 08/10/1976
No stockholders' equity

APPLIED LOGIC INC (NV)
Each share Common 3¢ par exchanged for (0.05) share Common $0.001 par 03/01/1995
Name changed to Thunderstone Group Inc. 03/01/1996

APPLIED MACHINING TECHNOLOGY INC (DE)
Charter cancelled and declared inoperative and void for non-payment of taxes 3/1/93

APPLIED MAGNETICS CORP (DE)
Reincorporated 03/16/1987
Common 25¢ par changed to 10¢ par and (1) additional share issued 03/01/1970
Stock Dividend - 10% 03/28/1980
State of incorporation changed from (CA) to (DE) 03/16/1987
Common 10¢ par split (2) for (1) by issuance of (1) additional share 12/03/1987
Plan of reorganization under Chapter 11 Federal Bankruptcy proceedings effective 11/16/2001
No stockholders' equity

APPLIED MGMT SCIENCES INC (OR)
Name changed to T.A.G. Inc. 02/26/1992
(See T.A.G. Inc.)

APPLIED MATLS INC (CA)
Common 1¢ par changed to no par and (0.5) additional share issued 04/01/1980
Common no par split (3) for (2) by issuance of (0.5) additional share 02/05/1981
Common no par split (2) for (1) by issuance of (1) additional share 05/15/1986
Reincorporated under the laws of Delaware and Common no par changed to 1¢ par 04/24/1987

APPLIED MED DEVICES INC (CO)
Common 1¢ par split (10) for (1) by issuance of (9) additional shares 02/07/1980
Common 1¢ par changed to no par 01/18/2005
Each share old Common no par exchanged for (0.00029411) share new Common no par 05/31/2007
Reincorporated under the laws of Delaware as Dalkeith Investments, Inc. and new Common no par changed to $0.0001 par 02/11/2008
Dalkeith Investments, Inc. name changed to Sino Shipping Holdings Inc. 03/31/2008
(See Sino Shipping Holdings Inc.)

APPLIED MICRO CIRCUITS CORP (DE)
Old Common 1¢ par split (2) for (1) by issuance of (1) additional share payable 09/09/1999 to holders of record 09/02/1999
Old Common 1¢ par split (2) for (1) by issuance of (1) additional share payable 03/23/2000 to holders of record 03/15/2000
Old Common 1¢ par split (2) for (1) by issuance of (1) additional share payable 10/30/2000 to holders of record 10/16/2000
Each share old Common 1¢ par exchanged for (0.25) share new Common 1¢ par 12/11/2007
Merged into MACOM Technology Solutions Holdings, Inc. 01/26/2017
Each share new Common 1¢ par exchanged for (0.1089) share Common $0.001 par and $3.25 cash

APPLIED MICROBIOLOGY INC (NY)
Name changed to AMBI, Inc. 01/02/1997
AMBI, Inc. name changed to Nutrition 21 Inc. 03/09/2001
(See Nutrition 21 Inc.)

APPLIED MICROSYSTEMS CORP (WA)
Liquidation completed
Each share Common 1¢ par received initial distribution of $0.08 cash payable 11/21/2003 to holders of record 06/30/2003 Ex date - 11/24/2003
Each share Common 1¢ par received second and final distribution of $0.0651 cash payable 07/01/2005 to holders of record 06/30/2003 Ex date - 07/05/2005
Note: Certificates were not required to be surrendered and are without value

APPLIED MOLECULAR EVOLUTION INC (DE)
Merged into Lilly (Eli) & Co. 02/12/2004
Each share Common $0.001 par exchanged for (0.2446) share Common no par

APPLIED NANOTECH HLDGS INC (TX)
Reincorporated under the laws of Delaware as PEN Inc. 09/03/2014

APPLIED NEUROSOLUTIONS INC (DE)
Each share old Common $0.0025 par exchanged for (0.03333333) share new Common $0.0025 par 07/01/2009
SEC revoked common stock registration 10/01/2014

APPLIED OPTICAL TECHNOLOGIES PLC (UNITED KINGDOM)
Name changed to OpSec Security Group PLC 10/16/2007
(See OpSec Security Group PLC)

APPLIED OPTICS INC (MD)
Each share Common $0.0001 par exchanged for (0.01) share Common 1¢ par 03/18/1986
Charter forfeited for failure to file annual reports 10/13/1988

APPLIED PHYSICS CORP. (CA)
Completely liquidated 07/29/1966
Each share Common $1 par exchanged for first and final distribution of (0.961538) share Varian Associates (CA) Common $1 par
Varian Associates (CA) reincorporated in Delaware as Varian Associates, Inc. 10/07/1976 which name changed to Varian Medical Systems Inc. 04/03/1999

APPLIED POLYTECHNIC RESEARCH CORP. (MD)
Charter cancelled for failure to file annual reports 11/18/1970

APPLIED PWR INC (WI)
Name changed 1/17/73
Name changed from Applied Power Industries, Inc. to Applied Power Inc. 01/17/1973
Conv. Preferred Ser. B $1 par called for redemption 10/10/1986
Common $1 par split (3) for (1) by issuance of (2) additional shares 05/20/1987
Common $1 par reclassified as Class A Common 20¢ par 08/12/1987
Class A Common 20¢ par split (2) for (1) by issuance of (1) additional share 05/31/1989
Class A Common 20¢ par split (2) for (1) by issuance of (1) additional share payable 02/03/1998 to holders of record 01/22/1998 Ex date - 02/04/1998
Each share Class A Common 20¢ par received distribution of (1) share APW Ltd. (Bermuda) Common 1¢ par payable 07/31/2000 to holders of record 07/21/2000 Ex date - 08/01/2000
Name changed to Actuant Corp. 01/12/2001

APPLIED RESEARCH LABORATORIES (CA)
Acquired by Bausch & Lomb Optical Co. 04/09/1958
Each share Capital Stock $1 par exchanged for (0.6113) share Common $10 par
Each share Class B $1 par exchanged for (0.6113) share Common $10 par
Bausch & Lomb Optical Co. name changed to Bausch & Lomb Inc. 03/31/1960
(See Bausch & Lomb Inc.)

APPLIED RESH CORP (CO)
Each share Common $0.0001 par exchanged for (0.2) share Common $0.0005 par 10/28/1988
Recapitalized as U.S. Wind Farming, Inc. 03/19/2004
Each share Common $0.0005 par exchanged for (0.005) share Common $0.0005 par

APPLIED RESH INC (NY)
Name changed to Applied Industries, Inc. 01/05/1970
(See Applied Industries, Inc.)

APPLIED SCIENCE & TECHNOLOGY INC (DE)
Common 1¢ par split (3) for (2) by issuance of (0.5) additional share payable 12/12/1997 to holders of record 11/28/1997
Merged into MKS Instruments, Inc. 01/26/2001
Each share Common 1¢ par exchanged for (0.7669) share Common no par

APPLIED SCIENCE CORP. OF PRINCETON (NJ)
Common $2 par changed to $1 par and (1) additional share issued 07/01/1957
Name changed to Mercer Controls Corp. 09/18/1959
(See Mercer Controls Corp.)

APPLIED SIGNAL TECHNOLOGY INC (CA)
Acquired by Raytheon Co. 01/31/2011
Each share Common no par exchanged for $38 cash

APPLIED SOLAR ENERGY CORP (CA)
Acquired by Westar Capital 03/16/1992
Each share Common no par exchanged for $6 cash

APPLIED SOLAR INC (NV)
Chapter 7 bankruptcy proceedings terminated 03/30/2015
No stockholders' equity

APPLIED SOLAR TECHNOLOGIES INC (CO)
Out of business 11/21/1990
Details not available

APPLIED SPECTRUM TECHNOLOGIES INC (DE)
Reincorporated 11/17/2005
Each share old Common 1¢ par exchanged for (0.01) share Common 1¢ par 03/23/1990
State of incorporation changed from (MN) to (DE) and Common 1¢ par changed to $0.001 par 11/17/2005
Name changed to Benda Pharmaceutical, Inc. 02/12/2007
(See Benda Pharmaceutical, Inc.)

APPLIED SYNTHETICS CORP (NY)
Charter cancelled and proclaimed dissolved for failure to pay taxes 06/24/1981

APPLIED SYSTEMATICS INC (NY)
Merged into Process Analytics Corp. 10/24/1979
Each share Common 1¢ par exchanged for $1 cash

APPLIED TECHNOLOGY, INC. (CA)
Stock Dividend - 50% 08/24/1966
Merged into Itek Corp. (DE) 09/20/1967
Each share Common 25¢ par exchanged for (0.43) share Common no par
(See Itek Corp. (DE))

APPLIED TECHNOLOGY CORP. (WA)
Charter cancelled and proclaimed dissolved for failure to pay fees 07/01/1978

APPLIED TECHNOLOGY INC (NV)
Each share old Common $0.001 par exchanged for (0.1) share new Common $0.001 par 03/03/1997
Recapitalized as Golden Panther Resources Ltd. 03/22/1997
Each share new Common $0.001 par exchanged for (0.05) share Common $0.001 par
Golden Panther Resources Ltd. name changed to Panther Resources Ltd. 03/13/1998 which recapitalized as PhantomFilm.Com 06/15/1999 which recapitalized as Komodo, Inc. 10/08/2001
(See Komodo, Inc.)

APPLIED TECHNOLOGY SYS INC (DE)
Charter dissolved 06/02/1995

APPLIED TERRAVISION SYS INC (AB)
Merged into Cognicase Inc. 03/15/2002
Each share Common no par exchanged for (0.147574) share Common no par
(See Cognicase Inc.)

APPLIED URBANOLOGY, INC. (CA)
Charter suspended for failure to file reports and pay taxes 11/01/1974

APPLIED VOICE RECOGNITION INC (DE)
Reincorporated 02/03/1998
State of incorporation changed from (UT) to (DE) 02/03/1998
Name changed to E-Docs.MD, Inc. 02/23/1999
(See E-Docs.MD, Inc.)

APPLIED VOICE TECHNOLOGY INC (WA)
Common 1¢ par split (2) for (1) by issuance of (1) additional share payable 05/11/1998 to holders of record 05/04/1998
Name changed to AVT Corp. 07/29/1998
AVT Corp. name changed to Captaris, Inc. 04/09/2001
(See Captaris, Inc.)

APPLIED WELLNESS CORP (NV)
SEC revoked common stock registration 01/13/2010

APPLIEDTHEORY CORP (DE)
Filed a petition under Chapter 11 Federal Bankruptcy Code 04/17/2002
No stockholders' equity

APPLIX INC (MA)
Common $0.025 par split (2) for (1) by issuance of (1) additional share 12/26/1995
Merged into Cognos Inc. 10/25/2007
Each share Common $0.025 par exchanged for $17.87 cash

APPNET INC (DE)
Name changed 10/01/1999
Name changed from Appnet Systems, Inc. to Appnet, Inc. 10/01/1999
Merged into Commerce One Inc. 09/13/2000
Each share Common $0.0005 par exchanged for (0.8) share Common $0.0001 par
(See Commerce One Inc.)

APPOINT TECHNOLOGIES INC (CA)
SEC revoked common stock registration 11/10/2010

APPONAUG CO., INC.
Acquired by Aspinook (The) Corp. 00/00/1950
Details not available

APPONLINE COM INC (DE)
Chapter 11 bankruptcy proceedings converted to Chapter 7 on 11/14/2005
No stockholders' equity

APPRAISAL GROUP INTL INC (DE)
Name changed to International Realty Group, Inc. 08/10/1989
International Realty Group, Inc. name changed to Qualton Inc. 10/17/2000
(See Qualton Inc.)

APPROACH RES INC (BC)
Name changed to Future Media Technologies Corp. (BC) 04/26/1994
Future Media Technologies Corp. (BC) reincorporated as Future Media Technologies Corp. (WY) 01/29/1999 which recapitalized as Future Link Systems Inc. 06/21/1999 which recapitalized as Cal-Star Inc. 09/28/2001 which name changed to Amanta Resources Ltd. (WY) 07/13/2004 which reincorporated in British Columbia 08/31/2004

APPROPRIATE HEALTH SVCS COM INC (NV)
Name changed to Stayhealthy Inc. 04/14/2000

APPROVED FINANCE, INC. (OH)
Name changed to Nationwide Consumer Services, Inc. 07/01/1968
(See Nationwide Consumer Services, Inc.)

APPROVED FINL CORP (VA)
Common $1 par split (2) for (1) by issuance of (1) additional share payable 11/21/1997 to holders of record 11/07/1997
Merged into Approved Acquisition Corp. 12/31/2003
Each share Common $1 par exchanged for $0.2827 cash

APPS DENTAL INC (DE)
Name changed to CompDent Corp. 08/04/1995
(See CompDent Corp.)

APPS GENIUS CORP (NV)
Recapitalized as FAL Exploration Corp. 07/22/2013
Each share Common $0.001 par exchanged for (0.001) share Common $0.001 par
FAL Exploration Corp. recapitalized as Vapir Enterprises Inc. 10/03/2014 which name changed to Gratitude Health, Inc. 03/23/2018

APR ENERGY PLC (UNITED KINGDOM)
ADR agreement terminated 03/14/2016
Each ADR for Ordinary exchanged for $2.3839 cash

APRIA HEALTHCARE GROUP INC (DE)
Merged into Sky Acquisition LLC 10/28/2008
Each share Common $0.001 par exchanged for $21 cash

APRIL ENERGY INC (NV)
Name changed to AE Holding I, Inc. 01/05/2011

APRIL INDS INC (DE)
Each share Common 5¢ par exchanged for (0.1) share Common 50¢ par 12/21/1988
Merged into A.I. Newco 04/02/1991
Each share Common 50¢ par exchanged for $15 cash

APR-AQU — FINANCIAL INFORMATION, INC.

APRIL INDS INC (UT)
Reorganized under the laws of Delaware 07/14/1971
Each share Common 5¢ par exchanged for (0.25) share Common 5¢ par
(See April Industries, Inc. (DE))

APROGENEX INC (DE)
Charter forfeited for failure to maintain a registered agent 11/26/1998

APROPOS TECHNOLOGY INC (IL)
Merged into Enghouse Systems Ltd. 11/28/2005
Each share Common 1¢ par exchanged for $2.76 cash

APS HLDG CORP (DE)
Plan of reorganization under Chapter 11 Federal Bankruptcy Code effective 10/29/1999
No stockholders' equity

APSB BANCORP (CA)
Common no par split (6) for (5) by issuance of (0.2) additional share 12/20/1989
Stock Dividends - 20% 12/19/1986; 20% 12/18/1987
Name changed to American Pacific State Bank (Sherman Oaks, CA) 12/27/1990
(See American Pacific State Bank (Sherman Oaks, CA))

APSLEY MGMT GROUP INC (AB)
Name changed to Resverlogix Corp. 04/25/2003

APT SATELLITE HLDGS LTD (HONG KONG)
ADR agreement terminated 11/05/2008
Each Sponsored ADR for Ordinary exchanged for $0.607886 cash

APTA HLDGS INC (DE)
Each share Common $0.001 par received distribution of (1) share Gavella Corp. Common $0.001 par payable 12/27/2000 to holders of record 12/01/2000 Ex date - 12/28/2000
Name changed to InteliSys Aviation Systems of America, Inc. 08/25/2003
InteliSys Aviation Systems of America, Inc. recapitalized as China Yida Holding, Co. (DE) 02/28/2008 which reorganized in Nevada 11/19/2012
(See China Yida Holding, Co.)

APTECH LTD OLD (INDIA)
Merged into Hexaware Technologies Ltd. 03/28/2003
Each 144A GDR for Ordinary exchanged for (0.4) 144A Sponsored GDR for Equity Shares and $0.2493 cash
Each Reg. S GDR for Ordinary exchanged for (0.4) Reg. S GDR for Equity shares and $0.2493 cash
(See Hexaware Technologies Ltd.)

APTEK TECHNOLOGIES, INC. (MN)
Each share old Common 10¢ par exchanged for (0.00001) share new Common 10¢ par 12/06/1991
Note: In effect holders received $0.10 cash per share and public interest was eliminated

APTILON CORP (CANADA)
Name changed to DMD Digital Health Connections Group Inc. 08/07/2014
(See DMD Digital Health Connections Group Inc.)

APTIMUS INC (WA)
Merged into Apollo Group, Inc. 10/30/2007
Each share Common no par exchanged for $6.25 cash

APW LTD (BERMUDA)
Plan of reorganization under Chapter 11 Federal Bankruptcy Code effective 07/31/2002
Each share Common 1¢ par received distribution of (0.00148367) Common Stock Purchase Warrant expiring 07/31/2009
Note: Certificates were not required to be surrendered and are without value

AQ CORP (OR)
Each share old Common exchanged for (0.00001) share new Common 06/13/2002
Involuntarily dissolved for failure to file reports and pay fees 06/06/2008

AQM AUTOMOTIVE CORP (AB)
Acquired by AQM Acquisition Corp. 05/23/2001
Each share Common no par exchanged for $0.25 cash

AQM COPPER INC (BC)
Acquired by Teck Resources Ltd. 01/16/2017
Each share Common no par exchanged for $0.23 cash
Note: Unexchanged certificates will be cancelled and become without value 01/18/2023

AQUA AIR SYS CORP (NY)
Charter cancelled and proclaimed dissolved for failure to pay taxes and file reports 12/15/1975

AQUA ALLIANCE INC (DE)
Merged into Vivendi S.A. 08/23/1999
Each share Common $0.001 par exchanged for $2.90 cash

AQUA-AURUM MINING CO. LTD. (BC)
Struck off register and declared dissolved for failure to file returns 12/00/1974

AQUA AUSTRALIS INC (NV)
Recapitalized as Network Systems International Inc. 04/22/1996
Each share Common $0.001 par exchanged for (0.5) share Common $0.001 par
Network Systems International Inc. name changed to OnSpan Networking, Inc. 02/15/2001 which recapitalized as Double Eagle Holdings, Ltd. 04/02/2007 which name changed to Fuse Science, Inc. 11/03/2011

AQUA-BUOY CORP (CO)
Each share Common $0.00001 par exchanged for (0.01) share Common $0.001 par 01/24/1990
Name changed to Chester Holdings, Ltd. 09/30/1993
Chester Holdings, Ltd. recapitalized as First Light Resources Inc. 11/09/2005 which name changed to Invercoal, Inc. 06/28/2006 which recapitalized as Core International Ltd. 04/02/2007 which recapitalized as Therma-Med, Inc. 12/31/2008

AQUA CAP CORP (BC)
Name changed to Texada Software Inc. (BC) 05/15/2002
Texada Software Inc. (BC) reorganized in Ontario 11/05/2008 which recapitalized as Noble Iron Inc. 07/23/2012

AQUA CARE SYS INC (DE)
Each share old Common $0.001 par exchanged for (0.25) share new Common $0.001 par 02/03/1998
Charter cancelled and declared inoperative and void for non-payment of taxes 03/01/2003

AQUA CHEM INC (WI)
Merged into Coca-Cola Co. 05/08/1970
Each share Common $1 par exchanged for (0.762485) share Common no par

AQUA CLARA BOTTLING & DISTR INC (CO)
Recapitalized as BEVsystems International Inc. (CO) 03/15/2002
Each share Common no par exchanged for (0.1) share Common no par
BEVsystems International Inc. (CO) reorganized in Florida 01/02/2003
(See BEVsystems International Inc.)

AQUA DYNE INC (DE)
Name changed to EESTech, Inc. 07/10/2006

AQUA FONTANEA INC (NV)
Each share old Common $0.001 par exchanged for (3) shares new Common $0.001 par 11/12/2004
Name changed to Budget Waste, Inc. 05/24/2005
Budget Waste, Inc. name changed to Codido, Inc. 12/12/2008 which name changed to Quad Energy Corp. 09/13/2010

AQUA-LECTRIC, INC. (MN)
Merged into Federal Hydronics, Inc. 02/28/1964
Each share Common 10¢ par exchanged for (0.1) share Capital Stock 10¢ par
(See Federal Hydronics, Inc.)

AQUA MINING CORP. LTD. (QC)
Charter annulled for failure to file annual reports 11/02/1974

AQUA 1 BEVERAGE INC (BC)
Name changed to PowerNova Technologies Corp. 09/11/2003

AQUA PURA INC (NM)
Involuntarily dissolved for failure to file reports and pay fees 01/26/1979

AQUA PURA TECHNOLOGIES INC (AB)
Struck from the register and dissolved 12/01/1993

AQUA-PURE VENTURES INC (AB)
Reincorporated 11/13/2001
Place of incorporation changed from (BC) to (AB) 11/13/2001
Placed in receivership 08/18/2015
Stockholders' equity unlikely

AQUA ROYALE INC (DE)
Name changed to Micro Poly Corp. 03/04/1994

AQUA SOC INC (NV)
SEC revoked common stock registration 12/01/2011

AQUA SOL INC (DE)
Charter cancelled and declared inoperative and void for non-payment of taxes 03/01/1986

AQUA THERM PRODS CORP (NJ)
Acquired by Horizon International Healthcare, Inc. 05/09/1991
Each share Common 1¢ par exchanged for $0.4828 cash

AQUA VIE BEVERAGE CORP (DE)
Each share old Common $0.001 par exchanged for (0.2) share new Common $0.001 par 11/13/1998
Each share new Common $0.001 par exchanged again for (0.05) share new Common $0.001 par 08/30/2002
SEC revoked common stock registration 12/02/2008

AQUABLAST INC (ON)
Filed petition in bankruptcy 08/02/1974
No stockholders' equity

AQUACARE INTERNATIONAL LTD. (BC)
Each share old Capital Stock no par exchanged for (4) shares new Capital Stock no par 06/18/1969
Struck off register and declared dissolved for failure to file returns 01/31/1977

AQUACELL TECHNOLOGIES INC (DE)
Each share Common $0.001 par received distribution of (0.25) share AquaCell Media Inc. Preferred $0.001 par payable 11/26/2001 to holders of record 10/25/2001
Each share Common $0.001 par received distribution of (1) share AquaCell Water, Inc. Common $0.001 par payable 04/03/2006 to holders of record 03/09/2006
Ex date - 03/21/2006
Assets sold for the benefit of creditors 12/08/2009
No stockholders' equity

AQUACELL WATER INC (DE)
Name changed to Believing Today, Inc. 02/18/2010
(See Believing Today, Inc.)

AQUAFILTER CORP. (DE)
Each share Common 10¢ par exchanged for (0.1) share Common $1 par 06/03/1966
Name changed to Allen Electronic Industries, Inc. and Common $1 par changed to 10¢ par 12/15/1967
(See Allen Electronic Industries, Inc.)

AQUAGEN INTL INC (NV)
Reincorporated 02/06/2004
Each share old Common $0.001 par exchanged for (0.33333333) share new Common $0.001 par 07/18/2003
State of incorporation changed from (AZ) to (NV) 02/06/2004
Each share new Common $0.001 par exchanged again for (0.05) share new Common $0.001 par 12/10/2004
Name changed to Hoodia International, Inc. 08/05/2005
Hoodia International, Inc. recapitalized as Oceanic Research & Recovery, Inc. 04/22/2008 which name changed to McCusker Holdings Corp. 11/13/2017

AQUAGENIX INC (DE)
Chapter 11 bankruptcy proceedings converted to Chapter 7 on 04/07/2000
Stockholders' equity unlikely

AQUAGOLD RES INC (CANADA)
Reincorporated 01/19/1989
Place of incorporation changed from (ON) to (Canada) 01/19/1989
Name changed to Atlantic Industrial Minerals Inc. 11/19/1992

AQUALIV TECHNOLOGIES INC (NV)
Recapitalized as Verity Corp. 04/04/2013
Each share Common $0.001 par exchanged for (0.01) share Common $0.001 par

AQUAMER MED CORP (DE)
Name changed from Aquamer, Inc. to Aquamer Medical Corp. 06/22/2007
Each share old Common $0.0001 par exchanged for (0.01149425) share new Common $0.0001 par 12/29/2010
Name changed to Urban Ag. Corp. 01/05/2011
(See Urban Ag. Corp.)

AQUAMERICA INC (UT)
Involuntarily dissolved 05/16/1991

AQUAMIN RES INC (BC)
Name changed to Peruvian Gold Ltd. 05/10/1994
Peruvian Gold Ltd. merged into Quest Investment Corp. 07/04/2002 which merged into Quest Capital Corp. (BC) 06/30/2003 which reincorporated in Canada 05/27/2008 which name changed to Sprott Resource Lending Corp. 09/10/2010 which merged into Sprott Inc. 07/24/2013

AQUANATURAL CO (DE)
Charter cancelled and declared inoperative and void for non-payment of taxes 03/01/1996

AQUANAUTICS, INC. (CA)
Each share Preferred $3 par

exchanged for (1) share Common
$1 par 07/00/1969
Charter suspended for failure to pay
taxes 10/01/1971

AQUANAUTICS CORP (DE)
Recapitalized as Advanced Oxygen
Technologies Inc. 10/27/1993
Each share Common 1¢ par
exchanged for (0.2) share Common
1¢ par
Each share 7% Conv. Preferred Ser.
1 $10 par exchanged for (8.9)
shares Common 1¢ par 06/12/1990

AQUANETICS INC (NY)
Dissolved by proclamation 03/26/1997

AQUANON CORP (DE)
Charter cancelled and declared
inoperative and void for
non-payment of taxes 03/01/1994

AQUANTIVE INC (WA)
Merged into Microsoft Corp.
08/10/2007
Each share Common 1¢ par
exchanged for $66.50 cash

AQUAPENN SPRING WTR INC (PA)
Merged into Groupe Danone
12/08/1998
Each share Common no par
exchanged for $13 cash

AQUAPLAN INC (WY)
Each share old Common $0.001 par
exchanged for (0.002) share new
Common $0.001 par 01/17/2006
Note: Holders of between (10) and
(4,999) shares received (10) shares
Holders of (9) shares or fewer were
not affected by the reverse split
Name changed to Oxford Funding
Corp. 05/18/2007
Oxford Funding Corp. recapitalized as
Emerging Healthcare Solutions, Inc.
08/12/2009

AQUAPRO CORP (TN)
SEC revoked common stock
registration 07/23/2010

AQUARION CO (DE)
Common no par split (3) for (2) by
issuance of (0.5) additional share
payable 03/22/1999 to holders of
record 03/01/1999 Ex date -
03/23/1999
Merged into Kelda Group plc
01/07/2000
Each share Common no par
exchanged for $37.05 cash

AQUARIUMS, INC. (DE)
Name changed to Metaframe Corp.
11/15/1966
Metaframe Corp. acquired by Mattel,
Inc. (DE) 12/15/1969

AQUARIUS CAP CORP (ON)
Issue Information - 2,619,500 shares
COM offered at $0.10 per share on
02/01/2010
Recapitalized as China Green Star
Agricultural Corp. 06/07/2011
Each share Common no par
exchanged for (0.1) share Common
no par
China Green Star Agricultural Corp.
name changed to GreenStar
Agricultural Corp. 07/05/2013

AQUARIUS COATINGS INC (ON)
Recapitalized as Aquarius Surgical
Technologies Inc. 02/24/2017
Each share Common no par
exchanged for (0.05) share Common
no par

AQUARIUS INTERNATIONAL CORP. (WV)
Proclaimed dissolved for
non-payment of taxes 06/24/1974

AQUARIUS PLATINUM LTD (BERMUDA)
ADR agreement terminated
07/02/2004
Each old Sponsored ADR for Ordinary
exchanged for $11.70 cash
New Sponsored ADR's for Ordinary
split (3) for (1) by issuance of (2)
additional ADR's payable
12/04/2007 to holders of record
12/04/2007 Ex date - 12/06/2007
ADR agreement terminated
04/26/2016
Each new Sponsored ADR for
Ordinary exchanged for $0.34 cash

AQUARIUS PORCUPINE GOLD MINES LTD. (ON)
Merged into Pardee Amalgamated
Mines Ltd. on a (1) for (5) basis
12/00/1954
Pardee Amalgamated Mines Ltd.
liquidated for Rio Lagom Mines Ltd.
11/09/1961 which name changed to
Rio Algom Ltd. 04/30/1975
(See Rio Algom Ltd.)

AQUARIUS RES LTD (BC)
Reincorporated 05/24/1984
Place of incorporation changed from
(AB) to (BC) 05/24/1984
Struck off register and declared
dissolved for failure to file returns
12/27/1991

AQUARIUS SEAFARMS LTD (BC)
Assets sold for the benefit of creditors
08/31/1990
No stockholders' equity

AQUARIUS VENTURES INC (BC)
Reincorporated under the laws of
Canada as Citotech Systems Inc.
10/30/2000
Citotech Systems Inc. recapitalized as
SmartCool Systems Inc. 07/21/2004

AQUASCIENCES INTL INC (NY)
Charter cancelled and proclaimed
dissolved for failure to pay taxes
09/28/1994

AQUASEARCH INC (CO)
Under plan of reorganization each
share Common $0.0001 par
automatically became (1) share
Mera Pharmaceuticals Inc. (DE)
Common $0.0001 par 09/16/2002

AQUASIL INTL INC (NV)
Recapitalized as Multi-Corp
International Inc. 06/22/2012
Each share Common $0.0001 par
exchanged for (0.001) share
Common $0.0001 par

AQUASITION CORP (MARSHALL ISLANDS)
Name changed to KBS Fashion
Group Ltd. 11/03/2014

AQUASOL ENVIROTECH LTD (CAYMAN ISLANDS)
Recapitalized as China Linen Textile
Industry, Ltd. 06/30/2018
Each share Common $0.002 par
exchanged for (0.5) share Common
$0.002 par

AQUASOL INTL GROUP INC (AB)
Struck off register for failure to file
annual returns 10/05/1999

AQUASOL TECHNOLOGIES INC (DE)
Reincorporated under the laws of
Nevada 06/29/1998
Aquasol Technologies Inc. (NV)
recapitalized as ilink Telecom, Inc.
02/16/1999 which name changed to
9278 Communications Inc. (NV)
12/29/1999 which reincorporated in
Delaware 04/24/2000
(See 9278 Communications Inc.)

AQUASOL TECHNOLOGIES INC (NV)
Recapitalized as ilink Telecom, Inc.
2/14/99
Each share Common $0.001 par
exchanged for (0.2) share Common
$0.001 par
ilink Telecom, Inc. name changed to
9278 Communications Inc. (NV)
12/29/99 which reincorporated in
Delaware 4/24/2000
(See 9278 Communications Inc.)

AQUASTAR HLDGS INC (NV)
Name changed to SUTIMCo
International, Inc. 06/17/2011

AQUATECH AMER INC (DE)
Charter cancelled and declared
inoperative and void for
non-payment of taxes 03/01/1989

AQUATECH SYS INC (BC)
Struck from the register and dissolved
12/08/1995

AQUATEK UK LTD (WV)
Name changed to Environmental
Technologies International Inc.
02/08/2002
Environmental Technologies
International Inc. recapitalized as
Atlantic Wind & Solar, Inc.
10/23/2008

AQUATERRE MINERAL DEV LTD (BC)
Recapitalized as Quaterra Resources
Inc. 11/14/1997
Each share Common no par
exchanged for (0.2) share Common
no par

AQUATIC CELLULOSE INTL CORP (NV)
Name changed to Valor Energy Corp.
06/02/2008
(See Valor Energy Corp.)

AQUAZYME INDUSTRIES, INC. (MN)
Statutorily dissolved 10/7/91

AQUEOUS CAP CORP (AB)
Name changed to Stoneset Equity
Development Corp. 04/05/2010

AQUEST ENERGY LTD (AB)
Recapitalized as Anderson Energy
Ltd. 09/01/2005
Each share Common no par
exchanged for (0.31) share Common
no par
Anderson Energy Ltd. name changed
to Anderson Energy Inc. 01/27/2015
which name changed to InPlay Oil
Corp. 11/10/2016

AQUEST EXPLORATIONS LTD (AB)
Reincorporated 07/22/2002
Place of incorporation changed from
(BC) to (AB) 07/22/2002
Recapitalized as Aquest Energy Ltd.
02/04/2004
Each share Common no par
exchanged for (0.25) share Common
no par
Aquest Energy Ltd. recapitalized as
Anderson Energy Ltd. 09/01/2005
which name changed to Anderson
Energy Inc. 01/27/2015 which name
changed to InPlay Oil Corp.
11/10/2016

AQUEST MINERALS CORP (BC)
Recapitalized as Aquest Explorations
Ltd. (BC) 01/08/2002
Each share Common no par
exchanged for (0.1) share Common
no par
Aquest Explorations Ltd. (BC)
reincorporated in Alberta 07/22/2002
which recapitalized as Aquest
Energy Ltd. 02/04/2004 which
recapitalized as Anderson Energy
Ltd. 09/01/2005 which name
changed to Anderson Energy Inc.
01/27/2015 which name changed to
InPlay Oil Corp. 11/10/2016

AQUESTA BK (CORNELIUS, NC)
Stock Dividend - 20% payable
05/15/2013 to holders of record
04/29/2013 Ex date - 04/25/2013
Reorganized as Aquesta Financial
Holdings, Inc. 04/01/2014
Each share Common $4.17 par
exchanged for (1) share Common
1¢ par

AQICULTURE GARDENS INC (DE)
Charter cancelled 03/01/1974

AQUIFER SPRINGS LTD (AB)
Name changed to Arrowhead Water
Products Ltd. (AB) 05/06/1996
Arrowhead Water Products Ltd. (AB)
reincorporated in British Columbia
as Captiva Verde Industries Ltd.
05/09/2014

AQUILA APARTMENTS, INC. (PA)
Completely liquidated 05/00/1972
Each share Capital Stock no par
exchanged for first and final
distribution of $161.90 cash

AQUILA BIOPHARMACEUTICALS INC (DE)
Merged into Antigenics, Inc.
11/16/2000
Each share Common 1¢ par
exchanged for (0.2898) share
Common 1¢ par
Antigenics, Inc. name changed to
Agenus Inc. 01/06/2011

AQUILA GAS PIPELINE CORP (DE)
Merged into UtiliCorp United Inc.
05/14/1999
Each share Common 1¢ par
exchanged for $8 cash

AQUILA INC NEW (DE)
Each 9.75% Premium Income Equity
Security converted into (1.173)
shares Common $1 par 11/16/2002
Each 6.75% Premium Income Equity
Security converted into (8.0386)
shares Common $1 par 09/14/2007
Acquired by Great Plains Energy Inc.
07/14/2008
Each share Common $1 par
exchanged for (0.0856) share
Common no par and $1.80 cash
Great Plains Energy Inc. merged into
Evergy, Inc. 06/05/2018

AQUILA INC OLD (DE)
Merged into UtiliCorp United Corp.
01/07/2002
Each share Class A Common 1¢ par
exchanged for (0.6896) share
Common $1 par
UtiliCorp United Corp. name changed
to Aquila, Inc. (New) 03/15/2002
which was acquired by Great Plains
Energy Inc. 07/14/2008 which
merged into Evergy, Inc. 06/05/2018

AQUILA LIFE INSURANCE CO. (IN)
Merged into Coastal States Life
Insurance Co. 12/31/1966
Each share Common $1 par
exchanged for (0.288093) share
Common $1 par
Coastal States Life Insurance Co.
reorganized as Coastal States Corp.
10/05/1972
(See Coastal States Corp.)

AQUILA RES LTD (BC)
Recapitalized as Aquila Energy Corp.
03/08/1995
Each share Common no par
exchanged for (0.5) share Common
no par

AQUILINE RES INC (ON)
Reincorporated 12/16/2002
Place of incorporation changed from
(BC) to (ON) 12/16/2002
Acquired by Pan American Silver
Corp. 01/22/2010
Each share Common no par
exchanged for (0.2495) share
Common no par and (0.1) Common
Stock Purchase Warrant expiring
12/07/2014

AQUILIUM SOFTWARE CORP (CANADA)
Merged into MDR Switchview Global
Networks Inc. 02/20/2001
Each share Common no par
exchanged for (0.03393296) share
Common no par
MDR Switchview Global Networks
Inc. name changed to Avotus Corp.
05/14/2002
(See Avotus Corp.)

AQUINO MLG INC (DE)
Common $0.0001 par split (70) for (1) by issuance of (69) additional shares payable 06/24/2013 to holders of record 06/24/2013
Ex date - 06/25/2013
Name changed to Code 2 Action, Inc. 07/01/2013
Code 2 Action, Inc. name changed to AV Therapeutics, Inc. 12/27/2013

AQUISTAR VENTURES USA INC (NV)
Name changed to Custom Branded Networks, Inc. 06/05/2001
Custom Branded Networks, Inc. name changed to Novastar Resources, Ltd. 05/10/2005 which name changed to Thorium Power, Ltd. 10/10/2006 which recapitalized as Lightbridge Corp. 09/29/2009

AQUITAINE CO CDA LTD (CANADA)
Acquired by Canada Development Corp. 10/28/1981
Each share Common no par exchanged for CAD $74 cash
Note: Option to receive USD $61.65125 cash expired 11/27/1981

AQUIX ADVANCED SYS CORP (NY)
Dissolved by proclamation 12/24/1991

AR ASSOCS INC (NV)
Each share old Common $0.001 par exchanged for (0.03333333) share new Common $0.001 par 04/12/1999
Each share new Common $0.001 par exchanged again for (0.01) share new Common $0.001 par 12/24/2001
Charter revoked for failure to file reports and pay fees 06/01/2005

AR CAP ACQUISITION CORP (DE)
Name changed to Axar Acquisition Corp. 10/07/2016
(See Axar Acquisition Corp.)

AR GROWTH FIN CORP (DE)
SEC revoked common stock registration 09/01/2010

ARA SVCS INC (DE)
Common 50¢ par split (3) for (2) by issuance of (0.5) additional share 07/16/1975
Acquired by ARA Holding Co. 12/19/1984
Each share Common 50¢ par exchanged for $71.75 cash

ARAB POTASH CO LTD (JORDAN)
GDR agreement terminated 08/14/2017
Each 144A Sponsored GDR for Ordinary exchanged for $24.003491 cash
Each Reg. S Sponsored GDR for Ordinary exchanged for $24.003491 cash

ARABEE OIL & GAS CO. LTD. (BC)
Recapitalized as Arawain Producers Ltd. 12/27/1957
Each share Capital Stock $1 par exchanged for (0.2) share Capital Stock no par
Arawain Producers Ltd. acquired by Western Allenbee Oil & Gas Co. Ltd. 04/06/1960 which name changed to Convoy Capital Corp. 04/28/1989 which recapitalized as Hariston Corp. 09/25/1992 which recapitalized as Midland Holland Inc. (Canada) 02/10/1999 which reincorporated in Yukon 03/11/1999 which name changed to Mercury Partners & Co. Inc. 02/22/2000 which name changed to Black Mountain Capital Corp. 05/02/2005 which recapitalized as Grand Peak Capital Corp. (YT) 11/20/2007 which reincorporated in British Columbia 04/27/2010

ARABEL RECORDS INTL INC (DE)
Common $0.001 par split (4) for (1) by issuance of (3) additional shares payable 09/25/2001 to holders of record 09/17/2001
Each share old Common $0.001 par exchanged for (0.25) share new Common par 04/30/2002
Recapitalized as Asia Pacific Engineering Solutions International, Inc. 06/01/2005
Each share new Common $0.001 par exchanged for (0.001) share Common $0.001 par

ARABESQUE RES LTD (BC)
Struck off register and declared dissolved for failure to file returns 07/20/1990

ARABIAN AMERN DEV CO (DE)
Name changed 07/21/2000
Name changed from Arabian Shield Development Co. to Arabian American Development Co. 07/21/2000
Name changed to Trecora Resources 06/18/2014

ARABIAN PETROLEUM CORP. (BC)
Merged into Equus Petroleum Corp. 11/09/1982
Each share Common no par exchanged for (0.33333333) share Common no par
Equus Petroleum Corp. recapitalized as Nuequus Petroleum Corp. 09/30/1997 which name changed to Equus Energy Corp. 11/28/2002 which recapitalized as Habibi Resources Corp. 08/27/2008 which recapitalized as One World Investments Inc. 10/07/2009 which name changed to One World Minerals Inc. 02/28/2017 which name changed to One World Lithium Inc. 01/19/2018

ARACRUZ CELULOSE S A (BRAZIL)
Sponsored ADR's for Class B split (3) for (2) by issuance of (0.5) additional ADR 05/18/1994
Sponsored ADR's for Class B split (4) for (3) by issuance of (0.33333333) additional ADR 04/05/1995
Each Sponsored ADR for Ordinary exchanged for (0.5) Sponsored ADR for Class B 03/17/1997
Merged into Fibria Celulose S.A. 11/18/2019
Each Sponsored ADR for Class B exchanged for (1.347) Sponsored ADR's for Common

"ARAD" QUARRIES & ROADS LTD. (ISRAEL)
Name changed to "Arad" Investment & Industrial Development Ltd. 01/10/1978

ARADYME CORP (UT)
Reincorporated 12/29/2006
State of incorporation changed from (DE) to (UT) 12/29/2006
SEC revoked common stock registration 12/07/2011

ARAGON, INC.
Reorganized as Aragon Realty Corp. 00/00/1951
Each share Common no par exchanged for (1) share Common $1 par and $47.50 cash
(See Aragon Realty Corp.)

ARAGON-BALDWIN MILLS
Merged into Stevens (J.P.) & Co., Inc. 00/00/1946
Each share Capital Stock exchanged for (9.82765) shares Capital Stock $15 par
(See Stevens (J.P.) & Co., Inc.)

ARAGON EXPLS LTD (BC)
Struck off register 03/31/1983

ARAGON FD INC (MD)
Completely liquidated 11/10/1972
Each share Common $1 par exchanged for $9.869 cash

ARAGON RLTY CORP (DE)
Liquidation completed

Each share Common $1 par exchanged for initial distribution of $25 cash 07/31/1968
Each share Common $1 par received second distribution of $65 cash 02/01/1969
Each share Common $1 par received third and final distribution of $5.50 cash 02/17/1971

ARAK RES LTD (BC)
Each share old Common no par exchanged for (0.1) share new Common no par 11/29/2016
Reorganized as Cobalt 27 Capital Corp. 04/10/2017
Each share new Common no par exchanged for (3) shares Common no par

ARAKIS ENERGY CORP (BC)
Name changed 10/17/1988
Name changed 01/04/1991
Name changed from Arakis Mining Corp. to Arakis Capital Corp. 10/17/1988
Name changed from Arakis Capital Corp. to Arakis Energy Corp. 01/14/1991
Merged into Talisman Energy Inc. 10/08/1998
Each share Common no par exchanged for (0.1) share Common no par
(See Talisman Energy Inc.)

ARALDICA WINERIES LTD (NV)
Recapitalized as Interactive Solutions Corp. (NV) 02/14/2000
Each share Common $0.001 par exchanged for (0.001) share Common $0.0001 par
Interactive Solutions Corp. (NV) reorganized in Wyoming as MyMedicalCD, Ltd. 11/24/2004 which recapitalized as United Treatment Centers, Inc. 01/30/2009 which name changed to PotNetwork Holdings, Inc. 07/24/2015 which reincorporated in Colorado 03/03/2017

ARAMARK CORP (DE)
Name changed 12/14/2001
Name changed from Aramark Worldwide Corp. to ARAMARK Corp. 12/14/2001
Acquired by Goldman Sachs Group, Inc. 01/26/2007
Each share Class B Common 1¢ par exchanged for $33.80 cash

ARAMARK HLDGS CORP (DE)
Name changed to Aramark 05/12/2014

ARAMED INC (DE)
Merged into Gensia, Inc. 11/21/1995
Each share Callable Common 1¢ par exchanged for approximately (0.6366) share Common 1¢ par, (1) Contingent Value Right and $8 cash
Gensia, Inc. name changed to Gensia Sicor Inc. 02/28/1997 which name changed to Sicor Inc. 06/18/1999 which merged into Teva Pharmaceutical Industries Ltd. 01/22/2004

ARAMEX INTERNATIONAL LTD (BERMUDA)
Acquired by Rasmala Partners Ltd. 04/08/2002
Each share Common 1¢ par exchanged for $12 cash

ARAMIS VENTURES INC (BC)
Name changed to Newera Capital Corp. 03/31/1994
Newera Capital Corp. name changed to ThrillTime Entertainment International, Inc. 08/12/1997 which name changed to Advanced Proteome Therapeutics Corp. 10/25/2006

ARAN ENERGY PLC (IRELAND)
Acquired by Den Norske Stats Oljeselskap A.S. 12/15/1995

Each Sponsored ADR for Ordinary exchanged for $35.744 cash

ARANKA GOLD INC (ON)
Merged into Guyana Goldfields Inc. 01/28/2009
Each share Common no par exchanged for (0.3076923) share Common no par

ARANLEE RES LTD (YT)
Reincorporated 11/15/1996
Place of incorporation changed from (BC) to (YT) 11/15/1996
Recapitalized as Southern Metals Corp. 08/07/1998
Each share Common no par exchanged for (0.14285714) share Common no par
Southern Metals Corp. name changed to EPICentrix Technologies, Inc. 11/22/2000 which name changed to Ventura Gold Corp. (YT) 07/05/2004 which reincorporated in British Columbia 10/07/2004 which merged into International Minerals Corp. 01/20/2010
(See International Minerals Corp.)

ARAPAHO CAP CORP (BC)
Common no par split (2) for (1) by issuance of (1) additional share payable 04/05/2004 to holders of record 03/31/2004
Reincorporated under the laws of Ontario as Malbex Resources Inc. 12/09/2009
Malbex Resources Inc. name changed to Coin Hodl Inc. 09/10/2018

ARAPAHO PETE INC (CO)
Stock Dividend - 10% 05/31/1975
Plan of reorganization under Chapter 11 Federal Bankruptcy proceedings confirmed 06/13/1988
No stockholders' equity

ARAPAHOE ACQUISITIONS INC (CO)
Name changed to Eagle Software Systems, Inc. 09/30/1988

ARAPAHOE BASIN INC (CO)
Class A Common $1 par reclassified as Common 10¢ par 00/00/1959
Name changed to Arapahoe Holdings Corp. 05/04/1984
(See Arapahoe Holdings Corp.)

ARAPAHOE CHEMICALS INC. (CO)
Liquidation completed
Each share Common no par received initial distribution of $19 cash 09/17/1965
Each share Common no par received second and final distribution of $1.69 cash 06/27/1966
Note: Certificates were not required to be surrendered and are without value

ARAPAHOE ENERGY CORP NEW (AB)
Name changed to Canadian Phoenix Resources Corp. 01/07/2008
Canadian Phoenix Resources Corp. recapitalized as Knol Resources Corp. 03/11/2013

ARAPAHOE ENERGY CORP OLD (AB)
Plan of arrangement effective 02/06/2004
Each share Common no par exchanged for (0.33333333) share Arapahoe Energy Corp. (New) Common no par
Arapahoe Energy Corp. (New) name changed to Canadian Phoenix Resources Corp. 01/07/2008 which recapitalized as Knol Resources Corp. 03/11/2013

ARAPAHOE HLDGS CORP (CO)
Charter suspended for failure to file annual reports 09/30/1990

ARAPAHOE MNG CORP (BC)
Recapitalized as Salus Resource Corp. 05/06/1996

Each share Common no par exchanged for (0.2) share Common no par
Salus Resource Corp. name changed to Brandon Gold Corp. 12/04/1996 which recapitalized as Redmond Ventures Corp. 09/16/1999 which recapitalized as Crown Point Ventures Ltd. (BC) 03/12/2002 which reincorporated in Alberta as Crown Point Energy Inc. 07/31/2012

ARAUCO RES CORP (BC)
Reincorporated under the laws of Canada as Kit Resources Ltd. 08/29/1997
Kit Resources Ltd. (Canada) reincorporated in Ontario 03/03/2000 which merged into Wheaton River Minerals Ltd. 03/06/2000 which merged into Goldcorp Inc. 04/15/2005

ARAWAIN PRODUCERS LTD. (BC)
Acquired by Western Allenbee Oil & Gas Co. Ltd. 04/06/1960
Each share Capital Stock no par exchanged for (0.5) share Capital Stock no par
Western Allenbee Oil & Gas Co. Ltd. name changed to Convoy Capital Corp. 04/28/1989 which recapitalized as Hariston Corp. 09/25/1992 which recapitalized as Midland Holland Inc. (Canada) 02/10/1999 which reincorporated in Yukon 03/11/1999 which name changed to Mercury Partners & Co. Inc. 02/22/2000 which name changed to Black Mountain Capital Corp. 05/02/2005 which recapitalized as Grand Peak Capital Corp. (YT) 11/20/2007 which reincorporated in British Columbia 04/27/2010

ARAWAK ENERGY CORP (BRITISH WEST INDIES)
Reincorporated under the laws of Channel Islands as Arawak Energy Ltd. 06/03/2008
(See Arawak Energy Ltd.)

ARAWAK ENERGY LTD (CHANNEL ISLANDS)
Acquired by Rosco S.A. 04/14/2009
Each share Common no par exchanged for CAD$1 cash

ARAWAK MINES LTD (ON)
Merged into Gerrard Realty Inc. 01/28/1976
Each share Common no par exchanged for (0.01111111) share Common no par

ARBATAX INTL INC (YT)
Reincorporated 08/06/1996
Place of incorporation changed from (Canada) to (YT) 08/06/1996
Name changed to MFC Bancorp Ltd. (YT) 03/03/1997
MFC Bancorp Ltd. (YT) reincorporated in British Columbia 11/03/2004 which name changed to KHD Humboldt Wedag International Ltd. 11/01/2005 which reorganized as Terra Nova Royalty Corp. 03/30/2010 which name changed to MFC Industrial Ltd. 09/30/2011 which name changed to MFC Bancorp Ltd. (BC) 02/16/2016
(See MFC Bancorp Ltd. (BC))

ARBEC FST PRODS INC (CANADA)
Acquired by Jolina Capital Inc. 05/29/2006
Each share Common no par exchanged for $0.35 cash

ARBED S A (LUXEMBOURG)
ADR agreement terminated 09/04/2001
Details not available

ARBINET CORP (DE)
Name changed 06/16/2009
Name changed from Arbinet-thexchange, Inc. to Arbinet Corp. 06/16/2009
Each share old Common $0.001 par exchanged for (0.25) share new Common $0.001 par 06/14/2010
Merged into Primus Telecommunications Group, Inc. 02/28/2011
Each share new Common $0.001 par exchanged for approximately (0.5817) share Common 1¢ par
Primus Telecommunications Group, Inc. name changed to PTGi Holding, Inc. 10/29/2013 which name changed to HC2 Holdings, Inc. 04/14/2014

ARBIOS SYS INC (DE)
Reincorporated 07/25/2005
State of incorporation changed from (NV) to (DE) 07/25/2005
Plan of reorganization under Chapter 11 Federal Bankruptcy proceedings effective 09/21/2009
Each share old Common $0.001 par received first and final distribution of (0.2053388) share new Common $0.001 par
Note: Certificates were not required to be surrendered and are without value
(Additional Information in Active)

ARBITRAGE EXPL INC (ON)
Name changed to Argo Gold Inc. 09/22/2016

ARBITRON INC (DE)
Acquired by Nielsen Holdings N.V. 09/30/2013
Each share Common 50¢ par exchanged for $48 cash

ARBOR CAP INC (ON)
Name changed to Arbor Memorial Services Inc. 03/31/1994
(See Arbor Memorial Services Inc.)

ARBOR CAPITAL RESOURCES INC./ARBOR RESSOURCES FINANCIERES INC. (ON)
Each share Common no par exchanged for (1) share Class A Common no par and (1) share Class B Common no par 09/20/1982
Name changed to Arbor Capital Inc. 05/15/1986
Arbor Capital Inc. name changed to Arbor Memorial Services Inc. 03/31/1994
(See Arbor Memorial Services Inc.)

ARBOR DRUGS INC (MI)
Common 1¢ par split (3) for (2) by issuance of (0.5) additional share 06/15/1989
Common 1¢ par split (3) for (2) by issuance of (0.5) additional share 05/07/1991
Common 1¢ par split (3) for (2) by issuance of (0.5) additional share 05/15/1995
Common 1¢ par split (3) for (2) by issuance of (0.5) additional share payable 12/17/1996 to holders of record 12/03/1996
Common 1¢ par split (3) for (2) by issuance of (0.5) additional share payable 12/16/1997 to holders of record 12/08/1997
Merged into CVS Corp. 03/31/1998
Each share Common 1¢ par exchanged for (0.3182) share Common $1 par
CVS Corp. name changed to CVS/Caremark Corp. 03/22/2007 which name changed to CVS Caremark Corp. 05/10/2007 which name changed to CVS Health Corp. 09/04/2014

ARBOR ENTECH CORP (DE)
Each share Common $0.0001 par exchanged for (0.01) share Common $0.001 par 11/02/1989
Name changed to Evergreen International Corp. 07/27/2018

ARBOR HEALTH CARE CO (DE)
Merged into Extendicare Inc. 11/26/1997
Each share Common 3¢ par exchanged for $45 cash

ARBOR INC (NV)
Each share old Common $0.001 par exchanged for (3) shares new Common $0.001 par 10/29/2001
Name changed to China Granite Corp. 02/20/2004
China Granite Corp. name changed to Strategic Rare Earth Metals, Inc. 06/30/2006 which name changed to Affinity Beverage Group, Inc. 04/13/2016

ARBOR MEM SVCS INC (ON)
Acquired by Scanfield Holdings Ltd. 11/27/2012
Each share Class A no par exchanged for $32 cash
Each share Non-Vtg. Class B no par exchanged for $32 cash

ARBOR NATL HLDGS INC (NY)
Merged into BankAmerica Corp. (Old) 01/31/1995
Each share Common 1¢ par exchanged for (0.4103) share Common $1.5625 par
BankAmerica Corp. (Old) merged into BankAmerica Corp. (New) 09/30/1998 which name changed to Bank of America Corp. 04/28/1999

ARBOR PPTY TR (DE)
Merged into Vornado Realty Trust 12/16/1997
Each share Common no par exchanged for (0.24381) share Common 4¢ par

ARBOR RES INC (BC)
Recapitalized as Klondike Gold Corp. 01/24/1996
Each share Common no par exchanged for (0.1) share Common no par

ARBOR SOFTWARE CORP (DE)
Under plan of merger name changed to Hyperion Solutions Corp. 08/24/1998
(See Hyperion Solutions Corp.)

ARBOREAL ASSOC INC (DE)
Out of business 12/09/1976
No stockholders' equity

ARBOUR ENERGY INC (AB)
Cease trade order effective 05/19/2006
Note: Company being investigated for fraud

ARBOUR ENERGY USA INC (NV)
Name changed to Globe Energy, Inc. 02/26/2007
(See Globe Energy, Inc.)

ARBUTUS FOOD CORP (BC)
Name changed to Sabre Marketing Corp. 02/20/1992
Sabre Marketing Corp. recapitalized as Sabre Pacific Equities Ltd. 08/10/1994
(See Sabre Marketing Corp.)

ARBUTUS RES INC (NV)
Name changed to Cromwell Uranium Corp. 06/29/2007
Cromwell Uranium Corp. name changed to US Uranium Inc. 08/24/2007 which name changed to California Gold Corp. 03/30/2009 which recapitalized as MV Portfolios, Inc. 09/08/2014

ARBYS INC (OH)
Merged into Royal Crown Cola Co. 10/28/1976
Each share Common no par exchanged for $11.70 cash

ARC CAP (CA)
Name changed to Advanced Machine Vision Corp. 04/21/1997
Advanced Machine Vision Corp. merged into Key Technology, Inc. 07/31/2000
(See Key Technology, Inc.)

ARC COMMUNICATIONS INC (FL)
Reorganized under the laws of New Jersey 11/21/1997
Each share Common $0.001 par exchanged for (1) share Common $0.001 par
ARC Communications Inc. (NJ) reorganized in Nevada as RoomLinX, Inc. 06/25/2004

ARC COMMUNICATIONS INC (NJ)
Reorganized under the laws of Nevada as RoomLinX, Inc. 06/25/2004
Each share Preferred 20¢ par exchanged for (1) share Preferred 20¢ par
Each share Common $0.001 par exchanged for (1) share Common $0.001 par

ARC ENERGY TR (AB)
Reorganized as ARC Resources Ltd. 01/06/2011
Each Trust Unit exchanged for (1) share Common no par

ARC HOME ENTERTAINMENT DIVERSIFIED LTD. (ON)
Name changed to Ahed Music Corp. Ltd. 06/26/1970
Ahed Music Corp. name changed to Ahed Corp. 08/30/1978 which name changed to Eco Corp. 07/30/1987 which recapitalized as American Eco Corp. 11/15/1993
(See American Eco Corp.)

ARC INTL CORP (ON)
Reincorporated under the laws of Colorado as Kompass Travel Ltd. 03/00/2003
Kompass Travel Ltd. recapitalized as Imagexpress, Inc. 08/19/2003 which name changed to Imagexpres Corp. 10/01/2003

ARC LIQUIDATING CORP. (IL)
Completed liquidation
Each share Common $1 par exchanged for initial distribution of (0.891) share LTV Ling Altec, Inc. Common 50¢ par 10/27/1967
Each share Common $1 par received second and final distribution of $0.0520 cash 03/29/1968
LTV Ling Altec, Inc. name changed to Altec Corp. 04/27/1972

ARC LOGISTICS PARTNERS LP (DE)
Acquired by Zenith Energy U.S., L.P. 12/21/2017
Each Common Unit exchanged for $16.50 cash

ARC PAC METALS LTD (BC)
Recapitalized as Rampart Ventures Ltd. 03/06/2000
Each share Common no par exchanged for (0.33333333) share Common no par
Rampart Ventures Ltd. name changed to RPT Uranium Corp. 02/23/2007 which name changed to RPT Resources Ltd. (BC) 06/05/2009 which reincorporated in Alberta as ArPetrol Ltd. 04/08/2011

ARC RES LTD (AB)
Exchangeable Shares no par reclassified as Ser. A Exchangeable Shares no par 06/16/2006
Each Ser. A Exchangeable Share no par exchanged for (2.89162) shares Common no par 01/06/2011
Each Ser. B Exchangeable Share no par exchanged for (2.89162) shares Common no par 01/06/2011
(Additional Information in Active)

ARC RES LTD (BC)
Struck off register and declared dissolved for failure to file returns 09/11/1978

ARC-ARC

ARC STRATEGIC ENERGY FD (AB)
Class A Trust Units reclassified as Trust Units 11/26/1999
Class B Trust Units reclassified as Trust Units 11/26/1999
Liquidation completed
Each Trust Unit received initial distribution of $2.80 cash payable 11/06/2001 to holders of record 10/31/2001
Each Trust Unit received second and final distribution of $0.0705 cash payable 12/21/2001 to holders of record 12/19/2001

ARC WIRELESS SOLUTIONS INC (UT)
Each share old Common $0.0005 par exchanged for (0.02) share new Common $0.0005 par 02/12/2007
Recapitalized as ARC Group Worldwide, Inc. 08/08/2012
Each share new Common $0.0005 par exchanged for (0.51282051) share Common $0.0005 par

ARCA BIOPHARMA INC (DE)
Each share Conv. Preferred Ser. A $0.001 par automatically became (100) shares new Common $0.001 par 12/00/2013
(Additional Information in Active)

ARCA CORP (NJ)
Reincorporated under the laws of Delaware as Agate Technologies Inc. 06/30/1999
Agate Technologies Inc. recapitalized as PowerHouse Technologies Group, Inc. 04/30/2003 which name changed to Migo Software, Inc. 08/14/2006
(See Migo Software, Inc.)

ARCA EXPLS INC (CANADA)
Recapitalized as Pro-Spect-Or Resources Inc. 08/12/2004
Each share Common no par exchanged for (0.125) share Common no par
Pro-Spect-Or Resources Inc. name changed to Uranium Bay Resources Inc. 07/12/2007 which name changed to Uragold Bay Resources Inc. 07/15/2009 which name changed to HPQ-Silicon Resources Inc. 07/25/2016

ARCADE ACQUISITION CORP (DE)
Liquidation completed
Each Unit exchanged for initial distribution of $7.89835797 cash 05/21/2009
Each Unit received second and final distribution of $0.08736003 cash payable 03/11/2011 to holders of record 05/21/2009
Each share Common $0.0001 par exchanged for initial distribution of $7.89835797 cash 05/21/2009
Each share Common $0.0001 par received second and final distribution of $0.08736003 cash payable 03/11/2011 to holders of record 05/21/2009

ARCADE COTTON MILLS (SC)
Acquired by Mount Vernon-Woodberry Mills, Inc. 06/29/1955
Each share Common $25 par exchanged for (3) shares Common $2.50 par
6% Preferred $100 par called for redemption 12/31/1955
Mount Vernon-Woodberry Mills, Inc. name changed to Mount Vernon Mills, Inc. 03/28/1956
(See Mount Vernon Mills, Inc.)

ARCADIA EXPLS LTD (BC)
Recapitalized as New Arcadia Explorations Ltd. 08/22/1983
Each share Common no par exchanged for (0.25) share Common no par
New Arcadia Explorations Ltd. name changed to New Arcadia Resources Ltd. 11/10/1992
(See New Arcadia Resources Ltd.)

ARCADIA FINL LTD (MN)
Merged into Associates First Capital Corp. 04/03/2000
Each share Common 1¢ par exchanged for (1) Residual Value Obligation and $4.90 cash
Note: Residual Value Obligation expired without value
Associates First Capital Corp. merged into Citigroup Inc. 11/30/2000

ARCADIA GOLD MINES, LTD. (ON)
Charter revoked for failure to file reports and pay fees 08/15/1960

ARCADIA METAL PRODUCTS (CA)
Acquired by Northrop Corp. (CA) 06/01/1961
Each (13.909) shares Capital Stock $1 par exchanged for (1) share Common $1 par
Northrop Corp. (CA) reincorporated in Delaware 06/18/1985 which name changed to Northrop Grumman Corp. 05/18/1994 which reorganized as Northrop Grumman Corp. (Holding Company) 04/02/2001

ARCADIA MINERALS LTD (QC)
Placed in receivership by Court Order 06/25/1975
Stockholders' equity unlikely

ARCADIA NATL BK (SECAUCUS, NJ)
Merged into National Community Bank of New Jersey (Rutherford, NJ) 06/30/1979
Each share Common $6.25 par exchanged for $25 cash

ARCADIA NICKEL CORP. LTD. (QC)
Recapitalized as Associated Arcadia Nickel Corp. Ltd. on a (1) for (2) basis 08/21/1959
Associated Arcadia Nickel Corp. Ltd. recapitalized as Arcadia Minerals Ltd. 04/30/1971
(See Arcadia Minerals Ltd.)

ARCADIAN CONSOLIDATED MINING CO.
Property sold 00/00/1936
Details not available

ARCADIAN CORP (DE)
Each share Conv. Preferred Ser. A 1¢ par exchanged for (0.948) share Common 1¢ par 03/06/1997
Merged into Potash Corp. of Saskatchewan, Inc. (SK) 03/06/1997
Each share Common 1¢ par exchanged for (0.17713) share Common no par and $12.25 cash
Potash Corp. of Saskatchewan, Inc. (SK) reincorporated in Canada 05/08/2002 which merged into Nutrien Ltd. 01/02/2018

ARCADIAN PARTNERS L P (DE)
Merged into Arcadian Corp. 08/10/1995
Each Preference Unit exchanged for $14.50 cash and (0.0935) share Preferred Ser. A 1¢ par
Arcadian Corp. merged into Potash Corp. of Saskatchewan, Inc. (SK) 03/06/1997 which reincorporated in Canada 05/08/2002 which merged into Nutrien Ltd. 01/02/2018

ARCAN CORP LTD (ON)
Charter cancelled for failure to file reports 10/24/1973

ARCAN RES LTD (AB)
Acquired by Aspenleaf Energy Ltd. 06/08/2015
Each share Common no par exchanged for $0.11 cash
Note: Unexchanged certificates will be cancelled and become without value 06/08/2021

ARCANA CORP (UT)
Involuntarily dissolved for failure to file annual reports 12/31/1984

ARCANNA INDS CORP (BC)
Merged into Mercana Industries Ltd. (BC) 12/17/1993
Each share Common no par exchanged for (1.34) shares Common no par
Mercana Industries Ltd. (BC) reincorporated in Ontario 06/28/1995
(See Mercana Industries Ltd.)

ARCAP DIVERSIFIED INC (ON)
Recapitalized as First United Capital Inc. 10/25/1982
Each share Common $1 par exchanged for (0.2) share Common no par
(See First United Capital Inc.)

ARCATA CORP (CA)
Name changed 11/30/1978
Common $1 par changed to 25¢ par and (3) additional shares issued 11/15/1968
Under plan of merger name changed from Arcata National Corp. to Arcata Corp. 11/30/1978
Name changed to Atacra Liquidating Corp. 06/04/1982
(See Atacra Liquidating Corp.)

ARCATA REDWOOD CO. (CA)
Recapitalized as Arcata National Corp. 04/25/1967
Each share Capital Stock $10 par exchanged for (10) shares Capital Stock $1 par
Arcata National Corp. name changed to Aracta Corp. 11/30/1978 which name changed to Atacra Liquidating Corp. 06/04/1982
(See Atacra Liquidating Corp.)

ARCATA RES CORP (YUKON)
Recapitalized as Goldrush Resources Ltd. (YT) 05/14/2003
Each share Common no par exchanged for (0.5) share Common no par
Goldrush Resources Ltd. (YT) reincorporated in British Columbia 08/10/2006 which merged into First Mining Finance Corp. 01/11/2016 which name changed to First Mining Gold Corp. 01/11/2018

ARCELOR MITTAL (LUXEMBOURG)
Reincorporated 09/03/2007
Place of incorporation changed from (Netherlands) to (Luxembourg) and Class A New York Registry Shares reclassified as New York Registry Shares 09/03/2007
Merged into ArcelorMittal S.A. 11/13/2007
Each New York Registry Share exchanged for (1) New York Registry Share

ARCELOR S A (LUXEMBOURG)
Each Sponsored ADR for Ordinary received distribution of $0.3499 cash payable 08/06/2004 to holders of record 07/26/2004
ADR agreement terminated 11/27/2006
Each Sponsored ADR for Ordinary exchanged for $84.13631 cash

ARCH CAP GROUP LTD (BERMUDA)
7.875% Non-Cum. Preferred Ser. A 1¢ par called for redemption at $25 on 05/02/2012
8% Non-Cum. Preferred Ser. A 1¢ par called for redemption at $25 on 05/02/2012
6.75% Non-Cum. Preferred Ser. C 1¢ par called for redemption at $25 plus $0.009375 accrued dividends on 01/02/2018
(Additional Information in Active)

ARCH CAP GROUP LTD (DE)
Reincorporated under the laws of Bermuda 11/08/2000

ARCH CHEMICALS INC (VA)
Acquired by Lonza Group AG 10/20/2011
Each share Common $1 par exchanged for $47.20 cash

ARCH COAL INC (DE)
Old Common 1¢ par split (2) for (1) by issuance of (1) additional share payable 05/15/2006 to holders of record 05/05/2006 Ex date - 05/16/2006
5% Perpetual Preferred 1¢ par called for redemption at $50 on 02/01/2008
Each share old Common 1¢ par exchanged for (0.1) share new Common 1¢ par 07/28/2015
Plan of reorganization under Chapter 11 Federal Bankruptcy proceedings effective 10/05/2016
No stockholders' equity
(Additional Information in Active)

ARCH COMMUNICATIONS GROUP INC (DE)
Each share old Class B Common 1¢ par exchanged for (0.33333333) share new Class B Common 1¢ par 06/28/1999
Each share old Common 1¢ par exchanged for (0.33333333) share new Common 1¢ par 06/28/1999
Name changed to Arch Wireless, Inc. 09/25/2000
(See Arch Wireless, Inc.)

ARCH DEV CORP (BC)
Name changed to American Digital Industries Ltd. 06/03/1998
(See American Digital Industries Ltd.)

ARCH GLOBAL TECHNOLOGIES INC. (BC)
Struck off register and declared dissolved for failure to file returns 02/21/1992

ARCH MGMT SVCS INC (NV)
Common $0.001 par split (7) for (1) by issuance of (6) additional shares payable 06/04/2006 to holders of record 05/04/2006 Ex date - 07/04/2006
Name changed to Tiger Ethanol International, Inc. 11/30/2006
Each share Common $0.001 par exchanged for (1) share Common $0.001 par
Tiger Ethanol International, Inc. name changed to Tiger Renewable Energy Ltd. 02/29/2008 which recapitalized as Cono Italiano, Inc. 08/10/2009

ARCH PETE INC (TX)
Merged into USENCO Inc. 06/01/1988
Each share Common 10¢ par exchanged for (0.8585) share Common 1¢ par
USENCO Inc. name changed to Arch Petroleum, Inc. (NV) 06/01/1988 which reincorporated in Delaware 12/31/1991 which merged into Pogo Producing Co. 08/14/1998 which merged into Plains Exploration & Production Co. 11/06/2007 which merged into Freeport-McMoRan Copper & Gold Inc. 05/31/2013 which name changed to Freeport-McMoRan Inc. 07/14/2014

ARCH PETE INC NEW (DE)
Reincorporated 12/31/1991
State of incorporation changed from (NV) to (DE) 12/31/1991
Common 1¢ par split (2) for (1) by issuance of (1) additional share 01/18/1994
Merged into Pogo Producing Co. 08/14/1998
Each share Common 1¢ par exchanged for (0.09615) share Common $1 par
Pogo Producing Co. merged into Plains Exploration & Production Co. 11/06/2007 which merged into Freeport-McMoRan Copper & Gold Inc. 05/31/2013

ARCH WIRELESS INC (DE)
Plan of reorganization under Chapter

11 Federal Bankruptcy Code effective 05/29/2002
No stockholders' equity
Each share new Common $0.001 par exchanged for (1) share Class A Common $0.001 par 06/13/2003
Merged into USA Mobility, Inc. 11/16/2004
Each share Class A Common $0.001 par exchanged for (1) share Common $0.0001 par
USA Mobility, Inc. name changed to Spok Holdings, Inc. 07/09/2014

ARCHANGEL DIAMOND CORP (YT)
Reincorporated 09/16/1996
Place of incorporation changed from (BC) to (YT) 09/16/1996
Plan of reorganization under Chapter 11 Federal Bankruptcy proceedings confirmed 12/17/2009
Holders are expected to receive an undetermined amount of Liquidating Trust Class B

ARCHEAN CORP (NV)
Charter revoked for failure to file reports and pay fees 03/01/1971

ARCHEAN EXPLORATION CORP. (NV)
Name changed to Archean Corp. 11/03/1965
(See Archean Corp.)

ARCHEAN OIL LTD (AUSTRALIA)
Name changed to Tri-Arc Energy Ltd. 12/05/1983
Tri-Arc Energy Ltd. name changed to Triarc Corp. Ltd. 09/03/1987 which name changed to Central Bore NL 12/20/1994 which name changed to Central Exchange Ltd. 12/21/1999 which name changed to Orion Equities Ltd. 12/13/2005

ARCHEAN STAR RES INC (BC)
Name changed to Transatlantic Mining Corp. 02/05/2014

ARCHER BK (CHICAGO, IL)
Name changed 06/14/1995
Name changed from Archer National Bank (Chicago, IL) to Archer Bank (Chicago, IL) 06/14/1995
Merged into North Community Bank (Chicago, IL) 06/29/2013
Details not available

ARCHER COMMUNICATIONS INC (BC)
Name changed to QSound Labs, Inc. (BC) 06/26/1993
QSound Labs, Inc. (BC) reincorporated in Alberta 07/00/1990
(See QSound Labs, Inc.)

ARCHER DANIELS MIDLAND CO (DE)
Each Corporate Unit automatically became (1.2618) shares Common no par 06/01/2011
(Additional Information in Active)

ARCHER INTL DEVS LTD (BC)
Name changed to Archer Communications Inc. 04/28/1989
Archer Communications Inc. name changed to QSound Labs, Inc. (BC) 06/26/1993 which reincorporated in Alberta 07/00/1990
(See QSound Labs, Inc.)

ARCHER MINERALS INC. (BC)
Name changed to Archer International Developments Ltd. 12/17/1986
Archer International Developments Ltd. name changed to Archer Communications Inc. 04/28/1989 which name changed to QSound Labs, Inc. (BC) 06/26/1993 which reincorporated in Alberta 07/00/1990
(See QSound Labs, Inc.)

ARCHER OIL CO. (CA)
Charter suspended for failure to pay taxes 11/01/1960

ARCHER PETE CORP (BC)
Each share old Common no par exchanged for (0.1) share new Common no par 09/26/2012
Each share new Common no par exchanged again for (0.05) share new Common no par 08/09/2016
Name changed to Atlas Engineered Products Ltd. 11/09/2017

ARCHER RES LTD (AB)
Acquired by Dominion Energy, Inc. 04/21/1998
Each share Common no par exchanged for $7.60 cash

ARCHER SYS INC (DE)
Recapitalized as Ocumed Group Inc. 01/14/2002
Each share Common $0.0001 par exchanged for (0.001) share Common $0.0001 par
(See Ocumed Group Inc.)

ARCHIE ENTERPRISES INC (NY)
Merged into S.G. Associates 01/17/1983
Each share Common 1¢ par exchanged for $6.75 cash

ARCHIPELAGO HLDGS INC (DE)
Merged into NYSE Group, Inc. 03/07/2006
Each share Common 1¢ par exchanged for (1) share Common 1¢ par
NYSE Group, Inc. merged into NYSE Euronext 04/04/2007 which merged into IntercontinentalExchange Group, Inc. 11/13/2013 which name changed to Intercontinental Exchange, Inc. 06/02/2014

ARCHIPELAGO LEARNING INC (DE)
Acquired by Plato Learning, Inc. 05/17/2012
Each share Common $0.001 par exchanged for $11.10 cash

ARCHITECTS & ENGINEERS BUILDING, INC. (GA)
Completely liquidated 00/00/1966
Company's attorneys advised no stockholders' equity

ARCHITECTURAL INDS INC (FL)
Reincorporated under the laws of Delaware as Imperial Industries, Inc. 07/08/1968
(See Imperial Industries, Inc.)

ARCHITECTURAL MARBLE CO (FL)
Involuntarily dissolved 12/05/1978

ARCHITECTURAL PLASTICS CORP. (OR)
Each share Capital Stock $10 par exchanged for (9) shares Capital Stock $1 par 09/18/1959
Involuntarily dissolved for failure to file reports and pay fees 11/18/1964

ARCHITEL SYS CORP (ON)
Merged into Nortel Networks Corp. (New) 07/03/2000
Each share Common no par exchanged for (0.38682) share Common no par
(See Nortel Networks Corp. (New))

ARCHIVE CORP (CA)
Merged into Conner Peripherals, Inc. 12/29/1992
Each share Common no par exchanged for $11.25 cash

ARCHON CORP (NV)
Conv. Exchangeable Preferred 1¢ par called for redemption at $2.14 plus $3.101 accrued dividends on 08/31/2007
(Additional Information in Active)

ARCHON INC (DE)
Merged into Iroquois Brands, Ltd. 01/31/1978
Each share Common $1.20 par exchanged for $23 cash

ARCHON PURE PRODUCTS CORP. (DE)
Recapitalized as Archon Inc. 05/17/1976
Each share Common 20¢ par exchanged for (0.166666) share Common $1.20 par
(See Archon Inc.)

ARCHROCK PARTNERS L P (DE)
Merged into Archrock, Inc. 04/26/2018
Each Common Unit exchanged for (1.4) shares Common 1¢ par

ARCHSTONE CMNTYS TR (MD)
9% Ser. B Preferred 1¢ par called for redemption at $25 plus $0.23125 accrued dividends on 05/07/2001
Name changed to Archstone-Smith Trust 10/29/2001
(See Archstone-Smith Trust)

ARCHSTONE-SMITH TR (MD)
Preferred Ser. C 1¢ par called for redemption at $25 on 08/20/2002
Conv. Preferred Ser. A 1¢ par called for redemption at $25 plus $0.39026 accrued dividends on 12/01/2003
8.75% Preferred Ser. D 1¢ par called for redemption at $25 plus $0.21875 accrued dividends on 08/06/2004
Each share Conv. Preferred Ser. J 1¢ par exchanged for (1.975) Common Units 1¢ par 07/13/2002
Each share Conv. Preferred Ser. H 1¢ par exchanged for (1.975) Common Units 1¢ par 05/13/2003
Each share Conv. Preferred Ser. K 1¢ par exchanged for an undetermined amount of Common Units 09/00/2004
Each share Conv. Preferred Ser. L 1¢ par exchanged for an undetermined amount of Common Units 1¢ par 12/00/2004
Acquired by Tishman Speyer Real Estate Venture VII, LP 10/05/2007
Each Common Unit 1¢ par exchanged for $60.75 cash

ARCIS CORP (AB)
Each share old Common no par exchanged for (0.25) share new Common no par 07/24/2000
Merged into ARX Acquisition Corp. 02/29/2004
Each share new Common no par exchanged for $1.26 cash

ARCLAND ENERGY CORP (UT)
Each share old Common $0.001 par exchanged for (0.1) share new Common $0.001 par 10/20/2008
SEC revoked common stock registration 11/16/2011

ARCO CHEM CO (DE)
Merged into Lyondell Petrochemical Co. 07/28/1998
Each share Common $1 par exchanged for $57.75 cash

ARCO ELECTRONICS, INC. (DE)
Merged into Loral Electronics Corp. 01/05/1962
Each share Class A Common 25¢ par exchanged for (0.33333333) share Common 25¢ par
Loral Electronics Corp. name changed to Loral Corp. 10/30/1964
(See Loral Corp.)

ARCO INDS INC (DE)
Adjudicated bankrupt 01/20/1971
Stockholders' equity unlikely

ARCO PHARMACEUTICALS INC (NY)
Merged into Nature's Bounty, Inc. 01/01/1980
Each share Common 10¢ par exchanged for (1.38) shares Common 1¢ par
Nature's Bounty, Inc. name changed to NBTY, Inc. 05/26/1995

ARCO RES CORP (BC)
Each share old Common no par exchanged for (0.1) share new Common no par 04/15/2014
Each share new Common no par exchanged again for (0.33333333) share new Common no par 05/14/2014
Each share new Common no par exchanged again for (0.15258645) share new Common no par 03/06/2018
Name changed to Cannex Capital Holdings Inc. 03/14/2018

ARCO URANIUM, INC. (CO)
Merged into Lisbon Valley Uranium Co. share for share 11/31/1955
(See Lisbon Valley Uranium Co.)

ARCOL OIL CO. (CO)
Dissolved 04/26/1967
Details not available

ARCON BASE METALS LTD. (BC)
Struck off register and declared involuntarily dissolved for failure to file reports 12/01/1960

ARCON INTL RES P L C (IRELAND)
Each old Sponsored ADR for Ordinary exchanged for (0.1) new Sponsored ADR for Ordinary 08/06/2004
Merged into Lundin Mining Corp. 08/19/2005
Each Sponsored ADR for Ordinary exchanged for $12.96853 cash

ARCONIC INC (PA)
Each share 5.375% Depositary Preferred Class B Ser. 1 automatically became (1.56996) shares Common $1 par 10/02/2017
Reincorporated under the laws of Delaware 12/31/2017

ARCOPLATE HLDGS PLC (UNITED KINGDOM)
ADR agreement terminated 10/19/2005
No ADR holders' equity

ARCS EQUITIES CORP (NY)
Name changed 03/29/1972
Name changed from Arcs Industries, Inc. to Arcs Equities Corp. 03/29/1972
Liquidation completed
Each share Common 10¢ par received initial distribution of (0.58193) share Bates Manufacturing Co., Inc. Common $5 par 09/11/1978
Each share Common 10¢ par exchanged for second and final distribution of $0.52 cash 10/06/1980
(See Bates Manufacturing Co., Inc.)

ARCSIGHT INC (DE)
Acquired by Hewlett-Packard Co. 10/22/2010
Each share Common $0.00001 par exchanged for $43.50 cash

ARCSYS INC (DE)
Name changed to Avant! Corp. 11/27/1995
Avant! Corp. merged into Synopsys, Inc. 06/06/2002

ARCTCO INC (MN)
Common 1¢ par split (3) for (2) by issuance of (0.5) additional share 04/26/1993
Common 1¢ par split (3) for (2) by issuance of (0.5) additional share 09/02/1994
Name changed to Arctic Cat Inc. 08/20/1996
(See Arctic Cat Inc.)

ARCTIC ALASKA FISHERIES CORP (WA)
Merged into Tyson Foods, Inc. 10/05/1992
Each share Common 1¢ par exchanged for (0.5686) share Class A Common 10¢ par and $2.23 cash

ARCTIC CAT INC (MN)
Acquired by Textron Inc. 03/06/2017
Each share Common 1¢ par exchanged for $18.50 cash

ARCTIC DAIRY PRODUCTS CO.
Acquired by National Dairy Products Corp. 00/00/1929
Details not available

ARCTIC ENTERPRISES INC (MN)
Common 10¢ par split (4) for (1) by

issuance of (3) additional shares 01/14/1969
Common 10¢ par split (2) for (1) by issuance of (1) additional share 02/19/1970
Reorganized under Chapter 11 bankruptcy proceedings and Common 10¢ par reclassified as Class A Common 10¢ par 12/04/1981
Name changed to Minstar Inc. (MN) 12/14/1982
Minstar, Inc. (MN) reorganized in Delaware 08/31/1985
(See Minstar, Inc. (DE))

ARCTIC GOLD & SILVER MINES LTD (BC)
Recapitalized as Azam Energy Corp. 09/20/1980
Each share Common no par exchanged for (0.1) share Common no par
(See Azam Energy Corp.)

ARCTIC GROUP INC (AB)
Plan of arrangement effective 03/22/2002
Each share Common no par exchanged for (0.16666666) Arctic Glacier Income Fund Trust Unit

ARCTIC HUNTER URANIUM INC (BC)
Name changed to Arctic Hunter Energy Inc. 12/15/2011

ARCTIC MINING & EXPLORATION LTD. (BC)
Name changed to Arctic Gold & Silver Mines Ltd. 02/08/1968
Arctic Gold & Silver Mines Ltd. recapitalized as Azam Energy Corp. 08/27/1979
(See Azam Energy Corp.)

ARCTIC MINING CO. (OH)
Voluntarily dissolved 07/28/1925
Details not available

ARCTIC OIL & GAS CORP (NV)
Common $0.00001 par split (20) for (1) by issuance of (19) additional shares payable 12/21/2007 to holders of record 12/21/2007
Name changed to Placer Gold Corp. 02/25/2009
(See Placer Gold Corp.)

ARCTIC RED RES CORP (BC)
Recapitalized as Chuska Resources Corp. 01/31/1991
Each share Common no par exchanged for (0.1) share Common no par
Chuska Resources Corp. merged into Harken Energy Corp. 02/15/1993 which recapitalized as HKN, Inc. 06/06/2007

ARCTIC STAR DIAMOND CORP (CANADA)
Recapitalized as Arctic Star Exploration Corp. 07/08/2011
Each share Common no par exchanged for (0.08333333) share Common no par

ARCTIC YELLOWKNIFE MINES LTD (ON)
Charter cancelled and declared dissolved for failure to file returns and pay fees 11/08/1977

ARCTOS PETE CORP (AB)
Recapitalized as Stetson Oil & Gas Ltd. (AB) 11/12/2007
Each share Common no par exchanged for (0.1) share Common no par
Stetson Oil & Gas Ltd. (AB) reincorporated in Ontario 08/21/2014 which name changed to Magnolia Colombia Ltd. 06/14/2017

ARCTURUS ELECTRONICS, INC. (NJ)
Name changed to General Electronics, Inc. 00/00/1956
(See General Electronics, Inc.)

ARCTURUS GROWTHSTAR TECHNOLOGIES INC (BC)
Name changed to Future Farm Technologies Inc. 02/02/2017

ARCTURUS INC (MA)
Proclaimed dissolved for failure to file reports and pay taxes 12/31/1990

ARCTURUS RADIO TUBE CO. (DE)
No longer in existence having become inoperative and void for non-payment of taxes 04/01/1943

ARCTURUS RES LTD (BC)
Recapitalized as Arcturus Ventures Inc. 12/19/2000
Each share Common no par exchanged for (0.2) share Common no par

ARCUS INC (NY)
Merged into United Acquisition Co. 07/31/1995
Each share Common 1¢ par exchanged for $6.42594 cash

ARCUS RLTY CORP (NY)
Name changed to Wood Harmon Corp. 00/00/1958
(See Wood Harmon Corp.)

ARDAY CO. (CA)
Voluntarily dissolved 06/27/1996
Details not available

ARDEA BIOSCIENCES INC (DE)
Acquired by AstraZeneca PLC 06/19/2012
Each share Common $0.001 par exchanged for $32 cash

ARDEEN GOLD MINES LTD.
Assets sold for the benefit of creditors 00/00/1937
No stockholders' equity

ARDELL MINES LTD. (ON)
Charter revoked for failure to file reports and pay fees 00/00/1957

ARDEN FARMS, INC. (MD)
Merged into Arden Farms Co. (New) 08/01/1940
Each share $6 Preference exchanged for (1.5) shares Preferred no par and (5) shares Common $1 par
Arden Farms Co. (New) name changed to Arden-Mayfair, Inc. 04/24/1965 which reorganized as Arden Group, Inc. 12/19/1978
(See Arden Group, Inc.)

ARDEN FARMS CO. OLD (DE)
Merged into Arden Farms Co. (New) 08/01/1940
Each share $4 Class A exchanged for (3.75) shares Common $1 par
Each share Class B exchanged for (0.5) shares Common $1 par
Arden Farms Co. (New) name changed to Arden-Mayfair, Inc. 04/24/1965 which reorganized as Arden Group, Inc. 12/19/1978
(See Arden Group, Inc.)

ARDEN FARMS CO NEW (DE)
Name changed to Arden-Mayfair, Inc. 04/24/1965
Arden-Mayfair, Inc. reorganized as Arden Group, Inc. 12/19/1978
(See Arden Group, Inc.)

ARDEN GROUP INC (DE)
Common 25¢ par reclassified as Class A Common 25¢ par 04/01/1987
$2.25 Preferred Ser. A $15 par called for redemption 12/17/1990
Class A Common 25¢ par split (4) for (1) by issuance of (3) additional shares payable 07/15/1998 to holders of record 06/29/1998
Class B Common 25¢ par split (4) for (1) by issuance of (3) additional shares payable 07/15/1998 to holders of record 06/29/1998
Class B Common 25¢ par reclassified as Class A Common 25¢ par 11/10/2004
Acquired by GRCY Holdings, Inc. 02/19/2014
Each share Class A Common 25¢ par exchanged for $126.50 cash

ARDEN HLDGS INC (QC)
Acquired by 9109-5901 Quebec Inc. 02/19/2002
Each share Common no par exchanged for $8 cash

ARDEN INDL PRODS INC (MN)
Merged into Park-Ohio Industries, Inc. (New) 07/25/1997
Each share Common 1¢ par exchanged for $6 cash

ARDEN INTL KITCHENS INC (MN)
Merged into Schreiber Foods, Inc. 12/01/1994
Each share Common 10¢ par exchanged for $3.90 cash

ARDEN MAYFAIR INC (DE)
Reorganized as Arden Group, Inc. 12/19/1978
Each share Preferred no par exchanged for (1) share $2.25 Preferred Ser. A $15 par
Each share Common $1 par became (1) share Common 25¢ par
(See Arden Group, Inc.)

ARDEN MED SYS INC (DE)
Acquired by Johnson & Johnson 12/30/1986
Each share Common 1¢ par exchanged for $4.42 cash

ARDEN PROTECTED MILK CO. (DE)
Merged into Arden Farms Co. (New) 08/01/1940
Each share Preferred exchanged for (1) share Preferred no par and (5) shares Common $1 par
Arden Farms Co. (New) name changed to Arden-Mayfair, Inc. 04/24/1965 which reorganized as Arden Group, Inc. 12/19/1978
(See Arden Group, Inc.)

ARDEN RLTY INC (MD)
Merged into General Electric Capital Corp. 05/02/2006
Each share Common 1¢ par exchanged for $45.428 cash

ARDEN SALT CO.
Merged into Leslie Salt Co. 00/00/1936
Details not available

ARDENT ACQUISITION CORP (DE)
Name changed to Avantair, Inc. 04/27/2007

ARDENT COMMUNICATIONS INC (DE)
Plan of reorganization under Chapter 11 Federal Bankruptcy Code effective 12/02/2002
No stockholders' equity

ARDENT MINES LTD (NV)
Recapitalized as Gold Hills Mining, Ltd. 02/20/2013
Each share Common $0.00001 par exchanged for (0.01) share Common $0.00001 par
(See Gold Hills Mining, Ltd.)

ARDENT SOFTWARE INC (DE)
Merged into Informix Corp. 03/01/2000
Each share Common 1¢ par exchanged for (3.5) shares Common 1¢ par
Informix Corp. name changed to Ascential Software Corp. 07/03/2001
(See Ascential Software Corp.)

ARDIEM HLDGS LTD (BC)
Merged into Ardiem Industrial Corp. 01/02/1976
Each share Class A Common $1 par exchanged for (5) shares Class A no par
(See Ardiem Industrial Corp.)

ARDIEM INDL CORP (BC)
Bankrupt 02/25/1983
No stockholders' equity

ARDIS TELECOM & TECHNOLOGIES INC (DE)
Name changed to Dial-Thru International Corp. 01/20/2000
Dial-Thru International Corp. name changed to Rapid Link, Inc. 11/28/2005 which name changed to Spot Mobile International Ltd. 06/10/2010
(See Spot Mobile International Ltd.)

ARDMORE GOLD MINES LTD. (ON)
Charter revoked for failure to file reports and pay taxes 00/00/1955

ARDMORE HLDG CORP (DE)
Name changed to Yayi International Inc. 09/25/2008
(See Yayi International Inc.)

ARDO MINES INC (BC)
Recapitalized as Arex Resources Inc. 11/17/1976
Each share Capital Stock no par exchanged for (0.2) share Capital Stock no par
Arex Resources Inc. recapitalized as Ohio Resources Corp. (BC) 06/16/1980 which reincorporated in Alberta 07/09/1997 which name changed to Causeway Energy Corp. 11/16/1998 which merged into Bushmills Energy Corp. 08/29/2001 which merged into Brooklyn Energy Corp. 02/03/2003
(See Brooklyn Energy Corp.)

ARDONBLUE VENTURES INC (BC)
Name changed to Juggernaut Exploration Ltd. 10/23/2017

ARDSLEY BUTTE CORP. (SD)
Company went out of existence 00/00/1931

ARDSLEY BUTTE MINES CORP. (SD)
Charter cancelled for failure to file annual reports 07/01/1970

AREA BANCSHARES CORP (KY)
Merged into ONB Corp. 12/31/1986
Each share Common $2.50 par exchanged for $60 cash

AREA BANCSHARES CORP NEW (KY)
Common no par split (5) for (1) by issuance of (4) additional shares 09/01/1992
Common no par split (3) for (2) by issuance of (0.5) additional share 04/20/1994
Common no par split (3) for (2) by issuance of (0.5) additional share payable 12/16/1996 to holders of record 12/04/1996
Merged into BB&T Corp. 03/20/2002
Each share Common no par exchanged for (0.55) share Common $5 par

AREA INVT & DEV CO (UT)
Each share old Common 1¢ par exchanged for (0.0167504) share new Common 1¢ par 03/15/1996
Name changed to Maxx International Inc. 04/17/2000
(See Maxx International Inc.)

AREA MINES LTD (QC)
Each share Common $1 par stamped to indicate par value changed to 25¢ and a distribution of (0.125) share Mattagami Lake Mines Ltd. Capital Stock $1 par 04/28/1965
Stamped Common 25¢ par reclassified as Class A no par 08/13/1969
Completely liquidated 04/30/1971
Each share Class A no par exchanged for first and final distribution of (0.33333333) share Teck Corp. Ltd. Class B Common no par
Teck Corp. Ltd. name changed to Teck Corp. 11/21/1978 which name changed to Teck Cominco Ltd. 09/12/2001 which name changed to Teck Resources Ltd. 04/27/2009

AREA RES CORP (UT)
Recapitalized as Golden Eagle Financial Corp. 10/19/1983
Each share Common $0.001 par exchanged for (0.05) share Common 1¢ par
(See Golden Eagle Financial Corp.)

AREAWIDE CELLULAR INC (DE)
Reincorporated 04/12/2002
State of incorporation changed from (FL) to (DE) 04/12/2002
Chapter 7 bankruptcy proceedings terminated 04/22/2009
No stockholders' equity

AREL COMMUNICATIONS & SOFTWARE LTD (ISRAEL)
Each share Ordinary ILS 0.001 par received distribution of (0.30733) share Arelnet Ltd. Ordinary payable 06/12/2000 to holders of record 05/28/2000
Acquired by CYMI Financing LLC 03/13/2006
Each share Ordinary ILS 0.001 par exchanged for $1.50 cash

AREMISSOFT CORP (DE)
Common $0.001 par split (2) for (1) by issuance of (1) additional share payable 01/08/2001 to holders of record 12/28/2000 Ex date - 01/09/2001
Plan of reorganization under Chapter 11 Federal Bankruptcy Code effective 08/02/2002
Each share Common $0.001 par exchanged for (0.44737) share SoftBrands, Inc. Common 1¢ par
Note: Unexchanged certificates were cancelled and became without value 07/02/2003
(See SoftBrands, Inc.)

AREMISSOFT CORP (NV)
Reorganized under the laws of Delaware 03/05/1999
Each (1.711772) shares Common $0.001 par exchanged for (1) share Common $0.001 par
AremisSoft Corp. (DE) reorganized as SoftBrands, Inc. 08/02/2002
(See SoftBrands, Inc.)

ARENA GROUP INC (NV)
Name changed to Elligent Consulting Group, Inc. 07/31/1998
Elligent Consulting Group, Inc. name changed to E-Vantage Solutions, Inc. 07/16/2000
(See E-Vantage Solutions, Inc.)

ARENA RES INC (NV)
Common $0.001 par split (2) for (1) by issuance of (1) additional share payable 10/26/2007 to holders of record 10/15/2007 Ex date - 10/29/2007
Merged into SandRidge Energy, Inc. 07/16/2010
Each share Common $0.001 par exchanged for (4.7771) shares old Common $0.001 par and $4.50 cash
(See SandRidge Energy, Inc.)

ARENA TWINE & CORDAGE MFG. CO., INC. (NY)
Charter forfeited 00/00/1935

AREOPTIX TECHNOLOGY CORP (DE)
Common 10¢ par split (3) for (1) by issuance of (2) additional shares 12/27/1971
Name changed to Prime Technology, Inc. 07/31/1984
Prime Technology, Inc. name changed to Prime Technology, Ltd. 11/18/1985

AREQUIPA RES LTD (BC)
Merged into Barrick Gold Corp. 10/30/1996
Each share Common no par exchanged for $30 cash

ARES MULTI-STRATEGY CR FD INC (MD)
Merged into Ares Dynamic Credit Allocation Fund, Inc. 08/31/2015
Each share Common $0.001 par exchanged for (1.2134709) shares Common $0.001 par

ARES VENTURES CORP (NV)
Name changed to CommerceTel Corp. 10/05/2010
CommerceTel Corp. name changed to Mobivity Holdings Corp. 08/23/2012

ARETHUSA (OFF-SHORE) LTD. (BERMUDA)
Merged into Diamond Offshore Drilling, Inc. 04/29/1996
Each share Common 10¢ par exchanged for (0.88) share Common 1¢ par

AREV NUTRITION SCIENCES INC (BC)
Name changed to AREV Brands International Ltd. 09/12/2018

AREVA SA (FRANCE)
Basis changed from (1:0.01) to (1:0.1) 12/30/2010
ADR agreement terminated 09/15/2017
Each ADR for Ordinary issued by Bank of New York exchanged for $0.48406 cash

AREX INDEMNITY CO. (NY)
Recapitalized as Citizens Life Insurance Co. of New York 02/00/1957
Each share Common $4 par exchanged for (0.5) share Common $4 par
Citizens Life Insurance Co. of New York name changed to Executive Life Insurance Co. of New York 09/11/1969
(See Executive Life Insurance Co. of New York)

AREX INDS INC (DE)
Merged into Arex Holdings, Inc. 04/05/1985
Each share Common $1 par exchanged for $2 cash

AREX MINN INC (MN)
Statutorily dissolved 12/31/1993

AREX RES INC (BC)
Recapitalized as Ohio Resources Corp. (BC) 06/16/1980
Each share Capital Stock no par exchanged for (0.33333333) share Capital Stock no par
Ohio Resources Corp. (BC) reincorporated in Alberta 07/09/1997 which name changed to Causeway Energy Corp. 11/16/1998 which merged into Bushmills Energy Corp. 08/29/2001 which merged into Brooklyn Energy Corp. 02/03/2003
(See Brooklyn Energy Ltd.)

ARGAN BEAUTY CORP (NV)
Common $0.001 par split (7) for (1) by issuance of (6) additional shares payable 08/19/2014 to holders of record 08/19/2014
Name changed to Science to Consumers, Inc. 12/24/2014

ARGCEN HLDGS INC (CANADA)
Merged into Hollinger Inc. 09/17/1985
Each share Common no par exchanged for (1) share Common no par
(See Hollinger Inc.)

ARGENT BK (THIBODAUX, LA)
Common 10¢ par split (4) for (1) by issuance of (3) additional shares 08/31/1993
Common 10¢ par split (2) for (1) by issuance of (1) additional share 11/15/1995
Merged into Hibernia Corp. 02/01/1998
Each share Common 10¢ par exchanged for (2.04) shares Class A Common no par
Hibernia Corp. merged into Capital One Financial Corp. 11/16/2005

ARGENT CAP CORP (NV)
Name changed to Sequoia Interests Corp. 12/08/2003
Sequoia Interests Corp. name changed to Baby Bee Bright Corp. (New) 05/02/2006 which name changed to Fusion Pharm, Inc. 04/08/2011

ARGENT FINANCIAL CORP.
Dissolved 00/00/1934
Details not available

ARGENT INDL CORP (NY)
Charter cancelled and proclaimed dissolved for failure to pay taxes and file reports 12/15/1975

ARGENT MNG CORP (BC)
Recapitalized as Avion Resources Corp. 06/21/2007
Each share Common no par exchanged for (0.33333333) share Common no par
Avion Resources Corp. name changed to Avion Gold Corp. (BC) 06/05/2009 which reincorporated in Ontario 06/14/2011 which merged into Endeavour Mining Corp. 10/18/2012

ARGENT RES LTD (BC)
Recapitalized as Argent Mining Corp. 04/07/2006
Each share Common no par exchanged for (0.33333333) share Common no par
Argent Mining Corp. recapitalized as Avion Resources Corp. 06/21/2007 which name changed to Avion Gold Corp. (BC) 06/05/2009 which reincorporated in Ontario 06/14/2011 which merged into Endeavour Mining Corp. 10/18/2012

ARGENTA OIL & GAS INC (CANADA)
Recapitalized as Azabache Energy Inc. 01/11/2010
Each share Common no par exchanged for (0.2) share Common no par

ARGENTA SYS INC (BC)
Name changed 02/13/1987
Name changed from Argenta Resources Ltd. to Argenta Systems Inc. 02/13/1987
Recapitalized as Illusion Systems Inc. (BC) 03/03/2000
Each share Common no par exchanged for (0.5) share Common no par
Illusion Systems Inc. (BC) reincorporated in Delaware 02/27/2001
(See Illusion Systems Inc.)

ARGENTARIA CAJA POSTAL Y BANCO HIPOTECARIO S A (SPAIN)
Sponsored ADR's for Common P125 par changed to EUR 0.75 par 04/30/1999
Merged into Banco Bilbao Vizcaya Argentaria S.A. 01/31/2000
Each Sponsored ADR for Common EUR 0.75 par exchanged for (0.3) Sponsored ADR for Ordinary

ARGENTEX MNG CORP (BC)
Merged into Austral Gold Ltd. 08/22/2016
Each share Common no par exchanged for (0.564676) share Ordinary
Note: Unexchanged certificates will be cancelled and become without value 08/22/2022

ARGENTEX MNG CORP (NV)
Reincorporated 11/05/2007
Common $0.001 par split (3) for (1) by issuance of (2) additional shares payable 03/16/2004 to holders of record 03/15/2004 Ex date - 03/17/2004
State of incorporation changed from (NV) to (DE) 11/05/2007
State of incorporation changed from (DE) back to (NV) 06/03/2011
Reincorporated under the laws of British Columbia and Common $0.001 par changed to no par 06/08/2011
Argentex Mining Corp. (BC) merged into Austral Gold Ltd. 08/22/2016

ARGENTEX RESOURCE EXPL CORP (ON)
Merged into AXR Resources Ltd. 06/28/1988
Each share Common no par exchanged for (0.25) share Common no par
AXR Resources Ltd. merged into Greater Lenora Resources Corp. 01/05/1989
(See Greater Lenora Resources Corp.)

ARGENTINA FD INC (MD)
Acquired by Scudder International Fund, Inc. 12/17/2001
Each share Common 1¢ par exchanged for (0.43092348) share Latin America Fund Class M 1¢ par
Scudder International Fund, Inc. name changed to DWS International Fund, Inc. 02/06/2006

ARGENTINA GOLD CORP (BC)
Common no par split (3) for (1) by issuance of (2) additional shares 09/08/1994
Merged into HomeStake Mining Co. 04/28/1999
Each share Common no par exchanged for (0.545) share Common $1 par
Homestake Mining Co. merged into Barrick Gold Corp. 12/14/2001

ARGENTIUM RES INC (CANADA)
Recapitalized as Northern Sphere Mining Corp. 08/24/2015
Each share Common no par exchanged for (0.05) share Common no par

ARGENTUM CONS MINES INC (NV)
Common 20¢ par changed to 1¢ par 09/11/1974
Charter dissolved for failure to file reports and pay fees 12/31/1990

ARGENTUM MINES, LTD. (ON)
Charter cancelled and declared dissolved for default in filing returns and paying fees 12/12/1960

ARGEX MNG INC (CANADA)
Name changed to Argex Titanium Inc. 07/20/2012

ARGEX SILVER CAP INC (CANADA)
Name changed to Argex Mining Inc. 07/28/2010
Argex Mining Inc. name changed to Argex Titanium Inc. 07/20/2012

ARGO BANCORP INC (DE)
Common 1¢ par split (4) for (1) by issuance of (3) additional shares payable 10/23/1998 to holders of record 10/16/1998
Name changed to Umbrella Bancorp, Inc. (DE) 04/30/2001
Umbrella Bancorp, Inc. (DE) reincorporated in Maryland 05/28/2002 which name changed to Terme Bancorp, Inc. 02/01/2007

ARGO CAP TR CO (DE)
11% Capital Securities called for redemption at $10 on 11/17/2006

ARGO DEV CORP (BC)
Merged into Tymar Resources Inc. 10/31/1989
Each share Common no par exchanged for (0.4) share Common no par
Tymar Resources Inc. recapitalized as Baja Gold, Inc. 01/25/1993 which merged into Viceroy Resource Corp. 05/30/1996 which merged into

Quest Capital Corp. (BC) 06/30/2003 which reincorporated in Canada 05/27/2008 which name changed to Sprott Resource Lending Corp. 09/10/2010 which merged into Sprott Inc. 07/24/2013

ARGO ENERGY LTD (CANADA)
Plan of Arrangement effective 04/26/2005
Each share Common no par exchanged for (0.17125) Sequoia Oil & Gas Trust Trust Unit and (0.17125) share White Fire Energy Ltd. Common no par
(See each company's listing)

ARGO GOLD MNG INC (BC)
Merged into Pegasus Gold Ltd. 06/02/1981
Each share Common no par exchanged for (1.1) shares Common no par
Pegasus Gold Ltd. merged into Pegasus Gold Inc. 08/20/1984
(See Pegasus Gold Inc.)

ARGO OIL CO.
Merged into Argo Oil Corp. on a share for share basis 00/00/1936
(See Argo Oil Corp.)

ARGO OIL CORP. (DE)
Stock Dividends - 200% 12/15/1948; 20% 09/15/1951
Liquidation completed
Each share Common $5 par stamped to indicate initial distribution of (0.017093289) share Continental Oil Co. (DE) Capital Stock $5 par, (0.005285526) share Gulf Oil Corp. Capital Stock $8.33333333 par, (0.066710524) share Midwest Oil Corp. Common $10 par, (0.011515262) share Royal Dutch Petroleum Co. New York Shares for Ordinary 20 Gldrs. par, (0.032182183) share Standard Oil Co. (NJ) Capital Stock $7 par and $70 cash 12/26/1961
(See each company's listing)
Each share Stamped Common $5 par exchanged for second distribution of $1.91 cash 10/02/1962
Each share Stamped Common $5 par received third distribution of $0.25 cash 10/24/1966
Each share Stamped Common $5 par received fourth and final distribution of $0.1867 cash 05/17/1968

ARGO PETE CORP (DE)
Common 10¢ par split (5) for (4) by issuance of (0.25) additional share 01/20/1981
Stock Dividend - 50% 04/07/1978
Reorganized as Fortune Petroleum Corp. 07/06/1987
Each share Common 10¢ par exchanged for (0.1) share Common 1¢ par
Fortune Petroleum Corp. name changed to Fortune Natural Resources Corp. 07/03/1997
(See Fortune Natural Resources Corp.)

ARGO ROYALTY CO.
Merged into Argo Oil Corp. 00/00/1936
Each share Capital Stock exchanged for (2.3) shares Capital Stock $5 par
(See Argo Oil Corp.)

ARGOMA URANIUM MINES LTD. (ON)
Charter revoked for failure to file reports and pay fees 10/05/1959

ARGON ST INC (DE)
Acquired by Boeing Co. 08/05/2010
Each share Common 1¢ par exchanged for $34.50 cash

ARGON WELDING INDUSTRIES LTD. (CANADA)
Dissolved 03/28/1961
No stockholders' equity

ARGONAUT CONSOLIDATED MINING CO.
Liquidated 00/00/1941
No stockholders' equity

ARGONAUT ENERGY CORP (TX)
Common no par split (2) for (1) by issuance of (1) additional share 06/30/1978
Stock Dividend - 10% 11/23/1984
Plan of reorganization under Chapter 11 Federal Bankruptcy proceedings confirmed 12/15/1987
No stockholders' equity

ARGONAUT GOLD LTD (ON)
Name changed to Argonaut Gold Inc. 10/22/2010

ARGONAUT GROUP INC (DE)
Common 10¢ par split (3) for (1) by issuance of (2) additional shares 06/04/1991
Merged into Argo Group International Holdings, Ltd. 08/07/2007
Each share Common 10¢ par exchanged for (0.6484) share Common $1 par

ARGONAUT INS CO (CA)
Merged into Teledyne, Inc. 04/11/1969
Each share Preferred $20 par exchanged for (0.2) share $6 Conv. Preferred $1 par
Each share Common $1 par exchanged for (0.2) share $6 Conv. Preferred $1 par and (0.23) share $3.50 Conv. Preferred $1 par
(See Teledyne, Inc.)

ARGONAUT INVT CORP (AB)
Recapitalized as Spray-Air International, Inc. 10/24/1990
Each share Common no par exchanged for (0.33333333) share Common no par
Spray-Air International, Inc. name changed to Epicore Networks Inc. 12/23/1991 which recapitalized as Epicore BioNetworks Inc. 08/28/2000
(See Epicore BioNetworks Inc.)

ARGONAUT MINING CO., LTD.
Liquidated 00/00/1948
Details not available

ARGONAUT RES LTD (BC)
Reorganized under the laws of Delaware as P.D.C. Industrial Coatings Inc. 07/28/1989
Each share Common no par exchanged for (0.5) share Common no par
P.D.C. Industrial Coatings Inc. recapitalized as Advanced Industrial Minerals Inc. 12/13/1993 which merged into Aim Group, Inc. 03/31/1995 which name changed to Cereus Technology Partners, Inc. 12/06/1999 which merged into Verso Technologies, Inc. 10/02/2000

ARGONAUT RES LTD (NV)
Name changed to Sailtech International, Inc. 12/16/2000
Sailtech International, Inc. name changed to Ecloclean Industries, Inc. 12/15/2003

ARGONAUT TECHNOLOGIES INC (DE)
Liquidation completed
Each share Common $0.0001 par received initial distribution of $0.70 cash payable 07/08/2005 to holders of record 06/22/2005
Each share Common $0.0001 par received second distribution of $0.27 cash payable 12/11/2006 to holders of record 11/24/2006 Ex date - 12/11/2006
Each share Common $0.0001 par exchanged for third and final distribution of $0.0888 cash 03/31/2011

ARGONAUT YELLOWKNIFE MINES LTD. (ON)
Charter cancelled 00/00/1956

ARGONAUTS GROUP LTD (AB)
Name changed to Cequel Energy Inc. 06/07/2002
(See Cequel Energy Inc.)

ARGOS ENERGY TEX INC (DE)
Name changed to First American Energy, Inc. 08/21/1990
(See First American Energy, Inc.)

ARGOSY CAP CORP (ON)
Delisted from Canadian Dealer Network 04/06/1992

ARGOSY ED GROUP INC (IL)
Merged into Education Management Corp. 12/21/2001
Each share Class A Common 1¢ par exchanged for $12 cash

ARGOSY ENERGY INC (AB)
Discharged from receivership 09/15/2014
No stockholders' equity

ARGOSY ENERGY INC (UT)
Each share Common $0.001 par exchanged for (0.02) share Common 5¢ par 12/01/1986
Acquired by Garnet Resources Corp. 09/22/1988
Each share Common 5¢ par exchanged for (0.2) share Common 1¢ par
Garnet Resources Corp. merged into Aviva Petroleum Inc. 10/28/1998
(See Aviva Petroleum Inc.)

ARGOSY GAMING CO (DE)
Merged into Penn National Gaming, Inc. 10/03/2005
Each share Common 1¢ par exchanged for $47 cash

ARGOSY GOLD MINES LTD.
Recapitalized as Jason Mines Ltd. 00/00/1938
Each share Capital Stock exchanged for (0.2) share Capital Stock
Jason Mines Ltd. recapitalized as New Jason Mines Ltd. 00/00/1948
(See New Jason Mines Ltd.)

ARGOSY MINERALS INC (BC)
Reincorporated 05/26/2005
Place of incorporation changed from (YT) to (BC) 05/26/2005
Reincorporated under the laws of Australia as Argosy Minerals Ltd. and Common no par reclassified as Ordinary 03/18/2011

ARGOSY MNG CORP (YT)
Reincorporated 08/12/1997
Common no par split (2) for (1) by issuance of (1) additional share 08/20/1993
Place of incorporation changed from (BC) to (YT) 08/12/1997
Merged into Argosy Minerals Inc. (YT) 05/07/1999
Each share Common no par exchanged for (0.6) share Common no par
Argosy Minerals Inc. (YT) reincorporated in British Columbia 05/26/2005
Argosy Minerals Inc. (BC) reincorporated in Australia as Argosy Minerals Ltd. 03/18/2011

ARGOSY MNG LTD (ON)
Capital Stock $1 par changed to no par 07/21/1971
Name changed to Argosy Capital Corp. 03/29/1989
(See Argosy Capital Corp.)

ARGOSY RES CORP (BC)
Name changed to Motion Works Corp. 10/24/1991
Motion Works Corp. name changed to Motion Works Group Ltd. 08/08/1995
(See Motion Works Group Ltd.)

ARGOSYSTEMS INC (CA)
Common $0.125 par changed to 1¢ par and (1) additional share issued 05/12/1983
Merged into Boeing Co. 06/30/1987

Each share Common 1¢ par exchanged for $37 cash

ARGREL RES LTD (BC)
Struck off register and declared dissolved for failure to file returns 11/05/1993

ARGUS, INC. (MI)
Name changed to Argus Cameras, Inc. 00/00/1950
Argus Cameras, Inc. acquired by Sylvania Electric Products, Inc. 01/02/1957 which merged into General Telephone & Electronics Corp. 03/05/1959 which name changed to GTE Corp. 07/01/1982 which merged into Verizon Communications Inc. 06/30/2000

ARGUS CAMERAS, INC. (MI)
Acquired by Sylvania Electric Products, 01/02/1957
Each share Common $1 par exchanged for (0.47619047) share Common $7.50 par
Sylvania Electric Products, Inc. merged into General Telephone & Electronics Corp. 03/05/1959 which name changed to GTE Corp. 07/01/1982 which merged into Verizon Communications Inc. 06/30/2000

ARGUS CONSOLIDATED MINES LTD. (BC)
Recapitalized as Cassiar Copperfields Ltd. 00/00/1957
Each share Capital Stock exchanged for (0.4) share Capital Stock
(See Cassiar Copperfields Ltd.)

ARGUS CORP. (DE)
Incorporated 06/06/1925
Common no par exchanged (5) for (1) 00/00/1930
Common no par changed to $1 par 00/00/1932
Common $1 par changed to 10¢ par 00/00/1935
Recapitalized 00/00/1936
Each share Preferred $100 par exchanged for (1) share Preferred $10 par and (1) share Common 10¢ par
Each (10) shares Common 10¢ exchanged for (1) share Common 10¢ par
No longer in existence having become inoperative and void for non-payment of taxes 04/01/1958

ARGUS INC (DE)
Common 50¢ par changed to 10¢ par 07/01/1964
Name changed to Spiratone International, Inc. 10/14/1988
(See Spiratone International, Inc.)

ARGUS INDS (MN)
Proclaimed dissolved for failure to file annual reports 11/13/1991

ARGUS INTERESTS, LTD.
Liquidated 00/00/1943
Details not available

ARGUS LTD (ON)
$2.40 Conv. 2nd Preference Ser. A $50 par reclassified as $2.40 Conv. Preference Ser. A $50 par 05/31/1955
4.5% 1st Preference $100 par called for redemption 06/13/1955
$2.40 Preference Ser. A $50 par called for redemption 07/26/1960
$2.50 Class B Preference $50 par reclassified as $2.50 Class A Preference $50 par 05/31/1962
$2.60 Class C Preference $50 par reclassified as $2.60 Class A Preference $50 par 05/31/1962
Each share Common no par received distribution of (4) shares Non-Vtg. Participating Preference no par 06/20/1962
Under plan of merger each share Class C Participating Preference no par and Common no par exchanged

for $19.75 cash respectively 01/17/1986
Discharged from receivership 04/24/2009
No stockholders' equity

ARGUS METALS CORP (BC)
Each share old Common no par exchanged for (0.05) share new Common no par 01/07/2013
Each share new Common no par received distribution of (1.1055) shares Banyan Gold Corp. Class A Common no par payable 03/28/2013 to holders of record 03/18/2013
Ex date - 04/01/2013
Name changed to ePower Metals Inc. 12/07/2017

ARGUS PHARMACEUTICALS INC (DE)
Name changed to Aronex Pharmaceuticals, Inc. 09/12/1995
Aronex Pharmaceuticals, Inc. merged into Antigenics Inc. 07/13/2001 which name changed to Agenus Inc. 01/06/2011

ARGUS RES INC (NV)
Reincorporated under the laws of Delaware as 1st Global Petroleum Group, Inc. and Common $0.001 par changed to 20¢ par 03/31/2005
1st Global Petroleum Group, Inc. name changed to Commonwealth American Financial Group, Inc. 05/13/2005 which name changed to James Monroe Capital Corp. 05/30/2006

ARGUS SOLUTIONS LTD (AUSTRALIA)
Name changed to Moore Australasia Holdings Ltd. 03/14/2011
(See Moore Australasia Holdings Ltd.)

ARGUS TECHNOLOGIES INC (UT)
Involuntarily dissolved 04/01/1988

ARGUSS COMMUNICATIONS INC (DE)
Name changed 05/19/2000
Name changed from Arguss Holdings, Inc. to Arguss Communications, Inc. 05/19/2000
Merged into Dycom Industries, Inc. 02/21/2002
Each share Common 1¢ par exchanged for (0.33333333) share Common $0.33333333 par

ARGYLE FDG INC (DE)
Recapitalized as Fountain Colony Holding Corp. (DE) 01/15/1991
Each share Common $0.001 par exchanged for (0.025) share Common $0.001 par
Fountain Colony Holding Corp. (DE) reincorporated in Colorado 02/16/1999 which name changed to Fountain Colony Ventures Inc. 07/23/1999 which recapitalized as SGT Ventures, Inc. 03/20/2006 which name changed to Stronghold Industries, Inc. 07/10/2006 which recapitalized as Image Worldwide, Inc. 11/30/2007 which recapitalized as STL Marketing Group, Inc. 09/03/2009

ARGYLE FORESTS, INC. (FL)
Liquidation completed
Each share Common $5 par received initial distribution of (2) shares Gulfstream Land & Development Corp. Common 10¢ par 10/08/1973
Each share Common $5 par received second distribution of $19.50 cash 01/11/1974
Each share Common $5 par received third distribution of (1.008922) shares Gulfstream Land & Development Corp. 10/24/1974
Each share Common $5 par received fourth and final distribution of $0.0325 cash 09/09/1977
Note: Certificates were not required to be surrendered and are without value

ARGYLE PROPERTIES LTD. (SK)
Charter revoked for failure to file reports and pay fees 09/30/1961

ARGYLE PUBLISHING CORP. (NY)
Acquired by Metromedia, Inc. 09/10/1968
Each share Common 1¢ par exchanged for (0.103305) share Capital Stock $1 par
(See Metromedia, Inc.)

ARGYLE SEC ACQUISITION CORP (DE)
Name changed to Argyle Security, Inc. 08/29/2007

ARGYLE SOUTHN CO (DE)
Capital Stock $10 par changed to $5 par and (1) additional share issued 06/10/1964
Completely liquidated 03/31/1972
Each share Capital Stock $5 par received first and final distribution of (0.1) share Argyle Forests, Inc. Common $5 par
Note: Certificates were not required to be surrendered and are without value
(See Argyle Forests, Inc.)

ARGYLE TELEVISION INC (DE)
Merged into Hearst-Argyle Television, Inc. 08/29/1997
Each share Ser. A Common 1¢ par exchanged for (0.8497) share Common 1¢ and $3.98 cash
(See Hearst-Argyle Television, Inc.)

ARGYLE TRUST
Liquidated 00/00/1942
Details not available

ARGYLE VENTURES INC (BC)
Name changed to Anglo-Andean Explorations, Inc. (BC) 05/11/1994
Anglo-Andean Explorations, Inc. (BC) reincorporated in Canada 05/20/1994
(See Anglo-Andean Explorations, Inc.)

ARGYLE VENTURES INC (NV)
SEC revoked common stock registration 10/01/2008

ARGYLL ENERGY CORP (ON)
Assets sold for the benefit of creditors 05/00/1992
No stockholders' equity

ARGYLL GOLD MINES LTD. (ON)
Charter cancelled for failure to pay taxes and file returns 03/16/1976

ARGYLL RES LTD (CANADA)
Reincorporated 09/22/1982
Place of incorporation changed from (BC) to (Canada) 09/22/1982
Merged into Argyll Energy Corp. 08/16/1983
Each share Common no par exchanged for (1) share Class A no par
(See Argyll Energy Corp.)

ARI AUTOMATED RECYCLING INC (BC)
Recapitalized as Envipco Automated Recycling Inc. 11/01/1994
Each share Common no par exchanged for (0.2) share Common no par
Envipco Automated Recycling Inc. name changed to Automated Recycling Inc. 08/20/1999 which name changed to OceanLake Commerce Inc. 03/01/2001

ARI HLDGS INC (NJ)
Liquidation completed
Each share Common 1¢ par received initial distribution of $7.25 cash 09/28/1995
Each share Common 1¢ par received second and final distribution of $1.28 cash 04/12/1996

ARI INDS INC (DE)
Merged into Ogazaki Manufacturing Co. 11/14/1980
Each share Common 1¢ par exchanged for $5.40 cash

ARI-MEX OIL & EXPL INC (NM)
Out of business 00/00/1989
Details not available

ARI NETWORK SVCS INC (WI)
Each share old Common $0.001 par exchanged for (0.25) share new Common $0.001 par 11/19/1997
Acquired by True Wind Capital, L.P. 08/29/2017
Each share new Common $0.001 par exchanged for $7.10 cash

ARIA INTL HLDGS INC (NV)
Charter permanently revoked 11/30/2012

ARIA WIRELESS SYS INC (DE)
Charter forfeited for failure to maintain a registered agent 04/21/2002

ARIAD PHARMACEUTICALS INC (DE)
Acquired by Takeda Pharmaceutical Co. Ltd. 02/16/2017
Each share Common $0.001 par exchanged for $24 cash

ARIAN RES CORP (ON)
Merged into Bema Gold Corp. (BC) 07/08/1998
Each share Common no par exchanged for (0.3030303) share Common no par
Bema Gold Corp. (BC) reincorporated in Canada 07/19/2002 which merged into Kinross Gold Corp. 02/27/2007

ARIAN SILVER CORP (BRITISH VIRGIN ISLANDS)
Each share old Common no par exchanged for (0.1) share new Common no par 09/03/2013
Shares transferred to British Virgin Islands register 02/01/2016

ARIANE GOLD CORP (CANADA)
Merged into Cambior Inc. 11/29/2003
Each share Common no par exchanged for (0.3436) share Common no par
Cambior Inc. acquired by Iamgold Corp. 11/08/2006

ARIANNE CO. (NV)
Reorganized as One E-Commerce Corp. 03/31/1999
Each share Common $0.001 par exchanged for (1.8) shares Common $0.001 par
One E-Commerce Corp. recapitalized as Islet Sciences, Inc. 02/23/2012

ARIANNE RES INC (QC)
Each share old Common no par exchanged for (0.2) share new Common no par 07/03/2009
Name changed to Arianne Phosphate Inc. 07/05/2013

ARIBA INC (DE)
Old Common $0.002 par split (2) for (1) by issuance of (1) additional share payable 12/17/1999 to holders of record 12/03/1999
Old Common $0.002 par split (2) for (1) by issuance of (1) additional share payable 03/31/2000 to holders of record 03/20/2000
Each share old Common $0.002 par exchanged for (0.16666666) share new Common $0.002 par 07/01/2004
Acquired by SAP America, Inc. 10/01/2012
Each share new Common $0.002 par exchanged for $45 cash

ARICANA RES INC (BC)
Struck off register and declared dissolved for failure to file returns 06/22/1990

ARIDTECH INC (CA)
Recapitalized as Pacific Agricultural Holdings, Inc. 05/09/1988
Each share Common no par exchanged for (0.33333333) share Common no par
Pacific Agricultural Holdings, Inc. reorganized as Cadiz Land Co. (DE) 05/26/1992 which name changed to Cadiz Inc. 09/01/1998

ARIEL CORP (DE)
Filed a petition under Chapter 7 Federal Bankruptcy Code 06/26/2003
No stockholders' equity

ARIEL GROWTH FD (MA)
Shares of Bene. Int. reclassified as Ariel Fund Investor Class 02/01/1999
Name changed to Ariel Investment Trust 11/10/2001

ARIEL RES LTD (BC)
Reincorporated 07/10/2002
Place of incorporation changed from (BC) to (WY) 07/10/2002
SEC revoked common stock registration 11/02/2010

ARIELY ADVERTISING LTD (ISRAEL)
Name changed to Publicis-Ariely Ltd. 09/17/1997
Publicis-Ariely Ltd. name changed to Oz Investments Co. Ltd. 04/11/2002
(See Oz Investments Co. Ltd.)

ARIES COPPER MINES LTD. (ON)
Charter revoked for failure to file reports and pay fees 04/01/1965

ARIES CORP (MN)
Adjudicated bankrupt 10/30/1975
Stockholders' equity unlikely

ARIES MARITIME TRANSPORT LTD (BERMUDA)
Name changed to NewLead Holdings Ltd. 12/21/2009

ARIES MIDWEST CORP (MN)
Merged into Resource Financial Corp. 12/26/1969
Each share Conv. Preferred 10¢ par or Common 10¢ par exchanged for (1) share Common 1¢ par
Resource Financial Corp. completely liquidated for Automation Technology, Inc. Common 1¢ par which name changed to Tax Corp. of America (MD) 03/11/1971
(See Tax Corp. of America (MD))

ARIES RESOURCE CORP (BC)
Recapitalized as Alderon Resource Corp. 09/24/2008
Each share Common no par exchanged for (0.1) share Common no par
Alderon Resource Corp. name changed to Alderon Iron Ore Corp. 10/05/2011

ARIES RES INC (BC)
Reincorporated under the laws of Yukon as Total Global Ventures Inc. 05/19/1999
Total Global Ventures Inc. recapitalized as JNB Developments Co. Ltd. 10/03/2001 which name changed to Cooper Minerals Inc. (YT) 07/14/2004 which reincorporated in British Columbia as United Coal Holdings Ltd. 05/28/2012

ARIES URANIUM INC (UT)
Reorganized under the laws of Texas as X-L Energy Co. 12/17/1982
Each share Common 1¢ par exchanged for (1) share Common 1¢ par

ARIES VENTURES INC (NV)
Reincorporated under the laws of Delaware as Cardium Therapeutics, Inc. and Common 1¢ par changed to $0.0001 par 01/23/2006
Cardium Therapeutics, Inc. name changed to Taxus Cardium Pharmaceuticals Group, Inc. 10/07/2014

ARIL GROUP INC (FL)
Proclaimed dissolved for failure to file reports and pay fees 08/25/1995

ARIMATHAEA RES INC (BC)
Reincorporated under the laws of Bermuda as Van Diemen's Co. Ltd. and Common no par changed to 10¢ par 06/29/1992
Van Diemen's Co. Ltd. recapitalized as VDC Corp. Ltd. 07/17/1995 which merged into VDC Communications, Inc. 11/06/1998
(See VDC Communications, Inc.)

ARIMETCO INTL INC (CANADA)
Plan of reorganization under Chapter 11 Federal Bankruptcy proceedings confirmed 04/01/1999
No stockholders' equity

ARIMEX MNG CORP (BC)
Recapitalized as International Arimex Resources Inc. 02/22/1999
Each share Common no par exchanged for (0.25) share Common no par
International Arimex Resources Inc. name changed to WestCan Uranium Corp. 09/10/2007

ARINCO COMPUTER SYS INC (NM)
Reincorporated under the laws of Delaware as Change Technology Partners, Inc. 09/12/2000
Change Technology Partners, Inc. name changed to Neurologix, Inc. 02/12/2004
(See Neurologix, Inc.)

ARIPEKA SAW MILLS
Dissolved 00/00/1933
Details not available

ARIS CDA LTD (AB)
Placed in receivership 01/10/2003
No stockholders' equity

ARIS CORP (DE)
Name changed to Lamonts Corp. 04/12/1991
Lamonts Corp. name changed to Lamonts Apparel, Inc. 11/02/1992
(See Lamonts Apparel, Inc.)

ARIS CORP (WA)
Merged into Ciber, Inc. 09/19/2001
Each share Common no par exchanged for (0.1937) share Common 1¢ par and $1.30 cash
Ciber, Inc. name changed to CMTSU Liquidation, Inc. 12/22/2017

ARIS INDS INC (NY)
Plan of reorganization under Chapter 11 Federal Bankruptcy proceedings confirmed 03/29/2007
No stockholders' equity

ARISE TECHNOLOGIES CORP (CANADA)
Reincorporated 07/30/2003
Place of incorporation changed from (BC) to Canada 07/30/2003
Deemed to have made an assignment in bankruptcy 04/11/2012
Stockholders' equity unlikely

ARISTA RES INC (BC)
Recapitalized as Patricia Mines Ltd. 01/15/1996
Each share Common no par exchanged for (0.33333333) share Common no par
Patricia Mines Ltd. recapitalized as Patricia Mining Corp. (BC) 09/13/1999 which reincorporated in Ontario 01/15/2003 which was acquired by Richmont Mines Inc. 12/16/2008 which merged into Alamos Gold Inc. (New) 11/24/2017

ARISTA TRUCK RENTING CORP. (NY)
Through tender offer 00/00/1963 and subsequent private acquisitions public interest was eliminated

ARISTAR INC (DE)
Merged into Gamble-Skogmo, Inc. 01/26/1979

Each share Common $1 par exchanged for $10 principal amount of 10% Senior Subord. Sinking Fund Debentures due 01/01/1989

ARISTECH CHEM CORP (DE)
Common $1 par split (3) for (2) by issuance of (0.5) additional share 04/17/1989
Merged into ACC Acquisition Corp. 03/23/1990
Each share Common $1 par exchanged for $27 cash

ARISTEK CMNTYS INC (DE)
Common 1¢ par changed to $0.001 par 09/23/1976
Stock Dividends - 10% 11/1/1982; 10% 05/10/1983; 10% 11/01/1983
Name changed to Homefree Village Resorts Inc. 11/05/1986
(See Homefree Village Resorts, Inc.)

ARISTEK CORP. (DE)
Name changed to Aristek Communities, Inc. 12/28/1981
Aristek Communities, Inc. name changed to Homefree Village Resorts, Inc. 11/05/1986
(See Homefree Village Resorts, Inc.)

ARISTO FOODS INC (MO)
Common $1 par changed to $0.66666666 par and (0.5) additional share issued 10/09/1967
Common $0.66666666 par changed to $0.445 par and (0.5) additional share issued 03/15/1968
Under plan of merger each (100) shares Common $0.445 par exchanged for $25 principal amount of 12% Subord. Debentures due 05/13/1986 and $25 cash 06/03/1981

ARISTO INTL CORP (DE)
Name changed to Playnet Technologies, Inc. 11/19/1996
(See Playnet Technologies, Inc.)

ARISTOCRAT APPAREL, INC. (DE)
Voluntarily dissolved 08/22/1975
No stockholders' equity

ARISTOCRAT GROUP CORP (FL)
Common $0.0001 par split (5) for (1) by issuance of (4) additional shares payable 05/15/2012 to holders of record 05/14/2012 Ex date - 05/16/2012
Reorganized under the laws of Nevada 04/17/2015
Each share Common $0.0001 par exchanged for (0.01) share Common $0.001 par 04/17/2015
Note: No holder will receive fewer than (5) shares

ARISTOCRAT TRAVEL PRODS (CA)
Acquired by Boise Cascade Corp. 07/24/1969
Each share Common $1 par exchanged for (0.435) share Common $2.50 par
Boise Cascade Corp. name changed to OfficeMax Inc. 11/01/2004 which merged into Office Depot, Inc. 11/05/2013

ARISTOTLE CORP (DE)
Each share Common $1 par exchanged for (0.1) share Common 1¢ par 05/11/1994
Each share Common 1¢ par received distribution of (1) share 11% Preferred Ser. I 1¢ par payable 06/17/2002 to holders of record 06/10/2002
Acquired by Geneve Corp. 11/18/2009
Each share 11% Ser. I Preferred 1¢ par exchanged for $7 cash
Each share Common 1¢ par exchanged for $5.50 cash

ARISTOTLE VENTURE CORP (DE)
Name changed to Parker Automotive Corp. 03/13/1989
(See Parker Automotive Corp.)

ARITECH CORP (DE)
Acquired by Sentrol Lifesafety Corp. 12/20/1993
Each share Common $2 par exchanged for $6.25 cash

ARIUS RESH INC (ON)
Acquired by F. Hoffmann-La Roche Ltd. 09/24/2008
Each share Common no par exchanged for $2.44 cash

ARIVACA SILVER MINES LTD (BC)
Delisted from Vancouver Stock Exchange 07/10/1990

ARIX CORP (DE)
Reincorporated 12/22/1989
State of incorporation changed from (CA) to (DE) and Common no par changed to 1¢ par 12/22/1989
Charter cancelled and declared inoperative and void for non-payment of taxes 03/01/1996

ARIZAKO MINES LTD (BC)
Merged into Goldrich Resources Inc. 10/22/1984
Each share Common no par exchanged for (1) share Common no par
(See Goldrich Resources Inc.)

ARIZIGON CORP (NV)
Recapitalized as Gocitylink.Com Inc. 10/10/2000
Each share Common $0.001 par exchanged for (2.5) shares Common $0.001 par
Gocitylink.Com Inc. recapitalized as Bell AZ Consultants, Inc. 12/08/2003 which name changed to Strategy X, Inc. 03/11/2004 which recapitalized as Alliance Transcription Services, Inc. 08/14/2007
(See Alliance Transcription Services, Inc.)

ARIZONA AGROCHEMICAL CORP. (AZ)
Completely liquidated 01/02/1969
Each share Common $2.50 par exchanged for first and final distribution of (1) share Early California Industries, Inc. Common $1 par
Early California Industries, Inc. name changed to Erly Industries, Inc. (CA) 10/31/1985 which reorganized in Delaware as Torchmail Communications, Inc. 05/24/2001 which name changed to Ohana Enterprises, Inc. 12/11/2002 which reorganized as Vinoble, Inc. 11/19/2004 which name changed to Matrixx Resource Holdings, Inc. 07/14/2003
(See Matrixx Resource Holdings, Inc.)

ARIZONA AIRCRAFT SPARES INC (NV)
Name changed to Cell Wireless Corp. 01/07/2005
(See Cell Wireless Corp.)

ARIZONA ANTLERS MINING CO. (UT)
Recapitalized as Antlers Oil, Mining & Milling Inc. 06/11/1953
Each share Common 10¢ par exchanged for (0.4) share Common 25¢ par
Antlers Oil, Mining & Milling, Inc. merged into American Mining & Development Co. 03/26/1959 which recapitalized as American International Corp. (NV) 06/01/1972 which recapitalized as American Diversified Corp. (NV) 01/10/1985 which recapitalized as Natural Pharmaceutical International Inc. 06/18/1990

ARIZONA APPETITOS STORES INC (AZ)
Charter revoked for failure to file reports or pay fees 11/10/1991

ARIZONA BANCORPORATION (DE)
Reincorporated 07/23/1963
State of incorporation changed from (AZ) to (DE) 07/23/1963
Merged into Signal Oil & Gas Co. 09/01/1967
Each share Common $10 par exchanged for (1) share $1 Conv. Preferred no par
Signal Oil & Gas Co. name changed to Signal Companies, Inc. 05/01/1968 which merged into Allied-Signal Inc. 09/19/1985 which name changed to AlliedSignal Inc. 04/26/1993 which name changed to Honeywell International Inc. 12/01/1999

ARIZONA BANCSHARES INC (AZ)
Company's sole asset placed in receivership 09/04/2009
Stockholders' equity unlikely

ARIZONA BANCWEST CORP (AZ)
Stock Dividend - 10% 11/20/1984
Acquired by Security Pacific Corp. 10/17/1986
Each share Common $2.50 par exchanged for $45 cash

ARIZONA BK (PHOENIX, AZ)
Capital Stock $5 par changed to $2.50 par and (1) additional share issued 04/10/1972
Stock Dividends - 15% 02/26/1971; 15% 02/25/1974; 10% 01/31/1975; 15% 11/28/1977; 15% 11/20/1978; 15% 09/14/1979; 10% 11/20/1980
Under plan of reorganization each share Capital Stock $2.50 par automatically became (1) share Arizona Bancwest Corp. Common $2.50 par 10/01/1982
(See Arizona Bancwest Corp.)

ARIZONA BK (TUCSON, AZ)
Merged into Compass Bancshares, Inc. 12/15/1998
Each share Preferred Ser. E $10.50 par exchanged for (1) share Preferred Ser. E $25 par
Each share Common $5 par exchanged for (2.9286) shares Common $2 par
Perpetual Preferred Ser. F called for redemption at $25.75 on 02/15/1999
Compass Bancshares, Inc. merged into Banco Bilbao Vizcaya Argentaria, S.A. 09/07/2007

ARIZONA BIOCHEMICAL CO (DE)
Name changed to National Environmental Controls, Inc. 10/15/1970
(See National Environmental Controls, Inc.)

ARIZONA BREWING CO., INC. (AZ)
Name changed to Brewery Liquidating Corp. 12/03/1964
(See Brewery Liquidating Corp.)

ARIZONA COLO LD & CATTLE CO (AZ)
Name changed to AZL Resources, Inc. 05/17/1977
(See AZL Resources, Inc.)

ARIZONA COLOR FILM PROCESSING LABORATORIES (AZ)
Common $1 par changed to 20¢ par 04/00/1960
Recapitalized as Multi-Color, Inc. 11/30/1964
Each share Common 20¢ par exchanged for (0.1) share Common $2 par
Multi-Color, Inc. recapitalized as Phototron Corp. (AZ) 08/28/1973 which reincorporated in Delaware 06/17/1976
(See Phototron Corp. (DE))

ARIZONA COMM BK (TUCSON, AZ)
Common no par changed to 1¢ par 11/01/1988
Declared insolvent by Superintendent of Banks 04/12/1991

ARIZONA COMMERCIAL MINING CO.
Stockholders' equity unlikely
Liquidated 00/00/1932
Details not available

ARIZONA COMSTOCK CORP.
Assets sold 00/00/1938
Details not available

ARIZONA COPPER BELT MINING CO. (AZ)
Charter revoked for failure to file reports and pay fees 05/13/1952

ARIZONA DIVIDE MINING CO. (NV)
Charter revoked for failure to file reports and pay fees 03/03/1929

ARIZONA EDISON CO.
Reorganized as Arizona Edison Co., Inc. 00/00/1935
Details not available

ARIZONA EDISON CO., INC.
Merged into Arizona Public Service Co. 00/00/1952
Each share $5 Preferred no par exchanged for (2) shares $2.50 Preferred $50 par
Each share Common $5 par exchanged for (1.75) shares new Common $5 par

ARIZONA FEEDS (AZ)
Acquired by Dekalb AgResearch Inc. 01/30/1974
Each share Common $3.33333333 par exchanged for (0.2596) share Class A Common no par
Dekalb AgResearch Inc. name changed to Dekalb Corp. 12/17/1985 which name changed to Dekalb Energy Co. 09/06/1988 which merged into Apache Corp. 05/17/1995

ARIZONA FERTILIZER & CHEMICAL CO. (AZ)
Under plan of merger name changed to Arizona Agrochemical Corp. 11/27/1961
Arizona Agrochemical Corp. acquired by Early California Industries, Inc. 01/02/1969 which name changed to Erly Industries, Inc. (CA) 10/31/1985 which reorganized in Delaware as Torchmail Communications, Inc. 05/24/2001 which name changed to Ohana Enterprises, Inc. 12/11/2002 which reorganized as Vinoble, Inc. 11/19/2004 which name changed to Matrixx Resource Holdings, Inc. 07/14/2003
(See Matrixx Resource Holdings, Inc.)

ARIZONA FLOUR MILLS CO. (AZ)
Name changed to Arizona Milling Co. 05/25/1960
Arizona Milling Co. recapitalized as Arizona Feeds 04/01/1969 which was acquired by Dekalb AgResearch Inc. 01/30/1974 which name changed to Dekalb Corp. 12/17/1985 which name changed to Dekalb Energy Co. 09/6/1988 which merged into Apache Corp. 05/17/1995

ARIZONA GLOBE URANIUM, INC. (AZ)
Charter revoked for failure to file reports and pay fees 04/10/1961

ARIZONA-GOLCONDA METALS, INC. (DE)
No longer in existence having become inoperative and void for non-payment of taxes 04/01/1962

ARIZONA GOLDEN PAC RES LTD (BC)
Struck off register and declared dissolved for failure to file returns 12/04/1992

ARIZONA HELIUM CORP. (AZ)
Adjudicated bankrupt 04/02/1971
No stockholders' equity

ARIZONA INSTR CORP (DE)
Each share old Common 1¢ par exchanged for (0.2) share new Common 1¢ par 02/16/1999
Merged into AZI LLC 06/27/2000
Each share new Common 1¢ par exchanged for $5 cash

ARIZONA JOJOBA INC (BC)
Struck off register and declared dissolved for failure to file returns 05/29/1992

ARIZONA JUNO RES INC (NV)
Name changed to WebGalaxy, Inc. 09/29/1997
WebGalaxy, Inc. recapitalized as Nanoforce, Inc. 04/11/2005

ARIZONA LAND CORP. (AZ)
Adjudicated bankrupt 07/24/1972
No stockholders' equity

ARIZONA LAND TITLE & TRUST CO. (AZ)
Name changed to Lawyers Title of Arizona 08/26/1969

ARIZONA LD INCOME CORP (AZ)
Reincorporated under the laws of Maryland as Pacific Office Properties Trust, Inc. and Class A Common no par reclassified as Common $0.0001 par 03/20/2008

ARIZONA MNG INC (BC)
Acquired by South32 Ltd. 08/10/2018
Each share Common no par exchanged for $6.20 cash
Note: Unexchanged certificates will be cancelled and become without value 08/10/2024

ARIZONA MLG CO (AZ)
Recapitalized as Arizona Feeds 04/01/1969
Each share Capital Stock $10 par exchanged for (3) shares Common $3.33333333 par
Arizona Feeds acquired by Dekalb AgResearch Inc. 01/30/1974 which name changed to Dekalb Corp. 12/17/1985 which name changed to Dekalb Energy Co. 09/06/1988 which merged into Apache Corp. 05/17/1995

ARIZONA MTG & INVT CO (AZ)
Out of business 06/30/1989
No stockholders' equity

ARIZONA NEV MNG CO (NV)
Recapitalized as International Texas Industries, Inc. 07/20/1982
Each share Common 10¢ par exchanged for (0.5) share Common 20¢ par
International Texas Industries, Inc. name changed to Kentex Energy Inc. 06/10/1998 which recapitalized as Home Financing Centers, Inc. 01/13/2000 which recapitalized as WorldWide Indoor Karting, Inc. 07/23/2003 which name changed to Vault Financial Services Inc. 10/08/2003 which name changed to Prime Restaurants, Inc. 04/18/2007 which name changed to BIH Corp. 03/19/2008
(See BIH Corp.)

ARIZONA-NEW MEXICO DEVELOPMENT CORP. (AZ)
Each share old Common 80¢ par exchanged for (5) shares new Common 80¢ par 12/18/1961
Name changed to Dinosaur Caverns, Inc. 07/14/1962
(See Dinosaur Caverns, Inc.)

ARIZONA NEWSPAPERS, INC. (AZ)
Charter revoked for failure to file reports and pay fees 01/26/1967

ARIZONA OPPORTUNITIES, INC. (AZ)
Incorporated 11/03/1954
Name changed to Horizons Unlimited 05/03/1956
(See Horizons Unlimited)

ARIZONA OPPORTUNITIES INC (AZ)
Incorporated 06/06/1956
Completely liquidated 08/07/1968
Each share Class A $2.50 par exchanged for first and final distribution of (0.5) share United States Mining Corp. Common 20¢ par and (0.5) shares A.O.I. Minerals Corp. Common $1 par
Each share Class B 50¢ par exchanged for first and final distribution of (0.1) share United States Mining Corp. Common 20¢ par and (0.1) share A.O.I. Minerals Corp. Common $1 par
(See each company's listing)

ARIZONA PUB SVC CO (AZ)
$2.40 Preferred called for redemption 06/05/1959
Common $5 par changed to $2.50 par and (1) additional share issued 06/01/1961
$2.75 Preferred Ser. B $50 par called for redemption 03/02/1965
$8.50 Preferred Ser. F $100 par called for redemption 12/01/1982
Under plan of reorganization each share Common $2.50 par automatically became (1) share AZP Group, Inc. Common no par 04/29/1985
$10.70 Preferred Ser. I $100 par called for redemption 06/02/1986
$11.95 Preferred Ser. M $100 par called for redemption 06/02/1986
$3.58 Preferred Ser. O $25 par called for redemption 06/01/1987
$8.32 Preferred Ser. J $100 par called for redemption 11/03/1993
$8.80 Preferred Ser K $100 par called for redemption 01/04/1994
$8.48 Preferred Ser. S $100 par called for redemption 10/24/1994
$7.875 Preferred Ser. V $100 par called for redemption 06/01/1997
7.25% Preferred Ser. W $25 par called for redemption at $25 on 12/01/1998
Adjustable Rate Preferred Ser. Q $100 par called for redemption at $100 on 03/01/1999
$1.10 Preferred $25 par called for redemption at $27.50 on 03/01/1999
$2.275 Preferred Ser. D $50 par called for redemption at $50.50 on 03/01/1999
$2.36 Preferred $50 par called for redemption at $51 on 03/01/1999
$2.40 Preferred Ser. A $50 par called for redemption at $50.50 on 03/01/1999
$2.50 Preferred $50 par called for redemption at $51 on 03/01/1999
$2.625 Preferred Ser. C $50 par called for redemption at $51 on 03/01/1999
$3.25 Preferred Ser. E $50 par called for redemption at $51 on 03/01/1999
$4.35 Preferred $100 par called for redemption at $102 on 03/01/1999
$10 Preferred Ser. U $100 par called for redemption at $100 on 03/01/1999
(Additional Information in Active)

ARIZONA RES INDS INC (FL)
Merged into Ridgeway Petroleum Corp. 10/29/1997
Each share Common exchanged for (1.1) shares Common no par
Ridgeway Petroleum Corp. name changed to Enhanced Oil Resources Inc. 06/11/2007 which name changed to Hunter Oil Corp. 08/16/2016

ARIZONA SILVER CORP (BC)
Common no par split (2) for (1) by issuance of (1) additional share 11/21/1980
Recapitalized as ASC Industries Ltd. 06/06/1995
Each share Common no par exchanged for (0.1) share Common no par
ASC Industries Ltd. name changed to Acero-Martin Exploration Inc. 11/24/2004 which name changed to AM Gold Inc. 06/08/2010
(See AM Gold Inc.)

ARIZONA STAR RESOURCE CORP (BC)
Merged into Barrick Gold Corp. 12/19/2007
Each share Common no par exchanged for $18 cash

ARIZONA VY DEV CO (DE)
Acquired by Fuqua Industries, Inc. 06/18/1971
Each share Common $1 par exchanged for (0.25) share Common $1 par
Fuqua Industries, Inc. name changed to Actava Group Inc. 07/21/1993 which name changed to Metromedia International Group, Inc. 11/01/1995
(See Metromedia International Group, Inc.)

ARIZONA VENTURES INC (NV)
Name changed to Fox River Holdings, Inc. 10/13/2003
Fox River Holdings, Inc. name changed to Zynex Medical Holdings, Inc. 12/23/2003 which name changed to Zynex, Inc. 07/08/2008

ARIZONA WELDING EQUIPMENT CO. INC. (AZ)
Recapitalized as Savage Industries, Inc. 00/00/1953
Each share 6% Preferred $100 par exchanged for (10) shares Preferred $1 par
Each share Common $1 par exchanged for (1) share Common $1 par
Savage Industries, Inc. acquired by Royal Properties, Inc. 02/11/1964
(See Royal Properties, Inc.)

ARIZUMA SILVER INC (ON)
Recapitalized as ASI Internet Inc. 10/13/1999
Each share Common no par exchanged for (0.33333333) share Common no par
ASI Internet Inc. recapitalized as HIP Interactive Corp. 12/10/1999
(See HIP Interactive Corp.)

ARJAY INTL INC (DE)
Recapitalized as Maxwell-Cox Group, Inc. 12/15/1989
Each share Common $0.0001 par exchanged for (1) share Common $0.0001 par
Maxwell-Cox Group, Inc. name changed to Digicom Corp. 06/18/1993 which name changed to Emery Ferron Energy Corp. 06/27/1994
(See Emery Ferron Energy Corp.)

ARJO WIGGINS APPLETON P L C (UNITED KINGDOM)
Acquired by Worms & Cie S.A. 07/26/2000
Each Sponsored ADR for Ordinary exchanged for $19.3785 cash

ARJON ENTERPRISES INC (ON)
Recapitalized 07/24/1995
Recapitalized from Arjon Gold Mines Ltd. to Arjon Enterprises Inc. 07/24/1995
Each share Common $1 par exchanged for (0.1) share Common no par
Recapitalized as Cotton Valley Resource Corp. (ON) 06/17/1996
Each share Common no par exchanged for (1/3) share Common no par
Cotton Valley Resource Corp. (ON) reincorporated in Yukon 02/09/1998 which name changed to Aspen Group Resources Corp. 02/28/2000
(See Aspen Group Resources Corp.)

ARK DEV INC (NV)
Name changed to Blackbird Petroleum Corp. 12/05/2008
Blackbird Petroleum Corp. name changed to Blackbird International Corp. 03/09/2011 which recapitalized as Romana Food Brands Corp. 10/04/2017

ARK ENERGY INC (NV)
Charter revoked for failure to file reports and pay fees 05/01/1989

ARK ENERGY LTD (BC)
Recapitalized as Arcanna Industries Corp. 06/27/1990
Each share Common no par exchanged for (0.2) share Common no par
Arcanna Industries Corp. merged into Mercana Industries Ltd. (BC) 12/17/1993 which reincorporated in Ontario 06/28/1995
(See Mercana Industries Ltd.)

ARK EXPLS LTD (ON)
Merged into Ranchmen's Resources (1976) Ltd. 01/31/1977
Each share Common no par exchanged for (0.07692307) share Class A Common no par
Ranchmen's Resources (1976) Ltd. name changed to Ranchmen's Resources Ltd. 05/31/1985 which merged into Crestar Energy Inc. 10/11/1995 which was acquired by Gulf Canada Resources Ltd. 11/13/2000
(See Gulf Canada Resources Ltd.)

ARK LA TEX INDS LTD (BC)
Recapitalized as Landstar Properties Inc. 06/17/1992
Each share Common no par exchanged for (0.14285714) share Common no par

ARKADIA INTL (NV)
Name changed to Freedom Leaf Inc. 02/25/2015

ARKADOS GROUP INC (DE)
Each share old Common $0.0001 par exchanged for (0.03333333) share new Common $0.0001 par 03/18/2015
Name changed to Solbright Group, Inc. 11/07/2017

ARKAM GOLD INC (NV)
Recapitalized as Silver State Mining & Exploration, Inc. 04/04/1994
Each shares Common $0.001 par exchanged for (0.00333333) share Common $0.001 par
Silver State Mining & Exploration, Inc. recapitalized as Trivest Equities Ltd. 11/24/2004 which name changed to MCN Multicast Networks, Inc. 02/11/2005 which name changed to Downtown America Funding Corp. 09/08/2005 which name changed to Savior Energy Corp. 12/22/2006

ARKANSAS BEST CORP NEW (DE)
$2.875 Conv. Exchangeable Preferred Ser. A 1¢ par called for redemption at $50.575 on 09/12/2001
Name changed to ArcBest Corp. 05/01/2014

ARKANSAS BEST CORP OLD (DE)
Common $1 par split (2) for (1) by issuance of (1) additional share 10/31/1986
Stock Dividend - 10% 01/20/1977
Merged into Best Acquisition Corp. 10/20/1988
Each share Common $1 par exchanged for $26 cash

ARKANSAS CENTRAL POWER CO.
Merged into Arkansas Power & Light Co. 00/00/1926
Details not available

ARKANSAS 1ST NATL BK (HOT SPRINGS, AR)
99.38% acquired by First Arkansas Bankstock Corp. through exchange offer which expired 10/22/1970
Public interest eliminated

ARKANSAS FREIGHTWAYS CORP (AR)
Common 1¢ par split (2) for (1) by issuance of (1) additional share 03/10/1992
Name changed to American Freightways Corp. 01/04/1993
American Freightways Corp. merged into FedEx Corp. 02/12/2001

ARKANSAS FUEL OIL CORP. (DE)
Liquidation completed 12/02/1960
Details not available

ARKANSAS LA GAS CO (DE)
Common $5 par changed to $2.50 par and (1) additional share issued 01/04/1960
90¢ Preference $20 par conversion privilege expired 05/10/1962
Common $2.50 par split (5) for (4) by issuance of (0.25) additional share 11/07/1975
Common $2.50 par changed to $1.25 par and (1) additional share issued 12/10/1979
Stock Dividends - 10% 12/23/1955; 10% 11/21/1956
Name changed to Arkla, Inc. and Common $1.25 par changed to $0.625 par 11/23/1981
Arkla, Inc. name changed to NorAm Energy Corp. 05/11/1994 which merged into Houston Industries Inc. 07/06/1997 which name changed to Reliant Energy Inc. 02/08/1999 which reorganized as CenterPoint Energy, Inc. 08/31/2002

ARKANSAS LIGHT & POWER CO.
Merged into Arkansas Power & Light Co. 00/00/1926
Details not available

ARKANSAS-MISSOURI POWER CO. OLD (AR)
Reorganized under the laws of Delaware as Arkansas-Missouri Power Co. 00/00/1937
Each share Preferred exchanged for (2) shares Common $1 par
No Common stockholders' equity
Arkansas-Missouri Power Corp. reorganized as Arkansas-Missouri Power Co. (AR) (New) 01/31/1947
(See Arkansas-Missouri Power Co. (AR) (New))

ARKANSAS-MISSOURI POWER CORP. (DE)
Common $1 par changed to $5 par 00/00/1946
Reorganized as Arkansas-Missouri Power Co. (AR) (New) 01/31/1947
Details not available

ARKANSAS MO PWR CO NEW (AR)
5.5% Preferred $25 par called for redemption 05/12/1955
6% Preferred $25 par called for redemption 05/12/1955
Common $5 par split (3) for (2) by issuance of (0.5) additional share 06/15/1957
Each share Common $5 par exchanged for (2) shares Common $2.50 par 05/31/1963
Common $2.50 par split (5) for (4) by issuance of (0.25) additional share 06/15/1966
Stock Dividend - 33.33333333% 05/15/1947
Under Court approved plan each share Common $2.50 par exchanged for (0.7) share Middle South Utilities, Inc. Common $5 par 05/01/1972
Note: Certificates surrendered after 05/01/1977 will receive the cash equivalent of that date's market value
After 05/01/1987 claim must be made through the Office of the United States Treasury
Middle South Utilities, Inc. name changed to Entergy Corp. (FL) 05/19/1989 which reincorporated in Delaware 12/31/1993

ARKANSAS NATURAL GAS CO.
Merged into Arkansas Natural Gas Corp. 00/00/1928
Details not available

ARKANSAS NATURAL GAS CORP. (DE)
Reorganized 00/00/1953
Each share Common no par or Class A Common no par exchanged for (0.5) share Arkansas Fuel Oil Corp. Common $5 par and (0.5) share Arkansas Louisiana Gas Co. Common $5 par
(See each company's listing)

ARKANSAS NATURAL RESOURCES CORP. (DE)
No longer in existence having become inoperative and void for non-payment of taxes 04/01/1958

ARKANSAS OIL VENTURES INC (DE)
Recapitalized as Trojan Industries, Inc. 06/23/1969
Each share Common 1¢ par exchanged for (0.05) share Common 5¢ par
Trojan Industries, Inc. name changed to Leisure Trends, Inc. 05/04/1970
(See Leisure Trends, Inc.)

ARKANSAS-OKLAHOMA GAS CO. (DE)
Liquidated 00/00/1954
Details not available

ARKANSAS PWR & LT CO (AR)
$6 Preferred no par called for redemption 05/28/1955
$7 Preferred no par called for redemption 05/28/1955
5.48% Preferred $100 par called for redemption 05/17/1965
11.04% Preferred $100 par called for redemption 09/17/1991
10.40% Preferred $25 par called for redemption 07/07/1992
10.60% Preferred $100 par called for redemption 07/01/1994
13.28% Preferred $25 par called for redemption 01/01/1995
Name changed to Entergy Arkansas, Inc. 04/22/1996

ARKANSAS VALLEY INDS INC (AR)
Reincorporated under the laws of Delaware as Valmac Industries, Inc. 07/28/1970
(See Valmac Industries, Inc.)

ARKANSAS VALLEY INTERURBAN RAILWAY
Property sold at auction 00/00/1939
Details not available

ARKANSAS WESTN GAS CO (AR)
Each share Common no par exchanged for (7.6545) shares Common $5 par 00/00/1943
Common $5 par changed to $6 par and (1/5) additional share distributed 00/00/1948
Common $6 par changed to $5 par and (0.5) additional share distributed 00/00/1952
Common $5 par changed to $2.50 par and (1) additional share issued 03/23/1961
Common $2.50 par split (4) for (3) by issuance of (1/3) additional share 12/13/1976
Common $2.50 par split (2) for (1) by issuance of (1) additional share 12/09/1977
Stock Dividend - 25% 10/15/1957
Under plan of reorganization each share Common $2.50 par automatically became (1) share Southwestern Energy Co. Common $2.50 par 10/01/1979

ARKAY INTERNATIONAL, INC. (NY)
Under plan of merger name changed to Comspace Corp. 11/01/1965
(See Comspace Corp.)

ARKEN GOLD MINES LTD. (ON)
Charter revoked for failure to file reports and pay fees 05/30/1960

ARKLA EXPL CO (DE)
Merged into Arkla, Inc. 01/28/1992
Each share Common $1 par exchanged for (0.95) share Common $0.625 par
Arkla, Inc. name changed to NorAm Energy Corp. 05/11/1994 which merged into Houston Industries Inc. 08/06/1997 which name changed to Reliant Energy Inc. 02/08/1999 which reorganized as CenterPoint Energy, Inc. 08/31/2002

ARKLA INC (DE)
Common $0.625 par split (2) for (1) by issuance of (1) additional share 12/10/1981
90¢ Preference $20 par called for redemption 03/13/1987
Name changed to NorAm Energy Corp. 05/11/1994
NorAm Energy Corp. merged into Houston Industries Inc. 08/06/1997 which name changed to Reliant Energy Inc. 02/08/1999 which reorganized as CenterPoint Energy, Inc. 08/31/2002

ARKLOW ASSOCS INC (NV)
Recapitalized as Ultimate Cigar Inc. 03/31/1997
Each share Common $0.001 par exchanged for (0.15384615) share Common $0.001 par
Ultimate Cigar Inc. name changed to Ultimate Direct, Inc. 07/22/1999 which recapitalized as Altadyne, Inc. 04/14/2005 which name changed to Stem Cell International, Inc. 10/14/2005 which name changed to Stem Cell Therapy International, Inc. 10/18/2005 which name changed to AmStem Corp. 02/23/2010

ARKONA INC (DE)
Merged into DealerTrack Holdings, Inc. 06/06/2007
Each share Common $0.001 par exchanged for $1.38 cash

ARKONA RES INC (BC)
Recapitalized as Action Minerals Inc. 08/12/2004
Each share Common no par exchanged for (0.33333333) share Common no par
Action Minerals Inc. recapitalized as Aroway Minerals Inc. 02/05/2009 which name changed to Aroway Energy Inc. 02/04/2011
(See Aroway Energy Inc.)

ARKSON NUTRACEUTICALS CORP (DE)
Each share old Common $0.0001 par exchanged for (0.05) share new Common $0.001 par 09/03/2008
Each share new Common $0.001 par exchanged again for (0.11111111) share new Common $0.001 par 12/23/2010
Name changed to First Surgical Partners Inc. 02/22/2011
(See First Surgical Partners Inc.)

ARKWIN INDS INC (NY)
Merged into Newark Properties Corp. 12/23/1980
Each share Common 10¢ par exchanged for $7 cash

ARLANS DEPT STORES INC (NY)
Common $1 par split (5) for (2) by issuance of (1.5) additional shares 06/18/1965
Assets assigned for the benefit of creditors 01/27/1975
No stockholders' equity

ARLEN CORP (NY)
Name changed 10/16/1985
Name changed from Arlen Realty & Development Corp. to Arlen Corp. 10/16/1985

SEC revoked preferred and common stock registration 06/15/2006

ARLEN PPTY INVS (MA)
Name changed to API Trust 09/17/1975
(See API Trust)

ARLEN SHOPPING CTRS INC (DE)
Merged into Arlen Realty & Development Corp. 06/15/1971
Each share Common 10¢ par exchanged for (1.25) shares Common $1 par
Arlen Realty & Development Corp. name changed to Arlen Corp. 10/16/1985
(See Arlen Corp.)

ARLEY MERCHANDISE CORP (MA)
Merged into ROPS Acquisition Co., Inc. 12/23/1986
Each share Common 1¢ par exchanged for $10 cash

ARLING RES LTD (BC)
Name changed to I.D. Internet Direct Ltd. 12/07/1995
I.D. Internet Direct Ltd. merged into Look Communications Inc. 10/31/1999 which name changed to ONEnergy Inc. 07/12/2013

ARLINGTON BK & TR CO (ARLINGTON, TX)
Acquired by Texas Commerce Bancshares, Inc. 08/23/1974
Each share Capital Stock $10 par exchanged for (3.34) shares Common $4 par
Texas Commerce Bancshares, Inc. acquired by Chemical New York Corp. 05/01/1987 which name changed to Chemical Banking Corp. 04/29/1988 which name changed to Chase Manhattan Corp. (New) 03/31/1996 which name changed to J.P. Morgan Chase & Co. 12/31/2000 which name changed to JPMorgan Chase & Co. 07/20/2004

ARLINGTON BANK (ARLINGTON, VA)
Merged into Citizens Bancorp (MD) 05/30/1989
Each share Capital Stock no par exchanged for (0.71) share Common $2.50 par
Citizens Bancorp (MD) merged into Crestar Financial Corp. 12/31/1996 which merged into SunTrust Banks, Inc. 12/31/1998

ARLINGTON-CLARK BUILDING, INC. (IL)
Liquidation completed 10/24/1956
Details not available

ARLINGTON CORP (PA)
Capital Voting Trust terminated and Capital Stock no par changed to 5¢ par 06/30/1955
Merged into National Apartment Leasing Corp. 08/27/1973
Each share Capital Stock 5¢ par exchanged for $132 cash

ARLINGTON COTTON MILLS
Merged into Textiles, Inc. 00/00/1931
Details not available

ARLINGTON FIN CORP (DE)
Remarketed Preferred called for redemption 06/28/1990
Remarketed Preferred Ser. G called for redemption 06/28/1990
Remarketed Preferred Ser. A called for redemption 07/05/1990
Remarketed Preferred Ser. B called for redemption 07/12/1990
Remarketed Preferred Ser. C called for redemption 07/19/1990
Remarketed Preferred Ser. D called for redemption 07/26/1990
Remarketed Preferred Ser. E called for redemption 08/02/1990
Remarketed Preferred Ser. F called for redemption 08/08/1990

ARLINGTON HOSPITALITY INC (DE)
Each share old Common $0.005 par exchanged for (1) share new Common $0.005 par to reflect a (1) for (100) reverse split followed by a (100) for (1) forward split 11/28/2003
Note: Holders of (99) or fewer pre-split shares received $3.83 cash per share
Chapter 11 bankruptcy proceedings dismissed 08/29/2011
No stockholders' equity

ARLINGTON MILLS (MA)
Name changed to Whitman (William) Co., Inc. (MA) 00/00/1946
Whitman (William) Co., Inc. (MA) name changed to Carolet Corp. 00/00/1952
(See Carolet Corp.)

ARLINGTON NATIONAL HOLDING CORP. (OH)
Charter cancelled for non-payment of taxes 11/30/1973

ARLINGTON OIL & GAS LTD (YUKON)
Recapitalized as Cypress Hills Resource Corp. (Yukon) 03/12/2003
Each share Common no par exchanged for (0.25) share Common no par
Cypress Hills Resource Corp. (Yukon) reincorporated in Alberta 07/26/2005

ARLINGTON RLTY INVS (TX)
In process of liquidation
Each Share of Bene. Int. $1 par received initial distribution of $7.50 cash 03/08/1985
Each Share of Bene. Int. $1 par received second distribution of $1.50 cash 03/07/1986
Each Share of Bene. Int. $1 par received third distribution of $0.75 cash 08/16/1989
Note: Details on subsequent distributions, if any, are not available

ARLINGTON RES INC (ON)
Delisted from Toronto Venture Stock Exchange 07/04/2003

ARLINGTON SILVER MINES LTD (BC)
Recapitalized as Western Arlington Resources Ltd. 10/07/1981
Each share Common $1 par exchanged for (0.2) share Common no par
Western Arlington Resources Ltd. recapitalized as Lightning Creek Mines Ltd. 12/19/1986
(See Lightning Creek Mines Ltd.)

ARLINGTON TANKERS LTD (BERMUDA)
Under plan of merger name changed to General Maritime Corp. (New) 12/16/2008
(See General Maritime Corp. (New))

ARLINGTON TRUST CO., INC. (HERNDON, VA)
Capital Stock $10 par split (2) for (1) by issuance of (1) additional share 01/01/1978
Stock Dividends - 100% 04/01/1970; 50% 04/01/1973
Under plan of merger each share Capital Stock $10 par automatically became (1) share First American Bank of Virginia (McLean, VA) Common $10 par 03/31/1978
(See First American of Virginia (McLean, VA))

ARLINGTON TR CO (LAWRENCE, MA)
Capital Stock $20 par changed to $50 par 01/08/1963
Capital Stock $50 par changed to $12.50 par and (3) additional shares issued 05/09/1968
Capital Stock $12.50 par changed to $25 par 03/28/1972
Reorganized as Arltru Bancorporation 09/20/1973
Each share Capital Stock $25 par exchanged for (4) shares Common $6.25 par
Arltru Bancorporation merged into Hartford National Corp. 08/01/1985 which merged into Shawmut National Corp. 02/29/1988 which merged into Fleet Financial Group Inc. (New) 11/30/1995 which name changed to Fleet Boston Corp. 10/01/1999 which name changed to FleetBoston Financial Corp. 04/18/2000 which merged into Bank of America Corp. 04/01/2004

ARLINGTON TR INC (ARLINGTON, VA)
Capital Stock $20 par changed to $10 par and (1) additional share issued 06/30/1964
Merged into Arlington Trust Co., Inc. (Herndon, VA) 06/30/1969
Each share Capital Stock $10 par exchanged for (3) shares Capital Stock $10 par
Arlington Trust Co., Inc. (Herndon, VA) name changed to First American Bank of Virginia (McLean, VA) 03/31/1978
(See First American Bank of Virginia (McLean, VA))

ARLINGTON VENTURES LTD CDA (BC)
Reincorporated under the laws of Yukon as Arlington Oil & Gas Ltd. 06/27/2001
Arlington Oil & Gas Ltd. recapitalized as Cypress Hills Resource Corp. (Yukon) 03/12/2003 which reincorporated in Alberta 07/26/2005

ARLISS PLASTICS CORP. (DE)
No longer in existence having become inoperative and void for non-payment of taxes 04/01/1960

ARLO RES LTD (YT)
Recapitalized as International Arlo Resources Ltd. 06/08/1998
Each share Common no par exchanged for (0.2) share Common no par
(See International Arlo Resources Ltd.)

ARLTRU BANCORPORATION (MA)
Merged into Hartford National Corp. 08/01/1985
Each share Common $6.25 par exchanged for (4.88) shares Common $6.25 par
Hartford National Corp. merged into Shawmut National Corp. 02/29/1988 which merged into Fleet Financial Group Inc. (New) 11/30/1995 which name changed to Fleet Boston Corp. 10/01/1999 which name changed to FleetBoston Financial Corp. 04/18/2000 which merged into Bank of America Corp. 04/01/2004

ARM FINL CORP (NV)
Each share old Common $0.002 par exchanged for (0.2) share new Common $0.002 par 12/27/1991
Name changed to RX Medical Services Corp. 06/19/1992
RX Medical Services Corp. recapitalized as Super Blue Domain Technologies, Inc. 12/20/2007 which name changed to Golden Energy Corp. 06/16/2009 which name changed to Golden Grail Technology Corp. 12/31/2014

ARM FINL GROUP INC (DE)
9.5% Perpetual Preferred 1¢ par called for redemption at $25 on 12/15/1998
Plan of reorganization under Chapter 11 Federal Bankruptcy Code effective 08/23/2000
No stockholders' equity

ARM HLDGS PLC (ENGLAND & WALES)
Sponsored ADR's for Ordinary split (4) for (1) by issuance of (3) additional ADR's payable 04/21/1999 to holders of record 04/20/1999
Sponsored ADR's for Ordinary split (5) for (1) by issuance of (4) additional ADR's payable 04/19/2000 to holders of record 04/18/2000 ADR's cancelled 09/22/2016
Each Sponsored ADR for Ordinary exchanged for $66.6019 cash

ARMAC ENTERPRISES INC (DE)
Adjudicated bankrupt 06/21/1977
Stockholders' equity unlikely

ARMADA GOLD & MINERALS LTD (BC)
Name changed to Armada Mercantile Ltd. 03/04/1992

ARMADA GOLD CORP (YT)
Recapitalized 01/06/1994
Reincorporated 07/05/1996
Recapitalized from Armada Financial Corp. to Armada Gold Corp. 01/06/1994
Each share Common no par exchanged for (0.25) share Class A Common no par
Class A Common no par reclassified as Common no par 06/28/1996
Place of incorporation changed from (AB) to (YT) 07/05/1996
Delisted from Toronto Stock Exchange 07/07/2000

ARMADA HLDGS LTD (BERMUDA)
Name changed to Great Wall Pan Asia Holdings Ltd. 01/20/2017
(See Great Wall Pan Asia Holdings Ltd.)

ARMADA PORCUPINE MINES LTD. (ON)
Charter revoked for failure to file reports and pay fees 11/07/1955

ARMAGH GROUP INC (DE)
Recapitalized as SmartVideo Technologies, Inc. 01/06/2003
Each share Common $0.001 par exchanged for (0.33333333) share Common $0.001 par
SmartVideo Technologies, Inc. name changed to uVuMobile, Inc. 06/04/2007
(See uVuMobile, Inc.)

ARMAS INTL MFG CO (NV)
Recapitalized as Inter-Link Communications Group, Inc. 10/23/1998
Each share Common $0.005 par exchanged for (0.16666666) share Common $0.001 par
Inter-Link Communications Group, Inc. name changed to EnterTech Media Group, Inc. 04/22/1999
(See EnterTech Media Group, Inc.)

ARMATRON INTL INC (MA)
Merged into Armatron Merger Corp. 10/27/1999
Each share Common $1 par exchanged for $0.27 cash

ARMBRO ENTERPRISES INC (CANADA)
Each share old Common no par exchanged for (0.12987012) share new Common no par 12/08/1993
Name changed to Aecon Group Inc. 06/18/2001

ARMCO CAP CORP (AB)
Merged into 3099477 Nova Scotia Ltd. 06/01/2005
Each share Common no par exchanged for $1.09 cash

ARMCO INC (OH)
Common $5 par split (3) for (2) by issuance of (0.5) additional share 09/15/1978
Common $5 par changed to $1 par 04/24/1987
Common $1 par changed to 1¢ par 04/23/1993

Merged into AK Steel Holding Corp. 09/30/1999
Each share $2.10 Conv. Preferred no par exchanged for either $40 cash or (0.4863) share Common 1¢ par
Each share $3.625 Conv. Preferred Class A no par exchanged for (1) share $3.625 Conv. Preferred Class B no par
Each share $4.50 Conv. Preferred no par exchanged for either $50 cash or (0.85) share Common 1¢ par
Each share Common 1¢ par exchanged for (0.3829) share Common 1¢ par
Note: Option to elect stock expired 10/29/1999

ARMCO STL CORP (OH)
Common $10 par split (2) for (1) by issuance of (1) additional share 06/13/1955
Common $10 par changed to $5 par and (1) additional share issued 06/13/1969
Name changed to Armco Inc. 07/01/1978
Armco Inc. merged into AK Steel Holding Corp. 09/30/1999

ARMEAU BRANDS INC (NV)
Name changed to SanSal Wellness Holdings, Inc. 11/07/2017

ARMED ALERT SEC INC (NV)
Recapitalized as Acquired Sales Corp. 03/01/2006
Each share Common $0.001 par exchanged for (0.1) share Common $0.001 par

ARMEL INC (FL)
Common $0.001 par split (3) for (2) by issuance of (0.5) additional share 04/09/1985
Acquired by Woolworth (F.W.) Co. 01/07/1988
Each share Common $0.001 par exchanged for $7.75 cash

ARMENEX RESOURCES CDA INC (BC)
Recapitalized 07/04/1990
Recapitalized from Armenian Express Canada Inc. to Armenex Resources Canada Inc. 07/04/1990
Each share Common no par exchanged for (0.2) share Common no par
Recapitalized as Ecuadorean Copperfields Inc. 08/31/1994
Each share Common no par exchanged for (0.2) share Common no par
Ecuadorean Copperfields Inc. recapitalized as Bronx Minerals Inc. 06/24/1996 which name changed to Las Vegas From Home.com Entertainment Inc. 09/07/1999 which name changed to Jackpot Digital Inc. 06/18/2015

ARMENO RES INC (BC)
Common no par split (2) for (1) by issuance of (1) additional share 07/30/1986
Recapitalized as AG Armeno Mines & Minerals Inc. 05/25/1992
Each share Common no par exchanged for (0.1) share Common no par
AG Armeno Mines & Minerals Inc. recapitalized as Golden Nugget Exploration, Inc. 04/27/2000 which recapitalized as Lucky 1 Enterprises Inc. 05/02/2002 which recapitalized as Bronx Ventures Inc. 01/24/2005 which reorganized as ZAB Resources Inc. 03/19/2007 which recapitalized as Kokomo Enterprises Inc. 04/15/2009 which recapitalized as High 5 Ventures Inc. 08/29/2012 which recapitalized as 37 Capital Inc. 07/07/2014

ARMIN CORP (NJ)
Name changed 03/27/1973
Stock Dividends - 50% 11/30/1970; 50% 11/15/1975
Name changed from Armin Poly Film Corp. to Armin Corp. 03/27/1973
Merged into Tyco Laboratories, Inc. 09/13/1979
Each share Common 5¢ par exchanged for $16 cash

ARMINGTON ASSET MANAGEMENT CORP. (UT)
Involuntarily dissolved 09/01/1990

ARMISTICE GOLD MINES LTD. (ON)
Merged into Pardee Amalgamated Mines Ltd. 12/00/1954
Each share Capital Stock $1 par exchanged for (0.13333333) share Capital Stock $1 par
Pardee Amalgamated Mines Ltd. liquidated for Rio Algom Mines Ltd. 11/09/1961 which name changed to Rio Algom Ltd. 04/30/1975
(See Rio Algom Ltd.)

ARMISTICE RES CORP (CANADA)
Name changed to Kerr Mines Inc. 01/15/2014

ARMISTICE RES LTD (CANADA)
Reincorporated 11/09/1987
Place of incorporation changed from (ON) to (Canada) 11/09/1987
Recapitalized as Armistice Resources Corp. 04/28/2006
Each share Common no par exchanged for (0.25) share Common no par
Armistice Resources Corp. name changed to Kerr Mines Inc. 01/15/2014

ARMITAGE MNG CORP (NV)
Name changed to Golden Autumn Holdings, Inc. 05/07/2007
(See Golden Autumn Holdings, Inc.)

ARMITEC INC (DE)
SEC revoked common stock registration 10/08/2010

ARMO BIOSCIENCES INC (DE)
Acquired by Lilly (Eli) & Co. 06/22/2018
Each share Common $0.0001 par exchanged for $50 cash

ARMOR ALL PRODS CORP (DE)
Merged into Clorox Co. 01/02/1997
Each share Common 1¢ par exchanged for $19.09 cash

ARMOR DEV CORP (BC)
Struck off register and declared dissolved for failure to file returns 04/06/1990

ARMOR ELEVATOR CO (NY)
Merged into Smith (A.O.) Corp. 04/10/1970
Each share Common $1 par exchanged for $11.60 cash

ARMOR ENTERPRISES INC (FL)
Name changed to Armor Electric Inc. 10/04/2004

ARMOR HLDGS INC (DE)
Merged into BAE Systems PLC 07/31/2007
Each share Common 3¢ par exchanged for $88 cash

ARMOR OIL, GAS & REFINING CO. (OK)
Charter cancelled for failure to pay taxes 10/15/1923

ARMOR RES LTD (CANADA)
Reincorporated 05/05/1982
Place of incorporation changed from (BC) to (Canada) 05/05/1982
Merged into New Penn Energy Corp. (BC) (New) 11/22/1982
Each share Common no par exchanged for (0.08333333) share Common no par
New Penn Energy Corp. (BC) (New) reincorporated in Canada 01/29/1982 which merged into International Interlake Industries Inc. 12/31/1986
(See International Interlake Industries Inc.)

ARMORE MINES LTD (BC)
Recapitalized as Marcana Resources Ltd. 07/17/1973
Each share Capital Stock $1 par exchanged for (0.33333333) share Capital Stock $1 par
Marcana Resources Ltd. reorganized in Canada as FMG Telecomputer Ltd. 04/04/1983 which name changed to SOK Properties Ltd. 07/04/1989 which name changed to Impact Telemedia International Ltd. 08/03/1990 which name changed to UC'NWIN Systems Ltd. (Canada) 07/17/1992 which reincorporated in Delaware as UC'NWIN Systems Corp. 12/11/1995 which recapitalized as Winner's Edge.com, Inc. 10/29/1999 which name changed to Sealant Solutions Inc. 08/06/2001 which name changed to PowerChannel, Inc. 07/28/2003 which recapitalized as Qualibou Energy Inc. 02/05/2008

ARMORED STORAGE INCOME INVS LTD PARTNERSHIP (AZ)
Completely liquidated 12/31/1999
Details not available

ARMORFLEX CHEM CORP (DE)
Charter revoked and proclaimed inoperative and void for non-payment of taxes 04/15/1971

ARMORITE, INC. (NV)
Capital Stock 10¢ par changed to 1¢ par 09/10/1963
Name changed to Coast to Coast Co., Inc. 10/10/1963
(See Coast to Coast Co., Inc.)

ARMOTEK INDS INC (NY)
Each share old Common 10¢ par exchanged for (0.001) share new Common 10¢ par 10/18/1983
Note: In effect holders received $8.25 cash per share and public interest was eliminated

ARMOUR & CO (DE)
Reincorporated 10/29/1960
Each share 7% Preferred $100 par exchanged for (1) share $6 Preferred no par and (2) shares Common $5 par 00/00/1934
Each share Class A $25 par exchanged for (1) share Common $5 par 00/00/1934
Each share Class B $25 par exchanged for (0.5) share Common $5 par 00/00/1934
State of incorporation changed from (IL) to (DE) 10/29/1960
Stock Dividends - 10% 02/08/1957; 10% 03/12/1959; 10% 02/01/1965
Merged into Greyhound Corp. (DE) 12/28/1970
Each share Common $5 par exchanged for (3.25) shares Common $1.50 par
Under plan of reorganization each share $4.75 Preferred $100 par exchanged for (1) share Greyhound Corp. (AZ) $4.75 Preferred $100 par 10/04/1982
Greyhound Corp. (AZ) name changed to Greyhound Dial Corp. 05/08/1990 which name changed to Dial Corp. (AZ) 05/14/1991 which reincorporated in Delaware 03/18/1992 which name changed to Viad Corp. 08/15/1996

ARMOUR DIAL INC (DE)
Merged into Greyhound Corp. (DE) 06/30/1972
Each share Common $1 par exchanged for (1) share Common $1.50 par and (1) Common Stock Purchase Warrant expiring 05/14/1980
Greyhound Corp. (DE) reincorporated in Arizona 03/03/1978 which name changed to Greyhound Dial Corp. 05/08/1990 which name changed to Dial Corp. (AZ) 05/14/1991 which reincorporated in Delaware 03/18/1992 which name changed to Viad Corp. 08/15/1996

ARMOUR ENTERPRISES, INC. (FL)
Involuntarily dissolved 12/05/1979

ARMOUR LEATHER CO.
Merged into Mosser (J.K.) Leather Corp. 00/00/1926
Details not available

ARMOUR URANIUM & COPPER MINES LTD. (ON)
Charter cancelled 04/07/1958

ARMSTRONG A J INC (NY)
Merged into Security Pacific Corp. 07/27/1981
Each share Common $1 par exchanged for $77.20 cash

ARMSTRONG CORK CO (PA)
Each share Common $100 par exchanged for (4) shares Common no par 00/00/1928
Each share Common no par exchanged for (3) shares Common $1 par 04/27/1955
Common $1 par split (2) for (1) by issuance of (1) additional share 06/05/1964
Common $1 par split (2) for (1) by issuance of (1) additional share 06/09/1969
Non-Transferable Ctfs. of Contingent Interest issued in exchange for Cryo-Therm, Inc. 00/00/1972 were deemed worthless as of 12/31/1976
Name changed to Armstrong World Industries, Inc. (Old) 05/15/1980
Armstrong World Industries, Inc. (Old) reorganized as Armstrong Holdings, Inc. 05/01/2000
(See Armstrong Holdings, Inc.)

ARMSTRONG CORP (ON)
Each share old Common no par exchanged for (0.02) share new Common no par 05/04/1999
Petitioned into bankruptcy 03/13/2003
Details not available

ARMSTRONG CNTY TR CO (KITTANNING, PA)
Merged into BT Financial Corp. 06/13/1996
Each share Common $50 par exchanged for (26.5) shares Common $5 par and $533.21 cash
BT Financial Corp. name changed to Promistar Financial Corp. 11/15/2000 which merged into F.N.B. Corp. (FL) 01/18/2002

ARMSTRONG ELECTRIC & MANUFACTURING CORP.
Sold in bankruptcy 00/00/1935
Details not available

ARMSTRONG HLDGS INC (PA)
Liquidation completed
Each share Common $1 par received first and final distribution of approximately $0.69 cash payable 12/12/2007 to holders of record 12/05/2007
Note: Certificates were not required to be surrendered and are without value

ARMSTRONG HOUSING INDUSTRIES LTD. (ON)
Charter revoked for failure to file reports and pay taxes 00/00/1954

ARMSTRONG LABS INC (DE)
Merged into ATI Pharmaceuticals Inc. 01/04/1990
Each share Common 1¢ par exchanged for (0.4) share Common 8¢ par
ATI Pharmaceuticals Inc. name changed to Armstrong Pharmaceuticals Inc. 05/15/1991 which merged into Medeva PLC

01/14/1993 which merged into Celltech Group PLC 01/26/2000
(See Celltech Group PLC)

ARMSTRONG PAINT & VARNISH WKS INC (IL)
Each share Common $50 par exchanged for (3) shares Common $25 par 09/24/1959
Each share Common $25 par exchanged for (5) shares Common $5 par 02/28/1961
Merged into Pacific Holding Corp. 07/24/1969
Each share Common $5 par exchanged for (0.667) share $1.20 Conv. Preferred $1 par and (0.4) share Common $1 par
(See Pacific Holding Corp.)

ARMSTRONG PAINT & VARNISH WORKS (IL)
Name changed to Armstrong Paint & Varnish Works, Inc. 01/24/1956
Armstrong Paint & Varnish Works, Inc. merged into Pacific Holding Corp. 07/24/1969
(See Pacific Holding Corp.)

ARMSTRONG PHARMACEUTICALS INC (NY)
Merged into Medeva PLC 01/14/1993
Each share Common 8¢ par exchanged for (1.072) Sponsored ADR's for Ordinary 10p par
Medeva PLC merged into Celltech Group PLC 01/26/2000
(See Celltech Group PLC)

ARMSTRONG RUBBER CO., INC. (NJ)
Reorganized under the laws of Connecticut as Armstrong Rubber Co. 10/15/1940
Each share Class A no par exchanged for (1) share Class A no par
Each share Common no par exchanged for (1) share Class B no par
Armstrong Rubber Co. (CT) reorganized in Delaware as Armtek Corp. 04/10/1987
(See Armtek Corp.)

ARMSTRONG RUBR CO (CT)
4.75% Preferred $50 par called for redemption 07/05/1955
Class A Common no par and Class B Common no par split (5) for (2) by issuance of (1.5) additional shares respectively 06/08/1956
Class A Common no par and Class B Common no par changed to $1 par 06/11/1956
Class A Common $1 par and Class B Common $1 par reclassified as Common $1 par 05/16/1960
Common $1 par split (2) for (1) by issuance of (1) additional share 04/01/1982
Common $1 par split (2) for (1) by issuance of (1) additional share 04/02/1984
Stock Dividend - 300% 04/10/1945
Reincorporated under the laws of Delaware as Armtek Corp. 04/10/1987
(See Armtek Corp.)

ARMSTRONG WORLD INDS INC OLD (PA)
$3.75 Preferred no par called for redemption 07/20/1989
Common $1 par split (2) for (1) by issuance of (1) additional share 12/01/1986
Under plan of reorganization each share Common $1 par automatically became (1) share Armstrong Holdings, Inc. Common $1 par 05/01/2000
(See Armstrong Holdings, Inc.)

ARMTEC INFRASTRUCTURE INC (ON)
Name changed to 2242749 Ontario Ltd. 06/17/2015

ARMTEC INFRASTRUCTURE INCOME FD (ON)
Under plan of reorganization each Trust Unit automatically became (1) share Armtec Infrastructure Inc. Common no par 01/04/2011
Armtec Infrastructure Inc. name changed to 2242749 Ontario Ltd. 06/17/2015

ARMTEK CORP (DE)
Merged into MIV Acquisition, Inc. 10/11/1988
Each share Common $1 par exchanged for $46 cash

ARNAV AIRCRAFT ASSOCIATES, INC.
Name changed to Arnav Industries Inc. 08/23/1961
(See Arnav Industries Inc.)

ARNAV INDS INC (DE)
Each share old Common 10¢ par exchanged for (0.5) share new Common 10¢ par 12/29/1961
Each share new Common 10¢ par exchanged for (0.1) share new Common 1¢ par 06/28/1966
Each share new Common 1¢ par exchanged for (0.0004) share new Common 1¢ par 11/12/1985
Note: In effect holders received $15 cash per share and public interest was eliminated

ARNCLIFFE MANCHESTER VENTURES LTD (DE)
Charter cancelled and declared inoperative and void for non-payment of taxes 03/01/1988

ARNCOEUR GOLD MINES LTD. (QC)
Charter annulled for failure to file reports 07/07/1973

ARNER CO., INC. (NY)
Merged into Strong Cobb Arner Inc. on a (4) for (1) basis 06/08/1959
(See Strong Cobb Arner Inc.)

ARNEX INDS CORP (DE)
Liquidation completed
Each share Common 1¢ par exchanged for initial distribution of $7 cash 11/07/1973
Each share Common 1¢ par received second and final distribution of $0.87 cash 04/19/1976

ARNEX INVT GROUP LTD (DE)
Recapitalized as Vector Environmental Technologies, Inc. 09/07/1993
Each share Common $0.0001 par exchanged for (0.02) share Common $0.0001 par
Vector Environmental Technologies, Inc. name changed to WaterPur International, Inc. 07/07/1997 which recapitalized as Aquentium, Inc. 05/22/2002

ARNGRE INC (FL)
Reincorporated under the laws of Delaware as Silver King Resources, Inc. 03/31/1999
Silver King Resources, Inc. recapitalized as eNexi Holdings Inc. 07/18/2000 which recapitalized as Trinity3 Corp. 03/31/2003
(See Trinity3 Corp.)

ARNHEM RES INC (BC)
Recapitalized as Duck Book Communications Ltd. 05/24/1985
Each share Common no par exchanged for (5) shares Common no par
(See Duck Book Communications Ltd.)

ARNICA RES LTD (BC)
Delisted from Vancouver Stock Exchange 06/06/1991

ARNO MINES LTD (ON)
Each share old Capital Stock no par exchanged for (0.2) share new Capital Stock no par 00/00/1932
Charter cancelled for failure to pay taxes and file returns 06/30/1980

ARNOLD ALTEX ALUMINUM CO. (FL)
Adjudicated bankrupt 05/04/1964
No stockholders' equity

ARNOLD BROTHERS, LTD.
Merged into Consolidated Food Products, Ltd. 00/00/1928
Details not available

ARNOLD CONSTABLE CORP (DE)
Capital Stock no par changed to $5 par 00/00/1933
Capital Stock $5 par reclassified as Common $5 par 06/17/1970
Reorganized as No Name Stores, Inc. 12/14/1994
Each share Common $5 par exchanged for (1) share Common $5 par
(See No Name Stores, Inc.)

ARNOLD GRAPHIC INDS INC (PA)
Merged into CM-Graphic Acquisition Corp. 01/20/1981
Each share Capital Stock $2 par exchanged for $49.50339 cash

ARNOLD INDS INC (PA)
Common $1 par split (2) for (1) by issuance of (1) additional share 04/30/1986
Common $1 par split (5) for (4) by issuance of (0.25) additional share 09/30/1987
Common $1 par split (3) for (2) by issuance of (0.5) additional share 06/21/1988
Common $1 par split (2) for (1) by issuance of (1) additional share 06/21/1991
Common $1 par split (2) for (1) by issuance of (1) additional share 12/17/1993
Merged into Roadway Corp. 12/03/2001
Each share Common $1 par exchanged for $21.75 cash

ARNOLD PRINT WORKS, INC.
Liquidation completed 00/00/1943
Details not available

ARNORA SULPHUR MINING CORP. (QC)
Name changed 00/00/1951
Name changed from Arnora Gold Mines Ltd. to Arnora Sulphur Mining Corp. 00/00/1951
Charter cancelled 08/00/1973

ARNORA SULPHUR MINING CORP. (QC)
Name changed 00/00/1951
Name changed from Arnora Gold Mines Ltd. to Arnora Sulphur Mining Corp. 00/00/1951
Charter cancelled 08/00/1973

ARNOUX CORP. (CA)
Dissolved 12/31/1967
No stockholders' equity

ARNOX CORP (DE)
Recapitalized as Telemetrix Inc. 03/31/1999
Each share Common $0.001 par exchanged for (0.08695652) share Common $0.001 par
(See Telemetrix Inc.)

ARNTFIELD GOLD MINES LTD.
Acquired by Arntfield Mining Corp. Ltd. 00/00/1944
Each share Capital Stock $1 par exchanged for (0.25) share Capital Stock $1 par
(See Arntfield Mining Corp. Ltd.)

ARNTFIELD GOLD SYNDICATE, LTD.
Acquired by Pennaque Mining Corp. Ltd. 00/00/1937
Details not available

ARNTFIELD MINING CORP., LTD.
Acquired by New Arntfield Mines Ltd. 00/00/1947
Each share Capital Stock $1 par exchanged for (0.5) share Capital Stock $1 par and (0.2) share Arncoeur Gold Mines Ltd. Common $1 par
(See each company's listing)

ARNTFIELD MINING SYNDICATE LTD.
Assets sold to Pennaque Mining Corp. Ltd. on a (2) for (1) basis 00/00/1937
Pennaque Mining Corp. Ltd. recapitalized as Lakeshore Minerals Inc. 04/30/1986 which recapitalized as Leggo Holdings Inc. 07/18/1990 which name changed to Transarctic Petroleum Corp. 09/29/1997 which name changed to ivyNET Corp. 03/26/1999 which recapitalized as Saratoga Capital Corp. 08/25/2000
(See Saratoga Capital Corp.)

ARO CORP (DE)
Reincorporated 10/30/1965
4.5% Conv. Preferred $50 par called for redemption 12/02/1963
State of incorporation changed from (OH) to (DE) 10/30/1965
Common $2.50 par split (3) for (2) by issuance of (0.5) additional share 02/01/1968
Stock Dividends - 10% 11/16/1964; 10% 10/15/1976; 10% 01/14/1978; 10% 07/16/1979; 10% 10/15/1981
Merged into Todd Shipyards Corp. (NY) 11/27/1985
Each share Common $2.50 par exchanged for $35 cash

ARO EQUIPMENT CORP. (OH)
Common $1 par changed to $2.50 par 00/00/1943
Common $2.50 par split (3) for (2) by issuance of (0.5) additional share 09/01/1961
Stock Dividends - 100% 08/05/1943; 10% 06/12/1952; 10% 11/26/1952; 10% 07/31/1953; 10% 06/15/1959
Name changed to Aro Corp. (OH) 11/30/1961
Aro Corp. (OH) reincorporated in Delaware 10/30/1965
(See Aro Corp. (DE))

ARO LIQ INC (DE)
Plan of reorganization under Chapter 11 Federal Bankruptcy proceedings effective 04/17/2018
ARO Plan Stock was issued to the Plan Administrator for the benefit of holders

AROC INC (DE)
Merged into MPAC Energy, LLC 09/28/2001
Each share Common 1¢ par exchanged for $0.06 cash

ARODIEN RES LTD (BC)
Capital Stock $1 par changed to no par 02/06/1975
Recapitalized as Manchester Oil Corp. 03/27/1978
Each share Capital Stock no par exchanged for (0.25) share Capital Stock no par
Manchester Oil Corp. name changed to Manchester Resources Corp. 03/07/1984 which recapitalized as Danoil Energy Ltd. 09/01/1995 which merged into Acclaim Energy Trust 04/20/2001
(See Acclaim Energy Trust)

ARONEX PHARMACEUTICALS INC (DE)
Each share old Common $0.001 par exchanged for (0.5) share new Common $0.001 par 07/01/1996
Merged into Antigenics, Inc. 07/13/2001
Each share new Common $0.001 par exchanged for (0.0594) share Common 1¢ par and (1) Contingent Value Right
Contingent Value Rights expired without value 07/06/2002
Antigenics, Inc. name changed to Agenus Inc. 01/06/2011

ARONOS MULTINATIONAL INC (ON)
Name changed to RDG Minerals Inc. 10/24/1996
RDG Minerals Inc. recapitalized as Netforfun.com, Inc. 08/09/2000

AROOSTOOK TELEPHONE & TELEGRAPH CO.
Merged into New England Telephone & Telegraph Co. 00/00/1932
Details not available

AROOSTOOK TR CO (CARIBOU, ME)
Common $10 par changed to $2.50 par and (3) additional shares issued 06/17/1983
Merged into Bank of New England Corp. 12/05/1986
Each share Common $2.50 par exchanged for (2.46) shares Common $5 par
(See Bank of New England Corp.)

AROS CORP (DE)
Name changed to ReGen Biologics, Inc. 11/20/2002
(See ReGen Biologics, Inc.)

AROWANA INC (CAYMAN ISLANDS)
Merged into VivoPower International PLC 12/29/2016
Each Unit exchanged for (1.15) Ordinary Shares $0.012 par
Each Ordinary Share $0.0001 par exchanged for (1) Ordinary Share $0.012 par

AROWAY ENERGY INC (BC)
Assets surrendered for the benefit of creditors 11/17/2017
No stockholders' equity

AROWAY MINERALS INC (BC)
Name changed to Aroway Energy Inc. 02/04/2011
(See Aroway Energy Inc.)

ARP CORP (IN)
Liquidation completed
Each share Common $1 par received initial distribution of $10 cash 04/30/1976
Each share Common $1 par received second distribution of $2.30 cash 03/31/1977
Each share Common $1 par exchanged for third and final distribution of $1.20 cash 01/31/1978

ARP INSTRS INC (DE)
Chapter 11 bankruptcy proceedings converted to Chapter 7 on 10/07/1981
No stockholders' equity

ARPEGGIO ACQUISITION CORP (DE)
Name changed to Hill International, Inc. 06/29/2006

ARPEJA CALIF INC (CA)
Stock Dividend - 25% 03/19/1973
Merged into Arpeja II 03/29/1979
Each share Common 10¢ par exchanged for $9.60 cash

ARRABBIATA CAP CORP (BC)
Common no par split (1.558) for (1) by issuance of (0.558) additional share payable 01/08/2007 to holders of record 01/05/2007 Ex date - 01/10/2007
Reorganized under the laws of Ontario as Olivut Resources Ltd. 01/10/2007
Each share Common no par exchanged for (1) share Common no par

ARRAYS INC (CA)
Charter cancelled for failure to file reports and pay taxes 11/05/1988

ARRHYTHMIA RESH TECHNOLOGY INC (DE)
Each share old Common 1¢ par exchanged for (0.5) share new Common 1¢ par 09/30/1989
Each share new Common 1¢ par exchanged again for (0.5) share new Common 1¢ par 08/06/1990
Name changed to Micron Solutions, Inc. 03/27/2017

ARRIS GROUP INC NEW (DE)
Merged into ARRIS International PLC 01/05/2016
Each share Common 1¢ par exchanged for (1) share Ordinary £0.01 par

ARRIS GROUP INC OLD (DE)
Under plan of reorganization each share Common 1¢ par automatically became (1) share ARRIS Group, Inc. (New) Common 1¢ par 04/16/2013
ARRIS Group, Inc. (New) merged into ARRIS International PLC 01/05/2016

ARRIS HLDGS INC (BC)
Each share Common no par received distribution of (1) share Cielo Gold Corp. Common no par payable 07/28/2011 to holders of record 05/02/2011
Common no par split (5) for (1) by issuance of (4) additional shares payable 02/26/2014 to holders of record 02/26/2014 Ex date - 02/24/2014
Name changed to Global Hemp Group, Inc. 03/25/2014

ARRIS PHARMACEUTICAL CORP (DE)
Name changed to AxyS Pharmaceuticals, Inc. 01/08/1998
AxyS Pharmaceuticals, Inc. merged into Applera Corp. 11/19/2001
(See Applera Corp.)

ARRIS RES INC (BC)
Each share old Common no par exchanged for (0.2) share new Common no par 07/16/2007
Each share new Common no par received distribution of (1) share InCana Investments Inc. Common no par payable 10/23/2009 to holders of record 07/06/2009 Ex date - 07/02/2009
Each share new Common no par received distribution of (1) share Arris Holdings Inc. Common no par, (1) share CLI Resources Inc. Common no par and (1) share QMI Seismic Inc. Common no par payable 01/05/2010 to holders of record 12/15/2009
Name changed to RTN Stealth Software Inc. 01/08/2010
RTN Stealth Software Inc. name changed to Quantitative Alpha Trading Inc. (BC) 04/29/2011 which reincorporated in Ontario 12/09/2011
(See Quantitative Alpha Trading Inc.)

ARRISCRAFT INTL INCOME FD (ON)
Liquidation completed
Each Trust Unit no par received initial distribution of $7.65 cash payable 07/24/2007 to holders of record 07/24/2007
Each Trust Unit no par received second and final distribution of $0.294 cash payable 08/14/2008 to holders of record 07/24/2007

ARRISYSTEMS INC (NV)
Each share old Common $0.001 par exchanged for (0.002) share new Common $0.001 par 08/10/1998
Charter permanently revoked 04/30/2000

ARRIVAL ENERGY LTD (AB)
Merged into Chain Energy Corp. 08/10/2000
Each share Class A no par exchanged for (1.2846) shares Common no par
Each share Class B no par exchanged for (3.2114) shares Common no par

ARRIVALS LTD (IL)
Stock Dividend - 10% 10/04/1971
Name changed to 2nd Debut Cosmetics, Inc. 06/07/1972
(See 2nd Debut Cosmetics, Inc.)

ARRO EXPANSION BOLT CO (OH)
Acquired by Mid-Continent Manufacturing Co. (OH) 08/00/1964
Each share Common no par exchanged for (2.5) shares Common $1 par
5.5% Preferred $25 par called for redemption 09/09/1964
Mid-Continent Manufacturing Co. (OH) reincorporated in Delaware as Mid-Con Inc. 10/31/1968 which merged into A-T-O Inc. 10/29/1969 which name changed to Figgie International Inc. (OH) 06/01/1981 which reorganized in Delaware as Figgie International Holdings Inc. 07/18/1983 which name changed to Figgie International Inc. 12/31/1986 which name changed to Scott Technologies, Inc. 05/20/1998 which merged into Tyco International Ltd. (Bermuda) 05/03/2001 which reincorporated in Switzerland 03/17/2009 which merged into Johnson Controls International PLC 09/06/2016

ARROW AIRCRAFT CORP.
Foreclosed 00/00/1940
No stockholders' equity

ARROW AUTOMOTIVE INDS INC (MA)
Stock Dividend - 20% 07/02/1979
Filed a petition under Chapter 7 Federal Bankruptcy Code 10/16/1998
Stockholders' equity unlikely

ARROW BK CORP (NY)
Common $8 par split (5) for (4) by issuance of (0.25) additional share 10/01/1985
Common $8 par split (2) for (1) by issuance of (1) additional share 06/01/1986
Common $8 par changed to $5 par and (1) additional share issued 09/01/1987
Stock Dividend - 10% 02/01/1984
Under plan of merger name changed to Arrow Financial Corp. 07/02/1990

ARROW-CAN NATURAL GAS LTD. (BC)
Acquired by Christal Natural Gas & Minerals Ltd. 00/00/1977
Each share Common no par exchanged for (0.12004801) share Preference $5 par
Note: Company is now private

ARROW DEVELOPERS INC (MN)
Recapitalized as Commonweal Holdings, Ltd. 12/18/1995
Each share Common 5¢ par exchanged for (0.25) share Common 1¢ par
Commonweal Holdings, Ltd. recapitalized as Sandy Steele Unlimited Inc. 10/15/2001

ARROW-DISTILLERS, INC.
Name changed to Arrow Liqueurs Corp. 00/00/1943
Arrow Liqueurs Corp. merged into Heublein, Inc. 07/01/1965 which merged into Reynolds (R.J.) Industries, Inc. 10/13/1982 which name changed to RJR Nabisco, Inc. 04/25/1986 which merged into RJR Holdings Group, Inc. 04/28/1989
(See RJR Holdings Group, Inc.)

ARROW ELECTRIC CO.
Merged into Arrow-Hart & Hegeman Electric Co. 00/00/1928
Details not available

ARROW ELECTRS INC (NY)
$19.375 Depositary Preferred called for redemption 09/18/1992
(Additional Information in Active)

ARROW ENERGY LTD (AB)
Recapitalized as Kallisto Energy Corp. 11/02/2009
Each share Common no par exchanged for (0.25) share Common no par
Kallisto Energy Corp. name changed to Toro Oil & Gas Ltd. 11/25/2014
(See Toro Oil & Gas Ltd.)

ARROW-HART & HEGEMAN ELECTRIC CO. (CT)
Stock Dividends - 100% 06/00/1947; 25% 01/21/1952; 20% 01/21/1957; 20% 01/21/1960; 25% 10/12/1966
Name changed to Arrow-Hart, Inc. 05/01/1968
Arrow-Hart, Inc. merged into Crouse-Hinds Co. 04/30/1975
(See Crouse-Hinds Co.)

ARROW HART INC (CT)
Merged into Crouse-Hinds Co. 04/30/1975
Each share Common $10 par exchanged for (0.425) share $3.35 Conv. Preferred no par
(See Crouse-Hinds Co.)

ARROW INSURANCE CO. (MN)
Common $2.50 par changed to $1 par 12/31/1967
99.9% held by Consolidated Financial Corp. as of 09/14/1970
Public interest eliminated

ARROW INTL INC (PA)
Common no par split (2) for (1) by issuance of (1) additional share payable 08/15/2003 to holders of record 08/01/2003 Ex date - 08/18/2003
Merged into Teleflex Inc. 10/01/2007
Each share Common no par exchanged for $45.50 cash

ARROW LIQUEURS CORP. (MI)
Merged into Heublein, Inc. 07/01/1965
Each share Common $1 par exchanged for (1.5) shares Common $1 par
Heublein, Inc. merged into Reynolds (R.J.) Industries, Inc. 10/13/1982 which name changed to RJR Nabisco, Inc. 04/25/1986 which merged into RJR Holdings Group, Inc. 04/28/1989
(See RJR Holdings Group, Inc.)

ARROW MAGNOLIA INTL INC (TX)
Merged into Arrow Acquisition L.P. 01/07/2005
Each share Common $1 par exchanged for $1.60 cash

ARROW MGMT INC (NV)
Name changed to W-Waves USA Inc. 01/26/2000
W-Waves USA Inc. recapitalized as China Titanium & Chemical Corp. 09/07/2004 which name changed to Far Vista Interactive Corp. 09/19/2008 which name changed to Far Vista Petroleum Corp. 05/30/2013

ARROW TRANSN CO (OR)
Assets sold for the benefit of creditors 09/25/1997
No stockholders' equity

ARROW TUNGSTEN MINES LTD. (ON)
Charter cancelled for failure to pay taxes and file returns 03/16/1976

ARROW URANIUM CORP. (UT)
Name changed to Control Metals Corp. 11/12/1968
(See Control Metals Corp.)

ARROWFIELD RES LTD (BC)
Recapitalized as ITL Capital Corp. 04/27/1992
Each share Common no par exchanged for (0.5) share Common no par
ITL Capital Corp. recapitalized as MPH Ventures Corp. 12/19/2005 which name changed to Cuba Ventures Corp. 03/21/2016 which name changed to CUV Ventures Corp. 03/01/2018

ARROWHEAD & PURITAS WTRS INC (CA)
Capital Stock $1 par reclassified as Common $1 par 05/07/1964
Stock Dividend - 100% 06/01/1961
Merged into Coca-Cola Bottling Co. of Los Angeles 04/01/1969
Each share Common $1 par exchanged for (1) share $2 Conv. Preferred Ser. A $5 par
(See Coca-Cola Bottling Co. of Los Angeles)

ARROWHEAD BRIDGE CO. (WI)
Acquired by States of Minnesota and Wisconsin at $22 per Common no par 03/12/1963

ARROWHEAD CAP INC (CO)
Name changed to American Catalina Capital, Inc. 04/25/1989
(See American Catalina Capital, Inc.)

ARROWHEAD CONSOLIDATED MINES LTD.
Bankrupt 00/00/1932
Details not available

ARROWHEAD ENERGY CORP (UT)
Name changed to Reliance Enterprises Inc. 06/06/1985
Reliance Enterprises Inc. reorganized as Capitol Television Network Inc. 07/21/1988 which name changed to Royal Casino Group Inc. 04/19/1994 which name changed to E-Commerce West Corp. 07/31/1998 which recapitalized as Interactive Broadcasting Network Group Inc. 01/28/2002 which name changed to Baymark Technologies Inc. 08/30/2002 which name changed to Implantable Vision, Inc. 01/03/2006 which name changed to Arcland Energy Corp. 08/25/2008
(See Arcland Energy Corp.)

ARROWHEAD GOLD CORP (BC)
Each share old Common no par exchanged for (0.25) share new Common no par 04/08/2014
Recapitalized as Kontrol Energy Corp. 08/09/2016
Each share new Common no par exchanged for (0.16666666) share Common no par

ARROWHEAD GOLD MINES LTD. (QC)
Acquired by Quebec Cobalt & Exploration Ltd. 05/00/1988
Each share Capital Stock exchanged for (0.15061351) share Capital Stock $1 par
Quebec Cobalt & Exploration Ltd. merged into Consolidated Thompson-Lundmark Gold Mines Ltd. 07/01/1989 which name changed to Consolidated Thompson Iron Mines Ltd. 08/24/2006
(See Consolidated Thompson Iron Mines Ltd.)

ARROWHEAD LAKE CORP.
Liquidation completed 00/00/1946
Details not available

ARROWHEAD MINERALS CORP (BC)
Recapitalized as Gemini Energy Corp. 10/25/1999
Each share Common no par exchanged for (0.1) share Common no par
Gemini Energy Corp. merged into Bucking Horse Energy Inc. 03/03/2008

ARROWHEAD PAC SVGS BK BLUE JAY CALIF
Placed in conservatorship 04/00/1989
No stockholders' equity

ARROWHEAD PETROLEUM CORP. (DE)
Each share Common $1 par exchanged for (4) shares Common 25¢ par 02/19/1957
Liquidation completed
Each share Common 25¢ par exchanged for initial distribution of $0.155 cash 12/07/1962
Each share Common 25¢ par received second and final distribution of $0.008 cash 10/04/1963

ARROWHEAD PETROLEUM CORP (UT)
Proclaimed dissolved for failure to pay taxes 00/00/1941

ARROWHEAD RESH CORP (DE)
Each share old Common $0.001 par exchanged for (0.1) share new Common $0.001 par 11/17/2011
Name changed to Arrowhead Pharmaceuticals, Inc. 04/07/2016

ARROWHEAD RES LTD (BC)
Recapitalized as Double Arrow Oil & Gas Ltd. 08/23/1995
Each share Common no par exchanged for (0.1) share Common no par
Double Arrow Oil & Gas Ltd. name changed to Arrowhead Minerals Corp. 12/02/1996 which recapitalized as Gemini Energy Corp. 10/25/1999 which merged into Bucking Horse Energy Inc. 03/03/2008

ARROWHEAD SVGS & LN ASSN BLUE JAY CALIF (CA)
Guarantee Stock $10 par changed to $3.33 par and (2) additional shares issued 08/31/1981
Name changed to Arrowhead Pacific Savings Bank (Blue Jay, CA) 03/28/1984
(See Arrowhead Pacific Savings Bank (Blue Jay, CA))

ARROWHEAD WTR PRODS LTD (AB)
Each share old Class A Common no par exchanged for (0.2) share new Class A Common no par 10/01/2010
Reincorporated under the laws of British Columbia as Captiva Verde Industries Ltd. 05/09/2014

ARROWLINK CORP (ON)
Name changed to Triarx Gold Corp. 04/24/1996
(See Triarx Gold Corp.)

ARROWPOINT COMMUNICATIONS INC (DE)
Merged into Cisco Systems, Inc. 06/26/2000
Each share Common $0.001 par exchanged for (2.1218) shares Common no par

ARS INTL INC (NV)
Reorganized as Incremental Data Inc. 08/10/1994
Each share Common $0.001 par exchanged for (3) shares Common $0.001 par
Incremental Data Inc. recapitalized as Golden Age Homes Inc. 09/15/1997 which name changed to American Health Systems Inc. 10/14/1998
(See American Health Systems Inc.)

ARS NETWORKS INC (NH)
Each share old Common $0.0001 par exchanged for (0.02) share new Common $0.0001 par 03/26/2003
Each share new Common $0.0001 par exchanged again for (0.02) share new Common $0.0001 par 06/21/2004
Recapitalized as Green Mountain Capital Inc. (NH) 09/24/2004
Each share new Common $0.0001 par exchanged for (0.001) share Common $0.0001 par
Green Mountain Capital Inc. (NH) reincorporated in Nevada 07/12/2005 which name changed to IT Group Holdings, Inc. 02/26/2007

ARSENAL CAP INC (AB)
Merged into Arsenal Energy Inc. (Old) 11/14/2002
Each share Common no par exchanged for (0.8) share Common no par
Arsenal Energy Inc. (Old) merged into Arsenal Energy Inc. (New) 05/29/2003 which merged into Prairie Provident Resources Inc. 09/16/2016

ARSENAL ENERGY INC NEW (AB)
Each share old Common no par exchanged for (0.1) share new Common no par 08/13/2013
Merged into Prairie Provident Resources Inc. 09/16/2016
Each share new Common no par exchanged for (1.1417218) shares Common no par

ARSENAL ENERGY INC OLD (AB)
Merged into Arsenal Energy Inc. (New) 05/29/2003
Each share Common no par exchanged for (0.72072072) share Common no par
Arsenal Energy Inc. (New) merged into Prairie Provident Resources Inc. 09/16/2016

ART ADVANCED RESH TECHNOLOGIES INC NEW (CANADA)
Proposal under Bankruptcy and Insolvency Act effective 12/11/2009
No stockholders' equity

ART ADVANCED RESH TECHNOLOGIES INC OLD (CANADA)
Reorganized as ART Advanced Research Technologies Inc. (New) 11/27/2006
Each share Common no par exchanged for (1) share Common no par

ART CARDS INC (CO)
Common $0.0001 par split (10) for (1) by issuance of (9) additional shares 10/17/1988
Recapitalized as uMember.com, Inc. 03/17/2000
Each share Common $0.0001 par exchanged for (0.0004878) share Common $0.0001 par

ART CINEMA CORP.
Dissolved 00/00/1935
Details not available

ART-CRAFT BRIAR PIPE CORP. (NY)
Each share Common 50¢ par exchanged for (0.2) share $0.35 Preferred $1 par 00/00/1946
Proclaimed dissolved for failure to file reports and pay taxes 12/15/1953

ART DESIGN INC (CO)
Each share Common $0.001 par received distribution of (0.1) share Art Dimensions, Inc. Common no par payable 12/30/2009 to holders of record 11/23/2009
Name changed to Rockdale Resources Corp. (CO) 05/25/2012
Rockdale Resources Corp. (CO) reincorporated in Texas as Petrolia Energy Corp. 09/02/2016

ART DIMENSIONS INC (CO)
Name changed to Southern Hospitality Development Corp. 11/23/2012
Southern HospitalityDevelopment Corp. name changed to Smokin Concepts Development Corp. 05/09/2013 which name changed to Bourbon Brothers Holding Corp. 01/29/2014 which name changed to Southern Concepts Restaurant Group, Inc. 03/13/2015

ART EXPLOSION INC (FL)
Merged into Decor Corp. 03/25/1986
Each share Common 1¢ par exchanged for (0.015) share Common 1¢ par
Note: Each share Common 1¢ par received additional distribution of (0.0082) share Common 1¢ par 07/16/1987
Decor Corp. acquired by Claire's Stores Inc. (DE) 12/15/1989 which reincorporated in Florida 06/30/2000
(See Claire's Stores Inc.)

ART FIND SYS INC (UT)
Involuntarily dissolved 03/31/1978

ART GUARD INC (NV)
Reorganized under the laws of Delaware as Computer Integration Corp. 04/27/1994
Each share Common $0.001 par exchanged for (0.05882352) share Common $0.001 par
(See Computer Integration Corp.)

ART IN MOTION INCOME FD (BC)
Acquired by Clarke Inc. 09/25/2008
Each Trust Unit exchanged for $0.75 cash

ART INTL CORP (ON)
Common no par split (2) for (1) by issuance of (1) additional share payable 11/05/2004 to holders of record 10/29/2004 Ex date - 11/08/2004
Name changed to Diamant Art Corp. 11/26/2004
Each share Common no par exchanged for (1) share Common no par
(See Diamant Art Corp.)

ART METAL, INC. (NY)
Completely liquidated 03/15/1968
Each share Capital Stock $1 par exchanged for first and final distribution of (0.5) share Heller (Walter E.) & Co. $4.07 Conv. Preferred no par
Heller (Walter E.) & Co. reorganized as Heller (Walter E.) International Corp. 07/28/1969 which name changed to Amerifin Corp. 01/26/1984
(See Amerifin Corp.)

ART METAL CONSTRUCTION CO. (MA)
Stock Dividends - 100% 05/08/1951; 50% 05/10/1956
Reincorporated under the laws of New York as Art Metal, Inc. and Capital Stock $10 par changed to $1 par 12/31/1959
Art Metal, Inc. liquidated for Heller (Walter E.) & Co. 03/15/1968 which reorganized as Heller (Walter E.) International Corp. 07/28/1969 which name changed to Amerifin Corp. 01/26/1984
(See Amerifin Corp.)

ART METAL U S A INC (NY)
Charter cancelled and proclaimed dissolved for failure to pay taxes 03/28/2001

ART METAL WORKS, INC.
Common no par changed to $5 par 06/00/1932
Name changed to Ronson Art Metal Works, Inc. 00/00/1945
Ronson Art Metal Works, Inc. name changed to Ronson Corp. 00/00/1954
(See Ronson Corp.)

ART MUSIC & ENTMT INC (FL)
Administratively dissolved for failure to file annual report 09/22/2000

ART OF ANIMATION GALLERIES LTD (AB)
Delisted from Alberta Stock Exchange 02/20/1997

ART TECHNOLOGY GROUP INC (DE)
Common 1¢ par split (2) for (1) by issuance of (1) additional share payable 03/24/2000 to holders of record 03/10/2000
Acquired by Oracle Corp. 01/05/2011
Each share Common 1¢ par exchanged for $6 cash

ART WORLD INDS INC (DE)
Each share old Common $0.001 par

exchanged for (0.1) share new
Common $0.001 par 04/26/2001
Recapitalized as ISSG Inc.
08/08/2002
Each share new Common $0.001 par
exchanged for (1/3) share Common
$0.001 par
Note: Holders of (99) or fewer
pre-split shares not affected by split
Holders of between (100) and (299)
shares will receive (100) shares only
ISSG Inc. name changed to Rubicon
Financial Inc. (DE) 09/15/2006
which reincorporated in Nevada
08/29/2011

**ART'S WAY MANUFACTURING CO
INC (IA)**
Common no par split (3) for (2) by
issuance of (0.5) additional share
11/15/1973
Common no par split (3) for (2) by
issuance of (0.5) additional share
07/02/1979
Stock Dividend - 10% 07/14/1972
Reincorporated under the laws of
Delaware and Common no par
changed to 1¢ par 02/15/1989

ARTA ENTERPRISES INC (AB)
Name changed to Committee Bay
Resources Ltd. 08/09/2002
Committee Bay Resources Ltd.
recapitalized as CBR Gold Corp.
03/02/2009 which name changed to
Niblack Mineral Development Inc.
04/15/2010 which merged into
Heatherdale Resources Ltd.
01/23/2012

ARTAFLEX INC (ON)
Each share old Common no par
exchanged for (0.0000004) share
new Common no par 04/30/2013
Note: In effect holders received $0.05
cash per share and public interest
was eliminated

**ARTAGRAPH REPRODUCTION
TECHNOLOGY INC (ON)**
Recapitalized as A.R.T. International
Inc. 09/14/1998
Each share Common no par
exchanged for (0.004) share
Common no par
Preference not affected except for
change of name
A.R.T. International Inc. recapitalized
as ART International Corp.
06/16/2003 which name changed to
Diamant Art Corp. 11/26/2004
(See Diamant Art Corp.)

ARTCO-BELL CORP. (TX)
Name changed to Artco Industries,
Inc. 08/28/1981
(See Artco Industries, Inc.)

ARTCO INDS INC (TX)
Stock Dividend - 50% 10/12/1981
Liquidation completed
Each share Common $1 par received
initial distribution of $6 cash
01/14/1983
Each share Common $1 par
exchanged for second and final
distribution of (1) share B & M
Investments, Inc. Common no par
02/16/1983
(See B & M Investments, Inc.)

ARTEC CONSULTING CORP (NV)
Name changed to Artec Global Media,
Inc. 06/30/2014

ARTEC INC (IN)
Plan of liquidation and dissolution
effective 12/11/1995
Each share Common no par received
first and final distribution of $0.4920
cash

ARTECH SYS INC (DE)
Reincorporated 10/25/1991
Name changed 04/06/1992
State of incorporation changed from
(WA) to (DE) 10/25/1991
Each share old Common $0.005 par
exchanged for (0.05) share new
Common $0.005 par 01/27/1992
Name changed from ARTECH
Recovery Systems, Inc. to ARTECH
Systems, Inc. 04/06/1992
Stock Dividend - 26.178% 04/22/1992
Voluntarily dissolved 12/22/2004
Details not available

ARTECON INC (DE)
Merged into Dot Hill Systems Corp.
(NY) 08/02/1999
Each share Common $0.005 par
exchanged for (0.4) share Common
1¢ par
Dot Hill Systems Corp. (NY)
reincorporated in Delaware
09/19/2001

ARTEK EXPL LTD NEW (AB)
Merged into Kelt Exploration Ltd.
04/21/2015
Each share Common no par
exchanged for (0.34) share Common
no par

ARTEK SYS CORP (NY)
Common 10¢ par changed to 1¢ par
01/21/1974
Each share Common 1¢ par
exchanged for (0.25) share Common
10¢ par 06/02/1977
Merged into Dynatech Corp. (Old)
(MA) 08/05/1982
Each share Common 10¢ par
exchanged for (0.125) share
Common 20¢ par
Dynatech Corp. (Old) (MA) merged
into Dynatech Corp. (New) (MA)
05/21/1998 which reincorporated in
Delaware 09/08/1999 which name
changed to Acterna Corp.
08/30/2000
(See Acterna Corp.)

**ARTEL COMMUNICATIONS CORP
(MA)**
Merged into Chipcom Corp.
02/14/1994
Each share Common 1¢ par
exchanged for (0.07203682) share
Common 2¢ par
Chipcom Corp. merged into 3Com
Corp. (CA) 10/13/1995 which
reincorporated in Delaware
06/11/1997
(See 3Com Corp.)

ARTEMIS DEVELOPMENT, INC. (UT)
Name changed to Vista Corp.
04/00/1987
(See Vista Corp.)

ARTEMIS ENERGY HLDGS INC (NV)
Name changed to Findit, Inc.
02/20/2015

**ARTEMIS INTL SOLUTIONS CORP
(DE)**
Each share old Common $0.001 par
exchanged for (0.04) share new
Common $0.001 par 02/07/2003
Merged into Trilogy, Inc. 07/03/2006
Each share new Common $0.001 par
exchanged for $1.60 cash

**ARTEMIS U S CAP APPRECIATION
FD (ON)**
Trust terminated 02/23/2015
Each Class A Unit received $12.5808
cash

ARTEMIS VENTURE INC (BC)
Recapitalized as Paradym Ventures
Inc. 01/04/1999
Each shares Common no par
exchanged for (0.66666666) share
Common no par
Paradym Ventures Inc. recapitalized
as Pacific Paradym Energy Inc.
10/01/2007

ARTEPHARM GLOBAL CORP (NV)
Each share old Common $0.001 par
exchanged for (0.04) share new
Common $0.001 par 12/16/2010
Name changed to Sharprock
Resources Inc. 07/20/2011
Sharprock Resources Inc.
recapitalized as Evergreen-Agra,
Inc. (NV) 10/23/2013 which
reincorporated in Delaware as
Evergreen-Agra Global Investments,
Inc. 11/14/2017

**ARTERIAL VASCULAR ENGR INC
(DE)**
Common $0.001 par split (2) for (1)
by issuance of (1) additional share
payable 03/02/1998 to holders of
record 02/17/1998 Ex date -
03/03/1998
Merged into Medtronic, Inc. (MN)
01/28/1999
Each share Common $0.001 par
exchanged for (0.76726) share
Common 10¢ par
Medtronic, Inc. (MN) reincorporated in
Ireland as Medtronic PLC
01/27/2015

ARTERIS S A (BRAZIL)
GDR agreement terminated
01/06/2016
No GDR's remain outstanding

ARTES MED INC (DE)
Filed a petition under Chapter 7
Federal Bankruptcy Code
12/01/2008
No stockholders' equity

ARTESANIAS CORP (NV)
Common $0.001 par split (12) for (1)
by issuance of (11) additional shares
payable 03/03/2015 to holders of
record 02/23/2015 Ex date -
03/04/2015
Name changed to SocialPlay USA,
Inc. 07/07/2015

ARTESCOPE INC (DE)
Common $0.001 par split (4) for (1)
by issuance of (3) additional shares
payable 05/28/2002 to holders of
record 05/27/2002 Ex date -
05/29/2002
Name changed to GlobeTrac, Inc.
07/29/2002
GlobeTrac, Inc. recapitalized as Poly
Shield Technologies Inc. 07/12/2012
which name changed to Triton
Emission Solutions Inc. 08/25/2014

ARTESIAN PETE CORP (BC)
Struck off register and declared
dissolved for failure to file returns
08/21/1987

ARTESIAN RES CORP (DE)
7% Preferred $25 par called for
redemption at $30 on 02/21/2003
(Additional Information in Active)

ARTESIAN WTR CO (DE)
Stock Dividend - 25% 09/01/1957
Name changed to Artesian Resources
Corp. 07/31/1984

ARTESYN TECHNOLOGIES INC (FL)
Merged into Emerson Electric Co.
04/28/2006
Each share Common 1¢ par
exchanged for $11 cash

ARTEVO CORP (AB)
Placed in receivership 12/18/2009
Stockholders' equity unlikely

ARTEX CORP (NV)
Reorganized as AgriEuro Corp.
09/10/2010
Each share Common $0.001 par
exchanged for (40) shares Common
$0.001 par

ARTEX GRAPHICS INC (CO)
Name changed to Holographic
Dimensions Inc. 01/02/1996
Holographic Dimensions Inc.
recapitalized as Creston Resources
Ltd. 08/24/2004

ARTEX HOBBY PRODS INC (OH)
7% Conv. Preferred $10 par called for
redemption 06/25/1971
Merged into Riviana Foods, Inc. (Old)
01/26/1973
Each share Common no par
exchanged for (0.375) share
Common $3.50 par
Riviana Foods, Inc. (Old) acquired by
Colgate-Palmolive Co. 06/14/1976

**ARTEX HOLDINGS &
EXPLORATIONS LTD. (ON)**
Merged into Boeing Holdings &
Explorations Ltd. 11/03/1970
Details not available

ARTEX MINES LTD. (BC)
Name changed to Tower Mines Ltd.
10/08/1968
Tower Mines Ltd. name changed to
Tower Resources Ltd. 08/03/1970
which recapitalized as Consolidated
Tower Resources Ltd. 01/18/1972
(See Consolidated Tower Resources
Ltd.)

ARTEX MINES LTD. (ON)
Merged into Boeing Holdings &
Explorations Ltd. 11/03/1970
Each share Common $1 par
exchanged for (0.5) share Common
no par
Note: On 06/29/1970 the company
recapitalized as Artex Holdings &
Explorations Ltd. on a (1) for (2)
basis, changing the Common $1 par
to no par
Certificates were not surrendered at
time of recapitalization
Artex Holdings & Explorations Ltd.
merged into Boeing Holdings &
Explorations Ltd. on a share for
share basis
Subsequently as a result of the
merger each share Artex Mines Ltd.
Common $1 par (which actually
represents (0.5) share Artex
Holdings & Explorations Ltd.
Common no par) is exchanged for
(0.5) share Boeing Holdings &
Explorations Ltd. Common no par
Boeing Holdings & Explorations Ltd.
recapitalized as Consolidated
Boeing Holdings & Explorations Ltd.
01/06/1972 which name changed to
Academy Explorations Ltd.
04/10/1980
(See Academy Explorations Ltd.)

ART4LOVE INC (NV)
Each share old Common $0.001 par
exchanged for (0.2) share new
Common $0.001 par 09/28/2005
Each share new Common $0.001 par
exchanged again for (0.005) share
new Common $0.001 par
12/23/2008
Name changed to Smartag
International, Inc. 02/25/2009

**ARTGALLERYLIVE COM MGMT LTD
(BC)**
Recapitalized as Adaptive Marketing
Solutions Inc. 01/18/2001
Each share Common no par
exchanged for (0.06666666) share
Common no par
Adaptive Marketing Solutions Inc.
recapitalized as Permission
Marketing Solutions Inc. 01/18/2002
which name changed to Pacific Asia
China Energy Inc. 01/04/2006
(See Pacific Asia China Energy Inc.)

ARTHA RES CORP (BC)
Each share old Common no par
exchanged for (0.1) share new
Common no par 02/03/2015
Name changed to Centenera Mining
Corp. 06/22/2015

ARTHRITIS CLINICS INTL INC (CA)
Charter suspended for failure to file
reports and pay fees 05/03/1976

**ARTHRO PHARMACEUTICALS INC
(NV)**
Reorganized as Pantera Petroleum
Inc. 09/28/2007
Each share Common $0.001 par
exchanged for (16) shares Common
$0.001 par
Pantera Petroleum Inc. recapitalized
as ESP Resources, Inc. 01/27/2009

ARTHROCARE CORP (DE)
Common $0.001 par split (2) for (1) by issuance of (1) additional share payable 07/03/2000 to holders of record 06/19/2000
Acquired by Smith & Nephew PLC 05/29/2014
Each share Common $0.001 par exchanged for $48.25 cash

ARTHUR KAPLAN COSMETICS INC (NV)
Name changed to Savoy Energy Corp. 04/22/2009

ARTHUR REALTY CORP.
Liquidated 00/00/1943
Details not available

ARTHUR TREACHERS INC (UT)
Each share Common $0.001 par exchanged for (0.1) share Common 1¢ par 03/20/1986
Name changed to Digital Creative Development Corp. 07/31/2000

ARTHURIAN RES LTD (BC)
Recapitalized as Pacific Copperfields Inc. 12/16/1991
Each share Common no par exchanged for (0.33333333) share Common no par
Pacific Copperfields Inc. name changed to Botswana Diamondfields, Inc. 12/09/1993 which merged into Crew Development Corp. 01/14/2000 which name changed to Crew Gold Corp. 01/26/2004
(See Crew Gold Corp.)

ARTHURS-JONES INC (ON)
Name changed to Invesprint Corp. 09/23/1998
(See Invesprint Corp.)

ARTILLERY RES LTD (BC)
Recapitalized as Ferber Mining Corp. 01/11/1985
Each share Capital Stock no par exchanged for (0.2) share Common no par
(See Ferber Mining Corp.)

ARTINA RES LTD (BC)
Name changed to Prophecy Entertainment Inc. 03/31/2000
(See Prophecy Entertainment Inc.)

ARTIO GLOBAL INVT FDS (MA)
Local Emerging Markets Debt Fund Class A and Class I $0.001 par reclassified as Emerging Markets Local Currency Debt Fund Class A or Class I $0.001 par respectively 05/01/2012
Global Equity Fund Inc. Class A and Class I $0.001 par reclassified as Select Opportunities Fund Inc. Class A or Class I $0.001 par respectively 07/27/2012
Completely liquidated
Each share US Microcap Fund Class A $0.001 par received first and final distribution of $10.46 cash payable 10/31/2012 to holders of record 10/04/2012
Each share US Microcap Fund Class I $0.001 par received first and final distribution of $10.63 cash payable 10/31/2012 to holders of record 10/04/2012
Each share US Midcap Fund Class A $0.001 par received first and final distribution of $10.57 cash payable 10/31/2012 to holders of record 10/04/2012
Each share US Midcap Fund Class I $0.001 par received first and final distribution of $10.70 cash payable 10/31/2012 to holders of record 10/04/2012
Each share US Multicap Fund Class A $0.001 par received first and final distribution of $9.34 cash payable 10/31/2012 to holders of record 10/04/2012
Each share US Multicap Fund Class I $0.001 par received first and final distribution of $9.38 cash payable 10/31/2012 to holders of record 10/04/2012
Each share US Smallcap Fund Class A $0.001 par received first and final distribution of $9.93 cash payable 10/31/2012 to holders of record 10/04/2012
Each share US Smallcap Fund Class I $0.001 par received first and final distribution of $10.03 cash payable 10/31/2012 to holders of record 10/04/2012
Emerging Markets Local Currency Debt Fund Class A and Class I $0.001 par reclassified as Emerging Markets Local Debt Fund Class A or Class I $0.001 par respectively 01/01/2013
Note: Select Opportunities Fund Inc. is incorporated in Maryland
Under plan of reorganization each share of Global High Income Fund Class A and I ,International Equity Fund Class A and I ,International Equity Fund II Class A and I, Select Opportunities Fund Inc. Class A and I and Total Return Bond Fund Class A and I $0.001 par automatically became (1) share Aberdeen Funds Global High Income Fund Class A or I, Select International Equity Fund Class A or I, Select International Equity Fund II Class A or I, Global Select Opportunities Fund Inc. Class A or I or Total Return Bond Fund Class A or I respectively 05/12/2013
Emerging Markets Local Debt Fund Class A and I $0.001 par completely liquidated 04/19/2013
Details not available

ARTIO GLOBAL INVS INC (DE)
Acquired by Aberdeen Asset Management PLC 05/21/2013
Each share Class A Common $0.001 par exchanged for $2.75 cash

ARTIS REAL ESTATE INVT TR (CANADA)
Preferred Unit Ser. C called for redemption at USD$25 plus $0.328125 accrued dividends on 03/31/2018
(Additional Information in Active)

ARTISAN COMPONENTS INC (DE)
Merged into ARM Holdings PLC 12/23/2004
Each share Common $0.001 par exchanged for $36.3246 cash

ARTISAN CORP (AB)
Name changed 09/26/1995
Name changed from Artisan Drilling Ltd. to Artisan Corp. 09/26/1995
Merged into Ensign Resource Service Group Inc. 05/19/1998
Each share Common no par exchanged for (0.1871) share Common no par and $4.7473 cash
Ensign Resource Service Group Inc. name changed to Ensign Energy Services Inc. 06/07/2005

ARTISAN ENERGY CORP (AB)
Filed an assignment in bankruptcy 06/22/2016
Stockholders' equity unlikely

ARTISOFT INC (DE)
Each share old Common 1¢ par exchanged for (0.16666666) share new Common 1¢ par 04/23/2003
Name changed to Vertical Communications, Inc. 04/21/2006
(See Vertical Communications, Inc.)

ARTISTIC GREETINGS INC (NY)
Common 10¢ par split (2) for (1) by issuance of (1) additional share 03/09/1984
Common 10¢ par split (3) for (2) by issuance of (0.5) additional share 06/10/1991
Merged into AGI Acquisition 05/19/1998
Each share Common 10¢ par exchanged for $5.70 cash

ARTISTIC PHOTO PLATE CREATIONS INC (WA)
Recapitalized as APC Ventures Inc. 02/02/1995
Each share Common no par exchanged for (0.1) share Common no par
APC Ventures Inc. name changed to Yukon Gold Corp. (WA) 12/15/1995 which reincorporated in (Yukon) as Alliance Pacific Gold Corp. 06/12/1997 which recapitalized as International Alliance Resources, Inc. 09/24/1998 which name changed to Bluenose Gold Corp. 07/25/2012

ARTISTRY PUBLICATIONS INC (DE)
Name changed to China Redstone Group, Inc. 04/07/2010

ARTISTS & PRODUCERS INTERNATIONAL (UT)
Charter suspended for failure to pay taxes 09/30/1974

ARTISTS ENTMT COMPLEX INC (NY)
Common 1¢ par split (2) for (1) by issuance of (1) additional share 12/14/1971
Common 1¢ par split (3) for (2) by issuance of (0.5) additional share 04/10/1973
Dissolved by proclamation 09/30/1981

ARTKO CORP (DE)
Adjudicated bankrupt 03/21/1974
No stockholders' equity

ARTKRAFT MANUFACTURING CORP.
Merged into Universal Major Elec Appliances, Inc. 00/00/1952
Each share 6% Conv. Preferred $5 par exchanged for $5 face amount of 6% Series B Debentures
Each share 6% Non-Conv. Class B Preferred $5 par exchanged for $5 principal amount of 6% Series A Debentures
Each share Common 10¢ par exchanged for (1) share new Common 10¢ par
Universal Major Elec Appliances, Inc. merged into Birdsboro Steel Foundry & Machine Co. (DE) 07/02/1956 which merged into Birdsboro Corp. 12/31/1959
(See Birdsboro Corp.)

ARTLOOM CARPET CO., INC. (PA)
Common no par changed to $1 par 11/04/1955
Name changed to Artloom Industries, Inc. 11/24/1958
Artloom Industries, Inc. name changed to Trans-United Industries, Inc. 12/10/1959
(See Trans-United Industries, Inc.)

ARTLOOM CORP. (PA)
Name changed to Artloom Carpet Co., Inc. 00/00/1948
Artloom Carpet Co., Inc. name changed to Artloom Industries, Inc. 11/24/1958 which name changed to Trans-United Industries, Inc. 12/10/1959
(See Trans-United Industries, Inc.)

ARTLOOM INDUSTRIES, INC. (PA)
Name changed to Trans-United Industries, Inc. 12/10/1959
(See Trans-United Industries, Inc.)

ARTRA GROUP INC (PA)
Merged into Entrade Inc. 09/23/1999
Each share Common no par exchanged for (1) share Common no par
(See Entrade Inc.)

ARTRUST HOLDINGS CORP. (ON)
Charter revoked for failure to file reports and pay taxes 04/15/1952

ARTS & CRAFTS MATERIALS CORP. NEW (MD)
Each share Common no par exchanged for (0.33333333) share Common no par 09/17/1966
Name changed to Algonquin Corp. 08/03/1968
(See Algonquin Corp.)

ARTS & CRAFTS MATERIALS CORP. OLD (MD)
Certificates dated prior to 06/20/1965
Stock Dividend - 10% 11/15/1963
Name changed to Sargent Art Corp. 05/18/1965
Sargent Art Corp. name changed to Beverages, Inc. (MD) 12/23/1966
(See Beverages, Inc. (MD))

ARTS & LEISURE CORP (DE)
Completely liquidated 03/26/1976
Each share Common 10¢ par exchanged for first and final distribution of (1) share Century Greetings, Inc. Common 1¢ par and (1) share Circle Fine Art Corp. Common 10¢ par
(See each company's listing)

ARTS & SCIENCE TECHNOLOGY INC (DE)
Capital Stock 5¢ par changed to 1¢ par 03/31/1981
Each share old Capital Stock 1¢ par exchanged for (0.01) share new Capital Stock 1¢ par 08/17/1995
Reorganized as Litex Energy Inc. 11/17/1995
Each share new Capital Stock 1¢ par exchanged for (3) shares Capital Stock 1¢ par
Litex Energy Inc. recapitalized as International Ostrich Corp. 11/24/1997
(See International Ostrich Corp.)

ARTUP COM NETWORKS INC (CO)
Reincorporated under the laws of Nevada as Deerbrook Publishing Group Inc. 12/10/1999
Deerbrook Publishing Group Inc. recapitalized as VOLT, Inc. 04/06/2001 which name changed to Kore Holdings, Inc. 10/20/2004
(See Kore Holdings, Inc.)

ARTURION ENTMT INC (DE)
Name changed to POW! Entertainment, Inc. 06/10/2004

ARTURUS CAP LTD (AUSTRALIA)
ADR agreement terminated 05/20/2014
No ADR holders' equity

ARTWORK & BEYOND INC (CO)
Recapitalized as Advance Nanotech, Inc. (CO) 12/02/2004
Each share Common no par exchanged for (0.01) share Common no par
Advance Nanotech, Inc. (CO) reincorporated in Delaware 06/19/2006
(See Advance Nanotech, Inc.)

ARUBA COMBINED GOLDFIELDS LTD. (ON)
Charter revoked for failure to file reports and pay fees 12/09/1957

ARUBA NETWORKS INC (DE)
Acquired by Hewlett-Packard Co. 05/18/2015
Each share Common $0.0001 par exchanged for $24.67 cash

ARUMA VENTURES INC (BC)
Recapitalized as dot.com Technologies Inc. 09/07/1999
Each share Common no par exchanged for (0.5) share Common no par
dot.com Technologies Inc. recapitalized as BCS Collaborative Solutions Inc. 07/12/2002 which recapitalized as BCS Global Networks Inc. 09/02/2003
(See BCS Global Networks Inc.)

ARUNDEL CORP (MD)
Common no par split (3) for (1) by issuance of (2) additional shares 06/26/1970
5% Conv. Preferred Ser. A $50 par called for redemption 03/11/1985
3.2% Conv. Preferred Ser. B $50 par called for redemption 03/11/1985
Stock Dividends - 10% 01/15/1960; 10% 12/02/1985
Acquired by Florida Rock Industries Inc. 01/26/1988
Each share Common no exchanged for $40 cash

ARURA PHARMA INC (CANADA)
Company's principal asset sold for the benefit of creditors 09/30/2008
Stockholders' equity unlikely

ARUS CORP (NY)
Proclaimed dissolved 03/25/1992

ARV ASSISTED LIVING INC (DE)
State of incorporation changed from (CA) to (DE) 05/01/1998
Merged into Prometheus Assisted Living, L.L.C. 04/23/2003
Each share Common no par exchanged for $3.90 cash

ARVAL HLDGS INC (DE)
Charter cancelled and declared inoperative and void for non-payment of taxes 03/01/1997

ARVIDA CORP (DE)
Class B Common $1 par reclassified as Class A Common $1 par 07/26/1965
Class A Common $1 par reclassified as Common $1 par 01/19/1966
Merged into Pennsylvania Co. 06/30/1976
Each share Common $1 par exchanged for $12 cash

ARVIDA EXPL LTD (BC)
Name changed to Jade International Industrial Group Ltd. 03/15/1995
(See Jade International Industrial Group Ltd.)

ARVIN INDS INC (IN)
Recapitalized 09/30/1992
Capital Stock $2.50 par split (3) for (2) by issuance of (0.5) additional share 10/31/1967
Capital Stock $2.50 par reclassified as Common $2.50 par 04/18/1968
Common $2.50 par split (2) for (1) by issuance of (1) additional share 07/27/1972
Common $2.50 par split (3) for (2) by issuance of (0.5) additional share 12/21/1984
Common $2.50 par split (4) for (3) by issuance of (0.33333333) additional share 12/20/1985
$2 Conv. Preferred no par called for redemption 06/30/1988
Recapitalized 09/30/1992
Each share $3.75 Conv. Exchangeable Preferred no par exchanged for $50 principal amount of 7.5% Conv. Subordinated Debentures due 09/30/2014
Stock Dividends - 25% 04/28/1959; 10% 04/29/1963; 10% 05/26/1964; 10% 05/24/1966
Merged into ArvinMeritor, Inc. 07/07/2000
Each share Common $2.50 par exchanged for (1) share Common $1 par and $2 cash
ArvinMeritor, Inc. name changed to Meritor, Inc. 03/30/2011

ARVIND LTD (INDIA)
Name changed 08/15/2008
Name changed from Arvind Mills Ltd. to Arvind Ltd. 08/15/2008
ADR agreement terminated 04/03/2014
Each 144A GDR for Equity Shares exchanged for $2.496558 cash

ARVINMERITOR INC (IN)
Name changed to Meritor, Inc. 03/30/2011

ARVONIA-BUCKINGHAM SLATE CO., INC. (VA)
Voluntarily dissolved 06/25/1987
Details not available

ARWAY MFG CORP (NY)
Charter cancelled and proclaimed dissolved for failure to pay taxes and file reports 12/15/1969

ARWICK INTL RES LTD (BC)
Recapitalized as Gincho International Ventures Inc. 05/13/1992
Each share Common no par exchanged for (0.33333333) share Common no par
Gincho International Ventures Inc. name changed to Banner Mining Corp. 08/09/1994
(See Banner Mining Corp.)

ARWOOD CORP (DE)
Stock Dividends - 10% 02/15/1967; 10% 02/15/1968
5.5% Preferred $25 par called for redemption 05/05/1969
Merged into Interlake, Inc. 04/29/1976
Each share Common no par exchanged for (0.33333333) share Common $1 par
Interlake, Inc. reorganized as Interlake Corp. 05/29/1986
(See Interlake Corp.)

ARWOOD PRECISION CASTING CORP. (NY)
Merged into Arwood Corp. 02/01/1960
Each share 5.5% Preferred $25 par exchanged for (1) share 5.5% Preferred $25 par
Each share Common no par exchanged for (5) shares Common no par
Arwood Corp. merged into Interlake, Inc. 04/29/1976 which reorganized as Interlake Corp. 05/29/1986
(See Interlake Corp.)

ARX INC (DE)
Common 10¢ par split (5) for (4) by issuance of (0.25) additional share 03/02/1987
Stock Dividends - 10% 11/22/1985; 10% 05/25/1988
Name changed to AeroFlex Inc. 11/10/1994
(See AeroFlex Inc.)

ARXA INTL ENERGY INC (DE)
Each share old Common $0.001 par exchanged for (0.2) share new Common $0.001 par 10/26/1998
Name changed to King Resources, Inc. 12/11/2000

ARYT INDS LTD (ISRAEL)
Under plan of arrangement each share Ordinary ILS 0.02 par held outside of Israel received ILS 0.2053 cash 11/01/2009

ARYT OPTRONICS INDS LTD (ISRAEL)
Recapitalized as Aryt Industries, Ltd. 08/10/1992
Each share Ordinary ILS 0.02 par exchanged for (0.02) share Ordinary ILS 1 par
(See Aryt Industries, Ltd.)

ARYX THERAPEUTICS INC (DE)
Assets assigned for the benefit of creditors 03/22/2011
Stockholders' equity unlikely

ARZAN INTL 1991 LTD (ISRAEL)
Company reported out of business 03/22/2001
Details not available

AS EESTI TELEKOM (ESTONIA)
GDR agreement terminated 01/21/2010
Each Sponsored Reg. S GDR for Ordinary exchanged for $25.7427 cash
Each Sponsored 144A GDR for Ordinary exchanged for $25.7427 cash

ASA HLDGS INC (GA)
Merged into Delta Air Lines, Inc. 05/11/1999
Each share Common 10¢ par exchanged for $34 cash

ASA INTL LTD (DE)
Each share Common $0.0001 par exchanged for (0.02) share old Common 1¢ par 05/04/1990
Each share old Common 1¢ par exchanged for (0.5) share new Common 1¢ par to reflect a (1) for (200) reverse split followed by a (100) for (1) forward split 06/02/2003
Note: Holders of (199) or fewer pre-split shares received $1.11 cash per share
Each share new Common 1¢ par exchanged again for (0.00166666) share new Common 1¢ par 11/12/2004
Note: Holders of (599) or fewer pre-split shares received $5 cash per share
Under plan of merger each share new Common 1¢ par exchanged for $5.50 cash 02/25/2010

ASA LTD. (BERMUDA)
Common $1 par split (3) for (1) by issuance of (2) additional shares payable 05/03/2010 to holders of record 04/15/2010 Ex date - 05/04/2010
Name changed to ASA Gold & Precious Metals Ltd. 03/28/2011

ASA LTD (SOUTH AFRICA)
Reincorporated 11/19/2004
Common ZAR 50 par split (2) for (1) by issuance of (1) additional share 05/31/1973
Common ZAR 50 par changed to ZAR 25 par and (1) additional share issued 05/31/1975
Reincorporated under the laws of Bermuda and Common ZAR 50 par changed to $1 par 11/19/2004
ASA Ltd. (Bermuda) name changed to ASA Gold & Precious Metals Ltd. 03/28/2011

ASAC CORP (UT)
Each share old Common $0.001 par exchanged for (0.09139606) share new Common $0.001 par 08/04/1994
Charter expired by time limitation 10/20/2004

ASAH CORP (DE)
Recapitalized as American Surgical Holdings, Inc. 01/23/2007
Each share Common $0.001 par exchanged for (0.57142857) share Common $0.001 par
(See American Surgical Holdings, Inc.)

ASAHI / AMER INC (MA)
Merged into Asahi Organic Chemicals Industry Co., Ltd. 12/01/1999
Each share Common no par exchanged for $9.584453 cash

ASAHI BK LTD (JAPAN)
ADR agreement terminated 05/22/2002
Each ADR for Ordinary exchanged for $6.3613 cash

ASAHI BREWERIES LTD (JAPAN)
Name changed to Asahi Group Holdings Ltd. 07/08/2011

ASAHI CHEM IND LTD (JAPAN)
Name changed to Asahi Kasei Corp. 05/21/2001

ASAHI GLASS (JAPAN)
ADR's for Common split (10) for (1) by issuance of (9) additional ADR's payable 12/19/2006 to holders of record 12/15/2006 Ex date - 12/20/2006
Basis changed from (1:10) to (1:1) 12/19/2006
Basis changed from (1:1) to (1:0.2) 07/03/2017
Stock Dividends - 10% 03/21/1975; 10% 04/21/1978
Name changed to AGC Inc. 07/02/2018

ASAMERA INC (CANADA)
Common no par split (3) for (1) by issuance of (2) additional shares 09/09/1983
Each share 7% Non-Vtg. Conv. 2nd Preferred Ser. D no par exchanged for (1) share Common no par 07/01/1987
Acquired by Gulf Canada Resources Ltd. 08/04/1988
Each share 8% Conv. 2nd Preferred Ser. C no par exchanged for (1.406) shares Ordinary Stock no par
Each share Common no par exchanged for (0.6397) share Ordinary Stock no par
(See Gulf Canada Resources Ltd.)

ASAMERA MINERALS INC (CANADA)
Merged into Asamera Inc. 08/01/1992
Each share Common no par exchanged for $1.40 cash

ASAMERA OIL CORP. LTD. (CANADA)
Capital Stock 40¢ par changed to no par 09/01/1978
Name changed to Asamera Inc. 10/01/1980
Asamera Inc. acquired by Gulf Canada Resources Ltd. 08/04/1988
(See Gulf Canada Resources Ltd.)

ASANTAE HLDGS INTL INC (BC)
Name changed to Avidus Management Group Inc. 05/31/2013

ASANTE TECHNOLOGIES INC (DE)
Assets acquired by TechnoConcepts, Inc. 06/02/2005
Details not available

ASAP EXPO INC (NV)
Name changed to GreenBox Pos LLC 06/01/2018

ASAP SHOW INC (NV)
Recapitalized as China Yili Petroleum Co. 10/23/2007
Each share Common $0.001 par exchanged for (0.03448275) share Common $0.001 par
(See China Yili Petroleum Co.)

ASARCO INC (NJ)
$2.25 Depositary Conv. Exchangeable Preferred called for redemption 07/09/1987
Conv. Exchangeable Preferred no par called for redemption in 1988
Non-Dividend Conv. Preferred Ser. C no par called for redemption 00/00/1988
Merged into Grupo Mexico, S.A de C.V. 11/17/1999
Each share Common no par exchanged for $29.75 cash

ASAT HLDGS LTD (CAYMAN ISLANDS)
Each old Sponsored ADR for Ordinary exchanged for (0.33333333) new Sponsored ADR for Ordinary 12/26/2006
Basis changed from (1:5) to (1:15) 12/26/2006
ADR agreement terminated 06/18/2010
No ADR holders' equity

ASB BANCORP INC (NC)
Merged into First Bancorp 10/01/2017
Each share Common 1¢ par exchanged for (0.53) share Common no par and $26.46 cash

ASB BANCSHARES INC (DE)
Merged into Colonial BancGroup, Inc. 02/05/1998
Each share Common 1¢ par

exchanged for (8.883) shares Common $2.50 par
(See Colonial BancGroup, Inc.)

ASB BANKCORP, INC. (MI)
Common $10 par split (2) for (1) by issuance of (1) additional share 03/24/1989
Stock Dividends - 10% 02/02/1987; 10% 08/05/1988; 10% 02/01/1991; 10% 02/03/1992; 10% 01/26/1994
Merged into Mid Am, Inc. 03/01/1995
Each share Common $10 par exchanged for (4.536) shares Common no par
Mid Am, Inc. merged into Sky Financial Group, Inc. 10/02/1998 which merged into Huntington Bancshares Inc. 07/02/2007

ASB CAP CORP (NV)
Adjustable Tender Preferred $1 par called for redemption 04/11/1990
Public interest eliminated

ASB FDG CORP (NV)
Dutch Auction Rate Transferable Securities Preferred no par called for redemption 04/16/1990

ASB FINL CORP (OH)
Each share old Common no par exchanged for (1) share new Common no par to reflect a (1) for (300) reverse split followed by a (300) for (1) forward split 07/08/2005
Note: Holders of (299) or fewer pre-split shares received $23 cash per share
Merged into Peoples Bancorp Inc. 04/13/2018
Each share new Common no par exchanged for (0.592) share Common no par

ASB HLDG CO (USA)
Reorganized under the laws of New Jersey as American Bancorp of New Jersey, Inc. 10/05/2005
Each share Common 10¢ par exchanged for (2.55102) shares Common 10¢ par
American Bancorp of New Jersey, Inc. acquired by Investors Bancorp, Inc. (Old) 05/31/2009 which reorganized as Investors Bancorp, Inc. (New) 05/07/2014

ASBC CAP I (DE)
7.625% Trust Originated Preferred Securities called for redemption at $25 on 10/01/2012

ASBESTEC INDS INC (UT)
Common no par split (3) for (2) by issuance of (0.5) additional share 04/17/1987
Reorganized under the laws of Delaware as PDG Environmental, Inc. 12/17/1990
Each share Common no par exchanged for (0.05) share Common 2¢ par

ASBESTOS & RUBBER PRODUCTS CORP.
Operations discontinued 00/00/1935
Details not available

ASBESTOS AWAY USA (NV)
Recapitalized as SCAC Holdings Corp. 12/17/1996
Each share Common 1¢ par exchanged for (0.00666666) share Common 1¢ par

ASBESTOS LLOYD MINES LTD. (ON)
Dissolved 12/08/1989
Details not available

ASBESTOS LTD (CANADA)
Each share Preferred $100 par exchanged for (1.5) shares Common no par 00/00/1932
Each share 4.5% Conv. Preferred $100 par exchanged for (4.5454) shares Common no par 02/25/1969
(Additional Information in Active)

ASC AVCAN SYS CORP (BC)
Recapitalized as Avcan Systems Inc. (BC) 09/07/2001
Each share Common no par exchanged for (0.1) share Common no par
Avcan Systems Inc. (BC) reincorporated in Canada as Optimal Geomatics Inc. 10/09/2003 which merged into Aeroquest International Ltd. 09/30/2009
(See Aeroquest International Ltd.)

ASC INC. (DE)
Liquidation completed
Each share Common $1 par stamped to indicate initial distribution of (0.0563) share Litton Industries, Inc. Common $1 par 01/12/1962
Each share Stamped Common $1 par exchanged for second and final distribution of (0.0582) share Litton Industries, Inc. Common $1 par 07/26/1965
(See Litton Industries, Inc.)

ASC INDS LTD (BC)
Name changed to Acero-Martin Exploration Inc. 11/24/2004
Acero-Martin Exploration Inc. name changed to AM Gold Inc. 06/08/2010
(See AM Gold Inc.)

ASCALADE COMMUNICATIONS INC (BC)
Plan of arrangement under Companies' Creditors Arrangement Act effective
Each share Common no par received first and final distribution of $0.159 cash payable 12/22/2009 to holders of record 12/08/2009

ASCEND ACQUISITION CORP (DE)
Each old Unit exchanged for (0.1) new Unit and $5.9606 cash 09/25/2008
Each share old Common $0.0001 par exchanged for (0.1) share new Common $0.0001 par and $5.9606 cash 09/25/2008
Units separated 05/10/2010
Name changed to Kitara Media Corp. 08/20/2013
Kitara Media Corp. reorganized as Kitara Holdco Corp. 01/28/2015 which name changed to Propel Media, Inc. 02/09/2015

ASCEND COMMUNICATIONS INC (DE)
Common $0.001 par split (2) for (1) by issuance of (1) additional share 05/11/1995
Common $0.001 par split (2) for (1) by issuance of (1) additional share 10/05/1995
Common $0.001 par split (2) for (1) by issuance of (1) additional share payable 01/05/1996 to holders of record 12/15/1995
Merged into Lucent Technologies Inc. 06/24/1999
Each share Common $0.001 par exchanged for (1.65) shares Common no par
Lucent Technologies Inc. merged into Alcatel-Lucent S.A. 11/30/2006

ASCENDANT COPPER CORP (BC)
Name changed to Copper Mesa Mining Corp. 07/11/2008
(See Copper Mesa Mining Corp.)

ASCENDANT SOLUTIONS INC (TX)
Stock Dividends - 1% payable 12/10/2014 to holders of record 12/03/2014 Ex date - 12/01/2014; 1% payable 12/14/2015 to holders of record 12/07/2015 Ex date - 12/03/2015; 1% payable 12/12/2016 to holders of record 12/05/2016 Ex date - 12/01/2016
Name changed to Dougherty's Pharmacy, Inc. 06/09/2017

ASCENDIA BRANDS INC (DE)
Chapter 11 bankruptcy proceedings dismissed 07/18/2012

No stockholders' equity

ASCENSION INTL INC (NV)
Recapitalized as Brody International, Inc. 08/26/1997
Each share Common 1¢ par exchanged for (0.33333333) share Common 1¢ par

ASCENT ASSURN INC (DE)
Name changed to USHEALTH Group, Inc. 03/03/2005
(See USHEALTH Group, Inc.)

ASCENT ENERGY INC (DE)
Each share 8% Conv. Preferred Ser. B $0.001 par exchanged for (0.1878395) share Common $0.001 par and $0.40 cash 08/14/2003
Merged into RAM Energy Resources, Inc. 11/29/2007
Each share Common $0.001 par exchanged for $0.01 cash

ASCENT ENTMT GROUP INC (MD)
Merged into Liberty Media Corp. 06/09/2000
Each share Common 1¢ par exchanged for $15.25 cash

ASCENT INC (NV)
Name changed to American Pizza Co., Inc. 12/06/1988
(See American Pizza Co., Inc.)

ASCENT MEDIA CORP (DE)
Name changed to Ascent Capital Group, Inc. 07/07/2011

ASCENT MEDIA GROUP INC (DE)
Merged into Liberty Media Corp. (New) 07/01/2003
Each share Class A Common 1¢ par exchanged for (0.1147) share Ser. A Common 1¢ par
Liberty Media Corp. (New) reorganized as Liberty Media Corp. (Incorporated 02/28/2006) 05/10/2006 which name changed to Liberty Interactive Corp. 09/26/2011 which name changed to Qurate Retail, Inc. 04/10/2018

ASCENT PEDIATRICS INC (DE)
Under plan of merger each share Common $0.00004 par exchanged for (1) Depositary Share 07/26/1999
Acquired by Medicis Pharmaceutical Corp. 11/15/2001
Each Depositary Share exchanged for $0.4516 cash
Note: An additional distribution of approximately $1.05 cash per share was made 02/15/2006

ASCENTEX ENERGY INC (AB)
Recapitalized 01/17/1992
Recapitalized from Ascentex Resources Ltd. to Ascentex Energy, Inc. 01/17/1992
Each share Common no par exchanged for (0.2) share Common no par
Recapitalized as Bonavista Petroleum Ltd. 03/03/1997
Each share new Common no par exchanged for (0.33333333) share Common no par
(See Bonavista Petroleum Ltd.)

ASCENTIAL SOFTWARE CORP (DE)
Each share old Common 1¢ par exchanged for (0.25) share new Common 1¢ par 06/18/2003
Merged into International Business Machines Corp. 04/29/2005
Each share new Common 1¢ par exchanged for $18.50 cash

ASCH, LIMITED, MONTREAL
Acquired by Claude Neon General Advertising Ltd. 00/00/1930
Details not available

ASCHE TRANSN SVCS INC (DE)
Filed a petition under Chapter 7 Federal Bankruptcy Code 12/22/2000
No stockholders' equity

ASCIANO LTD (AUSTRALIA)
Each Unsponsored ADR for Ordinary exchanged for (1) Sponsored ADR for Ordinary 02/10/2014
ADR agreement terminated 08/29/2016
Each Sponsored ADR for Ordinary exchanged for $12.56 cash

ASCLA INC (FL)
Name changed to Amerdyne Industries, Inc. and Common 1¢ par changed to $0.005 par 07/15/1970
Amerdyne Industries, Inc. name changed to Leisure Capital Corp. of America 06/27/1985
(See Leisure Capital Corp. of America)

ASCO LIQUIDATING CORP (DE)
Company liquidated 11/20/1990
No stockholders' equity

ASCO LTD (DE)
Recapitalized back as Anderson-Stokes, Inc. 11/20/1984
Each share Common 1¢ par exchanged for (0.2) share Common 5¢ par
(See Anderson-Stokes, Inc.)

ASCONI CORP (NV)
Each share old Common $0.0001 par exchanged for (0.1) share new Common $0.0001 par 04/22/2003
SEC revoked common stock registration 07/22/2010

ASCOPEX EXPLS LTD (QC)
Charter annulled for failure to file reports or pay fees 05/25/1985

ASCOT ENERGY CORPORATION OF CANADA LTD. (ON)
Name changed to Crosscut Explorations Inc. 10/29/1981
Crosscut Explorations Inc. recapitalized as Renaissance Industrial Corp. 12/19/1984 which name changed to D.A.S. Electronics Industries, Inc. 01/29/1988 which recapitalized as Pace Corp. 09/30/1993
(See Pace Corp.)

ASCOT ENERGY RES LTD (AB)
Recapitalized as Great Northern Exploration Ltd. 09/26/2002
Each share Common no par exchanged for (0.2) share Common no par
Great Northern Exploration Ltd. acquired by APF Energy Trust 06/04/2004
(See APF Energy Trust)

ASCOT INVT CORP (BC)
1st Conv. Preferred Ser. A no par called for redemption 06/15/1990
Recapitalized as Pacific Western Investments Inc. 08/03/1990
Each share Common no par exchanged for (0.16666666) share Common no par
Pacific Western Investments Inc. merged into Revenue Properties Co. Ltd. 01/01/1992 which merged into Morguard Corp. 12/01/2008

ASCOT METALS CORP. LTD. (QC)
Recapitalized as Quebec Ascot Copper Corp. Ltd. 05/24/1957
Each share Common $1 par exchanged for (0.33333333) share Common $1 par
(See Quebec Ascot Copper Corp. Ltd.)

ASCOT PETE CORP (BC)
Merged into Consolidated Ascot Petroleum Corp. 02/08/1982
Each share Common no par exchanged for (0.85) share Common no par
Consolidated Ascot Petroleum Corp. name changed to Ascot Investment Corp. 03/03/1987 which recapitalized as Pacific Western Investments Inc. 08/03/1990 which which merged into Revenue

Properties Co. Ltd. 01/01/1992 which merged into Morguard Corp. 12/01/2008

ASCOT SOLUTIONS INC (NY)
Company went private 00/00/2004
Each share Class A Common 4¢ par exchanged for $0.25 cash

ASCOT TEXTILE CORP (NY)
Adjudicated bankrupt 06/04/1976
Stockholders' equity unlikely

ASCUTNEY FUND, INC. (MA)
Reincorporated 07/10/1964
State of incorporation changed from (VT) to (MA) 07/10/1964
Completely liquidated 06/12/1967
Each share Capital Stock $20 par exchanged for first and final distribution of (1.9846683) shares Loomis-Sayles Mutual Fund, Inc. Capital Stock $1 par
Loomis-Sayles Mutual Fund, Inc. name changed to CGM Trust 03/01/1991

ASD GROUP INC (DE)
Recapitalized as Alliant Diagnostics, Inc. 11/18/2005
Each share Common 1¢ par exchanged for (0.1) share Common 1¢ par
Alliant Diagnostics, Inc. name changed to Navicus, Inc. 03/05/2008 which name changed to Super Nova Resources, Inc. 11/13/2008

ASD SYS INC (TX)
Reincorporated under the laws of Delaware as Ascendant Solutions Inc. 10/20/2000
Ascendant Solutions Inc. name changed to Dougherty's Pharmacy, Inc. 06/09/2017

ASDAR GROUP (NV)
Name changed 12/10/1987
Name changed from Asdar Corp. to Asdar Group, Inc. 12/10/1987
Each share old Common $0.001 par exchanged for (0.01) share new Common $0.001 par 06/21/1996
Name changed to Precise Life Sciences Ltd. 05/02/2002
Precise Life Sciences Ltd. name changed to Iceberg Brands Corp. 03/03/2003 which recapitalized as Avalon Gold Corp. 09/08/2003 which name changed to Avalon Energy Corp. 03/22/2005 which recapitalized as Shotgun Energy Corp. 09/25/2007 which name changed to Organa Gardens International Inc. 04/07/2009 which recapitalized as Bravo Enterprises Ltd. 06/08/2012

ASE INDL HLDG CO LTD (TAIWAN)
Name changed to ASE Technology Holding Co., Ltd. 06/22/2018

ASE TEST LTD (TAIWAN)
Ordinary TWD $1 par split (2) for (1) by issuance of (1) additional share payable 02/08/1998 to holders of record 01/26/1998
Merged into ASE Inc. 05/30/2008
Each share Ordinary TWD $1 par exchanged for $14.78 cash

ASE TR II (DE)
Guaranteed Term Conv. Securities 144A called for redemption at $52.292 on 12/15/2000
Guaranteed Term Conv. Securities Ser. B called for redemption at $52.392 on 12/15/2000

ASEA AB (SWEDEN)
Name changed to ABB AB 05/23/1996
(See ABB BB)

ASEAN CYBERNETICS INC (BC)
Acquired by TransGlobe Internet & Telecom Co., Ltd. 07/28/2003
Each share Common no par exchanged for (0.3175) share Common no par and (0.3175) Common Stock Purchase Warrant expiring 04/16/2005
(See Transglobe Internet & Telecom Co., Ltd.)

ASEAN ENERGY CORP (BC)
Each share old Common no par exchanged for (0.1) share new Common no par 04/15/2015
Name changed to Genovation Capital Corp. 08/20/2015
Genovation Capital Corp. name changed to Valens Groworks Corp. 11/24/2016

ASEAN HLDGS INC (BC)
Delisted from Canadian Venture Exchange 05/31/2000

ASECO CORP (DE)
Merged into Micro Component Technology, Inc. 02/01/2000
Each share Common 1¢ par exchanged for (0.633) share Common 1¢ par
Micro Component Technology, Inc. name changed to MCT, Inc. 11/26/2008

ASECO INC (MI)
Common $5 par changed to $1 par and (2) additional shares issued 07/12/1968
Completely liquidated 00/00/1981
Details not available

ASELO INDS LTD (BC)
Recapitalized as Fairmont Gas & Oil Corp. 10/15/1979
Each share Common no par exchanged for (1) share Common no par
Fairmont Gas & Oil Corp. recapitalized as Cater Energy, Inc. 05/23/1984 which recapitalized as Houston Metals Corp. 10/27/1986 which recapitalized as Pacific Houston Resources, Inc. 03/30/1989
(See Pacific Houston Resources, Inc.)

ASF GROUP INC (FL)
Reincorporated under the laws of Georgia as American Seniors Association Holding Group, Inc. 04/28/2010

ASFE MINES LTD. (ON)
Charter revoked for failure to file reports and pay fees 09/21/1959

ASG INDS INC (DE)
Each share 5% Preferred $25 par exchanged for (3) shares Common $1 par 01/15/1973
Name changed to AFG Industries, Inc. 10/22/1979
(See AFG Industries, Inc.)

ASGA INC (NV)
Each share old Common $1 par exchanged for (0.005) share new Common $1 par 03/18/2002
Each share new Common $1 par exchanged for (0.02) share Common $0.001 par 12/31/2002
Name changed to ElectraCapital Inc. 09/02/2003
(See ElectraCapital Inc.)

ASGARD ALLIANCE CORP (NV)
Each share old Common $0.001 par exchanged for (0.02) share new Common $0.001 par 03/13/2007
Name changed to Santa Fe Holding Co., Inc. 06/26/2007
(See Santa Fe Holding Co., Inc.)

ASGARD HLDGS INC (NV)
Each share old Common $0.001 par exchanged for (0.00066666) share new Common $0.001 par 02/27/2006
Recapitalized as Principal Capital Group, Inc. (Old) 02/26/2008
Each share Common $0.001 par exchanged for (0.00001) share Common $0.001 par
(See Principal Capital Group, Inc. (Old))

ASGROW SEED CO. (CT)
Each share Common $25 par exchanged for (3) shares Common $10 par to effect a (2.5) for (1) split and 20% stock dividend 03/30/1961
Common $10 par changed to $5 par and (1) additional share issued 09/10/1965
Completely liquidated 05/01/1968
Each share Common $5 par exchanged for first and final distribution of (0.386) share Upjohn Co. (DE) Common $1 par
Upjohn Co. (DE) merged into Pharmacia & Upjohn Inc. 11/02/1995 which merged into Pharmacia Corp. 03/31/2000 which merged into Pfizer Corp. 04/16/2003

ASH GROVE CEM CO (DE)
Common no par split (2) for (1) by issuance of (1) additional share 03/03/1978
Acquired by CRH PLC 06/20/2018
Each share Common no par exchanged for $447.23 cash
Each share Class B no par exchanged for $447.23 cash

ASH GROVE LIME & PORTLAND CEM CO (DE)
Name changed to Ash Grove Cement Co. 03/22/1968

ASH TEMPLE LTD (ON)
Each share 6% Preference $100 par exchanged for (1) share 6% Class A Preference $100 par 01/31/1956
Each share Common no par exchanged for (0.28) share 6.5% Class B Preference $10 par and (1) share new Common no par 01/31/1956
6.5% Class B Preference $10 par called for redemption 04/30/1972
6% Class A Preference $100 par called for redemption 05/30/1973
Through purchase offer all but (222) shares Common no par acquired by Stern Metals Corp. as of 07/10/1970
Public interest eliminated

ASHA CORP (DE)
Each share old Common $0.00001 par exchanged for (0.0117647) share new Common $0.00001 par 02/01/1994
Name changed to McLaren Automotive Group, Inc. 04/03/1999
McLaren Automotive Group, Inc. name changed to McLaren Performance Technologies, Inc. 04/20/2000
(See McLaren Performance Technologies, Inc.)

ASHA VENTURES INC (BC)
Name changed to Cost Miser Coupons (International) Inc. 09/28/1992
Cost Miser Coupons (International) Inc. recapitalized as Integrated Media Communications Inc. 02/24/1994 which recapitalized as IMC Ventures, Inc. (BC) 09/29/1998 which reincorporated in Yukon Territory as Triumph Gold Corp. 03/29/2004 which reincorporated in British Columbia 08/26/2004 which recapitalized as Kenai Resources Ltd. 05/01/2007 which merged into Serabi Gold PLC 07/22/2013

ASHANTI GOLDFIELDS LTD (GHANA)
Merged into AngloGold Ashanti Ltd. 04/26/2004
Each 144A GDR for Ordinary exchanged for (0.29) 144A ADR for Ordinary
Each Reg. S GDR for Ordinary exchanged for (0.29) ADR for Ordinary

ASHBURTON OIL LTD (BC)
Delisted from Vancouver Stock Exchange 03/02/1989

ASHBURTON VENTURES INC (BC)
Each share old Common no par exchanged for (0.1) share new Common no par 08/30/2012
Each share new Common no par exchanged again for (0.1) share new Common no par 01/26/2017
Name changed to Progressive Planet Solutions Inc. 06/08/2018

ASHCROFT HOMES CORP (CO)
Company terminated registration of common stock and is no longer public as of 09/30/2004

ASHCROFT RES LTD (BC)
Recapitalized as Tchaikazan Enterprises Ltd. 12/05/1986
Each share Common no par exchanged for (0.25) share Common no par
(See Tchaikazan Enterprises Ltd.)

ASHDOD SYS LTD (AB)
Name changed to TER Thermal Retrieval Systems Ltd. 01/06/2000
(See TER Thermal Retrieval Systems Ltd.)

ASHE FED BK (WEST JEFFERSON, NC)
Name changed to AF Bank (West Jefferson, NC) 12/08/1997
AF Bank (West Jefferson, NC) reorganized as AF Bankshares, Inc. 06/16/1998 which name changed to AF Financial Group, Inc. 11/04/2002 which name changed to LifeStore Financial Group 12/22/2009 which name changed to LifeStore Financial Group, Inc. 06/01/2018

ASHER GOLD MINES LTD. (ON)
Charter revoked for failure to file reports and pay fees 03/04/1965

ASHER OIL CO. LTD. (AB)
Merged into Merrill Petroleums Ltd. 00/00/1953
Each (25) shares Capital Stock no par exchanged for (9) shares Capital Stock $1 par
Merrill Petroleums Ltd. merged into Pacific Petroleums Ltd. 01/24/1958
(See Pacific Petroleums Ltd.)

ASHER RES CORP (DE)
Recapitalized as Drone Delivery Canada Corp. 06/16/2016
Each share Common no par exchanged for (0.25) share Common no par

ASHERXINO CORP (DE)
SEC revoked common stock registration 11/19/2014

ASHEVILLE POWER & LIGHT CO.
Merged into Carolina Power & Light Co. 00/00/1926
Details not available

ASHFORD COM INC (DE)
Merged into Global Sports, Inc. 03/14/2002
Each share Common $0.001 par exchanged for (0.0076) share Common 1¢ par and $0.125 cash
Global Sports, Inc. name changed to GSI Commerce, Inc. 05/24/2002
(See GSI Commerce, Inc.)

ASHFORD HOSPITALITY PRIME INC (MD)
Name changed to Braemar Hotel & Resorts Inc. 04/24/2018

ASHFORD HOSPITALITY TR INC (MD)
9% Preferred Ser. E 1¢ par called for redemption at $25 plus $0.23125 accrued dividends on 08/08/2016
(Additional Information in Active)

ASHFORD INC (DE)
Reincorporated under the laws of Maryland 10/31/2016

ASHGROVE ENERGY LTD (NS)
Recapitalized 08/19/1993
Recapitalized from Ashsgrove

Resources Ltd. to Ashgrove Energy Ltd. 08/19/1993
Each share Common no par exchanged for (0.16666666) share Common no par
Name changed to Search Energy Inc. 08/29/1995
Search Energy Inc. merged into Search Energy Corp. 01/09/1997 which merged into Advantage Energy Income Fund 05/24/2001 which reorganized as Advantage Oil & Gas Ltd. 07/09/2009

ASHIKAGA BK LTD (JAPAN)
ADR agreement terminated 03/11/2003
Each ADR for Ordinary exchanged for $2.45322 cash
Note: Due to ADR's being unsponsored exchange rate may vary dependent upon depositary agent

ASHLAND BANKSHARES INC (KY)
Merged into Fifth Third Bancorp 04/16/1999
Each share Common no par exchanged for (9.754) shares Common no par

ASHLAND CANADIAN OILS LTD. (CANADA)
Name changed to Canadian Ashland Exploration Ltd. 09/08/1970
(See Canadian Ashland Exploration Ltd.)

ASHLAND CAP GROUP INC (CO)
Each share old Common no par exchanged for (0.00353711) share new Common no par 10/09/1991
Recapitalized as Visual Design Industries Inc. 09/24/1992
Each share new Common no par exchanged for (0.37037037) share Common no par

ASHLAND CO (DE)
Name changed to Hart Technologies, Inc. 06/03/1988
Hart Technologies, Inc. name changed to Lifschultz Industries Inc. 02/01/1991
(See Lifschultz Industries Inc.)

ASHLAND COAL INC (DE)
Merged into Arch Coal Inc. 07/01/1997
Each share Common 1¢ par exchanged for (1) share Common 1¢ par
(See Arch Coal Inc.)

ASHLAND INC NEW (KY)
Reincorporated under the laws of Delaware as Ashland Global Holdings Inc. 09/20/2016

ASHLAND INC OLD (KY)
$3.125 Conv. Preferred $1 par called for redemption at $51.88 plus $0.191 accrued dividends on 04/07/1997
Each share Common $1 par received distribution of (0.246097) share Arch Coal Inc. Common 1¢ par payable 03/29/2000 to holders of record 03/24/2000 Ex date - 03/30/2000
Merged into Marathon Oil Corp. 06/30/2005
Each share Common $1 par exchanged for (0.2364) share Common $1 par and (1) share Ashland Inc. (New) Common 1¢ par
(See each company's listing)

ASHLAND OIL & REFNG CO (KY)
$1.50 2nd Preferred 1952 Ser no par called for redemption 09/15/1962
$5 Preferred no par called for redemption 01/18/1966
$5 2nd Preferred 1956 Ser. no par called for redemption 09/15/1962
Common $1 par split (2) for (1) by issuance of (1) additional share 03/18/1966
Stock Dividends - 10% 06/15/1951; 100% 04/07/1952
Name changed to Ashland Oil, Inc. 02/02/1970
Ashland Oil, Inc. name changed to Ashland Inc. (Old) 01/27/1995
(See Ashland Inc. (Old))

ASHLAND OIL CDA LTD (AB)
6% Conv. Preferred $25 par called for redemption 12/22/1977
Name changed to Kaiser Petroleum Ltd. 03/23/1979
(See Kaiser Petroleum Ltd.)

ASHLAND OIL INC (KY)
$2.40 Conv. Preferred 1966 Ser. no par called for redemption 03/16/1977
Common $1 par split (3) for (2) by issuance of (0.5) additional share 01/12/1979
$5 Conv. Preferred 1969 Ser. no par called for redemption 05/18/1979
$2.40 Conv. Preferred 1970 Ser. no par called for redemption 09/28/1979
$5 Conv. Preferred 1970 Ser. no par called for redemption 12/10/1979
$3.96 Conv. Preferred 1981 Ser. no par called for redemption 03/17/1986
$4.50 Preferred 1980 Ser. no par called for redemption 05/05/1986
$8.375 Preferred 1974 Ser. no par called for redemption 12/15/1986
8.50% Preferred 1976 Ser. no par called for redemption 12/15/1986
Common $1 par split (2) for (1) by issuance of (1) additional share 07/28/1988
Name changed to Ashland Inc. (Old) 01/27/1995
(See Ashland Inc. (Old))

ASHLAND OPTICAL CORP (NY)
Assets sold at auction 06/07/1981
No stockholders' equity

ASHLAR FINL SVCS CORP (BC)
Cease trade order effective 10/25/2002
Stockholders' equity unlikely

ASHLEY APARTMENTS, INC.
Liquidated 00/00/1940
Details not available

ASHLEY GOLD & OIL MINERALS LTD.
Recapitalized as Western Ashley Minerals Ltd. 00/00/1949
Each share Capital Stock $1 par exchanged for (0.25) share Capital Stock $1 par
Western Ashley Minerals Ltd. recapitalized as Consolidated Ashley Minerals Ltd. 03/29/1956 which name changed to Daering Explorers Corp. Ltd. 08/20/1956 which recapitalized as Consolidated Daering Enterprises & Mining Inc. 08/20/1971 which recapitalized as Sim-Tek Enterprises & Exploration Inc. 12/11/1981 which name changed to Bonaventure Technologies Inc. 09/14/1983
(See Bonaventure Technologies Inc.)

ASHLEY GOLD MINING CORP. LTD.
Name changed to Ashley Gold & Oil Minerals Ltd. 00/00/1947
Ashley Gold & Oil Minerals Ltd. recapitalized as Western Ashley Minerals Ltd. 00/00/1949 which recapitalized as Consolidated Ashley Minerals Ltd. 03/29/1956 which name changed to Daering Explorers Corp. Ltd. 08/20/1956 which recapitalized as Consolidated Daering Enterprises & Mining Inc. 08/20/1971 which recapitalized as Sim-Tek Enterprises & Exploration Inc. 12/11/1981 which name changed to Bonaventure Technologies Inc. 09/14/1983
(See Bonaventure Technologies Inc.)

ASHLEY MARKETING CORP (NV)
Charter revoked for failure to file reports and pay fees 12/01/1998

ASHLEY MINERALS INC (UT)
Recapitalized as Cancer Detection, Inc. (UT) 09/21/1972
Each share Common 1¢ par exchanged for (3) shares Common $0.33333333 par
Cancer Detection, Inc. (UT) reincorporated in Nevada as Commercial Technology, Inc. 05/11/1973 which liquidated for Electric & Gas Technology, Inc. 10/00/1989
(See Electric & Gas Technology, Inc.)

ASHLEY VALLEY OIL CO (UT)
Charter dissolved for failure to pay taxes 09/28/1974

ASHLIN DEV CORP (FL)
Each share old Common $0.001 par exchanged for (0.80037163) share new Common $0.001 par 11/21/2005
Reincorporated under the laws of Delaware as Gales Industries, Inc. 02/15/2006
Gales Industries, Inc. name changed to Air Industries Group, Inc. (DE) 07/16/2007 which reincorporated in Nevada 09/03/2013

ASHLOO GOLD MINES LTD. (BC)
Charter revoked for failure to file reports and pay fees 06/12/1952

ASHLU EXPL LTD (AB)
Recapitalized as Rhodes Energy Corp. 07/10/1987
Each share Common no par exchanged for (0.1) share Common no par
Rhodes Energy Corp. merged into Accord Capital Corp. 09/01/1989 which recapitalized as Consolidated Accord Capital Corp. 12/17/1991 which merged into Peak Energy Services Ltd. (Old) 06/14/1996 which reorganized as Peak Energy Services Trust 05/01/2004 which reorganized as Peak Energy Services Ltd. (New) 01/06/2011
(See Peak Energy Services Ltd. (New))

ASHMONT PETROLEUMS LTD. (AB)
Merged into Pathfinder Petroleums Ltd. 00/00/1954
Each share Common no par exchanged for (0.5) share Capital Stock 50¢ par
Pathfinder Petroleums Ltd. merged into Medallion Petroleums Ltd. 09/11/1956 which merged into Canadian Industrial Gas & Oil Ltd. 03/08/1965 which merged into Norcen Energy Resources Ltd. (AB) 10/28/1975 which reincorporated in Canada 04/15/1977 which merged into Union Pacific Resources Group Inc. 04/17/1998 which merged into Andarko Petroleum Corp. 07/14/2000

ASHMORE GOLD MINES LTD. (ON)
Name changed to Murray Watts Explorations Ltd. 12/28/1968
(See Murray Watts Explorations Ltd.)

ASHNOLA MNG LTD (BC)
Reorganized as Tower Hill Mines Ltd. 06/01/1988
Each share Common no par exchanged for (1.7) shares Common no par
Tower Hill Mines Ltd. recapitalized as International Tower Hill Mines Ltd. (Old) 03/15/1991
(See International Tower Hill Mines Ltd. (Old))

ASHOK LEYLAND LTD (INDIA)
GDR agreement terminated 00/00/2002
No GDR's remain outstanding

ASHTABULA BOW SOCKET CO (OH)
Name changed to ABS Industries, Inc. (OH) 08/25/1975
ABS Industries, Inc. (OH) reincorporated in Delaware 08/17/1979
(See ABS Industries, Inc.)

ASHTABULA TEL CO (OH)
Acquired by Mid-Continent Telephone Corp. 12/01/1961
Each share Capital Stock no par exchanged for (5.3) shares Common no par
Mid-Continent Telephone Corp. name changed to Alltel Corp. (OH) 10/25/1983 which reincorporated in Delaware 05/15/1990
(See Alltel Corp.)

ASHTON LONG LAC GOLD MINES LTD. (ON)
Charter revoked for failure to file reports and pay fees 00/00/1951

ASHTON MNG CDA INC (CANADA)
Acquired by Stornoway Diamond Corp. (BC) 01/16/2007
Each share Common no par exchanged for (1) share Common no par and $0.01 cash
Stornoway Diamond Corp. (BC) reincorporated in Canada 10/28/2011

ASHTON MNG LTD (AUSTRALIA)
Unsponsored ADR's for Ordinary reclassified as Sponsored ADR's for Ordinary 10/18/1993
Acquired by Rio Tinto Ltd. 12/13/2000
Each Sponsored ADR for Ordinary exchanged for $5.439 cash

ASHTON MNG N L (AUSTRALIA)
Name changed to Ashton Mining Ltd. 01/15/1981
(See Ashton Mining Ltd.)

ASHTON TATE (CA)
Common no par split (2) for (1) by issuance of (1) additional share 01/12/1987
Acquired by Borland International, Inc. 10/11/1991
Each share Common no par exchanged for (0.361) share Common 1¢ par
Borland International, Inc. name changed to Inprise Corp. 06/05/1998 which name changed to Borland Software Corp. 01/22/2001
(See Borland Software Corp.)

ASHTON TECHNOLOGY GROUP INC (DE)
Name changed to Vie Financial Group Inc. 10/09/2002
(See Vie Financial Group Inc.)

ASHUELOT GAS & ELECTRIC CO.
Merged into Public Service Co. of New Hampshire 00/00/1926
Details not available

ASHURST TECHNOLOGY LTD. (BERMUDA)
Cease trade order effective 07/31/1998
Stockholders' equity unlikely

ASHWORTH INC (DE)
Acquired by adidas AG 11/20/2008
Each share Common $0.001 par exchanged for $1.90 cash

ASI (NV)
Recapitalized as ASI Technolgy Corp. 09/01/2000
Each share Common 10¢ par exchanged for (0.1) share Common 2¢ par
ASI Technology Corp. recapitalized as Robertson Global Health Solutions Corp. 08/06/2010

ASI COMMUNICATIONS INC (DE)
Each share Common 2¢ par exchanged for (0.2) share Common 10¢ par 02/09/1976
Voluntarily dissolved 12/19/1986
Details not available

ASI ENTMT INC (DE)
Name changed to AS-IP Tech, Inc. 07/30/2014

ASI INTL (UT)
Merged into American Scientific Industries International 06/19/1972
Each share Capital Stock 5¢ par exchanged for (0.16666666) share Common 10¢ par
(See American Scientific Industries International)

ASI INTERNET INC (ON)
Recapitalized as HIP Interactive Corp. 12/10/1999
Each share Common no par exchanged for (0.58651026) share Common no par
(See HIP Interactive Corp.)

ASI LIQUIDATING CORP (DE)
Liquidation completed
Each share Common $0.001 par received first and final distribution of $0.15 cash payable 05/27/2008 to holders of record 05/12/2008
Note: Certificates were not required to be surrendered and are without value

ASI SOLUTIONS INC (DE)
Merged into Aon Corp. (DE) 05/10/2001
Each share Common 1¢ par exchanged for (0.436226) share Common $1 par
Aon Corp. (DE) reorganized in England & Wales as Aon PLC 04/02/2012

ASI TECHNOLOGY CORP (NV)
Recapitalized as Robertson Global Health Solutions Corp. 08/06/2010
Each share Common 2¢ par exchanged for (0.06666666) share Common $0.001 par

ASIA-AMER CORP (NV)
Recapitalized as First American Railways Inc. 04/26/1996
Each shares Common $0.001 par exchanged for (0.00925925) share Common $0.001 par
First American Railways Inc. name changed to Spectrum Acquisition Holdings, Inc. 12/03/2007 which recapitalized as Nouveau Holdings, Ltd. 04/30/2013

ASIA AMERN INDS INC (NY)
Dissolved by proclamation 06/29/1994

ASIA AUTOMOTIVE ACQUISITION CORP (DE)
Reincorporated under the laws of British Virgin Islands as Tongxin International, Ltd. and Common $0.001 par reclassified as Ordinary $0.001 par 04/23/2008

ASIA BIO-CHEM GROUP CORP (BC)
Company announced insolvency 03/11/2016
Stockholders' equity unlikely

ASIA CARBON INDS INC (MD)
Charter forfeited 10/01/2015

ASIA CORK INC (DE)
SEC revoked common stock registration 12/18/2014

ASIA ELECTRICAL PWR INTL GROUP INC (NV)
Each share old Common $0.001 par exchanged for (0.002) share new Common $0.001 par 12/14/2010
Note: Holders of (499) or fewer pre-split shares received $0.068 cash per share
Each share new Common $0.001 par exchanged again for (0.00005714) share new Common $0.001 par 08/16/2011
Note: In effect holders received $2.90 cash per share and public interest was eliminated

ASIA ELECTRONICS HLDG INC (BRITISH VIRGIN ISLANDS)
In process of liquidation
Each share Common 1¢ par received initial distribution of $0.33 cash payable 09/28/2001 to holders of record 09/10/2001 Ex date - 10/01/2001
Each share Common 1¢ par received second distribution of $0.01 cash payable 10/01/2001 to holders of record 09/10/2001 Ex date - 10/02/2001
Note: Details on subsequent distribution(s), if any, are not available

ASIA ENTERTAINMENT & RESOURCES LTD (CAYMAN ISLANDS)
Name changed to Iao Kun Group Holding Co. 10/02/2013
Iao Kun Group Holding Co. Ltd. name changed to LiNiu Technology Group 04/27/2017

ASIA FIBER HLDGS LTD (DE)
Common 1¢ par split (5) for (2) by issuance of (1.5) additional shares payable 02/28/2001 to holders of record 02/26/2001
Charter cancelled and declared inoperative and void for non-payment of taxes 03/01/2001

ASIA FIBER LTD (THAILAND)
ADR agreement terminated 11/30/2015
Each Sponsored ADR for Ordinary exchanged for $0.375272 cash

ASIA 4 SALE COM INC (NV)
Common $0.001 par split (2) for (1) by issuance of (1) additional share payable 12/11/2000 to holders of record 12/01/2000 Ex date - 12/12/2000
Recapitalized as Asia8, Inc. 04/27/2007
Each share Common $0.001 par exchanged for (0.5) share Common $0.001 par

ASIA GLOBAL CROSSING LTD (BERMUDA)
Chapter 11 bankruptcy proceedings converted to Chapter 7 on 06/10/2003
Stockholders' equity unlikely

ASIA GLOBAL HLDGS CORP (NV)
SEC revoked common stock registration 08/13/2014

ASIA GOLD CORP (CANADA)
Reincorporated under the laws of British Columbia as SouthGobi Energy Resources Ltd. 05/29/2007
SouthGobi Energy Resources Ltd. name changed to SouthGobi Resources Ltd. 05/17/2010

ASIA GREEN AGRICULTURE CORP (NV)
Acquired by Asia Green Food Enterprise Ltd. 09/26/2014
Each share Common $0.001 par exchanged for $0.60 cash

ASIA MEDIA COMMUNICATIONS LTD (NV)
Each share old Common 1¢ par exchanged for (0.01) share new Common 1¢ par 02/23/1999
Name changed to MyWeb Inc.com 04/28/1999
(See MyWeb Inc.com)

ASIA MEDIA GROUP CORP (ON)
Delisted from CNQ 10/13/2000

ASIA MINERALS CORP (BC)
Reincorporated 06/07/1994
Place of incorporation changed from (AB) to (BC) 06/07/1994
Name changed to American Bonanza Gold Mining Corp. 10/16/2000
American Bonanza Gold Mining Corp. (BC) merged into American Bonanza Gold Corp. 03/31/2005 which merged into Kerr Mines Inc. 07/07/2014

ASIA NOW RES CORP (ON)
Discharged from receivership 04/22/2016
No stockholders' equity

ASIA OIL & MINERALS LTD (AUSTRALIA)
ADR agreement terminated 09/10/2003
No ADR holders' equity

ASIA ORIENT LTD (HONG KONG)
Each ADR for Ordinary USD $0.001 par exchanged for (0.16666666) ADR for Ordinary USD $0.006 par 01/28/1992
ADR agreement terminated 09/23/1996
Each ADR for Ordinary USD $0.006 par exchanged for $11.9305 cash
Each ADR for Ordinary USD $0.06 par exchanged for $119.305 cash

ASIA PAC BOILER CORP (NV)
Common $0.00001 par split (4) for (1) by issuance of (3) additional shares payable 11/09/2012 to holders of record 11/09/2012
Name changed to Wunong Asia Pacific Co. Ltd. 09/07/2018

ASIA PAC CAP CORP (CANADA)
Recapitalized as Asiatel Media Corp. 06/28/1989
Each share Common no par exchanged for (0.25) share Common no par
Asiatel Media Corp. recapitalized as Consolidated Asiatel Resources Ltd. (Canada) 09/10/1991 which reincorporated in Yukon Territory as Sino Foods Corp. 12/21/1994 which recapitalized as G.R. Pacific Resource Corp. (Yukon) 01/23/1997 which reincorporated in British Columbia as Pacific GeoInfo Corp. 02/03/2003

ASIA PAC CHEM ENGR CORP (UT)
Name changed to Interactive Objects, Inc. 09/15/1997
Interactive Objects, Inc. name changed to Fullplay Media Systems, Inc. 01/07/2002
(See Fullplay Media Systems, Inc.)

ASIA PAC COMMUNICATIONS INC (HI)
Name changed to EIF Holdings Inc. (HI) 12/28/1992
EIF Holdings Inc. (HI) reorganized in Delaware as U.S. Industrial Services Inc. 05/04/1998 which name changed to Nextgen Communications Corp. 08/07/2001 which name changed to Home Solutions of America, Inc. 12/23/2002
(See Home Solutions of America, Inc.)

ASIA PAC CONCRETE INC (AB)
Name changed to IVG Corp. 06/19/2000
IVG Corp. recapitalized as IVG Enterprises Ltd. 07/24/2002
(See IVG Enterprises Ltd.)

ASIA PAC ENTERPRISES INC (DE)
Name changed to E-VideoTV Inc. 08/05/1999
E-VideoTV Inc. name changed to Hi Score Corp. (DE) 07/02/2008 which reincorporated in Florida 07/01/2010

ASIA PAC ENTMT INC (NV)
Each share old Common $0.001 par exchanged for (0.01) share new Common $0.001 par 11/05/2008
Name changed to Access Beverage Inc. 01/06/2009
Access Beverage Inc. name changed to Unity Auto Parts Inc. 09/22/2009 which name changed to Unity Management Group, Inc. 01/08/2010 which name changed to Petrotech Oil & Gas, Inc. 03/26/2013

ASIA PAC GROUP INC (DE)
Name changed to IVAT Industries Inc. 09/13/2001

ASIA PAC RES INTL HLDGS LTD (BERMUDA)
Each share Class A 1¢ par received distribution of (0.8539) P.T. Inti Indorayon Utama Tbk Sponsored ADR for Ordinary payable 02/15/1999 to holders of record 01/18/1999 Ex date - 02/17/1999
Acquired by Gold Leaf Holdings Ltd. 06/30/2004
Each share Class A 1¢ par exchanged for $0.15 cash

ASIA PAC TRADING INC (DE)
Name changed to Novus Laboratories Inc. and (2) additional shares issued 06/20/2000
Novus Laboratories Inc. recapitalized as World Golf League, Inc. 02/12/2003 which name changed to WGL Entertainment Holdings, Inc. 08/29/2006 which recapitalized as Heathrow Natural Food & Beverage Inc. 03/09/2009

ASIA PACIFIC RES LTD (BC)
Name changed 09/22/1995
Name changed from Asia-Pacific Resources Ltd. to Asia Pacific Resources Ltd. 09/22/1995
Merged into Italian-Thai Development Public Company Ltd. 08/11/2006
Each share Common no par exchanged for $0.1425 cash

ASIA PACKAGING GROUP INC (BC)
All Canadian officers and directors resigned 11/27/2013

ASIA PMT SYS INC (NV)
Name changed to Cardtrend International, Inc. 08/16/2007
Cardtrend International, Inc. name changed to Mezabay International Inc. 09/10/2009

ASIA PREM TELEVISION GROUP INC (NV)
Each share old Common $0.001 par exchanged for (0.001) share new Common $0.001 par 03/26/2007
Recapitalized as China Grand Resorts, Inc. 11/17/2009
Each share new Common $0.001 par exchanged for (0.05) share Common $0.001 par

ASIA PULP & PAPER LTD (SINGAPORE)
Each Sponsored ADR for Ordinary received distribution of (0.2) Sponsored ADR for Warrants expiring 07/27/2000 payable 05/10/1999 to holders of record 04/19/1999
SEC revoked ADR registration 04/01/2005

ASIA RES HLDGS LTD (DE)
Name changed to Asia Fiber Holdings Ltd. 03/14/2000
(See Asia Fiber Holdings Ltd.)

ASIA SAPPHIRES LTD (YT)
Delisted from Canadian Venture Stock Exchange 05/31/2001

ASIA SATELLITE TELECOMMUNICATIONS HLDGS LTD (BERMUDA)
ADR agreement terminated 02/28/2008
Each Sponsored ADR for Common exchanged for $15.93123 cash

ASIA SCIENTIFIC CORP (NV)
Charter revoked for failure to file reports and pay fees 08/31/2008

ASIA SPECIAL SITUATION ACQUISITION CORP. (CAYMAN ISLANDS)
Name changed to GEROVA Financial Group, Ltd. (Cayman Islands) 01/22/2010
GEROVA Financial Group, Ltd. (Cayman Islands) reincorporated in Bermuda 09/20/2010
(See GEROVA Financial Group, Ltd.)

ASIA SUPERNET CORP (CO)
Administratively dissolved 02/28/2005

ASIA TIGERS FD INC (MD)
Stock Dividend - 24.2703% payable 01/31/2012 to holders of record 12/27/2011 Ex date - 12/22/2011
Under plan of reorganization each share Common $0.001 par automatically became (1.2088) shares Aberdeen Emerging Markets Equity Income Fund, Inc. Common $0.001 par 04/30/2018

ASIA TRAINING INST INC (NV)
Name changed to Po Yuen Cultural Holdings (Hong Kong) Co., Ltd. 12/06/2017

ASIA TRAVEL CORP (NV)
Name changed to Square Chain Corp. 04/11/2018

ASIA VENTURES CORP (DE)
SEC revoked common stock registration 11/08/2011

ASIA WEB HLDGS INC (DE)
Name changed to Case Financial, Inc. 05/22/2002
(See Case Financial, Inc.)

ASIACONTENT COM LTD (BRITISH VIRGIN ISLANDS)
Liquidation completed
Each share Class A 1¢ par received initial distribution of $1.46 cash payable 04/04/2003 to holders of record 07/10/2002
Each share Class A 1¢ par received second and final distribution of $0.28 cash payable 10/29/2004 to holders of record 07/10/2002
Note: Certificates were not required to be surrendered and are without value

ASIAINFO-LINKAGE INC (DE)
Name changed 07/01/2010
Name changed from AsiaInfo Holdings, Inc. to AsiaInfo-Linkage, Inc. 07/01/2010
Acquired by Skipper Ltd. 01/15/2014
Each share Common 1¢ par exchanged for $12 cash

ASIAMART INC (DE)
Chapter 7 bankruptcy proceedings terminated 07/24/2014
No stockholders' equity

ASIAMERICA EQUITIES LTD (WA)
Each share old Common $1 par exchanged for (2) shares new Common $1 par 01/12/1988
Name changed to Mercer International Inc. 01/01/1992

ASIAMERICA HLDGS LTD (CANADA)
Name changed to Stone Mark Capital Inc. (Canada) 11/17/1989
Stone Mark Capital Inc. (Canada) reincorporated in Yukon 06/21/1993
(See Stone Mark Capital Inc.)

ASIAMET RES LTD (BERMUDA)
Shares transferred to Bermuda share register 03/31/2017

ASIAN ALLIANCE VENTURES INC (NV)
Name changed to Asia Payment Systems Inc. 11/25/2003
Asia Payment Systems Inc. name changed to Cardtrend International, Inc. 08/16/2007 which name changed to Mezabay International Inc. 09/10/2009

ASIAN AMERN BK & TR CO (BOSTON, MA)
Stock Dividend - 3% payable 11/14/2004 to holders of record 10/01/2004 Ex date - 09/29/2004
Merged into UCBH Holdings, Inc. 11/29/2005
Each share Class A Common no par exchanged for (1.108) shares Common 1¢ par
(See UCBH Holdings, Inc.)

ASIAN-AMERICAN INTL INC (UT)
Each share old Common $0.001 par exchanged for (0.005) share new Common $0.001 par 10/31/1994
Name changed to International Marketing Dynamics Inc. 07/18/1995
International Marketing Dynamics Inc. name changed to Two Dog Net, Inc. 12/30/1998
(See Two Dog Net, Inc.)

ASIAN BAMBOO AG (GERMANY)
ADR agreement terminated 12/03/2015
Each Sponsored ADR for Ordinary exchanged for (0.5) share Ordinary
Note: Unexchanged ADR's will be sold and the proceeds, if any, held for claim after 06/03/2016

ASIAN CDN RES LTD (BC)
Recapitalized as Victorian Enuretic Services Ltd. 07/15/1990
Each share Common no par exchanged for (0.23809523) share Common no par
(See Victorian Enuretic Services Ltd.)

ASIAN DEV FRONTIER INC (NV)
Name changed to Unifunds Ltd. 03/23/2018

ASIAN DRAGON GROUP INC NEW (NV)
SEC revoked common stock registration 12/18/2014

ASIAN DRAGON GROUP INC OLD (NV)
Name changed to Angkor Minerals, Inc. 08/22/2006
Angkor Minerals, Inc. name changed to Hemisphere Gold Inc. 11/29/2006
(See Hemisphere Gold Inc.)

ASIAN EQUITIES INC (NV)
Recapitalized as International Apparel Marketing Inc. 10/21/1987
Each share Common 1¢ par exchanged for (0.66666666) share Common 1¢ par
International Apparel Marketing Inc. name changed to Statewide Corp. 10/19/1990
(See Statewide Corp.)

ASIAN MINERAL RES LTD (NEW ZEALAND)
Reincorporated under the laws of British Columbia 12/31/2004

ASIAN PAC LTD (NV)
Charter permanently revoked 10/31/2005

ASIAN RESOURCE GLOBAL STRATEGIES INC (ON)
Name changed to Nesscap Energy Inc. 01/24/2011
(See Nesscap Energy Inc.)

ASIAN STAR DEV INC (NV)
Each share old Common $0.001 par exchanged for (0.5) share new Common $0.001 par 11/27/2001
SEC revoked common stock registration 07/23/2010

ASIAN TRENDS MEDIA HLDGS INC (NV)
Recapitalized as YUS International Group Ltd. 05/20/2013
Each share Common $0.001 par exchanged for (0.01) share Common $0.001 par

ASIAN UN NEW MEDIA GROUP LTD (CAYMAN ISLANDS)
Name changed to China Jiuhao Health Industry Corp. Ltd. 05/30/2014
(See China Jiuhao Health Industry Corp. Ltd.)

ASIANA BK (SUNNYVALE, CA)
Merged into Nara Bancorp, Inc. 08/25/2003
Each share Common exchanged for (0.44482) share Common $0.001 par

ASIANA DRAGONS INC (DE)
Each share old Common $0.001 par exchanged for (0.08333333) share new Common $0.001 par 06/14/2010
Recapitalized as Annabidiol Corp. 01/08/2018
Each share new Common $0.001 par exchanged for (0.2) share Common $0.001 par

ASIANADA INC (DE)
Reincorporated 09/27/2007
State of incorporation changed from (NV) to (DE) 09/27/2007
Name changed to Lateral Media, Inc. 12/04/2008

ASIATEL MEDIA CORP (CANADA)
Recapitalized as Consolidated Asiatel Resources Ltd. (Canada) 09/10/1991
Each share Common no par exchanged for (0.2) share Common no par
Consolidated Asiatel Resources Ltd. (Canada) reincorporated in Yukon Territory as Sino Foods Corp. 12/21/1994 which recapitalized as G.R. Pacific Resource Corp. (YT) 01/23/1997 which reincorporated in British Columbia as Pacific GeoInfo Corp. 02/03/2003

ASIF GLOBAL FING XIX (DE)
144A Auction Market Equity Securities called for redemption at $1,000 plus $0.18 accrued dividends on 01/17/2013

ASIF GLOBAL FING XX
144A Auction Market Equity Securities called for redemption at $100 on 01/17/2006

ASITKA RES CORP (BC)
Name changed to Orenda Forest Products Ltd. 11/07/1989
Orenda Forest Products Ltd. merged into Repap Enterprises Inc. 09/05/1996
(See Repap Enterprises Inc.)

ASIYA PEARLS INC (NV)
Name changed to QPAGOS 06/03/2016

ASK CORP (TX)
Each share old Common no par exchanged for (0.25) share new Common no par 01/11/1991
Charter forfeited for failure to pay taxes 08/25/2000

ASK FDG LTD (AUSTRALIA)
ADR agreement terminated 05/11/2012
No ADR's remain outstanding

ASK GROUP INC (CA)
Name changed 11/23/1992
Common no par split (2) for (1) by issuance of (1) additional share 09/02/1983
Name changed from ASK Computer Systems, Inc. to ASK Group, Inc. 11/23/1992
Merged into Speedbird Merge, Inc. 09/20/1994
Each share Common no par exchanged for $13.25 cash

ASK JEEVES INC (DE)
Merged into IAC/InterActiveCorp 07/19/2005
Each share Common $0.001 par exchanged for (1.2668) shares Common 1¢ par

ASKIN SVC CORP (NY)
Common $1 par changed to 10¢ par 07/31/1974
Stock Dividend - 50% 04/15/1969
Name changed to White River Petroleum Corp. 02/22/1982
(See White River Petroleum Corp.)

ASKMENOW INC (DE)
SEC revoked common stock registration 06/28/2012

ASM LITHOGRAPHY HOLDING N.V. (NETHERLANDS)
Ordinary NLG 0.50 par split (2) for (1) by issuance of (1) additional share payable 05/13/1998 to holders of record 05/07/1998
Name changed to ASML Holding N.V. 06/00/2001

ASN TECHNOLOGIES INC (NV)
Common $0.001 par split (12) for (1) by issuance of (11) additional shares payable 11/09/2015 to holders of record 11/09/2015 Ex date - 11/10/2015
Reincorporated under the laws of Delaware as Senseonics Holdings, Inc. 12/22/2015

ASNAZU GOLD DREDGING LTD. (BC)
Liquidation completed
Capital Stock $1 par changed to 80¢ par and $0.20 cash distributed 00/00/1954
Capital Stock 80¢ par changed to 60¢ par and $0.20 cash distributed 08/17/1955
Capital Stock 60¢ par changed to 30¢ par and $0.30 cash distributed 07/05/1956
Capital Stock 30¢ par changed to 10¢ par and $0.20 cash distributed 10/07/1958
Each share Capital Stock received final distribution of $0.09365 cash 09/22/1959

ASP VENTURES CORP (FL)
SEC revoked common stock registration 04/03/2012

ASPAC COMMUNICATIONS, INC OLD (DE)
Merged into Aspac Communications, Inc. (New) 06/20/2000
Each share Common $0.00001 par exchanged for (1) share Common $0.00001 par

ASPEC TECHNOLOGY INC (DE)
Name changed to Ingenuus Corp. 05/08/2000
(See Ingenuus Corp.)

ASPECT COMMUNICATIONS INC (CA)
Merged into Concerto Software, Inc. 9/22/2005
Each share Common 1¢ par exchanged for $11.60 cash

ASPECT DEV INC (DE)
Common $0.001 par split (2) for (1) by issuance of (1) additional share payable 08/14/1998 to holders of record 07/31/1998
Common $0.001 par split (2) for (1) by issuance of (1) additional share payable 03/10/2000 to holders of record 02/25/2000
Merged into i2 Technologies, Inc. 06/12/2000
Each share Common $0.001 par exchanged for (0.55) share Common $0.00025 par
i2 Technologies, Inc. merged into JDA Software Group, Inc. 01/28/2010
(See JDA Software Group, Inc.)

ASPECT MED SYS INC (DE)
Acquired by Covidien PLC 11/06/2009
Each share Common 1¢ par exchanged for $12 cash

ASPECT TELECOMMUNICATIONS CORP (CA)
Common 1¢ par split (2) for (1) by issuance of (1) additional share 09/22/1995
Common 1¢ par split (2) for (1) by issuance of (1) additional share payable 01/22/1997 to holders of record 01/06/1997
Name changed to Aspect Communications, Inc. 10/01/1999
(See Aspect Communications, Inc.)

ASPEN BANCSHARES INC (CO)
Common 1¢ par split (5) for (4) by issuance of (0.25) additional share 10/03/1994
Common 1¢ par split (5) for (4) by

ASPEN (cont.)
issuance of (0.25) additional share 10/10/1995
Merged into Zions Bancorporation 05/16/1997
Each share Common 1¢ par exchanged for (0.738704) share Common no par
Zions Bancorporation merged into Zions Bancorporation, N.A. (Salt Lake City, UT) 10/01/2018

ASPEN ENERGY CORP (AB)
Recapitalized as Aspen Resources Corp. (New) 04/21/2003
Each share Common no par exchanged for (0.125) share Common no par
(See Aspen Resources Corp. (New))

ASPEN EXPL CORP (DE)
Each share Common $0.001 par exchanged for (0.2) share Common $0.005 par 03/17/1994
Stock Dividend - 10% 06/30/1988
Name changed to Enservco Corp. 01/04/2011

ASPEN GLOBAL CORP (DE)
Name changed to Diversified Mortgage Workout Corp. 08/08/2008
Diversified Mortgage Workout Corp. recapitalized as Arem Pacific Corp. 07/29/2013

ASPEN GROUP RES CORP (YT)
Each share Common no par exchanged for (0.14285714) share new Common no par 02/12/2001
SEC revoked common stock registration 04/14/2010

ASPEN GROVE COPPER MINES LTD. (BC)
Name changed to Aspen Grove Mines Ltd. 07/07/1965
Aspen Grove Mines Ltd. name changed to Legion Resources Ltd. (BC) 05/08/1986 which reorganized in Cayman Islands as Earl Resources Ltd. 06/02/1998 which reorganized in British Columbia 03/02/2018

ASPEN GROVE MINES LTD (BC)
Capital Stock $1 par reclassified as Common no par 12/18/1983
Name changed to Legion Resources Ltd. (BC) 05/08/1986
Legion Resources Ltd. (BC) reorganized in Cayman Islands as Earl Resources Ltd. 06/02/1998 which reorganized in British Columbia 03/02/2018

ASPEN IMAGING INTL INC (CO)
Name changed 12/03/1990
Name changed from Aspen Ribbons, Inc. to Aspen Imaging International, Inc. 12/03/1990
Under plan of liquidation each share Common no par exchanged for (0.1428571) share Pubco Corp. new Common 1¢ par 06/28/1996
(See Pubco Corp.)

ASPEN INS HLDGS LTD (BERMUDA)
Each 5.625% Perpetual Preferred Income Equity Replacement Security $0.0015144558 par exchanged for (0.3991) share Ordinary $0.15144558 par and $50 cash 05/30/2013
7.401% Non-Cum. Perpetual Preference Shares $0.15144558 par called for redemption at $25 on 01/01/2017
7.25% Non-Cum. Perpetual Preference Shares $0.15144558 par called for redemption at $25 on 07/01/2017
(Additional Information in Active)

ASPEN LEAF INC (DE)
Company went private 00/00/1993
Details not available

ASPEN MARINE GROUP INC (CO)
Each share old Common no par exchanged for (0.05) share new Common no par 01/21/1993
Declared defunct and inoperative for failure to pay taxes and file annual reports 06/03/1996

ASPEN RACING STABLES INC (NV)
Name changed to Kun Run Biotechnology, Inc. 11/06/2008
(See Kun Run Biotechnology, Inc.)

ASPEN RES CORP NEW (AB)
Acquired by 1148534 Alberta Ltd. 03/06/2006
Each share Common no par exchanged for $0.22 cash

ASPEN RES CORP OLD (AB)
Recapitalized as Aspen Energy Corp. 01/25/1996
Each share Common no par exchanged for (0.2) share Common no par
Aspen Energy Corp. recapitalized as Aspen Resources Corp. (New) 04/21/2003
(See Aspen Resources Corp. (New))

ASPEN SKIING CORP (CO)
Common $1 par split (3) for (1) by issuance of (2) additional shares 12/18/1969
Merged into Twentieth Century Fox-Film Corp. 06/28/1978
Each share Common $1 par exchanged for (1) share $3 Conv. Preferred Ser. A no par
(See Twentieth Century Fox-Film Corp.)

ASPEN SYS CORP (PA)
Merged into USICU Inc. 09/12/1978
Each share Capital Stock no par exchanged for $1.32 cash

ASPEN TECHNOLOGY INC (MA)
Common 10¢ par split (2) for (1) by issuance of (1) additional share payable 02/28/1997 to holders of record 02/14/1997 Ex date - 03/03/1997
Reincorporated under the laws of Delaware 03/12/1998

ASPEN WEST GROUP INC (DE)
Name changed to United Golf Products, Inc. 02/12/1997
United Golf Products, Inc. recapitalized as Order Logistics, Inc. 12/13/2005 which name changed to World Logistics Services, Inc. 12/21/2007

ASPEN WIND INC (CO)
Each share old Common no par exchanged for (0.02127659) share new Common no par 11/25/1989
Name changed to Aspen Marine Group, Inc. 03/27/1992
(See Aspen Marine Group, Inc.)

ASPENBIO PHARMA INC (CO)
Name changed 11/15/2005
Name changed from AspenBio Inc. to AspenBio Pharma, Inc. 11/15/2005
Each share old Common no par exchanged for (0.2) share new Common no par 07/29/2011
Each share new Common no par exchanged again for (0.16666666) share new Common no par 06/20/2012
Name changed to Venaxis, Inc. 12/20/2012
Venaxis, Inc. name changed to Bioptix, Inc. (CO) 12/12/2016 which reincorporated in Nevada 09/28/2017 which name changed to Riot Blockchain, Inc. 10/19/2017

ASPEON INC (DE)
Each share old Common 1¢ par exchanged for (0.06666666) share new Common 1¢ par 01/13/2009
Name changed to ASPI, Inc. 09/24/2009
ASPI, Inc. name changed to JV Group, Inc. 05/25/2012

ASPER-LAX, INC.
Out of business 00/00/1935
Details not available

ASPHALT ASSOCS INC (NV)
Reorganized as Pacific WebWorks, Inc. 01/09/1999
Each share Common $0.001 par exchanged for (4) shares Common $0.001 par
Pacific WebWorks, Inc. name changed to Heyu Biological Technology Corp. 06/28/2018

ASPHALT OILS LTD. (AB)
Struck off register and declared dissolved for failure to file reports 01/15/1963

ASPHALT PAV INTL INC (FL)
Merged into Mobile Reach International, Inc. 08/04/2003
Each share Common $0.001 par exchanged for (0.704162) share Common $0.001 par
Mobile Reach International, Inc. name changed to Crystal International Travel Group, Inc. 05/22/2006
(See Crystal International Travel Group, Inc.)

ASPI EUROPE INC (DE)
Reincorporated 12/19/2000
State of incorporation changed from (FL) to (DE) 12/19/2000
Name changed to Sharps Elimination Technologies Inc. 05/06/2002
Sharps Elimination Technologies Inc. name changed to Armagh Group Inc. 09/19/2002 which recapitalized as SmartVideo Technologies, Inc. 01/06/2003 which name changed to uVuMobile, Inc. 06/04/2007
(See uVuMobile, Inc.)

ASPI INC (DE)
Name changed to JV Group, Inc. 05/25/2012

ASPINOOK CO. (CT)
Liquidated 00/00/1937
Holders received only right to purchase bonds and common of Aspinook (The) Corp.

ASPINOOK CORP. (DE)
Completely liquidated 04/01/1955
Each share Common $1 par exchanged for first and final distribution of $500 cash

ASPINOOK CORP. (THE) (DE)
Each share old Common $1 par exchanged for (0.5) share new Common $1 par and $16 cash 06/09/1952
Recapitalized as Ambrook Industries, Inc. (DE) 12/15/1952
Each share new Common $1 par exchanged for (4) shares Common 25¢ par
Ambrook Industries, Inc. (DE) merged into Ambrook Industries, Inc. (RI) 06/01/1956 which merged into Barker Bros. Corp. (RI) 03/14/1958 which name changed to Larchfield Corp. 10/05/1960
(See Larchfield Corp.)

ASPIR-AIR, INC. (DE)
Charter cancelled and declared inoperative and void for non-payment of taxes 03/01/1991

ASPIRE CAP INC (AB)
Name changed to CalStar Oil & Gas Ltd. 04/25/2007
(See CalStar Oil & Gas. Ltd.)

ASPIRE JAPAN INC (DE)
SEC revoked common stock registration 09/24/2015

ASPREVA PHARMACEUTICALS CORP (BC)
Merged into Galenica AG 01/03/2008
Each share Common no par exchanged for USD$26 cash

ASPRO INC (DE)
Name changed to Dyneer Corp. 11/29/1978
Dyneer Corp. name changed to DYR Liquidating Corp. 07/31/1986
(See DYR Liquidating Corp.)

ASQUITH RES INC (ON)
Reincorporated under the laws of Canada as AXMIN Inc. 11/23/2001

ASR INVTS CORP (MD)
Each share old Common 1¢ par exchanged for (0.2) share new Common 1¢ par 07/07/1995
Merged into United Dominion Realty Trust, Inc. (VA) 03/27/1998
Each share new Common 1¢ par exchanged for (1.575) shares Common $1 par
United Dominion Realty Trust, Inc. (VA) reincorporated in Maryland 06/11/2003 which name changed to UDR, Inc. 03/14/2007

ASSANTE CORP (CANADA)
Subordinate no par reclassified as Common no par 11/01/2001
Each share Common no par received distribution of (1) share Loring Ward International Ltd. Common no par payable 11/24/2003 to holders of record 10/06/2003
Merged into CI Fund Management Inc. 11/14/2003
Each share Common no par exchanged for $8.25 cash

ASSECO POLAND S A (POLAND)
GDR agreement terminated 04/30/2010
Each Sponsored Reg. S GDR for Common exchanged for (1) Unsponsored ADR for Common
Note: Unexchanged GDR's will be sold and the proceeds, if any, held for claim after 04/30/2010
(Additional Information in Active)

ASSEMBLY & MFG SYS CORP (UT)
Recapitalized as American Ship Inc. 09/05/1997
Each share Common 50¢ par exchanged for (0.001) share Common 50¢ par
American Ship Inc. name changed to Petshealth, Inc. 05/20/1998
(See Petshealth, Inc.)

ASSEMBLY ENGINEERS, INC. (CA)
Completely liquidated 08/30/1967
Each share Common 50¢ par exchanged for first and final distribution of (0.125) share Rucker Co. Common no par
Rucker Co. merged into N L Industries, Inc. 01/21/1977

ASSEMBLY PRODS INC (OH)
Stock Dividend - 200% 05/15/1959
Name changed to API Instruments Co. 01/13/1965
API Instruments Co. merged into LFE Corp. 04/03/1970
(See LFE Corp.)

ASSET ACCEP CAP CORP (DE)
Merged into Encore Capital Group, Inc. 06/13/2013
Each share Common 1¢ par exchanged for $6.50 cash

ASSET CAP GROUP INC (NV)
Old Common $0.001 par split (5) for (1) by issuance of (4) additional shares payable 08/01/2007 to holders of record 07/25/2007 Ex date - 08/02/2007
Each share old Common $0.001 par exchanged for (0.02) share new Common $0.001 par 09/19/2008
Note: No holder will receive fewer than (100) post-split shares
Name changed to Solutions Group, Inc. 12/15/2008

ASSET DEV CORP (NV)
Name changed to Franklin (Joe) Productions, Inc. 08/10/1987
Franklin (Joe) Productions, Inc. recapitalized as Universal Medical Systems Inc. 10/10/1995
(See Universal Medical Systems Inc.)

ASSET EQUITY GROUP INC (UT)
SEC revoked common stock registration 01/19/2005

ASSET GROWTH PARTNERS INC (NJ)
Name changed to AGP & Co. Inc. 12/10/1990
(See AGP & Co. Inc.)

ASSET HLDG CO (UT)
Each share Common $0.001 par exchanged for (0.1) share Common 1¢ par 12/26/1989
Involuntarily dissolved 10/01/1992

ASSET INVS CORP (DE)
Under plan of merger name changed to American Land Lease, Inc. 08/11/2000
(See American Land Lease, Inc.)

ASSET INVS CORP (MD)
Each share old Common 1¢ par exchanged for (0.2) share new Common 1¢ par 11/21/1997
Reincorporated under the laws of Delaware 05/25/1999
Asset Investors Corp. (DE) name changed to American Land Lease, Inc. 08/11/2000
(See American Land Lease, Inc.)

ASSET INVS FD INC (DE)
In process of liquidation
Each share Common $1 par exchanged for initial distribution of $7.50 cash 12/04/1979
Note: In addition holders of (100) shares or more received shares of Castle (A.M.) Co. Common $5 par, Schenuit Industries, Inc. Common no par, Circle F. Industries, Inc. Common $1 par, Caribbean Finance Co., Inc. Common $1 par, Hawthorne Financial Corp. Common $1 par, Kewaunee Scientific Equipment Corp. Common $2.50 par, Greif Bros. Corp. Class A Common no par and National Silver Industries, Inc. Common $1 par
Holders of fewer than (100) shares received cash 02/01/1980
Details on subsequent distribution(s), if any are not available

ASSET MGMT INTL FING & SETTLEMENT LTD (DE)
Charter cancelled and declared inoperative and void for non-payment of taxes 03/01/1991

ASSET MGMT SOFTWARE SYS INC (ON)
Delisted from Toronto Venture Stock Exchange 06/30/2003

ASSET PROTN AMER INC (NV)
Name changed to BCI Holding, Inc. 02/09/2017

ASSET REALIZATION INC (NV)
Recapitalized as World Assurance Group, Inc. 10/08/2008
Each share Common $0.001 par exchanged for (0.03333333) share Common no par
World Assurance Group, Inc. name changed to Power Clouds Inc. 04/24/2015

ASSET RETRIEVAL SVCS INC (DE)
Recapitalized as Creditgroup.Com Inc. 02/01/1999
Each share Preferred $0.001 par exchanged for (0.25) share Preferred $0.001 par
Each share Common $0.001 par exchanged for (0.25) share Common $0.001 par
Creditgroup.Com Inc. recapitalized as Tradex Global Financial Services Inc. 07/18/2006
(See Tradex Global Financial Services Inc.)

ASSET SERVICING CORP (NV)
Name changed to Omni Park Pass Inc. and (7) additional shares issued 07/21/2000
Omni Park Pass Inc. recapitalized as Invvision Capital Inc. 04/25/2001 which name changed to RG America, Inc. (NV) 08/30/2004 which reorganized in Colorado as Sprout Tiny Homes, Inc. 04/21/2015

ASSET SOLUTIONS INC (NV)
Name changed to Mega Bridge Inc. 03/13/2017
Mega Bridge Inc. name changed to HypGen Inc. 08/01/2017

ASSET VENTURES, INC. (CO)
Charter suspended for failure to file annual reports 09/30/1987

ASSETRONICS INC (DE)
Name changed to Main St. & Main Inc. 06/22/1990
Main St. & Main Inc. name changed to Main Street Restaurant Group, Inc. 07/15/2004
(See Main Street Restaurant Group, Inc.)

ASSETS CORP. (CA)
Dissolved 12/16/1949
No stockholders' equity

ASSISTED CARE CORP (MN)
Each share old Common $0.001 par exchanged (0.05) share new Common $0.001 par 12/02/1999
Name changed to Quality One Wireless, Inc. 08/27/2002
(See Quality One Wirless, Inc.)

ASSISTED LIVING CONCEPTS INC (NV)
Ctfs. dated after 11/10/2006
Each share old Class A Common 1¢ par exchanged for (0.2) share new Class A Common 1¢ par 03/16/2009
Each share old Class B Common 1¢ par exchanged for (0.2) share new Class B Common 1¢ par 03/16/2009
New Class A Common 1¢ par split (2) for (1) by issuance of (1) additional share payable 06/15/2011 to holders of record 05/20/2011 Ex date - 06/16/2011
New Class B Common 1¢ par split (2) for (1) by issuance of (1) additional share payable 06/15/2011 to holders of record 05/20/2011
Acquired by TPG Capital L.P. 07/11/2013
Each share new Class A Common 1¢ par exchanged for $12 cash
Each share new Class B Common 1¢ par exchanged for $12.90 cash

ASSISTED LIVING CONCEPTS INC NEW (NV)
Merged into Extendicare Health Services, Inc. 01/31/2005
Each share Common 1¢ par exchanged for $18.50 cash

ASSISTED LIVING CONCEPTS INC OLD (NV)
Common 1¢ par split (2) for (1) by issuance of (1) additional share payable 07/09/1997 to holders of record 06/30/1997 Ex date - 07/10/1997
Plan of reorganization under Chapter 11 Federal Bankruptcy Code effective 01/01/2002
Each share Common 1¢ par exchanged for (0.015186) share Assisted Living Concepts, Inc. (New) Common 1¢ par
(See Assisted Living Concepts, Inc. (New))

ASSISTED LIVING CORP (MN)
Name changed to Stealth Industries Inc. (MN) 12/13/1999
Stealth Industries Inc. (MN) reincorporated in Nevada 11/22/2000 which recapitalized as Precious Metals Exchange Corp. 01/23/2009 which name changed to Legends Food Corp. 07/19/2011 which name changed to Republic of Texas Brands, Inc. 11/07/2011 which name changed to Totally Hemp Crazy Inc. 08/05/2014 which name changed to Rocky Mountain High Brands Inc. 10/16/2015

ASSISTGLOBAL TECHNOLOGIES CORP (BC)
Recapitalized as Bassett Ventures Inc. 07/08/2005
Each share Common no par exchanged for (0.25) share Common no par
Bassett Ventures Inc. name changed to Arris Resources Inc. 06/25/2007 which name changed to RTN Stealth Software Inc. 01/08/2010 which name changed to Quantitative Alpha Trading Inc. (BC) 04/29/2011 which reincorporated in Ontario 12/09/2011
(See Quantitative Alpha Trading Inc.)

ASSIX INTL INC (DE)
Name changed to Excal Enterprises, Inc. 05/31/1995
(See Excal Enterprises, Inc.)

ASSOCIATED APPAREL INDUSTRIES, INC.
Name changed to Gossard (H.W.) Co. 00/00/1937
Gossard (H.W.) Co. merged into Wayne-Gossard Corp. 01/31/1967 which name changed to Signal Apparel Co., Inc. 02/12/1987
(See Signal Apparel Co., Inc.)

ASSOCIATED ARCADIA NICKEL LTD (QC)
Recapitalized as Arcadia Minerals Ltd. 04/30/1971
Each share Common $1 par exchanged for (0.2) share Common $1 par
(See Arcadia Minerals Ltd.)

ASSOCIATED ARTISTS PRODUCTIONS CORP. (DE)
Common $1 par changed to 25¢ par and (3) additional shares issued 05/17/1957
Name changed to P.R.M., Inc. 11/26/1958
P.R.M., Inc. name changed to World-Wide Artists Inc. 05/11/1961
(See World-Wide Artists Inc.)

ASSOCIATED AUTOMOTIVE GROUP INC (FL)
Name changed to Motor Cars Auto Group, Inc. 12/30/2002
(See Motor Cars Auto Group, Inc.)

ASSOCIATED BABY SVCS INC (DE)
Common no par changed to $4 par and (0.2) additional share issued 11/15/1967
Common $4 par changed to $3.20 par and (0.25) additional share issued 03/01/1971
Name changed to Blessings Corp. 07/26/1972
(See Blessings Corp.)

ASSOCIATED BANC CORP (WI)
8% Depositary Preferred Ser. B called for redemption at $25 on 09/15/2016
(Additional Information in Active)

ASSOCIATED BANK CHICAGO (CHICAGO, IL)
Acquired by Associated Bank, N.A. (Chicago, IL) 07/16/2005
Details not available

ASSOCIATED BK CORP (IA)
Merged into Central National Bancshares, Inc. 02/27/1978
Each share Common $1 par exchanged for $2.45 cash

ASSOCIATED BK SVCS INC (WI)
Name changed to Associated Banc-Corp. 06/15/1977

ASSOCIATED BATTERIES (CANADA) LTD. (CANADA)
Name changed to Associated Landterre Ltd. 09/04/1964
(See Associated Landterre Ltd.)

ASSOCIATED BOWLING CENTERS, INC. (NY)
Merged into National Sports Centers, Inc. on a (0.125) for (1) basis 03/02/1960
National Sports Centers, Inc. name changed to Federal Bowling Centers, Inc. 06/23/1960
(See Federal Bowling Centers, Inc.)

ASSOCIATED BRANDS INCOME FD (ON)
Completely liquidated
Each Unit of Bene. Int. no par received first and final distribution of $0.82 cash payable 05/10/2007 to holders of record 05/10/2007

ASSOCIATED BREWERIES OF CANADA, LTD. (CANADA)
Name changed to Sicks' Breweries, Ltd. 07/11/1944
Sicks' Breweries, Ltd. name changed to Molson's Western Breweries Ltd. 02/01/1963

ASSOCIATED BREWING CO (MI)
Under plan of merger each share old Common $1 par exchanged for (0.4) share new Common $1 par 12/31/1965
Name changed to Armada Corp. 03/02/1973

ASSOCIATED CALITALO HOLDINGS, LTD. (DE)
Common no par changed to 10¢ par 00/00/1932
Name changed to Pacific Empire Holdings Inc. 00/00/1934
(See Pacific Empire Holdings, Inc.)

ASSOCIATED CAP INSTL TR (MA)
Trust terminated 06/05/1991
Details not available

ASSOCIATED CEM CO LTD (INDIA)
No GDR's remain outstanding as of 00/00/2005

ASSOCIATED CHAIN STORE REALTY CO., INC. (DE)
Liquidation completed 00/00/1952
Details not available

ASSOCIATED CO. (NJ)
Liquidation completed 00/00/1953
Details not available

ASSOCIATED COCA COLA BOTTLING INC (DE)
Common $1 par changed to 50¢ par and (1) additional share issued 05/14/1971
Common 50¢ par split (2) for (1) by issuance of (1) additional share 07/07/1972
Stock Dividend - 100% 01/20/1982
Acquired by Coca-Cola Co. 07/30/1982
Each share Common 50¢ par exchanged for $35.93 cash

ASSOCIATED COMMUNICATIONS CORP (DE)
Class A Common $2.50 par changed to 10¢ par 07/22/1982
Class B Common $2.50 par changed to 10¢ par 07/22/1982
Class A Common 10¢ par split (2) for (1) by issuance of (1) additional share 07/01/1986
Class B Common 10¢ par split (2) for (1) by issuance of (1) additional share 07/01/1986
Class A Common 10¢ par split (3) for (2) by issuance of (0.5) additional share 04/12/1988
Class B Common 10¢ par split (3) for (2) by issuance of (0.5) additional share 04/12/1988
Class A Common 10¢ par split (3) for (2) by issuance of (0.5) additional share 01/31/1989
Class B Common 10¢ par split (3) for (2) by issuance of (0.5) additional share 01/31/1989
Class A Common 10¢ par split (2) for (1) by issuance of (1) additional share 05/28/1991
Class B Common 10¢ par split (2) for (1) by issuance of (1) additional share 05/28/1991
Each share Class A Common 10¢ par or Class B Common 10¢ par received distribution of (0.25) share

Associated Group, Inc. Class A Common 10¢ par or Class B Common 10¢ par respectively 12/15/1994
Stock Dividend - In Class B Common to holders of Class A Common - 100% 07/14/1983
Merged into Southwestern Bell Corp. 12/15/1994
Each share Class A Common 10¢ par exchanged for (0.36) share Common $1 par
Each share Class B Common 10¢ par exchanged for (0.36) share Common $1 par
Southwestern Bell Corp. name changed to SBC Communications, Inc. 04/28/1995 which name changed to AT&T Inc. 11/18/2005

ASSOCIATED COMMUNICATIONS LTD (ENGLAND)
Acquired by TVW Enterprises Ltd. 08/19/1982
Each ADR for A Ordinary exchanged for 1.859 cash

ASSOCIATED COMPANIES
Reorganized as Postal Telegraph, Inc. 00/00/1940
Each share Preferred exchanged for (0.5) share Preferred no par and (2) shares Common $1 par
Postal Telegraph, Inc. acquired by Western Union Telegraph Co. 00/00/1943
(See Western Union Telegraph Co.)

ASSOCIATED COMPUTER SVCS INC (TX)
Completely liquidated 05/27/1971
Each share Common 10¢ par exchanged for first and final distribution of (0.181644) share Seaco Computer-Display Inc. Common no par
(See Seaco Computer-Display Inc.)

ASSOCIATED COS INC (IN)
Stock Dividends - 10% 03/31/1976; 10% 10/27/1978; 10% 11/30/1979; 10% 03/24/1980
Merged into Acap Corp. 07/05/1989
Each share Common no par exchanged for (3.076984) shares Common 10¢ par
Acap Corp. merged into UTG, Inc. 11/14/2011

ASSOCIATED DATA & MGMT CORP (DE)
Merged into Consolidated Recreation Corp. 08/31/1972
Each share Common 1¢ par exchanged for (0.3) share Common 1¢ par
(See Consolidated Recreation Corp.)

ASSOCIATED DENTAL PRODUCTS, INC.
Out of business 00/00/1933
Details not available

ASSOCIATED DEV & RESH CORP (NY)
Completely liquidated 11/05/1969
Each share Capital Stock $1 par exchanged for first and final distribution of (0.33333333) share General-Gilbert Corp. Common $1 par and (0.11) share Simplex Development Corp. Common $1 par
(See each company's listing)

ASSOCIATED DEVELOPMENTS LTD. (QC)
Acquired by New Associated Developments Ltd. 04/17/1963
Each share Capital Stock $1 par exchanged for (0.16666666) share Capital Stock $1 par
New Associated Developments Ltd. recapitalized as Consolidated Developments Ltd. 05/10/1971
(See Consolidated Developments Ltd.)

ASSOCIATED DRY GOODS CORP (VA)
Common no par changed to old Common $1 par 00/00/1932
Old Common $1 par split (2) for (1) by issuance of (1) additional share 06/03/1946
Each share 7% 2nd Preferred $100 par exchanged for (1.225) shares 6% 2nd Preferred $100 par 00/00/1951
Each share 6% Preferred $100 par exchanged for (1.2) shares 5.25% 1st Preferred $100 par 00/00/1951
Each share old Common $1 par exchanged for (1) share new Common $1 par 08/24/1951
6% 2nd Preferred $100 par called for redemption 10/01/1954
5.25% 1st Preferred $100 par reclassified as 5.25% Preferred $100 par 06/13/1955
New Common $1 par changed to 50¢ par and (1) additional share issued 06/20/1962
5.25% Preferred $100 par called for redemption 05/01/1963
Common 50¢ par split (3) for (2) by issuance of (0.5) additional share 06/22/1965
Common 50¢ par split (3) for (2) by issuance of (0.5) additional share 06/24/1968
Common 50¢ par split (2) for (1) by issuance of (1) additional share 08/30/1985
$4.75 Conv. Preferred Ser. A $50 par called for redemption 08/29/1986
Merged into May Department Stores Co. 10/04/1986
Each share Common 50¢ par exchanged for (1.72) shares Common $1 par
May Department Stores Co. merged into Federated Department Stores, Inc. 08/30/2005 which name changed to Macy's, Inc. 06/01/2007

ASSOCIATED DYEING & PRINTING CORP.
Reorganized as Associated Dyeing & Printing Co., Inc. 00/00/1930
Details not available

ASSOCIATED EDL SVCS INC (AZ)
Charter revoked for failure to pay taxes and pay fees 03/15/1974

ASSOCIATED ELECTRICAL INDS LTD (ENGLAND)
Stock Dividend - 100% 10/08/1953
ADR agreement terminated 05/01/1968
Details not available

ASSOCIATED EMPLOYEES INVESTMENTS, INC. (DE)
No longer in existence having become inoperative and void for non-payment of taxes 04/01/1934

ASSOCIATED ENERGY CORP (UT)
Involuntarily dissolved 08/01/1989

ASSOCIATED ESTATES RLTY CORP (OH)
9.75% Depositary Preferred Class A called for redemption at $25 plus $0.60938 accrued dividends on 01/06/2003
8.7% Depositary Preferred Class B called for redemption at $25 plus $0.5075 accrued dividends on 06/09/2010
Acquired by BSREP II Aries Pooling LLC 08/07/2015
Each share Common no par exchanged for $28.75 cash

ASSOCIATED FD TR (MO)
Name changed to Steadman Associated Fund (MO) 02/01/1971
Steadman Associated Fund (MO) reincorporated in the District of Columbia 12/27/1974 which name changed to Ameritor Security Trust 09/23/1998
(See Ameritor Security Trust)

ASSOCIATED FOOD STORES INC (NY)
Capital Stock $1 par changed to 10¢ par 02/25/1977
Merged into Harira, Inc. 07/22/1985
Each share Capital Stock 10¢ par exchanged for $2 cash

ASSOCIATED FREEZERS INCOME TR (ON)
Name changed to ACS Freezers Income Trust 08/11/2000
ACS Freezers Income Trust name changed to Atlas Cold Storage Income Trust 06/25/2001
(See Atlas Cold Storage Income Trust)

ASSOCIATED FREIGHTWAYS INC (MI)
Merged into American Natural Resources Co. (MI) 03/31/1977
Each share Common $3 par exchanged for (0.5) share Common $1 par
American Natural Resources Co. (MI) reincorporated in Delaware 06/30/1983
(See American Natural Resources Co. (DE))

ASSOCIATED GARAGES INC (MO)
Company went private 00/00/1980
Details not available

ASSOCIATED GAS & ELECTRIC CO. (NY)
Reorganized as General Public Utilities Corp. (NY) 00/00/1946
Note: Unexchanged certificates were cancelled and became without value 11/01/1951
(See General Public Utilities Corp. (NY))

ASSOCIATED GENERAL UTILITIES CO. (DE)
Common no par changed to $1 par 00/00/1941
Liquidation completed 02/24/1959
Details not available

ASSOCIATED GOLF MGMT INC (NV)
Name changed to Vidmar Acquisitions Inc. 08/15/2001
Vidmar Acquisitions Inc. recapitalized as Online Transaction Systems, Inc. 08/05/2003 which name changed to Delta Mining & Exploration Corp. 01/28/2004
(See Delta Mining & Exploration Corp.)

ASSOCIATED GRAPHICS & COMMUNICATIONS INC (AZ)
Recapitalized as Associated Growth Capital, Inc. 12/07/1977
Each share Common no par exchanged for (0.002) share Common no par
(See Associated Growth Capital, Inc.)

ASSOCIATED GROUP INC (DE)
Class A Common 10¢ par split (2) for (1) by issuance of (1) additional share payable 10/27/1997 to holders of record 10/17/1997
Class B Common 10¢ par split (2) for (1) by issuance of (1) additional share payable 10/27/1997 to holders of record 10/17/1997
Merged into AT&T Corp. 01/18/2000
Each share Class A Common 10¢ par exchanged for (1.20711) shares Common Liberty Media Group Class A $1 par and (0.49634) share Common $1 par
Each share Class B Common 10¢ par exchanged for (1.20711) shares Common Liberty Media Group Class A $1 par and (0.49634) share Common $1 par
AT&T Corp. merged into AT&T Inc. 11/18/2005

ASSOCIATED GROWTH CAPITAL, INC. (AZ)
Under plan of merger each share Common no par exchanged for $650 cash 04/22/1983

ASSOCIATED HEALTH STUDIOS, INC. (VA)
Charter revoked for failure to file reports and pay fees 01/03/1962

ASSOCIATED HEALTHCARE INDS INC (NV)
Recapitalized as Contour Medical Inc. 06/30/1993
Each share Common $0.001 par exchanged for (0.0769233) share Common $0.001 par
Contour Medical Inc. merged into Sun Healthcare Group, Inc. (Old) 06/30/1998
(See Sun Healthcare Group, Inc. (Old))

ASSOCIATED HOSTS INC (DE)
Reincorporated 11/07/1977
Common 10¢ par split (2) for (1) by issuance of (1) additional share 04/16/1975
Common 10¢ par split (5) for (4) by issuance of (0.25) additional share 07/03/1978
Stock Dividends - 10% 09/12/1973; 25% 09/24/1974
State of incorporation changed from (CA) to (DE) 11/07/1977
Common 10¢ par split (3) for (2) by issuance of (0.5) additional share 07/01/1983
Merged into IEP 12/30/1988
Each share Common 10¢ par exchanged for $11 cash

ASSOCIATED INDUSTRIALS CORP.
Liquidated 00/00/1951
Details not available

ASSOCIATED INNS & RESTAURANTS CO OF AMER (DE)
Name changed to Aircoa Hospitality Services, Inc. 11/25/1987
(See Aircoa Hospitality Services, Inc.)

ASSOCIATED INSURANCE FUND, INC.
Liquidated 00/00/1944
Details not available

ASSOCIATED INVENTIONS, INC. (DE)
Charter cancelled and declared inoperative and void for non-payment of taxes 04/01/1934

ASSOCIATED INVS SECS INC (AR)
Merged into Norin Corp. (DE) 11/03/1972
Each share Common 10¢ par exchanged for (0.03333333) share Common $1 par
Norin Corp. (DE) reorganized in Florida 05/31/1979
(See Norin Corp. (FL))

ASSOCIATED LANTERRE LTD. (CANADA)
Company went out of business 00/00/1981
Details not available

ASSOCIATED LAUNDRIES AMER INC (MD)
Each share Class A Part. no par exchanged for (2) shares Common no par 00/00/1929
Each share Class B Common no par exchanged for (1.5) shares Common no par 00/00/1929
Common no par changed to $1 par 00/00/1954
Name changed to Vanguard International, Inc. 03/24/1969
Vanguard International, Inc. recapitalized as C L Financial Corp. 07/14/1972 which name changed to California Life Corp. 05/20/1974
(See California Life Corp.)

ASSOCIATED LEISURE ENTERPRISES INC (DE)
Charter cancelled and declared inoperative and void for non-payment of taxes 03/01/1977

ASSOCIATED LIFE INS CO (IL)
Each share Common 50¢ par exchanged for (0.5) share Common $1 par 03/16/1964
Acquired by Hawkeye National Investment Co. 06/24/1969
Each share Common $1 par exchanged for (3.9) shares Common $1 par
Hawkeye National Investment Co. liquidated for Hawkeye National Life Insurance Co. 12/22/1978
(See Hawkeye National Life Insurance Co.)

ASSOCIATED MADISON COS INC (NY)
Conv. Preferred Ser. A 50¢ par called for redemption 04/27/1973
Common 50¢ par changed to 40¢ par and (0.25) additional share issued 06/22/1973
Merged into American Can Co. 04/08/1982
Each share Common 40¢ par exchanged for (0.4545) share Common $12.50 par
American Can Co. name changed to Primerica Corp. (NJ) 04/28/1987 which was acquired by Primerica Corp. (DE) 12/15/1988 which name changed to Travelers Inc. 12/31/1993 which name changed to Travelers Group Inc. 04/26/1995 which name changed to Citigroup Inc. 10/08/1998

ASSOCIATED MANUFACTURERS CO., INC. (NV)
Capital Stock $1 par changed to 10¢ par 01/27/1962
Name changed to Armorite, Inc. 03/01/1963
Armorite, Inc. name changed to Coast to Coast Co., Inc. 10/10/1963
(See Coast to Coast Co., Inc.)

ASSOCIATED MARINER FINL GROUP INC (MI)
Merged into InterSecurities, Inc. 02/07/1994
Each share Common $0.001 par exchanged for $0.40 cash

ASSOCIATED MATLS INC (DE)
Merged into Associated Holdings Inc. 04/19/2002
Each share Common $0.0025 par exchanged for $50 cash

ASSOCIATED MED DEVICES INC (NV)
Each share old Common $0.001 par exchanged for (0.2) share new Common $0.001 par 04/21/1999
Each share new Common $0.001 par exchanged again for (0.002) share new Common $0.001 par 07/12/1999
Reorganized as Yournet, Inc. (NV) 11/08/1999
Each share new Common $0.001 par exchanged for (3.5) shares Common $0.001 par
Yournet, Inc. (NV) reincorporated in Delaware as Global Path Inc. 08/14/2001 which name changed to Swiss Medica, Inc. 06/27/2003

ASSOCIATED MEDIA HLDGS INC (NV)
Recapitalized as N I S Holdings, Corp. 03/16/2010
Each share Common $0.001 par exchanged for (0.01) share Common $0.00025 par
N I S Holdings, Corp. name changed to E-Rewards Network Inc. 08/16/2013 which name changed to Rewards Nexus Inc. 10/02/2013 which recapitalized as One Step Vending, Corp. 04/06/2015

ASSOCIATED METALS CORP. (DE)
Charter cancelled and declared inoperative and void for non-payment of taxes 04/01/1931

ASSOCIATED MILLS CO.
Liquidated for benefit of creditors 00/00/1942
No stockholders' equity

ASSOCIATED MORTGAGE & INVESTMENT CO. (DE)
Reincorporated under the laws of Arizona as Arizona Mortgage & Investment Co. 09/19/1979
(See Arizona Mortgage & Investment Co.)

ASSOCIATED MTG COS INC (DE)
Each share Common $1 par exchanged for (0.001) share Common no par 09/15/1971
Note: In effect holders received $15 cash per share and public interest was eliminated

ASSOCIATED MTG INVS (MA)
Reorganized under the laws of Florida as ProCom Group, Inc. 06/01/1991
Each Share of Bene. Int. no par exchanged for (1.195) shares Common $0.0001 par
(See ProCom Group, Inc.)

ASSOCIATED MOTION PICTURE INDUSTRIES, INC. (DE)
Name changed to Seaboard Associates, Inc. 08/19/1960

ASSOCIATED MOTOR INNS CORP. (TN)
Merged into Highland Inns Corp. 07/11/1972
Each share Common 10¢ par exchanged for (1) share Common 10¢ par
Highland Inns Corp. name changed to Advantage Companies, Inc. 04/28/1980 which merged into LDDS Communications, Inc. (DE) 08/11/1989 which merged into Resurgens Communications Group, Inc. 09/15/1993 which name changed to LDDS Communications, Inc. (GA) 09/15/1993 which name changed to WorldCom, Inc. 05/26/1995 which name changed to MCI WorldCom, Inc. 09/18/1998 which name changed to WorldCom Inc. (New) 05/01/2000
(See WorldCom Inc. (New))

ASSOCIATED MOTOR TERMINALS CO.
Succeeded by Associated Garages, Inc. 00/00/1936
No stockholders' equity

ASSOCIATED NAT GAS CORP (DE)
Merged into Panhandle Eastern Corp. 12/15/1994
Each share Common 10¢ par exchanged for (1.875) shares Common $1 par
Panhandle Eastern Corp. name changed to Panenergy Corp. 04/26/1996 which merged into Duke Energy Corp. (NC) 06/18/1997 which merged into Duke Energy Corp. (DE) 04/03/2006

ASSOCIATED NATIONAL SHARES SERIES A
Trust terminated 00/00/1941
Details not available

ASSOCIATED NATURAL GAS CORP. (CO)
Charter revoked for failure to file reports and pay fees 10/10/1925

ASSOCIATED OIL & GAS CO. LTD. (CANADA)
Deemed not to be a subsisting company by the Dominion Secretary of State 12/15/1955

ASSOCIATED OIL & GAS CO (DE)
Capital Stock 1¢ par reclassified as Common 1¢ par 01/15/1968
Name changed to AO Industries, Inc. 05/05/1969
AO Industries, Inc. name changed to Aegis Corp. 06/01/1974
(See Aegis Corp.)

ASSOCIATED OIL CO., INC. (LA)
Charter revoked for failure to file annual reports 05/13/1982

ASSOCIATED OIL CO. (CA)
Merged into Tide Water Associated Oil Co. 00/00/1937
Each share Capital Stock exchanged for (2.25) shares Common $10 par
Tide Water Associated Oil Co. name changed to Tidewater Oil Co. 05/04/1956 which merged into Getty Oil Co. 09/30/1967
(See Getty Oil Co.)

ASSOCIATED PHARMACISTS, INC. (DE)
No longer in existence having become inoperative and void for non-payment of taxes 03/18/1925

ASSOCIATED PLASTIC COMPANIES, INC. (DE)
Reorganized as Commercial Plastics Co. 10/03/1955
Each share Preferred $10 par exchanged for (1) share Common $1 par
Class A & B Common no par had no equity

ASSOCIATED PORCUPINE MINES LTD (ON)
Merged into American Reserve Mining Corp. 02/27/1989
Each share Capital Stock no par held by Non-U.S. residents exchanged for (0.75) share Common no par, (3/16) Common Stock Purchase Warrant expiring 02/28/1994 and $5 cash
Each share Capital Stock no par held by U.S. residents exchanged for $5 cash and proceeds from the sale of stock and warrants to which they are entitled
American Reserve Mining Corp. recapitalized as AMI Resources Inc. 12/21/1994 which name changed to Ashanti Sankofa Inc. 01/19/2017

ASSOCIATED PORTLAND CEM MFRS LTD (ENGLAND)
Name changed to Blue Circle Industries Ltd. 06/01/1978
(See Blue Circle Industries PLC)

ASSOCIATED PRODS INC (IL)
Merged into Nabisco Inc. 10/12/1973
Each share Common $1 par exchanged for (0.725) share Common $5 par
Nabisco Inc. merged into Nabisco Brands, Inc. 07/06/1981
(See Nabisco Brands, Inc.)

ASSOCIATED PRODUCING & REFINING CORP. (DE)
Charter cancelled and declared inoperative and void for non-payment of taxes 03/18/1925

ASSOCIATED PUBLIC UTILITIES CORP.
Acquired by General Telephone Corp. 00/00/1946
Each (1.75) shares Common no par exchanged for (1) share Common $20 par
General Telephone Corp. name changed to General Telephone & Electronics Corp. 03/05/1959 which name changed to GTE Corp. 07/01/1982 which merged into Verizon Communications Inc. 06/30/2000

ASSOCIATED PUBLISHERS CO. (DE)
Charter cancelled for non-payment of taxes 00/00/1916

ASSOCIATED QUALITY CANNERS, LTD.
Liquidated 00/00/1936
No stockholders' equity

ASSOCIATED RAYON CORP.
Liquidated 00/00/1936
Details not available

ASSOCIATED RE-INSURANCE CO.
Liquidated 00/00/1933
Details not available

ASSOCIATED REC CORP (ON)
Name changed to ARC International Corp. (ON) 10/31/1983
ARC International Corp. (ON) reincorporated in Colorado as Kompass Travel Ltd. 03/00/2003 which recapitalized as Imagexpress, Inc. 08/19/2003 which name changed to Imagexpres Corp. 10/01/2003

ASSOCIATED SALES ANALYSTS, INC. (NY)
Class A 5¢ par reclassified as Common 5¢ par 03/29/1962
Completely liquidated 06/01/1965
Each share Common 5¢ par exchanged for first and final distribution of (0.166666) share Computer Applications Inc. Common 10¢ par 06/02/1965
(See Computer Applications Inc.)

ASSOCIATED SCRANTON INDS INC (PA)
Each share Common 1¢ par exchanged for (0.25) share Common 4¢ par 07/18/1969
Stock Dividend - 100% 01/18/1971
Merged into SWCC, Inc. 04/27/1981
Each share Common 4¢ par exchanged for $2.15 cash

ASSOCIATED SEED GROWERS, INC. (CT)
Name changed to Asgrow Seed Co. 11/18/1959
Asgrow Seed Co. liquidated for Upjohn Co. (DE) 05/01/1968 which merged into Pharmacia & Upjohn Inc. 11/02/1995 which merged into Pharmacia Corp. 03/31/2000 which merged into Pfizer Corp. 04/16/2003

ASSOCIATED SIMMONS HARDWARE COMPANIES
Reorganized as Simmons Hardware & Paint Corp. 00/00/1935
Details not available

ASSOCIATED SMELTERS INTL (NV)
Name changed to ASI 09/01/1978
ASI recapitalized as ASI Technology Corp. 09/01/2000 which recapitalized as Robertson Global Health Solutions Corp. 08/06/2010

ASSOCIATED SPRING CORP (DE)
Each share Common $25 par exchanged for (2.5) shares Common $10 par 00/00/1946
Common $10 par changed to $6.66-2/3 par and (0.5) additional share issued 04/29/1966
Stock Dividends - 50% 12/10/1957; 10% 01/16/1969; 10% 12/31/1970
Name changed to Barnes Group Inc. 04/07/1976

ASSOCIATED STANDARD OILSTOCKS SERIES A
Trust terminated 00/00/1949
Details not available

ASSOCIATED STANDARD WIRE & CABLE LTD. (ON)
Name changed to Industrial Wire & Cable Co. Ltd. 06/18/1962
Industrial Wire & Cable Co. Ltd. name changed to IWC Industries, Ltd. 04/25/1969 which name changed to IWC Communications Ltd. 12/05/1972 which recapitalized as Radio IWC Ltd. 04/07/1978
(See Radio IWC Ltd.)

ASSOCIATED STATIONERS SUPPLY CO., INC. (IL)
Common no par split (3) for (1) by issuance of (2) additional shares 02/15/1960
Acquired by Boise Cascade Corp. 09/30/1964
Each share Common no par exchanged for (0.25) share Common $5 par

Boise Cascade Corp. name changed to OfficeMax Inc. 11/01/2004 which merged into Office Depot, Inc. 11/05/2013

ASSOCIATED TELEPHONE CO., LTD. (CA)
Name changed to General Telephone Co. of California 12/31/1952
General Telephone Co. of California name changed to GTE California Inc. 01/01/1988
(See GTE California Inc.)

ASSOCIATED TELEPHONE UTILITIES CO. (DE)
Reorganized as General Telephone Corp. 00/00/1935
Prior Preferred, $6 Conv. Preferred and Common were exchanged for various amounts of 60 day rights and warrants which expired 11/01/1948 07/22/1940 was last day to effect exchange

ASSOCIATED TELEVISION CORP. LTD. (ENGLAND)
Stock Dividend - 10% 11/17/1972
Name changed to Associated Communications Corp. PLC 09/21/1978
(See Associated Communications Corp. PLC)

ASSOCIATED TELEVISION LTD (ENGLAND)
Stock Dividend - 100% 09/28/1964
Name changed to Associated Television Corp. Ltd. 10/19/1967
Associated Television Corp. Ltd. name changed to Associated Communications Corp. PLC 09/21/1978
(See Associated Communications Corp. PLC)

ASSOCIATED TESTING LABORATORIES, INC. (NJ)
Merged into Kidde (Walter) & Co., Inc. (NY) 03/02/1965
Each share Common 10¢ par exchanged for (0.36) share Common $2.50 par
Kidde (Walter) & Co., Inc. (NY) reincorporated in Delaware 07/02/1968 which name changed to Kidde, Inc. 04/18/1980 which merged into Hanson Trust PLC 12/31/1987 which name changed to Hanson PLC (Old) 01/29/1988 which reorganized as Hanson PLC (New) 10/15/2003
(See Hanson PLC (New))

ASSOCIATED TEXTILE COMPANIES (MA)
Liquidation completed
Each share Common no par exchanged for initial distribution of $16.90 cash 08/22/1960
Each share Common no par received second and final distribution of $1.77 cash 11/24/1964

ASSOCIATED TRAFFIC CLUBS INS CORP (DE)
Common 80¢ par changed to 50¢ par 06/21/1963
Common 50¢ par changed to 25¢ par 02/18/1965
Name changed to Associated Traffic Clubs Life Insurance Co. and Common 25¢ par changed to 7¢ par 09/27/1968
Associated Traffic Clubs Life Insurance Co. merged into Union Fidelity Corp. (PA) 03/02/1972 which merged into Filmways, Inc. (DE) 02/03/1978 which name changed to Orion Pictures Corp. 07/30/1982 which name changed to Metromedia International Group, Inc. 11/01/1995
(See Metromedia International Group, Inc.)

ASSOCIATED TRAFFIC CLUBS LIFE INS CO (DE)
Common 7¢ par changed to 15¢ par 06/30/1970
Merged into Union Fidelity Corp. (PA) 03/02/1972
Each share Common 15¢ par exchanged for (0.016476) share Common 10¢ par
Union Fidelity Corp. (PA) merged into Filmways, Inc. (DE) 02/03/1978 which name changed to Orion Pictures Corp. 07/30/1982 which merged into Metromedia International Group, Inc. 11/01/1995
(See Metromedia International Group, Inc.)

ASSOCIATED TRANS INC (DE)
6% Conv. Preferred $100 par called for redemption 06/25/1965
Common no par split (2) for (1) by issuance of (1) additional share 11/18/1965
Adjudicated bankrupt 04/28/1976
No stockholders' equity

ASSOCIATED TRUCK LINES INC (MI)
Each share Class B Common $1.50 par exchanged for (0.5) share Class A Common $3 par 12/21/1965
Class A Common $3 par split (3) for (2) by issuance of (0.5) additional share 04/01/1966
6% Preferred $100 par called for redemption 03/31/1973
Stock Dividends - Class A & B 10% 03/15/1962; Class A 100% 06/01/1963; 10% 12/29/1972
Reorganized as Associated Freightways, Inc. 08/06/1976
Each share Class A Common $3 par exchanged for (1) share Common $3 par
Associated Freightways, Inc. merged into American Natural Resources Co. (MI) 03/31/1977 which reincorporated in Delaware 06/30/1983
(See American Natural Resources Co. (DE))

ASSOCIATED UTILITIES, INC.
Bankrupt 00/00/1932
Stockholders' equity unlikely

ASSOCIATED WOMEN INVESTORS, INC. (FL)
Liquidation completed
Each share Common $2 par exchanged for initial distribution of $0.75 cash 07/28/1965
Each share Common $2 par received second distribution of $0.30 cash 07/14/1966
Each share Common $2 par received third distribution of $0.25 cash 05/11/1967
Each share Common $2 par received fourth distribution of $0.10 cash 05/31/1968
Each share Common $2 par received fifth distribution of $0.50 cash 07/01/1969
Each share Common $2 par received sixth distribution of $0.20 cash 12/31/1969
Each share Common $2 par received seventh distribution of $0.12 cash 01/08/1971
Each share Common $2 par received eighth and final distribution of $0.40 cash 03/17/1972

ASSOCIATES FIRST CAP CORP (DE)
Class A Common 1¢ par split (2) for (1) by issuance of (1) additional share payable 12/23/1998 to holders of record 12/09/1998 Ex date - 12/24/1998
Merged into Citigroup Inc. 11/30/2000
Each share Class A Common 1¢ par exchanged for (0.7334) share Common 1¢ par

ASSOCIATES INTL INC (UT)
Proclaimed dissolved for failure to pay taxes 09/30/1975

ASSOCIATES INVT CO (DE)
Reincorporated 06/26/1969
Each share Common $100 par exchanged for (7) shares Common no par 00/00/1926
Common no par split (5) for (1) by issuance of (4) additional shares 00/00/1935
5% Preferred $100 par called for redemption 06/29/1946
Each share Common no par exchanged for (2) shares Common $10 par 00/00/1947
Common $10 par split (3) for (1) by issuance of (2) additional shares 00/00/1953
Common $10 par changed to $5 par and (1) additional share issued 08/14/1964
State of incorporation changed from (IN) to (DE) 06/26/1969
Merged into Gulf & Western Industries, Inc. 07/01/1969
Each share Common $5 par exchanged for $45 principal amount of 5.5% Conv Subord. Debentures due 07/01/1993

ASSOCIATES LIFE INS CO (IN)
Stock Dividend - 10% 05/17/1965
Acquired by Alexander National Group, Inc. 12/13/1971
Each share Common $1 par exchanged for (1) share Conv. Preferred Ser. A $3 par
Alexander National Group, Inc. name changed to ANG, Inc. 02/02/1981
(See ANG, Inc.)

ASSOCIATES PROTECTIVE ASS'N (CA)
Charter revoked for failure to file reports and pay fees 00/00/1952

ASSOCIATION CORP (WI)
Merged into International Harvester Co. (DE) 03/09/1973
Each share Common 30¢ par exchanged for (0.1095) share Common $20 par
International Harvester Co. (DE) name changed to Navistar International Corp. 02/21/1986

ASSOCIATION LIQUID RESV FD INC (MD)
Name changed to National Liquid Reserves, Inc. 09/15/1975
National Liquid Reserves, Inc. name changed to Smith Barney Money Funds, Inc. 07/11/1991
(See Smith Barney Money Funds, Inc.)

ASSOCIATION OF ARMY & NAVY STORES INC. (NY)
Charter revoked for failure to file reports and pay fees 12/16/1957

ASSOCIATIONS INVESTMENT FUND, INC. (DE)
Name changed to Babson (David L.) Investment Fund, Inc. 02/21/1968
Babson (David L.) Investment Fund, Inc. name changed to Babson (David L.) Growth Fund, Inc. (DE) 10/03/1983 which reincorporated in Maryland 00/00/1978
(See Babson (David L.) Growth Fund, Inc.)

ASSUMPTION BANCSHARES INC (LA)
Merged into Argent Bank (Thibodaux, LA) 06/30/1997
Each share Common $25 par exchanged for either (6.3883) shares Common 10¢ par or $134.375 cash
Note: Option to make a definitive election expired 08/11/1997
Note: Holders of (15) shares or fewer received cash
Argent Bank (Thibodaux, LA) merged into Hibernia Corp. 02/01/1998 which merged into Capital One Financial Corp. 11/16/2005

ASSURANCE NETWORK INC (UT)
Recapitalized as Ult-I-Med Health Centers, Inc. (UT) 12/22/1993
Each share Common $0.001 par exchanged for (0.00650753) share Common $0.001 par
Ult-I-Med Health Centers, Inc. (UT) reincorporated in Delaware as Youthline USA, Inc. 08/17/1999
(See Youthline USA, Inc.)

ASSURE DATA INC (NV)
Name changed to Frontier Beverage Co., Inc. (NV) 02/08/2010
Frontier Beverage Co., Inc. (NV) reorganized in Wyoming as FBEC Worldwide, Inc. 12/23/2014

ASSURE ENERGY INC (AB)
Reincorporated 09/11/2003
Reincorporated 02/10/2004
Common $0.001 par split (3) for (2) by issuance of (0.5) additional share payable 09/17/2002 to holders of record 09/10/2002 Ex date - 09/18/2002
State of incorporation changed from (DE) to (NV) 09/11/2003
Place of incorporation changed from (NV) to (AB) 02/10/2004
Acquired by GEOCAN Energy Inc. 09/08/2005
Each share Common $0.001 par exchanged for (0.7) share Common no par
Note: Unexchanged certificates were cancelled and became without value 09/08/2010
GEOCAN Energy Inc. merged into Arsenal Energy Inc. (New) 10/08/2008 which merged into Prairie Provident Resources Inc. 09/16/2016

ASSURED CREDIT CORP. (CO)
Merged into Colorado Insurance Service Co. 03/00/1962
Each share Common 25¢ par exchanged for (0.0666666) share Common no par
Colorado Insurance Service Co. name changed to Cisco Group Inc. 05/13/1964
(See Cisco Group Inc.)

ASSURED GUARANTY LTD (BERMUDA)
Each share 8.5% Conv. Preferred exchanged for (3.8924) shares Common 1¢ par 06/01/2012
(Additional Information in Active)

ASSURED INVESTORS, INC. (PA)
Acquired by Equity Growth of America, Inc. 03/31/1971
Each share Common 1¢ par exchanged for (1) share Common 1¢ par
Equity Growth of America, Inc. name changed to Diversified Growth Corp. 05/01/1976
(See Diversified Growth Corp.)

ASSURED PHARMACY INC (NV)
Each share old Common $0.001 par exchanged for (0.00555555) share new Common $0.001 par 04/15/2011
Plan of reorganization under Chapter 11 Federal Bankruptcy proceedings effective 04/16/2015
No stockholders' equity

ASSURED TRAVEL SVCS INC (MA)
Voluntarily dissolved 08/04/1977
No stockholders' equity

AST GROUP INC (DE)
Each share old Common $0.000001 par exchanged for (0.005) share new Common $0.000001 par 06/01/1989
Charter cancelled and declared inoperative and void for non-payment of taxes 03/01/1989

AST RESH INC (CA)
Common 1¢ par split (2) for (1) by issuance of (1) additional share 02/25/1991
Merged into Samsung Electronics Co., Ltd. 08/11/1997
Each share Common 1¢ par exchanged for $5.40 cash

ASTA GROUP INC (NY)
Recapitalized 06/19/1984
Recapitalized from Asta Credit Corp. to Asta Group Inc. 06/19/1984
Each share Common 1¢ par exchanged for (4) shares Common 1¢ par
Merged into RES Servicing Inc. 01/09/1996
Each share Common 1¢ par exchanged for $2.80 cash

ASTA HLDGS CORP (NV)
Common $0.001 par split (13.8) for (1) by issuance of (12.8) additional shares payable 07/31/2015 to holders of record 07/27/2015 Ex date - 08/03/2015
Name changed to CSA Holdings Inc. 08/07/2015

ASTA-KING INDUSTRIES, INC. (DE)
No longer in existence having become inoperative and void for non-payment of taxes 04/01/1965

ASTA-KING PETROLEUM, INC. (DE)
Name changed to Asta-King Industries, Inc. 04/03/1963
(See Asta-King Industries, Inc.)

ASTAIRE (FRED) DANCE STUDIOS (METROPOLITAN NEW YORK) INC. (NY)
Charter cancelled and proclaimed dissolved for failure to pay taxes and file reports 12/15/1971

ASTAR MINERALS LTD (BC)
Name changed to FinCanna Capital Corp. 12/29/2017

ASTEC BSR PLC (UNITED KINGDOM)
Merged into Emerson Electric Co. 04/07/1999
Each ADR for Ordinary exchanged for $1.3192 cash

ASTEK INSTRUMENT CORP. (DE)
Completely liquidated 12/09/1966
Each share Common 10¢ par exchanged for first and final distribution of $1.75 cash

ASTER DEV ENTERPRISES LTD (DE)
Name changed to P A N Environmental Services Inc. 04/00/1993
P A N Environmental Services Inc. name changed to PAN Environmental Corp. 02/22/1994 which name changed to PAN International Gaming Inc. 12/30/1998 which name changed to SearchHound.com, Inc. 06/07/2000 which recapitalized as Coach Industries Group, Inc. 08/25/2003
(See Coach Industries Group, Inc.)

ASTER VENTURES CORP (BC)
Recapitalized as Knight Petroleum Corp. 03/22/2001
Each share Common no par exchanged for (0.5) share Common no par
Knight Petroleum Corp. name changed to Knight Resources Ltd. 03/07/2003 which recapitalized as Knight Metals Ltd. 05/25/2011 which name changed to Africa Hydrocarbons Inc. (BC) 02/02/2012 which reincorporated in Alberta 04/25/2013 which name changed to Blockchaink2 Corp. 05/30/2018

ASTERIKO CORP (NV)
Name changed to Star Alliance International Corp. 03/20/2017

ASTERISK, INC. (UT)
Name changed to Aztec Communications Group, Inc. (UT) 08/31/1987
Aztec Communications Group, Inc. (UT) reincorporated in Nevada 11/21/2003 which reorganized as Aztec Oil & Gas Inc. 08/13/2004

ASTEX PHARMACEUTICALS INC (DE)
Acquired by Otsuka Pharmaceutical Co., Ltd. 10/11/2013
Each share Common $0.001 par exchanged for $8.50 cash

ASTHMA DISEASE MGMT INC (DE)
Charter cancelled and declared inoperative and void for non-payment of taxes 03/01/2003

ASTIC VENTURES INC (BC)
Struck off register and declared dissolved for failure to file returns 07/15/1994

ASTON HILL ADVANTAGE BD FD (ON)
Name changed to LOGiQ Advantage Bond Fund 05/12/2017
(See LOGiQ Advantage Bond Fund)

ASTON HILL ADVANTAGE OIL & GAS INCOME FD (ON)
Name changed to LOGiQ Advantage Oil & Gas Income Fund 05/12/2017
LOGIQ Advantage Oil & Gas Income Fund name changed to Redwood Energy Income Fund 12/20/2017
(See Redwood Energy Income Fund)

ASTON HILL ADVANTAGE VIP INCOME FD (ON)
Name changed to LOGiQ Advantage VIP Income Fund 05/12/2017
LOGiQ Advantage VIP Income Fund name changed to Redwood Advantage Monthly Income Fund 12/20/2017 which merged into Purpose Multi-Asset Income Fund 05/04/2018

ASTON HILL FINL INC (AB)
Name changed to LOGiQ Asset Management Inc. 12/16/2016

ASTON HILL GLOBAL AGRIBUSINESS FD (ON)
Name changed to Aston Hill Global Resource & Infrastructure Fund and Trust Units reclassified as Series X 03/21/2013
Aston Hill Global Resource & Infrastructure Fund merged into Aston Hill Global Resource Fund (New) 11/06/2015

ASTON HILL GLOBAL RESOURCE & INFRASTRUCTURE FUND (ON)
Under plan of merger each Ser. A, Ser. F, Ser. I and Ser. X Unit automatically became (1) Aston Hill Global Resource Fund (New) Ser. A, Ser. F, Ser. I or Ser. X Unit respectively 11/06/2015

ASTON HILL GLOBAL RESOURCE FUND OLD (ON)
Trust terminated 08/20/2012
Each Class A, F and X Unit received net asset value

ASTON HILL GLOBAL URANIUM FD INC (ON)
Under plan of merger each share Common no par automatically became Aston Hill Global Resource & Infrastructure Fund Series X on a net asset basis 04/05/2013
Aston Hill Global Resource & Infrastructure Fund merged into Aston Hill Global Resource Fund (New) 11/06/2015

ASTON HILL OIL & GAS INCOME FD (ON)
Under plan of reorganization each Trust Unit automatically became (0.33333333) Aston Hill Global Resource Fund (New) Ser. X Unit 08/31/2015

ASTON HILL SR GOLD PRODUCERS INCOME CORP (ON)
Under plan of merger each share Class A no par automatically became Aston Hill Global Resource & Infrastructure Fund Series Y on a net asset basis 04/05/2013
Aston Hill Global Resource & Infrastructure Fund merged into Aston Hill Global Resource Fund (New) 11/06/2015

ASTON HILL VIP INCOME FD (ON)
Name changed to LOGiQ VIP Income Fund 05/12/2017
LOGiQ VIP Income Fund name changed to Redwood Monthly Income Fund 12/20/2017 which merged into Purpose Multi-Asset Income Fund 05/04/2018

ASTON RES LTD NEW (BC)
Recapitalized as Consolidated Aston Resources Ltd. 06/13/1996
Each share Common no par exchanged for (0.33333333) share Common no par
(See Consolidated Aston Resources Ltd.)

ASTON RES LTD OLD (BC)
Recapitalized as New Aston Resources Inc. 06/30/1977
Each share Common no par exchanged for (0.2) share Common no par
New Aston Resources Inc. merged into Atlantic Energy Corp. 11/03/1981 which merged into Bowtex Energy (Canada) Corp. 06/01/1987 which name changed to Luscar Oil & Gas Ltd. 10/21/1993 which merged into Encal Energy Ltd. 07/13/1994 which merged into Calpine Canada Holdings Ltd. 04/19/2001 which was exchanged for Calpine Corp. 05/27/2002
(See Calpine Corp.)

ASTONISH LAKE URANIUM MINING CORP. LTD. (ON)
Charter cancelled for failure to pay taxes and file returns 03/16/1976

ASTOR HANDPRINTS INC (NJ)
Stock Dividend - 20% 07/01/1977
Merged into Pantasote Co. 01/04/1978
Each share Common 1¢ par exchanged for $6.15 cash

ASTOR RESTAURANT GROUP INC (NJ)
Name changed to Blimpie International Inc. 04/30/1992
(See Blimpie International Inc.)

ASTORAND MINES LTD. (ON)
Charter revoked for failure to file reports and pay taxes 07/00/1951

ASTORIA FINL CORP (DE)
COM (1¢) 046265 10 4
Common 1¢ par split (2) for (1) by issuance of (1) additional share payable 06/03/1996 to holders of record 05/15/1996
Common 1¢ par split (2) for (1) by issuance of (1) additional share payable 12/03/2001 to holders of record 11/15/2001 Ex date - 12/04/2001
12% Non-Cum Perpetual Preferred Ser. B 1¢ par called for redemption at $27.25 plus $1 accrued dividends on 10/01/2003
Common 1¢ par split (3) for (2) by issuance of (0.5) additional share payable 03/01/2005 to holders of record 02/15/2005 Ex date - 03/02/2005
Merged into Sterling Bancorp 10/02/2017
Each share 6.5% Depositary Preferred Ser. C exchanged for (1) share 6.5% Depositary Preferred Ser. A
Each share Common 1¢ par exchanged for (0.875) share Common 1¢ par

ASTORIA INC (DE)
Recapitalized as Trans-Ad International, Inc. 07/27/1990
Each share Common $0.001 par exchanged for (0.05) share Common 2¢ par

ASTORIA QUEBEC MINES, LTD. (QC)
Recapitalized as Consolidated Astoria Mines Ltd. 09/28/1948
Each share Capital Stock $1 par exchanged for (0.2) share Capital Stock $1 par
Consolidated Astoria Mines, Ltd. recapitalized as Canadian Astoria Minerals Ltd. 06/30/1955 which recapitalized as Cam Mines Ltd. 12/02/1963 which recapitalized as Energy & Resources (Cam) Ltd./Energy & Resources (Cam) Ltee. 01/21/1980 which name changed to ERG Resources Inc. 10/09/1986
(See ERG Resources Inc.)

ASTORIA ROUYN MINES LTD.
Succeeded by Astoria Quebec Mines Ltd. 00/00/1938
Each share Capital Stock $1 par exchanged for (0.5) share Capital Stock $1 par
Astoria Quebec Mines Ltd. recapitalized as Consolidated Astoria Mines Ltd. 09/28/1948 which recapitalized as Canadian Astoria Minerals Ltd. 06/30/1955 which recapitalized as Cam Mines Ltd. 12/02/1963 which recapitalized as Energy & Resources (Cam) Ltd./Energy & Resources (Cam) Ltee. 01/21/1980 which name changed to ERG Resources Inc. 0/09/1986
(See ERG Resources Inc.)

ASTOUND INC (ON)
Merged into Genesys S.A. 03/27/2001
Each share Common no par exchanged for (1.61) Sponsored ADR's for Ordinary
(See Genesys S.A.)

ASTRA AB (SWEDEN)
Merged into AstraZeneca PLC 04/06/1999
Each Sponsored ADR for A Shares exchanged for (0.5045) Sponsored ADR for Ordinary
Each Sponsored ADR for B Shares exchanged for (0.5045) Sponsored ADR for Ordinary
Stock Dividend - 166.666666% payable 05/29/1997 to holders of record 05/28/1997

ASTRA CORP (MA)
Common no par changed to 10¢ par 06/24/1968
Stock Dividend - 10% 09/10/1968
Involuntarily dissolved for failure to file reports 08/31/1998

ASTRA FIN LTD (BERMUDA)
Series 1 Preferred called for redemption at $25 on 01/03/1998

ASTRA HLDGS PLC (UNITED KINGDOM)
ADR agreement terminated 12/31/1990
Details not available

ASTRA OIL & GAS CORP (DE)
Name changed to KGA Industries, Inc. 04/12/1972
(See KGA Industries, Inc.)

ASTRA RES LTD (BC)
Struck off register and declared dissolved for failure to file annual returns 11/18/1983

ASTRA VENTURES INC (NV)
Name changed to CEFC Global Strategic Holdings, Inc. 12/10/2013

ASTRABRUN MINES LTD (ON)
Charter cancelled and declared dissolved for failure to file reports and pay fees 03/17/1976

ASTRADYNE COMPUTER INDS INC (DE)
Charter cancelled and declared inoperative and void for non-payment of taxes 03/01/1990

ASTRAL BELLEVUE PATHE LTD. (ON)
Name changed to Astral Bellevue Pathe Inc. 01/28/1981
Astral Bellevue Pathe Inc. name changed to Astral Inc. 11/26/1990 which name changed to Astral Communications Inc. 09/04/1992 which name changed to Astral Media Inc. 02/25/2000

ASTRAL COMMUNICATIONS LTD (ON)
Merged into Astral Bellevue Pathe Ltd. 11/17/1973
Each share Common no par exchanged for (1) share Common no par
Astral Bellevue Pathe Ltd. name changed to Astral Bellevue Pathe Inc. 01/28/1981 which name changed to Astral Inc. 11/26/1990 which name changed to Astral Communications Inc. 09/04/1992 which name changed to Astral Media Inc. 02/25/2000
(See Astral Media Inc.)

ASTRAL INDUSTRIES, INC. (CO)
Name changed to Pace Industries, Inc. (CO) 02/27/1969
Pace Industries, Inc. (CO) reincorporated in Delaware 05/29/1969
(See Pace Industries, Inc. (DE))

ASTRAL MEDIA INC (ON)
Name changed 11/26/1990
Name changed 09/04/1992
Name changed 02/25/2000
Each share Common no par exchanged for (0.5) share Class A no par and (0.5) share Conv. Class B no par 01/16/1984
Name changed from Astral Bellevue Pathe Inc. to Astral Inc. 11/26/1990
Name changed from Astral Inc. to Astral Communications Inc. 09/04/1992
Name changed from Astral Communications Inc. to Astral Media Inc. 02/25/2000
Class A no par split (2) for (1) by issuance of (1) additional share payable 04/11/2002 to holders of record 04/11/2002
Class B no par split (2) for (1) by issuance of (1) additional share payable 04/11/2002 to holders of record 04/11/2002
Acquired by BCE Inc. 07/09/2013
Each share Class A Common no par exchanged for $50 cash
Each share Class B Common no par exchanged for $54.83 cash
Note: Unexchanged certificates will be cancelled and become without value 07/09/2019

ASTRAL MINING & RESOURCES LTD. (ON)
Recapitalized as New Astral Mining & Resources Ltd. 10/00/1962
Each share Capital Stock no par exchanged for (0.1) share Capital Stock no par
(See New Astral Mining & Resources Ltd.)

ASTRAL MNG CORP (BC)
Each share old Common no par exchanged for (0.25) share new Common no par 01/17/2006
Each share new Common no par exchanged again for (0.1) share new Common no par 03/26/2009

Merged into Orex Minerals Inc. (Old) 02/12/2013
Each share new Common no par exchanged for (0.0834) share new Common no par
Note: Unexchanged certificates were cancelled and became without value 02/12/2016
Orex Minerals Inc. (Old) reorganized as Orex Minerals Inc. (New) 09/29/2015

ASTRALIS LTD (DE)
Name changed 12/10/2001
Name and state of incorporation changed from Astralis Pharmaceuticals, Ltd. (CO) to Astralis, Ltd. (DE) 12/10/2001
SEC revoked common stock registration 10/05/2011

ASTRATA GROUP INC (NV)
Plan of reorganization under Chapter 11 Federal Bankruptcy proceedings effective 12/30/2009
No stockholders' equity

ASTREX INC (NY)
Common 50¢ par changed to $0.33333333 and (0.5) additional share issued 01/12/1962
Common $0.33333333 par changed to $0.16666666 par and (1) additional share issued 09/24/1980
Plan of reorganization under Chapter 11 Federal Bankruptcy Code effective 03/31/1992
Each share Common $0.16666666 par exchanged for (0.126) share Common 1¢ par
Note: Unexchanged certificates were cancelled and deemed without value 10/01/1993
Each share new Common 1¢ par received distribution of (0.33333333) share Non-Transferable Conv. Preferred Ser. B payable 07/17/2000 to holders of record 07/07/2000
Reorganized under the laws of Delaware as newAX, Inc. 09/06/2006
Each share new Common 1¢ par exchanged for (0.00016666) share Common 1¢ par

ASTRIDON DEV CORP (BC)
Struck off register and declared dissolved for failure to file returns 03/25/1994

ASTRIS ENERGI INC (AB)
Name changed to Carthew Bay Technologies Inc. 08/22/2007

ASTRIX NETWORKS INC (AB)
Name changed to Memex Inc. 07/22/2015

ASTRO CIRCUIT CORP (MA)
Name changed to Astro Technology Corp. 06/19/1969
Astro Technology Corp. merged into Eastern Air Devices, Inc. 10/25/1972 which name changed to Electro Audio Dynamics, Inc. 12/19/1974
(See Electro Audio Dynamics, Inc.)

ASTRO CTLS INC (DE)
Merged into Golconda Corp. 09/15/1970
Each share $1 Conv. Preferred $1 par exchanged for (1) share Conv. Preferred $1 par
Each share Common no par exchanged for (1.5) shares Common no par
Golconda Corp. reincorporated in Delaware as Rego Co. 06/17/1977 which name changed to Rego Group, Inc. 02/07/1978
(See Rego Group, Inc.)

ASTRO DRILLING CO (OK)
Name changed to Astro Communications, Inc. 04/16/1991

ASTRO ENTERPRISES INC (UT)
Recapitalized as Prime Air, Inc. (UT) 07/05/1994
Each share Common $0.001 par exchanged for (0.01) share Common $0.001 par
Prime Air, Inc. (UT) reincorporated in Delaware 11/10/1996 which reincorporated in Nevada 11/26/1997
(See Prime Air, Inc.)

ASTRO MED INC NEW (RI)
Common 5¢ par split (3) for (2) by issuance of (0.5) additional share 08/15/1988
Common 5¢ par split (3) for (2) by issuance of (0.5) additional share 05/15/1992
Common 5¢ par split (5) for (4) by issuance of (0.25) additional share payable 06/30/2006 to holders of record 06/16/2006 Ex date - 07/03/2006
Stock Dividend - 10% payable 05/26/2004 to holders of record 05/04/2004
Name changed to AstroNova, Inc. 05/26/2016

ASTRO MED INC OLD (RI)
Under plan of merger each share Common 5¢ par automatically became (1) share Astro-Med, Inc. (New) Common 5¢ par 01/31/1985
Astro-Med, Inc. (New) name changed to AstroNova, Inc. 05/26/2016

ASTRO MNG NL (AUSTRALIA)
ADR agreement terminated 02/03/2012
No ADR's remain outstanding

ASTRO OIL CORP. (DE)
No longer in existence having become inoperative and void for non-payment of taxes 04/01/1965

ASTRO-SCIENCE CORP. (CA)
Completely liquidated 06/30/1967
Each share Common $1 par exchanged for first and final distribution of (0.25) share Tracor, Inc. (TX) Common $0.33333333 par
Tracor, Inc. (TX) reincorporated in Delaware 06/20/1973
(See Tracor, Inc. (DE))

ASTRO SCIENCES CORP (CA)
Name changed to Chatcom Inc. 02/23/1996
Chatcom Inc. recapitalized as Southern Energy Co. Inc. (CA) 11/19/2007 which reincorporated in Nevada 12/13/2007
(See Southern Energy Co. Inc.)

ASTRO SPACE CORP (NV)
Name changed to Danmont Corp. (NV) 05/14/1970
Danmont Corp. (NV) reorganized in Delaware 04/27/1972
(See Danmont Corp. (NV))

ASTRO STREAM CORP (DE)
Each share old Common $0.001 par exchanged for (0.00333333) share new Common $0.001 par 03/05/1990
Name changed to Aristo International Corp. 05/03/1995
Aristo International Corp. name changed to Playnet Technologies, Inc. 11/19/1996
(See Playnet Technologies, Inc.)

ASTRO TECHNOLOGY CORP (MA)
Merged into Eastern Air Devices, Inc. 10/25/1972
Each share Common 10¢ par exchanged for (0.16666666) share Common $1 par
Eastern Air Devices, Inc. name changed to Electro Audio Dynamics, Inc. 12/19/1974
(See Electro Audio Dynamics, Inc.)

ASTROCOM CORP (MN)
Common 10¢ par split (3) for (2) by issuance of (0.5) additional share 03/15/1984
Plan of reorganization under Chapter 11 Federal Bankruptcy Code effective 09/29/2004
No stockholders' equity

ASTRODATA INC (CA)
Capital Stock no par reclassified as old Common no par and (1) additional share issued 11/10/1966
Each share old Common no par exchanged for (0.1) share new Common no par 08/17/1972
Name changed to Adacorp, Inc. (CA) 08/14/1978
Adacorp, Inc. (CA) reincorporated in Delaware 01/06/1987
(See Adacorp, Inc.)

ASTRODINE FOOD SYS INC (NY)
Name changed to National Communications Group Inc. 10/19/1970
National Communications Group Inc. name changed to Schulman Coin & Mint Inc. 04/09/1971
(See Schulman Coin & Mint Inc.)

ASTRON CORP. (NJ)
Merged into Renwell Industries, Inc. 11/26/1962
Each share 4% Preferred $10 par exchanged for (1.5) shares Common 1¢ par
Each share Common 10¢ par exchanged for (0.11111111) share Common 1¢ par
(See Renwell Industries, Inc.)

ASTRON FD INC (WA)
Capital Stock $1 par changed to $0.33333333 par and (2) additional shares issued 07/18/1969
Liquidation completed
Each share Capital Stock $0.33333333 par received initial distribution of $2.55 cash 06/01/1974
Each share Capital Stock $0.33333333 par received second distribution of $0.80 cash 12/21/1976
Each share Capital Stock $0.33333333 par received third and final distribution of $0.0189 cash 12/28/1978

ASTRON INDL ASSOC INC (FL)
Declared dissolved and charter cancelled for non-payment of taxes 06/28/1971

ASTRON INNOVATIONS INC (UT)
Name changed to Astron Energy Co., Inc. 07/13/1977

ASTRON RES CORP (YT)
Reincorporated under the laws of British Columbia as Nevada Copper Corp. 11/16/2006

ASTRONAUTICS ENGINEERING CORP. (FL)
Declared bankrupt 00/00/1960
Stockholders' equity unlikely

ASTRONETIC RESEARCH, INC. (NH)
Charter revoked for failure to file reports and pay fees 07/01/1965

ASTROP FAMILY OF FUNDS TRUST (MA)
Trust terminated 05/19/1988
Each Cash Reserve Fund Share of Bene. Int. received net asset value
Each Emerging Growth Fund Share of Bene. Int. received net asset value
Each Established Growth Fund Share of Bene. Int. received net asset value
Each Global Growth Fund Share of Bene. Int. received net asset value
Each High Yield Bond Fund Share of Bene. Int. received net asset value
EachNew South Fund Share of Bene. Int. received net asset value
Each OTC Fund Share of Bene. Int. received net asset value
Each U.S. Government Securities Fund Share of Bene. received net asset value
Each Utility Fund Share of Bene. Int. received net asset value

ASTROPHYSICS RESH CORP (CA)
Merged into EG&G, Inc. 11/01/1988
Each share Common 10¢ par exchanged for (0.2376158) share Common $1 par
EG&G, Inc. name changed to PerkinElmer, Inc. 10/25/1999

ASTROPOWER INC (DE)
Common 1¢ par split (3) for (2) by issuance of (0.5) additional share payable 05/31/2002 to holders of record 05/20/2002 Ex date - 06/03/2002
Plan of reorganization under Chapter 11 Federal Bankruptcy Code effective 12/27/2004
No stockholders' equity

ASTROSONICS, INC. (NY)
Dissolved 02/03/1970
No stockholders' equity

ASTROSYSTEMS INC (NY)
Common 10¢ par changed to 5¢ par and (1) additional share issued 01/24/1969
Under plan of partial liquidation each share Common 5¢ par exchanged for (1) share Common 3¢ par and $2.14 cash 12/14/1977
Common 3¢ par changed to 10¢ par and (3) additional shares issued 12/19/1980
Liquidation completed
Each share Common 10¢ par received initial distribution of $5 cash payable 09/08/1997 to holders of record 08/15/1997
Each share Common 10¢ par exchanged for second and final distribution of $0.845 cash 08/11/2003

ASTROSYSTEMS INTERNATIONAL INC (DE)
Name changed 04/30/1962
Reincorporated 09/14/1967
Name changed from Astrosystems, Inc. to Astrosystems International, Inc. 04/30/1962
State of incorporation changed from (NJ) to (DE) 09/14/1967
Name changed to Fairfield Technology Corp. 02/28/1969
(See Fairfield Technology Corp.)

ASTROTECH CORP (WA)
Each share old Common no par exchanged for (0.2) share new Common no par 10/16/2017
Reincorporated under the laws of Delaware and new Common no par changed to $0.001 par 12/22/2017

ASTROTECH INTL CORP NEW (DE)
Each share $1.20 Conv. Preferred 10¢ par exchanged for (4.7) shares Common 1¢ par 10/00/1992
Merged into Iteq Inc. 10/28/1997
Each share Common 1¢ par exchanged for (0.93) share Common $0.001 par
(See Iteq Inc.)

ASTROTECH INTL CORP OLD (DE)
Recapitalized as Astrotech International Corp. (New) 08/19/1988
Each share $1.80 Preference 10¢ par exchanged for (1) share $1.20 Conv. Preferred 10¢ par
Each share Common 30¢ par exchanged for (0.01666666) share Common 1¢ par and (0.03333333) Common Stock Purchase Warrant expiring 03/31/1993
Astrotech International Corp. (New) merged into Iteq Inc. 10/28/1997
(See Iteq Inc.)

ASTROTHERM CORP. (DE)
Bankrupt 12/26/1962
Stockholders' equity unlikely

ASTRUM INTL CORP (DE)
Name changed to Samsonite Corp. (New) 07/14/1995
(See Samsonite Corp. (New))

ASTUR GOLD CORP (BC)
Name changed to Black Dragon Gold Corp. 10/14/2016

ASYA KATILIM BANKASI AS (TURKEY)
ADR agreement terminated 04/17/2017
Each Sponsored ADR for Ordinary exchanged for (2) shares Ordinary
Notes: Unexchanged ADR's will be sold and the proceeds, if any, held for claim after 08/08/2017
Turkish Banking Regulation and Supervision Agency cancelled company's permit 07/22/2016 and shares were delisted on local market

ASYMETRIX LEARNING SYS INC (DE)
Name changed to Click2learn.com, Inc. 11/23/1999
Click2learn.com, Inc. name changed to Click2learn, Inc. 05/30/2001 which merged into SumTotal Systems, Inc. 03/19/2004
(See SumTotal Systems, Inc.)

ASYST CORP (UT)
Each share old Common $0.001 par exchanged for (3) shares new Common $0.001 par 12/10/2003
Each share new Common $0.001 par exchanged again for (0.125) share new Common $0.001 par 2/12/2004
Name changed to Amazon Biotech, Inc. 03/10/2004
Each share Common $0.001 par exchanged for (1) share Common $0.001 par

ASYST TECHNOLOGIES INC (CA)
Common no par split (2) for (1) by issuance of (1) additional share payable 08/22/1997 to holders of record 08/01/1997
Common no par split (2) for (1) by issuance of (1) additional share payable 02/04/2000 to holders of record 01/07/2000
Plan of reorganization under Chapter 11 Federal Bankruptcy Code effective 03/05/2010
No stockholders' equity

AT & T LATIN AMER CORP (DE)
Plan of reorganization under Chapter 11 Federal Bankruptcy Code effective 02/25/2004
No stockholders' equity

AT COMM CORP (DE)
Plan of reorganization under Chapter 11 Federal Bankruptcy Code effective 12/31/2002
No stockholders' equity

AT ENTMT INC (DE)
Merged into United Pan-Europe Communications N.V. 08/09/1999
Each share Common 1¢ par exchanged for $19 cash

AT HOME CORP (DE)
Common Ser. A 1¢ par split (2) for (1) by issuance of (1) additional share payable 06/16/1999 to holders of record 05/28/1999
Plan of reorganization under Chapter 11 Federal Bankruptcy Code effective 09/30/2002
No stockholders' equity

AT HOME HLDGS INC (NV)
Name changed to Dover Petroleum Corp. 08/27/2001
(See Dover Petroleum Corp.)

AT PLASTICS INC (ON)
Merged into Acetex Corp. 08/05/2003
Each share Common no par exchanged for (0.16666666) share Common no par
(See Acetex Corp.)

AT PLAY VACATIONS INC (NV)
Name changed to Axiom Holdings, Inc. 11/23/2015

AT POS COM INC (DE)
Merged into Symbol Technologies, Inc. 09/19/2002
Each share Preferred Ser. B exchanged for $0.46 cash
Each share Common $0.001 par exchanged for $0.46 cash

@ROAD INC (DE)
Name changed 07/28/2004
Name changed from At Road, Inc. to @Road, Inc. 07/28/2004
Merged into Trimble Navigation Ltd. (CA) 02/16/2007
Each share Common $0.0001 par exchanged for (0.0447) share Common no par and $5 cash
Trimble Navigation Ltd. (CA) reincorporated in Delaware as Trimble Inc. 10/03/2016

AT TRACK COMMUNICATIONS INC (DE)
Each share old Common 1¢ par exchanged for (0.2) share new Common 1¢ par 06/05/2001
Name changed to Minorplanet Systems USA, Inc. 07/23/2002
Minorplanet Systems USA, Inc. reorganized as Remote Dynamics, Inc. 07/02/2004

AT VENTUREWORKS INC (NV)
Name changed to Underground Solutions, Inc. 01/30/2001
(See Underground Solutions, Inc.)

AT&T CDA INC NEW (CANADA)
Name changed to Allstream Inc. 06/18/2003
Allstream Inc. acquired by Manitoba Telecom Services Inc. 06/04/2004 which merged into BCE Inc. 03/20/2017

AT&T CAP CORP (DE)
Merged into Hercules Ltd. 10/01/1996
Each share Common 1¢ par exchanged for $45 cash

AT&T WIRELESS SVCS INC (DE)
Acquired by Cingular Wireless LLC 10/26/2004
Each share Common 1¢ par exchanged for $15 cash

ATA / RESH PROFUTURES DIVERSIFIED FD L P (DE)
Name changed to ProFutures Diversified Fund, L.P. 06/01/2000
(See ProFutures Diversified Fund, L.P.)

ATA HLDGS CORP (IN)
Plan of reorganization under Chapter 11 Federal Bankruptcy Code effective 02/28/2006
No stockholders' equity

ATACAMA MINERALS CORP (BC)
Name changed to Sirocco Mining Inc. 01/30/2012
Sirocco Mining Inc. merged into RB Energy Inc. 02/05/2014

ATACAMA PAC GOLD CORP (CANADA)
Merged into Rio2 Ltd. (New) 07/27/2018
Each share Common no par exchanged for (0.6601) share Common no par
Note: Unexchanged certificates will be cancelled and become without value 07/27/2024

ATACAMA RES LTD (BC)
Merged into KAP Resources Ltd. 11/14/1990
Each share Common no par exchanged for (0.75) share Common no par
(See KAP Resources Ltd.)

ATACRA LIQUIDATING CORP. (CA)
Liquidation completed
Each share $1.15 Conv. Preferred Ser. E $5 par exchanged for first and final distribution of $42 cash 06/07/1982
Each share $2 Conv. Preferred Ser. C $5 par exchanged for first and final distribution of $60 cash 06/07/1982
Each share $2.16 Conv. Preferred Ser. A $5 par exchanged for first and final distribution of $28.50 cash 06/07/1982
Each share Common 25¢ par exchanged for initial distribution of $37.50 cash 06/07/1982
Each share Common 25¢ par received second distribution of $0.65 cash 09/23/1983
Each share Common 25¢ par received third distribution of $27.50 cash 05/31/1988
Each share Common 25¢ par received fourth and final distribution of $1.33 cash 11/07/1988
Note: An additional $1.50 cash per share was distributed in settlement of litigation 07/00/1989

ATALANTA CORP (NY)
Under plan of merger each share Common $1 par exchanged for $9.50 cash 06/09/1980

ATALANTA SOSNOFF CAP CORP (DE)
Merged into Atalanta Acquisition Co. 07/14/2003
Each share Common 1¢ par exchanged for $13.95 cash

ATAPA MINERALS LTD (CANADA)
Dissolved for non-compliance 08/15/2006

ATARI CORP (NV)
Common 1¢ par split (2) for (1) by issuance of (1) additional share 06/19/1987
Merged into JTS Corp. 07/30/1996
Each share Common 1¢ par exchanged for (1) share Common 1¢ par
(See JTS Corp.)

ATARI INC (DE)
Each share Common 1¢ par exchanged for (0.1) share Common 10¢ par 01/04/2007
Merged into Infogrames Entertainment S.A. 10/08/2008
Each share Common 10¢ par exchanged for $1.68 cash

ATC CAP GROUP LTD (DE)
Each share Common $0.0001 par exchanged for (0.5) share Common $0.0002 par 03/26/1996
Name changed to Cyphercom Solutions Inc. 08/06/1996

ATC COMMUNICATIONS GROUP INC (DE)
Name changed to Aegis Communications Group, Inc. 07/09/1998
(See Aegis Communications Group, Inc.)

ATC GROUP SVCS INC (DE)
Name changed 10/15/1996
Name changed from ATC Environmental Inc. to ATC Group Services Inc. 10/15/1996
Merged into WPG Corporate Development Associates V, L.P. 02/05/1998
Each share Common 1¢ par exchanged for $12 cash

ATC HEALTHCARE INC (DE)
SEC revoked common stock registration 02/09/2011

ATC-ONLANE INC (AZ)
Name changed to Openlane, Inc. 11/25/2008
(See Openlane, Inc.)

ATC PETE SVCS INTL INC (AB)
Name changed 09/25/2001
Name changed from ATC Environmental Group Inc. to ATC Petroleum Services International Inc. 09/25/2001
Recapitalized as Tiger Pacific Mining Corp. (AB) 02/03/2004

Each share Common no par exchanged for (0.11111111) share Common no par
Tiger Pacific Mining Corp. (AB) reincorporated in British Columbia 07/29/2004 which recapitalized as Chantrell Ventures Corp. 08/31/2010

ATC TECHNOLOGIES CORP (BC)
Delisted from Toronto Venture Stock Exchange 06/05/2002

ATC TECHNOLOGY CORP (DE)
Acquired by GENCO Distribution System, Inc. 10/22/2010
Each share Common 1¢ par exchanged for $25 cash

ATC II INC (DE)
Name changed 07/27/1993
Name changed from ATC, Inc. to ATC II, Inc. 07/27/1993
Each share old Common 1¢ par exchanged for (0.025) share new Common 1¢ par 08/25/1994
SEC revoked common stock registration 08/24/2004

ATCAN CAP CORP (CANADA)
Dissolved for non-compliance 06/17/2005

ATCHISON & EASTERN BRIDGE CO.
Liquidated 00/00/1945
Details not available

ATCHISON CASTING CORP (KS)
Reincorporated 01/01/1995
State of incorporation changed from (DE) to (KS) 01/01/1995
Chapter 11 bankruptcy proceedings converted to Chapter 7 on 01/22/2004
Stockholders' equity unlikely

ATCHISON TOPEKA & SANTA FE RY CO (KS)
Each share 5% Preferred $100 par or Common $100 par exchanged for (2) shares 5% Preferred $50 par or Common $50 par respectively 08/01/1951
5% Preferred $50 par and Common $50 par changed to $10 par and (4) additional shares issued respectively 08/01/1956
Merged into Santa Fe Industries, Inc. 03/24/1970
Each share 5% Preferred $10 par exchanged for (1) share 50¢ Conv. Preferred no par
Each share Common $10 par exchanged for (1) share Common $10 par
Santa Fe Industries, Inc. merged into Santa Fe Southern Pacific Corp. 12/23/1983 which name changed to Santa Fe Pacific Corp. 04/25/1989 which merged into Burlington Northern Santa Fe Corp. 09/22/1995
(See Burlington Northern Santa Fe Corp.)

ATCO CHEM INDL PRODS INC (ME)
Name changed to Atco Industries, Inc. 08/16/1973
(See Atco Industries, Inc.)

ATCO INDS INC (ME)
Charter suspended for failure to maintain a registered agent 04/08/1988

ATCO INDUSTRIES LTD. (AB)
Common no par reclassified as Conv. Class A no par 12/10/1973
Conv. Class A no par and Conv. Class B no par split (2) for (1) by issuance of (1) additional share respectively 08/27/1975
Name changed to ATCO Ltd. 11/08/1978

ATCO LTD (AB)
11.5% Conv. Jr. Preferred Ser. 2 no par called for redemption 01/17/1986
5.75% Preferred Ser. 3 called for redemption at $25.50 plus

$0.086644 accrued dividends on 03/23/2010
(Additional Information in Active)

ATCO NATL BK (ATCO, NJ)
Under plan of reorganization each share $2.40 Conv. Preferred and Common $5 par automatically became an undetermined amount of Atcorp Inc. Common $5 par 12/31/1988
Atcorp Inc. merged into Susquehanna Bancshares, Inc. 02/28/1997 which merged into BB&T Corp. 08/01/2015

ATCOR INC (DE)
Merged into Tyco Laboratories, Inc. 10/07/1987
Each share Common 10¢ par exchanged for $23 cash

ATCOR RES LTD (CANADA)
Merged into Forest Oil Corp. 01/16/1996
Each share Non-Vtg. Class A no par exchanged for $4.88 cash
Each share Class B no par exchanged for $4.88 cash
Note: Unexchanged certificates were cancelled and became without value 01/31/2002

ATCORP INC (NJ)
Merged into Susquehanna Bancshares, Inc. 02/28/1997
Each share Common $5 par exchanged for (1) share Common $2 par
Susquehanna Bancshares, Inc. merged into BB&T Corp. 08/01/2015

ATE ENTERPRISES INC (DE)
Completely liquidated 12/08/1986
Each share Common $1 par exchanged for first and final distribution of $6.50 cash

ATEBA MINES INC (ON)
Recapitalized as Ateba Technology & Environmental Inc. 03/08/2001
Each share Common no par exchanged for (0.33333333) share Common no par
Ateba Technology & Environmental Inc. recapitalized as Ateba Resources Inc. 10/16/2008

ATEBA TECHNOLOGY & ENVIRONMENTAL INC (ON)
Recapitalized as Ateba Resources Inc. 10/16/2008
Each share Common no par exchanged for (0.2) share Common no par

ATEC GROUP INC (DE)
Each share old Common 1¢ par exchanged for (0.2) share new Common 1¢ par 11/19/1997
Name changed to Interpharm Holdings, Inc. 06/02/2003
(See Interpharm Holdings, Inc.)

ATECH ENTERPRISES, INC. (NY)
Ceased operations 00/00/1975
No stockholders' equity

ATEK INDS INC (DE)
Adjudicated bankrupt 02/01/1973
Stockholders' equity unlikely

ATEK METALS CTR INC (OH)
Merged into Rolled Alloys, Inc. 10/20/1993
Each share Common no par exchanged for $4.51 cash

ATEL CASH DISTRIBUTION FUND (CA)
Partnership terminated
Each Unit of Ltd. Partnership received final distribution of $8.50 cash 00/00/1997
Note: Prior distributions paid quarterly amounted to $53.24 per Unit 00/00/1993; $49.76 00/00/1994; $15.05 00/00/1995; $10 00/00/1996; and $7.50 00/00/1997

ATEL CASH DISTRIBUTION FUND II (CA)
Partnership terminated
Each Unit of Ltd. Partnership received final distribution of $45 cash 12/00/1998
Note: Prior distributions paid quarterly amounted to $43.75 per Unit 00/00/1995; $26 00/00/1996; $15 00/00/1997 and $22.50 00/00/1998

ATF BK KAZAKSTAN JSC (KAZAKHSTAN)
GDR agreement terminated 08/30/2017
Each Sponsored Reg. S GDR for Ordinary exchanged for (1) share Ordinary
Note: Unexchanged GDR's will be sold and the proceeds, if any, held for claim after 09/03/2018

ATG INC (CA)
Assets sold for the benefit of creditors 12/31/2002
No stockholders' equity

ATHABASCA COLUMBIA RES LTD (AB)
Class A Common no par reclassified as Common no par 12/20/1968
Class B Common no par reclassified as 12/20/1968
Name changed to Taro Industries Ltd. 12/27/1978
Taro Industries Ltd. merged into EVI, Inc. 01/15/1998 which name changed to EVI Weatherford, Inc. 05/27/1998 which name changed to Weatherford International Inc. (New) (DE) 09/21/1998 which reincorporated in Bermuda as Weatherford International Ltd. 06/26/2002 which reincorporated in Switzerland 02/25/2009 which reincorporated in Ireland as Weatherford International PLC 06/18/2014

ATHABASCA EXPLORATION & MINING LTD. (AB)
Struck off register 12/31/1981

ATHABASCA NUCLEAR CORP (BC)
Reincorporated 11/10/2015
Place of incorporation changed from (AB) to (BC) 11/10/2015
Name changed to Clean Commodities Corp. 06/10/2016

ATHABASCA OIL SANDS CORP (AB)
Name changed to Athabasca Oil Corp. 05/15/2012

ATHABASCA OIL SANDS TR (AB)
Under plan of merger name changed to Canadian Oil Sands Trust (New) 07/05/2001
Canadian Oil Sands Trust (New) reorganized as Canadian Oil Sands Ltd. 01/06/2011 which merged into Suncor Energy Inc. (New) 03/23/2016

ATHABASCA POTASH INC (SK)
Acquired by BHP Billiton Canada Inc. 03/23/2010
Each share Common no par exchanged for $8.35 cash
Note: Unexchanged certificates were cancelled and became without value 03/23/2016

ATHABASCA URANIUM INC (BC)
Each share old Common no par exchanged for (0.1) share new Common no par 09/19/2014
Name changed to Atom Energy Inc. 11/18/2014

ATHABASCA URANIUM MINES LTD. (DE)
Completely liquidated 08/18/1958
Each share Common 10¢ par exchanged for first and final distribution of (1) share Pippin Mining & Uranium Corp. Ltd. Capital Stock no par
(See Pippin Mining & Uranium Corp. Ltd.)

ATHABASKA GOLD RES LTD (BC)
Delisted from Toronto Stock Exchange 08/31/2001

ATHABASKA GOLDFIELDS & URANIUM LTD. (ON)
Charter cancelled and declared dissolved for default in filing returns 12/02/1970

ATHANOR GROUP INC (CA)
Each share old Common 1¢ par exchanged for (1/3) share new Common 1¢ par to reflect a (1) for (240) reverse split followed by a (80) for (1) forward split 09/11/1989
Each share new Common 1¢ par exchanged again for (0.5) share new Common 1¢ par to reflect a (1) for (800) reverse split followed by a (400) for (1) forward split 01/31/2000
Note: Holders of (799) shares or fewer received $2.51 cash per share
Company terminated common stock registration and is no longer public as of 06/12/2002

ATHENA COMMUNICATIONS CORP (DE)
Merged into Tele-Communications, Inc. 08/31/1983
Each share Common $1 par exchanged for $12.50 cash

ATHENA GOLD CORP (BC)
Acquired by Miramar Mining Corp. 01/30/1995
Each share Common no par exchanged for (0.35714285) share Common no par
(See Miramar Mining Corp.)

ATHENA INDS INC (UT)
Recapitalized as Q-Tronics, Inc. 04/17/1982
Each share Common $0.005 par exchanged for (2) shares Common $0.001 par
(See Q-Tronics, Inc.)

ATHENA MED CORP (NV)
Name changed to A Fem Medical Corp. 07/10/1997
A Fem Medical Corp. name changed to Quantrx Biomedical Corp. 12/23/2005

ATHENA MINES LTD (BC)
Recapitalized as Saturn Energy & Resources Ltd. 08/13/1975
Each share Common 50¢ par exchanged for (0.25) share Common no par
(See Saturn Energy & Resources Ltd.)

ATHENA NEUROSCIENCES INC (DE)
Merged into Elan Corp., PLC 07/01/1996
Each share Common 1¢ par exchanged for (0.2956) Sponsored ADR for Ordinary
Elan Corp., PLC merged into Perrigo Co. PLC 12/18/2013

ATHENA VENTURES INC (NV)
Each share old Common $0.001 par exchanged for (0.01) share new Common $0.001 par 10/21/1993
Name changed to Channel I Ltd. 11/15/1993
Channel I Ltd. name changed to Channel I Inc. 03/02/1995 which name changed to WaveRider Communications Inc. 05/27/1997 which merged into Wave Wireless Corp. 03/30/2006
(See Wave Wireless Corp.)

ATHENS BANCSHARES CORP (TN)
Merged into CapStar Financial Holdings, Inc. 10/01/2018
Each share Common 1¢ par exchanged for (2.864) shares Common $1 par

ATHENS FED SVGS BK (ATHENS, GA)
Common $1 par split (3) for (2) by

issuance of (0.5) additional share 08/29/1985
Acquired by Bankers First Corp. 09/02/1986
Each share Common $1 par exchanged for (1.39) shares Common 1¢ par
Bankers First Corp. merged into SouthTrust Corp. 03/15/1996 which merged into Wachovia Corp. (Ctfs. dated after 09/01/2001) 11/01/2004 which merged into Wells Fargo & Co. (New) 12/31/2008

ATHENS RAILWAY & ELECTRIC CO.
Merged into Georgia Power Co. 00/00/1927
Details not available

ATHEROGENICS INC (GA)
Plan of reorganization under Chapter 11 Federal Bankruptcy proceedings effective 06/22/2009
No stockholders' equity

ATHERON INC (NV)
Name changed to New America Energy Corp. 12/01/2010

ATHEROS COMMUNICATIONS INC (DE)
Acquired by Qualcomm Inc. 05/24/2011
Each share Common $0.0005 par exchanged for $45 cash

ATHEY PRODS CORP (IL)
Capital Stock $4 par changed to $2 par and (1) additional share issued 12/31/1963
Capital Stock $2 par split (5) for (4) by issuance of (0.25) additional share 03/07/1973
Capital Stock $2 par split (2) for (1) by issuance of (1) additional share 04/26/1985
Capital Stock $2 par split (3) for (2) by issuance of (0.5) additional share 07/01/1986
Stock Dividends - 20% 01/16/1981; 20% 01/11/1982; 10% 01/13/1986; 10% 07/01/1987; 10% 01/15/1988; 10% 07/15/1988; 10% 07/21/1989
Plan of reorganization under Chapter 11 Federal Bankruptcy Code effective 12/05/2001
Each share Common $2 par received initial distribution of $0.25 cash payable 05/21/2002 to holders of record 05/15/2002
Each share Common $2 par received second and final distribution of $0.025487 cash payable 04/22/2003 to holders of record 03/31/2003
Note: Certificates were not required to be surrendered and are without value

ATHEY TRUSS WHEEL CO. (IL)
Name changed to Athey Products Corp. 09/17/1945
(See Athey Products Corp.)

ATHLODGE URANIUM MINES LTD. (ON)
Charter revoked for failure to file reports and pay fees 08/03/1964

ATHLON ENERGY INC (DE)
Acquired by Encana Corp. 11/13/2014
Each share Common 1¢ par exchanged for $58.50 cash

ATHLONE ENERGY LTD (BC)
Recapitalized 05/04/1999
Name changed 02/14/2005
Recapitalized from Athlone Resources Ltd. to Athlone Minerals Ltd. 05/04/1999
Each share Common no par exchanged for (0.1) share Common no par
Name changed from Athlone Minerals Ltd. to Athlone Energy Ltd. 02/14/2005
Acquired by Daylight Resources Trust 09/17/2008
Each share Common no par exchanged for $0.85 cash

ATHLONE INDS INC (DE)
Common 10¢ par split (3) for (1) by issuance of (2) additional shares 09/24/1974
Common 10¢ par split (2) for (1) by issuance of (1) additional share 04/24/1989
Merged into Allegheny Ludlum Corp. 11/10/1993
Each share Common 10¢ par exchanged for (0.84726) share Common 10¢ par
Allegheny Ludlum Corp. merged into Allegheny Teledyne Inc. 08/15/1996 which name changed to Allegheny Technolgies Inc. 11/29/1999

ATHOL INDS INC (NY)
Name changed to A.R.C. Toys Inc. 01/01/1990
(See A.R.C. Toys Inc.)

ATHONA MINES (1937) LTD. (ON)
Recapitalized as New Athona Mines Ltd. 11/00/1954
Each share Capital Stock no par exchanged for (0.25) share Capital Stock no par
New Athona Mines Ltd. recapitalized as Lakota Resources Inc. 11/21/1994 which recapitalized as Tembo Gold Corp. 09/26/2011

ATHONA MINES LTD. (ON)
Recapitalized as Athona Mines (1937) Ltd. 00/00/1937
Each share Capital Stock no par exchanged for (0.6) share Capital Stock no par
Athona Mines (1937) Ltd. recapitalized as New Athona Mines Ltd. 11/00/1954 which recapitalized as Lakota Resources Inc. 11/21/1994 which recapitalized as Tembo Gold Corp. 09/26/2011

ATI, INC. (NY)
Name changed to ATI Pharmaceuticals Inc. 12/29/1987
ATI Pharmaceuticals Inc. name changed to Armstrong Pharmaceuticals Inc. 05/15/1991 which merged into Medeva PLC 01/14/1993 which merged into Celltech Group PLC 01/26/2000
(See Celltech Group PLC)

ATI CORP (ON)
Name changed to Prairie Capital Inc. (ON) 06/30/1999
Prairie Capital Inc. (ON) reorganized in Canada as Continental (CBOC) Corp. 08/30/2002 which name changed to Stonington Capital Corp. 06/22/2004 which merged into Pyxis Capital Inc. 02/27/2006
(See Pyxis Capital Inc.)

ATI INC (DE)
Name changed to WorldWide Demolition Derby Production Inc. 08/22/2001

ATI INC (UT)
Name changed to XRF Inc. 07/11/1991
XRF Inc. name changed to NDS Software, Inc. 07/26/1994 which name changed to HomeSeekers.com Inc. 07/01/1998
(See HomeSeekers.com Inc.)

ATI MED INC (CA)
Common no par changed to $0.001 par 01/08/1990
Acquired by Mediq Inc. 06/01/1992
Each share Common $0.001 par exchanged for $4 cash

ATI MODULAR TECHNOLOGY CORP (NV)
Recapitalized as AmericaTowne Holdings, Inc. 03/08/2018
Each share Common $0.001 par exchanged for (0.02) share Common $0.001 par

ATI NETWORKS INC (CO)
Administratively dissolved 04/01/2003

ATI PHARMACEUTICALS INC (NY)
Name changed to Armstrong Pharmaceuticals Inc. 05/15/1991
Armstrong Pharmaceuticals Inc. merged into Medeva PLC 01/14/1993 which merged into Celltech Group PLC 01/26/2000
(See Celltech Group PLC)

ATI TECHNOLOGIES INC (CANADA)
Reincorporated 01/31/2005
Common no par split (4) for (1) by issuance of (3) additional shares payable 04/28/1998 to holders of record 04/23/1998 Ex date - 04/21/1998
Place of incorporation changed from (ON) to (Canada) 01/31/2005
Merged into Advanced Micro Devices, Inc. 10/25/2006
Each share Common no par exchanged for (0.9596) share Common no par

ATICO FINL CORP (DE)
Ctfs. dated prior to 08/30/1973
Stock Dividend - 10% 12/28/1965
Merged into Pan American Bancshares, Inc. 08/30/1973
Each share Common $1 par exchanged for (1.5) shares Common $1 par
Pan American Bancshares, Inc. name changed to Pan American Banks Inc. 05/01/1981 which merged into NCNB Corp. 12/31/1985 which name changed to NationsBank Corp. 12/31/1991 which reincorporated in Delaware as BankAmerica Corp. (Old) 09/25/1998 which merged into BankAmerica Corp. (New) 09/30/1998 which name changed to Bank of America Corp. 04/28/1999
ATICO FINANCIAL CORP. (DE)
Ctfs. dated after 01/04/1980
Merged into Intercontinental Bank (Miami, FL) 03/30/1991
Each share Common $1 par exchanged for (1) share Common $2 par
Intercontinental Bank (Miami, FL) merged into NationsBank Corp. 12/13/1995 which reincorporated in Delaware as BankAmerica Corp. (Old) 09/25/1998 which merged into BankAmerica Corp. (New) 09/30/1998 which name changed to Bank of America Corp. 04/28/1999

ATICO MTG INVS (MA)
Name changed to South Atlantic Trust (MA) 05/25/1978
South Atlantic Trust (MA) reorganized in Florida as South Atlantic Financial Corp. 08/01/1979 which merged into Stamford Capital Group, Inc. 11/04/1987 which name changed to Independence Holding Co. (New) 09/10/1990

ATIKOKAN RES INC (ON)
Recapitalized as Silvermet Inc. 07/10/2006
Each share Common no par exchanged for (0.2) share Common no par
Silvermet Inc. recapitalized as Global Atomic Corp. 12/27/2017

ATIKWA MINERALS CORP (ON)
Name changed to Atikwa Resources Inc. (ON) 11/18/2009
Atikwa Resources Inc. (ON) reincorporated in Alberta 04/26/2010
(See Atikwa Resources Inc.)

ATIKWA RES INC (AB)
Reincorporated 04/26/2010
Place of incorporation changed from (ON) to (AB) 04/26/2010
Discharged from receivership 06/30/2015
Stockholders' equity unlikely

ATKINS & DURBROW, LTD. (BC)
Each share Preferred no par exchanged for 35¢ principal amount of 2% 30-year Debentures 12/13/1962
Merged into Tatramar Holdings Ltd. 10/19/1990
Each share Common no par exchanged for $2.50 cash

ATKINSON CORP (DE)
Reincorporated 10/06/1971
State of incorporation changed from (WI) to (DE) and Common $5 par changed to $1 par 10/06/1971
Merged into JMN Corp. 01/01/1973
Each share 5% 1st Preferred $100 par exchanged for $102 cash
Each share Common $1 par exchanged for $3 cash

ATKINSON-DEACON-ELLIOTT CO.
Assets reduced to cash and liquidation completed 06/23/1947
Details not available

ATKINSON DREDGING CO., LTD. (BC)
Charter cancelled 00/00/1952

ATKINSON FINANCE CORP. (WI)
Name changed to Atkinson Corp. (WI) 04/20/1962
Atkinson Corp. (WI) reincorporated in Delaware 10/06/1971
(See Atkinson Corp.)

ATKINSON GUY F CO CALIF (DE)
Reincorporated 04/22/1994
State of incorporation changed from (CA) to (DE) 04/22/1994
Plan of reorganization under Chapter 11 Federal Bankruptcy Code effective 04/17/2000
Stockholders' equity unlikely

ATL PRODS INC (DE)
Merged into Quantum Corp. 09/28/1998
Each share Common $0.0001 par exchanged for (1.7554) shares Common 1¢ par

ATL ULTRASOUND INC (WA)
Each share Common 1¢ par received distribution of (0.33333333) share SonoSight, Inc. Common 1¢ par payable 04/06/1998 to holders of record 03/30/1998
Merged into Royal Philips Electronics 10/02/1998
Each share Common 1¢ par exchanged for $50.50 cash

ATLAN TOL INDS INC (RI)
Common 5¢ par split (2) for (1) by issuance of (1) additional share 07/11/1983
Under plan of merger name changed to Astro-Med, Inc. (New) 01/31/1985
Astro-Med, Inc. (New) name changed to AstroNova, Inc. 05/26/2016

ATLANFED BANCORP INC (MD)
Common $1 par split (5) for (4) by issuance of (0.25) additional share 06/25/1993
Stock Dividends - 10% 06/15/1990; 10% 06/17/1991; 15% 06/22/1992
Merged into Susquehanna Bancshares, Inc. 03/31/1995
Each share Common $1 par exchanged for (0.802) share Common $2 par
Susquehanna Bancshares, Inc. merged into BB&T Corp. 08/01/2015

ATLANTA & WEST POINT RR CO (GA)
Each Ctf. of Participation no par exchanged for (1) share Capital Stock $100 par 01/29/1981
Merged into Blue Berry Corp. 03/20/1984
Each share Capital Stock $100 par exchanged for $210 cash

ATLANTA BRAVES INC (DE)
Merged into Atlanta/La Salle Corp. 05/17/1974
Each share Common $1 par exchanged for $24.19 cash

ATLANTA EXPRESS AIRL CORP (DE)
Name changed to Air Transportation Holding Co., Inc. 03/09/1984
Air Transportation Holding Co., Inc name changed to Air T, Inc. 09/30/1999

ATLANTA GAS LT CO (GA)
Common $10 par changed to $5 par and and (1) additional share issued 09/15/1961
Common $5 par split (3) for (2) by issuance of (0.5) additional share 06/22/1964
Common $5 par split (2) for (1) by issuance of (1) additional share 12/01/1986
Common $5 par split (2) for (1) by issuance of (1) additional share 12/01/1995
Under plan of reorganization each share Common $5 par automatically became (1) share AGL Resources Inc. Common $5 par 03/06/1996
4.5% Preferred $100 par called for redemption at $105.25 on 08/15/1997
4.72% Preferred $100 par called for redemption at $103 on 08/15/1997
5% Preferred $100 par called for redemption at $105 on 08/15/1997
7.84% Preferred $100 par called for redemption at $101.96 on 08/15/1997
8.32% Preferred $100 par called for redemption at $102.08 on 08/15/1997
$1.925 Depositary Preferred called for redemption at $25 on 12/01/1997
(See AGL Resources Inc.)

ATLANTA GOLD CORP (BC)
Merged into Twin Gold Corp. 04/04/1997
Each share Common no par exchanged for (1) share Common no par
Twin Gold Corp. name changed to Twin Mining Corp. 03/15/2000 which recapitalized as Atlanta Gold Inc. 03/28/2007

ATLANTA INTL RACEWAY INC (GA)
Acquired by BND, Inc. 10/23/1990
Each share Capital Stock $1 par exchanged for $17.40 cash

ATLANTA LA SALLE CORP (DE)
Liquidation completed
Each share Common $1 par received initial distribution of (0.04) share Columbia General Corp. Common 50¢ par, (0.01) share MCI Communications Corp. Common 10¢ par and $1 cash 11/19/1981
Each share Common $1 par received second distribution of $0.50 cash 01/04/1983
Each share Common $1 par received third and final distribution of $0.66 cash 12/17/1986
Note: Certificates were not required to be surrendered and are without value

ATLANTA MINES LTD (QC)
Merged into Albarmont Mines Corp. 10/12/1971
Each share Capital Stock $1 par exchanged for (0.5) share Common no par
Albarmont Mines Corp. recapitalized as Albarmont (1985) Inc. 07/19/1985
(See Albarmont (1985) Inc.)

ATLANTA MTR LODGES INC (GA)
Completely liquidated 03/07/1969
Each share Common $1 par exchanged for (0.82143) share U.S. Realty Investments Ctfs. of Bene. Int. no par
(See U.S. Realty Investments)

ATLANTA NATL REAL ESTATE TR (MD)
Reorganized as Anret, Inc. 10/15/1979
Each Share of Bene. Int. $1 par exchanged for (0.4) share Common $1 par
Anret, Inc. name changed to Sunlite Inc. 12/13/1983
(See Sunlite Inc.)

ATLANTA PAPER CO. (GA)
Stock Dividends - 10% 12/20/1951; 10% 12/20/1952
Merged into Mead Corp. 05/06/1957
Each share Common exchanged for (0.5) Common $5 par
Mead Corp. merged into MeadWestvaco Corp. 01/29/2002 which merged into WestRock Co. 07/01/2015

ATLANTA TECHNOLOGY GROUP INC (DE)
Name changed to Docplus.net Corp. (DE) 12/28/1998
Docplus.net Corp. (DE) reorganized in Nevada as Sucre Agricultural Corp. 04/21/2006 which recapitalized as Bluefire Ethanol Fuels, Inc. 06/22/2006 which name changed to BlueFire Renewables, Inc. 10/25/2010

ATLANTA TIMES, INC. (GA)
Adjudicated bankrupt 01/17/1966
No stockholders' equity

ATLANTA TRANSIT CO. (GA)
Name changed to Fulton Investment Co. 12/17/1954
Fulton Investment Co. merged into Southeastern Capital Corp. (TN) 03/16/1965 which reincorporated in Georgia 07/31/1976
(See Southeastern Capital Corp. (GA))

ATLANTECH RESOURCES CORP (NY)
Common $0.001 par split (16) for (1) by issuance of (15) additional shares payable 09/17/1999 to holders of record 07/19/1999
Ex date - 11/04/1999
Name changed to Elderpower.com, Inc. 11/05/1999

ATLANTIC & DANVILLE RAILWAY CO. (VA)
Common $100 par changed to no par 00/00/1949
Assets sold to Norfolk & Western Railway 09/28/1962
No stockholders' equity

ATLANTIC & N C RR CO (NC)
Merged into North Carolina Railroad Co. 09/29/1989
Details not available

ATLANTIC & PAC FOOD SALES INC (UT)
Common 50¢ par changed to 1¢ par 06/11/1970
Recapitalized as Aegean Corp. 10/06/1972
Each share Common 1¢ par exchanged for (0.01) share Common $1 par
(See Aegean Corp.)

ATLANTIC & PAC LIFE INS CO AMER (GA)
Merged into First American Corp. (GA) 12/31/1974
Each share Capital Stock $1 par exchanged for (4) shares Class A Common 25¢ par
(See First American Corp. (GA))

ATLANTIC & PACIFIC INTERNATIONAL CORP.
Dissolved 00/00/1936
Details not available

ATLANTIC ACCEPTANCE CORP. LTD. (ON)
2nd Conv. Preference no par reclassified as 3rd Conv. Preference no par 09/25/1962
Placed in receivership and assets sold 00/00/1966
No stockholders' equity

ATLANTIC ACQUISITION CORP (DE)
Units separated 08/23/2018
Name changed to HF Foods Group Inc. 08/23/2018

ATLANTIC AIR SERVICE, INC.
Liquidated 00/00/1930
No stockholders' equity

ATLANTIC AIRCRAFT CORP. (DE)
No longer in existence having become inoperative and void for non-payment of taxes 04/01/1955

ATLANTIC ALLIANCE PARTNERSHIP CORP (BRITISH VIRGIN ISLANDS)
Completely liquidated 11/06/2017
Each share Ordinary no par exchanged for $10.58 cash

ATLANTIC AMERN LIFE INS CO (GA)
Under plan of reorganization each share Common $1 par automatically became (1) share Atlantic American Corp. Common $1 par 08/11/1970

ATLANTIC APPLIANCE INC (DE)
Each share Common 10¢ par exchanged for (0.0001) share Common $1,000 par 12/22/1978
Note: In effect holders received 10¢ cash per share and public interest was eliminated

ATLANTIC AVIATION CORP (DE)
Merged into AAC Acquisition Corp. 09/12/1997
Each share Common exchanged for $16.2195 cash

ATLANTIC BANCGROUP INC (FL)
Stock Dividend - 20% payable 06/16/2003 to holders of record 05/30/2003 Ex date - 05/28/2003
Merged into Jacksonville Bancorp, Inc. 11/17/2010
Each share Common 1¢ par exchanged for (0.2) share Common 1¢ par and $0.67 cash
Jacksonville Bancorp, Inc. merged into Ameris Bancorp 03/11/2016

ATLANTIC BANCORPORATION (FL)
Common $1 par split (2) for (1) by issuance of (1) additional share 09/06/1983
Acquired by First Union Corp. 11/15/1985
Each share Common $1 par exchanged for (1.05) shares Common $3.33-1/3 par
First Union Corp. name changed to Wachovia Corp. (Ctfs. dated after 09/01/2001) 09/01/2001 which merged into Wells Fargo & Co. (New) 12/31/2008

ATLANTIC BANCORPORATION (NJ)
Common $2.50 par split (3) for (2) by issuance of (0.5) additional share 08/08/1986
Common $2.50 par split (5) for (4) by issuance of (0.25) additional share 01/21/1987
Common $2.50 par split (5) for (4) by issuance of (0.25) additional share 07/14/1989
Stock Dividend - 10% 07/22/1988
Name changed to Glendale Bancorporation 07/28/1989
(See Glendale Bancorporation)

ATLANTIC BANCSHARES INC (SC)
Reclassification effective 01/19/2011
Common holders of (1,000) shares or fewer reclassified as Ser. AAA Preferred no par
Merged into South Atlantic Bancshares, Inc. 04/02/2018
Each share Ser. AAA Preferred exchanged for (0.2452) share Common $1 par
Each share Common no par exchanged for (0.2452) share Common $1 par

ATLANTIC BK & TR CO (BOSTON, MA)
Name changed to Capital Crossing Bank (Boston, MA) 09/02/1999
(See Capital Crossing Bank (Boston, MA))

ATLANTIC BANK OF SOUTH JACKSONVILLE (JACKSONVILLE, FL)
97.92% held by Atlantic Bancorporation through exchange offer which expired 10/22/1973
Public interest eliminated

ATLANTIC BEACH DEV CORP (DE)
Liquidation completed
Each share Common $1 par exchanged for initial distribution of $8 cash 12/07/1968
Preferred $1 par called for redemption 12/17/1968
Each share Common $1 par received second distribution of $7.80 cash 04/03/1969
Each share Common $1 par received third and final distribution of $1.90 cash 10/31/1972

ATLANTIC BEVERAGE INC (DE)
Name changed to Atlantic Premium Brands, Ltd. 06/01/1997
(See Atlantic Premium Brands, Ltd.)

ATLANTIC BOWLING CORP. (DE)
Adjudicated bankrupt 08/24/1964
No stockholders' equity

ATLANTIC BUILDING CO., INC. (VA)
Liquidation completed
Each share Capital Stock $100 par exchanged for initial distribution of (1) Ctf. of Participation and $25 cash 09/28/1976
Each Ctf. of Participation received second distribution of $5.33 cash 03/00/1977
Each Ctf. of Participation received third distribution of $5.33 cash 06/00/1977
Each Ctf. of Participation received fourth distribution of $5.33 cash 09/00/1977
Each Ctf. of Participation received fifth and final distribution of $234.83 cash 12/09/1977

ATLANTIC BUSINESS FORMS CO (OH)
Merged into Printing Acquisitions Inc. 05/31/1978
Each share Common $1 par exchanged for $5.25 cash

ATLANTIC CAP I (DE)
8.25% Guaranteed Quarterly Income Preferred Securities called for redemption at $25 on 02/28/2003

ATLANTIC CAP II (DE)
7.375% Guaranteed Trust Preferred Capital Securities called for redemption at $25 plus $0.358307 accrued dividend on 03/11/2004

ATLANTIC CARIBBEAN PRODS INC (FL)
Reincorporated under the laws of Delaware as Multi-Tool Technologies, Inc. 07/14/1988
(See Multi-Tool Technologies, Inc.)

ATLANTIC CASPIAN RES PLC (UNITED KINGDOM)
Basis changed from (1:10) to (1:0.001) 07/09/2004
ADR agreement terminated 09/18/2009
ADR holders' equity unlikely

ATLANTIC CASUALTY INSURANCE CO. (NJ)
Common $6 par changed to $10 par 12/30/1955
Name changed to Motor Club of America Insurance Co. 12/01/1956
(See Motor Club of America Insurance Co.)

ATLANTIC CITY & OCEAN CITY CO.
Dissolved 00/00/1946
Details not available

ATLANTIC CITY & SHORE CO.
Liquidation completed 00/00/1948

Details not available

ATLANTIC CITY AMBASSADOR HOTEL CORP (NJ)
Each share Common 10¢ par exchanged for (0.1) share Common $30 par 00/00/1951
Completely liquidated 12/29/1974
Each share Common $30 par exchanged for first and final distribution of $692.84 cash

ATLANTIC CITY ELEC CO (NJ)
Common $10 par changed to $6.50 par and (0.5) additional share issued 10/14/1955
Common $6.50 par changed to $4.33333333 par and (0.5) additional share issued 10/09/1959
Common $4.33333333 par changed to $3 par and (0.5) additional share issued 05/14/1964
8.4% Preferred $100 par called for redemption 08/01/1985
5.875% Conv. Preferred $100 par called for redemption 04/30/1987
Under plan of reorganization each share Common $3 par automatically became (1) share Atlantic Energy, Inc. Common no par 11/02/1987
Atlantic Energy, Inc. merged into Conectiv, Inc. 03/01/1998 which merged into Pepco Holdings Inc. 08/01/2002
$9.45 Preferred no par called for redemption 11/01/1989
9.96% Preferred $100 par called for redemption 05/14/1993
8.53% Preferred no par called for redemption 02/01/1996
7.52% Preferred $100 par called for redemption 09/16/1996
$8.25 Preferred no par called for redemption 09/16/1996
$8.20 Preferred $100 par called for redemption at $100 on 08/01/1998
$7.80 Preferred no par called for redemption at $100 on 05/01/2002
4% Preferred $100 par called for redemption at $105.50 on 02/25/2011
4.1% Preferred $100 par called for redemption at $101 on 02/25/2011
4.35% Preferred $100 par called for redemption at $101 on 02/25/2011
4.35% Preferred 2nd Ser. $100 par called for redemption at $101 on 02/25/2011
4.75% Preferred $100 par called for redemption at $101 on 02/25/2011
5% Preferred $100 par called for redemption at $100 on 02/25/2011

ATLANTIC CITY FIRE INSURANCE CO.
Dissolved 00/00/1946
Details not available

ATLANTIC CITY PPTY INVESTORS INC (NY)
Dissolved by proclamation 09/25/1991

ATLANTIC CO (GA)
Class B Common no par reclassified as Common no par 00/00/1945
Common no par changed to $1 par and (1) additional share issued 05/01/1966
Merged into Jackson-Atlantic, Inc. 11/15/1968
Each share Common $1 par exchanged for (1) share 4% Conv. Preferred $10 par and (1) share Common $1 par
Jackson-Atlantic Inc. name changed to Munford, Inc. 05/11/1971
(See Munford, Inc.)

ATLANTIC COAL PLC (UNITED KINGDOM)
ADR agreement terminated 07/17/2017
No ADR's remain outstanding

ATLANTIC COAST AIRLS HLDGS INC (CA)
Name changed 05/08/1998
Name changed from Atlantic Coast Airlines, Inc. to Atlantic Coast Airlines Holdings, Inc. 05/08/1998
Common 2¢ par split (2) for (1) by issuance of (1) additional share payable 02/23/2001 to holders of record 02/09/2001 Ex date - 02/26/2001
Name changed to FLYi, Inc. 08/04/2004
(See FLYi, Inc.)

ATLANTIC COAST COPPER LTD (ON)
Merged into Hunter Brook Holdings Ltd. 01/01/1999
Each share Common no par exchanged for $9 cash

ATLANTIC COAST ENTMT HLDGS INC (DE)
Merged into Icahn Enterprises L.P. 11/15/2007
Each share Common 1¢ par exchanged for $21.19 cash

ATLANTIC COAST FED CORP (USA)
Reorganized under the laws of Maryland as Atlantic Coast Financial Corp. 02/04/2011
Each share Common 1¢ par exchanged for (0.196) share Common 1¢ par
Atlantic Coast Financial Corp. merged into Ameris Bancorp 05/25/2018

ATLANTIC COAST FINL CORP (MD)
Merged into Ameris Bancorp 05/25/2018
Each share Common 1¢ par exchanged for (0.17) share Common $1 par and $1.39 cash

ATLANTIC COAST FISHERIES CO. (ME)
Common no par changed to $1 par 00/00/1940
Recapitalized as Atlantic Coast Industries, Inc. and Common $1 par changed to 10¢ par 01/14/1958
Atlantic Coast Industries, Inc. name changed to Atco Chemical-Industrial Products, Inc. 09/06/1960 which name changed to Atco Industries, Inc. 08/16/1973
(See Atco Industries, Inc.)

ATLANTIC COAST INDUSTRIES, INC. (ME)
Name changed to Atco Chemical-Industrial Products, Inc. 09/06/1960
Atco Chemical-Industrial Products, Inc. name changed to Atco Industries, Inc. 08/16/1973
(See Atco Industries, Inc.)

ATLANTIC COAST LINE CO (CT)
Each share Capital Stock $50 par exchanged for (3) shares Capital Stock no par 03/21/1955
Capital Stock no par split (3) for (1) by issuance of (2) additional shares 04/08/1966
Liquidation completed
Each share Capital Stock no par received initial distribution of $0.30 cash 03/26/1971
Each share Capital Stock no par exchanged for second distribution of (0.62807) share Seaboard Coast Line Industries, Inc. Common $20 par and (0.44085) share Alico Land Development Co. Common $1 par 06/04/1971
(See each company's listing)
Each share Capital Stock no par received third and final distribution of $0.67 cash 12/27/1971

ATLANTIC COAST LINE RR CO (VA)
Common $100 par changed to no par 05/06/1946
Common no par split (3) for (1) by issuance of (2) additional shares 02/23/1955
Merged into Seaboard Coast Line Railroad Co. 07/01/1967
Each share 5% Non-Cum. Preferred $100 par exchanged for (3) shares Common $20 par
Each share Common no par exchanged for (1.42) shares Common $20 par
Seaboard Coast Line Railroad Co. merged into Seaboard Coast Line Industries, Inc. 05/14/1971 which merged into CSX Corp. 11/01/1980

ATLANTIC CMNTY BANCORP INC (NC)
Merged into Triangle Bancorp Inc. 05/12/1995
Each share Common $2.50 par exchanged for (0.6) share Common no par
Triangle Bancorp Inc. merged into Centura Banks, Inc. 02/18/2000 which merged into Royal Bank of Canada (Montreal, QC) 06/05/2001

ATLANTIC CONSOLIDATED, INC. (FL)
Proclaimed dissolved for failure to file reports and pay fees 10/21/1974

ATLANTIC CREOSOTING CO (MD)
Name changed to Atlantic Wood Industries, Inc. 08/15/1978
(See Atlantic Wood Industries, Inc.)

ATLANTIC CTL SYS INC (NY)
Each share old Common 5¢ par exchanged for (0.00002) share new Common 5¢ par 04/11/1991
Note: In effect holders received $4.50 cash per share and public interest was eliminated

ATLANTIC DATA SVCS INC (MA)
Merged into ADS Parent Acquisition LLC 11/12/2003
Each share Common 1¢ par exchanged for $3.25 cash

ATLANTIC DEPT STORES INC (NY)
Merged into ARDC Retail Corp. 07/31/1974
Each share Common $1 par exchanged for $1 cash

ATLANTIC DEV INC (NV)
Name changed to IMS, Inc. (NV) 08/11/1986
IMS, Inc. (NV) reorganized in Massachusetts as IMSCO, Inc. 07/01/1987 which reincorporated in Delaware as IMSCO Technologies, Inc. 09/19/1996 which recapitalized as Global Sports & Entertainment Inc. 08/28/2001 which name changed to GWIN, Inc. 09/24/2002 which name changed to Winning Edge International, Inc. 09/27/2006 which assets were transferred to W Technologies, Inc. 10/20/2007

ATLANTIC ELECTROTYPE & STEREOTYPE CO. OF NEW YORK
Acquired by Rapid Electrotype Co. 00/00/1932
Details not available

ATLANTIC ELEVATOR CO. (PA)
Acquired by Westinghouse Electric & Manufacturing Co. 02/00/1945
Details not available

ATLANTIC ENERGY CORP (BC)
Merged into Bowtex Energy (Canada) Corp. 06/01/1987
Each share Common no par exchanged for for (0.00958497) share Common no par
Bowtex Energy (Canada) Corp. name changed to Luscar Oil & Gas Ltd. 10/21/1993 which merged into Encal Energy Ltd. 07/13/1994 which merged into Calpine Canada Holdings Ltd. 04/19/2001 which was exchanged for Calpine Corp. 05/27/2002
(See Calpine Corp.)

ATLANTIC ENERGY INC (NJ)
Common no par split (2) for (1) by issuance of (1) additional share 05/14/1992
Merged into Conectiv, Inc. 03/01/1998 which $100 par exchanged for (3) shares Common $20 par
Each share Common no par exchanged for (0.75) share Common 1¢ par and (0.125) share Class A Common 1¢ par
Conectiv, Inc. merged into Pepco Holdings Inc. 08/01/2002

ATLANTIC ENERGY INC (NV)
Name changed to Cherokee Atlantic Corp. 03/03/1988

ATLANTIC EXPRESS INC (CO)
Each share old Common $0.0001 par exchanged for (0.5) share new Common $0.0001 par 01/26/1987
Each share new Common $0.0001 par exchanged again for (0.0060606) share new Common $0.0001 par 09/13/1988
Each share new Common $0.0001 par exchanged for (0.5) share Common 1¢ par 08/20/1990
Plan of reorganization under Chapter 11 Federal Bankruptcy proceedings confirmed 08/23/1993
Each share Common 1¢ par exchanged for $0.25 cash

ATLANTIC FD INVT U S GOVT SECS INC (DE)
Completely liquidated 01/13/1972
Each share Common $5 par exchanged for first and final distribution of (2.34334) shares Fund for U.S. Government Securities, Inc. Capital Stock $1 par
Fund for U.S. Government Securities, Inc. name changed to Federated Fund for U.S. Government Securities, Inc. 03/31/1996 which reorganized as Federated Income Securities Trust 10/07/2002

ATLANTIC FED SVGS & LN ASSN FT LAUDERDALE FLA (USA)
Under plan of reorganization each share Common 1¢ par automatically became (1) share BankAtlantic, A Federal Savings Bank (Fort Lauderdale, FL) Common 1¢ par 01/04/1988
BankAtlantic, A Federal Savings Bank (Fort Lauderdale, FL) reorganized as BankAtlantic Bancorp, Inc. 07/14/1994 which name changed to BBX Capital Corp. (Old) 08/06/2012
(See BBX Capital Corp. (Old))

ATLANTIC FED SVGS BK (BALTIMORE, MD)
Stock Dividend - 10% 03/31/1987
Under plan of reorganization each share Common $1 par automatically became (1) share Atlanfed Bancorp, Inc. Common $1 par 11/07/1988
Atlanfed Bancorp, Inc. merged into Susquehanna Bancshares, Inc. 03/31/1995 which merged into BB&T Corp. 08/01/2015

ATLANTIC FINL CORP (VA)
Merged into F & M National Corp. 02/26/2001
Each share Common $5 par exchanged for (0.753) share Common $2 par
F & M National Corp. merged into BB&T Corp. 08/09/2001

ATLANTIC FINL FED (USA)
Placed in receivership by RTC
No stockholders' equity effective 03/15/1991

ATLANTIC FRUIT & SUGAR CO.
Dissolved 00/00/1932
Details not available

ATLANTIC GAS & ELECTRIC CORP.
Reorganized as Northwestern Pennsylvania Gas Corp. 00/00/1933
No stockholders' equity

ATLANTIC GEN CORP (PA)
On 12/21/1976 SEC determined control of company was fraudulently obtained with the intent of looting assets
Stockholders' equity unlikely

ATLANTIC GOLD MINES LTD (CANADA)
Reincorporated 07/26/1994
Place of incorporation changed from (NS) to (Canada) and Common no par reclassified as (4) Class A Multiple Shares and (1) Class B Multiple Shares 07/26/1994
Name changed to Delwood Capital Corp. Ltd. 02/19/1996
Delwood Capital Corp. name changed to Indostar Gold Corp. 07/10/1996 which name changed to Petroflow Energy Ltd. 10/28/1997

ATLANTIC GOLDFIELDS INC (ON)
Recapitalized as Dexus Inc. 06/22/1990
Each share Common no par exchanged for (0.1) share Non-Vtg. Class A Common no par and (0.1) share Class B Common no par
Dexus Inc. acquired by Trimin Enterprises Inc. (BC) 06/30/1993 which reorganized as Trimin Enterprises Inc. (Canada) 07/27/1998
(See Trimin Enterprises Inc.)

ATLANTIC GREEN PWR HLDG CO (DE)
Recapitalized as Southern USA Resources Inc. 04/23/2012
Each share Common $0.000001 par exchanged for (0.001) share Common $0.000001 par

ATLANTIC GUARANTY & TITLE INSURANCE CO.
Dissolution approved 00/00/1937
Details not available

ATLANTIC GULF & WEST INDIES STEAMSHIP LINES (ME)
Common no par changed to $1 par 00/00/1940
Completely liquidated 12/23/1966
Details not available

ATLANTIC GULF COMMUNITIES CORP (DE)
Chapter 11 Federal Bankruptcy proceedings converted to Chapter 7 on 06/18/2002
Stockholders' equity unlikely

ATLANTIC GULF ENERGY INC (DE)
Name changed to British American Petroleum Corp. 03/30/1983
British American Petroleum Corp. name changed to Crest Energy Resources Corp. 07/01/1987
(See Crest Energy Resources Corp.)

ATLANTIC GULF OIL CORP.
Dissolved 00/00/1934
Details not available

ATLANTIC GULFSTREAM CORP (FL)
Merged into Financial Industries Corp. (OH) 03/01/1977
Each share Class A Common 10¢ par exchanged for (0.35) share Common $1 par
Financial Industries Corp. (OH) reincorporated in Texas 12/31/1980
(See Financial Industries Corp.)

ATLANTIC GYPSUM PRODUCTS CO.
Acquired by National Gypsum Co. 00/00/1936
Details not available

ATLANTIC ICE & COAL CO.
Name changed to Atlantic Co. 00/00/1936
Atlantic Co. merged into Jackson-Atlantic, Inc. 11/15/68 which name changed to Munford, Inc. 05/11/1971
(See Munford, Inc.)

ATLANTIC IMPT CORP (DE)
Charter cancelled and declared inoperative and void for non-payment of taxes 06/25/1987

ATLANTIC INDS INC (FL)
Common 10¢ par changed to $0.095 par 10/15/1970
Completely liquidated 12/10/1979
Each share Common $0.095 par exchanged for first and final distribution of $0.22 cash

ATLANTIC INFORMATION SYS INC (GA)
Ceased operations 08/00/1971
No stockholders' equity

ATLANTIC INTL ENTMT LTD (DE)
Name changed to Online Gaming Systems, Ltd. 10/01/1999
Online Gaming Systems, Ltd. name changed to Advanced Resources Group Ltd. 02/15/2007

ATLANTIC INVESTMENTS, INC.
Acquired by Massachusetts Investors Trust 00/00/1932
Details not available

ATLANTIC LIBERTY FINL CORP (DE)
Merged into Flushing Financial Corp. 06/30/2006
Each share Common 10¢ par exchanged for (1.43) shares Common 1¢ par

ATLANTIC LOBOS OIL CO.
Dissolved 00/00/1933
Details not available

ATLANTIC MARINE INDS INC (DE)
Charter cancelled and declared inoperative and void for non-payment of taxes 03/01/2001

ATLANTIC MED CORP (DE)
Each share Common 1¢ par exchanged for (0.25) share Common $0.001 par 07/15/1990
Recapitalized as I-Rock Industries, Inc. 04/05/1999
Each share Common $0.001 par exchanged (0.22222222) shares Common $0.001 par
I-Rock Industries, Inc. name changed to IR Operating Corp. 04/26/1999 which name changed to Digi Link Technologies, Inc. 02/12/2001
(See Digi Link Technologies, Inc.)

ATLANTIC MET CORP (DE)
Merged into Hallwood Group Inc. 04/30/1984
Each share Common 10¢ par exchanged for (1) share Common 10¢ par
(See Hallwood Group Inc.)

ATLANTIC MICROFILM CORP (NY)
Completely liquidated 10/03/1969
Each share Common 10¢ par exchanged for first and final distribution of (0.4) share Arcata National Corp. Common 25¢ par
Arcata National Corp. name changed to Arcata Corp. 11/30/1978 which name changed to Atacra Liquidating Corp. 06/04/1982
(See Atacra Liquidating Corp.)

ATLANTIC NATL BK (ATLANTIC CITY, NJ)
Common $10 par changed to $6.66 par and (0.5) additional share issued 05/21/1973
Merged into Midlantic Banks Inc. 03/01/1980
Each share $1.50 Conv. Preferred $25 par exchanged for (1.76) shares $2 Conv. Preferred 2nd Ser. no par or (1.56) shares $2 Conv. Preferred 2nd Ser. no par plus $8.38 cash or $8.30 principal amount of 9.25% Sinking Fund Notes due 12/31/1989
Each share Common $6.66 par exchanged for (1.2) shares $2 Conv. Preferred 2nd Ser. no par or (1.06) shares $2 Conv. Preferred 2nd Ser. no par plus $5.70 cash or $5.70 principal amount of 9.25% Sinking Fund Notes due 12/31/1989
Note: Option to receive Preferred Stock plus cash or Notes expired 03/31/1980
Midlantic Banks Inc. merged into Midlantic Corp. 01/30/1987 which merged into PNC Bank Corp. 12/31/1995 which name changed to PNC Financial Services Group, Inc. 03/15/2000

ATLANTIC NATL BK (JACKSONVILLE, FL)
Stock Dividends - 33.33333333% 05/12/1954; 10% 06/02/1960; 50% 02/05/1964; 33.33333333% 10/14/1966
99% acquired by Atlantic Bancorporation through exchange offer which expired 09/16/1968
Public interest eliminated

ATLANTIC NATL BK (STAMFORD, CT)
Merged into Connecticut National Bank (Bridgeport, CT) 04/18/1970
Each share Common $5 par exchanged for (2) shares Common Capital Stock $5 par
Connecticut National Bank (Bridgeport, CT) merged into Hartford National Corp. 10/30/1982 which merged into Shawmut National Corp. 02/29/1988 which merged into Fleet Financial Group Inc. (New) 11/30/1995 which name changed to Fleet Boston Corp. 10/01/1999 which name changed to FleetBoston Financial Corp. 04/18/2000 which merged into Bank of America Corp. 04/01/2004

ATLANTIC NATL LIFE INS CO (MD)
Name changed to American Centennial Life Insurance Co. 12/31/1978
(See American Centennial Life Insurance Co.)

ATLANTIC NICKEL MINES LTD (ON)
Name changed to Syngold Exploration Inc. 06/27/1983
Syngold Exploration Inc. merged into Thunderwood Resources Inc.-Les Ressources Thunderwood Inc. 06/01/1989 which merged into Thundermin Ressources Inc. 11/01/1998 which merged into Rambler Metals & Mining PLC 01/12/2016

ATLANTIC NORTHERN RAILWAY CO.
Dissolved 00/00/1937
Details not available

ATLANTIC OIL CO., LTD. (AB)
Merged into Canadian Atlantic Oil Co. 10/00/1951
Each share Common $1 par exchanged for (0.5) share Common $2 par
Canadian Atlantic Oil Co. Ltd. acquired by Pacific Petroleums Ltd. 12/25/1958
(See Pacific Petroleums Ltd.)

ATLANTIC OIL CORP (DE)
Common $10 par changed to $5 par 00/00/1947
Each share Common $5 par exchanged for (5) shares Common $1 par 11/22/1955
Common $1 par changed to 1¢ par 11/01/0973
Merged into Stephen's Inc. 03/16/1983
Each share Common 1¢ par exchanged for $12 cash

ATLANTIC OIL INVESTMENT CORP.
Name changed to Atlantic Oil Corp. 00/00/1942
(See Atlantic Oil Corp.)

ATLANTIC OIL ROYALTY CORP.
Merged into Atlantic Keystone Petroleum Co., Ltd. 00/00/1931
Details not available

ATLANTIC PAC BK (SANTA ROSA, CA)
Name changed to AltaPacific Bank (Santa Rosa, CA) 08/19/2009
AltaPacific Bank (Santa Rosa, CA) reorganized as AltaPacific Bancorp 11/19/2010

ATLANTIC PAC INTL INC (WA)
Reorganized under the laws of Nevada as API Dental, Inc. 07/30/1999
Each share Common no par exchanged for (0.25) share Common no par
(See API Dental, Inc.)

ATLANTIC PEPSI COLA BOTTLING INC (SC)
Common 25¢ par changed to $0.125 par and (1) additional share issued 06/30/1978
Under plan of merger each share Common $0.125 par exchanged for (0.1) share Atlantic Telecasting Corp. Common no par and $33.0475 cash 03/29/1979
(See Atlantic Telecasting Corp.)

ATLANTIC PERM SVGS BK F S B (NORFOLK, VA)
Name changed 12/17/1986
Name changed from Atlantic Permanent Federal Savings & Loan Association to Atlantic Permanent Savings Bank, F.S.B. (Norfolk, VA) 12/17/1986
Placed in receivership by RTC and deposits subsequently purchased 07/12/1991
No stockholders' equity

ATLANTIC PETROLEUM CORP. (DE)
No longer in existence having become inoperative and void for non-payment of taxes 03/19/1924

ATLANTIC PFD CAP CORP (MA)
Name changed to Capital Crossing Preferred Corp. 03/22/2001
(See Capital Crossing Preferred Corp.)

ATLANTIC PHARMACEUTICALS INC (DE)
Name changed to Atlantic Technology Ventures, Inc. 03/22/2000
Atlantic Technology Ventures, Inc. name changed to Manhattan Pharmaceuticals, Inc. 02/21/2003 which recapitalized as TG Therapeutics, Inc. 04/30/2012

ATLANTIC PORT RAILWAY CORP.
Ceased operations 00/00/1933
Details not available

ATLANTIC PWR CORP (ON)
Reincorporated under the laws of British Columbia 07/08/2005

ATLANTIC PREM BRANDS LTD (DE)
Completely liquidated
Each share Common 1¢ par received first and final distribution of $0.0175 cash payable 12/05/2016 to holders of record 11/28/2016

ATLANTIC PUBLIC SERVICE ASSOCIATES, INC.
Reorganized as Northeastern Public Service Co. and Northeastern Utilities Co. 00/00/1931
Details not available

ATLANTIC PUBLIC UTILITIES, INC.
Reorganized as Northeastern Public Service Co. and Northeastern Utilities Co. 00/00/1931
Details not available

ATLANTIC RAYON CORP. (RI)
Name changed to Textron Inc. (RI) 05/18/1944
Textron Inc. (RI) name changed to Textron American, Inc. 02/24/1955 which name changed to Textron Inc. (RI) 05/15/1956 reincorporated in Delaware 01/02/1968

ATLANTIC RLTY CO (GA)
$6 Preferred called for redemption at $105 on 01/02/2003

ATLANTIC RLTY TR (MA)
Merged into Kimco Realty Corp. 03/31/2006
Each Share of Bene. Int. 10¢ par

exchanged for (0.568) share Common 1¢ par

ATLANTIC REFNG CO (PA)
Each share Common $100 par exchanged for (4) shares Common $25 par 00/00/1928
3.6% Ser. B Preferred $100 par reclassified as 3.75% Ser. B, Preferred $100 par 00/00/1947
4% Preferred Ser. A $100 par called for redemption 12/05/1950
Each share Common $25 par exchanged for (2.5) shares Common $10 par 00/00/1952
Stock Dividend - 20% 01/15/1951
Name changed to Atlantic Richfield Co. (PA) 05/03/1966
Atlantic Richfield Co. (PA) reincorporated in Delaware 05/07/1985 which merged into BP Amoco PLC 04/18/2000

ATLANTIC REGISTER CO. (OH)
Name changed to Atlantic Business Forms Co. 03/15/1961
(See Atlantic Business Forms Co.)

ATLANTIC RESEARCH CORP. (VA)
Common 5¢ par changed to $1 par and (1) additional share issued 06/30/1961
Merged into Susquehanna Corp. 12/04/1967
Each share Common $1 par exchanged for (1) share Class A Conv. Preferred $5 par
(See Susquehanna Corp.)

ATLANTIC RESH CORP (DE)
Common 10¢ par split (5) for (4) by issuance of (0.25) additional share 06/11/1982
Common 10¢ par split (3) for (2) by issuance of (0.5) additional share 06/13/1983
Common 10¢ par split (3) for (2) by issuance of (0.5) additional share 06/21/1985
Merged into Sequa Corp. 01/05/1988
Each share Common 10¢ par exchanged for $31.01 cash

ATLANTIC RES INC (NV)
Reorganized as Patriot Minefinders Inc. 04/19/2012
Each share Common $0.001 par exchanged for (24) shares Common $0.001 par
Patriot Minefinders Inc. recapitalized as Rise Resources Inc. 02/09/2015 which name changed to Rise Gold Corp. 04/07/2017

ATLANTIC RESTAURANT VENTURES INC (VA)
Acquired by Arvi Acquisition 07/29/1994
Each share Common 1¢ par exchanged for $0.65 cash

ATLANTIC RICHFIELD CO (DE)
Reincorporated 05/07/1985
Common $10 par changed to $5 par and (1) additional share issued 08/02/1968
Common $5 par split (2) for (1) by issuance of (1) additional share 09/13/1976
Common $5 par changed to $2.50 par and (1) additional share issued 06/30/1980
State of incorporation changed from (PA) to (DE) 05/07/1985
3.75% Preferred Ser. B $100 par called for redemption 09/30/1985
Common Stock Purchase Rights declared for Common stockholders of record 06/09/1986 were redeemed at $0.10 per right 09/15/1995 for holders of record 08/18/1995
Common $2.50 par split (2) for (1) by issuance of (1) additional share payable 06/13/1997 to holders of record 05/16/1997 Ex date - 06/16/1997

Merged into BP Amoco p.l.c. 04/18/2000
Each share Common $2.50 par exchanged for (0.82) Sponsored ADR for Ordinary
$3 Conv. Preference $1 par called for redemption at $70 on 04/27/2001
$2.80 Conv. Preference $1 par called for redemption at $82 on 04/27/2001
Public interest eliminated

ATLANTIC SECURITIES CO. OF BOSTON
Merged into Standard Equities Corp. 05/00/1941
No stockholders' equity

ATLANTIC SVCS INC (DE)
Each share Common $1 par exchanged for (0.25) share Common 10¢ par 09/01/1967
Charter cancelled and declared inoperative and void for non-payment of taxes 03/01/1971

ATLANTIC SHOPPING CENTRES LTD (NS)
Merged into Empire Co. Ltd. 08/29/1989
Each share Non-Vtg. Class A no par exchanged for (0.9) share Non-Vtg. Class A no par
Each share Class B Common no par exchanged for (0.9) share Non-Vtg. Class A no par
Note: Unexchanged certificates were cancelled and became without value 08/25/1999
9.25% Retractable Preferred Ser. 1 $25 par called for redemption 12/30/1996
Public interest eliminated

ATLANTIC SOUTHEAST AIRLS INC (GA)
Common 10¢ par split (3) for (2) by issuance of (0.5) additional share 11/20/1984
Common 10¢ par split (2) for (1) by issuance of (1) additional share 04/16/1985
Common 10¢ par split (4) for (3) by issuance of (0.33333333) additional share 08/23/1985
Common 10¢ par split (2) for (1) by issuance of (1) additional share 02/18/1993
Stock Dividend - 50% 11/26/1991
Under plan of reorganization each share Common 10¢ par automatically became (1) share ASA Holdings, Inc. Common 10¢ par 12/31/1996
(See ASA Holdings, Inc.)

ATLANTIC SOUTHN FINL GROUP INC (GA)
Company's principal asset placed in receivership 05/20/2011
Stockholders' equity unlikely

ATLANTIC STAMPING CO (NY)
Dissolved 11/28/1969
Details not available

ATLANTIC STATE BANK (POINT PLEASANT, NJ)
Acquired by Citizens State Bank of New Jersey (Lacey Township, NJ) 01/21/1977
Each share Common $5 par exchanged for $16.25 cash

ATLANTIC STEEL BOILER CO., INC. (DE)
Bankrupt 12/00/1953
Stockholders' equity unlikely

ATLANTIC STEWARDSHIP BK N J (MIDLAND PARK, NJ)
Under plan of reorganization each share Common no par automatically became (1) share Stewardship Financial Corp. Common no par 11/22/1996

ATLANTIC STL CO (DE)
Each share Common $100 par exchanged for (10) shares Common no par 00/00/1937

Each share Common no par exchanged for (2) shares Common $5 par 01/00/1955
Common $5 par split (3) for (2) by issuance of (0.5) additional share 01/01/1972
7% Preferred $100 par called for redemption 05/02/1975
Stock Dividend - 100% 01/01/1975
Merged into Ivaco Ltd.-Ivaco Ltee. 10/15/1979
Each share Common $5 par exchanged for $40 cash

ATLANTIC STS INDS INC (DE)
Reincorporated 01/14/1970
Common 10¢ par changed to 2¢ par and (4) additional shares issued 11/01/1963
State of incorporation changed from (NY) to (DE) 01/14/1970
Name changed to ASI Communications, Inc. 04/30/1970
(See ASI Communications, Inc.)

ATLANTIC SUGAR REFINERIES LTD (ON)
Common no par split (3) for (1) by issuance of (2) additional shares 08/05/1966
Merged into Jannock Corp. Ltd. 07/04/1973
Each share 5% Preference $100 par exchanged for (1) share 6% Preference 1st Ser. $100 par
Each share Class A no par exchanged for (1) share $1.20 Class A no par
Each share Common no par exchanged for (1) share Conv. Special no par
Jannock Corp. Ltd. reorganized as Jannock Ltd. 07/05/1977
(See Jannock Ltd.)

ATLANTIC SYNDICATION NETWORK INC (NV)
Name changed to Zealous Trading Group, Inc. 10/05/2007
Zealous Trading Group, Inc. name changed to Adult Entertainment Capital, Inc. 08/25/2008 which name changed to Zealous, Inc. 03/05/2009 which name changed to CoreStream Energy Inc. 09/03/2010
(See CoreStream Energy Inc.)

ATLANTIC SYNERGY INC (NV)
Name changed to Acies Corp. 11/16/2004
(See Acies Corp.)

ATLANTIC SYS GROUP INC (NB)
Company received a notice of foreclosure 09/03/2002
Stockholders' equity unlikely

ATLANTIC TECHNOLOGY CORP (NJ)
Adjudicated bankrupt 05/13/1977
No stockholders' equity

ATLANTIC TECHNOLOGY VENTURES INC (DE)
Name changed to Manhattan Pharmaceuticals, Inc. 02/21/2003
Manhattan Pharmaceuticals, Inc. recapitalized as TG Therapeutics, Inc. 04/30/2012

ATLANTIC TEL EQUIP INC (NY)
Attorney advised company out of business 05/06/1977
Stockholders' equity unlikely

ATLANTIC TELE-NETWORK INC (DE)
Each share old Common 1¢ par received distribution of (1) share Emerging Communications, Inc. Common 1¢ par payable 12/30/1997 to holders of record 11/18/1997
Each share old Common 1¢ par exchanged for (0.4) share new Common 1¢ par 11/18/1997
New Common 1¢ par split (5) for (2) by issuance of (1.5) additional shares payable 03/31/2006 to holders of record 03/20/2006 Ex date - 04/03/2006

Name changed to ATN International, Inc. 06/21/2016

ATLANTIC TELECASTING CORP (NC)
Administratively dissolved 10/16/1995

ATLANTIC THRIFT CENTERS, INC. (DE)
Merged into Spartans Industries, Inc. (DE) 03/12/1966
Each share (4.5) shares Common $1 par exchanged for $50 principal amount of 5% Conv. Subord. Debentures due 06/01/1986
(See Spartans Industries, Inc. (DE))

ATLANTIC TURNKEY CORP (UT)
Reorganized under the laws of Nevada as NuVoci, Inc. 01/28/2005
Each share Common $0.001 par exchanged for (0.005) share Common $0.001 par
Note: Holders of between (101) and (19,999) shares will receive (100) shares only
Holders of (100) or fewer shares will not be affected by the reverse split
NuVoci, Inc. reorganized as Cyberhand Technologies International, Inc. 05/13/2005 which name changed to ChromoCure, Inc. 07/09/2009

ATLANTIC UTILITIES CORP. (FL)
Merged into Southern Gulf Utilities, Inc. 11/17/1966
Each share Common $1 par exchanged for (0.5) share Common 5¢ par
Southern Gulf Utilities, Inc. name changed to Ecological Science Corp. 06/19/1968 which name changed to Amicor Inc. 05/20/1974 which recapitalized as Keystone Camera Products Corp. 06/20/1984
(See Keystone Camera Products Corp.)

ATLANTIC WHITEHALL FDS TR (DE)
Growth & Income Fund reclassified as Balanced Fund 04/24/2003
Completely liquidated
Each share Balanced Fund received first and final distribution of $11.55 cash payable 03/31/2005 to holders of record 03/30/2005
Each share Income Fund received first and final distribution of $9.81 cash payable 03/31/2005 to holders of record 03/30/2005
Each International Fund Institutional Class Share received first and final distribution of $7.10 cash payable 07/13/2009 to holders of record 07/02/2009
Each Multi-Cap Global Value Fund Institutional Class Share received first and final distribution of $6.08 cash payable 07/13/2009 to holders of record 07/02/2009
Under plan of reorganization each share Equity Income Fund Institutional Class automatically became AIM Equity Funds Disciplined Equity Fund Class Y $0.001 par on a net asset basis 09/21/2009
Under plan of reorganization each share Growth Fund automatically became AIM Equity Funds Large Cap Growth Fund Class Y $0.001 par on a net asset basis 09/21/2009
Under plan of reorganization each share Mid-Cap Growth Fund Institutional Class automatically became AIM Growth Series Mid Cap Core Equity Fund Class Y $0.001 on a net asset basis 09/21/2009

ATLANTIC WHSLRS LTD (NB)
5.5% Preferred $20 par called for redemption 08/16/1976
Merged into Loblaw Companies Ltd. 11/04/1976
Each share Class A no par exchanged for $100 cash

ATLANTIC WINE AGYS INC (FL)
Each share old Common $0.00001 par exchanged for (0.005) share new Common $0.00001 par 03/01/2004
Each share new Common $0.00001 par exchanged again for (0.04) share new Common $0.00001 par 05/19/2008
Reorganized as Novo Energies Corp. 06/24/2009
Each share Common $0.00001 par exchanged for (3) shares Common $0.00001 par
Novo Energies Corp. name changed to Immunovative, Inc. 05/08/2012 which name changed to Tauriga Sciences, Inc. 04/09/2013

ATLANTIC WOOD INDUSTRIES, INC. (MD)
Involuntarily dissolved 01/07/1987

ATLANTIS BUSINESS DEV CORP (NV)
Reincorporated 11/15/2004
Place of incorporation changed from (DE) to (NV) 11/15/2004
Each share old Common $0.001 par exchanged for (0.01) share new Common $0.001 par 11/26/2004
Each share new Common $0.001 par received distribution of (2) shares E-Direct Inc. Common $0.001 par payable 02/04/2005 to holders of record 01/21/2005 Ex date - 02/04/2005
Each share new Common $0.001 par exchanged again for (3) shares new Common $0.001 par 04/12/2005
Each share new Common $0.001 par received distribution of (1) share COR Equity Holdings Inc. Common $0.001 par payable 10/21/2005 to holders of record 09/16/2005
Each share new Common $0.001 par exchanged again for (0.01) share new Common $0.001 par 08/21/2006
Each share new Common $0.001 par exchanged again for (0.00333333) share new Common $0.001 par 05/30/2007
Reorganized as Atlantis Technology Group 10/11/2007
Each share new Common $0.001 par exchanged for (100) shares Common $0.001 par

ATLANTIS COMMUNICATIONS INC (ON)
Merged into Alliance Atlantis Communications Inc. 09/21/1998
Each share Subordinate no par exchanged for either (0.5) share Non-Vtg. Class B no par or (0.5) share Class C no par
(See Alliance Atlantis Communications Inc.)

ATLANTIS DEV CO (SC)
Involuntarily dissolved for failure to pay taxes 01/04/1980

ATLANTIS DEVELOPMENT CORP. (AB)
Merged into Triad Oil Co. Ltd. 00/00/1952
Each share Capital Stock $1 par exchanged for (0.4) share Capital Stock no par
Triad Oil Co. Ltd. name changed to BP Oil & Gas Ltd. 07/02/1970 which merged into BP Canada Ltd. (ON) 10/18/1972 which name changed to BP Canada Ltd.-BP Canada Ltee. 04/27/1973 which reincorporated in Canada as BP Canada Inc. 07/06/1979
(See BP Canada Inc.)

ATLANTIS ENTERPRISES INTL LTD (BC)
Delisted from Vancouver Stock Exchange 03/04/1991

ATLANTIS EXPL INC (CANADA)
Recapitalized as Noveko Echographs Inc. 02/04/2004
Each share Common no par exchanged for (0.33333333) share Common no par
Noveko Echographs Inc. name changed to Noveko International Inc. 01/11/2006

ATLANTIS GROUP INC (DE)
Ctfs. dated prior to 05/31/1994
Reincorporated under the laws of Florida as Atlantis Plastics, Inc. 05/31/1994
Atlantis Plastics, Inc. (FL) reincorporated in Delaware 03/15/2005
(See Atlantis Plastics, Inc.)

ATLANTIS GROUP INC NEW (DE)
Certificates dated after 11/02/1995
Charter cancelled and declared inoperative and void for non-payment of taxes 03/01/1997

ATLANTIS HLDG CORP (NV)
Recapitalized as Medical Institutional Services Holdings, Inc. 01/09/2008
Each share Common $0.001 par exchanged for (0.001) share Common $0.001 par
Medical Institutional Services Holdings, Inc. name changed to In Control Security, Inc. 09/10/2008 which recapitalized as Envirotek 10/28/2009 which name changed to Suffer 06/21/2010 which recapitalized as Ophir Resources Co. 01/23/2013
(See Ophir Resources Co.)

ATLANTIS INTL CORP (NJ)
Each share Common 5¢ par exchanged for (0.2) share Common 25¢ par 03/19/1969
Plan of arrangement effective 04/26/1969
Each share Common 25¢ par exchanged for (0.5) share Chauncey Enterprises, Inc. Common, (0.5) share Delanair, Inc. Common, Eleven Eleven Corp. Common, Knoxfort Corp. Common, Roark Enterprises, Inc. Common and Scientifacts Corp. Common
(See each company's listing)

ATLANTIS INTL LTD (AB)
Name changed to Atlantis Resources Ltd. 07/19/1988
(See Atlantis Resources Ltd.)

ATLANTIS MINES LTD (BC)
Struck off register and declared dissolved for failure to file returns 06/26/1977

ATLANTIS MNG & MFG INC (ID)
Administratively dissolved 02/06/1998

ATLANTIS PLASTICS INC (DE)
State of incorporation changed from (FL) to (DE) and Class A Common 10¢ par changed to $0.0001 par 03/15/2005
Chapter 11 bankruptcy proceedings converted to Chapter 7 on 12/19/2008
Stockholders' equity unlikely

ATLANTIS RES INTL LTD (AB)
Recapitalized as International Atlantis Resources Ltd. 12/06/1983
Each share Common no par exchanged for (0.25) share Common no par
International Atlantis Resources Ltd. name changed to Atlantis International Ltd. 11/03/1986 which name changed to Atlantis Resources Ltd. 07/19/1988
(See Atlantis Resources Ltd.)

ATLANTIS RES LTD (AB)
Merged into Grad & Walker Energy Corp. 01/01/1995
Each share Common no par held by Canadian residents exchanged for (0.185) share Common no par
Each share Common no par held by non-Canadian residents exchanged for $1.5921 cash plus the proceeds from the sale of Grad & Walker shares equivalent to (0.0541) share Common no par per share
(See Grad & Walker Energy Corp.)

ATLANTIS SYS CORP (CANADA)
Each share old Common no par exchanged for (0.05) share new Common no par 11/30/2010
Acquired by Bluedrop Performance Learning Inc. 12/31/2013
Each share new Common no par exchanged for $0.02759915 cash

ATLAS ACCEP CORP (DE)
Class A Common $1 par and Class B Common $1 par changed to 10¢ par 00/00/1933
Recapitalized 03/03/1964
Each share Preferred $100 par exchanged for (24) shares Common 10¢ par
Class A Common 10¢ par and Class B Common 10¢ par reclassified as Common 10¢ par share for share
Stock Dividend - 10% 03/12/1969
Name changed to Oppenheimer Industries, Inc. 03/21/1969
(See Oppenheimer Industries, Inc.)

ATLAS ACQUISITION HLDG CORP (DE)
Completely liquidated 03/16/2010
Each Unit exchanged for first and final distribution of $10 cash
Each share Common $0.001 par exchanged for first and final distribution of $10 cash

ATLAS AIR WORLDWIDE HLDGS INC (DE)
Reorganized 02/16/2001
Common 1¢ par split (3) for (2) by issuance of (0.5) additional share payable 02/08/1999 to holders of record 01/25/1999 Ex date - 02/09/1999
Under plan of reorganization each share Atlas Air, Inc. Common 1¢ par automatically became (1) share Atlas Air Worldwide Holdings, Inc. Common 1¢ par 02/16/2001
Plan of reorganization under Chapter 11 Federal Bankruptcy code effective 07/27/2004
No stockholders' equity
(Additional Information in Active)

ATLAS AMER INC (DE)
Common 1¢ par split (3) for (2) by issuance of (0.5) additional share payable 03/10/2006 to holders of record 02/28/2006 Ex date - 03/13/2006
Common 1¢ par split (3) for (2) by issuance of (0.5) additional share payable 05/25/2007 to holders of record 05/15/2007 Ex date - 05/29/2007
Common 1¢ par split (3) for (2) by issuance of (0.5) additional share payable 05/30/2008 to holders of record 05/21/2008 Ex date - 06/02/2008
Under plan of merger name changed to Atlas Energy, Inc. 09/29/2009
(See Atlas Energy, Inc.)

ATLAS AMERN CORP (DE)
100% reacquired 05/00/1982
Public interest eliminated

ATLAS AMERICAN OIL CORP. (TX)
Charter forfeited for non-payment of taxes 07/18/1966

ATLAS BOWLING CENTERS, INC. (DE)
No longer in existence having become inoperative and void for non-payment of taxes 04/01/1964

ATLAS BRADFORD CO (TX)
Liquidation completed
Each share Preferred $100 par exchanged for first and final distribution of (4.6) shares Rucker Co. Common no par 04/15/1969
Each share Common $1 par exchanged for initial distribution of (0.047614) share Rucker Co. Common no par 04/29/1969
Each share Common $1 par received second and final distribution of (0.015678) share Rucker Co. Common no par 06/23/1969
Rucker Co. merged into N L Industries, Inc. 01/21/1977

ATLAS BREWING CO.
Merged into Drewry's Limited, U.S.A., Inc. 00/00/1951
Each share Common $3 par exchanged for (0.2) share 5.75% Preferred $50 par
(See Drewry's Limited, U.S.A., Inc.)

ATLAS CAP HLDGS INC (NV)
Each share old Common $0.0001 par exchanged for (0.001) share new Common $0.0001 par 01/26/2012
Name changed to Home Health International Inc. 03/26/2012
Home Health International Inc. recapitalized as American Transportation Holdings, Inc. 04/29/2014

ATLAS CHAIN & PRECISION PRODS INC (PA)
99.612% acquired by Bucyrus-Erie Co. through purchase offer which expired 02/23/1968
Public interest eliminated

ATLAS CHEM INDS INC (DE)
Merged into Imperial Chemical Industries Ltd. 07/21/1971
Each share Common $1 par exchanged for $40 cash

ATLAS CHIBOUGAMAU MINES LTD. (ON)
Charter revoked for failure to file reports and pay fees 04/22/1965

ATLAS CLOUD ENTERPRISES INC (AB)
Reincorporated under the laws of British Columbia as Atlas Blockchain Group Inc. 07/27/2018

ATLAS COLD STORAGE INCOME TR (ON)
Acquired by Avion Group HF 11/03/2006
Each Trust Unit exchanged for $7.50 cash

ATLAS CORP (CO)
SEC revoked common stock registration 12/18/2014

ATLAS CORP (DE)
Each share $3 Preference Ser. A exchanged for (1) share 6% Preferred $50 par 10/31/1936
Each share Common no par exchanged for (1) share Common $5 par 10/31/1936
6% Preferred $50 par called for redemption 00/00/1946
Each share Common $5 par exchanged for (4) shares Common $1 par 05/31/1956
Each share old Common $1 par exchanged for (0.2) share new Common $1 par 12/03/1976
5% Preferred $20 par called for redemption 09/15/1980
Common $1 par split (2) for (1) by issuance of (1) additional share 04/24/1989
New Common $1 par changed to 1¢ par 07/29/1998
Reorganized under the laws of Colorado as Atlas Minerals Inc. 01/10/2000
For holdings of (1,000) or more shares each (30) shares new Common 1¢ par exchanged for (1) share Common 1¢ par
Holdings of (999) shares or fewer were cancelled and are without value

Atlas Minerals Inc. name changed to Atlas Corp. 05/07/2007
(See Atlas Corp.)

ATLAS CR CORP (PA)
20¢ Preferred called for redemption 05/15/1958
Class B Common 10¢ par reclassified as Common 10¢ par 05/31/1963
Merged into Sunasco Inc. 04/30/1966
Each share Common 10¢ par exchanged for (0.306783) share $1.65 Conv. Preferred 10¢ par
Sunasco Inc. name changed to Scientific Resources Corp. 10/11/1968
(See Scientific Resources Corp.)

ATLAS CROMWELL LTD (BC)
Reincorporated 05/02/2006
Place of incorporation changed from (ON) to (BC) 05/02/2006
Name changed to Terrane Metals Corp. 07/27/2006
Terrane Metals Corp. merged into Thompson Creek Metals Co., Inc. 10/20/2010

ATLAS CROMWELL RES LTD (AB)
Name changed to Polycorp Inc. (AB) 06/30/1998
Polycorp Inc. (AB) reincorporated in Ontario as Atlas Cromwell Ltd. 12/27/2001 which reincorporated in British Columbia 05/02/2006 which name changed to Terrane Metals Corp. 07/27/2006 which merged into Thompson Creek Metals Co., Inc. 10/20/2010

ATLAS DIESEL ENGINE CORP.
Dissolved 00/00/1947
Details not available

ATLAS DROP FORGE CO.
Name changed to A.D.F. Co. 09/15/1945
(See A.D.F. Co.)

ATLAS ELECTRONICS, INC. (NJ)
Completely liquidated 11/20/1967
Each share Common 10¢ par exchanged for first and final distribution of (0.0625) share Sterling Electronics Corp. 75¢ Conv. Preferred Ser. A $2.50 par
(See Sterling Electronics Corp.)

ATLAS ENERGY INC (DE)
Merged into Chevron Corp. 02/18/2011
Each share Common 1¢ par exchanged for (0.5203) Atlas Pipeline Holdings, L.P. Common Unit and $38.25 cash
Note: Each share Common 1¢ par received an additional $0.10 cash from litigation 11/29/2011

ATLAS ENERGY L P (DE)
Each Common Unit received distribution of (0.1021) Atlas Resource Partners, L.P. Common Unit payable 03/13/2012 to holders of record 02/28/2012 Ex date - 03/14/2012
Each Common Unit received distribution of (0.5) Atlas Energy Group, LLC Common Unit payable 02/27/2015 to holders of record 02/25/2015
Merged into Targa Resources Partners L.P. 02/27/2015
Each Common Unit exchanged for (0.1809) Common Unit and $9.12 cash
Targa Resources Partners L.P. merged into Targa Resources Corp. 02/17/2016

ATLAS ENERGY LTD (AB)
Merged into Pearl Exploration & Production Ltd. 12/26/2006
Each share Common no par exchanged for (0.82) share Common no par
Pearl Exploration & Production Ltd. name changed to BlackPearl Resources Inc. 05/14/2009

ATLAS ENERGY RES LLC (DE)
Merged into Atlas Energy, Inc. 09/29/2009
Each Common Unit exchanged for (1.16) shares Common 1¢ par
(See Atlas Energy, Inc.)

ATLAS ENVIRONMENTAL INC (CO)
Assets sold for the benefit of creditors 06/25/1999
No stockholders' equity

ATLAS EXPLS LTD (BC)
Recapitalized as Cima Resources Ltd. 07/26/1974
Each share Common 50¢ par exchanged for (0.25) share Common no par
Cima Resources Ltd. recapitalized as Consolidated Cima Resources Ltd. (BC) 08/23/1984 which reincorporated in Canada as Hankin Atlas Industries Ltd. 08/15/1989 which name changed to Hankin Water Technologies Ltd. 03/26/1999
(See Hankin Water Technologies Ltd.)

ATLAS FERTILIZER CORP. (PHILIPPINES)
Each share Common PHP 10 par exchanged for (10) shares Common PHP 1 par 06/19/1973
Name changed to Leisure & Resorts World Corp. 04/12/1999

ATLAS FINANCE CO., INC. (GA)
Each share Common $50 par exchanged for (5.2) shares Common $10 par 00/00/1951
Each share Common $10 par exchanged for (2) shares Common $5 par 00/00/1952
Stock Dividend - 10% 02/25/1953
Prior Preferred called for redemption 05/09/1959
Completely liquidated 07/15/1966
Each share 6% Conv. Preferred $20 par exchanged for first and final distribution of (0.7009) share Transamerica Corp. Common $2 par
Each share 5.75% Preferred $100 par exchanged for first and final distribution of (3.785) shares Transamerica Corp. Common $2 par
Each share Common $5 par exchanged for (0.4495) share Transamerica Corp. Common $2 par
Transamerica Corp. merged into Aegon N.V. 07/21/1999

ATLAS FINANCE CORP.
Dissolved 00/00/1943
Details not available

ATLAS GENERAL INDUSTRIES, INC. (MA)
Merged into Consolidated Electronics Industries Corp. 09/14/1964
Each share $1.25 Preferred $20 par exchanged for (0.8) share Common $5 par
Each share Common $1 par exchanged for (0.5) share Common $5 par
Consolidated Electronics Industries Corp. name changed to North American Philips Corp. 02/14/1969
(See North American Philips Corp.)

ATLAS GOLD MINES, INC.
Out of business 00/00/1952
Details not available

ATLAS GYPSUM CORP. LTD. (ON)
Charter revoked for failure to file reports and pay fees 00/00/1961

ATLAS HEALTHCARE INC (FL)
Recapitalized as MyGlobal Concierge, Inc. (FL) 09/30/2000
Each share Common $0.0001 par exchanged for (0.1) share Common $0.0001 par
MyGlobal Concierge.com, Inc. (FL) reincorporated in Delaware 08/21/2008

ATLAS HOTELS INC (DE)
Common no par split (3) for (1) by issuance of (2) additional shares 09/20/1968
Merged into AH Merger Co., Inc. 02/22/1988
Each share Common no par exchanged for $75 cash

ATLAS IMPERIAL DIESEL ENGINE CO.
Name changed to United Can & Glass Co. 00/00/1951
United Can & Glass Co. merged into Hunt Foods & Industries, Inc. 12/05/1958 which merged into Simon (Norton), Inc. 07/17/1968 which merged into Esmark, Inc. (Inc. 03/14/1969) 09/09/1983
(See Esmark, Inc. (Inc. 03/14/1969))

ATLAS INDUSTRIES, INC. (FL)
Proclaimed dissolved for failure to file reports and pay fees 05/22/1970

ATLAS LIFE INS CO (OK)
Capital Stock $5 par split (4) for (3) by issuance of (0.33333333) additional share 03/11/1987
Stock Dividends - 50% 00/00/1956; 33.33333333% 00/00/1957; 42.86% 00/00/1960; 10% 00/00/1963; 25% 04/18/1973; 10% 04/06/1977
Company reported as inactive 06/01/1998
Details not available

ATLAS MALTING CO.
Apparently out of business 00/00/1941
Details not available

ATLAS MANAGEMENT CO. (NV)
Merged into Duesenberg Corp. 06/22/1971
Each share Common $5 par exchanged for (0.25) share Capital Stock 10¢ par
(See Duesenberg Corp.)

ATLAS MEGLIO CORP (NY)
Recapitalized as Eastern Diversified Corp. 05/11/1970
Each share Common 10¢ par exchanged for (5) shares Common 2¢ par
(See Eastern Diversified Corp.)

ATLAS MINERALS INC (AB)
Reorganized under the laws of British Columbia as Cliffmont Resources Ltd. 02/22/2010
Each share Common no par exchanged for (0.1) share Common no par

ATLAS MINERALS INC (CO)
Name changed to Atlas Corp. 05/07/2007
(See Atlas Corp.)

ATLAS MINING & MILLING CORP. (UT)
Name changed to Coronado Corp. and
Common 10¢ par changed to no par 07/31/1961
(See Coronado Corp.)

ATLAS MNG CO (ID)
Common $1 par changed to 10¢ par 00/00/1953
Common 10¢ par changed to no par 00/00/1999
Reincorporated under the laws of Delaware as Applied Minerals, Inc. 10/30/2009

ATLAS NICKEL CORP. (QC)
Charter annulled for failure to file annual reports 00/00/1973

ATLAS OIL & GAS INC (NV)
Each share old Common $0.001 par exchanged for (0.01) share new Common $0.001 par 07/16/2009
Name changed to Cheyenne Resources Corp. 09/02/2009

ATLAS OIL & REFINING CORP.
Assets sold 00/00/1948
Details not available

ATLAS PAC LTD (AUSTRALIA)
Name changed to Atlas South Sea Pearl, Ltd. 06/07/2006
(See Atlas South Sea Pearl, Ltd.)

ATLAS PIPE, INC. (TX)
Name changed to Atlas Bradford Co. 00/00/1960
Atlas Bradford Co. liquidated for Rucker Co. 04/15/1969 which merged into N L Industries, Inc. 01/21/1977

ATLAS PIPE LINE CO., INC.
Reorganized as Atlas Pipe Line Corp. 00/00/1935
(See Atlas Pipe Line Corp.)

ATLAS PIPE LINE CORP.
Reorganized as Atlas Oil & Refining Corp. 00/00/1942
No stockholders' equity

ATLAS PIPELINE HLDGS L P (DE)
Name changed to Atlas Energy, L.P. 02/23/2011
Atlas Energy, L.P. merged into Targa Resources Partners L.P. 02/27/2015 which merged into Targa Resources Corp. 02/17/2016

ATLAS PIPELINE PARTNERS L P (DE)
8.25% Perpetual Preferred Units Class E called for redemption at $25 plus $0.246354 accrued dividends on 02/27/2015
Merged into Targa Resources Partners L.P. 02/27/2015
Each Unit of Ltd. Partnership Int. exchanged for (0.5846) Common Unit and $1.26 cash
Targa Resources Partners L.P. merged into Targa Resources Corp. 02/17/2016

ATLAS PLYWOOD CORP. (MA)
Each share old Common no par exchanged for (2) shares new Common no par 00/00/1929
Each share new Common no par exchanged for (2) shares Common $1 par 00/00/1943
Name changed to Atlas General Industries, Inc. 10/10/1960
Atlas General Industries, Inc. merged into Consolidated Electronics Industries Corp. 09/14/1964 which name changed to North American Philips Corp. 02/14/1969
(See North American Philips Corp.)

ATLAS PORTLAND CEMENT CO.
Acquired by United States Steel Corp. (NJ) 00/00/1930
Details not available

ATLAS POWDER CO. (DE)
5% Preferred $100 par changed to 4% Preferred $100 par 00/00/1946
Each share Common no par exchanged for (2) shares Common $20 par 00/00/1950
Recapitalized as Atlas Chemical Industries, Inc. 05/31/1961
Each share Common $20 par exchanged for (4) new shares Common $1 par
(See Atlas Chemical Industries, Inc.)

ATLAS PRESS CO (MI)
Common $1 par split (4) for (1) by issuance of (3) additional shares 10/31/1966
Stock Dividend - 100% 07/00/1947
Reincorporated under the laws of Delaware as Clausing Corp. 08/30/1969
(See Clausing Corp.)

ATLAS RAINBOW MINES LTD (ON)
Charter cancelled for failure to pay taxes and file returns 03/16/1976

ATLAS-REPUBLIC CORP (CO)
Reincorporated under the laws of Delaware as AMCO Transport Holdings, Inc. 11/27/2002
AMCO Transport Holdings, Inc. recapitalized as Business

Development Solutions, Inc. 02/28/2006
(See Business Development Solutions, Inc.)

ATLAS RESOURCE PARTNERS L P (DE)
Plan of reorganization under Chapter 11 Federal Bankruptcy proceedings effective 09/01/2016
No stockholders' equity

ATLAS RES INC (NV)
Recapitalized as Globaltech Holdings, Inc. 08/01/2007
Each share Common $0.001 par exchanged for (0.02) share $0.001 par

ATLAS SVGS & LN ASSN SAN FRANCISCO (CA)
Charter suspended for failure to file reports and pay fees 05/01/1989

ATLAS SEWING CENTERS, INC. (DE)
Stock Dividend - 10% 02/15/1957
Adjudicated bankrupt 10/27/1967
No stockholders' equity

ATLAS SOUTH SEA PEARL LTD (AUSTRALIA)
ADR agreement terminated 01/14/2008
Each Sponsored ADR for Ordinary exchanged for $7.58703 cash

ATLAS STAR CORP (AB)
Placed in receivership 07/00/2003
Details not available

ATLAS STEEL CORP.
Merged into Ludlum Steel Co. 00/00/1928
Details not available

ATLAS STEELS, LTD. (CANADA)
Common no par exchanged (5) for (1) 00/00/1946
Acquired by Rio Algom Mines, Ltd. 02/28/1963
Each share Common no par exchanged for $37.7438 cash

ATLAS STL CASTING INC (NY)
Charter 11 bankruptcy proceedings converted to Chapter 7 on 10/25/1985
Stockholders' equity unlikely

ATLAS STORES CORP. (DE)
Name changed to Davega Stores Corp. (DE) 00/00/1932
Davega Stores Corp. (DE) merged into Davega Stores Corp. (NY) 01/14/1946
(See Davega Stores Corp. (NY))

ATLAS SULPHUR & IRON CO. LTD. (QC)
Recapitalized as International Atlas Development & Exploration Ltd. 06/26/1963
Each share Capital Stock $1 par exchanged for (0.06666666) share Capital Stock $1 par
(See International Atlas Development & Exploration Ltd.)

ATLAS TACK CORP (MA)
Reincorporated 10/11/1967
State of incorporation changed from (NY) to (MA) 10/11/1967
Out of business 00/00/1985
Stockholders' equity unlikely

ATLAS TELEFILM LTD. (ON)
Recapitalized as Allied Telemedia Ltd. 01/24/1964
Each share Capital Stock no par exchanged for (1) share Common no par and (0.04) share 6% Preferred $10 par
(See Allied Telemedia Ltd.)

ATLAS THERAPEUTICS CORP (NV)
Common $0.001 par split (14) for (1) by issuance of (13) additional shares payable 07/14/2010 to holders of record 07/14/2010
Name changed to MYOS Corp. 05/21/2012

MYOS Corp. name changed to MYOS RENS Technology Inc. 03/22/2016

ATLAS URANIUM CORP. (UT)
Name changed to Atlas Mining & Milling Corp. 07/30/1957
Atlas Mining & Milling Corp. name changed to Coronado Corp. 07/31/1961
(See Coronado Corp.)

ATLAS URANIUM CORP. LTD. (AB)
Name changed to Aabro Mining & Oils Ltd. and Capital Stock 5¢ par reclassified as Common no par 05/10/1968
(See Aabro Mining & Oils Ltd.)

ATLAS UTILITIES CORP. (DE)
Name changed to Atlas Corp. 07/13/1932
(See Atlas Corp.)

ATLAS VAN LINES INC (DE)
Common no par split (3) for (2) by issuance of (0.5) additional share 06/08/1981
Common no par split (3) for (2) by issuance of (0.5) additional share 06/24/1983
Acquired by Wesray Transportation Inc. 10/15/1984
Each share Common no par exchanged for $18.85 cash

ATLAS YELLOWKNIFE MINES LTD. (ON)
Common $1 par changed to no par 10/13/1976
Name changed to Altas Yellowknife Resources Ltd. 02/20/1980
Atlas Yellowknife Resources Ltd. recapitalized as Panatlas Energy Inc. 02/08/1988 which was acquired by Velvet Exploration Ltd. 07/17/2000
(See Velvet Exploration Ltd.)

ATLAS YELLOWKNIFE RES LTD (ON)
Recapitalized as Panatlas Energy Inc. 02/08/1988
Each share Common no par exchanged for (0.083333333) share Common no par
Panatlas Energy Inc. acquired by Velvet Exploration Ltd. 07/17/2000
(See Velvet Exploration Ltd.)

ATLED CORP (DE)
Liquidation completed
Each share Capital Stock $50 par exchanged for initial distribution of $90,000 cash 04/30/1968
Each share Capital Stock $50 par received second and final distribution of $6,100 cash 10/24/1968

ATLEE CORP (MA)
Each share old Common no par exchanged for (4) shares new Common no par 02/24/1960
Each share new Common no par exchanged for (0.142857) share Common $1 par 03/05/1963
Merged into Spencer-Kennedy Laboratories, Inc. 05/01/1968
Each share Common $1 par exchanged for (1.33333333) shares Common $1 par
Spencer-Kennedy Laboratories, Inc. liquidated for Computer Devices, Inc. (MA) 11/21/1979 which reorganized in Maryland 06/30/1986
(See Computer Devices, Inc. (MD))

ATLIN MINERAL EXPL CORP (NV)
Common $0.001 par split (6) for (1) by issuance of (5) additional shares payable 04/23/2007 to holders of record 04/17/2007 Ex date - 04/24/2007
Name changed to Soltera Mining Corp. 05/30/2007

ATLIN-RUFFNER MINES (BC) LTD. (BC)
Recapitalized as Armore Mines Ltd. 02/22/1965

Each share Capital Stock $1 par exchanged for (0.2) share Capital Stock $1 par
Armore Mines Ltd. recapitalized as Marcana Resources Ltd. 07/17/1973 which recapitalized as FMG Telecomputer Ltd. 04/04/1983 which name changed to SOK Properties Ltd. 07/04/1989 which name changed to Impact Telemedia International Ltd. 08/03/1990 which name changed to UC'NWIN Systems Ltd. (BC) 07/17/1992 which reincorporated in Delaware as UC'NWIN Systems Corp. 12/11/1995 which recapitalized as Winner's Edge.com, Inc. 10/29/1999 which name changed to Sealant Solutions Inc. 08/06/2001 which name changed to PowerChannel, Inc. 07/28/2003

ATLIN-RUFFNER MINES LTD.
Merged into Atlin-Ruffner Mines (BC) Ltd. 00/00/1949
Each share Capital Stock $1 par exchanged for (0.25) share Capital Stock $1 par
Atlin-Ruffner Mines (BC) Ltd. recapitalized as Armore Mines Ltd. 02/22/1965 which recapitalized as Marcana Resources Ltd. 07/17/1973 which recapitalized as FMG Telecomputer Ltd. 04/04/1983 which name changed to SOK Properties Ltd. 07/04/1989 which name changed to Impact Telemedia International Ltd. 08/30/1990 which name changed to UC'NWIN Systems Ltd. (BC) 07/17/1992 which reincorporated in Delaware as UC'NWIN Systems Corp. 12/11/1995 which recapitalized as Winner's Edge.com, Inc. 10/29/1999 which name changed to Sealant Solutions Inc. 08/06/2001 which name changed to PowerChannel, Inc. 07/28/2003 which recapitalized as Qualibou Energy Inc. 02/05/2008

ATM CAPITOL CORP (NV)
Reincorporated under the laws of Delaware as ATM Capitol Co. 04/24/2000

ATM FINL CORP (NV)
Common $0.0001 par split (7) for (1) by issuance of (6) additional shares payable 02/05/2008 to holders of record 02/04/2008 Ex date - 02/06/2008
Name changed to Prime Sun Power Inc. 04/15/2008
Prime Sun Power Inc. name changed to 3Power Energy Group Inc. 03/31/2011

ATM HLDGS INC (NV)
SEC revoked common stock registration 03/02/2007

ATMANCO INC (CANADA)
Name changed to ATW Tech Inc. 06/12/2018

ATMEL CORP (DE)
Reincorporated 10/18/1999
Common no par split (2) for (1) by issuance of (1) additional share 04/11/1994
Common no par split (2) for (1) by issuance of (1) additional share 08/08/1995
Place of incorporation changed from (CA) to (DE) and Common no par changed to $0.001 par 10/18/1999
Common $0.001 par split (2) for (1) by issuance of (1) additional share payable 12/17/1999 to holders of record 12/03/1999
Common $0.001 par split (2) for (1) by issuance of (1) additional share payable 08/25/2000 to holders of record 08/11/2000
Merged into Microchip Technology Inc. 04/04/2016
Each share Common $0.001 par

exchanged for (0.0237) share Common $0.001 par and $7 cash

ATMI INC (DE)
Acquired by Entegris, Inc. 04/30/2014
Each share Common 1¢ par exchanged for $34 cash

ATMOS-PAK, INC. (DE)
Adjudicated bankrupt 11/08/1965
No stockholders' equity

ATMOSPHERIC CTL INDS INC (NY)
Charter cancelled and proclaimed dissolved for failure to pay taxes 12/15/1975

ATMOSPHERIC GLOW TECHNOLOGIES INC (DE)
Chapter 11 bankruptcy proceedings converted to Chapter 7 on 10/23/2008
No stockholders' equity

ATMOSPHERIC HEAT & POWER CO. (ME)
Charter suspended for failure to pay taxes 00/00/1928

ATN INC (UT)
Name changed to American Telemedia Network, Inc. 07/02/1987
American Telemedia Network, Inc. name changed to ATNN, Inc. 12/22/1989 which recapitalized as EuroTelecom Communications, Inc. 08/11/1997 which recapitalized as Bene Io, Inc. 07/24/2006

ATNA RES LTD (BC)
Plan of reorganization under Chapter 11 Federal Bankruptcy proceedings effective 12/31/2016
No stockholders' equity

ATNG INC (NV)
Reincorporated 09/06/2003
State of incorporation changed from (TX) to (NV) 09/06/2003
Recapitalized as Zann Corp. 12/03/2004
Each share Common $0.001 par exchanged for (0.00111111) share Common $0.001 par

ATNN INC (UT)
Reorganized under the laws of Delaware as EuroTelecom Communications, Inc. 08/11/1997
Each share Common no par exchanged for (0.00854267) share Common 1¢ par
EuroTelecom Communications, Inc. recapitalized as BENE IO, Inc. 07/24/2006
(See BENE IO, Inc.)

ATOCHA RES INC (BC)
Recapitalized as Durango Resources Inc. 02/12/2013
Each share Common no par exchanged for (0.05) share Common no par

ATOHM ELECTRONICS (CA)
Name changed to Technical Industries, Inc. 01/22/1965
Technical Industries, Inc. acquired by Thermal Systems, Inc. 11/28/1969 which name changed to Axial Corp. 10/05/1970 which name changed to Axial Liquidating Corp. 05/31/1973 which liquidated for Sierracin Corp. (CA) 06/06/1973 which reincorporated in Delaware 05/31/1977
(See Sierracin Corp. (DE))

ATOK GOLD MINING CO., INC.
Merged into Atok-Big Wedge Mining Co., Inc. 00/00/1948
Details not available

ATOM GOLD MINES LTD. (ON)
Dissolved 09/18/1961
Details not available

ATOM INC (NM)
98% acquired by Consolidated Oil & Gas, Inc. as of 03/00/1981
Public interest eliminated

ATOMIC BURRITO INC (OK)
SEC revoked common stock registration 10/03/2008

ATOMIC DEV CORP (NY)
Name changed to A D C Medical Instruments Corp. 06/27/1978
(See A D C Medical Instruments Corp.)

ATOMIC DEVELOPMENT & MACHINE CORP. (NY)
Name changed to Atomic Development Corp. 03/24/1971
Atomic Development Corp. name changed to A D C Medical Instruments Corp. 06/27/1978
(See A D C Medical Instruments Corp.)

ATOMIC DEVELOPMENT MUTUAL FUND INC. (DE)
Capital Stock $1 par changed to $0.33333333 par and (2) additional shares issued 08/12/1957
Name changed to Atomics, Physics & Science Fund, Inc. 10/05/1960
Atomics, Physics & Science Fund, Inc. name changed to Steadman Science & Growth Fund, Inc. 10/08/1965 which was acquired by Steadman American Industry Fund, Inc. 09/14/1970 which name changed to Ameritor Industry Fund 09/23/1998
(See Ameritor Industry Fund)

ATOMIC ENERGY CORP. (UT)
Name changed to Olidan Energy Corp. 06/04/1980
Olidan Energy Corp. recapitalized as Columbine Capital Corp. 07/15/1988
(See Columbine Capital Corp.)

ATOMIC FUEL EXTRACTION CORP (DE)
Merged into New Products Corp. 12/29/1969
Each share Common $1 par exchanged for (0.137931) share Common 10¢ par
New Products Corp. recapitalized as Commodore Resources Corp. 12/29/1978 which name changed to Commodore Environmental Services, Inc. (UT) 06/26/1987 which reincorporated in Delaware 08/00/1998
(See Commodore Environmental Services, Inc.)

ATOMIC GUPPY INC (NV)
Recapitalized as Quamtel, Inc. 09/09/2009
Each share Common $0.001 par exchanged for (0.1) share Common $0.001 par
Quamtel, Inc. name changed to DataJack, Inc. 12/31/2012 which name changed to Unified Signal, Inc. 11/28/2014

ATOMIC INSTRUMENT CO. (MA)
Merged into Baird Associates-Atomic Instrument Co. 06/01/1956
Each share Common $1 par exchanged for (0.45) share Common $1 par
Baird Associates-Atomic Instrument Co. name changed to Baird-Atomic, Inc. 12/04/1956 which name changed to Baird Corp. 02/28/1978
(See Baird Corp.)

ATOMIC MINERALS CORP., INC. (NV)
Name changed to Geo Resources Corp. 09/04/1958
(See Geo Resources Corp.)

ATOMIC MINERALS INC (BC)
Name changed to Arco Resources Corp. 05/11/2009
Arco Resources Corp. name changed to Cannex Capital Holdings Inc. 03/14/2018

ATOMIC MNG & OIL CORP (UT)
Recapitalized as Hollywood International Studios 01/15/1971
Each share Common 10¢ par exchanged for (0.1) share Common 1¢ par
Hollywood International Studios recapitalized as Utah Libra Corp. 12/24/1972
(See Utah Libra Corp.)

ATOMIC MINING CORP. (QC)
Declared bankrupt 00/00/1959
No stockholders' equity

ATOMIC PAINTBALL INC (TX)
SEC revoked common stock registration 10/04/2017

ATOMIC POWER URANIUM CORP. (DE)
Merged into American Duchess Uranium & 04/10/1956
Each share Common 5¢ par exchanged for (0.25) share Common 5¢ par
American Duchess Uranium & Oil Co. name changed to American Duchess Oil & Metals Corp. 07/01/1957 which merged into International Land & Development Corp. 05/03/1965 which name changed to International Chemical Development Corp. 10/25/1968 which recapitalized as Columbia Autocar, Inc. 04/15/1980 which name changed to American Peat Co. 04/22/1982 which name changed to American National Hydrocarbon, Inc. 11/15/1982
(See American National Hydrocarbon, Inc.)

ATOMIC RESEARCH CORP. (CO)
Charter revoked for failure to file reports and pay fees 10/01/1958

ATOMIC RESERVE URANIUM CORP. (UT)
Recapitalized as Atomic Mining & Oil Corp. 02/29/1968
Each share Common 1¢ par exchanged for (0.1) share Common 10¢ par
Atomic Mining & Oil Corp. recapitalized as Hollywood International Studios 01/15/1971 which recapitalized as Utah Libra Corp. 12/24/1972
(See Utah Libra Corp.)

ATOMIC URANIUM, INC. (UT)
Merged into Sterling Uranium Corp. on a (1) for (8-1/3) basis 03/01/1955
Sterling Uranium Corp. recapitalized as Sterling Beryllium & Oil Co. 02/04/1958 which merged into Elgin Gas & Oil Co. 06/12/1959
(See Elgin Gas & Oil Co.)

ATOMIC URANIUM CORP. (DE)
Charter cancelled and declared inoperative and void for non-payment of taxes 10/01/1957

ATOMICGIANT COM INC (UT)
Name changed to Datigen.com, Inc. (UT) 04/12/2000
Datigen.com, Inc. (UT) reincorporated in Nevada as Smart Energy Solutions, Inc. 09/02/2005 which name changed to CannaPowder, Inc. 07/11/2018

ATOMICS, PHYSICS & SCIENCE FUND, INC. (DE)
Name changed to Steadman Science & Growth Fund, Inc. 10/08/1965
Steadman Science & Growth Fund, Inc. acquired by Steadman American Industry Fund, Inc. 09/14/1970 which name changed to Ameritor Industry Fund 09/23/1998
(See Ameritor Industry Fund)

ATOURS INC (FL)
Name changed to Cache, Inc. (FL) 05/04/1983
Cache, Inc. (FL) reincorporated in Delaware 08/15/2013

ATP OIL & GAS CORP (TX)
13.5% Accredited Investor Preferred Ser. A $0.001 par called for redemption at $1,227.31 on 12/11/2006
12.5% Accredited Investor Preferred Ser. B $0.001 par called for redemption at $1,120.72 on 12/11/2006
Chapter 11 bankruptcy proceedings converted to Chapter 7 on 06/26/2014
Stockholders' equity unlikely

ATPLAN INC (TN)
Merged into DoubleClick Inc. 02/02/2001
Each share Common no par exchanged for (0.2829) share Common $0.001 par and $3.45 cash

ATR INDS INC (NV)
Each share old Common $0.001 par exchanged for (0.1) share new Common $0.001 par 01/27/1999
Name changed to Beautymerchant.com Inc. 09/17/1999
Beautymerchant.com Inc. name changed to National Beauty Corp. 03/30/2001 which recapitalized as Hairmax International, Inc. 08/01/2003 which name changed to China Digital Media Corp. 03/31/2005
(See China Digital Media Corp.)

ATR SEARCH CORP (NV)
Name changed to CareDecision Corp. 08/08/2002
CareDecision Corp. name changed to instaCare Corp. 04/18/2005 which recapitalized as Decision Diagnostics Corp. 12/01/2011

ATRATECH INC (NY)
Each share old Common $0.001 par exchanged for (0.1) share new Common $0.001 par 06/25/1990
Dissolved by proclamation 09/27/1995

ATREITES DEV CORP (FL)
Administratively dissolved for failure to file annual report 10/11/1991

ATREO MFG INC (NY)
Dissolved by proclamation 09/24/1980

ATRIA CMNTYS INC (DE)
Merged into Lazard Freres & Co. 09/15/1998
Each share Common 10¢ par exchanged for $20.25 cash

ATRIA SOFTWARE INC (MA)
Common 1¢ par split (2) for (1) by issuance of (1) additional share 09/18/1995
Merged into Pure Atria Corp. 08/26/1996
Each share Common 1¢ par exchanged for (1.544615) shares Common $0.0001 par
Pure Atria Corp. merged into Rational Software Corp. 07/30/1997
(See Rational Software Corp.)

ATRINSIC INC (DE)
Each share old Common 1¢ par exchanged for (0.25) share new Common 1¢ par 12/03/2010
New Common 1¢ par changed to $0.0000001 par 07/12/2013
Recapitalized as Protagenic Therapeutics, Inc. 07/27/2016
Each share Common $0.000001 par exchanged for (0.00006466) share Common $0.0001 par

ATRION CORP (AL)
Common 10¢ par split (3) for (2) by issuance of (0.5) additional share payable 12/02/1996 to holders of record 11/20/1996
Reincorporated under the laws of Delaware 02/25/1997

ATRIUM BIOTECHNOLOGIES INC (CANADA)
Name changed to Atrium Innovations Inc. and Subordinate Shares no par reclassified as Common no par 06/15/2007
(See Atrium Innovations Inc.)

ATRIUM INNOVATIONS INC (CANADA)
Acquired by Acquisition Glacier II Inc. 02/14/2014
Each share Common no par exchanged for $24 cash

ATRIUM RES LTD (BC)
Name changed to McCulloch's Canadian Beverages Ltd. 07/08/1992
McCulloch's Canadian Beverages Ltd. recapitalized as MCB Investments Corp. 10/06/1994

ATRIX INTL INC (MN)
Each share old Common 1¢ par exchanged for (0.25) share new Common 1¢ par 12/16/1997
Merged into Atrix Acquisition Corp. 07/01/1999
Each share new Common 1¢ par exchanged for $2 cash

ATRIX LABS INC (DE)
Acquired by QLT Inc. 11/19/2004
Each share Common $0.001 par exchanged for (1) share Common no par and $14.61 cash
QLT Inc. name changed to Novelion Therapeutics Inc. 12/01/2016

ATRON CORP (MN)
Merged into Mohawk Data Sciences Corp. 04/30/1971
Each share Common 20¢ par exchanged for (0.25) share Common 10¢ par
Mohawk Data Sciences Corp. name changed to Qantel Corp. 09/17/1987
(See Qantel Corp.)

ATRONIC INC (WY)
Charter revoked 03/15/1994

ATRONIX INC (NV)
Charter revoked for failure to file reports and pay fees 03/01/1983

ATS ANDLAUER INCOME FD (ON)
Acquired by Andlauer Management Group Inc. 12/11/2008
Each Trust Unit received $10.75 cash

ATS CORP (DE)
Acquired by Salient Federal Solutions, Inc. 03/30/2012
Each share Common $0.0001 par exchanged for $3.20 cash

ATS MED INC (MN)
Acquired by Medtronic, Inc. 08/13/2010
Each share Common 1¢ par exchanged for $4 cash

ATS MONEY SYS INC (NV)
Merged into De La Rue Inc. 05/25/2001
Each share Common $0.001 par exchanged for $1.98 cash
Note: A final distribution of approximately $0.1875 cash per share was made 11/00/2002

ATS WHEEL INC (BC)
Name changed to JSS Resources, Inc. 07/20/1998
JSS Resources, Inc. name changed to WSI Interactive Corp. 07/26/1999 which recapitalized as iaNett International Systems Ltd. 05/07/2001 which name changed to Data Fortress Systems Group Ltd. 09/03/2002
(See Data Fortress Systems Group Ltd.)

ATSI COMMUNICATIONS INC (NV)
Reorganized 05/24/2004
Reorganized from Delaware to under the laws of Nevada 05/24/2004
Each share Common $0.001 par exchanged for (0.1) share Conv. Preferred Ser. H $0.001 par and (0.01) share Common $0.001 par
Each share Conv. Preferred Ser. H $0.001 par exchanged for (1) share Common $0.001 par 04/26/2007

Name changed to Digerati Technologies, Inc. 03/21/2011

ATTACHE HLDGS LTD (CO)
Name changed to Consolidated Data, Inc. 11/16/1998
Consolidated Data, Inc. name changed to Your Bank Online.com, Inc. 02/18/2000 which name changed to Secure Sign, Inc. 10/31/2000 which name changed to SVC Financial Services, Inc. 02/03/2004
(See SVC Financial Services, Inc.)

ATTAPULGUS MINERALS & CHEMICALS CORP. (MD)
Merged into Minerals & Chemicals Corp. 06/23/1954
Each share Common $1 par exchanged for (1) share Common $1 par
Minerals & Chemicals Corp. of America name changed to Minerals & Chemicals-Philipp Corp. 07/21/1960 which merged into Engelhard Minerals & Chemicals Corp. 09/27/1967 which name changed to Phibro Corp. 05/20/1981 which name changed to Phibro-Salomon Inc. 05/20/1982 which name changed to Salomon Inc. 05/07/1986 which merged into Travelers Group Inc. 11/28/1997 which name changed to Citigroup Inc. 10/08/1998

ATTENDU ENGINES CO., LTD.
Liquidated 00/00/1929
Details not available

ATTENTION MED CO (NV)
Each share old Common 1¢ par exchanged for (0.1) share new Common 1¢ par 09/27/1990
Merged into Taylor Medical, Inc. 06/30/1993
Each share new Common 1¢ par exchanged for $2 cash

ATTILA RES LTD (BC)
Recapitalized as Klondex Mines Ltd. 11/19/1974
Each share Common no par exchanged for (0.2) share Common no par
(See Klondex Mines Ltd.)

ATTLEBORO GAS LIGHT CO.
Merged into Taunton Gas Light Co. 00/00/1950
Each share Common $100 par exchanged for (2) shares Common $50 par
Taunton Gas Light Co. merged into Brockton Taunton Gas Co. 00/00/1952 which merged into Bay State Gas Co. (New) 11/19/1974 which merged into Nipsco Industries, Inc. 02/12/1999 which name changed to NiSource Inc. (IN) 04/14/1999 which reincorporated in Delaware 11/01/2000

ATTN AVECA ENTMT CORP (CANADA)
Recapitalized as American Transportation Television Network, Inc. 03/04/1993
Each share Common no par exchanged for (0.33333333) share Common no par
(See American Transportation Television Network, Inc.)

ATTOCK ENERGY CORP (AB)
Recapitalized 08/02/1995
Recapitalized from Attock Oil Corp. to Attock Energy Corp. 08/02/1995
Each share Class A Common no par exchanged for (0.25) share Common no par
Merged into Cypress Energy Inc. 01/17/1997
Each share Class A Common no par exchanged for $0.83 cash

ATTORNEYS COM INC (FL)
Name changed to 1-800-Attorney, Inc. 06/01/2001

ATTWELL CAP INC (ON)
Recapitalized as Citation Resources Inc. 03/25/2014
Each share Common no par exchanged for (0.416666666) share Common no par
Citation Resources Inc. merged into Inlet Resources Ltd. 07/08/2014 which name changed to Guerrero Ventures Inc. 08/19/2014

ATTWOOD COPPER MINES LTD. (ON)
Charter cancelled for failure to pay taxes and file returns 03/16/1973

ATTWOOD GOLD CORP (BC)
Recapitalized as Dynasty Motorcar Corp. (BC) 06/02/2000
Each share Common no par exchanged for (0.5) share Common no par
Dynasty Motorcar Corp. (BC) reincorporated in Canada 11/29/2002 which recapitalized as Comwest Capital Corp. 06/29/2004 which merged into ComWest Enterprise Corp. 12/12/2005 which name changed to Unisync Corp. 08/01/2014

ATTWOODS PLC (UNITED KINGDOM)
Sponsored ADR's for Ordinary split (2) for (1) by issuance of (1) additional ADR 12/24/1990
Acquired by Browning-Ferris Industries, Inc. 00/00/1995
Details not available

ATV SYS INC (CA)
Charter suspended for failure to file reports and pay fees 04/15/1994

ATVROCKN (NV)
Each share old Common $0.001 par exchanged for (0.1) share new Common $0.001 par 02/16/2016
Name changed to Ameritek Ventures 07/24/2017

ATW GOLD CORP (BC)
Name changed to Redhill Resources Corp. 01/14/2011
Redhill Resources Corp. recapitalized as Millennial Lithium Corp. 06/24/2016

ATW VENTURE CORP (BC)
Name changed to ATW Gold Corp. 10/21/2008
ATW Gold Corp. name changed to Redhill Resources Corp. 01/14/2011 which recapitalized as Millennial Lithium Corp. 06/24/2016

A21 INC (DE)
Reincorporated 07/31/2006
State of incorporation changed from (TX) to (DE) 07/31/2006
Plan of liquidation under Chapter 11 Federal Bankruptcy proceedings effective 06/24/2009
No stockholders' equity

A2 ACQUISITION CORP (AB)
Recapitalized as Medicenna Therapeutics Corp. 03/03/2017
Each share Common no par exchanged for (0.07142857) share Common no par

ATWOOD FABRICS INC (DE)
Ceased operations and declared insolvent 06/20/1974
No stockholders' equity

ATWOOD MACHINE CO.
Liquidated 00/00/1945
Details not available

ATWOOD MINERALS & MNG CORP (NV)
Common $0.001 par split (7) for (1) by issuance of (6) additional shares payable 09/28/2009 to holders of record 09/28/2009
Name changed to Phreadz, Inc. 06/21/2010
Phreadz, Inc. name changed to Bizzingo, Inc. 05/02/2011
(See Bizzingo, Inc.)

ATWOOD OCEANICS INC (TX)
Common $1 par split (2) for (1) by issuance of (1) additional share payable 11/19/1997 to holders of record 11/12/1997 Ex date - 11/20/1997
Common $1 par split (2) for (1) by issuance of (1) additional share payable 04/07/2006 to holders of record 03/24/2006 Ex date - 04/10/2006
Common $1 par split (2) for (1) by issuance of (1) additional share payable 07/11/2008 to holders of record 06/27/200 Ex date - 07/14/2008
Stock Dividend - 100% 12/15/1980
Merged into Ensco PLC 10/06/2017
Each share Common $1 par exchanged for (1.6) share Class A Ordinary USD $0.10 par

ATX COMMUNICATIONS INC (DE)
Plan of reorganization under Chapter 11 Federal Bankruptcy Code effective 04/22/2005
No stockholders' equity

AU BON PAIN INC (DE)
Name changed to Panera Bread Co. 05/16/1999
(See Panera Bread Co.)

AU MARTINIQUE SILVER INC (ON)
Reincorporated under the laws of Canada as Aura Silver Resources Inc. 08/21/2006

AU RES LTD (BC)
Recapitalized as Texas T Resources Inc. (BC) 09/21/1994
Each share Common no par exchanged for (0.2) share Common no par
Texas T Resources Inc. (BC) reincorporated in Alberta 08/23/2001 which recapitalized as Texas T Minerals Inc. 02/19/2004 which was acquired by Grandcru Resources Corp. 05/23/2006 which merged into Bell Copper Corp. (Old) 05/12/2008 which reorganized as Bell Copper Corp. (New) 07/23/2013

AUBAY URANIUM MINES LTD. (ON)
Charter revoked for failure to file reports and pay fees 01/10/1968

AUBELLE MINES LTD. (ON)
Merged into Hydra Explorations Ltd. 11/16/1959
Each share Capital Stock $1 par exchanged for (0.64) share Capital Stock $1 par
Hydra Explorations Ltd. name changed to Hydra Capital Corp. 12/30/1992 which name changed to Waterford Capital Management Inc. 11/12/1996 which merged into CPI Plastics Group Ltd. 09/21/1998
(See CPI Plastics Group Ltd.)

AUBET EXPLORATIONS LTD (ON)
Name changed to Visa Gold Explorations Inc. 08/25/1999
(See Visa Gold Explorations Inc.)

AUBET RES INC (ON)
Recapitalized as Aubet Explorations Ltd. 09/30/1998
Each share Common no par exchanged for (0.36496350) share Common no par
Aubet Explorations Ltd. name changed to Visa Gold Explorations Inc. 08/25/1999
(See Visa Gold Explorations Inc.)

AUBRY CORP (DE)
Name changed to Standard Drilling Co. 07/15/1983
Standard Drilling Co. recapitalized as Standard Systems & Technology, Inc. 09/09/1983
(See Standard Systems & Technology, Inc.)

AUBRYN INTL INC (MN)
Recapitalized as Pacific Sunset Investments, Inc. 01/21/2004
Each share Common no par exchanged for (0.04) share Common no par
Pacific Sunset Investments, Inc. name changed to Gen-ID Lab Services, Inc. 10/10/2005 which recapitalized as Adventura Corp. 11/01/2009

AUBURN & SYRACUSE ELECTRIC RAILWAY CO.
Sold at auction 00/00/1930
Details not available

AUBURN AUTOMOBILE CO.
Reorganized as Auburn Central Manufacturing Corp. 00/00/1940
Each share Common exchanged for (0.1) share Common
Auburn Central Manufacturing Corp. name changed to American Central Manufacturing Corp. 00/00/1942 which was acquired by Aviation Corp. 00/00/1946 which name changed to Avco Manufacturing Corp. 00/00/1947 which name changed to Avco Corp. 04/10/1959
(See Avco Corp.)

AUBURN BANCORP (CA)
Merged into ValliCorp Holdings, Inc. 09/13/1996
Each share Common no par exchanged for (0.8209) share Common 1¢ par
ValliCorp Holdings, Inc. merged into Westamerica Bancorporation 04/12/1997

AUBURN CENTRAL MANUFACTURING CORP.
Name changed to American Central Manufacturing Corp. 00/00/1942
American Central Manufacturing Corp. acquired by Aviation Corp. 00/00/1946 which name changed to Avco Manufacturing Corp. 00/00/1947 which name changed to Avco Corp. 04/10/1959
(See Avco Corp.)

AUBURN EQUITIES INC (CO)
Reincorporated under the laws of Nevada as Turner Group, Inc. 05/29/1997
Turner Group, Inc. recapitalized as AutoAuction.com, Inc. (NV) 05/04/1999 which reorganized in Wyoming as HLV Trading Corp. 02/08/2005 which name changed to X-tra Petroleum 08/30/2006 which recapitalized as Xtra Energy Corp. 11/05/2010

AUBURN MINES, LTD. (ON)
Charter cancelled 11/00/1958

AUCAN RES LTD (BC)
Struck off register and declared dissolved for failure to file returns 08/17/1990

AUCKLAND EXPLS LTD (BC)
Recapitalized as Coromandel Resources Ltd. 02/15/1996
Each share Common no par exchanged for (0.33333333) share Common no par
Coromandel Resources Ltd. recapitalized as International Coromandel Resources Ltd. 05/05/2000 which name changed to Sonora Gold Corp. 08/17/2004 which recapitalized as MetalQuest Minerals Inc. 10/17/2007 which recapitalized as Canada Gold Corp. 09/01/2009 which name changed to STEM 7 Capital Inc. 07/12/2013 which name changed to South Star Mining Corp. 12/22/2017

AUCONDA PORCUPINE GOLD MINES, LTD. (ON)
Charter cancelled 05/00/1958

AUCOURT MINES LTD. (ON)
Charter cancelled 08/28/1961

AUCTION BRIDGE MAGAZINE, INC.
Out of business 00/00/1935
Details not available

AUCTION FLOOR INC (NV)
Each share old Common $0.001 par exchanged for (0.04) share new Common $0.001 par 04/07/2008
Charter permanently revoked 11/30/2010

AUCTION TV NETWORK INC (AR)
Name changed 12/23/1997
Name changed from Auction Television Network, Inc. to Auction TV Network, Inc. 12/23/1997
Name changed to Bidnow.com, Inc. 02/03/1999
Bidnow.com, Inc. recapitalized as Frontera Investment, Inc. 04/15/2008

AUCTIONANYTHING COM INC (DE)
Name changed to Disease Sciences Inc. 07/16/2001
Disease Sciences Inc. name changed to IceWEB, Inc. 05/30/2002 which recapitalized as UnifiedOnline, Inc. 01/05/2015

AUCTIONDINER COM INC (NV)
SEC revoked common stock registration 02/15/2006

AUCTIONS INTL INC (NV)
Name changed to Rangemore Film Productions Corp. 04/25/2013
Rangemore Film Productions Corp. recapitalized as Cre8tive Works, Inc. 01/16/2014 which name changed to Optium Cyber Systems, Inc. 10/03/2017

AUCXIS CORP (NV)
SEC revoked common stock registration 03/21/2012

AUDAX FD INC (DE)
Merged into Nicholas Fund, Inc. 12/05/1977
Each share Common $1 par exchanged for (0.481278) share Capital Stock $1 par

AUDAX GAS & OIL LTD NEW (AB)
Assets sold for the benefit of creditors 11/25/1992
No stockholders' equity

AUDAX GAS & OIL LTD OLD (AB)
Merged into Financial Trustco Capital Ltd. 06/25/1985
Each share Common no par exchanged for (0.082) share 10.25% 1st Preferred $10 par and (0.041) Common Stock Purchase Warrant expiring 06/15/1988
Financial Trustco Capital Ltd. name changed to FT Capital Ltd. 07/25/1989
(See FT Capital Ltd.)

AUDEC CORP (NJ)
Charter declared void for non-payment of taxes 07/30/1993

AUDIBLE INC (DE)
Each share old Common 1¢ par exchanged for (0.33333333) share new Common 1¢ par 06/16/2004
Acquired by Amazon.com, Inc. 03/18/2008
Each share new Common 1¢ par exchanged for $11.50 cash

AUDIENCE INC (DE)
Merged into Knowles Corp. 07/01/2015
Each share Common $0.001 par exchanged for (0.13207) share Common 1¢ par and $2.51 cash

AUDIO & VIDEO PRODUCTS CORP. (NY)
Proclaimed dissolved by the Secretary of State of New York 12/16/1963

AUDIO BOOK CLUB INC (FL)
Name changed to MediaBay, Inc. 10/20/1999
(See MediaBay, Inc.)

AUDIO COMMUNICATIONS NETWORK INC (FL)
Merged into Diverse Media Acquisition 10/06/1998
Each share Common 25¢ par exchanged for $6.40 cash

AUDIO DEVICES, INC. (NY)
Each share Common $10 par exchanged for (10) shares Common 10¢ par 00/00/1950
Stock Dividend - 10% 07/20/1954
Name changed to Capitol Industries, Inc. 02/27/1968
Capitol Industries, Inc. name changed to Capitol Industries-EMI, Inc. 01/02/1974
(See Capitol Industries-EMI, Inc.)

AUDIO-DYNAMICS CORP. (DC)
Acquired by Teletray Electronic Systems, Inc. 12/21/1960
Each share Common exchanged for (0.7) share Common
(See Teletray Electronic Systems, Inc.)

AUDIO DYNAMICS CORP (NY)
Common 10¢ par changed to 5¢ par and (1) additional share issued 09/18/1972
Merged into Discus (International) Ltd. 01/02/1973
Each share Common 5¢ par exchanged for $9 cash

AUDIO FID RECORDS INC (NY)
Name changed to Audiofidelity Enterprises, Inc. 10/06/1970
(See Audiofidelity Enterprises, Inc.)

AUDIO GRAPHICS INC (UT)
Recapitalized as Uranium International 12/03/1976
Each share Common 1¢ par exchanged for (0.1) share Common 10¢ par
(See Uranium International)

AUDIO KING CORP (MN)
Merged into Ultimate Electronics, Inc. 06/27/1997
Each share Common $0.001 par exchanged for either (0.7) share Common 1¢ par or $1.75 cash
Note: Option to receive stock expired 07/28/1997
(See Ultimate Electronics, Inc.)

AUDIO MAGNETICS INC (NV)
Charter revoked for failure to file reports and pay fees 01/01/1992

AUDIO MEDIA CORP (NY)
Dissolved by proclamation 09/23/1992

AUDIO VIDEO AFFILIATES INC (DE)
Common 1¢ par split (3) for (2) by issuance of (0.5) additional share 06/24/1985
Common 1¢ par split (3) for (2) by issuance of (0.5) additional share 04/18/1986
Name changed to REX Stores Corp. 08/02/1993
REX Stores Corp. name changed to REX American Resources Corp. 06/09/2010

AUDIO VISUAL EDL SYS INC (TX)
Merged into Jayark Corp. 03/11/1976
Each share Common 10¢ par exchanged for (2) shares Common 30¢ par
(See Jayark Corp.)

AUDIO VISUAL ELECTRS CORP (NY)
Dissolved by proclamation 06/24/1992

AUDIO VISUAL INTL CORP (DE)
Name changed to A V I Industries, Inc. 05/18/1970
(See A V I Industries, Inc.)

AUDIO VISUAL SVCS CORP (DE)
Plan of reorganization under Chapter 11 Federal Bankruptcy Code effective 03/05/2002
No stockholders' equity

AUDIOFAX INC (AZ)
Charter revoked for failure to file reports or pay fees 09/05/1974

AUDIOFIDELITY ENTERPRISES INC (NY)
Common 10¢ par split (10) for (1) by issuance of (9) additional shares 01/10/1980
Dissolved by proclamation 12/23/1992

AUDIOGENESIS SYS INC (NJ)
Name changed to Allstates WorldCargo, Inc. 11/30/1999

AUDIOGRAPHIC INC. (NY)
Adjudicated bankrupt 04/10/1963
No stockholders' equity

AUDIOHIGHWAY COM (CA)
Chapter 11 bankruptcy proceedings converted to Chapter 7 on 11/27/2001
No stockholders equity

AUDIOMONSTER ONLINE INC (NV)
Name changed to Lockwave Technologies, Inc. 03/15/2001
Lockwave Technologies, Inc. recapitalized as Edison Renewables, Inc. 05/19/2003 which name changed to NextPhase Wireless, Inc. 01/26/2005 which name changed to MetroConnect Inc. 02/02/2009
(See MetroConnect Inc.)

AUDION-EMENEE CORP. (NY)
Name changed to Emenee Corp. 11/16/1961
Emenee Corp. merged into Ohio Art Co. 04/30/1973

AUDIOPHONICS INC (FL)
Reincorporated under the laws of Delaware as Phoenix Industries Corp. 03/29/1974
(See Phoenix Industries Corp.)

AUDIOSCIENCE INC (MN)
Each share old Common 1¢ par exchanged for (0.5) share new Common 1¢ par 04/18/1994
Chapter 7 bankruptcy proceedings terminated 09/19/1997
Stockholders' equity unlikely

AUDIOSTOCKS INC (DE)
Name changed to Shrink Nanotechnologies, Inc. 06/24/2009
(See Shrink Nanotechnologies, Inc.)

AUDIOTECH HEALTHCARE CORP (BC)
Reincorporated 05/02/2008
Place of incorporation changed from (AB) to (BC) 05/02/2008
Acquired by AHC Acquisition Inc. 12/04/2012
Each share Common no par exchanged for $0.35 cash

AUDIOTRONICS CORP (DE)
Reincorporated 11/22/1976
Stock Dividends - 10% 12/21/1973; 10% 12/16/1974
State of incorporation changed from (CA) to (DE) 11/22/1976
Each share Common $1 par exchanged for (0.08) share Common 1¢ par 09/30/1994
Charter forfeited for failure to maintain a registered agent 08/09/2000

AUDIOVENTURES CORP (UT)
Involuntarily dissolved 02/01/1999

AUDIOVOX CORP (DE)
Name changed to VOXX International Corp. 12/05/2011

AUDISCAN INC (WA)
Name changed to Gemtec Corp. 06/21/1979
(See Gemtec Corp.)

AUDIT RES INC (AB)
Struck off register for failure to file annual returns 01/01/1989

AUDITORIUM HOTEL CO (OH)
Completely liquidated 01/18/1972
Each share Capital Stock no par exchanged for (1) share Vika Corp. Common $5 par
(See Vika Corp.)

AUDITS & SURVEYS WORLDWIDE INC (DE)
Merged into United Information Group, Inc. 03/23/1999
Each share Common 50¢ par exchanged for $3.24 cash

AUDLEY GOLD MINES LTD. (ON)
Dissolved by default 10/21/1963
No stockholders' equity

AUDN CORP (NY)
Assets sold for benefit of creditors 07/17/1975
No stockholders' equity

AUDORA PORCUPINE MINES, LTD. (ON)
Charter cancelled 00/00/1949

AUDRE RECOGNITION SYS INC (BC)
Reorganized under the laws of Delaware as eXtr@ct, Inc. 04/17/2000
Each share Common no par exchanged for (0.48) share Common
(See eXtr@ct, Inc.)

AUDREY RES INC (CANADA)
Acquired by Cambior Inc. 11/15/1995
Each share Common no par exchanged for (0.09523809) share Common no par
Cambior Inc. acquired by Iamgold Corp. 11/08/2006

AUDUBON PARK RACEWAY, INC. (DE)
No longer in existence having become inoperative and void for non-payment of taxes 04/01/1960

AUDUBON RACEWAY INC (KY)
Charter revoked for failure to file annual reports 03/15/1987

AUDUBON VILLAGE, INC. (NY)
Charter cancelled and proclaimed dissolved for failure to pay taxes 12/16/1935

AUEX VENTURES INC (BC)
Merged into Fronteer Gold Inc. 11/05/2010
Each share Common no par exchanged for (0.645) share Common no par, (0.5) share Renaissance Gold Inc. Common no par and $0.66 cash
Note: Unexchanged certificates were cancelled and became without value 11/05/2016
(See each company's listing)

AUFRON MINES LTD. (ON)
Declared dissolved by default 09/18/1961
No stockholders' equity

AUG CORP (DE)
Name changed to Biometrics Security Technology, Inc. 12/20/2002
(See Biometrics Security Technology, Inc.)

AUGAT INC (MA)
Common 10¢ par split (3) for (2) by issuance of (0.5) additional share 03/29/1971
Common 10¢ par split (3) for (2) by issuance of (0.5) additional share 04/13/1972
Common 10¢ par split (5) for (4) by issuance of (0.25) additional share 07/31/1978
Common 10¢ par split (3) for (2) by issuance of (0.5) additional share 05/31/1979
Common 10¢ par split (3) for (2) by issuance of (0.5) additional share 06/19/1981
Merged into Thomas & Betts Corp. 12/11/1996
Each share Common 10¢ par

AUG-AUL

exchanged for (0.6356) share Common 50¢ par
(See Thomas & Betts Corp.)

AUGDOME LTD (ON)
Recapitalized 02/08/1966
Recapitalized from Augdome Exploration Ltd. to Augdome Corp. Ltd. and Capital Stock $1 par changed to no par 02/08/1966
Cease trade order effective 05/21/1992

AUGEN CAP CORP (ON)
Reincorporated 11/19/2004
Place of incorporation changed from (AB) to (ON) 11/19/2004
Name changed to Gensource Capital Corp. 08/02/2012
Gensource Capital Corp. name changed to Gensource Potash Corp. 07/02/2013

AUGEN GOLD CORP (ON)
Acquired by Trelawney Mining & Exploration Inc. 11/04/2011
Each share Common no par exchanged for (0.0862) share Common no par
(See Trelawney Mining & Exploration Inc.)

AUGITE PORCUPINE MINES LTD.
Acquired by Aunor Gold Mines Ltd. 00/00/1939
Each share Capital Stock exchanged for (0.33333333) share Capital Stock $1 par
Aunor Gold Mines Ltd. merged into Pamour Porcupine Mines Ltd. 11/17/1972 which name changed to Pamour Inc. 07/11/1986 which merged into Royal Oak Mines Inc. 07/23/1991 which recapitalized as Royal Oak Ventures Inc. 02/14/2000
(See Royal Oak Ventures Inc.)

AUGME TECHNOLOGIES INC (DE)
Name changed to Hipcricket, Inc. 08/26/2013
(See Hipcricket, Inc.)

AUGMENT SYS INC (DE)
Each share Common 1¢ par exchanged for (0.25) share Common $0.0001 par 02/06/2001
Recapitalized as AUG Corp. 10/29/2001
Each share Common $0.0001 par exchanged for (0.01) share Common $0.0001 par
AUG Corp. name changed to Biometrics Security Technology, Inc. 12/20/2002
(See Biometrics Security Technology, Inc.)

AUGMITTO EXPLS LTD (ON)
Common $1 par changed to no par 09/12/1972
Placed in receivership 03/00/1989
No stockholders' equity

AUGRID CORP (NV)
Name changed 08/16/2002
Name changed from AuGRID of Nevada, Inc. to AuGRID Corp. 08/16/2002
Each share old Common $0.001 par exchanged for (0.02) share new Common $0.001 par 07/24/2002
Each share old Common $0.001 par exchanged for (0.01) share new Common $0.001 par 10/07/2004
Each share new Common $0.001 par exchanged again for (0.001) share new Common $0.001 par 10/27/2005
Name changed to AuGRID Global Holdings Corp. 01/30/2007
AuGRID Global Holdings Corp. recapitalized as GuanHua Corp. 02/11/2016

AUGRID GLOBAL HLDGS CORP (NV)
Each share old Common $0.001 par exchanged for (0.03333333) share new Common $0.001 par 03/14/2007
Each share new Common $0.001 par exchanged again for (0.0002) share new Common $0.001 par 10/03/2007
Each share new Common $0.001 par exchanged again for (0.001) share new Common $0.001 par 06/04/2008
Each share new Common $0.001 par exchanged again for (0.0002) share new Common $0.001 par 12/03/2008
Each share new Common $0.001 par exchanged again for (0.0004) share new Common $0.001 par 05/06/2009
Recapitalized as GuanHua Corp. 02/11/2016
Each share new Common $0.001 par exchanged for (0.001) share Common $0.001 par

AUGUST BIOMEDICAL CORP (NV)
Name changed to Pan American Energy Corp. and (4) additional shares issued 03/22/2004
Pan American Energy Corp. name changed to Morgan Beaumont, Inc. 08/06/2004 which recapitalized as nFinanSe Inc. 12/26/2006

AUGUST ENERGY CORP (DE)
Common $0.0001 par split (3) for (1) by issuance of (2) additional shares payable 03/28/2005 to holders of record 03/21/2005 Ex date - 03/29/2005
Recapitalized as Canyon Gold Corp. 05/02/2011
Each share Common $0.0001 par exchanged for (0.002) share Common $0.0001 par
Canyon Gold Corp. name changed to Defense Technologies International Corp. 06/15/2016

AUGUST FINL HLDG INC (NV)
Voluntarily dissolved 05/05/2004
Stockholders' equity unlikely

AUGUST METAL CORP (BC)
Recapitalized as Ardonblue Ventures Inc. 11/20/2013
Each share Common no par exchanged for (0.1) share Common no par
Ardonblue Ventures Inc. name changed to Juggernaut Exploration Ltd. 10/23/2017

AUGUST PETES LTD (BC)
Recapitalized as Cheyenne Petroleum Corp. 10/13/1976
Each share Common no par exchanged for (0.2) share Common no par
(See Cheyenne Petroleum Corp.)

AUGUST PORCUPINE GOLD MINES, LTD. (ON)
Charter cancelled for failure to pay taxes and file returns 10/18/1978

AUGUST PROJ I CORP (FL)
Name changed to Alliance Towers Inc. (FL) 02/06/2003
Alliance Towers Inc. (FL) reincorporated in Delaware as Enclaves Group, Inc. 07/29/2005
(See Enclaves Group, Inc.)

AUGUST PROJ II CORP (FL)
Name changed to Traffic Engine Holdings Inc. 05/11/2001
Traffic Engine Holdings Inc. name changed to Syndeos Group Inc. 01/15/2002 which recapitalized as Air Media Now!, Inc. 04/10/2002

AUGUST PROJ IV CORP (FL)
Name changed to Strategic Land Management, Inc. 09/13/2000
Strategic Land Management, Inc. recapitalized as China Now, Inc. 07/13/2006
(See China Now, Inc.)

AUGUST PROJ III CORP (FL)
Name changed to Trinity Medical Group USA, Inc. 04/24/2000

AUGUST TECHNOLOGY CORP (MN)
Merged into Rudolph Technologies, Inc. 02/15/2006
Each share Common 1¢ par exchanged for $10.50 cash

AUGUST THYSSEN-HUETTE AG (GERMANY)
Name changed to Thyssen AG 04/16/1977
(See Thyssen AG)

AUGUSTA & SAVANNAH RAILROAD
Liquidation completed 00/00/1951
Details not available

AUGUSTA CHEMICAL CO. (GA)
Acquired by Synalloy Corp. (SC) 09/29/1967
Each share Common $1 par exchanged for (0.081234) share Common $1 par
Synalloy Corp. (SC) reincorporated in Delaware 06/03/1988

AUGUSTA CORP (BC)
Recapitalized as Canley Developments Inc. 08/03/2001
Each share Class A Common no par exchanged for (0.06666666) share Class A Common no par
Canley Developments Inc. name changed to Sargold Resource Corp. 07/03/2003 which merged into Buffalo Gold Ltd. 10/30/2007
(See Buffalo Gold Ltd.)

AUGUSTA DOCTORS MEDICAL CENTER, INC. (GA)
Common $10 par changed to $3.33333333 par and (2) additional shares issued 08/31/1972
Common $3.33333333 par changed to $1.66666666 par and (1) additional share issued 02/27/1974
Name changed to First Medical Corp. and Common $1.66666666 par changed to 1¢ par 12/01/1982
(See First Medical Corp.)

AUGUSTA FINL INC (CO)
Name changed to On-Site Toxic Control, Inc. 01/09/1989
(See On-Site Toxic Control, Inc.)

AUGUSTA GOLD CORP (CANADA)
Recapitalized as Pulse Data Inc. 10/15/1999
Each share Class A Common no par exchanged for (0.4) share Class A Common no par
Pulse Data Inc. name changed to Pulse Seismic Inc. 05/28/2009

AUGUSTA GROCERY CO. INC. (GA)
6% Preferred $20 par called for redemption 03/01/1965
Public interest eliminated

AUGUSTA INDS INC (DE)
Recapitalized as IntellaEquity Inc. 10/04/2018
Each share Common 1¢ par exchanged for (0.1) share Common 1¢ par

AUGUSTA METALS INC (BC)
Each share old Common no par exchanged for (0.1) share new Common no par 08/25/1998
Name changed to CyberCom Systems Inc. 09/14/2000
(See CyberCom Systems Inc.)

AUGUSTA NEWSPAPERS, INC. (GA)
Class A Common $1 par changed to 50¢ par and (1) additional share issued 12/27/1955
Name changed to Southeastern Newspapers Corp. 08/01/1963
(See Southeastern Newspapers Corp.)

AUGUSTA RES CORP (CANADA)
Reincorporated 06/28/1999
Place of incorporation changed from (ON) to (Canada) 06/28/1999
Each share old Common no par exchanged for (0.33333333) share new Common no par 04/08/2003
Merged into HudBay Minerals Inc. 09/23/2014
Each share new Common no par exchanged for (0.315) share Common no par and (0.17) Common Stock Purchase Warrant expiring 07/20/2018

AUGUSTA RES INC (NV)
Name changed to Access Group, Inc. 11/20/1990
Access Group, Inc. name changed to Zipnet, Inc. 12/31/1998

AUGUSTA TECHNOLOGIES LTD (AB)
Reorganized under the laws of Ontario as Danbel Industries Corp. 12/21/1998
Each share Common no par exchanged for (0.25) share Common no par
Danbel Industries Corp. recapitalized as Danbel Ventures Inc. 12/01/2011 which recapitalized as Maricann Group Inc. 04/24/2017

AUGUSTINE VENTURES INC (ON)
Merged into Red Pine Exploration Inc. 02/06/2017
Each share Common no par exchanged for (0.76) share Common no par
Note: Unexchanged certificates will be cancelled and become without value 02/06/2023

AUGUSTUS EXPLORATION LTD. (ON)
Merged into Consolidated Canadian Faraday Ltd. 05/04/1967
Each share Capital Stock $1 par exchanged for (0.2) share Capital Stock no par
Consolidated Canadian Faraday Ltd. name changed to Faraday Resources Inc. 08/02/1983 which merged into Conwest Exploration Co. Ltd. (New) (AB) 09/01/1993 which merged into Alberta Energy Co. Ltd. 01/31/1996 which merged into EnCana Corp. 01/03/2003

AUGUSTUS RES LTD (BC)
Recapitalized as Croesus Resources Inc. 03/18/1987
Each share Common no par exchanged for (0.5) share Common no par
Croesus Resources Inc. recapitalized as International Croesus Ventures Corp. 11/10/1995 which name changed to Zinco Mining Corp. 01/29/2007

AUGYVA MNG RES (QC)
Recapitalized as Automotive Finco Corp. 03/08/2017
Each share Common no par exchanged for (0.06666666) share Common no par

AUKEKO GOLD MINES LTD. (ON)
Charter revoked for failure to file reports and pay fees 10/22/1962

AULD DAVID INC (DE)
Merged into Newport Chemical Industries, Inc. 07/01/1969
Each share Common 10¢ par exchanged for (1) share Common $1 par
Newport Chemical Industries, Inc. name changed to Newport General Corp. 08/07/1972
(See Newport General Corp.)

AULL METAL MINES LTD. (ON)
Charter revoked for failure to file reports and pay fees 02/00/1962

AULORE MINES LTD. (ON)
Charter revoked for failure to file reports and pay fees 11/00/1961

AULT & WIBORG PROPRIETARY, LTD. (ON)
Acquired by Interchemical Corp. 00/00/1963
Details not available

AULT FOODS LTD (CANADA)
Merged into Parmalat Food Inc. 07/23/1997
Each share Common no par exchanged for $34 cash

AULT GLAZER & CO INC (CO)
Name changed to Tytan Holdings Inc. 10/02/2009

AULT INC (MN)
Merged into SL Industries, Inc. 01/26/2006
Each share Common no par exchanged for $2.90 cash

AULT WILLIAMSON SHOE CO.
Liquidated 00/00/1941
Details not available

AULTRA GOLD INC (NV)
Each share Common $0.001 par exchanged for (0.01) share Common $0.00001 par 08/24/2010
Name changed to Shamika 2 Gold, Inc. 02/02/2011
(See Shamika 2 Gold, Inc.)

AUMAC EXPLORATIONS LTD. (ON)
Merged into Branly Enterprises Inc. 12/09/1976
Each share Capital Stock no par exchanged for (1.5) shares Capital Stock no par
Branly Enterprises Inc. recapitalized as Consolidated Branly Resources Inc. 02/27/1984 which name changed to CBR Holdings Inc. 06/20/1985

AUMACHO RIVER MINES, LTD. (ON)
Recapitalized as Urban Quebec Mines Ltd. 12/05/1962
Each share Capital Stock $1 par exchanged for (0.33333333) share Capital Stock $1 par
Urban Quebec Mines Ltd. name changed to Urban Resources Ltd. 04/18/1982 which recapitalized as Urbana Corp. 06/06/1985

AUMAQUE GOLD MINES LTD. (ON)
Recapitalized as Bounty Exploration Ltd. 06/15/1964
Each share Capital Stock $1 par exchanged for (0.153846) share Capital Stock $1 par
Bounty Exploration Ltd. name changed to Gulfstream Resources Canada Ltd. 02/01/1974
(See Gulfstream Resources Canada Ltd.)

AUMEGA DISCOVERIES LTD (BC)
Recapitalized as Fortress Base Metals Corp. 01/10/2007
Each share Common no par exchanged for (0.2) share Common no par
Fortress Base Metals Corp. name changed to Lions Gate Metals Inc. 07/21/2008 which name changed to Block X Capital Corp. 01/25/2018

AUMENTO CAP V CORP (ON)
Name changed to WeedMD Inc. 04/27/2017

AUMENTO CAP VI CORP (ON)
Name changed to CryptoStar Corp. 10/02/2018

AUMENTO CAP III CORP (CANADA)
Reincorporated 06/24/2013
Place of incorporation changed from (ON) to (Canada) 06/24/2013
Each share Common no par exchanged for (0.3125) shave Common no par
Name changed to EXO U Inc. 08/14/2013

AUMENTO CAP CORP (ON)
Name changed to Annidis Corp. 06/13/2011

AUMENTO CAP II CORP (ON)
Recapitalized as Intertain Group Ltd. (Old) 02/18/2014
Each share Common no par exchanged for (0.05) share Common no par
(See Intertain Group Ltd. (Old))

AUMENTO CAP IV CORP (ON)
Recapitalized as GreenSpace Brands Inc. 05/04/2015
Each share Common no par exchanged for (0.5) share Common no par

AUMINE RES LTD (BC)
Name changed to PetroReal Oil Corp. 08/06/1998
PetroReal Oil Corp. recapitalized as International PetroReal Oil Corp. (BC) 09/13/2002 which reorganized in Alberta 06/28/2007 which name changed to PetroReal Energy Inc. 09/15/2008

AUMO EXPLS INC (ON)
Recapitalized as RTO Enterprises Inc. 07/31/1993
Each share Common no par exchanged for (0.25) share Common no par
RTO Enterprises Inc. name changed to easyhome Ltd. 07/08/2003 which name changed to goeasy Ltd. 09/17/2015

AUMO PORCUPINE MINES LTD. (ON)
Charter revoked for failure to file reports and pay fees 04/22/1965

AUNITE MINING CORP. LTD. (ON)
Declared dissolved by default 03/02/1959

AUNOR GOLD MINES LTD (ON)
Merged into Pamour Porcupine Mines Ltd. 11/17/1972
Each share Capital Stock $1 par exchanged for (1) share Capital Stock no par and $0.25 cash
Pamour Porcupine Mines Ltd. name changed to Pamour Inc. 07/11/1986 which merged into Royal Oak Mines Inc. 07/23/1991 which recapitalized as Royal Oak Ventures Inc. 02/14/2000
(See Royal Oak Ventures Inc.)

AUNORE RES INC (CANADA)
Recapitalized as Denyvan Resources Inc. 05/06/1991
Each share Common no par exchanged for (0.14285714) share Common no par
Denyvan Resources Inc. merged into Minorca Resources Inc. 12/30/1994 which merged into McWatters Mining Inc. 10/26/1998
(See McWaters Mining Inc.)

AUNT JANE'S FOODS, INC. (MI)
Acquired by Borden Co. on a (1) for (4.6931) basis 04/30/1963
Borden Co. name changed to Borden, Inc. 04/17/1968 which merged into RJR Nabisco Holdings Corp. 03/14/1995 which name changed to Nabisco Group Holdings Corp. 06/15/1999
(See Nabisco Group Holdings Corp.)

AUNT MYRAS INC (UT)
Recapitalized as Torreon Holdings, Inc. 12/15/1999
Each share Common $0.001 par exchanged for (0.01666666) share Common $0.001 par
Torreon Holdings, Inc. recapitalized as Natvan Inc. 05/22/2001 which name changed to Prime Multimedia, Inc. 07/02/2003 which recapitalized as Eagle Rock Enterprises Inc. 07/01/2008 which name changed to Worldwide Food Services, Inc. 08/19/2009 which name changed to Global Holdings, Inc. 10/29/2013 which name changed to Element Global, Inc. 08/06/2015

AUNTEL CAP INC (FL)
Merged into Royce Laboratories, Inc. 02/15/1991
Each share Common $0.0001 par exchanged for (0.4065) share Common $0.005 par
Royce Laboratories, Inc. merged into Watson Pharmaceuticals Inc. 04/16/1997 which name changed to Actavis, Inc. (NV) 01/24/2013 which reorganized in Ireland as Actavis PLC 10/01/2013 which name changed to Allergan PLC 06/15/2015

AUR RES INC (CANADA)
Common no par split (2) for (1) by issuance of (1) additional share 04/20/1990
Acquired by Teck Cominco Ltd. 09/28/2007
Each share Common no par exchanged for (0.08607) share Class B Subordinate no par and $36.97 cash

AURA BIO CORP (NV)
Common $0.001 par split (20) for (1) by issuance of (19) additional shares payable 12/04/2009 to holders of record 12/04/2009
Name changed to Global Resource Energy, Inc. 12/10/2010

AURA GOLD INC (CANADA)
Reincorporated 04/20/2006
Place of incorporation changed from (ON) to (Canada) 04/20/2006
Name changed to Aura Minerals Inc. (Canada) 08/16/2007
Aura Minerals Inc. (Canada) reorganized in British Virgin Islands 01/05/2017

AURA INDS LTD (BC)
Name changed to Nycal (Canada) Inc. (BC) 07/25/1991
Nycal (Canada) Inc. (BC) reincorporated in Yukon 04/05/1995
(See Nycal (Canada) Inc.)

AURA INTL ENTERPRISES (UT)
Involuntarily dissolved 10/31/1987

AURA MINERALS INC (CANADA)
Each share old Common no par exchanged for (0.2) share new Common no par 07/23/2009
Reorganized under the laws of British Virgin Islands 01/05/2017
Each share new Common no par exchanged for (0.1) share Common no par

AURA SYS INC (DE)
Reincorporated 03/27/1987
State of incorporation changed from (UT) to (DE) 03/27/1987
Plan of reorganization under Chapter 11 Federal Bankruptcy Code effective 01/31/2006
Each share Common $0.005 par received (0.00295857) share Common $0.0001 par
Note: Holders of (337) shares or fewer will not receive any distribution
(Additional Information in Active)

AURACLE RES LTD (BC)
Recapitalized as Four River Ventures Ltd. 06/16/2015
Each share Common no par exchanged for (0.05) share Common no par
Four River Ventures Ltd. recapitalized as Canabo Medical Inc. 11/09/2016 which name changed to Aleafia Health Inc. 03/28/2018

AURADO ENERGY INC (ON)
Reincorporated 07/29/2003
Name and place of incorporation changed from Aurado Exploration Ltd. (ON) to Aurado Energy Inc. (NB) 07/29/2003
Delisted from Toronto Venture Stock Exchange 01/23/2006

AURALEE GOLD MINES LTD. (ON)
Charter revoked for failure to file reports and pay fees 09/30/1957

AURANTHETIC CORP (UT)
Proclaimed dissolved for failure to file reports 03/31/1978

AUREA MNG INC (BC)
Acquired by Newstrike Capital Inc. 06/26/2008
Each share Common no par exchanged for (0.18181818) share Common no par
Newstrike Capital Inc. merged into Timmins Gold Corp. 05/28/2015 which recapitalized as Alio Gold Inc. 05/16/2017

AUREAL INC (DE)
Plan of reorganization under Chapter 11 Federal Bankruptcy Code effective 09/07/2001
No stockholders' equity

AUREAL SEMICONDUCTOR (DE)
Recapitalized as Aureal Inc. 06/10/1999
Each share Common $0.001 par exchanged for (0.06666666) share Common $0.001 par
(See Aureal Inc.)

AURELIAN DEVELOPERS LTD (ON)
Delisted from TSXV 06/20/2003

AURELIAN RES INC (CANADA)
Common no par split (4) for (1) by issuance of (3) additional shares payable 07/13/2007 to holders of record 07/12/2007 Ex date - 07/10/2007
Acquired by Kinross Gold Corp. 10/03/2008
Each share Common no par exchanged for (0.317) share Common no par and (0.1429) Common Stock Purchase Warrant expiring 09/03/2013

AURELIAN SMALL BUSINESS DEVELOPERS LTD. (ON)
Name changed to Aurelian Developers Ltd. 07/28/1980
(See Aurelian Developers Ltd.)

AURELIO RES CORP (NV)
SEC revoked common stock registration 07/06/2012

AUREUS MNG INC (CANADA)
Name changed to Avesoro Resource Inc. 12/12/2016

AUREUS VENTURES INC (CANADA)
Name changed to Velo Energy Inc. 08/17/2006
Velo Energy Inc. recapitalized as Canadian Overseas Petroleum Ltd. 08/03/2010

AUREX RES CORP (BC)
Recapitalized as Cobre Mining Co., Inc. 03/10/1997
Each share Common no par exchanged for (0.1) share Common no par
(See Cobre Mining Co., Inc.)

AUREX RES INC (BC)
Merged into Galveston Resources Ltd. 07/29/1986
Each share Common no par exchanged for for (0.28571428) share Common no par
Galveston Resources Ltd. merged into Corona Corp. 07/01/1988 which recapitalized as International Corona Corp. 06/11/1991
(See International Corona Corp.)

AURGENT GOLD CORP (BC)
Name changed to Argent Resource Corp. 03/10/2014
Argent Resource Corp. name changed to First Cobalt Corp. (BC) 09/23/2016 which reincorporated in Canada 09/04/2018

AURGENT RES CORP (BC)
Name changed to First Cobalt Corp. (BC) 09/23/2016

First Cobalt Corp. (BC) reincorporated in Canada 09/04/2018

AURIAC MINES LTD.
Acquired by Union Mining Corp. 00/00/1945
Each share Common exchanged for (0.33333333) share Common no par
Union Mining Corp. name changed to Union Gold Inc. 03/05/1993 which merged into Jubilee Gold Inc. 01/01/2010 which merged into Jubilee Gold Exploration Ltd. 01/25/2013

AURIC CORP (DE)
Merged into OM Group, Inc. 01/30/1998
Each share Common 10¢ par exchanged for $195.93 cash
Each share Common 10¢ par received an additional initial distribution of approximately $2.54 cash 03/31/2000
Each share Common 10¢ par received second and final distribution of approximately $3.37 cash 02/08/2001

AURIC ENTERPRISES INC (NV)
Name changed to Freedom Golf Corp. 12/20/1999
(See Freedom Golf Corp.)

AURIC INTL INC (DE)
Liquidation completed
Each share Common $1.50 par exchanged for initial distribution of $43 cash 03/06/1984
Each share Common $1.50 par received second and final distribution of $8 cash 08/06/1985

AURIC METALS CORP (NV)
Reincorporated 04/01/1986
Each share old Common 1¢ par exchanged for (0.05) share new Common 1¢ par 09/24/1983
State of incorporation changed from (UT) to (NV) 04/01/1986
Name changed to Brainworks Ventures, Inc. 11/16/2000
Brainworks Ventures, Inc. name changed to AssuranceAmerica Corp. 07/02/2003

AURIC MNG CO (DE)
Stock Dividend - 3% payable 05/18/2012 to holders of record 05/14/2012 Ex date - 05/10/2012
Recapitalized as Enterra Corp. (Old) 12/18/2013
Each share Common $0.001 par exchanged for (0.00014285) share Common $0.001 par
Enterra Corp. (Old) name changed to VinCompass Corp. 04/27/2015 which name changed to Enterra Corp. (New) 11/13/2015

AURIC MNG CORP (NV)
Each share old Common 1¢ par exchanged for (0.16666666) share new Common 1¢ par 01/18/1996
Recapitalized as Pinnacle Oil International Inc. 02/05/1996
Each share new Common 1¢ par exchanged for (0.16666666) share Common $0.001 par
Pinnacle Oil International Inc. name changed to Energy Exploration Technologies (NV) 06/15/2000 which reincorporated in Alberta 10/24/2003 which name changed to NXT Energy Solutions Inc. 09/22/2008

AURIC RES LTD (BAHAMAS)
Reorganized under the laws of Yukon as Lalo Ventures Ltd. 11/02/2001
Each share Common no par exchanged for (0.1) share Common no par
Lalo Ventures Ltd. (YT) reincorporated in British Columbia 07/29/2005 which name changed to Sunrise Minerals Inc. 12/20/2005 which recapitalized as Cronus Resources Ltd. (BC) 03/10/2008 which reincorporated in Ontario 06/25/2009 which merged into Continental Gold Ltd. (New) (Bermuda) 03/30/2010 which reorganized in Ontario as Continental Gold Inc. 06/12/2015

AURIC RES LTD (ON)
Recapitalized as Chancellor Energy Resources Inc. 05/01/1978
Each share Capital Stock no par exchanged for (0.25) share Capital Stock no par
Chancellor Energy Resources Inc. merged into HCO Energy Ltd. 04/02/1996 which merged into Pinnacle Resources Ltd. (New) 10/20/1997 which merged into Renaissance Energy Ltd. 07/16/1998 which merged into Husky Energy Inc. 08/25/2000

AURICLE BIOMEDICAL CORP (BC)
Merged into Aztech Innovations Inc. 04/16/2010
Each share Common no par exchanged for (0.66666666) share Common no par

AURICO GOLD INC (ON)
Merged into Alamos Gold Inc. (New) 07/06/2015
Each share Common no par exchanged for (0.5046) share Class A Common no par, (0.2219) share AuRico Metals Inc. Common no par
(See each company's listing)
Note: Unexchanged certificates will be cancelled and become without value 07/06/2021

AURICO METALS INC (ON)
Acquired by Centerra Gold Inc. 01/09/2018
Each share Common no par exchanged for $1.80 cash
Note: Unexchanged certificates will be cancelled and become without value 01/09/2021

AURIDIAM CONS N L (AUSTRALIA)
ADR agreement terminated 10/22/2004
No ADR holders' equity

AURIFER CAP CORP (BC)
Name changed to Jaxon Minerals Inc. 12/01/2008
Jaxon Minerals Inc. reorganized as Jaxon Mining Inc. 08/30/2017

AURIGA GEOSCIENCES, INC. (UT)
Recapitalized as Deltek Intertrade Corp. 09/15/1986
Each share Common $0.001 par exchanged for (0.05) share Common $0.001 par
(See Deltek Intertrade Corp.)

AURIGA GOLD CORP (ON)
Each share old Common no par exchanged for (0.1) share new Common no par 01/15/2014
Name changed to Minnova Corp. 06/27/2014

AURIGA LABORATORIES INC (DE)
SEC revoked common stock registration 09/14/2011

AURIGA RES LTD (BC)
Struck off register and declared dissolved for failure to file returns 03/29/1996

AURIGA YELLOWKNIFE MINES LTD.
Merged into Aurlando Consolidated Mining Corp., Ltd. 00/00/1947
Each share Capital Stock $1 par exchanged for (0.2) share Capital Stock $1 par
(See Aurlando Consolidated Mining Corp., Ltd.)

AURIS MEDICAL HOLDING AG OLD (SWITZERLAND)
Merged into Auris Medical Holding AG (New) 03/14/2018
Each share Common CHF 0.40 par exchanged for (0.1) share Common CHF 0.40 par

AURIUM RESH CORP (NY)
Stock Dividends - 100% 07/19/1973; 10% 11/14/1975
Merged into Pioneer Dental Manufacturing Co. 10/19/1993
Each share Common 1¢ par exchanged for $0.25 cash

AURIZON MINES LTD (BC)
Merged into Hecla Mining Co. 06/01/2013
Each share Common no par exchanged for (0.9953) share Common 25¢ par

AURLANDO CONSOLIDATED MINING CORP., LTD. (ON)
Charter revoked for failure to file reports and pay fees 00/00/1954

AURLANDO GOLD MINES LTD.
Merged into Aurlando Consolidated Mining Corp., Ltd. 00/00/1947
Each share Capital Stock $1 par exchanged for (0.2) share Capital Stock $1 par
(See Aurlando Consolidated Mining Corp., Ltd.)

AURLODE GOLD MINES LTD. (ON)
Name changed to Embury Lake Mining Co. Ltd. 00/00/1948
(See Embury Lake Mining Co. Ltd.)

AURO RES LTD (BC)
Recapitalized as Tesoro Minerals Corp. 08/26/2013
Each share Common no par exchanged for (0.1) share Common no par

AUROFINA RESOURCE CORP. (BC)
Name changed to Asitka Resource Corp. 09/16/1983
Asitka Resource Corp. name changed to Orenda Forest Products Ltd. 11/07/1989 which merged into Repap Enterprises Inc. 09/05/1996
(See Repap Enterprises Inc.)

AUROGIN RES LTD (CANADA)
Merged into Castle Gold Corp. 08/28/2007
Each share Common no par exchanged for (0.5) share Common no par
(See Castle Gold Corp.)

AUROMAR DEV CORP (BC)
Merged into Casmyn Corp. (CO) 07/30/1996
Each share Common no par exchanged for (2.6) shares Common 4¢ par
Casmyn Corp. (CO) reorganized in Nevada as Aries Ventures Inc. 04/11/2000 which reincorporated in Delaware as Cardium Therapeutics, Inc. 01/23/2006 which name changed to Taxus Cardium Pharmaceuticals Group, Inc. 10/07/2014

AUROR CAP CORP (NV)
Name changed to Mount Knowledge Holdings, Inc. 02/09/2010
Mount Knowledge Holdings, Inc. name changed to Cybergy Holdings, Inc. 01/21/2015

AURORA ACQUISITIONS INC (CO)
SEC revoked common stock registration 10/12/2007

AURORA BANCSHARES CORP (IL)
Name changed to GreatBanc, Inc. and
Common $10 par changed to 1¢ par 07/15/1986
(See GreatBanc, Inc.)

AURORA BIOSCIENCES CORP (DE)
Merged into Vertex Pharmaceuticals Inc. 07/18/2001
Each share Common $0.001 par exchanged for (0.62) share Common 1¢ par

AURORA BULB CORP (WA)
Chapter 11 Federal Bankruptcy proceedings converted to Chapter 7 on 05/23/1990
Stockholders' equity unlikely

AURORA CORP ILL (IL)
Common $1 par changed to no par 05/27/1971
Each share old Common no par exchanged for (0.1) share new Common no par 04/24/1974
Merged into Aurora Merging Co. 06/30/1976
Each share new Common no par exchanged for $1 cash

AURORA DOWNS, INC. (OH)
Name changed to Grandview Raceway, Inc. 00/00/1957
(See Grandview Raceway, Inc.)

AURORA ELECTRS INC (DE)
Common 3¢ par split (5) for (4) by issuance of (0.25) additional share 12/10/1992
Under plan of merger name changed to Cerplex Group, Inc. and Common 3¢ par changed to $0.001 par 04/30/1998
(See Cerplex Group, Inc.)

AURORA ENERGY LTD (NV)
Merged into Cadence Resources Corp. 10/31/2005
Each share Common $0.001 par exchanged for (1.8) shares Common 1¢ par
Note: An additional (0.2) share will be held in escrow for possible future distribution
Cadence Resources Corp. name changed to Aurora Oil & Gas Corp. 05/24/2006
(See Aurora Oil & Gas Corp.)

AURORA ENERGY RES INC (NL)
Acquired by Fronteer Development Group Inc. 04/21/2009
Each share Common no par exchanged for (0.825) share Common no par
Fronteer Development Group Inc. name changed to Fronteer Gold Inc. 05/13/2010 which merged into Pilot Gold Inc. 04/08/2011 which name changed to Liberty Gold Corp. 05/12/2017

AURORA ENVIRONMENTAL INC (DE)
Merged into ATC Environmental Inc. 06/29/1995
Each share Common $0.001 par exchanged for (0.545) share Common 1¢ par
ATC Environmental Inc. name changed to ATC Group Services Inc. 10/15/1996
(See ATC Group Services Inc.)

AURORA FOODS INC (DE)
Plan of reorganization under Chapter 11 Federal Bankruptcy Code effective 03/19/2004
No stockholders' equity

AURORA GOLD LTD (AB)
Merged into Canadian Frobisher Resources Ltd. 11/21/1991
Each share Common no par exchanged for (0.16) share Common no par
Canadian Frobisher Resources Ltd. merged into Orbit Oil & Gas Ltd. 08/26/1994
(See Orbit Oil & Gas Ltd.)

AURORA INC (SD)
Reincorporated under the laws of Delaware as Aurora Environmental Inc. 12/24/1987
Aurora Environmental Inc. merged into ATC Environmental Inc. 06/29/1995 which name changed to ATC Group Services Inc. 10/15/1996
(See ATC Group Services Inc.)

AURORA LABORATORIES, INC.
Liquidated 00/00/1947
Details not available

AURORA MED TECHNOLOGY INC (FL)
Administratively dissolved 09/26/2008

AURORA METALS BVI LIMITED (BRITISH VIRGIN ISLANDS)
Reincorporated under the laws of British Columbia as Aurora Platinum Exploration Inc. 05/20/2008
Aurora Platinum Exploration Inc. merged into Nevoro Inc. 06/10/2008 which was acquired by Starfield Resources, Inc. 10/08/2009

AURORA NATL BK (AURORA, IL)
Common $25 par changed to $10 par and (2) additional shares issued plus a 20% stock dividend paid 02/14/1967
Stock Dividends - 25% 03/01/1976; 50% 04/02/1979
Reorganized as Aurora Bancshares Corp. 05/21/1981
Each share Common $10 par exchanged for (1) share Common $10 par
Aurora Bancshares Corp. name changed to GreatBanc, Inc. 07/15/1986
(See GreatBanc, Inc.)

AURORA OIL & GAS CORP (UT)
Plan of reorganization under Chapter 11 Federal Bankruptcy Code effective 12/22/2009
No stockholders' equity

AURORA OIL & GAS LTD (AUSTRALIA)
Acquired by Baytex Energy Corp. 06/11/2014
Each share Ordinary exchanged for $4.20 cash

AURORA PLASTICS CORP (NY)
Common $1 par split (3) for (2) by issuance of (0.5) additional share 07/06/1964
Common $1 par split (3) for (2) by issuance of (0.5) additional share 02/01/1966
Name changed to Aurora Products Corp. 06/04/1970
(See Aurora Products Corp.)

AURORA PLATINUM CORP (BC)
Reincorporated 06/30/2004
Place of incorporation changed from (YT) to (BC) 06/30/2004
Merged into FNX Mining Co. Inc. 07/01/2005
Each share Common no par exchanged for (0.1918) share Common no par
FNX Mining Co. Inc. merged into Quadra FNX Mining Ltd. 05/27/2010
(See Quadra FNX Mining Ltd.)

AURORA PLATINUM EXPL INC (BC)
Merged into Nevoro Inc. 06/10/2008
Each share Common no par exchanged for (1) share Common no par
Nevoro Inc. acquired by Starfield Resources, Inc. 10/08/2009

AURORA PRECIOUS METALS INC (NV)
Name changed to V-Net Beverage, Inc. 09/03/2003
V-Net Beverage, Inc. name changed to RushNet, Inc. 07/08/2005
(See RushNet, Inc.)

AURORA PRODS CORP (NY)
Merged into Nabisco Inc. 05/28/1971
Each share Common $1 par exchanged for $10.50 cash

AURORA URANIUM & GOLD MINES LTD. (ON)
Merged into Pardee Amalgamated Mines Ltd. 12/00/1954
Each share Common exchanged for (0.2) share Common $1 par
Pardee Amalgamated Mines Ltd. liquidated for Rio Algom Mines Ltd. 11/09/1961 which name changed to Rio Algom Ltd. 04/30/1975
(See Rio Algom Ltd.)

AURORA YELLOWKNIFE MINES, LTD. (ON)
Name changed to Aurora Uranium & Gold Mines Ltd. 00/00/1951
Aurora Uranium & Gold Mines Ltd. merged into Pardee Amalgamated Mines Ltd. 12/00/1954 which liquidated for Rio Algom Mines Ltd. 11/09/1961 which name changed to Rio Algom Ltd. 04/30/1975
(See Rio Algom Ltd.)

AUROX MINES LTD. (QC)
Company reported as inactive 00/00/1981
Details not available

AURQUEST RES INC (ON)
Name changed to Xanthic Biopharma Inc. 04/19/2018

AURRE MGMT INC (DE)
Reincorporated 08/03/1972
State of incorporation changed from (NY) to (DE) 08/03/1972
Name changed to Fluid Lift International Inc. 02/01/1982
Fluid Lift International Inc. recapitalized as Odessa Foods International, Inc. 01/23/1995
(See Odessa Foods International, Inc.)

AURRERA S A DE C V (MEXICO)
ADR's for Ser. B, P10 par split (8) for (5) by issuance of (0.6) additional share 09/30/1983
Stock Dividend - 100% 09/25/1985
Name changed to Cifra S.A. de C.V. 07/23/1986
Cifra S.A. de C.V. name changed to Wal-Mart de Mexico, S.A. de C.V. 03/09/2000 which name changed to Wal-Mart de Mexico, S.A.B. de C.V. 03/09/2007
(See Wal-Mart de Mexico, S.A. de C.V.)

AURTEX INC (NV)
Recapitalized as Sector Communications Inc. 06/17/1996
Each share Common $0.001 par exchanged for (0.16921518) share Common $0.001 par
Sector Communications Inc. name changed to Options Talent Group 01/11/2002 which name changed to Trans Continental Entertainment Group Inc. 01/16/2003
(See Trans Continental Entertainment Group Inc.)

AURUM EXPLORATIONS INC (NV)
Recapitalized as Greatmat Technology Corp. (NV) 12/28/2010
Each share Common $0.001 par exchanged for (0.2) share Common $0.001 par
Greatmat Technology Corp. (NV) reincorporated in Cayman Islands 10/27/2011

AURUM RESOURCE & ASSET MGMT INC (NV)
Name changed to Innovest Global, Inc. 03/13/2017

AURUM RES CORP (NV)
Name changed to North Springs Resources Corp. 07/07/2011

AURUM SOFTWARE INC (DE)
Merged into Baan Co. N.V. 08/26/1997
Each share Common no par exchanged for (0.355932) New York Registry Share NLG 0.01 par
(See Baan Co. N.V.)

AURUN MINES LTD (CANADA)
Struck off register and declared dissolved for failure to file returns 08/01/1991

AURUS CORP (DE)
Stock Dividend - 10% payable 10/12/2007 to holders of record 02/15/2007 Ex date - 10/02/2007
Company hijacked corporate identity of Black Rock Golf Corp. 10/27/2005
Note: Shares were not registered with the SEC and company is not a legitimate successor

AURUS MNG LTD (BC)
Recapitalized as Aucan Resources Ltd. 02/09/1982
Each share Common no par exchanged for (0.2) share Common no par
(See Aucan Resources Ltd.)

AURVISTA GOLD CORP (CANADA)
Name changed to Maple Gold Mines Ltd. 11/20/2017

AURYX GOLD CORP (BC)
Merged into B2Gold Corp. 12/21/2011
Each share Common no par exchanged for (0.23) share Common no par and $0.001 cash

AUSABLE MINES LTD (QC)
Charter annulled for failure to file reports or pay fees 02/02/1974

AUSAM ENERGY CORP (AB)
Each share old Common no par exchanged for (0.2) share new Common no par 09/27/2007
Chapter 7 bankruptcy proceedings terminated 11/28/2016
Stockholders' equity unlikely

AUSEX CAP CORP (BC)
Merged into Tasman Metals Ltd. 11/03/2009
Each share Common no par exchanged for (1) share Common no par
Tasman Metals Ltd. merged into Leading Edge Materials Corp. 08/26/2016

AUSIC MINING & REDUCTION CO., LTD. (ON)
Recapitalized as United Cobalt Mines Ltd. on a (1) for (2) basis 00/00/1951
United Cobalt Mines Ltd. merged into Langis Silver & Cobalt Mining Co. Ltd. 04/30/1980 which name changed to Aranka Gold Inc. 07/27/2005 which merged into Guyana Goldfields Inc. 01/28/2009

AUSIMONT N V (NETHERLANDS)
Name changed 05/08/1987
Name changed from Ausimont Compo N.V. to Ausimont N.V. 05/08/1987
98.5% owned by Montedison S.p.A. as of 00/00/1989
Public interest eliminated

AUSNORAM HLDGS LTD (ON)
Name changed to Batavia Energy Corp. and Class A no par and Class B no par reclassified as Common no par 02/23/2010
Batavia Energy Corp. name changed to Victory Gold Mines Inc. 02/18/2011 which merged into Northern Gold Mining Inc. 02/06/2013 which merged into Oban Mining Corp. 12/24/2015 which name changed to Osisko Mining Inc. 06/21/2016

AUSPEX MINERALS LTD (BC)
Name changed 12/04/1995
Name changed from Auspex Gold Ltd. to Auspex Minerals Ltd. 12/04/1995
Merged into EuroZinc Mining Corp. 04/21/1999
Each share Common no par exchanged for (0.75) share Common no par
EuroZinc Mining Corp. merged into Lundin Mining Corp. 11/01/2006

AUSPEX PHARMACEUTICALS INC (DE)
Acquired by Teva Pharmaceutical Industries Ltd. 05/05/2015
Each share Common $0.0001 par exchanged for $101 cash

AUSPEX SYS INC (DE)
Plan of reorganization under Chapter 11 Federal Bankruptcy proceedings effective 11/28/2003
Each share Common $0.001 par received initial distribution of $0.03 cash payable 06/11/2004 to holders of record 11/28/2003
Each share Common $0.001 par received second and final distribution of $0.0213 cash payable 03/10/2006 to holders of record 11/28/2003 Ex date - 03/22/2006
Note: Certificates were not required to be surrendered and are without value

AUSSIE APPAREL GROUP LTD (NV)
Each share old Common $0.001 par exchanged for (3) shares new Common $0.001 par 04/07/2003
Each share new Common $0.001 par exchanged again for (5) shares new Common $0.001 par 05/27/2003
Name changed to Bluetorch Inc. 11/03/2003
Bluetorch Inc. name changed to Pacific Crest Investments 04/25/2005 which name changed to Pacific Peak Investments 05/16/2005 which name changed to Global Beverage Solutions, Inc. 10/26/2005 which recapitalized as Real Brands, Inc. 10/22/2013

AUSSIE SOLES GROUP INC (NV)
Each share old Common $0.001 par exchanged for (0.1) share new Common $0.001 par 11/28/2008
Recapitalized as Global Housing Group 07/29/2010
Each share new Common $0.001 par exchanged for (0.1) share Common $0.001 par
Global Housing Group name changed to Global Enterprises Group, Inc. 03/12/2014 which name changed to Predictive Technology Group, Inc. 07/16/2015

AUSTAR RES INC (BC)
Recapitalized as Austpro Energy Corp. 01/31/1996
Each share Common no par exchanged for (0.25) share Common no par

AUSTIN & FIFTH BLDG. CORP. (TX)
Liquidation completed
Each share Capital Stock no par exchanged for initial distribution of $100 cash 12/01/1967
Each share Capital Stock no par received second and final distribution of $3.663 cash 05/01/1970

AUSTIN BANCSHARES CORP (TX)
Merged into InterFirst Corp. 04/01/1982
Each share Common $1 par exchanged for (1.6) shares Common $5 par
InterFirst Corp. merged into First RepublicBank Corp. 06/06/1987
(See First RepublicBank Corp.)

AUSTIN BK (CHICAGO, IL)
Each share old Capital Stock $10 par exchanged for (0.00066666) share new Capital Stock $10 par 11/27/1987
Note: In effect holders received $22.50 cash per share and public interest was eliminated

AUSTIN BOULEVARD APARTMENTS, INC. (IL)
Liquidated 00/00/1957
Details not available

AUSTIN CHALK OIL & GAS LTD (NV)
Recapitalized as Mercantile Resources, Ltd. 07/08/2010
Each share Common $0.001 par exchanged for (0.01) share Common $0.001 par
Mercantile Resources, Ltd. recapitalized as Sharewell Capital Group, Inc. 03/25/2011 which name changed to Artemis Energy Holdings

Inc. 04/11/2013 which name changed to Findit, Inc. 02/20/2015

AUSTIN DEVS CORP (BC)
Recapitalized as Universal Wing Technologies Inc. 12/11/2009
Each share Common no par exchanged for (0.05) share Common no par
Universal Wing Technologies Inc. recapitalized as Red Oak Mining Corp. 03/21/2014

AUSTIN EQUITIES INC (DE)
Each share Common $0.0001 par exchanged for (0.08333333) share Class A Common $0.0001 par 09/09/1988
Charter cancelled and declared void for failure to pay franchise taxes 03/01/1993

AUSTIN EXPL LTD (AUSTRALIA)
Each old Sponsored ADR for Ordinary exchanged for (0.1) new Sponsored ADR for Ordinary 11/14/2014
Basis changed from (1:100) to (1:10) 06/08/2017
ADR agreement terminated 08/07/2017
Each new Sponsored ADR for Ordinary exchanged for $0.045848 cash

AUSTIN INVT LTD (BC)
Struck off register and declared dissolved for failure to file returns 09/20/1985

AUSTIN LD & DEV INC (NV)
Reorganized as Merlin Software Technologies International, Inc. 01/13/2000
Each share Common no par exchanged for (1.23468) shares Common no par
(See Merlin Software Technologies International, Inc.)

AUSTIN MANOR APARTMENTS
Trust terminated 00/00/1950
Details not available

AUSTIN MED TECHNOLOGIES INC (NV)
Each share old Common $0.001 par exchanged for (0.1) share new Common $0.001 par 07/25/2003
Each share new Common $0.001 par exchanged again for (0.001) share new Common $0.001 par 07/10/2006
Name changed to Las Vegas Central Reservations Corp. 08/03/2006

AUSTIN MINES INC (BC)
Reincorporated under the laws of Alberta as Nighthawk Resources Inc. 03/13/1995
(See Nighthawk Resources Inc.)

AUSTIN NATL BK (AUSTIN, TX)
Each share Common $100 par exchanged for (8) shares Common $25 par to effect a (4) for (1) split and a 100% stock dividend 00/00/1945
Common $25 par changed to $10 par and (1.5) additional shares issued plus a 10% stock dividend paid 01/28/1966
Common $10 par changed to $5 par and (1) additional share issued plus a 15% stock dividend paid 03/01/1972
Stock Dividends - 10% 02/24/1965; 20% 11/14/1966; 15% 01/26/1968; 15% 01/31/1969
Under plan of reorganization each share Common $5 par automatically became (1) share Austin Bancshares Corp. Common $1 par 04/20/1973
Austin Bancshares Corp. merged into InterFirst Corp. 04/01/1982 which merged into First RepublicBank Corp. 06/06/1987
(See First RepublicBank Corp.)

AUSTIN NICHOLS & CO INC (VA)
Each share 7% Preferred $100 par exchanged for (1) share Prior Preferred Ser. A no par and (1.2) shares new Common no par in 1930
Each share old Common no par exchanged for (0.5) share new Common no par in 1930
$1.20 Conv. Prior Preference no par changed to $20 par 11/6/64
New Common no par changed to $1 par and (0.5) additional share issued 11/27/64
$1.20 Conv. Prior Preference $20 par called for redemption 11/1/67
Merged into Liggett & Myers Inc. 1/24/69
Each share Common $1 par exchanged for (0.4) share $5.25 Conv. Preference $1 par
Liggett & Myers Inc. name changed to Liggett Group Inc. 4/28/76
(See Liggett Group Inc.)

AUSTIN POWDER CO (OH)
Acquired by W.J.D. Investments Inc. 05/24/1995
Each share Capital Stock $100 par exchanged for $1,700 cash

AUSTIN RESOURCES, INC. (NV)
Charter revoked for failure to file reports and pay fees 03/01/1989

AUSTIN RES INC (BC)
Common no par split (2) for (1) by issuance of (1) additional share 09/26/1983
Acquired by Lincoln Resources Inc. 08/00/1984
Each share Common no par exchanged for (0.66666666) share Common no par
Lincoln Resources Inc. recapitalized as United Lincoln Resources Inc. 06/21/1988 which merged into Continental Gold Corp. (New) 03/15/1989
(See Continental Gold Corp. (New))

AUSTIN SILVER MINING CO.
Bankrupt 00/00/1939
Details not available

AUSTIN UNDERGROUND INC (NV)
Name changed to SaleOutlet.Com 02/26/1999
SaleOutlet.Com recapitalized as Gatlin Holdings Inc. 02/05/2001 which recapitalized as Bio Venture Holdings Inc. 06/11/2002 which name changed to Midwest Venture Holdings, Inc. 08/16/2002 which name changed to Inspiration Products Group, Inc. 02/03/2003 which name changed to MB-Tech, Inc. 05/18/2003
(See MB-Tech, Inc.)

AUSTIN YOUNG INC (UT)
Each share old Common $0.001 par exchanged for (0.33333333) share new Common $0.001 par 04/20/1992
Proclaimed dissolved for failure to pay taxes 11/01/1994

AUSTINS INTL INC (DE)
SEC revoked common stock registration 05/30/2008

AUSTINS STEAKS & SALOON INC (DE)
Each share old Common 1¢ par exchanged for (0.03189792) share new Common 1¢ par 07/08/1999
Name changed to Western Sizzlin Corp. 10/01/2003
(See Western Sizzlin Corp.)

AUSTONIA RED LAKE MINES LTD. (ON)
Charter cancelled 12/10/1962

AUSTRA RES CORP (BC)
Name changed to Austar Resources Inc. 11/01/1990
Austar Resources Inc. recapitalized as Austpro Energy Corp. 01/31/1996

AUSTRAK INTL CDA CORP (AB)
Struck off register for failure to file annual returns 12/01/1994

AUSTRAL OIL INC (DE)
Liquidation completed
Each share Common 25¢ par exchanged for initial distribution of $35 cash 04/24/1978
Each share Common 25¢ par received second distribution of $2.50 cash 08/28/1978
Each share Common 25¢ par received third distribution of $0.65 cash 03/23/1979
Each share Common 25¢ par received fourth distribution of $0.25 cash 04/14/1980
Each share Common 25¢ par received fifth distribution of $0.85 cash 11/24/1980
Each share Common 25¢ par received sixth and final distribution of $0.43477 cash 03/26/1982

AUSTRAL PAC ENERGY CORP (NV)
Name changed to Verida Internet Corp. 03/11/1999
(See Verida Internet Corp.)

AUSTRAL PAC ENERGY LTD (BC)
Reincorporated 10/16/2006
Place of incorporation changed from (YT) to (BC) 10/16/2006
Placed in receivership 04/30/2009
Stockholders' equity unlikely

AUSTRALAMERICA CORP. (DE)
Merged into Australamerica Corp. (TX) 06/05/1961
Each share Common exchanged for (1) share Common
(See Australamerica Corp. (TX))

AUSTRALAMERICA CORP. (TX)
Charter cancelled 11/02/1965

AUSTRALIA & NEW ZEALAND BKG GROUP LTD (AUSTRALIA)
9.125% Capital Securities called for redemption at $25 on 03/04/2003 (Additional Information in Active)

AUSTRALIA ACQUISITION CORP (CAYMAN ISLANDS)
Completely liquidated
Each Unit received first and final distribution of $10.10 cash payable 11/27/2012 to holders of record 11/20/2012
Each share Ordinary $0.001 par received first and final distribution of $10.10 cash payable 11/27/2012 to holders of record 11/20/2012

AUSTRALIA WIDE INDS LTD (AUSTRALIA)
ADR agreement terminated 10/22/1993
Each ADR for Ordinary exchanged for (0.2) share Ordinary

AUSTRALIAN AGRIC & PPTY DEV CORP (DE)
Name changed to Global Realty Development Corp. 07/11/2005

AUSTRALIAN AGRIC & PPTY DEV INC (DE)
Name changed to WorldSource, Inc. 06/21/2005
(See WorldSource, Inc.)

AUSTRALIAN BANC CAP SECS TR (ON)
Merged into Global Capital Securities Trust 02/04/2016
Each Class A Unit automatically became (0.413485) Class A Unit
Each Class F Unit automatically became (0.391346) Class F Unit
Global Capital Securities Trust name changed to Redwood Global Financials Income Fund 12/20/2017
(See Redwood Global Financials Income Fund)

AUSTRALIAN BANC INCOME FD (ON)
Name changed to Purpose Global Financials Income Fund 06/18/2018

AUSTRALIAN CANADIAN OIL ROYALTIES LTD (BC)
Reincorporated under the laws of Alberta as Chelsea Oil & Gas Ltd. 10/07/2013

AUSTRALIAN CANCER TECHNOLOGY LTD (AUSTRALIA)
Name changed to Avantogen Ltd. 06/14/2005
(See Avantogen Ltd.)

AUSTRALIAN CONS INVTS LTD (AUSTRALIA)
ADR agreement terminated 07/07/1993
Each Sponsored ADR for Ordinary exchanged for $0.9004875 cash

AUSTRALIAN FST INDS (NV)
Recapitalized as Lone Pine Holdings, Inc. 02/11/2009
Each share Common $0.001 par exchanged for (0.01) share Common $0.001 par
Lone Pine Holdings, Inc. name changed to Flux Power Holdings, Inc. 06/11/2012

AUSTRALIAN GOLD MINES CORP (BC)
Name changed to Blue Sun Resource Corp. 08/23/1990
Blue Sun Resource Corp. recapitalized as International Blue Sun Resource Corp. 12/17/1991 which name changed to Dalton Enterprises Ltd. (BC) 05/26/1994 which reincorporated in Wyoming 01/17/1995 which reincorporated in Delaware as Dalton Specialties, Ltd. 03/01/1996
(See Dalton Specialties, Ltd.)

AUSTRALIAN GOLDFIELDS NL (AUSTRALIA)
Liquidators declared Ordinary shares worthless 11/19/2001

AUSTRALIAN HYDROCARBONS LTD (AUSTRALIA)
ADR agreement terminated 01/23/1997
Each ADR for Ordinary exchanged for $1.2117165 cash

AUSTRALIAN NATL INDS LTD (AUSTRALIA)
Each Unsponsored ADR for Ordinary exchanged for (1) Sponsored ADR for Ordinary 10/15/1992
Stock Dividend - 80% 07/06/1987
ADR agreement terminated 06/28/1999
Each Sponsored ADR for Ordinary exchanged for $3.0116 cash

AUSTRALIAN OIL & GAS LTD (AUSTRALIA)
Each old ADR for Ordinary exchanged for (0.2) ADR for Ordinary and $3.54 cash 06/21/1991
Each new ADR for Ordinary exchanged for (0.2) Sponsored ADR for Ordinary 06/13/1997
ADR agreement terminated 11/27/2001
Each Sponsored ADR for Ordinary exchanged for $7.4079 cash

AUSTRALIAN OIL CORP. (DE)
Name changed to International Energy Co. and Common $1 par changed to 10¢ par 03/14/1968
International Energy Co. name changed to International Energy Co. of America 00/00/1980 which name changed to AMX International, Inc. 05/08/1987
(See AMX International, Inc.)

AUSTRALIAN OILFIELDS PTY LTD (BC)
Reincorporated under the laws of Alberta as Equatorial Energy Inc. 09/15/1997
Equatorial Energy Inc. name changed to Resolute Energy Inc. 11/14/2002
(See Resolute Energy Inc.)

AUSTRALIAN PAPER MFRS LTD (AUSTRALIA)
Name changed to APM Ltd. 11/01/1984
APM Ltd. recapitalized as Amcor Ltd. 01/22/1987

AUSTRALIAN SHALE & COAL N L (AUSTRALIA)
Each old ADR for Ordinary exchanged for (0.4) new ADR for Ordinary 04/16/1982
Each new ADR for Ordinary exchanged for (0.25) ADR for Ordinary 11/19/1982
Name changed to Charter Mining N.L. 04/12/1984
(See Charter Mining N.L.)

AUSTRALIAN SOLOMONS GOLD LTD (AUSTRALIA)
Acquired by Allied Gold Ltd. (Australia) 03/04/2010
Each share Ordinary exchanged for (0.85) share Ordinary
Allied Gold Ltd. (Australia) reorganized in England and Wales as Allied Gold Mining PLC 06/30/2011
(See Allied Gold Mining PLC)

AUSTRALIS AQUACULTURE LTD (AUSTRALIA)
Sponsored ADR's for Ordinary split (10) for (1) by issuance of (9) additional ADR's payable 05/01/2007 to holders of record 04/26/2007
Basis changed from (1:10) to (1:1) 05/01/2007
ADR agreement terminated 11/20/2012
Each Sponsored ADR for Ordinary exchanged for $0.000236 cash

AUSTRIA FD INC (MD)
Liquidation completed
Each share Common 1¢ par received initial distribution of $5.88 cash payable 03/1/2002 to holders of record 02/12/2002
Each share Common 1¢ par received second distribution of $0.47 cash payable 04/18/2002 to holders of record 04/05/2002
Each share Common 1¢ par received third and final distribution of $0.13 cash payable 05/03/2002 to holders of record 04/26/2002

AUSTRIAN TRADING SVCS INC (DE)
SEC revoked common stock registration 11/02/2007

AUSTRO-CAN EXPLORATIONS LTD. (BC)
Recapitalized as Agio Resources Corp. 12/31/1979
Each share Common 50¢ par exchanged for (0.5) share Common no par
(See Agio Resources Corp.)

AUSTRON INC (TX)
Acquired by Datum Inc. 06/24/1988
Each share Common $0.0125 par exchanged for $3.25 cash

AUTEC ASSOCS INC (NV)
Name changed to Capital Hill Gold, Inc. and Common no par changed to $0.001 par 02/19/2004
Capital Hill Gold, Inc. name changed to Amerimine Resources, Inc. 09/03/2005 which name changed to American Unity Investments, Inc. 08/09/2006
(See American Unity Investments, Inc.)

AUTEO MEDIA INC (NV)
Name changed to WorldStar Energy, Corp. 04/01/2005

AUTERRA MINES LTD. (ON)
Charter cancelled 09/18/1961
No stockholders' equity

AUTERRA VENTURES INC (BC)
Name changed to Global Hunter Corp. 02/24/2005

AUTEX INC (MA)
Merged into Itel Corp. (Old) 12/20/1976
Each share Common 10¢ par exchanged for (1.39) shares Common $1 par
Itel Corp. (Old) reorganized as Itel Corp. (New) 09/19/1983 which name changed to Anixter International Inc. 09/01/1995

AUTHENTEC INC (DE)
Acquired by Apple Inc. 10/04/2012
Each share Common 1¢ par exchanged for $8 cash

AUTHENTEX SOFTWARE LTD PARTNERSHIP (ON)
Reorganized under the laws of Alberta as Ophir Ventures Inc. 06/28/2005
Each Unit of Ltd. Partnership exchanged for (1) share Common no par
Ophir Ventures Inc. recapitalized as Consolidated Ophir Ventures Inc. (AB) 12/02/2005 which reorganized in British Virgin Islands as CIC Energy Corp. 03/14/2006
(See CIC Energy Corp.)

AUTHENTIC FITNESS CORP (DE)
Common 1¢ par split (2) for (1) by issuance of (1) additional share 02/10/1994
Merged into Warnaco Group, Inc. 12/16/1999
Each share Common 1¢ par exchanged for $20.80 cash

AUTHENTIC SPECIALTY FOODS INC (TX)
Merged into Authentic Acquisition Corp. 06/16/1998
Each share Common $1 par exchanged for $17 cash

AUTHENTIC TEAS INC (NV)
Reincorporated under the laws of Puerto Rico as MOJO Data Solutions, Inc. 09/16/2013

AUTHENTIDATE HLDG CORP (DE)
Each share old Common $0.001 par exchanged for (0.5) share new Common $0.001 par 08/31/2012
Each share new Common $0.001 par exchanged again for (0.11111111) share new Common $0.001 par 01/25/2016
Name changed to Aeon Global Health Corp. 02/01/2018

AUTHORISZOR INC (DE)
Recapitalized as GreenGro Technologies, Inc. 02/10/2010
Each share Common 1¢ par exchanged for (0.01) share Common 1¢ par

AUTHORIZE NET HLDGS INC (DE)
Acquired by CyberSource Corp. 11/01/2007
Each share Common 1¢ par exchanged for (1.1611) shares Common $0.001 par and $4.42 cash
(See CyberSource Corp.)

AUTHORIZED DISTR NETWORK INC (DE)
Charter cancelled and declared inoperative and void for non-payment of taxes 03/01/1991

AUTO AMER INC (WA)
Reorganized as Charter Equities, Inc. (WA) 06/04/2007
Each share Common no par exchanged for (0.01) share Common $0.001 par
Charter Equities, Inc. (WA) reincorporated in Arizona 01/23/2008 which reorganized in Nevada as Global Recycle Energy, Inc. 04/15/2008 which name changed to ATI Modular Technology Corp. 06/13/2017 which recapitalized as AmericaTowne Holdings, Inc. 03/08/2018

AUTO AUCTION COM INC (NV)
Reorganized under the laws of Wyoming as HLV Trading Corp. 02/08/2005
Each share Common $0.000001 par exchanged for (0.00285714) share Common $0.0001 par
HLV Trading Corp. name changed to X-tra Petroleum 08/30/2006 which recapitalized as Xtra Energy Corp. 11/05/2010

AUTO CENTRIX INC (FL)
Each share old Common $0.0001 par exchanged for (0.1) share new Common $0.0001 par 07/13/2005
Recapitalized as Greenstone Holdings, Inc. 01/03/2006
Each share new Common $0.0001 par exchanged for (0.66666666) share Common $0.0001 par
(See Greenstone Holdings, Inc.)

AUTO CHEK CTRS INC (DE)
Plan of reorganization under Chapter 11 Federal Bankruptcy Code effective 05/05/1995
Stockholders' equity unlikely

AUTO CITY BREWING CO.
Dissolved 00/00/1945
Details not available

AUTO CLUB AMER CORP (CO)
Each share old Common $0.0001 par exchanged for (0.005) share new Common $0.0001 par 12/15/1989
Name changed to Auto Club Marketing Corp. 04/01/2002
Auto Club Marketing Corp. reorganized as Evolution Solar Corp. 05/23/2008

AUTO CLUB MARKETING CORP (CO)
Reorganized as Evolution Solar Corp. 05/23/2008
Each share Common $0.0001 par exchanged for (2) shares Common $0.0001 par

AUTO-CONTROL LABORATORIES, INC. (CA)
Completely liquidated 09/26/1967
Each share Common 10¢ par exchanged for first and final distribution of (0.05) share Rucker Co. Common no par
Rucker Co. merged into N L Industries, Inc. 01/21/1977

AUTO DATA NETWORK INC (DE)
Each share Common $0.001 par received distribution of (0.6864782) share Aftersoft Group, Inc. Common no par payable 11/24/2008 to holders of record 11/17/2008
Ex date - 11/25/2008
SEC revoked common stock registration 06/13/2012

AUTO-DATA SYSTEMS, INC. (DE)
Charter cancelled and declared inoperative and void for non-payment of taxes 03/01/1980

AUTO DEALERS CREDIT CORP. (NY)
Completely liquidated 12/31/1965
Each share Preferred $20 par exchanged for first and final distribution of $20 cash
Each share Common $1 par exchanged for first and final distribution of $1 cash

AUTO DEPOT INC (DE)
Charter cancelled and declared inoperative and void for non-payment of taxes 03/01/2001

AUTO ELEC SVC LTD (ON)
Common no par changed to Capital Stock no par and (2) additional shares issued 04/11/1960
Name changed to Autolec Inc. 01/02/1975
Autolec Inc. name changed to Centurion Equities Corp. 04/06/1976 which name changed to Amcan Industries Corp. 08/17/1979
(See Amcan Industries Corp.)

AUTO FABRIC PRODUCTS CO., LTD. (CANADA)
Name changed to Autofab Ltd. 06/29/1961
(See Autofab Ltd.)

AUTO FINANCE CO. (SC)
Each share Common $10 par exchanged for (2) shares Common $5 par 00/00/1951
Common $5 par changed to $2.50 par and (1) additional share issued 06/19/1955
Stock Dividends - 10% 02/01/1948; 10% 01/10/1949; 10% 03/01/1954
Merged into American Discount Co. 10/02/1961
Each share Common $2.50 par exchanged for (1) share Common no par
American Discount Co. merged into American Credit Corp. 12/31/1964 which merged into Wachovia Corp. 07/01/1970
(See Wachovia Corp.)

AUTO GRAPHICS INC (CA)
Common no par split (3) for (1) by issuance of (2) additional shares payable 02/25/2000 to holders of record 02/11/2000
Reincorporated under the laws of Nevada as Agent Information Software, Inc. 03/02/2010

AUTO HOME LOCK INC (NV)
Name changed to Eclipse Identity Recognition Corp. 01/17/2013
Eclipse Identity Recognition Corp. name changed to Nudg Media Inc. 03/14/2014

AUTO ITALIA HLDGS LTD (BERMUDA)
ADR agreement terminated 12/23/2015
Each Sponsored ADR for Ordinary exchanged for $0.263467 cash

AUTO KNITTER HOSIERY CO.
Bankrupt 00/00/1926
No stockholders' equity

AUTO LEC STORES INC (MO)
Adjudicated bankrupt 06/02/1975
Stockholders' equity unlikely

AUTO MAGIC CAR WASH INC (DE)
Charter cancelled and declared inoperative and void for non-payment of taxes 03/01/1974

AUTO-MARINE ACCEPTANCE CORP. LTD. (AB)
Liquidation completed 07/21/1967
Each share Ordinary Stock $2 par exchanged for initial distribution of (0.2037) share Chieftain Development Co. Ltd. Common 50¢ par
Each share Ordinary Stock $2 par received second and final distribution of (0.04067) share Chieftain Development Co. Ltd. Common 50¢ par 12/12/1968
(See Chieftain Development Co. Ltd.)

AUTO MARINE ELEC LTD (BC)
3% Preference $1 par called for redemption 06/29/1973
Acquired by UAP Inc. 01/03/1991
Each share Common no par exchanged for $28 cash

AUTO MATE INC (DE)
Merged into Transcontinental Industries, Inc. (DE) 10/09/1970
Each share Common 1¢ par exchanged for (0.5) share Common 10¢ par
(See Transcontinental Industries, Inc.)

AUTO MAX GROUP HLDGS INC (FL)
Name changed to Biocentric Energy Holdings, Inc. 10/15/2008

AUTO METREKS INC (FL)
Recapitalized as Online Hearing.com Co. 04/06/1999
Each share Common no par exchanged for (0.03333333) share Common $0.0001 par
Online Hearing.com Co. name changed to Rompus Interactive Corp. 07/30/1999
(See Rompus Interactive Corp.)

AUTO-MISSION, INC. (FL)
Proclaimed dissolved for failure to file reports and pay fees 07/11/1972

AUTO N CORP (WY)
Name changed to Advanced Gaming Technology Inc. 07/17/1996
Advanced Gaming Technology Inc. name changed to Mediaworx, Inc. 07/17/2003
(See Mediaworx, Inc.)

AUTO NETWORK GROUP INC (AZ)
Name changed 10/22/1998
Name changed from Auto Network USA, Inc. to Auto Network Group, Inc. 10/22/1998
Name changed to Autotradecenter.Com, Inc. 04/30/1999
Autotradecenter.Com, Inc. merged into AutoTradeCenter, Inc. 10/10/2002 which name changed to ATC-Onlane, Inc. 08/20/2006 which name changed to Openlane, Inc. 11/25/2008
(See Openlane, Inc.)

AUTO-ORDNANCE CORP.
Name changed to Maguire Industries Inc. 00/00/1944
Maguire Industries, Inc. name changed to Components Corp. of America 04/03/1961
(See Components Corp. of America)

AUTO PHOTO TECHNOLOGIES INC (NV)
Common $0.001 par split (44) for (1) by issuance of (43) additional shares payable 09/17/2007 to holders of record 09/17/2007
Name changed to Raven Biofuels International Corp. 10/02/2007
(See Raven Biofuels International Corp.)

AUTO-Q INTL INC (DE)
Common $0.0001 par split (3) for (1) by issuance of (2) additional shares payable 10/10/2002 to holders of record 10/08/2002 Ex date - 10/11/2002
Recapitalized as Entertainment Is Us, Inc. 05/02/2005
Each share Common $0.001 par exchanged for (0.005) share Common $0.001 par
(See Entertainment Is Us, Inc.)

AUTO SEARCH CARS INC (NV)
Common $0.001 par split (91) for (1) by issuance of (90) additional shares payable 01/11/2010 to holders of record 12/09/2009 Ex date - 01/12/2010
Name changed to Curaxis Pharmaceutical Corp. 09/03/2010
(See Curaxis Pharmaceutical Corp.)

AUTO-SOLER CO. (GA)
Stock Dividend - 100% 11/14/1947
Acquired by Textron Inc. 03/31/1971
Each share Common $1 par exchanged for (0.415) share Common 25¢ par

AUTO STACK INTL (NV)
Name changed to BTC Financial Services 04/30/1999
BTC Financial Services name changed to First Equity Holding Corp. 09/19/2000 which recapitalized as Chilmark Entertainment Group, Inc. 06/23/2003 which recapitalized as Integrated Bio Energy Resources, Inc. 03/13/2007 which name changed to Onslow Holdings, Inc. 01/30/2014

AUTO SWAP U S A INC (DE)
Each share Common 1¢ par exchanged for (0.2) share Common $0.001 par 06/14/1993
Name changed to Water Chef Inc. 08/02/1993
Water Chef Inc. name changed to PureSafe Water Systems, Inc. 06/16/2009

AUTO TOOL TECHNOLOGIES INC (NV)
Name changed to AFC Building Technologies Inc. 01/14/2014
AFC Building Technologies Inc. name changed to First Colombia Development Corp. 04/26/2018

AUTO TRADE CTR CDA LTD (AB)
Delisted from Toronto Venture Stock Exchange 06/22/2006

AUTO TRAIN CORP (FL)
Liquidated by court order 05/29/1981
No stockholders' equity

AUTO TROL TECHNOLOGY CORP (CO)
Each share Common no par exchanged for (0.1) share Common 2¢ par 01/31/1996
Merged into ATTC, Inc. 07/30/2002
Each share Common 2¢ par exchanged for $0.20 cash

AUTO UNDERWRITERS OF AMER INC (CA)
SEC revoked common stock registration 12/15/2011

AUTO WHSL SPECIALISTS INC (FL)
Common $0.001 par split (2) for (1) by issuance of (1) additional share payable 11/08/1999 to holders of record 10/27/1999
SEC revoked common stock registration 02/20/2007

AUTOBAHN INTL INC (DE)
Each share old Common no par exchanged for (0.01) share new Common no par 10/07/2005
Name changed to Global Developments, Inc. 06/05/2006

AUTOBALE AMER CORP (UT)
Proclaimed dissolved for failure to pay taxes 12/31/1975

AUTOBANC INC (VA)
Acquired by private investors 10/20/2000
Each share Common no par exchanged for $1.16 cash

AUTOBIDXL INC (FL)
Name changed to Trophy Resources, Inc. 02/28/2006

AUTOBITTER GROUP INC (NJ)
Each share old Common $0.0001 par automatically became (2/3) share new Common $0.0001 par 05/00/1995
Charter revoked for failure to file annual reports 11/07/1995

AUTOBOND ACCEP CORP (TX)
Name changed to Agility Capital, Inc. 05/31/2001
(See Agility Capital, Inc.)

AUTOBYTE SYS CORP (BC)
Struck off register and declared dissolved for failure to file reports 06/11/1993

AUTOBYTE TECHNOLOGIES INC (BC)
Delisted from Toronto Venture Stock Exchange 12/27/2001

AUTOBYTEL INC (DE)
Name changed 08/15/2001
Under plan of merger name changed from Autobytel, Inc. to Autobytel, Inc. 08/15/2001
Each share old Common $0.001 par exchanged for (0.2) share new Common $0.001 par 07/12/2012
Name changed to AutoWeb, Inc. 10/09/2017

AUTOCAFE SYS INC (DE)
Charter cancelled and declared inoperative and void for non-payment of taxes 03/12/2000

AUTOCAM CORP (MI)
Common no par split (3) for (2) by issuance of (0.5) additional share 01/10/1994
Stock Dividends - 5% payable 11/28/1996 to holders of record 11/12/1996; 5% payable 11/17/1997 to holders of record 11/03/1997; 5% payable 11/16/1998 to holders of record 11/02/1998
Merged into Aurora Capital Group 02/07/2000
Each share Common no par exchanged for $18.75 cash

AUTOCANADA INCOME FD (AB)
Reincorporated under the laws of Canada as AutoCanada Inc. and Units no par reclassified as Common no par 12/31/2009

AUTOCAPITAL (NV)
Name changed to Wapro Group, Inc. 08/27/1999
Wapro Group, Inc. recapitalized as Royal Waterlily, Inc. 07/20/2000 which name changed to Royal Acquisitions & Development, Inc. 03/28/2005 which recapitalized as Innovative Health Sciences, Inc. (NV) 06/11/2008 which reincorporated in Delaware 02/24/2011 which name changed to Innovative Holdings Alliance, Inc. 05/27/2011

AUTOCAR CO. (PA)
Each share Common $100 par exchanged for (3) shares Common no par 00/00/1929
Common no par changed to $10 par 00/00/1932
Recapitalized 00/00/1936
Each share 8% Preferred $100 par exchanged for (1) share $3 Preferred $100 par and (5) shares Common 10¢ par
Each share Common $10 par exchanged for (0.5) share Common 10¢ par
Each share Common 10¢ par exchanged for (2) shares Common 5¢ par 00/00/1942
Stock Dividend - 10% 10/22/1945
Merged into White Motor Co. 00/00/1953
Each share 5% Preferred Ser. A, B or C $20 par exchanged for (49/200) share 5-1/4% Preferred $100 par
Each share Common 5¢ par exchanged for (24/200) share 5-1/4% Preferred $100 par of White Motor Co. and (0.6) share Common 5¢ par of Highway Trailer Co. (DE)
(See each company's listing)

AUTOCARBON INC (DE)
Name changed 11/01/2002
Each share old Common $0.0001 par exchanged for (0.02) share new Common $0.0001 par 10/08/2002
Name changed from Autocarbon.com, Inc. to AutoCarbon, Inc. 11/01/2002
Recapitalized as Global Pharmatech, Inc. 02/03/2005
Each share new Common $0.0001 par exchanged for (0.1) share Common $0.0001 par

AUTOCARE CORP (NV)
Charter revoked for failure to file reports and pay fees 04/01/1997

AUTOCENTRAL USA INC (FL)
Name changed to General Defense Systems, Inc. (FL) 03/07/2002
General Defense Systems, Inc. (FL) reorganized in Nevada 11/06/2003 which name changed to GenMedx Inc. 03/15/2005 which name changed to Pyramidion Technology Group, Inc. 06/19/2013

AUTOCHEM LABS INC (NY)
Name changed to ACL Laboratories International Inc. 01/18/1973
(See ACL Laboratories International Inc.)

AUTOCHINA INTL LTD (CAYMAN ISLANDS)
Units separated 01/21/2010
Name changed to Fincera Inc. 08/05/2015 which changed back to AutoChina International Ltd. 09/02/2015
Name changed back to Fincera Inc. 08/31/2017

AUTOCLAVE ENGINEERS INC (PA)
Stock Dividends - 10% 05/16/1988; 10% 09/15/1989
Reincorporated under the laws of California as Unit Instruments Inc. 11/17/1995
Unit Instruments Inc. merged into United States Filter Corp. (New) 01/22/1999
(See United States Filter Corp. (New))

AUTOCOMP INC (MD)
Filed for bankruptcy 06/24/1977
No stockholders' equity

AUTOCORP EQUITIES INC (NV)
Each share old Common 10¢ par exchanged for (0.03333333) share new Common 10¢ par 04/03/1997
Name changed to Homeland Security Network, Inc. 03/16/2005
Homeland Security Network, Inc. name changed to Global Ecology Corp. 01/05/2010

AUTOCRAT RES LTD (BC)
Recapitalized as Criswell (Jack) Resources Ltd. 06/15/1984
Each share Common no par exchanged for (0.2) share Common no par
(See Criswell (Jack) Resources Ltd.)

AUTOCROWN LTD (ON)
Name changed to Microbix Biosystems Inc. 10/01/1990

AUTOCYTE INC (DE)
Under plan of merger name changed to TriPath Imaging, Inc. 09/30/1999
(See TriPath Imaging, Inc.)

AUTODESK INC (CA)
Common no par split (3) for (1) by issuance of (2) additional shares 03/27/1987
Reincorporated under the laws of Delaware 08/04/1994

AUTODIE CORP (MI)
Chapter 11 bankruptcy proceedings converted to Chapter 7 on 03/09/1993
No stockholders' equity

AUTODYNAMICS INC (NJ)
Common 10¢ par reclassified as Conv. Class B Common 10¢ par 05/15/1981
Each share Conv. Class B Common 10¢ par received distribution of (1) share Class A Common 10¢ par 05/30/1981
Class A Common 10¢ par reclassified as Common 10¢ par 06/15/1984
Conv. Class B Common 10¢ par reclassified as Common 10¢ par 06/15/1984
Merged into Gilbert Associates, Inc. 03/11/1985
Each share Common 10¢ par exchanged for $0.66 cash

AUTOEYE INC (DE)
Name changed to forestindustry.com, Inc. 02/25/2000
forestindustry.com, Inc. name changed to Global Golf Holdings, Inc. 01/07/2003 which recapitalized as Vitasti, Inc. 12/09/2004 which

name changed to Welwind Energy International Corp. 10/31/2006
(See Welwind Energy International Corp.)

AUTOFAB LTD. (CANADA)
Placed in bankruptcy 11/00/1964
No stockholders' equity

AUTOFINANCE GROUP INC (CA)
Acquired by KeyCorp (New) 09/27/1995
Each share Common no par exchanged for (0.5) share Common $1 par

AUTOFUND SERVICING INC (NV)
Recapitalized as Intrepid Holdings, Inc. 07/26/2004
Each share Common $0.001 par exchanged for (0.5) share Common $0.001 par
Intrepid Holdings, Inc. recapitalized as My Healthy Access, Inc. 03/12/2008

AUTOGEN LTD (AUSTRALIA)
Name changed to AGT Biosciences Ltd. 03/19/2003
AGT Biosciences Ltd. name changed to ChemGenex Pharmaceuticals Ltd. 07/07/2004
(See ChemGenex Pharmaceuticals Ltd.)

AUTOIMMUNE INC (DE)
Liquidation completed
Each share Common 1¢ par received initial distribution of $0.48 cash payable 12/30/2010 to holders of record 06/30/2010 Ex date - 01/10/2011
Each share Common 1¢ par received second and final distribution of $0.023 cash payable 12/15/2013 to holders of record 06/30/2010 Ex date - 12/16/2013

AUTOINFO INC (DE)
Reincorporated 01/14/1987
Common 1¢ par split (3) for (2) by issuance of (0.5) additional share 01/14/1987
State of incorporation changed from (NY) to (DE) 06/04/1987
Acquired by AutoInfo Holdings, LLC 04/26/2013
Each share Common 1¢ par exchanged for $1.05 cash

AUTOLEASECHECK COM INC (FL)
Name changed to Gatelinx Global Corp. (FL) 03/15/2005
Gatelinx Global Corp. (FL) reincorporated in Nevada as GTX Global Corp. 10/12/2005 which recapitalized as Vision Technology Corp. 07/31/2006
(See Vision Technology Corp.)

AUTOLEC INC (ON)
Name changed to Centurion Equities Corp. 04/06/1976
Each share Capital Stock no par exchanged for (1) share Capital Stock no par
Centurion Equities Corp. name changed to Amcan Industries Corp. 08/17/1979
(See Amcan Industries Corp.)

AUTOLEND GROUP INC (DE)
Plan of reorganization effective 03/05/1999
Each share old Common $0.002 par exchanged for (1) Common Stock Purchase Right expiring 03/18/2000
Company terminated registration of common stock and is no longer public as of 06/09/2006

AUTOLINE GROUP INC (UT)
Name changed to GeNOsys, Inc. 10/10/2005

AUTOLINE OIL CO (MD)
Out of business 00/00/1987
Stockholders' equity not determined

AUTOLIV AB (SWEDEN)
Sponsored ADR's for Capital Stock split (2) for (1) by issuance of (1) additional ADR payable 06/04/1996 to holders of record 05/31/1996
Merged into Autoliv, Inc. 05/01/1997
Each 144A Sponsored ADR for Capital Stock exchanged for (1) share Common $1 par

AUTOLOGIC INFORMATION INTL INC (DE)
Merged into AGFA-Gevaert N.V. 12/03/2001
Each share Common 1¢ par exchanged for $7.127 cash

AUTOLOGOUS WOUND THERAPY INC (DE)
Name changed to Cytomedix, Inc. 03/30/2000
Cytomedix, Inc. name changed to Nuo Therapeutics, Inc. 11/14/2014

AUTOMATA INTERNATIONAL, INC. (CA)
Adjudicated bankrupt 01/20/1965
No stockholders' equity

AUTOMATED BENEFITS CORP (AB)
Name changed to Symbility Solutions Inc. 09/24/2012

AUTOMATED BLDG COMPONENTS INC (FL)
Common 50¢ par split (4) for (3) by issuance of (0.33333333) additional share 03/01/1968
Common 50¢ par split (2) for (1) by issuance of (1) additional share 10/31/1968
Stock Dividends - 15% 01/31/1963; 15% 01/31/1966
Merged into Redland Ltd. 01/04/1979
Each share Common 50¢ par exchanged for $12.50 cash

AUTOMATED BUSINESS CTLS INC (FL)
Name changed to Investex, Inc. 06/30/1977
(See Investex, Inc.)

AUTOMATED COMPLIANCE & TRAINING INC (TX)
Reincorporated under the laws of Utah as Chequemate International Inc. 08/30/1996
Chequemate International Inc. name changed to C-3D Digital, Inc. 01/08/2002
(See C-3D Digital, Inc.)

AUTOMATED DATA ASSOC INC (DE)
Common 10¢ par split (2) for (1) by issuance of (1) additional share 06/23/1973
Charter cancelled and declared inoperative and void for non-payment of taxes 03/01/1984

AUTOMATED DATA SCIENCES INC (DE)
Name changed to Delta States Oil, Inc. 01/28/1974
Delta States Oil, Inc. name changed to WindsorTech Inc. 01/30/2002 which name changed to QSGI, Inc. 10/18/2005
(See QSGI, Inc.)

AUTOMATED ENVIRONMENTAL SYS INC (NY)
Name changed to Unifi, Inc. 06/21/1971

AUTOMATED FINL SYS INC (DE)
Voluntarily dissolved 06/04/1996
Details not available

AUTOMATED GOVT MONEY TR (MA)
Merged into Money Market Obligations Trust 04/30/1999
Each Share of Bene. Int. received shares of Automated Government Money Trust at net asset value

AUTOMATED INDS INC (DE)
Each share Common 10¢ par exchanged for (5) shares Common 2¢ par 08/13/1969
Charter cancelled and declared inoperative and void for non-payment of taxes 04/15/1973

AUTOMATED INFORMATION INDS INC (DE)
Each share old Common 10¢ par exchanged for (0.25) share new Common 10¢ par 01/12/1978
Name changed to Standard Oil & Exploration Delaware, Inc. and new Common 10¢ par changed to Common $0.001 par 11/30/1987
(See Standard Oil & Exploration Delaware, Inc.)

AUTOMATED INFORMATION SYS INC (MA)
Proclaimed dissolved for failure to file reports and pay fees 01/10/1979

AUTOMATED LABELS & FORMS INC (NY)
Recapitalized as Automated Propulsion Systems, Inc. 02/05/1971
Each share Common 10¢ par exchanged for (0.5) share Common 10¢ par
Automated Propulsion Systems, Inc. merged into ALF Industries, Inc. 05/31/1974
(See ALF Industries, Inc.)

AUTOMATED LANGUAGE PROCESSING SYS INC (UT)
Name changed to Alpnet Inc. 08/17/1989
(See Alpnet Inc.)

AUTOMATED LEARNING INC (CO)
Merged into Automated Information Industries, Inc. 01/26/1973
Each share Common 10¢ par exchanged for (1) share Common 10¢ par
Automated Information Industries, Inc. name changed to Standard Oil & Exploration Delaware, Inc. 11/30/1987
(See Standard Oil & Exploration Delaware, Inc.)

AUTOMATED MGMT RES LTD (NV)
Recapitalized as RealTime Cars Inc. (NV) 12/19/2000
Each share Common $0.001 par exchanged for (0.05) share Common $0.001 par
RealTime Cars Inc. (NV) reorganized in Florida as Siteworks, Inc. 10/25/2002 which name changed to SiteWorks Building & Development Co. (FL) 04/15/2005 which reincorporated in Nevada as SBD International, Inc. 08/03/2006 which recapitalized as Solargy Systems Inc. 10/27/2008
(See Solargy Systems Inc.)

AUTOMATED MGMT SYS INC (MS)
Merged into Intersystems, Inc. 08/19/1969
Each share Common $1 par exchanged for (0.4) share Common $2 par
Intersystems, Inc. name changed back to School Pictures, Inc. 06/30/1975
(See School Pictures, Inc.)

AUTOMATED MANUFACTURING PRODUCTS, INC. (MN)
Name changed to Kinnard Companies, Inc. (MN) 01/27/1971
Kinnard Companies, Inc. (MN) reincorporated in Kansas 09/11/1980 which merged into Kelly-Johnston Enterprises, Inc. 12/28/1981
(See Kelly-Johnston Enterprises, Inc.)

AUTOMATED MARKETING SYS INC (DE)
Merged into Newsam, Inc. 12/05/1983
Each share Common 50¢ par exchanged for $10 cash

AUTOMATED MED LABS INC (FL)
Stock Dividend - 100% 04/14/1975
Name changed to Medicore Inc. 03/19/1986
Medicore Inc. merged into Dialysis Corp. of America 09/21/2005
(See Dialysis Corp. of America)

AUTOMATED MERCHANDISING CAPITAL CORP. (DE)
Name changed to A.M. Capital Corp. 10/02/1963
(See A.M. Capital Corp.)

AUTOMATED MICROSYSTEMS INC (NY)
Charter cancelled and proclaimed dissolved for failure to pay taxes 06/23/1993

AUTOMATED PLAYER MACHS INC (DE)
Name changed to Practice Tennis Centers, Inc. 10/27/1972
Practice Tennis Centers, Inc. name changed to Energy Control Systems of America, Inc. 04/06/1979 which recapitalized as National Tax Accounting Inc. 02/28/1997

AUTOMATED PRINTS, INC. (DE)
Merged into Universal Automated Industries, Inc. 03/26/1963
Each share Common exchanged for (4) shares Common 10¢ par
Universal Automated Industries, Inc. acquired by Castleton Industries, Inc. 10/11/1967
(See Castleton Industries, Inc.)

AUTOMATED PROCEDURES CORP (NY)
Charter cancelled and proclaimed dissolved for failure to pay taxes 12/29/1982

AUTOMATED PRODS CORP (MN)
Statutorily dissolved 09/25/1991

AUTOMATED PROFESSIONAL SYS INC (FL)
Name changed to Advanced Professional Sales Inc. (NY) 07/09/1985
Advanced Professional Sales Inc. (NY) reincorporated in Delaware as Omnicorp Ltd. 03/11/1987
(See Omnicorp Ltd.)

AUTOMATED PROPULSION SYS INC (NY)
Merged into ALF Industries, Inc. 05/31/1974
Each share Common 10¢ par exchanged for (1) share Common 10¢ par
(See ALF Industries, Inc.)

AUTOMATED RECYCLING INC (BC)
Name changed to OceanLake Commerce Inc. 03/01/2001

AUTOMATED REFERENCE CORP (NY)
Charter cancelled and proclaimed dissolved for failure to pay taxes 06/24/1981

AUTOMATED SEC HLDGS PLC (UNITED KINGDOM)
Merged into ADT Ltd. 09/05/1996
Each ADR for Ordinary exchanged for (0.06521739) share Common 10¢ par
ADT Ltd. merged into Tyco International Ltd. (Bermuda) 07/02/1997 which reincorporated in Switzerland 03/17/2009 which merged into Johnson Controls International PLC 09/06/2016

AUTOMATED SERVICES, INC. (OR)
Involuntarily dissolved 09/01/1989

AUTOMATED SVCS INC (MN)
Name changed to Dameron, Inc. 11/02/1971
(See Dameron, Inc.)

AUTOMATED SPORTS CENTERS, INC. (CA)
Adjudicated bankrupt 11/04/1966
No stockholders' equity

AUT-AUT — FINANCIAL INFORMATION, INC.

AUTOMATED SYS INC (WI)
Merged into Cadence Design Systems Inc. 07/12/1990
Each share Common 10¢ par exchanged for (0.3) share Common 1¢ par

AUTOMATED TECHNOLOGY CORP (DE)
Charter cancelled and declared inoperative and void for non-payment of taxes 03/01/1984

AUTOMATED TEL MGMT SYS INC (TX)
Charter forfeited for failure to pay taxes 02/14/1995

AUTOMATED TRANSFER SYS CORP (CO)
Name changed to Synergy Technologies Corp. 03/02/1999
(See Synergy Technologies Corp.)

AUTOMATED VENDING TECHNOLOGIES INC (DE)
Stock Dividend - 1% payable 05/08/2007 to holders of record 04/08/2007 Ex date - 04/05/2007
Reorganized under the laws of Nevada as AVT, Inc. 01/17/2008
Each share Common 1¢ par exchanged for (0.33333333) share Common $0.001 par
(See AVT, Inc.)

AUTOMATED-X INC (UT)
Common $0.005 par split (5) for (1) by issuance of (4) additional shares payable 12/03/2014 to holders of record 12/03/2014
Name changed to Saddle Ranch Media, Inc. 10/07/2015

AUTOMATIC BOOKKEEPING REGISTER CO. (DE)
Charter cancelled and declared inoperative and void for non-payment of taxes 03/18/1925

AUTOMATIC CAFETERIAS FOR INDUSTRY, INC. (DE)
Name changed to American Caduceus Industries Inc. 04/17/1967
(See American Caduceus Industries Inc.)

AUTOMATIC CANTEEN CO AMER (DE)
Each share Common no par exchanged for (3) shares Common $5 par 00/00/1945
Common $5 par changed to $2.50 par and (1) additional share issued 08/01/1958
Common $2.50 par split (2) for (1) by issuance of (1) additional share 12/17/1959
Name changed to Canteen Corp. 02/16/1966
Canteen Corp. merged into International Telephone & Telegraph Corp. (DE) 04/25/1969 which name changed to ITT Corp. 12/31/1983 which reorganized in Indiana as ITT Industries, Inc. 12/19/1995 which name changed to ITT Corp. 07/01/2006

AUTOMATIC CASH REGISTER CO. (OK)
Charter revoked for failure to file reports and pay fees 12/15/30

AUTOMATIC COM EXCHANGE SEC TR II (DE)
Each $1.55 Trust Automatic Common Exchange Security exchanged for (1) share Autonation Inc. Common 1¢ par 05/15/2000

AUTOMATIC COMPACTOR CORP (NY)
Dissolved by proclamation 3/25/81

AUTOMATIC CONCESSIONS CORP. (NY)
Acquired by American Univend Corp. on a (0.038) for (1) basis 06/07/1962
(See American Univend Corp.)

AUTOMATIC CTL CORP (NV)
Reincorporated under the laws of Utah as Sionix Corp. 04/22/1996
Sionix Corp. (UT) reincorporated back in Nevada 07/03/2003

AUTOMATIC DIALING CORP.
Bankrupt 00/00/1951
Details not available

AUTOMATIC DRILLING MACHS INC (TX)
Name changed to Advanced Drilling Systems, Inc. 03/15/1979
(See Advanced Drilling Systems, Inc.)

AUTOMATIC FILM PROCESSOR CORP (NY)
Name changed to AFP Imaging Corp. 11/01/1982

AUTOMATIC FIRE ALARM CO (NY)
Under plan of merger each share Common $25 par exchanged for (1.0944) shares Common $10 par in 1948
Common $10 par changed to no par 4/26/68
Name changed to AFA Protective Systems, Inc. and Common no par changed to $1 par 7/2/69

AUTOMATIC FIRE ALARM CO DEL (DE)
Capital Stock $25 par changed to $10 par and (1.4714) additional shares issued 01/26/1968
Merged into Automatic Fire Alarm Co. 04/26/1968
Each share Capital Stock $10 par exchanged for (2) shares Common no par
Automatic Fire Alarm Co. name changed to AFA Protective Systems, Inc. 07/02/1969

AUTOMATIC FIRING CORP. (MO)
Adjudicated bankrupt 06/16/1959
Stockholders' equity unlikely

AUTOMATIC INSTRUMENT CO. (MI)
Name changed to A M I, Inc. (MI) 06/01/1946
A M I, Inc. (MI) reorganized in Delaware 01/02/1952 which merged into Automatic Canteen Co. of America 03/27/1959 which name changed to Canteen Corp. 02/16/1966 which merged into International Telephone & Telegraph Corp. (DE) 04/25/1969 which name changed to ITT Corp. 12/31/1983 which reorganized in Indiana as ITT Industries, Inc. 12/19/1995 which name changed to ITT Corp. 07/01/2006

AUTOMATIC MERCHANDISING INC (FL)
Each share old Common 50¢ par exchanged for (0.4) share new Common 50¢ par 03/27/1969
Voluntarily dissolved 12/20/1979
No stockholders' equity

AUTOMATIC MUSICAL INSTRUMENT CO., LTD.
Name changed to Automatic Sales Co. of Canada Ltd. 00/00/1930
(See Automatic Sales Co. of Canada Ltd.)

AUTOMATIC MUSICAL INSTRUMENT CO. (DE)
Acquired by Automatic Musical Instruments Co. (MI) 00/00/1933
Details not available

AUTOMATIC MUSICAL INSTRUMENT CO. (MI)
Name changed to Automatic Instrument Co. 00/00/1937
Automatic Instrument Co. name changed to A M I, Inc. (MI) 06/01/1946 which reorganized in Delaware 01/02/1952 which merged into Automatic Canteen Co. of America 03/27/1959 which name changed to Canteen Corp. 02/16/1966 which merged into International Telephone & Telegraph Corp. (DE) 04/25/1969 which name changed to ITT Corp. (DE) 12/31/1983 which reorganized in Indiana as ITT Industries, Inc. 12/19/1995 which name changed to ITT Corp. 07/01/2006

AUTOMATIC NUT CO., INC. (NY)
Liquidation completed 05/23/1962
Details not available

AUTOMATIC PHONE INC (DE)
Name changed to Jero, Inc. 01/30/1987
(See Jero, Inc.)

AUTOMATIC PINSETTER CO., INC. (NJ)
Acquired by American Machine & Foundry Co. 02/04/1947
Each share Common $10 par exchanged for (0.33333333) share Common no par and (1/75,000) Automatic Pinsetter Co., Inc. Part. Ctf. no par
Liquidation completed 12/31/1966
Each (1/75,000) Part. Ctf. no par exchanged for final distribution of $3.355979866 cash
American Machine & Foundry Co. name changed to AMF Inc. 04/30/1970
(See AMF Inc.)

AUTOMATIC PRODUCTS CORP. (DE)
Reincorporated 00/00/1941
State of incorporation changed from (IL) to (DE) and Common $5 par changed to $1 par 00/00/1941
Name changed to Automatic Steel Products, Inc. 00/00/1947
Automatic Steel Products, Inc. name changed to Aspro, Inc. 11/26/1969 which name changed to Dyneer Corp. 11/29/1978 which name changed to DYR Liquidating Corp. 07/31/1986
(See DYR Liquidating Corp.)

AUTOMATIC RADIO MFG INC (MA)
5% Preferred $100 par called for redemption 01/31/1966
Name changed to Armatron International Inc. 02/12/1980
(See Armatron International Inc.)

AUTOMATIC REDUCTION SYS INC (MN)
Adjudicated bankrupt 07/19/1971
Stockholders' equity unlikely

AUTOMATIC REGISTERING MACHINE CO., INC. (DE)
Name changed to Automatic Voting Machine Corp. (Old) 00/00/1929
(See Automatic Voting Machine Corp. (Old))

AUTOMATIC REMOTE SYSTEMS, INC. (MD)
Voluntarily dissolved 11/30/1973
Details not available

AUTOMATIC RETAILERS AMER INC (DE)
Common $1 par changed to 50¢ par and (1) additional share issued 01/23/1961
Name changed to ARA Services, Inc. 03/10/1969
(See ARA Services, Inc.)

AUTOMATIC SAFETY DEVICES, INC. (NV)
Charter revoked for failure to file reports and pay fees 03/02/1964

AUTOMATIC SAFETY TRAFFIC SIGNAL CO. (DE)
Charter cancelled and declared inoperative and void for non-payment of taxes 03/16/1927

AUTOMATIC SALES CO. OF CANADA LTD.
Out of business 00/00/1934
Details not available

AUTOMATIC SVC CO (NC)
Name changed to Disson, Inc. 01/03/1969 which name changed back to Automatic Service Co. 05/19/1969
Name changed to Bowen Investment Co. 09/29/1976
(See Bowen Investment Co.)

AUTOMATIC SIGNAL CORP.
Merged into Eastern Industries, Inc. (Incorporated 10/02/1946) 00/00/1946
Each share Common $1 par exchanged for (1/3) share Common 50¢ par
Eastern Industries, Inc. (Incorporated 10/02/1946) merged into Laboratory for Electronics, Inc. 03/15/1961 which name changed to LFE Corp. 11/03/1969
(See LFE Corp.)

AUTOMATIC SPRINKLER CORP AMER (OH)
Common 50¢ par changed to 10¢ par and (4) additional shares issued 10/19/1965
Common 10¢ par split (5) for (2) by issuance of (1.5) additional shares 10/03/1969
Under plan of merger name changed to A-T-O Inc. 10/29/1969
A-T-O Inc. name changed to Figgie International Inc. (OH) 06/01/1981 which reorganized in Delaware as Figgie International Holdings Inc. 07/18/1983 which name changed to Figgie International Inc. 12/31/1986 which name changed to Scott Technologies, Inc. 05/20/1998 which merged into Tyco International Ltd. (Bermuda) 05/03/2001 which reincorporated in Switzerland 03/17/2009 which merged into Johnson Controls International PLC 09/06/2016

AUTOMATIC STL PRODS INC (DE)
Under plan of merger each share 30¢ Preferred $1 par exchanged for (1.5) shares Common $1 par 07/17/1963
Stock Dividend - 100% 01/12/1948
Name changed to Aspro, Inc. 11/26/1969
Aspro, Inc. name changed to Dyneer Corp. 11/29/1978 which name changed to DYR Liquidating Corp. 07/31/1986
(See DYR Liquidating Corp.)

AUTOMATIC SWITCH CO (DE)
Common $5 par changed to $2.50 par and (1) additional share issued 08/01/1978
Common $2.50 par changed to $1.25 par and (1) additional share issued 02/20/1981
Merged into Emerson Electric Co. 05/17/1985
Each share Common $1.25 par exchanged for (0.6429) share Common $1 par

AUTOMATIC TELEPHONE DIALER, INC. (DE)
No longer in existence having become inoperative and void for non-payment of taxes 10/01/1963

AUTOMATIC TOP CO. (DE)
No longer in existence having become inoperative and void for non-payment of taxes 03/16/1921

AUTOMATIC VENDORS OF AMERICA, INC. (DE)
Class A Common $1 par called for redemption 01/09/1970
Completely liquidated 12/29/1970
Each share Common $1 par exchanged for first and final distribution of (0.5) share Automatic Service Co. Common $1 par
Automatic Service Co. name changed to Bowen Investment Co. 09/26/1976
(See Bowen Investment Co.)

AUTOMATIC VOTING MACHINE CORP. OLD (DE)
Liquidation completed 12/23/1958
Details not available

AUTOMATIC VTG MACH CORP NEW (DE)
Name changed to AVM Corp. 03/24/1965
AVM Corp. name changed to American Locker Group Inc. 05/01/1985

AUTOMATIC WASHER CO. (DE)
Reorganized 00/00/1938
Each share Preference no par exchanged for (3) shares Common $3 par
Each (10) shares Common no par exchanged for (1) share Common $3 par and the right to purchase (1.5) shares Common at $4 a share
Common $3 par changed to $1.50 par and (1) additional share issued 11/03/1955
Under plan of reorganization each share Common $1.50 par exchanged for first and final liquidating distribution of $0.22 cash 07/27/1965
Note: Unexchanged certificates were cancelled and became without value 10/28/1970

AUTOMATION BUSINESS SYS INC (NC)
Merged into American Business Products, Inc. (DE) 11/17/1968
Each share Common 50¢ par exchanged for (0.133333) share Common $2 par
American Business Products, Inc. (DE) reincorporated in Georgia 04/30/1986
(See American Business Products, Inc. (GA))

AUTOMATION DEVELOPMENT, INC. (NY)
Adjudicated bankrupt 00/00/1962
No stockholders' equity

AUTOMATION ENGINEERING CORP. (DE)
No longer in existence having become inoperative and void for non-payment of taxes 04/01/1961

AUTOMATION INDUSTRIES, INC. (MD)
Charter revoked for failure to file reports and pay taxes 11/27/1963

AUTOMATION INDS INC (CA)
Common $1 par split (6) for (5) by issuance of (0.2) additional share 06/30/1967
Common $1 par split (2) for (1) by issuance of (1) additional share 05/26/1969
Conv. Preferred Ser. B $3 par called for redemption 11/01/1969
Conv. Preferred Ser. A $3 par called for redemption 03/01/1971
Acquired by General Cable Corp. 05/26/1978
Each share Common $1 par exchanged for $20 cash

AUTOMATION INSTRUMENTS, INC. (CA)
Name changed to Automation Industries, Inc. (CA) 12/14/1959
(See Automation Industries, Inc. (CA))

AUTOMATION INTL INC (CO)
Declared defunct and inoperative for failure to pay taxes and file annual reports 12/06/1977

AUTOMATION LABORATORIES, INC. (NY)
Acquired by Marquardt Corp. 10/31/1964
Each share Common exchanged for (0.25) share Capital Stock $1 par
Marquardt Corp. merged into CCI Marquardt Corp. 06/12/1968 which name changed to CCI Corp. 09/26/1969
(See CCI Corp.)

AUTOMATION SCIENCES INC (NY)
Charter cancelled and proclaimed dissolved for failure to pay taxes and file reports 12/15/1975

AUTOMATION SHARES, INC. (DE)
Name changed to Pioneer Enterprise Fund, Inc. 10/15/1962
Pioneer Enterprise Fund, Inc. acquired by Pioneer II, Inc. 06/28/1974 which name changed to Pioneer Value Fund 04/02/2001

AUTOMATION TECHNOLOGY INC (MD)
Stock Dividend - 100% 03/11/1970
Name changed to Tax Corp. of America (MD) 03/11/1971
(See Tax Corp. of America (MD))

AUTOMATIQUE INC (DE)
Name changed to Ambassador Food Services Corp. 08/01/1989

AUTOMATIX INC (DE)
Recapitalized as Acuity Imaging Inc. 01/26/1994
Each share Common 5¢ par exchanged for (0.05) share Common 5¢ par
Acuity Imaging Inc. merged into Robotic Vision Systems, Inc. 09/20/1995
(See Robotic Vision Systems, Inc.)

AUTOMAX GROUP INC (FL)
Each share old Common $0.001 par exchanged for (0.01) share new Common $0.001 par 05/24/2002
Recapitalized as Heritage Capital Credit Corp. 04/01/2004
Each share Common $0.001 par exchanged for (0.002) share Common $0.001 par
Heritage Capital Credit Corp. recapitalized as Protective Capital Structures Corp. 12/11/2008

AUTOMEDIX SCIENCES INC (IL)
Recapitalized as COMC, Inc. (IL) 11/06/1996
Each share Common 1¢ par exchanged for (0.1) share Common 1¢ par
COMC, Inc. (IL) reincorporated in Delaware 12/27/2000 which recapitalized as ICF Corp. 06/27/2005
(See ICF Corp.)

AUTOMOBILE BKG CORP (DE)
Liquidation completed
Each share 6% Preferred Ser. A $10 par or 6% Preferred Ser. B $10 par exchanged for first and final distribution of (0.4) share Liberty Loan Corp. $1.25 Conv. Preference $25 par 09/20/1968
Each share $1.50 Preferred $25 par exchanged for first and final distribution of (1) share Liberty Loan Corp. $1.25 Conv. Preference $25 par 09/20/1968
Each share Class A Common 25¢ par or Common 25¢ par stamped to indicate initial distribution of (0.0384) share Liberty Loan Corp. $1.25 Conv. Preference $25 par 05/02/1969
Each share Stamped Class A Common 25¢ par or Stamped Common 25¢ par exchanged for second and final distribution of (0.0096) share Liberty Loan Corp. $1.25 Conv. Preference $25 par and $0.0024243 cash 01/16/1974
Liberty Loan Corp. name changed to LLC Corp. 03/14/1980 which name changed to Valhi, Inc. 03/10/1987

AUTOMOBILE FINANCE CO.
Name changed to Continental Commercial Corp. 00/00/1943
Continental Commercial Corp. acquired by General Acceptance Corp. (New) 10/18/1967 which name changed to GAC Corp. (PA) 07/01/1968 which reincorporated in Delaware 12/20/1973
(See GAC Corp. (DE))

AUTOMOBILE INSURANCE CO. (CT)
Each share Capital Stock $100 par exchanged for (10) shares Capital Stock $10 par 00/00/1929
Merged into Aetna Casualty & Surety Co. share for share 12/31/1955
Aetna Casualty & Surety Co. acquired by Aetna Life Insurance Co. 12/29/1964 which name changed to Aetna Life & Casualty Co. 12/27/1967 which name changed to Aetna, Inc. (CT) 07/19/1996 which merged into ING Groep N.V. 12/13/2000

AUTOMOBILE PROTN CORP-APCO (GA)
Merged into Ford Motor Co. 07/17/1999
Each share Common $0.001 par exchanged for $13 cash

AUTOMOCO CORP (CA)
Merged into Spar Enterprises 12/20/1982
Each share Common 10¢ par exchanged for $2.625 cash

AUTOMODULAR CORP (ON)
Merged into HLS Therapeutics Inc. 03/14/2018
Each share Common no par exchanged for (1) share Preferred no par and (0.165834) share Common no par
Note: Unexchanged certificates will be cancelled and become without value 03/14/2024

AUTOMOTIVE CAP GROUP INC (NV)
Name changed to NowAuto, Inc. 11/05/2004

AUTOMOTIVE DEVICES CORP. (DE)
Incorporated 10/06/1928
No longer in existence having become inoperative and void for non-payment of taxes 04/01/1932

AUTOMOTIVE DEVICES CORP. (DE)
Incorporated 12/21/1932
No longer in existence having become inoperative and void for non-payment of taxes 04/01/1940

AUTOMOTIVE FAN & BEARING CO.
Assets sold for the benefit of creditors 00/00/1935
No stockholders' equity

AUTOMOTIVE FINL CORP IND INC (IN)
Plan of liquidation under Chapter 11 Federal Bankruptcy Act confirmed 01/28/1985
No stockholders' equity

AUTOMOTIVE FRANCHISE CORP (TN)
Plan of reorganization under Chapter 11 Federal Bankruptcy proceedings confirmed 11/13/1992
No stockholders' equity

AUTOMOTIVE HARDWARE LTD (ON)
Common no par reclassified as Conv. Participating Class A no par 09/24/1973
Conv. Part. Class A no par split (2) for (1) by issuance of (1) additional share 02/15/1979
Conv. Part. Class B no par split (2) for (1) by issuance of (1) additional share 02/15/1979
Conv. Part. Class A no par reclassified as Class X no par 02/20/1984
Conv. Part. Class B no par reclassified as Class X no par 02/20/1984
Each share Class X no par received distribution of (0.5) share Conv. Class Y no par 02/22/1984
Name changed to AHL Group Ltd. 01/23/1985
AHL Group Ltd. acquired by Ivaco Inc. 08/27/1985
(See Ivaco Inc.)

AUTOMOTIVE INDS HLDG INC (DE)
Merged into Lear Seating Corp. 08/22/1995
Each share Class A Common 1¢ par exchanged for $33.50 cash

AUTOMOTIVE INDS INC (DE)
Plan of reorganization under Chapter 11 Federal Bankruptcy proceedings confirmed 02/08/1990
No stockholders' equity

AUTOMOTIVE INVESTMENTS, INC.
Liquidated 00/00/1936
Details not available

AUTOMOTIVE PARTS CO. (OH)
Merged into Genuine Parts Co. 04/01/1964
Each share Class A and/or Class B Common no par exchanged for (0.66666666) share Common $5 par

AUTOMOTIVE REPLACEMENTS, INC. (IL)
Name changed to Reiland & Bree, Inc. 04/10/1954
(See Reiland & Bree, Inc.)

AUTOMOTIVE SPECIALTY CONCEPTS INC (NV)
Common 2¢ par split (10) for (1) by issuance of (9) additional shares payable 12/20/2005 to holders of record 12/16/2005 Ex date - 12/21/2005
Name changed to Drake Gold Resources, Inc. 02/13/2006
Drake Gold Resources, Inc. name changed to Universal Apparel & Textile Co. 04/27/2015

AUTOMOTIVE TECHNOLOGIES INC (CO)
Name changed to Integrated Homes Inc. 05/20/1999
(See Integrated Homes Inc.)

AUTONATION INC OLD (DE)
Merged into Republic Industries Inc. 01/16/1997
Each share Common $0.001 par exchanged for (0.217796) share Common 1¢ par
Republic Industries Inc. name changed to AutoNation, Inc. (New) 04/06/1999

AUTONAVI HLDGS LTD (CAYMAN ISLANDS)
Acquired by Alibaba Investment Ltd. 07/17/2014
Each Sponsored ADR for Ordinary exchanged for $20.95 cash

AUTONOMOUS TECHNOLOGIES CORP (FL)
Merged into Summit Technology, Inc. 04/30/1999
Each share Common 1¢ par exchanged for (0.7271904) share Common 1¢ par and $3.04 cash
Summit Technology, Inc. name changed to Summit Autonomous, Inc. 05/19/2000
(See Summit Autonomous, Inc.)

AUTONOMY CORP PLC (ENGLAND & WALES)
Old ADR's for Ordinary split (3) for (1) by issuance of (2) additional ADR's payable 08/02/2000 to holders of record 08/01/2000 Ex date - 08/01/2000
Each old ADR for Ordinary exchanged for (0.2) new ADR for Ordinary 10/21/2002
Basis changed from (1:1) to (1:5) 10/21/2002
ADR agreement terminated 02/02/2005
Each new ADR for Ordinary exchanged for $18.8859 cash
Acquired by Hewlett-Packard Co. 10/03/2011

Each ADR for Ordinary exchanged for $39.967845 cash

AUTONUMERICS INC (NY)
Plan of reorganization under Chapter 11 Federal Bankruptcy proceedings confirmed 07/27/1984
No stockholders' equity

AUTOPOINT PENCIL CO. (IL)
Proclaimed dissolved for failure to pay taxes and file reports 07/23/1926

AUTOSALES CORP. (DE)
Assets sold 00/00/1934
No stockholders' equity

AUTOSALES CORP. (NY)
Assets sold to Autosales Corp. (DE) 00/00/1932
Details not available

AUTOSPA AUTOMALLS INC (DE)
Charter cancelled and declared inoperative and void for non-payment of taxes 03/01/1990

AUTOSPA CORP (DE)
Charter cancelled and declared inoperative and void for non-payment of taxes 05/25/1995

AUTOSTOCK INC (QC)
Acquired by Belron International 12/31/1997
Each share Common no par exchanged for $5.50 cash

AUTOSTRADA MTRS INC (UT)
Each share old Common $0.001 par exchanged for (8) shares new Common $0.001 par 05/16/2006
Name changed to Waterbank of America (USA) Inc. 10/26/2006
Waterbank of America (USA) Inc. recapitalized as Global Water Asset Corp. (UT) 01/14/2010 which reincorporated in Delaware 10/26/2010

AUTOSTRADA TORINO-MILANO SPA (ITALY)
ADR agreement terminated 12/26/2017
No ADR's remain outstanding

AUTOSTROP SAFETY RAZOR CO.
Acquired by Gillette Safety Razor Co. 00/00/1930
Details not available

AUTOTOTE CORP (DE)
Class A Common 1¢ par split (3) for (2) by issuance of (0.5) additional share 06/30/1993
Class A Common 1¢ par split (2) for (1) by issuance of (1) additional share 10/25/1993
Name changed to Scientific Games Corp. (DE) 04/27/2001
Scientific Games Corp. (DE) reincorporated in Nevada 01/10/2018

AUTOTOTE SYS INC (DE)
Merged into UT Acquisition Corp. 12/11/1989
Each share Common 1¢ par exchanged for $42.88 cash

AUTOTRADECENTER INC (AZ)
Merged 10/10/2002
Merged from AutoTradeCenter.Com, Inc. into AutoTradeCenter, Inc. 10/10/2002
Each share Common no par exchanged for (1) share Common $0.00001 par
Each share Common $0.00001 par received additional distribution of (1.1303352) shares Ser. D Preferred payable 06/27/2003 to holders of record 10/10/2002
Each share Common $0.00001 par received additional distribution of (0.1255928) share Ser. D Preferred payable 12/10/2003 to holders of record 10/10/2002
Each share old Ser. D Preferred exchanged for (0.01) share new Ser. D Preferred 08/02/2004
Each share old Common $0.00001 par exchanged for (0.01) share new Common $0.00001 par 08/02/2004
Name changed to ATC-Onlane Inc. 08/20/2006
ATC-Onlane Inc. name changed to Openlane, Inc. 11/25/2008
(See Openlane, Inc.)

AUTOTROL CORP (WI)
Stock Dividend - 50% 03/15/1977
Merged into Osmonics, Inc. 10/15/1993
Each share Common 10¢ par exchanged for (0.77) share Common 1¢ par
Osmonics, Inc. merged into General Electric Co. 02/28/2003

AUTOVATIVE PRODS INC (NV)
Common $0.001 par split (7.5) for (1) by issuance of (6.5) additional shares payable 08/02/2013 to holders of record 07/23/2013
Ex date - 08/05/2013
Name changed to GlassesOff Inc. 08/12/2013
GlassesOff Inc. name changed to InnoVision Labs, Inc. 01/22/2016

AUTOVEND TECHNOLOGY CORP (CANADA)
Struck off register and declared dissolved for failure to file returns 03/13/1992

AUTOWEB COM INC (DE)
Merged into Autobytel, Inc. 08/15/2001
Each share Common $0.001 par exchanged for (0.3553) share Common $0.001 par
Autobytel, Inc. name changed to AutoWeb, Inc. 10/09/2017

AUTOZONE INC (DE)
Reincorporated under the laws of Nevada 12/22/1991

AUTREX INC (ON)
Merged into Basis 100 Inc. 10/29/1999
Each share Class A no par exchanged for (0.10373207) share Common no par
Each share Class B no par exchanged for (0.10373207) share Common no par
Note: An additional distribution of $0.40 cash per share was made to holders of record 10/19/1999
(See Basis 100 Inc.)

AUTROL CORP. (CO)
Charter revoked for failure to file reports and pay fees 10/17/1963

AUTUMN INDS INC (BC)
Name changed to Altek Power Corp. 03/07/2001

AUXELLENCE HEALTH CORP (BC)
Recapitalized as EVITRADE Health Systems Corp. 09/19/2016
Each share Common no par exchanged for (0.06666666) share Common no par

AUXER GROUP INC (DE)
Recapitalized as Viva International, Inc. (DE) 06/23/2003
Each share Common $0.001 par exchanged for (0.00125) share Common $0.001 par
Viva International, Inc. (DE) reincorporated in Nevada 03/14/2005 which recapitalized as River Hawk Aviation, Inc. 02/27/2007

AUXER INDS INC (ID)
Reorganized under the laws of Delaware as Auxer Group Inc. 10/15/1997
Each share Common $0.001 par exchanged for (1) share Common $0.001 par and (0.1) Common Stock Purchase Warrant expiring 10/31/1998
Auxer Group Inc. recapitalized as Viva International, Inc. (DE) 06/23/2003 which reincorporated in Nevada 03/14/2005 which recapitalized as River Hawk Aviation, Inc. 02/27/2007

AUXILIO INC (NV)
Each share old Common $0.001 par exchanged for (0.33333333) share new Common $0.001 par 01/13/2017
Reincorporated under the laws of Delaware as CynergisTek, Inc. 09/08/2017

AUXILIUM PHARMACEUTICALS INC (DE)
Merged into Endo International PLC 01/29/2015
Each share Common 1¢ par exchanged USD $0.0001 par and $16.625 cash

AUXILLIUM ENERGY INC (NV)
Charter revoked 11/30/2015

AUXTON COMPUTER ENTERPRISES INC (NJ)
Common 1¢ par split (2) for (1) by issuance of (1) additional share 11/07/1972
Common 1¢ par split (2) for (1) by issuance of (1) additional share 08/12/1983
Stock Dividends - 50% 10/01/1982; 50% 12/03/1982
Merged into Cincinnati Bell Inc. (Old) 06/15/1987
Each share Common 1¢ par exchanged for $15.75 cash

AV HOMES INC (DE)
Merged into Taylor Morrison Home Corp. 10/02/2018
Each share Common $1 par exchanged for (0.4034) share Class A Common $0.00001 par and $12.64 cash

AVA GOLD MNG LTD (ON)
Charter cancelled for failure to pay taxes and file returns 07/10/1973

AVA RESOURCES CORP (BC)
Each share old Common no par exchanged for (0.1) share new Common no par 07/04/2011
Completely liquidated 03/31/2014
Each share new Common no par received pro rata distribution of Tasman Metals Ltd. Units consisting of (1) share Common no par and (1) Common Stock Purchase Warrant expiring 02/11/2017
Note: U.S. holders received cash

AVACARE INC (TX)
Name changed to Carrington Laboratories, Inc. 04/28/1986
Carrington Laboratories, Inc. name changed to DelSite, Inc. 07/31/2008
(See DelSite, Inc.)

AVADO BRANDS INC (GA)
Plan of reorganization under Chapter 11 Federal Bankruptcy Code effective 05/19/2005
No stockholders' equity

AVADO FING I (DE)
Plan of reorganization under Chapter 11 Federal Bankruptcy Code effective 05/19/2005
No stockholders' equity

AVAGENESIS CORP (AB)
Reincorporated under the laws of British Columbia as Liberty Biopharma Inc. 01/06/2017
Liberty Biopharma Inc. name changed to HooXi Network Inc. 10/11/2018

AVAGO TECHNOLOGIES LTD (SINGAPORE)
Under plan of merger name changed to Broadcom Ltd. 02/01/2016
Broadcom Ltd. reorganized as Broadcom Inc. 04/05/2018

AVALA RES LTD (BC)
Each share old Common no par exchanged for (0.1) share new Common no par 10/09/2014
Merged into Dundee Precious Metals Inc. 04/12/2016
Each share new Common no par exchanged for (0.044) share Common no par
Note: Unexchanged certificates will be cancelled and become without value 04/12/2022

AVALANCHE BIOTECHNOLOGIES INC. (DE)
Name changed to Adverum Biotechnologies, Inc. 05/12/2016

AVALANCHE CAP VENTURE INC (CANADA)
Name changed to Syncom Image Display Systems Inc. 03/16/1998
Syncom Image Display Systems Inc. recapitalized as Syncom Imaging Systems Inc. 10/08/1998
(See Syncom Imaging Systems Inc.)

AVALANCHE INDS LTD (BC)
Recapitalized as CTG Compression Technology Group Inc. 06/13/1986
Each share Common no par exchanged for (0.25) share Common no par
(See CTG Compression Technology Group Inc.)

AVALANCHE MINERALS LTD (CANADA)
Recapitalized as OroAndes Resource Corp. 07/03/2008
Each share Common no par exchanged for (0.25) share Common no par
OroAndes Resource Corp. name changed to Fort St. James Nickel Corp. 12/02/2011

AVALANCHE NETWORKS CORP (CANADA)
Name changed to Avalanche Minerals Ltd. 09/14/2007
Avalanche Minerals Ltd. recapitalized as OroAndes Resource Corp. 07/03/2008 which name changed to Fort St. James Nickel Corp. 12/02/2011

AVALARD MINES, LTD. (ON)
Charter cancelled 00/00/1954

AVALITE INC (AB)
Recapitalized as Innovative Wireline Solutions Inc. 07/22/2010
Each share Common no par exchanged for (0.53333333) share Common no par
(See Innovative Wireline Solutions Inc.)

AVALLIN MINES LTD. (BC)
Struck off register and declared dissolved for failure to file returns 03/17/1975

AVALON BAY CMNTYS INC (MD)
Name changed to AvalonBay Communities, Inc. 10/02/1998

AVALON-BORDEN COS INC (DE)
SEC revoked common stock registration 07/22/2010

AVALON CAP HLDGS CORP (DE)
Each share old Common $0.001 par exchanged for (0.05) share new Common $0.001 par 10/28/2008
SEC revoked common stock registration 07/21/2010

AVALON CAP INC (MD)
Completely liquidated
Each share Common $0.001 par received first and final distribution of $15.2782 cash payable 11/24/2003 to holders of record 11/17/2003
Ex date - 11/25/2003
Note: Certificates were not required to

be surrendered and are without value

AVALON CMNTY SVCS INC (NV)
Name changed to Avalon Correctional Services, Inc. 06/22/1999
(See Avalon Correctional Services, Inc.)

AVALON CORP (CA)
Merged into Dundee Bancorp Inc. 02/02/1993
Each share Preferred $7.50 par exchanged for $3.75 cash
Each share Common $1 par exchanged for $3.75 cash

AVALON CORRECTIONAL SVCS INC (NV)
Each share old Common no par exchanged for (0.00004166) share new Common no par 12/05/2014
Note: Holders of (23,999) or fewer pre-split shares received approximately $4.49 cash per share
Acquired by Corrections Corp. of America 10/29/2015
Details not available
Preferred Ser. B $0.001 par called for redemption at $1.75 plus $0.014767 accrued dividends on 11/13/2015

AVALON DEV ENTERPRISES INC (FL)
Name changed to GuangZhou Global Telecom, Inc. 03/30/2007
GuangZhou Global Telecom, Inc. name changed to China Teletech Holding, Inc. 03/20/2012

AVALON DIGITAL MARKETING SYS INC (DE)
Plan of reorganization under Chapter 11 Federal Bankruptcy Code effective 11/18/2004
Each share Common $0.001 par received distribution of (0.00832317) share Common $0.0001 par
Note: Certificates were not required to be surrendered and are without value
(Additional Information in Active)

AVALON ENERGY CORP. (CA)
Under plan of merger name changed to Avalon Corp. 04/15/1985
(See Avalon Corp.)

AVALON ENERGY CORP (NV)
Recapitalized as Shotgun Energy Corp. 09/25/2007
Each share Common $0.001 par exchanged for (0.33333333) share Common $0.001 par
Shotgun Energy Corp. name changed to Organa Gardens International Inc. 04/07/2009 which recapitalized as Bravo Enterprises Ltd. 06/08/2012

AVALON ENTERPRISES INC (NV)
Name changed to Avalon Community Services Inc. 06/24/1992
Avalon Community Services Inc. name changed to Avalon Correctional Services, Inc. 06/22/1999
(See Avalon Correctional Services, Inc.)

AVALON GOLD CORP (NV)
Name changed to Avalon Energy Corp. 03/22/2005
Avalon Energy Corp. recapitalized as Shotgun Energy Corp. 09/25/2007 which name changed to Organa Gardens International Inc. 04/07/2009 which recapitalized as Bravo Enterprises Ltd. 06/08/2012

AVALON GROUP INC (NV)
Merged into Appropriate Health Services.Com, Inc. 06/15/1999
Each share Common $0.001 par exchanged for (0.125) share Common $0.001 par
Appropriate Health Services.Com, Inc. name changed to Stayhealthy Inc. 04/14/2000

AVALON OIL & GAS INC (NV)
Each share old Common $0.001 par exchanged for (0.05) share new Common $0.001 par 05/15/2007
Each share new Common $0.001 par exchanged again for (0.00333333) share new Common $0.001 par 07/23/2012
Name changed to Groove Botanicals, Inc. 05/14/2018

AVALON PARTNERS HLDGS INC (WY)
Name changed to Vision Airships, Inc. 10/02/2006

AVALON PHARMACEUTICALS INC (DE)
Merged into Clinical Data, Inc. (New) 05/28/2009
Each share Common 1¢ par exchanged for (0.047) share Common 1¢ par and (1) Contingent Value Right
Each Contingent Value Right exchanged for (0.009398) share Common 1¢ par 07/06/2010
(See Clinical Data, Inc. (New))

AVALON PPTYS INC (MD)
Merged into Avalon Bay Communities, Inc. 06/04/1998
Each share 8.96% Preferred Ser. B 1¢ par exchanged for (1) share 8.96% Ser. G 1¢ par
Each share 9% Preferred Ser. A 1¢ par exchanged for (1) share 9% Preferred Ser. F 1¢ par
Each share Common 1¢ par exchanged for (0.7683) share Common 1¢ par
Avalon Bay Communities, Inc. name changed AvalonBay Communities, Inc. 10/02/1998

AVALON RARE METALS INC (CANADA)
Reincorporated 02/09/2011
Place of incorporation changed from (BC) to (Canada) 02/09/2011
Name changed to Avalon Advanced Materials Inc. 03/03/2016

AVALON RES INC (BC)
Recapitalized as Twin Tires Systems Inc. 06/12/1989
Each share Common no par exchanged for (0.2) share Common no par
(See Twin Tires Systems Inc.)

AVALON STORES INC (MN)
Recapitalized as Ergonomic Enterprises, Inc. (MN) 05/15/2006
Each share Common no par exchanged for (0.01) share Common no par
Ergonomic Enterprises, Inc. (MN) reincorporated in Texas as Ecarfly, Inc. 07/17/2006 which reincorporated in Nevada as Market 99 Ltd. 12/06/2007

AVALON TECHNOLOGY GROUP INC (NV)
Common $0.0001 par split (2) for (1) by issuance of (1) additional share payable 07/25/2008 to holders of record 07/11/2008 Ex date - 07/28/2008
SEC revoked common stock registration 07/20/2010

AVALON TEL LTD (NL)
5% Conv. Preferred $25 par called for redemption 10/31/1964
5.5% Preference $25 par called for redemption 10/31/1964
5.5% Preference 1958 Ser. $25 par called for redemption 10/31/1964
5.5% Preference 1959 Ser. $25 par called for redemption 10/31/1964
6% Preference 1961 Ser. $25 par called for redemption 10/31/1964
6% Conv. Preferred $25 par called for redemption 10/31/1964
7% Conv. Preferred $25 par called for redemption 10/31/1964
Each share Ordinary $25 par exchanged for (5) shares Ordinary $5 par 00/00/1956
Name changed to Newfoundland Telephone Co. Ltd. 01/01/1970
Newfoundland Telephone Co. Ltd. reorganized as NewTel Enterprises Ltd. 10/15/1985 which merged into Aliant Inc. (Canada) 06/01/1999 which reorganized in Ontario as Bell Aliant Regional Communications Income Fund 07/10/2006 which reorganized in Canada as Bell Aliant Inc. 01/04/2011 which merged into BCE Inc. 10/31/2014

AVALON VENTURES LTD (BC)
Name changed to Avalon Rare Metals Inc. (BC) 02/18/2009
Avalon Rare Metals Inc. (BC) reincorporated in Canada 02/09/2011 which name changed to Avalon Advanced Materials Inc. 03/03/2016

AVALONBAY CMNTYS INC (MD)
9% Preferred Ser. F 1¢ par called for redemption at $25 plus $0.1625 accrued dividends on 06/11/2001
8.96% Preferred Ser. G 1¢ par called for redemption at $25 plus $0.4418 accrued dividends on 10/26/2001
8.50% Preferred Ser. C 1¢ par called for redemption at $25 plus $0.1417 accrued dividends on 07/12/2002
8% Preferred Ser. D 1¢ par called for redemption at $25 plus $0.0167 accrued dividends on 03/20/2003
8.70% Preferred Ser. H 1¢ par called for redemption at $25 plus $$0.1752 accrued dividends on 10/15/2008
(Additional Information in Active)

AVANCE INTL INC (BC)
Recapitalized as Avance Venture Corp. 10/21/1999
Each share Common no par exchanged for (0.2) share Common no par
Avance Venture Corp. recapitalized as Santa Cruz Ventures Inc. 02/09/2004 which name changed to Lignol Energy Corp. 01/23/2007

AVANCE VENTURE CORP (BC)
Recapitalized as Santa Cruz Ventures Inc. 02/09/2004
Each share Common no par exchanged for (0.1) share Common no par
Santa Cruz Ventures Inc. name changed to Lignol Energy Corp. 01/23/2007

AVANCO CAP CORP (BC)
Name changed to Hill Street Beverage Co. Inc. 07/31/2018

AVANEX CORP (DE)
Each share old Common $0.001 par exchanged for (0.06666666) share new Common $0.001 par 08/13/2008
Merged into Oclaro, Inc. 04/27/2009
Each share Common $0.001 par exchanged for (5.426) shares Common 1¢ par

AVANI INTL GROUP INC (NV)
Each share old Common $0.001 par exchanged for (0.1) share new Common $0.001 par 07/26/2001
SEC revoked common stock registration 06/17/2013

AVANIR PHARMACEUTICALS INC (DE)
Reincorporated 03/23/2009
Each share old Class A Common no par exchanged for (0.25) share new Class A Common no par 01/18/2006
Name and state of incorporation changed from Avanir Pharmaceutical (CA) to Avanir Pharmaceuticals, Inc. (DE) and Class A Common no par reclassified as Common $0.0001 par 03/23/2009
Acquired by Otsuka Pharmaceutical Co., Ltd. 01/13/2015

Each share Common $0.0001 par exchanged for $17 cash

AVANT CORP (DE)
Merged into Synopsys, Inc. 06/06/2002
Each share Common $0.0001 par exchanged for (0.371) share Common 1¢ par

AVANT GARDE COMPUTING INC (NJ)
Liquidating Plan of Reorganization under Chapter 11 Federal Bankruptcy proceedings confirmed 01/22/1990
Each share Common no par exchanged for initial distribution of $0.375 cash 01/31/1990
Each share Common no par received second and final distribution of $0.338 cash 04/30/1991

AVANT IMMUNOTHERAPEUTICS INC (DE)
Each share old Common no par exchanged for (0.08333333) share new Common no par 03/10/2008
Name changed to Celldex Therapeutics, Inc. 10/01/2008

AVANTE SEC CORP (ON)
Name changed to Avante Logixx Inc. 10/13/2010

AVANTE TECHNOLOGIES INC (AB)
Delisted from Toronto Venture Stock Exchange 06/30/2003

AVANTEC TECHNOLOGIES INC (BC)
Recapitalized as Harmony Gold Corp. 08/17/2009
Each share Common no par exchanged for (0.11111111) share Common no par
Harmony Gold Corp. name changed to Pure Energy Minerals Ltd. 10/22/2012

AVANTEK INC (CA)
Common no par split (2) for (1) by issuance of (1) additional share 02/29/1980
Common no par split (2) for (1) by issuance of (1) additional share 02/02/1981
Common no par split (2) for (1) by issuance of (1) additional share 07/02/1981
Acquired by Hewlett-Packard Co. (CA) 11/04/1991
Each share Common no par exchanged for $4.60 cash

AVANTGO INC (DE)
Merged into Sybase, Inc. 02/26/2003
Each share Common $0.0001 par exchanged for $1.0294797 cash

AVANTI CAP CORP (ON)
Recapitalized as AvantiCorp International Inc. 04/30/1992
Each share Common no par exchanged for (0.2) share Common no par
AvantiCorp International Inc. name changed to Micromem Technologies Inc. 02/01/1999

AVANTI MNG INC (BC)
Name changed to Alloycorp Mining Inc. 12/04/2014
(See Alloycorp Mining Inc.)

AVANTI PRODTNS INC (BC)
Company went private 12/05/1989
Details not available

AVANTICORP INTL INC (ON)
Name changed to Micromem Technologies Inc. 02/01/1999

AVANTOGEN LTD (AUSTRALIA)
ADR agreement terminated 09/09/2011
No ADR's remain outstanding

AVANTOGEN ONCOLOGY INC (NV)
Charter revoked for failure to file reports 01/01/2010

AVAPECIA LIFE SCIENCES CORP (BC)
Merged into Liberty Biopharma Inc. 01/06/2017
Each share Common no par exchanged for (0.33333333) share Common no par
Liberty Biopharma Inc. name changed to HooXi Network Inc. 10/11/2018

AVARANTA RES LTD (CANADA)
Reincorporated under the laws of British Columbia as Evrim Resources Corp. 01/25/2011

AVASOFT INC (NV)
SEC revoked common stock registration 07/23/2010

AVASTRA SLEEP CENTRES LTD (AUSTRALIA)
ADR agreement terminated 09/11/2009
No ADR's remain outstanding

AVATAR ENERGY INC (QC)
Merged into Neutrino Resources Inc. 11/26/1996
Each share Common no par exchanged for (0.38) share Common no par
(See Neutrino Resources Inc.)

AVATAR ENERGY LTD (AB)
Received Notice of Intention to Enforce Security 02/04/2013
Stockholders' equity unlikely

AVATAR HLDGS INC (DE)
Name changed to AV Homes, Inc. 02/16/2012
AV Homes, Inc. merged into Taylor Morrison Home Corp. 10/02/2018

AVATAR PETE INC (BC)
Merged into Quest Capital Corp. (BC) 06/30/2003
Each share Common no par exchanged for (0.2825) share Class A Subordinate no par
Note: Non-electing holders entitled to (99) shares or fewer received $1.10 cash per share
No payment of less than $10 cash will be made
Quest Capital Corp. (BC) reincorporated in Canada 05/27/2008 which name changed to Sprott Resource Lending Corp. 09/10/2010 which merged into Sprott Inc. 07/24/2013

AVATAR RESOURCE CORP (BC)
Recapitalized as Blackline Oil Corp. (BC) 12/21/1993
Each share Common no par exchanged for (0.2) share Common no par
Blackline Oil Corp. (BC) reincorporated in Alberta as Resourcexplorer Inc. 02/19/2001 which recapitalized as Exchequer Resource Corp. (AB) 07/24/2002 which reincorporated in British Columbia 10/25/2004 which recapitalized as CBD MED Research Corp. 07/18/2014

AVATECH SOLUTIONS INC (DE)
Common 1¢ par split (3) for (1) by issuance of (2) additional shares payable 10/01/2003 to holders of record 09/15/2003 Ex date - 10/02/2003
Name changed to Rand Worldwide, Inc. 12/30/2010

AVATERRA COM INC (NV)
Recapitalized as Xtreme Motorsports of California, Inc. 02/17/2006
Each share Common $0.001 par exchanged for (0.01) share Common $0.001 par
Xtreme Motorsports of California, Inc. name changed to Extreme Motorsports of California, Inc. 05/21/2007

AVATEX CORP (DE)
Each share $4.20 Exchangeable Preferred Ser. A no par exchanged for (7.253) shares Class A Common 1¢ par and (1) Class A Common Stock Warrant expiring 03/07/2005 on 12/07/1999
Each share $5 Conv. Preferred $5 par exchanged for (9.134) shares Class A Common 1¢ par and (1) Class A Common Stock Purchase Warrant expiring 03/07/2005 on 12/07/1999
Each share Common $5 par exchanged for (0.5) share Class A Common 1¢ par 12/07/1999
Plan of reorganization under Chapter 11 Federal Bankruptcy proceedings confirmed 04/14/2003
Holders who filed proofs of interest received an undetermined amount of Avatex Liquidating Trust Shares of Jr. Bene. Int.
Additional details not available

AVAYA INC (DE)
Merged into Sierra Holdings Corp. 10/26/2007
Each share Common 1¢ par exchanged for $17.50 cash

AVC VENTURE CAP CORP (BC)
Name changed to Lateral Gold Corp. 06/15/2012
Lateral Gold Corp. recapitalized as Trakopolis IoT Corp. 10/26/2016

AVCAN GLOBAL SYS INC (BC)
Recapitalized as ASC Avcan Systems Corp. 04/21/1999
Each share Common no par exchanged for (0.25) share Common no par
ASC Avcan Systems Corp. recapitalized as Avcan Systems Inc. (BC) 09/07/2001 which reincorporated in Canada as Optimal Geomatics Inc. 10/09/2003 which merged into Aeroquest International Ltd. 09/30/2009
(See Aeroquest International Ltd.)

AVCAN SYS INC (BC)
Reincorporated under the laws of Canada as Optimal Geomatics Inc. 10/09/2003
Optimal Geomatics Inc. merged into Aeroquest International Ltd. 09/30/2009
(See Aeroquest International Ltd.)

AVCO CMNTY DEVELOPERS INC (CA)
Merged into Avco Corp. 11/07/1980
Each share Common no par exchanged for (0.48) share Common $3 par
(See Avco Corp.)

AVCO CORP (DE)
$4.20 Conv. Preferred no par called for redemption 03/12/1981
$3.20 Conv. Preferred no par called for redemption 02/28/1985
Merged into Textron Inc. 02/28/1985
Each share Common $3 par exchanged for $50 cash

AVCO DELTA CORP CDA LTD (ON)
5.25% Conv. Preferred Ser. B $100 par called for redemption 02/15/1969
Merged into Avco Financial Services Canada Ltd. 05/05/1971
Each share 5.5% 1st Preference Ser. D $100 par exchanged for (1) share Class A Preference $100 par

AVCO FINL SVCS INC (DE)
$4.75 Preferred no par called for redemption 04/10/1974
Public interest eliminated

AVCO MFG CORP (DE)
$2.25 Conv. Preferred no par called for redemption 03/27/1959
Name changed to Avco Corp. 04/10/1959
(See Avco Corp.)

AVCOM INTL INC (DE)
Merged into Signature Resorts, Inc. 02/07/1997
Each share Common 1¢ par exchanged for (0.1625) share Common 1¢ par
Note: Each share Common 1¢ par received an additional distribution of approximately (0.012) share Common 1¢ par 00/00/1999
Signature Resorts, Inc. name changed to Sunterra Corp. 07/14/1998
(See Sunterra Corp.)

AVE INC (NV)
Each share old Common $0.001 par exchanged for (0.005) share new Common $0.001 par 07/11/1995
Recapitalized as Cyco.net, Inc. 08/12/1999
Each share new Common $0.001 par exchanged for (0.40485829) share Common $0.001 par
Cyco.net, Inc. name changed to Nexicon, Inc. 01/25/2005
(See Nexicon, Inc.)

AVEC CORP (NV)
SEC revoked common stock registration 03/08/2012

AVECIA GROUP PLC (ENGLAND)
16% Pay-In-Kind Preference called for redemption at $25 on 06/06/2008

AVECOR CARDIOVASCULAR INC (MN)
Merged into Medtronic, Inc. (MN) 03/08/1999
Each share Common 1¢ par exchanged for (0.17005) share Common 10¢ par
Medtronic, Inc. (MN) reincorporated in Ireland as Medtronic PLC 01/27/2015

AVEDA TRANSN & ENERGY SVCS INC (AB)
Merged into Daseke, Inc. 06/08/2018
Each share Common no par exchanged for (0.0751) share Common no par
Notes: Holders may receive an additional cash distribution subject to certain conditions
Unexchanged certificates will be cancelled and become without value 06/08/2024

AVEENO PHARMACEUTICALS, INC. (NY)
Completely liquidated 03/28/1963
Each share Common 1¢ par exchanged for $1 principal amount of Cooper, Tinsley Laboratories, Inc. (now Cooper Laboratories, Inc.) Subordinated Notes due 04/30/1968 with warrants and $4 cash

AVEMCO CORP (DE)
Common 10¢ par split (3) for (2) by issuance of (0.5) additional share 05/28/1986
Common 10¢ par split (2) for (1) by issuance of (1) additional share 06/05/1987
Common 10¢ par split (3) for (2) by issuance of (0.5) additional share 06/14/1991
Merged into HCC Insurance Holdings, Inc. 06/17/1997
Each share Common 10¢ par exchanged for (1) share Common $1 par
(See HCC Insurance Holdings, Inc.)

AVEMCO FINANCE CORP. (DE)
Under plan of liquidation each share Common 50¢ par exchanged for (3.5) shares Aviation Employees Corp. Common 10¢ par 06/07/1963
Aviation Employees Corp. name changed to Avemco Corp. 10/01/1963 which merged into HCC Insurance Holdings, Inc. 06/17/1997
(See HCC Insurance Holdings, Inc.)

AVENEX ENERGY CORP (AB)
Acquired by Spyglass Resources Corp. 04/04/2013
Each share Common no par exchanged for (1) share Common no par

AVENGER CORP (CO)
Recapitalized as Golden Burro Corp. 09/25/1993
Each share Common $0.0001 par exchanged for (0.01) share Common $0.0001 par

AVENIR DIVERSIFIED INCOME TR (AB)
Each old Trust Unit exchanged for (0.06666666) new Trust Unit no par 06/14/2004
Each new Trust Unit received distribution of (0.5) Essential Energy Services Trust, Trust Unit payable 05/31/2006 to holders of record 05/31/2006 Ex date - 05/26/2006
Reorganized as AvenEx Energy Corp. 01/07/2011
Each new Trust Unit exchanged for (1) share Common no par
Note: Unexchanged certificates were cancelled and became without value 01/07/2014
AvenEx Energy Corp. merged into Spyglass Resources Corp. 04/04/2013

AVENIR EXCHANGE CORP (AB)
Each Exchangeable Share no par exchanged for (1.00958) shares AvenEx Energy Corp. Common no par 01/07/2011
Note: Unexchanged certificates were cancelled and became without value 01/07/2014
AvenEx Energy Corp. merged into Spyglass Resources Corp. 04/04/2013

AVENIRA LTD (AUSTRALIA)
Shares transferred to Australian share register 03/24/2016

AVENOR INC (CANADA)
Merged into Bowater Inc. 07/24/1998
Each share Common no par exchanged for either (0.482053) share Common $1 par, (0.482053) Bowater Canada Inc. Exchangeable Share no par, $35 cash or a combination of stock and cash
Note: Option to receive Common, cash, or combination of stock and cash expired 07/20/1998
(See each company's listing)

AVENSYS CORP (NV)
Name changed to Manaris (2010) Corp. 08/23/2010

AVENTERRA EXPLORATIONS INC (NV)
Common $0.00001 par split (23) for (2) by issuance of (10.5) additional shares payable 09/25/2008 to holders of record 09/25/2008
Name changed to AM Oil Resources & Technology Inc. 01/13/2009
AM Oil Resources & Technology Inc. name changed to Medical Care Technologies Inc. 11/20/2009

AVENTINE RENEWABLE ENERGY HLDGS INC (DE)
Plan of reorganization under Chapter 11 Federal Bankruptcy proceedings effective 03/15/2010
Each share old Common $0.001 par exchanged for (0.02) share new Common $0.001 par 09/24/2012
Each share new Common $0.001 par received distribution of (4.714871) Common Stock Purchase Warrants expiring 09/18/2013 payable 10/15/2012 to holders of record 10/12/2012
Each share new Common $0.001 par exchanged for approximately (0.001) Common Stock Purchase Warrant expiring 03/15/2015
Merged into Pacific Ethanol, Inc. 07/01/2015
Each share new Common $0.001 par exchanged for (1.25) shares Common $0.001 par

FINANCIAL INFORMATION, INC. AVE-AVI

AVENTINE VENTURES INC (BC)
Recapitalized as Pacific Northwest Partners Ltd. (BC) 04/30/2004
Each share Common no par exchanged for (0.2) share Common no par
Pacific Northwest Partners Ltd. (BC) name changed to Enablence Technologies Inc. (Canada) 07/24/2006

AVENTIS (FRANCE)
Each Sponsored ADR for Partial Entitlement Shares exchanged for (1) Sponsored ADR for Ordinary 06/25/2001
Merged into Sanofi-Aventis 01/03/2005
Each Sponsored ADR for Ordinary exchanged for approximately (2.3478) Sponsored ADR's for Ordinary

AVENTURA ENERGY INC (AB)
Each share old Common no par exchanged for (0.1) share new Common no par 03/10/2003
Acquired by BG Energy Holding Ltd. 05/13/2004
Each share new Common no par exchanged for $5.10 cash

AVENTURA HLDGS INC (FL)
Recapitalized as Zolon Corp. 03/15/2010
Each share Common $0.001 par exchanged for (0.001) share Common $0.001 par
Zolon Corp. name changed to Quadrant 4 Systems Corp. (FL) 05/31/2011 which reincorporated in Illinois 04/25/2013
(See Quadrant 4 Systems Corp.)

AVENTURA RESORTS INC (NV)
Recapitalized as Borneo Resource Investments Ltd. 08/05/2011
Each share Common $0.001 par exchanged for (0.01) share Common $0.001 par

AVENUE A INC (WA)
Name changed to aQuantive, Inc. 03/21/2003
(See aQuantive, Inc.)

AVENUE AMER RECORDING LTD (ON)
Charter cancelled for failure to pay taxes and file returns 10/18/1978

AVENUE BK & TR CO (OAK PARK, IL)
Merged into First Colonial Bankshares Corp. 07/21/1986
Each share Capital Stock $10 par exchanged for $121 cash

AVENUE ENTMT GROUP INC (DE)
Name changed to alpha-En Corp. 07/22/2008

AVENUE EXCHANGE CORP (DE)
Each share old Common $0.000001 par exchanged for (0.05) share new Common $0.000001 par 11/19/2009
Note: No holder will receive fewer than (100) post-split shares
Each share new Common $0.000001 par exchanged again for (0.002) share new Common $0.000001 par 03/05/2010
Name changed to Eyes on the Go, Inc. 06/27/2011

AVENUE FINL CORP (ON)
Name changed to Mantis Mineral Corp. 06/20/2007
Mantis Mineral Corp. name changed to Gondwana Oil Corp. 02/26/2014 which name changed to European Metals Corp. 11/07/2014

AVENUE FINL HLDGS INC (TN)
Merged into Pinnacle Financial Partners, Inc. 07/01/2016
Each share Common no par exchanged for (0.36) share Common $1 par and $2 cash

AVENUE GROUP INC (DE)
SEC revoked common stock registration 06/13/2012

AVENUE HLDGS INC (FL)
Recapitalized as Global Prospecting Ventures, Inc. (FL) 01/12/2004
Each share Common $0.00066 par exchanged for (0.002) share Common 4¢ par
Global Prospecting Ventures, Inc. (FL) reincorporated in Nevada 06/04/2004 which name changed to Competitive Games International, Inc. 01/22/2007 which recapitalized as PacWest Equities, Inc. 05/07/2010
(See PacWest Equities, Inc.)

AVENUE INCOME CR STRATEGIES FD (DE)
Name changed to Aberdeen Income Credit Strategies Fund 12/01/2017

AVENUE INDS INC (BC)
Name changed 07/29/1992
Name changed from Avenue Resources Inc. to Avenue Industries Inc. 07/29/1992
Name changed to Black Tusk Energy Inc. 08/29/1997
(See Black Tusk Energy Inc.)

AVENUE LINE MUTUAL WATER CO. (CA)
Charter suspended for failure to pay taxes 07/01/1969

AVENUE SOUTH LTD (NV)
Each share old Common $0.001 par exchanged for (29) shares new Common $0.001 par 09/07/2011
Name changed to TBSS International 11/08/2011

AVENUE STATE BANK (OAK PARK, IL)
Capital Stock $40 par changed to $10 par and (3) additional shares issued 01/07/1974
Stock Dividend - 200% 02/14/1969
Name changed to Avenue Bank & Trust Co. (Oak Park, IL) 09/17/1974
(See Avenue Bank & Trust Co. (Oak Park, IL))

AVERE ENERGY INC (BC)
Name changed to East West Petroleum Corp. 08/10/2010

AVERION INTL CORP (DE)
Each share old Common $0.001 par exchanged for (1) share new Common $0.001 par to reflect a (1) for (20,500) reverse split followed by a (20,500) for (1) forward split 12/15/2009
Note: Holders of (20,499) or fewer pre-split shares received $0.01 cash per share
Each share new Common $0.001 par exchanged for (0.00104152) share Ser. A Participating Preferred $0.001 par 09/07/2010
Note: Company is now private

AVERT INC (CO)
Merged into Automatic Data Processing, Inc. 08/17/2001
Each share Common no par exchanged for $22 cash

AVERY ADHESIVE PRODUCTS, INC. (CA)
Name changed to Avery Products Corp. 04/01/1964
Avery Products Corp. name changed to Avery International Corp. (CA) 03/31/1976 which reincorporated in Delaware 04/01/1977 which name changed to Avery Dennison Corp. 10/16/1990

AVERY (B.F.) & SONS CO. (DE)
Common no par changed to $5 par 06/01/1937
Merged into Minneapolis-Moline Co. on a (2/3) for (1) basis 03/01/1951
6% Preferred $25 par called for redemption 04/01/1951
Minneapolis-Moline Co. name changed to Motec Industries, Inc. 02/21/1961 which name changed to Dolly Madison Foods, Inc. 09/27/1963 which name changed to Dolly Madison Industries, Inc. (MN) 02/15/1966 which reincorporated in Delaware 03/13/1969
(See Dolly Madison Industries, Inc. (DE))

AVERY COAL INC (PA)
Merged into Trafalgar Industries, Inc. 04/20/1982
Each share Common 10¢ par exchanged for (3.5) shares Common 10¢ par
Trafalgar Industries, Inc. merged into Triangle Industries, Inc. (Old) 05/16/1984
(See Triangle Industries, Inc. (Old))

AVERY COMMUNICATIONS INC (DE)
Each share old Common 1¢ par exchanged for (0.125) share new Common 1¢ par 12/12/2001
Each share new Common 1¢ par exchanged again for (0.0002) share new Common 1¢ par 07/07/2003
Note: In effect holders received $1.27 cash per share and public interest was eliminated

AVERY INC (DE)
Merged into NPM Acquisition Corp. 03/28/1991
Each share Common 1¢ par exchanged for $0.43 cash

AVERY INTL CORP (DE)
Reincorporated 4/1/77
5% Conv. Preferred Ser. A $1 par called for redemption 12/31/1976
State of incorporation changed from (CA) to (DE) 04/01/1977
Common $1 par split (2) for (1) by issuance of (1) additional share 12/28/1983
Common $1 par split (2) for (1) by issuance of (1) additional share 03/16/1987
Name changed to Avery Dennison Corp. 10/16/1990

AVERY PRODUCTS CORP. (CA)
Common $1 par split (5) for (4) by issuance of (0.25) additional share 01/31/1967
Common $1 par split (3) for (2) by issuance of (0.5) additional share 05/31/1968
Common $1 par split (2) for (1) by issuance of (1) additional share 11/21/1969
Name changed to Avery International Corp. (CA) 03/31/1976
Avery International Corp. (CA) reincorporated in Delaware 04/01/1977 which name changed to Avery Dennison Corp. 10/16/1990

AVERY RES INC (AB)
Recapitalized as Bengal Energy Ltd. 07/22/2008
Each share Common no par exchanged for (0.2) share Common no par

AVERY SPORTS TURF INC (DE)
Name changed to ECash, Inc. 05/15/2006
ECash, Inc. recapitalized as Pacific Green Technologies Inc. 06/13/2012

AVESIS INC (DE)
$10 Non-Vtg. Conv. Class A Preferred Ser. 2 1¢ par called for redemption at $10 plus $3.95 accrued dividends on 05/30/2008
Each share Common 1¢ par received distribution of (1) share AbsoluteCare, Inc. Restrictred Common payable 01/29/2016 to holders of record 01/15/2016
Acquired by Guardian Life Insurance Company of America 01/29/2016
Each share Common 1¢ par exchanged for $16.45 cash
Note: Each share Common 1¢ par received an initial additional distribution of $0.50 cash 06/10/2016
Each share Common 1¢ par received a second additional distribution of $0.10 cash 11/22/2016

AVEX ELECTRONICS INC. (CANADA)
Company declared inactive 06/01/1997
Details not available

AVEXIS INC (DE)
Acquired by Novartis AG 05/15/2018
Each share Common $0.0001 par exchanged for $218 cash

AVG TECHNOLOGIES N V (NETHERLANDS)
97% acquired through purchase offer which expired 10/28/2016
Note: Minority shares received approximately $24.70 cash per share through squeeze-out proceedings 03/16/2017

AVGOLD LTD (SOUTH AFRICA)
Acquired by Harmony Gold Mining Co. Ltd. 05/24/2004
Each Sponsored ADR for Ordinary exchanged for $10.1275 cash

AVI BIOPHARMA INC (OR)
Recapitalized as Sarepta Therapeutics, Inc. (OR) 07/12/2012
Each share Common $0.0001 par exchanged for (0.16666666) share Common $0.0001 par
Sarepta Therapeutics, Inc. (OR) reincorporated in Delaware 06/10/2013

AVI SOFTWARE INC (CANADA)
Acquired by COGNICASE Inc. 06/18/2002
Each share Common no par exchanged for either (0.0668316) share Common no par and $0.675 cash or (0.1336633) share Common no par
Note: Non-Canadian residents received CAD $1.35 cash
(See COGNICASE Inc.)

AVIALL INC NEW (DE)
Merged into Boeing Co. 09/20/2006
Each share Common 1¢ par exchanged for $48 cash

AVIALL INC OLD (DE)
Acquired by Ryder System, Inc. 11/12/1985
Each share Common 1¢ par exchanged for $25 cash

AVIAN CAP INC (BC)
Name changed to Aegis Investment Management (Golf) Inc. 01/04/2010

AVIANA CORP (NV)
Common $0.001 par split (6.56793) for (1) by issuance of (6.56793) additional shares payable 10/11/2013 to holders of record 10/07/2013 Ex date - 10/15/2013
Name changed to Staffing Group Ltd. 10/21/2013

AVIATION & TRANSPORTATION CORP.
Acquired by Aviation Corp. 00/00/1941
Each share Capital Stock exchanged for (1.06) shares new Capital Stock and cash
Aviation Corp. name changed to Avco Manufacturing Corp. 03/25/1947 which name changed to Avco Corp. 04/10/1959
(See Avco Corp.)

AVIATION ACTIVITIES INC. (TX)
Recapitalized as Dynamic Computer Systems, Inc. 03/12/1971
Each share Common 10¢ par exchanged for (1.5) shares Common 10¢ par
(See Dynamic Computer Systems, Inc.)

AVIATION CAPITAL, INC.
Dissolved 00/00/1942
Details not available

AVIATION CORP. (DE)
Name changed to Avco Manufacturing Corp. 03/25/1947
Avco Manufacturing Corp. name changed to Avco Corp. 04/10/1959
(See Avco Corp.)

AVIATION CORP. OF CALIFORNIA
Company sold 00/00/1930
Details not available

AVIATION CORP. OF THE AMERICAS (DE)
Name changed to Pan American Airways Corp. 04/00/1931
Pan American Airways Corp. recapitalized as Pan American World Airways, Inc. (NY) 00/00/1949 which reorganized in Delaware as Pan Am Corp. 09/14/1984
(See Pan Am Corp.)

AVIATION CREDIT CORP.
Acquired by Commercial Credit Co. 00/00/1933
Details not available

AVIATION DISTRS INC (DE)
Company terminated registration of common stock and is no longer public as of 03/21/2002

AVIATION ED SYS INC (DE)
Each share old Common 1¢ par exchanged for (0.05) share new Common 1¢ par 06/30/1996
Name changed to Setech, Inc. 02/06/1997
(See Setech, Inc.)

AVIATION EMPLOYEES CORP. (DE)
Name changed to Avemco Corp. 10/01/1963
Avemco Corp. merged into HCC Insurance Holdings, Inc. 06/17/1997
(See HCC Insurance Holdings, Inc.)

AVIATION GEN INC (DE)
Ceased operations 02/01/2005
Stockholders' equity unlikely

AVIATION GROUP INC (NC)
Common 10¢ par split (3) for (2) by issuance of (0.5) additional share 07/29/1983
Merged into Primark Corp. 01/31/1986
Each share Common 10¢ par exchanged for $23 cash

AVIATION GROUP INC (TX)
Recapitalized as Travelbyus, Inc. 01/25/2001
Each share Common 1¢ par exchanged for (0.2) share Common 1¢ par
(See Travelbyus, Inc.)

AVIATION HLDGS GROUP INC (DE)
Chapter 11 bankruptcy proceedings converted to Chapter 7 on 03/20/2001
Stockholders' equity unlikely

AVIATION HLDG CORP (DE)
Charter cancelled and declared inoperative and void for non-payment of taxes 04/15/1972

AVIATION INDS CORP (NV)
Recapitalized Jordyn Taylor Properties, Inc. 03/24/2005
Each share Common no par exchanged for (0.05) share Common no par
Jordyn Taylor Properties, Inc. name changed to Rent Finders USA, Inc. 04/26/2006 which recapitalized as Church & Crawford Inc. 03/30/2007

AVIATION INNOVATIONS & RESH INC (NV)
Recapitalized as Immune-Tree International, Inc. 10/26/2004
Each share Common $0.001 par exchanged for (0.06666666) share Common $0.001 par

AVIATION INVESTMENTS LTD. (ON)
Charter revoked for failure to file reports and pay fees 03/11/1965

AVIATION MAINTENANCE CORP.
Dissolved 00/00/1950
No stockholders' equity

AVIATION SALES CO (DE)
Recapitalized as TIMCO Aviation Services, Inc. 02/28/2002
Each share Common $0.001 par exchanged for (0.1) share Common $0.001 par
(See TIMCO Aviation Services, Inc.)

AVIATION SECURITIES CORP. (IL)
Dissolved 00/00/1933
Details not available

AVIATION SECURITIES CORP. OF NEW ENGLAND
Dissolved 00/00/1939
Details not available

AVIATION SIMULATION TECHNOLOGY INC (MA)
Acquired by AST Acquisition Corp. 12/28/1984
Holdings of (999) shares or fewer received $0.10 cash per share
Holdings of (1,000) shares or more received initial distribution of $0.329 cash 10/15/1986
Certificates were not required to be surrendered and are without value
Note: Details on subsequent distributions, if any, are not available

AVIATION SURVEILLANCE SYS INC (NV)
Common $0.001 par split (1.6) for (1) by issuance of (0.6) additional share payable 05/11/2009 to holders of record 05/11/2009
Name changed to Harmonic Energy, Inc. 07/29/2010
Harmonic Energy, Inc. name changed to THC Therapeutics, Inc. 02/07/2017 which name changed to Millennium BlockChain, Inc. 02/07/2018

AVIATION UPGRADE TECHNOLOGIES INC (NV)
Common $0.001 par split (1.4739739) for (1) by issuance of (0.4739739) additional share payable 10/26/2007 to holders of record 10/22/2007
Ex date - 10/29/2007
Name changed to OncoVista Innovative Therapies, Inc. 01/14/2008

AVIATO INTL INC (DE)
Name changed to Navigato International Inc. 03/03/1994
Navigato International Inc. name changed to Businessnet International Inc. 06/10/1996 which recapitalized as Businessnet Holdings Corp. 08/28/1998 which name changed to Invicta Corp. 06/30/2000 which name changed to Executive Hospitality Corp. 05/02/2005 which recapitalized as Forest Resources Management Corp. 08/09/2006
(See Forest Resources Management Corp.)

AVIATOR PETE CORP (AB)
Reincorporated under the laws of Ontario as Critical Outcome Technologies Inc. 10/30/2006
Critical Outcome Technologies Inc. name changed to Cotinga Pharmaceuticals Inc. 01/10/2018

AVIC GROUP INTL INC (DE)
Reincorporated 07/10/1996
State of incorporation changed from (CO) to (DE) 07/10/1996
Name changed to AmTec, Inc. 07/14/1997
AmTec, Inc. name changed to Terremark Worldwide, Inc. 05/01/2000
(See Terremark Worldwide, Inc.)

AVIC TECHNOLOGIES INC (AB)
Name changed to Ginger Beef Corp. 09/30/2002

AVIC TECHNOLOGIES LTD (DE)
Name changed to East Delta Resources Corp. 05/05/2004
(See East Delta Resources Corp.)

AVICENA GROUP INC (DE)
SEC revoked common stock registration 11/15/2011

AVICHINA IND & TECHNOLOGY CO LTD (CHINA)
ADR agreement terminated 08/06/2018
No ADR's remain outstanding

AVICI SYS INC (DE)
Each share old Common $0.0001 par exchanged for (0.25) share new Common $0.0001 par 11/08/2002
Name changed to Soapstone Networks Inc. 03/19/2008
(See Soapstone Networks Inc.)

AVID OIL & GAS LTD (AB)
Acquired by Husky Energy Inc. 06/28/2001
Each share Class A no par exchanged for $5.85 cash
Each share Class B no par exchanged for $10 cash

AVID SPORTSWEAR & GOLF CORP (NV)
Recapitalized as United Companies Corp. 09/18/2003
Each share Common 1¢ par exchanged for (0.02) share Common $0.001 par
United Companies Corp. recapitalized as Brownie's Marine Group, Inc. (NV) 08/22/2007 which reincorporated in Florida 12/07/2015

AVIDO CORP (DE)
Charter forfeited for failure to maintain a registered agent 12/30/1973

AVIDYN INC (DE)
Merged into Fiserv, Inc. 01/13/2003
Each share Common 1¢ par exchanged for (0.0856) share Common 1¢ par

AVIEN INC (NY)
Class B 10¢ par reclassified as Class A 10¢ par 07/01/1957
Class A 10¢ par reclassified as Common 10¢ par 01/10/1962
Adjudicated bankrupt 02/19/1976
Stockholders' equity unlikely

AVIGEN INC (DE)
Merged into MediciNova, Inc. 12/18/2009
Each share Common $0.001 par exchanged for $0.593945 principal amount of Floating Rate Conv. Notes due 06/18/2011 and $0.593945 cash

AVIGILON CORP (CANADA)
Acquired by Motorola Solutions, Inc. 04/02/2018
Each share Common no par exchanged for $27 cash
Note: Unexchanged certificates will be cancelled and become without value 04/02/2024

AVIGO RES CORP (CANADA)
Name changed to Carbon Friendly Solutions Inc. 08/08/2008
Carbon Friendly Solutions name changed to MicroCoal Technologies Inc. 07/22/2013 which reorganized as Targeted Microwave Solutions Inc. 05/22/2015

AVILA LIGNERIS GOLD MINES LTD. (ON)
Declared dissolved 09/18/1961
No stockholders' equity

AVILDSEN TOOLS & MACHS INC (DE)
6% Preferred $5 par called for redemption 12/31/1969
Plan of reorganization under Chapter 11 Federal Bankruptcy proceedings confirmed 06/29/1982
No stockholders' equity

AVILLA INTL EXPLS LTD (CANADA)
Company dissolved 00/00/1984
Stockholders' equity unlikely

AVILLABONA MINES LTD. (ON)
Merged into Hydra Explorations Ltd. on a (0.04) for (1) basis 11/16/1959
Hydra Explorations Ltd. name changed to Hydra Capital Corp. 12/30/1992 which name changed to Waterford Capital Management Inc. 11/12/1996 which merged into CPI Plastics Group Ltd. 09/21/1998
(See CPI Plastics Group Ltd.)

AVINCI MEDIA CORP (DE)
SEC revoked common stock registration 01/17/2014

AVINDA VIDEO INC (ON)
Placed in receivership 10/00/1991
No stockholders' equity

AVINO MINES & RES LTD (BC)
Recapitalized as International Avino Mines Ltd. 05/12/1995
Each share Common no par exchanged for (0.2) share Common no par
International Avino Mines Ltd. name changed to Avino Silver & Gold Mines Ltd. 08/29/1997

AVION GOLD CORP (ON)
Reincorporated 06/14/2011
Place of incorporation changed from (BC) to (ON) 06/14/2011
Merged into Endeavour Mining Corp. 10/18/2012
Each share Common no par exchanged for either (0.365) share Ordinary USD $0.01 par or (0.365) Avion Gold Corp. Non-Vtg. Preferred Exchangeable Share
Note: Option to receive Exchangeable Shares expired 10/10/2012
Unexchanged certificates were cancelled and became without value 10/18/2018
(Additional Information in Active)

AVION RES CORP (BC)
Name changed to Avion Gold Corp. (BC) 06/05/2009
Avion Gold Corp. (BC) reincorporated in Ontario 06/14/2011 which merged into Endeavour Mining Corp. 10/18/2012

AVIONICS CORP AMER (PA)
Charter cancelled for failure to file reports 01/29/1979

AVIRAGEN THERAPEUTICS INC (DE)
Recapitalized as Vaxart, Inc. 02/14/2018
Each share Common 10¢ par exchanged for (0.09090909) share Common 10¢ par

AVIRON (DE)
Merged into MedImmune, Inc. 01/15/2002
Each share Common $0.001 par exchanged for (1.075) shares Common 1¢ par
(See MedImmune, Inc.)

AVIS, INC. (ME)
Merged into International Telephone & Telegraph Corp. (MD) 07/22/1965
Each share Common $5 par exchanged for (0.1) share 4% Conv. Preferred Ser. F $100 par and (0.1375) share Common no par
International Telephone & Telegraph Corp. (MD) reincorporated in Delaware 01/31/1968 which name changed to ITT Corp. 12/31/1983 which reorganized in Indiana as ITT Industries, Inc. 12/19/1995 which name changed to ITT Corp. 07/01/2006

AVIS APTS., INC. (NY)
Dissolved 11/14/1962
Details not available

AVIS EUROPE PLC (UNITED KINGDOM)
ADR agreement terminated 00/00/2000
No ADR's remain outstanding

AVIS FLOWERS WORLDWIDE INC (UT)
Proclaimed dissolved for failure to pay taxes 04/01/1997

AVIS GROUP HLDGS INC (DE)
Name changed 03/27/2000
Name changed from Avis Rent A Car, Inc. to Avis Group Holdings Inc. 03/27/2000
Common 1¢ par reclassified as Class A Common 1¢ par 07/14/2000
Merged into Cendant Corp. 03/01/2001
Each share Class A Common 1¢ par exchanged for $33 cash

AVIS INC (DE)
Merged into Simon (Norton), Inc. 07/25/1977
Each share Common $1 par exchanged for $22 cash

AVIS INDL CORP (DE)
Reincorporated 06/05/1961
State of incorporation changed from (MI) to (DE) 06/05/1961
Common $5 par split (2) for (1) by issuance of (1) additional share 06/30/1965
Common $5 par changed to $1 par 12/11/1969
Stock Dividend - 10% 01/29/1964
Merged into International General Industries, Inc. 04/06/1971
Each share Common $1 par exchanged for (0.5) share Common 50¢ par
International General Industries, Inc. merged into International Bank (Washington, DC) 12/31/1979 which merged into USLICO Corp. 12/31/1985 which merged into NWNL Companies, Inc. 01/17/1995 which name changed to ReliaStar Financial Corp. 02/13/1995
(See ReliaStar Financial Corp.)

AVISIO INC (NV)
Recapitalized as Deal A Day Group Corp. 11/03/2011
Each share Common $0.001 par exchanged for (0.5) share Common $0.001 par

AVISTA CAP I (DE)
7.875% Trust Originated Preferred Securities Ser. A called for redemption at $25 on 04/28/2004

AVISTA CORP (WA)
Each $12.40 Depositary Preferred Ser. L exchanged for (0.7566) share Common no par plus $0.21 accrued dividends 02/16/2000
$6.95 Preferred Ser. K no par called for redemption at $100 on 09/14/2007
(Additional Information in Active)

AVISTA REAL ESTATE INVT TR (ON)
Each Installment Receipt plus final payment of $4 cash received (1) Unit prior to 11/02/1999
Merged into Summit Real Estate Investment Trust 11/02/1999
Each Unit exchanged for (0.8) Trust Unit
(See Summit Real Estate Investment Trust)

AVITAR INC OLD (DE)
Merged into Avitar, Inc. (New) 05/19/1995
Each share Common $0.001 par exchanged for (0.0247) share Common 1¢ par, (0.0589) Common Stock Purchase Warrant expiring 08/10/1996, (0.0723) Common Stock Purchase Warrant, Class A expiring 05/19/2000 and (0.0289) Common Stock Purchase Warrant, Class B expiring 09/19/1995

AVIV REIT INC (MD)
Merged into Omega Healthcare Investors, Inc. 04/01/2015
Each share Common 1¢ par exchanged for (0.9) share Common 10¢ par

AVIV REIT INC (MD)
Merged into Omega Healthcare Investors, Inc. 04/01/2015
Each share Common 1¢ par exchanged for (0.9) share Common 10¢ par

AVIVA PETE CDA INC (AB)
Name changed to Pero Development Group Inc. 06/06/1994
Pero Development Group Inc. merged into Canadiana Genetics Inc. 04/30/1996
(See Canadiana Genetics Inc.)

AVIVA PETE INC (TX)
Each share old Common no par exchanged for (0.0002) share new Common no par 08/12/2003
Note: In effect holders received $0.03 cash per share and public interest was eliminated

AVIVA RES INC (BC)
Name changed to VSC Technology Inc. 11/25/1987
(See VSC Technology Inc.)

AVIX TECHNOLOGIES INC (NV)
Plan of reorganization under Chapter 11 Federal Bankruptcy Code effective 08/04/2003
Holders of old Common $0.001 par who opted to retain their interests received new Common $0.001 par at approximately $0.015 per share
Note: Certificates were not required to be exchanged and are without value
(Additional Information in Active)

AVIZA TECHNOLOGY INC (DE)
Plan of reorganization under Chapter 11 Federal Bankruptcy proceedings confirmed 04/09/2010
Stockholders' equity unlikely

AVL GLOBAL INC (NV)
Each share old Common $0.0001 par exchanged for (0.02) share new Common $0.0001 par 10/01/2004
Name changed to China Northwest Biotech Corp. 02/15/2006
China Northwest Biotech Corp. recapitalized as LGM Biopharma, Inc. 06/29/2007 which name changed to Syncronys International, Inc. 12/11/2007 which name changed to Seeker Tec International, Inc. 04/24/2013

AVL INFORMATION SYS LTD (ON)
Recapitalized 07/31/1996
Recapitalized from AVL Information Systems Inc. to AVL Information Systems Ltd. 07/31/1996
Each share Common no par exchanged for (0.2) share Common no par
Recapitalized as AVL Ventures Inc. 02/17/2003
Each share Common no par exchanged for (0.1) share Common no par
(See AVL Ventures Inc.)

AVL VENTURES INC (ON)
Delisted from Toronto Venture Stock Exchange 06/16/2004

AVM CORP (DE)
Common $1 par split (2) for (1) by issuance of (1) additional share 08/16/1968
Name changed to American Locker Group Inc. 05/01/1985

AVMIN LTD (SOUTH AFRICA)
Each Unsponsored ADR for Ordinary exchanged for (0.6) Sponsored ADR for Ordinary 04/07/1997
Acquired by Anglovaal Ltd. 12/21/1998
Details not available

AVNEL GOLD MNG LTD (CHANNEL ISLANDS)
Merged into Endeavour Mining Corp. 09/18/2017
Each share Ordinary no par exchanged for (0.0187) share Ordinary USD $0.10 par

AVNET ELECTRONICS CORP. (NY)
Common 10¢ par changed to 5¢ par and (1) additional share issued 05/27/1960
Name changed to Avnet, Inc. 12/02/1964

AVNET INC (NY)
$3 Conv. Preferred Ser. B $1 par called for redemption 07/31/1978
$1 Conv. Preferred $1 par called for redemption 11/30/1988
$2.50 Conv. Preferred Ser. C $1 par called for redemption 11/30/1988
(Additional Information in Active)

AVOCA INC (LA)
Old Common no par split (5) for (1) by issuance of (4) additional shares 09/25/1981
Each share old Common no par exchanged for (0.01) share new Common no par 12/16/2004
Note: Holders of (99) or fewer pre-split shares received $28 cash per share
Name changed to Avoca LLC and Common no par reclassified as Units of Membership Ints. 01/22/2016

AVOCA MINES CDA LTD (ON)
Struck off register and declared dissolved for failure to file returns 10/29/1994

AVOCALON MINING SYNDICATE LTD (ON)
Charter revoked for failure to file reports and pay taxes 00/00/1947

AVOCENT CORP (DE)
Acquired by Emerson Electric Co. 12/11/2009
Each share Common $0.001 par exchanged for $25 cash

AVOCET MNG PLC (UNITED KINGDOM)
ADR agreement terminated 05/21/2018
No ADR's remain outstanding

AVOCET VENTURES INC (BC)
Acquired by Avocet Mining PLC 04/08/1996
Each share Common no par exchanged for (1) Ordinary share

AVOCET VENTURES INC (NV)
SEC revoked common stock registration 12/03/2007

AVOLA INDS INC (BC)
Recapitalized as Auramex Resource Corp. 01/16/2003
Each share Common no par exchanged for (0.33333333) share Common no par

AVOLON HLDGS LTD (CAYMAN ISLANDS)
Acquired by Bohai Leasing Co., Ltd. 01/08/2016
Each share Common $0.000004 par exchanged for $31 cash

AVON ALLIED PRODUCTS, INC.
Name changed to Avon Products, Inc. 00/00/1950

AVON CO.
Merged into Connecticut Investment Management Corp. 00/00/1931
Details not available

AVON GOLD MINES LTD. (QC)
Charter cancelled 10/00/1973

AVON PRODS INC (NY)
4% Preferred $50 par called for redemption 11/14/1962
$2 Equity Redemption Preferred $1 par called for redemption 06/03/1991
(Additional Information in Active)

AVON RENT-A-CAR & TRUCK CORP (DE)
Filed a petition under Chapter 11 Federal Bankruptcy Code 10/26/1990
No stockholders' equity

AVONDALE CORP. (KY)
Liquidation completed
Each share Common $10 par exchanged for initial distribution of $12.50 cash 05/15/1964
Each share Common $10 par received second distribution of $3.25 cash 04/12/1967
Each share Common $10 par received third and final distribution of $0.7275 cash 08/24/1968

AVONDALE FINL CORP (DE)
Under plan of merger name changed to MB Financial, Inc. (DE) 02/26/1999
MB Financial, Inc. (DE) merged into MB Financial, Inc. (MD) 11/07/2001

AVONDALE INDS INC (DE)
Merged into Litton Industries Inc. 08/02/1999
Each share Common $1 par exchanged for $39.50 cash

AVONDALE INVT TR (MA)
Reorganized as Professionally Managed Portfolios 06/01/1991
Details not available

AVONDALE MLS (AL)
Each share Common $100 par exchanged for (1) share Class A $5 par and (1) share Class B $5 par 00/00/1934
Each share Class A $5 par or Class B $5 par exchanged for (5) shares Common $1 par 00/00/1937
$4.50 Preferred Ser. A $1 par called for redemption 11/15/1971
Common $1 par split (2) for (1) by issuance of (1) additional share 03/23/1984
Stock Dividends - 10% 12/14/1961; 10% 05/15/1963; 10% 08/17/1964; 10% 06/01/1965; 10% 02/15/1966; 10% 02/15/1967; 10% 09/03/1968; 10% 05/15/1969; 10% 08/14/1970; 10% 08/13/1971; 10% 08/11/1972; 10% 08/10/1973; 10% 08/09/1974; 10% 12/05/1980
Merged into AM Acquisition, Inc. 07/02/1986
Each share Common $1 par exchanged for $28.20 cash

AVONDALE RES INC (BC)
Recapitalized as Portman Explorations Ltd. (BC) 09/18/1992
Each share Common no par exchanged for (0.1) share Common no par
Portman Explorations Ltd. (BC) reorganized in Yukon as Daytona Energy Corp. 01/18/1999 which reincorporated in British Columbia 01/29/2005 which reincorporated in Alberta 02/02/2007 which recapitalized as Riata Resources Corp. 09/01/2010 which name changed to Petroforte International Ltd. 11/02/2011 which recapitalized as Canamax Energy Ltd. 02/21/2014
(See Canamax Energy Ltd.)

AVONLEE CAP CORP (ON)
Recapitalized as Internet Liquidators International Inc. 05/28/1996
Each share Common no par exchanged for (0.4) share Common no par
Internet Liquidators International Inc. name changed to to Bid.Com International, Inc. 07/17/1998 which recapitalized as ADB Systems International Inc. 10/18/2001 which name changed to ADB Systems International Ltd. 11/01/2002 which

name changed to Northcore Technologies Inc. 07/18/2006

AVONMORE DEL L P
Guaranteed Preferred Securities Ser. A called for redemption at $1,054,366.2629 on 06/15/2005

AVONMORE WATERFORD GROUP PLC (IRELAND)
Name changed to Glanbia PLC 03/18/1999

AVOTUS CORP (CANADA)
Each (1,850,000) shares old Common no par exchanged for (1) share new Common no par 05/25/2005
Note: In effect holders received $0.25 cash per share and public interest was eliminated

AVP INC (DE)
Each share old Common $0.001 par exchanged for (0.1) share new Common $0.001 par 12/19/2005
Chapter 11 bankruptcy proceedings dismissed 02/13/2013
Stockholders' equity unlikely

AVRADA INC (NV)
Reincorporated 09/20/2004
Place of incorporation changed from (ON) to (NV) and Common no par changed to $0.001 par 09/20/2004
Name changed to Dakshidin Corp. 02/14/2007

AVRO ENERGY INC (NV)
Recapitalized as Rango Energy Inc. 03/30/2012
Each share Common $0.001 par exchanged for (0.02) share Common $0.001 par
Rango Energy Inc. name changed to Verde Science, Inc. 05/07/2014

AVSTAR AVIATION GROUP INC (CO)
Recapitalized as Spotlight Capital Holdings, Inc. 11/06/2014
Each share Common $0.001 par exchanged for (0.02) share Common $0.001 par

AVT CORP (WA)
Common 1¢ par split (2) for (1) by issuance of (1) additional share payable 01/10/2000 to holders of record 12/27/1999
Name changed to Captaris, Inc. 04/09/2001
(See Captaris, Inc.)

AVT INC (NV)
Each share old Common $0.001 par exchanged for (0.1) share new Common $0.001 par 03/02/2011
Each share new Common $0.001 par exchanged again for (2) shares new Common $0.001 par 08/18/2011
Chapter 11 bankruptcy proceedings converted to Chapter 7 on 07/29/2016
Stockholders' equity unlikely

AVTEAM INC (FL)
Plan of reorganization under Chapter 11 Federal Bankruptcy Code proceedings effective 09/22/2002
No stockholders' equity

AVTEK CORP (RI)
Adjudicated bankrupt 05/23/1974
No stockholders' equity

AVTEL COMMUNICATIONS INC (DE)
Reincorporated 12/01/1997
State of incorporation changed from (UT) to (DE) 12/01/1997
Each share Common $0.001 par exchanged for (0.25) share Common $0.001 par
Name changed to Netlojix Communications Inc. 09/15/1999
(See Netlojix Communications Inc.)

AVTOKRAZ (UKRAINE)
GDR agreement terminated 08/24/2017
Each Reg. S Sponsored GDR for Ordinary exchanged for (100) shares Ordinary

Note: Unexchanged GDR's will be sold and the proceeds, if any, held for claim after 08/27/2018

AVTOVAZ O A O (RUSSIA)
Sponsored Reg. S GDR's for Ordinary split (30) for (1) by issuance of (29) additional GDR's payable 07/15/2002 to holders of record 07/12/2002 Ex date - 07/10/2002
Basis changed from (1:30) to (1:1) 07/15/2002
Sponsored Reg. S GDR's for Ordinary split (20) for (1) by issuance of (19) additional GDR's payable 10/05/2007 to holders of record 10/04/2007
Basis changed from (1:1) to (1:5) 10/05/2007
Name changed to Avtovaz PJSC 11/16/2017

AVTR SYS INC (DE)
Each share old Common $0.00005 par exchanged for (0.025) share new Common $0.00005 par 03/19/1999
Name changed to Independent Music Group, Inc. 04/09/1999
Independent Music Group, Inc. name changed to Falcon Entertainment Corp. 12/14/1999
(See Falcon Entertainment Corp.)

AVUSA LTD (SOUTH AFRICA)
Name changed to Element One Ltd. 06/04/2008
(See Element One Ltd.)

AVVA TECHNOLOGIES INC (AB)
Acquired by Carmanah Technologies Corp. (AB) 10/01/2003
Each share Common no par exchanged for (0.125) share Common no par
Carmanah Technologies Corp. (AB) reincorporated in British Columbia 08/24/2010

AVWORKS AVIATION CORP (NV)
Reincorporated under the laws of Florida as Vapor Group, Inc. 04/29/2014

AVX CORP OLD (DE)
Name changed 08/22/1973
Under plan of merger name changed from AVX Ceramics Corp. to AVX Corp. (Old) 08/22/1973
Common $1 par split (2) for (1) by issuance of (1) additional share 09/14/1979
Common $1 par split (3) for (2) by issuance of (0.5) additional share 07/21/1983
Stock Dividend - 25% 04/24/1978
Acquired by Kyocera Corp. 01/18/1990
Each share Common $1 par exchanged for (0.43) ADR's for Common JPY 50 par

AW COMPUTER SYS INC (NJ)
Class A Common 1¢ par split (3) for (2) by issuance of (0.5) additional share 03/01/1985
Chapter 11 Federal Bankruptcy proceedings converted to Chapter 7 on 02/11/1999
Stockholders' equity unlikely

AW LIQUIDATING CO. (DE)
Liquidation completed
Each share Common $1 par exchanged for initial distribution of $8 cash 06/12/1970
Each share Common $1 par received second distribution of $0.75 cash 06/05/1972
Each share Common $1 par received third and final distribution of $8.55 cash 04/30/1980

AWARD RES LTD (BC)
Recapitalized as Tomco Developments Inc. 06/16/1990
Each share Common no par exchanged for (0.33333333) share Common no par

AWARD SOFTWARE INTL INC (CA)
Merged into Phoenix Technologies Ltd. 09/25/1998
Each share Common no par exchanged for (1.225) shares Common $0.001 par
(See Phoenix Technologies Ltd.)

AWARD VENTURES LTD (BC)
Name changed to Auracle Resources Ltd. 05/28/2010
Auracle Resources Ltd. recapitalized as Four River Ventures Ltd. 06/15/2015 which recapitalized as Canabo Medical Inc. 11/09/2016 which name changed to Aleafia Health Inc. 03/28/2018

AWEC RES INC (NY)
Reorganized under the laws of Nevada as Capitol Communities Corp. 02/07/1996
Each share Common $0.001 par exchanged for (0.2) share Common 1¢ par
Capitol Communities Corp. name changed to Capitol First Corp. 10/16/2003
(See Capitol First Corp.)

AWESOME RES LTD (BC)
Name changed to Santiago Capital Corp. 06/09/1987
Santiago Capital Corp. recapitalized as Fresh Ideas Food Corp. 04/04/1990 which recapitalized as Bobby Cadillac's Food Corp. 09/30/1992 which recapitalized as Immune Network Research Ltd. 04/29/1996 which name changed to Immune Network Ltd. 08/16/2000
(See Immune Network Ltd.)

AWFUL FRESH MACFARLANE
Name changed to Mac Farlanes Candies and Common no par changed to $1 par 06/22/1949
Mac Farlanes Candies merged into Riviana Foods Inc. (Old) 10/01/1971 which was acquired by Colgate-Palmolive Co. 06/14/1976

AWG AMERICAN-WESTJAVA INC (ON)
Reincorporated 01/04/1995
Reorganized 11/13/1995
Place of incorporation changed from (ON) to (BC) 01/04/1995
Reorganized from AWG American-WestJava Gold Corp. (BC) to under the laws of Ontario as AWG American-WestJava Gold Inc. 11/13/1995
Each share Common no par exchanged for (0.1) share Common no par
Recapitalized as Kalimantan Gold Corp. (ON) 05/03/1996
Each share Common no par exchanged for (0.33333333) share Common no par
Kalimantan Gold Corp. (ON) reincorporated in Bermuda as Kalimantan Gold Corp. Ltd. 12/19/1997 which name changed to Asiamet Resources Ltd. 07/27/2015
(See Asiamet Resources Ltd.)

AWG INTL WTR CORP (NV)
Name changed to Ambient Water Corp. 07/01/2014

AWG LTD (NV)
Each share old Common $0.001 par exchanged for (0.05) share new Common $0.001 par 09/14/2005
Company terminated common stock registration and is no longer public as of 06/19/2007

AWR-AMERICA WEST RES INC (NV)
Each share old Common 1¢ par exchanged for (0.05) share new Common 1¢ par 07/11/1997
Name changed to Integrated

Information International Group Co. Ltd. 10/08/1999
Integrated Information International Group Co. Ltd. name changed to Intervest Group, Ltd. 04/21/2001
(See Intervest Group, Ltd.)

AXA ASIA PAC HLDGS (AUSTRALIA)
ADR agreement terminated 03/14/2012
No ADR's remain outstanding

AXA FINL INC (DE)
Common 1¢ par split (2) for (1) by issuance of (1) additional share payable 10/01/1999 to holders of record 09/27/1999 Ex date - 10/04/1999
Merged into AXA S.A. 01/02/2001
Each share Common 1¢ par exchanged for (0.295) Sponsored ADR for Ordinary no par and $35.75 cash

AXA S A (FRANCE)
Name changed 07/11/1997
Name changed from AXA S.A. to AXA-UAP 07/11/1997
Name changed to AXA 07/26/1999

AXAGON RES LTD (BC)
Struck off register and declared dissolved for failure to file returns 01/12/1996

AXAR ACQUISITION CORP (DE)
Each share Common $0.0001 par received distribution of (0.5) Common Stock Purchase Warrant expiring 12/31/2022 payable 10/17/2016 to holders of record 10/11/2016 Ex date - 10/11/2016
Completely liquidated 10/02/2017
Each Unit exchanged for first and final distribution of $10.14 cash
Each share Common $0.0001 par exchanged for first and final distribution of $10.14 cash

AXB VENTURES INC (UT)
Name changed to Stari, Ltd. 03/31/1986
(See Stari, Ltd.)

AXCAN PHARMA INC (CANADA)
Acquired by 4445660 Canada Inc. 02/25/2008
Each share Common no par exchanged for USD$23.35 cash

AXCENSION CAP CORP (ON)
Reorganized under the laws of Bermuda as Caspian Oil Tools Ltd. 08/30/1999
Each share Common no par exchanged for (0.25) share Common no par
(See Caspian Oil Tools Ltd.)

AXCESS INC (DE)
Name changed to Axcess International, Inc. 04/15/2003

AXE HOUGHTON FD A INC. OLD (DE)
Merged into Axe-Houghton Fund, Inc. on net asset basis 10/31/1940
Axe-Houghton Fund, Inc. name changed to Axe-Houghton Fund A, Inc. (DE) (New) 02/23/1951 which reincorporated in Maryland 00/00/1973 which name changed to Axe-Houghton Income Fund, Inc. 09/24/1976 which reorganized as Axe-Houghton Funds, Inc. Income Fund 10/31/1990
(See Axe-Houghton Funds, Inc.)

AXE HOUGHTON FD A INC NEW (DE)
Capital Stock $1 par split (2) for (1) by issuance of (1) additional share 10/07/1955
Reincorporated under the laws of Maryland 00/00/1973
Axe-Houghton Fund A, Inc. (MD) name changed to Axe-Houghton Income Fund, Inc. 09/24/1976 which reorganized as Axe-Houghton

Funds, Inc. Income Fund 10/31/1990
(See Axe-Houghton Funds, Inc.)

AXE HOUGHTON FD B INC (MD)
Under plan of reorganization each share Capital Stock $1 par automatically became (1) share Axe-Houghton Funds, Inc. Fund B Common $1 par 10/31/1990
(See Axe-Houghton Funds, Inc.)

AXE HOUGHTON FDS INC (MD)
Completely liquidated 03/04/1991
Each share Fund B $1 par received Price (T. Rowe) Balanced Fund shares on a net asset basis
Each share Growth Fund $1 par received Price (T. Rowe) New America Growth Fund on a net asset basis
Each share Income Fund $1 par received Price (T. Rowe) New Income Fund on a net asset basis
Core International ADR Fund $1 par acquired by Bank of New York Co., Inc. 02/00/2002
Details not available

AXE-HOUGHTON FUND, INC. (DE)
Name changed to Axe-Houghton Fund A, Inc. (DE) (New) 02/23/1951
Axe-Houghton Fund A, Inc. (DE) (New) reincorporated in Maryland 00/00/1973 which name changed to Axe-Houghton Income Fund, Inc. 09/24/1976 which reorganized as Axe-Houghton Funds, Inc. Income Fund 10/31/1990

AXE-HOUGHTON FUND A, INC. (MD)
Name changed to Axe-Houghton Income Fund, Inc. 09/24/1976
Axe-Houghton Income Fund, Inc. reorganized as Axe-Houghton Funds, Inc. Income Fund 10/31/1990
(See Axe-Houghton Funds, Inc.)

AXE-HOUGHTON FUND B, INC. (DE)
Capital Stock $5 par split (3) for (1) by issuance of (2) additional shares 03/21/1956
Capital Stock $5 par changed to $1 par 01/23/1957
Reincorporated under the laws of Maryland 00/00/1973
Axe-Houghton Fund B, Inc. (MD) reorganized as Axe-Houghton Funds, Inc. Fund B 10/31/1990
(See Axe-Houghton Funds, Inc.)

AXE HOUGHTON INCOME FD INC (MD)
Under plan of reorganization each share Capital Stock $1 par automatically became (1) share Axe-Houghton Funds, Inc. Income Fund Common $1 par 10/31/1990
(See Axe-Houghton Funds, Inc.)

AXE HOUGHTON MONEY MKT FD INC (MD)
Fund terminated 06/10/1991
Details not available

AXE HOUGHTON STK FD INC (MD)
Under plan of reorganization each share Common $1 par automatically became (1) share Axe-Houghton Funds, Inc. Growth Fund Common $1 par 10/31/1990
(See Axe-Houghton Funds, Inc.)

AXE-HOUGHTON STOCK FUND, INC. (DE)
Reincorporated under the laws of Maryland 09/13/1974
Axe-Houghton Stock Fund, Inc. (MD) reorganized as Axe-Houghton Funds, Inc. Growth Fund 10/31/1990
(See Axe-Houghton Funds, Inc.)

AXE SCIENCE & ELECTRONICS CORP. (MD)
Name changed to Axe Science Corp. 01/30/1964
Axe Science Corp. merged into Axe-Houghton Stock Fund, Inc. (MD) 12/09/1974 which reorganized as Axe-Houghton Funds, Inc. Growth Fund 10/31/1990
(See Axe-Houghton Funds, Inc.)

AXE SCIENCE CORP (MD)
Capital Stock 1¢ par split (3) for (1) by issuance of (2) additional shares 05/08/1968
Merged into Axe-Houghton Stock Fund, Inc. (MD) 12/09/1974
Each share Capital Stock 1¢ par exchanged for (0.6919) share Common $1 par
Axe-Houghton Stock Fund, Inc. (MD) reorganized as Axe-Houghton Funds, Inc. Growth Fund 10/31/1990
(See Axe-Houghton Funds, Inc.)

AXE-TEMPLETON GROWTH FUND OF CANADA LTD. (CANADA)
Common $1 par changed to 25¢ par and (3) additional shares issued 09/14/1959
Name changed to Templeton Growth Fund of Canada Ltd. 07/03/1963
Templeton Growth Fund of Canada Ltd. name changed to Templeton Growth Fund, Ltd. 07/02/1964

AXEA CAP CORP (BC)
Recapitalized as MCW Enterprises Ltd. (BC) 10/22/2012
Each share Common no par exchanged for (0.16666666) share no par
MCW Enterprises Ltd. (BC) reincorporated in Ontario as MCW Energy Group Ltd. 12/20/2012 which recapitalized as Petroteq Energy Inc. 05/05/2017

AXEA ENERGY INC (BC)
Name changed to AgriMarine Holdings Inc. 06/03/2009
(See AgriMarine Holdings Inc.)

AXEDA SYS INC (DE)
Name changed to ITA Holdings, Inc. 12/05/2005
(See ITA Holdings, Inc.)

AXELSON MANUFACTURING CO. (CA)
Acquired by Pressed Steel Car Co., Inc. (PA) 00/00/1952
Each share Capital Stock $3 par exchanged for (1.18) shares Common $1 par
Pressed Steel Car Co., Inc. (PA) reincorporated in Delaware 00/00/1953 which name changed to U.S. Industries, Inc. 00/00/1954
(See U.S. Industries, Inc.)

AXENT TECHNOLOGIES INC (DE)
Merged into Symantec Corp. 12/18/2000
Each share Common 2¢ par exchanged for (0.5) share Common 1¢ par

AXESS MEDIA GROUP LTD (NV)
Recapitalized as MEDIA GLOBO Corp. 03/12/2007
Each share Common $0.001 par exchanged for (0.0001) share Common $0.001 par

AXIA GROUP INC (NV)
Each share old Common $0.001 par received distribution of (26) shares Nexia Holdings Inc. Common $0.001 par payable 01/08/2003 to holders of record 12/09/2002 Ex date - 12/05/2002
Each share old Common $0.001 par received distribution of (0.1) share Bottomline Home Loan, Inc. Common $0.001 par payable 05/15/2003 to holders of record 02/10/2003 Ex date - 02/06/2003
Each share old Common $0.001 par exchanged for (0.03333333) share new Common $0.001 par 05/19/2003
Each share new Common $0.001 par exchanged again for (0.001) share new Common $0.001 par 10/18/2004
Each share new Common $0.001 par exchanged again for (0.002) share new Common $0.001 par 02/01/2005
Each share new Common $0.001 par exchanged again for (0.001) share new Common $0.001 par 08/23/2005
Each share new Common $0.001 par exchanged again for (0.02) share new Common $0.001 par 04/17/2006
Each share new Common $0.001 par exchanged again for (0.0001) share new Common $0.001 par 05/23/2007
Each share new Common $0.001 par exchanged again for (0.0002) share new Common $0.001 par 08/26/2008
Recapitalized as Artistmss International Group, Inc. 12/11/2012
Each share new Common $0.001 par exchanged for (0.000125) share Common $0.00001 par

AXIA INC (DE)
Merged into New Able Holding Corp. 10/30/1984
Each share Common $2.50 par exchanged for $27 cash

AXIA MULTIMEDIA CORP (AB)
Name changed to Axia NetMedia Corp. 10/15/1998
(See Axia NetMedia Corp.)

AXIA NETMEDIA CORP (AB)
Acquired by Digital Connection (Canada) Corp. 08/03/2016
Each share Common no par exchanged for $4.25 cash
Note: Unexchanged certificates were cancelled and became without value 08/03/2018

AXIAL LIQUIDATING CORP. (CA)
Name changed 05/31/1973
Name changed from Axial Corp. to Axial Liquidating Corp. 05/31/1973
Completely liquidated 06/06/1973
Each share Common 10¢ par exchanged for first and final distribution of (0.22) share Sierracin Corp. (CA) Common $1 par
Sierracin Corp. (CA) reincorporated in Delaware 05/31/1977
(See Sierracin Corp. (DE))

AXIAL VECTOR ENGINE CORP (NV)
Recapitalized as AVEC Corp. 03/07/2011
Each share Common $0.001 par exchanged for (0.00666666) share Common $0.001 par
(See AVEC Corp.)

AXIALL CORP (DE)
Acquired by Westlake Chemical Corp. 08/31/2016
Each share Common 1¢ par exchanged for $33 cash

AXIM INTL INC (NV)
Name changed to AXIM Biotechnologies, Inc. 07/31/2014

AXIOHM TRANSACTION SOLUTIONS INC (CA)
Plan of reorganization under Chapter 11 Federal Bankruptcy Code effective 05/31/2000
No stockholders' equity

AXIOLOGIX ED CORP (NV)
Common $0.001 par split (5) for (1) by issuance of (4) additional shares payable 10/15/2010 to holders of record 10/04/2010 Ex date - 10/18/2010
Name changed to Axiologix, Inc. 09/14/2012

AXIOM GOLD & SILVER CORP (NV)
Recapitalized as Axiom Oil & Gas Corp. 10/16/2013
Each share Common $0.001 par exchanged for (0.04) share Common $0.001 par

AXIOM INC (DE)
Name changed to Telesciences Inc. 03/30/1999
(See Telesciences Inc.)

AXIOM INTL DEV CORP (BC)
Name changed 11/06/1985
Name changed from Axiom Explorations Inc. to Axiom International Development Corp. 11/06/1985
Common no par split (2) for (1) by issuance of (1) additional share 07/02/1986
Common no par split (2) for (1) by issuance of (1) additional share 02/04/1987
Delisted from Vancouver Stock Exchange 03/04/1992

AXIOM MGMT INC (NV)
Name changed to Potential Holdings, Inc. 07/24/2007
Potential Holdings, Inc. name changed to RightSmile, Inc. 08/28/2009

AXIOM MGMT INC (PA)
Chapter 7 bankruptcy proceedings terminated 01/12/2012
No stockholders' equity

AXIOM PHARMACEUTICALS INC (NV)
Name changed to AXM Pharma, Inc. 10/03/2003

AXIOM RESH CORP (FL)
Common $0.001 par changed to $0.0001 par and (2) additional shares issued 02/27/1987
Reorganized under the laws of Delaware as I B Net, Ltd. 09/27/2001
Each (305.6794) shares Common $0.0001 par exchanged for (1) share Common $0.001 par
(See I B Net, Ltd.)

AXIOM SEC SOLUTIONS INC (UT)
Proclaimed dissolved for failure to pay taxes 10/01/1996

AXIOM SYS INC (DE)
Chapter 11 bankruptcy proceedings converted to Chapter 7 on 09/25/1990
No stockholders' equity

AXIOM III INC (NV)
Name changed to SmartPay Express, Inc. 01/25/2008
SmartPay Express, Inc. name changed to Blue Water Ventures International, Inc. 07/03/2012

AXION COMMUNICATIONS INC (BC)
Merged into Technovision Systems Inc. 12/01/2002
Each share Common no par exchanged for (0.603) share new Common no par
Technovision Systems Inc. merged into Uniserve Communications Corp. 11/20/2003

AXION INTL HLDGS INC (CO)
Plan of reorganization under Chapter 11 Federal Bankruptcy proceedings effective 06/08/2016
No stockholders' equity

AXION SPATIAL IMAGING INC NEW (NV)
Recapitalized as Alco Advanced Technologies, Inc. 04/01/2009
Each share Common no par exchanged for (0.00071428) share Common $0.001 par
Alco Advanced Technologies, Inc. recapitalized as Southern ITS International, Inc. 04/11/2012

AXION SPATIAL IMAGING INC OLD (NV)
Reorganized as Axion Spatial Imaging, Inc. (New) 09/28/2007
Each share Common no par exchanged for (0.00166666) share Common no par
Axion Spatial Imaging, Inc. (New)

recapitalized as Alco Advanced
Technologies, Inc. 04/01/2009 which
recapitalized as Southern ITS
International, Inc. 04/11/2012

AXION SYS SCIENCE INC (CA)
Recapitalized as Wordcraft Systems,
Inc. (CA) 06/15/1994
Each share Common 1¢ par
exchanged for (0.1) share Common
5¢ par
Wordcraft Systems, Inc. (CA)
reorganized in Delaware as Wake
Up Now, Inc. 12/01/2010

AXIOS MOBILE ASSETS CORP (ON)
Each share old Common no par
exchanged for (0.1) share new
Common no par 10/22/2015
Discharged from receivership
04/10/2018
No stockholders' equity

AXIS CAP HLDGS LTD (BERMUDA)
7.25% Preferred Ser. A $0.0125 par
called for redemption at $25 plus
$0.0125 accrued dividends on
06/19/2013
7.5% Preferred Ser. B $0.0125 par
called for redemption at $100 plus
$1.187499 accrued dividends on
01/27/2016
6.875% Preferred Ser. C $0.0125 par
called for redemption at $25 on
04/17/2017
(Additional Information in Active)

AXIUM TECHNOLOGIES INC (NV)
Each share old Common $0.001 par
exchanged for (0.001) share new
Common $0.001 par 01/13/2014
Note: No holder will receive fewer
than (100) post-split shares
Name changed to Wincash
Resources, Inc. 01/05/2016
Wincash Resources, Inc. name
changed to Fovea Jewelry Holdings,
Ltd. 02/06/2018

AXIUS INC (NV)
Common $0.001 par split (5) for (1)
by issuance of (4) additional shares
payable 03/23/2012 to holders of
record 03/12/2012 Ex date -
03/26/2012
SEC revoked common stock
registration 09/25/2013

AXLON INC (CA)
Charter suspended for failure to file
reports and pay fees 04/01/1998

AXOGEN LTD (BERMUDA)
Units separated 12/31/1998
Acquired by Elan Corp., PLC
12/31/1999
Each share Common 1¢ par
exchanged for $34.56 cash

AXONYX INC (NV)
Common $0.001 par split (2) for (1)
by issuance of (1) additional share
payable 03/05/1999 to holders of
record 02/23/1999
Reorganized under the laws of
Delaware as TorreyPines
Therapeutics, Inc. 10/04/2006
Each share Common $0.001 par
exchanged for (0.125) share
Common $0.001 par
TorreyPines Therapeutics, Inc.
recapitalized as Raptor
Pharmaceutical Corp. 09/29/2009
(See Raptor Pharmaceutical Corp.)

AXP PROGRESSIVE FD INC (MN)
Name changed to AXP Progressive
Series, Inc. 11/13/2002

AXP SELECTIVE FD INC (MN)
Name changed to AXP Income
Series, Inc. 11/13/2002

AXP STK FD INC (MN)
Name changed to AXP Stock Series,
Inc. 11/13/2002

AXP UTILITIES INCOME FD INC (MN)
Name changed to AXP Sector Series,
Inc. 11/13/2002

AXQP INC (AB)
Reincorporated under the laws of
British Columbia as Canamex Silver
Corp. 10/07/2009
Canamex Silver Corp. name changed
to Canamex Resources Corp.
10/18/2010 which name changed to
Canamex Gold Corp. 11/08/2017

AXR DEV CORP (NV)
Recapitalized as Advanced Coating
Technologies, Inc. 12/11/1998
Each share Common $0.001 par
exchanged for (0.04347826) share
Common $0.001 par
Advanced Coating Technologies, Inc.
name changed to VitroSeal Inc.
01/19/1999 which name changed to
VitriSeal Inc. 02/18/1999 which
name changed to Liquitek
Enterprises Inc. 07/31/2000
(See Liquitek Enterprises Inc.)

AXR RES LTD (ON)
Merged into Greater Lenora
Resources Corp. 01/05/1989
Each share Common no par
exchanged for (0.2) share Common
no par
(See Greater Lenora Resources
Corp.)

AXS BLOCKCHAIN SOLUTIONS INC (BC)
Name changed to Litelink
Technologies Inc. 08/21/2018

AXS-ONE INC (DE)
Merged into Unify Corp. 06/30/2009
Each share Common 1¢ par
exchanged for (0.019442) share
Common $0.001 par
Unify Corp. name changed to Daegis
Inc. 07/07/2011
(See Daegis Inc.)

AXSYS TECHNOLOGIES INC (DE)
$1.20 Exchangeable Preferred 1¢ par
called for redemption at $7.70 on
06/04/1997
Common 1¢ par split (3) for (2) by
issuance of (0.5) additional share
payable 06/30/2004 to holders of
record 06/15/2004 Ex date -
07/01/2004
Acquired by General Dynamics
Advanced Information Systems, Inc.
09/03/2009
Each share Common 1¢ par
exchanged for $54 cash

AXTEL S A DE C V (MEXICO)
Name changed to Axtel, S.A.B. de
C.V. 01/09/2007

AXTION FOODS INC (CA)
Name changed to S3I Holdings, Inc.
04/02/2003
S3I Holdings, Inc. name changed to
S3 Investment Co., Inc. 10/21/2004
which name changed to Redwood
Group International 05/09/2011

AXTON-FISHER TOBACCO CO., INC.
Liquidation completed 00/00/1950
Details not available

AXXENT INC (ON)
Assets sold for the benefit of creditors
07/26/2001
No stockholders' equity

AXXENT MEDIA CORP (NV)
Name changed to UFood Franchise
Co. 08/31/2007
UFood Franchise Co. name changed
to UFood Restaurant Group, Inc.
10/04/2007
(See UFood Restaurant Group, Inc.)

AXXESS INC (NV)
Name changed to Financialweb.Com,
Inc. 01/01/1999
(See Financialweb.Com, Inc.)

AXXESS PHARMA INC (NV)
Reincorporated 12/06/2012
Each share old Common $0.0001 par
exchanged for (0.00133333) share
Common $0.0001 par 04/12/2012

State of incorporation changed from
(DE) to (NV) 12/06/2012
Each share old Common $0.0001 par
exchanged for (0.0004) share new
Common $0.0001 par 03/09/2016
Recapitalized as Allstar Health
Brands, Inc. 06/27/2017
Each share new Common $0.0001
par exchanged for (0.00005) share
Common $0.0001 par

AXXESS UNLIMITED INC (FL)
Name changed to Encompass
Compliance Corp. 06/22/2015

AXXEXS CAP INC (NJ)
Each share old Common no par
received distribution of (0.242) share
American DebtWorks, Inc.
Restricted Common payable
05/15/2003 to holders of record
05/15/2003
Each share old Common no par
exchanged for (0.06666666) share
new Common no par 01/27/2004
New Common no par split (2) for (1)
by issuance of (1) additional share
payable 10/14/2004 to holders of
record 09/30/2004 Ex date -
10/15/2004
Name changed to U.S. Shanghai
Chemical Corp. 10/14/2004
U.S. Shanghai Chemical Corp. name
changed to AmeriWorks Financial
Services, Inc. 12/16/2010 which
recapitalized as AmeriWorks, Inc.
01/29/2014

AXYN CORP (CO)
Each share old Common $0.0001 par
exchanged for (0.1) share new
Common $0.0001 par 02/12/2004
Name changed to Chef Selections,
Inc. 04/27/2004
Chef Selections, Inc. recapitalized as
Talisman Holdings, Inc. 04/14/2010
which recapitalized as Fidelity
Holding Corp. 08/20/2014

AXYS PHARMACEUTICALS INC (DE)
Merged into Applera Corp. 11/19/2001
Each share Common $0.001 par
exchanged for (0.135) share Celera
Genomics Group Common 1¢ par
(See Applera Corp.)

AYALA CORP (PHILIPPINES)
144A GDR's for Class B Common
split (3) for (2) by issuance of (0.5)
additional GDR payable 09/26/1996
to holders of record 08/14/1996
Stock Dividends - 25% payable
07/28/1997 to holders of record
05/14/1997; 20% payable
07/13/1998 to holders of record
05/14/1998; 20% payable
08/25/2000 to holders of record
07/21/2000 Ex date - 07/19/2000;
20% payable 06/11/2004 to holders
of record 04/15/2004
GDR agreement terminated
02/09/2005
Each 144A GDR for Class B Common
exchanged for $0.992911 cash
(Additional Information in Active)

AYDIN CORP (DE)
Common $1 par split (3) for (2) by
issuance of (0.5) additional share
06/10/1980
Common $1 par split (4) for (3) by
issuance of (0.33333333) additional
share 09/07/1982
Common $1 par split (3) for (2) by
issuance of (0.5) additional share
12/23/1988
Stock Dividend - 100% 02/26/1969
Merged into L-3 Communications
Holdings, Inc. 04/29/1999
Each share Common $1 par
exchanged for (13.5) shares
Common 1¢ par
L-3 Communications Holdings, Inc.
name changed to L3 Technologies,
Inc. 01/03/2017

AYDON INCOME PPTYS INC (BC)
Reorganized under the laws of

Canada as Delma Group Inc.
03/23/2018
Each share Common no par
exchanged for (0.005) share
Common no par

AYEROK PETE LTD (BC)
Recapitalized as Westrok Capital Inc.
(BC) 06/05/1987
Each share Common no par
exchanged for (0.1) share Common
no par
Westrok Capital Inc. (BC)
reincorporated in Alberta 01/25/1988
which recapitalized as Merit Energy
Ltd. 01/08/1996
(See Merit Energy Ltd.)

AYLEN MINES LTD. (ON)
Charter revoked for failure to file
reports and pay fees 09/21/1959

AYLETTE CHIBOUGAMAU GOLD MINES LTD. (ON)
Charter cancelled 03/26/1956

AYLMER MINES LTD (QC)
Name changed to Heron Exploration
Inc. 03/05/1997
(See Heron Exploration Inc.)

AYOTTE MUSIC INC (CANADA)
Reincorporated 05/16/2000
Place of incorporation changed from
(AB) to (Canada) 05/16/2000
Recapitalized as Verb Exchange Inc.
11/12/2002
Each share Common no par
exchanged for (0.2) share Common
no par
Verb Exchange Inc. recapitalized as
Seymour Ventures Corp. 07/05/2010
which name changed to Rare Earth
Industries Ltd. 07/13/2011 which
recapitalized as Ackroo Inc.
10/10/2012

AYR MINES LTD. (CANADA)
Involuntarily dissolved 07/27/1976
No stockholders' equity

AYRE HLDGS INC (DE)
Each share old Common $0.001 par
exchanged for (0.414422) share
new Common $0.001 par
06/05/2006
Name changed to HC Innovations,
Inc. 06/20/2006
(See HC Innovations, Inc.)

AYRES L S & CO (IN)
Each share Common $100 par
exchanged for (20) shares Common
$5 par 00/00/1954
Common $5 par changed to $2.50 par
and (1) additional share issued
07/10/1964
Stock Dividend - 50% 06/03/1966
4.5% Preferred $100 par called for
redemption 03/15/1972
4.5% Preferred 1947 Ser. called for
redemption 03/15/1972
Completely liquidated 04/20/1972
Each share Common $2.50 par
exchanged for first and final
distribution of (0.925) share
Associated Dry Goods Corp.
Common 50¢ par
Associated Dry Goods Corp. merged
into May Department Stores Co.
10/04/1986 which merged into
Federated Department Stores, Inc.
08/30/2005 which name changed to
Macy's, Inc. 06/01/2007

AYRETRADE INC (CN)
Name changed to Rocky Mountain
Ayre, Inc. 02/05/2015

AYREX RES LTD (AB)
Recapitalized as Yangarra Resources
Inc. 07/21/2003
Each share Class A no par
exchanged for (0.25) share Common
no par
Yangarra Resources Inc. merged into
Yangarra Resources Ltd. 10/09/2005

AYRHART MNG INC (QC)
Name changed to Meston Lake

Resources Inc./Les Ressources Du Lac Meston Inc. 04/30/1977
Meston Lake Ressources Inc./Les Ressources Du Lac Meston Inc. merged into Campbell Resources Inc. (New) 12/08/1987
(See Campbell Resources Inc. (New))

AYRSHIRE COLLIERIES CORP (IN)
Reincorporated 06/30/1965
Each share Common $1 par exchanged for (4) shares Common $3 par 00/00/1947
State of incorporation changed from (DE) to (IN) 06/30/1965
Merged into American Metal Climax, Inc. 10/31/1969
Each share Common $3 par exchanged for (1) share Conv. Preferred Ser. A $1 par
American Metal Climax, Inc. name changed to Amax Inc. 07/01/1974
(See Amax Inc.)

AYRSHIRE PATOKA COLLIERIES CORP. (DE)
Name changed to Ayrshire Collieries Corp. (DE) 00/00/1944
Ayrshire Collieries Corp. (DE) reincorporated in Indiana 06/30/1965 which merged into American Metal Climax, Inc. 10/31/1969 which name changed to Amax Inc. 07/01/1974
(See Amax Inc.)

AYUBOWAN CAP LTD (BC)
Name changed to Discovery Metals Corp. 06/13/2017

AZ MNG INC (BC)
Name changed to Arizona Mining Inc. 10/28/2015
(See Arizona Mining Inc.)

AZALEA HOMES, INC. (FL)
Liquidation completed 04/06/1960
Details not available

AZAM ENERGY CORP (BC)
Struck off register and declared dissolved for failure to file returns 12/06/1985

AZATECH INC (NY)
Dissolved by proclamation 09/28/1994

AZCAR TECHNOLOGIES INC (ON)
Class A no par reclassified as Common no par 10/28/1996
Ceased operations 03/23/2011
Details not available

AZCO MNG INC (DE)
Reincorporated 08/27/1991
State of incorporation changed from (CO) to (DE) 08/27/1991
Name changed to Santa Fe Gold Corp. 09/12/2007

AZCO MNG INC (WY)
Merged into Azco Mining Inc. (DE) 07/31/1992
Details not available

AZCON CORP (ME)
Merged into Consolidated Gold Fields Ltd. 03/01/1978
Each share Common $1 par exchanged for $13.50 cash

AZEL ENTERPRISES INC (NV)
SEC revoked common stock registration 01/18/2008

AZEN MINES LTD. (ON)
Charter cancelled for failure to pay taxes and file returns 11/08/1977

AZIA CORP (FL)
Name changed to Axxess Unlimited Inc. 03/20/2013
Axxess Unlimited Inc. name changed to Encompass Compliance Corp. 06/22/2015

AZIMUTH ENERGY INC (AB)
Name changed to C-Tech Energy Services Inc. 03/04/1999
(See C-Tech Energy Services Inc.)

AZIMUTH RES LTD (AUSTRALIA)
Acquired by Troy Resources Ltd. 07/18/2013
Each share Ordinary exchanged for (0.17559262) share Ordinary
(See Troy Resources Ltd.)

AZINCOURT RES INC (BC)
Name changed to Azincourt Uranium Inc. 06/24/2013
Azincourt Uranium Inc. name changed to Azincourt Energy Corp. 10/16/2017

AZINCOURT URANIUM INC (BC)
Each share old Common no par received distribution of (1.31415) shares Macusani Yellowcake Inc. Common no par payable 10/03/2014 to holders of record 09/17/2014 Ex date - 10/06/2014
Each share old Common no par exchanged for (0.25) share new Common no par 02/18/2015
Each share new Common no par exchanged again for (0.5) share new Common no par 10/01/2015
Name changed to Azincourt Energy Corp. 10/16/2017

AZKAN TECHNOLOGY INC (DE)
Common 10¢ par changed to 5¢ par and (1) additional share issued 08/29/1983
Charter cancelled and declared inoperative and void for non-payment of taxes 06/25/1987

AZL RES INC (AZ)
48¢ Conv. Preferred Ser. A no par called for redemption 11/18/1982
Merged into Tosco Corp. 01/03/1983
Each share Common no par exchanged for $10 cash

AZONIC CORP (NV)
Each share old Common $0.001 par exchanged for (4) shares new Common $0.001 par 03/23/2004
Name changed to Midland International Corp. 07/21/2005
Midland International Corp. name changed to Lumonall, Inc. 08/17/2007
(See Lumonall, Inc.)

AZORA MINERALS INC (BC)
Recapitalized as International Azora Minerals Inc. (BC) 09/22/1989
Each share Common no par exchanged for (0.25) share Common no par
International Azora Minerals Inc. (BC) reincorporated in Wyoming 00/00/1990 which name changed to Power Battery Holdings Corp. (WY) 03/05/1991 which reincorporated Washington 12/14/1992 which recapitalized as Consolidated Power Battery Corp. 07/09/1998

AZOT OJSC (UKRAINE)
GDR agreement terminated 04/21/2017
No GDR's remain outstanding

AZOVSTAL IRON & STL WKS OPEN JT STK CO (UKRAINE)
ADR agreement terminated 06/11/2012
Each Sponsored ADR for Common exchanged for (10) shares Common
Note: Unexchanged ADR's were sold and the proceeds, if any, held for claim after 10/31/2013

AZP GROUP INC (AZ)
Name changed to Pinnacle West Capital Corp. 04/27/1987

AZS CORP. (GA)
Merged into Toyo Soda Manufacturing Co., Ltd. 06/12/1980
Each share Common $1 par exchanged for $17.50 cash

AZTAR CORP (DE)
Merged into Columbia Sussex Corp. 01/03/2007
Each share Common 1¢ par exchanged for $54.3996 cash

AZTEC COMMUNICATIONS GROUP INC (NV)
Reincorporated 11/21/2003
Each share old Common $0.001 par exchanged for (0.5) share new Common $0.001 par 01/18/2001
State of incorporation changed from (UT) to (NV) 11/21/2003
Reorganized as Aztec Oil & Gas Inc. 08/13/2004
Each share new Common $0.001 par exchanged for (3) shares Common $0.001 par

AZTEC ENERGY CORP (CO)
Recapitalized as Noarko Resources, Inc. 10/31/1983
Each share Common no par exchanged for (0.2) share Common no par
(See Noarko Resources, Inc.)

AZTEC ENERGY CORP (UT)
Reorganized under the laws of Delaware as Blaze Energy Corp. 06/26/2007
Each share Common 1¢ par exchanged for (0.0083333333) share Common $0.001 par
(See Blaze Energy Corp.)

AZTEC EXPLORATION & DEVELOPMENT CO., INC. (AZ)
Charter revoked for failure to file reports and pay fees 02/14/1978

AZTEC EXPLORATION LTD. (BC)
Charter revoked for failure to file reports and pay fees 04/20/1961

AZTEC MFG CO (TX)
Each share old Common $1 par exchanged for (1) share new Common $1 par 09/10/1970
New Common $1 par split (4) for (3) by issuance of (0.33333333) additional share 04/28/1978
New Common $1 par split (2) for (1) by issuance of (1) additional share 04/27/1979
New Common $1 par split (5) for (4) by issuance of (0.25) additional share 05/02/1980
New Common $1 par split (4) for (3) by issuance of (0.33333333) additional share 05/01/1981
Stock Dividends - 10% 04/07/1975; 25% 04/30/1976; 25% 04/29/1977; 10% 04/30/1982
Name changed to AZZ Inc. 07/11/2000

AZTEC MINING CO., LTD.
Acquired by B.R.X. (1935) Consolidated Mines Ltd. 00/00/1935
Each share Capital Stock exchanged for (0.5) share Capital Stock 50¢ par
(See B.R.X. (1935) Consolidated Mines Ltd.)

AZTEC MNG CORP (DE)
Reincorporated 09/30/1970
State of incorporation changed from (AZ) to (DE) 09/30/1970
Merged into Southland Oil Co. 06/30/1976
Each share Common 10¢ par exchanged for $32 cash

AZTEC OIL & GAS CO (DE)
Merged into Southland Royalty Co. 06/30/1976
Each share Common $1 par exchanged for $32 cash

AZTEC PRODS INC (DE)
Name changed to Golden Girl Industries, Inc. 06/14/1974
(See Golden Girl Industries, Inc.)

AZTEC RES CORP (CO)
Merged into WEPCo Energy Co. 12/15/1986
Each share Common 1¢ par exchanged for (0.45) share Common 1¢ par and (0.2345116) Common Stock Purchase Warrant expiring 12/15/1991
WEPCo Energy Co. recapitalized as American Atlas Resources Corp. 08/09/1993
(See American Atlas Resources Corp.)

AZTEC RES LTD (AB)
Recapitalized as Pursuit Resources Inc. (New) 02/13/1997
Each share Common no par exchanged for (1) share Common no par and (0.25) Common Stock Purchase Warrant expiring 06/30/1998
Pursuit Resources Inc. (New) merged into EnerMark Income Fund 04/11/2000 which merged into Enerplus Resources Fund 06/22/2001 which reorganized as Enerplus Corp. 01/03/2011

AZTEC TECHNOLOGY PARTNERS INC (DE)
Recapitalized as Ultimate Lifestyle Corp. 03/24/2010
Each share Common $0.001 par exchanged for (0.001) share Common $0.001 par

AZTECA, INC. (FL)
Name changed to Energy Gas Saver, Inc. 09/25/1980
Energy Gas Saver, Inc. name changed to Fun Time International, Inc. 06/10/1983

AZTECA ACQUISITION CORP (DE)
Merged into Hemisphere Media Group, Inc. 04/05/2013
Each Unit exchanged for (1) share Class A Common $0.0001 par and (1) Class A Common Stock Purchase Warrant expiring 04/04/2018
Each share Common $0.0001 par exchanged for (1) share Class A Common $0.0001 par

AZTECH INTL LTD (NM)
Stock Dividends - 25% 08/17/1981; 10% 12/16/1983
Plan of reorganization under Chapter 11 Federal Bankruptcy Code effective 01/20/1995
No stockholders' equity

AZTECH NEW MEDIA CORP (ON)
Recapitalized as Star Navigation Systems Group Ltd. 08/29/2002
Each share Common no par exchanged for (0.07251266) share Common no par

AZTEK ENERGY LTD (AB)
Each share old Common no par exchanged for (0.1) share new Common no par 06/11/2009
Merged into Spartan Exploration Ltd. 01/18/2010
Each share new Common no par exchanged for (0.0805) share Common no par
Note: Unexchanged certificates were cancelled and became without value 01/18/2014
Spartan Exploration Ltd. merged into Spartan Oil Corp. 06/03/2011 which merged into Bonterra Energy Corp. (New) 01/29/2013

AZTEK RESOURCE DEV INC (BC)
Delisted from CNQ 11/15/2006

AZTEK TECHNOLOGIES INC (BC)
Recapitalized as Aztek Resource Development Inc. 11/19/2004
Each share Common no par exchanged for (0.33333333) share Common no par
(See Aztek Resource Development Inc.)

AZTEK VENTURES INC (NV)
Each share old Common $0.001 par exchanged for (2.5) shares new Common $0.001 par 07/09/2007
Name changed to Genesis Uranium Corp. 11/13/2007

Genesis Uranium Corp. name changed to Vault Technology, Inc. 05/02/2008 which recapitalized as Modern Renewable Technologies, Inc. 09/17/2009 which name changed to Eco Ventures Group, Inc. 05/16/2011 which recapitalized as Petlife Pharmaceuticals, Inc. (Old) 08/12/2014 which reorganized as Petlife Pharmaceuticals, Inc. (New) 09/12/2016

AZTERRA CORP (AB)
Delisted from Toronto Venture Stock Exchange 06/26/2002

AZTORE HLDGS INC (AZ)
Each share old Common no par exchanged for (0.00045454) share new Common no par 03/09/2009
Note: Holders of (2,199) or fewer pre-split shares received $0.15 cash per share
Merged into Visitalk Capital Corp. 08/31/2012
Each share new Common no par exchanged for (9,365) shares Common
Note: Company is now privately held

AZUL HLDGS INC (DE)
Assets sold for the benefit of creditors 12/28/2001
No stockholders' equity

AZUL STUDIOS INTL INC (WA)
Each share old Common $0.0001 par exchanged for (0.5) share new Common $0.0001 par 06/08/2006
Name changed to Modern City Entertainment, Inc. 04/27/2007
(See Modern City Entertainment, Inc.)

AZUL VENTURES INC (AB)
Recapitalized as Austin Resources Ltd. 09/24/2014
Each share Common no par exchanged for (0.33333333) share Common no par

AZUR HLDGS INC (DE)
SEC revoked common stock registration 07/22/2010

AZUR INTL INC (NV)
SEC revoked common stock registration 02/19/2008

AZURA VENTURES LTD (NB)
Reincorporated under the laws of Canada as Excellium Inc. 06/19/2012
Excellium Inc. name changed to XL-ID Solutions Inc. 01/24/2014
(See XL-ID Solutions Inc.)

AZURE DYNAMICS CORP. (AB)
Each share old Common no par exchanged for (0.025) share new Common no par 03/21/2012
Discharged from receivership 11/25/2015
Stockholders' equity unlikely

AZURE INTL INC (NV)
Name changed to Air Transport Group Holdings, Inc. 11/10/2008
Air Transport Group Holdings Inc. recapitalized as Pharmagreen Biotech Inc. 07/02/2018

AZURE MIDSTREAM PARTNERS LP (DE)
Plan of reorganization under Chapter 11 Federal Bankruptcy proceedings effective 06/02/2017
Common Units cancelled and a custodian formed to hold and single new Common Unit for the benefit of former Unitholders

AZURE RES CORP (BC)
Recapitalized as Panorama Petroleum Inc. 06/13/2014
Each share Common no par exchanged for (0.1) share Common no par
Panorama Petroleum Inc. recapitalized as Stamper Oil & Gas Corp. 04/06/2017

AZURE RES CORP (BC)
Recapitalized as Pencari Mining Corp. 08/09/2005
Each share Common no par exchanged for (0.28571428) share Common no par
Pencari Mining Corp. recapitalized as Pencari Resource Corp. 02/02/2009
Pencari Resource Corp. recapitalized as Sheen Resources Ltd. 08/27/2009

AZURE RES LTD (BC)
Recapitalized as Consolidated Azure Resources Ltd. 04/23/1987
Each share Capital Stock no par exchanged for (0.25) share Common no par
Consolidated Azure Resources Ltd. name changed to Caltech Data Ltd. 02/05/1988 which recapitalized as Roraima Gold Corp. 09/14/1994 which recapitalized as International Roraima Gold Corp. 06/13/1996
(See International Roraima Gold Corp.)

AZUREL LTD (DE)
Recapitalized as National Stem Cell Holding, Inc. 10/03/2006
Each share Common $0.001 par exchanged for (0.02702702) share Common $0.0001 par
National Stem Cell Holding, Inc. name changed to Proteonomix, Inc. 08/19/2008

AZURITE GOLD INC (WA)
Charter cancelled and proclaimed dissolved for failure to pay fees 09/24/1990

AZURIX CORP (DE)
Merged into Enron Corp. 03/16/2001
Each share Common 1¢ par exchanged for $8.375 cash

B

B & A RESH & SVCS INC (CO)
Name changed to Richard Group, Inc. 09/11/1987

B & B RESOURCE INC. (BC)
Merged into Viceroy Resource Corp. 04/06/1984
Each share Common no par exchanged for (1) share Common no par
Viceroy Resource Corp. merged into Quest Capital Corp. (BC) 06/30/2003 which reincorporated in Canada 05/27/2008 which name changed to Sprott Resource Lending Corp. 09/10/2010 which merged into Sprott Inc. 07/24/2013

B & C REALTY CORP. (FL)
Charter revoked for failure to file reports and pay fees 05/01/1962

B & D FOOD CORP (DE)
Recapitalized as Latteno Food Corp. 10/19/2009
Each share Common $0.001 par exchanged for (0.05) share Common $0.001 par

B & G FOODS HLDGS CORP (DE)
Name changed to B&G Foods, Inc. 10/14/2004

B & H BULK CARRIERS LTD (LIBERIA)
Name changed to Bulk Associates Ltd. 02/02/1996
(See Bulk Associates Ltd.)

B & J AVIATION, INC. (CA)
Name changed to B & J Consolidated, Inc. 11/06/1981
(See B & J Consolidated, Inc.)

B & J CONS INC (CA)
Charter suspended for failure to file reports and pay fees 02/01/1983

B & M INVTS INC (TX)
Merged into Chartwell Industries, Inc. 12/16/1983

Each share Common no par exchanged for $3.50 cash

B & P BRDG CO (TX)
Through purchase offer majority shares reacquired 00/00/1983
Public interest eliminated

B & S CO. (CT)
Liquidation completed
Each share Common $10 par exchanged for initial distribution of $28 cash 05/15/1963
Each share Common $10 par received second distribution of $4.50 cash 08/01/1963
Each share Common $10 par received third distribution of $6 cash 11/15/1963
Each share Common $10 par received fourth and final distribution of $0.57 cash 03/20/1964
In addition holders are entitled to receive pro rata liquidating benefits from remaining assets which were assigned to B & S Co. Stockholders Trust
(See B & S Co. Stockholders Trust)

B & S CO. STOCKHOLDERS TRUST
Liquidation completed
Each share Common $10 par received initial distribution of $0.90 cash 06/12/1964
Each share Common $10 par received second distribution of $0.46 cash 11/19/1964
Each share Common $10 par received third distribution of $0.75 cash 02/16/1965
Each share Common $10 par received fourth and final distribution of $1.782014 cash 12/30/1965

B & W INTL INC (CO)
Administratively dissolved 06/01/2000

B A COPPER MINES (BC)
Name changed to B.A. Resources Ltd. (BC) 06/17/1982
B.A. Resources Ltd. (BC) reincorporated in Canada 03/17/1995 which name changed to United China International Enterprises Group Ltd. (Canada) which reincorporated in Bermuda 10/31/1995

B A RES LTD (CANADA)
Reincorporated 03/17/1995
Place of incorporation changed from (BC) to (Canada) 03/17/1995
Name changed to United China International Enterprises Group Ltd. (Canada) 10/24/1995
United China International Enterprises Group Ltd. (Canada) reincorporated in Bermuda 10/31/1995

B A T INDS P L C (ENGLAND)
ADR's for Deferred Ordinary Reg. reclassified as ADR's for Ordinary Reg. 07/10/1980
ADR's for Ordinary Reg. split (4) for (1) by issuance of (3) additional ADR's 06/17/1983
ADR's for Ordinary Reg. split (2) for (1) by issuance of (1) additional ADR 05/26/1993
Each Unsponsored ADR for Ordinary exchanged for (0.5) Sponsored ADR for Ordinary 03/15/1994
Plan of Arrangement effective 09/08/1998
Each Sponsored ADR for Ordinary exchanged for (0.49291) Allied Zurich PLC ADR for Ordinary and (0.49295) British American Tobacco PLC ADR for Ordinary
(See each company's listing)

B A T INTL INC (UT)
Name changed to Green Star Products Inc. 07/25/2002

B&H OCEAN CARRIERS LTD (LIBERIA)
Each share old Common 1¢ par exchanged for (1) share new Common 1¢ par to reflect a (1) for

(101) reverse split followed by a (101) for (1) forward split 11/29/2011
Note: Holders of (100) or fewer pre-split shares received $4 cash per share
Plan of reorganization under Chapter 11 Federal Bankruptcy proceedings effective 05/03/2013
No stockholders' equity

B B REAL ESTATE INVT CORP (DE)
Acquired by California Real Estate Investment Trust 07/18/1989
Each share Class A Common 1¢ par exchanged for (0.9) Share of Bene. Int. $1 par
California Real Estate Investment Trust name changed to Capital Trust (CA) 07/15/1997 which reorganized as Capital Trust, Inc. (MD) 01/28/1999 which recapitalized as Blackstone Mortgage Trust, Inc. 05/07/2013

B B S STUDIOS INC (NC)
Recapitalized as Fisher-Harrison Corp. 10/13/1969
Each share Common $1 par exchanged for (0.1) share Common no par
(See Fisher-Harrison Corp.)

B.C. COAL LTD. (BC)
Name changed to Westar Mining Ltd. 06/00/1983
(See Westar Mining Ltd.)

B.C. METAL MINES LTD. (BC)
Acquired by Castle Oil & Gas Ltd. 00/00/1956
Each share Capital Stock $1 par exchanged for (0.066666) share Capital Stock no par
(See Castle Oil & Gas Ltd.)

B.C. PEAT CO., LTD. (BC)
Name changed to Atkins & Durbrow, Ltd. 00/00/1948
(See Atkins & Durbrow, Ltd.)

B.C. PLACER MINING & REFINING LTD. (BC)
Name changed to Sterling Silver Mines Ltd. 06/05/1963
Sterling Silver Mines Ltd. acquired by Gem Explorations Ltd. 11/00/1964 which recapitalized as Consolidated Gem Explorations Ltd. 01/08/1968 which recapitalized as Brendon Resources Ltd. 02/13/1973 which recapitalized as Brendex Resources Ltd. 09/10/1976
(See Brendex Resources Ltd.)

B.C. TURF & COUNTRY CLUB LTD. (BC)
Name changed to B.C. Turf Ltd. 05/16/1966
(See B.C. Turf Ltd.)

B C BANCORP (BC)
$2.22 Conv. Preferred Ser. B no par called for redemption 07/07/1992
$2.28 Preference Ser. A no par called for redemption 07/07/1992
Merged into Canadian Western Bank (Edmonton, AB) 11/01/1996
Each share Common no par exchanged for (0.035) share Class A Common no par

B C BANKSHARES INC (GA)
Merged into Wachovia Corp. (New) (Ctfs. dated between 05/20/1991 and 09/01/2001) 02/05/2000
Each share Common $5 par exchanged for (2.914) shares Common $5 par
Wachovia Corp. (New) (Ctfs. dated between 05/20/1991 and 09/01/2001) merged into Wachovia Corp. (Ctfs. dated after 09/01/2001) 09/01/2001 which merged into Wells Fargo & Co. (New) 12/31/2008

B C PACIFIC CAP CORP (BC)
Merged into Brookfield Asset Management Inc. 03/30/2007
Each share Class A Subordinate no par exchanged for $0.80 cash

Each share Class B Common no par exchanged for $0.80 cash

B C RLTY PARTNERS INC (FL)
Name changed to Weather All Manufacturing USA Inc. 11/23/1998
Weather All Manufacturing USA Inc. recapitalized as Cerro Dorado, Inc. (FL) 03/29/1999 which reincorporated in Nevada 07/14/1999 which recapitalized as AURYN Mining Corp. 08/14/2018

B C REPORT MAGAZINE LTD (BC)
Name changed to Glass Earth Ltd. 04/07/2005
Glass Earth Ltd. name changed to Glass Earth Gold Ltd. 12/28/2007 which recapitalized as Antipodes Gold Ltd. 03/24/2014 which recapitalized as Chatham Rock Phosphate Ltd. 02/24/2017

B C S INC (CO)
Name changed to Triple Co. 09/30/1990

B C SUGAR REFINERY LTD (CANADA)
Common no par split (4) for (1) by issuance of (3) additional shares 02/01/1956
Common no par split (3) for (1) by issuance of (2) additional shares 07/05/1969
Common no par reclassified as Conv. Class A Common no par 11/08/1973
Conv. Class A Common no par split (2) for (1) by issuance of (1) additional share 02/20/1981
Conv. Class B Common no par split (2) for (1) by issuance of (1) additional share 02/20/1981
Conv. Class A Common no par split (2) for (1) by issuance of (1) additional share 03/31/1989
Conv. Class B Common no par split (2) for (1) by issuance of (1) additional share 03/31/1989
5% Preferred $20 par called for redemption 08/16/1996
Acquired by BCS Acquisition Corp. 08/05/1997
Each share Conv. Class A no par exchanged for $16.50 cash
Each share Conv. Class B no par exchanged for $16.50 cash

B C TURF LTD (BC)
Merged into Diamond (J.) & Sons, Ltd. 12/22/1976
Each share Capital Stock $1 par exchanged for $7 cash

B C YUKON EXPL LTD (BC)
Struck off register and declared dissolved for failure to file returns 01/10/1977

B CORP (ON)
Each Installment Receipt exchanged for (1) share BCE Inc. Common no par and $30 cash 04/14/1992
Non-Dividend Retractable Preferred no par called for redemption 05/25/1992

B D M FD LTD (CANADA)
Completely liquidated 04/27/1978
Each share Capital Stock $1 par exchanged for first and final distribution of $10.39 cash

B/E AEROSPACE INC (DE)
Name changed 08/07/2012
Name changed from BE Aerospace, Inc. to B/E Aerospace, Inc. 08/07/2012
Each share Common 1¢ par received distribution of (0.5) share KLX Inc. Common 1¢ par payable 12/16/2014 to holders of record 12/05/2014
Ex date - 12/17/2014
Merged into Rockwell Collins, Inc. 04/13/2017
Each share Common 1¢ par exchanged for (0.3101) share Common $1 par and $34.10 cash

B-E HLDGS INC (DE)
Reorganized as Bucyrus-Erie Co. (New) 12/14/1994
Each share $3.125 Exchangeable Preferred Ser. A 1¢ par exchanged for (0.066477) share Common 1¢ par
Bucyrus-Erie Co. (New) name changed to Bucyrus International Inc. (Old) 05/24/1996
(See Bucyrus International Inc. (Old))

B-ETTES CORP. (DE)
No longer in existence having become inoperative and void for non-payment of taxes 04/01/1941

B-FAST CORP (LA)
Charter revoked 08/17/2012

B G FOODS INC (DE)
Class A Common $10 par called for redemption 06/03/1960
Charter cancelled and declared inoperative and void for non-payment of taxes 03/01/1984

B/G SANDWICH SHOPS, INC.
Name changed to B/G Foods, Inc. 00/00/1935
(See B/G Foods, Inc.)

B GREEN INNOVATIONS INC (NJ)
Each share old Class A Common no par exchanged for (0.0001) share new Class A Common no par 09/26/2014
Name changed to 024 Pharma, Inc. 11/10/2016

B H I T INC (DE)
Name changed to Banyan Rail Services Inc. 01/29/2010
Banyan Rail Services Inc. recapitalized as MedAmerica Properties Inc. 06/20/2017

B H SOUTH LTD (AUSTRALIA)
ADR agreement terminated 01/06/1983
Details not available

B.I. CORP. (CT)
Liquidation completed
Each share Common $1 par exchanged for initial distribution of $21 cash 07/06/1965
Each share Common $1 par received second and final distribution of $0.40 cash 12/17/1965

B-I-F INDUSTRIES, INC. (RI)
Capital Stock no par changed to $10 par 02/12/1957
Name changed to High Street Investment Fund, Inc. 11/17/1961
(See High Street Investment Fund, Inc.)

B.I.G. ENTERPRISES, INC. (NV)
Name changed to Itex Barter Systems, Inc. 05/19/1986
Itex Barter Systems, Inc. recapitalized as Itex Corp. 04/05/1991

B I INC (CO)
Each share old Common no par exchanged for (0.06666666) share new Common no par 03/25/1987
Merged into KBII Holdings, Inc. 10/16/2000
Each share new Common no par exchanged for $8.25 cash

B I VENTURES LTD (BC)
Dissolved 06/16/1989
Details not available

B I Z HLDGS INC (FL)
Administratively dissolved 09/19/2003

B J B GRAPHICS INC (NY)
Stock Dividend - 25% 06/02/1969
Name changed to Computer Capital Corp. 01/01/1975
Computer Capital Corp. name changed to Talbryn Financial Corp. 01/16/1985 which name changed to Zuccarelli Holophonics Corp. 02/17/1988

B L C BANK S A L (LEBANON)
GDR agreement terminated 08/21/2006
Each Regulation S GDR for Ordinary exchanged for $0.7082 cash
Each 144A GDR for Ordinary exchanged for $0.7082 cash

B.M.C. DURFEE SAFE DEPOSIT & TRUST CO. (FALL RIVER, MA)
Name changed to B.M.C. Durfee Trust Co. (Fall River, MA) 00/00/1916
(See B.M.C. Durfee Trust Co. (Fall River, MA))

B M C DURFEE TR CO (FALL RIVER, MA)
Capital Stock $100 par changed to $25 par and (3) additional shares issued plus a 25% stock dividend paid 02/27/1961
Capital Stock $25 par changed to $8.33333333 par and (2) additional shares issued 02/10/1967
Capital Stock $8.33333333 par changed to $12 par 10/22/1971
Capital Stock $12 par changed to $16.50 par 03/07/1973
Stock Dividends - 20% 11/00/1945; 20% 11/19/1951; 20% 11/23/1956; 10% 04/01/1965
99.9% held by Multibank Financial Corp. as of 10/05/1973
Public interest eliminated

B M C INDS INC (NY)
Charter cancelled and proclaimed dissolved for failure to pay taxes 12/16/1974

B-M HOLDING CORP. (DE)
Merged into Norton Co. 08/07/1962
Each share Preferred $100 par exchanged for (4) shares Common $10 par
Each share Class A Common no par and/or Class B Common no par exchanged for (7.91098) shares Common $10 par
(See Norton Co.)

B M I CAP INC (ON)
Charter cancelled for failure to file reports and pay taxes 09/12/1988

B M I CORP. (MI)
Liquidation completed 04/18/1961
In addition to previous cash distribution holders received Chatsworth Apartments Ctfs. of Bene. Int. upon exchange
(See Chatsworth Apartments)

B M J FINL CORP (NJ)
Common $5 par split (2) for (1) by issuance of (1) additional share 04/25/1985
Common $5 par changed to $1 par and (1) additional share issued 06/16/1986
Merged into Summit Bancorp 03/01/1997
Each share Common $1 par exchanged for (0.56) share Common $1.20 par
Summit Bancorp merged into FleetBoston Financial Corp. 03/01/2001 which merged into Bank of America Corp. 04/01/2004

B M P TECHNOLOGIES LTD (BC)
Name changed to Palomar Capital Corp. 05/26/1988
(See Palomar Capital Corp.)

B-MAVEN INC (NV)
Common $0.001 par split (40) for (1) by issuance of (39) additional shares payable 06/24/2015 to holders of record 06/01/2015
Ex date - 06/25/2015
Name changed to PureSnax International, Inc. 09/18/2015
PureSnax International, Inc. name changed to iQSTEL Inc. 08/30/2018

B-N-B ENTERPRISES INC (NV)
Recapitalized as Allwest Systems International, Inc. 03/20/1998

Each share Common $0.001 par exchanged for (0.66666666) share Common $0.001 par
Allwest Systems International, Inc. name changed to Lyon Capital Venture Corp. 09/10/2004 which name changed to UTEC, Inc. 03/21/2007 which name changed to Tiger Oil & Energy, Inc. 09/23/2010

B O A BANCSHARES INC (TX)
Merged into Sterling Bancshares, Inc. 06/01/1999
Each share Common $1 par exchanged for (1.1) shares Common $1 par
Sterling Bancshares, Inc. merged into Comerica, Inc. 07/28/2011

B O P CORP (PA)
Common $5 par split (2) for (1) by issuance of (1) additional share 04/20/1977
Stock Dividends - 10% 10/01/1969; 10% 06/27/1979
Name changed to Bancorp of Pennsylvania 03/25/1981
(See Bancorp of Pennsylvania)

B O S S ENTERPRISES (UT)
Proclaimed dissolved for failure to pay taxes 12/31/1985

B-1 BEVERAGE CORP.
Out of business 00/00/1942
Details not available

B.P.C. LIQUIDATING CO. (OH)
Liquidation completed
Each share Common no par received initial distribution of $19.60 cash 01/14/1965
Each share Common no par received second distribution of $0.75 cash 10/26/1965
Each share Common no par received third and final distribution of $0.17 cash 09/30/1968
Note: Certificates were not required to be surrendered and are without value

B.P.I. LIQUIDATING CORP. (DE)
Liquidation completed
Each share Common $1 par exchanged for initial distribution of (0.3111) share Bristol-Myers Co. Common $1 par 12/02/1968
Each share Common $1 par received second and final distribution of (0.04186) share Bristol-Myers Co. Common $1 par and $0.0303 cash 04/09/1971
Bristol-Myers Co. name changed to Bristol-Myers Squibb Co. 10/04/1989

B R RES LTD (BC)
Struck off register 02/02/1983

B.R.X. GOLD MINES LTD.
Assets sold to B.R.X. (1935) Consolidated Mines Ltd. 00/00/1935
Details not available

B R X 1935 CONS MINES LTD (BC)
Struck off register and declared dissolved for failure to file returns 12/02/1971

B.S.F. CO. (PA)
Reorganized under the laws of Delaware 09/30/1955
Each share Capital Stock no par exchanged for (2) shares Capital Stock $1 par
B.S.F. Co. (DE) merged into ELT, Inc. 03/31/1975 which name changed to Dutch Boy, Inc. 02/23/1977 which name changed to Artra Group Inc. 12/31/1980 which merged into Entrade Inc. 09/23/1999
(See Entrade Inc.)

B S F CO (DE)
Capital Stock $1 par changed to $0.66666666 par and (0.5) additional share issued 09/28/1959
Merged into ELT, Inc. 03/31/1975
Each share Capital Stock

$0.66666666 par exchanged for (1) share Common no par
ELT, Inc. name changed to Dutch Boy, Inc. 02/23/1977 which name changed to Artra Group Inc. 12/31/1980 which merged into Entrade Inc. 09/23/1999
(See Entrade Inc.)

B S FDG INC (DE)
Name changed to Adamson Brothers Holding Corp. 05/10/2004
Adamson Brothers Holding Corp. name changed to Red Mountain Pharmaceuticals, Inc. 06/07/2005 which name changed to Zalemark Holding Co., Inc. 12/24/2008

B.S.R. PLC (ENGLAND)
Each ADR for Ordinary Reg. exchanged for (3) ADR's for Ordinary 11/10/1972
Stock Dividends - 25% 06/29/1964; 25% 12/30/1968; 20% 05/22/1970; 10% 05/14/1971; 20% 06/07/1972; 25% 05/18/1973
Name changed to BSR International PLC 06/03/1983
BSR International PLC name changed to Astec (BSR) PLC 06/07/1989
(See Astec (BSR) PLC)

B SPLIT CORP (ON)
Preferred no par called for redemption at $25 on 11/29/2002
Capital Shares no par called for redemption at $3.14 on 11/29/2002

B SPLIT II CORP (ON)
Class A Preferred no par called for redemption at $18.23 on 06/01/2005
Class B Preferred no par called for redemption at $9.75 on 06/01/2010
Capital Shares no par called for redemption at $11.0074 on 06/01/2010

B SQUARED ART COM INC (NV)
Charter permanently revoked 03/31/2003

B SQUARED TECHNOLOGIES INC (NV)
Each share old Common $0.001 par received distribution of (0.01) share B Squared Art.com Inc. Common $0.001 par payable 06/27/2001 to holders of record 06/27/2001
Each share old Common $0.001 par received distribution of (0.09903881) share Inkstream Inc. Common $0.001 par payable 09/03/2002 to holders of record 06/20/2002 Ex date - 07/19/2002
Each share old Common $0.001 par exchanged for (0.005) share new Common $0.001 par 07/15/2002
Recapitalized as Metropolis Technologies Corp. 02/20/2003
Each share new Common $0.001 par exchanged for (0.002) share Common $0.001 par
Metropolis Technologies Corp. recapitalized as Impact E-Solutions Corp. 02/08/2007
(See Impact E-Solutions Corp.)

B T B CORP (NY)
Name changed to International Banknote Co., Inc. 01/02/1973
International Banknote Co., Inc. merged into United States Banknote Corp. (NY) 07/25/1990 which reincorporated in Delaware 09/21/1993 which name changed to American Banknote Corp. 07/03/1995
(See American Banknote Corp.)

B.T.L. CORP. (IL)
$6 Prior Preferred called for redemption 04/01/1946
Merged into McCrory Corp. 07/16/1960
Each share Common $15 par exchanged for (3) shares Common 50¢ par
McCrory Corp. merged into Rapid-American Corp. 03/12/1976

(See Rapid-American Corp.)

B T U ENGR CORP (DE)
Merged into Helec N.V. 07/27/1979
Each share Common 10¢ par exchanged for $8 cash

B-TELLER INC (WA)
Name changed to Congo Crest Mineral Corp. 08/01/2006
Congo Crest Mineral Corp. reorganized as New Wave Mobile, Inc. 11/22/2006 which name changed to New Wave Media, Inc. 03/26/2007 which name changed to CA Goldfields, Inc. 04/08/2008

B U D CORP (UT)
Recapitalized as Tecon, Inc. 01/05/1987
Each share Common 10¢ par exchanged for (0.5) share Common $0.001 par
Tecon, Inc. name changed to Buyit.com Inc. 05/06/1999 which name changed to Craftclick.com, Inc. (UT) 01/10/2000 which reorganized in Delaware 05/07/2000 which name changed to Mobilepro Corp. 06/19/2001

B U M INTL INC (MN)
Assets sold for the benefit of creditors 09/08/1997
Stockholders' equity unlikely

B.V.D., INC. (DE)
Name changed to B.V.D. Corp. 12/01/1937
B.V.D. Corp. name changed to B.V.D. Industries, Inc. 04/02/1951 which name changed to Erlanger Mills Corp. 10/01/1951
(See Erlanger Mills Corp.)

B.V.D. CO., INC. (DE)
Completely liquidated 05/19/1967
Each share Common $1 par exchanged for first and final distribution of (0.33333333) share Glen Alden Corp. (DE)
$3.15 Conv. Preferred no par
Glen Alden Corp. (DE) merged into Rapid-American Corp. (DE) 11/06/1972
(See Rapid-American Corp. (DE))

B.V.D. CORP. (DE)
Name changed to B.V.D. Industries, Inc. 04/02/1951
B.V.D. Industries, Inc. name changed to Erlanger Mills Corp. 10/01/1951
(See Erlanger Mills Corp.)

B.V.D. INDUSTRIES, INC. (DE)
Name changed to Erlanger Mills Corp. 10/01/1951
(See Erlanger Mills Corp.)

B.W. GROUP, INC. (DE)
Charter cancelled and declared inoperative and void for non-payment of taxes 03/01/1988

B.W.I.L., INC. (VA)
Liquidation completed
Each share Capital Stock $5 par received initial distribution of $10 cash 08/03/1965
Each share Capital Stock $5 par received second distribution of $4.50 cash 01/14/1966
Each share Capital Stock $5 par exchanged for third and final distribution of $0.50 cash 06/14/1966

B.X. MINING CO. LTD. (BC)
Acquired by Trojan Consolidated Mines Ltd. 12/08/1964
Each share Capital Stock $1 par exchanged for (1) share Common $1 par
Trojan Consolidated Mines Ltd. recapitalized as B.X. Development Ltd. 11/01/1972 which merged into Brent Petroleum Industries Ltd. 10/07/1981 which recapitalized as B.P.I. Resources Ltd. 05/20/1983

which name changed to Brent Resources Group Ltd. 03/22/1985
(See Brent Resources Group Ltd.)

B X DEV LTD (BC)
Merged into Brent Petroleum Industries Ltd. 10/07/1981
Each share Common no par exchanged for (3) shares Common no par
Brent Petroleum Industries Ltd. recapitalized as B.P.I. Resources Ltd. 05/20/1983 which name changed to Brent Resources Group Ltd. 03/22/1985
(See Brent Resources Group Ltd.)

B Y G NAT RES INC (ON)
Placed in receivership 04/06/2004
Stockholders' equity unlikely

BA BA CAP INC (ON)
Recapitalized as Imex Systems Inc. 05/13/2016
Each share Common no par exchanged for (0.09090909) share Common no par

BA MERCHANT SVCS INC (DE)
Merged into BankAmerica Corp. (New) 04/28/1999
Each share Class A Common 1¢ par exchanged for $20.50 cash

BAA PLC (UNITED KINGDOM)
Acquired by Airport Development & Investment Ltd. 10/11/2006
Each Sponsored ADR for Ordinary exchanged for $17.43384 cash

BAAN CO N V (NETHERLANDS)
New York Registry Shares NLG 0.02 par changed to NLG 0.01 par and (1) additional share issued payable 05/29/1996 to holders of record 05/15/1996
New York Registry Shares NLG 0.01 par changed to NLG 0.06 par and (1) additional share issued payable 12/17/1997 to holders of record 12/10/1997
91.69% acquired for approximately $2.80 cash per share by Invensys Holdings Ltd. through purchase offer which expired 08/16/2002
Liquidation completed
Each New York Registry Share NLG 0.06 par received initial distribution of $3.39282 cash payable 10/29/2010 to holders of record 10/15/2010
Each New York Registry Share NLG 0.06 par exchanged for second and final distribution of $0.49791 cash 08/08/2011

BAB HLDGS INC (IL)
Common no par split (3) for (2) by issuance of (0.5) additional share payable 04/26/1996 to holders of record 04/12/1996
Each share old Common no par exchanged for (0.16666666) share new Common no par 12/14/1999
Each share new Common no par received distribution of (1) share BAB Inc. Common no par payable 10/30/2000 to holders of record 10/17/2000
Reincorporated under the laws of Delaware as Planet Zanett, Inc. and Common no par changed to $0.001 par 10/31/2000
Planet Zanett, Inc. name changed to Zanett, Inc. 10/16/2002
(See Zanett, Inc.)

BAB SOL RES EXPLS LTD (ON)
Name changed to HWI Industries, Inc. 10/14/1983
(See HWI Industries, Inc.)

BABA ENTERPRISES INC (DE)
Name changed to Steiner Optics International, Inc. 04/26/1989
(See Steiner Optics International, Inc.)

BABBAGES INC (TX)
Merged into NeoStar Retail Group, Inc. 12/19/1994
Each share Common 10¢ par

exchanged for (1.3) shares Common 1¢ par
(See NeoStar Retail Group, Inc.)

BABBIT B T INC (NY)
Name changed to B.T.B. Corp. 12/05/1969
B.T.B. Corp. name changed to International Banknote Co., Inc. 01/02/1973 which merged into United States Banknote Corp. (NY) 07/25/1990 which reincorporated in Delaware 09/21/1993 which namechanged to American Banknote Corp. 07/03/1995

BABCOCK & BROWN AIR LTD (BERMUDA)
Name changed to Fly Leasing Ltd. 06/30/2010

BABCOCK & BROWN LTD (AUSTRALIA)
Placed in liquidation 06/11/2009
No stockholders' equity

BABCOCK & WILCOX CO (DE)
Each share Common 1¢ par received distribution of (0.5) share Babcock & Wilcox Enterprises, Inc. Common 1¢ par payable 06/30/2015 to holders of record 06/18/2015 Ex date - 07/01/2015
Name changed to BWX Technologies, Inc. 07/01/2015

BABCOCK & WILCOX CO (NJ)
Capital Stock $100 par changed to Capital Stock no par 00/00/1934
Each share old Capital Stock no par exchanged for (3) shares new Capital Stock no par 00/00/1938
New Capital Stock no par changed to $9 par and (2) additional shares issued 04/30/1956
Capital Stock $9 par changed to $4.50 par and (1) additional share issued 05/22/1964
Capital Stock $4.50 par reclassified as Common $4.50 par 04/24/1968
Stock Dividend - 100% 11/27/1950
Merged into McDermott (J. Ray) & Co., Inc. 03/31/1978
Each share Common $4.50 par exchanged for (1) share $2.20 Conv. Preferred Ser. A $1 par and (1) share $2.60 Preferred Ser. B $1 par
McDermott (J. Ray) & Co., Inc. name changed to McDermott Inc. 08/15/1980 which merged into McDermott International, Inc. 03/15/1983

BABCOCK ELECTRONICS CORP. (CA)
Completely liquidated 07/19/1968
Each share Capital Stock $1 par exchanged for first and final distribution of (0.57) share Esterline Corp. Common 20¢ par
Esterline Corp. name changed to Esterline Technologies Corp. 03/07/1991

BABCOCK INDS INC (NY)
Merged into Robins (A.H.) Co. Inc. 12/29/1977
Each share Common $1 par exchanged for $6 cash

BABCOCK RADIO ENGINEERING, INC. (CA)
Capital Stock $1 par split (4) for (3) by issuance of (0.33333333) additional share 07/05/1960
Name changed to Babcock Electronics Corp. 10/10/1960
Babcock Electronics Corp. liquidated for Esterline Corp. 07/19/1968 which name changed to Esterline Technologies Corp. 03/07/1991

BABINE INTL RES LTD (BC)
Merged into Seneca Developments Ltd. 12/08/1972
Each share Capital Stock 50¢ par exchanged for (0.166666) share Common no par
Senaca Developments Ltd. recapitalized as Award Resources Ltd. 02/08/1982 which recapitalized as Tomco Developments Inc. 06/16/1990

BABSON CAP CORPORATE INVS (MA)
Name changed to Barings Corporate Investors 09/12/2016

BABSON CAP GLOBAL SHORT DURATION HIGH YIELD FD (MA)
Name changed to Barings Global Short Duration High Yield Fund 09/12/2016

BABSON CAP PARTN INVS TR (MA)
Name changed to Barings Participation Investors 09/12/2016

BABSON D L BD TR (MO)
Merged into RBC Funds, Inc. 04/16/2004
Details not available

BABSON D L INCOME TR (MO)
Name changed to Babson (D.L.) Bond Trust 02/14/1984
(See Babson (D.L.) Bond Trust)

BABSON D L MONEY MKT FD INC (MD)
Merged into Great Hall Investment Funds, Inc. 04/16/2004
Details not available

BABSON D L TAX FREE INCOME FD INC (MD)
Merged into Tamarack Funds Trust 04/16/2004
Details not available

BABSON DAVID L GROWTH FD INC (MD)
Reincorporated 00/00/1978
State of incorporation changed from (DE) to (MD) 00/00/1978
Merged into RBC Funds, Inc. 04/16/2004
Details not available

BABSON DAVID L INVT FD INC (DE)
Name changed to Babson (David L.) Growth Fund, Inc. (DE) 10/03/1983
Babson (David L.) Growth Fund, Inc. (DE) reincorporated in Maryland 00/00/1978
(See Babson (David L.) Growth Fund, Inc.)

BABSON ENTERPRISE FD INC (MD)
Merged into Tamarack Funds Trust 04/16/2004
Details not available

BABSON-STEWART IVORY INTL FD INC (MD)
Completely liquidated 03/31/2004
Each share Common $1 par received net asset value

BABSON VALUE FD INC (MD)
Merged into Tamarack Funds Trust 04/16/2004
Details not available

BABY ALL CORP (DE)
Common $0.0001 par split (12) for (5) by issuance of (1.4) additional shares payable 04/03/2012 to holders of record 04/03/2012
Name changed to Santa Fe Petroleum, Inc. 09/20/2012

BABY BEE BRIGHT CORP NEW (NV)
Each share Common $0.001 par exchanged for (0.06666666) share old Common $0.0001 par 05/25/2006
Each share old Common $0.0001 par exchanged for (0.005) share new Common $0.0001 par 02/15/2008
Each share new Common $0.0001 par exchanged again for (0.005) share new Common $0.0001 par 03/01/2011
Stock Dividend - 5% payable 04/16/2007 to holders of record 03/30/2007
Name changed to Fusion Pharm, Inc. 04/08/2011

BABY BEE BRIGHT CORP OLD (NV)
Name changed to Lab Holdings, Inc. 05/02/2006
Lab Holdings, Inc. name changed to Mountain Top Properties, Inc. 12/13/2006

BABY FOX INTL INC (NV)
Name changed to Wonhe High-Tech International, Inc. 05/02/2012

BABY SUPERSTORE INC (SC)
Common no par split (3) for (2) by issuance of (0.5) additional share 02/22/1995
Merged into Toys R Us, Inc. 02/03/1997
Each share Common no par exchanged for (0.8121) share Common 10¢ par
(See Toys R Us, Inc.)

BABYDOT CO (NV)
Name changed to Capital City Energy Group, Inc. 01/31/2008

BABYKINS INTL INC (BC)
Name changed 10/10/1990
Name changed from Babykins Products Canada Ltd. to Babykins International Inc. 10/10/1990
Company dissolved 05/00/1993
No stockholders' equity

BABYLAND INDS INC (BC)
Struck from the register and dissolved 03/31/1995

BABYSTAR INC (DE)
Name changed to Datatrend Services Inc. 11/27/1995
(See Datatrend Services Inc.)

BABYUNIVERSE INC (FL)
Reincorporated under the laws of Colorado as Parent Co. 01/08/2008
(See Parent Co.)

BAC CAP TR I (DE)
7% Capital Securities called for redemption at $25 plus $0.243056 accrued dividends on 11/05/2012

BAC CAP TR II (DE)
7% Capital Securities called for redemption at $25 plus $0.019444 accrued dividends on 11/05/2012

BAC CAP TR III (DE)
7% Capital Securities called for redemption at $25 plus $0.388889 accrued dividends on 11/05/2012

BAC CAP TR IV (DE)
5.875% Capital Securities called for redemption at $25 plus $0.016319 accrued dividends on 11/05/2012

BAC CAP TR V (DE)
6% Capital Securities called for redemption at $25 plus $0.008333 accrued dividends on 11/05/2012

BAC CAP TR VIII (DE)
6% Capital Securities called for redemption at $25 plus $0.333333 accrued dividends on 08/15/2016

BAC CAP TR X (DE)
6.25% Capital Securities called for redemption at $25 plus $0.112847 accrued dividends on 07/25/2012

BAC CAP TR XII (DE)
6.875% Capital Securities called for redemption at $25 plus $0.014323 accrued dividends on 11/05/2012

BAC DEV CORP (DE)
Reincorporated 12/31/1970
State of incorporation changed from (NY) to (DE) 12/31/1970
Completely liquidated 06/19/1972
Each share Common 1¢ par exchanged for first and final distribution of (0.2) share Preferred Ser. A $1 par and (1) share Common $1 par of First Realty Investment Corp. (DE) First Realty Investment Corp. (DE) name changed to Thor Corp. (DE) 06/08/1976 which name changed to Thor Energy Resources, Inc. 07/31/1981
(See Thor Energy Resources Inc.)

BACA RES LTD (AB)
Name changed to CORDEX Petroleums Ltd. 07/11/1994
(See CORDEX Petroleums Ltd.)

BACANORA MINERALS LTD (AB)
Reorganized under the laws of the United Kingdom as Bacanora Lithium PLC 03/26/2018
Each share Common no par exchanged for (1) share Ordinary £0.10 par

BACARDI CORP (DE)
Common $10 par split (3) for (2) by issuance of (0.5) additional share 04/25/1972
Stock Dividends - 25% 04/16/1965; 33.33333333% 04/18/1967; 33.33333333% 04/21/1969
Recapitalized 11/07/1980
For holdings owned by U.S. citizens or permanent residents: Common $10 par reclassified as Class A Common $10 par
For holdings owned by Non-U.S. citizens or permanent residents: Each share Common $10 par exchanged for (1) share Class B Common $10 par
Class A Common $10 par changed to $2 par and (4) additional shares issued 07/01/1981
Class B Common $10 par changed to $2 par and (4) additional shares issued 07/01/1981
Each share Class A Common $2 par exchanged for (0.001) share Class A Common $1,000 par 05/14/1987
Each share Class B Common $2 par exchanged for (0.001) share Class B Common $1,000 par 05/14/1987
Public interest eliminated

BACCARAT CAP CORP (DE)
Reorganized under the laws of Nevada as Visitel Network, Inc. 05/23/1990
Each share Common $0.001 par exchanged for (0.5) share Common $0.002 par
Visitel Network, Inc. recapitalized as PRG Group, Inc. 08/11/2006
(See PRG Group, Inc.)

BACH-HAUSER INC (NV)
Old Common $0.001 par split (2) for (1) by issuance of (1) additional share payable 04/24/2000 to holders of record 04/24/2000 Ex date - 05/01/2000
Each share old Common $0.001 par exchanged for (0.1) share new Common $0.001 par 06/06/2001
Each share new Common $0.001 par exchanged again for (0.16666666) share new Common $0.001 par 09/15/2004
Name changed to Financial Access Solutions Technology, Inc. 02/11/2005
Financial Access Solutions Technology, Inc. name changed to ABV Gold, Inc. 01/22/2007 which recapitalized as PharmaCom BioVet Inc. 09/10/2008

BACHARACH INDUSTRIAL INSTRUMENT CO. (PA)
Stock Dividend - 100% 09/30/1965
Merged into American Bosch Arma Corp. 12/30/1966
Each share Common $1 par exchanged for $25 cash
American Bosch Arma Corp. merged into United Technologies Corp. 07/14/1978

BACHE & CO INC (DE)
Under plan of reorganization each share Common $2 par automatically became (1) share Bache Group Inc. Common $2 par 02/01/1975
(See Bache Group Inc.)

BACHE GROUP INC (DE)
Stock Dividend - 10% 10/17/1980
Acquired by Prudential Insurance Co. of America 06/12/1981
Each share Common $2 par exchanged for $32 cash

BACHE HUNTOON PAIGE GINNY MAE TR (NY)
Name changed to Bache Ginny Mae Trust, Series 1 on 09/11/1979

BACHELOR LAKE GOLD MINES INC (QC)
Merged into Espalau Mining Corp. 05/02/1994
Each share Common no par exchanged for (0.06666666) share Common no par
Espalau Mining Corp. name changed to CED-Or Corp. 12/15/1998

BACHELOR LAKE GOLD MINES LTD. (ON)
Charter surrendered 11/28/1969
No stockholders' equity

BACHMAN INFORMATION SYS INC (MA)
Name changed to Cayenne Software, Inc. 07/19/1996
(See Cayenne Software, Inc.)

BACHMAN UXBRIDGE WORSTED CORP. (DE)
Merged into Amerace Corp. 05/29/1957
Each share Common $1 par exchanged for (0.11111111) share Common $12.50 par
Amerace Corp. name changed to Amerace Esna Corp. 08/30/1968 which name changed back to Amerace Corp. 04/27/1973
(See Amerace Corp.)

BACHMANN, EMMERICH & CO., INC.
Acquired by Commercial Investment Trust Corp. 00/00/1937
Details not available

BACK & NECK MGMT CORP (DE)
Each share old Common $0.001 par exchanged for (0.05) share new Common $0.001 par 11/28/1997
Recapitalized as NNZ America Inc. 06/18/1998
Each share new Common $0.001 par exchanged for (0.05) share Common $0.001 par
NNZ America Inc. name changed to GTrade.Network, Inc. 04/20/1999 which name changed to VS2, Inc. 01/12/2001 which recapitalized as EuroWork Global, Ltd. 11/08/2004 which name changed to Quintessence Holdings, Inc. 07/25/2007 which name changed to Terminus Energy, Inc. 12/04/2009

BACK BAY REALTY ASSOCIATES
Property foreclosed 00/00/1942
Details not available

BACK BAY RESTAURANT GROUP INC (DE)
Merged into SRC Holdings, Inc. 04/05/1999
Each share Common 1¢ par exchanged for $10.25 cash

BACK YD BURGERS INC (DE)
Merged into BBAC LLC 11/05/2007
Each share Common 1¢ par exchanged for $6.50 cash

BACKER PETE CORP (BC)
Acquired by Allied Oil & Gas Corp. 09/01/2000
Each share Common no par exchanged for $1.75 cash

BACKER RES LTD (BC)
Common no par split (2) for (1) by issuance of (1) additional share 11/20/1982
Common no par reclassified as Class A Common no par 05/18/1984
Merged into Backer Petroleum Corp. 12/30/1988
Each share 10% Conv. Preferred Class B $5 par exchanged for (1)

share 10% Conv. Preferred Class B $5 par
Each share Class A Common no par exchanged for (1) share Class A Common no par
(See Backer Petroleum Corp.)

BACKSTAY WELT CO (IN)
Each share Common no par exchanged for (3) shares Class A Common no par and (1) share Class B Common no par 12/11/1961
Acquired by Essex International, Inc. 12/29/1969
Each share Class A Common no par or Class B Common no par exchanged for (0.25) share $2.84 Conv. Preferred Ser. A $1 par and (0.2375) share Common $1 par
Essex International, Inc. merged into United Aircraft Corp. 02/05/1974 which name changed to United Technologies Corp. 04/30/1975

BACM INDS LTD (MB)
Through exchange offer over 99% acquired by Genstar Ltd. as of 02/12/1972
Public interest eliminated

BACNOTAN CONS INDS INC (PHILIPPINES)
Stock Dividends - 20% payable 09/06/2006 to holders of record 08/11/2006; 15% payable 06/30/2007 to holders of record 06/15/2007; 10% payable 07/08/2008 to holders of record 06/13/2008
Name changed to Phinma Corp. 05/27/2010

BACOLA MINING EXPLORATIONS LTD. (ON)
Declared dissolved 11/27/1961
No stockholders' equity

BACOU USA INC (DE)
Merged into Christian Dalloz S.A. 09/06/2001
Each share Common $0.001 par exchanged for $28.50 cash

BACTECH ENVIROMET CORP (CANADA)
Name changed to BacTech Mining Corp. 01/22/2004
BacTech Mining Corp. name changed to REBgold Corp. 12/02/2010 which merged into Aquila Resources Inc. 01/22/2014

BACTECH METALLURGICAL SOLUTIONS LTD (CANADA)
Name changed to BacTech Enviromet Corp. 04/07/2000
BacTech Enviromet Corp. name changed to BacTech Mining Corp. 01/22/2004 which name changed to REBgold Corp. 12/02/2010 which merged into Aquila Resources Inc. 01/22/2014

BACTECH MINING CORP (CANADA)
Name changed to REBgold Corp. 12/02/2010
REBgold Corp. merged into Aquila Resources Inc. 01/22/2014

BACTERIN INTL HLDGS INC (DE)
Each share old Common $0.000001 par exchanged for (0.1) share new Common $0.000001 par 07/28/2014
Name changed to Xtant Medical Holdings, Inc. 08/05/2015

BACTOLAC PHARMACEUTICAL INC (TX)
Each share old Common 1¢ par exchanged for (0.002) share new Common 1¢ par 04/28/2008
Note: In effect holders received $4 cash per share and public interest was eliminated

BACTROL TECHNOLOGIES INC (NY)
Each share old Common $0.0001 par exchanged for (0.05) share new Common $0.0001 par 10/08/1999

Name changed to Military Resale Group, Inc. 01/02/2002
(See Military Resale Group, Inc.)

BAD AXE DRIVING PARK ASSOCIATION (MI)
Name changed to Bad Axe Fair 05/20/1922
(See Bad Axe Fair)

BAD AXE FAIR (MI)
Charter expired by time limitation 02/28/1936

BAD BOY APPLIANCES & FURNITURE LTD (ON)
Common no par split (2) for (1) by issuance of (1) additional share 08/30/1973
Filed voluntary assignment in bankruptcy 08/18/1977
No stockholders' equity

BAD TOYS HLDGS INC (NV)
Each share Common 1¢ par received distribution of (0.9825) share Southland Health Services, Inc. Common $0.001 par payable 02/01/2007 to holders of record 01/31/2007 Ex date - 02/02/2007
Reincorporated under the laws of Florida as Paladin Holdings, Inc. 08/17/2007
(See Paladin Holdings, Inc.)

BAD TOYS INC (NV)
Name changed to Bad Toys Holdings, Inc. (NV) 09/03/2004
Each share Common 1¢ par exchanged for (1) share Common 1¢ par
Bad Toys Holdings, Inc. (NV) reincorporated in Florida as Paladin Holdings, Inc. 08/17/2007
(See Paladin Holdings, Inc.)

BAD TOYS INC (OH)
Reincorporated under the laws of Nevada as MYCOM Group, Inc. 08/23/2000
MYCOMM Group, Inc. name changed to SARS Corp. 10/08/2007
(See SARS Corp.)

BADEN BK (ST. LOUIS, MO)
Each share Capital Stock $100 par exchanged for (5) shares Captial Stock $20 par 04/05/1945
Stock Dividend - 40% 04/25/1956
Merged into General Bank (St. Louis, MO) 07/09/1984
Details not available

BADEN EXPLS LTD (BC)
Reorganized under the laws of Canada as Reymont Gold Mines Ltd. 08/09/1988
Each share Common no par exchanged for (0.1) share Common no par
Reymont Gold Mines Ltd. recapitalized as Pallaum Minerals Ltd. 11/20/1991
(See Pallaum Minerals Ltd.)

BADEN GOLD MINES LTD. (ON)
Declared dissolved 10/22/1962
No stockholders' equity

BADEN TECHNOLOGIES INC (AB)
Name changed to FSI Energy Services Inc. 07/23/2010
FSI Energy Services Inc. name changed to FSI Energy Group Inc. 06/08/2012

BADGER DAYLIGHTING INC (AB)
Recapitalized as Badger Income Fund 04/01/2004
Each share Common no par exchanged for (0.5) Trust Unit
Badger Income Fund reorganized as Badger Daylighting Ltd. 01/10/2011

BADGER INCOME FD (AB)
Reorganized as Badger Daylighting Ltd. 01/10/2011
Each Trust Unit exchanged for (1) share Common no par
Note: Unexchanged certificates were cancelled and became without value 01/10/2016

BADGER METER MFG CO (WI)
Each share old Common $5 par exchanged for (3) shares Common $10 par 00/00/1946
Each share Common $10 par exchanged for (5) shares new Common $5 par 05/04/1964
New Common $5 par changed to $1 par and (2) additional shares issued 08/30/1968
Name changed to Badger Meter, Inc. 04/13/1971

BADGER NORTHLAND, INC. (WI)
Name changed to BN Liquidating Co., Inc. 06/02/1965
BN Liquidating Co., Inc. acquired by Massey-Ferguson Ltd. 06/07/1965 which name changed to Varity Corp. (Canada) 06/19/1986 which reorganized in Delaware 08/01/1991 which merged into LucasVarity PLC 09/06/1996
(See LucasVarity PLC)

BADGER PAINT & HARDWARE STORES, INC. (WI)
Acquired by Household Finance Corp. 06/24/1963
Each share Common $10 par exchanged for (1.08) shares Common no par and (0.1449) share 4.4% Preferred $100 par
Household Finance Corp. reorganized as Household International, Inc. 06/26/1981
(See Household International, Inc.)

BADGER PAPER MLS INC (WI)
Common no par split (4) for (1) by issuance of (3) additional shares 10/22/1985
Stock Dividends - 300% 11/01/1963; 100% 10/19/1988
Assets sold for the benefit of creditors 11/14/2005
Stockholders' equity unlikely

BADGER STATE CASH CREDIT CORP.
Merged into Franklin Plan Corp. 00/00/1932
Details not available

BADISCHE ANILIN & SODA FABRIK AG (GERMANY)
Name changed to BASF A.G. 06/20/1973
BASF A.G. name changed to BASF SE 01/14/2008

BAE SYS CDA INC (CANADA)
Merged into Oncap L.P. 04/11/2001
Each share Common no par exchanged for $25.25 cash

BAFFINLAND IRON MINES CORP (ON)
Acquired by ArcelorMittal S.A. 03/25/2011
Each share Common no par exchanged for $1.50 cash

BAGAMAC MINES LTD. (ON)
Recapitalized as Tribag Mining Co. Ltd. 09/27/1956
Each share Capital Stock $1 par exchanged for (0.2) share Capital Stock $1 par
Tribag Mining Co. Ltd. recapitalized as Great Northern Financial Corp. 08/01/1975 which reorganized as Embassy Resources Ltd. 08/12/1983 which merged into Unicorp Canada Corp. 03/02/1984 which recapitalized as Unicorp Energy Corp. 06/25/1991 which name changed to Unicorp Inc. 05/28/1999 which name changed to Wilmington Capital Management Inc. 03/08/2002

BAGAMAC ROUYN MINES LTD.
Recapitalized as Bagamac Mines Ltd. 00/00/1937
Each share Capital Stock $1 par exchanged for (0.25) share Capital Stock $1 par
Bagamac Mines Ltd. recapitalized as Tribag Mining Co. Ltd. 09/27/1956 which recapitalized as Great Northern Financial Corp. 08/01/1975 which reorganized as Embassy Resources Ltd. 08/12/1983 which merged into Unicorp Canada Corp. 03/02/1984 which recapitalized as Unicorp Energy Corp. 06/25/1991 which name changed to Unicorp Inc. 05/28/1999 which name changed to Wilmington Capital Management Inc. 03/08/2002

BAGDAD CHASE CONSOLIDATED MINES CO. (NV)
Name changed to Roosevelt Mines, Inc. 06/14/1929
Roosevelt Mines, Inc. name changed to Bagdad Chase Mining Co. 02/23/1949 which recapitalized as Bagdad Chase, Inc. 05/04/1968
(See Bagdad Chase, Inc.)

BAGDAD CHASE MINING CO. (NV)
Recapitalized as Bagdad Chase, Inc. 05/04/1968
Each share Common $1 par exchanged for (0.25) share Common $1 par
(See Bagdad Chase, Inc.)

BAGDAD COPPER CORP (AZ)
Reincorporated 04/19/1967
Each share Capital Stock $1 par exchanged for (0.2) share Capital Stock $5 par 00/00/1935
State of incorporation changed from (DE) to (AZ) 04/19/1967
Capital Stock $5 par changed to $2.50 par and (1) additional share issued 04/28/1967
Merged into Cyprus Mines Corp. 06/08/1973
Each share Capital Stock $2.50 par exchanged for (1.2) shares Common $4 par
Cyprus Mines Corp. merged into Standard Oil Co. (IN) 09/21/1979 which name changed to Amoco Corp. 04/23/1985 which merged into BP Amoco PLC 12/31/1998 which name changed to BP PLC 05/01/2001

BAGDAD LAND & LUMBER CO.
Dissolved 00/00/1939
Details not available

BAGEL MASTER INC (MD)
Acquired by JCC Acquisition Corp. 01/09/1990
Details not available

BAGELS U S A INC (FL)
Charter cancelled for non-payment of taxes 06/28/1971

BAGGS URANIUM CORP. (UT)
Merged into Sun Tide Corp. 11/15/1957
Each share Capital Stock 1¢ par exchanged for (0.4) share Capital Stock 10¢ par
Sun Tide Corp. name changed to Maxa Corp. 04/13/1974
(See Maxa Corp.)

BAGHDAD-LARDER MINES LTD. (ON)
Charter cancelled and company declared dissolved for default in filing returns 08/03/1964

BAGLEY BUILDING CO., A LIMITED PARTNERSHIP (MI)
Charter declared inoperative and void for failure to file reports 12/29/1988

BAGLEY BUILDING CORP. (MI)
Capital Stock no par changed to $4 par 00/00/1946
Completely liquidated 05/18/1977
Each share Capital Stock $4 par exchanged for first and final distribution of (1) Unit of Interest of Bagley Building Co., A Limited Partnership and $15 cash

(See Bagley Building Co., A Limited Partnership)

BAGLEY-CLIFFORD CORP.
Reorganized as Bagley Building Corp. 00/00/1937
Each share Preferred exchanged for (2) shares Common no par
(See Bagley Building Corp.)

BAGLEY CORP (UT)
Each share Common $0.025 par exchanged for (0.1) share Common 25¢ par 01/01/1983
Proclaimed dissolved for failure to pay taxes 09/30/1986

BAGPRINT LTD (NY)
Acquired by R&H Paper Co., Inc. 07/29/1985
Each share Common 1¢ par exchanged for $1 cash

BAGUIO GOLD HOLDINGS CORP (PHILIPPINES)
Name changed to PAL Holdings, Inc. 01/19/2007

BAGUIO GOLD MNG INC (PHILIPPINES)
Capital Stock P0.01 par reclassified as Class A P0.01 par and Class B P0.01 par 07/23/1976
Note: 60% Class A can be owned by Philippine Nationals only; 40% Class B can be owned by both Philippine Nationals and foreign nationals
Name changed to Baguio Gold Holdings Corp. 09/23/1996
Baguio Gold Holdings Corp. name changed to PAL Holdings, Inc. 01/19/2007

BAHA RES LTD (BC)
Struck off register and declared dissolved for failure to file returns 04/16/1993

BAHAMA RES LTD (BC)
Name changed to American Lightwave Corp. 02/03/1987
(See American Lightwave Corp.)

BAHAMA TERRACE DEVELOPMENT CO. LTD. (BAHAMAS)
Liquidated and subsequently struck off register 02/10/1967

BAHAMAS CARIBBEAN DEV LTD (ON)
Recapitalized as Oceanus Industries (Bahamas) Ltd. 03/24/1972
Each share Common no par exchanged for (0.05) share Common no par
(See Oceanus Industries (Bahamas) Ltd.)

BAHAMAS HELICOPTERS LTD. (BAHAMAS)
Name changed to World Wide Helicopters, Ltd. 07/27/1957
(See World Wide Helicopters, Ltd.)

BAHAMAS PETE CO PLC (ISLE OF MAN)
ADR agreement terminated 06/09/2017
Each Sponsored ADR for Ordinary exchanged for $0.505645 cash

BAHIA SUL CELULOSE S A (BRAZIL)
ADR agreement terminated 12/30/2002
Each Sponsored ADR for Preferred Ser. A exchanged for $2.762514 cash

BAHN FOODS INC (BC)
Recapitalized as Consolidated Bahn Foods Inc. 10/21/1996
Each share Common no par exchanged for (0.1) share Common no par
(See Consolidated Bahn Foods Inc.)

BAHUI USA INC (WA)
Name changed to A G Holdings, Inc. 04/06/1998
A G Holdings, Inc. name changed to Wasatch Interactive Learning Corp.

01/20/2000 which merged into Plato Learning, Inc. 04/05/2001
(See Plato Learning, Inc.)

BAIDU COM INC (CAYMAN ISLANDS)
Name changed to Baidu, Inc. 12/16/2008

BAIFIELD INDUSTRIES, INC. (DE)
Completely liquidated 07/12/1967
Each share Common 10¢ par exchanged for first and final distribution of (1.25) shares Automatic Sprinkler Corp. of America (OH) Common 10¢ par
Automatic Sprinkler Corp. of America (OH) name changed to A-T-O Inc. 10/29/1969 which name changed to Figgie International Inc. (OH) 06/01/1981 which reorganized in Delaware as Figgie International Holdings Inc. 07/18/1983 which name changed to Figgie International Inc. 12/31/1986 which name changed to Scott Technologies, Inc. 05/20/1998 which merged into Tyco International Ltd. (Bermuda) 05/03/2001 which reincorporated in Switzerland 03/17/2009 which merged into Johnson Controls International PLC 09/06/2016

BAIKAL FST CORP (BC)
Acquired by Far East Forest Industry Inc. 07/11/2014
Each share Common no par exchanged for $0.40 cash
Note: Unexchanged certificates were cancelled and became without value 07/11/2016

BAILEY & BARON INC (FL)
Name changed to Star Services Group, Inc. 06/23/1999
(See Star Services Group, Inc.)

BAILEY CORP (DE)
Each share Common $0.0001 par exchanged for (0.03076923) share Common 10¢ par 12/03/1986
Merged into Vemco Acquisition Corp. 08/29/1996
Each share Common 10¢ par exchanged for $8.75 cash

BAILEY FINL CORP (SC)
Merged into Anchor Financial Corp. 04/09/1999
Each share Common no par exchanged for (16.32) shares Common no par
Anchor Financial Corp. merged into South Financial Group, Inc. 06/07/2000 which merged into Toronto-Dominion Bank (Toronto, ON) 09/30/2010

BAILEY SELBURN OIL & GAS LTD (CANADA)
5% Preferred 1st Ser. $25 par called for redemption 05/03/1965
5.75% Preferred 2nd Ser. $25 par called for redemption 05/03/1965
Class A $1 par reclassified as Common $1 par 06/30/1969
Acquired by Pacific Petroleums Ltd. 10/07/1977
Each share Common $1 par exchanged for $17 cash

BAILLARGEON (J.B.) EXPRESS, LTD. (CANADA)
Name changed to Gestion Albanel Inc. 10/15/1979
(See Gestion Albanel Inc.)

BAIRD & WARNER MTG & RLTY INVS (IL)
Name changed to Bayswater Realty & Investment Trust (IL) 05/31/1979
Bayswater Realty & Investment Trust (IL) reorganized in Delaware as Bayswater Realty & Capital Corp. 07/02/1981
(See Bayswater Realty & Capital Corp.)

BAIRD ASSOCIATES-ATOMIC INSTRUMENT CO. (MA)
Name changed to Baird-Atomic, Inc. 12/04/1956
Baird-Atomic, Inc. name changed to Baird Corp. 02/28/1978
(See Baird Corp.)

BAIRD ATOMIC INC (MA)
Common $1 par split (2) for (1) by issuance of (1) additional share 06/29/1959
Name changed to Baird Corp. 02/28/1978
(See Baird Corp.)

BAIRD CASE FUNERAL HOMES INC (FL)
Under plan of merger each share Common 10¢ par exchanged for $12 cash 03/31/1981

BAIRD CORP (MA)
Merged into Imo Delaval Inc. 11/06/1987
Each share Common $1 par exchanged for $22 cash

BAIRD TELEVISION, LTD. (ENGLAND)
Completely liquidated 06/08/1964
Each American Unit Ser. A exchanged for first and final distribution of $1.7908 cash

BAIRNCO CORP (DE)
Reincorporated 05/01/1991
Common 5¢ par split (3) for (2) by issuance of (0.5) additional share 06/29/1984
State of incorporation changed from (NY) to (DE) 05/01/1991
Merged into Steel Partners II, L.P. 04/24/2007
Each share Common 5¢ par exchanged for $13.50 cash

BAITEX MED TECHNOLOGIES INC (ON)
Recapitalized as Stockguard Corp. 03/11/1992
Each share Common no par exchanged for (0.1) share Common no par
(See Stockguard Corp.)

BAIXO RELOCATION SVCS INC (NV)
Name changed to Gripevine Inc. 01/05/2017

BAJA GOLD INC (BC)
Merged into Viceroy Resource Corp. 05/30/1996
Each share Common no par exchanged for (0.297) share Common no par
Viceroy Resource Corp. merged into Quest Capital Corp. (BC) 06/30/2003 which reincorporated in Canada 05/27/2008 which name changed to Sprott Resource Lending Corp. 09/10/2010 which merged into Sprott Inc. 07/24/2013

BAJA MNG CORP (BC)
Recapitalized as Camrova Resources Inc. 10/17/2016
Each share Common no par exchanged for (0.05) share Common no par

BAJA PACIFIC INTERNATIONAL, INC. (UT)
Name changed to Taig Ventures, Inc. 10/07/1998
Taig Ventures, Inc. recapitalized as Viper Networks, Inc. (UT) 01/11/2001 which reincorporated in Nevada 05/18/2005

BAJAJ AUTO LTD NEW (INDIA)
GDR agreement terminated 02/01/2017
Each Reg. S Sponsored GDR for Equity Shares exchanged for (1) Equity Share

BAJAJ FINSERV LTD (INDIA)
GDR agreement terminated 02/01/2017
Each Reg. S Sponsored GDR for Equity Shares exchanged for (1) Equity Share

BAJAJ HINDUSTAN LTD (INDIA)
GDR agreement terminated 09/18/2014
Each Sponsored 144A GDR for Ordinary exchanged for (1) share Ordinary
Each Sponsored Reg. S GDR for Ordinary exchanged for (1) share Ordinary
Note: Unexchanged GDR's will be sold and the proceeds, if any, held for claim after 03/23/2015

BAJAJ HLDGS & INVT LTD (INDIA)
Name changed 03/31/2008
144A GDR's for Ordinary split (3) for (2) by issuance of (0.5) additional GDR payable 12/22/1997 to holders of record 10/09/1997
Name changed from Bajaj Auto Ltd. (Old) to Bajaj Holdings & Investment Ltd. 03/31/2008
Each Sponsored Reg. S GDR for Ordinary received (1) Bajaj Auto Ltd. (New) Sponsored GDR for Ordinary and (1) Bajaj Finserv Ltd. Sponsored GDR for Ordinary payable 08/21/2008 to holders of record 03/25/2008
GDR agreement terminated 11/21/2008
Each 144A GDR for Ordinary exchanged for approximately $15.787 cash
GDR agreement terminated 03/20/2017
Each Sponsored Reg. S GDR for Ordinary exchanged for $18.377846 cash

BAKBONE SOFTWARE INC (CANADA)
Reincorporated 08/11/2003
Place of incorporation changed from (AB) to (Canada) 08/11/2003
Acquired by Quest Software, Inc. 01/14/2011
Each share Common no par exchanged for USD$0.33 cash
Note: Unexchanged certificates were cancelled and became without value 01/14/2017

BAKCO ACCEP INC (GA)
Name changed to Perry & Co. 04/12/1982

BAKELITE CORP.
Acquired by Union Carbide & Carbon Corp. 00/00/1939
Details not available

BAKER (B.J.) & CO., INC.
Liquidation completed 00/00/1950
Details not available

BAKER (WALTER) & CO., LTD.
Acquired by Postum Co., Inc. 00/00/1927
Details not available

BAKER-BOYER NATIONAL BANK (WALLA WALLA, WA)
Name changed to Baker Boyer Bancorp 11/26/1986

BAKER BROS INC (DE)
Dissolved 11/15/1979
Details not available

BAKER BROS INC (FL)
Stock Dividend - 100% 05/17/1972
Merged into Roth-Baker Corp. 05/31/1982
Each share Common 10¢ par exchanged for $10.50 cash

BAKER BROTHERS INC. (CA)
Reincorporated under the laws of Delaware and Capital Stock $1 par reclassified as Common 50¢ par 06/25/1970
(See Baker Brothers Inc. (DE))

BAKER CO.
Reorganized as Baker Hotel of Dallas, Inc. 00/00/1935
Details not available

BAKER COMMUNICATIONS INC (CA)
Recapitalized as China Adnet Enterprises, Inc. 04/05/2006
Each share Common no par exchanged for (0.00526315) share Common no par
(See China Adnet Enterprises, Inc.)

BAKER (MORRIS T.) CO.
Merged into Baker Properties, Inc. (MN) 00/00/1938
Details not available

BAKER CORP.
Dissolved 00/00/1936
Details not available

BAKER ENGINEERING CORP. (MN)
Through voluntary exchange offer majority acquired by Magna-Tek, Inc. as of 12/01/1961
Note: Unexchanged shares became valueless due to the failure of Baker Engineering Corp. 00/00/1962

BAKER EVANS ICE CREAM
Acquired by National Dairy Products Corp. 00/00/1928
Details not available

BAKER FENTRESS & CO (DE)
Old Common $1 par split (3) for (1) by issuance of (2) additional shares 05/04/1983
Old Common $1 par split (2) for (1) by issuance of (1) additional share 07/26/1988
Each share old Common $1 par received distribution of (0.1281098) share Consolidated-Tomoka Land Co. Common $1 par payable 09/24/1999 to holders of record 08/30/1999 Ex date - 09/27/1999
Each share old Common $1 par exchanged for (1/6) share new Common $1 par 01/10/2000
Name changed to BKF Capital Group, Inc. 04/19/2000

BAKER GOLD LTD (BC)
Merged into U.S. Precious Metals, Inc. 03/20/1985
Each share Common no par exchanged for (1) share Common no par
U.S. Precious Metals, Inc. merged into Siskon Gold Corp. 08/23/1991
(See Siskon Gold Corp.)

BAKER HOTEL DALLAS INC (TX)
Common no par changed to $1 par 00/00/1949
Voluntarily dissolved 04/18/1977
Details not available

BAKER HUGHES INC (DE)
$3.50 Conv. Exchangeable Preferred $1 par called for redemption 08/31/1990
Preferred Stock Purchase Rights declared for Common stockholders of record 05/06/1988 were redeemed at $0.03 per right 05/24/1996 for holders of record 05/06/1996
Merged into Baker Hughes, a GE company 07/05/2017
Each share Common $1 par exchanged for (1) share Class A Common $0.0001 par

BAKER INDS INC (DE)
Common $1 par split (2) for (1) by issuance of (1) additional share 07/13/1956
Common $1 par split (3) for (2) by issuance of (0.5) additional share 03/15/1968
Common $1 par split (2) for (1) by issuance of (1) additional share 02/11/1969
Stock Dividends - 100% 05/18/1962; 10% 07/30/1962; 50% 07/30/1971
Merged into BWA Corp. 04/03/1978
Each share Common $1 par exchanged for $20 cash

BAKER INTL CORP (DE)
Reincorporated 01/27/1983
Common $1 par split (2) for (1) by issuance of (1) additional share 05/25/1978
Common $1 par split (2) for (1) by issuance of (1) additional share 05/23/1980
State of incorporation changed from (CA) to (DE) 01/27/1983
Merged into Baker Hughes Inc. 04/03/1987
Each share Common $1 par exchanged for (1) share Common $1 par
Baker Hughes Inc. merged into Baker Hughes, a GE company 07/05/2017

BAKER J INC (MA)
Common 50¢ par split (3) for (2) by issuance of (0.5) additional share 04/17/1987
Name changed to Casual Male Corp. 02/26/2001
(See Casual Male Corp.)

BAKER MFG CO (WI)
Preferred $10 par called for redemption 04/01/1964
Each share Common $100 par exchanged for (10) shares Common $10 par 09/22/1964
Stock Dividends - 10% 11/30/1966; 10% 02/01/1968; 10% 02/15/1969; 10% 02/15/1970; 10% 02/15/1971; 10% 02/15/1972; 10% 02/15/1973; 10% 02/15/1974; 10% 02/15/1975; 10% 02/15/1976; 10% 11/01/1976; 10% 02/14/1977; 10% 10/01/1977; 10% 02/15/1978; 10% 02/15/1979; 10% 02/15/1980
Merged into Sears Co. 05/13/2002
Each share Common $10 par exchanged for $96.40 cash

BAKER MICHAEL CORP (PA)
Common $1 par split (2) for (1) by issuance of (1) additional share 06/10/1992
Conv. Class B Common $1 par split (2) for (1) by issuance of (1) additional share 06/10/1992
Each share Conv. Class B Common $1 par automatically became (1) share Common $1 par 12/14/2001
Stock Dividend - 100% 06/08/1987
Acquired by Integrated Mission Solutions, LLC 10/11/2013
Each share Common $1 par exchanged for $40.50 cash

BAKER MICHAEL JR INC (PA)
Name changed to Euthenics Systems Corp. 05/01/1972
Euthenics Systems Corp. name changed to Baker (Michael) Corp. 04/16/1975
(See Baker (Michael) Corp.)

BAKER MINING & MILLING CO. LTD.
Succeeded by Baker Talc Ltd. 00/00/1952
Each share Preferred exchanged for (50) shares new Capital Stock
Each share Common exchanged for (5) shares new Capital Stock
Baker Talc Ltd. name changed to Bakertalc Inc. 09/23/1978 which name changed to Palace Explorations Inc. 12/05/1994 which recapitalized as X-Chequer Resources Inc. 12/02/1996 which recapitalized as International X-Chequer Resources Inc. (QC) 09/29/2004 which reorganized in British Columbia as Passport Metals Inc. 10/18/2007 which name changed to Passport Potash Inc. 11/10/2009

BAKER-MOISE HOISERY MILLS, INC. (TX)
Name changed to Vanette Hoisery Mills 00/00/1937
(See Vanette Hoisery Mills)

BAKER OIL TOOLS INC (CA)
Preferred $1 par called for redemption 11/25/1958
Common $1 par split (2) for (1) by issuance of (1) additional share 02/23/1973
Name changed to Baker International Corp. (CA) 01/28/1976
Baker International Corp. (CA) reincorporated in Delaware 01/27/1983 which merged into Baker Hughes Inc. 04/03/1987 which merged into Baker Hughes, a GE company 07/05/2017

BAKER PERKINS INC (NY)
Common no par changed to $20 par 00/00/1957
Common $20 par changed to $5 par and (1) additional share issued 05/28/1963
Common $5 par changed to $2.50 par and (1) additional share issued 10/15/1969
Merged into Baker Perkins Interim, Inc. 03/09/1977
Each share Common $2.50 par exchanged for $10.35 cash

BAKER PROPERTIES, INC. (DE)
Acquired by Baker Properties, Inc. (MN) 00/00/1938
Details not available

BAKER PROPERTIES, INC. (MN)
Each share Class A Common $1 par or Class B Common $1 par exchanged for (1) share Common $1 par 00/00/1943
Each share Common $1 par exchanged for (3) shares $5 Preferred $1 par 09/20/1955
Completely liquidated 01/15/1968
Each share $5 Preferred $1 par exchanged for first and final distribution of $106.04 cash

BAKER-RAULANG CO. (OH)
Common $100 par changed to no par 00/00/1929
Common no par changed to $1 par 00/00/1943
Stock Dividend - 100% 03/15/1952
Acquired by Otis Elevator Co. 00/00/1954
Each share Common $1 par exchanged for (0.26041666) share Common no par
Otis Elevator Co. merged into United Technologies Corp. 07/08/1976

BAKER STAGE RES INC (NV)
Recapitalized as Summary Corp. 06/21/1995
Each share Common $0.001 par exchanged for (0.05714285) share Common $0.001 par
Summary Corp. name changed to Luma Net Corp. 09/13/1996 which recapitalized as Riviera International Casinos Inc. 08/22/1997 which name changed to International Casino Cruises Inc. 11/21/1997 which name changed to Mountain Energy, Inc. 05/26/1998
(See Mountain Energy, Inc.)

BAKER TALC LTD (QC)
Name changed to Bakertalc Inc. 09/23/1978
Bakertalc Inc. name changed to Palace Explorations Inc. 12/05/1994 which recapitalized as X-Chequer Resources Inc. 12/02/1996 which recapitalized as International X-Chequer Resources Inc. (QC) 09/29/2004 which reorganized in British Columbia as Passport Metals Inc. 10/18/2007 which name changed to Passport Potash Inc. 11/10/2009

BAKER VAWTER CO.
Assets acquired by Remington Rand, Inc. 00/00/1927
Details not available

BAKERS FOOTWEAR GROUP INC (MO)
Chapter 11 bankruptcy proceedings converted to Chapter 7 on 01/18/2013
Stockholders' equity unlikely

BAKERSFIELD HACIENDA INC (CA)
Name changed to Barr Financial Ltd. 06/05/1970
(See Barr Financial Ltd.)

BAKERTALC INC (QC)
Name changed to Palace Explorations Inc. 12/05/1994
Palace Explorations Inc. recapitalized as X-Chequer Resources Inc. 12/02/1996 which recapitalized as International X-Chequer Resources Inc. (QC) 09/29/2004 which reorganized in British Columbia as Passport Metals Inc. 10/18/2007 which name changed to Passport Potash Inc. 11/10/2009

BAKRA RES LTD (BC)
Recapitalized as Northpoint Resources Ltd. 06/14/1994
Each share Common no par exchanged for (0.22222222) share Common no par
Northpoint Resources Ltd. recapitalized as Glacier Resources Ltd. 11/02/1998 which recapitalized as Bayfield Ventures Corp. 05/18/2001 which merged into New Gold Inc. 01/02/2015

BAKRIE MINARAK ENERGY INC (AB)
Name changed to Pertacal Energy Inc. 05/24/2000

BALA CYNWYD CORP (NJ)
SEC revoked common stock registration 12/16/2015

BALA INDUSTRIES, INC. (DE)
Merged into Babbitt (B.T.), Inc. 01/02/1968
Each share Common 10¢ par exchanged for (1.333333) shares Common $1 par
Babbitt (B.T.), Inc. name changed to B.T.B. Corp. 12/05/1969 which name changed to International Banknote Co., Inc. 01/02/1973 which merged into United States Banknote Corp. (NY) 07/25/1990 which reincorporated in Delaware 09/21/1993 which name changed to American Banknote Corp. 07/03/1995
(See American Banknote Corp.)

BALA RLTY INC (DE)
Under plan of merger each share Common 1¢ par exchanged for (0.5) share Sun Real Estate Investment Trust Common 1¢ par 04/05/1994

BALABAN & KATZ CORP. (DE)
Name changed to ABC Great States, Inc. 05/17/1968
(See ABC Great States, Inc.)

BALACLAVA MINES INC (BC)
Name changed 11/08/1996
Name changed from Balaclava Industries Ltd. to Balaclava Mines Inc. 11/08/1996
Recapitalized as Pillar Resources Inc. 06/07/2001
Each share Common no par exchanged for (0.1) share Common no par
Pillar Resources Inc. name changed to PilaGold Inc. 10/21/2003 which merged into Radius Gold Inc. 07/02/2004

BALANCE BAR CO (DE)
Merged into Kraft Foods, Inc. 03/03/2000
Each share Common 1¢ par exchanged for $19.40 cash

BALANCE COMPUTER CORP (MD)
Assets acquired by New Gen System, Inc. 05/31/1987
No stockholders' equity

BALANCE RES LTD (BC)
Name changed to International Topaz Business Development Corp. 02/01/1991
International Topaz Business

Development Corp. name changed to Leopardus Resources Ltd. 08/09/1996 which merged into Zarara Oil & Gas Ltd. (Channel Islands) 02/12/1999 which reorganized in Wyoming as Zara Trading, Inc. 03/05/2007
(See Zara Trading, Inc.)

BALANCED CARE CORP (DE)
Merged into IBC Acquisition Corp. 08/19/2002
Each share Common $0.001 par exchanged for $0.25 cash

BALANCED ENVIRONMENTAL SVCS TECH INC (NV)
Recapitalized as United States Indemnity & Casualty, Inc. 07/08/1993
Each share Common $0.001 par exchanged for (0.1) share Common $0.001 par
United States Indemnity & Casualty, Inc. name changed to Birch Financial, Inc. 01/20/2000

BALANCED INCOME FD INC (MD)
Name changed to Supervised Investors Income Fund, Inc. 01/21/1972
Supervised Investors Income Fund, Inc. name changed to Kemper Total Return Fund, Inc. (MD) 02/17/1977 which reincorporated in Massachusetts as Kemper Total Return Fund 01/31/1986 which name changed to Scudder Total Return Fund 06/08/2001 which name changed to DWS Balanced Fund 02/06/2006

BALANCED LIVING INC (CO)
Reorganized as Wizzard Software Corp. 02/09/2001
Each share Common $0.001 par exchanged for (1.65) shares Common $0.001 par
Wizzard Software Corp. name changed to FAB Universal Corp. 10/09/2012

BALANCED MUTUAL FUND OF CANADA LTD. (CANADA)
Each share Common $1 par exchanged for (4) shares Common 25¢ par 00/00/1953
Merged into Commonwealth International Corp. Ltd. 00/00/1957
Each share Common 25¢ par exchanged for (0.6096) share Common $1 par
Commonwealth International Corp. Ltd. name changed to Eaton Commonwealth Fund Ltd. 04/15/1974 which name changed to Eaton Bay Commonwealth Fund Ltd. 04/12/1978 which name changed back to Eaton Commonwealth Fund Ltd. 04/16/1986 which name changed to Viking Commonwealth Fund Ltd. 04/16/1987 which name changed to Laurentian Commonwealth Fund Ltd. 05/31/1993 which name changed to Strategic Value Commonwealth Fund Ltd. 06/05/1997 which name changed to StrategicNova Commonwealth Fund Ltd. 09/26/2000
(See StrategicNova Commonwealth Fund Ltd.)

BALATOC, INC. (PHILIPPINES)
Liquidation completed 03/26/1961
Each share Capital Stock PHP 1 par exchanged for first and final distribution of (0.25) share Benguet Consolidated, Inc. Capital Stock PHP 2 par and $0.02 cash
Benguet Consolidated, Inc. name changed to Benguet Corp. 06/30/1980

BALATOC MINING CO. (PHILIPPINES)
Name changed to Balatoc, Inc. 05/31/1958

Balatoc, Inc. acquired by Benguet Consolidated, Inc. 03/26/1961 which name changed to Benguet Corp. 06/30/1980

BALATON PWR INC (BC)
SEC revoked common stock registration 11/10/2014

BALBOA DEV INC (OR)
Involuntarily dissolved for failure to file annual report 11/06/1986

BALBOA EXPLORATION, LTD.
Acquired by Cortez Explorations, Ltd. 00/00/1946
Each share Capital Stock no par exchanged for (1) share Capital Stock no par
Cortez Explorations, Ltd. recapitalized as Marpic Explorations Ltd. 09/27/1957
(See Marpic Explorations Ltd.)

BALBOA EXPL CO (CO)
Proclaimed dissolved for failure to file reports 01/01/1992

BALBOA MINING & DEVELOPMENT CO. (CO)
Common 10¢ par changed to 1¢ par 04/12/1957
Completely liquidated 06/16/1965
Each share Common $1 par exchanged for first and final distribution of $0.98591 cash

BALBOA MNG & INVTS LTD (ON)
Name changed 10/31/1968
Name changed from Balboa U Mines Ltd. to Balboa Mining & Investments Ltd. 10/31/1968
Charter cancelled for failure to pay taxes and file returns 02/20/1980

BALBOA NATL BK (NATIONAL CITY, CA)
Common $2.50 par split (5) for (4) by issuance of (0.25) additional share 10/02/1987
Voluntarily dissolved 01/15/1988
Details not available

BALCO ENERGY CORP (GA)
Merged into Houston Oil Fields Co. (DE) 06/24/1983
Each share Common 10¢ par exchanged for (1.5) shares Common $10 par
Houston Oil Fields Co. (DE) merged into Plains Resources Inc. 04/22/1987
(See Plains Resources Inc.)

BALCO FOREST PRODUCTS LTD. (BC)
Name changed to Balco Industries Ltd. 07/05/1972
(See Balco Industries Ltd.)

BALCO INDS LTD (BC)
Common no par split (2) for (1) by issuance of (1) additional share 10/15/1973
Common no par split (2) for (1) by issuance of (1) additional share 09/21/1979
Acquired by Timber Investments Ltd. 07/00/1987
Details not available

BALCON, INC. (UT)
Recapitalized as Shared Technologies Inc. 03/00/1988
Each share Common $0.001 par exchanged for (0.25) share Common $0.004 par
Shared Technologies Inc. name changed to Shared Technologies Fairchild Inc. 03/18/1996
(See Shared Technologies Fairchild Inc.)

BALCOR/COLONIAL STORAGE INCOME FD L P (IL)
Completely liquidated 10/31/1996
Each Unit of Ltd. Partnership Int.-86 received first and final distribution of $0.56 cash
Units of Ltd. Partnership Int.-85 completely liquidated 09/30/1998

Details not available

BALCOR EQUITY PENSION INS L P (IL)
Units of Ltd. Partnership Tax Exempt 1 completely liquidated 12/22/1999
Details not available
Units of Ltd. Partnership Tax Exempt 2 completely liquidated 12/22/1999
Details not available
Units of Ltd. Partnership Tax Exempt 3 completely liquidated 12/22/1999
Details not available
Units of Ltd. Partnership Tax Exempt 4 completely liquidated 12/18/2000
Details not available

BALCOR INTL (NV)
Name changed to Dimension House Inc. 12/10/1998
Dimension House Inc. name changed to Presidents Telecom Inc. 10/28/1999 which name changed to VoIP Telecom Inc. 04/19/2000 which name changed to Diversified Thermal Solutions Inc. 07/01/2002
(See Diversified Thermal Solutions Inc.)

BALCOR MOBILE HOME INCOME FD LTD PARTNERSHIP (DE)
Filed Certificate of Cancellation 09/29/1993
Details not available

BALCOR PENSION INVS L P (IL)
Units of Ltd. Partnership completely liquidated 09/30/1997
Details not available
Units of Ltd. Partnership II completely liquidated 12/22/1999
Details not available
Units of Ltd. Partnership III completely liquidated 12/22/1999
Details not available
Units of Ltd. Partnership IV completely liquidated 12/22/1999
Details not available
Units of Ltd. Partnership V completely liquidated 12/22/1999
Details not available
Units of Ltd. Partnership VI completely liquidated 12/22/1999
Details not available
Units of Ltd. Partnership VII completely liquidated 12/22/1999
Details not available

BALCOR PFD PENSION LTD PARTNERSHIP (IL)
Completely liquidated 02/00/1997
Each Unit of Ltd. Partnership received first and final distribution of $1.40 cash

BALCOR RLTY INVS LTD L P (IL)
Units of Ltd. Partnership Int-81 completely liquidated 02/08/1991
Details not available
Units of Ltd. Partnership Int-80 completely liquidated 04/23/1991
Details not available
Units of Ltd. Partnership Int-82 completely liquidated 12/18/2000
Details not available
Units of Ltd. Partnership Int-83 completely liquidated 12/18/2000
Details not available

BALCOR RES CORP (BC)
Recapitalized as Preston Resource Corp. 02/12/1990
Each share Common no par exchanged for (0.1) share Common no par
Preston Resource Corp. recapitalized as Golden Treasure Explorations Ltd. 05/04/1993 which recapitalized as Foundry Holdings Corp. 06/21/2001 which name changed to Yangtze Telecom Corp. 09/08/2003

BALCRANK, INC. (OH)
Name changed to Disney Street Corp. 11/30/1962
(See Disney Street Corp.)

BALD BUTTE GOLD MINES CO (MT)
Charter expired 07/18/1974

No stockholders' equity

BALD BUTTE MINING & MILLING CO.
Dissolved 00/00/1937
Details not available

BALD EAGLE GOLF CORP (MB)
Cease trade order effective 07/14/2003

BALD MOUNTAIN HOMESTAKE MINES CORP.
Out of business 00/00/1935

BALDOR ELEC CO (MO)
Each share Class A Common $10 par exchanged for (11) shares Common 10¢ par 02/20/1973
Common 10¢ par split (2) for (1) by issuance of (1) additional share 06/05/1978
5% Preferred $10 par called for redemption 12/31/1978
Common 10¢ par split (3) for (2) by issuance of (0.5) additional share 09/21/1979
Common 10¢ par split (3) for (2) by issuance of (0.5) additional share 09/20/1989
Common 10¢ par split (3) for (2) by issuance of (0.5) additional share 12/17/1992
Common 10¢ par split (6) for (5) by issuance of (0.2) additional share 01/07/1994
Common 10¢ par split (3) for (2) by issuance of (0.5) additional share 09/06/1995
Common 10¢ par split (4) for (3) by issuance of (0.33333333) additional share payable 12/15/1997 to holders of record 12/01/1997
Acquired by ABB Ltd. 01/27/2011
Each share Common 10¢ par exchanged for $63.50 cash

BALDT CORP (DE)
Name changed to Delton Industries, Inc. 02/07/1977
(See Delton Industries, Inc.)

BALDWIN & LYONS INC (IN)
Common no par split (5) for (4) by issuance of (0.25) additional share 03/21/1972
Common no par reclassified as Class A Common no par 05/21/1986
Each share Class A Common no par received distribution of (4) shares Class B Common no par 06/11/1986
Class A Common no par split (3) for (1) by issuance of (2) additional shares 12/01/1993
Class B Common no par split (3) for (1) by issuance of (2) additional shares 12/01/1993
Class A Common no par split (5) for (4) by issuance of (0.25) additional share payable 03/03/2003 to holders of record 02/17/2003 Ex date - 03/04/2003
Class B Common no par split (5) for (4) by issuance of (0.25) additional share payable 03/03/2003 to holders of record 02/17/2003 Ex date - 03/04/2003
Name changed to Protective Insurance Corp. 08/01/2018

BALDWIN AIRCRAFT INTL INC (UT)
Involuntarily dissolved 12/01/1993

BALDWIN BANCSHARES INC (GA)
Merged into GB&T Bancshares, Inc. 08/29/2003
Each share Common exchanged for (2.895) shares Common $5 par
GB&T Bancshares, Inc. merged into SunTrust Banks, Inc. 05/01/2008

BALDWIN CHAIN & MANUFACTURING CO.
Merged into Baldwin Duckworth Chain Corp. 00/00/1930
Details not available

BALDWIN CO. (OH)
Common $20 par changed to $8 par 00/00/1932

Name changed to Baldwin Piano Co. 00/00/1954
Baldwin Piano Co. name changed to Baldwin (D.H.) Co. (OH) 04/01/1963
(See Baldwin (D.H.) Co. (OH))

BALDWIN CONS MINES LTD (ON)
Recapitalized as Canadian Baldwin Holdings Ltd. 07/11/1989
Each share Capital Stock $1 par exchanged for (0.2) share Common no par
Canadian Baldwin Holdings Ltd. recapitalized as Canadian Baldwin Resources Ltd. 07/25/2005 which name changed to Aura Gold Inc. (ON) 03/22/2006 which reincorporated in Canada 04/20/2006 which reorganized in British Virgin Islands 01/05/2017

BALDWIN D H CO (DE)
Reincorporated 12/09/1977
Common $8 par changed to $4 par and (1) additional share issued 04/30/1964
Common $4 par split (2) for (1) by issuance of (1) additional share 01/18/1965
Common $4 par changed to no par 04/05/1965
Common no par split (2) for (1) by issuance of (1) additional share 06/21/1971
Common no par split (2) for (1) by issuance of (1) additional share 04/30/1973
State of incorporation changed from (OH) to (DE) 12/09/1977
Note: 8% Preferred Ser. B and 8% Class D Preferred were not affected by reincorporation and remain outstanding under the Ohio company
Reorganized as PHLCorp, Inc. (DE) 11/13/1986
Each (100) shares 8% Preferred Ser. B $100 par exchanged for (86.93) shares Common $1 par and (86.93) Common Stock Purchase Warrants expiring 11/12/1991
Each (100) shares 8% Class D Preferred $100 par exchanged for (86.93) shares Common $1 par and (86.93) Common Stock Purchase Warrants expiring 11/12/1991
Note: Unexchanged certificates became without value 12/13/1989
PHLCorp, Inc. (DE) merged into PHLCorp, Inc. (PA) 04/22/1987 which merged into Leucadia National Corp. 12/31/1992 which name changed to Jefferies Financial Group Inc. 05/24/2018

BALDWIN (D.H.) CO. (DE)
Merged into Baldwin-United Corp. 01/27/1978
Each share 4% Class C Conv. Preferred Ser. 2 $100 par exchanged for (1) share 4% Class C Conv. Preferred Ser. 2 $100 par
Each share 4% Class C Conv. Preferred Ser. 3 $100 par exchanged for (1) share 4% Class C Conv. Preferred Ser. 3 $100 par
Each share 5% Conv. Preferred Ser. A $108 par exchanged for (1) share 5% Conv. Preferred Ser. A $108 par
Each share Common no par became (1) share Baldwin-United Corp. Common no par
Baldwin-United Corp. reorganized as PHLCorp, Inc. (DE) 11/13/1986 which merged into PHLCorp, Inc. (PA) 04/22/1987 which merged into Leucadia National Corp. 12/31/1992

BALDWIN DUCKWORTH CHAIN CORP.
Acquired by Chain Belt Co. 00/00/1939
Each share Capital Stock exchanged for (1.25) shares Capital Stock no par
Chain Belt Co. name changed to Rex Chainbelt Inc. 01/23/1964 which name changed to Rexnord Inc. 01/26/1973
(See Rexnord Inc.)

BALDWIN EHRET HILL INC (PA)
Merged into Keene Corp. (DE) (Old) 08/26/1969
Each share Common $1 par exchanged for $12.25 cash

BALDWIN ENCLOSURES INC (NY)
Charter cancelled and proclaimed dissolved for failure to pay taxes 12/15/1971

BALDWIN GOLD MINING CO. LTD. (ON)
Recapitalized as Baldwin Consolidated Mines Ltd. 00/00/1946
Each share Capital Stock $1 par exchanged for (0.05) share Capital Stock $1 par
Baldwin Consolidated Mines Ltd. recapitalized as Canadian Baldwin Holdings Ltd. 07/11/1989 which recapitalized as Canadian Baldwin Resources Ltd. 07/25/2005 which name changed to Aura Gold Inc. (ON) 03/22/2006 which reincorporated in Canada 04/20/2006 which name changed to Aura Minerals Inc. (Canada) 08/16/2007 whcih reorganized in British Virgin Islands 01/05/2017

BALDWIN-HILL CO. (NJ)
Merged into Baldwin-Ehret-Hill, Inc. 07/31/1959
Each share Common exchanged for (1) share Common $1 par
(See Baldwin-Ehret-Hill, Inc.)

BALDWIN HOTELS LTD (BC)
Struck off register 11/20/1987

BALDWIN KIRKLAND GOLD MINES LTD.
Recapitalized as Baldwin Consolidated Mines Ltd. 00/00/1946
Each share Capital Stock $1 par exchanged for (0.1) share Capital Stock $1 par
Baldwin Consolidated Mines Ltd. recapitalized as Canadian Baldwin Holdings Ltd. 07/11/1989 which recapitalized as Canadian Baldwin Resources Ltd. 07/25/2005 which name changed to Aura Gold Inc. (ON) 03/22/2006 which reincorporated in Canada 04/20/2006 which name changed to Aura Minerals Inc. (Canada) 08/16/2007 which reorganized in British Virgin Islands 01/05/2017

BALDWIN-LIMA-HAMILTON CORP. (PA)
Acquired by Armour & Co. 07/02/1965
Each share Common $13 par exchanged for (0.13) share $4.75 Preferred $100 par and (1/6) share Common $5 par
Armour & Co. merged into Greyhound Corp. (DE) 12/28/1970 which reincorporated in Arizona 03/03/1978 which name changed to Greyhound Dial Corp. 05/08/1990 which name changed to Dial Corp. (AZ) which reincorporated in Delaware 03/18/1992 which name changed to Viad Corp. 08/15/1996

BALDWIN LOCOMOTIVE WORKS
7% Preferred called for redemption 09/01/1950
Name changed to Baldwin-Lima-Hamilton Corp. and dividend of (1) share Baldwin Securities Corp. Common 75¢ par distributed 00/00/1950
Baldwin-Lima-Hamilton Corp. was acquired by Armour & Co. (DE) 07/02/1965 which merged into Greyhound Corp. (DE) 12/28/1970 which reincorporated in Arizona 03/03/1978 which name changed to Greyhound Dial Corp. 05/08/1990 which name changed to Dial Corp. (AZ) 05/14/1991 which reincorporated in Delaware 03/18/1992 which name changed to Viad Corp. 08/15/1996

BALDWIN MONTROSE CHEM INC (IN)
Merged into Chris-Craft Industries, Inc. 06/19/1968
Each share $1 Conv. Preferred no par exchanged for (1) share $1 Conv. Prior Preferred no par
Each share Common 50¢ par exchanged for (0.5) share $1.40 Conv. Preferred $1 par
Chris-Craft Industries, Inc. merged into News Corp., Ltd. 07/31/2001 which reorganized as News Corp. (Old) 11/03/2004 which name changed to Twenty-First Century Fox, Inc. 07/01/2013

BALDWIN PIANO & ORGAN CO (DE)
Assets sold for the benefit of creditors 10/31/2001
Stockholders' equity unlikely

BALDWIN PIANO CO. (OH)
Stock Dividend - 100% 01/13/1956
Name changed to Baldwin (D.H.) Co. (OH) 04/01/1963
(See Baldwin (D.H.) Co. (OH))

BALDWIN PROPERTIES, INC (TX)
Merged into Alaska Interstate Co. (AK) 01/31/1967
Each share Common $1 par exchanged for (1.25) shares Common $1 par
Alaska Interstate Co. (AK) reincorporated in Delaware as Enstar Corp. 06/04/1982
(See Enstar Corp. (DE))

BALDWIN RUBBER CO. (MI)
Each share Class A no par exchanged for (4) shares Common $1 par 00/00/1936
Each share Class B no par exchanged for (0.535) share Common $1 par 00/00/1936
Stock Dividends - 25% 01/26/1948; 10% 07/31/1952
Merged into Baldwin-Montrose Chemical Co., Inc. 06/26/1961
Each share Common $1 par exchanged for (1) share $1 Conv. Preferred no par
Baldwin-Montrose Chemical Co., Inc. merged into Chris-Craft Industries, Inc. 06/19/1968 which merged into News Corp., Ltd. 07/31/2001 which reorganized as News Corp. (Old) 11/03/2004 which name changed to Twenty-First Century Fox, Inc. 07/01/2013

BALDWIN SECS CORP (DE)
Reincorporated 03/29/1957
Common 75¢ par changed to 1¢ par 00/00/1952
State of incorporation changed from (PA) to (DE) 03/29/1957
Charter cancelled and declared inoperative and void for non-payment of taxes 03/01/1993

BALDWIN TECHNOLOGY INC (DE)
Class A Common 1¢ par split (2) for (1) by issuance of (1) additional share 08/15/1988
Class A Common 1¢ par split (2) for (1) by issuance of (1) additional share 09/15/1989
Acquired by Forsyth Capital Investors, L.L.C. 03/20/2012
Each share Class A Common 1¢ par exchanged for $0.96 cash
Each share Class B Common 1¢ par exchanged for $0.96 cash

BALDWIN UTD CORP (DE)
Common no par split (2) for (1) by issuance of (1) additional share 06/30/1982
Reorganized as PHLCorp, Inc. (DE) 11/13/1986
Each (100) shares $2.06 Conv. Class U Preferred $25 par exchanged for (21.73) shares Common $1 par and (21.73) Common Stock Purchase Warrants expiring 11/12/1991
Each (100) shares 4% Conv. Class C Preferred Ser. 2 $100 par exchanged for (86.93) shares Common $1 par and (86.93) Common Stock Purchase Warrants expiring 11/12/1991
Each (100) shares 4% Conv. Class C Preferred Ser. 3 $100 par exchanged for (86.93) shares Common $1 par and (86.93) Common Stock Purchase Warrants expiring 11/12/1991
Each (100) shares 5% Conv. Preferred Ser. A $108 par exchanged for (93.88) shares Common $1 par and (93.88) Common Stock Purchase Warrants expiring 11/12/1991
Each (100) shares Common no par exchanged for (6.42) shares Common $1 par and (6.42) Common Stock Purchase Warrants expiring 11/12/1991
Note: Unexchanged certificates became valueless 12/13/1989
PHLCorp, Inc. (DE) merged into PHLCorp, Inc. (PA) 04/22/1987 which merged into Leucadia National Corp. 12/31/1992 which name changed to Jefferies Financial Group Inc. 05/24/2018

BALDWINS MONTREAL LTD. (CANADA)
Name changed to Canadian Sheet Galvanizers Ltd. 00/00/1952
Canadian Sheet Galvanizers Ltd. name changed to Canadian Sheet Galvanizers (1962) Ltd. 11/01/1962
(See Canadian Sheet Galvanizers (1962) Ltd.)

BALFOUR BUILDING, INC. (CA)
Liquidation completed
Each share Common no par exchanged for initial distribution of $120 cash 00/00/1951
Each share Common no par received second distribution of $5 cash 12/21/1951
Each share Common no par received third and final distribution of $25.10 cash 09/21/1953

BALFOUR MACLAINE CORP (DE)
Recapitalized as Anti Aging Medical Group Corp. 01/23/2006
Each share Common $1 par exchanged for (0.001) share Common $0.001 par
Anti Aging Medical Group Corp. name changed to Innolife Pharma, Inc. 05/02/2007

BALFOUR MILLS, INC.
Acquired by International Cellucotton Products Co. 00/00/1946
Details not available

BALFOUR MNG LTD (BC)
Recapitalized as International Balfour Resources Ltd. 02/20/1978
Each share Common 50¢ par exchanged for (0.2) share Common no par
International Balfour Resources Ltd. name changed to Quartet Energy Resources Ltd. (BC) 08/28/1980 which reincorporated in Ontario 07/09/1981 which name changed to Oiltex International Ltd. 04/26/1984 which merged into International Oiltex Ltd. 10/01/1989 which merged into Aztec Resources Ltd. 09/02/1994 which recapitalized as Pursuit Resources Inc. (New) 02/13/1997 which merged into EnerMark Income Fund 04/11/2000 which merged into Enerplus Resources Fund 06/22/2001 which reorganized as Enerplus Corp. 01/03/2011

BALI EXPL LTD (BC)
Struck off register 09/16/1983

BALI INC (DE)
Common $1 par split (1.333) for (1) by issuance of (0.333) additional share 05/05/1968
Stock Dividend - 10% 06/20/1967
Merged into Hanes Corp. 12/31/1971
Each share Common $1 par exchanged for (0.3636) share Common $1 par
(See Hanes Corp.)

BALI JEWELRY LTD (NY)
Each share Common $0.001 par exchanged for (0.5) share Common $0.002 par 08/21/1992
Charter dissolved by proclamation 06/26/1996

BALIUS CORP (NV)
Reorganized as Apptigo International, Inc. 04/30/2014
Each share Common $0.001 par exchanged for (3.5) shares Common $0.001 par

BALL & SOCKET FASTENER CO.
Dissolved 00/00/1946
Details not available

BALL & SOCKET MFG CO (CT)
Became private 06/13/1983
Details not available

BALLAD ENTERPRISES LTD (BC)
Recapitalized as Ballad Ventures Ltd. 11/16/2001
Each share Common no par exchanged for (0.33333333) share Common no par
Ballad Ventures Ltd. recapitalized as Ballad Gold & Silver Ltd. 07/21/2003 which recapitalized as Goldbank Mining Corp. 01/14/2009

BALLAD GOLD & SILVER LTD (BC)
Recapitalized as Goldbank Mining Corp. 01/14/2009
Each share Common no par exchanged for (0.25) share Common no par

BALLAD VENTURES LTD (BC)
Recapitalized as Ballad Gold & Silver Ltd. 07/21/2003
Each share Common no par exchanged for (0.5) share Common no par
Ballad Gold & Silver Ltd. recapitalized as Goldbank Mining Corp. 01/14/2009

BALLANTYNE LONG LAC MINES LTD (ON)
Charter revoked for failure to file reports and pay taxes 00/00/1957

BALLANTYNE OMAHA INC (DE)
Common 1¢ par split (3) for (2) by issuance of (0.5) additional share payable 03/05/1997 to holders of record 02/10/1997 Ex date - 03/06/1997
Common 1¢ par split (3) for (2) by issuance of (0.5) additional share payable 06/12/1998 to holders of record 05/29/1998 Ex date - 06/15/1998
Stock Dividends - 10% payable 03/08/1996 to holders of record 02/09/1996; 5% payable 03/01/1999 to holders of record 02/15/1999
Name changed to Ballantyne Strong, Inc. 06/04/2009

BALLARD & BALLARD
Dissolved 00/00/1951
Details not available

BALLARD MED PRODS (UT)
Common 10¢ par split (3) for (2) by issuance of (0.5) additional share 02/19/1987
Common 10¢ par split (4) for (3) by issuance of (0.33333333) additional share 01/06/1989
Common 10¢ par split (3) for (2) by issuance of (0.5) additional share 11/01/1990
Common 10¢ par split (3) for (2) by issuance of (0.5) additional share 08/02/1991
Common 10¢ par split (3) for (2) by issuance of (0.5) additional share 02/21/1992
Common 10¢ par split (4) for (3) by issuance of (0.33333333) additional share 02/26/1993
Merged into Kimberly-Clark Corp. 09/23/1999
Each share Common 10¢ par exchanged for (0.4439) share Common $1.25 par

BALLARD OIL & GAS LTD (AB)
Struck off register and declared dissolved for failure to file returns 11/01/1989

BALLARD PWR SYS INC NEW (CANADA)
Reincorporated under the laws of British Columbia 08/24/2016

BALLARD PWR SYS INC OLD (CANADA)
Common no par split (3) for (1) by issuance of (2) additional shares payable 06/08/1998 to holders of record 06/05/1998
Plan of arrangement effective 01/07/2009
Each share Common no par exchanged for (1) share Ballard Power Systems Inc. (New) (Canada) Common no par
Ballard Power Systems Inc. (New) (Canada) reincorporated in British Columbia 08/24/2016

BALLARPUR INDS LTD (INDIA)
ADR agreement terminated 12/13/2003
No GDR's remain outstanding (Additional Information in Active)

BALLATAR EXPLS LTD (BC)
Recapitalized as International Ballater Resources Inc. 08/15/1995
Each share Common no par exchanged for (0.14285714) share Common no par
International Ballater Resources Inc. merged into First Quantum Minerals Ltd. (YT) 12/12/1997 which reincorporated in Canada 08/11/2003 which reincorporated in British Columbia 06/03/2005

BALLINDERRY EXPLS LTD (BC)
Recapitalized as Prairie Pacific Energy Corp. 03/06/1979
Each share Common $1 par exchanged for (0.2) share Common no par
(See Prairie Pacific Energy Corp.)

BALLISTIC ENERGY CORP (AB)
Merged into Stampeder Exploration Ltd. 06/13/1996
Each share Common no par exchanged for $5 cash

BALLISTIC RECOVERY SYS INC (MN)
Company terminated common stock registration and is no longer public as of 12/30/2008

BALLISTIC VENTURES INC (DE)
Each share old Common $0.001 par exchanged for (0.25) share new Common $0.001 par 01/21/2003
Name changed to River Capital Group, Inc. 06/07/2004
River Capital Group, Inc. recapitalized as Sonterra Resources, Inc. 02/14/2008 which name changed to Velocity Energy Inc. 04/14/2009

BALLISTIVET INC (MN)
Statutorily dissolved 08/01/1997

BALLMAN-CUMMINGS FURNITURE CO. (AR)
Voluntarily dissolved 02/04/1991
Details not available

BALLOONIES INC. (NV)
Name changed to Imagex Services, Inc. 06/29/1993
(See Imagex Services, Inc.)

BALLROOM DANCE FITNESS INC (FL)
Name changed to ZOOM Companies, Inc. 12/15/2015

BALLSTON BANCORP INC (VA)
Merged into MainStreet Financial Corp. 07/20/1998
Each share Common no par exchanged for (0.431) share Common $5 par
MainStreet Financial Corp. merged into BB&T Corp. 03/08/1999

BALLSTON SPA NATL BK (BALLSTON SPA, NY)
Reorganized as Ballston Spa Bancorp, Inc. 04/18/1983
Each share Common $25 par exchanged for (1) share Common $25 par

BALLY ENTMT CORP (DE)
Each share Common $0.66666666 par received distribution of (0.25) share Bally Total Fitness Holding Corp. Common 1¢ par payable 01/09/1996 to holders of record 11/15/1995 Ex date - 01/10/1996
$4 Conv. Exchangeable Preferred Ser. D $1 par called for redemption 06/24/1996
Merged into Hilton Hotels Corp. 12/18/1996
Each share 8% Conv. Increased Dividend Equity Security Preferred $1 par exchanged for (1) share 8% Conv. Increased Dividend Equity Security Preferred no par
Each share Common $0.66666666 par exchanged for (1) share Common $2.50 par
(See Hilton Hotels Corp.)

BALLY GAMING INTL INC (DE)
Merged into Alliance Gaming Corp. 06/18/1996
Each share Common 1¢ par exchanged for (0.0492) share 15% Sr. Pay-in-Kind Special Preferred Ser. B 10¢ par and (0.0789) share Common 10¢ par
Alliance Gaming Corp. name changed to Bally Technologies, Inc. 03/08/2006
(See Bally Technologies, Inc.)

BALLY MFG CORP (DE)
Common $1 par changed to $0.66666666 par and (0.5) additional share issued 02/24/1970
Common $0.66666666 par split (2) for (1) by issuance of (1) additional share 02/28/1977
Common $0.66666666 par split (2) for (1) by issuance of (1) additional share 06/07/1979
Stock Dividend - 100% 03/07/1972
Preferred Ser. E $1 par called for redemption 08/01/1987
Name changed to Bally Entertainment Corp. 05/17/1994
Bally Entertainment Corp. merged into Hilton Hotels Corp. 12/18/1996
(See Hilton Hotels Corp.)

BALLY TECHNOLOGIES INC (NV)
Acquired by Scientific Games Corp. 11/21/2014
Each share Common 10¢ par exchanged for $83.30 cash

BALLY TOTAL FITNESS HLDG CORP (DE)
Plan of reorganization under Chapter 11 Federal Bankruptcy Code effective 10/01/2007
Each share old Common 1¢ par exchanged for $0.31 cash
Acquired by Bally Merger Corp. 02/10/2017
Each share new Common 1¢ par exchanged for $1.05 cash

BALLYLIFFIN CAP CORP (AB)
Completely liquidated
Each share Common no par received first and final distribution of (0.32) share Ironside Resources Inc.
Common no par payable 07/10/2015 to holders of record 07/09/2015

BALLYNAGEE ACQUISITION CORP (DE)
Common $0.001 par split (5) for (1) by issuance of (4) additional shares payable 10/25/1999 to holders of record 10/14/1999
Name changed to e-Financial Depot.com, Inc. 11/02/1999
e-Financial Depot.com, Inc. name changed to Collaborative Financial Network Group, Inc. 06/28/2001
(See Collaborative Financial Network Group, Inc.)

BALLYS GRAND INC (DE)
Merged into Hilton Hotels Corp. 03/26/1998
Each share Common 1¢ par exchanged for $51.37 cash

BALLYS PK PL INC (DE)
Merged into Bally Manufacturing Corp. 06/12/1986
Each share Common 10¢ par exchanged for (1) share Common $0.66666666 par
Bally Manufacturing Corp. name changed to Bally Entertainment Corp. 05/17/1994 which merged into Hilton Hotels Corp. 12/18/1996
(See Hilton Hotels Corp.)

BALMORAL CAP CORP (AB)
Recapitalized as Commercial Consolidators Corp. 11/14/1999
Each share Common no par exchanged for (0.33333333) share Common no par
(See Commercial Consolidators Corp.)

BALMORAL FX SYS INC (FL)
Recapitalized as Amalgamated Gold & Silver, Inc. 08/01/2012
Each share Common no par exchanged for (0.02) share Common no par
Amalgamated Gold & Silver, Inc. recapitalized as Rainforest Resources Inc. 03/15/2016

BALMORAL INC (CO)
Each share old Common no par exchanged for (0.01) share new Common no par 03/13/1989
Name changed to Professional Health Care of America, Inc. 04/03/1989
(See Professional Health Care of America, Inc.)

BALMORAL PORCUPINE GOLD MINES LTD. (ON)
Charter revoked for failure to file reports and pay taxes 11/07/1955

BALOIL RES LTD (AB)
Name changed 03/21/1989
Name changed from Baloil Lassiter Petroleum Ltd. to Baloil Resources Ltd. 03/21/1989
Merged into Kuma Resources Ltd. 08/27/1993
Each share Common no par exchanged for (0.24067388) share Common no par
Kuma Resources Ltd. name changed to Algonquin Petroleum Corp. 03/18/1997 which recapitalized as Algonquin Oil & Gas Ltd. 04/10/2000 which recapitalized as PetroShale Inc. 03/19/2012

BALOISE HLDG (SWITZERLAND)
Name changed to Baloise Holding AG 01/22/2010

BALRAMPUR CHINI MLS LTD (INDIA)
GDR agreement terminated 03/20/2015
No GDR's remain outstanding

BALSA WOOD CO., INC.
Bankrupt 00/00/1939
Stockholders' equity unlikely

BALSAM RES INC (BC)
Recapitalized as Consolidated Balsam Resources Inc. 01/18/1990
Each share Common no par exchanged for (0.5) share Common no par
Consolidated Balsam Resources Inc. recapitalized as Bluebird Explorations Ltd. 10/01/1991 which recapitalized as Spire Ventures Ltd. 10/24/1995 which recapitalized as Consolidated Spire Ventures Ltd. 01/04/2001 which recapitalized as Berkwood Resources Ltd. 12/01/2010

BALSAM VENTURES INC (BC)
Name changed to Staccato Gold Resources Ltd. 11/12/2003
Staccato Gold Resources Ltd. acquired by Timberline Resources Corp. 06/02/2010

BALTEK CORP (DE)
Common $1 par split (2) for (1) by issuance of (1) additional share 01/25/1985
Common $1 par split (5) for (4) by issuance of (0.25) additional share 01/26/1987
Stock Dividend - 10% 01/20/1988
Merged into Alcan Inc. 07/01/2003
Each share Common $1 par exchanged for $15.17 cash

BALTIC MINES LTD. (ON)
Charter surrendered 02/05/1963
No stockholders' equity

BALTIC RES INC (AB)
Plan of arrangement effective 03/10/2008
Each share Common no par exchanged for (1) share Canadian Orebodies Inc. Common no par and (1.4) shares PhosCan Chemical Corp. Common no par
(See each company's listing)

BALTIC TRADING LTD (MARSHALL ISLANDS)
Merged into Genco Shipping & Trading Ltd. 07/17/2015
Each share Common 1¢ par exchanged for (0.216) share Common 1¢ par

BALTIMORE & OHIO RR CO (MD)
Each share Stamped 4% Preferred $100 par exchanged for (1) share Chesapeake & Ohio Railway Co. Common $25 par 02/04/1963
Each share Stamped Common $100 par exchanged for (0.571428) share Chesapeake & Ohio Railway Co. Common $25 par 02/04/1963
(See Chesapeake & Ohio Railway Co.)
Through voluntary exchange offer each share 4% Non-Cum. Preferred $100 par could be exchanged for (1) share Chessie System, Inc. Common $25 par and each share Common $100 par could be exchanged for (0.571428) share Chessie System, Inc. Common $25 par. This offer expired 05/07/1974.
By Court ruling both Preferred and Common shares which were not exchanged by 05/07/1974 were cancelled and would be thereafter exchangeable at the same rate but would not be entitled to receive cash for fractional interest nor dividends declared if record date was prior to date of surrender.
Merged into CSX Corp. 05/06/1993
Each share Common no par exchanged for (5.538) shares Common $1 par

BALTIMORE ACCEPTANCE CORP.
Liquidated 00/00/1932
Details not available

BALTIMORE AIRCOIL INC (MD)
Common $1.66666666 par changed to $0.83333333 par and (1) additional share issued 04/22/1965
Common $0.83333333 par changed to $0.66666666 par and (0.25) additional share issued 11/13/1967
Merged into Merck & Co., Inc. (Old) 05/28/1970
Each share Common $0.66666666 par exchanged for (0.7) share Common $0.05555555 par
Merck & Co., Inc. (Old) merged into Merck & Co., Inc. (New) 11/03/2009

BALTIMORE AMERICAN INSURANCE CO.
Merged into Home Insurance Co. 00/00/1948
Each share Capital Stock $2.50 par exchanged for (0.268) share Common $5 par
(See Home Insurance Co.)

BALTIMORE BANCORP (MD)
Common $5 par split (2) for (1) by issuance of (1) additional share 09/08/1986
Preferred Stock Purchase Rights declared for Common stockholders of record 07/06/1989 were redeemed at $0.01 per right 10/01/1991 for holders of record 09/16/1991
Merged into First Fidelity Bancorporation (New) 11/29/1994
Each share Common $5 par exchanged for $20.75 cash

BALTIMORE BK & TR CO (KANSAS CITY, MO)
Stock Dividend - 33.33333333% 12/21/1966
Through voluntary exchange offer 100% held by Boatmen's Bancshares, Inc. as of 12/18/1974
Public interest eliminated

BALTIMORE BANK (KANSAS CITY, MO)
Capital Stock $100 par changed to $25 par and (3) additional shares issued plus a 25% stock dividend paid 06/10/1963
Name changed to Baltimore Bank & Trust Co. (Kansas City, MO) 12/21/1966
(See Baltimore Bank & Trust Co. (Kansas City, MO))

BALTIMORE BASEBALL CLUB INC (MO)
Common no par changed to $1 par 11/16/1954
Name changed to Bird Fund, Inc. 11/27/1979
(See Bird Fund, Inc.)

BALTIMORE BRICK CO. (DE)
Merged into Arundel Corp. 05/02/1968
Each share 5% 1st Preferred $100 par exchanged for (2) shares 5% Conv. Preferred Ser. A $50 par
Each share Common $100 par exchanged for (10) shares 3.2% Conv. Preferred Ser. B $50 par
(See Arundel Corp.)

BALTIMORE BUSINESS FORMS INC (MD)
Each share old Common no par exchanged for (10) shares new Common no par 06/29/1961
Merged into CM-Graphic Acquisition Corp. 01/16/1981
Each share 4% Preferred $25 par exchanged for $5.50 cash
Each share Common no par exchanged for $1.40 cash

BALTIMORE CAMAS, INC. (ID)
Charter forfeited for failure to file reports and pay fees 11/30/1970

BALTIMORE CAMAS MINES, INC. (ID)
Name changed to Baltimore Camas, Inc. 08/07/1969
(See Baltimore Camas, Inc.)

BALTIMORE CO. (DE)
Liquidation completed 10/20/1952
Details not available

BALTIMORE CONTRACTORS INC (DC)
Charter cancelled and proclaimed dissolved for failure to file reports 09/12/1983

BALTIMORE GAS & ELEC CO (MD)
Common no par split (2) for (1) by issuance of (1) additional share 11/21/1959
6.5% Conv. Preference $100 par called for redemption 12/03/1982
Common no par split (2) for (1) by issuance of (1) additional share 08/31/1985
8.75% Preference 1970 Ser. $100 par called for redemption 10/01/1986
Common no par split (3) for (2) by issuance of (0.5) additional share 05/15/1992
7.64% Preferred Ser. 1988 $100 par called for redemption 07/01/1993
7.88% Preference 1971 Ser. $100 par called for redemption 09/01/1993
7.75% Preferred Ser. 1972 $100 par called for redemption 11/08/1993
6.95% Preferred $100 par called for redemption 10/01/1995
4% Preferred Ser. C $100 par called for redemption 05/28/1996
4.5% Preferred Ser. B $100 par called for redemption 05/28/1996
5.4% Preferred Ser. D $100 par called for redemption 05/28/1996
7.8% Preference Ser. 1989 $100 par called for redemption at $100 on 07/01/1997
8.25% Preference Ser. 1989 $100 par called for redemption at $100 on 10/01/1997
8.625% Preference Ser. 1990 $100 par called for redemption at $100 on 07/01/1998
6.75% Preference Ser. 1987 $100 par called for redemption at $102.25 on 07/17/1998
7.78% Preference Ser. 1973 $100 par called for redemption at $101 on 07/17/1998
7.5% Preference Ser. 1986 $100 par called for redemption at $102.50 on 10/01/1999
7.85% Preference Ser. 1991 $100 par called for redemption at $100 on 07/01/1999
Under plan of reorganization each share Common no par automatically became (1) share Constellation Energy Group, Inc. Common no par 05/03/1999
Constellation Energy Group, Inc. merged into Exelon Corp. 03/12/2012
6.99% Preference Ser. 1995 $100 par called for redemption at $100 plus $0.038833 accrued dividends on 07/03/2016
7.125% Preference Ser. 1993 $100 par called for redemption at $100 plus $0.039583 accrued dividends on 07/03/2016
6.7% Preference Ser. 1993 $100 par called for redemption at $100 plus $1.433055 accrued dividends on 09/18/2016
6.97% Preference Ser. 1993 $100 par called for redemption at $100 plus $1.490805 accrued dividends on 09/18/2016
(Additional Information in Active)

BALTIMORE ICE SPORTS, INC. (MD)
Completely liquidated 09/08/1975
No stockholders' equity

BALTIMORE NATIONAL BANK (BALTIMORE, MD)
Merged into Fidelity-Baltimore National Bank & Trust Co. (Baltimore, MD) 07/16/1954
Each share Capital Stock $10 par exchanged for (1.15) shares Capital Stock $10 par
Fidelity-Baltimore National Bank & Trust Co. (Baltimore, MD) name changed to Fidelity-Baltimore National Bank (Baltimore, MD) 01/15/1957 which merged into Baltimore National Bank (Baltimore, MD) 06/24/1960 name changed to Maryland National Bank (Baltimore, MD) 11/14/1961 which reorganized as Maryland National Corp. 05/01/1969 which name changed to MNC Financial, Inc. 04/29/1987 which merged into NationsBank Corp. 10/01/1993 which reincorporated in Delaware as BankAmerica Corp. (Old) 09/25/1998 which merged into BankAmerica Corp. (New) 09/30/1998 which name changed to Bank of America Corp. 04/28/1999

BALTIMORE OIL CORP.
Acquired by North American Oil Co. 00/00/1942
Details not available

BALTIMORE ORIOLES INC (MD)
Name changed to Bird Holding, Inc. 11/27/1979
(See Bird Holding, Inc.)

BALTIMORE PAINT & CHEM CORP (MD)
6.5% Preferred $20 par called for redemption 03/15/1972
Stock Dividend - 10% 11/15/1971
Merged into ELT, Inc. 11/19/1975
Each share Common 50¢ par exchanged for $14 cash

BALTIMORE PORCELAIN STEEL CORP.
Merged into Universal Major Elec Appliances, Inc. 00/00/1952
Each share 7% Preferred $5 par exchanged for $5 face amount of 6% Ser. B Debentures
Each share old Common 10¢ par exchanged for (0.5) share new Common 10¢ par
Universal Major Elec Appliances, Inc. merged into Birdsboro Steel Foundry & Machine Co. (DE) 07/02/1956 which merged into Birdsboro Corp. 12/31/1959
(See Birdsboro Corp.)

BALTIMORE RADIO SHOW INC (MD)
Each share Common $1 par exchanged for (5) shares Common 20¢ par 00/00/1937
Merged into Pittsburgh Radio Partners, Inc. 12/01/1994
Details not available

BALTIMORE SALESBOOK CO. (MD)
Name changed to Baltimore Business Forms, Inc. 06/01/1960
(See Baltimore Business Forms, Inc.)

BALTIMORE TECHNOLOGIES PLC (ENGLAND & WALES)
Sponsored ADR's for Ordinary split (4) for (1) by issuance of (3) additional ADR's payable 05/18/2000 to holders of record 05/11/2000
Basis changed from (1:2) to (1:0.2) 02/03/2003
Basis changed from (1:0.2) to (1:0.0016) 12/24/2004
ADR agreement terminated 01/03/2005
Each Sponsored ADR for Ordinary exchanged for $0.002 cash

BALTIMORE TRAN CO (MD)
Recapitalized in 1953
Each share 5% Preferred $100 par exchanged for (1) share $2.50 Preferred $50 par and (3) shares Common $1 par
Each share Common no par exchanged for (1) share Common $1 par
Recapitalized 6/21/57
Each share $2.50 Preferred $50 par exchanged for $30 principal amount of 6-2/3% Income Subord. Debentures due 1/1/77 and (1) share Common $1 par

Common $1 par reclassified as Ctfs. of Bene. Int. $1 par 4/14/71 Liquidation completed
Each Ctf. of Bene. Int. $1 par received initial distribution of $7 cash 4/17/71
Each Ctf. of Bene. Int. $1 par received second distribution of $0.07 cash 6/24/74
Each Ctf. of Bene. Int. $1 par received third and final distribution of $0.1825 cash 12/23/76

BALTIMORE TROTTING RACES INC (MD)
Name changed to BTR Realty, Inc. 05/19/1972
BTR Realty, Inc. merged into Mid-Atlantic Realty Trust 09/13/1993
(See Mid-Atlantic Realty Trust)

BALTIMORE TUBE CO.
Property sold to Revere Copper & Brass Inc. 00/00/1935
Details not available

BALVERNE CELLARS INC (CA)
Charter suspended for failure to file reports and pay fees 11/21/2000

BAM ENTMT INC (DE)
SEC revoked common stock registration 10/23/2008

BAM INVTS CORP (ON)
Common no par split (10) for (1) by issuance of (9) additional shares payable 05/31/2007 to holders of record 05/24/2007 Ex date - 05/22/2007
Name changed to Partners Value Fund Inc. 06/10/2013
Partners Value Fund Inc. name changed to Partners Value Investments Inc. 05/25/2015 which reorganized as Partners Value Investments L.P. 07/04/2016

BAM SPLIT CORP (ON)
Name changed 12/15/2006
Name changed from BNN Split Corp. to BAM Split Corp. 12/15/2006
Class A Preferred no par called for redemption at $25.25 on 07/27/2009
Name changed to Partners Value Split Corp. 08/28/2013

BAMA GOLD CORP (BC)
Each share old Common no par exchanged for (0.2) share new Common no par 12/30/2014
Recapitalized as Whattozee Networks Inc. 01/25/2017
Each share new Common no par exchanged for (0.33333333) share Common no par
Whattozee Networks Inc. name changed to Chemistree Technology Inc. 08/04/2017

BAMBERGER POLYMERS INC (DE)
Common 1¢ par split (5) for (4) by issuance of (0.25) additional share 09/23/1987
Common 1¢ par split (5) for (4) by issuance of (0.25) additional share 08/03/1988
Name changed to InterSystems, Inc. 04/28/1993
InterSystems, Inc. name changed to EquiFin, Inc. 11/15/2001

BAMBI MINES LTD. (ON)
Charter cancelled and declared dissolved for failure to file returns and pay fees 12/07/1977

BAMBOO COM INC (DE)
Name changed to Internet Pictures Corp. 01/21/2000
Internet Pictures Corp. name changed to IPIX Corp. 03/24/2004
(See IPIX Corp.)

BAMBOO CREEK GOLD MINES LTD (ON)
Charter revoked for failure to file reports and pay taxes 10/01/1972

BAMCO INDUSTRIES, INC. (WA)
Ceased operations 00/00/1973
No stockholders' equity

BAMCO MACHINE, INC. (WA)
Name changed to Bamco Industries, Inc. 01/06/1972
(See Bamco Industries, Inc.)

BAMCO MINERALS CORP (AB)
Name changed to Signet Industries Ltd. 02/01/1996

BAMM CORP (DE)
Charter cancelled and declared inoperative and void for non-payment of taxes 04/15/1971

BAMOCOR INC (MN)
Name changed to Palm Springs Lifestyle, Inc. 05/25/1988
(See Palms Springs Lifestyle, Inc.)

BAMOOS LAKE MINES LTD. (ON)
Charter revoked for failure to file reports and pay taxes 00/00/1959

BANBURY GOLD MINES LTD (BC)
Recapitalized as Enerwaste Minerals Corp. 07/06/1992
Each share Common no par exchanged for (0.25) share Common no par
Enerwaste Minerals Corp. name changed to Universal Gun-Loc Industries Ltd. 02/11/1994 which recapitalized as UGL Enterprises Ltd. 04/25/2002 which name changed to Red Hill Energy Inc. 05/31/2006
(See Red Hill Energy Inc.)

BANC AMER DUTCH AUCTION PFD CORP (DE)
Dividends Received Eligible Auction Market Stock called for redemption at $100,000 on 09/07/2007
Dividends Received Eligible Auction Market Stock Accredited Investors called for redemption at $100,000 on 09/12/2007
Dividends Received Eligible Auction Market Stock Accredited Investors called for redemption at $100,000 on 09/14/2007
Dividends Received Eligible Auction Market Stock Accredited Investors called for redemption at $100,000 on 09/19/2007
Dividends Received Eligible Auction Market Stock Accredited Investors called for redemption at $100,000 on 09/21/2007

BANC CALIF INC (MD)
Each 8% Equity Unit automatically became (4.447742) shares Common 1¢ par 05/15/2017
8% Depositary Preferred Ser. C called for redemption at $25 on 09/17/2018 (Additional Information in Active)

BANC CORP (DE)
Name changed to Superior Bancorp 05/19/2006
(See Superior Bancorp)

BANC MAINE CORP (ME)
Common $20 par changed to $15 par and (0.33333333) additional share issued 06/26/1973
Common $15 par changed to $6 par and (1.5) additional shares issued 02/09/1977
Merged into Norstar Bancorp Inc. 02/01/1985
Each share Common $6 par exchanged for $55 cash

BANC ONE CORP (OH)
Reincorporated 05/01/1989
Common no par split (3) for (2) by issuance of (0.5) additional share 12/14/1982
Common no par split (3) for (2) by issuance of (0.5) additional share 09/06/1983
Common no par split (3) for (2) by issuance of (0.5) additional share 08/30/1985
$5.50 Conv. Preferred Ser. A no par called for redemption 06/09/1987
State of incorporation changed from (DE) to (OH) 05/01/1989
$3 Conv. Preferred Ser. B no par called for redemption 06/04/1993
Common no par split (5) for (4) by issuance of (0.25) additional share 08/31/1993
$3.50 Conv. Preferred Ser. C no par called for redemption at $51.05 plus $0.15 accrued dividend on 04/16/1998
Stock Dividends - 10% 03/13/1980; 10% 03/12/1982; 10% 03/12/1984; 10% 03/12/1986; 10% 03/04/1988; 10% 03/02/1990; 10% 03/02/1992; 10% 03/04/1994; 10% payable 03/06/1996 to holders of record 02/21/1996; 10% payable 02/26/1998 to holders of record 02/12/1998
Merged into Bank One Corp. 10/02/1998
Each share Common no par exchanged for (1) share Common 1¢ par
Bank One Corp. merged into J.P. Morgan Chase & Co. 07/01/2004 which name changed to JPMorgan Chase & Co. 07/20/2004

BANC SVCS CORP (OH)
Common $10 par split (2) for (1) by issuance of (1) additional share payable 10/15/97 to holders of record 10/1/97
Merged into Wayne Bancorp, Inc. (OH) 5/31/2003
Each share Common $10 par exchanged for (1.391) shares Common $1 par and $14.40 cash
(See Wayne Bancorp, Inc. (OH))

BANC STK GROUP INC (FL)
Name changed to Diamond Hill Investment Group, Inc. (FL) 04/27/2001
Diamond Hill Investment Group, Inc. (FL) reincorporated in Ohio 05/06/2002

BANCA CARIGE S P A (ITALY)
ADR agreement terminated 12/26/2017
No ADR's remain outstanding

BANCA COMMERCIALE ITALIANA S P A (ITALY)
ADR agreement terminated 00/00/2001
Details not available

BANCA POPLARE DELL EMILIA ROMAGNA (ITALY)
Name changed to BPER BANCA S.p.A. 12/09/2016

BANCA POPOLARE DI MILANO (ITALY)
ADR agreement terminated 01/24/2017
Each ADR for Ordinary exchanged for $2.159661 cash

BANCA QUADRUM S A (MEXICO)
ADR agreement terminated 12/07/2006
No ADR holders' equity

BANCA TURCO ROMANA S A (ROMANIA)
GDR agreement terminated 04/27/2004
No GDR holders' equity

BANCAL TRI ST CORP (DE)
Merged into Mitsubishi Bank, Ltd. 06/18/1984
Each share Common $15 par exchanged for $50 cash

BANCALABAMA INC (DE)
Merged into Union Planters Corp. 10/01/1996
Each share Common $1 par exchanged for (0.5907) share Common $5 par
Union Planters Corp. merged into Regions Financial Corp. (New) 07/01/2004

BANCAMERICA-BLAIR CORP. (NY)
Capital Stock $10 par changed to $1 par 06/21/1932
Name changed to Blair & Co., Inc. 00/00/1939
Blair & Co., Inc. name changed to Blair Holdings Corp. 00/00/1947 which name changed to Pepsi-Cola United Bottlers, Inc. 04/10/1958 which name changed to PUB United Corp. 05/29/1964 which name changed to Rheingold Corp. 04/27/1965 which merged into Pepsico, Inc. 12/31/1973

BANCAPITAL FINL CORP (NV)
Merged into Texas Commerce Bancshares, Inc. 05/16/1977
Each share Common $1 par exchanged for (0.6797) share Common $4 par
Texas Commerce Bancshares, Inc. acquired by Chemical New York Corp. 05/01/1987 which name changed to Chemical Banking Corp. 04/29/1988 which name changed to Chase Manhattan Corp. (New) 03/31/1996 which name changed to J.P. Morgan Chase & Co. 12/31/2000 which name changed to JPMorgan Chase & Co. 07/20/2004

BANCFIRST CORP (DE)
Name changed to BNF Bancorp, Inc. 03/02/1994
BNF Bancorp, Inc. acquired by Union Planters Corp. 09/01/1994 which merged into Regions Financial Corp. (New) 07/01/2004

BANCFIRST OHIO CORP (OH)
Common 10¢ par split (2) for (1) by issuance of (1) additional share 05/24/1994
Common 10¢ par changed to no par 00/00/1977
Common no par split (2) for (1) by issuance of (1) additional share payable 05/19/1998 to holders of record 04/28/1998
Stock Dividend - 5% payable 10/31/2000 to holders of record 10/10/2000
Merged into Unizan Financial Corp. 03/08/2002
Each share Common 10¢ par exchanged for (1.325) shares Common no par
Unizan Financial Corp. merged into Huntington Bancshares Inc. 03/01/2006

BANCFLORIDA FINL CORP (FL)
Merged into First Union Corp. 08/01/1994
Each share Common 1¢ par exchanged for (0.665) share Common $3.33333333 par
First Union Corp. name changed to Wachovia Corp. (Ctfs. dated after 09/01/2001) 09/01/2001 which merged into Wells Fargo & Co. (New) 12/31/2008

BANCINSURANCE CORP (OH)
Common no par split (2) for (1) by issuance of (1) additional share 11/23/1984
Stock Dividend - 5% payable 06/18/1999 to holders of record 05/25/1999
Acquired by Fenist, LLC 12/09/2010
Each share Common no par exchanged for $8.50 cash

BANCITALY CORP.
Acquired by Transamerica Corp. 00/00/1928
Details not available

BANCO BHIF (CHILE)
Name changed to BBV Banco BHIF 10/01/1999
BBV Banco BHIF name changed to BBVA Banco BHIF 11/08/2000 which name changed to Banco Bilbao Vizcaya Argentaria 03/29/2003

(See Banco Bilbao Vizcaya Argentaria)

BANCO BILBAO VIZCAYA ARGENTARIA (CHILE)
ADR agreement terminated 10/20/2005
Each Sponsored ADR for Ser. G exchanged for $27.62017 cash

BANCO BILBAO VIZCAYA INTL GIBRALTAR LTD (SPAIN)
Sponsored ADR's for Guaranteed Preference Ser. A called for redemption at $25 plus $0.338542 accrued dividends on 11/19/2001
Name changed to BBVA Privanza International (Gibraltar) Ltd. 12/17/2001

BANCO BILBAO VIZCAYA S A (SPAIN)
Sponsored ADR's for Ordinary split (3) for (1) by issuance of (2) additional ADR's payable 07/21/1997 to holders of record 07/18/1997 Ex date - 07/22/1997
Sponsored ADR's for Ordinary split (3) for (1) by issuance of (2) additional ADR's payable 07/13/1998 to holders of record 07/10/1998 Ex date - 07/14/1998
Under plan of merger name changed to Banco Bilbao Vizcaya Argentaria, S.A. 01/31/2000

BANCO BISA S A (BOLIVIA)
ADR agreement terminated 11/13/2009
No ADR's remain outstanding

BANCO CENT HISPANO - USA (NEW YORK, NY)
Name changed 10/01/1992
Each share Capital Stock 40¢ par exchanged for (0.04) share Capital Stock $10 par 03/26/1982
Name changed from Banco Central of New York (New York, NY) to Banco Central Hispano - USA (New York, NY) 10/01/1992
Common $10 par split (3) for (1) by issuance of (2) additional shares payable 08/07/1998 to holders of record 07/31/1998
Stock Dividends - 11% 03/01/1985; 14.41441% 02/26/1986
Name changed to BCH - USA (New York, NY) 12/04/1998
(See BCH - USA (New York, NY))

BANCO CENTRAL S A (SPAIN)
Each old ADR for Ordinary exchanged for (1) new ADR for Ordinary 05/29/1987
New ADR's for Ordinary split (3) for (1) by issuance of (2) additional ADR's payable 08/07/1998 to holders of record 07/31/1998 Ex date - 08/10/1998
Stock Dividends - 10% 06/30/1988; 15% 10/31/1988
Merged into Banco Central Hispano S.A. 04/17/1999
Each new ADR for Ordinary exchanged for (0.6) ADR for Ordinary

BANCO COMERCIAL PORTUGUES S A (PORTUGAL)
Each old Sponsored ADR for Nominative Shares exchanged for (1) new Sponsored ADR for Nominative Shares 08/17/1992
Stock Dividends - (1) for (6) 06/25/1992; 20% 06/18/1993; 2.71% payable 05/24/2001 to holders of record 04/18/2001
ADR agreement terminated 09/15/2003
Each Sponsored ADR for Ordinary exchanged for $12.0363 cash (Additional Information in Active)

BANCO COMERCIAL S A (URUGUAY)
GDR agreement terminated 07/30/2002
No GDR holders' equity

BANCO DAYCOVAL S A (BRAZIL)
ADR agreement terminated 10/06/2016
Each Sponsored ADR for Preferred exchanged for $5.631122 cash

BANCO DE A EDWARDS (CHILE)
Merged into Banco de Chile 01/01/2002
Each Sponsored ADR for Ser. A exchanged for (0.86235223) Sponsored ADR for Ser. F

BANCO DE COLOMBIA (COLOMBIA)
Common 1 Peso par changed to 100 Peso par 02/06/1995
Merged into BanColombia S.A. 04/03/1998
Each share Common P100 par exchanged for either (9.59) shares Preference P127.98 par or (9.59) shares Common P127.98 par
Each GDR for Common exchanged for (1.763788) shares Preference P127.98 par or (1.763788) shares Common P127.98 par
Note: Preference or Common shares will only be issued to non-U.S. residents
U.S. residents received approximately $2.45 cash per GDR

BANCO DE GALICIA Y BUENOS AIRES S A (ARGENTINA)
Each old Sponsored ADR for Class B exchanged for (0.5) new Sponsored ADR for Class B 06/17/1993
Stock Dividends - 15% 11/30/1993; 15% 12/02/1994; 18% 11/22/1995; 17.5% payable 01/22/1998 to holders of record 01/20/1998; 9% payable 12/16/1998 to holders of record 12/14/1998; 15.6% payable 11/19/1999 to holders of record 11/12/1999
ADR agreement terminated 08/31/2000
Each new Sponsored ADR for Class B exchanged for $10.719 cash

BANCO DE LAS AMERICAS (TUCSON, AZ)
Name changed to Banco Internacional de Arizona (Tucson, AZ) 06/03/1974
Banco International de Arizona (Tucson, AZ) name changed to Southwestern Bank (Tucson, AZ) 06/06/1978
(See Southwestern Bank (Tucson, AZ))

BANCO DE ORO UNIBANK INC (PHILIPPINES)
Name changed 07/05/2007
Name changed 03/04/2008
Name changed from Banco de Oro Universal Bank to Banco de Oro-EPCI, Inc. 07/05/2007
Name changed from Banco de Oro-EPCI, Inc. to Banco De Oro Unibank, Inc. 03/04/2008
Name changed to BDO Unibank Inc. 09/26/2011

BANCO DE PONCE (PONCE, PR)
Common $100 par changed to $25 par and (3) additional shares issued 05/16/1966
Under plan of reorganization each share Common $25 par automatically became (1) share BanPonce Corp. (New) Common $5 par 08/01/1985
BanPonce Corp. (New) name changed to Popular Inc. 04/25/1997 (Additional Information in Active)

BANCO DE SAN JOSE (SAN JOSE, CA)
Name changed to California Security Bank (San Jose, CA) and Capital Stock $3.50 par changed to $10 par 11/01/1978
(See California Security Bank (San Jose, CA))

BANCO DE SAN JUAN (SANTURCE, PR)
Under plan of merger each share Capital Stock $10 par exchanged for (1) share 8.5% Preferred $10 par 09/16/1980
8.5% Preferred $10 par called for redemption 12/16/1980
Public interest eliminated

BANCO DE SANTIAGO (CHILE)
Name changed to Banco Santiago 08/20/1997
Banco Santiago name changed to Banco Santander Chile (New) 08/01/2002

BANCO DEL PUEBLO COML BK (SANTA ANA, CA)
Name changed to Santa Ana State Bank (Santa Ana, CA) 07/01/1977
Santa Ana State Bank (Santa Ana, CA) name changed to Pan American Bank (Los Angeles, CA) 11/02/1981
(See Pan American Bank (Los Angeles, CA))

BANCO ESPANOL DE CREDITO (SPAIN)
Reorganized as Banesto S.A. 05/25/1990
Each Unsponsored ADR for Ordinary exchanged for (2) Sponsored ADR's for Ordinary
(See Banesto S.A.)

BANCO FIN LTD (BC)
Name changed to First Western Capital Ltd. 06/28/1978

BANCO FRANCES DEL RIO DE LA PLATA S A (ARGENTINA)
Stock Dividends - 15% payable 12/22/1996 to holders of record 12/18/1995; 15% payable 12/19/1996 to holders of record 12/13/1996 Ex date - 12/11/1996
Name changed to BBVA Banco Frances S.A. 10/04/2000

BANCO GANADERO S A (COLOMBIA)
ADR agreement terminated 10/31/2006
Each Sponsored ADR for Class C Preferred exchanged for $12.413966 cash
Each Sponsored ADR for Class B exchanged for $10.28526 cash

BANCO INDL COLOMBIANO S A (COLOMBIA)
Name changed to BanColombia S.A. 04/03/1998

BANCO INDL S A (BOLIVIA)
Name changed to Banco Bisa S.A. 05/30/2000
(See Banco Bisa S.A.)

BANCO INTERNACIONAL DE ARIZONA (TUCSON, AZ)
Name changed to Southwestern Bank (Tucson, AZ) 06/06/1978
(See Southwestern Bank (Tucson, AZ))

BANCO ITAU HLDG FINANCEIRA S A (BRAZIL)
Name changed 02/27/2003
Each Sponsored ADR for Preferred exchanged for (0.2) Sponsored ADR for Preferred 02/21/2002
Name changed from Banco Itau S.A. to Banco Itau Holding Financeira S.A. 02/27/2003
ADR basis changed from (1:500) to (1:0.5) 10/20/2004
Sponsored ADR's for Preferred split (5) for (1) by issuance of (4) additional ADR's payable 10/06/2005 to holders of record 10/05/2005 Ex date - 10/07/2005
ADR basis changed from (1:0.5) to (1:1) 10/06/2005
Sponsored ADR's for Preferred split (2) for (1) by issuance of (1) additional ADR payable 10/05/2007 to holders of record 10/03/2007 Ex date - 10/09/2007
Sponsored ADR's for Preferred split (5) for (4) by issuance of (0.25) additional ADR payable 06/09/2008 to holders of record 06/04/2008 Ex date - 06/10/2008
Under plan of merger name changed to Itau Unibanco Banco Multiplo S.A. 03/30/2009
Itau Unibanco Banco Multiplo S.A. name changed to Itau Unibanco Holding S.A. 08/31/2009

BANCO LATINOAMERICANO DE EXPORTACIONES, S.A. (PANAMA)
Name changed to Banco Latinoamericano de Comercio Exterior, S.A. 07/08/2009

BANCO MACRO BANSUD S A (ARGENTINA)
Name changed to Banco Macro S.A. 08/14/2006

BANCO MERCANTIL C A S A C A BANCO UNIVERSAL (VENEZUELA)
Stock Dividend - 100% payable 10/10/1997 to holders of record 10/03/1997
ADR agreement terminated 10/15/1997
Details not available

BANCO MERCANTIL P R RIO (RIO PIEDRAS, PR)
Each share Capital Stock $10 par exchanged for (2) shares Capital Stock $5 par 02/19/1971
Capital Stock $5 par split (2) for (1) by issuance of (1) additional share 10/30/1971
Acquired by Bank of Nova Scotia 00/00/1979
Details not available

BANCO MERCANTIL S A (BOLIVIA)
ADR agreement terminated 11/13/2009
No ADR's remain outstanding

BANCO O HIGGINS (CHILE)
Merged into Banco de Santiago 01/13/1997
Each Sponsored ADR for Ordinary exchanged for (1) Sponsored ADR for Ser. D Preferred
Banco de Santiago name changed to Banco Santiago 08/20/1997 which name changed to Banco Santander Chile (New) 08/01/2002

BANCO OSORNO Y LA UNION (CHILE)
Name changed to Banco Santander Chile (Old) 07/01/1996
Banco Santander Chile (Old) merged into Banco Santander Chile (New) 08/01/2002

BANCO PATAGONIA SA (ARGENTINA)
Basis changed from (1:1) to (1:20) 11/23/2010
ADR agreement terminated 05/25/2017
No ADR's remain outstanding

BANCO POPOLARE SOCIETA COOP (ITALY)
Each old ADR for Ordinary exchanged for (0.1) new ADR for Ordinary 03/21/2014
ADR agreement terminated 01/24/2017
Each new ADR for Ordinary exchanged for $1.361091 cash

BANCO POPULAR DE P R (SAN JUAN, PR)
Common $20 par changed to $10 par and (1) additional share issued 04/23/1966
Common $10 par split (3) for (2) by issuance of (0.5) additional share 11/30/1981
Common $10 par changed to $5 par and (1) additional share issued 04/22/1985
Common $5 par split (2) for (1) by

issuance of (1) additional share 04/03/1989
Stock Dividends - 12.5% 05/20/1964; 10% 01/03/1967; 10% 01/02/1969; 10% 12/31/1970; 10% 12/31/1973
Merged into BanPonce Corp. (New) 12/31/1990
Each share Common $5 par exchanged for (1) share Common $6 par
BanPonce Corp. (New) name changed to Popular Inc. 04/25/1997

BANCO POPULAR ESPANOL S A (SPAIN)
Basis changed from (1:20) to (1:4) 07/17/2013
Stock Dividends - 0.42372% payable 02/18/2015 to holders of record 01/20/2015 Ex date - 01/15/2015; 0.38023% payable 05/27/2015 to holders of record 04/27/2015 Ex date - 04/23/2015; 0.55248% payable 10/15/2015 to holders of record 09/21/2015 Ex date - 09/17/2015; 0.649935% payable 03/02/2016 to holders of record 01/19/2016 Ex date - 01/14/2016; 0.9434% payable 03/23/2016 to holders of record 03/07/2016 Ex date - 03/03/2016
ADR agreement terminated 05/14/2018
No ADR holders' equity

BANCO RES LTD (BC)
Struck off register and declared dissolved for failure to file returns 04/16/1992

BANCO RIO DE LA PLATA S A (ARGENTINA)
ADR agreement terminated 11/30/2001
Each Sponsored ADR for Class B exchanged for $0.0094 cash

BANCO SANTANDER CENT HISPANO S A (SPAIN)
ADR's for Ordinary P500 par split (2) for (1) by issuance of (1) additional ADR payable 06/18/1999 to holders of record 06/11/1999 Ex date - 06/21/1999
Name changed to Banco Santander, S.A. 08/24/2007

BANCO SANTANDER CHILE (CHILE)
Sponsored ADR's for Ser. A Preferred split (2) for (1) by issuance of (1) additional ADR payable 07/02/1998 to holders of record 06/26/1998
Merged into Banco Santander Chile (New) 08/01/2002
Each Sponsored ADR for Ser. A exchanged for (0.75245999) new Sponsored ADR for Common

BANCO SANTANDER P R (SAN JUAN, PR)
Common $5 par changed to $2.50 par and (1) additional share issued 04/07/1998
Stock Dividend - 10% payable 02/22/2000 to holders of record 01/31/2000
Under plan of reorganization each share Common $2.50 par automatically became (1) share Santander BanCorp Common $2.50 par 05/01/2000
(See Santander BanCorp)
7% Perpetual Monthly Income Preferred Stock Ser. A $25 par called for redemption at $25 on 12/26/2003

BANCO SANTANDER S A (SPAIN)
Name changed 06/30/1992
Name changed from Banco de Santander, S.A. de Credito to Banco Santander S.A. 06/30/1992
ADR's for Ordinary P500 par split (3) for (1) by issuance of (2) additional ADR's payable 06/20/1997 to holders of record 06/06/1997 Ex date - 06/23/1997
ADR's for Ordinary P500 par split (2) for (1) by issuance of (1) additional ADR payable 07/02/1998 to holders of record 06/26/1998 Ex date - 07/06/1998
Stock Dividend - 2% payable 10/28/1998 to holders of record 08/20/1998 Ex date - 08/18/1998
Merged into Banco Santander Central Hispano S.A. 04/17/1999
Each ADR for Ordinary P500 par exchanged for (1) ADR for Ordinary P500 par
Banco Santander Central Hispano S.A. name changed to Banco Santander, S.A. 08/24/2007

BANCO SANTIAGO (CHILE)
Name changed to Banco Santander Chile (New) 08/01/2002

BANCO VENEZOLANO DE CREDITO S A C A (VENEZUELA)
Stock Dividends - 12.5% payable 01/09/1998 to holders of record 01/06/1998; 16.66666% payable 07/17/1998 to holders of record 07/07/1998; 20% payable 06/14/1999 to holders of record 06/01/1999; 14.29% payable 02/23/2000 to holders of record 02/11/2000; 20% payable 11/09/2000 to holders of record 10/23/2000 Ex date - 10/24/2000; 16.6666% payable 06/07/2001 to holders of record 05/23/2001 Ex date - 05/21/2001; 12.7217% payable 07/11/2002 to holders of record 07/09/2002 Ex date - 07/05/2002; 20% payable 11/23/2004 to holders of record 11/08/2004 Ex date - 11/04/2004; 4% payable 02/28/2007 to holders of record 02/13/2007 Ex date - 02/13/2007; 33.3333% payable 07/16/2007 to holders of record 05/25/2007 Ex date - 07/17/2007
Basis changed from (1:1) to (1:0.001) 08/11/2008
ADR agreement terminated 08/31/2016
Each Sponsored ADR for Common exchanged for (0.001) share Common
Note: Unexchanged ADR's will be sold and the proceeds, if any, held for claim after 09/04/2017

BANCO WIESE (PERU)
Sponsored ADR's for Common split (2.06192) for (1) by issuance of (1.06192) additional ADR's 03/03/1995
ADR agreement terminated 06/15/2001
Each Sponsored ADR for Ordinary exchanged for $0.1503 cash

BANCOHIO CORP (OH)
Capital Stock $20 par changed to $15 par 00/00/1933
Capital Stock $15 par changed to $20 par 00/00/1946
Capital Stock $20 par changed to $6.66666666 par and (2) additional shares issued 01/24/1966
Merged into National City Corp. 11/09/1984
Each share Capital Stock $6.66666666 par exchanged for $37 cash

BANCOKENTUCKY CO. (DE)
No longer in existence having become inoperative and void for non-payment of taxes 04/01/1934

BANCOKLAHOMA CORP (DE)
Common $4 par changed to $2 par and (1) additional share issued 08/19/1981
Common $2 par changed to $0.0001 par 11/16/1986
Each share $2.50 Conv. Preferred Ser. A $1 par exchanged for (1.25) shares Common $0.0001 par 09/26/1989
Plan of reorganization under Chapter 11 Federal Bankruptcy Code effective 12/31/1991
No stockholders' equity

BANCOMIT CORP.
Dissolved 00/00/1932
Details not available

BANCORP BK (WILMINGTON, DE)
Merged into Bancorp, Inc. (The) 12/22/2004
Each share Common $1 par exchanged for (1.15) shares Common $1 par

BANCORP CONN INC (DE)
Common $1 par split (2) for (1) by issuance of (1) additional share payable 12/01/1997 to holders of record 11/10/1997
Stock Dividend - 20% payable 06/19/1996 to holders of record 06/05/1996
Merged into Banknorth Group, Inc. (ME) 08/31/2002
Each share Common $1 par exchanged for $28 cash

BANCORP FINL GROUP INC (AB)
Merged into Rivera Enterprises Ltd. 09/04/2003
Each share Common no par exchanged for $0.12 cash

BANCORP HAWAII INC (HI)
$2.25 Conv. Preferred Ser. A $1 par called for redemption 07/08/1983
Common $2 par split (3) for (2) by issuance of (0.5) additional share 09/13/1991
Common $2 par split (3) for (2) by issuance of (0.5) additional share 03/15/1994
Stock Dividends - 50% 11/16/1988; 10% 05/04/1990
Name changed to Pacific Century Financial Corp. (HI) 04/25/1997
Pacific Century Financial Corp. (HI) reincorporated in Delaware 04/24/1998 which name changed to Bank of Hawaii Corp. 04/26/2002

BANCORP HUNTINGDON INC (TN)
Acquired by First South Bancorp, Inc. (TN) 01/27/2001
Each share Common $10 par exchanged for $333.47 cash

BANCORP INC (DE)
Each share Ser. A Preferred 1¢ par exchanged for (1.0854109) shares Common $1 par 09/00/2009
Each share Mandatorily Conv. Non-Vtg. Perpetual Preferred Ser. C 1¢ par exchanged for (222.222222) shares Common $1 par 09/29/2016
(Additional Information in Active)

BANCORP INC (KY)
Merged into S.Y. Bancorp, Inc. 05/01/2013
Each share Common no par exchanged for (12.7557) shares Common no par and $185.81 cash
S.Y. Bancorp, Inc. name changed to Stock Yards Bancorp, Inc. 04/25/2014

BANCORP INTL GROUP (NV)
Common $0.001 par changed to $0.0001 par 08/19/2005
Reorganized as Energy Source, Inc. 06/27/2008
Each share Common $0.0001 par exchanged for (0.005) share Common $0.001 par
(See Energy Source, Inc.)

BANCORP MISS INC (MS)
Common $5 par changed to $2.50 par and (1) additional share issued 12/18/1985
Common $2.50 par split (2) for (1) by issuance of (1) additional share 10/06/1986
Name changed to BancorpSouth, Inc. 10/06/1992
BancorpSouth, Inc. reorganized as BancorpSouth Bank (Tupelo, MS) 11/01/2017

BANCORP N J INC (DE)
Merged into UJB Financial Corp. 07/14/1995
Each share Common 1¢ par exchanged for (1.5441) shares Common $1.20 par
UJB Financial Corp. name changed to Summit Bancorp 03/01/1996 which merged into FleetBoston Financial Corp. 03/01/2001 which merged into Bank of America Corp. 04/01/2004

BANCORP PA (PA)
Merged into Dauphin Deposit Corp. 09/12/1983
Each share Common $5 par exchanged for $25.50 cash

BANCORP RHODE ISLAND INC (RI)
Merged into Brookline Bancorp, Inc. 01/03/2012
Each share Common 1¢ par exchanged for (4.686) shares Common 1¢ par

BANCORP III INC (MO)
Company's sole asset placed in receivership 09/04/2009
Stockholders' equity unlikely

BANCORPORATION MONT (MT)
Name changed to Bank of Montana System 01/18/1978
Bank of Montana System merged into Norwest Corp. 04/15/1994 which name changed to Wells Fargo & Co. (New) 11/02/1998

BANCORPORATION WIS INC (WI)
Merged into Citizens Bancorporation 07/02/1984
Each share Capital Stock $1 par exchanged for $38 principal amount of Variable Rate Conv. Notes due 07/01/1993

BANCORPSOUTH CAP TR I (DE)
8.15% Trust Preferred Securities called for redemption at $25 plus $0.237708 accrued dividends on 08/12/2013

BANCORPSOUTH INC (MS)
Common $2.50 par split (2) for (1) by issuance of (1) additional share 11/20/1995
Common $2.50 par split (2) for (1) by issuance of (1) additional share payable 05/15/1998 to holders of record 05/01/1998 Ex date - 05/18/1998
Stock Dividend - 15% 12/01/1993
Under plan of reorganization each share Common $2.50 par automatically became (1) share BancorpSouth Bank (Tupelo, MS) Common $2.50 par 11/01/2017

BANCROFT (JOSEPH) & SONS CO. (DE)
Common no par changed to $8 par 00/00/1948
Each share Common $8 par exchanged for (2) shares Common $4 par 00/00/1953
Stock Dividend - 200% 12/27/1946
Merged into Pequot Mills, Inc. 04/10/1962
Each share Common $4 par exchanged for $20 cash

BANCROFT CONV FD INC (DE)
Name changed to Bancroft Fund Ltd. and Common 1¢ par reclassified as Trust Shares 03/17/2006

BANCROFT HLDG CORP (DE)
Charter cancelled and declared void for failure to pay franchise taxes 03/01/1997

BANCROFT HOTEL CORP. (MA)
Liquidated 00/00/1952
Details not available

BANCROFT MINES LTD. (ON)
Charter cancelled and declared dissolved for failure to file returns and pay fees 07/27/1976

BANCROFT MINES LTD (ZAMBIA)
Merged into Zambia Copper Investments Ltd. 06/25/1970
Each ADR for Ordinary ZMK 50 par exchanged for either (0.684454) share Ordinary ZMK 24 par and (1.611788) Units of Loan Stock or $1.10 cash
Note: Option to receive stock expired 09/15/1970
Zambia Copper Investments Ltd. name changed to ZCI Ltd. 05/24/2010

BANCROFT REALTY CO. (MA)
Reorganized as Bancroft Hotel Corp. 00/00/1936
Each share old Preferred exchanged for (0.33333333) share new Class B Common no par
(See Bancroft Hotel Corp.)

BANCROFT URANIUM INC (NV)
Common $0.001 par split (52) for (1) by issuance of (51) additional shares payable 10/01/2007 to holders of record 10/01/2007
SEC revoked common stock registration 12/07/2011

BANCROFT URANIUM MINES LTD. (ON)
Name changed to Bancroft Mines Ltd. (ON) 11/01/1971
(See Bancroft Mines Ltd. (ON))

BANCSECURITY CORP (IA)
Merged into F&M Bancorporation, Inc. 07/01/1998
Each share Common exchanged for (93.6064) shares Common $1 par
F&M Bancorporation, Inc. merged into Citizens Banking Corp. 07/01/1997 which name changed to Citizens Republic Bancorp, Inc. 04/26/2007 which merged into FirstMerit Corp. 04/12/2013 which merged into Huntington Bancshares Inc. 08/16/2016

BANCSERVE GROUP INC (DE)
Common $5 par split (2) for (1) by issuance of (1) additional share 10/15/1986
Acquired by First of America Bank Corp. 06/30/1987
Each share Common $5 par exchanged for (0.2907) share Common $10 par and $3.04 cash
First of America Bank Corp. merged into National City Corp. 03/31/1998 which was acquired by PNC Financial Services Group, Inc. 12/31/2008

BANCSHARE PORTFOLIO CORP (ON)
Adjustable Rate Preferred no par called for redemption 10/01/1992
Public interest eliminated

BANCSHARES, LTD. (DE)
Charter cancelled and declared inoperative and void for non-payment of taxes 04/01/1938

BANCSHARES FLA INC (FL)
Name changed to Bank of Florida Corp. 12/21/2006
(See Bank of Florida Corp.)

BANCSHARES NEW JERSEY (NJ)
Name changed to Northern National Corp. 05/28/1981
Northern National Corp. merged into Horizon Bancorp 10/01/1983
(See Horizon Bancorp)

BANCSHARES N C INC (NC)
Stock Dividend - 100% 08/01/1972
Merged into NCNB Corp. 12/23/1982
Each share Common $5 par exchanged for (0.9696) share Common $2.50 par
NCNB Corp. name changed to NationsBank Corp. (NC) 12/31/1991 which reincorporated in Delaware as BankAmerica Corp. (Old) 09/25/1998 which merged into BankAmerica Corp. (New) 09/30/1998 which name changed to Bank of America Corp. 04/28/1999

BANCSHARES 2000, INC. (DE)
Name changed to Suburban Bancshares, Inc. 03/01/1991
Suburban Bancshares, Inc. merged into Columbia Bancorp 03/08/2000 which merged into Fulton Financial Corp. 02/01/2006

BANCSTOCK CORP AMER (FL)
Stock Dividend - 100% 07/22/1969
Name changed to General Financial Systems, Inc. 02/28/1970
General Financial Systems, Inc. name changed to First Marine Banks, Inc. 03/01/1976
(See First Marine Banks, Inc.)

BANCTEC INC (DE)
Common 1¢ par split (3) for (2) by issuance of (0.5) additional share 03/11/1993
Merged into Colonial Acquisition Corp. 07/22/1999
Each share Common 1¢ par exchanged for $18.50 cash

BANCTENN CORP (TN)
Each share old Common $8 par exchanged for (0.00014285) share new Common $8 par 01/15/2002
Note: In effect holders received $25.85 cash per share and public interest was eliminated

BANCTEXAS GROUP INC (DE)
Each share $1.4625 Conv. Preferred $1 par exchanged for (12) shares Common 1¢ par and $1.46 cash 07/17/1987
Each share Class A Conv. Preferred $8 par exchanged for (10) shares Common 1¢ par and $0.775 cash 07/17/1987
Each share Common $1 par exchanged for (0.02) share Common 1¢ par 07/17/1987
Recapitalized as First Banks America, Inc. 08/31/1995
Each share Common 1¢ par exchanged for (0.06666666) share Common 15¢ par
(See First Banks America, Inc.)

BANCTRUST FINL GROUP INC (AL)
Merged into Trustmark Corp. 02/15/2013
Each share Common 1¢ par exchanged for (0.125) share Common no par

BANCUS RICHMOND INC (TX)
Charter forfeited for failure to pay taxes 11/18/1991

BANCWEST CAP I (DE)
9.5% Quarterly Income Preferred Securities called for redemption at $25 on 12/01/2005

BANCWEST CORP (DE)
Ctfs. dated after 11/01/1998
Adjustable Rate Preferred Class A 144A called for redemption at $716.92 plus $479.36 accrued interest on 10/26/1998
Accredited Investors Adjustable Rate Preferred Class A called for redemption at $716.92 plus $479.36 accrued interest on 10/26/1998
Common $5 par split (2) for (1) by issuance of (1) additional share payable 12/15/1999 to holders of record 12/01/1999 Ex date - 12/16/1999
Merged into BNP Paribas 12/20/2001
Each share Common $5 par exchanged for $35 cash

BANCWEST CORP (DE)
Ctfs. dated prior to 03/18/1980
Name changed to BWC Liquidating Corp. 03/18/1980
(See BWC Liquidating Corp.)

BANCWIS CORP (WI)
Merged into Valley Bancorporation 03/31/1985
Each share Common $2.50 par exchanged for $29 cash

BAND LTD (NV)
Charter revoked for failure to file reports and pay fees 05/01/1997

BAND ORE RES LTD (ON)
Recapitalized 09/26/1991
Recapitalized from Band-Ore Gold Mines Ltd. to Band Ore Resources Ltd. 09/26/1991
Each share Common no par exchanged for (0.5) share new Common no par
Merged into West Timmins Gold Corp. 09/18/2006
Each share new Common no par exchanged for (0.9) share Common no par
West Timmins Gold Corp. merged into Lake Shore Gold Corp. 11/05/2009 which merged into Tahoe Resources Inc. 04/07/2016

BAND REP MGMT INC (NV)
Each share old Common $0.001 par exchanged for (187) shares new Common $0.001 par 05/23/2014
Name changed to Sky Century Investment Inc. 05/11/2017

BANDAG INC (IA)
Common no par changed to $1 par and (2) additional shares issued 01/22/1969
Common $1 par split (2) for (1) by issuance of (1) additional share 04/05/1973
Restricted Class B Common $1 par reclassified as Common $1 par 01/16/2007
Stock Dividends - 100% 12/10/1970; 50% 10/15/1971; in Restricted Class B Common 100% 01/16/1987; in Class A Common 100% 06/10/1992; in Class A Common to holders of Restricted Class B Common 100% 06/10/1992
Merged into Bridgestone Corp. 05/31/2007
Each share Common $1 par exchanged for $50.75 cash
Each share Class A Common $1 par exchanged for $50.75 cash

BANDAI LTD (JAPAN)
Sponsored ADR's for Common split (2) for (1) by issuance of (1) additional ADR payable 11/26/2003 to holders of record 09/29/2003 Ex date - 11/28/2003
ADR agreement terminated 08/01/2005
Each Sponsored ADR for Common exchanged for $5.38452 cash

BANDAR RAYA DEVS BERHAD (MALAYSIA)
ADR agreement terminated 02/15/2013
Each ADR for Ordinary exchanged for $0.9138 cash

BANDERA GOLD LTD (AB)
Each share old Common no par exchanged for (0.1) share new Common no par 02/02/2017
Name changed to Jaeger Resources Corp. 07/09/2018

BANDESS, INC. (MA)
Completely liquidated 04/12/1955
Details not available

B&H MARITIME CARRIERS LTD (LIBERIA)
Recapitalized as Excel Maritime Carriers Ltd. 05/27/1998
Each share Common 1¢ par exchanged for (0.05) share Common 1¢ par
(See Excel Maritime Carriers Ltd.)

BANDINI PETROLEUM CO. (CA)
Merged into Westates Petroleum Co. 12/24/1959
Details not available

BANDO MCGLOCKLIN CAP CORP (WI)
Each share Common $0.06666666 par received distribution of (0.23854051) share InvestorsBancorp, Inc. Common 1¢ par payable 09/06/1997 to holders of record 09/05/1997
Stock Dividend - 10% payable 01/31/2000 to holders of record 12/31/1999
Name changed to Middleton Doll Co. 05/04/2001
Middleton Doll Co. recapitalized as FirsTime Design Ltd. 02/22/2011

BANDOLAC MNG LTD (ON)
Name changed to Schyan Exploration Inc. 10/29/2008

BANDON CAP CORP (AB)
Name changed to Bandon Capital Resources Ltd. 06/15/2007
Bandon Capital Resources Ltd. name changed to Kierland Resources Ltd. 11/11/2008 which recapitalized as PetroSands Resources (Canada) Inc. 11/30/2010 which name changed to CanRock Energy Corp. 01/03/2012 which merged into Alston Energy Inc. 07/24/2012
(See Alston Energy Inc.)

BANDON CAP RES LTD (AB)
Name changed to Kierland Resources Ltd. 11/11/2008
Kierland Resources Ltd. recapitalized as PetroSands Resources (Canada) Inc. 11/30/2010 which name changed to CanRock Energy Corp. 01/03/2012 which merged into Alston Energy Inc. 07/24/2012
(See Alston Energy Inc.)

BANDOWAN MINES LTD. (ON)
Reincorporated under the laws of Quebec as Vanguard Explorations Ltd. 04/16/1958
Vanguard Exploratons Ltd. recapitalized as Guardian Mines Ltd. 09/20/1965 which recapitalized as Green Coast Resources Ltd. 07/20/1971 which recapitalized as Ridgepoint Resources Ltd. 06/15/1988 which recapitalized as Ridgepoint Mineral Corp. 10/31/1997 which name changed to Jet Drill Canada, Inc. 09/15/2000
(See Jet Drill Canada, Inc.)

BANESTO HLDGS LTD (SPAIN)
144A Preference Ser. A called for redemption at $25 plus $0.1458 accrued dividends on 07/02/2012

BANESTO S A (SPAIN)
ADR agreement terminated 05/13/2013
Each Sponsored ADR for Ordinary exchanged for $2.755177 cash

BANFF BREWERY CO (AB)
Recapitalized as Peak Brewing Group Inc. 09/23/1999
Each share Common no par exchanged for (0.2) share Common no par
(See Peak Brewing Group Inc.)

BANFF BREWING CAP CORP (AB)
Name changed to Banff Brewery Corp. 03/31/1995
Banff Brewery Corp. recapitalized as Peak Brewing Group Inc. 09/23/1999

BANFF MINES LTD. (BC)
Merged into Camela Mines & Oils Ltd. 07/00/1971
Each share Common $1 par exchanged for (1) share Common 25¢ par
(See Camela Mines & Oils Ltd.)

BANFF OIL LTD (AB)
Completely liquidated 02/26/1971
Each share Common 50¢ exchanged for first and final distribution of (0.52) share Aquitaine Co. of

Canada Ltd.-Societe Aquitaine du Canada Ltee. Common no par
(See Aquitaine Co. of Canada Ltd.-Societe Aquitaine du Canada Ltee.)

BANFF RES LTD (YT)
Reincorporated 03/06/1996
Place of incorporation changed from (BC) to (YT) 03/06/1996
Struck off register 01/26/2007

BANG SERVICE STATIONS
Sold to Shell Eastern Petroleum Products 00/00/1928
Details not available

BANGLA PPTY MGMT INC (CO)
Name changed to China Properties Developments, Inc. 12/01/2005
(See China Properties Developments, Inc.)

BANGOR & AROOSTOOK CORP. (ME)
Merged into Bangor Punta Alegre Sugar Corp. 10/15/1964
Each share Common $1 par exchanged for (0.4) share $1.25 Conv. Preference $1 par and (1.1) shares Common $1 par
Bangor Punta Alegre Sugar Corp. name changed to Bangor Punta Corp. 01/20/1967
(See Bangor Punta Corp.)

BANGOR & AROOSTOOK RR CO (ME)
5% Preferred $100 par called for redemption 11/02/1955
Assets sold for the benefit of creditors 01/09/2003
No stockholders' equity

BANGOR AMER INC (NY)
Charter cancelled and proclaimed dissolved for failure to pay taxes 01/08/1993

BANGOR HYDRO ELEC CO (ME)
Each share Common $100 par exchanged for (4) shares Common $25 par 00/00/1929
Common $25 par changed to $15 par 00/00/1944
Common $15 par changed to $5 par and (2) additional shares issued 06/01/1961
8.76% Preferred called for redemption 01/02/2001
Merged into Emera Inc. 10/10/2001
Each share Common $5 par exchanged for $26.806 cash
4% Preferred $100 par called for redemption at $110 plus $1.67 accrued dividends on 03/01/2003
4.25% Preferred $100 par called for redemption at $100 plus $0.106 accrued dividends on 03/01/2003
Name changed to Emera Maine 11/05/2015

BANGOR INVTS II INC (CO)
Each share old Common no par exchanged for (0.005) share new Common no par 06/30/1990
Merged into BI Acquisition Corp. 07/20/1992
Each share new Common no par exchanged for $1.10 cash

BANGOR INVTS INC (CO)
Name changed to E'Prime Aerospace Corp. 10/26/1987

BANGOR PUNTA ALEGRE SUGAR CORP. (DE)
Stock Distribution - (0.1) share $1.25 Conv. Preference $1 par for each share Common 10/13/1964
Name changed to Bangor Punta Corp. 01/20/1967
(See Bangor Punta Corp.)

BANGOR PUNTA CORP (DE)
$1.25 Conv. Preference $1 par called for redemption 06/15/1979
Common $1 par split (3) for (2) by issuance of (0.5) additional share 04/06/1981

Merged into Lear Siegler, Inc. 02/24/1984
Each share $2 Conv. Preference Ser. C $1 par exchanged for $58.03 cash
Each share Common $1 par exchanged for $27.50 cash

BANGOR WATER CO. (PA)
All owned by Pennsylvania State Water Corp. a subsidiary of American Water Works Co., Inc. as of 06/01/1965

BANISTER CONTL CORP (PA)
Acquired by Banister Continental, Ltd. (AB) 04/02/1973
Each share Common no par exchanged for (1) share Common no par
Banister Continental, Ltd. (AB) reincorporated in Canada 01/10/1978 which name changed to Banister Inc. 06/04/1990 which name changed to Banister Foundation Inc. 06/13/1994 which name changed to BFC Construction Corp. 06/10/1997
(See BFC Construction Corp.)

BANISTER FDNTN INC (CANADA)
Reincorporated 01/10/1978
Name changed 06/04/1990
Name changed 06/13/1994
Place of incorporation changed from (AB) to (Canada) 01/10/1978
Name changed from Banister Continental Ltd. to Banister Inc. 06/04/1990
Name changed from Banister Inc. to Banister Foundation Inc. 06/13/1994
Name changed to BFC Construction Corp. 06/10/1997
(See BFC Construction Corp.)

BANK & TRUST CO. OF NORTH BRANFORD (NORTH BRANFORD, CT)
Name changed to Community Banking Co. (North Branford, CT) 01/23/1968
Community Banking Co. (North Branford, CT) merged into State National Bancorp Inc. 09/28/1981
(See State National Bancorp Inc.)

BANK & TR CO OLD YORK ROAD (WILLOW GROVE, PA)
Stock Dividends - 10% 10/15/1971; 10% 12/20/1972; 10% 11/23/1973; 10% 11/01/1974; 10% 03/01/1984; 10% 03/01/1985; 10% 02/28/1986; 10% 03/10/1987
Reorganized as Old York Road Bancorp, Inc. 01/02/1991
Each share Common $2.50 par exchanged for (1) share Common $1 par
Old York Road Bancorp, Inc. merged into Midlantic Corp. 06/28/1995 which merged into PNC Bank Corp. 12/31/1995 which name changed to PNC Financial Services Group, Inc. 03/15/2000

BANK & TR PUERTO RICO (SAN JUAN, PR)
Merged into EuroBancshares, Inc. 05/03/2004
Each share 9.625% Monthly Income Preferred Ser. B $10 par held by U.S. residents exchanged for $26.34 cash
Shares held by residents of the Commonwealth of Puerto Rico or non-U.S. residents exchanged for (1) share Preferred Ser. A 1¢ par and $1.34 cash
(See EuroBancshares, Inc.)

BANK A LEVY (OXNARD, CA)
Common $100 par split (3) for (1) by issuance of (2) additional shares 01/27/1960
Common $100 par changed to $10 par and (9) additional shares issued plus a 50% stock dividend paid 12/14/1962
Stock Dividend - 50% 06/01/1965

Reorganized as Levy Bancorp 06/30/1969
Each share Common $10 par exchanged for (2) shares Capital Stock $5 par
Levy Bancorp merged into First Interstate Bancorp 01/31/1995 which merged into Wells Fargo & Co. (Old) 04/01/1996 which merged into Wells Fargo & Co. (New) 11/02/1998

BANK ABBEVILLE (ABBEVILLE, SC)
Under plan of reorganization each share Common $5 par automatically became (1) share Abbeville Capital Corp. Common $5 par 07/01/1997
Abbeville Capital Corp. merged into Community Capital Corp. 03/04/2004 which merged into Park Sterling Corp. 11/01/2011

BANK ALAMEDA (ALAMEDA, CA)
Common no par split (3) for (2) by issuance of (0.5) additional share payable 02/26/2001 to holders of record 02/05/2001 Ex date - 02/27/2001
Under plan of reorganization each share Common no par automatically became (1) share NorCal Community Bancorp Common no par 06/21/2002
(See NorCal Community Bancorp)

BANK ALEXANDRIA (ALEXANDRIA, VA)
Stock Dividend - 5% payable 02/18/1998 to holders of record 01/27/1998
Merged into F & M National Corp. 06/08/1998
Each share Common $5 par exchanged for (0.942) share Common $2 par
F & M National Corp. merged into BB&T Corp. 08/09/2001

BANK ALMA (ALMA, MI)
Stock Dividends - 25% 03/21/1974; 10% 03/00/1975; 25% 03/19/1976; 20% 03/00/1977; 20% 03/00/1978; 20% 03/00/1979; 20% 04/30/1980; 10% 05/28/1982
Reorganized as Firstbank Corp. 12/31/1985
Each share Common $10 par exchanged for (1) share Common $10 par
FirstBank Corp. merged into Mercantile Bank Corp. 06/01/2014

BANK ALTA CALGARY (EDMONTON, AB)
Name changed to Canadian Western Bank (Edmonton, AB) 05/09/1988

BANK AMER NATL TR & SVGS ASSN (SAN FRANCISCO, CA)
Capital Stock $12.50 par changed to $6.25 par and (1) additional share issued 00/00/1950
Stock Dividends - 66.66666666% 06/30/1945; 20% 04/15/1949; 20% 12/30/1968
Under plan of reorganization each share Capital Stock $6.25 par automatically became (1) share BankAmerica Corp. (Old) Common $6.25 par 04/01/1969
BankAmerica Corp. (Old) merged into BankAmerica Corp. (New) 09/30/1998 which name changed to Bank of America Corp. 04/28/1999

BANK ANAHEIM N A (ANAHEIM, CA)
Merged into California State Bank (Covina, CA) 09/16/1994
Each share Common $5 par exchanged for $14.7574 cash

BANK ARLINGTON (ARLINGTON, VA)
Acquired by Northern Virginia Bankshares Inc. 04/30/1973
Each share Common $5 par exchanged for (1.2) shares Common $1 par
Northern Virginia Bankshares Inc. liquidated for Central National Corp.

(VA) 01/02/1975 which merged into Commonwealth Banks, Inc. 12/31/1978 which name changed to Central Fidelity Banks, Inc. 06/01/1979 which merged into Wachovia Corp. (New) (Ctfs. dated between 05/20/1991 and 09/01/2001) 12/15/1997 which merged into Wachovia Corp. (Ctfs. dated after 09/01/2001) 09/01/2001 which merged into Wells Fargo & Co. (New) 12/31/2008

BANK ASHEVILLE NEW (ASHEVILLE, NC)
Under plan of reorganization each share Common $5 par automatically became (1) share Weststar Financial Services Corp. Common $1 par 01/29/2001
(See Westar Financial Services Corp.)

BANK ASHEVILLE OLD (ASHEVILLE, NC)
Capital Stock $10 par changed to $5 par and (1) additional share issued 07/28/1964
Capital Stock $5 par split (3) for (1) by issuance of (2) additional shares 03/23/1973
Stock Dividend - 45.45454545% 04/10/1959
Merged into NCNB Corp. 12/03/1979
Each share Capital Stock $5 par exchanged for (2.625) shares Common $2.50 par
NCNB Corp. name changed to NationsBank Corp. 12/31/1991 which reincorporated in Delaware as BankAmerica Corp. (Old) 09/25/1998 which merged into BankAmerica Corp. (New) 09/30/1998 which name changed to Bank of America Corp. 04/28/1999

BANK ASTORIA (ASTORIA, OR)
Common $1.25 par split (2) for (1) by issuance of (1) additional share payable 12/05/1997 to holders of record 12/01/1997
Acquired by Columbia Banking Systems, Inc. 10/01/2004
Each share Common $1.25 par exchanged for $20.78 cash

BANK ATLANTA (DECATUR, GA)
Merged into Premier Bancshares Inc. (New) 10/27/1999
Each share Common exchanged for (1.4375) shares Common $1 par Premier Bancshares Inc. (New) merged into BB&T Corp. 01/13/2000

BANK ATMORE (ATMORE, AL)
Stock Dividends - 25% 09/10/1975; 100% 04/15/1981
Reorganized as United Bancorporation of Alabama, Inc. 02/28/1983
Each share Common $10 par exchanged for (1) share Common 1¢ par

BANK AUSTRIA A G (AUSTRIA)
Merged into Bayerische Hypo-Und Vereinsbank AG 02/08/2001
Each Sponsored ADR for Bearer exchanged for (0.2) Sponsored ADR for Bearer
(See Bayerische Hypo-und Vereinsbank AG)

BANK AVOCA (AVOCA, NY)
Merged into Financial Institutions, Inc. 05/01/2002
Each share Common $20 par exchanged for (9.411) shares Common 1¢ par

BANK B C (VANCOUVER, BC)
Common $10 par changed to $5 par and (1) additional share issued 03/30/1982
Common $5 par changed to no par 04/30/1984
Name changed to B.C. Bancorp 04/09/1987
B.C. Bancorp merged into Canadian

Western Bank (Edmonton, AB) 11/01/1996

BANK BABYLON (BABYLON, NY)
Capital Stock $10 par changed to $5 par and (1) additional share issued plus a 10% stock dividend paid 01/20/1961
Stock Dividends - 10% 01/26/1959; 10% 01/22/1960
Merged into Charter New York Corp. 05/01/1972
Each share Capital Stock $5 par exchanged for (1) share Common $10 par
Charter New York Corp. name changed to Irving Bank Corp. 10/17/1979 which merged into Bank of New York Co., Inc. 12/30/1988 which merged into Bank of New York Mellon Corp. 07/01/2007

BANK BETHESDA (BETHESDA, MD)
Stock Dividend - 66.66666666% 02/15/1971
Under plan of reorganization each share Common $25 par automatically became (1) share Bethesda Bancorporation Common $25 par 08/02/1982
(See Bethesda Bancorporation)

BANK BEVERLY HILLS (BEVERLY HILLS, CA)
Taken over by the FDIC 04/03/1992
Stockholders' equity undetermined

BANK BLDG & EQUIP CORP AMER (DE)
Capital Stock $3 par changed to $2 par and (0.66666666) additional share issued 03/24/1952
Capital Stock $2 par changed to $1.33333333 par and (0.5) additional share issued 12/30/1963
Capital Stock $1.33333333 par reclassified as Common $1.33333333 par 02/17/1970
Common $1.33333333 par split (5) for (4) by issuance of (0.25) additional share 07/21/1981
Stock Dividends - 100% 01/05/1950; 50% 01/15/1951; 10% 12/15/1960; 50% 12/28/1972
Plan of reorganization under Chapter 11 Federal Bankruptcy Code effective 07/22/1991
No stockholders' equity

BANK BLOOMFIELD (BLOOMFIELD, NJ)
Reorganized as TransJersey Bancorp 07/03/1974
Each share Common $5 par exchanged for (1) share Common $5 par
(See TransJersey Bancorp)

BANK BPH S A (POLAND)
Each 144A GDR for Ordinary received distribution of $154.01353 cash payable 01/31/2008 to holders of record 01/22/2008
Each Reg. S GDR for Ordinary received distribution of $154.01353 cash payable 01/31/2008 to holders of record 01/22/2008
ADR agreement terminated 12/31/2010
Each 144A GDR for Ordinary exchanged for $4.407981 cash
Each Reg. S GDR for Ordinary exchanged for $4.407981 cash

BANK BUFFALO (BUFFALO, NY)
99.31% acquired by Bank of New York Co., Inc. through purchase offer as of 03/26/1976
Public interest eliminated

BANK BURLINGTON (BURLINGTON, WI)
Merged into Marshall & Ilsley Corp. (Old) 02/01/1995
Each share Common $20 par exchanged for (1.65) shares Common $1 par
(See Marshall & Ilsley Corp. (Old))

BANK CALIF N A (SAN FRANCISCO, CA)
Common Capital Stock $80 par changed to $100 par 00/00/1946
Each share Common Capital Stock $100 par exchanged for (5) shares Common Capital Stock $20 par 00/00/1949
Common Capital Stock $20 par changed to $10 par and (1) additional share issued 04/15/1957
Common Capital Stock $10 par changed to $15 par and (0.5) additional share issued 04/14/1970
Under plan of reorganization each share Common Capital Stock $15 par automatically became (1) share BanCal Tri-State Corp. Common $15 par 05/01/1972
(See BanCal Tri-State Corp.)

BANK CALUMET, N.A. (CHICAGO HEIGHTS, IL)
Acquired by Bank Calumet, N.A. (Hammond, IN) 06/06/1997
Details not available

BANK CALUMET INC (IN)
Merged into First Midwest Bancorp, Inc. 03/31/2006
Each share Common exchanged for $153.59 cash

BANK CENT PA (MONTOURSVILLE, PA)
Merged into Commonwealth Bancshares Corp. 12/30/1985
Each share Common $5 par exchanged for $74 cash

BANK CHARLES TOWN (CHARLES TOWN, WV)
Merged into Potomac Bancshares, Inc. 07/29/1994
Each share Common $1 par exchanged for (2) shares Common $1 par

BANK CHICAGO (CHICAGO, IL)
Acquired by TCF Financial Corp. 01/16/1997
Details not available

BANK CLARKSDALE (CLARKSDALE, MS)
Common $100 par changed to $20 par and (4) additional shares issued 11/05/1971
Common $20 par changed to $10 par and (1) additional share issued plus a 20% stock dividend paid 07/12/1973
Stock Dividends - 50% 12/01/1954; 66.66666666% 05/16/1961; 20% 03/01/1966; 20% 12/09/1970; 10% 03/31/1978
Name changed to United Southern Bank (Clarksdale, MS) 01/01/1980
United Southern Bank (Clarksdale, MS) reorganized as United Southern Corp. 01/30/1984 which was acquired by Union Planters Corp. 02/28/1989 which merged into Regions Financial Corp. (New) 07/01/2004

BANK CLEARWATER (CLEARWATER, FL)
Acquired by First Florida Banks, Inc. 01/14/1985
Each share Capital Stock $10 par exchanged for $125 cash

BANK COMM & TR CO (LEXINGTON, KY)
Capital Stock $25 par changed to $50 par 01/12/1981
Acquired by First Kentucky National Corp. 07/22/1985
Each share Capital Stock $50 par exchanged for $465 cash

BANK COMM & TR CO (ST FRANCISVILLE, LA)
Merged into Hancock Holding Co. 07/15/1997
Each share Common no par exchanged for (0.1202) share Common $3.33 par and $0.6137 cash
Hancock Holding Co. name changed to Hancock Whitney Corp. 05/25/2018

BANK COMM (CHARLOTTE, NC)
Acquired by HomeTrust Bancshares, Inc. 07/31/2014
Each share Common $5 par exchanged for $6.25 cash

BANK COMM (HAMTRAMCK, MI)
Common $100 par changed to $10 par and (9) additional shares issued plus a 25% stock dividend paid 01/31/1964
Stock Dividends - 33.33333333% 01/16/1946; 56.25% 01/31/1956; 50% 06/10/1958; 33.33333333% 04/29/1970; 10% 05/01/1972; 10% 05/01/1975; 20% 05/01/1980
Merged into Commerce Bancorp, Inc. (MI) 04/01/1983
Each share Common $10 par exchanged for (1) share Common no par
Commerce Bancorp, Inc. (MI) merged into Security Bancorp, Inc. 10/31/1985 which merged into First of America Bank Corp. 05/01/1992 which merged into National City Corp. 03/31/1998 which was acquired by PNC Financial Services Group, Inc. 12/31/2008

BANK COMM (LAREDO, TX)
Name changed to International Bank of Commerce (Laredo, TX) 04/01/1973
International Bank of Commerce (Laredo, TX) reorganized as International Bancshares Corp. (TX) 07/28/1980 which reincorporated in Delaware 05/18/1995

BANK COMM (NEW YORK, NY)
Capital Stock $10 par changed to $5 par and (1) additional share issued 02/11/1965
Capital Stock $5 par changed to $2.50 par and (1) additional share issued 08/17/1981
Stock Dividends - 10% 06/27/1967; 10% 09/30/1969; 10% 04/20/1971; 10% 04/30/1979
Merged into Norstar Bancorp Inc. 06/01/1983
Each share Capital Stock $2.50 par exchanged for $34 cash

BANK COMM (NEWARK, NJ)
Under plan of merger each share Capital Stock $10 par exchanged for (0.4) share Capital Stock $25 par 11/21/1956
Capital Stock $25 par changed to $12.50 par and (1) additional share issued plus a 5% stock dividend paid 09/06/1968
Merged into First Jersey National Corp. 12/29/1969
Each share Capital Stock $12.50 par exchanged for (2) shares Common $5 par
(See First Jersey National Corp.)

BANK COMM (SAN DIEGO, CA)
10% Conv. Preferred Ser. A no par called for redemption 12/31/1992
Floating Rate Conv. Preferred Ser. B no par called for redemption 11/15/1996
Common no par split (5) for (2) by issuance of (1.5) additional shares payable 05/05/1997 to holders of record 04/15/1997
Common no par split (2) for (1) by issuance of (1) additional share payable 12/10/1997 to holders of record 11/04/1997
Stock Dividends - 10% 08/19/1991; 10% 06/01/1992
Merged into U.S. Bancorp 07/15/1999
Each share Common no par exchanged for (0.6) share Common $1.25 par

BANK COMM FLA (FORT LAUDERDALE, FL)
Each share Common $80 par exchanged for (4) shares Common $20 par 01/01/1963
Each share Common $20 par exchanged for (2) shares Common $10 par 10/06/1964
Name changed to Florida Bank at Fort Lauderdale (Fort Lauderdale, FL) 10/22/1973
(See Florida Bank at Fort Lauderdale (Fort Lauderdale, FL))

BANK COMWLTH (DETROIT, MI)
Common $50 par changed to $16.66666666 par and (2) additional shares issued 02/01/1962
Common $16.66666666 par split (3) for (2) by issuance of (0.5) additional share 06/01/1966
Common $16.66666666 par changed to $11.11111111 par and (0.5) additional share issued 05/10/1967
Common $11.11111111 par changed to $7.04 par and (0.5) additional share issued 05/06/1968
Common $7.04 par changed to $4.9383 par and (0.5) additional share issued 02/13/1969
Common $4.9383 par changed to $3.292181 par and (0.5) additional share issued 07/15/1970
5.82% Preferred $100 par changed to $25 par and Common $3.292181 par changed to 5¢ par 02/28/1972
Each share 5.82% Preferred $25 par exchanged for (5) shares Common 50¢ par 01/25/1977
Each share Common 5¢ par exchanged for (0.1) share Common 50¢ par 01/25/1977
Stock Dividends - 10% 02/01/1945; 20% 06/25/1947; 25% 02/15/1949; 11.11111111% 02/01/1951; 20% 02/15/1954; 16.66666666% 02/15/1956; 12.5% 02/01/1961
Merged into Comerica, Inc. 11/23/1983
Each share Common 50¢ par exchanged for $3.57 principal amount of 11% Unsecured Subordinated Notes due 06/21/1985

BANK COMWLTH (NORFOLK, VA)
Reorganized as Commonwealth Bankshares, Inc. 11/07/1988
Each share Common exchanged for (2) shares Common $2.50 par
(See Commonwealth Bankshares, Inc.)

BANK COMPUTER NETWORK CORP (DE)
Name changed to Bankcom Corp. 01/01/1981
(See Bankcom Corp.)

BANK CORONADO (CORONADO, CA)
Under plan of reorganization each share Common no par automatically became (1) share Crown Bancorp Common no par 01/03/1983 which reorganized back as Bank of Coronado (Coronado, CA) 07/06/1994
Stock Dividend - 100% 04/23/1981
Merged into First Community Bancorp 01/09/2003
Each share Common no par exchanged for $14.15 cash

BANK CORP GA (GA)
Merged into Century South Banks, Inc. 12/16/1997
Each share Common $1 par exchanged for (1.35) shares Common $1 par
Century South Banks, Inc. merged into BB&T Corp. 06/07/2001

BANK COSTA MESA (COSTA MESA, CA)
Capital Stock $6 par changed to $3 par and (1) additional share issued 09/19/1974

Name changed to Citizens Bank (Costa Mesa, CA) 04/24/1975
(See Citizens Bank (Costa Mesa, CA))

BANK DALLAS TEX (DALLAS, TX)
Common $10 par changed to $4 par 07/12/1978
Acquired by Dallas Bancshares, Inc. 11/21/1980
Details not available

BANK DARIEN (DARIEN, CT)
Reorganized under the laws of Delaware as Hometown Bancorporation, Inc. and Common $5 par changed to $1 par 07/20/1987
(See Hometown Bancorporation, Inc.)

BANK DAVIE (MOCKSVILLE, NC)
Common $5 par split (6) for (5) by issuance of (0.2) additional share payable 12/21/2000 to holders of record 12/07/2000 Ex date - 12/13/2000
Under plan of merger name changed to Bank of the Carolinas (Mocksville, NC) 12/31/2001
Bank of the Carolinas (Mocksville, NC) reorganized as Bank of the Carolinas Corp. 08/18/2006 which merged into Bank of the Ozarks, Inc. 08/05/2015 which reorganized as Bank of the Ozarks (Little Rock, AR) 06/27/2017 which name changed to Bank OZK (Little Rock, AR) 07/16/2018

BANK DEARBORN (DEARBORN, MI)
Stock Dividends - 14.28571428% 09/26/1956; 10% 03/03/1966; 10% 05/08/1967; 10% 04/30/1969
Name changed to Dearborn Bank & Trust Co. (Dearborn, MI) 03/19/1974
Dearborn Bank & Trust Co. (Dearborn, MI) reorganized as Alliance Financial Corp. 10/01/1983
(See Alliance Financial Corp.)

BANK DEL (WILMINGTON, DE)
Capital Stock $25 par changed to $10 par and (1.5) additional shares issued 04/10/1959
Stock Dividends - 60% 09/29/1961; 10% 09/30/1963; 10% 04/14/1967
Under plan of reorganization each share Capital Stock $10 par automatically became (1) share Bank of Delaware Corp. Common 10¢ par 01/21/1983
Bank of Delaware Corp. acquired by PNC Financial Corp 03/31/1989 which name changed to PNC Bank Corp. 02/08/1993 which name changed to PNC Financial Services Group, Inc. 03/15/2000

BANK DEL CORP (DE)
Common 10¢ par split (5) for (2) by issuance of (1.5) additional shares 01/28/1985
Common 10¢ par split (2) for (1) by issuance of (1) additional share 08/11/1987
Acquired by PNC Financial Corp 03/31/1989
Each share Common 10¢ par exchanged for (0.7) share Common $5 par
PNC Financial Corp name changed to PNC Bank Corp. 02/08/1993 which name changed to PNC Financial Services Group, Inc. 03/15/2000

BANK DELMAR (DELMAR, MD)
Reorganized as Delmar Bancorp 07/01/1988
Each share Common $10 par exchanged for (1) share Common 1¢ par

BANK DENVER (DENVER, CO)
Capital Stock $10 par split (3) for (2) by issuance of (0.5) additional share 02/20/1969
Stock Dividend - 50% 02/04/1976
Under plan of reorganization each share Common $10 par automatically became (1) share Denver Bankshares Inc. Common $10 par 09/13/1994

BANK DOWNEY (DOWNEY, CA)
Stock Dividends - 10% 08/03/1972; 10.23% 07/30/1973; 10.31% 07/31/1974; 10% 07/25/1975; 11.1112% 06/30/1976; 10% 06/29/1977; 10% 07/14/1978; 10% 02/20/1979; 11% 07/18/1980
Merged into S C Bancorp 10/01/1981
Each share Capital Stock $10 par exchanged for (5) shares Common no par
S C Bancorp merged into Western Bancorp 10/10/1997 which merged into U.S. Bancorp 11/15/1999

BANK EAST (HARTFORD, CT)
Closed by the Connecticut Banking Commisioner and the FDIC was appointed receiver 12/13/1991
Stockholders' equity undetermined

BANK EAST TENNESSEE (KNOXVILLE, TN)
Acquired by Union Planters Corp. 05/03/1993
Each share Common $2 par exchanged for (0.387234) share Conv. Preferred Ser. E no par
(See Union Planters Corp.)

BANK EASTN IDAHO (IDAHO FALLS, ID)
Under plan of reorganization each share Common no par automatically became (1) share Bank of Idaho Holding Co. Common no par 09/15/1997

BANK EASTN ORE (ARLINGTON, OR)
Under plan of reorganization each share Common $5 par automatically became (1) share BEO Bancorp Common $5 par 12/08/1997

BANK EASTN SHORE (CAMBRIDGE, MD)
Common no par split (3) for (1) by issuance of (2) additional shares payable 05/30/1996 to holders of record 04/30/1996
Bank closed and FDIC appointed receiver 04/27/2012
Stockholders' equity unlikely

BANK EDMONDS (LYNNWOOD, WA)
Stock Dividend - 20% payable 05/19/2000 to holders of record 04/14/2000 Ex date - 07/28/2000
Name changed to Bank of Washington (Lynnwood, WA) 04/11/2001
Bank of Washington (Lynnwood, WA) reorganized as Washington Bancorp Inc. 07/25/2005

BANK EL PASO (EL PASO, TX)
Stock Dividend - 15.955% 02/16/1971
Merged into First International Bancshares, Inc. 08/06/1973
Each share Common $10 par exchanged for (2.2) shares Common $5 par
First International Bancshares, Inc. name changed to InterFirst Corp. 12/31/1981 which merged into First RepublicBank Corp. 06/06/1987
(See First RepublicBank Corp.)

BANK ESSEX (TAPPAHANNOCK, VA)
Stock Dividend - 100% 03/31/1995
Name changed to BOE Financial Services of Virginia Inc. 07/03/2000
BOE Financial Services of Virginia Inc. merged into Community Bankers Acquisition Corp. 05/31/2008 which name changed to Community Bankers Trust Corp. (DE) 06/02/2008 which reincorporated in Virginia 01/01/2014

BANK EVANSVILLE N A (EVANSVILLE, IN)
Merged into American Community Bancorp, Inc. 09/14/2004

Each share Common $5 par exchanged for (1) share Common no par
American Community Bancorp, Inc. merged into German American Bancorp, Inc. 01/03/2011

BANK FIN (LOS ANGELES, CA)
Capital Stock $10 par changed to $5 par 06/30/1967
Declared insolvent by FDIC 02/10/1984
No stockholders' equity

BANK FLA (FORT LAUDERDALE, FL)
Each share Common $80 par exchanged for (8) shares Common $10 par 05/15/1967
Through voluntary exchange offer Southeast Banking Corp. acquired 100% as of 06/27/1973
Public interest eliminated

BANK FLA CORP (FL)
Voluntarily dissolved 06/27/2011
Stockholders' equity unlikely

BANK FLOYD (FLOYD, VA)
Under plan of reorganization each share Common $10 par automatically became (1) share Cardinal Bankshares Corp. Common $10 par 07/01/1996
Cardinal Bankshares Corp. merged into Parkway Acquisition Corp. 07/01/2016

BANK FOR SAVINGS & TRUSTS (BIRMINGHAM, AL)
Capital Stock $50 par changed to $25 par and (1) additional share issued 09/23/1952
Each share Capital Stock $25 par exchanged for (5) shares Capital Stock $5 par 04/11/1957
Stock Dividends - 10% 01/02/1953; 10% 01/02/1954; 10% 01/03/1955; 100% 01/02/1956; 100% 01/02/1957; 12.9% 01/15/1959; 10% 12/28/1960
Merged into Birmingham Trust National Bank (Birmingham, AL) 12/06/1963
Each share Capital Stock $5 par exchanged for (0.555555) share Common $10 par
Birmingham Trust National Bank (Birmingham, AL) reorganized as BTNB Corp. 12/31/1968 which recapitalized as Alabama Financial Group, Inc. 03/10/1972 which name changed to Southern Bancorporation 04/17/1974 which name changed to Southern Bancorporation of Alabama 04/21/1975 which name changed to SouthTrust Corp. 09/18/1981 which merged into Wachovia Corp. (Ctfs. dated after 09/01/2001) 11/01/2004 which merged into Wells Fargo & Co. (New) 12/31/2008

BANK FOUR OAKS (FOUR OAKS, NC)
Name changed to Four Oaks Bank & Trust Co. (Four Oaks, NC) 06/25/1990
Four Oaks Bank & Trust Co. (Four Oaks, NC) reorganized as Four Oaks Fincorp, Inc. 07/01/1997 which merged into United Community Banks, Inc. 11/01/2017

BANK 1440 (PHOENIX, AZ)
Reorganized 11/13/2009
Each share Common $1 par held by holders of (1,000) or fewer shares exchanged for (1) share Class A Preferred $1 par
Merged into Alamogordo Financial Corp. (USA) 08/29/2014
Each share Class A Preferred $1 par exchanged for (0.17064) share Common 10¢ par and $0.94 cash
Each share Common $1 par exchanged for (0.17064) share Common 10¢ par and $0.94 cash
Alamogordo Financial Corp. (USA)

reorganized in Maryland as Bancorp 34, Inc. 10/12/2016

BANK FRANKLIN (FRANKLIN, VA)
Reorganized as United Community Bankshares, Inc. 08/01/1996
Each share Common $1 par exchanged for (4.806) shares Common $1 par
United Community Bankshares, Inc. merged into Atlantic Financial Corp. 12/01/1998 which merged into F & M National Corp. 02/26/2001 which merged into BB&T Corp. 08/09/2001

BANK FREMONT (FREMONT, CA)
Under plan of reorganization each share Common $20 par automatically became (1) share Fremont Bancorporation Common $20 par 10/15/1969
(See Fremont Bancorporation)

BANK FRUITLAND (FRUITLAND, MD)
Common $10 par split (2) for (1) by issuance of (1) additional share payable 09/25/1998 to holders of record 02/24/1998
Common $10 par split (2) for (1) by issuance of (1) additional share payable 10/28/1999 to holders of record 09/28/1999
Common $10 par split (2) for (1) by issuance of (1) additional share payable 02/25/2000 to holders of record 01/25/2000
Merged into Mercantile Bankshares Corp. 12/01/2000
Each share Common $10 par exchanged for (2.5) shares Common $2 par
Mercantile Bankshares Corp. merged into PNC Financial Services Group, Inc. 03/02/2007

BANK FT VALLEY (FORT VALLEY, GA)
Each share Common $20 par exchanged for (6.66666666) shares Common $3 par 06/01/1965
Stock Dividends - 50% 04/16/1965; 50% 05/19/1971; 10% 04/14/1973
Reorganized as Bank Corporation of Georgia 10/30/1980
Each share Common $3 par exchanged for (1) share Common $1 par
Bank Corporation of Georgia merged into Century South Banks, Inc. 12/16/1997 which merged into BB&T Corp. 06/07/2001

BANK FUKUOKA LTD (JAPAN)
ADR agreement terminated 04/30/2007
Each ADR for Common exchanged for $78.62539 cash

BANK FULTON CNTY (EAST POINT, GA)
Common $10 par changed to $5 par and (1) additional share issued 02/10/1967
Acquired by First Georgia Bancshares, Inc. 08/01/1973
Details not available

BANK GA (WATKINSVILLE, GA)
Merged into Synovus Financial Corp. 11/30/1998
Each share Common exchanged for (6.41805) shares Common $1 par

BANK GALVESTON N A (GALVESTON, TX)
Common Capital Stock $2.50 par changed to $1 par and (1.5) additional shares issued 01/24/1969
Name changed to Hometown Bank N.A. (Galveston, TX) 04/13/1999

BANK GEORGIA JT STK CO (GEORGIA)
GDR agreement terminated 06/06/2012
Each Reg. S GDR for Ordinary exchanged for (1) share Ordinary
Each 144A GDR for Ordinary exchanged for (1) share Ordinary

BANK GODFREY (GODFREY, IL)
Acquired by Reliance Bancshares Inc. 05/28/2003
Details not available

BANK GONZALES (GONZALES, LA)
Reorganized as Bank of Gonzales Holding Co., Inc. 06/01/1983
Each share Common $10 par exchanged for (1) share Common $10 par
Bank of Gonzales Holding Co., Inc. merged into Deposit Guaranty Corp. 06/28/1996 which merged into First American Corp. (TN) 05/01/1998 which merged into AmSouth Bancorporation 10/01/1999 which merged into Regions Financial Corp. (New) 11/04/2006

BANK GONZALES HLDG INC (LA)
Merged into Deposit Guaranty Corp. 06/28/1996
Each share Common $10 par exchanged for (1.1706) shares Common no par
Deposit Guaranty Corp. merged into First American Corp. (TN) 05/01/1998 which merged into AmSouth Bancorporation 10/01/1999 which merged into Regions Financial Corp. (New) 11/04/2006

BANK GRANADA HILLS (GRANADA HILLS, CA)
Stock Dividends - 10% payable 05/08/2000 to holders of record 04/17/2000; 10% payable 11/22/2000 to holders of record 11/01/2000 Ex date - 10/30/2000
Name changed to First State Bank of California (Granada Hills, CA) 11/13/2001
First State Bank of California (Granada Hills, CA) reorganized as First State Bancorp 03/10/2003 which merged into Boston Private Financial Holdings, Inc. 02/17/2004

BANK GRANITE CORP (DE)
Reorganized 06/01/1987
Common $5 par split (5) for (4) by issuance of (0.25) additional share 11/20/1985
Reorganized from Bank of Granite (Granite Falls, NC) to under the laws of Delaware as Bank of Granite Corp. 06/01/1987
Common $5 par split (2) for (1) by issuance of (1) additional share 08/21/1987
Common $5 par split (5) for (4) by issuance of (0.25) additional share 11/17/1989
Common $5 par changed to $1 par 03/28/1991
Common $1 par split (5) for (4) by issuance of (0.25) additional share 05/29/1992
Common $1 par split (5) for (4) by issuance of (0.25) additional share 05/31/1994
Common $1 par split (3) for (2) by issuance of (0.5) additional share payable 05/31/1996 to holders of record 05/10/1996
Common $1 par split (5) for (4) by issuance of (0.25) additional share payable 05/29/1998 to holders of record 05/08/1998
Common $1 par split (5) for (4) by issuance of (0.25) additional share payable 05/31/2002 to holders of record 05/10/2002 Ex date - 06/03/2002
Common $1 par split (5) for (4) by issuance of (0.25) additional share payable 09/25/2006 to holders of record 09/11/2006 Ex date - 09/26/2006
Merged into FNB United Corp. 10/24/2011
Each share Common $1 par exchanged for (3.375) shares Common $2.50 par

FNB United Corp. name changed to CommunityOne Bancorp 07/10/2013 which merged into Capital Bank Financial Corp. 10/26/2016

BANK GRAYS HBR (ABERDEEN, WA)
Merged into Harbor Bancorp Inc. 05/31/1997
Each share Common no par exchanged for (1) share Common no par
Harbor Bancorp Inc. merged into Pacific Financial Corp. 12/15/1999

BANK GREENVILLE (GREENVILLE, WV)
Reorganized under the laws of Delaware as Monroe Financial Inc. 04/05/1997
Each share Common 10¢ par exchanged for (5) shares Common 10¢ par
(See Monroe Financial Inc.)

BANK GREER (GREER, SC)
Merged into United Carolina Bancshares Corp. 10/01/1986
Each share Common $5 par exchanged for (2.39) shares Common $4 par
United Carolina Bancshares Corp. merged into BB&T Corp. 07/01/1997

BANK HALLANDALE & TR CO (HALLANDALE, FL)
Stock Dividends - 10% 02/12/1979; 20% 02/12/1981; 25% 02/14/1983
Acquired by Barnett Banks of Florida, Inc. 07/24/1984
Each share Common $10 par exchanged for $133.28 cash

BANK HAMPTON RDS (CHESAPEAKE, VA)
Under plan of reorganization each share Common $0.625 par automatically became (1) share Hampton Roads Bankshares, Inc. Common $0.625 par 07/01/2001
Hampton Roads Bankshares, Inc. name changed to Xenith Bankshares, Inc. (New) 08/01/2016

BANK HAMPTONS N A (EAST HAMPTON, NY)
Reorganized as Hamptons Bancshares, Inc. 09/04/1984
Each share Common $4 par exchanged for (1) share Common $4 par
Hamptons Bancshares, Inc. merged into Suffolk Bancorp 04/11/1994 which merged into People's United Financial, Inc. 04/01/2017

BANK HANDLOWY W WARSZAWIE SA (POLAND)
GDR agreement terminated 08/10/2017
Each 144A GDR for Ordinary exchanged for $18.801601 cash
Each Reg. S GDR for Ordinary exchanged for $18.801601 cash

BANK HANOVER & TR CO (HANOVER, PA)
Reorganized as Hanover Bancorp Inc. 08/02/1983
Each share Common no par exchanged for (1) share Common $2.50 par
Hanover Bancorp Inc. merged into Sterling Financial Corp. 07/27/2000
(See Sterling Financial Corp.)

BANK HAWAII (HONOLULU, HI)
Each share Capital Stock $100 par exchanged for (5) shares Capital Stock $20 par 00/00/1944
Capital Stock $20 par changed to $8 par and (1.5) additional shares issued 08/28/1961
Stock Dividends - 100% 03/15/1946; 33.33333333% 09/26/1957; 10% 01/23/1959; 18% 01/15/1969
Through purchase offer 99.675% acquired by Hawaii Bancorporation as of 08/00/1978

Public interest eliminated

BANK HAYWARD (HAYWARD, CA)
Acquired by MCB Financial Corp. 07/29/1994
Each share Common no par exchanged for $0.35 cash

BANK HEMET (HEMET, CA)
Under plan of reorganization each share Common no par automatically became (1) share Hemet Bancorp Common no par 11/23/2001
(See Hemet Bancorp)

BANK HOLLYWOOD (HOLLYWOOD, CA)
Stock Dividend - 10% payable 04/08/1996 to holders of record 03/15/1996
Merged into PBOC Holdings 01/31/2000
Each share Common no par exchanged for $19 cash

BANK HONOLULU N A (HONOLULU, HI)
Discharged from receivership 03/25/2005
No stockholders' equity

BANK HOUSTON (HOUSTON, TX)
Merged into Whitney Holding Corp. 02/18/2000
Each share Common $10 par exchanged for $109.545 cash

BANK HUNTSVILLE (HUNTSVILLE, AL)
Merged into Colonial BancGroup, Inc. 02/29/1984
Each share Common $1 par exchanged for (0.66667) share Class A Common $2.50 par
(See Colonial BancGroup, Inc.)

BANK IDAHO N A (BOISE, ID)
Stock Dividend - 100% 02/03/1972
Name changed to Bank of Idaho, N.A. (Boise, ID) 12/11/1973
Bank of Idaho, N.A., (Boise, ID) merged into Western Bancorporation 07/01/1980 which name changed to First Interstate Bancorp 06/01/1981 which merged into Wells Fargo & Co. (Old) 04/01/1996 which merged into Wells Fargo & Co. (New) 11/02/1998

BANK INICJATYW GOSPODARCZYCH BIG S A (POLAND)
Name changed to Big Bank Gdanski S.A. 10/22/1997
Big Bank Gdanski S.A. name changed to Bank Millennium S.A. 01/08/2003
(See Bank Millennium S.A.)

BANK IRVINE (IRVINE, CA)
Closed by Superintendent of Banks 05/18/1984

BANK ISLE OF WIGHT (SMITHFIELD, VA)
Merged into James River Bankshares, Inc. 02/29/1996
Each share Common $5 par exchanged for (4) shares Common $5 par
James River Bankshares, Inc. merged into First Virginia Banks, Inc. 07/02/2001 which merged into BB&T Corp. 07/01/2003

BANK JAMESTOWN (JAMESTOWN, NY)
Each share Preferred Ser. B $25 par exchanged for (20) shares Common $5 par 00/00/1945
Preferred Ser. A called for redemption 00/00/1947
Common $5 par changed to $6.66666666 par 00/00/1951
Common $6.66666666 par changed to $10 par 01/17/1962
Stock Dividends - 20% 01/25/1949; (3) for (22) 02/10/1951
Acquired by Bankers Trust New York Corp. 07/18/1969

Each share Common $10 par exchanged for (0.95) share Common $10 par
Bankers Trust New York Corp. name to Bankers Trust Corp. 04/23/1998
(See Bankers Trust Corp.)

BANK JONESBORO (JONESBORO, GA)
Name changed to Central Bank & Trust Co. (Jonesboro, GA) 06/12/1970
(See Central Bank & Trust Co. (Jonesboro, GA))

BANK KING PRUSSIA (KING OF PRUSSIA, PA)
Stock Dividends - 10% 07/15/1970; 10% 07/15/1971; 10% 07/15/1972
Name changed to Royal Bank of Pennsylvania (King of Prussia, PA) 12/00/1980
Royal Bank of Pennsylvania (King of Prussia, PA) reorganized as Royal Bancshares of Pennsylvania 06/29/1995 which merged into Bryn Mawr Bank Corp. 12/15/2017

BANK KY FINL CORP (KY)
Merged into BB&T Corp. 06/19/2015
Each share Common no par exchanged for (1.0126) shares Common $5 par and $9.40 cash

BANK LA (NEW ORLEANS, LA)
Acquired by BOL Bancshares, Inc. 04/29/1988
Details not available

BANK LANCASTER (LANCASTER, SC)
Each share Capital Stock $10 par exchanged for (5) shares Capital Stock $20 par 10/01/1947
Stock Dividends - 20% 03/09/1949; 33% 02/08/1961; 50% 02/08/1966; 33.33333333% 03/03/1970
Liquidation completed
Each share Capital Stock $20 par exchanged for initial distribution of $189.50 cash 02/07/1983
Each share Capital Stock $20 par received second and final distribution of $5.42 cash 06/30/1983

BANK LANSING (LANSING, MI)
Each share Capital Stock $100 par exchanged for (5) shares Capital Stock $20 par 02/05/1962
Capital Stock $20 par changed to $5 par and (3) additional shares issued 03/06/1967
Capital Stock $5 par changed to $3.75 par and (1/3) additional share issued 03/21/1969
Capital Stock $3.75 par changed to $2 par 12/30/1970
Stock Dividends - 50% 01/13/1942; 33.33333333% 01/09/1945; 50% 02/20/1948; 50% 10/22/1951; 33.33333333% 06/23/1954; 25% 02/17/1959
Acquired by Northern States Financial Corp. 12/31/1972
Holders had option to exchange each share Capital Stock $2 par for either (0.27464) share Common $5 par or (0.20872) share Common $5 par and (0.01351) share 6.5% Conv. Preferred no par
Note: Option to receive Preferred and Common expired 12/30/1972
Northern States Financial Corp. name changed to Northern States Bancorporation, Inc. 03/27/1973 which merged into First American Bank Corp. 10/09/1981 which name changed to First of America Bank Corp. 01/14/1983
(See First of America Bank Corp.)

BANK LAS VEGAS (LAS VEGAS, NV)
Under plan of merger name changed to Valley Bank of Nevada (Las Vegas, NV) 07/01/1969
Valley Bank of Nevada (Las Vegas,

NV) reorganized as Valley Capital Corp. 07/29/1982 which merged into BankAmerica Corp. (Old) 03/13/1992 which merged into BankAmerica Corp. (New) 09/30/1998 which name changed to Bank of America Corp. 04/28/1999

BANK LEIPSIC (LEIPSIC, OH)
Merged into United Bancshares Inc. 02/01/2000
Each share Common $20 par exchanged for (54.25) shares Common no par

BANK LENAWEE CNTY (ADRIAN, MI)
Stock Dividends - 10% 02/19/1970; 20% 12/30/1972; 20% 02/05/1973; 25% 03/15/1976; 20% 03/15/1978; 16.66666666% 03/31/1983
Under plan of reorganization each share Common $10 par automatically became (1) share Lenawee Bancorp Inc. Common $10 par 06/07/1993
Lenawee Bancorp Inc. name changed to Pavilion Bancorp, Inc. 04/22/2002 which merged into First Defiance Financial Corp. 03/17/2008

BANK LONG BEACH N A (LONG BEACH, CA)
Merged into Unionamerica, Inc. (CA) 07/23/1971
Each share Capital Stock $10 par exchanged for (1.5) shares Common no par
(See Unionamerica, Inc. (CA))

BANK LONG IS N A (EAST ISLIP, NY)
Merged into Norstar Bancorp Inc. 12/03/1984
Each share Common $2.50 par exchanged for $15 cash

BANK LOS ANGELES (LOS ANGELES, CA) Established 10/30/1980
Under plan of reorganization each share Common no par automatically became (1) share BKLA Bancorp Common no par 09/19/1984
BKLA Bancorp merged into Bank of Los Angeles (New) (Los Angeles, CA) 10/23/1995 which merged into Western Bancorp 10/23/1998 which merged into U.S. Bancorp 11/15/1999

BANK LOS ANGELES NEW (LOS ANGELES, CA)
Merged into Western Bancorp 10/23/1998
Each share Common no par exchanged for (0.4224) share Common no par
Western Bancorp merged into U.S. Bancorp 11/15/1999

BANK LOUISVILLE & TR CO (LOUISVILLE, KY)
Stock Dividend - 25% 05/20/1980
Reorganized as Mid-America Bancorp 03/25/1983
Each share Common $12.50 par exchanged for (1.5) shares Common no par
Mid-America Bancorp merged into BB&T Corp. 03/08/2002

BANK MADERA CNTY (OAKHURST, CA)
Merged into Central Valley Community Bancorp 12/31/2004
Each share Common no par exchanged for $26.2169 cash

BANK MADISON (MADISON, WI)
Each share Common $20 par exchanged for (2.2) shares Common $10 par to effect a (2) for (1) split and 10% stock dividend 03/25/1967
Through voluntary exchange offer of (2) shares Affiliated Bank Corp. Common $5 par for each share Common $10 par, 100% was acquired as of 03/31/1970
Affiliated Bank Corp. merged into Marshall & Ilsley Corp. (Old) 12/31/1980
(See Marshall & Ilsley Corp. (Old))

BANK MAINE N A (AUGUSTA, ME)
Reorganized as Banc of Maine Corp. 02/01/1973
Each share Common $20 par exchanged for (1) share Common $20 par
(See Banc of Maine Corp.)

BANK MARIN (CORTE MADERA, CA)
Common no par split (3) for (2) by issuance of (0.5) additional share payable 05/03/1999 to holders of record 04/19/1999
Common no par split (3) for (2) by issuance of (0.5) additional share payable 05/24/2004 to holders of record 05/19/2004
Stock Dividends - 7% payable 05/05/1997 to holders of record 04/21/1997; 7% payable 05/04/1998 to holders of record 04/20/1998; 5% payable 05/02/2001 to holders of record 04/23/2001 Ex date - 04/19/2001; 5% payable 05/06/2002 to holders of record 04/22/2002; 5% payable 05/05/2003 to holders of record 04/21/2003 Ex date - 04/16/2003; 5% payable 05/02/2005 to holders of record 04/18/2005; 5% payable 05/02/2006 to holders of record 04/24/2006 Ex date - 04/20/2006
Under plan of reorganization each share Common no par automatically became (1) share Bank of Marin Bancorp Common no par 07/02/2007

BANK MARIN (SAN RAFAEL, CA)
Reorganized as Independent Bankshares Corp. 12/31/1972
Each share Capital Stock $15 par exchanged for (1.63) shares Common $5 par
Independent Bankshares Corp. name changed to Westamerica Bancorporation 07/01/1983

BANK MARSHALL CNTY (BENTON, KY)
Under plan of reorganization each share Common $10 par automatically became (1) share BMC Bankcorp, Inc. Common no par 09/07/1982
BMC Bankcorp, Inc. merged into CBT Corp. (KY) 05/31/1994 which merged into Mercantile Bancorporation, Inc. which merged into Firstar Corp. (New) 09/20/1999 which merged into U.S. Bancorp (New) 02/27/2001

BANK MARYVILLE (MARYVILLE, TN)
Reorganized as Mountain Financial Co. 07/01/1980
Each share Common $10 par exchanged for (1) share Common $10 par or $50 principal amount 12.5% 10-Yr. Promissory Notes due 07/01/1990 or a combination of stock and notes
Note: Option to receive notes or combination of stock and notes expired 07/31/1980
(See Mountain Financial Co.)

BANK MCKENNEY (MCKENNEY, VA)
Old Common $2 par split (3) for (1) by issuance of (2) additional shares payable 08/30/2002 to holders of record 08/13/2002 Ex date - 09/02/2002
Each share old Common $2 par held by holders of (450) or fewer shares exchanged for (1) share Ser. A Preferred $2 par 05/11/2010
Name changed to Touchstone Bank (McKenney, VA) 11/28/2017

BANK MD (HILLCREST HEIGHTS, MD)
Acquired by Maryland National Corp. 06/01/1984
Each share Capital Stock $10 par exchanged for $62 cash

BANK MD CORP (MD)
Merged into Mason-Dixon Bancshares, Inc. 07/17/1995
Each share Common 5¢ par exchanged for (0.854) share Common $10 par or $12.81 cash or (0.409407) share Common $10 par and $0.66889 cash
Note: Option to receive either stock or cash only expired 08/14/1995
Mason-Dixon Bancshares, Inc. merged into BB&T Corp. 07/14/1999

BANK MECKLENBURG (CHARLOTTE, NC)
Common $5 par split (5) for (4) by issuance of (0.25) additional share 05/16/1995
Merged into Triangle Bancorp Inc. 10/03/1997
Each share Common $5 par exchanged for (1) share Common no par
Triangle Bancorp Inc. merged into Centura Banks, Inc. 02/18/2000 which merged into Royal Bank of Canada (Montreal, QC) 06/05/2001

BANK MIAMI (MIAMI, FL)
Merged into Southeast Banking Corp. 04/15/1987
Details not available

BANK MID-JERSEY (BORDENTOWN, NJ)
Common $10 par changed to $5 par and (0.5) additional share issued 05/01/1971
Stock Dividend - 100% 11/10/1982
Reorganized as B.M.J. Financial Corp. 02/06/1984
Each share Common $5 par exchanged for (1) share Common $5 par
B.M.J. Financial Corp. merged into Summit Bancorp. 02/28/1997 which merged into FleetBoston Financial Corp. 03/01/2001 which merged into Bank of America Corp. 04/01/2004

BANK MILLENNIUM SPOLKA AKCYJNA (POLAND)
GDR agreement terminated 11/29/2017
Each 144A GDR for Common exchanged for (15) shares Common
Each Reg. S GDR for Common exchanged for (15) shares Common
Note: Unexchanged GDR's will be sold and the proceeds, if any, held for claim after 12/03/2018

BANK MINNEAPOLIS & TR CO (MINNEAPOLIS, MN)
Merged into Metropolitan Bank (Bloomington, MN) 06/22/1987
Each share Capital Stock $10 par exchanged for $16.09 cash

BANK MONROE (UNION, WV)
Merged into Union Bankshares, Inc. 10/30/1998
Each share Common exchanged for $3 cash

BANK MONROVIA (MONROVIA, CA)
Name changed to Granite State Bank (Monrovia, CA) 04/20/1994
(See Granite State Bank (Monrovia, CA))

BANK MONT SYS (MT)
Common $10 par changed to $2.50 par and (3) additional shares issued 07/20/1984
Each share old Common $2.50 par exchanged for (0.008) share new Common $2.50 par 06/04/1985
Merged into Norwest Corp. 04/15/1994
Each share new Common $2.50 par exchanged for (2.0719) shares Common $1.66666666 par
Norwest Corp. name changed to Wells Fargo & Co. (New) 11/02/1998

BANK MONTICELLO (MONTICELLO, GA)
Recapitalized as Monticello Bancshares Inc. 07/01/1996
Each share Common $100 par exchanged for (0.05) share Common $100 par

BANK MONTREAL (MONTREAL, QC)
$2.85 Class A Preferred Ser. 1 no par called for redemption 03/27/1987
$2.50 Class A Preferred Ser. 2 no par called for redemption 12/18/1989
Non-Vtg. Class A Preferred Ser. 3 no par called for redemption 02/25/1992
7.625% Class A Preferred Ser. 5 no par called for redemption 12/05/1998
Adjustable Dividend Class A Preferred Ser. 4 no par called for redemption at $25 on 09/24/1999
Adjustable Dividend Class B Preferred Ser. 1 no par called for redemption at $25 on 02/25/2001
Adjustable Dividend Class B Preferred Ser. 2 no par called for redemption at $25 plus $0.0094 accrued dividends on 08/25/2001
Adjustable Dividend Class B Preferred Ser. 3 no par called for redemption at $25.50 plus $0.13573 accrued dividends on 09/30/2004
Adjustable Rate Class B Preferred Ser. 4 no par called for redemption at $25 plus $0.006575 accrued dividends on 08/27/2007
Adjustable Rate Class B Preferred Ser. 6 no par called for redemption at $25 plus $0.296875 accrued dividends on 11/25/2008
Class B Preferred Ser. 10 no par called for redemption at $25 plus $0.371875 accrued dividends on 02/25/2012
Adjustable Rate Class B Preferred Ser. 5 no par called for redemption at $25 plus $0.33125 accrued dividends on 02/25/2013
Non-Cum 5-Yr. Rate Reset Class B Preferred Ser. 18 no par called for redemption at $25 plus $0.40625 accrued dividends on 02/25/2014
Non-Cum 5-Year Rate Reset Class B Preferred Ser. 21 no par called for redemption at $25 on 05/25/2014
Non-Cum 5-Yr. Rate Reset Class B Preferred Ser. 23 no par called for redemption at $25 on 02/25/2015
Non-Cum Perpetual Class B Preferred Ser. 13 no par called for redemption at $25.25 on 05/25/2015
Non-Cum Perpetual Class B Preferred Ser. 14 no par called for redemption at $25 on 05/25/2017
Perpetual Class B Preferred Ser. 15 no par called for redemption at $25 on 05/25/2017
Non-Cum 5-Yr. Rate Reset Class B Preferred Ser. 16 no par called for redemption at $25 on 08/25/2018
Preferred Ser. 17 no par called for redemption at $25 on 08/25/2018
(Additional Information in Active)

BANK MUT CORP (USA)
Reorganized under the laws of Wisconsin 10/29/2003
Each share Common 1¢ par exchanged for (3.6686) shares Common 1¢ par
Bank Mutual Corp. (WI) merged into Associated Banc-Corp 02/01/2018

BANK MUT CORP (WI)
Merged into Associated Banc-Corp 02/01/2018
Each share Common 1¢ par exchanged for (0.422) share Common 1¢ par

BANK MYSTIC (MYSTIC, CT)
Merged into Norwich Financial Corp. 04/01/1995
Each share Common $5 par

exchanged for (0.541) share Common 1¢ par and $2.40 cash
Norwich Financial Corp. merged into People's Bank (Bridgeport, CT) 02/23/1998 which reorganized as People's United Financial, Inc. 04/16/2007

BANK N J (CAMDEN, NJ)
Reorganized as Bancshares of New Jersey 12/30/1972
Each share Capital Stock $5 par exchanged for (1) share Common $5 par
Bancshares of New Jersey name changed to Northern National Corp. 05/28/1981 which merged into Horizon Bancorp 10/01/1983
(See Horizon Bancorp)

BANK N MEX (ALBUQUERQUE, NM)
Each share Capital Stock $100 par exchanged for (4) shares Capital Stock $25 par 00/00/1954
Name changed to First Interstate Bank of Albuquerque (Albuquerque, NM) 06/01/1981
(See First Interstate Bank of Albuquerque (Albuquerque, NM))

BANK N S (HALIFAX, NS)
Adjustable Dividend Preferred Ser. 3 no par called for redemption 11/29/1994
Adjustable Dividend Preferred Ser. 4 no par called for redemption 05/19/1995
Floating Rate Preferred Ser. 1 no par called for redemption 12/05/1996
Adjustable Dividend Preferred Ser. 5 no par called for redemption at $25 on 10/29/1997
Adjustable Dividend Preferred Ser. 7 no par called for redemption at $26 on 07/29/2002
Adjustable Dividend Preferred Ser. 6 no par called for redemption at $25 on 10/29/2002
Adjustable Dividend Preferred Ser. 8 no par called for redemption at $26 on 01/29/2003
Adjustable Dividend Preferred Ser. 9 no par called for redemption at $26 on 04/28/2003
Adjustable Dividend Preferred Ser. 12 no par called for redemption at $25 on 10/29/2013
Preferred Ser. 24 no par called for redemption at $25 on 01/26/2014
5-Year Reset Preferred Ser. 26 no par called for redemption at $25 on 04/26/2014
Preferred Ser. 28 no par called for redemption at $25 on 04/26/2014
Preferred Ser. 13 no par called for redemption at $25 on 07/29/2014
Preferred Ser. 14 no par called for redemption at $25 on 04/27/2016
Preferred Ser. 15 no par called for redemption at $25 on 07/27/2016
Preferred Ser. 16 no par called for redemption at $25 on 01/27/2017
Non-Cum. Preferred Ser. 17 no par called for redemption at $25 on 04/26/2017
Non-Cum. 5-Yr. Rate Reset Preferred Ser. 18 no par called for redemption at $25 on 04/26/2018
Non-Cum. 5-Yr. Rate Reset Preferred Ser. 19 no par called for redemption at $25 on 04/26/2018
(Additional Information in Active)

BANK NAPA N A (NAPA, CA)
Merged into Bank of Marin Bancorp 11/21/2017
Each share Common $5 par exchanged for (0.307) share Common no par

BANK NASHVILLE (NASHVILLE, TN)
Under plan of reorganization each share Common $6 par automatically became (1) share Community Financial Group, Inc. Common $6 par 04/30/1996
Community Financial Group, Inc.

merged into Synovus Financial Corp. 07/31/2002

BANK NEV (LAS VEGAS, NV)
Merged into Western Bancorporation 10/01/1979
Each share Capital Stock $100 par exchanged for (20) shares Capital Stock $2 par
Western Bancorporation name changed to First Interstate Bancorp 06/01/1981 which merged into Wells Fargo & Co. (Old) 04/01/1996 which merged into Wells Fargo & Co. (New) 11/02/1998

BANK NEW CANAAN (NEW CANAAN, CT)
Under plan of reorganization each share Common no par automatically became (1) share BNC Financial Group, Inc. Common no par 12/17/2007
BNC Financial Group, Inc. name changed to Bankwell Financial Group, Inc. 09/11/2013

BANK NEW ENGLAND CORP (MA)
Common $5 par split (1.75) for (1) by issuance of (0.75) additional share 05/17/1985
Common $5 par split (2) for (1) by issuance of (1) additional share 05/16/1986
Adjustable Rate Preferred Ser. 1982 no par called for redemption 02/01/1988
Filed petition under Chapter 7 Federal Bankruptcy Code 01/07/1991
No stockholders' equity

BANK NEW HAMPSHIRE CORP (NH)
Common no par split (2) for (1) by issuance of (1) additional share 07/01/1983
Common no par split (2) for (1) by issuance of (1) additional share 10/01/1985
Stock Dividend - 10% 10/01/1980
Merged into Peoples Heritage Financial Group, Inc. 04/02/1996
Each share Common no par exchanged for (2) shares Common 1¢ par
Peoples Heritage Financial Group, Inc. name changed to Banknorth Group, Inc. (ME) 05/10/2000 which merged into TD Banknorth Inc. 03/01/2005
(See TD Banknorth Inc.)

BANK NEW HAMPSHIRE N A (MANCHESTER, NH)
Reorganized as Bank of New Hampshire Corp. 04/30/1980
Each share Common Capital Stock $10 par exchanged for (2) shares Common no par
Bank of New Hampshire Corp. merged into Peoples Heritage Financial Group, Inc. 04/02/1996 which name changed to Banknorth Group, Inc. (ME) 05/10/2000 which merged into TD Banknorth Inc. 03/01/2005
(See TD Banknorth Inc.)

BANK NEW HAVEN (NEW HAVEN, CT)
Capital Stock $8 par changed to $4 par and (1) additional share issued 12/20/1982
Stock Dividends - 10% 10/15/1981; 10% 06/14/1982; 10% 01/15/1985
Under plan of reorganization each share Capital Stock $4 par automatically became (1) share BNH Bancshares, Inc. Common $4 par 08/01/1985
(See BNH Bancshares, Inc.)

BANK NEW JERSEY (FT LEE, NJ)
Stock Dividend - 10% payable 01/15/2007 to holders of record 01/15/2007
Under plan of reorganization each share Common $10 par automatically became (1) share

Bancorp of New Jersey, Inc. Common no par 07/19/2007

BANK NEW ORLEANS & TR CO (NEW ORLEANS, LA)
Stock Dividend - 10% 02/15/1966
Reorganized as New Orleans Bancshares, Inc. 05/12/1970
Each share Capital Stock $12.50 par exchanged for (1) share Common $12.50 par
New Orleans Bancshares, Inc. merged into First Commerce Corp. 05/23/1983 which merged into Banc One Corp. 06/12/1998 which merged into Bank One Corp. 10/02/1998 which merged into J.P. Morgan Chase & Co. 12/31/2000 which name changed to JPMorgan Chase & Co. 07/20/2004

BANK NEW SOUTH WALES (AUSTRALIA)
Stock Dividend - 20% 09/10/1979
Name changed to Westpac Banking Corp. Ltd. 10/01/1982

BANK NEW YORK (NEW YORK, NY)
Name changed 07/01/1938
Name changed from Bank of New York & Trust Co. (New York, NY) to Bank of New York (New York, NY) 07/01/1938
Capital Stock $100 par changed to $40 par and (1.5) additional shares issued plus an 11.11111111% stock dividend paid 07/24/1963
Capital Stock $40 par changed to $20 par and (1) additional share issued 07/08/1966
Capital Stock $20 par reclassified as Common $15 par 12/07/1966
Stock Dividends - 100% 03/25/1955; 50% 10/01/1958
Reorganized as Bank of New York Co., Inc. 05/29/1969
Each share $4 Conv. Preferred $75 par exchanged for $60 principal amount of 6.25% Conv. Debentures due 09/01/1994 and (0.25) share Common $15 par
Each share Common $15 par exchanged for (1) share Common $15 par
Bank of New York Co., Inc. merged into Bank of New York Mellon Corp. 07/01/2007

BANK NEW YORK INC (NY)
• Common $15 par changed to $7.50 par and (1) additional share issued 10/22/1969
Common $7.50 par split (2) for (1) by issuance of (1) additional share 10/07/1983
Common $7.50 par split (3) for (2) by issuance of (0.5) additional share 11/06/1986
Fixed/Adjustable Rate Non-Cum. Preferred no par called for redemption 09/01/1988
Fixed/Adjustable Rate Preferred Ser. A no par called for redemption 12/01/1992
Adjustable Rate Preferred no par called for redemption 06/01/1993
Convertible Auction Dividend Preferred no par called for redemption 04/14/1993
Adjustable Rate Preferred no par called for redemption 02/22/1994
Adjustable Rate Preferred no par called for redemption 03/07/1994
Common $7.50 par split (2) for (1) by issuance of (1) additional share 05/13/1994
Common $7.50 par split (2) for (1) by issuance of (1) additional share payable 08/08/1996 to holders of record 07/19/1996
8.60% Depositary Preferred called for redemption at $25 on 12/01/1997
Common $7.50 par split (2) for (1) by issuance of (1) additional share payable 08/13/1998 to holders of

record 07/24/1998 Ex date - 08/14/1998
Preferred Stock Purchase Rights declared for Common stockholders of record 12/24/1985 were redeemed at $0.05 per right 03/25/2005 for holders of record 03/11/2005
7.75% Conv. Preferred $2 par called for redemption at $25 plus $0.11302 accrued dividends on 01/22/2007
Merged into Bank of New York Mellon Corp. 07/01/2007
Each share Common $7.50 par exchanged for (0.9434) share Common 1¢ par

BANK NEWNAN (BULLSBORO, GA)
Under plan of reorganization each share Common $10 par automatically became (1) share Bullsboro Bancshares, Inc. Common $43.37 par 10/04/1996
Bullsboro Bancshares, Inc. merged into Regions Financial Corp. (Old) 01/01/1999 which merged into Regions Financial Corp. (New) 07/01/2004

BANK NEWPORT (NEWPORT BEACH, CA)
Common $5 par changed to $2.50 par and (1) additional share issued 05/06/1976
Common $2.50 par changed to no par 03/00/1979
Common no par split (2) for (1) by issuance of (1) additional share 12/17/1979
Stock Dividends - 10% 07/04/1976; 15% 05/01/1978; 10% 03/30/1979; 10% 02/12/1981; 200% 04/19/1984
Bank failed 08/12/1994
Stockholders' equity unlikely

BANK NORTH (LAS VEGAS, NV)
Name changed to Valley Bank (Las Vegas, NV) 08/04/2011

BANK NORTH CAROLINA (THOMASVILLE, NC)
Common $2.50 par split (5) for (4) by issuance of (0.25) additional share payable 10/29/1997 to holders of record 09/16/1997
Common $2.50 par split (5) for (4) by issuance of (0.25) additional share payable 11/30/1998 to holders of record 11/17/1998
Common $2.50 par split (5) for (4) by issuance of (0.25) additional share payable 10/01/1999 to holders of record 09/15/1999
Common $2.50 par split (5) for (4) by issuance of (0.25) additional share payable 09/15/2000 to holders of record 09/01/2000 Ex date - 09/25/2000
Under plan of reorganization each share Common $2.50 par automatically became (1) share BNC Bancorp Common no par 12/16/2002
BNC Bancorp merged into Pinnacle Financial Partners, Inc. 06/16/2017

BANK NORTHUMBERLAND INC (HEATHSVILLE, VA)
Under plan of merger name changed to Eastern Virginia Bankshares, Inc. 12/29/1997
Eastern Virginia Bankshares, Inc. merged into Southern National Bancorp of Virginia, Inc. 06/23/2017

BANK NORTHWEST (BELLINGHAM, WA)
Common no par split (11) for (10) by issuance of (0.1) additional share payable 07/20/2000 to holders of record 07/14/2000
Under plan of reorganization each share Common no par automatically became (1) share BNW Bancorp Inc. Common no par 03/26/2003
BNW Bancorp Inc. acquired by Pacific Financial Corp. 02/27/2004

BANK OAK RIDGE (OAK RIDGE, NC)
Common $5 par changed to $3 par 06/30/2004
Common $3 par split (5) for (4) by issuance of (0.25) additional share payable 12/15/2004 to holders of record 12/10/2004 Ex date - 12/16/2004
Reorganized as Oak Ridge Financial Services, Inc. 04/20/2007
Each share Common $3 par exchanged for (1) share Common no par

BANK OAKLAND (OAKLAND, CA)
Acquired by Innovative Bancorp 04/02/2001
Each share Common exchanged for $1.96 cash

BANK OF AKRON CO. (AKRON, OH)
Merged into Akron-Dime Bank (Akron, OH) 11/01/1960
Each share Common exchanged for (0.1) share Capital Stock $10 par
Akron-Dime Bank (Akron, OH) name changed to Akron National Bank & Trust Co. (Akron, OH) 12/01/1966
(See Akron National Bank (Akron, OH))

BANK OF ALEX BROWN (WALNUT CREEK, CA)
Reorganized as Alex Brown Financial Group 04/14/1982
Each share Capital Stock $5 par exchanged for (1) share Common no par
(See Alex Brown Financial Group)

BANK OF AMADOR (JACKSON, CA)
Merged into American River Bankshares 12/03/2004
Each share Common no par exchanged for (0.5394) share Common no par and $5.878 cash
Each share Common no par received a final distribution of $0.947 cash from escrow 06/29/2005

BANK AMER CORP (DE)
$2.50 Conv. Preferred Ser. BB called for redemption at $25 per share on 10/01/1999
Depositary Preferred Ser. VII called for redemption at $50 plus $0.875 accrued dividends on 07/03/2006
6.75% Depositary Perpetual Preferred called for redemption at $50 plus $0.84375 accrued dividends on 07/14/2006
Each Common Equivalent Security 1¢ par exchanged for (1) share Common 1¢ par 02/24/2010
8.2% Depositary Preferred Ser. H called for redemption at $25 plus $0.5125 accrued dividends on 05/01/2013
8.625% Depositary Preferred Ser. 8 called for redemption at $25 plus $0.539063 accrued dividends on 05/28/2013
6.25% Depositary Preferred Ser. 7 called for redemption at $25 on 06/28/2013
6.7% Depositary Preferred Ser. 6 called for redemption at $25 on 06/28/2013
7.25% Depositary Preferred Ser. J called for redemption at $25 on 08/01/2013
Depositary Preferred Ser. M called for redemption at $1,000 on 05/15/2018
6.625% Depositary Preferred Ser. I called for redemption at $25 on 07/02/2018
Depositary Preferred Ser. K called for redemption at $1,000 on 07/30/2018
6.375% Depositary Preferred Ser. 3 called for redemption at $25 on 08/28/2018
6.204% Depositary Preferred Ser. D called for redemption at $25 on 09/14/2018
(Additional Information in Active)

BANK BEAUFORT (BEAUFORT, SC)
Common $3.75 par changed to $1.25 par and (2) additional shares issued 10/30/1974
Stock Dividends - 20% 11/01/1978; 10% 11/15/1979; 10% 12/19/1980; 10% 11/30/1981
Merged into First National Bank of South Carolina (Columbia, SC) 08/01/1983
Each share Common $1.25 par exchanged for $17 cash

BANK OF BOSTON CORP (MA)
Common $4.50 par changed to $2.25 par and (1) additional share issued 04/11/1986
Common $2.25 par split (3) for (2) by issuance of (0.5) additional share 01/26/1987
Name changed to BankBoston Corp. 04/25/1997
BankBoston Corp. merged into Fleet Boston Corp. 10/01/1999 which name changed to FleetBoston Financial Corp. 04/18/2000 which merged into Bank of America Corp. 04/01/2004

BANK OF BRANDYWINE VY (WEST CHESTER, PA)
Taken over by the FDIC 02/21/1992
Stockholders' equity undetermined

BANK OF CASEY (CASEY, IL)
Reorganized as Lincolnland Bancshares, Inc. 12/01/1982
Each share Common $10 par exchanged for (1) share Common $10 par
Lincolnland Bancshares, Inc. merged into AMBANC Corp. 06/01/1994 which merged into Union Planters Corp. 08/31/1998 which merged into Regions Financial Corp. (New) 07/01/2004

BANK OF COLUMBIA, N.A. (WASHINGTON, DC)
Name changed to National Bank of Commerce (Washington, DC) 10/15/1981
National Bank of Commerce (Washington, DC) reorganized in Delaware as Commerce Bancorp, Inc. 01/31/1985
(See Commerce Bancorp, Inc. (DE))

BANK OF COMMERCE & SAVINGS (WASHINGTON, DC)
Name changed to Bank of Commerce (Washington, DC) 03/01/1955
Bank of Commerce (Washington, DC) merged into National Savings & Trust Co. (Washington, DC) 09/09/1966 which reorganized in Delaware as NS&T Bankshares, Inc. 11/16/1981
(See NS&T Bankshares, Inc.)

BANK OF COMMERCE (MILWAUKEE, WI)
Each share Common $2 par exchanged for (0.02) share Common $100 par 07/20/1978
Acquired by Associated Banc-Corp. 08/30/1982
Each share Common $100 par exchanged for $1,410 cash

BANK OF COMMERCE (OAKLAND, CA)
Name changed to Oakland Bank of Commerce (Oakland, CA) 08/30/1944
Oakland Bank of Commerce (Oakland, CA) acquired by Union Bancorp 04/25/1969 which name changed to Unionamerica, Inc. (CA) 05/09/1969
(See Unionamerica, Inc. (CA))

BANK OF COMMERCE (TULSA, OK)
Name changed to Bank of Commerce & Trust Co. (Tulsa, OK) 11/21/1977

BANK OF COMMERCE (WASHINGTON, DC)
Capital Stock $100 par changed to $10 par and (9) additional shares issued 03/06/1964
Stock Dividend - 50% 03/07/1966
Merged into National Savings & Trust Co. (Washington, DC) 09/09/1966
Each share Capital Stock $10 par exchanged for (1.05) shares Capital Stock $10 par
National Savings & Trust Co. (Washington, DC) reorganized in Delaware as NS&T Bankshares, Inc. 11/16/1981
(See NS&T Bankshares, Inc.)

BANK OF COMMERCE LIQUIDATING CO. (MO)
Liquidation completed 03/15/1957
Details not available

BANK OF CRESTWOOD (CRESTWOOD, MO)
Name changed to Crestwood Metro Bank (Crestwood, MO) 01/24/1979
Crestwood Metro Bank (Crestwood, MO) reorganized as Metro Bancholding Corp. 09/02/1980
(See Metro Bancholding Corp.)

BANK OF CYPRUS PUBLIC CO LTD (CYPRUS)
Name changed 05/19/2004
Stock Dividends - 10% payable 05/21/1999 to holders of record 05/04/1999; 20% payable 12/28/2000 to holders of record 12/06/2000 Ex date - 12/07/2000
Name changed from Bank of Cyprus Ltd. to Bank of Cyprus Public Co. Ltd. 05/19/2004
GDR agreement terminated 11/23/2004
No GDR holders' equity
Each old ADR for Common exchanged for (0.0002) new ADR for Common 05/15/2015
Basis changed from (1:1) to (1:50) 05/15/2015
ADR agreement terminated 02/06/2017
Each new ADR for Common exchanged for $8.997753 cash

BANK OF DOUGLAS (PHOENIX, AZ)
Each share Capital Stock $100 par exchanged for (4) shares Capital Stock $25 par 00/00/1950
Each share Capital Stock $25 par exchanged for (5) shares Capital Stock $5 par 01/18/1957
Stock Dividend - 14.28571428% 05/01/1956
Name changed to Arizona Bank (Phoenix, AZ) 08/02/1960
Arizona Bank (Phoenix, AZ) reorganized as Arizona Bancwest Corp. 10/01/1982
(See Arizona Bancwest Corp.)

BANK OF EUROPE TRUST CO. (NY)
Liquidation completed 00/00/1945
No stockholders' equity

BANK FT WORTH (FORT WORTH, TX)
Each share Common $20 par exchanged for (2) shares Common $10 par 01/22/1976
Acquired by Texas American Bancshares Inc. 12/04/1978
Each share Common $10 par exchanged for (1.5) shares Common $5 par
(See Texas American Bancshares Inc.)

BANK OF FUQUAY (FUQUAY, NC)
Merged into Fidelity Bank (Fuquay-Varina, NC) 06/01/1970
Each share Common $50 par exchanged for (3) shares Common $25 par
Fidelity Bank (Fuquay-Varina, NC) reorganized as Fidelity Bancshares (N.C.), Inc. 04/01/1988

BANK OF GEORGIA (ATLANTA, GA)
Each share Capital Stock $100 par exchanged for (10) shares Capital Stock $10 par 12/00/1946
Stock Dividends - 33.33333333% 04/01/1958; (1) for (6.5) 12/31/1963
Name changed to National Bank of Georgia (Atlanta, GA) 09/01/1965
(See National Bank of Georgia (Atlanta, GA))

BANK OF HAITI
Liquidated 00/00/1935
Details not available

BANK OF HALLANDALE (HALLANDALE, FL)
Name changed to Bank of Hallandale & Trust Co. (Hallandale, FL) 01/26/1971
(See Bank of Hallandale & Trust Co. (Hallandale, FL))

BANK OF HAMTRAMCK (HAMTRAMCK, MI)
Stock Dividend - 50% 12/03/1941
Name changed to Bank of Commerce (Hamtramck, MI) 01/08/1946
Bank of Commerce (Hamtramck, MI) merged into Commerce Bancorp, Inc. (MI) 04/01/1983 which merged into Security Bancorp, Inc. 10/31/1985 which merged into First of America Bank Corp. 05/01/1992 which merged into National City Corp. 03/31/1998 which was acquired by PNC Financial Services Group, Inc. 12/31/2008

BANK OF HARRIS COUNTY, N.A. (HOUSTON, TX)
Bank failed 02/26/1988
No stockholders' equity

BANK OF HUNTINGTON (HUNTINGTON, NY)
Merged into Meadow Brook National Bank (West Hempstead, NY) 12/14/1962
Each share Common $10 par exchanged for (3.5) shares Capital Stock $5 par
Meadow Brook National Bank merged into National Bank of North America (West Hempstead, NY) 05/08/1967
(See National Bank of North America (West Hempstead, NY))

BANK OF IDAHO, N.A. (BOISE, ID)
Merged into Western Bancorporation 07/01/1980
Each share Capital Stock $10 par exchanged for (1.25) shares Capital Stock $2 par
Western Bancorporation name changed to First Interstate Bancorp 06/01/1981 which merged into Wells Fargo & Co. (Old) 04/01/1996 which merged into Wells Fargo & Co. (New) 11/02/1998

BANK OF INDIAN ROCKS (INDIAN ROCKS, FL)
Name changed to Ellis Bank of Indian Rocks (Indian Rocks, FL) 07/29/1982
Ellis Bank of Indian Rocks (Indian Rocks, FL) location changed to (Tampa, FL) 09/30/1983 which name changed to NCNB National Bank of Florida (Tampa, FL) 06/22/1984 which name changed to NationsBank of Florida, N.A. (Tampa, FL) 09/04/1992
(See NationsBank of Florida, N.A. (Tampa, FL))

BANK OF INDIANA, N.A. (GARY, IN)
Name changed 12/24/1964
Name changed from Bank of Indiana (Gary, IN) to Bank of Indiana, N.A. (Gary, IN) 12/24/1964
Common $10 par changed to $5 par and (2) additional shares issued plus a 50% stock dividend paid 03/30/1971
Stock Dividends - 11.1111111% 03/01/1966; 20% 08/23/1967
99.164% owned by Money Management Corp. as of 03/31/1980
Public interest eliminated

BANK OF INDUSTRY (CITY OF INDUSTRY, CA)
Stock Dividend - 10% 02/12/1987
Under plan of merger name changed to InBancshares 04/01/1988
(See InBancshares)

BANK OF KOBE, LTD. (JAPAN)
Merged into Mitsui Taiyo Kobe Bank, Ltd. 04/01/1990
Each ADR for Dollar Validated Common JPY 50 par exchanged for (1) ADR for Common JPY 50 par
Mitsui Taiyo Kobe Bank, Ltd. name changed to Sakura Bank, Ltd. 04/01/1992 which merged into Sumitomo Mitsui Banking Corp. 06/12/2001 which merged into Sumitomo Mitsui Financial Group, Inc. 01/15/2003

BANK OF LA JOLLA (LA JOLLA, CA)
Merged into Southern California First National Bank (San Diego, CA) 11/20/1968
Each share Capital Stock $10 par exchanged for (0.8) share Common $5 par
Southern California First National Bank (San Diego, CA) reorganized as Southern California First National Corp. 02/28/1969
(See Southern California First National Corp.)

BANK OF LAKEWOOD (LAKEWOOD, CA)
Merged into Gateway Bancorp 11/30/2001
Each share Common no par exchanged for $6 cash

BANK OF LANCASTER (KILMARNOCK, VA)
Under plan of reorganization each share Common $5 par automatically became (1) share Bay Banks of Virginia Inc. Common $5 par 07/01/1997

BANK OF LEXINGTON (LEXINGTON, KY)
Reorganized as Kentucky Bank-Shares of Lexington, Inc. 04/30/1982
Each share Common $10 par exchanged for (6) shares Common no par

BANK OF LOS ANGELES (LOS ANGELES, CA)
Ctfs. dated prior to 12/30/1965
Merged into United States National Bank (San Diego, CA) 12/30/1965
Each share Capital Stock $10 par or VTC for Capital Stock $10 par exchanged for (0.625) share Capital Stock $10 par
(See United States National Bank (San Diego, CA))

BANK OF LOUISVILLE-ROYAL BANK & TRUST CO. (LOUISVILLE, KY)
Common $10 par changed to $5 par and (2) additional shares issued 03/11/1969
Common $5 par changed to $7.50 par 07/26/1972
Common $7.50 par changed to $10 par 03/24/1976
Common $10 par changed to $12.50 par 03/23/1977
Stock Dividend - 19.047% 08/06/1963
Name changed to Bank of Louisville & Trust Co. (Louisville, KY) 03/26/1980
Bank of Louisville & Trust Co. (Louisville, KY) reorganized as Mid-America Bancorp 03/25/1983 which merged into BB&T Corp. 03/08/2002

BANK OF MAMMOTH (BISHOP LAKES, CA)
Reorganized 01/01/1985
Location changed from Mammoth Lakes, CA to Bishop, CA 01/01/1985
Name changed to First Sierra Bank (Bishop, CA) 03/22/1985
(See First Sierra Bank (Bishop, CA))

BANK OF MARINA DEL REY (MARINA DEL REY, CA)
Name changed to Marina State Bank (Marina Del Rey, CA) 01/25/1985
Marina State Bank (Marina Del Rey, CA) name changed to Marina Bank (Marina Del Rey, CA) 06/30/1995
(See Marina Bank (Marina Del Rey, CA))

BANK OF MONTECITO (MONTECITO, CA)
Merged into Montecito Bancorp 03/17/1983
Each share Common $5 par exchanged for $21 cash

BANK OF NEW YORK & FIFTH AVENUE BANK (NEW YORK, NY)
Name changed to Bank of New York (New York, NY) 05/01/1952
Bank of New York (New York, NY) reorganized as Bank of New York Co., Inc. 05/29/1969 which merged into Bank of New York Mellon Corp. 07/01/2007

BANK OF NEW YORK & TRUST CO. (NEW YORK, NY)
Name changed to Bank of New York (New York, NY) 07/01/1938
Bank of New York (New York, NY) merged into Bank of New York & Fifth Avenue Bank (New York, NY) 04/30/1948 which name changed to Bank of New York (New York, NY) 05/01/1952 which reorganized as Bank of New York Co., Inc. 05/29/1969 which merged into Bank of New York Mellon Corp. 07/01/2007

BANK OF NORTH AMERICA (NEW YORK, NY)
Certificates dated after 03/11/1965
Merged into National Bank of North America (New York, NY) 05/08/1967
Each share Common $5 par exchanged for (0.33333333) share of C.I.T. Financial Corp. $5.50 Conv. Preference 1967 Ser. no par
(See C.I.T. Financial Corp.)

BANK OF NORTH AMERICA OLD (NEW YORK, NY)
Certificates dated prior to 09/05/1958
Merged into Commercial Bank of North America (New York, NY) 09/05/1958
Each share Capital Stock $5 par exchanged for (1) share Capital Stock $5 par
Commercial Bank of North America (New York, NY) name changed to Bank of North America (New York, NY) (New) 03/11/1965
(See Bank of North America (New York, NY) (New))

BANK OF NORTH BAY VILLAGE (NORTH BAY VILLAGE, FL)
Name changed to Capital Bank of North Bay Village (North Bay Village, FL) 05/01/1975
Capital Bank of North Bay Village (North Bay Village, FL) merged into Capital Bank (North Bay Village, FL) 12/30/1977 which was acquired by Capital Bancorp 09/00/1982 which merged into Union Planters Corp. 12/31/1997 which merged into Regions Financial Corp. (New) 07/01/2004

BANK OF NORTH TAMPA (TAMPA, FL)
Through voluntary exchange offer Landmark Banking Corp. of Florida held 99.94% as of 02/20/1975
Public interest eliminated

BANK OF NORTHERN ILLINOIS (GLENVIEW, IL)
Acquired by Bank of Northern Illinois, N.A. (Glenview, IL) 08/01/1995
Details not available

BANK OF NT BUTTERFIELD & SON LTD (BERMUDA)
8% Non-Cum. Ltd. Vtg. Perpetual Preference USD $0.01 par called for redemption at $1,180 on 12/15/2016
(Additional Information in Active)

BANK OF NUTLEY (NUTLEY, NJ)
Capital Stock $25 par changed to $12.50 par and (1) additional share issued 01/28/1963
Capital Stock $12.50 par changed to $5 par and (1.5) additional shares issued plus a 20% stock dividend paid 02/04/1966
Stock Dividends - 10% 12/19/1944; 40% 01/19/1945; 25% 01/08/1946; 18.75% 11/27/1950; 11.5384% 12/14/1953
Merged into First National State Bank of New Jersey (Newark, NJ) 05/12/1967
Each share Capital Stock $5 par exchanged for (1) share Common $6.25 par
First National State Bank of New Jersey (Newark, NJ) reorganized as First National State Bancorporation 01/15/1970 which name changed to First Fidelity Bancorporation (Old) 05/01/1985 which merged into First Fidelity Bancorporation (New) 02/29/1988 which merged into First Union Corp. 01/01/1996 which name changed to Wachovia Corp. (Ctfs. dated after 09/01/2001) 09/01/2001 which merged into Wells Fargo & Co. (New) 12/31/2008

BANK OF OHIO CO. (CLEVELAND, OH)
Stock Dividend - 60% 10/01/1946
Liquidation completed
Each share Capital Stock $10 par stamped to indicate initial distribution of $43.50 cash 08/00/1954
Each share Stamped Capital Stock $10 par received second distribution of $5.60 cash 03/04/1955
Each share Stamped Capital Stock $10 par exchanged for third and final distribution of $0.45 cash 06/14/1957

BANK OF OKLAHOMA, CITY PLAZA (TULSA, OK)
Acquired by Bank of Oklahoma, N.A. (Tulsa, OK) 10/14/1989
Details not available

BANK OF PALM SPRINGS (PALM SPRINGS, CA)
Merged into Bank of California, N.A. (San Francisco, CA) 10/01/1987
Each share Common $6 par exchanged for $25.50 cash

BANK OF PARK RIDGE (STEVENS POINT, WI)
Through exchange offer 98.1% acquired by First Affiliated Bancorporation, Inc. as of 04/20/1979
First Affiliated Bancorporation, Inc. merged into Marshall & Ilsley Corp. (Old) 11/28/1986
(See Marshall & Ilsley Corp. (Old))

BANK OF PASSAIC & CLIFTON (PASSAIC, NJ)
Location changed 06/06/1969
Location changed from (Clifton, NJ) to (Passaic, NJ) 06/06/1969
Common $10 par changed to $5 par and (1) additional share issued 07/01/1969
Name changed to Bank of Passaic & Clifton, N.A. (Passaic, NJ) 03/16/1970
Bank of Passaic & Clifton, N.A. (Passaic, NJ) name changed to Valley National Bank (Passaic, NJ) 05/10/1976 which reorganized as Valley National Bancorp 05/02/1983

BANK OF PHILADELPHIA & TRUST CO. (PHILADELPHIA, PA)
Acquired by Bankers Trust Co. (Philadelphia, PA) 07/22/1930
Details not available

BANK OF ROCKVILLE CENTRE TRUST CO. (ROCKVILLE CENTRE, NY)
Stock Dividends - 100% 07/13/1948; 50% 03/22/1950
Acquired by Chemical Bank New York Trust Co. (New York, NY) 06/04/1963
Each share Capital Stock $100 par exchanged for (14) shares Capital Stock $12 par
Chemical Bank New York Trust Co. (New York, NY) reorganized as Chemical New York Corp. 02/17/1969 which name changed to Chemical Banking Corp. 04/29/1988 which name changed to Chase Manhattan Corp. (New) 03/31/1996 which name changed to J.P. Morgan Chase & Co. 12/31/2000 which name changed to JPMorgan Chase & Co. 07/20/2004

BANK ST ANN (ST ANN, MO)
Stock Dividend - 100% 01/25/1974
Name changed to Mega Bank of St. Ann (St. Ann, MO) 01/01/1985
Mega Bank of St. Ann (St. Ann, MO) name changed to Mega Bank (St. Ann, MO) 10/29/1993
(See Mega Bank (St. Ann, MO))

BANK OF SALEM (SALEM, OR)
Common $1.25 par split (4) for (1) by issuance of (3) additional shares payable 02/27/1998 to holders of record 02/01/1998
Stock Dividends - 5% payable 04/19/1999 to holders of record 03/31/1999; 5% payable 04/01/2000 to holders of record 03/31/2000 Ex date - 04/19/2000; 5% payable 04/16/2001 to holders of record 03/31/2001 Ex date - 03/28/2001; 5% payable 04/15/2002 to holders of record 03/31/2002 Ex date - 03/26/2002; 5% payable 04/15/2003 to holders of record 03/31/2003 Ex date - 03/27/2003; 5% payable 04/19/2004 to holders of record 03/15/2004 Ex date - 03/11/2004
Merged into Frontier Financial Corp. 11/30/2004
Each share Common $1.25 par exchanged for (0.99) share Common no par

BANK OF SAN CLEMENTE (CA)
Under plan of reorganization each share Common $2.50 par became (1) share San Clemente Bancorp Common no par 05/11/1982
(See San Clemente Bancorp)

BANK OF SAN DIEGO (SAN DIEGO, CA)
Under plan of reorganization each share Common no par automatically became (1) share BSD Bancorp., Inc. (CA) Common no par 03/23/1981
BSD Bancorp, Inc. (CA) reincorporated in Delaware 09/02/1987
(See BSD Bancorp, Inc.)

BANK OF SCOTTSDALE (SCOTTSDALE, AZ)
Merged into Pioneer Bank of Arizona (Phoenix, AZ) 01/20/1966
Each share Common $5 par exchanged for (1) share Common $10 par
Pioneer Bank of Arizona (Phoenix, AZ) reorganized as Western American Industries 06/19/1969 which merged into Great Western Corp. (DE) 12/31/1969 which name changed to Patagonia Corp. 06/09/1970
(See Patagonia Corp.)

BANK OF SOUTH HAVEN (SOUTH HAVEN, MI)
Stock Dividend - 33:33333333% 02/18/1954
Name changed to Citizens Trust & Savings Bank (South Haven, MI) 10/24/1963
Citizens Trust & Savings Bank (South Haven, MI) merged into Shoreline Financial Corp. 12/24/1987 which merged into Chemical Financial Corp. 01/09/2001

BANK SUFFOLK CNTY (STONY BROOK, NY)
Capital Stock $10 par changed to $5 par and (1) additional share issued 01/27/1965
Stock Dividends - 10% 01/26/1967; 20% 01/25/1968; 20% 03/26/1969; 20% 03/25/1970; 20% 03/25/1971; 100% 06/08/1971; 20% 04/01/1972; 20% 04/04/1973; 20% 04/03/1974
Merged into Banco Exterior de Espana 06/30/1980
Each share Capital Stock $5 par exchanged for $17 cash

BANK OF TACOMA (TACOMA, WA)
Merged into West One Bancorp 08/31/1990
Each share Common $15 par exchanged for (2.019) shares Common $1 par
West One Bancorp merged into U.S. Bancorp (OR) 12/26/1995 which merged into U.S. Bancorp (DE) 08/01/1997

BANK OF TENNESSEE (KINGSPORT, TN)
Under plan of reorganization each share Common $8 par automatically became (1) share BancTenn Corp. Common $8 par 11/01/1985
(See BancTenn Corp.)

BANK OF THE CAROLINAS (MOCKSVILLE, NC)
Common $5 par split (6) for (5) by issuance of (0.2) additional share payable 10/28/2005 to holders of record 10/14/2005 Ex date - 10/12/2005
Stock Dividend - 20% payable 06/27/2003 to holders of record 06/02/2003 Ex date - 05/29/2003
Reorganized as Bank of the Carolinas Corp. 08/18/2006
Each share Common $5 par exchanged for (1) share Common $5 par
Bank of the Carolinas Corp. merged into Bank of the Ozarks, Inc. 08/05/2015 which reorganized as Bank of the Ozarks (Little Rock, AR) 06/27/2017 which name changed to Bank OZK (Little Rock, AR) 07/16/2018

BANK OF THE CAROLINAS CORP (NC)
Common $5 par changed to no par 05/28/2014
Merged into Bank of the Ozarks, Inc. 08/05/2015
Each share Common no par exchanged for (0.00313515) share Common 1¢ par
Bank of the Ozarks, Inc. reorganized as Bank of the Ozarks (Little Rock, AR) 06/27/2017 which name changed to Bank OZK (Little Rock, AR) 07/16/2018

BANK OF THE JAMES (LYNCHBURG, VA)
Under plan of reorganization each share Common $4 par automatically became (1) share James Financial Group Inc. Common $4 par 01/01/2004

BANK OF THE MANHATTAN CO. (NEW YORK, NY)
Merged into Chase Manhattan Bank (New York, NY) 03/31/1955
Each share Capital Stock $10 par exchanged for (1) share Capital Stock $12.50 par
Chase Manhattan Bank (New York, NY) name changed to Chase Manhattan Bank (N.A.), (New York, NY) 09/23/1965 which reorganized as Chase Manhattan Corp. (Old) 06/04/1969 which merged into Chase Manhattan Corp. (New) 03/31/1996 which name changed to J.P. Morgan Chase & Co. 12/31/2000 which name changed to JPMorgan Chase & Co. 07/20/2004

BANK OF THE NORTHWEST (PORTLAND, OR)
Common $5 par split (11) for (10) by issuance of (0.1) additional share payable 07/26/2001 to holders of record 07/12/2001 Ex date - 07/10/2001
Common $5 par split (5) for (4) by issuance of (0.25) additional share payable 05/24/2002 to holders of record 05/10/2002 Ex date - 05/28/2002
Merged into Pacific Northwest Bancorp 11/13/2002
Each share Common $5 par exchanged for $21.08 cash

BANK OF THE OCEAN (OCEANSIDE, CA)
Merged into Home Group, Inc. 12/24/1986
Each share Common no par exchanged for $8.50 cash

BANK OF THE OZARKS (AR)
Reorganized 06/27/2017
Common 1¢ par split (2) for (1) by issuance of (1) additional share payable 06/17/2002 to holders of record 06/03/2002 Ex date - 06/18/2002
Common 1¢ par split (2) for (1) by issuance of (1) additional share payable 12/10/2003 to holders of record 11/26/2003 Ex date - 12/11/2003
Common 1¢ par split (2) for (1) by issuance of (1) additional share payable 08/16/2011 to holders of record 08/05/2011 Ex date - 08/17/2011
Common 1¢ par split (2) for (1) by issuance of (1) additional share payable 06/23/2014 to holders of record 06/13/2014 Ex date - 06/24/2014
Under plan of reorganization each share Bank of the Ozarks, Inc. Common 1¢ par automatically became (1) share Bank of the Ozarks (Little Rock, AR) Common 1¢ par 06/27/2017
Name changed to Bank OZK (Little Rock, AR) 07/16/2018

BANK OF THE POTOMAC (HERNDON, VA)
Acquired by F & M National Corp. 04/06/1995
Each share Common $10 par exchanged for (2.5168) shares Common $2 par
F & M National Corp. merged into BB&T Corp. 08/09/2001

BANK OF TORONTO (TORONTO, ON)
Each share Capital Stock $100 par exchanged for (10) shares Capital Stock $10 par 00/00/1944
Merged into Toronto-Dominion Bank (Toronto, ON) 02/01/1955
Each share Capital Stock $10 par exchanged for (1.333333) shares Capital Stock $10 par

BANK OF TULSA (TULSA, OK)
Reorganized as Tulbancorp, Inc. 12/29/1978
Each share Common $10 par exchanged for (1) share Common $1 par
(See Tulbancorp, Inc.)

BANK OF VENTURA (VENTURA, CA)
Merged into First Banks Inc. 08/31/2000
Each share Common $5 par exchanged for $26.47 cash

BANK OF VIENNA (VIENNA, VA)
Merged into Bank of Virginia Co. 04/29/1983
Each share Common no par exchanged for $40 cash

BANK OF VILLA PARK (VILLA PARK, IL)
Reorganized under the laws of Delaware as Duco Bancshares, Inc. 10/21/1986
Each share Common $10 par exchanged for (1) share Common $10 par
(See Duco Bancshares, Inc.)

BANK OF VIRGINIA (RICHMOND, VA)
Common $16.66666666 par changed to $20 par 00/00/1949
Each share Common $20 par exchanged for (3) shares Common $10 par 00/00/1954
Stock Dividend - 11.11111111% 12/29/1950
99.5% acquired by Virginia Commonwealth Bankshares, Inc. through exchange offer which expired 03/24/1971
Public interest eliminated

BANK OF WALNUT CREEK (WALNUT CREEK, CA)
Under plan of reorganization each share Common no par automatically became (1) share BWC Financial Corp. Common no par 08/26/1982
BWC Financial Corp. merged into First Republic Bank (San Franciso, CA) 10/16/2006 which merged into Merrill Lynch & Co., Inc. 09/21/2007 which was acquired by Bank of America Corp. 01/02/2009

BANK OF WESTCHESTER (YONKERS, NY)
Merged into County Trust Co. (White Plains, NY) 07/30/1947
Each share Common $10 par exchanged for (0.66666666) share Capital Stock $16 par
County Trust Co. (White Plains, NY) merged into Bank of New York Co., Inc. 05/29/1969 which merged into Bank of New York Mellon Corp. 07/01/2007

BANK OF WESTMINSTER (WESTMINSTER, CA)
Merged into Bank of Yorba Linda (Yorba Linda, CA) 06/14/1996
Each share Common $10 par exchanged for (6.52) shares Common no par
Bank of Yorba Linda (Yorba Linda, CA) reorganized as BYL Bancorp 11/19/1997
(See BYL Bancorp)

BANK OF WINSTON-SALEM (WINSTON-SALEM, NC)
Merged into Bancshares of North Carolina, Inc. 05/08/1972
Each share Common $10 par exchanged for (1.22) shares Common $5 par
Bancshares of North Carolina, Inc. merged into NCNB Corp. 12/23/1982 which name changed to NationsBank Corp. 12/31/1991 which reincorporated in Delaware as BankAmerica Corp. (Old) 09/25/1998 which merged into BankAmerica Corp. (New) 09/30/1998 which name changed to Bank of America Corp. 04/28/1999

BANK OF YUCCA VALLEY (YUCCA VALLEY, CA)
Name changed to First Community Bank of the Desert (Yucca Valley, CA) 10/30/1989
First Community Bank of the Desert (Yucca Valley, CA) merged into First Community Bancorp (CA) 05/31/2000 which reincorporated in Delaware as PacWest Bancorp 05/14/2008

BANK ON IT INC (CA)
Stock Dividends - 5% payable 12/29/2005 to holders of record 12/15/2005 Ex date - 12/20/2005; 5% payable 12/29/2006 to holders of record 12/15/2006 Ex date - 12/13/2006; 5% payable 12/31/2007 to holders of record 12/14/2007 Ex date - 12/13/2007; 5% payable 12/31/2008 to holders of record 12/15/2008 Ex date - 12/17/2008; 5% payable 01/29/2010 to holders of record 01/15/2010 Ex date - 01/15/2010
Acquired by Bay Commercial Bank (Walnut Creek, CA) 04/28/2014
Each share Common no par exchanged for $2.57 cash

BANK ONE CAP I (DE)
8% Preferred Securities called for redemption at $25 on 11/01/2004

BANK ONE CAP II (DE)
8.5% Preferred Security called for redemption at $25 on 08/15/2005

BANK ONE CAP V (DE)
8% Preferred Securities called for redemption at $25 on 02/05/2006

BANK ONE CAP VI (DE)
7.20% Preferred Securities called for redemption at $25 on 05/08/2013

BANK ONE CORP (DE)
7.5% Preferred Purchase Unit called for redemption at $25 on 08/10/1999
Adjustable Dividend Preferred Ser. B 1¢ par called for redemption at $100 plus $1 accrued dividend on 11/01/2001
Adjustable Dividend Preferred Ser. C 1¢ par called for redemption at $100 plus $1.083 accrued dividends on 11/01/2001
Merged into J.P. Morgan Chase & Co. 07/01/2004
Each share Common 1¢ par exchanged for (1.32) shares Common $1 par
J.P. Morgan Chase & Co. name changed to JPMorgan Chase & Co. 07/20/2004

BANK ORANGE CNTY (FOUNTAIN VALLEY, CA)
Reorganized as Orange Bancorp 02/05/1982
Each share Common no par exchanged for (1) share Common no par
Orange Bancorp merged back into Bank of Orange County (Fountain Valley, CA) 11/30/1996
Merged into CFB Merger Co. 01/22/1999
Each share Common no par exchanged for $37.537 cash

BANK ORE (WOODBURN, OR)
Reorganized as Banore Bancshares, Inc. 06/05/1981
Each share Common $2.50 par exchanged for (2) shares Common $2.50 par
(See Banore Bancshares, Inc.)

BANK PA (READING, PA)
Reorganized as B O P Corp. 08/12/1969
Each share Common $5 par exchanged for (1) share Common $5 par
B O P Corp. name changed to Bancorp of Pennsylvania 03/25/1981
(See Bancorp of Pennsylvania)

BANK PALM BEACH & TR CO (PALM BEACH, FL)
Stock Dividends - 50% 01/20/1964; 10% 01/18/1965
Through voluntary exchange offer over 99% acquired by Florida

Commercial Banks, Inc. as of 06/20/1967
Public interest eliminated

BANK PALMETTO (PALMETTO, FL)
Name changed to Palmetto Bank & Trust Co. (Palmetto, FL) 02/01/1971

BANK PASSAIC & CLIFTON N A (PASSAIC, NJ)
Name changed 10/08/1958
Name changed 03/16/1970
Each share Common $25 par exchanged for (2.75) shares Common $10 par to effect a (2.5) for (1) split and a 10% stock dividend 02/29/1956
Name changed from Bank of Passaic & Trust Co. (Passaic, NJ) to Bank of Passaic & Clifton (Clifton, NJ) 10/08/1958
Stock Dividends - 20% 02/01/1961; 10% 01/04/1965; 100% 05/19/1967
Location changed to from (Clifton, NJ) to (Passaic, NJ) 06/06/1969
Name changed from Bank of Passaic & Clifton (Passaic, NJ) to Bank of Passaic & Clifton, N.A. (Passaic, NJ) 03/16/1970
Name changed to Valley National Bank (Passaic, NJ) 05/10/1976
Valley National Bank (Passaic, NJ) reorganized as Valley National Bancorp 05/02/1983

BANK PETALUMA (PETALUMA, CA)
Common 1¢ par split (2) for (1) by issuance of (1) additional share payable 05/06/1998 to holders of record 04/28/1998
Stock Dividend - 5% payable 12/19/1997 to holders of record 11/29/1997
Merged into Greater Bay Bancorp 10/13/2000
Each share Common 1¢ par exchanged for (0.5731) share Common no par
Greater Bay Bancorp merged into Wells Fargo & Co. 10/01/2007

BANK PLUS CORP (DE)
Merged into FBOP Corp. 01/02/2002
Each share Common $1 par exchanged for $7.25 cash

BANK PRZEMYSLOWO HANDLOWY S A (POLAND)
Name changed to Bank BPH S.A. 07/15/2004
(See Bank BPH S.A.)

BANK RALEIGH (BECKLEY, WV)
Capital Stock $25 par changed to $12.50 par and (1) additional share issued 00/00/1968
Capital Stock $12.50 par changed to $6.25 par and (1) additional share issued 01/18/1972
Capital Stock $6.25 par changed to $2.08333333 par and (2) additional shares issued 11/21/1978
Reorganized as Raleigh Bankshares, Inc. 01/03/1984
Each share Capital Stock $2.08333333 par exchanged for (1) share Common $1 par
Raleigh Bankshares, Inc. name changed to Horizon Bancorp, Inc. 05/01/1985 which merged into City Holding Co. 12/31/1998

BANK RAVENSWOOD (CHICAGO, IL)
Reorganized as Ravenswood Financial Corp. 08/17/1983
Each share Common $1 par exchanged for $4.75 principal amount of 15% 15-yr. Debentures due 8/17/98 and (1) share Common $1 par
Ravenswood Financial Corp. acquired by First Chicago Corp. 10/31/1989 which merged into First Chicago NBD Corp. 12/01/1995 which merged into Bank One Corp. 10/02/1998 which merged into J.P. Morgan Chase & Co. 07/01/2004

which name changed to JPMorgan Chase & Co. 07/20/2004

BANK REALE (PASCO, WA)
Acquired by BEO Bancorp 02/28/2015
Each share Common held by holders of (400) or more shares exchanged for either (0.25) share Common $5 par, $6.42 cash or a combination thereof
Holders of (399) shares or fewer exchanged for $6.42 cash per share
Note: Option to make an election expired 04/29/2015 after which holders received 50% stock and 50% cash for their holdings

BANK REDDING (REDDING, CA)
Completely liquidated 10/29/1971
Each share Capital Stock $12 par exchanged for first and final distribution of (0.91) share Bank of California, N.A. (San Francisco, CA) Common Capital Stock $15 par
Bank of California, N.A. (San Francisco, CA) reorganized as BanCal Tri-State Corp. 05/01/1972
(See BanCal Tri-State Corp.)

BANK REDLANDS (REDLANDS, CA)
Common $5 par changed to $2.50 par and (1) additional share issued 07/07/1977
Common $2.50 par changed to $1.25 par and (1) additional share issued 07/20/1979
Common $1.25 par split (3) for (2) by issuance of (0.5) additional share 02/18/1988
Merged into Community Bank (Pasadena, CA) 06/05/1989
Each share Common $1.25 par exchanged for $9.55 cash

BANK RHODE IS (PROVIDENCE, RI)
Ser. B Preferred called for redemption at $25 on 04/27/1998
Under plan of reorganization each share Common 1¢ par automatically became (1) share Bancorp Rhode Island, Inc. Common 1¢ par 09/01/2000
Bancorp Rhode Island, Inc. merged into Brookline Bancorp, Inc. 01/03/2012

BANK RICHMOND N A (RICHMOND, VA)
Stock Dividend - 20% payable 04/12/2002 to holders of record 04/03/2002
Merged into Gateway Financial Holdings, Inc. 06/01/2007
Each share Common $4 par exchanged for either (2.08381857) shares Common no par and $0.3973211 cash or $30.05 cash
Note: Option to receive stock and cash expired 06/20/2007
Gateway Financial Holdings, Inc. merged into Hampton Roads Bankshares, Inc. 12/31/2008 which name changed to Xenith Bankshares, Inc. (New) 08/01/2016 which merged into Union Bankshares Corp. 01/01/2018

BANK ROCKBRIDGE (RAPHINE, VA)
Under plan of reorganization each share Common $1 par automatically became (1) share Summit Bankshares, Inc. Common $1 par 10/01/1996
Summit Bankshares, Inc. merged into One Valley Bancorp, Inc. 08/07/1998 which merged into BB&T Corp. 07/06/2000

BANK SACRAMENTO (SACRAMENTO, CA)
Capital Stock $20 par changed to $16 par and (0.25) additional share issued 04/01/1964
Capital Stock $16 par changed to $10 par 08/15/1968
Merged into Security Pacific National Bank (Los Angeles, CA) 08/03/1970
Each share Capital Stock $10 par

exchanged for (1) share Capital Stock $10 par
Security Pacific National Bank (Los Angeles, CA) reorganized as Security Pacific Corp. 06/30/1972 which merged into BankAmerica Corp. (Old) 04/22/1992 which merged into BankAmerica Corp. (New) 09/30/1998 which name changed to Bank of America Corp. 04/28/1999

BANK SACRAMENTO CALIF NEW (SACRAMENTO, CA)
Reorganized as Greater Sacramento Bancorp 10/30/2002
Each share Common no par exchanged for (1) share Common no par
(See Greater Sacramento Bancorp)

BANK ST PETERSBURG OJSC (RUSSIA)
GDR agreement terminated 12/10/2007
Each GDR for Ordinary exchanged for $20.9685 cash

BANK SALINAS (SALINAS, CA)
Under plan of reorganization each share Common no par automatically became (1) share Central Coast Bancorp Common no par 12/31/1994
(See Central Coast Bancorp)

BANK SALT LAKE (SALT LAKE CITY, UT)
Name changed to Commercial Security Bank of Salt Lake (Salt Lake City, UT) 03/18/1975
(See Commercial Security Bank of Salt Lake (Salt Lake City, UT))

BANK SAN BERNARDINO (SAN BERNARDINO, CA)
Stock Dividends - 20% 05/25/1990; 20% 08/31/1991
Name changed to Business Bank of California (San Bernadino, CA) 08/15/1996
Business Bank of California (San Bernardino, CA) reorganized as Business Bancorp (New) 01/21/2000
(See Business Bancorp (New))

BANK SAN FRANCISCO (SAN FRANCISCO, CA)
Reorganized as Bank of San Francisco Holding Co. 01/31/1982
Each share Common no par exchanged for (2.1) shares Common no par
Bank of San Francisco Holding Co. recapitalized as San Francisco Co. 06/27/1994
(See San Francisco Co.)

BANK SAN FRANCISCO HLDG CO (DE)
Reincorporated 07/00/1988
State of incorporation changed from (CA) to (DE) 07/00/1988
Recapitalized as San Francisco Co. 06/27/1994
Each share Class A Common no par exchanged for (0.05) share Class A Common 1¢ par
(See San Francisco Co.)

BANK SAN PEDRO (SAN PEDRO, CA)
Common $6 par changed to no par and (1) additional share issued 06/08/1979
Stock Dividends - 10% 11/24/1978; 10% 11/17/1980; 10% 11/23/1981; 15% 01/18/1983; 10% 12/22/1983; 15% 10/08/1984; 10% 12/09/1990
Closed by the California State Banking Superintendent and the FDIC named receiver 07/15/1994
Stockholders' equity undetermined

BANK SANTA ANA (SANTA ANA, CA)
Merged into United States National Bank (San Diego, CA) 12/29/1969
Each share Capital Stock $10 par

exchanged for (1.2) shares Capital Stock $10 par
(See United States National Bank (San Diego, CA))

BANK SANTA CLARA (SANTA CLARA, CA)
Stock Dividends - 6% payable 09/16/1997 to holders of record 09/02/1997; 6% payable 05/29/1998 to holders of record 05/15/1998
Merged into Greater Bay Bancorp 07/21/2000
Each share Common $4 par exchanged for (0.8499) share Common no par
Greater Bay Bancorp merged into Wells Fargo & Co. 10/01/2007

BANK SANTA MARIA CALIF (SANTA MARIA, CA)
Under plan of reorganization each share Common no par automatically became (1) share BSM Bancorp Common no par 03/11/1997
BSM Bancorp merged into Mid-State Bancshares 07/10/1998
(See Mid-State Bancshares)

BANK SECS INC (NM)
Each share Common $10 par exchanged for (2) shares Common $5 par 04/25/1975
Name changed to United New Mexico Financial Corp. 03/01/1984
United New Mexico Financial Corp. merged into First United Bank Group, Inc. 03/26/1993 which merged into Norwest Corp. 01/14/1994 which name changed to Wells Fargo & Co. (New) 11/02/1998

BANK SVCS & TRS (DALLAS, TX)
Name changed to Dallas International Bank (Dallas, TX) 06/09/1971
Dallas International Bank (Dallas, TX) name changed to Northwest Bank (Dallas, TX) 01/15/1987
(See Northwest Bank (Dallas, TX))

BANK SHS INC (MN)
Class B Common 1¢ par changed to no par 07/01/1955
Each share Class A Common $20 par exchanged for (2) shares 6% Prior Preferred Ser. A $10 par 06/11/1956
Each share Class B Common no par exchanged for (1) share Common no par 06/11/1956
Each share Common no par exchanged for (40) shares Common 20¢ par 03/02/1971
Acquired by First Bank System, Inc. 12/31/1992
Details not available

BANK SIERRA (PORTERVILLE, CA)
Common $6.25 par split (2) for (1) by issuance of (1) additional share payable 06/01/1996 to holders of record 05/01/1996
Common $6.25 par split (2) for (1) by issuance of (1) additional share payable 11/14/1997 to holders of record 10/14/1997
Under plan of reorganization each share Common $6.25 par automatically became (1) share Sierra Bancorp Common no par 08/10/2001

BANK SIERRA BLANCA (SIERRA BLANCA, TX)
Discharged from receivership 02/01/2004
No stockholders' equity

BANK SMITHTOWN (SMITHTOWN, NY)
Capital Stock $100 par changed to $10 par and (9) additional shares issued 10/06/1960
Capital Stock $10 par changed to $5 par and (1) additional share issued plus a 10% stock dividend paid 06/19/1964
Stock Dividends - 100% 07/01/1970; 25% 04/29/1974
Under plan of reorganization each

share Capital Stock $5 par automatically became (1) share Smithtown Bancorp, Inc. Common $5 par 11/01/1984
Smithtown Bancorp, Inc. merged into People's United Financial, Inc. 11/30/2010

BANK SOUTH (MT JULIET, TN)
Merged into Mid-America Bancshares, Inc. 09/01/2006
Each share Common $1 par exchanged for (2.1814) shares Common $1 par
Mid-America Bancshares, Inc. merged into Pinnacle Financial Partners, Inc. 11/30/2007

BANK SOUTH CAROLINA (CHARLESTON, SC)
Merged into Bank of South Carolina Corp. 04/17/1995
Each share Common $10 par exchanged for (2) shares Common no par

BANK SOUTH CORP (GA)
Common $5 par split (2) for (1) by issuance of (1) additional share 06/15/1983
Common $5 par split (5) for (4) by issuance of (0.25) additional share 06/01/1985
Common $5 par split (3) for (2) by issuance of (0.5) additional share 06/02/1986
Common $5 par split (5) for (4) by issuance of (0.25) additional share 06/01/1987
Stock Dividends - 25% 06/01/1981; 10% 06/01/1984; 10% 06/01/1988
Merged into NationsBank Corp. 01/09/1996
Each share Common $5 par exchanged for (0.44) share Common no par
NationsBank Corp. reincorporated in Delaware as BankAmerica Corp. (Old) 09/25/1998 which merged into BankAmerica Corp. (New) 09/30/1998 which name changed to Bank of America Corp. 04/28/1999

BANK SOUTH WINDSOR (SOUTH WINDSOR, CT)
Merged into New England Community Bancorp, Inc. 08/14/1998
Each share Common $5 par exchanged for (1.3539) shares Class A Common 10¢ par
New England Community Bancorp, Inc. merged into Webster Financial Corp. 12/01/1999

BANK SOUTHINGTON (SOUTHINGTON, CT)
Common $8 par changed to $6 par and (0.33333333) additional share issued 01/20/1988
Stock Dividend - 10% 01/28/1994
Merged into HUBCO, Inc. 01/08/1998
Each share Common $6 par exchanged for (0.618) share Common no par
HUBCO, Inc. name changed to Hudson United Bancorp 04/21/1999 which merged into TD Banknorth Inc. 01/31/2006
(See TD Banknorth Inc.)

BANK SOUTHN CALIF (SAN DIEGO, CA)
Name changed 07/19/1990
Name changed from Bank of Southern California, N.A. (San Diego, CA) to Bank of Southern California (San Diego, CA) 07/19/1990
Merged into First National Bank (San Diego, CA) 09/30/1996
Each share Common $4 par exchanged for (0.007103) share Common $100 par
(See First National Bank (San Diego, CA))

BANK SOUTHN ORE (MEDFORD, OR)
Common $5 par split (2) for (1) by issuance of (1) additional share payable 01/02/1996 to holders of record 12/01/1995
Under plan of merger each share Common $5 par automatically became (1) share PremierWest Bancorp Common no par 05/08/2000
(See PremierWest Bancorp)

BANK SOUTHWEST N A (HOUSTON, TX)
Each share Common $20 par exchanged for (2.2) shares Common $10 par to effect a (2) for (1) split and 10% stock dividend 01/06/1964
Stock Dividends - 10% 08/27/1956; 15% 01/20/1959; 15% 07/14/1961
Under plan of reorganization each share Common $10 par exchanged for (1) share Southwest Bancshares, Inc. Common $10 par 12/10/1970
Southwest Bancshares, Inc. merged into MCorp 10/11/1984
(See MCorp)

BANK ST GEORGE (ST. GEORGE, UT)
Acquired by Zions First National Bank, N.A. (Salt Lake City, UT) 06/30/1970
Each share Capital Stock $1 par exchanged for $5.55 cash

BANK STAMFORD (STAMFORD, CT)
Stock Dividend - 25% 04/15/1987
Under plan of reorganization each share Common $1 par automatically became (1) share Fairfield County Bancorp, Inc. Common $1 par 12/30/1988

BANK STK FD INC (CO)
Company reported out of business 05/18/1987
Details not available

BANK STK FD LTD (CO)
Name changed to Bank Stock Fund, Inc. 01/03/1969
(See Bank Stock Fund, Inc.)

BANK STOCK CORP. OF MILWAUKEE (WI)
Name changed to Marshall & Ilsley Bank Stock Corp. 08/01/1962
Marshall & Ilsley Bank Stock Corp. name changed to Marshall & Ilsley Corp. (Old) 12/30/1971
(See Marshall & Ilsley Corp. (Old))

BANK STOCK TRUST SHARES, SERIES C-1 BANK STOCK TRUST SHARES, SERIES C-2
Trusts terminated 00/00/1942
No stockhoders' equity

BANK STOCKDALE FSB (BAKERSFIELD, CA)
Merged into VIB Corp. 01/28/1999
Each share Common $4 par exchanged for (1.943) shares Common no par
(See VIB Corp.)

BANK STOCKTON (STOCKTON, CA)
Each share Capital Stock $100 par exchanged for (10) shares Capital Stock $10 par 03/09/1960
Stock Dividend - 50% 12/30/1960
Merged into 1867 Western Financial Corp. 10/02/1989
Each share Capital Stock $10 par exchanged for (1) share Preferred Ser. A no par and (1) share Common no par

BANK STORE (NY)
Name changed to Banker's Store Inc. 09/18/2001
(See Banker's Store Inc.)

BANK STRATFORD (STRATFORD, CT)
Merged into North American Bank & Trust Co. (Old) (Stratford, CT) 01/01/1978
Each share Common Capital Stock $5 par exchanged for (0.233) share Capital Stock $5 par
North American Bank & Trust Co. (Old) (Stratford, CT) reorganized as North American Bancorporation, Inc. 06/01/1982 which reorganized as North American Bank & Trust Co. (New) (Stratford, CT) 09/30/1994 which merged into Webster Financial Corp. 11/07/2003

BANK SUNSET & TR CO (SUNSET, LA)
Under plan of reorganization each share Common automatically became (1) share Sunset Bancorp, Inc. Common 04/01/1997

BANK SUSSEX CNTY (FRANKLIN, NJ)
Merged into National Community Bank (Rutherford, NJ) 01/02/1970
Each share Common $5 par exchanged for (2.333333) shares Common $6.25 par
National Community Bank (Rutherford, NJ) name changed to National Community Bank of New Jersey (Rutherford, NJ) 02/07/1975 which reorganized as National Community Banks, Inc. 02/28/1989 which merged into Bank of New York Co., Inc. 08/11/1993 which merged into Bank of New York Mellon Corp. 07/01/2007

BANK TANGLEWOOD NATL ASSN (HOUSTON, TX)
Merged into BOK Financial Corp. 10/25/2002
Each share Common exchanged for (1.73) shares Common $0.00006 par
Note: Each share Common received an additional distribution of (0.0202) share Common $0.00006 par 01/21/2004

BANK TAZEWELL CNTY (TAZEWELL, VA)
Merged into National Bankshares, Inc. 05/31/1996
Each share Common $1 par exchanged for (1) share Common $2.50 par

BANK TERREBONNE & TR CO (HOUMA, LA)
Capital Stock $100 par changed to $10 par and (9) additional shares issued 00/00/1962
Stock Dividends - 100% 11/00/1949; 100% 12/00/1954
Reorganized as Terrebonne Corp. 01/03/1972
Each share Capital Stock $10 par exchanged for (2) shares Capital Stock $5 par
Terrebonne Corp. merged into Louisiana Bancshares, Inc. 01/17/1986 which name changed to Premier Bancorp, Inc. 04/15/1987 which merged into Banc One Corp. 01/02/1996 which merged into Bank One Corp. 10/02/1998 which merged into J.P. Morgan Chase & Co. 12/31/2000 which name changed to JPMorgan Chase & Co. 07/20/2004

BANK TEX (HOUSTON, TX)
Stock Dividends - 10% 01/20/1961; 10% 01/25/1962
Reorganized as Houston Financial Corp. 09/30/1969
Each share Capital Stock $10 par exchanged for (1) share Common $10 par
Houston Financial Corp. reorganized as Houston First Corp. 12/15/1969 which name changed to Houston First Financial Group, Inc. 04/17/1970 which name changed to M.A.G. Liquidating Corp. 06/30/1978
(See M.A.G. Liquidating Corp.)

BANK TIDEWATER (VIRGINIA BEACH, VA)
Common $5 par split (5) for (4) by issuance of (0.25) additional share payable 03/12/1997 to holders of record 03/10/1997 Ex date - 03/13/1997
Common $5 par split (5) for (4) by issuance of (0.25) additional share payable 06/29/1998 to holders of record 06/15/1998
Acquired by SouthTrust Corp. 11/21/2001
Each share Common $5 par exchanged for (1.0691) share Common $2.50 par
SouthTrust Corp. merged into Wachovia Corp. (Ctfs. dated after 09/01/2001) 11/01/2004

BANK TOKYO CALIF (SAN FRANCISCO, CA)
Common $100 par changed to $20 par and (4) additional shares issued 05/03/1963
Common $20 par changed to $10 par and (1) additional share issued 04/30/1971
Common $10 par changed to $5 par and (1) additional share issued 12/29/1972
Name changed to California First Bank (San Francisco, CA) 09/30/1975
California First Bank (San Francisco, CA) name changed to Union Bank (San Francisco, CA) 11/01/1988 which merged into UnionBanCal Corp. (CA) 04/01/1996 which reincorporated in Delaware 09/30/2003
(See UnionBanCal Corp. (DE))

BANK TOKYO LTD (JAPAN)
Merged into Bank of Tokyo-Mitsubishi Ltd. 04/01/1996
Each Unsponsored ADR for Common exchanged for approximately $138 cash

BANK TOKYO-MITSUBISHI LTD (JAPAN)
Merged into Mitsubishi Tokyo Financial Group Inc. 04/05/2001
Each Sponsored ADR for Ordinary exchanged or (1) Sponsored ADR for Ordinary
Mitsubishi Tokyo Financial Group Inc. name changed to Mitsubishi UFJ Financial Group, Inc. 09/30/2005

BANK TRADE (SAN FRANCISCO, CA)
Capital Stock $10 par changed to $5 par 10/00/1966
Each share Capital Stock $5 par exchanged for (0.2) share Capital Stock $5 par 12/06/1989
Name changed to Lippobank (San Francisco, CA) 01/18/1990
(See Lippobank (San Francisco, CA))

BANK TURANALEM O J S C (KAZAKHSTAN)
GDR agreement terminated 03/14/2008
Each Sponsored Reg. S GDR for Ordinary exchanged for (1) Ordinary share
Note: Unexchanged GDR's will be sold and proceeds, if any, held for claim after 03/14/2009

BANK UN (MONROE, NC)
Merged into First Charter Corp. 12/21/1995
Each share Common $1.25 par exchanged for (0.75) share Common $5 par
First Charter Corp. merged into Fifth Third Bancorp 06/06/2008

BANK UTD (HOUSTON, TX)
Name changed 07/15/1996
Name changed from Bank United of Texas FSB (Houston, TX) to Bank United (Houston, TX) 07/15/1996
9.6% Preferred Ser. B $25 par called

for redemption at $26.25 plus $0.253 accrued dividends on 02/08/2001
10.12% Preferred Ser. A 1¢ par called for redemption at $25.50 plus $0.267 accrued dividends on 02/08/2001
Public interest eliminated

BANK UTD CORP (DE)
Merged into Washington Mutual, Inc. 02/09/2001
Each Premium Income Equity Security exchanged for (1) Premium Income Equity Security
Each Premium Income Equity Treasury Security exchanged for (1) Premium Income Equity Treasury Security
Each share Preferred exchanged for (1) share 7.25% Preferred Ser. H
Each share Class A Common 1¢ par exchanged for (1.3) shares Common no par and (1) Bank United Corp. Litigation Contingent Payment Rights Trust Contigent Payment Right
(See each company's listing)

BANK UTD CORP LITIGATION CONTINGENT PMT RTS TR (DE)
Litigation concluded 10/04/2004
No stockholders' equity

BANK UPSON (THOMASTON, GA)
Under plan of reorganization each share Common $1 par automatically became (1) share Upson Bankshares, Inc. Common no par 02/07/1997
Upson Bankshares, Inc. merged into SouthCrest Financial Group, Inc. 09/30/2004

BANK USA N.A. (PHOENIX, AZ)
Name changed 01/01/2007
Name changed from Bank USA, FSB (Phoenix, AZ) to Bank USA, N.A. (Phoenix, AZ) 01/01/2007
Bank closed and FDIC appointed receiver 10/30/2009
Stockholders' equity unlikely

BANK VA (CHESTERFIELD, VA)
Common $5 par changed to $2.50 par and (1) additional share issued payable 09/13/2005 to holders of record 09/06/2005 Ex date - 09/14/2005
Each share old Common $2.50 par exchanged for (0.2) share new Common $2.50 par 04/10/2012
Merged into Cordia Bancorp Inc. 04/01/2013
Each share new Common $2.50 par exchanged for (0.664) share Common 1¢ par
(See Cordia Bancorp Inc.)

BANK VA BEACH (VIRGINIA BEACH, VA)
Merged into Dominion Bank of Greater Hampton Roads, N.A. (Norfolk, VA) 07/01/1985
Each share Capital Stock $5 par exchanged for $44 cash
Note: An additional $3.50 cash per share was placed in escrow for possible future distribution

BANK VA CO (VA)
$1.20 Conv. Preferred Ser. A $20 par called for redemption 01/31/1974
$1.20 Preferred Ser. B $20 par called for redemption 07/01/1978
Common $5 par split (2) for (1) by issuance of (1) additional share 07/19/1984
Name changed to Signet Banking Corp. 07/14/1986
Signet Banking Corp. merged into First Union Corp. 11/28/1997 which name changed to Wachovia Corp. (Ctfs. dated after 09/01/2001) 09/01/2001 which merged into Wells Fargo & Co. (New) 12/31/2008

BK VENTURES INC (DE)
Name changed to Heavenly Hot Dogs, Inc. (DE) 06/15/1988
Heavenly Hot Dogs, Inc. (DE) reincorporated in Nevada 07/13/2000 which name changed to B4MC Gold Mines, Inc. 11/12/2013 which name changed to RocketFuel Blockchain, Inc. 09/28/2018

BANK VERONA (VERONA, WI)
Under plan of reorganization each share Common $25 par automatically became (1) share Verona Bankshares Ltd. Common $25 par 12/31/1997
(See Verona Bankshares Ltd.)

BANK VISALIA (VISALIA, CA)
Stock Dividends - 5% payable 06/08/1998 to holders of record 05/08/1998; 5% payable 05/20/2000 to holders of record 05/05/2000 Ex date - 05/03/2000; 5% payable 05/07/2001 to holders of record 04/24/2001 Ex date - 04/30/2001; 5% payable 05/10/2002 to holders of record 04/23/2002 Ex date - 04/25/2002
Under plan of reorganization each share Common no par automatically became (1) share Valley Commerce Bancorp Common no par 11/21/2002
Valley Commerce Bancorp merged into CVB Financial Corp. 03/10/2017

BANK VOZROZHDENIE (RUSSIA)
Name changed to Vozrozhdenie Bank 02/12/2016

BANK WASH (LYNNWOOD, WA)
Stock Dividends - 20% payable 05/24/2002 to holders of record 04/19/2002; 20% payable 05/15/2003 to holders of record 04/11/2003; 15% payable 05/14/2004 to holders of record 04/16/2004 Ex date - 06/15/2004
Under plan of reorganization each share Common 83¢ par automatically became (1) share Washington Bancorp Inc. Common no par 07/25/2005

BANK WATERBURY (WATERBURY, CT)
Acquired by Centerbank (Waterbury, CT) 03/18/1994
Each share Common $5 par exchanged for (0.17361) share Common $1 par
Centerbank (Waterbury, CT) reorganized as Center Financial Corp. 07/07/1995 which merged into First Union Corp. 11/13/1996 which name changed to Wachovia Corp. (Ctfs. dated after 09/01/2001) 09/01/2001 which merged into Wells Fargo & Co. (New) 12/31/2008

BANK WAUKEGAN (WAUKEGAN, IL)
Reorganized as Northern States Financial Corp. 10/01/1984
Each share Common $10 par exchanged for (1) share Common $10 par

BANK WAYNE N A (WAYNE, NJ)
Merged into Valley National Bank (Passaic, NJ) 06/11/1976
Each share Capital Stock $4 par exchanged for (0.5) share Common $5 par
Valley National Bank (Passaic, NJ) reorganized as Valley National Bancorp 05/02/1983

BANK WEIRTON (WEIRTON, WV)
Merged into Wesbanco, Inc. 08/30/1996
Each share Common $100 par exchanged for (130) shares Common $2.0833 par

BANK WEST (BELLEVUE, WA)
Acquired by Old National Bank of Washington (Spokane, WA) 03/04/1976
Each share Capital Stock $10 par exchanged for $26 cash

BANK WEST BATON ROUGE (PORT ALLEN, LA)
Stock Dividend - 5% payable 02/10/2002 to holders of record 12/31/2001 Ex date - 02/26/2002
Under plan of reorganization each share Common automatically became (1) share West Baton Rouge Bancshares Inc. Common $10 par 10/12/2001
West Baton Rouge Bancshares, Inc. name changed to American Gateway Financial Corp. 11/18/2004 which merged into Business First Bancshares, Inc. 03/31/2015

BANK WEST FINL CORP (MI)
Common 1¢ par split (3) for (2) by issuance of (0.5) additional share payable 12/02/1997 to holders of record 11/14/1997
Merged into Chemical Financial Corp. 09/14/2001
Each share Common 1¢ par exchanged for $11.50 cash

BANK WEST JERSEY (RIVERSIDE, NJ)
Reorganized as Fidelity Union Bancorporation 01/04/1971
Each share Capital Stock $10 par exchanged for (2.5) shares Common $5 par
Fidelity Union Bancorporation merged into First National State Bancorporation 04/05/1984 which name changed to First Fidelity Bancorporation (Old) 05/01/1985 which merged into First Fidelity Bancorporation (New) 02/29/1988 which merged into First Union Corp. 01/01/1996 which name changed to Wachovia Corp. (Ctfs. dated after 09/01/2001) 09/01/2001 which merged into Wells Fargo & Co. (New) 12/31/2008

BANK WESTBURY TR CO (WESTBURY, NY)
Capital Stock $12.50 par changed to $6.25 par and (1) additional share issued 07/10/1964
Stock Dividends - 20% 04/08/1967; 10% 05/18/1970
Merged into Long Island Trust Co. (Garden City, NY) 10/30/1970
Each share Capital Stock $6.25 par exchanged for (1.85) shares Capital Stock $5 par
Long Island Trust Co. (Garden City, NY) reorganized as Litco Corp. of New York 04/06/1973 which name changed to Litco Bancorporation of New York, Inc. 05/04/1979
(See Litco Bancorporation of New York, Inc.)

BANK WESTMORELAND (COLONIAL BEACH, VA)
Merged into First Virginia Bankshares Corp. 01/03/1972
Each share Common $25 par exchanged for (28) shares Common $1 par
First Virginia Bankshares Corp. name changed to First Virginia Banks, Inc. 09/01/1978 which merged into BB&T Corp. 07/01/2003

BANK WESTPORT (WESTPORT, CT)
Merged into Fairfield County Bank Corp. 06/21/2004
Each share Common $1 par exchanged for $12 cash

BANK WHEELING (WHEELING, WV)
Capital Stock $10 par changed to $5 par and (1) additional share issued 12/01/1978
Merged into Sunrise Bancorp, Inc. 07/01/1991
Each share Capital Stock $5 par exchanged for (2) shares Common 10¢ par
Sunrise Bancorp, Inc. merged into PNC Financial Corp 09/04/1992 which name changed to PNC Bank Corp. 02/08/1993 which name changed to PNC Financial Services Group, Inc. 03/15/2000

BANK WILMINGTON (WILMINGTON, NC)
Common $5 par split (5) for (4) by issuance of (0.25) additional share payable 06/15/2001 to holders of record 06/01/2001 Ex date - 06/18/2001
Common $5 par split (5) for (4) by issuance of (0.25) additional share payable 06/30/2005 to holders of record 06/22/2005 Ex date - 07/01/2005
Under plan of reorganization each share Common $5 par automatically became (1) share Bank of Wilmington Corp. Common $5 par 09/01/2005
Bank of Wilmington Corp. name changed to Cape Fear Bank Corp. 10/01/2006
(See Cape Fear Bank Corp.)

BANK WILMINGTON CORP (NC)
Stock Dividend - 5% payable 06/30/2006 to holders of record 06/22/2006 Ex date - 06/20/2006
Name changed to Cape Fear Bank Corp. 10/01/2006
(See Cape Fear Bank Corp.)

BANK WINTER PK (WINTER PARK, FL)
Merged into Huntington Bancshares, Inc. 10/31/1997
Each share Common no par exchanged for (0.8751) share Common no par

BANK WOODLAND (WOODLAND, CA)
Common no par split (2) for (1) by issuance of (1) additional share 02/01/1990
Name changed to Business & Professional Bank (Woodland, CA) 10/07/1992
(See Business & Professional Bank (Woodland, CA))

BANK WOODSTOCK (WOODSTOCK, VT)
Name changed to First Community Bank (Woodstock, VT) 04/15/1999
First Community Bank (Woodstock, VT) merged into New Hampshire Thrift Bancshares, Inc. 10/01/2007 which name changed to Lake Sunapee Bank Group 06/01/2015 which merged into Bar Harbor Bankshares 01/13/2017

BANK YAKIMA (YAKIMA, WA)
Liquidation completed
Each share Capital Stock $10 par exchanged for initial distribution of $54 cash 03/24/1977
Each share Capital Stock $10 par received second distribution of $2.50 cash 02/03/1978
Each share Capital Stock $10 par received third and final distribution of $0.18 cash 08/01/1978

BANK YOKOHAMA LTD (JAPAN)
ADR's for Common split (5) for (2) by issuance of (1.5) additional ADR's payable 11/30/2011 to holders of record 11/28/2011 Ex date - 12/01/2011
Basis changed from (1:10) to (1:4) 12/01/2011
ADR agreement terminated 04/25/2016
Each ADR for Ordinary issued by Bank of New York exchanged for $19.233823 cash

BANK YORBA LINDA (YORBA LINDA, CA)
Common no par split (4) for (3) by issuance of (0.33333333) additional share payable 06/30/1997 to holders of record 06/06/1997

Under plan of reorganization each share Common no par automatically became (1) share BYL Bancorp Common no par 11/19/1997
(See BYL Bancorp)

BANK ZACHARY (ZACHARY, LA)
Reorganized as Zachary Bancshares, Inc. 05/01/1984
Each share Common $10 par exchanged for (1) share Common $10 par

BANK ZACHODNI WBK SA (POLAND)
Name changed to Santander Bank Polska S.A. 10/02/2018

BANKAMERICA CAP I (DE)
7.75% Trust Originated Preferred Securities called for redemption at $25 on 03/15/2002

BANKAMERICA CAP IV (DE)
7% Trust Originated Preferred Securities called for redemption at $25 on 05/30/2003

BANKAMERICA CORP NEW (DE)
Name changed to Bank of America Corp. 04/28/1999

BANKAMERICA CORP OLD (DE)
Common $6.25 par changed to $3.125 par and (1) additional share issued 04/11/1972
Common $3.125 par changed to $1.5625 par and (1) additional share issued 09/07/1976
9.5% Conv. Preferred Ser. D no par called for redemption 08/24/1989
Special Ser. Preferred no par called for redemption 09/01/1990
Ser. 2 Depositary Preferred called for redemption 12/05/1994
Adjustable Rate Preferred Ser. 1 no par called for redemption 05/31/1995
6.50% Conv. Preferred Ser. G no par called for redemption 05/31/1995
Ser. I Depositary Preferred called for redemption 09/30/1995
11% Ser. I Preferred no par called for redemption 09/30/1995
Ser. J Depositary Preferred called for redemption 03/31/1996
11% Preferred Ser. J no par called for redemption 03/31/1996
9.625% Preferred Ser. F no par called for redemption 04/16/1996
9% Preferred Ser. H no par called for redemption 01/15/1997
8.375% Preferred Ser. K no par called for redemption 02/15/1997
Common $1.5625 par split (2) for (1) by issuance of (1) additional share payable 06/18/1997 to holders of record 06/02/1997 Ex date - 06/19/1997
8.16% Depositary Preferred called for redemption at $25 on 07/13/1997
7.875% Depositary Preferred Ser. M called for redemption at $25 on 09/30/1997
8.50% Depositary Preferred Ser. N called for redemption 12/15/1997
Adjustable Rate Preferred Ser. A no par called for redemption at $50 on 06/29/1998
Adjustable Rate Preferred Ser. B no par called for redemption at $100 on 06/29/1998
Merged into BankAmerica Corp. (New) 09/30/1998
Each share Common $1.5625 par exchanged for (1.1316) shares Common 1¢ par
BankAmerica Corp. (New) name changed to Bank of America Corp. 04/28/1999

BANKAMERICA RLTY INVS (CA)
Shares of Bene. Int. $1 par split (3) for (2) by issuance of (0.5) additional share 03/25/1983
Reorganized under the laws of Delaware as BRE Properties, Inc. and Shares of Bene. Int. $1 par reclassified as Class A Common 1¢ par 09/30/1987
BRE Properties, Inc. (DE) reincorporated in Maryland 03/15/1996 which merged into Essex Property Trust, Inc. 04/01/2014

BANKATLANTIC BANCORP INC (FL)
12.25% Preferred Ser. A 1¢ par called for redemption 10/07/1995
10% Preferred Ser. B 1¢ par called for redemption 10/07/1995
8% Preferred Ser. C 1¢ par called for redemption 10/07/1995
Common 1¢ par reclassified as Class B Common 1¢ par 03/12/1996
Each share Class B Common 1¢ par received distribution of (0.25) share old Class A Common 1¢ par payable 07/31/1996 to holders of record 07/19/1996
Old Class A Common 1¢ par split (5) for (4) by issuance of (0.25) additional share payable 07/31/1996 to holders of record 07/19/1996
Each share Class B Common 1¢ par received distribution of (0.25) share old Class A Common 1¢ par payable 03/04/1997 to holders of record 02/17/1997
Old Class A Common 1¢ par split (5) for (4) by issuance of (0.25) additional share payable 08/18/1997 to holders of record 08/01/1997
Each share Class B Common 1¢ par received distribution of (0.25) share old Class A Common 1¢ par payable 08/18/1997 to holders of record 08/01/1997
Old Class A Common 1¢ par split (5) for (4) by issuance of (0.25) additional share payable 02/18/1998 to holders of record 02/04/1998 Ex date - 02/19/1998
Each share Class B Common 1¢ par received distribution of (0.25) share old Class A Common 1¢ par payable 02/18/1998 to holders of record 02/04/1998 Ex date - 02/19/1998
Each share Class B Common 1¢ par received distribution of (0.15) share old Class A Common 1¢ par payable 08/26/1999 to holders of record 08/16/1999 Ex date - 08/12/1999
Each share old Class A Common 1¢ par received distribution of (0.25) share Levitt Corp. Class A Common 1¢ par payable 12/31/2003 to holders of record 12/18/2003 Ex date - 01/02/2004
Each share old Class A Common 1¢ par exchanged for (0.2) share new Class A Common 1¢ par 09/26/2008
Each share new Class A Common 1¢ par exchanged again for (0.2) share new Class A Common 1¢ par 10/17/2011
Stock Dividends - in Common to holders of Common 25% 07/19/1995; 25% payable 02/01/1996 to holders of record 01/22/1996; in Class A Common to holders of Class A Common 15% payable 08/26/1999 to holders of record 08/16/1999 Ex date - 08/12/1999
Merged into BFC Financial Corp. 08/18/2000
Each share Class B Common 1¢ par exchanged for $6 cash
Name changed to BBX Capital Corp. 08/06/2012
(See BBX Capital Corp.)

BANKATLANTIC FED SVGS BK (FORT LAUDERDALE, FL)
Under plan of reorganization each share 12.25% Preferred Ser. A 1¢ par, 10% Preferred Ser. B 1¢ par, 8% Preferred Ser. C 1¢ par or Common 1¢ par automatically became (1) share BankAtlantic Bancorp Inc. 12.25% Preferred Ser. A 1¢ par, 10% Preferred Ser. B 1¢ par, 8% Preferred Ser. C 1¢ par or Common 1¢ par respectively 07/14/1994
(See BankAtlantic Bancorp Inc.)

BANKATLANTIC FINL CORP (FL)
Each share old Common 1¢ par exchanged for (0.5) share new Common 1¢ par 01/03/1989
Name changed to BFC Financial Corp. 03/27/1992
BFC Financial Corp. name changed to BBX Capital Corp. (New) 02/03/2017

BANKBOSTON CORP (MA)
Depositary Preferred Ser. E called for redemption 09/15/1997
Adjustable Rate Preferred Ser. A no par called for redemption at $50 plus $0.23 accrued dividend on 07/13/1998
Adjustable Rate Preferred Ser. B no par called for redemption at $50 plus $0.23 accrued dividend on 07/13/1998
Adjustable Rate Preferred Ser. C no par called for redemption at $100 plus $0.42 accrued dividend on 07/13/1998
Depositary Preferred Ser. F called for redemption at $25 on 07/15/1998
Common no par split (2) for (1) by issuance of (1) additional share payable 06/22/1998 to holders of record 06/01/1998 Ex date - 06/23/1998
Merged into Fleet Boston Corp. 10/01/1999
Each share Common no par exchanged for (1.1844) shares Common 1¢ par
Fleet Boston Corp. name changed to FleetBoston Financial Corp. 04/18/2000 which merged into Bank of America Corp. 04/01/2004

BANKCHICAGO (CHICAGO, IL)
Acquired by Standard Bancshares, Inc. 05/15/2003
Details not available

BANKCOM CORP (DE)
Charter cancelled and declared inoperative and void for non-payment of taxes 03/01/1987

BANKEAST CORP (NH)
Common $5 par changed to $1 par 05/25/1982
Common $1 par split (3) for (2) by issuance of (0.5) additional share 12/15/1983
Common $1 par split (2) for (1) by issuance of (1) additional share 03/01/1985
Common $1 par split (2) for (1) by issuance of (1) additional share 12/01/1986
Plan of reorganization under Chapter 11 Federal Bankruptcy proceedings confirmed 08/30/1991
No stockholders' equity

BANKENGINE TECHNOLOGIES INC (DE)
Reincorporated 05/23/2002
State of incorporation changed from (FL) to (DE) 05/23/2002
Recapitalized as Syscan Imaging, Inc. 04/02/2004
Each share Common $0.001 par exchanged for (0.1) share Common $0.001 par
Syscan Imaging, Inc. name changed to Sysview Technology, Inc. 06/27/2006 which name changed to Document Capture Technologies, Inc. 01/08/2008
(See Document Capture Technologies, Inc.)

BANKENO MINES LTD (AB)
Reincorporated 01/30/1979
Place of incorporation changed from (ON) to (AB) 01/30/1979
Name changed to Bankeno Resources Ltd. 01/28/1987
(See Bankeno Resources Ltd.)

BANKENO RES LTD (AB)
Acquired by North Canadian Oils Ltd. 07/12/1990
Each share Common $1 par exchanged for $4.25 cash

BANKERS & SHIPPERS INSURANCE CO. OF NEW YORK (NY)
Each share Capital Stock $100 par exchanged for (4) shares Capital Stock $25 par 00/00/1929
Each share Capital Stock $25 par exchanged for (2.5) shares Capital Stock $10 par 00/00/1952
Stock Dividend - 50% 05/27/1955
Through offers or market purchases 100% held by Firemen's Insurance Co. of Newark, NJ as of 07/06/1968
Public interest eliminated

BANKERS & TELEPHONE EMPLOYEES INSURANCE CO. (PA)
Common $2.50 par changed to $1.25 par 11/24/1965
Dissolved by court decree 03/30/1967
No stockholders' equity

BANKERS ACCEP CORP (AZ)
Charter revoked for failure to file reports or pay fees 12/26/1972

BANKERS ACCEP CORP (IN)
Adjudicated bankrupt 01/21/1972
No stockholders' equity

BANKERS AGY INC (MN)
Name changed to Mobile Americana Corp. 01/30/1970
Mobile Americana Corp. name changed to MoAmCo Corp. 02/15/1972
(See MoAmCo. Corp.)

BANKERS BANK OF FLORIDA (FORT LAUDERDALE, FL)
Name changed to Southeast Bank of Galt Ocean Mile (Fort Lauderdale, FL) 06/14/1973
(See Southeast Bank of Galt Ocean Mile (Fort Lauderdale, FL))

BANKERS BD & MTG GTY CO AMER (DE)
Capital Stock no par reclassified as Common 1¢ par 06/08/1976
Merged into GBM Inc. 05/18/1983
Each share Common 1¢ par exchanged for $0.50 cash

BANKERS BLDG CORP (IL)
Voluntarily dissolved 02/15/1974
No stockholders' equity

BANKERS BOND & SHARE CORP. (IN)
Voluntarily dissolved 07/14/1966
Details not available

BANKERS BUILDING CORP. (MA)
Dissolved 00/00/1932
Details not available

BANKERS BUILDING LAND TRUST (IL)
Equitable Ownership Certificates no par called for redemption 00/00/1999

BANKERS CAPITAL LIFE INSURANCE CO. (MN)
Completely liquidated 09/30/1971
Each share Common $1 par exchanged for first and final distribution of (0.75) share Pacific Standard Life Co. (AZ) Common $1 par
Pacific Standard Life Co. (AZ) reincorporated in Delaware 05/13/1974
(See Pacific Standard Life Co. (DE))

BANKERS CORP (DE)
Common 1¢ par split (2) for (1) by issuance of (1) additional share 11/15/1993
Stock Dividends - 10% 01/30/1993; 20% 07/30/1994
Merged into Sovereign Bancorp, Inc. 08/29/1997
Each share Common 1¢ par

exchanged for (1.854) shares
Common no par
Sovereign Bancorp, Inc. merged into Banco Santander, S.A. 01/30/2009

BANKERS CREDIT LIFE INSURANCE CO. OF BIRMINGHAM, ALA
Merged into Old Republic Credit Life Insurance Co. 00/00/1931
Details not available

BANKERS DISCOUNT CORP. (TX)
Bankrupt 00/00/1953
Details not available

BANKERS DISPATCH CORP. (DE)
Common $1 par split (6) for (5) by issuance of (0.2) additional share 01/18/1963
Common $1 par split (6) for (5) by issuance of (0.2) additional share 12/16/1963
Name changed to Bankers Utilities Corp. 06/20/1967
Bankers Utilities Corp. name changed to International Couriers Corp. 05/02/1974
(See International Couriers Corp.)

BANKERS FID LIFE INS CO (GA)
Common 50¢ par changed to $1 par 06/17/1986
Merged into Atlantic America Corp. 04/01/1996
Each share Common $1 par exchanged for $6.25 cash

BANKERS FINANCIAL CORP. (WI)
Name changed to Mortgage Associates, Inc. (WI) 02/26/1965
Mortgage Associates, Inc. (WI) merged into Industrial National Corp. 03/15/1974 which name changed to Fleet Financial Group, Inc. (Old) 04/14/1982 which merged into Fleet/Norstar Financial Group, Inc. 01/01/1988 which name changed to Fleet Financial Group, Inc. (New) 04/15/1992 which name changed to Fleet Boston Corp. 10/01/1999 which name changed to FleetBoston Financial Corp. 04/18/2000 which merged into Bank of America Corp. 04/01/2004

BANKERS FINL LIFE CO (OK)
Capital Stock $10 par changed to $2.50 par and (3) additional shares issued 03/09/1967
Capital Stock $2.50 par changed to $4.60 par 03/02/1972
Stock Dividends - 33.33333333% 11/17/1966; 20% 11/17/1967
Name changed to United Services General Life Co. 06/06/1974
(See United Services General Life Co.)

BANKERS FINL SVCS CORP (PA)
Merged into Heritage Bancorp Inc. 03/01/1995
Each share Common $1 par exchanged for (1.02) shares Common $5 par
Heritage Bancorp Inc. merged into Main Street Bancorp, Inc. 05/01/1998 which merged into Sovereign Bancorp, Inc. 03/08/2002 which merged into Banco Santander, S.A. 01/30/2009

BANKERS FIRE & CASUALTY INSURANCE CO. (FL)
Completely liquidated 05/12/1976
No stockholders' equity

BANKERS FIRE & CASUALTY INSURANCE CO. (NC)
Common $10 par changed to $6 par 11/26/1965
Merged into Bankers Fire & Casualty Insurance Co. (FL) 03/13/1969
Each share Common $6 par exchanged for (1) share Common $4 par
(See Bankers Fire & Casualty Insurance Co. (FL))

BANKERS FIRE & MARINE INSURANCE CO. (AL)
Each share Preferred $1 par exchanged for (2) shares Common $1.25 par 10/29/1959
Common $5 par changed to $1.25 par 10/29/1959
Common $1.25 par changed to $1 par 08/06/1963
Stock Dividend - 10% 09/01/1952
Name changed to Washington Trust Life Insurance Co. 02/10/1966
Washington Trust Life Insurance Co. name changed to Washington Trust Insurance Co. 08/18/1967 which name changed to National Capitol Life Insurance Co. (AL) 04/15/1968
(See National Capitol Life Insurance Co. (AL))

BANKERS FIRE INSURANCE CO. (NC)
Name changed to Bankers Fire & Casualty Insurance Co. (NC) 12/04/1958
Bankers Fire & Casualty Insurance Co. (NC) merged into Bankers Fire & Casualty Insurance Co. (FL) 03/13/1969
(See Bankers Fire & Casualty Insurance Co. (FL))

BANKERS FIRST CORP (GA)
Merged into SouthTrust Corp. 03/15/1996
Each share Common 1¢ par exchanged for (1.126) shares Common $2.50 par
SouthTrust Corp. merged into Wachovia Corp. (Ctfs. dated after 09/01/2001) 11/01/2004 which merged into Wells Fargo & Co. (New) 12/31/2008

BANKERS INDUSTRIAL SERVICE CO.
Liquidated 00/00/1942
Details not available

BANKERS INVESTMENT CO. (CA)
Liquidated 00/00/1954
Details not available

BANKERS INVT CO (KS)
Merged into Security Pacific Corp. 08/31/1976
Each share Common $2 par exchanged for (1.055) shares Common $10 par
Security Pacific Corp. merged into BankAmerica Corp. (Old) 04/22/1992 which merged into BankAmerica Corp. (New) 09/30/1998 which name changed to Bank of America Corp. 04/28/1999

BANKERS INVT CORP (IN)
Common $3 par changed to $1 par 03/05/1964
Completely liquidated 08/19/1975
Each share Common $1 par exchanged for first and final distribution of $0.739 principal amount of Centura Petroleum Corp. 12% Conv. Subord. Debentures Ser. A due 06/30/1985, $0.739 principal amount of Centura Petroleum Corp. 12% Subord. Debentures Ser. B due 06/30/1985 and (0.5) share Centura Petroleum Corp. Common 5¢ par
Centura Petroleum Corp. liquidated for Centura Energy Corp. 08/31/1979 which merged into Minden Oil & Gas Inc. 02/11/1983 which name changed to Castle Energy Corp. 11/16/1986 which merged into Delta Petroleum Corp. 05/01/2006

BANKERS INVESTMENT TRUST OF AMERICA
Liquidated 00/00/1949
Details not available

BANKERS LIFE HLDG CORP (DE)
Merged into Conseco, Inc. 12/31/1996
Each share Common $0.001 par exchanged for (0.3983) share Common no par
(See Conseco, Inc.)

BANKERS LIFE INSURANCE CO. OF INDIANAPOLIS (IN)
Each share Common 25¢ par exchanged for (0.25) share Common $1 par 10/21/1963
Merged into Bankers United Life Assurance Co. 02/09/1967
Each share Common $1 par exchanged for (0.412371) share Common $1 par
(See Bankers United Life Assurance Co.)

BANKERS LIFE INSURANCE CO. OF NEBRASKA
Mutualization approved 00/00/1941
Details not available

BANKERS LOAN & INVESTMENT CO.
Liquidation completed 00/00/1943
Details not available

BANKERS LOAN & TRUST CO. OF AMERICA (DE)
No longer in existence having become inoperative and void for non-payment of taxes 04/01/1931

BANKERS MTG CORP (MN)
Name changed to Bamocor, Inc. 12/21/1979
Bamocor, Inc. name changed to Palm Springs Lifestyle, Inc. 05/25/1988
(See Palm Springs Lifestyle, Inc.)

BANKERS NATIONAL CORP. (UT)
Name changed to Northwest Pacific Enterprises Inc. 09/02/1971
(See Northwest Pacific Enterprises Inc.)

BANKERS NATIONAL INVESTING CORP.
Merged into Beneficial Corp. (Old) 00/00/1945
Each share Common $1 par exchanged for (1.5) shares Common $1 par
Beneficial Corp. (Old) acquired by Beneficial Finance Co. 03/15/1968 which name changed to Beneficial Corp. (New) 05/01/1970 which merged into Household International, Inc. 06/30/1998 which merged into HSBC Holdings PLC 03/28/2003

BANKERS NATL LIFE INS CO (NJ)
Each (42) shares old Capital Stock $10 par exchanged for (25) shares new Capital Stock $10 par 00/00/1932
New Capital Stock $10 par changed to $2 par and (4) additional shares issued 07/27/1956
Stock Dividends - 14.28571428% 12/20/1946; 25% 12/23/1948; 16.66666666% 12/27/1949; 14.28571428% 12/27/1950; 10% 10/17/1955; 7.5% 10/28/1969
Merged into Equity Funding Corp. of America 10/15/1971
Each share Capital Stock $2 par exchanged for (0.859156) share Common 30¢ par
(See Equity Funding Corp. of America)

BANKERS NATL SVC CORP (CO)
Name changed to Red Carpet Financial Corp. 08/22/1984 which name changed back to Bankers National Service Corp. 07/12/1985
Completely liquidated 12/31/1985
Each share Common no par exchanged for first and final distribution of $0.0048 cash

BANKERS NT INC (TX)
Common 1¢ par split (3) for (2) by issuance of (0.5) additional share 05/30/1986
Reincorporated under the laws of Georgia as VSI Holdings, Inc. 04/22/1997
(See VSI Holdings, Inc.)

BANKERS OIL & MINING, INC. (UT)
Name changed to Bankers National Corp. 12/15/1965
Bankers National Corp. name changed to Northwest Pacific Enterprises Inc. 09/02/1971
(See Northwest Pacific Enterprises Inc.)

BANKERS PETE LTD (AB)
Reincorporated 03/07/2014
Each share old Common no par received distribution of (0.1) share BNK Petroleum Inc. Common no par payable 07/17/2008 to holders of record 07/14/2008
Each share old Common no par exchanged for (0.33333333) share new Common no par 07/30/2008
Place of incorporation changed from (BC) to (AB) 03/07/2014
Acquired by Geo-Jade Petroleum Corp. 10/04/2016
Each share new Common no par exchanged for $2.20 cash
Note: Unexchanged certificates will be cancelled and become without value 10/04/2019

BANKERS PETES 1975 LTD (AB)
Recapitalized 10/13/1975
Recapitalized from Bankers Petroleum Ltd. to Bankers Petroleum (1975) Ltd. 10/13/1975
Each share Common no par exchanged for (0.2) share Common no par
Struck off register for failure to file annual returns 02/01/1989

BANKERS RESERVE DEPOSIT CO. (CO)
Declared defunct and inoperative for failure to pay taxes and file annual reports 09/17/1929

BANKERS SVGS BK (MIAMI, FL)
Merged into Republic Bancshares, Inc. 11/05/1998
Each share Common $4 par exchanged for (0.5749) share Common $2 par
Republic Bancshares, Inc. merged into BB&T Corp. 04/14/2004

BANKERS SEC LIFE INS SOC (NY)
Under plan of merger each share Common $25 par exchanged for (18) shares Common $1 par 12/31/1962
Common $1 par split (5) for (4) by issuance of (0.25) additional share 06/01/1973
Common $1 par changed to $2 par 07/23/1973
Stock Dividend - 10% 06/01/1967
Merged into United Services Life Insurance Co. 12/20/1979
Each share Common $2 par exchanged for (1.5) shares Common $1 par
United Services Life Insurance Co. reorganized in Virginia as USLICO Corp. 08/15/1984 which merged into NWNL Companies, Inc. 01/17/1995 which name changed to ReliaStar Financial Corp. 02/13/1995
(See ReliaStar Financial Corp.)

BANKERS SECS CORP (PA)
Each share Preferred $50 par exchanged for (1) share 6% Sr. Preferred $50 par and (4) shares Class A Common $1 par 07/01/1969
Each share Common $50 par exchanged for (1) share 6% Jr. Preferred $50 par and (7.13528) shares Common $1 par 07/01/1969
Common $1 par changed to no par 07/12/1983
Class A Common $1 par changed to no par 07/12/1983
Merged into BSC Corp. 02/01/1986
Each share 6% Jr. Preferred $50 par exchanged for $60 cash

Each share 6% Sr. Preferred $50 par exchanged for $60 cash
Each share Common no par exchanged for $51.50 cash
Each share Class A Common no par exchanged for $51.50 cash

BANKERS SERVICE LIFE INSURANCE CO. (OK)
Merged into Union Bankers Insurance Co. 06/30/1964
Each share Common exchanged for (0.16) share Common $1 par
(See Union Bankers Insurance Co.)

BANKERS SOUTHERN, INC. (KY)
Liquidation completed
Each share Common $100 par exchanged for initial distribution of $35 cash 03/04/1968
Each share Common $100 par received second and final distribution of (5) shares Seymour Water Co. (KY) Common no par and $25.50 cash 05/07/1969
(See Seymour Water Co. (KY))

BANKERS STORE INC (NY)
SEC revoked common stock registration 10/04/2011

BANKERS TRUST CO. (NEW YORK, NY)
Stock Dividends - 20% 12/29/1944; 100% 03/01/1960; 11.11111111% 03/10/1962
Acquired by BT New York Corp. 05/31/1966
Each share Capital Stock $10 par exchanged for (1) share Common $10 par
BT New York Corp. name changed to Bankers Trust New York Corp. 09/15/1967 which name changed to Bankers Trust Corp. 04/23/1998
(See Bankers Trust Corp.)

BANKERS TRUST CO. (PHILADELPHIA, PA)
Liquidated 09/24/1931
No stockholders' equity

BANKERS TR CO (DES MOINES, IA)
Stock Dividends - 50% 02/01/1940; 20% 12/29/1941; 11.111111111% 12/01/1943; 25% 01/15/1953; 20% 01/18/1957
Each (631.6) shares old Common $25 par exchanged for (1.2761) shares new Common $25 par 02/25/1994
Note: In effect holders received $501.56 cash per share and public interest was eliminated

BANKERS TR CORP (NY)
Name changed 04/23/1998
Common $10 par split (2) for (1) by issuance of (1) additional share 01/26/1981
Common $10 par split (2) for (1) by issuance of (1) additional share 01/27/1986
$2.50 Preferred Ser. A no par called for redemption 11/01/1986
$4.225 Preferred Ser. B no par called for redemption 11/01/1986
Common $10 par changed to $1 par 05/13/1988
Fixed/Adjustable Rate Preferred Ser. D no par called for redemption 00/00/1994
Adjustable Dividend Money Market Preferred Ser. E no par called for redemption 00/00/1994
Adjustable Dividend Money Market Preferred Ser. F no par called for redemption 00/00/1994
Adjustable Dividend Money Market Preferred Ser. G no par called for redemption 00/00/1994
Adjustable Dividend Money Market Preferred Ser. H no par called for redemption 00/00/1994
8.55% Depositary Preferred Ser. I called for redemption 03/01/1997
8.55% Preferred Ser. I no par called for redemption 03/01/1997
Depositary Preferred Ser. J called for redemption at $50 on 12/01/1997
Name changed from Bankers Trust New York Corp. to Bankers Trust Corp. 04/23/1998
Conv. Capital Securities no par called for redemption 06/01/1998
7.652% Depositary Preferred Ser. O called for redemption at $25 on 06/01/1998
7.652% Preferred Ser. O no par called for redemption at $250 on 06/01/1998
Conv. Capital Securities no par called for redemption at $25 on 08/15/1998
7.50% Depositary Preferred called for redemption at $25 plus $0.01042 accrued dividend on 08/17/1998
Merged into Deutsche Bank Aktiengesellschaft 06/04/1999
Each share Common $1 par exchanged for $93 cash
Adjustable Depositary Preferred Ser. Q called for redemption at $25 on 09/28/2000
Adjustable Depositary Preferred Ser. R called for redemption at $25 on 09/28/2000
7.750% Depositary Preferred Ser. S called for redemption at $25 on 09/28/2000

BANKERS TRUST LIFE INSURANCE CO. (AZ)
Merged into Security National Life Insurance Co. (UT) 12/30/1967
Each share Common $1 par exchanged for (0.25) share Class A Common $1.50 par
Security National Life Insurance Co. (UT) merged into S.N.L. Financial Corp. 03/24/1980 which name changed to Security National Financial Corp. 12/27/1990

BANKERS TR S C (COLUMBIA, SC)
Name changed 12/10/1974
Common $10 par split (2) for (1) by issuance of (1) additional share 07/01/1984
Each share $1.80 Conv. Preferred Ser. A $18 par exchanged for (1.815) shares Common $10 par 10/05/1984
Stock Dividends - 10% 11/21/1969; 20% 10/01/1978; 10% 10/10/1979; 10% 04/11/1980
Under plan of merger name changed to Bankers Trust of South Carolina, N.A. (Columbia, SC) 10/15/1973 which changed back to Bankers Trust of South Carolina (Columbia, SC) 12/10/1974
Acquired by NCNB Corp. 01/02/1986
Each share Common $10 par exchanged for (0.4139) share Common $2.50 par and $33.15 cash
NCNB Corp. name changed to NationsBank (NC) Corp. 12/31/1991 which reincorporated in Delaware 09/25/1998

BANKERS UN LIFE INS CO (CO)
Each share Class A $10 par exchanged for (2) shares Common $5 par 10/27/1972
Each share Class B $10 par exchanged for (3) shares Common $5 par 10/27/1972
Each share Class C $10 par exchanged for (2) shares Common $5 par 10/27/1972
Merged into I.C.H. Corp. 10/14/1982
Each share Common $5 par exchanged for (4.8186) shares Common $1 par
I.C.H. Corp. name changed to Southwestern Life Corp. (New) 06/15/1994 which name changed to I.C.H. Corp. (New) 10/10/1995
(See I.C.H. Corp. (New))

BANKERS UNITED LIFE ASSURANCE CO. (IL)
Under plan of exchange each share Common $1 par exchanged for (1) share Bankers United Management Corp. Common 50¢ par 02/15/1969

BANKERS UTD MGMT CORP (DE)
Name changed to Midwest Management Corp. 06/30/1972
(See Midwest Management Corp.)

BANKERS URANIUM, INC. (UT)
Name changed to Bankers Oil & Mining, Inc. 00/00/1959
Bankers Oil & Mining, Inc. name changed to Bankers National Corp. 12/15/1965 which name changed to Pacific Enterprises Inc. 09/02/1971
(See Pacific Enterprises Inc.)

BANKERS UTILS CORP (DE)
Common $1 par split (3) for (2) by issuance of (0.5) additional share 02/16/1970
Common $1 par split (3) for (2) by issuance of (0.5) additional share 03/15/1971
Common $1 par split (3) for (2) by issuance of (0.5) additional share 04/17/1972
Stock Dividend - 10% 02/23/1968
Name changed to International Couriers Corp. 05/02/1974
(See International Couriers Corp.)

BANKERSTRUST ALA INC (DE)
Merged into Banc Corp. 07/13/1999
Each share Common 1¢ par exchanged for $3 cash

BANKFIELD CONS MINES LTD (ON)
Charter cancelled and declared dissolved for failure to file returns and pay fees 03/16/1976

BANKFIELD GOLD MINES LTD. (ON)
Reorganized as Bankfield Consolidated Mines Ltd. 00/00/1936
Each share Capital Stock $1 par exchanged for (0.66666666) share Capital Stock $1 par
(See Bankfield Consolidated Mines Ltd.)

BANKFIRST CORP (TN)
Merged into BB&T Corp. 12/27/2000
Each share Common $2.50 par exchanged for (0.4554) share Common $5 par

BANKGREENVILLE FINL CORP (SC)
Acquired by HomeTrust Bancshares, Inc. 07/31/2013
Each share Common no par exchanged for $6.63 cash
Note: Each share Common no par received an additional distribution of $0.41 cash from escrow 10/30/2015

BANKHEAD HOTEL, INC. (AL)
Liquidation completed 04/20/1956
Details not available

BANKILLINOIS FINL CORP (DE)
Stock Dividends - 5% payable 06/08/1998 to holders of record 05/22/1998; 5% payable 06/04/1999 to holders of record 05/24/1999
Under plan of merger each share Common 1¢ par automatically became (1) share Main Street Trust, Inc. (IL) Common 1¢ par 03/23/2000
Main Street Trust, Inc. (IL) merged into First Busey Corp. 08/01/2007

BANKING CTR (WATERBURY, CT)
Name changed to Centerbank (Waterbury, CT) 05/09/1988
Centerbank (Waterbury, CT) reorganized as Center Financial Corp. 07/07/1995 which merged into First Union Corp. 11/13/1996 which name changed to Wachovia Corp. (Ctfs. dated after 09/01/2001) 09/01/2001 which merged into Wells Fargo & Co. (New) 12/31/2008

BANKINSTOCKS HOLDING CORP.
Dissolved 00/00/1935
Details not available

BANKIT CORP (WI)
Name changed to Farm House Foods Corp. 09/28/1971
(See Farm House Foods Corp.)

BANKIT RESOURCE CORP (BC)
Struck off register and declared dissolved for failure to file returns 10/08/1993

BANKLINE OIL CO. (CA)
5.5% Conv. Preferred called for redemption 05/01/1959
Merged into Signal Oil & Gas Co. 07/10/1959
Each share Common $1 par exchanged for (0.181818) share Class A Common $2 par
Signal Oil & Gas Co. name changed to Signal Companies, Inc. 05/01/1968 which merged into Allied-Signal Inc. 09/19/1985 which name changed to AlliedSignal Inc. 04/26/1993 which name changed to Honeywell International Inc. 12/01/1999

BANKNORTH CAP TR II (DE)
8% Guaranteed Trust Preferred Securities called for redemption at $25 on 06/29/2007

BANKNORTH FDS (DE)
Merged into Federated Equity Funds 08/31/2004
Details not available

BANKNORTH GROUP INC (DE)
Common $1 par split (2) for (1) by issuance of (1) additional share payable 04/06/1998 to holders of record 03/20/1998
Merged into Banknorth Group, Inc. (ME) 05/10/2000
Each share Common $1 par exchanged for (1.825) shares Common 1¢ par
Banknorth Group, Inc. (ME) merged into TD Banknorth Inc. 03/01/2005
(See TD Banknorth Inc.)

BANKNORTH GROUP INC (ME)
Under plan of merger each share Common 1¢ par exchanged for (0.49) share TD Banknorth Inc. Common 1¢ par, (0.2351) share Toronto-Dominion Bank (Toronto, ON) new Common no par and $12.24 cash 03/01/2005
(See each company's listing)

BANKNORTH GROUP INC NEW (VT)
Merged into BankNorth Group, Inc. (DE) 12/01/1989
Each share Common $3 par exchanged for (1.61) shares Common $1 par
BankNorth Group, Inc. (DE) merged into Banknorth Group, Inc. (ME) 05/10/2000

BANKNORTH GROUP INC OLD (VT)
Common $1 par split (3) for (1) by issuance of (2) additional shares 03/01/1984
Merged into First Vermont Financial Corp. 12/31/1985
Each share Common $1 par exchanged for (0.9) share Common $3 par
First Vermont Financial Corp. name changed to BankNorth Group, Inc. (VT) (New) 05/13/1986 which merged into BankNorth Group, Inc. (DE) 12/01/1989 which merged into Banknorth Group, Inc. (ME) 05/10/2000 which merged into TD Banknorth Inc. 03/01/2005
(See TD Banknorth Inc.)

BANKPLUS FSB (MORTON, IL)
Each share old Common 10¢ par exchanged for (1) share new Common 10¢ par to reflect a (1) for (150) reverse split followed by a (150) for (1) forward split 09/29/2003
Note: Holders of (149) or fewer pre-split shares received $20 cash per share
Stock Dividends - 10% payable 12/22/1997 to holders of record 10/31/1997; 10% payable

12/14/1998 to holders of record 10/31/1998; 10% payable 12/20/2001 to holders of record 10/31/2001 Ex date - 12/04/2001; 10% payable 12/19/2002 to holders of record 10/31/2002 Ex date - 01/09/2003; 7.5% payable 12/18/2003 to holders of record 10/31/2003 Ex date - 12/08/2003; 5% payable 12/16/2004 to holders of record 10/29/2004 Ex date - 11/30/2004; 6% payable 12/22/2005 to holders of record 10/31/2005 Ex date - 12/02/2005; 6% payable 12/21/2006 to holders of record 12/01/2006 Ex date - 11/29/2006 Merged into Heartland Bancorp Inc. 07/31/2007 Each share new Common 10¢ par exchanged for $21.79 cash

BANKRATE INC (DE)
Acquired by Red Ventures Holdco, LP 11/08/2017
Each share Common 1¢ par exchanged for $14 cash

BANKRATE INC (FL)
Merged into BEN Holdings, Inc. 09/25/2009
Each share Common 1¢ par exchanged for $28.50 cash

BANKS COM INC (FL)
Merged into Remark Media, Inc. 07/06/2012
Each share Common $0.001 par exchanged for (0.0258) share Common $0.001 par
Remark Media, Inc. name changed to Remark Holdings, Inc. 04/11/2017

BANKS ENERGY INC (YUKON)
Merged into Arapahoe Energy Corp. (New) 10/20/2005
Each share Common no par exchanged for (0.5) share Common no par
Arapahoe Energy Corp. (New) name changed to Canadian Phoenix Resources Corp. 01/07/2008 which recapitalized as Knol Resources Corp. 03/11/2013

BANKS IOWA INC (IA)
Common $5 par changed to no par and (1) additional share issued 12/05/1969
Stock Dividends - 10% 06/15/1979; 10% 03/15/1981
Merged into Firstar Corp. 04/29/1991
Each share Common no par exchanged for (2.7) shares Common $1.25 par
Firstar Corp. merged into Firstar Corp. (New) 11/20/1998 which merged into U.S. Bancorp (DE) 02/27/2001

BANKS IS GOLD LTD (BC)
Placed in receivership 01/15/2016
Stockholders' equity unlikely

BANKS MID AMER INC (DE)
Each share Adjustable Rate Preferred Ser. A $1 par exchanged for (9.4748) shares Common 10¢ par 10/17/1988
Each share $2.50 Conv. Preferred $1 par exchanged for (4.7374) shares Common 10¢ par 10/17/1988
Each share Common $1 par exchanged for (0.1) share Common 10¢ par 10/17/1988
Reincorporated under the laws of Oklahoma as Liberty Bancorp Inc. 05/26/1992
Liberty Bancorp Inc. (OK) merged into Banc One Corp. 06/01/1997 which merged into Bank One Corp. 10/02/1998 which merged into J.P. Morgan Chase & Co. 12/31/2000 which name changed to JPMorgan Chase & Co. 07/20/2004

BANKS-MILLER SUPPLY CO. (WV)
6% Preferred $100 par called for redemption 12/31/1946
Voluntarily dissolved 10/01/1977

Details not available

BANKS VENTURES LTD (YUKON)
Name changed to Banks Energy Inc. 07/26/2004
Banks Energy Inc. merged into Arapahoe Energy Corp. (New) 10/20/2005 which name changed to Canadian Phoenix Resources Corp. 01/07/2008 which recapitalized as Knol Resources Corp. 03/11/2013

BANKSHARE CORP. (VA)
Dissolved 00/00/1936
Details not available

BANKSHARES CORP. OF THE UNITED STATES (NJ)
Liquidated 00/00/1930
No stockholders' equity

BANKSHARES FAYETTEVILLE INC (AR)
Preferred called for redemption at $10 on 01/31/2010
Acquired by Farmers & Merchants Bancshares, Inc. (AR) 12/07/2015
Each share Common exchanged for $51.36 cash

BANKSHARES IND INC (IN)
Name changed to Money Management Corp. 12/31/1975
Money Market Corp. merged into Banc One Corp. (DE) 07/01/1986 which reincorporated in Ohio 05/01/1989 which merged into Bank One Corp. 10/02/1998 which merged into J.P. Morgan Chase & Co. 12/31/2000 which name changed to JPMorgan Chase & Co. 07/20/2004

BANKUNITED A SVGS BK (MIAMI, FL)
Stock Dividends - 10% 05/26/1992; 15% 11/30/1992
Under plan of reorganization each share Class A Common 1¢ par automatically became (1) share BankUnited Financial Corp. Class A Common 1¢ par 03/05/1993
(See BankUnited Financial Corp.)

BANKUNITED CAP (DE)
Each 10.25% Trust Preferred Security Ser. A exchanged for (1) 10.25% Trust Preferred Security Ser. B 05/00/1997
10.25% Trust Preferred Securities Ser. B called for redemption at $1,051.25 on 03/26/2007

BANKUNITED CAP II (DE)
9.60% Trust Preferred Securities called for redemption at $25 on 03/28/2003

BANKUNITED CAP III (DE)
9% Trust Preferred Securities called for redemption at $25 on 06/30/2003

BANKUNITED FINL CORP (FL)
8% Conv. Preferred 1996 Ser. 1¢ par called for redemption at $15 on 10/10/1997
8% Conv. Preferred 1993 Ser. 1¢ par called for redemption at $10 on 02/20/1998
9% Prepetual Preferred 1¢ par called for redemption at $10 on 08/15/2001
Each Corporate Hi-Med Unit exchanged for $50 principal amount of 6.37% Sr. Notes due 05/17/2012 on 10/22/2009
Stock Dividend - in Class A to holders of Class A 15% 04/13/1993
Plan of reorganization under Chapter 11 Federal Bankruptcy proceedings effective 03/09/2012
No stockholders' equity

BANKUR PATRICIA GOLD MINES LTD. (ON)
Charter cancelled 00/00/1956

BANKUS CORP. (NY)
Proclaimed dissolved for failure to file reports and pay fees 12/16/1935

BANKVERMONT CORP (VT)
Acquired by Bank of Boston Corp. 12/30/1988
Each share Common $1 par exchanged for (0.976) share Common $2.25 par and $1.12 cash
Bank of Boston Corp. name changed to BankBoston Corp. 04/25/1997 which merged into Fleet Boston Corp. 10/01/1999 which name changed to FleetBoston Financial Corp. 04/18/2000 which merged into Bank of America Corp. 04/01/2004

BANKVEST INC.
Merged into First Fidelity Bancorporation 03/25/1994
Each share Common no par exchanged for $214 cash

BANKWORCESTER CORP (DE)
Acquired by BBC Delaware Holdings, Inc. 05/27/1994
Each share Common 10¢ par exchanged for $34 cash

BANLIFE CORP. (DE)
Each share Capital Stock $1 par exchanged for (10) shares Capital Stock 10¢ par 01/22/1962
Stock Dividend - 25% 04/07/1964
Completely liquidated 01/28/1966
Each share Capital Stock 10¢ par received first and final distribution of (1.2258) shares Bankers National Life Insurance Co. Capital Stock $2 par
Note: Certificates were not required to be surrendered and are without value

BANNER AEROSPACE INC (DE)
Merged into Fairchild Corp. 04/08/1999
Each share Common $1 par exchanged for (0.7885) share Common 10¢ par
(See Fairchild Corp.)

BANNER CENT FIN CO (DE)
Company terminated common stock registration and is no longer public as of 06/28/2002

BANNER CORP (WA)
Fixed Rate Perpetual Preferred Ser. A 1¢ par called for redemption at $1,000 on 12/24/2012
(Additional Information in Active)

BANNER ENTMT INC (BC)
Recapitalized as Windsor Court Holdings Inc. 06/15/1990
Each share Common no par exchanged for (0.2) share Common no par
Windsor Court Holdings Inc. recapitalized as Teledata Ventures Corp. (BC) 10/01/1996 which reincorporated in Yukon as CTF Technologies Inc. 04/06/1998 which reincorporated in British Columbia 08/11/2008
(See CTF Technologies Inc.)

BANNER FD (ON)
Name changed to Bullock American Fund 04/10/1985
(See Bullock American Fund)

BANNER HLDG CORP (FL)
SEC revoked common stock registration 01/08/2009

BANNER-IDAHO MINES, INC. (ID)
Administratively dissolved 10/06/2003

BANNER INDS INC (BC)
Name changed to Banner Entertainment Inc. 09/25/1987
Banner Entertainment Inc. recapitalized as Windsor Court Holdings Inc. 06/15/1990 which recapitalized as Teledata Ventures Corp. (BC) 10/01/1996 which reincorporated in Yukon as CTF Technologies Inc. 04/06/1998 which reincorporated in British Columbia 08/11/2008
(See CTF Technologies Inc.)

BANNER INDS INC (DE)
Reincorporated 11/13/1970
State of incorporation changed from (MO) to (DE) 11/13/1970
Common 10¢ par reclassified as Class A Common 10¢ par 01/16/1987
Class A Common 10¢ par split (3) for (2) by issuance of (0.5) additional share 10/04/1988
Class A Common 10¢ par split (2) for (1) by issuance of (1) additional share 06/30/1989
Conv. Class B Common 10¢ par split (2) for (1) by issuance of (1) additional share 06/30/1989
8% Conv. Preferred 10¢ par called for redemption 03/01/1990
Name changed to Fairchild Corp. 11/15/1990
(See Fairchild Corp.)

BANNER MNG CO (NV)
Common $1 par changed to 50¢ par and (1) additional share issued 09/30/1964
Common 50¢ par changed to 25¢ par and (1) additional share issued 04/25/1968
Common 25¢ par changed to $0.08333333 par and (2) additional shares issued 03/16/1970
Merged into American Metal Climax, Inc. 06/27/1973
Each share Common $0.08333333 par exchanged for (0.139479) share Conv. Preferred Ser. A $1 par
American Metal Climax, Inc. name changed to Amax, Inc. 07/01/1974
(See Amax Inc.)

BANNER MNG CORP (BC)
Delisted from Canadian Venture Stock Exchange 10/13/2000

BANNER PETROLEUM CORP. (AB)
Merged into Consolidated Mic Mac Oils Ltd. 00/00/1953
Each share Common no par exchanged for (0.18181818) share new Common no par
(See Consolidated Mic Mac Oils Ltd.)

BANNER PORCUPINE MINES LTD (ON)
Merged into Broulan Resources Inc. 04/26/1983
Each share Capital Stock no par exchanged for (0.1) share Common no par
Broulan Resources Inc. merged into Cabre Exploration Ltd. 11/24/1989 which was acquired by EnerMark Income Fund 01/10/2001 which merged into Enerplus Resources Fund 06/22/2001 which reorganized as Enerplus Corp. 01/03/2011

BANNER RES LTD (BC)
Capital Stock no par split (3) for (1) by issuance of (2) additional shares 09/17/1981
Recapitalized as Angus Resources Ltd. 03/05/1984
Each share Capital Stock no par exchanged for (0.1) share Common no par
Angus Resources Ltd. recapitalized as Canadian Angus Resources Ltd. (BC) 12/31/1987 which reincorporated in Alberta 08/29/1988 which merged into Abacan Resource Corp. (New) 02/10/1995
(See Abacan Resource Corp. (New))

BANNERMAN RES LTD (AUSTRALIA)
Shares transferred to Australian share register 06/10/2016

BANNOCKBURN RES INC (CO)
Reorganized under the laws of British Columbia as Bannockburn Resources Ltd. 04/02/2004
Each share Common $0.001 par exchanged for (0.25) share Common $0.001 par
Bannockburn Resources Ltd. name

changed to Lucara Diamond Corp. 08/14/2007

BANNOCKBURN RES LTD (AB)
Struck from the register 07/01/1987

BANNOCKBURN RES LTD (BC)
Name changed to Lucara Diamond Corp. 08/14/2007

BANORE BANCSHARES INC (OR)
Completely liquidated 12/31/1988
Each share Common $2.50 par exchanged for first and final distribution of $1.38 cash

BANPAIS S A (MEXICO)
Assets acquired by Mercantil del Norte 00/00/1997
No ADR holders' equity

BANPONCE CORP NEW (PR)
Common $6 par split (2) for (1) by issuance of (1) additional share payable 07/01/1996 to holders of record 06/14/1996
Name changed to Popular Inc. 04/25/1997

BANPONCE CORP OLD (PR)
Common $5 par split (3) for (1) by issuance of (2) additional shares 08/30/1985
Merged into BanPonce Corp. (New) 12/31/1990
Each share Common $5 par exchanged for (2.717) shares Common $6 par
BanPonce Corp. (New) name changed to Popular Inc. 04/25/1997

BANQUE AUDI S A L (LEBANON)
GDR agreement terminated 02/26/1998
Each 144A GDR for Class B shares exchanged for approximately $30 cash
144A GDR's for Class B split (10) for (1) by issuance of (9) additional GDR's payable 05/24/2010 to holders of record 05/21/2010
Ex date - 05/25/2010
Reg. S GDR's for Class B split (10) for (1) by issuance of (9) additional GDR's payable 05/24/2010 to holders of record 05/21/2010
Ex date - 05/25/2010
Name changed to Bank Audi SAL 04/02/2014

BANQUE CANADIENNE NATIONALE (MONTREAL, QC)
Each share Capital Stock $100 par exchanged for (10) shares Capital Stock $10 par 00/00/1944
Each share Capital Stock $10 par received (5) shares Capital Stock $2 par 08/07/1967
Note: Certificates were not required to be surrendered and are without value
Merged into National Bank of Canada (Montreal, QC) 11/01/1979
Each share Capital Stock $2 par exchanged for (1) share Common $2 par

BANQUE INTERNATIONALE ARABE DE TUNISIE (TUNISIA)
Stock Dividend - 4.17% payable 01/06/2000 to holders of record 12/30/1999
GDR agreement terminated 10/31/2017
Each 144A Sponsored GDR for Ordinary exchanged for (0.5) share Ordinary
Each Reg. S Sponsored GDR for Ordinary exchanged for (0.5) share Ordinary
Note: Unexchanged GDR's will be sold and the proceeds, if any, held for claim after 11/05/2018

BANQUE LIBANAISE POUR LE COMM S A L (LEBANON)
Each old Regulation S GDR for Ordinary exchanged for (1/9) new Regulation S GDR for Ordinary 07/22/2002
Each old 144A GDR for Ordinary exchanged for (0.11111111) new 144A GDR for Ordinary 07/22/2002
Each old Regulation S GDR for Ordinary exchanged for (1) new Regulation S GDR for Ordinary 08/01/2003
Name changed to BLC Bank s.a.l. 08/01/2005
(See BLC Bank s.a.l.)

BANQUE NATIONALE DE PARIS (FRANCE)
Name changed to BNP Paribas 06/19/2000

BANQUE PROVINCIALE DU CANADA OLD (MONTREAL, QC)
Each share Capital Stock $100 par exchanged for (10) shares Capital Stock $10 par 00/00/1944
Each share Capital Stock $10 par exchanged for (5) shares Capital Stock $2 par 08/01/1967
Under plan of merger each share Common $2 par automatically became (1) share Banque Provinciale du Canada (Montreal, QC) (New) Common $2 par 06/16/1977
Banque Provinciale du Canada (Montreal, QC) merged into National Bank of Canada (Montreal, QC) 11/01/1979

BANQUE PROVINCIALE DU QUE MONTREAL (MONTREAL, QC)
Merged into National Bank of Canada (Montreal, QC) 11/01/1979
Each share Common $2 par exchanged for (1) share Common $2 par

BANQWEST RES LTD (BC)
Recapitalized as Universal Pre-Vent Inc. 11/04/1986
Each share Common 50¢ par exchanged for (0.2) share Common no par
(See Universal Pre-Vent Inc.)

BANRO CAP GROUP INC (ON)
Name changed to International Infopet Systems Ltd. 01/08/1990
International Infopet Systems Ltd. recapitalized as New International Infopet Systems Ltd. 02/26/1997 which
Name changed to SponsorsOne Inc. 01/13/2014

BANRO CORP (ON)
Reincorporated 04/02/2004
Place of incorporation changed from (ON) to (Canada) 04/02/2004
Old Common no par split (2) for (1) by issuance of (1) additional share payable 12/23/2004 to holders of record 12/16/2004
Each share Preference Ser. A no par exchanged for (209.95004) shares Common no par 04/19/2017
Each share old Common no par exchanged for (0.1) share new Common no par 05/26/2017
Amended Consolidated Plan of Compromise and Reorganization effective 05/03/2018
No stockholders' equity

BANRO RES CORP (ON)
Name changed 05/06/1996
Reincorporated 10/24/1996
Name changed from Banro International Capital Inc. to Banro Resources Corp. 05/06/1996
Place of incorporation changed from (Canada) to (ON) 10/24/1996
Recapitalized as Banro Corp. (ON) 01/22/2001
Each share Common $1 par exchanged for (0.33333333) share Common $1 par
Banro Corp. (ON) reincorporated in Canada 04/02/2004

BANSICILIA CORP.
Dissolved 00/00/1933

Details not available

BANTA CORP (WI)
Name changed 04/11/1989
Common 10¢ par split (3) for (2) by issuance of (0.5) additional share 02/01/1980
Common 10¢ par split (2) for (1) by issuance of (1) additional share 04/11/1983
Common 10¢ par split (2) for (1) by issuance of (1) additional share 04/30/1985
Name changed from Banta (George) Co., Inc. to Banta Corp. 04/11/1989
New Common Purchase Rights declared for Common stockholders of record 11/15/1991 were redeemed at $0.05 per right 12/13/1991
Common 10¢ par split (3) for (2) by issuance of (0.5) additional share 04/30/1993
Common 10¢ par split (3) for (2) by issuance of (0.5) additional share payable 03/01/1996 to holders of record 02/16/1996
Merged into Donnelley (R.R.) & Sons Co. 01/09/2007
Each share Common 10¢ par exchanged for $36.50 cash

BANTAM BOOKS INC (DE)
Merged into National General Corp. 02/11/1974
Each share Common $1 par exchanged for $25 cash

BANTEX BANCSHARES INC (TX)
Out of business 05/05/1987
Details not available

BANYAN COAST CAP CORP (AB)
Name changed to Banyan Gold Corp. 02/19/2013

BANYAN CORP (DE)
Chapter 11 bankrputcy proceedings converted to Chapter 7 on 07/17/1992
No stockholders' equity

BANYAN CORP (OR)
Each share old Common no par exchanged for (0.5) share new Common no par 08/23/1996
Each share new Common no par exchanged again for (0.05) share new Common no par 12/09/1996
Each share new Common no par exchanged again for (0.01) share new Common no par 09/13/2007
Each share new Common no par exchanged again for (0.01) share new Common no par 03/18/2010
Administratively dissolved 08/27/2010

BANYAN HEALTHCARE SVCS INC (DE)
Each share old Common $0.001 par exchanged for (0.04) share new Common $0.001 par 11/02/1998
Recapitalized as Netoy.com Corp. 03/15/1999
Each share new Common $0.001 par exchanged for (0.1) share Common $0.001 par
Netoy.com Corp. name changed to SafePay Solutions, Inc. 03/03/2006 which name changed to Emaji, Inc. 03/11/2008 which name changed to Broadside Enterprises, Inc. 12/01/2016

BANYAN HOTEL INVT FD (DE)
Name changed to B.H.I.T. Inc. 01/04/2008
B.H.I.T. Inc. name changed to Banyan Rail Services Inc. 01/29/2010 which recapitalized as MedAmerica Properties Inc. 06/20/2017

BANYAN INDS INTL INC (BC)
Name changed to Incentive Design Group Ltd. 11/19/1991
Incentive Design Group Ltd. name changed to Envoy Communications Group Inc. 01/22/1996 which name changed to Envoy Capital Group

Inc. 04/05/2007 which merged into Merus Labs International Inc. (New) 12/22/2011
(See Merus Labs International Inc. (New))

BANYAN MTG INVT FD (DE)
Recapitalized as Legend Properties, Inc. 12/31/1996
Each share Common 1¢ par exchanged for (0.04) share Common 1¢ par
(See Legend Properties, Inc.)

BANYAN MTG INVS L P (DE)
Plan of complete liquidation and termination of partnership adopted 09/21/1995
Details not available

BANYAN MTG INVS L P II (DE)
Plan of liquidation approved 08/19/1992
Details not available

BANYAN MTG INVS L P III (DE)
Merged into THSP Associates Limited Partnership 10/31/1994
Each Depositary Unit no par exchanged for $2.50 cash

BANYAN RAIL SVCS INC (DE)
Each share old Common 1¢ par exchanged for (0.1) share new Common 1¢ par 04/07/2010
Each share new Common 1¢ par exchanged again for (0.2) share new Common 1¢ par 09/19/2013
Recapitalized as MedAmerica Properties Inc. 06/20/2017
Each share new Common 1¢ par exchanged for (0.1) share Common 1¢ par

BANYAN SHORT TERM INCOME TR (MA)
Liquidation completed
Each Share of Bene. Int. no par received initial distribution of $3.95 cash payable 12/22/1995 to holders of record 12/11/1995
Each Share of Bene. Int. no par exchanged for second and final distribution of $0.50 cash 12/16/1996

BANYAN STRATEGIC LD FD II (DE)
Name changed to Semele Group Inc. 11/14/1997
(See Semele Group Inc.)

BANYAN STRATEGIC RLTY TR (MA)
Name changed 05/01/1993
Name changed from Banyan Strategic Land Trust to Banyan Strategic Realty Trust 05/01/1993
Liquidation completed
Each Share of Bene. Int. no par received initial distribution of $4.75 cash payable 06/28/2001 to holders of record 06/13/2001
Each Share of Bene. Int. no par received second distribution of $0.20 cash payable 10/24/2001 to holders of record 09/24/2001
Each Share of Bene. Int. no par received third distribution of $0.30 cash payable 05/31/2002 to holders of record 05/16/2002
Each Share of Bene. Int. no par received fourth distribution of $0.20 cash payable 07/15/2002 to holders of record 07/01/2002
Assets transferred to BSRT Liquidating Trust 01/02/2003
Each Share of Bene. Int. no par received fifth and final distribution of $0.3425 cash payable 09/30/2003 to holders of record 09/18/2003
Ex date - 10/01/2003
Note: Certificates were not required to be surrendered and are without value

BANYAN SYS INC (MA)
Name changed to ePresence, Inc. 05/25/2000
(See ePresence, Inc.)

BANYANTREE HEALTHCARE CORP (MD)
Charter forfeited 10/06/1998

BANYU PHARMACEUTICAL LTD (JAPAN)
Basis changed from (1:20) to (1:2) 07/15/2002
Stock Dividends - 12.5% 06/28/1974; 20% 07/17/1979; 10% 06/12/1984; 900% payable 07/15/2002 to holders of record 07/12/2002
ADR agreement terminated 06/10/2004
Each ADR for Common exchanged for $24.55 cash

BAOA INC (CA)
Recapitalized as Call-Solutions Inc. 10/06/2000
Each share Common $0.001 par exchanged for (0.05) share Common $0.001 par
Call-Solutions Inc. recapitalized as ProCoreGroup, Inc. (CA) 11/17/2003 which reorganized in Nevada as Universal Property Development & Acquisition Corp. 07/11/2005
(See Universal Property Development & Acquisition Corp.)

BAOSHINN CORP (NV)
Each share Common $0.001 par exchanged for (0.1) share Common $0.0001 par 10/19/2011
Name changed to Green Standard Technologies, Inc. 07/06/2015
Green Standard Technologies, Inc. name changed to ZZLL Information Technology, Inc. 06/02/2016

BAP ACQUISITION CORP (DE)
Name changed to REII Inc. 05/01/1998
REII Inc. name changed to B&D Food Corp. 07/08/2005 which recapitalized as Latteno Food Corp. 10/19/2009

BAPCO URANIUM & OIL INC (UT)
Recapitalized as Southwest Border Corp. 01/06/1989
Each share Capital Stock 2¢ par exchanged for (0.05) share Common 2¢ par
Southwest Border Corp. reorganized as EFO, Inc. 04/30/1993 which name changed to Think.com, Inc. 03/03/1999 which name changed to Go Think.com, Inc. 06/14/1999 which recapitalized as Knowledge Transfer Systems Inc. 04/24/2001 which name changed to Global General Technologies, Inc. 07/08/2005 which recapitalized as Turbine Aviation, Inc. 12/19/2014

BAR-FIN MINING CORP. LTD. (ON)
Charter cancelled for default in filing reports and paying fees 11/00/1964

BAR HARBOR BKG & TR CO (BAR HARBOR, ME)
Common $100 par changed to $20 par and (4) additional shares issued plus a 20% stock dividend paid 01/02/1963
Common $20 par split (2) for (1) by issuance of (1) additional share 10/24/1983
Stock Dividends - 25% 01/01/1936; 100% 11/22/1974
Reorganized as Bar Harbor Bankshares 06/29/1984
Each share Common $20 par exchanged for (2) shares Common $10 par

BAR-LAN GOLD MINES LTD. (ON)
Acquired by Gibson Mines Ltd. 03/24/1958
Each share Capital Stock $1 par exchanged for (0.16666666) share Capital Stock $1 par
(See Gibson Mines Ltd.)

BAR-LE-DUC CHIBOUGAMAU MINES LTD. (ON)
Charter cancelled and dissolved 11/09/1964

BAR-MANITOU MINES LTD. (QC)
Acquired by Courville Mines, Ltd. 12/31/1964
Each share Capital Stock $1 par exchanged for (0.1) share Capital Stock $1 par
(See Courville Mines, Ltd.)

BAR RES LTD (ON)
Recapitalized as Southern Bar Minerals Corp. 02/06/1995
Each share Common $1 par exchanged for (0.28571428) share Common no par
Southern Bar Minerals Corp. name changed to Texas Gulf Petroleum Corp. (ON) 01/26/1996 which reincorporated in British Columbia 06/11/1996 which recapitalized as Portrush Petroleum Corp. 03/15/2000 which recapitalized as Westbridge Energy Corp. 12/11/2009

BARADERO RES LTD (BC)
Reincorporated 11/23/2004
Place of incorporation changed from (YT) to (BC) 11/23/2004
Name changed to Centrasia Mining Corp. 09/16/2005
Centrasia Mining Corp. name changed to Kola Mining Corp. 03/27/2008 which name changed to Mitchell Resources Ltd. 05/27/2015 which name changed to Hannan Metals Ltd. 01/10/2017

BARAHONA SUGAR CO.
Acquired by West Indies Sugar Corp. 00/00/1940
Details not available

BARANDIUM RES LTD (BC)
Name changed to IGC International Golf Corp. 03/14/1990
IGC International Golf Corp. recapitalized as Medilase Industries Inc. 03/02/1992
(See Medilase Industries Inc.)

BARBADOS GOLD MINES LTD. (ON)
Charter cancelled 08/29/1960
No stockholders' equity

BARBADOS UNIT TRUST (BARBADOS)
Trust terminated 00/00/1993
Details not available

BARBANA MINING CORP, LTD. (ON)
Charter revoked for failure to file reports and pay taxes 00/00/1956

BARBARA LYNN STORES INC (DE)
Merged into Lynbar Corp. 01/24/1975
Each share Common 10¢ par exchanged for $4 cash
Note: An additional 40¢ per Common 10¢ par was paid simultaneously to holders who participated in a class action which was settled prior to merger date

BARBARY COAST NATIONAL BANK (SAN FRANCISCO, CA)
Taken over by the FDIC 05/19/1994
Stockholders' equity undetermined

BARBARY GOLD MINES, LTD. (ON)
Charter cancelled 00/00/1959

BARBASOL CO. (DE)
Name changed to Wasecowl Co. 08/31/1962
(See Wasecowl Co.)

BARBECON INC (ON)
Common no par split (4) for (1) by issuance of (3) additional shares 01/03/1979
7% Preference $50 par called for redemption 03/05/1979
Common no par split (2) for (1) by issuance of (1) additional share 06/20/1980
Each share Common no par exchanged for (1) share Conv. Class A Special no par and (0.5) share Conv. Class B Special no par 12/22/1981
Through exchange offer 100% Conv. Class A Special no par and Conv. Class B Special no par acquired by Abitibi-Price Inc. as of 04/15/1985
Public interest eliminated

BARBECUE INNS INTL INC (MN)
Name changed to Basic Investments, Inc. 08/17/1970
Basic Investments, Inc. name changed to Premier Investments, Inc. 01/26/1972
(See Premier Investments, Inc.)

BARBEQUE CAP CORP (NV)
Name changed 04/27/1990
Name changed from Barbecue Capital Corp. to Barbeque Capital Corp. 04/27/1990
Reincorporated under the laws of Wyoming as Consolidated Energy Inc. 10/14/2002
(See Consolidated Energy Inc.)

BARBEQUES GALORE LTD (AUSTRALIA)
Merged into BBG Australia Property Ltd. 10/17/2005
Each Sponsored ADR for Ordinary exchanged for $9.7442 cash

BARBER ASPHALT CORP. (DE)
Name changed to Barber Oil Corp. 00/00/1948
(See Barber Oil Corp.)

BARBER ASPHALT CORP. (NJ)
Reincorporated under the laws of Delaware 00/00/1947
Barber Asphalt Corp. (DE) name changed to Barber Oil Corp. 00/00/1948
(See Barber Oil Corp.)

BARBER CO., INC.
Name changed to Barber Asphalt Corp. (NJ) 00/00/1938
Barber Asphalt Corp. (NJ) reincorporated in Delaware 00/00/1947 which name changed to Barber Oil Corp. 00/00/1948
(See Barber Oil Corp.)

BARBER (W.H.) CO. (DE)
Each share Class A no par exchanged for (2) shares Common $1 par 00/00/1936
Each share Common no par exchanged for (2) shares Common $1 par 00/00/1936
Acquired by Pure Oil Co. 01/24/1955
Each share Common $1 par exchanged for (0.777148) share Common no par
Pure Oil Co. merged into Union Oil Co. of California 07/16/1965
(See Union Oil Co. of California)

BARBER ELLIS CDA LTD (ON)
Each share Common $10 par exchanged for (10) shares Common no par 04/22/1969
Common no par reclassified as Conv. Class A Common no par 11/18/1974
Name changed to Barbecon Inc. and Conv. Class A Common no par and Conv. Class B Common no par reclassified as Common no par 06/01/1978
(See Barbecon Inc.)

BARBER GREENE CO (DE)
Reincorporated 01/02/1969
Stock Dividend - 10% 09/16/1966
State of incorporation changed from (IL) to (DE) 01/02/1969
Common $5 par split (3) for (2) by issuance of (0.5) additional share 09/08/1978
Stock Dividend - 50% 12/10/1975
Merged into Astec Industries, Inc. 12/29/1986
Each share Common $5 par exchanged for (0.1218955) share Common 20¢ par and (0.1)

Common Stock Purchase Warrant expiring 12/29/1991

BARBER-LARDER GOLD MINES LTD.
Recapitalized 00/00/1942
Each share Capital Stock exchanged for (0.16666666) share Amalgamated Larder Mines Ltd. Capital Stock $1 par and (0.16666666) share New Barber-Larder Mines Ltd. Capital Stock
(See each company's listing)

BARBER OIL CORP. LIQUIDATING TRUST (DE)
Liquidation completed
Each Unit of Bene. Int. received initial distribution of $2 cash 01/12/1982
Each Unit of Bene. Int. received second distribution of $2 cash 08/06/1982
Each Unit of Bene. Int. received third distribution of $1.80 cash 10/08/1982
Each Unit of Bene. Int. received fourth distribution of $1.50 cash 04/22/1983
Each Unit of Bene. Int. received fifth and final distribution of $1.4473 cash 03/22/1985
Note: No Units were issued but holders received a statement showing the number of Units owned
(See Barber Oil Corp.)

BARBER OIL CORP (DE)
Capital Stock $10 par changed to $5 par and (1) additional share issued 08/15/1966
Each share Capital Stock $5 par exchanged for (1) share Common no par 05/20/1980
Stock Dividend - 100% 10/01/1952
Liquidation completed
Each share Common no par received initial distribution of $40 cash 01/30/1981
Each share Common no par received second distribution of $22 cash 04/08/1981
Each share Common no par received third and final distribution of $5 cash 06/30/1981
Assets transferred to Barber Oil Corp. Liquidating Trust and Common no par reclassified as Units of Bene. Int. 06/30/1981
(See Barber Oil Corp. Liquidating Trust)

BARBERS HAIRSTYLING FOR MEN INC (MN)
Common 10¢ par split (3) for (2) by issuance of (0.5) additional share payable 10/31/1996 to holders of record 10/15/1996
Common 10¢ par split (3) for (2) by issuance of (0.5) additional share payable 04/17/1998 to holders of record 04/03/1998
Stock Dividend - 100% 02/15/1982
Merged into Regis Corp. 05/20/1999
Each share Common 10¢ par exchanged for (0.5) share Common 5¢ par

BARBERTON ST BK (BARBERTON, OH)
Common $10 par changed to $7 par 05/02/1969
Name changed to American Bank of Commerce (Akron, OH) 07/10/1969
American Bank of Commerce (Akron, OH) name changed to Centran Bank (Akron, OH) 07/01/1974
(See Centran Bank (Akron, OH))

BARBI LAKE COPPER MINES LTD (ON)
Name changed to Bar Resources Ltd. 09/06/1978
Bar Resources Ltd. recapitalized as Southern Bar Minerals Corp. 02/06/1995 which name changed to Texas Gulf Petroleum Corp. (ON)

01/26/1996 which reincorporated in British Columbia 06/11/1996 which recapitalized as Portrush Petroleum Corp. 03/15/2000 which recapitalized as Westbridge Energy Corp. 12/11/2009

BARBICAN FINL CORP (BC)
Cease trade order effective 08/17/1995

BARBIZON INTL INC (DE)
Each share old Common 1¢ par exchanged for (0.25) share new Common 1¢ par 06/30/1975
Stock Dividend - 50% 02/27/1970
Merged into BII Corp. 06/30/1976
Each share new Common 1¢ par exchanged for $3.75 cash

BARBON CORP.
Liquidated 00/00/1941
Details not available

BARC RAY HOLDING CORP.
Bankrupt 00/00/1932
Details not available

BARCALO MANUFACTURING CO. (NY)
Each share Common $50 par exchanged for (1) share Common no par 00/00/1938
Common no par changed to $8.33 par 00/00/1940
Stock Dividend - 25% 07/25/1952
Liquidation completed
Each share Common $8.33 par exchanged for initial distribution of $7 cash 09/15/1965
Each share Common $8.33 par received second and final distribution of $1.15 cash 01/24/1966

BARCAN COMMUNICATIONS INC (CANADA)
Struck off register and declared dissolved for failure to file returns 06/04/1997

BARCELONA TRACTION LT & PWR LTD (CANADA)
Each share 7% Preference $100 par exchanged for (6) Ordinary Shares no par 00/00/1930
Each Ordinary Share $50 par exchanged for (1) Ordinary Share no par 00/00/1930
Dissolved 12/15/1980
No stockholders' equity

BARCHRIS CONSTR CORP (NY)
Common $1 par changed to 50¢ par and (1) additional share issued 05/09/1961
Petition in bankruptcy under Chapter XI filed 00/00/1962 and then transferred to Chapter X 11/08/1963
Assets sold for benefit of creditors 12/09/1971
No stockholders' equity

BARCLAY FUND, INC. (NY)
Name changed to Barclay Growth Fund, Inc. 04/07/1972
Barclay Growth Fund, Inc. acquired by National Investors Corp. (MD) 04/30/1974 which name changed to Seligman Growth Fund, Inc. 05/01/1982

BARCLAY GROWTH FD INC (NY)
Acquired by National Investors Corp. (MD) 04/30/1974
Each share Common 10¢ par exchanged for (1.1227) shares Capital Stock $1 par
National Investors Corp. (MD) name changed to Seligman Growth Fund, Inc. 05/01/1982

BARCLAY HOTEL CORP.
Property sold under plan of reorganization 00/00/1943
No stockholders' equity

BARCLAY INDS INC (DE)
Common $1 par split (3) for (2) by issuance of (0.5) additional share 10/22/1971

Common $1 par split (2) for (1) by issuance of (1) additional share 04/07/1972
Chapter 11 Federal Bankruptcy proceedings converted to Chapter 7 on 01/23/1989
Stockholders' equity unlikely

BARCLAY OILS LTD. (ON)
Name changed to Claybar Uranium & Oil Ltd. 03/08/1954
Claybar Uranium & Oil Ltd. recapitalized as Canbridge Oil Exploration Ltd. 01/21/1965 which merged into Thomson Drilling Co. Ltd. 12/31/1970 which name changed to Thomson Industries Ltd. 07/01/1973
(See Thomson Industries Ltd.)

BARCLAY PARK CORP.
Reorganized as Barclay Hotel Corp. 00/00/1939
No stockholders' equity

BARCLAY RES LTD (AB)
Name changed to Ballard Oil & Gas Ltd. 05/22/1981
(See Ballard Oil & Gas Ltd.)

BARCLAYS ADVANTAGED CORPORATE BD FD (ON)
Name changed to BG Advantaged Corporate Bond Fund 11/01/2006
BG Advantaged Corporate Bond Fund merged into Brompton Advantaged VIP Income Fund 07/14/2008 which name changed to Aston Hill Advantage VIP Income Fund 09/16/2011 which name changed to LOGiQ Advantage Income Fund 05/12/2017 which merged into Purpose Multi-Asset Income Fund 05/04/2018

BARCLAYS ADVANTAGED S&P/TSX INCOME TR INDEX FD (ON)
Name changed to BG Advantaged S&P/TSX Income Trust Index Fund 11/01/2006
BG Advantaged S&P/TSX Income Trust Index Fund merged into Brompton Advantaged VIP Income Fund 07/14/2008 which name changed to Aston Hill Advantage VIP Income Fund 09/16/2011 which name changed to LOGiQ Advantage VIP Income Fund 05/12/2017 which name changed to Redwood Advantage Monthly Income Fund 12/20/2017 which name changed to Redwood Advantage Monthly Income Fund 12/20/2017 which merged into Purpose Multi-Asset Income Fund 05/04/2018

BARCLAYS AFRICA GROUP LTD (SOUTH AFRICA)
Name changed to Absa Group Ltd. 07/16/2018

BARCLAYS BK PLC (ENGLAND)
ADR's for Preference Ser. A called for redemption 12/19/1994
ADR's for Preference Ser. B called for redemption 12/19/1994
Sponsored ADR's for Ser. C Units called for redemption at $25 plus $0.2039 accrued dividends on 06/30/2000
ADR's for Ser. C1 called for redemption at $20 plus $0.1359 accrued dividends on 06/30/2000
ADR's for Ser. C2 called for redemption at $5 plus $0.068 accrued dividends on 06/30/2000
ADR's for Ser. D1 called for redemption at $20 plus $0.1342 accrued dividends on 03/29/2001
ADR's for Ser. D2 called for redemption at $5 plus $0.067 accrued dividends on 03/29/2001
ADR's for Ser. D Units called for redemption at $25 plus $0.2012 accrued dividends on 03/29/2001
ADR's for Notes called for redemption at $25 on 06/01/2003

BARCLAYS GLOBAL INVESTORS FUNDS (DE)
Name changed 01/11/2002
Name and state of incorporation changed from Barclays Global Investors Funds, Inc. (MD) to Barclays Global Investors Funds (DE) 01/11/2002
Name changed to BlackRock Funds III 12/01/2009

BARCLAYS INCOME PLUS GROWTH SPLIT TR (ON)
Name changed to BG Income + Growth Split Trust 11/01/2006
BG Income + Growth Split Trust merged into Brompton VIP Income Fund 07/04/2008 which name changed to Aston Hill VIP Income Fund 09/16/2011 which name changed to LOGiQ VIP Income Fund 05/12/2017 which name changed to Redwood Monthly Income Fund 12/20/2017 which merged into Purpose Multi-Asset Income Fund 05/04/2018

BARCLAYS TOP 100 EQUAL WEIGHTED INCOME FD (ON)
Name changed to BG Top 100 Equal Weighted Income Fund 11/01/2006
BG Top 100 Equal Weighted Income Fund merged into Brompton VIP Income Fund 07/04/2008 which name changed to Aston Hill VIP Income Fund 09/16/2011 which name changed to LOGiQ VIP Income Fund 05/12/2017 which name changed to Redwood Monthly Income Fund 12/20/2017 which merged into Purpose Multi-Asset Income Fund 05/04/2018

BARCLAYS WEST INC (CO)
Name changed to Delta-Omega Technologies, Inc. 12/22/1989

BARCLIFF APARTMENTS
Trust terminated 00/00/1949
Details not available

BARCO CALIF (CA)
Common $1 par split (5) for (2) by issuance of (1.5) additional shares 06/26/1974
Each share old Common $1 par exchanged for (0.00001179) share new Common $1 par 03/19/1997
Note: In effect holders received $1.63 cash per share and public interest was eliminated

BARCO GASOLINE CO. (OK)
Charter cancelled for failure to file reports and pay fees 01/15/1935

BARCODE HLDGS LTD (AB)
Name changed to iSCOPE Inc. 05/12/2005
(See iSCOPE Inc.)

BARD C R INC (NY)
Reincorporated 04/17/1972
Capital Stock 25¢ par split (3) for (2) by issuance of (0.5) additional share 01/10/1966
Capital Stock 25¢ par split (2) for (1) by issuance of (1) additional share 09/15/1967
State of incorporation changed from (NY) to (NJ) 04/17/1972
Common 25¢ par split (2) for (1) by issuance of (1) additional share 04/28/1972
Common 25¢ par split (3) for (2) by issuance of (0.5) additional share 12/01/1982
Common 25¢ par split (2) for (1) by issuance of (1) additional share 05/30/1986
Common 25¢ par split (2) for (1) by issuance of (1) additional share 09/30/1988
Common 25¢ par split (2) for (1) by issuance of (1) additional share payable 05/28/2004 to holders of record 05/17/2004 Ex date - 06/01/2004

Merged into Becton, Dickinson & Co. 12/29/2017
Each share Common 25¢ par exchanged for (0.5077) share Common $1 par and $222.93 cash

BARD SILVER & GOLD LTD (BC)
Recapitalized as Consolidated Bard Silver & Gold Ltd. 05/14/1999
Each share Common no par exchanged for (0.2) share Common no par

BARD SPORTS CORP (DE)
Each (29) shares old Common $0.001 par exchanged for (1) share new Common $0.001 par 10/15/1988
Name changed to USA Sports Group Inc. 04/16/1994
USA Sports Group Inc. name changed to Collectible Concepts Group Inc. 06/29/1999
(See Collectible Concepts Group Inc.)

BARDEN CORP (CT)
Common $1 par split (2) for (1) by issuance of (1) additional share 12/16/1977
Common $1 par split (6) for (5) by issuance of (0.2) additional share 03/15/1989
Stock Dividend - 25% 03/17/1981
Merged into FAG Finance Corp. 12/21/1990
Each share Common $1 par exchanged for $66.50 cash

BARDINE OILS LTD (BC)
Struck off register and declared dissolved for failure to file returns 07/24/1992

BARDSTOWN DISTILLERY, INC.
Name changed to Barbon Corp. 00/00/1941
(See Barbon Corp.)

BARDSTOWN PARTNERS LTD (IL)
Liquidation completed
Each Unit of Ltd. Partnership received initial distribution of $16.60 cash 11/15/1982
Each Unit of Ltd. Partnership received second and final distribution of $0.9809 cash 02/21/1984
Note: Certificates were not required to be surrendered and are without value

BARE ESCENTUALS INC (DE)
Acquired by Shiseido Co., Ltd. 03/12/2010
Each share Common $0.001 par exchanged for $18.20 cash

BARECO INVESTMENT CO. (DE)
Merged into American Mutual Fund, Inc. (DE) 05/02/1958
Each share Common $1 par exchanged for (0.9326084) share Capital Stock $1 par
American Mutual Fund, Inc. (DE) reincorporated in Maryland 09/20/1983 which reincorporated in Delaware as American Mutual Fund 01/01/2011

BARECO OIL CO. (DE)
Each share Common $1 par exchanged for (0.1) share Common $5 par 00/00/1940
Common $5 par changed to $1 par and $4 in cash distributed 00/00/1946
Name changed to Bareco Investment Co. 05/09/1957
Bareco Investment Co. merged into American Mutual Fund, Inc. (DE) 05/02/1958 which reincorporated in Maryland 09/30/1983 which reincorporated in Delaware as American Mutual Fund 01/01/2011

BAREFOOT INC (DE)
Common 1¢ par split (2) for (1) by issuance of (1) additional share 07/15/1994
Merged into ServiceMaster Limited Partnership 02/24/1997

Each share Common 1¢ par exchanged for $16 cash

BAREL DUC CHIBOUGAMAU LTD. (ON)
Name changed to Bar-Le-Duc Chibougamau Mines Ltd. 00/00/1953
(See Bar-Le-Duc Chibougamau Mines Ltd.)

BARETTA MNG LTD (AB)
Merged into American Chromium Ltd. 01/01/1982
Each share Common no par exchanged for (1) share Conv. Class A Common no par and (1) share Class B Common no par
American Chromium Ltd. merged into Rhonda Mining Corp. 01/31/1992 which name changed to Rhonda Corp. 06/26/2000
(See Rhonda Corp.)

BAREXOR MINERALS INC (QC)
Company ceased operations 09/30/1997
Details not available

BARGAIN CENTER, INC. (VA)
Merged into ALT Corp. 09/24/1976
Each share Common $1 par exchanged for $7 cash

BARGAIN CENTERS, INC. (DE)
Merged into Bargain Center, Inc. (VA) 10/10/1962
Each share Common 10¢ par exchanged for (0.5) share Common $1 par
(See Bargain Center, Inc.)

BARGAIN CITY, U.S.A., INC. (PA)
Adjudicated bankrupt 05/08/1968
No stockholders' equity

BARGAIN PRODS INC (NV)
Each share Common 1¢ par exchanged for (0.01) share Common 10¢ par 07/29/1997
Each share old Common 10¢ par exchanged for (0.1) share new Common 10¢ par 04/27/1998
Name changed to Blini Hut, Inc. 05/11/1999
Blini Hut, Inc. recapitalized as UDS Group, Inc. 02/22/2005

BARGAIN TOWN, U.S.A. INC. (NY)
Name changed to Retail Centers of the Americas, Inc. 01/21/1965
Retail Centers of the Americas, Inc. merged into National Industries, Inc. (KY) 07/01/1968 which merged into Fuqua Industries, Inc. 01/03/1978 which name changed to Actava Group Inc. 07/21/1993 which name changed to Metromedia International Group, Inc. 11/01/1995
(See Metromedia International Group, Inc.)

BARGAINCITY COM INC (NV)
Charter revoked for failure to file reports and pay fees 07/05/2000

BARGIS MINES LTD. (ON)
Charter revoked for failure to file reports and pay taxes 12/16/1957

BARGNESI MINES LTD. (ON)
Charter cancelled for failure to pay taxes and file returns 05/00/1976

BARGO ENERGY CO (TX)
Merged into Mission Resources Corp. 05/16/2001
Each share Common 1¢ par exchanged for (0.09577326) share Common 1¢ par and $0.4517146 cash
(See Mission Resources Corp.)

BARGOLD MINES LTD. (ON)
Recapitalized as Ontex Mining Ltd. 01/02/1970
Each share Capital Stock $1 par exchanged for (0.25) share Common $1 par
Ontex Mining Ltd. recapitalized as Ontex Resources Ltd. 05/04/1981 which recapitalized as Goldstone Resources Inc. 12/22/2009 which merged into Premier Gold Mines Ltd. 08/16/2011

BARGOLD RES LTD (BC)
Name changed to Indusmin Energy Corp. 11/07/2000
Indusmin Energy Corp. name changed to Transeuro Energy Corp. 10/07/2004

BARIMA GOLD MINING CO. (CANADA) LTD. (ON)
Name changed to Barima Minerals Ltd. 09/26/1955
(See Barima Minerals Ltd.)

BARIMA MINERALS LTD (ON)
Charter cancelled for failure to pay taxes and file returns 02/14/1973

BARISAN GOLD CORP (BC)
Recapitalized as Lithion Energy Corp. 05/02/2017
Each share Common no par exchanged for (0.2) share Common no par

BARIUM STAINLESS STEEL CORP. (DE)
Name changed to Barium Steel Corp. (DE) 00/00/1944
Barium Steel Corp. (DE) name changed to Phoenix Steel Corp. 05/04/1959
(See Phoenix Steel Corp.)

BARIUM STEEL CORP. (DE)
Each share Common $1 par exchanged for (0.25) share Common $4 par 05/09/1958
Name changed to Phoenix Steel Corp. 05/04/1959
(See Phoenix Steel Corp.)

BARIUM STEEL CORP. (OH)
Acquired by Barium Stainless Steel Corp. 00/00/1936
Details not available

BARK GROUP INC (NV)
Common $0.001 par split (20) for (1) by issuance of (19) additional shares payable 08/17/2009 to holders of record 08/13/2009
Ex date - 08/18/2009
Name changed to United Communications Partners Inc. 03/25/2011

BARKENTE INC (UT)
Reorganized under the laws of Delaware as Desktop Broker, Inc. 04/02/1985
Each share Common $0.001 par exchanged for (0.2) share Common $0.001 par
(See Desktop Broker, Inc. (DE))

BARKER BROS. CORP. (MD)
Each share 6.5% Preferred $100 par exchanged for (2.33333333) shares 5.5% Preferred $50 par, (1) share Common no par and $10 cash 01/00/1937
5.5% Preferred $50 par reclassified as 4.5% Preferred $50 par 11/00/1945
Each share Common no par exchanged for (2) shares Common $10 par 04/25/1946
Common $10 par changed to $5 par and (1) additional share issued 09/21/1956
Merged into Barker Bros. Corp. (RI) 03/14/1958
Each share Common $5 par exchanged for (1.2) shares Common $1 par
Barker Bros. Corp. (RI) name changed to Larchfield Corp. 10/05/1960
(See Larchfield Corp.)

BARKER BROS. CORP. (RI)
Name changed to Larchfield Corp. 10/05/1960
(See Larchfield Corp.)

BARKER DOME OIL & GAS CO.
Merged into Delhi Oil Corp. on a share for share basis 00/00/1947
Delhi Oil Corp. merged into Delhi-Taylor Oil Corp. 00/00/1955
(See Delhi-Taylor Oil Corp.)

BARKER RES LTD (BC)
Name changed to Nortek Engines Ltd. 07/26/1977
Nortek Engines Ltd. name changed to Nortek Energy Corp. 09/24/1979 which name changed to Nortek Capital Corp. 10/03/1988 which recapitalized as Brigdon Resources Inc. 11/05/1991 which name changed to Tikal Resources Inc. 02/05/1999 which merged into Tikal Resources Corp. 05/31/1999 which was acquired by BelAir Energy Corp. 12/14/2001 which merged into Purcell Energy Ltd. (New) 09/04/2003
(See Purcell Energy Ltd. (New))

BARKER'S BAKERIES LTD.
Assets sold to Canadian Food Products, Ltd. 00/00/1945
Details not available

BARKER'S BREAD, LTD.
Name changed to Barker's Bakeries, Ltd. 00/00/1945
(See Barker's Bakeries, Ltd.)

BARKERVILLE MNG LTD (BC)
Merged into Austar Resources Inc. 11/01/1990
Each share Capital Stock $1 par exchanged for (0.25) share Common no par
Austar Resources Inc. recapitalized as Austpro Energy Corp. 01/31/1996

BARKHOR RES INC (BC)
Recapitalized as Latigo Resources Inc. 12/01/1998
Each share Common no par exchanged for (0.2) share Common no par
Latigo Resources Inc. name changed to LGO Net.Com Inc. (BC) 07/05/1999 which reincorporated in Alberta as Prolific Technology Inc. 01/26/2001 which recapitalized as Klad Enterprises Ltd. 03/18/2002 which merged into Diamond Hawk Mining Inc. (AB) 02/09/2005 which reincorporated in British Columbia 07/04/2005

BARKLEY-GROW AIRCRAFT CORP.
Acquired by Aviation Corp. 00/00/1940
Details not available

BARKLEY VY MINES LTD (BC)
Struck off register and declared dissolved for failure to file returns 07/22/1974

BARLOW & SEELIG MANUFACTURING CO.
Name changed to Speed Queen Corp. 00/00/1949
Speed Queen Corp. acquired by McGraw Electric Co. 09/30/1956 which name changed to McGraw-Edison Co. 01/02/1957
(See McGraw-Edison Co.)

BARLOW (SOUTH AFRICA)
Stock Dividends - 0.76302% payable 07/31/1997 to holders of record 06/13/1997; 2.2529% payable 01/30/1998 to holders of record 12/05/1997; 1.1398% payable 07/27/1998 to holders of record 06/12/1998
Name changed to Barloworld Ltd. 10/02/2000

BARLOW RAND LTD. (SOUTH AFRICA)
Name changed to Barlow Ltd. 01/24/1994
Barlow Ltd. name changed to Barloworld Ltd. 10/02/2000

BARLUM TOWER CORP. (MI)
Completely liquidated 12/29/1961
Each share Common $1 par exchanged for first and final distribution of $10 principal amount 6% Notes due 01/15/1982 and $3.013 cash

BARNABUS ENERGY INC (NV)
Name changed 05/12/2005
Each share old Common $0.001 par exchanged for (15) shares new Common $0.001 par 03/03/2004
Name changed from Barnabus Enterprises Ltd. to Barnabus Energy Inc. 05/12/2005
Name changed to Open Energy Corp. 04/21/2006
Open Energy Corp. name changed to Applied Solar, Inc. 01/20/2009
(See Applied Solar, Inc.)

BARNARD AVIATION EQUIPMENT CO., INC. (DE)
Name changed to General Aviation Equipment Co., Inc. 00/00/1941
General Aviation Equipment Co., Inc. name changed to General Aviation Corp. 00/00/1952
(See General Aviation Corp.)

BARNARD MANUFACTURING CO.
Bankrupt 00/00/1939
Details not available

BARNAT MINES LTD (QC)
Merged into Lake Shore Mines, Ltd. 03/31/1970
Each share Capital Stock $1 par exchanged for (0.2) share Capital Stock $1 par
Lake Shore Mines, Ltd. merged into LAC Minerals Ltd. (New) 07/29/1985 which was acquired by American Barrick Resources Corp. 10/17/1994 which name changed to Barrick Gold Corp. 01/18/1995

BARNES CORP (PA)
Merged into Bunker Ramo Corp. (New) 05/07/1971
Each share Common no par exchanged for (0.4156) share Common no par
Bunker Ramo Corp. (New) merged into Allied Corp. 07/31/1981 which merged into Allied-Signal Inc. 09/19/1985 which name changed to AlliedSignal Inc. 04/26/1993 which name changed to Honeywell International Inc. 12/01/1999

BARNES CREEK OIL CO., INC. (LA)
Charter revoked for failure to file annual reports 05/13/1982

BARNES ENGR CO (DE)
Merged into EDO Corp. 06/28/1986
Each share Common $1 par exchanged for $5.75 cash

BARNES HIND PHARMACEUTICALS INC (CA)
Merged into Revlon, Inc. 12/31/1976
Each share Common no par exchanged for (1.4666) share Common $1 par
(See Revlon, Inc.)

BARNES JAMES T WASH D C INC (DC)
Under plan of merger each share Common 10¢ par exchanged for $0.30 cash 12/30/1986

BARNES MTG INVT TR (MA)
Merged into Homac-Barnes, Inc. 09/28/1979
Each Share of Bene. Int. no par exchanged for (1) share Common $1 par
Homac-Barnes, Inc. name changed to Homac Inc. 04/10/1981 which name changed to Oxidyne Group, Inc. 05/27/1988
(See Oxidyne Group, Inc.)

BARNES REALTY LIQUIDATING CO.
Liquidated 00/00/1941
Details not available

BARNESANDNOBLE COM INC (DE)
Merged into Barnes & Noble, Inc. 05/27/2004
Each share Class A Common $0.001 par exchanged for $3.05 cash

BARNET LEATHER CO., INC.
Liquidation completed 00/00/1944
Details not available

BARNETT BANK AT WESTCHESTER, N.A. (MIAMI, FL)
95% held by Barnett Banks of Florida, Inc. as of 10/01/1972
Public interest eliminated

BARNETT BK JACKSONVILLE N A (JACKSONVILLE, FL)
Merged into Barnett Banks of Florida, Inc. 01/04/1982
Each share Common $20 par exchanged for (6.75) shares Common $2 par
Barnett Banks of Florida, Inc., name changed to Barnett Banks, Inc. 04/24/1987 which merged into NationsBank Corp. 01/09/98 which reincorporated in Delaware as BankAmerica Corp. (Old) 09/25/1998 which merged into BankAmerica Corp. (New) 09/30/1998 which name changed to Bank of America Corp. 04/28/1999

BARNETT BKS INC (FL)
Name changed 04/24/1987
Common $4 par changed to $2 par and (1) additional share issued 10/15/1969
Common $2 par split (3) for (2) by issuance of (0.5) additional share 07/01/1981
$2.375 Conv. Preferred Ser. A 10¢ par called for redemption 03/05/1985
Common $2 par split (3) for (2) by issuance of (0.5) additional share 05/24/1985
Common $2 par split (3) for (2) by issuance of (0.5) additional share 08/25/1986
$2.50 Conv. Preferred Ser. C 10¢ par called for redemption 11/04/1986
$3.88 Conv. Preferred Ser. D 10¢ par called for redemption 03/10/1987
Name changed from Barnett Banks of Florida, Inc. to Barnett Banks, Inc. 04/24/1987
$4.25 Conv. Preferred Ser. E 10¢ par called for redemption 05/08/1987
$4 Conv. Preferred Ser. C 10¢ par called for redemption 10/16/1995
$4.50 Conv. Preferred Ser. A 10¢ par called for redemption 04/15/1996
Common $2 par split (2) for (1) by issuance of (1) additional share payable 09/16/1996 to holders of record 09/06/1996 Ex date - 09/17/1996
Merged into NationsBank Corp. (NC) 01/09/1998
Each share $2.50 Conv. Preferred Ser. B 10¢ par exchanged for (1) share $2.50 Conv. Preferred Ser. B no par
Each share Common $2 par exchanged for (1.1875) shares Common no par
NationsBank Corp. (NC) reincorporated in Delaware as BankAmerica Corp. (Old) 09/25/1998 which merged into BankAmerica Corp. (New) 09/30/1998 which name changed to Bank of America Corp. 04/28/1999

BARNETT ENERGY CORP (NV)
Recapitalized as WorldWide Strategies Inc. 07/08/2005
Each share Common $0.001 par exchanged for (0.5) share Common $0.001 par

BARNETT FINL CORP (WA)
Believed out of business 00/00/1990
Details not available

BARNETT 1ST NATL BK (JACKSONVILLE, FL)
Name changed to Barnett Bank of Jacksonville, N.A. (Jacksonville, FL) 05/31/1971
Barnett Bank of Jacksonville, N.A. (Jacksonville, FL) merged into Barnett Banks of Florida, Inc. 01/04/1982 which name changed to Barnett Banks, Inc. 04/24/1987 which merged into NationsBank Corp. (NC) 01/09/1998 which reincorporated in Delaware as BankAmerica Corp. (Old) 09/25/1998 which merged into BankAmerica Corp. (New) 09/30/1998 which name changed to Bank of America Corp. 04/28/1999

BARNETT INC (DE)
Merged into Wilmar Industries, Inc. 10/02/2000
Each share Common 1¢ par exchanged for $13.15 cash

BARNETT J S & SON INC (WA)
Name changed to Barnett Financial Corp. 11/12/1970
(See Barnett Financial Corp.)

BARNETT MTG TR (FL)
Name changed to TRECO 07/05/1978
TRECO reincorporated in Delaware as Treco, Inc. 05/03/1979 which reincorporated in Florida 06/25/1980 which merged into Sunstates Corp. (FL) 01/30/1985 which merged into Acton Corp. 05/01/1988 which name changed to Sunstates Corp. (New) 01/03/1994
(See Sunstates Corp. (New))

BARNETT NATIONAL BANK (JACKSONVILLE, FL)
Each share Common $100 par exchanged for (6) shares Common $20 par to effect a (5) for (1) split and a 20% stock dividend 10/03/1955
Stock Dividends - 33.33333333% 01/25/1951; 25% 01/28/1954; 14.28571428% 02/02/1959; 25% 02/02/1961; 20% 02/01/1965
Name changed to Barnett First National Bank (Jacksonville, FL) 04/01/1965
Barnett First National Bank (Jacksonville, FL) name changed to Barnett Bank of Jacksonville, N.A. (Jacksonville, FL) 05/31/1971 which merged into Barnett Banks of Florida, Inc. 01/04/1982 which name changed to Barnett Banks, Inc. 04/24/1987 which merged into NationsBank Corp. (NC) 01/09/1998 which reincorporated in Delaware as BankAmerica Corp. (Old) 09/25/1998 which merged into BankAmerica Corp. (New) 09/30/1998 which name changed to Bank of America Corp. 04/28/1999

BARNETT NATIONAL BANK (ST. PETERSBURG, FL)
Through voluntary exchange offer Barnett Banks of Florida, Inc. held 98% excluding directors qualifying shares as of 04/19/1971
Public interest eliminated

BARNETT NATL SECS CORP (FL)
Name changed to Barnett Banks of Florida, Inc. 10/03/1969
Barnett Banks of Florida, Inc. name changed to Barnett Banks, Inc. 04/24/1987 which merged into NationsBank Corp. (NC) 01/09/1998 which reincorporated in Delaware as BankAmerica Corp. (Old) 09/25/1998 which merged into BankAmerica Corp. (New) 09/30/1998 which name changed to Bank of America Corp. 04/28/1999

BARNETT WINSTON INVT TR (FL)
Name changed to Compass Investment Group 12/04/1978
Compass Investment Group reorganized as American Pacific Corp. 03/30/1981
(See American Pacific Corp.)

BARNEYS N Y INC (DE)
Merged into Jones Apparel Group, Inc. 12/20/2004
Each share Common 1¢ par exchanged for $19 cash

BARNSDALL CORP.
Name changed to Barnsdall Oil Co. 00/00/1936
(See Barnsdall Oil Co.)

BARNSDALL OIL CO.
Merged into Sunray Oil Corp. 00/00/1950
Each share Common $5 par exchanged for (3) shares 5.5% 2nd Preferred $20 par
(See Sunray Oil Corp.)

BARNSDALL REFINING CORP.
Name changed to Bareco Oil Co. 00/00/1940
Bareco Oil Co. name changed to Bareco Investment Co. 05/09/1957 which merged into American Mutual Fund, Inc. (DE) 05/02/1958 which reincorporated in Maryland 09/20/1983 which reincorporated in Delaware as American Mutual Fund 01/01/2011

BARNSTABLE WTR CO (MA)
Merged into Connecticut Water Service, Inc. 02/23/2001
Each share Common $100 par exchanged for (19.21) shares Common no par
6% Preferred $100 par called for redemption at $105 on 11/01/2006

BARNWELL OFFSHORE, INC. (DE)
Name changed to Barnwell Industries, Inc. 09/01/1961

BAROID CORP (OLD) (DE)
Name changed to Tremont Corp. 10/29/1990
Tremont Corp. merged into Valhi, Inc. 02/07/2003

BAROID CORP NEW (DE)
Merged into Dresser Industries, Inc. (New) 01/21/1994
Each share Common 10¢ par exchanged for (0.4) share Common 25¢ par
Dresser Industries, Inc. (New) merged into Halliburton Co. 09/29/1998

BAROMA INC (NV)
Recapitalized as GoooGreen, Inc. 01/20/2016
Each share Common $0.001 par exchanged for (0.00125) share Common $0.001 par

BARON CAP PPTYS L P (DE)
Plan of reorganization under Chapter 11 Federal Bankruptcy Code effective 11/01/2005
Each Unit of Ltd. Partnership exchanged for initial distribution of $2.25 cash
Note: Upon surrender holders will receive a written notice of their respective trust interest

BARON CAP TR (DE)
Plan of reorganization under Chapter 11 Federal Bankruptcy Code effective 11/01/2005
Each share Common no par exchanged for initial distribution of $2.25 cash

BARON DATA SYS (CA)
Merged into Convergent Inc. 05/27/1987
Each share Common 10¢ par exchanged for $15 cash

BARON GOLD CORP (BC)
Name changed to BG Baron Group Inc. 03/20/1998
BG Baron Group Inc. recapitalized as Consolidated BG Baron Group Inc. 10/25/1999 which name changed to In.Sync Industries Inc. 04/03/2000 which name changed to Jet Gold Corp. 05/27/2003 which recapitalized as Deep-South Resources Inc. 11/16/2016

BARON INDS CORP (DE)
Reincorporated 12/30/1969
State of incorporation changed from (AZ) to (DE) 12/30/1969
Out of business and assets sold for benefit of note holder 06/00/1972
No stockholders' equity

BARONET PRODUCTS, INC. (UT)
Name changed to Continental Properties, Inc. 06/10/1963
(See Continental Properties, Inc.)

BARONS OIL LTD (AB)
Merged into Conwest Exploration Co. Ltd. (Old) 06/03/1990
Each share Common no par exchanged for (0.25) share Class B no par
Conwest Exploration Co. Ltd. (Old) merged into Conwest Exploration Co. Ltd. (New) (AB) 09/01/1993 which merged into Alberta Energy Co. Ltd. 01/31/1996 which merged into EnCana Corp. 01/03/2003

BARONY COPPER MINES LTD. (ON)
Charter cancelled 04/08/1965
No stockholders' equity

BAROQUE RES LTD (BC)
Recapitalized as Greenfields Industries Inc. 02/09/1990
Each share Common no par exchanged for (0.2) share Common no par
Greenfields Industries Inc. recapitalized as Oracle Minerals Inc. 12/06/1993 which recapitalized as Prophet Minerals Corp. 05/02/1997 which name changed to Meridex Network Corp. 12/21/1999 which recapitalized as Meridex Software Corp. 02/13/2003 which name changed to Cannabis Technologies Inc. 05/21/2014 which name changed to InMed Pharmaceuticals Inc. 10/21/2014

BAROSSA COFFEE CO INC (NV)
Name changed to eCareer Holdings, Inc. 05/22/2013
(See eCareer Holdings, Inc.)

BAROTEX TECHNOLOGY CORP (NV)
Charter revoked 04/30/2013

BARPOINT COM INC (DE)
Stock Dividends - 3.252% payable 10/20/1999 to holders of record 06/02/1999; 42.9% payable 03/02/2004 to holders of record 02/17/2004 Ex date - 02/20/2004
Name changed to LoyaltyPoint, Inc. 04/21/2004
(See LoyaltyPoint, Inc.)

BARR CORP. (NY)
Assets liquidated for benefit of creditors 12/22/1965
No stockholders' equity

BARR FINL LTD (CA)
Charter cancelled for failure to file reports and pay taxes 08/01/1972

BARR PHARMACEUTICALS INC (DE)
Reincorporated 12/31/2003
Common 1¢ par split (3) for (2) by issuance of (0.5) additional share 09/30/1986
Common 1¢ par split (3) for (2) by issuance of (0.5) additional share payable 03/25/1996 to holders of record 03/04/1996 Ex date - 03/26/1996
Common 1¢ par split (3) for (2) by issuance of (0.5) additional share payable 05/07/1997 to holders of record 04/24/1997 Ex date - 05/08/1997
Common 1¢ par split (3) for (2) by issuance of (0.5) additional share

payable 06/28/2000 to holders of record 06/12/2000
Common 1¢ par split (3) for (2) by issuance of (0.5) additional share payable 03/17/2003 to holders of record 02/28/2003 Ex date - 03/18/2003
Name and state of incorporation changed from Barr Laboratories, Inc. (NY) to Barr Pharmaceuticals, Inc. (DE) 12/31/2003
Common 1¢ par split (3) for (2) by issuance of (0.5) additional share payable 03/15/2004 to holders of record 02/23/2004 Ex date - 03/16/2004
Acquired by Teva Pharmaceutical Industries Ltd. 12/23/2008
Each share Common 1¢ par exchanged for (0.6272) ADR for Ordinary NIS 0.001 par and $39.90 cash

BARRA INC (DE)
Reincorporated 08/14/1998
Common no par split (3) for (2) by issuance of (0.5) additional share payable 10/13/1997 to holders of record 09/22/1997
State of incorporation changed from (CA) to (DE) and Common no par changed to $0.0001 par 08/14/1998
Acquired by Morgan Stanley 06/03/2004
Each share Common $0.0001 par exchanged for $41 cash

BARRACK TECHNOLOGY LTD (AUSTRALIA)
ADR agreement terminated 08/23/2013
No ADR holders' equity

BARRACUDA NETWORKS INC (DE)
Acquired by Thoma Bravo, LLC 02/12/2018
Each share Common $0.001 par exchanged for $27.55 cash

BARRACUDA RES LTD (BC)
Common no par split (3) for (2) by issuance of (2) additional shares 05/08/1984
Name changed to International Laser Tech Inc. 07/18/1985
(See International Laser Tech Inc.)

BARRAMUNDI GOLD LTD (BC)
Reorganized under the laws of Canada as PacRim Resources Ltd. 11/12/2002
Each share Common no par exchanged for (0.1) share Common no par
(See PacRim Resources Ltd.)

BARRANCO RES CORP (BC)
Name changed to Goldeneye Resources Corp. 10/31/2012

BARRET BANCORP INC (TN)
Merged into Trustmark Corp. 04/06/2001
Each share Common exchanged for (457.0841) shares Common $2.50 par

BARRETT BILL CORP (DE)
Name changed to HighPoint Resources Corp. 03/20/2018

BARRETT INDS INC (DE)
Completely liquidated 09/26/1975
Each share Common 1¢ par exchanged for first and final distribution of $1.80 cash

BARRETT RES CORP (DE)
Reincorporated 07/22/1987
State of incorporation changed from (CO) to (DE) 07/22/1987
Each share Common $0.001 par exchanged for (0.05) share Common 1¢ par 09/20/1987
Merged into Williams Companies, Inc. 08/02/2001
Each share Common 1¢ par exchanged for (1.767) shares Common $1 par

BARRETVILLE BK & TR CO (BARRETVILLE, TN)
Under plan of reorganization each share Common $100 par automatically became (1) share Barret Bancorp Inc. Common $100 par 02/17/1999
Barret Bancorp Inc. merged into Trustmark Corp. 04/06/2001

BARRICINI FOODS INC (DE)
Reincorporated 07/29/1987
State of incorporation changed from (NY) to (DE) 07/29/1987
Charter cancelled and declared inoperative and void for non-payment of taxes 09/27/1995

BARRICK GOLD INC (AB)
Reincorporated 05/09/2006
Place of incorporation changed from (ON) to (AB) 05/09/2006
Each Exchangeable Share no par exchanged for (0.53) share Barrick Gold Corp. Common no par 03/02/2009

BARRICK KENTUCKY OIL & GAS CO. (DE)
Charter cancelled and declared inoperative and void for non-payment of franchise taxes 03/16/1927

BARRICK RES CORP (ON)
Recapitalized as American Barrick Resources Corp. 12/06/1985
Each share $0.114 Conv. 1st Preferred Ser. A no par automatically became (1) share $0.114 Conv. 1st Preferred Ser. A no par
Each share $0.222 Conv. Exchangeable 2nd Preferred Ser. A no par became (1) share $0.222 Conv. Exchangeable 2nd Preferred Ser. A no par
Each share Common no par exchanged for (0.2) share Common no par
American Barrick Resources Corp. name changed to Barrick Gold Corp. 01/18/1995

BARRICODE INC (NV)
Common $0.001 par split (2) for (1) by issuance of (1) additional share payable 03/05/2009 to holders of record 03/05/2009
Common $0.001 par split (10) for (1) by issuance of (9) additional shares payable 12/30/2009 to holders of record 11/26/2009 Ex date - 12/31/2009
Name changed to Polar Wireless Corp. 06/21/2010

BARRIE MILTON R & CO INC (NY)
Charter cancelled and proclaimed dissolved for failure to pay taxes 12/30/1981

BARRIE RICHARD FRAGRANCES INC (NV)
Each share old Common $0.005 par exchanged for (0.33333333) share Common $0.005 par 03/09/1994
Name changed to FBR Capital Corp. 06/30/1996
FBR Capital Corp. name changed to Vitrix, Inc. 10/07/1999 which name changed to Time America, Inc. 12/09/2003 which name changed to NETtime Solutions, Inc. 05/11/2007 which name changed to Tempco, Inc. 10/14/2008 which name changed to Esio Water & Beverage Development Corp. 01/18/2013 which name changed to UPD Holding Corp. 03/01/2017

BARRIER EXPL N L (AUSTRALIA)
Name changed to Helm Corp. Ltd. 07/15/1985
(See Helm Corp. Ltd.)

BARRIER INTL CORP (NV)
Recapitalized as MATCO Enterprises Inc. 07/30/1998
Each share Common $0.0005 par exchanged for (0.005) share Common $0.0005 par
MATCO Enterprises Inc. recapitalized as PetroQuest Resources, Inc. 11/30/2005

BARRIER MNG CORP (BC)
Delisted from Vancouver Stock Exchange 05/31/2001

BARRIER REEF RES LTD (BC)
Capital Stock 50¢ par changed to no par 05/14/1979
Recapitalized as Consolidated Barrier Reef Resources Ltd. 10/01/1984
Each share Capital Stock no par exchanged for (0.2) share Common no par
Consolidated Barrier Reef Resources Ltd. name changed to M F C Mining Finance Corp. 05/05/1986 which merged into MinVen Gold Corp. 08/12/1988 which reorganized as Dakota Mining Corp. 09/15/1993
(See Dakota Mining Corp.)

BARRIER SCIENCE & TECHNOLOGY INC (DE)
Charter cancelled and declared inoperative and void for non-payment of taxes 03/01/1989

BARRIER TECHNOLOGY INC (BC)
Recapitalized as International Barrier Technology Inc. 03/11/1996
Each share Common no par exchanged for (0.1) share Common no par
(See International Barrier Technology Inc.)

BARRIER THERAPEUTICS INC (DE)
Merged into Stiefel Laboratories, Inc. 08/06/2008
Each share Common $0.0001 par exchanged for $4.15 cash

BARRIERE LAKE MINERALS LTD. (BC)
Name changed to Geneva Resources Ltd. 07/00/1972
Geneva Resources Ltd. name changed to Pacific Jade Industries Inc. 12/00/1973
(See Pacific Jade Industries Inc.)

BARRIERE LAKE MINES LTD. (BC)
Recapitalized as Barriere Lake Minerals Ltd. 09/18/1967
Each share Capital Stock no par exchanged for (0.1) share Capital Stock no par
Barriere Lake Minerals Ltd. name changed to Geneva Resources Ltd 07/00/1972 which name changed to Pacific Jade Industries Inc. 12/00/1983
(See Pacific Jade Industries Inc.)

BARRINCORP INDS INC (ON)
Merged into DBC Acquisition Corp. 11/17/1989
Each share Subordinate no par exchanged for $5.55 cash

BARRINGER LABS INC (DE)
Company terminated registration of common stock and is no longer public as of 08/11/2000

BARRINGER RESEARCH INC. (DE)
Stock Dividend - 100% 03/25/1980
Name changed to Barringer Resources, Inc. 05/22/1980
Barringer Resources, Inc. name changed to Barringer Technologies Inc. 02/12/1991
(See Barringer Technologies Inc.)

BARRINGER TECHNOLOGIES INC (DE)
Name changed 02/12/1991
Name changed from Barringer Resources, Inc. to Barringer Technologies, Inc. 02/12/1991
Each share old Common 1¢ par exchanged for (0.25) share new Common 1¢ par 09/25/1995
Merged into Smiths Group PLC 05/11/2001
Each share Conv. Preferred $2 par exchanged for $3.93 cash
Each share Class A Conv. Preferred $1 par exchanged for $4 cash
Each share new Common 1¢ par exchanged for $11.05 cash

BARRINGTON BANCORP INC (IL)
Merged into First Chicago NBD Corp. 06/06/1996
Each share Common $10 par exchanged for (0.589) share Common $1 par
First Chicago NBD Corp. merged into Bank One Corp. 10/02/1998 which merged into Morgan Chase & Co. 12/31/2000 which J.P. name changed to JPMorgan Chase & Co. 07/20/2004

BARRINGTON COURT, INC. (MA)
Reorganized as Barrington Court Trust 00/00/1949
Each share Common exchanged for (1) share Common
(See Barrington Court Trust)

BARRINGTON COURT TRUST (MA)
Liquidated 02/29/1956
Details not available

BARRINGTON ENTERPRISES LTD (AB)
Recapitalized as Phonettix Intellecom Ltd. 07/29/1994
Each share Common no par exchanged for (0.25) share Common no par
Phonettix Intellecom Ltd. name changed to Minacs Worldwide Inc. 07/21/1999
(See Minacs Worldwide Inc.)

BARRINGTON EXPL LTD (ON)
Charter cancelled for failure to pay taxes and file returns 03/16/1976

BARRINGTON FOODS INTL INC (NV)
Recapitalized as U.S. Canadian Minerals, Inc. 01/20/2004
Each share Common $0.001 par exchanged for (0.008) share Common $0.001 par
U.S. Canadian Minerals, Inc. name changed to Noble Consolidated Industries Corp. 01/15/2010
(See Noble Consolidated Industries Corp.)

BARRINGTON INDS INC (DE)
Class A Common 10¢ par and Class B Common 10¢ par reclassified as Common 10¢ par 08/21/1970
Merged into Wilson Brothers 09/20/1974
Each share Common 10¢ par exchanged for (0.125) share Common $1 par
Wilson Brothers name changed to Wilson Brothers USA, Inc. 08/20/1997
(See Wilson Brothers USA, Inc.)

BARRINGTON LABORATORIES INC (NV)
Name changed to ModernGroove Entertainment, Inc. 01/01/2001
ModernGroove Entertainment, Inc. name changed to Immediatek, Inc. 12/09/2002

BARRINGTON LAKE COPPER MINES, LTD. (ON)
Liquidated 00/00/1955
Details not available

BARRINGTON PETE LTD (BC)
Name changed 02/07/1985
Name changed from Barrington Properties Ltd. to Barrington Petroleum Ltd. 02/07/1985
Each share Common no par exchanged for (1) share Common no par
Merged into Petrobank Energy & Resources Ltd. (Old) 07/18/2001
Each share Common no par

exchanged for (0.33333333) share Common no par
Petrobank Energy & Resources Ltd. (Old) reorganized as Petrobank Energy & Resources Ltd. (New) 01/07/2013 which recapitalized as Touchstone Exploration Inc. 05/20/2014

BARRINGTON PPTYS LTD (AB)
Name changed Barrington Enterprises Ltd. 04/11/1988
Barrington Enterprises Ltd. recapitalized as Phonettix Intellecom Ltd. 07/29/1994 which name changed to Minacs Worldwide Inc. 07/21/1999
(See Minacs Worldwide Inc.)

BARRIS INDS INC (DE)
Common 50¢ par split (4) for (3) by issuance of (0.33333333) additional share 07/25/1985
Name changed to Guber-Peters Entertainment Co. 09/07/1989
(See Guber-Peters Entertainment Co.)

BARRIS KLEIN HLDGS INC (ON)
Recapitalized as London Strauss Capital Corp. 05/14/1991
Each share Common no par exchanged for (0.11111111) share Common no par
London Strauss Capital Corp. name changed to Viking Gold Corp. 09/05/1996
(See Viking Gold Corp.)

BARRIS (CHUCK) PRODUCTIONS, INC. (DE)
Common 50¢ par split (3) for (2) by issuance of (0.5) additional share 01/04/1971
Common 50¢ par split (2) for (1) by issuance of (1) additional share 10/30/1978
Common 50¢ par split (2) for (1) by issuance of (1) additional share 09/13/1979
Stock Dividends - 10% 08/03/1973; 50% 02/16/1978
Name changed to Barris Industries Inc. 10/19/1981
Barris Industries Inc. name changed to Guber-Peters Entertainment Co. 09/07/1989
(See Guber-Peters Entertainment Co.)

BARRISTER GLOBAL SERVICES NETWORK INC (DE)
Reincorporated 10/07/1997
Name changed 06/02/2000
Common 24¢ par split (3) for (2) by issuance of (0.5) additional share 05/20/1986
Each share old Common 24¢ par exchanged for (0.16666666) share new Common 24¢ par 12/20/1991
State of incorporation changed from (NY) to (DE) 10/07/1997
Name changed from Barrister Information Systems Corp. to Barrister Global Services Network, Inc. 06/02/2000
Each share old Common 24¢ par exchanged for (0.002) share new Common 24¢ par 07/26/2004
Note: In effect holders received an undetermined amount of cash and public interest was eliminated

BARRISTERS HALL TRUST (MA)
Liquidation completed 00/00/1953
Details not available

BARRON HUNTER HARGRAVE STRATEGIC RES INC (BC)
Struck off register and declared dissolved for failure to file returns 08/05/1997

BARRY BUILDING CORP.
Liquidation completed 00/00/1951
Details not available

BARRY CONTROLS, INC. (MA)
Stock Dividend - 16.66666666% 04/20/1960
Merged into Barry-Wright Corp. 08/31/1960
Each share Class A Common $1 par or Class B Common $1 par exchanged for (1) share Common $1 par
(See Barry-Wright Corp.)

BARRY MARTIN PHARMACEUTICAL INC (FL)
Completely liquidated 03/01/1981
Each share Class A Common 10¢ par exchanged for first and final distribution of $1.70 cash

BARRY R G CORP (DE)
Reincorporated 05/08/1975
Common $1 par split (5) for (4) by issuance of (0.25) additional share 08/15/1968
Common $1 par split (5) for (4) by issuance of (0.25) additional share 06/18/1969
Common $1 par split (3) for (2) by issuance of (0.5) additional share 06/01/1972
Common $1 par split (3) for (2) by issuance of (0.5) additional share 06/01/1979
Stock Dividends - 10% 06/01/1965; 10% 06/01/1966; 10% 05/15/1967; 25% 01/18/1968; 10% 06/25/1970; 10% 06/15/1971
State of incorporation changed from (OH) to (DE) 05/08/1975
Reincorporated back under the laws of Ohio 06/22/1984
(See Barry (R.G.) Corp. (OH))

BARRY R G CORP (OH)
Common $1 par split (4) for (3) by issuance of (0.33333333) additional share 06/22/1994
Common $1 par split (4) for (3) by issuance of (0.33333333) additional share 09/15/1995
Common $1 par split (5) for (4) by issuance of (0.25) additional share payable 06/17/1996 to holders of record 06/03/1996 Ex date - 06/18/1996
Acquired by Mill Road Capital II, L.P. 09/04/2014
Each share Common $1 par exchanged for $19 cash

BARRY S JEWELERS INC (DE)
Merged into Unimax Group, Inc. 03/17/1977
Each share Common 10¢ par exchanged for (1.5) shares Common 75¢ par
Unimax Group, Inc. name changed to Unimax Corp. 09/11/1980
(See Unimax Corp.)

BARRY WRIGHT CORP (MA)
Common $1 par split (2) for (1) by issuance of (1) additional share 09/28/1967
Common $1 par split (2) for (1) by issuance of (1) additional share 02/01/1979
Common $1 par split (2) for (1) by issuance of (1) additional share 10/01/1980
Merged into Applied Power Inc. 09/28/1989
Each share Common $1 par exchanged for $12.40 cash

BARRYS JEWELERS INC NEW (CA)
Under plan of reorganization each share old Common no par exchanged for (0.1399) share new Common no par and (0.1599) Common Stock Purchase Warrant expiring 06/18/2002 on 06/30/1992
Each share new Common no par exchanged exchanged again for (0.2) share new Common no par 11/16/1994
Stock Dividend - 25% 12/20/1988
Reorganized under Chapter 11 Federal Bankruptcy Code as Samuels Jewelers, Inc. 10/02/1998
Each share new Common no par exchanged for (0.06530996) Common Stock Purchase Warrant expiring 09/29/2003
(See Samuels Jewelers, Inc.)

BARSAND RES INC (BC)
Name changed to Harvest-Spring Nutritional Systems (1981) Corp. 08/30/1990
Harvest-Spring Nutritional Systems (1981) Corp. recapitalized as Xemac Resources Inc. 05/21/1996 which recapitalized as Abitex Resources Inc. 03/26/2004 which recapitalized as ABE Resources Inc. 04/16/2013 which name changed to Vision Lithium Inc. 03/27/2018

BARSTAN ELECTRS CORP (DE)
Adjudicated bankrupt 05/08/1973
Stockholders' equity unlikely

BART MINES LTD (BC)
Struck off register and declared dissolved for failure to file returns 04/22/1983

BART PRODUCTS CO. (DE)
Voluntarily dissolved 03/23/1939
Details not available

BART RES LTD (BC)
Name changed to Thermo Tech International Inc. 05/12/1988
Thermo Tech International Inc. recapitalized as Consolidated Thermo Tech International Inc. 09/08/1989 which recapitalized as Thermo Tech Technologies Inc. (BC) 06/09/1992 which reincorporated in Yukon 04/11/2000

BARTACO INDS LTD (ON)
Under plan of merger name changed to Redlaw Industries Inc. 07/13/1979
(See Redlaw Industries Inc.)

BARTEL FINL GROUP INC (CO)
Recapitalized as Desert Springs Acquisition Corp. (CO) 03/01/1996
Each share Common $0.0001 par exchanged for (0.005) share Common $0.0001 par
Desert Springs Acquisiton Corp. (CO) reincorporated in Nevada as iDial Networks, Inc. 01/14/2000 which name changed to GlobalNet Corp. 12/19/2003
(See GlobalNet Corp.)

BARTELL BROADCASTING CORP. (DE)
Capital Stock $1 par changed to 50¢ par 05/25/1961
Under plan of merger name changed to MacFadden-Bartell Corp. 02/09/1962
MacFadden-Bartell Corp. name changed to Bartell Media Corp. 06/18/1965
(See Bartell Media Corp.)

BARTELL MEDIA CORP (DE)
Merged into Downe Communications, Inc. 02/04/1977
Each share Capital Stock 50¢ par exchanged for $1.25 cash

BARTEP INDS INC (CO)
Recapitalized as Douglas Pharmacal Industries, Inc. 12/15/1969
Each share Common 10¢ par exchanged for (0.33333333) share Common 10¢ par
Douglas Pharmacal Industries, Inc. name changed to Douglas Industries, Inc. 08/18/1976
(See Douglas Industries, Inc.)

BARTER OF AMER PLUS CORP (NV)
Name changed to Digilava Inc. 07/31/2002
Digilava Inc. recapitalized as WGE Holdings Corp. 05/27/2015

BARTER RES INC (UT)
Proclaimed dissolved for failure to pay taxes 08/01/1989

BARTGIS BROTHERS CO.
Merged into New Haven Board & Carton Co., Inc. 07/01/1957
Each share Common $1 par exchanged for (1.33333333) shares Common $10 par
New Haven Board & Carton Co., Inc. name changed to Simkins Industries, Inc. 09/01/1967
(See Simkins Industries, Inc.)

BARTH SPENCER CORP (NY)
Class A $1 par reclassified as Common $1 par 02/20/1968
Common $1 par split (5) for (4) by issuance of (0.25) additional share 03/31/1972
Merged into Darby Drug Co., Inc. 07/02/1981
Each share Common $1 par exchanged for $6 cash

BARTH VITAMIN CORP. (NY)
Stock Dividend - 50% 01/11/1966
Name changed to Barth-Spencer Corp. 02/09/1966
(See Barth-Spencer Corp.)

BARTHOLOMEW HOUSE LTD (DE)
Liquidated 04/27/1979
Details not available

BARTIZAN CAP CORP (AB)
Discharged from receivership 00/00/2006
No stockholders' equity

BARTLES-MAGUIRE OIL CO.
Acquired by Vacuum Oil Co. 00/00/1930
Details not available

BARTLETT CAP TR (MA)
Merged into Legg Mason Global Trust 09/23/1999
Details not available

BARTLETT MGMT TR (OH)
Enhanced Cash Reserves Fund reclassified as Cash Reserves Fund 07/30/1991
Under plan of reorganization each Cash Reserves Fund Share of Bene. Int. automatically became Legg Mason Cash Reserve Trust Shares of Bene. Int. on a net asset basis 12/00/1996
(See Legg Mason Cash Reserve Trust)
Under plan of reorganization each Fixed Income Fund Share of Bene. Int. automatically became Legg Mason U.S. Government Intermediate-Term Portfolio Shares of Bene. Int. on a net asset basis 12/00/1996

BARTLETT MUNROE MINES LTD. (ON)
Charter revoked for failure to file reports and pay fees 05/19/1958

BARTON BAY RES INC (ON)
Delisted from Toronto Venture Stock Exchange 06/20/2003

BARTON BRANDS INC (DE)
In process of liquidation
Each share Common $1 par exchanged for initial distribution of (1) Barton Brands, Ltd. Limited Partnership Unit 08/01/1972
Barton Brands, Ltd. name changed to Bardstown Partners, Ltd. 10/31/1982
(See Bardstown Partners, Ltd.)

BARTON BRANDS LTD (IL)
Name changed to Bardstown Partners, Ltd. 10/31/1982
(See Bardstown Partners, Ltd.)

BARTON DISTILLING CO (DE)
Name changed to Barton Brands, Inc. 01/15/1970
(See Barton Brands, Inc.)

BARTON INDS INC (OK)
Plan of reorganization under Chapter 11 Federal Bankruptcy proceedings confirmed 02/01/1992
Each share old Common 1¢ par

exchanged for (0.24213075) share new Common 1¢ par
Plan of reorganization under Chapter 11 Federal Bankruptcy proceedings confirmed 11/15/1993
No stockholders' equity

BARTON INSTRUMENT CORP. (CA)
Merged into International Telephone & Telegraph Corp. (MD) 11/30/1964
Each share Common no par exchanged for (0.2922) share Capital Stock no par
International Telephone & Telegraph Corp. (MD) reincorporated in Delaware 01/31/1968 which name changed to ITT Corp. 12/31/1983 which reorganized in Indiana as ITT Industries, Inc. 12/19/1995 which name changed to ITT Corp. 07/01/2006

BARTON VALVE INC (OK)
Common 1¢ par split (3) for (2) by issuance of (0.5) additional share 01/08/1982
Name changed to Barton Industries Inc. 02/26/1987
(See Barton Industries Inc.)

BARTONS CANDY CORP (NY)
Merged into American Safety Razor Co. 08/06/1981
Each share Common $1 par exchanged for $4 cash

BARUCH FOSTER CORP (DE)
Merged into BFC Acquisition Inc. 12/27/1990
Each share Common 50¢ par exchanged for $6.24 cash

BARUCH KENILIND OIL CORP. (DE)
Merged into Baruch-Foster Corp. 01/11/1960
Each share Capital Stock 10¢ par exchanged for (0.29069767) share Capital Stock 50¢ par
(See Baruch-Foster Corp.)

BARUCH OIL CORP. (DE)
Merged into Baruch Kenilind Oil Corp. 10/09/1956
Each share Capital Stock 10¢ par exchanged for (1) share Capital Stock 10¢ par
Baruch Kenilind Oil Corp. merged into Baruch-Foster Corp. 01/11/1960
(See Baruch-Foster Corp.)

BARVALLEE MINES LTD (QC)
Merged into Albarmont Mines Corp. 10/12/1971
Each share Capital Stock $1 par exchanged for (0.2) share Common no par
Albarmont Mines Corp. recapitalized as Albarmont (1985) Inc. 07/19/1985
(See Albarmont (1985) Inc.)

BARVUE EXTENSION LTD. (QC)
Company is defunct and charter was surrendered 04/30/1960

BARVUE MINES, LTD. (ON)
Merged into Manitou-Barvue Mines Ltd. 03/23/1959
Each share Capital Stock $1 par exchanged for (0.1) share Capital Stock $1 par
Manitou-Barvue Mines Ltd. name changed to Terratech Resources Inc. 08/31/1983
(See Terratech Resources Inc.)

BARWICK E T INDS INC (GA)
Assets foreclosed upon 00/00/1980
No stockholders' equity

BARYMIN CO. LTD. (ON)
Liquidation completed 11/23/1956
Details not available

BARYMIN EXPLS LTD (ON)
Capital Stock $1 par changed to 50¢ par and (1) Ctf. of Bene. Int. no par of Barex Trust distributed 11/09/1961
Capital Stock 50¢ par changed to no par 02/17/1971

Cease trade order effective 10/10/1985

BARYTEX RES CORP (BC)
Recapitalized as International Barytex Resources Ltd. 07/06/1993
Each share Common no par exchanged for (0.25) share Common no par
International Barytex Resources Ltd. merged into Kobex Minerals Inc. 09/30/2009 which name changed to Kobex Capital Corp. 08/29/2014 which name changed to Itasca Capital Ltd. 06/23/2016

BARZEL INDS INC (DE)
Plan of reorganization under Chapter 11 Federal Bankruptcy proceedings effective 09/07/2012
Stockholders' equity unlikely

BAS CONSULTING INC (NV)
Each share old Common $0.001 par exchanged for (0.15544513) share new Common $0.001 par 11/30/2005
Name changed to AIDA Pharmaceuticals, Inc. 03/06/2006

BASABA ENTERPRISES INC (BC)
Struck off register and declared dissolved for failure to file returns 05/08/1992

BASALT BAY MINES LTD (ON)
Charter cancelled for failure to pay taxes and file returns 05/18/1976

BASALT ROCK CO., INC. (CA)
Each share Common $25 par exchanged for (48) shares Common $1 par 00/00/1951
Common $1 par changed to 50¢ par and $8 cash distributed 07/21/1955
Acquired by Dillingham Corp. 09/30/1968
Each share Common 50¢ par exchanged for (0.15) share $2 Conv. Preferred October 1968 Ser. no par and (0.72) share Common no par
(See Dillingham Corp.)

BASALT URANIUM & EXPLORATION CO. LTD. (ON)
Recapitalized as Basalt Bay Mines Ltd. 05/00/1955
Each share Common $1 par exchanged for (0.5) share Common $1 par
(See Basalt Bay Mines Ltd.)

BASCO INC (DE)
Merged into Best Products Co., Inc. 06/28/1982
Each share Common 10¢ par exchanged for (0.33333333) share Common $1 par
(See Best Products Co., Inc.)

BASCO OIL & GAS LTD. (BC)
Acquired by Provo Gas Producers 11/23/1959
Each share Capital Stock no par exchanged for (0.33333333) share Capital Stock no par
Provo Gas Producers Ltd. acquired by Dome Petroleum Ltd. 06/28/1967
(See Dome Petroleum Ltd.)

BASCOM HILL INVS INC (WI)
Under plan of reorganization each share Common $1 par automatically became Mosaic Equity Trust Investors Fund on a net asset basis 06/13/1997

BASE INDUSTRIES, INC. (TX)
Charter forfeited for failure to pay taxes 01/18/1967

BASE METALS MNG CORP LTD (CANADA)
Charter dissolved 12/15/1980

BASE OF BRDG TECHNOLOGY LTD (AB)
Cease trade order 07/11/2007

BASE OIL & GAS LTD (AB)
Name changed to Marquee Petroleum Ltd. 09/20/2011

Marquee Petroleum Ltd. merged into SkyWest Energy Corp. 12/09/2011 which recapitalized as Marquee Energy Ltd. (Old) 12/09/2011 which merged into Marquee Energy Ltd. (New) 12/08/2016

BASE TEN SYS INC (NJ)
Common 50¢ par reclassified as Class B Common $1 par 12/05/1980
Each share Class B Common $1 par received distribution of (2) shares Class A Common $1 par 12/20/1980
Class A Common $1 par split (2) for (1) by issuance of (1) additional share 02/11/1983
Class B Common $1 par split (2) for (1) by issuance of (1) additional share 02/11/1983
Each share old Class A Common $1 par exchanged for (0.2) share new Class A Common $1 par 09/24/1999
Each share old Class B Common $1 par exchanged for (0.2) share new Class B Common $1 par 09/24/1999
Stock Dividends - 10% 02/22/1980; 10% 01/29/1982; 10% 02/24/1984
Each share new Class A Common $1 par exchanged again for (0.001) share new Class A Common $1 par 11/15/2002
Each share new Class B Common $1 par exchanged again for (0.001) share new Class B Common $1 par 11/15/2002
Note: In effect holders received $0.034 cash and public interest was eliminated

BASEBALL CARD SOCIETY INC (DE)
Each share old Common $0.0001 par exchanged for (0.02) share new Common $0.0001 par 04/06/1989
Charter cancelled and declared inoperative and void for non-payment of taxes 03/01/1994

BASEBALL PPTYS INC (DE)
Recapitalized as Therma Freeze Inc. 12/03/1996
Each share Common $0.001 par exchanged for (0.25) share Common $0.001 par
Therma Freeze Inc. name changed to Enviro-Energy Corp. 07/03/2001
(See Enviro-Energy Corp.)

BASELINE MINES LTD. (ON)
Charter cancelled 00/00/1970

BASELINE OIL & GAS CORP (NV)
Plan of reorganization under Chapter 11 Federal Bankruptcy proceedings effective 10/01/2009
No stockholders' equity

BASF AG (GERMANY)
Each old ADR for Common exchangend for (5) new ADR's for Common 01/30/1987
Each new ADR for Common exchanged for for (1) Sponsored ADR for Common 12/06/1999
Name changed to BASF SE 01/14/2008

BASHAW CAP CORP (CANADA)
Name changed to Dynamite Resources Ltd. (Old) 03/27/2006
Dynamite Resources Ltd. (Old) reorganized as Dynamite Resources Ltd. (New) 09/17/2007 which merged into Avion Resources Corp. 05/08/2009 which name changed to Avion Gold Corp. (BC) 06/05/2009 which reincorporated in Ontario 06/14/2011

BASHAW HLDGS LTD (AB)
Name changed to Bluestar Battery Systems International Corp. 07/27/1995
(See Bluestar Battery Systems International Corp.)

BASHAW LEDUC OIL & GAS LTD (AB)
Recapitalized as Canadian Bashaw Leduc Oil & Gas Ltd. 09/17/1979

Each share Capital Stock no par exchanged for (0.2) share Capital Stock no par
Canadian Bashaw Leduc Oil & Gas Ltd. recapitalized as Erskine Resources Corp. 06/23/1987 which was acquired by Mark Resources Inc. 01/01/1989 which was acquired by EnerMark Income Fund 04/09/1996 which merged into Enerplus Resources Fund 06/22/2001 which reorganized as Enerplus Corp. 01/03/2011

BASHINFORMSVYAZ OPEN JT STK CO (RUSSIA)
Each ADR agreement terminated 12/07/2015
Each Sponsored ADR for Ordinary exchanged for $8.020974 cash

BASHNEY BISCUIT INC (FL)
Recapitalized as Magna Technologies Inc. 03/08/1985
Each share Common 10¢ par exchanged for (0.25) share Common $0.004 par
(See Magna Technologies Inc.)

BASIC AMERN CORP (UT)
Merged into Dynamic American Corp. 12/21/1982
Each share Common $5 par exchanged for (5) shares Common $1 par
(See Dynamic American Corp.)

BASIC AMERN MED INC (IN)
Stock Dividends - 10% 06/28/1985; 10% 06/27/1986; 10% 06/26/1987
Acquired by Columbia Hospital Corp. (NV) 07/15/1992
Each share Common no par exchanged for either (1.1) shares new Common 1¢ par or (0.7372) share new Common 1¢ par and $6 cash
Note: Option to elect to receive stock and cash expired 08/31/1992
Columbia Hospital Corp. (NV) reincorporated in Delaware as Columbia Healthcare Corp. 09/01/1993 which merged into Columbia/HCA Healthcare Corp. 02/10/1994 which name changed to HCA - The Healthcare Co. 05/25/2000 which name changed to HCA Inc. (Ctfs. dated after 06/29/2001) 06/29/2001
(See HCA Inc. (Ctfs. dated after 06/29/2001))

BASIC ATOMICS, INC. (DE)
Stock Dividend - 200% 09/07/1955
Name changed to Tudor Industries Corp. 05/07/1964
(See Tudor Industries Corp.)

BASIC COMMODITY TRUST
Liquidated 00/00/1953
Details not available

BASIC CONS INC (PHILIPPINES)
Name changed to Basic Energy Corp. 06/10/2013

BASIC COSMETICS LTD (DE)
Name changed to Brecht Medical, Inc. 09/08/1982
(See Brecht Medical, Inc.)

BASIC DOLOMITE, INC.
Name changed to Basic Refractories, Inc. 00/00/1941
Basic Refractories, Inc. name changed to Basic, Inc. 03/28/1956
(See Basic, Inc.)

BASIC EARTH SCIENCE SYS INC (DE)
Common 10¢ par split (2) for (1) by issuance of (1) additional share 05/26/1981
Common 10¢ par changed to $0.001 par 10/06/1995
Name changed to Earthstone Energy, Inc. 07/12/2010

BASIC EMPIRE CORP (DE)
Recapitalized 01/06/1977
Reincorporated 08/10/2004
Recapitalized from Basic Empire to Basic Empire Corp. 01/06/1977
Each share Capital Stock 10¢ par exchanged for (0.033333) share Capital Stock 10¢ par
Each (5.6) shares new Common 10¢ par exchanged for (1) share Common $0.001 par 05/25/2004
State of incorporation changed from (NV) to (DE) 08/10/2004
Reorganized as China Agritech, Inc. 06/14/2005
Each share Common $0.001 par exchanged for (1.14) shares Common $0.001 par

BASIC ENERGY INC (UT)
Each share old Common 10¢ par exchanged for (0.01) share new Common 10¢ par 02/18/2003
Name changed to Skyframes, Inc. 03/24/2003
(See Skyframes, Inc.)

BASIC FOOD INDS INC (DE)
Merged into Eastern Shores Food Corp. of Delaware, Inc. 11/01/1978
Each share Common 1¢ par exchanged for $3.75 cash

BASIC GROWTH FD INC (MD)
Charter forfeited for failure to file annual reports 10/15/1986

BASIC INC (OH)
Stock Dividends - 25% 04/16/1956; 33.33333333% 12/23/1959
Merged into Combustion Engineering, Inc. 04/30/1979
Each share 5% Conv. Preference $50 par exchanged for $104.55 cash
Each share Common $1 par exchanged for for $46 cash

BASIC INDS CORP (DE)
Charter cancelled and declared inoperative and void for non-payment of taxes 03/01/1976

BASIC INSURANCE SHARES
Trust terminated and liquidated 00/00/1936
Details not available

BASIC INVTS INC (MN)
Name changed to Premier Investments, Inc. 01/26/1972
(See Premier Investments, Inc.)

BASIC LEAD & ZINC MINES LTD. (ON)
Charter cancelled 07/29/1963
No stockholders' equity

BASIC LEASING CORP (NY)
Common 1¢ par split (3) for (1) by issuance of (2) additional shares 09/22/1988
Plan of reorganization under Chapter 11 Federal Bankruptcy proceedings confirmed 10/03/2001
No stockholders' equity

BASIC MATERIALS, INC. (NM)
Name changed to General Energy Corp. 02/01/1966

BASIC METALS INC (UT)
Charter suspended for failure to file annual reports 06/30/1984

BASIC MINERALS LTD. (SK)
Acquired by Basic Lead & Zinc Mines Ltd. 00/00/1958
Each share Common exchanged for (1) share Capital Stock
(See Basic Lead & Zinc Mines Ltd.)

BASIC NAT RES INC (CO)
Each share Common $0.00005 par exchanged for (0.2) share Common 1¢ par 06/30/1994
Each share Common 1¢ par exchanged for (0.01666666) share Common $0.003 par 01/10/1997
Name changed to Synaptix Systems Corp. 03/27/1997
Synaptix Systems Corp. name changed to Affiliated Resources Corp. 01/12/1999

BASIC ORES CO. (NV)
Charter revoked for failure to file reports and pay fees 03/01/1954

BASIC PETE & MINERALS INC (PHILIPPINES)
Name changed to Basic Consolidated Inc. 07/20/1996
Basic Consolidated Inc. name changed to Basic Energy Corp. 06/10/2013

BASIC PETE INTL LTD (BAHAMAS)
Ordinary Stock BSD$3 par split (3) for (1) by issuance of (2) additional shares 07/05/1994
Merged into Norcen Energy Resources Ltd. 09/30/1997
Each share Ordinary BSD$3 par exchanged for CAD$40 cash

BASIC PPTYS INC (DE)
Class A $1 par reclassified as Class A Common $1 par and Common $1 par reclassified as Class B $1 par 04/17/1962
10% of Class B $1 par converted to Class A Common $1 par on a (0.33333333) for (1) basis 12/31/1964
11.11111111% of Class B $1 par converted to Class A Common $1 par on a (0.33333333) for (1) basis 12/31/1965
28.57142857% of Class B $1 par converted to Class A Common $1 par on a (0.33333333) for (1) basis 12/31/1966
Remainder of Class B $1 par converted to Class A Common $1 par on a (0.33333333) for (1) basis 12/31/1967
Reorganized under the laws of Massachusetts as North American Mortgage Investors 12/31/1968
Each share Class A Common $1 par exchanged for (1) Share of Bene. Int. no par
North American Mortgage Investors merged into Southmark Corp. 05/10/1984
(See Southmark Corp.)

BASIC PRODUCTS CORP. (WI)
Name changed to Sola Basic Industries, Inc. 10/29/1965
Sola Basic Industries, Inc. merged into General Signal Corp. 09/30/1977 which merged into SPX Corp. 10/06/1998

BASIC RLTY INVT CORP (AB)
Recapitalized as Uni-Invest Ltd. 11/17/2000
Each share Common no par exchanged for (0.2) share Common no par
Uni-Invest Ltd. name changed to Homburg Invest Inc. 01/11/2001
(See Homburg Invest Inc.)

BASIC REFRACTORIES, INC. (OH)
Stock Dividend - 20% 09/15/1955
Name changed to Basic, Inc. 03/28/1956
(See Basic, Inc.)

BASIC RES CORP (NY)
Name changed to Basix Corp. 01/03/1984

BASIC RES CORP (UT)
Proclaimed dissolved for failure to pay taxes 11/09/1974

BASIC RES INTL BAHAMAS LTD (BAHAMAS)
Recapitalized as Basic Petroleum International Ltd. 08/04/1989
Each share Ordinary BSD$0.03 par exchanged for (0.01) share Ordinary BSD$3 par
(See Basic Petroleum International Ltd.)

BASIC RES INTL LTD (ON)
Completely liquidated 07/31/1972
Each share Common no par exchanged for first and final distribution of (1) share Basic Resources International S.A. Common $3.30 par
Basic Resources International S.A. recapitalized as BRISA International S.A. 12/08/1983
(See BRISA International S.A.)

BASIC RES INTL S A (LUXEMBOURG)
Recapitalized as BRISA International S.A. 12/08/1983
Each share Common USD$3.30 par exchanged for (0.1) share Common USD$1.10 par
(See BRISA International S.A.)

BASIC SCIENCE ASSOCS INC (DE)
Name changed to Sound Source Interactive Inc. 04/27/1994
Sound Source Interactive Inc. name changed to TDK Mediactive Inc. 12/01/2000
(See TDK Mediative Inc.)

BASIC SCIENCES INC (DE)
Common 1¢ par split (3) for (1) by issuance of (2) additional shares 02/15/1972
Charter cancelled and declared inoperative and void for non-payment of taxes 03/01/1976

BASIC SVCS INC (NV)
Each share Common $0.001 par received distribution of (1) share Generic Marketing Services, Inc. Common $0.001 par payable 10/19/2007 to holders of record 08/13/2007 Ex date - 10/22/2007
Name changed to Adrenalina 12/14/2007
Adrenalina name changed to ID Perfumes, Inc. 02/07/2013

BASIC TECHNOLOGIES INC (CO)
Reorganized under the laws of Delaware as StarCom Wireless Networks, Inc. 05/07/2003
Each share Common $0.00001 par exchanged for (0.14285714) share Common $0.0001 par
StarCom Wireless Networks, Inc. name changed to SkyLynx Communications, Inc. 09/29/2003 which recapitalized as PawsPlus, Inc. 01/29/2009
(See PawsPlus, Inc.)

BASIC TRADES HOLDING CO., INC. (NY)
Proclaimed dissolved for failure to file reports and pay fees 12/15/1937

BASIC-WITZ FURNITURE INDUSTRIES INC. (VA)
Capital Stock $10 par changed to $5 par and (1) additional share issued 08/10/1964
Name changed to B.W.I.L., Inc. 08/02/1965
(See B.W.I.L., Inc.)

BASICGOV SYSTEMS INC (BC)
Name changed to Pedro Resources Ltd. 09/30/2010

BASIN ENERGY CORP NEW (UT)
Name changed to Eurodynamics Corp. 03/12/1990
Eurodynamics Corp. recapitalized as U-Ship Inc. 06/16/1992 which name changed to United Shipping & Technology, Inc. (UT) 05/03/1999 which reincorporated in Delaware as Velocity Express Corp. 01/14/2002
(See Velocity Express Corp.)

BASIN EXPL & MNG CO (UT)
Name changed to Bonneville-West Corp. 06/22/1984
Bonneville-West Corp. merged into Bonneville Pacific Corp. 11/01/1987
(See Bonneville Pacific Corp.)

BASIN EXPL INC (DE)
Merged into Stone Energy Corp. 02/01/2001
Each share Common 1¢ par exchanged for (0.3974) share Common 1¢ par
Stone Energy Corp. name changed to Talos Energy Inc. 05/10/2018

BASIN GOLD MINES CORP.
Bankrupt 00/00/1938
Details not available

BASIN GOLDFIELDS, LTD. (MT)
Charter expired by time limitation 05/19/1973

BASIN INDS INC (OK)
Charter suspended for failure to pay taxes 03/05/1992

BASIN MONTANA TUNNEL CO. (DE)
Common $1 par changed to no par 00/00/1930
Common no par changed to $1 par 00/00/1933
Each share Common $1 par exchanged for (0.2) share new Common 50¢ par 00/00/1942
No longer in existence having become inoperative and void for non-payment of taxes 04/01/1958

BASIN NATURAL GAS CORP. (NM)
Charter revoked for failure to file reports and pay fees 00/00/1960

BASIN OIL CO. OF CALIFORNIA (CA)
Liquidation completed 05/27/1957
Details not available

BASIN OIL CORP. (DE)
Acquired by Texota Oil Co. 01/13/1961
Each share Common exchanged for (0.285714285) share Common 1¢ par
Texota Oil Co. name changed to North America Resources Corp. 12/15/1968

BASIN PETE CORP (NY)
Merged into Reserve Oil & Gas Co. 01/20/1976
Each share Common 2¢ par exchanged for (0.4) Class A Stock Purchase Warrants expiring 01/20/1981 and $8.50 cash

BASIN PETE RES LTD (BC)
Name changed to Gametek Systems Inc. 05/01/1987
(See Gametek Systems Inc.)

BASIN WTR INC (DE)
Plan of reorganization under Chapter 11 Federal Bankruptcy proceedings effective 02/01/2010
No stockholders' equity

BASINVIEW ENERGY INC (AB)
Recapitalized 02/10/2000
Recapitalized from Basinview Energy Ltd. to Basinview Energy Inc. 02/10/2000
Each share Common no par exchanged for (0.5) share Common no par
Acquired by Danoil Energy Ltd. 01/04/2001
Each share Common no par exchanged for $1.15 cash

BASIS INC (UT)
Involuntarily dissolved 12/31/1986

BASIS100 INC (ON)
Merged into First American Corp. 09/08/2004
Each share Common no par exchanged for $1 cash

BASIX CORP (NY)
Reorganized 11/17/1989
Basix Corp. reorganized under Chapter 11 Federal Bankruptcy Code as Basix Corp. 11/17/1989
Each (100) shares Common 5¢ par exchanged for approximately (1.023997) Units consisting of (1) share Common $0.001 par, (1) Common Stock Purchase Warrant expiring 11/15/1999 and (1) Common Stock Purchase

Anti-Dilution Warrant expiring 11/15/1999
(Additional Information in Active)

BASKA URANIUM MINES LTD. (SK)
Recapitalized as Norbaska Mines Ltd. 08/08/1966
Each share Capital Stock no par exchanged for (0.2) share Capital Stock no par
Norbaska Mines Ltd. merged into Dore-Norbaska Resources Inc. 12/23/1987 which merged into Griffin Corp. 02/23/1998
(See Griffin Corp.)

BASKIN ROBBINS ICE CREAM CO (DE)
Merged into J. Lyons (U.S. Holdings) Inc. 12/26/1974
Each share Common $1 par exchanged for $17.50 cash

BASLEN PETES LTD (ON)
Recapitalized as International Baslen Enterprises Ltd. 09/25/1972
Each share Capital Stock $1 par exchanged for (0.25) share Common no par
(See International Baslen Enterprises Ltd.)

BASQUE MINING & MILLING CO. (UT)
Name changed to Golf Card International, Inc. 11/14/1978
Golf Card International, Inc. name changed to GCI Industries Inc. 06/11/1982
(See GCI Industries Inc.)

BASS CAP CORP (AB)
Name changed to Shear Minerals Ltd. 01/19/1998
Shear Minerals Ltd. recapitalized as Shear Diamonds Ltd. 12/30/2010

BASS CHARRINGTON PLC (ENGLAND)
Reorganized as Bass PLC 02/07/1990
Each Unsponsored ADR for Ordinary exchanged for (5) Sponsored ADR's for Ordinary
Bass PLC name changed to Six Continents PLC 07/31/2001
(See Six Continents PLC)

BASS FINL CORP (DE)
Company went private 08/13/1982
Details not available

BASS MTG INCOME FD I LTD PARTNERSHIP (OH)
Terminated SEC registration 12/26/1995
Stockholders' equity unlikely

BASS PUB LTD CO (ENGLAND)
Each Sponsored ADR for Ordinary received distribution of (0.785714) additional Sponsored ADR for Ordinary and approximately $3.1409 cash payable 02/20/1998 to holders of record 02/06/1998 Ex date - 02/09/1998
Name changed to Six Continents PLC 07/31/2001
(See Six Continents PLC)

BASS REAL ESTATE FUND-84 (NC)
Terminated SEC registration 08/09/1996

BASS STRAIT OIL & GAS HLDGS N L (AUSTRALIA)
Name changed to Federation Resources N.L. 10/20/1988
(See Federation Resources N.L.)

BASSETT J R OPTICAL INC (DE)
Recapitalized as Samurai Energy Corp. (DE) 11/28/2005
Each share old Common $0.001 par exchanged for (0.02777777) share Common $0.001 par
Samurai Energy Corp. (DE) reincorporated in Nevada as ECCO Energy Corp. 09/01/2006 which recapitalized as Eagle Ford Oil & Gas, Corp. 07/27/2010

BASSETT VENTURES INC (BC)
Name changed to Arris Resources Inc. 06/25/2007
Arris Resources Inc. name changed to RTN Stealth Software Inc. 01/08/2010 which name changed to Quantitative Alpha Trading Inc. (BC) 04/29/2011 which reincorporated in Ontario 12/09/2011
(See Quantitative Alpha Trading Inc.)

BASSETT WALKER INC (VA)
Common $1 par split (3) for (1) by issuance of (0.5) additional share 02/28/1984
Acquired by V.F. Corp. 12/18/1984
Each share Common $1 par exchanged for $29 cash

BASSIQUE MINES, LTD. (ON)
Charter cancelled 00/00/1960

BASSONS INDUSTRIES CORP. (NY)
Bankrupt 01/12/1958
No stockholders' equity

BASTA CORP. (CA)
Charter suspended for failure to file reports and pay fees 04/06/1971

BASTA HLDGS CORP (NV)
Recapitalized as BlackPoll Fleet International, Inc. 07/28/2015
Each share Common $0.001 par exchanged for (0.1) share Common $0.001 par

BASTIAN BLESSING CO (IL)
Common no par split (4) for (1) by issuance of (3) additional shares 04/24/1961
Stock Dividend - 10% 01/02/1965
Merged into Astro Controls, Inc. 05/06/1969
Each share Common no par exchanged for (1) share $1 Conv. Preferred $1 par
Astro Controls, Inc. merged into Golgonda Corp. 09/15/1970 which reincorporated in Delaware as Rego Co. 06/17/1977 which name changed to Rego Group, Inc. 02/07/1978
(See Rego Group, Inc.)

BASTIAN BLESSING INC (DE)
Merged into Bastian Industries, Inc. 11/24/1980
Each share Capital Stock 10¢ par exchanged for (0.1) share $0.815 Conv. Preferred $1 par and (0.15) share Common 1¢ par
(See Bastian Industries, Inc.)

BASTIAN BROS CO (NY)
Each share Common $1 par exchanged for (5) shares Common $10 par 04/06/1951
89% held by company as of 00/00/1978
Public interest eliminated

BASTIAN INDS INC (DE)
Merged into Bastian Acquiring Corp. 07/24/1986
Each share $0.815 Conv. Preferred $1 par exchanged for $7 principal amount of 10% Sr. Subord. Debentures due 05/01/1996 and $22.50 principal amount of Zero Coupon Subord. Debentures due 11/01/2000
Each share $0.815 Conv. Preferred Ser. A $1 par exchanged for $15 principal amount of 10% Sr. Subord. Debentures due 05/01/1996 and $64.50 principal amount of Zero Coupon Subord. Debentures due 11/01/2000
Each share Common 1¢ par exchanged for $5 principal amount of 10% Sr. Subord. Debentures due 05/01/1996 and $21.50 principal amount of Zero Coupon Subord. Debentures due 11/01/2000

BASTIAN MORLEY INC (IN)
Each share Common no par exchanged for (15) shares Common $1 par 00/00/1946

Charter revoked for failure to file annual reports 06/01/1970

BASTION RES LTD (BC)
Recapitalized as Pan American Fertilizer Corp. (Old) 05/23/2012
Each share Common no par exchanged for (0.4) share Common no par
Pan American Fertilizer Corp. (Old) merged into Pan American Fertilizer Corp. (New) 08/07/2013

BASTOGI I R B S (ITALY)
ADR agreement terminated 10/30/2008
No ADR's remain outstanding

BATA PETROLEUMS LTD. (SK)
Recapitalized as Bata Resources Ltd. 03/31/1965
Each share Common no par exchanged for (0.16666666) share Common no par
Bata Resources Ltd. merged into United Bata Resources Ltd. 03/24/1969
(See United Bata Resources Ltd.)

BATA RES LTD (SK)
Merged into United Bata Resources Ltd. 03/24/1969
Each share Common no par exchanged for (1) share Common 50¢ par
(See United Bata Resources Ltd.)

BATAVIA ENERGY CORP (ON)
Name changed to Victory Gold Mines Inc. 02/18/2011
Victory Gold Mines Inc. merged into Northern Gold Mining Inc. 02/06/2013 which merged into Oban Mining Corp. 12/24/2015 which name changed to Osisko Mining Inc. 06/21/2016

BATAVIA FINL CORP (DE)
Acquired by Pinnacle Banc Group, Inc. 12/31/1992
Each share Common 1¢ par exchanged for initial distribution of $25.91 cash
Each share Common 1¢ par received second and final distribution of $1.13 cash 09/30/1993

BATCH RIVER GOLD MINES LTD. (ON)
Charter cancelled for failure to pay taxes and file returns 01/10/1973

BATCHAWANA URANIUM MINES LTD. (ON)
Charter cancelled 09/18/1961

BATCHELDER & SNYDER CO., INC.
Name changed to Bandess, Inc. 00/00/1946
(See Bandess, Inc.)

BATCHELDER SNYDER DORR & DOE
Reorganized as Batchelder & Snyder Co., Inc. 00/00/1934
Details not available

BATEAUX RES INC (BC)
Cease trade order effective 10/04/1989
Stockholders' equity unlikely

BATEMAN BAY MNG INC (QC)
Name changed 12/30/1978
Name changed from Bateman Bay Mining Co. to Bateman Bay Mining Co. Inc.-Compagnie Miniere Baie Bateman Inc. 12/30/1978
Cease trade order effective 10/29/1991
Stockholders' equity unlikely

BATEMAN ISLAND, INC. (DE)
Liquidation completed
Each share Common $1 par exchanged for initial distribution of (18) shares Louisiana Land & Exploration Co. Capital Stock 15¢ par and $3 cash 10/08/1965
Each share Common $1 par received second and final distribution of $2.07 cash 03/15/1967
Louisiana Land & Exploration Co. merged into Burlington Resources Inc. 10/22/1997 which merged into ConocoPhillips 03/31/2006

BATES & INNES, LTD. (CANADA)
Adjudicated bankrupt 08/15/1963
No stockholders' equity

BATES CO. (MN)
Charter expired by time limitation 11/25/1957

BATES FINL CORP (DE)
Charter cancelled and declared inoperative and void for non-payment of taxes 04/15/1973

BATES-GREAT WESTN ENERGY INC (UT)
Charter suspended for failure to file annual reports 06/01/1990

BATES MANUFACTURING CO. (ME)
Each share Common $100 par exchanged for (5) shares Common $10 par 00/00/1945
4.5% Preferred $100 par called for redemption 04/15/1963
Stock Dividend - 350% 03/14/1951
Merged into Bates Manufacturing Co., Inc. 05/15/1965
Each share Common $10 par exchanged for (1) share Capital Stock $5 par
(See Bates Manufacturing Co., Inc.)

BATES MFG INC (DE)
Capital Stock $5 par reclassified as Common $5 par 08/07/1969
$1 Conv. Preferred Ser. A $7.50 par called for redemption 05/27/1975
In process of liquidation
Each share Common $5 par received initial distribution of $52 cash 07/05/1979
Name changed to BAV Liquidating Corp. 07/27/1979
(See BAV Liquidating Corp.)

BATES VALVE BAG CORP.
Dissolved 00/00/1929
Details not available

BATH AIR SYS INC (DE)
Charter forfeited for failure to maintain a registered agent 10/19/1975

BATH INDS INC (DE)
Common $10 par changed to $1 par and (1.5) additional shares issued 06/23/1967
$5 Conv. Preferred Ser. A no par changed to $2.50 Conv. Preferred Ser. A no par and (1) additional share issued 09/12/1969
Common $1 par changed to 50¢ par and (1) additional share issued 09/12/1969
$2.50 Conv. Preferred Ser. A no par called for redemption 06/11/1971
Common 50¢ par split (3) for (2) by issuance of (0.5) additional share 01/24/1972
Name changed to Congoleum Corp. 04/25/1975
(See Congoleum Corp.)

BATH IRON WORKS CORP. (ME)
Common $1 par changed to $10 par 00/00/1950
Under plan of merger reincorporated under the laws of Delaware as Bath Industries, Inc. 06/01/1967
Bath Industries, Inc. name changed to Congoleum Corp. 04/25/1975
(See Congoleum Corp.)

BATH NATL BK (BATH, NY)
Under plan of reorganization each share Common $10 par automatically became (1) share Bath National Corp. Common $10 par 03/11/1983
(See Bath National Corp.)

BATH NATL CORP (NY)
Common $10 par changed to $5 par

and (1) additional share issued 00/00/1992
Common $5 par split (2) for (1) by issuance of (1) additional share payable 06/07/1996 to holders of record 04/24/1996
Merged into Financial Institutions, Inc. 05/01/2001
Each share Common $5 par exchanged for $48 cash

BATHROOMS BEAUTIFUL CDA LTD (CANADA)
Company wound up 00/00/1991
No stockholders' equity

BATHURST BASE METALS INC (CANADA)
Acquired by Breakwater Resources Ltd. (BC) 09/04/1990
Each share Common no par exchanged for (0.26666666) share Common no par
Breakwater Resources Ltd. (BC) reincorporated in Canada 05/11/1992
(See Breakwater Resources Ltd.)

BATHURST MINING CORP. LTD. (NB)
Merged into Maritimes Mining Corp. Ltd. share for share 12/30/1955
Maritimes Mining Corp. Ltd. recapitalized as First Maritime Mining Corp. Ltd. 05/22/1964
(See First Maritime Mining Corp. Ltd.)

BATHURST NORSEMINES LTD (BC)
Capital Stock 50¢ par changed to no par 07/24/1985
Recapitalized as Etruscan Enterprises Ltd. (BC) 09/12/1986
Each share Capital Stock no par exchanged for (0.33333333) share Capital Stock no par
Etruscan Enterprises Ltd. (BC) reincorporated in Nova Scotia as Etruscan Resources Inc. 09/11/1997 which merged into Endeavour Financial Corp. 09/14/2010 which name changed to Endeavour Mining Corp. 09/20/2010

BATHURST PAPER LTD (CANADA)
Acquired by Consolidated Paper Corp. Ltd. 06/23/1967
Each share Class A no par exchanged for (2) shares 6% Preferred 1966 Ser. $25 par and (1) Common Stock Purchase Warrant
Each share Common no par exchanged for (1) share 6% Preferred 1966 Ser. $25 par and (0.5) Common Stock Purchase Warrant
(See Consolidated Paper Corp. Ltd.)
5.25% Preferred 1963 Ser. $20 par reclassified as $1.05 Preferred 1963 Ser. no par 11/27/1980
$1.05 Preferred 1963 Ser. no par called for redemption 06/30/1988
Public interest eliminated

BATHURST PWR & PAPER LTD (CANADA)
Each share Class A no par exchanged for (1) new share Class A no par 11/06/1961
Each share Class B no par exchanged for (2) shares Common no par 11/06/1961
Name changed to Bathurst Paper Ltd. 05/19/1965
(See Bathurst Paper Ltd.)

BATHWICK MINES LTD. (ON)
Name changed to Farcroft Mines Ltd. 10/01/1954
(See Farcroft Mines Ltd.)

BATIK WINE & SPIRITS INC (CA)
Name changed to Comprehensive Health Systems, Inc. 02/16/1972
(See Comprehensive Health Systems, Inc.)

BATON BROADCASTING INC (ON)
Old Common no par split (2) for (1) by issuance of (1) additional share 11/07/1972
Each share old Common no par exchanged for (1) share Class A Common no par 06/12/1981
Each share Class A Common no par exchanged for (1) share new Common no par 01/24/1986
Each share Conv. Class B Common no par exchanged for (1) share new Common no par 01/27/1986
New Common no par split (2) for (1) by issuance of (1) additional share 01/21/1987
Name changed to CTV Inc. 12/21/1998
(See CTV Inc.)

BATON ROUGE BANCSHARES INC (LA)
Completely liquidated 07/30/1991
Each share Common $5 par exchanged for first and final distribution of $0.3688 cash

BATON ROUGE BK & TR CO (BATON ROUGE, LA)
Reorganized as Baton Rouge Bancshares, Inc. 06/30/1983
Each share Common $5 par exchanged for (1) share Common Capital Stock $5 par
(See Baton Rouge Bancshares, Inc.)

BATORI MINES LTD. (ON)
Property and assets sold to Bagamac Mines Ltd. 00/00/1946
Details not available

BATS GLOBAL MKTS INC (DE)
Merged into CBOE Holdings, Inc. 02/28/2017
Each share Common 1¢ par exchanged for (0.3201) share Common 1¢ par and $10 cash
CBOE Holdings, Inc. name changed to Cboe Global Markets, Inc. 10/18/2017

BATTANI LTD (NY)
Out of business 03/00/1975
No stockholders' equity

BATTERIES BATTERIES INC (DE)
Name changed to Wireless Xcessories Group, Inc. 03/20/2000

BATTERY CO.
Dissolved 00/00/1937
Details not available

BATTERY CTL CORP (DE)
Common $0.0001 par split (5) for (1) by issuance of (4) additional shares payable 12/02/2008 to holders of record 12/01/2008 Ex date - 12/03/2008
Common $0.0001 par split (2) for (1) by issuance of (1) additional share payable 03/16/2009 to holders of record 03/13/2009 Ex date - 03/17/2009
Name changed to Ecologix Resource Group, Inc. 06/15/2009

BATTERY ONE INC (AB)
Name changed 12/29/1994
Name changed from Battery One-Stop Inc. to Battery One, Inc. 12/29/1994
Recapitalized as Power Plus Corp. 10/28/1996
Each share Common no par exchanged for (0.05) share Common no par and (1) Right to purchase Exchange Units which expired 01/31/1997
Power Plus Corp. name changed to PPC Capital Corp. 08/03/1999
(See PPC Capital Corp.)

BATTERY TECHNOLOGIES INC (ON)
Filed a notice of intention to make a proposal under the Bankruptcy and Insolvency Act 03/31/2003
Stockholders' equity unlikely

BATTERY WORLD INC (NV)
Each share old Common $0.001 par exchanged for (0.00588235) share new Common $0.001 par 10/31/1997

Name changed to Essex Acquisition Corp. 12/05/1997
Essex Acquisition Corp. name changed to B Squared Technologies Inc. 10/07/1999 which recapitalized as Metropolis Technologies Corp. 02/20/2003 which recapitalized as Impact E-Solutions Corp. 02/08/2007
(See Impact E-Solutions Corp.)

BATTLE CREEK DEVS LTD (AB)
Merged into Strike Energy Inc. 07/01/1994
Each share Common no par exchanged for (1.2) shares Common no par
Strike Energy merged into Tarragon Oil & Gas Ltd. 05/01/1996 which merged into Marathon Oil Canada Ltd. 09/11/1998
(See Marathon Oil Canada Ltd.)

BATTLE CREEK GAS CO (MI)
Each share Common $100 par exchanged for (10) shares Common no par 00/00/1926
Stock Dividends - 25% 08/13/1954; 25% 05/20/1957; 10% 07/20/1966; 20% 12/06/1976
Acquired by Southeastern Michigan Gas Enterprises, Inc. 05/20/1985
Each share Common no par exchanged for $83.78 cash

BATTLE ENERGY CORP (BC)
Merged into United Tri-Star Resources Ltd. (BC) 12/31/1986
Each share Common no par exchanged for (0.0468384) share Common no par
United Tri-Star Resources Ltd. (BC) reincorporated in Canada 10/27/1994 which merged into UTS Energy Corp. 06/30/1998 which merged into SilverBirch Energy Corp. 10/01/2010 which merged into SilverWillow Energy Corp. 04/04/2012
(See SilverWillow Energy Corp.)

BATTLE MTN CDA INC (ON)
Merged into Newmont Mining Corp. 01/10/2001
Each Exchangeable Share no par exchanged for (0.105) share Common $1.60 par

BATTLE MTN GOLD CO (NV)
Non-Transferable Class B Common 10¢ par converted to Class A Common 10¢ par 06/30/1987
Class A Common 10¢ par split (3) for (2) by issuance of (0.5) additional share 10/21/1987
Class A Common 10¢ par reclassified as Common 10¢ par 07/01/1988
Merged into Newmont Mining Corp. 01/10/2001
Each share $3.25 Conv. Preferred $1 par exchanged for (1) share $3.25 Conv. Preferred $1 par
Each share Common $1 par exchanged for (0.105) share Common $1.60 par

BATTLE MTN GOLD EXPL CORP (NV)
Merged into Royal Gold, Inc. 10/25/2007
Each share Common $0.001 par exchanged for (0.016578) share Common 1¢ par
Each share Common $0.001 par received an additional distribution of (0.00032715) share Common 1¢ par from escrow 05/22/2009

BATTLE MTN GOLD INC (BC)
Merged into Gold Standard Ventures Corp. 06/15/2017
Each share Common no par exchanged for (0.1891) share Common no par and $0.08 cash
Note: Unexchanged certificates will be cancelled and become without value 06/15/2023

BATTLEFIELD MINERALS CORP (YT)
Recapitalized as BM Diamondcorp Inc. 11/21/2001
Each share Common no par exchanged for (0.14285714) share Common no par
BM Diamondcorp Inc. name changed to BDI Mining Corp. (Yukon) 07/26/2004 which reincorporated in British Virgin Islands 08/08/2005
(See BDI Mining Corp.)

BATTLEFORD CAP INC (AB)
Name changed to Sahara Energy Ltd. 12/16/2005

BATTLEFORD OIL CO. LTD. (ON)
Charter cancelled and declared dissolved for failure to file returns 09/22/1966

BATTRIX INVTS LTD (AB)
Recapitalized as Maxxcapp Corp. 03/09/2004
Each share Class A Common no par exchanged for (0.5) share Class A Common no par

BAUER ALUMINUM CO. (TX)
Name changed to Republic Aluminum Co. 04/30/1965
(See Republic Aluminum Co.)

BAUER EDDIE HLDGS INC (DE)
Plan of reorganization under Chapter 11 Federal Bankruptcy proceedings effective 04/06/2010
No stockholders' equity

BAUER EDDIE INC (WA)
Merged into General Mills, Inc. 03/08/1971
Each share Common $1 par exchanged for (0.37384) share Common $1.50 par

BAUER PARTNERSHIP INC (NV)
Name changed to Harbour Front Holdings, Inc. 01/27/2003
Harbour Front Holdings, Inc. recapitalized as American Eagle Manufacturing Co. 10/20/2003 which name changed to No Borders, Inc. 10/27/2004

BAUER PATENT CORP. (NY)
Charter cancelled and proclaimed dissolved for failure to pay taxes 12/15/1964

BAUER PERFORMANCE SPORTS LTD (BC)
Name changed to Performance Sports Group Ltd. 06/19/2014
Performance Sports Group Ltd. name changed to Old PSG Wind-down Ltd. 03/20/2017

BAUKOL NOONAN INC (ND)
Common $1 par split (3) for (1) by issuance of (2) additional shares 09/16/1983
Merged into Minnesota Power & Light Co. 11/17/1988
Each share Common $1 par exchanged for (0.8) share Common no par
Minnesota Power & Light Co. name changed to Minnesota Power, Inc. 05/27/1998 which name changed to Allete 09/01/2000 which name changed to Allete, Inc. 05/07/2001

BAUMAN LUDWIG & CO (NY)
Recapitalized 00/00/1946
Each share 7% 1st Preferred $100 par exchanged for $150 in Debentures, (1) share Common $1 par and $10 cash
Each share Common no par exchanged for (1) share Common $1 par
Merged into Acme-Hamilton Manufacturing Corp. 12/27/1962
Each share Common $1 par exchanged for $3 cash

BAUMRITTER CORP (NY)
Class A $1 par and Class B $1 par split (2) for (1) by issuance of (1)

additional share respectively 07/02/1971
Name changed to Allen (Ethan), Inc. 03/10/1972
Allen (Ethan), Inc. merged into Interco Inc. (Old) 01/28/1980
(See Interco Inc. (Old))

BAUR INTERNATIONAL, INC. (IL)
Proclaimed dissolved for failure to pay taxes and file reports 11/20/1972

BAUSCH & LOMB INC (NY)
Common $10 par changed to $5 par and (1) additional share issued 04/08/1966
Common $5 par changed to $2.50 par and (1) additional share issued 05/26/1972
Common $2.50 par changed to $1 par 04/30/1979
Common $1 par split (2) for (1) by issuance of (1) additional share 09/28/1979
Common $1 par changed to 40¢ par 04/23/1981
Common 40¢ par split (2) for (1) by issuance of (1) additional share 11/10/1983
4% Preferred $100 par called for redemption 07/16/1984
Common 40¢ par split (2) for (1) by issuance of (1) additional share 06/28/1991
Merged into WP Prism Inc. 10/26/2007
Each share Common 40¢ par exchanged for $65 cash

BAUSCH & LOMB OPTICAL CO (NY)
Stock Dividend - 20% 01/31/1958
Name changed to Bausch & Lomb Inc. 03/31/1960
(See Bausch & Lomb Inc.)

BAUSH MACH TOOL CO (DE)
Reincorporated 00/00/1962
Each share Preferred $100 par exchanged for (25) shares Common no par 00/00/1951
State of incorporation changed from (MA) to (DE) 00/00/1962
Company became private 03/28/1983
Details not available

BAUSKA MFG B C LTD (BC)
Cease trade order effective 07/27/1988
Stockholders' equity unlikely

BAV LIQUIDATING CORP (DE)
In process of liquidation
Each share Common $5 par exchanged for initial distribution of (1) share Avery Coal Co., Inc. Common 10¢ par 05/14/1980
Converted to a trust as BAV Liquidating Trust 05/15/1980
(See BAV Liquidating Trust)

BAV LIQUIDATING TRUST (DE)
Liquidation completed
Each Share of Bene. Int. received initial distribution of $1.218 cash 06/01/1981
Each Share of Bene. Int. received second distribution of $1.2857 cash 02/26/1982
Each Share of Bene. Int. received third distribution of $1.2832 cash 03/31/1983
Each Share of Bene. Int. received fourth distribution of (0.14167) share Trafalgar Industries, Inc. Common 10¢ par 01/20/1984
(See Trafalgar Industries, Inc.)
Each Share of Bene. Int. received fifth distribution of $0.787 cash 04/12/1984
Each Share of Bene. Int. received sixth distribution of $0.21 cash 06/08/1984
Each Share of Bene. Int. received seventh distribution of $0.50 cash 10/17/1985
Each Share of Bene. Int. received eighth distribution of $1 cash 10/24/1986
Each Share of Bene. Int. received ninth and final distribution of $0.3022 cash 10/20/1987

BAVARIAN LION INDS LTD (BC)
Name changed to First West Canada Capital Corp. 11/25/1991
First West Canada Capital Corp. recapitalized as Caring Products International, Inc. 01/14/1994 which name changed to US Global Aerospace, Inc. 09/26/2002 which name changed to US Global Nanospace, Inc. 07/24/2003

BAVARIAN PPTYS INC (DE)
Name changed 05/24/1989
Name changed from Bavarian Technologies Inc. to Bavarian Properties Inc. 05/24/1989
Charter cancelled and declared inoperative and void for non-payment of taxes 03/01/1992

BAWLF (N.) GRAIN CO., LTD.
Dissolved 00/00/1941
Details not available

BAXALTA INC (DE)
Merged into Shire PLC 06/03/2016
Each share Common 1¢ par exchanged for (0.1482) Sponsored ADR for Ordinary and $18 cash

BAXANO SURGICAL INC (DE)
Plan of reorganization under Chapter 11 Federal Bankruptcy proccedings effective 08/10/2015
No stockholders' equity

BAXL HLDGS INC (NV)
Charter revoked for failure to file reports and pay fees 06/01/2009

BAXLEY FED SVGS BK (BAXLEY, GA)
Merged into PAB Bankshares, Inc. 11/30/1999
Each share Common 1¢ par exchanged for (2.4) shares Common no par
(See PAB Bankshares, Inc.)

BAXTER INTL INC (DE)
Conv. Exchangeable Preferred no par called for redemption 11/25/1990
Adjustable Rate Preferred no par called for redemption 04/01/1992
Each 7% Corporate Unit received (1.4011) shares Common $1 par 02/16/2006
(Additional Information in Active)

BAXTER LABS INC (DE)
Common $1 par split (2) for (1) by issuance of (1) additional share 12/31/1959
Common $1 par split (2) for (1) by issuance of (1) additional share 12/08/1961
Common $1 par split (2) for (1) by issuance of (1) additional share 02/04/1966
Common $1 par split (2) for (1) by issuance of (1) additional share 09/30/1967
Common $1 par split (2) for (1) by issuance of (1) additional share 10/30/1969
Name changed to Baxter Travenol Laboratories, Inc. 05/03/1976
Baxter Travenol Laboratories, Inc. name changed to Baxter International Inc. 05/18/1988

BAXTER LAUNDRIES, INC.
Reorganized as Baxter Laundries Corp. 00/00/1934
Details not available

BAXTER LAUNDRIES CORP (MI)
Charter declared inoperative and void for failure to file reports 05/15/1975

BAXTER RES CORP (ON)
Merged into Baxter Technologies Corp. 12/31/1981
Each share Common no par exchanged for (1) share Common no par
Baxter Technologies Corp. name changed to Standard-Modern Technologies Corp. 10/08/1985
(See Standard-Modern Technologies Corp.)

BAXTER ROYALTY CO. (WY)
Dissolved 00/00/1953
Details not available

BAXTER TECHNOLOGIES CORP (ON)
Name changed to Standard-Modern Technologies Corp. 10/08/1985
(See Standard-Modern Technologies Corp.)

BAXTER TRAVENOL LABS INC (DE)
Common $1 par split (2) for (1) by issuance of (1) additional share 11/06/1981
Common $1 par split (2) for (1) by issuance of (1) additional share 11/17/1983
Name changed to Baxter International Inc. 05/18/1988

BAY ADELAIDE GARAGE LTD (ON)
Each share 7% Preferred exchanged for (5.8) shares new Common no par 00/00/1948
Each share old Common no par exchanged for (0.1) share new Common no par 00/00/1948 Wound up 00/00/1969
Each share new Common no par exchanged for approximately $19 cash

BAY ANN RES INC (BC)
Name changed to Zorah Media Corp. 06/21/1985
(See Zorah Media Corp.)

BAY APT CMNTYS INC (CA)
Reincorporated 07/12/1995
State of incorporation changed from (CA) to (MD) 07/12/1995
Under plan of merger name changed to Avalon Bay Communities, Inc. 06/04/1998
Avalon Bay Communities, Inc. name changed to AvalonBay Communities, Inc. 10/02/1998

BAY AREA BANCSHARES (CA)
Merged into Greater Bay Bancorp 05/21/1999
Each share Common no par exchanged for (1.38682) shares Common no par
Greater Bay Bancorp merged into Wells Fargo & Co. (New) 10/01/2007

BAY AREA HLDGS INC (CA)
SEC revoked preferred and common stock registration 10/15/2008

BAY AREA SPORTS ENTERPRISES (CA)
Capital Stock $100 par changed to $10 par and (9) additional shares issued 04/13/1971
Company went private 01/03/1989
Details not available

BAY BANCORP INC (MD)
Merged into Old Line Bancshares, Inc. 04/13/2018
Each share Common $1 par exchanged for (0.4088) share Common 1¢ par

BAY BANCSHARES INC (TX)
Merged into SouthTrust Corp. 03/30/2001
Each share Common $1 par exchanged for $26.42 cash

BAY CITIES NATL BK (REDONDO BEACH, CA)
Merged into Peninsula Banking Group, Inc. 11/30/1995
Each share Common $5 par exchanged for $13.25 cash

BAY CITIES PROPERTIES CORP.
Liquidation completed 00/00/1946
Details not available

BAY CITY BK & TR CO (BAY CITY, MI)
Stock Dividend - 33.33333333% 05/01/1969
Merged into Manufacturers National Corp. 09/30/1975
Each share Capital Stock $20 par exchanged for $75 principal amount of 9% Conv. Sub. Notes due serially (10) to (12) years from issuance date

BAY CITY BANK (BAY CITY, MI)
Capital Stock $100 par changed to $20 par and (4) additional shares issued 10/14/1959
Stock Dividends - 66.66666666% 06/09/1953; 50% 10/12/1959; 20% 10/12/1964
Name changed to Bay City Bank & Trust Co. (Bay City, MI) 09/14/1968
(See Bay City Bank & Trust Co. (Bay City, MI))

BAY COLONY PPTY INC (MA)
Reorganized under the laws of Delaware as Bay Financial Corp. and Shares of Bene. Int. no par reclassified as Common $1 par 03/03/1980
(See Bay Financial Corp.)

BAY COML BK (WALNUT CREEK, CA)
Under plan of reorganization each share Common no par automatically became (1) share BayCom Corp Common no par 01/27/2017

BAY COML SVCS (CA)
Merged into Greater Bay Bancorp 10/15/1999
Each share Common no par exchanged for (0.6833) share Common no par
Greater Bay Bancorp merged into Wells Fargo & Co. (New) 10/01/2007

BAY COPPER MINES LTD. (CANADA)
Voluntarily dissolved 01/29/1985
Details not available

BAY FINL CORP (DE)
Reorganized under Chapter 11 Federal Bankruptcy Code 06/27/1991
Each share Common $1 par exchanged for $0.10 cash

BAY HALL TRUST LTD. (ENGLAND)
Ordinary 10s par changed to 50p par per currency change 02/15/1971
Acquired by Union Corp. Ltd. 12/18/1972
Each share Ordinary 50p par exchanged for (1) share Ordinary Rand 6.25 par

BAY HEAD VENTURES INC (DE)
Each share old Common $0.00001 par exchanged for (4) shares new Common $0.00001 par 02/26/1988
Name changed to Air Brook Airport Express, Inc. 05/29/1989
Air Brook Airport Express, Inc. name changed to SportsQuest, Inc. 09/20/2007

BAY LAKE GOLD MINES LTD. (ON)
Charter revoked for failure to file reports and pay fees 01/27/1966

BAY MEADOWS OPER CO (DE)
(Issued and transferred only in Non-Separable Units of (1) share of (1) share Bay Meadows Operating Co. Common 1¢ par and (1) share California Jockey Club Common 1¢ par) Units split (2) for (1) by issuance of (1) additional Unit 11/14/1986
Merged into Patriot American Hospitality, Inc. 07/01/1997
Each Unit exchanged for (1) Unit consisting of (1) share Patriot American Hospitality, Inc. (DE) Common 1¢ par and (1) share

Patriot American Hospitality Operating Co. Common 1¢ par
(See each company's listing)

BAY MLS LTD (CANADA)
6% 1st Preferred Ser. A $10 par called for redemption 02/14/1978
Common no par split (3) for (1) by issuance of (2) additional shares 12/21/1979
Common no par split (3) for (1) by issuance of (2) additional shares 12/07/1984
Common no par split (3) for (1) by issuance of (2) additional shares 06/10/1986
Merged into CertainTeed Canada Inc. 10/07/1987
Each share Common no par exchanged for $13 cash

BAY NATL CORP (MD)
Stock Dividend - 10% payable 06/29/2007 to holders of record 06/18/2007 Ex date - 06/14/2007
Charter forfeited 10/01/2013

BAY NETWORKS INC (DE)
Common 1¢ par split (3) for (2) by issuance of (0.5) additional share payable 11/24/1995
Merged into Northern Telecom Ltd.-Northern Telecom Ltee. 08/31/1998
Each share Common 1¢ par exchanged for (0.6) share Common no par
Northern Telecom Ltd.-Northern Telecom Ltee. name changed to Nortel Networks Corp. (Old) 04/30/1999 which reorganized as Nortel Networks Corp. (New) 05/01/2000
(See Nortel Networks Corp. (New))

BAY PAC HEALTH CORP (DE)
Merged into Bay Acquisition Corp. 08/14/1986
Each share Common 1¢ par exchanged for $7.375 cash

BAY PETROLEUM CORP. (DE)
Liquidation completed 11/22/1955
Details not available

BAY PORT ST BK (BAY PORT, MI)
Stock Dividend - 20% 06/24/1977
Under plan of reorganization each share Common automatically became (1) share Bay Port Financial Corp. Common 07/14/1999

BAY RES LTD (BC)
Name changed to Frecom Communications Co. Inc. 04/19/1990
Frecom Communications Co. Inc. recapitalized as International Frecom Communications Inc. 07/02/1992
(See International Frecom Communications Inc.)

BAY RES LTD (DE)
Name changed to Golden River Resources Corp. 04/11/2006
(See Golden River Resources Corp.)

BAY RESSOURCES & SVCS INC (QC)
Merged into Exploration SEG Inc./SEG Exploration Inc. 01/01/1992
Each share Common no par exchanged for (0.19083969) share Common no par
Exploration SEG Inc./SEG Exploration Inc. name changed to West Africa Mining Exploration Inc. 07/06/1995 which name changed to Semafo Inc. 05/13/1997

BAY RIDGE BANCORP INC (NY)
Merged into Independence Savings Bank (Brooklyn, NY) 01/03/1996
Each share Common 10¢ par exchanged for $22 cash

BAY SHORE MINING LTD. (NB)
Charter forfeited for failure to file reports 11/16/1977

BAY ST BANCORP INC (DE)
Common 1¢ par split (3) for (1) by issuance of (2) additional shares payable 09/03/2002 to holders of record 08/19/2002 Ex date - 09/04/2002
Merged into Seacoast Financial Services Corp. 05/31/2003
Each share Common 1¢ par exchanged for (1.257) shares Common 1¢ par
Seacoast Financial Services Corp. merged into Sovereign Bancorp, Inc. 07/23/2004

BAY ST GAS CO NEW (MA)
Name changed 11/19/1974
Under plan of merger name changed from Bay State Gas Co. (Old) to Bay State Gas Co. (New) and each share 4.70% Preferred $100 par, 8.70% Preferred $100 par or 9.95% Preferred $100 par exchanged for (1) share 9.95% Preferred $100 par and each share Common $10 par exchanged for (1) share Common $10 par 11/19/1974
Common $10 par changed to $5 par and (1) additional share issued 07/18/1986
9.95% Preferred $100 par called for redemption 10/19/1986
Each share Common $5 par exchanged for (1.5) shares Common $3.333 par 05/18/1989
$3.80 Preferred $50 par called for redemption at $83 on 03/01/1998
5% Preferred $100 par called for redemption at $105 on 03/01/1998
7.2% Preferred $50 par called for redemption at $50 on 03/01/1998
Merged into Nipsco Industries, Inc. 02/12/1999
Each share Common $3.33 par exchanged for either (1.4414) shares Common no par or $40 cash
Note: Option to receive cash expired 03/01/1999

BAY ST MERCHANTS NATL BK (LAWRENCE, MA)
Capital Stock $17.50 par changed to $25 par 00/00/1950
Capital Stock $25 par changed to $12.50 par and (1) additional share issued 01/28/1958
Name changed to Bay State National Bank (Lawrence, MA) 03/19/1971
Bay State National Bank (Lawrence, MA) merged into Massachusetts Bay Bancorp, Inc. 12/29/1972 which merged into New England Merchants Co., Inc. 05/31/1980 which name changed to Bank of New England Corp. 05/01/1982
(See Bank of New England Corp.)

BAY ST NATL BK (LAWRENCE, MA)
Merged into Massachusetts Bay Bancorp, Inc. 12/29/1972
Each share Capital Stock $12.50 par exchanged for (2) shares Common $1 par
Massachusetts Bay Bancorp, Inc. merged into New England Merchants Co., Inc. 05/31/1980 which name changed to Bank of New England Corp. 05/01/1982
(See Bank of New England Corp.)

BAY STAKES CORP (DE)
Name changed to Chill N Out Cryotherapy, Inc. 01/25/2018

BAY STATE FISHING CO. (MA)
Liquidation completed 10/21/1938
Details not available

BAY STATE FUND, INC.
Liquidated 00/00/1940
Details not availbale

BAY STATE OIL & GAS CO. (OK)
Common $1 par changed to 10¢ par 00/00/1932

Liquidation completed 00/00/1955
Details not available

BAY STR CAP INC (NV)
Name changed to Los Angeles Syndicate of Technology, Inc. 10/14/2010
Los Angeles Syndicate of Technology, Inc. name changed to Invent Ventures, Inc. 09/19/2012

BAY STR SYS LTD (BC)
Recapitalized as Pacific Bay Street Systems, Inc. 08/17/1993
Each share Common no par exchanged for (0.2) share Common no par
Pacific Bay Street Systems, Inc. name changed to Pacific Bay Minerals Ltd. (Old) 07/17/1995 which recapitalized as Consolidated Pacific Bay Minerals Ltd. 08/29/2000 which name changed to Pacific Bay Minerals Ltd. (New) 07/22/2008

BAY VIEW CAP CORP (DE)
Old Common 1¢ par split (2) for (1) by issuance of (1) additional share payable 06/02/1997 to holders of record 05/09/1997
Each share old Common 1¢ par exchanged for (0.1) share new Common 1¢ par 07/01/2004
Under plan of merger name changed to Great Lakes Bancorp, Inc. (New) 05/01/2006
Great Lakes Bancorp, Inc. (New) merged into First Niagara Financial Group, Inc. (New) 02/15/2008 which merged into KeyCorp (New) 08/01/2016

BAY VIEW CAP I (DE)
9.76% Guaranteed Capital Securities called for redemption at $25 on 06/30/2004

BAY VIEW FED SVGS & LN ASSN SAN MATEO CALIF (USA)
Reorganized under the laws of Delaware as Bay View Capital Corp. 07/31/1989
Bay View Capital Corp. name changed to Great Lakes Bancorp, Inc. (New) 05/01/2006 which merged into First Niagara Financial Group, Inc. (New) 02/15/2008 which merged into KeyCorp (New) 08/01/2016

BAYAMON FED SVGS & LN ASSN P R (PR)
Common $1 par split (2) for (1) by issuance of (1) additional share 03/14/1986
Common $1 par split (2) for (1) by issuance of (1) additional share 08/22/1986
Name changed to Federal Savings Bank of Puerto Rico (Bayamon, PR) 07/13/1987
(See Federal Savings Bank of Puerto Rico (Bayamon, PR))

BAYARD DRILLING TECHNOLOGIES INC (DE)
Merged into Nabors Industries, Inc. (DE) 04/07/1999
Each share Common 1¢ par exchanged for (0.3375) share Common 10¢ par and $0.30 cash
Nabors Industries, Inc. (DE) reincorporated in Bermuda as Nabors Industries Ltd. 06/24/2002

BAYARD RES LTD (QC)
Cease trade order effective 07/26/1978
Stockholders' equity unlikely

BAYAURA MINES LTD (AB)
Cease trade order effective 05/14/1992
Stockholders' equity unlikely

BAYBANK (GLADSTONE, MI)
Under plan of reorganization each share Common $1 par automatically became (1) share Baybank Corp. Common $1 par 06/18/1997

BAYBANK HARVARD TRUST CO. (CAMBRIDGE, MA)
Capital Stock $10 par changed to $20 par 00/00/1977
99% held by BayBanks, Inc. as of 12/31/1979
Public interest eliminated

BAYBANK MIDDLESEX, N.A. (BURLINGTON, MA)
Capital Stock $10 par changed to $25 par 02/09/1977
Merged into BayBank Middlesex (Burlington, MA) 11/09/1979
Each share Capital Stock $25 par exchanged for (1.62) shares Common $22.50 par
BayBank Middlesex (Burlington, MA) name changed to BayBank Trust Co. (Burlington, MA) 06/30/1983 which name changed back to BayBank Middlesex (Burlington, MA) 12/08/1983

BAYBANK NEWTON-WALTHAM TRUST CO. (WALTHAM, MA)
Under plan of merger name changed to BayBank Middlesex (Burlington, MA) and Capital Stock $10 par reclassified as Common $22.50 par 11/09/1979
BayBank Middlesex (Burlington, MA) name changed to BayBank Trust Co. (Burlington, MA) 06/30/1983 which name changed back to BayBank Middlesex (Burlington, MA) 12/08/1983

BAYBANK NORFOLK CNTY TR CO (DEDHAM, MA)
Capital Stock $10 par changed to $15 par 07/10/1978
Acquired by Baybank (Burlington, MA) 10/24/1991
Details not available

BAYBANK TRUST CO. (BURLINGTON, MA)
Name changed back to BayBank Middlesex (Burlington, MA) 12/06/1983

BAYBANKS INC (MA)
Common $7.50 par changed to $3.75 par and (1) additional share issued 05/10/1982
Common $3.75 par changed to $2 par and (1) additional share issued 05/15/1986
Merged into Bank of Boston Corp. 07/29/1996
Each share Common $2 par exchanged for (2.2) shares Common $2.25 par
Bank of Boston Corp. name changed to BankBoston Corp. 04/25/1997 which merged into Fleet Boston Corp. 10/01/1999 which name changed to FleetBoston Financial Corp. 04/18/2000 which merged into Bank of America Corp. 04/01/2004

BAYCORP HLDGS LTD (DE)
Acquired by Sloan Group Ltd. 11/16/2005
Each share Common 1¢ par exchanged for $14.19 cash

BAYERISCHE HYPO-UND VEREINSBANK AG (GERMANY)
Each Sponsored ADR for Bearer no par received distribution of (0.25) Hypo Real Estate Holding AG Sponsored ADR for Ordinary payable 10/09/2003 to holders of record 10/02/2003
Acquired by UniCredit S.p.A. 09/15/2008
Each Sponsored ADR for Bearer no par exchanged for $51.2261 cash

BAYERISCHE HYPOTHEKEN-UND WECHSEL BK (GERMANY)
Merged into Bayerische Hypo-und Vereinsbank AG 09/01/1998
Each Sponsored ADR for Bearer Shares DM50 par exchanged for

(0.75) Sponsored ADR for Bearer Shares no par and DM0.26 cash
(See Bayerische Hypo-und Vereinsbank AG)

BAYERISCHE VEREINSBANK AG (GERMANY)
Merged into Bayerische Hypo-und Vereinsbank AG 09/01/1998
Each ADR for Ordinary exchanged for (1) Sponsored ADR for Bearer Shares
(See Bayerische Hypo-und Vereinsbank AG)

BAYFIELD TECHNOLOGIES, INC. (MN)
Assets sold for the benefit of creditors 00/00/1971
No stockholders' equity

BAYFIELD VENTURES CORP (BC)
Common no par split (2) for (1) by issuance of (1) additional share payable 02/15/2005 to holders of record 02/11/2005
Merged into New Gold Inc. 01/02/2015
Each share Common no par exchanged for for (0.0477) share Common no par
Note: Unexchanged certificates will be cancelled and become without value 01/02/2021

BAYFOR CORP. INC. (ON)
Charter cancelled for failure to pay taxes and file returns 02/20/1980

BAYHILL CAP CORP (DE)
Name changed to Agricon Global Corp. 06/01/2012
Agricon Global Corp. recapitalized as StrategaBiz, Inc. 12/16/2014 which name changed to CryptoSign, Inc. 07/06/2015 which name changed to NABUfit Global, 12/10/2015 which name changed to NewBridge Global Ventures, Inc. 12/12/2017

BAYLAKE CAP TR I (DE)
10% Trust Preferred Securities called for redemption at $10 on 03/31/2006

BAYLAKE CORP (WI)
Common $5 par split (2) for (1) by issuance of (1) additional share 09/00/1989
Common $5 par split (3) for (2) by issuance of (0.5) additional share payable 05/15/1998 to holders of record 05/01/1998
Common $5 par split (2) for (1) by issuance of (1) additional share payable 11/15/1999 to holders of record 10/15/1999 Ex date - 11/16/1999
Merged into Nicolet Bankshares, Inc. 04/29/2016
Each share Common $5 par exchanged for (0.4517) shares Common 1¢ par

BAYLESS A J MKTS INC (AZ)
Each share Class B Common $1 par exchanged for (1) share Common $1 par 12/22/1969
Stock Dividend - 10% 04/12/1971
Merged into RFS (Arizona) Merger Corp. 05/10/1984
Each share Common $1 par exchanged for $36 cash

BAYLY CORP (DE)
Name changed 03/01/1972
Common $4 par changed to $1 par and (3) additional shares issued 01/18/1965
Common $1 par split (3) for (2) by issuance of (0.5) additional share 03/01/1968
Name and state of incorporation changed from Bayly Manufacturing Co. (CO) to Bayly Corp. (DE) 03/01/1972
Common $1 par split (4) for (1) by issuance of (3) additional shares 04/07/1983
Stock Dividend - 50% 04/03/1972
Filed petition under Chapter 11 Federal Bankruptcy Code 12/14/1990
No stockholders' equity

BAYMARK TECHNOLOGIES INC (UT)
Each share old Common $0.001 par exchanged for (0.1) share new Common $0.001 par 10/07/2005
Name changed to Implantable Vision, Inc. 01/03/2006
Implantable Vision, Inc. name changed to Arcland Energy Corp. 08/25/2008
(See Arcland Energy Corp.)

BAYMONT CORP (NV)
Common $0.001 par split (6) for (1) by issuance of (5) additional shares payable 03/12/2004 to holders of record 02/28/2004 Ex date - 03/15/2004
Name changed to American Goldfields Inc. 03/31/2004
American Goldfields Inc. recapitalized as Goldfields International Inc. 06/07/2012

BAYNET LTD (DE)
Name changed 02/02/2000
Each share Common 15¢ par exchanged for (0.05) share Common no par 08/31/1999
Name changed from Bayou International Ltd. to Baynet Ltd. 02/02/2000
Name changed to Bay Resources Ltd. 10/23/2000
Bay Resources Ltd. name changed to Golden River Resources Corp. 04/11/2006
(See Golden River Resources Corp.)

BAYNTON ELECTRS CORP (PA)
Company voluntarily dissolved 07/23/1979
Details not available

BAYONNE BANCSHARES INC (DE)
Merged into Richmond County Financial Corp. 03/22/1999
Each share Common 1¢ par exchanged for (1.05) shares Common 1¢ par
Richmond County Financial Corp. merged into New York Community Bancorp, Inc. 07/31/2001

BAYONNE CMNTY BK (BAYONNE, NJ)
Stock Dividends - 10% payable 01/29/2002 to holders of record 01/15/2002; 10% payable 01/29/2003 to holders of record 01/15/2003 Ex date - 01/13/2003
Under plan of reorganization each share Common $5 par automatically became (1) share BCB Bancorp, Inc. Common no par 05/01/2003

BAYONNE MINE LTD. (BC)
Each share Capital Stock $2 par exchanged for (4) shares Capital Stock 50¢ par 10/02/1963
Struck off register and declared dissolved for failure to file returns 09/14/1972

BAYOU BEND PETE LTD
Name changed to ShaMaran Petroleum Corp. 10/21/2009

BAYOU CITY EXPL INC (NV)
Each share old Common $0.005 par exchanged for (0.01) share new Common $0.005 par 07/26/2012
Each share new Common $0.005 par exchanged again for (1) share new Common $0.005 par to reflect a (1) for (20,000) reverse split followed by a (20,000) for (1) forward split 03/11/2014
Note: In effect holders received $1.43 cash per share and public interest was eliminated

BAYOU DELTA INTERNATIONAL INC. (DE)
Name changed to Pecos Western Corp. of Delaware 09/09/1975
Pecos Western Corp. of Delaware name changed to Pecos Western Corp. 06/20/1980

BAYOU OIL & GAS INC (MN)
Each share old Common 1¢ par exchanged for (0.2) share new Common 1¢ par 12/31/1986
Reincorporated under the laws of Delaware as Bayou International, Ltd. and new Common 1¢ par changed to Common 15¢ par 03/06/1987
Bayou International, Ltd. name changed Baynet Ltd. 02/02/2000 which name changed to Bay Resources Ltd. 10/23/2000 which name changed to Golden River Resources Corp. 04/11/2006
(See Golden River Resources Corp.)

BAYOU RES INC (DE)
Merged into Patrick Petroleum Co. 08/04/1987
Each share Common 1¢ par exchanged for (1.282) shares Common 20¢ par
Note: An additional distribution of approximately $2.06 per share in stock or cash may be made at a later date
Patrick Petroleum Co. merged into Goodrich Petroleum Corp. 08/15/1995
(See Goodrich Petroleum Corp.)

BAYOU STL CORP LA PLACE (DE)
Plan of reorganization under Chapter 11 Federal Bankruptcy Code effective 02/18/2004
No Class A stockholders' equity
Acquired by Black Diamond Capital Management, L.L.C. 06/05/2006
Each share Common 1¢ par exchanged for $78.31 cash

BAYPORT RESTAURANT GROUP INC (FL)
Each share old Common $0.001 par exchanged for (0.25) share new Common $0.001 par 08/18/1993
Merged into Landry's Seafood Restaurants, Inc. 08/09/1996
Each share new Common $0.001 par exchanged for (0.189) share Common 1¢ par
Landry's Seafood Restaurants, Inc. name changed to Landry's Restaurants, Inc. 06/05/2001
(See Landry's Restaurants, Inc.)

BAYRIDGE, INC. (OH)
Charter revoked for failure to file reports and pay fees 10/15/1952

BAYRIDGE DEVS INC (BC)
Struck off register and declared dissolved for failure to file returns 08/19/1974

BAYROCK FD INC (MD)
Acquired by Affiliated Fund, Inc. (DE) 09/03/1975
Each share Common $1 par exchanged for (0.7477985) share Capital Stock $1.25 par
Affiliated Fund, Inc. (DE) reincorporated in Maryland 11/26/1975 which name changed to Lord Abbett Affiliated Fund, Inc. 03/01/1996

BAYROCK GROWTH FD INC (FL)
Acquired by Affiliated Fund, Inc. (DE) 09/03/1975
Each share Common 10¢ par exchanged for (0.6200771) share Capital Stock $1.25 par
Affiliated Fund, Inc. (DE) reincorporated in Maryland 11/26/1975 which name changed to Lord Abbett Affiliated Fund, Inc. 03/01/1996

BAYROCK UTIL SECS INC (MD)
Name changed to American Utility Shares, Inc. 08/01/1975
American Utility Shares, Inc. merged into Lord Abbett Income Fund, Inc. 07/31/1978 which name changed to Lord Abbett U.S. Government Securities Fund, Inc. 09/23/1985
(See Lord Abbett U.S. Government Securities Fund, Inc.)

BAYSHORE FLOATING RATE SR LN FD (ON)
Completely liquidated
Each Unit received first and final distribution of $0.42662009 cash payable 03/27/2009 to holders of record 03/27/2009

BAYSHORE ZINC & COPPER MINES, LTD. (ON)
Charter cancelled and company declared dissolved for failure to file returns 04/01/1965

BAYSIDE CAP CORP (AB)
Recapitalized as Pearl River Holdings Ltd. 07/02/1997
Each share Common no par exchanged for (0.5) share Common no par

BAYSIDE PETE CO INC (NV)
Common $0.001 par changed to $0.0001 par 05/12/2010
Recapitalized as Bayside Corp. 06/20/2011
Each share Common $0.0001 par exchanged for (0.004) share Common $0.0001 par

BAYSTAR PETE CORP (DE)
Charter cancelled and declared inoperative and void for non-payment of taxes 03/01/1988

BAYSTATE CORP (MA)
Common $15 par changed to $7.50 par and (1) additional share issued 02/27/1956
$2 Conv. Preferred $10 par called for redemption 07/31/1972
Stock Dividend - 100% 03/31/1965
Name changed to Baybanks, Inc. 04/09/1976
Baybanks, Inc. merged into Bank of Boston Corp. 07/29/1996 which name changed to BankBoston Corp. 04/25/1997 which merged into Fleet Boston Corp. 10/01/1999 which name changed to FleetBoston Financial Corp. 04/18/2000 which merged into Bank of America Corp. 04/01/2004

BAYSWATER RLTY & CAP CORP (DE)
Each share Common $1 par exchanged for $11 cash 12/30/1986

BAYSWATER RLTY & INVT TR (IL)
Reorganized under the laws of Delaware as Bayswater Realty & Capital Corp. and Shares of Bene. Int. no par reclassified as Common $1 par 07/02/1981
(See Bayswater Realty & Capital Corp.)

BAYSWATER URANIUM CORP NEW (BC)
Each share old Common no par exchanged for (0.1) share new Common no par 01/07/2010
Recapitalized as Green Thumb Industries Inc. 06/13/2018
Each share new Common no par exchanged for (0.1) Subordinate Share

BAYSWATER URANIUM CORP OLD (BC)
Merged into Bayswater Uranium Corp. (New) 07/24/2007
Each share Common no par exchanged for (1) share Common no par
Bayswater Uranium Corp. (New) recapitalized as Green Thumb Industries Inc. 06/13/2018

BAYSWATER VENTURES CORP (BC)
Merged into Bayswater Uranium Corp. (Old) 08/15/2006
Each share Common no par

exchanged for (1) share Common no par
Bayswater Uranium Corp. (Old) merged into Bayswater Uranium Corp. (New) 07/24/2007

BAYTEX ENERGY LTD (AB)
Each share Non-Vtg. Class B no par exchanged for (0.0721) share Class A Common no par 04/15/1997
Class A Common no par reclassified as Common no par 06/10/1999
Plan of arrangement effective 09/02/2003
Each share Common no par exchanged for (1) Baytex Energy Trust Trust Unit no par and (0.33333333) share Crew Energy Inc. Common no par
(See each company's listing)

BAYTEX ENERGY TR (AB)
Reorganizaed as Baytex Energy Corp. 01/03/2011
Each Trust Unit no par exchanged for (1) share Common no par
Note: Unexchanged certificates were cancelled and became without value 01/03/2014

BAYUK CIGARS INC. LIQUIDATING TRUST (MD)
Liquidation completed
Each share Common no par exchanged for third distribution of $1.50 cash 03/15/1983
Each share Common no par received fourth distribution of $1.25 cash 12/15/1983
Each share Common no par received fifth distribution of $0.50 cash 01/21/1985
Each share Common no par received sixth and final distribution of $0.84 cash 04/15/1986
(See Bayuk Cigars, Inc. for previous distributions)

BAYUK CIGARS INC (MD)
Each share old Common no par exchanged for (4) shares new Common no par 00/00/1936
New Common no par split (2) for (1) by issuance of (1) additional share 05/20/1964
New Common no par split (2) for (1) by issuance of (1) additional share 12/17/1973
New Common no par split (2) for (1) by issuance of (1) additional share 06/16/1980
Stock Dividend - 100% 10/03/1946
Liquidation completed
Each share new Common no par received initial distribution of $8 cash 04/06/1982
Each share new Common no par received second distribution of $4 cash 06/29/1982
Assets transferred to Bayuk Cigars Inc. Liquidating Trust 10/21/1982

BAYVIEW CORP (NV)
Reorganized as XPention Genetics Inc. 04/12/2005
Each share Common $0.001 par exchanged for (13) shares Common $0.001 par
XPention Genetics Inc. recapitalized as Cancer Detection Corp. 10/14/2008 which name changed to Tremont Fair, Inc. 09/18/2009 which name changed to Vican Resources, Inc. 06/10/2011

BAYVIEW OIL CORP. (DE)
6% Class A Common called for redemption 12/01/1964
Liquidation completed
Each share Common 25¢ par exchanged for initial distribution of $1.50 cash 12/01/1964
Each share Common 25¢ par received second and final distribution of $0.47 cash 05/20/1965

BAYVIEW PUB VENTURES INC (ON)
Reorganized under the laws of Delaware as Catch the Wind Ltd. 09/23/2008
Each (4.99) shares Common no par exchanged for (1) share Common $0.0001 par
Catch the Wind Ltd. (DE) reincorporated in Cayman Islands 06/28/2010 which recapitalized as BlueScout Technologies Ltd. 11/07/2012
(See BlueScout Technologies Ltd.)

BAYVIEW RED LAKE GOLD MINES, LTD.
Acquired by Red Poplar Gold Mines Ltd. 00/00/1947
Each share Capital Stock $1 par exchanged for (0.25) share Capital Stock $1 par
Red Poplar Gold Mines Ltd. recapitalized as Consolidated Red Poplar Minerals Ltd. 03/01/1955 which recapitalized as New Dimension Resources Ltd. 11/09/1971 which recapitalized as New Dimension Industries Ltd. 09/19/1989 which recapitalized as Toxic Disposal Corp. 02/15/1994 which recapitalized as Global Disposal Corp. 03/29/1996
(See Global Disposal Corp.)

BAYVIEW RES LTD (BC)
Recapitalized as Alamo Developments Ltd. 05/29/1984
Each share Common no par exchanged for (0.5) share Common no par
Alamo Developments Ltd. name changed to United Beverages Ltd. 01/14/1988
(See United Beverages Ltd.)

BAYWAY TERMINAL
Reorganized as Bayway Terminal Corp. 00/00/1937
No stockholders' equity

BAYWAY TERMINAL CORP. (NJ)
Merged into Penn-Texas Corp. 00/00/1954
Each share Common $1 par exchanged for (0.33333333) share Capital Stock $10 par
Penn-Texas Corp. name changed to Fairbanks Whitney Corp. 05/29/1959 which recapitalized as Colt Industries Inc. 05/15/1964
(See Colt Industries Inc.)

BAYWEST CAP EQUITIES CORP (CANADA)
Recapitalized as Diversified Baywest Capital Corp. 06/25/1990
Each share Common no par exchanged for (0.13333333) share Common no par
Diversified BayWest Capital Corp. name changed to Nextwave Software Corp. 11/01/1991 which recapitalized as Stox Infolink Systems Inc. 07/21/1994 which name changed to stox.com Inc. 02/24/1999
(See stox.com Inc.)

BAYWOOD INTL INC (NV)
Name changed 03/16/1992
Name changed from Baywood Financial, Inc. to Baywood International, Inc. 03/16/1992
Each share old Common $0.001 par exchanged for (0.05) share new Common $0.001 par 12/18/2007
Name changed to New Leaf Brands, Inc. 10/19/2009
(See New Leaf Brands, Inc.)

BAYWOOD PROPERTIES, INC.
Liquidated 00/00/1945
Details not available

BAZ RES LTD (BC)
Name changed to CHoPP Computer Corp., Inc. 04/25/1985
(See CHoPP Computer Corp., Inc.)

BAZAAR DE LA CUISINE INTERNATIONALE INC (DE)
Name changed to Cellular Telephone Enterprises, Inc. 04/07/1989
(See Cellular Telephone Enterprises, Inc.)

BAZAARVOICE INC (DE)
Acquired by Marlin Equity Partners 02/01/2018
Each share Common $0.0001 par exchanged for $5.50 cash

BAZI INTL INC (NV)
Recapitalized as True Drinks Holdings, Inc. 01/22/2013
Each share Common $0.001 par exchanged for (0.01) share Common $0.001 par

BB HLDGS LTD (BELIZE)
Each share Ordinary Stock 1¢ par received distribution of (0.4) share Carlisle Group Ltd. Ordinary Stock payable 09/09/2005 to holders of record 08/19/2005
Each share Ordinary Stock 1¢ par received distribution of (0.0625) OneSource Services Inc. Ordinary share payable 02/24/2006 to holders of record 02/17/2006 Ex date - 02/16/2006
Reorganized 05/12/2006
Each share Ordinary Stock 1¢ par of U.S. resident holders of (4,000) shares or fewer exchanged for $3.956 cash

BB LIQUIDATING INC (DE)
Chapter 7 bankruptcy proceedings terminated 06/29/2017
Stockholders' equity unlikely

BB&T CAP TR V (DE)
Enhanced Trust Preferred Securities called for redemption at $25 on 07/18/2012

BB&T CAP TR VI (DE)
Enhanced Trust Preferred Securities called for redemption at $25 on 07/18/2012

BB&T CAP TR VII (DE)
Enhanced Trust Preferred Securities called for redemption at $25 on 07/18/2012

BB&T FINL CORP (NC)
Merged into Southern National Corp. 02/28/1995
Each share Common $2.50 par exchanged for (1.45) shares Common $5 par
Southern National Corp. merged into BB&T Corp. 05/19/1997

BBC BROWN BOVERI LTD (SWITZERLAND)
Each old Sponsored ADR for Ordinary exchanged for (0.25) new Sponsored ADR for Ordinary 05/12/1993
Name changed to ABB AG 05/09/1996
(See ABB AG)

BBC CAP MGMT INC (BC)
Name changed to Cornerstone Industries International Inc. 09/23/2005
(See Cornerstone Industries International Inc.)

BBC CAP TR I (DE)
9.5% Trust Preferred Securities called for redemption at $25 on 01/21/2003

BBC CAP TR II (DE)
8.5% Guaranteed Trust Preferred Securities called for redemption at $25 on 09/12/2012

BBC GRAPHICS OF PALM BEACH INC (FL)
Name changed to HASCO Medical, Inc. 07/07/2009
(See HASCO Medical, Inc.)

BBC INDUSTRIES, INC. (DE)
Name changed to Yoo-Hoo Chocolate Beverage Corp. 02/17/1964

Yoo-Hoo Chocolate Beverage Corp. merged into Iroquois Brands, Ltd. 05/06/1976
(See Iroquois Brands, Ltd.)

BBC RLTY INVS (BC)
Merged into Bank of British Columbia (Vancouver, BC) 11/26/1984
Each Trust Unit exchanged for (1) share Common no par and $0.25 cash
Bank of British Columbia (Vancouver, BC) name changed to B.C. Bancorp 04/09/1987 which merged into Canadian Western Bank (Edmonton, AB) 11/01/1996

BBC STK MKT INC (FL)
Name changed to Environmental Solutions Worldwide, Inc. 03/11/1999

BBCN BANCORP INC (DE)
Under plan of merger name changed to Hope Bancorp, Inc. 08/01/2016

BBDO INTL INC (NY)
Common 10¢ par split (2) for (1) by issuance of (1) additional share 02/11/1983
Common 10¢ par split (2) for (1) by issuance of (1) additional share 04/04/1986
Merged into Omnicom Group Inc. 08/29/1986
Each share Common 10¢ par exchanged for (1.23) shares Common 50¢ par

BBF GROUP INC (MA)
Merged into AB Bofors 06/25/1976
Each share Common 10¢ par exchanged for $11 cash

BBF RES INC (AB)
Name changed to Western Energy Services Corp. 07/27/2005

BBI INC (DE)
Charter cancelled and declared inoperative and void for non-payment of taxes 03/01/1974

BBJ ENVIRONMENTAL TECHNOLOGIES INC (NV)
SEC revoked common stock registration 03/09/2009

BBM HLDGS INC (UT)
Reincorporated under the laws of Delaware as Ohr Pharmaceutical, Inc. and Common no par changed to $0.0001 par 09/24/2009

BBM PHOTOCOPY MANUFACTURING CORP. (NY)
Name changed to Bohn Business Machines, Inc. 11/06/1961
(See Bohn Business Machines, Inc.)

BBN CORP (MA)
Merged into GTE Corp. 08/15/1997
Each share Common $1 par exchanged for $29 cash

BBN GLOBAL CONSULTING INC (NV)
Name changed to Evolution Resources, Inc. 07/09/2009
Evolution Resources, Inc. recapitalized as Tapinator, Inc. 11/14/2013

BBOOTH INC (NV)
Common $0.0001 par split (2) for (1) by issuance of (1) additional share payable 10/16/2014 to holders of record 10/16/2014
Name changed to nFusz, Inc. 04/24/2017

BBV VIETNAM S E A ACQUISITION CORP (MARSHALL ISLANDS)
Units separated 02/08/2012
SEC revoked common stock registration 10/18/2013

BBVA BANCO BHIF (CHILE)
Name changed 11/08/2000
Name changed from BBV Banco BHIF to BBVA Banco BHIF 11/08/2000

Name changed to Banco Bilbao
Vizcaya Argentaria 03/29/2003
*(See Banco Bilbao Vizcaya
Argentaria)*

BBVA PFD CAP LTD (SPAIN)
7.8% Non-Cumulative Guaranteed
Preference Ser. A called for
redemption at $25 on 06/30/2002
7.75% Guaranteed Preferred Ser. B
called for redemption at $25 plus
$0.13 accrued dividends on
07/24/2006

**BBVA PRIVANZA INTL GIBRALTAR
LTD (SPAIN)**
Sponsored ADR's for Preference Ser.
E called for redemption at $25 plus
$0.50 accrued dividends on
06/30/2002
Sponsored ADR's for Preference Ser.
B called for redemption at $25 on
12/15/2002
Sponsored ADR's for Preference Ser.
C called for redemption at $25 plus
$0.50 accrued dividends on
06/30/2003
Sponsored ADR's for Preference Ser.
D reacquired at $1,000,000 per ADR
through cash purchase offer which
expired 01/30/2006

BBX CAP CORP OLD (FL)
Acquired by BFC Financial Corp.
12/16/2016
Each share Class A Common 1¢ par
exchanged for $20 cash

BC COMMUNICATIONS INC (DE)
Recapitalized as Cathel Partners, Ltd.
11/00/1994
Each share Common $0.00001 par
exchanged for (0.001) share
Common $0.00001 par
(See Cathel Partners, Ltd.)

BC GAS INC NEW (BC)
Reorganized 07/02/1993
Reorganized from BC Gas Inc. (Old)
to BC Gas Inc. (New) 07/02/1993
Name changed to Terasen Inc.
05/05/2003
Terasen Inc. was acquired by Kinder
Morgan, Inc. (KS) 11/30/2005
(See Kinder Morgan, Inc. (KS))

BC GAS UTIL LTD (BC)
7.1% Retractable 1st Preference
called for redemption at $25 plus
$0.44375 accrued dividends on
09/30/1999
6.32% 1st Preference called for
redemption at $25 plus $0.395
accrued dividends on 10/31/2000

BC RAIL LTD (BC)
Each $2.3125 Retractable 1st
Preferred Ser. A exchanged for (1)
share $2.3125 Legended
Guaranteed Retractable 1st
Preferred Ser. A 00/00/1992
$2.3125 Legended Guaranteed
Retractable 1st Preferred Ser. A $25
par called for redemption
05/12/1994
Public interest eliminated

BC TEL (CANADA)
$1.70 Preferred $25 par called for
redemption 04/01/1994
$1.76 Preferred $25 par called for
redemption 04/01/1994
Name changed to Telus
Communications BC Inc. 10/18/1999
Telus Communications BC Inc. name
changed to Telus Communications
Inc. 01/22/2001
(See Telus Communications Inc.)

BC TELECOM INC (CANADA)
Merged into BCT.TELUS
Communications Inc. 01/31/1999
Each share Common no par
exchanged for (0.75) share Common
no par and (0.25) share Non-Vtg. no
par
Note: Unexchanged certificates were
cancelled and became without value
01/31/2005

BCAM INTL INC (NY)
Recapitalized as CellMetrix, Inc.
05/24/2000
Each share Common 1¢ par
exchanged for (0.06666666) share
Common 1¢ par
(See CellMetrix, Inc.)

BCB FINL SVCS CORP (PA)
Common $2.50 par split (6) for (5) by
issuance of (0.2) additional share
payable 11/19/1996 to holders of
record 11/05/1996
Merged into Main Street Bancorp, Inc.
05/01/1998
Each share Common $2.50 par
exchanged for (1.3335) shares
Common $1 par
Main Street Bancorp, Inc. merged into
Sovereign Bancorp, Inc. 03/08/2002
which merged into Banco
Santander, S.A. 01/30/2009

BCB HLDGS INC (ON)
Reincorporated 10/01/1996
Place of incorporation changed from
(AB) to (ON) 10/01/1996
Recapitalized as BCB Voice Systems
Inc. 08/17/1998
Each share Common no par
exchanged for (0.1) share Common
no par
BCB Voice Systems Inc. name
changed to VoiceIQ Inc. (ON)
10/04/2000 which reorganized in
Alberta as Yoho Resources Inc.
(Old) 12/23/2004 which reorganized
as Yoho Resources Inc. (New)
03/21/2014
(See Yoho Resources Inc. (New))

BCB VOICE SYS INC (ON)
Name changed to VoiceIQ Inc. (ON)
10/04/2000
VoiceIQ Inc. (ON) reorganized in
Alberta as Yoho Resources Inc.
(Old) 12/23/2004 which reorganized
as Yoho Resources Inc. (New)
03/21/2014
(See Yoho Resources Inc. (New))

BCC INC (DE)
Name changed to Technicare Corp.
08/30/1973
Technicare Corp. merged into
Johnson & Johnson 02/21/1979

BCC INDUSTRIES, INC. (MA)
Reincorporated under the laws of
Delaware as BCC, Inc. 12/05/1972
BCC, Inc. name changed to
Technicare Corp. 08/30/1973 which
merged into Johnson & Johnson
02/21/1979

**BCD SEMICONDUCTOR MFG LTD
(CAYMAN ISLANDS)**
Merged into Diodes Inc. 03/04/2013
Each Sponsored ADR for Ordinary
exchanged for $8 cash

BCE DEV CORP (BC)
Each share 8.625% Sr. Preference
Ser. B $10 par reclassified as
9.125% Retractable Sr. Preference
Ser. A $10 par 02/01/1987
Each share 9.5% Sr. Preference Ser.
B $10 par reclassified as 9.75%
Retractable Sr. Preference Ser. B
$10 par 02/01/1987
75¢ Class A no par called for
redemption 05/25/1987
Name changed to BF Realty Holdings
Ltd. 08/19/1991
(See BF Realty Holdings Ltd.)

BCE EMERGIS INC (CANADA)
Name changed to Emergis Inc.
12/01/2004
(See Emergis Inc.)

BCE INC (CANADA)
$2.70 Conv. 1st Preferred Ser. I no
par called for redemption
03/16/1988
$1.96 Conv. 1st Preferred Ser. G no
par called for redemption 11/01/1991
$2.05 Conv. 1st Preferred Ser. H no
par called for redemption
04/16/1992
Adjustable Dividend 1st Preferred
Ser. O no par called for redemption
07/14/1995
$1.95 1st Preferred Ser. M no par
called for redemption 10/31/1995
$1.60 1st Preferred Ser. P no par
called for redemption at $25 plus
$0.40 accrued dividends on
01/15/2004
(Additional Information in Active)

**BCE MOBILE COMMUNICATIONS
INC (CANADA)**
Under plan of amalgamation each
share Common no par exchanged
for $58.75 cash 10/22/1999

BCE PL FIN CORP (QC)
Acquired by BF Realty Holdings Ltd.
06/03/1994
Each share 7.375% Retractable
Preferred Ser. 1 no par exchanged
for $25.75 cash
Each share 7.75% Retractable
Preferred Ser. 2 no par exchanged
for $26 cash

BCED CAP I CORP (QC)
Name changed to Brookfield Capital 1
Corp. 04/14/1992
(See Brookfield Capital 1 Corp.)

BCGOLD CORP (BC)
Each share old Common no par
exchanged for (0.1) share new
Common no par 11/05/2012
Each share new Common no par
exchanged again for (0.2) share new
Common no par 02/29/2016
Name changed to Pan Andean
Minerals Ltd. 03/16/2017

BCH - USA (NEW YORK, NY)
Liquidated 06/05/2001
Details not available

BCH CAPITAL LTD. (SPAIN)
10.5% Non-Cum. Guaranteed
Preference Ser. A called for
redemption at $25.7875 on
02/26/2002
9.43% Preference Ser. B called for
redemption at $25 plus $0.078583
accrued dividends on 07/12/2005

**BCH EUROCAPITAL LTD
(CAYMAN ISLANDS)**
Ser. B Preference called for
redemption at $25 on 04/22/2004

**BCH INTL-PUERTO RICO INC
(SPAIN)**
9.875% Guaranteed Monthly Income
Preferred Stock Ser. A called for
redemption at $25.75 plus $0.192
accrued dividends on 03/28/2002

BCH SYS INC (TX)
Reincorporated under the laws of
Nevada as National Healthcare
Logistics, Inc. 04/25/2005

BCI GEONETICS INC (DE)
Name changed to Integrated Water
Technologies, Inc. 01/31/1994
Integrated Water Technologies, Inc.
name changed to Integrated Water
Resources Inc. 03/06/2000

BCI HLDGS CORP (DE)
Each share 15.25% Exchangeable
Preferred 1¢ par exchanged for $25
principal amount of 15.25% Jr.
Subordinated Exchange Debentures
due 05/01/2002 on 08/01/1986

BCI MGMT LTD (CANADA)
Name changed to Unicap Commercial
Corp. 08/19/1993
Unicap Commercial Corp.
recapitalized as Unavest Capital
Corp. 08/19/1998 which merged into
Genterra Investment Corp.
04/30/1999 which merged into
Genterra Inc. 12/31/2003 which
merged into Genterra Capital Inc.
(New) 05/10/2010 which merged
into Gencan Capital Inc. 10/30/2015

BCMETALS CORP (AB)
Acquired by Imperial Metals Corp.
(New) 03/22/2007
Each share Common no par
exchanged for $1.70 cash

BCO HYDROCARBON LTD (NV)
Common $0.0001 par split (3.25) for
(1) by issuance of (2.25) additional
shares payable 06/07/2010 to
holders of record 06/06/2010
Ex date - 06/08/2010
Name changed to Sauer Energy, Inc.
10/20/2010

BCP ESSEX HLDGS INC (DE)
15% Exchangeable Preferred Ser. B
called for redemption at $27.041 on
07/15/1996

**BCS COLLABORATIVE SOLUTIONS
INC (BC)**
Recapitalized as BCS Global
Networks Inc. 09/02/2003
Each share Common no par
exchanged for (0.33333333) share
Common no par
(See BCS Global Networks Inc.)

BCS GLOBAL NETWORKS INC (BC)
Acquired by 2073832 Ontario Inc.
09/15/2005
Each share Common no par
exchanged for $0.20 cash

BCS INVT CORP (CO)
Recapitalized as Crossnet
Communications Inc. 12/18/2000
Each share Common no par
exchanged for (0.1) share Common
no par
Crossnet Communications Inc.
recapitalized as Cirond Technologies
Inc. 07/01/2002 which name
changed to Seaside Holdings Inc.
03/17/2003

BCS SOLUTIONS INC (FL)
Common $0.0001 par split (17) for (1)
by issuance of (16) additional
shares payable 03/28/2011 to
holders of record 03/25/2011
Ex date - 03/29/2011
Reincorporated under the laws of
Nevada as Grizzly Gold Corp.
08/01/2011

BCSB BANCORP INC (MD)
Merged into F.N.B. Corp. 02/15/2014
Each share Common 1¢ par
exchanged for (2.08) shares
Common $0.001 par

BCSB BANKORP INC (USA)
Reorganized under the laws of
Maryland as BCSB Bancorp, Inc.
04/11/2008
Each share Common 1¢ par
exchanged for (0.5264) share
Common 1¢ par
BCSB Bancorp, Inc. merged into
F.N.B. Corp. 02/15/2014

BCT INTL INC (DE)
Merged into Phoenix Group of
Florida, Inc. 12/05/2003
Each share Common 4¢ par
exchanged for $2 cash

**BCT TELUS COMMUNICATIONS INC
(CANADA)**
Name changed to Telus Corp.
05/08/2000

BCU INDS INC (CANADA)
Struck off register and declared
dissolved for failure to file returns
06/10/2004

BCV CORP (UT)
Name changed to Starich Inc.
04/28/1988
(See Starich Inc.)

BCX SPLIT CORP (ON)
Preferred Shares no par called for
redemption at $15.71 on 08/05/2008
Capital Shares no par called for
redemption at $23.277 on
08/05/2008

BCY LIFESCIENCES INC (CANADA)
Name changed 01/04/2001
Name changed from BCY Ventures Inc. to BCY LifeSciences Inc. 01/04/2001
Name changed to BCY Resources Inc. (Canada) 08/21/2007
BCY Resources Inc. (Canada) reincorporated in British Columbia 12/23/2010 which recapitalized as Mexigold Corp. 03/16/2011 which recapitalized as Savannah Gold Corp. 08/22/2016 which name changed to E3 Metals Corp. 05/19/2017

BCY RES INC (BC)
Reincorporated 12/23/2010
Place of incorporation changed from (Canada) to (BC) 12/23/2010
Recapitalized as Mexigold Corp. 03/16/2011
Each share Common no par exchanged for (0.25) share Common no par
Mexigold Corp. recapitalized as Savannah Gold Corp. 08/22/2016 which name changed to E3 Metals Corp. 05/19/2017

BDC CAP INC (MN)
Each share old Common 1¢ par exchanged for (0.01333333) share new Common 1¢ par 10/04/2006
Name changed to DigitalTown, Inc. 03/01/2007

BDC INDS CORP (BC)
Name changed to Jolt Beverage Co., Ltd. 09/04/1986
Jolt Beverage Co., Ltd. name changed to International Beverage Corp. 05/13/1988 which recapitalized as Clearly Canadian Beverage Corp. 05/14/1990
(See Clearly Canadian Beverage Corp.)

BDCA VENTURE INC (MD)
Name changed to Crossroads Capital, Inc. 12/03/2015

BDG PAC RES INC (BC)
Recapitalized as Southern Nites Petroleum Corp. 09/29/1999
Each share Common no par exchanged for (0.25) share Common no par
Southern Nites Petroleum Corp. name changed to Oracle Energy Corp. 07/11/2000

BDI INVT CORP (NJ)
Completely liquidated
Each share Common 10¢ par received first and final distribution of $10.0602 cash payable 04/20/2005 to holders of record 04/06/2005 Ex date - 04/21/2005
Note: Certificates were not required to be surrendered and are without value

BDI MNG CORP (BRITISH VIRGIN ISLANDS)
Acquired by Gem Diamonds Ltd. 06/07/2007
Each share Common no par exchanged for 37p cash

BDI MNG CORP (YT)
Reincorporated under the laws of British Virgin Islands 08/08/2005
(See BDI Mining Corp.)

BDM CORP. (DE)
Name changed to BDM International, Inc. (Old) 01/01/1980
(See BDM International, Inc. (Old))

BDM INTL INC NEW (DE)
New Common 1¢ par split (2) for (1) by issuance of (1) additional share payable 03/20/1997 to holders of record 03/06/1997
Merged into TRW Inc. 12/29/1997
Each share new Common 1¢ par exchanged for $29.50 cash

BDM INTL INC OLD (DE)
Common 10¢ par changed to 5¢ par and (1) additional share issued 08/29/1980
Common 5¢ par changed to $0.025 par and (1) additional share issued 05/16/1983
Common $0.025 par reclassified as Conv. Class B Common $0.025 par 12/15/1983
Class A Common $0.025 par split (2) for (1) by issuance of (1) additional share 06/03/1985
Conv. Class B Common $0.025 par split (2) for (1) by issuance of (1) additional share 06/03/1985
Acquired by Ford Motor Co. 07/01/1988
Each share Class A Common $0.025 par exchanged for $34.75 cash
Each share Conv. Class B Common $0.025 par exchanged for $34.75 cash

BDO UNIBANK INC (PHILIPPINES)
Stock Dividends - In Sponsored GDR's to holders of Reg. S Sponsored GDR's 3% payable 06/14/2012 to holders of record 05/25/2012 Ex date - 05/23/2012
In 144A Sponsored GDR's to holders of 144A Sponsored GDR's 3% payable 06/14/2012 to holders of record 05/25/2012 Ex date - 05/23/2012
GDR agreement terminated 05/14/2013
Each Sponsored Reg. S GDR for Ordinary exchanged for $44.8492 cash
Each Sponsored 144A GDR for Ordinary exchanged for $44.8492 cash
(Additional Information in Active)

BDR INDS INC (CO)
Name changed to Conectisys Corp. 10/16/1995

BDS INDS INC (AB)
Name changed to New-View Industries Inc. 08/30/1990
New-View Industries Inc. merged into Home Products, Inc. 09/28/1992
(See Home Products, Inc.)

BDW HLDGS LTD (CA)
Reorganized under the laws of Florida as International Energy Group, Inc. 03/08/2006
Each share Common no par exchanged for (0.001) share Common $0.0001 par
International Energy Group, Inc. name changed to International Energy Ltd., Inc. 11/06/2009 which name changed to Standard Oil Company USA, Inc. 05/13/2010 which name changed to Gold Mining USA Inc. 05/24/2012 which name changed to Vita Mobile Systems, Inc. 01/31/2018

BE AT TV INC (NV)
Common $0.0001 par split (33) for (2) by issuance of (15.5) additional shares payable 12/26/2013 to holders of record 12/26/2013
Recapitalized as Epic Stores Corp. 08/18/2015
Each share Common $0.0001 par exchanged for (0.41666666) share Common $0.0001 par

BE AVIONICS INC (DE)
Name changed to BE Aerospace, Inc. 05/29/1992
BE Aerospace, Inc. name changed to B/E Aerospace, Inc. 08/07/2012 which merged into Rockwell Collins, Inc. 04/13/2017

BE FREE INC (DE)
Common 1¢ par split (2) for (1) by issuance of (1) additional share payable 03/08/2000 to holders of record 03/01/2000
Merged into ValueClick, Inc. 05/23/2002
Each share Common 1¢ par exchanged for (0.65882) share Common $0.001 par
ValueClick, Inc. name changed to Conversant, Inc. 02/05/2014 which merged into Alliance Data Systems Corp. 12/11/2014

BE INC (DE)
Liquidation completed
Each share Common $0.001 par exchanged for initial distribution of $0.58 cash 05/19/2004
Each share Common $0.001 par received second and final distribution of $0.08304015 cash payable 04/13/2009 to holders of record 04/13/2009

BE MAC TRANS INC (MO)
Through voluntary purchase offer 98.95% acquired by U.S. Truck Lines, Inc. in 1972
Public interest eliminated

BE SAFE SVCS INC (DE)
SEC revoked common stock registration 01/08/2009

BEA INCOME FD INC (MD)
Name changed to Credit Suisse Asset Management Income Fund, Inc. 05/11/1999

BEA STRATEGIC GLOBAL INCOME FD INC (MD)
Name changed 05/13/1997
Name changed from BEA Strategic Income Fund, Inc. to BEA Strategic Global Income Fund, Inc. 05/13/1997
Name changed to Credit Suisse Asset Management Strategic Global Income Fund, Inc. 05/11/1999
Credit Suisse Asset Management Strategic Global Income Fund, Inc. merged into Credit Suisse Asset Management Income Fund, Inc. 05/14/2001

BEA SYS INC (DE)
Common $0.001 par split (2) for (1) by issuance of (1) additional share payable 12/19/1999 to holders of record 11/19/1999
Common $0.001 par split (2) for (1) by issuance of (1) additional share payable 04/24/2000 to holders of record 04/07/2000
Merged into Oracle Corp. 04/29/2008
Each share Common $0.001 par exchanged for $19.375 cash

BEACH BANK OF VERO BEACH (VERO BEACH, FL)
Reorganized as Beach ONE Financial Services, Inc. 02/01/1983
Each share Common $25 par exchanged for (1) share Common 1¢ par
(See Beach ONE Financial Services, Inc.)

BEACH BUSINESS BK (MANHATTAN BEACH, CA)
Merged into First PacTrust Bancorp, Inc. 07/02/2012
Each share Common no par exchanged for (1) Common Stock Purchase Warrant expiring 06/30/2013 and $9.21 cash

BEACH COUCH INC (DE)
Common $0.0001 par split (10) for (1) by issuance of (9) additional shares payable 04/04/2000 to holders of record 04/03/2000
Name changed to VIPC Communications Inc. 09/25/2000
(See VIPC Communications Inc.)

BEACH FIRST NATL BANCSHARES INC (SC)
Common $1 par split (3) for (2) by issuance of (0.5) additional share payable 12/21/2006 to holders of record 12/1/2006 Ex date - 12/22/2006
Chapter 7 bankruptcy proceedings terminated 05/05/2017
Stockholders' equity unlikely

BEACH FIRST NATL BK (POMPANO BEACH, FL)
Through voluntary exchange offer 99.94% held by First National Bankshares of Florida, Inc. and bank directors as of 11/30/1973
Public interest eliminated

BEACH GOLD MINES LTD (BC)
Recapitalized as Perron Gold Mines Ltd. 05/19/1983
Each share Common $1 par exchanged for (0.5) share Common no par
Perron Gold Mines Ltd. merged into Aurizon Mines Ltd. 08/24/1988 which merged into Hecla Mining Co. 06/01/2013

BEACH HAVEN NATL BK & TR CO (BEACH HAVEN, NJ)
Common $100 par changed to $10 par and (9) additional shares issued 03/00/1953
Common $10 par changed to $5 par and (1) additional share issued 01/22/1971
Stock Dividends - 28% 12/18/1970; 33.33333333% 07/19/1955; 12.5% 04/25/1957; 10% 11/27/1961; 33.33333333% 11/23/1966; 25% 00/00/1969, 33.33333333% 00/00/1973
Acquired by Bancshares of New Jersey 06/30/1976
Each share Common $5 par exchanged for (0.8) share Common $5 par
Bancshares of New Jersey name changed to Northern National Corp. 05/28/1981 which merged into Horizon Bancorp 10/01/1983
(See Horizon Bancorp)

BEACH HOTEL CO. (IL)
Merged into Chicago Beach Hotel, Inc. 00/00/1936
Details not available

BEACH NATIONAL BANK (POMPANO BEACH, FL)
Name changed to Beach First National Bank (Pompano Beach, FL) 12/31/1969
(See Beach First National Bank (Pompano Beach, FL))

BEACH ONE FINANCIAL SERVICES, INC. (FL)
Acquired by Northern Trust Corp. 03/31/1995
Details not available

BEACH SOAP CO. (MA)
Common $100 par changed to $50 par 00/00/1941
Acquired by National Industrial Products Co. 01/00/1960
Details not available
Preferred $100 par called for redemption 09/30/1964

BEACHPORT ENTMT CORP (UT)
Each share old Common $0.002 par exchanged for (0.2) share new Common $0.002 par 06/26/1995
SEC revoked common stock registration 08/05/2004

BEACON ASSOCIATES, INC. (RI)
Common no par changed to $10 par 00/00/1948
Liquidation completed 07/25/1958
Details not available

BEACON BOOK SHOP, INC. (NY)
Charter cancelled and proclaimed dissolved for failure to pay taxes and file reports 11/15/1947

BEACON BUILDING CORP. (IL)
Common no par changed to $1 par 00/00/1941
Liquidation completed 02/04/1958
Details not available

BEACON ENERGY CORP (AB)
Merged into Consolidated Beacon Resources Ltd. (AB) 11/14/1990
Each share Common no par exchanged for (0.5348) share Common no par
Consolidated Beacon Resources Ltd. (AB) reorganized in British Columbia as Zone Resources Inc. 07/24/2009

BEACON ENERGY HLDGS INC (DE)
Recapitalized as EQM Technologies & Energy, Inc. 02/10/2011
Each share Common $0.001 par exchanged for (0.2) share Common $0.001 par

BEACON ENERGY INC (UT)
Merged into Team-Beacon Energy, Inc. 10/04/1982
Each share Common $0.001 par exchanged for $0.6114 cash

BEACON ENTERPRISE SOLUTIONS GROUP INC (NV)
Name changed to FTE Networks, Inc. 03/18/2014

BEACON FED BANCORP INC (MD)
Merged into Berkshire Hills Bancorp, Inc. 10/19/2012
Each share Common 1¢ par exchanged for $20.50 cash

BEACON FINL INC (UT)
Name changed to Interwest Home Medical Inc. 05/02/1995
(See Interwest Home Medical Inc.)

BEACON HILL CO.
Liquidated 00/00/1943
Details not available

BEACON HILL MUT FD INC (MA)
Proclaimed dissolved for failure to file reports and pay taxes 06/27/1997

BEACON HOTEL CORP (NY)
Assets sold for benefit of creditors 10/22/1964
No stockholders' equity

BEACON INCOME FD INC (DE)
Charter cancelled and declared inoperative and void for non-payment of taxes 03/01/1985

BEACON LIFE INSURANCE CO. (MD)
Merged into Williamsburg Life Insurance Co (MD) 09/14/1966
Each share Capital Stock $1 par exchanged for (1) share Capital Stock $1 par
Williamsburg Life Insurance Co. (MD) merged into Independent Liberty Life Insurance Co. 12/30/1967
(See Independent Liberty Life Insurance Co.)

BEACON LT HLDG CORP (NV)
Reincorporated 11/18/1997
Name changed 02/18/1998
Common $0.125 par changed to 10¢ par 08/00/1979
Each share Common 10¢ par exchanged for (0.1) share Common $0.001 par 08/11/1997
State of incorporation changed from (ID) to (NV) 11/18/1997
Name changed from Beacon Light Mining Inc. to Beacon Light Holding Corp. 02/18/1998
Name changed to Wellux International Inc. 08/03/2001
Wellux International Inc. name changed to Readen Holding Corp. 08/22/2011

BEACON MANOR BUILDING CORP. (IL)
Property sold 00/00/1947
Details not available

BEACON MINING CO., LTD. (QC)
Merged into Highland-Crow Resources Ltd. 09/25/1978
Each share Capital Stock $1 par exchanged for (0.025) share Capital Stock no par
Highland-Crow Resources Ltd. merged into Noramco Mining Corp.

01/01/1988 which name changed to Quest Capital Corp. 01/03/1995 which name changed to Quest Oil & Gas Inc. 11/15/1996 which merged into EnerMark Income Fund 04/18/1997 which merged into Enerplus Resources Fund 06/22/2001 which reorganized as Enerplus Corp. 01/03/2011

BEACON PETROLEUMS LTD. (AB)
Recapitalized as Beacon Placers Ltd. 05/31/1961
Each share Capital Stock no par exchanged for (0.1) share Capital Stock no par no par
(See Beacon Placers Ltd.)

BEACON PHOTO SVC INC OLD (NY)
Completely liquidated 01/05/1984
Each share Common 1¢ par exchanged for first and final distribution of (1) share Beacon Photo Service, Inc. (New) Common 1¢ par and (1) share Imprint Products Inc. Common 1¢ par
(See each company's listing)

BEACON PHOTO SVCS INC NEW (NY)
Merged into a private company 11/18/1985
Each share Common 1¢ par exchanged for $4.61 cash

BEACON PLACERS LTD. (AB)
Struck off register for failure to file annual returns 10/31/1968

BEACON PWR CORP (DE)
Each share old Common 1¢ par exchanged for (0.1) share new Common 1¢ par 02/25/2011
Chapter 11 bankruptcy proceedings dismissed 05/12/2014
Company is a shell

BEACON PPTYS CORP (MD)
Merged into Equity Office Properties Trust 12/19/1997
Each share 8.98% Preferred Ser. A 1¢ par exchanged for (1) share 8.98% Preferred Ser. A 1¢ par
Each share Common 1¢ par exchanged for (1.4063) shares Common 1¢ par
(See Equity Office Properties Trust)

BEACON RES CORP (DE)
Name changed to Energy Sources, Inc. 04/30/1974
(See Energy Sources, Inc.)

BEACON STL CORP (DE)
Charter cancelled and declared inoperative and void for non-payment of taxes 06/24/1992

BEACON TRUST
Trust terminated and Participating Certificates exchanged for stock of 4716 Beacon Building Corp. 00/00/1942

BEACONEYE INC (CANADA)
Merged into TLC The Laser Center Inc. 04/27/1998
Each share Common no par exchanged for (0.08) share Common no par
TLC The Laser Center Inc. name changed to TLC Laser Eye Centers Inc. 11/11/1999 which reincorporated in New Brunswick as TLC Vision Corp. 05/16/2002
(See TLC Vision Corp.)

BEAM (JAMES B.) DISTILLING CO. (IL)
Common $2 par split (5) for (4) by issuance of (0.25) additional share 10/01/1963
Stock Dividends - 10% 12/28/1951; 100% 04/20/1961
Completely liquidated 04/03/1967
Each share Common $2 par exchanged for first and final distribution of $42.50 cash

BEAM INC (DE)
$2.67 Conv. Preferred no par called

for redemption at $30.50 plus $0.52 accrued dividends on 11/20/2012
Acquired by Suntory Holdings Ltd. 04/30/2014
Each share Common $3.125 par exchanged for $83.50 cash

BEAM-MATIC HOSPITAL SUPPLY, INC. (NY)
Completely liquidated 06/27/1967
Each share Common 10¢ par exchanged for first and final distribution of (0.24) share Vernitron Corp. (Old) (NY) Common 10¢ par
Vernitron Corp. (Old) (NY) reincorporated in Delaware 06/28/1968 which reorganized as Vernitron Corp. (New) 08/28/1987 which name changed to Axsys Technologies, Inc. 12/04/1996
(See Axsys Technologies, Inc.)

BEAMALLOY CORP (OH)
Plan of reorganization under Chapter 11 Federal Bankruptcy proceedings confirmed 03/24/2000
Stockholders' equity unlikely

BEAMAN CORP (NC)
Capital Stock $1 par split (2) for (1) by issuance of (1) additional share 06/26/1984
Capital Stock $1 par split (2) for (1) by issuance of (1) additional share 07/25/1985
Stock Dividend - 100% 09/22/1971
Merged into Condor Group PLC 10/27/1989
Each share Capital Stock $1 par exchanged for $7 cash

BEAMAN'S ENGINEERING CO. (NC)
Name changed to Beaman Corp. 07/28/1961
(See Beaman Corp.)

BEAMSCOPE CDA INC (ON)
Discharged from receivership 10/13/2005
No stockholders' equity

BEAN (JOHN) MANUFACTURING CO. (DE)
Name changed to Food Machinery Corp. 07/20/1929
Food Machinery Corp. name changed to Food Machinery & Chemical Corp. 09/10/1948 which name changed to FMC Corp. 06/30/1961

BEAN SPRAY PUMP CO. (DE)
Succeeded by Bean (John) Manufacturing Co. 08/10/1928
Details not available

BEANLAND MINING CO. LTD.
Recapitalized as Clenor Mining Co. Ltd. on a (1) for (2) basis in 1950

BEANSTALK CAP CORP (BC)
Recapitalized as Compliance Energy Corp. 08/30/2002
Each share Common no par exchanged for (0.5) share Common no par

BEANSTALK CAP INC (BC)
Name changed to Gold Mountain Mining Corp. 07/27/2011
Gold Mountain Mining Corp. merged into JDL Gold Corp. 10/07/2016 which name changed to Trek Mining Inc. 03/31/2017 which name changed to Equinox Gold Corp. 12/22/2017

BEAR AEROSPACE INC (NV)
Each share old Common $0.001 par exchanged for (0.25) share new Common $0.001 par 09/18/2002
SEC revoked common stock registration 10/15/2008

BEAR AUTOMOTIVE SVC EQUIP CO (DE)
Acquired by SPX Corp. 09/14/1988
Each share Common 1¢ par exchanged for $11 cash

BEAR BODY INC (CO)
Chapter 11 Federal Bankruptcy Code

converted to Chapter 7 on 07/26/1984
No stockholders' equity

BEAR CREEK CORP (DE)
Merged into Reynolds (R.J.) Development Corp. 01/03/1984
Each share Common 10¢ par exchanged for $39 cash

BEAR CREEK ENERGY LTD (AB)
Under plan of merger each share Common no par exchanged for (0.2) share Bear Ridge Resources Ltd. Common no par, (0.2) share Kereco Energy Ltd. Common no par, and (0.5) Ketch Resources Trust, Trust Unit 01/18/2005
(See each company's listing)

BEAR CREEK MNG CORP (YT)
Reincorporated under the laws of British Columbia 07/16/2004

BEAR EXPLORATION & RADIUM, LTD.
Merged into Yellowknife Bear Mines, Ltd. (ON) 00/00/1948
Each (100) shares Capital Stock $1 par exchanged for (60) shares Capital Stock $1 par
Yellowknife Bear Mines Ltd. (ON) reincorporated in Canada 10/12/1978 which name changed to Yellowknife Bear Resources Inc. 03/06/1981 which merged into Rayrock Yellowknife Resources Inc. 02/03/1986 which name changed to Rayrock Resources Inc. 11/27/1998
(See Rayrock Resources Inc.)

BEAR INTERNATIONAL INDUSTRIES LTD. (BC)
Recapitalized as Consolidated Bear Industries Ltd. 03/14/1972
Each share Capital Stock no par exchanged for (0.2) share Capital Stock no par
Consolidated Bear Industries Ltd. merged into Resource Service Group Ltd. 07/01/1977
(See Resource Service Group Ltd.)

BEAR LAKE GOLD LTD (ON)
Each share old Common no par exchanged for (0.5) share new Common no par 09/24/2008
Merged into Kerr Mines Inc. 05/26/2014
Each share new Common no par exchanged for (1) share Common no par and (0.5) Common Stock Purchase Warrant expiring 05/22/2016
Note: Unexchanged certificates were cancelled and became without value 05/26/2016

BEAR LAKE MINES LTD. (CANADA)
Charter cancelled 04/00/1969
No stockholders' equity

BEAR LAKE REC INC (NV)
Each share old Common $0.001 par exchanged for (0.28571428) share new Common $0.001 par 10/23/2006
Name changed to Modular Medical, Inc. 06/29/2017

BEAR LAKE RES LTD (BC)
Recapitalized as Consolidated Bear Lake Resources Ltd. 04/17/1990
Each share Common no par exchanged for (0.33333333) share Common no par
Consolidated Bear Lake Resources Ltd. name changed to Advance Tire Systems Inc. 11/29/1990 which recapitalized as ATS Wheel Inc. 11/17/1993 which name changed to JSS Resources, Inc. 07/20/1998 which name changed to WSI Interactive Corp. 07/26/1999 which recapitalized as iaNett International Systems Ltd. 05/07/2001 which name changed to Data Fortress Systems Group Ltd. 09/03/2002

(See Data Fortress Systems Group Ltd.)

BEAR NECESSITIES INC (DE)
Charter cancelled and declared inoperative and void for non-payment of taxes 03/01/1987

BEAR RIDGE RES LTD (AB)
Merged into Sabretooth Energy Ltd. 08/21/2007
Each share Common no par exchanged for (0.28171756) share Common no par and $0.97312972 cash
Sabretooth Energy Ltd. name changed to Cequence Energy Ltd. 08/17/2009

BEAR RIV RES INC (NV)
Reorganized as Omnicity Corp. 10/21/2008
Each share Common $0.001 par exchanged for (7.7) shares Common $0.001 par
(See Omnicity Corp.)

BEAR ST FINL INC (AR)
Stock Dividend - 11% payable 12/15/2014 to holders of record 12/01/2014 Ex date - 11/26/2014
Acquired by Arvest Acquisition Sub, Inc. 04/20/2018
Each share Common 1¢ par exchanged for $10.28 cash

BEAR STEARNS CAP TR II (DE)
7.5% Guaranteed Trust Issued Preferred Securities called for redemption at $25 on 12/15/2003

BEAR STEARNS CAP TR III (DE)
7.8% Trust Preferred Securities $1 par called for redemption at $25 on 11/30/2009

BEAR STEARNS COS INC (DE)
7.88% Depositary Preferred Ser. B called for redemption at $25 on 05/05/1998
7.60% Depositary Preferred Ser. C called for redemption at $25 plus $0.475 accrued dividend on 07/15/1998
Adjustable Rate Preferred Ser. A no par called for redemption at $50 on 01/15/2004
Common $1 par split (3) for (2) by issuance of (0.5) additional share 07/15/1986
Stock Dividends - 5% payable 05/31/1996 to holders of record 05/17/1996; 5% payable 02/28/1997 to holders of record 02/14/1997; 5% payable 02/26/1999 to to holders of record 02/12/1999; 5% payable 11/26/1999 to holders of record 11/12/1999
Merged into JPMorgan Chase & Co. 05/30/2008
Each share Common $1 par exchanged for (0.21753) share Common $1 par
Each 5.49% Depositary Preferred Ser. G exchanged for (1) JPMorgan Chase & Co. 5.49% Depositary Preferred Ser. G 07/15/2008
Each 5.72% Depositary Preferred Ser. F exchanged for (1) JPMorgan Chase & Co. 5.72% Depositary Preferred Ser. F 07/15/2008
Each 6.15% Depositary Preferred Ser. E exchanged for (1) JPMorgan Chase & Co. 6.15% Depositary Preferred Ser. E 07/15/2008

BEARCAT EXPLS LTD (BC)
Assets sold for the benefit of creditors 12/19/2006
No stockholders' equity

BEARD CO (DE)
Name changed 09/23/1986
Common 10¢ par changed to 5¢ par and (1) additional share issued 11/30/1979
Common 5¢ par changed to $0.03333333 par and (0.5) additional share issued 06/30/1981
Name changed from Beard Oil Co. (Old) to Beard Co. (DE) 09/23/1986
Merged into Beard Oil Co. (New) 06/28/1988
Each share Common $0.03333333 par exchanged for (1) share Common 5¢ par and $10 cash
Note: Beard Oil Co. (New) is a subsidiary of Union Pacific Corp.
Beard Oil Co. (New) (DE) reorganized as Beard Co. (OK) 10/26/1993

BEARD OIL CO NEW (DE)
Reorganized under the laws of Oklahoma as Beard Co. 10/26/1993
Each share Common 5¢ par exchanged for (0.33333333) share Common $0.001 par

BEARDMORE GOLD MINES LTD.
Sold to Northern Empire Mines Co., Ltd. 00/00/1932
No stockholders' equity

BEARDMORE RES LTD (BC)
Struck off register and declared dissolved for failure to file returns 08/27/1993

BEARDSLEY & WOLCOTT MANUFACTURING CO.
Liquidated 00/00/1938
Details not available

BEAREHAVEN RECLAMATION INC (CO)
Administratively dissolved 02/01/2003

BEARFOOT CORP (OH)
Chapter 11 Federal Bankruptcy Code converted to Chapter 7 on 00/00/1988
No stockholders' equity

BEARFOOT SOLE CO., INC. (OH)
Name changed to Bearfoot Corp. 01/27/1969
(See Bearfoot Corp.)

BEARING LITHIUM CORP OLD (BC)
Plan of arrangement effective 07/20/2018
Each share Common no par exchanged for (1) share Bearing Lithium Corp. (New) Common no par and (0.049921) share Lions Bay Mining Corp. Common no par
Note: Unexchanged certificates will be cancelled and become without value 07/20/2024

BEARING MINERAL EXPL INC (NV)
Name changed to Petrosonic Energy, Inc. 05/16/2012

BEARING PWR CDA LTD (ON)
Acquired by Wajax Ltd. 03/27/1998
Each share Common no par exchanged for $1.40 cash

BEARING RES LTD (BC)
Each share old Common no par exchanged for (0.25) share new Common no par 08/22/2016
Name changed to Bearing Lithium Corp. (Old) 05/11/2017
Bearing Lithium Corp. (Old) reorganized as Bearing Lithium Corp. (New) 07/20/2018

BEARING SPECIALISTS, INC. (DE)
Name changed to Bearings, Inc. (DE) 00/00/1953
Bearings, Inc. (DE) reincorporated in (OH) 10/18/1988 which name changed to Applied Industrial Technologies, Inc. 01/01/1997

BEARINGPOINT INC (DE)
Each share old Common 1¢ par exchanged for (0.02) share new Common 1¢ par 12/11/2008
Plan of reorganization under Chapter 11 Federal Bankruptcy proceedings effective 12/30/2009
No stockholders' equity

BEARINGS CO. OF AMERICA (DE)
Recapitalized 00/00/1946
Each share 1st Preferred $100 par exchanged for (1) share 4.50% Preferred Ser. A $100 par, (1) share 5% Preferred Ser. B $50 par and a bearer Special Certificate for (0.125) share 5% Preferred Ser. B
Each share 2nd Preferred $100 par exchanged for (50) shares Common $1 par
Each share Common no par exchanged for (1) share Common $1 par
Merged into Federal-Mogul Corp. (MI) 00/00/1954
Each shares Common $1 par exchanged for (0.25) share Common $5 par
Federal-Mogul Corp. (MI) name changed to Federal-Mogul-Bower Bearings, Inc. 07/29/1955 which name changed back to Federal-Mogul Corp. (MI) 04/30/1965
(See Federal-Mogul Corp. (MI))

BEARINGS INC (OH)
Reincorporated 10/18/1988
Each share Common 25¢ par exchanged for (0.33333333) share Common no par 04/06/1962
Common no par split (2) for (1) by issuance of (1) additional share 09/01/1971
Common no par split (2) for (1) by issuance of (1) additional share 11/14/1973
Common no par split (3) for (2) by issuance of (0.5) additional share 06/03/1988
State of incorporation changed from (DE) to (OH) 10/18/1988
Each share Common no par exchanged for (1) share Common no par
Common no par split (3) for (2) by issuance of (0.5) additional share 06/02/1989
Common no par split (3) for (2) by issuance of (0.5) additional share 12/04/1995
Name changed to Applied Industrial Technologies, Inc. 01/01/1997

BEARTOOTH PLATINUM CORP (ON)
Reincorporated 08/11/2004
Place of incorporation changed from (YT) to (ON) 08/11/2004
Recapitalized as Kria Resources Ltd. 07/24/2009
Each share Common no par exchanged for (0.05) share Common no par
Kria Resources Ltd. merged into Trevali Mining Corp. 04/07/2011

BEASLEY INDS INC (OH)
Merged into BI Interim Corp. 01/04/1984
Each share Common no par exchanged for $25 cash

BEATH (W.D.) & SON, LTD.
Acquired by Eastern Steel Products. Ltd. 00/00/1946
Details not available

BEATRICE COS INC (DE)
Name changed 06/05/1984
Each share Common $25 par exchanged for (2) shares Common $12.50 par 00/00/1949
Common $12.50 par split (3) for (2) by issuance of (0.5) additional share 03/05/1957
Common $12.50 par split (5) for (4) by issuance of (0.25) additional share 03/03/1960
3.375% Conv. Prior Preferred $100 par called for redemption 08/01/1962
Common $12.50 par changed to no par and (0.33333333) additional share issued 03/05/1963
Common no par split (4) for (3) by issuance of (0.33333333) additional share 03/01/1965
4.5% Preferred $100 par called for redemption 05/15/1967
Common no par split (2) for (1) by issuance of (1) additional share 03/03/1969
Common no par split (2) for (1) by issuance of (1) additional share 12/04/1972
$2.70 Conv. Preference no par called for redemption 02/17/1984
$4 Conv. Preference 2nd Ser. no par called for redemption 02/17/1984
$4.50 Conv. Preference 2nd Ser. no par called for redemption 02/17/1984
Name changed from Beatrice Foods Co. to Beatrice Companies, Inc. 06/05/1984
Acquired by BCI Holdings Corp. 04/17/1986
Each share Common no par exchanged for (0.4) share 15.25% Exchangeable Preferred 1¢ par and $40 cash
$3.38 Conv. Preference Ser. A no par called for redemption 08/08/1986
Public interest eliminated

BEATRICE CREAMERY CO.
Name changed to Beatrice Foods Co. 00/00/1946
Beatrice Foods Co. name changed to Beatrice Companies, Inc. 06/05/1984
(See Beatrice Companies, Inc.)

BEATRICE NATL BK & TR CO (BEATRICE, NE)
Reorganized as Beatrice National Corp. 06/07/1975
Each share Capital Stock $20 par exchanged for (1) share Common $20 par
(See Beatrice National Corp.)

BEATRICE NATL CORP (NE)
Acquired by Cook Investment, Inc. 00/00/1989
Details not available

BEATRICE RED LAKE MINES LTD. (ON)
Recapitalized as Interprovincial Dredging & Mining Co., Ltd. 04/17/1962
Each share Capital Stock $1 par exchanged for (0.2) share Capital Stock no par
Interprovincial Dredging & Mining Co., Ltd. recapitalized as Interprovincial Allied Enterprises Ltd. 09/28/1970 which name changed to Comac Communications Ltd. 07/12/1972
(See Comac Communications Ltd.)

BEATRIX MINES LTD (SOUTH AFRICA)
Merged into Gold Fields Ltd. (Old) 02/02/1998
Each ADR for Ordinary no par exchanged for (1) Sponsored ADR for Ordinary 1¢ par
Gold Fields Ltd. (Old) merged into Gold Fields Ltd. (New) 05/10/1999

BEATRIX VENTURES INC (BC)
Each share old Common no par exchanged for (0.5) share new Common no par 10/30/2012
Reincorporated under the laws of Ontario as Emerge Resources Corp. 09/11/2013
Emerge Resources Corp. recapitalized as Vaxil Bio Ltd. 03/10/2016

BEATTIE DUQUESNE MINES LTD (QC)
Recapitalized as Donchester-Duquesne Mines Ltd. 07/11/1972
Each share Capital Stock $1 par exchanged for (0.05) share Capital Stock $1 par
Donchester-Duquesne Mines Ltd. merged into Fundy Chemical International Ltd. 10/01/1973
(See Fundy Chemical International Ltd.)

BEATTIE GOLD MINES, LTD.
Succeeded by Beattie Gold Mines (Quebec), Ltd. 00/00/1937
Details not available

BEATTIE GOLD MINES (QUEBEC), LTD.
Recapitalized as Consolidated Beattie Mines Ltd. 00/00/1946
Each share Common $1 par exchanged for (0.5) share Common $2 par
Consolidated Beattie Mines Ltd. merged into Beattie-Duquesne Mines Ltd. 00/00/1952 which recapitalized as Donchester-Duquesne Mines Ltd. 07/11/1972 which merged into Fundy Chemical International Ltd. 10/01/1973
(See Fundy Chemical International Ltd.)

BEATTIE SUGAR CO.
Reorganized as Vicana Sugar Co. 00/00/1932
No stockholders' equity

BEATTY BROS LTD (CANADA)
Class A Common no par and Class B Common no par changed to Common no par 00/00/1947
Common no par exchanged (3) for (1) 00/00/1949
5% Preferred $10 par called for redemption 07/15/1964
Each share Class A no par exchanged for $0.35 cash and (1) share Preference Stock 05/31/1965 which was called for redemption 06/30/1965
Stock Distribution - (1) share Class A no par for each share of Common no par 10/18/1961
Merged into GSW Ltd.-GSW Ltee. 07/01/1970
Each share Common no par exchanged for (1.1) shares Class A Common no par and (2.2) shares Class B Common no par
GSW Ltd.-GSW Ltee. name changed to GSW Inc. 10/01/1980
(See GSW Inc.)

BEAU BRUMMELL, INC.
Name changed to Beau Brummel Ties, Inc. 00/00/1940
Beau Brummell Ties, Inc. merged into B.V.D. Co., Inc. 02/28/1962 which was acquired by Glen Alden Corp. (DE) 05/19/1967 which merged into Rapid-American Corp. (DE) 11/06/1972
(See Rapid-American Corp. (DE))

BEAU BRUMMELL TIES, INC. (OH)
Stock Dividend - 100% 07/24/1946
Merged into B.V.D. Co., Inc. 02/28/1962
Each share Common exchanged for (1) share Common $1 par
B.V.D. Co., Inc. acquired by Glen Alden Corp. (DE) 05/19/1967 which merged into Rapid-American Corp. (DE) 11/06/1972
(See Rapid-American Corp. (DE))

BEAU CDA EXPL LTD (CANADA)
Class A no par reclassified as Common no par 08/06/1993
Each share Common no par received distribution of (0.16666666) share Genoil Inc. Common no par payable 09/05/2000 to holders of record 08/25/2000
Acquired by Murphy Oil Corp. 11/13/2000
Each share Common no par exchanged for $2.15 cash

BEAU CHIBOUGAMAU MINES LTD. (ON)
Merged into Amalgamated Beau-Belle Mines Ltd. 06/29/1961
Each share Capital Stock $1 par exchanged for (1) share Capital Stock $1 par
(See Amalgamated Beau-Belle Mines Ltd.)

BEAU ELECTRONICS, INC. (CT)
Acquired by UMC Electronics Co. 10/01/1962
Each share Common no par exchanged for (0.4) share Capital Stock $1 par
(See UMC Electronics Co.)

BEAU PETE GOLD MINES LTD. (ON)
Charter revoked for failure to file reports and pay taxes 00/00/1958

BEAU PRE EXPLS LTD (BC)
Delisted from NEX 06/22/2006

BEAU RAND GOLD MINES LTD. (ON)
Charter revoked for failure to file reports and pay taxes 00/00/1958

BEAU VAL MINES LTD (BC)
Recapitalized as Bullion Reef Resources Ltd. 01/16/1991
Each share Capital Stock no par exchanged for (0.33333333) share Common no par
Bullion Reef Resources Ltd. recapitalized as Consolidated Bullion Reef Resources Ltd. 03/27/1995 which name changed to Canada Payphone Corp. 03/08/1996
(See Canada Payphone Corp.)

BEAUBRAN INC (PEI)
Name changed 12/28/1984
Name changed from Beaubran Canagex Inc. to Beaubran Inc. 12/28/1984
Name changed to Timvest Growth Fund Inc. 01/27/1986
Timvest Growth Fund Inc. name changed to Talvest Funds and Common no par reclassified as Growth Fund 03/23/1988
(See Talvest Funds)

BEAUCAGE MINES LTD. (ON)
Recapitalized as Nova Beaucage Mines Ltd. 11/17/1958
Each share Common $1 par exchanged for (0.2) share Common $1 par
Nova Beaucage Mines Ltd. recapitalized as Nova Beaucage Resources Ltd. 08/14/1996 which merged into Canuc Resources Corp. (New) 12/31/1996

BEAUCAMP YELLOWKNIFE MINES LTD.
Merged into Aurlando Consolidated Mining Corp., Ltd. 00/00/1947
Each share Capital Stock $1 par exchanged for (0.2) share Capital Stock $1 par
(See Aurlando Consolidated Mining Corp., Ltd.)

BEAUCE INVTS INC (QC)
Name changed to Novik Inc. 10/04/2005
(See Novik Inc.)

BEAUCHAMPS EXPL INC (BC)
Cease trade order effective 04/04/1995

BEAUCHANCE MINES, LTD. (ON)
Charter surrendered 10/11/1965
No stockholders' equity

BEAUCOEUR YELLOWKNIFE MINES LTD. (ON)
Charter cancelled 11/27/1961

BEAUCOUP RES LTD (CANADA)
Reincorporated 07/28/1987
Place of incorporation changed from (BC) to (Canada) 07/28/1987
Name changed to BCU Industries Inc. 09/13/1988
(See BCU Industries Inc.)

BEAUDALAIR MINES, LTD. (ON)
Charter cancelled 00/00/1960

BEAUFIELD CONSOLIDATED RES INC (BC)
Recapitalized 10/14/1992
Recapitalized from Beaufield Resources Inc. to Beaufield Consolidated Resources Inc. 10/14/1992
Each share old Common no par exchanged for (0.1) share new Common no par 10/14/1992
Name changed to Beaufield Resources Inc. (BC) 05/25/2006
Beaufield Resources Inc. (BC) reincorporated in Canada 04/04/2013 which merged into Osisko Mining Inc. 10/22/2018

BEAUFIELD RES INC (CANADA)
Reincorporated 04/04/2013
Place of incorporation changed from (BC) to (Canada) 04/04/2013
Merged into Osisko Mining Inc. 10/22/2018
Each share Common no par exchanged for (0.0482) share Common no par
Note: Unexchanged certificates will be cancelled and become without value 10/22/2024

BEAUFOR MINING CORP. (QC)
Assets sold to Cournor Mining Co. Ltd. 00/00/1939
Each share Common $1 par exchanged for (0.741176) share Common $1 par
Cournor Mining Co. Ltd. recapitalized as Courvan Mining Co. Ltd. 08/17/1960 which name changed to Courvan Mining Co. Ltd./ Societe Miniere Courvan Ltee. 02/24/1982 which recapitalized as Rutter Technologies Inc. (QC) 07/25/2002 which reorganized in Canada as Rutter Inc. 03/31/2004
(See Rutter Inc.)

BEAUFORD RES LTD (BC)
Delisted from Vancouver Stock Exchange 04/07/1986

BEAUFORT ENERGY LTD (CANADA)
Recapitalized as Venstone Ventures Corp. 02/17/1998
Each share Common no par exchanged for (0.33333333) share Common no par
Venstone Ventures Corp. recapitalized as iWave.com, Inc. 02/02/1999 which recapitalized as iWave Information Systems Inc. 06/28/2002 which name changed First Factor Developments Inc. 07/22/2005 which name changed to Millrock Resources Inc. (Canada) 08/14/2007 which reincorporated in British Columbia 07/24/2008

BEAUFORT EXPLS LTD (CANADA)
Merged into Equisure Financial Network Inc. 12/11/1996
Each share Class A Preferred no par exchanged for $0.5266567 cash
Each share Class A Common no par exchanged for $0.5266567 cash

BEAUFORT HILLS RES INC (ON)
Recapitalized as InterRent Properties Ltd. 11/01/1999
Each share Common no par exchanged for (0.33333333) share Common no par
InterRent Properties Ltd. recapitalized as InterRent International Properties Inc. 03/05/2001 which reorganized as InterRent Real Estate Investment Trust 12/07/2006

BEAUFORT PETE INVT LTD (CANADA)
Each share Class A Preferred 75¢ par exchanged for (2) shares new Common 75¢ par 09/05/1995
Each share Class C Preferred 75¢ par exchanged for (2) shares new Common 75¢ par 09/05/1995
Each share Class A Common 75¢ par exchanged for (2) shares new Common 75¢ par 09/05/1995
Each share Class C Common 75¢ par exchanged for (2) shares new Common 75¢ par 09/05/1995

Name changed to gronArctic Energy Inc. 02/22/1996 gronArctic Energy Inc. recapitalized as gronArctic Resources Inc. 12/10/1997 which merged into Kicking Horse Resources Ltd. 08/13/1999 which name changed to Launch Resources Inc. 10/02/2003
(See Launch Resources Inc.)

BEAUHARNOIS LIGHT, HEAT & POWER CO.
Taken over by Quebec Hydro-Electric Commission 00/00/1944
Details not available

BEAUHARNOIS POWER CORP. LTD.
Acquired by Beauharnois Light Heat & Power Co. 00/00/1940
Details not available

BEAULIEU YELLOWKNIFE MINES LTD.
Recapitalized as Consolidated Beaulieu Mines Ltd. 00/00/1949
Each share Capital Stock exchanged for (0.2) share Capital Stock
(See Consolidated Beaulieu Mines Ltd.)

BEAUMONT MANUFACTURING CO.
Acquired by Spartan Mills 00/00/1941
Details not available

BEAUMONT MINING CORP. LTD. (QC)
Completely liquidated 12/00/1971
Each share Capital Stock $1 par exchanged for (0.05) share Albarmont Mines Corp. Common no par
Albarmont Mines Corp. recapitalized as Albarmont (1985) Inc. 07/19/1985
(See Albarmont (1985) Inc.)

BEAUMONT RES LTD (BC)
Recapitalized as Consolidated Beaumont Resources Ltd. 07/23/1973
Each share Common no par exchanged for (0.2) share Common no par
Consolidated Beaumont Resources Ltd. recapitalized as Conbeau Resources Ltd. 09/18/1979 which recapitalized as Inlet Resources Ltd. 12/03/1984 which name changed to Guerrero Ventures Inc. 08/19/2014

BEAUMONT SELECT CORPS INC (AB)
Acquired by 1842492 Alberta Ltd. 10/20/2014
Each share Class A Common no par exchanged for $2.05 cash
Note: Unexchanged certificates will be cancelled and become without value 10/20/2019

BEAUNIT CORP (NY)
Name changed 06/29/1962
Each share Common $10 par exchanged for (4) shares Common $2.50 par 03/29/1946
Stock Dividend - 20% 03/25/1956
Name changed from Beaunit Mills, Inc. to Beaunit Corp. 06/29/1962
$5 Preferred no par called for redemption 09/01/1962
Common $2.50 par changed to $1.25 par and (1) additional share issued 07/21/1966
Merged into El Paso Natural Gas Co. 10/11/1967
Each share Common $1.25 par exchanged for (0.8) share Common $3 par
El Paso Natural Gas Co. reorganized as El Paso Co. 06/13/1974 which merged into Burlington Northern Inc. 12/13/1983
(See Burlington Northern Inc.)

BEAUNORM MINES LTD. (ON)
Charter revoked for failure to file reports and pay taxes 03/11/1957

BEAUPAS MINES LTD. (QC)
Declared dissolved for failure to file reports or pay taxes 08/13/1977

BEAUPORT GOLDFIELDS LTD. (ON)
Charter cancelled 03/14/1960

BEAUPORT HLDGS LTD (CANADA)
Recapitalized as Beauport Investors Ltd.-Investisseurs Beauport Ltee. 03/20/1972
Each share Common no par exchanged for (0.2) share Common no par
(See Beauport Investors Ltd.-Investisseurs Beauport Ltee.)

BEAUPORT INVS LTD (CANADA)
Bankruptcy proceedings completed 00/00/1979
No stockholders' equity

BEAUPRE BASE METALS MINES LTD. (ON)
Charter cancelled for default in filing returns 10/15/1969

BEAURIV YELLOWKNIFE MINES LTD. (ON)
Charter cancelled 04/21/1958
No stockholders' equity

BEAUTEC CORP. (IA)
Out of business 07/01/1982
No stockholders' equity

BEAUTICONTROL COSMETICS INC (DE)
Common 10¢ par split (3) for (2) by issuance of (0.5) additional share 06/15/1989
Common 10¢ par split (3) for (2) by issuance of (0.5) additional share 07/31/1991
Merged into Tupperware Corp. 10/18/2000
Each share Common 10¢ par exchanged for $7 cash

BEAUTIFUL LIFE FOODS INC (NV)
Reorganized as Diamond Bay Holdings, Inc. 01/07/2005
Each share Common $0.001 par exchanged for (2) shares Common $0.001 par
Diamond Bay Holdings, Inc. recapitalized as Shaan Xi Ding Cheng Science Holding Co., Ltd. 01/31/2007 which name changed to China Ding Cheng Science Holdings Co., Ltd. 03/22/2007 which name changed to China Transportation International Holdings Group Ltd. 04/23/2010
(See China Transportation International Holdings Group Ltd.)

BEAUTY BRANDS GROUP INC (FL)
Each shares old Common 10¢ par exchanged for (0.00666666) share new Common 10¢ par 11/10/2006
SEC revoked common stock registration 03/11/2013

BEAUTY COUNSELORS CDA LTD (ON)
Name changed to Beauty Counselors International, Inc. 09/22/1982
Beauty Counselors International, Inc. recapitalized as Century Technologies Inc. 01/10/1989
(See Century Technologies Inc.)

BEAUTY COUNSELORS INC (MI)
Common $1 par split (3) for (1) by issuance of (2) additional shares 12/15/1958
Merged into Rexall Drug & Chemical Co. 05/20/1968
Each share Common $1 par exchanged for (0.825) share Common $1.25 par
Rexall Drug & Chemical Co. name changed to Dart Industries, Inc. 04/22/1969 which reorganized as Dart & Kraft, Inc. 09/25/1980 which name changed to Kraft, Inc. (New) 11/21/1986
(See Kraft, Inc. (New))

BEAUTY COUNSELORS INTL INC (ON)
Recapitalized as Century Technologies Inc. 01/10/1989
Each share Common no par exchanged for (0.2) share Common no par
(See Century Technologies Inc.)

BEAUTY INDS INC (NY)
Name changed to Strathmore Industries, Inc. 05/09/1969
Strathmore Industries, Inc. merged into Transworld Investment Corp. 01/08/1971
(See Transworld Investment Corp.)

BEAUTY LABS INC (DE)
Merged into Robern Industries, Inc. 12/23/1992
Each share Common 1¢ par exchanged for (0.1676) share Common 1¢ par, (0.0838) Common Stock Purchase Warrant Class B expiring 04/03/1994 and (0.0838) Common Stock Purchase Warrant Class C expiring 06/30/1995
Robern Industries, Inc. name changed to WinStar Communications Inc. 12/02/1993
(See WinStar Communications Inc.)

BEAUTY MASTERS INC (NY)
Recapitalized as Nu-Mode Industries, Inc. 05/30/1972
Each share Common 1¢ par exchanged for (0.4) share Common 1¢ par
(See Nu-Mode Industries, Inc.)

BEAUTYMERCHANT COM (NV)
Name changed to National Beauty Corp. 03/30/2001
National Beauty Corp. recapitalized as Hairmax International, Inc. 08/01/2003 which name changed to China Digital Media Corp. 03/31/2005
(See China Digital Media Corp.)

BEAUVERNY GOLD MINES, LTD. (QC)
Charter surrendered and company declared dissolved 12/15/1959

BEAUX-ARTS APARTMENTS, INC. (NY)
Recapitalized 00/00/1939
Each share 1st Preferred no par exchanged for (1) share $3 Prior Preferred $15 par, (1) share Common $1 par and $3 in cash
Each share 2nd Preferred no par exchanged for (0.5) share Common $1 par
Each share Common no par exchanged for (0.01) share Common $1 par
Name changed to Beaux-Arts Properties, Inc. 12/17/1958
(See Beaux-Arts Properties, Inc.)

BEAUX ARTS PPTYS INC (NY)
Liquidation completed
Each share Common $1 par received initial distribution of $65 cash 08/23/1973
Each share Common $1 par received second distribution of $55 cash 11/01/1973
Each share Common $1 par exchanged for third and final distribution of $15 cash 06/17/1974

BEAVER BOARD COMPANIES
Acquired by Certain-Teed Products Corp. 00/00/1928
Details not available

BEAVER COAL CORP (DE)
Liquidated 12/29/1967
Company would not provide details

BEAVER CONSOLIDATED MINES LTD.
Name changed to Northern Canada Mining Corp. Ltd. 00/00/1928
(See Northern Canada Mining Corp. Ltd.)

BEAVER COPPER CO.
Name changed to Beaver Gold & Copper Co. 00/00/1932
(See Beaver Gold & Copper Co.)

BEAVER CREEK DISTILLERY INC. (IA)
Name changed to Beaver Creek Industries, Inc. (IA) 05/13/1968
Beaver Creek Industries, Inc. (IA) reincorporated in Delaware 05/01/1969 which name changed to Xacron Corp. 12/28/1973
(See Xacron Corp.)

BEAVER CREEK INDS INC (DE)
Reincorporated 05/01/1969
State of incorporation changed from (IA) to (DE) 05/01/1969
Name changed to Xacron Corp. 12/28/1973
(See Xacron Corp.)

BEAVER CREEK SILVER INC (DE)
Company believed out of business 00/00/1990
Details not available

BEAVER ENERGY RES INC (CANADA)
Merged into Barron Hunter Hargrave Strategic Resources Inc. 09/12/1985
Each share Common no par exchanged for (0.33333333) share Common no par
(See Barron Hunter Hargrave Strategic Resources Inc.)

BEAVER ENGR LTD (ON)
Common no par reclassified as Conv. Class A Common no par 11/06/1974
Merged into Beaver Executive Holdings Ltd. 03/09/1978
Each share Conv. Class A Common no par exchanged for $6.25 cash
Each share Conv. Class B Common no par exchanged for $6.25 cash

BEAVER GOLD & COPPER CO. (UT)
Charter revoked for failure to file reports and pay fees 03/31/1958

BEAVER GOLD RES INC (BC)
Name changed to Beaver Resources Inc. (Old) 09/09/1982
Beaver Resources Inc.(Old) merged into Beaver Resources Inc. (New) 06/13/1983
(See Beaver Resources Inc. (New))

BEAVER LAKE ENERGY CORP (AB)
Name changed to Beaver Lake Resources Corp. 04/01/1996
Beaver Lake Resources Corp. merged into GREKA Energy Corp. 09/13/1999
(See GREKA Energy Corp.)

BEAVER LAKE RES CORP (AB)
Merged into GREKA Energy Corp. 09/13/1999
Each share Common no par exchanged for (74.4) shares Common no par
(See GREKA Energy Corp.)

BEAVER LMBR LTD (CANADA)
Each share 7% Preferred $100 par exchanged for (5) shares $1.40 Preferred $20 par 00/00/1946
Each share Common no par exchanged for (1) share Common no par and (0.5) share Class A no par 00/00/1946
Each share Common no par exchanged for (5) shares Common no par 02/23/1955
Common no par split (4) for (1) by issuance of (3) additional shares 03/01/1968
Merged into Molson Companies Ltd.-Les Compagnies Molson Ltee. 07/13/1982
Each share $1.40 Preferred $20 par exchanged for (1.75) shares Class A Common no par
Each share $1 Class A no par exchanged for (1.75) shares Class A Common no par
Each share Common no par exchanged for (1.75) shares Class A Common no par
Molson Companies Ltd.-Les Compagnies Molson Ltee. name changed to Molson Inc. 06/29/1999 which merged into Molson Coors Brewing Co. 02/09/2005

BEAVER LODGE MINES LTD. (BC)
Name changed 00/00/1959
Name changed from Beaver Lodge Uranium Mines Ltd. to Beaver Lodge Mines Ltd. 00/00/1959
Recapitalized as Western Beaver Lodge Mines Ltd. 10/05/1962
Each share Common no par exchanged for (0.33333333) share Common no par
Western Beaver Lodge Mines Ltd. recapitalized as Portcomm Communications Corp. Ltd. 08/19/1969 which name changed to Roach (Hal) Studios Corp. 11/01/1977 which merged into H.R.S. Industries, Inc. 05/21/1982 which merged into International H.R.S. Industries Inc. 05/15/1984 which name changed to Glenex Industries Inc. 05/25/1987 which merged into Quest Investment Corp. 07/04/2002 which merged into Quest Capital Corp. (BC) 06/30/2003 which reincorporated in Canada 05/27/2008 which name changed to Sprott Resource Lending Corp. 09/10/2010 which merged into Sprott Inc. 07/24/2013

BEAVER LODGE OIL CORP. (DE)
Merged into Stekoll Petroleum Corp. on a (1) for (2) basis 05/15/1959
Stekoll Petroleum Corp. name changed to Sunac Petroleum Corp. 06/11/1962
(See Sunac Petroleum Corp.)

BEAVER MESA EXPL CO (NV)
Each share Capital Stock 25¢ par exchanged for initial distribution of $2 cash 06/15/1979
Each share Capital Stock 25¢ par received second and final distribution of $0.216484 cash 12/10/1981
Note: Each share Capital Stock 25¢ par received an additional $0.02082974541 cash Contingency Shareholder Interest payment

BEAVER MESA URANIUM INC (NV)
Name changed to Beaver Mesa Exploration Co. 03/10/1970
(See Beaver Mesa Exploration Co.)

BEAVER MNG CORP (QC)
Charter annulled for failure to file reports or pay fees 12/00/1977

BEAVER PORTLAND CEMENT CO.
Acquired by Pacific Portland Cement Co. 00/00/1936
Details not available

BEAVER RES INC NEW (BC)
Merged 06/13/1983
Merged from Beaver Resources Inc. (Old) to Beaver Resources Inc. (New) 06/13/1983
Each share Common no par exchanged for (1) share Common no par
Delisted from Toronto Stock Exchange 07/06/1992

BEAVER RIVER SILVER-LEAD MINES LTD. (ON)
Charter revoked for failure to file reports and pay taxes 08/00/1961

BEAVER TR CO (BEAVER, PA)
Capital Stock $20 par changed to $10 par and (1) additional share issued plus a 100% stock dividend paid 03/20/1973
Stock Dividend - 25% 03/18/1966
Merged into First Western Bancorp, Inc. 02/28/1986
Each share Capital Stock $10 par exchanged for (1.025) share Common $5 par
First Western Bancorp, Inc. merged into Sky Financial Group, Inc. 08/06/1999 which merged into

Huntington Bancshares Inc. 07/02/2007

BEAVER VALLEY COMMUNITY HOTEL CO. (PA)
Completely liquidated 12/31/1965
No stockholders' equity

BEAVER VALLEY OIL & REFINING CO. (TX)
Charter forfeited for failure to pay taxes 00/00/1920

BEAVER VALLEY WATER CO.
Dissolved 00/00/1940
Details not available

BEAVERBRIDGE MINES LTD (ON)
Charter cancelled for failure to pay taxes and file returns 03/16/1976

BEAVERHEAD RES LTD (BC)
Merged into International Interlake Industries Inc. 12/31/1986
Each share Common no par exchanged for (0.08368200) share Common no par
(See International Interlake Industries Inc.)

BEAVERHOUSE LAKE GOLD MINES LTD. (ON)
Name changed to Lake Beaverhouse Mines Ltd. and Capital Stock $1 par exchanged (2) for (5) 00/00/1950
(See Lake Beaverhouse Mines Ltd.)

BEAVERMOUTH DREDGING CO. LTD.
Dissolved 00/00/1950
Details not available

BEAVERTON BANKING CO. (OR)
Name changed to Business Banking Co. 06/03/1981
Business Banking Co. merged into Valley National Corp. (OR) 08/01/1985 which was acquired by U.S. Bancorp (OR) 06/01/1987 which merged into U.S. Bancorp (Old) (DE) 08/01/1997 which merged into U.S Bancorp (New) 02/27/2001

BEAZER HOMES USA INC (DE)
Conv. Exchangeable Preferred Ser. A 1¢ par called for redemption at $26.25 on 05/19/1999
Each 7.50% Tangible Equity Unit received (0.8606) share new Common 1¢ par 08/15/2013
(Additional Information in Active)

BEAZER PLC (ENGLAND)
Name changed 02/15/1988
Name changed from Beazer (C.H.) Holdings PLC to Beazer PLC 02/15/1988
Acquired by Hanson PLC (Old) 02/18/1992
Each Sponsored ADR for Ordinary exchanged for (5.52) Warrants expiring 09/30/1997 and £3.60 cash

BEB RES LTD (BC)
Name changed to Migent Software Corp. (BC) 06/27/1984
Migent Software Corp. (BC) reincorporated in Canada 03/18/1988
(See Migent Software Corp.)

BEBIDA BEVERAGE CO (NV)
Reincorporated under the laws of Wyoming 12/03/2009

BEC ENERGY (MA)
Merged into NSTAR 08/25/1999
Each share Common $1 par exchanged for either (1) share Common $1 par, $44.10 cash, or a combination thereof
Note: Cash electors received 26.172% of of total holdings in cash and the remaining 73.828% in stock
Holdings of (99) shares or fewer received cash only
Option to receive stock and cash or cash only expired 09/21/1999
NSTAR merged into Northeast Utilities 04/10/2012 which name changed to Eversource Energy 02/19/2015

BEC GROUP INC (DE)
Each share Common 1¢ par received distribution of (1/3) share Bolle Inc.
Common 1¢ par payable 03/12/1998 to holders of record 03/11/1998
Recapitalized as Lumen Technologies, Inc. 03/12/1998
Each share Common 1¢ par exchanged for (0.5) share Common 1¢ par
(See Lumen Technologies, Inc.)

BEC, INC. (MN)
Name changed to Gran Prix Enterprises, Inc. 12/02/1988
(See Gran Prix Enterprises, Inc.)

BECHTOLD ENGINEERING CO. (FL)
Completely liquidated 12/16/1966
Each share Common 5¢ par exchanged for first and final distribution of $3.03 cash

BECK & CO (NV)
Common $0.001 par split (10) for (1) by issuance of (9) additional shares payable 03/31/2000 to holders of record 03/31/2000 Ex date - 05/15/2000
Name changed to Greenvolt Power Corp. 08/29/2000
Greenvolt Power Corp. recapitalized as Satellite Enterprises Corp. 09/15/2002 which name changed to Satellite Newspapers Corp. 11/30/2005 which recapitalized as Genmed Holding Corp. 01/28/2008
(See Genmed Holding Corp.)

BECK ARNLEY CORP (NY)
Common 25¢ par split (5) for (3) by issuance of (0.16666666) additional share 09/23/1983
Acquired by Guest Keen & Nettlefolds PLC 08/23/1984
Each share Common 25¢ par exchanged for $15 cash

BECK GROUP INC (DE)
Merged into International Avionics Inc. 12/11/1998
Each share Common 1¢ par exchanged for $0.01 cash

BECK INDS INC (DE)
Common $1 par split (4) for (1) by issuance of (3) additional shares 01/07/1969
4.75% Preferred $100 par called for redemption 02/18/1969
Declared insolvent by Court order 10/24/1979
No stockholders' equity

BECK (A.S.) SHOE CORP. (DE)
Name changed to Beck Industries Inc. 10/29/1968
(See Beck Industries Inc.)

BECK'S INC. (MN)
Merged into Control Data Corp. (MN) on a (1) for (20.7) basis 06/28/1963
Control Data Corp. (MN) merged into Control Data Corp. (DE) 08/17/1968 which name changed to Ceridian Corp. (Old) 06/03/1992
(See Ceridian Corp. (Old))

BECKER CRANE & CONVEYOR CO. (OH)
Voluntarily dissolved 06/24/1964
Details not available

BECKER GOLD MINES LTD (BC)
Reincorporated 01/15/2007
Place of incorporation changed from (ON) to (BC) 01/15/2007
Each share old Common no par exchanged for (0.16666666) share new Common no par 02/02/2009
Name changed to Sonoro Metals Corp. 01/09/2012

BECKER MILK LTD (ON)
Class A Preferred $100 par called for redemption at $100 on 06/30/2006
(Additional Information in Active)

BECKETT INDUSTRIES INC. (NV)
Name changed to International Supercell Ltd. 05/11/1995
International Supercell Ltd. name changed to Bargaincity.com, Inc. 03/25/1999
(See Bargaincity.com, Inc.)

BECKETT TECHNOLOGIES CORP (ON)
Class A no par reclassified as Common no par 09/06/1994
Delisted from Alberta Stock Exchange 05/04/1998

BECKLEY BANCORP INC (DE)
Merged into Horizon Bancorp, Inc. 09/30/1997
Each share Common 10¢ par exchanged for $25.64 cash

BECKLEY INDS INC (CO)
Involuntarily dissolved for failure to pay taxes and file annual reports 01/01/1981

BECKLEY NATL BK (BECKLEY, WV)
Reorganized as Southern Bankshares Inc. 07/01/1983
Each share Capital Stock $25 par exchanged for (1) share Common $2.50 par
(See Southern Bankshares Inc.)

BECKMAN COULTER INC (DE)
Common 10¢ par split (2) for (1) by issuance of (1) additional share payable 12/07/2000 to holders of record 11/15/2000 Ex date - 12/08/2000
Acquired by Danaher Corp. 06/30/2011
Each share Common 10¢ par exchanged for $83.50 cash

BECKMAN INSTRS INC (CA)
Common $1 par split (2) for (1) by issuance of (1) additional share 12/28/1965
Common $1 par split (2) for (1) by issuance of (1) additional share 02/23/1976
Common $1 par split (2) for (1) by issuance of (1) additional share 11/27/1978
Merged into SmithKline Beckman Corp. 03/04/1982
Each share Common $1 par exchanged for (0.7535) share Common 25¢ par
SmithKline Beckman Corp. merged into SmithKline Beecham PLC 07/26/1989 which merged into GlaxoSmithKline PLC 12/27/2000

BECKMAN INSTRS INC (DE)
Name changed to Beckman Coulter, Inc. 04/02/1998
(See Beckman Coulter, Inc.)

BECKONS INDS LTD (INDIA)
GDR agreement terminated 04/22/2014
No GDR's remain outstanding

BECKS CITY BAKERY INC (VA)
Foreclosed by creditors and went out of business 06/30/1972
No stockholders' equity

BECKWITH-CHANDLER CO.
Acquired by Devoe & Raynolds Co., Inc. 00/00/1945
Details not available

BECO INDS CORP (DE)
Merged into Baldwin Securities Corp. 06/22/1972
Each share Common $1 par exchanged for (3.9) shares Common 1¢ par
(See Baldwin Securities Corp.)

BECOR COMMUNICATIONS INC (DE)
Name changed to Enhance Biotech Inc. 03/25/2003
(See Enhance Biotech Inc.)

BECOR WESTN INC (DE)
Acquired by B-E Holdings, Inc. 02/04/1988
Each share Common $5 par exchanged for $3 principal amount of 12.5% Sr. Notes due 02/04/1989, $10 principal amount of 12.5% Sr. Debentures due 09/15/2002, (0.6) Common Stock Purchase Warrants expiring 11/15/1992 and (0.2) share 12.5% Exchangeable Preferred Ser. A 1¢ par
B-E Holdings, Inc. reorganized as Bucyrus-Erie Co. (New) 12/14/1994 which name changed to Bucyrus International Inc. (Old) 05/24/1996
(See Bucyrus International Inc. (Old))

BECOS INDS INC (NV)
Reorganized 10/31/1984
Reorganized from (UT) to under the laws of (NV) 10/31/1984
Each share Common 1¢ par exchanged for (0.1) share Common 1¢ par
Name changed to Softpoint Inc. 09/01/1989
Softpoint Inc. recapitalized as Acquest Corp. 11/04/1996

BED & BISCUIT INNS AMER INC (NV)
Name changed to Dogs International 03/24/2003
Dogs International name changed to AFV Solutions, Inc. 02/11/2005 which recapitalized as Pure Transit Technologies, Inc. 06/18/2008

BED ROCK PETE CO (TX)
Charter cancelled and declared inoperative and void for non-payment of taxes 04/15/1972

BEDDIS INTL LTD (DE)
Recapitalized as Quantex Capital Corp. 05/05/2005
Each share Common $0.0001 par exchanged for (0.18181818) share Common $0.0001 par

BEDELIA CORP. (NV)
Name changed to Pollution Solutions, Inc. 06/30/1970
Pollution Solutions, Inc. name changed to Amerecen Industries 03/01/1972 which name changed to Amrec Industries Inc. 02/23/1973
(See Amrec Industries Inc.)

BEDERRA CORP (TX)
Each share old Common $0.001 par exchanged for (0.0025) share new Common $0.001 par 12/31/2008
Reorganizaed under the laws of Nevada as Zicix Corp. 02/09/2011
Each share new Common $0.001 par exchanged for (0.002) share Common $0.0001 par

BEDFORD BANCSHARES INC (VA)
Common 10¢ par split (2) for (1) by issuance of (1) additional share payable 06/15/1998 to holders of record 06/01/1998
Merged into FNB Corp. 08/01/2003
Each share Common 10¢ par exchanged for either (0.8793) share Common $5 par or $23.99 cash
Note: Option to receive stock expired 08/15/2003
FNB Corp. merged into StellarOne Corp. 02/28/2008 which merged into Union First Market Bankshares Corp. 01/02/2014 which name changed to Union Bankshares Corp. 04/28/2014

BEDFORD HLDGS INC (NJ)
Ceased doing business 07/28/2003
No stockholders' equity

BEDFORD LN & DEP BK (BEDFORD, KY)
Recapitalized as Bedford Loan & Deposit Bancorp Inc. 01/31/1997
Each share Common $50 par exchanged for (0.1) share Common $50 par

BEDFORD MINES LTD.
Acquired by Ventures Ltd. through exchange of (2) shares Sherritt Gordon Mines Ltd. for each (17)

shares of Bedford Mines Ltd. 00/00/1930
Sherritt Gordon Mines Ltd. name changed to Sherritt Gordon Ltd. 06/24/1988 which name changed to Sherritt Inc. 07/05/1993 which name changed to Viridian, Inc. 04/22/1996 which merged into Agrium Inc. 12/10/1996

BEDFORD NATIONAL CORP. (NY)
Charter revoked for failure to file reports and pay fees 12/15/1939

BEDFORD PORCUPINE GOLD MINES LTD.
Bankrupt 00/00/1949
Stockholders' equity unlikely

BEDFORD PPTY INVS INC (MD)
Common $1 par reclassified as Legended Common $1 par 02/21/1995
Common Stock Purchase Rights declared for Common stockholders of record 07/18/1989 were redeemed at $0.01 par right 09/29/1995 for holders of record 09/22/1995
Each share Legended Common $1 par exchanged for (0.5) share Common 2¢ par 03/29/1996
Merged into LBA Realty Fund II - WBP I LLC 05/05/2006
Each share 8.75% Ser. A Preferred 1¢ par exchanged for (1) share 8.75% Ser. A Preferred
Each share 7.625% Ser. B Preferred 1¢ par exchanged for (1) share 7.625% Ser. B Preferred
Each share Common $2 par exchanged for $27 cash

BEDFORD SOFTWARE LTD (BC)
Name changed to Stratford Software Corp. 07/28/1989
Stratford Software Corp. merged into Bow-Flex, Inc. 01/26/1993 which name changed to Direct Focus, Inc. 06/17/1998 which name changed to Nautilus Group, Inc. 05/21/2002 which name changed to Nautilus, Inc. 03/14/2005

BEDMINSTER NATL CORP (NV)
Reincorporated 10/20/2006
State of incorporation changed from (DE) to (NV) 10/20/2006
Each share Common $0.0001 par received distribution of (1) share Bedminster Capital Corp. Class A Common $0.0001 par payable 08/31/2007 to holders of record 08/31/2007
Each share Common $0.0001 par received distribution of (1) share Bedminster Capital Corp. Class B Common $0.0001 par payable 08/31/2007 to holders of record 08/31/2007
SEC revoked common stock registration 04/18/2012

BEDROCAN CANNABIS CORP (ON)
Merged into Tweed Marijuana Inc. 08/31/2015
Each share Common no par exchanged for (0.465) share Common no par
Note: Unexchanged certificates will be cancelled and become without value 08/31/2021
Tweed Marijuana Inc. name changed to Canopy Growth Corp. 09/22/2015

BEDROCK RES LTD (BC)
Name changed to Talemon Investments Ltd. 05/24/1985
Each share Common no par exchanged for (1) share Common no par
(See Talemon Investments Ltd.)

BEDROCS BRANDON INC (FL)
Name changed to World-Am Communications, Inc. (FL) 09/21/1998
World-Am Communications, Inc. (FL) reincorporated in Nevada

12/19/2002 which name changed to World Am, Inc. 08/02/2004

BEE VECTORING TECHNOLOGIES INTL INC (BC)
Reincorporated under the laws of Ontario 08/25/2016

BEEBAS CREATIONS INC (CA)
Name changed to Nitches, Inc. (CA) 12/31/1995
Nitches, Inc. (CA) reincorporated in Nevada 11/05/2008

BEECH AIRCRAFT CORP (DE)
Common $1 par split (3) for (1) by issuance of (2) additional shares 11/23/1960
Common $1 par split (3) for (2) by issuance of (0.5) additional share 07/22/1968
Common $1 par split (3) for (2) by issuance of (0.5) additional share 11/21/1973
Common $1 par split (3) for (2) by issuance of (0.5) additional share 05/24/1978
Stock Dividends - 50% 01/20/1949; 25% 08/24/1955; 10% 02/28/1957
Merged into Raytheon Co. 02/08/1980
Each share Common $1 par exchanged for (0.775) share Common $1.25 par

BEECH CREEK RR CO (PA)
Merged into Penn Central Corp. 10/24/1978
Each share Common $50 par exchanged for (0.37) share Common $1 par and $10.65 principal amount of non-interest bearing Certificates of Beneficial Interest no par
Note: a) Distribution is certain only for certificates surrendered prior to 05/01/1985 b) Distribution may also be made for certificates surrendered between 05/01/1985 and 12/31/1986 c) No distribution will be made for certificates surrendered after 12/31/1986
Penn Central Corp. name changed to American Premier Underwriters, Inc. 03/25/1994 which merged into American Premier Group, Inc. 04/03/1995 which name changed to American Financial Group, Inc. 06/09/1995 which merged into American Financial Group, Inc. (Holding Co.) 12/02/1997

BEECH-NUT LIFE SAVERS, INC. (NY)
Common $10 par changed to $5 par and (1) additional share issued 08/03/1962
Merged into Squibb Beech-Nut, Inc. 01/15/1968
Each share $2 Conv. Preferred $4.75 par exchanged for (1.03) shares $2 Conv. Preferred $1 par
Each share Common $5 par exchanged for (1) share Common $1 par
Squibb Beech-Nut, Inc. name changed to Squibb Corp. 04/30/1971 which merged into Bristol-Myers Squibb Co. 10/04/1989

BEECH-NUT PACKING CO. (NY)
Each share Common $20 par exchanged for (3.5) shares Common $10 par 00/00/1947
Merged into Beech-Nut Life Savers, Inc. 08/01/1956
Each share Common $10 par exchanged for (1.2) shares Common $10 par
Beech-Nut Life Savers, Inc. merged into Squibb Beech-Nut, Inc. 01/15/1968 which name changed to Squibb Corp. 04/30/1971 which merged into Bristol-Myers Squibb Co. 10/04/1989

BEECHAM GROUP PLC (ENGLAND)
ADR's for Ordinary Reg. 5s par changed to 25p par per currency change 02/15/1971

Each Unsponsored ADR for Ordinary Reg. 25p par exchanged for (0.5) Sponsored ADR for Ordinary Reg. 25p par 08/07/1987
Stock Dividends - 100% 04/07/1964; 50% 03/17/1968; 300% 09/05/1979
Merged into SmithKline Beecham PLC 07/26/1989
Each Sponsored ADR for Ordinary Reg. 25p par exchanged for (0.35136) Sponsored ADR for A Ordinary 25p par
Note: ADR holders will also receive the net proceeds from the sale of the Floating Rate Unsecured Loan Stock 1990/1992 of SmithKline Beecham PLC
SmithKline Beecham PLC merged into GlaxoSmithKline PLC 12/27/2000

BEECHAM INC (NJ)
Merged into Beecham-Massengill Corp. 08/31/1971
Each share Common $1 par exchanged for $35 cash

BEECHER ENERGY LTD (BC)
Name changed to Rising Phoenix Development Group Ltd. 12/04/1995
(See Rising Phoenix Development Group Ltd.)

BEECHPORT CAP INC (CO)
Common no par split (1.35) for (1) by issuance of (0.35) additional share payable 08/26/1999 to holders of record 08/20/1999
Reincorporated under the laws of Delaware as ITec Environmental Group, Inc. and Common no par changed to 1¢ par 10/11/2002
ITec Environmental Group, Inc. name changed to Eco2 Plastics, Inc. 03/26/2007
(See Eco2 Plastics, Inc.)

BEEF & BISON BREEDERS INC (DE)
Name changed to Camelot International, Inc. 10/22/1980
Camelot International, Inc. merged into American Leisure Corp. (DE) 11/24/1982 which merged into American Midland Corp. 07/06/1984
(See American Midland Corp.)

BEEF INDS INC (TX)
Merged into Cyclone Entertainment Ltd., Inc. 02/27/1987
Each share Common 5¢ par exchanged for (0.275) share Common 1¢ par
(See Cyclone Entertainment Ltd., Inc.)

BEEFLAND INTL INC (DE)
Reincorporated 07/07/1970
State of incorporation changed from (NE) to (DE) 07/07/1970
Merged into American Beef Packers, Inc. (DE) 12/22/1971
Each share Common $1 par exchanged for (0.66666666) share Common $1 par
American Beef Packers, Inc. (DE) name changed to Sudbury Holdings, Inc. 08/18/1983 which reorganized as Sudbury, Inc. 05/27/1987
(See Sudbury, Inc.)

BEEFSTEAK CHARLIES INC (DE)
Name changed to Lifestyle Restaurants, Inc. 04/29/1985
Lifestyle Restaurants, Inc. merged into Bombay Palace Restaurants, Inc. 09/14/1987
(See Bombay Palace Restaurants, Inc.)

BEEFY KING INTL INC (DE)
Merged into IEA Corp. (DE) 06/21/1971
Details not available

BEEHIVE INTL (NV)
Merged 04/01/1981
Reincorporated 06/07/1994
Common 2¢ par split (2) for (1) by

issuance of (1) additional share 02/12/1981
Merged from Beehive International (Old) (UT) to Beehive International (New) (UT) 04/01/1981
Each share Common 2¢ par exchanged for (1) Non-Separable Unit of (1) share Beehive International (New) Common 2¢ par and (1) share Beehive International, Ltd. Common 2¢ par
Pairing agreement rejected 08/13/1985
Each share Beehive International (New) old Common 2¢ par exchanged for (1) share new Common 2¢ par
Note: Assets of Beehive International, Ltd. will be used to retire debt no certificates will be issued
State of incorporation changed from (UT) to (NV) 06/07/1994
Charter revoked for failure to file reports and pay fees 07/01/2002

BEEHIVE MEDICAL ELECTRONICS, INC. (UT)
Name changed to Beehive International (Old) 10/25/1976
Beehive International (Old) merged into Beehive International (New) 04/01/1981
(See Beehive International (New))

BEEHIVE ST BK (SALT LAKE CITY, UT)
Merged into Commercial Security Bank (Ogden, UT) 12/31/1968
Each share Common $10 par exchanged for $19 principal amount of 4-yr. 7% Debentures

BEEHIVE URANIUM CORP (UT)
Recapitalized as Energy Fuels & Minerals Exploration Corp. 06/23/1971
Each share Common 1¢ par exchanged for (0.05) share Common 1¢ par
Energy Fuels & Minerals Exploration Corp. name changed to Texas Western, Inc. 04/26/1972
(See Texas Western, Inc.)

BEEKIST INC (NV)
Charter revoked 09/30/2016

BEELINE FASHIONS INC (IL)
Common no par split (2) for (1) by issuance of (1) additional share 06/20/1966
Reincorporated under laws of Delaware as Beeline, Inc. 01/28/1977
(See Beeline, Inc. (DE))

BEELINE INC (DE)
Acquired by employees 09/25/1984
Each share Common no par exchanged for $10 cash

BEEMAC INC (MI)
Completely liquidated 01/31/2000
Each share Common $1 par exchanged for first and final distribution of $1 cash

BEEP COMMUNICATIONS SYS INC (NY)
Merged into Metromedia, Inc. 01/04/1983
Each share Common 1¢ par exchanged for $6 cash

BEEPER PLUS INC (NV)
Each share old Common $0.001 par exchanged for (0.1) share new Common $0.001 par 04/28/1989
Name changed to Western Gaming Corp. 10/14/2003
Western Gaming Corp. recapitalized as InRob Tech, Ltd. 09/01/2005

BEERE FINL EQUITY CORP (MD)
Charter forfeited 10/06/2006

BEERE FINL GROUP INC (NV)
Recapitalized as Steadfast Holdings Group, Inc. 10/01/2007
Each share Common $0.001 par

exchanged for (0.0004) share Common $0.001 par
Steadfast Holdings Group, Inc. recapitalized as Scorpex, Inc. 05/20/2011

BEERMASTER DISTRS LTD (BC)
Recapitalized as Sunatco Development Corp. 06/06/1977
Each share Capital Stock no par exchanged for (0.2) share Capital Stock no par
Sunatco Development Corp. recapitalized as International Sunatco Industries Ltd. 01/14/1991

BEETZ EXPLS LTD (ON)
Merged into Consolidated Goldsec Explorations Ltd. 12/05/1980
Each share Common no par exchanged for (0.2) share Common no par
(See Consolidated Goldsec Explorations Ltd.)

BEFIRST COM INC (NV)
Name changed to FindWhat.com (NV) 09/03/1999
FindWhat.com (NV) reincorporated in Delaware 09/03/2004 which name changed to MIVA, Inc. 06/13/2005 which name changed to Vertro, Inc. 06/09/2009 which merged into Inuvo, Inc. 03/01/2012

BEFUT INTL CO LTD (NV)
Each share old Common $0.001 par exchanged for (1) share new Common $0.001 par to reflect a (1) for (150) reverse split followed by a (150) for (1) forward split 05/10/2012
Note: Holders of (149) or fewer pre-split shares received $0.65 cash per share
Name changed to Befut Global, Inc. 10/06/2017

BEGAMA TECHNOLOGIES INC (CANADA)
Name changed to Victhom Human Bionics Inc. 01/13/2003
(See Victhom Human Bionics Inc.)

BEGLEY CO (KY)
Name changed 08/31/1984
Common $5 par changed to $2.50 par and (1) additional share issued 07/22/1966
Common $2.50 par changed to $1.66666666 par and (0.5) additional share issued 02/03/1969
6% Preferred $25 par called for redemption 11/15/1979
Stock Dividend - 10% 01/16/1979
Name changed from Begley Drug Co. to Begley Co. 08/31/1984
Merged into Rite Aid Corp. 08/19/1988
Each share Common $1.66666666 par exchanged for $28 cash

BEHAVIORAL RESH LABS INC (CA)
Name changed 01/29/1971
Name changed from Behavioral Research Laboratories to Behavioral Research Laboratories, Inc. 01/29/1971
Adjudicated bankrupt 09/06/1979
No stockholders' equity

BEHAVIOUR COMMUNICATIONS INC (CANADA)
Name changed to MDP Worldwide Entertainment Inc. 06/05/2000
MDP Worldwide Entertainment Inc. name changed to M8 Entertainment Inc. 04/14/2004

BEHLEN MFG CO (NE)
Completely liquidated 03/14/1969
Each share Class A Ser. 1 thru 10 $1 par exchanged for first and final distribution of (0.5) share Wickes Corp. (MI) Common $2.50 par
Each share Common $1 par exchanged for first and final distribution of (0.5) share Wickes Corp. (MI) Common $2.50 par
Wickes Corp. (MI) reincorporated in Delaware 07/02/1971 which merged into Wickes Companies, Inc. 08/13/1980 which merged into WCI Holdings Corp. 04/13/1989 which name changed to Collins & Aikman Group Inc. 07/17/1992
(See Collins & Aikman Group Inc.)

BEHRENS DRUG CO. (TX)
Name changed to Behrens Inc. 09/01/1971

BEHRING CORP (DE)
Name changed to Leadership Housing Inc. 09/01/1972
(See Leadership Housing Inc.)

BEHRINGER HARVARD OPPORTUNITY REIT II INC (MD)
Name changed to Lightstone Value Plus Real Estate Investment Trust V, Inc. 07/20/2017

BEI HLDGS LTD (DE)
Name changed to Amresco Inc. 05/23/1994
(See Amresco Inc.)

BEI MED SYS INC (DE)
Name changed 11/04/1997
Each share Common $0.001 par received distribution of (1) share BEI Technologies Inc. Common $0.001 par payable 10/07/1997 to holders of record 09/24/1997
Name changed from BEI Electronics, Inc. to 11/04/1997
Merged into Boston Scientific Corp. 07/08/2002
Each share Common $0.001 par exchanged for $6.8426 cash

BEI TECHNOLOGIES INC (DE)
Each share Common $0.001 par received distribution of (0.5) share OpticNet Inc. Common $0.0001 par payable 11/21/2000 to holders of record 10/30/2000
Common $0.001 par split (2) for (1) by issuance of (1) additional share payable 11/21/2000 to holders of record 10/30/2000
Acquired by Schneider Electric S.A. 10/6/2005
Each share Common $0.001 par exchanged for $35 cash

BEICANG IRON & STL INC (NV)
SEC revoked common stock registration 08/20/2012

BEIJING BEIDA JADE BIRD UNVL SCI-TECH CO LTD (CHINA)
ADR agreement terminated 03/10/2017
Each Sponsored ADR for Ordinary exchanged for $6.8478 cash

BEIJING DATANG PWR GENERATION LTD (CHINA)
Name changed to Datang International Power Generation Co., Ltd. 03/15/2004

BEIJING MARVEL CLEANSING SUPPLIES CO LTD (BC)
Name changed to Brand Marvel Worldwide Consumer Products Corp. 02/11/2009

BEIJING MED-PHARM CORP (DE)
Name changed to BMP Sunstone Corp. 02/19/2008
(See BMP Sunstone Corp.)

BEIJING YANHUA PETROCHEMICAL LTD (CHINA)
Name changed to Sinopec Beijing Yanhua Petrochemical Co. Ltd. 03/30/2001
(See Sinopec Beijing Yanhua Petrochemical Co. Ltd.)

BEIRUT MINING CO. LTD. (ON)
Dissolved 00/00/1959
Details not available

BEISINGER INDS CORP (DE)
Merged into Beisin Corp. 09/17/1979
Each share Common 1¢ par exchanged for $0.35 cash

BEKEEN COMPUTER CORP (ON)
Cease trade offer effective 06/11/1991
Stockholders' equity unlikely

BEKER INDS CORP (DE)
Charter forfeited for failure to maintain a registered agent 02/25/1991

BEKINS CO (CA)
Common $5 par changed to no par and (1) additional share issued 07/14/1979
Merged into Minstar, Inc. 07/08/1983
Each share Common no par exchanged for $23 cash

BEKINS VAN & STORAGE CO. (CA)
Each share Common $50 par exchanged for (10) shares Common $5 par 01/16/1961
Name changed to Bekins Co. 01/02/1969
(See Bekins Co.)

BEKLAND RES CORP (DE)
Each share Common 10¢ par exchanged for (0.2) share Common 50¢ par 09/19/1975
Assets foreclosed upon 09/26/1986
No stockholders' equity

BEKS CHARBROILERS INTL INC (DE)
Name changed to Bekland Resources Corp. 01/27/1971
(See Bekland Resources Corp.)

BEKS FOOD INTL INC (DE)
Recapitalized as American Healthcare Providers, Inc. 03/12/1999
Each share Common $0.001 par exchanged for (0.02) share Common $0.001 par
(See American Healthcare Providers, Inc.)

BEL AIR RES LTD (BC)
Recapitalized as Consolidated Bel-Air Resources Ltd. 10/11/1985
Each share Common no par exchanged for (0.25) share Common no par
Consolidated Bel-Air Resources Ltd. recapitalized as Blue Sky Resources Ltd. 12/13/1991 which name changed to Axion Communications Inc. 02/28/1996 which merged into Technovision Systems Inc. 12/01/2002 which merged into Uniserve Communications Corp. 11/20/2003

BEL PAC INDS LTD (BC)
Struck off register and declared dissolved for failure to file returns 11/05/1993

BELAIR ENERGY CORP (AB)
Each share old Common no par exchanged for (0.125) share new Common no par 09/27/1999
Merged into Purcell Energy Ltd. (New) 09/04/2003
Each share new Common no par exchanged for (0.354) share Common no par and $0.10 cash
(See Purcell Energy Ltd. (New))

BELAIR ENTERPRISES INC (NV)
Name changed to Tenkom Group, Inc. 04/27/2005
Tenkom Group, Inc. recapitalized as VMT Scientific, Inc. 08/15/2005

BELAIR FINL CORP (DE)
Charter cancelled and declared inoperative and void for non-payment of taxes 03/01/1974

BELAIR HOTEL CORP.
Liquidated 00/00/1947
Details not available

BELAIRRE INC. (UT)
Name changed to Lambert Consolidated Industries Inc. 12/17/1985

BELAMOSE CORP.
Name changed to Hartford Rayon Corp. 00/00/1935
Hartford Rayon Corp. acquired by Bigelow-Sanford Carpet Co., Inc. (DE) 00/00/1951 which name changed to Bigelow-Sanford, Inc. 05/04/1960
(See Bigelow-Sanford, Inc.)

BELANGER (A.) LTEE. (QC)
Class A $1 par called for redemption 06/30/1976
Public interest eliminated

BELCARRA EXPLS LTD (BC)
Recapitalized as Karin Lake Explorations Ltd. 04/04/1978
Each share Common no par exchanged for (0.2) share Common no par
(See Karin Lake Explorations Ltd.)

BELCARRA MTRS LTD (BC)
Name changed 10/05/1994
Name changed from Belcarra Resources Ltd. to Belcarra Motors Ltd. 10/05/1994
Name changed to Predator Ventures Ltd. (BC) 09/10/1997
Predator Ventures Ltd. (BC) reincorporated in Wyoming 07/14/1999 which recapitalized as wwbroadcast.net Inc. 11/18/1999 which name changed to Luna Gold Corp. (WY) 08/12/2003 which reincorporated in Canada 12/01/2005 which merged into Trek Mining Inc. 03/31/2017 which name changed to Equinox Gold Corp. 12/22/2017

BELCHER EXTENSION CONSOLIDATED MINES CO. (NV)
Charter revoked for failure to file reports and pay fees 03/06/1933

BELCHER IRON ORES LTD. (ON)
Name changed to Vulcan Mines Ltd. 00/00/1955
Vulcan Mines Ltd. merged into Little Long Lac Gold Mines Ltd. (The) 04/27/1967 which merged into Little Long Lac Mines Ltd. 01/08/1971 which name changed to Little Long Lac Gold Mines Ltd. (New) 07/03/1975 which merged into LAC Minerals Ltd. (New) 07/29/1985 which was acquired by American Barrick Resources Corp. 10/17/1994 which name changed to Barrick Gold Corp. 01/18/1995

BELCHER MNG LTD (ON)
Merged into Little Long Lac Mines Ltd. (Old) 01/08/1971
Each share Capital Stock $1 par exchanged for (0.22222222) share Capital Stock no par
Little Long Lac Mines Ltd. name changed to Little Long Lac Gold Mines Ltd. (New) 07/03/1975 which merged into LAC Minerals Ltd. (New) 07/29/1985 which was acquired by American Barrick Resources Corp. 10/17/1994 which name changed to Barrick Gold Corp. 01/18/1995

BELCHER OIL CO (FL)
Through purchase offer 100% acquired by Coastal States Gas Corp. as of 03/30/1977
Public interest eliminated

BELCLAIR MARKET, INC. (NY)
Charter revoked for failure to file reports and pay fees 12/15/1939

BELCO OIL & GAS CORP (NV)
Merged into Westport Resources Corp. (NV) 08/21/2001
Each share 6.5% Preferred 1¢ par exchanged for (0.465795) share Common 1¢ par
Each share Common 1¢ par exchanged for (0.4125) share Common 1¢ par
Westport Resources Corp. merged into Kerr-McGee Corp. 06/25/2004

BELCO PETE CORP (DE)
Common $1 par split (3) for (2) by

issuance of (0.5) additional share 01/31/1979
Common $1 par split (2) for (1) by issuance of (1) additional share 03/05/1981
Merged into InterNorth, Inc. 08/01/1983
Each share Common $1 par exchanged for (0.315) share $10.50 2nd Preferred $100 par
InterNorth, Inc. name changed to Enron Corp. (DE) 05/12/1986 which reincorporated in Oregon 07/01/1997
(See Enron Corp. (OR))

BELCO POLLUTION CTL CORP (DE)
Merged into Foster Wheeler Corp. (NY) 10/24/1979
Each share Common 10¢ par exchanged for (0.33333333) share Common $1 par
Foster Wheeler Corp. (NY) reincorporated in Bermuda as Foster Wheeler Ltd. 05/25/2001 which reorganized in Switzerland as Foster Wheeler AG 02/09/2009 which merged into Amec Foster Wheeler PLC 01/19/2015
(See Amec Foster Wheeler PLC)

BELCO SYS TECHNOLOGIES INC (DE)
Each share old Common $0.001 par exchanged for (0.33333333) share new Common $0.001 par 03/04/1998
Name changed to SJI Group Inc. 03/05/1998
SJI Group Inc. name changed to iCommerce Group, Inc. 06/10/1999
(See iCommerce Group, Inc.)

BELCOR INC (CA)
Each share old Common 10¢ par exchanged for (0.2) share new Common 10¢ par 02/15/1990
Name changed to Silver Assets Inc. 08/19/1998
(See Silver Assets Inc.)

BELCROFT RADIUM MINES LTD. (ON)
Charter revoked for failure to file reports and pay fees 02/25/1965

BELDEN & BLAKE CORP (OH)
Merged into Texas Pacific Group 06/27/1997
Each share Common no par exchanged for $27 cash

BELDEN & BLAKE DRILLING PROGRAM 1986 (OH)
Partnership dissolved 00/00/1990
Details not available

BELDEN & BLAKE DRILLING PROGRAM 1987 (OH)
Partnership dissolved 00/00/1990
Details not available

BELDEN & BLAKE ENERGY CO (OH)
Merged into Belden & Blake Corp. 03/27/1992
Each Unit of Ltd. Partnership Int. exchanged for (0.13800717) share Common no par
(See Belden & Blake Corp.)

BELDEN ARMS APARTMENTS
Trust terminated and liquidated 00/00/1950
Details not available

BELDEN CDT INC (DE)
Name changed to Belden Inc. (New) 05/24/2007

BELDEN CORP (DE)
Name changed 05/02/1967
Reincorporated 05/06/1975
Each share Common $100 par exchanged for (10) shares Common $10 par 00/00/1936
Stock Dividends - 20% 06/01/1955; 100% 06/01/1960; 10% 12/06/1965
Name changed from Belden Manufacturing Co. to Belden Corp. 05/02/1967

State of incorporation changed from (IL) to (DE) 05/06/1975
Common $5 par split (3) for (2) by issuance of (0.5) additional share 06/16/1980
Merged into Crouse-Hinds Co. 12/10/1980
Each share Common $5 par exchanged for (1.24) shares Common $1.66666666 par
Crouse-Hinds Co. merged into Cooper Industries, Inc. (OH) 04/29/1981 which reincorporated in Bermuda as Cooper Industries, Ltd. 05/22/2002 which reincorporated in Ireland as Cooper Industries PLC 09/08/2009 which merged into Eaton Corp. PLC 11/30/2012

BELDEN INC OLD (DE)
Merged into Belden CDT Inc. 07/16/2004
Each share Common 1¢ par exchanged for (1) share Common 1¢ par
Belden CDT Inc. name changed to Belden Inc. (New) 05/24/2007

BELDING CORTICELLI LTD (CANADA)
Name changed 11/15/1979
Each share Preferred $100 par exchanged for (10) shares 7% Preferred $10 par 00/00/1951
Each share Common $100 par exchanged for (10) shares Common no par 00/00/1951
Common no par split (2) for (1) by issuance of (1) additional share 03/15/1965
Common no par split (2) for (1) by issuance of (1) additional share 10/10/1969
7% Preferred $10 par reclassified as 7% Conv. Class A Preferred $10 par 07/19/1974
Common no par reclassified as Conv. Class A Common no par 07/19/1974
Stock Dividend - 10% 06/30/1959
Name changed from Belding-Corticelli Ltd. to Belding-Corticelli Inc., 7% Conv. Class A Preferred $10 par, 7% Conv. Class B Preferred $10 par reclassified as Preferred no par and Conv. Class A Common no par and Conv. Class B Common no par reclassified as Common no par respectively 11/15/1979
Placed in receivership 04/22/1982
No stockholders' equity

BELDING HALL ELECTRIC CORP.
Out of business 00/00/1929
Details not available

BELDING HEMINWAY INC NEW (DE)
Name changed to Carlyle Industries, Inc. 03/27/1997
Carlyle Industries, Inc. merged into Levcor International, Inc. 01/07/2003

BELDING HEMINWAY INC OLD (DE)
Reorganized 00/00/1947
Reorganized from Belding Heminway Co. (CT) to Belding Heminway Co., Inc. (Old) (DE) 00/00/1947
Each share Common no par exchanged for (1) share Common $1 par
Capital Stock $1 par reclassified as Common $1 par 04/28/1960
Common $1 par split (3) for (2) by issuance of (0.5) additional share 01/17/1969
Common $1 par split (2) for (1) by issuance of (1) additional share 12/20/1971
Merged into Noel Group, Inc. 10/29/1993
Each share Common $1 par exchanged for $30.25 cash

BELEC COURVILLE MINES LTD. (ON)
Charter cancelled in 09/00/1962

BELFAST & MOOSEHEAD LAKE RR CO (ME)
Sold to private investors 00/00/1991
Details not available

BELFAST MINES LTD. (ON)
Acquired by Goldale Ltd. 06/18/1964
Each share Capital Stock $1 par exchanged for (0.1) share Capital Stock no par
Goldale Ltd. recapitalized as Canadian Goldale Corp. Ltd. 06/16/1965 which name changed to Hambro Canada (1972) Ltd. 01/09/1973 which name changed to Hambro Canada Ltd. 05/28/1974 which name changed to Hatleigh Corp. (Old) 08/03/1978 which merged into Hatleigh Corp. (New) 08/31/1978 which merged into Dexleigh Corp. 06/30/1984
(See Dexleigh Corp.)

BELFAST PETE INC (AB)
Acquired by Merit Energy Ltd. 08/17/2000
Each share Common no par exchanged for (0.2667) share Common no par
(See Merit Energy Ltd.)

BELFONT STEEL & WIRE CO.
Sold to American Rolling Mill Co. 00/00/1934
Details not available

BELGACOM SA (BELGIUM)
Name changed to Proximus Group 07/09/2015

BELGIAN NATL RYS CO (BELGIUM)
Deposit Agreement terminated 10/28/1966
Each American Share for Part. Preferred 500 Fcs. par exchanged for $48.09 cash

BELGIUM GLOVE & HOSIERY CO. OF CANADA, LTD. (CANADA)
Name changed to Belgium Stores Ltd. 00/00/1951
Belgium Stores Ltd. name changed to Belgium Standard Ltd. 04/01/1965 which name changed to Amertek Inc. (Canada) 11/14/1985 which reincorporated in Ontario 06/27/1989
(See Amertek Inc. (ON))

BELGIUM STD LTD (CANADA)
Common no par split (2) for (1) by issuance of (1) additional share 05/14/1970
Common no par split (3) for (1) by issuance of (2) additional shares 05/11/1971
Common no par split (2) for (1) by issuance of (1) additional share 01/23/1973
Name changed to Amertek Inc. (Canada) 11/14/1985
Amertek Inc. (Canada) reincorporated in Ontario 06/27/1989
(See Amertek Inc. (ON))

BELGIUM STORES LTD. (CANADA)
Name changed to Belgium Standard Ltd. 04/01/1965
Belgium Standard Ltd. name changed to Amertek Inc. (Canada) 11/14/1985 which reincorporated in Ontario 06/27/1989
(See Amertek Inc. (ON))

BELGO CANADIAN PAPER CO. LTD.
Merged into Consolidated Paper Corp. Ltd. 00/00/1931
Details not available

BELGOLD MINES LTD. (ON)
Charter revoked for failure to file reports and pay taxes 00/00/1957

BELIEVING TODAY INC (DE)
SEC revoked common stock registration 08/27/2010

BELINDA MINES LTD (BC)
Name changed to Goldfever Resources Ltd. 06/21/1982
(See Goldfever Resources Ltd.)

BELIZE AMERN CORP INTERNATIONALE (NV)
Common $0.001 par split (5) for (1) by issuance of (4) additional shares 12/03/1991
Common $0.001 par split (2) for (1) by issuance of (1) additional share 04/01/1992
Name changed to American Energy Group, Ltd. 12/05/1994
(See American Energy Group, Ltd.)

BELIZE HOLDINGS INC. (BELIZE)
Name changed to BHI Corp. 07/06/1995
BHI Corp. name changed to Carlisle Holdings Ltd. 06/02/1999 which name changed to BB Holdings Ltd. 08/18/2005
(See BB Holdings Ltd.)

BELK INC (DE)
Acquired by Bear Parent Inc. 12/10/2015
Each share Class B Common 1¢ par exchanged for $68 cash

BELK INC (DE)
Acquired by Bear Parent Inc. 12/10/2015
Each share Class A Common 1¢ par exchanged for $68 cash

BELKIN INC (BC)
Acquired by Paperboard Industries Corp. Inc. 09/01/1987
Each share Common no par exchanged for $23.50 cash
Each share Non-Vtg. Common no par exchanged for $23.50 cash

BELKNAP HARDWARE & MANUFACTURING CO. (KY)
Each share Common $10 par exchanged for (3) shares Common no par 00/00/1947
Name changed to Belknap, Inc. 07/22/1968
(See Belknap, Inc.)

BELKNAP INC (KY)
4% Preferred $20 par called for redemption 04/30/1984
Acquired by a group of investors 07/02/1984
Each share Common no par exchanged for $24 cash

BELKNAP REALTY CO. (TX)
Merged into United States National Bancshares, Inc. 05/01/1972
Each share Capital Stock no par exchanged for (0.0658) share Common $1 par
United States National Bancshares, Inc. acquired by Cullen/Frost Bankers, Inc. 05/03/1982

BELKOR MINES LTD. (ON)
Charter cancelled 00/00/1955

BELL & GOSSETT CO. (IL)
Each share Common $5 par exchanged for (3) shares Common $2 par 00/00/1954
Stock Dividends - 25% 10/01/1950; 20% 07/02/1951
Acquired by International Telephone & Telegraph Corp. (MD) 09/27/1963
Each share Common $2 par exchanged for (0.07) share 4% Conv. Preferred Ser. D $100 par and (0.335) share Capital Stock no par
International Telephone & Telegraph Corp. (MD) reincorporated in Delaware 01/31/1968 which name changed to ITT Corp. 12/31/1983 which reorganized in Indiana as ITT Industries, Inc. 12/19/1995 which name changed to ITT Corp. 07/01/2006

BELL & HOWELL CO (DE)
Reincorporated 05/06/1977
Each share Common $25 par exchanged for (25) shares Common $10 par 00/00/1945
Common $10 par changed to $5 par and (1) additional share issued 05/08/1959

Common $5 par changed to no par and (0.75) additional share issued 01/15/1960
4.25% Preferred $100 par called for redemption 09/01/1961
4.75% Preferred $100 par called for redemption 09/01/1961
4.25% Conv. Preferred $50 par called for redemption 07/01/1972
Stock Dividend - 10% 11/01/1955
State of incorporation changed from (IL) to (DE) 05/06/1977
$2.50 Conv. Preferred $50 par called for redemption 08/22/1983
Each share $12 Preferred no par exchanged for (20) shares Conv. Preferred Ser. A no par 11/10/1983
Acquired by Bell & Howell Group, Inc. 05/17/1988
Each share Conv. Preferred Ser. A no par exchanged for $64 cash
Each share Common no par exchanged for $64 cash

BELL & HOWELL CO NEW (DE)
Name changed to ProQuest Co. 06/05/2001
ProQuest Co. name changed to Voyager Learning Co. 07/02/2007 which merged into Cambium Learning Group, Inc. 12/09/2009

BELL & HOWELL HLDGS CO (DE)
Name changed to Bell & Howell Co. (New) 11/16/1995
Bell & Howell Co. (New) name changed to ProQuest Co. 06/05/2001 which name changed to Voyager Learning Co. 07/02/2007 which merged into Cambium Learning Group, Inc. 12/09/2009

BELL AIRCRAFT CORP. (NY)
Each share Preferred no par exchanged for (10) shares new Common $1 par 00/00/1936
Each share old Common $1 par exchanged for (10) shares new Common $1 par 00/00/1936
Common $1 par split (2) for (1) by issuance of (1) additional share 00/00/1954
Stock Dividends - 10% 12/02/1943; 10% 12/13/1945; 100% 02/29/1952
Reincorporated under the laws of Delaware as Bell Intercontinental Corp. 07/02/1960
Bell Intercontinental Corp. merged into Wheelabrator-Frye Inc. 11/04/1971 which merged into Signal Companies, Inc. 02/01/1983 which merged into Allied-Signal Inc. 09/19/1985 which name changed to AlliedSignal Inc. 04/26/1993 which name changed to Honeywell International Inc. 12/01/1999

BELL ALIANT INC (CANADA)
Merged into BCE Inc. 10/31/2014
Each share Common no par exchanged for (0.4778) share Common no par and $7.75 cash

BELL ALIANT PFD EQUITY INC (CANADA)
Merged into BCE Inc. 10/31/2014
Each share 5-Yr. Rate Reset Preferred Ser. A no par exchanged for (1) share 1st Preferred Ser. AM no par
Each share 5-Yr. Rate Reset Preferred Ser. C no par exchanged for (1) share 1st Preferred Ser. AO no par
Each share 5-Yr. Rate Reset Preferred Ser. E no par exchanged for (1) share 1st Preferred Ser. AQ no par

BELL ALIANT REGL COMMUNICATIONS INCOME FD (ON)
Reorganized under the laws of Canada as Bell Aliant Inc. 01/04/2011
Each Unit no par exchanged for (1) share Common no par

Bell Aliant Inc. merged into BCE Inc. 11/10/2014 which merged into BCE Inc. 10/31/2014

BELL ATLANTIC CORP (DE)
Common $1 par split (2) for (1) by issuance of (1) additional share 04/17/1986
Common $1 par split (2) for (1) by issuance of (1) additional share 05/01/1990
Common $1 par changed to 10¢ par and (1) additional share issued payable 06/29/1998 to holders of record 06/01/1998 Ex date - 06/30/1998
Under plan of merger name changed to Verizon Communications Inc. 06/30/2000

BELL AZ CONSULTANTS INC (NV)
Name changed to Strategy X, Inc. 03/11/2004
Strategy X, Inc. recapitalized as Alliance Transcription Services, Inc. 08/14/2007
(See Alliance Transcription Services, Inc.)

BELL BANCORP INC (DE)
Common 1¢ par split (2) for (1) by issuance of (1) additional share 09/08/1994
Merged into Standard Federal Bancorporation, Inc. 06/07/1996
Each share Common 1¢ par exchanged for $37.50 cash

BELL CABLEMEDIA PLC (ENGLAND & WALES)
Merged into Cable & Wireless Communications PLC 12/10/1997
Each Sponsored ADR for Ordinary exchanged for (0.69389) Sponsored ADR for Ordinary
(See Cable & Wireless Communications PLC)

BELL CANADA
See - Bell Telephone Co. of CanadaLa Compagnie De Telephone Bell Du Canada (Canada)

BELL CDA ENTERPRISES INC (CANADA)
$2.25 1st Conv. Preferred Ser. C no par called for redemption 10/31/1985
$1.80 1st Conv. Preferred Ser. F no par called for redemption 11/04/1986
Name changed to BCE Inc. 01/04/1988

BELL CDA INTL INC (CANADA)
Each share old Common no par exchanged for (0.00833799) share new Common no par 07/22/2002
Each share Class A Preferred Ser. 15 no par exchanged for (1) share BCE Inc. 1st Preferred Ser. AE no par 01/23/2007
Liquidation completed
Each share new Common no par received initial distribution of $6.25 cash payable 06/20/2006 to holders of record 05/25/2006
Each share new Common no par received second and final distribution of $1.0245 cash payable 06/27/2007 to holders of record 06/13/2007
Note: Certificates were not required to be surrendered and are without value

BELL CAPTAIN, INC. (PA)
Plan of arrangement under Chapter 11 Federal Bankruptcy proceedings confirmed 11/30/1983
No stockholders' equity

BELL CO. (MA)
Common $5 par changed to $1 par 06/08/1956
Merged into Pacific Coast Co. (DE) on a share for share basis 04/20/1962
(See Pacific Coast Co. (DE))

BELL COAST CAP CORP (BC)
Name changed to Uranium Power Corp. 03/22/2005
Uranium Power Corp. merged into Titan Uranium Inc. 07/31/2009 which merged into Energy Fuels Inc. 02/24/2012

BELL COPPER CORP OLD (BC)
Reorganized as Bell Copper Corp. (New) 07/23/2013
Each share Common no par exchanged for (0.2) share Common no par

BELL EARTH SCIENCES INC (BC)
Delisted from Vancouver Stock Exchange 03/01/1999

BELL ELECTR CORP (CA)
Common no par split (5) for (2) by issuance of (1.5) additional shares 09/30/1968
Name changed to Bell Industries (CA) 11/02/1971
Bell Industries (CA) reorganized as Bell Industries, Inc. (DE) 10/30/1979 which reincorporated in California 06/30/1995 which reorganized in Delaware 03/23/2011

BELL INDS INC (CA)
Reorganized 10/30/1979
Reincorporated 06/30/1995
Reorganized from Bell Industries (CA) to Bell Industries, Inc. (DE) and Common no par changed to 25¢ par 10/30/1979
Common 25¢ par split (6) for (5) by issuance of (0.2) additional share 08/13/1987
State of incorporation changed from (DE) to (CA) and Common 25¢ par changed to no par 06/30/1995
Each share old Common no par exchanged for (0.05) share new Common no par 12/26/2008
Stock Dividends - 5% payable 06/05/1996 to holders of record 05/24/1996; 20% payable 06/11/1997 to holders of record 05/30/1997 Ex date - 06/12/1997
Reorganized under the laws of Delaware 03/23/2011
Each share new Common no par exchanged for (0.05) share Common 1¢ par
Note: Holders of (19) or fewer pre-split shares received $1.85 cash per share

BELL INTERCONTINENTAL CORP (DE)
Merged into Wheelabrator-Frye Inc. 11/04/1971
Each share Common $1 par exchanged for (3) shares Common 10¢ par
Wheelabrator-Frye Inc. merged into Signal Companies, Inc. 02/01/1983 which merged into Allied-Signal Inc. 09/19/1985 which name changed to AlliedSignal Inc. 04/26/1993 which name changed to Honeywell International Inc. 12/01/1999

BELL KNIT INDS LTD (CANADA)
Completely liquidated 00/00/1983
Each share Common no par received first and final distribution of approximately $0.80 cash

BELL KO FILM CORP (DE)
Completely liquidated 12/18/1972
Each share Common 1¢ par exchanged for first and final distribution of (1) share Industries International Inc. Common 1¢ par
(See Industries International, Inc.)

BELL MANITOU GOLD MINE LTD. (QC)
Charter revoked for failure to file reports and pay fees 00/00/1946

BELL MICROPRODUCTS INC (CA)
Common 1¢ par split (3) for (2) by issuance of (0.5) additional share payable 08/31/2000 to holders of record 08/11/2000 Ex date - 09/01/2000
Acquired by Avnet, Inc. 07/06/2010
Each share Common 1¢ par exchanged for $7 cash

BELL MOLYBDENUM MINES INC (BC)
Name changed to Bell Earth Sciences Inc. 08/08/1997
(See Bell Earth Sciences Inc.)

BELL MOLYBDENUM MINES LTD (BC)
Merged into Bell Molybdenum Mines Inc. 04/12/1995
Each share Common no par exchanged for (1) share Common no par
Bell Molybdenum Mines Inc. name changed to Bell Earth Sciences Inc. 08/08/1997
(See Bell Earth Sciences Inc.)

BELL MTN SILVER MINES INC (NV)
Charter revoked for failure to file reports and pay fees 04/01/1991

BELL NATL CORP (CA)
Common $2 par split (2) for (1) by issuance of (1) additional share 01/03/1983
Common $2 par split (3) for (2) by issuance of (0.5) additional share 06/03/1983
Reincorporated under the laws of Delaware as Ampersand Medical Corp. and new Common no par changed to $0.001 par 05/26/1999
Ampersand Medical Corp. name changed to Molecular Diagnostics, Inc. 09/17/2001 which name changed to CytoCore, Inc. 08/17/2006 which name changed to Medite Cancer Diagnostics, Inc. 12/11/2014

BELL NORDIQ GROUP INC (QC)
1st Preferred Shares Ser. 8 called for redemption at $25 plus $0.359275 accrued dividends on 07/01/2006

BELL NORDIQ INCOME FD (QC)
Merged into Bell Aliant Regional Communications Income Fund (ON) 01/30/2007
Each Unit no par received (0.4113) Unit no par and $4 cash
Note: U.S. holders will receive cash from the sale of Units
Bell Aliant Regional Communications Income Fund (ON) reorganized in Canada as Bell Aliant Inc. 01/04/2011 which merged into BCE Inc. 10/31/2014

BELL PETE SVCS INC (TX)
Merged into Regal International, Inc. 11/20/1987
Each share 50¢ par exchanged for (1.1780596) shares Common 10¢ par
Regal International, Inc. recapitalized as Asia Resources Holdings Ltd. 02/19/1999 which name changed to Asia Fiber Holdings Ltd. 03/14/2000
(See Asia Fiber Holdings Ltd.)

BELL RES CORP (BC)
Merged into Bell Copper Corp. (Old) 05/12/2008
Each share Common no par exchanged for (0.5) share Common no par
Bell Copper Corp. (Old) reorganized as Bell Copper Corp. (New) 07/23/2013

BELL RES LTD (AUSTRALIA)
Name changed to Australian Consolidated Investments Ltd. 02/12/1991
(See Australian Consolidated Investments Ltd.)

BELL SVGS BK PASA (UPPER DARBY, PA)
Under plan of reorganization each share Common $1 par automatically became (1) share Bell Savings

Holdings, Inc. Common $1 par 01/31/1989
(See Bell Savings Holdings, Inc.)

BELL SVGS HLDGS INC (DE)
Holding company for Bell Savings Bank PaSA (Upper Darby, PA) which failed 03/21/1992
No stockholders' equity

BELL SPORTS CORP (DE)
Merged into HB Acquisition Corp. 08/17/1998
Each share Common 1¢ par exchanged for $10.25 cash

BELL TECHNOLOGY GROUP LTD (DE)
Name changed to Globix Corp. 06/01/1998
Globix Corp. name changed to NEON Communications Group, Inc. 03/01/2007
(See NEON Communications Group, Inc.)

BELL TEL CO CDA-BELL CDA (CANADA)
Each share Common $100 par exchanged for (4) shares Common $25 par 10/01/1948
Common $25 par changed to $8.33333333 par and (2) additional shares issued 05/09/1979
$1.80 Class B Preferred Ser. F $20 par, $1.96 Class D Conv. Preferred Ser. G $25 par, $2.05 Class E Conv. Preferred Ser. H $20 par, $2.25 Class B Preferred Ser. C $30 par, $2.28 Class C Conv. Preferred Ser. E $25 par, $2.70 Class E Conv. Preferred Ser. I $20 par, $3.20 Preferred $47 par, $3.34 Class B Conv. Preferred Ser. B $52 par, $4.23 Class C Conv. Preferred Ser. D $47 par and Common $8.33333333 par changed to no par respectively 04/21/1982
$3.20 Preferred no par called for redemption 08/01/1982
$3.34 Class B Conv. Preferred Ser. B no par called for redemption 08/15/1982
$4.23 Class C Conv. Preferred Ser. D no par called for redemption 09/01/1982
$2.28 Class C Conv. Preferred Ser. E no par called for redemption 10/02/1982
Under plan of reorganization each share $1.80 Class B Preferred Ser. F no par, $1.96 Class D Conv. Preferred Ser. G no par, $2.05 Class E Conv. Preferred Ser. H no par, $2.25 Class B Preferred Ser. C no par, $2.70 Class E Conv. Preferred Ser. I no par and Common no par automatically became (1) share Bell Canada Enterprises Inc. $1.80 Class B Conv. Preferred Ser. F no par, $1.96 Class D Conv. Preferred Ser. G no par, $2.05 Class E Conv. Preferred Ser. H no par, $2.25 Class B Conv. Preferred Ser. C no par, $2.70 Class E Conv. Preferred Ser. I no par and Common no par respectively 04/28/1983
Bell Canada Enterprises Inc. name changed to BCE Inc. 01/04/1988
Class A Ser. 10 Retractable Reset Dividend Preferred called for redemption at $25 plus $0.465 accrued dividends on 08/15/2000
Each share Class A Preferred Ser. 15 no par exchanged for (1) share BCE Inc. 1st Preferred Ser. AF no par 02/01/2007
Each share Class A Preferred Ser. 16 no par exchanged for (1) share BCE Inc. 1st Preferred Ser. AF no par 02/01/2007
Each share Class A Preferred Ser. 17 no par exchanged for (1) share BCE Inc. 1st Preferred Ser. AG no par 02/01/2007
Each share Class A Preferred Ser. 18 no par exchanged for (1) share BCE Inc. 1st Preferred Ser. AH no par 02/01/2007
Each share Class A Preferred Ser. 19 no par exchanged for (1) share BCE Inc. 1st Preferred Ser. AI no par 02/01/2007

BELL TELEPHONE CO. OF CANADA (CANADA)
Each share Common $100 par exchanged for (4) shares Common $25 par 00/00/1948
Name changed to Bell Telephone Co. of Canada - La Compagnie de Telephone Bell du Canada 06/30/1948
Bell Telephone Co. of Canada-La Compagnie de Telephone Bell du Canada reorganized as Bell Canada Enterprises Inc. 04/28/1983 which name changed to BCE Inc. 01/04/1988

BELL TELEVISION INC (NY)
Name changed to Holmes Protection Services Corp. 01/07/1972
Holmes Protection Services Corp. merged into National Kinney Corp. 10/13/1972 which name changed to Andal Corp. 11/07/1983
(See Andal Corp.)

BELL W & CO INC (DC)
Common 10¢ par split (5) for (4) by issuance of (0.25) additional share 03/26/1990
Stock Dividends - 20% 12/12/1980; 50% 12/11/1981; 10% 11/30/1983; 10% 12/14/1984
Charter revoked for failure to file reports 09/13/1993

BELL WESTN CORP (WY)
Each share old Common no par exchanged for (0.125) share new Common no par 07/02/1976
Merged into Vanderbilt Energy Corp. 10/25/1978
Each share new Common no par exchanged for (0.4759) share Common 10¢ par
(See Vanderbilt Energy Corp.)

BELLA COSTA DESIGNS INC (NV)
Name changed to China Crawfish, Ltd. 11/02/2017

BELLA PASTA INC (FL)
Name changed to Power Capital Partnership, Inc. 09/18/1997
(See Power Capital Partnership, Inc.)

BELLA PETRELLAS HLDGS INC (FL)
Name changed to Big Three Restaurants, Inc. 06/28/2012
Big Three Restaurants, Inc. recapitalized as Sports Venues of Florida, Inc. 05/19/2014

BELLA RES INC (AB)
Recapitalized as Angel Bioventures Inc. (AB) 08/28/2013
Each share Common no par exchanged for (0.25) share Common no par
Angel Bioventures Inc. (AB) reorganized in British Columbia as AbraPlata Resource Corp. 03/28/2017

BELLA TRADING CO INC (CO)
Common $0.001 par split (15) for (1) by issuance of (14) additional shares payable 06/25/2007 to holders of record 06/22/2007 Ex date - 06/26/2007
Name changed to Jayhawk Energy, Inc. (CO) 06/22/2007
Jayhawk Energy, Inc. (CO) reincorporated in Nevada 10/08/2015

BELLA VIAGGIO INC (NV)
Name changed to Kat Gold Holdings Corp. 08/26/2010
Kat Gold Holdings Corp. recapitalized as RemSleep Holdings, Inc. 03/26/2015

BELLA VISTA RANCHES, INC. (AZ)
Each share Capital Stock no par exchanged for (0.01) share Capital Stock $100 par 03/13/1978
Charter revoked for failure to file reports or pay fees 10/18/1988

BELLABON RES CORP (BC)
Struck off register and declared dissolved for failure to file returns 09/18/1992

BELLACASA PRODUCTIONS INC (NV)
Each share Common $0.0001 par received distribution of (0.721996) share Aquamer, Inc. Common $0.0001 par payable 03/05/2007 to holders of record 02/02/2007 Ex date - 01/31/2007
Recapitalized as WiFiMed Holdings Co., Inc. 03/06/2007
Each share Common $0.0001 par exchanged for (0.1) share Common $0.0001 par

BELLAIR VENTURES INC (CANADA)
Name changed to SustainCo Inc. 07/15/2013

BELLAMONT EXPL LTD (AB)
Each share Class B Common no par reclassified as (10) shares Class A Common no par 12/15/2011
Merged into Storm Resources Ltd. 03/23/2012
Each share Class A Common no par exchanged for (0.1445) share Common no par
Note: Unexchanged certificates were cancelled and became without value 03/23/2016

BELLANCA AIRCRAFT CORP. (DE)
Name changed to Bellanca Corp. 05/15/1956
Bellanca Corp. name changed to Olson Brothers, Inc. 12/01/1961 which name changed to Olson Farms, Inc. 06/28/1971 which name changed to Olson Industries, Inc. 09/05/1985 which merged into Dolco Packaging Corp. 07/29/1991
(See Dolco Packaging Corp.)

BELLANCA AIRCRAFT CORP (MN)
Chapter 11 bankruptcy proceedings converted to Chapter 7 on 04/27/1981
Stockholders' equity unlikely

BELLANCA CORP. (DE)
Name changed to Olson Brothers, Inc. 12/01/1961
Olson Brothers, Inc. name changed to Olson Farms, Inc. 06/28/1971 which name changed to Olson Industries, Inc. 09/05/1985 which merged into Dolco Packaging Corp. 07/29/1991
(See Dolco Packaging Corp.)

BELLAS HESS & CO.
Merged into National Bellas Hess Co., Inc. 00/00/1927
Details not available

BELLATOR EXPL INC (AB)
Merged into Baytex Energy Ltd. 06/07/2000
Each share Common no par exchanged for (0.165) share Common no par and $0.75 cash
(See Baytex Energy Ltd.)

BELLATRIX INTL INC (DE)
Name changed 08/18/1989
Name changed from Bellatrix Corp. to Bellatrix International, Inc. 06/18/1989
SEC revoked common stock registration 11/28/2008

BELLBROOK BANCORP INC (OH)
Acquired by BancFirst Ohio Corp. 07/01/1995
Each share Common no par exchanged for (1.11) shares Common 10¢ par
BancFirst Ohio Corp. merged into Unizan Financial Corp. 03/08/2002 which merged into Huntington Bancshares Inc. 03/01/2006

BELLCO ENERGY CORP (BC)
Name changed to Ocutech Canada Inc. 08/14/1987
(See Ocutech Canada Inc.)

BELLE AIRE RES EXPLS LTD (ON)
Name changed to Sprint Resources Ltd. 09/23/1982
Sprint Resources Ltd. name changed to Meacon Bay Resources Inc. 03/09/1987 which recapitalized as Advantex Marketing International Inc. 09/16/1991

BELLE ALKALI CO. (WV)
Acquired by Diamond Alkali Co. 00/00/1953
Details not available

BELLE-BRY YELLOWKNIFE MINES, LTD. (ON)
Merged into Pardee Amalgamated Mines Ltd. 00/00/1954
Each share Capital Stock $1 par exchanged for (0.2) share Common $1 par
Pardee Amalgamated Mines Ltd. liquidated for Rio Algom Mines Ltd. 11/09/1961 which name changed to Rio Algom Ltd. 04/30/1975
(See Rio Algom Ltd.)

BELLE-CHIBOUGAMAU MINES, LTD. (ON)
Merged into Amalgamated Beau-Belle Mines Ltd. 06/29/1961
Each share Capital Stock $1 par exchanged for (0.33333333) share Capital Stock $1 par
(See Amalgamated Beau-Belle Mines Ltd.)

BELLE-ELDRIDGE GOLD MINES (SD)
Charter cancelled for failure to file annual reports 07/01/1970

BELLE INTL HLDGS LTD (CAYMAN ISLANDS)
ADR's for Ordinary split (5) for (1) by issuance of (4) additional ADR's payable 08/23/2012 to holders of record 08/20/2012 Ex date - 08/24/2012
Basis changed from (1:50) to (1:10) 08/24/2012
ADR agreement terminated 08/11/2017
Each ADR for Ordinary exchanged for $8.007399 cash

BELLE ISLE CORP (DE)
Under plan of liquidation each share Common 20¢ par exchanged for (1) Belle Isle Net Profits Unit and $0.80 cash 03/31/1965

BELLE MINING & OIL EXPLORATION, INC. (PHILIPPINES)
Name changed to Belle Corp. 08/00/1994

BELLE TAHSIS MINES LTD. (BC)
Name changed to Bellex Mines Ltd. 10/03/1966
(See Bellex Mines Ltd.)

BELLEAIR INTERNATIONAL, INC. (FL)
Proclaimed dissolved for failure to file reports and pay fees 12/08/1980

BELLECHASSE METALS CO. LTD. (QC)
Charter annulled for failure to file reports 06/08/1974

BELLECHASSE MNG LTD (QC)
Delisted from Montreal Stock Exchange 06/05/1986

BELLEFIELD CO (PA)
Capital Stock no par changed to $1 par 00/00/1951
Completely liquidated 07/10/1961
Each share Capital Stock $1 par exchanged for first and final distribution of $22.27738 cash

BELLEFONTAINE NATL BK (BELLEFONTAINE, OH)
Merged into Huntington Bancshares Inc. 10/11/1977
Each share Common $25 par exchanged for $135.50 cash

BELLEFONTE CENT RR CO (PA)
In process of liquidation 00/00/1976
Stockholders' equity unlikely

BELLEGRAND MINES LTD. (ON)
Charter cancelled and company declared dissolved for default in filing returns 00/00/1952

BELLEKENO MINES LTD. (ON)
Recapitalized as Consolidated Bellekeno Mines Ltd. 03/29/1955
Each share Capital Stock $1 par exchanged for (0.33333333) share Capital Stock $1 par
(See Consolidated Bellekeno Mines Ltd.)

BELLEROCHE MINES LTD (ON)
Name changed to Bellerroche Resources Ltd. and Capital Stock $1 par changed to no par 01/11/1978

BELLES-LETTRES PRESS INC. (MD)
Charter annulled for failure to file annual reports 02/23/1939

BELLETERRE QUE MINES LTD (QC)
Name changed 00/00/1937
Name changed from Belleterre Mines Ltd. to Belleterre Quebec Mines Ltd. 00/00/1937
Capital Stock $1 par changed to 95¢ par 03/07/1966
Company reported out of business 00/00/1959
Details not available

BELLEVIEW CAP CORP (CO)
Name changed to Medical Ancillary Services, Inc. 03/05/1987
(See Medical Ancillary Services, Inc.)

BELLEVILLE NATL SVGS BK (BELLEVILLE, IL)
Capital Stock $12.50 par changed to $5 par and (1) additional share issued plus a stock dividend paid 04/14/1978
Stock Dividends - 20% 12/15/1960; 42.86% 01/19/1971
Reorganized as Mid-Continent Bancshares, Inc. 01/01/1980
Each share Capital Stock $5 par exchanged for (1) share Common $5 par
Mid-Continent Bancshares, Inc. merged into General Bancshares Corp. 11/01/1982 which merged into Boatmen's Bancshares, Inc. 03/29/1986 which merged into NationsBank Corp. 01/07/1997 which reincorporated in Delaware as BankAmerica Corp. (Old) 09/25/1998 which merged into BankAmerica Corp. (New) 09/30/1998 which name changed to Bank of America Corp. 04/28/1999

BELLEVUE CAP CORP (AB)
Reorganized under the laws of British Columbia as CMC Metals Ltd. 07/05/2005
Each share Common no par exchanged for (0.5) share Common no par

BELLEVUE GOLD MINES, LTD. (ON)
Charter cancelled and declared dissolved for failure to file reports 11/12/1969

BELLEVUE OIL & MINERALS LTD (BC)
Merged into Bellevue Ventures Ltd. 10/03/1984
Each share Common no par exchanged for (1) share Common no par
Bellevue Ventures Ltd. recapitalized as International Bellevue Ltd. 02/07/1985
(See International Bellevue Ltd.)

BELLEVUE RES LTD (AB)
Acquired by Elk Point Resources Inc. 09/29/1995
Each share Common no par exchanged for (0.2935) share Common no par
(See Elk Point Resources Inc.)

BELLEVUE VENTURES LTD (BC)
Recapitalized as International Bellevue Ventures Ltd. 02/07/1985
Each share Common no par exchanged for (0.33333333) share Common no par
(See International Bellevue Ventures Ltd.)

BELLEX MINES LTD (BC)
Struck off register and declared dissolved for failure to file returns 01/18/1979

BELLEX MNG CORP (BC)
Merged into Adex Mining Corp. 01/07/1993
Each share Common no par exchanged for (1) share Common no par
Adex Mining Corp. recapitalized as Adex Mining Inc. 07/15/1996

BELLEZONE MINES LTD. (ON)
Charter revoked for failure to file reports and pay taxes 00/00/1956

BELLHAVEN COPPER & GOLD INC (BC)
Each share old Common no par exchanged for (0.1) share new Common no par 02/20/2015
Merged into GoldMining Inc. 05/30/2017
Each share new Common no par exchanged for (0.25) share Common no par
Note: Unexchanged certificates will be cancelled and become without value 05/30/2023

BELLHAVEN VENTURES INC (BC)
Name changed to Bellhaven Copper & Gold Inc. 10/06/2006
Bellhaven Copper & Gold Inc. merged into GoldMining Inc. 05/30/2017

BELLHELEN DEVELOPMENT CORP. (ME)
Charter revoked for failure to file reports and pay fees 00/00/1930

BELLINGHAM BANCORPORATION (WA)
Merged into Horizon Financial Corp. (WA) 06/19/1999
Each share Common no par exchanged for (2.74) shares Common 1¢ par
(See Horizon Financial Corp. (WA))

BELLINGHAM NATL BK (BELLINGHAM, WA)
Capital Stock $100 par changed to $10 par and (9) additional shares issued plus a 50% stock dividend paid 02/03/1959
Capital Stock $10 par changed to $3.33333333 par and (2) additional shares issued 08/20/1982
Stock Dividends - 100% 01/26/1951; 100% 09/01/1968; 50% 01/09/1976
Merged into Puget Sound Bancorp 07/01/1984
Each share Capital Stock $3.33333333 held by holders of (199) or fewer shares exchanged for $16.25 cash
Holdings of (200) or more shares exchanged for $16.25 principal amount of Notes due 07/01/1989

BELLINGHAM PLYWOOD CORP.
Merged into Georgia-Pacific Plywood & Lumber Co. 00/00/1949
Each share Common no par exchanged for (0.75) share $2.25 Preferred no par and (4) shares Common $1 par
Georgia-Pacific Plywood & Lumber Co. name changed to Georgia-Pacific Plywood Co.

00/00/1951 which name changed to Georgia-Pacific Corp. 04/27/1956
(See Georgia-Pacific Corp.)

BELLMORE CORP (NV)
Name changed to MobileBits Holdings Corp. 02/18/2010

BELLOWS & CO., INC.
Acquired by National Distillers Products Corp. share for share 07/31/1941
National Distillers Products Corp. name changed to National Distillers & Chemical Corp. 05/01/1957 which name changed to Quantum Chemical Corp. 01/04/1988 which merged into Hanson PLC (Old) 10/01/1993 which reorganized as Hanson PLC (New) 10/15/2003

BELLOWS FALLS TR CO (BELLOWS FALLS, VT)
Common $20 par changed to $13.33 par and (0.5) additional share issued 12/01/1981
Merged into VerBanc Financial Corp. 09/30/1985
Each share Common $13.33 par exchanged for (1) share Common $1 par
VerBanc Financial Corp. acquired by Chittenden Corp. 04/28/1993
(See Chittenden Corp.)

BELLRINGER RES LTD (AB)
Struck off register for failure to file annual returns 11/02/2000

BELLSOUTH CORP (GA)
Common $1 par split (3) for (1) by issuance of (2) additional shares 05/22/1984
Common $1 par split (3) for (2) by issuance of (0.5) additional share 02/23/1987
Common $1 par split (2) for (1) by issuance of (1) additional share 11/08/1995
Common $1 par split (2) for (1) by issuance of (1) additional share payable 12/24/1998 to holders of record 12/03/1998 Ex date - 12/28/1998
Merged into AT&T Inc. 12/29/2006
Each share Common $1 par exchanged for (1.325) shares Common $1 par

BELLSOUTH PERU S A (PERU)
ADR agreement terminated 10/12/2001
No ADR holders' equity

BELLTECH VENTURES LTD (BC)
Name changed to Welichem Biotech Inc. 11/01/2004
(See Welichem Biotech Inc.)

BELLUS HEALTH INC OLD (CANADA)
Reorganized as BELLUS Health Inc. (New) 05/29/2012
Each share Common no par exchanged for (0.03333333) share Common no par

BELLWETHER CAP CORP (BC)
Recapitalized as FirstWeb Internet Solutions Inc. 03/19/2001
Each share Common no par exchanged for (0.33333333) share Common no par
(See FirstWeb Internet Solutions Inc.)

BELLWETHER EXPL CO (DE)
Reorganized 04/04/1994
Stock Dividends - 10% 01/31/1983; 10% 01/31/1984; 10% 03/31/1985
Reorganized from under the laws of (CO) to (DE) 04/04/1994
Each share Common no par exchanged for (0.125) share Common 1¢ par
Under plan of merger name changed to Mission Resources Corp. 05/16/2001
(See Mission Resources Corp.)

BELLWETHER INVT CORP (UT)
Recapitalized as Siliwood Entertainment Corp. 02/21/1996
Each share Common $0.001 par exchanged for (0.5) share Common $0.001 par
Siliwood Entertainment Corp. name changed to New Visual Entertainment, Inc. 10/27/1996 which name changed to New Visual Corp. 07/02/2001 which name changed to Rim Semiconductor Co. 09/19/2005
(See Rim Semiconductor Co.)

BELLWETHER RES LTD (BC)
Recapitalized as Eurocontrol Technics Inc. (BC) 03/20/1992
Each share Common no par exchanged for (0.33333333) share Common no par
Eurocontrol Technics Inc. (BC) reincorporated in Ontario 10/11/2006 which name changed to Eurocontrol Technics Group Inc. 08/22/2011

BELMAC CORP (FL)
Each share old Common 2¢ par exchanged for (0.1) share new Common 2¢ par 07/24/1995
Name changed to Bentley Pharmaceuticals, Inc. (FL) 01/02/1996
Bentley Pharmaceuticals, Inc. (FL) reincorporated in Delaware 11/03/1999
(See Bentley Pharmaceuticals, Inc.)

BELMONT AVENUE CORP.
Liquidation completed 00/00/1946
Details not available

BELMONT BANCORP (OH)
Common $25 par changed to $12.50 par 00/00/1994
Common $12.50 par changed to $3.57 par and (0.25) additional share issued 07/22/1994
Common $3.57 par changed to 50¢ par and (1) additional share issued 05/08/1995
Common 50¢ par changed to 25¢ par and (0.25) additional share issued 07/01/1997
Common 25¢ par split (2) for (1) by issuance of (1) additional share payable 05/22/1998 to holders of record 05/01/1998
Stock Dividend - 10% 02/02/1994
Merged into Sky Financial Group, Inc. 06/01/2005
Each share Common 25¢ par exchanged for (0.119215) share Common no par and $2.80218 cash
Sky Financial Group, Inc. merged into Huntington Bancshares Inc. 07/02/2007

BELMONT COPPER MINING CO. (AZ)
Liquidation completed
Each share Capital Stock $1 par exchanged for initial distribution of $0.10 cash 05/01/1977
Each share Capital Stock $1 par received second and final distribution of $0.43 cash 01/17/1978

BELMONT CNTY NATL BK (ST. CLAIRSVILLE, OH)
Reorganized as Belmont Bancorp 04/02/1984
Each share Capital Stock $25 par exchanged for (1) share Capital Stock $25 par
Belmont Bancorp merged into Sky Financial Group, Inc. 06/01/2005 which merged into Huntington Bancshares Inc. 07/02/2007

BELMONT FRANCHISING CORP (DE)
Charter cancelled and declared inoperative and void for non-payment of taxes 04/15/1973

BELMONT GOLD MINES LTD. (ON)
Charter revoked for failure to file reports and pay taxes 00/00/1954

BELMONT GROUP INC (NY)
Charter cancelled and proclaimed dissolved for failure to pay taxes 06/23/1993

BELMONT HERITAGE CORP. (NC)
Merged into Parkdale Mills, Inc. 08/02/1989
Each share Common $5 par exchanged for $18.5969 cash

BELMONT HOLDING CO.
Bankrupt 00/00/1939
Stockholders' equity unlikely

BELMONT HOMES INC (MS)
Common 10¢ par split (3) for (2) by issuance of (0.5) additional share payable 11/01/1996 to holders of record 10/15/1996
Merged into Cavalier Homes, Inc. 12/31/1997
Each share Common 10¢ par exchanged for (0.8) share Common 10¢ par
(See Cavalier Homes, Inc.)

BELMONT HOTEL CO. (OH)
Adjudicated bankrupt 02/20/1962
No stockholders' equity

BELMONT INDS INC (DE)
Charter cancelled and declared inoperative and void for non-payment of taxes 03/01/1975

BELMONT INDS INC (PA)
Common $0.33333333 par split (3) for (1) by issuance of (2) additional shares 09/17/1968
Each share Common $0.33333333 par exchanged for (0.02) share Common $16.66666666 par 06/20/1979
Merged into EXBI Corp. 04/16/1980
Each share Common $16.66666666 par exchanged for $175 cash

BELMONT IRON WORKS (PA)
Each share Common $50 par exchanged for (1) share $2.50 Preferred $35 par and (3) shares Common $5 par 00/00/1941
Common $5 par changed to $1 par 11/15/1967
Stock Dividend - 700% 12/02/1946
Name changed to Belmont Industries, Inc. (PA) and Common $1 par changed to $0.33333333 par 09/03/1968
(See Belmont Industries, Inc. (PA))

BELMONT METALS CORP.
Bankrupt 00/00/1936
Stockholders' equity unlikely

BELMONT MINING & EXPLORATION CO. LTD. (QC)
Acquired by Amalgamated Mining Development Corp. Ltd. 00/00/1960
Each share Capital Stock $1 par exchanged for (0.25) share Capital Stock $1 par
Amalgamated Mining Development Corp. Ltd. acquired by Amalgamated Mining Western Ltd. 12/20/1984 which name changed to Westall Resources Ltd. 07/12/1994
(See Westall Resources Ltd.)

BELMONT NATL BK (CHICAGO, IL)
Stock Dividends - 20% 02/08/1967; 20% 02/14/1968; 10% 02/12/1969
Acquired by Water Tower Bancorp, Inc. 00/00/1987
Details not available

BELMONT OIL CORP. (NV)
Charter revoked for failure to file reports and pay fees 03/07/1960

BELMONT OSBORN GOLD MINING CO. (CA)
Name changed to Transierra Gold Mining Co. 00/00/1944
Transierra Gold Mining Co. name changed to Transierra Exploration Corp. 00/00/1953 which name changed to Belcor Inc. 07/01/1985 which name changed to Silver Assets Inc. 08/19/1998
(See Silver Assets Inc.)

BELMONT RADIO CORP.
Acquired by Raytheon Manufacturing Co. 00/00/1945
Each share Common no par exchanged for (0.9) share new Common 50¢ par
Raytheon Manufacturing Co. name changed to Raytheon Co. 05/04/1959

BELMONT SVGS & LN ASSN (CA)
Name changed to Great Western Savings & Loan Association of Southern California 08/05/1970
(See Great Western Savings & Loan Association of Southern California)

BELMORAL MINES LTD (CANADA)
Reincorporated 12/20/1985
Common 50¢ par changed to no par 06/29/1983
Place of incorporation changed from (BC) to (Canada) 12/20/1985
Merged into Beau Canada Exploration Ltd. 11/04/1993
Each share Common no par exchanged for (0.05333333) share Common no par
(See Beau Canada Exploration Ltd.)

BELO CORP (DE)
Reincorporated 05/13/1987
Name changed 01/01/2001
$5 Preferred no par called for redemption 04/01/1959
Each share Common $5 par exchanged for (0.05) share Common $100 par 12/14/1978
Each share Common $100 par exchanged for (0.2) share Common $500 par 12/28/1978
Each share Common $500 par exchanged for (300) shares Common $1.67 par 06/29/1981
State of incorporation changed from (TX) to (DE) 05/13/1987
Common $1.67 par reclassified as Ser. A Common $1.67 par 05/13/1988
Each share Common Ser. A $1.67 par received distribution of (1) share Conv. Common Ser. B $1.67 par 05/19/1988
Common Ser. A $1.67 par split (2) for (1) by issuance of (1) additional share 06/09/1995
Conv. Common Ser. B $1.67 par split (2) for (1) by issuance of (1) additional share 06/09/1995
Common Ser. A $1.67 par split (2) for (1) by issuance of (1) additional share payable 06/05/1998 to holders of record 05/22/1998 Ex date - 06/08/1998
Conv. Common Ser. B $1.67 par split (2) for (1) by issuance of (1) additional share payable 06/05/1998 to holders of record 05/22/1998 Ex date - 06/08/1998
Name changed from Belo (A.H.) Corp. to Belo Corp. 01/01/2001
Each share Ser. A Common $1.67 par received distribution of (0.2) share A.H. Belo Corp. Ser. A Common 1¢ par payable 02/08/2008 to holders of record 01/25/2008 Ex date - 02/11/2008
Ser. A Common $1.67 par changed to 1¢ par 05/09/2012
Ser. B Common $1.67 par changed to 1¢ par 05/09/2012
Acquired by Gannett Co., Inc. 12/23/2013
Each share Ser. A Common 1¢ par exchanged for $13.75 cash
Each share Ser. B Common 1¢ par exchanged for $13.75 cash

BELOCK INSTRUMENT CORP. (NY)
Name changed to Applied Devices Corp. 03/01/1967
(See Applied Devices Corp.)

BELOIT TOOL CORP (DE)
Stock Dividends - 10% 09/15/1971; 10% 12/01/1972
Name changed to Regal-Beloit Corp. (DE) 04/27/1973
Regal-Beloit Corp. (DE) reincorporated in Wisconsin 04/18/1994 which name changed to Regal Beloit Corp. 04/28/2015

BELOIT WATER GAS & ELECTRIC CO.
Acquired by Wisconsin Power & Light Co. 00/00/1926
Details not available

BELORE MINES LTD (ON)
Merged into Golden Hart Exploration Inc. 06/05/1998
Each share Common $1 par exchanged for (0.2) share Common no par
Golden Hart Exploration Inc. recapitalized as Beaufort Hills Resources Inc. 06/30/1999 which recapitalized as InterRent Properties Ltd. 11/01/1999 which recapitalized as InterRent International Properties Inc. 03/05/2001 which reorganized as InterRent Real Estate Investment Trust 12/07/2006

BELRA EXPLS LTD (ON)
Charter cancelled and declared dissolved for failure to file returns and pay fees 05/14/1977

BELRIDGE OIL CO (CA)
Merged into Shell Oil Co. 12/11/1979
Each share Common $1 par exchanged for $3,665 cash

BELROSA MINES LTD. (ON)
Charter surrendered 03/00/1961
No stockholders' equity

BELSCOT RETAILERS INC (DE)
Merged into Group Investors Corp. 08/25/1981
Each share Common $1 par exchanged for $3.50 cash

BELT RAIL ROAD & STOCK YARDS CO. (IN)
Name changed to Indianapolis Stockyards Co., Inc. 02/21/1961
Indianapolis Stockyards Co., Inc. acquired by Lilly (Eli) & Co. 04/12/1968

BELTEC ENTERPRISES LTD (BC)
Recapitalized as First Choice Industries Ltd. 10/02/1992
Each share Common no par exchanged for (0.4) share Common no par
First Choice Industries Ltd. recapitalized as Glen Hawk Minerals Ltd. 11/21/2003 which recapitalized as Oronova Resource Corp. 11/24/2009 which name changed to Oronova Energy Inc. 12/16/2016

BELTECO KIRKLAND MINES LTD. (ON)
Company believed out of business 00/00/1990
Details not available

BELTONE RECORDING CORP (NY)
Dissolved by proclamation 06/27/2001

BELTRAN CORP (DE)
Each share Common $0.06666666 par exchanged for (0.33333333) share Common 20¢ par 06/21/1982
Chapter 11 Federal Bankruptcy proceedings converted to Chapter 7 on 01/28/1988
Stockholders' equity unlikely

BELTRON COMPUTER CORP (MN)
Statutorily dissolved 12/30/1994

BELUGA COMPOSITES CORP (DE)
Company terminated common stock registration and is no longer public as of 03/16/2006

BELVAC INTL INDS LTD (NY)
Acquired by Saslow (D.L.) Co. Inc. 00/00/1985
Each share Common 1¢ par exchanged for $1.39 cash

BELVEDERE COPPER CORP. LTD. (QC)
Completely liquidated 05/10/1969
No stockholders' equity

BELVEDERE CORP (DE)
Acquired by Christiania General Insurance Corp. 06/19/1992
Each share Common 10¢ par exchanged for $6.30 cash

BELVEDERE HOTEL CO. OF BALTIMORE
Reorganized as Belvedere Hotel Corp. 00/00/1936
Each share Capital Stock $100 par exchanged for (5) shares Common $1 par
(See Belvedere Hotel Corp.)

BELVEDERE HOTEL CORP. (MD)
Preferred $10 par called for redemption 09/01/1952
Completely liquidated 12/04/1952
Each share Common $1 par or VTC for Common $1 par exchanged for first and final distribution of $7.50 cash

BELVEDERE RES CORP (NV)
Recapitalized as Global Security Agency Inc. 06/28/2010
Each share Common $0.00001 par exchanged for (0.1) share Common $0.00001 par

BELVEDERE SOCAL (CA)
Company terminated common stock registration and is no longer public as of 05/14/2009

BELVILLE GOLD MINES LTD. (QC)
Name changed to Virginia Mining Corp. 00/00/1954
Virginia Mining Corp. recapitalized as Consolidated Virginia Mining Corp. 02/24/1964
(See Consolidated Virginia Mining Corp.)

BELZBERG FINL MKTS & NEWS INTL INC (ON)
Recapitalized as Belzberg Technologies Inc. 07/14/2000
Each share Common no par exchanged for (0.2) share Common no par
Belzberg Technologies Inc. name changed to Frontline Technologies Inc. 04/18/2011
(See Frontline Technologies Inc.)

BELZBERG TECHNOLOGIES INC (ON)
Common no par split (5) for (1) by issuance of (4) additional shares payable 07/15/2000 to holders of record 07/15/2000
Name changed to Frontline Technologies Inc. 04/18/2011
(See Frontline Technologies Inc.)

BEMA GOLD CORP (CANADA)
Reincorporated 07/19/2002
Place of incorporation changed from (BC) to (Canada) 07/19/2002
Merged into Kinross Gold Corp. 02/27/2007
Each share Common no par exchanged for (0.4447) share Common no par and $0.01 cash

BEMA INTL RES INC (BC)
Merged into Bema Gold Corp. (BC) 12/08/1988
Each share Common no par exchanged for (0.5) share Common no par
Bema Gold Corp. (BC) reincorporated in Canada 07/19/2002 which merged into Kinross Gold Corp. 02/27/2007

BEMAX CORP (CA)
Each share old Common no par exchanged for (0.2) share new Common no par 01/14/1991
Each share new Common no par

exchanged again for (0.5) share new Common no par 04/20/1993
Reorganized under the laws of Nevada as M T Financial Group, Inc. 03/31/1995
Each share new Common no par exchanged for (0.5) share Common $0.001 par
M T Financial Group, Inc. name changed to Photogen Technologies, Inc. 05/16/1997 which name changed to IMCOR Pharmaceutical Co. 02/05/2004

BEMIDJI ELECTRIC MANUFACTURING CO.
Merged into Interstate Power Co. 00/00/1927
Details not available

BEMIS BRO. BAG CO. (MO)
Common $100 par changed to $25 par and (3) additional shares issued 03/08/1957
Common $25 par changed to $10 par and (1.5) additional shares issued 10/14/1964
Stock Dividend - 50% 12/15/1948
Name changed to Bemis Co., Inc. 10/01/1965

BEMIS INC (MO)
8.5% Preferred 1974 Ser. $1 par called for redemption 06/01/1978
Each share Conv. Preferred Ser. B $100 par exchanged for (3.6834) shares Common $5 par 03/01/1984
Conv. Preferred Ser. A $100 par called for redemption 10/01/1984
Conv. Preferred Ser. C $100 par called for redemption 10/01/1984
Conv. Preferred Ser. D $100 par called for redemption 10/01/1984
(Additional Information in Active)

BEMPORAD CARPET MILLS, INC. (TN)
Bankrupt 00/00/1964
No stockholders' equity

BEN & JERRYS HOMEMADE INC (VT)
Common $0.033 par reclassified as Class A Common $0.033 par 07/24/1987
Each share Class A Common $0.033 par received distribution of (0.5) share Non-Transferable Conv. Class B Common $0.033 par 08/17/1987
Class A Common $0.033 par split (2) for (1) by issuance of (1) additional share 06/12/1992
Non-Transferable Conv. Class B Common $0.033 par split (2) for (1) by issuance of (1) additional share 06/12/1992
Each share Non-Transferable Conv. Class B Common $0.033 par exchanged for (1) share Class A Common $0.033 par 05/25/2000
Merged into Unilever N.V. 08/04/2000
Each share Class A Common $0.033 par exchanged for $43.60 cash

BEN ABRAHAM TECHNOLOGIES INC (ON)
Name changed to BioSante Pharmaceuticals, Inc. (WY) 12/17/1999
BioSante Pharmaceuticals, Inc. (WY) reincorporated in Delaware 06/26/2001 which recapitalized as ANI Pharmaceuticals, Inc. 07/18/2013

BEN EZRA WEINSTEIN & CO INC (NM)
Each share old Common $1 par exchanged for (0.08333333) share new Common $1 par 06/18/1998
Each share new Common $1 par received distribution of (0.1) share Compass Data Systems, Inc. Common $0.001 par payable 07/30/1999 to holders of record 07/10/1999
Each share new Common $1 par received distribution of (0.1) share Netstrat Inc. Common, (0.1) share International Thoughts Inc. Common, and (0.1) share American Software Inc. Class A Common 10¢ par payable 10/15/1999 to holders of record 07/24/1999
Charter revoked 10/26/2007

BEN FRANKLIN FINL INC (USA)
Reorganized under the laws of Maryland 01/23/2015
Each share Common 1¢ par exchanged for (0.3562) share Common 1¢ par

BEN FRANKLIN RETAIL STORES INC (DE)
Chapter 11 bankruptcy proceedings converted to Chapter 7 on 06/24/1997
Stockholders' equity unlikely

BEN-HUR PRODUCTS, INC. (DE)
Common $1 par changed to 10¢ par 00/00/1946
Merged into McCormick & Co., Inc. 00/00/1954
Each share $1.75 Prior Preferred no par exchanged for (0.2) share 5% Preferred $100 par
Each share Common 10¢ par exchanged for (0.03448275) share Non-Vtg. Common no par

BEN MINING CORP. (MT)
Merged into Eastern Pacific Corp. 01/20/1970
Each share Capital Stock $1 par exchanged for (1) share Common 1¢ par
Eastern Pacific Corp. name changed to Dmytrijk-Boyd Productions, Inc. 09/17/1973 which name changed to E-Z 8 Motels, Inc. 06/20/1974
(See E-Z 8 Motels, Inc.)

BEN TAM INC (FL)
Merged into Corporate Innovations, Inc. 09/23/2005
Details not available

BEN WA INTL INC (DE)
Name changed to CEC Properties, Inc. 03/01/1996
(See CEC Properties, Inc.)

BENACO INC (NV)
Common $0.001 split (21) for (1) by issuance of (20) additional shares payable 12/31/2012 to holders of record 11/06/2012 Ex date - 01/02/2013
Name changed to International Safety Group, Inc. 01/08/2013

BENACQUISTA GALLERIES INC (NV)
Each share old Common $0.001 par exchanged for (0.1) share new Common $0.001 par 01/08/2007
Name changed to Vibe Records, Inc. Nevada 07/30/2008

BENAFUELS INC (WV)
Chapter 11 Federal Bankruptcy Code converted to Chapter 7 on 10/24/1989
Stockholders' equity unlikely

BENBOW ASTRONAUTICS INC (DE)
Name changed to Multimedia Communications Group, Inc. 07/01/1994
Multimedia Communications Group, Inc. name changed to Satellite Communication Corp. 10/14/1994
(See Satellite Communication Corp.)

BENBOW MANUFACTURING CO. (CA)
Name changed to Insul-8-Corp. 00/00/1954
Insul-8-Corp. liquidated for Rucker Co. 11/04/1966 which merged into N L Industries, Inc. 01/21/1977

BENCH CRAFT INC (DE)
Common 1¢ par split (3) for (2) by issuance of (0.5) additional share 02/13/1987
Merged into Universal Furniture Ltd. 12/31/1987
Each share Common 1¢ par exchanged for (0.76) share Ordinary 1¢ par 12/31/1987
Universal Furniture Ltd. merged into Masco Corp. 05/30/1989

BENCH GROUP INC (DE)
Each share old Common $0.001 par exchanged for (0.33333333) share new Common $0.001 par 12/01/2003
Name changed to Qualmax, Inc. 12/23/2005
Qualmax, Inc. merged into New World Brands, Inc. 02/20/2009

BENCH PORTFOLIOS FD (MA)
Trust terminated 03/27/1991
Details not available

BENCHMARK ASSOCS INC (AZ)
Name changed to Rotherwood Group Inc. 01/28/1998
Rotherwood Group Inc. recapitalized as Entrada Software Inc. 09/01/1999 which recapitalized as Medlink Technologies, Inc. 04/04/2006 which name changed to Cambridge Resources Corp. 06/21/2006
(See Cambridge Resources Corp.)

BENCHMARK ENERGY CORP (CANADA)
Name changed to Bolivar Energy Corp. (Canada) 10/29/2010
Bolivar Energy Corp. (Canada) reorganized in Alberta as Anatolia Energy Corp. 12/13/2011 which merged into Cub Energy Inc. 07/01/2013

BENCHMARK ENTERPRISES INC (UT)
Recapitalized as Coconino SMA Inc. 06/19/1995
Each share Common $0.001 par exchanged for (0.02) share Common $0.001 par
Coconino SMA Inc. name changed to Veltex Corp. 04/01/1999

BENCHMARK FED SVGS BK (CINCINNATI, OH)
Merged into Winton Financial Corp. 06/11/1999
Each share Common $1 par exchanged for (3.35) shares Common $1 par
(See Winton Financial Corp.)

BENCHMARK TECHNOLOGY CORP (NV)
Name changed to Absolute Glass Protection Inc. 02/20/2003
Absolute Glass Protection Inc. name changed to Jagged Peak, Inc. 07/18/2005
(See Jagged Peak, Inc.)

BENCHMARQ MICROELECTRONICS INC (DE)
Merged into Unitrode Corp. 08/03/1998
Each share Common no par exchanged for (1) share Common 1¢ par
Unitrode Corp. merged into Texas Instruments Inc. 10/15/1999

BENCKISER N V (NETHERLANDS)
Merged into Reckitt Benckiser plc 12/03/1999
Each share Class B exchanged for (5) shares Ordinary
Note: 99.5% of outstanding shares were surrendered; remaining 0.5% received approximately USD $115.75 per share 06/05/2008

BENCO INDS INC (TN)
Proclaimed dissolved for failure to file annual reports 06/19/1992

BENCO PLASTICS INC (TN)
Name changed to Benco Industries, Inc. 06/01/1976
(See Benco Industries, Inc.)

BENCORP INDS LTD (CANADA)
Name changed to Doverton Oils Ltd. 05/16/1984
(See Doverton Oils Ltd.)

BENDA PHARMACEUTICAL INC (DE)
SEC revoked common stock registration 06/27/2013

BENDER BODY CO.
Bankrupt 00/00/1941
Details not available

BENDIGO & ADELAIDE BK LTD (AUSTRALIA)
ADR agreement terminated 08/06/2018
No ADR's remain outstanding

BENDIX AVIATION CORP. (DE)
Common no par changed to $5 par 00/00/1932
Common $5 par split (2) for (1) by issuance of (1) additional share 03/19/1955
Name changed to Bendix Corp. (DE) 06/02/1960
Bendix Corp. (DE) merged into Allied Corp. 01/31/1983 which merged into AlliedSignal Corp. 09/19/1985 which name changed to AlliedSignal Inc. 04/26/1993 which name changed to Honeywell International Inc. 12/01/1999

BENDIX CORP. (IL)
Acquired by Bendix Aviation Corp. 00/00/1929
Details not available

BENDIX CORP (DE)
Common $5 par split (2) for (1) by issuance of (1) additional share 09/23/1966
Common $5 par split (4) for (3) by issuance of (0.33333333) additional share 04/15/1976
$3 Conv. Preferred Ser. A no par called for redemption 01/28/1983
Merged into Allied Corp. 01/31/1983
Each share Common $5 par exchanged for $11.096 principal amount of 6% Notes due 12/15/1988, $6.985 principal amount of 6% Notes due 12/15/1990, (0.25) share Adjustable Rate Preferred Ser. F no par and (1.3) shares Common $1 par
9.75% Conv. Preferred Ser. B no par called for redemption 04/01/1985
Allied Corp. merged into Allied-Signal Inc. 09/19/1985 which name changed to AlliedSignal Inc. 04/26/1993 which name changed to Honeywell International Inc. 12/01/1999

BENDIX HELICOPTER, INC. (DE)
Name changed to Helicopters, Inc. (DE) 00/00/1948
(See Helicopters, Inc. (DE))

BENDIX HOME APPLIANCES, INC.
Merged into Avco Manufacturing Corp. 12/18/1950
Each share Common $0.33333333 par exchanged for (2) shares Common $3 par
Avco Manufacturing Corp. name changed to Avco Corp. 04/10/1959
(See Avco Corp.)

BENDIX SERVICE CORP.
Dissolved 00/00/1931
Details not available

BENE IO INC (DE)
SEC revoked common stock registration 07/23/2010

BENEDEK COMMUNICATIONS CORP (DE)
15% Sr. Exchangeable Preferred called for redemption at $115 on 06/08/1998

BENEDICT NUCLEAR PHARMACEUTICALS INC (CO)
Name changed to North American Chemical Corp. 10/09/1992
North American Chemical Corp. name

changed to Golden Pharmaceuticals, Inc. 03/04/1994 which recapitalized as docsales.com, inc. 07/12/1999 which name changed to Docplanet.com Inc. 10/19/1999
(See Docplanet.com Inc.)

BENEFICIAL CAP FINL SVCS CORP (CO)
Each share old Common $0.0001 par exchanged for (0.00666666) share new Common $0.0001 par 11/04/1994
Name changed to Golden Eagle International, Inc. 02/06/1995
Golden Eagle International, Inc. recapitalized as Advantego Corp. 02/22/2018

BENEFICIAL CORP NEW (DE)
Common $1 par split (3) for (2) by issuance of (0.5) additional share 01/31/1972
Common $1 par split (2) for (1) by issuance of (1) additional share 12/15/1993
Merged into Household International, Inc. 06/30/1998
Each share $4.30 Preferred no par exchanged for (1) share $4.30 Preferred no par
Each share $4.50 Preferred $100 par exchanged for (1) share $4.50 Preferred no par
Each share 5% Preferred $50 par exchanged for (1) share 5% Preferred no par
Each share $5.50 Conv. Preferred no par exchanged for (27.5994) shares Common $1 par
Each share Common $1 par exchanged for (3.0666) shares Common $1 par

BENEFICIAL CORP OLD (DE)
Stock Dividend - 40% 11/19/1952; 10% 08/31/1955
Completely liquidated 03/15/1968
Each share Common $1 par exchanged for first and final distribution of (0.28) share Beneficial Finance Co. $5.50 Conv. Preferred no par
Beneficial Finance Co. name changed to Beneficial Corp. (New) 05/01/1970 which merged into Household International, Inc. 06/30/1998

BENEFICIAL FIN CO (DE)
Common $4 par changed to $1 par and (0.06) share 5% Preferred $50 par distributed 05/13/1957
4.5% Preferred $100 par called for redemption 12/31/1967
Stock Dividend - 10% 11/20/1961; 10% 05/15/1964
Name changed to Beneficial Corp. (New) 05/01/1970
Beneficial Corp. (New) merged into Household International, Inc. 06/30/1998

BENEFICIAL INDUSTRIAL LOAN CORP.
Stock Dividend - 10% 12/30/1949
Name changed to Beneficial Loan Corp. 00/00/1951
Beneficial Loan Corp. name changed to Beneficial Finance Co. 04/29/1955 which name changed to Beneficial Corp. (New) 05/01/1970 which merged into Household International, Inc. 06/30/1998

BENEFICIAL LABS INC (NY)
Common 1¢ par split (2) for (1) by issuance of (1) additional share 02/21/1973
Common 1¢ par split (2) for (1) by issuance of (1) additional share 10/03/1975
Charter cancelled and proclaimed dissolved for failure to pay taxes 03/25/1981

BENEFICIAL LOAN CORP. (DE)
Common $10 par changed to $4 par and (1.5) additional shares issued 01/28/1955
Name changed to Beneficial Finance Co. 04/29/1955
Beneficial Finance Co. name changed to Beneficial Corp. (New) 05/01/1970 which merged into Household International, Inc. 06/30/1998 which merged into HSBC Holdings PLC 03/28/2003

BENEFICIAL LOAN SOCIETY
Merged into Beneficial Corp. (Old) 00/00/1945
Each share Preferred 1st Ser. exchanged for (1) share Preferred no par
Each share Common exchanged for (2.5) shares Common $1 par
Beneficial Corp. (Old) acquired by Beneficial Finance Co. 03/15/1968 which name changed to Beneficial Corp. (New) 05/01/1970 which merged into Household International, Inc. 06/30/1998 which merged into HSBC Holdings PLC 03/28/2003

BENEFICIAL MUT BANCORP INC (USA)
Reorganized under the laws of Maryland as Beneficial Bancorp, Inc. 01/13/2015
Each share Common 1¢ par exchanged for (1.0999) shares Common 1¢ par

BENEFICIAL NATL CORP (RI)
Merged into Associated Madison Companies, Inc. 10/30/1979
Each share Common 25¢ par exchanged for (3.4) shares Common 40¢ par
Associated Madison Companies, Inc. merged into American Can Co. 04/08/1982 which name changed to Primerica Corp. (NJ) 04/28/1987 which was acquired by Primerica Corp. (DE) 12/15/1988 which name changed to Travelers Inc. 12/31/1993 which name changed to Travelers Group Inc. 04/26/1995 which name changed to Citigroup Inc. 10/08/1998

BENEFICIAL NATL LIFE INS CO (NY)
Stock Dividend - 25% 01/10/1969
Name changed to National Benefit Life Insurance Co. 12/31/1980
(See National Benefit Life Insurance Co.)

BENEFICIAL SAVINGS BANK OF JACKSONVILLE (JACKSONVILLE, FL)
Merged into Beneficial Savings Bank, F.S.B. (Orlando, FL) 04/07/1986
Details not available

BENEFICIAL STANDARD LIFE INSURANCE CO. (CA)
Recapitalized 10/30/1962
Common $1 par reclassified as Class B Common $1 par and a 50% stock dividend in Class A Common $1 par paid 11/21/1962
Class A Common $1 par and Class B Common $1 par reclassified as Common $1 par 06/17/1968
Stock Dividend - 100% 10/01/1956
Merged into Beneficial Standard Corp. 02/11/1969
Each share Common $1 par exchanged for (1) share Class A Common $1 par
(See Beneficial Standard Corp.)

BENEFICIAL STD CORP (DE)
Class A Common $1 par changed to 80¢ par and (0.25) additional share issued 06/20/1979
Class B Common $1 par changed to 80¢ par and (0.25) additional share issued 06/20/1979
Class A Common 80¢ par changed to 50¢ par and (0.5) additional share issued 06/20/1980
Class B Common 80¢ par changed to 50¢ par and (0.5) additional share issued 06/20/1980
In process of liquidation
Each share Class A Common 50¢ par received initial distribution of $0.10 cash 06/15/1984
Each share Class B Common 50¢ par received initial distribution of $0.10 cash 06/15/1984
Each share Class A Common 50¢ par received second distribution of $0.10 cash 09/14/1984
Each share Class B Common 50¢ par received second distribution of $0.10 cash 9/14/84
Each share Class A Common 50¢ par received third distribution of $0.10 cash 12/13/84
Each share Class B Common 50¢ par received third distribution of $0.10 cash 12/13/1984
Each share Class A Common 50¢ par received fourth distribution of $0.10 cash 03/15/1985
Each share Class B Common 50¢ par received fourth distribution of $0.10 cash 03/15/1985
Each share Class A Common 50¢ par exchanged for fifth distribution of (1) Benequity Holdings Unit of Ltd. Partnership and $13.50 cash 05/15/1985
Each share Class B Common 50¢ par exchanged for fifth distribution of (1) Benequity Holdings Unit of Ltd. Partnership and $13.50 cash 05/15/1985
(See Benequity Holdings)
Assets transferred to BSC Note Liquidating Trust 05/15/1985
(See BSC Note Liquidating Trust)

BENEFICIAL STD MTG INVS (CA)
Shares of Bene. Int. $1 par reclassified as Common $1 par 12/10/1973
Reincorporated under the laws of Delaware as Alamand Corp. 06/16/1978
Alamand Corp. name changed to Moraga Corp. 12/26/1978
(See Moraga Corp.)

BENEFIT PERFORMANCES AMER INC (FL)
Each share Common $0.0001 par exchanged for (10) shares Common $0.00001 par 08/01/1988
Name changed to Triangle Group, Inc. 11/18/1988
Triangle Group, Inc. recapitalized as Triangle Imaging Group, Inc. (FL) 04/13/1995 which reincorporated in Delaware as Electronic Business Services Inc. 10/08/1999 which name changed to Tangent Solutions, Inc. 09/07/2001
(See Tangent Solutions, Inc.)

BENEFIT SOLUTIONS OUTSOURCING CORP (FL)
Common $0.0001 par split (17) for (1) by issuance of (16) additional shares payable 06/01/2011 to holders of record 05/31/2011
Ex date - 06/02/2011
Name changed to Buckeye Oil & Gas, Inc. (FL) 06/02/2011
Buckeye Oil & Gas, Inc. (FL) reincorporated in Nevada as Brisset Beer International, Inc. 07/24/2014

BENEFUND INC (CO)
SEC revoked common stock registration 01/08/2009

BENEM VENTURES INC (AB)
Name changed to Velocity Minerals Ltd. 05/08/2008

BENEQUITY HLDGS (CA)
Merged into Renouf Corp. International 07/30/1987

Each Unit of Ltd. Partnership exchanged for $31 cash

BENESSE CORP (JAPAN)
Name changed to Benesse Holdings, Inc. 10/15/2009

BENETTON GROUP SPA (ITALY)
Each old Sponsored ADR for Ordinary exchanged for (0.5) new Sponsored ADR for Ordinary 06/12/1989
ADR basis changed from (1:20) to (1:2) 05/21/2001
ADR agreement terminated 06/11/2012
Each new Sponsored ADR for Ordinary exchanged for $11.3811 cash

BENEV CAP INC (CANADA)
Name changed to Diversified Royalty Corp. 10/07/2014

BENEVENTUM MINING CO. LTD. (AB)
Struck off register for failure to file annual returns 05/15/1972

BENFIELD GROUP LTD (BERMUDA)
Acquired by Aon Corp. 11/28/2008
Each Unsponsored ADR for Ordinary exchanged for $10.3237 cash
Note: Due to ADR's being unsponsored exchange rate may vary dependent upon depositary agent

BENGAL OIL & GAS CORP (CO)
Each share Capital Stock 1¢ par exchanged for (0.01) share Common $1 par 07/23/1985
Merged into Gulf Exploration Consultants, Inc. 09/15/1988
Each share Common $1 par exchanged for (1) share Common 1¢ par
(See Gulf Exploration Consultants, Inc.)

BENGUET CONSOLIDATED MINING CO. (PHILIPPINES)
Capital Stock 10 Centavos par changed to PHP 1 par 00/00/1934
Name changed to Benguet Consolidated, Inc. 06/26/1956
Benguet Consolidated, Inc. name changed to Benguet Corp. 06/30/1980

BENGUET CORP (PHILIPPINES)
Name changed 06/30/1980
Capital Stock P1 par changed to P2 par 11/25/1960
Capital Stock P2 par changed to P3 par 11/09/1964
Capital Stock P3 par reclassified as Common P3 par 03/14/1969
Common P3 par reclassified as Class B Common P3 par 03/11/1974
Name changed from Benguet Consolidated, Inc. to Benguet Corp. 06/30/1980
Class B Common P3 par split (2) for (1) by issuance of (1) additional share 10/09/1989
Class B Common P3 par split (5) for (4) by issuance of (0.25) additional share 07/19/1990
Stock Dividends - 10% 09/01/1988; 15% 07/24/1989
SEC revoked Class B Common stock registration 07/17/2008

BENHAM BLAIR & AFFILIATES INC (DE)
Name changed to Benham Group Inc. 02/28/1978
Benham Group Inc. name changed to Benham Companies, Inc. 09/16/1985
(See Benham Companies, Inc.)

BENHAM COMPANIES, INC. (DE)
Acquired by SAIC, Inc. 08/02/2007
Details not available

BENHAM GROUP INC. (DE)
Name changed to Benham Companies, Inc. 09/16/1985
(See Benham Companies, Inc.)

BENIHANA INC (DE)
Class A Common 10¢ par split (3) for (2) by issuance of (0.5) additional share payable 06/15/2007 to holders of record 06/01/2007 Ex date - 06/18/2007
Common 10¢ par split (3) for (2) by issuance of (0.5) additional share payable 06/15/2007 to holders of record 06/01/2007 Ex date - 06/18/2007
Each share Class A Common 10¢ par exchanged for (1) share Common 10¢ par 11/30/2011
Stock Dividend - 15% payable 08/12/2002 to holders of record 07/15/2002 Ex date - 07/11/2002
Acquired by Safflower Holdings Corp. 08/21/2012
Each share Common 10¢ par exchanged for $16.30 cash

BENIHANA NATL CORP (DE)
Under plan of merger each share Class A Common 10¢ par or Common 10¢ par automatically became (1) share Benihana Inc. Class A Common 10¢ par or Common 10¢ par respectively 05/26/1995
(See Benihana Inc.)

BENJ FRANKLIN FED SVGS & LN ASSN PORTLAND ORE (USA)
Completely liquidated 08/10/2006
Each share Common $1 par exchanged for first and final distribution of $4.02 cash
Note: Shareholder lawsuit to obtain additional distribution dismissed 04/12/2011

BENJAMIN ELECTRIC MANUFACTURING CO. (IL)
Assets sold and company liquidated 01/02/1959
Details not available

BENJAMIN FRANKLIN BANCORP INC (MA)
Acquired by Independent Bank Corp. 04/10/2009
Each share Common no par exchanged for (0.59) share 1¢ par

BENJAMIN W A INC (NY)
Merged into Addison-Wesley Publishing Co., Inc. 02/26/1971
Each share Common 10¢ par exchanged for (0.74) share Class B Common no par
(See Addison-Wesley Publishing Co., Inc.)

BENJO MINERALS, INC. (NV)
Name changed to Murphy Hot Springs Land Corp. 02/15/1961
(See Murphy Hot Springs Land Corp.)

BENJOE MINES LTD (ON)
Name changed to Medipak Corp. Ltd. and Capital Stock $1 par changed to no par 04/07/1970
Medipak Corp. Ltd. recapitalized as Crown-Meakins Inc. 02/14/1975 which reorganized as Medicorp Technology Ltd. 01/05/1976 which merged into North American Combustion Technology Corp. 08/19/1980
(See North American Combustion Technology Corp.)

BENKOR GOLD MINES LTD.
Acquired by Belkor Mines Ltd. 00/00/1948
Each share Capital Stock exchanged for (0.16666666) share Capital Stock
(See Belkor Mines Ltd.)

BENMAC EXPLORATIONS LTD. (ON)
Merged into Drope Lake Explorations Ltd. 02/10/1967
Each share Capital Stock no par exchanged for (0.2) share Common no par
Drope Lake Explorations Ltd. name changed to Drope Lake Metals & Holdings Ltd. 12/22/1970
(See Drope Lake Metals & Holdings Ltd.)

BENN EXPLS LTD (BC)
Name changed to Allwest Industries Ltd. 01/16/1978
(See Allwest Industries Ltd.)

BENNETT (F.H.) BISCUIT CO.
Succeeded by Wheatsworth Inc. 00/00/1927
Details not available

BENNETT ENVIRONMENTAL INC (CANADA)
Common no par split (3) for (2) by issuance of (0.5) additional share payable 07/15/2002 to holders of record 07/09/2002 Ex date - 07/05/2002
Name changed to BENEV Capital Inc. 07/05/2012
BENEV Capital Inc. name changed to Diversified Royalty Corp. 10/07/2014

BENNETT PETE CORP (CO)
Merged into Abraxas Petroleum Corp. 08/14/1992
Each share Conv. Class A Preferred 1¢ par exchanged for (0.02) share Common 1¢ par
Each share Conv. Class B Preferred 1¢ par exchanged for (0.02) share Common 1¢ par
Each share Common 1¢ par exchanged for (0.1) share Common 1¢ par

BENNION CORP (NV)
Name changed to IDI Global, Inc. 01/14/2002
(See IDI Global, Inc.)

BENOS (CA)
Merged into Soneb Inc. 11/15/1980
Each share Common 10¢ par exchanged for $2 cash

BENPEL INDS LTD (BC)
Recapitalized as Palmer Industries Ltd. 12/18/1984
Each share Capital Stock no par exchanged for (0.5) share Common no par
Palmer Industries Ltd. name changed to Palmer Resources Ltd. 09/18/1996 which merged into Lyon Lake Mines Ltd. 02/05/1999
(See Lyon Lake Mines Ltd.)

BENPRES HLDGS CORP (PHILIPPINES)
Name changed to Lopez Holdings Corp. 11/12/2010
(See Lopez Holdings Corp.)

BENQ CORP (TAIWAN)
Stock Dividends - 12% payable 08/20/2002 to holders of record 06/28/2002 Ex date - 06/26/2002; 20% payable 08/18/2003 to holders of record 06/23/2003; 10% payable 08/02/2004 to holders of record 06/17/2004; 5% payable 08/17/2005 to holders of record 06/22/2005
Recapitalized as Qisda Corp. 10/15/2007
Each 144A Sponsored GDR for Common exchanged for (0.6) 144A Sponsored GDR for Common
Each Reg. S Sponsored GDR for Common exchanged for (0.6) Reg. S Sponsored GDR for Common

BENROY GOLD MINES LTD. (ON)
Charter cancelled and company declared dissolved for default in filing returns 11/09/1964

BENRUS CORP (DE)
Name changed to Wells Benrus Corp. 08/18/1977
(See Wells Benrus Corp.)

BENRUS WATCH INC (NY)
Reincorporated under the laws of Delaware as Benrus Corp. 12/20/1968
Benrus Corp. name changed to Wells Benrus Corp. 08/18/1977
(See Wells Benrus Corp.)

BENSEN AIRCRAFT CORP (NC)
Administratively dissolved 07/14/1993

BENSON EYECARE CORP (DE)
Merged into BEC Group, Inc. 05/03/1996
Each share Common 1¢ par exchanged for (0.5) share Common 1¢ par and $6.60 cash
BEC Group, Inc. recapitalized as Lumen Technologies, Inc. 03/12/1998
(See Lumen Technologies, Inc.)

BENSON FINL CORP (TX)
Merged into Norwest Corp. 05/31/1996
Each share Common 10¢ par exchanged for (0.554785) share Common $1.66666666 par
Norwest Corp. name changed to Wells Fargo & Co. (New) 11/02/1998

BENSON INDUSTRIES LTD. (BC)
Reorganized under the laws of Canada as Bencorp Industries Ltd. 09/00/1977
Each share Common no par exchanged for (0.5) share Common no par
Bencorp Industries Ltd. name changed to Doverton Oils Ltd. 05/16/1984
(See Doverton Oils Ltd.)

BENSON IRON ORE TR (NY)
Name changed 06/08/1961
Each share 1st Preferred $10 par exchanged for (10.5) shares Common $1 par 02/01/1956
Each share 2nd Preferred $10 par exchanged for (10.2) shares Common $1 par 02/01/1956
Each share Common $10 par exchanged for (10) shares Common $1 par 02/01/1956
Name changed from Benson Iron Ore Corp. to Benson Iron Ore Trust 06/08/1961
Each share Common $1 par exchanged for (1) Unit of Bene. Int.
Reorganized as Benson Mines Inc. 07/09/1980
Each Unit of Bene. Int. exchanged for (1) share Common 1¢ par

BENSON-LEHNER CORP. (CA)
Name changed to International Datatronics, Inc. 09/01/1964
International Datatronics, Inc. acquired by Udico Electric Co. 06/17/1966 which name changed to Udico Corp. 08/17/1966 which name changed to UDO Pacific Corp. 02/16/1972 which reorganized as Winkler/Scheid Corp. 08/30/1972 which name changed to Winkler Scheid Vineyards Inc. 07/29/1974 which name changed to Winkler Scheid Inc. 05/19/1977 which name changed to HS Group Inc. 05/28/1980 which assets were transferred to HS Group Inc. Liquidating Trust 08/23/1985
(See HS Group Inc. Liquidating Trust)

BENSON MFG CO (MO)
Merged into Electronic Communications, Inc. 11/23/1965
Each share Common $1 par exchanged for (0.1) share Common $1 par
(See Electronic Communications, Inc.)

BENSON MINES LTD (BC)
Recapitalized as Can Am Gold Resources Ltd. 10/05/1982
Each share Common 50¢ par exchanged for (0.25) share Common no par
Can Am Gold Resources Ltd. recapitalized as Golden Quail Resources Ltd. 09/23/1985 which recapitalized as Consolidated Golden Quail Resources Ltd. 11/24/1997
(See Consolidated Golden Quail Resources Ltd.)

BENSON PETE LTD (AB)
Acquired by Southward Energy Ltd. 03/20/2001
Each share Common no par exchanged for $3.05 cash

BENSON SUPER POWER CORP. (DE)
Liquidation completed
Each share Common 10¢ par exchanged for initial distribution of $18.75 cash 03/11/1966
Each share Common 10¢ par received second distribution of $10.95 cash 12/22/1971
Each share Common 10¢ par received third and final distribution of $1.73 cash 03/23/1972

BENSONHURST NATIONAL BANK (BROOKLYN, NY)
Each share Capital Stock $50 par exchanged for (6.25) shares Capital Stock $10 par to effect a (5) for (1) split and 25% stock dividend 01/15/1957
Stock Dividends - 25% 03/31/1945; 10% 06/27/1946; 25% 11/30/1948; 20% 05/29/1953; 25% 01/17/1961
Merged into Chemical Bank New York Trust Co. (New York, NY) 02/25/1964
Each share Capital Stock $10 par exchanged for (0.33333333) share Capital Stock $12 par
Chemical Bank New York Trust Co. (New York, NY) reorganized as Chemical New York Corp. 02/17/1969 which name changed to Chemical Banking Corp. 04/29/1988 which name changed to Chase Manhattan Corp. (New) 03/31/1996 which name changed to J.P. Morgan Chase & Co. 12/31/2000 which name changed to JPMorgan Chase & Co. 07/20/2004

BENTALL CAP CORP (BC)
9% Retractable 1st Preferred Ser. 1 no par called for redemption 02/23/1989
Public interest eliminated

BENTALL CORP (CANADA)
Merged into SITQ Vancouver Inc. 04/04/2001
Each share Common no par exchanged for $20 cash

BENTECH INDS INC (BC)
Struck from the register and dissolved 06/18/1993

BENTHOS INC (MA)
Common $0.06666666 par split (3) for (2) by issuance of (0.5) additional share payable 12/04/1997 to holders of record 11/18/1997
Merged into Teledyne Technologies Inc. 01/27/2006
Each share Common $0.06666666 par exchanged for $17.50 cash

BENTLEY COMMERCE CORP (FL)
Each share old Common $0.0001 par exchanged for (0.002) share new Common $0.0001 par 06/26/2007
SEC revoked common stock registration 09/11/2007

BENTLEY COMMUNICATIONS CORP (FL)
Stock Dividend - 20% payable 12/01/2003 to holders of record 11/05/2003 Ex date - 11/03/2003
Name changed to Bentley Commerce Corp. 01/12/2004
(See Bentley Commerce Corp.)

BENTLEY INTL INC (MO)
Common 18¢ par split (5) for (1) by issuance of (4) additional shares payable 10/22/1997 to holders of record 09/24/1997
In process of liquidation

Each share Common 18¢ par received initial distribution of $1.55 cash payable 02/02/2000 to holders of record 11/05/1999
Note: Number or amount of subsequent distributions, if any, are not available

BENTLEY LABS INC (DE)
Stock Dividend - 100% 06/22/1981
Merged into American Hospital Supply Corp. 12/15/1981
Each share Common 10¢ par exchanged for (1.2) shares Common no par
American Hospital Supply Corp. merged into Baxter Travenol Laboratories, Inc. 11/25/1985 which name changed to Baxter International Inc. 05/18/1988

BENTLEY NATL CORP (FL)
Name changed to Sunshine Resources International, Inc. 09/24/1975
(See Sunshine Resources International, Inc.)

BENTLEY PHARMACEUTICALS INC (DE)
Reincorporated 11/03/1999
State of incorporation changed from (FL) to (DE) 11/03/1999
Each share Common 2¢ par received distribution of (0.1) share CPEX Pharmaceuticals, Inc. Common 1¢ par payable 06/30/2008 to holders of record 06/20/2008 Ex date - 07/01/2008
Merged into Teva Pharmaceutical Industries Ltd. 07/22/2008
Each share Common 2¢ par exchanged for $14.8165 cash

BENTLEY RES LTD (BC)
Delisted from Vancouver Stock Exchange 03/04/1991

BENTLEYCAPITALCORP COM INC (WA)
Name changed to Proton Laboratories, Inc. 04/14/2004
Proton Laboratories, Inc. recapitalized as Good Water Co., Inc. 05/23/2013

BENTLEYTEL COM INC (NV)
Common $0.001 par split (4) for (1) by isssuance of (3) additional shares payable 04/23/2001 to holders of record 04/16/2001
Name changed back to 20 / 20 Web Design Inc. 07/12/2001
20 / 20 Web Design Inc. recapitalized as 20/20 Networks Inc. 02/14/2003 which name changed to Micro Bio-Medical Waste Systems, Inc. 01/02/2004 which name changed to Crown Equity Holdings Inc. 10/05/2006

BENTON CAP CORP (BC)
Each share old Common no par received distribution of (1) share Coro Mining Corp. Common no par payable 07/24/2014 to holders of record 07/11/2014 Ex date - 07/09/2014
Each share old Common no par exchanged for (0.5) share new Common no par 01/30/2015
Name changed to Alset Energy Corp. 05/02/2016
Alset Energy Corp. name changed to Alset Minerals Corp. 05/04/2017 which name changed to OrganiMax Nutrient Corp. 08/28/2018

BENTON HARBOR MALLEABLE INDS (MI)
Each share old Common $1 par exchanged for (3) shares new Common $1 par 00/00/1937
Stock Dividend - 100% 08/15/1966
Adjudicated bankrupt 01/21/1975
Stockholders' equity unlikely

BENTON OIL & GAS CO (DE)
Common 1¢ par split (2) for (1) by issuance of (1) additional share 07/25/1990
Common 1¢ par split (2) for (1) by issuance of (1) additional share 02/26/1991
Name changed to Harvest Natural Resources, Inc. 05/20/2002

BENTON RES CORP (BC)
Each share Common no par received distribution of (1) share Benton Resources Inc. Common no par payable 07/31/2012 to holders of record 07/26/2012 Ex date - 08/01/2012
Name changed to Benton Capital Corp. 08/01/2012
Benton Capital Corp. name changed to Alset Energy Corp. 05/02/2016 which name changed to Alset Minerals Corp. 05/04/2017 which name changed to OrganiMax Nutrient Corp. 08/28/2018

BENTON RES LTD (BC)
Struck off register and declared dissolved for failure to file returns 12/02/1994

BENTON-SPRY, INC. (DE)
Merged into Spector Industries, Inc. 12/31/1975
Each share Common $1 par exchanged for (0.50012) share Common $1 par
Spector Industries, Inc. merged into Telecom Corp. 12/31/1980 which name changed to TCC Industries, Inc. 06/01/1994
(See TCC Industries, Inc.)

BENVEST CAP INC (CANADA)
Under plan of reorganization each share Ser. A Common no par automatically became either (1) Benvest New Look Income Fund Trust Unit no par or (1) New Look Eyewear Inc. (Old) Exchangeable Share no par 05/02/2005
(See each company's listing)

BENVEST NEW LOOK INCOME FD (ON)
Under plan of reorganization each Trust Unit automatically became (1) share New Look Eyewear Inc. (New) Common no par 03/04/2010
New Look Eyewear Inc. (New) name changed to New Look Vision Group Inc. 06/01/2015

BENZ CAP CORP (BC)
Name changed to Benz Mining Corp. 01/28/2015

BENZ ENERGY INC (DE)
Chapter 11 bankruptcy proceedings converted to Chapter 7 on 03/08/2001
Stockholders' equity unlikely

BENZ ENERGY LTD (BC)
Name changed 03/01/1990
Name changed 07/02/1997
Name changed from Benz Gold Resources Ltd. to Benz Equities Ltd. 03/01/1990
Name changed from Benz Equities Ltd. to Benz Energy Ltd. 07/02/1997
Reincorporated under the laws of Delaware as Benz Energy, Inc. 05/00/1999
(See Benz Energy, Inc.)

BENZAC GOLD MINES LTD. (ON)
Charter revoked for failure to file reports and pay taxes 00/00/1957

BENZAI CAP CORP (BC)
Recapitalized as Redline Resources Inc. 02/11/2013
Each share Common no par exchanged for (0.5) share Common no par
Redline Resources Inc. name changed to Nickel One Resources Inc. 02/29/2016

BEPARIKO BIOCOM (NV)
Name changed to BPK Resources, Inc. 11/15/2002
BPK Resources, Inc. recapitalized as iCarbon Corp. 07/25/2006
(See iCarbon Corp.)

BER RES LTD (BC)
Struck off register and declared dissolved for failure to file returns 05/26/1993

BERACHAH SECS CORP (FL)
Proclaimed dissolved for failure to file reports and pay fees 10/11/1991

BERCOR INC (CA)
Merged into Berel Industries Inc. 08/31/1989
Each share Common no par exchanged for (1) share Common no par
(See Berel Industries Inc.)

BEREL INDS INC (DE)
Incorporated 02/05/1962
Charter cancelled and declared inoperative and void for non-payment of taxes 03/01/1979

BEREL INDS INC (DE)
Incorporated 06/21/1989
Merged into BJRM, Inc. 12/02/1992
Each share Common 1¢ par exchanged for $0.50 cash

BERENS ENERGY LTD (AB)
Merged into PetroBakken Energy Ltd. 02/25/2010
Each share Common no par exchanged for $2.70 cash

BERENS INDS INC (NV)
Recapitalized as Crescent Communications, Inc. 09/25/2001
Each share Common $0.001 par exchanged for (0.2) share Common $0.001 par
Crescent Communications, Inc. recapitalized as Bluegate Corp. 11/23/2004 which recapitalized as Logicquest Technology, Inc. 03/19/2015

BERENS REAL ESTATE INVT CORP (DE)
Dissolved 05/26/1978
Details not available

BERENS RIVER MINES LTD. (ON)
Liquidated 01/27/1956
Details not available

BERES INDS INC (NJ)
SEC revoked common stock registration 10/01/2008

BERETTA RESOURCE CORP (BC)
Name changed to Optimark Data Systems, Inc. 04/24/1992
(See Optimark Data Systems, Inc.)

BERG ELECTRS CORP (DE)
Common 1¢ par split (2) for (1) by issuance of (1) additional share payable 10/20/1997 to holders of record 09/29/1997 Ex date - 10/21/1997
Merged into Framatome Connectors International S.A. 10/23/1998
Each share Common 1¢ par exchanged for $35 cash

BERG ELECTRS HLDG CORP (DE)
Recapitalized as Berg Electronics Corp. 02/29/1996
Each share Common 1¢ par exchanged for (0.243309) share Common 1¢ par
(See Berg Electronics Corp.)

BERG ENTERPRISES INC (DE)
Common 10¢ par split (3) for (2) by issuance of (0.5) additional share 03/10/1983
Common 10¢ par split (2) for (1) by issuance of (1) additional share 12/09/1983
Acquired by American Can Co. 05/17/1985
Each share Common 10¢ par exchanged for $24 cash

BERG ENTERPRISES RLTY GROUP (MA)
Name changed to BRT Realty Trust (MA) 06/23/1975
BRT Realty Trust (MA) reorganized as BRT Apartments Corp. (MD) 03/18/2017

BERG WINFRED M INC (NY)
Acquired by Clarkson Industries, Inc. 10/01/1980
Each share Common 25¢ par exchanged for $17.427 cash

BERGEN BANK OF COMMERCE (PARAMUS, NJ)
Acquired by Horizon Bancorp 07/23/1979
Each share Common $10 par exchanged for (1.2) shares Common $4 par
(See Horizon Bancorp)

BERGEN BRUNSWIG CORP (NJ)
$1.15 Conv. Preferred Ser. 1 no par called for redemption 07/27/1981
Each share Class B Common $1.50 par exchanged for (9.5285) shares Class A Common $1.50 par 02/21/1994
Class A Common $1.50 par split (3) for (2) by issuance of (0.5) additional share 07/31/1969
Class B Common $1.50 par split (3) for (2) by issuance of (0.5) additional share 07/31/1969
Class A Common $1.50 par split (5) for (4) by issuance of (0.25) additional share 12/01/1980
Class B Common $1.50 par split (5) for (4) by issuance of (0.25) additional share 12/01/1980
Class A Common $1.50 par split (3) for (2) by issuance of (0.5) additional share 03/01/1982
Class B Common $1.50 par split (3) for (2) by issuance of (0.5) additional share 03/01/1982
Class A Common $1.50 par split (5) for (4) by issuance of (0.25) additional share 03/01/1983
Class B Common $1.50 par split (5) for (4) by issuance of (0.25) additional share 03/01/1983
Class A Common $1.50 par split (5) for (4) by issuance of (0.25) additional share 09/01/1989
Class A Common $1.50 par split (5) for (4) by issuance of (0.25) additional share 09/03/1991
Class A Common $1.50 par split (5) for (4) by issuance of (0.25) additional share payable 06/02/1997 to holders of record 05/05/1997 Ex date - 06/03/1997
Class A Common $1.50 par split (2) for (1) by issuance of (1) additional share payable 12/01/1998 to holders of record 11/02/1998 Ex date - 12/02/1998
Stock Dividends - 37% 06/01/1988; In Class A Common to holders of Class B Common 25% 09/01/1989; 25% 09/03/1991
Merged into AmeriSourceBergen Corp. 08/29/2001
Each share Class A Common $1.50 par exchanged for (0.37) share Common 1¢ par

BERGEN CAP TR I (DE)
7.8% Trust Originated Preferred Securities called for redemption at $25 on 05/28/2004

BERGEN CNTY NATL BK (HACKENSACK, NJ)
Completely liquidated 06/25/1971
Each share Common $25 par exchanged for first and final distribution of $800 cash

BERGEN DRUG CO (NJ)
Class A Capital Stock no par and Class B Capital Stock no par split (3) for (2) by issuance of (0.5)

additional share respectively 07/01/1965
Under plan of merger name changed to Bergen Brunswig Corp. and Class A Capital Stock no par reclassified as Class A Common $1.50 par and Class B Capital Stock no par reclassified as Class B Common $1.50 par 03/26/1969
Bergen Brunswig Corp. merged into AmeriSourceBergen Corp. 08/29/2001

BERGEN PACKAGING INC (NJ)
Adjudicated bankrupt 01/02/1973
Stockholders' equity unlikely

BERGEN POLLY CO (CA)
Recapitalized as Sega Enterprises, Inc. 03/25/1974
Each share Common 10¢ par exchanged for (0.1) share Common $1 par
(See Sega Enterprises, Inc.)

BERGEN ST BK (BERGENFIELD, NJ)
Merged into Citizens First Bancorp, Inc. 10/01/1983
Each share Capital Stock $2.50 par exchanged for (1) share $2.50 Conv. Preferred Ser. A no par
(See Citizens First Bancorp, Inc.)

BERGER GROWTH & INCOME FD INC (MD)
Name changed to Berger Large Cap Growth Fund, Inc. 01/29/2001
Berger Large Cap Growth Fund, Inc. merged into Janus Investment Fund 04/21/2003

BERGER GROWTH FD INC (MD)
Merged into Janus Investment Fund 04/21/2003
Each share Capital Stock 1¢ par exchanged for Olympus Fund on a net asset basis

BERGER HLDGS LTD (PA)
Each share $4.25 Conv. Preferred Ser. A 1¢ par exchanged for (4) shares Common 1¢ par 12/29/1992
Each share old Common 1¢ par exchanged for (0.1) share new Common 1¢ par 07/21/1993
Merged into Euramax International, Inc. 11/21/2003
Each share new Common no par exchanged for $3.90 cash

BERGER INDS INC (NY)
Chapter 11 Federal Bankruptcy proceedings converted to Chapter 7 in 01/00/1996
Stockholders' equity undetermined

BERGER KENT SPL FD INC (DE)
Name changed to Fleming Berger Fund, Inc. 10/10/1973
Fleming Berger Fund, Inc. acquired by One Hundred Fund, Inc. 09/30/1975 which name changed to Berger Growth Fund, Inc. 01/28/2000 which merged into Janus Investment Fund 04/21/2003

BERGER LARGE CAP GROWTH FD INC (MD)
Merged into Janus Investment Fund 04/21/2003
Each share Capital Stock 1¢ par exchanged for Growth & Income Fund 1¢ par on a net asset basis

BERGER OMNI INVT TR (MA)
Merged into Janus Investment Fund 04/21/2003
Each share Small Cap Value Fund Investor Class exchanged for Small Cap Value Fund Investor Class on a net asset basis
Each share Small Cap Value Fund Institutional Class exchanged for Small Cap Value Fund Institutional Class on a net asset basis

BERGER ONE HUNDRED & ONE FD INC (MD)
Name changed to Berger Growth & Income Fund, Inc. 01/31/2000

Berger Growth & Income Fund, Inc. name changed to Berger Large Cap Growth Fund, Inc. 01/29/2001 which merged into Janus Investment Fund 04/21/2003

BERGESEN D Y A S (NORWAY)
Sponsored ADR's for Ordinary A Shares split (2) for (1) by issuance of (1) additional ADR 05/13/1988
Sponsored ADR's for Non-Vtg. Ordinary B Shares split (2) for (1) by issuance of (1) additional ADR 05/13/1988
Sponsored ADR's for Ordinary A Shares split (2) for (1) by issuance of (1) additional ADR 06/02/1989
Sponsored ADR's for Non-Voting Ordinary B Shares split (2) for (1) by issuance of (1) additional ADR 06/02/1989
Sponsored ADR's for Ordinary A Shares split (2) for (1) by issuance of (1) additional ADR 06/06/1990
Sponsored ADR's for Non-Voting Ordinary B Shares split (2) for (1) by issuance of (1) additional ADR 06/06/1990
Acquired by World Nordic ApS 06/20/2003
Each Sponsored ADR for Ordinary A Shares exchanged for $22.86542 cash
Each Sponsored ADR for Ordinary B Shares exchanged for $19.55394 cash

BERGHOFF BREWING CORP. (IN)
Name changed to Napco Industries, Inc. 03/31/1955
Napco Industries, Inc. name changed to Mass Merchandisers, Inc. (IN) 05/11/1984 which was acquired by McKesson Corp. (MD) 10/29/1985 which reincoporated in Delaware 07/31/1987
(See McKesson Corp. (Old) (DE))

BERGLYNN RES INC (BC)
Common no par split (2) for (1) by issuance of (1) additional share 12/11/1987
Recapitalized as Arkona Resources Inc. 03/11/1992
Each share Common no par exchanged for (0.5) share Common no par
Arkona Resources Inc. recapitalized as Action Minerals Inc. 08/12/2004 which recapitalized as Aroway Minerals Inc. 02/05/2009 which name changed to Aroway Energy Inc. 02/04/2011
(See Aroway Energy Inc.)

BERGNER & ENGEL BREWING CO.
Acquired by Parkside Realty Co. 00/00/1928
Details not available

BERGSTROM CAP CORP (DE)
Liquidation completed
Each share Common $1 par received distribution of (0.2) share Adams Express Co. Common $1 par payable 09/20/1996 to holders of record 08/22/1996
Each share Common $1 par received initial distribution of $122.75 cash payable 04/11/2003 to holders of record 04/04/2003 Ex date - 04/14/2003
Each share Common $1 par received second and final distribution of $0.18 cash payable 06/06/2003 to holders of record 06/02/2003 Ex date - 06/09/2003
Note: Certificates were not required to be surrendered and are without value

BERGSTROM PAPER CO (WI)
Each share Class A Common $1 par or Class B Common $1 par received (0.5) share Class A Common $1 par 09/15/1959
Class A Common $1 par and Class B

Common $1 par reclassified as Common $1 par 03/01/1967
Stock Dividend - 10% 03/15/1967
Merged into Glatfelter (P.H.) Co. 01/30/1979
Each share Common $1 par exchanged for $31.75 cash

BERING EXPL INC (NV)
Each share old Common $0.001 par exchanged for (0.1) share new Common $0.001 par 02/27/2012
Name changed to Breitling Energy Corp. 01/22/2014

BERINGER GOLD CORP (BC)
Merged into Lions Gate Entertainment Corp. 11/13/1997
Each share Common no par exchanged for (0.1) share Common no par

BERINGER WINE ESTATES HLDGS INC (DE)
Merged into Foster's Brewing Group Ltd. 10/04/2000
Each share Class A Common 1¢ par exchanged for $55.75 cash
Each share Class B Common 1¢ par exchanged for $55.75 cash

BERITH HLDGS CORP (FL)
Name changed to Syntrol Corp. 11/29/2017

BERK & CO INC (MA)
Proclaimed dissolved for failure to file reports and pay fees 12/31/1990

BERK TEK INC (PA)
Reorganized 09/25/1987
Reorganized from Maryland to under the laws of (PA) 09/25/1987
Each share Common $0.001 par exchanged for (0.5) share Common $0.001 par
Merged into Nexans Inc. 12/26/1995
Details not available

BERKANA ENERGY CORP (AB)
Acquired by Quatro Resources Inc. 01/17/2008
Each share Common no par exchanged for $1.96 cash

BERKDALE MINES LTD. (ON)
Merged into Berkwater Explorations Ltd. 07/28/1976
Each share Capital Stock no par exchanged for (1.2) shares Capital Stock no par
Berkwater Explorations Ltd. merged into Branly Enterprises Inc. 12/09/1976 which recapitalized as Consolidated Branly Resources Inc. 02/27/1984 which name changed to CBR Holdings Inc. 06/20/1985

BERKELEY BIO MED INC (DE)
Reincorporated 02/14/1977
Name and state of incorporation changed from Berkeley Bio-Engineering, Inc. (CA) to Berkeley Bio-Medical, Inc. (DE) 02/14/1977
Common 5¢ par split (3) for (2) by issuance of (0.5) additional share 11/17/1971
Common 5¢ par split (3) for (2) by issuance of (0.5) additional share 07/31/1972
Each (70,615) shares Common 5¢ par exchanged for (1) share Common 1¢ par 06/29/1982
Note: In effect holders received $14.25 cash per share and public interest was eliminated

BERKELEY CAP CORP I
Recapitalized as iLOOKABOUT Corp. 04/07/2008
Each share Common no par exchanged for (0.2083) share Common no par

BERKELEY CAP CORP II (ON)
Completely liquidated
Each share Common no par received first and final distribution of (0.7052) share Med BioGene Inc. Common

no par and (0.3526) Common Stock Purchase Warrant expiring 06/05/2011 payable 06/16/2009 to holders of record 05/11/2009

BERKELEY COFFEE & TEA INC (NV)
Name changed to DTS8 Coffee Company, Ltd. 02/04/2013

BERKELEY HOTEL TR (MA)
Through purchase offer 100% acquired by Perry (A.W.), Inc. 00/00/1974
Public interest eliminated

BERKELEY IMAGING TECHNOLOGIES (UT)
Recapitalized as U.S. Motor & Safety Inc. 02/02/1992
Each share Common $0.001 par exchanged for (0.33333333) share Common $0.001 par

BERKELEY MINES LTD (ON)
Charter cancelled for failure to file reports and pay taxes 09/03/1994

BERKELEY TECHNOLOGY LTD (CHANNEL ISLANDS)
ADR agreement terminated 04/20/2010
Each Sponsored ADR for Ordinary exchanged for $0.29 cash

BERKEY & GAY FURNITURE CO.
Bankrupt 00/00/1948
Stockholders' equity unlikely

BERKEY INC (DE)
Name changed 09/20/1985
Common $1 par split (3) for (2) by issuance of (0.5) additional share 05/20/1966
Common $1 par split (3) for (2) by issuance of (0.5) additional share 05/23/1968
Name changed from Berkey Photo, Inc. to Berkey, Inc. 09/20/1985
Charter cancelled and declared inoperative and void for non-payment of taxes 05/30/1996

BERKLEY CENTER, INC. (MI)
Adjudicated bankrupt 09/23/1968
No stockholders' equity

BERKLEY DEAN SPL FD INC (MD)
Name changed to New York Hedge Fund, Inc. 09/15/1972
(See New York Hedge Fund, Inc.)

BERKLEY OIL & GAS LTD (AB)
Merged into Page Petroleum Ltd. 08/13/1971
Each share Capital Stock no par exchanged for (0.5) share Common no par
(See Page Petroleum Ltd.)

BERKLEY PETE CORP (AB)
Common no par split (3) for (1) by issuance of (2) additional shares payable 06/20/1997 to holders of record 06/18/1997 Ex date - 06/16/1997
Merged into Anadarko Petroleum Corp. 03/16/2001
Each share Common no par exchanged for $11.40 cash

BERKLEY RES INC NEW (BC)
Recapitalized as Berkley Renewables Inc. 04/16/2012
Each share Common no par exchanged for (0.1) share Common no par

BERKLEY RES INC OLD (BC)
Merged into Berkley Resources Inc. (New) 08/18/1986
Each share Common no par exchanged for (1) share Common no par
Berkley Resources Inc. (New) recapitalized as Berkley Renewables Inc. 04/16/2012

BERKLEY W R CAP TR II (DE)
6.75% Trust Originated Preferred Securities called for redemption at $25 plus $0.121875 accrued dividends on 05/26/2013

FINANCIAL INFORMATION, INC.

BERKLEY W R CORP (DE)
7.375% Depositary Preferred Ser. A called for redemption at $25 on 01/25/1999
Common Stock Purchase Rights declared for Common stockholders of record 05/21/1999 were redeemed at $0.01 per right on 03/04/1999 to holders of record 02/15/1999
(Additional Information in Active)

BERKLEY WALLCOVERINGS INC (QC)
Acquired by WCA Canada Inc. 11/23/1990
Each share Common no par exchanged for $6.35 cash

BERKLINE CORP (DE)
Merged into Corber Merger Co. 09/30/1988
Each share Common $1 par exchanged for $6.75 principal amount of 8-year Subordinated Notes and $10 cash

BERKS COUNTY TRUST CO. (READING, PA)
Stock Dividend - 10% 05/27/1963
Name changed to American Bank & Trust Co. of Pennsylvania (Reading, PA) 08/17/1964
American Bank & Trust Co. of Pennsylvania (Reading, PA) reorganized as American Bancorp, Inc. 09/02/1981 which merged into Meridian Bancorp, Inc. 06/30/1983 which merged into CoreStates Financial Corp 04/09/1996 which merged into First Union Corp. 04/28/1998 which name changed to Wachovia Corp. (Ctfs. dated after 09/01/2001) 09/01/2001 which merged into Wells Fargo & Co. (New) 12/31/2008

BERKSHIRE APPAREL CORP. (MA)
Stock Dividend - 10% 01/30/1967
Liquidation completed
Each share Common $1 par exchanged for initial distribution of (0.154278) share Genesco Inc. $6 Conv. Preference Ser. C no par 11/03/1967
Each share Common $1 par received second and final distribution of (0.02747) share Genesco Inc. $6 Conv. Preference Ser. C no par 04/15/1970

BERKSHIRE ASSET MGMT INC (NV)
Each share old Common $0.001 par exchanged for (0.02) share new Common $0.001 par 04/24/2003
Recapitalized as Greater Sooner Holdings, Inc. 10/11/2005
Each share new Common $0.001 par exchanged for (0.5) share Common $0.001 par
Greater Sooner Holdings, Inc. recapitalized as Dovarri Inc. 01/07/2008
(See Dovarri Inc.)

BERKSHIRE BANCORP INC (MA)
Stock Dividend - 40% 05/28/1971
Name changed to Conifer Group Inc. (Old) and Common $10 par changed to $1 par 09/29/1973
Conifer Group Inc. (Old) merged into Conifer/Essex Group, Inc. 02/17/1983 which name changed back to Conifer Group Inc. (New) 01/01/1985 which merged into Bank of New England Corp. 04/22/1987
(See Bank of New England Corp.)

BERKSHIRE BK & TR CO (PITTSFIELD, MA)
Stock Dividend - 50% 04/25/1969
Reorganized as Berkshire Bancorp Inc. 11/27/1970
Each share Common $10 par exchanged for (1) share Common $10 par
Berkshire Bancorp Inc. name changed to Conifer Group Inc. (Old) 09/29/1973 which merged into Conifer/Essex Group, Inc. 02/17/1983 which name changed back to Conifer Group Inc. (New) 01/01/1985 which merged into Bank of New England Corp. 04/22/1987
(See Bank of New England Corp.)

BERKSHIRE BOTTLING CO., INC. (MA)
Dissolved by Supreme Judicial Court 12/12/1951
No stockholders' equity

BERKSHIRE CAP CORP (AB)
Name changed to Minaean International Corp. (AB) 04/24/2003
Minaean International Corp. (AB) reorganized in British Columbia as Minaean SP Construction Corp. 08/28/2015

BERKSHIRE CAP FD INC (MA)
Merged into Massachusetts Financial Development Fund, Inc. 12/04/1979
Each share Common $1 par exchanged for (0.48607741) share Common $1 par
Massachusetts Financial Development Fund, Inc. name changed to MFS Research Fund 02/01/1992

BERKSHIRE COLLECTION INC (OR)
Reorganized 06/09/2005
Reorganized from under the laws of (ON) to (OR) 06/09/2005
Each share Common no par exchanged for (0.001) share new Common no par
Name changed to Mynewpedia Corp. 03/06/2007
Mynewpedia Corp. name changed to Club Vivanet, Inc. 06/11/2008 which name changed to Medical Marijuana, Inc. 04/28/2009

BERKSHIRE COTTON MANUFACTURING CO.
Merged into Berkshire Fine Spinning Associates, Inc. 00/00/1929
Details not available

BERKSHIRE DISTRS INC (MA)
Merged into Miracle Mart Inc. 07/06/1974
Each share Common $1 par received $5 cash
Note: Certificates were not required to be surrendered and are without value

BERKSHIRE ENERGY RES (MA)
Acquired by Energy East Corp. 09/05/2000
Each share Common no par exchanged for $38 cash

BERKSHIRE FINE SPINNING ASSOCIATES, INC. (MA)
Each share 7% Preferred $100 par exchanged for (1) share $5 Preferred no par and (2.5) shares Common no par 00/00/1937
Common no par split (3) for (1) by issuance of (2) additional shares 00/00/1947
Common no par changed to $5 par 00/00/1952
Under plan of merger name changed to Berkshire Hathaway Inc. (MA) 03/14/1955
Berkshire Hathaway Inc. (MA) reincorporated in Delaware 08/27/1973

BERKSHIRE FROCKS, INC. (MA)
Name changed to Berkshire Apparel Corp. 03/03/1966
Berkshire Apparel Corp. acquired by Genesco Inc. 11/03/1967

BERKSHIRE GAS CO (MA)
5% Preferred $100 par called for redemption 10/25/1965
5.875% Preferred $100 par called for redemption 10/25/1965
6% Preferred $100 par called for redemption 10/25/1965
Common $10 par changed to $5 par and (1) additional share issued 03/17/1980
Under plan of reorganization each share Common $5 par automatically became (1) share Berkshire Energy Resources Common no par 01/01/1999
(See Berkshire Energy Resources)

BERKSHIRE GRIFFIN INC (ON)
Name changed to China Wind Power International Corp. 08/05/2009
(See China Wind Power International Corp.)

BERKSHIRE GROWTH FD INC (MA)
Merged into Berkshire Capital Fund, Inc. 04/28/1975
Each share Common $1 par exchanged for (0.4487) share Common $1 par
Berkshire Capital Fund, Inc. merged into Massachusetts Financial Development Fund, Inc. 12/04/1979 which name changed to MFS Research Fund 02/01/1992

BERKSHIRE HATHAWAY INC (MA)
Reincorporated under the laws of Delaware 08/27/1973

BERKSHIRE INCOME RLTY INC (MD)
9% Preferred Ser. A no par called for redemption at $25 plus $0.462499 accrued dividends on 10/28/2015

BERKSHIRE INTL INC (FL)
Recapitalized as Rockstar Industries, Inc. (FL) 07/31/2006
Each share Common $0.001 par exchanged for (0.00333333) share Common $0.001 par
Rockstar Industries, Inc. (FL) reincorporated in Nevada as Monster Motors, Inc. 09/22/2006 which name changed to Eco2 Forests, Inc. 09/08/2009 which recapitalized as International Display Advertising, Inc. 03/20/2013

BERKSHIRE INTL MNG LTD (BC)
Recapitalized as Tyner Resources Ltd. 01/24/2002
Each share Common no par exchanged for (0.1) share Common no par

BERKSHIRE LMBR CO
Completely liquidated 04/20/2000
Each share Common exchanged for first and final distribution of $80 cash

BERKSHIRE RLTY INC (DE)
Merged into BRI Acquisition, LLC 10/15/1999
Each share Common 1¢ par exchanged for $12.25 cash

BERKSHIRE TEL CORP
4.5% Preferred called for redemption at $100 on 01/01/2001

BERKWATER EXPLS LTD (ON)
Merged into Branly Enterprises Inc. 12/09/1976
Each share Capital Stock no par exchanged for (0.52) share Capital Stock no par
Branly Enterprises Inc. recapitalized as Consolidated Branly Resources Inc. 02/27/1984 which name changed to CBR Holdings Inc. 06/20/1985

BERLAND RES LTD (BC)
Reorganized under the laws of Canada as Lithic Resources Ltd. 06/07/2002
Each share Common no par exchanged for (0.5) share Common no par
Lithic Resources Ltd. name changed to InZinc Mining Ltd. 02/19/2014

BERLAND SHOE STORES, INC. (DE)
Common no par changed to 50¢ par 00/00/1940
Stock Dividend - (1) share 6% Preferred and (1) share Common for each share Common 11/01/1950
Acquired by General Shoe Corp. 00/00/1953
Each (4.54545454) shares 6% Preferred A $20 par exchanged for (1) share $5 Preference B no par or each (2.0227) shares 6% Preferred A $20 par exchanged for (1) share Common $1 par
Each share Common 50¢ par exchanged for (1) share Common $1 par
General Shoe Corp. name changed to Genesco Inc. 03/02/1959

BERLANT AUTOMONITOR CORP (NY)
Name changed to Recreational Vehicles, Inc. 10/06/1970

BERLE OIL CORP. (BC)
Name changed to Berle Resources Ltd. 06/01/1983
Berle Resources Ltd. recapitalized as Eagle Pass Resources Ltd. 08/04/1987 which recapitalized as Starcore Resources Ltd. 09/18/1992 which recapitalized as Starcore International Ventures Ltd. 02/02/2004 which name changed to Starcore International Mines Ltd. 02/01/2008

BERLE RES LTD (BC)
Recapitalized as Eagle Pass Resources Ltd. 08/04/1987
Each share Common no par exchanged for (0.2) share Common no par
Eagle Pass Resources Ltd. recapitalized as Starcore Resources Ltd. 09/18/1992 which recapitalized as Starcore International Ventures Ltd. 02/02/2004 which name changed to Starcore International Mines Ltd. 02/01/2008

BERLIN CITY NATL BK (BERLIN, NH)
Reorganized 04/30/1974
Reorganized from Berlin City National Bank (Berlin, NH) to Berlin City Bank (Berlin, NH) 04/30/1974
Each share Common $15 par exchanged for (3) shares Capital Stock $5 par
Merged into Northway Financial Inc. 09/30/1997
Each share Capital Stock $5 par exchanged for (16) shares Common $1 par

BERLIN DOMAN HELICOPTERS INC (DE)
Name changed back to Doman Helicopters, Inc. 11/14/1969
(See Doman Helicopters, Inc.)

BERLINER COMMUNICATIONS INC (DE)
Name changed to UniTek Global Services, Inc. 07/06/2010
(See UniTek Global Services, Inc.)

BERLINER HANDELS-UND FRANKFURTER BK (GERMANY)
Name changed to BHF-Bank Aktiengesellschaft 07/01/1995
(See BHF-Bank Aktiengesellschaft)

BERLINER-JOYCE AIRCRAFT CORP.
Acquired by North American Aviation, Inc. 00/00/1930
Details not available

BERLITZ INTL INC (NY)
Merged into Berlitz International, Inc. (New) 02/08/1993
Each share Common 10¢ par exchanged for (0.165) share Common 10¢ par and $20.99 cash
(See Berlitz International, Inc. (New))

BERLITZ INTL INC NEW (NY)
Merged into Benesse Corp. 07/02/2001
Each share Common 10¢ par exchanged for $16.50 cash

BERMAN CTR INC (GA)
SEC revoked common stock registration 06/05/2012

BERMAN HLDGS INC (NV)
Name changed to Prepaid Card Holdings Inc. 05/16/2008
Prepaid Card Holdings Inc. name changed to PrepaYd, Inc. 05/12/2011

BERMAN LEASING CO. (PA)
Name changed to Bermec Corp. 09/03/1968
(See Bermec Corp.)

BERMEC CORP (PA)
Common $1 par split (3) for (2) by issuance of (2) additional shares 01/07/1969
Plan of reorganization under Chapter X Federal Bankruptcy Act confirmed 06/15/1979
No stockholders' equity

BERMUDA RES LTD (BC)
Name changed to Ameritel Management Inc. (BC) 09/01/1988
Ameritel Management Inc. (BC) reincorporated in Washington 02/13/1992 which recapitalized as WCT Communications, Inc. 06/04/1992
(See WCT Communications, Inc.)

BERMUDA SCHWORTZ INDS INC (CANADA)
Delisted from Vancouver Stock Exchange 04/03/1987

BERMUDA STAR LINE INC (CAYMAN ISLANDS)
Name changed to Norex America, Inc. 12/11/1989
Norex America, Inc. name changed to Norex Industries Inc. 07/23/1996 which name changed to Siem Industries Inc. 06/01/1998

BERN ENTERPRISES, INC. (UT)
Name changed to Garbalizer Machinery Corp. 04/12/1977
Garbalizer Machinery Corp. recapitalized as RecycleNet Corp. 04/01/1999 which recapitalized as Maydao Corp. 01/20/2010
(See Maydao Corp.)

BERN RES LTD (BC)
Name changed to Pachena Industries Ltd. (Old) 03/26/1985
Pachena Industries Ltd. (Old) merged into Pachena Industries Ltd. (New) 06/02/1997
Pachena Industries Ltd. (New) merged into AimGlobal Technologies Co., Inc. 03/31/1999

BERNADETTE TUNNEL MINING & MILLING CO. (CO)
Charter revoked for failure to file reports and pay fees 09/27/1915

BERNARD ALLAN & EDWARDS INC (FL)
Administratively dissolved 09/25/2009

BERNARD HALDANE ASSOC INC (FL)
Merged into Bernard Haldane Acquisition Corp. 04/09/1999
Each share Common 1¢ par exchanged for $3 cash

BERNARD SCREEN PRTG CORP (NY)
Dissolved by proclamation 09/29/1982

BERNCAM INTL INDS LTD (CANADA)
Common no par split (2) for (1) by issuance of (1) additional share 01/25/1973
Declared bankruptcy 06/07/1985
Details not available

BERNER & CO., INC. (NY)
Charter revoked for failure to file reports and pay fees 12/15/1938

BERNHARDT GOLD MINES LTD. (ON)
Charter cancelled 02/00/1963
No stockholders' equity

BERNS AIR KING CORP (IL)
Class A $2 par and Class B $2 par split (5) for (4) by issuance of (0.25) additional share respectively 12/15/1969
Stock Dividend - In Class A & B - 25% 04/30/1965
Name changed to Air King Corp. 09/16/1970
(See Air King Corp.)

BERNSTEIN/LEIBSTONE ASSOC INC (NY)
Name changed to Safetech Industries, Inc. 04/30/1997
(See Safetech Industries, Inc.)

BERNVILLE BK (BERNVILLE, PA)
Under plan of reorganization each share Common $5 par automatically became (1) share Community Independent Bank, Inc. Common $5 par 07/03/1985
Community Independent Bank, Inc. merged into National Penn Bancshares Inc. 01/03/2001

BERNZ (OTTO) CO., (NY)
Name changed to Bernz O Matic Corp. 09/05/1962
(See Bernz O Matic Corp.)

BERNZ O MATIC CORP (NY)
Class A $1 par reclassified as Common $1 par 10/10/1973
Merged into Newell Companies, Inc. 04/01/1982
Each share Common $1 par exchanged for $2.50 principal amount of 10% Conv. Subordinated Debentures due 04/01/1997

BERRY & BOYLE DEVELOPMENT PARTNERS (MA)
Name changed to Development Partners 09/22/1995
(See Development Partners)

BERRY & BOYLE DEVELOPMENT PARTNERS II (MA)
Name changed to Development Partners II 09/22/1995
(See Development Partners II)

BERRY ASPHALT CO. (AR)
Name changed to Berry Petroleum Co. 02/04/1965
Berry Petroleum Co. acquired by Commonwealth United Corp. 10/31/1968 which recapitalized as Iota Industries, Inc. 12/29/1972
(See Iota Industries, Inc.)

BERRY BROTHERS, INC.
Acquired by American-Marietta Co. 00/00/1947
Details not available

BERRY DOOR CORP. (MI)
Name changed to Berry Industries, Inc. 04/19/1962
Berry Industries, Inc. name changed to POM Corp. 06/15/1970
(See POM Corp.)

BERRY INDS CORP 1962 OLD (DE)
Merged into Berry Industries Corp. (New) 07/01/1979
Each share Common $1 par exchanged for (1) share Common $1 par
Berry Industries Corp. (New) name changed to Strata Search, Inc. 12/23/1987
(See Strata Search, Inc.)

BERRY INDS CORP 1979 NEW (DE)
Name changed to Strata Search, Inc. 12/23/1987
(See Strata Search, Inc.)

BERRY INDS INC (MI)
Name changed to POM Corp. 06/15/1970
(See POM Corp.)

BERRY MOTOR CAR CO.
Liquidation completed 09/18/1958
Details not available

BERRY MOTORS, INC.
Merged into Oliver Iron & Steel Corp. 00/00/1951
Each share Class C Preferred $5 par exchanged for (0.25) share Common $1 par
Each share Common no par exchanged for (0.25) share Common $1 par
Oliver Iron & Steel Corp. merged into Oliver Tyrone Corp. 12/31/1956
(See Oliver Tyrone Corp.)

BERRY ONLY INC (NV)
Common $0.001 par split (3.389831) for (1) by issuance of (2.389831) additional shares payable 01/18/2013 to holders of record 01/18/2013 Ex date - 01/22/2013
Name changed to DelMar Pharmaceuticals, Inc. 01/30/2013

BERRY PETE CO (DE)
Class A Common 1¢ par split (2) for (1) by issuance of (1) additional share 10/27/1989
Class A Common 1¢ par split (2) for (1) by issuance of (1) additional share payable 06/02/2006 to holders of record 05/17/2006 Ex date - 06/05/2006
Merged into LinnCo, LLC 12/16/2013
Each share Class A Common 1¢ par exchanged for (1.68) Common Shares
(See LinnCo, LLC)

BERRY PETROLEUM CO. (AR)
Liquidation completed 10/31/1968
Each share Common $2.50 par exchanged for first and final distribution of (0.8177) share Commonwealth United Corp. Common $1 par and (1) Berry Petroleum Co. Ctf. of Contingent Interest
Each Ctf. of Contingent Interest exchanged for first and final distribution of (0.108062) share Commonwealth United Corp. Common $1 par 01/22/1970
Commonwealth United Corp. recapitalized as Iota Industries, Inc. 12/29/1972
(See Iota Industries, Inc.)

BERRY PLASTICS GROUP INC (DE)
Name changed to Berry Global Group, Inc. 04/13/2017

BERSCHAM ENERGY & MINERALS INC (UT)
Name changed to Champion Energy Corp. 12/09/1983
Champion Energy Corp. recapitalized as Champion Financial Corp. (UT) 11/15/1989 which reorganized in Delaware as HealthStar Corp. 11/16/1998 which name changed to BlueStone Holding Corp. 09/05/2001
(See BlueStone Holding Corp.)

BERT LOGIC INC (WA)
Name changed to Tissera, Inc. 11/04/2003
(See Tissera, Inc.)

BERTEA CORP (CA)
Common no par split (3) for (2) by issuance of (0.5) additional share 03/26/1976
Merged into Parker-Hannifin Corp. 12/02/1978
Each share Common no par exchanged for (0.53) share Common no par

BERTEN USA HLDGS INC (FL)
Each share Common $0.001 par received distribution of (1) share Berten USA Inc. Common $0.001 par payable 06/30/2001 to holders of record 04/30/2001
Recapitalized as Digitalreach Holdings Inc. 07/13/2001
Each share Common $0.001 par exchanged for (0.02) share Common $0.001 par
Digitalreach Holdings Inc. name changed to People Dynamics Holdings Inc. 06/10/2003
(See People Dynamics Holdings Inc.)

BERTEN USA INC (NV)
Charter revoked for failure to file reports and pay fees 11/30/2005

BERTON GOLD MINES LTD (BC)
Struck off register and declared dissolved for failure to file returns 03/19/1975

BERTON INDUSTRIES LTD. (BC)
Reorganized as British Western Industries Ltd. 05/10/1971
Each share Class A no par exchanged for (0.2) share Common no par
(See British Western Industries Ltd.)

BERTRAM PORCUPINE MINES LTD. (ON)
Charter revoked for failure to file reports and pay taxes 00/00/1958

BERTUCCIS INC (MA)
Common $0.005 par split (3) for (2) by issuance of (0.5) additional share 03/16/1992
Merged into NE Restaurant Co., Inc. 07/21/1998
Each share Common $0.005 par exchanged for $10.50 cash

BERU AG (GERMANY)
ADR agreement terminated 01/31/2006
Each Sponsored ADR for Ordinary exchanged for (0.5) share Ordinary

BERVEN CARPETS CORP (CA)
Common 10¢ par split (3) for (2) by issuance of (0.5) additional share 11/01/1971
Common 10¢ par split (2) for (1) by issuance of (1) additional share 06/05/1972
Filed a petition under Chapter 7 Bankruptcy Code 09/06/1985
No stockholders' equity

BERWICK GOLD MINES LTD.
Acquired by Joburke Gold Mines Ltd. 00/00/1947
Each share Capital Stock $1 par exchanged for (0.5) share Capital Stock $1 par
Joburke Gold Mines Ltd. recapitalized as New Joburke Explorations Ltd. 08/21/1973 which name changed to Cenex Ltd. 08/16/1977
(See Cenex Ltd.)

BERWICK RETIREMENT CMNTYS LTD (BC)
Merged into Denford Holdings Ltd. 11/01/2005
Each share Common no par exchanged for $1.13 cash

BERYLLIUM CORP. (DE)
Common no par changed to $1 par 00/00/1953
Common $1 par changed to 50¢ par and (1) additional share issued 10/15/1959
Stock Dividend - 100% 05/06/1953
Merged into Kawecki Berylco Industries, Inc. 10/15/1968
Each share Common 50¢ par exchanged for (1) share Common $1 par
(See Kawecki Berylco Industries, Inc.)

BERYLLIUM INTL CORP (UT)
Reorganized under the laws of Florida as Wallstreet-Review Inc. 11/17/2000
Each share Common 1¢ par exchanged for (0.0033333) share Common 1¢ par
(See Wallstreet-Review Inc.)

BERYLLIUM INTL INC (DE)
Merged into U.S. Beryllium Corp. 01/25/1969
Each share Common 25¢ par exchanged for (0.25) share Common 1¢ par
(See U.S. Beryllium Corp.)

BERYLLIUM MFG CORP (DE)
Stock Dividend - 10% 05/20/1969
Name changed to Newspan, Inc. 03/06/1974
(See Newspan, Inc.)

BESCO ENTERPRISES INC (CA)
Acquired by Hartfield-Zodys, Inc. 03/28/1969
Each share Common $1 par exchanged for (0.094322) share Common $1 par
Hartfield-Zodys, Inc. reorganized as HRT Industries, Inc. 12/22/1981
(See HRT Industries, Inc.)

BESCO MERCHANDISING CORP (MN)
Name changed to WesPac Technologies Corp. (MN) 07/30/1987
WesPac Technologies Corp. (MN) reincorporated in Nevada 08/21/2001 which name changed to Strata Coal Co. 09/27/2002 which name changed to Delmar Management Inc. 11/26/2002 which name changed to 2energia Inc. 01/31/2003 which name changed to Coastal Holdings, Inc. 07/02/2003 which name changed to Canadian Blue Gold, Inc. 10/18/2007 which recapitalized as Boreal Water Collection, Inc. 03/19/2008
(See Boreal Water Collection, Inc.)

BESICORP GROUP INC (NY)
Each share Common 1¢ par exchanged for (0.1) share Common 10¢ par 04/24/1991
Merged into BGI Acquisition Corp. 03/22/1999
Each share Common 10¢ par exchanged for $36.97 cash

BESICORP LTD (NY)
Each share Common 1¢ par received distribution of (1) share WOM Corp. Common 1¢ par payable 04/25/2000 to holders of record 03/06/2000
Merged into Besicorp Acquisition 04/25/2000
Each share Common 1¢ par exchanged for (1) Combined Deferred Payment Right and $58.83 cash
Each share Common 1¢ par received an initial distribution of $35.08 cash from escrow payable 12/24/2001 to holders of record 04/25/2000
Each share Common 1¢ par received a second distribution of $0.80188 cash from escrow payable 02/21/2002 to holders of record 04/25/2000
Each share Common 1¢ par received third and final distribution of $20.29 cash from escrow payable 05/15/2008 to holders of record 04/25/2000

BESPAK PLC (UNITED KINGDOM)
Name changed to Consort Medical PLC 12/04/2007

BESPOKE TRICYCLES INC (NV)
Common $0.001 par split (18) for (1) by issuance of (17) additional shares payable 09/18/2015 to holders of record 09/17/2015
Ex date - 09/21/2015
Name changed to Biotech Products Services & Research, Inc. 11/04/2015

BESSEMER & LAKE ERIE RR CO (OH & PA)
$1.50 Preferred $50 par called for redemption 12/15/1988
$3 Preferred $50 par called for redemption 12/15/1988
Public interest eliminated

BESSEMER-AMERICAN MOTORS CORP. (DE)
Charter cancelled and declared inoperative and void for non-payment of taxes 03/17/1926

BESSEMER COAL & COKE CORP.
Merged into Hanna (M.A.) Co. 00/00/1945
Details not available

BESSEMER COAL IRON & LD CO (DE)
Through purchase offer over 99% acquired by MYCA, Inc. as of 06/02/1978
Public interest eliminated

BESSEMER GAS ENGINE CO.
Merged into Cooper-Bessemer Corp. 00/00/1929
Details not available

BESSEMER LIMESTONE & CEMENT CO. (DE)
Acquired by Bessemer Limestone & Cement Co. (OH) 00/00/1935
Details not available

BESSEMER LIMESTONE & CEMENT CO. (OH)
Common $1 par split (2) for (1) by issuance of (1) additional share 01/04/1960
Stock Dividends - 100% 05/10/1950; 10% 01/03/1956; 10% 01/02/1957; 10% 01/02/1958
Merged into Diamond Alkali Co. 09/12/1961
Each share Common $1 par exchanged for (0.33333333) share $4 Preferred Initial Ser. no par
Diamond Alkali Co. merged into Diamond Shamrock Corp. 12/19/1967 which name changed to Maxus Energy Corp. 04/30/1987
(See Maxus Energy Corp.)

BESSEMER MORTGAGE & SECURITIES CO.
Merged into Bessemer Coal, Iron & Land Co. 00/00/1943
Each share Common exchanged for (1) share Common
(See Bessemer Coal, Iron & Land Co.)

BESSEMER SECURITIES CO. (OH)
Liquidation completed 04/01/1957
Details not available

BEST & BELCHER GOLD & SILVER MINING CO. (CA)
Merged into Industrial Enterprises, Inc. (NV) 12/11/1961
Each share Common no par exchanged for (1) share Common no par
Industrial Enterprises, Inc. (NV) name changed to International Postal Systems, Inc. 08/31/1971
(See International Postal Systems, Inc.)

BEST & CO. INC. (NY)
Common no par changed to $1 par and (1) additional share issued 00/00/1945
Common $1 par split (1.4) for (1) by issuance of (0.4) additional share 04/28/1967
Reincorporated under the laws of Delaware as Beco Industries Corp. 05/02/1967
Beco Industries Corp. merged into Baldwin Securities Corp. 06/22/1972
(See Baldwin Securities Corp.)

BEST ACQUISITIONS INC (NV)
Name changed to Associated Healthcare Industries, Inc. 12/00/1991
Associated Healthcare Industries, Inc. recapitalized as Contour Medical Inc. 06/30/1993 which merged into Sun Healthcare Group, Inc. (Old) 06/30/1998
(See Sun Healthcare Group, Inc. (Old))

BEST BUY CAP L P (DE)
6.5% Guaranteed Conv. Monthly Income Preferred $1 par called for redemption at $50 on 06/30/1998
Public interest eliminated

BEST BUY DRUGS INC NEW (FL)
Reorganized 01/04/1989
Best Buy Drugs, Inc. (Old) reorganized under Chapter 11 Federal Bankruptcy Code as Best Buy Drugs, Inc. (New) 01/04/1989
Each share Common 1¢ par exchanged for (0.2) share Common $0.0001 par and (1) Common Stock Purchase Warrant expiring 07/03/1990
Proclaimed dissolved for failure to file annual reports 08/13/1993

BEST COLL INC (CO)
Each (30,000) shares old Common 10¢ par exchanged for (1) share new Common 3¢ par 10/23/2000
Note: In effect holders received $0.425 cash per share and public interest was eliminated

BEST ENERGY SVCS INC (NV)
Chapter 7 bankruptcy proceedings terminated 04/06/2016
No stockholders' equity

BEST ENERGY SYS INC (ON)
Name changed to DeNovo Corp. 06/28/1991
Denovo Corp. recapitalized as Princeton Media Group Inc. 10/29/1996
(See Princeton Media Group Inc.)

BEST FRANK E INC (WA)
Each share Common $1 par exchanged for (0.0000086) share Common 1¢ par 03/24/1998
Note: In effect holders received $53.61 cash per share and public interest was eliminated

BEST LOCK CORP (DE)
Each share Common no par exchanged for (0.0000006) share Common no par 03/24/1998
Note: In effect holders received $525.43 cash per share and public interest was eliminated

BEST MED TREATMENT GROUP INC (NV)
Name changed to Jenson International Inc. 06/12/1998
(See Jenson International Inc.)

BEST OF AMER CORP (CO)
Name changed to J. Rish Group, Inc. 09/28/1999
(See J. Rish Group, Inc.)

BEST ORE MINES LTD. (ON)
Charter revoked for failure to file reports and pay taxes 00/00/1956

BEST PAC RES LTD (AB)
Acquired by Advantage Energy Income Fund 11/19/2002
Each share Common no par exchanged for $1.25 cash

BEST PHOTO SVC INC (OH)
Acquired by Nashua Corp. (DE) 10/15/1971
Each share Common no par exchanged for (0.32605) share Common $1 par
Nashua Corp. (DE) reincorporated in Massachusetts 06/12/2002 which was acquired by Cenveo, Inc. 09/15/2009
(See Cenveo, Inc.)

BEST PLASTIC CONTAINER CORP. (CO)
Name changed to Best Quality Plastics, Inc. 03/03/1964
Best Quality Plastics, Inc. name changed to B Q P Industries Inc. 08/24/1973

BEST PLASTICS CORP (NY)
Charter cancelled and proclaimed dissolved for failure to pay taxes 12/20/1977

BEST PWR TECHNOLOGY INC (DE)
Merged into General Signal Corp. 06/14/1995
Each share Common 1¢ par exchanged for $21 cash

BEST PRODS INC (VA)
Common $1 par split (2) for (1) by issuance of (1) additional share 11/15/1971
Common $1 par split (3) for (2) by issuance of (0.5) additional share 02/01/1972
Common $1 par split (3) for (2) by issuance of (0.5) additional share 06/23/1978
Common $1 par split (3) for (2) by issuance of (0.5) additional share 12/14/1983
Stock Dividend - 100% 05/06/1976
Merged into BAC Holdings Corp. 03/03/1989
Each share Common $1 par exchanged for $27.50 cash

BEST PRODS INC NEW (VA)
Assets sold for the benefit of creditors 11/00/1996
Stockholders' equity unlikely

BEST QUALITY PLASTICS CO (CO)
Each share Common 10¢ par exchanged for (0.05) share Common $2 par 06/07/1968
Reorganized as B Q P Industries Inc. 10/15/1973
Each share Common $2 par exchanged for (10) shares Common 20¢ par

BEST RATE TRAVEL INC (NV)
Each share old Common $0.001 par exchanged for (0.001) share new Common $0.001 par 09/25/2006
Name changed to Yora International, Inc. 07/27/2007

BEST RES INC (BC)
Name changed to Cariana International Industries Inc. 06/13/1985
Each share Common no par exchanged for (1) share Common no par
(See Cariana International Industries Inc.)

BEST RES INC (NV)
Each share old Common $0.001 par exchanged for (0.1) share new Common $0.001 par 04/01/1993
Each share new Common $0.001 par exchanged again for (0.2) share new Common $0.001 par 05/20/1994
Name changed to Diversified Concepts, Inc. 08/27/1996
Diversified Concepts, Inc. name changed to Medsearch Inc. (NV) 07/09/1998 which reincorporated in Delaware as Medsearch Technologies Inc. 08/11/1999
(See Medsearch Technologies Inc.)

BEST SOFTWARE INC (VA)
Merged into Sage Group PLC 02/16/2000
Each share Common no par exchanged for $35 cash

BEST UNVL LOCK CO (WA)
Each share Class A Common no par exchanged for (0.0000366) share Common 1¢ par 03/24/1998
Note: In effect holders received $120.69 cash per share and public interest was eliminated

BEST WAY USA INC (NV)
Recapitalized as Ziasun Technologies Inc. 09/10/1998
Each share Common $0.001 par exchanged for (0.5) share Common $0.001 par
Ziasun Technologies Inc. merged into INVESTools Inc. 12/06/2001 which name changed to thinkorswim Group Inc. 06/06/2008 which merged into TD AMERITRADE Holding Corp. 06/11/2009

BEST WESTERN PROPERTIES, INC. (UT)
Reincorporated under the laws of

Colorado as Western Royalty Corp. 09/01/1983

BESTAR INC (QC)
Acquired by 9310-1574 Quebec Inc. 01/06/2015
Each share Common no par exchanged for $0.25 cash

BESTAR INTERNATIONAL GROUP LTD (CAYMAN ISLANDS)
Delisted from Toronto Venture Stock Exchange 06/05/2002

BESTFOODS (DE)
Common 25¢ par split (2) for (1) by issuance of (1) additional share payable 04/24/1998 to holders of record 03/31/1998 Ex date - 04/27/1998
Merged into Unilever United States, Inc. 10/04/2000
Each share Common 25¢ par exchanged for $73 cash

BESTFOODS (NJ)
Merged into Corn Products Co. (NJ) on a (1.6) for (1) basis 09/30/1958
Corn Products Co. (NJ) reincorporated in Delaware 04/30/1959 which name changed to CPC International Inc. 04/23/1969 which name changed to BestFoods (DE) 01/01/1998
(See BestFoods (DE))

BESTNET COMMUNICATIONS CORP (NV)
Name changed to Oncologix Tech, Inc. 02/07/2007

BESTOP INC (DE)
Acquired by Douglas & Lomason Co. 06/12/1995
Each share Common $0.002 par exchanged for $12.75 cash

BESTQUIPT SPORTS INC (ON)
Recapitalized as Big Hammer Group Inc. 08/29/2000
Each share Common no par exchanged for (0.25) share Common no par
(See Big Hammer Group Inc.)

BESTWALL GYPSUM CO. (MD)
Common $1 par changed to Common 40¢ par and (1.5) additional shares issued 06/05/1959
Merged into Georgia-Pacific Corp. 04/29/1965
Each share Common exchanged for (1) share $1.64 Conv. Preferred no par
(See Georgia-Pacific Corp.)

BESTWAY INC (DE)
Reorganized 06/07/1995
Each share old Common 1¢ par exchanged for (0.002) share new Common 1¢ par 06/06/1995
Reorganized from Bestway Rental, Inc. to Bestway Inc. 06/07/1995
Each share new Common 1¢ par exchanged for (10) shares Common 1¢ par
Each share old Common 1¢ par exchanged for (1) share new Common 1¢ par to reflect a (1) for (100) reverse split followed by a (100) for (1) forward split 06/02/2005
Note: Holders of (99) or fewer pre-split shares received $13 cash per share
Merged into Bestway Merger, Inc. 11/24/2010
Each share new Common 1¢ par exchanged for $19 cash
Each share new Common 1¢ par received an additional $6.85 cash from class action settlement 02/27/2012

BET HLDGS INC (DE)
Merged into Tele-Communications, Inc. 07/31/1998
Each share Class A Common 2¢ par exchanged for $63 cash

BET PUB LTD CO (ENGLAND)
ADR's for Auction Market Preferred Ser. B called for redemption 09/09/1992
ADR's for Auction Market Preferred Ser. C called for redemption 09/16/1992
ADR's for Auction Market Preferred Ser. D called for redemption 09/23/1992
Acquired by Rentokil Group PLC 07/23/1996
Each Sponsored ADR for Ordinary exchanged for $13.81 cash

BETA BRANDS INC (YT)
Reincorporated 09/20/1999
Place of incorporation changed from (ON) to (YT) 09/20/1999
Assets foreclosed upon 05/02/2003
No stockholders' equity

BETA ENGINEERING CORP. (CA)
Each share Capital Stock $1 par exchanged for (0.25) share Capital Stock no par 12/20/1966
Completely liquidated 04/12/1968
Each share Capital Stock no par exchanged for first and final distribution of (0.2) share Aero-Chatillon Corp. Common 10¢ par
Aero-Chatillon Corp. merged into Macrodyne-Chatillon Corp. 04/01/1969 which merged into Macrodyne Industries, Inc. 01/01/1974
(See Macrodyne Industries, Inc.)

BETA GAMMA EXPLORATION & DEVELOPMENT LTD. (SK)
Acquired by General Petroleums Drilling Ltd. 11/03/1969
Each share Common no par exchanged for $0.11 cash

BETA GAMMA MINES LTD. (SK)
Recapitalized as Consolidated Beta Gamma Mines Ltd. on a (1) for (3) basis 00/00/1956
Consolidated Beta Gamma Mines Ltd. recapitalized as Beta Gamma Exploration & Development Ltd. 01/20/1969
(See Beta Gamma Exploration & Development Ltd.)

BETA INSTR CORP (MA)
Common 1¢ par reclassified as Class A Common 1¢ par 09/00/1970
Acquired by Gould, Inc. 12/30/1971
Each share Class A Common 1¢ par exchanged for (0.043) share Common $4 par
(See Gould Inc.)

BETA MINERALS INC (ON)
Name changed to Advanced Primary Minerals Corp. (ON) 03/06/2009
Advanced Primary Minerals Corp. (ON) reincorporated in Canada 07/18/2012 which recapitalized as Morien Resources Corp. 11/09/2012

BETA OIL & GAS INC (NV)
Each share old Common $0.001 par exchanged for (0.5) share new Common $0.001 par 05/26/2004
Reincorporated under the laws of Delaware as Petrohawk Energy Corp. 07/16/2004
(See Petrohawk Energy Corp. (DE))

BETA PHASE INC (DE)
Reincorporated 05/22/1987
State of incorporation changed from (CA) to (DE) 05/22/1987
Acquired by Molex, Inc. 10/20/1995
Each share Common no par exchanged for $0.05 cash

BETA TECH ROBOTICS INC (NV)
Name changed to Axion Spatial Imaging Inc. (Old) 08/28/1996
Axion Spatial Imaging Inc. (Old) reorganized as Axion Spatial Imaging, Inc. (New) 09/28/2007 which recapitalized as Alco Advanced Technologies, Inc.

04/01/2009 which recapitalized as Southern ITS International, Inc. 04/11/2012

BETA WELL SVC INC (AB)
Common no par split (3) for (2) by issuance of (0.5) additional share 06/22/1993
Merged into Bonus Resource Services Corp. 07/15/1997
Each share Common no par exchanged for $5 cash

BETACOM CORP (ON)
Declared bankruptcy 12/00/2003
No stockholders' equity

BETAFOX CORP (NV)
Name changed to Future World Group, Inc. 11/20/2015
Future World Group, Inc. name changed to Global Entertainment Clubs, Inc. 03/20/2017 which name changed to Wewards, Inc. 01/29/2018

BETAMED PHARMACEUTICALS INC (IN)
Merged into Par Pharmaceutical, Inc. 11/28/1986
Each share Common no par exchanged for $0.50 cash

BETAPRO S&P 500 VIX SHORT TERM FUTURES 2X DAILY BULL ETF (ON)
Each old Class A unit automatically became (0.33333333) new Class A Unit 05/29/2017
Each new Class A Unit automatically became (0.2) new Class A Unit 1/15/2018
Trust terminated 06/11/2018
Each new Class A Unit received $13.222 cash

BETAPRO S&P 500 VIX SHORT-TERM FUTURES DAILY INVERSE ETF (ON)
Class A Units split (2) for (1) by issuance of (1) additional Unit payable 05/26/2017 to holders of record 05/25/2017 Ex date - 05/29/2017
Trust terminated 06/11/2018
Each Class A Unit received $2.4187 cash

BETAPRO US 30 YR BD 2X DAILY BEAR ETF (ON)
Trust terminated 02/28/2017
Each Class A Unit received $9.805984 cash

BETHEL BANCORP (ME)
Common $1 par split (2) for (1) by issuance of (1) additional share 12/15/1995
Name changed to Northeast Bancorp 07/01/1996

BETHEL GOLD MINES LTD. (ON)
Charter revoked for failure to file reports and pay taxes 06/09/1958

BETHEL HLDGS INC (NV)
Reorganized as Direct Pet Health Holdings, Inc. 06/28/2006
Each share Common $0.0001 par exchanged for (2) shares Common $0.001 par
Direct Pet Health Holdings, Inc. recapitalized as Core Resource Management, Inc. 11/13/2012

BETHESDA BANCORPORATION (DE)
Acquired by United Virginia Bankshares, Inc. 04/01/1986
Each share Common $25 par exchanged for $465 cash

BETHEX EXPLS LTD (BC)
Completely liquidated 01/23/1969
Each share Capital Stock 50¢ par exchanged for first and final distribution of (0.03) share Bethlehem Copper Corp. Ltd. Common 50¢ par and (0.174) share Valley Copper Mines Ltd. Common no par
(See each company's listing)

BETHLEHEM COPPER CORP (BC)
Name changed 07/15/1974
Name changed from Bethlehem Copper Corp. Ltd. to Bethlehem Copper Corp. and Common 50¢ par reclassified as Conv. Class A Common no par 07/15/1974
Conv. Class A Common no par reclassified as Common no par 08/20/1979
Conv. Class B Common no par reclassified as Common no par 08/20/1979
Merged into Worwill Investments Inc. 08/17/1981
Each share Common no par exchanged for $37.50 cash

BETHLEHEM CORP (PA)
Under plan of merger each share old Common no par exchanged for (11) shares new Common no par 08/31/1962
Stock Dividends - 10% 01/15/1970; 10% 01/15/1971; 10% 04/19/1982; 10% 04/25/1983; 10% 04/23/1984; 10% 04/18/1985; 10% 04/11/1986
SEC revoked common stock registration 10/01/2008

BETHLEHEM FOUNDRY & MACHINE CO. (PA)
Name changed to Bethlehem Corp. 04/17/1961
(See Bethlehem Corp.)

BETHLEHEM RES CORP (BC)
Merged into Imperial Metals Corp. (Old) 04/03/1995
Each share Common no par exchanged for (0.33333333) share Common no par
Imperial Metals Corp. (Old) reorganized as Imperial Metals Corp. (New) 04/30/2002

BETHLEHEM STEEL CORP (NJ)
Recapitalized under the laws of Delaware 00/00/1936
Each share 7% Preferred $100 par exchanged for (1) share new 7% Preferred $100 par, (1) share 5% Preferred $20 par and $1 cash
Common no par exchanged for new Common no par

BETHLEHEM STL CORP (DE)
Common no par split (3) for (1) by issuance of (2) additional shares 12/00/1947
Common no par changed to $8 par and (3) additional shares issued 02/06/1957
Recapitalized 12/02/1964
Each share 7% Preferred $100 par exchanged for $175 principal amount of 4-1/2% Subord. Debentures due 01/01/1990
Common $8 par changed to $1 par 04/28/1988
Plan of reorganization under Chapter 11 Federal Bankruptcy Code effective 12/31/2003
No stockholders' equity

BETHSAIDA COPPER MINES LTD. (BC)
Recapitalized as New Bethsaida Mines Ltd. 10/28/1963
Each share Common no par exchanged for (0.25) share Common no par
New Bethsaida Mines Ltd. acquired by Western Beaver Lodge Mines Ltd. 04/30/1964 which recapitalized as Portcomm Communications Corp. 08/19/1969 which name changed to Roach (Hal) Studios Corp. 11/01/1977 which merged into H.R.S. Industries, Inc. 05/21/1982 which merged into International H.R.S. Industries Inc. 05/15/1984 which name changed to Glenex Industries Inc. 05/25/1987 which merged into Quest Investment Corp. 07/04/2002 which merged into Quest Capital Corp. (BC)

06/30/2003 which reincorporated in Canada 05/27/2008 which name changed to Sprott Resource Lending Corp. 09/10/2010 which merged into Sprott Inc. 07/24/2013

BETHURUM LABS INC (UT)
Each share old Common $0.001 par exchanged for (0.1) share new Common $0.001 par 08/14/2000
Reorganized under the laws of British Virgin Islands as GSL Group, Inc. 01/18/2002
Each share new Common $0.001 par exchanged for (0.25) share Common no par
(See GSL Group, Inc.)

BETHWAIN OILS LTD. (CANADA)
Deemed not to be a subsisting company by the Dominion Secretary of State 01/10/1954

BETINA RES INC (BC)
Recapitalized as Nevcal Resources Ltd. 09/06/1983
Each share Capital Stock no par exchanged for (0.25) share Common no par
Nevcal Resources Ltd. recapitalized as Arapahoe Mining Corp. 12/31/1986 which recapitalized as Salus Resource Corp. 05/06/1996 which name changed to Brandon Gold Corp. 12/04/1996 which recapitalized as Redmond Ventures Corp. 09/16/1999 which recapitalized as Crown Point Ventures Ltd. (BC) 03/12/2002 which reincorporated in Alberta as Crown Point Energy Inc. 07/31/2012

BETNER (BENJAMIN C.) CO.
Merged into Continental Can Co. Inc. 00/00/1953
Each share Common no par exchanged for (0.37735849) share Common $20 par
Continental Can Co., Inc. name changed to Continental Group, Inc. 04/27/1976
(See Continental Group, Inc.)

BETTA ORTHODONTIC SUPPLIES INC (NY)
Stock Dividend - 50% 09/15/1972
Name changed to HMK Beta Ltd. 06/07/1976
(See HMK Beta Ltd.)

BETTER BIODIESEL INC (CO)
Name changed to GeoBio Energy, Inc. 02/15/2008

BETTER BUSINESS COMMUNICATIONS INC (CANADA)
Acquired by Maclean-Hunter Ltd. 06/01/1988
Each share Common no par exchanged for $3 cash

BETTER HEALTH NUTRACEUTICALS INC (DE)
Reorganized as Altera Holdings Corp. (DE) 10/25/2005
Each share Common $0.001 par exchanged for (10) shares Common $0.001 par
Altera Holdings Corp. (DE) reorganized in Nevada as Nurovysn Biotech Corp. 01/18/2006
(See Nurovysn Biotech Corp.)

BETTER RES LTD (BC)
Recapitalized as BlueRock Resources Ltd. 10/20/2005
Each share Common no par exchanged for (0.33333333) share Common no par
BlueRock Resources Ltd. recapitalized as Argus Metals Corp. 05/07/2009 which name changed to ePower Metals Inc. 12/07/2017

BETTERU ED CORP (BC)
Reincorporated under the laws of Canada 10/13/2017

BETTERWAY TELECOM LTD (DE)
Recapitalized as KDW Telecom, Inc. 12/31/2004
Each share Common exchanged for (0.001) share Common
KDW Telecom, Inc. recapitalized as KSW Industries, Inc. 09/12/2005

BETTING INC (MO)
Reincorporated under the laws of Nevada as eConnect and Common 1¢ par changed to $0.001 par 06/04/1999
eConnect name changed to EyeCashNetworks, Inc. 01/24/2003
(See EyeCashNetworks, Inc.)

BETTINGER CORP (MA)
Reorganized 10/19/1961
Each share old Common $1 par plus $3 cash exchanged for (1) share new Common $1 par which privilege expired 09/18/1961
Adjudicated bankrupt 10/24/1975
No stockholders' equity

BETTINGER ENAMEL CORP. (MA)
Name changed to Bettinger Corp. 00/00/1951
(See Bettinger Corp.)

BETTIS CORP (DE)
Merged into Daniel Industries, Inc. 12/12/1996
Each share Common 1¢ par exchanged for (0.58) share Common $1.25 par
Daniel Industries, Inc. merged into Emerson Electric Co. 06/24/1999

BETZ (JOHN F.) & SON, INC.
Property sold 00/00/1939
Details not available

BETZDEARBORN INC (PA)
Name changed 09/06/1996
Common 10¢ par split (2) for (1) by issuance of (1) additional share 03/30/1967
Common 10¢ par split (2) for (1) by issuance of (1) additional share 11/06/1969
Common 10¢ par split (2) for (1) by issuance of (1) additional share 07/17/1972
Common 10¢ par split (2) for (1) by issuance of (1) additional share 08/09/1990
Stock Dividend - 100% 12/18/1981
Name changed from Betz Laboratories, Inc. to BetzDearborn Inc. 09/06/1996
Merged into Hercules Inc. 10/15/1998
Each share Common 10¢ par exchanged for $72 cash

BEULAH YELLOWKNIFE MINES LTD.
Name changed to Fab Metal Mines Ltd. 00/00/1951
(See Fab Metal Mines Ltd.)

BEV CAL MINES LTD (BC)
Name changed to New Chemcrude Resources Ltd. 08/22/1975
(See New Chemcrude Resources Ltd.)

BEV-TYME INC (DE)
Each share old Common $0.0001 par exchanged for (0.1) share new Common $0.0001 par 07/17/1996
Filed a petition under Chapter 11 Federal Bankruptcy Code 04/09/1998
Stockholders' equity unlikely

BEVCON MINES LTD. (QC)
Merged into Malartic Gold Fields (Quebec) Ltd. 10/05/1965
Each share Capital Stock $1 par exchanged for (0.1) share Capital Stock $1 par
Malartic Gold Fields (Quebec) Ltd. name changed to Les Terrains Auriferes Malartic (Quebec) Ltee. 09/13/1979 which merged into Lac Minerals Ltd. (Old) 12/31/1982 which merged into LAC Minerals Ltd. (New) 07/29/1985 which was acquired by American Barrick Resources Corp. 10/17/1994 which name changed to Barrick Gold Corp. 01/18/1995

BEVCOURT GOLD MINES LTD. (QC)
Recapitalized as Bevcon Mines Ltd. 06/17/1955
Each share Capital Stock $1 par exchanged for (0.14285714) share Capital Stock $1 par
Bevcon Mines Ltd. merged into Malartic Gold Fields (Quebec) Ltd. 10/05/1965 which name changed to Les Terrains Auriferes Malartic (Quebec) Ltee. 09/13/1979 which merged into Lac Minerals Ltd. (Old) 12/31/1982 which merged into LAC Minerals Ltd. (New) 07/29/1985 which was acquired by American Barrick Resources Corp. 10/17/1994 which name changed to Barrick Gold Corp. 01/18/1995

BEVERAGE CANNERS INC (DE)
Merged into Wilson Bottling Corp. 08/03/1983
Each share Common 10¢ par exchanged for $23 cash

BEVERAGE FRANCHISES, INC. (NY)
Reincorporated under the laws of New Jersey as Beverage Franchises of New Jersey, Inc. 04/21/1957
(See Beverage Franchises of New Jersey, Inc.)

BEVERAGE FRANCHISES OF NEW JERSEY, INC. (NJ)
Charter revoked for failure to file reports and pay fees 02/05/1962

BEVERAGE LIQUIDATING CORP. (DE)
Liquidation completed
Each share Common $1 par received initial distribution of $4.88 cash 01/24/1979
Each share Common $1 par exchanged for second and final distribution of $0.6346 cash 12/11/1979

BEVERAGE MGMT INC (DE)
Common 10¢ par split (3) for (2) by issuance of (0.5) additional share 12/23/1977
Common 10¢ par split (3) for (2) by issuance of (0.5) additional share 05/21/1979
Merged into New BMI Co. 01/25/1983
Each share Common 10¢ par exchanged for $24 cash

BEVERAGE STORE INC (NV)
Each share old Common $0.001 par exchanged for (0.4) share new Common $0.001 par 08/15/1997
Recapitalized as Fortune Oil & Gas Inc. (NV) 04/17/1998
Each share new Common $0.001 par exchanged for (0.05) share Common $0.001 par
Fortune Oil & Gas Inc. (NV) reorganized in Wyoming as Manzo Pharmaceuticals, Inc. 09/17/2014

BEVERAGES, INC. (MD)
Completely liquidated 07/20/1967
Each share Common no par exchanged for first and final distribution of $0.115 cash

BEVERAGES BOTTLING CORP. (DE)
Name changed to BBC Industries, Inc. 08/18/1960
BBC Industries, Inc. name changed to Yoo-Hoo Chocolate Beverage Corp. 02/17/1964 which merged into Iroquois Brands, Ltd. 05/06/1976
(See Iroquois Brands, Ltd.)

BEVERLY BANCORPORATION INC (DE)
Reincorporated 7/24/96
Common no par split (2) for (1) by issuance of (1) additional share 01/10/1989
State of incorporation changed from (IL) to (DE) 07/24/1996
Common no par split (5) for (1) by issuance of (4) additional shares payable 08/21/1996 to holders of record 08/16/1996
Stock Dividends - 10% 01/15/1988; 5% payable 04/15/1996 to holders of record 04/05/1996; 5% payable 04/14/1997 to holders of record 04/01/1997; 5% payable 04/14/1998 to holders of record 04/01/1998
Merged into St. Paul Bancorp, Inc. 07/01/1998
Each share Common no par exchanged for (1.063) shares Common 1¢ par
St. Paul Bancorp, Inc. merged into Charter One Financial, Inc. 10/01/1999
(See Charter One Financial, Inc.)

BEVERLY BK (CHICAGO, IL)
Stock Dividend - 50% 08/01/1961
Reorganized as Beverly Bancorporation, Inc. (IL) 11/21/1969
Each share Capital Stock $25 par exchanged for (1) share Common no par
Beverly Bancorporation, Inc. (IL) reincorporated in Delaware 07/24/1996 which merged into St. Paul Bancorp, Inc. 07/01/1998 which merged into Charter One Financial, Inc. 10/01/1999
(See Charter One Financial, Inc.)

BEVERLY DEV INC (BC)
Common no par split (3) for (1) by issuance of (2) additional shares 08/27/1986
Delisted from Canadian Dealer Network 01/03/1995

BEVERLY ENTERPRISES INC (DE)
Reorganized 7/31/87
Common 10¢ par split (2) for (1) by issuance of (1) additional share 01/15/1969
Common 10¢ par split (3) for (2) by issuance of (0.5) additional share 02/02/1983
Common 10¢ par split (2) for (1) by issuance of (1) additional share 06/16/1986
Reorganized from Beverly Enterprises (CA) to Beverly Enterprises, Inc. (DE) 07/31/1987
Each share $2.75 Conv. Exchangeable Preferred $1 par exchanged for $50 principal amount of 5.5% Conv. Subordinated Debentures due 08/01/2018 on 11/01/1995
Each share old Common 10¢ par received distribution of (1) share new Common 10¢ par payable 12/15/1997 to holders of record 12/03/1997
Merged into PharMerica, Inc. 12/03/1997
Each share old Common 10¢ par exchanged for (0.4551) share Common 1¢ par
PharMerica, Inc. merged into Bergen Brunswig Corp. 04/26/1999 which merged into AmeriSourceBergen Corp. 08/29/2001
Acquired by Fillmore Capital Partners LLC 03/14/2006
Each share new Common 10¢ par exchanged for $12.50 cash

BEVERLY GAS & ELECTRIC CO. (MA)
Under plan of merger each share Common $25 par exchanged for (1.1) shares Common $10 par of North Shore Gas Co. (Mass.) and (2.1) shares Common $10 par of Essex County Electric Co. in 1953
(See each company's listing)

BEVERLY HILLS BANCORP (CA)
Common $2 par changed to $1 par and (0.5) additional share issued 05/20/1971
Common $1 par split (3) for (2) by issuance of (0.5) additional share 06/05/1972

Conditionally dissolved 12/19/1996
Stockholders' equity unlikely

BEVERLY HILLS BANCORP INC (DE)
Plan of reorganization under Chapter 11 Federal Bankruptcy proceedings effective 11/24/2014
Stockholders' equity unlikely

BEVERLY HILLS CTRY CLUB INC (UT)
Name changed to Beverly Hills Inc. 08/14/1998
Beverly Hills Inc. name changed to Aladdin Trading & Co. (UT) 08/01/2006 which reincorporated in Florida as Caribbean Casino & Gaming Corp. 05/15/2009 which recapitalized as Caribbean International Holdings, Inc. 01/17/2013

BEVERLY HILLS FAN CO (DE)
Charter cancelled and declared inoperative and void for non-payment of taxes 03/01/1996

BEVERLY HILLS FILM CORP (CA)
Capital Stock $27.50 par changed to $1.10 par and (24) additional shares issued 10/11/1968
Recapitalized as Contemporary Environments, Inc. 06/26/1970
Each share Capital Stock $1.10 par exchanged for (0.25) share Capital Stock $4.40 par
(See Contemporary Environments, Inc.)

BEVERLY HILLS FILM STUDIOS (NV)
Name changed to China Bio Health Group, Inc. 10/16/2003
China Bio Health Group, Inc. name changed to Emerging Media Holdings Inc. 07/18/2006 which name changed to Lifestyle Medical Network Inc. 07/31/2012

BEVERLY HILLS FILM STUDIOS INC (NV)
Name changed to Big Screen Entertainment Group, Inc. 04/01/2005

BEVERLY HILLS GROUP INC (NV)
Each share old Common $0.001 par exchanged for (0.01) share new Common $0.001 par 10/17/2016
Name changed to Full Alliance Group, Inc. 04/11/2017

BEVERLY HILLS INC (UT)
Name changed to Aladdin Trading & Co. (UT) 08/01/2006
Aladdin Trading & Co. (UT) reincorporated in Florida as Caribbean Casino & Gaming Corp. 05/15/2009 which recapitalized as Caribbean International Holdings, Inc. 01/17/2013 which name changed to BioStem Technologies, Inc. 12/09/2014

BEVERLY HILLS NATL BK (BEVERLY HILLS, CA)
Each share Common $2 par exchanged for (0.02) share Common $100 par 04/08/1970
Note: In effect holders received $13.50 cash per share and public interest was eliminated

BEVERLY HILLS PRODUCTIONS (CA)
Acquired by Beverly Hills Film Corp. on a (1) for (55) basis 05/01/1964
Beverly Hills Film Corp. recapitalized as Contemporary Environments, Inc. 06/26/1970
(See Contemporary Environments, Inc.)

BEVERLY HILLS SVGS & LN ASSN (CA)
Capital Stock no par split (3) for (2) by issuance of (0.5) additional share 08/08/1983
Charter suspended for failure to file reports and pay fees 02/01/2001

BEVERLY HILLS WEIGHT LOSS & WELLNESS INC (NV)
Each share old Common $0.0001 par exchanged for (0.005) share new Common $0.0001 par 11/28/2005
Reorganized under the laws of Delaware as Cardiovascular Sciences, Inc. 05/30/2006
Each share new Common no par exchanged for (0.2) share Common $0.0001 par

BEVERLY HLDGS INC (NV)
Each share old Common 40¢ par exchanged for (0.25) share new Common 40¢ par 08/21/2001
Charter revoked for failure to file reports and pay fees 07/31/2008

BEVERLY INVT PPTYS INC (MD)
Name changed to Nationwide Health Properties, Inc. 05/08/1989
Nationwide Health Properties, Inc. merged into Ventas, Inc. 07/01/2011

BEVERLY MANOR INC. (CA)
Common 20¢ par changed to 10¢ par and (1) additional share issued 08/18/1968
Stock Dividend - 100% 04/04/1968
Name changed to Beverly Enterprises (CA) 04/11/1968
Beverly Enterprises (CA) reorganized in Delaware as Beverly Enterprises, Inc. 07/31/1987
(See Beverly Enterprises, Inc.)

BEVERLY NATL CORP (MA)
Common $25 par changed to $2.50 par and (9) additional shares issued 03/17/1987
Common $2.50 par split (2) for (1) by issuance of (1) additional share payable 04/07/1998 to holders of record 03/31/1998
Stock Dividend - 5% payable 06/21/2002 to holders of record 06/05/2002 Ex date - 06/03/2002
Merged into Danvers Bancorp, Inc. 10/30/2009
Each share Common $2.50 par exchanged for (1.66) shares Common 1¢ par
Danvers Bancorp, Inc. merged into People's United Financial, Inc. 07/01/2011

BEVERLY PROPERTY, INC.
Liquidated 00/00/1941
Details not available

BEVERLY SVGS BK (BEVERLY, MA)
Acquired by Warren Five Cents Savings Bank (Peabody, MA) 08/01/1988
Each share Common 10¢ par exchanged for $13 cash

BEVEX INC (UT)
Recapitalized as GTG Ventures, Inc. 11/01/2005
Each share Common $0.001 par exchanged for (0.01666666) share Common $0.001 par

BEVIS INDS INC (RI)
Reincorporated 06/29/1970
Each share old Common 10¢ par exchanged for (0.2) share new Common 10¢ par 06/18/1969
State of incorporation changed from (FL) to (RI) 06/29/1970
Liquidation completed
Each share Common 10¢ par exchanged for initial distribution of $7.60 cash 02/23/1988
Each share Common 10¢ par received second distribution of $0.50 cash 12/15/1988
Each share Common 10¢ par received third distribution of $0.02 cash 12/23/1989
Each share Common 10¢ par received fourth distribution of $0.38 cash 02/20/1991
Each share Common 10¢ par received fifth and final distribution of $0.0686 cash 11/08/1991

BEVIS SHELL HOMES INC (FL)
Reorganized as Bevis Industries, Inc. (FL) 08/27/1964
Each share Common 50¢ par exchanged for (0.2) share Common 10¢ par plus a Purchase Warrant for (0.33333333) additional share
Bevis Industries, Inc. (FL) reincorporated in Rhode Island 06/29/1970
(See Bevis Industries, Inc. (RI))

BEVSYSTEMS INTL INC (FL)
Reorganized 01/02/2003
Reorganized from (CO) to under the laws of (FL) 01/02/2003
Each share old Common no par exchanged for (0.005) share new Common no par
Plan of reorganization under Chapter 11 Federal Bankruptcy Code effective 10/20/2006
No stockholders' equity

BEXAR CNTY NATL BK (SAN ANTONIO, TX)
Each share Common $50 par exchanged for (4) shares Common $12.50 par 05/26/1955
Common $12.50 par changed to $5 par and (1.5) additional shares issued plus a 20% stock dividend paid 05/01/1967
Stock Dividends - 20% 09/20/1954; 25% 06/30/1969
Merged into Republic of Texas Corp. 07/31/1978
Each share Common $5 par exchanged for $46.35 cash

BEXHILL GOLD MINES, LTD. (ON)
Charter cancelled 01/17/1955

BEXY COMMUNICATIONS INC (DE)
Each share old Common 1¢ par exchanged for (0.16666666) share new Common 1¢ par 07/18/1994
Each share new Common 1¢ par received distribution of (0.25) additional share payable 07/03/1996 to holders of record 05/15/1996
Recapitalized as Cheniere Energy, Inc. 07/03/1996
Each share new Common 1¢ par exchanged for (0.33333333) share Common 1¢ par

BEYOND COM CORP (DE)
Each share old Common $0.001 par exchanged for (0.06666666) share new Common $0.001 par 07/02/2001
Plan of reorganization under Chapter 11 Federal Bankruptcy Code effective 08/09/2004
No stockholders' equity

BEZENET INC (DE)
Each share old Common $0.0005 par exchanged for (0.05) share new Common $0.0005 par 08/27/2001
Recapitalized as Allarae Healthcare, Inc. 11/15/2007
Each share new Common $0.0005 par exchanged for (0.004) share Common $0.001 par
Allarae Healthcare, Inc. recapitalized as MP2 Technologies, Inc. 09/12/2007 which recapitalized as The Kiley Group, Inc. 11/03/2009

BF ENTERPRISES INC (DE)
Each share old Common 10¢ par exchanged for (0.00033333) share new Common 10¢ par 08/29/2005
Note: Holders of (2,999) or fewer pre-split shares received $8.95 cash per share
Note: An additional distribution of $2.386472 cash per share was made to holders who surrendered shares prior to 08/31/2006
Reincorporated under the laws of Florida as BFE Corp. 12/29/2015

BF MINERALS LTD (ON)
Recapitalized as Mukuba Resources Ltd. 06/27/2008
Each share Common no par exchanged for (0.24397979) share Common no par
Mukuba Resources Ltd. recapitalized as FogChain Corp. 05/29/2018

BF RLTY HLDGS LTD (BC)
Cease trade order effective 09/16/1994
Stockholders' equity unlikely

BFC CONSTR CORP (CANADA)
Merged into 3674053 Canada Inc. 12/21/1999
Each share Common no par exchanged for $12.50 cash

BFC FINL CORP (FL)
Common 1¢ par reclassified as Class B Common 1¢ par 10/06/1997
Class A Common 1¢ par split (5) for (4) by issuance of (0.25) additional share payable 10/21/1997 to holders of record 10/06/1997
Each share Class B Common 1¢ par received distribution of (0.25) share Class A Common 1¢ par payable 10/21/1997 to holders of record 10/06/1997
Class A Common 1¢ par split (3) for (1) by issuance of (2) additional shares payable 02/10/1998 to holders of record 01/27/1998 Ex date - 02/11/1998
Each share Class B Common 1¢ par received distribution of (0.2) share Class A Common 1¢ par payable 02/10/1998 to holders of record 01/27/1998 Ex date - 02/11/1998
Each share Class B Common 1¢ par received distribution of (0.15) share Class A Common 1¢ par payable 06/17/2003 to holders of record 06/03/2003
Class A Common 1¢ par split (5) for (4) by issuance of (0.25) additional share payable 12/01/2003 to holders of record 11/17/2003
Each share Class B Common 1¢ par received distribution of (0.25) share Class A Common 1¢ par payable 12/01/2003 to holders of record 11/17/2003 Ex date - 12/02/2003
Class A Common 1¢ par split (5) for (4) by issuance of (0.25) additional share payable 03/01/2004 to holders of record 02/20/2004 Ex date - 03/02/2004
Each share Class B Common 1¢ par received distribution of (0.25) share Class A Common 1¢ par payable 03/01/2004 to holders of record 02/20/2004 Ex date - 03/02/2004
Class A Common 1¢ par split (5) for (4) by issuance of (0.25) additional share payable 05/25/2004 to holders of record 05/17/2004
Each share Class B Common 1¢ par received distribution of (0.25) share Class A Common 1¢ par payable 05/25/2004 to holders of record 05/17/2004
Class A Common 1¢ par split (5) for (4) by issuance of (0.25) additional share payable 03/14/2005 to holders of record 03/07/2005 Ex date - 03/15/2005
Each share Class B Common 1¢ par received distribution of (0.25) share Class A Common 1¢ par payable 03/14/2005 to holders of record 03/07/2005 Ex date - 03/15/2005
Stock Dividend - In Class A to holders of Class A 15% payable 06/17/2003 to holders of record 06/03/2003 Ex date - 05/30/2003
Name changed to BBX Capital Corp. (New) 02/03/2017

BFD CAP GROUP INC (DE)
Name changed to Convergent Energy Systems, Inc. 12/23/1987
Convergent Energy Systems, Inc. recapitalized as National Transtech Corp. 12/26/1994
(See National Transtech Corp.)

BFD CAP GROUP INC (NV)
Name changed to Metronet Communications Co. 07/05/2000 Metronet Communications Co. name changed to FlashPoint International Inc. 10/26/2001 which name changed to Navitrak International Corp. 05/28/2004 which recapitalized as VECTr Systems, Inc. 05/21/2007
(See VECTr Systems, Inc.)

BFD INDS INC (BC)
Reincorporated under the laws of Delaware as Alpha Pro Tech, Ltd. and Common no par changed to 1¢ par 06/24/1994

BFGOODRICH CAP (DE)
8.3% Guaranteed Quarterly Income Preferred Securities A called for redemption at $25 on 03/02/2004

BFI CDA INCOME FD (ON)
Reorganized as BFI Canada Ltd. 10/02/2008
Each Trust Unit no par received (1) share Common no par
BFI Canada Ltd. name changed to IESI-BFC Ltd. 06/01/2009 which name changed to Progressive Waste Solutions Ltd. 05/11/2011 which recapitalized as Waste Connections, Inc. 06/01/2016

BFI CDA LTD (ON)
Name changed to IESI-BFC Ltd. 06/01/2009
IESI-BFC Ltd. name changed to Progressive Waste Solutions Ltd. 05/11/2011 which recapitalized as Waste Connections, Inc. 06/01/2016

BFI COMMUNICATIONS SYS INC (NY)
Dissolved by proclamation 03/24/1993

B52 INVTS INC (CANADA)
Name changed to DEQ Systems Corp. 09/09/2003
(See DEQ Systems Corp.)

BFK CAP CORP (ON)
Recapitalized as Hydropothecary Corp. 03/21/2017
Each share Common no par exchanged for (0.66666666) share Common no par
Hydropothecary Corp. name changed to HEXO Corp. 09/05/2018

BFORG CAP INC (AB)
Recapitalized as Parkbridge Lifestyle Communities Inc. 12/23/2004
Each share Common no par exchanged for (0.03000003) share Common no par
(See Parkbridge Lifestyle Communities Inc.)

B4MC GOLD MINES INC (NV)
Old Common $0.001 par split (3) for (1) by issuance of (2) additional shares payable 11/12/2013 to holders of record 11/12/2013
Each share old Common $0.001 par exchanged for (0.02) share new Common $0.001 par 08/21/2015
Name changed to RocketFuel Blockchain, Inc. 09/28/2018

BFS BANCORP INC (DE)
Merged into Eagle Financial Corp. 07/29/1988
Each share Common 1¢ par exchanged for (1.1) shares Common 1¢ par
Eagle Financial Corp. merged into Webster Financial Corp. 04/15/1998

BFS BANKORP INC (DE)
Merged into Dime Bancorp, Inc. (New) 04/30/1997
Each share Common 1¢ par exchanged for $52 cash

BFS ENTMT & MULTIMEDIA LTD (ON)
Filed an assignment in bankruptcy 02/29/2016
Stockholders' equity unlikely

BFX HOSPITALITY GROUP INC (DE)
Merged into American Hospitaity, LLC 12/22/2000
Each share Common 5¢ par exchanged for $2.25 cash

BG ADVANTAGED CORPORATE BD FD (ON)
Merged into Brompton Advantaged VIP Income Fund 07/14/2008
Each Unit no par received either (0.577987) Unit no par or $7.5974 cash
Note: Option to receive cash expired 07/31/2008
Brompton Advantaged VIP Income Fund name changed to Aston Hill Advantage VIP Income Fund 09/16/2011 which name changed to LOGiQ Advantage VIP Income Fund 05/12/2017 which name changed to Redwood Advantage Monthly Income Fund 12/20/2017 which merged into Purpose Multi-Asset Income Fund 05/04/2018

BG ADVANTAGED EQUAL WEIGHTED INCOME FD (ON)
Merged into Brompton Advantaged VIP Income Fund 07/14/2008
Each Unit no par received either (0.845594) Unit no par or $11.115 cash
Note: Option to receive cash expired 07/31/2008
Brompton Advantaged VIP Income Fund name changed to Aston Hill Advantage VIP Income Fund 09/16/2011 which name changed to LOGiQ Advantage VIP Income Fund 05/12/2017 which name changed to Redwood Advantage Monthly Income Fund 12/20/2017 which merged into Purpose Multi-Asset Income Fund 05/04/2018

BG ADVANTAGED S&P/TSX INCOME TR INDEX FD (ON)
Merged into Brompton Advantaged VIP Income Fund 07/14/2008
Each Unit no par received either (1.13986) Units no par or $14.983 cash
Note: Option to receive cash expired 07/31/2008
Brompton Advantaged VIP Income Fund name changed to Aston Hill Advantage VIP Income Fund 09/16/2011 which name changed to LOGiQ Advantage VIP Income Fund 05/12/2017 which name changed to Redwood Advantage Monthly Income Fund 12/20/2017 which merged into Purpose Multi-Asset Income Fund 05/04/2018

BG BARON GROUP INC (BC)
Recapitalized as Consolidated BG Baron Group Inc. 10/25/1999
Each share Common no par exchanged for (0.2) share Common no par
Consolidated BG Baron Group Inc. name changed to In.Sync Industries Inc. 04/03/2000 which name changed to Jet Gold Corp. 05/27/2003 which recapitalized as Deep-South Resources Inc. 11/16/2016

BG GROUP PLC (ENGLAND & WALES)
Reorganized 12/13/1999
Each ADR for Ordinary received distribution of (0.76) additional ADR payable 11/02/1997 to holders of record 10/31/1997
Scheme of arrangement effective 12/13/1999
Each (9) BG PLC ADR's for Ordinary exchanged for (8) BG Group PLC ADR's for Ordinary
Note: Holders of record 12/10/1999 received for every (1,568) ADR's held a distribution of $3.04586 cash per ADR from the proceeds of bond package sale 12/29/1999
Each new ADR for Final Installment par received distribution of (5) shares Lattice Group PLC Ordinary payable 10/27/2000 to holders of record 10/20/2000 Ex date - 10/23/2000
New ADR's for Final Installment split (5) for (1) by issuance of (4) additional ADR's payable 02/13/2012 to holders of record 02/10/2012 Ex date - 02/14/2012
Basis changed from (1:5) to (1:1) 02/13/2012
ADR agreement terminated 03/17/2016
Each New ADR for Final Installment exchanged for $15.192261 cash

BG INCOME + GROWTH SPLIT TR (ON)
Merged into Brompton VIP Income Fund 07/04/2008
Each Preferred Security no par received either (1) 6% Preferred Security or $10 cash
Each Capital Unit no par received either (1.013) Trust Units no par or $13.7612 cash
Note: Option to receive cash expired 07/31/2008
Brompton VIP Income Fund name changed to Aston Hill VIP Income Fund 09/16/2011 which name changed to LOGiQ VIP Income Fund 05/12/2017 which name changed to Redwood Monthly Income Fund 12/20/2017 which merged into Purpose Multi-Asset Income Fund 05/04/2018

BG TOP 100 EQUAL WEIGHTED INCOME FD (ON)
Merged into Brompton VIP Income Fund 07/04/2008
Each Unit no par received either (0.736385) Trust Unit or $10.0035 cash
Note: Option to receive cash expired 07/31/2008
Brompton VIP Income Fund name changed to Aston Hill VIP Income Fund 09/16/2011 which name changed to LOGiQ VIP Income Fund 05/12/2017 which name changed to Redwood Monthly Income Fund 12/20/2017 which merged into Purpose Multi-Asset Income Fund 05/04/2018

BGE CAP TR I (DE)
7.16% Trust Originated Preferred Securities called for redemption at $25 on 12/21/2003

BGI CORP (DE)
Name changed to Frontier U.S.A. Corp. 06/07/1976

BGM DIVERSIFIED ENERGY INC (BC)
Delisted from Toronto Venture Stock Exchange 06/05/2002

BGNX INC (FL)
Proclaimed dissolved for faliure to file reports and pay fees 11/14/1986

BGR CORP (NV)
Each share old Common $0.0001 par exchanged for (1.333) shares new Common $0.0001 par 05/15/2004
Recapitalized as Franchise Capital Corp. 01/12/2005
Each share Common $0.0001 par exchanged for (0.1) share Common $0.0001 par
Franchise Capital Corp. name changed to Aero Performance Products, Inc. 01/24/2008
(See Aero Performance Products, Inc.)

BGR PRECIOUS METALS INC (CANADA)
Name changed to Dundee Precious Metals Inc. 06/23/1999

BGS ACQUISITION CORP (BRITISH VIRGIN ISLANDS)
Completely liquidated 12/17/2013
Each Unit exchanged for first and final distribution of $10.15 cash
Each share Ordinary no par exchanged for first and final distribution of $10.15 cash

BGS ENERGY INC (NV)
Recapitalized as Dini Products, Inc. 11/06/1989
Each share Common $0.0001 par exchanged for (0.03333333) share Common $0.0001 par
(See Dini Products, Inc.)

BGS SYS INC (MA)
Common 10¢ par split (2) for (1) by issuance of (1) additional share payable 11/01/1996 to holders of record 11/01/1996
Merged into BMC Software, Inc. 03/26/1998
Each share Common 10¢ par exchanged for (0.566) share Common 1¢ par
(See BMC Software, Inc.)

BHA GROUP HLDGS INC (DE)
Name changed 02/18/1997
Common 1¢ par reclassified as Class A Common 1¢ par 04/21/1988
Class A Common 1¢ par split (3) for (2) by issuance of (0.5) additional share 08/31/1988
Class A Common 1¢ par split (3) for (2) by issuance of (0.5) additional share 05/22/1989
Conv. Class B Common 1¢ par split (3) for (2) by issuance of (0.5) additional share 05/22/1989
Class B Common 1¢ par reclassified as Class A Common 1¢ par 04/21/1993
Name changed from BHA Group, Inc. to BHA Group Holdings, Inc. 02/18/1997
Stock Dividends - 10% payable 07/10/1996 to holders of record 06/30/1996; 10% payable 06/27/1997 to holders of record 06/16/1997; 10% payable 06/11/1998 to holders of record 05/26/1998
Merged into General Electric Co. 09/01/2004
Each share Class A Common 1¢ par exchanged for $38 cash

BHARAT HOTELS LTD (INDIA)
GDR agreement terminated 07/29/2015
Each GDR for Ordinary exchanged for (2) shares Ordinary

BHC COMMUNICATIONS INC (DE)
Merged into News Corp., Ltd. 07/31/2001
Each share Class A Common 1¢ par exchanged for either (2.2278) ADR's for Ltd. Vtg. Preferred and $66 cash (Mixed election) or (1.5962) ADR's for Ltd. Vtg. Preferred and $85.27 cash (All cash election)
Note: All Stock or Non-electors received (4.3912) ADR's per share
News Corp., Ltd. reorganized as News Corp. 11/03/2004

BHC FINL INC (DE)
Common $0.001 par split (5) for (4) by issuance of (0.25) additional share 10/01/1993
Merged into Fiserv, Inc. 05/30/1997
Each share Common $0.001 par exchanged for (0.87446) share Common 1¢ par

BHF-BANK AKTIENGESELLSCHAFT (GERMANY)
ADR agreement terminated 12/17/1999
Each Sponsored ADR for Ordinary exchanged for $36.1014 cash

BHG SA - BRAZIL HOSPITALITY GROUP (BRAZIL)
ADR agreement terminated 02/23/2015
Each Sponsored ADR for Common exchanged for $5.228414 cash

BHI CORP (BELIZE)
Ordinary 1¢ par split (3) for (1) by issuance of (2) additional shares payable 05/24/1999 to holders of record 05/21/1999
Stock Dividends - 1.3% payable 09/03/1996 to holders of record 08/09/1996; 1.4% payable 03/03/1997 to holders of record 02/07/1997
Name changed to Carlisle Holdings Ltd. 06/02/1999
Carlisle Holdings Ltd. name changed to BB Holdings Ltd. 08/18/2005
(See BB Holdings Ltd.)

BHIRUD FDS INC (MD)
Bhirud Mid Cap Growth Fund reclassified as Apex Mid Cap Growth Fund 12/02/1996
Completely liquidated
Each share Apex Mid Cap Growth Fund received first and final distribution of $0.90 cash payable 11/15/2012 to holders of record 11/14/2012

BHK INC (KOREA)
GDR agreement terminated 04/30/2010
GDR holders' equity unlikely

BHK RES INC (BC)
Name changed to BHK Mining Corp. 01/28/2015

BHM INDS INC (DE)
Acquired by Schenley Industries, Inc. 12/15/1969
Each share Common 50¢ par exchanged for (1) share $1.40 Conv. Preferred $1 par
(See Schenley Industries, Inc.)

BHP GOLD MINES LTD (AUSTRALIA)
Merged into Newmont Australia Ltd. 02/15/1991
Each Sponsored ADR for Ordinary exchanged for $3.42 cash

BHP LTD (AUSTRALIA)
Each Sponsored ADR for Ordinary received distribution of (0.5) share Onesteel Ltd. Ordinary payable 12/05/2000 to holders of record 10/26/2000
Note: Non-electing holders received $0.2281 cash per ADR
Name changed to BHP Billiton Ltd. 06/29/2001

BHP OPERATIONS INC
Auction Market Preferred Ser. A called for redemption at $250,000 on 05/27/1998
Auction Market Preferred Ser. B called for redemption at $250,000 on 05/27/1998
Auction Market Preferred Ser. C called for redemption at $250,000 on 05/27/1998
Auction Market Preferred Ser. D called for redemption at $250,000 on 05/27/1998
Auction Market Preferred Ser. J called for redemption at $250,000 on 11/24/1999
Auction Market Preferred Ser. M called for redemption at $250,000 on 12/18/2000
Auction Market Preferred Ser. I called for redemption at $250,000 on 12/18/2000
Auction Market Preferred Ser. L called for redemption at $250,000 on 12/18/2000
Auction Market Preferred Ser. K called for redemption at $250,000 on 02/14/2006
Auction Market Preferred Ser. N called for redemption at $250,000 on 02/14/2006

BHP RES INC
Auction Market Preferred Ser. A called for redemption at $250,000 on 11/24/1999
Auction Market Preferred Ser. C called for redemption at $250,000 on 11/24/1999
Auction Market Preferred Ser. D called for redemption at $250,000 on 11/24/1999
Auction Market Preferred Ser. E called for redemption at $250,000 on 11/24/1999
Auction Market Preferred Ser. F called for redemption at $250,000 on 11/24/1999

BHR BUFFALO-HEAD RES LTD (BC)
Recapitalized as White Tiger Mining Corp. 07/03/2008
Each share Common no par exchanged for (0.25) share Common no par
White Tiger Mining Corp. name changed to Copper Lake Resources Ltd. 09/24/2014

BI-LO INC (SC)
Common 50¢ par changed to $0.33333333 par and (0.5) additional share issued 08/23/1972
Merged into Ahold N.V. 08/20/1977
Each share Common $0.33333333 par exchanged for $35 cash

BI-OPTIC VENTURES INC (BC)
Each share old Common no par exchanged for (0.1) share new Common no par 10/22/2014
Name changed to Arcturus Growthstar Technologies Inc. 02/17/2016
Arcturus Growthstar Technologies Inc. name changed to Future Farm Technologies Inc. 02/02/2017

BI-ORE MINES LTD. (ON)
Acquired by Consolidated Bi-Ore Mines Ltd. 06/08/1956
Each share Common no par exchanged for (0.2) share Common no par
(See Consolidated Bi-Ore Mines Ltd.)

BI-PETRO RES INC (BC)
Struck off register and declared dissolved for failure to file returns 05/28/1993

BI STATE INDS CORP (NY)
Majority of shares reacquired 00/00/1984
Public interest eliminated

BI-WEEKLY MTG ACCEP CORP (UT)
Involuntarily dissolved 11/01/1992

BIACORE INTL AB (SWEDEN)
ADR agreement terminated 05/21/2004
Each Sponsored ADR for Ordinary exchanged for $19.8271 cash

BIANCA RES LTD (BC)
Completely liquidated 11/19/1981
Each share Common no par exchanged for first and final distribution of (1.5) shares Action Resources Ltd. Common no par
Action Resources Ltd. merged into Interaction Resources Ltd. (BC) 12/22/1982 which reincorporated in Alberta 04/28/1994 which recapitalized as Ketch Energy Ltd. 06/16/2000 which merged into Acclaim Energy Trust 10/01/2002
(See Acclaim Energy Trust)

BIB CORP. (FL)
Acquired by Mead Johnson & Co. 04/01/1958
Each share Common $1 par exchanged for (0.1) share Common $1 par
Mead Johnson & Co. merged into Bristol-Myers Co. 12/22/1967 which name changed to Bristol-Myers Squibb Co. 10/04/1989

BIB HLDGS LTD (NV)
Name changed to Incode Technologies Corp. (NV) 02/07/2005
Incode Technologies Corp. (NV) reincorporated in Delaware as Inseq Corp. 07/13/2005 which name changed to GS Energy Corp. 07/19/2006 which recapitalized as EcoSystem Corp. 02/12/2008 which recapitalized as Adarna Energy Corp. 07/07/2011
(See Adarna Energy Corp.)

BIB NET CORP (GA)
Recapitalized as Obee's Franchise Systems, Inc. 10/29/2004
Each share Common $0.001 par exchanged for (0.002) share Common $0.001 par
(See Obee's Franchise Systems, Inc.)

BIBB CO (DE)
Merged into Dan River Inc. 10/14/1998
Each share Common 1¢ par exchanged for either (0.84615) share Class A Common 1¢ par, $16.50 cash, or a combination of stock and cash
Note: Non-electors will receive a combination of stock and cash to be determined upon surrender of certificates

BIBB CO (GA)
Common no par split (4) for (3) by issuance of (0.33333333) additional share 12/28/1984
Merged into National Textile Corp. 10/25/1985
Each share Common no par exchanged for $25 cash

BIBB CORP (NV)
Common $0.001 par split (6) for (1) by issuance of (5) additional shares payable 10/08/2010 to holders of record 09/27/2010 Ex date - 10/12/2010
Name changed to Z3 Enterprises, Inc. 10/13/2010
Z3 Enterprises, Inc. name changed to HPEV, Inc. 04/23/2012 which name changed to Cool Technologies, Inc. 04/12/2016

BIBB MFG CO (GA)
Each share Common $100 par exchanged for (4) shares Common $25 par 00/00/1946
Common $25 par changed to $12.50 par and (1) additional share issued 10/23/1959
Common $12.50 par changed to no par 12/21/1970
Stock Dividend - 10% 10/01/1966
Name changed to Bibb Co. 12/13/1971
(See Bibb Co.)

BIBIS YUKON MINES, LTD. (ON)
Recapitalized as International Bibis Tin Mines Ltd. 03/05/1965
Each share Capital Stock $1 par exchanged for (0.2) share Capital Stock $1 par
International Bibis Tin Mines Ltd. recapitalized as Laurasia Resources Ltd. 11/29/1973 which merged into StarTech Energy Inc. 02/09/1998 which merged into Impact Energy Inc. (Canada) 01/31/2001 which merged into Thunder Energy Inc. 04/30/2004
(See Thunder Energy Inc.)

BIC CORP (NY)
Name changed 05/19/1982
Common $1 par split (2) for (1) by issuance of (1) additional share 09/07/1972
Name changed from BIC Pen Corp. to BIC Corp. 05/19/1982
Common $1 par split (2) for (1) by issuance of (1) additional share 11/25/1985
Common $1 par split (2) for (1) by issuance of (1) additional share 12/15/1992
Merged into Societe BIC S.A. 12/06/1995
Each share Common $1 par exchanged for $40.50 cash

BICC PHILLIPS INC (CANADA)
Acquired by BICC plc 04/02/1996
Each share Common no par exchanged for $10 cash

BICE VENTURES CORP (BC)
Recapitalized as Pol-Invest Holdings Ltd. 09/24/1999
Each share Common no par exchanged for (0.33333333) share Common no par
Pol-Invest Holdings Ltd. name changed to Net Soft Systems Inc. 03/19/2003 which recapitalized as Rhys Resources Ltd. 02/24/2011 which recapitalized as Pacific Rim Cobalt Corp. 10/24/2017

BICER MED SYS LTD (BC)
Struck off register and declared dissolved for failure to file returns 10/14/1994

BICKFORD CORP (DE)
Merged into Northeast Management Corp. 06/02/1982
Each share Common 10¢ par exchanged for $2.25 cash

BICKFORD'S INC. (NY)
Merged into Bickford's Inc. (MD) 00/00/1943
Each share $2.50 Preference exchanged for $38 principal amount of 6.5% Debentures due 10/01/1962
Each share Common exchanged for (1) share Common $1 par
Bickford's Inc. (MD) merged into LaTouraine-Bickford's Foods, Inc. 11/30/1970 which name changed to Bickford Corp. 05/02/1978
(See Bickford Corp.)

BICKFORDS INC (MD)
Merged into LaTouraine-Bickford's Foods, Inc. 11/30/1970
Each share Common $1 par exchanged for (6.243) shares Common 10¢ par
LaTouraine-Bickford's Foods, Inc. name changed to Bickford Corp. 05/02/1978
(See Bickford Corp.)

BICKLE SEAGRAVE LTD. (ON)
Bankrupt 02/22/1956
Stockholders' equity unlikely

BICKS CDA LTD (ON)
Through purchase offer 100% acquired by Robin Hood Flour Mills Ltd. 00/00/1966
Public interest eliminated

BICO INC (PA)
Each share old Common 10¢ par exchanged for (0.00066666) share new Common $0.0001 par 08/11/2006
Name changed to MobiClear Inc. 11/30/2006
MobiClear Inc. name changed to Intelligent Communication Enterprise Corp. 12/22/2009 which name changed to One Horizon Group, Inc. (PA) 01/31/2013 which reorganized in Delaware 08/29/2013

BICO PPTYS CORP (DE)
Voluntarily dissolved 10/12/1984
Details not available

BICOASTAL COMMUNICATIONS INC (DE)
SEC revoked common stock registration 02/06/2007

BICOASTAL CORP (DE)
Charter cancelled and declared inoperative and void for non-payment of taxes 03/01/2004

BICOR AUTOMATION INDS (NJ)
Reincorporated under the laws of

Delaware as Key Biscayne Enterprises Inc. and Class A Common 10¢ par reclassified as Common 10¢ par 05/09/1972
(See Key Biscayne Enterprises Inc.)

BICROFT URANIUM MINES LTD. (ON)
Merged into Macassa Gold Mines Ltd. 11/01/1961
Each share Capital Stock $1 par exchanged for (0.2) share Capital Stock $1 par
Macassa Gold Mines Ltd. merged into Willroy Mines Ltd. 01/08/1971 which merged into Lac Minerals Ltd. (Old) 12/31/1982 which merged into LAC Minerals Ltd. (New) 07/29/1985 which was acquired by American Barrick Resources Corp. 10/17/1994 which name changed to Barrick Gold Corp. 01/18/1995

BID, INC. (MI)
Liquidation completed
Each share Common no par exchanged for initial distribution of $10.75 cash 01/10/1969
Each share Common no par received second and final distribution of $0.72 cash 11/14/1969

BID COM INTL INC (ON)
Recapitalized as ADB Systems International Inc. 10/18/2001
Each share Common no par exchanged for (0.5) share Common no par
ADB Systems International Inc. name changed to ADB Systems International Ltd. 11/01/2002 which name changed to Northcore Technologies Inc. 07/18/2006

BIDBAY COM INC (NV)
Name changed to AuctionDiner.com, Inc. 04/16/2002
(See AuctionDiner.com, Inc.)

BIDCOP MINES LTD (ON)
Recapitalized as Consolidated Bidcop Mines Ltd. on a (1) for (4) basis 06/25/1969
Note: Certificates were not surrendered at time of recapitalization
Consolidated Bidcop Mines Ltd. recapitalized as Consolidated Bidcop Mining Corp. Ltd. on a (1) for (4) basis 09/30/1970
Exchange of Bidcop Mines Ltd. was actually effected 12/17/1970 and as a result of both recapitalizations each share Capital Stock $1 par was exchangeable for (0.0625) share Consolidated Bidcop Mining Corp. Ltd. Capital Stock $1 par
Consolidated Bidcop Mining Corp. Ltd. recapitalized as Yorkshire Resources Ltd. 10/01/1974 which merged into Dolly Varden Minerals Inc. 12/21/1979 which recapitalized as New Dolly Varden Minerals Inc. 11/16/1992 which recapitalized as Dolly Varden Resources Inc. 04/17/2000 which name changed to DV Resources Ltd. 01/31/2012 which name changed to DLV Resources Ltd. 11/27/2017

BIDCRAWLER COM ONLINE INC (BC)
Recapitalized as TradeRadius Online Inc. 08/21/2001
Each share Common no par exchanged for (0.25) share Common no par
TradeRadius Online Inc. recapitalized as Jalna Resources Ltd. (New) 04/10/2003 which reorganized as Jalna Minerals Ltd. 06/01/2006 which recapitalized as Papuan Precious Metals Corp. 10/01/2010 which name changed to Ironside Resources Inc. 04/21/2015

BIDD CONSOLIDATED MINES LTD. (ON)
Charter cancelled 04/00/1958

BIDD YELLOWKNIFE EXPLORATION CO. LTD.
Succeeded by Bidd Consolidated Mines Ltd. on a (1) for (20) basis 00/00/1946
(See Bidd Consolidated Mines Ltd.)

BIDDEFORD & SACO DEVELOPMENT CORP (ME)
Completely liquidated 08/02/1973
Each share Common $10 par received first and final distribution of $0.32 cash
Note: Certificates were not required to be surrendered and are without value

BIDDEFORD & SACO WTR CO (ME)
Each share Common $100 par exchanged for (4.4) shares Common $25 par to effect a (4) for (1) split and a 10% stock dividend 08/31/1962
Stock Dividends - 10% 06/29/1960; 10% 04/01/1968; 10% 09/02/1971; 10% 03/18/1975; 10% 12/03/1981
Merged into Connecticut Water Service, Inc. 12/10/2012
Each share Common $25 par exchanged for (3.14) shares Common no par

BIDDER COMMUNICATIONS INC (NV)
Name changed to Energy & Engine Technology Corp. 12/26/2001
(See Energy & Engine Technology Corp.)

BIDFISH COM INC (NV)
Each share old Common $0.00001 par exchanged for (0.16666666) share new Common $0.00001 par 11/07/2011
Name changed to DYM Energy Corp. 04/23/2012
DYM Energy Corp. name changed to Four G Holdings Corp. 09/09/2015

BIDGIVE INTL INC (DE)
Each share old Common $0.001 par exchanged for (0.06666666) share new Common $0.001 par 01/20/2010
Recapitalized as Med One Oak, Inc. 12/06/2012
Each share new Common $0.001 par exchanged for (0.1) share Common $0.001 par

BIDGOOD CONSOLIDATED MINES LTD.
Succeeded by Bidgood Kirkland Gold Mines Ltd. on a (1) for (60) basis of $1 par or (1) for (12) basis of no par 00/00/1933
Bidgood Kirkland Gold Mines Ltd. recapitalized as Bidcop Mines Ltd. 04/12/1956
(See Bidcop Mines Ltd.)

BIDGOOD GOLD MINES LTD.
Succeeded by Bidgood Kirkland Gold Mines Ltd. on a (1) for (120) basis 00/00/1933
Bidgood Kirkland Gold Mines Ltd. recapitalized as Bidcop Mines Ltd. 04/12/1956
(See Bidcop Mines Ltd.)

BIDGOOD KIRKLAND GOLD MINES LTD. (ON)
Recapitalized as Bidcop Mines Ltd. on a (1) for (5) basis 04/12/1956
(See Bidcop Mines Ltd.)

BIDHIT COM INC (NV)
Name changed to U.S. National Commercial Partners Inc. 09/11/2001
U.S. National Commerical Partners Inc. recapitalized as Data-Fit, Inc. 09/10/2003 which recapitalized as Real Security Co., Inc. 12/12/2005
(See Real Security Co., Inc.)

BIDLAMAQUE GOLD MINES LTD. (ON)
Reincorporated 00/00/1944
Place of incorporation changed from (QC) to (ON) 00/00/1944
Recapitalized as New Bidlamaque Gold Mines Ltd. (ON) 00/00/1945
Each share Capital Stock no par exchanged for (0.5) share Capital Stock $1 par
New Bidlamaque Gold Mines Ltd. (ON) reincorporated in Canada 00/00/1987 which recapitalized as New Bidlamaque Enterprises Inc. 10/31/1995 which reorganized in British Virgin Islands as Chivor Emerald Corp. Ltd. 06/05/1996
(See Chivor Emerald Corp. Ltd.)

BIDNOW COM INC (AR)
Each share old Common no par exchanged for (0.1) share new Common no par 04/25/2000
Recapitalized as Frontera Investment, Inc. 04/15/2008
Each share Common no par exchanged for (0.06666666) share Common no par

BIDVILLE INC (NV)
Name changed to PrimEdge, Inc. 08/17/2006
(See PrimEdge, Inc.)

BIDZ COM INC (DE)
Acquired by Glendon Group, Inc. 11/26/2012
Each share Common $0.001 par exchanged for $0.78 cash

BIECIUK (HANK), INC. (TX)
Charter revoked for failure to file reports and pay fees 03/15/1967

BIEDERMAN FURNITURE CO. (ME)
Reorganized 09/03/1963
Reorganized from under the laws of (MO) to (ME) 09/03/1963
Each share Class A Common $1 par exchanged for (1) share Common $1 par
Name changed to K.H.T. Corp. 04/01/1966
(See K.H.T. Corp.)

BIF LTD (ON)
Name changed to York Centre Corp. 06/29/1978
York Centre Corp. name changed to Georgian Bancorp Inc. 04/12/1995
(See Georgian Bancorp Inc.)

BIFFS INC (DE)
Charter cancelled and declared inoperative and void for non-payment of taxes 03/01/1978

BIFLEX PRODUCTS CO.
Dissolved 00/00/1933
Details not available

BIFS TECHNOLOGIES CORP (FL)
SEC revoked common stock registration 07/28/2005

BIG A STORES (CA)
Name changed to Newport Western Inc. and Common no par changed to 1¢ par 11/05/1970
Newport Western Inc. name changed to Pride N Joy Industries, Inc. 07/18/1972
(See Pride N Joy Industries, Inc.)

BIG AGAUNICO MINES LTD. (ON)
Merged into Consolidated Professor Mines Ltd. 03/09/1964
Each share Capital Stock no par exchanged for (0.2) share Capital Stock no par
(See Consolidated Professor Mines Ltd.)

BIG APPLE CAP CORP (NY)
Dissolved by proclamation 12/24/1991

BIG APPLE FARMS INC (DE)
Each share old Common $0.005 par exchanged for (0.01428574) share new Common $0.005 par 10/16/1995

Name changed to Austrian Trading Services Inc. 12/06/1995
(See Austrian Trading Services Inc.)

BIG APPLE SUPERMARKETS INC (NY)
Merged into Foodarama Supermarkets, Inc. 05/15/1970
Each share Common 10¢ par exchanged for (0.7) share Common $1 par
(See Foodarama Supermarkets, Inc.)

BIG APPLE WORLDWIDE INC (DE)
Each share old Common $0.0000001 par exchanged for (0.004) share new Common $0.0000001 par 08/10/2007
Each share new Common $0.0000001 par exchanged again for (0.01) share new Common $0.0000001 par 11/10/2010
Name changed to Fusion Restaurant Group, Inc. 02/24/2011

BIG B INC (AL)
Common 10¢ par changed to 5¢ par and (1) additional share issued 09/20/1983
Common 5¢ par changed to 1¢ par 04/24/1984
Common 1¢ par split (2) for (1) by issuance of (1) additional share 10/01/1993
Merged into Revco (D.S.) Inc. (New) 12/23/1996
Each share Common 1¢ par exchanged for $17.25 cash

BIG BK BIG OIL SPLIT CORP (ON)
Completely liquidated 12/30/2016
Each Class A Preferred Share received $10 cash
Each Class A Capital Share received $7.589323 cash

BIG BANK GDANSKI S A (POLAND)
Name changed to Bank Millennium S.A. 01/08/2003
(See Bank Millennium S.A.)

BIG BAR GOLD CORP (BC)
Name changed to Big Bar Resources Corp. 10/19/2007
Big Bar Resources Corp. name changed to CVR Medical Corp. 09/27/2016

BIG BAR RES CORP (BC)
Each share old Common no par exchanged for (0.2) share new Common no par 03/26/2012
Name changed to CVR Medical Corp. 09/27/2016

BIG BEAR DEVELOPMENT CO. (CA)
Liquidation completed
Each share Common no par received initial distribution of $9.35 cash 01/22/1969
Each share Common no par received second distribution of $2.65 cash 07/25/1969
Each share Common no par received third and final distribution of $2.81 cash 11/01/1969
Note: Certificates were not required to be surrendered and are without value

BIG BEAR EXPL LTD (AB)
Each share old Common no par exchanged for (0.09090909) share new Common no par 01/27/1999
Merged into Avid Oil & Gas Ltd. 02/02/2000
Each share new Common no par exchanged for (0.06666666) share Class A Common no par
Note: Holders of (750) shares or fewer received $0.15 cash per share
(See Avid Oil & Gas Ltd.)

BIG BEAR INC (DE)
Stock Dividends - 10% 02/21/1986; 15% 02/20/1987; 15% 02/18/1988
Merged into Penn Traffic Co. (New) 06/28/1989
Each share Common 1¢ par exchanged for $38.60 cash

BIG BEAR MARKETS OF MICHIGAN, INC. (MI)
Merged into ACF-Wrigley Stores, Inc. 12/30/1955
Each share Common $1 par exchanged for (1.1875) shares Common $1 par
ACF-Wrigley Stores, Inc. name changed to Allied Supermarkets, Inc. (DE) 11/10/1961 which reincorporated in Michigan 08/18/1982 which name changed to Vons Companies, Inc. 07/22/1987 which merged into Safeway Inc. 04/08/1997
(See Safeway Inc.)

BIG BEAR MNG CORP (NV)
Common $0.001 par split (50) for (1) by issuance of (49) additional shares payable 02/18/2010 to holders of record 02/18/2010
SEC revoked common stock registration 10/01/2013

BIG BEAR OIL & GAS LTD (AB)
Name changed to Renata Resources Ltd. 01/06/1997
Renata Resources Ltd. merged into Rio Alto Exploration Ltd. 06/21/2000 which merged into Canadian Natural Resources Ltd. 07/01/2002

BIG BEAR RES INC (NV)
Name changed to Uranium Plus Resource Corp. 03/24/2008
Uranium Plus Resource Corp. reorganized as Artventive Medical Group, Inc. 02/16/2010

BIG BEAR STORES CO (DE)
Merged into Penn Traffic Co. 04/16/1993
Each share Common 1¢ par exchanged for either (0.662624) share old Common $1.25 par, $36 cash, or a combination thereof
(See Penn Traffic Co. (DE))

BIG BEAR STORES CO (OH)
5% Preferred $100 par called for redemption 07/10/1950
Each share Class A Common $1 par exchanged for (3) shares Class A Common $0.33333333 par 01/16/1957
Name changed to Scioto Investment Co. 08/30/1976
(See Scioto Investment Co.)

BIG BELL MINES LTD. (AUSTRALIA)
Completely liquidated 09/06/1956
Each share Capital Stock £1 par received first and final distribution of USD$2.78 cash
Note: Certificates were not required to be surrendered and are without value

BIG BEN RES INC (BC)
Recapitalized as M.I.T. Ventures Corp. 05/19/1993
Each share Common no par exchanged for (0.28571428) share Common no par

BIG BEND OIL & GAS CO. (KS)
Name changed to Fidelity Oil & Refining Co. 11/05/1919
(See Fidelity Oil & Refining Co.)

BIG BEND URANIUM CO. (UT)
Merged into Consolidated Oil & Resources, Inc. on a (1) for (20) basis 05/24/1956
Consolidated Oil & Resources, Inc. merged into Randex Consolidated Oil Co. 00/00/1956 which recapitalized as American-Caribbean Oil Co. 03/21/1958 which merged into Elgin Gas & Oil Co. 06/30/1959
(See Elgin Gas & Oil Co.)

BIG BITE INC (OH)
Common no par split (5) for (4) by issuance of (0.25) additional share 07/17/1982
Name changed to First National Corp. (OH) 04/24/1985
First National Corp. (OH) name changed to C.A. Short International, Inc. 06/07/1990 which name changed to Pages, Inc. (OH) 11/16/1992 which reincorporated in Delaware 10/13/1994 which recapitalized as Media Source Inc. 03/09/1999
(See Media Source Inc.)

BIG BLACKFOOT RES LTD (AB)
Recapitalized as BBF Resources Inc. 10/21/2002
Each share Common no par exchanged for (0.5) share Common no par
BBF Resources Inc. name changed to Western Energy Services Corp. 07/27/2005

BIG BOULDER CORP (PA)
Merged into Blue Ridge Real Estate Co. 11/01/2013
Each share Common no par exchanged for (0.5) share Common no par

BIG BOY PROPERTIES, INC. (CA)
Completely liquidated 06/30/1967
Each share Common $10 par exchanged for first and final distribution of (0.6066) share Marriott-Hot Shoppes, Inc. Common $1 par
Marriott-Hot Shoppes, Inc. name changed to Marriott Corp. 11/21/1967 which name changed to Host Marriott Corp. (DE) 10/08/1993 which reorganized in Maryland 12/29/1998 which name changed to Host Hotels & Resorts, Inc. 04/17/2006

BIG BRAKE SOUTHN CALIF INC (CA)
Charter suspended for failure to file reports and pay taxes 01/02/1975

BIG BUCK BREWERY & STEAKHOUSE INC (MI)
Each share old Common 1¢ par exchanged for (0.14285714) share new Common 1¢ par 09/16/2002
Each share new Common 1¢ par exchanged again for (0.1) share new Common 1¢ par 03/25/2004
Note: In effect holders received $0.25 cash per share and public interest was eliminated

BIG C STORES INC (OR)
Name changed to Baza'r, Inc. 08/02/1968

BIG C SUPERCENTER PUB CO LTD (THAILAND)
ADR agreement terminated 05/21/2018
No ADR's remain outstanding

BIG CAT ENERGY CORP (NV)
Each share Common $0.0001 par received distribution of (0.3328784) share Sterling Oil & Gas Co. Common $0.00001 par payable 04/02/2008 to holders of record 03/03/2008 Ex date - 03/31/2008
Recapitalized as Bridgegate Pictures Corp. 05/11/2016
Each share Common $0.0001 par exchanged for (0.01) share Common $0.0001 par

BIG CAT MINES LTD (BC)
Dissolved 06/13/1977

BIG CAT MNG CORP (NV)
Name changed to Big Cat Energy Corp. 05/03/2006
Big Cat Energy Corp. recapitalized as Bridgegate Pictures Corp. 05/11/2016

BIG CHIEF SAVINGS STAMPS, INC. (NM)
Charter revoked for failure to file reports and pay fees 08/17/1961

BIG CITY BAGELS INC (NY)
Each share old Common $0.001 par exchanged for (0.2) share new Common $0.001 par 06/23/1998
Name changed to Villageworld.com, Inc. 12/31/1999
Villageworld.com, Inc. name changed to Biometrics 2000 Corp. 03/04/2004
(See Biometrics 2000 Corp.)

BIG CITY RADIO INC (DE)
Liquidation completed
Each share Class A Common 1¢ par received initial distribution of (0.14321591) share Entravision Communications Corp. Class A Common $0.0001 par payable 02/09/2004 to holders of record 02/06/2004 Ex date - 02/10/2004
Each share Class A Common 1¢ par received second and final distribution of $0.19 cash payable 06/03/2005 to holders of record 05/24/2005 Ex date - 06/06/2005
Note: Certificates were not required to be surrendered and are without value

BIG CLIX CORP (FL)
Common $0.0001 par split (13) for (1) by issuance of (12) additional shares payable 02/02/2012 to holders of record 01/24/2012 Ex date - 02/03/2012
Name changed to HydroPhi Technologies Group, Inc. 10/07/2013

BIG COMSTOCK GOLD MINES, INC.
Apparently out of business 00/00/1941
Details not available

BIG CREEK APEX MNG CO (ID)
Merged into Sunshine Mining Co. 12/30/1981
Each share Capital Stock 5¢ par exchanged for (0.715) share Capital Stock 50¢ par
Sunshine Mining Co. name changed to Sunshine Mining & Refining Co. 06/20/1994
(See Sunshine Mining & Refining Co.)

BIG CREEK RES LTD (BC)
Merged into Pacific Sentinel Gold Corp. 12/01/1992
Each share Common no par exchanged for (1) share Common no par
Pacific Sentinel Gold Corp. merged into Great Basin Gold Ltd. 12/18/1997
(See Great Basin Gold Ltd.)

BIG DADDYS AUTO SALES INC (FL)
Name changed to Sweets & Eats, Inc. 04/19/2000
Sweets & Eats, Inc. name changed to Safe Transportation Systems, Inc. 01/23/2001
(See Safe Transportation Systems, Inc.)

BIG DADDYS BBQ RACING CO (NV)
Common $0.001 par split (10) for (1) by issuance of (9) additional shares payable 03/27/2000 to holders of record 03/20/2000
Name changed to Ehydrogen Solutions, Inc. 12/14/2009

BIG DADDYS LOUNGES INC (FL)
Name changed to Flanigan's Enterprises Inc. 01/03/1978

BIG DAN MINES LTD. (ON)
Charter cancelled 05/00/1960

BIG DIAMOND OIL & REFINING CO. (AZ)
Charter revoked for failure to file reports or pay fees 09/27/1927

BIG DOG HLDGS INC (DE)
Name changed to Walking Company Holdings, Inc. 05/07/2008
(See Walking Company Holdings, Inc.)

BIG DOLLAR FOOD STORES, INC. (DE)
Merged into Mayfair Supermarkets, Inc. 08/29/1956
Each share Common $1 par exchanged for (1) share Common $1 par
(See Mayfair Supermarkets, Inc.)

BIG DRUM INC (OH)
Stock Dividends - 10% 01/24/1969; 10% 09/15/1971; 100% 09/29/1972; 10% 09/16/1974; 10% 06/23/1978; 10% 06/22/1979
Merged into Alco Standard Corp. 05/14/1980
Each share Class A Common no par exchanged for (0.5) share Common no par or $18 cash
Each share Common no par exchanged for (0.5) share Common no par or $18 cash
Note: Option to receive cash expired 06/13/1980
Alco Standard Corp. name changed to IKON Office Solutions, Inc. 01/24/1997
(See IKON Office Solutions, Inc.)

BIG EDDY TELEPHONE CO. (NY)
5.5% Preferred $50 par called for redemption 01/01/1972
Merged into Continental Telephone Corp. 01/02/1973
Each share Common $5 par exchanged for (2) shares Common $1 par
Continental Telephone Corp. name changed to Continental Telecom Inc. 05/06/1982 which name changed to Contel Corp. 05/01/1986 which merged into GTE Corp. 03/14/1991 which merged into Verizon Communications Inc. 06/30/2000

BIG 8 SPLIT INC (ON)
Preferred Shares called for redemption at $25 on 12/15/2008
Stock Dividend - In Capital Shares to holders of Capital Shares 60% payable 12/15/2009 to holders of record 12/15/2009
Class B Preferred Shares Ser. 1 no par called for redemption at $12 plus $0.21 accrued dividends on 12/13/2013
Class C Preferred Shares Ser. 1 no par called for redemption at $12 plus $0.1725 accrued dividends on 12/13/2013
Capital Shares no par called for redemption at $27.0359 plus $0.1275 accrued dividends on 12/13/2013
(Additional Information in Active)

BIG ENTMT INC (FL)
Name changed to Hollywood.com Inc. 12/23/1999
Hollywood.com Inc. name changed to Hollywood Media Corp. 12/18/2000 which name changed to NovelStem International Corp. 09/26/2018

BIG EQUIP SVCS INC (NV)
Recapitalized as Epic Financial Corp. 02/25/2003
Each share Common $0.001 par exchanged for (0.05) share Common $0.001 par
(See Epic Financial Corp.)

BIG FIVE CAP CORP (AB)
Reorganized under the laws of Ontario as Lorne Park Capital Partners Inc. 11/07/2013
Each share Common no par exchanged for (0.5) share Common no par

BIG FLOWER HLDGS INC (DE)
Merged into BFH Merger Corp. 12/07/1999
Each share Common 1¢ par exchanged for $31.50 cash

BIG FLOWER PRESS HLDGS INC (DE)
Name changed to Big Flower Holdings Inc. 10/17/1997
(See Big Flower Holdings Inc.)

BIG FOOT FINL CORP (IL)
Merged into Midwest Banc Holdings, Inc. 01/06/2003
Each share Common 1¢ par exchanged for (1.104) shares Common 1¢ par
(See Midwest Banc Holdings, Inc.)

BIG 4 CONSOLIDATED OIL CO., INC. (NM)
Charter forfeited for failure to file reports 09/29/1932

BIG FOUR MNG & DEV CO (UT)
Completely liquidated and dissolved 12/15/1998
Each share Common no par exchanged for first and final distribution of $0.23 cash

BIG 4 RANCH INC (DE)
Company advised it has no assets and is insolvent 12/04/2002
No stockholders' equity

BIG FOUR SILVER MINES LTD. (BC)
Acquired by Cassiar Consolidated Mines, Ltd. 00/00/1952
Each share Capital Stock 50¢ par exchanged for (0.22222222) share Capital Stock 50¢ par
Cassiar Consolidated Mines, Ltd. recapitalized as Pacific Cassiar Mines Ltd. 10/22/1976 which name changed to Pacific Cassiar Ltd. 11/20/1978
(See Pacific Cassiar Ltd.)

BIG GAME MINES, LTD. (ON)
Merged into Consolidated Frederick Mines Ltd. on a (4) for (11) basis 09/09/1957
(See Consolidated Frederick Mines Ltd.)

BIG GLEN MINES LTD. (ON)
Charter cancelled for default in filing reports 07/09/1969

BIG HAMMER GROUP INC (ON)
Delisted from Canadian Dealer Network 10/13/2000

BIG HERB LAKE MINING & EXPLORATION LTD. (ON)
Charter cancelled and declared dissolved for failure to file returns and pay fees 03/16/1976

BIG HILL MNG CO (UT)
Merged into North Lily Mining Co. 12/01/1976
Each share Capital Stock 10¢ par exchanged for (0.0214) share Capital Stock 10¢ par
(See North Lily Mining Co.)

BIG HORN CORP (UT)
Proclaimed dissolved for failure to pay taxes 12/31/1976

BIG HORN MINING CORP. (UT)
Name changed to Big Horn Corp. 02/09/1971
(See Big Horn Corp.)

BIG HORN MT. GOLD & URANIUM CO. (CO)
Charter revoked for failure to file reports and pay fees 10/10/1962

BIG HORN NAT GAS OIL & MNG CORP (UT)
Name changed to Big Horn Mining Corp. 12/14/1968
Big Horn Mining Corp. name changed to Big Horn Corp. 02/09/1971
(See Big Horn Corp.)

BIG HORN NATL LIFE INS CO (WY)
Common $2 par changed to $1 par 11/20/1964
Completely liquidated 06/01/1970
Each share Common $1 par exchanged for first and final liquidating distribution of (1) share Western Resources Corp. Common $1 par
Western Resources Corp. name changed to Western Resources Life Insurance Co. 01/08/1980 which merged into Tidelands Capital Corp. 06/06/1980 which merged into Western Preferred Corp. 03/06/1981
(See Western Preferred Corp.)

BIG HORN OIL INC (UT)
Recapitalized as Nova Technology Corp. 12/30/1986
Each share Common $0.001 par exchanged for (0.05) share Common $0.001 par
(See Nova Technology Corp.)

BIG HORN POWDER RIV CORP (CO)
Each share Capital Stock $1 par exchanged for (10) shares Capital Stock 10¢ par 00/00/1952
Name changed to Plaza Petroleum, Inc. and Capital Stock 10¢ par reclassified as Common 10¢ par 12/28/1972
Plaza Petroleum, Inc. merged into Brock Exploration Corp. 10/01/1973 which merged into Key Production Co., Inc. 03/28/1996 which merged into Cimarex Energy Co. 09/30/2002

BIG HORN RES LTD (CANADA)
Merged into Westlinks Resources Ltd. 08/16/2001
Each share Common no par exchanged for (0.74) share Preferred Ser. I no par and $0.22 cash
Westlinks Resources Ltd. name changed to Enterra Energy Corp. 12/18/2001
(See Enterra Energy Corp.)

BIG HORN URANIUM CORP. (UT)
Name changed to Big Horn Natural Gas, Oil & Mining Corp. 00/00/1958
Big Horn Natural Gas, Oil & Mining Corp. name changed to Big Horn Mining Corp. 12/14/1968 which name changed to Big Horn Corp. 02/09/1971
(See Big Horn Corp.)

BIG I DEVS LTD (BC)
Recapitalized as Nustar Resources Inc. 05/19/1998
Each share Common no par exchanged for (0.2) share Common no par
Nustar Resources Inc. merged into Canstar Resources Inc. 04/07/2005

BIG I MINES LTD (BC)
Struck off register and declared dissolved for failure to file returns 11/05/1993

BIG INDIAN MINES, INC.
Merged into Standard Uranium Corp. 04/30/1955
Each share Common exchanged for (6) shares Common 1¢ par
Standard Uranium Corp. name changed to Standard Metals Corp. 05/19/1960 which name changed to American Holdings, Inc. 11/22/2005
(See American Holdings, Inc.)

BIG INDIAN OIL & GAS CO (WY)
Charter revoked for failure to pay corporate taxes 07/19/1927

BIG INDIAN PETROLEUM CO. (WY)
Charter forfeited for non-payment of taxes 07/19/1927

BIG INDIAN RES INC (UT)
Name changed 04/25/1983
Name changed from Big Indian Uranium Corp. to Big Indian Resources, Inc. 04/25/1983
Involuntarily dissolved 09/01/1987

BIG ISLAND COPPER MINES LTD. (ON)
Liquidated 12/23/1958
Details not available

BIG JACKPOT MINES LTD (ON)
Charter cancelled for failure to pay taxes and file returns 07/00/1973

BIG JOE GOLD MINES LTD. (ON)
Name changed to Big Joe Mines Ltd. 00/00/1955
(See Big Joe Mines Ltd.)

BIG JOE MINES LTD. (ON)
Charter revoked for failure to file reports and pay fees 11/11/1965

BIG LAKE FINL CORP (FL)
Stock Dividends - 2.5% payable 03/01/2000 to holders of record 02/18/2000; 2.5% payable 04/20/2001 to holders of record 02/18/2000; 2.5% payable 04/20/2001 to holders of record 02/28/2001 Ex date - 05/02/2001; 2.5% payable 04/02/2002 to holders of record 02/28/2005 Ex date - 05/02/2002; 2.5% payable 04/01/2003 to holders of record 02/28/2003 Ex date - 04/28/2003; 2.5% payable 04/01/2004 to holders of record 02/27/2004 Ex date - 03/11/2004
Each share Common 1¢ par held by holders of (199) or fewer shares exchanged for (1) share Ser. A Preferred 03/16/2005
Merged into Seacoast Banking Corp. of Florida 04/03/2006
Each share Ser. A Preferred $1 par exchanged for (2.95427) shares Common 10¢ par
Each share Common 1¢ par exchanged for (2.95427) shares Common 10¢ par

BIG LONG LAC GOLD MNG LTD (ON)
Recapitalized as Commstar Ltd. 12/08/1988
Each share Capital Stock no par exchanged for (0.1) share Common no par
(See Commstar Ltd.)

BIG M RES LTD (BC)
Name changed 08/17/1990
Name changed from Big M Petroleum Inc. to Big M Resources Ltd. 08/17/1990
Recapitalized as Nickelodeon Minerals Inc. 07/17/1992
Each share Common no par exchanged for (0.33333333) share Common no par
Nikelodeon Minerals Inc. name changed to Strongbow Resources Inc. (BC) 08/18/2000 which reorganized in Canada as Strongbow Exploration Inc. 05/03/2004

BIG MARSH OIL CO. (WV)
Merged into Columbia Natural Resources, Inc. 09/16/1988
Details not available

BIG MERGERS INC (NV)
Name changed to Self Insurers Services & Underwriters, Inc. 01/11/1988
(See Self Insurers Services & Underwriters, Inc.)

BIG MESA URANIUM, INC. (UT)
Merged into Graytex Oil & Chemical Co. Inc. 11/28/1955
Each share Common exchanged for (0.00666666) share Common
(See Graytex Oil & Chemical Co., Inc.)

BIG MISSOURI MINES CORP. (QC)
Charter annulled for failure to file annual reports 07/22/1972

BIG MISSOURI MINING CO.
Reorganized as Big Missouri Mines Corp. 00/00/1933
Each share Common exchanged for (0.5) share Common
(See Big Missouri Mines Corp.)

BIG MOJO CAP INC (BC)
Name changed to CapGain Properties Inc. (BC) 01/09/2013
CapGain Properties Inc. (BC) reincorporated in Alberta 03/27/2013

BIG NAMA CREEK MINES LTD (ON)
Recapitalized as York Consolidated Exploration Ltd. 07/29/1977
Each share Capital Stock $1 par exchanged for (0.5) share Capital Stock no par
York Consolidated Exploration Ltd. name changed to Amco Industrial Holdings Ltd. 09/09/1983 which recapitalized as International Amco Corp. (ON) 11/04/1985 which reorganized in England & Wales as Amco Corp. PLC 11/10/1989 which name changed to Billington Holdings Plc 03/31/2009

BIG NELL MINES LTD (QC)
Recapitalized as EP 2000 Conservation Inc. 12/18/1997
Each share Common no par exchanged for (0.33333333) share Common no par
(See EP 2000 Conservation Inc.)

BIG NET HLDGS INC (DE)
Chapter 7 bankruptcy proceedings terminated 05/13/2008
No stockholders' equity

BIG NET INC (MI)
Reincorporated under the laws of Delaware as Big Net Holdings, Inc. 03/22/1999
(See Big Net Holdings, Inc.)

BIG NORTH CAP INC (BC)
Name changed to Big North Graphite Corp. 04/09/2012
Big North Graphite Corp. name changed to CobalTech Mining Inc. 11/24/2016 which merged into First Cobalt Corp. (BC) 12/04/2017 which reincorporated in Canada 09/04/2018

BIG NORTH GRAPHITE CORP (BC)
Each share old Common no par exchanged for (0.1) share new Common no par 05/01/2015
Name changed to CobalTech Mining Inc. 11/24/2016
CobalTech Mining Inc. merged into First Cobalt Corp. (BC) 12/04/2017 which reincorporated in Canada 09/04/2018

BIG O TIRES INC (NV)
Common 2¢ par split (3) for (1) by issuance of (2) additional shares 09/25/1987
Each share Common 2¢ par exchanged for (0.2) share Common 10¢ par 06/15/1992
Merged into TBC Corp. (Old) 07/10/1996
Each share Common 10¢ par exchanged for $16.47 cash

BIG PICTURE MULTIMEDIA INC (AB)
Name changed to Big Picture Technologies Inc. 08/24/1998
(See Big Picture Technologies Inc.)

BIG PICTURE TECHNOLOGIES INC (AB)
Assets sold for the benefit of creditors 06/00/2002
No stockholders' equity

BIG PINEY OIL & GAS CO (UT)
Name changed 03/29/1957
Name changed from Big Piney Oil & Uranium Co. to Big Piney Oil & Gas Co. 03/29/1957
Merged into National Energy Group, Inc. 06/11/1991
Each share Common 5¢ par exchanged for (0.1) share Class A Common 1¢ par
(See National Energy Group, Inc.)

BIG PINEY OIL & REFINING CO. (UT)
Merged into Big Piney Oil & Uranium Co. on a share for share basis 07/01/1955
Big Piney Oil & Uranium Co. name changed to Big Piney Oil & Gas Co. 03/29/1957 which merged into National Energy Group, Inc. 06/11/1991
(See National Energy Group, Inc.)

BIG PONY GOLD INC (UT)
Each share old Common $0.001 par

exchanged for (0.33333333) share new Common $0.001 par 03/01/1996
Name changed to Pan American Motorsports Inc. 04/29/1998
Pan American Motorsports Inc. name changed to Queench Inc. 11/07/2002

BIG RED DIAMOND CORP (CANADA)
Name changed to Northcore Resources Inc. 07/28/2011

BIG RED GOLD INC (UT)
Proclaimed dissolved for failure to pay taxes 03/01/1990

BIG ROCK BREWERY INCOME TR (AB)
Reorganized as Big Rock Brewery Inc. 01/07/2011
Each Trust Unit exchanged for (1) share Common no par
Note: Unexchanged certificates were cancelled and became without value 01/07/2014

BIG ROCK BREWERY LTD (AB)
Recapitalized as Big Rock Brewery Income Trust 01/10/2003
Each share Common no par exchanged for (1) Trust Unit
Big Rock Brewery Income Trust reorganized as Big Rock Brewery Inc. 01/07/2011

BIG ROCK GOLD LTD (BC)
Reorganized as International Cruiseshipcenters Corp. 04/04/1988
Each share Common no par exchanged for (1) share Common no par
International Cruiseshipcenters Corp. recapitalized as Riley Resources Ltd. 06/24/1991 which recapitalized as International Riley Resources Ltd. 01/23/1998 which recapitalized as Wind River Resources Ltd. 11/22/2001 which recapitalized as Teslin River Resources Corp. 01/03/2008 which recapitalized as Siyata Mobile Inc. 07/29/2015

BIG ROCK LABS INC (BC)
Recapitalized as Blox Labs Inc. 11/21/2017
Each share Common no par exchanged for (0.5) share Common no par

BIG ROCK OIL & GAS INC (NY)
Name changed to Resort Resource Group, Inc. 10/03/1986
Resort Resource Group, Inc. name changed to Asia American Industries, Inc. 03/20/1990
(See Asia American Industries, Inc.)

BIG SALMON URANIUM, INC. (ID)
Dissolved 00/00/1957
Details not available

BIG SANDY CO. (ME)
Common $100 par changed to $1 par 00/00/1938
Reorganized under the laws of Massachusetts as Big Sandy Co., Inc. 12/31/1967
Each share Common $1 par exchanged for (10) shares Common $1 par
Big Sandy Co., Inc. (MA) reorganized in Delaware as Big Sandy Co., Inc. L.P. 07/16/1984

BIG SANDY GOLD MINES LTD. (ON)
Charter cancelled 01/04/1960

BIG SANDY HLDG CO (CO)
Filed a petition under Chapter 11 Federal Bankruptcy Code 09/27/2012
Stockholders' equity unlikely

BIG SANDY INC (MA)
Reorganized under the laws of Delaware as Big Sandy Co., L.P. 07/16/1984
Each share Common $1 par exchanged for (1) Unit of Ltd. Partnership

BIG SAVE FURNITURE INC (MN)
Name changed to Sklar's Inc. 04/08/1977
(See Sklar's Inc.)

BIG SKY BANCORP INC (DE)
Merged into Sterling Financial Corp. 11/13/1998
Each share Common 1¢ par exchanged for (1.384) shares Common $5 par
(See Sterling Financial Corp.)

BIG SKY CTRY APPAREL INC (MT)
Name changed to Big Sky USA Inc. (MT) 07/31/1988
Big Sky USA Inc. (MT) reincorporated in Washington 12/17/1991 which name changed to Organik Technologies, Inc. 12/01/1993 which recapitalized as Telemax Global Communications, Inc. 02/08/2002 which name changed to ICBS, Ltd. 06/01/2006

BIG SKY ENERGY CORP (NV)
SEC revoked common stock registration 03/10/2010

BIG SKY SAPPHIRE INC (UT)
Proclaimed dissolved for failure to pay taxes 06/01/1992

BIG SKY TRANSN CO (MT)
Class A Common 10¢ par reclassified as Common 10¢ par 02/06/1984
Plan of recapitalization effective 08/23/1996
Each share Common 10¢ par exchanged for (0.00333333) share Common no par plus (59) additional shares for each full share held
Note: Holders of (299) or fewer shares received $0.21875 cash per share
Merged into Mesaba Holdings, Inc. 12/03/2002
Each share Common no par exchanged for $2.60 cash

BIG SKY USA INC (WA)
Reincorporated 12/17/1991
Common 5¢ par split (11) for (10) by issuance of (0.1) additional share 07/31/1988
State of incorporation changed from (MT) to (WA) 12/17/1991
Name changed to Organik Technologies, Inc. 12/01/1993
Organik Technologies, Inc. recapitalized as Telemax Global Communications, Inc. 02/08/2002 which name changed to ICBS, Ltd. 06/01/2006

BIG SKY WESTN BK (BIG SKY, MT)
Merged into Glacier Bancorp, Inc. (Old) 01/20/1999
Each share Common no par exchanged for (10.917) shares Common $0.0044 par
Glacier Bancorp, Inc. (Old) reorganized as Glacier Bancorp, Inc. (New) (DE) 07/08/1998 which reincorporated in Montana 04/30/2004

BIG SMITH BRANDS INC (DE)
Each share Common 1¢ par exchanged for (0.5) share Common $0.001 par 10/18/1999
Recapitalized as Pacific East Advisors, Inc. 01/12/2007
Each share Common $0.001 par exchanged for (0.01) share Common $0.001 par
Pacific East Advisors, Inc. name changed to Pacific Asia Petroleum, Inc. 06/06/2007 which name changed to CAMAC Energy Inc. 04/07/2010 which recapitalized as Erin Energy Corp. 04/23/2015

BIG SMOKE URANIUM, INC. (WA)
Merged into Spokane National Mines, Inc. 06/02/1958
Each (6.41) shares Common 10¢ par exchanged for (1) share Common $1 par

BIG SPRINGS EXPL INC (TX)
Acquired by MGF Oil Corp. 03/16/1979
Each share Common $1 par exchanged for (0.21165) share Capital Stock $1 par
(See MGF Oil Corp.)

BIG STAR ENERGY INC (BC)
Recapitalized as Arcland Resources Inc. 02/19/2004
Each share Common no par exchanged for (0.16666666) share Common no par

BIG STAR MEDIA GROUP INC (DE)
Each share Common $0.001 par exchanged for (0.0004) share Common $0.025 par 10/18/2010
Name changed to Pharmstar Pharmaceuticals, Inc. (DE) 04/08/2011
Pharmstar Pharmaceuticals, Inc. (DE) reorganized in Nevada as Nexus Energy Services, Inc. 10/15/2013 which name changed to Illegal Restaurant Group, Inc. 06/02/2015 which name changed back to Nexus Energy Services, Inc. 08/13/2015

BIG STEER, INC. (MN)
Name changed to Woody's Inc. 11/17/1972
(See Woody's Inc.)

BIG STICK MEDIA CORP (ON)
Each share old Common no par exchanged for (0.2) share new Common no par 05/19/2009
Acquired by 2242823 Ontario Inc. 07/15/2010
Each share new Common no par exchanged for $0.10 cash

BIG STRIKE RES LTD (BC)
Struck off register and declared dissolved for failure to file returns 03/05/1993

BIG TEX ENTERPRISES (NV)
Name changed to Kanakaris Communications, Inc. 11/26/1997
Kanakaris Communications, Inc. recapitalized as Wi-Fi TV, Inc. 04/20/2004

BIG THREE INDUSTRIAL GAS & EQUIPMENT CO. (TX)
Capital Stock $2.50 par split (5) for (4) by issuance of (0.25) additional share 01/12/1966
Capital Stock $2.50 par split (5) for (4) by issuance of (0.25) additional share 02/09/1967
Name changed to Big Three Industries Inc. 04/06/1970
(See Big Three Industries Inc.)

BIG THREE INDS INC (TX)
Capital Stock $2.50 par split (5) for (4) by issuance of (0.25) additional share 06/24/1971
Capital Stock $2.50 par split (3) for (2) by issuance of (0.5) additional share 02/15/1975
Capital Stock $2.50 par split (2) for (1) by issuance of (1) additional share 07/30/1976
Capital Stock $2.50 par split (2) for (1) by issuance of (1) additional share 03/16/1981
Merged into American Air Liquide, Inc. 02/25/1987
Each share Capital Stock $2.50 par exchanged for $29 cash

BIG THREE RESTAURANTS INC (FL)
Recapitalized as Sports Venues of Florida, Inc. 05/19/2014
Each share Common 1¢ par exchanged for (0.0002) share Common 1¢ par

BIG THREE WELDING EQUIPMENT CO. (TX)
Recapitalized as Big Three Industrial Gas & Equipment Co. 11/06/1964
Each share Capital Stock $5 par exchanged for (2) shares Capital Stock $2.50 par

Big Three Industrial Gas & Equipment Co. name changed to Big Three Industries Inc. 04/06/1970
(See Big Three Industries Inc.)

BIG TURTLE INC (ID)
Name changed 02/26/1986
Name changed from Big Turtle Mines, Inc. to Big Turtle, Inc. 02/26/1986
Charter forfeited 12/02/1996

BIG V SUPERMARKETS INC (NY)
Common 10¢ par split (2) for (1) by issuance of (1) additional share 02/01/1979
Common 10¢ par split (3) for (2) by issuance of (0.5) additional share 11/16/1982
Common 10¢ par reclassified as Class A 10¢ par 04/03/1986
Stock Dividends - 10% 05/27/1977; 10% 02/15/1978; 20% 02/26/1981; 20% 11/11/1983
Acquired by BV Holdings Corp. 10/30/1987
Each share Class A Stock 10¢ par exchanged for $21 cash
Each share Class B Stock 10¢ par exchanged for $21 cash

BIG VALLEY EXPLORATIONS LTD. (BC)
Name changed to Explorer Petroleum Corp. and Common $1 par changed to no par 01/14/1981
Explorer Petroleum Corp. recapitalized as Consolidated Explorer Petroleum Corp. 01/10/1986 which name changed to PEC Energy Corp. (BC) 07/14/1989 which reorganized in Delaware as Perennial Energy, Inc. 10/18/1991

BIG VALLEY MINING CO. LTD.
Dissolved 00/00/1948
Details not available

BIG VALLEY PETROLEUMS LTD. (BC)
Recapitalized as Big Valley Explorations Ltd. 07/11/1972
Each share Common $1 par exchanged for (0.5) share Common $1 par
Big Valley Explorations Ltd. name changed to Explorer Petroleum Corp. 01/14/1981 which recapitalized as Consolidated Explorer Petroleum Corp. 01/10/1986 which name changed to PEC Energy Corp. 07/14/1989 which reorganized in Delaware as Perennial Energy, Inc. 10/18/1991

BIG VALLEY RES INC (BC)
Recapitalized as Consolidated Big Valley Resources Inc. 09/09/2003
Each share Common no par exchanged for (0.1) share Common no par
Consolidated Big Valley Resources Inc. name changed to Gold Bullion Development Corp. 01/31/2007 which name changed to Granada Gold Mine Inc. 01/16/2017

BIG WEDGE MINING CO., INC.
Merged into Atok-Big Wedge Mining Co., Inc. 00/00/1948
Details not available

BIG WIND CAP INC (BC)
Name changed to Hilltop Cybersecurity Inc. 02/26/2018

BIGBAND NETWORKS INC (DE)
Acquired by ARRIS Group, Inc. 11/21/2011
Each share Common $0.001 par exchanged for $2.24 cash

BIGBREWS HLDGS INC (DE)
Common $0.001 par split (10) for (1) by issuance of (9) additional shares payable 02/18/2003 to holders of record 02/14/2003
Reorganized under the laws of Nevada as Patriot Energy Corp. 09/09/2003
Each share Common $0.001 par

exchanged for (0.1) share Common $0.001 par
Patriot Energy Corp. name changed to Healing Hand Network International, Inc. 12/22/2003 which name changed to Patriot Energy Corp. (NV) 10/10/2005

BIGELOW CO. (CT)
Completely liquidated 04/29/1963
Details not available

BIGELOW-HARTFORD CARPET CO. (MA)
Name changed to Bigelow-Sanford Carpet Co., Inc. (MA) 00/00/1929
Bigelow-Sanford Carpet Co., Inc. (MA) reorganized under the laws of Delaware 00/00/1951 which name changed to Bigelow-Sanford, Inc. 05/04/1960
(See Bigelow-Sanford, Inc.)

BIGELOW-SANFORD, INC. (DE)
4.5% Preferred $100 par called for redemption 12/01/1963
Common $5 par split (5) for (4) by issuance of (0.25) additional share 12/04/1964
Common $5 par split (2) for (1) by issuance of (1) additional share 05/24/1966
Merged into Sperry & Hutchinson Co. 10/31/1968
Each share Common $5 par exchanged for $27 cash

BIGELOW-SANFORD CARPET CO., INC. (DE)
Name changed to Bigelow-Sanford, Inc. 05/04/1960
(See Bigelow-Sanford, Inc.)

BIGELOW-SANFORD CARPET CO., INC. (MA)
Reorganized under the laws of Delaware 00/00/1951
Each share 6% Preferred $100 par exchanged for (1.5) shares 4.5% Preferred $100 par
Each share Common no par exchanged for (1.5) shares Common $5 par
Bigelow-Sanford Carpet Co., (DE) name changed to Bigelow-Sanford, Inc. 05/04/1960
(See Bigelow-Sanford, Inc.)

BIGGER MERGERS INC (NV)
Name changed to Modern Chemical Technology Inc. 02/02/1988

BIGHART OIL & GAS LTD (AB)
Merged into Westar Petroleum Ltd. 10/01/1982
Each share Common no par exchanged for $15 cash

BIGHORN DEV CORP (BC)
Struck off register and declared dissolved for failure to file returns 12/16/1994

BIGHORN PETE LTD (BC)
Recapitalized as Sunset Pacific Petroleum Ltd. 05/07/2009
Each share Common no par exchanged for (0.1) share Common no par

BIGHUB COM INC (FL)
SEC revoked common stock registration 11/14/2011

BIGI INC (FL)
Reorganized as View Systems, Inc. (FL) 09/30/1998
Each share Common $0.001 par exchanged for (2) shares Common $0.001 par
View Systems, Inc. (FL) reincorporated in Nevada 07/31/2003

BIGMAR INC (DE)
SEC revoked common stock registration 12/01/2004

BIGSKY PRODUCTIONS INC (NV)
Name changed to Autris 01/14/2014

BIGSKY RES CORP (YT)
Recapitalized as International BigSky Resources Corp. 09/18/2000
Each share Common no par exchanged for (0.125) share Common no par
(See International BigSky Resources Corp.)

BIGSTAR ENTMT INC (DE)
Recapitalized as USA Synthetic Fuel Corp. 02/23/2010
Each share Common $0.001 par exchanged for (0.02) share Common $0.001 par

BIGSTONE MINERALS LTD (BC)
Recapitalized as Adamas Resources Corp. 08/30/1993
Each share Common no par exchanged for (0.2) share Common no par
Adamas Resources Corp. recapitalized as Britannica Resources Corp. 08/27/2002 which name changed to Trinity Valley Energy Corp. 10/08/2013 which recapitalized as Smooth Rock Ventures Corp. 11/15/2017

BIGSTRING CORP (DE)
Company terminated common stock registration and is no longer public as of 08/14/2012

BIGWAY INC (NV)
Name changed to Miracom Industries, Inc. 05/10/1999
Miracom Industries, Inc. recapitalized as Axesstel Inc. 09/16/2002

BIGWEST ENVIRONMENTAL INC (NV)
Name changed to BookMerge Technology, Inc. 02/22/2010
BookMerge Technology, Inc. name changed to Extreme Biodiesel, Inc. 02/12/2013

BIH CORP (NV)
Common $0.001 par split (2) for (1) by issuance of (1) additional share payable 01/29/2009 to holders of record 01/21/2009 Ex date - 01/30/2009
Charter revoked for failure to file reports and pay taxes 05/31/2011

BIHAR TUBES LTD (INDIA)
Name changed to APL Apollo Tubes Ltd. 09/17/2010

BII ENTERPRISES INC (ON)
Name changed to OSF Inc. (ON) 09/02/1993
(See OSF Inc. (ON))

BIJENKORF BEHEER N V (NETHERLANDS)
Name changed to Koninklijke Bijenkorf Beheer KBB N.V. 09/03/1971
(See Koninklijke Bijenkorf Beheer KBB N.V.)

BIJOU RESOURCE CORP (ON)
Recapitalized 08/27/1985
Recapitalized from Bijou Mines & Oils Ltd. to Bijou Resource Corp. 08/27/1985
Each share Common no par exchanged for (0.25) share new Common no par
Recapitalized as Kingscross Communities Inc. 09/11/1998
Each share new Common no par exchanged for (0.2) share Common no par
(See Kingscross Communities Inc.)

BIKERS DREAM INC (CA)
Each share old Common no par exchanged for (0.2) share new Common no par 02/05/1994
Name changed to Ultra Motorcycle Co. (CA) 01/17/2001
Ultra Motorcycle Co. (CA) reincorporated in Delaware as New Dover Capital Corp. 08/02/2007
(See Ultra Motorcycle Co.)

BIKESTAR INC (AB)
Recapitalized as Adventurx.Com, Inc. 08/23/1999
Each share Common no par exchanged for (0.2) share Common no par
Adventurx.Com, Inc. name changed to Nettron.Com, Inc. 09/28/1999 which recapitalized as Valcent Products Inc. 05/03/2005 which name changed to Alterrus Systems Inc. 06/12/2012

BIKINI TEAM INTL INC (UT)
Name changed to Logistical Support, Inc. 06/02/2004

BIL INTL LTD (NEW ZEALAND)
Name changed to GuocoLeisure Ltd. (New Zealand) 11/13/2007
GuocoLeisure Ltd. (New Zealand) reincorporated in Bermuda as GL Ltd. 11/18/2015

BILBO ENERGY INC (ID)
Name changed to Hydrocarbon Technologies Corp. 12/05/1983
(See Hydrocarbon Technologies Corp.)

BILDNER J & SONS INC (DE)
Plan of reorganization under Chapter 11 Federal Bankruptcy proceedings confirmed 08/29/1989
Each share Common 1¢ par exchanged for $0.03 cash

BILFINGER BERGER SE (GERMANY)
Name changed 11/04/2010
Name changed from Bilfinger Berger AG to Bilfinger Berger S.E. 11/04/2010
Name changed to Bilfinger S.E. 10/05/2012

BILL THE BUTCHER INC (NV)
Common $0.001 par split (3.8) for (1) by issuance of (2.8) additional shares payable 06/04/2010 to holders of record 06/04/2010
SEC revoked common stock registration 01/30/2017

BILLABONG INTL LTD (AUSTRALIA)
Each old ADR for Ordinary exchanged for (0.2) new ADR for Ordinary 12/01/2015
ADR agreement terminated 05/04/2018
Each new ADR for Ordinary issued by Bank of New York exchanged for $1.53802 cash

BILLBOARDS, INC. (FL)
Name changed back to Photovoltaics, Inc. 06/03/1985
Photovoltaics, Inc. name changed to Tri-Texas, Inc. 03/17/1986 which name changed to Enviromint International Inc. 06/30/1992
(See Enviromint International Inc.)

BILLERUD AB (SWEDEN)
Name changed to BillerudKorsnas AB 12/15/2014

BILLIARD CHANNEL INC (DE)
Charter cancelled and declared inoperative and void for non-payment of taxes 03/01/2001

BILLIKIN RES INC (BC)
Recapitalized as Cora Resources Ltd. 03/28/1991
Each share Common no par exchanged for (0.25) share Common no par
Cora Resources Ltd. recapitalized as Boss Gold Corp. 11/19/2003 which recapitalized as Boss Gold International Corp. 07/11/2005 which name changed to Boss Power Corp. 06/15/2007 which name changed to Eros Resources Corp. 07/29/2015

BILLING CONCEPTS CORP (DE)
Name changed 02/27/1998
Common 1¢ par split (2) for (1) by issuance of (1) additional share payable 01/30/1998 to holders of record 01/20/1998
Name changed from Billing Information Concepts Corp. to Billing Concepts Corp. 02/27/1998
Name changed to New Century Equity Holdings Corp. 02/12/2001
New Century Equity Holdings Corp. name changed to Wilhelmina International, Inc. 02/19/2009

BILLINGS & SPENCER CO. (CT)
Name changed to B & S Co. 10/09/1962
(See B & S Co.)

BILLINGS CORP (UT)
Name changed to Hydrogen Energy Corp. 08/21/1985
(See Hydrogen Energy Corp.)

BILLINGS ENERGY CORP. (UT)
Name changed to Billings Corp. 08/04/1981
Billings Corp. name changed to Hydrogen Energy Corp. 08/21/1985
(See Hydrogen Energy Corp.)

BILLINGS ENERGY RESEARCH CORP. (UT)
Name changed to Billings Energy Corp. 06/10/1976
Billings Energy Corp. name changed to Billings Corp. 08/04/1981 which name changed to Hydrogen Energy Corp. 08/21/1985
(See Hydrogen Energy Corp.)

BILLINGTON THERMAL SONIC ENERGY CTL CORP (NV)
Charter revoked for failure to file reports and pay fees 08/01/2002

BILLITON PLC (UNITED KINGDOM)
Name changed to BHP Billiton PLC 07/29/2001

BILLMYPARENTS INC (CO)
Name changed to SpendSmart Payments Co. (CO) 02/28/2013
SpendSmart Payments Co. (CO) reincorporated in Delaware as SpendSmart Networks, Inc. 06/20/2014

BILLSERV INC (NV)
Name changed 05/24/2001
Name changed from Billserv.com, Inc. to Billserv, Inc. 05/24/2001
Name changed to Payment Data Systems, Inc. 08/06/2003

BILLUPS EASTERN PETROLEUM CO. (DE)
Completely liquidated 10/01/1965
Each share Common $1 par exchanged for (0.25) share Hess Oil & Chemical Corp. Common 50¢ par
Hess Oil & Chemical Corp. merged into Amerada Hess Corp. 06/20/1969 which name changed to Hess Corp. 05/03/2006

BILLUPS WESTN PETE CO (DE)
Merged into Charter Co. 09/07/1971
Each share Common $1 par exchanged for (0.33333333) share $1.75 Conv. Ser. E Conv. Preferred $1 par
(See Charter Co.)

BILLY BLUES FOOD CORP (TX)
Name changed to Watermarc Food Management Co. 03/28/1995
(See Watermarc Food Management Co.)

BILLY GOAT CREEK MINES LTD (BC)
Recapitalized as Circle Builders Corp. 06/21/1976
Each share Common 50¢ par exchanged for (0.25) share Common no par
Circle Builders Corp. name changed to Miromit Solar Corp. 09/09/1977
(See Miromit Solar Corp.)

BILLY MARTINS USA INC (DE)
Each share old Common $0.0001 par exchanged for (0.02) share new Common $0.0001 par 07/19/2002
Each share new Common $0.0001 par exchanged again for (12) shares

new Common $0.0001 par 06/09/2004
Name changed to Real American Brands, Inc. 01/14/2008
Real American Brands, Inc. recapitalized as Real American Capital Corp. 06/17/2011

BILLY THE KID INC (DE)
Common 10¢ par split (5) for (4) by issuance of (0.25) additional share 03/26/1976
Stock Dividends - 20% 04/01/1977; 10% 01/02/1980; 10% 11/26/1980; 10% 11/04/1981
Name changed to BTK Industries, Inc. 03/01/1982
(See BTK Industries, Inc.)

BILLYWEB CORP (FL)
Each share old Common $0.0001 par exchanged for (0.1) share new Common $0.0001 par 04/02/2001
Each share new Common $0.0001 par exchanged again for (0.1) share new Common $0.0001 par 05/10/2002
Name changed to Poseidis, Inc. 08/28/2002
(See Poseidis, Inc.)

BILOXI YELLOWKNIFE MINES LTD. (ON)
Charter revoked for failure to file reports and pay taxes 00/00/1954

BILTMORE BK CORP (AZ)
Each share old Common no par exchanged for (0.008) share new Common no par 12/19/1996
Note: In effect holders received $1 cash per share and public interest was eliminated

BILTMORE INDS LTD (CANADA)
Name changed 10/30/1973
Each share Common no par exchanged for (0.5) share $1 Class A Preferred no par and (0.5) share Common no par 00/00/1946
Recapitalized 06/12/1972
Each share $1 Class A Preferred no par exchanged for (4) shares Class A Conv. Preferred no par and (1) share Class B Non-Cum. Preferred no par
Each share old Common no par exchanged for (4) shares new Common no par and (1) share Class B Non-Cum. Preferred no par
Name changed from Biltmore Hats Ltd. to Biltmore Industries Ltd. and Class B Preferred no par reclassified as new Common no par 10/30/1973
Assets sold 06/00/1982
No stockholders' equity

BILTMORE VACATION RESORTS INC (NV)
Each share old Common $0.001 par exchanged for (0.1) share new Common $0.001 par 12/07/1999
Recapitalized as AbsoluteSKY Inc. 04/05/2006
Each share new Common $0.001 par exchanged for (0.001) share Common $0.001 par
(See AbsoluteSKY Inc.)

BILTRITE CORP (DE)
Merged into Chelsea Merger Co. 04/29/1985
Each share Common 1¢ par exchanged for $6.75 cash

BILTRITE NIGHTINGALE INC (QC)
Merged into Canam Manac Group Inc. 09/30/1988
Each share Common no par exchanged for (0.5) share Class A Subordinate no par and $1 cash
Canam Manac Group Inc. name changed to Canam Group Inc. 01/01/2005

BIM BIRLESIK MAGAZALAR A S JT STK CO (TURKEY)
Reg. S GDR's for Ordinary split (3) for (1) by issuance of (2) additional GDR's payable 07/01/2008 to holders of record 06/30/2008
Reg. S GDR's for Ordinary split (2) for (1) by issuance of (1) additional GDR payable 06/10/2010 to holders of record 05/28/2010
144A GDR's for Ordinary split (2) for (1) by issuance of (1) additional GDR payable 06/10/2010 to holders of record 05/28/2010 Ex date - 06/11/2010
Reg. S GDR's for Ordinary split (2) for (1) by issuance of (1) additional GDR payable 07/02/2013 to holders of record 07/01/2013
144A GDR's for Ordinary split (2) for (1) by issuance of (1) additional GDR payable 07/02/2013 to holders of record 07/01/2013
GDR agreement terminated 12/15/2014
Each Reg. S GDR for Ordinary exchanged for $21.2443 cash
Each 144A GDR for Ordinary exchanged for $21.2443 cash

BIM HOMES INC (DE)
Under plan of reorganization each share Common $0.0001 par automatically became (1) Armada Enterprises, L.P. Ltd. Partnership Unit 12/27/2017

BIMA ENTMT LTD (DE)
Each share Common $0.00001 par exchanged for (0.02) share $0.0005 par 01/31/1989
Charter cancelled and declared inoperative and void for non-payment of taxes 03/01/1991

BIMAR CORP. (MA)
Liquidation completed
Each share Capital Stock $5 par stamped to indicate initial distribution of $20 cash 06/16/1966
Each share Stamped Capital Stock $5 par stamped to indicate second distribution of $20 cash 12/30/1966
Each share Stamped Capital Stock $5 par exchanged for third and final distribution of $0.51 cash 05/22/1967

BIMINI MTG MGMT INC (MD)
Name changed to Opteum, Inc. 02/10/2006
Opteum, Inc. name changed to Bimini Capital Management, Inc. 09/28/2007

BIMS RENEWABLE ENERGY INC (FL)
Recapitalized as Tung Ding Resources, Inc. 04/18/2007
Each share Common $0.001 par exchanged for (0.00666666) share Common $0.001 par
(See Tung Ding Resources, Inc.)

BIN-DICATOR CO. (MI)
Name changed to BID, Inc. 12/16/1968
(See BID, Inc.)

BINARY SYS INC (NY)
Reorganized under Chapter 11 Bankruptcy Code 01/26/1982
New Common 1¢ par issued to Debentureholders only
Old Common 1¢ par declared valueless
Name changed to Hemocare, Inc. 04/24/1986
Hemocare, Inc. name changed to Mediware Information Systems, Inc. 05/00/1991
(See Mediware Information Systems, Inc.)

BIND THERAPEUTICS INC (DE)
Name changed to DNIB Unwind, Inc. 08/31/2016
(See DNIB Unwind, Inc.)

BINDLEY WESTN INDS INC (IN)
Common $1 par split (2) for (1) by issuance of (1) additional share 04/30/1985
Common $1 par split (4) for (3) by issuance of (0.33333333) additional share payable 06/03/1998 to holders of record 05/21/1998 Ex date - 06/04/1998
Each share Common $1 par received distribution of (0.448) share Priority Healthcare Corp. Class B Common 1¢ par payable 12/31/1998 to holders of record 12/15/1998 Ex date - 01/04/1999
Common $1 par split (4) for (3) by issuance of (0.33333333) additional share payable 06/25/1999 to holders of record 06/11/1999 Ex date - 06/28/1999
Merged into Cardinal Health, Inc. 02/14/2001
Each share Common $1 par exchanged for (0.4275) share Common no par

BINDVIEW DEV CORP (TX)
Common no par split (2) for (1) by issuance of (1) additional share payable 02/16/2000 to holders of record 02/09/2000
Merged into Symantec Corp. 01/06/2006
Each share Common no par exchanged for $4 cash

BING & BING, INC. (NY)
Each share Common $5 par exchanged for (4) shares Common $1.25 par 00/00/1948
Each share Common $1.25 par exchanged for (3) shares Common $1 par 00/00/1951
Liquidation declared effective 08/29/1956
Details not available

BINGHAM CANYON CORP (NV)
Name changed to PCT Ltd. 05/22/2018

BINGHAM DEVELOPMENT CO. (UT)
Charter expired 01/01/1998

BINGHAM FINL SVCS CORP (MI)
Completely liquidated 09/29/2005
Each share Common no par exchanged for first and final distribution of $0.0113 cash

BINGHAM-HERBRAND CORP. (OH)
Acquired by Van Norman Industries, Inc. 12/05/1956
Each share Common $1 par exchanged for (0.5) share $2.28 Preferred $5 par
Van Norman Industries, Inc. merged into Universal American Corp. (DE) (Ctfs. dated prior to 01/12/1968) 01/31/1962 which merged into Gulf & Western Industries, Inc. (DE) 01/12/1968
(See Gulf & Western Industries, Inc. (DE))

BINGHAM LIQUIDATING CO. (DE)
Each share Common no par exchanged for initial distribution of $36 cash and non-negotiable receipt 06/25/1965
Assets transferred to Bingham Liquidating Co. Stockholders' Trust 01/31/1966
(See Bingham Liquidating Co. Stockholders' Trust)

BINGHAM LIQUIDATING CO. STOCKHOLDERS' TRUST (DE)
Distribution of income: $0.114 paid 12/28/1966 and $0.096 04/06/1967
Second and final liquidating payment of $3.51165 per share to holders of receipts for Common no par 04/06/1967

BINGHAM MINES CO.
Absorbed by United States Smelting Refining & Mining Co. (Old) 00/00/1929
Details not available

BINGHAM SILVER LEAD CO (UT)
Each share Common 10¢ par exchanged for (0.2) share Common no par 02/23/1972
Charter revoked for failure to file reports and pay fees 05/01/1990

BINGHAM STAMPING CO. (OH)
Name changed to Bingham-Herbrand Corp. 08/21/1947
Bingham-Herbrand Corp. acquired by Van Norman Industries, Inc. 12/05/1956 which merged into Universal American Corp. (DE) (Ctfs. dated prior to 01/12/1968) 01/31/1962 which merged into Gulf & Western Industries, Inc. (DE) 01/12/1968
(See Gulf & Western Industries, Inc. (DE))

BINGHAMTON LIGHT HEAT & POWER CO.
Acquired by New York State Electric & Gas Corp. 00/00/1929
Details not available

BINGHAMTON SVGS BK (BINGHAMTON, NY)
Reorganized under the laws of Delaware as BSB Bancorp, Inc. and Common $1 par changed to 1¢ par 10/03/1988
BSB Bancorp, Inc. merged into Partners Trust Financial Group, Inc. (DE) 07/14/2004 which merged into M&T Bank Corp. 11/30/2007

BINGHAMTON WASHING MACHINE CORP.
Dissolved 00/00/1939
Details not available

BINGO & GAMING INTL INC (DE)
Name changed to BGI Inc. 10/19/1999

BINGO COM INC (FL)
Reincorporated under the laws of British West Indies as Bingo.com Ltd. and Common $0.001 par changed to no par 04/06/2005
Bingo.com Ltd. name changed to Shoal Games Ltd. 01/27/2015

BINGO COM INC (FL)
Reincorporated under the laws of British West Indies as Bingo.com Ltd. 04/06/2005

BINGO COM LTD (BRITISH WEST INDIES)
Name changed to Shoal Games Ltd. 01/27/2015

BINGO GOLD COM INC (NV)
Name changed to Gameweaver.com Inc. 11/26/1999
Gameweaver.com Inc. name changed to Inform Media Group, Inc. 03/15/2002 which name changed to Acquisition Media, Inc. 08/12/2002 which name changed to Actionview International, Inc. 08/20/2003 which recapitalized as AVEW Holdings, Inc. 07/31/2015

BINGO KING INC (DE)
Reincorporated 01/21/1987
State of incorporation changed from (CO) to (DE) 01/21/1987
Name changed to Stuart Entertainment Inc. 07/01/1991
(See Stuart Entertainment Inc.)

BINGO U S A CORP (UT)
Recapitalized as Full Circle, Inc. (UT) 02/15/1989
Each share Common $0.001 par exchanged for (0.2) share Common $0.005 par
Full Circle, Inc. (UT) reorganized in Nevada as Hydro Grow Inc. 12/08/1998 which name changed to Asgard Alliance Corp. 09/22/1999 which name changed to Santa Fe Holding Co., Inc. 06/26/2007
(See Santa Fe Holding Co., Inc.)

BINKS-SAMES CORP (DE)
Name changed 05/19/1997
Each share Class A no par exchanged for (1) share Capital Stock $1 par 00/00/1936
Each share Class B no par exchanged for (0.25) share Capital Stock $1 par 00/00/1936
Capital Stock $1 par split (2) for (1) by issuance of (1) additional share 02/10/1961
Capital Stock $1 par and VTC's for Capital Stock $1 par split (2) for (1) by issuance of (1) additional share respectively 02/28/1966
Voting Trust Agreement expired 12/14/1974
Each old VTC for Capital Stock $1 par exchanged for (1) new VTC for Capital Stock $1 par expiring 12/14/1976 or (1) share Capital Stock $1 par
Stock Dividends - 19% 02/28/1951; 20% 02/28/1964; 10% 02/25/1965; 10% 02/03/1977; 20% 02/23/1978; 10% 02/26/1979; 10% 02/27/1980
Name changed from Binks Manufacturing Co. to Binks Sames Corp. 05/19/1997
Name changed to Sames Corp. 06/01/1999
(See Sames Corp.)

BINNEY & SMITH CO. (NJ)
Merged into Binney & Smith, Inc. 12/31/1953
Details not available

BINNEY & SMITH INC (DE)
Common $2.50 par split (2) for (1) by issuance of (1) additional share 12/08/1972
Common $2.50 par split (5) for (4) by issuance of (0.25) additional share 12/08/1978
Stock Dividend - 25% 06/10/1977
Acquired by Hallmark Cards Inc. 08/10/1984
Each share Common $2.50 par exchanged for $56 cash

BINNINGS INC (NC)
Merged into National Gypsum Co. 05/07/1974
Each share Common $1 par exchanged for (0.23259) share Common 50¢ par
(See National Gypsum Co.)

BINOPTIC INTL CORP (DE)
Reincorporated 03/22/1994
Place of incorporation changed from (AB) to (DE) 03/22/1994
Charter cancelled and declared inoperative and void for non-payment of taxes 11/03/1997

BINSCARTH PVC VENTURES INC (ON)
Name changed to DoveCorp Enterprises Inc. 07/13/2005
(See DoveCorp Enterprises Inc.)

BINSWANGER GLASS CO. (VA)
Acquired by National Gypsum Co. 03/00/1969
Details not available

BIO-AMERICAN CAP CORP (NV)
Each share old Common $0.001 par exchanged for (0.05) share new Common $0.001 par 11/25/1998
Note: No holder of (100) shares or more will receive fewer than (100) post-split shares
Holders of (99) shares or fewer will be rounded up to (100) post-split shares
Each share new Common $0.001 par exchanged again for (0.005) share new Common $0.001 par 02/24/2004
Name changed to Cheetah Oil & Gas Ltd. 05/26/2004

BIO ANALYTIC LABS INC (FL)
Name changed to Eutro Group Holdings, Inc. 09/06/1991
Eutro Group Holdings, Inc. name changed to Strategic Alliance Group Inc. 10/18/1999 which name changed to CruiseCam International, Inc. 07/30/2004

BIO ANGEL I CORP (CANADA)
Recapitalized as Omnitech Consultant Group Inc. 02/03/2005
Each share Common no par exchanged for (0.28571428) share Common no par
(See Omnitech Consultant Group Inc.)

BIO-AQUA SYS INC (FL)
Name changed to New Dragon Asia Corp. 12/11/2001
(See New Dragon Asia Corp.)

BIO BLAST PHARMA LTD (ISRAEL)
Name changed to Bioblast Pharma Ltd. 08/09/2016

BIO CAL INSTR CO (CA)
Merged into Bio-Rad Laboratories (CA) 05/31/1974
Each share Capital Stock no par exchanged for (0.1) share Common no par
Bio-Rad Laboratories (CA) reincorporated in Delaware as Bio-Rad Laboratories Inc. 04/25/1975

BIO-CARBON SOLUTIONS INTL INC (NV)
Name changed to NSU Resources Inc. 12/22/2011
NSU Resources Inc. recapitalized as Hemcare Health Services Inc. 05/05/2015 which recapitalized as DLT Resolution Inc. 12/20/2017

BIO-CHEM TECHNOLOGY INC (FL)
Name changed to Triton Asset Management, Inc. (FL) 09/24/1997
Triton Asset Management, Inc. (FL) reincorporated in Nevada as Triton Acquisition Corp. 12/28/1998 which name changed to Light Management Group, Inc. 05/20/1999

BIO-CLEAN INC (NV)
Name changed to Global NuTech, Inc. 10/08/2010
Global NuTech, Inc. name changed to Texas Gulf Energy, Inc. 03/07/2012

BIO DATA INC (MN)
Statutorily dissolved 06/15/1995

BIO DENTAL TECHNOLOGIES CORP (CO)
Merged into Zila, Inc. 01/08/1997
Each share Common 1¢ par exchanged for (0.825) share Common $0.001 par
(See Zila, Inc.)

BIO DERIVATIVES CORP (NY)
Charter cancelled and proclaimed dissolved for failure to pay taxes and file reports 12/20/1977

BIO DYNAMICS INC (IN)
Common Capital Stock no par split (2) for (1) by issuance of (1) additional share 07/15/1967
Common Capital Stock no par split (3) for (2) by issuance of (0.5) additional share 12/29/1971
Merged into ABM Corp. 05/01/1975
Each share Common Capital Stock no par exchanged for $13.75 cash

BIO-DYNE CORP (GA)
Recapitalized as No Good TV, Inc. 01/26/2005
Each share Common 1¢ par exchanged for (0.002) share Common 1¢ par
No Good TV, Inc. name changed to LB Center, Inc. 05/03/2005 which name changed to Berman Center, Inc. 09/16/2005
(See Berman Center, Inc.)

BIO-ELECTRO SYS INC (DE)
Merged into Alza Corp. 02/07/1992
Each share Class A Common 1¢ par exchanged for (0.5772) share Class A Common 1¢ par
Alza Corp. merged into Johnson & Johnson 06/22/2001

BIO ENERGY INC (UT)
Name changed to Bio-Ten Energy, Inc. 02/24/1982

BIO ENERGY SYS INC (NY)
Name changed to Besicorp Group Inc. 11/19/1982
(See Besicorp Group Inc.)

BIO-EXTRACTION INC (ON)
Name changed to BioExx Specialty Proteins Ltd. 01/04/2010
(See BioExx Specialty Proteins Ltd.)

BIO FEED INDS LTD (BC)
Delisted from Vancouver Stock Exchange 03/04/1991

BIO FLORESCENT TECHNOLOGIES INC (NV)
Each share old Common $0.001 par exchanged for (0.33333333) share new Common $0.001 par 12/02/1996
Each share new Common $0.001 par exchanged again for (0.01) share new Common $0.001 par 03/06/1998
Name changed to Ranes International Holdings Inc. 03/11/1998
Ranes International Holdings Inc. name changed to Whatsforfree Technologies Inc. 01/10/2000 which recapitalized as Krifter Holdings Inc. 04/18/2005
(See Krifter Holdings Inc.)

BIO GAS COLO INC (CO)
Chapter 11 Federal Bankruptcy Code converted to Chapter 7 on 12/30/1988
No stockholders' equity

BIO GENEX LABORATORIES INC (WY)
Each share Common $0.001 par received distribution of (10) shares Restricted Common $0.001 payable 08/19/2009 to holders of record 07/19/2009
Administratively dissolved for failure to pay taxes 04/12/2010

BIO GRAPHICS INC (DE)
Name changed to Original Diet Pizza Co., Inc. 10/07/1988
(See Original Diet Pizza Co., Inc.)

BIO-HELIX INC (NV)
Name changed to Concept Gold Inc. 09/25/1990
Concept Gold Inc. recapitalized as Environmental Plasma Arc Technology Inc. 09/25/1992 which name changed to Earth Products & Technologies Inc. 11/07/1997 which name changed to China Shen Zhou Mining & Resources, Inc. 10/20/2006

BIO IMAGING TECHNOLOGIES INC (DE)
Stock Dividend - 60% 03/27/1992
Name changed to BioClinica, Inc. 07/13/2009
(See BioClinica, Inc.)

BIO ISOLATES HLDGS PLC (ENGLAND)
ADR agreement terminated 00/00/1991
Details not available

BIO-KEY INTL INC (MN)
Reincorporated under the laws of Delaware and Common 1¢ par changed to $0.0001 par 01/01/2005

BIO KINETICS CORP (DE)
Charter cancelled and declared inoperative and void for non-payment of taxes 03/01/1976

BIO-LIFE LABS INC (NV)
Charter permanently revoked 06/29/2012

BIO-LIFE SYS INC (MI)
Recapitalized as Educational Services International Inc. (MI) 11/08/2001
Each share Common 10¢ par exchanged for (0.02857142) share Common 10¢ par
Educational Services International Inc. (MI) reorganized in Wyoming as WindPower Innovations, Inc. 11/18/2009 which name changed to NexGen Holdings Corp. 01/10/2014

BIO LOGIC SYS CORP (DE)
Common 1¢ par split (3) for (2) by issuance of (0.5) additional share 12/11/1985
Common 1¢ par split (3) for (2) by issuance of (0.5) additional share 05/28/1991
Common 1¢ par split (3) for (2) by issuance of (0.5) additional share payable 02/11/2005 to holders of record 01/26/2005 Ex date - 02/14/2005
Stock Dividend - 50% 06/07/1985
Merged into Natus Medical Inc. 01/05/2006
Each share Common 1¢ par exchanged for $8.77 cash

BIO-LOGICS SYSTEMS, INC. (UT)
Merged into Healthgarde Corp. 11/08/1974
Each share Common 5¢ par exchanged for (1) share Common 1¢ par
Healthgarde Corp. name changed to Allscope Resources International, Inc. 04/09/1982
(See Allscope Resources International, Inc.)

BIO MFG INC (MN)
Each share old Common 1¢ par exchanged for (0.22222222) share new Common 1¢ par 03/16/1990
Merged into Bioplasty Inc. 05/29/1992
Each share new Common 1¢ par exchanged for (0.1) share Common 1¢ par
(See BioPlasty Inc.)

BIO-MATRIX SCIENTIFIC GROUP INC OLD (DE)
Each share old Class A Common 50¢ par exchanged for (0.1) share new Class A Common 50¢ par 05/31/2005
Each share Class A Common 50¢ par received distribution of (1) share Frezer, Inc. Common $0.0001 payable 06/15/2005 to holders of record 05/31/2005
Name changed to BMXP Holdings, Inc. 08/28/2006
BMXP Holdings, Inc. recapitalized as Freedom Environmental Services, Inc. 06/11/2008

BIO MECHANICAL SYS CORP (UT)
Each share Common $1 par exchanged for (5) shares Common 20¢ par 04/13/1972
Involuntarily dissolved for failure to maintain a registered agent 09/30/1975

BIO MED INFORMATION SYS INC (UT)
Name changed to DiEnco 05/01/1975
(See DiEnco)

BIO MED LABORATORIES INC (CANADA)
Ceased operations 04/20/2005
Details not available

BIO MED SCIENCES INC (NY)
Common 10¢ par changed to 1¢ par 01/02/1979
Recapitalized as Oak Hill Sportswear Corp. 07/07/1983
Each share Common 1¢ par exchanged for (0.5) share Common 2¢ par
Oak Hill Sportswear Corp. name changed to Rexx Environmental Corp. 02/17/1998 which recapitalized as Newtek Capital Inc.

09/19/2000 which name changed to Newtek Business Services, Inc. (NY) 11/26/2002 which reincorporated in Maryland as Newtek Business Services Corp. 11/13/2014

BIO-MED TECHNOLOGIES INC (WY)
Administratively dissolved 06/17/2009

BIO-MEDICAL AUTOMATION INC (CO)
Name changed to Ridgefield Acquisition Corp. (CO) 01/14/2003
Ridgefield Acquisition Corp. (CO) reincorporated in Nevada 06/23/2006

BIO MEDICUS INC (MN)
Common 5¢ par changed to 1¢ par and (2) additional shares issued 09/15/1972
Merged into Medtronic, Inc. (MN) 09/21/1990
Each share Common 1¢ par exchanged for (0.32258064) share Common 10¢ par
Medtronic, Inc. (MN) reincorporated in Ireland as Medtronic PLC 01/27/2015

BIO METALLICS INC (DE)
Recapitalized as Sparta Surgical Corp. 06/29/1990
Each share Common $0.001 par exchanged for (0.5) share Common $0.002 par
(See Sparta Surgical Corp.)

BIO-MONITOR INC (DE)
Each share old Common $0.001 par exchanged for (0.1) share new Common $0.001 par 03/05/1990
Charter cancelled and declared inoperative and void for non-payment of taxes 03/01/1992

BIO MULTIMIN INC (NV)
Charter revoked 07/31/2014

BIO NITROGEN CORP (NJ)
Name changed to BioNitrogen Holdings Corp. 10/15/2013

BIO-NUCLEAR LABORATORIES INC. (CA)
Charter suspended for failure to file reports and pay fees 01/02/1981

BIO-NUTRIONICS INC (DE)
Charter cancelled and declared inoperative and void for non-payment of taxes 03/01/1989

BIO-ONE CORP (NV)
Charter revoked for failure to file reports and pay fees 02/28/2008

BIO 1 INC (CANADA)
Name changed to Aurelian Resources Inc. 06/02/2003
Aurelian Resources Inc. acquired by Kinross Gold Corp. 10/03/2008

BIO PAPPEL S A B DE C V (MEXICO)
ADR agreement terminated 12/07/2017
Each Sponsored ADR for Ordinary exchanged for (2) shares Ordinary
Note: Unexchanged ADR's will be sold and the proceeds, if any, held for claim after 12/10/2019

BIO-PATH HLDGS INC (UT)
Reincorporated under the laws of Delaware and Common no par changed to $0.001 par 12/31/2014

BIO PHYSICS INTL INC (UT)
Involuntarily dissolved 01/01/1991

BIO-PLEXUS INC (CT)
Reorganized under the laws of Delaware 07/19/2001
Each share Common no par exchanged for (0.1) share Common $0.001 par
(See Bio-Plexus, Inc. (DE))

BIO-PLEXUS INC (DE)
Merged into ICU Medical, Inc. 11/01/2002
Each share Common $0.001 par exchanged for $0.66 cash

BIO-PRESERVE INTL CORP (NV)
Recapitalized as Life Systems Corp. 11/27/2000
Each share Common $0.001 par exchanged for (0.04) share Common $0.001 par
(See Life Systems Corp.)

BIO PURE INC (OR)
Name changed to Howard Corp. of Oregon 08/30/1973 which name changed back to Bio-Pure, Inc. 10/29/1974
Adjudicated bankrupt 08/18/1975
Stockholders' equity unlikely

BIO-QUANT INC (UT)
Each share old Common no par exchanged for (0.00025) share new Common no par 04/27/2009
Acquired by NexMed, Inc. 12/14/2009
Details not available

BIO RAD LABS (CA)
Reincorporated under the laws of Delaware as Bio-Rad Laboratories, Inc. and Common no par changed to $1 par 04/25/1975

BIO RECOVERY TECHNOLOGY INC (NV)
Merged into Electronic Clearing House, Inc. 01/17/1986
Each share Common 2/7¢ par exchanged for (0.5) share Common $0.001 par
(See Electronic Clearing House, Inc.)

BIO-REFERENCE LABS INC (NJ)
Each share Common $0.001 par exchanged for (0.1) share old Common 1¢ par 10/04/1991
Each share old Common 1¢ par exchanged for (0.33333333) share new Common 1¢ par 08/23/1993
New Common 1¢ par split (2) for (1) by issuance of (1) additional share payable 04/21/2010 to holders of record 04/19/2010 Ex date - 04/22/2010
Merged into OPKO Health, Inc. 08/20/2015
Each share new Common 1¢ par exchanged for (2.75) shares Common 1¢ par

BIO RESH LAB INC (UT)
Charter suspended for failure to file annual reports 12/31/1974

BIO RESPONSE INC (DE)
Each share old Common $0.004 par exchanged for (0.03269202) share new Common $0.004 par 04/09/1999
Name changed to Liberty Group Holdings Inc. 11/23/1999

BIO-SAFE NAT TECHNOLOGIES INC (NV)
Name changed to Equal Trading, Inc. 12/08/2004

BIO-SAFE TECHNOLOGIES INC (NV)
Common $0.001 par split (4) for (1) by issuance of (3) additional shares payable 07/07/2000 to holders of record 07/07/2000 Ex date - 07/10/2000
Recapitalized as Nubio Ventures Inc. 08/31/2001
Each share Common $0.001 par exchanged for (0.03333333) share Common $0.001 par
Nubio Ventures Inc. recapitalized as County Line Resources Inc. 03/18/2005 which reorganized as County Line Energy Corp. 05/15/2006

BIO SCIENCE RES INC (NJ)
Charter declared void for non-payment of taxes 06/26/1990

BIO-SHIELD TECHNOLOGY CORP (NV)
Charter permanently revoked 06/29/2007

BIO SOLUTIONS CORP (NV)
Stock Dividend - 20% payable 07/01/2010 to holders of record 06/29/2010 Ex date - 06/25/2010
Each share old Common $0.001 par exchanged for (0.1) share new Common $0.001 par 02/26/2014
Recapitalized as Glucose Health, Inc. 11/17/2014
Each share Common $0.001 par exchanged for (0.02) share Common $0.001 par

BIO-SOLUTIONS INTL INC (NV)
Each share old Common $0.0001 par exchanged for (0.002) share new Common $0.0001 par 08/31/2004
Each share new Common $0.0001 par exchanged again for (0.1) share new Common $0.0001 par 06/14/2005
Name changed to Omnimed International, Inc. 11/23/2005
Omnimed International, Inc. name changed to MedeFile International, Inc. 01/17/2006 which recapitalized as Tech Town Holdings Inc. 11/02/2017 which name changed to Hash Labs Inc. 03/06/2018

BIO SOLUTIONS MFG INC (NV)
Reorganized 11/20/2008
Reorganized from (NY) to under the laws of Nevada 11/20/2008
Each share Common $0.001 par exchanged for (0.001) share Common $0.00001 par
Name changed to Todays Alternative Energy Corp. 06/21/2010

BIO STD CORP (FL)
Each share old Common 1¢ par exchanged for (0.02) share new Common 1¢ par 05/22/2003
Name changed to Nettel Holdings, Inc. 05/23/2003
(See Nettel Holdings, Inc.)

BIO-STUFF (NV)
Common $0.001 par split (18) for (1) by issuance of (17) additional shares payable 12/22/2010 to holders of record 12/21/2010 Ex date - 12/23/2010
Name changed to 5Barz International Inc. 12/29/2010

BIO-SYS LTD (DE)
Reorganized under the laws of Nevada as Equity Systems Ltd. 05/05/1995
Each share Common $0.001 par exchanged for (1) share Common $0.001 par
Equity Systems Ltd. recapitalized as North American Graphics Ltd. 11/25/1996 which name changed to Environmental Technology Systems Inc. 08/18/1997 which recapitalized as Tombao Antiques & Art Group 04/05/2012

BIO-TECH INDS INC (UT)
Involuntarily dissolved for failure to file annual reports 06/01/1998

BIO TECHNOLOGY GEN CORP (DE)
Common 1¢ par split (5) for (4) by issuance of (0.25) additional share 11/29/1993
Name changed to Savient Pharmaceuticals, Inc. 06/23/2003
(See Savient Pharmaceuticals, Inc.)

BIO TEL WESTN INC (UT)
Involuntarily dissolved 03/31/1977

BIO-THRUST INC (UT)
Reorganized under the laws of Nevada as Easy Golf Corp. 04/22/2005
Each share Common $0.001 par exchanged for (0.08333333) share Common $0.001 par
Easy Golf Corp. name changed to China Bio-Immunity Corp. 02/25/2018

BIO-TRACKING SEC INC (FL)
Recapitalized as Nord Oil International Inc. 10/25/2005
Each share Common $0.001 par exchanged for (0.08333333) share Common $0.001 par
Nord Oil International Inc. name changed to North West Oil Group, Inc. 11/16/2006

BIO TRONICS INC (NV)
Name changed to Theratech, Inc. 02/27/1981
(See Theratech, Inc.)

BIO VASCULAR INC (MN)
Each share Common 1¢ par received distribution of (0.5) share Vital Images Inc. Common 1¢ par payable 05/13/1997 to holders of record 05/05/1997
Name changed to Synovis Life Technologies, Inc. 05/01/2002
(See Synovis Life Technologies, Inc.)

BIO VENTURE HLDGS INC (NV)
Reorganized as Midwest Venture Holdings, Inc. 08/16/2002
Each share Common $0.001 par exchanged for (1) share Common $0.001 par
Midwest Venture Holdings, Inc. name changed to Inspiration Products Group, Inc. 02/03/2003 which name changed to MB-Tech, Inc. 05/18/2003
(See MB-Tech, Inc.)

BIO VITA INC (QC)
Charter cancelled for failure to file reports and pay fees 08/00/1977

BIO-WARM CORP (NV)
Recapitalized as DDC Industries, Inc. 04/23/2007
Each share Common $0.001 par exchanged for (0.02) share Common $0.001 par
DDC Industries, Inc. name changed to PHI Mining Group, Inc. 12/19/2008 which name changed to PHI Gold Corp. 01/28/2011

BIOAB STRATEGIES LTD (BC)
Name changed to Invictus MD Strategies Corp. 12/23/2014

BIOACCELERATE HLDGS INC (NV)
Name changed to Gardant Pharmaceuticals, Inc. 04/11/2006
(See Gardant Pharmaceuticals, Inc.)

BIOANALOGICS INC (CA)
Charter suspended for failure to file reports and pay fees 01/02/1991

BIOANALOGICS SYS INC (OR)
Reincorporated 03/13/1992
Reincorporated 11/05/1992
Place of incorporation changed from (BC) to (WY) 03/13/1992
State of incorporation changed from (WY) to (OR) 11/05/1992
Recapitalized as International Bioanalogics Systems, Inc. (OR) 08/16/1993
Each share Common no par exchanged for (0.33333333) share Common no par
International Bioanalogics Systems, Inc. (OR) reincorporated in Canada 09/29/2006 which recapitalized as reWORKS Environmental Corp. 05/11/2007 which name changed to Forterra Environmental Corp. 02/22/2008

BIOASSAY SYS CORP (DE)
Charter cancelled and declared inoperative and void for non-payment of taxes 03/01/1990

BIOCAPITAL INVTS LTD PARTNERSHIP (QC)
Reorganized as Fonds de solidarite des travailleurs du Quebec 04/16/2001
Each Unit of Ltd. Partnership exchanged for (0.343502) Unit of Ltd. Partnership
Note: Non-Canadian residents received $10.40 cash

BIOCELL TECHNOLOGY CORP (DE)
Charter cancelled and declared

inoperative and void for non-payment of taxes 03/01/1985

BIOCHEM INTL INC (DE)
Merged into BCI Merger Corp. 01/11/1999
Each share Common 2¢ par exchanged for $6.28 cash

BIOCHEM PHARMA INC (QC)
Common no par split (2) for (1) by issuance of (1) additional share payable 04/07/1997 to holders of record 04/07/1997
Each share Common no par received distribution of (0.025) share CliniChem Development Inc. Class A Common no par payable 06/26/1998 to holders of record 06/22/1998
Merged into Shire Pharmaceuticals Group PLC 05/11/2001
For Canadian Residents: Each share Common no par exchanged for (0.75856666) Exchangeable Shares
For Non-Canadian Residents: Each share Common no par exchanged for (2.2757) shares Ordinary 5p par
Shire Pharmaceuticals Group PLC name changed to Shire PLC (England & Wales) 11/25/2005 which reincorporated in Channel Islands as Shire Ltd. 05/23/2008 which name changed to Shire PLC 10/01/2008

BIOCHEM SOLUTIONS INC (FL)
Name changed to Balmoral FX Systems Inc. 07/29/2010
Balmoral FX Systems Inc. recapitalized as Amalgamated Gold & Silver, Inc. 08/01/2012 which recapitalized as recapitalized as Rainforest Resources Inc. 03/15/2016

BIOCHEMICAL PROCEDURES, INC. (DE)
Name changed to B.P.I. Liquidating Corp. 11/19/1968
B.P.I. Liquidating Corp. liquidated for Bristol-Myers Co. 04/09/1971 which name changed to Bristol-Myers Squibb Co. 10/04/1989

BIOCIRCUITS CORP (DE)
Each share old Common $0.001 par exchanged for (0.25) share new Common $0.001 par 01/02/1996
Each share new Common $0.001 par exchanged again for (0.4) share new Common $0.001 par 02/23/1998
Recapitalized as Beluga Composites Corp. 02/07/2005
Each share new Common $0.001 par exchanged for (0.005) share Common $0.001 par
(See Beluga Composites Corp.)

BIOCLINICA INC (DE)
Acquired by BioCore Holdings, Inc. 03/13/2013
Each share Common $0.00025 par exchanged for $7.25 cash

BIOCOLL MEDICAL CORP (BC)
Merged into GenSci Regeneration Sciences Inc. 08/12/1997
Each share Common no par exchanged for (1) share Common no par
(See GenSci Regeneration Sciences Inc.)

BIOCONTROL TECHNOLOGY INC (PA)
$10 Conv. 1986 Preferred Ser. 1 $10 par called for redemption 09/13/1996
Name changed to BICO, Inc. 10/11/2000
BICO, Inc. name changed to MobiClear Inc. 11/30/2006 which name changed to Intelligent Communication Enterprise Corp. 12/22/2009 which name changed to One Horizon Group, Inc. (PA) 01/31/2013 which reorganized in Delaware 08/29/2013

BIOCORAL INC (DE)
Each share Common $0.001 par exchanged for (0.02) share new Common $0.001 par 04/17/2001
Each share new Common $0.001 par exchanged again for (0.06666666) share new Common $0.001 par 12/24/2002
SEC revoked common stock registration 08/19/2015

BIOCORP GLOBAL INC (CO)
Proclaimed dissolved for failure to file reports and pay fees 01/01/1992

BIOCRAFT LABS INC (DE)
Common 1¢ par split (3) for (2) by issuance of (0.5) additional share 01/15/1986
Merged into Teva Pharmaceutical Industries Ltd. 05/31/1996
Each share Common 1¢ par exchanged for (0.461) ADR for Ordinary NIS 0.001 par

BIODEL INC (DE)
Each share old Common 1¢ par exchanged for (0.25) share new Common 1¢ par 06/11/2012
Recapitalized as Albireo Pharma, Inc. 11/04/2016
Each share new Common 1¢ par exchanged for (0.03333333) share Common 1¢ par

BIODRAIN MED INC (MN)
Name changed to Skyline Medical Inc. (MN) 08/08/2013
Skyline Medical Inc. (MN) reincorporated in Delaware 12/18/2013 which name changed to Precision Therapeutics Inc. 02/02/2018

BIODYNAMICS INTL INC (FL)
Each share old Common no par exchanged for (0.1) share new Common no par 11/10/1997
Name changed to Tutogen Medical, Inc. 04/15/1998
Tutogen Medical, Inc. merged into RTI Biologics, Inc. 02/27/2008 which name changed to RTI Surgical, Inc. 07/18/2013

BIODYNE DEV CO (TX)
Name changed to Signal Advance, Inc. 08/14/2007

BIODYNETICS INC (NV)
Name changed to Futura Automotive Group, Inc. 04/02/1992
Futura Automotive Group, Inc. name changed to Spa International Inc. 10/09/1992
(See Spa International Inc.)

BIOELECTRIC, INC. (NV)
Recapitalized as NexMed, Inc. 10/02/1995
Each share Common $0.001 par exchanged for (0.05) share Common $0.001 par
NexMed, Inc. name changed to Apricus Biosciences, Inc. 09/14/2010

BIOENERGY INC (NV)
Common $0.001 par split (7.5) for (1) by issuance of (6.5) additional shares payable 10/20/2008 to holders of record 10/10/2008 Ex date - 10/21/2008
Name changed to Cavitation Technologies, Inc. 10/21/2008

BIOENERGY NUTRIENTS INC (CO)
Each share Common $0.00001 par exchanged for (0.0090909) share Common $0.0011 par 03/27/1992
Name changed to Amrion Inc. 03/26/1993
Amrion Inc. merged into Whole Foods Market, Inc. 09/11/1997
(See Whole Foods Market, Inc.)

BIOENVELOP TECHNOLOGIES CORP (CANADA)
Filed a notice of intention to make a proposal under the Bankruptcy and Insolvency Act and all board of directors resigned 08/16/2006
Stockholders' equity unlikely

BIOENVISION INC (DE)
Merged into Genzyme Corp. 10/23/2007
Each share Ser. A Preferred $0.001 par exchanged for $11.20 cash
Each share Common $0.001 par exchanged for $5.60 cash

BIOEXX SPECIALTY PROTEINS LTD (ON)
CCAA proceedings terminated 01/15/2014
Stockholders' equity unlikely

BIOFARM INC (NV)
Name changed to friendlyway Corp. 04/22/2005
friendlyway Corp. name changed to PSI Corp. 10/02/2006 which name changed to Coupon Express, Inc. 01/26/2012

BIOFEEDBACK MGMT CO AMER INC (FL)
Reorganized under the laws of Delaware as TMI Technical Management, Inc. 02/22/1978
Each share Common 1¢ par exchanged for (0.1) share Common 2¢ par
(See TMI Technical Management, Inc.)

BIOFIELD CORP (DE)
Each share old Common $0.001 par exchanged for (0.1) share new Common $0.001 par 06/20/2008
Name changed to MacKay Life Sciences, Inc. 05/03/2011
(See MacKay Life Sciences, Inc.)

BIOFILTRATION SYS INC (FL)
Common $0.001 par split (100) for (1) by issuance of (99) additional shares payable 04/15/2000 to holders of record 03/31/2000
Name changed to BIFS Technologies Corp. 10/04/2000
(See BIFS Technologies Corp.)

BIOFLAMEX CORP (WY)
Reincorporated 02/20/2013
Each share old Common $0.0001 par exchanged for (0.025) share new Common $0.0001 par 12/31/2012
State of incorporation changed from (NV) to (WY) 02/20/2013
Each share new Common $0.0001 par exchanged again for (0.01) share new Common $0.0001 par 09/04/2014
Name changed to Canamed4Pets, Inc. 03/25/2015

BIOFLEX TECHNOLOGIES INC (CANADA)
Name changed to Relevium Technologies Inc. 12/23/2015

BIOFLOW ENVIRONMENTAL TECHNOLOGIES INC (BC)
Recapitalized as Strategic Merchant Bancorp Inc. 05/15/1997
Each share Common no par exchanged for (0.33333333) share Common no par
Strategic Merchant Bancorp Inc. name changed to Strategic Nevada Resources Corp. 08/03/2006 which name changed to SNS Silver Corp. 02/26/2007 which name changed to SNS Precious Metals Inc. 05/17/2010 which recapitalized as Gold Finder Explorations Ltd. 10/08/2010 which recapitalized as Venzee Technologies Inc. 01/05/2018

BIOFOREST PAC INC (ON)
Recapitalized as Byron Resources Inc. 04/15/2003
Each share Common no par exchanged for (0.00714285) share Common no par
Byron Resources Inc. recapitalized as Byron Global Corp. 08/11/2004 which recapitalized as Byron Americor Inc. 07/30/2007 which name changed to Ungava Mines Inc. 10/12/2007

BIOFORM MED INC (DE)
Merged into Merz GmbH & Co. KGaA 02/19/2010
Each share Common 1¢ par exchanged for $5.45 cash

BIOFUEL ENERGY CORP (DE)
Each share old Common 1¢ par exchanged for (0.05) share new Common 1¢ par 06/15/2012
Name changed to Green Brick Partners, Inc. 10/28/2014

BIOFUEL INC (CA)
Name changed to Biflyx 01/18/1982

BIOGAN INTL INC (DE)
Name changed 9/5/97
Name changed from Biogan Medical International, Inc. to Biogan International Inc. 09/05/1997
Each share Common $0.001 par received distribution of (0.05) share R-Tec Holding, Inc. Common no par payable 09/27/1999 to holders of record 09/15/1999
Plan of reorganization under Chapter 11 Federal Bankruptcy Code effective
Each share Common $0.001 par received distribution of (0.08333333) share HMZ Metals Inc. Common no par payable 04/06/2005 to holders of record 04/05/2005
Note: Certificates were not required to be surrendered and are without value

BIOGEN IDEC INC (DE)
Name changed to Biogen Inc. 03/24/2015

BIOGEN INC (MA)
Name changed 07/01/1988
Reincorporated 09/30/1988
Name changed from Biogen N.V. (Netherlands Antilles) to Biogen, Inc. (DE) 07/01/1988
State of incorporation changed from (DE) to (MA) 09/30/1988
$2.125 Conv. Exchangeable Preferred 1¢ par called for redemption 06/20/1991
Common 1¢ par split (2) for (1) by issuance of (1) additional share payable 11/15/1996 to holders of record 11/04/1996 Ex date - 11/18/1996
Common 1¢ par split (2) for (1) by issuance of (1) additional share payable 06/25/1999 to holders of record 06/11/1999
Merged into Biogen Idec Inc. 11/13/2003
Each share Common 1¢ par exchanged for (1.15) shares Common $0.0005 par
Biogen Idec Inc. name changed to Biogen Inc. (DE) 03/24/2015

BIOGENERICS LTD (NV)
Common $0.001 par split (10) for (1) by issuance of (9) additional shares payable 05/11/2005 to holders of record 05/06/2005 Ex date - 05/12/2005
Each share Common $0.001 par received distribution of (0.03333) share WW Oil & Gas, Inc. Common $0.001 par payable 03/13/2007 to holders of record 01/02/2007
Name changed to Diversified Oil & Gas Holdings, Ltd. 07/09/2007

BIOGENETIC TECHNOLOGIES INC (NV)
Each share old Common no par exchanged for (0.5) share new Common no par 11/26/1997
Cease trade order effective 06/30/1999

BIOGENIX INC (FL)
Name changed to BGNX, Inc. 03/10/1986
(See BGNX, Inc.)

BIOGENIX INC (NV)
Charter revoked for failure to file reports and pay fees 11/01/1987

BIOGENTECH CORP (NV)
Name changed to Cobalis Corp. 07/08/2004
Each share Common $0.001 par exchanged for (1) share Common $0.001 par
(See Cobalis Corp.)

BIOHEART INC (FL)
Recapitalized as U.S. Stem Cell, Inc. 11/04/2015
Each share Common $0.001 par exchanged for (0.001) share Common $0.001 par

BIOIMMUNE INC (FL)
SEC revoked common stock registration 05/04/2010

BIOJECT MED SYS LTD (BC)
Reorganized under the laws of Oregon as Bioject Medical Technologies Inc. 12/17/1992
Each share Common no par exchanged for (1) share Common no par
(See Bioject Medical Technologies Inc.)

BIOJECT MED TECHNOLOGIES INC (OR)
Each share old Common no par exchanged for (0.2) share new Common no par 10/13/1999
Voluntarily dissolved 11/28/2016
No stockholders' equity

BIOKEYS PHARMACEUTICALS INC (DE)
Name changed to ADVENTRX Pharmaceuticals, Inc. 06/13/2003
ADVENTRX Pharmaceuticals, Inc. name changed to Mast Therapeutics, Inc. 03/11/2013 which recapitalized as Savara Inc. 04/28/2017

BIOKRONIX INC (NV)
Recapitalized as Innosuisse Corp. 12/31/2004
Each share Common $0.001 par exchanged for (0.002) share Common $0.001 par
Innosuisse Corp. name changed to Noxel Corp. 01/13/2012

BIOLAB CORP. (MO)
Charter forfeited for failure to file reports 01/01/1975

BIOLABMART INC (WY)
Name changed to Qrons Inc. 08/10/2017

BIOLABS INC (NY)
Name changed to Genesis Bioventures, Inc. (NY) 11/05/2001
Genesis Bioventures, Inc. (NY) reincorporated in Nevada 10/30/2007 which name changed to Abviva, Inc. 12/18/2007
(See Abviva, Inc.)

BIOLASE TECHNOLOGY INC (DE)
Stock Dividends - 1% payable 03/31/2011 to holders of record 03/15/2011 Ex date - 03/11/2011; 1% payable 06/30/2011 to holders of record 06/10/2011 Ex date - 06/08/2011; 1% payable 09/15/2011 to holders of record 08/29/2011 Ex date - 08/25/2011; 1% payable 12/05/2011 to holders of record 11/25/2011 Ex date - 11/22/2011; 0.5% payable 03/30/2012 to holders of record 03/15/2012 Ex date - 03/13/2012
Name changed to Biolase, Inc. 05/29/2012

BIOLECTRONICS CORP (UT)
Reorganized under the laws of Michigan 04/16/1991
Each share Common $0.001 par exchanged for (0.04) share Common 10¢ par
Biolectronics Corp. (MI) name changed to Bio-Life Systems, Inc. 06/22/1992 which recapitalized as Educational Services International Inc. (MI) 11/08/2001 which reorganized in Wyoming as WindPower Innovations, Inc. 11/18/2009 which name changed to NexGen Holdings Corp. 01/10/2014

BIOLECTRONICS CORP NEW (MI)
Name changed to Bio-Life Systems, Inc. 06/22/1992
Bio-Life Systems, Inc. recapitalized as Educational Services International Inc. (MI) 11/08/2001 which reorganized in Wyoming as WindPower Innovations, Inc. 11/18/2009

BIOLIGHT LIFE SCIENCES LTD (ISRAEL)
Name changed 02/23/2016
Basis changed from (1:100) to (1:10) 08/03/2015
Name changed from Bio Light Israeli Life Sciences Investments Ltd. to BioLight Life Sciences Ltd. 02/23/2016
Basis changed from (1:10) to (1:0.4) 02/29/2016
ADR agreement terminated 02/29/2016
Each Sponsored ADR for Ordinary exchanged for $1.261626 cash

BIOLINK CORP (ON)
Recapitalized as First Empire Entertainment.com Inc. 03/31/2000
Each share Common no par exchanged for (0.25) share Common no par
First Empire Entertainment.com Inc. recapitalized as First Empire Corp. 08/14/2003 which reorganized as Noble House Entertainment Inc. (ON) 11/01/2004 which reincorporated in Canada as LiveReel Media Corp. 12/01/2006

BIOLOGICAL PRESERVATION INC (DE)
Name changed to Fenley Ltd. 03/14/1978
(See Fenley Ltd.)

BIOLOGISTICS INC (DE)
Recapitalized as Skintek Labs, Inc. 05/12/1999
Each share Common $0.001 par exchanged for (0.16666666) share Common $0.001 par
Skintek Labs, Inc. name changed to Hunno Technologies Inc. 09/18/2002 which name changed to Abazias, Inc. 10/08/2003 which was acquired by OmniReliant Holdings, Inc. 08/27/2009

BIOLOGIX B C LTD (BC)
Reincorporated under the laws of Utah as Hemisphere Ltd. 04/21/1993
Hemisphere Ltd. name changed to Biologix International Ltd. (UT) 04/21/1993 which reincorporated in Nevada as Axess Media Group 03/31/2001 which recapitalized as MEDIA GLOBO Corp. 03/12/2007

BIOLOGIX INTL LTD (UT)
Reincorporated under the laws of Nevada as Axess Media Group, Ltd. 03/31/2001
Axess Media Group, Ltd. recapitalized as MEDIA GLOBO Corp. 03/12/2007

BIOLOK INTL INC (DE)
Each share old Common 1¢ par exchanged for (0.1) share new Common 1¢ par 07/20/1998
Acquired by HealthpointCapital Partners II, L.P. 11/03/2006
Each share new Common 1¢ par exchanged for $2.15 cash

BIOMAG CORP (NV)
Name changed to Biomagnetics Diagnostics Corp. 12/18/2006

BIOMAGNETIC TECHNOLOGIES (CA)
Name changed to 4-D Neuroimaging 03/27/2000
(See 4-D Neuroimaging)

BIOMASS RES CORP (DE)
Recapitalized as Eagle Resource Holdings, Inc. 05/31/2007
Each share Common $0.001 par exchanged for (0.01818181) share Common $0.001 par

BIOMASSE INTL INC (FL)
Recapitalized as BIMS Renewable Energy, Inc. 08/01/2003
Each share Common $0.001 par exchanged for (0.01666666) share Common $0.001 par
BIMS Renewable Energy, Inc. recapitalized as Tung Ding Resources, Inc. 04/18/2007
(See Tung Ding Resources, Inc.)

BIOMATRIX INC (DE)
Common $0.0001 par split (2) for (1) by issuance of (1) additional share payable 04/23/1999 to holders of record 04/16/1999 Ex date - 04/26/1999
Merged into Genzyme Corp. 12/18/2000
Each share Common $0.0001 par exchanged for (0.7162) share Common-Biosurgery Division 1¢ par and $10.50 cash
(See Genzyme Corp.)

BIOMAX TECHNOLOGIES INC (BC)
Delisted from Toronto Venture Stock Exchange 12/23/2005

BIOMECHANICS CORP AMER (NY)
Name changed to BCAM International, Inc. 06/22/1995
BCAM International, Inc. recapitalized as CellMetrix, Inc. 05/24/2000
(See CellMetrix, Inc.)

BIOMED RLTY TR INC (MD)
7.375% Preferred Ser. A 1¢ par called for redemption at $25 plus $0.30217 accrued dividends on 03/15/2013
Acquired by Blackstone Group L.P. 01/27/2016
Each share Common 1¢ par exchanged for $23.8239 cash

BIOMED RESH INC (UT)
Involuntarily dissolved for failure to pay taxes 03/01/1988

BIOMEDICAL COMMUNICATIONS SYSTEMS, INC. (MN)
Statutorily dissolved 10/04/1991

BIOMEDICAL COMPUTER SVCS INC (MN)
Recapitalized as Biomedical Communications Systems, Inc. 04/14/1972
Each share Capital Stock 5¢ par exchanged for (0.33333333) share Capital Stock $0.025 par

BIOMEDICAL DEV CORP (DE)
Capital Stock 5¢ par changed to $0.0167 par and (2) additional shares issued 06/11/1971
Name changed to Center for Laboratory Medicine, Inc. 03/30/1973
Center for Laboratory Medicine, Inc. merged into Damon Corp. 06/01/1977
(See Damon Corp.)

BIOMEDICAL DYNAMICS CORP (MN)
Common no par split (3) for (2) by issuance of (0.5) additional share 04/01/1986
Merged into Vital Signs, Inc. 04/16/1992
Each share Common no par exchanged for (0.359) share Common no par
(See Vital Signs, Inc.)

BIOMEDICAL INDS INC (FL)
Completely liquidated 10/15/1996
Each share Class A Common 10¢ par exchanged for first and final distribution of $1.24 cash

BIOMEDICAL REFERENCE LABS INC (NC)
Stock Dividends - 50% 10/31/1980; 50% 06/19/1981
Merged into Hofmann-La Roche Inc. 06/08/1982
Each share Common 10¢ par exchanged for $28 cash

BIOMEDICAL RES CORP (DE)
Merged into International Clinical Laboratories, Inc. (New) 08/31/1977
Each share Common 10¢ par exchanged for (0.33333333) share Common $0.33333333 par
(See International Clinical Laboratories, Inc. (New))

BIOMEDICAL TECHNOLOGIES INC (UT)
Recapitalized as Southern Cross Ventures Inc. (UT) 08/29/1984
Each share Common $0.001 par exchanged for (0.1) share Common 1¢ par
Southern Cross Ventures Inc. (UT) reorganized in Nevada as Centra Corp. 01/20/1989 which recapitalized as Greenway Environmental Systems, Inc. 05/10/1991 which recapitalized as Travel Dynamics, Inc. 01/13/1999 which name changed to TRU Dynamics International, Inc. 02/14/2001
(See TRU Dynamics International, Inc.)

BIOMEDICAL WASTE SYS INC (DE)
Chapter 11 bankruptcy proceedings closed 07/22/1999
Stockholders' equity unlikely

BIOMEDTEX INC (FL)
Administratively dissolved 09/23/2011

BIOMERGE INDS LTD (AB)
Reincorporated 04/15/2009
Place of incorporation changed from (BC) to (AB) 04/15/2009
Merged into Total Energy Services Inc. 05/20/2009
Each share Common no par exchanged for (0.00023707) share Common no par and $0.00282112 cash
Note: Unexchanged certificates were cancelled and became without value 05/20/2014

BIOMET INC (IN)
Common no par split (2) for (1) by issuance of (1) additional share 03/15/1983
Common no par split (2) for (1) by issuance of (1) additional share 07/22/1983
Common no par split (2) for (1) by issuance of (1) additional share 04/30/1986
Common no par split (3) for (2) by issuance of (0.5) additional share 08/19/1988
Common no par split (3) for (2) by issuance of (0.5) additional share 05/08/1989
Common no par split (2) for (1) by issuance of (1) additional share 01/14/1991
Common no par split (2) for (1) by issuance of (1) additional share 12/16/1991
Common no par split (3) for (2) by issuance of (0.5) additional share payable 08/08/2000 to holders of record 07/18/2000
Common no par split (3) for (2) by issuance of (0.5) additional share payable 08/06/2001 to holders of

record 07/30/2001 Ex date - 08/07/2001
Merged into LVB Acquisition, Inc. 09/25/2007
Each share Common no par exchanged for $46 cash

BIOMET TECHNOLOGY INC (BC)
Struck off register and declared dissolved for failure to file returns 12/02/1994

BIOMETRIC ACCESS TECHNOLOGIES INC (DE)
Recapitalized as Polar Cargo Systems Inc. 04/16/1999
Each share Common $0.0001 par exchanged for (0.02) share Common $0.001 par
Polar Cargo Systems Inc. name changed to Coldwall, Inc. 06/02/2004
(See Coldwall, Inc.)

BIOMETRIC SEC CORP (WY)
Recapitalized as Safeguard Biometric Corp. (WY) 12/29/1999
Each share Common no par exchanged for (0.2) share Common no par
Safeguard Biometric Corp. (WY) reincorporated in British Columbia 11/30/2001 which name changed to Devon Ventures Corp. 02/11/2002 which name changed to Pender Financial Group Corp. 06/23/2004
(See Pender Financial Group Corp.)

BIOMETRIC TESTING INC (DE)
Adjudicated bankrupt 02/19/1980
Stockholders' equity unlikely

BIOMETRIC VERIFICATION HLDGS INC (FL)
Name changed to Vadda Energy Corp. 09/02/2003
(See Vadda Energy Corp.)

BIOMETRICS INC (OR)
Involuntarily dissolved for failure to pay fees 11/30/1981

BIOMETRICS SECURITY TECHNOLOGY INC (DE)
SEC revoked common stock registration 03/10/2010

BIOMETRICS 2000 CORP (NY)
SEC revoked common stock registration 10/03/2008

BIOMETRX INC (DE)
Each share Common 1¢ par exchanged for (0.25) share Common $0.001 par 03/14/2006
Each share old Common $0.001 par exchanged for (0.005) share new Common $0.001 par 03/19/2009
SEC revoked common stock registration 09/07/2011

BIOMEX CORP (NV)
Charter revoked for failure to file annual reports and pay fees 02/01/1986

BIOMIMETIC THERAPEUTICS INC (DE)
Merged into Wright Medical Group, Inc. 03/01/2013
Each share Common $0.001 par exchanged for (0.2482) share Common 1¢ par, (1) Contingent Value Right and $1.50 cash
Wright Medical Group, Inc. merged into Wright Medical Group N.V. 10/02/2015

BIOMIN THERAPEUTIC CORP (BC)
Name changed to Pharmex Industries Inc. 11/06/1996
Pharmex Industries Inc. name changed to PanGeo Pharma Inc. (BC) 08/21/2000 which reincorporated in Canada 09/21/2000 which recapitalized as Silvio Ventures Inc. 01/09/2006 which name changed to Regency Gold Corp. 07/17/2008

BIOMIRA INC (CANADA)
Reorganized under the laws of Delaware as Oncothyreon Inc. 12/11/2007
Each share Common no par exchanged for (0.16666666) share Common $0.0001 par
Oncothyreon Inc. name changed to Cascadian Therapeutics, Inc. 06/09/2016
(See Cascadian Therapeutics, Inc.)

BIOMMUNE TECHNOLOGIES INC (BC)
Name changed to Pascal Biosciences Inc. 03/31/2017

BIOMODA INC (NM)
Plan of reorganization under Chapter 11 Federal Bankruptcy proceedings effective 04/14/2014
No stockholders' equity

BIOMS MED CORP (AB)
Name changed to Medwell Capital Corp. (AB) 07/08/2010
Medwell Capital Corp. (AB) reorganized in Canada as GDI Integrated Facility Services Inc. 05/14/2015

BIOMUNE SYS INC (NV)
Each share old Common $0.0001 par exchanged for (0.01) share new Common $0.0001 par 03/22/1993
Each share new Common $0.0001 par exchanged again for (0.1) share new Common $0.0001 par 12/10/1997
Each share new Common $0.0001 par received distribution of (0.1) share Volu-Sol, Inc. Common $0.0001 par payable 01/20/1998 to holders of record 03/05/1997
Each share new Common $0.0001 par exchanged again for (0.1) share new Common $0.0001 par 12/30/1998
Each share new Common $0.0001 par exchanged for (0.2) share new Common $0.0001 par 10/31/2000
Name changed to Donlar Biosyntrex Corp. 06/15/2001
Donlar Biosyntrex Corp. merged into Donlar Corp. 03/05/2003
(See Donlar Corp.)

BIONAIRE INC (CANADA)
Merged into Rival Co. (MO) 04/02/1996
Each share Common no par exchanged for $2.25 cash

BIONEBRASKA INC (DE)
Name changed to Restoragen, Inc. 08/20/2001
(See Restoragen, Inc.)

BIONET TECHNOLOGIES INC (NV)
Charter revoked for failure to file reports and pay fees 09/01/2002

BIONETICS RESH LABS INC (MD)
Class B Common 20¢ par reclassified as Class A Common 20¢ par 08/31/1967
Name changed to 101 West Jefferson Liquidating Corp. 06/25/1968
101 West Jefferson Liquidating Corp. liquidation for Litton Industries, Inc. completed 09/21/1971
(See Litton Industries, Inc.)

BIONEX CORP (ON)
Charter cancelled for failure to file reports and pay taxes 02/04/1995

BIONIC ENTERPRISES INC (BC)
Name changed to Hymex Diamond Corp. (BC) 10/18/1994
Hymex Diamond Corp. (BC) reincorporated in Yukon 09/04/1996
(See Hymex Diamond Corp. (Yukon))

BIONIC INSTRS DEL INC (DE)
Reorganized 10/19/1978
Reorganized from Bionic Instruments, Inc. (PA) to under the laws of Delaware as Bionic Instruments of Delaware, Inc. 10/19/1979
Each share Common 1¢ par exchanged for (0.25) share Common 5¢ par
Charter cancelled and declared inoperative and void for non-payment of taxes 03/01/1981

BIONIC PRODS INC (NV)
Each share old Common $0.001 par exchanged for (0.0002) share new Common $0.001 par 02/25/2010
Recapitalized as Texas Oil & Minerals Inc. 02/01/2012
Each share new Common $0.001 par exchanged for (0.1) share Common $0.001 par

BIONIC SCIENCES CORP (TX)
Adjudicated bankrupt 04/20/1977
Stockholders' equity unlikely

BIONICHE INC (CANADA)
Merged into Bioniche Life Sciences Inc. 09/01/1999
Each share Common no par exchanged for (0.2) share Common no par
Bioniche Life Sciences Inc. name changed to Telesta Therapeutics Inc. 12/01/2014 which merged into ProMetic Life Sciences Inc. 11/01/2016

BIONICHE LIFE SCIENCES INC (CANADA)
Name changed to Telesta Therapeutics Inc. 12/01/2014
Telesta Therapeutics Inc. merged into ProMetic Life Sciences Inc. 11/01/2016

BIONICS MED SVCS CORP (UT)
Name changed to Western Pacific Energy Ltd. 01/16/1978
Western Pacific Energy Ltd. name changed to Technedyne, Inc. 04/19/1980
(See Technedyne, Inc.)

BIONOMIC SCIENCES INTL INC (NV)
Each share Common $0.001 par exchanged for (0.05) share old Common 2¢ par 06/27/1984
Each share old Common 2¢ par exchanged for (0.002) share new Common 2¢ par 03/03/1998
Name changed to Icon Financial Inc. 04/27/1998
Icon Financial Inc. name changed to International Gaming Group, Inc. 06/04/1999 which name changed to American Standard Energy Inc. 04/16/2002 which name changed to Sports Wheels, Inc. 04/17/2003 which recapitalized as Automotive Specialty Concepts, Inc. 02/01/2005 which name changed to Drake Gold Resources, Inc. 02/13/2006 which name changed to Universal Apparel & Textile Co. 04/27/2015

BIONOMICS LTD (AUSTRALIA)
ADR agreement terminated 05/21/2015
Each Sponsored ADR for Ordinary exchanged for $4.677975 cash

BIONOR PHARMA ASA (NORWAY)
Name changed to Solon Eiendom ASA 01/31/2017

BIONOVA HLDG CORP (DE)
Merged into Savia S.A. de C.V. 03/29/2004
Each share Common 1¢ par exchanged for $0.09 cash

BIONOVA U S INC (DE)
Under plan of merger name changed to DNAP Holding Corp. 09/26/1996
DNAP Holding Corp. name changed to Bionova Holding Corp. 04/29/1999
(See Bionova Holding Corp.)

BIONOVO INC (DE)
Each share old Common $0.0001 par exchanged for (0.2) share new Common $0.0001 par 08/31/2010
Filed a petition under Chapter 7 Federal Bankruptcy Code 10/26/2012
Stockholders' equity unlikely

BIONUTRICS INC (NV)
Each share old Common $0.001 par exchanged for (0.2) share new Common $0.001 par 05/30/2001
Name changed to Synovics Pharmaceuticals, Inc. 04/11/2006

BIONX IMPLANTS INC (DE)
Merged into CONMED Corp. 03/10/2003
Each share Common $0.0019 par exchanged for $4.35 cash

BIOPAC INDS INC (BC)
Recapitalized as BPI Industries Inc. 01/18/1995
Each share Common no par exchanged for (0.25) share Common no par
BPI Industries Inc. name changed to BPI Energy Holdings, Inc. 02/09/2006
(See BPI Energy Holdings, Inc.)

BIOPACK ENVIRONMENTAL SOLUTIONS INC (NV)
Each share old Common $0.0001 par exchanged for (0.1) share new Common $0.0001 par 06/11/2008
Recapitalized as Tristar Wellness Solutions Inc. 01/18/2013
Each share new Common $0.0001 par exchanged for (0.001) share Common $0.0001 par

BIOPAT CAP INC (CANADA)
Name changed to Colt Energy Inc. 12/04/1997
Colt Energy Inc. merged into KeyWest Energy Corp. 12/17/1998
(See KeyWest Energy Corp.)

BIOPETROL INC (UT)
Common 1¢ par split (6) for (1) by issuance of (5) additional shares 07/17/1982
Reincorporated under the laws of Nevada as Kensington International, Inc. 04/17/1996
(See Kensington International, Inc.)

BIOPHARM ASIA INC (NV)
SEC revoked common stock registration 06/04/2013

BIOPHARMACEUTICS INC (DE)
Each share old Common $0.001 par exchanged for (0.25) share new Common $0.001 par 06/25/1997
Name changed to Feminique Corp. 06/28/1999
Feminique Corp. recapitalized as Receivable Acquisition & Management Corp. 05/11/2004 which name changed to PwrCor, Inc. 03/29/2017

BIOPHARMX CORP (NV)
Reincorporated under the laws of Delaware 05/16/2014

BIOPHYSICAL ELECTRONICS, INC. (PA)
Merged into Communications Industries, Inc. 02/06/1961
Each share Common 10¢ par exchanged for (0.33333333) share Common 10¢ par
(See Communications Industries, Inc.)

BIOPLASTY INC (MN)
Plan of reorganization under Chapter 11 Federal Bankruptcy Code effective 01/31/1994
No stockholders' equity

BIOPONIC INTL (CA)
Reincorporated under the laws of Delaware as MR3 Systems Inc. and Common no par changed to 1¢ par 06/07/2000
(See MR3 Systems Inc.)

BIOPOOL INTL INC (DE)
Name changed to Xtrana, Inc. 06/22/2001

Xtrana, Inc. recapitalized as Alpha Innotech Corp. 10/06/2005
(See Alpha Innotech Corp.)

BIOPORE INC (DE)
Charter cancelled and declared inoperative and void for non-payment of taxes 06/24/1991

BIOPOTENTIAL CAP INC (AB)
Name changed to Osta Biotechnologies Inc. 07/18/2005

BIOPROGRESS PLC (ENGLAND & WALES)
Name changed to Meldex International PLC 09/28/2007
(See Meldex International PLC)

BIOPROGRESS TECHNOLOGY INTL INC (NV)
Reincorporated under the laws of England & Wales as BioProgress PLC and Common $0.001 par reclassified as Ordinary 1p par 05/21/2003
BioProgress PLC name changed to Meldex International PLC 09/28/2007

BIOPSYS MED INC (DE)
Merged into Johnson & Johnson 08/01/1997
Each share Common $0.001 par exchanged for (0.4393) share Common $1 par

BIOPTIX INC (NV)
Reincorporated 09/28/2017
State of incorporation changed from (CO) to (NV) 09/28/2017
Name changed to Riot Blockchain, Inc. 10/19/2017

BIOPULSE INTERNATIONAL INC (NV)
Recapitalized as Only You, Inc. 01/17/2006
Each share Common $0.001 par exchanged for (0.03333333) share Common $0.001 par
Note: Holders of between (20) and (599) shares will receive (20) shares
Holders of (19) or fewer shares were not affected by the reverse split

BIOPURE CORP (DE)
Each share old Class A Common 1¢ par exchanged for (0.16666666) share new Class A Common 1¢ par 05/27/2005
Each share new Class A Common 1¢ par exchanged again for (0.2) share new Class A Common 1¢ par 10/02/2007
Under Chapter 11 Federal Bankruptcy reorganization each share new Class A Common 1¢ par received distribution of $0.029 cash payable 07/07/2011 to holders of record 04/21/2010

BIOQUEST INC (DE)
Each shares old Common $0.001 par exchanged for (0.5025252) share new Common $0.001 par 07/26/2000
Name changed to Biokeys Pharmaceuticals Inc. 10/12/2000
Biokeys Pharmaceuticals Inc. name changed to ADVENTRX Pharmaceuticals, Inc. 06/13/2003 which name changed to Mast Therapeutics, Inc. 03/11/2013 which recapitalized as Savara Inc. 04/28/2017

BIOQUEST TECHNOLOGIES INC (NV)
Each share old Common $0.001 par exchanged for (0.0025) share new Common $0.001 par 12/07/2007
Name changed to Texas Hill Country Barbecue Inc. 06/28/2010
Texas Hill Country Barbecue Inc. name changed to South American Properties, Inc. 04/10/2013 which name changed to USA Restaurant Funding Inc. 11/17/2014 which name changed to Chron Organization, Inc.

03/24/2016 which name changed to Zenergy Brands, Inc. 12/01/2017

BIORA AB (SWEDEN)
ADR agreement terminated 12/09/2002
Each Sponsored ADR for Ordinary exchanged for $4.7246 cash

BIORELEASE CORP (DE)
Recapitalized as BRL Holdings, Inc. 07/02/2001
Each share Common $0.0001 par exchanged for (0.08) share Common $0.0001 par
BRL Holdings, Inc. name changed to Element 21 Golf Co. (DE) 10/18/2004 which reincorporated in Nevada as American Rare Earths & Materials, Corp. 07/20/2010

BIORELIANCE CORP (DE)
Merged into Invitrogen Corp. 02/10/2004
Each share Common 1¢ par exchanged for $48 cash

BIORESTORATIVE THERAPIES INC (NV)
Each share old Common $0.001 par exchanged for (0.02) share new Common $0.001 par 04/15/2013
Reincorporated under the laws of Delaware 01/01/2015

BIOREX CORP (NY)
Merged into Ashley American Co. 06/30/1982
Each share Common 1¢ par exchanged for $2.50 cash

BIOREX GROUPE CONSEIL INC (CANADA)
Reorganized as ACSI-BIOREX Inc. 01/01/1989
Details not available

BIOSAFE INTL INC (NV)
Reincorporated under the laws of Delaware as Waste Systems International, Inc. 10/27/1997
(See Waste Systems International, Inc.)

BIOSAFETY SYS INC (DE)
Merged into HVB, Inc. 12/20/1995
Each share Common 1¢ par exchanged for $3.16 cash

BIOSANTE PHARMACEUTICALS INC (DE)
Reincorporated 12/19/1996
Reincorporated 06/26/2001
Place of incorporation changed from (ON) to (WY) 12/19/1996
State of incorporation changed from (WY) to (DE) and Common no par changed to $0.0001 par 06/26/2001
Each share old Common $0.0001 par exchanged for (0.1) share new Common $0.0001 par 05/31/2002
Each share new Common $0.0001 par exchanged again for (0.16666666) share new Common $0.0001 par 06/04/2012
Recapitalized as ANI Pharmaceuticals, Inc. 07/18/2013
Each share Common $0.0001 par exchanged for (0.16666666) share Common $0.0001 par

BIOSCRYPT INC (CANADA)
Acquired by L-1 Identity Solutions, Inc. 03/05/2008
Each share Common no par exchanged for (0.0324) share Common $0.001 par
(See L-1 Identity Solutions, Inc.)

BIOSEARCH MED PRODS INC (NJ)
Each share old Common no par exchanged for (0.2) share new Common no par 06/22/1995
Stock Dividend - 50% 02/10/1983
Merged into Hydromer, Inc. 02/03/2000
Each share new Common no par exchanged for $0.20 cash

BIOSECURE CORP (NV)
SEC revoked common stock registration 05/07/2010

BIOSENSOR CORP (MN)
Recapitalized as Biotel Inc. 05/25/1999
Each share Common 5¢ par exchanged for (0.125) share Common 1¢ par
(See Biotel Inc.)

BIOSENSORS INTL GROUP LTD (BERMUDA)
ADR agreement terminated 05/04/2016
Each ADR for Common exchanged for $12.519208 cash

BIOSHIELD TECHNOLOGIES INC (GA)
Each share Common no par received distribution of (0.1) share Healthcare Network Solutions, Inc. Common $0.0001 par payable 12/03/2001 to holders of record 11/12/2001
Ex date - 12/04/2001
Name changed to International BioChemical Industries, Inc. 09/25/2002
(See International BioChemical Industries, Inc.)

BIOSIGN TECHNOLOGIES INC (ON)
Each share old Common no par exchanged for (0.1) share new Common no par 08/28/2015
Ceased operations 04/13/2016
Stockholders' equity unlikely

BIOSITE INC (DE)
Name changed 06/14/2001
Name changed from Biosite Diagnostics Inc. to Biosite Inc. 06/14/2001
Merged into Inverness Medical Innovations, Inc. 06/29/2007
Each share Common 1¢ par exchanged for $92.50 cash

BIOSONICS INC (PA)
SEC revoked common stock registration 08/05/2004

BIOSOURCE INDS INC (BC)
Merged into BioSource International, Inc. 05/19/1993
Each share Common no par exchanged for (0.5) share Common no par
(See BioSource International, Inc.)

BIOSOURCE INTL INC (DE)
Merged into Invitrogen Corp. 10/06/2005
Each share Common $0.001 par exchanged for $12.50 cash

BIOSOURCE SOLUTIONS INC (NV)
Common $0.001 par split (4) for (1) by issuance of (3) additional shares payable 03/09/2007 to holders of record 03/01/2007 Ex date - 03/12/2007
Charter revoked for failure to file reports and pay fees 07/30/2010

BIOSPHERE MED INC (DE)
Name changed 05/18/1999
Name changed from BioSepra Inc. to BioSphere Medical, Inc. 05/18/1999
Acquired by Merit Medical Systems, Inc. 09/10/2010
Each share Common 1¢ par exchanged for $4.38 cash

BIOSPHERICS INC (DE)
Common 1¢ par changed to $0.005 par and (1) additional share issued payable 05/30/1996 to holders of record 05/15/1996
Stock Dividends - 100% 10/12/1979; 33.33333333% 06/15/1981; 100% 04/04/1983
Name changed to Spherix Inc. 05/15/2001

BIOSTEM INC (NV)
Recapitalized as Joytoto USA, Inc. 10/31/2007
Each share Common $0.001 par exchanged for (0.025) share Common $0.001 par
Joytoto USA, Inc. recapitalized as Pollex, Inc. 10/24/2008 which name changed to eMARINE Global Inc. 09/12/2017

BIOSTEM U S CORP (NV)
Old Common $0.001 par split (4) for (1) by issuance of (3) additional shares payable 01/04/2012 to holders of record 12/22/2011
Ex date - 01/05/2012
Each share old Common $0.001 par exchanged for (0.001) share new Common $0.001 par 11/05/2012
SEC revoked common stock registration 01/15/2016

BIOSTIM INC (DE)
Charter cancelled and declared inoperative and void for non-payment of taxes 06/25/1987

BIOSURFACE TECHNOLOGY INC (DE)
Acquired by Genzyme Corp. 12/16/1994
Each share Common no par exchanged for (0.575) share Common-Tissue Repair Division 1¢ par
(See Genzyme Corp.)

BIOSYNTECH INC (CANADA)
Reincorporated 03/28/2006
Place of incorporation changed from (NV) to (Canada) 03/28/2006
Dissolved for non-compliance 02/07/2013

BIOSYS (DE)
Reincorporated 05/23/1994
Reincorporated from Biosys (CA) to under the laws of Delaware as Biosys Inc. and Common no par changed to $0.001 par 05/23/1994
Each share old Common $0.001 par exchanged for (0.4) share new Common $0.001 par 03/15/1996
Plan of reorganization under Chapter 11 Federal Bankruptcy Code effective 04/29/1998
No stockholders' equity

BIOTA HLDGS LTD (AUSTRALIA)
Acquired by Biota Pharmaceuticals, Inc. 01/04/2013
Each Sponsored ADR for Ordinary exchanged for (0.37486196) share Common 10¢ par
Biota Pharmaceuticals, Inc. name changed to Aviragen Therapeutics, Inc. 04/13/2016 which recapitalized as Vaxart, Inc. 02/14/2018

BIOTA PHARMACEUTICALS INC (DE)
Name changed to Aviragen Therapeutics, Inc. 04/13/2016
Aviragen Therapeutics, Inc. recapitalized as Vaxart, Inc. 02/14/2018

BIOTECH CAP CORP (DE)
Name changed to Infotechnology Inc. 09/17/1987
(See Infotechnology Inc.)

BIOTECH ELECTRS LTD (CANADA)
Name changed to Bionaire Inc. 01/03/1989
(See Bionaire Inc.)

BIOTECH HLDGS LTD (AB)
Deemed bankrupt 11/06/2009
Stockholders' equity unlikely

BIOTECH HOLDRS TR (DE)
Trust terminated
Each Depositary Receipt received first and final distribution of $153.084657 cash payable 01/07/2013 to holders of record 12/20/2012

BIOTECH INDS INC (CO)
Recapitalized as ValuShip Ltd. (CO) 06/01/2001
Each share Common no par

exchanged for (0.002) share Common no par
ValuShip Ltd. (CO) reincorporated in Bahamas 01/04/2002 which reorganized in Delaware as Vorsatech Ventures Inc. 03/03/2004 which name changed to Synutra International, Inc. 09/12/2005
(See Synutra International, Inc.)

BIOTECH MED SCIENCES INC (AB)
Merged into CAPVEST Income Corp. 01/05/2005
Each share Common no par exchanged for (0.88) share Common no par
(See CAPVEST Income Corp.)

BIOTECH PATENT INC (NY)
Completely liquidated 04/16/2003
Each share Common 1¢ par exchanged for first and final distribution of $0.001841 cash

BIOTECH RESH LABS INC (MD)
Stock Dividend - 100% 12/10/1982
Merged into Cambridge Biotech Corp. 09/10/1990
Each share Common 1¢ par exchanged for (1) share Common 1¢ par
Cambridge Biotech Corp. reorganized as Aquila Biopharmaceuticals, Inc. 10/22/1996 which merged into Antigenics, Inc. 11/16/2000 which name changed to Agenus Inc. 01/06/2011

BIOTECHNA ENVIRONMENTAL TECHNOLOGIES CORP (BRITISH WEST INDIES)
Name changed 09/13/1996
Reincorporated 05/08/1998
Name changed from Biotechna Environmental Ltd. (AB) to Biotechna Environmental Technologies Corp. (AB) 09/13/1996
Each share Common no par exchanged for (0.06666666) share new Common no par
Place of incorporation changed from (AB) to British West Indies 05/08/1998
Recapitalized as Biotechna Environmental (2000) Corp. 05/12/2000
Each share Common no par exchanged for (0.05) share Common no par
(See Biotechna Environmental (2000) Corp.)

BIOTECHNA ENVIRONMENTAL (2000) CORP (BRITISH WEST INDIES)
Assets assigned to creditors 07/11/2001
Stockholders' equity unlikely

BIOTECHNICA INTL INC (DE)
Merged into LG Corp. 01/08/1999
Each share Common 1¢ par exchanged for $0.05 cash

BIOTECHNOLOGY DEV CORP (DE)
Name changed to Microfluidics International Corp. (Old) 06/09/1993
Microfluidics International Corp. (Old) name changed to MFIC Corp. 06/25/1999 which name changed to Microfluidics International Corp. (New) 06/18/2008
(See Microfluidics International Corp. (New))

BIOTECHNOLOGY TOOLS INC (DE)
Merged into Ventana Acquisition 10/15/1998
Each share Common 1¢ par exchanged for $1.5193 cash
Note: An additional distribution of $0.08 cash per share was made 06/15/1999

BIOTEL INC (MN)
Acquired by CardioNet, Inc. 12/20/2010
Each share Common 1¢ par exchanged for $4.055 cash

BIOTELEMETRIC SIGNALING INC (ANTIGUA)
Name changed to Flirty Girl International Inc. 12/27/2005
Flirty Girl International Inc. name changed to PlayStar Corp. (Antigua) (New) 07/27/2006
(See PlayStar Corp. (Antigua) (New))

BIOTEQ ENVIRONMENTAL TECHNOLOGIES INC (BC)
Name changed to BQE Water Inc. 03/01/2017

BIOTHERAPEUTICS CORP (NV)
Name changed to Granite Development Corp. 01/14/1997
Granite Development Corp. recapitalized as Technology Logistics Systems Inc. 04/15/1999 which recapitalized as Interactive Business Development, Inc. (New) 01/03/2006 which name changed to American BioDiesel Fuels Corp. 02/02/2007 which name changed to Planet Resource Recovery, Inc. 03/09/2007

BIOTHERAPEUTICS INC (TN)
Name changed to Response Technologies, Inc. 11/01/1989
Response Technologies Inc. recapitalized as Response Oncology Inc. 11/02/1995
(See Response Oncology Inc.)

BIOTIE THERAPIES OYJ (FINLAND)
ADR agreement terminated 02/07/2017
Each Sponsored ADR for Ordinary exchanged for $25.109908 cash

BIOTONIX 2010 INC (CANADA)
Recapitalized as AtmanCo Inc. 12/11/2012
Each share Common no par exchanged for (0.5) share Common no par
AtmanCo Inc. name changed to ATW Tech Inc. 06/12/2018

BIOTRANSPLANT INC (MA)
Plan of reorganization under Chapter 11 Federal Bankruptcy Code effective 04/26/2004
No stockholders' equity

BIOTRONIC ENERGY ENGR INC (UT)
Each share old Common $0.001 par exchanged for (0.01) share new Common $0.001 par 09/01/1991
Recapitalized as Sonoran Group, Inc. 01/16/1994
Each share new Common $0.001 par exchanged for (0.066) share Common $0.001 par
Sonoran Group, Inc. recapitalized as Zorro International Inc. 04/29/1994 which recapitalized as Health & Wealth Inc. 07/12/1994 which recapitalized as Twenty First Century Health Inc. 05/23/1995 which name changed to Bio-Tech Industries Inc. 05/21/1997
(See Bio-Tech Industries Inc.)

BIOTRONICS, INC. (MN)
Completely liquidated 05/24/1962
Each share Common 10¢ par received first and final distribution of (1) share Diginamics Corp. Common 10¢ par
Note: Certificates were not required to be surrendered and are without value

BIOVAIL CORP (CANADA)
Common no par split (2) for (1) by issuance of (1) additional share payable 10/13/2000 to holders of record 10/10/2000 Ex date - 10/16/2000
Under plan of merger name changed to Valeant Pharmaceuticals International, Inc. (Canada) 09/28/2010
Valeant Pharmaceuticals International, Inc. (Canada) reincorporated in British Columbia 08/09/2013 which name changed to Bausch Health Companies Inc. 07/16/2018

BIOVAIL CORP INTL NEW (ON)
Common no par split (3) for (1) by issuance of (2) additional shares payable 01/16/1996 to holders of record 01/10/1996
Common no par split (2) for (1) by issuance of (1) additional share payable 01/19/2000 to holders of record 01/12/2000
Name changed to Biovail Corp. 02/18/2000
Biovail Corp. merged into Valeant Pharmaceuticals International, Inc. (Canada) 09/28/2010 which reincorporated in British Columbia 08/09/2013 which name changed to Bausch Health Companies Inc. 07/16/2018

BIOVAIL CORP INTL OLD (ON)
Merged into Biovail Corp. International (New) 03/29/1994
Each share Common no par exchanged for (1) share Common no par
Biovail Corp. International (New) name changed to Biovail Corp. 02/18/2000 which merged into Valeant Pharmaceuticals International, Inc. (Canada) 09/28/2010 which reincorporated in British Columbia 08/09/2013 which name changed to Bausch Health Companies Inc. 07/16/2018

BIOVERATIV INC (DE)
Acquired by Sanofi 03/08/2018
Each share Common $0.001 par exchanged for $105 cash

BIOVERIS CORP (DE)
Acquired by Roche Holding Ltd. 06/26/2007
Each share Common $0.001 par exchanged for $21.50 cash

BIOVEST CORP I (CANADA)
Name changed to Magor Corp. 03/15/2013

BIOVEST INTL INC (DE)
Plan of reorganization under Chapter 11 Federal Bankruptcy proceedings effective 07/09/2013
No stockholders' equity

BIOVITRUM AB (SWEDEN)
Name changed to Swedish Orphan Biovitrum AB 05/13/2010

BIOWEST THERAPEUTICS INC (BC)
Name changed to Carrus Capital Corp. 08/22/2011
Carrus Capital Corp. name changed to Global Blockchain Technologies Corp. 10/05/2017

BIOWHITTAKER INC (DE)
Merged into Cambrex Corp. 10/03/1997
Each share Common 1¢ par exchanged for $11.625 cash

BIOX CORP (CANADA)
Acquired by CFFI Ventures Inc. 09/27/2017
Each share Common no par exchanged for $1.23 cash
Note: Unexchanged certificates will be cancelled and become without value 09/27/2023

BIOXEL PHARMA INC (CANADA)
Declared bankrupt 04/30/2009
No stockholders' equity

BIOZHEM COSMECEUTICALS INC (TX)
Recapitalized as Islet Holdings, Inc. 05/28/2009
Each share Common $0.001 par exchanged for (0.002) share Common $0.001 par

BIOZONE PHARMACEUTICALS INC (NV)
Common $0.001 par split (10) for (1) by issuance of (9) additional shares payable 03/14/2011 to holders of record 03/11/2011 Ex date - 03/15/2011
Reincorporated under the laws of Delaware as Cocrystal Pharma, Inc. 04/15/2014

BIOZYMES INTL LTD (CANADA)
Declared dissolved for failure to file annual reports 12/15/1980

BIP INVT PARTNERS SA (LUXEMBOURG)
ADR agreement terminated 04/25/2011
No ADR's remain outstanding

BIP OIL INC (NV)
Reorganized under the laws of Delaware as Clear Skies Holdings, Inc. 01/07/2008
Each share Common $0.001 par exchanged for (9.19231) shares Common $0.001 par
Clear Skies Holdings, Inc. name changed to Clear Skies Solar, Inc. 02/27/2008
(See Clear Skies Solar, Inc.)

BIPER S A DE C V (MEXICO)
Stock Dividend - 2.9657% payable 04/03/2000 to holders of record 03/30/2000
ADR agreement terminated 11/10/2003
Each Sponsored ADR for Class B exchanged for $114.9476 cash

BIPOP-CARIRE S P A (ITALY)
Name changed to Fineco S.p.A. 07/11/2002
Fineco S.p.A. name changed to FinecoGroup S.p.A. 12/04/2002
(See FinecoGroup S.p.A.)

BIRCH BRH INC (CO)
Each share old Common no par exchanged for (0.33333333) share new Common no par 06/04/2007
Acquired by Birch Branch Acquisition Corp. 04/08/2013
Each share new Common no par exchanged for $0.10 cash

BIRCH CAP INC (ON)
Name changed to Breckenridge Technologies Inc. 04/02/1996
Breckenridge Technologies Inc. name changed to Breckenridge Minerals Inc. 10/23/1996 which reorganized as Wavepower Systems International Inc. 07/06/2005 which name changed to Delta Uranium Inc. 06/06/2007

BIRCH HILL GOLD CORP (BC)
Merged into Canoe Mining Ventures Corp. 06/04/2014
Each share Common no par exchanged for (0.4) share Common no par

BIRCH MTN RES LTD (AB)
Name changed 12/31/1995
Name changed from Birch Mountain Minerals Ltd. to Birch Mountain Resources Ltd. 12/31/1995
Placed in receivership pursuant to the Bankruptcy and Insolvency Act 11/06/2009
No stockholders' equity

BIRCH POINT MINES LTD. (ON)
Merged into Great Molly Explorations & Enterprises Ltd. 01/29/1968
Each share Common no par exchanged for (0.25) share Common no par
Great Molly Explorations & Enterprises Ltd. merged into Great Eagle Explorations & Holdings Ltd. 07/07/1969 which merged into Belle Aire Resource Explorations Ltd. 08/29/1978 which name changed to Sprint Resources Ltd. 09/23/1982 which name changed to Meacon Bay Resources Ltd. 03/09/1987 which recapitalized as Advantex

Marketing International Inc. 09/16/1991

BIRCH TREE CAP CORP (FL)
Name changed to Internet Sports Network Inc. 02/01/1999
Internet Sports Network Inc. name changed to Reibanc USA, Inc. 03/26/2003 which name changed to Flair Petroleum Corp. 06/30/2006

BIRCHCLIFF ENERGY LTD OLD (AB)
Merged into Birchcliff Energy Ltd. (New) 05/31/2005
Each share Common no par exchanged for (1) share Common no par

BIRCHPOINT CAP INC (AB)
Name changed to Ucore Uranium Inc. 10/10/2006
Ucore Uranium Inc. name changed to Ucore Rare Metals Inc. 06/29/2010

BIRCHWOOD VENTURES LTD (BC)
Recapitalized as Oromin Explorations Ltd. (Old) 09/30/1997
Each share Common no par exchanged for (0.2) share Common no par
Oromin Explorations Ltd. (Old) merged into Oromin Explorations Ltd. (New) 02/25/2002 which merged into Teranga Gold Corp. 10/08/2013

BIRD & SON INC (MA)
Each share Common no par exchanged for (0.1) share Common no par 02/00/1933
Each share Common no par exchanged for (15) shares Common no par 10/00/1933
Common no par split (3) for (1) by issuance of (2) additional shares 05/17/1972
Common no par split (2) for (1) by issuance of (1) additional share 05/17/1976
$2.75 Conv. Preference no par called for redemption 12/31/1976
Common no par changed to $4 par and (0.33333333) additional share issued 12/11/1978
Name changed to Bird, Inc. 07/08/1983
Bird, Inc. reorganized as Bird Corp. 05/24/1990
(See Bird Corp.)

BIRD-ARCHER CO. (NY)
Acquired by American Cyanamid Co. 12/00/1968
Details not available

BIRD CONSTR INCOME FD (ON)
Under plan of reorganization each Unit no par automatically became (1) share Bird Construction Inc. Common no par 01/04/2011

BIRD CONSTR LTD (SK)
Common no par split (20) for (1) by issuance of (19) additional shares payable 05/16/2001 to holders of record 05/11/2001
Merged into Bird Construction Income Fund 02/27/2006
Each share Common no par exchanged for (3) Trust Units no par
Bird Construction Income Fund reorganized as Bird Construction Inc. 01/04/2011

BIRD CORP (MA)
Merged into Compagnie de Saint-Gobain 07/29/1998
Each share $1.85 Conv. Preference $1 par exchanged for $20 cash
Each share Common $4 par exchanged for $5.50 cash
5% Preferred $100 par called for redemption at $110 on 09/24/1998
Public interest eliminated

BIRD FD INC (MO)
Liquidation completed
Each share Common $1 par received initial distribution of $32 cash 01/06/1981
Each share Common $1 par received second distribution of $12.50 cash 01/07/1982
Each share Common $1 par received third and final distribution of $5.10 cash 10/20/1982
Note: Certificates were not required to be surrendered and are without value

BIRD GROCERY STORES, INC.
Merged into Safeway Stores, Inc. 00/00/1928
Details not available

BIRD HLDG INC (MD)
Liquidation completed
Each share Common $10 par received initial distribution of $25.50 cash 01/12/1981
Each share Common $10 par received second distribution of $10 cash 01/13/1982
Each share Common $10 par received third and final distribution of $5.80 cash 10/22/1982
Note: Certificates were not required to be surrendered and are without value

BIRD INC (MA)
Under plan of reorganization each share $1.85 Conv. Preference $1 par, 5% Preferred $100 par and Common $4 par automatically became (1) share Bird Corp. $1.85 Conv. Preference $1 par, 5% Preferred $100 par and Common $4 par respectively 05/24/1990
(See Bird Corp.)

BIRD MACH CO (MA)
Merged into Bird & Son, Inc. 03/01/1972
Each share Common no par exchanged for (1) share $2.75 Conv. Preference no par
(See Bird & Son, Inc.)

BIRD MED TECHNOLOGIES INC (CA)
Merged into Thermo Electron Corp. 10/18/1995
Each share Common 1¢ par exchanged for $9.25 cash

BIRD RIV MINES INC (MB)
Name changed 02/13/2001
Name changed from Bird River Mines Ltd. to Bird River Mines Inc. 02/13/2001
Name changed to Bird River Resources Inc. 02/07/2011

BIRDAIR STRUCTURES INC (NY)
Common 10¢ par split (2) for (1) by issuance of (1) additional share 05/15/1970
Merged into Chemical Fabrics Corp. 08/01/1979
Each share Common 10¢ par exchanged for $25 cash

BIRDFINDER CORP (FL)
Name changed to Non-Invasive Monitoring Systems, Inc. 11/10/1989

BIRDSBORO CORP (PA)
Common $4 par changed to 10¢ par and (4) additional shares issued 10/31/1971
Common 10¢ par split (1.75) for (1) by issuance of (0.75) additional share 07/30/1976
Reported out of business 00/00/1987
Details not available

BIRDSBORO STEEL FOUNDRY & MACHINE CO. (DE)
Merged into Birdsboro Corp. (PA) 12/31/1959
Each share Capital Stock 50¢ par exchanged for (0.33333333) share Common $4 par
(See Birdsboro Corp.)

BIRDSBORO STEEL FOUNDRY & MACHINE CO. (PA)
Each share Common $50 par exchanged for (11) shares Common no par 00/00/1937
Name changed to B.S.F. Co. (PA) 00/00/1954
B.S.F. Co. (PA) reorganized in Delaware 09/30/1955 which merged into ELT, Inc. 03/31/1975 which name changed to Dutch Boy, Inc. 02/23/1977 which name changed to Artra Group Inc. 12/31/1980 which merged into Entrade Inc. 09/23/1999
(See Entrade Inc.)

BIRDSBORO WATER CO. (PA)
Liquidation completed
Each share Capital Stock $100 par received initial distribution of $200 cash 01/03/1963
Each share Capital Stock $100 par received second distribution of $45 cash 05/10/1963
Each share Capital Stock $100 par received third and final distribution of $3 cash 04/18/1967
Note: Certificates were not required to be surrendered and are without value

BIRDVIEW SATELLITE COMMUNICATIONS INC (DE)
Each share Common $0.001 par exchanged for (0.1) share Common 1¢ par 09/09/1983
Plan of reorganization under Chapter 11 Federal Bankruptcy proceedings confirmed 11/14/1988
No stockholders' equity

BIRELEY'S INC.
Completely liquidated 02/22/1943
Each share Common received first and final distribution of (0.15) share General Foods Corp. Common no par
(See General Foods Corp.)

BIRIM GOLDFIELDS INC (ON)
Class A Common no par reclassified as Common no par 00/00/1998
Merged into Volta Resources Inc. 03/31/2008
Each share Common no par exchanged for (0.38461538) share Common no par
Volta Resources Inc. merged into B2Gold Corp. 12/27/2013

BIRK BROTHERS BREWING CO.
Business discontinued 00/00/1950
Details not available

BIRKA CAP CORP (AB)
Name changed to Qnetix Inc. 03/30/1998
(See Qnetix Inc.)

BIRKS & MAYORS INC (CANADA)
Name changed to Birks Group Inc. 10/01/2013

BIRMAN MANAGED CARE INC (DE)
Each share old Common no par exchanged for (0.33333333) share new Common no par 07/15/1999
Recapitalized as Hackerproof, Ltd. 10/27/2005
Each share new Common no par exchanged for (0.001) share Common $0.001 par
Hackerproof, Ltd. name changed to Alcard Chemicals Group, Inc. 03/14/2006 which name changed to Alcar Chemicals Group, Inc. 04/03/2006

BIRMINGHAM & NORTHWESTERN RAILWAY
Merged into Gulf, Mobile & Northern Railroad Co. 09/00/1929
Details not available

BIRMINGHAM BLOOMFIELD BANCSHARES INC (MI)
Acquired by Arbor Bancorp, Inc. 01/06/2017
Each share Common no par exchanged for $16.50 cash

BIRMINGHAM BLOOMFIELD BK (BIRMINGHAM, MI)
Common $10 par changed to $7.50 par and (0.33333333) additional share issued 04/23/1968
Placed in receivership 02/13/1971
Note: Receiver opined no stockholders' equity

BIRMINGHAM ELEC CO (AL)
Merged into Alabama Power Co. 00/00/1952
Each share 4.20% Preferred $100 par exchanged for (1) share 4.2% Preferred $100 par
Each share Common no par received $22.75 cash

BIRMINGHAM FIRE & CASUALTY CO. (AL)
Merged into St. Paul Fire & Marine Insurance Co. 01/01/1962
Each share Common exchanged for (0.44) share Capital Stock $6.25 par
St. Paul Fire & Marine Insurance Co. name changed to St. Paul Companies, Inc. 01/01/1968 which name changed to St. Paul Travelers Companies, Inc. 04/01/2004 which name changed to Travelers Companies, Inc. 02/27/2007

BIRMINGHAM FIRE INSURANCE CO. (AL)
Stock Dividend - 75% 10/01/1951
Name changed to Birmingham Fire & Casualty Co. 01/01/1957
Birmingham Fire & Casualty Co. merged into St. Paul Fire & Marine Insurance Co. 01/01/1962 which name changed to St. Paul Companies, Inc. 01/01/1968 which name changed to St. Paul Travelers Companies, Inc. 04/1/2004 which name changed to Travelers Companies, Inc. 02/27/2007

BIRMINGHAM GAS CO.
Name changed to Alabama Gas Corp. 00/00/1949
Alabama Gas Corp. name changed to Alagasco Inc. 01/18/1979 which name changed to Energen Corp. 10/01/1985

BIRMINGHAM LEAD & SMELTING CO., INC. (AL)
Each share Preferred $1 par exchanged for $1 principal amount of 6% Debentures
Each share Common 1¢ par exchanged for (0.02) share Common 50¢ par
Completely liquidated 00/00/1967
Each share Common 50¢ par exchanged for first and final distribution of $0.50 cash

BIRMINGHAM NATIONAL BANK (BIRMINGHAM, MI)
Stock Dividend - 10% 12/29/1954
Merged into Detroit Bank & Trust Co. (Detroit, MI) 08/31/1956
Each share Capital Stock $10 par exchanged for (1) share Common $10 par
Detroit Bank & Trust Co. (Detroit, MI) reorganized as Detroitbank Corp. 06/01/1973 which name changed to Comerica, Inc. 07/01/1982

BIRMINGHAM SOUND REPRODUCERS LTD. (ENGLAND)
Stock Dividend - 50% 12/15/1960
Name changed to B.S.R. Ltd. 06/19/1962
B.S.R. PLC name changed to BSR International PLC 06/03/1983 which name changed to Astec (BSR) PLC 06/07/1989
(See Astec (BSR) PLC)

BIRMINGHAM STL CORP (DE)
Common 1¢ par split (3) for (2) by issuance of (0.5) additional share 06/30/1988
Common 1¢ par split (3) for (2) by issuance of (0.5) additional share 12/16/1992
Plan of reorganization under Chapter 11 Federal Bankruptcy Code effective 12/09/2002

Each share Common 1¢ par received first and final distribution of $0.4675 cash payable 12/27/2002 to holders of record 12/10/2002 Ex date - 12/30/2002
Note: Certificates were not required to be surrendered and are without value

BIRMINGHAM TR NATL BK (BIRMINGHAM, AL)
Each share Common $50 par exchanged for (2) shares Common $25 par 00/00/1952
Each share Common $25 par exchanged for (3.125) shares Common $10 par to effect a (2.5) for (1) split and 25% stock dividend 01/10/1956
Stock Dividends - 66.66666666% 12/24/1946; 20% 01/20/1958; 33.33333333% 04/20/1959; 25% 05/26/1961; 20% 06/21/1963; 12.5% 07/19/1966; 11.11111111% 05/21/1968
Reorganized as BTNB Corp. 12/31/1968
Each share Common $10 par exchanged for (1) share Common $10 par
BTNB Corp. recapitalized as Alabama Financial Group, Inc. 03/10/1972 which name changed to Southern Bancorporation 04/17/1974 which name changed to Southern Bancorporation of Alabama 04/21/1975 which name changed to SouthTrust Corp. 09/18/1981 which merged into Wachovia Corp. (Ctfs. dated after 09/01/2001) 11/01/2004 which merged into Wells Fargo & Co. (New) 12/31/2008

BIRMINGHAM TURF CLUB, LTD. (AL)
Dissolved 12/31/1992
Details not available

BIRMINGHAM UTILS INC (CT)
Common no par split (2) for (1) by issuance of (1) additional share payable 03/31/1999 to holders of record 03/18/1999
Name changed to BIW Ltd. 07/01/2002
(See BIW Ltd.)

BIRMINGHAM WTR CO (CT)
Merged into Ansonia Derby Water Co. 01/01/1972
Each share Capital Stock $25 par exchanged for (5.14) shares Common no par
Ansonia Derby Water Co. name changed to Birmingham Utilities, Inc. 07/19/1993 which name changed to BIW Ltd. 07/01/2002
(See BIW Ltd.)

BIRNAYE OIL & URANIUM CO. (NV)
Dissolved 01/09/1959
Details not available

BIROCO KIRKLAND MINES LTD (ON)
Acquired by Inter.tain.net Inc. 03/08/1996
Each share Common no par exchanged for $0.10 cash

BIRON BAY RES LTD (ON)
Recapitalized 03/12/1981
Recapitalized from Biron Bay Gold Mines Ltd. to Biron Bay Resources Ltd. 03/12/1981
Each share Capital Stock $1 par exchanged for (0.2) share Common no par
Merged into Royal Ecoproducts Ltd. 05/01/1997
Each share new Common no par exchanged for (0.34246575) share Subordinate no par
Royal Ecoproducts Ltd. merged into Royal Group Technologies Ltd. 07/23/1998
(See Royal Group Technologies Ltd.)

BIRR WILSON MONEY FD (CA)
Fund terminated 01/01/1989

Each share Common no par received net asset value

BIRTCHER MED SYS INC (CA)
Name changed 11/15/1990
Name changed from Birtcher Corp. to Birtcher Medical Systems, Inc. 11/15/1990
Merged into CONMED Corp. 03/15/1995
Each share 6% Conv. Participating Preferred Ser. A no par exchanged for (0.5) share Conv. Preferred 1¢ par
Each share Common no par exchanged for (0.0833) share Common 1¢ par

BIRTMAN ELECTRIC CO. (IL)
Stock Dividend - 200% 04/21/1950
Merged into Whirlpool Corp. (DE) 04/01/1957
Each share Common $5 par exchanged for (0.71428571) share Common $5 par

BIRZAI MILK JOINT-STK CO (LITHUANIA)
Company placed in bankruptcy 10/24/2005
GDR holders' equity unlikely

BIS COMMUNICATIONS CORP (NY)
Dissolved by proclamation 12/24/1991

BISASSIST INC (NV)
Name changed to Cody Ventures Corp. 10/11/2004
Cody Ventures Corp. recapitalized as Paw4mance Pet Products International, Inc. 07/28/2011 which recapitalized as Fearless Films, Inc. 11/19/2014

BISCAYNE APPAREL INC (FL)
Recapitalized as El Apparel, Inc. 08/29/2005
Each share Common 1¢ par exchanged for (0.001) share Common 1¢ par
El Apparel, Inc. recapitalized as NutriOne Corp. 07/27/2006
(See NutriOne Corp.)

BISCAYNE FED SVGS & LN ASSN MIAMI FLA (USA)
Capital Stock 1¢ par reclassified as Common 1¢ par 10/12/1979
Common 1¢ par split (3) for (2) by issuance of (0.5) additional share 10/26/1979
Declared insolvent 04/06/1983
No stockholders' equity

BISCAYNE HLDGS INC (FL)
Reorganized 07/01/1990
Each share Class A Common 50¢ par exchanged for (0.33333333) share Class A Common 1¢ par 06/29/1987
Under plan of reorganization state of incorporation changed from (DE) to (FL) 07/01/1990
Each share Class A Common 1¢ par exchanged for (1) share Common 1¢ par
Each share Non-Vtg. Conv. Class B 50¢ par exchanged for (1/3) share Common no par
Name changed to Biscayne Apparel, Inc. 05/31/1994
Biscayne Apparel, Inc. recapitalized as El Apparel, Inc. 08/29/2005 which recapitalized as NutriOne Corp. 07/27/2006
(See NutriOne Corp.)

BISCAYNE NATL CORP (FL)
Administratively dissolved 09/28/2012

BISCHOFF CHEM CORP (NY)
Ceased operations 11/00/1974
Company has no assets

BISHOP & BABCOCK CORP. (OH)
5% Conv. Preferred $10 par called for redemption 08/20/1963
Acquired by Valley Mould & Iron Corp. 03/26/1965
Each share Common no par exchanged for (0.1888) share Common $5 par
Each share Common no par received distribution of (0.0112) additional share Common $5 par 03/13/1968
Valley Mould & Iron Corp. name changed to Vare Corp. 12/04/1967 which merged into Microdot Inc. (CA) 01/31/1969 which reincorporated in Delaware 07/02/1971
(See Microdot Inc. (DE))

BISHOP & BABCOCK MANUFACTURING CO. (OH)
Common no par split (3) for (1) by issuance of (2) additional shares 04/28/1960
Common no par split (2) for (1) by issuance of (1) additional share 05/10/1961
Under plan of merger name changed to Bishop & Babcock Corp. 04/30/1962
Bishop & Babcock Corp. acquired by Valley Mould & Iron Corp. 03/26/1965 which name changed to Vare Corp. 12/04/1967 which merged into Microdot Inc. (CA) 01/31/1969 which reincorporated in Delaware 07/02/1971
(See Microdot Inc. (DE))

BISHOP CANYON OIL & GAS CORP. (NM)
Charter revoked for failure to file reports and pay fees 08/17/1961

BISHOP CANYON URANIUM CORP. (NM)
Name changed to Bishop Canyon Oil & Gas Corp. 05/13/1959
(See Bishop Canyon Oil & Gas Corp.)

BISHOP CAP CORP (BC)
Reincorporated under the laws of Alberta as Bishop Resources Inc. 03/19/1996
Bishop Resources Inc. recapitalized as Bishop Gold Inc. (AB) 08/16/2004 which reincorporated in British Columbia 09/19/2006 which recapitalized as First Pursuit Ventures Ltd. 11/21/2007 which name changed to Silver Pursuit Resources Ltd. 06/03/2011 which name changed to Golden Pursuit Resources Ltd. 06/15/2018

BISHOP CO.
Acquired by National Biscuit Co. 00/00/1930
Details not available

BISHOP EQUITIES INC (NV)
Name changed to Aethlon Medical, Inc. 04/03/2000

BISHOP GOLD INC (BC)
Reincorporated 09/19/2006
Place of incorporation changed from (AB) to (BC) 09/19/2006
Recapitalized as First Pursuit Ventures Ltd. 11/21/2007
Each share Common no par exchanged for (0.05) share Common no par
First Pursuit Ventures Ltd. name changed to Silver Pursuit Resources Ltd. 06/03/2011 which name changed to Golden Pursuit Resources Ltd. 06/15/2018

BISHOP INC. (DE)
Name changed 01/28/1988
Common 1¢ par changed to $0.00666 par and (0.5) additional share issued 07/11/1983
Common $0.00666 par changed to 10¢ par 04/01/1985
Stock Dividends - 10% 12/23/1977; 10% 06/15/1979; 10% 04/24/1981; 10% 04/22/1983; 10% 04/22/1985
Name and state of incorporation changed from Bishop Graphics, Inc. (CA) to Bishop Inc. (DE) 01/28/1988
Charter cancelled and declared inoperative and void for non-payment of taxes 03/01/1995

BISHOP (HAZEL) INC. (NY)
Under plan of merger each share old Common 10¢ par exchanged for (0.25) share new Common 10¢ par 01/23/1962
Name changed to Bishop Industries Inc. (NY) 05/19/1967
(See Bishop Industries Inc. (NY))

BISHOP INDS INC (CT)
Merged into United Equities, Inc. 12/28/1968
Each share Common $1 par exchanged for (1) share Common 1¢ par
(See United Equities, Inc.)

BISHOP INDS INC (NY)
Adjudicated bankrupt 12/20/1974
Stockholders' equity unlikely

BISHOP INVESTMENT CORP (DE)
Merged into Crocker National Corp. 01/23/1980
Each share Common no par exchanged for (1) share Common 10¢ par
(See Crocker National Corp.)

BISHOP NATIONAL BANK OF HAWAII (HONOLULU, HI)
Stock Dividend - 25% 07/23/1958
Name changed to First National Bank of Hawaii (Honolulu, HI) 04/15/1960
First National Bank of Hawaii (Honolulu, HI) name changed to First Hawaiian Bank (Honolulu, HI) 01/02/1969 which reorganized as First Hawaiian, Inc. 07/01/1974 which name changed to BancWest Corp. (New) 11/01/1998
(See BancWest Corp. (New))

BISHOP OIL CO. (CA)
Liquidation completed 08/15/1962
Details not available

BISHOP OIL CORP.
Merged into Bishop Oil Co.00/00/1939
Each share Common exchanged for (1) share Common
(See Bishop Oil Co.)

BISHOP RES DEV LTD (BC)
Name changed 10/12/1982
Name changed from Bishop Mines Ltd. to Bishop Resources Development Ltd. 10/12/1982
Cease trade order effective 07/19/1989
Stockholders' equity unlikely

BISHOP RES INC (AB)
Recapitalized as Bishop Gold Inc. (AB) 08/16/2004
Each share Common no par exchanged for (0.33333333) share Common no par
Bishop Gold Inc. (AB) reincorporated in British Columbia 09/19/2006 which recapitalized as First Pursuit Ventures Ltd. 11/21/2007 which name changed to Silver Pursuit Resources Ltd. 06/03/2011 which name changed to Golden Pursuit Resources Ltd. 06/15/2018

BISHOP RES INTL EXPL INC (QC)
Recapitalized as Caldera Resources Inc. 11/30/1995
Each share Common no par exchanged for (0.1) share Common no par

BISHOP TR LTD (HONOLULU, HI)
Reorganized as Bishop Investment Corp. 04/01/1970
Each share Common $10 par exchanged for (2) shares Common no par
Bishop Investment Corp. merged into Crocker National Corp. 01/23/1980
(See Crocker National Corp.)

BISHOPSGATE PLATINUM LTD (SOUTH AFRICA)
Recapitalized as Impala Platinum Holdings Ltd. 10/30/1978

Each ADR for Ordinary exchanged for (0.5) ADR for Ordinary

BISHU MINES LTD. (ON)
Declared dissolved 06/03/1963
No stockholders' equity

BISI INC (NY)
Charter cancelled and proclaimed dissolved for failure to pay taxes and file reports 12/20/1977

BISMARCK BREWING CORP.
Assets acquired by Croft Brewing Co. 00/00/1938
Details not available

BISMARCK HOTEL CO (IL)
Voluntarily dissolved 07/14/1998
Details not available

BISMARCK MNG CO (ID)
Recapitalized as Western Goldfields Inc. (ID) 07/17/2002
Each share Common 10¢ par exchanged for (0.33333333) share Common 1¢ par
Western Goldfields Inc. (ID) reincorporated in Ontario 06/29/2007 which merged into New Gold Inc. 06/04/2009

BISMILLAH VENTURES INC (BC)
Recapitalized as Royal Rock Ventures Inc. 11/10/1997
Each share Common no par exchanged for (0.2) share Common no par
Royal Rock Ventures Inc. recapitalized as Bi-Optic Ventures Inc. 04/06/2001 which name changed to Arcturus Growthstar Technologies Inc. 02/17/2016 which name changed to Future Farm Technologies Inc. 02/02/2017

BISON GOLD EXPL INC (ON)
Recapitalized as Bison Gold Resources Inc. 05/11/2009
Each share Common no par exchanged for (0.33333333) share Common no par
Bison Gold Resources Inc. merged into Klondex Mines Ltd. 10/20/2017
(See Klondex Mines Ltd.)

BISON GOLD RES INC (ON)
Each share old Common no par exchanged for (0.04) share new Common no par 02/24/2016
Merged into Klondex Mines Ltd. 10/20/2017
Each share new Common no par exchanged for (0.1242) share Common no par
Note: Unexchanged certificates will be cancelled and become without value 10/20/2023
(See Klondex Mines Ltd.)

BISON MFG CORP (NY)
Name changed to New Bison, Inc. 05/31/1967
(See New Bison, Inc.)

BISON PETE & MINERALS LTD (ON)
Recapitalized as United Bison Resources Ltd. 12/22/1987
Each share Capital Stock $1 par exchanged for (0.01) share Class A no par
United Bison Resources Ltd. merged into Nalcap Holdings Inc. 04/25/1991 which recapitalized as Arbatax International Inc. (Canada) 03/28/1996 which reincorporated in Yukon 08/06/1996 which name changed to MFC Bancorp Ltd. (YT) 03/03/1997 which reincorporated in British Columbia 11/03/2004 which name changed to KHD Humboldt Wedag International Inc. 11/01/2005 which reorganized as Terra Nova Royalty Corp. 03/30/2010 which name changed to MFC Industrial Ltd. 09/30/2011 which name changed to MFC Bancorp Ltd. 02/16/2016
(See MFC Bancorp Ltd. (BC))

BISON PETE CORP (NV)
Common $0.001 par split (8) for (1) by issuance of (7) additional shares payable 06/19/2013 to holders of record 06/19/2013
Recapitalized as Yinhang Internet Technologies Development, Inc. 09/01/2015
Each share Common $0.001 par exchanged for (0.01) share Common $0.001 par

BISON PETROLEUMS LTD. (ON)
Acquired by Saskalon Uranium & Oils Ltd. 00/00/1954
Each share Common $1 par exchanged for (0.2) share Capital Stock $1 par
(See Saskalon Uranium & Oils Ltd.)

BISON RES LTD (AB)
Merged into Mission Oil & Gas Inc. 01/05/2006
Each share Class A Common no par exchanged for (0.3284) share Common no par and $6.055 cash
Mission Oil & Gas Inc. merged into Crescent Point Energy Trust 02/14/2007 which reorganized as Crescent Point Energy Corp. 07/07/2009

BISSETT GOLD MINES LTD (MB)
Charter cancelled 05/00/1972

BISYS GROUP INC (DE)
Common 2¢ par split (2) for (1) by issuance of (1) additional share payable 10/20/2000 to holders of record 10/06/2000
Common 2¢ par split (2) for (1) by issuance of (1) additional share payable 02/22/2002 to holders of record 02/08/2002 Ex date - 02/25/2002
Merged into Citigroup Inc. 08/01/2007
Each share Common 2¢ par exchanged for $11.85 cash

BIT INTEGRATION TECHNOLOGY INC (ON)
Name changed to Smartcardesolutions.com Ltd. 09/21/2000
(See Smartcardesolutions.com Ltd.)

BITCO CORP (DE)
Common $1 par split (5) for (4) by issuance of (0.25) additional share 03/14/1980
Common $1 par split (5) for (4) by issuance of (0.25) additional share 03/12/1982
Common $1 par split (3) for (2) by issuance of (0.5) additional share 06/22/1983
Merged into Old Republic International Corp. 03/11/1985
Each share Common $1 par exchanged for (0.4) share Conv. Preferred Ser. E no par

BITCOIN COLLECT INC (NV)
Name changed to Good Vibrations Shoes Inc. 09/09/2014

BITCOIN SHOP INC (NV)
Name changed to BTCS Inc. 08/03/2015

BITEC DEV CORP (BC)
Struck off register and declared dissolved for failure to file returns 03/31/1994

BITECH PETE CORP (CANADA)
Name changed 08/11/1989
Reorganized 11/20/1996
Name changed from Bitech Energy Resources Ltd. to Bitech Corp. 08/11/1989
Reorganized from Bitech Corp. (ON) to under the laws of Canada as Bitech Petroleum Corp. 11/20/1996
Each share old Common no par exchanged for (0.0666) share new Common no par
Merged into LUKOIL Overseas Canada Ltd. 10/09/2001

Each share new Common no par exchanged for $1.55 cash

BITEX CORP (DE)
Adjudicated bankrupt 10/31/1974
Stockholders' equity unlikely

BITGOLD INC (CANADA)
Name changed to GoldMoney Inc. 07/30/2015

BITSTREAM INC (DE)
Each share Class A Common 1¢ par received distribution of (1) share Marlborough Software Development Holdings Inc. Common 1¢ par payable 03/14/2012 to holders of record 03/08/2012
Acquired by Monotype Imaging Holdings Inc. 03/19/2012
Each share Class A Common 1¢ par exchanged for $4.36197 cash

BITTERROOT MNG CO (ID)
Recapitalized as Advanced Process Technologies Inc. 09/20/2000
Each share Common 10¢ par exchanged for (0.25) share Common 10¢ par
Advanced Process Technologies Inc. name changed to Integrated Pharmaceuticals, Inc. 12/12/2000
(See Integrated Pharmaceuticals, Inc.)

BITUMEN CAP INC (CANADA)
Recapitalized as Goliath Resources Ltd. 10/18/2017
Each share Common no par exchanged for (0.59880239) share Common no par

BITUMINOUS CAS CORP (IL)
Capital Stock $25 par changed to $12.50 par and (1) additional share issued 05/24/1957
Capital Stock $12.50 par changed to $4.16666666 par and (2) additional shares issued 05/24/1972
Stock Dividends - 100% 05/22/1963; 100% 05/26/1967; 100% 06/02/1971
Reincorporated under the laws of Delaware as Bitco Corp. and Capital Stock $4.16666666 par reclassified as Common $1 par 06/01/1973
Bitco Corp. merged into Old Republic International Corp. 03/11/1985

BITWISE DESIGNS INC (DE)
Name changed to AuthentiDate Holding Corp. 03/23/2001
AuthentiDate Holding Corp. name changed to Aeon Global Health Corp. 02/01/2018

BITX FINL CORP (BC)
Recapitalized as Digatrade Financial Corp. 06/22/2016
Each share Common no par exchanged for (0.02) share Common no par

BIW CABLE SYS INC (MA)
Merged into Draka Holding B.V. 06/30/1988
Each share Common 40¢ par exchanged for $5.85 cash

BIW LTD (CT)
Merged into South Central Connecticut Regional Water Authority 01/16/2008
Each share Common no par exchanged for $23.75 cash

BIZ OUTSOURZING INC (NV)
Name changed to Mobile Entertainment, Inc. 05/25/2007

BIZAUCTIONS INC (DE)
Each share old Common $0.001 par exchanged for (0.00005882) share new Common $0.001 par 02/21/2012
Name changed to CannaGrow Holdings, Inc. 11/05/2014

BIZCAP INC (DE)
Each share Common $1 par exchanged for (0.005) share Common $200 par 01/29/1986

Note: Holders of (199) or fewer pre-split shares received $41 cash per share
Name changed to Caribbean Marine Inc. 12/03/1986
(See Caribbean Marine Inc.)

BIZMART INC (DE)
Merged into IEI Acquisition Corp. 06/18/1991
Each share Common 1¢ par exchanged for $16.50 cash

BIZNESSONLINE COM INC (DE)
Each (3,000,000) shares old Common 1¢ par exchanged for (1) share new Common 1¢ par 03/24/2004
Note: In effect holders received $0.01 cash per share and public interest was eliminated

BIZNET GROUP INC (FL)
Each share old Common $0.001 par exchanged for (0.004) share new Common $0.001 par 05/06/2003
Recapitalized as ProMed Alliance International, Inc. 02/21/2006
Each share new Common $0.001 par exchanged for (0.1) share Common $0.001 par
ProMed Alliance International, Inc. name changed to Biomedtex, Inc. 10/09/2007
(See Biomedtex, Inc.)

BIZZINGO INC (NV)
SEC revoked common stock registration 04/22/2016

BJ SVCS CO (DE)
Common 10¢ par split (2) for (1) by issuance of (1) additional share payable 02/20/1998 to holders of record 01/30/1998 Ex date - 02/23/1998
Common 10¢ par split (2) for (1) by issuance of (1) additional share payable 05/31/2001 to holders of record 05/17/2001 Ex date - 06/01/2001
Common 10¢ par split (2) for (1) by issuance of (1) additional share payable 09/01/2005 to holders of record 08/18/2005 Ex date - 09/02/2005
Merged into Baker Hughes Inc. 04/28/2010
Each share Common 10¢ par exchanged for (0.40035) share Common $1 par and $2.69 cash
Baker Hughes Inc. merged into Baker Hughes, a GE company 07/05/2017

BJB INVT FDS (MA)
Name changed to Julius Baer Investment Funds 07/01/1998
Julius Baer Investment Funds name changed to Artio Global Investment Funds 10/13/2008
(See Artio Global Investment Funds)

BJS WHSL CLUB INC (DE)
Common 1¢ par split (2) for (1) by issuance of (1) additional share payable 03/02/1999 to holders of record 02/16/1999 Ex date - 03/03/1999
Acquired by Beacon Holding Inc. 09/30/2011
Each share Common 1¢ par exchanged for $51.25 cash

BKC SEMICONDUCTORS INC (MA)
Merged into Micro BKC Acquisition Corp. 05/14/1998
Each share Common no par exchanged for $9.17 cash

BKF CAP GROUP INC (DE)
Common Stock Purchase Rights declared for Common stockholders of record 06/18/2001 were redeemed at $0.01 per right 07/29/2005 for holders of record 07/15/2005
(Additional Information in Active)

BKL INC (CO)
Recapitalized as Tahoe Co., Inc. 08/18/1988

Each share Common no par exchanged for (0.02) share Common no par

BKLA BANCORP (CA)
Common no par split (5) for (4) by issuance of (0.25) additional share 08/05/1985
Stock Dividends - 10% 06/30/1987; 10% 02/28/1990
Merged into Bank of Los Angeles (New) (Los Angeles, CA) 10/23/1995
Each share Common no par exchanged for (0.2) share Common no par
Bank of Los Angeles (New) (Los Angeles, CA) merged into Western Bancorp 10/26/1998 which merged into U.S. Bancorp 11/15/1999

BKW SYS INC (DE)
Name changed 11/04/1985
Name and state of incorporation changed from BKW, Inc. (NH) to BKW Systems, Inc. 11/04/1985
Trustee appointed 12/18/1989
No stockholders' equity

BLACK & DECKER CORP (MD)
Name changed 01/28/1985
Common no par changed to $1 par 02/01/1955
Common $1 par split (2) for (1) by issuance of (1) additional share 10/17/1955
Common $1 par changed to 50¢ par and (1) additional share issued 09/11/1959
Common 50¢ par split (2) for (1) by issuance of (1) additional share 09/04/1964
Common 50¢ par split (3) for (2) by issuance of (0.5) additional share 10/17/1967
Common 50¢ par split (3) for (2) by issuance of (0.5) additional share 07/28/1970
Common 50¢ par split (3) for (1) by issuance of (2) additional shares 02/15/1974
Name changed from Black & Decker Manufacturing Co. to Black & Decker Corp. 01/28/1985
Merged into Stanley Black & Decker, Inc. 03/12/2010
Each share Common 50¢ par exchanged for (1.275) shares Common $2.50 par

BLACK ANGUS FRANCHISE SYS INC (FL)
Name changed to Black Angus Systems, Inc. 05/19/1970
(See Black Angus Systems, Inc.)

BLACK ANGUS SYS INC (FL)
Merged into Black Angus Management Corp. 07/21/1987
Each share Common 10¢ par exchanged for $2 cash

BLACK ART BEVERAGE INC (NV)
Recapitalized as VoxPop Worldwide, Inc. 12/15/2010
Each share Common $0.001 par exchanged for (0.01) share Common 1¢ par
VoxPop Worldwide, Inc. name changed to Renovate Neighborhoods, Inc. 01/06/2014

BLACK BAY URANIUM LTD (AB)
Recapitalized as New Black Bay Minerals Ltd. 07/18/1974
Each share Common no par exchanged for (0.005) share Common no par
(See New Black Bay Minerals Ltd.)

BLACK BEAR CONSOLIDATED MINING CO. (NV)
Each share Common 20¢ par exchanged for (0.1) share Common $1 par 11/02/1959
Name changed to Black Bear Industries, Inc. and Common $1 par changed to 15¢ par 05/24/1960
(See Black Bear Industries, Inc.)

BLACK BEAR INDUSTRIES, INC. (NV)
Charter revoked for failure to pay fees 03/05/1962

BLACK BEAR MINING CO. (CA)
Charter revoked for failure to pay taxes 02/28/1920

BLACK BEAVER (UT)
Name changed to Casino Systems, Inc. 09/10/1979
Casino Systems, Inc. name changed to Black Beaver, Inc. 01/02/1981 which merged into Nevaco Systems, Inc. 10/09/1982

BLACK BEAVER INC (UT)
Common $0.005 par split (2) for (1) by issuance of (1) additional share 02/06/1981
Merged into Nevaco Systems Inc. 10/09/1982
Each share Common $0.005 par exchanged for (0.1) share Common 10¢ par

BLACK BIRCH CAP ACQUISITION I CORP (ON)
Name changed to Oremex Gold Inc. 09/20/2011

BLACK BIRCH CAP ACQUISITION II CORP (CANADA)
Reincorporated under the laws of British Columbia as Chinapintza Mining Corp. 06/19/2013

BLACK BIRCH CAP ACQUISITION III CORP (BC)
Reincorporated 07/28/2017
Each share old Common no par exchanged for (0.33333333) share new Common no par 06/13/2017
Place of incorporation changed from (Canada) to (BC) 07/28/2017
Recapitalized as GTEC Holdings Ltd. 06/22/2018
Each share new Common no par exchanged for (0.08333333) share Common no par

BLACK BOURGON MINES LTD. (ON)
Charter cancelled 07/10/1961

BLACK BULL RES INC (AB)
Reincorporated under the laws of Canada 06/12/2008

BLACK CANYON RES INC (AB)
Merged into Cannon Oil & Gas Ltd. 07/23/1999
Each share Common no par exchanged for (0.210526) share Common no par
Cannon Oil & Gas Ltd. acquired by G2 Resources Inc. 01/29/2007 which merged into Regal Energy Ltd. 07/10/2008 which recapitalized as Novus Energy Inc. 08/05/2009
(See Novus Energy Inc.)

BLACK CASTLE DEVS HLDGS INC (NV)
Recapitalized as ingXabo Corp. 01/28/2015
Each share Common $0.0001 par exchanged for (0.0002) share Common $0.0001 par
(See ingXabo Corp.)

BLACK CASTLE DEVS INC (NV)
Reincorporated 06/01/2011
State of incorporation changed from (FL) to (NV) 06/01/2011
Name changed to Black Castle Developments Holdings, Inc. 08/02/2011
Black Castle Developments Holdings, Inc. recapitalized as ingXabo Corp. 01/28/2015
(See ingXabo Corp.)

BLACK CAT ENTMT CORP (CO)
Name changed to Mobile Airwaves Corp. 08/15/2005
Mobile Airwaves Corp. recapitalized as American Community Development, Inc. 11/04/2009 which recapitalized as UMF Group Inc. 02/23/2017

BLACK CLAWSON CO (OH)
Each share Common $100 par exchanged for (10) shares old Common no par 00/00/1940
Each share old Common no par exchanged for (2) shares new Common no par 00/00/1946
Merged into Parsons & Whittemore, Inc. 11/16/1979
Each share Common no par exchanged for $50 cash
Preferred $1 par acquired 00/00/1984
Details not available

BLACK CLIFF MINES LTD (ON)
Common $1 par changed to no par 06/12/1979
Name changed to Altai Resources Inc. 07/28/1992

BLACK CREEK IMPROVEMENT CO. (PA)
Liquidation completed
Each share Common $1 par exchanged for initial distribution of $6 cash 02/15/1968
Each share Common $1 par received second distribution of $0.95 cash 10/29/1968
Each share Common $1 par received third and final distribution of $0.68 cash 12/29/1969

BLACK CRICKET MINES LTD (ON)
Charter cancelled for failure to pay taxes and file returns 03/16/1976

BLACK CROW MINES LTD. (ON)
Charter cancelled and declared dissolved 02/11/1965

BLACK DIAMOND BRANDS CORP (BC)
Name changed to Rainchief Energy Inc. 01/23/2009
Rainchief Energy Inc. name changed to Bit-X Financial Corp. 02/19/2015 which recapitalized as Digatrade Financial Corp. 06/22/2016

BLACK DIAMOND ENERGY INC (WY)
Name changed to Causeway Technologies, Inc. 08/23/1999

BLACK DIAMOND INC (DE)
Name changed to Clarus Corp. (New) 08/14/2017

BLACK DIAMOND INCOME FD (AB)
Reorganized as Black Diamond Group Ltd. 12/31/2009
Each Trust Unit exchanged for (1) share Common no par
Note: Unexchanged certificates were cancelled and became without value 12/31/2014

BLACK DIAMOND INDS LTD (AB)
Name changed to RPV Industries (Canada) Inc. 09/07/1988
(See RPV Industries (Canada) Inc.)

BLACK DIAMOND RES LTD (BC)
Name changed to Com-Air Containers (Canada) Inc. 01/14/1987
(See Com-Air Containers (Canada) Inc.)

BLACK DIAMOND SVGS BK FSB (NORTON, VA)
Merged into FNB Financial Services Corp. 08/31/1999
Each share Common $1 par exchanged for (1.3333) shares Common $1 par
FNB Financial Services Corp. merged into NewBridge Bancorp 07/31/2007 which merged into Yadkin Financial Corp. 03/01/2016 which merged into F.N.B. Corp. 03/11/2017

BLACK DOME ENERGY CORP (CO)
Each share old Common no par exchanged for (0.00099999) share new Common no par 10/31/1994
Completely liquidated
Each share new Common no par received first and final distribution of approximately $11.70 cash payable 05/15/1998 to holders of record 04/30/1998
Note: Certificates were not required to be surrendered and are without value

BLACK DRAGON ENTMT INC (DE)
Common $0.0001 par split (4) for (1) by issuance of (3) additional shares payable 09/26/2000 to holders of record 09/21/2000 Ex date - 09/27/2000
Recapitalized as Vita Biotech Corp. 08/10/2002
Each share Common $0.0001 par exchanged for (0.05) share Common $0.0001 par
Vita Biotech Corp. name changed to August Energy Corp. 07/02/2004 which recapitalized as Canyon Gold Corp. 05/02/2011 which name changed to Defense Technologies International Corp. 06/15/2016

BLACK DRAGON RES INC (DE)
Recapitalized as Black Dragon Resource Companies, Inc. 01/05/2005
Each share Common $0.001 par exchanged for (0.002) share Common $0.001 par

BLACK GIANT MINES LTD (BC)
Recapitalized as Alcina Development Corp. 08/22/1984
Each share Capital Stock no par exchanged for (0.2) share Common no par
(See Alcina Development Corp.)

BLACK GIANT OIL CO (NV)
Common 5¢ par changed to $1.25 par and (3) additional shares issued 04/25/1980
Name changed to Broadband Wireless International Corp. 02/16/2000
(See Broadband Wireless International Corp.)

BLACK GOLD MINES LTD. (ON)
Charter revoked for failure to file reports and pay taxes 00/00/1958

BLACK GOLD OIL & GAS LTD (AB)
Merged into Intensity Resources Ltd. 09/17/1990
Each share Common no par exchanged for (0.34418) share Common no par
Intensity Resources Ltd. merged into Renata Resources Inc. 04/25/1997 which merged into Rio Alto Exploration Ltd. 06/21/2000 which merged into Canadian Natural Resources Ltd. 07/01/2002

BLACK GOLD RES INC (UT)
Reorganized as Souvall-Page & Co., Inc. 00/00/1987
Details not available

BLACK GOLD RES 1973 LTD (AB)
Name changed to Black Gold Oil & Gas Ltd. 08/29/1980
Black Gold Oil & Gas Ltd. merged into Intensity Resources Ltd. 09/17/1990 which merged into Renata Resources Inc. 04/25/1997 which merged into Rio Alto Exploration Ltd. 06/21/2000 which merged into Canadian Natural Resources Ltd. 07/01/2002

BLACK GREGOR EXPLORATIONS LTD. (ON)
Name changed to Gregor Goldfields Corp. 08/11/1993
Gregor Goldfields Corp. recapitalized as Aavdex Corp. 02/24/1998 which name changed to Richmond Minerals Inc. 11/17/2005

BLACK HAT CAP INC (AB)
Name changed to Castle Resources Inc. (AB) 04/10/2007
Castle Resources Inc. (AB) reincorporated in Ontario 08/12/2011
(See Castle Resources Inc.)

BLACK HAWK EXPL INC (NV)
Ceased all activity and operations 08/29/2013

BLACK HAWK GAMING & DEV INC (CO)
Merged into Gameco, Inc. 02/22/2002
Each share Common $0.001 par exchanged for $12 cash

BLACK HAWK HLDGS INC (MN)
Reincorporated 10/09/1989
State of incorporation changed from (IA) to (MN) 10/09/1989
Each share old Common 1¢ par exchanged for (0.25) share new Common 1¢ par 04/26/1991
Name changed to Eagle Pacific Industries, Inc. 07/11/1995
Eagle Pacific Industries, Inc. name changed to PW Eagle, Inc. 06/19/2000
(See PW Eagle, Inc.)

BLACK HAWK MNG INC (QC)
Name changed 02/11/1982
Name changed from Black Hawk Mining Ltd. to Black Hawk Mining Inc.-Compagnie Miniere Black Hawk Inc. 02/11/1982
Common $1 par changed to no par 02/16/1988
Merged into Glencairn Gold Corp. 10/20/2003
Each share Common $1 par exchanged for (0.33333333) share Common no par
Glencairn Gold Corp. recapitalized as Central Sun Mining Inc. 12/05/2007 which was acquired by B2Gold Corp. 03/31/2009

BLACK HAWK PORCUPINE MINES LTD. (ON)
Charter cancelled 00/00/1957

BLACK HAWK RES CO (UT)
Name changed to Trionics, Inc. 07/02/1990

BLACK HAWK URANIUM & METALS CO. (UT)
Name changed to Black Hawk Resources Co. and Common 2¢ par changed to no par 11/21/1961
Black Hawk Resources Co. name changed to Trionics, Inc. 07/02/1990

BLACK HILL MINERALS LTD (AUSTRALIA)
ADR's for Ordinary split (5) for (2) by issuance of (1.5) additional ADR 03/06/1992
Name changed to DeepGreen Minerals Corp. N.L. 12/05/1996
(See DeepGreen Minerals Corp. N.L.)

BLACK HILL NICKEL MINES LTD. (ON)
Dissolved 12/29/2000
Details not available

BLACK HILL RES LTD (BC)
Name changed to Texcan Technology Corp. 05/15/1985
Texcan Technology Corp. recapitalized as International Texcan Technology Corp. 01/29/1987
(See International Texcan Technology Corp.)

BLACK HILLS PWR & LT CO (SD)
4.56% Preferred $25 par called for redemption 02/24/1959
5.65% Preferred $100 par called for redemption 02/28/1966
Common $1 par split (2) for (1) by issuance of (1) additional share 05/31/1983
Common $1 par split (2) for (1) by issuance of (1) additional share 02/28/1986
Stock Dividend - 100% 02/19/1986
Name changed to Black Hills Corp. 03/27/1996

BLACK HILLS UTILITIES CO.
Name changed to Montana-Dakota Utilities Co. 00/00/1930
Montana-Dakota Utilities Co. name changed to MDU Resources Group, Inc. 04/25/1985

BLACK INDS INC (NC)
Merged into Tri-Star Acquisition of North Carolina 10/09/1991
Each share Common $1 par exchanged for $13 cash

BLACK JADE RES LTD (BC)
Name changed to International Magnetics Corp. 00/00/1985
International Magnetics Corp. name changed to United Southern Minerals Corp. 11/01/1988
(See United Southern Minerals Corp.)

BLACK LABEL RES INC (BC)
Name changed to Autobyte Technologies Inc. 06/03/1992
(See Autobyte Technologies Inc.)

BLACK LAKE URANIUM MINES, LTD. (ON)
Charter cancelled and proclaimed dissolved for failure to pay taxes and file returns 11/05/1962

BLACK LIME OIL CO. (TX)
Dissolved 04/29/1924
No stockholders' equity

BLACK MAMMOTH CONSOLIDATED MINING CO. (NV)
Capital Stock 10¢ par changed to 5¢ par 01/17/1955
Recapitalized as Terex Corp. 10/29/1962
Each share Capital Stock 5¢ par exchanged for (0.1) share Common Capital Stock no par
(See Terex Corp.)

BLACK MARLIN ENERGY CORP (BC)
Cease trade order effective 02/08/1985
Stockholders' equity unlikely

BLACK MARLIN ENERGY HLDGS LTD (BRITISH VIRGIN ISLANDS)
Merged into Afren PLC 10/08/2010
Each share Common no par exchanged for (0.3647) share Ordinary
Note: Unexchanged certificates were cancelled and became without value 10/08/2016

BLACK MTN CAP CORP (YT)
Recapitalized as Grand Peak Capital Corp. (YT) 11/20/2007
Each share Common no par exchanged for (0.2) share Common no par
Grand Peak Capital Corp. (YT) reincorporated in British Columbia 04/27/2010

BLACK MTN MINERALS INC (ON)
Recapitalized as Augustine Ventures Inc. 11/30/2006
Each share Common no par exchanged for (0.02) share Common no par
Augustine Ventures Inc. merged into Red Pine Exploration Inc. 02/06/2017

BLACK OWL RES LTD (BC)
Struck off register and declared dissolved for failure to file returns 12/14/1990

BLACK PANTHER MNG CORP (BC)
Each share old Common no par exchanged for (0.33333333) share new Common no par 06/13/2013
Name changed to Canadian International Pharma Corp. 06/22/2015

BLACK PEARL MINERALS CONS INC (ON)
Name changed to Canada Lithium Corp. (ON) 01/19/2009
Canada Lithium Corp. (ON) reorganized in Canada as RB Energy Inc. 02/05/2014

BLACK PEARL MINERALS INC (ON)
Recapitalized as Black Pearl Minerals Consolidated Inc. 06/22/2000
Each share Common no par exchanged for (0.2) share Common no par
Black Pearl Minerals Consolidated Inc. name changed to Canada Lithium Corp. (ON) 01/19/2009 which reorganized in Canada as RB Energy Inc. 02/05/2014

BLACK PEARL PETROLEUMS LTD. (BC)
Recapitalized as Signet Resources Inc. 08/02/1983
Each share Capital Stock no par exchanged for (1) share Common no par
Signet Resources Inc. recapitalized as New Signet Resources Inc. 03/11/1987 which recapitalized as Amir Ventures Corp. (BC) 06/29/1993 which reorganized in Yukon Territory as America Mineral Fields Inc. 08/08/1995 which name changed to Adastra Minerals Inc. 05/12/2004 which merged into First Quantum Minerals Ltd. 08/11/2006

BLACK PEARL RES LTD (BC)
Reorganized under the laws of Delaware as Wizan Productions, Inc. 02/11/1987
Each share Common no par exchanged for (1) share Common no par
(See Wizan Productions, Inc.)

BLACK PHOTO LTD (ON)
Common no par reclassified as Conv. Class A no par 08/22/1973
Conv. Class A no par reclassified as Common no par 02/26/1980
Conv. Class B no par reclassified as Common no par 02/26/1980
Common no par split (3) for (1) by issuance of (2) additional shares 10/20/1981
Stock Dividend - 40% 03/20/1980
Merged into Scott's Hospitality Inc. 05/28/1985
Each share Common no par exchanged for $22 cash

BLACK POINT RES LTD (ON)
Recapitalized as InfoUtility Corp. 06/15/2000
Each share Common no par exchanged for (0.25) share Common no par
InfoUtility Corp. recapitalized as Lynden Ventures Ltd. (ON) 01/19/2004 which reincorporated in British Columbia 02/02/2006 which name changed to Lynden Energy Corp. 01/17/2008 which merged into Earthstone Energy, Inc. 05/19/2016

BLACK PT CAP INC (CANADA)
Merged into Mistral Pharma Inc. 04/29/2005
Each share Common no par exchanged for (1) share Common no par
(See Mistral Pharma Inc.)

BLACK RAVEN ENERGY INC (NV)
Merged into EnerJex Resources, Inc. 10/01/2013
Each share Common $0.001 par exchanged for (0.34971) share Common $0.001 par
EnerJex Resources, Inc. recapitalized as AgEagle Aerial Systems, Inc. 03/27/2018

BLACK RIDGE OIL & GAS INC (DE)
Reincorporated under the laws of Nevada 12/10/2012

BLACK RIV PETE CORP (NV)
Name changed to Viva Entertainment Group, Inc. 08/02/2016

BLACK RIVER MINING LTD. (QC)
Recapitalized as Menorah Mines Ltd. 03/04/1968
Each share Capital Stock no par exchanged for (0.33333333) share Capital Stock no par
Menorah Mines Ltd. name changed to Menora Resources Inc. 04/28/1983 which recapitalized as Mengold Resources Inc. 12/04/2003 which recapitalized as MGold Resources Inc. (QC) 09/22/2010 which reincorporated in Alberta 07/25/2013 which name changed to Tanager Energy Inc. 09/23/2013

BLACK ROCK GOLF CORP (DE)
SEC revoked common stock registration 11/08/2011
Note: Corporate identity hijacked by Aurus Corp. which is not a legitimate successor

BLACK ROCK NEV MINES LTD (BC)
Name changed to Argosy Mining Corp. (BC) 07/26/1993
Argosy Mining Corp. (BC) reincorporated in Yukon 08/12/1997 which merged into Argosy Minerals Inc. (YT) 05/07/1999 which reincorporated in British Columbia 05/26/2005 which reincorporated in Australia as Argosy Minerals Ltd. 03/18/2011

BLACK SEA ENERGY LTD (YT)
Name changed to Ivanhoe Energy Inc. 06/30/1999
(See Ivanhoe Energy Inc.)

BLACK SEA OIL INC NEW (NV)
Common $0.001 par changed to $0.0001 par and (16.5) additional shares issued payable 12/26/2006 to holders of record 12/19/2006
Ex date - 12/27/2006
Recapitalized as Clearview Acquisitions, Inc. 11/14/2008
Each share Common $0.0001 par exchanged for (0.001) share Common $0.0001 par
Clearview Acquisitions, Inc. name changed to Helix Wind, Corp. 04/24/2009

BLACK SEA OIL INC OLD (NV)
Charter revoked for failure to file reports and pay fees 09/01/2003

BLACK SHEEP VENTURES INC (BC)
Name changed to Ameroil Energy Corp. (BC) 07/11/1985
Ameroil Energy Corp. (BC) reincorporated in Alberta 08/00/1989 which reincorporated in Oklahoma as ALN Resources Corp. 11/07/1990 which recapitalized as American Natural Energy Corp. (Ctfs. dtd. prior to 07/19/1994) 12/01/1992 which was acquired by Alexander Energy Corp. 07/19/1994 which merged into National Energy Group, Inc. 08/30/1996
(See National Energy Group, Inc.)

BLACK, SIVALLS & BRYSON, INC. (DE)
4.25% Preferred $100 par called for redemption 01/23/1952
Each share Common $1 par exchanged for (0.5) share Houston Oil Field Material Co., Inc. $1.50 Part. Preferred no par 11/22/1965
(See Houston Oil Field Material Co., Inc.)
4.75% Preferred $100 par reclassified as 7% Preferred $100 par 06/12/1969
5.75% Preferred $100 par reclassified as 7.5% Preferred $100 par 06/12/1969
7% Preferred $100 par called for redemption 12/19/1974
Stock Dividend - 20% 12/23/1949
7.5% Preferred $100 par called for redemption 12/00/1975
Public interest eliminated

BLACK SMOKER VENTURES INC (BC)
Recapitalized as Jager Resources Inc. 11/28/2012
Each share Common no par

exchanged for (0.07692307) share Common no par
Jager Resources Inc. recapitalized as Sora Capital Corp. 02/20/2014 which name changed to ProSmart Enterprises Inc. 07/12/2017

BLACK SPARROW CAP CORP (AB)
Recapitalized as Aphria Inc. 12/08/2014
Each share Common no par exchanged for (0.1) share Common no par

BLACK SPRINGS CAP CORP (BC)
Reorganized under the laws of Quebec as Kintavar Exploration Inc. 04/03/2017
Each share Common no par exchanged for (0.5) share Common no par
Note: Unexchanged certificates will be cancelled and become without value 04/03/2023

BLACK STALLION MGMT INC (NV)
Each share old Common $0.001 par exchanged for (1.25) shares new Common $0.001 par 01/31/2000
Name changed to Digital Bridge, Inc. 03/16/2000
Digital Bridge, Inc. recapitalized as Tantivy Group, Inc. 03/25/2002 which recapitalized as Oretech, Inc. 04/01/2003
(See Oretech, Inc.)

BLACK, STARR & GORHAM, INC. (DE)
Acquired by Black, Starr & Frost, Ltd. 04/09/1962
Each share Class A Common no par exchanged for $21.50 cash

BLACK STEER AMER INC (UT)
Common 5¢ par split (5) for (2) by issuance of (1.5) additional shares 03/15/1971
Completely liquidated 05/00/1972
Each share Common 5¢ par exchanged for first and final distribution of (1) share Water Wonderland Corp. Capital Stock no par
Water Wonderland Corp. name changed to Progressive National Industries, Inc. 08/17/1972
(See Progressive National Industries, Inc.)

BLACK STURGEON GOLD MINES LTD. (ON)
Charter revoked for failure to file reports and pay taxes 00/00/1954

BLACK SWAN RES LTD (YT)
Name changed 11/01/1999
Reincorporated 00/00/2001
Each share old Common no par exchanged for (0.2) share new Common no par 03/06/1997
Name changed from Black Swan Gold Mines Ltd. to Black Swan Resources Ltd. 11/01/1999
Place of incorporation changed from (BC) to (YT) 00/00/2001
Reincorporated under the laws of British Columbia as Brazilian Diamonds Ltd. 09/23/2003
Brazilian Diamonds Ltd. name changed to Kincora Copper Ltd. 07/18/2011

BLACK (ALBERT) TELEVISION PRODUCTIONS, INC. (DE)
Recapitalized as American & Foreign Productions, Inc. 00/00/1953
Each share Common 1¢ par exchanged for (0.2) share Common 5¢ par
(See American & Foreign Productions, Inc.)

BLACK THUNDER OIL, INC. (SD)
Name changed to Black Thunde Oil-Uranium Inc. 06/30/1950
Black Thunder Oil-Uranium Inc. merged into Mountain Valley Oil Corp. 09/09/1955
(See Mountain Valley Oil Corp.)

BLACK THUNDER OIL-URANIUM INC. (SD)
Merged into Mountain Valley Oil Corp. 09/09/1955
Details not available

BLACK THUNDER PETE CORP (BC)
Recapitalized as Conley Resources Corp. 06/28/1990
Each share Common no par exchanged for (0.2) share Common no par
(See Conley Resources Corp.)

BLACK TIE AFFAIR INC (NV)
Name changed to Pitts & Spitts of Texas Inc. 07/26/1996
Pitts & Spitts of Texas Inc. name changed to Energy Drilling Industries, Inc. 12/22/1997 which name changed to American International Industries Inc. 06/30/1998

BLACK TIGER COPPER MINING CO. (WY)
Charter revoked for non-payment of taxes 07/19/1927

BLACK TUSK ENERGY INC (BC)
Assets sold for the benefit of creditors 03/31/2004
Stockholders' equity unlikely

BLACK TUSK MINERALS INC (NV)
Each share old Common $0.001 par exchanged for (2) shares new Common $0.001 par 09/12/2007
New Common $0.001 par split (2) for (1) by issuance of (1) additional share payable 02/12/2010 to holders of record 02/01/2010 Ex date - 02/16/2010
Each share new Common $0.001 par exchanged again for (0.02) share new Common $0.001 par 10/12/2010
Completely liquidated
Each share new Common $0.001 par received distribution of (1) share Minera Bonanza Peru S.A. Common payable 09/16/2013 to holders of record 09/03/2013

BLACK WARRIOR WIRELINE CORP (DE)
Each share Common $0.00001 par exchanged for (0.005) share old Common $0.0005 par 05/01/1990
Each share old Common $0.0005 par exchanged again for (0.005) share new Common $0.0005 par 10/30/1995
Each share new Common $0.0005 par exchanged again for (0.1) share new Common $0.0005 par 12/27/2005
Name changed to Warrior Energy Services Corp. 02/08/2006
Warrior Energy Services Corp. merged into Superior Energy Services, Inc. 12/12/2006

BLACK WIDOW RES INC (CANADA)
Name changed to BWR Exploration Inc. 10/03/2016

BLACKBERRY GOLD RES INC (BC)
Struck off register and declared dissolved for failure to file returns 05/01/1992

BLACKBIRD INTL CORP (NV)
Each share old Common $0.001 par exchanged for (0.05) share new Common $0.001 par 10/27/2014
Recapitalized as Romana Food Brands Corp. 10/04/2017
Each share new Common $0.001 par exchanged for (0.01) share Common $0.001 par

BLACKBIRD INVTS INC (BC)
Name changed to Blackbird Energy Inc. 03/25/2010

BLACKBIRD PETE CORP (NV)
Common $0.001 par split (3) for (1) by issuance of (2) additional shares payable 12/05/2008 to holders of record 11/25/2008 Ex date - 12/08/2008
Common $0.001 par split (2) for (1) by issuance of (1) additional share payable 02/09/2009 to holders of record 02/03/2009 Ex date - 02/10/2009
Name changed to Blackbird International Corp. 03/09/2011
Blackbird International Corp. recapitalized as Romana Food Brands Corp. 10/04/2017

BLACKBOARD INC (DE)
Acquired by Bulldog Holdings, L.L.C. 10/04/2011
Each share Common 1¢ par exchanged for $45 cash

BLACKBOX SEMICONDUCTOR INC (NV)
Each share old Common $0.001 par exchanged for (20) shares new Common $0.001 par 06/13/2011
Name changed to Vision Dynamics Corp. 01/16/2013
Vision Dynamics Corp. recapitalized as Secured Technology Innovations Corp. 02/14/2014

BLACKBRIDGE CAP CORP (BC)
Name changed to Rupert Resources Ltd. 11/01/1994

BLACKCHAIN SOLUTIONS INC (BC)
Recapitalized as Trackloop Analytics Corp. 09/25/2018
Each share Common no par exchanged for (0.5) share Common no par

BLACKDOG RES LTD (AB)
Name changed to StonePoint Energy Inc. 11/06/2014
(See StonePoint Energy Inc.)

BLACKDOME MNG CORP (BC)
Name changed 05/01/1986
Common no par reclassified as Class A Common no par 02/29/1980
Class A Common no par reclassified as Common no par 04/08/1982
Class B Common no par reclassified as Common no par 04/08/1982
Name changed from Blackdome Exploration Ltd. to Blackdome Mining Corp. 05/01/1986
Merged into MinVen Gold Corp. 08/23/1989
Each share Common no par exchanged for (1) share Common no par
MinVen Gold Corp. reorganized as Dakota Mining Corp. 09/15/1993
(See Dakota Mining Corp.)

BLACKEAGLE DEV CORP (BC)
Name changed to EVI Global Group Developments Corp. 07/13/2016

BLACKFOOT ENTERPRISES INC (NV)
Common $0.001 par split (15) for (1) by issuance of (14) additional shares payable 09/07/2005 to holders of record 09/06/2005 Ex date - 09/08/2005
Name changed to Tower Tech Holdings, Inc. 02/07/2006
Tower Tech Holdings, Inc. name changed to Broadwind Energy, Inc. (NV) 03/04/2008 which reincorporated in Delaware 06/20/2008

BLACKGOLD ENERGY RES INC (CO)
Completely liquidated 10/08/1987
Each share Common no par exchanged for first and final distribution of (0.006357) Snyder Oil Partners L.P. Unit of Ltd. Partnership
(See Snyder Oil Partners L.P.)

BLACKHAWK AMERICAN CORP. (IA)
Charter cancelled for failure to file annual reports 11/24/1975

BLACKHAWK BREWING CO. (IA)
Adjudicated bankrupt 00/00/1953
No stockholders' equity

BLACKHAWK CAP GROUP BDC INC (DE)
SEC revoked common stock registration 10/01/2013

BLACKHAWK FD (NV)
Each share old Common $0.001 par exchanged for (0.00125) share new Common $0.001 par 11/17/2005
New Common $0.001 par changed to $0.0001 par 08/07/2008
Recapitalized as Vidable, Inc. 07/01/2011
Each share Common $0.0001 par exchanged for (0.0002) share Common $0.0001 par
Vidable, Inc. recapitalized as Vibe I, Inc. 08/03/2015 which name changed to Coresource Strategies, Inc. (NV) 10/26/2015 which reincorporated in Oklahoma as NUGL, Inc. 12/11/2017

BLACKHAWK FINL INC (NV)
Name changed to Jedi Mind, Inc. 04/29/2009
Jedi Mind, Inc. name changed to Mind Technologies, Inc. 05/09/2011
(See Mind Technologies, Inc.)

BLACKHAWK HLDG CO (IL)
Proclaimed dissolved for failure to pay taxes and file reports 04/01/2004

BLACKHAWK NETWORK HLDGS INC (DE)
Class A Common $0.001 par reclassified as Common $0.001 par 05/22/2015
Class B Common $0.001 par reclassified as Common $0.001 par 05/22/2015
Acquired by BHN Holdings, Inc. 06/15/2018
Each share Common $0.001 par exchanged for $45.25 cash

BLACKHORN GOLD MINES LTD (CANADA)
Name changed to Oremex Resources Inc. 10/16/2003
Oremex Resources Inc. name changed to Oremex Silver Inc. 09/09/2011 which name changed to Monarca Minerals Inc. 08/24/2016

BLACKICE ENTERPRISE RISK MANAGMENT INC (BC)
Recapitalized as Blackchain Solutions Inc. 12/28/2017
Each share Common no par exchanged for (0.5) share Common no par
Blackchain Solutions Inc. recapitalized as Trackloop Analytics Corp. 09/25/2018

BLACKJACK URANIUM CO. (UT)
Merged into Apache Uranium Corp. 00/00/1954
Each share Common 1¢ par exchanged for (8.33333333) share Common 1¢ par
Apache Uranium Corp. merged into International Oil & Metals Corp. 03/29/1956 which liquidated for Perfect Photo, Inc. 03/24/1965 which was acquired by United Whelan Corp. 06/30/1966 which name changed to Perfect Film & Chemical Corp. 05/31/1967 which name changed to Cadence Industries Corp. 10/22/1970
(See Cadence Industries Corp.)

BLACKLINE GPS CORP (AB)
Each share old Common no par exchanged for (0.1) share new Common no par 06/24/2011
Name changed to Blackline Safety Corp. 07/09/2015

BLACKLINE OIL CORP (BC)
Reincorporated under the laws of Alberta as Resourcexplorer Inc. 02/19/2001
Resourcexplorer Inc. recapitalized as

Exchequer Resource Corp. (AB) 07/24/2002 which reincorporated in British Columbia 10/25/2004 which recapitalized as CBD MED Research Corp. 07/18/2014

BLACKMAN MERCHANDISING CORP (MO)
Stock Dividend - Class A & B Common - 100% 07/15/1961
Name changed to Green Cross Industries, Inc. 03/04/1970
(See Green Cross Industries, Inc.)

BLACKMAN-UHLER CHEMICAL CO. (SC)
Name changed to Blackman-Uhler Industries, Inc. 03/01/1965
Blackman-Uhler Industries, Inc. name changed to Synalloy Corp. (SC) 07/31/1967 which reincorporated in Delaware 06/03/1988

BLACKMAN-UHLER INDUSTRIES, INC. (SC)
Common $1 par split (5) for (4) by issuance of (0.25) additional share 04/01/1965
Name changed to Synalloy Corp. (SC) 07/31/1967
Synalloy Corp. (SC) reincorporated in Delaware 06/03/1988

BLACKMIST RES INC (BC)
Recapitalized as Stray Horse Resources Inc. 01/18/1985
Each share Capital Stock no par exchanged for (0.2) share Common no par
Stray Horse Resources Inc. name changed to Oriole Communications Inc. 07/28/1987 which recapitalized as Consolidated Oriole Communications Inc. 09/10/1993 which name changed to Oriole Systems Inc. 03/26/1996
(See Oriole Systems Inc.)

BLACKPOOL EXPL LTD (AB)
Merged into Western Canada Energy Ltd. 04/07/2008
Each share Common no par exchanged for (0.46000064) share Common no par
(See Western Canada Energy Ltd.)

BLACKRIDGE HLDGS INC (AB)
Name changed to Lifestart Multimedia Corp. 05/03/1995
Lifestart Multimedia Corp. recapitalized as GLK Strategies Inc. 11/20/2000 which recapitalized as Yankee Hat Industries Corp. (ALTA) 02/18/2003 which reincorporated in British Columbia as Yankee Hat Minerals Ltd. 02/09/2005

BLACKROCK ADVANTAGE TERM TR INC (MD)
Completely liquidated
Each share Common 1¢ par received first and final distribution of $10.23 cash payable 12/29/2005 to holders of record 12/15/2005

BLACKROCK APEX MUN FD INC (MD)
Merged into BlackRock MuniAssets Fund, Inc. 02/25/2011
Each share Common 10¢ par exchanged for (0.72861057) share Common 10¢ par

BLACKROCK BROAD INVT GRADE 2009 TERM TR INC (MD)
Completely liquidated 10/29/2009
Each share Common 1¢ par exchanged for first and final distribution of $12.569731 cash

BLACKROCK BUILD AMER BD TR (DE)
Name changed to BlackRock Taxable Municipal Bond Trust 08/25/2015

BLACKROCK CALIF INDS MUN 2008 TERM TR INC (MD)
Auction Rate Municipal Preferred Ser. W7 1¢ par split (2) for (1) by issuance of (1) additional share 07/24/1995
Auction Rate Municipal Preferred Ser. W28 no par split (2) for (1) by issuance of (1) additional share 07/24/1995
Auction Rate Municipal Preferred Ser. W7 1¢ par called for redemption at $25,000 on 10/26/2006
Auction Rate Municipal Preferred Ser. W28 1¢ par called for redemption at $25,000 on 11/09/2006
Trust terminated 12/30/2008
Each share Common 1¢ par received first and final distribution of $14.6109 cash

BLACKROCK CALIF INSD MUN INCOME TR (DE)
Merged into BlackRock California Municipal Income Trust 02/01/2010
Each share Auction Rate Preferred Ser. F7 $0.001 par automatically became (1) share Auction Rate Preferred Ser. F7 $0.001 par
Each share Common $0.001 par exchanged for (0.97546003) Share of Bene. Int. $0.001 par

BLACKROCK CALIF INVT QUALITY MUN TR INC (MD)
Auction Rate Municipal Preferred Ser. W7 no par split (2) for (1) by issuance of (1) additional share 07/24/1995
Auction Rate Municipal Preferred Ser. W7 no par called for redemption at $25,000 on 09/30/2010
Liquidation completed
Each share Common 1¢ par received initial distribution of $13.9081 cash payable 09/30/2010 to holders of record 09/10/2010
Each share Common 1¢ par received second and final distribution of $0.063075 cash payable 11/23/2011 to holders of record 09/10/2010

BLACKROCK CALIF MUN BD TR (DE)
Merged into BlackRock California Municipal Income Trust 02/01/2010
Each share Auction Rate Preferred Ser. F7 $0.001 par automatically became (1) share Auction Rate Preferred Ser. F7 $0.001 par
Each share Common $0.001 par exchanged for (1.04505055) Shares of Bene. Int. $0.001 par

BLACKROCK CALIF MUN INCOME TR (DE)
Municipal Auction Rate Preferred Ser. R7 $0.001 par called for redemption at $25,000 on 04/13/2012
Municipal Auction Rate Preferred Ser. F7 $0.001 par called for redemption at $25,000 on 04/16/2012
Municipal Auction Rate Preferred Ser. T7 $0.001 par called for redemption at $25,000 on 04/18/2012
(Additional Information in Active)

BLACKROCK CALIF MUN INCOME TR II (DE)
Merged into BlackRock California Municipal Income Trust 02/01/2010
Each share Auction Rate Preferred Ser. R7 $0.001 par automatically became (1) share Auction Rate Preferred Ser. R7 $0.001 par
Each share Auction Rate Preferred Ser. T7 $0.001 par automatically became (1) share Auction Rate Preferred Ser. T7 $0.001 par
Each share Common $0.001 par exchanged for (0.99301767) Share of Bene. Int. $0.001 par

BLACKROCK CALIF MUN 2018 TERM TR (DE)
Auction Market Preferred Ser. M-7 $0.001 par called for redemption at $25,000 on 06/10/2014
(Additional Information in Active)

BLACKROCK CAPITAL & INCOME STRATEGIES FD INC (MD)
Name changed to BlackRock Enhanced Capital & Income Fund, Inc. 05/09/2007

BLACKROCK CORPORATE HIGH YIELD FD INC (MD)
Merged into BlackRock Corporate High Yield Fund VI, Inc. 11/18/2013
Each share Common 10¢ par exchanged for (0.59633674) share Common 10¢ par
BlackRock Corporate High Yield Fund VI, Inc. name changed to BlackRock Corporate High Yield Fund, Inc. 03/03/2014

BLACKROCK CORPORATE HIGH YIELD FD III INC (MD)
Merged into BlackRock Corporate High Yield Fund VI, Inc. 11/18/2013
Each share Common 10¢ par exchanged for (0.61218457) share Common 10¢ par
BlackRock Corporate High Yield Fund VI, Inc. name changed to BlackRock Corporate High Yield Fund, Inc. 03/03/2014

BLACKROCK CORPORATE HIGH YIELD FD V INC (MD)
Merged into BlackRock Corporate High Yield Fund VI, Inc. 11/18/2013
Each share Common 10¢ par exchanged for (1.0266581) shares Common 10¢ par
BlackRock Corporate High Yield Fund VI, Inc. name changed to BlackRock Corporate High Yield Fund, Inc. 03/03/2014

BLACKROCK CORPORATE HIGH YIELD FD VI INC (MD)
Name changed to BlackRock Corporate High Yield Fund, Inc. 03/03/2014

BLACKROCK CREDIT ALLOCATION INCOME TR I INC (MD)
Name changed 11/13/2009
Name changed from BlackRock Preferred & Corporate Income Strategies Fund, Inc. to BlackRock Credit Allocation Income Trust I, Inc. 11/13/2009
Auction Market Preferred Ser. M7 10¢ par called for redemption at $25,000 on 12/07/2010
Auction Market Preferred Ser. T7 10¢ par called for redemption at $25,000 on 12/08/2010
Merged into BlackRock Credit Allocation Income Trust IV 12/10/2012
Each share Common 10¢ par exchanged for (0.74476327) share Common $0.001 par
BlackRock Credit Allocation Income Trust IV name changed to BlackRock Credit Allocation Income Trust 02/11/2013

BLACKROCK CREDIT ALLOCATION INCOME TR II INC (MD)
Name changed 11/13/2009
Name changed from BlackRock Preferred Income Strategies Fund Inc. to BlackRock Credit Allocation Income Trust II, Inc. 11/13/2009
Auction Market Preferred Ser. M7 10¢ par called for redemption at $25,000 on 01/04/2011
Auction Market Preferred Ser. T7 10¢ par called for redemption at $25,000 on 01/05/2011
Auction Market Preferred Ser. W7 10¢ par called for redemption at $25,000 on 01/06/2011
Auction Market Preferred Ser. TH7 10¢ par called for redemption at $25,000 on 01/07/2011
Auction Market Preferred Ser. F7 10¢ par called for redemption at $25,000 on 01/10/2011
Auction Market Preferred Ser. W28 10¢ par called for redemption at $25,000 on 01/13/2011
Auction Market Preferred Ser. TH28 10¢ par called for redemption at $25,000 on 01/28/2011
Merged into BlackRock Credit Allocation Income Trust IV 12/10/2012
Each share Common 10¢ par exchanged for (0.80162384) share Common $0.001 par
BlackRock Credit Allocation Income Trust IV name changed to BlackRock Credit Allocation Income Trust 02/11/2013

BLACKROCK CR ALLOCATION INCOME TR III (DE)
Name changed 11/13/2009
Name changed from BlackRock Preferred Opportunity Trust to BlackRock Credit Allocation Income Trust III 11/13/2009
Auction Market Preferred Shares Ser. T7 10¢ par called for redemption at $25,000 on 12/08/2010
Auction Market Preferred Shares Ser. W7 10¢ par called for redemption at $25,000 on 12/09/2010
Auction Market Preferred Shares Ser. R7 10¢ par called for redemption at $25,000 on 12/10/2010
Merged into BlackRock Credit Allocation Income Trust IV 12/10/2012
Each Common Share 10¢ par exchanged for (0.85922134) share Common $0.001 par
BlackRock Credit Allocation Income Trust IV name changed to BlackRock Credit Allocation Income Trust 02/11/2013

BLACKROCK CR ALLOCATION INCOME TR (DE)
Name changed 11/13/2009
Name changed from BlackRock Preferred & Equity Advantage Trust to BlackRock Credit Allocation Income Trust IV 11/13/2009
Auction Market Preferred Ser. T7 $0.001 par called for redemption at $25,000 on 01/05/2011
Auction Market Preferred Ser. W7 $0.001 par called for redemption at $25,000 on 01/06/2011
Auction Market Preferred Ser. R7 $0.001 par called for redemption at $25,000 on 01/07/2011
Auction Market Preferred Ser. F7 $0.001 par called for redemption at $25,000 on 01/10/2011
Name changed to BlackRock Credit Allocation Income Trust 02/11/2013

BLACKROCK DEFINED OPPORTUNITY CREDIT TR (DE)
Trust terminated 08/18/2017
Each Common Share of Bene. Int. $0.001 par received (1) BHL Liquidating Trust Common Share of Bene. Int. and $8.755 cash

BLACKROCK DIVERSIFIED INCOME STRATEGIES FD INC (MD)
Merged into BlackRock Floating Rate Income Strategies Fund, Inc. 10/08/2012
Each share Common 10¢ par exchanged for (0.72423797) share Common 10¢ par

BLACKROCK DIVIDEND INCOME TR (DE)
Name changed 08/13/2013
Name changed from BlackRock S&P Quality Rankings Global Equity Managed Trust to BlackRock Dividend Income Trust 08/13/2013
Merged into BlackRock Enhanced Equity Dividend Trust 12/08/2014
Each Common Share of Bene. Int. $0.001 par exchanged for (1.57393059) Common Shares of Bene. Int. $0.001 par

BLACKROCK ECOSOLUTIONS INVT TR (DE)
Merged into BlackRock Resources & Commodities Strategy Trust 12/08/2014
Each Common Share of Bene. Int. $0.001 par exchanged for (0.73620796) Common Share of Bene. Int. $0.001 par

BLACKROCK ENHANCED DIVID ACHIEVERS TR (DE)
Name changed to BlackRock Enhanced Equity Dividend Trust 05/09/2011

BLACKROCK ENHANCED EQUITY YIELD & PREM FD INC (MD)
Merged into BlackRock Enhanced Capital & Income Fund, Inc. 11/03/2008
Each share Common 10¢ par exchanged for (0.81144752) share Common 10¢ par

BLACKROCK ENHANCED EQUITY YIELD FD INC (MD)
Merged into BlackRock Enhanced Capital & Income Fund, Inc. 11/03/2008
Each share Common 10¢ par exchanged for (0.80653563) share Common 10¢ par

BLACKROCK EQUITY DIVID TR (DE)
Name changed 05/09/2011
Name changed from BlackRock Dividend Achievers Trust to BlackRock Equity Dividend Trust 05/09/2011
Merged into BlackRock Enhanced Equity Dividend Trust 02/27/2012
Each Common Share of Bene. Int. $0.001 par exchanged for (1.27840257) Common Shares of Bene. Int. $0.001 par

BLACKROCK EUROPE FD INC (MD)
Merged into BlackRock EuroFund 11/06/2006
Each share Common 10¢ par exchanged for (0.54963775) share Class A

BLACKROCK FLA INSD MUN 2008 TERM TR (MA)
Auction Rate Preferred Ser. R7 1¢ par split (2) for (1) by issuance of (1) additional share 07/24/1995
Auction Rate Municipal Preferred Shares Ser. R7 1¢ par called for redemption at $25,000 on 10/27/2006
Trust terminated 12/30/2008
Each share Common 1¢ par received first and final distribution of $14.4387 cash

BLACKROCK FLOATING RATE INCOME STRATEGIES FD II INC (MD)
Merged into BlackRock Floating Rate Income Strategies Fund, Inc. 10/08/2012
Each share Common 10¢ par exchanged for (0.91462449) share Common 10¢ par

BLACKROCK FLOATING RATE INCOME TR (DE)
Name changed 03/09/2009
Name changed from BlackRock Global Floating Rate Income Trust to BlackRock Floating Rate Income Trust 03/09/2009
Auction Preferred Shares Ser. T7 $0.001 par called for redemption at $25,000 on 12/08/2010
Auction Preferred Shares Ser. W7 $0.001 par called for redemption at $25,000 on 12/09/2010
Auction Preferred Shares Ser. R7 $0.001 par called for redemption at $25,000 on 12/10/2010
(Additional Information in Active)

BLACKROCK FLA MUN 2020 TERM TR (DE)
Auction Preferred Ser. F7 $0.001 par called for redemption at $25,000 on 11/10/2014
(Additional Information in Active)

BLACKROCK FOCUS TWENTY FD INC (MD)
Name changed to BlackRock Focus Growth Fund, Inc. 12/17/2007

BLACKROCK GLOBAL ENERGY & RES TR (DE)
Name changed to BlackRock Energy & Resources Trust 03/09/2009

BLACKROCK GLOBAL EQUITY INCOME TRUST (DE)
Merged into BlackRock Global Opportunities Equity Trust 07/27/2009
Each Common Share of Bene. Int. $0.001 par exchanged for (0.55125638) Common Share of Bene. Int. $0.001 par
BlackRock Global Opportunites Equity Trust name changed to BlackRock Enhanced Global Dividend Trust 06/12/2017

BLACKROCK GLOBAL OPPORTUNITIES EQUITY TR (DE)
Name changed to BlackRock Enhanced Global Dividend Trust 06/12/2017

BLACKROCK HIGH INCOME SHS (MA)
Merged into BlackRock Corporate High Yield Fund VI, Inc. 11/18/2013
Each share Common no par exchanged for (0.17536312) share Common 10¢ par

BLACKROCK HIGH YIELD TR (DE)
Merged into BlackRock Corporate High Yield Fund VI, Inc. 11/18/2013
Each share Common $0.001 par exchanged for (0.58941105) share Common 10¢ par
BlackRock Corporate High Yield VI Fund, Inc. name changed to BlackRock Corporate High Yield Fund, Inc. 03/03/2014

BLACKROCK INCOME OPPORTUNITY TR INC (MD)
Name changed 08/28/2002
Name changed from BlackRock North American Government Income Trust Inc. to BlackRock Income Opportunity Trust Inc. 08/28/2002
Merged into BlackRock Core Bond Trust 11/10/2014
Each share Common 1¢ par exchanged for (0.78050585) Share of Bene. Int. $0.001 par

BLACKROCK INDEX FDS INC (DE)
Completely liquidated 03/29/2007
Each share Aggregate Bond Index Fund Class A $0.001 par exchanged for $10.49 cash
Each share Aggregate Bond Index Fund Institutional Class $0.001 par exchanged for $10.48 cash
Merged into BlackRock Funds III 04/19/2013
Each share S&P 500 Index Fund Class A $0.001 par exchanged for (0.10150342) S&P 500 Stock Fund Investor A Share $0.001 par
Each share S&P 500 Index Fund Institutional Class $0.001 par exchanged for (0.10163775) S&P 500 Stock Fund Institutional Share $0.001 par
(Additional Information in Active)

BLACKROCK INSD MUN 2008 TERM TR INC (MD)
Auction Rate Municipal Preferred Ser. R28 1¢ par split (2) for (1) by issuance of (1) additional share 07/24/1995
Old Auction Rate Municipal Preferred Ser. T7 1¢ par split (2) for (1) by issuance of (1) additional share 07/24/1995
Auction Rate Municipal Preferred Ser. R7 1¢ par split (2) for (1) by issuance of (1) additional share 07/24/1995
Auction Rate Municipal Preferred Ser. T28 1¢ par split (2) for (1) by issuance of (1) additional share 07/24/1995
Auction Rate Municipal Preferred Ser. R28 called for redemption at $25,000 on 07/14/2006
Auction Rate Municipal Preferred Ser. T28 called for redemption at $25,000 on 07/26/2006
Auction Rate Municipal Preferred Ser. T7 1¢ par called for redemption at $25,000 on 04/04/2007
Auction Rate Municipal Preferred Ser. R7 1¢ par called for redemption at $25,000 on 04/09/2007
Trust terminated 12/30/2008
Each share Common 1¢ par received first and final distribution of $14.7325 cash

BLACKROCK INSD MUN INCOME TR (DE)
Name changed 11/09/2010
Name changed from BlackRock Insured Municipal Income Trust to BlackRock Municipal Income Quality Trust 11/09/2010
Auction Rate Municipal Preferred Ser. F $0.001 par called for redemption at $25,000 on 01/09/2012
Auction Rate Municipal Preferred Ser. M $0.001 par called for redemption at $25,000 on 01/10/2012
Auction Rate Municipal Preferred Ser. TH $0.001 par called for redemption at $25,000 on 01/13/2012
(Additional Information in Active)

BLACKROCK INSD MUN TERM TR INC (MD)
Auction Rate Preferred Ser. M28 1¢ par split (2) for (1) by issuance of (1) additional share 07/24/1995
Old Auction Rate Municipal Preferred Ser. M7 1¢ par split (2) for (1) by issuance of (1) additional share 07/24/1995
New Auction Rate Municipal Preferred Ser. M7 1¢ par reclassified as old Auction Rate Municipal Preferred Ser. M7 1¢ par 03/21/2000
Auction Rate Municipal Preferred Ser. M28 1¢ par called for redemption at $25,000 on 03/02/2007
Old Auction Rate Municipal Preferred Ser. M7 1¢ par called for redemption at $25,000 on 11/28/2008
Liquidation completed
Each share Common 1¢ par received initial distribution of $10.01 cash payable 12/31/2010 to holders of record 12/15/2010
Each share Common 1¢ par received second and final distribution of $0.0347 cash payable 12/24/2012 to holders of record 12/15/2010

BLACKROCK INTL GROWTH & INCOME TR (DE)
Name changed to BlackRock Enhanced International Dividend Trust 06/12/2017

BLACKROCK INVT QUALITY MUN INCOME TR (MA)
Name changed 09/18/2008
Auction Rate Municipal Preferred split (2) for (1) by issuance of (1) additional share 07/24/1995
Name changed from BlackRock Florida Investment Quality Municipal Trust to BlackRock Investment Quality Municipal Income Trust 09/18/2008
Auction Rate Municipal Preferred called for redemption at $25,000 on 06/29/2012
Completely liquidated
Each share Common 1¢ par received initial distribution of $13.3561 cash payable 06/29/2012 to holders of record 06/15/2012
Each share Common 1¢ par received second and final distribution of $0.044671 cash payable 12/27/2012 to holders of record 06/15/2012

BLACKROCK INVT QUALITY MUN TR INC (MD)
Auction Rate Municipal Preferred Ser. T7 no par split (2) for (1) by issuance of (1) additional share 07/24/1995
Auction Rate Municipal Preferred Ser. T28 no par split (2) for (1) by issuance of (1) additional share 07/24/1995
Each new Auction Rate Municipal Preferred Ser. T7 no par exchanged for (1) Auction Rate Municipal Preferred Ser. T7 no par 03/22/2000
Auction Rate Municipal Preferred Ser. T7 no par called for redemption at $25,000 on 01/11/2012
Auction Rate Municipal Preferred Ser. T28 no par called for redemption at $25,000 on 01/18/2012
(Additional Information in Active)

BLACKROCK INVT QUALITY TERM TR INC (MD)
Trust terminated 12/30/2004
Each share Common 1¢ par exchanged for $10 cash

BLACKROCK KELSO CAP CORP (DE)
Name changed to BlackRock Capital Investment Corp. 03/09/2015

BLACKROCK MD MUN BD TR (DE)
Municipal Auction Rate Preferred Ser. R7 $0.001 par called for redemption at $25,000 on 07/06/2012
(Additional Information in Active)

BLACKROCK MULTI-STRATEGY HEDGE ADVANTAGE (DE)
Completely liquidated 12/08/2008
Each Share of Bene. Int. 1¢ par received net asset value

BLACKROCK MUN BD INVT TR (DE)
Name changed 09/16/2008
Name changed from BlackRock Florida Municipal Bond Trust to BlackRock Municipal Bond Investment Trust 09/16/2008
Municipal Auction Rate Preferred Ser. W-7 $0.001 par called for redemption at $25,000 on 10/06/2011
Under plan of reorganization each share 144A Variable Rate Demand Preferred Ser. W-7 $0.001 par or Common Share of Bene. Int. $0.001 par automatically became (1) share BlackRock Municipal Income Investment Trust 144A Variable Rate Demand Preferred Ser. W-7 $0.001 par or (1.04878696) Common Shares of Bene. Int. $0.001 par respectively 05/16/2016

BLACKROCK MUN BD TR (DE)
Auction Rate Preferred Ser. T7 $0.001 par called for redemption at $25,000 on 01/11/2012
Auction Rate Preferred Ser. R7 $0.001 par called for redemption at $25,000 on 01/13/2012
(Additional Information in Active)

BLACKROCK MUN INCOME INVT QUALITY TR (DE)
Name changed 09/16/2008
Name changed 11/09/2010
Name changed from BlackRock Florida Insured Municipal Income Trust to BlackRock Insured Municipal Income Investment Trust 09/16/2008
Name changed from BlackRock Insured Municipal Income Investment Trust to BlackRock Municipal Income Investment Quality Trust 11/09/2010
Auction Rate Municipal Preferred Ser. M7 $0.001 par called for redemption at $25,000 on 01/10/2012
(Additional Information in Active)

BLACKROCK MUN INCOME INVT TR (DE)
Name changed from BlackRock Florida Municipal Income Trust to BlackRock Municipal Income Investment Trust 09/16/2008
Municipal Auction Rate Preferred Ser. T7 $0.001 par called for redemption at $25,000 on 10/12/2011
(Additional Information in Active)

BLACKROCK MUN INCOME TR (DE)
Auction Rate Municipal Preferred Ser. F7 $0.001 par called for redemption at $25,000 on 01/09/2012
Auction Rate Municipal Preferred Ser. M7 $0.001 par called for redemption at $25,000 on 01/10/2012
Auction Rate Municipal Preferred Ser. T7 $0.001 par called for redemption at $25,000 on 01/11/2012
Auction Rate Municipal Preferred Ser. W7 $0.001 par called for redemption at $25,000 on 01/12/2012
Auction Rate Municipal Preferred Ser. R7 $0.001 par called for redemption at $25,000 on 01/12/2012
(Additional Information in Active)

BLACKROCK MUN TARGET TERM TR (DE)
Name changed to Blackrock Municipal 2030 Target Term Trust 03/01/2016

BLACKROCK MUN TARGET TERM TR INC (MD)
Auction Rate Preference Ser. F7 no par split (2) for (1) by issuance of (1) additional share 07/24/1995
Old Auction Rate Preferred Ser. W7 no par split (2) for (1) by issuance of (1) additional share 07/24/1995
Auction Rate Preference Ser. W28 no par split (2) for (1) by issuance of (1) additional share 07/24/1995
Each old Auction Rate Preferred Ser. W7 no par exchanged for (1) new Auction Rate Municipal Preferred Ser W7 no par 03/16/2000
Auction Rate Preferred Ser. W28 no par called for redemption at $25,000 on 03/10/2005
Auction Rate Preferred Stock Ser. F7 no par called for redemption at $25,000 on 11/07/2005
Each new Auction Rate Municipal Preferred Ser. W7 exchanged for (1) Auction Rate Preferred Ser. W7 03/16/2000
Auction Rate Municipal Preferred Ser. W7 called for redemption at $25,000 on 02/02/2006
Trust terminated 12/28/2006
Each share Common 1¢ par received $9.72 cash

BLACKROCK MUNI INTERMEDIATE DURATION FD INC (MD)
Auction Market Preferred Ser. F7 10¢ par called for redemption at $25,000 on 04/04/2011
Auction Market Preferred Ser. M7 10¢ par called for redemption at $25,000 on 04/05/2011
Auction Market Preferred Ser. T7 10¢ par called for redemption at $25,000 on 04/06/2011
Auction Market Preferred Ser. W7 10¢ par called for redemption at $25,000 on 04/07/2011
Auction Market Preferred Ser. TH7 10¢ par called for redemption at $25,000 on 04/08/2011
Auction Market Preferred Ser. TH28 10¢ par called for redemption at $25,000 on 04/08/2011
Variable Rate Demand Preferred Ser W-7 called for redemption at $100,000 on 12/21/2012
(Additional Information in Active)

BLACKROCK MUNI NEW YORK INTER DURATION FD INC (MD)
Auction Market Preferred Ser. F-7 10¢ par called for redemption at $25,000 on 10/03/2011
(Additional Information in Active)

BLACKROCK MUN INCOME TR II (DE)
Auction Market Preferred Ser. M7 $0.001 par called for redemption at $25,000 on 01/10/2012
Auction Market Preferred Ser. T7 $0.001 par called for redemption at $25,000 on 01/11/2012
Auction Market Preferred Ser. W7 $0.001 par called for redemption at $25,000 on 01/12/2012
Auction Market Preferred Ser. R7 $0.001 par called for redemption at $25,000 on 01/13/2012
(Additional Information in Active)

BLACKROCK MUN 2018 TERM TR (DE)
Auction Market Preferred Ser. R-7 called for redemption at $25,000 on 01/02/2015
Auction Market Preferred Ser. W-7 called for redemption at $25,000 on 01/02/2015
(Additional Information in Active)

BLACKROCK MUNIENHANCED FD INC (MD)
Auction Market Preferred Ser. C 10¢ par called for redemption at $25,000 on 05/31/2011
Auction Market Preferred Ser. D 10¢ par called for redemption at $25,000 on 06/10/2011
Auction Market Preferred Ser. A 10¢ par called for redemption at $25,000 on 06/14/2011
Auction Market Preferred Ser. B 10¢ par called for redemption at $25,000 on 06/21/2011
(Additional Information in Active)

BLACKROCK MUNIHOLDINGS CALIF QUALITY FD INC (MD)
Name changed from BlackRock MuniHoldings California Insured Fund, Inc. to BlackRock MuniHoldings California Quality Fund, Inc. 11/09/2010
Auction Market Preferred Ser. D 10¢ par called for redemption at $25,000 on 04/12/2012
Auction Market Preferred Ser. C 10¢ par called for redemption at $25,000 on 04/13/2012
Auction Market Preferred Ser. B 10¢ par called for redemption at $25,000 on 04/16/2012
Auction Market Preferred Ser. A 10¢ par called for redemption at $25,000 on 04/17/2012
Auction Market Preferred Ser. E 10¢ par called for redemption at $25,000 on 04/18/2012
(Additional Information in Active)

BLACKROCK MUNIHOLDINGS FD INC (MD)
Auction Market Preferred Ser. B 10¢ par called for redemption at $25,000 on 01/06/2012
Auction Market Preferred Ser. C 10¢ par called for redemption at $25,000 on 01/10/2012
Auction Market Preferred Ser. A 10¢ par called for redemption at $25,000 on 01/11/2012
(Additional Information in Active)

BLACKROCK MUNIHOLDINGS FD II INC (MD)
Auction Market Preferred Ser. B 10¢ par called for redemption at $25,000 on 01/09/2012
Auction Market Preferred Ser. A 10¢ par called for redemption at $25,000 on 01/11/2012
(Additional Information in Active)

BLACKROCK MUNIHOLDINGS INSD INVT FD INC (MA)
Name changed 09/16/2008
Name changed 11/09/2010
Name changed from BlackRock MuniHoldings Florida Insured Fund, Inc. to BlackRock MuniHoldings Insured Investment Fund 09/16/2008
Name changed from BlackRock MuniHoldings Insured Investment Fund to BlackRock MuniHoldings Investment Quality Fund 11/09/2010
Auction Market Preferred Ser. B 10¢ par called for redemption at $25,000 on 07/18/2011
Auction Market Preferred Ser. C 10¢ par called for redemption at $25,000 on 07/19/2011
Auction Market Preferred Ser. A 10¢ par called for redemption at $25,000 on 07/20/2011
Auction Market Preferred Ser. D 10¢ par called for redemption at $25,000 on 07/21/2011
Auction Market Preferred Ser. E 10¢ par called for redemption at $25,000 on 07/22/2011
(Additional Information in Active)

BLACKROCK MUNIHOLDINGS N J QUALITY FD INC (MD)
Name changed 11/09/2010
Name changed from BlackRock MuniHoldings New Jersey Insured Fund, Inc. to BlackRock MuniHoldings New Jersey Quality Fund, Inc. 11/09/2010
Auction Market Preferred Ser. E 10¢ par called for redemption at $25,000 on 07/18/2011
Auction Market Preferred Ser. A 10¢ par called for redemption at $25,000 on 07/19/2011
Auction Market Preferred Ser. C 10¢ par called for redemption at $25,000 on 07/20/2011
Auction Market Preferred Ser. D 10¢ par called for redemption at $25,000 on 07/21/2011
Auction Market Preferred Ser. B 10¢ par called for redemption at $25,000 on 07/22/2011
(Additional Information in Active)

BLACKROCK MUNIHOLDINGS N Y QUALITY FD INC (MD)
Name changed 11/09/2010
Name changed from BlackRock MuniHoldings New York Insured Fund, Inc. to BlackRock MuniHoldings New York Quality Fund, Inc. Inc. 11/09/2010
Auction Market Preferred Ser. D 10¢ par called for redemption at $25,000 on 07/18/2011
Auction Market Preferred Ser. C 10¢ par called for redemption at $25,000 on 07/19/2011
Auction Market Preferred Ser. E 10¢ par called for redemption at $25,000 on 07/20/2011
Auction Market Preferred Ser. A 10¢ par called for redemption at $25,000 on 07/21/2011
Auction Market Preferred Ser. B 10¢ par called for redemption at $25,000 on 07/22/2011
(Additional Information in Active)

BLACKROCK MUNIHOLDINGS QUALITY FD INC (NJ)
Name changed 11/09/2010
Name changed from BlackRock MuniHoldings Insured Fund, Inc. to BlackRock MuniHoldings Quality Fund, Inc. 11/09/2010
Auction Market Preferred Ser. A 10¢ par called for redemption at $25,000 on 01/06/2012
Auction Market Preferred Ser. B 10¢ par called for redemption at $25,000 on 01/10/2012
(Additional Information in Active)

BLACKROCK MUNIHOLDINGS QUALITY FD II INC (MD)
Name changed 11/09/2010
Name changed from BlackRock MuniHoldings Insured Fund II, Inc. to BlackRock MuniHoldings Quality Fund II, Inc. 11/09/2010
Auction Market Preferred Ser. B 10¢ par called for redemption at $25,000 on 01/05/2012
Auction Market Preferred Ser. A 10¢ par called for redemption at $25,000 on 01/06/2012
Auction Market Preferred Ser. C 10¢ par called for redemption at $25,000 on 01/11/2012
(Additional Information in Active)

BLACKROCK MUNIVEST FD INC (MD)
Auction Market Preferred Ser. D 10¢ par called for redemption at $25,000 on 01/03/2012
Auction Market Preferred Ser. E 10¢ par called for redemption at $25,000 on 01/03/2012
Auction Market Preferred Ser. A 10¢ par called for redemption at $25,000 on 01/09/2012
Auction Market Preferred Ser. F 10¢ par called for redemption at $25,000 on 01/11/2012
Auction Market Preferred Ser. B 10¢ par called for redemption at $25,000 on 01/17/2012
Auction Market Preferred Ser. C 10¢ par called for redemption at $25,000 on 01/23/2012
(Additional Information in Active)

BLACKROCK MUNIVEST FD II INC (MD)
Auction Market Preferred Ser. D 10¢ par called for redemption at $25,000 on 01/10/2012
Auction Market Preferred Ser. A 10¢ par called for redemption at $25,000 on 01/12/2012
Auction Market Preferred Ser. C 10¢ par called for redemption at $25,000 on 01/12/2012
Auction Market Preferred Ser. B 10¢ par called for redemption at $25,000 on 01/19/2012
(Additional Information in Active)

BLACKROCK MUNIYIELD ARIZONA FD INC NEW (MD)
Auction Market Preferred Ser. C 10¢ par called for redemption at $25,000 on 06/06/2011
Auction Market Preferred Ser. A 10¢ par called for redemption at $25,000 on 06/09/2011
Auction Market Preferred Ser. B 10¢ par called for redemption at $25,000 on 06/14/2011
(Additional Information in Active)

BLACKROCK MUNIYIELD CALIF FD INC (MD)
Auction Market Preferred Ser. B 10¢ par called for redemption at $25,000 on 06/02/2011
Auction Market Preferred Ser. D 10¢ par called for redemption at $25,000 on 06/07/2011
Auction Market Preferred Ser. A 10¢ par called for redemption at $25,000 on 06/09/2011
Auction Market Preferred Ser. C 10¢ par called for redemption at $25,000 on 06/30/2011
(Additional Information in Active)

BLACKROCK MUNIYIELD CALIF QUALITY FD INC (MD)
Name changed 11/09/2010
Name changed from BlackRock MuniYield California Insured Fund, Inc. to BlackRock MuniYield California Quality Fund, Inc. 11/09/2010
Auction Market Preferred Ser. F 10¢ par called for redemption at $25,000 on 05/12/2011
Auction Market Preferred Ser. D 10¢ par called for redemption at $25,000 on 05/13/2011
Auction Market Preferred Ser. E 10¢ par called for redemption at $25,000 on 05/13/2011
Auction Market Preferred Ser. B 10¢ par called for redemption at $25,000 on 05/16/2011

Auction Market Preferred Ser. C 10¢ par called for redemption at $25,000 on 05/18/2011

Auction Market Preferred Ser. A 10¢ par called for redemption at $25,000 on 06/06/2011

(Additional Information in Active)

BLACKROCK MUNIYIELD FD INC (MD)

Auction Market Preferred Ser. D 10¢ par called for redemption at $25,000 on 07/13/2011

Auction Market Preferred Ser. E 10¢ par called for redemption at $25,000 on 07/13/2011

Auction Market Preferred Ser. G 10¢ par called for redemption at $25,000 on 07/18/2011

Auction Market Preferred Ser. C 10¢ par called for redemption at $25,000 on 07/20/2011

Auction Market Preferred Ser. F 10¢ par called for redemption at $25,000 on 07/21/2011

Auction Market Preferred Ser. A 10¢ par called for redemption at $25,000 on 07/27/2011

Auction Market Preferred Ser. B 10¢ par called for redemption at $25,000 on 08/03/2011

(Additional Information in Active)

BLACKROCK MUNIYIELD FLA FD (MA)

Name changed to BlackRock MuniYield Investment Fund 09/16/2008

BLACKROCK MUNIYIELD INVT QUALITY FD (MA)

Name changed 09/16/2008

Name changed 11/09/2010

Name changed from BlackRock MuniYield Florida Insured Fund Inc. to BlackRock MuniYield Insured Investment Fund 09/16/2008

Name changed from BlackRock MuniYield Insured Investment Fund to BlackRock MuniYield Investment Quality Fund 11/09/2010

Auction Market Preferred Ser. B 10¢ par called for redemption at $25,000 on 01/05/2012

Auction Market Preferred Ser. A 10¢ par called for redemption at $25,000 on 01/10/2012

BLACKROCK MUNIYIELD MICH QUALITY FD INC (MD)

Name changed 11/09/2010

Name changed from BlackRock MuniYield Michigan Insured Fund, Inc. to BlackRock MuniYield Michigan Quality Fund, Inc. 11/09/2010

Auction Market Preferred Ser. C 10¢ par called for redemption at $25,000 on 05/12/2011

Auction Market Preferred Ser. B 10¢ par called for redemption at $25,000 on 05/16/2011

Auction Market Preferred Ser. D 10¢ par called for redemption at $25,000 on 05/17/2011

Auction Market Preferred Ser. A 10¢ par called for redemption at $25,000 on 05/18/2011

(Additional Information in Active)

BLACKROCK MUNIYIELD MICH QUALITY FD II INC (MD)

Name changed 11/09/2010

Name changed from BlackRock MuniYield Michigan Insured Fund II, Inc. to BlackRock MuniYield Michigan Quality Fund II, Inc. 11/09/2010

Auction Market Preferred Ser. A 10¢ par called for redemption at $25,000 on 05/31/2011

Auction Market Preferred Ser. B 10¢ par called for redemption at $25,000 on 06/08/2011

Auction Market Preferred Ser. C 10¢ par called for redemption at $25,000 on 06/09/2011

Merged into BlackRock MuniYield Michigan Quality Fund, Inc. 09/14/2015

Each share 144A Variable Rate Demand Preferred Ser. W-7 10¢ par exchanged for (1) share 144A Variable Rate Demand Preferred Ser. W-7 10¢ par

Each share Common 10¢ par exchanged for (0.93643508) share Common 10¢ par

BLACKROCK MUNIYIELD N J FD INC (MD)

Auction Market Preferred Ser. C 10¢ par called for redemption at $25,000 on 05/17/2011

Auction Market Preferred Ser. B 10¢ par called for redemption at $25,000 on 05/18/2011

Auction Market Preferred Ser. A 10¢ par called for redemption at $25,000 on 05/19/2011

(Additional Information in Active)

BLACKROCK MUNIYIELD N J QUALITY FD INC (MD)

Name changed from BlackRock MuniYield New Jersey Insured Fund, Inc. to BlackRock MuniYield New Jersey Quality Fund, Inc. 11/09/2010

Auction Market Preferred Ser. B 10¢ par called for redemption at $25,000 on 07/22/2011

Auction Market Preferred Ser. A 10¢ par called for redemption at $25,000 on 07/25/2011

Merged into BlackRock MuniHoldings New Jersey Quality Fund, Inc. 04/13/2015

Each 144A Variable Rate Demand Preferred Share Ser. W-7 10¢ par exchanged for (1) 144A Variable Rate Demand Preferred Share Ser. W-7 5¢ par

Each share Common 10¢ par exchanged for (0.99469981) Common Share of Bene. Int. 10¢ par

BLACKROCK MUNIYIELD N Y INSD FD INC (MD)

Name changed to BlackRock MuniYield New York Quality Fund, Inc. 11/09/2010

Auction Market Preferred Ser. B 10¢ par called for redemption at $25,000 on 05/10/2011

Auction Market Preferred Ser. F 10¢ par called for redemption at $25,000 on 05/13/2011

Auction Market Preferred Ser. C 10¢ par called for redemption at $25,000 on 05/16/2011

Auction Market Preferred Ser. D 10¢ par called for redemption at $25,000 on 05/18/2011

Auction Market Preferred Ser. E 10¢ par called for redemption at $25,000 on 05/19/2011

Auction Market Preferred Ser. A 10¢ par called for redemption at $25,000 on 05/24/2011

BLACKROCK MUNIYIELD PA INSD FD (MA)

Name changed to BlackRock MuniYield Pennsylvania Quality Fund 11/09/2010

BLACKROCK MUNIYIELD QUALITY FD INC (MD)

Auction Market Preferred Ser. E 10¢ par called for redemption at $25,000 on 10/03/2011

Auction Market Preferred Ser. C 10¢ par called for redemption at $25,000 on 10/07/2011

Auction Market Preferred Ser. D 10¢ par called for redemption at $25,000 on 10/07/2011

Auction Market Preferred Ser. B 10¢ par called for redemption at $25,000 on 10/11/2011

Auction Market Preferred Ser. A 10¢ par called for redemption at $25,000 on 10/25/2011

(Additional Information in Active)

BLACKROCK MUNIYIELD QUALITY FD II INC (MD)

Auction Market Preferred Ser. C 10¢ par called for redemption at $25,000 on 01/09/2012

Auction Market Preferred Ser. D 10¢ par called for redemption at $25,000 on 01/10/2012

Auction Market Preferred Ser. A 10¢ par called for redemption at $25,000 on 01/17/2012

Auction Market Preferred Ser. A 10¢ par called for redemption at $25,000 on 01/23/2012

(Additional Information in Active)

BLACKROCK MUNIYIELD QUALITY FD III INC (MD)

Name changed 11/09/2010

Name changed from BlackRock MuniYield Insured Fund, Inc. to BlackRock MuniYield Quality Fund III, Inc. 11/09/2010

Auction Market Preferred Ser. I 10¢ par called for redemption at $25,000 on 06/06/2011

Auction Market Preferred Ser. F 10¢ par called for redemption at $25,000 on 06/07/2011

Auction Market Preferred Ser. C 10¢ par called for redemption at $25,000 on 06/09/2011

Auction Market Preferred Ser. E 10¢ par called for redemption at $25,000 on 06/09/2011

Auction Market Preferred Ser. H 10¢ par called for redemption at $25,000 on 06/10/2011

Auction Market Preferred Ser. G 10¢ par called for redemption at $25,000 on 06/14/2011

Auction Market Preferred Ser. D 10¢ par called for redemption at $25,000 on 06/16/2011

Auction Market Preferred Ser. A 10¢ par called for redemption at $25,000 on 06/23/2011

Auction Market Preferred Ser. B 10¢ par called for redemption at $25,000 on 06/30/2011

BLACKROCK N J INVT QUALITY MUN TR INC (MA)

Auction Rate Market Preferred Ser. T7 no par split (2) for (1) by issuance of (1) additional share 07/24/1995

Auction Rate Market Preferred Ser. T7 no par called for redemption at $25,000 on 07/25/2012

Completely liquidated

Each share Common 1¢ par received initial distribution of $13.7558 cash payable 07/26/2012 to holders of record 07/16/2012

Each share Common 1¢ par received second and final distribution of $0.049871 cash payable 12/27/2012 to holders of record 07/16/2012

BLACKROCK N J MUN INCOME TR (DE)

Municipal Auction Rate Preferred Ser. R7 $0.001 par called for redemption at $25,000 on 04/13/2012

Under plan of reorganization each Common Share of Bene. Int. $0.001 par automatically became (0.97444747) BlackRock MuniYield New Jersey Fund, Inc. Common Share of Bene. Int. 10¢ par 06/11/2018

BLACKROCK N Y INVT QUALITY MUN TR INC (MD)

Auction Rate Municipal Preferred Ser. F7 no par split (2) for (1) by issuance of (1) additional share 07/24/1995

Auction Rate Municipal Preferred Ser. F7 no par called for redemption at $25,000 on 07/23/2012

Completely liquidated

Each share Common 1¢ par received initial distribution of $15.2804 cash payable 07/26/2012 to holders of record 07/16/2012

Each share Common 1¢ par received second and final distribution of $0.036629 cash payable 12/27/2012 to holders of record 07/16/2012

BLACKROCK NEW JERSEY MUN BD TR (DE)

Municipal Auction Rate Preferred Ser. M7 $0.001 par called for redemption at $25,000 on 07/10/2012

Under plan of reorganization each Common Share of Bene. Int. $0.001 par automatically became (0.97922768) BlackRock MuniYield New Jersey Fund, Inc. Common Share of Bene. Int. 10¢ par 06/11/2018

BLACKROCK N Y INDS MUN 2008 TERM TR INC (MD)

Auction Rate Municipal Preferred Ser. F7 1¢ par split (2) for (1) by issuance of (1) additional share 07/24/1995

Auction Rate Municipal Preferred Ser. F28 1¢ par split (2) for (1) by issuance of (1) additional share 07/24/1995

Auction Rate Municipal Preferred Ser. F28 1¢ par called for redemption at $25,000 on 07/10/2006

Auction Rate Municipal Preferred Ser. F7 1¢ par called for redemption at $25,000 on 10/23/2006

Trust terminated 12/30/2008

Each share Common 1¢ par received $14.6463 cash

BLACKROCK NEW YORK MUN BD TR (DE)

Municipal Auction Rate Preferred Ser. T7 $0.001 par called for redemption at $25,000 on 10/12/2011

(Additional Information in Active)

BLACKROCK NEW YORK MUN INCOME QUALITY TR (DE)

Name changed from BlackRock New York Insured Municipal Income Trust to BlackRock New York Municipal Income Quality Trust 11/09/2010

Municipal Auction Rate Preferred Ser. R-7 $0.001 par called for redemption at $25,000 on 10/07/2011

(Additional Information in Active)

BLACKROCK NEW YORK MUN INCOME TR II (DE)

Auction Market Preferred Ser. W-7 $0.001 par called for redemption at $25,000 on 10/06/2011

(Additional Information in Active)

BLACKROCK N Y MUN INCOME TR (DE)

Municipal Auction Rate Preferred Ser. W7 $0.001 par called for redemption at $25,000 on 04/12/2012

Municipal Auction Rate Preferred Ser. F7 $0.001 par called for redemption at $25,000 on 04/16/2012

(Additional Information in Active)

BLACKROCK NY MUN 2018 TERM TR (DE)

Auction Rate Municipal Preferred Ser. T7 $0.001 par called for redemption at $25,000 on 03/18/2015

(Additional Information in Active)

BLACKROCK 1998 TERM TR INC (MD)

Trust terminated 12/23/1998

Each share Common 1¢ par exchanged for $10.02 cash

BLACKROCK 1999 TERM TR INC (MD)

Trust terminated 12/16/1999

Each share Common 1¢ par exchanged for first and final distribution of $10.15 cash

BLACKROCK PA STRATEGIC MUN TR (DE)

Municipal Auction Rate Preferred Ser.

W $0.001 par called for redemption at $25,000 on 07/05/2012
Merged into BlackRock MuniYield Pennsylvania Quality Fund 04/13/2015
Each Variable Rate Demand Preferred Share $0.001 par exchangd for (1) Variable Rate Demand Preferred Share Ser. W-7 5¢ par
Each share Common $0.001 par exchanged for (0.90936725) Common Share of Bene. Int. 10¢ par

BLACKROCK PETE CORP (NV)
Common $0.001 par split (15) for (1) by issuance of (14) additional shares payable 09/20/2007 to holders of record 09/20/2007
Name changed to Nexgen Petroleum Corp. 06/09/2008
Nexgen Petroleum Corp. recapitalized as Hubei Minkang Pharmaceutical Ltd. 10/21/2010

BLACKROCK REAL ASSET EQUITY TR (DE)
Merged into BlackRock Resources & Commodities Strategy Trust 12/08/2014
Each Common Share of Bene. Int. $0.001 par exchanged for (0.75619994) Common Share of Bene. Int. $0.001 par

BLACKROCK RES INC (NV)
Name changed to Artepharm Global Corp. 01/14/2010
Artepharm Global Corp. name changed to Sharprock Resources Inc. 07/20/2011 which recapitalized as Evergreen-Agra, Inc. (NV) 10/23/2013 which reincorporated in Delaware as Evergreen-Agra Global Investments, Inc. 11/14/2017

BLACKROCK SR FLOATING RATE FD INC (MD)
Under plan of merger each share Class I 10¢ par received (0.76034411) BlackRock Funds II Floating Rate Income Portfolio Investor A Share $0.001 par 03/18/2011

BLACKROCK SR FLOATING RATE FD II INC (MD)
Under plan of merger each share Class II 10¢ par received (0.82468294) BlackRock Funds II Floating Rate Income Portfolio Investor C1 Share $0.001 par 03/18/2011

BLACKROCK SILVER BULLION TR (ON)
Name changed to iShares Silver Bullion Fund and Hedged Units and Non-Hedged Units reclassified as Hedged Common Units or Non-Hedged Common Units respectively 11/05/2012
iShares Silver Bullion Fund name changed to iShares Silver Bullion ETF 10/30/2013

BLACKROCK SR HIGH INCOME FD INC (MD)
Merged into BlackRock Debt Strategies Fund Inc. 12/09/2013
Each share Common 10¢ par exchanged for (0.9743718) share Common 10¢ par

BLACKROCK STRATEGIC BD TR (DE)
Merged into BlackRock Debt Strategies Fund Inc. 12/09/2013
Each share Common $0.001 par exchanged for (3.26403638) shares Common 10¢ par

BLACKROCK STRATEGIC EQUITY DIVID TR (DE)
Name changed 05/09/2011
Name changed from BlackRock Strategic Dividend Achievers Trust to BlackRock Strategic Equity Dividend Trust 05/09/2011
Merged into BlackRock Enhanced Equity Dividend Trust 02/27/2012
Each Common Share of Bene. Int $0.001 par exchanged for (1.41137167) Common Shares of Bene. Int $0.001 par

BLACKROCK STRATEGIC MUN TR (DE)
Municipal Auction Rate Preferred Ser. W $0.001 par called for redemption at $25,000 on 01/12/2012
(Additional Information in Active)

BLACKROCK STRATEGIC TERM TR INC (MD)
Trust terminated 12/30/2002
Each share Common 1¢ par exchanged for $10 cash

BLACKROCK TARGET TERM TR INC (MD)
Trust terminated 12/29/2000
Each share Common 1¢ par exchanged for $10 cash

BLACKROCK 2001 TERM TR INC (MD)
Trust terminated 06/29/2001
Each share Common 1¢ par exchanged for $10 cash

BLACKROCK UTIL & INFRASTRUCTURE TR (DE)
Name changed to BlackRock Utilities, Infrastructure, & Power Opportunities Trust 11/27/2017

BLACKROCK VA MUN BD TR (DE)
Municipal Auction Rate Preferred Ser. R7 $0.001 par called for redemption at $25,000 on 07/06/2012
(Additional Information in Active)

BLACKROCK VENTURES INC (CANADA)
Acquired by Shell Canada Ltd. 07/11/2006
Each share Common no par exchanged for $24 cash

BLACKROCK WORLD INVT TR (DE)
Merged into BlackRock Global Opportunities Equity Trust 07/27/2009
Each Common Share of Bene. Int. $0.001 par exchanged for (0.59681881) Common Share of Bene. Int. $0.001 par
BlackRock Global Opportunites Equity Trust name changed to BlackRock Enhanced Global Dividend Trust 06/12/2017

BLACKRUN MINERALS INC (BC)
Recapitalized 06/10/1999
Recapitalized from Blackrun Ventures Inc. to Blackrun Minerals Inc. 06/10/1999
Each share Common no par exchanged for (0.25) share Common no par
Name changed to Diversified Industries Ltd. 03/29/2000
(See Diversified Industries Ltd.)

BLACKSANDS PETE INC (NV)
Old Common $0.001 par split (30) for (1) by issuance of (29) additional shares payable 06/21/2006 to holders of record 06/21/2006
Each share old Common $0.001 par exchanged for (0.33333333) share new Common $0.001 par 01/05/2011
SEC revoked common stock registration 02/23/2018

BLACKSTAR ENERGY GROUP INC (NV)
Name changed to BlackStar Enterprise Group, Inc. 09/30/2016

BLACKSTONE / GSO SR FLOATING RATE TERM FD (DE)
Floating Rate Term Preferred Ser. A called for redemption at $1,000 plus $2.41429 accrued dividends on 10/08/2014
(Additional Information in Active)

BLACKSTONE ADVANTAGE TERM TR INC (MD)
Name changed to Blackrock Advantage Term Trust Inc. 06/22/1992
(See Blackrock Advantage Term Trust Inc.)

BLACKSTONE CIGAR CO. (NJ)
Name changed back to Waitt & Bond, Inc. 01/10/1967

BLACKSTONE EQUITIES CORP (CO)
Merged into Pyrocap International Corp. 05/27/1993
Each share Common $0.001 par exchanged for (1) share Common $0.001 par
(See Pyrocap International Corp.)

BLACKSTONE INCOME TR INC (MD)
Name changed to Blackrock Income Trust Inc. 06/22/1992

BLACKSTONE INDUSTRIES, INC. (CA)
Merged into Bevis Industries, Inc. (FL) 07/22/1968
Each share Common no par exchanged for (0.4059287) share Common 10¢ par
Bevis Industries, Inc. (FL) reincorporated in Rhode Island 06/29/1970

BLACKSTONE INSD MUN TERM TR INC (MD)
Name changed to BlackRock Insured Municipal Term Trust Inc. 06/22/1992
(See BlackRock Insured Municipal Term Trust Inc.)

BLACKSTONE INVT QUALITY TERM TR INC (MD)
Name changed to Blackrock Investment Quality Term Trust Inc. 06/22/1992
(See Blackrock Investment Quality Term Trust Inc.)

BLACKSTONE LAKE MINERALS INC (NV)
Name changed to Caleco Pharma Corp. 08/31/2009
(See Caleco Pharma Corp.)

BLACKSTONE MUN TARGET TERM INC (MD)
Name changed to Blackrock Municipal Target Term Trust Inc. 06/22/1992
(See Blackrock Municipal Target Term Trust Inc.)

BLACKSTONE 1998 TERM TR INC (MD)
Name changed to Blackrock 1998 Term Trust Inc. 06/22/1992
(See Blackrock 1998 Term Trust Inc.)

BLACKSTONE NORTH AMERN GOVT INCOME TR INC (MD)
Name changed to BlackRock North American Government Income Trust Inc. 06/22/1992
BlackRock North American Government Income Trust Inc. name changed to BlackRock Income Opportunity Trust Inc. 08/28/2002 which merged into BlackRock Core Bond Trust 11/10/2014

BLACKSTONE RES INC (BC)
Recapitalized as Blackstone Ventures Inc. 04/23/2001
Each share Common no par exchanged for (0.4) share Common no par
Blackstone Ventures Inc. recapitalized as Lattice Biologics Ltd. 01/04/2016

BLACKSTONE STRATEGIC TERM TR INC (MD)
Name changed to Blackrock Strategic Term Trust Inc. 06/22/1992
(See Blackrock Strategic Term Trust Inc.)

BLACKSTONE TARGET TERM TR INC (MD)
Name changed to Blackrock Target Term Trust Inc. 06/22/1992
(See Blackrock Target Term Trust Inc.)

BLACKSTONE URANIUM MINES, INC. (DE)
Recapitalized as Scenic Developers Inc. 03/00/1970
Each share Common 1¢ par exchanged for (0.05) share Common 20¢ par
(See Scenic Developers Inc.)

BLACKSTONE VALLEY ELEC CO (RI)
Name changed 03/02/1965
Name changed from Blackstone Valley Gas & Electric Co. to Blackstone Valley Electric Co. 03/02/1965
Merged into Eastern Utilities Associates 06/30/1967
Each share Common $50 par exchanged for (3.5) shares Eastern Utilities Associates Common $10 par
Note: Unexchanged certificates were cancelled and became without value 06/30/1972
4.25% Preferred $100 par called for redemption at $104.40 on 03/28/2000
5.6% Preferred $100 par called for redemption at $103.82 on 03/28/2000
(See Eastern Utilities Associates)

BLACKSTONE VENTURES INC (BC)
Each share old Common no par exchanged for (0.05) share new Common no par 09/23/2015
Recapitalized as Lattice Biologics Ltd. 01/04/2016
Each share new Common no par exchanged for (0.33333333) share Common no par

BLACKSTRAP CAP CORP (SK)
Name changed to Blackstrap Hospitality Corp. 05/20/1999
(See Blackstrap Hospitality Corp.)

BLACKSTRAP HOSPITALITY CORP (SK)
Merged into 6385842 Canada Ltd. 06/02/2005
Each share Common no par exchanged for $0.30 cash

BLACKSTREAM ENERGY CORP (BC)
Name changed to SunOil Ltd. 10/11/2013

BLACKWATCH ENERGY SVCS CORP (AB)
Name changed to Calmena Energy Services Inc. 06/15/2010

BLACKWATCH ENERGY SVCS LTD PARTNERSHIP (AB)
Plan of arrangement effective 12/31/2008
Each Trust Unit no par exchanged for (1) share BlackWatch Energy Services Corp. Common no par
BlackWatch Energy Services Corp. name changed to Calmena Energy Services Inc. 06/15/2010

BLACKWATCH ENERGY SVCS TR (AB)
Plan of arrangement effective 12/31/2008
Each Trust Unit no par exchanged for (1) share BlackWatch Energy Services Corp. Common no par
BlackWatch Energy Services Corp. name changed to Calmena Energy Services Inc. 06/15/2010

BLACKWATER CAP CORP (AB)
Merged into Cumberland Oil & Gas Ltd. 02/26/2010
Each share Common no par exchanged for (0.2875) share Common no par

FINANCIAL INFORMATION, INC.

BLA-BLA

Note: Unexchanged certificates were cancelled and became without value 02/26/2015
Cumberland Oil & Gas Ltd. merged into Kallisto Energy Corp. 10/15/2012 which name changed to Toro Oil & Gas Ltd. 11/25/2014
(See Toro Oil & Gas Ltd.)

BLACKWATER GOLD CORP (BC)
Recapitalized as Bonaventure Enterprises Inc. 03/20/2002
Each share Common no par exchanged for (0.33333333) share Common no par
Bonaventure Enterprises Inc. recapitalized as Iconic Minerals Ltd. 03/03/2011

BLACKWATER MIDSTREAM CORP (NV)
Acquired by ArcLight Capital Partners, L.L.C. 10/10/2012
Each share Common $0.001 par exchanged for $0.64 cash

BLACKWATER MINES LTD. (ON)
Merged into Staple Mining Co. Ltd. 08/11/1972
Each share Capital Stock no par exchanged for (0.222222) share Capital Stock no par
Staple Mining Co. Ltd. merged into Gerrard Realty Inc. 01/28/1976

BLACKWELL CAP INC (AB)
Name changed to WellPoint Systems Inc. 07/04/2001
(See WellPoint Systems Inc.)

BLACKWELL OIL & GAS CO. (OK)
Liquidation completed
Each share Common $1 par exchanged for initial distribution of $1.25 cash 12/11/1961
Each share Common $1 par received second distribution of $0.13 cash 04/26/1962
Each share Common $1 par received third and final distribution of $0.0366399872 cash 07/24/1964

BLACKWOOD APARTMENT CO.
Liquidated 00/00/1948
Details not available

BLACKWOOD HODGE CDA LTD (CANADA)
Name changed 12/01/1980
Name changed from Blackwood Hodge (Canada) Ltd. to Blackwood Hodge (Canada) Ltd.-Blackwood Hodge (Canada) Ltee. and Class A Conv. Common no par and Class B Conv. Common no par reclassified as Common no par respectively 12/01/1980
Acquired by Blackwood Hodge Overseas Holdings Ltd. 06/11/1987
Each share Common no par exchanged for $15.50 cash

BLADE YELLOWKNIFE GOLD MINES LTD. (ON)
Charter revoked for failure to file reports and pay taxes 00/00/1954

BLADELOGIC INC (DE)
Merged into BMC Software, Inc. 04/18/2008
Each share Common $0.001 par exchanged for $28 cash

BLAGMAN MEDIA INTL INC (NV)
Recapitalized as Innovation Holdings, Inc. 03/05/2003
Each share Common 1¢ par exchanged for (0.0002) share Common 1¢ par
Innovation Holdings, Inc. name changed to Marketing Concepts International 10/20/2006

BLAGOVNO TRGOVINSKI CTR D D (SLOVENIA)
GDR agreement terminated 08/21/2001
Details not available

BLAIR & CO., INC. (NY)
Name changed to Blair Holdings Corp. 00/00/1947
Blair Holdings Corp. name changed to Pepsi-Cola United Bottlers, Inc. 04/10/1958 which name changed to PUB United Corp. 05/29/1964 which name changed to Rheingold Corp. 04/27/1965 which merged into Pepsico, Inc. 12/31/1973

BLAIR CORP (DE)
Merged into Appleseed's Topco, Inc. 04/30/2007
Each share Common no par exchanged for $42.50 cash

BLAIR HOLDINGS CORP. (NY)
Name changed to Pepsi-Cola United Bottlers, Inc. 04/10/1958
Pepsi-Cola United Bottlers, Inc. name changed to PUB United Corp. 05/29/1964 which name changed to Rheingold Corp. 04/27/1965 which merged into Pepsico, Inc. 12/31/1973

BLAIR JOHN & CO (DE)
Common $1 par split (2) for (1) by issuance of (1) additional share 02/14/1969
Common $1 par split (3) for (2) by issuance of (0.5) additional share 06/22/1979
Common $1 par split (2) for (1) by issuance of (1) additional share 06/22/1983
Merged into JB Acquisition Corp. 12/24/1986
Each share Common $1 par exchanged for $38.11 principal amount of 12% 15-Yr. Jr. Subordinated Discount Debentures due 12/24/2001

BLAIR VENEER CO.
Acquired by Owens-Illinois Glass Co. 00/00/1948
Details not available

BLAIR WILLIAM READY RESVS INC (MD)
Name changed to Blair (William) Mutual Funds, Inc., Bond Portfolio reclassified as Income Shares and Money Market Portfolio reclassified as Ready Reserve Shares 04/23/1991
Blair (William) Mutual Funds, Inc. name changed to Blair (William) Funds (MD) 01/12/1996 which reincorporated in Delaware 12/08/1999

BLAKE & WALTER CORP. (WA)
Name changed to Sea Galley Stores, Inc. (WA) 11/04/1976
Sea Galley Stores, Inc. (WA) reincorporated in Delaware 11/24/1980
(See Sea Galley Stores, Inc.)

BLAKE CHIBOUGAMAU MINING CORP.
In process of liquidation 00/00/1950
Details not available

BLAKE RES LTD (CANADA)
Dissolved for failure to file annual return 05/02/2002

BLAKE RIV EXPLORATIONS LTD (ON)
Delisted from Canadian Dealer Network 10/13/2000

BLAKE STEPHENS & KITTREDGE INC (CA)
Name changed to Innova, Inc. 12/18/1973
(See Innova, Inc.)

BLAMM CORP. (UT)
Name changed to Ion Holding, Inc. 07/09/1985
Ion Holding, Inc. name changed to Laser Holding, Inc. 05/13/1986 which name changed to Ion Laser Technology, Inc. (New) 08/22/1988 which name changed to BriteSmile, Inc. 08/24/1998 which name changed to BSML, Inc. 11/01/2006
(See BSML, Inc.)

BLANCA CORP (NV)
Name changed to Transglobal Mining Corp. 05/03/2007
Transglobal Mining Corp. recapitalized as Ring Energy, Inc. 06/02/2008

BLANCH E W HLDGS INC (DE)
Merged into Benfield Greig Group plc 05/31/2001
Each share Common 1¢ par exchanged for $13.50 cash

BLANCHARD FDS (MA)
Short Term Bond Fund 1¢ par reclassified as Short-Term Flexible Income Fund 1¢ par 10/10/1995
American Equity Fund 1¢ par merged into Virtus Funds 06/00/1996
Details not available
Merged into Evergreen Funds 02/20/1998
Details not available

BLANCHARD GOLD MINES LTD. (ON)
Charter surrendered 11/22/1954

BLANCHARD PRECIOUS METALS FD INC (MD)
Under plan of merger each share Common $0.001 par automatically became Evergreen International Trust Precious Metals Fund A on a net asset basis 02/27/1998

BLANCHARD PRESS INC (NY)
Name changed to Rumford Press Inc. 07/28/1970
(See Rumford Press Inc.)

BLANCHARD STRATEGIC GROWTH FD (MA)
Reorganized as Blanchard Funds Global Growth Fund 1¢ par 00/00/1993
Details not available

BLANCHE ERNEST E & ASSOC INC (MD)
6% Preferred $100 par called for redemption 12/31/1965
Merged into Levin-Townsend Service Corp. 12/31/1968
Each share Class A Common 10¢ par exchanged for (0.118906) share Common 25¢ par
Levin-Townsend Service Corp. name changed to Tolley International Corp. (NJ) 01/12/1971 which reincorporated in Delaware 03/31/1976 which name changed to TIC International Corp. 11/06/1981
(See TIC International Corp.)

BLANCHE RIVER KIRKLAND GOLD MINES LTD.
Succeeded by North American Land & Minerals Ltd. on a (1) for (4) basis 00/00/1935
North American Land & Minerals Ltd. name changed to Kelly-Kirkland Mines Ltd. 00/00/1937
(See Kelly-Kirkland Mines Ltd.)

BLANDINGS CAP LTD (AB)
Name changed to AMG Bioenergy Resources Holdings Ltd. 05/14/2010

BLANDY CORP. (UT)
Charter suspended for failure to pay taxes 09/02/1969

BLANE (J.G.) CO., INC. (LA)
Charter revoked for failure to file annual reports 05/13/1982

BLASIUS INDS INC (DE)
Name changed to Lexington Precision Corp. 01/13/1989
(See Lexington Precision Corp.)

BLASKE LINES, INC. (DE)
Each share Common $10 par exchanged for (5) shares Common $2 par 01/00/1954
5% Preferred called for redemption 05/31/1956
Merged into American Barge Line Co. 00/00/1956
Each share Common exchanged for (0.14285714) share Common
American Barge Line Co. merged into American Commercial Barge Line Co. 08/01/1957 which name changed to American Commercial Lines Inc. 04/30/1964 which merged into Texas Gas Transmission Corp. 05/15/1968
(See Texas Gas Transmission Corp.)

BLAST APPLICATIONS INC (DE)
Name changed to Italian Food & Beverage Corp. 03/17/2015

BLAST ENERGY SVCS INC (TX)
Reincorporated 02/27/2008
State of incorporation changed from (CA) to (TX) 02/27/2008
Recapitalized as PEDEVCO Corp. 08/03/2012
Each share Common $0.001 par exchanged for (0.00892857) share Common $0.001 par

BLASTGARD INTL INC (CO)
Name changed to HighCom Global Security, Inc. 08/03/2017

BLATCHFORD CALF MEAL CO (IL)
Acquired by Peter Hand Brewery Co. 08/20/1965
Each share Common no par exchanged for $10 cash

BLATT M CO (NJ)
Completely liquidated 05/26/1972
Each share Common 25¢ par exchanged for first and final distribution of (1) share American World Travel Corp. Common 1¢ par
(See American World Travel Corp.)

BLAU BARRY & PARTNERS INC (CT)
Company went private 00/00/1995
Details not available

BLAUNER'S (PA)
Each share Common no par exchanged for (2) shares Common $3 par 00/00/1946
Common $3 par changed to 50¢ par 12/13/1961
Name changed to Gale Industries, Inc. 11/11/1963
(See Gale Industries, Inc.)

BLAW-KNOX CO. (DE)
Reincorporated 00/00/1952
State of incorporation changed from (NJ) to (DE) 00/00/1952
Capital Stock $10 par reclassified as Common $10 par 04/20/1967
Merged into White Consolidated Industries, Inc. 05/03/1968
Each share Common $10 par exchanged for (0.55) share $3 Preferred Ser. C $50 par and (0.5) share Common $1 par
(See White Consolidated Industries, Inc.)

BLAZE ENERGY CORP (DE)
SEC revoked common stock registration 09/30/2014

BLAZE SOFTWARE INC (DE)
Merged into Brokat AG 10/02/2000
Each share Common $0.0001 par exchanged for (0.3652) Sponsored ADR for Ordinary
Brokat AG name changed to Brokat Technologies AG 08/28/2001
(See Brokat Technologies AG)

BLAZEDALE RES INC (ON)
Merged into Southern Eagle Petroleum Corp. 04/23/1986
Each share Common no par exchanged for (1) share Conv. Preference Ser. Y no par, (0.5) share Non-Vtg. Class A no par and (0.5) share Common no par
Southern Eagle Petroleum Corp. merged into Southern Eagle Enterprises Inc. 10/01/1987 which merged into Equican Ventures Corp. 12/04/1987 which recapitalized as

Equican Capital Corp. 01/27/1988 which name changed to Genterra Capital Corp. (Old) 08/23/1995 which merged into Genterra Capital Corp. (New) 02/28/1997 which recapitalized as Genterra Capital Inc. 06/30/1998 which name changed to Genterra Investment Corp. 04/30/1999 which merged into Genterra Inc. 12/31/2003

BLAZO CORP (DE)
Charter cancelled and declared inoperative and void for non-payment of taxes 03/01/1992

BLAZON CORP. (AZ)
Charter revoked for failure to file reports and pay fees 07/10/1982

BLAZOON SYS INC (CO)
Reincorporated under the laws of Nevada as USA Digital, Inc. 03/09/1999
USA Digital, Inc. name changed to Avix Technologies, Inc. 01/02/2002
(See Avix Technologies, Inc.)

BLC CAP ACCUMULATION FD INC (DE)
Name changed to Princor Capital Accumulation Fund, Inc. (DE) 11/01/1986
Princor Capital Accumulation Fund, Inc. (DE) reincorporated in Maryland 11/01/1989 which name changed to Principal Capital Value Fund, Inc. 01/01/1998
(See Principal Capital Value Fund, Inc.)

BLC CASH MGMT FD INC (MD)
Name changed to Princor Cash Management Fund, Inc. 11/01/1986
Princor Cash Management Fund, Inc. name changed to Principal Cash Management Fund, Inc. 01/01/1998
(See Principal Cash Management Fund, Inc.)

BLC FD INC (MD)
Name changed to Princor Fund, Inc. 11/01/1986
Princor Fund, Inc. name changed to Princor Investment Fund, Inc. 11/01/1987 which name changed to Principal Capital Accumulation Fund, Inc. (DE) 11/01/1988 which reincorporated in Maryland 05/26/1989
(See Principal Capital Accumulation Fund, Inc.)

BLC FINL SVCS INC (DE)
Merged into Allied Capital Corp. (New) 01/02/2001
Each share Common 1¢ par exchanged for (0.18) share Common $0.0001 par
Allied Capital Corp. (New) merged into Ares Capital Corp. 04/01/2010

BLC GOVT SECS INCOME FD (MD)
Name changed to Princor Federal Government Securities Fund 11/01/1986
Princor Federal Government Securities Fund name changed to Princor Government Securities Income Fund, Inc. 11/01/1987 which name changed to Principal Government Securities Income Fund, Inc. 01/01/1998
(See Principal Government Securities Income Fund, Inc.)

BLC GROWTH FD INC (DE)
Name changed to Princor Growth Fund, Inc. (DE) 11/01/1986
Princor Growth Fund, Inc. (DE) reincorporated in Maryland 11/01/1989 which name changed to Principal Growth Fund, Inc. 01/01/1998
(See Principal Growth Fund, Inc.)

BLC INCOME FD INC (DE)
Name changed to BLC Capital Accumulation Fund, Inc. 11/01/1985
BLC Capital Accumulation Fund, Inc. name changed to Princor Capital Accumulation Fund, Inc. (DE) 11/01/1986 which reincorporated in Maryland 11/01/1989 which name changed to Principal Capital Value Fund, Inc. 01/01/1998
(See Principal Capital Value Fund, Inc.)

BLC TAX EXEMPT BD FD INC (MD)
Name changed to Princor Tax-Exempt Bond Fund, Inc. 11/01/1986
Princor Tax-Exempt Bond Fund, Inc. name changed to Principal Tax-Exempt Bond Fund, Inc. 01/01/1998
(See Principal Tax-Exempt Bond Fund, Inc.)

BLDRS INDEX FDS TR (NY)
Asia 50 ADR Index Fund split (3) for (1) by issuance of (2) additional shares payable 07/07/2006 to holders of record 06/22/2006 Ex date - 07/10/2006
Developed Markets 100 ADR Index Fund split (3) for (1) by issuance of (2) additional shares payable 07/07/2006 to holders of record 06/22/2006 Ex date - 07/10/2006
Emerging Markets 50 ADR Index Fund split (4) for (1) split by issuance of (3) additional shares payable 07/07/2006 to holders of record 06/22/2006 Ex date - 07/10/2006
Europe 100 ADR Index Fund split (3) for (1) by issuance of (2) additional shares payable 07/07/2006 to holders of record 06/22/2006 Ex date - 07/10/2006
Europe 100 ADR Index Fund reclassified as Europe Select ADR Index Fund 09/19/2011
Name changed to Invesco BLDRS Index Funds Trust 06/04/2018

BLENHEIM EXHIBS GROUP PLC (UNITED KINGDOM)
Sponsored ADR's for Ordinary split (3) for (1) by issuance of (2) additional ADR's 09/17/1991
ADR agreement terminated 02/28/1997
Each Sponsored ADR for Ordinary exchanged for $16.1922 cash

BLESSINGS CORP (DE)
4% Preferred $10 par called for redemption 06/01/1977
Common $3.20 par changed to $2.13 par and (0.5) additional share issued 05/31/1985
Common $2.13 par split (2) for (1) by issuance of (1) additional share 06/02/1986
Common $2.13 par changed to $1.42 par and (0.5) additional share issued 05/31/1991
Common $1.42 par changed to 71¢ par and (1) additional share issued 12/15/1994
Stock Dividends - 10% 06/01/1978; 15% 06/01/1984
Merged into Huntsman Packaging Corp. 05/19/1998
Each share Common 71¢ par exchanged for $21 cash

BLF REAL ESTATE INVT TR (QC)
Acquired by Cogir Apartments L.P. 08/11/2014
Each Trust Unit exchanged for $7.50 cash

BLI-RIV URANIUM & COPPER CORP. LTD. (QC)
Name changed to Upper Ungava Mining Corp. Ltd. 09/06/1957
(See Upper Ungava Mining Corp. Ltd.)

BLIMPIE INTL INC (NJ)
Common 1¢ par split (3) for (2) by issuance of (0.5) additional share 03/11/1994
Merged into X2Y1, Inc. 01/24/2002

Each share Common 1¢ par exchanged for $2.80 cash

BLINCO IMPORT & EXPORT CORP. (NV)
Name changed to Refractory Minerals & Mining, Inc. 06/08/1970
(See Refractory Minerals & Mining, Inc.)

BLIND RIVER URANIUM MINES LTD. (ON)
Charter revoked for failure to file reports and pay fees 12/08/1966

BLINDER INTL ENTERPRISES INC (CO)
Name changed to Intercontinental Enterprises, Inc. 10/16/1989
(See Intercontinental Enterprises, Inc.)

BLINDSPOT ALERT INC (NV)
Name changed to WebSafety, Inc. 09/25/2009

BLING CAP CORP (AB)
Name changed to Kestrel Gold Inc. 06/28/2010

BLING MARKETING INC (NV)
Common $0.0001 par split (15.04) for (1) by issuance of (14.04) additional shares payable 01/26/2015 to holders of record 01/17/2015 Ex date - 01/27/2015
Name changed to NuGene International, Inc. 02/03/2015

BLINI HUT INC (NV)
Recapitalized as UDS Group, Inc. 02/22/2005
Each share Common 10¢ par exchanged for (0.001) share Common 1¢ par

BLINK COUTURE INC (DE)
Each share old Common $0.0001 par exchanged for (0.01904761) share new Common $0.0001 par 11/23/2009
Name changed to Toga Ltd. 12/16/2016

BLINK LOGIC INC (NV)
Each share old Common $0.001 par exchanged for (0.14285714) share new Common $0.001 par 02/08/2008
Ceased operations 09/18/2009
Stockholders' equity unlikely

BLINKX PLC (ENGLAND & WALES)
Name changed to RhythmOne PLC 07/08/2016

BLIS INTL INC (AB)
Name changed to Millennia Foods Inc. 10/01/1994
(See Millennia Foods Inc.)

BLISS & LAUGHLIN INDS INC NEW (DE)
Merged into BRW Steel Corp. 04/02/1996
Each share Common 1¢ par exchanged for $9.50 cash

BLISS & LAUGHLIN INDS INC OLD (DE)
Name changed 05/07/1965
Each share Common $5 par exchanged for (2) shares Common $2.50 par 00/00/1946
Common $2.50 par split (3) for (2) by issuance of (0.5) additional share 11/28/1956
Name changed from Bliss & Laughlin, Inc. to Bliss & Laughlin Industries Inc. (Old) 05/07/1965
Common $2.50 par split (2) for (1) by issuance of (1) additional share 05/29/1968
Common $2.50 par split (5) for (4) by issuance of (0.25) additional share 07/03/1978
Common $2.50 par split (5) for (4) by issuance of (0.25) additional share 07/01/1980
Stock Dividend - 10% 04/14/1967; 10% 06/30/1973; 20% 11/21/1975; 20% 07/01/1977
Name changed to Axia Inc. 05/06/1982
(See Axia Inc.)

BLISS A T & CO INC (MA)
Common 1¢ par split (3) for (2) by issuance of (0.5) additional share 09/30/1981
Common 1¢ par split (2) for (1) by issuance of (1) additional share 10/15/1983
Stock Dividend - In Preferred to holders of Common 10% 01/30/1984
Recapitalized as Omni Equities, Inc. 09/30/1985
Each share Preferred 1¢ par exchanged for (1) share Preferred 1¢ par
Each share Common 1¢ par exchanged for (0.33333333) share Common 1¢ par
(See Omni Equities, Inc.)

BLISS COAL CORP (DE)
Charter forfeited for failure to maintain a registered agent 08/01/1975

BLISS (E.W.) CO. (DE)
Recapitalized 00/00/1937
Each share 8% 1st Preferred $50 par exchanged for (2) shares 6% Preferred $25 par and $18 cash
Each share 7% 2nd Preferred $50 par exchanged for (2) shares 5% Preferred $25 par and $20.15 cash
Each share 6% 2nd Preferred $10 par exchanged for (0.4) share 5% Preferred $25 par and $3.45 cash
Each share Common no par exchanged for (1) share Common $1 par
Common $1 par changed to 50¢ par and (1) additional share issued 05/11/1962
Stock Dividends - 100% 08/18/1948; 20% 02/02/1953
$1.80 Conv. Preferred no par called for redemption 11/03/1967
Merged into Gulf & Western Industries, Inc. (DE) 01/11/1968
Each share Common 50¢ par exchanged for (1/3) share $3.875 Conv. Preferred Ser. C $2.50 par

BLIZZARD ENERGY INC (AB)
Under plan of merger each share Common no par exchanged for (0.0777) Shiningbank Energy Income Fund Trust Unit no par, (0.16666666) share Zenas Energy Corp. Common no par and (1) Zenas Energy Corp. Common Stock Purchase Warrant expiring 09/01/2005 on 08/02/2005
(See each company's listing)

BLIZZARD RES LTD (BC)
Struck off register and declared dissolved for failure to file returns 12/05/1986

BLOC DEV CORP (DE)
Name changed 12/01/1989
Name changed and state of incorporation changed from Bloc Development Technologies, Inc. (NY) to Bloc Development Corp. (DE) 12/01/1989
Name changed to Tiger Direct Inc. 01/03/1995
Tiger Direct Inc. merged into Global DirectMail Corp. 11/30/1995 which name changed to Systemax Inc. 05/19/1999

BLOCH BROTHERS TOBACCO CO. (WV)
Recapitalized 00/00/1951
Each share 6% Preferred $100 par exchanged for (2) shares 6% Preferred $50 par
Each share Common $20 par exchanged for (2) shares Common $12.50 par
Common $12.50 par changed to

$6.25 par and (1) additional share issued 08/03/1964
Merged into Helme Products, Inc. (DE) 08/01/1968
Each share 6% Conv. Preference $50 par exchanged for (4.1248) shares Common $5 par
Each share 6% Preferred $50 par exchanged for (4.1248) shares Common $5 par
Each share Common $6.25 par exchanged for (0.5156) share Common $5 par
(See Helme Products, Inc. (DE))

BLOCK BROS INDS LTD (BC)
Common no par split (3) for (1) by issuance of (2) additional shares 06/20/1969
Each share old Common no par exchanged for (0.001) share new Common no par 07/09/1979
Note: In effect holders received $9 cash per share and public interest was eliminated

BLOCK DRUG INC (NJ)
Class A Common 10¢ par split (2) for (1) by issuance of (1) additional share 12/02/1985
Stock Dividends - 3% payable 01/02/1996 to holders of record 12/01/1995; 3% payable 01/02/1997 to holders of record 12/02/1996; 3% payable 01/02/1998 to holders of record 12/01/1997; 3% payable 01/04/1999 to holders of record 12/01/1998; 3% payable 01/03/2000 to holders of record 12/01/1999
Merged into GlaxoSmithKline PLC 01/16/2001
Each share Non-Vtg. Class A Common 10¢ par exchanged for $53 cash

BLOCK ENGR INC (DE)
Merged into New Block, Inc. 07/26/1978
Each share Common 10¢ par exchanged for $4.25 cash

BLOCK OF ATLANTA, INC. (GA)
Merged into Block (H & R), Inc. 07/30/1970
Each share Common no par exchanged for (0.083423) share Common no par

BLOCKBUSTER ENTMT CORP (DE)
Common 10¢ par split (2) for (1) by issuance of (1) additional share 03/29/1988
Common 10¢ par split (2) for (1) by issuance of (1) additional share 08/10/1988
Common 10¢ par split (2) for (1) by issuance of (1) additional share 05/30/1989
Common 10¢ par split (2) for (1) by issuance of (1) additional share 03/08/1991
Merged into Viacom Inc. (Old) 09/30/1994
Each share Common 10¢ par exchanged for (0.08) share Class A Common 1¢ par, (0.60615) share Non-Vtg. Class B Common 1¢ par and (1) Variable Common Right
(See Viacom Inc. (Old))

BLOCKBUSTER INC (DE)
Name changed to BB Liquidating Inc. 10/13/2011

BLOCKCHAIN MNG LTD (ISRAEL)
ADR agreement terminated 07/26/2018
Each Sponsored ADR for Ordinary exchanged for (2) shares Ordinary
Note: Unexchanged ADR's will be sold and the proceeds, if any, held for claim after 11/26/2018

BLOCKER ENERGY CORP (TX)
Reincorporated under the laws of Delaware as Energy Service Co., Inc. 09/22/1987
Energy Service Co., Inc. name changed to ENSCO International

Inc. (DE) 05/26/1995 which reorganized in England & Wales as Ensco International PLC 12/23/2009 which name changed to Ensco PLC 03/31/2010

BLOCKSON CHEMICAL CO. (DE)
Merged into Olin Mathieson Chemical Corp. 06/30/1955
Each share Class B $7.50 par or Common $7.50 par exchanged for (0.75) share Common $5 par
Olin Mathieson Chemical Corp. name changed to Olin Corp. 09/01/1969

BLOG 8 INC (DE)
Name changed to SecuritEYES International, Inc. 12/02/2004
SecuritEYES International, Inc. name changed to Medify Solutions Ltd. 02/17/2005 which name changed to Petel Inc. 05/08/2007 which recapitalized as Gleeworks, Inc. 12/14/2009 which name changed to Capital Art, Inc. 05/09/2011 which name changed to Globe Photos, Inc. 06/25/2018

BLOND BEAR HLDGS INC (AB)
Recapitalized as Grey Island Systems International Inc. 06/25/2002
Each share Common no par exchanged for (0.25) share Common no par
Grey Island Systems International Inc. merged into Webtech Wireless Inc. 10/28/2009 which merged into BSM Technologies Inc. 10/05/2015

BLONDEAU MINES LTD. (ON)
Recapitalized as New Blondeau Nickel Mines Ltd. 02/18/1963
Each share Capital Stock $1 par exchanged for (0.5) share Capital Stock $1 par
(See New Blondeau Nickel Mines Ltd.)

BLONDEAU NICKEL MINES LTD. (ON)
Name changed to Blondeau Mines Ltd. 02/12/1960
Blondeau Mines Ltd. recapitalized as New Blondeau Nickel Mines Ltd. 02/18/1963
(See New Blondeau Nickel Mines Ltd.)

BLONDOR QUEBEC MINES LTD. (ON)
Declared dissolved 04/01/1963
No stockholders' equity

BLOOD BROS. MACHINE CO.
Merged into Standard Steel Spring Co. 00/00/1936
Details not available

BLOOD KNITTING CO.
Assets sold 00/00/1938
Details not available

BLOODHOUND SEARCH TECHNOLOGIES INC (NV)
Each share old Common $0.0001 par exchanged for (0.5) share new Common $0.0001 par 01/17/2006
SEC revoked common stock registration 06/16/2011

BLOOM INCOME & GROWTH CDN FD (ON)
Under plan of merger each Trust Unit automatically became (0.69309357) Bloom Select Income Fund Unit 10/26/2015

BLOOM U S ADVANTAGED INCOME & GROWTH FD (ON)
Name changed to Bloom U.S. Income & Growth Fund 05/19/2013

BLOOMFIELD BLDG INDS INC (DE)
Class B Common 10¢ par reclassified as Class A Common 10¢ par 01/21/1970
Stock Dividend - 10% 09/24/1963
Name changed to BBI, Inc. 02/19/1971
(See BBI, Inc.)

BLOOMFIELD BUILDING CO., INC.
Bankrupt 00/00/1933
Details not available

BLOOMFIELD INDUSTRIES, INC. (DE)
Common $1 par split (4) for (3) by issuance of (0.33333333) additional share 02/20/1963
Name changed to Hardan Liquidating Co. 12/15/1964
(See Hardan Liquidating Co.)

BLOOMFIELD RTY CORP (TX)
Name changed to Financial Technology, Inc. 12/29/1969
Financial Technology, Inc. name changed to Texon Energy Corp. 05/14/1974
(See Texon Energy Corp.)

BLOOMFIELD SVGS & LN ASSN BIRMINGHAM MICH (USA)
Name changed 03/31/1984
Name changed from Bloomfield Savings & Loan Association to Bloomfield Savings & Loan Association, F.A. 03/31/1984
Company placed in receivership due to insolvency 05/12/1989
Details not available

BLOOMFIELD STATE BANK (BLOOMFIELD, CT)
Name changed to Security Bank & Trust Co. (Bloomfield, CT) 06/04/1979
Security Bank & Trust Co. (Bloomfield, CT) merged into Northeast Bancorp, Inc. 01/24/1983 which merged into First Fidelity Bancorporation (New) 05/03/1993 which merged into First Union Corp. 01/01/1996 which name changed to Wachovia Corp. (Ctfs. dated after 09/01/2001) 09/01/2001 which merged into Wells Fargo & Co. (New) 12/31/2008

BLOOMINGDALE BROTHERS, INC.
Acquired by Federated Department Stores, Inc. 00/00/1949
Each share Common exchanged for (1.5) shares Common $5 par
Federated Department Stores, Inc. name changed to Macy's, Inc. 06/01/2007

BLOOMSBURG & SULLIVAN RAILROAD
Acquired by Reading Co. 10/23/1928
Details not available

BLOSSBURG MERCANTILE CO.
Liquidated 00/00/1935
Details not available

BLOSSMAN HYDRATANE GAS INC (LA)
Merged into Petrosub Corp. 01/28/1974
Each share Common $1 par exchanged for $7.50 cash

BLOUGH MANUFACTURING CO., INC.
Name changed to Blough-Wagner Manufacturing Co., Inc. 00/00/1950

BLOUIN LAKE GOLD MINES, LTD. (CANADA)
Dissolved 00/00/1960
No stockholders' equity

BLOUNT INC (DE)
Each share Common 10¢ par exchanged for (0.33333333) share Common $1 par 06/28/1976
Common $1 par split (2) for (1) by issuance of (1) additional share 07/01/1981
Common $1 par reclassified as Class B Common $1 par 07/08/1983
Each share Class B Common $1 par received distribution of (1) share Class A Common $1 par 07/15/1983
Merged into Blount International, Inc. (Old) 11/03/1995
Each share Class A Common $1 par exchanged for (1.5) shares Class A Common 1¢ par
Each share Class B Common $1 par exchanged for (1.5) shares Class B Common 1¢ par
Blount International, Inc. (Old) merged into Blount International, Inc. (New) 08/19/1999
(See Blount International Inc. (New))

BLOUNT INTL INC NEW (DE)
Acquired by ASP Blade Intermediate Holdings, Inc. 04/12/2016
Each share Common 1¢ par exchanged for $10 cash

BLOUNT INTL INC OLD (DE)
Class A Common 1¢ par split (2) for (1) by issuance of (1) additional share payable 12/08/1997 to holders of record 11/24/1997 Ex date - 12/09/1997
Class B Common 1¢ par split (2) for (1) by issuance of (1) additional share payable 12/08/1997 to holders of record 11/24/1997 Ex date - 12/09/1997
Merged into Blount International, Inc. (New) 08/19/1999
Each share Class A Common 1¢ par exchanged for $30 cash
Each share Class B Common 1¢ par exchanged for $30 cash

BLOWING ROCK SKI LODGE, INC. (NC)
Assets sold for benefit of creditors 11/15/1968
No stockholders' equity

BLOWOUT ENTMT INC (DE)
Assets sold for the benefit of creditors 05/17/1999
No stockholders' equity

BLS MEDIA INC (NV)
Name changed to Coyote Resources, Inc. 09/02/2010
(See Coyote Resources, Inc.)

BLU-DUK INC (NV)
Each share old Common $0.001 par exchanged for (0.1) share new Common $0.001 par 12/07/1989
Name changed to Ingleby Communications Corp. 03/12/1990
(See Ingleby Communications Corp.)

BLUE ARROW PLC (UNITED KINGDOM)
Name changed to Manpower PLC (United Kingdom) 04/09/1990
Manpower PLC (United Kingdom) reorganized in Wisconsin as Manpower Inc. 05/13/1991 which name changed to ManpowerGroup 04/18/2011

BLUE BALL NATL BANK (BLUE BALL, PA)
Common $2.50 par split (2) for (1) by issuance of (1) additional share 08/01/1986
Stock Dividend - 10% 07/16/1985
Under plan of reorganization each share Common $2.50 par automatically became (1) share PennRock Financial Services Corp. $2.50 par 08/01/1986
PennRock Financial Services Corp. merged into Community Banks, Inc. 07/01/2005 which merged into Susquehanna Bancshares, Inc. 11/16/2007 which merged into BB&T Corp. 08/01/2015

BLUE BELL, INC. (NC)
Reincorporated under the laws of Delaware 04/02/1962
(See Blue Bell, Inc. (DE))

BLUE BELL GLOBE MANUFACTURING CO.
Name changed to Blue Bell, Inc. (NC) 00/00/1943
Blue Bell, Inc. (NC) reincorporated in Delaware 04/02/1962
(See Blue Bell, Inc. (DE))

BLUE BELL INC (DE)
Common $5 par changed to $3.33333333 par and (0.5) additional share issued 02/27/1970
4.75% Conv. Preferred $100 par called for redemption 07/30/1971
Common $3.33333333 par split (2) for (1) by issuance of (1) additional share 10/01/1971
Common $3.33333333 par split (2) for (1) by issuance of (1) additional share 09/17/1976
Stock Dividend - 20% 09/29/1964
Acquired by Blue Bell Holding Co. Inc. 11/27/1984
Each share Common $3.33333333 par exchanged for $47.65 cash

BLUE BELL MINING CO., LTD. (ID)
Charter revoked for failure to file reports and pay fees 11/30/1923

BLUE BIRD MINES CORP. (CO)
Declared defunct and inoperative for failure to pay taxes and file annual reports 02/28/1934

BLUE BONNETS RACEWAY INC (QC)
Each share Common $1 par exchanged for (5) shares Common 20¢ par 06/14/1963
Acquired by Campeau Corp. Ltd. 11/24/1972
Each share Common 20¢ par exchanged for $3 cash

BLUE BUFFALO PET PRODS INC (DE)
Acquired by General Mills, Inc. 04/24/2018
Each share Common 1¢ par exchanged for $40 cash

BLUE CALYPSO INC (NV)
Common $0.0001 par split (3.4) for (1) by issuance of (2.4) additional shares payable 08/11/2011 to holders of record 08/11/2011
Reincorporated under the laws of Delaware 10/17/2011

BLUE CHIP COMPUTERWARE INC (DE)
Recapitalized as Anviron Holding Co. 05/08/2008
Each share Common 1¢ par exchanged for (0.001) share Common 1¢ par

BLUE CHIP GOLD MINES LTD. (ON)
Charter cancelled and declared dissolved for failure to file returns in December 1962

BLUE CHIP RES INC (BC)
Cease trade order effective 02/26/1991

BLUE CHIP SVGS ASSN (CINCINNATI, OH)
Merged into Winton Financial Corp. 01/05/1996
Each share Common no par exchanged for (2.1015) shares Common $1 par
(See Winton Financial Corp.)

BLUE CHIP STAMPS (CA)
Common $0.33333333 par changed to $1 par and (4) additional shares issued 11/04/1969
Merged into Berkshire Hathaway Inc. 07/28/1983
Each share Common $1 par exchanged for (0.077) share Common $5 par

BLUE CHIP VALUE FD INC (MD)
Merged into Westcore Trust 03/28/2011
Each share Common 1¢ par exchanged for (0.34421093) share Blue Chip Fund Retail Class no par

BLUE CIRCLE INDS PLC (ENGLAND)
Each Unsponsored ADR for Ordinary £1 par exchanged for (1) Sponsored ADR for Ordinary £1 par 03/10/1989
Sponsored ADR's for Ordinary £1 par changed to 50p par and (1) additional ADR issued 08/07/1989
Each old Sponsored ADR for Ordinary 50p par exchanged for (0.88) new Sponsored ADR for Ordinary 50p par 12/19/2000
Merged into Lafarge S.A. 07/11/2001
Each Sponsored ADR for Ordinary 50p par exchanged for $6.989 cash

BLUE COAT SYS INC (DE)
Each share old Common $0.0001 par exchanged for (0.2) share new Common $0.0001 par 09/16/2002
New Common $0.0001 par split (2) for (1) by issuance of (1) additional share payable 10/03/2007 to holders of record 09/13/2007 Ex date - 10/04/2007
Acquired by Project Barbour Holdings Corp. 02/15/2012
Each share new Common $0.0001 par exchanged for $25.81 cash

BLUE COVE CAP CORP (BC)
Name changed to CuOro Resources Corp. 04/18/2011
CuOro Resources Corp. name changed to Rockshield Capital Corp. 05/30/2014

BLUE CREEK COAL & LAND CO.
Property sold 00/00/1943
No stockholders' equity

BLUE CROWN INC (NV)
Liquidation completed
Each share Common 10¢ par exchanged for initial distribution of $1.35 cash 12/29/1976
Each share Common 10¢ par received second distribution of $0.21 cash 09/15/1977
Each share Common 10¢ par received third and final distribution of $0.1537 cash 12/15/1977

BLUE CROWN PETES LTD (AB)
Acquired by Blue Crown, Inc. 09/14/1970
Each share Common 20¢ par exchanged for (1) share Common 20¢ par
(See Blue Crown, Inc.)

BLUE DATA GROUP INC (NV)
Name changed to Expert Group, Inc. 11/07/2007
Expert Group, Inc. name changed to American Premium Water Corp. 12/19/2013

BLUE DESERT MNG INC (BC)
Recapitalized as Canada Fluorspar Inc. 05/25/2000
Each share Common no par exchanged for (0.33333333) share Common no par
Canada Fluorspar Inc. name changed to Continental Ridge Resources Inc. 02/05/2001 which name changed to Nevada Geothermal Power Inc. 05/13/2003 which recapitalized as Alternative Earth Resources Inc. 04/02/2013 which recapitalized as Black Sea Copper & Gold Corp. 09/28/2016

BLUE DIAMOND COAL CO (DE)
Capital Stock $100 par changed to $50 par and (1) additional shares issued 03/04/1966
Merged into J River MergerSub Inc. 05/05/1998
Each share Capital Stock $50 par exchanged for $60.413 cash
Note: An initial additional payment of $8.54 cash per share was made 04/28/2000
A second additional payment of $0.321 cash per share was made 09/00/2002

BLUE DIAMOND CORP. (DE)
Stock Dividend - 100% 01/24/1949
Acquired by Flintkote Co. 05/14/1959
Each share Capital Stock $2 par exchanged for (0.802) share Common $5 par
(See Flintkote Co.)

BLUE DIAMOND ENERGY RES INC (BC)
Recapitalized as Nippon Investments Corp. 12/14/1988
Each share Common no par exchanged for (0.2) share Common no par
(See Nippon Investments Corp.)

BLUE DIAMOND MNG CORP (BC)
Recapitalized as Colossal Resources Corp. (BC) 06/07/2010
Each share Common no par exchanged for (0.04) share Common no par
Colossal Resources Corp. (BC) reincorporated in Alberta as Top Strike Resources Corp. 12/13/2012

BLUE EARTH INC (NV)
Each share Common $0.001 par received distribution of (0.5) Common Stock Purchase Warrant expiring 12/31/2013 payable 12/31/2010 to holders of record 12/31/2010
Plan of reorganization under Chapter 11 Federal Bankruptcy proceedings effective 08/01/2016
No stockholders' equity

BLUE EARTH REFINERIES INC (BRITISH VIRGIN ISLANDS)
Ordinary no par changed to $1 par 10/27/2006
Liquidation completed
Each share Ordinary $1 par received initial distribution of $0.25 cash payable 09/22/2006 to holders of record 09/18/2006 Ex date - 09/14/2006
Each share Ordinary $1 par received second distribution of $0.25 cash payable 04/12/2007 to holders of record 04/02/2007
Each share Ordinary $1 par received third distribution of $1 cash payable 10/08/2007 to holders of record 10/03/2007 Ex date - 10/09/2007
Each share Ordinary $1 par received fourth distribution of $1.04 cash payable 01/03/2008 to holders of record 12/31/2007 Ex date - 01/04/2008
Each share Ordinary $1 par received fifth distribution of $0.41 cash payable 01/07/2010 to holders of record 12/29/2009 Ex date - 01/08/2010
Each share Ordinary $1 par received sixth and final distribution of $0.44 cash payable 05/25/2012 to holders of record 05/15/2012 Ex date - 06/07/2012

BLUE EMERALD RES INC (BC)
Recapitalized as Saville Resources Inc. 01/17/2003
Each share Common no par exchanged for (0.06666666) share Common no par

BLUE FASHION CORP (NV)
Name changed to Vopia, Inc. 08/29/2014
Vopia, Inc. name changed to Drone Guarder, Inc. 03/24/2017

BLUE FISH CLOTHING INC (PA)
Recapitalized as Monogram Energy, Inc. 05/11/2007
Each share Common $0.001 par exchanged for (0.05) share Common $0.001 par
Monogram Energy, Inc. reorganized as Marquis Tech Holdings, Inc. 07/19/2011 which recapitalized as Tritent Int'l Agriculture, Inc. 07/11/2012

BLUE FISH ENTMT INC (NV)
Name changed to Pacific Gold Corp. 09/08/2003

BLUE FLAG GOLD MINING CO. (CO)
Charter expired by time limitations 12/09/1922

BLUE FOX INDS INC (NY)
Adjudicated bankrupt 04/18/1974
Stockholders' equity unlikely

BLUE FYRE ONE INC (CANADA)
Name changed to Soltoro Ltd. 09/08/2006
Soltoro Ltd. merged into Agnico Eagle Mines Ltd. 06/10/2015

BLUE GOLD BEVERAGES INC (NV)
Recapitalized as Dragon Polymers Inc. 04/27/2012
Each share Common $0.001 par exchanged for (0.03333333) share Common $0.001 par
Dragon Polymers Inc. name changed to Hitec Corp. 11/04/2015 which recapitalized as Lead Innovation Corp. 03/27/2018

BLUE GOLD INTL INC (ON)
Cease trade order effective 05/25/2001
Stockholders' equity unlikely

BLUE GOLD MNG INC (BC)
Merged into Riverstone Resources Inc. 12/17/2012
Each share Common no par exchanged for (0.801) share Common no par
Riverstone Resources Inc. name changed to True Gold Mining Inc. 02/25/2013 which merged into Endeavour Mining Corp. 04/27/2016

BLUE GOLD RES LTD (BC)
Recapitalized as International Blue Gold Corp. 08/15/1994
Each share Common no par exchanged for (0.33333333) share Common no par
International Blue Gold Corp. recapitalized as Buddha Resources Inc. 01/16/1998
(See Buddha Resources Inc.)

BLUE GOLD WTR TECHNOLOGIES LTD (BC)
Name changed to NanoStruck Technologies Inc. 10/02/2013
NanoStruck Technologies Inc. name changed to Fineqia International Inc. 11/01/2016

BLUE GRASS BREEDERS INC (CO)
Each share old Common 1¢ par exchanged for (0.05) share new Common 1¢ par 05/07/1984
Recapitalized as Southwestern Environmental Corp. 07/07/1993
Each share new Common 1¢ par exchanged for (0.1) share Common 1¢ par
Southwestern Environmental Corp. name changed to CITA Biomedical, Inc. (CO) 11/30/1998 which reincorporated in Delaware 05/29/2002 which recapitalized as Xino Corp. 01/07/2005 which reorganized as AsherXino Corp. 08/19/2009
(See AsherXino Corp.)

BLUE GRIZZLY TRUCK INC (NV)
Name changed to Music & Entertainment Network Inc. (NV) 12/29/1995
Music & Entertainment Network Inc. (NV) reorganized under the laws of Delaware as Informatix Holdings, Inc. 06/30/1998 which recapitalized as Autologous Wound Therapy, Inc. 11/08/1999 which name changed to Cytomedix, Inc. 03/30/2000 which name changed to Nuo Therapeutics, Inc. 11/14/2014

BLUE GULCH EXPLS LTD (BC)
Name changed to Pacific Resources Development Ltd. and Capital Stock 50¢ par changed to no par 07/25/1973
Pacific Resources Development Ltd. recapitalized as Nu Pacific Resources Ltd. 04/04/1984 which recapitalized as Iron Lady Resources Inc. 03/11/1988 which

recapitalized as Takepoint Ventures Ltd. (BC) 08/03/1994 which reorganized in Yukon as Consolidated Takepoint Ventures Ltd. 06/25/2002 which name changed to Lake Shore Gold Corp. (YT) 12/18/2002 which reincorporated in British Columbia 06/30/2004 which reincorporated in Canada 07/18/2008 which merged into Tahoe Resources Inc. 04/07/2016

BLUE HAVEN POOLS (CA)
Through purchase offer company reacquired over 99% as of 03/26/1973
Public interest eliminated

BLUE HAWK VENTURES INC (NV)
Name changed to Molecular Pharmacology (USA) Ltd. 08/29/2005

BLUE HERON FINL CORP (ON)
Recapitalized as Avenue Financial Corp. 05/21/2002
Each share Common no par exchanged for (0.5) share Common no par
Avenue Financial Corp. name changed to Mantis Mineral Corp. 06/20/2007 which name changed to Gondwana Oil Corp. 02/26/2014 which name changed to European Metals Corp. 11/07/2014

BLUE HILLS BK COMM (KANSAS CITY, MO)
Stock Dividend - 20% 07/01/1964
Name changed to Commerce Bank of Blue Hills (Kansas City, MO) 03/01/1972
Each share Capital Stock $20 par exchanged for (1) share Capital Stock $20 par
(See Commerce Bank of Blue Hills (Kansas City, MO))

BLUE ICE MINERALS LTD (AB)
Recapitalized as Monroe Minerals Inc. 11/27/2001
Each share Common no par exchanged for (0.33333333) share Common no par
Monroe Minerals Inc. recapitalized as Kirrin Resources Inc. 05/26/2009
(See Kirrin Resources Inc.)

BLUE INDS INC (NV)
Each share old Common $0.001 par exchanged for (0.05) share new Common $0.001 par 10/28/2002
Each share new Common $0.001 par exchanged again for (0.005) share new Common $0.0001 par 05/20/2005
Note: Holders of between (100) to (19,999) pre-split shares received (100) shares
Holders of (99) shares or fewer were not affected
Name changed to Pegasus Wireless Corp. 06/06/2005
(See Pegasus Wireless Corp.)

BLUE JACKET MNG CO (NV)
Name changed to United Casino Corp. 01/00/1995
United Casino Corp. name changed to United Trading.com 08/03/2000 which name changed to Global Links Corp. (Old) 02/04/2003 which name changed to Global Links Corp. (New) 08/04/2003

BLUE JAY ENTERPRISES INC (DE)
Name changed 07/01/1988
Name changed from Blue Jay Energy Corp. to Blue Jay Enterprises, Inc. 07/01/1988
Each share old Common 1¢ par exchanged for (0.05) share new Common 1¢ par 02/27/1995
Name changed to Unidyne Corp. 09/03/1996
(See Unidyne Corp.)

BLUE LAGOON VENTURES INC (BC)
Recapitalized as VMX Resources Inc. 12/08/2004
Each share Common no par exchanged for (0.25) share Common no par
VMX Resources Inc. name changed to Monster Uranium Corp. 09/07/2007

BLUE LAKE RES LTD (BC)
Name changed to Lake Ventures Ltd. 01/21/1986
(See Lake Ventures Ltd.)

BLUE LIGHTNING VENTURES INC (BC)
Name changed to Universal Uranium Ltd. 05/03/2005
Universal Uranium Ltd. name changed to Expedition Mining Inc. 07/07/2010 which name changed to Imagin Medical Inc. 02/24/2016

BLUE LIST PUBLISHING CO., INC. (DE)
Acquired by Standard & Poor's Corp. 04/01/1963
Each share Common 50¢ par exchanged for (0.45) share Common $1 par
Standard & Poor's Corp. merged into McGraw-Hill, Inc. 02/15/1966 which name changed to McGraw-Hill Companies, Inc. 04/28/1995 which name changed to McGraw Hill Financial, Inc. 05/02/2013 which name changed to S&P Global Inc. 04/28/2016

BLUE LIZARD MINES INC (UT)
Name changed to International Tungsten & Minerals, Corp. (UT) 09/22/1969
International Tungsten & Minerals, Corp. (UT) reorganized in Nevada 10/01/1982
(See International Tungsten & Minerals, Corp. (NV))

BLUE MARBLE MEDIA CORP (BC)
Name changed to KBridge Energy Corp. 01/31/2012

BLUE MARTINI SOFTWARE INC (DE)
Each share old Common $0.001 par exchanged for (0.14285714) share new Common $0.001 par 11/14/2002
Acquired by Multi-Channel Holdings Inc. 05/13/2005
Each share new Common $0.001 par exchanged for $4 cash

BLUE MOON FOODS, INC. (DE)
Acquired by Foremost Dairies, Inc. (NY) 03/11/1955
Each share Capital Stock $1 par exchanged for (0.12) share 4.5% Preferred $50 par and (0.4) share Common $2 par
Foremost Dairies, Inc. (NY) merged into Foremost-McKesson, Inc. 07/19/1967 which name changed to McKesson Corp. (MD) 07/27/1983 which reincorporated in Delaware 07/31/1987
(See McKesson Corp. (DE))

BLUE MOON GROUP INC (DE)
Common $0.001 par split (3) for (1) by issuance of (2) additional shares payable 12/15/2003 to holders of record 12/05/2003 Ex date - 12/16/2003
Recapitalized as One Punch Productions, Inc. 12/07/2005
Each share Common $0.001 par exchanged for (0.01) share Common $0.001 par
One Punch Productions, Inc. name changed to Caltas Fitness, Inc. 08/21/2006 which name changed to Cinemaya Media Group, Inc. 02/06/2007 which recapitalized as SNM Global Holdings 11/14/2008

BLUE MOON MINING CORP. (OR)
Dissolved 00/00/1961

No stockholders' equity

BLUE MOOSE MEDIA INC (NV)
Each share old Common $0.001 par exchanged for (3) shares new Common $0.001 par 06/27/2011
Name changed to LiqTech International, Inc. 10/14/2011

BLUE MOUNTAIN EXPLORATION, INC. (UT)
Name changed to Blue Mountain Corp. 10/06/1981
Blue Mountain Corp. name changed to OGC Corp. 02/24/1985

BLUE MOUNTAIN URANIUM MINES, INC. (DE)
Merged into Midwest Consolidated Uranium Corp. 06/10/1955
Each share Common exchanged for (0.3) share Common
Midwest Consolidated Uranium Corp. merged into COG Minerals Corp. 05/01/1956
(See COG Minerals Corp.)

BLUE MTN BEVERAGES INC (ON)
Delisted from Canadian Dealer Network 12/31/1997

BLUE MTN CORP (UT)
Name changed to OGC Corp. and Common $0.001 par changed to $0.0001 par 02/24/1985

BLUE MTN ENERGY LTD (AB)
Acquired by Trilogy Energy Trust 10/27/2006
Each share Common no par exchanged for $5.50 cash

BLUE MTN MINES INC (MT)
Merged into Almar Supply Co., Inc. 01/18/1971
Each share Common 5¢ par exchanged for (1) share Common 1¢ par
Almar Supply Co., Inc. recapitalized as Almar-Shields Corp. 04/06/1971 which merged into Uni-Shield International Corp. 09/20/1972
(See Uni-Shield International Corp.)

BLUE MTN RES INC (NV)
Name changed to Patient Access Solutions Inc. 06/02/2008

BLUE MTN RES LTD (AB)
Recapitalized as Blue Mountain Energy Ltd. 07/18/2002
Each share Common no par exchanged for (0.08) share Common no par
(See Blue Mountain Energy Ltd.)

BLUE NILE INC (DE)
Acquired by Bain Capital Private Equity 02/17/2017
Each share Common $0.001 par exchanged for $40.75 cash

BLUE NT METALS INC (CANADA)
Name changed to Blue Note Mining Inc. 10/04/2006
(See Blue Note Mining Inc.)

BLUE NT MNG INC (CANADA)
Plan of arrangement effective 08/31/2009
Each share old Common no par exchanged for (0.03333333) share new Common no par 08/31/2009
Each share new Common no par received distribution of (0.02503) share GeoVenCap Inc. Common no par payable 07/31/2012 to holders of record 07/27/2012 Ex date - 07/25/2012
Deemed to have filed an assignment in bankruptcy 11/16/2013
Stockholders' equity unlikely

BLUE OCEAN NUTRASCIENCES INC (ON)
Each share old Common no par exchanged for (0.1) share new Common no par 09/27/2016
Name changed to CO2 Gro Inc. 04/12/2018

BLUE PARROT ENERGY INC (BC)
Recapitalized as RIA Resources Corp. 05/19/2009
Each share Common no par exchanged for (0.05) share Common no par
RIA Resources Corp. reorganized as Qwest Diversified Capital Corp. 06/05/2013

BLUE PEARL MNG LTD (ON)
Name changed to Thompson Creek Metals Co., Inc. (ON) 05/15/2007
Thompson Creek Metals Co., Inc. (ON) reincorporated in British Columbia 07/29/2008 which merged into Centerra Gold Inc. 10/21/2016

BLUE PINES INC (NV)
Name changed to Netvoice Technologies Corp. 08/11/1998
(See Netvoice Technologies Corp.)

BLUE PWR ENERGY CORP (ON)
Recapitalized as Cadillac Ventures Inc. 04/20/2006
Each share Common no par exchanged for (0.2) share Common no par

BLUE RANGE ENERGY CORP (AB)
Recapitalized as Blue Range Resource Corp. 06/08/1990
Each share Class A Common no par exchanged for (0.125) share Class A Common no par
Blue Range Resource Corp. merged into Big Bear Exploration Ltd. 02/12/1999 which merged into Avid Oil & Gas Ltd. 02/02/2000
(See Avid Oil & Gas Ltd.)

BLUE RANGE RESOURCE CORP (AB)
Merged into Big Bear Exploration Ltd. 02/12/1999
Each share Class A no par exchanged for (11) shares new Common no par
Big Bear Exploration Ltd. merged into Avid Oil & Gas Ltd. 02/02/2000
(See Avid Oil & Gas Ltd.)

BLUE REGAL RES LTD (ON)
Name changed to Unique Capital Corp. 01/16/1996
Unique Capital Corp. recapitalized as Pele Mountain Resources Inc. 09/30/1997

BLUE RHINO CORP (DE)
Merged into Ferrell Companies, Inc. 04/20/2004
Each share Common $0.001 par exchanged for $17 cash

BLUE RIBBON ACADEMIES, INC. (OH)
Out of business 09/00/1982
Details not available

BLUE RIBBON BEEF (IA)
Merged into Iowa Beef Packers, Inc. (DE) 08/01/1969
Each share Common no par exchanged for $10 principal amount of 6.25% Conv. Subord. Debentures due 02/01/1984

BLUE RIBBON CAP CORP (ON)
Recapitalized as Kilo Goldmines Ltd. 04/21/2009
Each share Common no par exchanged for (0.25) share Common no par

BLUE RIBBON CORP. LTD. (CANADA)
6.5% Preference $50 par changed to 5% Preference $50 par 00/00/1938
Assets acquired by Brooke Bond Canada (1959) Ltd. 00/00/1959
Each share Preference exchanged for $62.08 cash
Each share Common exchanged for $62.08 cash

BLUE RIBBON INTL INC (NY)
Recapitalized as Puritan Financial Group, Inc. (NY) 12/27/2005
Each share Common $0.001 par

exchanged for (0.04) share Common $0.001 par
Puritan Financial Group, Inc. (NY) reincorporated in Maryland as Concordis Group, Inc. 04/27/2009

BLUE RIBBON LTD.
Merged into Blue Ribbon Corp. Ltd. 00/00/1930
Details not available

BLUE RIBBON RES LTD (BC)
Recapitalized as New Blue Ribbon Resources Ltd. 03/09/1998
Each share Common no par exchanged for (0.2) share Common no par
New Blue Ribbon Resources Ltd. recapitalized as Blue Diamond Mining Corp. 01/28/2003 which recapitalized as Colossal Resources Corp. (BC) 06/07/2010 which reincorporated in Alberta as Top Strike Resources Corp. 12/13/2012

BLUE RIDGE BK (SPARTA, NC)
Merged into FCFT, Inc. 04/09/1997
Each share Common $2.50 par exchanged for $19.50 cash

BLUE RIDGE BK N A (FLOYD, VA)
Common $8.50 split (3) for (1) by issuance of (2) additional shares payable 10/31/2003 to holders of record 09/30/2003 Ex date - 11/03/2003
Stock Dividends - 10% payable 06/30/2000 to holders of record 05/31/2000; 10% payable 07/31/2001 to holders of record 06/30/2001 Ex date - 07/20/2001; 10% payable 07/31/2002 to holders of record 06/28/2002 Ex date - 07/29/2002
Merged into Carter Bank & Trust (Martinsville, VA) 12/29/2006
Each share Common $8.50 par exchanged for (2.474) shares Common

BLUE RIDGE CORP. (DE)
Common no par changed to $1 par 11/00/1932
Merged into Blue Ridge Mutual Fund, Inc. 00/00/1951
Each share old Common $1 par exchanged for (0.385047) share new Common $1 par
Blue Ridge Mutual Fund, Inc. name changed to Sigma Investment Shares, Inc. 04/24/1969 which name changed to ProvidentMutual Investment Shares, Inc. 03/01/1990
(See ProvidentMutual Investment Shares, Inc.)

BLUE RIDGE ENERGY INC (NV)
Name changed to Bayou City Exploration, Inc. 06/22/2005
(See Bayou City Exploration, Inc.)

BLUE RIDGE GOLD CORP (CO)
Common no par reclassified as Class A Common 1¢ par 04/17/1987
Declared defunct and inoperative for failure to pay taxes and file annual reports 01/01/1996

BLUE RIDGE INC (UT)
Name changed to Vencor International, Inc. 03/14/1986
Vencor International, Inc. recapitalized as PLAD, Inc. 11/06/2015 which name changed to Elev8 Brands, Inc. 12/28/2016

BLUE RIDGE INDUSTRIES, INC. (DE)
No longer in existence having become inoperative and void for non-payment of taxes 04/15/1968

BLUE RIDGE MIDWAY GOLD MINES CO. LTD. (NV)
Name changed to American Helium & Mining Corp. 04/09/1963
American Helium & Mining Corp. name changed to "999" 10/30/1980 which reincorporated in Delaware as 999 Inc. 05/01/1991

BLUE RIDGE MUT FD INC (DE)
Name changed to Sigma Investment Shares, Inc. 04/24/1969
Sigma Investment Shares, Inc. name changed to ProvidentMutual Investment Shares, Inc. 03/01/1990
(See ProvidentMutual Investment Shares, Inc.)

BLUE RIDGE NATURAL GAS & OIL CORP. (DE)
Recapitalized as Blue Ridge Industries, Inc. 07/29/1960
Each share Common no par exchanged for (0.06666666) share Common no par
(See Blue Ridge Industries, Inc.)

BLUE RIDGE RES LTD (BC)
Name changed to International Trans Asia Trading Corp. 07/13/1988
International Trans Asia Trading Corp. recapitalized as ITC International Trading Corp. 07/20/1989
(See ITC International Trading Corp.)

BLUE RIV FED SVGS BK (EDINBURGH, IN)
Merged into Salin Bank & Trust Co. (Indianapolis, IN) 11/23/2002
Each share Common 1¢ par exchanged for $38 cash

BLUE RIVER BANCSHARES INC (IN)
Administratively dissolved 07/14/2014

BLUE ROCK CERIUM MINES LTD. (ON)
Name changed to Rare Earth Mining Co. Ltd. 03/05/1956
Rare Earth Mining Co. Ltd. merged into Amalgamated Rare Earth Mines Ltd. 05/27/1957
(See Amalgamated Rare Earth Mines Ltd.)

BLUE SKIES URANIUM INC. (UT)
Merged into National Uranium Corp. 00/00/1955
Each share Common 5¢ par exchanged for (0.00588235) share Common 5¢ par
National Uranium Corp. name changed to Industries & Mines, Inc. 01/27/1956 which merged into General Utilities & Industries, Inc. (UT) 08/29/1960 which reorganized in Florida as General Utilities, Inc. 05/04/1962
(See General Utilities, Inc. (FL))

BLUE SKY MEDIA CORP (WY)
Name changed to Life Clips, Inc. 12/15/2015

BLUE SKY PETE INC (NV)
Common $0.001 par split (3) for (1) by issuance of (2) additional shares payable 07/31/2012 to holders of record 07/31/2012
Name changed to Asian Development Frontier Inc. 07/09/2015
Asian Development Frontier Inc. name changed to Unifunds Ltd. 03/23/2018

BLUE SKY RES LTD (BC)
Name changed to Axion Communications Inc. 02/28/1996
Axion Communications Inc. merged into Technovision Systems Inc. 12/01/2002 which merged into Uniserve Communications Corp. 11/20/2003

BLUE SPA INC (NV)
Name changed to Sustainable Petroleum Group Inc. 12/19/2016
Sustainable Petroleum Group Inc. name changed to Sustainable Projects Group Inc. 10/26/2017

BLUE SQUARE - ISRAEL LTD (ISRAEL)
Name changed to Alon Holdings Blue Square - Israel Ltd. 07/16/2010
Alon Holdings Blue Square - Israel Ltd. name changed to Alon Blue Square Israel Ltd. 05/06/2013
(See Alon Blue Square Israel Ltd.)

BLUE STAR COFFEE INC (NV)
Name changed to Consumer Direct of America 04/05/2002
Consumer Direct of America name changed to Shearson Financial Network, Inc. 07/06/2006
(See Shearson Financial Network, Inc.)

BLUE STAR ENERGY INC (CO)
Name changed to Brishlin Resources, Inc. 01/24/2008
Brishlin Resources, Inc. recapitalized as Synergy Resources Corp. 09/22/2008 which name changed to SRC Energy Inc. 03/06/2017

BLUE STAR INVT LTD (BC)
Struck off register and declared dissolved for failure to file returns 06/19/1992

BLUE STAR MARITIME S A (GREECE)
Acquired by Attica Holdings S.A. 06/30/2008
Each 144A Sponsored GDR for Ordinary exchanged for $22.52983 cash
Each Reg. S Sponsored GDR for Ordinary exchanged for $22.52983 cash

BLUE STAR MINES, LTD. (ON)
Charter cancelled and company declared dissolved for default in filing returns 12/00/1952

BLUE STAR MINES LTD (BC)
Struck off register and declared dissolved for failure to file returns 11/03/1980

BLUE SUMMIT GROUP INC (NV)
Reorganized as INREEX, Inc. 03/15/2006
Each share Common $0.001 par exchanged for (55) shares Common $0.001 par
INREEX, Inc. name changed to Northern Potash Co. 07/29/2008

BLUE SUN MEDIA INC (NV)
Name changed to Apple Green Holding, Inc. 03/19/2014

BLUE SUN RESOURCE CORP (BC)
Recapitalized as International Blue Sun Resource Corp. 12/17/1991
Each share Common no par exchanged for (0.33333333) share Common no par
International Blue Sun Resource Corp. name changed to Dalton Enterprises Ltd. (BC) 05/26/1994 which reincorporated in Wyoming 01/17/1995 which reincorporated in Delaware as Dalton Specialties, Ltd. 03/01/1996
(See Dalton Specialties, Ltd.)

BLUE TREE WIRELESS DATA INC (CANADA)
Merged into Sixnet Holdings, LLC 11/07/2007
Each share Common no par exchanged for $0.21 cash

BLUE VISTA TECHNOLOGIES INC (ON)
Recapitalized as Arbitrage Exploration Inc. 01/16/2015
Each share Common no par exchanged for (0.25) share Common no par
Arbitrage Exploration Inc. name changed to Argo Gold Inc. 09/22/2016

BLUE WATER DRILLING CORP. (DE)
Acquired by Santa Fe Drilling Co. 03/24/1965
Each share Common 10¢ par exchanged for $6 cash

BLUE WAVE SYS INC (DE)
Merged into Motorola, Inc. 07/02/2001
Each share Common 1¢ par exchanged for (0.443) share Common $3 par
Motorola, Inc. recapitalized as Motorola Solutions, Inc. 01/04/2011

BLUE WILLOW HLDG INC (CO)
Reincorporated under the laws of Delaware as Americana Gold & Diamond Holdings, Inc. 02/02/1993
Americana Gold & Diamond Holdings, Inc. recapitalized as MineCore International, Inc. (DE) 06/29/2004 which reincorporated in Nevada 04/09/2008
(See MineCore International, Inc.)

BLUE WIRELESS & DATA INC (DE)
Each share Common 1¢ par exchanged for (0.02) share Common $0.001 par par 05/09/2006
Name changed to Big Star Media Group, Inc. 10/02/2009
Big Star Media Group, Inc. name changed to Pharmstar Pharmaceuticals, Inc. (DE) 04/08/2011 which reorganized in Nevada as Nexus Energy Services, Inc. 10/15/2013 which name changed to Illegal Restaurant Group, Inc. 06/02/2015 which name changed back to Nexus Energy Services, Inc. 08/13/2015

BLUE WOLF MONGOLIA HLDGS CORP (BRITISH VIRGIN ISLANDS)
Completely liquidated 07/23/2013
Each Unit exchanged for first and final distribution of $9.96069099 cash
Each share Ordinary no par exchanged for first and final distribution of $9.96069099 cash

BLUE WTR BAR & GRILL INC (CO)
Name changed to Tiger Reef, Inc. 02/01/2017

BLUE WTR RESTAURANT GROUP INC (NV)
Name changed to Blue Water Global Group, Inc. 07/12/2013

BLUE ZONE INC (NV)
Charter revoked for failure to file reports and pay fees 03/31/2006

BLUEBEAR NETWORKS INTL INC (NV)
Each share Common $0.0001 par received distribution of (1) share BlueBear, Inc. Common payable 05/14/2007 to holders of record 05/14/2007
Reorganized under the laws of Wyoming as Pinpinhao, Inc. 05/29/2007
Each share Common $0.0001 par exchanged for (0.01818181) share Common $0.0001 par

BLUEBERRY HLDGS INC (NY)
Reincorporated under the laws of Nevada as Alentus Corp. 03/25/2008
Alentus Corp. recapitalized as Areti Web Innovations, Inc. 07/05/2012

BLUEBIRD EXPL CO (DE)
Name changed to Xcellink International Inc. and (7) additional shares issued 12/19/2008
Xcellink International Inc. recapitalized as Trxade Group, Inc. 02/06/2014

BLUEBIRD EXPLS LTD (BC)
Recapitalized as Spire Ventures Ltd. 10/24/1995
Each share Common no par exchanged for (0.25) share Common no par
Spire Ventures Ltd. recapitalized as Consolidated Spire Ventures Ltd. 01/04/2001 which recapitalized as Berkwood Resources Ltd. 12/01/2010

BLUEBIRD INC (PA)
Reincorporated 08/03/1970
State of incorporation changed from (NY) to (PA) 08/03/1970

Merged into Northern Foods Ltd. 01/04/1980
Each share Common 25¢ par exchanged for $14.875 cash

BLUEBIRD MINERALS LTD (AB)
Recapitalized as Blue Ice Minerals Ltd. 11/02/1999
Each share Common no par exchanged for (0.33333333) share Common no par
Blue Ice Minerals Ltd. recapitalized as Monroe Minerals Inc. 11/27/2001 which recapitalized as Kirrin Resources Inc. 05/26/2009
(See Kirrin Resources Inc.)

BLUEBIRD OIL CORP. (DE)
Charter cancelled for non-payment of taxes 01/26/1926

BLUEBOOK INTL HLDG CO (DE)
Old Common $0.0001 par split (3) for (1) by issuance of (2) additional shares payable 11/08/2001 to holders of record 11/07/2001
Each share old Common $0.0001 par exchanged for (0.05) share new Common $0.0001 par 11/18/2004
SEC revoked common stock registration 05/23/2011

BLUEBOY INC (DE)
Charter cancelled and declared inoperative and void for non-payment of taxes 03/01/1985

BLUEFIELD ENTERPRISES (UT)
Recapitalized as Optical Express Inc. (UT) 07/03/1992
Each share Common $0.001 par exchanged for (0.03090234) share Common $0.001 par
Optical Express Inc. (UT) reorganized in Delaware as Bassett (J.R.) Optical Inc. 09/23/1994 which recapitalized as Samurai Energy Corp. (DE) 11/28/2005 which reincorporated in Nevada as ECCO Energy Corp. 09/01/2006 which recapitalized as Eagle Ford Oil & Gas, Corp. 07/27/2010

BLUEFIELD GAS CO (WV)
Merged into Roanoke Gas Co. 05/15/1987
Each share Common 20¢ par exchanged for (0.143) share Common $5 par
Roanoke Gas Co. reorganized as RGC Resources, Inc. 07/29/1998

BLUEFIELD SUPPLY CO (VA)
Reincorporated 06/03/1983
Each share Common $100 par exchanged for (5) shares Common $20 par 00/00/1947
Common $20 par changed to $4 par and (4) additional shares issued 11/28/1956
Common $4 par changed to $2 par and (1) additional share issued 05/07/1971
Stock Dividend - 100% 12/30/1944
State of incorporation changed from (WV) to (VA) 06/03/1983
Liquidation completed
Each share Common $2 par received initial distribution of $15.75 cash 01/08/1987
Each share Common $2 par received second distribution of $1.71 cash 03/16/1987
Each share Common $2 par received third distribution of $2 cash 05/13/1987
Each share Common $2 par received fourth distribution of $1 cash 03/25/1988
Each share Common $2 par received fifth and final distribution of $1.04 cash 08/20/1988
Note: Certificates were not required to be surrendered and are without value

BLUEFIRE ETHANOL FUELS INC (NV)
Name changed to BlueFire Renewables, Inc. 10/25/2010

BLUEFIRE MNG CORP (BC)
Name changed to Royalty North Partners Ltd. 02/17/2016

BLUEFLASH COMMUNICATIONS INC (FL)
Reorganized under the laws of Nevada as Neurotrope, Inc. 08/09/2013
Each share Common $0.0001 par exchanged for (2.242) shares Common $0.0001 par

BLUEFLY INC (DE)
Reincorporated 02/02/2001
State of incorporation changed from (NY) to (DE) 02/02/2001
Each share old Common 1¢ par exchanged for (0.1) share new Common 1¢ par 04/04/2008
Acquired by Clearlake Capital Group 05/23/2013
Each share new Common 1¢ par exchanged for $0.10 cash

BLUEGATE CORP (NV)
Recapitalized as Logicquest Technology, Inc. 03/19/2015
Each share Common $0.001 par exchanged for (0.05) share Common $0.001 par

BLUEGRASS PETE INC (BC)
Name changed to Superburn Systems Ltd. 11/12/1985
(See Superburn Systems Ltd.)

BLUEGRASS RAYMOND MINES LTD. (ON)
Name changed to Bluegrass Uranium Mines Ltd. 12/07/1954
(See Bluegrass Uranium Mines Ltd.)

BLUEGRASS URANIUM MINES LTD (ON)
Charter cancelled and declared dissolved for failure to file returns and pay fees 05/18/1976

BLUEGREEN CORP (MA)
Stock Dividend - 5% payable 03/28/1996 to holders of record 03/07/1996
Acquired by Woodbridge Holdings, LLC 04/02/2013
Each share Common 1¢ par exchanged for $10 cash

BLUEGROUSE SEISMIC SOLUTIONS LTD (AB)
Acquired by Divestco Inc. 05/03/2007
Each share Common no par exchanged for (0.3125) share Common no par

BLUELAND CAP INC (AB)
Name changed to Nicer Canada Corp. 02/25/2003
(See Nicer Canada Corp.)

BLUENOSE PERSHING MINES, LTD. (ON)
Charter cancelled and company declared dissolved for default in filing returns 12/03/1962

BLUEPHOENIX SOLUTIONS LTD (ISRAEL)
Each share Ordinary ILS 0.01 par exchanged for (0.25) share Ordinary ILS 0.04 par 12/28/2011
Name changed to ModSys International Ltd. 01/23/2015

BLUEPOINT DATA INC (YT)
Assets sold 11/20/2012
Details not available

BLUEPOINT DATA STORAGE INC (YT)
Name changed to BluePoint Data, Inc. 07/27/2009
(See BluePoint Data, Inc.)

BLUERIDGE BK (FREDERICK, MD)
Merged into Revere Bank (Laurel, MD) 03/23/2016

Each share Common $1.25 par exchanged for (0.6245) share Common $5 par

BLUEROCK ACQUISITION CORP (BC)
Reorganized under the laws of Jersey as PetroKamchatka PLC 12/09/2009
Each share Common no par exchanged for (0.46837) share Common no par
PetroKamchatka PLC recapitalized as EastSiberian PLC 10/02/2012
Note: Unexchanged certificates were cancelled and became without value 12/09/2014

BLUEROCK RES LTD (BC)
Recapitalized as Argus Metals Corp. 05/07/2009
Each share Common no par exchanged for (0.06666666) share Common no par
Argus Metals Corp. name changed to ePower Metals Inc. 12/07/2017

BLUERUSH MEDIA GROUP CORP (ON)
Name changed to BlueRush Inc. 04/30/2018

BLUESCOUT TECHNOLOGIES LTD (CAYMAN ISLANDS)
Chapter 7 bankruptcy proceedings terminated 07/13/2018
Stockholders' equity unlikely

BLUESKY INDS INC (AB)
Recapitalized as Firelight Corp. 09/07/1991
Each share Common no par exchanged for (0.33333333) share Common no par
(See Firelight Corp.)

BLUESKY OIL & GAS LTD (AB)
Reincorporated 10/27/1980
Place of incorporation changed from (BC) to (AB) 10/27/1980
7% Conv. Preferred Ser. A $5 par called for redemption 09/30/1984
Recapitalized as Mark Resources Inc. 11/13/1986
Each share Common no par exchanged for (0.33333333) share Common no par
Mark Resources Inc. acquired by EnerMark Income Fund 04/09/1996 which merged into Enerplus Resources Fund 06/22/2001 which reorganized as Enerplus Corp. 01/03/2011

BLUESKY SYS CORP (PA)
Reorganized under the laws of Nevada as Bluesky Systems Holdings, Inc. 09/01/2011
Each share Common $0.001 par exchanged for (0.03333333) share Common $0.001 par
(See Bluesky Systems Holdings, Inc.)

BLUESKY SYS HLDGS INC (NV)
SEC revoked common stock registration 12/18/2014

BLUESTAR BATTERY SYS INTL CORP (AB)
Each share old Common no par exchanged for (0.04602991) share new Common no par 12/14/2000
Ceased operations 06/29/2001
No stockholders' equity

BLUESTAR FINL GROUP INC (NV)
Name changed to YouChange Holdings Corp. 06/25/2010
YouChange Holdings Corp. recapitalized as Infinity Resources Holdings Corp. 11/13/2012 which name changed to Quest Resource Holding Corp. 10/28/2013

BLUESTAR HEALTH INC (CO)
SEC revoked common stock registration 06/16/2011

BLUESTAR LEASING INC (NV)
Name changed to Sterling Equity Holdings, Inc. 03/14/2003
(See Sterling Equity Holdings, Inc.)

BLUESTEEL NETWORKS INC (CA)
Merged into Broadcom Corp. 03/01/2000
Each share Preferred Ser. A exchanged for (0.04331553) share Class B Common $0.0001 par
Broadcom Corp. merged into Broadcom Ltd. 02/01/2016 which reorganized as Broadcom Inc. 04/05/2018

BLUESTONE CAP CORP (CO)
Reorganized under the laws of Delaware as Dialogue Inc. 07/09/1990
Each share Common $0.00001 par exchanged for (0.05) share Common 1¢ par

BLUESTONE HLDG CORP (DE)
SEC revoked common stock registration 03/22/2010

BLUESTONE SOFTWARE INC (DE)
Merged into Hewlett-Packard Co. 01/18/2001
Each share Common no par exchanged for (0.4866) share Common $0.001 par
Hewlett-Packard Co. name changed to HP Inc. 11/02/2015

BLUESTONE VENTURES INC (NV)
Common $0.001 par split (15.508328) for (1) by issuance of (14.508328) additional shares payable 01/21/2005 to holders of record 01/11/2005 Ex date - 01/24/2005
Name changed to Electronic Sensor Technology, Inc. 02/01/2005
(See Electronic Sensor Technology, Inc.)

BLUETORCH INC (NV)
Each share old Common $0.001 par exchanged for (0.0004) share new Common $0.001 par 04/18/2005
Name changed to Pacific Crest Investments 04/25/2005
Pacific Crest Investments name changed to Pacific Peak Investments 05/16/2005 which name changed to Global Beverage Solutions, Inc. 10/26/2005 which recapitalized as Real Brands, Inc. 10/22/2013

BLUEWATER HOLDING CORP. (MN)
Name changed to Cache Technologies Corp. 09/09/1988

BLUEWATER OIL & GAS LTD (AB)
Reincorporated 00/00/1972
Place of incorporation changed from (ON) to (AB) 00/00/1972
Acquired by a private corporation 01/11/1985
Each share Capital Stock no par exchanged for $6 cash

BLUEWAVE GROUP INC (NV)
Recapitalized as Green & Hill Industries, Inc. 08/06/2013
Each share Common $0.001 par exchanged for (0.00133333) share Common $0.001 par

BLUGRASS ENERGY INC (NV)
Common $0.001 par split (15) for (1) by issuance of (14) additional shares payable 10/01/2008 to holders of record 10/01/2008
Each share old Common $0.001 par exchanged for (0.2) share new Common $0.001 par 05/17/2011
Recapitalized as Nogal Energy, Inc. 08/12/2013
Each new share Common $0.001 par exchanged for (0.005) share Common $0.001 par
Nogal Energy, Inc. name changed to Novamex Energy, Inc. 12/23/2014

BLUM (PHILIP) & CO., INC.
In process of liquidation 00/00/1948
Details not available

BLUM'S (CA)
Voting Trust Agreement terminated 05/26/1952

Each VTC for Common $2 par exchanged for (1) share Common $2 par
Merged into Uncle John's Restaurants, Inc. 12/10/1965
Each share 5% Conv. Preferred $20 par exchanged for (4) shares Common 50¢ par
Each share Common $2 par exchanged for (0.66666666) share Common 50¢ par
Uncle John's Restaurants, Inc. name changed to Envirofood, Inc. 09/29/1969
(See Envirofood, Inc.)

BLUMENTHAL (SIDNEY) & CO., INC. (NY)
7% Preferred $100 par called for redemption 10/01/1946
Common no par changed to $1 par 03/30/1956
Stock Dividend - 50% 04/14/1947
Merged into Burlington Industries, Inc. 11/06/1961
Each share Common $1 exchanged for (0.5) share Common $1 par
(See Burlington Industries, Inc.)

BLUMONT CANADIAN OPPORTUNITIES FUND (ON)
Merged into BluMont Core Hedge Fund 08/07/2009
Each Class A Unit automatically became (1.1642) Class A Units

BLUMONT CAP INC (ON)
Acquired by Integrated Asset Management Corp. 03/02/2007
Each share Common no par exchanged for (0.35714285) share Common no par

BLUMONT HIRSCH LONG/SHORT FUND (ON)
Merged into BluMont Core Hedge Fund 08/07/2009
Each Class A Unit automatically became (1.2021) Class A Units
Each Class F Unit automatically became (1.2445) Class F Units

BLUMONT MAN ALTERNATIVE YIELD FD (ON)
Completely liquidated
Each Unit no par received first and final distribution of $8.94803499 cash payable 08/24/2007 to holders of record 08/24/2007

BLUMONT MINES LTD. (AB)
Struck off register for failure to file annual returns 08/31/1964

BLUMONT STRATEGIC PARTNERS HEDGE FD (ON)
Merged into BluMont Canadian Opportunities Fund 12/31/2006
Each Trust Unit no par received (0.0762974) Trust Unit no par
BluMont Canadian Opportunities Fund merged into BluMont Core Hedge Fund 08/07/2009

BLUTIP PWR TECHNOLOGIES LTD (AB)
Assets sold for the benefit of creditors 05/03/2013
Stockholders' equity unlikely

BLVD HLDGS INC (NV)
Name changed to A.C. Simmonds & Sons Inc. 08/18/2014
(See A.C. Simmonds & Sons Inc.)

BLYE INTL LTD (DE)
Charter cancelled and declared inoperative and void for non-payment of taxes 03/01/1981

BLYTH HLDGS INC (DE)
Recapitalized as Omnis Technology Corp. 04/10/1997
Each share Common 1¢ par exchanged for (0.1) share Common 1¢ par
Omnis Technology Corp. name changed to Raining Data Corp. 12/04/2000 which name changed to TigerLogic Corp. 04/17/2008

(See TigerLogic Corp.)

BLYTH INC (DE)
Name changed 06/14/2000
Common 2¢ par split (2) for (1) by issuance of (1) additional share 12/27/1995
Common 2¢ par split (3) for (2) by issuance of (0.5) additional share payable 06/26/1997 to holders of record 06/16/1997 Ex date - 06/27/1997
Name changed from Blyth Industries, Inc. to Blyth, Inc. 06/14/2000
Each share old Common 2¢ par exchanged for (0.25) share new Common 2¢ par 01/30/2009
New Common 2¢ par split (2) for (1) by issuance of (1) additional share payable 06/15/2012 to holders of record 06/01/2012 Ex date - 06/18/2012
Acquired by Carlyle U.S. Equity Opportunity Fund, L.P. 10/14/2015
Each share new Common 2¢ par exchanged for $6 cash

BLYVOORUITZICHT GOLD MNG LTD (SOUTH AFRICA)
Each Unsponsored ADR for Ordinary exchanged for (1) Sponsored ADR for Ordinary 08/12/1996
Merged into Durban Roodepoort Deep Ltd. 09/15/1997
Each Sponsored ADR for Ordinary exchanged for (0.75) Sponsored ADR for Ordinary
Durban Roodepoort Deep Ltd. name changed to DRDGOLD Ltd. 12/06/2004

BM DIAMONDCORP INC (YT)
Name changed to BDI Mining Corp. (Yukon) 07/26/2004
BDI Mining Corp. (Yukon) reincorporated in British Virgin Islands 08/08/2005
(See BDI Mining Corp.)

BM RT RLTY INVTS (ON)
Under plan of reorganization each Trust Unit exchanged for $10.33 principal amount of Bank of Montreal Mortgage Corp. 11.75% Debentures due 09/08/1991 and $0.1525 cash 09/25/1981

BMA ASSOC INC (NY)
Adjudicated bankrupt 10/14/1970
No stockholders' equity

BMA CORP (MO)
Certificates dated prior to 02/28/1977
Merged into Business Men's Assurance Co. of America 02/28/1977
Each share Common $2 par exchanged for (1) share Common $2 par
Business Men's Assurance Co. of America reorganized as BMA Corp. 06/01/1988 which name changed to Seafield Capital Corp. 05/20/1991 which name changed to Lab Holdings, Inc. 10/20/1997 which merged into LabOne, Inc. (New) 08/10/1999
(See LabOne, Inc. (New))

BMA CORP NEW (MO)
Certificates dated after 06/01/1988
Name changed to Seafield Capital Corp. 05/20/1991
Seafield Capital Corp. name changed to Lab Holdings, Inc. 10/20/1997 which merged into LabOne, Inc. (New) 08/10/1999
(See LabOne, Inc. (New))

BMA HOLDING CORP. (MO)
Name changed to BMA Corp. 04/10/1968
BMA Corp. merged into Business Men's Assurance Co. of America 02/28/1977 which reorganized as BMA Corp. 06/01/1968 which name changed to Seafield Capital Corp. 05/20/1991 which name changed to Lab Holdings, Inc. 10/20/1997 which

merged into LabOne, Inc. (New) 08/10/1999
(See LabOne, Inc. (New))

BMA MNG CORP (BC)
Recapitalized as Dasher Energy Corp. 05/26/1999
Each share Common no par exchanged for (0.2) share Common no par
Dasher Energy Corp. name changed to Dasher Resources Corp. 10/03/2002 which recapitalized as Dasher Exploration Ltd. 04/16/2003 which name changed to New World Resource Corp. 06/27/2005

BMB CAP CORP (BC)
Name changed to Maritime Resources Corp. 10/06/2010

BMB COMPUSCIENCE CDA LTD (CANADA)
Name changed to Systems Xcellence Inc. (Canada) 01/09/1995
Systems Xcellence Inc. (Canada) reincorporated in Yukon as SXC Health Solutions Corp. 08/01/2007 which name changed to Catamaran Corp. 07/11/2012
(See Catamaran Corp.)

BMB MUNAI INC (NV)
Reincorporated 01/13/2005
State of incorporation changed from (DE) to (NV) 01/13/2005
Recapitalized as Freedom Holding Corp. 09/05/2017
Each share Common $0.001 par exchanged for (0.04) share Common $0.001 par

BMC BANKCORP, INC. (KY)
Merged into CBT Corp. (KY) 05/31/1994
Each share Common no par exchanged for (2) shares Common no par
CBT Corp. (KY) merged into Mercantile Bancorporation, Inc. 07/01/1998 which merged into Firstar Corp. (New) 09/20/1999 which merged into U.S. Bancorp (New) 02/27/2001

BMC INDS INC (MN)
Common no par split (2) for (1) by issuance of (1) additional share 09/08/1994
Common no par split (2) for (1) by issuance of (1) additional share 11/13/1995
Plan of reorganization under Chapter 11 Federal Bankruptcy proceedings effective 08/21/2006
No stockholders' equity

BMC INTL CORP (DE)
Charter cancelled and declared inoperative and void for non-payment of taxes 03/01/1988

BMC SOFTWARE INC (DE)
Common 1¢ par split (3) for (2) by issuance of (0.5) additional share 03/07/1990
Common 1¢ par split (2) for (1) by issuance of (1) additional share 08/14/1995
Common 1¢ par split (2) for (1) by issuance of (1) additional share payable 11/18/1996 to holders of record 11/04/1996
Common 1¢ par split (2) for (1) by issuance of (1) additional share payable 05/15/1998 to holders of record 05/01/1998
Acquired by Boxer Parent Co. Inc. 09/10/2013
Each share Common 1¢ par exchanged for $46.25 cash

BMC WEST CORP (DE)
Common $0.001 par split (3) for (2) by issuance of (0.5) additional share 03/04/1994
Reincorporated under the laws of California as Building Materials Holding Corp. 09/24/1997

(See Building Materials Holding Corp.)

BMD ENTERPRISES LTD (BC)
Delisted from Toronto Venture Stock Exchange 07/03/2002

BMI EDL SVCS INC (NJ)
Merged into BMI Acquisition Co. 12/07/1998
Each share Common no par exchanged for $4.30 cash

BMJ MED MGMT INC (DE)
Charter cancelled and declared inoperative and void for non-payment of taxes 03/01/2001

BMO AGRICULTURE COMMODITIES INDEX ETF (ON)
Trust terminated 12/06/2013
Each Unit received $10.62439 cash

BMO BASE METALS COMMODITIES ETF (ON)
Trust terminated 12/06/2013
Each Unit received $9.19435 cash

BMO CDN GOVT BD FD (ON)
Name changed to BMO Mid Federal Bond Index ETF 06/01/2010

BMO CHINA EQUITY HEDGED TO CAD INDEX ETF (ON)
Name changed to BMO China Equity Index ETF 10/02/2012

BMO DOW JONES CDN TITANS 60 INDEX ETF (ON)
Name changed to BMO S&P/TSX Capped Composite Index ETF 09/25/2012

BMO DOW JONES DIAMONDS INDEX ETF (ON)
Name changed to BMO Dow Jones Industrial Average Hedged to CAD Index ETF 10/26/2009

BMO EMERGING MKTS EQUITY ETF (ON)
Name changed to BMO MSCI Emerging Markets Index ETF 04/03/2013

BMO ENERGY COMMODITIES ETF (ON)
Trust terminated 12/06/2013
Each Unit received $15.57528 cash

BMO EQUITY LINKED CORPORATE BD ETF (ON)
Trust terminated 01/06/2017
Each Unit received $20.45113 cash

BMO II FINL CORP (CANADA)
Adjustable Rate Preferred no par called for redemption at $22.50 on 09/30/1992

BMO INDIA EQUITY HEDGED TO CAD INDEX ETF (ON)
Name changed to BMO India Equity Index ETF 10/02/2012

BMO INTL EQUITY HEDGED TO CAD INDEX ETF (ON)
Name changed to BMO MSCI EAFE Hedged CAD Index ETF 04/03/2013

BMO NT FINL CORP (CANADA)
Capital Stock no par called for redemption 08/31/1992
Public interest eliminated

BMO PRECIOUS METALS COMMODITIES ETF (ON)
Trust terminated 12/06/2013
Each Unit received $12.51435 cash

BMO S&P/TSX EQUAL WEIGHT BANKS INDEX ETF (ON)
Name changed to BMO Equal Weight Banks Index ETF 09/15/2017

BMO S&P/TSX EQUAL WEIGHT GLOBAL BASE METALS HEDGED TO CAD INDEX ETF (ON)
Name changed to BMO Equal Weight Global Base Metals Hedged to CAD Index ETF 09/15/2017

BMO S&P / TSX EQUAL WEIGHT GLOBAL GOLD INDEX ETF (ON)
Name changed to BMO Equal Weight Global Gold Index ETF 09/15/2017

BMO S&P / TSX EQUAL WEIGHT INDUSTRIALS INDEX ETF (ON)
Name changed to BMO Equal Weight Industrials Index ETF 09/15/2017

BMO S&P/TSX EQUAL WEIGHT OIL & GAS INDEX ETF (ON)
Name changed to BMO Equal Weight Oil & Gas Index ETF 09/15/2017

BMO S&P/TSX LADDERED PFD SH INDEX ETF (ON)
Name changed to BMO Laddered Preferred Share Index ETF 10/19/2015

BMO 2015 CORPORATE BD TARGET MAT ETF (ON)
Trust terminated 08/07/2015
Each Unit received $14.59 cash

BMO 2013 CORPORATE BD TARGET MAT ETF (ON)
Under plan of reorganization each Unit automatically became (0.25) BMO Ultra Short-Term Bond ETF Unit 01/07/2014

BMO 2020 CORPORATE BD TARGET MAT ETF (ON)
Trust terminated 08/07/2015
Each Unit received $16.33 cash

BMO 2025 CORPORATE BD TARGET MAT ETF (ON)
Trust terminated 08/07/2015
Each Unit received $16.73 cash

BMO US EQUITY HEDGED TO CAD INDEX ETF (ON)
Name changed 10/26/2009
Name changed from BMO US Equity Index ETF to BMO US Equity Hedged to CAD Index ETF 10/26/2009
Name changed to BMO S&P 500 Hedged to CAD Index ETF 09/25/2012

BMONT SPLIT CORP (ON)
Preferred Shares called for redemption at $27.45 on 08/05/2009
Capital Shares called for redemption at $12.6596 on 08/05/2009

BMP HLDGS INC (DE)
Common $0.0001 par split (10) for (1) by issuance of (9) additional shares payable 10/12/2016 to holders of record 10/06/2016 Ex date - 10/13/2016
Name changed to PixarBio Corp. 11/01/2016

BMP SUNSTONE CORP (DE)
Acquired by Sanofi-Aventis 02/25/2011
Each share Common $0.001 par exchanged for $10 cash

BMR FINL GROUP INC (GA)
Acquired by SouthTrust Corp. 12/15/1993
Each share Common 1¢ par exchanged for $6.30 cash

BMR GOLD CORP (BC)
Reincorporated 05/22/1990
Place of incorporation changed from (ALTA) to (BC) and Class A Common no par reclassified as Common no par 05/22/1990
Delisted from Toronto Stock Exchange 08/13/1999

BMS DATA PROCESSING CORP (DE)
Charter cancelled and declared inoperative and void for non-payment of taxes 04/15/1972

BMX DEV CORP (FL)
Name changed to Panache Beverage Inc. (FL) 10/05/2011
Panache Beverage Inc. (FL) reincorporated in Delaware 11/04/2013

BMX HLDGS INC (NV)
Common $0.001 par split (4) for (1) by issuance of (3) additional shares payable 05/14/2002 to holders of record 04/20/2002 Ex date - 05/15/2002
Recapitalized as Direct Music Group Inc. 02/07/2003
Each share Common $0.001 par exchanged for (0.08) share Common $0.001 par
Direct Music Group Inc. name changed to Cell Bio-Systems, Inc. 04/14/2004 which name changed to Tulip BioMed, Inc. (NV) 06/02/2006 which reorganized in Florida as Bitcoin Services, Inc. 03/21/2016

BMXP HLDGS INC (DE)
Recapitalized as Freedom Environmental Services, Inc. 06/11/2008
Each share Common 50¢ par exchanged for (0.05) share Common $0.001 par

BN LIQUIDATING CO., INC. (WI)
Completely liquidated 06/07/1965
Each share Common $1 par exchanged for first and final distribution of (0.3288) share Massey-Ferguson Ltd. Common no par
Massey-Ferguson Ltd. name changed to Varity Corp. (Canada) 06/19/1986 which reorganized in Delaware 08/01/1991 which merged into LucasVarity PLC 09/06/1996
(See LucasVarity PLC)

BNB BANCORP (CA)
Charter suspended for failure to file reports and pay fees 09/18/1992

BNB BANCORP INC (OH)
Merged into LCNB Corp. 04/30/2015
Each share Common no par exchanged for (2.005) shares Common no par and $15.75 cash

BNB CAP TR (DE)
Trust Preferred Securities called for redemption at $10 on 06/30/2002

BNB FINL SVCS CORP (NY)
Stock Dividends - 6% payable 03/12/1998 to holders of record 01/30/1998; 7% payable 03/01/1999 to holders of record 01/15/1999; 7% payable 03/31/2000 to holders of record 01/15/2000; 8% payable 03/07/2001 to holders of record 01/31/2001 Ex date - 04/05/2001; 8% payable 03/28/2003 to holders of record 01/31/2003 Ex date - 04/07/2003; 8% payable 03/15/2004 to holders of record 01/31/2004 Ex date - 03/26/2004
Name changed to Hana Bancorp, Inc. 09/24/2013

BNB SUNGWON CO LTD (KOREA)
ADR agreement terminated 12/17/2012
Each Sponsored ADR for Common exchanged for (10) shares Common
Note: Unexchanged ADR's will be sold and the proceeds, if any, held for claim after 04/17/2013

BNC BANCORP (NC)
Common no par split (5) for (4) by issuance of (0.25) additional share payable 11/15/2005 to holders of record 10/31/2005 Ex date - 11/16/2005
Fixed Rate Perpetual Preferred Ser. A no par called for redemption at $1,000 plus $10.27 accrued dividends on 04/29/2013
Stock Dividends - 10% payable 09/15/2003 to holders of record 09/01/2003 Ex date - 08/27/2003; 10% payable 01/22/2007 to holders of record 01/05/2007 Ex date - 01/03/2007
Merged into Pinnacle Financial Partners, Inc. 06/16/2017
Each share Common no par exchanged for (0.5235) share Common $1 par

BNC FINL GROUP INC (CT)
Name changed to Bankwell Financial Group, Inc. 09/11/2013

BNC MTG INC (DE)
Merged into BNCM Acquisition Co. 07/26/2000
Each share Common $0.001 par exchanged for $10 cash

BNF BANCORP INC (DE)
Acquired by Union Planters Corp. 09/01/1994
Each share Common 1¢ par exchanged for (1.078) shares Common $5 par
Union Planters Corp. merged into Regions Financial Corp. (New) 07/01/2004

BNH BANCSHARES INC (CT)
Common $4 par split (5) for (4) by issuance of (0.25) additional share 11/05/1985
Common $4 par split (2) for (1) by issuance of (1) additional share 05/15/1986
Common $4 par changed to $1 par 04/21/1992
Common $1 par changed to no par 04/27/1993
Each share old Common no par exchanged for (0.25) share new Common no par 05/01/1996
Stock Dividend - 10% 01/08/1990
Merged into Citizens Financial Group Inc. 08/28/1997
Each share new Common no par exchanged for $15.50 cash

BNH INC (NV)
Reorganized as BEESFREE, Inc. 10/27/2011
Each share Common $0.001 par exchanged for (2) shares Common $0.001 par

BNL FINL CORP (IA)
Acquired by Ameritas Life Insurance Corp. 01/04/2012
Each share Common no par exchanged for $2.31 cash

BNN CORP (NV)
Reincorporated under the laws of Delaware as Kaleidoscope Media Group, Inc. 12/05/1997
(See Kaleidoscope Media Group, Inc.)

BNN INVTS LTD (ON)
Name changed to BAM Investments Corp. 07/05/2006
BAM Investments Corp. name changed to Partners Value Fund Inc. 06/10/2013 which name changed to Partners Value Investments Inc. 05/25/2015 which reorganized as Partners Value Investments L.P. 07/04/2016

BNN SPLIT CORP (ON)
Name changed to BAM Split Corp. 12/15/2006

BNP PETE CORP (DE)
Name changed to Pilgrim Petroleum Corp. 07/01/2005

BNP RESIDENTAL PPTYS INC (MD)
Merged into Babcock & Brown Bravo Holdings LLC 02/28/2007
Each share Common 1¢ par exchanged for $24 cash

BNS CO (DE)
Each share Class A Common $1 par exchanged for (0.2) share Class A Common 1¢ par 05/10/2001
Each share Class B Common $1 par exchanged for (0.2) share Class B Common 1¢ par 05/10/2001
Name changed to BNS Holding, Inc. 12/14/2004
(See BNS Holding, Inc.)

BNS HLDG INC (DE)
Class B Common 1¢ par reclassified as old Class A Common 1¢ par 05/02/2005
Each share old Class A Common 1¢ par exchanged for (1) share new Class A Common 1¢ par to reflect a (1) for (200) reverse split followed by a (200) for (1) forward split 08/13/2007
Note: Holders of (199) or fewer pre-split shares held in their name received $13.62 cash per share
Each share new Class A Common 1¢ par exchanged again for (0.05) share new Class A Common 1¢ par to reflect a (1) for (1,000) reverse split followed by a (50) for (1) forward split 08/31/2010
Note: Holders of (999) or fewer pre-split shares held in their name received $12.25 cash per share Completely liquidated
Each share new Class A Common 1¢ par received first and final distribution of $473.48 cash payable 06/18/2012 to holders of record 06/15/2012
Note: Certificates were not required to be surrendered and are without value

BNS SPLIT CORP (ON)
Preferred no par called for redemption at $23 on 08/02/2007
Capital Shares no par called for redemption at $38.4892 on 08/02/2007

BNS SPLIT CORP II (ON)
Class A Preferred Shares called for redemption at $20.83 on 09/22/2010
Class B Preferred Ser. B called for redemption at $18.85 on 09/22/2015
(Additional Information in Active)

BNT LTD (ON)
Capital Shares no par called for redemption at $15.55 on 04/20/1995
Equity Dividend Shares no par called for redemption at $27.50 on 04/20/1995

BNW BANCORP INC (WA)
Acquired by Pacific Financial Corp. 02/27/2004
Each share Common no par exchanged for (0.85) share Common $1 par

BNY CAP II (DE)
7.8% Trust Preferred Securities Ser. C called for redemption at $25 on 09/01/2002

BNY CAP III (DE)
7.05% Preferred Securities Ser. D called for redemption at $25 plus $0.440625 accrued dividend on 06/01/2003

BNY CAP IV (DE)
6.875% Trust Preferred Securities Ser. E called for redemption at $25 plus $0.40582 accrued dividends on 11/26/2012

BNY CAP V (DE)
5.95% Trust Preferred Securities Ser. F called for redemption at $25 plus $0.1033 accrued dividends on 11/26/2012

BOARD OF TRADE BUILDING TRUST (MA)
Liquidation completed
Each share Common $100 par received initial distribution of $30 cash 07/26/1960
Each share Common $100 par exchanged for second and final distribution of $9.70 cash 07/10/1963

BOARDROOM BUSINESS PRODS INC (UT)
Proclaimed dissolved for failure to file annual report 05/01/1990

BOARDWALK BANCORP INC (NJ)
Merged into Cape Bancorp, Inc. 01/31/2008

Each share Common $5 par exchanged for (0.347775) share Common 1¢ par and $19.5245 cash
Cape Bancorp, Inc. merged into OceanFirst Financial Corp. 05/02/2016

BOARDWALK BK (LINWOOD, NJ)
Stock Dividend - 5% payable 12/09/2004 to holders of record 11/29/2004
Reorganized as Boardwalk Bancorp, Inc. 07/03/2006
Each share Common $5 par exchanged for (1) share Common $5 par
Boardwalk Bancorp, Inc. merged into Cape Bancorp, Inc. 01/31/2008 which merged into OceanFirst Financial Corp. 05/02/2016

BOARDWALK CASINO INC (NV)
Merged into Mirage Resorts, Inc. 06/30/1998
Each share Common $0.001 par exchanged for $5 cash

BOARDWALK EQUITIES INC (AB)
Common no par split (2) for (1) by issuance of (1) additional share payable 12/03/1997 to holders of record 12/01/1997
Reorganized as Boardwalk Real Estate Investment Trust 05/03/2004
Each share Common no par received (1) Trust Unit no par
Note: New York residents received approximately U.S. $11.60 cash

BOARDWALK NATL BK (ATLANTIC CITY, NJ)
Capital Stock $100 par changed to $25 par and (3) additional shares issued 05/09/1958
Capital Stock $25 par changed to $10 par and (1.5) additional shares issued 02/03/1963
Stock Dividends - (2) for (13) 02/16/1955; 20% 07/16/1957; 10% 09/28/1960
Name changed to First National Bank of South Jersey (Pleasantville, NJ) 12/01/1969
First National Bank of South Jersey (Pleasantville, NJ) merged into First National State Bancorporation 12/31/1980 which name changed to First Fidelity Bancorporation (Old) 05/01/1985 which merged into First Fidelity Bancorporation (New) 02/29/1988 which merged into First Union Corp. 01/01/1996 which name changed to Wachovia Corp. (Ctfs. dated after 09/01/2001) 09/01/2001 which merged into Wells Fargo & Co. (New) 12/31/2008

BOARDWALK PETE INVT INC (UT)
Name changed to Boardwalk Petroleum, Inc. 09/21/1977
Boardwalk Petroleum, Inc. merged into Ambra Oil & Gas Co. 08/31/1979
(See Ambra Oil & Gas Co.)

BOARDWALK PETROLEUM, INC. (UT)
Merged into Ambra Oil & Gas Co. 08/31/1979
Each share Common 1¢ par exchanged for (2) shares Common 10¢ par
(See Ambra Oil & Gas Co.)

BOARDWALK PIPELINE PARTNERS LP (DE)
Acquired by Boardwalk GP, LP 07/18/2018
Each Common Unit exchanged for $12.06 cash

BOARDWALK SECS CORP (NJ)
Merged into a private company 03/20/1998
Each share Common $100 par exchanged for $9,815.72 cash

BOATMEN'S TRUST CO. (ST. LOUIS, MO)
Acquired by Nationsbank Corp. 03/13/1998
Details not available

BOATMENS BANCSHARES INC (MO)
Common $10 par split (4) for (3) by issuance of (0.33333333) additional share 01/09/1984
Common $10 par changed to $1 par 04/23/1991
Common $1 par split (2) for (1) by issuance of (1) additional share 10/01/1993
Stock Dividends - 25% 01/17/1977; 25% 01/09/1981; 10% 01/09/1982; 25% 01/08/1983
Merged into NationsBank Corp. (NC) 01/07/1997
Each share Adjustable Preferred Ser. A no par exchanged for (1) share Adjustable Preferred Ser. A no par
Each 7% Depositary Share Class A exchanged for (1) 7% Depositary Share Class A
Each share 7% Preferred Ser. B no par exchanged for (1) share 7% Preferred Ser. B no par
Each share Common $1 par exchanged for (0.6525) share Common no par
NationsBank Corp. (NC) reincorporated in Delaware as BankAmerica Corp. (Old) 09/25/1998 which merged into BankAmerica Corp. (New) 09/30/1998 which name changed to Bank of America Corp. 04/28/1999

BOATMENS NATL BK (ST LOUIS, MO)
Common $20 par changed to $10 par and (1) additional share issued 02/25/1963
Stock Dividends - 25% 10/21/1941; 20% 05/01/1945; 12.5% 10/15/1951; 10% 11/22/1954; 12.5% 01/15/1960
Under plan of reorganization each share Common $10 par automatically became (1) share Boatmen's Bancshares, Inc. Common $10 par 09/09/1969
Boatmen's Bancshares, Inc. merged into NationsBank Corp. (NC) 01/07/1997 which reincorporated in Delaware as BankAmerica Corp. (Old) 09/25/1998 which merged into BankAmerica Corp. (New) 09/30/1998 which name changed to Bank of America Corp. 04/28/1999

BOATRACS INC (CA)
Name changed to Advanced Remote Communication Solutions Inc. 07/26/1999
(See Advanced Remote Communication Solutions Inc.)

BOB EVANS FARMS INC (OH)
Common no par split (4) for (3) by issuance of (0.33333333) additional share 05/13/1968
Common no par split (5) for (4) by issuance of (0.25) additional share 06/03/1974
Common no par split (3) for (2) by issuance of (0.5) additional share 04/16/1976
Common no par split (3) for (2) by issuance of (0.5) additional share 04/15/1977
Common no par split (4) for (3) by issuance of (0.33333333) additional share 12/16/1977
Common no par split (2) for (1) by issuance of (1) additional share 09/29/1978
Common no par split (3) for (2) by issuance of (0.5) additional share 09/18/1981
Common no par split (4) for (3) by issuance of (0.33333333) additional share 01/17/1983
Common no par split (5) for (4) by issuance of (0.25) additional share 09/16/1983
State of incorporation changed from (OH) to (DE) and Common no par changed to 1¢ par 12/27/1985
Common 1¢ par split (5) for (4) by issuance of (0.25) additional share 09/19/1986
Common 1¢ par split (5) for (4) by issuance of (0.25) additional share 09/11/1987
Common 1¢ par split (4) for (3) by issuance of (0.33333333) additional share 04/24/1992
Stock Dividends - 10% 10/02/1967; 10% 09/01/1970; 10% 09/17/1982; 10% 09/06/1985; 10% 09/29/1989
Acquired by Post Holdings, Inc. 01/12/2018
Each share Common 1¢ par exchanged for $77 cash

BOBBIE BROOKS INC (OH)
issuance of (1) additional share 03/11/1960
Common no par split (2) for (1) by issuance of (1) additional share 09/14/1962
Each share old Common no par exchanged for (0.1) share new Common no par 08/14/1990
Merged into Pubco Corp. 06/28/1996
Each share new Common no par exchanged for (0.16666666) share new Common 1¢ par
(See Pubco Corp.)

BOBBS MERRILL CO (IN)
Voluntary purchase offer 00/00/1958 by Howard W. Sams & Co., Inc.; held 96.99% as of 11/27/1958 and 100% acquired by 06/15/1969

BOBBY CADILLACS FOOD CORP (BC)
Recapitalized as Immune Network Research Ltd. 04/29/1996
Each share Common no par exchanged for (0.66666666) share Common no par
Immune Network Research Ltd. name changed to Immune Network Ltd. 08/16/2000
(See Immune Network Ltd.)

BOBCAM MINES, LTD. (ON)
Charter cancelled and company declared dissolved for default in filing returns 12/00/1962

BOBCAT OIL CO (CO)
Each share Capital Stock 1¢ par exchanged for (0.1) share Capital Stock 10¢ par 06/03/1974
Liquidation completed
Each share Capital Stock 10¢ par exchanged for initial distribution of $1.17 cash 01/07/1977
Each share Capital Stock 10¢ par received second and final distribution of $0.0413 cash 03/21/1978

BOBERNCO INC (NV)
Recapitalized as GTC Telecom Corp. 09/14/1998
Each share Common $0.001 par exchanged for (0.5) share Common $0.001 par
(See GTC Telecom Corp.)

BOBJO MINES LTD. (ON)
Merged into Jowsey (R.J.) Mining Co. Ltd. 00/00/1956
Each share Capital Stock $1 par exchanged for (0.33333333) share Capital Stock $1 par
Jowsey (R.J.) Mining Co. Ltd. name changed to Open End Mines Ltd. 08/04/1971 which liquidated for New York Oils Ltd. (BC) 04/28/1972 which reincorporated in Alberta 07/19/1982 which was acquired by Sceptre Resources Ltd. 03/14/1989 which merged into Canadian Natural Resources Ltd. 08/15/1996

BOBS LAKE GOLD MINES LTD. (ON)
Name changed to New Bobs Lake Gold Mines Ltd. 07/07/1952
(See New Bobs Lake Gold Mines Ltd.)

BOC FINL CORP (NC)
Merged into Bank of the Carolinas (Mocksville, NC) 12/31/2001
Each share Common $1 par exchanged for (0.92) share Common $5 par
Bank of the Carolinas (Mocksville, NC) reorganized as Bank of the Carolinas Corp. 08/18/2006 which merged into Bank of the Ozarks, Inc. 08/05/2015 which reorganized as Bank of the Ozarks (Little Rock, AR) 06/27/2017 which name changed to Bank OZK (Little Rock, AR) 07/16/2018

BOC GROUP PLC (UNITED KINGDOM)
Name changed 02/17/1982
Name changed from BOC International Group to BOC Group PLC 02/17/1982
Each Unsponsored ADR for Ordinary exchanged for (0.5) Sponsored ADR for Ordinary 09/18/1996
Merged into Linde AG 09/05/2006
Each Sponsored ADR for Ordinary exchanged for $60.18241 cash

BOCA BANCORP INC (DE)
Merged into Intercontinental Bank (Miami, FL) 12/30/1994
Each share Class A $3.85 par exchanged for either (0.9662) share Common $2 par or $1.903 cash
Each share Class B $3.85 par exchanged for either (0.9662) share Common $2 par or $1.903 cash
Note: Option to elect to receive stock expired 02/06/1995

BOCA RATON CAP CORP (FL)
Each share old Common $0.001 par exchanged for (0.04) share new Common $0.001 par 05/12/1992
Each share new Common $0.001 par exchanged again for (0.1) share new Common $0.001 par 06/11/1993
Name changed to CRP Holding Corp. 10/24/1997
CRP Holding Corp. recapitalized as American Food Holdings, Inc. 05/02/2007 which name changed to Plateau Mineral Development, Inc. 09/15/2008

BOCA RATON FIRST NATL BK FLA (BOCA RATON, FL)
Merged into First Union Corp. 04/11/1997
Each share Common no par exchanged for $7.41 cash

BOCA RATON NATL BK (BOCA RATON, FL)
Capital Stock $10 par changed to $5 par and (1) additional share issued plus a 5% stock dividend paid 03/28/1969
Capital Stock $5 par changed to $2.50 par and (1) additional share issued 06/08/1973
Stock Dividend - 10% 03/15/1977
97% acquired by First Bankers Corp. of Florida through exchange offer which expired 05/28/1982
Public interest eliminated

BOCA RESH INC (FL)
Name changed to Inprimis, Inc. 10/10/2000
Inprimis, Inc. name changed to Ener1, Inc. 10/28/2002
(See Ener1, Inc.)

BOCA RESORTS INC (FL)
Acquired by Blackstone Group 12/13/2004
Each share Class A Common 1¢ par exchanged for $24 cash

BOCA RES LTD (AB)
Name changed to Canadian Fortune Resources Inc. (Old) 10/28/1987
Canadian Fortune Resources Inc. (Old) merged into Consolidated Canadian Fortune Resources Inc. 12/07/1990 which name changed to Canadian Fortune Resources Inc. (New) 03/15/1993 which merged into Fortune Energy Inc. 09/01/1993
(See Fortune Energy Inc.)

BOCABOIS GOLD MINES, LTD. (ON)
Dissolved 01/05/1970
No stockholders' equity

BOCH & LIMOGES LTD (BC)
Recapitalized as Vannessa Ventures Ltd. 07/21/1994
Each share Common no par exchanged for (0.45454545) share Common no par
Vannessa Ventures Ltd. name changed to Infinito Gold Ltd. 05/28/2008

BODCAW CO. (DE)
Merged into International Paper Co. 09/21/1979
Each share Capital Stock $1 par exchanged for $3,539.33 cash

BODDIE-NOELL PPTYS INC (MD)
Name changed 10/03/1994
Reincorporated 07/31/1997
Name changed from Boddie-Noell Restaurant Properties Inc. to Boddie-Noell Properties Inc. 10/03/1994
State of incorporation changed from (DE) to (MD) 07/31/1997
Name changed to BNP Residential Properties, Inc. 04/24/2000
(See BNP Residential Properties, Inc.)

BODEGA VENTURES INC (AB)
Recapitalized as Leader Oil & Gas Ltd. 06/22/1993
Each share Common no par exchanged for (0.25) share Common no par
Leader Oil & Gas Ltd. name changed to Canadian Leader Energy Inc. 07/18/1994 which merged into Centurion Energy International Inc. 05/20/1997
(See Centurion Energy International Inc.)

BODEKER DRUG CO. (VA)
Acquired by Owens, Minor & Bodeker, Inc. 06/10/1955
Details not available

BODI GARD CDA LTD (CANADA)
Merged into Bodi-Gard Canada (1977) Ltd. 12/08/1977
Each share Common no par exchanged for $2.25 cash

BODIN APPAREL INC (DE)
Reincorporated 12/16/1982
Common 10¢ par split (3) for (2) by issuance of (0.5) additional share 03/01/1973
State of incorporation changed from (FL) to (DE) 12/16/1982
Name changed to JSN Industries, Inc. 03/01/1983
JSN Industries, Inc. name changed to Johnston Acquisition Corp. 03/14/2006
(See Johnston Acquisition Corp.)

BODISEN BIOTECH INC (DE)
Common no par split (4) for (1) by issuance of (3) additional shares payable 03/02/2004 to holders of record 02/27/2004 Ex date - 03/03/2004
SEC revoked common stock registration 08/26/2016

BODY CONCEPTS INC (NV)
Common $0.001 par split (5) for (2) by issuance of (1.5) additional shares payable 07/03/2000 to holders of record 05/16/2000 Ex date - 07/05/2000
Name changed to Digital Village World Technologies Inc. 07/03/2000
Digital Village World Technologies Inc. name changed to Super Energy Investments Corp. 09/23/2002 which recapitalized as USA Signal Technology, Inc. 04/17/2006 which name changed to Icon Media Inc. 06/10/2011

BODY DRAMA INC (CA)
Merged into Beeba's Creations, Inc. 11/30/1994
Each share Common no par exchanged for $2.93 cash

BODY SHOP INTL PLC (UNITED KINGDOM)
ADR agreement terminated 11/18/2002
Each Sponsored ADR for Ordinary exchanged for $10.33212141 cash

BODYSCAN CORP (NV)
Charter revoked for failure to file reports and pay fees 11/01/2006

BODYSONIC CO LTD (JAPAN)
Name changed to Omega Project Inc. 07/01/2000
Omega Project Inc. name changed to Omega Project Holdings Co., Ltd. 04/01/2005
(See Omega Project Holdings Co., Ltd.)

BODYTEL SCIENTIFIC INC (NV)
Common $0.001 par split (13) for (1) by issuance of (12) additional shares payable 01/03/2007 to holders of record 01/02/2007 Ex date - 01/04/2007
SEC revoked common stock registration 08/09/2012

BOE CAP CORP (BC)
Name changed to Athabasca Uranium Inc. 07/21/2010
Athabasca Uranium Inc. name changed to Atom Energy Inc. 11/18/2014

BOE FINL SVCS VA INC (VA)
Merged into Community Bankers Acquisition Corp. 05/31/2008
Each share Common $5 par exchanged for (5.7278) shares Common 1¢ par
Community Bankers Acquisition Corp. name changed to Community Bankers Trust Corp. (DE) 06/02/2008 which reincorporated in Virginia 01/01/2014

BOECKH CO., LTD. (ON)
Name changed to Amberley Industries Ltd. 03/17/1966
(See Amberley Industries Ltd.)

BOEING AIRPLANE & TRANSPORT CORP. OF SEATTLE
Name changed to United Aircraft & Transport Corp. 00/00/1929
(See United Aircraft & Transport Corp.)

BOEING AIRPLANE CO (DE)
Capital Stock $5 par split (2) for (1) by issuance of (1) additional share 00/00/1954
Capital Stock $5 par split (2) for (1) by issuance of (1) additional share 08/06/1956
Name changed to Boeing Co. 05/04/1961

BOEING HOLDINGS & EXPLORATIONS LTD. (ON)
Recapitalized as Consolidated Boeing Holdings & Explorations Ltd. 01/06/1972
Each share Common no par exchanged for (0.5) share Common no par
Consolidated Boeing Holdings & Explorations Ltd. name changed to Academy Explorations Ltd. 04/10/1980
(See Academy Explorations Ltd.)

BOEING MINES LTD. (ON)
Merged into Boeing Holdings & Explorations Ltd. 12/13/1968
Each share Common $1 par exchanged for (0.33333333) share Common no par
Note: on 12/10/1968 the company recapitalized as Boeing Mines (1968) Ltd. on a (0.33333333) for (1) basis changing the Common $1 par to no par
Certificates were not surrendered at time of recapitalization
Boeing Mines (1968) Ltd. merged into Boeing Holdings & Explorations Ltd. on a share for share basis
Subsequently as a result of the merger each share Boeing Mines Ltd. Common $1 par (which actually represents (0.33333333) share Boeing Mines (1968) Ltd. Common no par) is exchangeable for (0.33333333) share Boeing Holdings & Explorations Ltd.
Boeing Holdings & Explorations Ltd. recapitalized as Consolidated Boeing Holdings & Explorations Ltd. 01/06/1972 which name changed to Academy Explorations Ltd. 04/10/1980
(See Academy Explorations Ltd.)

BOEING MINES (1968) LTD. (ON)
Merged into Boeing Holdings & Explorations Ltd. 12/13/1968 (For complete details see listing for Boeing Mines Ltd.)

BOELITE, INC. (WA)
Adjudicated bankrupt 02/01/1966
No stockholders' equity

BOFI HLDG INC (DE)
Each share 6% Conv. Perpetual Preferred Ser. B 1¢ par exchanged for (61.92) shares Common 1¢ par 09/11/2012
Common 1¢ par split (4) for (1) by issuance of (3) additional shares payable 11/17/2015 to holders of record 11/06/2015 Ex date - 11/18/2015
Name changed to Axos Financial, Inc. 09/13/2018

BOGALUSA PAPER CO., INC. (LA)
Merged into Gaylord Container Corp. 00/00/1937
Details not available

BOGALUSA TUNG OIL CO (LA)
Name changed to Money Hill Plantation, Inc. 07/06/1970

BOGERT OIL CO (OK)
Each share Common 1¢ par exchanged for (0.1) share Common 10¢ par 04/02/1986
Merged into LDEC Acquisition Corp. 07/19/1990
Each share Common 10¢ par exchanged for $13.20 cash

BOGUE ELEC MFG CO (NJ)
Recapitalized as Bogue International Inc. 06/23/2006
Each share Common $1 par exchanged for (0.05) share Common $1 par
(See Bogue International Inc.)

BOGUE INTL INC (NJ)
SEC revoked common stock registration 10/01/2008

BOHACK CORP (NY)
Common $1 par split (3) for (2) by issuance of (0.5) additional share 01/29/1971
Merged into Key International Manufacturing, Inc. 12/28/1979
Each share 5.5% Prior Preferred $100 par automatically became (1) share 5.5% Prior Preferred $100 par
Each share Common $1 par exchanged for (0.1) share Common 1¢ par
(See Key International Manufacturing, Inc.)

BOHACK H C INC (NY)
Each share Common $100 par exchanged for (4) shares old Common no par 00/00/1928
Each share 7% 1st Preferred $100 par exchanged for (1.4) shares 5.5% Prior Preferred $100 par and $7.50 cash 00/00/1948
Each share old 6% 2nd Preferred $100 par exchanged for (1) share new 6% 2nd Preferred $100 par 00/00/1948
Each share old Common no par exchanged for (1) share new Common no par 00/00/1948
New 6% 2nd Preferred $100 par exchanged for new Common no par 00/00/1963
New Common no par changed to $1 par 10/18/1968
Stock Dividend - 300% 03/29/1951
Name changed to Bohack Corp. 06/06/1969
Bohack Corp. merged into Key International Manufacturing, Inc. 12/28/1979
(See Key International Manufacturing, Inc.)

BOHACK REALTY CORP. (NY)
Each share 7% Preferred $100 par with accrued dividends of $94 per share exchanged for (2) shares 5% Prior Preference $100 par and $3 in cash 00/00/1950
5% Prior Preference $100 par called 07/10/1967

BOHEMIA INC (OR)
Common no par split (3) for (2) by issuance of (0.5) additional share 06/26/1979
Stock Dividend - 10% 07/10/1978
Merged into B Acquisition Corp. 09/26/1991
Each share Common no par exchanged for $24 cash

BOHEMIA LUMBER CO., INC. (OR)
Common no par split (2) for (1) by issuance of (1) additional share 10/31/1969
Name changed to Bohemia Inc. 09/27/1972
(See Bohemia Inc.)

BOHEMIAN BREWERY CORP. (CA)
Charter revoked for failure to file reports and pay fees 08/01/1958

BOHLER UDDEHOLM AG (AUSTRIA)
Sponsored 144A ADR's for Ordinary ATS 100 par changed to EUR 2 par and (4.3333333) additional ADR's issued payable 06/07/2006 to holders of record 06/06/2006
Sponsored ADR's for Ordinary ATS 100 par changed to EUR 2 par and (4.3333333) additional ADR's issued payable 06/07/2006 to holders of record 06/06/2006
ADR basis changed from (1:0.3333) to (1:0.25) 06/07/2006
Acquired by Voestalpine AG 11/24/2008
Each Sponsored 144A ADR for Ordinary EUR 2 par exchanged for $22.906316 cash
Each Sponsored ADR for Ordinary EUR 2 par exchanged for $22.906316 cash
Note: Each Sponsored ADR for Ordinary EUR 2 par received an additional distribution of $2.486047 cash 06/15/2012

BOHN ALUMINUM & BRASS CORP. (MI)
Common no par changed to $5 par 00/00/1933
Stock Dividend - 50% 06/20/1952
Merged into Universal American Corp. (DE) 08/31/1963
Each share Common $5 par exchanged for (1) share 2nd Conv. Preferred 1st Ser. $35 par and (1) share Common 25¢ par

BOH-BOL FINANCIAL INFORMATION, INC.

Universal American Corp. (DE) merged into Gulf & Western Industries, Inc. (DE) 01/12/1968 which name changed to Gulf + Western Inc. 05/01/1986 which name changed to Paramount Communications Inc. 06/05/1989 which merged into Viacom Inc. (Old) 07/07/1994
(See Viacom Inc. (Old))

BOHN BENTON INC (NY)
Merged into Bohn (Leon) Inc. 06/19/1975
Each share Common 50¢ par exchanged for $1.50 cash

BOHN BUSINESS MACHINES, INC. (NY)
Merged into Victoreen Instrument Co. 03/28/1967
Each share Capital Stock 5¢ par exchanged for $10 cash

BOILERMAKER VENTURES INC (NV)
Name changed to Venkoren International Inc. 12/03/1992
Venkoren International Inc. name changed to Vivante Internationale Inc. 01/14/1994 which name changed to Viva Pharmaceutical Inc. 05/16/1995
(See Viva Pharmaceutical Inc.)

BOIS D ARC ENERGY INC (NV)
Merged into Stone Energy Corp. 08/28/2008
Each share Common 1¢ par exchanged for (0.165) share Common 1¢ par and $13.65 cash
Stone Energy Corp. name changed to Talos Energy Inc. 05/10/2018

BOISE CASCADE CORP (DE)
Conv. Preferred $50 par called for redemption 04/30/1959
Common $10 par changed to $5 par and (1) additional share issued 05/27/1960
Common $5 par changed to $2.50 par and (1) additional share issued 04/27/1966
$1.40 Conv. Preferred no par called for redemption 05/29/1969
$5 Conv. Exchangeable Preferred Ser. B no par called for redemption 04/11/1986
$3 Conv. Preferred Ser. A no par called for redemption 04/30/1987
Common $2.50 par split (5) for (3) by issuance of (0.66666666) additional share 01/15/1988
Each share $3.50 Conv. Exchangeable Preferred Ser. C no par exchanged for $50 principal amount of 7% Conv. Subordinated Debentures due 05/01/2016 effective 05/01/1988
Each $1.79 Depositary Preferred Ser. E exchanged for (1) share Common $2.50 par 01/15/1995
$1.58 Depositary Preferred Ser. G called for redemption at $21.225 on 07/15/1997
$1.58 Conversion Preferred Ser. G no par called for redemption at $212.25 on 07/15/1997
9.4% Depositary Preferred Ser. F called for redemption at $25 on 02/17/1998
Name changed to OfficeMax Inc. 11/01/2004
Each Adjustable Conversion Rate Equity Security received (1.5689) shares OfficeMax Inc. Common $2.50 par 12/16/2004
OfficeMax Inc. merged into Office Depot, Inc. 11/05/2013

BOISE CASCADE OFFICE PRODS CORP (DE)
Merged into Boise Cascade Corp. 04/19/2008
Each share Common 1¢ par exchanged for $16.50 cash

BOISE CREEK RES LTD (BC)
Struck off register and declared dissolved for failure to file returns 07/28/1995

BOISE GAS LIGHT & COKE CO.
Property sold 00/00/1944
No Common stockholders' equity

BOISE INC (DE)
Acquired by Packaging Corp. of America 10/25/2013
Each share Common $0.0001 par exchanged for $12.55 cash

BOISE PAYETTE LUMBER CO. (DE)
Each share Common no par exchanged for (10) shares Common $10 par 00/00/1950
Name changed to Boise Cascade Corp. 00/00/1957
Boise Cascade Corp. name changed to OfficeMax Inc. 11/01/2004 which merged into Office Depot, Inc. 11/05/2013

BOISE WTR CORP (ID)
Name changed to United Water Idaho Inc. 03/20/1995
(See United Water Idaho Inc.)

BOJO URANIUM CO. (NV)
Merged into Republic Uranium Co. on a (2) for (1) basis 02/06/1956
Republic Uranium Co. name changed to Republic Oil & Mining Corp. 00/00/1957 which merged into Entrada Corp. 01/17/1958 which recapitalized as Pacific Energy Corp. 01/14/1976 which name changed to Aimco, Inc. 09/01/1977 which recapitalized as Colt Technology, Inc. 03/31/1983

BOKUM CORP (NM)
Liquidation completed
Each share Common no par received initial distribution of $10.50 cash 06/03/1971
Each share Common no par exchanged for second and final distribution of $2.6157 cash 04/27/1972

BOKUM RES CORP (DE)
Assets sold for the benefit of creditors 11/04/1991
No stockholders' equity

BOL ENERGY LTD (AB)
Name changed to American Environmental Enterprises Corp. 03/13/1987
(See American Environmental Enterprises Corp.)

BOL-INCA MINING CORP. (NY)
Completely liquidated 00/00/1958
Each share Common $1 par exchanged for first and final distribution of (3) shares Bol-Inca Mining Corp. (NV) Common 40¢ par
(See Bol-Inca Mining Corp. (NV))

BOL INCA MNG CORP (NV)
Voluntarily dissolved 10/22/1982
Details not available

BOLACK OIL & GAS CO. (NM)
Merged into Albuquerque Associated Oil Co. 07/11/1955
Each share Capital Stock 10¢ par exchanged for (0.33333333) share Common $1 par
Albuquerque Associated Oil Co. merged into Atlas Corp. 05/31/1956
(See Atlas Corp.)

BOLAR PHARMACEUTICAL INC (NY)
Common 1¢ par split (3) for (2) by issuance of (0.5) additional share 03/09/1979
Common 1¢ par split (2) for (1) by issuance of (1) additional share 02/11/1980
Common 1¢ par split (2) for (1) by issuance of (1) additional share 08/05/1985
Common 1¢ par split (2) for (1) by issuance of (1) additional share 10/22/1987
Stock Dividends - 100% 06/30/1972; 100% 11/10/1980
Name changed to Circa Pharmaceuticals Inc. 03/26/1993
Circa Pharmaceuticals Inc. merged into Watson Pharmaceuticals, Inc. 07/17/1995 which name changed to Actavis, Inc. (NV) 01/24/2013 which reorganized in Ireland as Actavis PLC 10/01/2013 which name changed to Allergan PLC 06/15/2015

BOLCAR ENERGIE INC (CANADA)
Name changed to AAER Inc. 11/07/2006
(See AAER Inc.)

BOLD ENERGY INC (NV)
Name changed to Lot78, Inc. 02/07/2013

BOLD VENTURES INC (BC)
Reincorporated under the laws of Ontario 08/31/2010

BOLD VIEW RES INC (NV)
Reorganized as SunSi Energies Inc. 04/21/2009
Each share Common $0.001 par exchanged for (12) shares Common $0.001 par
SunSi Energies Inc. name changed to ForceField Energy Inc. 02/28/2013

BOLDER TECHNOLOGIES CORP (DE)
Chapter 11 Federal Bankruptcy proceedings converted to Chapter 7 on 02/08/2002
Stockholders' equity unlikely

BOLEN HOLDING CO. (OH)
Dissolved and completely liquidated 07/26/1993
Details not available

BOLERO MINES LTD (BC)
Recapitalized as Michael Resources Ltd. 03/13/1984
Each share Common no par exchanged for (0.2) share Common no par
(See Michael Resources Ltd.)

BOLERO RES CORP (ON)
Each share old Common no par exchanged for (0.1) share new Common no par 07/29/2009
Name changed to Canada Carbon Inc. 10/05/2012

BOLERO RES INC (BC)
Recapitalized as United Bolero Development Corp. (BC) 02/12/1992
Each share Common no par exchanged for (0.33333333) share Common no par
United Bolero Development Corp. (BC) reincorporated in Ontario as Bolero Resources Corp. 09/18/2007 which name changed to Canada Carbon Inc. 10/05/2012

BOLGO GOLD MINES LTD.
Charter cancelled 08/00/1974

BOLIDEN LTD (CANADA)
Each Instalment Receipt no par exchanged for (1) share 144A Common no par 06/17/1998
Plan of arrangement effective 12/07/2001
Each Conv. Preferred Ser. 1 received (1.8875) shares Boliden AB Ordinary
Each share 144A Common no par received (0.05) share Ordinary
Note: Boliden AB shares are book entry only. Surrender of certificates is required only upon effecting a trade.

BOLIVAR ENERGY CORP (CANADA)
Reorganized under the laws of Alberta as Anatolia Energy Corp. 12/13/2011
Each share Common no par exchanged for (0.05) share Common no par
Anatolia Energy Corp. merged into Cub Energy Inc. 07/01/2013

BOLIVAR GOLD CORP (YT)
Each share old Common no par exchanged for (1) share new Common no par to reflect a (1) for (100) reverse split followed by a (100) for (1) forward split 06/29/2004
Note: Holders of (99) or fewer pre-split shares received $1.37 cash per share
Merged into Gold Fields Ltd. (New) 03/03/2006
Each share new Common no par exchanged for $3.20 cash

BOLIVAR GOLDFIELDS LTD (YT)
Each share old Common no par exchanged for (0.2) share new Common no par 06/25/1997
Name changed to Storage @ccess Technologies Inc. 02/09/2001
Storage @ccess Technologies Inc. recapitalized as BluePoint Data Storage, Inc. 01/31/2003 which name changed to BluePoint Data, Inc. 07/27/2009
(See BluePoint Data, Inc.)

BOLIVAR MINES LTD. (ON)
Charter revoked for failure to file reports and pay taxes 00/00/1955

BOLIVAR URANIUM CORP. (DE)
No longer in existence having become inoperative and void for non-payment of taxes 04/01/1958

BOLIVIAN AMERICAN OIL CO. (DE)
Merged into Perfect Fit Industries, Inc. 09/27/1961
Each share Common 20¢ par exchanged for (0.5) share Class A 10¢ par
Perfect Fit Industries, Inc. (PA) reincorporated in Delaware 04/00/1965 which name changed to PRF Corp. 07/15/1969 which name changed to XYZ Liquidating Corp. 05/14/1981
(See XYZ Liquidating Corp.)

BOLIVIAN GOLD MINES LTD (ON)
Charter cancelled for failure to pay taxes and file returns 07/27/1976

BOLIVIAN POWER CO., LTD. (NS)
Name changed to Compania Boliviana De Energia Electrica S.A. - Bolivian Power Co., Ltd. 07/20/1965

BOLLE AMER INC (DE)
Merged into Benson Eyecare Corp. 11/02/1995
Each share Common 1¢ par exchanged for (0.775) share Common 1¢ par
Benson Eyecare Corp. merged into BEC Group, Inc. 05/03/1996 which recapitalized as Lumen Technologies, Inc. 03/12/1998
(See Lumen Technologies, Inc.)

BOLLE INC (DE)
Merged into Worldwide Sports & Recreation, Inc. 02/09/2000
Each share Common 1¢ par exchanged for $5.25 cash

BOLLENTE COS INC (NV)
Each share Common $0.001 par received distribution of (0.05) share Nuvola, Inc. Restricted Common $0.001 par payable 11/24/2014 to holders of record 10/20/2014
Name changed to Trutankless, Inc. 07/02/2018

BOLLINGER CORP (PA)
Adjucated bankrupt 03/14/1977
Stockholders' equity unlikely

BOLSA CHICA CO (DE)
Name changed to Koll Real Estate Group Inc. 09/30/1993
Koll Real Estate Group Inc. name changed to California Coastal Communities Inc. 05/29/1998
(See California Coastal Communities Inc.)

BOLSA CHICA OIL CORP. (DE)
Recapitalized 00/00/1941

Each share Class A Common $10 par exchanged for (2) shares Common $1 par
Each share Class B Common $10 par exchanged for (1) share Common $1 par
Name changed to U.S. Natural Gas Corp. 08/06/1962
U.S. Natural Gas Corp. name changed to U.S. Natural Resources, Inc. 11/01/1968
(See U.S. Natural Resources, Inc.)

BOLSA-GRANDE CORP. (CA)
Liquidation completed
Each share Capital Stock $1 par received initial distribution of $71.2821 cash 03/02/1970
Each share Capital Stock $1 par received second and final distribution of $2.16060 cash 11/25/1975
Note: Certificates were not required to be surrendered and are without value

BOLSA-HUNTINGTON CORP. (CA)
Liquidation completed
Each share Capital Stock $1 par received initial distribution of $30.2564 cash 03/02/1970
Each share Capital Stock $1 par received second and final distribution of $2.21553 cash 11/25/1975
Note: Certificates were not required to be surrendered and are without value

BOLSA-LAGUNA CORP. (CA)
Liquidation completed
Each share Capital Stock $1 par received initial distribution of $128.9744 cash 03/02/1970
Each share Capital Stock $1 par received second and final distribution of $1.66603 cash 11/25/1975
Note: Certificates were not required to be surrendered and are without value

BOLSA LAND CO.
Dissolved 00/00/1941
Details not available

BOLSA-LOS PATOS CORP. (CA)
Liquidation completed
Each share Capital Stock $1 par received initial distribution of $131.5385 cash 03/02/1970
Each share Capital Stock $1 par received second and final distribution of $2.84407 cash 11/25/1975
Note: Certificates were not required to be surrendered and are without value

BOLSA-MESA CORP. (CA)
Liquidation completed
Each share Capital Stock $1 par received initial distribution of $125.1282 cash 03/02/1970
Each share Capital Stock $1 par received second and final distribution of $1.63671 cash 11/25/1975
Note: Certificates were not required to be surrendered and are without value

BOLSA-PACIFIC CORP. (CA)
Liquidation completed
Each share Capital Stock $1 par received initial distribution of $38 cash 07/16/1971
Each share Capital Stock $1 par received second and final distribution of $1.47697 cash 11/25/1975
Note: Certificates were not required to be surrendered and are without value

BOLT BERANEK & NEWMAN INC (MA)
Common no par changed to $1 par 11/08/1979
Common $1 par split (3) for (2) by issuance of (0.5) additional share 05/01/1981
Common $1 par split (3) for (2) by issuance of (0.5) additional share 07/19/1983
Common $1 par split (2) for (1) by issuance of (1) additional share 11/30/1983
Common $1 par split (2) for (1) by issuance of (1) additional share 07/24/1987
Name changed to BBN Corp. 11/27/1995
(See BBN Corp.)

BOLT ENERGY LTD (AB)
Acquired by Blue Mountain Energy Ltd. 09/18/2002
Each share Common no par exchanged for (0.3125) share Common no par
(See Blue Mountain Energy Ltd.)

BOLT TECHNOLOGY CORP (CT)
Common no par split (3) for (2) by issuance of (0.5) additional share payable 01/30/2008 to holders of record 01/16/2008 Ex date - 01/31/2008
Acquired by Teledyne Technologies Inc. 11/18/2014
Each share Common no par exchanged for $22 cash

BOLTON ELECTRIC CO.
Merged into Connecticut Power Co. 00/00/1936
Details not available

BOLTON GROUP LTD (NY)
Recapitalized as Richton Industries, Ltd. 02/11/1974
Each share Common 1¢ par exchanged for (0.33333333) share Common 1¢ par
Richton Industries, Ltd. name changed to Parker Rich Group Ltd. 04/20/1981 which recapitalized as Project 80's Holding Corp. 03/25/1983 which recapitalized as Titan Resources Inc. 06/27/1994 which recapitalized as Palm Works Inc. 09/28/1999 which name changed to Zydant Corp. 10/17/2000

BOLTON TREMBLAY EQUITY FD LTD (CANADA)
Merged into Planned Resources Fund Ltd.-Fonds de Planification des Ressources Ltee. 07/26/1978
Each Mutual Fund Share no par exchanged for (1.191) Mutual Fund Shares $2 par

BOLTON TREMBLAY FD LTD (CANADA)
Merged into Bolton, Tremblay Equity Fund Ltd.-Fonds d'Actions Bolton, Tremblay, Ltee. 07/02/1975
Each Mutual Fund Share $1 par exchanged for (2) Mutual Fund Shares no par
Each share Founders Common 1¢ par exchanged for (1.73) Mutual Fund Shares no par
Bolton, Tremblay Equity Fund Ltd.-Fonds d'Actions Bolton, Tremblay, Ltee. merged into Planned Resources Fund Ltd.-Fonds de Planification des Ressources Ltee. 07/26/1978

BOLTON TREMBLAY INTL FD (MB)
Fund terminated 00/00/1999
Details not available

BOLTONS CAP CORP (YT)
Recapitalized as Valterra Wines Ltd. 02/05/2003
Each share Common no par exchanged for (0.1) share Common no par
Valterra Wines Ltd. name changed to Valterra Resource Corp. (Yukon) 01/22/2007 which reincorporated in British Columbia 02/22/2008

BOLY GROUP HLDGS CORP (DE)
Name changed to US VR Global.com Inc. 02/07/2018

BOLYARD OIL & GAS LTD (CO)
Name changed to Camelot Corp. (CO) 06/29/1989
Camelot Corp. (CO) reorganized in Nevada 05/23/2011 which name changed to Comjoyful International Co. 01/30/2013

BOM HLDGS PLC (UNITED KINGDOM)
ADR agreement terminated 00/00/1989
No ADR's remain outstanding

BOMAC BATTEN LTD (CANADA)
Name changed to Principal Neo-Tech Inc. 05/02/1984
Principal Neo-Tech Inc. name changed to Laird Group Inc. 07/15/1988 which merged into Printera Corp. 11/22/1996
(See Printera Corp.)

BOMAINE CORP (CA)
Reincorporated 12/08/1978
Each share $5 Conv. Class A Preference no par exchanged for (4) shares Common $1 par 04/20/1972
State of incorporation changed from (DE) to (CA) 12/08/1978
Acquired by BGK Group Inc. 08/29/1984
Each share Common $1 par exchanged for $11 cash

BOMARC INC. (WI)
Common $1 par called for redemption 12/30/1966

BOMARC MINING CO. LTD. (BC)
Merged into Anglo-Bomarc Mines Ltd. 05/28/1970
Each share Common no par exchanged for (1) share Common no par

BOMARKO INC (DE)
Each share old Common no par exchanged for (0.01) share new Common no par 07/18/1988
Acquired by Azzar Inc. 07/21/1989
Each share new Common no par exchanged for $1,800 cash

BOMAX RESOURCE CORP (BC)
Delisted from Canadian Dealer Network 06/07/2001

BOMBARDIER INC (CANADA)
Adjustable Rate Preferred Ser. 1 no par called for redemption at $25 plus $0.3108 accrued dividend on 06/30/1997
(Additional Information in Active)

BOMBARDIER LTD (CANADA)
Acquired by MLW-Worthington Ltd./MLW-Worthington Ltee. 05/07/1976
Each share Class A Common no par exchanged for (0.190476) share Capital Stock no par
MLW-Worthington Ltd./MLW-Worthington Ltee. name changed to Bombardier-MLW Ltd./Bombardier-MLW Ltee. 09/28/1976 which name changed to Bombardier Inc. 07/20/1978

BOMBARDIER MLW LTD (CANADA)
Name changed to Bombardier Inc. 07/20/1978

BOMBAY INC (DE)
Common $1 par split (3) for (2) by issuance of (0.5) additional share 03/02/1992
Common $1 par split (3) for (2) by issuance of (0.5) additional share 12/04/1992
Common $1 par split (3) for (2) by issuance of (0.5) additional share 07/01/1993
Common $1 par split (3) for (2) by issuance of (0.5) additional share 12/31/1993
Plan of reorganization under Chapter 11 Federal Bankruptcy Code effective 09/12/2008
No stockholders' equity

BOMBAY PALACE RESTAURANTS INC (DE)
Charter cancelled and declared inoperative and void for non-payment of taxes 03/01/1994

BOMED MED MFG LTD (CA)
Name changed to CardioDynamics International Corp. 10/00/1993
(See CardioDynamics International Corp.)

BOMONT MINES LTD. (ON)
Dissolved 04/18/1966
Details not available

BOMPRECO S A SUPERMERCADOS DO NORDESTE (BRAZIL)
ADR agreement terminated 12/11/2001
Each 144A GDR for Ordinary exchanged for $10.72534 cash
Each Reg. S GDR for Ordinary exchanged for $10.72534 cash

BOMPS MNG INC (DE)
Name changed to China Chemical Corp. 10/06/2010

BON AIRE INDS INC (DE)
Voluntarily dissolved 08/21/1978
Details not available

BON AMI CO. (DE)
Recapitalized 12/27/1960
Each share Class A no par exchanged for (1.75) shares Common no par
Each share Class B no par exchanged for (1) share Common no par
Merged into Lestoil Products, Inc. 07/24/1964
Each share Common no par exchanged for (1.5) shares Common 50¢ par
Lestoil Products, Inc. merged into Standard International Corp. 11/19/1964 which name changed to Standex International Corp. (OH) 07/24/1973 which reincorporated in Delaware 06/30/1975

BON VAL MINES LTD (BC)
Recapitalized as Cameron Resources Ltd. 11/30/1978
Each share Common 50¢ par exchanged for (0.2) share Common no par
Cameron Resources Ltd. name changed to Jafta International Inc. 10/29/1982 which recapitalized as Dornoch International Inc. 10/05/1987 which name changed to DNI Holdings Inc. 04/28/1988
(See DNI Holdings Inc.)

BONA COFFEE HLDGS CORP (NY)
Common $0.001 par split (10) for (1) by issuance of (9) additional shares payable 11/12/2008 to holders of record 11/12/2008 Ex date - 11/13/2008
Name changed to VuQo Holdings Corp. 05/09/2011
VuQo Holdings Corp. name changed to WMAC Holdings Corp. (NY) 07/08/2013 which reincorporated in Nevada as Lighthouse Global Holdings Inc. 05/03/2018

BONA FILM GROUP LTD (CAYMAN ISLANDS)
Acquired by Mountain Tiger International Ltd. 04/08/2016
Each Sponsored ADR for Ordinary exchanged for $13.65 cash

BONAMOUR PAC INC (NV)
Each share old Common $0.001 par exchanged for (0.001) share new Common $0.001 par 08/02/2012
Note: No holder will receive fewer than (100) post-split shares
Name changed to TexStar Oil Corp. 12/03/2012

BONANZA AIR LINES INC (NV)
Merged into Air West, Inc. 04/17/1968
Each share Common $1 par exchanged for (1) share Common $1 par
Air West, Inc. name changed to AW Liquidating Co. 04/01/1970
(See AW Liquidating Co.)

BONANZA BLUE CORP (ON)
Recapitalized as CannaRoyalty Corp. 12/08/2016
Each share Common no par exchanged for (0.2) share Common no par

BONANZA CENTRAL MINING CO. (AZ)
Merged into Bonanza Mining Co. (AZ) 09/17/1952
Each share Common $1 par exchanged for (1) share Common 09/17/1952
(See Bonanza Mining Co. (AZ))

BONANZA CHIEF GOLD MINING CO. (MT)
Charter expired by time limitation 10/23/1899

BONANZA CONSOLIDATED MINING CO. (UT)
Charter expired 01/21/2004

BONANZA ENTERPRISES (CA)
Name changed to Land Dynamics 04/27/1971
(See Land Dynamics)

BONANZA EXPLORATIONS INC (BC)
Recapitalized as Bonanza Resources Corp. 05/29/2002
Each share Common no par exchanged for (0.33333333) share Common no par
Bonanza Resources Corp. name changed to BRS Resources Ltd. 02/18/2011

BONANZA EXPLORATIONS LTD. (BC)
Name changed to Panama Mines Ltd. 07/20/1971
Panama Mines Ltd. recapitalized as Panama Resources Ltd. 06/04/1980 which merged into Freedom Marine Ltd. 04/07/1986
(See Freedom Marine Ltd.)

BONANZA GOLD CORP (NV)
Ctfs. dated after 12/29/2010
Each share old Common $0.001 par exchanged for (0.00666666) share new Common $0.001 par 03/04/2011
Name changed to Brightlane Corp. 09/23/2015

BONANZA GOLD CORP (NV)
Ctfs. dated prior to 08/28/1998
Each share old Common $0.001 par exchanged for (0.1) share new Common $0.001 par 02/20/1998
Name changed to Goldeye USA Inc. 08/28/1998
Goldeye USA Inc. recapitalized as Sierra Diamond International, Inc. 02/10/2004 which recapitalized as ITOS, Inc. 04/12/2004 which recapitalized as Satellite Phone Source Inc. (NV) 08/10/2004 which reincorporated in Delaware as Vision Works Media Group, Inc. 04/06/2005 which name changed to Perihelion Global, Inc. (DE) 10/25/2006 which reincorporated in Nevada 04/01/2008 which recapitalized as Nymet Holdings Inc. 04/21/2009

BONANZA GOLD INC (WA)
Common 10¢ par changed to $0.001 par 02/02/2004
Each share old Common $0.001 par exchanged for (0.25) share new Common $0.001 par 02/07/2006
Name changed to Left Behind Games, Inc. (WA) 05/05/2006
Left Behind Games, Inc. (WA) reincorporated in Nevada 11/29/2010
(See Left Behind Games, Inc. (NV))

BONANZA GOLD MINES CORP. (UT)
Proclaimed dissolved for failure to pay taxes 11/09/1974

BONANZA INTL INC (NV)
Acquired by a group of investors 02/28/1984
Each share Common no par exchanged for $1.25 principal amount of Bonanza International, Inc. 12% Secured Subordinated Notes due 05/01/1994

BONANZA INTL PETES LTD (AB)
Merged into Amalgamated Bonanza Petroleum Ltd. 04/15/1974
Each share Capital Stock no par exchanged for (0.8) share Capital Stock no par
(See Amalgamated Bonanza Petroleum Ltd.)

BONANZA LAND & LIVESTOCK CO. (NM)
Name changed to Santa Fe Downs, Inc. and Capital Stock 25¢ par changed to Common 50¢ par 09/00/1971
(See Santa Fe Downs, Inc.)

BONANZA LD HLDGS INC (NV)
Name changed to VLinx Technology, Inc. 11/08/2011
VLinx Technology, Inc. name changed to Vision Plasma Systems, Inc. 04/03/2012

BONANZA METALS INC (QC)
Recapitalized as Consolidated Bonanza Metals Inc. 08/26/1992
Each share Common no par exchanged for (0.2) share Common no par
Consolidated Bonanza Metals Inc. name changed to Mincor Resources Inc. 02/19/1995
(See Mincor Resources Inc.)

BONANZA MINES, INC. (OR)
Name changed to Bonanza Oil & Mine Corp. 00/00/1951
Bonanza Oil & Mine Corp. merged into Industrial Minerals, Inc. 03/11/1961 which name changed to Danbourne Corp. 06/25/1971
(See Danbourne Corp.)

BONANZA MINING CO. (AZ)
Incorporated 04/05/1900
Charter revoked 03/20/1926

BONANZA MINING CO. (AZ)
Incorporated 10/19/1948
Charter revoked 10/29/1959

BONANZA MINING CO. (UT)
Name changed to Bonanza Oil & Mining Co. 00/00/1952
Bonanza Oil & Mining Co. recapitalized as Diamond-B Industries, Inc. 02/14/1961

BONANZA OIL & GAS INC (NV)
Common $0.001 par split (2.1) for (1) by issuance of (1.1) additional shares payable 01/10/2008 to holders of record 01/10/2008
Common $0.001 par split (2) for (1) by issuance of (1) additional share payable 01/20/2010 to holders of record 01/20/2010 Ex date - 01/21/2010
SEC revoked common stock registration 08/19/2013

BONANZA OIL & GAS LTD NEW (AB)
Acquired by Poco Petroleums Ltd. 01/01/1992
Each share Common no par exchanged for $0.60 cash

BONANZA OIL & GAS LTD OLD (AB)
Merged into Bonanza Resources Ltd. 10/07/1983
Each share Common no par exchanged for (0.875) share Common no par
Bonanza Resources Ltd. recapitalized as CanCapital Corp. (AB) 02/09/1987 which reincorporated in British Columbia 05/12/1993 which recapitalized as Prada Holdings Ltd. (BC) 07/14/1994 which reincorporated in Yukon 07/26/1996
(See Prada Holdings Ltd.)

BONANZA OIL & MINE CORP. (OR)
Merged into Industrial Minerals, Inc. 03/11/1961
Each share Capital Stock 10¢ par exchanged for (0.125) share Capital Stock 25¢ par
Industrial Minerals, Inc. name changed to Danbourne Corp. 06/25/1971
(See Danbourne Corp.)

BONANZA OIL & MINING CO., INC. (UT)
Recapitalized as Diamond-B Industries, Inc. 02/14/1961
Each share Common 5¢ par exchanged for (0.2) share Common 25¢ par

BONANZA RED LAKE EXPLS INC (ON)
Recapitalized as Eugenic Corp. 08/15/2000
Each share Common no par exchanged for (0.33333333) share Common no par
Eugenic Corp. name changed to Eagleford Energy Inc. 12/01/2009 which recapitalized as Eagleford Energy Corp. 08/25/2014 which recapitalized as Intelligent Content Enterprises Inc. 02/05/2016 which recapitalized as Novicius Corp. 05/29/2017

BONANZA RES CORP (BC)
Each share old Common no par exchanged for (0.1) share new Common no par 08/23/2010
Name changed to BRS Resources Ltd. 02/18/2011

BONANZA RES LTD (AB)
Recapitalized as CanCapital Corp. (AB) 02/09/1987
Each share Common no par exchanged for (0.5) share Common no par
CanCapital Corp. (AB) reincorporated in British Columbia 05/12/1993 which recapitalized as Prada Holdings Ltd. (BC) 07/14/1994 which reincorporated in Yukon 07/26/1996
(See Prada Holdings Ltd.)

BONANZA SILVER CORP (BC)
Recapitalized as Bonanza Explorations Inc. 09/07/2001
Each share Common no par exchanged for (0.33333333) share Common no par
Bonanza Explorations Inc. recapitalized as Bonanza Resources Corp. 05/29/2002 which name changed to BRS Resources Ltd. 02/18/2011

BONAPARTE CAP CORP (BC)
Name changed to Bonaparte Resources Inc. 08/11/2010
Bonaparte Resources Inc. name changed to BlackIce Enterprise Risk Management Inc. 06/04/2014 which recapitalized as Blackchain Solutions Inc. 12/21/2017 which recapitalized as Trackloop Analytics Corp. 09/25/2018

BONAPARTE RES INC (BC)
Incorporated 07/10/2007
Name changed to BlackIce Enterprise Risk Management Inc. 06/04/2014
BlackIce Enterprise Risk Management Inc. recapitalized as Blackchain Solutions Inc. 12/21/2017 which recapitalized as Trackloop Analytics Corp. 09/25/2018

BONAPARTE RES INC (BC)
Incorporated 00/00/1981
Acquired by Veronex Resources Ltd. 08/31/1984
Each share Capital Stock no par exchanged for (0.33333333) share Common no par
Veronex Resources Ltd. recapitalized as International Veronex Resources Ltd. 10/20/1992 which name changed to Veronex Technologies Inc. 12/04/1997
(See Veronex Technologies Inc.)

BONAR INC (CANADA)
Merged into Low & Bonar Canada Inc. 10/10/1995
Each share Common no par exchanged for $38 cash

BONAVENTURE ENTERPRISES INC (BC)
Recapitalized as Iconic Minerals Ltd. 03/03/2011
Each share Common no par exchanged for (0.1) share Common no par

BONAVENTURE MNG LTD (QC)
Name changed to Venturbon Enterprises Inc. 10/04/1996
Venturbon Enterprises Inc. recapitalized as Java Joe's International Corp. 10/08/1997
(See Java Joe's International Corp.)

BONAVENTURE RES LTD (BC)
Delisted from Canadian Venture Stock Exchange 06/07/2001

BONAVENTURE TECHNOLOGIES INC (ON)
Delisted from Alberta Stock Exchange 11/21/1988

BONAVISTA ENERGY TR (AB)
Reorganized as Bonavista Energy Corp. 01/07/2011
Each Trust Unit no par exchanged for (1) share Common no par
Note: Unexchanged certificates were cancelled and became without value 01/07/2014

BONAVISTA MNG LTD (BC)
Merged into Eaton Mining & Exploration Ltd. 07/15/1976
Each share Common 50¢ par exchanged for (0.33333333) share Common no par
Eaton Mining & Exploration Ltd. recapitalized as Synco Development Corp. 07/27/1982
(See Synco Development Corp.)

BONAVISTA PETE LTD (AB)
Plan of arrangement effective 07/02/2003
Each share Common no par exchanged for (1) share NuVista Energy Ltd. Common no par and (2) Bonavista Energy Trust Units no par
Note: Option to receive Exchangeable Shares in lieu of Trust Units expired 06/23/2003
(See each company's listing)
Each Exchangeable Share no par exchanged for (2.40917) Bonavista Energy Corp. Exchangeable Shares no par 01/07/2011
Note: Unexchanged certificates were cancelled and became without value 01/07/2014

BOND & MORTGAGE GUARANTEE CO.
Liquidation ordered by court 00/00/1937
Details not available

BOND & SHARE CO. LTD.
Liquidated 00/00/1934
Details not available

BOND & SHARE TRADING CORP.
Liquidated 00/00/1939
Details not available

BOND ACCUMULATION FD INC (IA)
Merged into Princor Bond Fund, Inc. 05/01/1990

Each share Common $0.001 par exchanged for (1.037) shares Common 1¢ par
Princor Bond Fund, Inc. name changed to Principal Bond Fund, Inc. 01/01/1998
(See Principal Bond Fund, Inc.)

BOND CLOTHING CO.
Merged into Bond Stores, Inc. 00/00/1937
Each share Class A exchanged for (0.6) share Common $1 par
Each share Class B exchanged for (2.53) shares Common $1 par
Bond Stores, Inc. reorganized as Bond Industries, Inc. 03/17/1970
(See Bond Industries, Inc.)

BOND CORP HLDGS LTD (AUSTRALIA)
Stock Dividends - 20% 03/05/1987; 20% 06/16/1987
Each ADR for Ordinary exchanged for (1) Sponsored ADR for Ordinary 11/17/1987
Each old Sponsored ADR for Ordinary exchanged for (0.05) new Sponsored ADR for Ordinary 08/30/1991
Liquidator declared Ordinary shares worthless 01/06/1994
No ADR holders' equity

BOND ELECTRIC CORP.
Declared insolvent by court 00/00/1937
Details not available

BOND FUND OF BOSTON, INC. (MA)
Merged into Boston Fund, Inc. 11/28/1958
Each share Capital Stock $1 par exchanged for (0.443089) share Common $1 par
Boston Fund, Inc. name changed to Vance, Sanders Investors Fund 06/28/1973 which name changed to Eaton Vance Investors Fund, Inc. 09/24/1982 which name changed to Eaton Vance Investors Trust 09/29/1993
(See Eaton Vance Investors Trust)

BOND INDS INC (DE)
Common $1 par split (3) for (2) by issuance of (0.5) additional share 04/29/1970
Merged into BND Holdings, Inc. 08/19/1981
Each share Common $1 par exchanged for $16.25 cash

BOND INTL GOLD INC (CAYMAN ISLANDS)
Acquired by LAC Minerals Ltd. (New) 08/30/1991
Each share Ordinary 1¢ par exchanged for (0.71) share Common no par
LAC Minerals Ltd. (New) acquired by American Barrick Resources Corp. 10/17/1994 which name changed to Barrick Gold Corp. 01/18/1995

BOND INVESTMENT TRUST OF AMERICA (MA)
Ctfs. of Bene. Int. $100 par changed to no par 00/00/1942
Ctfs. of Bene. Int. no par changed to $1 par 00/00/1945
Stock Dividend - 400% 06/30/1950
Merged into Colonial Fund, Inc. (DE) 05/01/1959
Each Ctf. of Bene. Int. $1 par exchanged for (1.85853) shares Common $1 par
Colonial Fund, Inc. (DE) merged into Colonial Fund, Inc. (MA) 08/18/1959 which reorganized as Colonial Fund 12/22/1986 which merged into Colonial Trust III 02/14/1992 which name changed to Liberty Funds Trust III 04/01/1999

BOND LABORATORIES INC (NV)
Each share old Common 1¢ par exchanged for (2) shares new Common 1¢ par 01/09/2008

Recapitalized as FitLife Brands, Inc. 09/30/2013
Each share Common 1¢ par exchanged for (0.1) share Common 1¢ par

BOND PORTFOLIO FOR ENDOWMENTS INC (DE)
Capital Stock $1 par split (50) for (1) by issuance of (49) additional shares 02/16/1988
Under plan of reorganization each share Capital Stock $1 par automatically became (1) share Endowments Bond Portfolio 07/31/1998
(See Endowments)

BOND STORES INC (MD)
Plan of merger effective 00/00/1937
Each share Class A $20 par exchanged for (0.553) share Common $1 par
Each share Class B no par exchanged for (0.506) share Common $1 par
Stock Dividend - 100% 06/06/1945
Under plan of reorganization each share Common $1 par automatically became (1) share Bond Industries, Inc. Common $1 par 03/17/1970
(See Bond Industries, Inc.)

BOND STR CORP (CO)
Recapitalized as Worldwide Forest Products Inc. 10/01/1990
Each share Common $0.0001 par exchanged for (0.02) share Common $0.0001 par

BOND WILLIAM INC (TN)
Stock Dividend - 25% 09/15/1974
Name changed to Care Inns, Inc. 08/04/1975
(See Care Inns, Inc.)

BONDED HOMES, INC. (FL)
Adjudicated bankrupt 06/12/1964
No stockholders' equity

BONDED MTRS INC (CA)
Assets foreclosed upon 04/21/2000
No stockholders' equity

BONDELL INDS INC (BC)
Name changed 05/12/1987
Name changed from Bondell Resources Inc. to Bondell Industries Inc. 05/12/1987
Recapitalized as Rift Resources Ltd. (BC) 12/29/1993
Each share Common no par exchanged for (0.33333333) share Common no par
Rift Resources Ltd. (BC) reincorporated in Ontario 09/05/1995
(See Rift Resources Ltd.)

BONDHOLDERS MANAGEMENT, INC. (MI)
Stock Dividend - 10% 12/15/1948
Reorganized as B M I Corp. 00/00/1953
Each share Class A Common no par exchanged for (5) shares Common $5 par
(See B M I Corp.)

BONDS COM GROUP INC (DE)
Each share old Common $0.0001 par exchanged for (0.0025) share new Common $0.0001 par 04/26/2013
Acquired by MTS Markets International, Inc. 05/08/2014
No stockholders' equity

BONDSTOCK CORP (DE)
Stock Dividends - 10% 05/15/1951; 10% 05/15/1953; 10% 05/20/1955; 10% 05/20/1959
Acquired by Security Equity Fund, Inc. 01/23/1980
Each share Common $1 par exchanged for (1.058) shares Common $25 par
Security Equity Fund, Inc. name changed to Security Equity Fund 12/11/1981

BONDUEL STATE BANK (BONDUEL, WI)
Under plan of reorganization each share Common $10 par automatically became (1) share Bonduel Bancorp, Inc. Common $2 par 01/01/1991

BONE CARE INTL INC (WI)
Common 1¢ par split (2) for (1) by issuance of (1) additional share payable 11/14/1997 to holders of record 10/27/1997
Merged into Genzyme Corp. 07/01/2005
Each share Common 1¢ par exchanged for $33 cash

BONE HEALTH INC (CANADA)
Merged into Draxis Health Inc. 07/01/1994
Each share Common no par exchanged for (1/6) share Common no par
(See Draxis Health Inc.)

BONE MED LTD (AUSTRALIA)
ADR agreement terminated 08/03/2017
No ADR's remain outstanding

BONETAL GOLD MINES LTD. (ON)
Merged into Broulan Reef Mines Ltd. 00/00/1951
Each share Capital Stock $1 par exchanged for (0.5) share $1 par
Broulan Reef Mines Ltd. merged into Broulan Resources Inc. 04/26/1983 which merged into Cabre Exploration Ltd. 11/24/1989 which was acquired by EnerMark Income Fund 01/10/2001 which merged into Enerplus Resources Fund 06/22/2001 which reorganized as Enerplus Corp. 01/03/2011

BONFIELD MINES LTD. (ON)
Charter revoked for failure to file reports and pay taxes 01/00/1958

BONFIRE PRODUCTIONS INC (NV)
Common $0.001 par split (10) for (1) by issuance of (9) additional shares payable 04/20/2009 to holders of record 04/15/2009 Ex date - 04/21/2009
Name changed to cMoney, Inc. 07/27/2010

BONGIOVI ENTMT INC (NV)
Each share old Common $0.001 par exchanged for (0.03333333) share new Common $0.001 par 05/06/2005
Name changed to NewGen Technologies, Inc. 08/11/2005
(See NewGen Technologies, Inc.)

BONIEBROOK INC (UT)
Proclaimed dissolved for failure to pay taxes 05/01/1987

BONITA CAP CORP (AB)
Name changed to Palmarejo Gold Corp. 04/04/2005
Palmarejo Gold Corp. name changed to Palmarejo Silver & Gold Corp. 12/19/2005 which merged into Coeur d'Alene Mines Corp. (ID) 12/21/2007 which reincorporated in Delaware as Coeur Mining, Inc. 05/17/2013

BONITA CORP (CO)
Recapitalized as European Securities & Trading Group, Inc. 07/05/1994
Each share Common no par exchanged for (0.08333333) share Common no par
(See European Securities & Trading Group, Inc.)

BONKERS INDOOR PLGDS INC (AB)
Recapitalized as Bonkers Ventures Inc. 09/30/1998
Each share Common no par exchanged for (0.2) share Common no par
(See Bonkers Ventures Inc.)

BONKERS VENTURES INC (AB)
Company became inactive 00/00/2002

BONMARTIC MINES LTD. (ON)
Charter revoked for failure to file reports and pay taxes 03/10/1958

BONN LITTMAN & CO INC (DE)
Charter cancelled and declared inoperative and void for non-payment of taxes 03/01/1991

BONNACORD EXPLS LTD (ON)
Recapitalized as Medina Energy Resources Corp. 04/14/1980
Each share Common no par exchanged for (0.2) share Common no par
Medina Energy Resources Corp. recapitalized as Meenreco Energy Corp. 01/19/1984 which name changed to Millers Cove Resources Inc. 08/30/1984
(See Millers Cove Resources Inc.)

BONNE BAY MINES LTD (ON)
Charter cancelled and declared dissolved for failure to file returns and pay fees 05/18/1976

BONNER CO.
Name changed 00/00/1929
Name changed from Bonner Oil Co. to Bonner Co. 00/00/1929
Merged into Stayton Oil Co. 00/00/1940
Details not available

BONNET MINES LTD. (BC)
Name changed to Bon-Val Mines Ltd. 08/06/1971
Bon-Val Mines Ltd. recapitalized as Cameron Resources Ltd. 11/30/1978 which name changed to Jafta International Inc. 10/29/1982 which recapitalized as Dornoch International Inc. 10/05/1987 which name changed to DNI Holdings Inc. 04/28/1988
(See DNI Holdings Inc.)

BONNETTS ENERGY CORP (AB)
Acquired by BEC Acquisition Ltd. 11/08/2013
Each share Common no par exchanged for $7.08 cash
Note: Unexchanged certificates were cancelled and became without value 11/08/2016

BONNETTS ENERGY SVCS TR (AB)
Reorganized as Bonnett's Energy Corp. 07/06/2011
Each Trust Unit exchanged for (1) share Common no par
Note: Unexchanged certificates were cancelled and became without value 11/08/2016
(See Bonnett's Energy Corp.)

BONNEVILLE BASIN URANIUM CORP. (UT)
Recapitalized as Bonneville Resources, Inc. 08/20/1958
Each share Capital Stock 2¢ par exchanged for (0.2) share Capital Stock 10¢ par
Bonneville Resources, Inc. recapitalized as Admiral Hospitals Inc. 05/06/1970
(See Admiral Hospitals Inc.)

BONNEVILLE CAPITAL CORP. (UT)
Liquidated 12/00/1966
Details must be obtained from the United States District Court Clerk, Salt Lake City

BONNEVILLE DEVS LTD (BC)
Recapitalized as Santana Petroleum Corp. 08/04/1981
Each share Common 50¢ par exchanged for (1) share Common no par
Santana Petroleum Corp. recapitalized as International Santana Resources Inc. 12/02/1985 which name changed to Image West Entertainment Corp. 12/19/1986

BONNEVILLE FINL INC (UT)
Merged into Professional Investors Corp. 03/31/1975
Each share Common $1 par exchanged for (0.7576) share Common $1 par
Professional Investors Corp. name changed to Professional Investors Insurance Group, Inc. 03/11/1985
(See Professional Investors Insurance Group, Inc.)

BONNEVILLE LIFE INSURANCE CO. (UT)
Each share Common $10 par exchanged for (10) shares Common $1 par 05/09/1962
Merged into Bonneville-Sylvan Life Insurance Co. 04/01/1965
Each share Common $1 par exchanged for (0.5) share Capital Stock $2 par
Bonneville-Sylvan Life Insurance Co. reorganized as Bonneville Financial Corp. Inc. 12/01/1972 which merged into Professional Investors Corp. 03/31/1975 which name changed to Professional Investors Insurance Group, Inc. 03/11/1985
(See Professional Investors Insurance Group, Inc.)

BONNEVILLE LTD. (DE)
Liquidation completed 02/25/1963
Details not available

BONNEVILLE MED PRODS INC (NV)
Recapitalized as Ametex Corp. 02/11/1974
Each share Common 10¢ par exchanged for (1) share Common 1¢ par
(See Ametex Corp.)

BONNEVILLE PAC CORP (DE)
Each share old Common 1¢ par exchanged for (0.25) share new Common 1¢ par 11/03/1998
Merged into El Paso Energy Corp. 01/18/2000
Each share Common 1¢ par exchanged for $11.4389 cash
Each share Common 1¢ par received an initial additional distribution of $0.1654 cash 12/19/2001
Each share Common 1¢ par received a second additional distribution of $0.26067 cash 01/08/2004
Each share Common 1¢ par received a third and final additional distribution of $0.0368 cash 12/18/2008

BONNEVILLE RACEWAY PK INC (NV)
Merged into International Teldata II Corp. 03/01/1981
Each share Common 1¢ par exchanged for (2.5) shares Common 1¢ par
International Teldata II Corp. name changed to International Teldata Corp. 06/12/1984
(See International Teldata Corp.)

BONNEVILLE RES INC (UT)
Recapitalized as Admiral Hospitals Inc. 05/06/1970
Each share Capital Stock 10¢ par exchanged for (0.05) share Capital Stock no par
(See Admiral Hospitals Inc.)

BONNEVILLE SYLVAN LIFE INS CO (UT)
Common Capital Stock $2 par changed to $1 par 12/15/1966
Reorganized as Bonneville Financial Corp., Inc. 12/01/1972
Each share Common Capital Stock $1 par exchanged for (1) share Common $1 par
Bonneville Financial Corp., Inc. merged into Professional Investors Corp. 03/31/1975 which name changed to Professional Investors Insurance Group, Inc. 03/11/1985

(See Professional Investors Insurance Group, Inc.)

BONNEVILLE WEST CORP (UT)
Merged into Bonneville Pacific Corp. 11/01/1987
Each share Capital Stock 1¢ par exchanged for (1) share Common 1¢ par
(See Bonneville Pacific Corp.)

BONNIE GOLD MINES LTD. (ON)
Charter cancelled 05/27/1965
No stockholders' equity

BONNYVILLE OIL & REFNG CORP (QC)
Recapitalized as Consolidated Bonnyville Ltd. 03/02/1963
Each share Common $1 par exchanged for (0.1) share Common $1 par
Consolidated Bonnyville Ltd. acquired by Cold Lake Pipe Line Co. Ltd. 02/26/1964 which recapitalized as Worldwide Energy Co. Ltd. 07/01/1967 which reincorporated under the laws of Delaware as Weco Development Corp. 07/17/1972 which name changed to Worldwide Energy Corp. 06/14/1977 which merged into Triton Energy Corp. (TX) 11/18/1986 which reincorporated in Delaware 05/12/1995 which merged into Triton Energy Ltd. 03/25/1996
(See Triton Energy Ltd.)

BONORE GOLD MINES LTD. (ON)
Charter revoked for failure to file reports and pay taxes 00/00/1955

BONRAY DRILLING CORP (DE)
Each share Common 10¢ par exchanged for (0.1) share Common $1 par 11/26/1985
Note: Holdings of (99) shares or fewer received $0.94 cash per share
Merged into DLB Oil & Gas, Inc. 02/10/1997
Each share new Common $1 par exchanged for $30 cash

BONRAY ENERGY CORP (DE)
Each share Common 50¢ par exchanged for (0.002) share Common $250 par 11/26/1985
Merged out of existence 11/01/1991
Details not available

BONSECOUR MINES, LTD. (ON)
Charter revoked for failure to file reports and pay taxes 00/00/1954

BONSTATE BANCSHARES INC (TX)
Reorganized 08/19/1997
Reorganized from Bonham State Bank (Bonham, TX) to Bonstate Bancshares, Inc. 08/19/1997
Each share Common no par exchanged for (1) share Common no par
Note: Holdings of (349) shares or fewer owned by non-residents of Texas will receive $3.40 cash per share
Acquired by Legend Bancorp, Inc. 10/10/2007
Each share Common no par exchanged for $12 cash

BONTAN CORP INC (ON)
Reincorporated under the laws of British Virgin Islands as Portage Biotech Inc. and Common no par reclassified as Ordinary no par 08/23/2013

BONTERA MINING CORP., LTD. (ON)
Charter revoked for failure to file reports and pay taxes 00/00/1957

BONTERRA ENERGY CORP OLD (AB)
Reorganized as Bonterra Energy Income Trust (Old) 06/28/2001
Each share Common no par exchanged for (0.25) share Trust Unit no par
Bonterra Energy Income Trust (Old) merged into Bonterra Energy Income Trust (New) 02/01/2002 which name changed to Bonterra Oil & Gas Ltd. 11/17/2008 which name changed to Bonterra Energy Corp. (New) 01/15/2010

BONTERRA ENERGY INCOME TR NEW (AB)
Name changed to Bonterra Oil & Gas Ltd. and Trust Unit no par reclassified as Common no par 11/17/2008

BONTERRA ENERGY INCOME TR OLD (AB)
Merged into Bonterra Energy Income Trust (New) 02/01/2002
Each Trust Unit no par exchanged for (0.885) Trust Unit no par
Bonterra Energy Income Trust (New) name changed to Bonterra Oil & Gas Ltd. 11/17/2008 which name changed to Bonterra Energy Corp. (New) 01/15/2010

BONTERRA OIL & GAS LTD (AB)
Name changed to Bonterra Energy Corp. (New) 01/15/2010

BONTEX INC (VA)
Charter terminated 09/30/2010

BONUS LTD (CO)
Recapitalized as Intelligent Financial Corp. 08/15/1991
Each share Common $0.0001 par exchanged for (0.025) share Common $0.001 par
Intelligent Financial Corp. name changed to Cell Robotics International Inc. 05/19/1995
(See Cell Robotics International Inc.)

BONUS PRODUCTS CO. (MO)
Charter revoked for failure to file reports and pay fees 01/01/1949

BONUS RES LTD (BC)
Name changed to Santa Sarita Mining Co. Ltd. 09/21/1973
Santa Sarita Mining Co. Ltd. recapitalized as Solid Gold Capital Corp. 08/28/1989 which merged into Consolidated Ruskin Developments Ltd. (New) 03/31/1992 which name changed to Leisureways Marketing Ltd. (BC) 11/23/1992 which reincorporated in Yukon 11/10/1997 which name changed to LML Payment Systems Inc. (YT) 07/15/1998 which reincorporated in British Columbia 09/07/2012
(See LML Payment Systems Inc.)

BONUS RES SVCS CORP (CANADA)
Name changed 06/06/1996
Name changed from Bonus Petroleum Corp. to Bonus Resource Services Corp. 06/06/1996
Recapitalized as Enserco Energy Service Co. Inc. 05/15/2001
Each share Common no par exchanged for (0.25) share Common no par
(See Enserco Energy Service Co. Inc.)

BONUSAMERICA WORLDWIDE CORP (NV)
Name changed to Asia Global Holdings Corp. 07/17/2006
(See Asia Global Holdings Corp.)

BONVILLE GOLD MINES LTD. (ON)
Merged into Hydra Explorations Ltd. 11/16/1959
Each share Capital Stock $1 par exchanged for (0.04) share Capital Stock $1 par
Hydra Explorations Ltd. name changed to Hydra Capital Corp. 12/30/1992 which name changed to Waterford Capital Management Inc. 11/12/1996 which merged into CPI Plastics Group Ltd. 09/21/1998
(See CPI Plastics Group Ltd.)

BONWIT, LENNON & CO., INC.
Assets sold to Consolidated Retail Stores, Inc. 00/00/1939
Details not available

BONWITHA MINING CO. LTD. (ON)
Charter cancelled and company declared dissolved for default in filing returns 01/06/1971

BOO KOO HLDGS INC (DE)
Reincorporated 12/17/2007
State of incorporation changed from (FL) to (DE) and Common no par changed to $0.0001 par 12/17/2007
Name changed to Performing Brands, Inc. 08/19/2008
(See Performing Brands, Inc.)

BOOHOO COM PLC (JERSEY)
Name changed to boohoo group PLC 07/27/2018

BOOK-CADILLAC CORP. (MI)
Name changed to Sheraton-Cadillac Corp. 00/00/1952
Sheraton-Cadillac Corp. merged into Sheraton Corp. of America 03/01/1960 which was acquired by International Telephone & Telegraph Corp. (DE) 02/29/1968 which name changed to ITT Corp. (MI) 12/31/1983 which reorganized in Indiana as ITT Industries Inc. 12/19/1996 which name changed to ITT Corp. 07/01/2006

BOOK-CADILLAC PROPERTIES, INC.
Reorganized 00/00/1941
No stockholders' equity

BOOK CORP OF AMER (UT)
Reincorporated under the laws of Nevada as Secured Diversified Investment Ltd. and Common $0.005 par changed to $0.001 par 09/09/2002
(See Secured Diversified Investment Ltd.)

BOOK CTRS INC (OR)
Each share old Common no par exchanged for (0.00001) share new Common no par 10/18/1996
Note: In effect holders received $0.09 cash per share and public interest was eliminated

BOOK IT LOC INC (NV)
Name changed to Blake Insomnia Therapeutics, Inc. 10/13/2015

BOOK MONTH CLUB INC (NY)
Capital Stock $1.25 par split (3) for (2) by issuance of (0.5) additional share 10/21/1968
Capital Stock $1.25 par split (3) for (2) by issuance of (0.5) additional share 07/01/1976
Merged into Time Inc. 11/30/1977
Each share Capital Stock $1.25 par exchanged for (1) share $1.575 Conv. Preferred Ser. A $1 par
Note: Prior to 11/29/1977 holders had the option to receive $30 cash in lieu of stock
(See Time Inc.)

BOOK PRESS INC. (DE)
Recapitalized as General Educational Services Corp. 07/24/1968
Each share Common $1 par exchanged for (10) shares Common 10¢ par
General Educational Services Corp. name changed to Devon Group, Inc. 07/23/1976
(See Devon Group, Inc.)

BOOK PRINTERS ACADEMIC MEDIA INC (NY)
Adjudicated bankrupt 01/29/1974
Stockholders' equity unlikely

BOOK TOWER CO. (MI)
Liquidation completed 00/00/1958
Details not available

BOOK TOWER GARAGE INC. (MI)
Liquidation completed 12/10/1953
Details not available

BOOKER GOLD EXPLS LTD (BC)
Recapitalized as Pacific Booker Minerals Inc. 02/09/2000
Each share Common no par exchanged for (0.2) share Common no par

BOOKER GROUP PLC (UNITED KINGDOM)
ADR agreement terminated 04/06/2018
Each ADR for Ordinary issued by Bank of New York exchanged for $31.185159 cash

BOOKER PLC (UNITED KINGDOM)
ADR agreement terminated 01/16/2001
Each Sponsored ADR for Ordinary exchanged for $10.0072 cash

BOOKFORTRAVEL COM INC (AB)
Delisted from Toronto Venture Stock Exchange 06/20/2003

BOOK4GOLF COM CORP (CANADA)
Reorganized under the laws of Alberta as B-for-G Capital Inc. 10/26/2004
Each share Common no par exchanged for (0.33333333) share Common no par
B-for-G Capital Inc. recapitalized as Parkbridge Lifestyle Communities Inc. 12/23/2004
(See Parkbridge Lifestyle Communities Inc.)

BOOKHAM INC (DE)
Under plan of merger name changed to Oclaro, Inc. 04/27/2009

BOOKHAM TECHNOLOGY PLC (ENGLAND & WALES)
Reorganized under the laws of Delaware as Bookham, Inc. 09/10/2004
Each Sponsored ADR for Ordinary exchanged for (0.1) share Common 1¢ par
Bookham, Inc. name changed to Oclaro, Inc. 04/27/2009

BOOKKEEPERS HLDG LTD (NV)
Each share Common 10¢ par exchanged for (0.1) share Common no par 04/10/1974
Merged into Bookkeepers Ltd. 11/30/1974
Each share Common no par exchanged for (0.01) share Common no par
(See Bookkeepers Ltd.)

BOOKKEEPERS LTD (DE)
Charter dissolved 04/29/1991

BOOKMERGE TECHNOLOGY INC (NV)
Common $0.0001 par split (7) for (1) by issuance of (6) additional shares payable 02/25/2010 to holders of record 02/25/2010 Ex date - 02/26/2010
Name changed to Extreme Biodiesel, Inc. 02/12/2013

BOOKS-A-MILLION INC (DE)
Common 1¢ par split (2) for (1) by issuance of (1) additional share 09/15/1994
Acquired by Family Acquisition Holdings, Inc. 12/10/2015
Each share Common 1¢ par exchanged for $3.25 cash

BOOKS MOBILE INC (NJ)
Name changed to BMI Educational Services Inc. 09/15/1998
(See BMI Educational Services Inc.)

BOOKSHELF AMER INC (NY)
Name changed to Anymed Service Corp. 11/18/1969
(See Anymed Service Corp.)

BOOKTECH COM INC (NV)
Charter permanently revoked 11/01/2007

BOOLE & BABBAGE INC (CA)
Common no par split (3) for (2) by issuance of (0.5) additional share 11/07/1994
Common no par split (3) for (2) by issuance of (0.5) additional share 12/06/1995
Common no par split (3) for (2) by issuance of (0.5) additional share payable 12/10/1996 to holders of record 11/18/1996
Common no par split (3) for (2) by issuance of (0.5) additional share payable 03/25/1998 to holders of record 03/06/1998
Merged into BMC Software, Inc. 03/30/1999
Each share Common no par exchanged for (0.675) share Common 1¢ par
(See BMC Software, Inc.)

BOOM CAP CORP (AB)
Recapitalized as Ranchero Oil & Gas Ltd. 12/17/1999
Each share Common no par exchanged for (0.4009) share Common no par
Ranchero Oil & Gas Ltd. acquired by Newquest Energy Inc. 04/14/2000 which recapitalized as Ranchero Energy Inc. 09/01/2000 which merged into Cypress Energy Inc. 03/26/2001 which merged into PrimeWest Energy Trust 05/29/2001

BOOMERANG RES INC (AB)
Merged into Laurasia Resources Ltd. 07/01/1994
Each share Common no par exchanged for (2.8) shares Common no par
Laurasia Resources Ltd. merged into StarTech Energy Inc. 02/09/1998 which merged into Impact Energy Inc. (Canada) 01/31/2001 which merged into Thunder Energy Inc. 04/30/2004
(See Thunder Energy Inc.)

BOOMERANG SYS INC (DE)
Each share old Common $0.001 par exchanged for (0.05) share new Common $0.001 par 06/22/2011
Plan of reorganization under Chapter 11 Federal Bankruptcy proceedings effective 03/31/2016
No stockholders' equity

BOOMERANG TRACKING INC (CANADA)
Acquired by LoJack Corp. 10/29/2004
Each share Common no par exchanged for either (0.2192) share Common 1¢ par or $2.95 cash
Note: Option to receive stock expired 10/27/2004
(See LoJack Corp.)

BOOMERS CULTURAL DEV INC (NV)
Common $0.001 par split (10) for (1) by issuance of (9) additional shares payable 09/12/2005 to holders of record 09/09/2005 Ex date - 09/13/2005
Name changed to Quantum Energy, Inc. 05/30/2006

BOOMJ INC (NV)
Name changed to Beyond Commerce, Inc. 02/23/2009

BOOMTOWN INC (DE)
Merged into Hollywood Park, Inc. (New) 06/30/1997
Each share Common 1¢ par exchanged for (0.625) share Common 10¢ par
Hollywood Park, Inc. (New) name changed to Pinnacle Entertainment, Inc. 02/23/2000

BOONE (DANIEL) FRIED CHICKEN, INC. (KY)
Filed Section 4 petition in bankruptcy 08/14/1970
Assets sold for benefit of creditors and on 02/18/1972 trustee's attorney advised there is no stockholders' equity

BOONE DANIEL CORP (WV)
Proclaimed dissolved for non-payment of taxes 06/24/1974

BOONE TIRE & RUBBER CO. (DE)
No longer in existence having become inoperative and void for non-payment of taxes 03/19/1924

BOONSHAFT & FUCHS, INC. (PA)
Name changed to East County Line Road Corp. 03/10/1964
(See East County Line Road Corp.)

BOONTON ELECTRS CORP (NJ)
Common 10¢ par split (3) for (2) by issuance of (0.5) additional share 02/14/1983
Stock Dividends - 10% 02/27/1970; 10% 02/24/1975; 10% 07/25/1977; 10% 07/27/1978; 10% 07/29/1982; 10% 06/01/1984; 10% 06/03/1985
Merged into Wireless Telecom Group, Inc. 07/10/2000
Each share Common 10¢ par exchanged for (0.79) share Common 1¢ par

BOORUM & PEASE CO (NY)
Each share First Preferred $100 par exchanged for (9) shares new Common $10 par 05/03/1966
Each share Second Preferred $100 par exchanged for (10) shares new Common $10 par 05/03/1966
Each share old Common $10 par exchanged for (3) shares new Common $10 par 05/03/1966
New Common $10 par changed to Common $5 par and (1) additional share issued 10/15/1969
Merged into Esselte Business Systems Inc. 12/31/1985
Each share Common $5 par exchanged for $39 cash

BOOSTER CORP (UT)
Name changed to Dion (Kenneth) of Scottsdale, Inc. (UT) 02/05/1988
Dion (Kenneth) of Scottsdale, Inc. (UT) reorganized in Delaware as Select Housing Associates, Inc. 02/02/1990

BOOT HILL MINES (ON)
Name changed to Boulder Gold Mines Ltd. 00/00/1947
(See Boulder Gold Mines Ltd.)

BOOTH (F.E.) CO., INC. (NV)
Each share Class A exchanged for (1) share Preferred $15 par and (1) share Common $2 par 00/00/1936
Each share Class B exchanged for (1) share Common $2 par 00/00/1936
Common $2 par changed to $1 par 00/00/1948
Liquidation completed
Each share Preferred $15 par exchanged for first and final distribution of $125.63 cash 04/15/1966
Each share Common $1 par exchanged for initial distribution of $3.64 cash 04/15/1966
Each share Common $1 par received second distribution of $0.864 cash 09/02/1966
Each share Common $1 par received third and final distribution of $0.2477 cash 07/21/1967

BOOTH FISHERIES CORP. (DE)
Name changed 00/00/1933
Name changed from Booth Fisheries Co. to Booth Fisheries Corp. 00/00/1933
Each share 2nd Preferred no par exchanged for (1) share 6% Preferred $100 par, (0.25) share Common $5 par and $23.50 cash 00/00/1943
Each share Class A Common no par exchanged for (1) share Common $5 par 00/00/1943
Each share Class B Common no par exchanged for (0.1) share Common $5 par 00/00/1943

Common $5 par split (3) for (2) by issuance of (0.5) additional share 03/08/1963
4% Preferred $100 par called for redemption 03/31/1964
Stock Dividends - 200% 02/20/1946; 10% 09/02/1952; 20% 05/02/1955; 10% 05/01/1956
Completely liquidated 05/02/1964
Each share Common $5 par exchanged for first and final distribution of $35 cash

BOOTH INC (TX)
Merged into Household Manufacturing, Inc. 02/23/1987
Each share Common 50¢ par exchanged for $5 cash

BOOTH MANUFACTURING CO.
Assets sold 00/00/1938
Details not available

BOOTH NEWSPAPERS INC (MI)
Capital Stock no par changed to $2.50 par and (3) additional shares issued 05/28/1969
Capital Stock $2.50 par changed to $1.25 par and (1) additional share issued 08/16/1971
Capital Stock $1.25 par changed to 50¢ par 05/01/1973
Stock Dividend - 50% 07/01/1976
Through purchase offer over 99.6% acquired by Herald Co. as of 01/07/1977
Public interest eliminated

BOOTHE COURIER CORP (CA)
Name changed 04/07/1977
Capital Stock $1 par reclassified as Common $1 par 07/01/1968
Conv. Preferred no par called for redemption 05/12/1976
Stock Dividends - 10% 06/10/1970; 10% 06/30/1972
Name changed from Boothe Computer Corp. to Boothe Courier Corp. 04/07/1977
Name changed to Boothe Financial Corp. (CA) 05/12/1978
Boothe Financial Corp. (CA) reincorporated in Delaware 10/19/1979 which name changed to Robert Half International Inc. 06/17/1987

BOOTHE DATA SYS INC (NY)
Name changed to Infonational Inc. 09/05/1972
(See Infonational Inc.)

BOOTHE FINL CORP (DE)
Reincorporated 10/19/1979
State of incorporation changed from (CA) to (DE) 10/19/1979
Common $1 par split (2) for (1) by issuance of (1) additional share 08/15/1983
Common $1 par split (2) for (1) by issuance of (1) additional share 05/21/1984
$2.80 Preferred Ser. A $1 par called for redemption 02/07/1985
Name changed to Robert Half International Inc. 06/17/1987

BOOTHE LEASING CORP. (CA)
Acquired by Greyhound Corp. (DE) 03/30/1962
Each share Common no par exchanged for (0.8) share 4.5% Conv. Preference $50 par
(See Greyhound Corp. (DE))

BOOTIE BEER CORP (FL)
Name changed to TMT Capital Corp. 06/08/2007

BOOTS & COOTS INC (DE)
Name changed 06/23/2009
Each share old Common $0.00001 par exchanged for (0.25) share new Common $0.00001 par 10/02/2003
Name changed from Boots & Coots International Well Control, Inc. to Boots & Coots, Inc. 06/23/2009
Merged into Halliburton Co. 09/17/2010

Each share new Common $0.00001 par exchanged for approximately (0.0412) share Common $2.50 par and $1.72 cash

BOOTS DRUG STORES CDA LTD (CANADA)
4% Preferred $50 par changed to no par 01/14/1981
Merged into Boots Drug Stores (Holdings) Ltd. 12/08/1983
Each share 4% Preferred no par exchanged for $64.50 cash

BOOTS GROUP PLC (UNITED KINGDOM)
Stock Dividend - 34.482% payable 02/13/2006 to holders of record 02/10/2006 Ex date - 02/14/2006
Name changed to Alliance Boots PLC 08/07/2006
(See Alliance Boots PLC)

BOOTS PLC (UNITED KINGDOM)
Scheme of arrangement effective 02/10/2003
Each ADR for Ordinary exchanged for (1) Boots Group PLC ADR for Ordinary
Boots Group PLC name changed to Alliance Boots PLC 08/07/2006
(See Alliance Boots PLC)

BOOTS PURE DRUG CO. LTD. (ENGLAND)
4% Preference A £7 par, 6% Preference B £100 par and 6% Preference C £1 par called for redemption 03/31/1965
4% Preferred Ordinary A, B, C & D £1 par called for redemption 03/31/1965
Ordinary 5s par and ADR's for Ordinary 5s par changed to 25p par per currency change 02/15/1971
Stock Dividend - Ordinary - 50% 08/28/1964; ADR's - 50% 09/11/1964
Name changed to Boots Co. PLC 09/01/1971
Boots Co. PLC reorganized as Boots Group PLC 02/10/2003 which name changed to Alliance Boots PLC 08/07/2006
(See Alliance Boots PLC)

BOOZ ALLEN & HAMILTON INC (DE)
Merged into BA & H Inc. 03/29/1976
Each share Common 25¢ par exchanged for $7.75 cash

BOPPERS HLDGS INC (NV)
Name changed to e-Smart Technologies, Inc. 12/22/2000
(See e-Smart Technologies, Inc.)

BORA CAP INC (CA)
Company went out of business 00/00/1984
Details not available

BORAL LTD OLD (AUSTRALIA)
Each Unsponsored ADR for Ordinary exchanged for (0.5) old Sponsored ADR for Ordinary 08/15/1989
Each old Sponsored ADR for Ordinary exchanged for (0.25) new Sponsored ADR for Ordinary 06/18/1992
Stock Dividends - 20% 10/11/1982; 20% 12/10/1984; 20% 12/16/1985; 25% 12/08/1986; 20% 10/14/1988; 10% 12/11/1989
Under plan of demerger each new Sponsored ADR for Ordinary received (0.5) Origin Energy Ltd. Sponsored ADR for Ordinary to reflect name change and distribution of (0.5) Boral Ltd. (New) Sponsored ADR for Ordinary 02/17/2000
(See each company's listing)

BORALEX PWR INCOME FD (QC)
Merged into Boralex Inc. 11/01/2010
Each Trust Unit automatically became $5 Principal Amount of 6.75% Conv. Unsecured Subordinate Debentures due 06/30/2017

BORAM OIL LTD (CANADA)
Name changed to Can-Tel Communications, Inc. 04/16/1984
Each share Common no par exchanged for (1) share Common no par
Can-Tel Communications, Inc. recapitalized as Euro-Asia Capital Ltd. 10/01/1986 which recapitalized as Asiamerica Holdings Ltd. 01/18/1989 which name changed to Stone Mark Capital Inc. (Canada) 11/17/1989 which reincorporated in Yukon 06/21/1993
(See Stone Mark Capital Inc. (Yukon))

BORAWAY MINES LTD. (BC)
Name changed to Able Explorations Ltd. 03/21/1972
Able Explorations Ltd. reorganized as Arrowhead Resources Ltd. 07/03/1979 which recapitalized as Double Arrow Oil & Gas Ltd. 08/23/1995 which name changed to Arrowhead Minerals Corp. 12/02/1996 which recapitalized as Gemini Energy Corp. 10/25/1999 which merged into Bucking Horse Energy Inc. 03/03/2008

BORAX CONSOLIDATED LTD. (ENGLAND)
Name changed to Borax (Holdings) Ltd. 07/02/1956
Borax (Holdings) Ltd. merged into Rio Tinto-Zinc Corp. Ltd. 08/05/1968 which name changed to RTZ Corp. PLC 08/26/1987 which name changed to Rio Tinto PLC 06/02/1997

BORAX (HOLDINGS) LTD. (ENGLAND)
Each share Deferred Reg. £1 par exchanged for (4) shares Deferred Reg. 5s par plus a 200% stock dividend paid 01/17/1957
Merged into Rio Tinto-Zinc Corp. Ltd. 08/05/1968
Each ADR for Deferred Reg. 5s par exchanged for (0.3) share ADR for Ordinary Reg. 10s par
Rio Tinto-Zinc Corp. PLC name changed to RTZ Corp. PLC 08/26/1987 which name changed to Rio Tinto PLC 06/02/1997

BORAXX TECHNOLOGIES INC (CO)
Reincorporated under the laws of Nevada as Quad X Sports.Com Inc. 03/03/1999
Quad X Sports.Com Inc. recapitalized as Bethel Holdings Inc. 09/17/2001 which reorganized as Direct Pet Health Holdings, Inc. 06/28/2006 which recapitalized as Core Resource Management, Inc. 11/13/2012

BORCAN RES LTD (BC)
Name changed to Le Groupe Opus Communications Inc. 02/26/1985
Each share Common no par exchanged for (1) share Common no par
(See Le Groupe Opus Communications Inc.)

BORDEAUX ENERGY INC (BC)
Recapitalized as Enterprise Energy Resources Ltd. 11/10/2008
Each share Common no par exchanged for (0.03333333) share Common no par
Enterprise Energy Resources Ltd. merged into LNG Energy Ltd. 08/20/2013 which recapitalized as Esrey Energy Ltd. 11/18/2013 which name changed to Esrey Resources Ltd. 10/16/2017

BORDEAUX GOLD MINES LTD. (ON)
Name changed to Lloydal Petroleum Ltd. 00/00/1949
Lloydal Petroleum Ltd. merged into Continental Consolidated Mines & Oils Co. Ltd. 10/04/1957
(See Continental Consolidated Mines & Oils Co. Ltd.)

BORDEAUX PETE CO (CO)
Name changed 09/19/1980
Name changed from Bordeaux Trading Co. to Bordeaux Petroleum Co. 09/19/1980
Recapitalized as Saba Petroleum Co. (CO) 08/08/1991
Each share Capital Stock 1¢ par exchanged for (0.01) share Capital Stock 1¢ par
Saba Petroleum Co. (CO) reincorporated in Delaware 06/10/1997 which merged into GREKA Energy Corp. 03/24/1999
(See GREKA Energy Corp.)

BORDEAUX RES LTD (BC)
Recapitalized as Visionary Industries Ltd. 09/03/1992
Each share Common no par exchanged for (0.4) share Common no par
Visionary Industries Ltd. name changed to Visionary Mining Corp. 07/25/1996 which recapitalized as Nu-Vision Resource Corp. 07/11/2001 which name changed to Vision Coatings Group Ltd. 02/16/2004
(See Vision Coatings Group Ltd.)

BORDEN CHEMS & PLASTICS LTD PARTNERSHIP (DE)
Depositary Preference Units reclassified as Depositary Common Units 02/16/1993
Plan of reorganization under Chapter 11 Federal Bankruptcy Code effective 03/13/2003
No stockholders' equity

BORDEN CO (NJ)
Each share Capital Stock $50 par exchanged for (2) shares Capital Stock $25 par 00/00/1929
Capital Stock $25 par changed to $15 par 00/00/1935
Capital Stock $15 par changed to $7.50 par and (1) additional share issued 01/27/1960
Capital Stock $7.50 par changed to $3.75 par and (1) additional share issued 06/11/1965
Stock Dividend - 10% 10/11/1954
Name changed to Borden, Inc. 04/17/1968
Borden, Inc. merged into RJR Nabisco Holdings Corp. 03/14/1995 which name changed to Nabisco Group Holdings Corp. 06/15/1999
(See Nabisco Group Holdings Corp.)

BORDEN INC (NJ)
Common $3.75 par changed to $1.875 par and (1) additional share issued 06/03/1985
Common $1.875 par changed to $1.25 par and (0.5) additional share issued 06/03/1986
Common $1.25 par changed to $0.625 par and (1) additional share issued 09/06/1989
Common Stock Purchase Rights declared for Common stockholders of record 02/10/1986 were redeemed at $0.01666 per right 12/29/1994 for holders of record 12/20/1994
$1.32 Conv. Preferred Ser. B no par called for redemption 01/25/1995
Merged into RJR Nabisco Holdings Corp. 03/14/1995
Each share Common $0.625 par exchanged for (2.29146) shares Common 1¢ par
RJR Nabisco Holdings Corp. name changed to Nabisco Group Holdings Corp. 06/15/1999
(See Nabisco Group Holdings Corp.)

BORDENTOWN BK CO (BORDENTOWN, NJ)
Name changed to Bank of Mid-Jersey (Bordentown, NJ) 10/26/1970

Bank of Mid-Jersey (Bordentown, NJ) reorganized as B.M.J. Financial Corp. 02/06/1984 which merged into Summit Bancorp 02/28/1997 which merged into FleetBoston Financial Corp. 03/01/2001 which merged into Bank of America Corp. 04/01/2004

BORDER & SOUTHN STOCKHOLDERS TR PLC (ENGLAND)
Each ADR for Ordinary exchanged for (5) ADR's for Ordinary Reg. 06/23/1978
Name changed to Govett Strategic Investment Trust PLC. 01/29/1986
(See Govett Strategic Investment Trust PLC)

BORDER CAP CORP (AB)
Name changed to iTV Games, Inc. 09/27/2000
(See iTV Games, Inc.)

BORDER MALARTIC GOLD MINES LTD. (ON)
Merged into Pardee Amalgamated Mines Ltd. 12/00/1954
Each share Capital Stock $1 par exchanged for (0.02) share Common $1 par
Pardee Amalgamated Mines Ltd. liquidated for Rio Algom Mines Ltd. 11/09/1961 which name changed to Rio Algom Ltd. 04/30/1975
(See Rio Algom Ltd.)

BORDER PETE CORP (AB)
Recapitalized as Border Petroleum Ltd. 03/24/2014
Each share Common no par exchanged for (0.1) share Common no par

BORDER PETE INC (BC)
Reorganized under the laws of Alberta as Border Petroleum Corp. 09/14/2010
Each share Common no par exchanged for (0.25) share Common no par
Border Petroleum Corp. recapitalized as Border Petroleum Ltd. 03/24/2014

BORDER STL ROLLING MLS INC (TX)
Acquired by Border Enterprises, Inc. 12/20/1977
Each share Common $2.50 par exchanged for $16 cash

BORDERFREE INC (DE)
Acquired by Pitney Bowes Inc. 06/10/2015
Each share Common 1¢ par exchanged for $14 cash

BORDERS GROUP INC (MI)
Reincorporated 08/31/1997
Common $0.001 par split (2) for (1) by issuance of (1) additional share payable 03/27/1997 to holders of record 03/11/1997 Ex date - 03/31/1997
State of incorporation changed from (DE) to (MI) 08/31/1997
Plan of reorganization under Chapter 11 Federal Bankruptcy proceedings effective 01/12/2012
No stockholders' equity

BORDESSA MINES LTD.
Merged into Aurlando Consolidated Mining Corp., Ltd. 00/00/1947
Each share Capital Stock $1 par exchanged for (0.2) share Capital Stock $1 par
(See Aurlando Consolidated Mining Corp., Ltd.)

BORDULAC MINES LTD. (ON)
Recapitalized as North Bordulac Mines Ltd. 04/19/1963
Each share Capital Stock $1 par exchanged for (0.25) share Capital Stock $1 par
North Bordulac Mines Ltd. recapitalized as Gold Hawk Exploration Ltd. 10/31/1969

(See Gold Hawk Exploration Ltd.)

BORDUN LTD (ON)
Name changed 10/04/1996
Name changed from Bordun Mining (Quebec) Ltd. to Bordun Ltd. 10/04/1996
Struck off register 05/10/2002

BORDUN MNG LTD (ON)
Acquired by Bordun Mining (Quebec) Ltd. 01/14/1971
Each share Capital Stock $1 par exchanged for (1) share Capital Stock $1 par
Bordun Mining (Quebec) Ltd. name changed to Bordun Ltd. 10/04/1996
(See Bordun Ltd.)

BOREAL EXPL INC (QC)
Each share old Common no par exchanged for (0.33333333) share new Common no par 05/06/1997
Recapitalized as TGW Corp. (QC) 01/08/2001
Each share new Common no par exchanged for (0.18326064) share Common no par
TGW Corp. (QC) reincorporated in Canada as GlobeStar Mining Corp. 12/18/2002
(See GlobeStar Mining Corp.)

BOREAL PRODUCTIONS INC (NV)
Common $0.001 par split (5) for (1) by issuance of (4) additional shares payable 06/24/2008 to holders of record 06/24/2008 Ex date - 06/24/2008
Recapitalized as DSG Global Inc. 02/23/2015
Each share Common $0.001 par exchanged for (0.33333333) share Common $0.001 par

BOREAL RARE METALS LTD. (QC)
Bankrupt 09/18/1957
Details not available

BOREAL WTR COLLECTION INC (NV)
SEC revoked common stock registration 12/05/2016

BOREALIS EXPL LTD (CANADA)
Reincorporated under the laws of Gibraltar on 10/19/1998

BOREALIS RETAIL REAL ESTATE INVT TR (ON)
Name changed to Primaris Retail Real Estate Investment Trust 05/17/2005
Primaris Retail Real Estate Investment Trust merged into H&R Real Estate Investment Trust/H&R Finance Trust 04/04/2013
(See H&R Real Estate Investment Trust/H&R Finance Trust)

BOREALIS TECHNOLOGY CORP (DE)
Name changed to Portivity, Inc. 04/23/1999
(See Portivity, Inc.)

BOREAS MINES LTD. (AB)
Name changed to Expander Mines & Petroleums Ltd. 06/00/1959
Expander Mines & Petroleums, Ltd. recapitalized as Northrim Mines Ltd. 11/28/1973
(See Northrim Mines Ltd.)

BOREL BK & TR CO (SAN MATEO, CA)
Common no par split (2) for (1) by issuance of (1) additional share 06/22/1983
Common no par split (2) for (1) by issuance of (1) additional share payable 07/31/1997 to holders of record 07/15/1997 Ex date - 08/01/1997
Merged into Boston Private Financial Holdings, Inc. 12/03/2001
Each share Common no par exchanged for (1.8996) share Common $1 par

BOREN OIL & GAS CORP. (DE)
Name changed to American Hydrocarbon Corp. 00/00/1958
(See American Hydrocarbon Corp.)

BOREXCO INC (UT)
Name changed to True Health, Inc. (UT) 02/23/1986
True Health, Inc. (UT) reorganized in Nevada as MediQuip Holdings, Inc. 05/01/2006 which name changed to Deep Down, Inc. 12/18/2006

BORG & BECK CO.
Merged into Borg-Warner Corp. (IL) 00/00/1928
Details not available

BORG (GEORGE W.) CORP. (DE)
Merged into Amphenol-Borg Electronics Corp. 01/01/1959
Each share Capital Stock $10 par exchanged for (1.3) shares Common $1 par
Amphenol-Borg Electronics Corp. name changed to Amphenol Corp. (Old) 05/11/1965 which merged into Bunker Ramo Corp. (New) 06/03/1968 which merged into Allied Corp. 07/31/1981 which merged into Allied-Signal Inc. 09/19/1985 which name changed to AlliedSignal Inc. 04/26/1993 which name changed to Honeywell International Inc. 12/01/1999

BORG WARNER AUTOMOTIVE INC (DE)
Name changed to BorgWarner Inc. 02/04/2000

BORG WARNER CORP (DE)
Reincorporated 10/31/1967
Each share Common $10 par exchanged for (2) shares Common $5 par 00/00/1937
Common $5 par split (3) for (1) by issuance of (2) additional shares 00/00/1955
3.5% Preferred $100 par called for redemption 10/23/1967
State of incorporation changed from (IL) to (DE) 10/31/1967
Common $5 par changed to $2.50 par and (1) additional share issued 11/22/1967
Common $2.50 par split (2) for (1) by issuance of (1) additional share 11/25/1981
Common $2.50 par split (2) for (1) by issuance of (1) additional share 11/23/1983
$4.50 Conv. Preferred called for redemption 06/04/1987
Merged into Borg-Warner Holding Corp. 07/30/1987
Each share Common $2.50 par exchanged for $54.25 principal amount of Jr. Subord. Discount Debentures due 07/15/2007 and $19.75 cash

BORG WARNER SEC CORP (DE)
Name changed to Burns International Services Corp. 07/07/1999
(See Burns International Services Corp.)

BORIN-VIVITONE CORP.
Bankrupt 00/00/1932
Details not available

BORKIN INDS CORP (BC)
Cease trade order effective 03/18/1987
Stockholders' equity unlikely

BORLAND INTL INC (DE)
Reorganized 10/06/1989
Reorganized from (CA) to under the laws of Delaware 10/06/1989
Each share Common no par exchanged for (0.2) share Common 1¢ par
Name changed to Inprise Corp. 06/05/1998
Inprise Corp. name changed to Borland Software Corp. 01/22/2001
(See Borland Software Corp.)

BORLAND SOFTWARE CORP (DE)
Acquired by Micro Focus International PLC 07/27/2009
Each share Common 1¢ par exchanged for $1.50 cash

BORMAN FOOD STORES INC (MI)
Common $1 par split (2) for (1) by issuance of (1) additional share 11/17/1961
Reincorporated under the laws of Delaware as Borman's Inc. 07/01/1969
(See Borman's Inc.)

BORMANS INC (DE)
Merged into Great Atlantic & Pacific Tea Co., Inc. 03/01/1989
Each share Common $1 par exchanged for $27 cash
Each share Non-Transferable Class B Common $1 par exchanged for $27 cash

BORNE, SCRYMSER CO. (NJ)
Each share Capital Stock $100 par exchanged for (4) shares Capital Stock $25 par 00/00/1926
Each share Capital Stock $25 par exchanged for (5) shares Capital Stock $5 par 00/00/1951
Name changed to Borne Chemical Co., Inc. (Old) 08/11/1956
Borne Chemical Co., Inc. (Old) merged into Borne Chemical Co., Inc. (New) 05/28/1974
(See Borne Chemical Co., Inc. (New))

BORNE CHEM CO NEW (NJ)
Merged 05/28/1974
Capital Stock $5 par changed to $1.50 par and (2) additional shares issued 05/18/1959
Capital Stock $1.50 par reclassified as Common 10¢ par 04/26/1967
Merged from Borne Chemical Co., Inc. (Old) to Borne Chemical Co., Inc. (New) 05/28/1974
Each share Common 10¢ par exchanged for (0.25) share Common 10¢ par
Liquidated 00/00/1984
Details not available

BORNEO ENERGY USA INC (DE)
Name changed to AAP, Inc. 09/28/2011

BORNEO GOLD CORP (BC)
Name changed to Nexttrip.com Travel Inc. 01/04/2000
Nexttrip.com Travel Inc. recapitalized as WorldPlus Ventures Inc. 05/26/2003 which recapitalized as New Global Ventures Ltd. 06/07/2007 which recapitalized as New Global Ventures International Ltd. 03/14/2008 which name changed to Auro Resources Corp. 10/15/2010 which recapitalized as Tesoro Minerals Corp. 08/26/2013

BORNEO INDL FISHERY CORP (NV)
Name changed to Shenzhen Yidian Double Way of Innovation Culture Media Corp. 04/26/2017

BORNITE COPPER & GOLD MINING CO. (WA)
Charter cancelled and proclaimed dissolved for failure to pay fees 08/23/1909

BORNITE COPPER CORP. LTD. (QC)
Name changed to Bornite Mines Ltd. 07/11/1963
Bornite Mines Ltd. recapitalized as Rouyn Exploration Ltd. 08/25/1966
(See Rouyn Exploration Ltd.)

BORNITE INTL MINES LTD (BC)
Name changed to International Bornite Mines Ltd. 02/22/1971
(See International Bornite Mines Ltd.)

BORNITE MINES LTD. (QC)
Recapitalized as Rouyn Exploration Ltd. 08/25/1966
Each share Capital Stock $1 par exchanged for (0.33333333) share Capital Stock $1 par
(See Rouyn Exploration Ltd.)

BORNITE RIDGE MINES LTD (BC)
Reorganized as Bornite International Mines Ltd. 01/18/1971
Each share Capital Stock 50¢ par exchanged for (0.2) share Capital Stock no par
Bornite International Mines Ltd. name changed to International Bornite Mines Ltd. 02/22/1971
(See International Bornite Mines Ltd.)

BORNOT, INC. (DE)
Each share Class A no par exchanged for (1.1) shares Common no par 00/00/1942
Each share Class B no par exchanged for (0.1) share Common no par 00/00/1942
Voluntarily dissolved 04/25/1967
Details not available

BORO ELECTRS INC (NY)
Name changed to Royal General Corp. and Common 35¢ par changed to 10¢ par 04/24/1972
(See Royal General Corp.)

BORO RECYCLING INC (NY)
Plan of reorganization under Chapter 11 Federal Bankruptcy proceedings confirmed 09/06/1988
No stockholders' equity

BORON CHEMS INTL LTD (BC)
Name changed to Atacama Minerals Corp. 08/08/1997
Atacama Minerals Corp. name changed to Sirocco Mining Inc. 01/30/2012 which merged into RB Energy Inc. 02/05/2014

BORON LEPORE & ASSOCS INC (DE)
Merged into Cardinal Health, Inc. 06/27/2002
Each share Common 1¢ par exchanged for $16 cash

BORREGO SPRINGS BK (BORREGO SPRINGS, CA)
Acquired by Viejas Band of Kumeyaay Indians 12/29/2004
Each share Common $2.50 par exchanged for $22 cash

BORROR CORP (OH)
Name changed to Dominion Homes Inc. 05/07/1997
(See Dominion Homes Inc.)

BORSODCHEM NYRT (HUNGARY)
Sponsored 144A GDR's for Ordinary split (5) for (1) by issuance of (4) additional GDR's payable 06/18/2004 to holders of record 06/11/2004
Sponsored Reg. S GDR's for Ordinary split (5) for (1) by issuance of (4) additional GDR's payable 06/18/2004 to holders of record 06/11/2004
Sponsored Reg. S GDR's for Euro Shares split (5) for (1) by issuance of (4) additional GDR's payable 06/18/2004 to holders of record 06/11/2004
Acquired by First Chemical Holding Kft. 03/29/2007
Each Sponsored 144A GDR for Ordinary exchanged for $15.9884 cash
Each Sponsored Reg. S GDR for Ordinary exchanged for $15.9884 cash
Each Sponsored Reg. S GDR for Euro Shares exchanged for $15.9884 cash

BORTON INC (KS)
In process of liquidation
Each share Common 1¢ par received initial distribution of $1.30 cash 06/30/2000
Note: Details on subsequent distribution(s), if any, are not available

BORU MNG LTD (BC)
Recapitalized as Gallahad Petroleum Ltd. 07/30/1976
Each share Common 50¢ par exchanged for (0.2) share Common no par
Gallahad Petroleum Ltd. merged into Backer Petroleum Corp. 12/30/1988
(See Backer Petroleum Corp.)

BOSCH (ROBERT) MAGNETO CO., INC. (NY)
Merged into United American Bosch Corp. 12/00/1930
Details not available

BOSCO FLOORING INC (NV)
Name changed to Bosco Holdings, Inc. 04/08/2008
Bosco Holdings, Inc. name changed to Caduceus Software Systems Corp. 03/03/2011

BOSCO HLDGS INC (NV)
Common $0.001 par split (5) for (1) by issuance of (4) additional shares payable 04/08/2008 to holders of record 04/04/2008 Ex date - 04/09/2008
Name changed to Caduceus Software Systems Corp. 03/03/2011

BOSCO RES CORP (DE)
Recapitalized as Appraisal Group International, Inc. 12/15/1986
Each share Common 10¢ par exchanged for (0.125) share Common $0.001 par
Appraisal Group International, Inc. name changed to International Realty Group, Inc. 08/10/1989 which name changed to Qualton Inc. 10/17/2000
(See Qualton Inc.)

BOSS ENERGY LTD (AB)
Merged into Canadian Leader Energy Inc. 11/02/1995
Each share Common no par exchanged for (0.26315789) share Common no par
Canadian Leader Energy Inc. merged into Centurion Energy International Inc. 05/20/1997
(See Centurion Energy International Inc.)

BOSS GOLD CORP (BC)
Recapitalized as Boss Gold International Corp. 07/11/2005
Each share Common no par exchanged for (0.33333333) share Common no par
Boss Gold International Corp. name changed to Boss Power Corp. 06/15/2007 which name changed to Eros Resources Corp. 07/29/2015

BOSS GOLD INTL CORP (BC)
Name changed to Boss Power Corp. 06/15/2007
Boss Power Corp. name changed to Eros Resources Corp. 07/29/2015

BOSS-LINCO LINES, INC. (NY)
Through voluntary exchange offer 100% acquired by Novo Industrial Corp. as of 08/08/1973
Public interest eliminated

BOSS MFG CO (DE)
Reincorporated 04/01/1963
Each share Common $100 par exchanged for (4) shares Common $25 par 00/00/1943
State of incorporation changed from (IL) to (DE) 04/01/1963
Common $25 par changed to no par and (1) additional share issued 06/29/1970
Stock Dividend - 10% 06/30/1964
Merged into ACPI Acquisition Subsidiary Inc. 10/19/1987
Each share Common no par exchanged for $17.802177 cash

BOSS MINERALS INC (NV)
Reorganized as Environmental Control Corp. 04/18/2006
Each share Common $0.001 par exchanged for (5) shares Common $0.001 par

BOSS PWR CORP (BC)
Name changed to Eros Resources Corp. 07/29/2015

BOSSERT CO., INC.
Acquired by Timken-Detroit Axle Co. 00/00/1946
Details not available

BOSSERT MFG CORP (NY)
Reported out of business 00/00/1985
Stockholders' equity unlikely

BOSSIER BK & TR CO LA (BOSSIER CITY, LA)
Placed in receivership and FDIC appointed receiver 06/13/1986
Stockholders' equity unlikely

BOST, INC. (DE)
No longer in existence having become inoperative and void for non-payment of taxes 04/01/1954

BOST TOOTH PASTE CORP. (NY)
Succeeded by Bost, Inc. 00/00/1946
Details not available

BOSTANA MINES CO. (MT)
Adjudicated bankrupt 06/09/1955
Stockholders' equity unlikely

BOSTIC CONCRETE INC (LA)
Merged into Transit Mix Concrete & Materials Co. 01/10/1996
Details not available

BOSTITCH, INC. (RI)
Stock Dividend - (0.5) share Class A Common for (1) Class A Common and/or Class B Common 11/24/1958
Completely liquidated 09/02/1966
Each share Class A Common $4 par or Class B Common $4 par exchanged for first and final distribution of (1.25) shares Textron Inc. (RI) Common 25¢ par
Textron Inc. (RI) reincorporated in Delaware 01/02/1968

BOSTON & ALBANY RAILROAD CO. (NY & MA)
Merged into New York Central Railroad Co. 04/03/1961
Each share Capital Stock $100 par exchanged for $150 of New York Central Coll. Trust 6's due 04/01/1980

BOSTON & CORBIN MINING CO.
Dissolved 00/00/1926
Details not available

BOSTON & ME CORP (DE)
Plan of reorganization confirmed 06/30/1983
No stockholders' equity

BOSTON & ME INDS INC (DE)
Name changed to Bomaine Corp. (DE) 05/26/1971
Bomaine Corp. (DE) reincorporated in California 12/08/1978
(See Bomaine Corp. (CA))

BOSTON & PROVIDENCE RR CORP (MA & RI)
Under plan of reorganization each share Capital Stock $100 par received (1) Ctf. of Cont. Bene. Interest 04/21/1971
Each share Capital Stock $100 par exchanged for $110 cash 05/28/1971
Each Ctf. of Cont. Bene. Interest received initial distribution of $277.50 cash 01/31/1973
Each Ctf. of Cont. Bene. Interest received second distribution of $19.738522 cash 12/31/1974
Involuntarily dissolved 08/31/1998

BOSTON & WORCESTER STREET RAILWAY
Succeeded by Boston, Worcester & New York Street Railway Co. 00/00/1927
Details not available

BOSTON ACCEP INC (MA)
Liquidation completed
Each share 7% Preferred $10 par exchanged for first and final distribution of $13.50 cash 06/30/1965
Each share Common no par exchanged for initial distribution of $18 cash 09/22/1965
Each share Common no par received second and final distribution of $3.25 cash 09/28/1967

BOSTON ACOUSTICS INC (MA)
Common 1¢ par split (2) for (1) by issuance of (1) additional share 10/18/1991
Common 1¢ par split (3) for (2) by issuance of (0.5) additional share payable 08/17/1998 to holders of record 07/31/1998
Merged into D&M Holdings U.S. Inc. 08/26/2005
Each share Common 1¢ par exchanged for $17.50 cash

BOSTON & MAINE RAILROAD (MA, ME, NH & NY)
Each share Prior Preference $100 par exchanged for (1.2) share new Preferred $100 par and (1) share new Common $100 par 00/00/1953
Each share 1st Preferred Ser. A $100 par exchanged for (0.65) share new Common $100 par 00/00/1953
Each share 1st Preferred Ser. B $100 par exchanged for (0.85) share new Common $100 par 00/00/1953
Each share 1st Preferred Ser. C $100 par exchanged for (0.79) share new Common $100 par 00/00/1953
Each share 1st Preferred Ser. D $100 par exchanged for (1.05) shares new Common $100 par 00/00/1953
Each share 1st Preferred Ser. E $100 par exchanged for (0.6) share new Common $100 par 00/00/1953
Each share 6% Preferred $100 par exchanged for (0.07) share new Common $100 par 00/00/1953
Each share Common $100 par exchanged for (0.05) share new Common $100 par
Common $100 par changed to no par 01/30/1957
Reincorporated under the laws of Delaware as Boston & Maine Corp. and Common no par changed to $1 par 04/30/1964
(See Boston & Maine Corp.)

BOSTON AUTOMATIC FIRE ALARM CO.
Merged into Automatic Fire Alarm Co. 00/00/1948
Details not available

BOSTON BANCORP (MA)
Common $1 par split (2) for (1) by issuance of (1) additional share 03/31/1987
Merged into Bank of Boston Corp. 06/28/1996
Each share Common $1 par exchanged for (0.8792) share Common $2.25 par
Bank of Boston Corp. name changed to BankBoston Corp. 04/25/1997 which merged into Fleet Boston Corp. 10/01/1999 which name changed to FleetBoston Financial Corp. 04/18/2000 which merged into Bank of America Corp. 04/01/2004

BOSTON BAY MINES LTD (QC)
Struck off register 05/02/2003

BOSTON BIOMEDICA INC (MA)
Name changed to Pressure BioSciences, Inc. 09/15/2004

BOSTON BLOCK TRUST OF MINNEAPOLIS (MA)
Trust terminated 00/00/1943
Details not available

BOSTON CAP CORP (MA)
Common $1 par changed to 50¢ par and (1) additional share issued 09/12/1969
Name changed to BCC Industries, Inc. (MA) 06/02/1971
BCC Industries, Inc. (MA) reincorporated in Delaware as BCC, Inc. 12/05/1972 which which name changed to Technicare Corp. 08/30/1973 which merged into Johnson & Johnson 02/21/1979

BOSTON CELTICS LTD PARTNERSHIP NEW (DE)
Name changed to Henley Limited Partnership 12/31/2002
(See Henley Limited Partnership)

BOSTON CELTICS LTD PARTNERSHIP OLD (DE)
Under plan of reorganization name changed to Boston Celtics Limited Partnership (New) and each Unit of Undivided Int. received distribution of $20 principal amount of 6% Subordinated Debentures due 06/30/2038 and $1 cash 06/30/1998
Boston Celtics Limited Partnership (New) name changed to Henley Limited Partnership 12/31/2002
(See Henley Limited Partnership)

BOSTON CHAMBER OF COMMERCE REALTY TRUST (MA)
1st & 2nd Preferred $100 par and Common no par declared valueless 06/01/1959
6% Prior Preference $100 par liquidated 00/00/1960
Details not available

BOSTON CHICKEN INC (DE)
Common 1¢ par split (2) for (1) by issuance of (1) additional share 08/31/1994
Plan of reorganization under Chapter 11 Federal Bankruptcy Code effective 05/26/2000
No stockholders' equity

BOSTON CO., INC. (MA)
Class A Common $1 par and Class B Common $1 par split (2) for (1) by issuance of (1) additional share respectively 05/28/1969
Stock Dividend - 50% 07/27/1972
Merged into Shearson/American Express Inc. 09/25/1981
Each share Class A Common $1 par exchanged for $42 cash
Each share Class B Common $1 par exchanged for $42 cash

BOSTON CO-OPERATIVE BLDG. CO.
Liquidation completed 00/00/1943
Details not available

BOSTON CO-OPERATIVE SHOE MANUFACTURING CO. (MA)
Proclaimed dissolved for failure to file reports and pay fees 00/00/1931

BOSTON COM STK FD INC (MA)
Name changed to Vance, Sanders Common Stock Fund, Inc. 12/29/1972
Vance, Sanders Common Stock Fund, Inc. name changed to Eaton Vance Growth Fund, Inc. 11/16/1981 which name changed to Eaton Vance Growth Trust 08/18/1992

BOSTON COMMUNICATIONS GROUP INC (MA)
Merged into Megasoft Ltd. 08/30/2007
Each share Common 1¢ par exchanged for $3.60 cash

BOSTON DEV CORP (AB)
Acquired by 101037490 Saskatchewan Ltd. 02/14/2003
Each share Common no par exchanged for $0.40 cash

BOSTON DIGITAL CORP (MA)
Stock Dividends - 50% 06/30/1979; 200% 03/17/1980
Merged into BDC Aquisition Corp. 05/25/1993
Each share Common 10¢ par exchanged for $3.75 cash

BOSTON DRY DOCK CO.
Adjudicated bankrupt 00/00/1940
Stockholders' equity unlikely

BOSTON DUCK CO.
Merged into Otis Co. 00/00/1926
Details not available

BOSTON EDISON CO (MA)
Each share Capital Stock $100 par exchanged for (4) shares Capital Stock $25 par 00/00/1940
Capital Stock $25 par reclassified as Common $25 par 06/21/1956
Common $25 par changed to $10 par and (1.5) additional shares issued 06/20/1962
Common $10 par changed to $5 par and (1) additional share issued 10/01/1986
$1.175 Preference $1 par called for redemption 03/30/1987
$1.46 Preference $1 par called for redemption 06/01/1992
8.88% Preferred $100 par called for redemption 05/01/1993
8.25% Depositary Preferred called for redemption at $25 on 06/01/1997
Depositary Preferred called for redemption at $25 on 07/01/1998
7.27% Preferred $100 par called for redemption at $101.94 on 07/01/1998
7.75% Preferred $100 par called for redemption at $25 on 07/01/1998
Under plan of reorganization each share Common $1 par automatically became (1) share BEC Energy Common $1 par 05/21/1998
BEC Energy merged into NSTAR 08/25/1999
(See NSTAR)
8% Preferred $100 par called for redemption at $100 on 12/01/2001
Name changed to NSTAR Electric Co. 02/26/2007

BOSTON ELEVATED RAILWAY CO. (MA)
Liquidation completed 00/00/1953
Details not available

BOSTON FD INC (MA)
Common $5 par changed to $1 par 00/00/1939
Common $1 par split (2) for (1) by issuance of (1) additional share 06/29/1962
Stock Dividend - 100% 04/30/1955
Name changed to Vance, Sanders Investors Fund 06/28/1973
Vance, Sanders Investors Fund name changed to Eaton Vance Investors Fund, Inc. 09/24/1982 which name changed to Eaton Vance Investors Trust 09/29/1993
(See Eaton Vance Investors Trust)

BOSTON FINL GROUP INC (AB)
Recapitalized as Jager (H.) Developments Inc. 11/28/1991
Each share Common no par exchanged for (0.1) share Common no par
Jager (H.) Developments Inc. name changed to Westbridge Land Development Corp. 10/15/1999
(See Westbridge Land Development Corp.)

BOSTON FISH MKT CORP (MA)
Name changed to Fulham, Maloney & Co., Inc. 06/22/1973
Fulham, Maloney & Co., Inc. name changed to Fulham (John) & Sons, Inc. 12/18/1979
(See Fulham (John) & Sons, Inc.)

BOSTON FISHING BOAT CO., INC. (MA)
Dissolved by court decree 07/17/1973
No stockholders' equity

BOSTON FIVE BANCORP INC (DE)
Reorganized 07/28/1988
Common 1¢ par split (3) for (2) by issuance of (0.5) additional share 06/24/1986
Common 1¢ par split (4) for (3) by issuance of (0.33333333) additional share 01/09/1987
Under plan of reorganization each share Boston Five Cents Savings Bank FSB (Boston, MA) Common 1¢ par automatically became (1) share Boston Five Bancorp, Inc. (DE) Common 1¢ par 07/28/1988
Merged into Citizens Financial Group, Inc. (DE) 10/13/1993
Each share Common 1¢ par exchanged for $13 cash

BOSTON FNDTN FD INC (MD)
Name changed to Federated Stock & Bond Fund, Inc. (Old) 01/01/1985
Federated Stock & Bond Fund, Inc. (Old) name changed to Stock & Bond Fund, Inc. 04/17/1993 which name changed to Federated Stock & Bond Fund, Inc. (New) (MD) 03/31/1996 which reincorporated in Massachusetts as Federated Stock & Bond Fund 09/05/2008

BOSTON GARDEN ARENA CORP (MA)
Common no par changed to $1 par 11/15/1946
Each share Common $1 par exchanged for (6) shares Common no par 06/05/1959
Stock Dividend - 100% 09/17/1958
Merged into Storer Broadcasting Co. 07/31/1973
Each share Common no par exchanged for (1.6) shares Common $1 par
Storer Broadcasting Co. name changed to Storer Communications, Inc. 01/01/1983
(See Storer Communications, Inc.)

BOSTON GAS CO (MA)
Variable Term Preferred Ser. A called for redemption at $25 plus $0.4013 accrued dividends on 09/01/2003

BOSTON GEAR WORKS, INC.
Acquired by Murray Co. 00/00/1947
Details not available

BOSTON GROUND RENT TRUST (IL)
Merged into Real Estate Investment Trust of America 06/01/1956
Each Trust Unit $100 par exchanged for (4) Ctfs. of Bene. Int. $1 par
(See Real Estate Investment Trust of America)

BOSTON HARBOR MARINA INC (MA)
Common no par changed to $1 par 08/29/1967
Name changed to Marina Industries, Inc. 09/18/1967
(See Marina Industries, Inc.)

BOSTON HERALD TRAVELER CORP (MA)
Name changed to WHDH Corp. 06/19/1972
(See WHDH Corp.)

BOSTON INC NEW (UT)
Name changed to Resource Technology Group, Inc. 11/28/1988

BOSTON INSURANCE CO. (MA)
Each share Capital Stock $100 par exchanged for (10) shares Capital Stock $10 par 00/00/1946
Each share Capital Stock $10 par exchanged for (2) shares Capital Stock $5 par 00/00/1952
Stock Dividends - 12.5% 12/21/1949; 11.11111111% 12/12/1950
Name changed to Bimar Corp. 06/06/1966
(See Bimar Corp.)

BOSTON INS EXCHANGE BLDG INC (MA)
Liquidation completed
Each share $5 Preferred no par exchanged for first and final distribution of $100 cash 06/21/1982
Each share Class A Common no par exchanged for initial distribution of $461 cash 06/21/1982
Each share Class A Common no par received second and final distribution of $21.50 cash 03/02/1983
Each share Class B Common no par exchanged for initial distribution of $461 cash 06/21/1982
Each share Class B Common no par received second and final distribution of $21.50 cash 03/02/1983
Each VTC for Class B Common no par received first and final distribution of $21.50 cash 03/02/1983

BOSTON INVTS INC (CO)
Recapitalized as Nostalgia Network, Inc. (CO) 01/27/1987
Each share Common $0.001 par exchanged for (0.025) share Common 4¢ par
Nostalgia Network, Inc. (CO) reincorporated in Delaware 10/09/1987
(See Nostalgia Network, Inc.)

BOSTON LIFE SCIENCES INC (DE)
Each share old Common 1¢ par exchanged for (0.1) share new Common 1¢ par 06/09/1997
Each share new Common 1¢ par exchanged again for (0.2) share new Common 1¢ par 02/04/2005
Name changed to Alseres Pharmaceuticals, Inc. 06/11/2007

BOSTON MANUFACTURING CO.
Liquidated 00/00/1930
Details not available

BOSTON MCCREA GOLD MINES, LTD.
Assets sold 00/00/1941
Details not available

BOSTON METAL INVESTORS, INC.
Liquidation completed 00/00/1946
Details not available

BOSTON METROPOLITAN BLDGS., INC.
Reorganized 00/00/1950
No stockholders' equity

BOSTON MINE (MI)
Liquidation completed 12/02/1960
Details not available

BOSTON MUT EQUITY GROWTH FD INC (MA)
Under plan of merger name changed to Boston Mutual Fund, Inc. 12/31/1974
(See Boston Mutual Fund, Inc.)

BOSTON MUT FD INC (MA)
Proclaimed dissolved for failure to file reports and pay taxes 05/20/1988

BOSTON PAC MED INC (MA)
Reorganized under the laws of Nevada as DirectView, Inc. 04/11/2003
Each share Common 1¢ par exchanged for (0.01) share Common $0.0001 par
DirectView, Inc. (NV) reorganized in Delaware as GC Carbon Corp. 12/08/2006 which name changed to Seaway Valley Capital Corp. 08/17/2007

BOSTON PATRIOTS FOOTBALL CLUB (MA)
Name changed to New England Patriots Football Club, Inc. 04/01/1971
(See New England Patriots Football Club, Inc.)

BOSTON PERS PPTY TR (MA)
Each share Capital Stock $100 par exchanged for (10) shares Capital Stock no par 00/00/1929
Capital Stock no par split (4) for (1) by issuance of (3) additional shares 10/21/1964
Completely liquidated 10/05/1972
Each share Capital Stock no par exchanged for first and final distribution of (2.61945) shares of Consolidated Investment Trust Capital Stock $1 par
(See Consolidated Investment Trust)

BOSTON PRIVATE FINL HLDGS INC (MA)
Name changed 04/22/1998
Name changed from Boston Private Bancorp, Inc. to Boston Private Financial Holdings Inc. 04/22/1998
6.95% Depositary Preferred Ser. D called for redemption at $25 on 06/15/2018
(Additional Information in Active)

BOSTON RAILROAD HOLDING CO.
Acquired by New York, New Haven & Hartford Railroad Co. under plan of reorganization 05/26/1948
Details not available

BOSTON REAL ESTATE TRUST (MA)
Capital Stock $1,000 par changed to $100 par 00/00/1929
Capital Stock $100 par changed to no par 00/00/1944
Merged into Real Estate Investment Trust of America 06/01/1956
Each share Capital Stock no par exchanged for (3) Ctfs. of Bene. Int. $1 par
(See Real Estate Investment Trust of America)

BOSTON RESTAURANT ASSOCS INC (DE)
Merged into Dolphin Direct Equity Partners, L.P. 12/22/2006
Each share Common 1¢ par exchanged for $0.70 cash

BOSTON STORAGE WAREHOUSE CO. (MA)
Dissolved 00/00/1953
Details not available

BOSTON TECHNOLOGY INC (CO)
Each share old Common $0.001 par exchanged for (0.1) share new Common $0.001 par 10/27/1989
Merged into Comverse Technology, Inc. 01/14/1998
Each share new Common $0.001 par exchanged for (0.65) share Common 10¢ par
Comverse Technology, Inc. merged into Verint Systems Inc. 02/05/2013

BOSTON TRANSCRIPT CO.
Publication suspended 00/00/1941
Details not available

BOSTON WHARF CO. (MA)
Common $100 par changed to $50 par and $50 principal amount of 5% Debentures distributed 00/00/1954
Completely liquidated 06/12/1963
Each share Common $50 par exchanged for first and final distribution of $75.50 cash

BOSTON WOVEN HOSE & RUBBER CO. (MA)
Common no par split (4) for (1) by issuance of (3) additional shares 00/00/1952
Common no par changed to $1 par 00/00/1953
Merged into American Biltrite Rubber Co., Inc. 04/25/1957
Each share 6% Preferred $100 par exchanged for (1) share 6.5% 1st Preferred $100 par
Each share Common $1 par exchanged for (1) share $0.80 2nd Preferred no par
American Biltrite Rubber Co., Inc. name changed to American Biltrite Inc. 05/03/1973

BOSTONFED BANCORP INC (DE)
Merged into Banknorth Group, Inc. (ME) 01/21/2005
Each share Common 1¢ par exchanged for (1.241) shares Common 1¢ par
Banknorth Group, Inc. (ME) merged into TD Banknorth Inc. 03/01/2005
(See TD Banknorth Inc.)

BOS-BOU

BOSTWICK STL LATH CO (OH)
Each share old Common no par exchanged for (10) shares new Common no par 07/00/1955
Common no par split (2) for (1) by issuance of (1) additional share 12/15/1980
Proclaimed dissolved 12/29/1988

BOSWELL INTL TECHNOLOGIES LTD (BC)
Cease trade order effective 01/22/1997
Stockholders' equity unlikely

BOSWELL RIV MINES LTD (BC)
Recapitalized as B.R. Resources Ltd. 09/00/1972
Each share Capital Stock no par exchanged for (0.2) share Common no par
(See B.R. Resources Ltd.)

BOSY HLDGS CORP (NV)
Name changed to United Royale Holdings Corp. 02/15/2018

BOTANECO CORP (CANADA)
Name changed to Natunola AgriTech Inc. 07/09/2013
(See Natunola AgriTech Inc.)

BOTANIEX INC (NV)
Name changed to HE-5 Resources Corp. 03/16/2006
HE-5 Resources Corp. recapitalized as Fansfrenzy Corp. 12/05/2017

BOTANY CONSOLIDATED MILLS, INC. (NJ)
Reorganized as Botany Worsted Mills 00/00/1937
Each share Class A exchanged for (0.4) share Class A $5 par
Each share Common exchanged for (0.05) share Class A $5 par
Botany Worsted Mills name changed to Botany Mills, Inc. 00/00/1947 which name changed to Botany Industries, Inc. (NJ) 04/21/1959 which reincorporated in Delaware 12/31/1966
(See Botany Industries, Inc. (DE))

BOTANY INDS INC (DE)
Reincorporated 12/31/1966
Each share Common $1 par exchanged for (0.5) share Common $2 par 04/20/1965
State of incorporation changed from (NJ) to (DE) 12/31/1966
Adjudicated bankrupt 10/30/1973
Stockholders' equity unlikely

BOTANY MILLS, INC. (NJ)
Each share $1.25 Preferred $10 par exchanged for (1) share 6% Prior Preferred $25 par 00/00/1948
Each share Class A $5 par exchanged for (1) share 5% Preferred $25 par and (0.5) share Common $1 par
Each share Class B $1 par exchanged for (4) shares Common $1 par
6% Prior Preferred $25 par changed to 5% Preferred $15 par 03/15/1956
5% Preferred $25 par changed to 4% Preferred $10 par 03/15/1956
Each share old Common $1 par exchanged for (1) share new Common $1 par 03/15/1956
Name changed to Botany Industries, Inc. (NJ) 04/21/1959
Botany Industries, Inc. (NJ) reincorporated in Delaware 12/31/1966
(See Botany Industries, Inc.)

BOTANY WORSTED MILLS (NJ)
Name changed to Botany Mills, Inc. 00/00/1947
Botany Mills, Inc. name changed to Botany Industries, Inc. (NJ) 04/21/1959 which reincorporated in Delaware 12/31/1966
(See Botany Industries, Inc.)

BOTAR CORP (DE)
Charter cancelled and declared inoperative and void for non-payment of taxes 03/01/1975

BOTETOURT BANKSHARES INC (VA)
Under plan of merger each share Common $1 par automatically became (1) share Bank of Botetourt (Buchanan, VA) Common $1 par 10/24/2013

BOTEX INDS CORP (BC)
Name changed to Radical Elastomers Inc. 08/02/2001
(See Radical Elastomers Inc.)

BOTSWANA DIAMOND FIELDS INC (BC)
Merged into Crew Development Corp. 01/14/2000
Each share Common no par exchanged for (0.66666666) share Common no par
Crew Development Corp. name changed to Crew Gold Corp. 01/26/2004
(See Crew Gold Corp.)

BOTTOMLINE HOME LN INC (NV)
SEC revoked common stock registration 11/17/2011

BOUCHARD-CLERICY GOLD MINES LTD.
Succeeded by Bouchard Gold Mines Ltd. 00/00/1946
Each share Capital Stock exchanged for (0.5) share Capital Stock
(See Bouchard Gold Mines Ltd.)

BOUCHARD GOLD MINES LTD. (ON)
Charter cancelled and company declared dissolved for default in filing returns 02/00/1958

BOUCHER-OEHMKE HLDGS INC (NV)
Reported out of business 00/00/1991
Details not available

BOUGAINVILLE COPPER LTD (PAPUA NEW GUINEA)
ADR agreement terminated 07/24/2009
Each ADR for Ordinary exchanged for $0.39975 cash

BOULDER ACCEPTANCE CORP. (CO)
Declared defunct and inoperative for non-payment of taxes 10/11/1963

BOULDER ACQUISITIONS INC (NV)
Each share old Common $0.001 par exchanged for (0.00666666) share new Common $0.001 par 06/20/2003
Each share new Common $0.001 par exchanged again for (0.5) share new Common $0.001 par 04/28/2004
New Common $0.001 par split (1.31722) for (1) issuance of (0.31722) additional share payable 06/22/2004 to holders of record 06/10/2004 Ex date - 06/23/2004
Name changed to China Digital Wireless, Inc. 08/06/2004
China Digital Wireless, Inc. name changed to China Recycling Energy Corp. 03/08/2007
Each share Common $0.001 par exchanged for (1) share Common $0.001 par

BOULDER BRANDS INC (DE)
Acquired by Pinnacle Foods Inc. 01/15/2016
Each share Common $0.0001 par exchanged for $11 cash

BOULDER BREWING CO (CO)
Reorganized under the laws of Nevada as Boulder Acquisitions, Inc. 09/24/2001
Each share Common $0.001 par exchanged for (0.2) share Common $0.001 par
Boulder Acquistions, Inc. name changed to China Digital Wireless, Inc. 08/06/2004 which name changed to China Recycling Energy Corp. 03/08/2007

BOULDER CAP OPPORTUNITIES INC (CO)
Common no par split (5) for (2) by issuance of (1.5) additional shares payable 07/16/1999 to holders of record 07/12/1999
Name changed to Stan Lee Media, Inc. 08/13/1999
(See Stan Lee Media, Inc.)

BOULDER CAP OPPORTUNITIES III INC (CO)
Name changed to Sonic Jet Performance, Inc. 11/06/1998
Sonic Jet Performance, Inc. name changed to Force Protection, Inc. (CO) 09/30/2003 which reorganized in Nevada 02/04/2005
(See Force Protection, Inc.)

BOULDER CREEK EXPLORATIONS INC (NV)
Each share old Common $0.001 par exchanged for (8) shares new Common $0.001 par 11/16/2006
Name changed to CanAm Uranium Corp. 11/28/2006
CanAm Uranium Corp. recapitalized as CleanPath Resources Corp. 11/12/2008

BOULDER CREEK MINES LTD. (AB)
Struck off register for failure to file annual returns 04/00/1978

BOULDER ENERGY LTD (AB)
Acquired by ARC Energy Fund 8 on 04/15/2016
Each share Common no par exchanged for $2.59 cash
Note: Unexchanged certificates will be cancelled and become without value 04/15/2019

BOULDER GOLD MINES LTD. (ON)
Charter cancelled and company declared dissolved for default in filing returns 04/14/1966

BOULDER GROUP NL (AUSTRALIA)
Name changed 11/22/1994
Name changed from Boulder Gold N.L. to Boulder Group N.L. 11/22/1994
Name changed to Boulder Steel Ltd. 01/21/2000
(See Boulder Steel Ltd.)

BOULDER GROWTH & INCOME FD INC (MD)
Auction Market Preferred Ser. M28 1¢ par called for redemption at $25,000 on 04/23/2013
(Additional Information in Active)

BOULDER HILL MINES LTD. (ON)
Acquired by Boulder Gold Mines Ltd. on a (1) for (3) basis 00/00/1948
(See Boulder Gold Mines Ltd.)

BOULDER MNG CORP (ON)
Reincorporated under the laws of British Columbia as Opal Energy Corp. 01/09/2007
Opal Energy Corp. name changed to Versus Systems Inc. 07/13/2016

BOULDER MTN RES LTD (BC)
Recapitalized as Consolidated Boulder Mountain Resources Ltd. 11/05/1987
Each share Common no par exchanged for (0.2) share Common no par
Consolidated Boulder Mountain Resources Ltd. merged into Rich Coast Resources Ltd. (BC) 01/25/1993 which reincorporated in Delaware as Rich Coast Inc. 09/16/1996 which reincorporated in Nevada 07/14/1998 which recapitalized as Media Pal Holdings, Corp. 03/16/2010

BOULDER SPECIALTY BRANDS INC (DE)
Name changed to Smart Balance, Inc. 05/21/2007
Smart Balance, Inc. name changed to Boulder Brands, Inc. 01/02/2013
(See Boulder Brands, Inc.)

BOULDER STL LTD (AUSTRALIA)
Each Sponsored ADR for Ordinary received distribution of $0.0651 cash payable 04/16/2002 to holders of record 04/02/2002
ADR agreement terminated 09/19/2014
Each Sponsored ADR for Ordinary exchanged for $0.002192 cash

BOULDER TOTAL RETURN FD INC (MD)
Money Market Preferred called for redemption at $100,000 on 08/15/2000
Taxable Auction Market Preferred 1¢ par called for redemption at $100,000 on 04/10/2013
Merged into Boulder Growth & Income Fund, Inc. 03/20/2015
Each share Common 1¢ par exchanged for (3.121182) shares Common 1¢ par

BOULDER TUNGSTEN PRODUCTION CO. (CO)
Charter suspended for failure to file annual reports 10/09/1923

BOULEVARD ACQUISITION CORP (DE)
Name changed to AgroFresh Solutions, Inc. 08/03/2015

BOULEVARD ACQUISITION CORP II (DE)
Units separated 12/22/2017
Merged into Estre Ambiental, Inc. 12/22/2017
Each share Class A Common $0.0001 par exchanged for (1) share Ordinary $0.0001 par

BOULEVARD BANCORP INC (DE)
Common $1 par changed to 4¢ par and (24) additional shares issued 08/05/1986
Merged into First Bank System, Inc. 03/25/1994
Each share Common 4¢ par exchanged for (0.8132) share Common $1.25 par
First Bank System, Inc. name changed to U.S. Bancorp 08/01/1997

BOULEVARD BANK (SEPULVEDA, CA)
Liquidation completed
Each share Capital Stock $15 par exchanged for initial distribution of $24.25 cash 07/26/1967
Each share Capital Stock $15 par received second and final distribution of $0.2264 cash 11/01/1967

BOULEVARD CAP LTD (BC)
Name changed to Urban Communications Inc. 06/28/2001
(See Urban Communications Inc.)

BOULEVARD INDL REAL ESTATE INVT TR (ON)
Plan of arrangement effective 10/02/2015
Each Trust Unit exchanged for (0.04651) PRO Real Estate Investment Trust, Trust Unit
Note: Unexchanged Units will be cancelled and become without value 10/02/2021

BOUNCEBACKTECHNOLOGIES COM INC (MN)
Reincorporated under the laws of Delaware as Name Dynamics, Inc. 11/05/2010
Name Dynamics, Inc. name changed to UBL Interactive, Inc. 07/03/2012

BOUND BROOK WTR CO (NJ)
Each share Capital Stock $10 par exchanged for (1) share Capital Stock $5 par and $5 of Debentures 00/00/1938

Merged into Elizabethtown Water Co. 01/01/1977
Each share Capital Stock $5 par exchanged for (1) share Common no par
Elizabethtown Water Co. reorganized as E'town Corp. 09/01/1985
(See E'town Corp.)

BOUNDARIES CAP INC (NV)
Name changed to Golden Patriot Corp. and (5) additional shares issued 09/29/2003
(See Golden Patriot Corp.)

BOUNDARY BAY RES INC (NV)
Recapitalized as Wave Technology Group Inc. 05/06/2010
Each share Common $0.001 par exchanged for (0.001) share Common $0.001 par
Wave Technology Group Inc. name changed to eMamba International Corp. 07/27/2011

BOUNDARY CREEK RES LTD (AB)
Acquired by Bow Valley Energy Ltd. 08/30/2002
Each share Common no par exchanged for either (1.5) shares Common no par or $2.40 cash
Note: Option to receive cash expired 09/23/2002
(See Bow Valley Energy Ltd.)

BOUNDARY EXPL LTD (BC)
Recapitalized as Consolidated Boundary Exploration Ltd. 08/22/1974
Each share Capital Stock no par exchanged for (0.33333333) share Capital Stock no par
Consolidated Boundary Exploration Ltd. recapitalized as Boundary Gold Corp. 03/07/1989
(See Boundary Gold Corp.)

BOUNDARY GOLD CORP (BC)
Struck off register and declared dissolved for failure to file returns 03/25/1994

BOUNDLESS CORP (DE)
Each share old Common 1¢ par exchanged for (0.1) share new Common 1¢ par 03/26/1998
Plan of reorganization under Chapter 11 Federal Bankruptcy Code effective 06/09/2006
No stockholders' equity

BOUNDLESS MTR SPORTS RACING INC (CO)
Reincorporated under the laws of Delaware as Dirt Motor Sports, Inc. 07/08/2005
Dirt Motor Sports, Inc. name changed to World Racing Group, Inc. 01/31/2008

BOUNTY EXPL LTD (ON)
Capital Stock $1 par changed to no par 12/16/1971
Name changed to Gulfstream Resources Canada Ltd. 02/01/1974
(See Gulfstream Resources Canada Ltd.)

BOUNTY GROUP INC (DE)
Each share old Common 1¢ par exchanged for (0.1) share new Common 10¢ par 10/30/1992
Each share new Common 10¢ par exchanged for (0.00001) share Common no par 12/27/1995
Note: In effect holders received $0.60 cash per share and public interest was eliminated

BOUNTY RES INC (BC)
Recapitalized as Starlight Energy Corp. 06/15/1982
Each share Common no par exchanged for (0.33333333) share Common no par
Starlight Energy Corp. recapitalized as Hansa International Resources Ltd. 07/23/1990
(See Hansa International Resources Ltd.)

BOUNTY VENTURES INC (UT)
Involuntarily dissolved 07/01/1987

BOURBEAU LAKE GOLD MINES LTD.
Succeeded by Bourbeau Lake Mines Ltd. on a (35) for (1) basis in 1938
(See Bourbeau Lake Mines Ltd.)

BOURBEAU LAKE MINES LTD (QC)
Charter annulled for failure to file annual reports 10/09/1982

BOURBON BANCSHARES INC (KY)
Name changed to Kentucky Bancshares, Inc. 07/15/2003

BOURBON BROS HLDG CORP (CO)
Name changed to Southern Concepts Restaurant Group, Inc. 03/13/2015

BOURBON MINES, LTD. (ON)
Charter revoked for failure to file reports and pay taxes 00/00/1956

BOURBON MINING CO. LTD. (QC)
Charter annulled for failure to file annual reports 11/18/1978

BOURBON OIL & DEVELOPMENT CO. (DE)
Charter cancelled for non-payment of taxes 00/00/1922

BOURBON STK YDS CO (KY)
Common $100 par changed to no par 00/00/1940
Merged into Lincoln International Corp. 07/31/1978
Each share Common no par exchanged for approximately $40 cash

BOURBON STR ORIGS INC (DE)
Adjudicated bankrupt 03/08/1973
No stockholders' equity

BOURJOIS INC (NY)
Common no par changed to $1 par 00/00/1950
Merged into Chanel, Inc. 06/07/1974
Each share Common $1 par exchanged for $1.65 cash

BOURLAMAQUE GOLD MINES, LTD.
Out of business 00/00/1942
Details not available

BOURNE-FULLER CO.
Merged into Republic Steel Corp. 00/00/1930
Details not available

BOURNS INC (CA)
Capital Stock 50¢ par reclassified as Common 50¢ par 05/01/1968
Stock Dividends - 50% 12/22/1961; 100% 06/01/1963
Each (23,761.44) shares Common 50¢ par exchanged for (1) share Common no par 05/31/1978
Note: In effect holders received $28.75 cash per share and public interest was eliminated

BOURSE DE MONTREAL INC (QC)
Merged into TSX Group Inc. 05/01/2008
Each share Common no par exchanged for (0.454) share Common no par and $16.26 cash
TSX Group Inc. name changed to TMX Group Inc. 06/18/2008 which merged into TMX Group Ltd. 09/14/2012

BOUSCADILLAC GOLD MINES, LTD. (ON)
Merged into Cadamet Mines Ltd. 11/17/1958
Each share Capital Stock exchanged for (0.25) share Capital Stock $1 par
Cadamet Mines Ltd. recapitalized as Terrex Mining Co. Ltd. 09/08/1966
(See Terrex Mining Co. Ltd.)

BOUTARI JOHN & SONS WINES & SPIRITS S A (GREECE)
ADR agreement terminated 12/19/2008
No ADR's remain outstanding

BOUTON CORP (DE)
Reincorporated 06/29/1992
Common 50¢ par changed to no par 01/00/1989
State of incorporation changed from (PA) to (DE) and Common no par changed to $0.001 par 06/29/1992
Each share Common $0.001 par exchanged for (0.00002) share Common $50 par 05/09/1996
Note: In effect holders received $0.12 cash per share and public interest was eliminated

BOUYGUES OFFSHORE S A (FRANCE)
Acquired by Saipem S.p.A. 11/26/2002
Each Sponsored ADR for Ordinary exchanged for $30.1702 cash

BOUZAN MINES LTD. (ON)
Name changed 00/00/1955
Name changed from Bouzan Gold Mines Ltd. to Bouzan Mines Ltd. 00/00/1955
Merged into Kerr Addison Mines Ltd. 11/18/1963
Each share Capital Stock exchanged for (0.1) share Capital Stock no par
Kerr Addison Mines Ltd. merged into Noranda Inc. 04/11/1996 which name changed to Falconbridge Ltd. (New) 2005 on 07/01/2005
(See Falconbridge Ltd. (New) 2005)

BOVAR INC (AB)
Common no par reclassified as Class A Common no par 11/20/1998
Each share Class A Common no par exchanged for (0.2) share Common no par 07/03/2002
Name changed to Orbus Pharma Inc. 05/23/2003

BOVERAN DIAGNOSTICS INC (NV)
Name changed to Thrive World Wide, Inc. 09/28/2009

BOVILLE RES LTD (BC)
Name changed to Torhsen Energy Corp. 02/29/1984
Torhsen Energy Corp. name changed to Niagara Capital Corp. 02/23/1987
(See Niagara Capital Corp.)

BOVIS LTD (ON)
Under plan of merger each Capital Stock no par received $0.75 cash 06/15/1979
Note: Certificates were not required to be surrendered and are without value

BOW-BILT BONDHOLDERS CORP.
Dissolved 00/00/1945
Details not available

BOW ENERGY LTD (AB)
Merged into Petrolia Energy Corp. 03/07/2018
Each share Common no par exchanged for (1.15) shares Common $0.001 par
Note: Unexchanged certificates will be cancelled and become without value 03/06/2021

BOW-FLEX INC (WA)
Name changed to Direct Focus, Inc. 06/17/1999
Direct Focus, Inc. name changed to Nautilus Group, Inc. 05/21/2002 which name changed to Nautilus, Inc. 03/14/2005

BOW KNOT URANIUM CORP. (UT)
Merged into Sun Uranium Mining Co. on a (1) for (14.5) basis 12/15/1954
Sun Uranium Mining Co. name changed to Sun Tide Corp. 07/22/1955 which name changed to Maxa Corp. 04/13/1974
(See Maxa Corp.)

BOW RIV RES LTD (BC)
Recapitalized as Suneva Resources Ltd. 04/06/1979
Each share Common no par exchanged for (0.33333333) share Common no par
Suneva Resources Ltd. recapitalized as International Suneva Resources Ltd. 01/20/1989 which recapitalized as Nevsun Resources Ltd. 12/19/1991

BOW RIVER EXPLORATION LTD. (AB)
Delisted from Alberta Stock Exchange 04/28/1992

BOW VY BREWING LTD (AB)
Acquired by Peak Brewing Group Inc. 10/06/1999
Each share Common no par exchanged for (0.1656) share Common no par
(See Peak Brewing Group Inc.)

BOW VY ENERGY INC (AB)
Name changed 06/07/1993
Each share Common no par exchanged for (4) shares Common no par 03/01/1963
Common no par split (2) for (1) by issuance of (1) additional share 11/25/1967
Each share old 5.5% Preferred Ser. A $20 par exchanged for (1) share new 5.5% Preferred Ser. A $20 par 04/30/1971
Common no par split (2) for (1) by issuance of (1) additional share 11/13/1978
5% 2nd Preference $100 par called for redemption 04/14/1980
5.5% Preferred Ser. A $20 par called for redemption 04/15/1980
Common no par split (3) for (1) by issuance of (2) additional shares 06/23/1980
7% Conv. Class B Preferred $60 par called for redemption 06/30/1983
Each share U.S. $2 Conv. Class D Preferred Ser. 2 no par exchanged for (1.47) shares Common no par 11/30/1989
Each share $2.05 Conv. Class D Preferred Ser. 1 no par exchanged for (1.2) shares Common no par 11/30/1989
$1.875 Conv. Class D Preferred Ser. 4 no par called for redemption 12/05/1991
$2.025 Conv. Preferred Class D Ser. 3 no par called for redemption 05/27/1993
Name changed from Bow Valley Industries Ltd. to Bow Valley Energy Inc. 06/07/1993
Acquired by Talisman Energy Inc. 08/11/1994
Each share Class Z Preferred Ser. 5 no par exchanged for (0.58721) share Common no par
Each share $0.56 Class Z Preferred Ser. 4 no par exchanged for (0.58721) share Common no par
Each share Common no par exchanged for (0.54982) share Common no par
$2 Conv. Preferred Class D Ser. 2 no par called for redemption 09/15/1994
$2.05 Conv. Preferred Class D Ser. 1 no par called for redemption 09/15/1994
(See Talisman Energy Inc.)

BOW VY ENERGY LTD (AB)
Acquired by Dana Petroleum PLC 04/30/2009
Each share Common no par exchanged for $0.50 cash

BOW VY FST PRODS LTD (AB)
Name changed to Flowing Energy Corp. 07/21/1998
Flowing Energy Corp. merged into Daylight Energy Trust 04/05/2000
(See Daylight Energy Trust)

BOW VY RES SVCS LTD (AB)
Reorganized as Bovar Inc. 06/09/1989

Each share $2.125 Conv. Class B Preferred Ser. 1 no par exchanged for (2.1675) shares Common no par
Each share Common no par exchanged for (0.1) share Common no par
Bovar Inc. name changed to Orbus Pharma Inc. 05/23/2003

BOWATER CDA INC (CANADA)
Recapitalized as AbitibiBowater Canada Inc. 10/29/2007
Each Exchangeable Share no par exchanged for (0.52) Exchangeable Share no par
(See AbitibiBowater Canada Inc.)

BOWATER INC (DE)
7% Depositary Preferred called for redemption at (0.82) share Common $1 par 01/09/1997
Adjustable Rate Libor Preferred Ser. A $1 par called for redemption 05/12/1997
8.4% Depositary Preferred Ser. C called for redemption 02/08/1999
Merged into AbitibiBowater Inc. 10/29/2007
Each share Common $1 par exchanged for (0.52) share Common $1 par
(See AbitibiBowater Inc.)

BOWATER INDS PLC (ENGLAND)
Name changed 05/01/1972
Demerged 07/23/1984
Stock Dividends - Ordinary - 25% 05/21/1951; 33% 01/28/1952; 33% 07/26/1954; 100% 12/16/1965; 20% 06/30/1960
Stock Dividend - ADR's - 20% 06/17/1960
Name changed from Bowater Paper Corp. Ltd. to Bowater Corp. Ltd. 05/01/1972
Canadian Registry closed 08/00/1978
Plan of demerger effective 07/23/1984
Each Bowater Corp. Ltd. ADR for Ordinary Reg. £1 par exchanged for (0.5) Bowater Industries PLC ADR for Ordinary Reg. £1 par
Note: Distribution of (0.121388) share Bowater Inc. Common $1 par per ADR was made 08/31/1984
Name changed to Bowater PLC 05/11/1990
Bowater PLC name changed to Rexam PLC 06/01/1995

BOWATER MERSEY PAPER LTD (NS)
5.5% Preferred $50 par called for redemption 10/01/1980
Public interest eliminated

BOWATER PLC NEW (ENGLAND)
Name changed to Rexam PLC 06/01/1995

BOWATER'S NEWFOUNDLAND PULP & PAPER MILLS, LTD. (NL)
Name changed to Bowaters Newfoundland Ltd. 09/19/1968

BOWATERS MERSEY PAPER LTD (NS)
Name changed to Bowater Mersey Paper Co. Ltd. 03/01/1976
(See Bowater Mersey Paper Co. Ltd.)

BOWDOIN GAS CO. (MT)
Involuntarily dissolved for failure to file reports 05/22/1971

BOWDOIN SQUARE GARAGE, INC. (MA)
Liquidated 04/01/1966
Details not available

BOWEN INVT CO (NC)
Completely liquidated 06/08/1979
Each share Common $1 par exchanged for first and final distribution of (0.99968377) share Fidelity Municipal Bond Fund, Inc. (MD) Capital Stock 1¢ par
Note: Unexchanged certificates will be sold and proceeds held by the Treasurer of North Carolina for claim after 09/07/1979

Fidelity Municipal Bond Fund, Inc. (MD) reorganized in Massachusetts as Fidelity Municipal Bond Fund 08/01/1984

BOWEN-ROGERS MANUFACTURING CO. (MO)
Charter forfeited for failure to file reports 01/01/1933

BOWER INDS INC (AZ)
Class A Common $1 par changed to 10¢ par 07/18/1980
Name changed to Metalclad Corp. (AZ) 05/29/1987
Metalclad Corp. (AZ) reincorporated in Delaware 11/24/1993 which name changed to Entrx Corp. 06/24/2002 which name changed to Entrprize Corp. (DE) 06/04/2012 which reincorporated in Indiana as Tprize, Inc. 08/18/2016

BOWER ROLLER BEARING CO. (MI)
Common $10 par changed to no par 00/00/1928
Common no par changed to $5 par 00/00/1933
Stock Dividends - 100% 11/01/1946; 100% 08/15/1950
Merged into Federal-Mogul-Bower Bearings, Inc. on a (10) for (9) basis 07/29/1955
Federal-Mogul-Bower Bearings, Inc. name changed to Federal-Mogul Corp. (MI) 04/30/1965
(See Federal-Mogul Corp. (MI))

BOWERS BATTERY & SPARK PLUG CO. (PA)
Name changed to General Battery & Ceramic Corp. (PA) 11/10/1960
General Battery & Ceramic Corp. (PA) reincorporated in New York 12/29/1961 which name changed to General Battery Corp. 10/03/1969
(See General Battery Corp.)

BOWES LTD (CANADA)
Name changed 00/00/1953
Name changed from Bowes (1950) Ltd. to Bowes Ltd. 00/00/1953
Common no par split (5) for (1) by issuance of (4) additional shares 05/21/1965
Preferred $1 par called for redemption 03/23/1967
Acquired by Weston (George) Ltd. 10/31/1972
Each share Common exchanged for $27.50 cash

BOWES LYON RES LTD (BC)
Struck off register and declared dissolved for failure to file returns 07/24/1992

BOWEY'S, INC. (DE)
Under plan of merger name changed to Capitol Food Industries, Inc. 10/22/1963
(See Capitol Food Industries, Inc.)

BOWFUND CORP (IL)
Merged into Baldwin (D.H.) Co. (OH) 12/31/1969
Each share Common $50 par exchanged for initial distribution of (0.449) share 5% Conv. Preferred Ser. A $108 par and (0.436) share 8% Conv. Preferred Ser. B $100 par
Each share Common $50 par received second and final distribution of (0.019137) share 8% Conv. Preferred Ser. B $100 par 08/12/1972
(See Baldwin (D.H.) Co. (OH))

BOWIE YELLOWKNIFE MINES, LTD. (ON)
Charter revoked for failure to file reports and pay taxes 00/00/1955

BOWL MOR INC (DE)
Adjudicated bankrupt 02/15/1967
No stockholders' equity

BOWLES FLUIDICS CORP (MD)
Each share old Common 10¢ par

exchanged for (0.001) share new Common 10¢ par 04/14/1999
Acquired by Morgenthaler Private Equity 12/31/2014
Each share new Common 10¢ par exchanged for $6,697.09 cash
Note: Each share new Common 10¢ par received an initial additional distribution of $69.0926 cash from escrow 08/13/2015
Each share new Common 10¢ par received a second additional distribution of $10.8349 cash from escrow 12/17/2015
Each share new Common 10¢ par received a third and final additional distribution of $414.48641 cash from escrow 07/19/2016

BOWLIN OUTDOOR ADVERTISING & TRAVEL CTRS INC (NV)
Each share Common $0.001 par received distribution of (1) share Bowlin Travel Centers Inc. Common $0.001 par payable 01/30/2001 to holders of record 01/20/2001
Merged into Lamar Advertising Co. (Old) 02/01/2001
Each share Common $0.001 par exchanged for (0.15818) share Class A Common $0.001 par Lamar Advertising Co. (Old) merged into Lamar Advertising Co. (New) 11/19/2014

BOWLINE CORP (NY)
Merged into Arrowhead Holdings Corp. 05/31/1996
Each share Common 2¢ par exchanged for $1.32 cash

BOWLING & CONSTRUCTION CORP. (DE)
Acquired by Haven Industries, Inc. 05/28/1962
Each share Class A Common $1 par exchanged for (5.5) shares Common 10¢ par
Haven Industries, Inc. name changed to Federated Communications Corp. 04/29/1975
(See Federated Communications Corp.)

BOWLING CORP AMER (NY)
Each share Common par exchanged for (0.25) share Common 40¢ par 04/01/1964
Name changed to Charan Industries, Inc. 12/24/1969
(See Charan Industries, Inc.)

BOWLING CORRAL LTD. (SK)
Struck off register for failure to file reports and pay taxes 10/18/1968

BOWLING GREEN FUND, INC. (DE)
Name changed to Winfield Growth Industries Fund, Inc. 12/30/1957
Winfield Growth Industries Fund, Inc. name changed to Winfield Growth Fund, Inc. 09/21/1966 which name changed to Research Equity Fund, Inc. (DE) 01/26/1973 which reincorporated in Maryland 09/09/1973 which reincorporated in California as Franklin Equity Fund 10/10/1984

BOWLING INVESTMENTS, INC. (CO)
Name changed to Bartep Industries, Inc. 05/06/1968
Bartep Industries, Inc. recapitalized as Douglas Pharmacal Industries, Inc. 12/15/1969 which name changed to Douglas Industries, Inc. 08/18/1976
(See Douglas Industries, Inc.)

BOWMAN-BILTMORE HOTELS CORP.
Reorganized as Commodore Hotel Inc. 00/00/1946
Each share 1st Preferred exchanged for (6) shares Common $1 par
Each shares 2nd Preferred exchanged for (0.28571428) share Common $1 par
Each share Common exchanged for

(0.14285714) share new Common $1 par
(See Commodore Hotel, Inc.)

BOWMAN DAIRY CO. (IL)
Name changed to Bowfund Corp. 01/20/1966
Bowfund Corp. merged into Baldwin (D.H.) Co. (OH) 12/31/1969
(See Baldwin (D.H.) Co. (OH))

BOWMAN GUM, INC.
Name changed to Haelan Laboratories, Inc. 00/00/1952
Haelan Laboratories, Inc. recapitalized as Connelly Containers, Inc. 04/29/1955
(See Connelly Containers, Inc.)

BOWMAN INDUSTRIES, INC. (AR)
Charter revoked for failure to pay taxes 02/20/1961

BOWMAN LEISURE INDS CORP (NJ)
Merged into Habanero Corp. 09/19/1972
Each share Common no par exchanged for (2.5) shares Common 1¢ par
Habanero Corp. name changed to Terra Linda Corp. 06/10/1988
(See Terra Linda Corp.)

BOWMAN PRODUCTS CO. (OH)
Name changed to B.P.C. Liquidating Co. 12/15/1964
(See B.P.C. Liquidating Co.)

BOWMAR INSTR CORP (IN)
Common no par split (2) for (1) by issuance of (1) additional share 01/10/1961
Common no par split (2) for (1) by issuance of (1) additional share 09/29/1972
Merged into White Electronic Designs Corp. 10/23/1998
Each share $3 Conv. Preferred no par exchanged for (1) share $3 Conv. Sr. Preferred no par
Each share Common no par exchanged for (1.275) shares Common no par
(See White Electronic Designs Corp.)

BOWMORE EXPL LTD (AB)
Recapitalized as Osisko Metals Inc. 06/26/2017
Each share Common no par exchanged for (0.33333333) share Common no par

BOWNE & CO INC (DE)
Common $1 par split (2) for (1) by issuance of (1) additional share 08/20/1980
Common $1 par split (2) for (1) by issuance of (1) additional share 06/10/1981
Common $1 par split (2) for (1) by issuance of (1) additional share 05/10/1987
Common $1 par changed to 1¢ par 03/16/1988
State of incorporation changed from (NY) to (DE) 07/06/1998
Common 1¢ par split (2) for (1) by issuance of (1) additional share payable 08/26/1998 to holders of record 08/14/1998 Ex date - 08/27/1998
Acquired by Donnelley (R.R.) & Sons Co. 11/24/2010
Each share Common 1¢ par exchanged for $11.50 cash

BOWOOD ENERGY INC (CANADA)
Recapitalized as LGX Oil + Gas Inc. (Canada) 08/22/2012
Each share Common no par exchanged for (0.05) share Common no par
LGX Oil + Gas Inc. (Canada) reincorporated in Alberta 06/27/2013

BOWRAM ENERGY INC (BC)
Merged into Terrace Resources Inc. (New) 06/02/2009
Each share Common no par

exchanged for (0.528426) share Common no par
Terrace Resources Inc. (New) name changed to Terrace Energy Corp. 06/24/2011

BOWRIDGE RES GROUP INC (AB)
Acquired by ESI Energy Serivces Inc. 11/19/2001
Each share Common no par exchanged for $1.15 cash

BOWSER (S.F.) & CO., INC. (IN)
Name changed to Bowser, Inc. (IN) 00/00/1943
Bowser, Inc. (IN) reincorporated in Delaware as Bowser Delaware Corp. 11/17/1969
(See Bowser Delaware Corp.)

BOWSER DELAWARE CORP. (DE)
Completely liquidated 07/02/1970
Each share Common $1 par and Class B Common $1 par exchanged for first and final distribution of $18.60 cash

BOWSER INC (IN)
$1.20 Preferred $25 par reclassified as $1.61 Preferred $28 par and (0.75) share Class B Common $1 par issued for each share of $1.20 Preferred held 12/01/1962
Recapitalized 12/28/1968
Each share $1.61 Preferred $28 par exchanged for $28 principal amount of 6% Subord. Notes due 07/01/1988
Reincorporated under the laws of Delaware as Bowser Delaware Corp. 11/17/1969
(See Bowser Delaware Corp.)

BOWSINQUE MINES LTD. (ON)
Charter cancelled 00/00/1959

BOWTEX ENERGY CDA CORP (AB)
Name changed to Luscar Oil & Gas Ltd. 10/21/1993
Luscar Oil & Gas Ltd. merged into Encal Energy Ltd. 07/13/1994 which merged into Calpine Canada Holdings Ltd. 04/19/2001 which was exchanged for Calpine Corp. 05/27/2002
(See Calpine Corp.)

BOWTHORPE PLC (UNITED KINGDOM)
Sponsored ADR's for Ordinary split (3) for (1) by issuance of (2) additional ADR's payable 05/16/2000 to holders of record 05/12/2000 Ex date - 05/15/2000
Name changed to Spirent PLC 05/12/2000
Spirent PLC name changed to Spirent Communications PLC 05/08/2006

BOX ELDER COUNTY BANK (BRIGHAM CITY, UT)
Merged into First Interstate Bank of Utah, N.A. (Salt Lake City, UT) 11/01/1982
Each share Capital Stock $10 par exchanged for $97.50 cash

BOX ENERGY CORP (DE)
Name changed to Remington Oil & Gas Corp. 12/05/1997
Remington Oil & Gas Corp. merged into Helix Energy Solutions Group, Inc. 07/01/2006

BOX WORLDWIDE INC (FL)
Merged into TCI Music, Inc. 12/17/1997
Each share Common $0.001 par exchanged for (0.07) share Conv. Preferred Ser. A 1¢ par
TCI Music, Inc. name changed to Liberty Digital Inc. 09/10/1999 which merged into Liberty Media Corp. (New) 03/14/2002 which reorganized as Liberty Media Corp. (Incorporated 02/28/2006) 05/10/2006 which name changed to Liberty Interactive Corp. 09/26/2011 which name changed to Qurate Retail, Inc. 04/10/2018

BOXADA MINES LTD. (ON)
Acquired by Argyll Gold Mines Ltd. 00/00/1946
Each share Capital Stock exchanged for (0.16666666) share Capital Stock
(See Argyll Gold Mines Ltd.)

BOXHILL SYS CORP (NY)
Name changed to Dot Hill Systems Corp. (NY) 08/02/1999
Dot Hill Systems Corp. (NY) reincorporated in Delaware 09/19/2001
(See Dot Hill Systems Corp.)

BOXWOODS INC (DE)
Name changed to Duke Mining Co., Inc. 07/13/2009
Duke Mining Co., Inc. reorganized as KaChing KaChing, Inc. 06/07/2010 which name changed to KS International Holdings Corp. 12/02/2013

BOXXER GOLD CORP (AB)
Name changed to ExGen Resources Inc. 12/18/2014

BOYCON PERSHING GOLD MINES LTD.
Recapitalized as Keyboycon Mines Ltd. on a (1) for (4) basis 00/00/1950
Keyboycon Mines Ltd. recapitalized as Con-Key Mines Ltd. 08/16/1956 which merged into Can-Con Enterprises & Explorations Ltd. 11/30/1970 which name changed to Aubet Resources Inc. 09/08/1981 which recapitalized as Aubet Explorations Ltd. 09/30/1998 which name changed to Visa Gold Explorations Inc. 08/25/1999
(See Visa Gold Explorations Inc.)

BOYD BROS TRANSN INC (DE)
Acquired by BBT Acquisition Corp. 09/13/2004
Each share Common $0.001 par exchanged for $9.18 cash

BOYD ENERGY CORP (NV)
Recapitalized as Barnett Energy Corp. 08/02/2001
Each share Common $0.001 par exchanged for (0.08333333) share Common $0.001 par
Barnett Energy Corp. recapitalized as WorldWide Strategies Inc. 07/08/2005

BOYD GROUP INC (MB)
Reorganized as Boyd Group Income Fund 02/28/2003
Each share Class A Common no par exchanged for (0.1624) Trust Unit and (0.0876) share Boyd Group Holdings Inc. Class A Common no par
(See each company's listing)

BOYD KIRKLAND GOLD MINES LTD.
Recapitalized as Belrosa Mines Ltd. 00/00/1944
Each share Capital Stock exchanged for (0.16666666) share Capital Stock
(See Belrosa Mines Ltd.)

BOYD-WELSH, INC.
Name changed to Missouri Shoe Co. 12/04/1951
(See Missouri Shoe Co.)

BOYD-WELSH SHOE CO.
Name changed to Boyd-Welsh, Inc. 00/00/1934
Boyd-Welsh, Inc. name changed to Missouri Shoe Co. 12/04/1951
(See Missouri Shoe Co.)

BOYDS COLLECTION LTD NEW (MD)
Assets transferred to Enesco, LLC 12/16/2010
Details not available

BOYDS COLLECTION LTD OLD (MD)
Plan of reorganization under Chapter 11 Federal Bankruptcy Code effective 06/28/2006
Each share Common $0.0001 par held by holders of (201) or more shares received an undetermined amount of Boyd's Collection, Ltd. (New) Common $0.0001 par
Holders of (200) or fewer shares received approximately $0.15 cash per share
(See Boyd's Collection, Ltd. (New))
Note: Certificates were not required to be surrendered and are without value

BOYDS WHEELS INC (CA)
Plan of reorganization under Chapter 11 Federal Bankruptcy proceedings confirmed 11/13/1998
No stockholders' equity

BOYERTOWN BURIAL CASKET CO (PA)
Capital Stock no par changed to $10 par 00/00/1954
Name changed to TB Holding Co. 05/15/1987
(See TB Holding Co.)

BOYERTOWN PACKAGING SERVICE CORP. (PA)
Acquired by Marden Packaging Corp. 01/03/1979
Each share Capital Stock no par exchanged for $26.675 cash

BOYKIN LODGING CO (OH)
Merged into Braveheart II Realty Corp. 09/21/2006
Each Class A Depositary Share no par exchanged for $25 cash
Each share Common no par exchanged for $8.23 cash

BOYLE INTL INC (FL)
Proclaimed dissolved for failure to file reports and pay fees 09/21/2001

BOYLE ROYALTIES CO.
Dissolved 00/00/1950
Details not available

BOYLES BROS. DRILLING CO. LTD. (BC)
Acquired by Inspiration Ltd. 00/00/1966
Each (7) shares Class A no par exchanged for $25 principal amount of a 5% Note and (3) shares $1.50 Conv. Preferred $25 par
Each share Class B no par exchanged for $11 principal amount of a Non-Interest Bearing Note, (4) shares Common no par, and $1 cash
(See Inspiration Ltd.)

BOYLSTON MARKET ASSOCIATION (MA)
Liquidation completed 00/00/1959
Details not available

BOYMAR GOLD MINES LTD. (ON)
Recapitalized as Marboy Mines Ltd. 09/20/1960
Each share Capital Stock exchanged for (0.2) share Capital Stock
(See Marboy Mines Ltd.)

BOYNE PRODUCTS, INC. (MI)
Completely liquidated 11/03/1967
Each share Common $1 par exchanged for first and final distribution of (0.5) share Essex Wire Corp. Common $1 par
Essex Wire Corp. name changed to Essex International, Inc. 12/19/1968 which merged into United Aircraft Corp. 02/05/1974 which name changed to United Technologies Corp. 04/30/1975

BOYS MKTS INC (DE)
Merged into American Breco Corp. 04/04/1988
Each share Common 1¢ par exchanged for $12.50 cash

BOYSTOYS COM INC (DE)
Recapitalized as Environmental Credits, Ltd. (DE) 10/23/2008
Each share Common 1¢ par exchanged for (0.005) share Common 1¢ par
Environmental Credits, Ltd. (DE) reincorporated in Nevada as GlyEco, Inc. 11/23/2011

BP 150 INC (UT)
Name changed to American Restaurant Management, Inc. 06/26/1987
American Restaurant Management, Inc. recapitalized as Global Web, Inc. 03/12/1999

BP AMOCO P L C (ENGLAND)
Sponsored ADR's for Ordinary 25p par split (2) for (1) by issuance of (1) additional ADR payable 10/01/1999 to holders of record 10/01/1999 Ex date - 10/04/1999
Name changed to BP PLC 05/01/2001

BP CDA INC (CANADA)
Ctfs. dated prior to 02/28/1983
Reincorporated 10/18/1972
Name changed 4/27/73
Reincorporated 07/06/1979
Place of incorporation changed from (Canada) to (ON) 10/18/1972
Name changed from BP Canada Ltd. to BP Canada-BP Canada Ltee. 04/27/1973
Name and place of incorporation changed from BP Canada Ltd.-BP Canada Ltee. (ON) to BP Canada Inc. (Canada) 07/06/1979
5% Sinking Fund Preference $100 par called for redemption 03/26/1979
Under plan of reorganization each share Common no par exchanged for (3) shares Class A no par and (1) share Class B no par of BP Refining & Marketing Canada Ltd. and (1) share Common no par of BP Resources Canada Ltd. 02/28/1983
(See each company's listing)

BP CDA INC (CANADA)
Ctfs. dated after 05/29/1984
Common no par split (2) for (1) by issuance of (1) additional share 05/22/1987
Name changed to Talisman Energy Inc. 12/31/1992
(See Talisman Energy Inc.)

BP CANADA LTD. (CANADA)
Under plan of merger reincorporated under the laws of Ontario 10/18/1972
BP Canada Ltd. (ON) name changed to BP Canada Ltd.-BP Canada Ltee. 04/27/1973 which reincorporated in Canada as BP Canada Inc. 07/06/1979
(See BP Canada Inc.)

BP CANADA LTD. (ON)
Name changed to BP Canada Ltd.-BP Canada Ltee. (ON) 04/27/1973
BP Canada Ltd.-BP Canada Ltee. (ON) reincorporated in Canada as BP Canada Inc. 07/06/1979
(See BP Canada Inc.)

BP CANADA LTD.-BP CANADA LTEE. (ON)
5% Sinking Fund Preference $100 par called for redemption 03/26/1979
Reincorporated under the laws of Canada as BP Canada Inc. 07/06/1979
(See BP Canada Inc.)

BP INTL INC (DE)
SEC revoked common stock registration 07/06/2011

BP OIL & GAS LTD (AB)
Merged into BP Canada Ltd. (ON) 10/18/1972
Each share Capital Stock no par exchanged for (0.4) share Common no par
BP Canada Ltd. (ON) name changed to BP Canada Ltd.-BP Canada Ltee.

(ON) 04/27/1973 which reincorporated in Canada as BP Canada Inc. 07/06/1979
(See BP Canada Inc.)

BP REFNG & MARKETING CDA LTD (CANADA)
Class A no par called for redemption 05/06/1983
Name changed to Petro Canada Products Inc. 10/21/1983
(See Petro-Canada Products Inc.)

BP RESOURCES CANADA LTD. (CANADA)
Name changed to BP Canada Inc. 05/29/1984
BP Canada Inc. name changed to Talisman Energy Inc. 12/31/1992
(See Talisman Energy Inc.)

BPC HLDGS CORP (DE)
Merged into BPC Mergerco, Inc. 06/18/1996
Each share Class A Common $0.00005 par exchanged for $58.55 cash

BPI ENERGY HLDGS INC (BC)
Name changed 02/09/2006
Name changed from BPI Industries Inc. to BPI Energy Holdings, Inc. 02/09/2006
Plan of reorganization under Chapter 11 Federal Bankruptcy proceedings effective 08/18/2009
No stockholders' equity

BPI FINL CORP (CANADA)
Merged into C.I. Fund Management Inc. 08/25/1999
Each share Common no par exchanged for either (0.25) share Common no par or $5 cash
Note: Option to receive cash expired 09/20/1999
C.I. Fund Management Inc. name changed to CI Fund Management Inc. 11/04/2002 which name changed to CI Financial Inc. 12/06/2005 which reorganized as CI Financial Income Fund 06/30/2006 which reorganized as CI Financial Corp. 01/01/2009

BPI GLOBAL OPPORTUNITIES II FD (ON)
Name changed 11/05/1998
Name changed from BPI Canadian Opportunities II Fund to BPI Global Opportunities II Fund 11/05/1998
Name changed to CI Global Opportunities II Fund 04/27/2005
(See CI Global Opportunities II Fund)

BPI PKG TECHNOLOGIES INC (DE)
Name changed 02/26/1993
Name changed from BPI Environmental, Inc. to BPI Packaging Technologies, Inc. 02/26/1993
Chapter 7 bankruptcy proceedings terminated 10/06/2005
Stockholders' equity unlikely

BPI RES LTD (BC)
Name changed to Brent Resources Group Ltd. 03/22/1985
(See Brent Resources Group Ltd.)

BPI SYS INC (TX)
Stock Dividend - 100% 03/01/1983
Merged into Computer Associates International, Inc. 08/12/1987
Each share Common 1¢ par exchanged for $1.92 cash

BPK RES INC (NV)
Common $0.001 par split (2) for (1) by issuance of (1) additional share payable 12/31/2002 to holders of record 12/30/2002 Ex date - 01/02/2003
Recapitalized as iCarbon Corp. 07/25/2006
Each share Common $0.001 par exchanged for (0.16666666) share Common $0.001 par
(See iCarbon Corp.)

BPL COMMUNICATIONS LTD (INDIA)
Name changed 00/00/2001
Name changed from BPL Cellular Holdings Ltd. to BPL Communications Ltd. 00/00/2001
ADR agreement terminated 04/07/2003
Each 144A Sponsored ADR for Equity Shares exchanged for (1) Equity Share

BPO MGMT SVCS INC (DE)
Merged into BPO Management Services, Inc. (PA) 12/30/2008
Each share Common 1¢ par exchanged for (0.2467) share Common 10¢ par
(See BPO Management Services, Inc. (DE))

BPO MGMT SVCS INC (PA)
SEC revoked common stock registration 05/21/2012

BPO PPTYS LTD (CANADA)
Common no par split (3) for (1) by issuance of (2) additonal shares payable 12/28/2009 to holders of record 12/08/2009 Ex date - 12/04/2009
Under plan of reorganization each share Common no par automatically became (1) Brookfield Office Properties Canada Trust Unit no par 05/05/2010
Brookfield Office Properties Canada Trust name changed to Brookfield Canada Office Properties 02/29/2012
Merged into Brookfield Office Properties Inc. 04/29/2013
Each share Adjustable Rate Preferred Ser. G no par exchanged for (1) share Class AAA Preference Ser. V no par
Each share Floating Rate Preferred Ser. J no par exchanged for (1) share Class AAA Preference Ser. W no par
Each share Adjustable Rate Preferred Ser. K no par exchanged for (1) share Class AAA Preference Ser. X no par
Each share Adjustable Rate Preferred Ser. M no par exchanged for (1) share Class AAA Preference Ser. Y no par
Each share Perpetual Preferred Ser. N no par exchanged for (1) share Class AAA Preference Ser. Z no par
(See Brookfield Office Properties Inc.)

BPP LIQUIDATING TRUST (MD)
Liquidation completed
Each Unit of Bene. Int. received initial distribution of $0.50 cash payable 10/30/2002 to holders of record 06/27/2002
Each Unit of Bene. Int. received second distribution of $0.30 cash payable 08/15/2003 to holders of record 06/27/2002 Ex date - 08/18/2003
Each Unit of Bene Int. received third distribution of $0.10 cash payable 10/15/2003 to holders of record 06/27/2002 Ex date - 08/18/2003
Each Unit of Bene Int. received fourth distribution of $0.10 cash payable 12/15/2003 to holders of record 06/27/2002 Ex date - 12/24/2003
Each Unit of Bene. Int. received fifth distribution of $0.15 cash payable 03/31/2004 to holders of record 06/27/2002 Ex date - 04/01/2004
Each Unit of Bene Int. received sixth distribution of $0.05 cash payable 03/07/2005 to holders of record 06/27/2002 Ex date - 03/08/2005
Each Unit of Bene Int. received seventh distribution of $0.05 cash payable 08/31/2005 to holders of record 06/27/2002 Ex date - 09/01/2005
Each Unit of Bene. Int. received eighth and final distribution of $0.1667073 cash payable 12/29/2005 to holders of record 06/27/2002
Note: Certificates were not required to be surrendered and are without value
(See Burnham Pacific Properties, Inc. for previous distributions)

BPW ACQUISITION CORP (DE)
Merged into Talbots, Inc. 04/07/2010
Each share Common $0.0001 par exchanged for (0.9853) share Common 1¢ par
(See Talbots, Inc.)

BPZ ENERGY INC (CO)
Reincorporated under the laws of Texas as BPZ Resources, Inc. 10/17/2007
(See BPZ Resources, Inc.)

BPZ RES INC (TX)
Plan of reorganization under Chapter 11 Federal Bankruptcy proceedings effective 12/31/2015
No stockholders' equity

BQ METALS CORP (BC)
Name changed to BeMetals Corp. 04/18/2018

BR COMMUNICATIONS (CA)
Acquired by Technology for Communication International Inc. 02/05/1988
Each share Common no par exchanged for $7.75 cash

BR PPTYS S A (BRAZIL)
ADR agreement terminated 06/17/2015
Each Sponsored ADR for Ordinary exchanged for $3.367929 cash

BRABAR METALS & HLDGS LTD (ON)
Charter cancelled for failure to pay taxes and file returns 02/20/1980

BRABAR MINES LTD. (ON)
Name changed to Brabar Metals & Holdings Ltd. 12/20/1970
(See Brabar Metals & Holdings Ltd.)

BRABEIA INC (BC)
Name changed to Seahawk Ventures Inc. 03/01/2016

BRACE RES LTD (BC)
Recapitalized as International Brace Resources Inc. 05/11/1988
Each share Capital Stock no par exchanged for (0.5) share Capital Stock no par
International Brace Resources Inc. recapitalized as Prescott Resources Inc. (BC) 04/04/1997 which reincorporated in Yukon as Asia Sapphires Ltd. 06/29/1998
(See Asia Sapphires Ltd.)

BRACELL PETES LTD (AB)
Acquired by Murphy Oil Co. Ltd. 12/03/1973
Each share Common no par exchanged for $3 cash

BRACEMAC MINES LTD (ON)
Charter cancelled and declared dissolved for failure to file returns and pay fees 11/09/1976

BRACH (E.J.) & SONS (IL)
Common no par split (6) for (1) by issuance of (5) additional shares 12/12/1960
Common no par split (2) for (1) by issuance of (1) additional share 03/15/1962
Merged into American Home Products Corp. 05/20/1966
Each share Common no par exchanged for (0.4) share $2 Conv. Preferred $2.50 par and (0.4) share Common $1 par
American Home Products Corp. name changed to Wyeth 03/11/2002 which was acquired by Pfizer Inc. 10/15/2009

BRACKEN EDDIE VENTURES FLA INC (DE)
Charter forfeited for failure to maintain a registered agent 05/02/1972

BRACKEN EXPLORATION CO. LIQUIDATING TRUST (DE)
In process of liquidation
Each Share of Bene. Int. 1¢ par received initial distribution of $0.20 cash 01/15/1991
Each Share of Bene. Int. 1¢ par received second and final distribution of approximately $0.07 cash 03/00/1995
(See Bracken Exploration Co. for previous distributions)

BRACKEN EXPL CO (DE)
In process of liquidation
Each share Common 1¢ par received initial distribution of $3 cash 05/30/1986
Each share Common 1¢ par received second distribution of $0.75 cash 12/16/1986
Each share Common 1¢ par received third distribution of $0.25 cash 05/08/1987
Assets transferred to Bracken Exploration Co. Liquidating Trust and Common 1¢ par reclassified as Shares of Bene. Int. 1¢ par 05/11/1987
(See Bracken Exploration Co. Liquidating Trust)

BRACKEN MINES LTD (SOUTH AFRICA)
Merged into Evander Gold Mines Ltd. 11/18/1996
Each ADR for Ordinary exchanged for (0.02564) ADR for Ordinary
Evander Gold Mines Ltd. merged into Harmony Gold Mining Co. Ltd. 08/28/1998

BRACKENRIDGE BREWING CO.
Bankrupt 00/00/1942
Details not available

BRACKNELL CORP. (ON)
Reincorporated 06/13/1989
Name and place of incorporation changed from Bracknell Resources Ltd. (AB) to Bracknell Corp. (ON) 06/13/1989
Lenders notified company of their intent to enforce their security interests and all officers and directors resigned 11/01/2001
No stockholders' equity

BRACO RES LTD (AB)
Recapitalized as Yogen Fruz World-Wide Inc. 09/08/1994
Each (13.9) shares Common no par exchanged for (1) share Common no par
Yogen Fruz World-Wide Inc. name changed to CoolBrands International Inc. (NS) 10/06/2000 which reincorporated in Canada 03/27/2006 which reorganized in Delaware as Swisher Hygiene Inc. 11/04/2010

BRAD FOOTE GEAR WKS INC (DE)
Acquired by Bucyrus-Erie Co. (Old) 05/19/1969
Each share Common 20¢ par exchanged for (1/3) share Common $5 par
Bucyrus-Erie Co. (Old) name changed to Becor Western Inc. 04/30/1985 which was acquired by B-E Holdings, Inc. 02/04/1988 which reorganized as Bucyrus-Erie Co. (New) 12/14/1994 which name changed to Bucyrus International Inc. (Old) 05/24/1996
(See Bucyrus International Inc. (Old))

BRADBURY INTL EQUITIES LTD (BC)
Recapitalized as Consolidated Bradbury International Equities Ltd. 10/05/1998
Each share Common no par

exchanged for (0.1) share Common no par
Consolidated Bradbury International Equities Ltd. recapitalized as Talus Ventures Corp. 04/17/2001 which name changed to SolutionInc Technologies Ltd. (BC) 06/26/2002 which reincorporated in Nova Scotia 02/24/2004

BRADDICK RES LTD (BC)
Recapitalized as Kingsman Resources Inc. 07/08/2002
Each share Common no par exchanged for (0.14285714) share Common no par
Kingsman Resources Inc. recapitalized as Contagious Gaming Inc. 09/23/2014

BRADDOCK, DUNN & MC DONALD, INC. (TX)
Merged into BDM Corp. 01/15/1975
Each share Common no par exchanged for (2) shares Common 10¢ par
BDM Corp. name changed to BDM International, Inc. (Old) 01/01/1980
(See BDM International, Inc. (Old))

BRADDOCK INVT CORP (DE)
Class B Common $1 par reclassified as Common $1 par 04/16/1970
Charter cancelled and declared inoperative and void for non-payment of taxes 03/01/1975

BRADEN-AERMOTOR CORP. (NY)
Name changed to Braden Industries, Inc. (NY) 12/13/1968
Braden Industries, Inc. (NY) reincorporated in Delaware 08/31/1973
(See Braden Industries, Inc. (DE))

BRADEN-BURRY EXPEDITING LTD (NT)
Merged into Stewart Holdings Ltd. 11/01/2004
Each share Common no par exchanged for $0.35 cash

BRADEN INDS INC (DE)
Reincorporated 08/31/1973
State of incorporation changed from (NY) to (DE) 08/31/1973
Stock Dividends - 20% 04/22/1974; 100% 06/30/1975
Liquidation completed
Each share Common $1 par exchanged for initial distribution of $7.52 cash 04/13/1977
Each share Common $1 par received second distribution of $0.40 cash 07/12/1979
Each share Common $1 par received third and final distribution of $0.66 cash 12/29/1980

BRADEN TECHNOLOGIES INC (NV)
Name changed to Lincoln Gold Corp. (NV) 03/26/2004
Lincoln Gold Corp. (NV) reincorporated in Canada 04/04/2008 which reincorporated in British Columbia 02/18/2009 which merged into Lincoln Mining Corp. 08/12/2009

BRADENS INC (DE)
Assets sold 00/00/1989
No stockholders' equity

BRADES RES CORP (BC)
Recapitalized as Canex Energy Corp. 05/12/2015
Each share Common no par exchanged for (0.33333333) share Common no par

BRADFORD & BINGLEY PLC (UNITED KINGDOM)
ADR agreement terminated 02/24/2010
No ADR's remain outstanding

BRADFORD AUDIO CORP. (NY)
Charter forfeited for failure to pay taxes and file reports 12/15/1966

BRADFORD COMPUTER & SYS INC (DE)
Common 10¢ par split (2) for (1) by issuance of (1) additional share 06/08/1970
Name changed to Bradford National Corp. 05/12/1976
Bradford National Corp. name changed to Fidata Corp. 03/06/1985 which merged into Advanced Medical Technologies, Inc. 03/27/1989 which name changed to Advanced Medical Inc. 09/07/1990 which name changed to ALARIS Medical, Inc. 04/30/1997 which name changed to ALARIS Medical Systems, Inc. 06/30/2003
(See ALARIS Medical Systems, Inc.)

BRADFORD CORP.
Assets sold 00/00/1935
No stockolders' equity

BRADFORD ELECTRIC LIGHT CO.
Merged into Central Vermont Public Service Corp. 00/00/1929
Details not available

BRADFORD INDUSTRIES, INC. (NJ)
Bankrupt 11/00/1962
No stockholders' equity

BRADFORD INDUSTRIES, INC. (NY)
Incorporated 03/05/1965
Charter cancelled and proclaimed dissolved for failure to pay taxes 03/26/1980

BRADFORD INDS INC (CA)
Charter revoked for failure to file reports and pay fees 06/01/1966

BRADFORD INDS INC (NY)
Incorporated 11/18/1987
Dissolved by proclamation 09/21/1992

BRADFORD NATIONAL BANK (BRADFORD, OH)
Merged into Miami Citizens National Bank & Trust Co. (Piqua, OH) 04/01/1968
Each share Capital Stock $10 par exchanged for (1.5) shares Common $10 par
Miami Citizens National Bank & Trust Co. (Piqua, OH) reorganized as Miami Citizens Bancorp 07/01/1984 which name changed to C&H Bancorp 12/31/1986 which was acquired by Fifth Third Bancorp 04/01/1988

BRADFORD NATL BK (BRADFORD, PA)
Each share Capital Stock $100 par exchanged for (8) shares Capital Stock $15 par 10/31/1958
Stock Dividend - 25% 01/29/1962
Merged into First Laurel Bank (St. Mary's, PA) 07/01/1972
Each share Capital Stock $15 par exchanged for (3.4) shares Capital Stock $5 par
First Laurel Bank (St. Mary's, PA) merged into Pennsylvania Bank & Trust Co. (Titusville, PA) 03/01/1975 which reorganized as Pennbancorp 12/31/1980 which merged into Integra Financial Corp. 01/26/1989 which merged into National City Corp. 05/03/1996 which was acquired by PNC Financial Services Group, Inc. 12/31/2008

BRADFORD NATL CORP (DE)
Name changed to Fidata Corp. 03/06/1985
Fidata Corp. merged into Advanced Medical Technologies, Inc. 03/27/1989 which name changed to Advanced Medical Inc. 09/07/1990 which name changed to ALARIS Medical, Inc. 04/30/1997 which name changed to ALARIS Medical Systems, Inc. 06/30/2003
(See ALARIS Medical Systems, Inc.)

BRADFORD OIL, GAS & DEVELOPMENT CO. (DE)
No longer in existence having become inoperative and void for non-payment of taxes 02/05/1908

BRADFORD OIL CO. (MA)
Dissolved 12/17/1958

BRADFORD OIL REFINING CO.
Sold 00/00/1941
No stockholders' equity

BRADFORD POOLS, INC. (NJ)
Name changed to Bradford Industries, Inc. (NJ) 06/13/1961
(See Bradford Industries, Inc. (NJ))

BRADFORD PRODUCING CO., INC.
Dissolved 00/00/1948
Details not available

BRADFORD SPEED PACKAGING & DEV CORP (DE)
Common $1 par changed to 50¢ par and (1) additional share issued 09/30/1969
Stock Dividend - 10% 07/29/1969
Under plan of merger name changed to International General Industries, Inc. 04/06/1971
International General Industries, Inc. merged into International Bank (Washington, DC) 12/31/1979 which merged into USLICO Corp. 12/31/1985 which merged into NWNL Companies, Inc. 01/17/1995 which name changed to ReliaStar Financial Corp. 02/13/1995
(See ReliaStar Financial Corp.)

BRADHILL MINES LTD. (ON)
Charter cancelled 04/01/1963

BRADIAN MINES LTD.
Merged into Bralorne Mines Ltd. 00/00/1935
Each share Capital Stock exchanged for (0.4) share Capital Stock no par
Bralorne Mines Ltd. name changed to Bralorne Pioneer Mines Ltd 03/19/1959 which name changed to Bralorne Can-Fer Resources Ltd. 12/03/1969 which name changed to Bralorne Resources Ltd. 05/29/1972 which recapitalized as BRL Enterprises Inc. 11/27/1990
(See BRL Enterprises Inc.)

BRADING BREWERIES, LTD.
Acquired by Brewing Corp. of Canada Ltd. 00/00/1930
Details not available

BRADLEE REAL ESTATE TRUST (MA)
Dissolved 00/00/1950
Details not available

BRADLEES INC (MA)
Plan of reorganization under Chapter 11 Federal Bankruptcy Code effective 02/02/1999
No old Common stockholders' equity
Plan of reorganization under Chapter 11 Federal Bankruptcy Code effective 12/28/2001
No new Common stockholders' equity

BRADLEY (WILLIAM) & SON
Dissolved 00/00/1942
Details not available

BRADLEY INDUSTRIES, INC. (IL)
Acquired by Richardson-Merrell Inc. 00/00/1965
Each share Common $1 par exchanged for $17.75 cash

BRADLEY KNITTING CO.
Liquidation completed 00/00/1942
Details not available

BRADLEY PHARMACEUTICALS INC (NJ)
Class A Common no par reclassified as Common no par 07/26/1999
Merged into Nycomed US Inc. 02/21/2008
Each share Common no par exchanged for $20 cash

BRADLEY REAL ESTATE INC (MD)
Merged into Heritage Property Investment Trust, Inc. 09/18/2000
Each share 8.4% Conv. Preferred Ser. A 1¢ par exchanged for $22.45814618 cash
Each share Common 1¢ par exchanged for $22 cash

BRADLEY REAL ESTATE TR (MA)
Trust Shares $1 par split (3) for (2) by issuance of (0.5) additional share 02/27/1987
Reorganized under the laws of Maryland as Bradley Real Estate, Inc. 10/17/1994
Each Share of Bene. Int. $1 par exchanged for (0.5) share Common 1¢ par
(See Bradley Real Estate, Inc.) merged 01/20/1961) (State Street

BRADLEY WASHFOUNTAIN CO (WI)
Name changed to Bradley Corp. 05/26/1972

BRADMAR PETE CORP (OK)
Merged into Alexander Energy Corp. 03/19/1992
Each share Common 10¢ par exchanged for (0.48) share Common 3¢ par and $2.57 cash
Alexander Energy Corp. merged into National Energy Group, Inc. 08/30/1996
(See National Energy Group, Inc.)

BRADMER PHARMACEUTICALS INC (ON)
Each share old Common no par exchanged for (0.055147) share new Common no par 02/16/2006
Reorganized under the laws of Cayman Islands as Galaxy Digital Holdings Ltd. 08/01/2018
Each share new Common no par exchanged for (0.00791264) share Ordinary CAD $0.001 par
Note: Unexchanged certificates will be cancelled and become without value 08/01/2024

BRADNER RES LTD (BC)
Recapitalized as Bradner Ventures Ltd. 12/14/1999
Each share Common no par exchanged for (0.14285714) share Common no par
Bradner Ventures Ltd. recapitalized as HIP Energy Corp. 11/19/2009
(See HIP Energy Corp.)

BRADNER VENTURES LTD (BC)
Each share old Common no par exchanged for (0.2) share new Common no par 04/20/2004
Recapitalized as HIP Energy Corp. 11/19/2009
Each share new Common no par exchanged for (0.2) share Common no par
(See HIP Energy Corp.)

BRADNOR MALARTIC MINES, LTD. (ON)
Charter revoked for failure to file reports and pay taxes 00/00/1958

BRADSHAW, INC. (CA)
Acquired by Speedee Mart, Inc. 09/10/1963
Each share 6% Preferred $25 par exchanged for (2.5) shares 6% Preferred $10 par
Each share Common $1 par exchanged for (0.6) share 6% Preferred $10 par
(See Speedee Mart, Inc.)

BRADSTONE EQUITY PARTNERS INC (AB)
Each share Common no par reclassified as (0.5) Multiple Share no par and (0.5) Subordinate Share no par 09/08/1997
Merged into Quest Investment Corp. 07/04/2002
Each Multiple Share no par exchanged for (1) Class B Multiple Share no par
Each Subordinate Share no par exchanged for (1) share Class A Subordinate no par

BRADSUE RES LTD (BC)
Quest Investment Corp. merged into Quest Capital Corp. (BC) 06/30/2003 which reincorporated in Canada 05/27/2008 which name changed to Sprott Resource Lending Corp. 09/10/2010 which merged into Sprott Inc. 07/24/2013

BRADSUE RES LTD (BC)
Name changed to E.T.C. Industries, Ltd. 08/27/1993
E.T.C. Industries, Ltd. recapitalized as Consolidated E.T.C. Industries Ltd. 01/28/2002 which name changed to Highbank Resources Ltd. 07/25/2003

BRADY CROSS LAKE SILVER MINES LTD (ON)
Charter cancelled and declared dissolved for failure to file returns and pay fees 07/27/1976

BRADY ENERGY CORP (DE)
Charter cancelled and declared inoperative and void for non-payment of taxes 03/01/1988

BRADY W H CO (WI)
Non-Vtg. Class A Common 1¢ par split (2) for (1) by issuance of (1) additional share 10/31/1986
Non-Vtg. Class A Common 1¢ par split (3) for (2) by issuance of (0.5) additional share 12/15/1995
Name changed to Brady Corp. 08/01/1998

BRAE-BREEST GOLD MINES LTD. (ON)
Name changed to Brae-Breest Uranium Mines & Metals Ltd. 00/00/1954
(See 'Brae-Breest Uranium Mines & Metals Ltd.)

BRAE-BREEST URANIUM MINES & METALS LTD. (ON)
Dissolved 12/01/1958
Details not available

BRAE CORP (DE)
Merged into Brae Acquisition Corp. 03/15/1990
Each share Common $1 par exchanged for $6.25 cash

BRAEBURN ALLOY STEEL CORP.
Assets sold 00/00/1944
Details not available

BRAEDEN VY MINES INC (NV)
Name changed to Zenosense, Inc. 11/26/2013

BRAEGAN ENERGY LTD (AB)
Acquired by Sunfire Energy Corp. 05/17/2000
Each share Common no par exchanged for $0.62 cash

BRAEMAR PETROLEUM LTD. (AB)
Struck off register for failure to file annual returns 05/13/1973

BRAEMAR SHIPPING SVCS PLC (UNITED KINGDOM)
ADR agreement terminated 06/14/2018
No ADR's remain outstanding

BRAEMOUNT RES LTD (BC)
Reincorporated 05/28/1993
Place of incorporation changed from (AB) to (BC) 05/28/1993
Recapitalized as Lumby Resources Corp. 07/28/1993
Each share Common no par exchanged for (0.5) share Common no par
Lumby Resources Corp. recapitalized as Rock Resources Inc. 10/01/1996 which recapitalized as Adroit Resources Inc. 02/10/2004 which recapitalized as iMetal Resources Inc. 11/09/2015

BRAEVAL MNG CORP (ON)
Recapitalized as Oban Mining Corp. 04/22/2014
Each share Common no par exchanged for (0.31847133) share Common no par
Oban Mining Corp. name changed to Osisko Mining Inc. 06/21/2016

BRAEWOOD DEV CORP (TX)
Merged into Lomas & Nettleton Financial Corp. 02/21/1984
Each share Common $1 par exchanged for $1.875 cash

BRAFOR CAP LTD (CANADA)
Name changed to Sonor Petroleum Corp. 03/28/1980
Sonor Petroleum Corp. name changed to Sonor Resources Corp. 04/17/1986 which name changed to Home Capital Group Inc. (Canada) 01/21/1987 which reincorporated in Ontario 07/18/1988

BRAGER EISENBERG INC (MD)
Liquidation completed
Each share Capital Stock $1 par received initial distribution of $125 cash 11/01/1978
Each share Capital Stock $1 par exchanged for second and final distribution of $8.7573 cash 09/18/1979

BRAHMA RES INC (BC)
Cease trade order effective 01/23/1991
Stockholders' equity unlikely

BRAIDEN RES LTD (BC)
Recapitalized as Pure Pioneer Ventures Ltd. 06/14/2002
Each share Common no par exchanged for (0.2) share Common no par

BRAIN TREE INTL INC (UT)
Each share old Common $0.001 par exchanged for (0.025) share new Common $0.001 par 01/13/2012
Reincorporated under the laws of Delaware as Trunity Holdings, Inc. and new Common $0.001 par changed to $0.0001 par 02/16/2012
Trunity Holdings, Inc. recapitalized as True Nature Holding, Inc. 01/20/2016

BRAINARD STEEL CORP.
Acquired by Sharon Steel Corp. 00/00/1946
Each (2.57) shares Common exchanged for (1) share new Common
(See Sharon Steel Corp.)

BRAINERD INTL INC (MN)
Each share Common no par exchanged for (0.1) share Common 1¢ par 10/09/1992
Merged into Colonel's International Inc. 12/31/1995
Each share Common 1¢ par exchanged for (1) share Common 10¢ par
Colonel's International Inc. name changed to Sports Resorts International Inc. 03/12/2001
(See Sports Resorts International Inc.)

BRAINHUNTER INC (ON)
Companies' Creditors Arrangement Act proceedings terminated 04/29/2011
No stockholders' equity

BRAINIUM TECHNOLOGIES INC (BC)
Cease trade order effective 05/29/2002
Stockholders' equity unlikely

BRAINSTORM CELL THERAPEUTICS INC (WA)
Reincorporated under the laws of Delaware 12/21/2006

BRAINTECH INC NEW (NV)
Each share old Common $0.001 par exchanged for (0.2) share new Common $0.001 par 09/09/2002
SEC revoked common stock registration 05/25/2012

BRAINTECH INC OLD (NV)
Merged into Nicolet Instrument Corp. 06/08/1987
Each share Common 1¢ par exchanged for $0.18 cash

BRAINTREE SVGS BK (BRAINTREE, MA)
Stock Dividends - 10% 02/28/1986; 50% 05/19/1986
Merged into Walden Bancorp Inc. 12/08/1995
Each share Common $1 par exchanged for (1) share Common $1 par
Walden Bancorp Inc. merged into UST Corp. 01/03/1997
(See UST Corp.)

BRAINWORKS VENTURES INC (NV)
Name changed to AssuranceAmerica Corp. 07/02/2003

BRAJDAS CORP (CA)
Reorganized under the laws of Delaware as Richey Electronics, Inc. 12/30/1993
Each share Common 10¢ par exchanged for (0.285714) share Common 10¢ par
(See Richey Electronics, Inc.)

BRAKE CHECK CDA INC (CANADA)
Assets sold for the benefit of creditors in 06/00/1991
No stockholders' equity

BRAKE HEADQUARTERS U S A INC (DE)
Each share old Common $0.001 par exchanged for (0.33333333) share new Common $0.001 par 01/29/1999
Chapter 11 bankruptcy proceedings converted to Chapter 7 on 09/07/2000
Stockholders' equity unlikely

BRAKE O INDS INC (NV)
In process of liquidation
Each share Common 10¢ par received initial distribution of $0.30 cash 03/03/1977
Each share Common 10¢ par exchanged for second distribution of $0.164 cash 04/08/1977
Each share Common 10¢ par received third distribution of $0.156 cash 09/16/1977
Each share Common 10¢ par received fourth distribution of $0.03 cash 12/15/1978
Details on subsequent distributions, if any, are not available

BRAKPAN VENTURES CORP (BC)
Common no par split (3) for (1) by issuance of (2) additional shares payable 03/23/2017 to holders of record 03/17/2017 Ex date - 03/15/2017
Name changed to International Cobalt Corp. 03/29/2017

BRALORNE CAN FER RES LTD (BC)
Name changed to Bralorne Resources Ltd. 05/29/1972
Bralorne Resources Ltd. recapitalized as BRL Enterprises Inc. 11/27/1990
(See BRL Enterprises Inc.)

BRALORNE GOLD MINES LTD (BC)
Merged into Avino Silver & Gold Mines Ltd. 10/20/2014
Each share Common no par exchanged for (0.14) share Common no par
Note: Unexchanged certificates will be cancelled and become without value 10/20/2020

BRALORNE MINES LTD. (BC)
Under plan of merger name changed to Bralorne Pioneer Mines Ltd. 03/19/1959
Bralorne Pioneer Mines Ltd. name changed to Bralorne Can-Fer Resources Ltd. 12/03/1969 which name changed to Bralorne Resources Ltd. 05/29/1972 which recapitalized as BRL Enterprises Inc. 11/27/1990
(See BRL Enterprises Inc.)

BRALORNE OIL & GAS LTD (AB)
Name changed to Bracell Petroleums Ltd. 05/08/1972
(See Bracell Petroleums Ltd.)

BRALORNE-PIONEER GOLD MINES LTD (BC)
Recapitalized as Bralorne Gold Mines Ltd. 08/25/2004
Each share Common no par exchanged for (0.1) share Common no par
Bralorne Gold Mines Ltd. merged into Avino Silver & Gold Mines Ltd. 10/20/2014

BRALORNE PIONEER MINES LTD (BC)
Under plan of merger name changed to Bralorne Can-Fer Resources Ltd. 12/03/1969
Bralorne Can-Fer Resources Ltd. name changed to Bralorne Resources Ltd. 05/29/1972 which recapitalized as BRL Enterprises Inc. 11/27/1990
(See BRL Enterprises Inc.)

BRALORNE RES LTD (BC)
Capital Stock no par split (3) for (1) by issuance of (2) additional shares 05/30/1980
Each share 8.75% Conv. First Preferred Ser. A $20 par exchanged for (12) shares Common no par 02/10/1988
Recapitalized as BRL Enterprises Inc. 11/27/1990
Each share Common no par exchanged for (0.04) share Common no par
(See BRL Enterprises Inc.)

BRALSAMAN PETES LTD (BC)
Merged into Ranger Oil Ltd. 07/11/1980
Each share Capital Stock $1 par exchanged for $7.36 cash

BRAMALEA INC (ON)
Name changed 12/07/1976
Recapitalized 08/08/1994
Common no par split (5) for (1) by issuance of (4) additional shares 08/30/1968
Name changed from Bramalea Consolidated Developments Ltd. to Bramalea Ltd. 12/07/1976
Common no par split (2) for (1) by issuance of (1) additional share 08/01/1980
Common no par split (2) for (1) by issuance of (1) additional share 08/08/1981
Common no par split (3) for (2) by issuance of (0.5) additional share 10/06/1989
Plan of reorganization under Canada Creditors Arrangement Act confirmed 03/22/1993
Each share Floating Rate Retractable 1st Preference Ser. B no par exchanged for (26.2662) shares Common no par
Recapitalized from Bramalea Ltd. to Bramalea Inc. 08/08/1994
Each share Common no par exchanged for (0.05) share Common no par
Involuntary petition for bankruptcy filed 03/26/1995
No stockholders' equity

BRAMALEA PPTYS INC (ON)
9.75% Retractable 1st Preferred Ser. 1 no par called for redemption 03/23/1992
Public interest eliminated

BRAMEDA RES LTD (BC)
Merged into Teck Corp. 02/08/1979
Each share Common no par exchanged for (0.2) share Class B Common no par
Teck Corp. name changed to Teck

Cominco Ltd. 09/12/2001 which name changed to Teck Resources Ltd. 04/27/2009

BRAMINCO ENTERPRISES INC (ON)
Name changed 04/18/1995
Common $1 changed to no par 09/26/1983
Name changed from Braminco Mines Ltd. to Braminco Enterprises Inc. 04/18/1995
Reorganized under the laws of New Brunswick as Q-Zar Inc. 06/27/1995
Each share Common no par exchanged for (0.16666666) share Common no par
Q-Zar Inc. name changed to Q-Entertainment, Inc. 07/31/1997
(See Q-Entertainment, Inc.)

BRANA OIL & GAS LTD (AB)
Struck off register for failure to file annual returns 03/01/1993

BRANCH BKG & TR (WILSON, NC)
Each share Common $100 par exchanged for (5) shares Common $25 par to effect a (4) for (1) split and 25% stock dividend 10/05/1948
Each share Common $25 par exchanged for (5) shares Common $5 par 01/22/1957
Stock Dividends - 100% 02/11/1953; 100% 12/16/1957; 100% 08/01/1967
Reorganized as Branch Corp. 07/01/1974
Each share Common $5 par exchanged for (2) shares Common $2.50 par
Branch Corp. name changed to BB&T Financial Corp. 05/10/1988 which merged into Southern National Corp. 02/28/1995 which merged into BB&T Corp. 05/19/1997

BRANCH CORP (NC)
Common $2.50 par split (2) for (1) by issuance of (1) additional share 12/15/1987
Stock Dividends - 10% 01/15/1979; 10% 10/19/1979
Name changed to BB&T Financial Corp. 05/10/1988
BB&T Financial Corp. merged into Southern National Corp. 02/28/1995 which merged into BB&T Corp. 05/19/1997

BRANCH CNTY BK (COLDWATER, MI)
Name changed 02/04/1964
Name changed from Branch County Savings Bank (Coldwater, MI) to Branch County Bank (Coldwater, MI) 02/04/1964
Common $20 par changed to $10 par and (2.4) additional shares issued to reflect a (2) for (1) split and 20% stock dividend 02/28/1969
Common $10 par split (2) for (1) by issuance of (1) additional share 11/15/1985
Stock Dividends - 50% 00/00/1954; 11.11111111% 00/00/1958; 10% 00/00/1960; 10% 07/20/1964; 10% 09/19/1966; 10% 02/23/1971; 50% 04/30/1976; 10% 04/30/1979; 10% 05/05/1988
Name changed to Century Bank & Trust (Coldwater, MI) 05/30/1989
Century Bank & Trust (Coldwater, MI) reorganized as Century Financial Corp. (MI) 12/13/1989

BRANCH INDS INC (DE)
Common $1 par split (2) for (1) by issuance of (1) additional share 12/17/1971
Plan of reorganization under Chapter 11 Federal Bankruptcy Code dismissed 03/08/1988
No stockholders' equity

BRANCH RIVER WOOL COMBING CO., INC. (DE)
Each share Preferred $100 par exchanged for (8) shares Common $20 par 00/00/1946

Each share Common no par exchanged for (6) shares Common $20 par 00/00/1946
Name changed to Framatex Corp. 02/01/1967
(See Framatex Corp.)

BRANCHEZ-VOUS INC (CANADA)
Name changed to BV! Media Inc. 06/09/2009
(See BV! Media Inc.)

BRANCO RES LTD (BC)
Name changed to Candelaria Mining Corp. 03/22/2016

BRAND & MILLEN, LTD.
Bankrupt 00/00/1951
Details not available

BRAND COS INC (DE)
Common 10¢ par split (2) for (1) by issuance of (1) additional share 07/09/1990
Merged into Rust International Inc. 05/10/1993
Each share Common 10¢ par exchanged for (1) share Common 1¢ par
Rust International Inc. merged into WMX Technologies, Inc. 07/12/1995 which name changed to Waste Management, Inc. (New) 05/12/1997 which merged into Waste Management, Inc. 07/16/1998

BRAND INSULATIONS INC (IL)
Reorganized under the laws of Delaware as Brand Companies, Inc. 03/27/1987
Each share $1.60 Preferred Ser. C no par exchanged for (1.1523) shares Common 10¢ par
Each Fractional Share Preferred Ser. E no par exchanged for (0.03731) share Common 10¢ par
Each share Common 10¢ par exchanged for (1) share Common 10¢ par
Brand Companies, Inc. merged into Rust International Inc. 05/10/1993 which merged into WMX Technologies, Inc. 07/12/1995 which name changed to Waste Management, Inc. (New) 05/12/1997 which merged into Waste Management, Inc. 07/16/1998

BRAND LEADERS PLUS INCOME ETF (ON)
Name changed to Harvest Leaders Plus Income ETF 06/19/2018

BRAND LEADERS PLUS INCOME FD (ON)
Under plan of reorganization each Class A and Class U Unit automatically became (1) Brand Leaders Plus Income ETF Class A or Class U Unit respectively 10/24/2016
Brand Leaders Plus Income ETF name changed to Harvest Leaders Plus Income ETF 06/19/2018

BRAND NEUE CORP (NV)
Name changed to Culture Medium Holdings Corp. (NV) 03/14/2011
Culture Medium Holdings Corp. (NV) reincorporated in Wyoming 07/01/2014 which recapitalized as Code Navy 02/13/2015 which name changed to Universal Power Industry Corp. 06/02/2016

BRAND'S RESTAURANT CONTROL CORP. (DE)
No longer in existence having become inoperative and void for non-payment of taxes 07/01/1947

BRANDAID MARKETING CORP (DE)
SEC revoked common stock registration 10/12/2005

BRANDALE FOOD SVCS INC (CANADA)
Name changed to Villaret Resources Ltd. 06/08/1999
Villaret Resources Ltd. recapitalized

as Kast Telecom Inc. (Canada) 05/23/2000 which reincorporated in Luxembourg as Kast Telecom Europe S.A. 04/25/2001

BRANDED BEVERAGES INC (NV)
Common $0.0001 par split (21) for (1) by issuance of (20) additional shares payable 12/14/2010 to holders of record 12/14/2010
Name changed to Raptor Technology Group, Inc. 01/06/2011
(See Raptor Technology Group, Inc.)

BRANDENBURG METALS CORP (BC)
Name changed to Brandenburg Energy Corp. 07/14/2011

BRANDERA COM INC (ON)
Recapitalized as BrandEra Inc. 04/23/2001
Each share Common no par exchanged for (0.1) share Common no par
BrandEra Inc. name changed to National Construction Inc. 05/16/2002 which name changed to E.G. Capital Inc. 03/16/2005 which recapitalized as Quantum International Income Corp. 03/14/2014

BRANDERA INC (ON)
Name changed to National Construction Inc. 05/16/2002
National Construction Inc. name changed to E.G. Capital Inc. 03/16/2005 which recapitalized as Quantum International Income Corp. 03/14/2014

BRANDEVOR ENTERPRISES LTD (BC)
Delisted from Toronto Stock Exchange 04/01/1999

BRANDON APPLIED SYS INC (NY)
Stock Dividend - 100% 07/19/1968
Name changed to Rand Information Systems, Inc. 07/27/1978

BRANDON ENERGY LTD (AB)
Merged into Cannon Oil & Gas Ltd. 07/23/1999
Each share Class A no par exchanged for (0.0712368) share Common no par
Cannon Oil & Gas Ltd. acquired by G2 Resources Inc. 01/29/2007 which merged into Regal Energy Ltd. 07/10/2008 which recapitalized as Novus Energy Inc. 08/05/2009
(See Novus Energy Inc.)

BRANDON GOLD CORP (BC)
Recapitalized as Redmond Ventures Corp. 09/16/1999
Each share Common no par exchanged for (0.5) share Common no par
Redmond Ventures Corp. recapitalized as Crown Point Ventures Ltd. (BC) 03/12/2002 which reincorporated in Alberta as Crown Point Energy Inc. 07/31/2012

BRANDON SYS CORP (DE)
Common 10¢ par split (5) for (4) by issuance of (0.25) additional share 03/01/1991
Common 10¢ par split (5) for (4) by issuance of (0.25) additional share 06/18/1992
Stock Dividend - 20% 01/17/1989
Merged into Interim Services Inc. 05/23/1996
Each share Common 10¢ par exchanged for (0.88) share Common 1¢ par
Interim Services Inc. name changed to Spherion Corp. 07/07/2001 which name changed to SFN Group, Inc. 03/01/2010
(See SFN Group, Inc.)

BRANDPARTNERS GROUP INC (DE)
SEC revoked common stock registration 04/18/2012

BRANDQUEST DEV GROUP INC (NV)
Name changed to Novus Acquisition & Development Corp. 07/27/2009

BRANDRAM-HENDERSON LTD. (CANADA)
Reorganized 00/00/1937
Each share Preferred $100 par exchanged for (5) shares Capital Stock no par
Each share Common $100 par exchanged for (1) share Capital Stock no par
Charter surrendered 03/08/1965
Each share Capital Stock no par exchanged for $17.55 cash

BRANDS SHOPPING NETWORK INC (NV)
Each share old Common $0.001 par exchanged for (0.125) share new Common $0.001 par 02/18/2002
Each share new Common $0.001 par exchanged again for (0.25) share new Common $0.001 par 04/10/2002
Recapitalized as United Fuel & Energy Corp. 01/31/2005
Each share Common $0.001 par exchanged for (0.025) share Common $0.001 par
(See United Fuel & Energy Corp.)

BRANDT-WARNER MANUFACTURING CO.
Name changed to York Axle & Forge Co. 00/00/1949
(See York Axle & Forge Co.)

BRANDY BROOK MINES LTD (ON)
Charter cancelled for failure to pay taxes and file returns 01/03/1983

BRANDY RES INC (BC)
Recapitalized as Vital Pacific Resources Ltd. (BC) 09/06/1984
Each share Common no par exchanged for (0.5) share Common no par
Vital Pacific Resources Ltd. (BC) reincorporated in Canada 05/26/1987 which reincorporated in Bahamas 08/21/1998 which reorganized in Yukon as First Majestic Resource Corp. 01/03/2002 which reincorporated in British Columbia 01/17/2005 which name changed to First Majestic Silver Corp. 11/22/2006

BRANDYWINE BUSINESS SVCS LTD (AR)
Reincorporated under the laws of Nevada as TeloVax Corp. 08/01/2005

BRANDYWINE RACEWAY ASSN INC (DE)
Common $1 par split (2) for (1) by issuance of (1) additional share 10/11/1962
Merged into Rollins International, Inc. 06/02/1970
Each share Common $1 par exchanged for (0.85) share Common $1 par
Rollins International, Inc. name changed to RLC Corp. 02/07/1975 which name changed to Rollins Truck Leasing Corp. 01/25/1990
(See Rollins Truck Leasing Corp.)

BRANDYWINE RLTY TR (MD)
7.50% Preferred Shares of Bene. Int. Ser. C 1¢ par called for redemption at $25 plus $0.09375 accrued dividends on 05/03/2012
7.375% Preferred Shares of Bene. Int. Ser. D 1¢ par called for redemption at $25 plus $0.36875 accrued dividends on 12/28/2012
6.9% Preferred Shares of Bene. Int. 1¢ par called for redemption at $25 plus $0.50792 accrued dividends 04/11/2017
(Additional Information in Active)

BRANDYWINE SVGS & LN ASSN DOWNINGTOWN (PA)
Acquired by Flagship Financial Corp. 06/15/1989
Each share Common $1 par exchanged for $21.50 cash

BRANDYWINE SHARES
Trust terminated and liquidated 00/00/1937
Details not available

BRANDYWINE SPORTS INC (DE)
Merged into Brandywine Enterprises, Inc. 10/15/1987
Each share Common $1 par exchanged for $5.25 cash

BRANER RES INC (BC)
Recapitalized as Consolidated Braner Ventures Inc. 02/14/1992
Each share Common no par exchanged for (0.33333333) share Common no par
Consolidated Braner Ventures Inc. name changed to Sunmakers Travel Group Inc. 05/13/1994 which name changed to Setanta Ventures Inc. 01/24/1996
(See Setanta Ventures Inc.)

BRANFORD SVGS BK (BRANFORD, CT)
Common $1 par changed to no par 11/21/1991
Each share old Common no par exchanged for (0.1) share new Common no par 10/21/1994
Merged into North Fork Bancorporation, Inc. 12/12/1997
Each share new Common no par exchanged for (0.1957) share Common $2.50 par
North Fork Bancorporation, Inc. merged into Capital One Financial Corp. 12/01/2006

BRANIFF AIRWAYS, INC. (OK)
Each share Common $10 par exchanged for (4) shares Common $2.50 par 00/00/1940
Common $2.50 par changed to $1.25 par and (1) additional share issued 06/01/1966
Stock Dividend - 50% 08/21/1943
Reincorporated under the laws of Nevada 08/31/1966
Braniff Airways, Inc. (NV) reorganized as Braniff International Corp. 11/28/1973 which reorganized as Dalfort Corp. 12/15/1983
(See Dalfort Corp.)

BRANIFF AWYS INC (NV)
Common $1.25 par changed to 50¢ par and (2) additional shares issued 05/03/1968
Reorganized as Braniff International Corp. 11/28/1973
Each share Conv. Class A Special 50¢ par exchanged for (1) share Common 50¢ par
Each share Common 50¢ par automatically became (1) share Common 50¢ par
Braniff International Corp. reorganized as Dalfort Corp. 12/15/1984
(See Dalfort Corp.)

BRANIFF INC (NV)
Each share old Common 1¢ par exchanged for (0.2) share new Common 1¢ par and $7 cash 10/24/1988
Liquidating Plan of Reorganization under Chapter 11 Federal Bankruptcy proceedings confirmed 07/23/1992
No stockholders' equity

BRANIFF INTL CORP (NV)
Plan of reorganization under Chapter 11 bankruptcy proceedings confirmed 12/15/1983
Each share Common 50¢ par exchanged for (0.008080983) share Dalfort Corp. Common 1¢ par
Note: Unexchanged certificates were cancelled and became without value 12/16/1985
Holdings of (123) shares or fewer did not participate in the plan
(See Dalfort Corp.)

BRANLY ENTERPRISES INC (ON)
Recapitalized as Consolidated Branly Resources Inc. 02/27/1984
Each share Common no par exchanged for (0.16666666) share Common no par
Consolidated Branly Resources Inc. name changed to CBR Holdings Inc. 06/20/1985

BRANSON INSTRUMENTS, INC. (CT)
Common $1 par split (3) for (1) by issuance of (2) additional shares 05/17/1961
Name changed to B.I. Corp. 06/03/1965
(See B.I. Corp.)

BRANTFORD CORDAGE CO. LTD. (CANADA)
Each share Common no par exchanged for (0.5) share new Common no par 00/00/1944
Each share Common no par exchanged for (0.75) share Class A no par and (1) share Class B no par 00/00/1950
Acquired by Trafalgar Investments Co. Ltd. 03/10/1959
Each share Class A no par exchanged for $24 cash
Each share Class B no par exchanged for $24 cash

BRANTLEY CAP CORP (MD)
Liquidation completed
Each share Common 1¢ par received initial distribution of $1.50 cash payable 03/14/2008 to holders of record 03/12/2008 Ex date - 03/17/2008
Each share Common 1¢ par received second distribution of $0.75 cash payable 05/28/2008 to holders of record 05/26/2008 Ex date - 05/29/2008
Each share Common 1¢ par received third distribution of $0.35 cash payable 09/05/2008 to holders of record 09/02/2008 Ex date - 09/08/2008
Each share Common 1¢ par received fourth distribution of approximately $0.28 cash payable 05/15/2012 to holders of record 05/12/2012
Each share Common 1¢ par received fifth and final distribution of $0.00787291 cash payable 10/21/2013 to holders of record 09/25/2013

BRAS-AMERN CORP (ON)
Cease trade order effective 06/21/1991
Stockholders' equity unlikely

BRAS D OR MINES LTD (QC)
Merged into Belmoral Mines Ltd. 12/20/1985
Each share Common no par exchanged for (0.66666666) share Common no par
Belmoral Mines Ltd. merged into Beau Canada Exploration Ltd. 11/04/1993
(See Beau Canada Exploration Ltd.)

BRASCADE CORP (ON)
Reincorporated 01/04/2007
Place of incorporation changed from (Canada) to (ON) 01/04/2007
Sr. Preferred Class 1 Ser. B called for redemption at $40 on 01/04/2007
Name changed to Brookfield Investments Corp. 02/21/2008

BRASCADE RES INC (CANADA)
Conv. Preferred Ser. A no par reclassified as Variable Rate Conv. Preferred Ser. A no par 06/29/1984
Variable Rate Conv. Preferred Ser. A no par called for redemption at $40 on 06/30/1999
Merged into Brascade Corp. 09/13/2004
Each share Variable Rate Conv. Preferred Ser. B no par exchanged for (1) share Class 1 Senior Preferred Ser. B no par
Each share Common no par exchanged for $34 cash

BRASCAN ADJ RATE TR I (ON)
Completely liquidated
Each Trust Unit no par received first and final distribution of $0.03 cash payable 08/15/2008 to holders of record 07/31/2008

BRASCAN CORP (CANADA)
Class A Limited Shares no par split (3) for (2) by issuance of (0.5) additional share payable 06/01/2004 to holders of record 05/21/2004 Ex date - 06/02/2004
Class A Preference Ser. 1 no par called for redemption at $25 plus $0.05039 accrued dividend on 07/30/2004
Class A Preference Ser. 3 no par called for redemption at $100,000 plus $211.56 accrued dividends on 11/08/2005
Name changed to Brookfield Asset Management, Inc. 11/10/2005

BRASCAN FINANCIAL CORP (CANADA)
Acquired by Brascan Corp. 07/12/2002
Each share Class A no par exchanged for (0.146368) share Ltd. Vtg. Class A no par and $11.9527616 cash
Each share Class I Preferred Ser. A no par exchanged for (1) share Brascan Corp. Class A Preference Ser. 13 no par 01/01/2005
Each share Class II Preferred Ser. 2 no par exchanged for (1) share Brascan Corp. Class A Preference Ser. 14 no par 01/01/2005
Each share Class II Preferred Ser. 3 no par exchanged for (1) share Brascan Corp. Class A Preference Ser. 13 no par 01/01/2005
(Additional Information in Active)

BRASCAN LTD (CANADA)
Ordinary no par split (6) for (5) by issuance of (0.2) additional share 06/27/1969
Ordinary no par reclassified as Conv. Class A Ordinary no par 12/18/1973
Each (3) shares 6% Preference $100 par exchanged for (20) shares Conv. Class A Ordinary no par 04/30/1985
Conv. Class A Ordinary no par split (2) for (1) by issuance of (1) additional share 04/11/1986
Conv. Class B Ordinary no par split (2) for (1) by issuance of (1) additional share 04/11/1986
Conv. Class C Ordinary no par split (2) for (1) by issuance of (1) additional share 04/11/1986
Conv. Class A Ordinary no par reclassified as Class A no par 07/08/1986
Conv. Class B Ordinary no par reclassified as Class A no par 07/08/1986
Conv. Class C Ordinary no par reclassified as Class A no par 07/08/1986
$2.6875 1981 Preferred Ser. A no par called for redemption 05/15/1987
Each share 8.50% Tax Deferred Preferred Ser. A $25 par exchanged for $25 cash 07/15/1996
10% Preferred Ser. B no par called for redemption 07/15/1996
Stock Dividends - Ordinary - 10% 01/29/1971; 10% 07/31/1972
Stock Dividend - Conv. Class A Ordinary and Conv. Class B Ordinary - in Conv. Class A Ordinary 10% 07/31/1974
Merged into EdperBrascan Corp. 08/01/1997
Each share Floating Rate Preferred 1981 Ser. D no par exchanged for (1) share Class A Preference Ser. 4 no par
Each share $1.875 Preferred 1981 Ser. F no par exchanged for (1) share Class A Preference Ser. 6 no par
Each share Floating Rate Preferred 1981 Ser. J no par exchanged for (1) share Class A Preference Ser. 8 no par
Each share Class A no par exchanged for (1.5) shares Class A Limited Vtg. no par
EdperBrascan Corp. name changed to Brascan Corp. 04/28/2000

BRASCAN SOUNDVEST DIVERSIFIED INCOME FD (ON)
Merged into Brookfield Soundvest Equity Fund 01/04/2010
Each Trust Unit no par automatically became (1.655611) Trust Units
Brookfield Soundvest Equity Fund name changed to Soundvest Equity Fund 02/21/2018
(See Soundvest Equity Fund)

BRASCAN SOUNDVEST FOCUSED BUSINESS TR (ON)
Under plan of merger name changed to Brookfield Soundvest Equity Fund 01/04/2010
Brookfield Soundvest Equity Fund name changed to Soundvest Equity Fund 02/21/2018
(See Soundvest Equity Fund)

BRASCAN SOUNDVEST RISING DISTR SPLIT TR (ON)
Name changed to Brookfield Soundvest Split Trust 04/30/2010
Brookfield Soundvest Split Trust name changed to Soundvest Split Trust 02/21/2018

BRASCAN SOUNDVEST TOTAL RETURN FD (ON)
Merged into Brookfield Soundvest Equity Fund 01/04/2010
Each Trust Unit no par automatically became (1.256327) Trust Units
Brookfield Soundvest Equity Fund name changed to Soundvest Equity Fund 02/21/2018
(See Soundvest Equity Fund)

BRASCO DRILLING & EXPLORATION CO. LTD.
Bankrupt 00/00/1938
Details not available

BRASEL VENTURES INC (DE)
Recapitalized as American Pharmaceutical Co. 07/27/1993
Each share Common $0.001 par exchanged for (0.1) share Common 1¢ par

BRASIL ECODIESEL INDUSTRIA E COMERCIO DE BIOCOMBUSTIVEIS E OLEOS VEGETAIS S A (BRAZIL)
Name changed to Vanguarda Agro S.A. 12/16/2011
Vanguarda Agro S.A. name changed to Terra Santa Agro S.A. 12/22/2016
(See Terra Santa Agro S.A.)

BRASIL GOLD RES LTD (BC)
Name changed to ARI Automated Recycling Inc. 10/05/1990
ARI Automated Recycling Inc. recapitalized as Envipco Automated Recycling Inc. 11/01/1994 which name changed to Automated Recycling Inc. 08/20/1999 which name changed to OceanLake Commerce Inc. 03/01/2001

BRASIL TELECOM PARTICIPACOES S A (BRAZIL)
ADR basis changed from (1:5,000) to (1:5) 06/05/2007
Merged into Brasil Telecom S.A. 11/16/2009

Each Sponsored ADR for Preferred exchanged for (1.516028) Sponsored ADR's for Preferred and (0.860033) Sponsored ADR's for Common
Brasil Telecom S.A. name changed to Oi S.A. 02/28/2012

BRASIL TELECOM S A (BRAZIL)
ADR basis changed from (1:3,000) to (1:3) 05/18/2007
Name changed to Oi S.A. 02/28/2012

BRASILCA MNG CORP (BC)
Delisted from NEX 06/29/2005

BRASS CAP CORP (AB)
Reorganized under the laws of British Columbia as Heatherdale Resources Ltd. 11/17/2009
Each share Common no par exchanged for (0.4) share Common no par

BRASS CRAFT MFG CO (MI)
Common $1 par split (5) for (4) by issuance of (0.25) additional share 06/21/1978
Merged into Masco Corp. 03/30/1983
Each share Common $1 par exchanged for $26 cash

BRASS EAGLE INC (DE)
Merged into K2 Inc. 12/16/2003
Each share Common 1¢ par exchanged for (0.6036) share Common $1 par
K2 Inc. merged into Jarden Corp. 08/08/2007

BRASS RING RES INC (BC)
Recapitalized as Oneida Resources Inc. 12/30/1987
Each share Common no par exchanged for (0.2) share Common no par
(See Oneida Resources Inc.)

BRASS SPLIT CORP (ON)
Name changed to BNN Split Corp. 08/02/2001
BNN Split Corp. name changed to BAM Split Corp. 12/15/2006

BRASSIE GOLF CORP (BC)
Reorganized under the laws of Delaware as Divot Golf Corp. 06/16/1998
Each share Common no par exchanged for (0.0666) share Common $0.001 par
Divot Golf Corp. name changed to orbitTRAVEL.com Corp. 04/20/2000 which name changed to Orbit Brands Corp. 10/12/2005
(See Orbit Brands Corp.)

BRASSNECK CAP CORP (AB)
Name changed to National Access Cannabis Corp. and (0.205) additional share issued 09/08/2017

BRATHENDALE ORIG SOUP KETTLE INC (NV)
Each share Common 5¢ par exchanged for (5) shares Common 1¢ par 01/06/1971
Adjudicated bankrupt 05/18/1972
Stockholders' equity unlikely

BRAUCH DATABASE SYS INC (ON)
Cease trade order effective 01/10/2002

BRAUN C F & CO (CA)
Merged into Santa Fe International Corp. 01/30/1980
Each share Common $1 par exchanged for $58.50 cash

BRAUN CONSULTING INC (DE)
Merged into Fair Issac Corporation 11/10/2004
Each share Common $0.001 par exchanged for $2.34 cash

BRAUN ENGR CO (MI)
Common $1 par split (2) for (1) by issuance of (1) additional share 06/23/1983
Common $1 par split (3) for (2) by issuance of (0.5) additional share 08/02/1984
Stock Dividend - 100% 04/03/1964
Merged into Masco Industries, Inc. 08/09/1985
Each share Common $1 par exchanged for $18 cash

BRAUNS FASHIONS CORP (DE)
Common 1¢ par split (3) for (2) by issuance of (0.25) additional share payable 12/14/1999 to holders of record 11/30/1999
Common 1¢ par split (3) for (2) by issuance of (0.5) additional share payable 07/11/2000 to holders of record 06/27/2000
Name changed to Christopher & Banks Corp. 07/26/2000

BRAUVIN HIGH YIELD FD L P (DE)
In process of liquidation
Each Unit of Ltd. Partnership Int. received initial distribution of $2.687 cash 00/00/2000
Each Unit of Ltd. Partnership Int. II received initial distribution of $287.05 cash 00/00/2000
Each Unit of Ltd. Partnership Int. received second distribution of $0.278 cash 11/01/2002
Note: Details on subsequent distribution(s), if any, are not available

BRAUVIN INCOME PPTYS L P (DE)
Terminated Partnership registration and is no longer public as of 06/30/2005
Details not available

BRAUVIN NET LEASE V INC (MD)
Liquidation completed 03/09/2007
Details not available

BRAUVIN REAL ESTATE FD L P (DE)
Completely liquidated
Each Unit of Ltd. Partnership Int. 1 received first and final distribution of $5.50 cash 12/28/1995
Partnership terminated 12/27/1995
No equity for holders of Units of Ltd. Partnership Int. 2 Partnership terminated 09/27/1996
Equity unlikely for holders of Units of Ltd. Partnership Int. 3
Terminated registration with SEC of Units of Ltd. Partnership 5 on 06/30/2008
Details not available
Units of Ltd. Partnership 4 filed Certificate of Cancellation with Secretary of State 08/07/2008
Details not available

BRAVADA GOLD CORP OLD (BC)
Under plan of merger each share Common no par automatically became (1) share Bravada Gold Corp. (New) Common no par 01/07/2011

BRAVE ENTMT CORP (DE)
Name changed to Sun Music Group Inc. 05/01/1997
Sun Music Group Inc. recapitalized as Banyan Healthcare Services Inc. 12/21/1997 which recapitalized as Netoy.com Corp. 03/15/1999 which name changed to SafePay Solutions, Inc. 03/03/2006 which name changed to Emaji, Inc. 03/11/2008 which name changed to Broadside Enterprises, Inc. 12/01/2016

BRAVO BRANDS INC (DE)
Name changed 04/09/2007
Name changed from Bravo! Foods International Corp. to Bravo! Brands, Inc. 04/09/2007
Chapter 7 bankruptcy proceedings terminated 04/09/2015
No stockholders' equity

BRAVO BRIO RESTAURANT GROUP INC (OH)
Acquired by GP Investments, Ltd. 05/24/2018

Each share Common no par exchanged for $4.05 cash

BRAVO GOLD CORP (BC)
Each share Common no par received distribution of (0.1) share Bravada Gold Corp. (Old) Common no par payable 03/29/2010 to holders of record 12/31/2009
Recapitalized as Homestake Resource Corp. 04/16/2012
Each share Common no par exchanged for (0.1) share Common no par
Homestake Resource Corp. merged into Auryn Resources Inc. 09/07/2016

BRAVO GOLD INC (BC)
Recapitalized as International Bravo Resource Corp. 09/22/1998
Each share Common no par exchanged for (0.5) share Common no par
International Bravo Resource Corp. recapitalized as Bravo Venture Group Inc. 03/15/2002 which name changed to Bravo Gold Corp. 02/22/2010 which recapitalized as Homestake Resource Corp. 04/16/2012 which merged into Auryn Resources Inc. 09/07/2016

BRAVO KNITS INC (NY)
Dissolved by proclamation 12/24/1991

BRAVO RESOURCE PARTNERS LTD (YT)
SEC revoked common stock registration 04/05/2016

BRAVO RES LTD (BC)
Recapitalized as Oro Bravo Resources Ltd. (BC) 05/06/1994
Each share Common no par exchanged for (0.28571428) share Common no par
Oro Bravo Resources Ltd. (BC) reorganized in Yukon as Bravo Resource Partners Ltd. 01/21/2000
(See Bravo Resource Partners Ltd.)

BRAVO RES LTD (NV)
Name changed to Woize International Ltd. 12/30/2005
Woize International Ltd. name changed to Smart Comm International Ltd. 10/17/2008
(See Smart Comm International Ltd.)

BRAVO VENTURE GROUP INC (BC)
Name changed to Bravo Gold Corp. 02/22/2010
Bravo Gold Corp. recapitalized as Homestake Resource Corp. 04/16/2012 which merged into Auryn Resources Inc. 09/07/2016

BRAVO YELLOWKNIFE MINES, LTD. (ON)
Charter revoked for failure to file reports and pay taxes 11/05/1956

BRAVURA SOLUTIONS LTD (AUSTRALIA)
ADR agreement terminated 10/25/2013
Each Sponsored ADR for Ordinary exchanged for $5.284 cash

BRAVURA VENTURES CORP NEW (BC)
Each share old Common no par exchanged for (0.5) share new Common no par 03/18/2015
Each share new Common no par exchanged again for (0.1) share new Common no par 05/04/2017
Name changed to Quantum Cobalt Corp. 11/07/2017

BRAVURA VENTURES CORP OLD (BC)
Each share old Common no par exchanged for (0.2) share new Common no par 03/05/2015
Plan of arrangement effective 03/11/2015
Each share new Common no par exchanged for (1) share Bravura Ventures Corp. (New) Common no par, (0.5) share NuRAN Wireless Inc. Common no par and (0.5) share 1014379 B.C. Ltd. Common no par Bravura Ventures Corp. (New) name changed to Quantum Cobalt Corp. 11/07/2017

BRAXTON INDS INC (MN)
Statutorily dissolved 12/31/1993

BRAZ DIAMOND MNG INC (NV)
Each share old Common $0.001 par for (0.05) share new Common $0.001 par 06/22/2005
Charter revoked for failure to file reports and pay fees 07/31/2010

BRAZALTA RES CORP (AB)
Name changed to Canacol Energy Ltd. 02/13/2009

BRAZAURO RES CORP (BC)
Merged into Eldorado Gold Corp. (New) 07/20/2010
Each share Common no par exchanged for (0.0675) share Common no par and (0.33333333) share TriStar Gold Inc. Common no par
(See each company's listing)
Note: Unexchanged certificates were cancelled and became without value 07/20/2016

BRAZIL FAST FOOD CORP (DE)
Each share old Common $0.0001 par exchanged for (0.25) share new Common $0.0001 par 07/09/1999
Acquired by Queijo Holding Corp. 05/05/2015
Each share new Common $0.0001 par exchanged for $18.30 cash

BRAZIL FD INC (MD)
Completely liquidated 06/02/2006
Each share Common 1¢ par exchanged for first and final distribution of approximately $61.19 cash

BRAZIL GOLD & DIAMOND MINES CORP. (DE)
No longer in existence having become inoperative and void for non-payment of taxes 04/01/1950

BRAZIL GOLD CORP (NV)
Each share old Common $0.001 par exchanged for (0.001) share new Common $0.001 par 01/07/2014
Recapitalized as Conexus Cattle Corp. 01/12/2015
Each share Common $0.001 par exchanged for (0.001) share Common $0.001 par
Conexus Cattle Corp. name changed to Connexus Corp. 12/02/2015

BRAZIL INTERACTIVE MEDIA INC (DE)
Name changed to American Cannabis Co., Inc. 10/10/2014

BRAZIL RAILWAY CO. (ME)
Declared defunct 01/01/1976
No stockholders' equity

BRAZIL RLTY S A PARTICIPACOES (BRAZIL)
Reg. S GDR's for Ordinary reclassified as Sponsored GDR's for Preferred 07/23/1998
Name changed to Cyrela Brazil Realty S.A. 06/29/2005

BRAZIL RES INC (BC)
Reincorporated under the laws of Canada as GoldMining Inc. 12/07/2016

BRAZILIAN DIAMONDS LTD (BC)
Each share old Common no par exchanged for (0.1) share new Common no par 09/30/2009
Each share new Common no par exchanged again for (1/3) share new Common no par 01/19/2011
Name changed to Kincora Copper Ltd. 07/18/2011

BRAZILIAN EQUITY FD INC (MD)
Completely liquidated
Each share Common $0.001 par received first and final distribution of $9.60 cash payable 05/02/2005 to holders of record 04/29/2005

BRAZILIAN GOLD CORP (BC)
Merged into Brazil Resources Inc. (BC) 11/22/2013
Each share Common no par exchanged for (0.172) shares Common no par
Note: Unexchanged certificates will be cancelled and become without value 11/22/2019
Brazil Resources Inc. (BC) reincorporated in Canada as GoldMining Inc. 12/07/2016

BRAZILIAN GOLDFIELDS LTD (BAHAMAS)
Recapitalized as Brazilian International Goldfields Ltd. 11/27/1998
Each share Common no par exchanged for (0.25) share Common no par
Brazilian International Goldfields Ltd. recapitalized as Aguila American Resources Ltd. (Bahamas) 03/08/2002 which reincorporated in British Columbia 01/14/2008 which name changed to Aguila American Gold Ltd. 05/26/2011

BRAZILIAN INTL GOLDFIELDS LTD (BAHAMAS)
Recapitalized as Aguila American Resources Ltd. (Bahamas) 03/08/2002
Each share Common no par exchanged for (0.05) share Common no par
Aguila American Resources Ltd. (Bahamas) reincorporated in British Columbia 01/14/2008 which name changed to Aguila American Gold Ltd. 05/26/2011

BRAZILIAN LT & PWR LTD (CANADA)
Name changed to Brascan Ltd. 06/23/1969
Brascan Ltd. merged into EdperBrascan Corp. 08/01/1997 which name changed to Brascan Corp. 04/28/2000 which name changed to Brookfield Asset Management, Inc. 11/10/2005

BRAZILIAN MNG CORP (NV)
Name changed to Sierra Desert Holdings Inc. 10/18/2010
Sierra Desert Holdings Inc. recapitalized as Telefix Communications Holdings, Inc. 03/12/2012

BRAZILIAN TRACTION LIGHT & POWER CO., LTD. (CANADA)
Each share Ordinary $100 par exchanged for (4) shares old Ordinary no par 00/00/1928
Each share old Ordinary no par exchanged for (2) shares new Ordinary no par 00/00/1951
Name changed to Brazilian Light & Power Co. Ltd. 07/04/1966
Brazilian Light & Power Co. Ltd. name changed to Brascan Ltd. 06/23/1969 which merged into EdperBrascan Corp. 08/01/1997 which name changed to Brascan Corp. 04/28/2000 which name changed to Brookfield Asset Management, Inc. 11/10/2005

BRAZMIN CORP (BRITISH VIRGIN ISLANDS)
Name changed to Talon Metals Corp. 07/09/2007

BRAZOS INTL EXPL INC (NV)
Common $0.001 par split (4) for (1) by issuance of (3) additional shares payable 09/15/2009 to holders of record 09/15/2009
Common $0.001 par split (20) for (1) by issuance of (19) additional shares payable 11/08/2010 to holders of record 08/17/2010
Ex date - 11/09/2010
Recapitalized as Scepter Holdings, Inc. 05/06/2015
Each share Common $0.001 par exchanged for (0.00125) share Common $0.001 par

BRAZOS PAC CORP (BC)
Name changed 04/17/1990
Name changed from Brazos Petroleum Corp. to Brazos Pacific Corp. 04/17/1990
Recapitalized as S.T.A. Resources Corp. 11/18/1994
Each share Common no par exchanged for (0.2) share Common no par
S.T.A. Resources Corp. recapitalized as T.T.A. Resources Corp. 10/03/1996 which name changed to Minefund Development Corp. 08/26/1999

BRAZOS RIVER GAS CO. (DE)
Liquidation completed 07/31/1962
Details not available

BRAZOS SPORTSWEAR INC (DE)
Recapitalized as Marinas International Inc. 08/29/2005
Each share Common no par exchanged for (0.001) share Common no par 08/29/2005
(See Marinas International Inc.)

BRC DIAMONDCORE LTD (CANADA)
Reincorporated 08/13/2004
Name changed 02/11/2008
Name and place of incorporation changed from BRC Development Corp. (ON) to BRC Diamond Corp. (Canada) 08/13/2004
Name changed from BRC Diamond Corp. to BRC DiamondCore Ltd. 02/11/2008
Recapitalized as Delrand Resources Ltd. 06/27/2011
Each share Common no par exchanged for (0.5) share Common no par
Delrand Resources Ltd. name changed to KuuHubb Inc. 06/16/2017

BRC HLDGS INC (DE)
Common 10¢ par split (2) for (1) by issuance of (1) additional share payable 04/06/1998 to holders of record 03/20/1998
Acquired by Affiliated Computer Services, Inc. 02/12/1999
Each share Common 10¢ par exchanged for $19 cash

BRE BK SA (POLAND)
Name changed to mBank S.A. 05/16/2016

BRE CONSULTING GROUP INC (CO)
SEC revoked common stock registration 03/14/2007

BRE PPTYS INC (MD)
Reincorporated 03/15/1996
State of incorporation changed from (DE) to (MD) and Class A Common 1¢ par reclassified as Common 1¢ par 03/15/1996
Common 1¢ par split (2) for (1) by issuance of (1) additional share payable 06/27/1996 to holders of record 06/07/1996 Ex date - 06/28/1996
Each share Common 1¢ par received distribution of (0.2) share VelocityHSI, Inc. Common 1¢ par payable 08/15/2000 to holders of record 08/07/2000 Ex date - 08/17/2000
8.5% Preferred Ser. A 1¢ par called for redemption at $25 on 01/29/2018
8.08% Preferred Ser. B 1¢ par called for redemption at $25 plus $0.42644 accrued dividends on 09/14/2007
6.75% Preferred Ser. C 1¢ par called for redemption at $25 plus $0.34688 accrued dividends on 06/13/2011
6.75% Preferred Ser. D 1¢ par called for redemption at $25 plus $0.23438 accrued dividends on 02/20/2014
Merged into Essex Property Trust, Inc. 04/01/2014
Each share Common 1¢ par exchanged for (0.2971) share Common $0.0001 par and $7.18 cash

BRE X MINERALS LTD (AB)
Common no par split (10) for (1) by issuance of (9) additional shares payable 06/07/1996 to holders of record 05/24/1996 Ex date - 05/22/1996
Each share Common no par received distribution of (0.1) share Bro-X Minerals Ltd. Common no par payable 10/24/1996 to holders of record 10/23/1996
Placed into bankruptcy by Alberta's Court of Queen's Bench 11/05/1997
No stockholders' equity

BREA CANON OIL CO (CA)
Completely liquidated 00/00/1972
Accountant advised all holders have received distribution

BREA CO. (CA)
Acquired by Thrifty Drug Stores Co. Inc. 05/28/1965
Each share Capital Stock $1 par exchanged for (1) share Common no par
Thrifty Drug Stores Co., Inc. name changed to Thrifty Corp. 02/05/1977 which was acquired by Pacific Lighting Corp. 08/05/1986 which name changed to Pacific Enterprises 02/16/1988
(See Pacific Enterprises)

BREA RES CORP (CANADA)
Recapitalized as Goldstream Minerals Inc. 09/21/2012
Each share Common no par exchanged for (0.4) share Common no par

BREAD MAN INTL INC (ON)
Name changed to B.M.I. Capital Inc. 06/00/1982
(See B.M.I. Capital Inc.)

BREADBASKET CORP (DE)
Charter cancelled and declared inoperative and void for non-payment of taxes 04/15/1973

BREAK-FREE CORP (DE)
Name changed to Hallamore Corp. 09/11/1989
(See Hallamore Corp.)

BREAKAWAY SOLUTIONS INC (DE)
Common $0.000125 par split (2) for (1) by issuance of (1) additional share payable 03/23/2000 to holders of record 03/07/2000
Chapter 11 bankruptcy proceedings dismissed 09/07/2006
Stockholders' equity unlikely

BREAKER ENERGY LTD (AB)
Each share Class B no par reclassified as (0.8675) share Class A no par 08/13/2008
Merged into NAL Oil & Gas Trust 12/11/2009
Each share Class A no par exchanged for (0.475) Trust Unit
Note: Unexchanged certificates were cancelled and became without value 12/11/2014
NAL Oil & Gas Trust reorganized as NAL Energy Corp. 01/06/2011 which merged into Pengrowth Energy Corp. 06/05/2012

BREAKTHROUGH ELECTRS INC (NV)
Each share old Common 40¢ par exchanged for (0.01) share new Common 40¢ par 04/09/1999
Name changed to Digital DJ Holdings Inc. 01/10/2000
Digital DJ Holdings Inc. recapitalized as Beverly Holdings Inc. 05/23/2001
(See Beverly Holdings Inc.)

BREAKTHROUGH TECHNOLOGY PARTNERS I INC (DE)
Reincorporated under the laws of Nevada as California Clean Air, Inc. 12/20/2002
(See California Clean Air, Inc.)

BREAKTHRU INDS GROUP INC (UT)
Reorganized under the laws of Delaware 05/24/1990
Each share Common $0.001 par exchanged for (0.1) share Common $0.001 par

BREAKWATER RES LTD (CANADA)
Reincorporated 05/11/1992
Common no par split (2) for (1) by issuance of (1) additional share 06/10/1983
Place of incorporation changed from (BC) to (Canada) 05/11/1992
Each share old Common no par exchanged for (0.05) share new Common no par 06/20/1995
Each share new Common no par exchanged again for (0.1) share new Common no par 06/11/2010
Acquired by Nyrstar N.V. 09/07/2011
Each share new Common no par exchanged for $7 cash

BREAM VENTURES INC (NV)
Common $0.001 par split (25) for (1) by issuance of (24) additional shares payable 11/18/2004 to holders of record 11/17/2004
Ex date - 11/19/2004
Name changed to Sino Silver Corp. 01/14/2005

BREARS TRUCKING LTD (AB)
Name changed to Allnet Secom Inc. 07/07/2000

BREATHE ECIG CORP (NV)
Recapitalized as White Fox Ventures, Inc. 06/22/2016
Each share Common $0.001 par exchanged for (0.01) share Common $0.001 par

BRECCIA INTL MINERALS INC (DE)
Name changed to Nano World Projects Corp. 03/01/2000
(See Nano World Projects Corp.)

BRECHT MED INC (DE)
Charter cancelled and declared inoperative and void for non-payment of taxes 03/01/1988

BRECK (JOSEPH) & SONS CORP. (MA)
Each share 1st Preferred exchanged for (1) share Class A Common no par 00/00/1936
Each share 2nd Preferred exchanged for (0.05) share Class A Common no par 00/00/1936
Involuntarily dissolved 01/10/1979

BRECKENRIDGE BANCSHARES CO (MO)
Merged into Commerce Bancshares, Inc. 03/01/2001
Each share Common $1 par exchanged for (0.8601) share Common $5 par

BRECKENRIDGE MINERALS INC (ON)
Reorganized as Wavepower Systems International Inc. 07/06/2005
Each share Common no par exchanged for (0.025) share Common no par
Wavepower Systems International Inc. name changed to Delta Uranium Inc. 06/06/2017

BRECKENRIDGE RES LTD (BC)
Recapitalized as GTO Resources Inc. 08/07/2003
Each share Common no par exchanged for (0.0625) share Common no par
GTO Resources Inc. recapitalized as

Ram Power, Corp. 10/20/2009 which recapitalized as Polaris Infrastructure Inc. 05/19/2015

BRECKENRIDGE TECHNOLOGIES INC (ON)
Name changed to Breckenridge Minerals Inc. 10/23/1996
Breckenridge Minerals Inc. reorganized as Wavepower Systems International Inc. 07/06/2005 which name changed to Delta Uranium Inc. 06/06/2007

BREECE (GEO. E.) LUMBER CO. (NM)
Liquidation completed 04/22/1961
Details not available

BREED TECHNOLOGIES INC (DE)
Plan of reorganization under Chapter 11 Federal Bankruptcy Code effective 12/26/2000
Stockholders' equity unlikely

BREEDIT CORP (DE)
Recapitalized as TechCare Corp. 10/21/2016
Each share Common $0.0001 par exchanged for (0.03333333) share Common $0.0001 par

BREEKO INDS INC (TN)
Merged into Hillsboro Enterprises, Inc. 06/09/1977
Each share Common $1 par exchanged for $19.75 cash

BREEZE CAP CORP (UT)
Reorganized under the laws of Delaware as Brushgard Systems, Inc. 07/17/1987
Each share Common no par exchanged for (0.01666666) share Common no par
(See Brushgard Systems, Inc.)

BREEZE CORPS INC (NJ)
Common no par changed to $1 par 00/00/1936
Stock Dividend - 100% 03/30/1951
Merged into TransTechnology Corp. (CA) 12/15/1982
Each share Common $1 par exchanged for (2.5) shares Common 50¢ par
TransTechnology Corp. (CA) reincorporated in Delaware 07/18/1986 which name changed to Breeze-Eastern Corp. 10/12/2006
(See Breeze-Eastern Corp.)

BREEZE-EASTERN CORP (DE)
Acquired by TransDigm Group Inc. 01/04/2016
Each share Common 1¢ par exchanged for $19.61 cash

BREEZECOM LTD (ISRAEL)
Under plan of merger name changed to Alvarion 08/01/2001

BREEZY LAKE GOLD MINING CO. LTD. (ON)
Charter revoked for failure to file reports and pay taxes 12/00/1970

BREISE-JOHNSTON FLYING SERVICE, INC. (CA)
Name changed to B & J Aviation Inc. 03/06/1975
B & J Aviation Inc. name changed to B & J Consolidated, Inc. 11/06/1981
(See B & J Consolidated, Inc.)

BREIT LABS INC (UT)
Proclaimed dissolved for failure to pay taxes 09/30/1986

BREITBURN ENERGY PARTNERS L P (DE)
Plan of reorganization under Chapter 11 Federal Bankruptcy proceedings effective 04/06/2018
No stockholders' equity

BREK ENERGY CORP (NV)
Each share Common $0.001 par received distribution of (0.10057706) share Rock City Energy Corp. Common $0.001 par payable 11/30/2007 to holders of record 10/29/2007 Ex date - 11/13/2007
Merged into Gasco Energy, Inc. 12/14/2007
Each share Common $0.001 par exchanged for (0.1356) share Common $0.0001 par
(See Gasco Energy, Inc.)

BREKFORD CORP (DE)
Name changed 07/21/2010
Name changed from Brekford International Corp. to Brekford Corp. 07/21/2010
Name changed to Brekford Traffic Safety, Inc. 06/08/2017
Brekford Traffic Safety, Inc. merged into Novume Solutions, Inc. 08/28/2017

BREKFORD TRAFFIC SAFETY INC (DE)
Merged into Novume Solutions, Inc. 08/28/2017
Each share Common $0.0001 par exchanged for (0.06666666) share Common $0.0001 par

BRELL MAR PRODS INC (MS)
Administratively dissolved 12/04/1996

BREMEN BANCORP INC (MO)
Acquired by Midwest BankCentre, Inc. 07/25/2016
Each share Common $1 par exchanged for $93.925 cash

BREMER CAP TR I (DE)
9% Capital Trust Preferred Securities called for redemption at $25 on 07/17/2006

BREMERTON BRIDGE CO.
Acquired by the State of Washington 00/00/1937
No stockholders' equity

BREN-MAR MINERALS LTD (BC)
Name changed to Canadian Metals Exploration Ltd. 09/22/2000
Canadian Metals Exploration Ltd. name changed to Hard Creek Nickel Corp. 06/28/2004 which recapitalized as Giga Metals Corp. 08/28/2017

BREN MAR RES LTD (BC)
Recapitalized as Bren-Mar Minerals Ltd. 03/15/2000
Each share Common no par exchanged for (0.2) share Common no par
Bren-Mar Minerals Ltd. name changed to Canadian Metals Exploration Ltd. 09/22/2000 which name changed to Hard Creek Nickel Corp. 06/28/2004 which recapitalized as Giga Metals Corp. 08/28/2017

BRENCO INC (VA)
Common $1 par split (2) for (1) by issuance of (1) additional share 09/30/1965
Common $1 par split (2) for (1) by issuance of (1) additional share 05/01/1972
Common $1 par split (5) for (3) by issuance of (0.66666666) additional share 07/11/1977
Common $1 par split (2) for (1) by issuance of (1) additional share 10/12/1979
Stock Dividend - 50% 04/10/1967
Merged into Varlen Corp. 08/23/1996
Each share Common $1 par exchanged for $16.125 cash

BRENDA MINES LTD (BC)
Merged into Noranda Inc. 04/10/1996
Each share Common no par exchanged for $21 cash

BRENDAN TECHNOLOGIES INC (NV)
SEC revoked common stock registration 12/30/2011

BRENDEX RES LTD (BC)
Recapitalized 09/13/1976
Recapitalized from Brendon Resources Ltd. to Brendex Resources Ltd. 09/13/1976
Each share Capital Stock no par exchanged for (0.2) share Capital Stock no par
Struck off the register 02/14/1983

BRENDLES INC (NC)
Filed a petition under Chapter 11 Federal Bankruptcy Code 04/16/1996
No stockholders' equity

BRENEX OIL CORP (UT)
Common 1¢ par changed to $0.0001 par 02/06/2000
Each share old Common $0.0001 par exchanged for (0.06666666) share new Common $0.0001 par 04/04/2003
Each share new Common $0.0001 par exchanged again for (0.06666666) share new Common $0.0001 par 09/04/2003
Name changed to CinemaElectric, Inc. 10/15/2003
(See CinemaElectric, Inc.)

BRENGOLD MINES LTD. (ON)
Charter revoked for failure to file reports and pay fees 02/24/1958

BRENHAM OIL & GAS CORP (NV)
Recapitalized as Africa Growth Corp. 01/30/2017
Each share Common $0.0001 par exchanged for (0.005) share Common no par

BRENMAC MINES LTD (BC)
Recapitalized as International BrenMac Development Corp. 11/28/1975
Each share Capital Stock no par exchanged for (0.2) share Capital Stock no par
International BrenMac Development Corp. recapitalized as Oberg Industries Ltd. 01/14/1986 which recapitalized as Consolidated Oberg Industries Ltd. 08/21/1990 which name changed to Hytec Flow Systems Inc. 01/16/1997
(See Hytec Flow Systems Inc.)

BRENMORE QUEBEC MINES LTD. (QC)
Charter annulled for failure to file reports 12/29/1973

BRENNA RES LTD (BC)
Recapitalized as Clearview Mineral Resources Corp. 05/20/1999
Each share Common no par exchanged for (0.1) share Common no par
Clearview Mineral Resources Corp. recapitalized as Mineral Hill Industries Ltd. 10/22/2004

BRENNAN & KENTY BROTHERS PROSPECTING CO., LTD. (ON)
Charter revoked for failure to file reports and pay taxes 00/00/1953

BRENNAN PACKING CO., INC.
Acquired by Wilson & Co., Inc. (Old) 00/00/1934
Details not available

BRENNAND PAIGE INDS INC (DE)
Common 10¢ par split (5) for (2) by issuance of (1.5) additional shares 07/19/1978
Common 10¢ par split (5) for (2) by issuance of (1.5) additional shares 11/18/1980
Merged into Thackeray Corp. 08/24/1983
Each share Common 10¢ par exchanged for $13.50 cash

BRENNER COS INC (NC)
Acquired by a private investor 10/27/1988
Each share Common 50¢ par exchanged for $18 cash

BRENNER INDS INC (NC)
Common $1 par split (3) for (2) by issuance of (0.5) additional share 05/31/1972
Stock Dividend - 50% 08/31/1971
Merged into Browning-Ferris Industries, Inc. 08/31/1978
Each (8.6725) shares Common $1 par exchanged for (1) share Ser. 7 Serial Preferred Subseries A no par and (1) share Ser. 7 Serial Preferred Subseries B no par
(See Browning-Ferris Industries, Inc.)

BRENNER INTL INC (DE)
Charter forfeited for failure to maintain a registered agent 02/25/1998

BRENT EXPLORATIONS LTD. (BC)
Name changed to Brent Petroleum Industries Ltd. and Common 50¢ par changed to no par 08/27/1979
Brent Petroleum Industries Ltd. recapitalized as B.P.I. Resources Ltd. 05/20/1983 which name changed to Brent Resources Group Ltd. 03/22/1985
(See B.P.I. Resources Ltd.)

BRENT PETE INDS LTD (BC)
Common no par split (3) for (1) by issuance of (2) additional shares 06/30/1981
Recapitalized as B.P.I. Resources Ltd. 05/20/1983
Each share Common no par exchanged for (0.2) share Common no par
B.P.I. Resources Ltd. name changed to Brent Resources Group Ltd. 03/22/1985
(See Brent Resources Group Ltd.)

BRENT RES GROUP LTD (BC)
Company went into receivership 08/31/1988
No stockholders' equity

BRENTON BKS INC (IA)
Common $25 par changed to $5 par and (4) additional shares issued 05/03/1972
Common $5 par split (3) for (2) by issuance of (0.5) additional share 05/05/1978
Common $5 par split (3) for (2) by issuance of (0.5) additional share 11/30/1983
Common $5 par split (2) for (1) by issuance of (1) additional share 01/30/1990
Common $5 par split (3) for (2) by issuance of (0.5) additional share 05/03/1994
Common $5 par changed to $2.50 par and (1) additional share issued payable 02/20/1998 to holders of record 02/10/1998
Stock Dividends - 50% 01/29/1982; 10% payable 10/29/1996 to holders of record 10/17/1996; 10% payable 05/28/1997 to holders of record 05/15/1997; 10% payable 06/18/1998 to holders of record 06/01/1998; 10% payable 06/18/1999 to holders of record 06/01/1999
Merged into Wells Fargo & Co. 12/01/2000
Each share Common $2.50 par exchanged for (0.276421) share Common $1.66666 par

BRENTWOOD BK (LOS ANGELES, CA)
Each share old Common no par exchanged for (0.1) share new Common no par 05/21/1999
Name changed to First Commerce Bank (Los Angeles, CA) 12/03/1999
First Commerce Bank (Los Angeles, CA) reorganized as First Commerce Bancorp 04/01/2004
(See First Commerce Bancorp)

BRENTWOOD FINANCIAL CORP. (DE)
Acquired by Walter (Jim) Corp. 01/06/1966
Each share Common $1 par

exchanged for (0.0963855) share Common $0.16666666 par and (0.266667) share $1.20 Conv. Preferred no par
(See Walter (Jim) Corp.)

BRENTWOOD FINL CORP (OH)
Acquired by PNC Bank Corp. 03/03/1995
Each share Common 1¢ par exchanged for $29 cash

BRENTWOOD INDS INC (DE)
Charter cancelled and declared inoperative and void for non-payment of taxes 03/01/1979

BRENTWOOD INSTRS INC (CA)
Charter cancelled for failure to file reports and pay fees 01/02/1991

BRENTWOOD ORIGS INC (DE)
Acquired by Bomaine Corp. 01/02/1979
Each share Common 10¢ par exchanged for $4.47 cash

BRENTWOOD RES LTD (BC)
Name changed to Maverick Naturalite Beef Corp. 12/19/1986
Maverick Naturalite Beef Corp. name changed to Golden Iskut Resources Inc. 09/06/1988 which merged into Aegis Resources Ltd. 08/01/1990 which recapitalized as New Aegis Resources Ltd. 03/17/1993 which was acquired by Norcan Resources Ltd. 08/19/1994 which recapitalized as Odyssey Exploration Inc. 06/07/2000 which recapitalized as Consolidated Odyssey Exploration Inc. 12/08/2000 which reorganized as Odyssey Petroleum Corp. 08/25/2005 which recapitalized as Petrichor Energy Inc. 03/03/2011

BRENWEST MNG LTD (BC)
Recapitalized as Ridgeway Petroleum Corp. 03/01/1990
Each share Common no par exchanged for (0.33333333) share Common no par
Ridgeway Petroleum Corp. name changed to Enhanced Oil Resources Inc. 06/11/2007 which name changed to Hunter Oil Corp. 08/16/2016

BRENZAC DEV CORP (BC)
Recapitalized as Consolidated Brenzac Development Corp. 04/20/1993
Each share Common no par exchanged for (0.33333333) share Common no par
Consolidated Brenzac Development Corp. name changed to Borneo Gold Corp. 04/16/1996 which name changed to Nexttrip.com Travel Inc. 01/04/2000 which recapitalized as WorldPlus Ventures Ltd. 05/26/2003 which recapitalized as New Global Ventures Ltd. 06/07/2007 which recapitalized as New Global Ventures International Ltd. 03/14/2008 which name changed to Auro Resources Corp. 10/15/2010 which recapitalized as Tesoro Minerals Corp. 08/26/2013

BREON (GEO. A.) & CO.
Acquired by Sterling Drug Inc. 00/00/1946
Details not available

BRESAGEN LTD (AUSTRALIA)
Acquired by Hospira, Inc. 12/11/2006
Each Sponsored ADR for Ordinary exchanged for $1.03066 cash

BRESEA RES LTD (CANADA)
Reincorporated 02/26/1990
Place of incorporation changed from (BC) to (Canada) 02/26/1990
Common no par split (10) for (1) by issuance of (9) additional shares payable 12/20/1995 to holders of record 12/18/1995
Recapitalized as Sasamat Capital Corp. 09/12/2001
Each share Common no par exchanged for (0.1) share Common no par
Sasamat Capital Corp. merged into KHD Humboldt Wedag International Ltd. 06/01/2007 which reorganized as Terra Nova Royalty Corp. 03/30/2010 which name changed to MFC Industrial Ltd. 09/30/2011 which name changed to MFC Bancorp Ltd. (BC) 02/16/2016
(See MFC Bancorp Ltd. (BC))

BRESKIN PUBLICATIONS, INC. (NY)
Merged into McGraw-Hill Publishing Co., Inc. 01/01/1964
Each share Common $1 par exchanged for (0.58) share Common $1 par
McGraw-Hill Publishing Co., Inc. name changed to McGraw-Hill, Inc. 01/02/1964 which name changed to McGraw-Hill Companies, Inc. 04/28/1995 which name changed to McGraw Hill Financial, Inc. 05/02/2013 which name changed to S&P Global Inc. 04/28/2016

BRESNAHAN COMPUTER CORP (DE)
Merged into New BCC, Inc. 10/31/1975
Each share Common $1 par exchanged for $2.375 cash

BRESNAHAN COMPUTER LEASING CORP. (IL)
Reincorporated under the laws of Delaware as Bresnahan Computer Corp. and Common no par changed to $1 par 05/01/1969
(See Bresnahan Computer Corp.)

BRETOONA CORP. (NY)
Reincorporated 00/00/1940
State of incorporation changed from (PA) to (NY) 00/00/1940
Dissolved 01/01/1957
No stockholders' equity

BRETT OILS LTD (AB)
Recapitalized as BRO Resources Ltd. (AB) 02/09/1978
Each share Common no par exchanged for (0.2) share Common no par
BRO Resources Ltd. (AB) reincorporated in British Columbia 10/08/1981 which recapitalized as Canadian Quantum Energy Corp. 12/06/1990

BRETT RES INC (BC)
Each share old Common no par exchanged for (0.33333333) share new Common no par 03/11/2003
Acquired by Osisko Mining Corp. 08/13/2010
Each share new Common no par exchanged for (0.34) share Common no par and $0.0001 cash
Note: Unexchanged certificates were cancelled and became without value 08/13/2016
(See Osisko Mining Corp.)

BRETT TRETHEWEY MINES LTD.
Completely liquidated 00/00/1952
Each share Common received first and final distribution of $0.001 cash

BRETTLAND MINES LTD (BC)
Recapitalized as Valdez Resource Industries Ltd. 03/26/1975
Each share Capital Stock no par exchanged for (0.2) share Capital Stock no par
Valdez Resource Industries Ltd. recapitalized as Goldera Resources Inc. 05/05/1980
(See Goldera Resources Inc.)

BRETTON MINES LTD. (ON)
Charter cancelled and declared dissolved for failure to file returns and pay fees 03/16/1976

BRETTON RED LAKE GOLD MINES LTD. (ON)
Name changed to Bretton Mines Ltd. 04/00/1958
(See Bretton Mines Ltd.)

BRETTON RESOURCE CORP (AB)
Recapitalized as Suncrest Capital Corp. 11/21/1991
Each share Common no par exchanged for (0.5) share Common no par
Suncrest Capital Corp. recapitalized as Suncrest Energy Inc. 07/06/1993 which recapitalized as Nextra Technologies Inc. 10/18/1994 which name changed to NUVO Network Management Inc. 06/27/1997
(See NUVO Network Management Inc.)

BREUNER JOHN CO (CA)
Merged into Field (Marshall) & Co. 09/29/1978
Each share Common no par exchanged for (1.625) shares Common $1 par
(See Field (Marshall) & Co.)

BREVEL PRODS CORP (NJ)
Completely liquidated 02/29/1972
Each share Common 10¢ par exchanged for first and final distribution of (0.3) share McGraw-Edison Co. Common $1 par
(See McGraw-Edison Co.)

BREW KETTLE CORP (ON)
Recapitalized as Lago Resources Ltd. 10/13/1995
Each share Common no par exchanged for (0.14285714) share Common no par
Lago Resources Ltd. recapitalized as RUX Resources Inc. 01/16/1997 which name changed to Galaxy Online Inc. 12/08/1999
(See Galaxy Online Inc.)

BREW RICHARD D & CO INC (NH)
Merged into New Hampshire Astro, Inc. 06/22/1984
Each share Common $1 par exchanged for $1.25 cash

BREWBAC RES INC (ON)
Charter cancelled for failure to file reports and pay taxes 02/28/1994

BREWER ALCOHOL FUELS CORP (DE)
Recapitalized as National Gas & Power Co., Inc. 11/21/1983
Each share Common 1¢ par exchanged for (0.1) share Common 1¢ par
(See National Gas & Power Co., Inc.)

BREWER C & CO LTD (HI)
Each share Capital Stock $100 par exchanged for (5) shares Capital Stock $20 par 00/00/1947
Capital Stock $20 par reclassified as Common no par 00/00/1952
Common no par split (2) for (1) by issuance of (1) additional share 12/24/1963
Common no par split (3) for (2) by issuance of (0.5) additional share 10/20/1972
Merged into IU International Corp. 08/14/1978
Each share Common no par exchanged for (1) share $1.36 Conv. Preferred no par
(See IU International Corp.)

BREWER C HOMES INC (DE)
Reincorporated 10/21/1994
State of incorporation changed from (HI) to (DE) 10/21/1994
Name changed to Hawaii Land & Farming Co., Inc. 12/02/1998
(See Hawaii Land & Farming Inc.)

BREWER (J.W.) CO., INC. (CA)
Out of business 11/29/1965
No stockholders' equity

BREWER TITCHENER CORP (NY)
Completely liquidated 02/26/1968
Details not available

BREWERS & DISTILLERS OF VANCOUVER, LTD. (CANADA)
Name changed to Western Canada Breweries Ltd. 00/00/1950
(See Western Canada Breweries Ltd.)

BREWERS BEST ASSOCIATES, INC.
Bankrupt 00/00/1949
Details not available

BREWERY INVESTMENTS, LTD. (AB)
Liquidation completed 00/00/1953
Details not available

BREWERY LIQUIDATING CORP. (AZ)
Liquidation completed
Each share Common no par exchanged for initial distribution of $14 cash 12/03/1964
Each share Common no par received second and final distribution of $0.665 cash 06/27/1966

BREWERY LIQUIDATION CO. (WA)
Liquidation completed 12/02/1959
Details not available

BREWING CORP. OF AMERICA (VA)
Each share Capital Stock $3 par exchanged for (0.2) share Capital Stock $15 par 00/00/1941
Name changed to Carling Brewing Co., Inc. 00/00/1954
(See Carling Brewing Co., Inc.)

BREWING CORP. OF CANADA LTD. (ON)
Name changed to Canadian Breweries Ltd. 04/00/1937
Canadian Breweries Ltd. name changed to Carling O'Keefe Ltd. 11/09/1973
(See Carling O'Keefe Ltd.)

BREWING CORP. OF ONTARIO LTD. (ON)
Name changed to Brewing Corp. of Canada Ltd. 10/00/1930
Brewing Corp. of Canada Ltd. name changed to Canadian Breweries Ltd. 11/03/1970 which name changed to Carling O'Keefe Ltd. 11/09/1973
(See Carling O'Keefe Ltd.)

BREWIS RED LAKE MINES LTD. (ON)
Recapitalized as DeCoursey-Brewis Minerals Ltd. 02/01/1955
Each share Capital Stock $1 par exchanged for (0.125) share Common $1 par
DeCoursey-Brewis Minerals Ltd. recapitalized as Consolidated Brewis Minerals Ltd. 01/20/1964 which merged into Beauty Counselors of Canada Ltd. 12/01/1981 which name changed to Beauty Counselors International, Inc. 09/22/1982 which recapitalized as Century Technologies Inc. 01/10/1989
(See Century Technologies Inc.)

BREWMASTER CALIFORNIA CORP. (CA)
Charter suspended for failure to pay taxes 07/03/1967

BREWMASTER SYS LTD (BC)
Merged into Jolt Beverage Co., Ltd. 12/14/1987
Each share Common no par exchanged for (0.2) share Common no par
Jolt Beverage Co., Ltd. name changed to International Beverage Corp. 05/13/1988 which recapitalized as Clearly Canadian Beverage Corp. 05/14/1990
(See Clearly Canadian Beverage Corp.)

BREWSERV CORP (NV)
Reincorporated 07/00/2001
Each share old Common no par exchanged for (0.66666666) shares new Common no par 08/10/1998

State of incorporation changed from (ID) to (NV) 07/00/2001
Recapitalized as Grant Ventures, Inc. 02/15/2002
Each share new Common no par exchanged for (0.5) share Common no par
Grant Ventures, Inc. name changed to Grant Life Sciences, Inc. 11/12/2004
(See Grant Life Sciences, Inc.)

BREWSTER AERONAUTICAL CORP. (NY)
Liquidation completed
Each share Common $1 par received initial distribution of $5.25 cash 12/24/1947
Each share Common $1 par received second distribution of $0.50 cash 07/27/1948
Each share Common $1 par received third and final distribution of $0.07 cash 12/29/1950

BREWSTER-BARTLE DRILLING CO., INC. (DE)
Merged into Kilroy Drilling & Production Co. 05/01/1965
Each share Common $2 par exchanged for $5 cash

BREWSTER IDEAL CHOCOLATE CO. (PA)
Name changed to Wilbur-Suchard Chocolate Co., Inc. 00/00/1932
Wilbur-Suchard Chocolate Co., Inc. name changed to Wilbur Chocolate Co. 12/31/1958 which name changed to W.C.C., Inc. 01/03/1966
(See W.C.C., Inc.)

BREWSTER INDS INC (DE)
Ceased operations 07/00/1976
No stockholders' equity

BREWSTER LAKE MINES LTD (BC)
Recapitalized as Mace Technology Inc. 09/14/1976
Each share Common 50¢ par exchanged for (0.2) share Common no par
(See Mace Technology Inc.)

BRF BRASIL FOODS S A (BRAZIL)
Sponsored ADR's for Common split (4) for (1) by issuance of (3) additional ADR's payable 04/07/2010 to holders of record 04/06/2010 Ex date - 04/08/2010
ADR basis changed from (1:2) to (1:1) 04/08/2010
Name changed to BRF S.A. 05/01/2013

BRI SON INDS INC (DE)
Adjudicated bankrupt 05/16/1973
Stockholders' equity unlikely

BRIA COMMUNICATIONS CORP (NJ)
Each share old Class A Common 10¢ par exchanged for (0.05) share new Class A Common 10¢ par 04/11/1997
Each share new Class A Common 10¢ par exchanged for (0.01) share Class A Common $0.001 par 11/16/1998
Name changed to Tianrong Internet Products & Services Inc. 04/09/1999

BRIALTO ENERGY CORP (AB)
Name changed to Highland Energy Inc. and Class A Common no par and Class B Common no par reclassified as Common no par 09/09/1999
Highland Energy Inc. merged into Interaction Resources Ltd. 05/30/2000 which recapitalized as Ketch Energy Ltd. 06/16/2000 which merged into Acclaim Energy Trust 10/01/2002
(See Acclaim Energy Trust)

BRIAN CAP INC (DE)
Name changed to Gump & Co., Inc. 08/29/1997
Gump & Co., Inc. name changed to CRD Holdings Inc. 06/24/2002

BRIAN LLOYD INC (NY)
Adjudicated bankrupt 03/22/1974
No stockholders' equity

BRIANA BIO-TECH INC (BC)
Name changed 09/25/1990
Name changed from Briana Resources Ltd. to Briana Bio-Tech Inc. 09/25/1990
Each share old Common no par exchanged for (0.4) share new Common no par 10/15/1997
Deemed bankrupt 04/27/1999
No stockholders' equity

BRIAR COURT MINES LTD (ON)
Charter cancelled for failure to pay taxes and file returns 03/16/1976

BRIARCLIFF CANDY CORP (NY)
Dissolved by proclamation 09/30/1981

BRIARCLIFF CAP CORP (DE)
Auction Rate 144A Preferred called for redemption at $100,000 on 11/17/1997

BRIARCLIFFE MINES, LTD. (ON)
Charter revoked for failure to file reports and pay taxes 05/13/1957

BRIARWOOD CAP CORP (CO)
Administratively dissolved for failure to file annual reports 01/01/1993

BRIAZZ INC (WA)
Filed a petition under Chapter 11 Federal Bankruptcy Code 06/07/2004
No stockholders' equity

BRICAN RES LTD (BC)
Recapitalized as International Brican Resources Ltd. 05/06/1991
Each share Common no par exchanged for (0.33333333) share Common no par
International Brican Resources Ltd. name changed to C & E Furniture Industries Inc. 02/06/1992
(See C & E Furniture Industries Inc.)

BRICK GROUP INCOME FD (AB)
Under plan of reorganization each Class A Unit no par automatically became (1) share Brick Ltd. (Canada) Common no par 01/05/2011
(See Brick Ltd.)

BRICK LTD (CANADA)
Acquired by Leon's Furniture Ltd. 03/28/2013
Each share Common no par exchanged for $5.40 cash

BRICK TOP PRODUCTIONS INC (FL)
Name changed to Carolco Pictures, Inc. 01/20/2015
Carolco Pictures, Inc. name changed to Recall Studios, Inc. 11/29/2017

BRICK TOWER CORP (NV)
Name changed to Whole Living, Inc. 03/22/1999
Whole Living, Inc. name changed to ForeverGreen Worldwide Corp. 12/29/2006

BRICKELL ENTERPRISES INC (NV)
Name changed to Road Wings Inc. 11/05/1999
Road Wings Inc. recapitalized as OneFi Technology Inc. 03/02/2009 which recapitalized as Seesmart Technologies, Inc. 02/17/2012
(See Seesmart Technologies, Inc.)

BRICKELL FORECLOSURE PPTYS INC (FL)
Name changed to Dynamic Imaging Systems Corp. 02/07/1997
Dynamic Imaging Systems Corp. name changed to Dynamic Media, Inc. 05/15/2000 which name changed to Holoco, Inc. 09/22/2004

BRICKELLBANC SVGS ASSN (FL)
Name changed 04/16/1982
Name changed from Brickellbanc Savings & Loan Association to Brickellbanc Savings Association 04/16/1982
Closed 06/09/1990
No stockholders' equity

BRICKLAND CORP (UT)
Each share Common $0.001 par exchanged for (0.1) share Common 1¢ par 11/20/1987
Recapitalized as Nature's Gift, Inc. 05/15/1991
Each share Common 1¢ par exchanged for (0.1) share Common 1¢ par
Nature's Gift, Inc. name changed to Imall Inc. 01/16/1996 which merged into At Home Corp. 10/27/1999
(See At Home Corp.)

BRICOL CAP CORP (AB)
Name changed to QSolar Ltd. 03/25/2011
(See QSolar Ltd.)

BRIDAL EXPOS INC (NY)
Under plan of merger each share Common 1¢ par exchanged for $0.06 cash 07/28/2000

BRIDGE & TANK CO CDA LTD (ON)
Common no par split (3) for (1) by issuance of (2) additional shares 05/04/1960
2.9% Preference $50 par called for redemption 04/20/1979
Merged into 39588 Ontario Ltd. 05/01/1979
Each share Common no par exchanged for $7.20 cash

BRIDGE BK N A (SANTA BARBARA, CA)
Name changed 03/27/2002
Name changed from Bridge Bank of Silicon Valley N.A. (Santa Barbara, CA) to Bridge Bank, N.A. (Santa Barbara, CA) 03/27/2002
Under plan of reorganization each share Common $2.50 par automatically became (1) share Bridge Capital Holdings Common no par 10/01/2004
Bridge Capital Holdings merged into Western Alliance Bancorporation 06/30/2015

BRIDGE CAP HLDGS (CA)
Merged into Western Alliance Bancorporation 06/30/2015
Each share Common no par exchanged for (0.8145) share Common $0.0001 par and $2.39 cash

BRIDGE COMMUNICATIONS INC (CA)
Merged into 3Com Corp. (CA) 09/29/1987
Each share Common no par exchanged for (1.4) shares Common no par
3Com Corp. (CA) reincorporated in Delaware 06/11/1997
(See 3Com Corp.)

BRIDGE ECHO LAKE MINES LTD. (ON)
Charter cancelled and company declared dissolved for default in filing returns 11/18/1963

BRIDGE HILL MINES LTD (ON)
Charter cancelled for failure to pay taxes and file returns 03/16/1976

BRIDGE OIL LTD (AUSTRALIA)
Each Unsponsored ADR for Ordinary exchanged for (0.2) Sponsored ADR for Ordinary 07/14/1989
Acquired by Parker & Parsley Petroleum Co. 08/10/1994
Each Sponsored ADR for Ordinary exchanged for AUD$4.50 cash

BRIDGE REALTY CO.
Liquidated 00/00/1938
Details not available

BRIDGE RES CORP (AB)
Recapitalized as Idaho Natural Resources Corp. 04/24/2012
Each share Common no par exchanged for (0.01) share Common no par
(See Idaho Natural Resources Corp.)

BRIDGE RES LTD (BC)
Recapitalized as Ravenroc Resources Ltd. 10/18/1984
Each share Common no par exchanged for (0.33333333) share Common no par
Ravenroc Resources Ltd. recapitalized as Rocraven Resources Ltd. 06/05/1990 which recapitalized as Lifetime Ventures Ltd. 10/22/2002

BRIDGE RIV DEV CORP (BC)
Struck off register and declared dissolved for failure to file returns 01/13/1995

BRIDGE RIVER CONSOLIDATED MINES (BC)
Recapitalized as Bridge River United Mines Ltd. 10/21/1958
Each share Class A or Class B no par exchanged for (0.1) share Class A or Class B no par
Bridge River United Mines Ltd. name changed to International Space Modules Ltd. 12/10/1970
(See International Space Modules Ltd.)

BRIDGE RIVER UNITED MINES LTD. (BC)
Name changed to International Space Modules Ltd. 12/10/1970
Each share Class A no par or Class B no par exchanged for (1) share Class A no par or Class B no par respectively
(See International Space Modules Ltd.)

BRIDGE STR FINL INC (DE)
Merged into Alliance Financial Corp. 10/06/2006
Each share Common 1¢ par exchanged for (0.7547) share Common $1 par
Alliance Financial Corp. merged into NBT Bancorp Inc. 03/08/2013

BRIDGE STR INC (DE)
Liquidation completed
Each share Common $1 par exchanged for initial distribution of $4.25 cash 01/21/1974
Each share Common $1 par received second distribution of $0.25 cash 11/06/1974
Each share Common $1 par received third and final distribution of $0.0292 cash 10/08/1976

BRIDGE TECHNOLOGY INC (NV)
Chapter 11 bankruptcy proceedings converted to Chapter 7 on 09/15/2004
Stockholders' equity unlikely

BRIDGE VIEW BANCORP (NJ)
Common no par split (2) for (1) by issuance of (1) additional share payable 12/01/1997 to holders of record 11/14/1997 Ex date - 12/02/1997
Stock Dividends - 5% payable 04/03/1998 to holders of record 03/16/1998; 5% payable 04/01/1999 to holders of record 03/15/1999; 5% payable 05/01/2000 to holders of record 04/14/2000; 10% payable 04/02/2001 to holders of record 03/15/2001 Ex date - 03/13/2001; 10% payable 04/01/2002 to holders of record 03/15/2002 Ex date - 03/13/2002
Merged into Interchange Financial Services Corp. 05/01/2003
Each share Common no par exchanged for $21.9891 cash

BRIDGE VIEW BK (ENGLEWOOD CLIFFS, NJ)
Merged into Bridge View Bancorp 12/09/1996

Each share Common no par exchanged for (2) shares Common no par
(See Bridge View Bancorp)

BRIDGEBANK CAP INC (ON)
Recapitalized as Aquarius Coatings Inc. 09/28/1992
Each share Common no par exchanged for (0.1) share Common no par
Aquarius Coatings Inc. recapitalized as Aquarius Surgical Technologies Inc. 02/24/2017

BRIDGEFILMS INC (NV)
Name changed to Utility Investment Recovery, Inc. 12/14/2007
Utility Investment Recovery, Inc. name changed to General Automotive Co. 03/07/2008 which name changed to MDCorp 05/26/2017 which name changed to Qian Yuan Baixing Inc. 05/01/2018

BRIDGEHAMPTON NATL BK (BRIDGEHAMPTON, NY)
Common $10 par changed to $5 par 00/00/1972
Under plan of reorganization each share Common $5 par automatically became (1) share Bridge Bancorp, Inc. Common $5 par 03/31/1989

BRIDGEHAMPTON RD RACES CORP (NY)
Sold at auction 06/00/1992
Details not available

BRIDGELINE SOFTWARE INC (DE)
Name changed to Bridgeline Digital, Inc. 03/23/2010

BRIDGEPOINT INTL INC (QC)
Acquired by Afcan Mining Corp. 11/03/2003
Each share Common no par exchanged for (0.07751937) share Common no par and (0.03875968) Common Stock Purchase Warrant expiring 10/01/2004
Afcan Mining Corp. merged into Eldorado Gold Corp. (New) 09/13/2005

BRIDGEPORT BRASS CO. (CT)
Each share Capital Stock $100 par exchanged for (15) shares Capital Stock no par 00/00/1934
Capital Stock no par changed to Common no par 00/00/1941
Common no par changed to $5 par 00/00/1952
Merged into National Distillers & Chemical Corp. 06/30/1961
Each share 4.5% Preferred $50 par exchanged for (1) share 4.5% Preferred $50 par
Each share Common $5 par exchanged for (1.35) shares Common $5 par
National Distillers & Chemical Corp. name changed to Quantum Chemical Corp. 01/04/1988 which merged into Hanson PLC (Old) 10/01/1993 which reorganized as Hanson PLC (New) 10/15/2003
(See Hanson PLC (New))

BRIDGEPORT COMMUNICATIONS INC (FL)
Reincorporated under the laws of Delaware as WealthHound.com, Inc. 07/23/1999
WealthHound.com, Inc. recapitalized as Eurosport Active World Corp. 04/07/2008

BRIDGEPORT GAS CO. (CT)
5.28% Preferred $25 par called for redemption 02/03/1964
Merged into Southern Connecticut Gas Co. 01/01/1967
Each share Common no par exchanged for (1.06) shares Common $20 par
Southern Connecticut Gas Co. reorganized as Connecticut Energy Corp. 05/01/1979 which merged into Energy East Corp. 02/08/2000
(See Energy East Corp.)

BRIDGEPORT GAS LIGHT CO. (CT)
Each share Capital Stock $100 par exchanged for (5) shares Capital Stock no par 00/00/1927
Name changed to Bridgeport Gas Co. 06/01/1955
Bridgeport Gas Co. merged into Southern Connecticut Gas Co. 01/01/1967 which reorganized as Connecticut Energy Corp. 05/01/1979 which merged into Energy East Corp. 02/08/2000
(See Energy East Corp.)

BRIDGEPORT HARDWARE MANUFACTURING CORP. (CT)
Acquired by Purolator Products, Inc. 10/16/1959
Each share Capital Stock no par exchanged for (0.9) share Common $1 par
Purolator Products, Inc. name changed to Purolator, Inc. (DE) 04/16/1968 which reincorporated in New York as Purolator Courier Corp 07/01/1984
(See Purolator Courier Corp. (NY))

BRIDGEPORT HYDRAULIC CO (CT)
Each share Common $100 par exchanged for (5) shares Capital Stock $20 par 00/00/1928
Common $20 par changed to $10 par and (1) additional share issued 05/02/1966
Reorganized under the laws of Delaware as Hydraulic Co. 08/12/1969
Each share Common $10 par exchanged for (1) share Common $10 par
Hydraulic Co. name changed to Aquarion Co. 04/23/1991
(See Aquarion Co.)

BRIDGEPORT MACHINE CO.
Name changed to Bridgeport Oil Co., Inc. 00/00/1943
(See Bridgeport Oil Co., Inc.)

BRIDGEPORT MACHS INC (DE)
Merged into Goldman Industrial Group, Inc. 08/20/1999
Each share Common 1¢ par exchanged for $10 cash

BRIDGEPORT METAL GOODS MFG CO (CT)
Assets sold for the benefit of creditors 08/00/2004
No stockholders' equity

BRIDGEPORT OIL CO., INC.
Dissolved 00/00/1949
Details not available

BRIDGEPORT VENTURES INC (ON)
Recapitalized as Premier Royalty Inc. 12/11/2012
Each share Common no par exchanged for (0.25) share Common no par
Premier Royalty Inc. merged into Sandstorm Gold Ltd. 10/09/2013

BRIDGER PETE LTD (AB)
Merged into Home Oil Co. Ltd. 07/27/1978
Each share Capital Stock no par exchanged for $12.60 cash

BRIDGER RES INC (BC)
Recapitalized as BDG Pacific Resources Inc. 08/20/1993
Each share Common no par exchanged for (0.33333333) share Common no par
BDG Pacific Resources Inc. recapitalized as Southern Nites Petroleum Corp. 09/29/1999 which name changed to Oracle Energy Corp. 07/11/2000

BRIDGERLAND ENTERPRISES, INC. (UT)
Proclaimed dissolved for failure to pay taxes 12/31/1977

BRIDGES COM INC (AB)
Name changed to Bridges Transitions Inc. 06/25/2004
(See Bridges Transitions Inc.)

BRIDGES ENERGY INC (AB)
Struck off register for failure to file annual reports 08/01/1995

BRIDGES INITIATIVES INC (AB)
Name changed to Bridges.Com Inc. 04/21/1999
Bridges.Com Inc. name changed to Bridges Transitions Inc. 06/25/2004
(See Bridges Transitions Inc.)

BRIDGES TRANSITIONS INC (AB)
Merged into Xap Corp. 07/21/2006
Each share Common no par exchanged for $0.98 cash

BRIDGESTONE CAP CORP (DE)
Recapitalized as Imagetrust Inc. 10/13/1992
Each share Common 5¢ par exchanged for (0.2) share Common 5¢ par
(See Imagetrust Inc.)

BRIDGESTONE CORP (DE)
Recapitalized as Intellectual Technology Inc. 04/10/1997
Each share Common $0.00001 par exchanged for (0.02) share Common $0.00001 par
(See Intellectual Technology Inc.)

BRIDGESTONE TIRE LTD (JAPAN)
Stock Dividends - 10% 03/22/1973; 22% 03/21/1974; 10% 03/16/1981; 10% 03/19/1982
Name changed to Bridgestone Corp. 04/01/1984

BRIDGESTREET ACCOMMODATIONS INC (DE)
Merged into Meristar Hotels & Resorts Inc. 06/01/2000
Each share Common 1¢ par exchanged for (0.5) share Common 1¢ par and $1.50 cash
MeriStar Hotels & Resorts Inc. merged into Interstate Hotels & Resorts, Inc. 07/31/2002
(See Interstate Hotels & Resorts, Inc.)

BRIDGETON GAS LIGHT CO.
Dissolved 00/00/1950
Details not available

BRIDGETON NATL BK (BRIDGETON, NJ)
Each share Capital Stock $100 par exchanged for (40) shares Capital Stock $2.50 par 00/00/1971
Merged into Citizens National Bank of South Jersey (Bridgeton, NJ) 01/26/1972
Each share Capital Stock $2.50 par exchanged for (1) share Common $3 par
Citizens National Bank of South Jersey (Bridgeton, NJ) acquired by Citizens Bancorp (NJ) 11/02/1972
(See Citizens Bancorp (NJ))

BRIDGETOWN ENERGY CORP (AB)
Acquired by Olympia Energy Inc. 08/30/2001
Each share Common no par exchanged for $1.95 cash

BRIDGEVILLE SVGS BK FSB (BRIDGEVILLE, PA)
Merged into Northwest Savings Bank (Warren, PA) 02/21/1997
Each share Common 10¢ par exchanged for $16 cash

BRIDGEWATER NATIONAL BANK (BRIDGEWATER, NJ)
Merged into United National Bank (Plainfield, NJ) 08/25/1975
Each share Capital Stock 10¢ par exchanged for $30 cash

BRIDGEWATER PLATFORMS INC (NV)
Name changed to Mirage Energy Corp. 11/28/2016

BRIDGEWATER SYS CORP (CANADA)
Acquired by Amdocs Ltd. 08/18/2011
Each share Common no par exchanged for $8.20 cash
Note: Unexchanged certificates were cancelled and became without value 08/18/2017

BRIDGEWEST DEV CORP (BC)
Recapitalized as BDC Industries Corp. 11/22/1984
Each share Common no par exchanged for (0.2) share Common no par
BDC Industries Corp. name changed to Jolt Beverage Co., Ltd. 09/04/1986 which name changed to International Beverage Corp. 05/13/1988 which recapitalized as Clearly Canadian Beverage Corp. 05/14/1990
(See Clearly Canadian Beverage Corp.)

BRIDGFORD PACKING CO. (CA)
Name changed to Bridgford Foods Corp. 03/13/1963

BRIEL INDS INC (IN)
Name changed to Ohio Valley Aluminum Co., Inc. 02/17/1971
(See Ohio Valley Aluminum Co., Inc.)

BRIER GLEN DEVS CORP (BC)
Recapitalized as Innova Technologies Corp. 09/07/1994
Each share Common no par exchanged for (0.5) share Common no par
Innova Technologies Corp. name changed to Innova Technologies Corporation 05/12/1998 which name changed to Innova LifeSciences Corp. 08/03/2000
(See Innova LifeSciences Corp.)

BRIER HILLS IRON & COAL CO.
Dissolved 00/00/1939
Details not available

BRIER RES CORP (BC)
Name changed to Ashlar Financial Services Corp. 08/02/2000
(See Ashlar Financial Services Corp.)

BRIERFIELD OPERATING CORP.
Liquidated 00/00/1949
No stockholders' equity

BRIERLEY INVTS LTD (NEW ZEALAND)
ADR's for Ordinary split (5) for (4) by issuance of (0.25) additional ADR 02/08/1988
Each old ADR for Ordinary exchanged for (0.1) new ADR for Ordinary 05/01/1995
Basis changed from (1:20) to (1:10) 05/10/2001
Stock Dividend - 10% 10/20/1989
Name changed to BIL International Ltd. 01/14/2002
BIL International Ltd. name changed to GuocoLeisure Ltd. (New Zealand) 11/13/2007 which reincorporated in Bermuda as GL Ltd. 11/18/2015

BRIGADE RES INC (BC)
Merged into Colossus Resource Equities Inc. 12/08/1987
Each share Common no par exchanged for (0.33333333) share Common no par
Colossus Resource Equities Inc. merged into Prime Resources Corp. (BC) 02/01/1989 which recapitalized as Prime Resources Group Inc. 01/26/1990 which merged into HomeStake Mining Co. 12/03/1998 which merged into Barrick Gold Corp. 12/14/2001

BRIGADIER ENERGY INC (AB)
Recapitalized 04/26/1995
Name changed 07/31/1997
Recapitalized from Brigadier Capital Corp to Brigadier Venture Capital Corp. 04/26/1995
Each share Common no par exchanged for (0.125) share Common no par
Name changed from Brigadier Venture Capital Corp. to Brigadier Energy Inc. 07/31/1997
Merged into Raider Resources Inc. 02/11/1999
Each share Common no par exchanged for (0.8) share Common no par
Raider Resources Inc. recapitalized as Raider Resources Ltd. 06/24/1994 which merged into Shiningbank Energy Income Fund 06/01/2000 which merged into PrimeWest Energy Trust 07/13/2007
(See PrimeWest Energy Trust)

BRIGADIER INDS CORP (SC)
Merged into Town & Country Mobile Homes, Inc. 09/02/1981
Each share Common 50¢ par exchanged for (2.46) shares Common 80¢ par
Town & Country Mobile Homes, Inc. name changed to Brigadier Industries Corp. (TX) 04/05/1982 which merged into U.S. Home Corp.(Old) 01/07/1983 which reorganized as U.S. Home Corp. (New) 06/21/1993 which merged into Lennar Corp. 05/02/2000

BRIGADIER INDS CORP (TX)
Merged into U.S. Home Corp. (Old) 01/07/1983
Each share Common 80¢ par exchanged for (0.14863) share Common 10¢ par
U.S. Home Corp. (Old) reorganized as U.S. Home Corp. (New) 06/21/1993 which merged into Lennar Corp. 05/02/2000

BRIGADIER RES LTD (BC)
Recapitalized as Parametric Ventures Inc. 04/04/1994
Each share Common no par exchanged for (0.3030303) share Common no par
Parametric Ventures Inc. recapitalized as Centura Resources Inc. 11/12/1999 which recapitalized as Polar Resources Corp. 02/14/2005

BRIGADOON CAP CORP (DE)
Charter cancelled and declared inoperative and void for non-payment of taxes 03/01/1974

BRIGDON RES INC (BC)
Name changed to Tikal Resources Inc. and Class A Common no par reclassified as Common no par 02/05/1999
Tikal Resources Inc. merged into Tikal Resources Corp. 05/31/1999 which was acquired by BelAir Energy Corp. 12/14/2001 which merged into Purcell Energy Ltd. (New) 09/04/2003
(See Purcell Energy Ltd. (New))

BRIGEDAN EQUITIES INC (AB)
Name changed to Everlast Filtration Systems Inc. 10/30/1989
(See Everlast Filtration Systems Inc.)

BRIGGS & STRATTON CORP (DE)
Capital Stock no par split (2) for (1) by Issuance of (1) additional share 04/25/1946
Capital Stock no par changed to $3 par and (2) additional shares issued 04/23/1956
Capital Stock $3 par split (2) for (1) by issuance of (1) additional share 10/05/1962
Capital Stock $3 par split (2) for (1) by issuance of (1) additional share 06/25/1971
Capital Stock $3 par reclassified as Common $3 par 09/15/1975
Common $3 par split (2) for (1) by issuance of (1) additional share 06/25/1976
Reincorporated under the laws of Wisconsin and Common $3 par changed to 1¢ par 10/31/1992

BRIGGS LEASING CORP (NY)
Stock Dividend - 100% 08/03/1970
Merged into Briggs Acquisition Corp. 02/26/1985
Each share Common $1 par exchanged for $1.50 cash

BRIGGS MFG CO (MI)
Common no par changed to $3.50 par and (2) additional shares issued 03/25/1955
Common $3.50 par changed to no par 11/27/1967
Name changed to Panacon Corp. and Common no par changed to $1 par 04/09/1970
(See Panacon Corp.)

BRIGGS TRANSN CO (MN)
Statutorily dissolved 12/31/1992

BRIGHAM EXPL CO (DE)
Acquired by Statoil A.S.A. 12/08/2011
Each share Common 1¢ par exchanged for $36.50 cash

BRIGHT HORIZONS FAMILY SOLUTIONS INC OLD (DE)
Common 1¢ par split (2) for (1) by issuance of (1) additional share payable 03/18/2005 to holders of record 03/04/2005 Ex date - 03/21/2005
Acquired by Bain Capital Partners LLC 05/29/2008
Each share Common 1¢ par exchanged for $48.25 cash

BRIGHT HORIZONS INC (DE)
Merged into Bright Horizons Family Solutions, Inc. (Old) 07/24/1998
Each share Common 1¢ par exchanged for (1.15022) shares Common 1¢ par
(See Bright Horizons Family Solutions, Inc. (Old))

BRIGHT MTN ACQUISITION CORP (FL)
Name changed 07/29/2014
Name changed from Bright Mountain Holdings Inc. to Bright Mountain Acquisition Corp. 07/29/2014
Name changed to Bright Mountain Media, Inc. 12/07/2015

BRIGHT MTN HLDGS INC (NV)
Name changed to Wall Street Media Co, Inc. 09/10/2013

BRIGHT RED LAKE MINES LTD (ON)
Charter cancelled for failure to pay taxes and file returns 10/18/1978

BRIGHT SCREENS INC (NV)
Old Common $0.001 par split (10) for (1) by issuance of (9) additional shares payable 03/06/2009 to holders of record 03/06/2009
Name changed to PrismOne Group, Inc. 07/15/2009

BRIGHT STA PLC (UNITED KINGDOM)
Name changed to Smartlogik Group PLC 07/09/2001
(See Smartlogik Group PLC)

BRIGHT STAR CORP. (IL)
Company ceased operations 07/00/1992
Details not available

BRIGHT STAR HLDG INC (NV)
Recapitalized as Food Safe International, Inc. (NV) 09/11/2003
Each share Common 1¢ par exchanged for (0.00125) share Common 1¢ par
Food Safe International, Inc. (NV) reorganized in Colorado as Produce Safety & Security International, Inc. 03/04/2005 which reincorporated in Nevada as Eco Green Team Inc. 01/29/2009 which name changed to Champion Investments, Inc. 06/28/2012

BRIGHT STAR METALS INC (AB)
Name changed to Jasper Mining Corp. 03/12/2001

BRIGHT STAR TRIO MNG LTD (BC)
Merged into Salem Mines Ltd. 06/15/1972
Each share Common $1 par exchanged for (1) share Common no par
Salem Mines Ltd. name changed to Salem Resources Ltd. 11/19/1973
(See Salem Resources Ltd.)

BRIGHT STAR VENTURES CORP (AB)
Name changed to Bright Star Metals Inc. 10/14/1999
Bright Star Metals Inc. name changed to Jasper Mining Corp. 03/12/2001

BRIGHT STAR VENTURES LTD (BC)
Delisted from Toronto Stock Venture Exchange 04/18/2006

BRIGHT STAR WORLD ENTMT INC (DE)
Each share old Common $0.00001 par exchanged for (0.05) share new Common $0.00001 par 01/25/1994
Name changed to Cyto Skin Care Corp. 03/15/1994
Cyto Skin Care Corp. name changed to Chantal Skin Care Corp. 08/01/1994 which recapitalized as Utix Group, Inc. 11/21/2003
(See Utix Group, Inc.)

BRIGHT T G & CO LTD (ON)
5% Preference $23 par called for redemption 03/29/1963
Common no par split (10) for (1) by issuance of (9) additional shares 06/22/1970
Common no par reclassified as Conv. Class A no par 07/18/1973
Conv. Class A no par split (2) for (1) by issuance of (1) additional share 08/07/1987
Conv. Class B no par split (2) for (1) by issuance of (1) additional share 08/07/1987
Acquired by Wine Acquisition Inc. 09/03/1993
Each share Conv. Class A no par exchanged for $20 cash
Each share Conv. Class B no par exchanged for $20 cash
Note: Unexchanged shares were cancelled and became without value 09/01/1999

BRIGHTEC INC (NV)
Charter revoked for failure to file reports and pay fees 12/31/2012

BRIGHTER CMNTY INC (DE)
Reincorporated 09/18/1989
State of incorporation changed from (NY) to (DE) 09/18/1989
Charter cancelled and declared inoperative and void for non-payment of taxes 03/01/1994

BRIGHTER MINDS MEDIA INC (ON)
Each share old Common no par exchanged for (0.1) share new Common no par 07/21/2008
Assets sold under Section 363 of the Bankruptcy Code 04/10/2009
No stockholders' equity

BRIGHTON APARTMENTS
Trust terminated 00/00/1949
Details not available

BRIGHTON INFORMATION SYS CORP (DE)
Each share old Common 2¢ par exchanged for (0.0625) share new Common 2¢ par 09/17/1992
Name changed to Greater China Corp. 11/14/1995
(See Greater China Corp.)

BRIGHTON MILLS, INC. (GA)
Acquired by Burlington Mills Corp. 08/00/1950
Details not available

BRIGHTON MILLS (NJ)
Merged into Brighton Mills, Inc. 12/15/1941
Each share Class A and/or B exchanged for (1) share 5% Preferred $100 par, (1) share $3 Preferred $50 par, (1) share Common $5 par and $2.50 in cash
(See Brighton Mills, Inc.)

BRIGHTON OIL & GAS INC (NV)
Each share old Common $0.001 par exchanged for (0.1) share new Common $0.001 par 12/12/2007
Recapitalized as Gulf Onshore Inc. 04/04/2008
Each share Common $0.001 par exchanged for (0.1) share Common $0.001 par
Gulf Onshore Inc. name changed to Cannabis Science, Inc. 05/07/2009

BRIGHTON STATE BANK (BRIGHTON, MI)
Merged into Pacesetter Financial Corp. (DE) 06/30/1978
Each share Common $10 par exchanged for (1.85) shares Common $10 par
Pacesetter Financial Corp. (DE) reincorporated in Michigan 03/10/1980
(See Pacesetter Financial Corp. (MI))

BRIGHTON TECHNOLOGIES CORP (DE)
Each share old Common $0.001 par exchanged for (0.33333333) share new Common $0.001 par 10/14/1997
Each share new Common $0.001 par exchanged again for (0.33333333) share new Common $0.001 par 01/26/1998
Each share new Common $0.001 par exchanged again for (3) shares new Common $0.001 par 04/15/1998
Name changed to Seedling Technologies Corp. 02/28/2001
Seedling Technologies Corp. name changed to Worldmodal Network Services Inc. 10/26/2001
(See Worldmodal Network Services Inc.)

BRIGHTPATH EARLY LEARNING INC (CANADA)
Acquired by Busy Bees Holdings Ltd. 07/28/2017
Each share Common no par exchanged for $0.80 cash
Note: Unexchanged certificates will be cancelled and become without value 07/28/2020

BRIGHTPOINT INC (IN)
Old Common 1¢ par split (5) for (4) by issuance of (0.25) additional share 09/20/1995
Old Common 1¢ par split (3) for (2) by issuance of (0.5) additional share payable 12/16/1996 to holders of record 11/25/1996
Old Common 1¢ par split (5) for (4) by issuance of (0.25) additional share payable 03/03/1997 to holders of record 02/11/1997
Old Common 1¢ par split (2) for (1) by issuance of (1) additional share payable 11/21/1997 to holders of record 11/06/1997
Each share old Common 1¢ par exchanged for (0.14285714) share new Common 1¢ par 06/27/2002
New Common 1¢ par split (3) for (2) by issuance of (0.5) additional share payable 08/25/2003 to holders of record 08/11/2003 Ex date - 08/26/2003
New Common 1¢ par split (3) for (2) by issuance of (0.5) additional share payable 10/15/2003 to holders of

record 09/30/2003 Ex date - 10/16/2003
State of incorporation changed from (DE) to (IN) 06/03/2004
Common 1¢ par split (3) for (2) by issuance of (0.5) additional share payable 09/15/2005 to holders of record 08/31/2005 Ex date - 09/16/2005
Common 1¢ par split (3) for (2) by issuance of (0.5) additional share payable 12/30/2005 to holders of record 12/16/2005 Ex date - 01/03/2006
Common 1¢ par split (6) for (5) by issuance of (0.2) additional share payable 05/31/2006 to holders of record 05/19/2006
Acquired by Ingram Micro Inc. 10/15/2012
Each share Common 1¢ par exchanged for $9 cash

BRIGHTWAVE VENTURES INC (CANADA)
Merged into SNB Capital Corp. 05/20/2003
Each share Common no par exchanged for (0.3424) share Common no par
SNB Capital Corp. name changed to Protox Therapeutics Inc. 07/14/2004 which name changed to Sophiris Bio Inc. 04/05/2012

BRIGHTWEST RESOURCE EXPLS INC (ON)
Recapitalized as CD ROM Network Corp. 09/09/1994
Each share Common no par exchanged for (0.66666666) share Common no par
(See CD ROM Network Corp.)

BRIGHTWIRE CORP (FL)
Each old share Common $0.001 par exchanged for (0.001) share new Common $0.001 par 05/19/2005
Name changed to Global Monitoring Systems, Inc. 04/13/2006
Each share new Common $0.001 par exchanged for (1) share Common $0.001 par
Global Monitoring Systems, Inc. name changed to Planet Signal, Inc. 11/21/2007
(See Planet Signal, Inc.)

BRIGHTWORK RES INC (BC)
Recapitalized as Consolidated Brightwork Resources Inc. 01/06/1992
Each share Common no par exchanged for (0.5) share Common no par
Consolidated Brightwork Resources Inc. name changed to Petra Resource Corp. 11/18/1997 which recapitalized as Olly Industries Inc. 01/20/2004 which name changed to Aurea Mining Inc. 06/16/2004 which was acquired by Newstrike Capital Inc. 06/26/2008 which merged into Timmins Gold Corp. 05/28/2015 which recapitalized as Alio Gold Inc. 05/16/2017

BRIGUS GOLD CORP (CANADA)
Reincorporated 06/09/2011
Place of incorporation changed from (YT) to (Canada) 06/09/2011
Merged into Primero Mining Corp. 03/05/2014
Each share Common no par exchanged for (0.175) share Common no par, (0.1) share Fortune Bay Corp. Common no par and $0.000001 cash
(See each company's listing)
Note: Unexchanged certificates will be cancelled and become without value 03/05/2020

BRILHART ELECTRONICS CORP. (NY)
Bankrupt 02/21/1963
No stockholders' equity

BRILHART (ARNOLD), LTD. (NY)
Name changed to Brilhart Plastics Corp. 00/00/1950
Brilhart Plastics Corp. name changed to Brilhart Electronics Corp. 04/24/1961
(See Brilhart Electronics Corp.)

BRILHART PLASTICS CORP. (NY)
Common $1 par changed to 5¢ par 00/00/1950
Each share Common 5¢ par exchanged for (0.2) share Common 25¢ par 00/00/1951
Common 25¢ par changed to $1 par 05/01/1957
Name changed to Brilhart Electronics Corp. 04/24/1961
(See Brilhart Electronics Corp.)

BRILL (J.G.) CO.
Acquired by ACF-Brill Motors Co. 00/00/1945
Details not available

BRILL CORP. (DE)
Merged into ACF-Brill Motors Co. 08/01/1944
Each share 7% Preferred exchanged for (8) shares Common $2.50 par, $70 principal amount of 6% Debentures and $12.25 cash
Each share Class A exchanged for (1.1) shares Common $2.50 par
Each (2) shares Class B exchanged for a warrant to purchase (1) share Common $2.50 par
ACF-Brill Motors Co. merged into ACFWrigley Stores, Inc. 12/30/1955 which name changed to Allied Supermarkets, Inc. (DE) 11/10/1961 which reincorporated in Michigan 08/18/1982 which name changed to Vons Companies, Inc. 07/22/1987 which merged into Safeway Inc. 04/08/1997
(See Safeway Inc.)

BRILLIAN CORP (DE)
Name changed to Syntax-Brillian Corp. 11/30/2005
(See Syntax-Brillian Corp.)

BRILLIANCE CHINA AUTOMOTIVE HLDGS LTD (BERMUDA)
Common 1¢ par split (3) for (2) by issuance of (0.5) additional share payable 07/12/1999 to holders of record 06/29/1999 Ex date - 07/13/1999
Common 1¢ par split (5) for (1) by issuance of (4) additional shares payable 10/01/1999 to holders of record 09/24/1999 Ex date - 10/04/1999
Each share Common 1¢ par exchanged for (0.2) Sponsored ADR for Ordinary 04/14/2000
ADR agreement terminated 08/31/2019
Each Sponsored ADR for Ordinary exchanged for $11.420186 cash

BRILLIANT MNG CORP (AB)
Each share old Class A Common no par exchanged for (0.5) share new Class A Common no par 06/01/2009
Each share new Class A Common no par received distribution of approximately (0.1639) share Panoramic Resources Ltd. Ordinary no par payable 11/26/2009 to holders of record 05/29/2009
Name changed to Brilliant Resources Inc. 11/24/2011
Brilliant Resources Inc. name changed to FCF Capital Inc. 06/29/2015 which recapitalized as Founders Advantage Capital Corp. 05/19/2016

BRILLIANT RES INC (AB)
Name changed to FCF Capital Inc. 06/29/2015
FCF Capital Inc. recapitalized as Founders Advantage Capital Corp. 05/19/2016

BRILLIANT SANDS INC (MT)
Name changed to NexGen Mining, Inc. 01/18/2018

BRILLO MANUFACTURING CO. (NY)
Common no par changed to $1 par and (2) additional shares issued 06/30/1959
Merged into Purex Corp., Ltd. 12/20/1963
Each share Common $1 par exchanged for (1) share $1.35 Conv. Preferred Ser. 1 $5 par
Purex Corp., Ltd. name changed to Purex Corp. (CA) 11/05/1973 which reincorporated in Delaware as Purex Industries, Inc. 10/31/1978
(See Purex Industries, Inc.)

BRIMAC DEV CORP (AB)
Name changed to Wintertherm Corp. 02/02/1993
Wintertherm Corp. recapitalized as Wintercrest Resources Ltd. 08/20/1997 which recapitalized as Mahdia Gold Corp. (AB) 12/02/2009 which reincorporated in Ontario 03/25/2013

BRIMM ENERGY CORP (CANADA)
Reincorporated 08/29/1994
Place of incorporation changed from (BC) to Canada 08/29/1994
Class A Conv. 1st Preferred Ser. 1 no par called for redemption 11/18/1996
Name changed to Odyssey Petroleum Corp. 03/07/1997
(See Odyssey Petroleum Corp.)

BRIMSTONE GOLD CORP (CANADA)
Recapitalized as Foxpoint Resources Ltd. 10/21/1999
Each share Common no par exchanged for (0.06666666) share Common no par
Foxpoint Resources Ltd. name changed to Kirkland Lake Gold Inc. 11/18/2002 which merged into Kirkland Lake Gold Ltd. 12/06/2016

BRINCO LTD (NL)
Each share Conv. Preferred Ser. B $5.50 par exchanged for (0.55) share Common no par 10/20/1980
Recapitalized 12/10/1985
Each share 7% Conv. Preferred Ser. A $5.50 par exchanged for (4) shares Common no par
Each share Common no par exchanged for (1) share Class 1 Common no par and (0.1) Cassiar Mining Corp. Unit consisting of (1) share Common no par and (1) Common Stock Purchase Warrant Series I expiring 04/30/1986
Merged into Consolidated Brinco Ltd. 05/30/1986
For holdings of (999) shares or fewer each share Class 1 Common no par exchanged for $0.35 cash
For holdings of (1,000) shares or more each share Class 1 Common no par exchanged for (0.1) share Class A Common no par and $0.10 cash
Consolidated Brinco Ltd. merged into Hillsborough Resources Ltd. (ON) 02/06/1992 which reincorporated in Canada 11/05/1997
(See Hillsborough Resources Ltd. (Canada))

BRINK'S INC. (IL)
Stock Dividend - 300% 09/18/1951
Merged into Pittston Co. (DE & VA) 02/10/1962
Each share Capital Stock $5 par exchanged for (1.0853) shares Common $1 par
Pittston Co. (DE & VA) Delaware incorporation rescinded 05/14/1986 which name changed to Brink's Co. 05/05/2003

BRINKMAN OUTDOORS INC (TX)
Reorganized under the laws of Florida as Auto Max Group Holdings, Inc. 01/10/2008

Each share Common $0.001 par exchanged for (0.03333333) share Common $0.001 par
Auto Max Group Holdings, Inc. name changed to Biocentric Energy Holdings, Inc. 10/15/2008

BRINKMANN INSTRS INC (NY)
Name changed to Cantiaque Capital Corp. 03/30/1979
(See Cantiaque Capital Corp.)

BRINKMANN INSTRS INC NEW (DE)
Merged into Beijer Industries AB 05/23/1989
Each share Common 1¢ par exchanged for $18.50 cash

BRINKS HOME SEC HLDGS INC (VA)
Merged into Tyco International Ltd. (Switzerland) 05/14/2010
Each share Common no par exchanged for (0.7666) share Common CHF 8.53 par and $12.75 cash
Tyco International Ltd. (Switzerland) reorganized in Ireland as Tyco International PLC 11/17/2014 which merged into Johnson Controls International PLC 09/06/2016

BRINKS INC (DE)
Common $1 par changed to 50¢ par and (1) additional share issued 06/15/1972
Merged into Pittston Co. (DE & VA) 06/25/1979
Each share Common 50¢ par exchanged for $9.625 cash

BRINKTUN, INC. (MN)
Completely liquidated 10/31/1967
Each share Common 70¢ par exchanged for first and final distibution of (0.2) share Larson Industries, Inc. Common 10¢ par
(See Larson Industries, Inc.)

BRINTEC CORP (DE)
Merged into BICC PLC 08/31/1989
Each share Common 1¢ par exchanged for $14.75 cash

BRINTON CARPETS LTD. (CANADA)
Acquired by Armstrong Cork Canada Ltd. 11/00/1966
Each share Capital Stock no par exchanged for $51 cash

BRIO GOLD INC (ON)
Merged into Leagold Mining Corp. 05/25/2018
Each share Common no par exchanged for (0.922) share Common no par and (0.4) Common Stock Purchase Warrant expiring 05/24/2020
Note: Unexchanged certificates will be cancelled and become without value 05/25/2024

BRIO INDS INC (BC)
Name changed to Leading Brands, Inc. 10/25/1999
Leading Brands, Inc. name changed to Liquid Media Group Ltd. 08/13/2018

BRIO SOFTWARE INC (DE)
Name changed 09/07/2001
Name changed from Brio Technology, Inc. to Brio Software, Inc. 09/07/2001
Merged into Hyperion Solutions Corp. 10/16/2003
Each share Common $0.001 par exchanged for (0.109) share Common $0.001 par and $0.363 cash
(See Hyperion Solutions Corp.)

BRIONOR RES INC (QC)
Name changed to Magna Terra Minerals Inc. 06/09/2017

BRISA-AUTO-ESTRADAS DE PORTUGAL S A (PORTUGAL)
ADR agreement terminated 10/30/2013
Each Sponsored ADR for Ordinary exchanged for $2.035543 cash

BRISA INTL S A (LUXEMBOURG)
Completely liquidated 09/10/1986
Each share Common $1.10 par received first and final distribution of (9) shares Basic Resources International (Bahamas) Ltd. Ordinary Stock no par
Note: Certificates were not required to be surrendered and are without value
Basic Resources International (Bahamas) Ltd. recapitalized as Basic Petroleum International Ltd. 08/04/1989
(See Basic Petroleum International Ltd.)

BRISAM CORP (NV)
Charter revoked for failure to file reports and pay fees 03/31/2010

BRISHLIN RES INC (CO)
Recapitalized as Synergy Resources Corp. 09/22/2008
Each share Common $0.001 par exchanged for (0.1) share Common $0.001 par
Synergy Resources Corp. name changed to SRC Energy Inc. 03/06/2017

BRISKER CORP. (LA)
Bankrupt 03/19/1962
No stockholders' equity

BRISTA CORP (NV)
Common $0.001 par split (5) for (1) by issuance of (4) additional shares payable 02/23/2015 to holders of record 02/23/2015
Name changed to MyDx, Inc. 04/24/2015

BRISTOL & PLAINVILLE ELECTRIC CO.
Merged into Connecticut Light & Power Co. 00/00/1927
Details not available

BRISTOL BANK & TRUST CO. (BRISTOL, CT)
Common $25 par changed to $10 par and (1.5) additional shares issued 05/01/1959
Stock Dividends - 100% 12/00/1941; 50% 09/00/1943
Merged into United Bank & Trust Co. (Hartford, CT) 06/14/1965
Each share Common $10 par exchanged for (0.9) share Common $10 par
United Bank & Trust Co. (Hartford, CT) reorganized as First Connecticut Bancorp, Inc. 11/12/1970 which merged into Fleet Financial Group, Inc. (Old) 03/17/1996 which merged into Fleet/Norstar Financial Group, Inc. 01/01/1988 which name changed to Fleet Financial Group, Inc. (New) 04/15/1992 which name changed to Fleet Boston Corp. 10/01/1999 which name changed to FleetBoston Financial Corp. 04/18/2000 which merged into Bank of America Corp. 04/01/2004

BRISTOL BK (BRISTOL, NH)
Merged into Bank of New Hampshire Corp. 05/16/1983
Each share Common $5 par exchanged for $16 cash

BRISTOL BAY PACKING CO. (CA)
Liquidation completed 04/30/1955
Details not available

BRISTOL BOAT CORP. (CA)
Charter suspended for non-payment of taxes 09/04/1962

BRISTOL BRASS CORP (CT)
Each share Common $25 par exchanged for (2.5) shares Common $10 par 00/00/1946
Stock Dividends - 66.66666666% 10/01/1950; 100% 01/15/1957
Name changed to Bristol Brass Liquidating Corp. 04/18/1980
(See Bristol Brass Liquidating Corp.)

BRISTOL BRASS LIQUIDATING CORP. (CT)
Liquidation completed
Each share Common $10 par exchanged for initial distribution of $28 cash 05/16/1980
Each share Common $10 par received second distribution of $3 cash 11/10/1981
Each share Common $10 par received third distribution of $0.50 cash 06/22/1982
Each share Common $10 par received fourth distribution of $0.50 cash 09/20/1983
Each share Common $10 par received fifth and final distribution of $0.315 cash 09/15/1984

BRISTOL CORP (IN)
Stock Dividend - 25% 06/29/1983
Acquired by W-H Corp. 06/08/1984
Each share Common no par exchanged for $16 cash

BRISTOL CNTY TR CO (TAUNTON, MA)
Merged into First Bristol County National Bank (Taunton, MA) 06/30/1970
Each share Capital Stock $12.50 par exchanged for (2) shares Common $10 par
First Bristol County National Bank (Taunton, MA) reorganized as First New England Bankshares Corp. 07/01/1985 which was acquired by Hartford National Corp. 11/14/1986 which merged into Shawmut National Corp. 02/29/1988 which merged into Fleet Financial Group Inc. (New) 11/30/1995 which name changed to Fleet Boston Corp. 10/01/1999 which name changed to FleetBoston Financial Corp. 04/18/2000 which merged into Bank of America Corp. 04/01/2004

BRISTOL DYNAMICS INC (NY)
Completely liquidated 12/12/1968
Each share Common 1¢ par exchanged for first and final distribution of (0.9) share Computer Equipment Corp. Common no par
Computer Equipment Corp. name changed to Cetec Corp. (CA) 05/29/1974 which reincorporated in Delaware 05/12/1986
(See Centec Corp. (DE))

BRISTOL EXPLS LTD (BC)
Recapitalized as Afrasia Mineral Fields Inc. 07/17/1996
Each share Common no par exchanged for (0.5) share Common no par
Afrasia Mineral Fields recapitalized as Westbay Ventures Inc. 01/24/2017 which name changed to Cryptanite Blockchain Technologies Corp. 03/12/2018

BRISTOL FED SVGS BK (BRISTOL, CT)
Under plan of reorganization each share Common 1¢ par automatically became (1) share BFS Bancorp, Inc. Common 1¢ par 12/16/1987
BFS Bancorp, Inc. reorganized as Eagle Financial Corp. 07/29/1988 which merged into Webster Financial Corp. 04/15/1998

BRISTOL HLDGS CORP (NV)
Recapitalized 01/30/1989
Capital Stock 10¢ par changed to 1¢ par 02/18/1975
Stock Dividend - 10% 07/11/1983
Recapitalized from Bristol Gaming Corp. to Bristol Holdings Inc. 01/30/1989
Each share Capital Stock 1¢ par exchanged for (0.4) share Common 1¢ par
Name changed to Sports-Tech, Inc. 04/20/1992
Sports-Tech, Inc. recapitalized as All-Comm Media Corp. 08/23/1995 which name changed to Marketing Services Group, Inc. 07/01/1997 which name changed to MKTG Services, Inc. 03/26/2002 which name changed to Media Services Group, Inc. 12/26/2003 which name changed to MSGI Security Solutions, Inc. 02/09/2005
(See MSGI Security Solutions, Inc.)

BRISTOL HOTEL CO (DE)
Common 1¢ par split (3) for (2) by issuance of (0.5) additional share payable 07/15/1997 to holders of record 06/30/1997 Ex date - 07/16/1997
Each share Common 1¢ par received distribution of (0.5) share Bristol Hotels & Resorts, Inc. Common 1¢ par payable 08/06/1998 to holders of record 07/27/1998
Merged into FelCor Lodging Trust Inc. 07/28/1998
Each share Common 1¢ par exchanged for (0.685) share Common 1¢ par
FelCor Lodging Trust Inc. merged into RLJ Lodging Trust 08/31/2017

BRISTOL HOTELS & RESORTS INC (DE)
Merged into Bass PLC 04/10/2000
Each share Common 1¢ par exchanged for $9.50 cash

BRISTOL MANUFACTURING CO.
Dissolved 00/00/1933
Details not available

BRISTOL MINES 1946 LTD (BC)
Recapitalized as Camero Developments Ltd. 09/28/1974
Each share Capital Stock 50¢ par exchanged for (0.1) share Capital Stock no par
(See Camero Developments Ltd.)

BRISTOL MYERS CO (DE)
Capital Stock $5 par reclassified as Common $5 par 07/00/1945
Each share Common $5 par exchanged for (2) shares Common $2.50 par 12/00/1945
Common $2.50 par changed to $1 par and (2) additional shares issued 07/27/1959
Common $1 par split (2) for (1) by issuance of (1) additional share 10/25/1963
3.75% Preferred $100 par called for redemption 10/15/1965
Common $1 par split (2) for (1) by issuance of (1) additional share 10/28/1966
Common $1 par split (2) for (1) by issuance of (1) additional share 05/27/1977
Common $1 par split (2) for (1) by issuance of (1) additional share 05/26/1983
Common $1 par changed to 10¢ par and (1) additional share issued 06/09/1987
Name changed to Bristol-Myers Squibb Co. 10/04/1989

BRISTOL OIL & GAS CORP (TX)
Reincorporated 10/09/1984
State of incorporation changed from (CO) to (TX) 10/09/1984
Charter forfeited for failure to pay taxes 04/26/1988

BRISTOL OIL & MINERALS PLC (UNITED KINGDOM)
Name changed to BOM Holdings PLC 11/06/1986
(See BOM Holdings PLC)

BRISTOL OILS LTD. (ON)
Recapitalized as New Bristol Oils Ltd. 00/00/1953
Each share Common $1 par exchanged for (0.25) share Common $1 par
New Bristol Oils Ltd. merged into Able Land & Minerals Ltd. 09/16/1959 which was acquired by Canaveral International Corp. 05/01/1963 which recapitalized as Madison Group Associates Inc. 02/02/1993
(See Madison Group Associates Inc.)

BRISTOL PRODS INC (IN)
Stock Dividends - 25% 07/01/1977; 25% 05/08/1978; 25% 06/29/1979
Name changed to Bristol Corp. 05/19/1980
(See Bristol Corp.)

BRISTOL RESH CORP (CA)
Charter suspended for failure to file reports and pay fees 08/02/1993

BRISTOL RETAIL SOLUTIONS INC (DE)
Name changed 07/21/1997
Name changed from Bristol Technology Systems Inc. to Bristol Retail Solutions Inc. 07/21/1997
Merged into VoiceFlash Networks, Inc. 06/26/2001
Each share Common $0.001 par exchanged for (0.65) share Common $0.001 par
(See VoiceFlash Networks, Inc.)

BRISTOL SILVER MINES CO (NV)
Name changed to Bristol Gaming Corp. 01/25/1980
Bristol Gaming Corp. recapitalized as Bristol Holdings Inc. 01/30/1989 which name changed to Sports-Tech, Inc. 04/20/1992 which recapitalized as All-Comm Media Corp. 08/23/1995 which name changed to Marketing Services Group, Inc. 07/01/1997 which name changed to MKTG Services, Inc. 03/26/2002 which name changed to Media Services Group, Inc. 12/26/2003 which name changed to MSGI Security Solutions, Inc. 02/09/2005

BRISTOL SOUND CTRS INC (NY)
Dissolved by proclamation 12/23/1992

BRISTOL-STERLING FINL CORP (DE)
Charter cancelled and declared inoperative and void for non-payment of taxes 03/01/1990

BRISTOL WEST HLDGS INC (DE)
Acquired by Zurich Financial Services 07/03/2007
Each share Common 1¢ par exchanged for $22.50 cash

BRISTOW GROUP INC (DE)
Each share 5.50% Mandatory Convertible Preferred 1¢ par automatically became (1.418) shares Common 1¢ par 09/15/2009
(Additional Information in Active)

BRIT-LEDUC OILS, LTD. (ON)
Dissolved 11/18/1963
Details not available

BRITALTA PETROLEUMS LTD. (BC)
Capital Stock no par changed to $1 par 00/00/1951
Acquired by Wilshire Oil Co. of Texas 10/12/1962
Each share Capital Stock $1 par exchanged for (1) share Common $1 par
Wilshire Oil Co. of Texas name changed to Wilshire Enterprises, Inc. 07/01/2003
(See Wilshire Enterprises, Inc.)

BRITANNIA MINERALS CORP (BC)
Recapitalized 06/14/1999
Recapitalized from Britannia Gold Corp. to Britannia Minerals Corp. 06/14/1999
Each share old Common no par exchanged for (0.14285714) share new Common no par
Name changed to Nanotek Inc. 08/07/2001
Nanotek Inc. name changed to Minterra Resource Corp. 10/25/2002
(See Minterra Resource Corp.)

BRITANNICA RES CORP (BC)
Each share old Common no par exchanged for (0.1) share new Common no par 10/05/2011
Name changed to Trinity Valley Energy Corp. 10/08/2013
Trinity Valley Energy Corp. recapitalized as Smooth Rock Ventures Corp. 11/15/2017

BRITAURA PORCUPINE MINES LTD. (ON)
Name changed to Luckridge Phosphate Mines Ltd. 07/04/1958
(See Luckridge Phosphate Mines Ltd.)

BRITCO INC (TX)
Charter forfeited for failure to pay taxes 03/19/1979

BRITCO OILS LTD. (ON)
Merged into Continental Consolidated Mines & Oils Co. Ltd. 10/04/1957
Each share Capital Stock exchanged for (0.2) share Capital Stock
(See Continental Consolidated Mines & Oils Co. Ltd.)

BRITCOL RES DEV LTD (BC)
Recapitalized as Coldspring Resources Ltd. 06/16/1987
Each share Common no par exchanged for (0.2) share Common no par
Coldspring Resources Ltd. recapitalized as Isleshaven Capital Corp. 07/14/1989 which name changed to Nortel Communications Inc. 06/17/1991 which recapitalized as American Nortel Communications Inc. (BC) 05/11/1992 which reincorporated in Wyoming 02/09/1993 which reincorporated in Nevada 08/03/2007

BRITE UNIVERSAL, INC. (DE)
Reincorporated 12/31/1961
State of incorporation changed from (NY) to (DE) 12/31/1961
No longer in existence having become inoperative and void for non-payment of taxes 04/01/1965

BRITE VOICE SYS INC (KS)
Merged into InterVoice-Brite, Inc. 08/12/1999
Each share Common no par exchanged for (0.957143) share Common no par
InterVoice-Brite, Inc. name changed to InterVoice, Inc. (New) 08/30/2002
(See InterVoice, Inc. (New))

BRITESHINE CORP (NY)
Name changed to Indentcorporation, Inc. 08/19/1971
(See Indentcorporation, Inc.)

BRITESMILE INC (UT)
Each share old Common $0.001 par exchanged for (0.06666666) share new Common $0.001 par 01/27/2003
New Common $0.001 par split (5) for (2) by issuance of (1.5) additional shares payable 01/30/2004 to holders of record 01/16/2004 Ex date - 02/02/2004
Name changed to BSML, Inc. 11/01/2006
(See BSML, Inc.)

BRITEX RES INC (DE)
Charter cancelled and declared inoperative and void for non-payment of taxes 06/26/1985

BRITISH AEROSPACE CAP CORP (DE)
Auction Preferred Ser. A called for redemption 02/10/1998
Auction Preferred Ser. B called for redemption 02/17/1998
Auction Preferred Ser. C called for redemption 02/17/1998

BRITISH AEROSPACE PUB LTD CO (UNITED KINGDOM)
Name changed to BAE Systems PLC 05/08/2000

BRITISH ALUM PLC (ENGLAND)
Each ADR for Ordinary Reg. exchanged for (4) ADR's for Ordinary Reg. to effect a (2) for (1) split and 100% stock dividend 05/08/1979
Acquired by Alcan Aluminum Ltd. (Old) 02/28/1983
Each ADR for Ordinary Reg. exchanged for $0.88 cash

BRITISH AMER CONSTR & MATLS LTD (MB)
Name changed to BACM Industries, Ltd. 07/05/1967
(See BACM Industries, Ltd.)

BRITISH AMERICAN BANK NOTE CO., LTD. (CANADA)
Common no par split (3) for (1) by issuance of (2) additional shares 10/10/1969
Name changed to British American Bank Note Inc. 10/30/1980
British American Bank Note Inc. merged into Bell Canada Enterprises Inc. 10/26/1984 which name changed to BCE Inc. 01/04/1988

BRITISH AMERN BK NT INC (CANADA)
Common no par split (4) for (1) by issuance of (3) additional shares 08/14/1981
Merged into Bell Canada Enterprises Inc. 10/26/1984
Each share Common no par exchanged for (0.85) share Common no par
Bell Canada Enterprises Inc. name changed to BCE Inc. 01/04/1988

BRITISH AMERN INS LTD (BAHAMAS)
Each share Ordinary B£5 par exchanged for (5) shares Ordinary B£1 par 10/22/1965
Each share Ordinary B£1 par exchanged for (1.886792) shares Ordinary B$2 par 09/28/1966
Each share Ordinary B$2 par exchanged for (5) shares Ordinary USD $1 par 06/12/1987
Stock Dividend - 100% 03/27/1969
Acquired by CL Financial 05/00/1998
Details not available

BRITISH AMERN OIL LTD (CANADA)
Each share Capital Stock $25 par exchanged for (4) shares old Capital Stock no par 00/00/1927
Each share old Capital Stock no par exchanged for (2) shares new Capital Stock no par 00/00/1930
New Capital Stock no par reclassified as old Common no par 00/00/1947
Each share old Common no par exchanged for (2) shares new Common no par 00/00/1951
Name changed to Gulf Oil Canada Ltd. 01/01/1969
Gulf Oil Canada Ltd. name changed to Gulf Canada Ltd.-Gulf Canada Ltee. 06/02/1978 which was acquired by Gulf Canada Corp. 02/10/1986 which reorganized reorganized as Gulf Canada Resources Ltd. 07/01/1987
(See Gulf Canada Resources Ltd.)

BRITISH AMERN PETE CORP (DE)
Name changed to Crest Energy Resources Corp. 07/01/1987
(See Crest Energy Resources Corp.)

BRITISH AMERICAN TIMBER CO. LTD.
Liquidated 00/00/1952
Details not available

BRITISH AMERN TOB PLC (ENGLAND)
Each share Ordinary Reg. £1 par exchanged for (2) shares Ordinary Reg. 10s par 00/00/1953
Each ADR for Ordinary Bearer 10s par or ADR's for Ordinary Reg. 10s par exchanged for (2) ADR's for Ordinary Bearer 5s par or (2) ADR's for Ordinary Reg. 5s par 01/11/1971
Ordinary Reg. 5s par, ADR's for Ordinary Reg. 5s par and ADR's for Bearer 5s par changed to 25p par per currency change 02/15/1971
Stock Dividends - in Ordinary to holders of Ordinary 33-1/3% 06/14/1957; 25% 06/21/1963; in ADR's to holders of ADR's 33-1/3% 06/21/1957; 25% 06/28/1963
Merged into B.A.T Industries PLC 08/06/1976
Each (10) shares Ordinary Reg. 25p par exchanged for (1) share Deferred Reg. 25p par and (12) shares Ordinary Reg. 25p par
Each (10) ADR's for Ordinary Bearer 25p par exchanged for (1) ADR for Deferred Reg. 25p par and (12) ADR's for Ordinary Reg. 25p par
Each (10) ADR's for Ordinary Reg. 25p par exchanged for (1) ADR for Deferred Reg. 25p par and (12) ADR's for Ordinary Reg. 25p par
(See B.A.T Industries PLC)
(Additional Information in Active)

BRITISH AWYS PLC (ENGLAND & WALES)
ADR's for Ordinary split (2) for (1) by issuance of (1) additional ADR payable 08/31/2010 to holders of record 08/25/2010 Ex date - 09/01/2010
Basis changed from (1:10) to (1:5) 09/01/2010
Merged into International Consolidated Airlines Group S.A. 01/21/2011
Each ADR for Ordinary exchanged for (1) Sponsored ADR for Ordinary

BRITISH BIOTECH P L C (UNITED KINGDOM)
Name changed 08/05/1994
Sponsored ADR's for Ordinary split (2) for (1) by issuance of (1) additional ADR payable 08/02/1996 to holders of record 07/26/1996
Name changed from British Bio-Technology Group PLC to British Bio-Tech, PLC 08/05/1994
Each old Sponsored ADR for Ordinary exchanged for (0.25) new Sponsored ADR for Ordinary 12/16/2002
Basis changed from (1:10) to (1:40) 12/16/2002
Basis changed from (1:40) to (1:2) 04/23/2003
Name changed to Vernalis PLC 10/01/2003

BRITISH BRASSES LTD (DE)
Name changed to Quantum Power Corp. 06/17/1999

BRITISH CAN CO., LTD.
Acquired by Metal Box Co. Ltd. 00/00/1931
Details not available

BRITISH CAN SHARES, INC.
Dissolved 00/00/1934
Details not available

BRITISH CANADIAN MINES LTD.
Acquired by Santa Fe Gold Mines Ltd. on a (1) for (7) basis 00/00/1937
(See Santa Fe Gold Mines Ltd.)

BRITISH CELANESE LTD. (ENGLAND)
Ordinary 10s par changed to £1 par 00/00/1954
Acquired by Courtaulds PLC 00/00/1957
Each share 7.5% Preference £1 par exchanged for (1.25) shares 6% 2nd Preference £1 par and £1 cash
Each share 7% Preference £1 par exchanged for (1.2) shares 6% 2nd Preference £1 par
Each share Ordinary £1 par exchanged for (0.66666666) share Ordinary £1 par
(See Courtaulds PLC)

BRITISH COLUMBIA ELEC LTD (BC)
Acquired by the Government of British Columbia 08/01/1961
Each share 4% Preferred $100 par exchanged for $100 principal amount of 4% Perpetual Bonds or 4% Ser. AA Bonds due 08/01/1986
Each share 4.25% Preferred $50 par exchanged for $50 principal amount of 4.25% Perpetual Bonds or 4.25% Ser. AB Bonds due 08/01/1986
Each share 4.25% Preferred $50 par exchanged for $50 principal amount of 4.25% Perpetual Bonds or 4.25% Ser. AC Bonds due 08/01/1986
Each share 4.75% Preferred $100 par exchanged for $100 principal amount of 4.75% Perpetual Bonds or 4.75% Ser. AD Bonds due 08/01/1986
Each share 5% Preferred $50 par exchanged for $50 principal amount of 5% Perpetual Bonds or 5% Ser. AE Bonds due 08/01/1986
Each share 5.5% Preferred $50 par exchanged for $50 principal amount of 5.5% Perpetual Bonds or 5.5% Ser. AF Bonds due 08/01/1986
Option to exchange Perpetual Bonds for 25-year Bonds due 08/01/1986 expired 08/01/1962

BRITISH COLUMBIA ELECTRIC POWER & GAS CO., LTD. (BC)
Name changed 00/00/1946
Name changed from British Columbia Electric Power & Gas Co., Ltd. to British Columbia Electric Co., Ltd. 00/00/1946
Acquired by the government of British Columbia 08/01/1961
Details not available

BRITISH COLUMBIA EXPLORERS (1953) LTD. (BC)
Completely liquidated 00/00/1962
Each share Capital Stock $1 par exchanged for first and final distribution of (7) shares Perlite Mining Corp. Ltd. Capital Stock $1 par and $2.25 cash
(See Perlite Mining Corp. Ltd.)

BRITISH COLUMBIA FISHING & PACKING CO. LTD.
Acquired by British Columbia Packers Ltd. and liquidated 00/00/1928
Details not available

BRITISH COLUMBIA FOREST PRODS LTD (BC)
Ordinary Stock no par reclassified as Common no par 04/22/1966
Common no par split (2) for (1) by issuance of (1) additional share 05/18/1973
Common no par split (2) for (1) by issuance of (1) additional share 09/12/1978
Common no par split (2) for (1) by issuance of (1) additional share 05/19/1980
6% Preferred 1966 Ser. $50 par called for redemption 08/01/1988
Name changed to Fletcher Challenge Canada Ltd. and Common no par reclassified as Class A Common no par 09/02/1988
Fletcher Challenge Canada Ltd. name changed to Norske Skog Canada Ltd. (BC) 01/02/2001 which reincorporated in Canada 08/27/2001 which name changed to Catalyst Paper Corp. (Old) 10/06/2005
(See Catalyst Paper Corp. (Old))

BRITISH COLUMBIA MOLYBDENUM LTD (BC)
Assets sold to Kennecott Copper Corp. 04/00/1973
Details not available

BRITISH COLUMBIA NICKEL MINES LTD. (BC)
Reorganized as Pacific Nickel Mines Ltd. on a (0.25) for (1) basis 02/00/1938
(See Pacific Nickel Mines Ltd.)

BRITISH COLUMBIA OIL LDS LTD (BC)
Acquired by BP Oil & Gas Investments Ltd. 03/03/1977
Each share Capital Stock $1 par exchanged for $20 cash

BRITISH COLUMBIA PACKERS LTD (CANADA)
Each share Preference $100 par exchanged for (2.5) shares new Common no par 00/00/1935
Each share old Common no par exchanged for (0.1) share new Common no par 00/00/1935
Each share new Common no par exchanged for (2) shares Class A no par and (2) shares Class B no par 00/00/1946
Acquired by Weston (George) Ltd. 00/00/1984
Each share Conv. Class A no par exchanged for $71.50 cash
Each share Class B no par exchanged for $65 cash

BRITISH COLUMBIA PWR LTD (CANADA)
Recapitalized 00/00/1953
Each share Class A no par exchanged for (2) shares Common no par
Each share Class B no par exchanged for (0.5) share Common no par
Liquidation completed
Each share Common no par received initial distribution of $25 cash 01/02/1964
Each share Common no par received second distribution of $0.50 cash 03/12/1965
Each share Common no par received third and final distribution of $0.0635 cash 04/29/1969
Note: Certificates were not required to be surrendered and are without value

BRITISH COLUMBIA RES INVT CORP (BC)
Name changed to Westar Group Ltd. 09/01/1988
(See Westar Group Ltd.)

BRITISH COLUMBIA TEL CO (CANADA)
Each share Ordinary Stock $100 par exchanged for (4) shares Ordinary Stock $25 par 00/00/1951
6.25% Preferred $100 par called for redemption 06/15/1965
Ordinary Stock $25 par changed to $5 par and (4) additional shares issued 03/25/1975
Ordinary Stock $5 par changed to no par 07/03/1975
10.16% Preferred $25 par called for redemption 04/01/1985
$2.32 Conv. Subord. Preferred $25 par called for redemption 07/02/1986
Ordinary Stock no par split (2) for (1) by issuance of (1) additional share 05/19/1989
11.24% Retractable Preferred $25 par called for redemption 06/15/1990
Under plan of reorganization name of Preference and Preferred stocks was changed to BC Tel and name of Ordinary Stock was changed to BC Telecom Inc. 05/01/1993
(See each company's listing)

BRITISH DOMINION OIL & DEVELOPMENT CORP. LTD.
Recapitalized as New British Dominion Oil Co. Ltd. on a (1) for (3) basis 00/00/1958
New British Dominion Oil Co. Ltd. name changed to Asamera Oil Corp. Ltd. 01/02/1958 which name changed to Asamera Inc. 10/01/1980 which was acquired by Gulf Canada Resources Ltd. 08/04/1988
(See Gulf Canada Resources Ltd.)

BRITISH ELEC TRACTION PLC (ENGLAND)
Stock Dividend - 100% 04/24/1987
Name changed to BET PLC 09/05/1985
(See BET PLC)

BRITISH EMPIRE OIL CO. LTD. (AB)
Class A $1 par exchanged for new Common $1 par 00/00/1953
Each share Class B $1 par exchanged for (1.5) shares new Common $1 par 00/00/1953
Recapitalized as Canadian British Empire Oil Co. Ltd. 00/00/1954
Each share Common $1 par exchanged for (0.2) share Common 10¢ par
Canadian British Empire Oil Co. Ltd. merged into Canadian Western Oil Co., Inc. 03/12/1958 which merged into Westates Petroleum Co. 12/24/1959 which assets were transferred to Westates Petroleum Co. Liquidating Trust 05/02/1977
(See Westates Petroleum Co. Liquidating Trust)

BRITISH EMPIRE OIL DEVELOPMENTS LTD.
Merged into Trans Empire Oils Ltd. on a (0.2) for (1) basis 12/30/1950
Trans Empire Oils Ltd. name changed to West Canadian Oil & Gas Ltd. 03/10/1958 which merged into Canadian Delhi Oil Ltd. 01/01/1962 which recapitalized as CanDel Oil Ltd. 01/10/1972
(See CanDel Oil Ltd.)

BRITISH EMPIRE STEEL CORP.
Merged into Dominion Steel & Coal Corp., Ltd. 00/00/1930
Details not available

BRITISH ENERGY PLC (UNITED KINGDOM)
Each (75) old Sponsored ADR's for Ordinary exchanged for (4) new Sponsored ADR's for Ordinary 03/18/2003
ADR agreement terminated 02/22/2005
Each new Sponsored ADR for Ordinary exchanged for $16.724 cash

BRITISH GAS PLC (ENGLAND & WALES)
Under plan of demerger name changed to BG PLC and each ADR for Ordinary received distribution of (1) Centrica PLC ADR for Ordinary 02/17/1997
BG PLC reorganized as BG Group PLC 12/13/1999
(See BG Group PLC)

BRITISH GROUP REAL ESTATE CORP (BC)
Name changed 10/15/1996
Name changed 10/28/1997
Each share Non-Vtg. Class B Common 65¢ par exchanged for (1) share Class A Common 65¢ par 04/22/1996
Name changed from British Group Holdings Inc. to British Group Resources Ltd. 10/15/1996
Name changed from British Group Resources Ltd. to British Group Real Estate Corp. 10/28/1997
Recapitalized as British Group Realty Corp. 12/14/1999

Each share Class A Common 65¢ par exchanged for (0.25) share Common no par
(See British Group Realty Corp.)

BRITISH GROUP RLTY CORP (BC)
Acquired by J. Block Acquisition Co. Ltd. 02/01/2002
Each share Common no par exchanged for $1.80 cash

BRITISH INDS CAP CORP (BC)
Name changed to British Group Holdings Inc. 04/16/1992
British Group Holdings Inc. name changed to British Group Resources Ltd. 10/15/1996 which name changed to British Group Real Estate Corp. 10/28/1997 which recapitalized as British Group Realty Corp. 12/14/1999
(See British Group Realty Corp.)

BRITISH INDUSTRIES CORP. (NY)
Common $1 par changed to 50¢ par 00/00/1951
Stock Dividend - 20% 12/21/1956
Under plan of merger name changed to Avnet Electronics Corp. and Capital Stock 50¢ par reclassified as Common 5¢ par 12/28/1960
Avnet Electronics Corp. name changed to Avnet, Inc. 12/02/1964

BRITISH INTL FIN LTD (ON)
Name changed to BIF Corp. Ltd. 08/15/1972
BIF Corp. Ltd. name changed to York Centre Corp. 06/29/1978 which name changed to Georgian Bancorp Inc. 04/12/1995
(See Georgian Bancorp Inc.)

BRITISH LD AMER INC (DE)
Reincorporated 12/15/1986
Name and state of incorporation changed from British Land of America (CA) to British Land of America Inc. (DE) 12/15/1986
Merged into Medical Management of America, Inc. 09/23/1988
Each share Common $1 par exchanged for (1.025) shares Common 1¢ par
(See Medical Management of America, Inc.)

BRITISH LEYLAND MTR LTD (ENGLAND)
ADR's for Ordinary 5s par changed to 25p par per currency change 02/15/1971
Reorganized as British Leyland PLC 10/20/1975
Each ADR for Ordinary 25p par issued by First National City Bank, New York exchanged for (1) ADR for Ordinary
Each ADR for Ordinary 25p par issued by Irving Trust Co., New York exchanged for $2.04 cash
British Leyland PLC name changed to Rover Group PLC 07/07/1986
(See Rover Group PLC)

BRITISH LEYLAND PLC (ENGLAND)
Name changed to Rover Group PLC 07/07/1986
(See Rover Group plc)

BRITISH LION MINES LTD (BC)
Delisted from Vancouver Stock Exchange 10/31/1994

BRITISH MATACHEWAN GOLD MINES LTD (ON)
Recapitalized as Saskuran Explorations Inc. 10/25/1977
Each share Capital Stock $1 par exchanged for (0.4) share Capital Stock no par
Saskuran Explorations Inc. name changed to Team Energy & Minerals Inc. 11/05/1980
(See Team Energy & Minerals Inc.)

BRITISH MED SVCS LTD (BC)
Recapitalized as BMD Enterprises Ltd. 10/05/1990
Each share Common no par exchanged for (0.33333333) share Common no par
(See BMD Enterprises Ltd.)

BRITISH MORTGAGE & TRUST CO. (STRATFORD, ON)
Capital Stock $100 par changed to $5 par and (19) additional shares issued 00/00/1962
Merged into Victoria & Grey Trust Co. (Lindsay, ON) 09/30/1965
Each share Capital Stock $5 par exchanged for (0.166666) share Common $2 par
Victoria & Grey Trust Co. (Lindsay, ON) name changed to Victoria & Grey Trust Co./La Compagnie de Fiducie Victoria et Grey (Lindsay, ON) 10/31/1978 which merged into Victoria Grey Metro Trust Co. (Stratford, ON) 10/31/1979 which name changed to Victoria & Grey Trust Co. (Stratford, ON) 04/07/1980 which merged into National Victoria & Grey Trust Co. (Toronto, ON) 08/31/1984 which name changed to National Trust Co. (Toronto, ON) 10/28/1985
(See National Trust Co. (Toronto, ON))

BRITISH MOTOR CORP. LTD. (ENGLAND)
Stock Dividend - 12.5 % 06/19/1964
Name changed to British Motor Holdings Ltd. 12/19/1966
British Motor Holdings Ltd. name changed to British Leyland Motor Corp. Ltd. 05/14/1968
(See British Leyland Motor Corp. Ltd.)

BRITISH MOTOR HOLDINGS LTD. (ENGLAND)
Name changed to British Leyland Motor Corp. Ltd. 05/14/1968
(See British Leyland Motor Corp. Ltd.)

BRITISH NFLD LTD (NL)
Each share Founders Stock no par exchanged for (1.05) shares Common no par 06/28/1967
Name changed to Brinco Ltd. 07/02/1971
Brinco Ltd. merged into Consolidated Brinco Ltd. 05/30/1986 which merged into Hillsborough Resources Ltd. (ON) 02/06/1992 which reincorporated in Canada 11/05/1997
(See Hillsborough Resources Ltd. (Canada))

BRITISH OXYGEN PLC (ENGLAND)
ADR's for Ordinary Reg. 5p par changed to 25p par per currency change 02/15/1971
Stock Dividend - 50% 06/12/1961
Name changed to BOC International PLC 04/16/1975
BOC International PLC name changed to BOC Group PLC 02/17/1982
(See BOC Group PLC)

BRITISH PAC FINL INC (BC)
Each share old Common no par exchanged for (4) shares new Common no par 02/17/1986
Recapitalized as Inter-Asia Equities Inc. 08/10/1988
Each share new Common no par exchanged for (0.1) share Common no par
(See Inter-Asia Equities Inc.)

BRITISH PAC INVT CORP (BC)
Struck off register and declared dissolved for failure to file returns 02/25/1983

BRITISH PACIFIC EXPLORATIONS LTD. (BC)
Name changed to British Pacific Investment Corp. 02/14/1975
(See British Pacific Investment Corp.)

BRITISH PACIFIC RESOURCES INC. (BC)
Name changed to British Pacific Financial Inc. 11/18/1985
British Pacific Financial Inc. recapitalized as Inter-Asia Equities Inc. 08/10/1988
(See Inter-Asia Equities Inc.)

BRITISH PETE PLC (ENGLAND)
Old depositary agreement terminated 03/16/1970
Each old ADR for Ordinary Reg. £1 par exchanged for (1) American Share for Ordinary Reg. 25p par
Note: Exchange for old ADR's for new American Shares effected until 02/26/1975 after which each ADR may be exchanged for $10.49 cash only
8% 1st Preference £1 par reclassified as 5.6% 1st Preference £1 par 04/05/1973
9% 2nd Preference £1 par reclassified as 6.3% Preference £1 par 04/05/1973
Ordinary Reg. Shares 25p par split (3) for (1) by issuance of (2) additional shares 04/30/1987
American Shares for Ordinary Reg. 25p par split (2) for (1) by issuance of (1) additional share payable 06/05/1997 to holders of record 05/29/1997
Stock Dividends - Ordinary Reg. 400% 12/10/1954; 100% 10/14/1958; 20% 11/10/1961; 20% 06/05/1964
Stock Dividends - ADR's for Ordinary Reg. 400% 12/28/1954; 100% 10/23/1958; 20% 11/28/1961; 20% 06/20/1964
Merged into BP Amoco PLC 12/31/1998
Each American Share for Ordinary Reg. 25p par exchanged for (1) Sponsored ADR for Ordinary 25p par
BP Amoco PLC name changed to BP PLC 05/01/2001

BRITISH PETROLEUMS LTD. (CANADA)
Name changed to Leamac Petroleums Ltd. 04/11/1957
Leamac Petroleums Ltd. recapitalized as Embassy Petroleums Ltd. 08/08/1961 which merged into Cavalier Energy Inc. (ON) 03/01/1974 which reincorporated in Alberta as Cavalier Energy Ltd. 02/07/1978
(See Cavalier Energy Ltd.)

BRITISH RUBBER CO. OF CANADA LTD.
Name changed to Mailman Corp. Ltd. 00/00/1948
(See Mailman Corp. Ltd.)

BRITISH SILBAK PREMIER MINES LTD (BC)
Each share Capital Stock no par exchanged for (0.5) share Class A Common no par and (0.5) share Class B Common no par 12/21/1982
Name changed to Silbak Premier Mines, Ltd. (New) 07/23/1987
Silbak Premier Mines Ltd (New) merged into Pioneer Metals Corp. (Old) 05/11/1988
(See Pioneer Metals Corp. (Old))

BRITISH SKY BROADCASTING GROUP PLC (UNITED KINGDOM)
Sponsored ADR's for Ordinary split (3) for (2) by issuance of (0.5) additional ADR payable 12/23/2002 to holders of record 12/20/2002 Ex date - 12/24/2002
ADR basis changed from (1:6) to (1:4) 12/23/2012
Name changed to Sky PLC 11/24/2014

BRITISH SOUTH AFRICA CO. (UNITED KINGDOM)
Merged into Charter Consolidated Ltd. 05/05/1965
Each ADR for Ordinary exchanged for (3) ADR's for Ordinary
(See Charter Consolidated Ltd.)

BRITISH STL PLC (ENGLAND)
Name changed to Corus Group PLC 10/06/1999
(See Corus Group PLC)

BRITISH SUGAR LTD (ENGLAND)
Acquired by Berisford International 00/00/1982
Details not available

BRITISH TELECOMMUNICATIONS P L C (ENGLAND)
Scheme of arrangement effective 11/16/2001
Each ADR for Final Installment exchanged for (1) mmO2 PLC Sponsored ADR for Ordinary
(See mmO2 PLC)

BRITISH TEXAN OILS LTD. (CANADA)
Proclaimed dissolved for failure to file reports 12/16/1980

BRITISH TYPE INVESTORS, INC. (DE)
Class A & B no par exchanged (4) for (1) and Class A no par exchanged again (2) for (1) 00/00/1929
Class A no par changed to $1 par 00/00/1931
Recapitalized 00/00/1937
Class A $1 par changed to 25¢ par
Class B no par changed to 10¢ par
Merged into Allied International Investing Corp. 02/29/1956
Each share Class A 25¢ par exchanged for (0.05) share Capital Stock $1 par
Each share Class B 10¢ par exchanged for (0.025) share Capital Stock $1 par and a 10-Year option to purchase (1) share at $7.35 for each (5) shares held
Allied International Investing Corp. name changed to Dorsey Corp. 03/26/1959 which name changed to Constar International Inc. 05/01/1987
(See Constar International Inc.)

BRITISH WESTERN AMERICA URANIUM CORP. (CO)
Charter revoked for failure to file reports and pay fees 09/30/1958

BRITISH WESTN INDS LTD (BC)
Acquired by a private co. 12/14/1978
Each share Common no par exchanged for $0.55 cash

BRITMAR CORP (DE)
100% acquired at $1.75 cash per share through purchase offer which expired 08/20/1990
Public interest eliminated

BRITOIL PLC (ENGLAND)
Merged into British Petroleum Co. PLC 10/21/1988
Each ADR for Ordinary exchanged for $44.277 cash

BRITT-MALARTIC GOLD MINES LTD. (ON)
Charter revoked for failure to file reports and pay fees 09/08/1966

BRITT RES LTD (BC)
Recapitalized as La Cieba Minerals Corp. (BC) 07/15/1992
Each share Common no par exchanged for (0.33333333) share Common no par
La Cieba Minerals Corp. (BC) reincorporated in Canada as Lowell Petroleum Inc. 09/26/1995 which recapitalized as Hedong Energy, Inc. 08/17/1998 which recapitalized as Benchmark Energy Corp. 02/09/2004 which name changed to Bolivar Energy Corp. 10/29/2010 which reorganized in Alberta as Anatolia Energy Corp. 12/13/2011 which merged into Cub Energy Inc. 07/01/2013

BRITT TECH CORP (IA)
Common $2 par changed to $1 par and (1) additional share issued 10/02/1972
Common $1 par changed to 50¢ par and (1) additional share issued 10/16/1976
Stock Dividend - 100% 10/23/1978
Completely liquidated 05/24/1989
Each share Common 50¢ par exchanged for first and final distribution of $0.26653918 cash

BRITTANY ENERGY INC (AB)
Name changed 07/18/1997
Name changed from Brittany Capital Corp. to Brittany Energy Inc. 07/18/1997
Merged into Diaz Resources Ltd. 06/08/1999
Each share no par exchanged for (0.75) share Class A Subordinate no par
Diaz Resources Ltd. merged into Tuscany Energy Ltd. (Old) 07/18/2013 which reorganized as Tuscany Energy Ltd. (New) 07/19/2013
(See Tuscany Energy Ltd. (New))

BRITTON & KOONTZ CAP CORP (MS)
Common $10 par changed to $2.50 par and (3) additional shares issued payable 05/15/1997 to holders of record 04/25/1997
Acquired by Home Bancorp, Inc. 02/14/2014
Each share Common $2.50 par exchanged for $16.14 cash

BRITTON ELECTRS CORP (NY)
Adjudicated bankrupt 03/25/1964
No stockholders' equity

BRITTON INTL INC (NV)
Each share old Common $0.0001 par exchanged for (30) shares new Common $0.0001 par 11/15/2007
Name changed to Belltower Entertainment Corp. 10/14/2008

BRITTON LEE INC (DE)
Reincorporated 03/09/1987
State of incorporation changed from (CA) to (DE) 03/09/1987
Name changed to Sharebase Corp. 05/15/1989
Sharebase Corp. merged into Teradata Corp. 06/27/1990 which merged into American Telephone & Telegraph Co. 02/28/1992 which name changed to AT&T Corp. 04/20/1994 which merged into AT&T Inc. 11/18/2005

BRIX MARITIME CO (DE)
Each share Common $1 par exchanged for (0.002) share Common no par 04/04/1989
Acquired by Brix Acquisition Co. 08/16/1990
Each share Common no par exchanged for $2,175 cash

BRIYANTE SOFTWARE CORP (BC)
Merged into Imagis Technologies Inc. (BC) 11/25/2003
Each share Common no par exchanged for (0.31111) share Common no par
Imagis Technologies Inc. (BC) reincorporated in Canada as Visiphor Corp. 07/07/2005

BRL ENTERPRISES INC (BC)
Acquired by B.C. Pacific Capital Corp. 06/26/1998
Each share Common no par exchanged for $6.75 cash

BRL HLDGS INC (DE)
Common 1¢ par split (2) for (1) by issuance of (1) additional share payable 12/10/2002 to holders of record 10/4/2002 Ex date - 12/11/2002
Name changed to Element 21 Golf Co. (DE) 10/18/2004
Element 21 Golf Co. (DE) reincorporated in Nevada as American Rare Earths & Materials, Corp. 07/20/2010

BRM CAP CORP (AB)
Name changed to Cartier Partners Financial Group Inc. 03/30/2001
Cartier Partners Financial Group Inc. merged into Dundee Wealth Management Inc. 12/30/2003 which name changed to DundeeWealth Inc. 06/28/2007 which was acquired by Bank of Nova Scotia (Halifax, NS) 03/09/2011

BRO DART INDS (NJ)
Capital Stock 10¢ par reclassified as Common 10¢ par 12/20/1968
Common 10¢ par split (2) for (1) by issuance of (1) additional share 01/06/1969
Name changed to BDI Investment Corp. 07/02/1983
(See BDI Investment Corp.)

BRO RES LTD (BC)
Reincorporated 10/08/1981
Place of incorporation changed from (ALTA) to (BC) 10/08/1981
Recapitalized as Canadian Quantum Energy Corp. 12/06/1990
Each share Common no par exchanged for (0.2) share Common no par

BRO-X MINERALS LTD (AB)
Company became inactive 05/00/1997
Details not available

BROAD & WALL CORP (NY)
Charter cancelled and proclaimed dissolved for failure to pay taxes 12/15/1973

BROAD-GRACE ARCADE CORP. (VA)
5% Preferred $100 par called for redemption 04/30/1963
Liquidation completed
Each share Preferred $3 par received initial distribution of $4.11 cash 02/09/1973
Each share Common $1 par received initial distribution of $10.25 cash 02/09/1973
Each share Preferred $3 par exchanged for second distribution of $7.8979 cash 06/28/1974
Each share Common $1 par exchanged for second distribution of $7.4447 cash 06/28/1974
Each share Preferred $3 par received third and final distribution of $0.3362 cash 12/15/1974
Each share Common $1 par received third and final distribution of $0.838 cash 12/15/1974

BROAD INC (MD)
$1.50 Conv. Preferred Ser. A no par called for redemption 09/06/1989
Name changed to SunAmerica Inc. 02/01/1993

BROAD NATL BANCORPORATION (NJ)
9% Class 1985 Preferred $15 par called for redemption 01/07/1996
8.5% 1992 Preferred $1 par called for redemption 04/08/1996
Common $10 par split (3) for (2) by issuance of (0.5) additional share 04/10/1986
Common $10 par split (2) for (1) by issuance of (1) additional share 04/09/1987
Common $10 par changed to $8 par and (0.25) additional share issued 04/15/1988
Common $8 par split (3) for (2) by issuance of (0.5) additional share 12/15/1988
Stock Dividends - 10% 12/15/1989;

10% payable 10/04/1996 to holders of record 10/03/1996; 5% payable 01/06/1998 to holders of record 12/30/1997; 5% payable 01/15/1999 to holders of record 01/11/1999
Merged into Independence Community Bank Corp. 07/30/1999
Each share Common $8 par exchanged for (1.9859) shares Common 1¢ par
(See Independence Community Bank Corp.)

BROAD NATL BK (NEWARK, NJ)
Reorganized as Broad National Bancorp 02/01/1983
Each share Common $10 par exchanged for (2) shares Common $10 par
Broad National Bancorp merged into Independence Community Bank Corp. 07/30/1999
(See Independence Community Bank Corp.)

BROAD RIVER POWER CO.
Name changed to South Carolina Electric & Gas Co. 00/00/1937
South Carolina Electric & Gas Co. reorganized as SCANA Corp. (Old) 12/31/1984 which merged into SCANA Corp. (New) 02/10/2000

BROAD SCOPE ENTERPRISES INC (NV)
Each share Common $0.001 par exchanged for (5.53846) shares Common $0.001 par 04/08/2004
Name changed to Xten Networks, Inc. 05/07/2004
Xten Networks, Inc. name changed to CounterPath Solutions, Inc. 09/16/2005 which name changed to CounterPath Corp. 10/17/2007

BROAD STR INVESTING CORP (MD)
Capital Stock $5 par changed to $1 par 03/31/1955
Capital Stock $1 par changed to 50¢ par and (1) additional share issued 04/01/1959
Stock Dividend - 50% 01/24/1955
Name changed to Seligman Common Stock Fund, Inc. 05/01/1982

BROAD STR NATL BK (TRENTON, NJ)
Each share Capital Stock $100 par exchanged for (5) shares Capital Stock $20 par 01/25/1955
Capital Stock $20 par changed to $5 par and (3) additional shares issued 09/15/1969
Stock Dividends - 100% 02/02/1948; 100% 06/01/1951; 20% 03/15/1968; 20% 04/02/1973; 20% 04/01/1982
Each share Capital Stock $5 par exchanged for (0.0008) share Capital Stock $100 par 01/31/1986
Note: In effect holders received $67 cash per share and public interest was eliminated

BROAD STREET INVESTING CO., INC.
Name changed to Broad Street Investing Corp. 00/00/1939
Broad Street Investing Corp. name changed to Seligman Common Stock Fund, Inc. 05/01/1982

BROAD STREET TRUST CO. (PHILADELPHIA, PA)
Each share Capital Stock $20 par exchanged for (2) shares Capital Stock $10 par 10/28/1955
Capital Stock $10 par changed to $5 par and (1) additional share issued 09/27/1961
Merged into Continental Bank & Trust Co. (Norristown, PA) 08/02/1965
Each share Capital Stock $5 par exchanged for (1) share Capital Stock $5 par
Continental Bank & Trust Co. (Norristown, PA) name changed to Continental Bank (Norristown, PA) 07/17/1969 which reorganized as Continental Bancorp, Inc. 05/01/1982 which merged into Midlantic Corp. 01/30/1987 which merged into PNC Bank Corp. 12/31/1995 which name changed to PNC Financial Services Group, Inc. 03/15/2000

BROADBACK MINES LTD. (ON)
Charter reported cancelled 12/00/1968

BROADBAND HOLDRS TR (DE)
Trust terminated
Each Depositary Receipt received first and final distribution of $14.044132 cash payable 01/08/2013 to holders of record 12/24/2012

BROADBAND LEARNING CORP (ON)
Ceased operations 08/27/2009
Stockholders' equity unlikely

BROADBAND TECHNOLOGIES INC (DE)
Name changed to Pliant Systems, Inc. 12/13/1999
(See Pliant Systems, Inc.)

BROADBAND WIRELESS INTL CORP (NV)
Stock Dividend - 10% payable 03/29/2004 to holders of record 03/16/2004
SEC revoked common stock registration 11/08/2011

BROADBASE SOFTWARE INC (DE)
Common $0.001 par split (2) for (1) by issuance of (1) additional share payable 04/07/2000 to holders of record 03/31/2000
Merged into Kana Software, Inc. 06/29/2001
Each share Common $0.001 par exchanged for (1.05) shares Common $0.001 par
Kana Software, Inc. name changed to SWK Holdings Corp. 12/23/2009

BROADCAST CAP CORP (AB)
Reincorporated under the laws of British Columbia as Pebble Creek Mining Ltd. 12/29/2006

BROADCAST COM INC (DE)
Common 1¢ par split (2) for (1) by issuance of (1) additional share payable 02/11/1999 to holders of record 02/01/1999
Merged into Yahoo! Inc. 07/20/1999
Each share Common 1¢ par exchanged for (0.7722) share Common $0.001 par
Yahoo! Inc. name changed to Altaba Inc. 06/19/2017

BROADCAST INDS CORP (DE)
Adjudicated bankrupt 06/12/1978
Stockholders' equity unlikely

BROADCAST INTL INC NEW (UT)
Merged into Wireless Ronin Technologies, Inc. 08/01/2014
Each share Common 1¢ par exchanged for (0.00535594) share new Common 1¢ par
Wireless Ronin Technologies, Inc. name changed to Creative Realities, Inc. 09/17/2014

BROADCAST INTL INC OLD (UT)
Each share Common $0.001 par exchanged for (0.02) share old Common 10¢ par 08/13/1987
Each share old Common 10¢ par exchanged for (0.4) share new Common 10¢ par 05/24/1990
Merged into Data Broadcasting Corp. 06/30/1995
Each share new Common 10¢ par exchanged for (1.01408) shares Common 1¢ par and $2.25 cash
Data Broadcasting Corp. name changed to Interactive Data Corp. 06/20/2001
(See Interactive Data Corp.)

BROADCASTER INC (DE)
Reincorporated 05/21/2007
State of incorporation changed from (CA) to (DE) and Common no par changed to $0.001 par 05/21/2007
Each share old Common $0.001 par exchanged for (0.5) share new Common $0.001 par 06/25/2007
SEC revoked common stock registration 02/07/2012

BROADCASTING CO. OF THE SOUTH (SC)
Name changed to Cosmos Broadcasting Corp. 05/01/1965
Cosmos Broadcasting Corp. acquired by Liberty Corp. (SC) 12/31/1968
(See Liberty Corp. (SC))

BROADCASTING PARTNERS INC (DE)
Merged into Evergreen Media Corp. 05/12/1995
Each share Class A Common 1¢ par exchanged for (0.46) share Class A Common 1¢ par and $12 cash
Evergreen Media Corp. name changed to Chancellor Media Corp. 09/15/1997 which name changed to AMFM, Inc. 07/13/1999 which merged into Clear Channel Communications, Inc. 08/30/2000
(See Clear Channel Communications, Inc.)

BROADCOM CORP (CA)
Class A Common $0.0001 par split (2) for (1) by issuance of (1) additional share payable 02/17/1999 to holders of record 02/05/1999
Class A Common $0.0001 par split (2) for (1) by issuance of (1) additional share payable 02/11/2000 to holders of record 01/31/2000
Class B Common $0.0001 par split (2) for (1) by issuance of (1) additional share payable 02/11/2000 to holders of record 01/31/2000
Class A Common $0.0001 par split (3) for (2) by issuance of (0.5) additional share payable 02/21/2006 to holders of record 02/06/2006
Ex date - 02/22/2006
Class B Common $0.0001 par split (3) for (2) by issuance of (0.5) additional share payable 02/21/2006 to holders of record 02/06/2006
Ex date - 02/22/2006
Merged into Broadcom Ltd. 02/01/2016
Each share Class A Common $0.0001 par exchanged for (0.02423599) share Ordinary no par and $51.482955 cash
Each share Class B Common $0.0001 par exchanged for (0.02423599) share Ordinary no par and $51.482955 cash
Broadcom Ltd. reorganized as Broadcom Inc. 04/05/2018

BROADCOM LTD (SINGAPORE)
Scheme of Arrangement effective 04/05/2018
Each share Ordinary no par exchanged for (1) share Broadcom Inc. Common $0.001 par

BROADENGATE SYS INC (NV)
Name changed to Otter Lake Resources, Inc. 11/06/2006
(See Otter Lake Resources, Inc.)

BROADLANDS RES LTD NEW (BC)
Recapitalized as Pinnacle Mines Ltd. (Ctfs. dated after 07/16/2003) 07/16/2003
Each share Common no par exchanged for (0.2) share Common no par
Pinnacle Mines Ltd. (Ctfs. dated after 07/16/2003) name changed to Jayden Resources Inc. (BC) 06/29/2010 which reincorporated in Cayman Islands 10/03/2012

BROADLANDS RES LTD OLD (BC)
Merged into International Broadlands Resources Ltd. 04/06/1995
Each share Common no par exchanged for (1) share Common no par
International Broadlands Resources Ltd. recapitalized as Broadlands Resources Ltd. (New) 03/15/1999 which recapitalized as Pinnacle Mines Ltd. (Ctfs. dated after 07/16/2003) 07/16/2003 which name changed to Jayden Resources Inc. (BC) 06/29/2010 which reincorporated in Cayman Islands 10/03/2012

BROADLEAF CAP PARTNERS INC (NV)
Recapitalized as EnergyTek Corp. 07/23/2014
Each share Common $0.001 par exchanged for (0.00666666) share Common $0.001 par
EnergyTek Corp. recapitalized as TimefireVR Inc. 11/22/2016

BROADLEAF INDS INC (UT)
Charter expired 02/26/2002

BROADMOOR APARTMENTS, INC. (IL)
Dissolved 10/25/1967
Details not available

BROADMOOR CORP. (NY)
Liquidation completed
Each share Capital Stock $1 par exchanged for initial distribution of $290 cash 02/21/1964
Each share Capital Stock $1 par received second distribution of $35 cash 02/02/1965
Each share Capital Stock $1 par received third distribution of $7 cash 02/01/1967
Each share Capital Stock $1 par received fourth and final distribution of $2.95 cash 11/06/1970

BROADPOINT GLEACHER SECURITIES GROUP INC (NY)
Reincorporated under the laws of Delaware as Gleacher & Co., Inc. 05/28/2010

BROADPOINT SECS GROUP INC (NY)
Name changed to Broadpoint Gleacher Securities Group, Inc. (NY) 06/05/2009
Broadpoint Gleacher Securities Group, Inc. (NY) reincorporated in Delaware as Gleacher & Co., Inc. 05/28/2010

BROADRELAY HLDGS INC (NV)
Name changed to Sivoo Holdings, Inc. 03/12/2007
(See Sivoo Holdings, Inc.)

BROADSOFT INC (DE)
Acquired by Cisco Systems, Inc. 02/01/2018
Each share Common 1¢ par exchanged for $55 cash

BROADSPOT WORLD WIDE WIRELESS INC (CANADA)
Each share old Common $0.001 par exchanged for (0.025) share new Common $0.001 par 04/23/2007
Dissolved for non-compliance 03/12/2007

BROADVIEW, INC. (IL)
Liquidation completed 04/07/1960
Details not available

BROADVIEW CAP CORP (AB)
Name changed to Broadview Press Inc. 05/23/2000

BROADVIEW FINL CORP (OH)
Merged into Broadview Savings Bank (Cleveland, OH) 11/06/1987
Each share Common no par exchanged for (1) share Capital Stock 10¢ par
(See Broadview Savings Bank (Cleveland, OH))

BROADVIEW INST INC (MN)
Each share old Common 1¢ par exchanged for (0.00000029) share new Common 1¢ par 06/29/2015
Note: In effect holders received $0.05 cash per share and public interest was eliminated

BROADVIEW LIQUIDATION TRUST
Liquidation completed
Each Ctf. of Bene. Int. no par received initial distribution of $4.52 cash 03/27/1961
Each Ctf. of Bene. Int. no par received second distribution of $4.92 cash 03/26/1962
Each Ctf. of Bene. Int. no par received third distribution of $4.93 cash 03/18/1963
Each Ctf. of Bene. Int. no par received fourth distribution of $5.38 cash 03/16/1964
Each Ctf. of Bene. Int. no par received fifth distribution of $5.56 cash 03/19/1965
Each Ctf. of Bene. Int. no par received sixth distribution of $6.09 cash 03/29/1966
Each Ctf. of Bene. Int. no par exchanged for seventh distribution of $51.50 cash 03/10/1967
Each Ctf. of Bene. Int. no par received eighth and final distribution of $1.07 cash 05/12/1970

BROADVIEW MEDIA INC (MN)
Name changed to Broadview Institute, Inc. 08/15/2006
(See Broadview Institute, Inc.)

BROADVIEW PRESS INC (AB)
Each share old Common no par exchanged for (0.00001333) share new Common no par 03/23/2010
Note: In effect holders received $0.10 cash per share and public interest was eliminated

BROADVIEW RES INC (AB)
Merged into Prime Petroleum Corp. 05/01/1989
Each share Common no par exchanged for (0.2857142) share Common no par
Prime Petroleum Corp. merged into Senex Petroleum Corp. 12/31/1989 which merged into Devran Petroleum Ltd. 03/01/1993 which name changed to Reserve Royalty Corp. 11/16/1995 which merged into PrimeWest Energy Trust 07/27/2000
(See PrimeWest Energy Trust)

BROADVIEW SVGS BK (CLEVELAND, OH)
Taken over by the RTC 03/30/1989
Stockholders' equity unlikely

BROADWATER DEVS INC (BC)
Recapitalized as Wyn Developments Inc. 04/18/2000
Each share Common no par exchanged for (0.33333333) share Common no par
(See Wyn Developments Inc.)

BROADWAY & 58TH STREET CORP. (NY)
Liquidation completed 07/01/1959
Details not available

BROADWAY & SEYMOUR INC (DE)
Name changed to Elite Information Group, Inc. 05/27/1999
(See Elite Information Group, Inc.)

BROADWAY ANGELS, INC. (NV)
Charter revoked for failure to file reports and pay fees 03/04/1957

BROADWAY BK & TR CO (PATERSON, NJ)
Capital Stock $6.25 par changed to $10 par and a 200% stock dividend paid 04/11/1968
Capital Stock $10 par changed to $5 par and (1) additional share issued 04/10/1972
Stock Dividend - 25% 08/01/1951
Reorganized as Broadway Financial Corp. 03/02/1983
Each share Capital Stock $5 par exchanged for (1) share Common no par
(See Broadway Financial Corp.)

BROADWAY BEVERAGES LTD (BC)
Struck off register and declared dissolved for failure to file returns 09/25/1990

BROADWAY DEPARTMENT STORE, INC. (DE)
Name changed to Broadway-Hale Stores, Inc. (DE) 05/15/1951
6% Conv. Preferred $25 par called for redemption 05/25/1951
Broadway-Hale Stores, Inc. (DE) merged into Broadway-Hale Stores, Inc. (CA) 08/27/1970 which name changed to Carter Hawley Hale Stores Inc. (CA) 05/30/1974 which reincorporated in Delaware 07/26/1984 which name changed to Broadway Stores, Inc. 06/17/1994 which merged into Federated Department Stores, Inc. 10/11/1995 which name changed to Macy's, Inc. 06/01/2007

BROADWAY ENGINEERING & DEVELOPMENT CORP. (PA)
Name changed to Broadway Research & Development Corp. 12/20/1963
Broadway Research & Development Corp. name changed to Environmental Services, Inc. (PA) 01/16/1968 which merged into Environmental Services, Inc. (NY) 03/26/1970

BROADWAY ENTERPRISES INC (CO)
Name changed to Hotel Rent-A-Car System, Inc. 09/20/1978
Hotel Rent-A-Car System, Inc. name changed to Red Carpet Inns International, Inc. 06/22/1979
(See Red Carpet Inns International, Inc.)

BROADWAY EXCHANGE CORP.
Reorganized as 61 Broadway Corp. 00/00/1944
No stockholders' equity

BROADWAY FINL CORP (NJ)
Common no par split (2) for (1) by issuance of (1) additional share 07/01/1985
Common no par split (2) for (1) by issuance of (1) additional share 06/16/1986
Placed in receivership with FDIC 03/13/1992
No stockholders' equity

BROADWAY HALE STORES INC (CA)
Reincorporated 08/27/1970
Common $10 par changed to $5 par and (1) additional share issued 07/17/1959
5% Preferred $25 par called for redemption 06/01/1963
Common $5 par split (3) for (2) by issuance of (0.5) additional share 03/08/1968
Under plan of merger state of incorporation changed from (DE) to (CA) 08/27/1970
Each share $2 Conv. Preferred Ser. A $5 par automatically became (1) share $2 Conv. Preferred Ser. A $5 par
Common $5 par split (9) for (8) by issuance of (0.125) additional share 09/18/1970
Common $5 par split (3) for (2) by issuance of (0.5) additional share 06/21/1972
Name changed to Carter Hawley Hale Stores, Inc. (CA) 05/30/1974
Carter Hawley Hale Stores Inc. reincorporated in Delaware 07/26/1984 which name changed to Broadway Stores, Inc. 06/17/1994 which merged into Federated Department Stores, Inc. 10/11/1995 which name changed to Macy's, Inc. 06/01/2007

BROADWAY HLDGS INC (DE)
Merged into American Midland Corp. 07/27/1988
Each share Common 1¢ par exchanged for (5) shares new Common 1¢ par
(See American Midland Corp.)

BROADWAY JOES INC (FL)
Declared bankrupt 08/16/1971
Stockholders' equity unlikely

BROADWAY NATL BK & TR CO (PITMAN, NJ)
Merged into Peoples National Bank of New Jersey (Westmont, NJ) 02/08/1971
Each share Capital Stock $100 par exchanged for (6) shares Common Capital Stock $3.375 par
Peoples National Bank of New Jersey (Westmont, NJ) name changed to First Peoples National Bank of New Jersey (Westmont, NJ) 06/30/1974 which name changed to First Peoples Bank of New Jersey (Westmont, NJ) 03/20/1978 which reorganized as First Peoples Financial Corp. 03/03/1987 which merged into CoreStates Financial Corp 09/03/1992 which merged into First Union Corp. 04/28/1998 which name changed to Wachovia Corp. (Ctfs. dated after 09/01/2001) 09/01/2001 which merged into Wells Fargo & Co. (New) 12/31/2008

BROADWAY NATL BK (BAYONNE, NJ)
Acquired by First National State Bancorporation 03/30/1982
Each share Common $10 par exchanged for $64.69 cash

BROADWAY NATIONAL BANK (NASHVILLE, TN)
Stock Dividends - 66.66666666% 07/20/1951; 50% 03/29/1957; 33.33333333% 06/05/1959
Merged into Commerce Union Bank (Nashville, TN) 05/22/1962
Each share Capital Stock $25 par exchanged for (1.625) shares Capital Stock $10 par
Commerce Union Bank (Nashville, TN) reorganized as Tennessee Valley Bancorp, Inc. 05/15/1972 which name changed to Commerce Union Corp. 04/20/1982 which merged into Sovran Financial Corp. 11/01/1987 which merged into C&S/Sovran Corp. 09/01/1990 which merged into NationsBank Corp. (NC) 12/31/1991 which reincorporated in Delaware as BankAmerica Corp. (Old) 09/25/1998 which merged into BankAmerica Corp. (New) 09/30/1998 which name changed to Bank of America Corp. 04/28/1999

BROADWAY NATL BK (SAN ANTONIO, TX)
Under plan of reorganization each share Capital Stock $10 par automatically became (1) share Broadway Bancshares, Inc. Common $10 par 05/31/1982

BROADWAY-NEW STREET CORP. (NY)
Liquidation completed 00/00/1953
Details not available

BROADWAY REALIZATION CORP. (NY)
Charter revoked for failure to file reports and pay fees 12/15/1950

BROADWAY RLTY CO (NY)
Name changed to 5085 Broadway Realty, LLC 11/30/1995
(See 5085 Broadway Realty, LLC)

BROADWAY RESEARCH & DEVELOPMENT CORP. (PA)
Name changed to Environmental Services, Inc. (PA) and Class A Common 10¢ par and Class B Common 10¢ par reclassified as Common 10¢ par 01/16/1968
Environmental Services, Inc. (PA) merged into Environmental Services, Inc. (NY) 03/26/1970

BROADWAY-SPRING ARCADE BUILDING CORP. (CA)
Dissolved 09/25/1964
Details not available

BROADWAY STORES INC (DE)
Merged into Federated Department Stores, Inc. 10/11/1995
Each share Exchangeable Preferred Ser. A 1¢ par exchanged for (0.001) share Broadway Stores Inc. Exchangeable Preferred Ser. A 1¢ par
Each share Common 1¢ par exchanged for (0.27) share Common 1¢ par
Each Exchangeable Preferred Share Ser. A exchanged for $0.50 cash 04/17/1996
Federated Department Stores, Inc. name changed to Macy's, Inc. 06/01/2007

BROADWAY TRINITY CORP (NY)
Charter cancelled and proclaimed dissolved for failure to pay taxes 03/26/1980

BROADWAY-TRINITY PLACE CORP. (NY)
Each share Capital Stock $1 par exchanged for (1) share Capital Stock 10¢ par and either $21 principal amount of Debentures or $21 cash 03/07/1955
Name changed to Broadway-Trinity Corp. 02/15/1956
(See Broadway-Trinity Corp.)

BROADWAY VENTURES INC (CO)
Name changed to Silicon Development Corp. 10/09/1987
(See Silicon Development Corp.)

BROADWIND ENERGY INC (NV)
Reincorporated under the laws of Delaware 06/20/2008

BROADWING COMMUNICATIONS INC (DE)
Merged into Cincinnati Bell Inc. (New) 09/08/2003
Each share 12.50% Jr. Exchangeable Preferred exchanged for (35.8) shares Common 1¢ par

BROADWING CORP (DE)
Acquired by Level 3 Communications, Inc. 01/03/2007
Each share Common 1¢ par exchanged for (1.3411) shares Common 1¢ par and $8.18 cash
Level 3 Communications, Inc. merged into CenturyLink, Inc. 11/01/2017

BROADWING INC (OH)
7.25% Jr. Conv. Preferred no par called for redemption at $104.83 on 04/06/2000
Name changed to Cincinnati Bell Inc. (New) 05/16/2003

BROCADE COMMUNICATIONS SYS INC (DE)
Old Common $0.001 par split (2) for (1) by issuance of (1) additional share payable 12/02/1999 to holders of record 11/18/1999
Old Common $0.001 par split (2) for (1) by issuance of (1) additional share payable 03/14/2000 to holders of record 02/28/2000
Old Common $0.001 par split (2) for (1) by issuance of (1) additional share payable 12/21/2000 to holders of record 12/11/2000 Ex date - 12/22/2000
Each share old Common $0.001 par exchanged for (1) share new

Common $0.001 par to reflect a (1) for (100) reverse split followed by a (100) for (1) forward split 06/27/2007
Note: Holders of (99) or fewer pre-split shares received $8.44 cash per share
Acquired by Broadcom Ltd. 11/17/2017
Each share new Common $0.001 par exchanged for $12.75 cash

BROCK CANDY CO (DE)
Merged into Brach (E.J.) Co. 11/01/1994
Each share Class A Common 1¢ par exchanged for $20 cash

BROCK CTL SYS INC (GA)
Name changed to Brock International, Inc. 02/05/1996
Brock International, Inc. name changed to Firstwave Technologies Inc. (GA) 03/01/1998 which reorganized in Nevada as Textmunication Holdings, Inc. 11/15/2013

BROCK EXPL CORP (DE)
Merged into Key Production Co., Inc. 03/28/1996
Each share Common 10¢ par exchanged for (0.6897) share Common 25¢ par
Key Production Co., Inc. merged into Cimarex Energy Co. 09/30/2002

BROCK GOLD MINES LTD.
Acquired by Upper Canada Mines Ltd. 00/00/1946
Each share Capital Stock $1 par exchanged for (0.06666666) share Capital Stock $1 par
Upper Canada Mines Ltd. name changed to Upper Canada Resources Ltd. 10/05/1972 which reorganized as Challenger International Services Ltd. 07/07/1978
(See Challenger International Services Ltd.)

BROCK HOTEL CORP (DE)
Each share old Common 10¢ par exchanged for (0.02) share new Common 10¢ par 06/25/1986
Name changed to Integra-A Hotel & Restaurant Co. 05/04/1988
(See Integra-A Hotel & Restaurant Co.)

BROCK INTL INC (GA)
Name changed to Firstwave Technologies Inc. (GA) 03/01/1998
Firstwave Technologies Inc. (GA) reorganized in Nevada as Textmunication Holdings, Inc. 11/15/2013

BROCK STANLEY LTD (CANADA)
Each share Class A Common no par exchanged for (1) share Common no par 05/17/1965
Each share Class B Common no par exchanged for (1) share Common no par 05/17/1965
Name changed to Slater, Walker of Canada Ltd. 07/23/1971
Slater, Walker of Canada Ltd. name changed to Talcorp Associates Ltd. 03/10/1976 which name changed to Talcorp Ltd. 09/14/1982 which reorganized as Consolidated Talcorp Ltd. 08/07/1986 which name changed to Sound Insight Enterprises Ltd. 12/07/1990 which merged into CamVec Corp. 09/11/1992 which name changed to AMJ Campbell Inc. 08/14/2001
(See AMJ Campbell Inc.)

BROCKER TECHNOLOGY GROUP INC (AB)
Name changed 12/03/1998
Name changed from Brocker Investments Ltd. to Brocker Technology Group, Inc. 12/03/1998
Each share old Common no par exchanged for (0.25) share new Common no par 04/30/2001

Name changed to Datec Group Ltd. (Old) 06/27/2003
(See Datec Group Ltd. (Old))

BROCKTON CAP CORP (BC)
Name changed to MegaWest Energy Corp. (BC) 03/06/2007
MegaWest Energy Corp. (BC) reincorporated in Alberta 02/12/2008 which recapitalized as Gravis Oil Corp. (AB) 06/20/2011 which reincorporated in Delaware 09/11/2012 which name changed to Petro River Oil Corp. 03/20/2013

BROCKTON EDISON CO (MA)
6.4% Preferred $100 par called for redemption 08/21/1961
5.48% Preferred $100 par called for redemption 11/06/1963
5.6% Preferred $50 par called for redemption 11/06/1963
Each share Common $25 par exchanged for (2.25) shares Eastern Utilities Associates Common $10 par 06/30/1967
(See Eastern Utilities Associates)
Name changed to Eastern Edison Co. 08/01/1979
(See Eastern Edison Co.)

BROCKTON GAS LIGHT CO.
Name changed to Brockton Taunton Gas Co. 00/00/1952
Brockton Taunton Gas Co. merged into Bay State Gas Co. (New) 11/19/1974 which merged into Nipsco Industries, Inc. 02/12/1999 which name changed to NiSource Inc. (IN) 04/14/1999 which reincorporated in Delaware 11/01/2000

BROCKTON NATIONAL BANK (BROCKTON, MA)
Stock Dividend - 66.66666666% 03/06/1940
Merged into National Bank of Plymouth County (Brockton, MA) 09/28/1956
Each share Capital Stock $20 par exchanged for (2.06666666) share Capital Stock $10 par
National Bank of Plymouth County (Brockton, MA) name changed to First County National Bank (Brockton, MA) 09/11/1966 which name changed to Shawmut First County Bank, N.A. (Brockton, MA) 04/01/1975
(See Shawmut First County Bank, N.A. (Brockton, MA))

BROCKTON RES INC (BC)
Name changed to Chartwell Ventures Ltd. (BC) 11/20/1992
Chartwell Ventures Ltd. (BC) reincorporated in Alberta 01/17/1996 which name changed to Chartwell Technology, Inc. 12/08/1998 which merged into Amaya Gaming Group Inc. 07/18/2011 which name changed to Amaya Inc. (QC) 12/04/2014 which reincorporated in Ontario as Stars Group Inc. 08/01/2017

BROCKTON TAUNTON GAS CO (MA)
Merged into Bay State Gas Co. (New) 11/19/1974
Each share $3.25 Preferred $50 par, $3.80 Preferred $50 par or 5.625% Preferred $50 par exchanged for (1) share $3.80 Preferred $50 par
Each share Common $10 par exchanged for (1.3) shares Common $10 par
Bay State Gas Co. (New) merged into Nipsco Industries, Inc. 02/12/1999 which name changed to NiSource Inc. (IN) 04/14/1999 which reincorporated in Delaware 11/01/2000

BROCKVILLE CHEMICALS LTD. (CANADA)
Merged into Sogemines Ltd. 10/18/1965

Each share 6% Part. Preferred $10 par exchanged for (0.57) share Common no par
Sogemines Ltd. name changed to Genstar Ltd. 02/25/1969 which name changed to Genstar Corp. 06/15/1981
(See Genstar Corp.)

BROCKWAY CTZNS BK (BROCKWAY, PA)
Each share Capital Stock $25 par exchanged for (5) shares Capital Stock $5 par 03/10/1975
Stock Dividends - 100% 03/01/1948; 100% 03/05/1969
Merged into UniBank (Brookville, PA) 09/29/1978
Each share Capital Stock $5 par exchanged for (1.75) shares Common $2.50 par
(See UniBank (Brookville, PA))

BROCKWAY GLASS CO., INC. (NY)
Each share Common $50 par exchanged for (7) shares Common $10 par to effect a (5) for (1) split and 40% stock dividend 03/01/1955
Common $10 par changed to $5 par and (1) additional share issued 11/30/1959
Common $5 par reclassified as Class A Common $5 par 10/20/1964
Class A Common $5 par reclassified as Common $2.50 par 05/08/1970
Common $2.50 par split (2) for (1) by issuance of (1) additional share 05/25/1970
5% Preferred $50 par called for redemption 09/30/1976
Common $2.50 par split (3) for (2) by issuance of (0.5) additional share 12/15/1978
Stock Dividends - 100% 11/29/1941; 25% 12/15/1943; 25% 02/19/1946; 40% 02/12/1948
Name changed to Brockway, Inc. 05/14/1982
(See Brockway, Inc.)

BROCKWAY INC (NY)
Common $2.50 par split (3) for (2) by issuance of (0.5) additional share 12/19/1986
Merged into Owens-Illinois, Inc. 04/12/1988
Each share Common $2.50 par exchanged for $60 cash

BROCKWAY MOTOR CO., INC. (NY)
Assets sold and name changed to Cortland Corp. 10/01/1956
(See Cortland Corp.)

BROCKWAY MOTOR TRUCK CORP.
Reorganized as Brockway Motor Co., Inc. 00/00/1938
Each (5) shares Preferred exchanged for (1.66666666) shares new Common and (1) 5-Yr. Common Stock Purchase Warrant
Each share Common received (0.1) 5-Yr. Common Stock Purchase Warrant
Brockway Motor Co., Inc. name changed to Cortland Corp. 10/01/1956
(See Cortland Corp.)

BROCKWAY PRESSED METALS INC (PA)
Merged into Inland Engineered 03/02/1998
Each share 5% Preferred exchanged for $50 cash
Each share Class A Common exchanged for $87.05 cash
Each share Class B Common exchanged for $87.05 cash

BROCKWAY STD HLDGS CORP (DE)
Name changed to Bway Corp. 03/04/1996
(See Bway Corp.)

BRODERBUND SOFTWARE INC (DE)
Common 1¢ par split (2) for (1) by issuance of (1) additional share 11/21/1994

Merged into Learning Co. Inc. 08/31/1998
Each share Common 1¢ par exchanged for (0.8) share Common 1¢ par
Learning Co. Inc. merged into Mattel, Inc. 05/13/1999

BRODERICK & BASCOM ROPE CO (MO)
Class A Common $1 par reclassified as Common $1 par 12/31/1956
Company liquidated 06/25/1984
Details not available

BRODHEAD GARRETT CO (OH)
Each share old Common $1 par exchanged for (20) shares new Common $1 par 06/15/1967
Merged into Taylor Woodcraft Inc. 11/30/1987
Each share new Common $1 par exchanged for $15.97 cash

BRODIE (RALPH N.) CO. (CA)
Stock Dividend - 100% 07/05/1963
Name changed to R.N.B. Co. 11/15/1963
(See R.N.B. Co.)

BRODIE EXPL CORP (CO)
SEC revoked common stock registration 11/08/2011

BRODY B SEATING CO (IL)
Common no par split (3) for (2) by issuance of (0.5) additional share 06/03/1966
Plan of reorganization under Chapter 11 bankruptcy proceedings confirmed 01/09/1981
No stockholders' equity

BROGAN ASSOC INC (NY)
Each share Common 1¢ par exchanged for (0.2) share Class A Common 1¢ par 05/13/1977
Recapitalized as American Gold Depository Corp. 02/15/1980
Each share Class A Common 1¢ par exchanged for (0.2) share Common 1¢ par
(See American Gold Depository Corp.)

BROHM RES INC (BC)
Merged into MinVen Gold Corp. 08/12/1988
Each share Common no par exchanged for (1) share Common no par
MinVen Gold Corp. reorganized as Dakota Mining Corp. 09/15/1993
(See Dakota Mining Corp.)

BROKAT TECHNOLOGIES AG (GERMANY)
Name changed 08/28/2001
Name changed from Brokat AG to Brokat Technologies AG 08/28/2001
ADR agreement terminated 12/19/2002
No stockholders' equity

BROKEN ARROW PETE CO (DE)
Reincorporated 06/13/1991
State of incorporation changed from (UT) to (DE) 06/13/1991
Recapitalized as 3eee, Inc. 05/31/2000
Each share Common $0.001 par exchanged for (0.016) share Common $0.001 par
3eee, Inc. recapitalized as Digital Utilities Ventures Inc. 05/12/2009

BROKEN HILL EXPLS LTD (ON)
Charter cancelled for failure to pay taxes and file returns 03/16/1976

BROKEN HILL PROPRIETARY LTD (AUSTRALIA)
Each Unsponsored ADR for Ordinary Reg. exchanged for (1) Sponsored ADR for Ordinary 11/09/1985
Each old Sponsored ADR for Ordinary Reg. exchanged for (0.5) new Sponsored ADR for Ordinary Reg. 06/04/1987
New Sponsored ADR's for Ordinary

split (2) for (1) by issuance of (1) additional ADR payable 06/24/1996 to holders of record 06/17/1996 Ex date - 06/25/1996
Stock Dividends - ADR's 10% 12/15/1971; 25% 04/12/1974; 20% 06/14/1979; 20% 06/20/1984; 12-1/2% 06/19/1985; 20% 03/24/1986; 20% 06/24/1987; 10% 05/26/1989; 10% 06/16/1995
Ordinary 10% 11/23/1971; 25% 03/15/1974; 20% 05/22/1979; 20% 05/22/1984; 12-1/2% 05/29/1985; 20% 03/03/1986; 20% 06/24/1987; 10% 06/07/1995
Name changed to BHP Ltd. 10/30/2000
BHP Ltd. name changed to BHP Billiton Ltd. 06/29/2001

BROKEN HILL SOUTH LTD (AUSTRALIA)
Name changed to BH South Ltd. 12/06/1973
(See BH South Ltd.)

BROKER DATA INC (MN)
Recapitalized as Nutrition World, Inc. 12/31/1971
Each share Common 1¢ par exchanged for (0.2) share Common 5¢ par
Nutrition World, Inc. name changed to Atlantic Group, Inc. 01/19/1988

BROKER PMT SYS WORLDWIDE INC (NV)
Name changed to Broker Processing Service, Inc. 12/23/2005
(See Broker Processing Service, Inc.)

BROKER PROCESSING SVC INC (NV)
Each share old Common $0.001 par exchanged for (0.1) share new Common $0.001 par 12/31/2007
Charter revoked for failure to file reports and pay fees 06/29/2012

BROKERAGE DATA PROCESSING CORP (NY)
Charter cancelled and proclaimed dissolved for failure to pay taxes 12/20/1977

BROKERS MTG SVC INC (NJ)
Merged into Travelers Corp. 04/30/1985
Each share Common no par exchanged for (0.28) share Common $1.25 par
Travelers Corp. merged into Travelers Inc. 12/31/1993 which name changed to Travelers Group Inc. 04/16/1995 which name changed to Citigroup Inc. 10/08/1998

BROKERS SECS INC (VA)
Name changed to BSI Holdings, Inc. 12/31/1988
BSI Holdings, Inc. name changed to Autobanc Inc. 06/12/1991
(See Autobanc Inc.)

BROMINCO INC (QC)
Merged into Aur Resources Inc. 05/16/1985
Each share Capital Stock no par exchanged for (2.5) shares Common no par
Aur Resources Inc. acquired by Teck Cominco Ltd. 09/28/2007 which name changed to Teck Resources Ltd. 04/27/2009

BROMLEY MARR ECOS INC (AB)
Assets sold for the benefit of creditors 00/00/2001
No stockholders' equity

BROMO CEDIN CORP. (DE)
No longer in existence having become inoperative and void for non-payment of taxes 04/01/1962

BROMO MINT CO. (DE)
Merged into Kenner Products Co. 03/14/1962
Each share Capital Stock $1 par exchanged for (8.067) shares Common $1 par
Kenner Products Co. name changed to Rennek Co. 12/20/1967 which was acquired by General Mills, Inc. 12/20/1967

BROMPTON ADVANTAGED EQUAL WEIGHT OIL & GAS INCOME FD (ON)
Name changed to Brompton Advantaged Oil & Gas Income Fund 06/24/2008
Brompton Advantaged Oil & Gas Income Fund name changed to Aston Hill Advantage Oil & Gas Income Fund 09/16/2011 which name changed to LOGiQ Advantage Oil & Gas Income Fund 05/12/2017 which name changed to Redwood Energy Income Fund 12/20/2017
(See Redwood Energy Income Fund)

BROMPTON ADVANTAGED OIL & GAS INCOME FD (ON)
Name changed to Aston Hill Advantage Oil & Gas Income Fund 09/16/2011
Aston Hill Advantage Oil & Gas Income Fund name changed to LOGiQ Advantage Oil & Gas Income Fund 05/12/2017 which name changed to Redwood Energy Income Fund 12/20/2017
(See Redwood Energy Income Fund)

BROMPTON ADVANTAGED TRACKER FD (ON)
Recapitalized as Brompton Advantaged VIP Income Fund 07/14/2008
Each Unit no par received (0.61892907) Unit no par
Brompton Advantaged VIP Income Fund name changed to Aston Hill Advantage VIP Income Fund 09/16/2011 which name changed to LOGiQ Advantage VIP Income Fund 05/12/2017 which name changed to Redwood Advantage Monthly Income Fund 12/20/2017 which merged into Purpose Multi-Asset Income Fund 05/04/2018

BROMPTON ADVANTAGED VIP INCOME FD (ON)
Name changed to Aston Hill Advantage VIP Income Fund 09/16/2011
Aston Hill Advantage VIP Income Fund name changed to LOGiQ Advantage VIP Income Fund 05/12/2017 which name changed to Redwood Advantage Monthly Income Fund 12/20/2017 which merged into Purpose Multi-Asset Income Fund 05/04/2018

BROMPTON EQUAL WEIGHT INCOME FD (ON)
Merged into Brompton VIP Income Fund 07/04/2008
Each Unit no par received either (0.85831) Trust Unit or $11.6598 cash
Note: Option to receive cash expired 07/31/2008
Brompton VIP Income Fund name changed to Aston Hill VIP Income Fund 09/16/2011 which name changed to LOGiQ VIP Income Fund 05/12/2017 which name changed to Redwood Monthly Income Fund 12/20/2017 which merged into Purpose Multi-Asset Income Fund 05/04/2018

BROMPTON EQUAL WEIGHT OIL & GAS INCOME FD (ON)
Name changed to Brompton Oil & Gas Income Fund 06/20/2008
Brompton Oil & Gas Income Fund name changed to Aston Hill Oil & Gas Income Fund 09/16/2011 which reorganized as Aston Hill Global Resource Fund (New) 08/31/2015

BROMPTON EQUITY SPLIT CORP (ON)
Merged into Dividend Growth Split Corp. 05/20/2011
Each share Preferred no par automatically became (1) Preferred Share
Each share Class A no par automatically became (1.493584) Class A Shares

BROMPTON MVP INCOME FD (ON)
Under plan of merger each Trust Unit no par automatically became (1.07245) Brompton VIP Income Fund Trust Units no par 12/31/2005
Brompton VIP Income Fund name changed to Aston Hill VIP Income Fund 09/16/2011 which name changed to LOGiQ VIP Income Fund 05/12/2017 which name changed to Redwood Monthly Income Fund 12/20/2017 which merged into Purpose Multi-Asset Income Fund 05/04/2018

BROMPTON OIL & GAS INCOME FD (ON)
Name changed to Aston Hill Oil & Gas Income Fund 09/16/2011
Aston Hill Oil & Gas Income Fund reorganized as Aston Hill Global Resource Fund (New) 08/31/2015

BROMPTON PPTY GROUP INC (AB)
Merged into Brompton Acquisition Corp. 09/14/2005
Each share Common no par exchanged for $0.54 cash

BROMPTON PULP & PAPER CO.
Merged into St. Lawrence Corp. Ltd. 00/00/1930
Details not available

BROMPTON STABLE INCOME FD (ON)
Merged into Brompton VIP Income Fund 07/04/2008
Each Trust Unit no par received either (0.965166) Trust Unit or $13.1114 cash
Note: Option to receive cash expired 07/31/2008
Brompton VIP Income Fund name changed to Aston Hill VIP Income Fund 09/16/2011 which name changed to LOGiQ VIP Income Fund 05/12/2017 which name changed to Redwood Monthly Income Fund 12/20/2017 which merged into Purpose Multi-Asset Income Fund 05/04/2018

BROMPTON TOP 50 COMPOUND GROWTH FD (ON)
Merged into Brompton Advantaged VIP Income Fund 07/14/2008
Each Unit no par received either (0.692406) Unit no par or $9.1014 cash
Note: Option to receive cash expired 07/31/2008
Brompton Advantaged VIP Income Fund name changed to Aston Hill Advantage VIP Income Fund 09/16/2011 which name changed to LOGiQ Advantage VIP Income Fund 05/12/2017 which name changed to Redwood Advantage Monthly Income Fund 12/20/2017 which merged into Purpose Multi-Asset Income Fund 05/04/2018

BROMPTON TRACKER FD (ON)
Merged into Brompton VIP Income Fund 07/04/2008
Each Unit no par received either (0.666423) Trust Unit or $9.0531 cash
Note: Option to receive cash expired 07/31/2008
Brompton VIP Income Fund name changed to Aston Hill VIP Income Fund 09/16/2011 which name changed to LOGiQ VIP Income Fund 05/12/2017 which name changed to Redwood Monthly Income Fund 12/20/2017 which merged into Purpose Multi-Asset Income Fund 05/04/2018

BROMPTON VIP INCOME FD (ON)
6% Preferred Securities no par called for redemption at $10 plus $0.026090 accrued dividends on 05/31/2009
Name changed to Aston Hill VIP Income Fund 09/16/2011
Aston Hill VIP Income Fund name changed to LOGiQ VIP Income Fund 05/12/2017 which name changed to Redwood Monthly Income Fund 12/20/2017 which merged into Purpose Multi-Asset Income Fund 05/04/2018

BROMPTON VIP INCOME TR (ON)
Under plan of merger each Trust Unit automatically became (1) Brompton VIP Income Fund Trust Unit 12/31/2005
Brompton VIP Income Fund name changed to Aston Hill VIP Income Fund 09/16/2011 which name changed to LOGiQ VIP Income Fund 05/12/2017 which name changed to Redwood Monthly Income Fund 12/20/2017 which merged into Purpose Multi-Asset Income Fund 05/04/2018

BRONCO DRILLING CO INC (DE)
Merged into Chesapeake Energy Corp. 06/06/2011
Each share Common 1¢ par exchanged for $11 cash

BRONCO ENERGY LTD (AB)
Merged into Legacy Oil + Gas Inc. 11/09/2010
Each share Common no par exchanged for (0.0182) share Common no par
Note: Unexchanged certificates were cancelled and became without value 11/09/2015
Legacy Oil + Gas Inc. merged into Crescent Point Energy Corp. 07/06/2015

BRONCO OIL & GAS CO (CO)
Each share Common 1¢ par exchanged for (0.1) share Common 10¢ par 09/08/1981
Declared defunct and inoperative for failure to pay taxes and file annual reports 01/01/1997

BRONCO PETES LTD (BC)
Recapitalized as Quorum Resource Corp. 09/05/1985
Each share Common no par exchanged for (0.14285714) share Common no par
Quorum Resource Corp. recapitalized as Mirage Resource Corp. 04/16/1992 which merged into Dayton Mining Corp. 04/06/2000 which merged into Pacific Rim Mining Corp. 04/11/2002 which merged into OceanaGold Corp. 12/02/2013

BRONSON MINES LTD (BC)
Recapitalized as Goliath Gold Mines Ltd. 10/21/1980
Each share Common no par exchanged for (0.5) share Common no par
Goliath Gold Mines Ltd. merged into Hemlo Gold Mines Inc. 02/03/1987 which merged into Battle Mountain Canada Inc. 07/19/1996 which merged into Newmont Mining Corp. 01/10/2001

BRONTE CHAMPAGNE & WINES INC (MI)
Assets sold for the benefit of creditors 00/00/1985
No stockholders' equity

BRONX FIRE INSURANCE CO. (NY)
Merged into New York Fire Insurance Co. 00/00/1931
Details not available

BRONX GAS & ELECTRIC CO.
Merged into Consolidated Edison Co. of New York, Inc. 00/00/1936
Details not available

BRONX MINERALS INC (BC)
Name changed to Las Vegas From Home.com Entertainment Inc. 09/07/1999
Las Vegas From Home.com Entertainment Inc. name changed to Jackpot Digital Inc. 06/18/2015

BRONX TITLE & MORTGAGE GUARANTEE CO. (NY)
Liquidated 00/00/1936
Details not available

BRONX VENTURES INC (BC)
Reorganized as ZAB Resources Inc. 03/19/2007
Each share Common no par exchanged for (50) shares Common no par
ZAB Resources Inc. recapitalized as Kokomo Enterprises Inc. 04/15/2009 which recapitalized as High 5 Ventures Inc. 08/29/2012 which recapitalized as 37 Capital Inc. 07/07/2014

BRONXVILLE-COMMODORE OPERATING CORP.
Dissolved 00/00/1950
Details not available

BRONZE MARKETING INC (NV)
Recapitalized as Sutor Technology Group Ltd. 03/08/2007
Each share Common $0.001 par exchanged for (0.1) share Common $0.001 par

BRONZINI, LTD. (NY)
Acquired by Rockower Brothers, Inc. 10/14/1969
Details not available

BROOK LABS. CO., INC. (NY)
Name changed to Central Instrument Corp. 06/15/1962
(See Central Instrument Corp.)

BROOKDALE LIVING CMNTYS INC (DE)
Merged into Fortress Brookdale Acquisition LLC 09/19/2000
Each share Common 1¢ par exchanged for $15.25 cash

BROOKE BD INC (CANADA)
Name changed 01/12/1981
Name changed from Brooke Bond Foods Ltd. to Brooke Bond Inc. 01/12/1981
4.16% Preferred no par called for redemption 04/15/1984
Public interest eliminated

BROOKE BOND CANADA (1959) LTD. (CANADA)
Name changed to Brooke Bond Canada Ltd. 07/09/1961
Brooke Bond Canada Ltd. name changed to Brooke Bond Foods Ltd. 11/07/1969 which name changed to Brooke Bond Inc. 01/12/1981
(See Brooke Bond Inc.)

BROOKE BOND CDA LTD (CANADA)
Name changed to Brooke Bond Foods Ltd. 11/07/1969
Brooke Bond Foods Ltd. name changed to Brooke Bond Inc. 01/12/1981
(See Brooke Bond Inc.)

BROOKE CAP CORP (KS)
Chapter 11 bankruptcy proceedings converted to Chapter 7 on 06/29/2009
Stockholders' equity unlikely

BROOKE CORP (KS)
Common $1 par split (6) for (1) by issuance of (5) additional shares payable 03/12/2003 to holders of record 03/03/2003 Ex date - 03/13/2003
Common $1 par changed to 1¢ par 04/22/2004
Common 1¢ par split (2) for (1) by issuance of (1) additional share payable 06/10/2004 to holders of record 05/26/2004 Ex date - 06/14/2004
Chapter 11 bankruptcy proceedings converted to Chapter 7 on 06/29/2009
Stockholders' equity unlikely

BROOKE CR CORP (DE)
Name changed to Aleritas Capital Corp. 08/19/2008
(See Aleritas Capital Corp.)

BROOKE E & G LD CO (PA)
Liquidation completed
Each share Capital Stock $50 par received initial distribution of $70 cash 05/15/1963
Each share Capital Stock $50 par received second distribution of $55 cash 09/16/1963
Each share Capital Stock $50 par received third distribution of $95 cash 01/02/1964
Each share Capital Stock $50 par received fourth distribution of $50 cash 05/15/1964
Each share Capital Stock $50 par received fifth distribution of $60 cash 01/21/1965
Each share Capital Stock $50 par received sixth distribution of $110 cash 07/01/1965
Each share Capital Stock $50 par received seventh distribution of $75 cash 05/30/1966
Each share Capital Stock $50 par received eighth distribution of $20 cash 10/24/1969
Each share Capital Stock $50 par received ninth and final distribution of $7.20 cash 04/01/1975
Note: Certificates were not required to be surrendered and are without value

BROOKE GROUP LTD (DE)
Stock Dividend - 5% payable 09/30/1999 to holders of record 09/24/1999
Name changed to Vector Group Ltd. 05/24/2000

BROOKE (E. & G.) IRON CO.
Acquired by Colorado Fuel & Iron Corp. 00/00/1952
Each share Common $2 par exchanged for (1/8) share 5% Preferred $50 par and (3/8) share Common no par
Colorado Fuel & Iron Corp. name changed to CF&I Steel Corp. 08/01/1966
(See CF&I Steel Corp.)

BROOKEMONT CAP INC (BC)
Recapitalized as Turbo Capital Inc. 11/17/2014
Each share Common no par exchanged for (0.5) share Common no par
Turbo Capital Inc. recapitalized as Cruz Capital Corp. 04/12/2016 which name changed to Cruz Cobalt Corp. 02/23/2017

BROOKFIELD ASSET MGMT INC (CANADA)
8.3% Preferred Securities no par called for redemption at $25 plus $0.017055 accrued dividends on 07/03/2007
Class A Preference Ser. 10 no par called for redemption at $25 plus $0.359375 accrued dividends on 04/05/2012
Class A Preference Ser. 11 no par called for redemption at $25 plus $0.34375 accrued dividends on 09/30/2012
Class A Preference Ser. 21 no par called for redemption at $25 on 06/30/2013
Class A Preference Ser. 12 no par called for redemption at $26 plus $0.0222 accrued dividends on 04/06/2014
Class A Preference Ser. 22 no par called for redemption at $25 on 09/30/2014
Class A Preference Ser. 14 no par called for redemption at $100 plus $0.1351 accrued dividends on 03/01/2016
(Additional Information in Active)

BROOKFIELD BANCSHARES CORP (DE)
Merged into CMI Acquisition Corp. 03/29/1991
Each share Common $1 par exchanged for $40.78 cash

BROOKFIELD BANK (BROOKFIELD, CT)
Closed by the FDIC 05/08/1992
Stockholders' equity unlikely

BROOKFIELD CDA OFFICE PPTYS (ON)
Name changed 02/29/2012
Name changed from Brookfield Office Properties Canada to Brookfield Canada Office Properties 02/29/2012
Acquired by Brookfield Property Partners L.P. 07/04/2017
Each Trust Unit exchanged for $32.50 cash
Note: Unexchanged certificates will be cancelled and become without value 06/29/2020

BROOKFIELD CAP 1 CORP (QC)
7.25% Rectractable Preferred Ser. 1 no par called for redemption 05/11/1994
Public interest eliminated

BROOKFIELD FED SVGS BK (BROOKFIELD, IL)
Reorganized under the laws of Delaware as Brookfield Bancshares Corp. 07/29/1988
Each share Common $1 par exchanged for (1) share Common $1 par
(See Brookfield Bancshares Corp.)

BROOKFIELD HIGH INCOME FD INC (MD)
Under plan of merger each share Common $0.001 par automatically became (0.32112) share Brookfield Real Assets Income Fund Inc. Common $0.001 par 12/05/2016

BROOKFIELD HIGH YIELD STRATEGIC INCOME FD (ON)
Trust terminated 06/22/2017
Each Unit received $8.03 cash

BROOKFIELD HOMES CORP (DE)
Each share Common 1¢ par received distribution of $4.50 principal amount of Sr. Subordinated Debentures due 06/30/2020 and $4.50 cash payable 04/30/2004 to holders of record 04/16/2004 Ex date - 05/03/2004
Merged into Brookfield Residential Properties Inc. 03/31/2011
Each share 8% Conv. Preferred Ser. A 1¢ par exchanged for (1) share 8% Conv. Preferred Ser. A no par
Each share Common 1¢ par exchanged for (0.76490053) share Common no par
(See Brookfield Residential Properties Inc.)

BROOKFIELD HOMES LTD (CANADA)
Merged into Brookfield Properties Corp. 05/08/1997
Each share Sr. Floating Rate Preferred Ser. A no par exchanged for (1.2) shares Class A Preferred Ser. A no par
Each share Common no par exchanged for (0.66666666) share Common no par
Brookfield Properties Corp. name changed to Brookfield Office Properties Inc. 05/09/2011
(See Brookfield Office Properties Inc.)

BROOKFIELD MTG OPPORTUNITY INCOME FD INC (MD)
Under plan of merger each share Common $0.001 par automatically became (0.65664) share Brookfield Real Assets Income Fund Inc. Common $0.001 par 12/05/2016

BROOKFIELD NEW HORIZONS INCOME FD (ON)
Trust terminated 07/31/2017
Each Unit received $8.2876 cash

BROOKFIELD OFFICE PPTYS INC (CANADA)
Name changed 05/09/2011
Each share Common no par received distribution of (0.2) share Brookfield Homes Corp. Common 1¢ par payable 01/06/2003 to holders of record 01/02/2003 Ex date - 01/07/2003
Common no par split (3) for (2) by issuance of (0.5) additional share payable 03/31/2005 to holders of record 03/15/2005 Ex date - 04/01/2005
Common no par split (3) for (2) by issuance of (0.5) additional share payable 05/22/2007 to holders of record 05/08/2007 Ex date - 05/23/2007
Name changed from Brookfield Properties Corp. to Brookfield Office Properties Inc. 05/09/2011
Class AAA Preference Ser. I no par called for redemption at $25 plus $0.325 accrued dividends on 03/30/2012
Class AAA Preference Ser. F no par called for redemption at $25 plus $0.1233 accrued dividends on 01/31/2013
Class A Preferred Ser. A no par called redemption at $1.11111 on 06/09/2014
Class A Preferred Ser. B no par called redemption at $1.11111 on 06/09/2014
Plan of arrangement effective 06/09/2014
Each share Common no par exchanged for (0.5735) Brookfield Property Partners L.P. Non-Vtg. Unit of Ltd. Partnership and USD$8.67501 cash
Note: Canadian holders option to receive Brookfield Office Properties Exchange LP Exchangeable Units of Ltd. Partnership in lieu of Non-Vtg. Units expired 03/30/2014
Class AAA Preference Ser. L no par called for redemption at $25 on 09/30/2014
Class AAA Preference Ser. H no par called for redemption at $25 plus $0.20816 accrued dividends on 05/23/2016
Class AAA Preference Ser. K no par called for redemption at $25 on 03/31/2017
Class AAA Preferred Ser. G no par called for redemption at $25 plus $0.2337 accrued dividends on 06/05/2017
Class AAA Preference Ser. J no par called for redemption at $25 plus $0.2226 accrued dividends on 06/05/2017
(Additional Information in Active)

BROOKFIELD REAL ESTATE SVCS FD (ON)
Under plan of reorganization each Trust Unit no par automatically became (1) share Brookfield Real Estate Services Inc. Common no par 01/04/2011

BROOKFIELD RENEWABLE ENERGY PARTNERS LP (BERMUDA)
Name changed to Brookfield Renewable Partners L.P. 05/10/2016

BROOKFIELD RENEWABLE PWR FD (QC)
Under plan of reorganization each Trust Unit automatically became (1) Brookfield Renewable Energy Partners L.P. (Bermuda) Unit of Ltd. Partnership 11/30/2011
Renewable Energy Partners L.P. (Bermuda) name changed to Brookfield Renewable Partners L.P. 05/10/2016

BROOKFIELD RESIDENTIAL PPTYS INC (ON)
Each share 8% Conv. Preferred Ser. A no par exchanged for (2.7317876) shares Common no par 08/01/2014
Acquired by Brookfield Asset Management Inc. 03/16/2015
Each share Common no par exchanged for USD$24.25 cash
Note: Unexchanged certificates were cancelled and became without value 03/16/2018

BROOKFIELD RES INC (NV)
Name changed to Broadcast Live Digital Corp. 08/02/2013

BROOKFIELD SOUNDVEST EQUITY FUND (ON)
Name changed to Soundvest Equity Fund 02/21/2018
(See Soundvest Equity Fund)

BROOKFIELD SOUNDVEST SPLIT TR (ON)
Name changed to Soundvest Split Trust 02/21/2018

BROOKFIELD TOTAL RETURN FD INC (MD)
Under plan of merger each share Common $0.001 par automatically became (0.9583) share Brookfield Real Assets Income Fund Inc. Common $0.001 par 12/05/2016

BROOKHAVEN BK & TR CO (BROOKHAVEN, MS)
Under plan of reorganization each share Common $5 par automatically became (1) share Brookhaven Financial Corp. Common $5 par 11/15/1982
(See Brookhaven Financial Corp.)

BROOKHAVEN FINANCIAL CORP. (MS)
Closed 09/30/1985
No stockholders' equity

BROOKINGS INTERNATIONAL LIFE INSURANCE CO. (SD)
Acquired by North American Corp. 00/00/1969
Each share Common exchanged for (0.66666666) share Common no par
North American Corp. merged into North American National Corp. 11/15/1974
(See North American National Corp.)

BROOKINGS RES LTD (BC)
Name changed to Cognoscente Software International Inc. 06/24/1993
(See Cognoscente Software International Inc.)

BROOKLINE BANCORP INC (MA)
Reorganized under the laws of Delaware 07/10/2002
Each share Common 1¢ par exchanged for (2.186964) shares Common 1¢ par

BROOKLINE INSTR INC (NY)
Merged into Neptune-Brookline, Inc. 11/13/1980
Each share Common 5¢ par exchanged for $0.21 cash

BROOKLINE MINERALS INC (CANADA)
Name changed to Ventel Inc. 12/15/1995
Ventel Inc. recapitalized as Fifty-Plus.Net International Inc. 07/09/1999 which name changed to ZoomerMedia Ltd. 07/02/2008

BROOKLINE OIL CO (CA)
Charter suspended for failure to file reports and pay taxes 08/02/1971

BROOKLINE SAVINGS & TRUST CO. (PITTSBURGH, PA)
Stock Dividend - 100% 02/01/1961
Merged into Western Pennsylvania National Bank (Pittsburgh, PA) 02/09/1968
Each share Capital Stock $12.50 par exchanged for (1) share $2.10 Conv. Preferred $35 par
Western Pennsylvania National Bank (Pittsburgh, PA) reorganized as WPNB Corp. 04/01/1969 which name changed to Equimark Corp. 05/10/1971
(See Equimark Corp.)

BROOKLINE TR CO (BROOKLINE, MA)
Capital Stock $100 par changed to $10 par and (9) additional shares issued plus a 66.66666666% stock dividend paid 03/05/1968
Merged into Patriot Bancorporation 12/05/1980
Each share Capital Stock $10 par exchanged for (1.3568) shares Common $10 par
Patriot Bancorporation acquired by Conifer Group Inc. 07/10/1986 which merged into Conifer/Essex Group, Inc. 02/17/1983 which name changed back to Conifer Group Inc. 01/01/1985 which merged into Bank of New England Corp. 04/22/1987
(See Bank of New England Corp.)

BROOKLYN & QUEENS TRANSIT CORP.
Acquired by the City of New York 00/00/1940
Liquidation completed 12/26/1956

BROOKLYN & RICHMOND FERRY CO. INC. (NY)
Liquidation completed
Each 465/154,000 Capital Stock Scrip ctf. received initial distribution of $0.34 cash 07/08/1957
Each 465/154,000 Capital Stock Scrip ctf. received second and final distribution of $0.044 cash 06/00/1968

BROOKLYN ASSETS CORP.
Liquidated 00/00/1948
Details not available

BROOKLYN ASSOCIATES (NY)
Dissolved 00/00/1952
Details not available

BROOKLYN BANCORP INC (DE)
Merged into Republic New York Corp. 02/29/1996
Each share Common 1¢ par exchanged for $41.50 cash

BROOKLYN BORO GAS CO (NY)
Common no par exchanged for (5) for (1) 01/26/1953
Merged into Brooklyn Union Gas Co. 06/01/1959
Each share Common no par exchanged for (0.75) share Common $10 par
$4.40 Preferred $100 par called for redemption 06/15/1959
Brooklyn Union Gas Co. reorganized as KeySpan Energy Corp. 09/30/1997 which merged into MarketSpan Corp. 05/29/1998 which name changed to KeySpan Energy 09/10/1998 which name changed to KeySpan Corp. 05/20/1999
(See KeySpan Corp.)

BROOKLYN CHEESECAKE & DESSERTS CO INC (NY)
Each share Common $0.001 par exchanged for (0.04) share old Common $0.025 par 03/22/2006
Each share old Common $0.025 par exchanged for (0.14285714) share new Common $0.025 par 11/18/2010
Name changed to Meridian Waste Solutions, Inc. 04/16/2015
Meridian Waste Solutions, Inc. name changed to Attis Industries Inc. 05/01/2018

BROOKLYN CITY RAILROAD CO.
Merged into Brooklyn-Manhattan Transit Corp. 00/00/1929
Details not available

BROOKLYN DRINK INC (UT)
Each share old Common $0.0005 par exchanged for (0.14285714) share new Common $0.0005 par 03/06/1995
Name changed to Net Tel International, Inc. 05/28/1996
(See Net Tel International, Inc.)

BROOKLYN EDISON CO.
Acquired by Consolidated Edison Co. of New York, Inc. 07/31/1945
Details not available

BROOKLYN ENERGY CORP (AB)
Merged into Lightning Energy Ltd. 06/01/2004
Each share Common no par exchanged for either (0.42) share Common no par or $2.10 cash
Note: Non-electors will receive cash
(See Lightning Energy Ltd.)

BROOKLYN FED BANCORP INC (USA)
Acquired by Investors Bancorp, Inc. 01/06/2012
Each share Common 1¢ par exchanged for $0.80 cash

BROOKLYN FIRE INSURANCE CO.
Merged into Knickerbocker Insurance Co. of New York 00/00/1931
Details not available

BROOKLYN FOX CORP. (NY)
Under plan of reorganization each share Common $1 par exchanged for (1) share 4% Preferred $2 par 10/01/1957
4% Preferred $2 par called for redemption 07/31/1958

BROOKLYN GARDEN APTS INC (NY)
Placed in receivership 09/00/1979
No stockholders' equity

BROOKLYN-LAFAYETTE CORP. (NY)
Name changed to Brookmont Corp. 01/18/1933
(See Brookmont Corp.)

BROOKLYN-MANHATTAN TRANSIT CORP.
Liquidation completed 12/26/1956
Details not available

BROOKLYN MORTGAGE GUARANTY & TITLE CO. (NY)
Acquired by Inter-County Title Guaranty & Mortgage Co. 05/19/1955
Details not available

BROOKLYN NATIONAL CORP.
Liquidation completed 00/00/1947
Details not available

BROOKLYN NATIONAL LIFE INSURANCE CO.
Merged into United States Life Insurance Co. in the City of New York 00/00/1935
Details not available

BROOKLYN POLY INDS INC (NY)
Common 10¢ par changed to 1¢ par 08/24/1970
Dissolved 09/08/2005
Details not available

BROOKLYN RES INC (BC)
Recapitalized as Stafford Industries Ltd. 04/14/1992
Each share Common no par exchanged for (0.4) share Common no par
Stafford Industries Ltd. recapitalized as New Stafford Industries Ltd. 07/21/1997 which name changed to Grandcru Resources Corp. 07/10/2003 which merged into Bell Copper Corp. (Old) 05/12/2008 which reorganized as Bell Copper Corp. (New) 07/23/2013

BROOKLYN SVGS BK (DANIELSON, CT)
Placed in receivership 10/19/1990
No stockholders' equity

BROOKLYN STEMWINDER GOLD MINES LTD. (BC)
Bankrupt 00/00/1951
Stockholders' equity unlikely

BROOKLYN TOWERS, INC. (NY)
Charter cancelled and proclaimed dissolved for failure to pay taxes and file reports 12/15/1967

BROOKLYN UN GAS CO (NY)
Common no par split (2) for (1) by issuance of (1) additional share 06/16/1952
5% Preferred $40 par called for redemption 08/01/1954
Common no par changed to $10 par 01/15/1957
Common $10 par split (2) for (1) by issuance of (1) additional share 11/25/1959
5.5% Preferred Ser. A $100 par called for redemption 03/01/1965
Common $10 par changed to $1 par 02/13/1976
Common $1 par changed to 50¢ par and (1) additional share issued 03/28/1986
$3.95 Preferred Ser. II $25 par called for redemption 09/01/1986
$2.47 Preferred Ser. I $25 par called for redemption 04/01/1992
8.6% Preferred Ser. C $100 par called for redemption 04/01/1992
8.92% Preferred Ser. D $100 par called for redemption 04/01/1992
Common 50¢ par changed to $0.33333333 par and (0.5) additional share issued 07/20/1993
4.6% Preferred Ser. B $100 par called for redemption 09/10/1997
Stock Dividend - 10% 10/09/1961
Under plan of reorganization each share Common $0.33333333 par automatically became (1) share KeySpan Energy Corp. Common $0.33333333 par 09/30/1997
KeySpan Energy Corp. merged into MarketSpan Corp. 05/29/1998 which name changed to KeySpan Energy 09/10/1998 which name changed to KeySpan Corp. 05/20/1999
(See KeySpan Corp.)

BROOKLYN VENTURES CORP (BC)
Name changed to World Famous Pizza Co. Ltd. 06/04/2009

BROOKMERE VENTURES INC (BC)
Name changed to Tegra Enterprises Inc. 09/21/1984
Tegra Enterprises Inc. recapitalized as Pacific Video Canada Ltd. 08/21/1989 which reorganized as Command Post & Transfer Corp. (BC) 05/01/1999 which reincorporated in Ontario 06/24/1999
(See Command Post & Transfer Corp. (ONT))

BROOKMIRE MANAGEMENT CORP. (AR)
Placed in receivership 09/16/1970
No stockholders' equity

BROOKMONT CORP. (NY)
Dissolved 08/31/1941
Details not available

BROOKPARK-ROYALON, INC. (OH)
Merged into Jeannette Glass Co. 12/28/1969
Each share Common $100 par exchanged for (13.06) shares Common $1 par
Jeannette Glass Co. name changed to Jeannette Corp. 05/14/1971
(See Jeannette Corp.)

BROOKRIDGE DEV CORP (DE)
Reorganized as Controlled Reaction Corp. 01/27/1969
Each share Common $1 par exchanged for (1/3) share Common 1¢ par
(See Controlled Reaction Corp.)

BROOKS & PERKINS INC (DE)
Common $1 par split (3) for (2) by issuance of (0.5) additional share 08/25/1972
Common $1 par split (5) for (4) by issuance of (0.25) additional share 10/28/1977
Common $1 par split (3) for (2) by issuance of (0.5) additional share 09/28/1979
Stock Dividend - 10% 07/12/1954
Acquired by AAR Corp. 08/12/1981
Each share Common $1 par exchanged for (1.58) shares Common $1 par and $8 cash

BROOKS (JAMES) & CO., INC. (NY)
Adjudicated bankrupt 06/00/1962
No stockholders' equity

BROOKS AUTOMATION CDA INC (CANADA)
Each share Non-Vtg. Exchangeable Preferred no par exchanged for (0.52) share Brooks Automation, Inc. (New) Common 1¢ par 07/23/2004

BROOKS AUTOMATION INC OLD (DE)
Under plan of merger name changed to Brooks-PRI Automation, Inc. 05/14/2002
Brooks-PRI Automation, Inc. name changed to Brooks Automation, Inc. (New) 02/27/2003

BROOKS BK & TR CO (TORRINGTON, CT)
Capital Stock $25 par changed to $12.50 par and (1) additional share issued 04/08/1968
Stock Dividend - 10% 11/25/1968
Merged into Colonial Bank & Trust Co. (Waterbury, CT) 12/31/1969
Each share Capital Stock $12.50 par exchanged for (3.25) shares Capital Stock $10 par
Colonial Bank & Trust Co. (Waterbury, CT) reorganized as Colonial Bancorp, Inc. (CT) 06/01/1970 which merged into Bank of Boston Corp. 06/20/1985 which name changed to BankBoston Corp. 04/25/1997 which merged into Fleet Boston Corp. 10/01/1999 which name changed to FleetBoston Financial Corp. 04/18/2004 which merged into Bank of America Corp. 04/01/2004

BROOKS BROTHERS
Merged into Brooks Brothers, Inc. on a (20) for (1) basis 02/29/1952
Brooks Brothers, Inc. merged into Garfinckel (Julius) & Co., Inc. 01/31/1957 which name changed to Garfinckel, Brooks Brothers, Miller & Rhoads, Inc. 12/05/1967
(See Garfinckel, Brooks Brothers, Miller & Rhoads, Inc.)

BROOKS BROTHERS, INC. (NY)
Merged into Garfinckel (Julius) & Co., Inc. 01/31/1957
Each share Common $1 par exchanged for (0.23076924) share Common 50¢ par
Garfinckel (Julius) & Co., Inc. name changed to Garfinckel, Brooks Brothers, Miller & Rhoads, Inc. 12/05/1967

(See Garfinckel, Brooks Brothers, Miller & Rhoads, Inc.)

BROOKS FASHION STORES INC (NY)
Common 10¢ par split (3) for (2) by issuance of (0.5) additional share 11/06/1978
Common 10¢ par split (2) for (1) by issuance of (1) additional share 08/01/1983
Merged into BR Acquisition Corp. 10/31/1984
Each share Common 10¢ par exchanged for $32 cash

BROOKS FIBER PPTYS INC (DE)
Merged into WorldCom, Inc. 01/29/1998
Each share Common 1¢ par exchanged for (1.85) shares Common 1¢ par
WorldCom, Inc. which name changed to MCI WorldCom, Inc. 09/14/1998 which name changed to WorldCom Inc. (New) 05/01/2000
(See WorldCom Inc. (New))

BROOKS FIELD NATL BK (SAN ANTONIO, TX)
Common $10 par changed to $5 par and (1) additional share issued 03/16/1967
Merged into National Bancshares Corp. of Texas 11/27/1978
Each share Common $5 par exchanged for (0.9375) share Common $10 par
(See National Bancshares Corp. of Texas)

BROOKS GODS LAKE MINES LTD. (ON)
Charter cancelled 08/00/1960

BROOKS INDS INC (CO)
Each share Common 10¢ par exchanged for (0.5) share Common 20¢ par 01/02/1973
Declared defunct and inoperative for failure to pay taxes and file annual reports 01/01/1981

BROOKS INSTRUMENT CO., INC. (PA)
Acquired by Emerson Electric Co. 11/30/1964
Each share Common 25¢ par exchanged for (0.14667) share Common $1 par

BROOKS INTL INC (TX)
Each share Common no par received distribution of (0.18181818) share Agri-Sul, Inc. Common no par 11/27/1972
Name changed to Incorporated Carriers Ltd. 11/21/1979
(See Incorporated Carriers Ltd.)

BROOKS-PRI AUTOMATION CDA INC (CANADA)
Name changed to Brooks Automation (Canada), Inc. 09/30/2003
Brooks Automation (Canada), Inc. exchanged for Brooks Automation, Inc. (New) 07/23/2004

BROOKS-PRI AUTOMATION INC (DE)
Name changed to Brooks Automation, Inc. (New) 02/27/2003

BROOKS REALTY CO. (PA)
Capital Stock $50 par changed to $25 par 00/00/1950
Liquidated 12/31/1969
Details not available

BROOKS RES CORP (OR)
Each share old Common no par exchanged for (0.1) share new Common no par 05/20/1985
Merged into BRC Merger Co. 08/25/1989
Each share new Common no par exchanged for $8 cash

BROOKS RES LTD (BC)
Recapitalized as International Brooks Petroleum Ltd. 09/01/1998
Each share Common no par exchanged for (0.1) share Common no par
International Brooks Petroleum Ltd. recapitalized as Flying A Petroleum Ltd. 08/14/2003

BROOKS SATELLITE INC (DE)
Charter cancelled and declared inoperative and void for non-payment of taxes 03/01/1988

BROOKS SCANLON INC (DE)
Each share Common $1 par exchanged for (1.04) shares Class A Common $1 par and (0.96) share Class B Common $1 par 10/11/1957
Class A Common $1 par and Class B Common $1 par reclassified as Common $1 par 05/13/1968
Common $1 par split (2) for (1) by issuance of (1) additional share 05/09/1969
Merged into Diamond International Corp. 06/17/1980
Each share Common $1 par exchanged for (1.2830) shares Common 50¢ par
(See Diamond International Corp.)

BROOKS TECH, INC. (DE)
Liquidation completed
Each share Common 10¢ par received initial distribution of $3.35 cash 10/08/1976
Each share Common 10¢ par received second and final distribution of $0.38 cash 02/14/1977
Note: Certificates were not required to be surrendered and are without value

BROOKSHIRE OIL CO.
Liquidated 00/00/1950
Details not available

BROOKSIDE DISTILLING PRODUCTS CORP. (DE)
Charter cancelled and declared inoperative and void for non-payment of taxes 04/01/1959

BROOKSIDE TECHNOLOGY HLDGS CORP (FL)
Common $0.001 par split (7) for (1) by issuance of (6) additional shares payable 07/06/2007 to holders of record 07/06/2007
Name changed to Blueprint Technologies, Inc. 03/24/2011

BROOKSTONE INC (DE)
Common $0.001 par split (3) for (2) by issuance of (0.5) additional share payable 09/23/2003 to holders of record 09/02/2003 Ex date - 09/24/2003
Common $0.001 par split (3) for (2) by issuance of (0.5) additional share payable 04/26/2004 to holders of record 04/19/2004 Ex date - 04/27/2004
Merged into Brookstone Holdings Corp. 10/04/2005
Each share Common $0.001 par exchanged for $20 cash

BROOKTREE CORP (CA)
Merged into Rockwell International Corp. 09/25/1996
Each share Common no par exchanged for $15 cash

BROOKTROUT INC (MA)
Name changed 05/13/1999
Common 1¢ par split (3) for (2) by issuance of (0.5) additional share payable 02/27/1996 to holders of record 02/09/1996
Common 1¢ par split (3) for (2) by issuance of (0.5) additional share payable 06/20/1996 to holders of record 06/10/1996
Name changed from Brooktrout Technology Inc. to Brooktrout Inc. 05/13/1999
Merged into EAS Group, Inc. 10/24/2005

Each share Common 1¢ par exchanged for $13.05 cash

BROOKVILLE GLASS AND TILE CO. (NJ)
Charter cancelled 00/00/1927

BROOKWATER VENTURES INC (ON)
Reincorporated 09/27/2013
Place of incorporation changed from (BC) to (ON) 09/27/2013
Each share old Common no par exchanged for (0.05263157) share new Common no par 12/31/2013
Name changed to Blue Sky Energy Inc. 07/15/2016

BROOKWOOD HEALTH SVCS INC (AL)
Merged into American Medical International, Inc. 06/30/1981
Each share Common $1 par exchanged for (1.169) shares Common $1 par
American Medical International, Inc. merged into American Medical Holdings, Inc. 04/12/1990 which merged into National Medical Enterprises, Inc. 02/28/1995 which name changed to Tenet Healthcare Corp. 06/23/1995

BROOME GENE SYS INC (DE)
Completely liquidated 10/26/1984
Each share Common 1¢ par exchanged for first and final distribution of $0.45702 cash

BROS HLDG CO (NV)
Recapitalized as Jufeel International Group 02/24/2017
Each share Common $0.001 par exchanged for (0.002) share Common $0.0001 par

BROSHIER PORCUPINE MINES LTD. (ON)
Charter surrendered 10/13/1966
No stockholders' equity

BROSNAN CANADIAN MINES LTD. (QC)
Name changed to Brosnan Mines Ltd.-Les Mines Brosnan Ltee. 02/07/1981
Brosnan Mines Ltd.-Les Mines Brosnan Ltee. recapitalized as Brosnor Exploration Inc. 09/24/1985 which recapitalized as Loubel Exploration Inc. 12/05/1990 which recapitalized as Lounor Exploration Inc. 04/17/2006

BROSNAN CHIBOUGAMAU MINES LTD. (QC)
Recapitalized as Brosnan Canadian Mines Ltd. 04/02/1968
Each share Capital Stock $1 par exchanged for (0.25) share Capital Stock $1 par
Brosnan Canadian Mines Ltd. name changed to Brosnan Mines Ltd.-Les Mines Brosnan Ltee. 02/07/1981 which recapitalized as Brosnor Exploration Inc. 09/24/1985 which recapitalized as Loubel Exploration Inc. 12/05/1990 which recapitalized as Lounor Exploration Inc. 04/17/2006

BROSNAN MINES LTD.-LES MINES BROSNAN LTEE. (QC)
Common $1 par changed to no par 03/29/1983
Recapitalized as Brosnor Exploration Inc. 09/24/1985
Each share Common no par exchanged for (0.2) share Common no par
Brosnor Exploration Inc. recapitalized as Loubel Exploration Inc. 12/05/1990 which recapitalized as Lounor Exploration Inc. 04/17/2006

BROSNOR EXPL INC (QC)
Recapitalized as Loubel Exploration Inc. 12/05/1990
Each share Common no par exchanged for (0.14285714) share Common no par

Loubel Exploration Inc. recapitalized as Lounor Exploration Inc. 04/17/2006

BROSS UTILS SVC CORP (CT)
Charter cancelled and proclaimed dissolved for failure to file annual reports 08/19/1988

BROTHEN INC (MN)
Liquidation completed
Each share Common 10¢ par exchanged for initial distribution of $16.32 cash 00/00/1985
Each share Common 10¢ par received second and final distribution of $5.845 cash 07/31/1986
Note: After 01/15/1988 holders must contact Minnesota Department of Commerce to receive payment

BROTHER INTL CORP (DE)
Common stock purchased by Brother Industries Ltd. (Japan) 00/00/1977
Details not available

BROTHERHOOD BANCSHARES INC (KS)
Name changed to Bank of Labor Bancshares, Inc. 11/21/2016

BROTHERHOOD BK & TR CO (KANSAS CITY, KS)
Name changed 01/24/1979
Name changed from Brotherhood State Bank (Kansas City, KS) to Brotherhood Bank & Trust Co. (Kansas City, KS) 01/24/1979
Each share Common $25 par exchanged for (5) shares Common $10 par 03/11/1981
Each share Common $10 par exchanged for (0.01666666) share Common $600 par 11/10/1989
Reorganized as Brotherhood Bancshares, Inc. 05/31/1990
Each share Common $600 par exchanged for (1) share Common $10 par
Brotherhood Bancshares, Inc. name changed to Bank of Labor Bancshares, Inc. 11/21/2016

BROTHERHOOD HOLDING CO. (OH)
Charter cancelled for failure to pay taxes 11/15/1933

BROTHERS CHEMICAL CO. (NJ)
Adjudicated bankrupt 08/17/1965
No stockholders' equity

BROTHERS GOURMET COFFEES INC (DE)
Plan of reoganization under Chapter 11 Federal Bankruptcy Code effective 02/18/2000
No stockholders' equity

BROTHERS TWO INTL INC (FL)
Proclaimed dissolved for failure to file reports and pay fees 10/13/1989

BROTT & CO., INC.
Acquired by City Union Corp. 00/00/1931
Details not available

BROUGHAM INDS INC (TX)
Stock Dividend - 10% 10/23/1978
Name changed to Alfa Leisure Inc. 12/29/1986
(See Alfa Leisure Inc.)

BROUGHER INS GROUP INC (IN)
Reacquired 08/16/1988
Each share Common no par exchanged for $8 cash

BROUGHTON COPPER LTD. (QC)
Charter surrendered 07/15/1968

BROUGHTON FOODS CO (OH)
Each share Class A Common $1 par exchanged for (1) share Common $1 par 02/28/1997
Each share Class B Common $1 par exchanged for (1) share Common $1 par 02/28/1997
Merged into Suiza Foods Corp. 06/23/1999

Each share Common $1 par exchanged for $16.50 cash

BROUGHTONS FARM DAIRY INC (OH)
Name changed to Broughton Foods Co. 05/27/1969
(See Broughton Foods Co.)

BROULAN PORCUPINE MINES LTD. (ON)
Merged into Broulan Reef Mines Ltd. 06/00/1951
Each share Capital Stock exchanged for (1) share Capital Stock $1 par
Broulan Reef Mines Ltd. merged into Broulan Resources Inc. 04/26/1983 which merged into Cabre Exploration Ltd. 11/24/1989 which was acquired by EnerMark Income Fund 01/10/2001 which merged into Enerplus Resources Fund 06/22/2001 which reorganized as Enerplus Corp. 01/03/2011

BROULAN REEF MINES LTD (ON)
Capital Stock $1 par changed to no par 06/12/1975
Merged into Broulan Resources Inc. 04/26/1983
Each share Capital Stock no par exchanged for (1) share Common no par
Broulan Resources Inc. merged into Cabre Exploration Ltd. 11/24/1989 which was acquired by EnerMark Income Fund 01/10/2001 which merged into Enerplus Resources Fund 06/22/2001 which reorganized as Enerplus Corp. 01/03/2011

BROULAN RES INC (ON)
Merged into Cabre Exploration Ltd. 11/24/1989
Each share Common no par exchanged for (0.4347826) share Common no par
Cabre Exploration Ltd. acquired by EnerMark Income Fund 01/10/2001 which merged into Enerplus Resources Fund 06/22/2001 which reorganized as Enerplus Corp. 01/03/2011

BROVAL, INC. (CA)
Charter suspended for failure to pay taxes 06/03/1957

BROWARD BANCORP (FL)
Acquired by Jefferson Bancorp, Inc. 09/30/1987
Each share Common $5 par exchanged for (1.1) shares Common $1 par
Jefferson Bancorp, Inc. merged into Colonial BancGroup, Inc. 01/03/1997
(See Colonial BancGroup, Inc.)

BROWARD BANCSHARES INC (FL)
Common $1 par split (3) for (1) by issuance of (2) additional shares 12/01/1972
Stock Dividend - 10% 01/25/1974
Under plan of merger name changed to Century Banks, Inc. 04/08/1976
Century Banks, Inc. merged into Sun Banks of Florida, Inc. 07/01/1982 which name changed to Sun Banks, Inc. 05/02/1983 which merged into SunTrust Banks, Inc. 07/01/1985

BROWARD BANK & TRUST CO. (FORT LAUDERDALE, FL)
Stock Dividend - 233% 02/17/1945
Name changed to Broward National Bank (Fort Lauderdale, FL) 06/01/1946
Broward National Bank (Fort Lauderdale, FL) acquired by Broward Bancshares, Inc. 05/28/1970 which name changed to Century Banks, Inc. 04/08/1976 which merged into Sun Banks of Florida, Inc. 07/01/1982 which name changed to Sun Banks, Inc. 05/02/1983 which merged into SunTrust Banks, Inc. 07/01/1985

BROWARD BANK (LAUDERDALE LAKES, FL)
Reorganized as Broward Bancorp 04/02/1984
Each share Common $5 par exchanged for (1) share Common $5 par
Broward Bancorp acquired by Jefferson Bancorp, Inc. 09/30/1987 which merged into Colonial BancGroup, Inc. 01/03/1997
(See Colonial BancGroup, Inc.)

BROWARD NATL BK (FORT LAUDERDALE, FL)
Each share Capital Stock $100 par exchanged for (5) shares Capital Stock $20 par 00/00/1946
Each share Capital Stock $20 par exchanged for (2) shares Capital Stock $10 par 02/07/1955
Stock Dividends - 100% 01/24/1951; 25% 03/13/1957; 10% 07/30/1959; 18% 03/01/1965
Acquired by Broward Bancshares, Inc. 05/28/1970
Each share Capital Stock $10 par exchanged for (2) shares Common $1 par
Broward Bancshares, Inc. name changed to Century Banks, Inc. 04/08/1976 which merged into Sun Banks of Florida, Inc. 07/01/1982 which name changed to Sun Banks, Inc. 05/02/1983 which merged into SunTrust Banks, Inc. 07/01/1985

BROWER EXPL INC (WY)
Reincorporated 12/29/1993
Place of incorporation changed from (BC) to (WY) 12/29/1993
Reorganized under the laws of Massachusetts as Stocker & Yale, Inc. (New) 05/11/1994
Each share Common no par exchanged for (0.2) share Common $0.001 par
Stocker & Yale, Inc. (New) name changed to StockerYale, Inc. 07/03/2000 which name changed to ProPhotonix Ltd. 07/23/2010

BROWN & BIGELOW (MN)
Each share Common no par exchanged for (10) shares Common $1 par 00/00/1947
Merged into Standard Packaging Corp. 04/06/1960
Each share Common $1 par exchanged for (0.625) share 6% Preferred $20 par
(See Standard Packaging Corp.)

BROWN & GRIST INC (DE)
Reincorporated 09/29/1969
State of incorporation changed from (VA) to (DE) 09/29/1969
Merged into Consulting Technology, Inc. 02/21/1973
Each share Common $1 par exchanged for (0.85) share Common 1¢ par

BROWN & SHARPE MFG CO (DE)
Reincorporated 01/24/1969
Each share Capital Stock $500 par exchanged for (10) shares Capital Stock $50 par 00/00/1937
Each share Capital Stock $50 par exchanged for (5) shares Capital Stock $10 par 00/00/1947
Voting Trust Agreement terminated 04/24/1961
Each VTC for Capital Stock $10 par exchanged for (1) share Capital Stock $10 par
Capital Stock $10 par split (2) for (1) by issuance of (1) additional share 07/07/1967
State of incorporation changed from (RI) to (DE) and Capital Stock $10 par reclassified as Common $10 par 01/24/1969
Common $10 par changed to $1 par 04/27/1979
Common $1 par reclassified as Class A Common $1 par 05/20/1988

Each share Class A Common $1 par received distribution of (1/3) share Non-Transferable Class B Common $1 par par 06/10/1988
Stock Dividends - 100% 07/01/1967; 20% 03/23/1979
Name changed to BNS Co. 04/27/2001
BNS Co. name changed to BNS Holding, Inc. 12/14/2004
(See BNS Holding, Inc.)

BROWN & WILLIAMSON TOBACCO CO.
Dissolved 00/00/1927
Details not available

BROWN (JOHN) DISTILLING CO., INC. (WV)
Recapitalized as Brown (John) Holding Corp. 01/28/1980
Each share Common $5 par exchanged for (3) shares Common 1¢ par
(See Brown (John) Holding Corp.)

BROWN-ALLEN CHEMICALS, INC. (NY)
Common $1 par changed to 10¢ par 09/25/1957
Under plan of merger name changed to Standard Magnesium Corp. (NY) 11/13/1961
Standard Magnesium Corp. (NY) reorganized in Delaware as Standard Magnesium & Chemical Co. 05/31/1963
(See Standard Magnesium & Chemical Co.)

BROWN BEAR PETROLEUMS LTD. (BC)
Merged into August Petroleums Ltd. 09/24/1973
Each share Common $1 par exchanged for (0.606061) share Common no par
August Petroleums Ltd. recapitalized as Cheyenne Petroleums Corp. 10/13/1976
(See Cheyenne Petroleums Corp.)

BROWN BRDG MLS INC (OH)
Merged into Kimberly-Clark Corp. 07/21/1971
Each share Common no par exchanged for (1.8457) shares Common $5 par

BROWN CO (DE)
Reincorporated 04/30/1965
Reorganized 00/00/1941
Each share 6% Preferred $100 par exchanged for (12.5) shares Common $1 par
Each share Common no par exchanged for (3.8) shares Common $1 par and (2.5) Common Stock Purchase Warrants expiring 00/00/1947
State of incorporation changed from (ME) to (DE) 04/30/1965
Recapitalized 06/09/1970
Each share $1.50 Conv. Preferred Ser. A $1 par exchanged for $19 principal amount of 9% Subord. Debentures due 06/01/1995 and (1.25) Common Stock Purchase Warrants expiring 05/15/1980
Common $1 par split (5) for (4) by issuance of (0.25) additional share 02/27/1976
Merged into James River Corp. of Virginia 10/28/1980
Each share Common $1 par exchanged for (0.12) share $5.40 Conv. Preferred Ser. G $10 par, (0.35) share Common 10¢ par and $21.62 cash
James River Corp. of Virginia name changed to Fort James Corp. 08/13/1997 which merged into Georgia-Pacific Corp. 11/27/2000
(See Georgia-Pacific Corp.)

BROWN CONSOLIDATED PETROLEUM LTD.
Name changed to Federated Petroleums Ltd. 00/00/1940
Federated Petroleums Ltd. merged into Home Oil Co. Ltd. 00/00/1955
(See Home Oil Co. Ltd.)

BROWN COUNTY SKI MOUNTAIN RESORT (IN)
Chapter 11 bankruptcy proceedings converted to Chapter 7 on 00/00/1988
No stockholders' equity

BROWN DISC PRODS INC (CO)
Each share old Common no par exchanged for (0.01) share new Common no par 04/29/1991
Name changed to Quartz Group Inc. 07/08/1997
Quartz Group Inc. recapitalized as Tenguy World International, Inc. 09/12/2005 which recapitalized as CMK Gaming International, Inc. 10/23/2013

BROWN DURRELL CO. (MA)
Each share Preferred $100 par exchanged for (1.78) shares new Preferred $100 par 00/00/1942
Common no par changed to $7.50 par 00/00/1942
Acquired by Hermes Electronics Co. 05/20/1960
Each share Common $7.50 par exchanged for (0.2) share Common 10¢ par and an undetermined amount of cash
Hermes Electronics Co. merged into Itek Corp. (DE) 07/26/1960
(See Itek Corp. (Del.))

BROWN ENGINEERING CO., INC. (AL)
Common $1 par split (3) for (2) by issuance of (0.5) additional share 03/31/1964
Completely liquidated 04/20/1967
Each share Common $1 par exchanged for first and final distribution of (0.15) share Teledyne, Inc. Common $1 par
Teledyne, Inc. merged into Allegheny Teledyne, Inc. 08/15/1996 which name changed to Allegheny Technologies Inc. 11/29/1999

BROWN ENTERPRISES INC (MO)
Adjudicated bankrupt 02/28/1972
No stockholders' equity

BROWN FD INC (HI)
Name changed to Franklin Option Fund, Inc. (HI) 05/26/1981
Franklin Option Fund, Inc. (HI) reincorporated in California as Franklin Option Fund 00/00/1983 which name changed to Franklin Premier Return Fund 04/12/1991

BROWN FENCE & WIRE CO.
Name changed to Brown (Jim) Stores, Inc. 00/00/1946
Brown (Jim) Stores, Inc. merged into Bearing Specialists, Inc. 00/00/1953 which name changed to Bearings, Inc. (DE) 00/00/1953 which reincorporated in (OH) 10/18/1988 which name changed to Applied Industrial Technologies, Inc. 01/01/1997

BROWN FINTUBE CO (OH)
Acquired by Ecological Science Corp. 03/25/1969
Each share Class A Common $1 par exchanged for (0.5) share Common 2¢ par and (0.625) Common Stock Purchase Warrant expiring 03/15/1972
Ecological Science Corp. name changed to Amicor Inc. 05/20/1974 which recapitalized as Keystone Camera Products Corp. 06/20/1984
(See Keystone Camera Products Corp.)

BROWN FORMAN CORP (DE)
Name changed 08/04/1987
Class A Common 15¢ par split (3) for (2) by issuance of (0.5) additional share 04/01/1987
Class B Common 15¢ par split (3) for (2) by issuance of (0.5) additional share 04/01/1987
Name changed from Brown-Forman Inc. to Brown-Forman Corp. 08/04/1987
4% Preferred $10 par called for redemption at $10.25 on 10/01/1998
(Additional Information in Active)

BROWN-FORMAN DISTILLERS CORP. (DE)
4% Jr. Preferred $10 par reclassified as 4% Preferred $10 par 00/00/1954
Common $1 par reclassified as Class A Common 30¢ par 10/26/1959 and (2) shares Class B Common 30¢ par issued 12/02/1959
Class A Common 30¢ par and Class B Common 30¢ par split (3) for (2) by issuance of (0.5) additional share respectively 03/04/1964
Class A Common 30¢ par and Class B Common 30¢ par split (5) for (4) by issuance of (0.25) additional share respectively 07/22/1965
Class A Common 30¢ par and Class B Common 30¢ par split (5) for (4) by issuance of (0.25) additional share respectively 08/15/1968
Class A Common 30¢ par changed to 15¢ par and (1) additional share issued 07/16/1981
Class B Common 30¢ par changed to 15¢ par and (1) additional share issued 07/16/1981
Stock Dividends - 100% 08/23/1946; 50% 12/15/1951; 15% 09/01/1956
Name changed to Brown-Forman Inc. 07/27/1984
Brown-Forman Inc. name changed to Brown-Forman Corp. 08/04/1987

BROWN-FORMAN DISTILLERY CO.
Name changed to Brown-Forman Distillers Corp. 00/00/1940
Brown-Forman Distillers Corp. name changed to Brown-Forman Inc. 07/27/1984 which name changed to Brown-Forman Corp. 08/04/1987

BROWN FUND OF HAWAII, LTD. (HI)
Common $1 par changed to 50¢ par and (1) additional share issued 05/08/1962
Name changed to Brown Fund Inc. 03/23/1977
Brown Fund Inc. name changed to Franklin Option Fund, Inc. (HI) 05/26/1981 which reincorporated in California as Franklin Option Fund 00/00/1983 which name changed to Franklin Premier Return Fund 04/12/1991

BROWN GROUP INC (NY)
Common $3.75 par split (3) for (2) by issuance of (0.5) additional share 07/01/1981
Common $3.75 par split (2) for (1) by issuance of (1) additional share 06/30/1983
Name changed to Brown Shoe Co., Inc. (New) 05/28/1999
Brown Shoe Co., Inc. (New) name changed to Caleres, Inc. 05/29/2015

BROWN GROWTH INCOME FD INC (HI)
Acquired by Brown Fund of Hawaii, Ltd. 12/14/1972
Each share Common $5 par exchanged for (1.9889) shares Common 50¢ par
Brown Fund of Hawaii Ltd. name changed to Brown Fund Inc. 03/23/1977 which name changed to Franklin Option Fund, Inc. (HI) 05/26/1981 which reincorporated in California as Franklin Option Fund 00/00/1983 which name changed to Franklin Premier Return Fund 04/12/1991

BROWN HOISTING MACHINERY CO.
Merged into Industrial Brownhoist Corp. 00/00/1927
Details not available

BROWN INSTL FD INC (HI)
Recapitalized as Brown Growth-Income Fund, Inc. 09/02/1971
Each share Common 25¢ par exchanged for (0.05) share Common $5 par
Brown Growth-Income Fund, Inc. acquired by Brown Fund of Hawaii, Ltd. 12/14/1972 which name changed to Brown Fund Inc. 03/23/1977 which name changed to Franklin Option Fund, Inc. (HI) 05/26/1981 which reincorporated in California as Franklin Option Fund 00/00/1983 which name changed to Franklin Premier Return Fund 04/12/1992

BROWN INTERNATIONAL, INC. (IN)
Name changed to Brown Rubber Co., Inc. 06/08/1965
(See Brown Rubber Co., Inc.)

BROWN INVESTMENT CO. LTD. (HI)
Name changed to Brown Fund of Hawaii Ltd. 05/03/1957
Brown Fund of Hawaii Ltd. name changed to Brown Fund Inc. 03/23/1977 which name changed to Franklin Option Fund, Inc. (HI) 05/26/1981 which reincorporated in California as Franklin Option Fund 00/00/1983 which name changed to Franklin Premier Return Fund 04/12/1991

BROWN J ADVERTISING LTD (NY)
Dissolved by proclamation 06/30/2004

BROWN JOHN HLDG CORP (WV)
Proclaimed dissolved for non-payment of taxes 05/15/1990

BROWN (J.W.) MANUFACTURING CO.
Acquired by Electric Auto-Lite Co. 00/00/1929
Details not available

BROWN (W.A.) MANUFACTURING CO. (IL)
Acquired by American Photocopy Equipment Co. (IL) 04/30/1964
Each share Common no par exchanged for (17/20) share Common no par
American Photocopy Equipment Co. (IL) reincorporated in Delaware 05/15/1969 which name changed to Apeco Corp. 04/13/1971 which recapitalized as Lori Corp. 08/29/1985 which name changed to COMFORCE Corp. 12/01/1995
(See COMFORCE Corp.)

BROWN MARTHA LTD (IL)
Recapitalized 10/10/1972
Recapitalized from Brown-Lynch-Scott Co., Inc. to Brown (Martha) Ltd. 10/10/1972
Each share Common $5 par exchanged for (0.05) share Common $100 par or $5 cash
Proclaimed dissolved for failure to pay taxes and file reports 12/27/1993

BROWN MCLAREN MANUFACTURING CO. (MI)
Stock Dividend - 10% 06/30/1958
Name changed to BeeMac, Inc. 06/26/1967
(See BeeMac, Inc.)

BROWN NATL BK (KENOSHA, WI)
Common $20 par changed to $10 par and (1) additional share issued 02/20/1973
Stock Dividends - 20% 02/16/1971; 100% 03/01/1974; 100% 03/01/1979

Acquired by Independence Bank Group 11/01/1983
Details not available

BROWN OIL CORP. LTD.
Reorganized as Coastal Oils Ltd. on a (0.2) for (1) basis 00/00/1944
Coastal Oils Ltd. was acquired by Federated Petroleums Ltd. 00/00/1951 which merged into Home Oil Co. Ltd. 00/00/1955
(See Home Oil Co. Ltd.)

BROWN OVERTON MINES LTD (BC)
Recapitalized as Oxbow Resources Ltd. 08/26/1974
Each share Common no par exchanged for (0.33333333) share Common no par
Oxbow Resources Ltd. recapitalized as Pasadena Energy Corp. 07/21/1981 which name changed to Pasadena Technology Corp. 06/03/1985 which name changed to EMS Systems Ltd. 08/11/1986
(See EMS Systems Ltd.)

BROWN PAPER MILL CO., INC. (DE)
Acquired by Olin Mathieson Chemical Corp. 00/00/1955
Details not available

BROWN ROBERT C & CO INC (CA)
Merged into Capitalcorp, Inc. 11/30/1989
Each share Common 1¢ par exchanged for $7 cash

BROWN RUBBER CO., INC. (IN)
Stock Dividend - 50% 05/15/1950
Name changed to Brown International, Inc. 07/02/1962 which name changed back to Brown Rubber Co., Inc. 06/08/1965
Completely liquidated 12/31/1967
Each share Common $1 par exchanged for first and final distribution of $1.25 cash

BROWN SHOE INC NEW (NY)
Common $3.75 par split (3) for (2) by issuance of (0.5) additional share payable 04/03/2006 to holders of record 03/17/2006 Ex date - 04/04/2006
Common $3.75 par split (3) for (2) by issuance of (0.5) additional share payable 04/02/2007 to holders of record 03/19/2007 Ex date - 04/03/2007
Common $3.75 par changed to 1¢ par 05/31/2007
Name changed to Caleres, Inc. 05/29/2015

BROWN SHOE INC OLD (NY)
Each share Common no par exchanged for (2) shares Common $15 par 00/00/1946
Common $15 par split (2) for (1) by issuance of (1) additional share 09/14/1956
Common $15 par changed to $7.50 par and (1) additional share issued 02/02/1965
Common $7.50 par changed to $3.75 par and (1) additional share issued 01/30/1968
Name changed to Brown Group, Inc. 01/14/1972
Brown Group, Inc. name changed to Brown Shoe Co., Inc. (New) 05/28/1999 which name changed to Caleres, Inc. 05/29/2015

BROWN (JIM) STORES, INC. (DE)
Recapitalized 00/00/1947
Each share Class A Preferred no par exchanged for (1) share Preference no par and (0.5) share new Common $1 par
Each share old Common $1 par exchanged for (0.33333333) share new Common $1 par
Merged into Bearing Specialists, Inc. 00/00/1953
Each share Preference no par exchanged for (3) shares Common 50¢ par

Each share Common $1 par exchanged for (1) share Common 50¢ par
Bearing Specialists, Inc. name changed to Bearings, Inc. (DE) 00/00/1953 which reincorporated in Ohio 10/18/1988 which name changed to Applied Industrial Technologies, Inc. 01/01/1997

BROWN TOM INC (DE)
Reincorporated 02/00/1987
Common 10¢ par split (3) for (1) by issuance of (2) additional shares 09/19/1980
Each share Common 10¢ par received distribution of (0.1) share TMBR Drilling Inc. Common 10¢ par 09/07/1984
Stock Dividends - 50% 08/02/1977; 100% 02/07/1978; 20% 03/17/1980
State of incorporation changed from (NV) to (DE) 02/00/1987
Each share old Common 10¢ par exchanged for (0.05) share new Common 10¢ par 09/07/1988
Acquired by EnCana Corp. 05/24/2004
Each share new Common 10¢ par exchanged for $48 cash

BROWN TRANS INC (GA)
Proclaimed dissolved for failure to pay annual fees 01/09/1992

BROWNIES MARINE GROUP INC (NV)
Common $0.001 par changed to $0.0001 par 02/22/2012
Each share old Common $0.0001 par exchanged for (0.00074074) share new Common $0.0001 par 07/15/2013
Reincorporated under the laws of Florida 12/07/2015

BROWNING (UT)
Merged into F.N. International Societe Anonyme Holding 06/30/1978
Each share Capital Stock $1 par exchanged for $13 cash

BROWNING ARMS CO. (UT)
Name changed to Browning 04/21/1972
(See Browning)

BROWNING COMMUNICATIONS INC (ON)
Delisted from Alberta Stock Exchange 08/21/1990

BROWNING ENTERPRISES INC (DE)
Recapitalized as Cabec Energy Corp. 04/01/1993
Each share Common 10¢ par exchanged for (0.2) share Common 10¢ par
Cabec Energy Corp. name changed to Palweb Corp. (DE) 04/19/1999 which reorganized in Oklahoma 06/25/2002 which name changed to Greystone Logistics Inc. 03/18/2005

BROWNING FERRIS INDS INC (DE)
Reincorporated 01/29/1971
Each share Common $0.33333333 par exchanged for (2) shares Common $0.16666666 par 12/02/1970
State of incorporation changed from (TX) to (DE) 01/29/1971
6% Preferred $10 par called for redemption 11/30/1971
Common $0.16666666 par split (2) for (1) by issuance of (1) additional share 12/01/1971
Common $0.16666666 par split (3) for (2) by issuance of (0.5) additional share 01/07/1983
Ser. 7 Serial Preferred Subseries A no par called for redemption 01/07/1985
Ser. 7 Conv. Serial Preferred Subseries B no par called for redemption 01/07/1985
Common $0.16666666 par split (2) for (1) by issuance of (1) additional share 12/26/1985
Common $0.16666666 par split (2) for (1) by issuance of (1) additional share 04/24/1987
Each share Automatic Common Exchangeable Securities exchanged for (1) share Common $0.16666666 par 06/30/1998
Merged into Allied Waste Industries, Inc. 07/30/1999
Each share Common $0.16666666 par exchanged for $45 cash

BROWNING FERRIS MACHY CO (TX)
Recapitalized as Browning-Ferris Industries, Inc. (TX) 09/09/1969
Each share Common $1 par exchanged for (3) shares Common 33-1/3¢ par
Preferred not affected except for change of name
Browning-Ferris Industries, Inc. (TX) reincorporated in Delaware 01/29/1971
(See Browning-Ferris Industries, Inc.)

BROWNING KING & CO.
Bankrupt 00/00/1934
Stockholders' equity unlikely

BROWNLEE MINES LTD. (ON)
Recapitalized as Brownlee Mines (1936) 00/00/1936
Each share Capital Stock $1 par exchanged for (0.2) share Capital Stock $1 par
Brownlee Mines (1936) Ltd. name changed to Joliet-Quebec Mines Ltd. 00/00/1939 which recapitalized as J-Q Resources Inc. 09/08/1978 which name changed to International Pursuit Corp. 09/21/1987 which recapitalized as Apollo Gold Corp. (ON) 06/24/2002 which reincorporated in Yukon 05/28/2003 which recapitalized as Brigus Gold Corp. (YT) 06/25/2010 which reincorporated in Canada 06/09/2011
(See Brigus Gold Corp.)

BROWNLEE MINES (1936) LTD. (ON)
Name changed to Joliet-Quebec Mines, Ltd. 00/00/1939
Joliet-Quebec Mines Ltd. recapitalized as J-Q Resources Inc. 09/08/1978 which name changed to International Pursuit Corp. 09/21/1987 which recapitalized as Apollo Gold Corp. (ON) 06/24/2002 which reincorporated in Yukon 05/28/2003 which recapitalized as Brigus Gold Corp. (YT) 06/25/2010 which reincorporated in Canada 06/09/2011
(See Brigus Gold Corp.)

BROWNS LIMOUSINE SVC INC (NY)
Adjudicated bankrupt 01/31/1978
Stockholders' equity unlikely

BROWNS ROGER MINIATURE HORSE FARMS INC (FL)
Name changed to Mini International Corp. 01/16/1985
(See Mini International Corp.)

BROWNSTAR VENTURES INC (BC)
Name changed to Longview Strategies Inc. 08/15/2005
Longview Strategies Inc. name changed to Longview Capital Partners Inc. 10/25/2006 which name changed to Resinco Capital Partners Inc. 11/30/2009

BROWNSTONE ENERGY INC (CANADA)
Reincorporated 12/01/2011
Place of incorporation changed from (BC) to (Canada) 12/01/2011
Recapitalized as ThreeD Capital Inc. 06/23/2016
Each share Common no par exchanged for (0.1) share Common no par

BROWNSTONE RES INC (WY)
Recapitalized as Pomsta Group, Inc. 10/12/2010
Each share Common no par exchanged for (0.00001) share Common no par
Pomsta Group, Inc. name changed to Oidon Co., Ltd. 12/31/2010

BROWNSTONE VENTURES INC (BC)
Name changed 01/20/1997
Name changed 12/23/2003
Name changed from Brownstone Investment Inc. to Brownstone Resources Inc. 01/20/1997
Name changed from Brownstone Resources Inc. to Brownstone Ventures Inc. 12/23/2003
Name changed to Brownstone Energy Inc. (BC) 01/18/2011
Brownstone Energy Inc. (BC) reincorporated in Canada 12/01/2011 which recapitalized as ThreeD Capital Inc. 06/23/2016

BROWNSVILLE CO (NV)
Each share old Common $0.001 par exchanged for (3) shares new Common $0.001 par 07/26/2006
Reorganized as Uranium Hunter Corp. 02/14/2007
Each share new Common $0.001 par exchanged for (2) shares Common $0.001 par
Uranium Hunter Corp. recapitalized as Resgreen Group International Ltd. 09/15/2016

BROWSESAFE COM INC (NV)
Name changed to PlanetGood Technologies, Inc. 07/20/2000
PlanetGood Technologies, Inc. name changed to American Diamond Corp. 06/02/2004 which recapitalized as All American Coffee & Beverage, Inc. 03/21/2006
(See All American Coffee & Beverage, Inc.)

BRS VENTURES LTD (BC)
Each share old Common no par exchanged for (0.33333333) share new Common no par 11/02/2011
Reorganized as Silver One Resources Inc. 09/01/2016
Each share new Common no par exchanged for (3) shares Common no par

BRT RLTY TR (MA)
Each Share of Bene. Int. $1 par exchanged for (0.33333333) Share of Bene. Int. $3 par 08/21/1986
Stock Dividend - 23.40824 % payable 10/30/2009 to holders of record 09/30/2009
Under plan of reorganization each Share of Bene. Int. $3 par automatically became (1) share BRT Apartments Corp. (MD) Common 1¢ par 03/18/2017

BRUBEC MINES LTD. (NB)
Charter forfeited for failure to file annual reports 11/16/1977

BRUCE (E.L.) CO. (DE)
Common no par changed to $5 par 00/00/1937
Each share Common $5 par exchanged for (2) shares Common $2.50 par 00/00/1948
Stock Dividends - 10% 04/03/1951; 10% 04/30/1955
Merged into Bruce (E.L.) Co., (Inc.) 09/22/1961
Each share Common $2.50 par exchanged for (2.25) share Common $1 par
Bruce (E.L.) Co., (Inc.) merged into Cook Industries, Inc. 03/21/1969 which name changed to Cook International Inc. 05/11/1981
(See Cook International Inc.)

BRUCE DOLOMITE LTD. (ON)
Charter cancelled and declared dissolved for default in filing returns 11/06/1970

BRUCE E L INC (NY)
Merged into Cook Industries, Inc. 03/21/1969
Each share Common $1 par exchanged for (1) share Common $1 par
Cook Industries, Inc. name changed to Cook International Inc. 05/11/1981
(See Cook International Inc.)

BRUCE MFG INC (WI)
Merged into Allegheny Ludlum Industries, Inc. 01/31/1974
Each share Common 10¢ par exchanged for (0.05) share Common $1 par
Allegheny Ludlum Industries, Inc. name changed to Allegheny International Inc. 04/29/1981
(See Allegheny International Inc.)

BRUCE NATIONAL ENTERPRISES, INC. (FL)
Charter cancelled and declared dissolved for non-payment of taxes 08/28/1964

BRUCE PRESTO MINES LTD (ON)
Bankrupt 02/03/1969
No stockholders' equity

BRUCE ROBERT INC (PA)
Merged into Consolidated Foods Corp. 02/28/1973
Each share Common 25¢ par exchanged for (0.453) share Common $1.33333333 par
Consolidated Foods Corp. name changed to Sara Lee Corp. 04/02/1985 which recapitalized as Hillshire Brands Co. 06/29/2012
(See Hillshire Brands Co.)

BRUCE ROBERT INDS INC (DE)
Plan of reorganization under Chapter 11 Federal Bankruptcy Code dismissed 09/20/1990
No stockholders' equity

BRUCETON & KINGWOOD TELEPHONE CO. (WV)
Completely liquidated 06/30/1959
Each share Capital Stock $10 par exchanged for first and final distribution of $10 cash

BRUCK MLS LTD (CANADA)
Each share Common no par exchanged for (1) share Class A no par and (2) shares Class B no par 00/00/1948
Class A no par reclassified as (10) shares Common no par 08/17/1978
Class B no par reclassified as Common no par 08/17/1978
Merged into Toyobo Co., Ltd. 09/00/1978
Each share Common no par exchanged for $0.50 cash

BRUCK SILK MILLS.
Name changed to Bruck Mills, Ltd. 00/00/1948
(See Bruck Mills, Ltd.)

BRUCKER INTL INC (NY)
These Certificates were issued as a result of a name change from International Hydrolines, Inc. which was reported as being effective 06/05/1972; but the change was not filed with the Secretary of State and is therefore not valid. Brucker International, Inc. certificates represent the same amount of shares of International Hydrolines, Inc., the company's legal title and need not be exchanged.
(See International Hydrolines, Inc.)

BRUIN GROUP INC (DE)
Recapitalized as Fusion Road, Inc. 07/30/2007
Each share Common 1¢ par exchanged for (0.001) share Common 1¢ par
Fusion Road, Inc. name changed to VZillion, Inc. (DE) 09/10/2007 which

reincorporated in Nevada 08/25/2008

BRUIN PT HELIUM CORP (BC)
Name changed to American Helium Inc. 05/11/2018

BRUIN YELLOWKNIFE GOLD MINES. LTD. (ON)
Charter revoked for failure to file reports and pay taxes 00/00/1956

BRUKER AXS INC (DE)
Merged into Bruker BioSciences Corp. 07/01/2003
Each share Common 1¢ par exchanged for (0.63) share Common 1¢ par
Bruker BioSciences Corp. name changed to Bruker Corp. 02/26/2008

BRUKER BIOSCIENCES CORP (DE)
Name changed to Bruker Corp. 02/26/2008

BRUKER DALTONICS INC (DE)
Under plan of merger name changed to Bruker BioSciences Corp. 07/01/2003
Bruker BioSciences Corp. name changed to Bruker Corp. 02/26/2008

BRUMMEL MANOR APARTMENTS, INC.
Liquidated 00/00/1941
Details not available

BRUN SENSOR SYS INC (DE)
Reincorporated 01/27/1969
State of incorporation change from (OH) to (DE) and Common no par changed to 10¢ par 01/27/1969
Merged into Industrial Nucleonics Corp. 01/30/1973
Each share Common 10¢ par exchanged for (0.0399) share Common $1 par
Each share Common 10¢ par received an additional and final distribution of (0.0114) share Common $1 par 05/31/1975
Industrial Nucleonics Corp. name changed to AccuRay Corp. 07/02/1979
(See AccuRay Corp.)

BRUNCOR INC (NB)
7.25% Retractable Preferred Ser. A no par called for redemption 06/30/1994
Common no par split (2) for (1) by issuance of (1) additional share payable 04/30/1998 to holders of record 04/17/1998
Merged into Aliant Inc. (Canada) 06/01/1999
Each share Common no par exchanged for (1.011) shares Common no par
Aliant Inc. (Canada) reorganized in Ontario as Bell Aliant Regional Communications Income Fund 07/10/2006

BRUNDAGE STORY & ROSE INVT TR (OH)
Growth & Income Fund no par reclassified as Equity Fund no par 04/01/1996
Merged into Old Westbury Funds, Inc. 06/08/2003
Details not available

BRUNEAU MINERALS INC (QC)
Recapitalized as Arianne Resources Inc. 02/28/2003
Each share Common $1 par exchanged for (0.16666666) share Common $1 par
Arianne Resources Inc. name changed to Arianne Phosphate Inc. 07/05/2013

BRUNEAU MINES LTD (QC)
Recapitalized as Bruneau Mining Corp. (1970)-Corporation Miniere Bruneau (1970) on 07/13/1970
Each share Common $1 par exchanged for (0.33333333) share Common $1 par

Bruneau Mining Corp. (1970)-Corporation Miniere Bruneau (1970) name changed to Bruneau Mining Corp. 02/26/1975 which recapitalized as Bruneau Minerals Inc. 12/30/1992 which recapitalized as Arianne Resources Inc. 02/28/2003 which name changed to Arianne Phosphate Inc. 07/05/2013

BRUNEAU MNG CORP (QC)
Name changed 02/26/1975
Name changed from Bruneau Mining Corp. (1970)-Corporation Miniere Bruneau (1970) to Bruneau Mining Corp. 02/26/1975
Recapitalized as Bruneau Minerals Inc. 12/30/1992
Each share Common $1 par exchanged for (0.16666666) share Common $1 par
Bruneau Minerals Inc. recapitalized as Arianne Resources Inc. 02/28/2003 which name changed to Arianne Phosphate Inc. 07/05/2013

BRUNETTE PORCUPINE GOLD MINES LTD. (ON)
Merged into Queensland Acceptance Corp. Ltd. 10/19/1963
Each share Capital Stock $1 par exchanged for (0.1) share Capital Stock no par
(See Queensland Acceptance Corp. Ltd.)

BRUNHURST MINES LTD. (ON)
Merged into Hydra Explorations Ltd. 11/16/1959
Each share Capital Stock $1 par exchanged for (0.04) share Capital Stock $1 par
Hydra Explorations Ltd. name changed to Hydra Capital Corp. 12/30/1992 which name changed to Waterford Capital Management Inc. 11/12/1996 which merged into CPI Plastics Group Ltd. 09/21/1998
(See CPI Plastics Group Ltd.)

BRUNING (CHARLES) CO., INC. (DE)
Reincorporated 03/31/1955
Common no par changed to $40 par 12/31/1954
State of incorporation changed from (NJ) to (DE) 03/31/1955
Each share Common $40 par exchanged for (15) shares Common $3 par 08/30/1955
Stock Dividends - 25% 12/14/1956; 100% 12/29/1959; 10% 12/15/1961
Merged into Addressograph-Multigraph Corp. 11/30/1963
Each share 5% Non-Cum. Preferred $100 par exchanged for (1.6161) shares Common $2.50 par
Each share Common $3 par exchanged for (0.6) share Common $2.50 par
Addressograph-Multigraph Corp. name changed to AM International, Inc. (Old) 01/02/1979 which reorganized as AM International, Inc. (New) 10/13/1993 which recapitalized as Multigraphics, Inc. 05/28/1997
(See Multigraphics, Inc.)

BRUNNER COS INCOME PPTYS L P (DE)
Units of Ltd. Partnership Int. II completely liquidated 00/00/1996
Details not available
Units of Ltd. Partnership Int. III completely liquidated 12/30/1999
Details not available
Company terminated registration of Units of Ltd. Partnership Int. I and is no longer public as of 03/28/2003

BRUNNER MANUFACTURING CO. (NY)
Each share Common $5 par exchanged for (13.5) shares Common $1 par and (2-5408/6296)

shares 4.5% Preferred $25 par 00/00/1945
Stock Dividend - 100% 03/23/1948
Name changed to Utica B.M.C., Inc. 03/29/1957
Utica B.M.C., Inc. merged into Dunham-Bush, Inc. 04/15/1957 which merged into Signal Oil & Gas Co. 12/29/1967 which name changed to Signal Companies, Inc. 05/01/1968 which merged into Allied-Signal Inc. 09/19/1985 which name changed to AlliedSignal Inc. 04/26/1993 which name changed to Honeywell International Inc. 12/01/1999

BRUNOS INC (AL)
Common 50¢ par changed to 25¢ par and (1) additional share issued 09/13/1977
Common 25¢ par changed to $0.125 par and (1) additional share issued 11/03/1978
Common $0.125 par changed to 5¢ par and (1) additional share issued 12/08/1980
Common 5¢ par changed to $0.025 par and (1) additional share issued 01/18/1983
Common $0.025 par changed to 1¢ par and (1) additional share issued 04/12/1985
Old Common 1¢ par split (2) for (1) by issuance of (1) additional share 11/17/1987
Merged into Crimson Acquisition Corp. 08/18/1995
Each share old Common exchanged for $12 cash
Plan of reorganization under Chapter 11 Federal Bankruptcy Code effective 01/20/2000
No new Common stockholders' equity

BRUNSMAN MINES LTD. (ON)
Merged into Hydra Explorations Ltd. 11/16/1959
Each share Capital Stock $1 par exchanged for (0.04) share Capital Stock $1 par
Hydra Explorations Ltd. name changed to Hydra Capital Corp. 12/30/1992 which name changed to Waterford Capital Management Inc. 11/12/1996 which merged into CPI Plastics Group Ltd. 09/21/1998
(See CPI Plastics Group Ltd.)

BRUNSTON MINING CO. LTD. (ON)
Recapitalized as Sunburst Exploration Ltd. 00/00/1956
Each share Capital Stock $1 par exchanged for (0.2) share Common no par
Sunburst Exploration Ltd. recapitalized as Sunburst Resources 1991 Inc. 11/14/1991 which name changed to Sunburst M.C. Ltd. 02/16/1994 which name changed to Channel I Canada Inc. 01/10/1997 which recapitalized as Zaurak Capital Corp. 12/01/1999
(See Zaurak Capital Corp.)

BRUNSWICK-BALKE-COLLENDER CO. (DE)
Common no par split (2) for (1) by issuance of (1) additional share 09/25/1957
Common no par split (4) for (3) by issuance of (0.33333333) share 12/01/1958
Common no par split (3) for (1) by issuance of (2) additional shares 11/12/1959
Name changed to Brunswick Corp. 04/18/1960

BRUNSWICK BK & TR CO (MANALAPAN, NJ)
Stock Dividend - 12% 02/01/1981
Reorganized as Brunswick Bancorp 01/15/1986
Each share Common $2 par exchanged for (1) share Common no par

BRUNSWICK CORP (DE)
$5 Preferred no par called for redemption 04/01/1962
$6 Preferred Ser. A no par called for redemption 12/31/1974
$2.40 Conv. Preferred Ser. A no par called for redemption 12/21/1983
(Additional Information in Active)

BRUNSWICK FED SVGS F A ME (USA)
Acquired by Bethel Bancorp 07/06/1990
Each share Common $1 par exchanged for $37 cash

BRUNSWICK-KROESCHELL CO.
Merged into Carrier Corp. 10/31/1930
Details not available

BRUNSWICK MNG & SMLT LTD (NB)
Capital Stock $1 par reclassified as Common $1 par 06/23/1967
Acquired by Noranda Inc. 10/13/1995
Each share Common $1 par exchanged for (0.5) share Common no par
Noranda Inc. name changed to Falconbridge Ltd. (New) 2005 on 07/01/2005
(See Falconbridge Ltd. (New) 2005)

BRUNSWICK N L (AUSTRALIA)
Unsponsored ADR's for Ordinary split (3) for (1) by issuance of (2) additional ADR 06/19/1987
Each Unsponsored ADR for Ordinary exchanged for (0.1) Sponsored ADR for Ordinary 08/29/1988
Stock Dividend - 10% 05/20/1988
Delisted from ASX 10/02/1991
No ADR holders' equity

BRUNSWICK OIL N L (AUSTRALIA)
Each old ADR for Ordinary exchanged for (0.2) new ADR for Ordinary 04/30/1982
Name changed to Brunswick N.L. 07/28/1986
(See Brunswick N.L.)

BRUNSWICK-QUEBEC DEVELOPMENT LTD. (QC)
Name changed to Abadex Mines Ltd. 00/00/1957
(See Abadex Mines Ltd.)

BRUNSWICK SITE CO. (NY)
Liquidation completed 06/26/1953
Details not available

BRUNSWICK TECHNOLOGIES INC (ME)
Common Stock Purchase Rights declared for Common stockholders of record 04/17/2000 were redeemed at $0.001 per right 06/12/2000 for holders of record 06/11/2000
Merged into Compagnie de Saint-Gobain 07/07/2000
Each share Common $0.0001 par exchanged for $8.50 cash

BRUNSWICK TERMINAL & RAILWAY SECURITIES CO.
Bankrupt 00/00/1933
Stockholders' equity unlikely

BRUNSWIG DRUG CO (CA)
Each share Common $4 par exchanged for (2) shares Common no par 00/00/1951
Common no par changed to $1 par 04/04/1955
Stock Dividends - 10% 04/01/1955; 10% 04/06/1956; 50% 03/08/1957
Merged into Bergen Brunswig Corp. 03/26/1969
Each share Common $1 par exchanged for (1) share $1.15 Conv. Preferred Ser. 1 no par
Bergen Brunswig Corp. merged into AmeriSourceBergen Corp. 08/29/2001

BRUNTON CO (WY)
Acquired by U.S. Energy Corp. of America, Inc. 05/18/1994
Each share Common 1¢ par

exchanged for (0.1) share Common 1¢ par

BRUNTON VINEYARDS HLDGS INC (NY)
SEC revoked common stock registration 02/19/2010

BRUSH CREEK MNG & DEV INC (NV)
Each share Common $0.0001 par exchanged for (0.1) share old Common no par 06/25/1985
Each share old Common no par exchanged for (0.0666666) share new Common no par 11/29/1993
Each share new Common no par exchanged for (0.1) share old Common $0.001 par 05/08/1998
Each share old Common $0.001 par exchanged for (0.08333333) share new Common $0.001 par 04/02/1999
Name changed to J.A.B. International, Inc. 05/26/1999
(See J.A.B. International, Inc.)

BRUSH ENGINEERED MATLS INC (OH)
Name changed 10/26/1971
Name changed 05/16/2000
Common $1 par split (2) for (1) by issuance of (1) additional share 04/22/1960
Name changed from Brush Beryllium Co. to Brush Wellman Inc. 10/26/1971
Common $1 par split (5) for (4) by issuance of (0.25) additional share 03/28/1977
Common $1 par split (2) for (1) by issuance of (1) additional share 09/28/1979
Common $1 par split (3) for (2) by issuance of (0.5) additional share 01/20/1983
Common $1 par split (2) for (1) by issuance of (1) additional share 06/22/1984
Name changed from Brush Wellman Inc. to Brush Engineered Materials Inc. and Common $1 par changed to no par 05/16/2000
Name changed to Materion Corp. 03/08/2011

BRUSHGARD SYS INC (DE)
Charter cancelled and declared inoperative and void for non-payment of taxes 03/01/1992

BRW LEASING SVCS INC
United States District Court, Los Angeles found 00/00/1998 stock was sold in fraudulent scheme
No stockholders' equity

BRX MNG & PETE LTD (BC)
Recapitalized as Consolidated BRX Mining & Petroleum Ltd. 04/30/1985
Each share Common no par exchanged for (0.25) share Common no par
(See Consolidated BRX Mining & Petroleum Ltd.)

BRYAN BANCORP INC (GA)
Merged into Savannah Bancorp, Inc. 12/15/1998
Each share Common no par exchanged for (1.85) shares Common $1 par
Savannah Bancorp, Inc. merged into SCBT Financial Corp. 12/14/2012 which name changed to First Financial Holdings, Inc. 07/30/2013 which name changed to South State Corp. 06/30/2014

BRYAN-COLLEGE STA FINL HLDG CO (DE)
Stock Dividend - 10% payable 03/01/1999 to holders of record 02/15/1999
Merged into Texas United Bancshares, Inc. 07/31/2002
Each share Common 1¢ par exchanged for (0.29211) share Common $1 par
Texas United Bancshares, Inc. merged into Prosperity Bancshares, Inc. 02/01/2007

BRYAN STEAM CORP (NM)
Merged into Burnham Corp. 03/12/1999
Each share Common no par exchanged for $152 cash

BRYAN STREET TRUST (MA)
Liquidation completed
Each Non-Negotiable Receipt received initial distribution of $1 cash 06/05/1984
Each Non-Negotiable Receipt received second and final distribution of $1.27 cash 06/00/1985

BRYANT & CHAPMAN CO.
Acquired by National Dairy Products Corp. 00/00/1929
Details not available

BRYANT PAPER CO.
Assets sold to Portage Liquidating Co. 00/00/1945
Details not available

BRYANT RES INC (BC)
Name changed to Outrider Energy Corp. 10/07/2013
Outrider Energy Corp. name changed to Pinedale Energy Ltd. 06/02/2017

BRYCE FINL INC (CO)
Recapitalized as Medical Innovations, Inc. 05/31/1989
Each share Common $0.0001 par exchanged for (0.01333333) share Common $0.0075 par
(See Medical Innovations, Inc.)

BRYCON EXPLORATIONS LTD. (BC)
Name changed to Brycon Industries, Ltd. 07/14/1971
Each share Capital Stock no par exchanged for (1) share Capital Stock no par
(See Brycon Industries, Ltd.)

BRYCON INDS LTD (BC)
Struck off register and declared dissolved for failure to file returns 08/09/1976

BRYHERN EXPLORATION, DEVELOPMENT & MINING LTD. (ON)
Merged into Pardee Amalgamated Mines Ltd. on a (2) for (15) basis 12/00/1954
Pardee Amalgamated Mines Ltd. liquidated for Rio Algom Mines Ltd. 11/09/1961 which name changed to Rio Algom Ltd. 04/30/1975
(See Rio Algom Ltd.)

BRYLANE INC (DE)
Merged into Pinault-Printemps-Redoute S.A. 04/23/1999
Each share Common 1¢ par exchanged for $24.50 cash

BRYMORE OIL & GAS LTD (AB)
Reincorporated 02/09/1995
Place of incorporation changed from (BC) to (AB) 02/09/1995
Name changed to BXL Energy Ltd. and Class A Common no par reclassified as Common no par 05/30/1996
BXL Energy Ltd. acquired by Viking Energy Royalty Trust 06/21/2001 which merged into Harvest Energy Trust 02/07/2006
(See Harvest Energy Trust)

BRYN MAWR CAMP RESORTS, INC. (PA)
Reincorporated under the laws of Delaware as Bryn Mawr Corp. 10/31/1979
Bryn Mawr Corp. name changed to Dixon Ticonderoga Co. 09/21/1983
(See Dixon Ticonderoga Co.)

BRYN MAWR CORP (DE)
Stock Dividend - 100% 07/28/1980
Under plan of merger name changed to Dixon Ticonderoga Co. 09/21/1983
(See Dixon Ticonderoga Co.)

BRYN MAWR GROUP, INC. (PA)
Name changed to Bryn Mawr Camp Resorts, Inc. (PA) 05/10/1973
Bryn Mawr Camp Resorts, Inc. (PA) reincorporated in Delaware as Bryn Mawr Corp. 10/31/1979 which name changed to Dixon Ticonderoga Co. 09/21/1983
(See Dixon Ticonderoga Co.)

BRYN MAWR TRUST
Liquidated 00/00/1948
Details not available

BRYN MAWR TR CO (BRYN MAWR, PA)
Common $5 par split (2) for (1) by issuance of (1) additional share 04/30/1985
Stock Dividends - 10% 11/01/1960; 10% 05/15/1968
Reorganized as Bryn Mawr Bank Corp. 01/02/1987
Each share Common $5 par exchanged for (3) shares Common $1 par

BRYNA COSMETICS INC (DE)
Charter cancelled and declared inoperative and void for non-payment of taxes 03/01/1977

BRYNA INDUSTRIES, INC. (DE)
Name changed to Bryna Cosmetics, Inc. 06/29/1971
(See Bryna Cosmetics, Inc.)

BRYNA INTERNATIONAL CORP. (NY)
Name changed to World Explorers/Sportsmen's Club, Inc. 05/10/1967
(See World Explorers/Sportsmen's Club, Inc.)

BRYNDON VENTURES INC (AB)
Reorganized under the laws of British Columbia as Conqueror Holdings Ltd. 03/16/1995
Each share Common no par exchanged for (0.2) share Common no par
Conqueror Holdings Ltd. merged into Med Net International Ltd. 07/31/2000
(See Med Net International Ltd)

BSA SATELLINK INC (DE)
Name changed to Affluence Corp. 01/07/2009

BSB BANCORP INC (DE)
Common 1¢ par split (3) for (2) by issuance of (0.5) additional share 12/17/1993
Common 1¢ par split (3) for (2) by issuance of (0.5) additional share 12/08/1995
Common 1¢ par split (3) for (2) by issuance of (0.5) additional share payable 09/10/1997 to holders of record 08/21/1997
Merged into Partners Trust Financial Group, Inc. (DE) 07/14/2004
Each share Common 1¢ par exchanged for (3.6) shares Common 10¢ par
Partners Trust Financial Group, Inc. (DE) merged into M&T Bank Corp. 11/30/2007

BSC NOTE LIQUIDATING TRUST (CA)
In process of liquidation
Each Unit of Bene. Int. received initial distribution of $1.74 cash 06/04/1985
Each Unit of Bene. Int. received second distribution of $1.50 cash 01/08/1987
Note: Details on subsequent distributions, if any, are not available

BSCH FINANCE LTD. (CAYMAN ISLANDS)
8.125% Guaranteed Preference Ser. F called for redemption at $25.8125 plus $0.4232 accrued dividends on 09/15/2003
7.35% Guaranteed Preference Ser. J called for redemption at $25 plus $0.2603 accrued dividends on 11/21/2003
7.79% Guaranteed Preference Ser. H called for redemption at $25 plus $0.2759 accrued dividends on 11/21/2003
8.625% Guaranteed Preference Ser. Q called for redemption at $25 plus $0.035938 accrued dividends on 10/06/2005

BSD BANCORP INC (DE)
Reincorporated 09/03/1987
Common no par split (4) for (3) by issuance of (0.33333333) additional share 03/15/1983
State of incorporation changed from (CA) to (DE) and Common no par changed to 10¢ par 09/02/1987
Charter cancelled and declared inoperative and void for non-payment of taxes 03/01/1995

BSD HEALTHCARE INDS INC (FL)
Name changed to BSD Software Inc. 12/17/2001
BSD Software Inc. merged into NeoMedia Technologies, Inc. 03/23/2006

BSD MED CORP (UT)
Reincorporated under the laws of Delaware and Common $0.0005 par changed to 1¢ par 07/29/1986
BSD Medical Corp. (DE) (Old) name changed to Perseon Corp. 02/25/2015 which name changed to BSD Medical Corp. (New) 10/28/2016
(See BSD Medical Corp. (New))

BSD MED CORP NEW (DE)
Plan of reorganization under Chapter 11 Federal Bankruptcy proceedings effective 01/13/2017
Holders are expected to receive pro rata share of the Company's assets
Distributions of less than $25 will not be made

BSD MED CORP OLD (DE)
Common 1¢ par changed to $0.001 par 04/18/2002
Name changed to Perseon Corp. 02/25/2015
Perseon Corp. name changed to BSD Medical Corp. (New) 10/28/2016
(See BSD Medical Corp. (New))

BSD SOFTWARE INC (FL)
Merged into NeoMedia Technologies, Inc. 03/23/2006
Each share Common $0.001 par exchanged for (0.2019) share Common 1¢ par

BSEL INFRASTRUCTURE RLTY LTD (INDIA)
GDR agreement terminated 06/12/2015
Each Sponsored Reg. S GDR for Ordinary exchanged for $0.124501 cash

BSES LTD (INDIA)
Name changed to Reliance Energy Ltd. 02/24/2004
Reliance Energy Ltd. name changed to Reliance Infrastructure Ltd. 05/12/2008

BSI HLDGS INC (VA)
Name changed to Autobanc Inc. 06/12/1991
(See Autobanc Inc.)

BSI2000 INC (DE)
SEC revoked common stock registration 05/13/2011

BSK & TECH INC (NV)
SEC revoked common stock registration 01/17/2012

BSL TECHNOLOGY (UT)
Each share old Common 1¢ par

exchanged for (0.25) share new
Common 1¢ par 05/02/1984
Name changed to Systemed, Inc.
(UT) 12/12/1985
Systemed, Inc. (UT) reincorporated in
Delaware as Knowledge Data
Systems, Inc. 03/16/1987
(See Knowledge Data Systems, Inc.)

BSM BANCORP (CA)
Merged into Mid-State Bancshares
07/10/1998
Each share Common no par
exchanged for (1) share Common
no par
(See Mid-State Bancshares)

BSML INC (UT)
Chapter 7 bankruptcy proceedings
terminated 06/20/2017
Stockholders' equity unlikely

BSN (FRANCE)
Each Unsponsored ADR for Bearer
Shares exchanged for (10)
Unsponsored ADR's for Bearer
Shares 02/07/1989
Each Unsponsored ADR for Bearer
Shares exchanged for (1)
Sponsored ADR for Bearer Shares
12/10/1990
Name changed to Groupe Danone
07/07/1994
Groupe Danone name changed to
Danone 05/01/2009

BSN CORP (DE)
Each share Common 1¢ par received
distribution of (0.1) share Tennis
Lady, Inc. Common 1¢ par
03/12/1984
Each share Common 1¢ par
exchanged for (0.33333333) share
Common 3¢ par 05/16/1985
Common 3¢ par split (5) for (4) by
issuance of (0.25) additional share
11/07/1986
Stock Dividend - 25% 05/15/1981
Name changed to Aurora Electronics
Inc. 12/03/1992
Aurora Electronics Inc. name
changed to Cerplex Group, Inc.
04/30/1998
(See Cerplex Group, Inc.)

BSP ONELINK INC (DE)
Name changed to One Link 4 Travel,
Inc. 01/20/2004
One Link 4 Travel, Inc. name
changed to OneLink Corp.
03/15/2006

BSR INTL PLC (ENGLAND)
Name changed to Astec (BSR) PLC
06/07/1989
(See Astec (BSR) PLC)

BT ENERGY CORP (DE)
Each share old Class A Common no
par exchanged for (0.1) share new
Class A Common no par 09/30/1991
Charter cancelled and declared
inoperative and void for
non-payment of taxes 03/01/1997

BT FINL CORP (PA)
Common $5 par split (2) for (1) by
issuance of (1) additional share
09/16/1986
Common $5 par split (2) for (1) by
issuance of (1) additional share
payable 05/01/1998 to holders of
record 04/08/1998
Stock Dividends - 10% payable
10/22/1996 to holders of record
09/20/1996; 10% payable
09/15/1997 to holders of record
08/27/1997; 5% payable 02/01/2000
to holders of record 01/04/2000
Name changed to Promistar Financial
Corp. 11/15/2000
Promistar Financial Corp. merged into
F.N.B. Corp. (FL) 01/18/2002

BT HLDGS EUROPE LTD
144A Money Market Preferred Ser. A
called for redemption at $100,000
on 11/03/1998
144A Money Market Preferred Ser. B
called for redemption at $100,000
on 11/10/1998
144A Money Market Preferred Ser. C
called for redemption at $100,000
on 11/17/1998
144A Money Market Preferred Ser. D
called for redemption at $100,000
on 11/24/1998

BT MTG INVS (MA)
Shares of Bene. Int. no par split (2)
for (1) by issuance of (1) additional
share 10/20/1971
Shares of Bene. Int. no par changed
to 50¢ par 02/18/1972
Merged into Charan Industries, Inc.
(DE) 06/18/1982
Each Share of Bene. Int. 50¢ par
exchanged for (1) share Common
50¢ par
(See Charan Industries, Inc. (DE))

BT N Y CORP (NY)
Name changed to Bankers Trust New
York Corp. 09/15/1967
Bankers Trust New York Corp. name
changed to Bankers Trust Corp.
04/23/1998
(See Bankers Trust Corp.)

BT NORTHEAST INC (DE)
Charter cancelled and declared
inoperative and void for
non-payment of taxes 12/09/1991

BT OFFICE PRODS INTL INC (NETHERLANDS)
Merged into Buhrmann NV
09/29/1998
Each share Common 1¢ par
exchanged for $13.75 cash

BT PREFERRED CAP TR I (DE)
8.125% Preferred Securities Ser. I
called for redemption at $25 on
02/28/2002

BT SHIPPING LTD (BERMUDA)
Each old Sponsored ADR for Ordinary
exchanged for (0.2) new Sponsored
ADR for Ordinary 03/31/1999
Each new Sponsored ADR for
Ordinary par exchanged again for
(0.2) new Sponsored ADR for
Ordinary 01/21/2000
ADR agreement terminated
04/26/2001
Each new Sponsored ADR for
Ordinary exchanged for $3.22 cash

BT TELECOM INC (DE)
Name changed to Versus Technology,
Inc. 10/25/1989
(See Versus Technology, Inc.)

BTC FINL SVCS (NV)
Name changed to First Equity Holding
Corp. 09/19/2000
First Equity Holding Corp.
recapitalized as Chilmark
Entertainment Group, Inc.
06/23/2003 which recapitalized as
Integrated Bio Energy Resources,
Inc. 03/13/2007 which name
changed to Onslow Holdings, Inc.
01/30/2014

BTHC VI INC (DE)
Each share old Common $0.001 par
exchanged for (0.59880239) share
new Common $0.001 par
06/05/2007
Name changed to Athersys, Inc.
09/06/2007

BTG COSMETICS INC (NV)
Reorganized as BioPharmetics, Inc.
04/03/2006
Each share Common $0.001 par
exchanged for (3) shares Common
$0.001 par

BTG INC (VA)
Merged into Titan Corp. 11/28/2001
Each share Common no par
exchanged for (0.43578) share
Common 1¢ par and $2.5365 cash
(See Titan Corp.)

BTHC III INC (DE)
Name changed to International Stem
Cell Corp. 01/29/2007

BTHC VII INC (DE)
Name changed to Whitehall Jewelers
Holdings, Inc. 09/07/2007
(See Whitehall Jewelers Holdings, Inc.)

BTHC VIII INC (DE)
Each share old Common $0.001 par
exchanged for (0.625) share new
Common $0.001 par 10/16/2007
New Common $0.001 par split (1.92)
for (1) by issuance of (0.92)
additional share payable 06/23/2009
to holders of record 06/15/2009
Ex date - 06/24/2009
Reincorporated under the laws of
Nevada as THT Heat Transfer
Technology, Inc. 12/15/2009

BTHC XV INC (DE)
SEC revoked common stock
registration 12/12/2014

BTK INDS INC (DE)
Merged into McGregor Corp.
03/28/1985
Each share Conv. Preferred Ser. A $1
par exchanged for $2.875 cash
Each share Common 10¢ par
exchanged for $0.50 cash

BTNB CORP (DE)
Recapitalized as Alabama Financial
Group, Inc. 03/10/1972
Each share Common $10 par
exchanged for (1) share Common
$10 par
Alabama Financial Group, Inc. name
changed to Southern Bancorporation
04/17/1974 which name changed to
Southern Bancorporation of
Alabama 04/21/1975 which name
changed to SouthTrust Corp.
09/18/1981 which merged into
Wachovia Corp. (Ctfs. dated after
09/01/2001) 11/01/2004 which
merged into Wells Fargo & Co.
(New) 12/31/2008

BTR PLC (ENGLAND)
Merged 10/30/1969
Name changed 04/18/1972
Merged from BTR Industries Ltd. to
BTR Leyland Industries Ltd.
10/30/1969
Each share Ordinary Reg. 5s par
exchanged for (0.866667) share
Ordinary Reg. 25p par
Ordinary Reg. 5s par changed to 25p
par per currency change 02/15/1971
Name changed from BTR Leyland
Industries Ltd. to BTR PLC
04/18/1972
Each Unsponsored ADR for Ordinary
Reg. exchanged for (0.25)
Sponsored ADR for Ordinary
06/30/1987
Each (16) old Sponsored ADR's for
Ordinary exchanged for (13) new
Sponsored ADR's for Ordinary
05/18/1998
Stock Dividends - Ordinary Reg.
100% 05/31/1985; 50% 06/11/1986;
ADR's for Ordinary 50% 12/12/1983;
100% 05/15/1985; 50% 06/11/1986;
66% 06/11/1993
Merged into BTR Siebe PLC
02/12/1999
Each new Sponsored ADR for
Ordinary exchanged for (1.066)
Sponsored ADR's for Ordinary
BTR Siebe PLC name changed to
Invensys PLC 04/16/1999

BTR RLTY INC (MD)
Common $1 par split (2) for (1) by
issuance of (1) additional share
09/04/1981
Common $1 par split (2) for (1) by
issuance of (1) additional share
12/31/1982
Common $1 par split (2) for (1) by
issuance of (1) additional share
04/01/1985
Common $1 par split (2) for (1) by
issuance of (1) additional share
04/23/1986
Merged into Mid-Atlantic Realty Trust
09/13/1993
Each share Common $1 par
exchanged for (0.33333333) Share
of Bene. Int. 1¢ par
(See Mid-Atlantic Realty Trust)

BTR SIEBE PLC (UNITED KINGDOM)
Name changed to Invensys PLC
04/16/1999
(See Invensys PLC)

BTU CAP CORP (BC)
Each share old Common no par
exchanged for (0.33333333) share
new Common no par 12/28/2012
Name changed to BTU Metals Corp.
08/29/2017

BTU INTL INC (DE)
Merged into Amtech Systems, Inc.
01/30/2015
Each share Common 1¢ par
exchanged for (0.3291) share
Common 1¢ par

B2 HEALTH INC (DE)
Name changed to Creative Learning
Corp. 07/27/2010

B2B INTERNET HOLDRS TR (DE)
Trust terminated
Each Depositary Receipt received
first and final distribution of
$0.084198 cash payable 01/10/2013
to holders of record 12/24/2012

B2B SOLUTIONS INC (BC)
Name changed to Timer Explorations
Inc. 08/12/2004
Timer Explorations Inc. name
changed to Potash North Resource
Corp. 05/30/2008 which merged into
Potash One Inc. 04/17/2009
(See Potash One Inc.)

B2B TR (CANADA)
Merged into Laurentian Bank of
Canada (Montreal, QC) 06/08/2004
Each share Common no par
exchanged for $9.50 cash

B2BSTORES COM INC (DE)
Name changed to Ivax Diagnostics,
Inc. 03/15/2001
Ivax Diagnostics, Inc. name changed
to ERBA Diagnostics, Inc.
06/18/2012

B2W-COMPANHIA GLOBAL DO VAREJO (BRAZIL)
Name changed to B2W-Companhia
Digital 07/30/2013

BTX HLDGS INC (FL)
Old Common $0.001 par split (5) for
(1) by issuance of (4) additional
shares payable 07/28/2006 to
holders of record 07/24/2006
Ex date - 07/31/2006
Each share old Common $0.001 par
exchanged for (0.1) share new
Common $0.001 par 07/09/2007
Each share new Common $0.001 par
exchanged again for (0.2) share new
Common $0.001 par 09/09/2008
Recapitalized as Rebornne (USA) Inc.
03/22/2010
Each share Common $0.001 par
exchanged for (0.70323488) share
Common $0.001 par

BU MAX GOLD CORP (BC)
Delisted from Vancouver Stock
Exchange 03/04/1991

BUBBEE VENTURES INC (ON)
Merged into Cash Store Australia
Holdings Inc. 03/13/2009
Each share Common no par
exchanged for (0.66666666) share
Common no par

BUCA INC (MN)
Merged into Planet Hollywood
International, Inc. (New) 09/30/2008
Each share Common 1¢ par
exchanged for $0.45 cash

BUCAN MINES LTD. (ON)
Declared dissolved 11/06/1961
No stockholders' equity

BUCCANEER CASINO & HOTEL CORP (UT)
Common $0.001 par split (2) for (1) by issuance of (1) additional share 01/22/1994
Name changed to Worthington Venture Fund Inc. (UT) 02/06/1995
Worthington Venture Fund Inc. (UT) reincorporated in Delaware 06/03/1998 which name changed to Admax Technology Inc. 08/16/1998 which name changed to Aamaxan Transport Group, Inc. 08/28/1998

BUCCANEER RES LTD (BC)
Struck off register and declared dissolved for failure to file returns 09/20/1985

BUCHANAN MINES LTD (AB)
Merged into Cord International Minerals Ltd. 02/09/1972
Each share Common no par exchanged for (0.1) share Common no par
(See Cord International Minerals Ltd.)

BUCHANAN REALTY CORP.
Dissolved 00/00/1943
Details not available

BUCHANAN STEEL PRODUCTS CORP. (MI)
Stock Dividend - 20% 09/15/1959
Acquired by National Standard Co. (DE) on a (1) for (5.5) basis 04/01/1964
National-Standard Co. (DE) reincorporated in Indiana 01/31/1994
(See National-Standard Co.)

BUCHANS MINERALS CORP (CANADA)
Merged into Minco PLC 07/16/2013
Each share Common no par exchanged for (0.826) share Ordinary

BUCHANS RIV LTD (CANADA)
Reincorporated 06/10/2008
Place of incorporation changed from (NL) to (Canada) 06/10/2008
Merged into Royal Roads Corp. (Canada) 07/25/2008
Each share Common no par exchanged for (1.55) shares Common no par
Royal Roads Corp. (Canada) name changed to Buchans Minerals Corp. 07/05/2010
(See Buchans Minerals Corp.)

BUCK A ROOS HLDG CORP (NV)
Company terminated common stock registration and is no longer public as of 03/23/2010

BUCK CREEK OIL CO. (WY)
Capital Stock $1 par changed to 25¢ par 00/00/1937
Completely liquidated 02/24/1964
Each share Capital Stock 25¢ par exchanged for first and final distribution of $0.70 cash

BUCK ENGR INC (NJ)
Stock Dividend - 200% 11/01/1967
Name changed to Lab-Volt Systems, Inc. 11/22/1995
(See Lab-Volt Systems, Inc.)

BUCK LAKE VENTURES LTD (BC)
Recapitalized as Ultra Uranium Corp. 05/11/2006
Each share Common no par exchanged for (0.2) share Common no par
Ultra Uranium Corp. recapitalized as Ultra Resources Corp. 11/14/2012 which recapitalized as Empire Rock Minerals Inc. 10/22/2015 which name changed to Empire Metals Corp. 02/02/2017

BUCK MAN ELECTRS INC (NY)
Name changed to Frequency Control Products, Inc. 01/05/1981
Frequency Control Products, Inc. name changed to FCP Inc. 07/08/1985
(See FCP Inc.)

BUCK TOOL CO. (MI)
Voluntarily dissolved 03/08/1996
Details not available

BUCKAROO STEAK RANCHES INC (DE)
Completely liquidated 02/28/1970
Each share Common 5¢ par exchanged for first and final distribution of (0.271846) share Downtowner Corp. Common $1 par
Downtowner Corp. name changed to Perkins Foods, Inc. 11/28/1973
(See Perkins Foods, Inc.)

BUCKBEE MEARS CO (MN)
Common 10¢ par split (3) for (2) by issuance of (0.5) additional share 10/26/1973
Name changed to BMC Industries Inc. and Common 10¢ par changed to no par 04/28/1983
(See BMC Industries Inc.)

BUCKEYE BREWING CO. (OH)
Each share Common no par exchanged for (2) shares Common $5 par 00/00/1946
Name changed to Toledo Management Co. 05/19/1966
(See Toledo Management Co.)

BUCKEYE CAP CORP II (DE)
Dutch Auction Rate Transferable Securities Preferred no par called for redemption 09/25/1989
Public interest eliminated

BUCKEYE CELLULOSE CORP (DE)
Name changed to Buckeye Technologies Inc. 11/01/1997
(See Buckeye Technologies Inc.)

BUCKEYE COMMUNICATIONS INC (DE)
Each share Common $0.00001 par exchanged for (0.2) share Common $0.0025 par 03/22/1993
Charter cancelled and declared inoperative and void for non payment of taxes 03/01/1997

BUCKEYE CORP. (DE)
Common $1 par changed to 10¢ par 07/11/1963
Recapitalized as Mount Clemens Corp. 07/15/1966
Each share 5% Preferred Ser. A $10 par exchanged for (1) share 5% Conv. Preferred Ser. A $10 par
Each share Common 10¢ par exchanged for (0.1) share Common 10¢ par
(See Mount Clemens Corp.)

BUCKEYE CRUDE EXPL INC (OH)
Stock Dividend - 25% 12/30/1986
Plan of reorganization under Chapter 11 Federal Bankruptcy proceedings confirmed 01/09/1990
No stockholders' equity

BUCKEYE ENERGY CORP (YT)
Reorganized under the laws of Alberta as Regal Energy Corp. 01/30/2004
Each share Common no par exchanged for (0.5) share Common no par
Regal Energy Corp. recapitalized as Regal Energy Ltd. 01/19/2006 which recapitalized as Novus Energy Inc. 08/05/2009
(See Novus Energy Inc.)

BUCKEYE EXPLS LTD (BC)
Struck off register and declared dissolved for failure to file returns 04/04/1977

BUCKEYE FED SVGS & LN ASSN OHIO (USA)
Stock Dividends - 25% 05/24/1978; 10% 03/15/1979
Merged into Buckeye Financial Corp. 10/31/1983
Each share Common 5¢ par exchanged for (1.1) shares Common no par
Buckeye Financial Corp. merged into National City Corp. 01/24/1991 which was acquired by PNC Financial Services Group, Inc. 12/31/2008

BUCKEYE FINL CORP (OH)
Stock Dividends - 10% 03/15/1981; 10% 03/17/1986; 10% 07/21/1986
Merged into National City Corp. 01/24/1991
Each share Common no par exchanged for (0.2) share Common $4 par and $3.08 cash
National City Corp. acquired by PNC Financial Services Group, Inc. 12/31/2008

BUCKEYE GP HLDGS L P (DE)
Merged into Buckeye Partners, L.P. 11/19/2010
Each Common Unit of Ltd. Partnership Int. exchanged for (0.705) Unit of Ltd. Partnership Int.

BUCKEYE INCUBATOR CO. (DE)
Common $2 par changed to $1 par 00/00/1953
Name changed to Buckeye Corp. 03/05/1956
Buckeye Corp. recapitalized as Mount Clemens Corp. 07/15/1966
(See Mount Clemens Corp.)

BUCKEYE INTL INC (OH)
Common no par split (3) for (1) by issuance of (2) additional shares 05/20/1968
Stock Dividends - 10% 12/27/1967; 10% 12/27/1968; 10% 12/02/1974; 10% 12/15/1978
Merged into Worthington Industries, Inc. (OH) 05/27/1980
Each share Common no par exchanged for (1.5) shares Common no par
Worthington Industries, Inc. (OH) reincorporated in Delaware 10/13/1998

BUCKEYE OIL & GAS INC (FL)
Each share old Common $0.0001 par exchanged for (0.01) share new Common $0.0001 par 07/08/2013
Reincorporated under the laws of Nevada as Brisset Beer International, Inc. 07/24/2014

BUCKEYE OIL CO. (WY)
Charter revoked for failure to pay taxes 07/19/1927

BUCKEYE PIPE LINE CO. (OH)
Under plan of unification 00/00/1943, each share Common $50 par exchanged for (5) shares Common no par
Common no par split (2) for (1) by issuance of (1) additional share 05/21/1963
Acquired by Pennsylvania Co. 07/24/1964
Each share Common no par exchanged for (0.385) share 4.625% Preferred $100 par
(See Pennsylvania Co.)

BUCKEYE SHERIFF STREET REALTY CO. (OH)
Liquidation completed 12/30/1950
Details not available

BUCKEYE STEEL CASTINGS CO. (OH)
Common $25 par changed to no par 00/00/1931
6% Preferred $100 par called for redemption 11/01/1959
Stock Dividends - 10% 09/22/1964; 10% 06/25/1965; 10% 04/15/1966; 10% 11/25/1966
Name changed to Buckeye International Inc. 10/10/1967
Buckeye International Inc. merged into Worthington Industries, Inc. (OH) 05/27/80 which reincorporated in Delaware 10/13/1998

BUCKEYE TECHNOLOGIES INC (DE)
Common 1¢ par split (2) for (1) by issuance of (1) additional share payable 02/17/1998 to holders of record 02/10/1998 Ex date - 02/18/1998
Acquired by Georgia-Pacific LLC 08/23/2013
Each share Common 1¢ par exchanged for $37.50 cash

BUCKEYE TOOLS CORP. (OH)
Dissolution completed
Each share Common 50¢ par exchanged for initial distribution of (0.3) share Rockwell Manufacturing Co. Common $2.50 par 07/09/1962
Each share Common received second and final distribution of (0.039633) share Rockwell Manufacturing Co. Common $2.50 par 07/12/1963
Rockwell Manufacturing Co. merged into Rockwell International Corp. (Old) 02/16/1973 which merged into Boeing Co. 12/06/1996

BUCKEYE UN OIL CO (CA)
Charter suspended for failure to file reports and pay taxes 02/03/1975

BUCKEYE UNION CASUALTY CO. (OH)
Each share Capital Stock $100 par exchanged for (5) shares Capital Stock $20 par plus a 66.66666666% stock dividend paid 11/28/1949
Capital Stock $20 par changed to $5 par and (4) additional shares issued 12/02/1958
Capital Stock $5 par changed to $2 par and (1.5) additional shares issued 06/01/1964
Liquidation completed
Each share Capital Stock $2 par exchanged for initial distribution of $25.30 cash 10/25/1965
Each share Capital Stock $2 par received second and final distribution of $11.22 cash and (1) Ctf. of Equitable Int. no par 01/14/1966
Each Ctf. of Equitable Int. no par received first and final distribution of $0.14168 cash 12/30/1971
Note: Certificates were not required to be surrendered and are without value

BUCKEYE UNION FIRE INSURANCE CO. (OH)
Capital Stock $20 par changed to $10 par and (1) additional share issued 03/13/1962
Stock Dividend - 100% 12/31/1954
Liquidation completed
Each share Capital Stock $10 par exchanged for initial distribution of $65 cash 10/25/1965
Each share Capital Stock $10 par received second and final distribution of $41.92 cash and (1) Ctf. of Equitable Int. no par 01/14/1966
Each Ctf. of Equitable Int. no par received first and final distribution of $0.72819 cash 12/30/1971
Note: Certificates were not required to be surrendered and are without value

BUCKEYE URANIUM CORP (UT)
Recapitalized as Graphic Arts Data Systems, Inc. 06/01/1971
Each share Capital Stock 1¢ par exchanged for (0.1) share Capital Stock 1¢ par
Graphic Arts Data Systems, Inc.

name changed to Central States Resources, Inc. 03/09/1972
(See Central States Resources, Inc.)

BUCKEYE VENTURES INC (NV)
Reincorporated 10/29/2007
State of incorporation changed from (MI) to (NV) 10/29/2007
Name changed to Energy King, Inc. 02/26/2008
Energy King, Inc. name changed to Godfather Media, Inc. 10/18/2011 which name changed to Embark Holdings, Inc. 08/20/2012 which name changed to Muscle Warfare International, Inc. 06/28/2013 which name changed to Cannabusiness Group, Inc. 02/18/2014

BUCKHEAD AMER CORP (GA)
Name changed to America's Best Franchising, Inc. 10/07/2005

BUCKHEAD CAP CORP (CO)
Name changed to Glacier Holdings, Inc. 01/25/1989
(See Glacier Holdings, Inc.)

BUCKHEAD INDL PPTYS INC (MD)
Completely liquidated 06/30/2014
Each share Ser. A Preferred exchanged for first and final distribution of $1,000 cash

BUCKHORN INC (DE)
Merged into Myers Industries, Inc. 08/27/1981
Each share Conv. Preferred Ser. A $1 par exchanged for $8.125 cash
Each share Common $1 par exchanged for $5.375 cash

BUCKHORN INC (OH)
Merged into Buckhorn Inc. (DE) 12/22/1981
Each share Common no par exchanged for (1) share Common $1 par
(See Buckhorn Inc. (DE))

BUCKHORN MINES LTD. (ON)
Charter cancelled 00/00/1956

BUCKHORN MINING SYNDICATE LTD.
Acquired by Buckhorn Mines Ltd. on a (5) for (1) basis 00/00/1942
(See Buckhorn Mines Ltd.)

BUCKINGHAM CORP (DE)
Class A Common $1 par changed to 50¢ par and (1) additional share issued 02/01/1966
Reorganized as BHM Industries, Inc. 05/15/1969
Each share Class A Common 50¢ par exchanged for (1) share Common 50¢ par
BHM Industries, Inc. acquired by Schenley Industries, Inc. 12/15/1969
(See Schenley Industries, Inc.)

BUCKINGHAM EXPL INC (NV)
Each share old Common $0.0001 par exchanged for (0.0025) share new Common $0.0001 par 07/23/2010
Name changed to Tierra Grande Resources Inc. 04/10/2013
Tierra Grande Resources Inc. name changed to VNUE, Inc. 07/20/2015

BUCKINGHAM FREIGHT LINES (SD)
Name changed to United-Buckingham Freight Lines 10/16/1961
United-Buckingham Freight Lines name changed to United-Buckingham Freight Lines, Inc. 06/24/1967
(See United-Buckingham Freight Lines, Inc.)

BUCKINGHAM INTL HLDGS LTD (AB)
Placed in liquidation 08/14/1986
Details not available

BUCKINGHAM MTR IMPORTS LTD (CA)
Name changed to David Jamison Carlyle Corp. 02/28/1981
(See David Jamison Carlyle Corp.)

BUCKINGHAM VENTURE CORP (CO)
Name changed to Physicians Dispensing RX, Inc. 03/14/1988
Physicians Dispensing RX, Inc. name changed to PD-RX Pharmaceuticals, Inc. 01/15/1991

BUCKLES ALGOMA URANIUM MINES LTD. (ON)
Merged into Spanish American Mines Ltd. on a (1) for (5) basis 03/19/1956
Spanish American Mines Ltd. merged into Northspan Uranium Mines Ltd. 07/05/1956 which merged into Rio Algom Mines Ltd. 06/30/1960 which name changed to Rio Algom Ltd. 04/30/1975
(See Rio Algom Ltd.)

BUCKLEY CORP. (NY)
Charter revoked for failure to file reports and pay fees 12/15/1961

BUCKNELL INDS INC (NY)
Company filed a petition under Chapter 11 Federal Bankruptcy Code 02/17/1987
Stockholders' equity unlikely

BUCKNER INDUSTRIES, INC. (CA)
Completely liquidated 09/07/1967
Each share Common $1 par exchanged for first and final distribution of $3.50 cash

BUCKS CNTY BK & TR CO (PERKASIE, PA)
Common $10 par changed to $2.50 par and (3) additional shares issued 11/10/1977
Reorganized as Independence Bancorp, Inc. (PA) 11/01/1982
Each share Common $2.50 par exchanged for (1) share Common $2.50 par
Independence Bancorp, Inc. (PA) merged into CoreStates Financial Corp 06/27/1994 which merged into First Union Corp. 04/28/1998 which name changed to Wachovia Corp. (Ctfs. dated after 09/01/2001) 09/01/2001 which merged into Wells Fargo & Co. (New) 12/31/2008

BUCKS CNTY BK (DOYLESTOWN, PA)
Merged into First Bank (Hamilton, NJ) 10/13/2017
Each share Common $1 par exchanged for (0.98) share Common $5 par

BUCKS CNTY LEATHER INC (PA)
Name changed to Chado Gold Mines, Inc. 08/31/1973

BUCKS COUNTY MORTGAGE & GUARANTEE CO.
Liquidation completed 00/00/1951
Details not available

BUCKS STOVE & RANGE CO.
Liquidated 00/00/1930
Details not available

BUCKTV COM INC (NV)
Recapitalized as Multi-Tech International Corp. 11/22/2002
Each share Common $0.001 par exchanged for (0.06884681) share Common $0.001 par
Multi-Tech International Corp. recapitalized as Australian Forest Industries 10/21/2004 which recapitalized as Lone Pine Holdings, Inc. 02/11/2009 which name changed to Flux Power Holdings, Inc. 06/11/2012

BUCS FINL CORP (MD)
Common 10¢ par split (2) for (1) by issuance of (1) additional share payable 05/02/2005 to holders of record 04/15/2005 Ex date - 05/03/2005
Stock Dividends - 10% payable 01/31/2004 to holders of record 01/15/2004 Ex date - 01/13/2004; 10% payable 01/01/2006 to holders of record 12/19/2005 Ex date - 12/15/2005
Merged into Community Banks, Inc. 04/02/2007
Each share Common 10¢ par exchanged for (0.9942) share Common $5 par
Community Banks, Inc. merged into Susquehanna Bancshares, Inc. 11/16/2007 which merged into BB&T Corp. 08/01/2015

BUCYRUS CO.
Merged into Bucyrus-Erie Co. 00/00/1927
Details not available

BUCYRUS ERIE CO OLD (DE)
Each share old 7% Preferred $100 par exchanged for (1) share Common $5 par and $5 cash 00/00/1936
Each share Common $10 par exchanged for (1) share Common $5 par 00/00/1936
Common $5 par split (2) for (1) by issuance of (1) additional share 05/23/1966
Common $5 par split (3) for (2) by issuance of (0.5) additional share 01/24/1968
Common $5 par split (4) for (3) by issuance of (0.33333333) additional share 12/27/1973
Common $5 par split (2) for (1) by issuance of (1) additional share 12/24/1975
Name changed to Becor Western Inc. 04/30/1985
Becor Western Inc. acquired by B-E Holdings, Inc. 02/04/1988 which reorganized as Bucyrus-Erie Co. (New) 12/14/1994 which name changed to Bucyrus International Inc. (Old) 05/24/1996
(See Bucyrus International Inc. (Old))

BUCYRUS INTL INC NEW (DE)
Class A Common 1¢ par split (3) for (2) by issuance of (0.5) additional share payable 03/29/2006 to holders of record 03/20/2006 Ex date - 03/30/2006
Class A Common 1¢ par reclassified as Common 1¢ par 04/30/2008
Common 1¢ par split (2) for (1) by issuance of (1) additional share payable 05/27/2008 to holders of record 05/13/2008 Ex date - 05/28/2008
Acquired by Caterpillar Inc. 07/08/2011
Each share Common 1¢ par exchanged for $92 cash

BUCYRUS INTL INC OLD (DE)
Name changed 05/24/1996
Name changed from Bucyrus-Erie Co. (New) to Bucyrus International, Inc. (Old) 05/24/1996
Merged into American Industrial Partners Capital Fund II, L.P. 09/26/1997
Each share Common 1¢ par exchanged for $18 cash

BUD FINL GROUP INC (NV)
Reincorporated 03/19/1999
Each share old Common $0.0001 par exchanged for (0.2) share new Common $0.0001 par 01/04/1995
Reorganized from (CO) to under the laws of Nevada 03/19/1999
Each share new Common $0.0001 par exchanged for (0.2) share Common $0.001 par
Name changed to Codestream Holdings Inc. 06/12/2000
(See Codestream Holdings Inc.)

BUDA CO. (DE)
Each share Common $100 par exchanged for (8) shares Common $12.50 par 00/00/1937
Each share Common $12.50 par exchanged for (2) shares Common $6.25 par 00/00/1946
Common $6.25 par changed to $15 par 00/00/1948
Merged into Allis-Chalmers Manufacturing Co. 00/00/1953
Each share Common $15 par exchanged for (0.46153846) share new Common $20 par
Allis-Chalmers Manufacturing Co. name changed to Allis-Chalmers Corp. 05/28/1971 which name changed to Allis-Chalmers Energy, Inc. 01/01/2005
(See Allis-Chalmers Energy, Inc.)

BUDBOIS GOLD MINES LTD. (ON)
Charter cancelled for failure to pay taxes and file returns 04/16/1976

BUDCO MINES LTD. (ON)
Charter revoked for failure to file reports and pay taxes 00/00/1956

BUDD AUTOMOTIVE CO. OF CANADA LTD. (ON)
Name changed to Budd Canada Inc. 05/30/1979
Budd Canada Inc. name changed to ThyssenKrupp Budd Canada Inc. 03/31/2003
(See ThyssenKrupp Budd Canada Inc.)

BUDD CDA INC (ON)
Name changed to ThyssenKrupp Budd Canada Inc. 03/31/2003
(See ThyssenKrupp Budd Canada Inc.)

BUDD CO (PA)
Common no par changed to $5 par 00/00/1954
Under plan of merger each share Common $5 par exchanged for $34 cash 04/25/1978
$5 Preferred no par called for redemption 05/25/1978
Public interest eliminated

BUDD INTERNATIONAL CORP.
Dissolved 00/00/1943
Details not available

BUDD (EDWARD G.) MANUFACTURING CO.
Name changed to Budd Co. 00/00/1946
(See Budd Co.)

BUDD WHEEL CO.
Merged into Budd Co. share for share 00/00/1946
(See Budd Co.)

BUDDHA RES INC (BC)
Cease trade order effective 03/01/2002
Stockholders' equity unlikely

BUDGET CAP CORP (CA)
Each share Common 50¢ par exchanged for (0.001) share Common $500 par 09/14/1973
Note: In effect holders received $10 cash per Common 50¢ par
Merged into Financial Corp. of America 05/04/1982
Each share 6% Ser. Preferred $10 par exchanged for (0.38) share Common 50¢ par
(See Financial Corp. of America)

BUDGET CTR INC (NV)
Recapitalized as Enabling Asia Inc. 11/08/2017
Each share Common $0.001 par exchanged for (0.00333333) share Common $0.001 par

BUDGET FINANCE PLAN (CA)
Class A Common $10 par reclassified as 7% Preferred $10 par 00/00/1952
Class B Common 50¢ par changed to Common 50¢ par 00/00/1952
Each share 7% Preferred $10 par exchanged for (1.16666666) shares 6% Ser. Preferred $10 par 10/16/1956
60¢ Conv. Preferred $9 par called for redemption 04/15/1963
Stock Dividends - 25% 08/21/1962; 25% 11/25/1963

Name changed to Budget Capital Corp. 12/20/1972
(See Budget Capital Corp.)

BUDGET FUNDING CORP. (DE)
Became inoperative and void for non-payment of taxes 04/01/1958

BUDGET GROUP CAP TR (DE)
Plan of reorganization under Chapter 11 Federal Bankruptcy Code effective 05/03/2004
Holders will receive an undetermined amount of cash

BUDGET GROUP INC (DE)
Plan of reorganization under Chapter 11 Federal Bankruptcy Code effective 05/03/2004
No stockholders' equity

BUDGET INDS INC (DE)
Name changed to Financial Corp. of America 03/08/1978
(See Financial Corp. of America)

BUDGET RENT A CAR CORP (DE)
Merged into Beech Holdings Corp. 03/30/1989
Each share Common 1¢ par exchanged for $30 cash

BUDGET SYS CORP (MN)
Statutorily dissolved 09/30/1991

BUDGET WASTE INC (NV)
Each share old Common $0.001 par exchanged for (0.03333333) share new Common $0.001 par 10/16/2006
New Common $0.001 par split (3) for (2) by issuance of (0.5) additional share payable 01/05/2007 to holders of record 12/20/2006 Ex date - 01/08/2007
New Common $0.001 par changed to $0.0001 par and (1) additional share issued payable 03/09/2007 to holders of record 02/19/2007 Ex date - 03/12/2007
Name changed to Codido, Inc. 12/12/2008
Codido, Inc. name changed to Quad Energy Corp. 09/13/2010

BUDGETHOTELS NETWORK INC (NV)
Name changed 08/14/2001
Name changed from Budgethotels.com, Inc. to Budgethotels Network Inc. 08/14/2001
Recapitalized as Edentify, Inc. 07/19/2005
Each share Common $0.001 par exchanged for (0.1) share Common $0.001 par
(See Edentify, Inc.)

BUDLOCK REFRIG SUPPLY INC (IN)
Merged into Temperature Control Centers of Indiana, Inc. 12/18/1973
Each share Capital Stock no par exchanged for $14 cash

BUECHE GIROD CORP (NY)
Dissolved by proclamation 09/29/1993

BUEHLER CORP (IN)
Merged into Maul Technology Corp. 09/30/1977
Each share Common no par exchanged for (1) share Common no par
(See Maul Technology Corp.)

BUEHRER OIL & GAS, INC. (IL)
Charter revoked for failure to file reports and pay fees 11/15/1968

BUELL DIE & MACHINE CO. (MI)
Stock Dividend - 10% 11/29/1956
Merged into Buell Industries, Inc. 03/01/1962
Each share Common $1 par exchanged for (0.33333333) share Common $1 par
Buell Industries, Inc. merged into Illinois Tool Works Inc. 07/18/1990

BUELL INDS INC (DE)
Common $1 par split (2) for (1) by issuance of (1) additional share 05/30/1986
Stock Dividends - 10% 10/30/1972; 12% 03/23/1973; 12% 10/30/1974; 12% 10/30/1975; 12% 10/29/1976
Merged into Illinois Tool Works Inc. 07/18/1990
Each share Common $1 par exchanged for (0.3218) share Common no par

BUENA EXPL LTD (BC)
Name changed to Hagensborg Resources Ltd. 07/29/1986
(See Hagensborg Resources Ltd.)

BUENA PARK HOTEL CORP (DE)
Charter cancelled and declared inoperative and void for non-payment of taxes 04/01/1966

BUENA SHORE APARTMENTS
Trust terminated 00/00/1950
Details not available

BUENA TERRACE CORP. (IL)
Liquidation completed 08/12/1969
Details not available

BUENA VENTURA INC (DE)
Name changed to Los Alamos Diagnostics, Inc. 04/26/1988

BUENO COEUR D ALENE INC (NV)
Recapitalized as Graly Resources, Inc. 03/31/1983
Each share Common 1¢ par exchanged for (0.1) share Common 1¢ par
Graly Resources, Inc. recapitalized as Graly Inc. 11/10/1986
(See Graly Inc.)

BUENOS AIRES EMBOTELLADORA S A (ARGENTINA)
ADR agreement terminated 11/09/2000
Each Sponsored ADR for Class B 0.01 Peso par exchanged for $0.0094 cash

BUF-GASPE MINES LTD. (ON)
Declared dissolved 12/03/1962
No stockholders' equity

BUFETE INDL S A (MEXICO)
ADR agreement terminated 04/13/2010
No ADR holders' equity

BUFF ARIO GOLD MINES LTD. (ON)
Charter revoked for failure to file reports and pay taxes 03/27/1957

BUFFADISON GOLD MINES LTD. (ON)
Recapitalized as United Buffadison Mines Ltd. on a (1) for (5) basis 02/26/1962
United Buffadison Mines Ltd. was acquired by Western-Buff Mines & Oils Ltd. 05/20/1969
(See Western-Buff Mines & Oils Ltd.)

BUFFALO & ERIE RAILWAY CO.
Sold at foreclosure 00/00/1937
Details not available

BUFFALO & LACKAWANNA TRACTION CO.
Succeeded by Buffalo & Lackawanna Traction Corp. 00/00/1931
(See Buffalo & Lackawanna Traction Corp.)

BUFFALO & LACKAWANNA TRACTION CORP.
Out of business 00/00/1939
Details not available

BUFFALO ANKERITE GOLD MINES LTD. (ON)
Capital Stock $1 par changed to no par 02/05/1962
Name changed to Buffalo Ankerite Holdings Ltd. 09/27/1962
Buffalo Ankerite Holdings Ltd. name changed to Romfield Building Corp. Ltd. 07/21/1964 which recapitalized as Dolphin Quest Inc. 09/30/1996 which name changed to Naftex Energy Corp. (ON) 04/10/1997 which reincorporated in Yukon 09/16/1998
(See Naftex Energy Corp.)

BUFFALO ANKERITE HOLDINGS LTD. (ON)
Name changed to Romfield Building Corp. Ltd. 07/21/1964
Romfield Building Corp. recapitalized as Dolphin Quest Inc. 09/30/1996 which name changed to Naftex Energy Corp. (ON) 04/10/1997 which reincorporated in Yukon 09/16/1998
(See Naftex Energy Corp.)

BUFFALO BOLT CO. (NY)
Name changed to Buffalo-Eclipse Corp. 00/00/1950
Buffalo-Eclipse Corp. acquired by Houdaille Industries, Inc. (MI) which reincorporated in Delaware 04/01/1968
(See Houdaille Industries, Inc. (DE))

BUFFALO CANADIAN GOLD MINES LTD. (CANADA)
Deemed no longer a subsisting corporation for non-compliance with Companies Act 09/21/1960

BUFFALO CAP INC (CANADA)
Name changed to Waverley Pharma Inc. 10/27/2017

BUFFALO CAP III LTD (CO)
Name changed to Heritage Organization Inc. 02/14/2000

BUFFALO CAP V LTD (CO)
Recapitalized as Aladdin Oil Corp. 06/21/1999
Each share Common no par exchanged for (0.5) share Common no par
(See Aladdin Oil Corp.)

BUFFALO CAP IV LTD (CO)
Name changed to M & A West Inc. 05/14/1999
(See M & A West Inc.)

BUFFALO CAP VI LTD (CO)
Name changed to Isolver.Com Inc. 08/23/1999
(See Isolver.Com Inc.)

BUFFALO CAP VII LTD (CO)
Name changed to Workfire.com, Inc. 06/00/1999
Workfire.com, Inc. name changed to BCS Investment Corp. 02/14/2000 which recapitalized as Crossnet Communications Inc. 12/18/2000 which recapitalized as Cirond Technologies Inc. 07/01/2002 which name changed to Seaside Holdings Inc. 03/17/2003

BUFFALO CAP VIII LTD (CO)
Reincorporated under the laws of Delaware as Momentum Holdings Corp. 07/14/2000
Momentum Holdings Corp. name changed to Cipher Holdings Corp. 11/25/2003 which name changed to Imagin Molecular Corp. 07/05/2005
(See Imagin Molecular Corp.)

BUFFALO DIAMONDS LTD (AB)
Recapitalized as Buffalo Gold Ltd. 02/17/2003
Each share Common no par exchanged for (0.1) share Common no par
(See Buffalo Gold Ltd.)

BUFFALO DONS ARTESIAN WELLS LTD (WI)
Merged into BDAC, Inc. 09/17/1993
Each share Common 1¢ par exchanged for $1 cash

BUFFALO-ECLIPSE CORP. (NY)
Stock Dividend - 10% 06/11/1956
Acquired by Houdaille Industries Inc. (MI) on a share for share basis 06/25/1962
Houdaille Industries, Inc. (MI) reincorporated in Delaware 04/01/1968
(See Houdaille Industries, Inc. (DE))

BUFFALO ELEVATORS, INC. (NY)
Charter revoked for failure to file reports and pay fees 12/15/1950

BUFFALO ENTERPRISES INC (NV)
Charter revoked for failure to file reports and pay fees 03/01/2001

BUFFALO EQUITY FD INC (MD)
Name changed to Buffalo Large Cap Fund Inc. 02/28/2002

BUFFALO FORGE CO (NY)
Common $1 par split (2) for (1) by issuance of (1) additional share 01/31/1968
Common $1 par split (2) for (1) by issuance of (1) additional share 01/31/1980
Stock Dividend - 100% 02/02/1954
Merged into Ampco-Pittsburgh Corp. 07/15/1981
Each share Common $1 par exchanged for $37.50 cash

BUFFALO GAS & OIL LTD (QC)
Dissolved 00/00/1972
Each share Common 1¢ par exchanged for first and final distribution of (1) share Guernsey Petroleum Corp. Common 1¢ par

BUFFALO GENERAL LAUNDRIES CORP. (NY)
Liquidation completed 02/15/1960
Common stockholders had no equity

BUFFALO GOLD LTD (AB)
Delisted from Toronto Venture Stock Exchange 07/12/2010

BUFFALO INC (FL)
Each share Common $0.001 par exchanged for (0.1) share Common 1¢ par 09/19/1986
Plan of reorganization under Chapter 11 Federal Bankruptcy proceedings effective 04/01/1992
Each share old Common 1¢ par exchanged for (0.1) share new Common 1¢ par
Voluntarily dissolved 03/21/2001
Details not available

BUFFALO INS CO (NY)
Each share Capital Stock $100 par exchanged for (10) shares Capital Stock $10 par 08/02/1955
Acquired by Assicurazioni Generali di Trieste e Venezia 00/00/1966
Details not available

BUFFALO LAKE MINES LTD (BC)
Struck off register and declared dissolved for failure to file returns 04/00/1975

BUFFALO MINES LTD (BC)
Name changed to Gulf Shores Resources Ltd. 03/22/1999
Gulf Shores Resources Ltd. name changed to Ashanti Gold Corp. 08/15/2016

BUFFALO NATIONAL CORP.
Dissolution approved 00/00/1949
Details not available

BUFFALO NIAGARA & EASTERN POWER CORP.
Reorganized as Buffalo Niagara Electric Corp. 11/01/1945
Each share $5 Preferred exchanged for (1) share 5% Preferred $100 par and $16.25 cash
(See Buffalo Niagara Electric Corp.)
$1.60 Preferred called for redemption 12/28/1945

BUFFALO NIAGARA ELEC CORP
5% Preferred $100 par called for 02/14/1946
Merged into Niagara Mohawk Power Corp. 01/05/1950
Each share 3.6% Preferred $100 par exchanged for like stock of new company

BUFFALO OIL CORP (AB)
Under plan of merger name changed

to Buffalo Resources Corp. 08/03/2007
Buffalo Resources Corp. merged into Twin Butte Energy Ltd. 10/15/2009

BUFFALO OIL LTD (AB)
Reincorporated 06/17/2004
Place of incorporation changed from (SK) to (AB) 06/17/2004
Recapitalized as Buffalo Oil Corp. 01/03/2005
Each share Common no par exchanged for (0.2) share Common no par
Buffalo Oil Corp. name changed to Buffalo Resources Corp. 08/03/2007 which merged into Twin Butte Energy Ltd. 10/15/2009

BUFFALO RED LAKE MINES LTD (ON)
Recapitalized as Consolidated Buffalo Red Lake Mines Ltd. 05/15/1969
Each share Capital Stock $1 par exchanged for (0.25) share Capital Stock $1 par
(See Consolidated Buffalo Red Lake Mines Ltd.)

BUFFALO RES CORP (AB)
Merged into Twin Butte Energy Ltd. 10/15/2009
Each share Common no par exchanged for (0.7) share Common no par

BUFFALO RES LTD (BC)
Recapitalized as Kruger Explorations Ltd. 09/18/1992
Each share Common no par exchanged for (0.25) share Common no par
Kruger Explorations Ltd. name changed to Kruger Capital Corp. 09/03/1993 which name changed to Nextraction Energy Corp. 11/05/2008

BUFFALO ROUYN MINES LTD.
Recapitalized as Buffalo Canadian Gold Mines Ltd. 00/00/1931
Each share Capital Stock exchanged for (0.17647058) share Capital Stock
(See Buffalo Canadian Gold Mines Ltd.)

BUFFALO-TEXAS OIL CO.
Company went out of business 00/00/1928
No stockholders' equity

BUFFALO VY TEL CO (PA)
Common $10 par changed to no par and (4) additional shares issued 05/01/1987
Merged into Conestoga Enterprises, Inc. 05/31/1996
Each share Common no par exchanged for either (1) share $3.42 Conv. Preferred Ser. A $65 par or (2.4) shares Common $5 par or $65 cash
Note: Option to receive Preferred or cash expired 06/28/1996
Conestoga Enterprises, Inc. merged into D&E Communications, Inc. 05/24/2002 which merged into Windstream Corp. 11/10/2009 which name changed to Windstream Holdings, Inc. 09/03/2013

BUFFALO WILD WINGS INC (MN)
Common no par split (2) for (1) by issuance of (1) additional share payable 06/15/2007 to holders of record 06/01/2007 Ex date - 06/18/2007
Acquired by Arby's Restaurant Group, Inc. 02/05/2018
Each share Common no par exchanged for $157 cash

BUFFANA URANIUM MINES LTD. (ON)
Name changed to Le Mans Explorations Ltd. 07/21/1961
(See Le Mans Explorations Ltd.)

BUFFELSFONTEIN GOLD MINES LTD (SOUTH AFRICA)
Name changed 04/29/1996
Name changed from Buffelsfontein Gold Mining Co. Ltd. to Buffelsfontein Gold Mines Ltd. 04/29/1996
Each Unsponsored ADR for Ordinary exchanged for (1) Sponsored ADR for Ordinary 08/12/1996
Merged into Durban Roodepoort Deep Ltd. 09/15/1997
Each Sponsored ADR for Ordinary exchanged for (1.1) Sponsored ADR's for Ordinary
Durban Roodepoort Deep Ltd. name changed to DRDGOLD Ltd. 12/06/2004

BUFFET CRAMPON INTL INC (NY)
Merged into Boosey & Hawkes Ltd. 10/05/1981
Each share Common 1¢ par exchanged for $0.96 cash

BUFFETS INC (MN)
Merged into Caxton-Iseman Capital, Inc. 10/02/2000
Each share Common 1¢ par exchanged for $13.85 cash

BUFFETS RESTAURANTS HLDGS INC (DE)
Plan of reorganization under Chapter 11 Federal Bankruptcy proceedings effective 07/18/2012
No stockholders' equity

BUFFS-N-PUFFS LTD (NV)
Name changed to TimeOne, Inc. 07/24/1997
TimeOne, Inc. name changed to SunGlobe Fiber Systems Corp. 07/07/2000
(See SunGlobe Fiber Systems Corp.)

BUFFTON CORP (DE)
Name changed 02/14/1983
Name changed from Buffton Oil & Gas, Inc. to Buffton Corp. 02/14/1983
Each share Common 1¢ par exchanged for (0.2) share Common 5¢ par 10/03/1985
Name changed to BFX Hospitality Group, Inc. 07/21/1997
(See BFX Hospitality Group, Inc.)

BUFFUMS (CA)
Each share Common $25 par exchanged for (5) shares Common $5 par 07/19/1961
Common $5 par split (5) for (4) by issuance of (0.25) additional share 02/23/1972
Common $5 par split (5) for (4) by issuance of (0.25) additional share 06/14/1973
Through purchase offer David Jones Ltd. acquired all but (230) shares as of 08/02/1974
Public interest eliminated

BUFORD (W.E.) & CO., INC. (VA)
Business discontinued 12/10/1954
No stockholders' equity

BUGABOO CREEK STEAK HSE INC (DE)
Merged into Longhorn Steaks, Inc. 09/13/1996
Each share Common 1¢ par exchanged for (0.5625) share Common no par
Longhorn Steaks, Inc. name changed to RARE Hospitality International, Inc. 01/13/1997
(See RARE Hospitality International, Inc.)

BUHNER FERTILIZER CO., INC. (IN)
5% Preferred called for redemption 10/01/1957
Liquidation completed 01/27/1961
Details not available

BUHRMANN NV (NETHERLANDS)
Stock Dividends - 2.08% payable 05/30/2003 to holders of record 05/08/2003; approximately 1% payable 06/01/2004 to holders of record 05/07/2004
Name changed to Corporate Express N.V. 04/19/2007
(See Corporate Express N.V.)

BUHRMANN-TETTERODE N V (NETHERLANDS)
Merged into N.V. Koninklijke KNP BT 00/00/1993
Each ADR for Ordinary exchanged for (1) Sponsored ADR for Ordinary
N.V. Koninklijke KNP BT reorganized as Buhrmann N.V. 08/31/1998 which name changed to Corporate Express N.V. 04/19/2007
(See Corporate Express N.V.)

BUI INC (DE)
Name changed to Buyersonline.com Inc. 04/20/2000
Buyersonline.com Inc. name changed to Buyers United Inc. 11/20/2001 which name changed to UCN, Inc. 07/15/2004 which name changed to inContact, Inc. 01/01/2009
(See inContact, Inc.)

BUILD AMER INVT GRADE BD FD (ON)
Name changed to Aston Hill Corporate Bond Fund and each Class A or Class F Unit reclassified as (2) Ser. X or Ser. F Units respectively 02/27/2015

BUILDERS DESIGN INC (DE)
Charter cancelled and declared inoperative and void for non-payment of taxes 03/01/1993

BUILDERS ENERGY SVCS TR (AB)
Merged into Essential Energy Services Trust 04/04/2008
Each Trust Unit no par exchanged for (1.25) Trust Units no par
Essential Energy Services Trust reorganized as Essential Energy Services Ltd. 05/05/2010

BUILDERS EXPRESS INC (DE)
Charter forfeited for failure to maintain a registered agent 02/25/1998

BUILDERS FED SVGS & LN ASSN ROCKY MT N C (USA)
Stock Dividend - 50% 04/30/1987
Acquired by RS Financial Corp. 11/30/1989
Each share Common $1 par exchanged for $13 cash

BUILDERS FINANCE & MORTGAGE CORP. (FL)
Name changed to Samson Realty & Development Corp. 05/28/1968
(See Samson Realty & Development Corp.)

BUILDERS INVT GROUP (FL)
Shares of Bene. Int. 10¢ par reclassified as Common Shares of Bene. Int. 10¢ par 12/01/1973
Name changed to Winn Enterprises 08/17/1983
(See Winn Enterprises)

BUILDERS IRON FOUNDRY (RI)
Name changed to B-I-F Industries, Inc. 11/00/1953
B-I-F Industries, Inc. name changed to High Street Investment Fund, Inc. 11/17/1961
(See High Street Investment Fund, Inc.)

BUILDERS TRANS INC (DE)
Common 1¢ par split (3) for (2) by issuance of (0.5) additional share 09/06/1985
Assets sold for the benefit of creditors 07/28/1998
No stockholders' equity

BUILDERS WHSE ASSN INC (CO)
Each share Common no par exchanged for (0.25) share old Common $0.008 par 03/10/1993
Each share old Common $0.008 par exchanged for (0.16666666) share new Common $0.008 par 04/10/1995
Each share new Common $0.008 par exchanged again for (0.5) share new Common $0.008 par 06/30/1995
Merged into Osicom Technologies, Inc. 09/30/1996
Each share new Common $0.008 par exchanged for (0.94) share Common 10¢ par
Osicom Technologies, Inc. name changed to Sorrento Networks Corp. (NJ) 01/17/2001 which reincorporated in Delaware 06/04/2003 which merged into Zhone Technologies, Inc. 07/01/2004 which name changed to DASAN Zhone Solutions, Inc. 09/12/2016

BUILDEX INC (DE)
Merged into Instrument Systems Corp. 09/15/1982
Each share Common 10¢ par exchanged for (3.75) shares 2nd Preferred Ser. I 25¢ par
Instrument Systems Corp. name changed to Griffon Corp. 03/03/1995
(See Griffon Corp.)

BUILDEX VENTURE CAP CORP (CANADA)
Name changed to Iledor Exploration Corp. 11/11/2011

BUILDING & LAND TECHNOLOGY LIQUIDATING TRUST (NJ)
Liquidation completed
Each Trust Participating Ctf. received initial distribution of $0.41 cash 02/21/1986
Each Trust Participating Ctf. exchanged for second and final distribution of $0.25 cash 04/14/1989

BUILDING & LD TECHNOLOGY CORP (NJ)
In process of liquidation
Each share Common 10¢ par received initial distribution of $0.15 cash 06/28/1985
Assets transferred to Building & Land Technology Liquidating Trust and Common 10¢ par reclassified as Trust Participating Ctf. 02/00/1986
(See Building & Land Technology Liquidating Trust)

BUILDING DYNAMICS INC (AZ)
Charter revoked for failure to file reports and pay fees 12/26/1972

BUILDING MATLS HLDG CORP (CA)
Common $0.001 par split (2) for (1) by issuance of (1) additional share payable 03/14/2006 to holders of record 02/28/2006 Ex date - 03/15/2006
Plan of reorganization under Chapter 11 Federal Bankruptcy proceedings effective 01/04/2010
No stockholders' equity

BUILDING ONE SVCS CORP (DE)
Merged into Encompass Services Corp. 02/22/2000
Each share Common $0.001 par exchanged for (1.25) shares Common $0.001 par
(See Encompass Services Corp.)

BUILDING PRODUCTS LTD. (CANADA)
Each share Class A or Class B no par exchanged for (4) shares Capital Stock no par 00/00/1938
Name changed to Probuild Proceeds Ltd. 08/20/1964
(See Probuild Proceeds Ltd.)

BUILDING SYND CO (OR)
Liquidation completed
Each share Common no par exchanged for initial distribution of $900 cash 01/27/1983
Each share Common no par received second distribution of $150 cash 04/11/1983

Each share Common no par received third and final distribution of $87.50 cash 12/14/1983

BUILDING SYS INC (OH)
Plan of reorganization under Chapter XI Bankruptcy Act confirmed 02/11/1976
Stockholders' equity unlikely

BUILDING TECHNOLOGIES INDS INC (DE)
Charter cancelled and declared inoperative and void for non-payment of taxes 03/01/1989

BUILDING TURBINES INC (NV)
Common $0.001 par changed to $0.0001 par 11/06/2014
Recapitalized as HempTech Corp. 03/31/2016
Each share Common $0.0001 par exchanged for (0.0002) share Common $0.0001 par
HempTech Corp. name changed to Nuvus Gro Corp. 04/12/2018

BUILDING VENTURES, INC. (NY)
Name changed to Ventex Corp. 07/13/1966
(See Ventex Corp.)

BUILTWELL HOMES INC (GA)
Liquidation completed
Each share Common 20¢ par received initial distribution of 8¢ cash 09/01/1968
Each share Common 20¢ par received second and final distribution of 1¢ cash 12/31/1971
Note: Certificates were not required to be surrendered and are without value

BUKA VENTURES INC (NV)
Name changed to Nutranomics, Inc. 09/19/2013

BUKIDNON ASSOCIATES (MA)
Liquidation completed
Each Trust Share no par exchanged for initial distribution of $13 cash 06/01/1965
Each Trust Share no par received second distribution of $2.55 cash 07/08/1965
Each Trust Share no par received third and final distribution of $0.825 cash 05/24/1967

BULB MISER CORP AMER (DE)
Name changed to BMC International Corp. 12/28/1983
(See BMC International Corp.)

BULGARI S P A (ITALY)
Acquired by LVMH Moet Hennessy Louis Vuitton S.A. 10/04/2011
Each Sponsored ADR for Ordinary exchanged for $65.4385 cash

BULGARTABAC HLDG GROUP (BULGARIA)
GDR agreement terminated 04/16/2018
No GDR's remain outstanding

BULK ASSOCIATES LTD. (LIBERIA)
Acquired by Bulk Acquisition Corp. 07/10/1997
Each share Common 1¢ par exchanged for $0.50 cash

BULK MATLS INC (NY)
Plan of liquidation under Chapter 11 Federal Bankruptcy Code filed 06/03/1997
No stockholders' equity

BULKLEY BLDG CO (OH)
Common $10 par changed to $1 par 00/00/1947
Merged into Millcapp Corp. 06/26/1970
Each share 7% Preferred $100 par exchanged for $258 cash
Each share Common $1 par exchanged for $3 cash

BULL & BEAR CAP GROWTH FD INC (MD)
Name changed to Bull & Bear Special Equities Fund 06/00/1992
Bull & Bear Special Equities Fund name changed to Midas Special Equities Fund 06/30/1999 which name changed to Midas Special Fund, Inc. 05/01/2006 which name changed to Midas Magic, Inc. (New) 04/29/2011 which reorganized as Midas Series Trust 10/12/2012

BULL & BEAR CORP (MD)
Under plan of reorganization each share Quality Growth Fund automatically became (1) share Midas U.S. & Overseas Fund Ltd. 06/28/1999
(See Midas U.S. & Overseas Fund Ltd.)

BULL & BEAR EQUITY INCOME FD INC (DE)
Merged into Bull & Bear Financial News Composite Fund Inc. 09/00/1992
Each share Common $1 par exchanged for (1) share Common 1¢ par
Bull & Bear Financial News Composite Fund Inc. merged into Bull & Bear Fund I, Inc. 01/21/1994 which name changed to Midas U.S. & Overseas Fund Ltd. 06/28/1999
(See Midas U.S. & Overseas Fund Ltd.)

BULL & BEAR FINL NEWS COMPOSITE FD INC (MD)
Merged into Bull & Bear Funds I, Inc. 01/21/1994
Each share Common 1¢ par exchanged for (1) share Quality Growth Fund 1¢ par
Bull & Bear Funds I, Inc. name changed to Midas U.S. & Overseas Fund Ltd. 06/28/1999
(See Midas U.S. & Overseas Fund Ltd.)

BULL & BEAR GLOBAL INCOME FD INC (MD)
Name changed to Global Income Fund, Inc. 11/24/1998
Global Income Fund, Inc. name changed to Self Storage Group, Inc. 11/15/2013 which name changed to Global Self Storage, Inc. 01/19/2016

BULL & BEAR GOLD INVS LTD (MD)
Name changed to Midas Investors Ltd. 06/30/1999
Midas Investors Ltd. merged into Midas Fund, Inc. (MD) 11/16/2001 which reorganized in Delaware as Midas Series Trust 10/12/2012

BULL & BEAR GROUP INC (DE)
Name changed to Winmill & Co. Inc. 06/30/1999

BULL & BEAR GROUP INC (NY)
25¢ Conv. Preferred 1¢ par called for redemption 10/31/1983
Reorganized under the laws of Delaware 12/03/1985
Each share Class A Common 1¢ par exchanged for (0.2) share Class A Common 1¢ par or $2 cash
Each share Class B Common 1¢ par exchanged for (0.2) share Class B Common 1¢ par or $2 cash
Note: Holdings of (4) or fewer shares received $2 cash per share
Option of holders of between (5) and (499) to receive stock expired 12/03/1985
Bull & Bear Group, Inc. (DE) name changed to Winmill & Co. Inc. 06/30/1999

BULL & BEAR MUN SECS INC (MD)
Name changed to Tuxis Corp. and Municipal Income Fund reclassified as Common 1¢ par 09/01/1998

BULL & BEAR OVERSEAS FD LTD (MD)
Common 1¢ par split (2) for (1) by issuance of (1) additional share 02/26/1992
Name changed to Midas U.S. & Overseas Fund Ltd. 06/30/1999
(See Midas U.S. & Overseas Fund Ltd.)

BULL & BEAR SPL EQUITIES FD INC (MD)
Name changed to Midas Special Equities Fund 06/30/1999
Midas Special Equities Fund name changed to Midas Special Fund, Inc. 05/01/2006 which name changed to Midas Magic, Inc. (New) 04/29/2011 which reorganized as Midas Series Trust 10/12/2012

BULL & BEAR U S & OVERSEAS FD LTD (MD)
Name changed to Bull & Bear Funds I, Inc. U.S. & Overseas Fund 09/23/1993

BULL & BEAR U S GOVT SECS FD INC (MD)
Name changed to Bexil Corp. 08/26/1999

BULL & BEAR FDS II INC (MD)
Name changed 10/29/1993
High Yield Fund Stock 1¢ par reclassified as Global Income Fund 1¢ par 10/29/1992
Name changed from Bull & Bear Inc. to Bull & Bear Funds II, Inc. 10/29/1993
Under plan of reorganization each Global Income Fund share 1¢ par automatically became (1) share Bull & Bear Global Income Fund Inc. Common 1¢ par 02/07/1997
(See Bull & Bear Global Income Fund Inc.)
Under plan of reorganization each Dollar Reserves Stock 1¢ par automatically became (1) share Dollar Reserves Inc. Common 1¢ par 06/30/1999

BULL EXPLS LTD (BC)
Name changed to Hardy International Developments Inc. 11/24/1982
Hardy International Developments Inc. recapitalized as Unisave Energy Ltd. 11/06/1986 which recapitalized as U.C. Valve Corp. 04/26/1989 which reorganized as Blackbridge Capital Corp. 12/01/1989 which name changed to Rupert Resources Ltd. 11/01/1994

BULL FIN CORP
Market Auction Preferred Ser. A called for redemption at $1,000,000 on 10/17/2002
Market Auction Preferred Ser. B called for redemption at $2,000,000 on 10/24/2002

BULL RED LAKE GOLD MINES LTD. (ON)
Charter cancelled and company declared dissolved by default in filing returns 10/07/1957

BULL RUN CORP (GA)
Name changed 12/22/1992
Old Common no par changed to 1¢ par 05/16/1981
Name changed from Bull Run Gold Mines, Ltd. (WA) to Bull Run Corp. (GA) 12/22/1992
Each share old Common 1¢ par exchanged for (0.1) share new Common 1¢ par 05/16/2003
Merged into Triple Crown Media, Inc. 12/30/2005
Each share new Common 1¢ par exchanged for (0.0289) share Common $0.001 par
(See Triple Crown Media, Inc.)

BULL RUN INC (NV)
SEC revoked common stock registration 11/21/2007

BULL SHIRT VENTURES LTD (BC)
Name changed to Pharaoh Capital Corp. 08/04/1989

BULL TROUT LAKE INC (NV)
Recapitalized as C.B. BioSciences, Inc. 03/12/2015
Each share Common $0.001 par exchanged for (0.04) share Common $0.001 par
C.B. BioSciences, Inc. name changed to ANGO World Holdings, Inc. 01/07/2016

BULLARD (R.D.) CORP. OF VERMONT (VT)
Charter revoked for failure to file annual reports 05/31/1972

BULLARD CO. (CT)
Each share old Common no par exchanged for (3) shares new Common no par 00/00/1929
New Common no par changed to $10 par and (1) additional share issued 00/00/1952
Stock Dividend - 10% 01/15/1954
Merged into White Consolidated Industries, Inc. 03/27/1968
Each share Common $10 par exchanged for (0.43) share $3 Preferred Ser. C $50 par and (0.4488) share Common $1 par
(See White Consolidated Industries, Inc.)

BULLARD MACHINE TOOL CO.
Name changed to Bullard Co. 00/00/1929
Bullard Co. merged into White Consolidated Industries, Inc. 03/27/1968
(See White Consolidated Industries, Inc.)

BULLDOG ENERGY INC (AB)
Plan of arrangement effective 11/29/2005
Each share Class A Common no par exchanged for (0.13) Crescent Point Energy Trust, Trust Unit no par and (0.5) share Bulldog Resources Inc. Common no par
Each share Class B Common no par exchanged for (0.42341) Crescent Point Energy Trust, Trust Unit no par and (1.6285) shares Bulldog Resources Inc. Common no par
(See each company's listing)

BULLDOG EXPLORATIONS LTD (AB)
Reincorporated under the laws of British Columbia as Green Arrow Resources Inc. 02/13/2013

BULLDOG FINL INC (NV)
Common $0.00001 par split (5) for (1) by issuance of (4) additional shares payable 07/31/2007 to holders of record 06/22/2007 Ex date - 08/01/2007
Name changed to Arctic Oil & Gas Corp. 12/21/2007
Arctic Oil & Gas Corp. name changed to Placer Gold Corp. 02/25/2009
(See Placer Gold Corp.)

BULLDOG RES INC (AB)
Acquired by TriStar Oil & Gas Ltd. (New) 02/07/2008
Each share Common no par exchanged for (0.59) share Common no par
TriStar Oil & Gas Ltd. (New) merged into PetroBakken Energy Ltd. (Old) 10/05/2009 which reorganized as PetroBakken Energy Ltd. (New) 01/07/2013 which name changed to Lightstream Resources Ltd. 05/28/2013

BULLDOG TECHNOLOGIES INC (NV)
Recapitalized as Next10, Inc. 03/25/2011
Each shares Common $0.001 par exchanged for (0.00333333) share Common $0.001 par

BULLDOG YELLOWKNIFE GOLD MINES LTD. (ON)
Recapitalized as Taurcanis Mines Ltd. 06/15/1956
Each share Capital Stock $1 par exchanged for (0.25) share Common $1 par
Taurcanis Mines Ltd. recapitalized as Tundra Gold Mines Ltd. (ON) 04/30/1963 which reincorporated in British Columbia 02/05/1982
(See Tundra Gold Mines Ltd.)

BULLET ENVIRONMENTAL TECHNOLOGIES INC (DE)
Name changed to ComCam, Inc. 07/24/2002
ComCam, Inc. recapitalized as Monkey Rock Group, Inc. 05/05/2010

BULLET GROUP INC (BC)
Name changed 03/08/1985
Name changed from Bullet Energy Ltd. to Bullet Group, Inc. 03/08/1985
Recapitalized as Consolidated Bullet Group, Inc. 08/07/1992
Each share Common no par exchanged for (0.25) share Common no par
Consolidated Bullet Group, Inc. recapitalized as New Bullet Group, Inc. (BC) 09/04/1996 which reincorporated in Ontario as Amerix Precious Metals Corp. 05/31/2004 which recapitalized as Eagle Graphite Inc. 01/22/2015

BULLET SPORTS INTERNATIONAL INC (DE)
Charter cancelled and declared inoperative and void for non-payment of taxes 03/01/1999

BULLFROG KEYSTONE GOLD MINING CO. (SD)
Charter expired by time limitation 00/00/1926

BULLHIDE LINER CORP (WA)
SEC revoked common stock registration 06/22/2006

BULLION BASIN MINES LTD. (ON)
Name changed to Alroy Kirkland Gold Mines Ltd. 11/03/1936
(See Alroy Kirkland Gold Mines Ltd.)

BULLION EXPL CO (UT)
Merged into Love Oil Co., Inc. 02/16/1970
Each share Capital Stock 10¢ par exchanged for (0.25) share Common 10¢ par
(See Love Oil Co., Inc.)

BULLION GOLD RES CORP (AB)
Reincorporated under the laws of British Columbia 02/01/2016

BULLION LODE SILVER MINING CO. (WA)
Acquired by Painted Desert Uranium & Oil Co., Inc. (WA) 08/01/1986
Each share Common no par exchanged for (0.66666666) share Common 1¢ par
Painted Desert Uranium & Oil Co., Inc. (WA) reincorporated in Nevada as Royal Pacific Resources Inc. 06/13/2003 which recapitalized as Great American Family Parks, Inc. 02/03/2004 which name changed to Parks! America, Inc. 06/25/2008

BULLION MINING CO. (UT)
Name changed to Bullion Exploration Co. 00/00/1959
Bullion Exploration Co. merged into Love Oil Co., Inc. 02/16/1970
(See Love Oil Co., Inc.)

BULLION MONARCH CO (UT)
Name changed 11/02/1966
Name changed from Bullion Monarch Uranium Co., Inc. to Bullion Monarch Co., Inc. 11/02/1966
Name changed to Bullion Monarch Mining Inc. 11/03/2006
Each share Common no par exchanged for (1) share Common no par
Bullion Monarch Mining Inc. merged into Eurasian Minerals Inc. 08/17/2012 which name changed to EMX Royalty Corp. 07/19/2017

BULLION MONARCH MINING CO. (UT)
Reorganized as Bullion Monarch Uranium Co., Inc. 10/12/1954
Each share Common no par exchanged for (2) shares Common no par
Bullion Monarch Uranium Co., Inc. name changed to Bullion Monarch Co., Inc. 11/02/1966 which name changed to Bullion Monarch Mining Inc. 11/03/2006 which merged into Eurasian Minerals Inc. 08/17/2012 which name changed to EMX Royalty Corp. 07/19/2017

BULLION MONARCH MNG INC (UT)
Merged into Eurasian Minerals Inc. 08/17/2012
Each share Common $0.001 par exchanged for (0.45) share Common no par and $0.11 cash
Eurasian Minerals Inc. name changed to EMX Royalty Corp. 07/19/2017

BULLION MTN MNG LTD (BC)
Recapitalized as Northern Bullion (Keno) Ltd. 07/23/1976
Each share Common 50¢ par exchanged for (0.33333333) share Common no par
Northern Bullion (Keno) Ltd. recapitalized as Jubilee Explorations Inc. 04/23/1979
(See Jubilee Explorations Inc.)

BULLION PLACERS LTD.
Bankrupt 00/00/1942
Details not available

BULLION RANGE EXPL CORP (BC)
Name changed to Maximusic North America Corp. 08/09/1991
Maximusic North America Corp. recapitalized as Trivalence Mining Corp. 03/02/1995 which name changed to Azure Resources Corp. 03/26/2008 which recapitalized as Panorama Petroleum Co. 06/13/2014 which recapitalized as Stamper Oil & Gas Corp. 04/06/2017

BULLION REEF RES LTD (BC)
Recapitalized as Consolidated Bullion Reef Resources Ltd. 03/27/1995
Each share Common no par exchanged for (0.16666666) share Common no par
Consolidated Bullion Reef Resources Ltd. name changed to Canada Payphone Corp. 03/08/1996
(See Canada Payphone Corp.)

BULLION RIV GOLD CORP (NV)
Plan of reorganization under Chapter 11 Federal Bankruptcy proceedings effective 03/03/2010
No stockholders' equity

BULLMAN VENTURES INC (BC)
Name changed to Bullman Minerals Inc. 07/17/2013

BULLOCHS LTD (MB)
Name changed to Inter-City Manufacturing Ltd. 07/12/1971
(See Inter-City Manufacturing Ltd.)

BULLOCK AGGRESSIVE GROWTH SHS INC (MD)
Under plan of reorganization each share Common $1 par automatically became (1) share Surveyor Fund, Inc. Common $1 par 03/13/1987
Surveyor Fund, Inc. name changed to Alliance Global Small Capital Fund, Inc. 09/17/1990 which name changed to AllianceBernstein Global Small Capital Fund, Inc. 03/31/2003
(See AllianceBernstein Global Small Capital Fund, Inc.)

BULLOCK AMERN FD (ON)
Reorganized as Spectrum United American Growth Fund 11/01/1996
Details not available

BULLOCK BALANCED SHS INC (MD)
Name changed to Alliance Balanced Shares, Inc. 03/13/1987
Alliance Balanced Shares, Inc. name changed to AllianceBernstein Balanced Shares, Inc. 03/31/2003

BULLOCK DIVID SHS INC (MD)
Name changed to Alliance Dividend Shares, Inc. 03/13/1987
Alliance Dividend Shares, Inc. name changed to Alliance Growth & Income Fund, Inc. 10/17/1989 which name changed to AllianceBernstein Growth & Income Fund, Inc. 03/31/2003

BULLOCK FD LTD (MD)
Stock Dividend - 200% 03/25/1955
Name changed to Bullock Growth Shares, Inc. 04/08/1985
Bullock Growth Shares, Inc. merged into Chemical Fund, Inc. 03/13/1987 which name changed to Alliance Fund, Inc. 04/01/1987 which name changed to Alliance Mid-Capital Growth Fund Inc. 02/01/2002 which name changed to AllianceBernstein Mid-Capital Growth Fund, Inc. 03/31/2003

BULLOCK GROWTH FD LTD (CANADA)
Reorganized as Spectrum United Canadian Growth Fund 11/01/1996
Details not available

BULLOCK GROWTH SHS INC (MD)
Capital Stock $1 par split (2) for (1) by issuance of (1) additional share 03/03/1986
Merged into Chemical Fund, Inc. 03/13/1987
Each share Capital Stock $1 par exchanged for (1) share Common $0.125 par
Chemical Fund, Inc. name changed to Alliance Fund, Inc. 04/01/1987 which name changed to Alliance Mid-Cap Growth Fund Inc. 02/01/2002 which name changed to AllianceBernstein Mid-Cap Growth Fund, Inc. 03/31/2003

BULLOCK HIGH INCOME SHS INC (MD)
Merged into Alliance Bond Fund, Inc. 03/13/1987
Each share Capital Stock $1 par exchanged for (1.012974) shares High-Yield Portfolio Common $0.001 par
Alliance Bond Fund, Inc. name changed to AllianceBernstein Bond Fund, Inc. 03/31/2003

BULLOCK INC (IL)
Reincorporated under the laws of Nevada as Curt Bullock Builders, Inc. 01/01/1978
(See Curt Bullock Builders, Inc.)

BULLOCK INSD CALIF TAX EXEMPT SHS INC (MD)
Name changed to Alliance Insured California Tax-Exempt Shares, Inc. 03/13/1987
Alliance Insured California Tax-Exempt Shares, Inc. reorganized as Alliance Tax-Free Income Fund 11/16/1987 which name changed to Alliance Municipal Income Fund, Inc. 09/27/1988 which name changed to AllianceBernstein Municipal Income Fund, Inc. 03/31/2003

BULLOCK MONTHLY INCOME SHS INC (MD)
Under plan of reorganization each share Capital Stock $1 par automatically became (1) share Alliance Bond Fund Monthly Income Portfolio Common $0.001 par 03/13/1987

BULLOCK TAX FREE SHS INC (MD)
Name changed to Alliance Tax-Free Shares, Inc. 03/13/1987
Alliance Tax-Free Shares, Inc. merged into Alliance Tax-Free Income Fund 07/10/1987 which name changed to Alliance Municipal Income Fund, Inc. 09/27/1988 which name changed to AllianceBernstein Municipal Income Fund, Inc. 03/31/2003

BULLOCK U S GOVT INC SHS INC (MD)
Name changed to Alliance Bond Fund, Inc. U.S. Government Portfolio 03/13/1987
Alliance Bond Fund, Inc. name changed to AllianceBernstein Bond Fund, Inc. 03/31/2003

BULLOCK'S, INC. (DE)
Each share Common no par exchanged for (3) shares Common no par 10/01/1945
Common no par changed to $10 par 04/04/1950
Common $10 par changed to $5 par and (1) additional share issued 09/25/1959
4% Preferred $100 par called for redemption 12/15/1961
Merged into Federated Department Stores, Inc. 08/29/1964
Each share Common $5 par exchanged for (1.4) shares Common $1.25 par
Federated Department Stores, Inc. name changed to Macy's, Inc. 06/01/2007

BULLS OFFERING CORP (CANADA)
Name changed to Merrill Lynch Mortgage Loans, Inc. 12/29/1998
Merrill Lynch Mortgage Loans, Inc. name changed to Merrill Lynch Financial Assets Inc. 03/15/2001
(See Merrill Lynch Financial Assets Inc.)

BULLS ON THE RUN PRODTNS CORP (NV)
Each share old Common $0.001 par exchanged for (0.01) share new Common $0.001 par 07/08/1992
Name changed to China Treasure, Inc. 04/18/1994
China Treasure, Inc. name changed to China Pacific, Inc. 01/25/1996
(See China Pacific, Inc.)

BULLSBORO BANCSHARES INC (GA)
Merged into Regions Financial Corp. (Old) 01/01/1999
Each share Common $43.37 par exchanged for (3.65) shares Common $0.625 par
Regions Financial Corp. (Old) merged into Regions Financial Corp. (New) 07/01/2004

BULLSEYE CORP. (NV)
Recapitalized as Natural Solutions Ltd. 02/00/1993
Each share Common $0.001 par exchanged for (0.005) share Common $0.001 par
Natural Solutions Ltd. recapitalized as Highseas Entertainment & Casino Ltd. 02/22/1994 which name changed to Phoenix Media Group Ltd. 03/24/1994 which recapitalized as TecScan International, Inc. 06/23/2003 which name changed to Bio-Labs, Inc. 05/19/2004
(See Bio-Life Labs, Inc.)

BULLSEYE MARKETING GROUP INC (NJ)
Reorganized under the laws of Delaware as Headstrong Group, Inc. 02/06/1995
Each share Common no par exchanged for (7) shares Class A Common no par

BUL-BUR

BULLSNBEARS COM INC (DE)
Name changed to Michael James Enterprises, Inc. 12/11/2015

BULLZI SEC INC (NV)
Name changed to Bullzi Holdings, Inc. 02/11/2014

BULOLO GOLD DREDGING LTD. (BC)
Merged into Placer Development Ltd. 04/26/1966
Each share Capital Stock $5 par exchanged for (0.4) share Common no par
Placer Development Ltd. merged into Placer Dome Inc. 08/13/1987 which merged into Barrick Gold Corp. 03/08/2006

BULORA LTD (CANADA)
Placed in receivership 11/28/1977
No stockholders' equity

BULOVA CORP (NY)
Name changed 06/17/1988
Each share Common no par exchanged for (2) shares Common $5 par 00/00/1945
Common $5 par split (3) for (2) by issuance of (0.5) additional share 08/08/1969
Stock Dividend - 200% 09/30/1955
Name changed from Bulova Watch Co. Inc. to Bulova Corp. 06/17/1988
Merged into Loews Corp. 01/18/2005
Each share Common no par exchanged for $35 cash

BUMBLEBERRY ENTERPRISES INC (UT)
Common 10¢ par changed to 5¢ par and (1) additional share issued 11/01/1971
Adjudicated bankrupt 09/30/1976
Stockholders' equity unlikely

BUN & BURGER INTL INC (DE)
Each share Common 1¢ par exchanged for (0.01) share Common $1 par 05/16/1978
Charter cancelled and declared inoperative and void for non-payment of taxes 03/01/1999

BUNDY CORP (MI)
Common $5 par split (3) for (2) by issuance of (0.5) additional share 11/30/1976
Merged into TI Group PLC 04/27/1988
Each share Common $5 par exchanged for $40 cash

BUNDY ELECTRS CORP (NJ)
Merged into Covington Corp. 01/10/1969
Each share Common 10¢ par exchanged for (1) share Common 10¢ par
(See Covington Corp.)

BUNGE LTD (BERMUDA)
Each share 5.125% Conv. Preference Share 1¢ par exchanged for (9.7596) shares Common 1¢ par 12/01/2010
(Additional Information in Active)

BUNING INTL INC (FL)
Name changed 05/30/1978
Name changed from Buning The Florist, Inc. to Buning International Inc. 05/30/1978
Merged into Gerald Stevens Inc. 08/27/1999
Each share Common 10¢ par exchanged for (0.1003) share Common $0.06666666 par and $12.2158 cash
(See Gerald Stevens Inc.)

BUNKER CHANCE MNG CO (ID)
Name changed to Silver Corp. of America 10/28/1983

BUNKER HILL & SULLIVAN MINING & CONCENTRATING CO. (DE)
Each share Common $10 par exchanged for (4) shares Common $2.50 par 00/00/1937
Name changed to Bunker Hill Co. 03/28/1956
Bunker Hill Co. merged into Gulf Resources & Chemical Corp. 05/31/1968 which name changed to Gulf USA Corp. 05/01/1992
(See Gulf USA Corp.)

BUNKER HILL CO. (DE)
6% Preferred $100 par called for redemption 03/31/1964
Merged into Gulf Resources & Chemical Corp. 05/31/1968
Each share Common $2.50 par exchanged for (1) share $1.30 Conv. Preferred Ser. B $1 par, (0.6) share Common 10¢ par and $0.2567 cash
Gulf Resources & Chemical Corp. name changed to Gulf USA Corp. 05/01/1992
(See Gulf USA Corp.)

BUNKER HILL EXTN MINES LTD (CANADA)
Each share old Capital Stock no par exchanged for (0.2) share new Capital Stock no par 00/00/1934
Recapitalized as Bunker Hill Resources, Inc. 12/17/1981
Each share Capital Stock no par exchanged for (0.2) share Capital Stock no par
Bunker Hill Resources Inc. recapitalized as Zacherra Holdings Inc. (Canada) 06/19/1987 which reincorporated in Ontario 08/01/1997 which name changed to First Interactive Inc. 01/18/2000
(See First Interactive Inc.)

BUNKER HILL INCOME SECS INC (MD)
Reorganized into Pacific Horizon Funds, Inc. 04/25/1994
Each share Common $1 par exchanged for (1) share Corporate Bond Fund $0.001 par
(See Pacific Horizon Funds, Inc.)

BUNKER HILL MNG INC (BC)
Struck off register and declared dissolved for failure to file returns 11/12/1993

BUNKER HILL RES INC (CANADA)
Recapitalized as Zacherra Holdings Inc. 06/19/1987
Each share Capital Stock no par exchanged for (0.25) share Capital Stock no par
Zacherra Holdings Inc. name changed to First Interactive Inc. 01/18/2000
(See First Interactive Inc.)

BUNKER-RAMO CORP. OLD (DE)
Merged into Bunker Ramo Corp. (New) 06/03/1968
Each share Common no par exchanged for (1) share Common no par
Bunker Ramo Corp. (New) merged into Allied Corp. 07/31/1981 which merged into Allied-Signal Inc. 09/19/1985 which name changed to Allied Signal Inc. 04/26/1993

BUNKER RAMO CORP NEW (DE)
Each share Common no par exchanged for (0.33333333) share Common Capital Stock no par 04/25/1973
$1.50 Conv. Preferred no par called for redemption 07/20/1981
Merged into Allied Corp. 07/31/1981
Each share Common Capital Stock no par exchanged for (1) share $6.74 Conv. Preferred Ser. C no par
Allied Corp. merged into Allied-Signal Inc. 09/19/1985 which name changed to AlliedSignal Inc. 04/26/1993 which name changed to Honeywell International Inc. 12/01/1999

BUNNINGTON CORP (DE)
Name changed to Magnetic Technologies Corp. 06/27/1983
Magnetic Technologies Corp. merged into SPS Technologies, Inc. 12/02/1997 which merged into Precision Castparts Corp. 12/09/2003
(See Precision Castparts Corp.)

BUNTE BROTHERS (IL)
Each share 7% Preferred $100 par exchanged for (1.2) shares 5% Preferred $100 par 00/00/1936
Stock Dividend - 200% 04/00/1947
Name changed to American Candy Co. 01/26/1954
American Candy Co. merged into Raymond-Commerce Corp. 12/31/1954
(See Raymond-Commerce Corp.)

BUNTE BROTHERS CHASE CANDY CO. (MO)
Name changed to Chase General Corp. 03/26/1962

BUNTIN REID PAPER LTD (ON)
Through purchase offer Domtar Ltd. held all but (15) shares as of 05/24/1974
Public interest eliminated

BUNTING INC (DE)
Name changed 06/16/1981
Name changed from Bunting Sterisystems, Inc. to Bunting Inc. 06/16/1981
Common 1¢ par split (2) for (1) by issuance of (1) additional share on 12/15/1984
Common 1¢ par split (3) for (2) by issuance of (0.5) additional share 01/03/1986
Stock Dividend - 10% 06/01/1985
Charter cancelled and declared inoperative and void for non-payment of taxes 03/01/1992

BUNYAN PAUL FD INC (MI)
Merged into GAC Growth Fund, Inc. 12/31/1970
Each share Common $1 par exchanged for (1) share Common 10¢ par
GAC Growth Fund, Inc. acquired by New York Venture Fund, Inc. 07/24/1972 which name changed to Davis New York Venture Fund, Inc. 10/01/1995

BUNYORO RES INC (BC)
Name changed to Friedrich Technologies, Inc. 03/24/1986
Friedrich Technologies, Inc. name changed to International Prime Technologies Inc. 05/13/1988
(See International Prime Technologies Inc.)

BUOY CLUB INC (FL)
Name changed to Identa Ltd. 01/23/2002
Identa Ltd. name changed to Identa Corp. 01/22/2002

BUR-LEY LONG LAC GOLD MINES LTD.
Name changed to Bur-Ley Porcupine Gold Mines Ltd. 00/00/1944
(See Bur-Ley Porcupine Gold Mines Ltd.)

BUR-LEY PORCUPINE GOLD MINES LTD. (ON)
Charter cancelled and dissolved 09/26/1960
No stockholders' equity

BURCHELL LAKE MINES LTD. (ON)
Charter cancelled and company declared dissolved for default in filing returns 08/03/1964

BURCO, INC. (DE)
Incorporated 09/13/1929
Merged into Investment Co. of America 07/07/1944 through an exchange of stock based on net asset value

BURCO, INC. (DE)
Ctfs. dated after 00/00/1953
Liquidated 03/31/1955
Details not available

BURCO CONSOLIDATED LEAD & SILVER MINES LTD.
Name changed to Burco Consolidated Mines Ltd. 00/00/1949
(See Burco Consolidated Mines Ltd.)

BURCO CONSOLIDATED MINES LTD. (ON)
Charter cancelled and dissolved 03/04/1963

BURCON CAP CORP (YT)
Name changed to Burcon NutraScience Corp. 10/18/1999

BURCON PPTYS LTD (BC)
Recapitalized 06/26/1995
Name changed 07/11/1997
Recapitalized from Burcon Developments Ltd. to Burcon International Developments Ltd. 06/26/1995
Each share Common no par exchanged for (0.05208333) share Common no par
Name changed from Burcon International Developments Ltd. to BurCon Properties Ltd. 07/11/1997
Each share Common no par received distribution of (0.7) share Concord Pacific Group Inc. Common no par payable 06/01/1998 to holders of record 05/27/1998
Merged into Oxford Properties Group Inc. 05/29/1998
Each share Common no par exchanged for (0.74377) share Common no par
(See Oxford Properties Group Inc.)

BURD PISTON RING CO.
Merged into Gabriel Co. 00/00/1951
Each share Common $1 par exchanged for (1.375) shares Common $1 par
(See Gabriel Co.)

BURDELLE MINES, INC. (NV)
Charter revoked for failure to file reports and fees 01/06/1958

BURDETT OXYGEN CO CLEVELAND INC (OH)
Common $1 par split (5) for (2) by issuance of (1.5) additional shares 03/15/1966
Name changed to Burdox, Inc. 06/26/1974
(See Burdox, Inc.)

BURDETT RES LTD (BC)
Recapitalized as AFF Automated Fast Foods Ltd. 11/19/1991
Each share Common no par exchanged for (0.33333333) share Common no par
AFF Automated Fast Foods Ltd. name changed to Brier Resources Corp. 07/31/1998 which name changed to Ashlar Financial Services Corp. 08/02/2000
(See Ashlar Financial Services Corp.)

BURDINES, INC. (FL)
Each share Preference no par exchanged for (1) share new Preference no par and (0.66666666) share Common no par 00/00/1929
Each share Common no par exchanged for (0.33333333) share new Common no par 00/00/1929
Each share Common no par exchanged for (3) shares Common $1 par 00/00/1937
Common $1 par changed to $10 par 00/00/1947
Merged into Federated Department Stores, Inc. 07/28/1956
Each share Common $10 par exchanged for (0.6) share Common $5 par
Federated Department Stores, Inc. name changed to Macy's, Inc. 06/01/2007

BURDOS MINES LTD (BC)
Recapitalized as Pentagon Resources Ltd. 05/02/1979
Each share Common 50¢ par

exchanged for (0.2) share Common no par
Pentagon Resources Ltd. recapitalized as Quintel Industries Ltd. 08/22/1983
(See Qunitel Industries Ltd.)

BURDOX INC (OH)
Merged into Gas Accumulator Corp. 04/27/1978
Each share Common $1 par exchanged for $25 cash

BUREAU ELECTR PUBG INC (DE)
Recapitalized as Pacific Chemical, Inc. 06/27/1997
Each share Common $0.001 par exchanged for (0.16666666) share Common $0.001 par
Pacific Chemical, Inc. recapitalized as RegalTech, Inc. 03/15/2005 which name changed to Asante Networks, Inc. 10/17/2005

BUREAU NATL AFFAIRS INC (DE)
Acquired by Bloomberg Inc. 09/30/2011
Each share Class A Common $1 par exchanged for $39.50 cash

BUREAU OF FUGITIVE RECOVERY INC (CO)
Name changed to Reven Housing REIT, Inc. (CO) 08/16/2012
Reven Housing REIT, Inc. (CO) reorganized in Maryland 11/07/2014

BUREL ENTERPRISES INC (DE)
Recapitalized as Research Resources, Inc. 09/26/1984
Each share Common $0.0001 par exchanged for (0.1) share Common $0.0001 par
(See Research Resources, Inc.)

BURETT, INC. (UT)
Name changed to Energy Motor Control, Inc. 06/07/1984
(See Energy Motor Control, Inc.)

BURGEMEISTER BREWING CO.
Reorganized as Warsaw Brewing Corp. 00/00/1936
Each share Preferred upon payment of $0.20 cash per share exchanged for (1) share new Common
Each share old Common exchanged for (0.025) share new Common
(See Warsaw Brewing Corp.)

BURGER BREWING CO (OH)
Name changed to Central Investment Corp. 04/02/1973
(See Central Investment Corp.)

BURGER BROTHERS CO.
Name changed to Burger Brewing Co. 00/00/1934
Burger Brewing Co. name changed to Central Investment Corp. 04/02/1973
(See Burger Brewing Co.)

BURGER KING HLDGS INC (DE)
Acquired by Blue Acquisition Holding Corp. 10/19/2010
Each share Common 1¢ par exchanged for $24 cash

BURGER KING INVS MASTER L P (DE)
Name changed to U.S. Restaurant Properties Master L.P. (DE) 11/11/1994
U.S. Restaurant Properties Master L.P. (DE) reincorporated in Maryland as U.S. Restaurants Properties, Inc. 10/15/1997 which name changed to Trustreet Properties, Inc. 02/25/2005
(See Trustreet Properties, Inc.)

BURGER KING WORLDWIDE INC (DE)
Merged into Restaurant Brands International Inc. 12/15/2014
Each share Common 1¢ par exchanged for (0.99) share Common no par and (1) Restaurant Brands International L.P. Exchangeable Unit

BURGERMEISTER BREWING CORP. (CA)
Name changed to San Francisco Liquidating Co. 12/29/1961
(See San Francisco Liquidating Co.)

BURGESS BATTERY CO. (OLD) (DE)
Reorganized as Burgess Vibrocrafters, Inc. and Burgess Battery Co. (New) 01/18/1950
Each share Common $10 par exchanged for (1) share Burgess Vibrocrafters, Inc. Common $3 par and (1) share Burgess Battery Co. (New) Capital Stock $6 par
(See each company's listing)

BURGESS BATTERY CO. (WI)
Reorganized under the laws of Delaware 11/20/1939
Each share Common $100 par exchanged for (10) shares Common $10 par
(See Burgess Battery Co. (DE) (Old))

BURGESS BATTERY CO. NEW (DE)
Capital Stock $6 par changed to $10 par and (1) additional share issued 06/21/1955
Name changed to Freeport Liquidating Co., Inc. 01/15/1959
(See Freeport Liquidating Co., Inc.)

BURGESS CELLULOSE CO (DE)
Completely liquidated 08/14/1968
Each share Capital Stock no par exchanged for first and final distribution of (0.4) share Minnesota Mining & Manufacturing Co. Common no par
Minnesota Mining & Manufacturing Co. name changed to 3M Co. 04/08/2002

BURGESS INDS INC (DE)
Common 50¢ par split (4) for (3) by issuance of (0.33333333) additional share 02/25/1970
Merged into Valley Industries, Inc. 10/19/1982
Each share Common 50¢ par exchanged for $4.95 cash

BURGESS MANNING CO (IL)
Common $10 par changed to $2.50 par and (2) additional shares Common $2.50 par plus (1) share Class A $2.50 par issued 05/24/1963
Class A $2.50 par called for redemption 07/05/1963
Common $2.50 par changed to $1 par and (1.5) additional shares issued 08/28/1967
Reincorporated under the laws of Delaware as Burgess Industries Inc. and Common $1 par changed to 50¢ par 01/31/1969
(See Burgess Industries Inc.)

BURGESS NORTON MFG. CO. (IL)
Each share Common $50 par exchanged for (16) shares Common $2.50 par 00/00/1947
Through purchase offer 100% acquired by Amsted Industries, Inc. as of 10/00/1969
Public interest was eliminated

BURGESS-PARR CO.
Name changed to Illium Corp. 00/00/1950
Illium Corp. name changed to Burco, Inc. 00/00/1954
(See Burco, Inc.)

BURGESS POINT RESOURCES INC. (ON)
Recapitalized as Metallica Resources Inc. 01/14/1994
Each share Common no par exchanged for (0.14285714) share Common no par
Metallica Resources Inc. merged into New Gold Inc. 06/30/2008

BURGESS VIBROCRAFTERS INC (DE)
Merged into Acme General Corp. 04/28/1977
Each share Common $3 par exchanged for $27 cash

BURGESS YELLOWKNIFE KIRKLAND MINES, LTD. (ON)
Charter revoked for failure to file reports and pay taxes 00/00/1955

BURGMASTER CORP. (CA)
Acquired by Houdaille Industries, Inc. (MI) 11/18/1965
Each share Common $1 par exchanged for (0.75585) share 4.5% Conv. Preferred Ser. A $25 par
Houdaille Industries, Inc. (MI) reincorporated in Delaware 04/01/1968
(See Houdaille Industries, Inc. (DE))

BURGUNDY BULL, INC. (MN)
Adjudicated bankrupt 06/04/1970
No stockholders' equity

BURIN EQUITIES CORP (AB)
Name changed to Starlink Communications Corp. 04/25/1997
Starlink Communications Corp. name changed to Starlink Capital Corp. 12/08/2000 which recapitalized as Nevis Energy Services Ltd. 10/05/2001 which was acquired by Phoenix Technology Services Inc. 11/01/2002 which recapitalized as Phoenix Technology Income Fund 07/01/2004 which reorganized as PHX Energy Services Corp. 01/06/2011

BURING FOOD GROUP INC (DE)
Merged into Riverside Foods Ltd. 10/28/1978
Each share Common $1 par exchanged for $16 cash

BURK-HALL CO (TN)
Completely liquidated 11/27/1989
No stockholders' equity

BURK LOUIS CO (PA)
Adjudicated bankrupt 03/18/1969
No stockholders' equity

BURKART (F.) MANUFACTURING CO. (MO)
Each share Common no par exchanged for (3) shares Common $1 par 00/00/1936
Common $1 par changed to $8 par 00/00/1949
Stock Dividend - 100% 07/20/1946
Name changed to Second Street Liquidating Corp. 00/00/1953
(See Second Street Liquidating Corp.)

BURKE GROCERY CO.
Bankrupt 00/00/1941
Details not available

BURKE-MARTIN MINES, INC. (CO)
Declared defunct and inoperative for failure to pay taxes and file annual reports 10/13/1966

BURKE MLS INC (NC)
Recapitalized as Fortran Corp. 02/20/2013
Each share Common no par exchanged for (0.1) share Common no par

BURKE OIL CO.
Dissolved 00/00/1931
Details not available

BURKE OIL CO. (UT)
Reincorporated under the laws of Nevada as Centre Capital Corp. 09/06/1988
Centre Capital Corp. name changed to Golden Health Holdings, Inc. 04/15/2004
(See Golden Health Holdings, Inc.)

BURKE PARSONS BOWLBY CORP (WV)
Stock Dividends - 100% 06/30/1975; 100% 01/15/1986
Merged into Stella-Jones Inc. 04/01/2008
Each share Common $2 par exchanged for $47.78 cash
Note: An additional initial distribution of approximately $4.92 cash per share was paid from escrow 07/23/2008

BURKE SEC INC (DE)
Charter cancelled and declared inoperative and void for non-payment of taxes 03/01/1991

BURKHART PETE CORP (NV)
Merged into ZG Energy Corp. (DE) 06/29/1987
Each share Common 1¢ par exchanged for (0.00202020) share Common 1¢ par
ZG Energy Corp. (DE) reorganized in Oklahoma as Vantage Point Energy, Inc. 04/30/1990
(See Vantage Point Energy, Inc.)

BURKINA CAP CORP (CANADA)
Name changed to Canada's Choice Spring Water, Inc. 04/27/1999
Canada's Choice Spring Water, Inc. recapitalized as Echo Springs Water Corp. 03/27/2002
(See Echo Springs Water Corp.)

BURKYARNS INC (NC)
Name changed to Burke Mills, Inc. 05/07/1979
Burke Mills, Inc. recapitalized as Fortran Corp. 02/20/2013

BURLING-CENTER TRUST
Liquidated 00/00/1956
Details not available

BURLINGAME BANCORP (CA)
Merged into Pacific Bank, N.A. (San Francisco, CA) 04/02/1996
Each share Common no par exchanged for $12.94 cash

BURLINGAME FOODS (CA)
Name changed to Burlingame-Western 06/07/1971
(See Burlingame-Western)

BURLINGAME FORMULA FUND (MA)
Name changed to Federated Fund of New England 00/00/1952
Federated Fund of New England name changed to Federated Fund 03/04/1956 which merged into Income Foundation Fund, Inc. 12/31/1956 which name changed to Boston Foundation Fund Inc. 09/22/1969 which name changed to Federated Stock & Bond Fund, Inc. (Old) 01/01/1985 which name changed to Stock & Bond Fund, Inc. 04/17/1993 which name changed to Federated Stock & Bond Fund, Inc. (New) (MD) 03/31/1996 which reincorporated in Massachusetts as Federated Stock & Bond Fund 09/05/2008

BURLINGAME WESTN (CA)
Charter suspended for failure to file reports and pay fees 05/01/1979

BURLINGTON BANK & TRUST CO. (BURLINGTON, NC)
Name changed to Burlington National Bank (Burlington, NC) 04/01/1976
(See Burlington National Bank (Burlington, NC))

BURLINGTON BK & TR CO (BURLINGTON, IA)
Name changed to Hawkeye Bank & Trust Co. (Burlington, IA) 07/20/1976
(See Hawkeye Bank & Trust Co. (Burlington, IA))

BURLINGTON BK & TR CO (BURLINGTON, NJ)
Merged into Fidelity Bank & Trust Co. of New Jersey (Pennsauken, NJ) 05/01/1970
Each share Common $5 par exchanged for (1) share Common $5 par
(See Fidelity Bank & Trust Co. of New Jersey (Pennsauken, NJ))

BURLINGTON COAT FACTORY WHSE CORP (DE)
Common $1 par split (3) for (2) by issuance of (0.5) additional share 03/23/1990
Common $1 par split (3) for (2) by issuance of (0.5) additional share 07/27/1992
Common $1 par split (3) for (2) by issuance of (0.5) additional share 10/04/1993
Common $1 par split (6) for (5) by issuance of (0.2) additional share payable 10/16/1997 to holders of record 10/01/1997 Ex date - 10/17/1997
Merged into Bain Capital Partners, LLC 04/13/2006
Each share Common $1 par exchanged for $45.50 cash

BURLINGTON CNTY BK N J (BURLINGTON, NJ)
Merged into Trenton Savings Bank, FSB (Trenton, NJ) 09/30/1996
Each share Common exchanged for $77 cash

BURLINGTON CNTY NATL BK (MEDFORD, NJ)
Merged into Midlantic Banks, Inc. 10/01/1981
Each share Common $1.25 par exchanged for $18 cash

BURLINGTON CNTY TR CO (MOORESTOWN, NJ)
Stock Dividend - 20% 10/15/1956
Merged into Fidelity Union Bancorporation 07/17/1978
Each share Common $5 par exchanged for (1) Common Stock Purchase Warrant expiring 01/15/1979 and $48 cash

BURLINGTON DEV & CONSTR CORP (NJ)
Charter declared void for non-payment of taxes 09/01/1988

BURLINGTON GOLD MINES LTD (BC)
Recapitalized as B.G.M. Diversified Energy Inc. 04/08/1986
Each share Capital Stock no par exchanged for (0.2) share Common no par
(See B.G.M. Diversified Energy Inc.)

BURLINGTON HOME BUILDING CO. (WI)
Sold out completely to Geo. Waller former Secretary and Treasurer 00/00/1933
Details not available

BURLINGTON INDS EQUITY INC (DE)
Name changed to Burlington Industries, Inc. (New) 02/03/1994
(See Burlington Industries, Inc. (New))

BURLINGTON INDS INC NEW (DE)
Plan of reorganization under Chapter 11 Federal Bankruptcy Code effective 11/10/2003
No stockholders' equity

BURLINGTON INDS INC OLD (DE)
3.5% Preferred $100 par called for redemption 07/15/1963
4% Preferred $100 par called for redemption 07/15/1963
4.2% Preferred $100 par called for redemption 07/15/1963
4.5% 2nd Preference $100 par called for redemption 07/15/1963
Common $1 par split (2) for (1) by issuance of (1) additional share 08/10/1965
Stock Dividend - 10% 09/16/1955
Merged into Burlington Holdings Inc. 09/03/1987
Each share Common $1 par exchanged for $78 cash

BURLINGTON LIGHT & POWER CO.
Acquired by Green Mountain Power Corp. 00/00/1928
Details not available

BURLINGTON MILLS CO., INC.
Acquired by Burlington Mills Corp. 02/00/1937
Details not available

BURLINGTON MILLS CORP. (DE)
Common $1 par split (2) for (1) by issuance of (1) additional share 03/15/1945
Common $1 par split (2) for (1) by issuance of (1) additional share 07/02/1946
Common $1 par split (3) for (2) by issuance of (0.5) additional share 03/26/1951
Name changed to Burlington Industries, Inc. (Old) 02/03/1955
(See Burlington Industries, Inc. (Old))

BURLINGTON MINES & ENTERPRISES LTD (BC)
Recapitalized as Burlington Gold Mines Ltd. 12/19/1974
Each share Capital Stock no par exchanged for (0.5) share Capital Stock no par
Burlington Gold Mines Ltd. recapitalized as B.G.M. Diversified Energy Inc. 04/08/1986
(See B.G.M. Diversified Energy Inc.)

BURLINGTON MINES LTD. (BC)
Name changed to Burlington Mines & Enterprises Ltd. 07/31/1970
Each share Capital Stock no par exchanged for (1) share Capital Stock no par
Burlington Mines & Enterprises Ltd. recapitalized as Burlington Gold Mines Ltd. 12/19/1974 which recapitalized as B.G.M. Diversified Energy Inc. 04/08/1986
(See B.G.M. Diversified Energy Inc.)

BURLINGTON NATIONAL BANK (BURLINGTON, NC)
Merged into Central Carolina Bank & Trust Co. (Durham, NC) 12/31/1980
Each share Common $5 par exchanged for $20 cash

BURLINGTON NORTHN INC (DE)
Common no par split (2) for (1) by issuance of (1) additional share 06/27/1980
$2.85 Conv. Preferred no par called for redemption 10/10/1980
Common no par split (2) for (1) by issuance of (1) additional share 02/24/1984
$2.125 Preferred no par called for redemption 06/01/1986
Adjustable Rate Preferred no par called for redemption 12/01/1986
5.5% Preferred $10 par called for redemption 07/15/1993
Under plan of merger name changed to Burlington Northern Santa Fe Corp. 09/22/1995
(See Burlington Northern Santa Fe Corp.)

BURLINGTON NORTHN SANTA FE CORP (DE)
6.25% Conv. Preferred Ser. A no par called for redemption 12/26/1995
Common 1¢ par split (3) for (1) by issuance of (2) additional shares payable 09/01/1998 to holders of record 08/17/1998 Ex date - 09/02/1998
Preferred Stock Purchase Rights declared for Common stockholders of record 12/31/1999 were redeemed at $0.01 per right 04/02/2001 to holders of record 03/12/2001
Merged into Berkshire Hathaway Inc. 02/12/2010
Each share Common 1¢ par exchanged for $100 cash

BURLINGTON RLTY CO (MA)
Proclaimed dissolved for failure to file reports and pay taxes 09/11/1969

BURLINGTON RES COAL SEAM GAS RTY TR (DE)
Completely liquidated
Each Unit of Bene. Int. received first and final distribution of $8.13 cash 04/13/1999

BURLINGTON RES INC (DE)
Common 1¢ par split (2) for (1) by issuance of (1) additional share payable 06/01/2004 to holders of record 05/05/2004 Ex date - 06/02/2004
Merged into ConocoPhillips 03/31/2006
Each share Common 1¢ par exchanged for (0.7214) share Common 1¢ par and $46.50 cash

BURLINGTON STEEL CO., LTD. (ON)
Each share Capital Stock no par exchanged for (2) shares Capital Stock no par 01/02/1957
Merged into Slater Steel Industries Ltd. 02/22/1962
Each share Capital Stock no par exchanged for (0.5) share 6.25% Preferred Ser. A $20 par and (1) share Common no par
Slater Steel Industries Ltd. name changed to Slater Steel Corp. 07/27/1984 which name changed to Slater Industries Inc. 10/02/1986 which name changed to Slater Steel Inc. 06/25/1996
(See Slater Steel Inc.)

BURLOCK INDS INC (NY)
Charter cancelled and proclaimed dissolved for failure to pay taxes 12/16/1974

BURMA CORP., LTD.
Under plan of liquidation each share was exchanged for (1) share Ordinary 3s6d par of Burma Mines Ltd. and (1) share Ordinary 1s par of Non Ferrous Metal Products Ltd. 00/00/1952
(See each company's listing)

BURMA DIP GOLD MINES LTD. (ON)
Name changed to Eldrich Mines Ltd. 07/13/1953
Eldrich Mines Ltd. name changed to Canadian-Australian Exploration Ltd. 04/01/1963 which recapitalized as Win-Eldrich Mines Ltd. 06/21/1965

BURMA MINES PLC (ENGLAND)
Name changed to Southwest Resources PLC 01/17/1983

BURMA SHORE MINES LTD. (ON)
Name changed 06/14/1956
Name changed from Burma Shore Uranium Mines Ltd. to Burma Shore Mines Ltd. 06/14/1956
Charter cancelled 05/06/1965
No stockholders' equity

BURMA SHORE URANIUM MINES LTD. (ON)
Name changed to Burma Shore Mines Ltd. 06/14/1956
(See Burma Shore Mines Ltd.)

BURMAC ELECTRONICS CO., INC. (NY)
Name changed to Victory Electronics, Inc. 10/10/1964
(See Victory Electronics, Inc.)

BURMAC ENERGY CORP (BC)
Recapitalized as Bus Holdings Corp. 02/07/1991
Each share Common no par exchanged for (0.14285714) share Common no par
Bus Holdings Corp. name changed to Savannah Ventures Ltd. 11/17/1997 which recapitalized as International Savannah Ventures Ltd. 12/01/1998 which name changed to Softcare EC.com, Inc. 06/10/1999 which name changed to Softcare EC Inc. 10/05/2001 which recapitalized as Open EC Technologies, Inc. 06/23/2003
(See Open EC Technologies, Inc.)

BURMAH CASTROL PLC (SCOTLAND)
Name changed 07/30/1990
Each Unsponsored ADR for Ordinary exchanged for (0.25) Sponsored ADR for Ordinary Reg. 11/16/1987
Stock Dividends - 100% 09/30/1955; 100% 08/12/1959
Name changed from Burmah Oil Co., PLC to Burmah Castrol PLC 07/30/1990
Acquired by BP Amoco PLC 07/07/2000
Each share Ordinary Reg. received GBP 16.75 cash
Each Sponsored ADR for Ordinary Reg. received approximately $40 cash

BURMIS ENERGY INC (AB)
Acquired by Baytex Energy Trust 06/04/2008
Each share Common no par exchanged for (0.1525) Trust Unit no par
Note: Unexchanged certificates were cancelled and became without value 06/04/2014
Baytex Energy Trust reorganized as Baytex Energy Corp. 01/03/2011

BURNABY PAPERBOARD LTD (BC)
All held by MacMillan Bloedel Ltd. as of 07/12/1974
Public interest eliminated

BURNDALE RES LTD (BC)
Name changed to Tai Energy Resources Corp. 09/14/1989
Tai Energy Resources Corp. merged into Tai Energy Corp. 06/30/1993 which was acquired by Maxx Petroleum Ltd. 03/17/1995 which was acquired by Provident Energy Trust 05/21/2001 which reorganized as Provident Energy Ltd. (New) 01/03/2011 which merged into Pembina Pipeline Corp. 04/02/2012

BURNDY CORP (NY)
Common $1 par split (2) for (1) by issuance of (1) additional share 06/03/1966
Common $1 par split (3) for (2) by issuance of (0.5) additional share 02/17/1976
Common $1 par split (3) for (2) by issuance of (0.5) additional share 01/17/1977
Common $1 par split (2) for (1) by issuance of (1) additional share 08/18/1981
Merged into Framatome S.A. 02/13/1989
Each share Common $1 par exchanged for $26 cash

BURNELL & CO., INC. (NY)
Merged into Nytronics, Inc. (NJ) 08/01/1966
Each share Common 25¢ par exchanged for (0.125) share Capital Stock $1 par
Nytronics, Inc. (NJ) reincorporated in Delaware 01/04/1968 which merged into Bastian Industries, Inc. 11/24/1980
(See Bastian Industries, Inc.)

BURNELL CORP. (DE)
Merged into DeWitt International Corp. 04/01/1969
Each share Capital Stock exchanged for (6) shares Common $1 par
DeWitt International Corp. name changed to DeWitt Drug & Beauty Products, Inc. 11/03/1969 which name changed back to DeWitt International Corp. 09/13/1974
(See DeWitt International Corp.)

BURNER EXPL LTD (AB)
Merged into Berkley Petroleum Corp. 03/31/1998
Each share Common no par exchanged for (0.071428) share Common no par
(See Berkley Petroleum Corp.)

BURNETT, LTD. (CANADA)
Adjudicated bankrupt 00/00/1955
No stockholders' equity

BURNHAM & MORRILL CO., INC. (ME)
Merged into Underwood (William) Inc. 06/02/1966
Each share Common $1 par exchanged for $25 cash

BURNHAM (E.S.) PACKING CO.
Property sold 00/00/1928
Details not available

BURNHAM AMERN PPTYS (CA)
Under plan of reorganization each Unit of Ltd. Partnership no par automatically became (1) share Burnham American Properties, Inc. Common no par 10/01/1987
Burnham American Properties, Inc. acquired by Burnham Pacific Properties, Inc. (CA) 06/14/1988 which reincorporated in Maryland 05/31/1997
(See Burnham Pacific Properties, Inc.)

BURNHAM AMERN PPTYS INC (CA)
Common no par split (2) for (1) by issuance of (1) additional share 10/15/1987
Acquired by Burnham Pacific Properties, Inc. (CA) 06/14/1988
Each share Common no par exchanged for (0.87) share Common no par
Burnham Pacific Properties, Inc. (CA) reincorporated in Maryland 05/31/1997
(See Burnham Pacific Properties, Inc.)

BURNHAM AVENUE APARTMENTS
Property sold 00/00/1948
Details not available

BURNHAM BOILER CORP.
Merged into Burnham Corp. (NY) 00/00/1947
Each share Common exchanged for (1) share 6% Preferred $50 par and (5) shares Common $15 par
Burnham Corp. (NY) reincorporated in Delaware 04/29/2002 which name changed to Burnham Holdings, Inc. 01/08/2003

BURNHAM CHEMICAL CO. (NV)
Charter revoked for failure to file reports and pay fees 03/01/1976

BURNHAM CORP (NY)
Reincorporated 04/29/2002
Common $15 par split (2) for (1) by issuance of (1) additional share 04/20/1964
Common $15 par split (5) for (4) by issuance of (0.25) additional share 01/01/1984
Common $15 par reclassified as Class A Common $1 par 04/28/1989
Each share Class A Common $1 par received distribution of (1) share Class B Common $1 par 06/05/1989
Class A Common $1 par split (2) for (1) by issuance of (1) additional share 03/10/1995
Class B Common $1 par split (2) for (1) by issuance of (1) additional share 03/10/1995
State of incorporation changed from (NY) to (DE) 04/29/2002
Stock Dividends - 50% 11/07/1975; 25% 12/22/1976; 25% 12/06/1977
Name changed to Burnham Holdings, Inc. 01/08/2003

BURNHAM FD (NJ)
Merged into Drexel Burnham Fund 06/16/1975
Each share Common $1 par exchanged for (1.016968) shares Common 10¢ par

BURNHAM-MUNGER-ROOT DRY GOODS CO.
Liquidated 00/00/1930
Details not available

BURNHAM PAC PPTYS INC (MD)
Reincorporated 05/31/1997
Common no par split (3) for (2) by issuance of (0.5) additional share 04/20/1987
State of incorporation changed from (CA) to (MD) and Common no par changed to 1¢ par 05/31/1997
In process of liquidation
Each share Common no par received initial distribution of $0.10 cash payable 12/29/2000 to holders of record 12/18/2000
Each share Common no par received second distribution of $0.10 cash payable 04/23/2001 to holders of record 04/13/2001
Each share Common no par received third distribution of $1.25 cash payable 01/08/2002 to holders of record 12/31/2001
Each share Common no par received fourth distribution of $0.45 cash payable 02/22/2002 to holders of record 02/14/2002
Each share Common no par received fifth distribution of (0.07525) share Developers Diversified Realty Corp. Common no par and $0.30 cash payable 03/12/2002 to holders of record 02/28/2002
Each share Common no par received sixth distribution of $0.30 cash payable 06/27/2002 to holders of record 06/19/2002
Assets transferred to BPP Liquidating Trust and Common no par reclassified as Units of Bene. Int. 06/28/2002
(See BPP Liquidating Trust)

BURNHAM SERVICE CORP. (GA)
Common no par split (3) for (2) by issuance of (0.5) additional share 06/17/1983
Reincorporated under the laws of Delaware and Common no par changed to 1¢ par 04/16/1987
(See Burnham Service Corp. (DE))

BURNHAM SVC CORP (DE)
Acquired by BVL Holdings Inc. 04/21/1988
Each share Common 1¢ par exchanged for $22 cash

BURNHAM SLEEPY HOLLOW LTD (CA)
Units of Ltd. Partnership split (2) for (1) by issuance of (1) additional Unit 12/07/1984
Reorganized as Burnham Pacific Properties, Inc. (CA) 04/01/1987
Each Unit of Ltd. Partnership exchanged for (1) share Common no par
Burnham Pacific Properties, Inc. (CA) reincorporated in Maryland 05/31/1997
(See Burnham Pacific Properties, Inc.)

BURNHAM TRADING CORP.
Out of business 00/00/1934
Details not available

BURNING BUSH REC CORP (CO)
Name changed to Edgerton Musical Amplifiers, Inc. 10/22/1996
(See Edgerton Musical Amplifiers, Inc.)

BURNLEY CORP (DE)
Each share Common 10¢ par exchanged for (0.1) share Common $1 par 06/15/1981
Each share Common $1 par exchanged for (0.002) share Common $500 par 03/08/1990
Note: Minority holders received an undetermined amount of cash and public interest was eliminated

BURNS & CO. LTD. (CANADA)
Recapitalized 00/00/1934
Each share old Preferred exchanged for (1.5) shares Class B no par
Each (20) shares old Common exchanged for (1) share Class B no par
Recapitalized 05/27/1955
Each share Class A no par exchanged for (6) shares Common no par
Each share Class B no par exchanged for (4) shares Common no par
Name changed to Burns Foods Ltd. 04/29/1965
(See Burns Foods Ltd.)

BURNS & TOWNE INC (DE)
Common 10¢ par changed to 1¢ par 10/26/1970
Each share Common 1¢ par exchanged for (0.06666666) share Common $0.015 par 05/27/1972
Name changed to Eastern York, Inc. 07/06/1976
(See Eastern York, Inc.)

BURNS FOODS LTD (CANADA)
Common no par split (3) for (1) by issuance of (2) additional shares 06/19/1970
Merged into WCB Holdings Ltd. 12/12/1978
Each share Common no par exchanged for $18 cash

BURNS INTL SEC SVCS INC (DE)
Class B Common 50¢ par reclassified as Class A Common 50¢ par 05/26/1982
Merged into Borg-Warner Corp. 06/01/1982
Each share Class A Common 50¢ par exchanged for $28 cash

BURNS INTL SVCS CORP (DE)
Merged into Securites AB 09/08/2000
Each share Common 1¢ par exchanged for $21.50 cash

BURNS PHILP & CO LTD (AUSTRALIA)
Stock Dividends - 20% 06/23/1988; 10% 12/15/1989
Acquired by Rank Group Ltd. 12/20/2006
Each Sponsored ADR for Ordinary exchanged for $5.1244 cash

BURNS R L CORP (DE)
Reincorporated 01/25/1974
State of incorporation changed from (NY) to (DE) 01/25/1974
Common 10¢ par split (3) for (2) by issuance of (0.5) additional share 12/31/1975
Stock Dividends - 50% 12/31/1973; 100% 04/15/1975
Name changed to Pyro Energy Corp. 12/15/1981
(See Pyro Energy Corp.)

BURNS WILLIAM J INTL DETECTIVE AGY INC (DE)
Class A Common $1.50 par and Class B Common $1.50 par changed to $1 par and (0.5) additional share issued respectively 12/29/1967
Class A Common $1 par and Class B Common $1 par changed to 50¢ par and (1) additional share issued respectively 03/07/1969
Name changed to Burns International Security Services, Inc. 05/04/1971
(See Burns International Security Services, Inc.)

BURNSIDE CORP. (DE)
Completely liquidated 01/25/1966
Each share Preferred $25 par exchanged for first and final distribution of (0.05) share Kinsford Co. Common $6.25 par and $0.05 cash
No Common stockholders' equity
Kingsford Co. merged into Clorox Co. (CA) 03/12/1973 which reincorporated in Delaware 10/22/1986

BURNT HILL TUNGSTEN & METALLURGICAL LTD (QC)
Charter annulled for failure to file annual reports 01/24/1981

BURNT HILL TUNGSTEN MINES LTD. (QC)
Name changed to Burnt Hill Tungsten & Metallurgical Ltd. 02/04/1956
(See Burnt Hill Tungsten & Metallurgical Ltd.)

BURNT IS GOLD LTD (BC)
Name changed to New Era Developments Ltd. 06/09/1987
(See New Era Developments Ltd.)

BURNT RIVER MINING SYNDICATE LTD.
Acquired by Cardiff Uranium Mines Ltd. on an (8) for (1) basis 00/00/1953
Cardiff Uranium Mines Ltd. merged into Insulblock Systems Inc. 09/01/1988
(See Insulblock Systems Inc.)

BURNT RIVER URANIUM MINES LTD. (ON)
Voluntarily wound up and liquidated 00/00/1957
Capital Stock $1 par exchanged for pro-rata distribution of Cardiff Uranium Mines Ltd. Common $1 par
Cardiff Uranium Mines Ltd. merged into Insulblock Systems Inc. 09/01/1988
(See Insulblock Systems Inc.)

BURNTSAND INC (CANADA)
Reincorporated 03/12/1998
Place of incorporation changed from (AB) to (Canada) 03/12/1998
Name changed from Burnt Sand Solutions Inc. to Burntsand Inc. 10/04/1999
Acquired by Open Text Corp. 05/31/2010
Each share Common no par exchanged for $0.15 cash

BURNUP & SIMS INC (DE)
Common 10¢ par split (3) for (2) by issuance of (0.5) additional share 04/24/1970
Common 10¢ par split (3) for (2) by issuance of (0.5) additional share 01/29/1971
Common 10¢ par split (2) for (1) by issuance of (1) additional share 07/02/1971
Common 10¢ par split (2) for (1) by issuance of (1) additional share 07/10/1972
Name changed to Mastec, Inc. (DE) 03/11/1994
Mastec, Inc. (DE) reincorporated in Florida 05/29/1998

BURR BROWN CORP (DE)
Common 1¢ par split (3) for (2) by issuance of (0.5) additional share 01/17/1986
Common 1¢ par split (5) for (4) by issuance of (0.25) additional share 12/12/1986
Common 1¢ par split (3) for (2) by issuance of (0.5) additional share 05/19/1995
Common 1¢ par split (3) for (2) by issuance of (0.5) additional share payable 04/08/1997 to holders of record 03/18/1997 Ex date - 04/09/1997
Common 1¢ par split (3) for (2) by issuance of (0.5) additional share payable 03/20/1998 to holders of record 03/06/1998
Common 1¢ par split (3) for (2) by issuance of (0.5) additional share payable 12/20/1999 to holders of record 12/10/1999
Merged into Texas Instruments Inc. 08/24/2000
Each share Common 1¢ par exchanged for (1.3) shares Common $1 par

BURRARD DRY DOCK LTD (CANADA)
Class A no par reclassified as Conv. Preferred no par 10/31/1969
Acquired by Cornat Industries Ltd. 08/01/1972
Each share Conv. Preferred exchanged for an undetermined amount of cash
Each share Common $1 par exchanged for $10 cash
Each share Class B exchanged for an undetermined amount of cash

BURRARD MTG INVTS LTD (BC)
Name changed to Canlan Investment Corp. 06/26/1978
Canlan Investment Corp. name changed to Canlan Ice Sports Corp. 06/25/1999

BURRARD TECHNOLOGIES INC (NV)
Common $0.001 par split (3) for (1) by issuance of (2) additional shares payable 10/01/2001 to holders of record 10/01/2001 Ex date - 10/02/2001
Name changed to Blue Industries Inc. 04/02/2002
Blue Industries Inc. name changed to Pegasus Wireless Corp. 06/06/2005
(See Pegasus Wireless Corp.)

BURRARD VENTURES INC (BC)
Struck off register and declared dissolved for failure to file returns 09/24/1993

BURREX MINES LTD (ON)
Recapitalized as Burrgold Mines Ltd. 12/00/1973
Each share Common no par exchanged for (0.33333333) share Common no par
(See Burrgold Mines Ltd.)

BURRGOLD MINES LTD. (ON)
Charter cancelled 03/00/1977

BURRILLVILLE RACING ASSN (RI)
Merged into Lincoln Greyhound Park 02/00/1989
Each share Class A Common no par exchanged for $400 cash

BURRIS CHEM INC (SC)
Merged into SOCO Chemical Inc. 01/03/1997
Details not available

BURRIS INDS INC (NC)
Merged into La-Z-Boy Chair Co. 12/19/1985
Each share Common $1 par exchanged for $0.75 cash

BURRITT INTERFINANCIAL BANCORPORATION (CT)
Common $1 par split (2) for (1) by issuance of (1) additional share 05/23/1986
Stock Dividend - 10% 06/01/1987
Placed in receivership 12/04/1992
No stockholders' equity

BURRO CREEK MINERALS LTD (BC)
Struck off register and declared dissolved for failure to file returns 10/01/1993

BURROUGHS ADDING MACHINE CO. (MI)
Common no par split (5) for (1) by issuance of (4) additional shares 08/01/1929
Name changed to Burroughs Corp. (MI) and Common no par changed to $5 par 00/00/1953
Burroughs Corp. (MI) reincorporated in Delaware 05/30/1984 which name changed to Unisys Corp. 11/13/1986

BURROUGHS CORP (DE)
Reincorporated 05/30/1984
Common $5 par split (2) for (1) by issuance of (1) additional share 04/28/1969
Common $5 par split (2) for (1) by issuance of (1) additional share 04/29/1974
State of incorporation changed from (MI) to (DE) 05/30/1984
Name changed to Unisys Corp. 11/13/1986

BURROUGHS J P & SONS INC (MI)
Each share old Common $1 par exchanged for (0.33333333) share new Common $1 par 04/01/1963
Merged into Blount, Inc. 07/10/1972
Each share new Common $1 par exchanged for (1) share Common 10¢ par
Blount, Inc. merged into Blount International, Inc. (Old) 11/03/1995 which merged into Blount International, Inc. (New) 08/19/1999
(See Blount International Inc. (New))

BURROW MNG INC (NV)
Common $0.001 par split (10) for (1) by issuance of (9) additional shares payable 05/14/2010 to holders of record 05/06/2010 Ex date - 05/17/2010
Name changed to True 2 Beauty Inc. 05/21/2010
True 2 Beauty Inc. name changed to LegacyXChange, Inc. 07/30/2015

BURRUS MLS INC (DE)
4.5% Preferred $100 par called for redemption 09/11/1972
Liquidation completed
Each share Common no par exchanged for initial distribution of $20 cash 02/01/1973
Each share Common no par received second distribution of $6 cash 06/15/1973
Each share Common no par received third distribution of $4.50 cash 09/30/1974
Each share Common no par received fourth and final distribution of $1.60 cash 01/18/1983

BURRY BISCUIT CORP. (DE)
Each share Common 50¢ par exchanged for (4) shares Common $0.125 par 00/00/1936
$1.25 Preferred called for redemption 10/14/1961
Acquired by Quaker Oats Co. 01/05/1962
Each share Common $0.125 par exchanged for (0.33333333) share Common $5 par
Quaker Oats Co. acquired by PepsiCo, Inc. 08/02/2001

BURSCOTT GOLD MINES LTD. (ON)
Charter revoked for failure to file reports and pay taxes 01/00/1971

BURST AGRITECH INC (DE)
Name changed 07/01/1983
Name changed from Burst Products, Inc. to Burst Agritech, Inc. 07/01/1983
Charter cancelled 03/01/1993

BURST COM INC (DE)
Name changed to Democrasoft, Inc. 04/27/2010
Democrasoft, Inc. name changed to Democrasoft Holdings, Inc. 04/22/2013

BURT (F.N.) CO. LTD.
Merged into Moore Corp. Ltd. 00/00/1939
Each share 7% Preference exchanged for (1) share 7% Conv. Preference Ser. A $100 par
Each share Common exchanged for (0.75) share Common $1 par
Moore Corp. Ltd. name changed to Moore Corp. Ltd.-Corporation Moore Ltee. (ON) 06/07/1976 which reincorporated in Canada 06/03/2002 which name changed to Moore Wallace Inc. 05/15/2003 which was acquired by Donnelley (R.R.) & Sons Co. 02/27/2004

BURT SPORTS TECHNOLOGY INC (DE)
Charter cancelled and declared inoperative and void for non-payment of taxes 03/01/1999

BURTON ADVERTISING INC (MI)
Plan of reorganization under Chapter 11 Federal Bankruptcy Act confirmed 07/08/1985
No stockholders' equity

BURTON DISTRIBUTING CO., INC. (NY)
Charter cancelled and proclaimed dissolved for failure to pay taxes 12/15/1954

BURTON DIXIE CORP (DE)
Merged into Bur-Dix Corp. 05/30/1981
Each share Common $12.50 par exchanged for $8 cash

BURTON ENERGY & SOLAR TECHNOLOGY INC (DE)
Charter forfeited for failure to maintain a registered agent 11/04/1990

BURTON (E.) ENTERPRISES, INC. (UT)
Name changed to Inducon Funding Corp. 10/09/1989
Inducon Funding Corp. name changed to U. S. International Group, Ltd. 02/11/1993

BURTON GROUP PLC (UNITED KINGDOM)
ADR agreement terminated 05/01/1995
Each ADR for Ordinary exchanged for approximately $8.47 cash

BURTON HAWKS INC (CO)
Reincorporated under the laws of Delaware as Hawks Industries, Inc. (DE) 12/29/1988
Hawks Industries, Inc. (DE) reincorporated in Wyoming 02/02/1998 which reincorporated in Nevada 02/18/2000 which name changed to Emex Corp. 02/20/2001
(See Emex Corp.)

BURTON MANUFACTURING CO. (IL)
Common $1 par split (2) for (1) by issuance of (1) additional share 01/20/1955
Common $1 par changed to 10¢ par 06/16/1961
Preferred $20 par called for redemption 07/01/1963
Adjudicated bankrupt 11/01/1966
No stockholders' equity

BURTON MOUNT CORP. (NY)
Name changed to Poly Repro International Ltd. 11/07/1962
(See Poly Repro International Ltd.)

BURTON SOHIGIAN INC (MI)
Stock Dividend - 100% 10/30/1974
Name changed to Burton Advertising Inc. 06/24/1977
(See Burton Advertising Inc.)

BURWELL GOLD MINES LTD.
Bankrupt 00/00/1939
Stockholders' equity unlikely

BURWILL HLDGS LTD (BERMUDA)
ADR agreement terminated 05/26/1998
Each Sponsored ADR for Ordinary exchanged exchanged for approximately $1.52 cash

BURYATZOLOTO PJSC (RUSSIA)
Name changed 10/21/2016
Name changed from Buryatzoloto JSC to Buryatzoloto PJSC 10/21/2016
ADR agreement terminated 08/07/2017
Each Sponsored ADR for Ordinary exchanged for $11.909985 cash

BUS BERZELIUS UMWELT SVC A G (GERMANY)
Merged into Nordag AG 06/10/2003
Details not available

BUS HLDGS CORP (BC)
Name changed to Savannah Ventures Ltd. 11/17/1997
Savannah Ventures Ltd. recapitalized as International Savannah Ventures Ltd. 12/01/1998 which name changed to Softcare EC.com, Inc. 06/10/1999 which name changed to Softcare EC Inc. 10/05/2001 which recapitalized as Open EC Technologies, Inc. 06/23/2003
(See Open EC Technologies, Inc.)

BUS SYS INC (CANADA)
Name changed to SUB Capital Inc. 12/29/2008
SUB Capital Inc. name changed to Inca One Metals Corp. 05/11/2011 which name changed to Inca One Resources Inc. 10/26/2011 which name changed to Inca One Gold Corp. 09/17/2014

BUSANDA EXPLORATIONS INC (NV)
Name changed to Image Innovations Holdings, Inc. 08/26/2003
(See Image Innovations Holdings, Inc.)

BUSCAR OIL INC (NV)
Name changed to Buscar Co. 06/15/2015

BUSH & RANK CINTEL LTD. (ENGLAND)
Name changed to Rank Radio & Television Ltd. 12/03/1962
(See Rank Radio & Television Ltd.)

BUSH ACQUISITION CORP. (MN)
Statutorily dissolved 04/14/2005

BUSH BOAKE ALLEN INC (VA)
Merged into International Flavors & Fragrances Inc. 11/08/2000
Each share Common $1 par exchanged for $48.50 cash

BUSH HOG, INC. (DE)
Acquired by Fulton Industries, Inc. (GA) 10/04/1966
Each share Common $1 par exchanged for (0.5) share $1 Class A Conv. Preferred $10 par
Fulton Industries, Inc. (GA) name changed to FII Liquidating Co. 04/30/1968
(See FII Liquidating Co.)

BUSH INDS INC (DE)
Class A Common 10¢ par split (3) for (2) by issuance of (0.5) additional share 02/05/1987
Class B Common 10¢ par split (3) for (2) by issuance of (0.5) additional share 02/05/1987
Class A Common 10¢ par split (3) for (2) by issuance of (0.5) additional share 04/18/1988
Class B Common 10¢ par split (3) for (2) by issuance of (0.5) additional share 04/18/1988
Class A Common 10¢ par split (3) for (2) by issuance of (0.5) additional share 01/07/1994
Class A Common 10¢ par split (5) for (4) by issuance of (0.25) additional share 01/20/1995
Class A Common 10¢ par split (3) for (2) by issuance of (0.5) additional share payable 06/28/1996 to holders of record 06/14/1996 Ex date - 07/01/1996
Plan of reorganization under Chapter 11 Federal Bankruptcy Code effective 11/12/2004
Each share Class A Common 10¢ par exchanged for approximately $0.062 cash
Note: Each share Class A Common 10¢ par received an additional distribution of approximately $0.054 cash 06/05/2006

BUSH MANUFACTURING CO. (CT)
Merged into Dunham-Bush, Inc. 06/29/1956
Each share Common $5 par exchanged for (3.5) shares Common $2 par
Dunham-Bush, Inc. merged into Signal Oil & Gas Co. 12/29/1967

which name changed to Signal Companies, Inc. 05/01/1968 which merged into Allied-Signal Inc. 09/19/1985 which name changed to AlliedSignal Inc. 04/26/1993 which name changed to Honeywell International Inc. 12/01/1999

BUSH TERMINAL BUILDINGS CO. (NY)
Reorganized 00/00/1939
Each share old 7% Preferred $100 par exchanged for (1) share new 7% Preferred $100 par and (0.2) share Bush Terminal Co. 6% Preferred $100 par
Recapitalized 00/00/1952
Each share Common $5 par exchanged for (50) shares Common 10¢ par
New 7% Preferred $100 par called for redemption 06/01/1954
5% Prior Preferred $50 par called for redemption 05/20/1955
Liquidation completed
Each share Common 10¢ par received initial distribution of $36 cash 06/14/1963
Each share Common 10¢ par exchanged for second distribution of $4.285 cash 02/31/1964
Each share Common 10¢ par received third and final distribution of $1.28131 cash 12/28/1966
(See listing for Bush Terminal Co.)

BUSH TERMINAL CO. (NY)
Reorganized 00/00/1938
Each share 7% Debenture Stock $100 par exchanged for (4) shares Common $1 par
Common no par exchanged for Common $1 par
Name changed to Bush Universal Inc. 07/22/1968
Bush Universal Inc. merged into Katy Industries, Inc. 10/01/1975

BUSH UNVL INC (NY)
Merged into Katy Industries, Inc. 10/01/1975
Each share Common $1 par exchanged for (0.555555) share $1.46 Class B Conv. Preferred no par
(See Katy Industries, Inc.)

BUSHMAN RESOURCES INC (BC)
Cease trade order effective 05/24/2002
Stockholders' equity unlikely

BUSHMILL WINE & PRODUCTS CO., INC.
Name changed to Brookside Distilling Products Corp. 00/00/1939
(See Brookside Distilling Products Corp.)

BUSHMILLS ENERGY CORP (AB)
Merged into Brooklyn Energy Corp. 02/03/2003
Each share Common no par exchanged for (0.6484214) share Common no par and $0.4412628 cash
Note: Unexchanged certificates were cancelled and became without value 02/03/2009
(See Brooklyn Energy Corp.)

BUSHNELL COMMUNICATIONS LTD (ON)
Class A no par reclassified as Common no par 04/30/1970
Merged into Standard Broadcasting Corp. Ltd. 09/05/1980
Each share Common no par exchanged for $16 cash

BUSHNELL TV CO. LTD. (ON)
Name changed to Bushnell Communications Ltd. 07/22/1969
(See Bushnell Communications Ltd.)

BUSINESS & PROFESSIONAL BK (WOODLAND, CA)
Stock Dividend - 5% payable 03/01/1996 to holders of record 01/31/1996
Merged into U.S. Bancorp 05/01/1997
Each share Common no par exchanged for $18 cash

BUSINESS ASSETS MGMT INC (OR)
Involuntarily dissolved for failure to file reports and pay fees 02/19/1998

BUSINESS AUTOMATION & SYS INC (CO)
Name changed to Jeremiah Corp. 05/22/1976
Jeremiah Corp. merged into October Oil Co. (New) 10/18/1982
(See October Oil Co. (New))

BUSINESS BANCORP NEW (CA)
Stock Dividends - 5% payable 06/28/2002 to holders of record 06/14/2002; 5% payable 06/27/2003 to holders of record 06/13/2003
Ex date - 06/11/2003
Merged into UnionBanCal Corp. 01/16/2004
Each share Common no par exchanged for $28.57 cash

BUSINESS BANCORP OLD (CA)
Merged into SJNB Financial Corp. 09/30/1994
Each share Common no par exchanged for (0.531323) share Common no par and $3.7125 cash
SJNB Financial Corp. merged into Greater Bay Bancorp 10/23/2001 which merged into Wells Fargo & Co. (New) 10/01/2007

BUSINESS BK CALIF (SAN BERNARDINO, CA)
Common no par split (5) for (4) by issuance of (0.25) additional share payable 08/27/1999 to holders of record 08/06/1999
Under plan of reorganization each share Common no par automatically became (1) share Business Bancorp (New) Common no par 01/21/2000
(See Business Bancorp (New))

BUSINESS BK CORP (NV)
Merged into City National Corp. 02/28/2007
Each share Common $1 par exchanged for $66.50 cash

BUSINESS BANKING CO. (OR)
Merged into Valley National Corp. (OR) 08/01/1985
Each share Common $4 par exchanged for (1.35) shares Common $1 par
Valley National Corp. (OR) acquired by U.S. Bancorp (OR) 06/01/1987 which merged into U.S. Bancorp (Old) (DE) 08/01/1997 which merged into U.S. Bancorp (New) 02/27/2001

BUSINESS CAP CORP (IL)
Reincorporated under the laws of Nevada as Dallas Business Capital Corp. 03/13/1973
Dallas Business Capital Corp. (NV) reincorporated in Delaware as Bizcap Inc. 03/29/1983 which name changed to Caribbean Marine Inc. 12/03/1986
(See Caribbean Marine Inc.)

BUSINESS CAPITAL CORP. (DE)
Liquidation completed 08/23/1951
Details not available

BUSINESS CARDS TOMORROW INC (DE)
Name changed to American Franchise Group, Inc. 10/06/1988
American Franchise Group, Inc. name changed to BCT International, Inc. 07/31/1992
(See BCT International, Inc.)

BUSINESS COMPUTER NETWORK INC (WY)
Charter revoked for non-payment of taxes 03/04/1987

BUSINESS COMPUTER SOLUTIONS INC (FL)
Proclaimed dissolved for failure to file reports and pay fees 09/11/1990

BUSINESS COMPUTING INTL INC (NY)
Dissolved by proclamation 01/25/2012

BUSINESS CONTINUITY SOLUTIONS INC (FL)
Name changed to Tall Trees LED Co. 08/05/2016
Tall Trees LED Co. recapitalized as Light Engine Design Corp. 12/21/2016

BUSINESS DATA GROUP INC (DE)
Each share Common $0.001 par exchanged for (0.1) share Common 1¢ par 10/31/1985
Name changed to Roadrunner Video Group, Inc. 08/31/1995
(See Roadrunner Video Group, Inc.)

BUSINESS DEV CORP S C (SC)
Each share old Common no par exchanged for (0.01) share new Common no par 06/17/1996
Note: In effect holders received $3.20 cash per share and public interest was eliminated

BUSINESS DEV SOLUTIONS INC (DE)
SEC revoked common stock registration 10/17/2013

BUSINESS ENGINEERING SCIENCE TECHNOLOGY DISCOVERIES FD INC (ON)
Reorganized as Tier One Capital L.P. 07/11/2014
Each Class L Share exchanged for (0.67717142) Unit of Ltd. Partnership

BUSINESS EXCHANGE INC (CA)
Charter cancelled for failure to file reports and pay taxes 10/01/1993

BUSINESS FDS INC (DE)
Reincorporated 06/04/1969
State of incorporation changed from (MD) to (DE) and Capital Stock $8 par reclassified as Common $1 par 06/04/1969
Name changed to Marathon Manufacturing Co. 12/08/1969
Marathon Manufacturing Co. merged into Penn Central Corp. 12/18/1979 which name changed to American Premier Underwriters, Inc. 03/25/1994 which merged into American Premier Group, Inc. 04/03/1995 which name changed to American Financial Group, Inc. 06/09/1995 which merged into American Financial Group, Inc. (Holding Co.) 12/02/1997

BUSINESS FIRST NATL BANK (SANTA BARBARA, CA)
Merged into Heritage Oaks Bancorp 10/12/2007
Each share Common $5 par exchanged for (0.5758) share Common no par and $3.44 cash
Heritage Oaks Bancorp merged into Pacific Premier Bancorp, Inc. 03/31/2017

BUSINESS JOURNAL N J INC (NJ)
Name changed to Corfacts Inc. 03/01/1990

BUSINESS LIQUIDATORS INC (DE)
Name changed to Cardiac Electronics, Inc. 06/03/1980
Cardiac Electronics, Inc. name changed to Digital Diagnostics Corp. 12/21/1989
(See Digital Diagnostics Corp.)

BUSINESS MENS ASSURN CO AMER (MO)
Each share Common $100 par exchanged for (10) shares Common $10 par 12/21/1954
Common $10 par changed to $4 par and (1.5) additional shares issued 01/07/1959
Common $4 par changed to $2 par and (1) additional share issued 04/30/1965
Common $2 par changed to $1 par and (1) additional share issued 06/07/1985
Stock Dividends - 33.5% 01/26/1922; 12.5% 06/21/1923; 10% 01/11/1926; 58.33333333% 08/22/1929; 100% 03/06/1941; 90% 12/31/1945; 100% 12/21/1950; 100% 12/21/1954; 25% 05/04/1961; 20% 04/25/1962
Under plan of reorganization each share Common $1 par automatically became (1) share BMA Corp. Common $1 par 06/01/1988
BMA Corp. name changed to Seafield Capital Corp. 05/20/1991 which name changed to Lab Holdings Inc. 10/20/1997 which name changed to LabOne, Inc. (New) 08/10/1999
(See LabOne, Inc. (New))

BUSINESS MOTIVATION INC (MN)
Common 5¢ par changed to 2¢ par 07/01/1969
Out of business 08/00/1975
No stockholders' equity

BUSINESS NEWS NETWORK INC (NV)
Name changed to BNN Corp. (NV) 11/08/1994
BNN Corp. (NV) reincorporated in Delaware as Kaleidoscope Media Group, Inc. 12/05/1997
(See Kaleidoscope Media Group, Inc.)

BUSINESS OBJECTS S A (FRANCE)
Sponsored ADR's for Ordinary split (2) for (1) by issuance of (1) additional ADR payable 05/14/1996 to holders of record 05/10/1996
Sponsored ADR's for Ordinary split (2) for (1) by issuance of (1) additional ADR payable 01/20/2000 to holders of record 01/19/2000
Sponsored ADR's for Ordinary split (3) for (2) by issuance of (0.5) additional ADR payable 03/12/2001 to holders of record 03/09/2001
Ex date - 02/22/2001
Acquired by SAP France S.A. 02/04/2008
Each Sponsored ADR no par exchanged for $62.14514 cash

BUSINESS OUTSOURCING SVCS INC (NV)
Name changed to Orgenesis Inc. 09/02/2011

BUSINESS PLUS INC (DE)
Recapitalized as Edgewater Petroleum Ltd. 08/03/1994
Each share Common $0.00001 par exchanged for (0.001) share Common $0.001 par
Edgewater Petroleum Ltd. recapitalized as English Furniture Industries, Inc. 06/30/1995
(See English Furniture Industries, Inc.)

BUSINESS PPTY ASSOC (MA)
Trust Shares $100 par changed to $5 par and (19) additional shares issued 01/31/1962
Merged into Bradley Real Estate Trust (MA) 09/27/1969
Each Trust Share $5 par exchanged for (2.05) Trust Shares $1 par
Bradley Real Estate Trust (MA) reorganized in Maryland as Bradley Real Estate, Inc. 10/17/1994
(See Bradley Real Estate, Inc.)

BUSINESS RECORDS CORP HLDG CO (DE)
Name changed to BRC Holdings Inc. 05/16/1996
(See BRC Holdings Inc.)

BUSINESS RECOVERY CORP.
Trust terminated 00/00/1936
Details not available

BUSINESS RESOURCE GROUP (CA)
Merged into BR Holdings LLC 08/18/2000
Each share Common 1¢ par exchanged for $9.25 cash

BUSINESS RES INC (NV)
Charter revoked for failure to file reports and pay fees 06/01/1989

BUSINESS SYS INTL INC (AB)
Assets sold for the benefit of creditors 04/00/1995
No stockholders' equity

BUSINESS TRAINING INTL INC (ID)
Name changed to Freiberg Silver Inc. 01/22/1990
Freiberg Silver Inc. name changed to Inter Stop Travel Centers, Inc. 05/06/1991
(See Inter Stop Travel Centers, Inc.)

BUSINESS TRANSLATION SVCS INC (NV)
Name changed to Muller Media Inc. 01/22/2002
Muller Media Inc. recapitalized as China Jiangsu Golden Horse Steel Ball, Inc. 10/05/2007 which recapitalized as Santana Mining Inc. 12/24/2008
(See Santana Mining Inc.)

BUSINESS TR EQUAL WEIGHT INCOME FD (ON)
Merged into Brompton VIP Income Fund 07/04/2008
Each Trust Unit no par received either (0.691945) Trust Unit no par or $9.3998 cash
Note: Option to receive cash expired 07/31/2008
Brompton VIP Income Fund name changed to Aston Hill VIP Income Fund 09/16/2011 which name changed to LOGiQ VIP Income Fund 05/12/2017 which name changed to Redwood Monthly Income Fund 12/20/2017 which merged into Purpose Multi-Asset Income Fund 05/04/2018

BUSINESS VALET SVCS CORP (NV)
Name changed to CTI Technology Inc. 06/06/2000
CTI Technology Inc. reorganized as Dover Holding Co. 02/10/2003

BUSINESS VENTURES CORP. (UT)
Name changed to Cherry Creek Gold Corp. 08/18/1993
Cherry Creek Gold Corp. name changed to Toner Systems International, Inc. (UT) 12/30/1994 which reincorporated in Nevada 02/09/1998 which reorganized as Trident Systems International, Inc. 01/25/2001 which name changed to AAMPRO Group, Inc. 01/07/2003
(See AAMPRO Group, Inc.)

BUSINESS VN INC (NV)
Recapitalized as Omni Global Technologies, Inc. 11/18/2016
Each share Common $0.001 par exchanged for (0.00666666) share Common $0.001 par
Note: No holder will receive fewer than (100) post-split shares
Omni Global Technologies, Inc. name changed to Blockchain Industries, Inc. 01/10/2018

BUSINESS WAY INTL CORP (FL)
Recapitalized as ICBS International Corp. (FL) 12/01/2004
Each share Common $0.001 par exchanged for (0.2) share Common $0.001 par
ICBS International Corp. (FL) reorganized in Delaware as Wah King Invest Corp. 06/09/2005 which name changed to Royal Invest International Corp. 03/01/2007

BUSINESSLAND INC (CA)
Merged into JWP Inc. 11/13/1991
Each share Common no par exchanged for (0.06557) share Common 10¢ par
(See JWP Inc.)

BUSINESSMALL COM (NV)
Charter revoked for failure to file a current list of officers 07/01/2002

BUSINESSMANS FD INC (NY)
Merged into MagnaCap Fund Inc. 09/22/1972
Each share Capital Stock 50¢ par exchanged for (1.2252) shares Capital Stock 10¢ par
MagnaCap Fund Inc. name changed to Pilgrim MagnaCap Fund, Inc. 06/20/1985
Pilgrim MagnaCap Fund, Inc. merged into Pilgrim Investment Funds, Inc. 07/03/1992 which name changed to Pilgrim America Investment Funds, Inc. 07/14/1995 which name changed back to Pilgrim Investment Funds, Inc. 11/16/1998 which name changed to ING Investment Funds, Inc. 03/01/2002

BUSINESSNET HLDGS CORP (DE)
Recapitalized 08/28/1998
Recapitalized from Businessnet International Inc. to Businessnet Holdings Corp. 08/28/1998
Each share old Common 1¢ par exchanged for (0.02) share new Common 1¢ par
New Common 1¢ par split (2) for (1) by issuance of (1) additional share payable 07/30/1999 to holders of record 07/23/1999
Name changed to Invicta Corp. 06/30/2000
Invicta Corp. name changed to Executive Hospitality Corp. 05/02/2005 which recapitalized as Forest Resources Management Corp. 08/09/2006
(See Forest Resources Management Corp.)

BUSSIERES MINING CO. LTD. (QC)
Recapitalized as Cournor Mining Co. Ltd. 00/00/1937
Each share Common no par exchanged for (0.2) share Common no par
Cournor Mining Co. Ltd. recapitalized as Courvan Mining Co. Ltd. 08/17/1960 which name changed to Courvan Mining Co. Ltd./ Societe Miniere Courvan Ltee. 02/24/1982 which recapitalized as Rutter Technologies Inc. (QC) 07/25/2002 which reorganized in Canada as Rutter Inc. 03/31/2004
(See Rutter Inc.)

BUSTOP SHELTERS NEV INC (NV)
Merged into a private company 05/12/2000
Each share Common no par exchanged for $9.636398 cash

BUSYBOX COM INC (DE)
Filed a petition under Chapter 7 Federal Bankruptcy Code 07/30/2001
Stockholders' equity unlikely

BUTALMA MINES LTD.
Dissolved 00/00/1948
Details not available

BUTE RES INC (BC)
Merged into American Pyramid Resources Inc. 07/24/1979
Each share Common no par exchanged for (0.5) share Common no par
(See American Pyramid Resources Inc.)

BUTEC INTL CHEM CORP (BC)
Recapitalized as International Butec Industries Corp. 05/05/1988
Each share Common no par exchanged for (0.33333333) share Common no par
International Butec Industries Corp. recapitalized as WebSmart.com Communications, Inc. 10/17/2000 which name changed to Gold Reach Resources Ltd. 10/13/2004 which name changed to Surge Copper Corp. 02/21/2018

BUTLER AVIATION INTL INC (DE)
Name changed to Butler International, Inc. (DE) 06/20/1974
Butler International, Inc. (DE) merged into North American Ventures, Inc. 02/02/1987 which recapitalized as Butler International Inc. (MD) 06/29/1992
(See Butler International Inc. (MD))

BUTLER BROTHERS (IL)
Common $20 par changed to $10 par 00/00/1933
Common $10 par changed to $15 par 12/00/1944
5% Conv. Preferred called for redemption 02/09/1945
Name changed to B.T.L. Corp. 02/11/1960
B.T.L. Corp. merged into McCrory Corp. 07/16/1960 which merged into Rapid-American Corp. 03/12/1976
(See Rapid-American Corp.)

BUTLER BUILDING LIQUIDATION TRUST
Liquidation completed 02/02/1959
Details not available

BUTLER CAP CORP (NY)
Name changed to Butler Publishing Corp. 05/22/1973
Butler Publishing Corp. name changed to Macro Communications, Inc. (NY) 01/27/1977 which reincorporated in Nevada as First Capital Holdings Corp. 04/27/1983
(See First Capital Holdings Corp.)

BUTLER (P.H.) CO.
Name changed to Thorofare Markets Inc. 00/00/1949
Thorofare Markets Inc. name changed to Thorofare Corp. 05/21/1982 which name changed to Casablanca Industries Inc. 01/31/1983
(See Casablanca Industries Inc.)

BUTLER CONS COAL CO (PA)
Dissolved 11/13/1974
Details not available

BUTLER DEVS CORP (BC)
Recapitalized as Butler Resource Corp. 02/12/2009
Each share Common no par exchanged for (0.125) share Common no par
Butler Resource Corp. name changed to Quantum Rare Earth Developments Corp. 03/04/2010 which name changed to NioCorp Developments Ltd. 03/04/2013

BUTLER ENGR INC (LA)
Merged into Butler Engineering Co., Inc. (NJ) 11/15/1977
Each share Capital Stock 10¢ par exchanged for $0.75 cash

BUTLER (JAMES) GROCERY CO.
Bankrupt 00/00/1936
Details not available

BUTLER INTL INC (DE)
Common $1 par split (5) for (4) by issuance of (0.25) additional share 08/27/1976
Common $1 par split (4) for (3) by issuance of (0.33333333) additional share 08/26/1977
Common $1 par split (4) for (3) by issuance of (0.33333333) additional share 02/27/1979
Common $1 par split (2) for (1) by issuance of (1) additional share 02/27/1980
Merged into North American Ventures, Inc. 02/02/1987
Each share Common $1 par exchanged for (0.2802) share Common $0.001 par and $16 cash
North American Ventures, Inc. recapitalized as Butler International Inc. (MD) 06/29/1992
(See Butler International Inc. (MD))

BUTLER INTL INC NEW (MD)
Common $0.001 par split (3) for (2) by issuance of (0.5) additional share payable 06/01/1999 to holders of record 05/16/1999
Chapter 11 bankruptcy proceedings dismissed 04/01/2010
No stockholders' equity

BUTLER JOHN O CO (DE)
Common 1¢ par split (3) for (2) by issuance of (0.5) additional share 05/23/1986
Common 1¢ par split (4) for (3) by issuance of (0.33333333) additional share 11/17/1986
Acquired by Sunstar Inc. 09/12/1988
Each share Common 1¢ par exchanged for $25 cash

BUTLER MFG CO (DE)
Reincorporated 12/15/1969
Reorganized 00/00/1937
Each share 7% Preferred $100 par exchanged for (1) share 6% Preferred $100 par, (1) share Common $25 par and $6 cash
Common stockholders surrendered (1) share for each (5) shares held (1) additional share issued 09/30/1966
Stock Dividends - 50% 06/30/1943; 50% 06/29/1946; 200% 09/24/1951; 100% 11/12/1954; 100% 01/24/1969
State of incorporation changed from (MO) to (DE) 12/15/1969
4.5% Class A Preferred $100 par called for redemption 12/01/1978
Common no par split (2) for (1) by issuance of (1) additional share 01/04/1974
Common no par split (3) for (2) by issuance of (0.5) additional share 10/19/1976
Common no par split (3) for (2) by issuance of (0.5) additional share 07/17/1995
Merged into BlueScope Steel Ltd. 04/27/2004
Each share Common no par exchanged for $22.50 cash

BUTLER MILLS
Merged into Hoosac Mills Corp. 00/00/1931
Details not available

BUTLER (JIM) MINING CO.
Out of existence 00/00/1949
Details not available

BUTLER MTN MINERALS CORP (BC)
Name changed 01/11/1983
Name changed from Butler Mountain Moly Corp. to Butler Mountain Minerals Corp. 01/11/1983
Struck off register and declared dissolved for failure to file returns 05/17/1991

BUTLER NATL CORP (DE)
Reincorporated under the laws of Kansas 01/29/2002

BUTLER PUBG CORP (NY)
Name changed to Macro Communications, Inc. (NY) 01/27/1977
Macro Communications, Inc. (NY) reincorporated in Nevada as First Capital Holdings Corp. 04/27/1983
(See First Capital Holdings Corp.)

BUTLER RAILWAYS CO.
In process of liquidation 00/00/1941
Details on amount of distributions, if any, are not available

BUTLER RESOURCE CORP (BC)
Name changed to Quantum Rare Earth Developments Corp. 03/04/2010
Quantum Rare Earth Developments Corp. name changed to NioCorp Developments Ltd. 03/04/2013

BUTLER SUBURBAN WATER CO.
Property sold to Butler Water Co.
00/00/1942
Details not available

BUTLERS SHOE CORP (FL)
Name changed 06/10/1959
Name changed from Butler's Inc. to
Butler's Shoe Corp. 06/10/1959
Common $1 par split (4) for (3) by
issuance of (0.33333333) additional
share 09/14/1959
Common $1 par split (4) for (3) by
issuance of (0.33333333) additional
share 03/01/1966
Common $1 par split (5) for (4) by
issuance of (0.25) additional share
12/30/1968
4.5% Preferred $25 par called for
redemption 03/01/1969
Merged into Zale Corp. 09/11/1969
Each share Common $1 par
exchanged for (1) share 80¢ Conv.
Preferred Ser. A $1 par
(See Zale Corp.)

BUTTE & SUPERIOR MINING CO.
Liquidated 00/00/1940
Details not available

BUTTE CMNTY BK (PARADISE, CA)
Common no par split (4) for (3) by
issuance of (0.33333333) additional
share 07/01/1995
Common no par split (4) for (3) by
issuance of (0.33333333) additional
share payable 07/08/1996 to holders
of record 07/01/1996
Common no par split (4) for (3) by
issuance of (0.33333333) additional
share payable 11/14/1997 to holders
of record 10/31/1997
Common no par split (4) for (3) by
issuance of (0.33333333) additional
share payable 11/15/1999 to holders
of record 11/01/1999
Under plan of reorganization each
share Common no par automatically
became (1) share Community Valley
Bancorp Common no par
06/17/2002
(See Community Valley Bancorp)

BUTTE COPPER & ZINC CO. (ME)
Acquired by Logan (Jonathan), Inc.
02/02/1960
Each share Capital Stock $5 par
exchanged for (1) share Common
50¢ par
(See Logan (Jonathan), Inc.)

BUTTE COPPER CONSOLIDATED MINES (SD)
Charter cancelled for failure to file
annual reports 00/00/1970

BUTTE COPPER CZAR MINING CO. (MT)
Charter expired by time limitation
03/24/1957

BUTTE ENERGY INC (AB)
Reincorporated under the laws of
British Columbia 06/19/2018

BUTTE HIGHLANDS MNG CO (DE)
Each share Capital Stock $1 par
exchanged for (0.66666666) share
Common 10¢ par 00/00/1937
Common 10¢ par reclassified as
Class A Common 1¢ par 10/20/1996
Note: Holders who could not be
located will have their interests
represented in Non-Vtg. Class B
Common 1¢ par held by a trustee
until valid claim is made
Class A Common 1¢ par changed to
$0.001 par 02/02/2012
Reincorporated under the laws of
Nevada as Ironclad Encryption
Corp. 03/02/2017
Ironclad Encryption Corp. (NV)
reincorporated in Delaware
10/16/2017

BUTTE PACIFIC COPPER CO. (MT)
Charter expired by time limitation
09/25/1932

BUTTE RES LTD (CANADA)
Recapitalized as Kingtron
International Inc. 09/22/1989
Each share Common no par
exchanged for (0.25) share Common
no par
(See Kingtron International Inc.)

BUTTER ROCK RES INC (BC)
Name changed to INN Investment
News Network Ltd. 09/25/1992
INN Investment News Network Ltd.
name changed to Interactive Telesis,
Inc. (BC) 03/01/1994 which
reincorporated in Delaware
09/23/1996
(See Interactive Telesis, Inc.)

BUTTERFIELD EQUITIES CORP (CA)
Chapter 11 Federal Bankruptcy Code
converted to Chapter 7 on
03/22/1990
Stockholders' equity unlikely

BUTTERFLY HOSIERY CO. LTD. (QC)
Acquired by Belding-Corticelli Ltd.
07/01/1962
Details not available

BUTTERICK CO., INC. (NY)
Reorganized 00/00/1936
Reorganized from Butterick
Publishing Co. to Butterick Co., Inc.
00/00/1936
Each share Common exchanged for
(0.05) share Common no par
Common no par changed to $1 par
04/30/1956
Preferred $50 par called for
redemption 04/30/1965
Common $1 par changed to 20¢ par
and (4) additional shares issued
06/11/1965
Stock Dividend - 50% 07/17/1967
Acquired by American Can Co.
01/19/1968
Each share Common 20¢ par
exchanged for (0.55) share Common
$12.50 par
American Can Co. name changed to
Primerica Corp. (NJ) 04/28/1987
which was acquired by Primerica
Corp. (DE) 12/15/1988 which name
changed to Travelers Inc.
12/31/1993 which name changed to
Travelers Group Inc. 04/16/1995
which name changed to Citigroup
Inc. 10/08/1998

BUTTERWORTH (H.W.) & SONS CO. (PA)
Merged into Van Norman Industries,
Inc. 00/00/1956
Each share Common $10 par
exchanged for (1.23) shares
Common $2.50 par
Van Norman Industries, Inc. merged
into Universal American Corp. (DE)
(Ctfs. dtd. prior to 01/12/1968)
01/31/1962 which merged into Gulf
& Western Industries, Inc. (DE)
01/12/1968
(See Gulf & Western Industries, Inc. (DE))

BUTTES GAS & OIL CO (PA)
Reincorporated 11/30/1977
Reorganized 02/16/1989
Common $1 par changed to no par
05/00/1960
5% Preferred $1 par called for
redemption 07/15/1962
State of incorporation changed from
(CA) to (DE) and Common no par
changed to 10¢ par 11/30/1977
Reorganized from Delaware to under
the laws of Pennsylvania 02/16/1989
Each share $2.10 Conv. Preferred
10¢ par exchanged for (1.695)
shares Common 1¢ par
Each share Common 10¢ par
exchanged for (1) share Common
1¢ par
Reorganized under the laws of
Delaware as Reunion Resources
Co. 06/28/1993
Each share new Common 1¢ par
exchanged for (0.003) share
Common 1¢ par
Reunion Resources Co. name
changed to Reunion Industries, Inc.
04/19/1996

BUTTES OILFIELDS, INC. (CA)
Merged into Buttes Gas & Oil Co.
(CA) 00/00/1954
Each share Class A Common $1 par
exchanged for (1) share 5%
Preferred $1 par and (1) share
Common $1 par
Buttes Gas & Oil Co. (CA)
reincorporated in Delaware
11/30/1977 which reorganized in
Pennsylvania 02/16/1989 which
reorganized in Delaware as Reunion
Resources Co. 06/28/1993 which
name changed to Reunion
Industries, Inc. 04/19/1996

BUTTLE LAKE MNG LTD (BC)
Merged into Stampede International
Resources Ltd. 05/25/1970
Each share Capital Stock 50¢ par
exchanged for (1) share Capital
Stock no par
Stampede International Resources
Ltd. merged into Stampede
International Resources Inc.
05/31/1982 which merged into
International H.R.S. Industries Inc.
05/15/1984 which name changed to
Glenex Industries Inc. 05/25/1987
which merged into Quest Investment
Corp. 07/04/2002 which merged into
Quest Capital Corp. (BC)
06/30/2003 which reincorporated in
Canada 05/27/2008 which name
changed to Sprott Resource Lending
Corp. 09/10/2010 which merged into
Sprott Inc. 07/24/2013

BUTTON GWINNETT BANCORP INC (GA)
Name changed to Button Gwinnett
Financial Corp. 01/25/1993
Button Gwinnett Financial Corp.
merged into Premier Bancshares,
Inc. (New) 07/01/1998 which
merged into BB&T Corp. 01/13/2000

BUTTON GWINNETT FINL CORP (GA)
Merged into Premier Bancshares, Inc.
(New) 07/01/1998
Each share Common 1¢ par
exchanged for (3.885) shares
Common $1 par
Premier Bancshares Inc. (New)
merged into BB&T Corp. 01/13/2000

BUTTONWOOD CAPITAL CORP. (DE)
Completely liquidated 02/01/1967
Each share Capital Stock $1 par
exchanged for first and final
distribution of $23.90 cash

BUTTONWOOD SECS INC (CA)
Charter suspended for failure to pay
06/00/1973

BUTTREY FOOD & DRUG STORES CO (DE)
Merged into Locomotive Acquisition
Corp. 10/05/1998
Each share Common 1¢ par
exchanged for $15.50 cash

BUTTREY FOODS, INC. (MT)
Merged into Jewel Companies, Inc.
06/15/1966
Each share Common no par
exchanged for (0.7) share Common
$1 par
Jewel Companies, Inc. merged into
American Stores Co. (New)
11/16/1984 which merged into
Albertson's, Inc. 06/23/1999 which
merged into Supervalu Inc.
06/02/2006

BUVAL EXECUTIVE MNG INDS (BC)
Struck off register and declared
dissolved for failure to file returns
10/22/1979

BUVAL MINES LTD. (BC)
Name changed to Buval Executive
Mining Industries Ltd. and Capital
Stock 50¢ par changed to no par
11/24/1969
(See Buval Executive Mining
Industries Ltd.)

BUY COM INC (DE)
Merged into SB Acquisition, Inc.
11/27/2001
Each share Common $0.0001 par
exchanged for $0.17 cash

BUY IT CHEAP COM INC (DE)
Recapitalized as Advanced Battery
Technologies, Inc. 07/12/2004
Each share Common $0.001 par
exchanged for (0.1) share Common
$0.001 par
(See Advanced Battery Technologies, Inc.)

BUY THE HOUR, INC. (UT)
Name changed to Manufacturers &
Investors Technologies Inc.
04/20/1988
(See Manufacturers & Investors
Technologies Inc.)

BUYER ONE INC (DE)
Charter cancelled and declared
inoperative and void for
non-payment of taxes 03/01/1989

BUYERS UNITED INC (DE)
Name changed to UCN, Inc.
07/15/2004
UCN, Inc. name changed to
inContact, Inc. 01/01/2009
(See inContact, Inc.)

BUYERS UTD INTL INC (UT)
Reorganized under the laws of
Delaware as BUI Inc. 04/09/1999
Each share Common no par
exchanged for (0.25) share Common
$0.0001 par
BUI Inc. name changed to
Buyersonline.com Inc. 04/20/2000
which name changed to Buyers
United Inc. 11/20/2001 which name
changed to UCN, Inc. 07/15/2004
which name changed to inContact,
Inc. 01/01/2009
(See inContact, Inc.)

BUYERSONLINE COM INC (DE)
Name changed to Buyers United Inc.
11/20/2001
Buyers United Inc. name changed to
UCN, Inc. 07/15/2004 which name
changed to inContact, Inc.
01/01/2009
(See inContact, Inc.)

BUYIT COM INC (UT)
Name changed to Craftclick.com, Inc.
(UT) 01/10/2000
Craftclick.com, Inc. (UT) reorganized
in Delaware 05/07/2000 which name
changed to Mobilepro Corp.
06/19/2001

BUYONATE INC (NV)
Name changed to China Electronics
Holdings, Inc. 08/23/2010

BUZZ MEDIA LTD (NV)
Name changed to Sinobiopharma,
Inc. 08/01/2008
(See Sinobiopharma, Inc.)

BUZZ TELECOMMUNICATIONS SVCS INC (CANADA)
Name changed to Knowlton Capital
Inc. (New) 01/21/2014
Knowlton Capital Inc. (New)
recapitalized as LGC Capital Ltd.
07/19/2016

BUZZARDS BAY GAS CO. (MA)
6% Prior Preferred $25 par called
03/25/1963

BUZZARDS BAY NATL BK (BUZZARDS BAY, MA)
Stock Dividends - 20% 03/11/1952;
13.33333333% 06/19/1959; 100%
09/01/1966; 50% 03/01/1971
Merged into Cape Cod Bank & Trust
Co. (Hyannis, MA) 05/15/1974
Each share Common $100 par

exchanged for (4) shares Common $10 par
Cape Cod Bank & Trust Co. (Hyannis, MA) reorganized as CCBT Bancorp Inc. 02/11/1999 which name changed to CCBT Financial Companies Inc. 09/23/1999 which merged into Banknorth Group, Inc. (ME) 04/30/2004 which merged into TD Banknorth Inc. 03/01/2005
(See TD Banknorth Inc.)

BV MEDIA INC (CANADA)
Acquired by Rogers Media Inc. 10/01/2010
Each share Common no par exchanged for $0.40 cash

BV PHARMACEUTICAL INC (NV)
Common $0.001 par split (4) for (1) by issuance of (3) additional shares payable 02/23/2006 to holders of record 02/20/2006
Name changed to Radial Energy Inc. 04/10/2006
Radial Energy Inc. recapitalized as iPure Labs Inc. 06/23/2014

BVBC CAP TR I (DE)
10.375% Guaranteed Trust Preferred Securities called for redemption at $8 on 9/30/2005

BVR SYSTEMS (1998) LTD. (ISRAEL)
Name changed to R.V.B. Holdings Ltd. 03/02/2010
R.V.B. Holdings Ltd. name changed to Eviation Aircraft Ltd. 03/02/2017

BVR TECHNOLOGIES LTD (ISRAEL)
Each share Ordinary NIS 0.50 par received distribution of (1) share B.V.R. Systems (1998) Ltd. Common NIS 1 par payable 10/29/1998 to holders of record 10/22/1998
Name changed to Technoprises Ltd. and Ordinary NIS 0.50 par changed to no par 04/25/2004
(See Technoprises Ltd.)

BW / IP INC (DE)
Name changed 05/11/1994
Name changed from BWIP Holding, Inc. to BW/IP Inc. and Common 1¢ par reclassified as Common 1¢ par 05/11/1994
Merged into Flowserve Corp. 07/22/1997
Each share Common 1¢ par exchanged for (0.6968) share Common $1.25 par

BW TECHNOLOGIES LTD (AB)
Acquired by First Technology Acquisition Canada Inc. 06/17/2004
Each share Common no par exchanged for $36 cash

BWANA M'KUBWA COPPER MINING CO., LTD.
Liquidated 00/00/1935
Details not available

BWAY CORP (DE)
Common 1¢ par split (3) for (2) by issuance of (0.5) additional share payable 09/22/1997 to holders of record 09/02/1997 Ex date - 09/23/1997
Merged into BCO Holding Co. 02/07/2003
Each share Common 1¢ par exchanged for $20 cash

BWAY HLDG CO (DE)
Acquired by Picasso Parent Co., Inc. 06/16/2010
Each share Common 1¢ par exchanged for $20 cash

BWC FINL CORP (CA)
Common no par split (2) for (1) by issuance of (1) additional share payable 07/20/1998 to holders of record 07/10/1998
Stock Dividends - 10% 06/30/1995; 10% payable 08/15/1996 to holders of record 07/31/1996; 10% payable 02/17/1998 to holders of record 02/03/1998; 10% payable 08/15/2000 to holders of record 08/01/2000; 10% payable 06/15/2001 to holders of record 05/25/2001 Ex date - 05/23/2001; 10% payable 07/31/2002 to holders of record 07/15/2002 Ex date - 07/11/2002; 10% payable 12/22/2003 to holders of record 12/05/2003; 10% payable 01/05/2005 to holders of record 12/27/2004 Ex date - 12/22/2004
Merged into First Republic Bank (San Francisco, CA) 10/16/2006
Each share Common no par exchanged for (0.97) share Common 1¢ par
First Republic Bank (San Francisco, CA) merged into Merrill Lynch & Co., Inc. 09/21/2007 which was acquired by Bank of America Corp. 01/02/2009

BWC LIQUIDATING CORP. (DE)
Liquidation completed
Each share Common $5 par exchanged for initial distribution of $48 cash 03/18/1980
Each share Common $5 par received second and final distribution of $0.07098 cash 07/16/1980

BWI HLDGS INC (NV)
Old Common $0.001 par split (5) for (1) by issuance of (4) additional shares payable 01/30/2009 to holders of record 01/20/2009 Ex date - 02/02/2009
Each share old Common $0.001 par exchanged for (0.1) share new Common $0.001 par 08/16/2014
Name changed to Aquasil International Inc. and Common $0.001 par changed to $0.0001 par 02/18/2011
Aquasil International Inc. recapitalized as Multi-Corp International Inc. 06/22/2012

BWI RES LTD (BC)
Recapitalized as Penteco Resources Ltd. 01/02/2001
Each share Common no par exchanged for (0.25) share Common no par
Penteco Resources Ltd. name changed to Pennant Energy Inc. 04/30/2004 which merged into Blackbird Energy Inc. 04/22/2014

BWIN INTERACTIVE (AUSTRIA)
Merged into PartyGaming PLC 03/31/2011
Each ADR for Common exchanged for $19.563608 cash

BWT AG (AUSTRIA)
ADR agreement terminated 05/01/2013
Each Sponsored ADR for Ordinary exchanged for $21.41481 cash

BXL ENERGY LTD (AB)
Acquired by Viking Energy Royalty Trust 06/21/2001
Each share Common no par exchanged for either (0.333) Trust Unit no par or (0.20852) Trust Unit no par and $1.12 cash
Note: Option to receive Trust Units and cash expired 08/24/2001
Viking Energy Royalty Trust merged into Harvest Energy Trust 02/07/2006
(See Harvest Energy Trust)

BXP CONSTRUCTION CORP. (DE)
Merged into Concept Housing Corp. 11/30/1970
Each share 7% Conv. Preferred $10 par exchanged for (1) VTC for Common $1 par
Each share Common $1 par exchanged for (2) VTC's for Common $1 par

BY & C MGMT INC (FL)
Common $0.001 par split (8.25) for (1) by issuance of (7.25) additional shares payable 01/18/2002 to holders of record 01/17/2002 Ex date - 01/22/2002
Name changed to Mediabus Networks Inc. 01/24/2002
Mediabus Networks Inc. name changed to Presidion Corp. 02/28/2003
(See Presidion Corp.)

BY & G VENTURES CORP (BC)
Recapitalized as Load Resources Ltd. 11/19/1997
Each share Common no par exchanged for (0.25) share Common no par
Load Resources Ltd. name changed to GIS Global Imaging Solutions, Inc. 05/31/2000 which name changed to Segami Images Inc. 02/05/2001
(See Segami Images Inc.)

BY DESIGN INC (NV)
Name changed to Global Gate Property Corp. 08/26/2010
(See Global Gate Property Corp.)

BY-PRODUCTS COKE CORP. (NY)
Name changed to Interlake Iron Corp. 00/00/1929
Interlake Iron Corp. name changed to Interlake Steel Corp. (NY) 12/22/1964 which reincorporated in Delaware as Interlake, Inc. 05/15/1970 which reorganized as Interlake Corp. 05/29/1986
(See Interlake Corp.)

BY WORD CORP (CT)
Common $1 par changed to 10¢ par 09/12/1973
Name changed to B.W. Group, Inc. 09/10/1984
(See B.W. Group, Inc.)

BYCOM SYS INC (GA)
Name changed to Superior Holding Corp. 08/22/1985
Superior Holding Corp. name changed to Superior TeleTec Inc. 08/21/1989 which merged into Alpine Group, Inc. 11/10/1993
(See Alpine Group, Inc.)

BYER-ROLNICK CORP. (DE)
Common $10 par changed to $5 par and (1) additional share issued 08/09/1966
Liquidation completed
Each share Common $5 par exchanged for initial distribution of $9.65 cash 12/27/1967
Each share Common $5 par received second and final distribution of $0.14972 cash 10/10/1968

BYER-ROLNICK HAT CORP. (DE)
Name changed to Byer-Rolnick Corp. 11/19/1963
(See Byer-Rolnick Corp.)

BYERS A M CO (PA)
Common no par changed to $10 par 07/03/1957
Common 10 par changed to $3.33333333 par and (2) additional shares issued 10/02/1959
Common $3.33333333 par changed to $2.50 par and (0.25) additional share issued 02/09/1965
Merged into General Tire & Rubber Co. 11/30/1970
Each share Common $2.50 par exchanged for (0.814) share Common 30¢ par
General Tire & Rubber Co. name changed to GenCorp Inc. (OH) 03/30/1984 which reincorporated in Delaware 04/14/2014 which name changed to Aerojet Rocketdyne Holdings, Inc. 04/27/2015

BYERS COMMUNICATIONS SYSTEMS, INC. (GA)
Common $1 par split (3) for (2) by issuance of (0.5) additional share 03/26/1984
Name changed to BYCOM Systems, Inc. 03/25/1985
BYCOM Systems, Inc. name changed to Superior Holding Corp. 08/22/1985 which name changed to Superior TeleTec Inc. 08/21/1989 which merged into Alpine Group, Inc. 11/10/1993
(See Alpine Group, Inc.)

BYERS INC (DE)
Charter cancelled and declared inoperative and void for non-payment of taxes 06/26/1990

BYERS MACHINE CO. (OH)
Liquidation completed 06/10/1955
Details not available

BYL BANCORP (CA)
Common no par split (4) for (3) by issuance of (0.33333333) additional share payable 06/30/1998 to holders of record 06/06/1998
Merged into First Banks America, Inc. 11/01/2001
Each share Common no par exchanged for $18.50 cash

BYLINE CORP (FL)
Proclaimed dissolved for failure to file reports and pay fees 11/10/1983

BYLLESBY (H.M.) & CO. (DE)
$2 Preferred no par changed to $10 par 00/00/1942
Class A and B Common no par changed to 10¢ par 00/00/1942
Each share $2 Preferred $10 par exchanged for (2) shares 5% Preferred $25 par and (2) shares Common 10¢ par 00/00/1952
Each share Class A Common 10¢ par exchanged for (1.5) shares Common 10¢ par 00/00/1952
Each share Class B Common 10¢ par exchanged for (1) share Common 10¢ par 00/00/1952
Common 10¢ par split (2) for (1) by issuance of (1) additional share 10/23/1961
Name changed to Advance Ross Corp. (Old) 04/23/1964
Advance Ross Corp. (Old) reorganized as Advance Ross Corp. (New) 06/17/1993 which merged into CUC International Inc. 01/10/1996 which name changed to Cendant Corp. 12/17/1997 which reorganized as Avis Budget Group, Inc. 09/01/2006

BYLLESBY CORP. (DE)
Merged into Byllesby (H.M.) & Co. 00/00/1952
Each share Common 10¢ par exchanged for (1) share new Common 10¢ par
Byllesby (H.M.) & Co. name changed to Advance Ross Corp. (Old) 04/23/1964 which reorganized as Advance Ross Corp. (New) 06/17/1993 which name changed to CUC International Inc. 01/10/1996 which name changed to Cendant Corp. 12/17/1997 which reorganized as Avis Budget Group, Inc. 09/01/2006

BYMART, INC.
Recapitalized as Bymart-Tintair, Inc. 00/00/1951
Each share 5% Preferred $100 par exchanged for (10) shares 5% Preferred $10 par
Each share Common $1 par exchanged for (2) shares Common 50¢ par
Bymart-Tintair, Inc. name changed to Tintair, Inc. 07/12/1966
(See Tintair, Inc.)

BYMART-TINTAIR, INC. (DE)
5% Preferred $10 par changed to $1 par 00/00/1952
Common 50¢ par changed to 1¢ par 00/00/1952
Name changed to Tintair, Inc. 07/12/1966
(See Tintair, Inc.)

BYNAMICS INC (ON)
Discharged from bankruptcy
03/24/1985
No stockholders' equity

BYNET INC (DE)
Charter cancelled and declared void for failure to pay franchise taxes
03/01/2001

BYRD OIL CORP. (DE)
Name changed to Bayview Oil Corp.
08/28/1957
(See Bayview Oil Corp.)

BYRNDUN CORP. (NY)
$3 Participating Preferred no par called for redemption 03/15/1960
$5 Class A Participating Preferred no par called for redemption 03/15/1960
7% 2nd Preferred $100 par called for redemption 05/02/1960
Merged into Hat Corp. of America 05/02/1960
Each share Class A Common $10 par or Common $1 par exchanged for (2.84) shares Common $1 par
Hat Corp. of America name changed to HCA Industries, Inc. 04/30/1970 which name changed to HCA-Martin, Inc. 05/11/1973 which name changed to Martin Processing, Inc. 05/16/1975
(See Martin Processing, Inc.)

BYRON AMERICOR INC (ON)
Name changed to Ungava Mines Inc.
10/12/2007

BYRON CORP. (NJ)
Name changed to Valley Industries, Inc. 07/03/1969
(See Valley Industries, Inc.)

BYRON GLOBAL CORP (ON)
Recapitalized as Byron Americor Inc.
07/30/2007
Each share Common no par exchanged for (0.1) share Common no par
Byron Americor Inc. name changed to Ungava Mines Inc. 10/12/2007

BYRON JACKSON CO. (DE)
Common no par changed to $10 par and (0.4) additional share issued
00/00/1951
Merged into Borg-Warner Corp. (IL)
09/01/1955
Each share Common $10 par exchanged for (0.8) share Common $5 par
Borg-Warner Corp. (IL) reincorporated in Delaware 10/31/1967
(See Borg-Warner Corp. (DE))

BYRON JACKSON PUMP CO.
Name changed to Byron Jackson Co.
00/00/1929
Byron Jackson Co. merged into Borg-Warner Corp. (IL) 09/01/1955 which reincorporated in Delaware 10/31/1967
(See Borg-Warner Corp. (DE))

BYRON RES INC (BC)
Recapitalized as Select Ventures Inc.
09/03/1992
Each share Common no par exchanged for (0.33333333) share Common no par
Select Ventures Inc. recapitalized as Majestic Gold Corp. 12/03/1996

BYRON RES INC (ON)
Recapitalized as Byron Global Corp.
08/11/2004
Each share Common no par exchangeda for (0.1) share Common no par
Byron Global Corp. recapitalized as Byron Americor Inc. 07/30/2007 which name changed to Ungava Mines Inc. 10/12/2007

BYTEC COMTERM INC (CANADA)
Name changed back to Comterm Inc.
07/25/1984
(See Comterm Inc.)

BYTEX CORP (DE)
Merged into Network Systems Corp.
11/24/1993
Each share Common 10¢ par exchanged for $6.80 cash

BZURA CHEMICAL CO., INC. (DE)
Adjudicated bankrupt 03/02/1964
No stockholders' equity

C

C / GRIP: INC (OK)
Name changed to Worldwide Energy Inc. 09/25/1998
Worldwide Energy Inc. name changed to Worldwide E Commerce Inc.
12/16/1999

C. & S. INVESTMENT CO. (CA)
Liquidation completed
Each share Common 50¢ par stamped to indicate initial distribution of $5 cash 11/17/1965
Each share Stamped Common 50¢ par stamped to indicate second distribution of $3.71 cash 08/29/1966
Each share Stamped Common 50¢ par exchanged for third and final distribution of $0.745 cash 10/04/1967

C. W. LIQUIDATING CO.
Liquidation completed
Each share Common no par received initial distribution of $8 cash 07/26/1943
Each share Common no par received second distribution of $2.75 cash 05/16/1944
Each share Common no par received third and final distribution of $0.105 cash 12/31/1945

C & A RESTAURANTS INC (NV)
Reorganized as USSE Corp. (NV)
07/08/2009
Each share Common $0.001 par exchanged for (3) shares Common $0.001 par
USSE Corp. (NV) reincorporated in Delaware as Quick Start Holdings, Inc. 10/12/2018

C & C INDS CORP LTD (BERMUDA)
Name changed to Xenex Minerals Ltd. 01/11/2008
(See Xenex Minerals Ltd.)

C & C INVTS INC (NJ)
Name changed to T.O.P.S. Medical, Corp. 12/22/1987

C & C SUPER CORP. (DE)
Name changed to C & C Television Corp. 08/05/1957
C & C Television Corp. recapitalized as Television Industries, Inc.
06/18/1958 which name changed to Trans-Beacon Corp. 05/05/1966
(See Trans-Beacon Corp.)

C & C TELEVISION CORP. (DE)
Recapitalized as Television Industries, Inc. 06/18/1958
Each share Common 10¢ par exchanged for (0.1) share Common $1 par
Television Industries, Inc. name changed to Trans-Beacon Corp.
05/05/1966
(See Trans-Beacon Corp.)

C & C YACHTS LTD (ON)
Merged into Delplax Holdings Ltd.
12/22/1991
Each share Common no par exchanged for $6 cash

C & E CONCEPTS INC (UT)
Name changed to Newcastle Financial Corp. 07/09/1985

C & E FURNITURE INDS INC (BC)
Cease trade order effective
05/28/1993
Stockholders' equity unlikely

C & F ELECTRONICS, INC. (UT)
Charter revoked for failure to file reports and pay fees 09/29/1961

C & G DEC CAP INC (FL)
Name changed to Energiz Renewable Inc. 06/02/2010
(See Energiz Renewable Inc.)

C & H BANCORP (OH)
Acquired by Fifth Third Bancorp 04/01/1988
Each share Common no par exchanged for (1) share Common no par

C & K PETE INC (DE)
Stock Dividend - 50% 07/15/1977
Merged into Alaska Interstate Co. (AK) 10/24/1980
Each share Common 10¢ par exchanged for $35 cash

C & M CAP CORP (CO)
Each share old Common no par exchanged for (0.001) share new Common no par 05/05/1993
Name changed to American Entertainment Group, Inc.
05/18/1993

C & R CLOTHIERS INC (DE)
Common 1¢ par split (3) for (1) by issuance of (2) additional share 01/18/1980
Stock Dividend - 50% 01/17/1973
Prepackaged Plan of Reorganization under Chapter 11 Federal Bankruptcy proceedings confirmed 01/13/1993
No stockholders' equity

C & R ENTERPRISES INC (CO)
Company believed out of business
07/28/1989
Details not available

C & S BANCORPORATION (GA)
Name changed to FCB Financial Corp. 01/23/2002

C & S SOVRAN CORP (DE)
Merged into NationsBank Corp. (NC)
12/31/1991
Each share Common $1 par exchanged for (0.84) share Common $2.50 par
NationsBank Corp. (NC) reincorporated in Delaware as BankAmerica Corp. (Old) 09/25/1998 which merged into BankAmerica Corp. (New) 09/30/1998 which name changed to Bank of America Corp. 04/28/1999

C & U COMMUNICATIONS CORP. (NY)
Common $10 par changed to $5 par and (1) additional share issued
05/02/1966
5% Class D Preferred $50 par called for redemption 04/30/1967
Acquired by Continental Telephone Corp. 01/18/1968
Each share 4.5% Class A Preferred $100 par or 4.5% Class B Ser. A Preferred $100 par exchanged for (4) shares 5% Preferred 1961 Ser. $25 par
Each share Common $5 par exchanged for (1) share Common $1 par
Continental Telephone Corp. name changed to Continental Telecom Inc. 05/06/1982 which name changed to Contel Corp. 05/01/1986 which merged into GTE Corp. 03/14/1991 which merged into Verizon Communications Inc. 06/30/2000

C & W PRECISION PRODS INC (NY)
Name changed to Supply Resources, Inc. 06/29/1972
(See Supply Resources, Inc.)

C A BANCORP CDN RLTY FIN CORP (ON)
Name changed to NorRock Realty Finance Corp. 05/30/2011
(See NorRock Realty Finance Corp.)

C A BANCORP INC (AB)
Each share old Common no par exchanged for (0.1) share new Common no par 04/30/2007
Name changed to Crosswinds Holdings Inc. 09/26/2014

C A BLOCKERS INC (DE)
Charter cancelled and declared inoperative and void for non-payment of taxes 03/01/1991

C A E INDS LTD (CANADA)
Common no par split (3) for (2) by issuance of (0.5) additional share
07/10/1965
Common no par reclassified as Conv. Class A Common no par 01/02/1975
Conv. Class A Common no par reclassified as Common no par and (2) additional shares issued
07/20/1979
Conv. Class B Common no par reclassified as Common no par and (2) additional shares issued
07/20/1979
Common no par split (3) for (1) by issuance of (2) additional shares
07/21/1981
Common no par split (2) for (1) by issuance of (1) additional share
07/10/1984
Common no par split (2) for (1) by issuance of (1) additional share
07/10/1986
Name changed to CAE Inc.
09/15/1993

C A LA ELECTRICIDAD DE CARACAS SACA CORPORACION EDC SACA (VENEZUELA)
Stock Dividend - 16.66666666% payable 03/24/1999 to holders of record 03/12/1999
ADR agreement terminated
02/04/2009
Each Sponsored ADR for Ordinary exchanged for (50) shares Ordinary
Note: Unexchanged ADR's will be sold and the proceeds, if any, held for claim after 02/04/2010

C A SHORT INTL INC (OH)
Name changed to Pages, Inc. (OH)
11/16/1992
Pages, Inc. (OH) reincorporated in Delaware 10/13/1994 which recapitalized as Media Source Inc.
03/09/1999
(See Media Source Inc.)

C A VENEZOLANA DE PULPA Y PAPEL S A C A (VENEZUELA)
Name changed to Venepal S.A.C.A.
04/15/1997
(See Venepal S.A.C.A.)

C ATS SOFTWARE INC (DE)
Merged into Moxie Acquisition Corp.
01/22/1999
Each share Common $0.001 par exchanged for $7.50 cash

C B & T INC (TN)
Merged into Union Planters Corp.
07/07/1998
Each share Common $2.50 par exchanged for (5.488) shares Common $5 par
Union Planters Corp. merged into Regions Financial Corp. (New)
07/01/2004

C B BIOSCIENCES INC (NV)
Name changed to ANGO World Holdings, Inc. 01/07/2016

C.B.M.I. CORP. (CO)
Liquidation completed
Each share Common 25¢ par exchanged for initial distribution of $4 cash 05/14/1976
Each share Common 25¢ par received second and final distribution of $0.80 cash
11/01/1977

C BRDG INTERNET SOLUTIONS INC (DE)
Merged into eXcelon Corp. 09/20/2001
Each share Common 1¢ par exchanged for (1.2517) shares Common $0.0001 par
(See eXcelon Corp.)

C.C. LIQUIDATING CO. (PA)
Liquidation completed
Each share Common $1 par stamped to indicate initial distribution of $4 cash 03/26/1973
Each share Stamped Common $1 par stamped to indicate second distribution of $3.50 cash 10/25/1963
Each share Stamped Common $1 par exchanged for third and final distribution of $0.63 cash 01/06/1964

C C C CODED COMMUNICATIONS CORP (BC)
Recapitalized as CCI Coded Communications Inc. (BC) 10/21/1992
Each share Common no par exchanged for (0.33333333) share Common no par
CCI Coded Communications Inc. (BC) reincorporated in Delaware as Coded Communications Corp. 08/27/1993
(See Coded Communications Corp.)

C C R VIDEO CORP (DE)
Charter cancelled and declared inoperative and void for non-payment of taxes 06/26/1990

C C W SYS LTD (BC)
Struck off register and declared dissolved for failure to file returns 08/11/1995

C-CHIP TECHNOLOGIES CORP (NV)
Name changed to Manaris Corp. 08/09/2005
Manaris Corp. name changed to Avensys Corp. 12/12/2007 which name changed to Manaris (2010) Corp. 08/23/2010

C-COR INC (PA)
Name changed 07/19/1999
Name changed 06/26/2004
Common 10¢ par split (2) for (1) by issuance of (1) additional share 03/30/1989
Common 10¢ par split (2) for (1) by issuance of (1) additional share 12/05/1994
Name changed from C-Cor Electronics, Inc. to C-Cor.net Corp. 07/19/1999
Common 10¢ par split (2) for (1) by issuance of (1) additional share payable 01/06/2000 to holders of record 12/22/1999
Name changed from C-Cor.net Corp. to C-Cor Inc. 06/26/2004
Merged into ARRIS Group, Inc. (Old) 12/14/2007
Each share Common 10¢ par exchanged for (1.0245) shares Common 1¢ par and $0.688 cash
ARRIS Group, Inc. (Old) reorganized as ARRIS Group, Inc. (New) 04/16/2013 which merged into ARRIS International PLC 01/05/2016

C-CUBE MICROSYSTEMS INC (DE)
Common $0.001 par split (2) for (1) by issuance of (1) additional share 12/19/1995
Each share Common $0.001 par received distribution of (1) share C-Cube Semiconductor Inc. Common $0.001 par payable 05/02/2000 to holders of record 04/25/2000
Merged into Harmonic Inc. 05/03/2000
Each share Common $0.001 par exchanged for (0.5427) share Common $0.001 par

C-CUBE MICROSYSTEMS INC NEW (DE)
Merged into LSI Logic Corp. 06/11/2001
Each share Common $0.001 par exchanged for (0.79) share Common 1¢ par
LSI Logic Corp. name changed to LSI Corp. 04/06/2007
(See LSI Corp.)

C-CUBE SEMICONDUCTOR INC (DE)
Name changed to C-Cube Microsystems Inc. (New) 05/02/2000
C-Cube Microsystems Inc. (New) merged into LSI Logic Corp. 06/11/2001 which name changed to LSI Corp. 04/06/2007
(See LSI Corp.)

C D & M CO (UT)
Proclaimed dissolved for failure to pay taxes 03/31/1979

C D I CORP (PA)
Common 10¢ par split (2) for (1) by issuance of (1) additional share 11/02/1984
Common 10¢ par split (3) for (2) by issuance of (0.5) additional share 08/20/1985
Common 10¢ par split (3) for (2) by issuance of (0.5) additional share 08/10/1987
Common 10¢ par split (3) for (2) by issuance of (0.5) additional share 01/18/1989
Common 10¢ par split (2) for (1) by issuance of (1) additional share 08/30/1989
Acquired by Nova Merger Sub, Inc. 09/13/2017
Each share Common 10¢ par exchanged for $8.25 cash

C D W CORP (IL)
Merged into VH Holdings, Inc. 10/12/2007
Each share Common 1¢ par exchanged for $87.75 cash

C E C INDS CORP (NV)
Common 5¢ par changed to $0.001 par 03/01/2002
Each share old Common $0.001 par exchanged for (0.1) share new Common $0.001 par 10/01/1992
Each share new Common $0.001 par exchanged again for (0.01) share new Common $0.001 par 12/03/2002
Recapitalized as Advantage Capital Development Corp. 09/01/2004
Each share new Common $0.001 par exchanged for (0.1) share Common $0.001 par
(See Advantage Capital Development Corp.)

C E ENTMT (NV)
Name changed to American Sierra Gold Corp. 05/19/2009

C-E-I-R INC. (DE)
Class A $1 par changed to $0.33333333 par and (2) additional shares issued 09/00/1959
Class A $0.33333333 par changed to $0.16666666 par and (1) additional share issued 04/07/1961
Acquired by Control Data Corp. (MN) 11/22/1967
Each share Class A $0.16666666 par exchanged for (0.15748) share Common 50¢ par
Control Data Corp. (MN) merged into Control Data Corp. (DE) 08/17/1968 which name changed to Ceridian Corp. (Old) 06/03/1992
(See Ceridian Corp. (Old))

C E L INDS LTD (BC)
Under plan of reorganization each share Common no par exchanged for (1) share Ordinary Stock no par and $0.445 cash 03/08/1991
Name changed to Pan Smak Pizza Inc. 07/20/1995
(See Pan Smak Pizza Inc.)

C E M CENTRY ELECTR MONITORING CORP (AB)
Reorganized under the laws of British Columbia as Metalex Ventures Ltd. 03/31/1997
Each share Common no par exchanged for (0.19230769) share Common no par

C88 CAP CORP (AB)
Name changed to Kam & Ronson Media Group Inc. 03/29/2006
(See Kam & Ronson Media Group Inc.)

C.F.C. FUNDING INC. (NY)
Name changed to CFC Industries, Inc. 05/14/1962
(See CFC Industries, Inc.)

C F GREEN CORP (DE)
Each share old Common $0.0001 par exchanged for (3) shares new Common $0.0001 par 06/15/2004
Name changed to Eco-Safe Systems USA, Inc. 11/13/2006

C-F-M CO. (OH)
Out of business 06/30/1967
No stockholders' equity

C/FUNDS GROUP INC (FL)
Completely liquidated
Each share C/Fund $0.001 par received first and final distribution of $13.35 cash payable 04/28/2008 to holders of record 04/28/2008
Each share C/Growth Stock Fund $0.001 par received first and final distribution of $10.20 cash payable 04/28/2008 to holders of record 04/28/2008

C.G. SPRING & BUMPER CO.
Acquired by General Spring & Bumper Corp. 00/00/1929
Details not available

C G FD INC (DE)
Reincorporated under the laws of Maryland as CIGNA Growth Fund, Inc. 04/28/1983
CIGNA Growth Fund, Inc. (MD) reorganized in Massachusetts as CIGNA Funds Group Growth Fund 04/30/1985 which reincorporated in Delaware as Aim Funds Group 06/30/1992

C G INCOME FD INC (DE)
Reincorporated under the laws of Maryland as CIGNA Income Fund, Inc. (MD) 04/28/1983
CIGNA Income Fund, Inc. (MD) reorganized in Massachusetts as CIGNA Funds Group Income Fund 04/30/1985 which reincorporated in Delaware as AIM Funds Group 06/30/1992

C G MONEY MKT FD INC (MD)
Name changed to CIGNA Money Market Fund, Inc. (MD) 04/28/1983
CIGNA Money Market Fund, Inc. (MD) reorganized in Massachusetts as CIGNA Funds Group Money Market Fund 04/30/1985 which reincorporated in Delaware as AIM Funds Group 06/30/1992

C G MUN BD FD INC (MD)
Name changed to CIGNA Municipal Bond Fund, Inc. (MD) 04/28/1983
CIGNA Municipal Bond Fund, Inc. (MD) reorganized in Massachusetts as CIGNA Funds Group Municipal Bond Fund 04/30/1985 which reincorporated in Delaware as AIM Funds Group 06/30/1992

C G S SCIENTIFIC CORP (PA)
SEC revoked common stock registration 11/11/2010

C G S UNITS INC (NY)
Recapitalized as DMS Industries, Inc. 06/14/1974
Each share Common 1¢ par exchanged for (0.02222222) share Common 1¢ par
DMS Industries, Inc. name changed to Swissray International, Inc. (NY) 06/01/1995 which reincorporated in Delaware 07/11/2002
(See Swissray International, Inc.)

C G SMITH LTD (SOUTH AFRICA)
ADR agreement terminated 10/19/2004
Details not available

C H B FOODS INC (CA)
Stock Dividends - 50% 12/19/1975; 10% 06/24/1977
Acquired by California Home Brands, Inc. 05/21/1985
Each share Common $1 par exchanged for $16 cash

C.H.W. CO. (KY)
Completely liquidated 07/02/1963
Each share Capital Stock $5 par exchanged for first and final distribution of $6.75 cash

C.I.B., INC. (MD)
Liquidation completed
Each share Common 25¢ par exchanged for initial distribution of (1) share Charg-It of Florida, Inc. Common 25¢ par and $6.50 cash 02/07/1968
Each share Common 25¢ par received second and final distribution of $0.422 cash 03/29/1968

C I CONV FD INC (DE)
Name changed to Castle Convertible Fund, Inc. 02/06/1974

C-I CREDIT CORP. LTD. (ON)
Name changed to Realty Capital Corp. Ltd. 01/24/1969
Realty Capital Corp. Ltd. name changed to Federal Trustco Inc. 06/01/1979 which name changed to Realcap Holdings Ltd. 10/02/1980

C I FD MGMT INC (ON)
Name changed 11/04/2002
Common no par split (2) for (1) by issuance of (1) additional share payable 04/24/1998 to holders of record 04/21/1998 Ex date - 04/17/1998
Common no par split (2) for (1) by issuance of (1) additional share payable 01/28/2000 to holders of record 01/25/2000
Common no par split (2) for (1) by issuance of (1) additional share payable 11/10/2000 to holders of record 11/07/2000
Name changed from C.I. Fund Management Inc. to CI Fund Management Inc. 11/04/2002
Name changed to CI Financial Inc. 12/06/2005
CI Financial Inc. reorganized as CI Financial Income Fund 06/30/2006 which reorganized as CI Financial Corp. 01/01/2009

C I L INC (CANADA)
Merged into ICI Investments Canada Inc. 04/22/1988
Each share Common no par exchanged for $47 cash

C I MTG GROUP (MA)
Name changed to Enterprise Development Group 05/29/1981
(See Enterprise Development Group)

C I P CORP (OH)
Filed petition under Chapter 7 Federal Bankruptcy Code 01/19/1991
No stockholders' equity

C I RLTY INVS (MA)
Name changed to Kenilworth Realty Trust 09/04/1979
Kenilworth Realty Trust assets transferred to Kenilworth Realty Liquidating Trust 08/04/1981
(See Kenilworth Realty Liquidating Trust)

C.I.T. FINANCIAL CORP. (DE)
Common no par split (2) for (1) by

issuance of (1) additional share 12/06/1961
$5.50 Conv. Preference 1967 Ser. no par reclassified as $5.50 Conv. Preferred 1967 Ser. no par 04/28/1969
$5 Preferred 1965 Ser. no par called for redemption 12/31/1970
$5.50 Preferred 1967 Ser. no par conversion privilege expired 12/31/1976
$5.50 Preferred 1967 Ser. no par called for redemption 06/30/1977
$5.50 Conv. Preferred 1970 Ser. no par called for redemption 06/30/1977
Stock Dividend - 150% 01/30/1953
Merged into RCA Corp. 01/31/1980
Each share Common no par exchanged for (1) share $2.125 Conv. Preference no par and (1) share $3.65 Preference no par
(See RCA Corp.)

C J C INDS INC (DE)
Each share Common $0.0001 par exchanged for (0.1) share Common $0.001 par 05/29/1986
Name changed to Federated Medical, Inc. 03/17/1989
Federated Medical, Inc. name changed to Medical Depot, Inc. 11/20/1989
(See Medical Depot, Inc.)

C J I INDS INC (DE)
Adjudicated bankrupt 01/21/1975
Stockholders' equity unlikely

C.K.P. DEVELOPMENTS, INC. (DE)
Name changed to Deltona Corp. 11/12/1963
(See Deltona Corp.)

C.K.P. DEVELOPMENTS, LTD. (CANADA)
Assets transferred to C.K.P. Developments, Inc. 10/22/1962
C.K.P. Developments, Inc. name changed to Deltona Corp. 11/12/1963
(See Deltona Corp.)

C.L.C. AUTO RENTAL, INC. (NY)
Liquidation completed 12/18/1958
Details not available

C L FINL CORP (MD)
Name changed to California Life Corp. 05/20/1974
(See California Life Corp.)

C L I CORP (MA)
Common $1 par changed to 10¢ par and (9) additional shares issued 07/21/1967
Reincorporated under the laws of Delaware as Tallman Industries, Inc. 06/02/1972
Tallman Industries, Inc. merged into Data-Design Laboratories (CA) 04/30/1980 which reincorporated in Delaware as Data-Design Laboratories, Inc. 12/01/1986 which name changed to DDL Electronics, Inc. 12/17/1993 which name changed to SMTEK International, Inc. 10/09/1998 which merged into CTS Corp. 02/01/2005

C-L LIQ. CO., INC. (IL)
Liquidating distribution of $1.60 per share paid and each share Common $2.50 par exchanged for (1) Ctf. of Beneficial Interest in C-L Liq. Co., Inc. Liquidating Trust 01/08/1960
(See C-L Liq. Co., Inc. Liquidating Trust)

C-L LIQ. CO., INC. LIQUIDATING TRUST (IL)
Liquidation completed
Each Ctf. of Bene. Int. received initial distribution of $1.25 cash 06/03/1960
Each Ctf. of Bene. Int. received second distribution of $1.25 cash 06/02/1961
Each Ctf. of Bene. Int. received third distribution of $1.25 cash 07/02/1962
Each Ctf. of Bene. Int. received fourth distribution of $1.25 cash 07/12/1963
Each Ctf. of Bene. Int. received fifth distribution of $1.30 cash 07/14/1964
Each Ctf. of Bene. Int. received sixth distribution of $0.15 cash 07/19/1965
Each Ctf. of Bene. Int. received seventh distribution of $1 cash 10/25/1965
Each Ctf. of Bene. Int. received eighth distribution of $1.45 cash 04/04/1969
Each Ctf. of Bene. Int. received ninth distribution of $0.4252 cash 12/31/1969
Each Ctf. of Bene. Int. received tenth distribution of $3.60 cash 12/26/1974
Each Ctf. of Bene. Int. received eleventh and final distribution of $0.93 cash 06/26/1976
Note: Certificates were not required to be surrendered and are without value

C LEVEL BIO INTL HLDG INC (QC)
Recapitalized as Nevada Exploration Inc. 03/05/2007
Each share Common no par exchanged for (0.5) share Common no par

C LEVEL III INC (CANADA)
Name changed to Canoe Mining Ventures Corp. 12/09/2013

C LEVEL II INTL HLDG INC (CANADA)
Recapitalized as Canadian Oil Recovery & Remediation Enterprises Ltd. 06/30/2008
Each share Common no par exchanged for (0.33333333) share Common no par

C.M. CO. (OH)
Liquidation completed
Each share Common $1 par received initial distribution of $10 cash 10/31/1967
Each share Common $1 par received second distribution of (1) share International Assemblix Corp. Common no par 12/20/1967
Each share Common $1 par received third distribution of $1 cash 10/07/1968
Each share Common $1 par exchanged for fourth and final distribution of (1) Ctf. of Bene. Int. no par 11/05/1968
Each Ctf. of Bene. Int. no par exchanged for first and final distribution of $0.246849929 cash 07/20/1970

C M C INDS (UT)
Name changed to Andersen 2000, Inc. (UT) 07/09/1970
Andersen 2000, Inc. (UT) reorganized in Delaware 09/30/1971 which merged into Crown Andersen Inc. 01/31/1986
(See Crown Andersen Inc.)

C M CORP (IA)
Stock Dividend - 10% 10/26/1972
99.817% acquired by Beverly Enterprises, Inc. as of 11/01/1984
Public interest eliminated

C.M.E., INC. (MN)
Statutorily dissolved 10/04/1991

C.M.F. CORP. (MI)
Liquidated 00/00/1953
Details not available

C M INDS (CA)
Charter suspended for failure to file reports and pay fees 12/01/1980

C M L GLOBAL CAP LTD (CANADA)
Merged into 6223711 Canada Inc. 01/01/2005

Each share Common no par exchanged for $2.10 cash

C M LABS INC (DE)
Name changed to Techco Holdings, Inc. 12/11/1975
(See Techco Holdings, Inc.)

C M MAGNETICS CORP (DE)
Charter cancelled and declared inoperative and void for non-payment of taxes 06/27/1989

C M OLIVER INC (BC)
Recapitalized as Datawest Solutions Inc. 02/22/2000
Each share Common no par exchanged for (0.5) share Common no par
(See Datawest Solutions Inc.)

C-MAC INDS INC (CANADA)
Common no par split (2) for (1) by issuance of (1) additional share 09/30/1993
Merged into Solectron Corp. 12/03/2001
Each share Common no par exchanged for (1.755) shares Common $0.001 par or (1.755) Solectron Global Services Canada Inc. Exchangeable Shares no par
Note: Non-Canadian residents received Common
Solectron Corp. merged into Flextronics International Ltd. 10/01/2007 which name changed to Flex Ltd. 09/28/2016

C MAR INSTR CORP (NJ)
Charter declared void for non-payment of taxes 01/03/1967

C ME RUN CORP (DE)
SEC revoked common stock registration 03/27/2007

C.N.B. DATA SERVICES CORP. (CA)
Charter suspended for failure to file reports and pay fees 02/02/1987

C.N.I. LIQUIDATING CO. (DE)
Liquidation completed 03/27/1957
Each share Common $1 par received second and final distribution of $4.01 cash
(See Clinton Foods Inc. for previous distribution)
Note: Certificates were not required to be surrendered and are without value

C O G ENERGY SVCS INC (DE)
Name changed to Arjay International, Inc. 03/13/1985
Arjay International, Inc. recapitalized as Maxwell-Cox Group, Inc. 12/15/1989 which name changed to Digicom Corp. 06/18/1993 which name changed to Emery Ferron Energy Corp. 06/27/1994
(See Emery Ferron Energy Corp.)

C O M B CO (MN)
Common no par split (2) for (1) by issuance of (1) additional share 06/20/1986
Name changed to CVN Companies, Inc. 08/31/1987
CVN Companies, Inc. acquired by QVC Network, Inc. 10/31/1989 which name changed to QVC, Inc. 06/29/1994
(See QVC, Inc.)

C1 ENERGY LTD (AB)
Acquired by Penn West Energy Trust 09/25/2007
Each share Common no par exchanged for $0.20 cash

C.P. LIQUIDATING CORP. (DE)
Liquidation completed
Each share Common 5¢ par received initial distribution of $0.23 cash 12/27/1972
Each share Common 5¢ par received second distribution of $0.10 cash 07/00/1973
Each share Common 5¢ par received third distribution of $0.22 cash 03/15/1974
Each share Common 5¢ par exchanged for fourth and final distribution of $0.12 cash 01/06/1975

C P CLARE CORP (MA)
Name changed to Clare, Inc. 03/14/2001
Clare, Inc. merged into IXYS Corp. 06/10/2002
(See IXYS Corp.)

C P L CORP (RI)
Stock Dividend - 100% 10/10/1976
Merged into Whittaker Corp. (CA) 01/10/1979
Each share Common $1 par exchanged for $23.25 cash

C P LOTUS CORP (CAYMAN ISLANDS)
ADR agreement terminated 01/24/2018
No ADR's remain outstanding

C P M TECHNOLOGIES INC (AB)
Name changed to Grace Resources Inc. 08/18/1998
(See Grace Resources Inc.)

C P PRODS CORP (IN)
Merged into Coachmen Industries, Inc. 11/14/1980
Each share Common no par exchanged for (0.1) share Common no par
Coachmen Industries, Inc. name changed to All American Group, Inc. 06/11/2010
(See All American Group, Inc.)

C P RLTY TR (CA)
Reported in liquidation 00/00/1980
Details not available

C P REHAB CORP (NY)
Stock Dividend - 100% 03/02/1983
Reincorporated under the laws of Delaware as Prime Medical Services, Inc. (Old) 07/01/1986
Prime Medical Services, Inc. (Old) merged into Prime Medical Services, Inc. (New) 10/18/1993 which merged into HealthTronics, Inc. 11/10/2004
(See HealthTronics, Inc.)

C P T HLDGS INC (MN)
Reorganized 07/23/1991
Common 5¢ par split (3) for (1) by issuance of (2) additional shares 07/02/1981
Stock Dividends - 25% 05/15/1975; 25% 12/01/1975; 50% 09/22/1978; 50% 10/31/1979
Reorganized under Chapter 11 Federal Bankruptcy proceedings from CPT Corp. to CPT Holdings, Inc. 07/23/1991
Each share Common 5¢ par exchanged for (0.1) share Class B Common 5¢ par
Each share old Class A Common 5¢ par exchanged for (0.09090909) share new Class A Common 5¢ par 09/11/1992
Each share old Class B Common 5¢ par exchanged for (0.09090909) share new Class B Common 5¢ par 09/11/1992
Each share new Class A Common 5¢ par exchanged for (1) share new Common 5¢ par 09/29/1992
Each share new Class B Common 5¢ par exchanged for (1) share new Common 5¢ par 09/29/1992
Plan of reorganization under Chapter 11 Federal Bankruptcy Code effective 12/27/2005
No stockholders' equity

C-PHONE CORP (NY)
Completely liquidated
Each share Common 1¢ par received first and final distribution of $0.0175 cash payable 06/04/2012 to holders of record 05/29/2012

C.R-CAB

Note: Certificates were not required to be surrendered and are without value

C.R. LIQUIDATING CO. (DE)
Liquidation completed 11/30/1960
Details not available

C R G CORP (DE)
Charter cancelled and declared inoperative and void for non-payment of taxes 06/21/1979

C R H CATERING INC (PA)
Each share Preferred exchanged for $1 principal amount of 10% Subordinated Debenture Promissory Notes due 07/01/2005

C.R.M. CO.
Liquidation completed 11/20/1956
Details not available

C R X INC (NV)
Merged into Allied Waste Industries, Inc. 04/10/1996
Each share Common $0.001 par exchanged for $0.08 cash

C S BANCSHARES INC (IN)
Merged into Fifth Third Bancorp 08/25/1989
Each share Common $10 par exchanged for (1.06182) share Common no par

C S C INC (MN)
Name changed to Maple Plain Co., Inc. 08/27/1973
(See Maple Plain Co., Inc.)

C S D SECS LTD (CANADA)
Voluntarily dissolved 11/17/2007
Details not available

C S FINL CORP (OH)
Merged into Charter One Financial, Inc. 10/16/1998
Each share Common $5 par exchanged for (63.37149) shares Common 1¢ par
(See Charter One Financial, Inc.)

C S HLDG (SWITZERLAND)
Sponsored ADR's for Ordinary split (5) for (1) by issuance of (4) additional ADR's 12/28/1993
Name changed to Credit Suisse Group 01/01/1997

C S I COMPUTER SYS INC (OH)
Merged into Automatic Data Processing, Inc. 12/18/1972
Each share Common no par exchanged for (0.06666666) share Common 10¢ par

C S I CORP. (VA)
Name changed to CDP Control Corp. (VA) 02/04/1969
CDP Control Corp. (VA) reincorporated in Delaware as Professional Associates, Inc. 05/15/1974
(See Professional Associates, Inc.)

C-S LIQUIDATING CO., INC. (MO)
Liquidation completed
Each share Common no par exchanged for initial distribution of (0.28) share Consolidated Foods Corp. Common $1.33333333 par 05/08/1968
Each share Common no par received second distribution of (0.0250189) share Consolidated Foods Corp. Common $1.33333333 par 04/25/1969
Each share Common no par received third and final distribution of (0.0250189) share Consolidated Foods Corp. Common $1.33333333 par 02/28/1970
Consolidated Foods Corp. name changed to Sara Lee Corp. 04/02/1985 which recapitalized as Hillshire Brands Co. 06/29/2012
(See Hillshire Brands Co.)

C SQUARE VENTURES INC (TX)
Each share Common $0.0001 par exchanged for (0.03333333) share Common $0.003 par 11/13/1989
Each share new Common $0.003 par exchanged again for (0.025) share new Common $0.003 par 08/27/1996
Name changed to ConSyGen, Inc. 09/06/1996
(See ConSyGen, Inc.)

C SQUARED DEVS INC (BC)
Name changed to Dynasty Gold Corp. 05/14/2003

C T EXPLORANDA LTD (BC)
Name changed to Izone International Ltd. 04/28/1986
(See Izone International Ltd.)

C T I TECHNOLOGIES CORP (BC)
Recapitalized as World Videophone Teleconferencing Technologies Ltd. 03/29/1990
Each share Common no par exchanged for (0.2) share Common no par
(See World Videophone Teleconferencing Technologies Ltd.)

C TEC CORP (PA)
Common $1 par split (3) for (1) by issuance of (2) additional shares 05/25/1989
Conv. Class B Common $1 par split (3) for (1) by issuance of (2) additional shares 05/25/1989
Each share Common $1 par and Class B Common $1 par received distribution of (0.25) share Cable Michigan, Inc. Common $1 par and (1) share RCN Corp. Common $1 par payable 09/30/1997 to holders of record 09/19/1997
Stock Dividend - In Conv. Class B Common to holders of Common - 100% 04/25/1986
Recapitalized as Commonwealth Telephone Enterprises Inc. (New) 10/10/1997
Each share Common $1 par exchanged for (0.66666666) share Common $1 par
Each share Class B Common $1 par exchanged for (0.66666666) share Class B Common $1 par
Commonwealth Telephone Enterprises Inc. (New) merged into Citizens Communications Co. 03/08/2007 which name changed to Frontier Communications Corp. 07/31/2008

C TECH ENERGY SVCS INC (AB)
Merged into Dover Corp. 06/08/2005
Each share Common no par exchanged for $0.44 cash

C-THRU PRODUCTS INC. (NY)
Name changed to CTP Industries Inc. 04/25/1967
(See CTP Industries Inc.)

C V AMERN CORP (DE)
Liquidation completed
Each share Common $0.66666666 par received initial distribution of $10 cash 12/31/1986
Each share Common $0.66666666 par received second distribution of $4 cash 07/01/1987
Each share Common $0.66666666 par received third distribution of $1.90 cash 10/00/1988
Each share Common $0.66666666 par received fourth and final distribution of $0.36 cash 03/00/1990
Note: Certificates were not required to be surrendered and are without value

C V INTL CORP (DE)
Chapter 11 bankruptcy proceedings converted to Chapter 7 on 10/14/1983
No stockholders' equity

C.V.M. CORP. (MA)
Completely liquidated 06/26/1964
Details not available

C.W.C. LIQUIDATING CORP. (NY)
Liquidation completed 08/24/1956
Details not available

C W INDS GROUP INC (NV)
Charter revoked for failure to file reports and pay fees 05/01/1988

C.W.S. WAVEGUIDE CORP. (DE)
No longer in existence having become inoperative and void for non-payment of taxes 04/01/1965

C W TRANS INC (DE)
Stock Dividends - 20% 11/08/1968; 66.66666666% 03/17/1972
Merged into Gerber Products Co. 08/24/1979
Each share Common $1 par exchanged for (1) share Common $2.50 par
(See Gerber Products Co.)

C WATRE INTL INC (DE)
Recapitalized as Biomimix, Inc. 04/13/2009
Each share Common 5¢ par exchanged for for (0.00142857) share Common 5¢ par

C&C ENERGIA LTD (AB)
Plan of arrangement effective 01/03/2013
Each share Common no par exchanged for (0.3528) share Pacific Rubiales Energy Corp. new Common no par, (1) share Platino Energy Corp. Common no par and $0.001 cash
(See each company's listing)
Note: Unexchanged certificates were cancelled and became without value 01/03/2016

C&C FOODS, INC. (OH)
Name changed to Charlie Chan Restaurants, Inc. 02/12/1981
(See Charlie Chan Restaurants, Inc.)

C&D PRODTN INC (NV)
Name changed to Planet Nutrition Holdings, Inc. 07/30/2007
Planet Nutrition Holdings, Inc. recapitalized as GT Legend Automotive Holdings, Inc. 11/26/2008

C&D TECHNOLOGIES INC (DE)
Old Common 1¢ par split (2) for (1) by issuance of (1) additional share payable 07/24/1998 to holders of record 07/10/1998 Ex date - 07/27/1998
Old Common 1¢ par split (2) for (1) by issuance of (1) additional share payable 06/16/2000 to holders of record 06/02/2000 Ex date - 06/19/2000
Old Common 1¢ par split (1.37335) for (1) by issuance of (0.37335) additional share payable 12/30/2010 to holders of record 12/21/2010 Ex date - 12/31/2010
Each share old Common 1¢ par exchanged for (0.02857142) share new Common 1¢ par 03/15/2011
Acquired by Angel Acquisition Corp. (DE) 01/13/2012
Each share new Common 1¢ par exchanged for $9.75 cash

C&F ENTERPRISES, INC. (MO)
Charter forfeited for failure to file reports 01/01/1979

C&J ENERGY SVCS INC OLD (DE)
Merged into C&J Energy Services Ltd. 03/24/2015
Each share Common 1¢ par exchanged for (1) share Common 1¢ par
(See C&J Energy Services Ltd.)

C&J ENERGY SVCS LTD (BERMUDA)
Under Chapter 11 plan of reorganization each share Common 1¢ par received distribution of (0.00994747) C&J Energy Services, Inc. Common Stock Purchase Warrant expiring 01/06/2024 payable 01/06/2017 to holders of record 01/06/2017

CA GOLDFIELDS INC (WA)
SEC revoked common stock registration 03/18/2011

CA SHORT CO (DE)
Stock Dividend - 8% payable 08/01/1997 to holders of record 07/16/1997
Name changed to Casco International Inc. 08/01/1997
(See Casco International Inc.)

CAARA VENTURES INC (BC)
Cease trade order effective 03/10/1988
Stockholders' equity unlikely

CAB-TIVE ADVERTISING INC (NV)
Common $0.001 par split (10) for (1) by issuance of (9) additional shares payable 10/25/2007 to holders of record 10/19/2007 Ex date - 10/26/2007
Name changed to BioGold Fuels Corp. 01/08/2008

CABALA YELLOWKNIFE MINES LTD. (ON)
Merged into Aurlando Consolidated Mining Corp., Ltd. 00/00/1947
Each share Capital Stock $1 par exchanged for (0.2) share Capital Stock $1 par
(See Aurlando Consolidated Mining Corp., Ltd.)

CABANA COACH CORP (TN)
Plan of arrangement under Chapter XI bankruptcy act approved 04/11/1975

CABANA POOLS INC (NJ)
Reorganized under the laws of Delaware as Anabac Industries, Inc. 05/15/1970
Each share Common 10¢ par exchanged for (0.2) share Common 10¢ par
(See Anabac Industries, Inc.)

CABANGA DEVELOPMENTS LTD. (ON)
Name changed to Palliser Petroleums Ltd. and Capital Stock no par changed to 20¢ par 06/10/1958
Palliser Petroleums Ltd. name changed to Dundee-Palliser Resources Inc. 05/17/1973 which recapitalized as Scorpion Minerals Inc. 04/01/1996 which which name changed to Nextair Inc. 03/05/2001 which recapitalized as NXA Inc. 02/23/2005 which recapitalized as Ellipsiz Communications Ltd. 11/26/2015

CABANO KINGSWAY INC (QC)
Name changed to TransForce Inc. (QC) 04/29/1999
TransForce Inc. (QC) reorganized as TransForce Income Fund (QC) 09/30/2002 which reorganized in Canada as TransForce Inc. 05/20/2008 which name changed to TFI International Inc. 12/30/2016

CABARET ROYALE CORP (DE)
Name changed to Exceptional Enterprises, Inc. 07/18/1997
(See Exceptional Enterprises, Inc.)

CABARRUS BK & TR CO (CONCORD, NC)
Merged into Northwestern Financial Corp. 04/01/1983
Each share Capital Stock $100 par exchanged for $4,250 cash

CABARRUS COTTON MILLS
Merged into Cannon Mills Co. 00/00/1928
Details not available

CABARRUS SVGS BK INC (CONCORD, NC)
Stock Dividend - 20% 08/15/1989

Merged into Carolina First Bancshares, Inc. 01/30/1992
Each share Common $1 par exchanged for (0.422) share Common $2.50 par
Carolina First Bancshares, Inc. merged into First Charter Corp. 04/04/2000 which merged into Fifth Third Bancorp 06/06/2008

CABCO TR FOR BELLSOUTH DEBS (DE)
6.75% Trust Certificates called for redemption at $25.8325 on 01/18/2005

CABCO TR FOR FLA P & L FIRST MTG BDS (DE)
Trust Certificates called for redemption at $25.6825 on 12/01/2003

CABEC ENERGY CORP (DE)
Name changed to Palweb Corp. (DE) 04/19/1999
Palweb Corp. (DE) reorganized in Oklahoma 06/25/2002 which changed name to Greystone Logistics Inc. 03/18/2005

CABELAS INC (DE)
Acquired by Bass Pro Group, LLC 09/25/2017
Each share Common 1¢ par exchanged for $61.50 cash

CABELL'S INC. (FL)
Reincorporated 00/00/1957
State of incorporation changed from (TX) to (FL) 00/00/1957
Merged into Southland Corp. of Texas 12/27/1960
Details not available

CABELTEL INTL CORP (NV)
Name changed to New Concept Energy, Inc. 06/03/2008

CABERFAE INC (MI)
Plan of reorganization under Chapter 11 Federal Bankruptcy proceedings confirmed 03/21/1985
No stockholders' equity

CABERFAE SKI AREA INC (MI)
Name changed to Caberfae, Inc. 01/16/1970
(See Caberfae, Inc.)

CABERNET CAP CORP (BC)
Name changed to Auralite Investments Inc. 09/07/2018

CABG MED INC (MN)
In process of liquidation
Each share Common no par exchanged for initial distribution of $1.49 cash 04/28/2006
Note: Details on subsequent distributions, if any, are not available

CABIN CREEK CONSOLIDATED COAL CO.
Acquired by Truax-Traer Coal Co. 00/00/1928
Details not available

CABINET GROW INC (NV)
Each share old Common $0.001 par exchanged for (0.004) share new Common $0.001 par 03/09/2017
Name changed to Blockchain Solutions Inc. 03/06/2018

CABLE & CO WORLDWIDE INC (DE)
Recapitalized as Market & Research Corp. 04/22/2008
Each share Common 1¢ par exchanged for (0.00666666) share Common 1¢ par

CABLE & WIRELESS COMMUNICATIONS PLC (ENGLAND & WALES)
Merged into Cable & Wireless PLC 05/12/2000
Each Sponsored ADR for Ordinary exchanged for (0.77083) Sponsored ADR for Ordinary, (0.28360155) share NTL Inc. Common 1¢ par and $14.1722136 cash
(See each company's listing)

ADR agreement terminated 05/31/2016
No ADR's remain outstanding

CABLE & WIRELESS HKT (HONG KONG)
Merged into Pacific Century CyberWorks Ltd. 08/17/2000
Each Sponsored ADR for Ordinary exchanged for (1.1) Sponsored ADR's for Ordinary
Pacific Century CyberWorks Ltd. name changed to PCCW Ltd. 08/09/2002

CABLE & WIRELESS HLDG LTD (ENGLAND)
Each share Ordinary £1 par exchanged for (4) shares Ordinary 5s par 03/26/1956
Ordinary 5s par changed to 25p par per currency change 02/15/1971
Name changed to Cable Trust Ltd. 05/05/1971
Cable Trust Ltd. merged into Globe Investment Trust plc 09/19/1977
(See Globe Investment Trust plc)

CABLE & WIRELESS PLC (UNITED KINGDOM)
ADR agreement terminated 04/16/2010
Each ADR for Ordinary issued by Bank of New York exchanged for $10.922954 cash
Each ADR for Ordinary issued by Citibank Shareholder Services exchanged for $10.890270 cash
Each ADR for Ordinary issued by Deutsche Bank Trust Company Americas exchanged for $10.906964 cash

CABLE & WIRELESS PUB LTD CO (UNITED KINGDOM)
Sponsored ADR's for Ordinary split (2) for (1) by issuance of (1) additional ADR 11/08/1993
ADR agreement terminated 12/13/2005
Each Sponsored ADR for Ordinary exchanged for $6.1189 cash

CABLE & WIRELESS WORLDWIDE PLC (ENGLAND & WALES)
ADR agreement terminated 09/10/2012
Each Sponsored ADR for Ordinary exchanged for $5.87982 cash

CABLE ADVERTISING SYS INC (DE)
Reincorporated 08/11/1987
State of incorporation changed from (TX) to (DE) 08/11/1987
Recapitalized as Frontier Oil & Gas Ltd. 08/19/2004
Each share Common 1¢ par exchanged for (0.0025) share Common 1¢ par
Frontier Oil & Gas Ltd. name changed to Alaska Oil & Gas Ltd. 11/16/2004 which name changed to Transworld Oil & Gas, Ltd. 07/29/2005 which recapitalized as Caribbean Exploration Ventures Inc. 01/16/2007 which name changed to Siguiri Basin Mining, Inc. (DE) 03/28/2007 which reorganized in Nevada as Anything Brands Online Inc. 01/17/2008 which name changed to MyFreightWorld Technologies, Inc. 05/13/2010

CABLE APPLICATIONS INC (NY)
Reorganized under Chapter 11 Federal Bankruptcy Code 10/02/1989
Each share old Common 1¢ par exchanged for (0.11111111) share new Common 1¢ par
Filed a petition under Chapter 11 Federal Code 04/00/1991
Stockholders' equity unlikely

CABLE CAR BEVERAGE CORP (DE)
Merged into Triarc Companies, Inc. 11/25/1997
Each share Common 1¢ par exchanged for (0.1722) share Class A Common 10¢ par
Triarc Companies, Inc. name changed to Wendy's/Arby's Group, Inc. 09/29/2008 which name changed to Wendy's Co. 07/11/2011

CABLE CAR BURGER INC (CO)
Recapitalized as Winthrop-Scott Corp. 11/03/1972
Each share Common 10¢ par exchanged for (0.2) share Common 15¢ par
(See Winthrop-Scott Corp.)

CABLE CARRIERS, INC. (DE)
No longer in existence having become inoperative and void for non-payment of taxes 04/01/1964

CABLE CO (MD)
Completely liquidated 09/10/1974
Each share Common $5 par exchanged for first and final distribution of $1.8474 cash

CABLE COMMUNICATIONS CORP (DE)
Charter cancelled and declared inoperative and void for non-payment of taxes 03/01/1987

CABLE DESIGN TECHNOLOGIES CORP (DE)
Common 1¢ par split (3) for (2) by issuance of (0.5) additional share 12/29/1995
Common 1¢ par split (3) for (2) by issuance of (0.5) additional share payable 01/09/1998 to holders of record 12/30/1997 Ex date - 01/12/1998
Common 1¢ par split (3) for (2) by issuance of (0.5) additional share payable 08/21/2000 to holders of record 08/07/2000 Ex date - 08/22/2000
Merged into Belden CDT Inc. 07/16/2004
Each share Common 1¢ par exchanged for (0.5) share Common 1¢ par
Belden CDT Inc. name changed to Belden Inc. (New) 05/24/2007

CABLE ELECTRIC PRODUCTS, INC. (DE)
Common no par changed to 50¢ par 00/00/1939
Liquidation completed 02/17/1959
Each share Common 50¢ par exchanged for first and final distribution of $6.604227 cash

CABLE EXCHANGE INC (CO)
Name changed to CBLX Holdings Inc. 09/25/1990
CBLX Holdings Inc. recapitalized as Evans Environmental Corp. 05/03/1993 which name changed to ECOS Group, Inc. (CO) 11/01/1996 which reincorporated in Florida 02/22/2000 which recapitalized as Third Millennium Telecommunications, Inc. (FL) 10/01/2001 which reincorporated in Delaware as TMTM Merger Co. 09/04/2009 which recapitalized as Green Processing Technologies, Inc. 06/16/2010 which recapitalized as Umbra Applied Technologies Group, Inc. 01/13/2014

CABLE FDG CORP (DE)
Name changed to Geneve Corp. 03/01/1976
(See Geneve Corp.)

CABLE GROUP SOUTH INC (DE)
Recapitalized as Softnet Industries, Inc. 12/10/1998
Each share Common 1¢ par exchanged for (0.125) share Common 1¢ par
Softnet Industries, Inc. name changed to I Crystal, Inc. 07/29/1999 which name changed to ICrystal, Inc. 06/15/2000 which name changed to ALL Fuels & Energy Co. 05/07/2007

which recapitalized as All Energy Corp. 01/17/2012

CABLE HLDGS INC (NY)
Each (22,870) shares old Common 1¢ par exchanged for (1) share new Common 1¢ par 11/20/1986
Note: In effect holders received $3.25 cash per share and public interest was eliminated

CABLE HYDROCARBONS INC (AB)
Name changed to Monte Carlo Gold Mines Ltd. (AB) 12/23/1986
Monte Carlo Gold Mines Ltd. (AB) reincorporated in Ontario 10/31/1987 which recapitalized as Exxadon Technology Corp. 07/12/1993 which name changed to EWMC International Inc. 12/03/1996 which name changed to Environmental Waste International Inc. 07/12/2001

CABLE LINK INC (OH)
Common no par split (2) for (1) by issuance of (1) additional share 11/10/1994
Common no par split (6) for (5) by issuance of (0.2) additional share payable 05/16/1996 to holders of record 05/06/1996
Common no par split (3) for (2) by issuance of (0.5) additional share payable 01/31/1997 to holders of record 01/21/1997
Reincorporated under the laws of Delaware as A Novo Broadband Inc. 02/16/2001
(See A Novo Broadband Inc.)

CABLE LIQUIDATION CORP. (DE)
Completely liquidated 03/04/1969
Each share Common 1¢ par exchanged for first and final distribution of (1) share 4% Conv. Preference $1 par and (0.6) share Babbitt (B.T.), Inc. Common $1 par
Babbitt (B.T.), Inc. name changed to B.T.B. Corp. 12/05/1969 which name changed to International Banknote Co., Inc. 01/02/1973 which merged into United States Banknote Corp. (NY) 07/25/1990 which reincorporated in Delaware 09/21/1993 which name changed to American Banknote Corp. 07/03/1995

CABLE MICH INC (PA)
Merged into Avalon Cable 11/06/1998
Each share Common $1 par exchanged for $40.50 cash

CABLE MINES & OILS LTD. (QC)
Merged into St. Fabien Copper Mines Ltd. 07/27/1967
Each share Capital Stock $1 par exchanged for (1) share Common $1 par
St. Fabien Copper Mines Ltd. name changed to St. Fabien Explorations Inc. 02/11/1981 which recapitalized as Fabien Explorations Inc. 07/18/1983
(See Fabien Explorations Inc.)

CABLE NEWS NETWORK, INC. (GA)
Exchangeable Preferred Class A 1¢ par called for redemption 10/26/1989
Public interest eliminated

CABLE RADIO TUBE CORP.
Name changed to Cable Electric Products, Inc. 00/00/1934
(See Cable Electric Products, Inc.)

CABLE-SAT SYS INC (FL)
Name changed to Compressent Corp. 03/07/1997
(See Compressent Corp.)

CABLE SATISFACTION INTL INC (CANADA)
Plan of Arrangement under Companies' Creditors Arrangement Act effective 08/01/2006
No stockholders' equity

CABLE TR LTD (ENGLAND)
Merged into Globe Investment Trust PLC 09/19/1977
Each (5) shares Ordinary 25p par exchanged for (7) shares Ordinary 25p par
(See Globe Investment Trust PLC)

CABLE TV INDS (CA)
Merged into Anixter Bros., Inc. 12/08/1988
Each share Common no par exchanged for $5.25 cash

CABLE WEST CORP (CO)
Charter suspended for failure to file annual reports 09/30/1987

CABLECASTING LTD (ON)
Class A 50¢ par called for redemption 03/09/1978
Class B 50¢ par called for redemption 03/09/1978
Public interest eliminated

CABLECOM GEN INC (OK)
Merged into Capital Cities Communications, Inc. 07/02/1981
Each share Common 3¢ par exchanged for $42 cash

CABLEGUARD INC (TX)
Merged into CG Merger Corp. 11/14/1989
Each share Common no par exchanged for $1.90 cash

CABLEMAXX INC (DE)
Merged into Heartland Wireless Communications, Inc. 02/23/1996
Each share Common 1¢ par exchanged for (0.3033) share Common $0.001 par
(See Heartland Wireless Communications, Inc.)

CABLES & WIRELESS, LTD.
Name changed to Cable & Wireless (Holding) Ltd. 00/00/1934
Cable & Wireless (Holding) Ltd. name changed to Cable Trust Ltd. 05/05/1971 which merged into Globe Investment Trust PLC 09/19/1977
(See Globe Investment Trust PLC)

CABLESERV INC (ON)
Acquired by Costeff Network Solutions Inc. 01/15/2007
Each share Common no par exchanged for $0.095 cash

CABLESHARE INC (ON)
Each share Common no par exchanged for (3) shares Class A no par and (1) share Class B no par 07/25/1986
Merged into Source Media, Inc. 01/14/1997
Each share Class A Subordinate no par exchanged for (0.19937794) share new Common $0.001 par
Each share Class B Multiple no par exchanged for (0.19937794) share new Common $0.001 par
(See Source Media, Inc.)

CABLETECH INC (FL)
Merged into Primages, Inc. 06/12/1986
Each share Common 1¢ par exchanged for (0.2) share Common 1¢ par
(See Primages, Inc.)

CABLETEL COMMUNICATIONS CORP (ON)
Assets sold for the benefit of creditors 00/00/2004
Stockholders' equity unlikely

CABLETRON SYS INC (DE)
Common 1¢ par split (5) for (2) by issuance of (1.5) additional share 09/09/1994
Common 1¢ par split (2) for (1) by issuance of (1) additional share payable 11/26/1996 to holders of record 11/07/1996 Ex date - 11/27/1996
Each share Common 1¢ par received distribution of (0.5131) share Riverstone Networks, Inc. Common 1¢ par payable 08/06/2001 to holders of record 07/27/2001 Ex date - 08/06/2001
Name changed to Enterasys Networks, Inc. 08/06/2001
(See Enterasys Networks, Inc.)

CABLEVISION SYS CORP (DE)
Under plan of merger name changed to CSC Holdings, Inc. 03/04/1998
(See CSC Holdings, Inc.)
Class A Common 1¢ par split (2) for (1) by issuance of (1) additional share payable 03/30/1998 to holders of record 03/19/1998 Ex date - 03/31/1998
Class A Common 1¢ par split (2) for (1) by issuance of (1) additional share payable 08/21/1998 to holders of record 08/10/1998 Ex date - 08/24/1998
Class A Common 1¢ par reclassified as Cablevision NY Group Class A Common 1¢ par 03/12/2001
Each share Cablevision NY Group Class A Common 1¢ par received distribution of (0.5) share Rainbow Media Group Common payable 03/29/2001 to holders of record 03/15/2001
Each share Rainbow Media Group Common exchanged for (1.19093) shares Cablevision New York Group Class A Common 1¢ par 08/20/2002
Each share Cablevision NY Group Class A Common 1¢ par received distribution of (0.25) share Madison Square Garden, Inc. Common 1¢ par payable 02/09/2010 to holders of record 01/25/2010 Ex date - 02/10/2010
Each share Cablevision NY Group Class A Common 1¢ par received distribution of (0.25) share AMC Networks Inc. Class A Common 1¢ par payable 06/30/2011 to holders of record 06/16/2011 Ex date - 07/01/2011
Acquired by Altice N.V. 06/21/2016
Each share Cablevision NY Group Class A Common 1¢ par exchanged for $34.90 cash

CABO MNG CORP (YT)
Reincorporated 02/01/1996
Recapitalized 07/15/1998
Reincorporated from Cabo Ventures Inc. (BC) to Cabo Exploration Ventures Inc. (Yukon) 02/01/1996
Recapitalized from Cabo Exploration Ventures Inc. to Cabo Mining Corp. 07/15/1998
Each share Common no par exchanged for (0.2) share Common no par
Recapitalized as Cabo Mining Enterprises Corp. 01/05/2004
Each share Common no par exchanged for (0.2) share Common no par
Cabo Mining Enterprises Corp. name changed to Cabo Drilling Corp. 01/12/2006

CABO MNG ENTERPRISES CORP (YT)
Name changed to Cabo Drilling Corp. 01/12/2006

CABO VERDE CAP INC (DE)
Reincorporated 07/23/2014
State of incorporation changed from (WA) to (DE) 07/23/2014
Reincorporated under the laws of Nevada and Common $0.0001 par changed to $0.00001 par 11/05/2015

CABOL ENTERPRISES LTD (ON)
Charter cancelled and declared dissolved for failure to file returns and pay fees 07/27/1976

CABOT CABOT & FORBES LD TR (MA)
Name changed to Bay Colony Property Co. (MA) 04/19/1977
Bay Colony Property Co. (MA) reorganized in Delaware as Bay Financial Corp. 03/03/1980
(See Bay Financial Corp.)

CABOT CORP (DE)
Preferred Stock Purchase Rights declared for Common stockholders of record 12/03/1986 were redeemed at $0.05 per right 12/08/1995 for holders of record 11/24/1994
(Additional Information in Active)

CABOT EXPLS LTD (QC)
Cease trade order effective 11/14/1980
Stockholders' equity unlikely

CABOT INDL TR (MD)
Merged into Calwest Industrial Properties, LLC 12/07/2001
Each Common Share of Bene. Int. 1¢ par exchanged for $24 cash

CABOT J P EQUITY CORP (NY)
Merged into Yavapai Hills, Inc. 08/14/1980
Each share Common 1¢ par exchanged for (1) share Common $1 par and $18.50 cash
Yavapai Hills, Inc. name changed to J.P. Cabot Realty, Inc. 10/26/2004

CABOT J P SHORT TERM FD INC (MD)
Liquidated 00/00/1975
Details not available

CABOT JOHN EXPLS LTD (BC)
Name changed to Antrim Resources Ltd. 01/17/1980
Antrim Resources Ltd. name changed to Kenridge Mineral Corp. 01/31/1984 which recapitalized as Pacific Kenridge Ventures Inc. 03/20/1987
(See Pacific Kenridge Ventures Inc.)

CABOT KNITTING MLS INC (NY)
Charter cancelled and proclaimed dissolved for failure to pay taxes 02/29/1984

CABOT MED CORP (NJ)
Stock Dividends - 10% 07/02/1993; 10% 01/14/1994; 10% 05/13/1994
Merged into Circon Corp. 08/28/1995
Each share Common no par exchanged for (0.415) share Common 1¢ par
Circon Corp. merged into Maxxim Medical, Inc. 01/08/1999

CABOT RES CORP (BC)
Merged into Emtech Technology Corp. 08/16/1993
Each share Common no par exchanged for (1) share Common no par
Emtech Technology Corp. reorganized as Emtech Ltd. (Bermuda) 07/18/1994 which name changed to Ashurst Technology Ltd. 07/09/1996
(See Ashurst Technology Ltd.)

CABOT YELLOWKNIFE GOLD MINES, LTD. (ON)
Charter revoked for failure to file annual reports 00/00/1957

CABRE CAP CORP (BC)
Recapitalized as Northcliff Resources Ltd. 06/08/2011
Each share Common no par exchanged for (0.2) share Common no par

CABRE CORP (TX)
Each share Common 10¢ par exchanged for (0.05) share Common $2 par 06/15/1994
Name changed to Antenna Products, Inc. 01/30/1998
Antenna Products, Inc. name changed to Phazar Corp. 03/12/2001
(See Phazar Corp.)

CABRE EXPL LTD (AB)
Each share Common no par received distribution of (2.488) shares Vanguard Oil Corp. Common no par payable 12/29/2000 to holders of record 12/20/2000 Ex date - 12/18/2000
Acquired by EnerMark Income Fund 01/10/2001
Each share Common no par exchanged for (3.25) Trust Units no par and (1) Trust Unit Purchase Warrant expiring 12/17/2001
EnerMark Income Fund merged into Enerplus Resources Fund 06/22/2001 which reorganized as Enerplus Corp. 01/03/2011

CABRILLO CAP CORP (AB)
Reincorporated 04/12/2002
Reincorporated 10/15/2009
Name changed to Indico Technologies Corp. (AB) 09/16/1998
Indico Technologies Corp. (AB) reincorporated in Bermuda 04/12/2002 which name changed to Indico Technologies Ltd. 05/23/2002 which name changed to Indico Resources Ltd. (Bermuda) 04/27/2007 which reincorporated in British Columbia 10/15/2009

CABRILLO ST BK (SAN FERNANDO, CA)
Merged into Santa Clarita National Bank (Newhall, CA) 05/30/1981
Each share Common $7.50 par exchanged for (0.27571) share Common $2.50 par
Santa Clarita National Bank (Newhall, CA) acquired by Security Pacific Corp. 11/16/1990 which merged into BankAmerica Corp. (Old) 04/22/1992 which merged into BankAmerica Corp. (New) 09/30/1998 which name changed to Bank of America Corp. 04/28/1999

CABRIOLET CORP (NV)
Charter revoked for failure to file reports and pay fees 06/01/2005

CAC HOMES CORP (DE)
Reincorporated under the laws of Wyoming as Ostashkov Industrial Inc. 11/20/2013
(See Ostashkov Industrial Inc.)

CAC INC (MI)
Name changed to Purification Systems, Inc. 04/30/1970

CACH FOODS INC (NV)
Recapitalized as U.S. Wireless Online, Inc. 05/19/2003
Each share Common $0.001 par exchanged for (0.48) share Common $0.001 par

CACHE BAY (CHIBOUGAMAU) MINES LTD. (QC)
Acquired by Obalski (1945) Ltd. 00/00/1955
Each share Capital Stock exchanged for (0.2) share Capital Stock
Obalski (1945) Ltd. recapitalized as United Obalski Mining Co. Ltd. 11/13/1961 which merged into Allied Mining Corp. 09/22/1969 which merged into United Asbestos Inc. 06/29/1973 which merged into Campbell Resources Inc. (New) 06/08/1983
(See Campbell Resources Inc. (New))

CACHE CAP CORP (UT)
Name changed to Pure Broadcast Corp. 04/04/2017

CACHE CREEK BANK (SACRAMENTO, CA)
Location changed 12/31/1981
Location changed from (Woodland, CA) to (Sacramento, CA) 12/31/1981

Name changed to Mercantile Bank (Sacramento, CA) 05/01/1982
Mercantile Bank (Sacramento, CA) merged into SierraWest Bancorp 06/30/1997 which merged into BancWest Corp. 07/01/1999
(See BancWest Corp. (New))

CACHE D OR RES INC (BC)
Name changed 11/21/1984
Name changed from Cache d'Or Resource Inc. to Cache d'Or Resources Inc. 11/21/1984
Recapitalized as Consolidated Cache d'Or Resources Inc./Ressources Unifiees Cache d'Or Inc. 12/29/1989
Each share Common no par exchanged for (0.2) share Common no par
Consolidated Cache d'Or Resources Inc./ Ressources Unifiees Cache d'Or Inc. name changed to Exploration Auriginor Inc. (BC) 03/19/1993 which reincorporated in Canada 03/03/1998
(See Exploration Auriginor Inc.)

CACHE D'OR GOLD MINES LTD. (ON)
Charter revoked for failure to file annual reports 09/30/1957

CACHE DRILLING, INC. (UT)
Name changed to Almur Cosmetics, Inc. 07/26/1988
Almur Cosmetics, Inc. recapitalized as Multi-Media Industries Corp. 06/19/1995 which recapitalized as Worldnet Resources Group Inc. 02/14/2000 which recapitalized as Asset Equity Group, Inc. 12/12/2001
(See Asset Equity Group, Inc.)

CACHE EXPLS INC (CANADA)
Merged into MSV Resources Inc. 10/16/1995
Each share Common no par exchanged for (0.25) share Common no par
MSV Resources Inc. merged into Campbell Resources Inc. (New) 07/05/2001
(See Campbell Resources Inc. (New))

CACHE INC (FL)
Each share old Common 1¢ par exchanged for (0.25) share new Common 1¢ par 09/15/1993
New Common 1¢ par split (3) for (2) by issuance of (0.5) additional share payable 06/18/2004 to holders of record 05/21/2004 Ex date - 06/21/2004
Stock Dividend - 10% 12/15/1983
Reincorporated under the laws of Delaware 08/15/2013

CACHE LA POUDRE CO.
Dissolved 00/00/1936
Details not available

CACHEFLOW INC (DE)
Name changed to Blue Coat Systems, Inc. 08/21/2002
(See Blue Coat Systems, Inc.)

CACHET COMMUNICATIONS INC (AB)
Delisted from Alberta Stock Exchange 11/22/1999

CACHET ENTERPRISES CORP (BC)
Name changed to Gold Star Resources Corp. 04/02/2004
Gold Star Resources Corp. name changed to Simba Energy Inc. 02/19/2010 which name changed to Simba Essel Energy Inc. 04/24/2017

CACHET FINL SOLUTIONS INC (DE)
Each share old Common $0.0001 par exchanged for (0.06666666) share new Common $0.0001 par 07/27/2016
Each share new Common $0.0001 par exchanged again for (0.66666666) share new Common $0.0001 par 03/10/2017
Name changed to Digiliti Money Group, Inc. 04/10/2017

CACI INC (DE)
Reincorporated 11/19/1976
State of incorporation changed from (CA) to (DE) 11/19/1976
Under plan of merger each share Common 10¢ par exchanged for (1) Paired Ctf. consisting of (1) share new Common 10¢ par and (1) CACI N.V. Share of Bene. Int. 10¢ par 02/27/1981
Under plan of merger each Paired Ctf. exchanged for (1) share Class A Common 10¢ par 06/02/1986
Stock Dividends - 200% 12/12/1982; 200% 04/29/1983; 30% 09/19/1986
Name changed to CACI International Inc. 12/23/1986

CACTUS NEW MEDIA I INC (DE)
Old Common $0.0001 par split (15) for (1) by issuance of (14) additional shares payable 07/13/2001 to holders of record 07/13/2001 Ex date - 07/16/2001
Each share old Common $0.0001 par exchanged for (0.01) share new Common $0.0001 par 10/31/2003
Name changed to Medical Makeover Corp. of America 04/06/2004
(See Medical Makeover Corp. of America)

CACTUS SPINA INC (NV)
Name changed to NoMatterWare, Inc. 10/18/2001
(See NoMatterWare, Inc.)

CACTUS URANIUM CO.
Merged into Sun Uranium Mining Co. on a (1) for (12.5) basis 12/15/1954
Sun Uranium Mining Co. name changed to Sun Tide Corp. 07/22/1955 which name changed to Maxa Corp. 04/13/1974
(See Maxa Corp.)

CACTUS VENTURES INC (NV)
Each share old Common 1¢ par exchanged for (0.5) share new Common 1¢ par 12/19/2007
Reincorporated under the laws of Delaware as Actinium Pharmaceuticals, Inc. and new Common 1¢ par changed to $0.001 par 04/18/2013

CACTUS WEST EXPLS LTD (BC)
Recapitalized as Cimarron Minerals Ltd. (BC) 04/29/1996
Each share Common no par exchanged for (0.2) share Common no par
Cimarron Minerals Ltd. (BC) reorganized in Canada as DiscFactories Corp. 05/01/2000 which name changed to Excalibur Resources Ltd. 02/20/2007 which recapitalized as Metalla Royalty & Streaming Ltd. (Canada) 12/07/2016 which reincorporated in British Columbia 11/16/2017

CAD-E-MOBILE CORP. OF AMERICA (DC)
Class A 5¢ par and Class B 5¢ par reclassified as Common 5¢ par 04/14/1969
Name changed to Aetna Development Corp. 10/29/1969
Aetna Development Corp. recapitalized as Israel International Corp. 06/22/1972
(See Israel International Corp.)

CADAMET MINES LTD. (ON)
Recapitalized as Terrex Mining Co. Ltd. 09/08/1966
Each share Capital Stock $1 par exchanged for (0.2) share Capital Stock $1 par
(See Terrex Mining Co. Ltd.)

CADAN RES CORP (BC)
Each share old Common no par exchanged for (0.2) share new Common no par 11/10/2009
Each share new Common no par exchanged again for (0.125) share new Common no par 12/01/2014
Name changed to Rizal Resources Corp. 10/07/2016

CADAPULT GRAPHIC SYS INC (DE)
Name changed to Media Sciences International, Inc. 04/29/2002
(See Media Sciences International, Inc.)

CADBURY PLC (ENGLAND & WALES)
Acquired by Kraft Foods Inc. 06/01/2010
Each Sponsored ADR for Ordinary exchanged for (0.7496) share Class A Common and $28.93 cash

CADBURY SCHWEPPES DEL LP (DE)
8.625% Guaranteed Quarterly Income Preferred Securities called for redemption at $25 on 4/18/2005

CADBURY SCHWEPPES P L C (ENGLAND & WALES)
ADR's for Auction Preferred Ser. 3 called for redemption 03/04/1997
ADR's for Auction Preferred Ser. 4 called for redemption 03/11/1997
ADR's for Auction Preferred Ser. 5 called for redemption 03/18/1997
ADR's for Auction Preferred Ser. 6 called for redemption 03/25/1997
Each old ADR for Ordinary exchanged for (0.1) new ADR for Ordinary 09/24/1984
New ADR's for Ordinary split (2) for (1) by issuance of (1) additional ADR issued payable 05/28/1999 to holders of record 05/21/1999 Ex date - 06/01/1999
Each new ADR for Ordinary received distribution of (0.48) share Dr Pepper Snapple Group, Inc. Common 1¢ par payable 05/06/2008 to holders of record 05/01/2008
Merged into Cadbury PLC 05/02/2008
Each new ADR for Ordinary exchanged for (0.64) Sponsored ADR for Ordinary
Cadbury PLC acquired by Kraft Foods Inc. 06/01/2010

CADDEV INDS INC (BC)
Delisted from Vancouver Stock Exchange 11/16/1990

CADDO CENTRAL OIL & REFINING CORP. (NY)
Assets sold for benefit of creditors 00/00/1926
No stockholders' equity

CADDO INTL INC (NV)
Each share Common 10¢ par received distibution of (0.05) share Petrolind Drilling Co., Inc. Restricted Common payable 07/16/2009 to holders of record 06/20/2009
SEC revoked common stock registration 10/27/2009

CADDYSTATS INC (DE)
Reorganized as Roadships Holdings Inc. 04/21/2009
Each share Common $0.001 par exchanged for (5) shares Common $0.001 par
Roadships Holdings Inc. name changed to Tautachrome Inc. 11/05/2015

CADE INDS INC (WI)
Merged into United Technologies Corp. 02/04/2000
Each share Common $0.001 par exchanged for $5.05 cash

CADE STRUKTUR CORP (YT)
Each share old Common no par exchanged for (1) share new Common no par to reflect a (1) for (500) reverse split followed by a (500) for (1) forward split 11/22/2002
Note: Holders of (499) or fewer pre-split shares received $0.000002 cash per share
Acquired by KHD Humboldt Wedag International Ltd. 10/23/2006
Each share new Common no par exchanged (0.0029163) share Common no par
KHD Humboldt Wedag International Ltd. reorganized as Terra Nova Royalty Corp. 03/30/2010 which name changed to MFC Industrial Ltd. 09/30/2011 which name changed to MFC Bancorp Ltd. (BC) 02/16/2016
(See MFC Bancorp Ltd. (BC))

CADEC SYS INC (MA)
Merged into Cummins Acquisition, Inc. 12/05/1986
Each share Common 1¢ par exchanged for $3.50 cash

CADEMA CORP (DE)
SEC revoked preferred and common stock registration 10/09/2008

CADENCE ENERGY INC (AB)
Merged into Barrick Gold Corp. 11/10/2008
Each share Common no par exchanged for $6.75 cash

CADENCE FINL CORP (MS)
Acquired by Community Bancorp L.L.C. 03/04/2011
Each share Common $1 par exchanged for $2.50 cash

CADENCE INDS CORP (DE)
Merged into CMG Management, Inc. 11/09/1983
Each share Common $1.20 par exchanged for $17.50 cash
$3.50 Conv. Preferred Ser. A $50 par called for redemption 01/31/1987
Public interest eliminated

CADENCE PHARMACEUTICALS INC (DE)
Acquired by Mallinckrodt PLC 03/20/2014
Each share Common $0.0001 par exchanged for $14 cash

CADENCE RES CORP (UT)
Name changed to Aurora Oil & Gas Corp. 05/24/2006
(See Aurora Oil & Gas Corp.)

CADET RES LTD (BC)
Charter cancelled 10/22/1979

CADGIE TAYLOR CO (MT)
Name changed to Carleton Enterprises (MT) 04/03/1984
Carleton Enterprises (MT) reincorporated in Nevada as SCN, Ltd. 11/13/1984 which recapitalized as Health Care Centers America Inc. 01/04/1994 which name changed to Hexagon Consolidated Companies of America Inc. 08/31/1999 which name changed to NMC Inc. 09/09/2003

CADHERIN BIOMEDICAL INC (CANADA)
Acquired by Adherex Technologies Inc. (Canada) 12/03/2004
Each share Class A Preferred no par exchanged for approximately (0.069) share Common no par
Adherex Technologies Inc. (Canada) reorganized in British Columbia 08/30/2011 which recapitalized as Fennec Pharmaceuticals Inc. 09/05/2014

CADILARTIC MINES LTD. (ON)
Charter revoked for failure to file annual reports 11/01/1954

CADILLAC CABLE CORP (NY)
Each share Preferred $10 par exchanged for (0.5) share Common 1¢ par 06/01/1973
Each share Common 10¢ par exchanged for (0.1) share Common 1¢ par 06/01/1973
Merged into Ag-Met, Inc. 08/29/1974
Each share Common 1¢ par exchanged for (0.174) share Common 50¢ par
Ag-Met, Inc. name changed to Refinemet International Co. 09/18/1980

CADILLAC CAP INC (NV)
Name changed to Cerx Entertainment Corp. 03/25/1998
Cerx Entertainment Corp. name changed to Cerxnet Inc. 05/10/1999 which name changed to GlobalNet Equities, Inc. 01/12/2001 which recapitalized as GlobalNet Energy Corp. 10/10/2001

CADILLAC CONDUIT CORP. (NY)
Name changed to Cadillac Cable Corp. 11/27/1968
Cadillac Cable Corp. merged into Ag-Met, Inc. 08/29/1974 which name changed to Refinemet International Co. 09/18/1980
(See Refinemet International Co.)

CADILLAC DEV LTD (ON)
Merged into Cadillac Fairview Corp. Ltd. 06/03/1974
Each share 6.5% Class B Preference 1st Ser. $25 par exchanged for (1) share 6.5% Preference 1st Ser. $25 par
Each share Common no par exchanged for (1) share Common no par
(See Cadillac Fairview Corp. Ltd.)

CADILLAC EXPLS LTD (BC)
Common 50¢ par changed to no par 07/08/1971
Struck off register and declared dissolved for failure to file returns 05/22/1987

CADILLAC FAIRVIEW CORP (ON)
Merged into Ontario Teachers' Pension Plan Board 03/17/2000
Each share Common no par exchanged for $34 cash

CADILLAC FAIRVIEW LTD (ON)
Each share 6.5% Preference 1st Ser. $25 par exchanged for (2) shares Preference Ser. A no par 08/31/1978
Each (2) shares old Common no par automatically became (1) share Preference Ser. A no par and (2) shares new Common no par 08/31/1978
New Common no par split (3) for (1) by issuance of (2) additional shares 08/17/1981
Stock Dividend - In Second Preference Ser. A to holders of Common 25% 07/26/1985
Acquired by JMB Institutional Realty Corp. 11/02/1987
Each share new Common no par exchanged for $34 cash
Preference Ser. A no par called for redemption 10/31/1988
Second Preference Ser. A no par called for redemption 10/31/1988
Public interest eliminated

CADILLAC KNITTING MLS INC (NJ)
Charter declared void for non-payment of taxes 03/27/1972

CADILLAC LIFE INSURANCE CO. (MI)
Merged into National Bankers Life Insurance Co. 05/13/1966
Each share Common $1 par exchanged for (0.2) share Common $1 par

CADILLAC MNG CORP (BC)
Reincorporated 05/22/2007
Place of incorporation changed from (ON) to (BC) 05/22/2007
Merged into Pilot Gold Inc. 08/29/2014
Each share Common no par exchanged for (0.12195) share Common no par and (0.12195) Common Stock Purchase Warrant expiring 08/29/2016
Pilot Gold Inc. name changed to Liberty Gold Corp. 05/12/2017

CADILLAC MOLY MINES LTD (QC)
Each share Preferred $1 par exchanged for (1) share Common no par 04/17/1969
Company is insolvent
Assets taken over by the Trustee for benefit of bondholders 00/00/1970
No stockholders' equity

CADISCOR RES INC (CANADA)
Acquired by North American Palladium Ltd. (Old) 05/26/2009
Each share Common no par exchanged for (0.33) share Common no par
North American Palladium Ltd. (Old) reorganized as North American Palladium Ltd. (New) 08/10/2015

CADISTA HLDGS INC (DE)
Acquired by Jubilant Life Sciences Ltd. 12/23/2014
Each share Common $0.001 par exchanged for $1.60 cash

CADITEC INTL INC (DE)
Name changed to AMC American Music Corp., Inc. 05/03/2004
AMC American Music Corp., Inc. recapitalized as Mercantile Gold Co. (DE) 10/05/2004 which reincorporated in Wyoming 09/23/2005 which recapitalized as Anglo Andean Mining Co. 02/07/2006 which name changed to MGM Mineral Resources Inc. 04/28/2006 which recapitalized as Brownstone Resources, Inc. 10/05/2007 which recapitalized as Pomsta Group, Inc. 10/12/2010 which name changed to Oidon Co., Ltd. 12/31/2010

CADIZ LD INC (DE)
Name changed to Cadiz Inc. 09/01/1998

CADMAN RES INC (BC)
Name changed to Matica Graphite Inc. 04/21/2014
Matica Graphite Inc. name changed to Matica Enterprises Inc. 07/04/2014

CADMUS COMMUNICATIONS CORP (VA)
Common 50¢ par split (4) for (3) by issuance of (0.33333333) additional share 03/05/1986
Common 50¢ par split (2) for (1) by issuance of (1) additional share 06/05/1987
Stock Dividend - 10% 09/05/1985
Merged into Cenveo, Inc. 03/08/2007
Each share Common 50¢ par exchanged for $24.75 cash

CADNETIX CORP (CO)
Merged into Daisy Systems Corp. (DE) 05/31/1989
Each share Common 1¢ par exchanged for $5.72 principal amount of 9% Conv. Debentures due 05/31/2014 and $3.78 cash

CADO SYS CORP (CA)
Merged into Continental Telecom Inc. 01/03/1983
Each share Common 10¢ par exchanged for (0.625) share Common $1 par
Continental Telecom Inc. name changed to Contel Corp. 05/01/1986 which merged into GTE Corp. 03/14/1991 which merged into Verizon Communications Inc. 06/30/2000

CADOMIN CAP CORP (ON)
Voluntarily dissolved 11/30/2012
Details not available

CADORNA RES INC (AB)
Name changed to Innicor Subsurface Technologies Inc. 05/18/2001
(See Innicor Subsurface Technologies Inc.)

CADRE INDUSTRIES CORP. (NY)
Common $5 par split (2) for (1) by issuance of (1) additional share 11/01/1960
Common $5 par changed to $2 par and (1.5) additional shares issued plus a 20% stock dividend paid 11/01/1961
Merged into Amphenol Corp. (Old) 05/11/1965
Each share Common $2 par exchanged for (0.25) share Common $1 par
Amphenol Corp. (Old) merged into Bunker Ramo Corp. (New) 06/03/1968 which merged into Allied Corp. 07/31/1981 which merged into Allied-Signal Inc. 09/19/1985 which name changed to AlliedSignal Inc. 04/26/1993 which name changed to Honeywell International Inc. 12/01/1999

CADRE RES LTD (CANADA)
Reincorporated 06/19/1995
Place of incorporation changed from (BC) to Canada 06/19/1995
Charter dissolved for non-compliance 07/16/2011

CADUS CORP (DE)
Name changed 06/20/2003
Name changed from Cadus Pharmaceutical Corp. to Cadus Corp.06/20/2003
Acquired by Starfire Holding Corp. 06/28/2018
Each share Common 1¢ par exchanged for $1.61 cash

CADY LUMBER CORP.
Assets sold to Southwest Lumber Mills, Inc. 00/00/1935
No stockholders' equity

CAERE CORP (DE)
Common $0.001 par split (2) for (1) by issuance of (1) additional share 12/04/1992
Merged into ScanSoft, Inc. 03/13/2000
Each share Common $0.001 par exchanged for (1.55779) shares Common $0.001 par
ScanSoft, Inc. name changed to Nuance Communications, Inc. (New) 11/21/2005

CAERUS RESOURCE CORP (BC)
Name changed to Angel Gold Corp. 10/04/2004

CAESAR SILVER MINES LTD. (BC)
Merged into Norex Resources Ltd. 04/01/1976
Each share Capital Stock 50¢ par exchanged for (1) share Common no par
Norex Resources Ltd. recapitalized as Consolidated Norex Resources Corp. 09/19/1983 which was acquired by Morgan Hydrocarbons Inc. 05/15/1992 which was acquired by Stampeder Exploration Ltd. 10/15/1996 which was acquired by Gulf Canada Resources Ltd. 09/10/1997
(See Gulf Canada Reources Ltd.)

CAESARS ACQUISITION CO (DE)
Merged into Caesars Entertainment Corp. 10/06/2017
Each share Class A Common $0.001 par exchanged for (1.625) shares Common 1¢ par

CAESARS ENTMT INC (DE)
Merged into Harrah's Entertainment, Inc. 06/13/2005
Each share Common $2.50 par exchanged for $17.75 cash

CAESARS EXPLORATIONS INC (BC)
Recapitalized 08/16/1999
Recapitalized from Caesar's Gold Ltd. to Caesar's Explorations Inc. 08/16/1999
Each share old Common no par exchanged for (0.5) share new Common no par
Name changed to Great Southern Enterprises Corp. 11/04/2002
Great Southern Enterprises Corp. recapitalized as Balmoral Resources Ltd. 03/29/2010

CAESARS N J INC (NJ)
Merged into Caesars World, Inc. 12/27/1990
Each share Common 10¢ par exchanged for $22.25 cash

CAESARS WORLD INC (FL)
Common 10¢ par split (3) for (2) by issuance of (0.5) additional share 11/10/1978
Common 10¢ par split (3) for (1) by issuance of (2) additional shares 06/05/1979
Merged into ITT Corp. 03/02/1995
Each share Common 10¢ par exchanged for $67.50 cash

CAESARSTONE SDOT YAM LTD (ISRAEL)
Name changed to Caesarstone Ltd. 06/20/2016

CAFE ODYSSEY INC (DE)
Name changed to Popmail.Com, Inc. 09/16/1999
(See Popmail.Com, Inc.)

CAFES ONE L P (DE)
Each Unit of Ltd. Partnership exchanged for initial distribution of $9.75 cash 12/13/1989
Each Unit of Ltd. Partnership received second distribution of $0.25 cash 02/28/1990
Each Unit of Ltd. Partnership received third and final distribution of $0.57339 cash 08/19/1994

CAFETERIAS INC (TX)
Common 40¢ par changed to 32¢ par and (0.25) additional share issued 02/03/1978
Common 32¢ par split (3) for (2) by issuance of (0.5) additional share 06/30/1978
Common 32¢ par split (5) for (4) by issuance of (0.25) additional share 08/15/1980
Stock Dividends - 10% 02/13/1976; 10% 02/08/1977
Name changed to Luby's Cafeterias, Inc. (TX) 01/07/1981
Luby's Cafeterias, Inc. (TX) reincorporated in Delaware 12/31/1991 which name changed to Luby's Inc. 01/08/1999

CAFFE DIVA GROUP LTD (DE)
Name changed to Autobahn International, Inc. 06/16/2005
Autobahn International, Inc. name changed to Global Developments, Inc. 06/05/2006

CAFFE ESPRESS CORP (NV)
Reincorporated 11/27/2002
State of incorporation changed from (NJ) to (NV) 11/27/2002
Name changed to M.POS, Inc. 03/10/2005

CAG CAP INC (BC)
Reincorporated 11/25/2009
Place of incorporation changed from (Canada) to (BC) 11/25/2009
Name changed to Stellar Biotechnologies, Inc. 04/19/2010

CAGIM REAL ESTATE CORP (CANADA)
Acquired by BTB Real Estate Investment Trust 06/08/2010
Each share Class A no par exchanged for $1.05 cash

CAGLES INC (GA)
Class A Common $1 par split (5) for (4) by issuance of (0.25) additional share 01/15/1994
Class A Common $1 par split (2) for (1) by issuance of (1) additional share 01/16/1995
Stock Dividends - 50% 11/03/1969; 25% 12/22/1972
Plan of reorganization under Chapter 11 Federal Bankruptcy proceedings effective

Each share Class A Common $1 par received initial distribution of $3.03 cash payable 02/11/2013 to holders of record 11/06/2012
Note: Name changed to CGLA Liquidation, Inc. 09/25/2012

CAGY INDUSTRIES, INC. (DE)
Each share old Common 50¢ par exchanged for (0.005) share new Common 50¢ par 08/15/1996
Note: In effect holders received $3 cash per share and public interest was eliminated

CAHABA PHARMACEUTICALS INC (NV)
Name changed to Visual Network Design, Inc. 07/21/2011
Visual Network Design, Inc. name changed to Rackwise, Inc. 10/27/2011

CAHOKIA DOWNS INC (DE)
Completely liquidated 01/01/1981
Each share Capital Stock $1 par exchanged for first and final distribution of $0.05 cash
Note: Unexchanged certificates were cancelled and became without value 12/31/1983

CAI WIRELESS SYS INC (CT)
Plan of reorganization under Chapter 11 Federal Bankruptcy proceedings confirmed 09/30/1998
No old Common stockholders' equity
Merged into MCI Worldcom, Inc. 08/31/1999
Each share new Common no par exchanged for $28 cash

CAIN CHEM INC (DE)
Merged into Occidental Petroleum Corp. 05/02/1988
Each share Class A Common 1¢ par exchanged for $73.958 cash

CAIN'S TRUCK LINES (CA)
Name changed to Transcon Lines 00/00/1947
Transcon Lines reorganized as Transcon Inc. 05/01/1981 which name changed to US 1 Industries, Inc. (CA) 09/21/1994 which reincorporated in Indiana 02/00/1995
(See US 1 Industries, Inc. (IN))

CAIO CAP CORP (AB)
Name changed to Battery One-Stop Inc. 03/30/1988
Battery One-Stop Inc. name changed to Battery One, Inc. 12/29/1994 which recapitalized as Power Plus Corp. 10/28/1996 which name changes to PPC Capital Corp. 08/03/1999
(See PPC Capital Corp.)

CAIRE INC (DE)
Acquired by MVE Holdings, Inc. 02/02/1998
Details not available

CAIRN ENERGY USA INC (DE)
Merged into Meridian Resource Corp. 11/05/1997
Each share Common 1¢ par exchanged for (1.08) shares Common 1¢ par
(See Meridian Resource Corp.)

CAIRN MINES LTD (BC)
Struck off register and declared dissolved for failure to file returns 11/17/1975

CAIRN PETES LTD (AB)
Acquired by Dynamar Energy Ltd. 00/00/1981
Details not available

CAIRNGLEN EXPLS LTD (ON)
Charter cancelled and declared dissolved for failure to file returns and pay fees 05/14/1975

CAIRO BRIDGE & TERMINAL CO.
Reorganized as Cairo Bridge Co. 00/00/1933
Details not available

CAIRO BRIDGE CO.
Liquidated 00/00/1942
Details not available

CAIS INTERNET INC (DE)
Name changed to Ardent Communications, Inc. 07/26/2001
(See Ardent Communications, Inc.)

CAIYSTANE CAP CORP (AB)
Name changed to Armada Financial Corp. 10/06/1992
Armada Financial Corp. recapitalized as Armada Gold Corp. (AB) 01/06/1994 which reincorporated in Yukon 07/05/1996
(See Armada Gold Corp.)

CAJUN OIL & GAS PRODUCERS INC (BC)
Recapitalized as Alto Industries Inc. 01/21/1994
Each share Common no par exchanged for (0.16666666) share Common no par
Alto Industries Inc. name changed to Alto Minerals Inc. 04/07/1997 which recapitalized as Alto Ventures Ltd. 04/19/2002

CAL ALTA AUTO GLASS INC (NV)
Each share old Common $0.001 par exchanged for (0.005) share new Common $0.001 par 10/20/2010
Name changed to Mining Minerals of Mexico Corp. 05/21/2012
Mining Minerals of Mexico Corp. recapitalized as Aurum Resource & Asset Management, Inc. 07/17/2014 which name changed to Innovest Global, Inc. 01/30/2017

CAL AM CORP (NY)
Filed a petition under Chapter 11 Federal Bankruptcy Code 11/08/1982
Stockholders' equity unlikely

CAL DENVER RES LTD (BC)
Recapitalized as Carson Gold Corp. (BC) 10/13/1987
Each share Common no par exchanged for (0.5) share Common no par
Carson Gold Corp. (BC) reincorporated in Yukon 08/11/1995 which name changed to Diamondworks Ltd. 10/20/1996 which name changed to Energem Resources Inc. (Yukon) 06/09/2004 which reincorporated in British Columbia 07/21/2005

CAL DIVE INTL INC (MN)
Common no par split (2) for (1) by issuance of (1) additional share payable 11/13/2000 to holders of record 10/30/2000 Ex date - 11/14/2000
Common no par split (2) for (1) by issuance of (1) additional share payable 12/08/2005 to holders of record 12/01/2005 Ex date - 12/09/2005
Name changed to Helix Energy Solutions Group, Inc. 03/06/2006

CAL DYNAMICS CORP (BC)
Recapitalized as Ridgecrest Resources Ltd. 08/17/1984
Each share Common no par exchanged for (0.2) share Common no par
Ridgecrest Resources Ltd. name changed to Hallicrafters Communications International Co. Ltd. 12/31/1985 which name changed to Johnston & Frye Securities Ltd. 12/01/1987
(See Johnston & Frye Securities Ltd.)

CAL DYNAMICS ENERGY CORP. (BC)
Name changed to Cal Dynamics Corp. 01/10/1984
Cal Dynamics Corp. recapitalized as Ridgecrest Resources Ltd. 08/17/1984 which name changed to Hallicrafters Communications International Co. Ltd. 12/31/1985 which name changed to Johnston & Frye Securities Ltd. 12/01/1987
(See Johnston & Frye Securities Ltd.)

CAL-FACTORS, INC. (CA)
Name changed to Certified Financial, Inc. 08/29/1962
Certified Financial, Inc. was acquired by Voss Corp. 05/19/1969
(See Voss Corp.)

CAL FED BANCORP INC (DE)
Merged into California Federal Bank, A Federal Savings Bank (Los Angeles, CA) 01/03/1997
Each share Common $1 par exchanged for (0.1) Secondary Contingent Litigation Recovery Participation Interest and $23.50 cash

CAL FED INCOME PARTNERS L P (DE)
Name changed to CF Income Partners L.P. 01/02/1990
(See CF Income Partners L.P.)

CAL GRAPHITE CORP (BC)
Common no par split (2) for (1) by issuance of (1) additional share 10/10/1986
Common no par split (3) for (2) by issuance of (0.5) additional share 07/09/1990
Reincorporated under the laws of Ontario as Applied Carbon Technology, Inc. 07/12/1993
Applied Carbon Technology, Inc. name changed to Merchant Capital Group Inc. 07/17/2000
(See Merchant Capital Group Inc.)

CAL-MOAB URANIUM CORP. (OK)
Name changed to Hydromotive Corp. 06/24/1961
(See Hydromotive Corp.)

CAL RAY BAKERIES, INC. (CA)
Acquired by Burry Biscuit Corp. 07/27/1961
Each share Common $1 par exchanged for (0.5) share Common $0.125 par
Burry Biscuit Corp. acquired by Quaker Oats Co. 01/05/1962 which was acquired by PepsiCo, Inc. 08/02/2001

CAL REP BANCORP INC (CA)
Common $1 par split (2) for (1) by issuance of (1) additional share 09/14/1987
Stock Dividends - 10% 10/14/1988; 10% 06/30/1989
Acquired by First Interstate Bancorp 12/10/1993
Each share Common $1 par exchanged for (0.432715) share Common $2 par
First Interstate Bancorp merged into Wells Fargo & Co. (Old) 04/01/1996 which merged into Wells Fargo & Co. (New) 11/02/1998

CAL STAR FINL SVCS INC (DE)
Common 1¢ par split (2) for (1) by issuance of (1) additional share 06/30/1984
Charter cancelled and declared inoperative and void for non-payment of taxes 03/01/1991

CAL-STAR INC (WY)
Name changed to Amanta Resources Ltd. (WY) 07/13/2004
Amanta Resources Inc. (WY) reincorporated in British Columbia 08/31/2004

CAL STAR RES CORP (BC)
Struck off register and declared dissolved for failure to file returns 06/05/1987

CAL-TECH SYSTEMS, INC. (DE)
Class A Common 50¢ par reclassified as Common 50¢ par 02/03/1961

Name changed to Fullview Industries, Inc. 08/31/1962
Fullview Industries, Inc. recapitalized as Darfield Industries, Inc. 03/09/1972
(See Darfield Industries, Inc.)

CAL-UTAH URANIUM, INC. (CA)
Charter suspended for non-payment of taxes 10/02/1961
No stockholders' equity

CAL UTE TECHNOLOGIES INC (UT)
Involuntarily dissolved 02/01/1989

CAL-VAL RESEARCH & DEVELOPMENT CORP. (DE)
Completely liquidated 03/15/1966
Each share Common 10¢ par exchanged for first and final distribution of $0.40 cash

CAL-WEST AVIATION, INC. (CA)
Placed in bankruptcy 10/30/1964
No stockholders' equity

CAL WEST PETES LTD (AB)
Recapitalized as Legacy Petroleum Ltd. 06/26/1985
Each share Common no par exchanged for (0.2) share Class A Common no par
(See Legacy Petroleum Ltd.)

CALA CORP (OK)
SEC revoked common stock registration 03/06/2017

CALA ENERGY CORP (NV)
Each share old Common $0.001 par exchanged for (0.00125) share new Common $0.001 par 03/25/2015
Name changed to Lingerie Fighting Championships, Inc. 04/29/2015

CALADESI NATL BK (DUNEDIN, FL)
Common $25 par changed to $10 par and (1.5) additional shares issued plus a 10% stock dividend paid 03/02/1970
Acquired by Southeast National Bank (Dunedin, FL) 11/15/1971
Each share Common $10 par exchanged for (0.52) share Common $10 par
(See Southeast National Bank (Dunedin, FL))

CALAHOO PETE LTD (AB)
Each share old Common no par exchanged for (0.33333333) share new Common no par 06/22/1998
Acquired by Samson Investment Co. 06/15/2000
Each share Class C Preferred Ser. 1 no par exchanged for $1.05 cash
Each share new Common no par exchanged for $2.90 cash

CALAIS CORP (MN)
Recapitalized as Braxton Industries, Inc. 06/05/1987
Each share Common no par exchanged for (0.33333333) share Common no par
(See Braxton Industries, Inc.)

CALAIS GROUP INC (AB)
Name changed to Airline Training International Ltd. 01/10/2000
(See Airline Training International Ltd.)

CALAIS RES INC (BC)
SEC revoked common stock registration 06/29/2012

CALAIS RES LTD (AB)
Acquired by Financial Trustco Capital Ltd. 06/04/1985
Each share Common no par exchanged for (0.045) share 10-1/4% 1st Preferred $10 par and $0.45 cash
Financial Trustco Capital Ltd. name changed to FT Capital Ltd. 07/25/1989
(See FT Capital Ltd.)

CALALTA PETROLEUMS LTD. (AB)
Acquired by Plains Petroleums Ltd. 06/15/1963

CAL-CAL

Each share Common 25¢ par exchanged for (1) share Common no par
(See Plains Petroleums Ltd.)

CALAMBA SUGAR ESTATE
Each share Common $20 par exchanged for (1) share Capital Stock $1 par of Calamba Sugar Estate, Inc. 00/00/1943
(See Calamba Sugar Estate, Inc.)

CALAMBA SUGAR ESTATE, INC. (CA)
Liquidation completed 03/15/1960 Details not available

CALAMITY CREEK URANIUM CORP. (UT)
Name changed to Transamerica Enterprises, Inc. 02/09/1960
(See Transamerica Enterprises, Inc.)

CALAMOS ASSET MGMT INC (DE)
Acquired by Calamos Partners LLC 02/21/2017
Each share Class A Common 1¢ par exchanged for $8.25 cash

CALAMOS CONV & HIGH INCOME FD (DE)
Preferred Shares Ser. M no par called for redemption at $25,000 on 07/21/2009
Preferred Shares Ser. TU no par called for redemption at $25,000 on 07/22/2009
Preferred Shares Ser. A no par called for redemption at $25,000 on 07/23/2009
Preferred Shares Ser. W no par called for redemption at $25,000 on 07/23/2009
Preferred Shares Ser. TH no par called for redemption at $25,000 on 07/24/2009
Preferred Shares Ser. F no par called for redemption at $25,000 on 07/27/2009
(Additional Information in Active)

CALAMOS CONV OPPORTUNITIES & INCOME FD (DE)
Auction Market Preferred Ser. W28 no par called for redemption at $25,000 on 08/13/2009
Auction Market Preferred Ser. M no par called for redemption at $25,000 on 08/18/2009
Auction Market Preferred Ser. TU no par called for redemption at $25,000 on 08/19/2009
Auction Market Preferred Ser. W no par called for redemption at $25,000 on 08/20/2009
Auction Market Preferred Ser. TH no par called for redemption at $25,000 on 08/21/2009
Auction Market Preferred Ser. TH7 no par called for redemption at $25,000 on 08/21/2009
Auction Market Preferred Ser. F7 no par called for redemption at $25,000 on 08/24/2009
(Additional Information in Active)

CALAMOS ETF TR (DE)
Trust terminated 08/02/2016
Each share Calamos Focus Growth ETF no par received $10.539048 cash

CALAMOS GLOBAL DYNAMIC INCOME FD (DE)
Auction Rate Preferred Ser. T no par called for redemption at $25,000 on 10/21/2009
Auction Rate Preferred Ser. W no par called for redemption at $25,000 on 10/22/2009
Auction Rate Preferred Ser. TH no par called for redemption at $25,000 on 10/23/2009
Auction Rate Preferred Ser. F no par called for redemption at $25,000 on 10/26/2009
Auction Rate Preferred Ser. M no par called for redemption at $25,000 on 10/27/2009

(Additional Information in Active)
CALAMOS GLOBAL TOTAL RETURN FD (DE)
Auction Rate Preferred Ser. T called for redemption at $25,000 on 05/13/2008
(Additional Information in Active)

CALAMOS INVT TR OLD (MA)
Under plan of reorganization each share Convertible Income Fund no par automatically became CFS Investment Trust Calamos Convertible Fund no par 05/01/1992

CALAMOS STRATEGIC TOTAL RETURN FD (DE)
Auction Rate Preferred Ser. M no par called for redemption at $25,000 on 06/23/2009
Auction Rate Preferred Ser. TU no par called for redemption at $25,000 on 06/24/2009
Auction Rate Preferred Ser. A no par called for redemption at $25,000 on 06/25/2009
Auction Rate Preferred Ser. W no par called for redemption at $25,000 on 06/25/2009
Auction Rate Preferred Ser. B no par called for redemption at $25,000 on 06/26/2009
Auction Rate Preferred Ser. TH no par called for redemption at $25,000 on 06/26/2009
Auction Rate Preferred Ser. F no par called for redemption at $25,000 on 06/29/2009
(Additional Information in Active)

CALANDRA INDS INC (DE)
Reincorporated 08/25/1971
Stock Dividends - Class A & B Common 100% 10/14/1968; 10% 05/10/1971
Name and state of incorporation changed from Calandra Photo, Inc. (NE) to Calandra Industries, Inc. (DE) 08/25/1971
Class A Common $1 par split (3) for (2) by issuance of (0.5) additional share 03/10/1972
Conv. Class B Common $1 par split (3) for (2) by issuance of (0.5) additional share 03/10/1972
Acquired by Fox-Stanley Photo Products, Inc. 06/19/1973
Each share Class A Common $1 par exchanged for $11.25 cash
Each share Conv. Class B Common $1 par exchanged for $11.25 cash
Note: An additional distribution of $0.80 cash per share was paid 04/01/1974

CALARIVADA SILVERS (AZ)
Charter expired by time limitation 10/06/1946

CALATLANTIC GROUP INC (DE)
Merged into Lennar Corp. 02/12/2018
Each share Common 1¢ par exchanged for (0.885) share Class A Common 10¢ par and (0.0177) share Class B Common 10¢ par

CALAVERAS CEMENT CO. (DE)
Common no par changed to $5 par 00/00/1950
Stock Dividend - 10% 12/26/1950
Merged into Flintkote Co. 09/30/1959
Each share Common $5 par exchanged for (1.7) shares Common $5 par
(See Flintkote Co.)

CALAVERAS EXPLS LTD (BC)
Recapitalized as Cardinal Mineral Corp. Ltd. 06/11/1986
Each share Common no par exchanged for (0.4) share Common no par
Cardinal Mineral Corp. Ltd. recapitalized as Connecticut Development Corp. 11/08/1990 which recapitalized as Mira Properties Ltd. 04/16/1999 which recapitalized as Resolve Ventures, Inc. 08/19/2003

CALAVERAS LAND & TIMBER CORP. (MI)
Liquidation completed
Each share Common $1 par exchanged for initial distribution of $28 cash 01/15/1962
Each share Common $1 par received second distribution of $4.25 cash 06/21/1962
Each share Common $1 par received third and final distribution of $0.19 cash 06/19/1964

CALBATECH INC (NV)
Recapitalized as LifeStem International, Inc. 05/02/2008
Each share Common $0.001 par exchanged for (0.00033333) share Common $0.001 par
LifeStem International, Inc. recapitalized as International Aerospace Enterprises, Inc. 04/30/2009
(See International Aerospace Enterprises, Inc.)

CALBIOCHEM (CA)
Common $1 par changed to 50¢ par and (1) additional share issued 06/22/1976
Merged into American Hoechst Corp. 11/30/1977
Each share Common 50¢ par exchanged for $10.25 cash

CALBRICO PETROLEUMS LTD. (AB)
Recapitalized as New Calbrico Petroleums Ltd. 02/09/1966
Each share Capital Stock no par exchanged for (0.01) share Capital Stock no par
(See New Calbrico Petroleums Ltd.)

CALCAP INVTS LTD (AB)
Delisted from Alberta Stock Exchange 02/07/1994

CALCASIEU MARINE NATL BK (LAKE CHARLES, LA)
Each share Capital Stock $100 par exchanged for (10) shares Capital Stock $10 par 09/01/1977
Stock Dividends - 38.9% 05/27/1941; 20% 02/26/1946; 25% 11/00/1948; 33.33333333% 12/12/1949; 50% 06/23/1952; 33.33333333% 03/26/1955; 25% 01/08/1957; 40% 06/22/1959; 50% 02/28/1964; 33.33333333% 02/28/1966; 50% 01/31/1973
Common $10 par reclassified as Class A Common $10 par 04/29/1988
Under plan of reorganization each share Class A Common $10 par and Class B Common $10 par automatically became (1) share CM Bank Holding Co. Class A Common $10 par or Class B Common $10 par respectively 10/21/1994
(See CM Bank Holding Co.)

CALCASIEU REAL ESTATE & OIL CO (LA)
Each share old Common no par exchanged for (50) shares new Common no par 07/14/1981
Name changed to CKX Lands, Inc. 05/14/2005

CALCO CHEMICAL CO.
Acquired by American Cyanamid Co. 00/00/1929
Details not available

CALCO ENTERPRISES INC (WA)
Merged into Realm Resources, Inc. (NV) 04/14/1983
Each share Common 5¢ par exchanged for (0.5) share Class A Common 1¢ par and (0.5) share Common 1¢ par
Realm Resources, Inc. (NV) reincorporated in Wyoming 10/30/1991
(See Realm Resources, Inc. (WY))

CALCO RES INC (BC)
Recapitalized as Berkshire International Mining Ltd. 02/19/1997
Each share Common no par exchanged for (0.1) share Common no par
Berkshire International Mining Ltd. recapitalized as Tyner Resources Ltd. 01/24/2002

CALCOMP TECHNOLOGY INC (DE)
Voluntarily dissolved 08/06/1999
Stockholders' equity unlikely

CALCORP RES LTD (BC)
Struck off register and declared dissolved for failure to file returns 01/31/1977

CALCULATOR COMPUTER LEASING CORP (DE)
Recapitalized as Electric M & R Inc. 03/28/1980
Each share Common 10¢ par exchanged for (0.1) share Common $1 par
(See Electric M & R Inc.)

CALDATA, INC. (CA)
No longer in existence having become inoperative and void for non-payment of taxes 04/01/1965

CALDER BOUSQUET GOLD MINES LTD. (ON)
Merged into Pardee Amalgamated Mines Ltd. 12/31/1954
Each share Common exchanged for (0.2) share Common $1 par
Pardee Amalgamated Mines Ltd. liquidated for Rio Algom Mines Ltd. 11/09/1961 which name changed to Rio Algom Ltd. 04/30/1975
(See Rio Algom Ltd.)

CALDERA CORP (FL)
Name changed to Level Jump Financial Group, Inc. 12/28/1999
(See Level Jump Financial Group, Inc.)

CALDERA CORP (NV)
Charter cancelled 09/30/2014

CALDERA INC (DE)
Recapitalized as Unistar Financial Service Corp. 08/17/1998
Each share Common 1¢ par exchanged for (0.06666666) share Common $0.001 par
(See Unistar Financial Service Corp.)

CALDERA INTL INC (DE)
Each share old Common $0.001 par exchanged for (0.25) share new Common $0.001 par 03/14/2002
Name changed to SCO Group, Inc. 05/16/2003
(See SCO Group, Inc.)

CALDERA MINES LTD (BC)
Name changed to MTC Electronic Technologies Co. Ltd. 04/30/1987
MTC Electronic Technologies Co. Ltd. name changed to GrandeTel Technologies Inc. (BC) 09/08/1995 which reincorporated in Canada 09/28/1995
(See GrandeTel Technologies Inc.)

CALDERA PHARMACEUTICALS INC (DE)
Name changed to XRpro Sciences, Inc. 12/04/2014
XRpro Sciences, Inc. name changed to Icagen, Inc. (New) 09/22/2015

CALDERA SYS INC (DE)
Name changed to Caldera International, Inc. 05/04/2001
Caldera International, Inc. name changed to SCO Group, Inc. 05/16/2003
(See SCO Group, Inc.)

CALDERA TECHNOLOGIES CORP (YT)
Name changed 12/02/1992
Reincorporated 08/16/1994
Recapitalized 06/18/1996
Name changed from Caldera

Resources Ltd. to Caldera Environmental Corp. 12/02/1992
Place of incorporation changed from (BC) to (Yukon) 08/16/1994
Recapitalized from Caldera Environmental Corp. to Caldera Technologies Corp. 06/18/1996
Each share Common no par exchanged for (0.1) share Common no par
Cease trade order effective 07/15/1997
Stockholders' equity unlikely

CALDERONE CORP (ON)
Name changed to Cardinal Factor Corp. 07/21/2000
(See Cardinal Factor Corp.)

CALDERONE CURRAN RANCHES INC (MI)
Charter declared inoperative and void for failure to file reports 08/11/1976

CALDINA OILS LTD. (ON)
Charter cancelled and proclaimed dissolved for failure to pay taxes and file returns 11/05/1962

CALDOR CORP NEW (DE)
Assets sold for the benefit of creditors 01/22/1999
No stockholders' equity

CALDOR INC OLD (DE)
Common 10¢ par changed to 5¢ par and (1) additional share issued 09/20/1963
Common 5¢ par split (5) for (4) by issuance of (0.25) additional share 10/22/1965
Common 5¢ par split (5) for (4) by issuance of (0.25) additional share 08/31/1966
5.5% Conv. Preferred $20 par called for redemption 04/11/1967
Common 5¢ par split (4) for (3) by issuance of (0.33333333) additional share 11/09/1979
Stock Dividends - 25% 04/16/1971; 25% 11/12/1976
Merged into Associated Dry Goods Corp. 05/27/1981
Each share Common 5¢ par exchanged for (0.4222) share $4.75 Conv. Preferred Ser. A $50 par and $15.89 cash
(See Associated Dry Goods Corp.)

CALDWELL (A. & G.J.), INC. (DE)
Each share Common $1 par exchanged for (0.01) share Common $100 par 11/30/1954
Merged into Felton & Son, Inc. 07/31/1957
Each share Common $100 par exchanged for (1) share 5% Preferred $100 par and $35 cash
(See Felton & Son, Inc.)

CALDWELL (J.E.) & CO. (PA)
Name changed to Caldwell (J.E.) Co. 01/25/1965
Caldwell (J.E.) Co. merged into Dayton Corp. 02/14/1969 which name changed to Dayton-Hudson Corp. 06/20/1969 which name changed to Target Corp. 01/31/2000

CALDWELL COMPUTER CORP (TX)
Name changed to Brooks International, Inc. 03/01/1971
Brooks International, Inc. name changed to Incorporated Carriers Ltd. 11/21/1979
(See Incorporated Carriers Ltd.)

CALDWELL CONSTR CORP (DE)
Charter cancelled and declared inoperative and void for non-payment of taxes 04/15/1972

CALDWELL FD INC (FL)
Name changed to C/Funds Group, Inc. 06/25/1992
(See C/Funds Group, Inc.)

CALDWELL INDS INC (DE)
Charter cancelled and declared inoperative and void for non-payment of taxes 04/15/1974

CALDWELL J E & CO (PA)
Merged into Dayton Corp. 02/14/1969
Details not available

CALDWELL SAVINGS & LOAN, INC. (LENOIR, NC)
Name changed to Caldwell Savings Bank, Inc. (Lenoir, NC) 05/28/1986
Caldwell Savings Bank, Inc. (Lenoir, NC) name changed to Caldwell Savings Bank, Inc., SSB (Lenoir, NC) 07/31/1992
(See Caldwell Savings Bank, Inc., SSB (Lenoir, NC))

CALDWELL SAVINGS BANK, INC., SSB (LENOIR, NC)
Acquired by First-Citizens Bank & Trust Co. (Raleigh, NC) 06/19/1993
Details not available

CALDWELL SAVINGS BANK, INC. (LENOIR, NC)
Name changed to Caldwell Savings Bank, Inc., SSB (Lenoir, NC) 07/31/1992
(See Caldwell Savings Bank, Inc., SSB (Lenoir, NC))

CALECO PHARMA CORP (NV)
SEC revoked common stock registration 11/24/2014

CALEDONIA FINL CORP (MI)
Common split (2) for (1) by issuance of (1) additional share payable 06/15/2000 to holders of record 06/01/2000 Ex date - 06/29/2000
Common split (2) for (1) by issuance of (1) additional share payable 04/03/2003 to holders of record 03/18/2003 Ex date - 04/04/2003
Merged into Chemical Financial Corp. 12/01/2000
Each share Common exchanged for $39 cash

CALEDONIA MNG CORP (CANADA)
Reincorporated 03/29/1995
Place of incorporation changed from (BC) to (Canada) 03/29/1995
Each share old Common no par exchanged for (0.1) share new Common no par 04/12/2013
Reincorporated under the laws of Jersey as Caledonia Mining Corp. PLC 03/24/2016

CALEDONIA RES LTD (BC)
Common no par split (2) for (1) by issuance of (1) additional share 09/22/1980
Recapitalized as Aston Resources Ltd. (New) 02/03/1988
Each share Common no par exchanged for (0.2) share Common no par
Aston Resources Ltd. (New) recapitalized as Consolidated Aston Resources Ltd. 06/13/1996
(See Consolidated Aston Resources Ltd.)

CALEDONIA SILVER LEAD MNG CO (ID)
Name changed to Nevada-Comstock Mining Co. 11/01/2004

CALEDONIAN PACIFIC MINERALS N L (AUSTRALIA)
Name changed to Quadtel Ltd. 07/27/2000
Quadtel Ltd. name changed to Wytomic Ltd. 03/17/2004 which name changed to Sultan Corp. Ltd. 12/06/2006 which name changed to Balamara Resources, Ltd. 02/07/2012

CALENDAR CAP INC (MN)
Each share old Common 1¢ par exchanged for (0.05) share new Common 1¢ par 02/16/2001
Name changed to IQUniverse, Inc. 04/11/2001
(See IQUniverse, Inc.)

CALENDAR DRAGON INC (NV)
Reorganized as North American Oil & Gas Corp. 11/16/2012
Each share Common $0.001 par exchanged for (19) shares Common $0.001 par
(See North American Oil & Gas Corp.)

CALENDAR PROFITS INC (BRITISH VIRGIN ISLANDS)
Name changed to Galaxy Strategy & Communications Inc. 03/09/2011

CALENERGY CAP TR II (DE)
6.25% Conv. Trust Preferred Securities called for redemption at $50 on 07/29/2010

CALENERGY CAP TR III (DE)
6.50% Conv. Preferred Securities called for redemption at $50 on 12/01/2011

CALENERGY INC (DE)
Merged into MidAmerican Energy Holdings Co. (New) 03/12/1999
Each share Common $0.001 par exchanged for (1) share Common no par
(See MidAmerican Energy Holdings Co. (New))

CALEX RES LTD (AB)
Merged into Beau Canada Exploration Ltd. 10/19/1994
Each share Common no par exchanged for (0.5132) share Common no par
(See Beau Canada Exploration Ltd.)

CALFED INC (DE)
$4.75 Conv. Preferred $1 par called for redemption 08/08/1986
Merged into California Federal Bank, A Federal Savings Bank (Los Angeles, CA) 12/16/1992
Each share Common $1 par exchanged for (1) share Common $1 par and (0.541) Common Stock Purchase Warrant expiring 06/30/1994
California Federal Bank, A Federal Savings Bank (Los Angeles, CA) name changed to Citibank (West) FSB (San Francisco, CA) 12/11/2002
(See Citibank (West) FSB (San Francisco, CA))

CALGARY & EDMONTON CORP. LTD. (CANADA)
Acquired by Canadian Superior Oil Ltd. 08/12/1965
Each share Capital Stock no par exchanged for (1.16) shares Common $1 par
(See Canadian Superior Oil Ltd.)

CALGARY CENTRE HLDGS LTD (AB)
8.125% Retractable 1st Preferred Ser. 1 no par called for redemption 07/20/1992
Public interest eliminated

CALGARY POWER CO. LTD.
Liquidation completed 00/00/1948
Details not available

CALGARY POWER INVESTMENTS, LTD. (CANADA)
Name changed to Canelco Services Ltd. 12/06/1962

CALGARY PWR LTD (CANADA)
Each share old Common no par exchanged for (5) shares new Common no par 11/30/1959
4% Preferred $100 par reclassified as 4% 1st Ser. 1st Preferred $100 par 10/31/1973
4.5% Preferred $100 par reclassified as 4.5% 2nd Ser. 1st Preferred $100 par 10/31/1973
5% Preferred $100 par reclassified as 5% 3rd Ser. 1st Preferred $100 par 10/31/1973
5.4% Conv. Preferred $100 par reclassified as 5.4% 4th Ser. Conv. 1st Preferred $100 par 10/31/1973
7% Preferred $100 par reclassified as 7% 5th Ser. 1st Preferred $100 par 10/31/1973
Common no par reclassified as Conv. Class A Common no par 06/41/1975
5.4% 4th Ser. 1st Preferred $100 par conversion privilege expired 11/30/1976
Par value of all classes of Preferred then outstanding changed to no par 05/03/1979
Conv. Class A Common no par split (3) for (1) by issuance of (2) additional shares 05/23/1980
Conv. Class B Common no par split (3) for (1) by issuance of (2) additional shares 05/23/1980
Stock Dividend - 200% 10/15/1953
Name changed to TransAlta Utilities Corp. 06/15/1981

CALGENE INC (DE)
Reincorporated 01/22/1987
State of incorporation changed from (CA) to (DE) and Common no par changed to $0.001 par 01/22/1987
$2.25 Conv. Exchangeable Preferred $0.001 par called for redemption 07/27/1992
Merged into Monsanto Co. 05/19/1997
Each share Common $0.001 par exchanged for $8 cash

CALGON CARBON CORP (DE)
Common 1¢ par split (2) for (1) by issuance of (1) additional share 11/14/1988
Common 1¢ par split (2) for (1) by issuance of (1) additional share 06/03/1991
Acquired by Kuraray Co., Ltd. 03/09/2018
Each share Common 1¢ par exchanged for $21.50 cash

CALGON CORP. (PA)
5.3% Conv. Preferred $50 par called for redemption 09/01/1964
Common $1 par split (5) for (2) by issuance of (1.5) additional shares 12/29/1964
Merged into Merck & Co., Inc. (Old) 01/31/1968
Each share Common $1 par exchanged for (0.85) share Common $0.05555555 par
Merck & Co., Inc. (Old) merged into Merck & Co., Inc. (New) 11/03/2009

CALGROUP GRAPHICS LTD (ON)
Struck off register and declared dissolved for failure to file reports 04/27/1992

CALHOUN INVT INC (SC)
Merged into Anco Corp. 06/09/1970
Each share Common $1 par exchanged for (1) share Common $1 par
Anco Corp. name changed to Appalachian National Corp. 05/02/1972
(See Appalachian National Corp.)

CALHOUN LIFE INSURANCE CO. (SC)
Common $2.50 par changed to $1 par 00/00/1956
Name changed to Calhoun Investment Co., Inc. 04/06/1967
Calhoun Investment Co., Inc. merged into Anco Corp. 06/09/1970 which name changed to Appalachian National Corp. 05/02/1972
(See Appalachian National Corp.)

CALHOUN-RUMSEY BRIDGE CO.
Sold to Kentucky State Highway Dept. 00/00/1937
Details not available

CALI COMPUTER SYS INC (NY)
Charter cancelled and proclaimed dissolved for failure to pay taxes 09/25/1991

CALI HLDGS INC (UT)
Name changed to Sovereign

Exploration Associates Interrnational, Inc. 10/27/2005

CALI RLTY CORP (MD)
Name changed to Mack-Cali Realty Corp. 12/12/1997

CALIAN TECHNOLOGIES LTD (CANADA)
Name changed to Calian Group Ltd. 04/05/2016

CALIAN TECHNOLOGY LTD (CANADA)
Name changed to Calian Technologies Ltd. 03/14/2005
Calian Technologies Ltd. name changed to Calian Group Ltd. 04/05/2016

CALIBER LEARNING NETWORK INC (MD)
Plan of reorganization under Chapter 11 Federal Bankruptcy Code effective 11/26/2004
No stockholders' equity

CALIBER SYS INC (OH)
Merged into FDX Corp. 01/27/1998
Each share Common no par exchanged for (0.8) share Common 10¢ par
FDX Corp. name changed to FedEx Corp. 01/19/2000

CALIBERT EXPLORATIONS LTD (NV)
Common $0.001 par split (15) for (1) by issuance of (14) additional shares payable 08/24/2010 to holders of record 08/24/2010
Common $0.001 par split (12) for (5) by issuance of (1.4) additional shares payable 11/29/2010 to holders of record 11/26/2010 Ex date - 12/01/2010
Name changed to Net Savings Link, Inc. (NV) 12/03/2010
Net Savings Link, Inc. (NV) reincorporated in Colorado 02/28/2017 which reincorporated in Delaware 05/17/2017

CALIBRE CORP (OH)
Name changed to Meret Inc. 02/28/1986
(See Meret Inc.)

CALIBRE ENERGY INC (AB)
Plan of arrangement effective 10/12/1999
Holdings of (11,200) shares or more exchanged for Trego Energy Inc. (a private company) Redeemable Class B Common no par on a (1) for (56) basis or $1 cash per share
Holdings of (11,199) or fewer shares exchanged for $1 cash per share
Note: Unredeemed Class B Common was reclassified as Class A Common 12/05/1999

CALIBRE TECHNOLOGIES CORP (BC)
Delisted from Vancouver Stock Exchange 12/10/1996

CALIBRUS INC (NV)
Name changed to Grow Condos, Inc. 10/08/2014

CALICO COMM INC (DE)
Under plan of reorganization each share Common $0.001 par received initial distribution of $0.46 cash payable 12/18/2003 to holders of record 08/26/2003
Each share Common $0.001 par received second distribution of $0.09 cash payable 05/17/2004 to holders of record 08/26/2003
Each share Common $0.001 par received third and final distribution of $0.03 cash payable 12/28/2004 to holders of record 08/26/2003
Note: Certificates were not required to be surrendered and are without value

CALICO EXPLORATION CORP. (UT)
Reincorporated under the laws of Nevada as Imperial Petroleum, Inc. 03/03/1981
Each share Common $0.001 par exchanged for (1) share Common $0.001 par

CALICO RES CORP (BC)
Merged into Paramount Gold Nevada Corp. 07/07/2016
Each share Common no par exchanged for (0.07) share Common 1¢ par
Note: Unexchanged certificates will be cancelled and become without value 07/07/2022

CALICO SEARCH CORP (DE)
Name changed to Interwest Communications Corp. 05/09/1989
Interwest Communications Corp. merged into Internet Communications Corp. 09/19/1996 which merged into Internet Commerce & Communications, Inc. 11/29/2000
(See Internet Commerce & Communications, Inc.)

CALICO SILVER MINES LTD (BC)
Recapitalized as Sable Resources Ltd. 02/06/1980
Each share Common no par exchanged for (0.2) share Common no par

CALIENTE CAP CORP (BC)
Reincorporated under the laws of Alberta as Webtech Wireless Inc. 03/25/2003
Webtech Wireless Inc. (AB) reincorporated in British Columbia 08/01/2006 which merged into BSM Technologies Inc. 10/05/2015

CALIENTE RES LTD (BC)
Struck from the register and declared dissolved 10/09/1992

CALIFORNIA AERO TOPO INC (CA)
Name changed to Earthdata, Inc. 12/31/1976
(See Earthdata, Inc.)

CALIFORNIA ALMOND INVESTORS I (CA)
Completely liquidated 12/20/2004
Details not available

CALIFORNIA AMPLIFIER INC (DE)
Reincorporated 12/31/1987
State of incorporation changed from (CA) to (DE) 12/31/1987
Common 1¢ par split (2) for (1) by issuance of (1) additional share payable 03/22/1996 to holders of record 03/01/1996
Name changed to CalAmp Corp. 08/04/2004

CALIFORNIA ASIC TECHNICAL SVCS INC (NV)
Old Common $0.001 par split (2) for (1) by issuance of (1) additional share 10/08/1993
Each share old Common $0.001 par exchanged for (1/3) share new Common $0.001 par 03/23/1995
Merged into JMAR Technologies, Inc. 05/01/1998
Each share new Common $0.001 par exchanged for (0.091) share Common $0.001 par 05/01/1998
(See JMAR Technologies, Inc.)

CALIFORNIA ASSETS CORP.
Out of business 00/00/1944
Details not available

CALIFORNIA ASSOCIATES, INC. (DE)
Dissolved 12/16/1936
Details not available

CALIFORNIA BAKING CO.
Acquired by Langendorf United Bakeries, Inc. 00/00/1928
Details not available

CALIFORNIA BANCORP INC (DE)
Common $5 par changed to $2.50 par and (1) additional share issued 05/15/1980
In process of liquidation
Each share Common $2.50 par received initial distribution of $8 cash 07/16/1982
Note: Details on subsequent distribution(s), if any, are not available

CALIFORNIA BANCSHARES INC (DE)
Merged into U.S. Bancorp (OR) 06/06/1996
Each share Common $2.50 par exchanged for (0.95) share Common $5 par
U.S. Bancorp (OR) merged into U.S. Bancorp (Old) (DE) 08/01/1997 which merged into U.S. Bancorp 02/27/2001

CALIFORNIA BANK (LOS ANGELES, CA)
Each share Common $25 par exchanged for (2) shares Common $12.50 par 00/00/1953
Stock Dividend - 40% 06/29/1959
Merged into United California Bank (Los Angeles, CA) 02/24/1961
Each share Common $12.50 par exchanged for (1.25) shares Capital Stock $12.50 par
United California Bank (Los Angeles, CA) merged into Western Bancorporation 01/16/1978 which name changed to First Interstate Bancorp 06/01/1981 which merged into Wells Fargo & Co. (Old) 04/01/1996 which merged into Wells Fargo & Co. (New) 11/02/1998

CALIFORNIA BK COMM (LAFAYETTE, CA)
Under plan of reorganization each share Common no par automatically became (1) share California BanCorp Common no par 07/03/2017

CALIFORNIA BIOTECHNOLOGY INC (DE)
Reincorporated 04/08/1988
State of incorporation changed from (CA) to (DE) and Common no par changed to 1¢ par 04/08/1988
Name changed to Scios Inc. 03/02/1992
Scios Inc. merged into Scios-Nova Inc. 09/04/1992 which name changed back to Scios Inc. 03/26/1996
(See Scios Inc.)

CALIFORNIA BUSINESS COMMUNICATIONS INC (CA)
Assets foreclosed on 00/00/1977
No stockholders' equity

CALIFORNIA CAMI Z INC (MN)
Recapitalized as Cami'z Inc. 02/09/1990
Each share Common no par exchanged for (0.1) share Common no par
Cami'z Inc. name changed to B.U.M. International Inc. 11/02/1994
(See B.U.M. International Inc.)

CALIFORNIA CASKET CO (CA)
Each share Capital Stock no par exchanged for (0.0002) share Capital Stock no par 11/01/1979
Note: In effect holders received $0.434 cash per share and public interest was eliminated

CALIFORNIA CTR BK (LOS ANGELES, CA)
Common no par split (2) for (1) by issuance of (1) additional share payable 02/08/2001 to holders of record 01/18/2001 Ex date - 02/09/2001
Stock Dividends - 7% payable 07/12/1996 to holders of record 06/28/1996; 11% payable 11/30/1998 to holders of record 11/13/1998; 12% payable 05/07/1999 to holders of record 04/19/1999; 13% payable 03/15/2000 to holders of record 02/25/2000; 13% payable 03/01/2001 to holders of record 03/01/2001 Ex date - 02/27/2001; 11% payable 03/18/2002 to holders of record 03/01/2002 Ex date - 02/27/2002
Under plan of reorganization each share Common no par automatically became (1) share Center Financial Corp. Common no par 10/28/2002
Center Financial Corp. merged into BBCN Bancorp, Inc. 12/01/2011 which name changed to Hope Bancorp, Inc. 08/01/2016

CALIFORNIA CENTRAL BANK (LOS ANGELES, CA)
Name changed to California Center Bank (Los Angeles, CA) 09/12/1986
California Center Bank (Los Angeles, CA) reorganized as Center Financial Corp. 10/28/2002 which merged into BBCN Bancorp, Inc. 12/01/2011 which name changed to Hope Bancorp, Inc. 08/01/2016

CALIFORNIA CENTRAL RAILROAD CO.
Acquired by Phelps Dodge Corp. 00/00/1931
Details not available

CALIFORNIA CENTURY STORES, INC. (CA)
Charter suspended for failure to pay taxes 06/01/1966

CALIFORNIA CHEMICAL CO.
Acquired by Westvaco Chlorine Products Corp. 00/00/1937
Each share Common exchanged for (27.2) shares Common
Westvaco Chlorine Products Corp. name changed to Westvaco Chemical Corp. 05/01/1948 which merged into Food Machinery & Chemical Corp. 09/10/1948 which name changed to FMC Corp. 06/30/1961

CALIFORNIA CLEAN AIR INC (NV)
Charter revoked for failure to file reports and pay fees 12/31/2008

CALIFORNIA COASTAL BANK (SAN DIEGO, CA)
Merged into Heritage Bank (Anaheim, CA) 06/29/1981
Each share Common $5 par exchanged for (1.22) shares Common no par
Heritage Bank (Anaheim, CA) reorganized as Heritage Bancorp 12/28/1981
(See Heritage Bancorp)

CALIFORNIA COASTAL CMNTYS INC (DE)
Each share old Common 5¢ par exchanged for (1) share new Common 5¢ par to reflect a (1) for (100) reverse split followed by a (100) for (1) forward split 06/18/1999
Note: Holders of (99) or fewer shares received $6.51 cash per share
Plan of reorganization under Chapter 11 Federal Bankruptcy proceedings effective 03/01/2011
No stockholders' equity

CALIFORNIA COLA DISTRG INC (DE)
Name changed to Rexford Inc. 10/01/1992
Rexford Inc. recapitalized as Lexon Technologies Inc. 07/21/1999 which name changed to Social Cube Inc. 03/28/2012

CALIFORNIA COLD STORAGE & DISTRG CO (CA)
Each share $1.50 Preferred no par exchanged for (3) shares $0.50 Preferred $1 par 00/00/1953
(Additional Information in Active)

CALIFORNIA COML BANKSHARES (CA)
Common no par split (3) for (2) by

issuance of (0.5) additional share 03/31/1989
Common no par split (3) for (2) by issuance of (0.5) additional share 07/16/1990
Merged into Western Bancorp 06/04/1997
Each share Common no par exchanged for (1) share Common no par
Western Bancorp merged into U.S. Bancorp 11/15/1999

CALIFORNIA CMNTY BANCSHARES CORP (CA)
Merged into SierraWest Bancorp 04/15/1998
Each share Common 10¢ par exchanged for (0.8283) share Common no par
SierraWest Bancorp merged into BancWest Corp. (New) 07/01/1999
(See BancWest Corp. (New))

CALIFORNIA CMNTY BANCSHARES INC (CA)
Merged into CCB Newco 12/28/2001
Each share Common 1¢ par exchanged for $4.50 cash

CALIFORNIA CMNTY BK (ESCONDIDO, CA)
Acquired by Grandpoint Capital, Inc. 11/30/2012
Each share Common no par exchanged for $14.167 cash

CALIFORNIA COMPUTER PRODS INC (CA)
Common 50¢ par split (2) for (1) by issuance of (1) additional share 12/05/1967
Stock Dividends - 50% 07/08/1964; 25% 06/15/1967
Merged into Sanders Associates, Inc. (DE) 02/19/1980
Each share Common 50¢ par exchanged for (0.34) share Common $1 par
(See Sanders Associates Inc. (DE))

CALIFORNIA CONSERVING CO.
Merged into Hunt Foods, Inc. 00/00/1945
Each share Common exchanged for (2) shares Preference $10 par and (2) shares Common $6.66666666 par
Hunt Foods, Inc. merged into Hunt Foods & Industries, Inc. 12/05/1958 which merged into Simon (Norton), Inc. 07/17/1968 which merged into Esmark, Inc. (Inc. 03/14/1969) 09/09/1983
(See Esmark, Inc. (Inc. 03/14/1969))

CALIFORNIA COPPER CORP.
Capital Stock $10 par changed to $1 par and Company merged into California-Engels Mining Co. 00/00/1936
Details not available

CALIFORNIA CORP. FOR BIOCHEMICAL RESEARCH (CA)
Stock Dividend - 20% 12/09/1960
Name changed to Calbiochem 05/08/1962
(See Calbiochem)

CALIFORNIA COTTON MILLS CO.
Merged into National Automotive Fibres, Inc. on a (0.7) for (1) basis 00/00/1949
National Automotive Fibres, Inc. name changed to Nafi Corp. 04/27/1959 which name changed to Chris-Craft Industries, Inc. 04/30/1962 which merged into News Corp., Ltd. 07/31/2001 which reorganized as News Corp. 11/03/2004

CALIFORNIA CRUSHED FRUIT CO.
Acquired by Mission Dry Corp. 00/00/1933
Details not available

CALIFORNIA CULINARY ACADEMY INC (CA)
Merged into Career Education Corp. 04/03/2000
Each share Common no par exchanged for $5.25 cash

CALIFORNIA CYBER DESIGN INC (DE)
Old Common $0.0001 par split (3.5) for (1) by issuance of (2.5) additional shares payable 03/14/2000 to holders of record 03/06/2000
Each share old Common $0.0001 par exchanged for (0.5) share new Common $0.0001 par 11/06/2001
Recapitalized as American Financial Holdings, Inc. 09/02/2004
Each share new Common $0.0001 par exchanged for (0.0025) share Common $0.0001 par
American Financial Holdings, Inc. recapitalized as Tactical Solution Partners, Inc. 01/19/2006 which name changed to Brekford International Corp. 05/13/2008 which name changed to Brekford Corp. 07/21/2010 which name changed to Brekford Traffic Safety, Inc. 06/08/2017 which merged into Novume Solutions, Inc. 08/28/2017

CALIFORNIA DAILY TAX FREE INCOME FD INC (MD)
Common $0.001 par reclassified as Class A $0.001 par 01/26/1995
California Tax Exempt Liquidity Fund Class $0.001 par reclassified as Advantage California Tax Exempt Liquidity Fund Class $0.001 par 04/29/2004
Completely liquidated 07/30/2015
Each share Class A $0.001 par received net asset value
Each share Class B $0.001 par received net asset value
Each share Advantage California Tax Exempt Liquidity Fund Class $0.001 par received net asset value

CALIFORNIA DAIRIES, INC. (MD)
Name changed to Western Dairy Products, Inc. 12/15/1929
Western Dairy Products, Inc. name changed to Arden Farms, Inc. 06/09/1936 which merged into Arden Farms Co. (New) 08/01/1940 which name changed to Arden-Mayfair, Inc. 04/24/1965 which reorganized as Arden Group, Inc. 11/19/1978
(See Arden Group, Inc.)

CALIFORNIA DATA SYSTEMS CORP. (MN)
Name changed to Interscan, Inc. and Common 10¢ par changed to $0.001 par 06/16/1971
(See Interscan, Inc.)

CALIFORNIA DELTA FARMS, INC.
Liquidated 00/00/1946
Details not available

CALIFORNIA DESIGN MANUFACTURING CORP. (CA)
Charter suspended for failure to pay taxes 04/01/1958

CALIFORNIA DRESSED BEEF CO.
Property sold to Bondholders Committee 00/00/1929
Details not available

CALIFORNIA EASTERN AIRWAYS, INC. (DE)
Common $1 par changed to 10¢ par 00/00/1949
Name changed to California Eastern Aviation, Inc. 02/10/1955
California Eastern Aviation, Inc. name changed to Dynalectron Corp. 06/19/1961 which name changed to DynCorp 05/11/1987
(See DynCorp)

CALIFORNIA EASTERN AVIATION, INC. (DE)
Name changed to Dynalectron Corp. 06/19/1961
Dynalectron Corp. name changed to DynCorp 05/11/1987
(See DynCorp)

CALIFORNIA EASTERN OIL CO.
Acquired by Sunset Pacific Oil Co. 00/00/1928
Details not available

CALIFORNIA ELEC PWR CO (DE)
Common $10 par changed to $1 par 00/00/1943
$2.50 Preferred $50 par called for redemption 11/06/1963
5.75% Preferred $50 par called for redemption 11/06/1963
6% Preferred $50 par called for redemption 11/06/1963
Merged into Southern California Edison Co. 12/31/1963
Each share $3 Preferred $50 par exchanged for (3) shares 4.78% Preferred $25 par
Each share Common $1 par exchanged for (0.95) share Common $8.33333333 par
Southern California Electric Power Co. reorganized as SCEcorp 07/01/1988 which name changed to Edison International 02/05/1996

CALIFORNIA ELECTRIC GENERATING CO.
Dissolved 00/00/1936
Details not available

CALIFORNIA ENERGY INC (DE)
Common $0.0675 par split (3) for (2) by issuance of (0.5) additional share 03/17/1989
Name changed to CalEnergy Co., Inc. 03/26/1996
CalEnergy Co., Inc. merged into MidAmerican Energy Holdings Co. (New) 03/12/1999

CALIFORNIA EXPL LTD (YT)
Recapitalized as Baradero Resources Ltd. (YT) 06/03/2004
Each share Common no par exchanged for (0.25) share Common no par
Baradero Resources Ltd. (YT) reincorporated in British Columbia 11/23/2004 which name changed to Centrasia Mining Corp. 09/16/2005 which name changed to Kola Mining Corp. 03/27/2008 which name changed to Mitchell Resources Ltd. 05/27/2015 which name changed to Hannan Metals Ltd. 01/10/2017

CALIFORNIA FED BK A FED SVGS BK (LOS ANGELES, CA)
Reorganized as Calfed, Inc. (DE) 12/23/1983
Each share Common $1 par exchanged for (1) share Common $1 par
(See Calfed, Inc.)
Each share Common 20¢ par exchanged for (0.2) share Common $1 par 02/28/1993
Under plan of reorganization each share Common $1 par automatically became (1) share Cal Fed Bancorp Inc. Common $1 par 01/01/1996
(See Cal Fed Bancorp Inc.)
7.75% Conv. Preferred Ser. A $25 par called for redemption 06/14/1996
10.625% Perpetual Preferred Ser. B $100 par called for redemption at $105.313 on 04/01/1999
11.5% Perpetual Preferred no par called for redemption at $105.75 on 09/01/1999
Name changed to Citibank (West) FSB (San Francisco, CA) 12/11/2002
(See Citibank (West) FSB (San Francisco, CA))

CALIFORNIA FED PFD CAP CORP (MD)
9.125% Exchangeable Preferred Ser. A 1¢ par called for redemption at $25.91 plus $0.54497 accrued dividends on 03/27/2003

CALIFORNIA FINL CORP (DE)
Stock Dividend - 200% 04/20/1962
Liquidation completed
Each share Capital Stock $1 par exchanged for initial distribution of $10.165 cash 10/19/1977
Each share Capital Stock $1 par received second distribution of $0.062319 cash 11/28/1977
Each share Capital Stock $1 par received third and final distribution of $0.005552 cash 04/20/1978

CALIFORNIA FINL HLDG CO (DE)
Stock Dividend - 10% 12/15/1993
Merged into Temple-Inland Inc. 06/27/1997
Each share Common 1¢ par exchanged for (0.5037) share Common $1 par
(See Temple-Inland Inc.)

CALIFORNIA FIRST BK (SAN FRANCISCO, CA)
Stock Dividend - 10% 01/08/1988
Name changed to Union Bank (San Francisco, CA) 11/01/1988
Union Bank (San Francisco, CA) merged into UnionBanCal Corp. (CA) 04/01/1996 which reincorporated in Delaware 09/30/2003
(See UnionBanCal Corp. (DE))

CALIFORNIA FOOD & VENDING, INC. (NV)
Name changed to Partners Financial Group, Inc. (New) 08/21/1992
(See Partners Financial Group, Inc. (New))

CALIFORNIA FUND, INC. (DE)
Name changed to Convertible Securities & Growth Stock Fund, Inc. 04/01/1964
Convertible Securities & Growth Stock Fund, Inc. name changed to Enterprise Fund, Inc. (DE) 03/31/1967 which reincorporated in Maryland as American General Enterprise Fund, Inc. 01/15/1979 which name changed to American Capital Enterprise Fund, Inc. (MD) 09/09/1983 which reincorporated in Delaware as Van Kampen American Capital Enterprise Fund 08/03/1995 which name changed to Van Kampen Enterprise Fund 08/31/1998

CALIFORNIA GEN INC (CA)
Completely liquidated 03/08/1978
Each share Capital Stock $1 par exchanged for first and final distribution of $1 cash

CALIFORNIA GIRL MFG INC (CA)
Merged into FCL Corp. 07/28/1980
Each share Common 25¢ par exchanged for $1.55 cash

CALIFORNIA GOLD CORP (NV)
Recapitalized as MV Portfolios, Inc. 09/08/2014
Each share Common $0.001 par exchanged for (0.01) share Common $0.001 par

CALIFORNIA GOLD MINES INC (BC)
Cease trade order effective 11/16/1992
Stockholders' equity unlikely

CALIFORNIA GOLD MINES LTD (BC)
Merged into Centurion Gold Ltd. 06/06/1988
Each share Common no par exchanged for (0.25) share Common no par
Centurion Gold Ltd. merged into Siskon Gold Corp. 08/23/1991
(See Siskon Gold Corp.)

CAL-CAL

CALIFORNIA GOLD MNG INC (AB)
Reorganized under the laws of Ontario 06/07/2016
Each share Common no par exchanged for (0.1) share Common no par

CALIFORNIA GROUP CORP.
Name changed to Group Corp. 00/00/1934
(See Group Corp.)

CALIFORNIA GROWTH CAP INC (CA)
Name changed to First Southern Capital Corp. and Common $5 par changed to 10¢ par 03/26/1973
(See First Southern Capital Corp.)

CALIFORNIA HEALTH CARE INC (CA)
Common 50¢ par split (3) for (2) by issuance of (0.5) additional share 04/21/1971
Name changed to Flagg Industries, Inc. 08/17/1971
(See Flagg Industries, Inc.)

CALIFORNIA HERITAGE BANK (SAN DIEGO, CA)
Through purchase offer 100% reacquired 00/00/1981
Public interest eliminated

CALIFORNIA ICE & COLD STORAGE CO.
Merged into California Cold Storage & Distributing Co. 00/00/1947
Each share Class A no par exchanged for (0.5) share Prior Preferred $25 par and (0.2) share Preferred no par
Each share Class B no par exchanged for (1.2) shares Common no par

CALIFORNIA INDPT BANCORP (CA)
Stock Dividends - 5% payable 09/20/1996 to holders of record 08/30/1996; 5% payable 09/12/1997 to holders of record 08/29/1997; 5% payable 09/18/1998 to holders of record 08/31/1998; 5% payable 09/17/1999 to holders of record 08/31/1999; 5% payable 09/15/2000 to holders of record 08/31/2000; 5% payable 09/25/2001 to holders of record 09/10/2001; 5% payable 09/20/2002 to holders of record 09/05/2002 Ex date - 09/03/2002
Merged into Humboldt Bancorp 01/06/2004
Each share Common no par exchanged for (0.4393) share Common no par and $31.032 cash
Humboldt Bancorp merged into Umpqua Holdings Corp. 07/10/2004

CALIFORNIA INK CO., INC. (DE)
Class A no par & Class B no par reclassified as Capital Stock no par 00/00/1932
Capital Stock no par changed to $5.50 par and (2) additional shares issued 00/00/1953
Stock Dividend - 10% 12/21/1953
Acquired by Tennessee Gas Transmission Co. 03/01/1965
Each share Capital Stock $5.50 par exchanged for (1.4) share Common $5 par
Tennessee Gas Transmission Co. name changed to Tenneco Inc. 04/11/1966 which merged into El Paso Natural Gas Co. 12/12/1996 which reorganized as El Paso Energy Corp. 08/01/1998 which name changed to El Paso Corp. 02/05/2001

CALIFORNIA INTL PPTYS INC (CA)
Charter cancelled for failure to file reports and pay taxes 04/01/1987

CALIFORNIA INTST TEL CO (CA)
5.25% Conv. Preferred $20 par called for redemption 05/01/1967
Name changed to Continental Telephone Co. of California 11/11/1969
Continental Telephone Co. of California name changed to Contel of California, Inc. 02/19/1988
(See Contel of California, Inc.)

CALIFORNIA INVT TR (MA)
Reincorporated 12/29/2006
State of incorporation changed from (MA) to (DE) 12/29/2006
Each share Tax-Free Income Fund no par automatically became (1) share Shelton Funds California Tax-Free Income Fund Class S no par 11/29/2011
Each share Tax-Free Money Market Fund no par automatically became (1) share Shelton Funds California Tax-Free Money Market Fund Class S no par 11/29/2011
Each share Equity Income Fund Class A no par automatically became (1) share Shelton Funds Shelton Core Value Fund Class S no par 01/01/2012
Each share Equity Income Fund Class B no par automatically became (1) share Shelton Funds Shelton Core Value Fund Class S no par 01/01/2012

CALIFORNIA INVT TR II (MA)
Merged into California Investment Trust (DE) 01/04/2007
Details not available

CALIFORNIA JAMAR INC (DE)
Name changed to JMAR Industries, Inc. 01/11/1993
JMAR Industries, Inc. name changed to JMAR Technologies, Inc. 05/27/1998
(See JMAR Technologies, Inc.)

CALIFORNIA JOCKEY CLUB (CA)
Each share old Common no par exchanged for (3) shares new Common no par 03/27/1963
New Common no par split (2) for (1) by issuance of (1) additional share 04/08/1966
New Common no par split (5) for (1) by issuance of (4) additional shares 08/20/1970
Reorganized under the laws of Delaware 03/30/1983
Each share new Common no par exchanged for (8) Units consisting of (1) share Bay Meadows Operating Co. Common 1¢ par and (1) share California Jockey Club (DE) Common 1¢ par
(See each company's listing)

CALIFORNIA LAND & PRODUCTS CORP. (CA)
Charter suspended for failure to pay fees 02/27/1926

CALIFORNIA LEISURE PRODS INC (DE)
Merged into Aero Systems Aviation Corp. 02/28/1990
Each share Common 10¢ par exchanged for $0.013128 cash

CALIFORNIA LIBERTY MINES CO. (NV)
Voluntarily dissolved 08/14/1956
Details not available

CALIFORNIA LIFE CORP (MD)
Common $1 par changed to 75¢ par and (0.33333333) additional share issued 06/24/1976
90¢ Conv. Preferred Ser. A $10 par reclassified as $0.925 Conv. Preferred Ser. A $10 par 07/01/1977
Merged into Bohana Corp. 01/25/1983
Each share $0.925 Conv. Preferred Ser. A $10 par exchanged for $1.10 cash
Each share $1.10 Preferred Ser. C $10 par exchanged for $1.25 cash
Each share $2.50 Preferred Ser. B $10 par exchanged for $3 cash
Each share Common 75¢ par exchanged for $0.40 cash

CALIFORNIA LIFE INS CO (CA)
Each share Class A Common $5 par exchanged for (0.2) share Common $1 par 08/29/1960
Common $1 par changed to 50¢ par and (1) additional share issued 10/23/1961
Common 50¢ par changed to $1 par 01/22/1963
Common $1 par changed to $2 par 03/26/1973
Common $2 par changed to $1.77 par 09/23/1974
Each share Common $1.77 par exchanged for (0.00066666) share Common $2,655 par 02/21/1978
Note: In effect holders received $12.58 cash per share and public interest eliminated

CALIFORNIA LIMESTONE PRODUCTS (CA)
Adjudicated bankrupt 08/15/1963
No stockholders' equity

CALIFORNIA LIQUID GAS CORP. (CA)
Stock Dividends - 100% 12/20/1960; 50% 10/20/1961
Merged into Dillingham Corp. 10/01/1968
Each share Capital Stock $1 par exchanged for (0.2) share $2 Conv. Preferred October 1968 Ser. no par and (0.7) share Common no par
(See Dillingham Corp.)

CALIFORNIA MAGNETIC CTL CORP (CA)
Charter cancelled for failure to file reports and pay taxes 08/01/1975

CALIFORNIA-MASON REALTY CO. (CA)
Liquidation completed
Each share Class A $1 par exchanged for initial distribution of $25 cash 02/05/1962
Each share Class B $1 par exchanged for initial distribution of $25 cash 02/05/1962
Each share Class A $1 par received second distribution of $5 cash 02/27/1962
Each share Class B $1 par received second distribution of $5 cash 02/27/1962
Each share Class A $1 par received third and final distribution of $3.005 cash 07/25/1962
Each share Class B $1 par received third and final distribution of $3.005 cash 07/25/1962

CALIFORNIA MED CTRS (CA)
Charter suspended for failure to file reports and pay fees 06/02/1975

CALIFORNIA MICH LD & WTR CO (CA)
Company advised SEC it is private 03/02/2015

CALIFORNIA MICRO DEVICES CORP (DE)
Reincorporated 09/15/2006
State of incorporation changed from (CA) to (DE) and Common no par changed to $0.001 par 09/15/2006
Merged into ON Semiconductor Corp. 01/27/2010
Each share Common $0.001 par exchanged for $4.70 cash

CALIFORNIA MICROWAVE INC (DE)
Reincorporated 11/00/1987
Common 25¢ par split (3) for (2) by issuance of (0.5) additional share 06/13/1983
Stock Dividends - 50% 03/10/1977; 50% 03/09/1978; 50% 03/08/1979; 100% 06/15/1981
State of incorporation changed from (CA) to (DE) and Common 25¢ par changed to 10¢ par 11/00/1987
Name changed to Adaptive Broadband Corp. 04/29/1999
(See Adaptive Broadband Corp.)

CALIFORNIA MODULAR HOMES, INC. (NV)
Charter revoked for failure to file reports and pay fees 03/06/1961

CALIFORNIA MUT FD (CA)
Name changed to Warren (Ted) Fund 07/13/1970 which name changed back to California Mutual Fund 05/09/1973
Charter suspended for failure to file reports and pay taxes 11/01/1974

CALIFORNIA NEWS TECH (NV)
Each share old Common $0.003 par received distribution of (1) share Media Sentiment, Inc. Restricted Common $0.001 par payable 11/27/2006 to holders of record 11/20/2006
Each share old Common $0.003 par exchanged for (0.1) share new Common $0.003 par 01/09/2007
Name changed to Debut Broadcasting Corp., Inc. 06/04/2007
(See Debut Broadcasting Corp., Inc.)

CALIFORNIA NORTHWEST CAPITAL CO. (CA)
Voluntarily dissolved 01/14/1980
Details not available

CALIFORNIA OAKS ST BK (THOUSAND OAKS, CA)
Merged into California United Bank (Encino, CA) 12/31/2010
Each share Common no par exchanged for either (0.61926011) share Common no par and $3.7744425 cash, (0.9278) share Common no par or $11.35 cash
Note: Option to receive stock or cash only expired 01/20/2011
California United Bank (Encino, CA) reorganized as CU Bancorp 08/01/2012 which merged into PacWest Bancorp 10/20/2017

CALIFORNIA OIL & GAS CORP (NV)
SEC revoked common stock registration 04/04/2012

CALIFORNIA OREGON POWER CO. (CA)
Merged into Pacific Power & Light Co. 06/21/1961
7% & 6% Preferred $100 par exchanged on a share for share basis
4.7% Preferred $100 par exchanged for for 5% Preferred $100 par; and 5.1% Preferred $100 par exchanged for 5.4% Preferred $100 par, on a share for share basis
Each share Common $20 par exchanged for (1.2) shares Common $6.50 par
Pacific Power & Light Co. name changed to PacifiCorp (ME) 06/15/1984 which reincorporated in Oregon 01/09/1989

CALIFORNIA OSBORN MINING CO.
Bankrupt 00/00/1938
Stockholders' equity unlikely

CALIFORNIA PAC BK (FULLERTON, CA)
Merged into Republic Bank (Gardena, CA) 12/31/1979
Each share Common $7.50 par exchanged for (0.3293) share Common $2.50 par
Republic Bank (Gardena, CA) reorganized as American Republic Bancorp 11/02/1981 which name changed to Republic Bank (Torrance, CA) 09/09/1992
(See Republic Bank (Torrance, CA))

CALIFORNIA PAC NATL BK (LOS ANGELES, CA)
Merged into Security Pacific Corp. 03/31/1987
Each share Common $5 par exchanged for $18.55 cash

CALIFORNIA PAC UTILS CO (CA)
Each share 5% Preferred $100 par exchanged for (5) shares 5% Preferred $20 par 00/00/1943
Each share Common $20 par exchanged for (2) shares Common $10 par 00/00/1951
5.5% Conv. Preferred $20 par called for redemption 04/11/1958
Common $10 par changed to $5 par and (1) additional share issued 01/15/1960
5.4% Conv. Preferred $20 par called for redemption 03/01/1963
5% 1955 Conv. Preferred called for redemption 12/01/1965
Name changed to CP National Corp. 05/08/1978
CP National Corp. acquired by Alltel Corp. (OH) 12/30/1988 which reincorporated in Delaware 05/15/1990
(See Alltel Corp.)

CALIFORNIA PACIFIC FINANCIAL CORP. (CA)
Merged into Standard-Pacific Corp. (CA) 06/28/1965
Each share Common no par exchanged for (1) share Common 25¢ par
Standard-Pacific Corp. (CA) reincorporated in Delaware 08/31/1981 which assets were transferred to Standard Pacific, L.P. 12/30/1986 which reorganized as Standard Pacific Corp. (New) 12/31/1991 which merged into CalAtlantic Group, Inc. 10/01/2015 which merged into Lennar Corp. 02/12/2018

CALIFORNIA PACIFIC TITLE & TRUST CO. (CA)
Name changed to California Pacific Title Insurance Co. 00/00/1942
California Pacific Title Insurance Co. merged into Title Insurance & Trust Co. 01/14/1959 which name changed to TI Corp. (of California) 06/28/1968 which name changed to Ticor 04/27/1977
(See Ticor)

CALIFORNIA PACIFIC TITLE INSURANCE CO. (CA)
Recapitalized 00/00/1933
Each share Preferred $100 par exchanged for (2) shares Preferred $50 par and (1) share Common $50 par
Each share Common $100 par exchanged for (2) shares Preferred $50 par and (1) share Common $50 par
Recapitalized 00/00/1946
Each share Preferred $50 par exchanged for (2) shares Preferred $25 par
Each share Common $50 par exchanged for (2) shares Common $25 par
Common $25 par changed to $12.50 par and (1) additional share issued 00/00/1953
Each share Common $12.50 par exchanged for (2) shares Common $6.25 par 06/21/1957
Merged into Title Insurance & Trust Co. 01/14/1959
Each share Preferred $25 par exchanged for (1) share 7% Preferred $25 par
Each share Common $6.25 par exchanged for (1) share Common $2.50 par
Title Insurance & Trust Co. name changed to TI Corp. (of California) 06/28/1968 which name changed to Ticor 04/27/1977
(See Ticor)

CALIFORNIA PACKING CORP. (NY)
Common no par reclassified as Capital Stock $5 par 00/00/1951
Capital Stock $5 par changed to $2.50 par and (1) additional share issued 09/15/1961
Stock Dividends - 100% 07/23/1951; 10% 06/26/1956
Name changed to Del Monte Corp. 06/28/1967
(See Del Monte Corp.)

CALIFORNIA PETROLEUM CORP.
Dissolved 00/00/1938
Details not available

CALIFORNIA PIZZA KITCHEN INC (DE)
Reincorporated 12/22/2004
State of incorporation changed from (CA) to (DE) 12/22/2004
Common 1¢ par split (3) for (2) by issuance of (0.5) additional share payable 06/18/2007 to holders of record 06/11/2007 Ex date - 06/19/2007
Acquired by CPK Holdings Inc. 07/07/2011
Each share Common 1¢ par exchanged for $18.50 cash

CALIFORNIA PORTLAND CEM CO (CA)
Each share Common $100 par exchanged for (10) shares Common $10 par 00/00/1950
Common $10 par changed to $5 par and (1) additional share issued 10/27/1970
Common $5 par changed to $2.50 par and (1) additional share issued 06/08/1981
Stock Dividend - 400% 04/30/1965
Merged into CalMat Co. 06/27/1984
Each share Common $2.50 par exchanged for (1) share Common $1 par
(See CalMat Co.)

CALIFORNIA PRESS BUR INC (WY)
Name changed to Atronic, Inc. 09/02/1981
(See Atronic, Inc.)

CALIFORNIA PRO SPORTS INC (DE)
Name changed to ImaginOn, Inc. 01/04/1999

CALIFORNIA PROPERTIES CO.
Liquidation completed 00/00/1949
Details not available

CALIFORNIA QUICKSILVER MINES, INC. (CA)
Acquired by COG Minerals Corp. on a (0.16) for (1) basis 08/07/1958
(See COG Minerals Corp.)

CALIFORNIA REAL ESTATE INVT TR (CA)
Name changed to Capital Trust (CA) and Shares of Bene. Int. $1 par reclassified as Class A Common Shares of Bene. Int. $1 par 07/15/1997
Capital Trust (CA) reorganized as Capital Trust, Inc. (MD) 01/28/1999 which recapitalized as Blackstone Mortgage Trust, Inc. 05/07/2013

CALIFORNIA REAL ESTATE PARTNERS (CA)
Majority interest acquired through purchase offer which expired 02/15/2003
Public interest eliminated

CALIFORNIA REAL ESTATE TRUST (CA)
Under plan of reorganization each Share of Bene. Int. $10 par automatically became (1) share Capistrano Group Common no par 05/30/1984
(See Capistrano Group)

CALIFORNIA REP BANCORP (CA)
Acquired by Coast Acquisition Corp. 10/01/2016
Each share Common 10¢ par exchanged for $37.19 cash

CALIFORNIA REP BK (BAKERSFIELD, CA)
Common $5 par changed to $1 par and (4) additional shares issued 04/06/1979
Under plan of reorganization each share Common $1 par automatically became (1) share Cal Rep Bancorp, Inc. Common $1 par 01/05/1983
Cal Rep Bancorp, Inc. acquired by First Interstate Bancorp 12/10/1993 which merged into Wells Fargo & Co. (Old) 04/01/1996 which merged into Wells Fargo & Co. (New) 11/02/1998

CALIFORNIA REPUBLIC BK (NEWPORT BEACH, CA)
Under plan of reorganization each share Common 10¢ par automatically became (1) share California Republic Bancorp Common 10¢ par 02/23/2012
(See California Republic Bancorp)

CALIFORNIA RISING LTD (CO)
Name changed to Nouveaux Corp. 08/06/1990
Nouveaux Corp. name changed to Persona Records, Inc. (CO) 04/29/1998 which reincorporated in Nevada as HIV-VAC Inc. 03/08/1999 which name changed to Grupo International, Inc. 10/28/2010

CALIFORNIA ROCK & QUARRY ENTERPRISES, INC. (NV)
Charter revoked for failure to pay fees 03/05/1962

CALIFORNIA SVGS BK (SAN FRANCISCO, CA)
Merged into FBOP Corp. 07/01/2004
Each share Common no par exchanged for $198.0808822 cash

CALIFORNIA SEC BK (SAN JOSE, CA)
Merged into Summit Bank Corp. 06/30/1998
Each share Common $10 par exchanged for $0.30166 cash

CALIFORNIA SECURE-UR-TRIP, INC. (CA)
Charter forfeited for failure to pay taxes 04/01/1964

CALIFORNIA SHOPPING CTRS INC (CA)
Name changed to McCombs Corp. 08/08/1978
(See McCombs Corp.)

CALIFORNIA SILVER LTD (BC)
Name changed to California Gold Mines Ltd. 05/27/1986
California Gold Mines Ltd. merged into Centurion Gold Ltd. 06/06/1988 which merged into Siskon Gold Corp. 08/23/1991
(See Siskon Gold Corp.)

CALIFORNIA SOFTWARE CORP (NV)
Old Common $0.001 par split (2) for (1) by issuance of (1) additional share payable 03/25/2000 to holders of record 03/15/2000
Each share old Common $0.001 par exchanged for (0.1) share new Common new Common $0.001 par 11/24/2003
Each share new Common $0.001 par exchanged again for (0.1) share new Common $0.001 par 12/27/2004
Name changed to Infinite Software Corp. 04/05/2007

CALIFORNIA ST BK (COVINA, CA)
Stock Dividend - 25% 03/15/1989
Merged into First Security Corp. 05/30/1998
Each share Common no par exchanged for (2.13) shares Common $1.25 par
First Security Corp. merged into Wells Fargo & Co. (New) 10/26/2004

CALIFORNIA STANDARD FINANCE CORP.
Liquidation completed 00/00/1945
Details not available

CALIFORNIA STANDARD GOLD MINES CORP.
Out of business 00/00/1940
Details not available

CALIFORNIA STREET CABLE R.R. CO. (CA)
Charter suspended for failure to file reports and pay fees 01/02/1953

CALIFORNIA TAX EXEMPT BD FDS INC (CA)
Completely liquidated 00/00/1990
Each Unit of Undivided Int. no par exchanged for net asset value

CALIFORNIA TIME PETE INC (DE)
Name changed to Petrominerals Corp. 09/17/1973
(See Petrominerals Corp.)

CALIFORNIA TUNGSTEN CORP. (DE)
Name changed to Uranium Mines of America Inc. 00/00/1953
Uranium Mines of America Inc. merged into Consolidated Uranium Mines, Inc. 11/30/1954
(See Consolidated Uranium Mines, Inc.)

CALIFORNIA UTD BK (ENCINO, CA)
Under plan of reorganization each share Common no par automatically became (1) share CU Bancorp Common no par 08/01/2012
CU Bancorp merged into PacWest Bancorp 10/20/2017

CALIFORNIA VY BK (FRESNO, CA)
Merged into Valley National Corp. (AZ) 12/30/1987
Each share Common $3 par exchanged for (0.03127) share Common $2.50 par
Valley National Corp. (AZ) merged into Banc One Corp. 03/31/1993 which merged into Bank One Corp. 10/02/1998 which merged into J.P. Morgan Chase & Co. 12/31/2000 which name changed to JPMorgan Chase & Co. 07/20/2004

CALIFORNIA VENTURE FD INC (CA)
Name changed to Cumulo Alternate Fund, Inc. 05/01/1973
(See Cumulo Alternate Fund, Inc.)

CALIFORNIA VENTURE GROUP (NV)
Recapitalized as Heartland, Inc. 12/23/1991
Each share old Common $0.001 par exchanged for (0.0025) share Common no par
Heartland, Inc. name changed back to California Venture Group. 08/18/1998
Charter revoked for failure to file reports and pay fees 04/01/2000

CALIFORNIA VENTURES INC (CO)
Reorganized under the laws of Delaware as AMDL, Inc. 06/12/1989
Each share Common $0.0001 par exchanged for (0.06666666) share Common $0.0001 par
AMDL, Inc. name changed to Radient Pharmaceuticals Corp. 09/22/2009
(See Radient Pharmaceuticals Corp.)

CALIFORNIA WATER & TELEPHONE CO. (CA)
Common $25 par changed to $12.50 par and (1) additional share issued 00/00/1953
Common $12.50 par changed to $6.25 par and (1) additional share issued 04/05/1962
Stock Dividend - 20% 03/10/1947
Merged into General Telephone & Electronics Corp. 06/30/1964
Each share Common $6.25 par exchanged for (1) share Common $3.33333333 par
General Telephone & Electronics Corp. name changed to GTE Corp. 07/01/1982 which merged into Verizon Communications Inc. 06/30/2000

CAL-CAL

CALIFORNIA WTR SVC CO (CA)
Each share Preferred $100 par exchanged for (4) shares Preferred Ser. A $25 par 00/00/1940
Each share Common $100 par exchanged for (4) shares Common $25 par 00/00/1940
Common $25 par changed to $12.50 par and (1) additional share issued 03/19/1959
5.8% Preferred Ser. I $25 par called for redemption 05/15/1961
Common $12.50 par changed to $6.25 par and (1) additional share issued 05/02/1984
Common $6.25 par changed to no par and (1) additional share issued 10/20/1987
5.2% Conv. Preferred Ser. H $25 par called for redemption 05/14/1988
5.2% Conv. Preferred Ser. G $25 par called for redemption 05/14/1988
5.28% Conv. Preferred Ser. E $25 par called for redemption 05/14/1988
5.3% Conv. Preferred Ser. D $25 par called for redemption 05/14/1988
5.36% Conv. Preferred Ser. F $25 par called for redemption 05/14/1988
9.25% Preferred Ser. K $25 par called for redemption 05/14/1988
Under plan of reorganization each share 4.4% Preferred Ser. C $25 par and Common no par automatically became (1) share California Water Service Group (CA) 4.4% Preferred Ser. C no par or Common no par respectively 12/31/1997
California Water Service Group (CA) reincorporated in Delaware 11/23/1999

CALIFORNIA WESTN GAS CO (DE)
Majority of shares acquired through purchase offer which expired 00/00/1995
Public interest eliminated 00/00/2001

CALIFORNIA WESTN STS LIFE INS CO (CA)
Capital Stock $10 par changed to $5 par 00/00/1934
Capital Stock $5 par changed to $7.50 par 00/00/1945
Capital Stock $7.50 par changed to $10 par 00/00/1946
Capital Stock $10 par changed to $5 par and (1) additional share issued 04/20/1960
Capital Stock $5 par changed to $2.50 par and (1) additional share issued plus a 10% stock dividend paid 04/18/1962
Stock Dividends - 100% 05/11/1950; 100% 10/30/1953; 10% 04/15/1958; 10% 04/15/1959; 10% 04/17/1961; 10% 04/17/1964; 10% 04/16/1965; 10% 05/21/1966
Merged into American General Insurance Co. 12/31/1975
Each share Capital Stock $2.50 par exchanged for (1) share 90¢ Conv. Preferred 1975 Ser. $1.50 par
American General Insurance Co. reorganized as American General Corp. 07/01/1980 which merged into American International Group, Inc. 08/29/2001

CALIFORNIA WHSL ELEC CO (CA)
Name changed to Chalet Gourmet Corp. 01/12/1982
(See Chalet Gourmet Corp.)

CALIFORNIA WINDSOR CO (CA)
Merged into Hutton (E.F.) Group Inc. 02/21/1978
Each share Capital Stock no par exchanged for (0.88) share Common $1 par
(See Hutton (E.F.) Group Inc.)

CALIFORNIA WINE ASSOCIATION
Dissolved 00/00/1936
Details not available

CALIFORNIA WORLD FINL CORP (CA)
Common no par split (5) for (4) by issuance of (0.25) additional share 02/18/1976
Common no par split (5) for (4) by issuance of (0.25) additional share 08/14/1978
Merged into Continental Group, Inc. 05/01/1979
Each share Common no par exchanged for (0.38) share $2.10 Conv. Preference Ser. B $1 par and (0.32) share Common $1 par
(See Continental Group, Inc.)

CALIFORNIA WTR SVC GROUP (DE)
Reincorporated 11/23/1999
Common no par split (2) for (1) by issuance of (1) additional share payable 01/23/1998 to holders of record 12/31/1997 Ex date - 01/26/1998
State of incorporation changed from (CA) to (DE) and Common no par changed to 1¢ par 11/23/1999
4.4% Preferred Ser. C $25 par called for redemption at $26.75 on 08/15/2008
(Additional Information in Active)

CALIMONT CORP (NV)
Each share old Common $0.001 par exchanged for (0.1) share new Common $0.001 par 09/24/2004
Dissolved 07/31/2006
Details not available

CALIPER DEVS LTD (QC)
Declared dissolved for failure to file reports and pay fees 07/15/1989

CALIPER LIFE SCIENCES INC (DE)
Acquired by PerkinElmer, Inc. 11/07/2011
Each share Common $0.001 par exchanged for $10.50 cash

CALIPER TECHNOLOGIES CORP (DE)
Name changed to Caliper Life Sciences, Inc. 01/12/2004
(See Caliper Life Sciences, Inc.)

CALIPSO INC (DE)
Name changed to Knowledge Foundations Inc. 09/21/2000
Knowledge Foundations Inc. name changed to BSI2000 Inc. 04/04/2003
(See BSI2000 Inc.)

CALITALO INVESTMENT CORP.
Dissolved 00/00/1931
Details not available

CALIVADA RES LTD (BC)
Recapitalized as Heritage Petroleums Inc. 06/25/1979
Each share Capital Stock no par exchanged for (0.33333333) share Common no par
Heritage Petroleums Inc. merged into Heritage American Resource Corp. 07/25/1994 which recapitalized as Heritage Explorations Ltd. 09/17/2001 which merged into St Andrew Goldfields Ltd. 08/22/2005 which merged into Kirkland Lake Gold Inc. 01/29/2016 which merged into Kirkland Lake Gold Ltd. 12/06/2016

CALIX CORP (NV)
Merged into Crandall Finance Corp. 12/29/1993
Details not available

CALIX GOLD MINES LTD. (BC)
Name changed to Calix Mines Ltd. 04/01/1966
Calix Mines Ltd. recapitalized as Bev-Cal Mines Ltd. 08/18/1972 which name changed to New Chemcrude Resources Ltd. 08/22/1975
(See New Chemcrude Resources Ltd.)

CALIX MINES LTD. (BC)
Recapitalized as Bev-Cal Mines Ltd. 08/18/1972
Each share Capital Stock 50¢ par exchanged for (0.125) share Capital Stock no par
Bev-Cal Mines Ltd. name changed to New Chemcrude Resources Ltd. 08/22/1975
(See New Chemcrude Resources Ltd.)

CALKINS INDUSTRIES, INC. (NV)
Each share old Common $0.001 par exchanged for (4) shares new Common $0.001 par 11/26/1986
Recapitalized as Compliance Industries, Inc. 11/23/1993
Each share new Common $0.001 par exchanged for (0.1) share Common $0.001 par
Compliance Industries, Inc. recapitalized as Vintage Properties Inc. 04/03/1995 which name changed to Xecom Corp. 10/24/1995 which name changed to AirStar Technologies, Inc. 04/28/1998
(See AirStar Technologies, Inc.)

CALL-AGE (OH)
Transfers terminated 03/18/1971
No stockholders' equity

CALL GENIE INC (AB)
Name changed to VoodooVox Inc. 01/17/2012
VoodooVox Inc. name changed to UpSnap, Inc. 07/25/2014

CALL-NET ENTERPRISES INC (CANADA)
Each share old Common no par exchanged for (0.05) share new Common no par 04/10/2002
Each share old Class B Common no par exchanged for (0.05) share new Class B Non-Vtg. Common 04/10/2002
Merged into Rogers Communications Inc. 07/01/2005
Each share new Common no par exchanged for (0.23529411) share Non-Vtg. Class B Common no par
Each share new Class B Common exchanged for (0.23529411) share Non-Vtg. Class B Common no par

CALL 900 INC (AB)
Name changed to Xentel Interactive Inc. 08/03/1995
Xentel Interactive Inc. recapitalized as Xentel DM Inc. 07/01/1998 which name changed to iMarketing Solutions Group Inc. 11/26/2010
(See iMarketing Solutions Group Inc.)

CALL-ONLINE INC (DE)
Each share old Common 1¢ par exchanged for (0.1) share new Common 1¢ par 12/31/1997
Name changed to Sino-City Gas Inc. 04/21/1998
Sino-City Gas Inc. name changed to Speechlink Communications Corp. 09/23/1999 which recapitalized as Eros Enterprises, Inc. 12/15/2005 which name changed to IQ Webquest, Inc. 03/03/2006

CALL-SOLUTIONS INC (CA)
Recapitalized as ProCoreGroup, Inc. (CA) 11/17/2003
Each share Common $0.001 par exchanged for (0.01315789) share Common $0.001 par
ProCoreGroup, Inc. (CA) reorganized in Nevada as Universal Property Development & Acquisition Corp. 07/11/2005
(See Universal Property Development & Acquisition Corp.)

CALLAHAN MNG CORP (AZ)
Capital Stock $1 par changed to $3 par 04/09/1973
Capital Stock $3 par reclassified as Common $3 par 05/09/1977
Common $3 par split (3) for (2) by issuance of (0.5) additional share 04/02/1980
Common $3 par changed to $1 par 05/06/1980
Merged into Coeur D'Alene Mines Corp. (ID) 12/31/1991
Each share Common $1 par exchanged for (0.435) share Common $1 par
Coeur D'Alene Mines Corp. (ID) reincorporated in Delaware as Coeur Mining, Inc. 05/17/2013

CALLAHAN ZINC LEAD CO. (AZ)
Capital Stock $10 par changed to $1 par 00/00/1934
Name changed to Callahan Mining Corp. 04/30/1958
Callahan Mining Corp. merged into Coeur D'Alene Mines Corp. (ID) 12/31/1991 which reincorporated in Delaware as Coeur Mining, Inc. 05/17/2013

CALLAN PUBG INC (MN)
Merged into Ratac Corp. 08/04/1978
Each share Common 10¢ par exchanged for $2.90 cash

CALLAWAY GOLF CO (DE)
Reincorporated 07/01/1999
Common 1¢ par split (2) for (1) by issuance of (1) additional share 03/19/1993
Common 1¢ par split (2) for (1) by issuance of (1) additional share 03/07/1994
Common 1¢ par split (2) for (1) by issuance of (1) additional share 03/10/1995
State of incorporation changed from (CA) to (DE) 07/01/1999
144A Conv. Perpetual Preferred Ser. B 1¢ par reclassified as 7.5% Conv. Perpetual Preferred Ser. B 1¢ par 06/15/2010
7.5% Conv. Perpetual Preferred Ser. B 1¢ par called for redemption at $100 plus $1.1875 accrued dividends on 11/13/2013
(Additional Information in Active)

CALLAWAY MILLS
Liquidation completed 00/00/1947
Details not available

CALLDIRECT CAP CORP (AB)
Recapitalized as Ocean Ventures Inc. 01/27/2000
Each share Common no par exchanged for (0.2) share Common no par
Ocean Ventures Inc. name changed to Digital Youth Network Corp. 07/28/2004
(See Digital Youth Network Corp.)

CALLEX ENTERPRISES LTD (BC)
Name changed 10/29/1985
Name changed from Callex Mineral Explorations Ltd. to Callex Enterprises Ltd. 10/29/1985
Name changed to Shephard Insurance Group Ltd. 10/12/1988
Shephard Insurance Group Ltd. recapitalized as Collingwood Capital Corp. 03/11/1999 which name changed to Rainy River Resources Ltd. 06/17/2005 which merged into New Gold Inc. 10/16/2013

CALLIDUS SOFTWARE INC (DE)
Acquired by SAP S.E. 04/05/2018
Each share Common $0.001 par exchanged for $36 cash

CALLINAN FLIN-FLON MINES LTD. (CANADA)
Each share old Capital Stock no par exchanged for (0.25) share new Capital Stock no par 00/00/1939
Recapitalized as Consolidated Callinan Flin-Flon Mines Ltd. 07/17/1956
Each share new Capital Stock no par exchanged for (0.5) share Common no par
Consolidated Callinan Flin-Flon Mines Ltd. name changed to Callinan

Mines Ltd. 03/10/1998 which name changed to Callinan Royalties Corp. 07/14/2011 which merged into Altius Minerals Corp. 05/07/2015

CALLINAN MINES LTD (CANADA)
Each share Common no par received distribution of (0.22222222) share Callinex Mines Inc. Common no par payable 07/14/2011 to holders of record 07/13/2011 Ex date - 07/11/2011
Name changed to Callinan Royalties Corp. 07/14/2011
Callinan Royalties Corp. merged into Altius Minerals Corp. 05/07/2015

CALLINAN ROYALTIES CORP (CANADA)
Merged into Altius Minerals Corp. 05/07/2015
Each share Common no par exchanged for (0.163) share Common no par and $0.203 cash
Note: Unexchanged certificates will be cancelled and become without value 05/07/2021

CALLIOPE METALS CORP (YT)
Reincorporated 06/17/1997
Place of incorporation changed from (Canada) to (YT) 06/17/1997
Under plan of merger name changed to Argosy Minerals Inc. (YT) 05/07/1999
Argosy Minerals Inc. (YT) reincorporated in British Columbia 05/26/2005 which reincorporated in Australia as Argosy Minerals Ltd. 03/18/2011

CALLISTO PHARMACEUTICALS INC (DE)
Merged into Synergy Pharmaceuticals, Inc. 01/18/2013
Each share Common $0.0001 par exchanged for (0.1799) share Common $0.0001 par

CALLISTO RES LTD (AB)
Merged into Alma Oil & Gas Ltd. 12/31/1996
Each share Common no par exchanged for (0.16666666) share Common no par
Alma Oil & Gas Ltd. merged into Hornet Energy Ltd. 12/31/1999
(See Hornet Energy Ltd.)

CALLITE TUNGSTEN CORP.
Bankrupt 00/00/1949
Stockholders' equity unlikely

CALLMATE TELECOM INTL INC (FL)
Name changed to BankEngine Technologies, Inc. (FL) 03/21/2001
BankEngine Technologies, Inc. (FL) reincorporated in Delaware 05/23/2002 which recapitalized as Syscan Imaging, Inc. 04/02/2004 which name changed to Sysview Technology, Inc. 06/27/2006 which name changed to Document Capture Technologies, Inc. 01/08/2008
(See Document Capture Technologies, Inc.)

CALLNOW COM INC (DE)
Charter cancelled and declared inoperative and void for non-payment of taxes 03/01/2003

CALLON CONS PARTNERS L P (CA)
Merged into Callon Petroleum Co. (DE) 09/14/1994
Each Unit of Ltd. Partnership Int. exchanged for (1/3) share Common 1¢ par

CALLON PETE CO (CA)
Capital Stock $0.33333333 par split (3) for (2) by issuance of (0.5) additional share 12/01/1980
Merged into CPC Acquisition Corp. 11/22/1988
Each share Capital Stock $0.33333333 par exchanged for $0.625 cash

CALLON PETE CO (DE)
$2.125 Conv. Exchangeable Preferred Ser. A 1¢ par called for redemption at $25.213 plus $0.525347 accrued dividends on 07/14/2005
Each share 18% Conv. Preferred 1¢ par exchanged for (10) shares Common 1¢ par 12/31/2009
(Additional Information in Active)

CALLOWAY PPTYS INC (AB)
Recapitalized as Calloway Real Estate Investment Trust 02/18/2002
Each share Common no par exchanged for (0.5) Trust Unit
Calloway Real Estate Investment Trust name changed to Smart Real Estate Investment Trust 07/08/2015 which name changed to SmartCentres Real Estate Investment Trust 10/24/2017

CALLOWAY REAL ESTATE INVT TR (AB)
Each old Trust Unit exchanged for (0.08905195) new Trust Unit 11/04/2002
Name changed to Smart Real Estate Investment Trust and Trust Units reclassified as Variable Units 07/08/2015
Smart Real Estate Investment Trust name changed to SmartCentres Real Estate Investment Trust 10/24/2017

CALLWRITER INC (NV)
Name changed to American Boardsports 07/09/1999
American Boardsports name changed to Sierra Pacific Gypsum Corp. 11/00/1999 which name changed to Sanitec Holdings USA 06/16/2000 which recapitalized as Co-Media Inc. 11/25/2000 which reorganized as Jarvis Group Inc. 01/18/2002 which name changed to Cash 4 Homes 247 on 05/21/2003 which name changed to Vegas Equity International Corp. 02/01/2006
(See Vegas Equity International Corp.)

CALMAC MINES LTD. (BC)
Struck off register and declared dissolved for failure to file returns 00/00/1974

CALMAR INC (DE)
Acquired by Kebo AB 09/24/1987
Each share Common 10¢ par exchanged for $32 cash

CALMAR WEST OILS LTD. (AB)
Recapitalized as Brett Oils Ltd. 06/29/1965
Each share Common no par exchanged for (0.25) share Common no par
Brett Oils Ltd. recapitalized as BRO Resources Ltd. (ALTA) 02/09/1978 which reincorporated in British Columbia 10/08/1981 which recapitalized as Canadian Quantum Energy Corp. 12/06/1990

CALMAT CO (DE)
Common $1 par split (2) for (1) by issuance of (1) additional share 04/02/1987
Merged into Vulcan Materials Co. 01/06/1999
Each share Common $1 par exchanged for $31 cash

CALMONT OILS LTD. (CANADA)
Each share old Capital Stock $1 par exchanged for (0.25) share new Capital Stock $1 par 00/00/1929
New Capital Stock $1 par changed to no par 00/00/1950
Acquired by Anglo-Canadian Oil Co. Ltd. 00/00/1953
Each share Capital Stock no par exchanged for (0.22222222) share Capital Stock no par 00/00/1953
Anglo-Canadian Oil Co. Ltd. acquired by Canadian Oil Companies Ltd. 11/03/1955

(See Canadian Oil Companies Ltd.)

CALMOR IRON BAY MINES LTD (ON)
Merged into Calmor Iron Bay Mines (1978) Ltd. 12/01/1978
Each share Capital Stock no par exchanged for $1.13 cash

CALMOR IRON BAY MINES (1978) LTD. (ON)
Merged into Calmor Iron Bay Mines (1979) Ltd. 06/22/1979
Each share Capital Stock no par exchanged for $1.17 cash

CALMOR MINES LTD. (ON)
Completely liquidated 08/22/1962
Each share Capital Stock $1 par exchanged for first and final distribution of (0.448) share Iron Bay Mines Ltd. Capital Stock $1 par and $0.09 cash
Iron Bay Mines Ltd. recapitalized as Calmor Iron Bay Mines Ltd. 12/14/1966
(See Calmor Iron Bay Mines Ltd.)

CALNET BUSINESS BK N A (SACRAMENTO, CA)
Merged into Commercial Capital Bancorp, Inc. 03/06/2006
Each share Common $5 par exchanged for (1.073) shares Common 1¢ par
(See Commercial Capital Bancorp, Inc.)

CALNETICS CORP (CA)
Merged into Summa Industries 10/28/1997
Each share Common 10¢ par exchanged for $7.35 cash

CALNEVA RES LTD (BC)
Recapitalized as International Calneva Gold Corp. 09/01/1994
Each share Common no par exchanged for (0.2) share Common no par
International Calneva Gold Corp. recapitalized as Tenacity Resources Corp. 09/30/1999
(See Tenacity Resources Corp.)

CALNOR RES LTD (BC)
Recapitalized as Norcal Resources Ltd. 08/23/1991
Each share Common no par exchanged for (0.33333333) share Common no par
Norcal Resources Ltd. recapitalized as Troon Ventures Ltd. (BC) 06/18/2002 which reorganized in Ontario as Grenville Strategic Royalty Corp. 02/21/2014 which merged into LOGiQ Asset Management Inc. (AB) 06/07/2018 which reorganized in British Columbia as Flow Capital Corp. 06/11/2018

CALNORTH OILS LTD. (AB)
Recapitalized as Northcal Oils Ltd. 07/31/1956
Each share Capital Stock no par exchanged for (0.25) share Capital Stock no par
Northcal Oils Ltd. name changed to Northcal Mines Ltd. 09/27/1963 which recapitalized as New Northcal Mines Ltd. 07/26/1971 which recapitalized as Venture Properties Ltd. 04/17/1974 which recapitalized as Allied Venture Properties Ltd. 09/02/1975 which recapitalized as Buckingham International Holdings Ltd. 03/22/1979
(See Buckingham International Holdings Ltd.)

CALNY FOOD SERVICES, INC. (DE)
Name changed to Calny, Inc. 10/08/1981
(See Calny, Inc.)

CALNY INC (DE)
Common 1¢ par split (3) for (2) by issuance of (0.5) additional share 11/21/1983
Stock Dividends - 50% 03/01/1982; 50% 11/23/1982
Acquired by PepsiCo, Inc. 03/02/1988
Each share Common 1¢ par exchanged for $11 cash

CALODE URANIUM MINING CO. LTD. (ON)
Charter cancelled 09/00/1961

CALOR LATERITE CORP (BC)
Name changed to Interstrat Resources Inc. 10/04/1982
(See Interstrat Resources Inc.)

CALOTTO CAP INC (ON)
Recapitalized as Hamilton Thorne Ltd. 11/06/2009
Each share Common no par exchanged for (0.12966376) share Common no par

CALPETRO RES INC (BC)
Recapitalized as Nucal Resources Ltd. 01/28/1985
Each share Common no par exchanged for (0.2) share Common no par
Nucal Resources Ltd. recapitalized as Captive Air International Inc. 06/30/1987 which recapitalized as Kik Tire Technologies Inc. 04/08/1996 which recapitalized as Kik Polymers Inc. 06/20/2006 which name changed to Edgewater Wireless Systems Inc. 02/01/2012

CALPIAN INC (TX)
Name changed to MoneyOnMobile, Inc. 10/26/2016

CALPINE CDA HLDGS LTD (AB)
Each Exchangeable Share no par exchanged for (1) share Calpine Corp. Common $0.001 par 05/27/2002
(See Calpine Corp.)

CALPINE CAP TR (DE)
Each Term Income Deferrable Equity Security called for redemption at $50 plus $0.6309 accrued dividends on 10/20/2004

CALPINE CAP TR II (DE)
5.5% Term Income Conv. Preferred called for redemption at $50 plus $0.6035 accrued dividends on 10/20/2004

CALPINE CAP TR III (DE)
5% Conv. Term Income Preferred called for redemption at $50 plus $0.50 accrued dividends on 07/13/2005

CALPINE CORP (DE)
Old Common $0.001 par split (2) for (1) by issuance of (1) additional share payable 10/07/1999 to holders of record 09/28/1999 Ex date - 10/08/1999
Old Common $0.001 par split (2) for (1) by issuance of (1) additional share payable 06/08/2000 to holders of record 05/29/2000 Ex date - 06/09/2000
Old Common $0.001 par split (2) for (1) by issuance of (1) additional share payable 11/14/2000 to holders of record 11/06/2000 Ex date - 11/15/2000
Plan of reorganization under Chapter 11 Federal Bankruptcy Code effective 01/31/2008
Each share old Common $0.001 par exchanged for (0.10118613) Common Stock Purchase Warrant, Ser. A expiring 08/26/2008
Acquired by Volt Parent, L.P. 03/08/2018
Each share new Common $0.001 par exchanged for $15.25 cash

CALPINE NAT GAS TR (AB)
Merged into Viking Energy Royalty Trust 02/01/2005
Each Trust Unit no par exchanged for (2) Trust Units no par
Viking Energy Royalty Trust merged

into Harvest Energy Trust 02/07/2006
(See Harvest Energy Trust)

CALPINE PWR INCOME FD (AB)
Acquired by Harbinger Capital Partners Special Situations Fund, L.P. 02/14/2007
Each Trust Unit exchanged for $13 cash

CALPINE RES INC (BC)
Merged into Prime Resources Group Inc. 04/12/1990
Each share Common no par exchanged for (1) share Common no par and (0.5) Common Stock Purchase Warrant expiring 04/12/1991
Prime Resources Group Inc. merged into HomeStake Mining Co. 12/03/1998 which merged into Barrick Gold Corp. 12/14/2001

CALPIS CO LTD (JAPAN)
Name changed 09/01/1997
Name changed from Calpis Food Industry Co., Ltd. to Calpis Co., Ltd. 09/01/1997
Acquired by Ajinomoto Co., Inc. 09/25/2007
No ADR's remain outstanding

CALPROP CORP (CA)
Reincorporated 6/5/86
Reincorporated 7/1/93
Stock Dividends - 10% 12/16/1978; 10% 12/28/1979; 10% 07/31/1981; 10% 12/22/1982; 10% 12/15/1983; 10% 12/17/1984; 10% 12/16/1985; 10% 12/19/1986; 10% 12/17/1987; 10% 12/09/1988; 10% 12/15/1989
State of incorporation changed from (CA) to (DE) 06/05/1986
State of incorporation changed from (DE) to (CA) and Common $1 par changed to no par 07/01/1993
Conv. Preferred no par called for redemption 07/12/1996
Merged into NewCal Corp. 10/08/2005
Each share Common no par exchanged for $0.65 cash

CALS REFINERIES LTD (INDIA)
Reg. S Sponsored GDR's for Equity Shares spilt (20) for (1) by issuance of (19) additional GDR's payable 06/05/2008 to holders of record 06/03/2008
Basis changed from (1:100) to (1:50) 06/05/2008
GDR agreement terminated 07/08/2014
Each Reg. S Sponsored GDR for Equity Shares exchanged for (50) Equity Shares INR 1 par 07/08/2014

CALSPAN CORP (NY)
Merged into Arvin Industries, Inc. 04/21/1978
Each share Common 50¢ par exchanged for $8 cash

CALSTAR OIL & GAS LTD (AB)
Cease trade order 02/06/2008

CALSTAR PETE CO (CA)
Each share Capital Stock $10 par exchanged for initial distribution of $100 cash 07/31/1976
Each share Capital Stock $10 par received second distribution of $175 cash 03/25/1977
Note: Details on subsequent distributions, if any, are not available

CALTA MINES LTD (BC)
Merged into Coralta Resources Ltd. 10/18/1973
Each share Capital Stock 50¢ par exchanged for (0.5) share Common $1 par
(See Coralta Resources Ltd.)

CALTAG INC (UT)
Each share old Common $0.008 par exchanged for (0.1) share new Common $0.008 par 01/04/1991

Merged into Invitrogen Corp. 05/23/2005
Each share new Common $0.008 par exchanged for $6.2907059 cash
Note: Each share new Common $0.008 par received an initial distribution from escrow of $0.6359592 cash 10/07/2005
Each share new Common $0.008 par received a second distribution of $0.02555649 cash payable 04/12/2006 to holders of record 05/23/2005
Each share new Common $0.008 par received a third and final distribution of $1.4461313 cash 03/30/2007

CALTAS FITNESS INC (DE)
Name changed to Cinemaya Media Group, Inc. 02/06/2007
Cinemaya Media Group, Inc. recapitalized as SNM Global Holdings 11/14/2008

CALTEC INVTS INC (AB)
Struck from the register and dissolved 08/08/1997

CALTECH DATA LTD (BC)
Recapitalized as Roraima Gold Corp. 09/14/1994
Each share Common no par exchanged for (0.5) share Common no par
Roraima Gold Corp. recapitalized as International Roraima Gold Corp. 06/13/1996
(See International Roraima Gold Corp.)

CALTEM LIQUIDATING, INC. (CA)
Liquidation completed
Each share Common 10¢ par exchanged for initial distribution of $1.88 cash 06/30/1980
Each share Common 10¢ par received second distribution of $0.15 cash 01/30/1981
Each share Common 10¢ par received third and final distribution of $0.12 cash 06/17/1981

CALTERRA FREEHOLD VENTURES INC (AB)
Name changed 04/24/2001
Name changed from Calterra Resources Ltd. to Calterra Freehold Ventures Inc. 04/24/2001
Reorganized under the laws of British Columbia as West Africa Energy Inc. 06/29/2006
Each share Common no par exchanged for (0.5) share Common no par
West Africa Energy Inc. name changed to Centric Energy Corp. 08/20/2007 which merged into Africa Oil Corp. 02/22/2011

CALTEX OIL CO. (NV)
Charter revoked for failure to pay taxes 03/06/1933

CALTO INDS INC (AB)
Name changed 12/29/1988
Name changed from Calto Resources Inc. to Calto Industries Inc. 12/29/1988
Delisted from Alberta Stock Exchange 11/22/1989

CALTON INC NEW (NJ)
Each share old Common 1¢ par received distribution of (1) share Non-transferable Conv. Class B Common 1¢ par 08/24/1987
Reorganized under Chapter 11 Federal Bankruptcy Code 05/28/1993
Each share old Common 1¢ par exchanged for (0.05) share new Common 1¢ par
Each share Non-transferable Conv. Class B Common 1¢ par exchanged for (0.05) share new Common 1¢ par
Each share new Common 1¢ par exchanged for (0.2) share Common 5¢ par to reflect a (1) for (25)

reverse split followed by a (5) for (1) forward split 05/31/2000
Note: Holders of (24) or fewer pre-split shares received $32.813 cash per share
Recapitalized as Second Street Capital, Inc. 01/26/2012
Each share Common 5¢ par exchanged for (0.1) share Common 5¢ par

CALTON INC OLD (NJ)
Each share Common 1¢ par exchanged for (0.5) share Common 2¢ par 01/21/1985
Merged into Calacq, Inc. 11/15/1985
Each share Common 2¢ par exchanged for $6 cash

CALTRAN SYS INC (DE)
Stock Dividend - 90% 10/26/1977
Charter cancelled and declared inoperative and void for non-payment of taxes 03/01/1979

CALTRON INC (PA)
Name changed to J-Bird Music Group Ltd. 10/15/1997
J-Bird Music Group Ltd. name changed to International Biofuel & Biochemical Corp. 12/09/2002
(See International Biofuel & Biochemical Corp.)

CALUMET & ARIZONA MINING CO.
Acquired by Phelps Dodge Corp. 00/00/1931
Details not available

CALUMET & GOLDFIELD MINING & DEVELOPMENT CO. (AZ)
Charter expired by time limitation 03/15/1931

CALUMET & HECLA, INC. (MI)
$4.75 Preferred Ser. A no par called for redemption 03/27/1968
Merged into Universal Oil Products Co. 04/30/1968
Each share Common $5 par exchanged for (0.6) share Capital Stock $1 par
Universal Oil Products Co. name changed to UOP Inc. 07/15/1975
(See UOP Inc.)

CALUMET & HECLA CONSOLIDATED COPPER CO. (MI)
Name changed to Calumet & Hecla, Inc. 00/00/1952
Calumet & Hecla, Inc. merged into Universal Oil Products Co. 04/30/1968 which name changed to UOP Inc. 07/15/1975
(See UOP Inc.)

CALUMET APARTMENTS, INC.
Liquidated 00/00/1940
Details not available

CALUMET BANCORP INC (DE)
Common 1¢ par split (3) for (2) by issuance of (0.5) additional share 11/18/1994
Common 1¢ par split (3) for (2) by issuance of (0.5) additional share payable 11/17/1997 to holders of record 11/03/1997
Merged into FBOP Acquisition Co. 04/30/1999
Each share Common 1¢ par exchanged for $32.04 cash

CALUMET CONTACT URANIUM MINES LTD. (QC)
Charter cancelled for failure to file reports 06/22/1974

CALUMET GAS & ELECTRIC CO.
Name changed to Northern Indiana Public Service Co. 00/00/1926
Northern Indiana Public Service Co. reorganized as Nipsco Industries, Inc. 03/03/1988 which name changed to NiSource Inc. (IN) 04/14/1999 which reincorporated in Delaware 11/01/2000

CALUMET GOLD MINES CO. (NV)
Name changed to Aeco Corp. 00/00/1950

Aeco Corp. recapitalized as Universal Services Alliance Inc. 09/17/1984
(See Universal Services Alliance Inc.)

CALUMET INDS INC (DE)
Common 25¢ par split (2) for (1) by issuance of (1) additional share 06/02/1980
Common 25¢ par split (2) for (1) by issuance of (1) additional share 03/02/1981
Chapter 11 bankruptcy proceedings converted to Chapter 7 on 01/16/1991
Stockholders' equity unlikely

CALUMET MINES LTD. (QC)
Reorganized as New Calumet Mines Ltd. 00/00/1942
Each (100) shares Capital Stock exchanged for (68) shares Capital Stock $1 par plus a $25 Note
(See New Calumet Mines Ltd.)

CALUMET NATL BK (HAMMOND, IN)
Capital Stock $100 par changed to $25 par and (3) additional shares issued plus a 50% stock dividend paid 12/14/1956
Stock Dividends - 14.28571428% 12/11/1946; 11.11111111% 01/31/1950; 33.33333333% 01/28/1960
Under plan of reorganization each share Common automatically became (1) share Calumet National Corp. Common 10/10/1996
Calumet National Corp. name changed to Bank Calumet Inc. 04/21/2000
(See Bank Calumet Inc.)

CALUMET NATL CORP (IN)
Name changed to Bank Calumet Inc. 04/21/2000
(See Bank Calumet Inc.)

CALUMET OIL CO. (CA)
Completely liquidated 06/19/1959
Each share Capital Stock $1 par exchanged for first and final distribution of (0.014380) share Monterey Oil Co. Common $1 par
(See Monterey Oil Co.)

CALUMET REFINING CO. (DE)
Each share Common $100 par exchanged for (8) shares Common $25 par 00/00/1954
Acquired by Calumet Industries, Inc. 11/20/1962
Details not available

CALUMET SILVER MNG CO (DE)
Name changed to Glenco International Corp. 10/05/1981
(See Glenco International Corp.)

CALUMET URANIUM MINES LTD. (QC)
Recapitalized as Atlanta Mines Ltd. 01/22/1965
Each share Capital Stock $1 par exchanged for (0.2) share Capital Stock $1 par
Atlanta Mines Ltd. merged into Albarmont Mines Corp. 10/12/1971 which recapitalized as Albarmont (1985) Inc. 07/19/1985
(See Albarmont (1985) Inc.)

CALUNITE CORP. (DE)
Charter cancelled and declared inoperative and void for non-payment of taxes 04/15/1969

CALVADA RES INC (BC)
Merged into Eurus Resource Corp. 05/01/1990
Each share Common no par exchanged for (0.4) share Common no par
Eurus Resource Corp. merged into Crystallex International Corp. (BC) 09/29/1995 which reincorporated in Canada 01/23/1998

CALVALLEY PETE INC NEW (CANADA)
Acquired by Calvalley Energy Ltd. 05/12/2015
Each share Class A Common no par exchanged for USD$0.75 cash
Each share Class A Common no par received an additional USD$0.057 cash per share from escrow 04/20/2016

CALVALLEY PETE INC OLD (CANADA)
Reorganized as Calvalley Petroleum Inc. (New) 08/09/1996
Each share Common no par exchanged for (0.25) share Class A Common no par
(See Calvalley Petroleum Inc. (New))

CALVAN CONSOLIDATED OIL & GAS CO. LTD. (CANADA)
Completely liquidated 11/30/1961
Each share Capital Stock $1 par exchanged for $4.59 cash

CALVAN PETROLEUMS LTD.
Merged into Calvan Consolidated Oil & Gas Co. Ltd. 00/00/1951
Each share Capital Stock no par exchanged for (1) share Capital Stock $1 par
(See Calvan Consolidated Oil & Gas Co. Ltd.)

CALVERITE MINING CO. (NV)
Charter revoked for failure to file reports and pay fees 00/00/1924

CALVERT CASH RESVS OLD (MA)
Name changed to Money Management Plus 09/10/1984
Money Management Plus name changed to Calvert Cash Reserves (New) 06/30/1996

CALVERT DALE ESTATES LTD (ON)
Each share Common no par exchanged for (0.5) share Class A no par and (0.5) share Class B no par 06/22/1981
Name changed to Argyll Energy Corp. 06/21/1983
(See Argyll Energy Corp.)

CALVERT DRILLING, INC. (IL)
Reincorporated under the laws of Delaware as Calvert Petroleum Co. 12/31/1959
(See Calvert Petroleum Co.)

CALVERT EXPL CO (DE)
6% Conv. Preferred $100 par called for redemption 01/11/1973
Merged into Sun Oil Co. (PA) 07/31/1974
Each share Common 10¢ par exchanged for (0.154559) share Common $1 par
Sun Oil Co. (PA) name changed to Sun Co., Inc. 04/27/1976 which name changed to Sunoco, Inc. 11/06/1998 which merged into Energy Transfer Partners, L.P. (Old) 10/05/2012 which merged into Energy Transfer Partners, L.P. (New) 05/01/2017 which merged into Energy Transfer L.P. 10/19/2018

CALVERT GAS & OILS LTD (CANADA)
Capital Stock no par changed to 5¢ par 07/16/1962
Capital Stock 5¢ par changed to no par 04/23/1976
Recapitalized as Heenan Petroleum Ltd. 08/08/1985
Each share Capital Stock no par exchanged for (0.2) share Capital Stock no par
Heenan Petroleum Ltd. merged into Heenan Senlac Resources Ltd. 08/07/1986 which merged into Mining & Allied Supplies (Canada) Ltd. 08/25/1992 which name changed to Bearing Power (Canada) Ltd. 03/28/1994
(See Bearing Power (Canada) Ltd.)

CALVERT PETROLEUM CO. (DE)
Liquidation completed 11/24/1961
Details not available

CALVERT TAX FREE RESVS (MA)
Under plan of reorganization each share Money Management Plus Tax-Free Portfolio no par automatically became Money Market Portfolio Class MMP no par shares on a net asset basis 10/02/1995
(Additional Information in Active)

CALVERT TELECOMMUNICATIONS CORP. (MD)
Merged into Comcast Corp. (Old) 02/15/1984
Each share Common 1¢ par exchanged for $25 principal amount of 8.75% Conv. Subordinated Debentures due 03/17/1999 or $25 cash
Note: Option to receive Debentures expired 03/07/1984

CALVIDEO ELECTRONICS, INC. (CA)
Charter suspended for non-payment of taxes 03/02/1964

CALVIN EXPL & DEV CORP (QC)
Completely liquidated 11/14/1974
Each share Capital Stock no par received first and final distribution of (0.5) share Calvin Oil Co. Ltd. Capital Stock no par
Note: Certificates were not required to be surrendered and are without value

CALVIN EXPL INC (CO)
Name changed to CLX Exploration Inc. 09/23/1991
CLX Exploration Inc. recapitalized as CLX Energy Inc. 04/09/1993 which name changed to CLX Investment Co., Inc. 09/02/2004 which name changed to CLX Medical, Inc. 04/30/2008

CALVIN OIL LTD (AB)
Struck off register for failure to file returns 03/15/1977

CALVISTA GOLD CORP (ON)
Acquired by AUX Acquisition 3 SARL 12/12/2012
Each share Common no par exchanged for $1.10 cash

CALVITAL PHARMACEUTICAL & COSMETIC CORP. (NY)
Name changed to Calvital Pharmaceutical Corp. 06/01/1972
(See Calvital Pharmaceutical Corp.)

CALVITAL PHARMACEUTICAL CORP. (NY)
Charter cancelled and proclaimed dissolved for failure to pay taxes 06/24/1981

CALWA CO.
Dissolved 00/00/1942
Details not available

CALWEST VENTURES INC (NV)
Name changed to Nationwide Capital Corp. 08/06/2002
(See Nationwide Capital Corp.)

CALYPSO ACQUISITION CORP (BC)
Name changed to Calypso Uranium Corp. 09/24/2007
Calypso Uranium Corp. merged into U308 Corp. 05/15/2013

CALYPSO DEV LTD (BC)
Recapitalized as Calypso Acquisition Corp. 11/18/2002
Each share Common no par exchanged for (0.1) share Common no par
Calypso Acquisition Corp. name changed to Calypso Uranium Corp. 09/24/2007 which merged into U308 Corp. 05/15/2013

CALYPSO ENTERPRISES INC (DE)
Name changed to Huron Ventures Inc. 06/18/2003
Huron Ventures Inc. name changed to Cano Petroleum, Inc. 06/01/2004

(See Cano Petroleum, Inc.)

CALYPSO FOOD & BEVERAGE CO., LTD. (ON)
Name changed to Grissol Foods Ltd. 09/19/1962
(See Grissol Foods Ltd.)

CALYPSO MEDIA SVCS GROUP INC (NV)
Name changed to Colorado Rare Earths, Inc. 02/03/2011
Colorado Rare Earths, Inc. name changed to U.S. Rare Earths Inc. 02/03/2011

CALYPSO URANIUM CORP (BC)
Merged into U308 Corp. 05/15/2013
Each share Common no par exchanged for (0.4) share Common no par

CALYPSO WIRELESS INC (DE)
Voluntarily dissolved 03/29/2016
No stockholders' equity

CALYX BIO-VENTURES INC (BC)
Name changed to Calyx Ventures Inc. 02/05/2018

CAM COMM SOLUTIONS INC (DE)
Merged into Vegas Holding Corp. 08/14/2008
Each share Common $0.001 par exchanged for $40.50 cash

CAM CORP (NC)
Adjudicated bankrupt 04/09/1970
No stockholders' equity

CAM DATA SYS INC (DE)
Name changed to CAM Commerce Solutions, Inc. 04/12/2000
(See CAM Commerce Solutions, Inc.)

CAM DESIGNS INC (DE)
Each share old Class A Common $0.001 par exchanged for (0.125) share new Class A Common $0.001 par 01/26/2000
Name changed to TheNETdigest.com, Inc. 05/18/2001
(See TheNETdigest.com, Inc.)

CAM MINES LTD (QC)
Recapitalized as Energy & Resources (Cam) Ltd./Energy & Resources (Cam) Ltee. 01/21/1980
Each share Capital Stock $1 par exchanged for (0.25) share Capital Stock no par
Energy & Resources (Cam) Ltd./Energy & Resources (Cam) Ltee. name changed to ERG Resources Inc. 10/09/1986
(See ERG Resources Inc.)

CAM-NET COMMUNICATIONS NETWORK INC (CANADA)
Reincorporated 02/01/1991
Place of incorporation changed from (BC) to (Canada) 02/01/1991
Name changed to Suncom Telecommunications Inc. 08/01/1997
Suncom Telecommunications Inc. name changed to VirtualSellers.com, Inc. 06/01/1999 which name changed to Healthtrac, Inc. 03/25/2002
(See Healthtrac, Inc.)

CAM-OR INC (IN)
5% Preferred $100 par called for redemption 12/15/1969
Common no par split (3) for (2) by issuance of (0.5) additional share 06/29/1981
Charter revoked for failure to file annual reports 07/31/1989

CAM TURF CORP (ON)
Delisted from Alberta Stock Exchange 11/22/1989

CAMABIE MINES LTD. (ON)
Charter dissolved 11/28/1973

CAMAC ENERGY INC (DE)
Stock Dividend - 143.48% payable 02/21/2014 to holders of record 02/13/2014 Ex date - 02/24/2014

Recapitalized as Erin Energy Corp. 04/23/2015
Each share Common $0.001 par exchanged for (0.16666666) share Common $0.001 par

CAMAGUEY SUGAR CO.
Reorganized as Vertientes-Camaguey Sugar Co. 00/00/1937
No stockholders' equity

CAMALLOY INC (PA)
Merged into CBH Corp. 03/31/1996
Each share Common no par exchanged for $0.15 cash

CAMAN GOLD MINES LTD. (ON)
Merged into Garrison Creek Consolidated Mines Ltd. on a (1) for (15) basis 12/09/1954
Garrison Creek Consolidated Mines Ltd. merged into QSR Ltd. 09/07/1993 which name changed to Coniagas Resources Ltd. 06/25/1999 which name changed to Lithium One Inc. 07/23/2009
(See Lithium One Inc.)

CAMARGO CORREA DESENVOLVIMENTO IMOBILIARIO (BRAZIL)
ADR agreement terminated 11/26/2012
Each Sponsored Reg. S ADR for Common exchanged for $2.267649 cash
Each Sponsored 144A ADR for Common exchanged for $2.267649 cash

CAMARILLO CMNTY BK (CAMARILLO, CA)
Stock Dividend - 13.50% payable 07/15/1996 to holders of record 06/19/1996
Name changed to First California Bank (Camarillo, CA) 10/25/2001
First California Bank (Camarillo, CA) reorganized as FCB Bancorp 09/20/2005 which merged into First California Financial Group, Inc. 03/12/2007 which merged into PacWest Bancorp 05/31/2013

CAMAS RES LTD (BC)
Name changed to Merlin Resources Inc. 01/17/1991
(See Merlin Resources Inc.)

CAMBER SPORTS INC (AB)
Recapitalized as Zycom Corp. 03/24/1993
Each share Common no par exchanged for (0.33333333) share Common no par
(See Zycom Corp.)

CAMBEX CORP (MA)
Common 10¢ par split (3) for (2) by issuance of (0.5) additional share 02/25/1991
Common 10¢ par split (2) for (1) by issuance of (1) additional share 02/14/1992
Company terminated common stock registration and is no longer public as of 08/02/2007

CAMBIO INC (DE)
Name changed to Telynx, Inc. 11/28/2000
(See Telynx, Inc.)

CAMBIOR INC (QC)
Acquired by Iamgold Corp. 11/08/2006
Each share Common no par exchanged for (0.42) share Common no par

CAMBODIAN VENTURES LTD (WY)
Each share old Common no par exchanged for (0.0002) share new Common no par 02/12/2007
Stock Dividend - 10% payable 04/28/2006 to holders of record 04/20/2006 Ex date - 04/18/2006
Reincorporated under the laws of Delaware as STS Evermedia Corp. 03/12/2007

CAM-CAM

CAMBORNE INDS LTD (BC)
Reorganized under the laws of the United Kingdom as Camborne Industries PLC 07/20/1990
Each share Common no par exchanged for (1) share Ordinary Stock 50p par
(See Camborne Industries PLC)

CAMBORNE INDS PLC (UNITED KINGDOM)
Discharged from receivership 12/04/2002
Stockholders' equity unlikely

CAMBORNE RESOURCES LTD. (BC)
Name changed to Camborne Industries Ltd. (BC) 05/23/1989
Camborne Industries Ltd. (BC) reorganized in United Kingdom as Camborne Industries PLC 07/20/1990
(See Camborne Industries PLC)

CAMBRI MINING & DEVELOPMENT LTD. (BC)
Struck off register and declared dissolved for failure to file reports 08/30/1973

CAMBRIA ETF TR (DE)
Trust terminated 06/30/2017
Each share Dhandho Junoon ETF no par received net asset value
(Additional Information in Active)

CAMBRIA INC (UT)
Each share old Common $0.001 par exchanged for (0.05) share new Common $0.001 par 03/18/1986
Charter cancelled for failure to file for renewal 11/01/1998

CAMBRIA IRON CO.
Merged into Bethlehem Steel Corp. (DE) 00/00/1942
Each share Capital Stock $50 par exchanged for $55 principal amount of 2% 5-Year Bonds

CAMBRIA RES LTD (BC)
Name changed to On Wah Investments Corp. 03/02/1989
(See On Wah Investments Corp.)

CAMBRIAN GOLD RES INC (UT)
Proclaimed dissolved for failure to pay taxes 06/01/1990

CAMBRIAN SYS INC (OR)
Reincorporated under the laws of Delaware as Cambrian Systems Corp. and Common no par changed to $0.001 par 09/29/2008

CAMBRIDGE ANALYTICAL ASSOC INC (MA)
Acquired by National Environmental Testing Inc. 09/08/1989
Each share Common 1¢ par exchanged for $3.48 cash

CAMBRIDGE ANTIBODY TECHNOLOGY GROUP PLC (UNITED KINGDOM)
Acquired by AstraZeneca PLC 09/20/2006
Each Sponsored ADR for Ordinary exchanged for $24.99089 cash

CAMBRIDGE APPRECIATION FD INC (DE)
Liquidated and closed 00/00/1982
Details not available

CAMBRIDGE BEVERAGE CORP (DE)
Charter cancelled and declared inoperative and void for non-payment of taxes 03/01/1976

CAMBRIDGE BIOCHEMICS INC (BC)
Name changed to Cambridge Softek Inc. 06/23/1993
Cambridge Softek Inc. recapitalized as Alantra Venture Corp. 11/21/1994
(See Alantra Venture Corp.)

CAMBRIDGE BIOMEDICAL CORP (DE)
Ceased operations 02/19/1975
No stockholders' equity

CAMBRIDGE BIOSCIENCE CORP (DE)
Name changed to Cambridge Biotech Corp. 09/07/1990
Cambridge Biotech Corp. reorganized as Aquila Biopharmaceuticals, Inc. 10/22/1996 which merged into Antigenics, Inc. 11/16/2000 which name changed to Agenus Inc. 01/06/2011

CAMBRIDGE BIOTECH CORP (DE)
Reorganized as Aquila Biopharmaceuticals, Inc. 10/22/1996
Each share Common 1¢ par exchanged for (7.569) shares Common 1¢ par
Aquila Biopharmaceuticals, Inc. merged into Antigenics, Inc. 11/16/2000 which name changed to Agenus Inc. 01/06/2011

CAMBRIDGE CAP ACQUISITION CORP (DE)
Merged into Ability Inc. 12/24/2015
Each Unit exchanged for (1) share Ordinary $0.0001 par and (1) Ordinary Stock Purchase Warrant expiring 12/17/2018
Each share Common $0.0001 par exchanged for (1) share Ordinary $0.0001 par

CAMBRIDGE CAP HLDGS INC (UT)
Charter expired 01/31/2011

CAMBRIDGE COFFEE TEA & SPICE HOUSE INC (MA)
Common 5¢ par changed to $0.005 par and (2) additional shares issued 07/15/1971
Assets sold for the benefit of creditors 00/00/1973
No stockholders' equity

CAMBRIDGE COLLEGES INC (AB)
Delisted from Canadian Dealer Network 05/31/2000

CAMBRIDGE COLLEGES LTD (AB)
Name changed to Cambridge Colleges Inc. 02/10/1999
(See Cambridge Colleges Inc.)

CAMBRIDGE COMPUTER CORP (DE)
Merged into I.M.S. International, Inc. 08/13/1974
Each share Common 1¢ par exchanged for (0.2) share Common 1¢ par
I.M.S. International, Inc. merged into Dun & Bradstreet Corp. 05/26/1988 which name changed to R.H. Donnelley Corp. 07/01/1998
(See R.H. Donnelley Corp.)

CAMBRIDGE CORP (MN)
Liquidation completed
Each share Common 5¢ par received initial distribution of (0.5) share Northwest Teleproductions, Inc. Common 1¢ par 07/01/1976
Each share Common 5¢ par received second distribution of $0.45 cash 08/10/1976
Each share Common 5¢ par exchanged for third and final distribution of $0.275 cash 03/16/1977

CAMBRIDGE DISPLAY TECHNOLOGY INC (DE)
Merged into Sumitomo Chemical Co., Ltd. 09/19/2007
Each share Common 1¢ par exchanged for $12 cash

CAMBRIDGE ENERGY CORP (NV)
Each share Common $0.0001 par received distribution of (0.06666666) share North American GeoPower, Inc. Common $0.0001 par payable 12/20/2002 to holders of record 06/15/2002 Ex date - 06/12/2002
Each share Common $0.0001 par received distribution of (0.01984) share J.W. Resources Exploration & Development Inc. Common payable 01/20/2005 to holders of record 09/30/2004

Name changed to EnviroXtract, Inc. (NV) 08/11/2009
EnviroXtract, Inc. (NV) reincorporated in Wyoming 08/19/2010 which recapitalized as Mission Mining Co. 01/04/2013

CAMBRIDGE ENVIRONMENTAL SYS INC (AB)
Reincorporated 12/09/1993
Place of incorporation changed from (BC) to (AB) 12/09/1993
Cease trade order effective 02/21/2002

CAMBRIDGE EQUITIES LTD (DE)
Charter cancelled and declared inoperative and void for non-payment of taxes 03/01/1985

CAMBRIDGE FD INC (DE)
Name changed to Asset Investors Fund, Inc. 5/3/76
(See Asset Investors Fund, Inc.)

CAMBRIDGE FDG GROUP INC (NV)
Name changed to Agriceuticals Technologies, Inc. 10/02/1998
Agriceuticals Technologies, Inc. name changed to Playandwin Inc. 07/13/1999

CAMBRIDGE FINL CORP (DE)
Merged into United Products International Inc. 10/08/1984
Each share Class A 1¢ par exchanged for (0.2) share Class A 5¢ par
United Products International Inc. recapitalized as Environmental Digital Services Inc. (FL) 12/30/1996 which reincorporated in Delaware 07/01/2008 which recapitalized as Sabre Industrial, Inc. 04/12/2010 which name changed to Tsingyuan Brewery Ltd. 01/19/2011
(See Tsingyuan Brewery Ltd.)

CAMBRIDGE GAS LIGHT CO.
Acquired by New England Gas & Electric Association 00/00/1927
Details not available

CAMBRIDGE GROWTH FD (DE)
Acquired by Pilgrim Financial & Growth Fund, Inc. 01/01/1966
Each share Capital Stock 10¢ par exchanged for (0.4292) share Common $1 par
Pilgrim Financial & Growth Fund, Inc. name changed to Pilgrim Fund, Inc. 07/28/1966 which merged into Pilgrim Magnacap Fund, Inc. 06/20/1985

CAMBRIDGE HLDGS LTD (CO)
Each share Common $0.001 par exchanged for (0.04) share Common $0.025 par 05/29/1990
Each share Common $0.025 par received distribution of (0.16393442) share AspenBio Inc. Common no par payable 08/26/2002 to holders of record 08/21/2002 Ex date - 08/27/2002
In process of liquidation
Each share Common $0.025 par received initial distribution of (0.11981) share Advanced Nutraceuticals, Inc. new Common 1¢ par, (0.13185) share A4S Security Inc. Restricted Common no par, and $0.1852 cash payable 12/02/2005 to holders of record 11/22/2005 Ex date - 12/05/2005
Each share Common $0.025 par received second and final distribution of approximately (0.07) share AspenBio Pharma, Inc. Common no par payable 12/31/2009 to holders of record 11/30/2009 Ex date - 11/25/2009

CAMBRIDGE INDS INC (DE)
Name changed to Cambridge Beverage Corp. 11/30/1971
(See Cambridge Beverage Corp.)

CAMBRIDGE INSTITUTE FOR MANAGEMENT EDUCATION, INC. (DE)
Charter cancelled and declared inperative and void for non-payment of taxes 03/01/1980

CAMBRIDGE INSTR PLC (UNITED KINGDOM)
Name changed to Leica PLC 04/04/1990
(See Leica PLC)

CAMBRIDGE INVESTMENT CORP.
Liquidated 00/00/1941
Details not available

CAMBRIDGE LEASEHOLDS LTD (ON)
Capital Stock no par split (2) for (1) by issuance of (1) additional share 07/24/1972
Each share Capital Stock no par exchanged for (0.005) share Capital Stock no par 08/21/1979
Note: In effect holders received $30 cash per share and public interest eliminated

CAMBRIDGE LIFE INSURANCE CO. (CO)
Merged into Colorado Credit Life, Inc. 12/31/1959
Details not available

CAMBRIDGE MARINE INDS INC (MA)
Merged into Herley Industries, Inc. 08/18/1992
Details not available

CAMBRIDGE MED TECHNOLOGY CORP (DE)
Reincorporated 12/31/1986
State of incorporation changed from (MA) to (DE) 12/31/1986
Charter cancelled and declared inoperative and void for non-payment of taxes 03/01/1994

CAMBRIDGE MEMORIES INC (MA)
Name changed to Cambex Corp. 08/08/1980
(See Cambex Corp.)

CAMBRIDGE MINERALS LTD (AB)
Name changed to Cambridge Ventures Ltd. 07/28/1999
Cambridge Ventures Ltd. name changed to VRX WorldWide Inc. 02/05/2001 which name changed to MediaValet Inc. 10/06/2014

CAMBRIDGE MINES LTD (BC)
Recapitalized as United Cambridge Mines Ltd. 03/15/1976
Each share Capital Stock no par exchanged for (0.2) share Capital Stock no par
United Cambridge Mines Ltd. recapitalized as Consolidated Cambridge Mines Ltd. 12/27/1989 which name changed to Cambridge Environmental Systems Inc. (BC) 07/20/1993 reincorporated in Alberta 12/09/1993
(See Cambridge Environmental Systems Inc.)

CAMBRIDGE MINING CORP. LTD. (ON)
Charter cancelled for failure to pay taxes and file returns 05/18/1976

CAMBRIDGE NEUROSCIENCE INC (DE)
Merged into CeNeS Pharmaeuticals plc 12/18/2000
Each share Common $0.001 par exchanged for (2.3472) Ordinary Shares 10p par

CAMBRIDGE NUCLEAR CORP (MA)
Common $1 par split (2) for (1) by issuance of (1) additional share 11/25/1968
Common $1 par changed to 10¢ par 10/27/1982
Common 10¢ par split (2) for (1) by issuance of (1) additional share 01/31/1983

Name changed to Cambridge Medical Technology Corp. (MA) 10/26/1983
Cambridge Medical Technology Corp. (MA) reincorporated in Delaware 12/31/1986
(See Cambridge Medical Technology Corp.)

CAMBRIDGE OIL & GAS LTD (AB)
Recapitalized as Riata Resources Ltd. 03/01/1995
Each share Common no par exchanged for (0.2) share Common no par
(See Riata Resources Ltd.)

CAMBRIDGE OIL CO.
Merged into Bailey Selburn Oil & Gas Ltd. 00/00/1952
Each Unit exchanged for (46) shares Class A $1 par
(See Bailey Selburn Oil & Gas Ltd.)

CAMBRIDGE OIL CO (DE)
Plan of reorganization under Chapter 11 Federal Bankruptcy proceedings effective 06/09/1990
Each share Common 3¢ par exchanged for (0.0125) Houston Operating Co. Participation Right

CAMBRIDGE PK LTD INC (FL)
Recapitalized as Family Entertainment Corp. 11/30/2007
Each share Common $0.001 par exchanged for (0.005) share Common $0.001 par
Family Entertainment Corp. recapitalized as Airborne Security & Protective Services, Inc. (Ctfs. dated prior to 09/30/2009) 09/16/2008 which name changed to Harbor Brewing Co., Inc. 09/30/2009 which name changed to CTGX Mining, Inc. 02/28/2013

CAMBRIDGE PROJS INC (NV)
Name changed to Ionix Technology, Inc. 02/04/2016

CAMBRIDGE RES CORP (NV)
Charter revoked for failure to file reports and pay fees 08/31/2008

CAMBRIDGE RES LTD (BC)
Name changed to Selkirk Springs International Corp. 12/02/1991
Selkirk Springs International Corp. name changed to Canadian Glacier Beverage Corp. 10/24/1995 which recapitalized as Glacier Ventures International Corp. (BC) 08/26/1997 which reincorporated in Canada 09/20/1999 which merged into Glacier Ventures International Corp. (Canada) (New) 04/28/2000 which name changed to Glacier Media Inc. 07/01/2008

CAMBRIDGE RTY CO (TX)
Common $1 par split (2) for (1) by issuance of (1) additional share 06/01/1982
6% Conv. Preferred $10 par called for redemption 09/08/1986
Stock Dividend - 10% 01/15/1982
Merged into Global Natural Resources, Inc. 09/10/1986
Each share Common $1 par exchanged for (0.69) share Common $1 par
Global Natural Resources, Inc. merged into Seagull Energy Corp. 10/03/1996 which name changed to Ocean Energy, Inc. (TX) 03/30/1999 which reincorporated in Delaware 05/09/2001 which merged into Devon Energy Corp. 04/25/2003

CAMBRIDGE RUBR CO (MD)
Each share Common $5 par exchanged for (1) share Common $2.50 par and (1) share Class A Common $2.50 par 00/00/1952
Proclaimed dissolved 03/15/1988

CAMBRIDGE SHOPPING CENTRES LTD (ON)
$1.625 Conv. 1st Preferred 1st Ser. no par called for redemption 02/13/1989
Acquired by Ivanho Inc. 08/30/2000
Each share Common no par exchanged for $12.50 cash

CAMBRIDGE SOFTEK INC (BC)
Recapitalized as Alantra Venture Corp. 11/21/1994
Each share Common no par exchanged for (0.2) share Common no par
(See Alantra Venture Corp.)

CAMBRIDGE SOUNDWORKS INC (MA)
Merged into Creative Technology Ltd. 12/05/1997
Each share Common no par exchanged for $10.68 cash

CAMBRIDGE TECHNOLOGY PARTNERS MASS INC (DE)
Common 1¢ par split (3) for (1) by issuance of (2) additional shares payable 06/19/1996 to holders of record 05/29/1996
Merged into Novell, Inc. 07/11/2001
Each share Common 1¢ par exchanged for (0.668) share Common 10¢ par
(See Novell, Inc.)

CAMBRIDGE TILE MFG CO (OH)
Acquired by private investors 06/29/1984
Each share Common no par exchanged for $8 cash

CAMBRIDGE TR CO (CAMBRIDGE, MA)
Capital Stock $100 par changed to $25 par and (3) additional shares issued 01/12/1960
Capital Stock $25 par changed to $10 par and (4) additional shares issued 03/16/1969
Stock Dividends - 33.33333333% 01/15/1945; 100% 01/21/1946; 25% 03/01/1955; 20% 03/01/1967; 25% 03/20/1981
Under plan of reorganization each share Capital Stock $10 par automatically became (1) share Cambridge Bancorp Common $1 par 07/01/1983

CAMBRIDGE UNVL CORP (CO)
Reorganized under the laws of Florida as Whitehall Limited, Inc. 06/23/1999
Each share Common no par exchanged for (0.33333333) share Common 10¢ par
(See Whitehall Limited, Inc.)

CAMBRIDGE VENTURES CORP (AB)
Recapitalized as Cartaway Container Corp. 10/18/1989
Each share Common no par exchanged for (0.33333333) share Common no par
Cartaway Container Corp. name changed to Cartaway Resources Corp. 04/24/1996
(See Cartaway Resources Corp.)

CAMBRIDGE VENTURES INC (CO)
Proclaimed dissolved for failure to file reports 09/30/1987

CAMBRIDGE VENTURES LTD (AB)
Name changed to VRX WorldWide Inc. 02/05/2001
VRX WorldWide Inc. name changed to MediaValet Inc. 10/06/2014

CAMBRO-KIRKLAND MINES LTD.
Acquired by Bidgood Kirkland Gold Mines Ltd. 00/00/1939
Each share Capital Stock $1 par exchanged for (0.08333333) share Capital Stock $1 par
Bidgood Kirkland Gold Mines Ltd. recapitalized as Bidcop Mines Ltd. 04/12/1956
(See Bidcop Mines Ltd.)

CAMCHIB RES INC (QC)
Merged into Campbell Resources Inc. (New) 06/08/1983
Each share Capital Stock no par exchanged for (0.6) share Common no par
(See Campbell Resources Inc. (New))

CAMCO FINL CORP (DE)
Common $1 par split (3) for (2) by issuance of (0.5) additional share payable 07/23/1998 to holders of record 07/10/1998
Stock Dividends - 5% payable 07/19/1996 to holders of record 07/10/1996; 5% payable 07/21/1997 to holders of record 07/11/1997; 5% payable 07/20/1999 to holders of record 07/12/1999
Acquired by Huntington Bancshares Inc. 03/01/2014
Each share Common $1 par exchanged for $6 cash

CAMCO INC (TX)
Common $1 par split (2) for (1) by issuance of (1) additional share 11/22/1968
Common $1 par split (3) for (2) by issuance of (0.5) additional share 09/12/1980
Common $1 par split (2) for (1) by issuance of (1) additional share 09/11/1981
Stock Dividend - 20% 09/11/1981
Acquired by Pearson PLC 09/10/1987
Each share Common $1 par exchanged for $29 cash

CAMCO INC ONT (CANADA)
Common no par split (2) for (1) by issuance of (1) additional share 05/20/1987
Merged into Controladora Mabe S.A. de C.V. 10/03/2005
Each share Common no par exchanged for $3.52 cash

CAMCO INTL INC (DE)
Merged into Schlumberger Ltd. 08/31/1998
Each share Common 1¢ par exchanged for (1.18) shares Common 1¢ par

CAMCO OIL CORP. (NY)
Proclaimed dissolved for failure to file reports and pay fees 12/15/1967

CAMDALE CORP. (DE)
Charter revoked for non-payment of taxes 04/01/1961

CAMDECK MINES LTD (ON)
Charter cancelled and declared dissolved for failure to file returns and pay fees 07/27/1976

CAMDEN & BURLINGTON COUNTY RAILWAY CO. (NJ)
Assets sold to Penndel Co. 12/31/1957
Each share exchanged for $31.50 cash

CAMDEN FIRE INS ASSN (NJ)
99.83% held by General Accident Group of Insurance Companies as of 05/22/1974
Public interest eliminated

CAMDEN FORGE CO. (NJ)
Completely liquidated 11/04/1964
Details not available

CAMDEN LEARNING CORP
Units separated 11/23/2009
Name changed to National American University Holdings, Inc. 01/12/2010

CAMDEN MINES LTD (NV)
Common $0.00001 par split (5) for (1) by issuance of (4) additional shares payable 05/17/2001 to holders of record 05/16/2001 Ex date - 05/18/2001
Common $0.00001 par split (3) for (1) by issuance of (2) additional shares payable 08/03/2004 to holders of record 07/28/2004 Ex date - 08/04/2004
Name changed to Xinhua China Ltd. 10/12/2004
Each share Common $0.00001 par exchanged for (1) share Common $0.00001 par

CAMDEN OIL CORP (BC)
Name changed to Maxwell Resources Inc. 12/02/1992
Maxwell Resources Inc. name changed to Maxwell Energy Corp. (BC) 05/12/1993 which reincorporated in Alberta 09/12/1996 which recapitalized as Maxwell Oil & Gas Ltd. 11/18/1996
(See Maxwell Oil & Gas Ltd.)

CAMDEN PPTY TR (TX)
$2.25 Conv. Preferred Ser. A 1¢ par called for redemption at $25 on 04/30/2001
(Additional Information in Active)

CAMDEN RAIL & HARBOR TERMINAL CORP. (NJ)
Reorganized as Camden Refrigerating & Terminals Co. 00/00/1939
Each share Preferred exchanged for (0.25) share Common no par
Each share Common exchanged for (0.001) share Common no par
(See Camden Refrigerating & Terminals Co.)

CAMDEN REFRIGERATING & TERMINALS CO. (NJ)
5% Preferred $100 par called for redemption 07/31/1961
Liquidation completed
Each share Common no par received initial distribution of $2 cash 07/31/1961
Each share Common no par received second distribution of $1 cash 11/29/1961
Each share Common no par received third distribution of $1.25 cash 05/15/1962
Each share Common no par received fourth distribution of $1.50 cash 11/16/1962
Each share Common no par received fifth distribution of $1.50 cash 05/15/1963
Each share Common no par received sixth distribution of $1.25 cash 11/15/1963
Each share Common no par received seventh distribution of $1.50 cash 05/15/1964
Each share Common no par received eighth distribution of $1.25 cash 11/12/1964
Each share Common no par received ninth distribution of $1 cash 06/04/1965
Each share Common no par received tenth distribution of $1 cash 02/11/1966
Each share Common no par received eleventh distribution of $1.50 cash 11/17/1966
Each share Common no par received twelfth distribution of $2 cash 05/02/1967
Each share Common no par received thirteenth and final distribution of $2 cash 06/21/1967
Each share Common no par exchanged for (1) Part. Ctf. no par of Camden Refrigerating & Terminals Co. Liquidating Trust 06/30/1967
(See Camden Refrigerating & Terminals Co. Liquidating Trust)

CAMDEN REFRIGERATING & TERMINALS CO. LIQUIDATING TRUST (NJ)
Liquidation completed
Each Part. Ctf. no par received initial distribution of $1.115570 cash 12/26/1967
Each Part. Ctf. no par received second distribution of $2.737855 cash 12/27/1968

Each Part. Ctf. no par received third
distribution of $1.308489 cash
12/30/1969
Each Part. Ctf. no par received fourth
distribution of $2.851751 cash
12/04/1970
Each Part. Ctf. no par received fifth
distribution of $2.513966 cash
12/10/1971
Each Part. Ctf. no par received sixth
distribution of $2.572421 cash
12/14/1972
Each Part. Ctf. no par received
seventh distribution of $2.464913
cash 12/10/1973
Each Part. Ctf. no par received eighth
distribution of $2.6423218 cash
12/11/1974
Each Part. Ctf. no par received ninth
distribution of $0.5085161 cash
12/05/1975
Each Part. Ctf. no par received tenth
distribution of $1.774833 cash
12/17/1976
Each Part. Ctf. no par received
eleventh distribution of $1.1088704
cash 12/19/1977
Each Part. Ctf. no par received twelfth
distribution of $1.1218149 cash
12/19/1978
Each Part. Ctf. no par received
thirteenth distribution of $1.1499523
cash 12/24/1979
Each Part. Ctf. no par received
fourteenth distribution of $32.992573
cash 12/19/1980
Each Part. Ctf. no par received
fifteenth and final distribution of
$2.791778 cash 09/03/1985

CAMDEN TR CO (CAMDEN, NJ)
Common $3 par changed to $4 par
00/00/1945
Common $4 par changed to $5 par
00/00/1952
Stock Dividend - 25% 08/20/1948
Name changed to Bank of New
Jersey (Camden, NJ) 12/01/1969
Bank of New Jersey (Camden, NJ)
reorganized as Bancshares of New
Jersey 12/30/1972 which name
changed to Northern National Corp.
05/28/1981 which merged into
Horizon Bancorp 10/01/1983
(See Horizon Bancorp)

CAMDEV CORP (ON)
Name changed to O&Y Properties
Corp. 07/31/1997
(See O&Y Properties Corp.)

CAMDON HLDGS, INC. (CO)
Name changed to American
Temperature Control, Inc.
11/03/1993
American Temperature Control, Inc.
name changed to Connectivity &
Technologies, Inc. 12/10/1993 which
recapitalized as Peacock Financial
Corp. (CO) 02/27/1996 which
reorganized in Nevada as Broadleaf
Capital Partners, Inc. 03/22/2002
which recapitalized as EnergyTek
Corp. 07/23/2014 which
recapitalized as TimefireVR Inc.
11/22/2016

CAMECO CORP (SK)
Each Installment Receipt exchanged
for (1) share Common no par
03/20/1997
8.75% Preferred Securities called for
redemption at USD$25 on
12/17/2004
(Additional Information in Active)

CAMEL MFG CO (TN)
Merged into Bower's, Inc. 05/01/1978
Each share Common 25¢ par
exchanged for $0.25 cash

CAMEL OIL & GAS LTD (AB)
Merged into Trans-Canada Resources
Ltd. (New) 11/01/1985
Each share Common no par
exchanged for (0.1) share Class A
Common no par

Note: Holdings of (99) shares or
fewer exchanged for cash
Trans-Canada Resources Ltd. (New)
recapitalized as Consolidated
Trans-Canada Resources Ltd.
09/22/1988 which merged into
Ranchmen's Resources Ltd.
09/30/1989 which merged into
Crestar Energy Inc. 10/11/1995
which was acquired by Gulf Canada
Resources Ltd. 11/13/2000
(See Gulf Canada Resources Ltd.)

CAMELA MINES & OILS LTD. (BC)
Stock Dividend - 10% 06/15/1976
Struck off register and declared
dissolved for failure to file returns
00/00/1976

CAMELBACK CAP INC (NV)
Recapitalized as NewCare Health
Corp. 04/14/1994
Each share Common $0.001 par
exchanged for (0.05) share Common
$0.001 par
(See NewCare Health Corp.)

CAMELION DEV CORP (AB)
Recapitalized as Great Northern
Gold, Inc. 01/17/1990
Each share Common no par
exchanged for (0.33333333) share
Common no par
Great Northern Gold, Inc. merged into
Ascentex Energy, Inc. 12/24/1991
which recapitalized as Bonavista
Petroleum Ltd. 03/03/1997
(See Bonavista Petroleum Ltd.)

CAMELOT CORP (CO)
Reincorporated 05/23/2011
Each share old Common 1¢ par
exchanged for (0.03333333) share
new Common 1¢ par 08/27/1990
Each share new Common 1¢ par
exchanged again for (0.025) share
new Common 1¢ par 07/15/1997
State of incorporation changed from
(CO) to (NV) 05/23/2011
Each share new Common 1¢ par
exchanged for (0.04) share Common
1¢ par
Note: Holders of between (25) and
(2,500) shares received (100)
shares
Holders of (24) of fewer pre-split
shares received $1 cash per share
Name changed to Comjoyful
International Co. 01/30/2013

CAMELOT ENTERPRISES INC (DE)
Charter cancelled and declared
inoperative and void for
non-payment of taxes 03/01/1977

CAMELOT INDS CORP (DE)
Acquired by Buckbee-Mears Co.
06/14/1982
Each share Common 10¢ par
exchanged for $9.50 cash

CAMELOT INDS INC (BC)
Merged into DC Diagnosticare, Inc.
07/15/1996
Each share Common no par
exchanged for (1.68) shares
Common no par
(See DC Diagnosticare, Inc.)

CAMELOT INFORMATION SYS INC (BRITISH VIRGIN ISLANDS)
Acquired by Camelot Employee
Scheme Inc. 03/28/2014
Each Sponsored ADR for Ordinary
exchanged for $2.05 cash

CAMELOT INTL INC (DE)
Merged into American Leisure Corp:
(DE) 11/24/1982
Each share Common 1¢ par
exchanged for (7) shares Class A
Common 1¢ par
American Leisure Corp. (DE) merged
into American Midland Corp.
07/06/1984
(See American Midland Corp.)

CAMELOT MUSIC HLDGS INC (DE)
Merged into Trans World
Entertainment Corp. 04/22/1999

Each share Common 1¢ par
exchanged for (1.9) shares Common
1¢ par

CAMELOT RES NL (AUSTRALIA)
Name changed to Pacmin Mining
Corp. Ltd. 02/25/1999
(See Pacmin Mining Corp. Ltd.)

CAMEO MINERALS INC (UT)
Merged into Hendon Exploration, Inc.
12/17/1982
Each share Common 3¢ par
exchanged for (1) share Common
no par
Hendon Exploration, Inc. name
changed to U.S. Energy Corp. of
America, Inc. 11/03/1989

CAMEO PKWY RECORDS INC (DE)
Class A Common 10¢ par reclassified
as Common 10¢ par 10/28/1966
Name changed to ABKCO Industries,
Inc. 02/18/1969
(See ABKCO Industries, Inc.)

CAMEO RES CORP (BC)
Each share old Common no par
exchanged for (0.04) share new
Common no par 02/21/2017
Name changed to Cameo Cobalt
Corp. 05/25/2018

CAMERA CORP AMER (DE)
Charter cancelled and declared
inoperative and void for
non-payment of taxes 01/12/1965

CAMERA CORP AMER CDA LTD (ON)
Charter cancelled for default in filing
returns and paying fees 09/06/1972

CAMERA ENTERPRISES INC (DE)
Charter cancelled and declared
inoperative and void for
non-payment of taxes 06/26/1990

CAMERA PLATFORMS INTL INC (DE)
Common $0.0005 par split (2) for (1)
by issuance of (1) additional share
04/24/1987
SEC revoked common stock
registration 11/02/2010

CAMERINA PETE CORP (DE)
Capital Stock no par changed to
$1.25 par 09/08/1961
Completely liquidated 01/10/1969
Each share Capital Stock $1.25 par
exchanged for first and final
distribution of $1.467015 cash

CAMERO DEVELOPMENTS LTD. (BC)
Charter cancelled 08/23/1982

CAMERO RESOURCE INDS LTD (BC)
Recapitalized as International Cameo
Resources Ltd. 10/03/1983
Each share Common no par
exchanged for (0.33333333) share
Common no par
International Camero Resources Ltd.
name changed to International
Pharmadyne Ltd. 03/05/1985
(See International Pharmadyne Ltd.)

CAMERON ASHLEY BLDG PRODS INC (GA)
Name changed 11/21/1995
Name changed from Cameron Ashley
Inc. to Cameron Ashley Building
Products Inc. 11/21/1995
Merged into Guardian Industries
Corp. 06/12/2000
Each share Common no par
exchanged for $18.35 cash

CAMERON BANCSHARES INC (LA)
Merged into IBERIABANK Corp.
05/31/2011
Each share Common $1 par
exchanged for (3.464) shares
Common $1 par

CAMERON BROWN INVT GROUP (MA)
Reorganized under the laws of
Delaware as Sunstates Corp. (Old)
and Shares of Bene. Int. no par

reclassified as Common $1 par
01/20/1981
Sunstates Corp. (Old) (DE) merged
into Sunstates Corp. (FL)
01/30/1985 which merged into Acton
Corp. 05/04/1988 which name
changed to Sunstates Corp. (New)
01/03/1994
(See Sunstates Corp. (New))

CAMERON CAP CORP (UT)
Involuntarily dissolved 04/01/1993

CAMERON COPPER MINES LTD. (QC)
Charter annulled for failure to file
reports 06/01/1974

CAMERON FINL CORP (DE)
Merged into Dickinson Financial Corp.
01/12/2001
Each share Common 1¢ par
exchanged for $20.75 cash

CAMERON FINL CORP (NC)
Common $5 par changed to
$3.33333333 par and (0.5)
additional share issued 06/19/1972
Name changed to First Union Corp.
04/23/1975
First Union Corp. name changed to
Wachovia Corp. (Ctfs. dated after
09/01/2001) 09/01/2001 which
merged into Wells Fargo & Co.
(New) 12/31/2008

CAMERON INTL CORP (DE)
Common 1¢ par split (2) for (1) by
issuance of (1) additional share
payable 12/28/2007 to holders of
record 12/17/2007 Ex date -
12/31/2007
Merged into Schlumberger Ltd.
04/01/2016
Each share Common 1¢ par
exchanged for (0.716) share
Common 1¢ par and $14.44 cash

CAMERON INTL INC (NV)
Common $0.001 par split (30) for (1)
by issuance of (29) additional
shares payable 11/09/2005 to
holders of record 11/08/2005
Ex date - 11/10/2005
Charter revoked for failure to file
reports and pay fees 01/01/2007

CAMERON IRON WKS INC (TX)
Common $2.50 par changed to
$0.625 par and (3) additional shares
issued 11/05/1976
Common $0.625 par changed to
$0.20833333 par and (2) additional
shares issued 03/25/1980
Each share $3.50 Conv.
Exchangeable Preferred 10¢ par
exchanged for $50 principal amount
of 7% Conv. Subordinated
Debentures due 06/15/2012 on
09/15/1989
Merged into Cooper Industries, Inc.
(OH) 11/29/1989
Each share Common $0.20833333
par exchanged for (0.2) share 8%
Conv. Exchangeable Preferred $1
par
Cooper Industries, Inc. (OH)
reincorporated in Bermuda as
Cooper Industries, Ltd. 05/22/2002
which reincorporated in Ireland as
Cooper Industries PLC 09/08/2009
which merged into Eaton Corp. PLC
11/30/2012

CAMERON MUSICAL INDS LTD (NY)
Dissolved by proclamation 12/27/2000

CAMERON RES LTD (BC)
Name changed to Jafta International
Inc. 10/29/1982
Jafta International Inc. recapitalized
as Dornoch International Inc.
10/05/1987 which name changed to
DNI Holdings Inc. 04/28/1988
(See DNI Holdings Inc.)

CAMETIN INDS LTD (BC)
Struck off register and declared
dissolved for failure to file returns
12/18/1978

CAMEX ENERGY CORP (BC)
Each share old Common no par exchanged for (0.2) share new Common no par 06/21/2012
Each share new Common no par exchanged again for (0.66666666) share new Common no par 12/21/2012
Reorganized under the laws of Ontario as Desert Lion Energy Inc. 02/26/2018
Each share new Common no par exchanged for (0.08315455) share Common no par
Note: Unexchanged certificates will be cancelled and become without value 02/26/2024

CAMEX MINES LTD. (ON)
Completely liquidated 07/23/1963
Each share Capital Stock $1 par exchanged for (0.1) share Braminco Mines Ltd. Capital Stock $1 par
Braminco Mines Ltd. name changed to Braminco Enterprises Inc. (ONT) 04/18/1995 which reorganized in New Brunswick as Q-Zar Inc. 06/27/1995 which name changed to Q-Entertainment, Inc. 07/31/1997
(See Q-Entertainment, Inc.)

CAMFLO INTL INC (YT)
Merged into Arctos Petroleum Corp. 10/04/2004
Each share Common no par exchanged for (0.75) share Common no par
Arctos Petroleum Corp. recapitalized as Stetson Oil & Gas Ltd. (AB) 11/12/2007 which reincorporated in Ontario 08/21/2014 which name changed to Magnolia Colombia Ltd. 06/14/2017

CAMFLO MATTAGAMI MINES LTD. (ON)
Name changed to CamFlo Mines Ltd. 08/05/1966
CamFlo Mines Ltd. merged into Barrick Resources Corp. 07/14/1984 which recapitalized as American Barrick Resources Corp. 12/06/1985 which name changed to Barrick Gold Corp. 01/18/1995

CAMFLO MINES LTD (ON)
Merged into Barrick Resources Corp. 07/14/1984
Each share Capital Stock $1 par exchanged for (7) shares Common no par
Barrick Resources Corp. recapitalized as American Barrick Resources Corp. 12/06/1985 which name changed to Barrick Gold Corp. 01/18/1995

CAMFLO RES LTD (AB)
Reorganized under the laws of Yukon as Camflo International Inc. 11/22/2001
Each share Common no par exchanged for (0.11111111) share Common no par
Camflo International Inc. merged into Arctos Petroleum Corp. 10/04/2004 which recapitalized as Stetson Oil & Gas Ltd. (AB) 11/12/2007 which reincorporated in Ontario 08/21/2014 which name changed to Magnolia Colombia Ltd. 06/14/2017

CAMFORD CAP CORP (BC)
Struck off register and dissolved 03/20/1992

CAMFREY RES LTD (BC)
Recapitalized as Brio Industries, Inc. 03/17/1993
Each share Common no par exchanged for (0.4) share Common no par
Brio Industries, Inc. name changed to Leading Brands, Inc. 10/25/1999 which name changed to Liquid Media Group Ltd. 08/13/2018

CAMI Z INC (MN)
Each share old Common no par exchanged for (0.5) share new Common no par 08/09/1991
Name changed to B.U.M. International Inc. 11/02/1994
(See B.U.M. International Inc.)

CAMILLE ST MORITZ INC (CA)
Charter suspended for failure to file reports and pay fees 01/02/2002

CAMIN INDS CORP (NY)
Liquidation completed
Each share Common 10¢ par exchanged for initial distribution of (0.412311) share Nuveen Municipal Bond Fund, Inc. Common 10¢ par 11/09/1979
Each share Common 10¢ par received second and final distribution of (0.06) share Nuveen Municipal Bond Fund, Inc. Common 10¢ par and $3.55 cash 11/07/1980
(See Nuveen Municipal Bond Fund, Inc.)

CAMIN LABORATORIES, INC. (NY)
Stock Dividend - 100% 02/28/1969
Name changed to Camin Industries Corp. 11/23/1971
Camin Industries Corp. liquidated for Nuveen Municipal Bond Fund, Inc. 11/09/1979
(See Nuveen Municipal Bond Fund, Inc.)

CAMINDEX MINES LTD (ON)
Acquired by MVP Capital Corp. 12/31/1989
Each share Common $1 par exchanged for (0.15) share Common no par
MVP Capital Corp. recapitalized as LatinGold Inc. 10/23/1996 which name changed to Travelbyus.Com Ltd. 06/11/1999
(See Travelbyus.Com Ltd.)

CAMINO-CALIFORNIA BANK (PALO ALTO, CA)
Name changed to America California Bank (Palo Alto, CA) 09/05/1980
America California Bank (Palo Alto, CA) location changed to (San Francisco, CA) 09/07/1982

CAMINO ENERGY CORP (BC)
Cease trade order effective 09/27/1984
Stockholders' equity unlikely

CAMINO INC (UT)
Reorganized under the laws of Delaware as City Auto Resources Services Inc. 09/24/1996
Each share Common $0.001 par exchanged for (0.25) share Common $0.001 par
City Auto Resources Services Inc. name changed to CyPro International, Inc. 08/15/1998

CAMINO RES LTD (BC)
Recapitalized as Advanced Projects Ltd. 03/08/1991
Each share Common no par exchanged for (0.25) share Common no par
Advanced Projects Ltd. recapitalized as Skye Resources Inc. 05/23/2001 which was acquired by HudBay Minerals Inc. 08/26/2008

CAMINOSOFT CORP (CA)
Reincorporated under the laws of Delaware as CMSF Corp. and Common no par changed to $0.000001 par 10/12/2010
CMSF Corp. recapitalized as Plures Technologies, Inc. 09/27/2011
(See Plures Technologies, Inc.)

CAMINUS CORP (DE)
Merged into SunGard Data Systems Inc. 04/10/2003
Each share Common 1¢ par exchanged for $9 cash

CAMISHA RES CORP (BC)
Name changed to Prima Fluorspar Corp. 04/19/2013
Prima Fluorspar Corp. name changed to Prima Diamond Corp. 07/03/2014 which recapitalized as Voltaic Minerals Corp. 04/14/2016

CAMLACHIE OILS EXPLORATION LTD. (ON)
Charter cancelled and company declared dissolved for default in filing returns 09/17/1962

CAMLAREN MINES LTD (CANADA)
Reorganized under the laws of Ontario as Stamford Bancorp Inc. 06/30/1987
Each share Common no par exchanged for (0.33333333) share Common no par
Stamford Bancorp Inc. recapitalized as Stamford International Inc. 04/15/1996
(See Stamford International Inc.)

CAMLOC FASTENER CORP. (NY)
Stock Dividend - 20% 08/31/1966
Completely liquidated 11/02/1967
Each share Common $2 par exchanged for first and final distribution of (0.458715) share Rex Chainbelt Inc. $2.50 Conv. Preferred Ser. A no par
Rex Chainbelt Inc. name changed to Rexnord Inc. 01/26/1973
(See Rexnord Inc.)

CAMNOR RES LTD (BC)
Recapitalized as Stornoway Ventures Ltd. 10/30/2000
Each share Common no par exchanged for (0.125) share Common no par
Stornoway Ventures Ltd. merged into Stornoway Diamond Corp. (BC) 07/16/2003 which reincorporated in Canada 10/28/2011

CAMOOSE MINES LTD. (ON)
Completely liquidated 03/31/1958
Each share Capital Stock $1 par exchanged for (1) share Camoose Uranium Mines of America, Inc. Common 1¢ par
Camoose Uranium Mines of America, Inc. reorganized as A.U.M. Corp. 08/03/1967
(See A.U.M. Corp.)

CAMOOSE URANIUM MINES AMER INC (DE)
Recapitalized as A.U.M. Corp. 08/03/1967
Each share Common 1¢ par exchanged for (0.05) share Common 1¢ par
(See A.U.M. Corp.)

CAMP AFFILIATES INC (NY)
Stock Dividend - 20% 06/17/1970
Adjudicated bankrupt 09/30/1977
Stockholders' equity unlikely

CAMP CHEM INC (NY)
Name changed to Camp Laboratories, Inc. 08/21/1969
Camp Laboratories, Inc. name changed to Camp Affiliates, Inc. 01/31/1970
(See Camp Affiliates, Inc.)

CAMP LABS INC (NY)
Stock Dividend - 10% 09/10/1969
Name changed to Camp Affiliates, Inc. 01/31/1970
(See Camp Affiliates, Inc.)

CAMP MANUFACTURING CO., INC. (VA)
Merged into Union Bag-Camp Paper Corp. 07/12/1956
Each share Common exchanged for (1.75) shares Common $1 par
Union Bag-Camp Paper Corp. name changed to Union Camp Corp. 04/27/1966 which merged into International Paper Co. 04/30/1999

CAMP NINE INC (NV)
Name changed to Relmada Therapeutics, Inc. 08/06/2014

CAMPANELLI INDS INC (DE)
Name changed to Realmark, Inc. (Old) 07/23/1987
(See Realmark, Inc. (Old))

CAMPAR CAP CORP (ON)
Under plan of merger each share Common no par automatically became (0.0138164) Starlight U.S. Multi-Family (No. 5) Core Fund Class A Ltd. Partnership Unit 10/18/2016

CAMPBELL, WYANT & CANNON FOUNDRY CO. (MI)
Capital Stock no par changed to $15 par 00/00/1954
Name changed to Ridgeway Corp. 04/20/1956
(See Ridgeway Corp.)

CAMPBELL (A.S.) CO., INC. (MA)
Common no par changed to $1 par 00/00/1939
Stock Dividend - 100% 02/14/1956
Liquidation completed 04/30/1959
Details not available

CAMPBELL (J.B.) MANUFACTURING CO., INC. (NJ)
Succeeded by Carthage Mills, Inc. 00/00/1928
Details not available

CAMPBELL (ROBERT) PROSPECTORS LTD. (ON)
Recapitalized as Emo Mines Ltd. 00/00/1954
Each share Capital Stock exchanged for (10) shares Capital Stock
(See Emo Mines Ltd.)

CAMPBELL APARTMENTS, INC.
Liquidated 00/00/1940
Details not available

CAMPBELL CAP CORP (DE)
Name changed to Dental Services of America, Inc. 08/09/1996
(See Dental Services of America, Inc.)

CAMPBELL CHAIN CO (DE)
Each share Common 10¢ par exchanged for (0.001) share Common $100 par 09/25/1980
Note: In effect holders received $7.50 cash per share and public interest was eliminated

CAMPBELL CHIBOUGAMAU MINES LTD (QC)
Common $1 par reclassified as Conv. Class A Common $1 par 04/03/1975
Name changed to Campbell Resources Inc. (Old) and Conv. Class A Common $1 par and Conv. Class B Common $1 par reclassified as Common $1 par 09/22/1980
Campbell Resources Inc. (Old) merged into Campbell Resources Inc. (New) 06/08/1983
(See Campbell Resources Inc. (New))

CAMPBELL-CRAWFORD COBALT SILVER MINING CO. LTD.
Bankrupt 00/00/1931
Details not available

CAMPBELL INDS (CA)
Stock Dividend - 10% 02/15/1975
Merged into Marine Construction & Design Co. 12/17/1979
Each share Common $1 par exchanged for $7.50 cash

CAMPBELL ISLAND MINES & EXPLORATIONS LTD. (ON)
Recapitalized as New Campbell Island Mines Ltd. (ON) 00/00/1958
Each share Capital Stock $1 par exchanged for (0.25) share Capital Stock $1 par
New Campbell Island Mines (ON) reincorporated in Canada 07/23/1984 which recapitalized as Minera Delta Inc. (Old) 03/12/1997 which recapitalized as Whitmore Resource Corp. 07/20/1999 which name changed to Minera Delta Inc. (New) 10/15/2001 which name

changed to Vector Wind Energy Inc. 11/26/2004
(See Vector Wind Energy Inc.)

CAMPBELL-LURIE PLASTICS, INC. (FL)
Charter cancelled for non-payment of taxes 06/30/1967

CAMPBELL MACHINE, INC. (CA)
Common $1 par split (2) for (1) by issuance of (1) additional share 10/17/1966
Stock Dividend - 10% 02/15/1964
Name changed to Campbell Industries 07/30/1971
(See Campbell Industries)

CAMPBELL MFG INC (TX)
Name changed to H.P. Campbell, Inc. 04/22/1985
(See H.P. Campbell, Inc.)

CAMPBELL RED LAKE MINES LTD (ON)
Capital Stock $1 par changed to 50¢ par and (1) additional share issued 05/24/1974
Capital Stock 50¢ par changed to no par and (1) additional share issued 06/01/1979
Capital Stock no par split (3) for (1) by issuance of (2) additional shares 06/01/1981
Merged into Placer Dome Inc. 08/13/1987
Each share Capital Stock no par exchanged for (1.702) shares Common no par
Placer Dome Inc. merged into Barrick Gold Corp. 03/08/2006

CAMPBELL RES INC NEW (CANADA)
Each share Preference Ser. 1 no par exchanged for (0.2) share Preference Ser. A no par 11/15/1984
Each share Preference Ser. A no par exchanged for (3.8) shares Common no par and (1) Common Stock Purchase Warrant expiring 12/31/1988 on 09/11/1985
Each share old Common no par exchanged for (0.1) share new Common no par 05/25/2000
Placed in receivership 12/10/2009
Stockholders' equity unlikely

CAMPBELL RES INC OLD (QC)
Common $1 par changed to no par 12/31/1981
Merged into Campbell Resources Inc. (New) 06/08/1983
Each share Common no par exchanged for (1) share Common no par
(See Campbell Resources Inc. (New))

CAMPBELL SOUP LTD (CANADA)
Acquired by Campbell Soup Co. 07/15/1991
Each share Common no par exchanged for $41 cash

CAMPBELL TAGGART ASSD BAKERIES INC (DE)
Each share Preferred exchanged for (5) shares new Capital Stock no par 00/00/1945
Each share old Capital Stock exchanged for (10) shares new Capital Stock no par 00/00/1945
Each share new Capital Stock no par exchanged for (5) shares Capital Stock $1 par 00/00/1953
Capital Stock $1 par reclassified as Common $1 par 06/25/1969
Name changed to Campbell Taggart, Inc. 03/23/1971
(See Campbell Taggart, Inc.)

CAMPBELL TAGGART INC (DE)
Common $1 par split (2) for (1) by issuance of (1) additional share 04/01/1971
Common $1 par split (3) for (2) by issuance of (0.5) additional share 03/24/1976
Common $1 par split (3) for (2) by issuance of (0.5) additional share 05/18/1977
Common $1 par split (3) for (2) by issuance of (0.5) additional share 10/01/1981
Merged into Anheuser-Busch Companies, Inc. 11/02/1982
Each share Common 1¢ par exchanged for $36 cash

CAMPBELL TECHNOLOGIES INC (NV)
Recapitalized as Elite Brands International, Inc. 02/06/2002
Each share Common $0.001 par exchanged for (0.001) share Common $0.001 par
Elite Brands International, Inc. name changed to Aviation Innovations & Research, Inc. 10/03/2002 which recapitalized as Immune-Tree International, Inc. 10/26/2004

CAMPBELL'S CREEK COAL CO.
Merged into Hatfield-Campbell Creek Coal Co. 00/00/1928
Details not available

CAMPCO CORP (FL)
Common 1¢ par split (3) for (2) by issuance of (0.5) additional share 07/14/1972
Proclaimed dissolved for failure to file reports and pay fees 10/21/1974

CAMPEAU CORP (ON)
Name changed 10/09/1973
Under plan of merger name changed from Campeau Corp Ltd. to Campeau Corp. and each share of Common no par exchanged for (1) share Class A Common no par 10/09/1973
3rd Preference $4.50 par called for redemption 12/18/1973
7% 1st Conv. Preference $10 par called for redemption 12/12/1977
Class A Common no par called for redemption 12/31/1977
Class B Common no par reclassified as Common no par 08/04/1979
Common no par split (4) for (1) by issuance of (3) additional shares 05/19/1981
Common no par reclassified as Subordinate no par 05/11/1983
Subordinate no par split (2) for (1) by issuance of (1) additional share 08/20/1987
Preference Ser. A no par called for redemption 06/25/1988
Subordinate no par reclassified as Ordinary no par 08/16/1988
Recapitalized as Camdev Corp. 02/14/1992
Each share Non-Vtg. Preference Ser. B no par exchanged for (0.04) share Common no par
Each share Non-Vtg. Preference Ser. C no par exchanged for (0.04) share Common no par
Each share 9% Non-Vtg. Preference Ser. D no par exchanged for (0.04) share Common no par
Each share Ordinary Stock no par exchanged for (0.02) share Common no par
Camdev Corp. name changed to O&Y Properties Corp. 07/31/1997
(See O&Y Properties Corp.)

CAMPHOR VENTURES INC (BC)
Acquired by Mountain Province Diamonds Inc. 04/19/2007
Each share Common no par exchanged for (0.41) share new Common no par

CAMPION RES LTD (AB)
Acquired by Progress Energy Ltd. 06/13/2002
Each share Common no par exchanged for (0.4) share Common no par
(See Progress Energy Ltd.)

CAMPO ELECTRS APPLIANCES & COMPUTERS INC (LA)
SEC revoked common stock registration 02/08/2011

CAMPO UNITED PETROLEUMS LTD. (AB)
Struck off register for failure to file annual returns 04/30/1969

CAMPTOWN INDS INC (MD)
Charter annulled for failure to file annual reports 10/13/1988

CAMPUS CASUALS CALIF (CA)
Stock Dividend - 100% 08/15/1975
Merged into Chromalloy American Corp. (DE) 06/30/1978
Each share Common $1 par exchanged for (3.5) shares $5 Conv. Preferred $1 par
Chromalloy American Corp. (DE) merged into Sun Chemical Corp. 12/23/1986 which name changed to Sequa Corp. 05/08/1987
(See Sequa Corp.)

CAMPUS CREST CMNTYS INC (MD)
Acquired by Harrison Street Real Estate Capital, LLC 03/02/2016
Each share Common 1¢ par exchanged for $7.018 cash
8% Preferred Ser. A 1¢ par called for redemption at $25 plus $2.256 accrued dividends on 03/03/2016

CAMPUS SWEATER & SPORTSWEAR CO. (OH)
Acquired by Interco Inc. (Old) 04/12/1968
Each share Common $1 par exchanged for (0.162159) share $5.25 Conv. 2nd Preferred Ser. C no par
(See Interco Inc. (Old))

CAMRAY MINES LTD. (ON)
Charter cancelled and company declared dissolved for default in filing returns 12/30/1965

CAMREAL CORP (ON)
Merged into Dundee Realty Corp. 04/30/1998
Each share Common no par exchanged for (1) share Common no par
Dundee Realty Corp. reorganized as Dundee Real Estate Investment Trust 06/30/2003 name changed to Dream Office Real Estate Investment Trust 05/08/2014

CAMRECO INC (ON)
Merged into Environmental Technologies International Inc. 11/29/1991
Each share Capital Stock no par exchanged for (0.05) share Common no par
Environmental Technologies International Inc. recapitalized as Eco Technologies International Inc. 04/24/1998
(See Eco Technologies International Inc.)

CAMRELCO RES GROUP LTD (BC)
Recapitalized as Canadian Beaver Resources Ltd. 01/06/1982
Each share Capital Stock no par exchanged for (0.25) share Common no par
(See Canadian Beaver Resources Ltd.)

CAMREX RES LTD (AB)
Name changed to Crispin Energy Inc. 08/20/1996
Crispin Energy Inc. was acquired by Pengrowth Energy Trust 04/29/2005 which reorganized as Pengrowth Energy Corp. 01/03/2011

CAMROCK MINES LTD. (ON)
Charter revoked for failure to file reports and pay taxes 00/00/1956

CAMROSE GOLD & METALS LTD. (ON)
Charter cancelled and proclaimed dissolved for failure to pay taxes and file annual reports 08/07/1956

CAMSEAL INC (DE)
Charter cancelled and declared inoperative and void for non-payment of taxes 03/01/1983

CAMSELL RIVER SILVER MINES, LTD. (ON)
Charter revoked for failure to file reports and pay taxes 00/00/1956

CAMTEX INDS INC (DE)
Charter cancelled and declared inoperative and void for non-payment of taxes 02/02/1988

CAMTEX OIL CORP. (DE)
Reorganized as Camtex Industries, Inc. 07/01/1968
Each share Class A 10¢ par exchanged for (1) share Class A 1¢ par
Each share Class B 10¢ par exchanged for (100) shares Class A 1¢ par
(See Camtex Industries, Inc.)

CAMVEC CORP (ON)
Name changed to AMJ Campbell Inc. 08/14/2001
(See AMJ Campbell Inc.)

CAN ALBION PETES LTD (BC)
Struck off register and declared dissolved for failure to file returns 08/09/1976

CAN/AM AUTO SALES INC (NV)
Common $0.001 par split (5) for (1) by issuance of (4) additional shares payable 07/12/2004 to holders of record 07/12/2004
Common $0.001 par split (16.5) for (1) by issuance of (15.5) additional shares payable 08/18/2004 to holders of record 08/18/2004
Name changed to LFG International, Inc. 09/03/2004
Each share Common $0.001 par exchanged for (1) share Common $0.001 par
LFG International, Inc. name changed to Nano-Jet Corp. 11/07/2006 which name changed to Hitor Group, Inc. 01/09/2008

CAN AM GOLD RES LTD (BC)
Recapitalized as Golden Quail Resources Ltd. 09/23/1985
Each share Common no par exchanged for (0.5) share Common no par
Golden Quail Resources Ltd. recapitalized as Consolidated Golden Quail Resources Ltd. 11/24/1997
(See Consolidated Golden Quail Resources Ltd.)

CAN AM INDS CORP (BC)
Recapitalized as Save-On Automotive Industries Corp. 04/05/1990
Each share Capital Stock no par exchanged for (0.33333333) share Common no par
Save-On Automotive Industries Corp. name changed to MIS Multimedia Interactive Services Inc. (BC) 09/08/1993 which reincorporated in Delaware as MIS International, Inc. 07/01/1997 which name changed to Cosmoz.Com, Inc. 12/07/1998 which name changed to Cosmoz Infrastructure Solutions, Inc. 04/16/2001 which recapitalized as FinancialContent, Inc. 11/13/2001
(See FinancialContent, Inc)

CAN AMERA EXPT REFNG LTD (AB)
Name changed to Can-Amera Oil Sands Inc. 06/00/1985
(See Can-Amera Oil Sands Inc.)

CAN-AMERA OIL SANDS DEVELOPMENT INC. (AB)
Each share Capital Stock no par exchanged for (0.1) share Capital Stock Ser. B no par 05/29/1962

Name changed to Can-Amera Export Refining Co. Ltd. 07/29/1963
Can-Amera Export Refining Co. Ltd. name changed to Can-Amera Oil Sands Inc. 06/00/1985
(See Can-Amera Oil Sands Inc.)

CAN-AMERA OIL SANDS INC. (AB)
Majority owned by Solv-Ex Corp. as of 00/00/1992
Public interest eliminated

CAN-AMERI AGRI CO (BC)
Each share old Common no par exchanged for (0.001) share new Common no par 04/27/2017
Note: In effect holders received $0.35 cash per share and public interest was eliminated

CAN-AMERICAN COPPER LTD. (BC)
Acquired by Eagle Plains Developments Ltd. 00/00/1959
Each share Capital Stock exchanged for (0.2) share Capital Stock
(See Eagle Plains Developments Ltd.)

CAN-AMERICAN NATURAL RESOURCES LTD. (BC)
Struck off register and declared dissolved for failure to file returns 09/27/1976

CAN AMERN PETES LTD (BC)
Recapitalized as Can-American Natural Resources Ltd. 06/20/1969
Each share Capital Stock no par exchanged for (0.166666) share Capital Stock no par
(See Can-American Natural Resources Ltd.)

CAN-BANC NT CORP (ON)
Equity Dividend Shares no par called for redemption 08/31/1998
Capital Shares no par called for redemption 08/31/1998
Class A Capital Shares no par called for redemption at $56.267073 on 09/02/2003
Preferred no par called for redemption at $25.70 on 09/02/2003

CAN BASE INDS LTD (BC)
Struck off register and declared dissolved for failure to file returns 12/18/1978

CAN-CHIN ENTMT GROUP CO LTD (BC)
Cease trade order effective 08/24/2007
Stockholders' equity unlikely

CAN-CON ENTERPRISES & EXPLS LTD (ON)
Name changed to Aubet Resources Inc. 09/08/1981
Aubet Resources Inc. recapitalized as Aubet Explorations Ltd. 09/30/1998 which name changed to Visa Gold Explorations Inc. 08/25/1999
(See Visa Gold Explorations Inc.)

CAN ENERGY COVERED CALL ETF (ON)
Name changed to First Asset Can-Energy Covered Call ETF 06/06/2012
(See First Asset Can-Energy Covered Call ETF)

CAN ENERGY INCOME ETF (ON)
Name changed to Can-Energy Covered Call ETF 10/26/2011
Can-Energy Covered Call ETF name changed to First Asset Can-Energy Covered Call ETF 06/06/2012
(See First Asset Can-Energy Covered Call ETF)

CAN-ERIN MINES LTD. (ON)
Recapitalized as Argosy Mining Corp. Ltd. 11/16/1964
Each share Capital Stock $1 par exchanged for (0.2) share Capital Stock $1 par
Argosy Mining Corp. name changed to Argosy Capital Corp. 03/29/1989
(See Argosy Capital Corp.)

CAN-EX MINERALS CORP (NV)
SEC revoked common stock registration 10/05/2007

CAN EX RES LTD (BC)
Recapitalized as Kintana Resources Ltd. 12/14/1990
Each share Common no par exchanged for (0.2) share Common no par
(See Kintana Resources Ltd.)

CAN FER MINES LTD (ON)
Capital Stock $1 par changed to no par 04/20/1967
Merged into Bralorne Can-Fer Resources Ltd. 12/03/1969
Each share Capital Stock no par exchanged for (1) share Capital Stock no par
Bralorne Can-Fer Resources Ltd. name changed to Bralorne Resources Ltd. 05/29/1972 which recapitalized as BRL Enterprises Inc. 11/27/1990
(See BRL Enterprises Inc.)

CAN FINANCIALS COVERED CALL ETF (ON)
Name changed to First Asset Can-Financials Covered Call ETF 06/06/2012
(See First Asset Can-Financials Covered Call ETF)

CAN-FINANCIALS INCOME CORP (ON)
Under plan of reorganization each Equity Share automatically became (0.37989) share First Asset Fund Corp. MSCI Canada Quality Index Class ETF 05/04/2016

CAN FINANCIALS INCOME ETF (ON)
Name changed to Can-Financials Covered Call ETF 10/26/2011
Can-Financials Covered Call ETF name changed to First Asset Can-Financials Covered Call ETF 06/06/2012
(See First Asset Can-Financials Covered Call ETF)

CAN MAC EXPL LTD (QC)
Delisted from Vancouver Stock Exchange 11/03/1992

CAN MATLS COVERED CALL ETF (ON)
Name changed to First Asset Can-Materials Covered Call ETF 06/06/2012

CAN MATLS INCOME ETF (ON)
Name changed to Can-Materials Covered Call ETF 10/26/2011
Can-Materials Covered Call ETF name changed to First Asset Can-Materials Covered Call ETF 06/06/2012

CAN-MED TECHNOLOGY INC (ON)
Cease trade order effective 11/15/1995
Stockholders' equity unlikely

CAN-MET EXPLORATIONS LTD. (ON)
Merged into Denison Mines Ltd. 04/07/1960
Each share Capital Stock $1 par exchanged for (0.005) share Capital Stock $1 par
Denison Mines Ltd. recapitalized as Denison Energy Inc. (ON) 05/30/2002 which reorganized in Alberta 03/08/2004 which name changed to Calfrac Well Services Ltd. 03/29/2004

CAN NATION RES LTD (BC)
Struck off register and declared dissolved for failure to file returns 09/30/1983

CAN PRO DEV LTD (BC)
Recapitalized as Cadre Resources Ltd. (BC) 05/19/1993
Each share Common no par exchanged for (0.16666666) share Common no par
Cadre Resources Ltd. (BC) reincorporated in Canada 06/19/1995
(See Cadre Resources Ltd.)

CAN 60 COVERED CALL ETF (ON)
Name changed to First Asset Can-60 Covered Call ETF 06/06/2012
(See First Asset Can-60 Covered Call ETF)

CAN-60 INCOME CORP (ON)
Under plan of reorganization each Non-Vtg. Equity Share automatically became (0.33333333) First Asset Core Fund Corp. Canadian Equity Income ETF 11/12/2015
First Asset Core Fund Corp. reorganized as First Asset Fund Corp. 05/04/2016

CAN 60 INCOME ETF (ON)
Name changed to Can-60 Covered Call ETF 10/26/2011
Can-60 Covered Call ETF name changed to First Asset Can-60 Covered Call ETF 06/06/2012
(See First Asset Can-60 Covered Call ETF)

CAN TEL COMMUNICATIONS INC (BC)
Recapitalized as Euro-Asia Capital Ltd. 10/01/1986
Each share Common no par exchanged for (0.33333333) share Common no par
Euro-Asia Capital Ltd. recapitalized as Asiamerica Holdings Ltd. 01/18/1989 which name changed to Stone Mark Capital Inc. (Canada) 11/17/1989 which reincorporated in Yukon 06/21/1993
(See Stone Mark Capital Inc. (Yukon))

CAN TRAC INDS LTD (BC)
Charter cancelled 09/27/1976

CANA PETROLEUM CORP (NV)
Name changed to XCana Petroleum Corp. 05/22/2007

CANA VENTURE CAP CORP (AB)
Merged into Arkadia Capital Corp. 03/14/2014
Each share Common no par exchanged for (0.60434) share Common no par

CANAAN ENERGY CORP (OK)
Merged into Chesapeake Energy Corp. 06/28/2002
Each share Common 1¢ par exchanged for $18 cash

CANAAN NATL BANCORP INC (DE)
Merged into Salisbury Bancorp Inc. 09/10/2004
Each share Common 1¢ par exchanged for (1.3371) shares Common 10¢ par and $31.20 cash

CANABO MED INC (BC)
Name changed to Aleafia Health Inc. 03/28/2018

CANABRAVA DIAMOND CORP (BC)
Acquired by Superior Diamonds Inc. (YT) 11/27/2003
Each share Common no par exchanged for (0.2) share Common no par
Note: Non-electing holders of (999) or fewer shares will receive $0.08 cash per share after 12/24/2003
Certificates were cancelled and became without value 11/27/2009
Superior Diamonds Inc. (YT) reincorporated in British Columbia 06/30/2004

CANACCORD FINL INC (BC)
Name changed 12/04/2009
Name changed from Canaccord Capital Inc. to Canaccord Financial Inc. 12/04/2009
Name changed to Canaccord Genuity Group Inc. 10/02/2013

CANACCORD GENUITY ACQUISITION CORP (ON)
Under plan of merger each Class A Restricted Unit automatically became (1) share Spark Power Group Inc. Common no par and (1) Common Stock Purchase Warrant expiring 08/31/2023 on 09/05/2018

CANACO RES INC (CANADA)
Each share Common no par received distribution of (0.2) share Tigray Resources Inc. Common no par payable 07/04/2011 to holders of record 07/04/2011 Ex date - 06/29/2011
Each share Common no par received distribution of (0.33333333) share East Africa Metals Inc. Common no par payable 04/04/2013 to holders of record 04/03/2013 Ex date - 04/05/2013
Recapitalized as Orca Gold Inc. 04/09/2013
Each share Common no par exchanged for (0.33333333) share Common no par

CANACO RES LTD (CANADA)
Recapitalized 06/17/1998
Recapitalized from Canaco Mining Resources Ltd. to Canaco Resources Ltd./ Ressources Canaco Ltee. 06/17/1998
Each share Common no par exchanged for (0.33333333) share Common no par
Recapitalized as Canaco Resources Inc. 11/10/2003
Each share Common no par exchanged for (0.1) share Common no par
Canaco Resources Inc. recapitalized as Orca Gold Inc. 04/09/2013

CANACORD RES INC (CANADA)
Merged into Prime Resources Corp. (BC) 08/31/1989
Each share Common no par exchanged for (0.1) share Common no par
Prime Resources Corp. (BC) recapitalized as Prime Resources Group Inc. 01/26/1990 which merged into HomeStake Mining Co. 12/03/1998 which merged into Barrick Gold Corp. 12/14/2001

CANADA & DOMINION SUGAR CO. LTD. (CANADA)
Each share Capital Stock no par exchanged for (3) shares Capital Stock no par 00/00/1938
Name changed to Redpath Industries Ltd.- Les Industries Redpath Ltee. 02/14/1973
(See Redpath Industries Ltd.-Les Industries Redpath Ltee.)

CANADA-AMERICAN TRUST SHARES, FIRST TRUST
Liquidated 00/00/1934
Details not available

CANADA BISCUIT CO., LTD.
Name changed to McCormick's Ltd. 00/00/1935
(See McCormick's Ltd.)

CANADA BREAD LTD (ON)
Each share Class B Preference $50 par exchanged for (1) share $2.75 Preference $49 par and (4) shares Common no par 12/10/1962
Name changed to Corporate Foods Ltd. 11/19/1969
Corporate Foods Ltd. name changed to Canada Bread Ltd. (New) 05/06/1997
(See Canada Bread Ltd. (New))

CANADA BREAD LTD NEW (ON)
Acquired by Grupo Bimbo, S.A.B. de C.V. 05/26/2014
Each share Common no par exchanged for $72 cash
Note: Unexchanged certificates were cancelled and became without value 05/25/2017

CANADA BROKERLINK INC (AB)
Merged into Allianz of Canada, Inc. 03/24/2000
Each share Common no par exchanged for $1.20 cash

CANADA BUD BREWERIES LTD.
Acquired by Canadian Breweries Ltd. 00/00/1943
Each share Common exchanged for (0.2) share Preference no par and (1) share Common no par
Canadian Breweries Ltd. name changed to Carling O'Keefe Ltd. 11/09/1973
(See Carling O'Keefe Ltd.)

CANADA CARTAGE DIVERSIFIED INCOME FD (ON)
Units no par called for redemption at $11.293509 on 07/09/2007

CANADA CEM LAFARGE LTD (CANADA)
Common no par split (4) for (1) by issuance of (3) additional shares 05/23/1973
Common no par reclassified as Conv. Class A Common no par 07/14/1976
Conv. Class A Common no par reclassified as Common no par 03/07/1979
Conv. Class B Common no par reclassified as Common no par 03/07/1979
Under plan of reorganization each share old $1.17 Conv. 2nd Preference Ser. A no par and Common no par automatically became (1.05) shares new $1.17 Conv. 2nd Preference Ser. A no par and (1.05) shares Exchangeable Preference no par respectively 05/17/1983
Note: Additional shares reflecting the recapitalization were mailed 05/19/1983
$1.30 Preference $20 par called for redemption 08/13/1984
New $1.14 Conv. 2nd Preference Ser. A no par reclassified as $1.17 Conv. Preference Ser. A no par 01/09/1986
$1.17 Conv. Preference Ser. A no par called for redemption 04/14/1986
Name changed to Lafarge Canada Ltd. 01/12/1988
(See Lafarge Canada Ltd.)

CANADA CEM LTD (CANADA)
Name changed to Canada Cement Lafarge Ltd.-Ciments Canada Lafarge Ltee. 05/01/1970
Canada Cement Lafarge Ltd.-Ciments Canada Lafarge Ltee. name changed to Lafarge Canada Inc. 01/12/1988
(See Lafarge Canada Inc.)

CANADA CEMENT CO. LTD. (CANADA)
Each share 6.5% Preference $100 par exchanged for (5) shares $1.30 Preference $20 par 00/00/1946
Each share old Common no par exchanged for (4) shares new Common no par 02/21/1955
Name changed to Canada Cement Co. Ltd.-Compagnie de Ciment Canada Ltee. 02/22/1967
Canada Cement Co. Ltd.-Compagnie de Ciment Canada Ltee. name changed to Canada Cement Lafarge Ltd.-Ciments Canada Lafarge Ltee. 05/01/1970 which name changed to Lafarge Canada Inc. 01/12/1988
(See Lafarge Canada Inc.)

CANADA CHIBOUGAMAU RESOURCES LTD. (QC)
Charter annulled for failure to file annual reports 10/28/1978

CANADA COSTA RICA MINES LTD (ON)
Charter cancelled for failure to file reports and pay taxes 08/28/1989

CANADA CROWN INVT CORP (NV)
Each share old Common $0.005 par exchanged for (0.5) share new Common $0.005 par 08/29/1991
Name changed to Global Aener/Cology Corp. 06/16/1996
(See Global Aener/Cology Corp.)

CANADA CRUSHED & CUT STONE LTD (ON)
Name changed to Steetley Industries Ltd. 04/24/1969
(See Steetley Industries Ltd.)

CANADA CRUSHED STONE CORP. LTD.
Name changed to Canada Crushed Stone Ltd. 00/00/1940
(See Canada Crushed Stone Ltd.)

CANADA CRUSHED STONE LTD.
Acquired by Canada Crushed & Cut Stone Ltd. 00/00/1951
Details not available

CANADA DEV CORP (CANADA)
Stock Dividend - In Common to holders of 8% Conv. Preferred Class B 100% 03/06/1981
8% Conv. Preferred Class B $100 par called for redemption 06/08/1987
Name changed to Polysar Energy & Chemical Corp. 01/01/1988
Polysar Energy & Chemical Corp. acquired by Nova Corp. of Alberta 09/07/1988 which name changed to Nova Gas Transmission Ltd. 05/11/1994
(See Nova Gas Transmission Ltd.)

CANADA DOMINION RES 2005 LTD PARTNERSHIP (ON)
Under plan of reorganization each Unit of Ltd. Partnership no par automatically became (0.9493) share Dynamic Managed Portfolios Ltd. DMP Resource Class no par 02/06/2007

CANADA DOMINION RES 2005 II LTD PARTNERSHIP (ON)
Under plan of reorganization each Unit of Ltd. Partnership no par automatically became (0.6047) share Dynamic Managed Portfolios Ltd. DMP Resource Class no par 02/06/2007

CANADA DRY BOTTLING CO. OF CUBA
Liquidated 00/00/1944
Details not available

CANADA DRY BOTTLING CO ST LOUIS (MO)
Charter forfeited for failure to file reports 04/19/1973

CANADA DRY BOTTLING CORP.
Dissolved 00/00/1944
Details not available

CANADA DRY CORP (DE)
Merged into Simon (Norton), Inc. 07/17/1968
Each share $4.25 Preferred no par exchanged for $95 principal amount of 6% Subord. Debentures due 07/01/1998
Each share Common $1.66666666 par exchanged for (0.3125) share $1.60 Conv. Preferred Ser. A $5 par and (0.6875) share Common $1 par
Simon (Norton), Inc. merged into Esmark, Inc. (Inc. 03/14/1969) 09/09/1983
(See Esmark, Inc. (Inc. 03/14/1969))

CANADA DRY-FROSTIE CORP. (MD)
Charter annulled for failure to pay taxes 12/30/1968

CANADA DRY GINGER ALE INC (DE)
Capital Stock no par changed to $5 par 00/00/1933
Capital Stock $5 par reclassified as Common $5 par 00/00/1942
Each share Common $5 par exchanged for (3) shares Common $1.66666666 par 00/00/1946
Name changed to Canada Dry Corp. 02/03/1958
Canada Dry Corp. merged into Simon (Norton), Inc. 07/17/1968 which merged into Esmark, Inc. (Inc. 03/14/1969) 09/09/1983
(See Esmark, Inc. (Inc. 03/14/1969))

CANADA FLOORING CO. LTD. (QC)
Acquired by Zodiac Ltd. 10/16/1963
Details not available

CANADA FLUORSPAR INC (AB)
Acquired by Golden Gate Capital Opportunity Fund, L.P. 05/30/2014
Each share Common no par exchanged for $0.35 cash

CANADA FLUORSPAR INC (BC)
Name changed to Continental Ridge Resources Inc. 02/05/2001
Continental Ridge Resources Inc. name changed to Nevada Geothermal Power Inc. 05/13/2003 which recapitalized as Alternative Earth Resources Inc. 04/02/2013 which recapitalized as Black Sea Copper & Gold Corp. 09/28/2016

CANADA FOILS LTD (ON)
99% of Common no par acquired at $45 per share through purchase offer 03/00/1969
98% of Class A no par acquired at $40 per share through purchase offer 03/00/1969
Public interest eliminated

CANADA FORGINGS LTD (CANADA)
Recapitalized 12/21/1970
Each share old Common no par exchanged for (0.1) share new Common no par
Each share Class A no par exchanged for (0.5) share new Common no par
Acquired by Toromont Industries Ltd. 06/28/1976
Each share new Common no par exchanged for $17 cash

CANADA FOUNDRIES & FORGINGS LTD. (CANADA)
Recapitalized 00/00/1928
Each share 7% Preferred $100 par exchanged for (4) shares Class A no par
Each share Common $100 par exchanged for (1) share Class B no par
Each share Class B no par exchanged for (4) shares Common no par 07/18/1955
Name changed to Canada Forgings Ltd. 12/09/1966
(See Canada Forgings Ltd.)

CANADA GAS CORP (BC)
Each share old Common no par exchanged for (0.33333333) share new Common no par 09/07/2010
Name changed to Canada Rare Earths Inc. 03/01/2011
Canada Rare Earths Inc. name changed to Canada Strategic Metals Inc. (BC) 08/01/2012 which reincorporated in Canada 11/29/2013 which recapitalized as Quebec Precious Metals Corp. 07/05/2018

CANADA GENERAL FUND, INC. (DE)
Merged into Canada General Fund (1954) Ltd. on a (1.224735) for (1) basis 00/00/1954
Canada General Fund (1954) Ltd. name changed to Canada General Fund Ltd. 00/00/1956 which reincorporated in Massachusetts as Canada General Fund, Inc. 02/17/1964 which name changed to Boston Common Stock Fund, Inc. 09/17/1968 which name changed to Vance, Sanders Common Stock Fund, Inc. 12/29/1972 which name changed to Eaton Vance Growth Fund, Inc. 11/16/1981 which name changed to Eaton Vance Growth Trust 08/18/1992

CANADA GENERAL FUND, INC. (MA)
Stock Dividend - 100% 01/10/1966
Name changed to Boston Common Stock Fund, Inc. 09/17/1968
Boston Common Stock Fund, Inc. name changed to Vance, Sanders Common Stock Fund, Inc. 12/29/1972 which name changed to Eaton Vance Growth Fund, Inc. 11/16/1981 which reorganized as Eaton Vance Growth Trust 07/01/2007

CANADA GENERAL FUND (1954) LTD. (CANADA)
Name changed to Canada General Fund Ltd. 00/00/1956
Canada General Fund Ltd. (Canada) reincorporated in Massachusetts as Canada General Fund, Inc. 02/17/1964 which name changed to Boston Common Stock Fund, Inc. 09/17/1968 which name changed to Vance, Sanders Common Stock Fund, Inc. 12/29/1972 which name changed to Eaton Vance Growth Fund, Inc. 11/16/1981 which reorganized as Eaton Vance Growth Trust 07/01/2007

CANADA GENERAL FUND LTD. (CANADA)
Reincorporated under the laws of Massachusetts as Canada General Fund, Inc. 02/17/1964
Canada General Fund, Inc: (MA) name changed to Boston Common Stock Fund, Inc. 09/17/1968 which name changed to Vance, Sanders Common Stock Fund, Inc. 12/29/1972 which name changed to Eaton Vance Growth Fund, Inc. 11/16/1981 which reorganized as Eaton Vance Growth Trust 07/01/2007

CANADA GEOTHERMAL OIL LTD (ON)
Discharged from receivership 04/04/1986
Stockholders' equity unlikely

CANADA GOLD CORP (BC)
Name changed to STEM 7 Capital Inc. 07/12/2013
STEM 7 Capital Inc. name changed to South Star Mining Corp. 12/22/2017

CANADA GRAPHITE MINES LTD. (ON)
Charter revoked for failure to file reports and pay fees 11/09/1967

CANADA GROWTH FD (MB)
Name changed to Bolton, Tremblay International Fund 04/14/1977
(See Bolton, Tremblay International Fund)

CANADA GYPSUM & ALABASTINE, LTD. (CANADA)
Name changed to Gypsum Lime & Alabastine Canada, Ltd. 00/00/1930
Gypsum Lime & Alabastine Canada, Ltd. acquired by Dominion Tar & Chemical Co. Ltd. 02/23/1959 which name changed to Domtar Ltd. 07/01/1965 which name changed to Domtar Ltd.-Domtar Ltee. 01/13/1972 which name changed to Domtar Inc. 02/23/1978 which reorganized as Domtar Corp. (DE) 03/07/2007

CANADA INCOME PLUS FD (ON)
Fund terminated 10/09/1992
Each Trust Unit exchanged for either $9.78 net asset value of any fund of Guardian Group of Funds Ltd. or $9.68 cash

CANADA INCOME PLUS FD 1986 (ON)
Trust Units reclassified as Special Mutual Fund Units 03/30/1988
Mutualized 04/26/1988
Details not available

CANADA INCOME PLUS FD 1987 (ON)
Trust Units reclassified as Special Mutual Fund Units 03/30/1988
Name changed to Guardian Group of Funds Ltd. Canada Bond Fund 01/01/1991

CDA INTL INC (ON)
Ceased operations 02/00/2005
No stockholders' equity

CANADA IRON FDRYS LTD (CANADA)
Each share 6% Preference $100 par exchanged for (10) shares 6% Preference $10 par 00/00/1944
Each share Common $100 par exchanged for (10) shares Common $10 par 00/00/1944
Common $10 par changed to no par and (2) additional shares issued 01/31/1966
Name changed to Canron Ltd.-Canron Ltee. 04/15/1968
Canron Ltd.-Canron Ltee. name changed to Canron Inc. 06/05/1978
(See Canron Inc.)

CANADA ISRAEL DEV LTD (CANADA)
Common no par reclassified as Conv. Class A Common no par 05/20/1974
Merged out of existence 10/23/1987
Details not available

CANADA KELP CO., LTD.
Bankrupt 00/00/1948
Details not available

CANADA LANDED & NATIONAL INVESTMENT CO., LTD.
Absorbed by Canada Permanent Mortgage Corp. 00/00/1928
Details not available

CANADA LIFE ASSURANCE CO.
Mutualization approved 05/15/1959
Details not available

CANADA LIFE FINL CORP (CANADA)
Acquired by Great-West Lifeco Inc. 07/10/2003
Each share Common no par exchanged for (0.17632335) share 4.8% 1st Preferred Ser. E $25 par, (0.05748811) share 5.9% 1st Preferred Ser. F $25 par and $38.6547131 cash
6.23% Preferred Ser. B called for redemption at $25 plus $0.390625 accrued dividends on 12/31/2010

CANADA LITHIUM CORP (ON)
Each share old Common no par exchanged for (1) share new Common no par to reflect a (1) for (100) reverse split followed by a (100) for (1) forward split 07/20/2010
Note: Holders of (99) or fewer pre-split shares received $0.51 cash per share
Reorganized under the laws of Canada as RB Energy Inc. 02/05/2014
Each share new Common no par exchanged for (0.33333333) share Common no par

CANADA MACHY LTD (CANADA)
Each share Common $10 par exchanged for (5) shares Common no par 00/00/1940
Acquired by Ingersoll-Rand Co. (NJ) 03/02/1976
Each share Common no par exchanged for (0.7) share Common $2 par
Ingersoll-Rand Co. (NJ) reorganized in Bermuda as Ingersoll-Rand Co. Ltd. 12/31/2001 which reincorporated in Ireland as Ingersoll-Rand PLC 07/01/2009

CANADA MALTING LTD (CANADA)
4.5% Preferred $26 par called for redemption 12/15/1960
Each share old Common no par exchanged for (4) shares new Common no par 06/25/1963
Each share new Common no par received stock distribution of (3) shares 6% Preferred Ser. B $1 par 03/15/1968
6% Preferred Ser. B $1 par called for redemption 06/15/1973
New Common no par reclassified as Conv. Class A Common no par 08/01/1973
Conv. Class A Common no par reclassified back as Common no par 12/27/1979
Conv. Class B Common no par reclassified as Common no par 12/27/1979
Common no par split (3) for (1) by issuance of (2) additional shares 05/20/1984
Common no par split (3) for (2) by issuance of (0.5) additional share 05/20/1988
Common no par split (2) for (1) by issuance of (1) additional share 06/15/1990
Common no par split (3) for (2) by issuance of (0.5) additional share 05/25/1992
Acquired by ConAgra, Inc. 12/05/1995
Each share Common no par exchanged for $20.50 cash

CANADA NATIONAL FIRE INSURANCE CO.
Liquidated 00/00/1932
Details not available

CANADA NATIONAL LIFE INSURANCE CO.
Liquidated 00/00/1932
Details not available

CANADA NORTH WEST LAND CO. LTD. (CANADA)
Name changed to Canada Northwest Land Ltd. 10/29/1969
Canada Northwest Land Ltd. name changed to Canada Northwest Energy Ltd. 05/14/1982 which merged into Sherritt Gordon Ltd. 10/15/1991 which name changed to Sherritt Inc. 07/05/1993 which name changed to Viridian, Inc. 04/22/1996 which merged into Agrium Inc. 12/10/1996

CANADA NORTHERN POWER CORP. LTD. (CANADA)
Each share old Common no par exchanged for (5) shares new Common no par 00/00/1929
Dissolution approved and each (2) shares Common no par received (1.0625) shares Common no par of Northern Quebec Power Co. Ltd. 12/09/1955
(See Northern Quebec Power Co. Ltd.)

CANADA NORTHWEST AUSTRALIA OIL N L (AUSTRALIA)
Recapitalized as National Venture Corp. N.L. 11/24/1986
Each share Common 25¢ par exchanged for (0.25) share Ordinary $1 par
National Venture Corp. N.L. name changed to Doral Mineral Industries Ltd. 03/28/1991
(See Doral Mineral Industries Ltd.)

CANADA NORTHWEST ENERGY LTD (CANADA)
Name changed 05/14/1982
Common $1 par changed to no par and (19) additional shares issued 11/04/1969
Name changed from Canada Northwest Land Ltd. to Canada Northwest Energy Ltd. 05/14/1982
Common no par split (2) for (1) by issuance of (1) additional share 03/11/1983
Merged into Sherritt Gordon Ltd. 10/15/1991
Each share 7.75% Conv. Preferred Ser. C no par exchanged for (0.96775) share Common $1 par
Each share 9% Retractable Preferred Ser. B $25 par exchanged for (0.96775) share Common $1 par
Each share Common no par exchanged for (0.0516) share Common $1 par
Sherritt Gordon Ltd. name changed to Sherritt Inc. 07/05/1993 which name changed to Viridian, Inc. 04/22/1996 which merged into Agrium Inc. 12/10/1996 which merged into Nutrien Ltd. 01/02/2018

CANADA OIL LANDS LTD. (AB)
Acquired by Great Plains Development Co. of Canada Ltd. 02/16/1965
Each share Capital Stock no par exchanged for $3.25 cash

CANADA ORIENT RES INC (BC)
Struck off register and declared dissolved for failure to file returns 03/25/1994

CANADA PAC CAP CORP (ON)
Voluntarily dissolved 07/04/2014
Each share Common no par received first and final distribution of approximately (0.54976) Lakeside Minerals Inc. Unit consisting of (1) share Common no par and (0.5) Common Stock Purchase Warrant expiring 06/24/2017
Lakeside Minerals Inc. name changed to Lineage Grow Co. Ltd. 07/25/2017

CANADA PACKERS INC (CANADA)
Common no par split (2) for (1) by issuance of (1) additional share 07/15/1983
Common no par split (3) for (1) by issuance of (2) additional shares 07/11/1986
Name changed to Maple Leaf Foods Inc. (Old) 07/01/1991
Maple Leaf Foods Inc. (Old) merged into Maple Leaf Foods Inc. (New) 04/26/1995

CANADA PACKERS LTD. (CANADA)
Each share Capital Stock no par exchanged for (2) shares Class A no par and (4) shares Class B no par 00/00/1944
Each share Class A no par or Class B no par exchanged for (5) shares Common no par 08/15/1968
Common no par reclassified as Conv. Class C Common no par 05/23/1973
Conv. Class C Common no par reclassified as Common no par 03/15/1979
Conv. Class D Common no par reclassified as Common no par 03/15/1979
Name changed to Canada Packers Inc. 05/06/1980
Canada Packers Inc. name changed to Maple Leaf Foods Inc. (Old) 07/01/1991 which merged into Maple Leaf Foods Inc. (New) 04/26/1995

CANADA PAVING & SUPPLY CORP. LTD.
Bankrupt 00/00/1946
Details not available

CANADA PAYPHONE CORP (BC)
Acquired by Globalive Communications Inc. 09/30/2004
Each share Common no par exchanged for $0.02 cash

CANADA PERM INCOME INVTS (ON)
Name changed to Canada Trust Income Investments 07/24/1986
(See Canada Trust Income Investments)

CANADA PERM MTG CORP (CANADA)
Each share Capital Stock $100 par exchanged for (5) shares Capital Stock $20 par 00/00/1950
Each share Capital Stock $25 par exchanged for (2) shares Capital Stock $10 par 10/16/1958
Capital Stock $10 par changed to $2 par and (4) additional shares issued 11/12/1965
Capital Stock $2 par reclassified as Common $2 par 07/22/1976
6.75% Tax Deferred Conv. Preference Ser. A $25 par called for redemption 00/00/1985
Merged into Canada Trustco Mortgage Co. 12/31/1985
Each share Adjustable Rate Preference Ser. C $25 par exchanged for (1.25) shares Adjustable Rate 1st Preference Ser. B $20 par
Each share 8% Preference Ser. B exchanged for (1) share 8% 1st Preference Ser. B $20 par
Each share Common $2 par exchanged for (0.52465) share Common no par
(See Canada Trustco Mortgage Co.)

CANADA POWER & PAPER CORP.
Merged into Consolidated Paper Corp. Ltd. 00/00/1931
Details not available

CANADA QATAR OIL & GAS INC (NV)
Recapitalized as Echo Resources Inc. 02/10/1997
Each share Common $0.001 par exchanged for (0.05) share Common $0.001 par
Echo Resources Inc. name changed to Big Daddy's BBQ Racing Co. 01/07/1999 which name changed to Ehydrogen Solutions, Inc. 12/14/2009

CANADA QUEBEC MINING CORP., LTD.
Succeeded by Quebec Gold Research Corp. Ltd. 00/00/1933
Details not available

CANADA RADIUM CORP. LTD. (ON)
Recapitalized as Santos Silver Mines Ltd. 04/30/1963
Each share Capital Stock no par exchanged for (0.1) share Capital Stock no par
Santos Silver Mines Ltd. acquired by Utica Mines Ltd. (New) 09/30/1964 which recapitalized as Dankoe Mines Ltd. 09/25/1971 which recapitalized as Emerald Dragon Mines Inc. 10/30/1996
(See Emerald Dragon Mines Inc.)

CANADA RARE EARTHS INC (BC)
Name changed to Canada Strategic Metals Inc. (BC) 08/01/2012
Canada Strategic Metals Inc. (BC) reincorporated in Canada 11/29/2013 which recapitalized as Quebec Precious Metals Corp. 07/05/2018

CANADA RENEWABLE BIOENERGY CORP (AB)
Reincorporated under the laws of British Columbia 09/27/2012

CANADA SAFEWAY LTD (CANADA)
4.4% Preferred $100 par called for redemption 10/01/1986
Public interest eliminated

CANADA SLATE PRODUCTS LTD.
Dissolved 00/00/1944
No stockholders' equity

CANADA SOUTHERN OILS LTD. (CANADA)
Plan of reorganization effective 04/20/1954
Each (8) shares Capital Stock $1 par exchanged for (8) shares Canada Southern Petroleum Ltd. Capital Stock $1 par, (5) shares Canso Natural Gas Ltd. Capital Stock $1 par and (4) shares Canso Oil Producers Ltd. Capital Stock $1 par
(See each company's listing)

CANADA SOUTHN PETE LTD (AB)
Reincorporated 05/29/1980
Reincorporated 03/09/2005
Place of incorporation changed from (Canada) to (NS) 05/29/1980
Each VTC for Capital Stock $1 par exchanged for (1) share Capital Stock $1 par 04/20/1964
Capital Stock $1 par reclassified as Limited Vtg. Stock $1 par 01/21/1986
Place of incorporation changed from (NS) to (AB) and Limited Vtg. Stock $1 par reclassified as Common no par 03/09/2005
Merged into Canadian Oil Sands Trust 10/25/2006
Each share Common no par exchanged for $13.10 cash

CANADA SOUTHN RY CO (CANADA)
Recapitalized 06/06/1985
Each share Capital Stock $100 par exchanged for $507 cash

CANADA SS LINES LTD (CANADA)
Reorganized 00/00/1937
Each share Preference $100 par exchanged for (1.25) shares new Common no par
Each share Common no par exchanged for (0.5) share new Common no par
Recapitalized 00/00/1954
Each share 5% Preference $50 par exchanged for (4) shares 5% Preference $12.50 par
Each share Common no par exchanged for (4) shares new Common no par
Recapitalized 05/06/1964
5% Preference $12.50 par changed to $6.25 par and (1) additional share issued
Common no par split (2) for (1) by issuance of (1) additional share
Each share new Common no par exchanged for $40 cash 05/09/1972
5% Preference $6.25 par called for redemption 12/19/1975
Public interest eliminated

CANADA STARCH CO. LTD. (CANADA)
Each share Common $100 par exchanged for (5) shares Common $5 par 00/00/1937
All but (100) shares of Preference $100 par acquired by Corn Products Refining Co. through voluntary purchase offer 12/00/1950
Common acquired by Corn Products Refining Co. 00/00/1956
Each share Common $5 par exchanged for $75 cash

CANADA STRATEGIC METALS INC (CANADA)
Reincorporated 11/29/2013
Place of incorporation changed from (BC) to (Canada) 11/29/2013
Recapitalized as Quebec Precious Metals Corp. 07/05/2018
Each share Common no par exchanged for (0.24038461) share Common no par

CANADA TALC LTD.
Assets acquired by Canada Talc Industries Ltd. 00/00/1951
No stockholders' equity

CANADA 3000 INC (AB)
Petition under Chapter 11 bankruptcy proceedings dismissed 02/24/2005
Stockholders' equity unlikely

CANADA TR INCOME INVTS (ON)
Trust terminated 10/31/2007
Each Trust Unit no par exchanged for $9.32447341 cash

CANADA TRUSTCO MTG CO (CANADA)
Conv. Class B Common no par reclassified as Common no par 06/14/1979
7.75% Preference Ser. C $20 par called for redemption 12/16/1981
7.25% Conv. Preference Ser. B $20 par called for redemption 12/29/1982
Reorganized as CT Financial Services Inc. 11/25/1987
Each share Common no par exchanged for (3) shares Common no par
Note: U.S. residents received CAD $57.30 cash
(See CT Financial Services Inc.)
11% 1st Preference Ser. G $20 par called for redemption 10/03/1989
8% 1st Preference Ser. B $20 par changed to no par 06/01/1993
Adjustable Rate 1st Preference Ser. C $20 par changed to no par 06/01/1993
Floating Rate 2nd Preference Ser. 1 $25 par changed to no par 06/01/1993
8% 1st Preference Ser. B no par called for redemption 12/29/1995
Adjustable Rate 1st Preference Ser. C no par called for redemption at $20 on 12/30/1997
Floating Rate 2nd Preference Ser. 1 no par called for redemption at $25 on 12/30/1997
Public interest eliminated

CANADA TUNGSTEN INC (CANADA)
Merged into Aur Resources Inc. 01/01/1997
Each share Common no par exchanged for (0.22222222) share Common no par
Aur Resources Inc. acquired by Teck Cominco Ltd. 09/28/2007 which name changed to Teck Resources Ltd. 04/27/2009

CANADA TUNGSTEN MNG LTD (ON)
Capital Stock $1 par changed to no par 04/00/1978
Merged into Canada Tungsten Inc. 01/01/1993
Each share Common no par exchanged for (1) share Common no par
Canada Tungsten Inc. merged into Aur Resources Inc. 01/01/1997 which was acquired by Teck Cominco Ltd. 09/28/2007 which name changed to Teck Resources Ltd. 04/27/2009

CANADA-UTE URANIUM CORP. (UT)
Merged into Globe Minerals, Inc. 03/07/1969
Each share Capital Stock $1 par exchanged for (1) share Common no par
Globe Minerals, Inc. recapitalized as Globe Inc. 10/16/1970
(See Globe Inc.)

CANADA WEST CAP CORP (AB)
Name changed to Insurcom Financial Corp. 09/24/1999
Insurcom Financial Corp. name changed to Omega World Inc. 09/17/2007

CANADA WEST CAP INC (CANADA)
Reorganized under the laws of Alberta as Canadian Sub-Surface Energy Services Corp. 02/14/2006
Each Special Share no par exchanged for (1) share Class A Common no par
Each share Common no par exchanged for (0.14285714) share Class A Common no par
Canadian Sub-Surface Energy Services Corp. merged into Pure Energy Services Ltd. 06/25/2009
(See Pure Energy Services Ltd.)

CANADA WEST TECHNOLOGY CORP (AB)
Recapitalized as Bellator Exploration Inc. 12/10/1993
Each share Common no par exchanged for (0.5) share Common no par
Bellator Exploration Inc. merged into Baytex Energy Ltd. 06/07/2000
(See Baytex Energy Ltd.)

CANADA WESTN CORDAGE LTD (BC)
Completely liquidated 08/31/1989
Each share 50¢ Class A Conv. Preference no par received first and final distribution of $13.539 cash
Each share Class B no par received first and final distribution of $13.539 cash
Note: Certificates were not required to be surrendered and are without value

CANADA WIRE & CABLE CO. LTD. (CANADA)
Class B Common no par exchanged (5) for (1) 05/15/1956
All Class A Common no par acquired by Noranda Mines Ltd. through exchange offer 04/21/1965
Acquired by Noranda Mines Ltd. 06/09/1965
Each share Class B Common no par exchanged for (0.4) share Capital Stock no par and $0.50 cash
Noranda Mines Ltd. name changed to Noranda Inc. 05/28/1984 which name changed to Falconbridge Ltd. (New) 2005 on 07/01/2005
(See Falconbridge Ltd. (New) 2005)

CANADA ZINC METALS CORP (BC)
Name changed to ZincX Resources Corp. 05/07/2018

CANADA ZINC MINES LTD. (ON)
Charter cancelled 00/00/1960

CANADAS CHOICE SPRING WTR INC (CANADA)
Recapitalized as Echo Springs Water Corp. 03/27/2002
Each share Common no par exchanged for (0.05) share Common no par
(See Echo Springs Water Corp.)

CANADAS PIZZA DELIVERY CORP (CANADA)
Each share old Common no par exchanged for (0.1) share new Common no par 03/01/2005
Under plan of arrangement each share new Common no par exchanged for $0.60 cash 08/21/2007
Note: Unexchanged certificates were cancelled and became without value 08/21/2013

CANADEX RES LTD (ON)
Name changed 09/22/1980
Common $1 par changed to no par 09/29/1971
Name changed from Canadex Mining Corp. Ltd. to Canadex Resources Ltd. 09/22/1980
Acquired by Student Transportation of America Ltd. 01/28/2008
Each share Common no par exchanged for $5.72 cash

CANADIAN ADDICKS MNG CORP (MN)
Mining claims forfeited 12/31/1976
No stockholders' equity

CANADIAN ADMIRAL CORP., LTD. (CANADA)
Over 99.7% acquired by York Lambton Inc. through purchase offer which expired 09/01/1979
Public interest eliminated

CANADIAN ADMIRAL OILS LTD. (CANADA)
Assets sold to Canadian Homestead Oils Ltd. on a (0.25) for (1) basis 11/22/1957
Canadian Homestead Oils Ltd. merged into Inter-City Gas Corp. (MB) 04/14/1980 which reorganized as Inter-City Products Corp. (MB) 04/18/1990 which reincorporated in Canada 06/05/1992 which name changed to International Comfort Products Corp. 07/09/1997
(See International Comfort Products Corp.)

CANADIAN AGRA FOODS INC (CANADA)
Discharged from receivership 00/00/2004
No stockholders' equity

CANADIAN AGTECHNOLOGY PARTNERS INC (AB)
Name changed to SportsMate International Inc. 01/04/1996
(See SportsMate International)

CANADIAN AIRLS CORP (AB)
Plan of reorganization under Chapter 11 Federal Bankruptcy Code effective 06/27/2000
No stockholders' equity

CANADIAN AIRWAYS, LTD.
Liquidation completed 00/00/1947
Details not available

CANADIAN ALLIED PPTY INVTS LTD (BC)
Acquired by Laing Investments Ltd. 09/12/1975
Each share Capital Stock $5 par exchanged for $12.50 cash

CANADIAN ALUMINA CORP. LTD. (NS)
Dissolution approved 02/00/1963
No stockholders' equity

CANADIAN ANACONDA OILS LTD. (CANADA)
Recapitalized as Anaconda Petroleum Ltd. 03/25/1957
Each share Capital Stock no par exchanged for (0.2) share Capital Stock 50¢ par
Anaconda Petroleum Ltd. name changed to Zebedee Oil Ltd. 01/20/1971 which name changed to Osias Resources Canada Ltd. 04/19/1971 which recapitalized as Troy Gold Industries Ltd. (Canada) 06/12/1974 which reincorporated in Alberta 09/06/1978
(See Troy Gold Industries Ltd. (AB))

CANADIAN ANAESTHETISTS MUT ACCUMULATING FD LTD (CANADA)
Name changed to Stone & Co. Corporate Funds Ltd. 09/01/2003

CANADIAN ANGUS RES LTD (AB)
Reincorporated 08/29/1988
Place of incorporation changed from (BC) to (AB) 08/29/1988
Merged into Abacan Resource Corp. (New) 02/10/1995
Each share Common no par exchanged for (0.3) share Common no par
(See Abacan Resource Corp. (New))

CANADIAN ARCTIC PETES LTD (AB)
Reincorporated 06/16/1995
Place of incorporation changed from (BC) to (AB) 06/16/1995
Recapitalized as Tekerra Gas Inc. 09/17/1996
Each share Common no par exchanged for (0.5) share Common no par
Tekerra Gas Inc. merged into Del Roca Energy Ltd. 10/31/1998 which merged into Tusk Energy Inc. 02/01/2003
(See Tusk Energy Inc.)

CANADIAN ARENA CO (QC)
4% Preferred $10 par called for redemption 06/30/1956
4% Preferred $100 par called for redemption 12/01/1964
4% Preferred $10 par called for redemption 11/01/1968
Common no par split (50) for (1) by issuance of (49) additional shares 10/29/1969
Name changed to Carena-Bancorp Inc. 11/30/1974

Carena-Bancorp Inc. acquired by Carena-Bancorp Holdings Inc. 03/12/1979 which name changed to Carena-Bancorp Inc. 11/13/1984 which name changed to Carena Developments Ltd. 03/07/1989 which recapitalized as Brookfield Properties Corp. 06/03/1996 which name changed to Brookfield Office Properties Inc. 05/09/2011
(See Brookfield Office Properties Inc.)

CANADIAN ARROW MINES LTD (ON)
Capital Stock $1 par changed to Common no par 05/29/1974
Merged into Tartisan Resources Corp. 02/02/2018
Each share Common no par exchanged for (0.05714285) share Common no par
Note: Unexchanged certificates will be cancelled and become without value 02/02/2024
Tartisan Resources Corp. name changed to Tartisan Nickel Corp. 03/23/2018

CANADIAN ASHLAND EXPL LTD (CANADA)
$2 Preferred $20 par called for redemption 10/06/1978
Public interest eliminated

CANADIAN ASSOCIATED GOLDFIELDS LTD.
Bankrupt 00/00/1928
Stockholders' equity unlikely

CANADIAN ASTORIA MINERALS LTD. (QC)
Recapitalized as Cam Mines Ltd. 12/02/1963
Each share Capital Stock $1 par exchanged for (0.25) share Capital Stock $1 par
Cam Mines Ltd. recapitalized as Energy & Resources (Cam) Ltd./Energy & Resources (Cam) Ltee. 01/21/1980 which name changed to ERG Resources Inc. 10/09/1986
(See ERG Resources Inc.)

CANADIAN ATLANTIC OIL CO. LTD. (AB)
Acquired by Pacific Petroleums Ltd. 12/25/1958
Each share Common $2 par exchanged for (0.33333333) share Common $1 par
(See Pacific Petroleums Ltd.)

CANADIAN ATLAS STEELS, LTD. (CANADA)
Name changed to Atlas Steels, Ltd. 00/00/1938
(See Atlas Steels, Ltd.)

CANADIAN-AUSTRALIAN EXPLORATION LTD. (ON)
Recapitalized as Win-Eldrich Mines Ltd. 06/21/1965
Each share Capital Stock $1 par exchanged for (0.2) share Capital Stock $1 par

CANADIAN AVIATION ELECTRONICS LTD. (CANADA)
Common no par split (3) for (1) by issuance of (2) additional shares 02/06/1963
Name changed to CAE Industries Ltd. 07/07/1965
CAE Industries Ltd. name changed to CAE Inc. 09/15/1993

CANADIAN BAKERIES LTD. (CANADA)
Each share 7% 1st Preferred $100 par exchanged for (1) share 5% Preferred $100 par 00/00/1939
Each share 7% 2nd Preferred $100 par exchanged for (9-739/1000) shares Common no par 00/00/1939
Each share Class A no par exchanged for (0.125) share Common no par
Through purchase offer Maple Leaf Mills Ltd. acquired all except (500) shares as of 03/25/1971
Public interest eliminated

CANADIAN BALDWIN RES LTD (ON)
Recapitalized 07/25/2005
Recapitalized from Canadian Baldwin Holdings Ltd. to Canadian Baldwin Resources Ltd. 07/25/2005
Each share Common no par exchanged for (0.57142857) share Common no par
Name changed to Aura Gold Inc. (ON) 03/22/2006
Aura Gold Inc. (ON) reincorporated in Canada 04/20/2006 which name changed to Aura Minerals Inc. (Canada) 08/16/2007 which reorganized in British Virgin Islands 01/05/2017

CANADIAN BANC CAP SECS TR (ON)
Merged into Global Capital Securities Trust 02/04/2016
Each Class A Unit automatically became (0.968751) Class A Unit
Each Class F Unit automatically became (0.970716) Class F Unit
Global Capital Securities Trust name changed to Redwood Global Financials Income Fund 12/20/2017
(See Redwood Global Financials Income Fund)

CANADIAN BANC RECOVERY CORP (ON)
Class A no par split (1.18045988) for (1) by issuance of (0.18045988) additional share payable 01/17/2012 to holders of record 01/17/2012
Ex date - 01/13/2012
Name changed to Canadian Banc Corp. 01/27/2012

CANADIAN BK NT LTD (ON)
Merged into Arends Holdings Inc. 07/13/2004
Each share Common no par exchanged for $3.50 cash

CANADIAN BANK OF COMMERCE (TORONTO, ON)
Each share Capital Stock $100 par exchanged for (10) shares Capital Stock $10 par 00/00/1944
Merged into Canadian Imperial Bank of Commerce (Toronto, ON) 06/01/1961
Each share Capital Stock $10 par exchanged for (1) share Capital Stock $10 par

CANADIAN BANK STOCK TRUST SHARES SERIES D
Trust terminated 00/00/1932
Details not available

CANADIAN BANKSTOCKS, INC.
Liquidated 00/00/1930
Details not available

CANADIAN BARRANCA CORP. LTD (AB)
Name changed 08/26/1970
Name changed from Canadian Barranca Mines Ltd. to Canadian Barranca Corp. Ltd. 08/26/1970
Struck off register and declared dissolved for failure to file returns 02/01/1987

CANADIAN BASHAW LEDUC OIL & GAS LTD (AB)
Recapitalized as Erskine Resources Corp. 06/23/1987
Each share Capital Stock no par exchanged for (0.125) share Common no par
Erskine Resources Corp. acquired by Mark Resources Inc. 01/01/1989 which was acquired by EnerMark Income Fund 04/09/1996 which merged into Enerplus Resources Fund 06/22/2001 which reorganized as Enerplus Corp. 01/03/2011

CANADIAN BEAVER RES LTD (BC)
Struck off register and declared dissolved for failure to file returns 12/30/1994

CANADIAN BIOCEUTICAL CORP (ON)
Name changed to MPX Bioceutical Corp. 11/06/2017

CANADIAN BLACK RIV PETE LTD (ON)
Reorganized under the laws of Alberta as Uruguay Goldfields Inc. 02/13/1998
Each share Common no par exchanged for (0.04) share Common no par
Uruguay Goldfields Inc. reincorporated in Yukon as Uruguay Mineral Exploration Inc. 02/11/2002 which name changed to Orosur Mining Inc. 01/08/2010

CANADIAN BLACKHAWK ENERGY INC (AB)
Acquired by TM Energy Ltd. 02/19/2003
Each share Common no par exchanged for $0.01 cash

CANADIAN BLUE GOLD INC (NV)
Recapitalized as Boreal Water Collection, Inc. 03/19/2008
Each share Common 1¢ par exchanged for (0.00333333) share Common 1¢ par
(See Boreal Water Collection, Inc.)

CANADIAN BONANZA PETES LTD (AB)
Merged into Amalgamated Bonanza Petroleum Ltd. 04/15/1974
Each share Common no par exchanged for (0.5) share Capital Stock no par
(See Amalgamated Bonanza Petroleum Ltd.)

CANADIAN BREWERIES LTD.-LES BRASSERIES CANADIENNES LTEE. (ON)
Name changed to Carling O'Keefe Ltd.-Carling O'Keefe Ltee. 11/09/1973
(See Carling O'Keefe Ltd.-Carling O'Keefe Ltee.)

CANADIAN BREWERIES LTD (ON)
Each share Preference no par exchanged for (3) shares Common no par 00/00/1945
$1.25 Preferred called for redemption 04/04/1960
Common no par split (5) for (1) by issuance of (4) additional shares 03/19/1962
Name changed to Carling O'Keefe Ltd. 11/09/1973
(See Carling O'Keefe Ltd.)

CANADIAN BRIT ALUM CO (QC)
Merged into Canadian Reynolds Metals Co., Ltd.-Societe Canadienne De Metaux Reynolds, Ltee. 07/31/1970
Each share Class A no par exchanged for (1) share 40¢ Preferred $12.78 par
(See Canadian Reynolds Metals Co., Ltd.- Societe Canadienne De Metaux Reynolds, Ltee.)

CANADIAN BRITISH EMPIRE OIL CO. LTD. (AB)
Merged into Canadian Western Oil Co., Inc. 03/12/1958
Each share Common exchanged for (0.33333333) share Common
Canadian Western Oil Co., Inc. merged into Westates Petroleum Co. 12/24/1959 which assets were transferred to Westates Petroleum Co. Liquidating Trust 05/02/1977
(See Westates Petroleum Co. Liquidating Trust)

CANADIAN BRONZE CO., LTD. (CANADA)
Common no par split (2) for (1) by issuance of (1) additional share 00/00/1928
Common no par split (2) for (1) by issuance of (1) additional share 00/00/1948
Acquired by Canadian Aviation Electronics Ltd. 05/15/1963
Each share Common no par exchanged for $25 cash
5% Preferred $100 par called for redemption 04/27/1989
Public interest eliminated

CANADIAN CABLESYSTEMS LTD (CANADA)
Common no par reclassified as Conv. Class A Common no par 08/15/1977
Each share Conv. Class A Common no par exchanged for (2) shares Class A no par 06/28/1979
Each share Conv. Class B Common no par exchanged for (2) shares Class A no par 06/28/1979
Stock Dividend - In Class B Non-Vtg. 100% 08/05/1980
Name changed to Rogers Cablesystems Inc. 02/13/1981
Rogers Cablesystems Inc. name changed to Rogers Communications Inc. 04/24/1986

CANADIAN CANNERS LTD (CANADA)
Each share 7% Preferred exchanged for (0.5) share 6% 1st Preference $100 par and (4) shares 5% Conv. Preferred no par 00/00/1927
Each share Common $100 par exchanged for (6) shares Common no par 00/00/1927
Each share 6% 1st Preference $100 par exchanged for (5) shares 5% 1st Preference $20 par 00/00/1936
5% 1st Preference $20 par called for redemption 04/01/1950
5% Conv. Preferred no par called for redemption 12/11/1950
Each share Common no par exchanged for (1) share Class A Common no par and (2) shares Class B Common no par 10/26/1956
Each share Class A Common no par exchanged for $12 cash 01/28/1975
Each share Class B Common no par exchanged for (1) share Common no par 01/02/1978
99.7% owned by Del Monte Corp. as of 01/02/1978
Public interest eliminated

CANADIAN CAR & FOUNDRY CO. LTD. (CANADA)
Recapitalized 00/00/1929
Each share Preference $100 par exchanged for (4) shares Preference $25 par
Each share Ordinary $100 par exchanged for (4) shares Ordinary no par
Class A $20 par and Ordinary no par purchased by A.V. Roe (Canada) Ltd. at $30 per share 00/00/1955

CANADIAN CARIBOO RES LTD (BC)
Struck off register and declared dissolved for failure to file returns 02/03/1995

CANADIAN CASEY COBALT CO. LTD.
Liquidated 00/00/1936
Details not available

CANADIAN CELANESE LTD. (CANADA)
Each share 7% Preferred $100 par exchanged for (4) shares $1.75 Preferred $25 par and (0.5) share Common no par 00/00/1945
Stock Dividend - 300% 12/18/1948
Merged into Chemcell (1963) Ltd. 10/08/1964
Each share Common no par exchanged for (6) shares Common no par $1 and $1.75 Preferred $25 par exchanged share for share
Chemcell (1963) Ltd. name changed to Chemcell Ltd. - Chemcell Ltee. 06/01/1966 which name changed to

Celanese Canada Ltd.-Celanese Canada Ltee. 01/07/1972 which name changed to Celanese Canada Inc. 01/08/1980
(See Celanesa Canada Inc.)

CANADIAN CELLULOSE LTD (BC)
Acquired by British Columbia Resources Investment Corp. 08/28/1980
Each share Common no par exchanged for $15 cash

CANADIAN CHANNING VENTURE FUND LTD. (ON)
Name changed to IOS International Fund Ltd. 05/04/1970
IOS International Fund Ltd. name changed to Commonwealth International Venture Fund Ltd. 05/04/1971 which name changed to Eaton International Fund Ltd. 04/15/1974 which name changed to Eaton Bay International Fund Ltd. (ONT) 04/12/1978 which reincorporated in Canada 04/16/1980 which name changed back to Eaton International Fund 04/16/1986 which name changed to Viking International Fund Ltd. 04/16/1987 which name changed to Laurentian International Fund Ltd. 05/31/1993 which name changed to Strategic Value International Fund Ltd. 06/05/1997 which name changed to StrategicNova World Large Cap Fund Ltd. 09/26/2000
(See StrategicNova World Large Cap Fund Ltd.)

CANADIAN CHARCOAL PRODUCTS LTD. (ON)
Reported bankrupt in 06/00/1959
No stockholders' equity

CANADIAN CHEM LTD (AB)
Merged into Chemcell (1963) Ltd. 10/08/1963
Each share Common no par exchanged for (1) share Common no par
Chemcell (1963) Ltd. name changed to Chemcell Ltd.-Chemcell Ltee. 06/01/1966 which name changed to Celanese Canada Ltd.-Celanese Canada Ltee. 01/07/1972 which name changed to Celanese Canada Inc. 01/08/1980
(See Celanese Canada Inc.)

CANADIAN CHEM RECLAIMING LTD (AB)
Name changed to CCR Technologies Ltd. 01/21/2000
(See CCR Technologies Ltd.)

CANADIAN CHEMICAL & CELLULOSE CO. LTD. (CANADA)
Completely liquidated 08/20/1959
Each share Common no par exchanged for first and final distribution of (1) share Canadian Chemical Co., Ltd. Common no par and (1) share Columbia Cellulose Co. Ltd. Common no par
(See each company's listing)

CANADIAN CHIEFTAN PETROLEUMS LTD. (AB)
Acquired by British Canadian Holding Corp. Ltd. 02/00/1963
Each share Capital Stock no par exchanged for $1.325 cash

CANADIAN COLLIERIES (DUNSMUIR) LTD. (CANADA)
Recapitalized 00/00/1947
Each share Preference $10 par exchanged for (2) shares Capital Stock no par
Each share Ordinary $1 par exchanged for (0.03) share Capital Stock no par
Capital Stock no par changed to $3 par 00/00/1952
Capital Stock $3 par reclassified as Common $3 par 02/17/1956
Name changed to Canadian Collieries Resources Ltd. 01/24/1957
(See Canadian Collieries Resources Ltd.)

CANADIAN COLLIERIES RESOURCES LTD. (CANADA)
Each share 5% Preferred Ser. B, C, D, E, F and G $1 par exchanged for (0.05) share 5% Preferred $20 par 05/31/1963
Acquired by Weldwood of Canada Ltd. 11/20/1964
Each share Common $3 par exchanged for $13 cash
5% Preferred $20 par called for redemption 03/31/1966
Public interest eliminated

CANADIAN COLONIAL AIRWAYS, INC.
Name changed to Colonial Airlines, Inc. 00/00/1942
Colonial Airlines, Inc. acquired by Eastern Air Lines, Inc. 05/31/1956 which merged into Texas Air Corp. 11/25/1986
(See Texas Air Corp.)

CANADIAN COLONIAL AIRWAYS LTD. (CANADA)
Completely liquidated 03/01/1960
Each share Capital Stock no par exchanged for first and final distribution of $0.5834068 cash

CANADIAN COML BK (EDMONTON, AB)
Became insolvent 09/03/1985
No stockholders' equity

CANADIAN COMSTOCK EXPL LTD (BC)
Recapitalized as American Comstock Exploration Ltd. 06/07/1995
Each share Common no par exchanged for (0.25) share Common no par
American Comstock Exploration Ltd. recapitalized as International Comstock Exploration Ltd. 01/09/1998 which recapitalized as Secureview Systems Inc. 09/27/2001 which name changed to Global Immune Technologies Inc. (BC) 05/03/2005 which reincorporated in Wyoming 05/12/2006

CANADIAN CONIAURUM INVTS LTD (ON)
Name changed to MTS International Services Ltd. 03/01/1971
MTS International Services Ltd. name changed to MTS International Services Inc. (ON) 10/06/1971 which reincorporated in Canada as Epitek International Inc. 12/07/1981 which recapitalized as International Epitek Inc. 08/01/1987 which name changed to CompAS Electronics Inc. 07/29/1993 which was acquired by AIM Safety Co., Inc. 12/08/1997 which name changed to AimGlobal Technologies Co., Inc. 01/29/1999
(See AimGlobal Technologies Co., Inc.)

CANADIAN CONQUEST EXPL INC (AB)
Merged into Cypress Energy Inc. 05/10/1999
Each share Common no par exchanged for (0.162) share Class A Common no par
Cypress Energy Inc. merged into PrimeWest Energy Trust 05/29/2001
(See PrimeWest Energy Trust)

CANADIAN CONTL OIL CORP (BC)
Recapitalized as CBO Resources Corp. 03/25/1987
Each share Common no par exchanged for (0.25) share Common no par
(See CBO Resources Corp.)

CANADIAN CONV DEB FD (ON)
Name changed to First Asset Canadian Convertible Debenture Fund and Units reclassified as Class A Units 06/04/2012

CANADIAN CONV LIQUID UNIVERSE ETF (ON)
Name changed to First Asset Canadian Convertible Bond ETF 06/07/2012

CANADIAN CONVERTERS LTD (CANADA)
Each share Capital Stock $100 par exchanged for (4) shares Class A $20 par and (1) share Class B no par 00/00/1945
Placed in bankruptcy 08/27/1973
No stockholders' equity

CANADIAN CONVERTIBLES FD (ON)
Name changed to First Asset Canadian Convertibles Fund 12/21/2015

CANADIAN CONVERTIBLES INCOME PLUS FD (ON)
Name changed to Canadian Convertibles Plus Fund 04/14/2011

CANADIAN COOL CLEAR WTAA INC (FL)
Name changed 02/05/1999
Name changed from Canadian Cool Clear Water, Inc. to Canadian Cool Clear Wtaa, Inc. 02/05/1999
Name changed to WTAA International, Inc. 10/27/1999
WTAA International, Inc. name changed to Gravitas International, Inc. (FL) 12/06/2001 which reorganized in Nevada as Formcap Corp. 10/12/2007

CANADIAN CORPORATE MGMT LTD (CANADA)
5% Preferred $1,000 par called for redemption 07/01/1964
Common no par split (4) for (1) by issuance of (3) additional shares 04/24/1970
Common no par reclassified as Conv. Class A Common no par 12/17/1971
Each share Conv. Class A Common no par exchanged for (1) share Class X Common no par and (1) share Conv. Class Y Common no par 05/27/1980
Each share Conv. Class B Common no par exchanged for (1) share Class X Common no par and (1) share Conv. Class Y Common no par 05/27/1980
6% Preferred $10 par called for redemption 06/02/1986
Merged into Federal Industries Ltd. 06/11/1986
Each share Class X Common no par exchanged for (2) shares Conv. Class A Common no par
Each share Conv. Class Y Common no par exchanged for (2) shares Conv. Class A Common no par
Federal Industries Ltd. name changed to Russel Metals Inc. 06/01/1995

CANADIAN CREW ENERGY CORP (BC)
Name changed to Crew Development Corp. (BC) 03/21/1997
Crew Development Corp. (BC) reincorporated in Yukon 01/26/2000 which name changed to Crew Gold Corp. 01/26/2004
(See Crew Gold Corp.)

CANADIAN CRUDE SEPARATORS INC (AB)
Recapitalized as CCS Income Trust 05/24/2002
Each share Common no par exchanged for (1) Trust Unit
Note: Canadian residents had the option to elect to receive (1) CCS Inc. Exchangeable Share prior to 05/22/2002
(See CCS Income Trust)

CANADIAN CURTISS WRIGHT LTD (ON)
Recapitalized as Curtiss-Wright of Canada Inc. 06/03/1985
Each share Common no par exchanged for (0.2) shares Common no par
(See Curtiss-Wright of Canada Inc.)

CANADIAN DATA PRESV INC (BC)
Name changed to AXS Blockchain Solutions Inc. 06/11/2018
AXS Blockchain Solutions Inc. name changed to Litelink Technologies Inc. 08/21/2018

CANADIAN DECALTA GAS & OILS LTD. (CANADA)
Recapitalized as Western Decalta Petroleum Ltd. 11/22/1956
Each share Capital Stock $1 par exchanged for (0.5) share Capital Stock $1 par
(See Western Decalta Petroleum Ltd.)

CANADIAN DELHI OIL LTD (CANADA)
Common 10¢ par changed to no par 01/19/1965
Recapitalized as CanDel Oil Ltd. 01/10/1972
Each share Common no par exchanged for (0.5) share Common $3 par
(See CanDel Oil Ltd.)

CANADIAN DELHI PETROLEUM LTD. (CANADA)
Assets sold to Canadian Delhi Oil Ltd. 06/21/1957
Each share Capital Stock 10¢ par exchanged for (1) share Common 10¢ par
Canadian Delhi Oil Ltd. recapitalized as CanDel Oil Ltd. 01/10/1972
(See CanDel Oil Ltd.)

CANADIAN DENTAL PARTNERS INC (AB)
Name changed to International Health Partners Inc. 12/19/2000
International Health Partners Inc. name changed to Patient Home Monitoring Corp. (AB) 06/08/2010 which reincorporated in British Columbia 12/30/2013
(See Patient Home Monitoring Corp.)

CANADIAN DEPARTMENT STORES
Liquidated 00/00/1928
Details not available

CANADIAN DESTINATION PPTYS INC (AB)
Cease trade order effective 01/20/2003
Stockholders' equity unlikely

CANADIAN DEVONIAN PETROLEUMS LTD. (CANADA)
Under plan of merger name changed to Teck Corp. Ltd. 09/11/1963
Teck Corp. Ltd. name changed to Teck Corp. 11/21/1978 which name changed to Teck Cominco Ltd. 09/12/2001 which name changed to Teck Resources Ltd. 04/27/2009

CANADIAN DREDGE & DOCK CO. LTD. (CANADA)
Each share old Common no par exchanged for (4) shares new Common no par 00/00/1954
New Common no par split (3) for (2) by issuance of (0.5) additional share 07/13/1959
Name changed to CDRH Ltd. 07/07/1967
CDRH Ltd. name changed to Foodex Systems Ltd. 05/09/1972 which merged into Foodex Inc. 06/30/178 which merged into Dexleigh Corp. 06/30/1984
(See Dexleigh Corp.)

CANADIAN DYNO MINES LTD. (ON)
Merged into International Mogul Mines Ltd. 11/20/1968
Each share Capital Stock $1 par

exchanged for (0.149253) share Capital Stock no par
International Mogul Mines Ltd. merged into Conwest Exploration Co. Ltd. (Old) (ON) 08/27/1982 which merged into Conwest Exploration Co. Ltd. (New) (AB) 09/01/1993 which merged into Alberta Energy Co. Ltd. 01/31/1996 which merged into EnCana Corp. 01/03/2003

CANADIAN EAGLE EXPL INC (CANADA)
Struck from the register and dissolved 10/04/1993

CANADIAN EAGLE EXPLS LTD (BC)
Recapitalized as Eaglecrest Explorations Ltd. 02/01/1993
Each share Common no par exchanged for (0.25) share Common no par
Eaglecrest Explorations Ltd. name changed to Colombia Crest Gold Corp. 02/14/2011

CANADIAN EAGLE OIL & GAS LTD (BC)
Name changed to Lifestyle Beverage Corp. 04/09/1986
Lifestyle Beverage Corp. name changed to Australian Corporate Holdings Ltd. 10/23/1987

CANADIAN EAGLE OIL CO. LTD. (CANADA)
Each share Part. Preference no par exchanged for (1.1) shares Ordinary no par 04/01/1955
Stock Dividend - 25% 09/15/1955
Assets sold and each share Ordinary no par exchanged for (0.16666666) share Royal Dutch Petroleum Co. Ordinary 20 Guilders par and (0.25) share Shell Transport & Trading Co. Ltd. Ordinary £1 par 07/22/1959
(See each company's listing)

CANADIAN EDL COURSEWARE INC (BC)
Name changed to Can West Exploration Inc. 08/28/1997
Can West Exploration Inc. recapitalized as Watch Resources Ltd. (BC) 10/13/2000 which reincorporated in Alberta 07/20/2006 which recapitalized as Watch Resources Ltd. (New) 01/17/2007 which merged into Pearl Exploration & Production Ltd. 10/21/2007 which name changed to BlackPearl Resources Inc. 05/14/2009

CANADIAN 88 ENERGY CORP (CANADA)
Each share old Class A Common no par exchanged for (0.1) share new Class A Common no par 08/06/1991
New Class A Common no par reclassified as Common no par 09/08/1994
Each share Common no par received distribution of (0.19230769) share Prize Energy Inc. Common no par payable 01/14/2000 to holders of record 01/04/2000
Name changed to Esprit Exploration Ltd. 05/26/2003
(See Esprit Exploration Ltd.)

CANADIAN EMJAY PETROLEUMS LTD. (AB)
Recapitalized as Consolidated Emjay Petroleums Ltd. 07/31/1957
Each share Capital Stock no par exchanged for (0.2) share Capital Stock 50¢ par
Consolidated Emjay Petroleums Ltd. recapitalized as New Emjay Petroleums Ltd. 02/04/1966
(See New Emjay Petroleums Ltd.)

CANADIAN EMPIRE EXPLORATION CORP (BC)
Recapitalized as X-Terra Resources Corp. (BC) 02/23/2007
Each share Common no par exchanged for (0.1) share Common no par
X-Terra Resources Corp. (BC) reincorporated in Canada 09/04/2008 which name changed to Norvista Capital Corp. 07/03/2014

CANADIAN ENERGY CONV DEB FD (ON)
Units reclassified as Ser. A Units 07/08/2011
Name changed to First Asset Canadian Energy Convertible Debenture Fund 06/04/2012

CANADIAN ENERGY EXPL INC (AB)
Acquired by Standard Exploration Ltd. 10/22/2012
Each share Common no par exchanged for (0.13986) share Common no par
Note: Unexchanged certificates were cancelled and became without value 10/22/2014

CANADIAN ENERGY SVCS & TECHNOLOGY CORP (CANADA)
Common no par split (3) for (1) by issuance of (2) additional shares payable 07/18/2011 to holders of record 07/13/2011 Ex date - 07/11/2011
Common no par split (3) for (1) by issuance of (2) additional shares payable 07/23/2014 to holders of record 07/18/2014 Ex date - 07/24/2014
Name changed to CES Energy Solutions Corp. 06/20/2017

CANADIAN ENERGY SVCS L P (ON)
Merged into Canadian Energy Services & Technology Corp. 01/01/2010
Each Class A Common Ltd. Partnership Unit exchanged for (1) share Common no par
Note: Unexchanged certificates were cancelled and became without value 01/01/2016
Canadian Energy Services & Technology Corp. name changed to CES Energy Solutions Corp. 06/20/2017

CANADIAN ENERGY SVCS LTD (BC)
Name changed to Industra Service Corp. 07/10/1992
Industra Service Corp. merged into American Eco Corp. 01/02/1997
(See American Eco Corp.)

CANADIAN ENTECH RES INC (BC)
Recapitalized 03/31/1995
Recapitalized from Canadian Entech Research Corp. to Canadian Entech Resources Inc. 03/31/1995
Each share Common no par exchanged for (0.2) share Common no par
Name changed to H20 Entertainment Corp. 07/15/1996
H20 Entertainment Corp. recapitalized as Consolidated H2O Entertainment Corp. 07/14/2005 which name changed to Tri-River Ventures Inc. 07/30/2007

CANADIAN EQUIP RENT FD LTD PARTNERSHIP (AB)
Reorganized as CERF Inc. 10/03/2011
Each Unit of Ltd. Partnership Int. exchanged for (1) share Common no par
Note: Unexchanged certificates were cancelled and became without value 10/03/2014
CERF Inc. name changed to Canadian Equipment Rentals Corp. 06/27/2016 which name changed to Zedcor Energy Inc. 06/30/2017

CANADIAN EQUIP RENTALS CORP (AB)
Name changed to Zedcor Energy Inc. 06/30/2017

CANADIAN EQUITY & DEV LTD (ON)
Merged into Cadillac Fairview Corp. Ltd. 06/03/1974
Each share Common no par exchanged for (1.2) shares Common no par
(See Cadillac Fairview Corp. Ltd.)

CANADIAN EQUITY SHARES
Trust terminated and liquidated 00/00/1941
Details not available

CANADIAN ESTATE LD CORP (ON)
Name changed to Silversword Corp. 03/16/1988
(See Silversword Corp.)

CANADIAN EVEROCK EXPLORATIONS INC (ON)
Recapitalized as Everock Inc. (ON) 11/22/2002
Each share Common no par exchanged for (0.10526315) share Common no par
Everock Inc. (ON) reorganized in Nevada 12/12/2005

CANADIAN EXPLOSIVES LTD.
Name changed to Canadian Industries Ltd. (Old) 00/00/1927
Canadian Industries Ltd. (Old) recapitalized as Canadian Industries Ltd. and DuPont of Canada Securities Ltd. 06/30/1954
(See each company's listing)

CANADIAN EXPRESS LTD NEW (ON)
Recapitalized as BNN Investments Ltd. 11/02/2001
Each share Common no par exchanged for (0.1) share Common no par
BNN Investments Ltd. name changed to BAM Investments Corp. 07/05/2006 which name changed to Partners Value Fund Inc. 06/10/2013 which name changed to Partners Value Investments Inc. 05/25/2015 which reorganized as Partners Value Investments L.P. 07/04/2016

CANADIAN EXPRESS LTD OLD (ON)
Recapitalized as Consolidated Canadian Express Ltd. 12/24/1990
Each share Common no par exchanged for (0.05) share Common no par
Consolidated Canadian Express Ltd. name changed to Canadian Express Ltd. (New) 05/18/2001 which recapitalized as BNN Investments Ltd. 11/02/2001 which name changed to BAM Investments Corp. 07/05/2006 which name changed to Partners Value Fund Inc. 06/10/2013 which name changed to Partners Value Investments Inc. 05/25/2015 which reorganized as Partners Value Investments L.P. 07/04/2016

CANADIAN EXPT GAS & OIL LTD (AB)
Acquired by Canex Placer Ltd. 07/29/1977
Each share Common $0.16666666 par exchanged for $6.45 cash

CANADIAN EXPT GAS LTD (CANADA)
Merged into Canadian Export Gas & Oil Ltd. 06/12/1958
Each share Common exchanged for (2.5) shares Common $0.16666666 par
(See Canadian Export Gas & Oil Ltd.)

CANADIAN FAIRBANKS MORSE CO. LTD. (CANADA)
Common no par exchanged (3) for (1) 00/00/1952
Each share Common no par exchanged for (2) shares Class A Common 50¢ par and (1) share Class B Common no par 12/01/1959
Class A Common 50¢ par changed to no par 09/26/1960
Name changed to Morse (Robert) Corp. Ltd. 06/28/1963

(See Morse (Robert) Corp. Ltd.)

CANADIAN FARADAY CORP LTD (ON)
Merged into Consolidated Canadian Faraday Ltd. 05/04/1967
Each share Capital Stock no par exchanged for (1) share Capital Stock no par
Consolidated Canadian Faraday Ltd. name changed to Faraday Resources Inc. 08/02/1983 which merged into Conwest Exploration Co. Ltd. (New) (AB) 09/01/1993 which merged into Alberta Energy Co. Ltd. 01/31/1996 which merged into EnCana Corp. 01/03/2003

CANADIAN FD INC (MD)
Stock Dividend - 100% 03/01/1974
Merged into Alliance Global Fund 03/13/1987
Details not available

CANADIAN FERRITE CORP (BC)
Name changed 10/25/1984
Name changed from Canadian Ferrites Corp. to Canadian Ferrite Corp. 10/25/1984
Name changed to Maghemite Inc. 02/26/1986
(See Maghemite Inc.)

CANADIAN FIBER FOODS INC (BC)
Recapitalized as Red Engine Resources Corp. 08/19/1996
Each share Common no par exchanged for (0.22222222) share Common no par
Red Engine Resources Corp. reorganized as Red Engine Exploration Ltd. 06/09/1997 which merged into Canmine Resources Corp. 11/30/1998
(See Canmine Resources Corp.)

CANADIAN 50 ADVANTAGED PFD SH FD (ON)
Under plan of merger each Class A or Class F Unit automatically became (0.701142) or (0.735713) Redwood Canadian Preferred Share Fund ETF Unit respectively 12/22/2017
Redwood Canadian Preferred Share Fund name changed to Purpose Canadian Preferred Share Fund 06/18/2018

CANADIAN FINANCE & INVESTMENTS LTD. (MB)
Completely liquidated 01/30/1967
Each share Class A no par or Common no par exchanged for first and final distribution of (1) share British International Finance (Canada) Ltd. Class A Non-Cum. Part. no par
British International Finance (Canada) Ltd. name changed to BIF Corp. 08/15/1972 which name changed to York Centre Corp. 06/29/1978 which name changed to Georgian Bancorp Inc. 04/12/1995
(See Georgian Bancorp Inc.)

CANADIAN FINL DIVID & INCOME FD (ON)
Merged into Canadian Financial Income Fund 01/16/2007
Each Class A Unit received (0.902969) Unit
Canadian Financial Income Fund name changed to Claymore Canadian Financial Monthly Income ETF 04/11/2007 which name changed to iShares Canadian Financial Monthly Income Fund 03/29/2012 which name changed to iShares Canadian Financial Monthly Income ETF 10/18/2013

CANADIAN FINL HLDGS CORP (ON)
Recapitalized as Calderone Corp. 07/10/1998
Each share Common no par exchanged for (0.1) share Common no par
Calderone Corp. name changed to Cardinal Factor Corp. 07/21/2000

(See Cardinal Factor Corp.)

CANADIAN FINL INCOME FD (ON)
Name changed to Claymore Canadian Financial Monthly Income ETF 04/11/2007
Claymore Canadian Financial Monthly Income ETF name changed to iShares Canadian Financial Monthly Income Fund 03/29/2012 which name changed to iShares Canadian Financial Monthly Income ETF 10/18/2013

CANADIAN FINL SVCS NT CORP (ON)
Completely liquidated 12/01/2005
Each Preferred Share exchanged for first and final distribution of $15 cash
Each Capital Share exchanged for first and final distribution of $62.52452 cash

CANADIAN FINANCIALS & UTILS SPLIT CORP (ON)
Preferred Shares called for redemption at $10.0361 on 01/31/2012
Class A Shares called for redemption at $5.4248 on 01/31/2012

CANADIAN FIRST FINL GROUP INC (ON)
Acquired by Dundee Wealth Management Inc. 08/21/2002
Each share Common no par exchanged for $1.26 cash

CANADIAN FIRST MORTGAGE CORP. (ON)
Merged into Victoria & Grey Trust Co. (Stratford, ON) 10/31/1980
Each share Common $10 par exchanged for (2) shares Common $3 par
Victoria & Grey Trust Co. (Stratford, ON) merged into National Victoria & Grey Trust Co. (Toronto, ON) 08/31/1984 which name changed to National Trust Co. (Toronto, ON) 10/28/1985
(See National Trust Co. (Toronto, ON))

CANADIAN FNDTN LTD (CANADA)
6% Preferred Ser. A $20 par reclassified as $1.20 Preference no par 07/21/1980
Merged into Banister Continental, Ltd. 05/01/1989
Each share $1.20 Preference no par exchanged for (1) share Foundation Co. of Canada (New) $1.20 Preference no par
Each share Common no par exchanged for (1.3) shares Banister Continental, Ltd. Common no par
(See each company's listing)

CANADIAN FOOD PRODS LTD (ON)
Each share old Common no par exchanged for (2) shares Class A no par and (4) shares new Common no par 00/00/1945
Each share 4.5% Preference $100 par exchanged for (1) share 1st Preference $50 par, (1) share 2nd Preference $50 par and (2) shares new Common no par 11/29/1960
Each share Class A no par exchanged for (4) shares new Common no par 11/29/1960
Cease trade order effective 06/24/1981
Stockholders' equity unlikely

CANADIAN FOREMOST LTD (AB)
Old Common no par reclassified as new Common no par 06/02/1981
Each share new Common no par received distribution of (1) share Special Stock no par 06/12/1981
New Common no par reclassified as Class A no par 08/25/1983
Special Stock no par reclassified as Class B no par 08/25/1983
Each share Class A no par exchanged for (1) share Common no par 10/30/1992
Each share Class B no par exchanged for (1.05) shares Common no par 10/30/1992
Name changed to Foremost Industries Inc. 06/01/1994
(See Foremost Industries Inc.)

CANADIAN FORTUNE OILS LTD (AB)
Merged into Page Petroleum Ltd. 08/13/1971
Each share Capital Stock 10¢ par exchanged for (0.071428) share Common no par
(See Page Petroleum Ltd.)

CANADIAN FORTUNE RES INC NEW (AB)
Merged into Fortune Energy Inc. 09/01/1993
Each share Common no par exchanged for (0.51) share Common no par
(See Fortune Energy Inc.)

CANADIAN FORTUNE RES INC OLD (AB)
Merged into Consolidated Canadian Fortune Resources Inc. 12/07/1990
Each share Common no par exchanged for (0.5) share Common no par
Consolidated Canadian Fortune Resources Inc. name changed to Canadian Fortune Resources Inc. (New) 03/15/1993 which merged into Fortune Energy Inc. 09/01/1993
(See Fortune Energy Inc.)

CANADIAN FRACMASTER LTD (AB)
Name changed to Fracmaster Ltd. 05/14/1998
(See Fracmaster Ltd.)

CANADIAN FROBISHER RES LTD (AB)
Merged into Orbit Oil & Gas Ltd. 08/26/1994
Each share Common no par exchanged for (1.025) shares Common no par
(See Orbit Oil & Gas Ltd.)

CANADIAN FUNDAMENTAL 100 INCOME FD (ON)
Name changed to Claymore Canadian Fundamental 100 Monthly Income ETF 04/11/2007
Claymore Canadian Fundamental 100 Monthly Income ETF merged into Claymore Canadian Fundamental Index ETF 10/01/2007 which name changed to iShares Canadian Fundamental Index Fund 03/29/2012 which name changed to iShares Canadian Fundamental Index ETF 06/04/2014

CANADIAN FUTURITY OILS LTD (AB)
Recapitalized as Baca Resources Ltd. 08/04/1989
Each share Class A no par exchanged for (0.2) share Class A no par
Baca Resources Ltd. name changed to CORDEX Petroleums Ltd. 07/11/1994
(See CORDEX Petroleums Ltd.)

CANADIAN GAMES NETWORK INC (ON)
Recapitalized as Northquest Ventures Inc. 01/14/1987
Each share Common no par exchanged for (0.33333333) share Common no par
(See Northquest Ventures Inc.)

CANADIAN GAS & ENERGY FD LTD (ON)
Part. Preference 20¢ par changed to 4¢ par and (4) additional shares issued 07/30/1979
Part. Preference 4¢ par reclassified as Mutual Fund Shares no par 06/08/1984
Name changed to AGF Canadian Resources Fund Ltd. 11/22/1989

CANADIAN GAS & ENERGY INVESTMENTS LTD. (ON)
Name changed to Canadian Gas & Energy Fund Ltd. 07/31/1963
Canadian Gas & Energy Fund Ltd. name changed to AGF Canadian Resources Fund Ltd. 11/22/1989

CANADIAN GEARY MNG LTD (ON)
Common $1 par changed to no par 06/17/1971
Charter cancelled 02/20/1980

CANADIAN GEN CAP (DE)
9.125% Trust Originated Preferred Securities called for redemption at $25 on 03/31/2001

CANADIAN GENERAL ELECTRIC CO., LTD. (CANADA)
Each share Common $50 par exchanged for (40) shares Common no par 02/01/1962
Name changed to Canadian General Electric Co. Ltd.-Compagnie Generale Electrique du Canada Ltee. 07/02/1965
Canadian General Electric Co. Ltd.-Compagnie Generale Electrique du Canada Ltee. name changed to General Electric Canada Inc. 08/19/1987
(See General Electric Canada Inc.)

CANADIAN GEN ELEC LTD (CANADA)
Each share $1.25 Conv. Preferred $28 par exchanged for (1) share Common no par 11/15/1975
Preferred $50 par called for redemption 00/00/1983
Common no par split (6) for (1) by issuance of (5) additional shares 03/06/1987
Name changed to General Electric Canada Inc. 08/19/1987
(See General Electric Canada Inc.)

CANADIAN GENERAL INVESTMENT TRUST LTD.
Merged into Canadian General Investments, Ltd. 00/00/1931
Details not available

CANADIAN GEN INVTS LTD (ON)
5.4% Class A Preference Ser. 1 no par called for redemption at $25 plus $0.07767 accrued dividends on 10/06/2008
4.65% Class A Preference Ser. 2 no par called for redemption at $25 plus $0.23887 accrued dividends on 05/29/2013
3.9% Class A Preference Ser. 3 no par called for redemption at $25 plus $0.2324 accrued dividends on 06/10/2016
 (Additional Information in Active)

CANADIAN GEN LIFE INS CO (ON)
Acquired by Westbury Canadian Life Insurance Co. 00/00/2000
Details not available

CANADIAN GEN SECS LTD (CANADA)
Acquired by Central Capital Corp. 03/00/1988
Details not available

CANADIAN GIANT EXPL LTD (BC)
Delisted from Vancouver Stock Exchange 03/06/1995

CANADIAN GIFT SALES LTD. (ON)
Adjudicated bankrupt 07/13/1964
No stockholders' equity

CANADIAN GLACIER BEVERAGE CORP (BC)
Recapitalized as Glacier Ventures International Corp. (BC) 08/26/1997
Each share Common no par exchanged for (0.2) share Common no par
Glacier Ventures International Corp. (BC) reincorporated in Canada 09/20/1999 which merged into Glacier Ventures International Corp. (Canada) (New) 04/28/2000 which name changed to Glacier Media Inc. 07/01/2008

CANADIAN GOLD & METALS MINING CO. LTD. (ON)
Charter cancelled and company declared dissolved for default in filing returns 04/14/1966

CANADIAN GOLD HUNTER CORP (CANADA)
Reincorporated 07/29/2004
Place of incorporation changed from (BC) to (Canada) 07/29/2004
Name changed to NGEx Resources Inc. 09/22/2009

CANADIAN GOLD MINES LTD (MB)
Merged into Consolidated Canadian Fortune Resources Inc. 12/07/1990
Each share Common no par exchanged for (1) share Common no par
Consolidated Canadian Fortune Resources Inc. name changed to Canadian Fortune Resources Inc. (New) 03/15/1993 which merged into Fortune Energy Inc. 09/01/1993
(See Fortune Energy Inc.)

CANADIAN GOLD PLACERS LTD.
Bankrupt 00/00/1933
Details not available

CANADIAN GOLD RES INC (ON)
Recapitalized as Strategic Vista International Inc. 03/27/1997
Each share Common no par exchanged for (0.04) share Common no par
Strategic Vista International Inc. name changed to Lorex Technology Inc. 03/20/2006
(See Lorex Technology Inc.)

CANADIAN GOLDALE LTD (ON)
Common no par split (3) for (1) by issuance of (2) additional shares 06/10/1969
Name changed to Hambro Canada (1972) Ltd. 01/09/1973
Hambro Canada (1972) Ltd. name changed to Hambro Canada Ltd. 05/28/1974 which name changed to Hatleigh Corp. (Old) 08/03/1978 which merged into Hatleigh Corp. (New) 08/31/1978 which merged into Dexleigh Corp. 06/30/1984
(See Dexleigh Corp.)

CANADIAN GOLDEN DRAGON RES LTD (BC)
Name changed to Trillium North Minerals Ltd. 11/05/2007
Trillium North Minerals Ltd. recapitalized as White Metal Resources Corp. 06/04/2014

CANADIAN GRAPHITE LTD (BC)
Name changed to BFD Industries, Inc. (BC) 07/06/1989
BFD Industries, Inc. (BC) reincorporated in Delaware as Alpha Pro Tech, Ltd. 06/24/1994

CANADIAN GRIDOIL LTD (AB)
Merged into Ashland Oil Canada Ltd. 09/14/1970
Each share Common 45¢ par exchanged for (1) share Common 45¢ par
Ashland Oil Canada Ltd. name changed to Kaiser Petroleum Ltd. 03/23/1979
(See Kaiser Petroleum Ltd.)

CANADIAN GROWTH PORTFOLIO (BC)
Completely liquidated 12/31/1975
Details not available

CANADIAN GYPSUM LTD (CANADA)
Name changed to CGC Inc. 09/11/1987
(See CGC Inc.)

CANADIAN HEARING CARE INC (AB)
Name changed to Audiotech Healthcare Corp. (AB) 04/07/1998
Each share Common no par exchanged for (1) share Common no par
Audiotech Healthcare Corp. (AB) reincorporated in British Columbia 05/02/2008
(See Audiotech Healthcare Corp.)

CANADIAN HELICOPTERS GROUP INC (CANADA)
Name changed to HNZ Group Inc. 09/25/2012
(See HNZ Group Inc.)

CANADIAN HELICOPTERS INCOME FD (QC)
Under plan of reorganization each Unit no par automatically became (1) share Canadian Helicopters Group Inc. (Canada) Common no par 01/04/2011
Note: Non-Canadian residents received Variable Voting Shares
Canadian Helicopters Group Inc. name changed to HNZ Group Inc. 09/25/2012
(See HNZ Group Inc.)

CANADIAN HERITAGE BREWING LTD (BC)
Cease trade order effective 10/04/1989
Stockholders' equity unlikely

CANADIAN HIDROGAS RES LTD (BC)
Acquired by Norcen Energy Resources Ltd. 03/28/1980
Each share Capital Stock $1 par exchanged for $15.50 cash

CANADIAN HIGH CREST OILS LTD. (AB)
Recapitalized as Canadian Tricentrol Oils Ltd. 06/01/1966
Each share Common 20¢ par exchanged for (0.1) share Common $2 par
Canadian Tricentrol Oils Ltd. name changed to Tricentrol Canada Ltd. (AB) 05/05/1972 which reincorporated in Ontario as Tricentrol Canada Ltd. (Old) 11/28/1972 which merged into Tricentrol Canada Ltd. (ON) (New) 12/28/1972
(See Tricentrol Canada Ltd. (ON))

CANADIAN HIGH YIELD FOCUS FD (ON)
Trust terminated 06/27/2016
Each Unit received net asset value

CANADIAN HOLLY MINERALS CORP (DE)
Name changed to Natural Resource & Land Development Corp. 07/14/1969
(See Natural Resource & Land Development Corp.)

CANADIAN HOME SHOPPING NETWORK CHSN LTD (CANADA)
Merged into Rogers Communications Inc. 09/01/1993
Each share Common no par exchanged for $0.895 cash

CANADIAN HOMESTEAD OILS LTD (AB)
6% Preferred $10 par called for redemption 12/30/1976
Merged into Inter-City Gas Corp. (MB) 04/14/1980
Each share Common 10¢ par exchanged for (1.4) shares Common no par
Inter-City Gas Corp. (MB) reorganized as Inter-City Products Corp. 04/18/1990

CANADIAN HOTEL INCOME PPTYS REAL ESTATE INVT TR (BC)
Each Instalment Receipt exchanged for (1) Unit 06/25/1998
Merged into British Columbia Investment Management Corp. 10/04/2007
Each Unit exchanged for $19.10 cash

CANADIAN HUNTER EXPL LTD (AB)
Acquired by Burlington Acquisition Corp. 12/11/2001
Each share Common no par exchanged for $53 cash

CANADIAN HUSKY OIL LTD. (CANADA)
Name changed to Husky Oil Canada Ltd. 05/13/1963
Husky Oil Canada Ltd. name changed to Husky Oil Ltd. 09/03/1968
(See Husky Oil Ltd.)

CANADIAN HYDRO DEVELOPERS INC (AB)
Acquired by TransAlta Corp. 11/09/2009
Each share Common no par exchanged for $5.25 cash

CANADIAN HYDRO-ELECTRIC CORP. LTD.
Acquired under Plan of Recapitalization by Gatineau Power Co. 00/00/1937
Each share First Preferred exchanged for (1) share 5% Preferred $100 par and (1.5) shares new Common no par
Each share Second Preferred exchanged for (5.27608) shares new Common no par
Each share old Common exchanged for (0.12) share new Common no par
Gatineau Power Co. name changed to Gatineau Powers Co.-Compagnie D'Electricite Gatineau 05/04/1962
(See Gatineau Powers Co.-Compagnie D-Electricite Gatineau)

CANADIAN HYDROCARBONS LTD (CANADA)
Common no par split (2) for (1) by issuance of (1) additional share 12/29/1967
Common no par split (2) for (1) by issuance of (1) additional share 08/15/1969
Merged into Inter-City Gas Ltd. (MB) 02/28/1979
Each share Common no par exchanged for (1.5) shares Common no par
(See Inter-City Gas Ltd. (MB))
5.5% Preferred Ser. A $20 par called for redemption 12/31/1987
Inter-City Gas Ltd. (MB) reincorporated in (Canada) 06/05/1992 which name changed to International Comfort Products Corp. (Canada) 07/09/1997
(See International Comfort Products Corp. (Canada))

CANADIAN ICE MACHINE CO., LTD. (CANADA)
Name changed to Cimco Ltd. 06/30/1967
(See Cimco Ltd.)

CANADIAN IMPERIAL BK COMM (TORONTO, ON)
$2.05 Conv. Class B Preferred Ser. 1 no par called for redemption 01/24/1986
$2.50 Class A Preferred Ser. 1 no par called for redemption 08/20/1986
$3.5625 Class A Preferred Ser. 2 no par called for redemption 02/16/1987
Adjustable Rate Class A Preferred Ser. 3 no par called for redemption 02/28/1992
Adjustable Rate Class A Preferred Ser. 6 no par called for redemption 00/00/1994
Adjustable Dividend Preferred Class A Ser. 8 no par called for redemption 02/20/1995
Adjustable Dividend Preferred Class A Ser. 10 no par called for redemption 12/02/1996
Adjustable Dividend Preferred Class A Ser. 11 no par called for redemption 12/02/1996
Adjustable Rate Preferred Class A Ser. 4 no par called for redemption at $100 on 10/31/1997
Floating Rate Preferred Class A Ser. 5 no par called for redemption at $25 on 10/31/1997
Adjustable Rate Preferred Class A Ser. 9 no par called for redemption at $26 plus $0.56875 accrued dividend on 04/30/1998
Adjustable Dividend Preferred Class A Ser. 12 no par called for redemption 10/31/2000
Adjustable Dividend Preferred Class A Ser. 13 no par called for redemption 10/31/2000
$0.371875 Preferred Class A Ser. 14 no par called for redemption at $26 on 07/31/2003
Adjustable Dividend Preferred Class A Ser. 15 no par called for redemption at $25 on 08/03/2004
Adjustable Dividend Preferred Class A Ser. 16 no par called for redemption at U.S. $25.50 on 10/29/2004
Adjustable Dividend Preferred Class A Ser. 17 no par called for redemption at $25.50 on 10/29/2004
Class A Preferred Ser. 21 no par called for redemption at $26 plus $0.008152 accured dividends on 08/02/2005
Class A Preferred Ser. 22 no par called for redemption at $26 plus $0.008492 accured dividends on 08/02/2005
Class A Adjustable Rate Preferred Ser. 20 no par called for redemption at $25.50 plus $0.321875 accrued dividends on 10/31/2005
Class A Preferred Ser. 24 no par called for redemption at $26 on 01/31/2007
Class A Preferred Ser. 25 no par called for redemption at $26 on 07/31/2007
Class A Preferred Ser. 19 no par called for redemption at $25.45 plus $0.309375 accrued dividends on 10/31/2010
Class A Preferred Ser. 23 no par called for redemption at $25 plus $0.331250 accrued dividends on 10/31/2010
Class A Preferred Ser. 28 no par called for redemption at $10 plus $0.02 accrued dividends on 04/28/2011
Class A Preferred Ser. 30 no par called for redemption at $25.75 on 07/31/2011
Class A Preferred Ser. 31 no par called for redemption at $26 on 01/31/2012
Class A Preferred Ser. 32 no par called for redemption at $26 plus $0.28125 accrued dividends on 04/30/2012
Class A Preferred Ser. 18 no par called for redemption at $25 plus $0.33811 accrued dividends on 10/29/2012
Non-Cum. Rate Reset Class A Preferred Ser. 35 no par called for redemption at $25 on 04/30/2014
Non-Cum. Rate Reset Class A Preferred Ser. 33 no par called for redemption at $25 on 07/31/2014
Rate Reset Class A Preferred Ser. 37 no par called for redemption at $25 on 07/31/2014
Class A Preferred Ser. 26 no par called for redemption at $25 on 10/31/2014
Class A Preferred Ser. 27 no par called for redemption at $25 on 01/31/2015
Non-Cum. Class A Preferred Ser. 29 no par called for redemption at $25 on 04/30/2015
(Additional Information in Active)

CANADIAN IMPERIAL GINSENG PRODS LTD (BC)
Each share old Common no par exchanged for (0.1) share new Common no par 10/02/1995
Name changed to Imperial Ginseng Products Ltd. 12/04/1995

CANADIAN IMPERIAL MINES INC (BC)
Recapitalized as Pacific Imperial Mines Inc. 12/15/1994
Each share Common no par exchanged for (0.4) share Common no par

CANADIAN INCOME MGMT TR (AB)
Trust terminated 09/07/2012
Each Trust Unit received $1.79 cash

CANADIAN INDUSTRIAL ALCOHOL CO., LTD. (CANADA)
Name changed to Corby (H.) Distillery Ltd. 00/00/1950
Corby (H.) Distillery Ltd. name changed to Corby Distilleries Ltd. - Les Distilleries Corby Ltee. 01/24/1969 which name changed to Corby Spirit & Wine Ltd. 11/12/2013

CANADIAN INDL GAS & OIL LTD (AB)
Each share old Common no par exchanged for (3) shares new Common no par 04/07/1969
5.5% Preferred $10 par called for redemption 09/30/1973
Merged into Norcen Energy Resources Ltd. (AB) 10/28/1975
Each share new Common no par exchanged for (0.7) share Common no par
Norcen Energy Resources Ltd. (AB) reincorporated in Canada 04/15/1977
(See Norcen Energy Resources Ltd.)

CANADIAN INDUSTRIAL GAS LTD. (ON)
Capital Stock $2.50 par reclassified as Common no par 06/07/1963
Merged into Canadian Industrial Gas & Oil Ltd. 05/31/1965
Each share 5.5% Conv. Preference $10 par exchanged for (1) share Preferred $10 par
Each share Common no par exchanged for (1) share Common no par
Canadian Industrial Gas & Oil Ltd. merged into Norcen Energy Resources Ltd. (AB) 10/28/1975 which reincorporated in Canada 04/15/1977 which merged into Union Pacific Resources Group Inc. 04/17/1998 which merged into Anadarko Petroleum Corp. 07/14/2000

CANADIAN INDL MINERALS CORP (AB)
Reincorporated 01/20/1995
Place of incorporation changed from (BC) to (AB) 01/20/1995
Merged into Abacan Resource Corp. (New) 02/10/1995
Each share Common no par exchanged for (0.51) share Common no par
(See Abacan Resource Corp. (New))

CANADIAN INDUSTRIES LTD. NEW (CANADA)
Name changed 12/30/1955
Name changed from Canadian Industries (1954) Ltd. to Canadian Industries Ltd. (New) 12/30/1955
Name changed to C-I-L Inc. 01/02/1980
(See C-I-L Inc.)

CANADIAN INDUSTRIES LTD. OLD (CANADA)
Each share Class A or B Common no

par exchanged for (10) shares Common no par 07/11/1946
Recapitalized as Canadian Industries (1954) Ltd. and DuPont of Canada Securities Ltd. 06/30/1954
Each share 7% Preferred $100 par exchanged for (1) share 7.5% Preferred $50 par in each of the new companies
Each share Common no par exchanged for (1.1) shares Common no par in each of the new companies
(See each company's listing)

CANADIAN INGERSOLL-RAND CO., LTD. (CANADA)
Common no par split (3) for (1) by issuance of (2) additional shares 08/31/1956
Through purchase offer 100% acquired by Ingersoll-Rand Co. (NJ) as of 02/00/1962
Public interest eliminated

CANADIAN INSULOCK CORP (BC)
Recapitalized as American Insulock Inc. 09/05/1995
Each share Common no par exchanged for (0.25) share Common no par
American Insulock Inc. name changed to Lexicon Building Systems Ltd. 04/27/2011

CANADIAN INTERNATIONAL GROWTH FUND LTD. (CANADA)
Reincorporated under the laws of Maryland as Channing International Growth Fund, Inc. and Common $1 par changed to 1¢ par 05/15/1964
Channing International Growth Fund, Inc. acquired by Channing Shares, Inc. (DE) 08/30/1966 which reincorporated in Maryland 10/09/1973 which merged into American General Shares, Inc. 09/02/1975 which merged into American General Enterprise Fund, Inc. 08/31/1979 which name changed to American Capital Enterprise Fund, Inc. (MD) 09/09/1983 which reincorporated in Delaware as Van Kampen American Capital Enterprise Fund 08/03/1995 which name changed to Van Kampen Enterprise Fund 08/31/1998

CANADIAN INTL INVT TR LTD (CANADA)
Common $20 par changed to no par 00/00/1932
Name changed to CIIT Inc. 06/30/1980
(See CIIT Inc.)

CANADIAN INTL LP (MB)
Plan of arrangement effective 01/01/2009
Each Class B Unit exchanged for (1) share CI Financial Corp. Common no par

CANADIAN INTL MINERALS INC (BC)
Each share old Common no par exchanged for (0.1) share new Common no par 02/10/2014
Each share new Common no par exchanged again for (0.05) share new Common no par 11/15/2017
Name changed to Canadian Energy Materials Corp. 04/12/2018

CANADIAN INTERNATIONAL POWER CO. LTD. LIQUIDATING TRUST (CANADA)
Each Trust Unit received sixth distribution of $0.10 cash 01/21/1980
Each Trust Unit received seventh distribution of $0.08 cash 01/21/1981
Each Trust Unit received eighth distribution of $0.18 cash 11/02/1981
Each Trust Unit received ninth distribution of $0.17 cash 07/30/1982
Note: Amount or number of additional distributions, if any, are not available
(See Canadian International Power Co. Ltd. for previous distribution)

CANADIAN INTL PWR LTD (CANADA)
6% Preferred $50 par called for redemption 01/05/1966
5.2% Preferred 1965 Ser. $20 par called for redemption 07/29/1977
Common no par split (5) for (4) by issuance of (0.25) additional share 07/10/1968
Common no par split (2) for (1) by issuance of (1) additional share 07/07/1972
Common no par reclassified as Conv. Class A Common no par 08/19/1975
In process of liquidation
Each share Conv. Class A Common no par or Conv. Class B Common no par received initial distribution of (0.5) share Compania Boliviana de Energia Electrica S.A.-Bolivian Power Co., Ltd. Common $100 par and (0.5) Compania de Alumbrado Electrico de San Salvador ADR for Common Colones 10 par 10/03/1977
(See each company's listing)
Each share Conv. Class A Common no par or Conv. Class B Common no par received second distribution of $20 cash 11/03/1977
Each share Conv. Class A Common no par received third distribution of $0.60 cash 06/29/1978
Each share Conv. Class B Common no par received third distribution of $0.51 cash 06/29/1978
Each share Conv. Class A Common no par received fourth distribution of $0.75 cash 01/15/1979
Each share Conv. Class B Common no par received fourth distribution of $0.75 cash 01/15/1979
Each share Conv. Class A Common no par received fifth distribution of $0.25 cash 04/30/1979
Each share Conv. Class B Common no par received fifth distribution of $0.25 cash 04/30/1979
Assets transferred to Canadian International Power Co. Ltd. Liquidating Trust 04/30/1979
(See Canadian International Power Co. Ltd. Liquidating Trust for additional distributions)

CANADIAN INTERNATIONAL TRUSTEE SHARES
Trust terminated 00/00/1955 and final liquidation payment made 06/04/1956
Details not available

CANADIAN INTERURBAN PPTYS LTD (ON)
Merged into Campeau Corp. 10/09/1973
Each share 7% Preference Ser. A $10 par exchanged for (1) share 7% 1st Conv. Preference $10 par
Each share Common no par exchanged for (1) share 3rd Preference $4.50 par
(See Campeau Corp.)

CANADIAN INVT FD LTD (CANADA)
Special Stock $1 par changed to $0.3333333 par and (2) additional shares issued 05/08/1964
Under plan of reorganization each Special Share $0.3333333 par automatically became (1) Spectrum United Canadian Investment Fund Share of Bene. Int. $0.3333333 par 10/31/1996

CANADIAN INVESTORS CORP. LTD.
Liquidated 00/00/1950
Details not available

CANADIAN JAMIESON MINES LTD (ON)
Name changed to Unicorp Financial Inc. 11/30/1972
Unicorp Financial Inc. merged into Unicorp Financial Corp. 07/11/1974 which name changed to Unicorp Canada Corp. 07/13/1982 which recapitalized as Unicorp Energy Corp. 06/25/1991 which name changed to Unicorp Inc. 05/28/1999 which name changed to Wilmington Capital Management Inc. 03/08/2002

CANADIAN JAVELIN FOUNDRIES & MACHINE WORKS LTD. (CANADA)
Name changed to Canadian Javelin Ltd. 04/00/1954
Canadian Javelin Ltd. name changed to Javelin International Ltd. 08/18/1981 which recapitalized as Nalcap Holdings Inc. 10/06/1987 which recapitalized as Arbatax International Inc. (Canada) 03/28/1996 which reincorporated in Yukon 08/06/1996 which name changed to MFC Bancorp Ltd. (YT) 03/03/1997 which reincorporated in British Columbia 11/03/2004 which name changed to KHD Humboldt Wedag International Ltd. 11/01/2005 which reorganized as Terra Nova Royalty Corp. 03/30/2010 which name changed to MFC Industrial Ltd. 09/30/2011 which name changed to MFC Bancorp Ltd. (BC) 02/16/2016
(See MFC Bancorp Ltd. (BC))

CANADIAN JAVELIN LTD (CANADA)
Name changed to Javelin International Ltd. 08/18/1981
Javelin International Ltd. recapitalized as Nalcap Holdings Inc. 10/06/1987 which recapitalized as Arbatax International Inc. (Canada) 03/28/1996 which reincorporated in Yukon 08/06/1996 which name changed to MFC Bancorp Ltd. (YT) 03/03/1997 which reincorporated in British Columbia 11/03/2004 which name changed to KHD Humboldt Wedag International Ltd. 11/01/2005 which reorganized as Terra Nova Royalty Corp. 03/30/2010 which name changed to MFC Industrial Ltd. 09/30/2011 which name changed to MFC Bancorp Ltd. 02/16/2016
(See MFC Bancorp Ltd. (BC))

CANADIAN JOREX LTD (CANADA)
Reincorporated 10/30/1984
Place of incorporation changed from (ON) to (Canada) 10/30/1984
Merged into Cypress Energy Inc. 09/17/1996
Each share Common no par exchanged for $0.72 cash

CANADIAN KEELEY MINES LTD (ON)
Reorganized under the laws of Canada as Keeley-Frontier Resources Ltd. 07/22/1981
Each share Capital Stock no par exchanged for (0.14285714) share Common no par and (0.14285714) Common Stock Purchase Warrant expiring 02/14/1982
Keeley-Frontier Resources Ltd. merged into Jamie Frontier Resources Inc. 02/15/1984
(See Jamie Frontier Resources Inc.)

CANADIAN KINETICS CORP (AB)
Struck from the register and dissolved 06/01/1995

CANADIAN KIRKLAND MINES LTD.
Succeeded by Amalgamated Kirkland Mines Ltd. on a (1) for (10) basis 00/00/1939
Amalgamated Kirkland Mines Ltd. merged into Mayfield Explorations & Developments Ltd. 06/21/1971 which merged into Microsolve Computer Capital Inc. 02/11/1998 which name changed to Homebank Technologies Inc. 12/20/2000 which name changed to Selient Inc. 06/15/2005
(See Selient Inc.)

CANADIAN KODIAK REFINERIES LTD. (AB)
Recapitalized as Kodiak Petroleums Ltd. 02/13/1963
Each share Capital Stock no par exchanged for (0.33333333) share Common no par
Kodiak Petroleums Ltd. was acquired by Manhattan Continental Development Corp. 10/02/1969
(See Manhattan Continental Development Corp.)

CANADIAN LEADER ENERGY INC (AB)
Merged into Centurion Energy International Inc. 05/20/1997
Each share Common no par exchanged for (0.5) share Common no par
(See Centurion Energy International Inc.)

CANADIAN LENCOURT MINES LTD (QC)
Capital Stock $1 par changed to no par 00/00/1983
Recapitalized as Lencourt Ltd./Lencourt Ltee. 05/22/1987
Each share Capital Stock no par exchanged for (0.2) share Common no par
(See Lencourt Ltd./Lencourt Ltee.)

CANADIAN LIBERTY DEV CORP (BC)
Struck off register and declared dissolved for failure to file returns 03/01/1996

CANADIAN LIGHT & POWER CO. (QC)
Liquidation completed
Each share Common received initial distribution of $20 cash 10/00/1949
Each share Common received second distribution of $5 cash 04/00/1951
Each share Common received third and final distribution of $1.67 cash 04/00/1954
Note: Certificates were not required to be surrendered and are without value

CANADIAN LITHIUM MINING CORP. LTD. (ON)
Merged into Augustus Exploration Ltd. 11/26/1958
Each share Capital Stock $1 par exchanged for (0.22222222) share Capital Stock $1 par
Augustus Exploration Ltd. merged into Consolidated Canadian Faraday Ltd. 05/04/1967 which name changed to Faraday Resources Inc. 08/02/1983 which merged into Conwest Exploration Co. Ltd. (New) (AB) 09/01/1993 which merged into Alberta Energy Co. Ltd. 01/31/1996 which merged into EnCana Corp. 01/03/2003

CANADIAN LOCOMOTIVE CO. LTD. (CANADA)
Recapitalized 00/00/1932
Each share 7% Preference $100 par exchanged for (1) share old Common no par
Each share Ordinary $100 par exchanged for (0.2) share old Common no par
Each share old Common no par exchanged for (4) shares new Common no par 00/00/1944
Name changed to Fairbanks Morse (Canada) Ltd. 07/26/1965
(See Fairbanks Morse (Canada) Ltd.)

CANADIAN LONG IS PETES LTD (AB)
Recapitalized as First Calgary Petroleums Ltd. 08/15/1979
Each share Common no par exchanged for (0.5) share Common no par
(See First Calgary Petroleums Ltd.)

CANADIAN LONGHORN PETE CORP (BC)
Name changed to Canadian Ferrites Corp. 08/01/1984
Canadian Ferrites Corp. name changed to Canadian Ferrite Corp. 10/25/1984 which name changed to Maghemite Inc. 02/26/1986
(See Maghemite Inc.)

CANADIAN LORRAIN SILVER MINES LTD.
Liquidated 00/00/1931
No stockholders' equity

CANADIAN LYNX PETE LTD (BC)
Reincorporated under the laws of Canada as Tanganyika Oil Co. Ltd. 09/19/1995
(See Tanganyika Oil Co. Ltd.)

CANADIAN MAGNESITE MINES LTD (ON)
Capital Stock $1 par changed to no par 05/03/1971
Name changed to EQ Resources Ltd. (ON) 08/19/1989
EQ Resources Ltd. (ON) reorganized in Delaware as Teton Petroleum Co. 11/23/1998 which name changed to Teton Energy Corp. 07/01/2005
(See Teton Energy Corp.)

CANADIAN MAJESTIC RES LTD (AB)
Merged into Chancellor Energy Resources Inc. 12/05/1988
Each share Common no par exchanged for (0.68965517) share Common no par
Chancellor Energy Resources Inc. merged into HCO Energy Ltd. 04/02/1996 which merged into Pinnacle Resources Ltd. (New) 10/20/1997 which merged into Renaissance Energy Ltd. 07/16/1998 which merged into Husky Energy Inc. 08/25/2000

CANADIAN MALARTIC GOLD MINES LTD (CANADA)
Merged into Canray Resources Ltd. 12/21/1976
Each share Capital Stock no par exchanged for (0.25) share Common no par
Canray Resources Ltd. recapitalized as Exall Resources Ltd. 12/09/1983 which merged into Gold Eagle Mines Ltd. 12/27/2006 which was acquired by Goldcorp Inc. 09/25/2008

CANADIAN MANOIR INDS LTD (CANADA)
Class A Preferred 10¢ par called for redemption 06/29/1972
6% Preferred 10¢ par called for redemption 12/29/1972
(Additional Information in Active)

CANADIAN MAPLE LEAF FINL CORP (CANADA)
Each share old Class A Common no par exchanged for (0.2) share new Class A Common no par 09/14/1994
New Class A Common no par reclassified as Common no par 01/29/1997
Name changed to CML Global Capital Ltd. 10/26/1999
(See CML Global Capital Ltd.)

CANADIAN MARCONI CO (CANADA)
Capital Stock $1 par changed to no par 05/14/1981
Capital Stock no par split (4) for (1) by issuance of (3) additional shares 09/14/1983
Name changed to BAE Systems Canada Inc. 02/08/2000
(See BAE Systems Canada Inc.)

CANADIAN MATACHEWAN LTD.
Acquired by Matachewan Consolidated Mines Ltd. 00/00/1933
Details not available

CANADIAN MAUSOLEUMS LTD. (CANADA)
Deemed not to be a subsisting company by the Dominion Secretary of State 01/17/1957

CANADIAN MED LABORATORIES LTD (ON)
Name changed to CML HealthCare Inc. (Old) 03/28/2003
(See CML HealthCare Inc. (Old))

CANADIAN MED LEGACY CORP (BC)
Name changed to Continental Home Healthcare Ltd. 10/16/1998

CANADIAN MEDIA ARTS CAP CORP (AB)
Recapitalized as CMA Capital Corp. (AB) 04/19/1990
Each share Common no par exchanged for (0.5) share Common no par
CMA Capital Corp. (AB) reincorporated in Canada 05/05/1995
(See CMA Capital Corp.)

CANADIAN MEM SVCS LTD (ON)
Name changed to Arbor Capital Resources Inc./Arbor Ressources Financieres Inc. 05/01/1975
Arbor Capital Resources Inc./Arbor Ressources Financieres Inc. name changed to Arbor Capital Inc. 05/15/1986 which name changed to Arbor Memorial Services Inc. 03/31/1994
(See Arbor Memorial Services Inc.)

CANADIAN MERRILL LTD (QC)
Merged into Francana Oil & Gas Ltd. 03/31/1980
Each share Capital Stock no par exchanged for (1.9) shares Common no par
Francana Oil & Gas Ltd. acquired by Sceptre Resources Ltd. 05/14/1982 which merged into Canadian Natural Resources Ltd. 08/15/1996

CANADIAN METALS EXPL LTD (BC)
Name changed to Hard Creek Nickel Corp. 06/28/2004
Hard Creek Nickel Corp. recapitalized as Giga Metals Corp. 08/28/2017

CANADIAN METALS SYNDICATE, INC. (NV)
Recapitalized as South Comstock Corp. 02/16/1970
Each share Common 25¢ par exchanged for (2.5) shares Common 10¢ par
South Comstock Corp. name changed to Comstock Industries, Inc. (NV) 08/18/1983 which reincorporated in Florida 07/21/2000
(See Comstock Industries, Inc.)

CANADIAN MICROCOOL CORP (BC)
Name changed to EI Environmental Engineering Concepts Ltd. 07/19/1990
(See EI Environmental Engineering Concepts Ltd.)

CANADIAN MINEFINDERS LTD. (ON)
Merged into Twentieth Century Explorations Ltd. (QC) 09/12/1969
Each share Capital Stock $1 par exchanged for (1) share Capital Stock no par
Twentieth Century Explorations Ltd. (QC) reincorporated in Ontario as Twentieth Century Explorations Inc. 03/01/1975 which recapitalized as Minefinders Corp. Ltd. 04/26/1979 which merged into Pan American Silver Corp. 04/02/2012

CANADIAN MINERAL CORP (BC)
Recapitalized as Canadian-United Minerals Inc. 07/14/1983
Each share Common no par exchanged for (0.2) share Common no par
Canadian-United Minerals Inc. recapitalized as Mansfield Minerals Inc. 09/10/1990 which name changed to Goldrock Mines Corp. 01/22/2013 which merged into Fortuna Silver Mines Inc. 07/28/2016

CANADIAN MINERAL DEVELOPMENT CO., LTD. (AZ)
Charter revoked for failure to file reports and pay fees 06/04/1952

CANADIAN MINERALS INC (CO)
Name changed to Continental Power Systems, Inc. 06/11/1986
(See Continental Power Systems, Inc.)

CANADIAN MINERALS 1960 LTD (AB)
Name changed to Canadian Minerals & Resources Ltd. 08/20/1970

CANADIAN MNG CO INC (AB)
Each share old Common no par exchanged for (0.16666666) share new Common no par 03/30/2015
Reincorporated under the laws of British Columbia as Canadian Zeolite Corp. 02/08/2016
Canadian Zeolite Corp. name changed to International Zeolite Corp. 03/06/2018

CANADIAN MNG CORP (BC)
Name changed to Chemesis International Inc. 07/18/2018

CANADIAN MNG LTD (AB)
Name changed to Zeo-Tech Enviro Corp. 05/19/2000
Zeo-Tech Enviro Corp. name changed to Canadian Mining Co. Inc. (AB) 02/08/2007 which reincorporated in British Columbia as Canadian Zeolite Corp. 02/08/2016 which name changed to International Zeolite Corp. 03/06/2018

CANADIAN MNG RES INC (AB)
Recapitalized as Axia Multimedia Corp. 06/28/1995
Each share Common no par exchanged for (0.5) share Common no par
Axia Multimedia Corp. name changed to Axia NetMedia Corp. 10/15/1998
(See Axia NetMedia Corp.)

CANADIAN MR BUILD INDS INC (BC)
Name changed to Socal Capital Corp. 02/18/1992
Socal Capital Corp. name changed to Empyrean Diagnostics Ltd. (BC) 08/05/1993 which reincorporated in Wyoming 12/31/1996 which name changed to Empyrean Bioscience, Inc. (WY) 02/08/1999 which reincorporated in Delaware 03/21/2001
(See Empyrean Bioscience, Inc. (DE))

CANADIAN MONO MINES INC (BC)
Delisted from Vancouver Stock Exchange 05/09/1994

CANADIAN MOTION PICTURE PRODUCTIONS, LTD. (ON)
Charter revoked for failure to file reports and pay taxes 02/10/1958

CANADIAN MTN MINERALS LTD (AB)
Merged into Cantex Mine Development Corp. 04/09/1998
Each share Common no par exchanged for (0.16666666) share Common no par

CANADIAN NAT GAS INDEX ETF (ON)
Trust terminated 03/23/2018
Each Class A Unit received $3.77 cash

CANADIAN NAT RES LTD (AB)
Incorporated 11/07/1973
Reincorporated 01/06/1982
Place of incorporation changed from (BC) to (AB) 01/06/1982
Each share 8.5% Conv. Preferred Ser. A Preferred Ser. A $20 par exchanged for (0.1) share Common no par 09/09/1988
(Additional Information in Active)

CANADIAN NATIONAL BANK (MONTREAL, QUE)
See - Banque Canadienne Nationale (Montreal, Que.)

CANADIAN NATIONAL FIRE INSURANCE CO.
In process of liquidation 00/00/1932
Details not available

CANADIAN NATL RY CO (CANADA)
Each 1st Installment Receipt exchanged for (1) share Common no par 11/26/1996
(Additional Information in Active)

CANADIAN NATURAL RESOURCES LTD. (BC)
Incorporated 00/00/1929
Name changed to AEX Minerals Corp. 11/07/1973
AEX Minerals Corp. name changed to Canadian Natural Resources Ltd. (BC) 12/16/1975 which reincorporated in Alberta 01/06/1982

CANADIAN NEWNORTH RES LTD (ON)
Charter cancelled 11/26/1994

CANADIAN NEWSCOPE RES LTD (CANADA)
Name changed to Newscope Resources Ltd. 07/11/1994
Newscope Resources Ltd. name changed to Denbury Resources Inc. (Canada) 12/21/1995 which reincorporated in Delaware 04/21/1999

CANADIAN NISTO MINES LTD (ON)
Charter cancelled for failure to pay taxes and file returns 03/16/1976

CANADIAN NORTH INCA MINES LTD (ON)
Recapitalized as Southmark Petroleum Ltd. 11/20/1968
Each share Capital Stock $1 par exchanged for (1) share Common $1 par
(See Southmark Petroleum Ltd.)

CANADIAN NORTHCOR ENERGY INC (AB)
Merged into Purcell Energy Ltd. (Old) 11/19/1993
Each share Class A Common no par exchanged for (1) share Common no par
Purcell Energy Ltd. (Old) recapitalized as Purcell Energy Ltd. (New) 03/07/1997
(See Purcell Energy Ltd. (New))

CANADIAN NORTHN LITES INC (TX)
Reorganized under the laws of Nevada as Leopard Capital, Inc. 12/01/2000
Each share Common $0.001 par exchanged for (0.04) share Common $0.001 par
Leopard Capital, Inc. name changed to China Expert Technology, Inc. 03/29/2004
(See China Expert Technology, Inc.)

CANADIAN NORTHSTAR CORP (AB)
Reorganized as First Chicago Investment Corp. 12/07/2001
Each share Common no par exchanged for (1) Dividend Share no par, (1) Subordinate Share no par and (0.25) Multiple Share no par
First Chicago Investment Corp. name changed to Graystone Corp. 02/25/2004 which merged into Pyxis Capital Inc. 02/27/2006
(See Pyxis Capital Inc.)

CAN-CAN

FINANCIAL INFORMATION, INC.

CANADIAN NORTHWEST MINES & OILS LTD. (ON)
Charter cancelled and declared dissolved for default in filing returns 01/10/1968

CANADIAN OCCIDENTAL PETE LTD (CANADA)
Common $1 par changed to $0.33333333 par and (2) additional shares issued 11/23/1979
Common $0.33333333 par changed to no par 06/04/1980
10% Class A Preferred 1st Ser. $25 par called for redemption 10/01/1985
Common no par split (2) for (1) by issuance of (1) additional share 10/02/1987
Common no par split (2) for (1) by issuance of (1) additional share payable 06/03/1996 to holders of record 05/28/1996 Ex date - 06/03/1996
Name changed to Nexen Inc. 11/02/2000
(See Nexen Inc.)

CANADIAN OIL & GAS RESERVES LTD. (AB)
Recapitalized as Canadusa Oil & Gas Reserves Ltd. 03/21/1956
Each share Common exchanged for (0.2) share Common
Canadusa Oil & Gas Reserves Ltd. merged into Titan Petroleum Corp. Ltd. 03/11/1957
(See Titan Petroleum Corp. Ltd.)

CANADIAN OIL CO. LTD. (ON)
8% Class A Preference $100 par all acquired by Shell Canada Ltd. through purchase offer as of 00/00/1964
Public interest eliminated

CANADIAN OIL COMPANIES LTD. (ON)
Each share Common $100 par exchanged for (6) shares Common no par 00/00/1927
Each share Common no par exchanged for (2) shares Common no par 00/00/1945
Each share Common no par exchanged for (2) shares Common no par 00/00/1952
Merged into Canadian Oil Co. Ltd. 01/31/1963
Each share 8% Preference $100 par exchanged for (1) share 8% Class A Preference $100 par
Each share Common no par exchanged for (1) share 6% Class B Preference $52 par plus a warrant to purchase Shell Canada Ltd. Class B Common no par to 09/30/1972
Class B Preference was not issued but was called 03/11/1963, so that upon presentation holders will receive the Class B Preference redemption price

CANADIAN OIL SANDS LTD (AB)
Merged into Suncor Energy Inc. (New) 03/23/2016
Each share Common no par exchanged for (0.28) share Common no par
Note: Unexchanged certificates will be cancelled and become without value 03/23/2021

CANADIAN OIL SANDS TR NEW (AB)
Units split (5) for (1) by issuance of (4) additional shares payable 05/07/2006 to holders of record 05/03/2006 Ex date - 05/01/2006
Reorganized as Canadian Oil Sands Ltd. 01/06/2011
Each Unit exchanged for (1) share Common no par
Note: Unexchanged certificates were cancelled and became without value 01/06/2017
Canadian Oil Sands Ltd. merged into Suncor Energy Inc. (New) 03/23/2016

CANADIAN OIL SANDS TR OLD (AB)
Merged into Canadian Oil Sands Trust (New) 07/05/2001
Each Trust Unit exchanged for (1) Unit
Canadian Oil Sands Trust (New) reorganized as Canadian Oil Sands Ltd. 01/06/2011 which merged into Suncor Energy Inc. (New) 03/23/2016

CANADIAN OILFIELD SOLUTIONS CORP (AB)
Name changed to Divergent Energy Services Corp. 06/09/2014

CDN OILFIELD TECHNOLOGIES & SOLUTIONS CORP (AB)
Name changed to Canadian Oilfield Solutions Corp. 10/17/2012
Canadian Oilfield Solutions Corp. name changed to Divergent Energy Services Corp. 06/09/2014

CANADIAN OREBODIES INC (AB)
Reincorporated under the laws of Ontario 07/21/2008

CANADIAN ORIENTAL HLDGS LTD (ON)
Name changed to Canalite Ltd. 12/20/1974
(See Canalite Ltd.)

CANADIAN OVERSEAS EXPL CORP (CANADA)
Reincorporated 05/26/1992
Place of incorporation changed from (BC) to (Canada) 05/26/1992
Charter dissolved 12/13/2004

CANADIAN PAC ENTERPRISES LTD (CANADA)
Common no par split (2) for (1) by issuance of (1) additional share 06/13/1980
4.75% Preferred Ser. A no par called for redemption 07/16/1980
Merged into Canadian Pacific Ltd. (Old) 12/06/1985
Each share Common no par exchanged for (1.675) shares Ordinary Stock no par
Canadian Pacific Ltd. (Old) reorganized as Canadian Pacific Ltd. (New) 07/03/1996 which recapitalized as Fairmont Hotels & Resorts Inc. 10/01/2001

CANADIAN PAC FOREST PRODS LTD (CANADA)
Reincorporated 01/01/1989
Place of incorporation changed from (ON) to (Canada) 01/01/1989
Name changed to Avenor Inc. 03/21/1994
(See Avenor Inc.)

CANADIAN PAC INVTS LTD (CANADA)
Name changed to Canadian Pacific Investments Ltd.-Investissements Canedien Pacifique Ltee. 06/12/1974
Canadian Pacific Investments Ltd.-Investissements Canedien Pacifique Ltee. name changed to Canadian Pacific Enterprises Ltd.-Les Entreprises Canedien Pacifique Ltee. 05/26/1980 which merged into Canadian Pacific Ltd. (Old) 12/06/1985 which reorganized as Canadian Pacific Ltd. (New) 07/03/1996 which recapitalized as Fairmont Hotels & Resorts Inc. 10/01/2001

CANADIAN PAC LTD NEW (CANADA)
Common no par split (2) for (1) by issuance of (1) additional share payable 09/27/1999 to holders of record 09/23/1999
Plan of arrangement effective 10/01/2001
Each share Common no par received distribution of (0.25) share CP Ships Ltd. Common no par, (0.5) share Canadian Pacific Railway Ltd. Common no par, (0.25) share Fairmont Hotels & Resorts Inc. Common no par, (0.166) share Fording Inc. Common no par, and (0.684) share PanCanadian Energy Corp. Common no par payable 10/9/2001 to holders of record 10/5/2001
Note: Certificates were not required to be surrendered and are without value
(See each Company's listing)

CANADIAN PAC LTD OLD (CANADA)
Each share Ordinary Stock $25 par exchanged for (5) shares Ordinary $5 par 10/01/1971
4% Preference £1 par changed to no par 05/02/1984
4% Canadian Dollar Preference $3 par changed to no par 05/02/1984
Ordinary Stock $5 par changed to no par 05/02/1984
4% Non-Cum. Preference no par reclassified as 4% Sterling Preference no par 05/10/1984
4% Non-Cum. Canadian Dollar Preference no par reclassified as 4% Canadian Dollar Preference no par 05/10/1984
7.25% Preferred Ser. A $10 par called for redemption 03/29/1985
4% Sterling Preference no par split (3) for (1) by issuance of (2) additional shares 06/07/1985
4% Canadian Dollar Preference no par split (3) for (1) by issuance of (2) additional shares 06/07/1985
Ordinary Stock no par split (3) for (1) by issuance of (2) additional shares 06/07/1985
Each share 4% Sterling Preference no par exchanged for (0.2345765) share Ordinary Stock no par 07/03/1996
Each share 4% Canadian Dollar Preference no par exchanged for (0.2345765) share Ordinary Stock no par 07/03/1996
Reorganized as Canadian Pacific Ltd. (New) 07/03/1996
Each share Ordinary Stock no par exchanged for (1) share Common no par
(See Canadian Pacific Ltd. (New))

CANADIAN PAC RY CO (CANADA)
Each share Ordinary $100 par exchanged for (4) shares Ordinary $25 par 00/00/1930
Name changed to Canadian Pacific Ltd. (Old) 07/05/1971
Canadian Pacific Ltd. (Old) reorganized as Canadian Pacific Ltd. (New) 07/03/1996
(See Canadian Pacific Ltd. (New))

CANADIAN PACER PETE CORP (BC)
Name changed to Providence Innovations Inc. 10/30/1989
Providence Innovations Inc. recapitalized as Providence Industries Inc. 10/04/1991 which merged into Gold City Mining Corp. 12/07/1994 which recapitalized as Consolidated Gold City Mining Corp. 10/24/1997 which recapitalized as Gold City Industries Ltd. (BC) 08/26/1998 which reincorporated in Manitoba 06/21/2005 which merged into San Gold Corp. 07/07/2005
(See San Gold Corp.)

CANADIAN PACIFIC INVESTMENTS LTD.- INVESTISSEMENTS CANADIEN PACIFIQUE LTEE. (CANADA)
4.75% Preferred Ser. A $20 par changed to no par 04/30/1979
Name changed to Canadian Pacific Enterprises Ltd.-Les Entreprises Canedien Pacifique Ltee. 05/26/1980
Canadian Pacific Enterprises Ltd.-Les Entreprises Canadien Pacifique Ltee. merged into Canadian Pacific Ltd.- Canadien Pacifique Ltee. 12/06/1985

CANADIAN PACIFIC LUMBER LTD. (AB)
Adjudicated bankrupt 06/14/1955
No stockholders' equity

CANADIAN PALMER STENDEL OIL CORP. (DE)
Name changed to Progas of Canada, Inc. 10/30/1953
(See Progas of Canada, Inc.)

CANADIAN PANDORA GOLD MINES LTD.
Assets acquired by Pandora Cadillac Gold Mines Ltd. 00/00/1936
Each share Common exchanged for (0.33333333) share Common
(See Pandora Cadillac Gold Mines Ltd.)

CANADIAN PAPERBOARD CO., LTD.
Reorganized as Canadian Paperboard Ltd. 00/00/1934
Details not available

CANADIAN PAPERBOARD LTD.
Liquidation approved 00/00/1940
Details not available

CANADIAN PATRICIA EXPL LTD (ON)
Recapitalized as In-Flight Phone Canada Inc. 04/30/1993
Each share Common no par exchanged for (0.09803921) share Common no par
In-Flight Phone Canada Inc. name changed to Normex Technologies Corp. 09/30/1996 which recapitalized as Cygnal Technologies Corp. 04/07/1998
(See Cygnal Technologies Corp.)

CANADIAN PAWNEE OIL CORP (BC)
Recapitalized as Britannia Gold Corp. 11/07/1989
Each share Common no par exchanged for (0.1) share Common no par
Britannia Gold Corp. recapitalized as Britannia Minerals Corp. 06/14/1999 which name changed to Nanotek Inc. 08/07/2001 which name changed to Minterra Resource Corp. 10/25/2002
(See Minterra Resource Corp.)

CANADIAN PETROFINA LTD (CANADA)
6% Non-Cum. Participating Preference $10 par reclassified as Common $10 par 08/12/1964
Name changed to Petrofina Canada Ltd. 08/01/1968
Petrofina Canada Ltd. name changed to Petrofina Canada Inc. 09/26/1979 which name changed to Petro-Canada Enterprises Inc./Entreprises Petro-Canada Inc. 11/16/1981
(See Petro-Canada Enterprises Inc./Entreprises Petro-Canada Inc.)

CANADIAN PHOENIX RES CORP (AB)
Each share old Common no par exchanged for (0.04) share new Common no par 11/18/2009
Each share new Common no par exchanged for (1) share Class A Common no par and (0.5985) share Renegade Petroleum Ltd. Common no par 12/20/2012
Note: Unexchanged certificates were cancelled and became without value 12/18/2015
Recapitalized as Knol Resources Corp. 03/11/2013
Each share Class A Common no par exchanged for (0.1) share Class A Common no par

CANADIAN PIONEER ENERGY INC (AB)
Each share 1st Preference Ser. A $10

par converted into (250) shares Class A Common no par 01/04/1991
Each share 2nd Preference Ser. A $10 par converted into (22) shares Class A Common no par 01/04/1991
Each share old Class A Common no par exchanged for (0.1) share new Class A Common no par 07/10/1992
Acquired by Cimarron Petroleum Ltd. 12/20/1995
Cimarron Petroleum Ltd. merged into Newport Petroleum Corp. 04/09/1997
(See Newport Petroleum Corp.)
Each (32.34) shares new Class A Common no par exchanged for (1) share Common no par

CANADIAN PIONEER MGMT LTD (CANADA)
Recapitalized as Pioneer Lifeco Inc. 08/18/1987
Each share Common no par exchanged for (0.1) share Common no par
Pioneer Lifeco Inc. name changed to Wokingham Capital Corp. 07/27/1992 which name changed to Coniston Capital Corp. 07/18/1994 which name changed to CPL Ventures Ltd. 08/08/1996 which recapitalized as Manfrey Capital Corp. 11/11/1996
(See Manfrey Capital Corp.)

CANADIAN PIONEER OILS LTD (AB)
Recapitalized as Canadian Pioneer Energy Inc. 10/26/1987
Each share Conv. 2nd Preference Ser. A $10 par automatically became (1) share Conv. 2nd Preference Ser. A $10 par
Each share Class A Common no par exchanged for (0.25) share Class A Common no par
Canadian Pioneer Energy Inc. acquired by Cimarron Petroleum Ltd. 12/20/1995 which merged into Newport Petroleum Corp. 04/09/1997
(See Newport Petroleum Corp.)

CANADIAN PIPE LINES PRODUCERS LTD. (BC)
Acquired by Canadian Pipelines & Petroleums Ltd. 00/00/1954
Each share Capital Stock $1 par exchanged for (1) share Capital Stock $1 par
Canadian Pipelines & Petroleums Ltd. merged into Scurry-Rainbow Oil Ltd. 05/09/1957 which was acquired by Home Oil Co. Ltd. (New) 11/08/1993 which merged into Anderson Exploration Ltd. 09/07/1995
(See Anderson Exploration Ltd.)

CANADIAN PIPELINES & PETROLEUMS LTD. (AB)
Merged into Scurry-Rainbow Oil Ltd. 05/09/1957
Each share Capital Stock $1 par exchanged for (1) share Capital Stock 50¢ par
Scurry-Rainbow Oil Ltd. acquired by Home Oil Co. Ltd. (New) 11/08/1993 which merged into Anderson Exploration Ltd. 09/07/1995
(See Anderson Exploration Ltd.)

CANADIAN PLATINUM REFINERIES INC (AB)
Struck off register for failure to file annual returns 10/01/1988

CANADIAN POWER & PAPER INVESTMENTS, LTD.
Acquired by Canadian Power & Paper Securities Ltd. 00/00/1952
Each share $5 Preferred no par exchanged for $57.50 cash
Each share Common no par exchanged for (1) share Common no par
Canadian Power & Paper Securities Ltd. merged into Warnock Hersey International Ltd. 07/02/1968 which

name changed to TIW Industries Ltd.-Les Industries TIW Ltee. 12/31/1977
(See TIW Industries Ltd.-Les Industries Ltee.)

CANADIAN POWER & PAPER SECURITIES LTD. (CANADA)
Merged into Warnock Hersey International Ltd. 07/02/1968
Each share $1.30 Preferred Ser. A $25 par exchanged for (1) share $1.50 Preferred Ser. A $25 par
Each share Common no par exchanged for (2) shares Common no par
Warnock Hersey International Ltd. name changed to TIW Industries Ltd.-Les Industries TIW Ltee. 12/31/1977
(See TIW Industries Ltd.-Les Industries TIW Ltee.)

CANADIAN PREM RES CORP (BC)
Merged into Mahogany Minerals Resources Inc. (New) 07/07/1987
Each share Common no par exchanged for (1) share Class B Subordinate no par
Mahogany Minerals Resources Inc. (New) recapitalized as International Mahogany Corp. 09/08/1988 which recapitalized as Reliant Ventures Ltd. 06/06/2000 which name changed to Esperanza Silver Corp. 05/14/2003 which name changed to Esperanza Resources Corp. 07/19/2010

CANADIAN PREM SELECT INCOME FD (ON)
Combined Units separated 12/07/2011
Merged into Harvest Canadian Income & Growth Fund 11/25/2013
Each Trust Unit received (0.8531) Ser. R Unit

CANADIAN PROGRAMMING CONCEPTS LTD (YUKON)
Name changed to GST Global Telecommunications Inc. 10/01/1996
GST Global Telecommunications Inc. name changed to Global Light Telecommunications Inc. 10/28/1998
(See Global Light Telecommunications Inc.)

CANADIAN PROPANE LTD. (AB)
Acquired by Canadian Hydrocarbons Ltd. 02/06/1961
Each share Capital Stock $1 par exchanged for $10 cash

CANADIAN PROSPECT LTD (AB)
Each share Common $1 par exchanged for (3) shares Common $0.33333333 par 00/00/1952
Each share Common $0.33333333 par exchanged for (2) shares Common $0.16666666 par 08/22/1955
Under plan of merger name changed to Canadian Export Gas & Oil Ltd. 06/12/1958
(See Canadian Export Gas & Oil Ltd.)

CANADIAN PUB VENTURE CAP I INC (AB)
Reincorporated under the laws of Canada as NordTech Aerospace Inc. 06/25/2004
NordTech Aerospace Inc. name changed to ExelTech Aerospace Inc. 04/19/2005
(See ExelTech Aerospace Inc.)

CANADIAN PUB VENTURE EQUITIES I INC (AB)
Reorganized under the laws of Ontario as Vanguard Response Systems Inc. 11/24/2003
Each share Common no par exchanged for (0.33333333) share Common no par
Vanguard Response Systems Inc. name changed to Allen-Vanguard Corp. 03/25/2005
(See Allen-Vanguard Corp.)

CANADIAN PUBLIC SERVICE CORP. LTD.
Liquidated 00/00/1938
Details not available

CANADIAN PUB VENTURE FIN 1 INC (AB)
Reorganized under the laws of Canada as Extenway Solutions Inc. 09/28/2005
Each share Common no par exchanged for (1) share Common no par
(See Extenway Solutions Inc.)

CANADIAN PUGET SOUND LMBR & TIMBER LTD (BC)
Preference $10 par changed to $1 par and (9) additional shares issued 06/06/1963
Common $10 par reclassified as Class B Common $1 par and (9) additional shares issued 06/06/1963
Preference $1 par called for redemption 11/20/1980
Merged into Puget Sound Holdings Ltd. 12/31/1980
Each share Class B Common $1 par exchanged for $8 cash
Each share Class D Common $1 par exchanged for $8 cash

CANADIAN RAIL & HARBOR TERMINALS LTD.
Property sold 00/00/1936
No stockholders' equity

CANADIAN REAL ESTATE INVT TR (ON)
Merged into Choice Properties Real Estate Investment Trust 05/07/2018
Each Trust Unit exchanged for $53.75 cash
Note: Unexchanged certificates will be cancelled and become without value 05/07/2024

CANADIAN REALTY CO. OF CANADA LTD.
Liquidation completed 12/05/1956
No stockholders' equity

CANADIAN RLTY INVS (ON)
Each Trust Unit exchanged for (0.225) share Crown Trust Co. 14.5% Preference Ser. B $20 par and $2 cash 04/29/1982

CANADIAN REFRACTORIES LTD (CANADA)
Merged into Dresser Industries Canada Ltd. 09/01/1971
Each share Common no par exchanged for $22 cash

CANADIAN REIT INCOME FD (ON)
Under plan of merger each Unit automatically became (0.7811) First Asset Canadian REIT Income Fund Class A Unit 10/01/2013
First Asset Canadian REIT Income Fund name changed to First Asset Canadian REIT ETF 07/14/2015

CANADIAN RESV GOLD CORP (BC)
Recapitalized as Christina Gold Resources Ltd. 04/18/1996
Each share Common no par exchanged for (0.2) share Common no par
Christina Gold Resources Ltd. recapitalized as PowerHouse Energy Corp. 12/11/1998 which recapitalized as International Powerhouse Energy Corp. 09/18/2001 which name changed to Sea Breeze Power Corp. 07/30/2003

CANADIAN RESOURCE OPPORTUNITIES INC (AB)
Merged into LHS Management Ltd. 12/30/2002
Each share Common no par exchanged for $0.10 cash

CANADIAN RES HSE LTD (BC)
Name changed to Nu Energy Uranium Corp. 01/26/2007
Nu Energy Uranium Corp. merged into Mega Uranium Ltd. 08/14/2007

CANADIAN RES INCOME TR II (ON)
Reorganized as Canadian Resources Income Trust 04/07/2002
Each Trust Unit no par exchanged for (1.1693) Units no par

CANADIAN RESV OIL & GAS LTD (AB)
Merged into Getty Oil Co. 07/29/1983
Each share Capital Stock $1 par exchanged for $26 cash

CANADIAN REYNOLDS METALS LTD (QC)
40¢ Preferred $12.78 par called for redemption 09/30/1980
Public interest eliminated

CANADIAN ROCKY MTN PPTYS INC (CANADA)
Reincorporated 07/00/2002
Place of incorporation changed from (AB) to (Canada) 07/00/2002
Acquired by Parkbridge L.P. 02/03/2004
Each share Common no par exchanged for $2 cash

CANADIAN ROXANA RES LTD (BC)
Delisted from Vancouver Stock Exchange 05/18/1995

CANADIAN ROXY PETE LTD (AB)
Merged into Numac Energy Inc. 04/01/1994
Each share Common no par exchanged for (0.634) share Common no par
(See Numac Energy Inc.)

CANADIAN ROYALTIES INC (CANADA)
Reincorporated 11/27/2002
Place of incorporation changed from (AB) to (Canada) 11/27/2002
Merged into Jilin Jien Nickel Industry Co., Ltd. 01/13/2010
Each share Common no par exchanged for $0.80 cash

CANADIAN SALT CO. LTD.
Capital Stock $100 par split (3) for (2) by issuance of (1) additional share 00/00/1920
Acquired by Canadian Industries, Ltd. (Old) 00/00/1928
Each share Capital Stock $100 par exchanged for $250 cash

CANADIAN SALT CO. LTD. (CANADA)
Capital Stock no par split (3) for (1) by issuance of (2) additional shares 11/20/1961
Name changed to Canadian Salt Co. Ltd.- La Societe Canadienne de Sel Ltee. 04/18/1966
(See Canadian Salt Co. Ltd.-La Societe Canadienne de Sel Ltee.)

CANADIAN SALT LTD (CANADA)
Common no par split (3) for (1) by issuance of (2) additional shares 02/09/1968
Common no par reclassified as Conv. Class A Common no par 06/09/1976
Under plan of merger each share Conv. Class A Common no par and Conv. Class B Common no par received $20 cash respectively 11/11/1977
Note: Certificates were not required to be surrendered and are without value
Preferred no par called for redemption 12/22/1977
Public interest eliminated

CANADIAN SATELLITE COMMUNICATIONS INC (CANADA)
Common no par split (2) for (1) by issuance of (1) additional share payable 03/28/2000 to holders of record 03/23/2000
Acquired by Shaw Communications Inc. 04/02/2001
Each share Common no par exchanged for (0.9) share Non-Vtg. Class B no par and $0.01 cash

CANADIAN SATELLITE RADIO HLDGS INC (ON)
Name changed to Sirius XM Canada Holdings Inc. 01/17/2013
(See Sirius XM Canada Holdings Inc.)

CANADIAN SCENIC OILS LTD (AB)
Merged into Conventures Ltd. 06/25/1973
Each share Common no par exchanged for (0.33333333) share Common no par
Conventures Ltd. merged into Oakwood Petroleums Ltd. 07/30/1985 which was acquired by Sceptre Resources Ltd. 03/14/1989 which merged into Canadian Natural Resources Ltd. 08/15/1996

CANADIAN SCOTIA LTD. (NS)
Acquired by Code Oil & Gas Ltd. 00/00/1958
Each share Capital Stock exchanged for (1.5) share Capital Stock
(See Code Oils & Gas Ltd.)

CANADIAN SCUDDER INVT FD LTD (CANADA)
Common $1 par changed to 25¢ par and (3) additional shares issued 08/18/1972
Merged into Bolton, Tremblay, Equity Fund Ltd.-Fonds d'Actions Bolton, Tremblay, Ltee. 07/02/1975
Each share Common 25¢ par exchanged for (0.7835049) Mutual Fund Share no par
Bolton, Tremblay, Equity Fund Ltd.-Fonds d'Actions Bolton, Tremblay, Ltee. merged into Planned Resources Fund Ltd.-Fonds de Planification des Ressources Ltee. 07/26/1978

CANADIAN SEC MGMT LTD (ON)
Merged into A.G.F. Management Ltd.-La Societe de Gestion A.G.F. Ltee. 07/31/1976
Each share Class A $1 par exchanged for (0.142857) share Class B Preference no par
A.G.F. Management Ltd.-La Societe de Gestion A.G.F. Ltee. name changed to AGF Management Ltd. 12/23/1994

CANADIAN SECURITY UNDERWRITERS GROWTH FUND LTD. (ON)
Name changed to Canadian Security Growth Fund Ltd. 04/18/1966

CANADIAN SECURITY UNDERWRITERS LTD. (ON)
Name changed to Canadian Security Management Ltd. 05/03/1966
Canadian Security Management Ltd. merged into A.G.F. Management Ltd.-La Societe De Gestion A.G.F. Ltee. 07/31/1976 which name changed to AGF Management Ltd. 12/23/1994

CANADIAN SHEET GALVANIZERS (1962) LTD. (CANADA)
Ceased operations and charter surrendered 03/00/1974
No stockholders' equity

CANADIAN SHEET GALVANIZERS LTD. (CANADA)
Name changed to Canadian Sheet Galvanizers (1962) Ltd. 11/01/1962
(See Canadian Sheet Galvanizers (1962) Ltd.)

CANADIAN SHIELD FUND (ON)
Combined Units separated 12/10/2009
Under plan of reorganization each Unit automatically became (1) Mackenzie Universal Canadian Shield Fund Ser. B Unit 07/08/2011

CANADIAN SHIELD RES INC (ON)
Recapitalized as Canadian Shield Resources Ltd. 03/12/2009
Each share Common no par exchanged for (0.05) share Common no par
Canadian Shield Resources Ltd. name changed to Estrella Gold Corp. 08/06/2010 which merged into Alianza Minerals Ltd. 04/30/2015

CANADIAN SHIELD RES LTD (ON)
Name changed to Estrella Gold Corp. 08/06/2010
Estrella Gold Corp. merged into Alianza Minerals Ltd. 04/30/2015

CANADIAN SILICA CORP. LTD. (ON)
Merged into Industrial Minerals of Canada Ltd. 06/30/1965
Each share Common no par exchanged for (0.0909091) share Capital Stock no par
Industrial Minerals of Canada Ltd. merged into Indusmin Ltd. 11/06/1968
(See Indusmin Ltd.)

CANADIAN SILK PRODS CORP (QC)
Charter annulled for failure to file reports or pay fees 10/13/1973

CANADIAN SOUTH AFRICAN GOLD FD LTD (CANADA)
Mutual Fund Shares 50¢ par split (2) for (1) by issuance of (1) additional share 06/25/1974
Name changed to Goldfund Ltd. 07/13/1977
(See Goldfund Ltd.)

CANADIAN SPIRIT RES INC (BC)
Reincorporated under the laws of Alberta 05/25/2012

CANADIAN-STAR INDS INC (AB)
Struck off register for failure to file annual returns 11/01/1993

CANADIAN STEVIA CORP (AB)
Delisted from NEX 10/01/2007

CANADIAN STRATEGIC HLDGS LTD (BC)
Struck off register and declared dissolved for failure to file returns 01/26/1996

CANADIAN STS RES INC (ON)
Name changed 10/26/1995
Name changed from Canadian States Gas Ltd. to Canadian States Resources Inc. 10/26/1995
Name changed to High North Resources Inc. 07/07/1997
High North Resources Inc. recapitalized as HNR Ventures Inc. 06/30/2000 which recapitalized as RMM Ventures Inc. (ON) 06/06/2006 which reorganized in Alberta as PowerComm Inc. 12/31/2006 which name changed to PetroCorp Group Inc. 12/23/2009

CANADIAN SUB-SURFACE ENERGY SVCS CORP (AB)
Merged into Pure Energy Services Ltd. 06/25/2009
Each share Class A Common no par exchanged for (0.3017) share Common no par
(See Pure Energy Services Ltd.)

CANADIAN SUMNER IRON WORKS LTD. (CANADA)
Acquired by Black-Clawson-Sumner Ltd. 11/09/1962
Each share Common exchanged for $6.62 cash
6% 1st Preferred $10 par called for redemption 12/31/1965

CANADIAN SUPER COMPOST (1963) LTD. (CANADA)
Involuntarily dissolved 06/24/1967

CANADIAN SUPERIOR ENERGY INC (AB)
Recapitalized as Sonde Resources Corp. 06/08/2010
Each share Common no par exchanged for (0.2) share Common no par
(See Sonde Resources Corp.)

CANADIAN SUPERIOR OIL LTD (CANADA)
Merged into Superior Oil Co. (NV) 01/24/1980
Each share Common $1 par exchanged for (1.145) shares Common 50¢ par and $25 cash
(See Superior Oil Co. (NV))

CANADIAN SUPERIOR OIL OF CALIFORNIA LTD. (CANADA)
Name changed to Canadian Superior Oil Ltd. 05/31/1961
Canadian Superior Oil Co. merged into Superior Oil Co. (NV) 01/24/1980
(See Superior Oil Co. (NV))

CANADIAN SUPREME ENERGY LTD (AB)
Recapitalized as Multi-Energies Developments Ltd. 02/18/1993
Each share Common no par exchanged for (0.5) share Common no par
Multi-Energies Developments Ltd. name changed to Sunalta Energy Inc. 06/20/1994
(See Sunalta Energy Inc.)

CANADIAN TACTICAL TRAINING ACADEMY INC (NV)
Recapitalized as Earth Life Sciences Inc. 06/02/2014
Each share Common $0.001 par exchanged for (0.025) share Common $0.001 par

CANADIAN TALON RES LTD (YT)
Name changed to TALON International Energy Ltd. (YT) 10/01/1999
TALON International Energy Ltd. (YT) reorganized in Alberta as Canadian Energy Exploration Inc. 01/20/2010 which was acquired by Standard Exploration Ltd. 10/22/2012

CANADIAN TASTY FRIES INC (NV)
Name changed to International Tasty Fries Inc. 04/13/1995
International Tasty Fries Inc. recapitalized as Filtered Souls Entertainment Inc. 11/25/1996 which name changed to Skyline Entertainment, Inc. 03/31/1999 which name changed to Quotemedia.Com Inc. 08/19/1999 which name changed to Quotemedia, Inc. 03/11/2003

CANADIAN THORIUM CORP. LTD. (ON)
Recapitalized as Quebec Mattagami Minerals Ltd. 10/11/1961
Each share Common $1 par exchanged for (0.25) share Common $1 par
Quebec Mattagami Minerals Ltd. name changed to Q.M.G. Holdings Inc. 10/03/1977
(See Q.M.G. Holdings Inc.)

CANADIAN TIRE LTD (ON)
5% Preference $20 par called for redemption 03/31/1960
(Additional Information in Active)

CANADIAN TOKAR LTD (QC)
Name changed to Interpublishing (Canada) Ltd.-Interpublication (Canada) Ltee. 04/21/1976
Interpublishing (Canada) Ltd.-Interpublication (Canada) Ltee. merged into Pagurian Corp. Ltd. 11/14/1979 which name changed to Edper Group Ltd. (Old) 05/10/1995 which merged into Edper Group Ltd. (New) 01/01/1997 which name changed to EdperBrascan Corp. 08/01/1997 which name changed to Brascan Corp. 04/28/2000 which name changed to Brookfield Asset Management, Inc. 11/10/2005

CANADIAN TRACE MINERALS LTD (BC)
Cease trade order effective 05/01/1989

CANADIAN TRANSCONTINENTAL AIRWAYS LTD.
Acquired by Canadian Airways, Ltd. 00/00/1931
Details not available

CANADIAN TRANSTECH INDS LTD (BC)
Struck off register and declared dissolved for failure to file returns 06/19/1992

CANADIAN TRICENTROL OILS LTD (AB)
Name changed to Tricentrol Canada Ltd. (AB) 05/05/1972
Tricentrol Canada Ltd. (AB) reincorporated in Ontario 11/28/1972 which merged into Tricentrol Canada Ltd. (ON) (New) 12/28/1972
(See Tricentrol Canada Ltd. (New))

CANADIAN TRUSTEED INCOME FD (CANADA)
Name changed to AGF Canadian Bond Fund 11/23/1989
AGF Canadian Bond Fund merged into AGF Group of Funds 05/20/2016

CANADIAN TURBO INC (AB)
Acquired by Pay Less Holdings Inc. 05/01/1992
Each share Common no par exchanged for $3.96 cash

CANADIAN UNIT BURIAL LTD. (CANADA)
Charter cancelled by the Provincial Secretary of Alberta for default 09/12/1961
No stockholders' equity

CANADIAN UTD MINERALS INC (BC)
Recapitalized as Mansfield Minerals Inc. 09/10/1990
Each share Common no par exchanged for (0.2) share Common no par
Mansfield Minerals Inc. name changed to Goldrock Mines Corp. 01/22/2013 which merged into Fortuna Silver Mines Inc. 07/28/2016

CANADIAN UTILS LTD (CANADA)
$1.25 Conv. 2nd Preferred $20 par reclassified as $1.25 Conv. Preferred $20 par 05/16/1974
$1.25 Conv. Preferred $20 par called for redemption 01/28/1977
10.25% 2nd Preferred Ser. A $25 par called for redemption 03/05/1984
2nd Preferred Ser. D no par called for redemption 10/16/1985
9.24% 2nd Preferred Ser. B $25 par called for redemption 12/23/1985
2nd Preferred Ser. E no par called for redemption 03/03/1986
14% 2nd Preferred Ser. F no par called for redemption 10/01/1986
2nd Preferred Ser. G no par called for redemption 05/01/1987
2nd Preferred Ser. H no par called for redemption 11/02/1987
$1.95 2nd Preferred Ser. K no par called for redemption 10/15/1993
7.08% 2nd Preferred Ser. M no par called for redemption 04/14/1994
8.74% 2nd Preferred Ser. I no par called for redemption 04/14/1994
$1.925 2nd Preferred Ser. L $25 par called for redemption at $25 plus $0.1688 accrued dividend on 10/03/1997
Adjustable Rate 2nd Preferred Ser. N $25 par called for redemption at $25 plus $0.1556 accrued dividend on 10/03/1997
$2 2nd Preferred Ser. P $25 par called for redemption at $25 plus $0.1753 accrued dividend on 10/03/1997
4.25% Preferred $100 par called for redemption at $102.50 plus $0.5705 accrued dividend on 10/03/1997
5% Preferred $100 par called for

redemption at $104 plus $0.6712 accrued dividend on 10/03/1997
6% Preferred $100 par called for redemption at $101 plus $1.0356 accrued dividend on 10/03/1997
7.3% 2nd Preferred Ser. C $25 par called for redemption at $25 plus $0.315 accrued dividend 10/03/1997
$1.475 2nd Preferred Ser. Q called for redemption at $25 plus $0.3152 accrued dividends on 05/18/2007
$1.325 2nd Preferred Ser. R called for redemption at $25 plus $0.2832 accrued dividends on 05/18/2007
2nd Preferred Ser. S $25 par called for redemption at $25 plus $0.3526 accrued dividends on 05/18/2007
4.35% 2nd Preferred Ser. O $25 par called for redemption at $25 plus $0.271875 accrued dividends on 12/02/2011
4.35% 2nd Preferred Ser. T $25 par called for redemption at $25 plus $0.271875 accrued dividends on 12/02/2011
4.35% 2nd Preferred Ser. U $25 par called for redemption at $25 plus $0.271875 accrued dividends on 12/02/2011
6% Preferred Ser. X $25 par called for redemption at $25 on 06/30/2012
5.8% 2nd Preferred Ser. W $25 par called for redemption at $25 plus $0.1907 accrued dividends on 07/19/2012
(Additional Information in Active)

CANADIAN VENTURE CORP (BC)
Recapitalized as Consolidated Canadian Venture Corp. (BC) 07/27/1990
Each share Common no par exchanged for (0.33333333) share Common no par
Consolidated Canadian Venture Corp. (BC) reorganized in Cayman Islands as Primeline Energy Holdings Inc. 06/30/1995

CANADIAN VICKERS LTD (CANADA)
Common no par exchanged (10) for (1) 00/00/1950
Name changed to Vickers Canada Inc. 11/17/1978
(See Vickers Canada Inc.)

CANADIAN WALLPAPER MFRS LTD (CANADA)
Class B Common $5 par changed to no par 00/00/1933
Class A Common no par and Class B Common no par reclassified as Common no par 08/15/1967
Acquired by Arthur Sanderson & Sons (Canada) Ltd. 05/15/1973
Each share Common no par exchanged for $200 cash

CANADIAN WEST RES LTD (BC)
Merged into Cantrell Capital Corp. 09/29/1995
Each share Common no par exchanged for (0.66666666) share Common no par
Cantrell Capital Corp. name changed to Petroamerica Oil Corp. 10/23/2009
(See Petroamerica Oil Corp.)

CANADIAN WESTERN GYPSUM CORP. LTD. (BC)
Name changed to United Gypsum Corp. Ltd. 00/00/1959
(See United Gypsum Corp. Ltd.)

CANADIAN WESTERN LUMBER CO. LTD. (CANADA)
Common $5 par changed to $2 par 00/00/1933
Common $2 par changed to no par 00/00/1945
Acquired by Crown Zellerbach Canada Ltd. share for share 00/00/1956
Crown Zellerbach Canada Ltd. name changed to Crown Forest Industries Ltd. 11/09/1983 which was acquired by Fletcher Challenge Canada Inc. 01/01/1988 which name changed to Fletcher Challenge Investments Inc. 09/14/1988
(See Fletcher Challenge Investments Inc.)

CANADIAN WESTERN NATURAL GAS, LIGHT, HEAT & POWER CO., LTD.
Recapitalized as Canadian Western Natural Gas Co., Ltd. 00/00/1947
Each share 6% Preference $100 par exchanged for (5) shares 4% Preference $20 par and $5 cash
(See Canadian Western Natural Gas Co., Ltd.)

CANADIAN WESTERN OIL CO., INC. (DE)
Merged into Westates Petroleum Co. 12/24/1959
Each share Common exchanged for (0.75) share Common $1 par
Westates Petroleum Co. assets transferred to Westates Petroleum Co. Liquidating Trust 05/02/1977
(See Westates Petroleum Co. Liquidating Trust)

CANADIAN WESTGROWTH LTD (AB)
Each share 12% Conv. 1st Preferred Ser. B $5 par exchanged for (0.7) share Common no par 11/18/1986
Merged into Ulster Petroleums Ltd. 10/27/1987
Each share Common no par exchanged for (1.5) shares Common no par
Ulster Petroleums Ltd. merged into Anderson Exploration Ltd. 05/23/2000
(See Anderson Exploration Ltd.)

CANADIAN WESTINGHOUSE LTD (CANADA)
Each share Capital Stock $100 par exchanged for (6) shares Capital Stock no par 00/00/1929
Capital Stock no par split (4) for (1) by issuance of (3) additional shares 05/06/1966
Name changed to Westinghouse Canada Ltd.-Westinghouse Canada Ltee. 05/06/1971
Westinghouse Canada Ltd.-Westinghouse Canada Ltee. name changed to Westinghouse Canada Inc. 05/15/1980
(See Westinghouse Canada Inc.)

CANADIAN WESTN BK (EDMONTON, AB)
Non-Cum. 5-Year Rate Reset 1st Preferred Ser. 3 $25 par called for redemption at $25 on 04/30/2014
(Additional Information in Active)

CANADIAN WESTN NAT GAS LTD (AB)
Acquired by Canadian Utilities Ltd. 06/19/1972
Each share Ordinary no par exchanged for (1) share $1.25 Conv. 2nd Preferred $20 par
4% Preferred $20 par called for redemption 12/30/1996
5.5% Preferred $20 par called for redemption 12/30/1996
Public interest eliminated

CANADIAN WM. A ROGERS, LTD.
Acquired by Oneida Community Ltd. 07/00/1929
Details not available

CANADIAN WILLISTON MINERALS LTD. (AB)
Capital Stock no par changed to 6¢ par 00/00/1954
Merged into Canadian Gridoil Ltd. 02/18/1966
Each share Capital Stock 6¢ par exchanged for (0.16) share Capital Stock 45¢ par
Canadian Gridoil Ltd. merged into Ashland Oil Canada Ltd. 09/14/1970 which name changed to Kaiser Petroleum Ltd. 03/23/1979
(See Kaiser Petroleum Ltd.)

CANADIAN WINERIES, LTD.
Name changed to Chateau-Gai Wines Ltd. 00/00/1941
(See Chateau-Gai Wines Ltd.)

CANADIAN WIRELESS TR (ON)
Trust terminated 01/02/2014
Each Trust Unit received $13.075 cash

CANADIAN WOOL CO., LTD. (ON)
Dissolved 02/00/1981
Details not available

CANADIAN WOOLENS, LTD.
Merged into Dominion Woollens & Worsteds Ltd. 00/00/1928
Details not available

CANADIAN WORLD FD LTD (ON)
Acquired by Third Canadian General Investment Trust Ltd. 05/07/2018
Each share Common no par exchanged for $9.25 cash
Note: Unexchanged certificates will be cancelled and become without value 05/07/2024

CANADIAN WORLDWIDE ENERGY LTD (AB)
Name changed to Triton Canada Resources, Ltd. 09/09/1987 Triton Canada Resources, Ltd. name changed to Transwest Energy Inc. 11/16/1993 which merged into Jordan Petroleum Ltd. 02/28/1997
(See Jordan Petroleum Ltd.)

CANADIAN WTR LTD (BC)
Recapitalized as Aumine Resources Ltd. 11/07/1996
Each share Common no par exchanged for (0.1) share Common no par
Aumine Resources Ltd. name changed to PetroReal Oil Corp. 08/06/1998 which recapitalized as International PetroReal Oil Corp. (BC) 09/13/2002 which reorganized in Alberta 06/28/2007 which name changed to PetroReal Energy Inc. 09/15/2008

CANADIAN ZEOLITE CORP (BC)
Name changed to International Zeolite Corp. 03/06/2018

CANADIAN ZEOLITE LTD (AB)
Name changed to Canadian Mining Co. Ltd. 01/08/1997
Canadian Mining Co. Ltd. name changed to Zeo-Tech Enviro Corp. 05/19/2000 which name changed to Canadian Mining Co. Inc. (AB) 02/08/2007 which reincorporated in British Columbia as Canadian Zeolite Corp. 02/08/2016 which name changed to International Zeolite Corp. 03/06/2018

CANADIAN ZINC CORP (BC)
Name changed to NorZinc Ltd. 09/11/2018

CANADIANA GENETICS INC (AB)
Cease trade order effective 10/09/1997
Stockholders' equity unlikely

CANADIANWIDE PPTYS LTD (ON)
Liquidation completed
Each share Capital Stock $1 par stamped to indicate initial distribution of $4.50 cash 12/27/1967
Each share Stamped Capital Stock $1 par received second and final distribution of $4.76 cash 06/07/1978

CANADORE MINES & RES LTD (QC)
Recapitalized 12/22/1972
Recapitalized from Canadore Mining & Development Corp. to Canadore Mines & Resources Ltd. 12/22/1972
Each share Common no par exchanged for (0.5) share Common no par
Charter annulled for failure to file reports or pay fees 01/13/1979

CANADREAM CORP (AB)
Acquired by ATL Canada Ltd. 07/17/2017
Each share Common no par exchanged for $1.85 cash
Note: Unexchnaged certificates will be cancelled and become without value 07/10/2020

CANADUSA OIL & GAS RESERVES LTD. (AB)
Merged into Titan Petroleum Corp. Ltd. 03/11/1957
Each share Common exchanged for (0.1) share Common $1 par
(See Titan Petroleum Corp. Ltd.)

CANAF GROUP INC (AB)
Name changed to Canaf Investments Inc. 07/27/2018

CANAFRICAN METALS & MNG CORP (AB)
Name changed to Canaf Group Inc. 06/01/2007
Canaf Group Inc. name changed to Canaf Investments Inc. 07/27/2018

CANAFUND LTD (CANADA)
Liquidation completed
Each share Common $1 par exchanged for first and final distribution of (1) Unit of Canafund (Luxembourg) and $1.23 cash 03/31/1971
Each share Deferred no par exchanged for first and final distribution of $1.20 cash 11/16/1971

CANAGAU MINES LTD (ON)
Charter cancelled for failure to pay taxes and file returns 03/16/1976

CANAL ASSETS INC (LA)
Each share Common $1 par exchanged for (10) shares Common 10¢ par 06/19/1958
Merged into Southdown, Inc. 08/21/1969
Each share Common 10¢ par exchanged for (1.2) shares Common $2.50 par
(See Southdown Inc.)

CANAL BK TR (NEW ORLEANS, LA)
Certificates of Bene. Int. no par called for redemption 03/20/1996

CANAL CONSTRUCTION CO. (DE)
Completely liquidated 11/00/1946
Each share Preference no par exchanged for first and final distribution of $0.45 cash
No stockholders' equity for Common

CANAL CORP (ME)
Merged into Depositors Corp. 08/31/1983
Each share Common $10 par exchanged for (1.107) shares Capital Stock $6.25 par
Depositors Corp. merged into Key Banks Inc. 02/29/1984 which name changed to KeyCorp (NY) 08/28/1985 which merged into KeyCorp (New) (OH) 03/01/1994

CANAL NATL BK (PORTLAND, ME)
Each share Capital Stock $100 par exchanged for (5) shares Capital Stock $25 par to effect a (4) for (1) split and 25% stock dividend 07/15/1949
Each share Capital Stock $25 par exchanged for (2.5) shares Capital Stock $10 par 01/10/1956
Under plan of merger each share Capital Stock $10 par received (3/105) additional share Capital Stock $10 par 06/21/1965
Stock Dividends - 33.33333333% 01/10/1950; 12.5% 01/15/1954; 25% 07/17/1964

Reorganized as United Bancorp of Maine 06/02/1969
Each share Capital Stock $10 par exchanged for (1) share Common $10 par
United Bancorp of Maine name changed to Canal Corp. 04/01/1976 which merged into Depositors Corp. 08/31/1983 which merged into Key Banks Inc. 02/29/1984 which name changed to KeyCorp (NY) 08/28/1985 which merged into KeyCorp (New) (OH) 03/01/1994

CANAL PLUS S A (FRANCE)
Sponsored ADR's for Ordinary split (4) for (1) by issuance of (3) additional ADR's payable 07/07/1999 to holders of record 07/01/1999
Each Sponsored ADR for Ordinary received distribution of (0.4) Vivendi Universal Sponsored ADR for Ordinary payable 12/13/2000 to holders of record 12/08/2000
Ex date - 12/11/2000
ADR agreement terminated 02/24/2006
Each ADR for Ordinary exchanged for $2.26643 cash

CANAL RANDOLPH CORP (DE)
In process of liquidation
Each share Common $1 par received initial distribution of (3) shares United Stockyards Corp. Common 1¢ par and $22 cash 06/01/1984
(See United Stockyards Corp.)
Each share Common $1 par received second distribution of $33 cash 07/17/1984
Each share Common $1 par received third distribution of $13 cash 01/10/1985
Assets transferred to Canal-Randolph Limited Partnership 03/06/1985
Each share Common $1 par exchanged for (1) Assignee Unit of Ltd. Partnership
(See Canal-Randolph Ltd. Partnership)

CANAL RANDOLPH LTD PARTNERSHIP (MD)
In process of liquidation
Each Assignee Unit of Ltd. Partnership received initial distribution of $4 cash 05/15/1985
Each Assignee Unit of Ltd. Partnership received second distribution of $3 cash 10/02/1986
Each Assignee Unit of Ltd. Partnership exchanged for third distribution of $2 cash 10/30/1987
Each Assignee Unit of Ltd. Partnership received fourth distribution of $2 cash 01/22/1991
Note: Details on subsequent distributions, if any, not available

CANALANDS RES CORP (CANADA)
Delisted from Alberta Stock Exchange 10/15/1992

CANALASK NICKEL MINES LTD. (ON)
Recapitalized as Northwest Canalask Nickel Mines Ltd. 09/11/1962
Each share Capital Stock $1 par exchanged for (0.25) share Capital Stock $1 par
Northwest Canalask Nickel Mines Ltd. recapitalized as New Canalask Minerals Ltd. 08/30/1973
(See New Canalask Minerals Ltd.)

CANALASKA RES LTD (BC)
Recapitalized as International CanAlaska Resources Ltd. 09/15/1993
Each share Common no par exchanged for (0.25) share Common no par
International CanAlaska Resources Ltd. recapitalized as CanAlaska Ventures Ltd. 12/03/1999 which name changed to CanAlaska Uranium Ltd. 10/11/2006

CANALASKA VENTURES LTD (BC)
Name changed to CanAlaska Uranium Ltd. 10/11/2006

CANALITE LTD (ON)
Charter cancelled for failure to pay taxes and file returns 11/08/1977

CANALTA MINERALS LTD (AB)
Name changed to New Energy West Corp. 11/14/1994
New Energy West Corp. acquired by Gastar Exploration Ltd. (AB) 11/20/2001 which reincorporated in Delaware as Gastar Exploration, Inc. (Old) 11/15/2013 which reorganized as Gastar Exploration, Inc. (New) 02/03/2014

CANALTA OIL CO. LTD. (ON)
Charter revoked for failure to file reports and pay taxes 09/08/1959

CANALTA RES LTD (BC)
Merged into Consolidated Ascot Petroleum Corp. 02/08/1982
Each share Common no par exchanged for (0.3) share Common no par
Consolidated Ascot Petroleum Corp. name changed to Ascot Investment Corp. 03/03/1987 which recapitalized as Pacific Western Investments Inc. 08/03/1990 which merged into Revenue Properties Co. Ltd. 01/01/1992 which merged into Morguard Corp. 12/01/2008

CANAM COAL CORP (AB)
Delisted from NEX 03/13/2017

CANAM COPPER CO. LTD. (CANADA)
Capital Stock $1 par changed to no par 03/01/1955
Completely liquidated 11/22/1966
Each share Capital Stock no par exchanged for first and final distribution of (0.125) share Giant Mascot Mines Ltd. Common $1 par
Giant Mascot Mines Ltd. recapitalized as G M Resources Ltd. (BC) 04/11/1977 which reincorporated in Canada 09/08/1982 which merged into Campbell Resources Inc. (New) 06/08/1983
(See Campbell Resources Inc. (New))

CANAM ENERGY INC (DE)
Recapitalized as Registered Express Corp. 06/29/2009
Each share Common 10¢ par exchanged for (0.00066666) share Common $0.001 par
Registered Express Corp. name changed to Proactive Pet Products, Inc. 02/20/2015 which recapitalized as GVCL Ventures, Inc. 11/02/2016 which recapitalized as Rain Forest International, Inc. 05/22/2018

CANAM GROUP INC (QC)
Name changed 01/01/2005
Name changed from Canam Manac Group Inc. to Canam Group Inc. 01/01/2005
Class A Subordinate no par reclassified as Common no par 08/28/2006
Acquired by Canaveral Acquisition Inc. 07/05/2017
Each share Common no par exchanged for $12.30 cash
Note: Unexchanged certificates will be cancelled and become without value 07/05/2023

CANAM URANIUM CORP (NV)
Recapitalized as CleanPath Resources Corp. 11/12/2008
Each share Common $0.001 par exchanged for (0.005) share Common $0.001 par

CANAMAX ENERGY LTD (AB)
Acquired by 1936003 Alberta Ltd. 01/19/2016
Each share Common no par exchanged for $0.67 cash
Note: Unexchanged certificates will be cancelled and become without value 01/18/2019

CANAMAX RES INC (CANADA)
Merged into Canada Tungsten Inc. 01/01/1993
Each share Common no par exchanged for (0.2) share Common no par
Canada Tungsten Inc. merged into Aur Resources Inc. 01/01/1997 which was acquired by Teck Cominco Ltd. 09/28/2007 which name changed to Teck Resources Ltd. 04/27/2009

CANAMCO RESOURCES LTD. (BC)
Recapitalized as Bermuda Resources Ltd. 06/21/1984
Each share Common no par exchanged for (0.33333333) share Common no par
Bermuda Resources Ltd. name changed to Ameritel Management Inc. (BC) 09/01/1988 which reincorporated in Washington 02/13/1992 which recapitalized as WCT Communications, Inc. 06/04/1992
(See WCT Communications, Inc.)

CANAMED VENTURES LTD (AB)
Recapitalized as VSM MedTech Ltd. (AB) 02/27/1998
Each share Common no par exchanged for (0.25) share Common no par
VSM MedTech Ltd. (AB) reincorporated in British Columbia 06/19/2006

CANAMER NICKEL LTD. (QC)
Declared dissolved for failure to file reports and pay fees 12/15/1959

CANAMERA EXPLS INC (BC)
Recapitalized as Wind River Resources Ltd. 05/03/1988
Each share Common no par exchanged for (0.33333333) share Common no par
Wind River Resources Ltd. recapitalized as Richlode Investments Corp. 05/03/1993 which recapitalized as Thundelarra Exploration Ltd. (BC) 07/30/1998 which reincorporated in Yukon 01/23/2001 which reincorporated in Western Australia 09/08/2003 which name changed to Thundelarra Ltd. 03/21/2013

CANAMERICA PRECIOUS METALS INC (AB)
Struck off register for failure to file annual returns 10/01/1992

CANAMEX INDS LTD (BC)
Name changed to International Cablecasting Technologies Inc. (BC) 11/06/1986
International Cablecasting Technologies Inc. (BC) reorganized in Delaware 09/28/1990 which name changed to DMX, Inc. 04/27/1995 which merged into TCI Music, Inc. 07/11/1997 which merged into Liberty Media Corp. (New) 03/14/2002 which reorganized as Liberty Media Corp. (Incorporated 02/28/2006) 05/10/2006 which name changed to Liberty Interactive Corp. 09/26/2011 which name changed to Qurate Retail, Inc. 04/10/2018

CANAMEX RES CORP (BC)
Each share old Common no par exchanged for (0.25) share new Common no par 10/20/2016
Name changed to Canamex Gold Corp. 11/08/2017

CANAMEX SILVER CORP (BC)
Name changed to Canamex Resources Corp. 10/18/2010
Canamex Resources Corp. name changed to Canamex Gold Corp. 11/08/2017

CANAMIN RES LTD (BC)
Recapitalized as New CanaMin Resources Ltd. 03/26/1991
Each share Common no par exchanged for (0.2) share Common no par
New CanaMin Resources Ltd. merged into Princeton Mining Corp. 07/03/1995
(See Princeton Mining Corp.)

CANANDAIGUA BRANDS INC (DE)
Name changed to Constellation Brands Inc. 09/19/2000

CANANDAIGUA ENTERPRISES CORP (NY)
Reorganized 08/21/1970
Each share Class A 1¢ par or Class B 1¢ par exchanged for (0.5) share Common 1¢ par and (0.5) Common Stock Warrant expiring 11/19/1970
Under plan of reorganization holders of Preferred $5 par had option to exchange each share for either (0.5) share Common 1¢ par or $5 cash until 02/23/1986 after which holders were entitled to receive Common Stock only
Merged into Delaware North Co. 08/07/1984
Each share Common 1¢ par exchanged for $2.25 cash

CANANDAIGUA NATL BK & TR (CANANDAIGUA, NY)
Name changed 02/15/1927
Stock Dividend - 150% 00/00/1927
Name changed from Canandaigua National Bank (Canandaigua, NY) to Canandaigua National Bank & Trust Co. (Canandaigua, NY) 02/15/1927
Capital Stock $100 par changed to $50 par and (1.5) additional shares issued 11/01/1967
Capital Stock $50 par split (5) for (2) by issuance of (1.5) additional shares 11/01/1976
Stock Dividend - 100% 00/00/1957
Under plan of reorganization each share Capital Stock $50 par automatically became (1) share Canandaigua National Corp. Capital Stock $50 par 05/31/1985

CANANDAIGUA WINE CO., INC. (DE)
Common 1¢ par reclassified as Conv. Class B Common 1¢ par 07/11/1986
Each share Conv. Class B Common 1¢ par received distribution of (1.5) shares Class A Common 1¢ par 07/15/1986
Class A Common 1¢ par split (3) for (2) by issuance of (0.5) additional share 11/08/1991
Conv. Class B Common 1¢ par split (3) for (2) by issuance of (0.5) additional share 11/08/1991
Class A Common 1¢ par split (3) for (2) by issuance of (0.5) additional share 07/20/1992
Conv. Class B Common 1¢ par split (3) for (2) by issuance of (0.5) additional share 07/20/1992
Name changed to Canandaigua Brands, Inc. 09/01/1997
Canandaigua Brands, Inc. name changed to Constellation Brands, Inc. 09/19/2000

CANARAMA LTD. (SK)
Acquired by Western Heritage Properties Ltd. 00/00/1963
Details not available

CANARCHON HLDGS LTD (ON)
Voluntarily dissolved 01/28/1991
For Canadian and Non-North American residents holding (200) shares or more, each share Common no par received first and final distribution of (0.50) share Ordinary Stock £1 par and (0.44) Nominal Variable Rate Unsecured

Loan Stock 1995/ 1998 of R.E.A.
Holdings plc 02/20/1991
For all U.S. holders regardless of
holding, Canadian and Non-North
American residents holding (199)
shares or fewer, each share
Common no par received first and
final distribution of $0.1648 cash
Note: Certificates were not required to
be exchanged and are without value

CANARCTIC RESOURCES LTD. (BC)
Recapitalized as Concept Resources
Ltd. (BC) 03/20/1972
Each share Capital Stock no par
exchanged for (0.1) share Capital
Stock no par
Concept Resources Ltd. (BC)
reincorporated in Alberta 08/21/1978
which name changed to Skyline
Natural Resources Ltd. 10/23/1987
which recapitalized as Stellarton
Energy Corp. 09/06/1996
(See Stellarton Energy Corp.)

CANARCTIC VENTURES LTD (BC)
Recapitalized as Consolidated
Canarctic Industries Ltd. 02/21/1985
Each share Class A Common no par
exchanged for (0.4) share Class A
Common no par
(See Consolidated Canarctic
Industries Ltd.)

CANARD RES LTD (CANADA)
Struck off register and declared
dissolved for failure to file returns
03/06/2000

CANARGO ENERGY CORP (DE)
Plan of reorganization under Chapter
11 Federal Bankruptcy Code
effective 01/08/2010
No stockholders' equity

CANARGO ENERGY INC (AB)
Merged into CanArgo Energy Corp.
07/15/1998
Each share Common no par
exchanged for (0.8) share Common
10¢ par
(See CanArgo Energy Corp.)

CANARGO OIL & GAS INC (DE)
Each Exchangeable Share
exchanged for (1) share CanArgo
Energy Corp. Common 10¢ par
05/23/2002
(See CanArgo Energy Corp.)

CANASIA INDS CORP (BC)
Recapitalized as Makena Resources
Inc. 01/23/2013
Each share Common no par
exchanged for (0.05) share Common
no par

CANASKA EXPLORERS LTD. (ON)
Charter revoked for failure to file
reports and pay taxes 10/17/1955

CANAUSTRA GOLD EXPL LTD (ON)
Merged into Cliff Resources Corp.
01/09/1989
Each share Common no par
exchanged for (0.75) share Common
no par
Cliff Resources Corp. name changed
to Mineral Resources Corp.
09/13/1995 which name changed to
Minroc Mines Inc. 06/10/1998 which
name changed to Cassiar Mines &
Metals, Inc. 06/10/1999 which name
changed to Cassiar Magnesium Inc.
04/25/2000 which name changed to
Cassiar Resources Inc. 07/25/2001
which name changed to Troutline
Investments Inc. (ON) 06/30/2003
which reorganized in Alberta as
Innova Exploration Ltd. 04/16/2004
(See Innova Exploration Ltd.)

CANAUSTRA RES INC (AB)
Reorganized under the laws of Yukon
as Oriental Minerals Inc. 08/15/2005
Each share Common no par
exchanged for (0.5) share Common
no par
Oriental Minerals Inc. (YT)
reincorporated in British Columbia
11/01/2007 which name changed to
Woulfe Mining Corp. 02/25/2010
which merged into Almonty
Industries Inc. 09/14/2015

CANAVERAL INTL CORP (DE)
Common $1 par changed to 50¢ par
and (1) additional share issued
07/10/1962
Recapitalized as Madison Group
Associates Inc. 02/02/1993
Each share Common 50¢ par
exchanged for (0.25) share Common
50¢ par
(See Madison Group Associates Inc.)

**CANAVERAL UTILITIES &
DEVELOPMENT CORP. (FL)**
Merged into Paradise Fruit Co., Inc.
08/26/1965
Each share Common 10¢ par
exchanged for (1) share Common
10¢ par
Paradise Fruit Co., Inc. name
changed to Paradise Inc.
08/12/1993

CANBAIKAL RES INC (AB)
Merged into Novation Trading Ltd.
02/05/2002
Each share Common no par
exchanged for $0.38 cash

CANBANC 8 INCOME CORP (ON)
Under plan of reorganization each
Equity Share automatically became
(0.98557) share First Asset Fund
Corp. CanBanc Income Class ETF
05/04/2016

CANBANC INCOME CORP (ON)
Name changed to First Asset
CanBanc Income ETF and Equity
Shares reclassified as ETF Shares
09/24/2013
First Asset CanBanc Income ETF
reorganized as First Asset Fund
Corp. 05/04/2016

CANBEC RES LTD (BC)
Delisted from Vancouver Stock
Exchange 12/05/1988

CANBRA FOODS LTD (AB)
10% Conv. Preferred Ser. 1 no par
called for redemption 04/04/1996
Acquired by James Richardson
International Ltd. 08/25/1999
Each share Common no par
exchanged for $23 cash

**CANBRAS COMMUNICATIONS
CORP (BC)**
Liquidation completed
Each share Common no par received
initial distribution of $0.21 cash
payable 08/23/2004 to holders of
record 08/23/2004
Each share Common no par received
second distribution of $0.18 cash
payable 12/22/2005 to holders of
record 12/09/2005
Each share Common no par received
third and final distribution of $0.0993
cash payable 05/28/2007 to holders
of record 05/11/2007
Note: Certificates were not required to
be surrendered and are without
value

CANBRIDGE OIL EXPL LTD (ON)
Merged into Thomson Drilling Co. Ltd.
12/31/1970
Each share Capital Stock 90¢ par
exchanged for (0.1) share Capital
Stock par
Thomson Drilling Co. Ltd. name
changed to Thomson Industries Ltd.
07/01/1973
(See Thomson Industries Ltd.)

CANBY LAND & LOT CO. (SD)
Charter expired by time limitation
12/15/1942

CANBY RES INC (BC)
Name changed to Bicer Medical
Systems Ltd. 06/15/1988
(See Bicer Medical Systems Ltd.)

CANCAL MINES, LTD. (BC)
Name changed to Cancal Resources
Ltd. 10/01/1981
(See Cancal Resources Ltd.)

CANCAL RES LTD (BC)
Struck off register and declared
dissolved for failure to file returns
01/10/1986

**CANCALL CELLULAR
COMMUNICATIONS INC (BC)**
Delisted from Vancouver Stock
Exchange 03/15/1999

CANCANA RES CORP (AB)
Reincorporated 08/12/2015
Place of incorporation changed from
(AB) to (BC) 08/12/2015
Plan of arrangement effective
11/28/2016
Each share Common no par
exchanged for (0.4) share Meridian
Mining S.E. Common EUR 0.01 par
Note: Unexchanged certificates will
be cancelled and become without
value 11/28/2022

CANCAP PFD CORP (QC)
5.4% Preferred no par called for
redemption at $25 on 07/03/2007

CANCAPITAL CORP (BC)
Reincorporated 05/12/1993
Place of incorporation changed from
(AB) to (BC) 05/12/1993
Recapitalized as Prada Holdings Ltd.
(BC) 07/14/1994
Each share Common no par
exchanged for (0.25) share Common
no par
Prada Holdings Ltd. (BC)
reincorporated in Yukon 07/26/1996
(See Prada Holdings Ltd.)

CANCEN OIL CDA INC (AB)
Reincorporated 12/20/2012
Place of incorporation changed from
(BC) to (AB) 12/20/2012
Name changed to Ceiba Energy
Services Inc. 07/29/2013
(See Ceiba Energy Services Inc.)

CANCER DETECTION CORP (NV)
Name changed to Tremont Fair, Inc.
09/18/2009
Tremont Fair, Inc. name changed to
Vican Resources, Inc. 06/10/2011

CANCER DETECTION INC (UT)
Reincorporated under the laws of
Nevada as Commercial Technology,
Inc. 05/11/1973
Commercial Technology, Inc.
liquidated for Electric & Gas
Technology, Inc. 10/00/1989
(See Electric & Gas Technology, Inc.)

CANCER DIAGNOSTICS INC (KS)
Charter forfeited for failure to file
reports 11/15/1987

**CANCER SCREENING SVCS INC
(CA)**
Merged into American Health
Industries, Inc. 09/25/1973
Each share Common 10¢ par
exchanged for (0.2) share 9%
Preferred $10 par
American Health Industries, Inc.
recapitalized as American Cytology
Services Corp. 07/21/1975 which
name changed to American
Cytogenetics, Inc. 09/30/1982
(See American Cytogenetics, Inc.)

CANCER THERAPEUTICS INC (DE)
Recapitalized as Nano Dimensions,
Inc. 11/08/2010
Each share Common $0.001 par
exchanged for (0.002) share
Common $0.001 par
Nano Dimensions, Inc. name changed
to Legal Life Plans, Inc. 02/07/2012
(See Legal Life Plans, Inc.)

**CANCER TREATMENT HLDGS INC
(NV)**
Each share old Common $0.003 par
exchanged for (0.25) share new
Common $0.003 par 09/01/1989
Company terminated registration of
common stock and is no longer
public as of 08/19/2003

CANCEROPTION COM INC (FL)
Name changed to BioImmune Inc.
06/22/2001
(See BioImmune Inc.)

CANCERVAX CORP (DE)
Recapitalized as Micromet, Inc.
05/08/2006
Each share Common $0.00004 par
exchanged for (0.33333333) share
Common $0.00004 par
(See Micromet, Inc.)

CANCHROME MINES INC (CANADA)
Name changed to Cancor Mines Inc.
12/14/1995
Cancor Mines Inc. merged into
Yorbeau Resources Inc. 05/28/2014

**CANCOIL INTEGRATED SVCS INC
(AB)**
Name changed to Technicoil Corp.
07/26/2002
Technicoil Corp. merged into
Essential Energy Services Ltd.
05/31/2011

CANCOM INC (MN)
Name changed to Computer Network
Technology Corp. 11/29/1983
Computer Network Technology Corp.
merged into McDATA Corp.
06/01/2005 which was acquired by
Brocade Communications Systems,
Inc. 01/29/2007
(See Brocade Communications
Systems, Inc.)

CANCOM INDS INC (BC)
Recapitalized as Strategic
Technologies Inc. 07/10/1990
Each share Common no par
exchanged for (0.28571428) share
Common no par
Strategic Technologies Inc. name
changed to Wireless2 Technologies,
Inc. 10/24/2006 which name
changed to Nanotech Security Corp.
04/15/2010

CANCOR MINES INC (CANADA)
Merged into Yorbeau Resources Inc.
05/28/2014
Each share Common no par
exchanged for (0.08333333) share
Class A Common no par and
(0.04166666) Class A Common
Stock Purchase Warrant expiring
12/31/2015
Note: Unexchanged certificates will
be cancelled and become without
value 05/28/2020

CANCORP ENTERPRISES INC (BC)
Name changed to G.E.M.
Environmental Management Inc.
(BC) 10/02/1989
G.E.M. Environmental Management
Inc. (BC) reincorporated in Delaware
07/13/1990
(See G.E.M. Environmental
Management Inc.)

**CANCRETE ENVIRONMENTAL
SOLUTIONS INC (AB)**
Delisted from Alberta Stock Exchange
11/23/1999

CANDAO ENTERPRISES INC (BC)
Delisted from NEX 12/21/2006

CANDAX ENERGY INC (BC)
Reincorporated 07/06/2011
Place of incorporation changed from
(ON) to (BC) 07/06/2011
Acquired by Geofinance N.V.
11/17/2015
Each share Common no par
exchanged for $0.002 cash
Note: Unexchanged certificates will
be cancelled and become without
value 11/17/2021

CANDEGO MINES LTD. (ON)
Recapitalized as Consolidated
Candego Mines Ltd. 00/00/1950
Each share Capital Stock $1 par

exchanged for (0.25) share Capital Stock $1 par
Consolidated Candego Mines Ltd. acquired by East MacDonald Mines Ltd. 00/00/1954
(See East MacDonald Mines Ltd.)

CANDEL OIL LTD (CANADA)
Common $3 par split (3) for (1) by issuance of (2) additional shares 05/20/1980
Acquired by Sulpetro Ltd. 11/02/1981
Each share Common $3 par exchanged for $44.55 cash

CANDELA CORP (DE)
Name changed 11/16/1995
Common 1¢ par split (2) for (1) by issuance of (1) additional share 07/16/1987
Name changed from Candela Laser Corp. to Candela Corp. 11/16/1995
Common 1¢ par split (3) for (2) by issuance of (0.5) additional share payable 02/28/2000 to holders of record 01/28/2000
Common 1¢ par split (2) for (1) by issuance of (1) additional share payable 03/16/2004 to holders of record 02/16/2004 Ex date - 03/17/2004
Merged into Syneron Medical Ltd. 01/05/2010
Each share Common 1¢ par exchanged for (0.2911) share Ordinary ILS 0.01 par
(See Syneron Medical Ltd.)

CANDELA RES LTD (BC)
Recapitalized as New Candela Resources Ltd. 04/03/1998
Each share Common no par exchanged for (0.25) share Common no par
New Candela Resources Ltd. recapitalized as Sherwood Petroleum Corp. (BC) 10/20/1999 which reincorporated in Alberta 07/20/2000 which name changed to Sherwood Mining Corp. 11/09/2001 which recapitalized as Sherwood Copper Corp. 09/12/2005 which merged into Capstone Mining Corp. 11/25/2008

CANDELARIA MINES CO. (NV)
Charter revoked for failure to pay taxes 03/02/1925

CANDEN CAP CORP (YT)
Reincorporated 06/12/2000
Place of incorporation changed from (BC) to (Yukon) 06/12/2000
Name changed to Superior Canadian Resources Inc. 05/25/2004

CANDENTE RESOURCE CORP (BC)
Reincorporated 03/09/2007
Place of incorporation changed from (BC) to (Canada) 09/27/2002 which reincorporated back in British Columbia 03/09/2007
Name changed to Candente Copper Corp. 12/31/2009

CANDEUB FLEISSIG & ASSOC (DE)
Name changed to Espre Solutions, Inc. 08/06/2004
(See Espre Solutions, Inc.)

CANDEV RESOURCE EXPL INC (NV)
Name changed to Del Toro Silver Corp. 08/14/2009

CANDIAC DEV CORP (QC)
Name changed to Candiac Urban Developments Inc.-Developpements Urbains Candiac Inc. 05/25/1978

CANDIAC NURSERIES LTD (QC)
Company believed out of business 00/00/1986
Details not available

CANDIES INC (DE)
Name changed to Iconix Brand Group, Inc. 07/01/2005

CANDLER CO (DE)
Adjudicated bankrupt 08/23/1974
Stockholders' equity unlikely

CANDLEWEALTH INTL INC (NV)
Recapitalized as Promethean Corp. 06/18/2007
Each share Common $0.001 par exchanged for (0.2) share Common 1¢ par

CANDLEWOOD BK & TR CO (NEW FAIRFIELD, CT)
Merged into New Milford Bank & Trust Co. (New Milford, CT) 04/29/1994
Each share Common $5 par exchanged for $10.06 cash

CANDLEWOOD HOTEL INC (DE)
Completely liquidated
Each share Common 1¢ par received first and final distribution of $0.0601 cash payable 09/22/2008 to holders of record 09/12/2008 Ex date - 09/23/2008
Note: Certificates were not required to be surrendered and are without value

CANDLEWOOD ISLE CORP. (CT)
Dissolved 09/22/1998
Details not available

CANDO CAP INC (AB)
Name changed to Trius Investments Inc. (Old) 11/10/1999
Trius Investments Inc. (Old) name changed to eCycling Technologies Inc. 10/18/2006 which name changed to Trius Investments Inc. (New) 10/18/2007

CANDOL DEVS LTD (BC)
Under plan of merger each share Common no par exchanged for (0.5) share Common no par 05/22/1985
Recapitalized as Terrastar Development Corp. 03/30/1993
Each share Common no par exchanged for (0.1) share Common no par
(See Terrastar Development Corp.)

CANDOO GOLD MINES LTD. (ON)
Name changed to Candoo Metals & Oils Ltd. 00/00/1951
(See Candoo Metals & Oils Ltd.)

CANDOO METALS & OILS LTD. (ON)
Charter cancelled for failure to pay taxes and file returns 06/13/1960

CANDOR VENTURES CORP (ON)
Merged into Canstar Resources Inc. 04/07/2005
Each share Common no par exchanged for (1) share Common no par

CANDORADO MINES LTD (BC)
Recapitalized as A.R.C. Resins International Corp. 12/10/1993
Each share Common no par exchanged for (0.33333333) share Common no par
(See A.R.C. Resins International Corp.)

CANDORADO OPER COMPANY LTD (BC)
Recapitalized as Sunrise Resources Ltd. 08/08/2012
Each share Common no par exchanged for (0.2) share Common no par

CANDORE EXPLS LTD (ON)
Recapitalized as Golden Crescent Resources Corp. 12/31/1987
Each share Capital Stock no par exchanged for (0.125) share Capital Stock no par
Golden Crescent Resources Corp. recapitalized as Golden Crescent Corp. 05/20/1998
(See Golden Crescent Corp.)

CANDY BRANDS, INC.
Liquidated 00/00/1934
No stockholders' equity

CANDY EXPRESS STORES LTD (BC)
Recapitalized as Patriots Venture Group Ltd. 09/21/1993
Each share Common no par exchanged for (0.33333333) share Common no par
Patriots Venture Group Ltd. recapitalized as Tearlach Resources Ltd. 05/22/1997

CANDY INVTS LTD (ON)
Name changed 12/08/1969
Name changed 04/05/1972
Name changed from Candy Mines Ltd. to Candy Mines & Investments Ltd. 12/08/1969
Name changed from Candy Mines & Investments Ltd. to Candy Investments Ltd. 04/05/1972
Completely liquidated
Each share Common $1 par received first and final distribution of $0.5358 cash payable 09/13/2005 to holders of record 03/14/2005

CANDY MTN GOLD MINES LTD (NV)
Charter revoked for failure to file reports and pay fees 08/01/1987

CANDY STRIPERS CANDY CORP (UT)
Recapitalized as Piedmont, Inc. 12/30/1997
Each share Common $0.001 par exchanged for (0.01) share Common $0.001 par
Piedmont, Inc. recapitalized as U.S. Biodefense, Inc. 06/20/2003 which name changed to Elysium Internet, Inc. 07/28/2008 which name changed to TheDirectory.com, Inc. 08/17/2011

CANDYMASTERS, INC. (MN)
Completely liquidated
Each share Common $1 par received first and final distribution of $0.006 cash 03/23/1967
Note: Certificates were not required to be surrendered and are without value

CANDYWYNE CORP (FL)
Proclaimed dissolved for failure to file reports and pay fees 09/03/1976

CANE CONSOLIDATED EXPLORATIONS LTD. (ON)
Name changed to Cane Resources Ltd. 07/08/1983
Cane Resources Ltd. recapitalized as Cane Corp. 09/20/1984 which recapitalized as Aurcana Corp. 06/18/1996

CANE CORP (ON)
Recapitalized 09/20/1984
Recapitalized from Cane Resources Ltd. to Cane Corp. 09/20/1984
Each share Common no par exchanged for (0.2) share Common no par
Recapitalized as Aurcana Corp. 06/18/1996
Each share Common no par exchanged for (0.5) share Common no par

CANE CREEK OIL & GAS CO. (UT)
Dissolved 02/19/1964
No stockholders' equity

CANE SILVER MINES LTD. (ON)
Recapitalized as Cane Consolidated Explorations Ltd. 08/22/1977
Each share Capital Stock $1 par exchanged for (0.125) share Common no par
Cane Consolidated Explorations Ltd. name changed to Cane Resources Ltd. 07/08/1983 which recapitalized as Cane Corp. 09/20/1984 which recapitalized as Aurcana Corp. 06/18/1996

CANE SPRINGS OIL & MINERALS CORP. (UT)
Name changed to Sharin 'O' The Green, Inc. 10/03/1967
Sharin 'O' The Green, Inc. liquidated for Western Recreation, Inc. 04/08/1971 which name changed to Charvet/Jackson & Co., Inc. 09/20/1972

(See Charvet/Jackson & Co., Inc.)

CANE SPRINGS URANIUM CORP. (UT)
Recapitalized as Cane Springs Oil & Minerals Corp. 08/16/1956
Each share Common 1¢ par exchanged for (0.2) share Capital Stock 5¢ par
Cane Springs Oil & Minerals Corp. name changed to Sharin 'O' The Green, Inc. 10/03/1967 which liquidated for Western Recreation, Inc. 04/08/1971 which name changed to Charvet/Jackson & Co., Inc. 09/20/1972
(See Charvet/Jackson & Co., Inc.)

CANECO AUDIO PUBLISHER INC (BC)
Name changed 01/20/1986
Name changed from Caneco Resources Inc. to Caneco Audio-Publishers Inc. 01/20/1986
Charter dissolved 08/18/1989

CANELCO SERVICES LTD. (CANADA)
6.5% 1st Preferred $10 par called for redemption 03/01/1967
(Additional Information in Active)

CANELSON DRILLING INC (AB)
Merged into Trinidad Drilling Ltd. 08/14/2015
Each share Common no par exchanged for (1.0631) shares Common no par
Note: Unexchanged certificates will be cancelled and become without value 08/14/2020

CANEONTI MINES LTD (ON)
Charter cancelled 03/00/1976

CANETIC RES TR (AB)
Acquired by Penn West Energy Trust 01/11/2008
Each Trust Unit exchanged for (0.515) Trust Unit
Penn West Energy Trust reorganized as Penn West Petroleum Ltd. (New) 01/03/2011 which name changed to Obsidian Energy Ltd. 06/29/2017

CANEUM INC (NV)
Chapter 7 bankruptcy proceedings terminated 11/03/2010
No stockholders' equity

CANEURO RES LTD (AB)
Merged into Attock Oil Corp. 02/04/1991
Each share Class A Common no par exchanged for (0.2) share Class A Common no par
Attock Oil Corp. recapitalized as Attock Energy Corp. 08/02/1995
(See Attock Energy Corp.)

CANEX ENERGY INC (AB)
Plan of arrangement effective 05/30/2006
Each share Common no par held by Canadian residents exchanged for (0.1003) Crescent Point Energy Trust, Trust Unit no par, (0.5) share Canext Energy Ltd. (Old) Common no par, (0.16666666) Common Stock Purchase Warrant expiring 06/29/2006 and $0.5876 cash
Each share Common no par held by non-Canadian residents exchanged for (0.1003) Crescent Point Energy Trust, Trust Unit no par, (0.66666666) share Canext Energy Ltd. (Old) Common no par and $0.4209 cash
(See each company's listing)
Note: Unexchanged certificates were cancelled and became without value 05/30/2010

CANEX RESOURCES CORP. (BC)
Delisted from Vancouver Stock Exchange 05/04/1994

CANEXT ENERGY LTD NEW (AB)
Merged into TriOil Resources Ltd. 04/21/2010

Each share Common no par exchanged for (0.1) share Class A Common no par
(See TriOil Resources Ltd.)

CANEXT ENERGY LTD OLD (AB)
Merged into Canext Energy Ltd. (New) 06/22/2007
Each share Common no par exchanged for (1.0309) shares Common no par
Canext Energy Ltd. (New) merged into TriOil Resources Ltd. 04/21/2010
(See TriOil Resources Ltd.)

CANEXUS CORP (AB)
Acquired by Chemtrade Logistics Income Fund 03/13/2017
Each share Common no par exchanged for $1.65 cash
Note: Unexchanged certificates will be cancelled and become without value 03/13/2019

CANEXUS INCOME FD (AB)
Under plan of reorganization each Trust Unit automatically became (1) share Canexus Corp. Common no par 07/13/2011
(See Canexus Corp.)

CANFE VENTURES LTD (BC)
Name changed to Golden Fame Resources Corp. 10/27/2010
Golden Fame Resources Corp. reorganized as Pan American Fertilizer Corp. (New) 08/07/2013

CANFIBRE GROUP LTD (ON)
Delisted from Toronto Venture Stock Exchange 06/20/2003

CANFIC RES LTD (BC)
Recapitalized as Delcorp Resources Inc. 05/06/1987
Each share Common no par exchanged for (0.4) share Common no par
Delcorp Resources Inc. recapitalized as Bahn Foods Inc. 11/20/1990 which recapitalized as Consolidated Bahn Foods Inc. 10/21/1996
(See Consolidated Bahn Foods Inc.)

CANFIC SILVER MINES LTD. (BC)
Name changed to Canfic Resources Ltd. 12/04/1981
Canfic Resources Ltd. recapitalized as Delcorp Resources Inc. 05/06/1987 which recapitalized as Bahn Foods Inc. 11/20/1990 which recapitalized as Consolidated Bahn Foods Inc. 10/21/1996
(See Consolidated Bahn Foods Inc.)

CANFIELD FINL LTD (AB)
Name changed to Learnco International Inc. 07/28/1998
(See Learnco International Inc.)

CANFIELD OIL CO.
Acquired by Standard Oil Co. (OH) 00/00/1945
Details not available

CANFOR CAP LTD (BC)
Floating Rate Retractable Sr. Preferred Ser. 1, $25 par called for redemption 10/15/1989
Public interest eliminated

CANFOR CORP OLD (BC)
$2.25 Class A Exchangeable Preferred Ser. 1 $25 par called for redemption 03/31/1994
Common no par split (2) for (1) by issuance of (1) additional share 05/16/1994
Plan of arrangement effective 07/01/2006
Each share Common no par held by Canadian residents exchanged for (0.1) Canfor Pulp Income Fund Trust Unit no par and $10.1384 cash
Each share Common no par held by non-Canadian residents exchanged for (1) share Canfor Corp. (New) Common no par and $10.1384 cash
(See each company's listing)

CANFOR INVTS LTD (BC)
11% Preferred $5 par called for redemption 11/01/1983
Public interest eliminated

CANFOR PULP INCOME FD (ON)
Under plan of reorganization each Unit no par automatically became (1) share Canfor Pulp Products Inc. (BC) Common no par 01/06/2011

CANFORD EXPLORATIONS LTD. (BC)
Merged into Consolidated Vigor Mines Ltd. 01/28/1969
Each share Capital Stock 50¢ par exchanged for (0.1) share Capital Stock no par
(See Consolidated Vigor Mines Ltd.)

CANGENE CORP (ON)
Acquired by Emergent BioSolutions Inc. 02/24/2014
Each share Common no par exchanged for USD$3.24 cash
Note: Unexchanged certificates will be cancelled and become without value 02/24/2020

CANGLOBE INTL INC (NV)
Name changed to Globetech Environmental, Inc. 11/07/2005
Globetech Environmental, Inc. recapitalized as Global Gold Corp. 03/09/2009 which recapitalized as Fernhill Corp. 01/20/2012

CANGOLD LTD (BC)
Reincorporated 12/22/2004
Place of incorporation changed from (YT) to (BC) 12/22/2004
Each share old Common no par exchanged for (0.2) share new Common no par 05/27/2011
Merged into Great Panther Silver Ltd. 05/27/2015
Each share new Common no par exchanged for (0.05) share Common no par
Note: Unexchanged certificates will be cancelled and become without value 05/27/2021

CANGOLD RES INC (BC)
Reorganized under the laws of Ontario as Amalgamated CanGold Inc. 07/31/1995
Each share 7% Conv. Retractable Preferred Ser. A no par exchanged for (1) share 7% Conv. Retractable Preferred Ser. A no par
Each share Common no par exchanged for (0.1) share Common no par
Amalgamated CanGold Inc. merged into Central Asia Goldfields Corp. 01/08/1996
(See Central Asia Goldfields Corp.)

CANGRO RESOURCES LTD. (CANADA)
Completely liquidated
Each share Special $1 par and Deferred $1 par received initial distribution of USD$17 cash payable 09/24/1965 to holders of record 06/23/1965
Each share Special $1 par and Deferred $1 par received second distribution of (0.1474896225) share Canadian Delhi Oil Ltd. Common no par, (1.38995366) shares Canadian Export Gas & Oil Ltd. Common $0.16666666 par, (0.1275830477) share Dome Petroleum Ltd. Capital Stock $2.50 par, (0.1332157035) share Home Oil Co. Ltd. Class A no par, (0.1980704195) share Marine Capital Corp. Common $1 par, (0.316105097) share Mortgage Associates, Inc. (WI) Common $1 par, (0.452422155) share Provo Gas Producers Ltd. Capital Stock no par, (0.08596020948) share Scurry-Rainbow Oil Ltd. Capital Stock $3.50 par, (0.775903996) share Westmount Financial Holdings Ltd. Ordinary $1 par and (0.0387951998) share Westmount Life Insurance Co. Capital Stock $10 par payable 12/02/1965 to holders of record 06/23/1965
(See each company's listing)
Each share Special $1 par and Deferred $1 par received third distribution of USD$2 cash payable 03/14/1966 to holders of record 06/23/1965
Each share Special $1 par or Deferred $1 par exchanged for fourth and final distribution of USD$0.31945 cash 06/03/1966

CANGUARD PHARMA INC (BC)
Name changed 07/16/1993
Name changed from Canguard Health Technologies Inc. to Canguard Pharma Inc. 07/16/1993
Recapitalized as GeriatRx Pharmaceutical Corp. 08/17/1994
Each share Common no par exchanged for (0.2) share Common no par
GeriatRx Pharmaceutical Corp. recapitalized as Paladin Labs Inc. (BC) 05/10/1996 which reincorporated in Canada 07/24/1998 which merged into Endo International PLC 03/03/2014

CANHART MINES LTD. (ON)
Charter cancelled for failure to pay taxes and file returns 03/25/1980

CANHORN CHEM CORP (ON)
Merged into Nayarit Gold Inc. 05/02/2005
Each share Common no par exchanged for (1) share Common no par
Nayarit Gold Inc. merged into Capital Gold Corp. 08/02/2010 which merged into Gammon Gold Inc. (QC) 04/08/2011 which reincorporated in Ontario as AuRico Gold Inc. 06/14/2011 which merged into Alamos Gold Inc. (New) 07/06/2015

CANHORN MNG CORP (ON)
Merged into Canhorn Chemical Corp. 04/26/1995
Each share Common no par exchanged for (0.5) share Common no par
Canhorn Chemical Corp. merged into Nayarit Gold Inc. 05/02/2005 which merged into Capital Gold Corp. 08/02/2010 which merged into Gammon Gold Inc. (QC) 04/08/2011 which reincorporated in Ontario as AuRico Gold Inc. 06/14/2011 which merged into Alamos Gold Inc. (New) 07/06/2015

CANICO RESOURCE CORP (BC)
Merged into Companhia Vale do Rio Doce 02/13/2006
Each share Common no par exchanged for $20.80 cash

CANIN INDL GROUP INC (AB)
Struck off register for failure to file annual returns 03/13/1999

CANISCO RES INC (DE)
Merged into Kenny Industrial Services, LLC 08/16/2000
Each share Common $0.0025 par exchanged $1 cash

CANLAN INVT CORP (BC)
Name changed to Canlan Ice Sports Corp. 06/25/1999

CANLEY DEVS INC (BC)
Name changed to Sargold Resource Corp. 07/03/2003
Sargold Resource Corp. merged into Buffalo Gold Ltd. 10/30/2007
(See Buffalo Gold Ltd.)

CANLORM RES INC (BC)
Reincorporated 08/01/1995
Place of incorporation changed from (ON) to (BC) 08/01/1995
Recapitalized as Oroperu Resources Inc. 09/05/1995
Each share Common no par exchanged for (0.14285714) share Common no par
Oroperu Resources Inc. recapitalized as New Oroperu Resources Inc. 06/06/2001

CANMARC REAL ESTATE INVT TR (QC)
Acquired by Cominar Real Estate Investment Trust 03/05/2012
Each Trust Unit received $16.50 cash

CANMARK INTL RES INC (BC)
Cease trade order effective 12/19/2003
Stockholders' equity unlikely

CANMAX INC (WY)
Each share old Common no par exchanged for (0.2) share new Common no par 12/21/1995
Reincorporated under the laws of Delaware as ARDIS Telecom & Technologies, Inc. 02/01/1999
ARDIS Telecom & Technologies, Inc. name changed to Dial-Thru International Corp. 01/20/2000 which name changed to Rapid Link, Inc. 11/28/2005 which name changed to Spot Mobile International Ltd. 06/10/2010
(See Spot Mobile International Ltd.)

CANMET RES LTD (BC)
Name changed to Archangel Diamond Corp. (BC) 06/30/1994
Archangel Diamond Corp. (BC) reincorporated in Yukon 09/16/1996
(See Archangel Diamond Corp.)

CANMEX MINERALS CORP (BC)
Each share old Common no par exchanged for (0.2) share new Common no par 09/22/1999
Name changed to Africa Oil Corp. 08/20/2007

CANMINE RES CORP (ON)
Placed in receivership 02/26/2003
No stockholders' equity

CANMORE MINES LTD (CANADA)
Each share Capital Stock $100 par exchanged for (4) shares Capital Stock no par 00/00/1947
Through voluntary exchange offer Dillingham Corp. acquired all Capital Stock no par shares of 06/10/1971
Public interest eliminated

CANNA BRANDS INC (NV)
Name changed to Canna Consumer Goods, Inc. 06/24/2015

CANNABIS CAP CORP (NV)
Name changed to Crown Baus Capital Corp. 07/25/2014

CANNABIS KINETICS CORP (NV)
Common $0.001 par split (3) for (1) by issuance of (2) additional shares payable 12/22/2014 to holders of record 12/18/2014 Ex date - 12/23/2014
Name changed to Monarch America, Inc. 12/26/2014

CANNABIS LEAF INC (NV)
Common $0.001 par split (6) for (1) by issuance of (5) additional shares payable 06/27/2017 to holders of record 06/27/2017
Name changed to Apotheca Biosciences, Inc. 08/24/2018

CANNABIS MED SOLUTIONS INC (DE)
Common 1¢ par split (10) for (1) by issuance of (9) additional shares payable 06/01/2010 to holders of record 05/14/2010 Ex date - 06/02/2010
Name changed to MediSwipe Inc. 07/08/2011
MediSwipe Inc. name changed to Agritek Holdings, Inc. 05/20/2014

CANNABIS-RX INC (DE)
Name changed to Praetorian Property, Inc. (DE) 10/26/2015

Praetorian Property, Inc. (DE)
reincorporated in Nevada
12/30/2015

CANNABIS TECHNOLOGIES INC (BC)
Name changed to InMed Pharmaceuticals Inc. 10/21/2014

CANNABIS THERAPY CORP (NV)
Stock Dividend - 50% payable 03/31/2014 to holders of record 03/28/2014 Ex date - 04/01/2014
Name changed to Peak Pharmaceuticals, Inc. 02/05/2015

CANNABIS WHEATON INCOME CORP (BC)
Name changed to Auxly Cannabis Group Inc. 06/08/2018

CANNAMED CORP (NV)
Name changed to Chuma Holdings, Inc. 08/29/2014

CANNASAT THERAPEUTICS INC (CANADA)
Name changed to Cynapsus Therapeutics Inc. 04/27/2010
(See Cynapsus Therapeutics Inc.)

CANNAVEST CORP (DE)
Reincorporated 08/13/2013
State of incorporation changed from (TX) to (DE) 08/13/2013
Name changed to CV Sciences, Inc. 06/08/2016

CANNELLE EXPL LTD (BC)
Name changed to RangeStar Telecommunications Ltd. 02/01/1996
(See RangeStar Telecommunications Ltd.)

CANNIMED THERAPEUTICS INC (CANADA)
Merged into Aurora Cannabis Inc. 05/01/2018
Each share Common no par exchanged for (3.4) shares Common no par

CANNON CRAFT CO (TX)
Each share Common 50¢ par received distribution of (1) share Cannon Craft Western Co. Class A Common 25¢ par 01/15/1971
Each share Common 50¢ par exchanged for (0.0001) share Common $5,000 par 11/01/1983
Note: In effect holders received $2.69 cash per share and public interest was eliminated

CANNON CRAFT WESTN CO (CA)
Each share Class A Common 25¢ par exchanged for (0.0001) share Common $2,500 par 11/15/83
Note: In effect holders received $2.19 cash per share and public interest was eliminated

CANNON ELECTRIC CO. (CA)
Stock Dividend - 10% 01/28/1963
Acquired by International Telephone & Telegraph Corp. (MD) 11/30/1963
Each share Common $1 par exchanged for (0.05) share 4% Conv. Preferred Ser. D $100 par and (0.3023) share Common no par
International Telephone & Telegraph Corp. (MD) reincorporated in Delaware 01/31/1968 which name changed to ITT Corp. 12/31/1983 which reorganized in Indiana as ITT Industries, Inc. 12/19/1995 which name changed to ITT Corp. 07/01/2006

CANNON EXPLS LTD (BC)
Name changed to U.T. Technologies Ltd. 09/23/1987
(See U.T. Technologies Ltd.)

CANNON EXPRESS INC (DE)
Common 1¢ par split (5) for (4) by issuance of (0.25) additional share 12/13/1991
Common 1¢ par reclassified as Class A Common 1¢ par 01/11/1993
Each share Class A Common 1¢ par received distribution of (1) share Non-Vtg. Class B Common 1¢ par 01/26/1993
Class A Common 1¢ par reclassified as Common 1¢ par 04/10/1996
Each share old Class B Common 1¢ par exchanged for (0.000002) share new Class B Common 1¢ par 04/10/1996
Note: Holders of fewer than (500,000) pre-split shares will receive $9 cash
Chapter 11 bankruptcy petition dismissed 06/08/2004
No stockholders' equity

CANNON GROUP INC (DE)
Reincorporated 05/03/1984
State of incorporation changed from (NY) to (DE) 05/03/1984
Name changed to Pathe Communications Corp. 03/20/1989
(See Pathe Communications Corp.)

CANNON INDS INC (NY)
Name changed to Pud Industries, Inc. 05/09/1977
(See Pud Industries, Inc.)

CANNON MANUFACTURING CO.
Succeeded by Cannon Mills Co. 00/00/1928
Details not available

CANNON MINERALS LTD (BC)
Name changed to Nevada Goldfields Corp. (BC) 12/23/1985
Nevada Goldfields Corp. (BC) reincorporated in Canada 04/27/1989 which recapitalized as Consolidated Nevada Goldfields Corp. 05/01/1991 which recapitalized as Real Del Monte Mining Corp. 05/14/1998
(See Real Del Monte Mining Corp.)

CANNON MINES LTD (ON)
Recapitalized as Dencal Development Corp. 08/29/1988
Each share Common no par exchanged for (0.25) share Common no par
Dencal Development Corp. recapitalized as Bestquipt Sports Inc. 02/04/1991 which recapitalized as Big Hammer Group Inc. 08/29/2000
(See Big Hammer Group Inc.)

CANNON MLS CO (NC)
Each share Common no par exchanged for (5) shares Common $5 par 05/25/1973
Each share Class B Common $25 par exchanged for (5) shares Common $5 par 05/25/1973
Stock Dividends - (1) share Class B for each share Common 11/10/1947; 10% 04/10/1980
Merged into Pacific Holding Corp. 03/30/1982
Each share Common $5 par exchanged for $44 cash

CANNON OIL & GAS LTD (AB)
Acquired by G2 Resources Inc. 01/29/2007
Each share Common no par exchanged for (0.95) share Class A Common no par
G2 Resources Inc. merged into Regal Energy Ltd. 07/10/2008 which recapitalized as Novus Energy Inc. 08/05/2009
(See Novus Energy Inc.)

CANNON PICTURES INC (DE)
SEC revoked common stock registration 10/10/2008

CANNON PT RES LTD (BC)
Each share old Common no par exchanged exchanged for (0.25) share new Common no par 11/16/2011
Merged into Northern Dynasty Minerals Ltd. 10/29/2015
Each share Common no par exchanged for (0.376) share Common no par

Note: Unexchanged certificates will be cancelled and become without value 10/29/2021

CANNON RES LTD (BC)
Recapitalized as Samson Gold Corp. 12/13/1983
Each share Capital Stock no par exchanged for (0.25) share Common no par
Samson Gold Corp. name changed to Kinghorn Energy Corp. 09/20/1989 which recapitalized as Kinghorn Petroleum Corp. 04/30/1991 which recapitalized as Triple 8 Energy Corp. (BC) 11/17/1992 which reincorporated in Alberta 02/24/1994 which name changed to Oilexco Inc. 03/01/1994 which recapitalized as ScotOil Petroleum Ltd. (AB) 06/09/2011 which reincorporated in British Columbia as 0915988 B.C. Ltd. 07/27/2011
(See 0915988 B.C. Ltd.)

CANNON SHOE CO (MD)
5.5% Preferred called for redemption 07/01/1943
Class A Common $1 par reclassified as Common $1 par 04/22/1959
Merged into BSR Associates 02/18/1981
Each share Common $1 par exchanged for $3.50 cash

CANNON TIME INC. (DE)
Name changed to Avcom International, Inc. 09/00/1993
Avcom International, Inc. merged into Signature Resorts, Inc. 02/07/1997 which name changed to Sunterra Corp. 07/14/1998
(See Sunterra Corp.)

CANNONDALE CORP (DE)
Plan of reorganization under Chapter 11 Federal Bankruptcy Code effective 12/20/2004
No stockholders' equity

CANO PETE INC (DE)
Plan of reorganization under Chapter 11 Federal Bankruptcy proceedings effective 08/02/2012
Stockholders' equity unlikely

CANOE CDN DIVERSIFIED INCOME FD (ON)
Under plan of merger each Unit automatically became (0.9600187) share Canoe 'GO CANADA!' Fund Corp. Equity Income Class Ser. Z 04/22/2016

CANOE GO CDA INCOME FD (AB)
Combined Units separated 02/11/2011
Merged into Canoe 'GO CANADA!' Fund Corp. 12/20/2012
Each Trust Unit received (0.89) share Equity Income Class Ser. A

CANOE STRATEGIC RES INCOME FD (AB)
Merged into Canoe 'GO CANADA!' Equity Income Class 12/18/2012
Each Trust Unit received (0.77) share Ser. A

CANOE U S STRATEGIC YIELD ADVANTAGE FD (ON)
Under plan of merger each Class A and Class U Trust Unit automatically became (0.86130395) or (1.08767508) Canoe 'GO CANADA!' Fund Corp. North American Monthly Income Class Ser. Z respectively 05/20/2016

CANOEL INTL ENERGY LTD (BC)
Each share old Common no par exchanged for (0.1) share new Common no par 09/06/2013
Name changed to Zenith Energy Ltd. 10/03/2014

CANOGA ELECTRS CORP (NV)
Name changed to Canoga Industries 04/01/1969
(See Canoga Industries)

CANOGA INDS (NV)
Merged into Zero Manufacturing Co. 04/08/1976
Each share Common no par exchanged for $2.50 principal amount of 10% Subord. Debentures due 02/01/1989 and $1.70 cash
Note: Holders of (99) shares or fewer received $3.40 cash per share

CANOIL EXPL CORP (BC)
Name changed to AMS Homecare Inc. 03/15/2002
(See AMS Homecare Inc.)

CANOL METAL MINES LTD (ON)
Charter cancelled for failure to pay taxes and file returns 03/16/1976

CANOL MINES LTD (BC)
Struck off register 09/20/1985

CANONCITO CORP. (NM)
Charter revoked for failure to file reports and pay fees 10/06/1965

CANONCITO URANIUM CORP. (NM)
Name changed to Canoncito Corp. 10/16/1957
(See Canoncito Corp.)

CANONIE COMPANIES, INC. (MI)
Name changed to Canonie, Inc. 11/01/1981
(See Canonie, Inc.)

CANONIE CONSTRUCTION CO. (MI)
Capital Stock $10 par changed to $5 par and (1) additional share issued plus a 100% stock dividend paid 12/01/1970
Reorganized as Canonie Companies, Inc. 08/09/1976
Each share Capital Stock $5 par exchanged for (5) shares Common $1 par
Canonie Companies, Inc. name changed to Canonie, Inc. 11/01/1981
(See Canonie, Inc.)

CANONIE ENVIRONMENTAL SVCS CORP (DE)
Name changed to Smith Environmental Technologies Corp. 02/28/1995
Smith Environmental Technologies Corp. name changed to Smith Technology Corp. 09/23/1996
(See Smith Technology Corp.)

CANONIE, INC. (MI)
Voluntarily dissolved 07/27/1990
Details not available

CANOP WORLDWIDE CORP (AB)
Recapitalized as Avery Resources Inc. 09/24/2002
Each share Common no par exchanged for (0.1) share Common no par
Avery Resources Inc. recapitalized as Bengal Energy Ltd. 07/22/2008

CANORA PUBLIC SERVICE CORP. (DE)
No longer in existence having become inoperative and void for non-payment of taxes 04/01/1932

CANORAMA EXPLORATIONS LTD. (ON)
Recapitalized as Consolidated Canorama Explorations Ltd. 10/08/1963
Each share Capital Stock $1 par exchanged for (0.25) share Capital Stock $1 par
(See Consolidated Canorama Explorations Ltd.)

CANOREX DEV LTD (BC)
Struck off register and declared dissolved for failure to file returns 03/31/1983

CANORO RES LTD (AB)
Reincorporated 09/21/2001
Place of incorporation changed from (BC) to (AB) 09/21/2001
Reincorporated under the laws of British Columbia 03/22/2011

CANOVA RES LTD (BC)
Struck off register and declared dissolved for failure to file returns 08/13/1993

CANPAR OIL & GAS LTD (CANADA)
Charter cancelled 05/25/1984

CANPLATS RES CORP (BC)
Acquired by Goldcorp Inc. (New) 02/04/2010
Each share Common no par exchanged for (1) share Camino Minerals Corp. Common no par and $4.60 cash

CANQUEST RESOURCE CORP (AB)
Delisted from Canadian Venture Exchange 05/31/2001

CANRAD-HANOVIA, INC. (DE)
Each share old Common 75¢ par exchanged for (0.5) share new Common 75¢ par 10/29/1976
Name changed to Canrad, Inc. 05/27/1985
(See Canrad, Inc.)

CANRAD INC (DE)
Merged into ARC International Corp. 12/29/1988
Each share Common 75¢ par exchanged for $13.75 cash

CANRAD PRECISION INDUSTRIES, INC. (DE)
Each share Common 25¢ par exchanged for (0.33333333) share Common 75¢ par 11/13/1968
Name changed to Canrad-Hanovia, Inc. 05/22/1973
Canrad-Hanovia, Inc. name changed to Canrad, Inc. 05/27/1985
(See Canrad, Inc.)

CANRAY RES LTD (ON)
Recapitalized as Exall Resources Ltd. 12/09/1983
Each share Common no par exchanged for (0.25) share Common no par
Exall Resources Ltd. merged into Gold Eagle Mines Ltd. 12/27/2006 which was acquired by Goldcorp Inc. 09/25/2008

CANREOS MINERALS 1980 LTD (CANADA)
Struck off register and declared dissolved for failure to file returns 12/06/1995

CANRISE RES LTD (AB)
Acquired by Poco Petroleums Ltd. 08/06/1998
Each share Commom no par exchanged for (0.3845) share Common no par
Poco Petroleums Ltd. merged into Burlington Resources Inc. 11/18/1999 which merged into ConocoPhillips 03/31/2006

CANROC OILS LTD. (AB)
Struck off register and declared dissolved for failure to file returns 00/00/1958

CANROCK ENERGY CORP (AB)
Merged into Alston Energy Inc. 07/24/2012
Each share Common no par exchanged for (2.321) shares Common no par
(See Alston Energy Inc.)

CANRON INC (CANADA)
Conv. Class A Common no par split (2) for (1) by issuance of (1) additional share 09/18/1979
Conv. Class B Common no par split (2) for (1) by issuance of (1) additional share 09/18/1979
$6 Preferred 1974 Ser. $100 par called for redemption 04/01/1985
Conv. Class A Common no par reclassified as Class A no par 10/08/1986
Conv. Class B Common no par reclassified as Class A no par 10/08/1986

Each share Conv. Class A no par received distribution of (0.1) share Class B Subordinate no par 10/10/1986
Merged into Ivaco Inc. 05/31/1990
Each share Class A no par exchanged for $20.50 cash
Each share Class B Subordinate no par exchanged for $20.50 cash

CANRON LTD.-CANRON LTEE. (CANADA)
4.25% Preferred 1956 Ser. $100 par called for redemption 03/31/1977
Name changed to Canron Inc. and Common no par reclassified as Conv. Class A Common no par 06/05/1978
(See Canron Inc.)

CANSCOPE MINING LTD. (ON)
Charter revoked for failure to file reports and pay fees 03/30/1967

CANSCOT RES LTD (AB)
Acquired by APF Energy Trust 09/26/2003
Each share Common no par exchanged for $2.60 cash

CANSHORE EXPL LTD (CANADA)
Each share Preferred no par exchanged for (1) share Common no par 09/11/1991
Charter dissolved 05/06/2004

CANSIB ENERGY INC (BC)
Delisted from Toronto Venture Stock Exchange 06/05/2002

CANSIL CONSOLIDATED MINES LTD.
Dissolved 00/00/1950
Details not available

CANSO EXPLS LTD (BC)
Name changed to Geonova Explorations Inc. 03/25/1994
Geonova Explorations Inc. merged into Campbell Resources Inc. (New) 06/30/2001
(See Campbell Resources Inc. (New))

CANSO MINING CORP. LTD. (NS)
Acquired by Canadian Alumina Co. Ltd. 00/00/1958
Each share Capital Stock no par exchanged for (1) share Capital Stock no par
(See Canadian Alumina Co. Ltd.)

CANSO NATURAL GAS LTD. (CANADA)
Merged into United Canso Oil & Gas Ltd. (Canada) 07/02/1958
Each VTC for Capital Stock $1 par exchanged for (0.5) share VTC for Capital Stock $1 par
United Canso Oil & Gas Ltd. (Canada) reincorporated in Nova Scotia 06/06/1980
(See United Canso Oil & Gas Ltd. (NS))

CANSO OIL PRODUCERS LTD. (CANADA)
Merged into United Canso Oil & Gas Ltd. (Canada) 07/02/1958
Each VTC for Capital Stock $1 par exchanged for (0.5) share VTC for Capital Stock $1 par
United Canso Oil & Gas Ltd. (Canada) reincorporated in Nova Scotia 06/06/1980
(See United Canso Oil & Gas Ltd. (NS))

CANSO SELECT OPPORTUNITIES FD (ON)
Under plan of merger each Class A and Class F Unit automatically became (1) Canso Select Opportunities Corp. Class A Multiple Share and (1) Class B Subordinate Share 09/04/2018

CANSORB INDS INC (BC)
Delisted from Vancouver Stock Exchange 11/11/1988

CANSTAR SPORTS INC (CANADA)
Merged into Nike Inc. 02/13/1995
Each share Common no par exchanged for $27.50 cash

CANSTAR VENTURES CORP (AB)
Merged into Abacan Resource Corp. (New) 02/10/1995
Each share Common no par exchanged for (0.45) share Common no par
(See Abacan Resource Corp. (New))

CANSTAT PETE CORP (BC)
Name changed 09/16/1986
Name changed from Canstat Petroleum Corp. to Canstat Petroleum Corp.-La Societe de Ressources Petrolieres Canstat Inc. 09/16/1986
Recapitalized as International Canstat Petroleum Corp.-La Societe de Ressources Petrolieres Canstat Internationale Inc. 05/29/1989
Each share Common no par exchanged for (0.2) share Common no par
International Canstat Petroleum Corp.-La Societe De Ressources Petrolieres Canstat Internationale Inc. recapitalized as Blackwater Gold Corp. 09/16/1993 which recapitalized as Bonaventure Enterprises Inc. 03/20/2002 which recapitalized as Iconic Minerals Ltd. 03/03/2011

CANTAB PHARMACEUTICALS PLC (ENGLAND)
Each Sponsored ADR for Ordinary exchanged for (0.8333) Sponsored ADR for Ordinary 05/26/1998
ADR agreement terminated 01/04/2002
Each Sponsored ADR for Ordinary exchanged for $2.5282 cash

CANTECH VENTURES INC (BC)
Recapitalized as New Cantech Ventures Inc. 08/22/2003
Each share Common no par exchanged for (0.1) share Common no par
New Cantech Ventures Inc. name changed to Nanika Resources Inc. 06/20/2008 which recapitalized as Goldbar Resources Inc. 07/06/2012

CANTEEN CORP. (DE)
Certificates dated prior to 04/25/1969
Merged into International Telephone & Telegraph Corp. (DE) 04/25/1969
Each share Common $2.50 par exchanged for (0.193) share $4 Conv. Preferred Ser. K no par, (0.2686) share Common $1 par and $0.12 cash
International Telephone & Telegraph Corp. (DE) name changed to ITT Corp. 12/31/1983 which reorganized in Indiana as ITT Industries, Inc. 12/19/1995

CANTEEN CORP (DE)
Certificates dated after 02/05/1973
Merged into Trans World Airlines, Inc. 08/10/1973
Each share Common $1 par exchanged for $22 cash

CANTEL INDS INC (DE)
Name changed to Cantel Medical Corp. 04/07/2000

CANTERBURY CONSULTING GROUP INC (PA)
Name changed 03/01/1994
Name changed 06/12/1997
Name changed 04/30/2001
Name changed from Canterbury Educational Services Inc. to Canterbury Corporate Services Inc. 03/01/1994
Name changed from Canterbury Corporate Services Inc. to Canterbury Information Technology Inc. 06/12/1997
Each share old Common $0.001 par

exchanged for (0.33333333) share new Common $0.001 par 04/14/1998
Name changed from Canterbury Information Technology, Inc. to Canterbury Consulting Group Inc. 04/30/2001
Each share new Common $0.001 par exchanged again for (0.14285714) share new Common $0.001 par 01/24/2003
Merged into CCG Group, Inc. 10/24/2005
Each share new Common $0.001 par exchanged for $0.32 cash

CANTERBURY PRESS INC (PA)
Name changed to Canterbury Educational Services, Inc. 05/15/1987
Canterbury Educational Services, Inc. name changed to Canterbury Corporate Services Inc. 03/01/1994 which name changed to Canterbury Information Technology, Inc. 06/12/1997 which name changed to Canterbury Consulting Group Inc. 04/30/2001
(See Canterbury Consulting Group Inc.)

CANTERBURY RES INC (BC)
Struck off register and declared dissolved for failure to file returns 08/17/1990

CANTERBURY RES INC (NV)
Common $0.001 par split (5) for (1) by issuance of (4) additional shares payable 08/27/2012 to holders of record 08/27/2012 Ex date - 08/28/2012
Name changed to Echo Automotive, Inc. 09/24/2012
(See Echo Automotive, Inc.)

CANTERRA DEV CORP. LTD (BC)
Struck off register and declared dissolved for failure to file returns 01/10/1983

CANTERRA ENERGY LTD. (AB)
Acquired by Husky Oil Ltd. 10/14/1988
Each share Common no par exchanged for $3 cash

CANTERRA ENERGY LTD (CANADA)
Merged into Canada Development Corp. 09/30/1987
Each share Common no par exchanged for (0.66666666) share Common no par
Canada Development Corp. name changed to Polysar Energy & Chemical Corp. 01/01/1988 which was acquired by Nova Corp. of Alberta 09/07/1988 which reorganized as Nova Corp. (Old) 05/10/1994 which merged into TransCanada PipeLines Ltd. 07/02/1998 which reorganized as TransCanada Corp. 05/15/2003

CANTEX ENERGY CORP (BC)
Name changed to Texacan Energy Ltd. 04/19/1983
(See Texacan Energy Ltd.)

CANTEX ENERGY CORP (NV)
Recapitalized as Arkose Energy Corp. 06/20/2014
Each share Common $0.001 par exchanged for (0.004) share Common no par

CANTEX ENERGY INC (ON)
Name changed to Outlook Resources Inc. 06/21/2001
(See Outlook Resources Inc.)

CANTEXAS ROYALTY CO., LTD. (CANADA)
Liquidation completed
Each share Class A no par received initial distribution of USD$1.30 cash 03/15/1966
Each share Class A no par received second and final distribution of USD$0.053 cash 09/15/1966

CANTIAQUE CAPITAL CORP. (NY)
Liquidation completed
Each share Common $1 par exchanged for initial distribution of $19.65 cash 04/11/1979
Each share Common $1 par received second distribution of $0.25 cash 03/00/1981
Each share Common $1 par received third and final distribution of $0.96 cash 12/23/1982

CANTITOE CORP.
Dissolved 00/00/1948
Details not available

CANTOL LTD (QC)
Name changed 10/15/1971
Name changed from Cantol Diversified Ltd. to Cantol Ltd.-Cantol Ltee. 10/15/1971
Each share old Common 20¢ par exchanged for (0.001) share new Common 20¢ par 12/23/2005
Note: In effect holders received $3.65 cash per share and public interest was eliminated

CANTON BANCORP INC (PA)
Merged into Chemung Financial Corp. 05/29/2009
Each share Common $1 par exchanged for $272 cash

CANTON EXPLORATIONS LTD. (ON)
Merged into New Force Crag Mines Ltd. 11/22/1974
Each share Common no par exchanged for (0.18181818) share Common no par
(See New Force Crag Mines Ltd.)

CANTON INDL CORP (NV)
Reincorporated 03/09/1993
Each share old Common no par exchanged for (0.25) share new Common no par 10/22/1992
State of incorporation changed from (OH) to (NV) 03/09/1993
Each share new Common no par exchanged for (0.1) share Common $0.001 par 08/01/1994
Name changed to Cyberamerica Corp. 06/18/1996
Cyberamerica Corp. name changed to Axia Group, Inc. 12/07/2000 which recapitalized as Artistmss International Group, Inc. 12/11/2012

CANTON NATL BK (CANTON, OH)
Each share Common $50 par exchanged for (2.5) shares Common $20 par 00/00/1944
Stock Dividends - 25% 08/00/1946; 33.33333333% 02/01/1965
Under plan of merger name changed to United National Bank & Trust Co. (Canton, OH) 10/02/1972
United National Bank & Trust Co. (Canton, OH) reorganized as UNB Corp. 10/01/1984 which name changed to Unizan Financial Corp. 03/08/2002 which merged into Huntington Bancshares Inc. 03/01/2006

CANTON TEA GARDEN CO. (IL)
Proclaimed dissolved for failure to pay taxes and file reports 05/17/1934

CANTON TIN PLATE CORP.
Acquired by Republic Steel Corp. 00/00/1936
Details not available

CANTON VENTURES LTD (BC)
Name changed to Seacorp Capital Corp. 03/01/1993
Seacorp Capital Corp. recapitalized as Seacorp Communications Inc. 04/07/1995
(See Seacorp Communications Inc.)

CANTOP INC (DE)
Charter forfeited for failure to maintain registered agent 01/07/1974

CANTOP INDS INC (DE)
Charter forfeited for failure to maintain a registered agent 02/10/1975

CANTOP VENTURES INC (NV)
Name changed to Wolf Resources, Inc. 05/09/2008
Wolf Resources, Inc. name changed to AISystems, Inc. 05/13/2010
(See AISystems, Inc.)

CANTOR CO. (DE)
Merged into Seaporcel, Inc. 02/02/1962
Each share Common $1 par exchanged for (5) shares Common 10¢ par
Seaporcel, Inc. name changed to Investment Property Builders, Inc. 11/16/1962 which name changed to Centree Corp. 10/05/1972 which name changed to Air Florida System, Inc. 12/26/1973 which name changed to Jet Florida System, Inc. 08/15/1985
(See Jet Florida System, Inc.)

CANTOR GROUP INC (CO)
Reincorporated under the laws of Wyoming as MedX Holdings, Inc. and Common $0.0001 par changed to $0.001 par 02/18/2016

CANTOR H & W ENTERPRISES INC (DE)
Name changed to Leisure & Learning, Inc. 10/07/1969
Leisure & Learning, Inc. merged into Majestic Penn State, Inc. (DE) 06/29/1973 which reincorporated in Pennsylvania 02/01/1976
(See Majestic Penn State, Inc. (PA))

CANTRELL CAP CORP (BC)
Name changed 06/19/1992
Name changed from Cantrell Resources Ltd. to Cantrell Capital Corp. 06/19/1992
Name changed to Petroamerica Oil Corp. 10/23/2009
(See Petroamerica Oil Corp.)

CANTREND INDS LTD (ON)
Class A no par and Class B no par reclassified as Class A Preference no par and Class B Preference no par respectively 05/17/1978
Class A Preference no par called for redemption 06/16/1978
Class B Preference no par called for redemption 06/16/1978
Public interest eliminated

CANTRI MINES LTD (ON)
Merged into Can-Con Enterprises & Explorations Ltd. 11/30/1970
Each share Capital Stock $1 par exchanged for (0.1) share Capital Stock no par
Can-Con Enterprises & Explorations Ltd. name changed to Aubet Resources Inc. 09/08/1981 which recapitalized as Aubet Explorations Ltd. 09/30/1998 which name changed to Visa Gold Explorations Inc. 08/25/1999
(See Visa Gold Explorations Inc.)

CANTRONIC SYS INC (BC)
Merged 11/30/2006
Merged from Cantronic Systems Inc. (YT) into Cantronic Systems Inc. (BC) 11/30/2006
Each share old Common no par exchanged for (1) share new Common no par
Note: Unexchanged certificates were cancelled and became without value 11/30/2013
Each share new Common no par exchanged again for (0.00000062) share new Common no par 02/01/2013
Note: In effect holders received $0.04 cash per share and public interest was eliminated

CANTY GOLD MINES (1945) LTD. (BC)
Completely liquidated 00/00/1954
Each share Common exchanged for first and final distribution of (0.5) share Nighthawk Gold Mines Ltd. Common $1 par
Nighthawk Gold Mines Ltd. recapitalized as High Point Mines Ltd. 03/07/1966 which recapitalized as Highhawk Mines Ltd. 05/18/1972 which recapitalized as Newhawk Gold Mines Ltd. 03/12/1979 which merged into Silver Standard Resources Inc. 09/30/1999

CANTY GOLD MINES (HEDLEY) LTD. (BC)
Succeeded by Canty Gold Mines (1945) Ltd. on a (1) for (3) basis 00/00/1945
Canty Gold Mines (1945) Ltd. liquidated for Nighthawk Gold Mines Ltd. 00/00/1954 which recapitalized as High Point Mines Ltd. 03/07/1966 which recapitalized as Highhawk Mines Mines Ltd. 05/18/1972 which recapitalized as Newhawk Gold Mines Ltd. 03/12/1979 which merged into Silver Standard Resources Inc. 09/30/1999

CANU RES LTD (BC)
Merged into Ican Minerals Ltd. (BC) 12/18/1986
Each share Common no par exchanged for (2) shares Common no par
Ican Minerals Ltd. (BC) reincorporated in Alberta 12/02/1992 which recapitalized as Net Resources Inc. 12/17/1998 which name changed to Bakbone Software Inc. (AB) 03/13/2000 which reincorporated in Canada 08/11/2003
(See BakBone Software Inc.)

CANUBA MANGANESE MINES LTD. (ON)
Charter cancelled and company declared dissolved for default in filing returns 09/08/1966

CANUC RES CORP OLD (ON)
Name changed 06/19/1980
Name changed from Canuc Mines Ltd. to Canuc Resources Corp. (Old) 06/19/1980
Each share old Common no par exchanged for (0.2) share new Common no par 07/02/1996
Merged into Canuc Resources Corp. (New) 12/31/1996
Each share new Common no par exchanged for (1) share Common no par

CANUCK EXPLORERS, LTD. (ON)
Charter cancelled and company declared dissolved for default in filing returns 09/18/1961

CANUCK RES CORP (BC)
Name changed to Intertel Communications Inc. 12/14/1990
Intertel Communications Inc. name changed to Intelcom Group Inc. 09/01/1993 which reorganized as ICG Communications, Inc. 08/02/1996
(See ICG Communications, Inc.)

CANUS LABS LTD (BC)
Cease trade order effective 12/05/1988
Stockholders' equity unlikely

CANUS MINES & EXPLORATION LTD.
Name changed to Canus Petroleum Corp. Ltd. 00/00/1948
(See Canus Petroleum Corp. Ltd.)

CANUS PETROLEUM CORP. LTD. (ON)
Charter cancelled and company declared dissolved for default in filing returns 01/27/1966

CANUSA CAP CORP (DE)
Reorganized as DecisionPoint Systems, Inc. (Old) 07/01/2009
Each share Common $0.001 par exchanged for (8) shares Common $0.001 par
DecisionPoint Systems, Inc. (Old) merged into Comamtech Inc. (ON) 06/15/2011 which reincorporated in Delaware as DecisionPoint Systems, Inc. (New) 06/22/2011

CANUSA CARIBOO GOLD MINES LTD. (BC)
Recapitalized as Canusa Mines Ltd. 00/00/1956
Each share Capital Stock 50¢ par exchanged for (0.2) share Capital Stock 50¢ par
Canusa Mines Ltd. recapitalized as Interplex Mining & Industrial Ltd. 05/20/1969 which name changed to Interplex Spa Industries Ltd. 09/15/1971
(See Interplex Spa Industries Ltd.)

CANUSA ENERGY LTD (BC)
Merged into Bonanza Resources Ltd. 10/07/1983
Each share Common no par exchanged for (0.5) share Common no par
Bonanza Resources Ltd. recapitalized as CanCapital Corp. (AB) 02/09/1987 which reincorporated in British Columbia 05/12/1993 which recapitalized as Prada Holdings Ltd. (BC) 07/14/1994 which reincorporated in Yukon 07/26/1996
(See Prada Holdings Ltd.)

CANUSA FINL CORP (BC)
Name changed to Micro Concepts Inc. 11/01/1989
(See Micro Concepts Inc.)

CANUSA GOLD MINES LTD. (ON)
Charter cancelled 08/11/1959

CANUSA HLDGS LTD (DE)
Name changed to Anusound Inc. 02/13/1973
(See Anusound Inc.)

CANUSA MINES LTD (BC)
Recapitalized as Interplex Mining & Industrial Ltd. 05/20/1969
Each share Capital Stock 50¢ par exchanged for (0.5) share Capital Stock no par
Interplex Mining & Industrial Ltd. name changed to Interplex Spa Industries Ltd. 09/15/1971
(See Interplex Spa Industries Ltd.)

CANUTILITIES HLDGS LTD (AB)
Each share Retractable Preferred Ser. A no par exchanged for (0.5) share Preferred Ser. A no par, (0.25) share Preferred Ser. B no par and (0.25) share Preferred Ser. C no par 10/17/1994
Ser. A Preferred no par called for redemption at $25 plus $0.37 accrued dividends on 07/01/2001
Ser. B Preferred no par called for redemption at $25 on 07/01/2001
Ser. C Preferred no par called for redemption at $25 on 07/01/2001

CANVEDO INDS LTD (ON)
Recapitalized as Corporate Master Ltd. 11/19/1973
Each share Common no par exchanged for (0.2) share Common no par
Preferred not affected except for change of name
(See Corporate Master Ltd.)

CANVEND VENTURE CAP INC (AB)
Recapitalized as Serenpet Energy Inc. 10/19/1990
Each share Common no par exchanged for (0.25) share Common no par

Serenpet Energy Inc. recapitalized as Serenpet Inc. 04/07/1992
(See Serenpet Inc.)

CANWEL BLDG MATLS INCOME FD (BC)
Each Unit no par exchanged for (1) share CanWel Holdings Corp. Common no par 02/04/2010
CanWel Holdings Corp. name changed to CanWel Building Materials Group Ltd. 05/11/2010

CANWEL BLDG MATLS LTD (BC)
Reorganized as CanWel Building Materials Income Fund 05/18/2005
Each share Common no par exchanged for (2) Trust Units no par
Note: Option for Canadian residents to receive (2) CanWel Operating Partnership Exchangeable Partnership Units in lieu of Trust Units expired 05/05/2005
CanWel Building Materials Income Fund exchanged for CanWel Holdings Corp. 02/04/2010

CANWEL HLDGS CORP (CANADA)
Reincorporated 02/01/2010
Place of incorporation changed from (BC) to (Canada) 02/01/2010
Name changed to CanWel Building Materials Group Ltd. 05/11/2010

CANWEL OPER PARTNERSHIP (BC)
Each Exchangeable Partnership Unit exchanged for (1) share CanWel Holdings Corp. Common no par 02/04/2010
CanWel Holdings Corp. name changed to CanWel Building Materials Group Ltd. 05/11/2010

CANWEST EXPL INC (BC)
Recapitalized as Watch Resources Ltd. (BC) 10/13/2000
Each share Common no par exchanged for (0.05) share Common no par
Watch Resources Ltd. (BC) reincorporated in Alberta 07/20/2006 which recapitalized as Watch Resources Ltd. (New) 01/17/2007 which merged into Pearl Exploration & Production Ltd. 10/21/2007 which name changed to BlackPearl Resources Inc. 05/14/2009

CANWEST FINL HLDGS LTD (CANADA)
$2.56 Retractable Preferred Ser. A no par called for redemption 01/09/1984
Public interest eliminated

CANWEST GLOBAL COMMUNICATIONS CORP (CANADA)
Subordinate Shares no par split (2) for (1) by issuance of (1) additional share 02/20/1995
Subordinate Shares no par split (3) for (1) by issuance of (2) additional shares payable 07/15/1996 to holders of record 06/04/1996
Non-Vtg. Shares no par split (3) for (1) by issuance of (2) additional shares payable 07/15/1996 to holders of record 06/04/1996
Stock Dividend - 1.24% payable 09/29/2000 to holders of record 09/15/2000
Sale of assets under Bankruptcy and Insolvency Act effective 10/27/2010
Each Subordinate Shares no par exchanged for $0.061921 cash
Each Non-Vtg. Share no par exchanged for $0.061921 cash

CANWEST MEDIAWORKS INCOME FD (ON)
Merged into CanWest MediaWorks LP 07/10/2007
Each Unit no par received $9 cash

CANWEST PETE CORP (CO)
Name changed to Oilsands Quest Inc. 11/01/2006
(See Oilsands Quest Inc.)

CANWEST TRUSTCO LTD (CANADA)
Plan of amalgamation effective 04/25/1996
Each share Class A Common no par exchanged for (67.2) shares Class B Preference no par which was subsequently redeemed at $0.01 cash per share

CANWEX EXPLS LTD (BC)
Struck off register and declared dissolved for failure to file returns 02/25/1983

CANYON CARIBOO GOLD MINES, LTD. (BC)
Struck off register and dissolved by default 04/11/1957
No stockholders' equity

CANYON CITY EXPLS LTD (BC)
Struck off register and declared dissolved for failure to file returns 12/18/1978

CANYON COPPER CORP (BC)
Reorganized 05/31/2013
Each share old Common $0.00001 par exchanged for (0.33333333) share new Common $0.00001 par 05/15/2009
Each share new Common $0.00001 par exchanged again for (0.79) share new Common $0.00001 par 11/24/2010
Reorganized from Nevada to under the laws of British Columbia 05/31/2013
Each share new Common $0.00001 par exchanged for (1) share Common no par
Each share old Common no par exchanged for (0.06666666) share new Common no par 01/21/2014
Each share new Common no par exchanged again for (0.33333333) share new Common no par 08/17/2017
Name changed to Searchlight Resources Inc. 07/27/2018

CANYON GOLD, INC. (CO)
Capital Stock 1¢ par changed to 5¢ par 00/00/1958
Declared defunct and inoperative for failure to pay franchise taxes and file annual reports 10/26/1960

CANYON GOLD CORP (DE)
Each share old Common $0.0001 par exchanged for (0.05) share new Common $0.0001 par 04/04/2014
Name changed to Defense Technologies International Corp. 06/15/2016

CANYON MTN THEATERS INC (NV)
Name changed to Consolidated Oil & Gas Inc. 10/03/2002
Consolidated Oil & Gas Inc. name changed to Hampden Group Inc. 03/17/2003 which recapitalized as myPhotoPipe.com, Inc. 10/06/2006
(See myPhotoPipe.com, Inc.)

CANYON NATL BK (PALM SPRINGS, CA)
Common $5 par changed to $2.50 and (1) additional share issued payable 05/12/2004 to holders of record 04/26/2004 Ex date - 05/13/2004
Stock Dividends - 5% payable 04/16/2002 to holders of record 04/05/2002 Ex date - 04/03/2002; 5% payable 04/14/2003 to holders of record 03/31/2003 Ex date - 03/27/2003; 5% payable 12/19/2003 to holders of record 12/05/2003 Ex date - 12/03/2003; 5% payable 05/24/2005 to holders of record 05/06/2005 Ex date - 05/04/2005; 5% payable 12/22/2005 to holders of record 12/07/2005 Ex date - 12/05/2005
Under plan of reorganization each share Common $2.50 par automatically became (1) share Canyon Bancorp Common no par 06/30/2006

CANYON REEF CARRIERS INC (TX)
Merged into Pennzoil Exploration & Production Co. 06/12/1997
Each share Common 1¢ par exchanged for $12.20 cash

CANYON RES CORP (DE)
Each share old Common 1¢ par exchanged for (0.25) share new Common 1¢ par 03/24/2000
Merged into Atna Resources Ltd. 03/19/2008
Each share Common 1¢ par exchanged for (0.32) share Common no par
(See Atna Resources Ltd.)

CANYON SVCS GROUP INC (AB)
Merged into Trican Well Service Co., Ltd. 06/07/2017
Each share Common no par exchanged for (1.7) shares Common no par
Note: Unexchanged certificates will be cancelled and become without value 06/07/2020

CANYON SILVER MINES INC (ID)
Charter forfeited for failure to file reports 03/01/1991

CANYON ST CORP (NV)
Name changed to American Pacific Mint, Inc. 07/15/1986
American Pacific Mint, Inc. name changed to Dallas Gold & Silver Exchange Inc. 06/18/1992 which name changed to DGSE Companies, Inc. 06/27/2001

CANYON STATE MINING CORP. (CO)
Charter suspended for failure to file annual reports 10/17/1974

CANYON STATE MINING CORP. OF NEVADA (NV)
Recapitalized as Canyon State Corp. 10/14/1981
Each share Common $1 par exchanged for (0.2) share Common 1¢ par
Canyon State Corp. name changed to American Pacific Mint, Inc. 07/15/1986 which name changed to Dallas Gold & Silver Exchange Inc. 06/18/1992 which name changed to DGSE Companies, Inc. 06/27/2001

CANYONLANDS URANIUM INC (NV)
Merged into M & D Development, Inc. 12/30/1982
Each share Common 5¢ par exchanged for $0.05 cash

CANZAC MINES LTD. (BC)
Merged into Wollaston Lake Mines Ltd. 04/15/1969
Each share Capital Stock 50¢ par exchanged for (0.33333333) share Capital Stock 50¢ par
Wollaston Lake Mines Ltd. recapitalized as Comaplex Resources International Ltd. (BC) 09/08/1971 which reincorporated in Alberta 00/00/1987
(See Comaplex Resources International Ltd.)

CANZONA MINERALS INC (BC)
Merged into American Energy Corp. 08/03/1982
Each share Common no par exchanged for (0.25) share Common no par
American Energy Corp. recapitalized as Nickling Resources Inc. 06/05/1984 which recapitalized as Florin Resources Inc. 05/09/1989 which merged into Crimsonstar Mining Corp. 06/19/1991 which recapitalized as Mountain View Ventures Inc. 05/21/1993 which recapitalized as Blackrun Ventures Inc. 04/08/1997 which recapitalized as Blackrun Minerals Inc. 06/10/1999 which name changed to Diversified Industries Ltd. 03/29/2000
(See Diversified Industries Ltd.)

CAP & GOWN CO. (DE)
Acquired by Cenco Instruments Corp. 05/02/1966
Each share Class A Common $1 par exchanged for (0.190006) share $3 Conv. Preferred $5 par
Cenco Instruments Corp. name changed to Cenco Inc. 10/06/1972
(See Cenco Inc.)

CAP CORP (NV)
Under plan of liquidation each share Common 1¢ par received first and final distribution of (1) Unit of Ltd. Partnership of Cap Ltd. 05/15/1983
(See Cap Ltd.)

CAP EX IRON ORE LTD (CANADA)
Each share old Common no par exchanged for (0.25) share new Common no par 09/22/2014
Name changed to ML Gold Corp. 11/03/2016

CAP-EX VENTURES LTD (CANADA)
Name changed to Cap-Ex Iron Ore Ltd. 03/20/2013
Cap-Ex Iron Ore Ltd. name changed to ML Gold Corp. 11/03/2016

CAP GEMINI S A (FRANCE)
ADR's for Ordinary split (5) for (2) by issuance of (1.5) additional ADR's payable 11/01/2016 to holders of record 10/31/2016 Ex date - 11/02/2016
Basis changed from (1:0.5) to (1:0.2) 11/02/2016
Name changed to Capgemini S.E. 06/20/2017

CAP-LINK VENTURES LTD (CANADA)
Name changed to Petrodorado Energy Ltd. 04/08/2010

CAP LTD. (OK)
Completely liquidated 12/21/1988
Each Unit of Ltd. Partnership received first and final distribution of $0.23 cash

CAP ROC INC (NY)
Merged into Duplan Corp. 09/30/1969
Each share Common $1 par exchanged for $31 principal amount of 5.5% Conv. Subord. Debentures due 02/01/1994

CAP ROCK ENERGY CORP (TX)
Merged into Lindsay Goldberg & Bessemer L.P. 05/11/2006
Each share Common 1¢ par exchanged for $21.75 cash

CAP RX LTD (BERMUDA)
Reincorporated under the laws of Delaware as Capx Corp. 02/26/1992
Capx Corp. name changed to Autolend Group, Inc. 02/13/1995
(See Autolend Group, Inc.)

CAPA SOFTWARE PUBG CORP (SK)
Delisted from Alberta Stock Exchange 01/12/1993

CAPAC BANCORP INC (MI)
Merged into County Bank Corp. 09/22/2016
Each share Common no par exchanged for (0.9) share new Common $5 par

CAPALTA INC (AB)
Acquired by CDK Services Ltd. 10/15/2002
Each share Common no par exchanged for (1) Unit consisting of (1) share Common no par and (1) Common Stock Purchase Warrant expiring 04/30/2002
CDK Services Ltd. name changed to EcoMax Energy Services Ltd. (AB) 07/05/2005 which reincorporated in British Columbia as Tasca Resources Ltd.10/19/2011

CAPAMERICA FD INC (DE)
Name changed to Bull & Bear Equity-Income Fund, Inc. 05/02/1983
Bull & Bear Equity-Income Fund, Inc. merged into Bull & Bear Financial News Composite Fund, Inc. 09/00/1992 which merged into Bull & Bear Fund I, Inc. 01/21/1994 which name changed to Midas U.S. & Overseas Fund Ltd. 06/28/1999
(See Midas U.S. & Overseas Fund Ltd.)

CAPBERTA ENTERPRISES INC (AB)
Struck off register for failure to file annual returns 11/01/1990

CAPCO AUTOMOTIVE PRODS CORP (MI)
Merged into Eaton Corp. 04/17/1996
Each share Common 1¢ par exchanged for $12.50 cash

CAPCO ENERGY INC (CO)
Each share old Common $0.001 par exchanged for (4) shares new Common $0.001 par 12/26/2003
Plan of reorganization under Chapter 11 Federal Bankruptcy proceedings effective 07/22/2009
No stockholders' equity

CAPE ANN BK & TR CO (GLOUCESTER, MA)
Reorganized as Yankee Bancorporation 01/22/1973
Each share Capital Stock $10 par exchanged for (2) shares Common $1 par
Yankee Bancorporation merged into Massachusetts Bay Bancorporation, Inc. 03/31/1976 which merged into New England Merchants Co., Inc. 05/31/1980 which name changed to Bank of New England Corp. 05/01/1982
(See Bank of New England Corp.)

CAPE BANCORP INC (MD)
Merged into OceanFirst Financial Corp. 05/02/2016
Each share Common 1¢ par exchanged for (0.6375) share Common 1¢ par and $2.25 cash

CAPE BRETON ELECTRIC CO. LTD.
Dissolved 00/00/1931
Details not available

CAPE CANAVERAL CORP (FL)
Name changed to Electronomic Industries, Inc. (FL) 11/17/1969
Electronomic Industries, Inc. (FL) reincorporated in New York as Electronomic Industries Corp. 02/23/1979 which name changed to Quantech Electronics Corp. (NY) 02/23/1983 which reincorporated in Colorado 12/15/2003 which name changed to Signal Bay, Inc. 10/24/2014 which recapitalized as EVIO, Inc. 09/06/2017

CAPE COASTAL TRADING CORP (DE)
Reorganized 12/15/2005
Reorganized from (NY) to under the laws of Delaware 12/15/2005
Each (1.6667) shares Common $0.001 par exchanged for (1) share $0.001 par
Name changed to uBid.com Holdings, Inc. 02/10/2006
uBid.com Holdings, Inc. name changed to Enable Holdings, Inc. 08/04/2008
(See Enable Holdings, Inc.)

CAPE COD AQUACULTURE CORP (NV)
Common $0.001 par split (9) for (1) by issuance of (8) additional shares payable 12/17/2009 to holders of record 12/03/2009 Ex date - 12/18/2009
Name changed to Bluewave Group, Inc. 03/18/2010
Bluewave Group, Inc. recapitalized as Green & Hill Industries, Inc. 08/06/2013

CAPE COD BK & TR CO (HYANNIS, MA)
Common $10 par changed to $5 par and (1) additional share issued 06/25/1982
Common $5 par changed to $2.50 par and (1) additional share issued 11/30/1984
Common $2.50 par split (2) for (1) by issuance of (1) additional share 06/25/1986
Common $2.50 par split (2) for (1) by issuance of (1) additional share payable 05/10/1996 to holders of record 04/24/1996
Common $2.50 par split (2) for (1) by issuance of (1) additional share payable 08/07/1998 to holders of record 07/20/1998
Under plan of reorganization each share Common $2.50 par automatically became (1) share CCBT Bancorp Inc. Common $2.50 par 02/11/1999
CCBT Bancorp Inc. name changed to CCBT Financial Companies Inc. 09/23/1999 which merged into Banknorth Group, Inc. (ME) 04/30/2004 which merged into TD Banknorth Inc. 03/01/2005
(See TD Banknorth Inc.)

CAPE CODDER SYS INC (KY)
Adjudicated bankrupt 03/08/1978
Stockholders' equity unlikely

CAPE COPPER MINES, LTD. (ON)
Charter cancelled 08/29/1960

CAPE CORAL ACQUISITION INC (CO)
Recapitalized as International Converter Corp. 11/21/1989
Each share Common no par exchanged for (0.04) share Common no par
International Converter Corp. name changed to V.I.P. Global Capital Inc. 11/03/1992
(See V.I.P. Global Capital Inc.)

CAPE CORAL BK & TR (CAPE CORAL, FL)
Merged into Sun Banks of Florida, Inc. 01/07/1980
Each share Capital Stock $5 par exchanged for $54.20 cash

CAPE CORAL BANK (CAPE CORAL, FL)
Each share Capital Stock $10 par exchanged for (2) shares Capital Stock $5 par 05/09/1973
Name changed to Cape Coral Bank & Trust (Cape Coral, FL) 01/25/1977
(See Cape Coral Bank & Trust (Cape Coral, FL))

CAPE CORAL FINL CORP (FL)
Name changed to South Florida Financial Corp. 05/16/1987
(See South Florida Financial Corp.)

CAPE FEAR BK CORP (NC)
Stock Dividend - 5% payable 06/29/2007 to holders of record 06/22/2007 Ex date - 06/20/2007
Plan of reorganization under Chapter 11 Federal Bankruptcy proceedings effective 12/21/2009
Stockholders' equity unlikely

CAPE GIRARDEAU BRIDGE CO.
Property sold 00/00/1935
No stockholders' equity

CAPE MAY CNTY NATL BK (OCEAN CITY, NJ)
Stock Dividends - 10% 05/24/1968; 100% 08/06/1962
Merged into First National Bank of South Jersey (Pleasantville, NJ) 05/31/1975
Each share Common $10 par exchanged for $50 cash

CAPE RANGE WIRELESS LTD (AUSTRALIA)
Name changed 06/07/2005
Name changed from Cape Range Ltd. to Cape Range Wireless Ltd. 06/07/2005
Each old Sponsored ADR for Ordinary exchanged for (0.01666666) new Sponsored ADR for Ordinary 02/11/2008
Each new Sponsored ADR for Ordinary exchanged again for (0.04) new Sponsored ADR for Ordinary 01/21/2011
ADR agreement terminated 11/20/2012
Each new Sponsored ADR for Ordinary exchanged for $0.236667 cash

CAPE RES INC (ON)
Merged into International Pagurian Corp. Ltd. 03/27/1987
Each share Common no par exchanged for (0.11111111) share Common no par
International Pagurian Corp. Ltd. name changed to Canadian Express Ltd. (Old) 05/12/1988 which recapitalized as Consolidated Canadian Express Ltd. 12/24/1990 which name changed to Canadian Express Ltd. (New) 05/18/2001 which recapitalized as BNN Investments Ltd. 11/02/2001 which name changed to BAM Investments Corp. 07/05/2006 which name changed to Partners Value Fund Inc. 06/10/2013 which name changed to Partners Value Investments Inc. 05/25/2015 which reorganized as Partners Value Investments L.P. 07/04/2016

CAPE SYS GROUP INC (NJ)
SEC revoked common stock registration 11/10/2010

CAPE VERDE EXPLORATIONS, LTD. (NV)
Charter permanently revoked 05/01/2005

CAPEHART, INC.
Assets acquired by Farnsworth Television & Radio Corp. 00/00/1939
Details not available

CAPEHART CORP. (NY)
Name changed to Clavier Corp. and Common 50¢ par changed to 5¢ par 08/31/1964
Clavier Corp. merged into Dero Research & Development Corp. 09/24/1969 which name changed to Dero Industries Inc. 02/10/1971
(See Dero Industries Inc.)

CAPEHART CORP (DE)
Stock Dividend - 100% 04/28/1972
Proceedings under Chapter XI dismissed 04/16/1981
No stockholders' equity

CAPELLA ED CO (MN)
Merged into Strategic Education, Inc. 08/01/2018
Each share Common 10¢ par exchanged for (0.875) share Common 1¢ par

CAPELLA RES LTD. (BC)
Incorporated 02/27/1987
Each share old Common no par exchanged for (0.1) share new Common no par 12/24/2008
Recapitalized as Cerro Mining Corp. 05/16/2012
Each share new Common no par exchanged for (0.16666666) share Common no par

CAPELLA RES LTD (BC)
Incorporated 00/00/1973
Struck from the register and dissolved 11/23/1990

CAPEQ CORP (AB)
Delisted from Alberta Stock Exchange 10/17/1997

CAPEWELL MFG INC (CT)
Common $5 par changed to $1 par and (4) additional shares issued 04/15/1966
Preferred $25 par called for redemption 03/31/1967
Stock Dividend - 100% 05/15/1967
Through purchase offer by Standard Screw Co. of $7 for each share Common $1 par less than (1,500) shares remained unexchanged as of 11/10/1970
Public interest eliminated

CAPEX S A (ARGENTINA)
Stock Dividends - 12.43236% payable 10/18/1999 to holders of record 10/08/1999; 17.27496% payable 11/03/2000 to holders of record 10/24/2000
GDR agreement terminated 10/23/2002
Each 144A GDR for Ordinary exchanged for $2.8736915 cash

CAPEZIO & THINGS INC (MD)
Each share old Common no par exchanged for (0.2) share new Common no par 12/13/1973
Company believed out of business 00/00/1996
Details not available

CAPFILM INC (DE)
Each share old Common $0.001 par exchanged for (0.2) share new Common $0.001 par 05/26/1992
Ceased operations 12/31/1997
Stockholders' equity unlikely

CAPGAIN PPTYS INC (BC)
Reincorporated under the laws of Alberta 03/27/2013

CAPGROW INC (AB)
Recapitalized as Oakhill Communications Inc. 07/25/1995
Each share Common no par exchanged for (0.33333333) share Common no par
(See Oakhill Communications Inc.)

CAPILANO INTL INC (CANADA)
Name changed to Kelman Technologies Inc. 08/14/1996
(See Kelman Technologies Inc.)

CAPILANO RES INC (BC)
Cease trade order effective 06/29/1989
Stockholders' equity unlikely

CAPISTRANO BANCORP (CA)
Charter cancelled for failure to file reports and pay taxes 04/01/1988

CAPISTRANO GROUP (CA)
Charter cancelled for failure to file reports and pay taxes 02/15/1994

CAPISTRANO NATIONAL BANK (SAN JUAN CAPISTRANO, CA)
Common $5 par changed to $2.50 par and (1) additional share issued 05/27/1980
Under plan of reorganization each share Common $2.50 par automatically became (1) share Capistrano Bancorp Common $2.50 par 12/07/1981
(See Capistrano Bancorp)

CAPITA GROUP (UNITED KINGDOM)
Name changed to Capita PLC 01/17/2012

CAPITA PFD TR (DE)
Trust Originated Preferred Securities called for redemption at $29.25 on 09/01/1998

CAPITA RESH GROUP INC (NV)
SEC revoked common stock registration 10/28/2008

CAPITAL & INCOME STRATEGIES FD INC (MD)
Name changed to BlackRock Capital & Income Strategies Fund, Inc. 10/02/2006
BlackRock Capital & Income Strategies Fund, Inc. name changed

to BlackRock Enhanced Capital & Income Fund, Inc. 05/09/2007

CAPITAL ABTB INC (CANADA)
Reorganized under the laws of Quebec as BTB Real Estate Investment Trust 10/03/2006
Each share Common no par exchanged for (0.2) Trust Unit no par

CAPITAL ACQUISITIONS HLDGS LTD (NV)
Name changed to Sun Peaks Energy, Inc. 02/13/2007
(See Sun Peaks Energy, Inc.)

CAPITAL ACQUISITIONS INC (DE)
Reincorporated under the laws of Florida as Capital Brands, Inc. 09/08/1994
Capital Brands, Inc. name changed to CompScript, Inc. 07/08/1996 which merged into Omnicare, Inc. 06/26/1998
(See Omnicare, Inc.)

CAPITAL ADMINISTRATION CO., LTD. (MD)
Recapitalized 00/00/1933
Preferred $50 par changed to $10 par
Class A no par changed to $1 par
Recapitalized 00/00/1937
Class B no par changed to 1¢ par
Merged into Tri-Continental Corp. 00/00/1953
Each share $3 Preferred $10 par exchanged for (0.5) share $6 Preferred no par
Each share Class A $1 par exchanged for (1.5) shares Common $1 par and (1) Common Stock Purchase Warrant
Each share Class B 1¢ par exchanged for (0.2) share Common $1 par and (0.5) Common Stock Purchase Warrant

CAPITAL ADVISORS ACQUISITION CORP (DE)
Each share old Common $0.0001 par exchanged for (0.01) share new Common $0.0001 par 11/05/1996
Name changed to Harvard Financial Services Corp. 12/11/1997
Harvard Financial Services Corp. recapitalized as e*machinery.net, inc. 02/09/2000

CAPITAL AIRLINES, INC. (DE)
Merged into United Air Lines, Inc. on a 06/01/1961
Each (70) shares Common $1 par exchanged for (10.3) shares Common $10 par
United Air Lines, Inc. reorganized as UAL, Inc. 08/01/1969 which name changed to Allegis Corp. 04/30/1987 which name changed to UAL Corp. 05/27/1988
(See UAL Corp.)

CAPITAL ALLIANCE CORP (DE)
Name changed to Mariners Financial Corp. 02/09/1976
(See Mariners Financial Corp.)

CAPITAL ALLIANCE GROUP INC (BC)
Name changed to CIBT Education Group Inc. 11/14/2007

CAPITAL ALLIANCE INCOME TR REAL ESTATE INVT TR (DE)
Each share old Preferred Ser. A 1¢ par exchanged for (0.33333333) share new Preferred Ser. A 1¢ par 05/11/2001
Each share old Common 1¢ par exchanged for (0.33333333) share new Common 1¢ par 05/11/2001
Name changed to Eastern Light Capital, Inc. 08/25/2008

CAPITAL AND SERVICES, INC. (KS)
Charter forfeited for failure to file annual report 03/15/1995

CAPITAL APPLICATIONS INC (DE)
Recapitalized as Ventura Entertainment Group Ltd. 09/12/1988
Each share Common $0.001 par exchanged for (0.05) share Common $0.001 par
Ventura Entertainment Group Ltd. name changed to Insight Entertainment Corp. 09/20/1995
(See Insight Entertainemnt Corp.)

CAPITAL ART INC (DE)
Name changed to Globe Photos, Inc. 06/25/2018

CAPITAL ASSOC INC (DE)
Each share old Common $0.008 par exchanged for (0.5) share new Common $0.008 par 11/02/1995
SEC revoked common stock registration 08/16/2000

CAPITAL ASSURN CORP (NV)
Each share old Common $0.001 par exchanged for (0.00125) share new Common $0.001 par 03/30/1999
Name changed to Phelps Engineered Plastics Corp. 05/17/1999
Phelps Engineered Plastics Corp. name changed to Clayton, Dunning Group Inc. 07/29/2005 which recapitalized as Carlton Companies, Inc. 07/09/2008

CAPITAL AUTOMOTIVE REIT (MD)
Merged into Flag Fun V LLC 12/16/2005
Each Common Share of Bene. Int. 1¢ par exchanged for $38.75 cash
7.5% Preferred Ser. A 1¢ par called for redemption at $25 on 04/02/2012
8% Preferred Ser. B 1¢ par called for redemption at $25 on 04/02/2012
Public interest eliminated

CAPITAL BANCORP (CA)
Company's principal asset closed by California Superintendent of Banks 08/26/1994
No stockholders' equity

CAPITAL BANCORP (FL)
Merged into Union Planters Corp. 12/31/1997
Each share Common $1 par exchanged for (0.8525) share Common $5 par
Union Planters Corp. merged into Regions Financial Corp. (New) 07/01/2004

CAPITAL BANCORP INC (TN)
Common $4 par split (2) for (1) by issuance of (1) additional share payable 08/16/2004 to holders of record 07/30/2004
Merged into Renasant Corp. 07/03/2007
Each share Common $4 par exchanged for (0.7304243) share Common $5 par and $16.074 cash

CAPITAL BANCORPORATION INC (MO)
Merged into Union Planters Corp. 12/31/1995
Each Depositary Share Ser. C exchanged for $20 cash
Each share Increasing Rate Preferred Ser. C no par exchanged for $20 cash
Each share Common 10¢ par exchanged for (1.185) shares Common $5 par
Union Planters Corp. merged into Regions Financial Corp. (New) 07/01/2004

CAPITAL BANCSHARES INC (FL)
Name changed to Capital General Corp. 11/03/1969
(See Capital General Corp.)

CAPITAL BANCSHARES INC (LA)
Stock Dividend - 15% 04/28/1981
Charter revoked for failure to file annual reports 08/18/1998

CAPITAL BANK, N.A. (WASHINGTON, DC)
Acquired by FCNB Bank (Frederick, MD) 11/20/1998
Details not available

CAPITAL BK & TR (BELTON, SC)
Acquired by Southern National Bank of South Carolina (Greenville, SC) 12/31/1986
Details not available

CAPITAL BANK & TRUST CO. (HARRISBURG, PA)
Stock Dividend - 33.33333333% 06/12/1946
Merged into Central Trust Capital Bank (Harrisburg, PA) 07/03/1958
Each share Capital Stock $10 par exchanged for (1.65) shares Capital Stock $10 par
Central Trust Capital Bank (Harrisburg, PA) merged into National Bank & Trust Co. of Central Pennsylvania (York, PA) 10/13/1961 which merged into National Central Bank (Lancaster, PA) 12/07/1970 which reorganized as National Central Financial Corp. 12/31/1972 which merged into CoreStates Financial Corp 05/02/1983 which merged into First Union Corp. 04/28/1998 which name changed to Wachovia Corp. (Ctfs. dated after 09/01/2001) 09/01/2001 which merged into Wells Fargo & Co. (New) 12/31/2008

CAPITAL BK & TR CO (ALBANY, NY)
6% Conv. Perpetual Preferred Ser. A called for redemption at $25 plus $0.375 accrued dividends on 12/30/2005
Under plan of reorganization each share Common $4 par automatically became (1) share Fort Orange Financial Corp. Common $4 par 12/04/2006
Fort Orange Financial Corp. merged into Chemung Financial Corp. 04/08/2011

CAPITAL BK & TR CO (BATON ROUGE, LA)
Stock Dividends - 10% 03/08/1977; 10% 03/14/1978; 10% 04/17/1979
Under plan of reorganization each share Common $10 par automatically became (1) share Capital Bancshares, Inc. Common $10 par 03/31/1980
(See Capital Bancshares, Inc.)

CAPITAL BK & TR CO (NASHVILLE, TN)
Under plan of reorganization each share Common $10 par automatically became (1) share Capital Bancorp, Inc. Common $4 par 07/02/2001
Capital Bancorp, Inc. merged into Renasant Corp. 07/03/2007

CAPITAL BANK (CLEVELAND, OH)
Stock Dividend - 20% 01/13/1960
Name changed to Capital National Bank (Cleveland, OH) 11/16/1964
(See Capital National Bank (Cleveland, OH))

CAPITAL BANK (DOWNEY, CA)
Reorganized as Capital Bancorp 01/27/1982
Each share Common Capital Stock $10 par exchanged for (1) share Common no par
(See Capital Bancorp)

CAPITAL BANK (NORTH BAY VILLAGE, FL)
Acquired by Capital Bancorp 09/00/1982
Each share Common $10 par exchanged for (1) share Common $1 par
Capital Bancorp merged into Union Planters Corp. 12/31/1997 which merged into Regions Financial Corp. (New) 07/01/2004

CAPITAL BK (RALEIGH, NC)
Under plan of reorganization each share Common $5 par automatically became (1) share Capital Bank Corp. Common $5 par 03/31/1999
Capital Bank Corp. merged into Capital Bank Financial Corp. 09/24/2012 which merged into First Horizon National Corp. 11/30/2017

CAPITAL BK (SAN JUAN CAPISTRANO)
Stock Dividend - 5% payable 11/23/2016 to holders of record 09/30/2016
Merged into Seacoast Commerce Banc Holdings 10/01/2017
Each share Common no par exchanged for (1.38376) shares Common no par and $6.40 cash

CAPITAL BK CALIF (LOS ANGELES, CA)
Bank closed by California Superintendent of Banks 06/18/1993
No stockholders' equity

CAPITAL BK CORP (NC)
Merged into Capital Bank Financial Corp. 09/24/2012
Each share Common no par exchanged for (0.1354) share Class A Common 1¢ par
Capital Bank Financial Corp. merged into First Horizon National Corp. 11/30/2017

CAPITAL BK FINL CORP (DE)
Merged into First Horizon National Corp. 11/30/2017
Each share Class A Common 1¢ par exchanged for (2.1732) shares Common $0.625 par

CAPITAL BK MIAMI N A (MIAMI, FL)
Merged into Capital Bank (North Bay Village, FL) 12/30/1977
Each share Common $4 par exchanged for (0.33333333) share Common $10 par
Capital Bank (North Bay Village, FL) acquired by Capital Bancorp 09/00/1982 which merged into Union Planters Corp. 12/31/1997 which merged into Regions Financial Corp. (New) 07/01/2004

CAPITAL BK N A (ROCKVILLE, MD)
Merged into FCNB Corp. 11/19/1998
Each share Common no par exchanged for (1.7382) shares Common no par
FCNB Corp. merged into BB&T Corp. 01/08/2001

CAPITAL BANK OF BROWARD COUNTY (OAKLAND PARK, FL)
Merged into Capitol Bancorp 12/31/1982
Each share Capital Stock $10 par exchanged for $21.61 cash

CAPITAL BANK OF KENDALE (KENDALE, FL)
Merged into Capital Bank (North Bay Village, FL) 12/30/1977
Each share Common $10 par exchanged for (1) share Common $10 par
Capital Bank (North Bay Village, FL) acquired by Capital Bancorp 09/00/1982 which merged into Union Planters Corp. 12/31/1997 which merged into Regions Financial Corp. (New) 07/01/2004

CAPITAL BANK OF NORTH BAY VILLAGE (NORTH BAY VILLAGE, FL)
Merged into Capital Bank (North Bay Village, FL) 12/30/1977
Each share Common $10 par exchanged for (1) share Common $10 par
Capital Bank (North Bay Village, FL) acquired by Capital Bancorp 09/00/1982 which merged into Union

Planters Corp. 12/31/1997 which merged into Regions Financial Corp. (New) 07/01/2004

CAPITAL BEVERAGE CORP OLD (DE)
Reorganized as Capital Beverage Corp. (New) 09/05/2018
Each share Common $0.001 par exchanged for (0.05) share Common $0.001 par

CAPITAL BLDG INDS LTD (ON)
Name changed to Capital Diversified Industries Ltd. 05/15/1969
Capital Diversified Industries Ltd. name changed to Action Traders Inc. 02/15/1978 which name changed to ATI Corp. 06/21/1988 which name changed to Prairie Capital Inc. (ON) 06/30/1999 which reorganized in Canada as Continental (CBOC) Corp. 08/30/2002 which name changed to Stonington Capital Corp. 06/22/2004 which merged into Pyxis Capital Inc. 02/27/2006
(See Pyxis Capital Inc.)

CAPITAL BLF INC (CANADA)
Reorganized under the laws of Quebec as BLF Real Estate Investment Trust 08/23/2013
Each share Common no par exchanged for (0.025) Trust Unit
Note: Unexchanged certificates will be cancelled and become without value 08/23/2019
(See BLF Real Estate Investment Trust)

CAPITAL BRANDS INC (FL)
Each share Common $0.0001 par exchanged for (0.125) share Common $0.0008 par 04/26/1996
Name changed to CompScript, Inc. 07/08/1996
CompScript, Inc. merged into Omnicare, Inc. 06/26/1998
(See Omnicare, Inc.)

CAPITAL BUILDERS DEVELOPMENT PROPERTIES, A CALIFORNIA LIMITED PARTNERSHIP (CA)
Terminated registration with SEC 03/28/2001
Details not available

CAPITAL BUILDERS DEVELOPMENT PROPERTIES, II, A CALIFORNIA LIMITED PARTNERSHIP (CA)
Terminated registration with SEC 12/31/2005
Details not available

CAPITAL BUILDING SYSTEMS, INC. (TX)
Charter forfeited for failure to pay taxes 03/21/1977

CAPITAL CABLE TV LTD (AB)
Name changed to Shaw Cablesystems Ltd. 06/12/1984
Shaw Cablesystems Ltd. name changed to Shaw Communications Inc. 05/26/1993

CHASE CAP IV (DE)
7.75% Capital Securities Ser. D called for redemption at $25 on 11/10/2003

CAPITAL CHARTER CORP (BC)
Reincorporated under the laws of Ontario as Zconnexx Corp. 03/24/2000
(See Zconnexx Corp.)

CAPITAL CITIES ABC INC (NY)
Common $1 par split (10) for (1) by issuance of (9) additional shares 06/17/1994
Merged into Disney (Walt) Co. 02/09/1996
Each share Common $1 par exchanged for either (1) share Common 1¢ par and $65 cash, (1.0493208) share Common 1¢ par and $61.9421106 cash or $127 cash
Note: Option to receive stock and cash expired 03/07/1996

CAPITAL CITIES BROADCASTING CORP. (NY)
Common $1 par split (2) for (1) by issuance of (1) additional share 02/03/1966
Common $1 par split (2) for (1) by issuance of (1) additional share 06/02/1969
Name changed to Capital Cities Communications, Inc. 05/07/1973
Capital Cities Communications, Inc. name changed to Capital Cities/ABC, Inc. 01/03/1986 which merged into Disney (Walt) Co. 02/09/1996

CAPITAL CITIES COMMUNICATIONS INC (NY)
50¢ Conv. Preferred $1 par called for redemption 06/20/1975
Common $1 par split (2) for (1) by issuance of (1) additional share 07/14/1978
Name changed to Capital Cities/ABC, Inc. 01/03/1986
Capital Cities/ABC, Inc. merged into Disney (Walt) Co. 02/09/1996

CAPITAL CITIES NURSING CENTRES INC (DE)
Charter cancelled and declared inoperative and void for non-payment of taxes 04/15/1972

CAPITAL CITIES TELEVISION CORP. (NY)
Name changed to Capital Cities Broadcasting Corp. 03/01/1960
Capital Cities Broadcasting Corp. name changed to Capital Cities Communications, Inc. 05/07/1973 which name changed to Capital Cities/ABC, Inc. 01/03/1986 which merged into Disney (Walt) Co. 02/09/1996

CAPITAL CITY BK (NASHVILLE, TN)
Merged into Nashville City Bank & Trust Co. (Nashville, TN) 11/20/1970
Each share Common $10 par exchanged for (4.87) shares Common $2 par
Nashville City Bank & Trust Co. (Nashville, TN) merged into Dominion Bankshares Corp. 01/30/1987 which merged into First Union Corp. 03/01/1993 which name changed to Wachovia Corp. (Ctfs. dated after 09/01/2001) 09/01/2001 which merged into Wells Fargo & Co. (New) 12/31/2008

CAPITAL CITY PRODUCTS CO. (DE)
Each share Common no par exchanged for (2) shares Common $5 par 00/00/1948
Common $5 par changed to $1 par and (1) additional share issued 11/21/1962
Merged into Stokely-Van Camp, Inc. 05/31/1964
Each share Common $1 par exchanged for (1) share Common $1 par
(See Stokely-Van Camp, Inc.)

CAPITAL CITY SURETY CO.
Liquidated 00/00/1930
Details not available

CAPITAL COLOR LABS INC (NY)
Dissolved by proclamation 09/29/1982

CAPITAL COM INC (AB)
Acquired by Pethealth Inc. 12/19/2000
Each share Common no par exchanged for (1) share Common no par
(See Pethealth Inc.)

CAPITAL COMPUTER INC (DE)
Charter cancelled and declared inoperative and void for non-payment of taxes 03/01/1986

CAPITAL CONSORTIUM INC (NV)
Name changed to Legend Sporting Goods, Inc. 11/14/1989

CAPITAL CORP OF THE WEST (CA)
Old Common no par split (3) for (2) by issuance of (0.5) additional share payable 05/02/1997 to holders of record 04/11/1997
Each share old Common no par exchanged for (1.8) shares new Common no par 04/08/2005
Stock Dividends - 5% payable 09/16/1996 to holders of record 08/16/1996; 5% payable 06/01/1998 to holders of record 05/07/1998; 5% payable 04/01/2001 to holders of record 03/09/2001 Ex date - 03/07/2001; 5% payable 04/26/2002 to holders of record 04/05/2002; 5% payable 04/25/2003 to holders of record 04/01/2003 Ex date - 03/28/2003
Plan of reorganization under Chapter 11 Federal Bankruptcy Code effective 02/04/2010
Stockholders' equity unlikely

CAPITAL CORP TEX (TX)
Texas State Securities Board revoked trading of stock 07/07/1970
Former president advised he will write off own holdings as worthless 00/00/1971

CAPITAL CORPORATE RES INC (NY)
Charter cancelled and proclaimed dissolved for failure to pay taxes 06/27/1979

CAPITAL CROSSING BK (BOSTON, MA)
Common $1 par split (2) for (1) by issuance of (1) additional share payable 08/09/2004 to holders of record 08/02/2004 Ex date - 08/10/2004
Merged into Lehman Brothers Holdings Inc. 02/15/2007
Each share Common $1 par exchanged for $30 cash

CAPITAL CROSSING PFD CORP (MA)
9.75% Non-Cumulative Exchangeable Preferred 1¢ par called for redemption at $10 on 03/23/2007
10.25% Non-Cumulative Exchangeable Preferred 1¢ par called for redemption at $10 on 03/23/2007
Name changed to EOS Preferred Corp. 07/13/2010
(See EOS Preferred Corp.)

CAPITAL DESBOG INC (CANADA)
Name changed to HLT Energies 2006 Inc. 04/18/2006
HLT Energies 2006 Inc. name changed to HLT Energies Inc. 02/28/2007
(See HLT Energies Inc.)

CAPITAL DEV GROUP INC (OR)
Each share old Common $0.0001 par exchanged for (0.0625) share new Common $0.0001 par 04/09/2002
Reincorporated under the laws of Florida as GSociety, Inc. and Common $0.0001 par changed to $0.001 par 05/28/2002
(See GSociety, Inc.)

CAPITAL DIAMOND & DEV CORP (NV)
Charter revoked for failure to file reports and pay fees 06/01/1985

CAPITAL DIRECTIONS INC (MI)
Common $5 par split (2) for (1) by issuance of (1) additional share payable 12/01/1997 to holders of record 11/03/1997
Merged into CDI Merger Co., Inc. 01/27/2004
Each share Common $5 par exchanged for $50 cash
Note: Holders of (225) shares or more retained their interests
Merged into Commercial National Financial Corp. 01/01/2017
Each share Common $5 par exchanged for (3.6998) shares Common no par and $18.04 cash

CAPITAL DIVERSIFIED INDS LTD (ON)
Name changed to Action Traders Inc. 02/15/1978
Action Traders Inc. name changed to ATI Corp. 06/21/1988 which name changed to Prairie Capital Inc. (ON) 06/30/1999 which reorganized in Canada as Continental (CBOC) Corp. 08/30/2002 which name changed to Stonington Capital Corp. 06/22/2004 which merged into Pyxis Capital Inc. 02/27/2006
(See Pyxis Capital Inc.)

CAPITAL DYNAMICS LTD (CANADA)
Struck off register and declared dissolved for failure to file returns 08/25/1995

CAPITAL ENDEAVORS CORP (BC)
Acquired by eMedia Networks International Corp. 02/25/2002
Each share Common no par exchanged for (0.48971596) Unit consisting of (1) share Common no par and (1) Common Stock Purchase Warrant expiring 02/22/2003
(See eMedia Networks International Corp.)

CAPITAL ENERGY & OPERATING CO. (NV)
Charter revoked for failure to file reports and pay fees 08/01/1985

CAPITAL ENERGY CORP (CA)
Name changed to Life Chemistry Inc. 11/28/1983
(See Life Chemistry Inc.)

CAPITAL ENTERPRISES INC. (UT)
Name changed to International Petroleum Holding Corp. 08/11/1959
International Petroleum Holding Corp. name changed to Federal Gold & Silver, Inc. 07/01/1968
(See Federal Gold & Silver, Inc.)

CAPITAL ENTERPRISES INC (CO)
Declared defunct and inoperative for failure to pay taxes and file annual reports 05/01/2002

CAPITAL ENVIRONMENTAL RESOURCE INC (ON)
Reorganized under the laws of Delaware as Waste Services, Inc. 07/31/2004
Each share Common no par exchanged for (1) share Common 1¢ par
Waste Services, Inc. merged into IESI-BFC Ltd. 07/02/2010 which name changed to Progressive Waste Solutions Ltd. 05/11/2011 which recapitalized as Waste Connections, Inc. 06/01/2016

CAPITAL EQUIP LEASING CORP (PA)
Common 1¢ par split (6) for (5) by issuance of (0.2) additional share 12/17/1973
Stock Dividend - 20% 12/29/1972
Name changed to Capital First Corp. 12/24/1973
Capital First Corp. name changed to Capitalcare Corp. 08/27/1984

CAPITAL EQUITY RES INC (DE)
Name changed to Asha Corp. 08/27/1986
Asha Corp. name changed to McLaren Automotive Group, Inc. 05/05/1999 which name changed to McLaren Performance Technologies, Inc. 04/20/2000
(See McLaren Performance Technologies, Inc.)

CAPITAL ESTATES INC (DE)
Capital Stock $6 par changed to $5 par 00/00/1945
Each share Capital Stock $5 par

exchanged for (5) shares Capital Stock $1 par 00/00/1954
100% acquired by Lucky Breweries, Inc. through purchase offer which expired 12/27/1971
Public interest eliminated

CAPITAL FACS CORP (NY)
Liquidation completed
Each share Common 1¢ par exchanged for initial distribution of $2.25 cash 11/20/1986
Each share Common 1¢ par received second and final distribution of $0.28 cash 02/24/1994

CAPITAL FACTORS HLDG INC (FL)
Merged into Union Planters & Asset Management 11/30/1998
Each share Common 1¢ par exchanged for $17.50 cash

CAPITAL FD AMER INC (DE)
Merged into New Perspective Fund, Inc. (MD) 11/03/1978
Each share Capital Stock $1 par exchanged for (1.277232) shares Common $1 par
New Perspective Fund, Inc. (MD) reincorporated in Delaware as New Perspective Fund 12/01/2012

CAPITAL FD INVT INC (NV)
Charter revoked for failure to file a list of officers 04/01/2002

CAPITAL FDG CORP (DE)
Common 25¢ par split (2) for (1) by issuance of (1) additional share 04/23/1969
Name changed to Amax Financial Corp. 06/01/1973
Amax Financial Corp. name changed to University Group, Inc. 07/01/1975 which merged into Southmark Corp. 02/08/1984
(See Southmark Corp.)

CAPITAL FED SVGS & LN ASSN SACRAMENTO CALIF (USA)
Acquired by San Francisco Federal Savings & Loan Association (USA) 02/29/1988
Each share Common $1 par exchanged for (1.2174) shares Common 1¢ par
San Francisco Federal Savings & Loan Association (USA) reorganized in Delaware as SFFED Corp. 07/01/1988
(See SFFED Corp.)

CAPITAL FILM LABS INC (DE)
Recapitalized 06/21/1965
Holders had option to exchange each share Class A Common $1 par for (6) shares Common no par or (3) shares Common no par and $1.25 cash
Final date for option was 09/07/1965, after which Class A Common $1 par became exchangeable for (3) shares Common no par and $1.25 cash
Each share Class B Common 50¢ par exchanged for (1) share Common no par
Common no par changed to 50¢ par 06/30/1966
Merged into CFL Holding Corp. 09/19/1977
Each share Common 50¢ par exchanged for $4.80 cash

CAPITAL FIN CORP (NM)
Completely liquidated 07/00/1977
No stockholders' equity

CAPITAL FINANCE CORP. (OH)
Preferred $100 par called for redemption 12/31/1968
Through voluntary exchange offer Continental Corp. (NY) acquired 100% of Common no par as of 08/05/1971
Public interest eliminated

CAPITAL FIRE & CASUALTY INSURANCE CO. (AL)
Completely liquidated 03/00/1964
Each share Capital Stock 50¢ par exchanged for (0.04) share American Life Insurance Co. Capital Stock $1 par
American Life Insurance Co. name changed to American-Amicable Life Insurance Co. 03/01/1965
(See American-Amicable Life Insurance Co.)

CAPITAL FIRST CORP (PA)
Name changed to Capitalcare Corp. 08/27/1984

CAPITAL FOR TECHNICAL INDUSTRIES, INC. (CA)
Completely liquidated 09/29/1967
Each share Common $1 par exchanged for first and final distribution of (1) share Cap Tech Inc. Common $1 par
(See Cap Tech Inc.)

CAPITAL FOUNDERS CORP. (DE)
Charter cancelled and declared inoperative and void for non-payment of taxes 03/01/1976

CAPITAL FRANCHISING INC (CO)
Reorganized under the laws of Delaware as Jubilee4 Gold, Inc. 05/27/2014
Each share Common $0.001 par exchanged for (0.02222222) share Common $0.001 par
Jubilee4 Gold, Inc. recapitalized as Helix TCS, Inc. 11/03/2015

CAPITAL FUNDING & DEVELOPMENT CORP. (NV)
Name changed to International Property Exchange, Inc. 05/03/1983
(See International Property Exchange, Inc.)

CAPITAL FUNDING CORP. (NY)
Proclaimed dissolved for failure to file reports and pay fees 12/15/1966

CAPITAL GAINS INCOME STREAMS CORP (ON)
Merged into Dividend 15 Split Corp. 12/01/2013
Each Capital Yield Share exchanged for (1.22352296) Preferred Shares no par and (1.22352296) Class A Shares no par
Each Equity Dividend Share exchanged for (0.19516249) Preferred Shares no par and (0.19516249) Class A Shares no par

CAPITAL GAMING INTL INC (NJ)
Plan of reorganization under Chapter 11 Federal Bankruptcy Code effective 05/28/1997
Each share old Common no par exchanged for (0.002587) share new Common no par
Note: Unexchanged certificates were cancelled and became without value 05/28/1999
Plan of reorganization under Chapter 11 Federal Bankruptcy Code effective 10/16/2000
Each share new Common no par exchanged for (0.0013) share Class B Common no par 10/16/2000
Company terminated registration of Class A and Class B Common stock and is no longer public as of 09/05/2001

CAPITAL GEN CORP (FL)
Proclaimed dissolved for failure to file reports and pay fees 10/11/1991

CAPITAL GOLD CORP (DE)
Reincorporated 11/21/2005
State of incorporation changed from (NV) to (DE) and Common $0.001 par changed to $0.0001 par 11/21/2005
Each share old Common $0.0001 par exchanged for (0.25) share new Common $0.0001 par 01/25/2010
Merged into Gammon Gold Inc. (QC) 04/08/2011
Each share new Common $0.0001 par exchanged for (0.5209) share Common no par and $1.09 cash
Gammon Gold Inc. (QC) reincorporated in Ontario as AuRico Gold Inc. 06/14/2011 which merged into Alamos Gold Inc. (New) 07/06/2015

CAPITAL GROWTH CORP. (IN)
Completely liquidated 07/20/1976
Each share Common no par exchanged for first and final distribution of $1.5174 cash

CAPITAL GROWTH CORP (DE)
Each share Common $0.001 par exchanged for (0.1) share Common 1¢ par 09/24/1986
Name changed to Integrated Labs, Inc. 08/04/1989
Integrated Labs, Inc. name changed to Multi-Platform Integrations Inc. 05/30/2002
(See Multi-Platform Integrations Inc.)

CAPITAL GROWTH HLDGS LTD (CO)
Name changed to MicroCap Financial Services, Inc. 11/05/1998
MicroCap Financial Services, Inc. name changed to GlobalNet Financial.Com, Inc. 04/16/1999
(See GlobalNet Financial.Com, Inc.)

CAPITAL GROWTH INC (NV)
Each share old Common $0.001 par exchanged for (0.05) share new Common $0.001 par 05/18/1999
Name changed to Imagenetix, Inc. 11/09/2000

CAPITAL GROWTH SYS INC (FL)
Plan of reorganization under Chapter 11 Federal Bankruptcy proceedings effective 10/01/2011
No stockholders' equity

CAPITAL GTY CORP (MD)
Merged into Financial Security Assurance Holdings Ltd. 12/20/1995
Each share Common 10¢ par exchanged for (0.6716) share Common 1¢ par and $5.69 cash

CAPITAL HILL GOLD INC (NV)
Each share old Common $0.001 par exchanged for (0.05) share new Common $0.001 par 03/01/2005
New Common $0.001 par split (4) for (1) by issuance of (3) additional shares payable 06/07/2005 to holders of record 05/31/2005
Ex date - 06/08/2005
Name changed to Amerimine Resources, Inc. 09/03/2005
Amerimine Resources, Inc. name changed to American Unity Investments, Inc. 08/09/2006
(See American Unity Investments, Inc.)

CAPITAL HLDGS GROUP, INC (OK)
Name changed to Avisana Corp. 11/07/2006

CAPITAL HLDGS INC (OH)
Merged into Fifth Third Bancorp 03/09/2001
Each share Common no par exchanged for (0.638) share Common no par

CAPITAL HOLDING LLC (TURKS & CAICOS ISLANDS)
Name changed to Providian LLC 07/14/1994
Providian LLC name changed to Commonwealth General LLC 11/24/1997
(See Commonwealth General LLC)

CAPITAL HLDG CORP (DE)
Common $1 par split (2) for (1) by issuance of (1) additional share 05/30/1972
Each share 24¢ Conv. Preferred Ser. A $5 par exchanged for (0.9662) share Common $1 par 07/15/1980
Common $1 par split (2) for (1) by issuance of (1) additional share 04/30/1985
Common $1 par split (2) for (1) by issuance of (1) additional share 04/30/1993
Each share Jr. Conv. Preferred Ser. J $5 par exchanged for (5.55) shares Common $1 par 06/16/1993
Adjustable Rate Preferred Ser. F $5 par called for redemption 03/02/1994
Name changed to Providian Corp. 05/12/1994
Providian Corp. merged into Aegon N.V. 06/10/1997

CAPITAL HSG & MTG PARTNERS INC (DE)
Completely liquidated 12/31/1993
Each share Common 1¢ par exchanged for first and final distribution of $5.23 cash

CAPITAL ICE REFRIGERATING CO.
Acquired by Capital Ice Refrigerating Co., Inc. 00/00/1938
Details not available

CAPITAL IDEAS INC (DE)
Name changed to Galleria Group, Inc. 02/27/1989
(See Galleria Group, Inc.)

CAPITAL INCOME FD INC (DE)
Name changed to Capamerica Fund, Inc. 09/03/1969
Capamerica Fund, Inc. name changed to Bull & Bear Equity-Income Fund, Inc. 05/02/1983 which merged into Bull & Bear Financial News Composite Fund, Inc. 09/00/1992 which merged into Bull & Bear Fund I, Inc. 01/21/1994 which name changed to Midas U.S. & Overseas Fund Ltd. 06/28/1999
(See Midas U.S. & Overseas Fund)

CAPITAL INDS INC (IN)
Each share old Common no par exchanged for (0.08333333) share new Common no par 11/19/1984
In process of liquidation
Each share new Common no par exchanged for initial distribution of $5.10 cash 04/24/1996
Assets transferred to Capital Industries Liquidating Trust 05/00/1996
(See Capital Industries Liquidating Trust)

CAPITAL INDUSTRIES LIQUIDATING TRUST (IN)
Liquidation completed
Each Share of Bene. Int. no par received initial distribution of $1.15 cash payable 01/14/1997 to holders of record 10/25/1996
Each Share of Bene. Int. no par received second distribution of $1.25 cash payable 01/30/1998
Each Share of Bene. Int. no par received third distribution of $1.05 cash payable 05/07/1998
Each Share of Bene. Int. no par received fourth distribution of $0.50 cash payable 12/01/1998
Each Share of Bene. Int. no par received fifth and final distribution of $0.33 cash payable 04/23/1999

CAPITAL INVT DEV CORP (FL)
Name changed to Graystone Financial Services, Inc. (FL) 10/10/1988
Graystone Financial Services, Inc. (FL) reorganized in Delaware as GS Financial Services, Inc. 12/01/1997
(See GS Financial Services, Inc.)

CAPITAL INVT LTD (HI)
Name changed to Capital Investment of Hawaii, Inc. 05/14/1968

CAPITAL INVS CORP (MT)
Voluntarily dissolved 06/30/1977
Details not available

CAPITAL INVS GROWTH FD INC (DE)
Merged into Capital Shares, Inc. 12/27/1974
Each share Common $1 par

exchanged for (0.66) share Capital Stock 1¢ par
Capital Shares, Inc. name changed to Bull & Bear Capital Growth Fund 05/02/1983 which name changed to Bull & Bear Special Equities Fund 06/00/1992 which name changed to Midas Special Equities Fund 06/30/1999 which name changed to Midas Special Fund, Inc. 05/01/2006 which name changed to Midas Magic, Inc. (New) 04/29/2011 which reorganized as Midas Series Trust 10/12/2012

CAPITAL INVTS INC (WI)
Common $5 par changed to $1 par and (1) additional share issued 05/22/1962
Common $1 par split (2) for (1) by issuance of (1) additional share 06/15/1971
Company went private 00/00/1992
Details not available

CAPITAL L ESTEREL INC (CANADA)
Recapitalized as iseemedia Inc. 04/12/2005
Each share Common no par exchanged for (0.25994281) share Common no par
iseemedia Inc. merged into Synchronica PLC 01/06/2011

CAPITAL LEASING CO (CA)
Merged into U.S. Financial (CA) 12/31/1968
Each share Class B Common $1 par exchanged for (0.038628) share Common $2.50 par
U.S. Financial (CA) reincorporated in Delaware as U.S. Financial Inc. 08/11/1972
(See U.S. Financial Inc.)

CAPITAL LIQUIDITY INC (MD)
Liquidated and subsequently dissolved 05/16/1977
Details not available

CAPITAL LITHIUM MINES LTD. (ON)
Acquired by Augustus Exploration Ltd. 02/05/1959
Each share Capital Stock $1 par exchanged for (1/6) share Capital Stock $1 par
Augustus Exploration Ltd. merged into Consolidated Canadian Faraday Ltd. 05/04/1967 which name changed to Faraday Resources Inc. 08/02/1983 which merged into Conwest Exploration Co. Ltd. (New) (AB) 09/01/1993 which merged into Alberta Energy Co. Ltd. 01/31/1996 which merged into EnCana Corp. 01/03/2003

CAPITAL MANAGEMENT CORP.
Dissolved 00/00/1937
Details not available

CAPITAL MANAGEMENT CORP (LA)
Incorporated 02/24/1960
Merged into Tidelands Capital Corp. 06/05/1964
Each share Common 25¢ par exchanged for (0.888888) share Common no par
Tidelands Capital Corp. merged into Western Preferred Corp. 03/06/1981
(See Western Preferred Corp.)

CAPITAL MINERAL INVS INC (NV)
SEC revoked common stock registration 05/21/2012

CAPITAL MKT SVCS CORP (NY)
100% reacquired 00/00/1985
Details not available

CAPITAL MKTS TECHNOLOGIES INC (FL)
SEC revoked common stock registration 04/02/2012

CAPITAL MKTS WEST INC (AB)
Company wound up
Each share Common no par received initial distribution of $0.43 cash 01/00/1991
Each share Common no par received second and final distribution of pro rata shares in private companies Nichols Advanced Technology Inc. and SPI Synthetic Peptides Inc. and $0.07 cash 06/30/1991
Note: Certificates were not required to be surrendered and are without value

CAPITAL MLB INC (QC)
Completely liquidated 09/09/2010
Each share Common no par exchanged for first and final distribution of (1.337) Nuvolt Corp. Inc. Units consisting of (1) share Common and (0.5) Common Stock Purchase Warrant expiring 08/23/2010

CAPITAL MTG INVTS (MD)
Name changed to Washington Corp. and Shares of Bene. Int. $1 par reclassified as Common $1 par 01/01/1980
(See Washington Corp.)

CAPITAL NATL BK (AUSTIN, TX)
Each share Common $25 par exchanged for (2.5) shares Common $10 par 00/00/1953
Common $10 par changed to $4 par and (1.5) additional shares issued 07/21/1972
Common $4 par changed to $5 par 07/21/1972
Stock Dividends - 25% 07/18/1966; 25% 08/20/1969
Under plan of reorganization each share Common $5 par automatically became (1) share Bancapital Finance Corp. Common $1 par 10/31/1973
Bancapital Financial Corp. merged into Texas Commerce Bancshares 05/16/1977 which was acquired by Chemical New York Corp. 05/01/1987 which name changed to Chemical Banking Corp. 04/29/1988 which name changed to Chase Manhattan Corp. (New) 03/31/1996 which name changed to J.P. Morgan Chase & Co. 12/31/2000 which name changed to JPMorgan Chase & Co. 07/20/2004

CAPITAL NATL BK (CLEVELAND, OH)
99% held by BancOhio Corp. as of 04/23/1973
Public interest eliminated

CAPITAL NATL BK (HOUSTON, TX)
Common $20 par changed to $10 par and (1) additional share issued 06/17/1968
Stock Dividend - 20% 02/14/1967
Recapitalized as Capital National Corp. 11/18/1968
Each share Common $10 par exchanged for (1) share Common $10 par
Capital National Corp. name changed to Federated Capital Corp. 01/29/1974 which merged into Mercantile Texas Corp. 12/30/1976 which name changed to MCorp 10/11/1984
(See MCorp)

CAPITAL NATL BK (MIAMI, FL)
Name changed to Peoples Downtown National Bank (Miami, FL) 06/01/1972
(See Peoples Downtown National Bank (Miami, FL))

CAPITAL NATL BK (TAMPA, FL)
Name changed to Pan American Bank of Tampa N.A. (Tampa, FL) 10/16/1972
(See Pan American Bank of Tampa N.A. (Tampa, FL))

CAPITAL NATL CORP (DE)
Common $10 par split (5) for (4) by issuance of (0.25) additional share 02/20/1970
Common $10 par changed to $5 par and (1) additional share issued 11/06/1972
Under plan of merger name changed to Federated Capital Corp. and Common $5 par changed to $4 par 01/29/1974
Federated Capital Corp. merged into Mercantile Texas Corp. 12/30/1976 which name changed to MCorp 10/11/1984
(See MCorp)

CAPITAL NATIONAL LIFE INSURANCE CO. (TX)
Merged into Alabama National Life Insurance Co. 12/31/1961
Each share Capital Stock no par exchanged for (1.333333) shares Common 25¢ par
(See Alabama National Life Insurance Co.)

CAPITAL NETWORK GROUP INC (NV)
Recapitalized as Princeton Fine Art, Inc. 02/05/1990
Each share Common 1¢ par exchanged for (0.2) share Common 1¢ par
Princeton Fine Art, Inc. recapitalized as Princeton-Tarryall, Inc. 12/09/1991

CAPITAL NOBEL INC (CANADA)
Reorganized under the laws of Quebec as Nobel Real Estate Investment Trust 05/30/2013
Each share Common no par exchanged for (1) Trust Unit
Note: Unexchanged certificates will be cancelled and become without value 05/30/2019
Nobel Real Estate Investment Trust merged into Nexus Real Estate Investment Trust 04/05/2017

CAPITAL OIL & GAS CORP (BC)
Struck off register and declared dissolved for failure to file returns 03/27/1986

CAPITAL OIL & GAS INC (DE)
Recapitalized as Southcorp Capital, Inc. 01/28/2009
Each share Common $0.001 par exchanged for (0.0001) share Common $0.001 par

CAPITAL ONE CAP II (DE)
7.5% Enhanced Trust Preferred Securities called for redemption at $25 on 01/02/2013

CAPITAL ONE FINL CORP (DE)
Each 6.25% Upper DECS received (0.6967) share Common 1¢ par 05/17/2025
(Additional Information in Active)

CAPITAL ONE INC (WY)
Name changed to Finance One, Us, Inc. 07/27/2005
Finance One, Us, Inc. name changed to PBC Inc. 11/16/2005
(See PBC Inc.)

CAPITAL ONE VENTURES CORP (DE)
Name changed to Cirus Telecom, Inc. 02/12/2001
Cirus Telecom, Inc. recapitalized as THC Communications Inc. 03/08/2002
(See THC Communications Inc.)

CAPITAL PAC BANCORP (OR)
Merged into Pacific Continental Corp. 03/06/2015
Each share Common no par exchanged for (1.132) shares Common no par
Pacific Continental Corp. merged into Columbia Banking System, Inc. 11/01/2017

CAPITAL PAC BANK (PORTLAND, OR)
Under plan of reorganization each share Common no par automatically became (1) share Capital Pacific Bancorp Common no par 05/23/2007
Capital Pacific Bancorp merged into Pacific Continental Corp. 03/06/2015 which merged into Columbia Banking System, Inc. 11/01/2017

CAPITAL PAC HLDGS INC (DE)
Merged into CPH Holding Inc. 05/26/2006
Each share Common 10¢ par exchanged for $11.25 cash

CAPITAL PETROLEUM BLDG., INC.
Name changed to Cravens Petroleum Bldg., Inc. 00/00/1952
(See Cravens Petroleum Bldg. Inc.)

CAPITAL PLACEMENT CORP (DE)
Each share old Common $0.000001 par exchanged for (0.01) new Common $0.000001 par 09/30/1989
Charter cancelled and declared inoperative and void for non-payment of taxes 03/01/1994

CAPITAL PLACEMENT SPECIALISTS INC (UT)
Name changed to Converge Global, Inc. (Old) 12/05/1998
Converge Global, Inc. (Old) recapitalized as Converge Global, Inc. (New) 09/03/2010 which name changed to Marijuana Co. of America, Inc. 12/01/2015

CAPITAL PLANNING RES (CA)
Name changed to Carlsberg Capital Corp. (CA) 08/21/1975
Carlsberg Capital Corp. (CA) reincorporated in Delaware as Carlsberg Corp. 07/01/1980 which merged into Southmark Corp. 02/25/1986
(See Southmark Corp.)

CAPITAL PLASTICS, INC. (NY)
Stock Dividends - 10% 10/17/1955; 10% 10/16/1957
Merged into Cap-Roc Inc. 02/20/1964
Each share Capital Stock $1 par exchanged for (0.58) share Common $1 par
(See Cap-Roc Inc.)

CAPITAL POWER INCOME L P (ON)
Merged into Atlantic Power Corp. 11/09/2011
Each Unit of Ltd. Partnership no par exchanged for (1.3) shares Common no par
Note: Unexchanged certificates were cancelled and became without value 11/09/2017

CAPITAL PPTYS INC (DE)
Common $1 par changed to 10¢ par and (19) additional shares issued 06/20/1962
Merged into Cap Prop, Inc. 10/10/1978
Each share Common 10¢ par exchanged for $2 cash

CAPITAL RE CORP (DE)
Common 1¢ par split (2) for (1) by issuance of (1) additional share payable 06/30/1998 to holders of record 06/15/1998 Ex date - 07/01/1998
Merged into ACE Ltd. (Cayman Islands) 12/30/1999
Each share Common 1¢ par exchanged for (0.65) share Ordinary $0.041666667 par and $3.4456 cash
ACE Ltd. (Cayman Islands) reincorporated in Switzerland 07/17/2008

CAPITAL RE LLC (TURKS & CAICOS ISLANDS)
7.65% Monthly Income Preferred Ser. A 1¢ par called for redemption at $25 on 07/12/2004

CAPITAL RLTY INVS LTD LP (DE)
Units of Ltd. Partnership 85 completely liquidated 12/31/2006
Details not available

(Additional Information in Active)

CAPITAL RLTY INVS TAX EXEMPT FD LTD PARTNERSHIP (DE)
Merged into Capital Apartment 12/04/1996
Each Bene. Assignee Certificate Ser. 1 no par exchanged for $15.42 cash
Each Bene. Assignee Certificate Ser. 2 no par exchanged for $15.11 cash

CAPITAL RLTY INVS TAX EXEMPT FD III LTD PARTNERSHIP (DE)
Merged into Capital Apartment 12/04/1996
Each Bene. Assignee Certificate Ser. A no par exchanged for $15.73 cash

CAPITAL RESERVE CORP. (DE)
Name changed to Capital Founders Corp. 04/30/1965
(See Capital Founders Corp.)

CAPITAL RESOURCE ALLIANCE INC (CO)
Common $0.001 par split (4) for (1) by issuance of (3) additional shares payable 02/01/2008 to holders of record 02/01/2008 Ex date - 02/04/2008
Common $0.001 par split (3) for (1) by issuance of (2) additional shares payable 12/18/2008 to holders of record 12/18/2008
Name changed to Nate's Food Co. 09/25/2014

CAPITAL RESOURCE FDG INC (NC)
Reincorporated under the laws of Delaware as China Sun Group High-Tech Co. and Common $0.00000005 par changed to $0.001 par 09/06/2007

CAPITAL RES INC (DE)
Name changed to Valor International Inc. 05/16/1988
(See Valor International Inc.)

CAPITAL RES INDS INC (DE)
Merged into Health Corp. of America 10/03/1972
Each share Common 1¢ par exchanged for (1) share Common 1¢ par
(See Health Corp. of America)

CAPITAL RESV CDA LTD (AB)
SEC revoked common stock registration 06/17/2013

CAPITAL RESV CORP (CA)
Capital Stock no par reclassified as Common no par 07/28/1967
Name changed to Capital Energy Corp. 12/14/1977
Capital Energy Corp. name changed to Life Chemistry Inc. 11/28/1983
(See Life Chemistry Inc.)

CAPITAL RESV CORP (CO)
Each share Class A Common 1¢ par exchanged for (0.1) share Class A Common no par 10/01/1990
Name changed to Fact Corp. 02/08/2002

CAPITAL RESV INC (BC)
Common no par split (3.5) for (1) by issuance of (2.5) additional shares 06/15/1988
Struck from the register and dissolved 06/19/1992

CAPITAL SAVINGS & LOAN ASSOCIATION (VA)
Merged into Heritage Financial Corp. (VA) 10/12/1982
Each share Capital Stock no par exchanged for (1) share Common $0.33333333 par
(See Heritage Financial Corp. (VA))

CAPITAL SVGS BANCORP INC (DE)
Common 1¢ par split (2) for (1) by issuance of (1) additional share payable 11/22/1996 to holders of record 11/08/1996
Merged into Union Planters Corp. 07/08/1998
Each share Common 1¢ par exchanged for (0.3812) share Common $5 par
Union Planters Corp. merged into Regions Financial Corp. (New) 07/01/2004

CAPITAL SAVINGS LIFE INSURANCE CO. (IL)
Through voluntary exchange offer Commonwealth Industries Corp. acquired 100% as of 00/00/1973
Public interest eliminated

CAPITAL-SEABOARD CORP. (TX)
Merged into Sawyer Resources Corp. on a share for share basis 10/21/1960
Sawyer Resources Corp. name changed to Union Petrochemical Corp. of Nevada 10/09/1967
(See Union Petrochemical Corp. of Nevada)

CAPITAL SEARCH REGISTRY INC (DE)
Charter cancelled and declared inoperative and void for non-payment of taxes 03/01/1989

CAPITAL SEC LIFE INS CO (IL)
Acquired by Georgetown Life Insurance Co. 12/30/1970
Each share Common 10¢ par exchanged for (0.125) share Common $1 par
Georgetown Life Insurance Co. merged into Exchange Investment Corp. 09/30/1975 which merged into Fiduciary & General Corp. 10/22/1981
(See Fiduciary & General Corp.)

CAPITAL SECURITIES CO., INC. (NJ)
Prior Preferred $100 par changed to $30 par 00/00/1928
Common $10 par changed to $1 par 00/00/1932
Prior Preferred $100 par called for redemption 04/00/1955
Liquidation completed 05/15/1958
Details not available

CAPITAL SHOPPING CENTRES GROUP (UNITED KINGDOM)
ADR agreement terminated 12/10/2010
Each Sponsored ADR for Ordinary exchanged for $4.638052 cash

CAPITAL SHS INC (MD)
Capital Life Insurance Shares and Growth Stock Fund Shares 1¢ par reclassified as Capital Stock 1¢ par 04/29/1969
Stock Dividend - 25% 02/07/1964
Name changed to Bull & Bear Capital Growth Fund 05/02/1983
Bull & Bear Capital Growth Fund name changed to Bull & Bear Special Equities Fund 06/00/1992 which name changed to Midas Special Equities Fund 06/30/1999 which name changed to Midas Special Fund, Inc. 05/01/2006 which name changed to Midas Magic, Inc. (New) 04/29/2011 which reorganized as Midas Series Trust 10/12/2012

CAPITAL SILVER-LEAD MINING CO. (ID)
Charter revoked for failure to file reports and pay fees 11/30/1966

CAPITAL SOLUTIONS I INC (DE)
Each share old Common $0.0000001 par exchanged for (0.1) share new Common $0.0000001 par 06/20/2005
Each share new Common $0.0000001 par exchanged again for (0.002) share new Common $0.0000001 par 01/31/2006
Name changed to Fuda Faucet Works, Inc. 01/03/2008

CAPITAL SOURCE L P (DE)
Merged into America First Real Estate Investment Partners L.P. 12/31/2000
Each Unit of Bene. Assignments Ltd. Partnership Int. exchanged for (1.3957) Units of Ltd. Partnership Int.
America First Real Estate Investment Partners L.P. merged into America First Apartment Investors, Inc. 06/03/2004
(See America First Apartment Investors, Inc.)

CAPITAL SOURCE II L P (DE)
Merged into America First Real Estate Investment Partners L.P. 12/31/2000
Each Unit of Bene. Assignments Ltd. Partnership Int. exchanged for (0.762) Unit of Ltd. Partnership Int.
America First Real Estate Investment Partners L.P. merged into America First Apartment Investors, Inc. 06/03/2004
(See America First Apartment Investors, Inc.)

CAPITAL SR LIVING CMNTYS L P (DE)
Partnership dissolved 12/31/1999
No stockholders' equity

CAPITAL ST BK INC (WV)
Merged into South Branch Valley Bancorp Inc. 03/31/1998
Each share Common exchanged for (3.95) shares Common $2.50 par
South Branch Valley Bancorp Inc. name changed to Summit Financial Group, Inc. 12/30/1999

CAPITAL ST-CHARLES INC (CANADA)
Name changed to CVTech Group Inc. 04/22/2005
Each share Common no par exchanged for (1) share Common no par
CVTech Group Inc. name changed to NAPEC Inc. 09/11/2014
(See NAPEC Inc.)

CAPITAL STAR PETE (CA)
Charter suspended for failure to file reports and pay fees 07/01/1983

CAPITAL SYS CORP (DE)
Reincorporated 03/31/1973
State of incorporation changed from (IL) to (DE) 03/31/1973
Each share Common 1¢ par exchanged for (0.009901) share Common $1.01 par 08/31/1973
Merged into Capital Building Systems, Inc. 02/28/1975
Details not available

CAPITAL SYSTEMS, INC. (LA)
Name changed to Commercial Capital Systems, Inc. 01/15/1969
Commercial Capital Systems, Inc. name changed to First National Corp. 03/31/1977
(See First National Corp.)

CAPITAL TITLE GROUP INC (DE)
Merged into LandAmerica Financial Group, Inc. 09/08/2006
Each share Common $0.001 par exchanged for either (0.024522) share Common no par and $6.40 cash or $8 cash
Note: Option to receive stock and cash expired 09/15/2006
(See LandAmerica Financial Group, Inc.)

CAPITAL TRACTION CO.
Acquired by Capital Transit Co. (DC) 00/00/1933
Details not available

CAPITAL TRANSIT CO. (DC)
Each share Capital Stock $100 par exchanged for (4) shares Capital Stock $19.50 par 00/00/1951
Name changed to Universal Corp. (DC) 08/17/1956
Universal Corp. (DC) name changed to Universal Marion Corp. (DC) 04/10/1957 which reincorporated in Florida 05/29/1959
(See Universal Marion Corp. (FL))

CAPITAL TRINITY FD INC (DE)
Merged into Fairfield Fund, Inc. 04/30/1974
Each share Capital Stock $1 par exchanged for (1.185) shares Capital Stock $1 par
Fairfield Fund, Inc. reorganized as National Aggressive Growth Fund Inc. (MA) 12/01/1989 which merged into National Worldwide Opportunities Fund 12/17/1990
(See National Worldwide Opportunities Fund)

CAPITAL TR (CA)
Under plan of reorganization each Class A Common Share of Bene. Int. $1 par automatically became (1) share Capital Trust, Inc. (MD) Class A Common 1¢ par 01/28/1999
Capital Trust, Inc. recapitalized as Blackstone Mortgage Trust, Inc. 05/07/2013

CAPITAL TR INC (MD)
Each share old Class A Common 1¢ par exchanged for (0.33333333) share new Class A Common 1¢ par 04/02/2003
Recapitalized as Blackstone Mortgage Trust, Inc. 05/07/2013
Each share new Class A Common 1¢ par exchanged (0.1) share Class A Common 1¢ par

CAPITAL TRUST SHARES, SERIES "A"
Trust terminated 00/00/1931
Details not available

CAPITAL 2000 INC (CO)
Name changed to United Shields Corp. 05/19/1997
(See United Shields Corp.)

CAPITAL VENTURES INC (DE)
Recapitalized as Hi-Tech Computer Products, Inc. 06/25/1992
Each share Common $0.0001 par exchanged for (0.05882352) share Common $0.0001 par
(See Hi-Tech Computer Products, Inc.)

CAPITAL VTECHLAB INC (CANADA)
Name changed to Capital DGMC Inc. 11/03/2011

CAPITAL WAPITI INC (CANADA)
Name changed to Investus Real Estate Inc. 06/20/2008
(See Investus Real Estate Inc.)

CAPITAL WIRE & CABLE CORP. OLD (TX)
Common $2 par changed to $1 par and (1) additional share issued 09/12/1966
Completely liquidated 10/04/1968
Each share Common $1 par exchanged for first and final distribution of (1) share U.S. Industries, Inc. Common $1 par and (1) Unit of Participation
(See U.S. Industries, Inc.)

CAPITAL WIRE & CABLE CORP NEW (TX)
Merged into Penn Central Corp. 08/23/1988
Each share Common no par exchanged for $13.75 cash

CAPITAL WIRE CLOTH LTD (ON)
Recapitalized 12/05/1962
Recapitalized from Capital Wire Cloth & Manufacturing Co. to Capital Wire Cloth Ltd. 12/05/1962
Each share Common exchanged for (0.1) share Common 90% acquired at $12.50 per share through purchase offer which expired 00/00/1964
Public interest eliminated

CAPITALISTICS INC (DE)
Name changed to Fossil Bay Holding Inc. 06/06/1989

CAPITALSOURCE INC (DE)
Merged into PacWest Bancorp 04/07/2014
Each share Common 1¢ par exchanged for (0.2837) share Common 1¢ par and $2.47 cash

CAPITALSOUTH BANCORP (DE)
Company's sole asset placed in receivership 08/21/2009
Stockholders' equity unlikely

CAPITOL ACQUISITION CORP II (DE)
Units separated 07/09/2015
Name changed to Lindblad Expeditions Holdings, Inc. 07/09/2015

CAPITOL ACQUISITION CORP III (DE)
Units separated 06/30/2017
Under plan of merger each share Common $0.0001 par automatically became (1) share Cision Ltd. Ordinary $0.0001 par 06/30/2017

CAPITOL ACQUISITION CORP (DE)
Units separated 10/28/2009
Reincorporated under the laws of Maryland as Two Harbors Investment Corp. and Common $0.0001 par changed to 1¢ par 10/28/2009

CAPITOL AIR INC (TN)
Chapter 11 Federal Bankruptcy Code converted to Chapter 7 on 12/15/1987
No stockholders' equity

CAPITOL AMERN FINL CORP (OH)
Merged into Conseco, Inc. 03/04/1997
Each share Common no par exchanged for (0.1647) share Common no par and $30.75 cash
(See Conseco, Inc.)

CAPITOL ASSOCIATED PRODUCTS, INC. (CT)
Name changed to Bishop Industries, Inc. (CT) 03/09/1962
Bishop Industries, Inc. (CT) merged into United Equities, Inc. 12/28/1968
(See United Equities, Inc.)

CAPITOL BANCORP LTD (MI)
Common no par split (11) for (10) by issuance of (0.1) additional share 11/01/1990
Common no par split (6) for (5) by issuance of (0.2) additional share payable 12/18/1998 to holders of record 12/04/1998
Stock Dividends - 10% payable 12/31/1996 to holders of record 12/02/1996; 10% payable 12/15/1997 to holders of record 12/01/1997
Plan of reorganization under Chapter 11 Federal Bankruptcy proceedings effective 02/03/2014
Stockholders' equity unlikely

CAPITOL BANCORPORATION (MA)
Common $1.25 par changed to $0.83333333 par and (0.5) additional share issued 05/31/1985
Common $0.83333333 par changed to $0.55555555 par and (0.5) additional share issued 05/30/1986
Each share Common $0.55555555 par exchanged for (0.002) share Common no par 07/14/1993
Proclaimed dissolved for failure to file reports and pay fees 08/31/1998

CAPITOL BK & TR CO (BOSTON, MA)
Common $25 par changed to $6.25 par and (3) additional shares issued 01/20/1969
Common $6.25 par changed to $1.25 par and (4) additional shares issued 06/05/1969
Stock Dividend - 20% 01/15/1968
Reorganized as Capitol Bancorporation 12/30/1972
Each share Common $1.25 par exchanged for (1) share Common $1.25 par
(See Capitol Bancorporation)

CAPITOL BANK OF COMMERCE (SACRAMENTO, CA)
Name changed to CapitolBank (Sacramento, CA) 09/00/1989
CapitolBank (Sacramento, CA) merged into Westamerica Bancorporation 06/06/1995

CAPITOL BREWING CO.
Out of business 00/00/1938
Details not available

CAPITOL CENTER CORP. (OH)
Charter revoked for failure to file reports and pay fees 11/10/1964

CAPITOL CITY BANCSHARES INC (ATLANTA, GA)
Reorganized 12/22/1998
Under plan of reorganization each share Capitol City Bank & Trust Co. (Atlanta, GA) Common $6 par automatically became (1) share Capitol City Bancshares, Inc. Common $6 par 12/22/1998
Common $6 par changed to $1.50 par and (3) additional shares issued payable 03/01/2005 to holders of record 03/01/2005
Common $1.50 par changed to $1 par and (3) additional shares issued payable 10/27/2010 to holders of record 06/22/2010
Administratively dissolved 12/31/2015

CAPITOL CMNTYS CORP (NV)
Name changed to Capitol First Corp. 10/16/2003
(See Capitol First Corp.)

CAPITOL CORP.
Dissolved 00/00/1933
Details not available

CAPITOL ENERGY RES LTD (AB)
Each share old Common no par exchanged for (0.2) share new Common no par 05/16/2005
Each share Non-Vtg. Common no par exchanged for (0.2) share new Common no par 05/16/2005
Acquired by Provident Energy Trust 06/22/2007
Each share new Common no par exchanged for $8.16 cash

CAPITOL FED FINL (USA)
Reorganized under the laws of Maryland as Capitol Federal Financial, Inc. 12/22/2010
Each share Common 1¢ par exchanged for (2.2637) shares Common 1¢ par

CAPITOL FED SVGS & LN ASSN DENVER COLO (USA)
Reorganized under the laws of Delaware as First Capitol Financial Corp. 06/30/1988
Each share Common 1¢ par exchanged for (1) share Common 1¢ par
(See First Capitol Financial Corp.)

CAPITOL FIRST CORP (NV)
Each share old Common 1¢ par exchanged for (0.0005) share new Common 1¢ par 06/08/2005
Note: In effect holders received $0.18 cash per share and public interest was eliminated

CAPITOL FOOD INDS INC (DE)
Merged into Vinco-CFI, Inc. 01/21/1983
Each share 6% Conv. Preferred $10 par exchanged for $6.25 cash
Each share Common $1 par exchanged for $4.75 cash

CAPITOL HILL ASSOC INC (DE)
Each share Founders Stock $100 par exchanged for (2) shares Class A Common no par 03/17/1967
Each share Common $50 par exchanged for (1) share Class B Common no par 03/17/1967
Liquidation completed
Each share Class A Common no par exchanged for initial distribution of $35 cash 09/15/1978
Each share Class B Common no par exchanged for initial distribution of $35 cash 09/15/1978
Each share Class A Common no par received second and final distribution of $23.14 cash 02/20/1979
Each share Class B Common no par received second and final distribution of $23.14 cash 02/20/1979

CAPITOL HILL OIL CORP. (DE)
Recapitalized as Inter-Global, Inc. of USA 12/16/1977
Each share Common 10¢ par exchanged for (0.5) share Common 10¢ par
(See Inter-Global, Inc. of USA)

CAPITOL HLDG CORP (DC)
Charter revoked for failure to file reports 09/13/1971

CAPITOL INDEMNITY INSURANCE CO. (IN)
Merged into Vernon Financial Corp. 12/31/1970
Each share Common $1 par exchanged for (1) share Common $1 par
(See Vernon Financial Corp.)

CAPITOL INDTY CORP (WI)
Common $1.40 par changed to $1.50 par 09/25/1962
Common $1.50 par changed to $1.86 par 10/15/1975
Each (1,200) shares Common $1.86 par exchanged for (1) share Common $2,232 par 12/14/1979
Note: In effect holders received $3.25 cash per share and public interest was eliminated

CAPITOL INDUSTRIES, INC. (NY)
Name changed to Capitol Industries-EMI, Inc. 01/02/1974
(See Capitol Industries-EMI, Inc.)

CAPITOL INDS EMI INC (NY)
Merged into EMI-North American Holdings Inc. 10/20/1978
Each share Common 10¢ par exchanged for $30.50 cash

CAPITOL INTL AWYS INC (TN)
Name changed to Capitol Air Inc. 01/06/1982
(See Capitol Air Inc.)

CAPITOL LAND TITLE INSURANCE, INC. (WI)
Each share old Common $1.50 par exchanged for (0.5) share new Common $1.50 par and $2.42 cash 12/03/1970
Each (1,300) shares new Common $1.50 par exchanged for (1) share Common $1,950 par 06/26/1979
Note: In effect holders received $1.75 cash per share and public interest was eliminated

CAPITOL LIFE INSURANCE CO. (TN)
Merged into Lincoln Income Life Insurance Co. 08/11/1961
Each share Common $1 par exchanged for (0.11111111) share Common $1 par
(See Lincoln Income Life Insurance Co.)

CAPITOL MINERAL RIGHTS CO. (IL)
Merged into Ladd Petroleum Corp. 10/26/1970
Each share Common 5¢ par exchanged for (1.25) shares Common 10¢ par
Ladd Petroleum Corp. merged into Utah International Inc. 11/30/1973 which merged into General Electric Co. 12/20/1976

CAPITOL MULTIMEDIA INC (DE)
Name changed to Celerity Solutions Inc. 09/02/1997
(See Celerity Solutions Inc.)

CAPITOL PETROLEUM CO. (CO)
Declared defunct and inoperative for failure to pay taxes and file annual reports 10/22/1925

CAPITOL PETROLEUMS LTD. (ON)
Acquired by Ellesmere Oil & Development Ltd. 00/00/1952
Each share Capital Stock no par exchanged for (0.1) share Capital Stock no par
Ellesmere Oil & Development Ltd. merged into New Concord Development Corp. Ltd. 00/00/1952
(See New Concord Development Corp. Ltd.)

CAPITOL PLASTICS OHIO INC (OH)
Merged into Dixico, Inc. 04/05/1976
Each share Common no par exchanged for (0.132) share Common $1 par
(See Dixico, Inc.)

CAPITOL PRODS CORP (PA)
Stock Dividend - 100% 06/04/1969
Merged into Ethyl Corp. 03/20/1970
Each share Capital Stock 50¢ par exchanged for $17 cash

CAPITOL RECLAMATION CORP (DE)
Liquidation completed
Each share Common 3¢ par received initial distribution of $1 cash 02/28/1979
Each share Common 3¢ par received second distribution of $0.50 cash 03/31/1980
Each share Common 3¢ par received third distribution of $0.50 cash 08/15/1981
Each share Common 3¢ par received fourth distribution of $1.35 cash 00/00/1986
Each share Common 3¢ par exchanged for fifth and final distribution of $0.19 cash 04/00/1990

CAPITOL RECORDS, INC. (CA)
Each share Common 25¢ par exchanged for (0.005) share Common $50 par 11/20/1969
Public interest eliminated

CAPITOL REEF URANIUM CORP. (NV)
Charter revoked for failure to file reports and pay fees 03/03/1958

CAPITOL REFINING CO., INC. (VA)
Dissolved 11/19/1928
Details not available

CAPITOL SILVER MINES INC NEW (NV)
Name changed to Capitol Toys, Inc. 08/17/2005
(See Capitol Toys, Inc.)

CAPITOL SILVER MINES INC OLD (ID)
Each share Common 10¢ par exchanged for (0.02) share Common $0.001 par 04/28/1999
Reincorporated under the laws of Nevada as Internet Culinary Corp. 09/00/1999
Internet Culinary Corp. name changed to Capitol Silver Mines Inc. (New) 03/01/2005 which name changed to Capitol Toys, Inc. 08/17/2005
(See Capitol Toys, Inc.)

CAPITOL SILVER MINES LTD.
Merged into Castle-Trethewey Mines Ltd. 00/00/1929
Each share Capital Stock $1 par exchanged for (0.2) share Capital Stock $1 par
Castle-Trethewey Mines Ltd. acquired by McIntyre Porcupine Mines Ltd. 12/16/1959 which name changed to McIntyre Mines Ltd. 05/31/1974

which merged into Falconbridge Ltd. 01/24/1989
(See Falconbridge Ltd.)

CAPITOL STATE BANK (TRENTON, NJ)
Acquired by Citizens Investments, Inc. 06/27/1986
Each share Common $1 par exchanged for $12 cash

CAPITOL STR CORP (MS)
Merged into CS Acquisition Corp. 05/16/1991
Each share Common $1 par exchanged for $117.62 cash
Each share Common $1 par received second and final distribution of $1.11 cash 07/01/1991

CAPITOL TELEVISION NETWORK INC (UT)
Name changed to Royal Casino Group Inc. 04/19/1994
Royal Casino Group Inc. name changed to E-Commerce West Corp. 07/31/1998 which recapitalized as Interactive Broadcasting Network Group Inc. 01/28/2002 which name changed to Baymark Technologies Inc. 08/30/2002 which name changed to Implantable Vision, Inc. 01/03/2006 which name changed to Arcland Energy Corp. 08/25/2008
(See Arcland Energy Corp.)

CAPITOL TOYS INC (NV)
SEC revoked common stock registration 07/25/2011

CAPITOL TRANSAMERICA CORP (WI)
Common $1 par split (4) for (3) by issuance of (0.33333333) additional share 05/27/1986
Common $1 par split (3) for (2) by issuance of (0.5) additional share 05/29/1987
Common $1 par split (5) for (4) by issuance of (0.25) additional share 06/30/1989
Common $1 par split (3) for (2) by issuance of (0.5) additional share 06/29/1990
Common $1 par split (5) for (4) by issuance of (0.25) additional share 07/01/1991
Common $1 par split (3) for (2) by issuance of (0.5) additional share 06/29/1992
Common $1 par split (3) for (2) by issuance of (0.5) additional share payable 01/15/1997 to holders of record 12/31/1996
Stock Dividends - 10% 06/06/1988; 10% payable 01/15/1996 to holders of record 12/28/1995
Merged into Alleghany Corp. 01/07/2002
Each share Common $1 par exchanged for $16.50 cash

CAPITOL URANIUM CO. (CO)
Merged into Capital-Seaboard Corp. 00/00/1957
Each share Capital Stock 10¢ par exchanged for (0.16666666) share Capital Stock 10¢ par
Capital-Seaboard Corp. merged into Sawyer Resources Corp. 10/20/1960 which name changed to Union Petrochemical Corp. of Nevada 10/09/1967
(See Union Petrochemical Corp. of Nevada)

CAPITOLBANK (SACRAMENTO, CA)
Merged into Westamerica Bancorporation 06/06/1995
Each share Common $1.5625 par exchanged for (0.0882) share Common no par

CAPLAN CORP (DE)
Each share old Common $0.001 par exchanged for (0.125) share new Common $0.001 par 02/07/1985
Each share new Common $0.001 par exchanged again for (0.33333333) share new Common $0.001 par 06/15/1987
Each share new Common $0.001 par exchanged again for (0.5) share new Common $0.001 par 04/09/2001
Recapitalized as Mid-Power Service Corp. (DE) 04/10/2001
Each share Common $0.001 par exchanged for (0.5) share Common $0.001 par
Mid-Power Service Corp. (DE) reincorporated in Nevada 07/31/2001 which reorganized as Caldera Corp. 03/05/2007
(See Caldera Corp.)

CAPLEASE INC (MD)
Name changed from Capital Lease Funding, Inc. to Caplease, Inc. 07/30/2007
Acquired by American Realty Capital Properties, Inc. 11/05/2013
Each share 8.125% Preferred Ser. A 1¢ par exchanged for $25 cash
Each share 8.375% Preferred Ser. B 1¢ par exchanged for $25 cash
Each share 7.25% Preferred Ser. C 1¢ par exchanged for $25 cash
Each share Common 1¢ par exchanged for $8.50 cash

CAPMAC HLDGS INC (DE)
Merged into MBIA Inc. 02/17/1998
Each share Common 1¢ par exchanged for (0.4675) share Common $1 par

CAPMARK FINL GROUP INC (NV)
Name changed to Bluestem Group Inc. 06/19/2015

CAPNIA INC (DE)
Name changed to Soleno Therapeutics, Inc. 05/12/2017

CAPO RES LTD (BC)
Name changed to Laurentian Goldfields Ltd. 05/16/2008
Laurentian Goldfields Ltd. name changed to Pure Gold Mining Inc. 06/27/2014

CAPOOSE MINERALS INC (BC)
Recapitalized as Tyler Resources Inc. (BC) 07/10/1986
Each share Common no par exchanged for (0.5) share Common no par
Tyler Resources Inc. (BC) reincorporated in Alberta 04/27/1995
(See Tyler Resources Inc.)

CAPPS GOLD MINES LTD. (ON)
Charter revoked for failure to file reports and pay taxes 00/00/1952

CAPRA MINERALS LTD (AB)
Recapitalized as Urban Resource Technologies Inc. 03/04/1994
Each share Common no par exchanged for (0.5) share Common no par
(See Urban Resource Technologies Inc.)

CAPRATE COML PPTYS INC (AB)
Liquidation completed
Each share Common no par received initial distribution of $0.2166 cash payable 09/15/2005 to holders of record 09/15/2005
Each share Common no par received second and final distribution of an undetermined amount 00/00/2006

CAPRI CORP (MN)
Each share Common 1¢ par received distribution of (1) share InterConexus.com, Inc. Restricted Common $0.0001 par payable 06/01/2000 to holders of record 05/30/2000
Merged into Made2Manage Systems Inc. 12/08/2005
Each share Common 1¢ par exchanged for $0.2231382 cash

CAPRI COSMETICS, INC. (TN)
Adjudicated bankrupt 04/16/1968
No stockholders' equity

CAPRI INDS INC (NC)
Stock Dividends - 20% 06/21/1971; 10% 06/30/1972
Completely liquidated 06/00/1977
Details not available

CAPRI MNG LTD (BC)
Struck from register and dissolved 02/25/1983

CAPRI RES LTD (BC)
Recapitalized as International Capri Resources Ltd. 12/24/1987
Each share Common no par exchanged for (0.33333333) share Common no par
International Capri Resources Ltd. name changed to Apiva.com Web Corp. 07/19/2000 which name changed to Apiva Ventures Ltd. 12/18/2001 which recapitalized as Mark One Global Industries, Inc. 08/13/2008
(See Mark One Global Industries, Inc.)

CAPRICE GREYSTOKE ENTERPRISES INC (BC)
Delisted from Vancouver Stock Exchange 09/30/1996

CAPRICE RES INC (BC)
Struck off register and declared dissolved for failure to file returns 12/30/1983

CAPRICO INTERNATIONAL, INC. (NY)
Adjudicated bankrupt 01/04/1965
No stockholders' equity

CAPRICORN RES LTD (BC)
Struck off register and declared dissolved for failure to file returns 11/12/1993

CAPRIUS INC (DE)
Each share old Common 1¢ par exchanged for (0.05) share new Common 1¢ par 04/05/2005
Acquired by Vintage Capital Group, L.L.C. 04/21/2011
Each share new Common 1¢ par exchanged for $0.065 cash

CAPRIVE INDS & RES LTD (QC)
Recapitalized as Consolidated Caprive Industries & Resources Ltd.-Industries & Ressources Caprive Consolides Ltee. 08/15/1974
Each share Capital Stock no par exchanged for (0.33333333) share Capital Stock no par
(See Consolidated Caprive Industries & Resources Ltd.-Industries & Ressources Caprive Consolides Ltee.)

CAPRIVE OIL & GAS LTD (QC)
Capital Stock $1 par changed to no par 04/17/1970
Name changed to Caprive Industries & Resources Ltd. 11/25/1970
Caprive Industries & Resources Ltd. recapitalized as Consolidated Caprive Industries & Resources Ltd.-Industries & Ressources Caprive Consolides Ltee. 08/15/1974
(See Consolidated Caprive Industries & Resources Ltd.-Industries & Ressources Caprive Consolides Ltee.)

CAPROCK COMMUNICATIONS CORP (TX)
Merged into McLeodUSA Inc. 12/08/2000
Each share Common 1¢ par exchanged for (0.3876) share Common 1¢ par
(See McLeodUSA Inc.)

CAPROCK CORP (CO)
Recapitalized as Striker Capital Corp. (CO) 05/05/2004
Each share Common $0.00001 par exchanged for (0.0005) share Common $0.00001 par
Striker Capital Corp. (CO) reincorporated in Nevada as Petro Plus USA Inc. 07/21/2006 which name changed to Petroleum Consolidators of America, Inc. (NV) 09/08/2006 which reincorporated in Delaware as CTX Virtual Technologies, Inc. 04/19/2010

CAPROCK ENERGY LTD (BC)
Recapitalized as Consolidated Caprock Resources Ltd. 09/14/1989
Each share Common no par exchanged for (0.2) share Common no par
Consolidated Caprock Resources Ltd. recapitalized as Minco Mining & Metals Corp. 03/12/1993 which name changed to Minco Gold Corp. 02/01/2007

CAPROCK OIL INC (NV)
Recapitalized as Stack-It Storage, Inc. 07/23/2015
Each share Common 1¢ par exchanged for (0.1) share Common 1¢ par
Stack-It Storage, Inc. name changed to Manufactured Housing Properties Inc. 12/08/2017

CAPSALUS CORP (NV)
Recapitalized as ForU Holdings, Inc. 07/03/2014
Each share Common $0.001 par exchanged for (0.0060606) share Common $0.001 par

CAPSEARCH INC (NY)
Charter cancelled and proclaimed dissolved for failure to pay taxes 03/24/1993

CAPSOURCE FINL INC (CO)
Company terminated common stock registration and is no longer public as of 11/13/2008

CAPSTAR BROADCASTING CORP (DE)
Merged into AMFM, Inc. 07/13/1999
Each share Class A Common 1¢ par exchanged for (0.4955) share Common 1¢ par
Each share Class C Common 1¢ par exchanged for (0.4955) share Common 1¢ par
AMFM, Inc. merged into Clear Channel Communications, Inc. 08/30/2000

CAPSTAR BROADCASTING PARTNERS INC (DE)
Each share 12% Exchangeable Sr. Preferred exchanged for $100 principal amount of 12% Exchangeable Subordinated Debentures due 07/01/2009 on 01/03/2000

CAPSTAR HOTEL CO (DE)
Each share Common 1¢ par received distribution of (1) share MeriStar Hotels & Resorts, Inc. Common 1¢ par payable 08/03/1998 to holders of record 07/31/1998
Merged into MeriStar Hospitality Corp. 08/03/1998
Each share Common 1¢ par exchanged for (1) share Common 1¢ par
(See MeriStar Hospitality Corp.)

CAPSTEAD MTG CORP (MD)
$1.60 Conv. Preferred Ser. A 10¢ par called for redemption at $16.40 plus $0.3165 accrued dividends on 06/13/2013
$1.26 Conv. Preferred Ser. B 10¢ par called for redemption at $12.50 plus $0.042 accrued dividends on 06/13/2013
(Additional Information in Active)

CAPSTOCK FINL INC (BC)
Name changed to Gespeg Copper Resources Inc. 06/11/2012

CAPSTONE BK (RALEIGH, NC)
Merged into NewBridge Bancorp 04/01/2014
Each share Common $5 par exchanged for (2.25) shares Class A Common no par
NewBridge Bancorp merged into Yadkin Financial Corp. 03/01/2016 which merged into F.N.B. Corp. 03/11/2017

CAPSTONE CAP CORP (MD)
Merged into Healthcare Realty Trust Inc. 10/15/1998
Each share 8.875% Preferred Ser. A $0.001 par exchanged for (1) share 8.875% Preferred Ser. A $1 par
Each share Common $0.001 par exchanged for (0.8518) share Common 1¢ par

CAPSTONE CASHMAN FARRELL VALUE FD INC (DE)
Ceased operations 05/06/1994
Details not available

CAPSTONE CORP (DE)
Name changed to Primavera Laboratories Inc. 06/13/1990
(See Primavera Laboratories Inc.)

CAPSTONE EQUITY SER INC (MD)
Ceased operations 05/06/1994
Details not available

CAPSTONE FIXED INCOME SER INC (MD)
Reorganized as Capstone Christian Values Fund, Inc. 03/13/2000
Details not available

CAPSTONE GOLD CORP (BC)
Name changed to Capstone Mining Corp. 02/13/2006

CAPSTONE GOVT INCOME FD INC (DE)
Reincorporated under the laws of Maryland as Capstone Fixed Income Series Inc. and Common reclassified as Government Income Fund 05/11/1992
(See Capstone Fixed Income Series Inc.)

CAPSTONE GROWTH FD INC (MD)
Name changed 08/26/1994
Name changed from Capstone U.S. Trend Fund, Inc. to Capstone Growth Fund, Inc. 08/26/1994
Name changed to Capstone Series Fund, Inc. and Common $0.001 par reclassified as Steward Small Cap Equity Fund Institutional Class $0.001 par 01/22/2002

CAPSTONE INFRASTRUCTURE CORP (BC)
Acquired by iCON Infrastructure Partners III, L.P. 05/04/2016
Each share Common no par exchanged for $4.90 cash
Note: Unexchanged certificates will be cancelled and become without value 05/04/2022
(Additional Information in Active)

CAPSTONE INTL CORP (DE)
Each share old Common $0.001 par exchanged for (5) shares new Common $0.001 par 05/07/2003
Each share new Common $0.001 par exchanged again for (7) shares new Common $0.001 par 01/12/2004
Name changed to First National Power Corp. (DE) 01/28/2004
First National Power Corp. (DE) reorganized in Nevada as First National Energy Corp. 02/11/2009

CAPSTONE INTL SER TR (MA)
European Plus Fund 1¢ par reclassified as Capstone European Fund 08/10/1992
New Zealand Fund 1¢ par reclassified as Capstone New Zealand Fund 1¢ par 08/10/1992
Nikko Japan Tilt Fund 1¢ par reclassified as Capstone Nikko Japan Fund 1¢ par 08/10/1992
Name changed to Commonwealth International Series Trust and Capstone European Fund 1¢ par reclassified as Global Fund 1¢ par, Capstone New Zealand Fund 1¢ par reclassified as Australia/New Zealand Fund 1¢ par and Capstone Nikko Japan Fund 1¢ par reclassified as Japan Fund 1¢ par 10/10/2000

CAPSTONE PHARMACY SVCS INC (DE)
Reincorporated 10/02/1995
State of incorporation changed from (NY) to (DE) 10/02/1995
Under plan of merger name changed to PharMerica, Inc. 12/03/1997
PharMerica, Inc. merged into Bergen Brunswig Corp. 04/26/1999 which merged into AmeriSourceBergen Corp. 08/29/2001

CAPSTONE SER INC (MD)
Merged into Capstone Growth Fund, Inc. 05/30/1995
Each Balanced Fund $1 par exchanged for Common $0.001 par on a net asset basis
Capstone Growth Fund, Inc. name changed to Capstone Series Fund, Inc. 01/22/2002

CAPSTREAM VENTURES INC (BC)
Name changed to Axion Ventures Inc. 03/10/2017

CAPSULE COMMUNICATIONS INC (DE)
Merged into Covista Communications, Inc. 02/08/2002
Each share Common $0.001 par exchanged for (0.0917) share Common 5¢ par

CAPSULE SYS INC (CO)
Administratively dissolved for failure to file reports 01/01/1992

CAPSULE TECHNOLOGY GROUP INC (ON)
Declared bankrupt 12/00/1989
No stockholders' equity

CAPSURE HLDGS CORP (OH)
Merged into CNA Surety Corp. 09/30/1997
Each share Common 5¢ par exchanged for (1) share Common 1¢ par
(See CNA Surety Corp.)

CAPT. CRAB'S TAKE-AWAY, INC. (FL)
Under plan of merger name changed to Capt. Crabs, Inc. 06/08/1984
Capt. Crabs, Inc. name changed to Bayport Restaurant Group, Inc. 06/04/1990 which merged into Landry's Seafood Restaurants, Inc. 08/09/1996 which name changed to Landry's Restaurants, Inc. 06/05/2001
(See Landry's Restaurants, Inc.)

CAPT CRABS INC (FL)
Name changed to Bayport Restaurant Group, Inc. 06/04/1990
Bayport Restaurant Group, Inc. merged into Landry's Seafood Restaurants, Inc. 08/09/1996 which name changed to Landry's Restaurants, Inc. 06/05/2001
(See Landry's Restaurants, Inc.)

CAPTAIN CONS RES LTD (ON)
Recapitalized as International Captain Industries Corp. 10/03/1990
Each share Common no par exchanged for (0.2) share Common no par
International Captain Industries Corp. recapitalized as Rocklite International Inc. 09/25/1992
(See Rocklite International Inc.)

CAPTAIN INTL INDS LTD (BC)
Recapitalized as Quaker Energy Inc. 03/12/1980
Each share Capital Stock no par exchanged for (0.5) share Capital Stock no par
Quaker Energy Inc. name changed to Quaker Resources Inc. 08/18/1983 which name changed to Comco Mining & Smelting Corp. 09/10/1984 which name changed to Quaker Resources Canada Ltd. 08/18/1986 which name changed to SPI Safety Packaging International Ltd. 04/25/1987
(See SPI Safety Packaging International Ltd.)

CAPTAIN MINES LTD (ON)
Recapitalized as Captain Consolidated Resources Ltd. 12/31/1980
Each share Capital Stock no par exchanged for (0.2) share Common no par
Captain Consolidated Resources Ltd. recapitalized as International Captain Industries Corp. 10/03/1990 which recapitalized as Rocklite International Inc. 09/25/1993
(See Rocklite International Inc.)

CAPTAIN TONYS PIZZA INC (NY)
Common $0.001 par split (2) for (1) by issuance of (1) additional share 07/20/1988
Reorganized under the laws of Nevada as Am-Pac International, Inc. 11/26/1996
Each share Common $0.001 par exchanged for (0.05) share Common $0.001 par
(See Am-Pac International, Inc. (NV))

CAPTAIN YELLOWKNIFE GOLD MINES, LTD. (ON)
Name changed to Captain Mines Ltd. 01/10/1957
Captain Mines Ltd. recapitalized as Captain Consolidated Resources Ltd. 12/31/1980 which recapitalized as International Captain Industries Corp. 10/03/1990 which recapitalized as Rocklite International Inc. 09/25/1993
(See Rocklite International Inc.)

CAPTAINS CLUB, INC. (DE)
Dissolved 03/15/1961
No stockholders' equity

CAPTARIS INC (WA)
Merged into Open Text Corp. 10/31/2008
Each share Common 1¢ par exchanged for $4.80 cash

CAPTEC NET LEASE RLTY INC (DE)
Merged into Commercial Net Lease Realty, Inc. 12/01/2001
Each share Common 1¢ par exchanged for (0.21034679) share 9% Preferred Ser. A, (0.4575) share Common 1¢ par and $1.27 cash

CAPTECH COMMUNICATION INC (CANADA)
Recapitalized as Captech Multicom Inc. 05/23/1997
Each share Common no par exchanged for (0.25) share Common no par
(See Captech Multicom Inc.)

CAPTECH FINL GROUP INC (FL)
Old Common no par split (2) for (1) by issuance of (1) additional share payable 08/09/2004 to holders of record 07/28/2004 Ex date - 08/10/2004
Each (75) shares old Common $0.001 par exchanged for (0.01) share new Common no par 02/20/2007
Each share new Common no par exchanged again for (0.2) share new Common no par 07/16/2007
Name changed to Boo Koo Holdings, Inc. (FL) 08/13/2007
Boo Koo Holdings, Inc. (FL) reincorporated in Delaware 12/17/2007 which name changed to Performing Brands, Inc. 08/19/2008
(See Performing Brands, Inc.)

CAPTECH INC (CA)
Stock Dividend - 10% 06/20/1973
Prior Preferred $100 par called for redemption 01/30/1978
Preferred $100 par called for redemption 01/30/1978
Merged into Texace Corp. 09/20/1978
Each share Common $1 par exchanged for $14.625 cash

CAPTECH INC NEW (CA)
Name changed to Matthews Studio Equipment Group 02/15/1989
(See Matthews Studio Equipment Group)

CAPTECH MULTICOM INC (CANADA)
Dissolved for non-compliance 09/19/2005

CAPTERRA FINL GROUP INC (CO)
Each share old Common $0.001 par exchanged for (0.5) share new Common $0.001 par 09/03/2010
Reincorporated under the laws of Delaware as NexCore Healthcare Capital Corp. 04/14/2011
(See NexCore Healthcare Capital Corp.)

CAPTIVA SOFTWARE CORP (DE)
Merged into EMC Corp. 12/30/2005
Each share Common 1¢ par exchanged for $22.25 cash

CAPTIVE AIR INC (NV)
Name changed to UTI Chemicals, Inc. 09/24/1987
UTI Chemicals, Inc. recapitalized as Urethane Technologies, Inc. 11/25/1991
(See Urethane Technologies, Inc.)

CAPTIVE AIR INTL INC (BC)
Recapitalized as Kik Tire Technologies Inc. 04/08/1996
Each share Common no par exchanged for (0.2) share Common no par
Kik Tire Technologies Inc. recapitalized as Kik Polymers Inc. 06/20/2006 which name changed to Edgewater Wireless Systems Inc. 02/01/2012

CAPTIVE VENTURE CAP INC (UT)
Name changed to Scan-Graphics, Inc. (UT) 03/18/1987
Scan-Graphics, Inc. (UT) reincorporated in Pennsylvania 06/15/1992 which name changed to Sedona Corp. 04/02/1999

CAPTURE NET TECHNOLOGIES INC (ON)
Name changed to Sea Green Capital Corp. 03/05/2003
Sea Green Capital Corp. recapitalized as Cava Resources Inc. 07/23/2012 which name changed to Gold Rush Cariboo Corp. 06/21/2018

CAPUCINOS INC (DE)
Recapitalized as Boston Restaurant Associates Inc. 06/24/1994
Each share Common 1¢ par exchanged for (0.1) share Common 1¢ par
(See Boston Restaurant Associates Inc.)

CAPVEST INCOME CORP (AB)
Each share old Common no par exchanged for (0.06666666) share new Common no par 03/26/2007
Completely liquidated
Each share new Common no par received first and final distribution of $0.73 cash payable 02/27/2009 to holders of record 02/26/2009
Note: Certificates were not required to be surrendered and are without value

CAPVEST INTERNATIONALE LTD (CO)
Declared defunct and inoperative for failure to pay taxes and file annual reports 01/01/1994

CAPWELL, SULLIVAN & FURTH (CA)
Liquidation completed 02/25/1955
Details not available

CAPX CORP (DE)
Name changed to Autolend Group, Inc. 02/13/1995
(See Autolend Group, Inc.)

CAR CHARGING GROUP INC (NV)
Each share old Common $0.001 par exchanged for (0.02) share new Common $0.001 par 02/25/2011
Recapitalized as Blink Charging Co. 08/29/2017
Each share new Common $0.001 par exchanged for (0.02) share Common $0.001 par

CAR MART INC (CO)
Name changed to Monaco Finance, Inc. 06/29/1993
(See Monaco Finance, Inc.)

CAR PLAN SYSTEMS, INC. (FL)
Recapitalized as Audiophonics, Inc. (FL) 01/08/1970
Each share Common 10¢ par exchanged for (0.25) share Common 1¢ par
Audiophonics, Inc. (FL) reincorporated in Delaware as Phoenix Industries Corp. 03/29/1974
(See Phoenix Industries Corp.)

CARA OPERATIONS LTD (ON)
Old Common no par split (3) for (1) by issuance of (2) additional shares 12/01/1978
Old Common no par reclassified as new Common no par 07/24/1980
Each share new Common no par received distribution of (1) share Non-Vtg.Class A no par 07/30/1980
Non-Vtg.Class A no par split (3) for (1) by issuance of (2) additional shares 07/12/1986
New Common no par split (3) for (1) by issuance of (2) additional shares 07/22/1986
Non-Vtg. Class A no par split (3) for (1) by issuance of (2) additional shares 07/22/1991
New Common no par split (3) for (1) by issuance of (2) additional shares
Acquired by 2034617 Ontario Inc. 02/25/2004
Each share Non-Vtg. Class A no par exchanged for $8 cash
Each share new Common no par exchanged for $8 cash
Name changed to Recipe Unlimited Corp. 05/16/2018

CARACAL ENERGY INC (CANADA)
Acquired by Glencore PLC 07/08/2014
Each share Common no par exchanged for USD$3.22637412 cash
Note: Unexchanged certificates were cancelled and became without value 07/06/2016

CARACO PHARMACUETICAL LABS LTD (MI)
Merged into Sun Pharmaceutical Industries Ltd. 06/14/2011
Each share Common no par exchanged for $5.25 cash

CARADA CAP CORP (AB)
Name changed to Norlana Energy Inc. 12/09/1991
Norlana Energy Inc. recapitalized as Norlana Resources Ltd. 12/02/1997
(See Norlana Resources Ltd.)

CARADON PLC (ENGLAND)
Each ADR for Ordinary exchanged for (0.9) ADR for Ordinary 05/20/1997
Name changed to Novar PLC 01/03/2001
(See Novar PLC)

CARAMAT GOLD MINES LTD. (ON)
Merged into Milestone Exploration Ltd. 07/23/1968
Each share Capital Stock $1 par exchanged for (4,124) shares Capital Stock no par
Milestone Exploration Ltd. merged into Jubilee Gold Inc. 01/01/2010 which merged into Jubilee Gold Exploration Ltd. 01/25/2013

CARAMORA PORCUPINE MINES, LTD. (ON)
Charter cancelled and declared dissolved for failure to file returns and pay fees 11/28/1973

CARAN ENGINEERING CORP. (TX)
Voluntarily dissolved 09/28/1972
Details not available

CARAT EXPL INC (BC)
Common no par split (5) for (1) by issuance of (4) additional shares payable 02/27/2006 to holders of record 02/23/2006 Ex date - 02/21/2006
Name changed to Stronghold Metals Inc. 04/12/2010
Stronghold Metals Inc. recapitalized as Eagle Mountain Gold Corp. 07/26/2012 which merged into Goldsource Mines Inc. 03/05/2014

CARATEL LTD (ON)
Recapitalized as Juritel Systems Inc. 08/24/1992
Each share Common no par exchanged for (0.16666666) share Common no par
Juritel Systems Inc. name changed to Huntington Rhodes Inc. 09/02/1993
(See Huntington Rhodes Inc.)

CARAUSTAR INDS INC (NC)
Plan of reorganization under Chapter 11 Federal Bankruptcy proceedings effective 08/20/2009
Each share received approximately $0.10 cash

CARAVAN DEV CORP (BC)
Cease trade order effective 08/17/1983

CARAVAN INTL LTD (BC)
Name changed to C.I. Resources International Ltd. 07/13/1981
(See C.I. Resources International Ltd.)

CARAVAN OIL & GAS LTD (AB)
Acquired by Ketch Energy Ltd. 11/30/2000
Each share Common no par exchanged for (0.477) share Common no par and $0.381 cash
Ketch Energy Ltd. merged into Acclaim Energy Trust 10/01/2002
(See Acclaim Energy Trust)

CARAVAN TRAILER LODGES B C LTD (BC)
Name changed to Caravan Development Corp. and Class A Common no par reclassified as Common no par 05/01/1977
(See Caravan Development Corp.)

CARAVAN TRAILER LODGES INTL LTD (BC)
Name changed to Caravan International Ltd. 04/30/1975
Caravan International Ltd. name changed to C.I. Resources International Ltd. 07/13/1981
(See C.I. Resources International Ltd.)

CARAVAN TRAILER LODGES ST LAWRENCE LTD (CANADA)
Name changed to Trevista Estates Ltd. 00/00/1978
(See Trevista Estates Ltd.)

CARAVATT COMMUNICATIONS INC (NY)
Proclaimed dissolved for failure to pay taxes 12/24/1991

CARAVELLE MINES LTD (ON)
Charter cancelled and declared dissolved for failure to file returns and pay fees 03/16/1976

CARAVELLE RES LTD (BC)
Name changed to STN Shop Television Network Ltd. (BC) 10/16/1986
STN Shop Television Network Ltd. (BC) reincorporated in Delaware as Shop Television Network Inc. 12/21/1987
(See Shop Television Network Inc.)

CARB A DRINK INTL INC (UT)
Name changed to Fountain Fresh International 04/26/1988
Fountain Fresh International name changed to Bevex, Inc. 08/17/1998 which recapitalized as GTG Ventures, Inc. 11/01/2005

CARBEC MINES LTD (QC)
Merged into Triton Explorations Ltd. 12/15/1969
Each share Capital Stock $1 par exchanged for (0.11111111) share Capital Stock $1 par
(See Triton Explorations Ltd.)

CARBEN ENERGY INC (BC)
Reincorporated under the laws of Delaware as American Medical Technologies, Inc. and Common no par changed to 1¢ par 11/06/1987
American Medical Technologies, Inc. name changed to Tidel Technologies, Inc. 08/04/1997 which name changed to Secure Alliance Holdings Corp. 06/19/2007 which recapitalized as aVinci Media Corp. 06/09/2008
(See aVinci Media Corp.)

CARBER CAP CORP (ON)
Recapitalized as Ba Ba Capital Inc. 08/17/2010
Each share Common no par exchanged for (0.1) share Common no par
Ba Ba Capital Inc. recapitalized as Imex Systems Inc. 05/13/2016

CARBIDE/GRAPHITE GROUP INC (DE)
Plan of reorganization under Chapter 11 Federal Bankruptcy Code effective 01/13/2005
No stockholders' equity

CARBITE GOLF INC (YT)
Reorganized 10/12/2001
Reorganized from under the laws of (BC) to (YT) 10/12/2001
Each share Common no par exchanged for (0.25) share Common no par
Dissolved and struck off register 05/25/2005

CARBIZ COM INC (ON)
Name changed to Carbiz Inc. 10/06/2003
(See Carbiz Inc.)

CARBIZ INC (ON)
Company transferred all assets to secured lenders and ceased operations 02/12/2010
Stockholders' equity unlikely

CARBO INDS INC (NY)
Under plan of merger each share Class A Common 5¢ par exchanged for $16.50 cash 07/01/1988

CARBO-OXYGEN CO., INC.
Merged into National Cylinder Gas Co. 00/00/1937
Details not available

CARBOCLOR S A (ARGENTINA)
ADR agreement terminated 10/18/2017
Each Sponsored ADR for Ordinary exchanged for (1) share Ordinary
Note: Unexchanged ADR's will be sold and the proceeds, if any, held for claim after 10/22/2018

CARBOLINE CO (MO)
Capital Stock $1 par split (3) for (2) by issuance of (0.5) additional share 03/15/1976
Stock Dividends - 15% 03/22/1965; 20% 03/15/1966; 20% 03/15/1967; 20% 03/20/1968
Merged into Sun Co., Inc. 01/07/1980
Each share Capital Stock $1 par exchanged for $30.75 cash

CARBON CREDITS INTL INC (NV)
Each share old Common $0.0001 par exchanged for (0.008) share new Common $0.0001 par 06/20/2011
Name changed to SinglePoint Inc. 07/01/2013

CARBON ENERGY CORP (CO)
Merged into Evergreen Resources, Inc. 10/29/2003
Each share Common no par exchanged for (0.55) share Common no par
Evergreen Resources, Inc. merged into Pioneer Natural Resources Co. 09/28/2004

CARBON ENERGY LTD (AUSTRALIA)
ADR agreement terminated 07/21/2017
Each Sponsored ADR for Ordinary exchanged for $0.015626 cash

CARBON FIBER PRODS INC (UT)
Recapitalized as Cyntech Technologies Inc. 01/21/1999
Each share Common $0.001 par exchanged for (0.06060606) share Common $0.001 par
(See Cyntech Technologies Inc.)

CARBON FRIENDLY SOLUTIONS INC (CANADA)
Name changed to MicroCoal Technologies Inc. 07/22/2013
MicroCoal Technologies Inc. reorganized as Targeted Microwave Solutions Inc. 05/22/2015

CARBON FUEL CO (WV)
Under plan of reorganization each share Common $2.50 par automatically became (1) share Carbon Industries, Inc. Common $2.50 par 11/08/1974
Carbon Industries, Inc. merged into International Telephone & Telegraph Corp. 02/11/1977 which name changed to ITT Corp. 12/31/1983 which reorganized as ITT Industries Inc. (IN) 12/19/1995 which name changed to ITT Corp. 07/01/2006

CARBON INC (UT)
Each share Capital Stock 20¢ par exchanged for (0.05) share Capital Stock 1¢ par 12/04/1968
Each share Capital Stock 1¢ par exchanged for (0.1) share Capital Stock 10¢ par 11/12/1969
Proclaimed dissolved for failure to pay taxes 09/28/1974

CARBON, INC. (DE)
Charter cancelled and declared inoperative and void for non-payment of taxes 04/01/1930

CARBON INDS INC (WV)
Common $2.50 par changed to no par 05/24/1976
Stock Dividend - 100% 09/02/1975
Merged into International Telephone & Telegraph Corp. 02/11/1977
Each share Common no par exchanged for (0.85) share $4 Conv. Preferred Ser. K no par
International Telephone & Telegraph Corp. name changed to ITT Corp. 12/31/1983
(See ITT Corp.)

CARBON JUNGLE INC (NV)
Recapitalized as Global New Energy Industries Inc. 01/17/2013
Each share Common $0.001 par exchanged for (0.001) share Common $0.001 par
Global New Energy Industries Inc. name changed to Coin Citadel 11/06/2014

CAR-CAR — FINANCIAL INFORMATION, INC.

CARBON MONOXIDE ELIMINATOR CORP.
Dissolved 03/15/1954
Details not available

CARBON NAT GAS CO (DE)
Each share old Common 1¢ par exchanged for (0.05) share new Common 1¢ par 03/17/2017
Name changed to Carbon Energy Corp. 06/07/2018

CARBON SCIENCES INC (NV)
Each share old Common $0.001 par exchanged for (0.025) share new Common $0.001 par 06/06/2011
Each share new Common $0.001 par exchanged again for (0.1) share new Common $0.001 par 04/01/2016
Name changed to Digital Locations, Inc. 11/21/2017

CARBON URANIUM CO. (UT)
Recapitalized as Carbon, Inc. 00/00/1959
Each share Capital Stock 20¢ par exchanged for (0.05) share Capital Stock 20¢ par
(See Carbon, Inc.)

CARBONIC CHEMS CORP (NM)
Common $2 par changed to $1 par 11/01/1965
Name changed to S.E.C. Corp. (NM) 05/01/1968
(See S.E.C. Corp. (NM))

CARBONIC PRODUCTS CORP.
Name changed to Globe Oil & Gas Corp. 00/00/1934
(See Globe Oil & Gas Corp.)

CARBONICS CAP CORP (DE)
Common $0.001 par changed to $0.0001 par 01/04/2010
Recapitalized as Westport Energy Holdings Inc. 12/03/2012
Each share Common $0.0001 par exchanged for (0.0002) share Common $0.0001 par

CARBONONE TECHNOLOGIES INC (BC)
Name changed to TekModo Industries Inc. 10/12/2016
TekModo Industries Inc. recapitalized as Lincoln Ventures Ltd. 07/16/2018

CARBONS CONS INC (DE)
Common no par changed to $7 par 00/00/1938
Common $7 par changed to $5 par and $2 cash distributed 00/00/1941
Common $5 par changed to $2 par and $2.50 cash distributed 00/00/1952
Liquidation completed
Each share Common $2 par exchanged for initial distribution of $4 cash 02/08/1974
Each share Common $2 par received second and final distribution of $0.2241 cash 03/30/1976

CARBON2GREEN CORP (CANADA)
Recapitalized as TomaGold Corp. 01/04/2012
Each share Class A Common no par exchanged for (0.2) share Class A Common no par 10/07/2009

CARBORUNDUM CO (DE)
Each share Common $100 par exchanged for (5) shares Common no par 00/00/1927
Each share Common no par exchanged for (3) shares Common $5 par 00/00/1951
Common $5 par changed to $3 par and (1) additional share issued 05/16/1966
Common $3 par changed to $1.50 par and (1) additional share issued 05/24/1976
Merged into Kennecott Industries, Inc. 01/12/1978
Each share Common $1.50 par exchanged for $66 cash

CARBYLAN THERAPEUTICS INC (DE)
Recapitalized as KalVista Pharmaceuticals, Inc. 11/22/2016
Each share Common $0.001 par exchanged for (0.07142857) share Common $0.001 par

CARCI COMPUTAB SYS INC (NY)
Merged into Cybermatics Inc. (NY) 05/22/1970
Each share Common 10¢ par exchanged for (0.55) share Common 1¢ par
Cybermatics Inc. (NY) reincorporated in Delaware 06/19/1974
(See Cybermatics Inc.)

CARCO ELECTRS (CA)
Class A no par and Class B no par split (2) for (1) by issuance of (1) additional share respectively 08/24/1964
Class A no par and Class B no par split (2) for (1) by issuance of (1) additional share respectively 11/01/1972
Class A no par and Class B no par split (2) for (1) by issuance of (1) additional share respectively 10/13/1981
Plan of reorganization under Chapter 11 Federal Bankruptcy proceedings effective 02/16/2005
No stockholders' equity

CARCO INDUSTRIES, INC. (DE)
Name changed to Deval Aerodynamics, Inc. 03/02/1962
(See Deval Aerodynamics, Inc.)

CARCORP USA CORP (DE)
Name changed to Elite Flight Solutions Inc. 06/26/2003
Elite Flight Solutions Inc. name changed to Home Energy Savings Corp. 07/21/2006

CARD LAKE COPPER MINES LTD (ON)
Recapitalized as Card Lake Resources Ltd. 10/31/1986
Each share Capital Stock $1 par exchanged for (0.2) share Common no par
Card Lake Resources Ltd. recapitalized as Franc-Or Resources Corp. (ON) 04/20/1994 which reincorporated in Yukon 08/25/1997 which recapitalized as Crocodile Gold Corp. (YT) 11/06/2009 which reincorporated in Ontario 12/04/2009 which merged into Newmarket Gold Inc. (ON) 07/14/2015 which recapitalized as Kirkland Lake Gold Ltd. 12/06/216

CARD LAKE RES LTD (ON)
Recapitalized as Franc-Or Resources Corp. (ON) 04/20/1994
Each share Common no par exchanged for (0.1) share Common no par
Franc-Or Resources Corp. (ON) reincorporated in Yukon 08/25/1997 which recapitalized as Crocodile Gold Corp. (YT) 11/06/2009 which reincorporated in Ontario 12/04/2009 which merged into Newmarket Gold Inc. (ON) 07/14/2015 which recapitalized as Kirkland Lake Gold Ltd. 12/06/2016

CARD TEL INC (DE)
Charter forfeited for failure to maintain a registered agent 12/08/1992

CARDCONNECT CORP (DE)
Acquired by First Data Corp. (New) 07/06/2017
Each share Common $0.001 par exchanged for $15 cash

CARDERO RES LTD (BC)
Recapitalized as International Cardero Resources Inc. 05/11/1983
Each share Common no par exchanged for (0.33333333) share Common no par
(See International Cardero Resources Inc.)

CARDIA BIOPLASTICS LTD (AUSTRALIA)
ADR agreement terminated 08/07/2015
Each Sponsored ADR for Ordinary exchanged for $0.393043 cash

CARDIAC CTL SYS INC (DE)
Each share old Common 10¢ par exchanged for (0.14285714) share new Common 10¢ par 12/12/1994
Plan of reorganization under Chapter 11 Federal Bankruptcy Code effective 07/02/2001
No stockholders' equity

CARDIAC ELECTRONICS, INC. (NY)
Adjudicated bankrupt 09/22/1976
Details not available

CARDIAC ELECTRS INC (DE)
Name changed to Digital Diagnostics Corp. 12/21/1989
(See Digital Diagnostics Corp.)

CARDIAC PACEMAKERS INC (MN)
Common 1¢ par split (2) for (1) by issuance of (1) additional share 09/21/1976
Stock Dividends - 100% 11/21/1973; 100% 05/17/1974
Merged into Lilly (Eli) & Co. 12/15/1978
Each share Common 1¢ par exchanged for (0.85) share Common $0.625 par

CARDIAC PATHWAYS CORP (DE)
Each share old Common $0.001 par exchanged for (0.2) share new Common $0.001 par 07/27/1999
Merged into Boston Scientific Corp. 08/14/2001
Each share new Common $0.001 par exchanged for $5.267 cash

CARDIAC RESUSCITATOR CORP. (OR)
Incorporated 04/06/1972
Name changed to Medical Electronics Investment Co. 09/00/1979
(See Medical Electronics Investment Co.)

CARDIAC RESUSCITATOR CORP (OR)
Incorporated 08/06/1979
Involuntarily dissolved 11/02/1993

CARDIAC SCIENCE CORP (DE)
Merged into Opto Circuits (India) Ltd. 12/03/2010
Each share Common $0.001 par exchanged for $2.30 cash

CARDIAC SCIENCE INC (DE)
Each share old Common $0.001 par exchanged for (0.08749999) share new Common $0.001 par 09/08/1997
Merged into Cardiac Science Corp. 09/01/2005
Each share new Common $0.001 par exchanged for (0.1) share Common $0.001 par
(See Cardiac Science Corp.)

CARDICA INC (DE)
Each share old Common $0.001 par exchanged for (0.1) share new Common $0.001 par 02/17/2016
Name changed to Dextera Surgical Inc. 06/22/2016

CARDIFF COMMUNICATIONS INC (NV)
Each share old Common $0.001 par exchanged for (0.01) share new Common $0.001 par 09/15/2005
Note: No holder received fewer than (100) post-split shares
Name changed to Liberator Medical Holdings, Inc. 06/14/2007
(See Liberator Medical Holdings, Inc.)

CARDIFF COMMUNICATIONS INC (UT)
Name changed 01/07/1981
Common $1 par changed to 1¢ par 12/31/1971
Each share Common 1¢ par exchanged for (0.25) share Common 4¢ par 09/12/1972
Name changed from Cardiff Industries, Inc. to Cardiff Communications, Inc. 01/07/1981
Completely liquidated 08/15/1991
Each share Common 4¢ par exchanged for first and final distribution of $0.39 cash

CARDIFF CORP (AB)
Struck off register for failure to file annual returns 01/01/1996

CARDIFF ENERGY CORP (BC)
Each share old Common no par exchanged for (0.14285714) share new Common no par 01/19/2017
Name changed to Cheetah Canyon Resources Corp. 07/19/2017

CARDIFF EQUITIES CORP (DE)
Merged into Leucadia Inc. 03/28/1986
Each share Common 67¢ par exchanged for $12.85 cash

CARDIFF FINL INC (CO)
Name changed to United American, Inc. 04/24/1989
United American, Inc. name changed to Cardiff International Inc. (CO) 12/04/1989 which reorganized in Florida 09/12/2014 which name changed to Cardiff Lexington Corp. 02/07/2018

CARDIFF FLUORITE MINES LTD. (ON)
Name changed to Cardiff Uranium Mines Ltd. 00/00/1953
Cardiff Uranium Mines Ltd. merged into Insulblock Systems Inc. 09/01/1988
(See Insulblock Systems Inc.)

CARDIFF FLUORITE MINING SYNDICATE LTD.
Acquired by Cardiff Uranium Mines Ltd. 00/00/1953
Each share Common exchanged for (0.125) share Common
Cardiff Uranium Mines Ltd. merged into Insulblock Systems Inc. 09/01/1988
(See Insulblock Systems Inc.)

CARDIFF INTL INC (FL)
Reorganized 09/12/2014
Common no par changed to $0.00001 par 10/22/2013
Reorganized from (CO) to under the laws of Florida 09/12/2014
Each share Common $0.00001 par exchanged for (0.00004) share Common $0.001 par
Name changed to Cardiff Lexington Corp. 02/07/2018

CARDIFF MINING & MILLING CO. (UT)
Name changed to Cardiff Industries, Inc. 10/28/1960
Cardiff Industries, Inc. name changed to Cardiff Communications, Inc. 01/07/1981
(See Cardiff Communications, Inc.)

CARDIFF MINING CO. LTD. (BC)
Charter revoked for failure to file reports and pay fees 01/27/1966

CARDIFF RES INC (AB)
Name changed to Hy-Drive Technologies Ltd. 04/26/2004
Hy-Drive Technologies Ltd. name changed to blutip Power Technologies Ltd. 06/01/2011
(See blutip Power Technologies Ltd.)

CARDIFF RES INC (UT)
Involuntarily dissolved 11/01/1988

CARDIFF URANIUM MINES LTD (ON)
Merged into Insulblock Systems Inc. 09/01/1988

Each share Common $1 par exchanged for (0.25) share Common no par
(See Insulblock Systems Inc.)

CARDIFF VENTURES CORP (AB)
Recapitalized as Cardiff Corp. 11/04/1992
Each share Common no par exchanged for (0.2) share Common no par
(See Cardiff Corp.)

CARDIGAN CAP CORP (AB)
Reincorporated under the laws of Canada as Icron Systems Inc. 01/25/1999
Icron Systems Inc. recapitalized as Icron Technologies Corp. 07/10/2001
(See Icron Technologies Corp.)

CARDIGAN DEV LTD (BC)
Recapitalized as United Cardigan Development Ltd. 08/15/1975
Each share Capital Stock no par exchanged for (0.1) share Capital Stock no par
(See United Cardigan Development Ltd.)

CARDIGANT MED INC (DE)
Name changed to Takung Art Co., Ltd. 11/12/2014

CARDILLO TRAVEL SYS INC (CA)
Charter suspended for failure to file reports and pay fees 06/01/1987

CARDIMA INC (DE)
Each share old Common $0.001 par exchanged for (0.1) share new Common $0.001 par 07/31/2007
Each share new Common $0.001 par exchanged again for (0.1) share new Common $0.001 par 05/11/2010
Plan of reorganization under Chapter 11 Federal Bankruptcy proceedings confirmed 10/28/2011
No stockholders' equity

CARDINAL BANCORP INC (PA)
Merged into Susquehanna Bancshares, Inc. 12/16/1998
Each share Common 50¢ par exchanged for (2.048) shares Common $2 par
Susquehanna Bancshares, Inc. merged into BB&T Corp. 08/01/2015

CARDINAL BANCSHARES INC (KY)
Each share Common no par received distribution of approximately (1.5) shares Security First Network Bank (Atlanta, GA) Common no par payable 05/23/1996 to holders of record 05/13/1996
Acquired by Area Bancshares Corp. (New) 09/30/1997
Each share Common no par exchanged for (2.7391) shares Common no par
Area Bancshares Corp. (New) merged into BB&T Corp. 03/20/2002

CARDINAL BANKSHARES CORP (VA)
Common $10 par split (3) for (1) by issuance of (2) additional shares payable 06/01/2001 to holders of record 04/25/2001 Ex date - 06/04/2001
Merged into Parkway Acquisition Corp. 07/01/2016
Each share Common $10 par exchanged for (1.3) shares Common no par

CARDINAL CAP CORP (NV)
Recapitalized as Capital Media Group Ltd. 01/11/1996
Each share Common $0.001 par exchanged for (0.1) share Common $0.001 par

CARDINAL COMMUNICATIONS INC (NV)
Each share old Common $0.0001 par exchanged for (0.03333333) share new Common $0.0001 par 01/23/2007

Chapter 11 bankruptcy proceedings terminated 03/29/2010
No stockholders' equity

CARDINAL COMPOUND FD (BC)
Completely liquidated 04/21/1975
Each Share no par received first and final distribution of (1.559531) shares Pacific Income Fund Shares no par
Note: Certificates were not required to be surrendered and are without value

CARDINAL CORP (NV)
Recapitalized as Communications Corp. of America 11/19/1976
Each share Common 10¢ par exchanged for (0.33333333) share Common 1¢ par
(See Communications Corp. of America)

CARDINAL CORP KY (KY)
Completely liquidated 02/07/1989
Each share Common $2 par exchanged for first and final distribution of $40.48719 cash

CARDINAL DISTR INC (OH)
Common no par split (5) for (4) by issuance of (0.25) additional share 09/30/1989
Common no par split (5) for (4) by issuance of (0.25) additional share 09/30/1990
Common no par split (5) for (4) by issuance of (0.25) additional share 09/30/1991
Stock Dividends - 10% 04/16/1985; 10% 03/17/1986; 10% 09/30/1987; 10% 09/30/1988
Name changed to Cardinal Health, Inc. 02/07/1994

CARDINAL DIVID FD (BC)
Name changed to Pacific Income Fund 01/01/1975

CARDINAL ENERGY CORP (UT)
Name changed to Check Rite International, Inc. 06/07/1984
Check Rite International, Inc. merged into Broadcast International, Inc. (Old) 12/03/1990 which merged into Data Broadcasting Corp. 06/30/1995 which name changed to Interactive Data Corp. 06/20/2001
(See Interactive Data Corp.)

CARDINAL ENTMT CORP (DE)
Filed for Chapter 7 bankruptcy proceedings 02/10/1986
Stockholders' equity unlikely

CARDINAL EXTRUSIONS CO. (KY)
Name changed to Cardinal Aluminum Co. 09/30/1981

CARDINAL FACTOR CORP (ON)
Delisted from CNQ 10/13/2000

CARDINAL FD INC (OH)
Common no par split (3) for (2) by issuance of (0.5) additional share 01/12/1990
Under plan of reorganization each share Common no par automatically became Cardinal Group Cardinal Fund Common no par on a net asset basis 05/01/1996

CARDINAL FDG INC (DE)
Name changed to Inferno Snuffers Inc. 09/16/1991
(See Inferno Snuffers Inc.)

CARDINAL FED SVGS BK (OWENSBORO, KY)
Reorganized under the laws of Delaware as Cardinal Financial Group, Inc. and Common $1 par changed to 10¢ par 08/31/1989
(See Cardinal Financial Group, Inc.)

CARDINAL FINL CORP (VA)
Each share 7.25% Conv. Preferred Ser. A $1 par exchanged for (0.7519) share Common $1 par 03/29/2004

Merged into United Bankshares, Inc. 04/24/2017
Each share Common $1 par exchanged for (0.71) share Common $2.50 par

CARDINAL FINL GROUP INC (DE)
Acquired by Great Financial Federal 04/30/1993
Each share Common 10¢ par exchanged for $17.50 cash

CARDINAL GNMA TR (NY)
Completely liquidated 01/31/2000
Details not available

CARDINAL GOLD MINING CO. (CA)
Charter suspended for failure to file reports and pay fees 12/01/1950

CARDINAL GOVT OBLIG FD (OH)
Name changed 02/01/1991
Name changed from Cardinal Government Guaranteed Fund to Cardinal Government Obligations Fund and Shares of Bene. Int. no par reclassified as Investor Shares no par 02/01/1991
Under plan of reorganization each Investor Share no par automatically became Cardinal Group Government Obligations Fund Investor Share no par on a net asset basis 05/01/1996

CARDINAL INDS INC (NV)
Reincorporated 09/21/1999
State of incorporation changed from (MA) to (NV) 09/21/1999
Name changed to Maxum Development, Inc. 06/01/2000
Maxum Development, Inc. name changed to Tropical Leisure Resorts, Inc. 09/10/2001 which recapitalized as eWorldMedia Holdings, Inc. 10/22/2002 which name changed to Liberty Diversified Holdings, Inc. 01/09/2006 which name changed to Nutripure Beverages, Inc. 01/17/2008

CARDINAL INSTRUMENTATION CORP. (CA)
Adjudicated bankrupt 10/14/1960
Stockholders' equity unlikely

CARDINAL INVESTOR FUND (NV)
Name changed to Coastal Security Investment Fund 01/08/1965
Coastal Security Investment Fund name changed to Hanover Fund 00/00/1968 which name changed to F-D Capital Fund 04/00/1970 which merged into Pine Tree Fund, Inc. 11/27/1972

CARDINAL LIFE INSURANCE CO. (KY)
Name changed to Cardinal Corp. Louisville Kentucky 12/31/1959
(See Cardinal Corp. Louisville Kentucky)

CARDINAL MINERAL CORP (BC)
Recapitalized as Connecticut Development Corp. 11/08/1990
Each share Common no par exchanged for (0.33333333) share Common no par
Connecticut Development Corp. recapitalized as Mira Properties Ltd. 04/16/1999 which recapitalized as Resolve Ventures, Inc. 08/19/2003

CARDINAL MINERALS INC (NV)
Recapitalized as Universal Food & Beverage Co. 03/04/2005
Each share Common no par exchanged for (0.1) share Common $0.001 par
(See Universal Food & Beverage Co.)

CARDINAL PETE CO (DE)
Common no par changed to $1 par 12/14/1964
Liquidation completed
Each share Common $1 par exchanged for initial distribution of $24.75 cash 04/01/1974
Each share Common $1 par received second distribution of $1.80 cash 02/24/1975
Each share Common $1 par received third and final distribution of $0.0441 cash 03/14/1979

CARDINAL PETROLEUMS LTD. (CANADA)
Merged into Consolidated Allenbee Oil & Gas Co. Ltd. 00/00/1952
Each share Capital Stock $1 par exchanged for (0.4) share Common $1 par
Consolidated Allenbee Oil & Gas Co. Ltd. recapitalized as Western Allenbee Oil & Gas Co. Ltd. 04/06/1960 which name changed to Convoy Capital Corp. 04/28/1989 which recapitalized as Hariston Corp. 09/25/1992 which recapitalized as Midland Holland Inc. (Canada) 02/10/1999 which reincorporated in Yukon 03/11/1999 which name changed to Mercury Partners & Co. Inc. 02/22/2000 which name changed to Black Mountain Capital Corp. 05/02/2005 which recapitalized as Grand Peak Capital Corp. (YT) 11/20/2007 which reincorporated in British Columbia 04/27/2010

CARDINAL RLTY SVCS INC (OH)
Name changed to Lexford, Inc. 10/07/1997
Lexford, Inc. merged into Lexford Residential Trust 03/18/1998 which merged into Equity Residential Properties Trust 10/01/1999 which name changed to Equity Residential 05/15/2002

CARDINAL SILVER INC (NV)
Merged into U.S. Silver & Mining Corp. 05/26/1970
Each share Common 10¢ par exchanged for (0.8) Common 1¢ par
U.S. Silver & Mining Corp. recapitalized as Diversified Resources Corp. 09/01/1972
(See Diversified Resources Corp.)

CARDINAL TAX EXEMPT BD FD (NY)
Name changed to Cardinal Tax-Exempt Bond Trust 10/08/1975

CARDINAL TECHNOLOGIES INC (UT)
SEC revoked common stock registration 10/10/2008

CARDINAL YELLOWKNIFE MINES, INC. (ON)
Charter cancelled and company declared dissolved 09/30/1957

CARDIO INFRARED TECHNOLOGIES INC (WY)
Reincorporated 07/15/2010
Each share old Common $0.001 par exchanged for (0.0002) share new Common $0.001 par 05/05/2009
Each share new Common $0.001 par exchanged again for (0.0005) share new Common $0.001 par 04/30/2010
Reorganized from Nevada to Wyoming 07/15/2010
Each share new Common $0.001 par exchanged for (0.0005) share Common $0.000001 par
Each share old Common $0.000001 par exchanged for (0.00033333) share new Common $0.000001 par 05/04/2011
Recapitalized as Enchanted World, Inc. 12/08/2014
Each share new Common $0.000001 par exchanged for (0.001) share Common $0.000001 par

CARDIO PACE MED INC (DE)
Name changed to Novacon Corp. 11/18/1987
Novacon Corp. recapitalized as NVCN Corp. 06/20/2002

CARDIO PET INC (NY)
Common 1¢ par split (2) for (1) by

issuance of (1) additional share 07/26/1984
Under plan of merger name changed to Animed, Inc. 06/07/1985
(See Animed, Inc.)

CARDIO PULMONARY SVCS INC (MN)
Out of business 10/00/1975
Details not available

CARDIO VASCULAR MED DEVICE CORP (DE)
Common $0.0001 par split (4) for (1) by issuance of (3) additional shares payable 12/19/2008 to holders of record 12/18/2008 Ex date - 12/22/2008
Reincorporated under the laws of Florida as Computer Vision Systems Laboratories, Corp. 06/27/2011
Computer Vision Systems Laboratories, Corp name changed to CVSL Inc. 05/28/2013 which name changed to JRjr33, Inc. 03/07/2016

CARDIOBIOSCIENCE CORP (NV)
Name changed to Secure Blue, Inc. 02/07/2003
Secure Blue, Inc. name changed to RedHand International, Inc. 10/06/2003 which name changed to African Diamond Co., Inc. 04/17/2006
(See African Diamond Co., Inc.)

CARDIODYNAMICS INC (NV)
Name changed to Vida Medical Systems, Inc. 10/16/1974
Vida Medical Systems, Inc. recapitalized as Oasis Oil Corp. 10/06/1997 which name changed to MVP Network, Inc. 09/07/2005
(See MVP Network, Inc.)

CARDIODYNAMICS INTL CORP (CA)
Each share old Common no par exchanged for (0.14285714) share new Common no par 05/09/2008
Merged into SonoSite, Inc. 08/14/2009
Each share Common no par exchanged for $1.35 cash

CARDIOGENESIS CORP (CA)
Acquired by CryoLife, Inc. 05/17/2011
Each share Common no par exchanged for $0.457 cash

CARDIOGENESIS CORP (DE)
Merged into Eclipse Surgical Technologies, Inc. 03/17/1999
Each share Common $0.001 par exchanged for (0.8) share Common no par
Eclipse Surgical Technologies, Inc. name changed to Cardiogenesis Corp. (CA) 06/21/2001
(See Cardiogenesis Corp. (CA))

CARDIOME PHARMA CORP (CANADA)
Reorganized 03/12/2002
Reorganized from British Columbia to under the laws of Canada 03/12/2002
Each share Common no par exchanged for (0.25) share Common no par
Each share old Common no par exchanged for (0.2) share new Common no par 04/12/2013
Name changed to Correvio Pharma Corp. 05/17/2018

CARDIOMETRICS INC (DE)
Merged into EndoSonics Corp. 07/23/1997
Each share Common 1¢ par exchanged for (0.35) share Common no par, (0.1364) share CardioVascular Dynamics, Inc. Common 1¢ par and $3 cash
(See each company's listing)

CARDIONET INC (DE)
Name changed to BioTelemetry, Inc. 08/01/2013

CARDIOPULMONARY TECHNOLOGIES INC (DE)
Name changed to American Heart & Lung Technologies, Inc. 09/04/1984
(See American Heart & Lung Technologies, Inc.)

CARDIOPULMONICS INC (DE)
Name changed to Innerdyne, Inc. 05/10/1994
Innerdyne, Inc. merged into Tyco International Ltd. (Bermuda) 12/06/2000 which reincorporated in Switzerland 03/17/2009 which merged into Johnson Controls International PLC 09/06/2016

CARDIOSEARCH INC (NJ)
Merged into Steritek, Inc. 12/26/1986
Each share Common no par exchanged for (0.42636) share Common no par
(See Steritek, Inc.)

CARDIOTECH INTL INC (DE)
Reincorporated 10/26/2007
State of incorporation changed from (MA) to (DE) and Common 1¢ par changed to $0.001 par 10/26/2007
Name changed to AdvanSource Biomaterials Corp. 10/16/2008

CARDIOTHORACIC SYS INC (DE)
Merged into Guidant Corp. 11/15/1999
Each share Common $0.001 par exchanged for (0.3611) share Common no par
Guidant Corp. merged into Boston Scientific Corp. 04/21/2006

CARDIOTRONICS SYS INC (CO)
Each share Common $0.0001 par exchanged for (0.04) share Common $0.003 par 08/30/1991
Each share Common $0.003 par exchanged for (0.25) share Common $0.012 par 06/21/1995
Merged into Ballard Acquisition Corp. 12/30/1996
Each share Common $0.012 par exchanged for $3.75 cash

CARDIOVASCULAR DIAGNOSTICS INC (NC)
Name changed to Pharmanetics Inc. 07/27/1998
(See Pharmanetics Inc.)

CARDIOVASCULAR DYNAMICS INC (DE)
Name changed to Radiance Medical Systems, Inc. 01/14/1999
Radiance Medical Systems, Inc. name changed to Endologix, Inc. 05/31/2002

CARDIOVASCULAR IMAGING SYS INC (CA)
Merged into Boston Scientific Corp. 03/09/1995
Each share Common no par exchanged for $10.50 cash

CARDIOVASCULAR LABORATORIES INC (NV)
Name changed to Clixhealth.Com Inc. 03/26/1999
Clixhealth.Com Inc. name changed to Clix Group Inc. (NV) 08/23/2000 which reorganized in Colorado as RCC Holdings Corp. 04/09/2003

CARDIS CORP (DE)
Reorganized under Chapter 11 Federal Bankruptcy Code 12/12/1989
Each share old Common 1¢ par exchanged for (0.17172) share new Common 1¢ par
Each share new Common 1¢ par exchanged again for (0.05) share Common 1¢ par 10/31/1991
Charter cancelled and declared inoperative and void for non-payment of taxes 03/01/1995

CARDIUM THERAPEUTICS INC (DE)
Each share old Common $0.0001 par exchanged for (0.05) share new Common $0.0001 par 07/18/2013
Name changed to Taxus Cardium Pharmaceuticals Group, Inc. 10/07/2014

CARDO MED INC (DE)
Name changed to Tiger X Medical, Inc. 07/13/2011
Tiger X Medical, Inc. name changed to BioCardia, Inc. 10/26/2016

CARDON PHONOCRAFT CORP.
Acquired by Sparks-Withington Co. 00/00/1930
Details not available

CARDTREND INTL INC (NV)
Name changed to Mezabay International Inc. 09/10/2009

CARDTRONICS INC (DE)
Reorganized under the laws of England & Wales as Cardtronics PLC 07/01/2016
Each share Common $0.0001 par exchanged for (1) share Class A Ordinary 1¢ par

CARDWELL RES LTD (BC)
Each share Capital Stock 50¢ par exchanged for (1) share Capital Stock no par 07/07/1972
Struck off register and declared dissolved for failure to file returns 07/28/1980

CARDY CORP., LTD.
Name changed to Sheraton Ltd. 00/00/1950
(See Sheraton Ltd.)

CARE CAP PPTYS INC (DE)
Merged into Sabra Health Care REIT, Inc. 08/17/2017
Each share Common 1¢ par exchanged for (1.123) shares Common 1¢ par

CARE CENTERS, INC. (OH)
Common 10¢ par changed to 5¢ par and (1) additional share issued 12/23/1968
Common 5¢ par changed to $0.025 par and (1) additional share issued 09/15/1969
Reorganized under the laws of Delaware 05/19/1977
Each (2) shares Common $0.025 par exchanged for (1) share Common $0.025 par and (1) share Class B Common $0.025 par
(See Care Centers, Inc. (DE) Ctfs. dated after 05/18/1977)

CARE CONCEPTS I INC (DE)
Reorganized 11/30/1992
Name changed 10/24/2002
Reorganized from under the laws of (NV) to Delaware 11/30/1992
Each share old Common $0.001 par exchanged for (0.25) share new Common $0.001 par
Each share new Common $0.001 par exchanged again for (0.2) share new Common $0.001 par 11/23/1994
Each share new Common $0.001 par exchanged again for (0.2) share new Common $0.001 par 10/23/2002
Name changed from Care Concepts, Inc. to Care Concepts I, Inc. 10/24/2002
Name changed to Interactive Brand Development, Inc. 12/01/2004
(See Interactive Brand Development, Inc.)

CARE CORP (MI)
Reincorporated 10/15/1981
State of incorporation changed from (DE) to (MI) 10/15/1981
Common 50¢ par split (4) for (1) by issuance of (3) additional shares 01/17/1983
Common 50¢ par reclassified as Class B Common 50¢ par 07/27/1983
Each share Class B Common 50¢ par received distribution of (1) share Class A Common 50¢ par 08/03/1983
Merged into Health Care & Retirement Corp. of America 10/03/1986
Each share Class A Common 50¢ par exchanged for $24.75 cash
Each share Class B Common 50¢ par exchanged for $24.75 cash

CARE CTRS INC (DE)
Ctfs. dated prior to 02/28/1969
Merged into Medic-Home Enterprises Inc. 02/28/1969
Each share Class A 10¢ par exchanged for (0.4) share Common 10¢ par
Each share Class B 10¢ par exchanged for (0.363636) share Common 10¢ par
Medic-Home Enterprises Inc. name changed to Ganot Corp. 05/16/1980
(See Ganot Corp.)

CARE CTRS INC (DE)
Ctfs. dated after 05/18/1977
Under plan of partial liquidation each share old Common $0.025 par and old Class B Common $0.025 par exchanged for $1.90 principal amount of Contract Rights and $0.63 cash 01/23/1984
Note: Above ratio applies to 64% of holdings. Balance of 36% was reissued in shares of new Common $0.025¢ par and new Class B Common $0.025 par respectively
Merged into Southmark Corp. 02/14/1985
Each share new Common $0.025 par and new Class B Common $0.025 par exchanged for $2.1287 beneficial interest in a Fort Vancouver Broadcasting Corp. promissory note and $7.9375 cash respectively

CARE ENTERPRISES (DE)
Reincorporated 06/19/1986
Common no par reclassified as Conv. Class B Common no par 09/25/1985
Each share Conv. Class B Common no par received distribution of (0.5) share Class A Common no par 09/25/1985
State of incorporation changed from (CA) to (DE) 06/19/1986
Reorganized under Chapter 11 Federal Bankruptcy Code 12/31/1990
Each (13.32) shares Class A Common no par exchanged for (1) share Common 1¢ par 12/31/1990
Each (13.32) shares Conv. Class B Common no par exchanged for (1) share Common 1¢ par 12/31/1990
Merged into Regency Health Services, Inc. 04/04/1994
Each share Common 1¢ par exchanged for (0.71) share Common 1¢ par
Regency Health Services, Inc. acquired by Sun Healthcare Group, Inc. (Old) 10/08/1997
(See Sun Healthcare Group, Inc. (Old))

CARE (ARTHUR) ENTERPRISES LTD. (ON)
Out of business 00/00/1961
No stockholders' equity

CARE FINL GROUP INC (NV)
Each share old Common $0.001 par exchanged for (0.004) share new Common $0.001 par 04/14/1997
Name changed to Trump Oil Corp. 05/16/1997
Trump Oil Corp. recapitalized as 20 / 20 Web Design Inc. 04/20/1999 which name changed to Bentleytel.com Inc. 04/16/2001 which name changed back to 20 / 20 Web Design Inc. 07/12/2001 which recapitalized as 20/20 Networks Inc. 02/14/2003 which name changed to Micro Bio-Medical

Waste Systems, Inc. 01/02/2004 which name changed to Crown Equity Holdings Inc. 10/05/2006

CARE FREE SWIMMING POOL MFG CORP (NY)
Dissolved by proclamation 12/23/1992

CARE GROUP INC (DE)
Plan of reorganization under Chapter 11 Federal Bankruptcy proceedings effective 02/01/1999
No stockholders' equity

CARE INNS INC (TN)
Merged into MBJ, Inc. 12/31/1979
Each share Common $1 par exchanged for $4.33 cash

CARE INVT TR INC (MD)
Common $0.001 par split (3) for (2) by issuance of (0.5) additional share payable 09/20/2010 to holders of record 09/13/2010
Name changed to Tiptree Financial Inc. and Common $0.001 par reclassified as Class A Common $0.001 par 07/03/2013
Tiptree Financial Inc. name changed to Tiptree Inc. 01/09/2017

CARE PLUS INC (FL)
Each share old Common 1¢ par exchanged for (1/7) share new Common 1¢ par 10/09/1987
Merged into New England Critical Care, Inc. 02/26/1991
Each share new Common 1¢ par exchanged for (0.775) share Common 10¢ par
New England Critical Care, Inc. name changed to Critical Care America, Inc. 03/29/1991 which merged into Medical Care America, Inc. 09/09/1992 which merged into Columbia/HCA Healthcare Corp. 09/16/1994 which name changed to HCA - The Healthcare Co. 05/25/2000 which name changed to HCA Inc. (Ctfs. dated after 06/29/2001) 06/29/2001
(See HCA Inc. (Ctfs. dated after 06/29/2001))

CARE PT MED CENTRES LTD (BC)
Recapitalized as Consolidated Care Point Medical Centres Ltd. 09/18/1991
Each share Common no par exchanged for (0.125) share Common no par
(See Consolidated Care Point Medical Centres Ltd.)

CARE-TRAN INC (NV)
Name changed to Claims Direct, Inc. 04/12/1996

CARE VETERINARY PHARMACEUTICALS LTD (BC)
Delisted from Vancouver Stock Exchange 03/04/1994

CARE VISIONS CORP (NV)
Merged into Care Visions Acquisition, Inc. 01/23/1992
Details not available

CAREADVANTAGE INC (DE)
Each share old Common 1¢ par exchanged for (0.16666666) share new Common 1¢ par 09/27/1996
SEC revoked common stock registration 11/24/2014

CAREAMERICA INC (DE)
Name changed to U.S. Technologies Inc. 07/17/1989
(See U.S. Technologies Inc.)

CARECENTRIC INC (DE)
Merged into Borden Associates, Inc. 09/04/2003
Each share Common $0.001 par exchanged $0.75 cash

CARECENTRIC INC NEW (DE)
Each share old Common $0.001 par exchanged for (1) share new Common $0.001 par 09/08/2003
Note: In effect holders received $0.75 cash per share and public interest was eliminated

CAREDATA COM INC (DE)
Filed a plan of liquidation under Chapter 7 Federal Bankruptcy Code 11/15/2000
No stockholders' equity

CAREDECISION CORP (NV)
Stock Dividend - 8% payable 10/15/2003 to holders of record 07/21/2003
Name changed to instaCare Corp. 04/18/2005 instaCare Corp. recapitalized as Decision Diagnostics Corp. 12/01/2011

CAREER ACADEMY INC (DE)
Common 10¢ par split (2) for (1) by issuance of (1) additional share 10/18/1968
Stock Dividends - 50% 07/30/1965; 50% 04/12/1966; 100% 10/27/1966; 100% 10/27/1967
Adjudicated bankrupt 04/15/1975
No stockholders' equity

CAREER BLAZERS INC (DE)
Name changed to Immedient Corp. 12/21/1999
Each share Common 1¢ par exchanged for (1) share Common 1¢ par
(See Immedient Corp.)

CAREER GUIDANCE CORP (NJ)
Charter declared void for non-payment of taxes 09/18/1978

CAREER HORIZONS INC (DE)
Common 1¢ par split (2) for (1) by issuance of (1) additional share payable 02/22/1996 to holders of record 02/08/1996
Merged into AccuStaff Inc. 11/14/1996
Each share Common 1¢ par exchanged for (1.53) shares Common $1 par
AccuStaff Inc. name changed to Modis Professional Services, Inc. 10/01/1998 which name changed to MPS Group, Inc. 01/01/2002
(See MPS Group, Inc.)

CAREER WORTH INC (NV)
Each share old Common $0.001 par exchanged for (0.01) share new Common $0.001 par 02/22/2002
Each share new Common $0.001 par exchanged again for (0.03333333) share new Common $0.001 par 03/06/2002
Name changed to U.S. Homes & Properties, Inc. 11/22/2002
(See U.S. Homes & Properties, Inc.)

CAREERBUILDER INC (DE)
Merged into Career Holdings, Inc. 08/24/2000
Each share Common $0.001 par exchanged for $8 cash

CAREERCOM CORP (PA)
Reincorporated 07/15/1987
State of incorporation changed from (NJ) to (PA) 07/15/1987
Common 1¢ par split (4) for (3) by issuance of (0.33333333) additional share 05/10/1988
Filed a petition under Chapter 11 Federal Bankruptcy Code 12/16/1992
Stockholders' equity unlikely

CAREERENGINE NETWORK INC (DE)
Name changed to CNE Group, Inc. 06/09/2003
CNE Group, Inc. name changed to Arrow Resources Development, Inc. 12/20/2005

CAREEREXCHANGE INTERACTIVE CORP (BC)
Name changed to Cytiva Software Inc. 06/21/2005
(See Cytiva Software Inc.)

CAREERSTAFF UNLIMITED INC (DE)
Acquired by Sun Healthcare Group, Inc. (Old) 06/21/1995
Each share Common $0.0001 par exchanged for (0.868) share Common 1¢ par
(See Sun Healthcare Group, Inc. (Old))

CAREFREE CUSTOM CYCLES INC (NV)
Name changed 09/10/2007
Name changed to Carefree Custom Developments Inc. 09/10/2007 which name changed back to Carefree Custom Cycles, Inc. 01/23/2008
Charter revoked for failure to file reports and pay fees 09/30/2010

CAREFREE CUSTOM DEVS INC (NV)
Name changed back to Carefree Custom Cycles, Inc. 01/23/2008

CAREFREE LIFE INS CORP AMER (AZ)
Stock Dividend - 10% 04/30/1969
Reorganized as Clica Industries 04/30/1969
Each share Common 5¢ par exchanged for (0.1) share Common 50¢ par
Clica Industries name changed back to Carefree Life Insurance Corp. of America 07/01/1977 which name changed to National Annuity Life Insurance Co. 05/19/1982
(See National Annuity Life Insurance Co.)

CAREFUSION CORP (DE)
Merged into Becton, Dickinson & Co. 03/17/2015
Each share Common 1¢ par exchanged for (0.0777) share Common $1 par and $49 cash

CAREINSITE INC (DE)
Merged into WebMD Corp. 09/12/2000
Each share Common 1¢ par exchanged for (1.3) shares Common $0.001 par
WebMD Corp. name changed to Emdeon Corp. 10/17/2005 which name changed to HLTH Corp. 05/21/2007 which merged into WebMD Health Corp. 10/23/2009
(See WebMD Health Corp.)

CARELINE INC (DE)
Merged into Laidlaw Inc. 10/27/1995
Each share Common $0.001 par exchanged for (1.1) shares Non-Vtg. Class B no par
(See Laidlaw Inc.)

CAREMARK INC (DE)
Common no par split (3) for (2) by issuance of (0.5) additional share 03/06/1987
Acquired by Baxter Travenol Laboratories, Inc. 08/03/1987
Each share Common no par exchanged for (0.871057) share Common $1 par
Baxter Travenol Laboratories, Inc. name changed to Baxter International Inc. 05/18/1988

CAREMARK INTL INC (DE)
Merged into MedPartners, Inc. (New) 09/05/1996
Each share Common $1 par exchanged for (1.21) shares Common $0.001 par
MedPartners, Inc. (New) name changed to Caremark Rx, Inc. 09/13/1999 which merged into CVS/Caremark Corp. 03/22/2007 which name changed to CVS Caremark Corp. 05/10/2007

CAREMARK RX CAP TR I (DE)
Shared Preference Redeemable Securities 144A called for redemption at $52 on 10/15/2002
7% Guaranteed Shared Preference Redeemable Securities called for redemption at $52 on 10/15/2002

CAREMARK RX INC (DE)
Merged into CVS/Caremark Corp. 03/22/2007
Each share Common $0.001 par exchanged for (1.67) shares Common 1¢ par
CVS/Caremark Corp. name changed to CVS Caremark Corp. 05/10/2007

CAREMATRIX CORP (DE)
Each share old Common 5¢ par exchanged for (0.0555555) share new Common 5¢ par 09/19/2000
Plan of reorganization under Chapter 11 Federal Bankruptcy Code effective 04/04/2002
No stockholders' equity

CARENA BANCORP INC (CANADA)
Name changed 11/13/1984
Common $20 par split (2) for (1) by issuance of (1) additional share 12/08/1980
Common $20 par split (3) for (1) by issuance of (2) additional shares 07/31/1984
Name changed from Carena-Bancorp Holdings Inc. to Carena-Bancorp Inc. 11/13/1984
Common no par split (3) for (2) by issuance of (0.5) additional share 03/31/1989
Stock Dividend - 50% 08/29/1986
Name changed to Carena Developments Ltd. 03/07/1989
Carena Developments Ltd. recapitalized as Brookfield Properties Corp. 06/03/1996 which name changed to Brookfield Office Properties Inc. 05/09/2011
(See Brookfield Office Properties Inc.)

CARENA BANCORP INC (QC)
Common no par split (2) for (1) by issuance of (1) additional share 11/05/1975
Acquired by Carena-Bancorp Holdings Inc. 03/12/1979
Each share Class A Preferred $2.50 par exchanged for (1) share Class A Preference $2.50 par
Each share Common no par exchanged for (1) share Common $20 par
Carena-Bancorp Holdings Inc. name changed to Carena-Bancorp Inc. 11/13/1984 which name changed to Carena Developments Ltd. 03/07/1989 which recapitalized as Brookfield Properties Corp. 06/03/1996 which name changed to Brookfield Office Properties Inc. 05/09/2011
(See Brookfield Office Properties Inc.)

CARENA DEVS LTD (CANADA)
Common no par split (3) for (2) by issuance of (0.5) additional share 03/31/1989
Recapitalized as Brookfield Properties Corp. 06/03/1996
Each share Common no par exchanged for (0.2) share Common no par
Preference not affected except for change of name
Brookfield Properties Corp. name changed to Brookfield Office Properties Inc. 05/09/2011
(See Brookfield Office Properties Inc.)

CARENETWORK INC (WI)
Acquired by Humana Inc. 12/21/1994
Each share Common 1¢ par exchanged for $25.25 cash

CARESCIENCE INC (PA)
Merged into Quovadx, Inc. 09/19/2003
Each share Common no par exchanged for (0.1818) share Common 1¢ par and $1.40 cash
(See Quovadx, Inc.)

CARESIDE INC (DE)
Chapter 11 bankruptcy proceedings

converted to Chapter 7 on 04/03/2003
Stockholders' equity unlikely

CARESSA GROUP INC (FL)
Acquired by Footwear Holdings Inc. 12/28/1984
Each share Common 1¢ par exchanged for $15.75 cash

CARESSA INC (FL)
Class B Common 50¢ par reclassified as Common 50¢ par 05/31/1968
Common 50¢ par split (3) for (2) by issuance of (0.5) additional share 06/21/1971
Common 50¢ par split (5) for (2) by issuance of (1.5) additional shares 05/01/1972
Common 50¢ par split (3) for (2) by issuance of (0.5) additional share 04/11/1983
Common 50¢ par split (4) for (3) by issuance of (1/3) additional share 01/09/1984
Under plan of reorganization each share Common 50¢ par automatically became (1) share Caressa Group, Inc. Common 1¢ par 07/01/1984
(See Caressa Group, Inc.)

CARETENDERS HEALTHCORP (DE)
Each share Common 2¢ par exchanged for (0.2) share Common 10¢ par 03/24/1995
Name changed to Almost Family Inc. 02/01/2000
Almost Family Inc. merged into LHC Group, Inc. 04/01/2018

CAREX INTL INC (DE)
Name changed to Medica USA, Inc. 09/13/1980
Medica USA, Inc. name changed to Pacific Realm, Inc. 07/06/1984 which name changed to aeroTelesis, Inc. 10/22/2003
(See aeroTelesis, Inc.)

CAREY BAXTER & KENNEDY, INC. (DE)
Name changed to CBK Industries, Inc. 04/17/1964
CBK Industries, Inc. name changed to CBK Agronomics, Inc. 04/24/1969 which name changed to General Energy Corp. (DE) 10/10/1972 which merged into Kirby Exploration Co. 07/15/1983 which reorganized as Kirby Exploration Co. Inc. 08/01/1984 which name changed to Kirby Corp. 05/01/1990

CAREY DIVERSIFIED LLC (DE)
Name changed to W.P. Carey & Co. L.L.C. (DE) 06/28/2000
W.P. Carey & Co. L.L.C. (DE) reorganized in Maryland as W.P. Carey Inc. 09/28/2012

CAREY INSTL PPTYS INC (MD)
Merged into Corporate Property Associates 15 Inc. 09/01/2004
Each share Ser. 11 Common $0.001 par exchanged for either (1.09) shares Common $0.001 par or $10.90 cash
Note: Holders also received an additional distribution of $3 cash per share
Corporate Property Associates 15 Inc. merged into W.P. Carey Inc. 09/28/2012

CAREY INTL INC (DE)
Merged into Ford Motor Co. 09/20/2000
Each share Common 1¢ par exchanged for $18.25 cash

CAREY (PHILIP) MANUFACTURING CO. (OH)
Each share Common $100 par exchanged for (5) shares Common no par 00/00/1937
Recapitalized 00/00/1945
Each share 6% Preferred $100 par exchanged for (1.25) shares new 5% Preferred $100 par
Each share old 5% Preferred $100 par exchanged for (1) share new 5% Preferred $100 par
Each share Common no par exchanged for (1) share Common $20 par
Recapitalized 00/00/1946
Each share Common $20 par exchanged for (2) shares Common $10 par
Stock Dividend - 20% 01/22/1960
Merged into Glen Alden Corp. (DE) 06/01/1967
Each share Common $10 par exchanged for (1) share $2.25 Sr. Conv. Preferred no par
Glen Alden Corp. (DE) merged into Rapid-American Corp. (DE) 11/06/1972
(See Rapid-American Corp. (DE))

CAREY OF NEW YORK TRUST
Acquired by Prugh Petroleum Co. 12/31/1953
Each Unit of Bene. Int. no par exchanged for (2.74) shares Common $5 par
Prugh Petroleum Co. merged into Livingston Oil Co. 09/01/1956 which name changed to LVO Corp. 09/24/1969 which merged into Utah International Inc. 10/31/1974 which merged into General Electric Co. 12/20/1976

CAREY TRUST
Acquired by Prugh Petroleum Co. 12/31/1953
Each Unit of Bene. Int. no par exchanged for (3.81) shares Common $5 par
Prugh Petroleum Co. merged into Livingston Oil Co. 09/01/1956 which name changed to LVO Corp. 09/24/1969 which merged into Utah International Inc. 10/31/1974 which merged into General Electric Co. 12/20/1976

CARFINCO FINL GROUP INC (AB)
Acquired by Banco Santander, S.A. 03/09/2015
Each share Common no par exchanged for $11.25 cash
Note: Unexchanged certificates will be cancelled and become without value 03/08/2021

CARFINCO INC (ON)
Name changed to Carfinco Income Fund (ON) and Common no par reclassified as Trust Units 12/06/2002
Carfinco Income Fund (ON) reorganized in Alberta as Carfinco Financial Group Inc. 01/05/2012
(See Carfinco Financial Group Inc.)

CARFINCO INCOME FD (ON)
Each Trust Unit received distribution of (0.007) additional Unit payable 12/29/2006 to holders of record 12/20/2006 Ex date - 12/18/2006
Stock Dividends - 0.0529% payable 12/31/2004 to holders of record 12/15/2004 Ex date - 12/13/2004; 2.57% payable 12/31/2009 to holders of record 12/18/2009 Ex date - 12/16/2009; 2.549% payable 12/31/2010 to holders of record 12/20/2010 Ex date - 12/16/2010
Under plan of reorganization each Trust Unit no par automatically became (1) share Carfinco Financial Group Inc. (AB) Common no par 01/05/2012
(See Carfinco Financial Group Inc.)

CARGILL BANCORP INC (DE)
Stock Dividends - 5% payable 01/00/1996; 5% payable 01/00/1997; 5% payable 01/26/1998 to holders of record 12/30/1997
Merged into Westbank Corp. 01/29/1999
Each share Common 1¢ par exchanged for (1.3655) shares Common $2 par
Westbank Corp. merged into NewAlliance Bancshares, Inc. 01/02/2007 which merged into First Niagara Financial Group, Inc. (New) 04/15/2011 which merged into KeyCorp (New) 08/01/2016

CARGILL BK CONN (PUTNAM, CT)
Under plan of reorganization each share Common $1 par automatically became (1) share Cargill Bancorp Inc. (DE) Common 1¢ par 09/29/1989
Cargill Bancorp Inc. merged into Westbank Corp. 01/29/1999 which merged into NewAlliance Bancshares, Inc. 01/02/2007 which merged into First Niagara Financial Group, Inc. (New) 04/15/2011 which merged into KeyCorp (New) 08/01/2016

CARGILL TRUST CO. (PUTNAM, CT)
Merged into Hartford National Bank & Trust Co. (Hartford, CT) 11/10/1964
Each share Capital Stock $100 par exchanged for (10) shares Capital Stock $10 par
Hartford National Bank & Trust Co. (Hartford, CT) reorganized in Delaware as Hartford National Corp. 04/30/1969 which merged into Shawmut National Corp. 02/29/1988 which merged into Fleet Financial Group Inc. (New) 11/30/1995 which name changed to Fleet Boston Corp. 10/01/1999 which name changed to FleetBoston Financial Corp. 04/18/2000 which merged into Bank of America Corp. 04/01/2004

CARGOJET INCOME FD (ON)
Reorganized as Cargojet Inc. 01/06/2011
Each Unit held by Canadians exchanged for (1) share Common no par
Each Unit held by non-Canadians exchanged for (1) Variable Voting Share no par

CARHART PHOTO INC (NY)
Class A Preferred 10¢ par reclassified as Class A 10¢ par 09/01/1967
Merged into National Consumer Products, Ltd. 04/18/1985
Each share Class A 10¢ par exchanged for $4.50 cash

CARIANA INTL INDS INC (BC)
Struck off register and declared dissolved for failure to file returns 07/09/1993

CARIB SYNDICATE, LTD.
Liquidation completed 00/00/1944
Details not available

CARIBBEAN AMERN HEALTH RESORTS INC (MN)
SEC revoked common stock registration 05/25/2010

CARIBBEAN ATLANTIC AIRLS INC (PR)
Adjudicated bankrupt 06/07/1973
No stockholders' equity

CARIBBEAN CASINO & GAMING CORP (FL)
Recapitalized as Caribbean International Holdings, Inc. 01/17/2013
Each share Common $0.001 par exchanged for (0.02857142) share Common $0.001 par
Caribbean International Holdings, Inc. name changed to BioStem Technologies, Inc. 12/09/2014

CARIBBEAN CEM LTD (JAMAICA)
Each share Ordinary £1 par exchanged for (4) shares Ordinary 5s par 06/14/1965
Each ADR for Ordinary exchanged for (4) ADR's for Ordinary 06/14/1965
Ordinary 5s par changed to J$0.50 par per currency change 00/00/1970
Debenture Stock J$2 par called for redemption 05/01/1972
Stock Dividend - Ordinary - 11.11111111% 05/31/1967 - ADR's for Ordinary - 11.11111111% 06/07/1967
99.4% of Ordinary owned by National Investment Corp. as of 00/00/1985
ADR agreement terminated 01/11/2010
No ADR's remain outstanding

CARIBBEAN CIGAR CO (FL)
Each share old Common $0.001 par exchanged for (0.125) share new Common $0.001 par 09/01/1998
Administratively dissolved for failure to maintain a registered agent 07/26/1999

CARIBBEAN CLUBS INTL INC (UT)
Name changed to CCI Group, Inc. 08/29/2003
(See CCI Group, Inc.)

CARIBBEAN CORP (LIBERIA)
Name changed to Antares Ltd. 07/08/1969
(See Antares Ltd.)

CARIBBEAN DEVS INC (DE)
Recapitalized as VShield Software Corp. 01/30/2007
Each share Common 1¢ par exchanged for (0.001) share Common 1¢ par

CARIBBEAN EXPL VENTURES INC (DE)
Name changed to Siguiri Basin Mining, Inc. (DE) 03/28/2007
Siguiri Basin Mining, Inc. (DE) reorganized in Nevada as Anything Brands Online Inc. 01/17/2008 which name changed to MyFreightWorld Technologies, Inc. 05/13/2010

CARIBBEAN FIN INC (PR)
Name changed to Altair Corp. 04/28/1981
(See Altair Corp.)

CARIBBEAN GOLD MINES, LTD. (ON)
Dissolved 11/25/1970
Details not available

CARIBBEAN HOTELS CORP. LTD. (BAHAMAS)
Charter revoked for failure to file reports and pay fees 09/16/1965

CARIBBEAN INTERNATIONAL CORP. (AZ)
Each share old Class A Common 1¢ par exchanged for (0.1) share new Class A Common 1¢ par 06/25/1973
Charter revoked for failure to file reports or pay fees 01/10/1983

CARIBBEAN INTL HLDGS INC (FL)
Name changed to BioStem Technologies, Inc. 12/09/2014

CARIBBEAN LEISUREWEAR INC (PR)
Common $1 par changed to $0.66666666 par and (0.5) additional share issued 07/21/1971
Common $0.66666666 par changed to $0.33333333 par and (1) additional share issued 03/08/1972
Common $0.33333333 par changed to $0.16666666 par and (1) additional share issued 08/15/1972
Adjudicated bankrupt 05/03/1978
No stockholders' equity

CARIBBEAN MARINE INC (DE)
Each share Common $200 par exchanged for (0.5) share Common $400 par 08/27/1991
Note: Minority holders received an undetermined amount of cash and public interest was eliminated

CARIBBEAN MARITIME OPERATIONS INC (NV)
Charter revoked for failure to file reports and pay fees 06/01/2009

CARIBBEAN MTR WKS U S A INC (DE)
Each share old Common $0.001 par exchanged for (0.05) share new Common $0.001 par 08/23/2002
Reorganized under the laws of Nevada as Homeland Security Corp. 10/17/2005
Each share new Common $0.001 par exchanged for (0.5) share Common $0.00001 par

CARIBBEAN RES CORP (BC)
Each share old Common no par exchanged for (0.000004) share new Common no par 04/01/2016
Note: In effect holders received $0.0052 cash per share and public interest was eliminated
Unexchanged certificates will be cancelled and become without value 04/01/2022

CARIBBEAN RES CORP (BC)
Merged into Mishibishu Gold Corp. 10/27/1989
Each share Common no par exchanged for (0.4215) share Common no par
Mishibishu Gold Corp. recapitalized as Messina Minerals Inc. 04/07/2003 which merged into Canadian Zinc Corp. 12/20/2013 which name changed to NorZinc Ltd. 09/11/2018

CARIBBEAN RES LTD (VIRGIN ISLANDS)
Struck off register for failure to file annual returns 12/31/1985

CARIBBEAN SELECT INC (CO)
Filed a petition under Chapter 11 Federal Bankruptcy Code 12/28/1990
Stockholders' equity unlikely

CARIBBEAN SHOE CORP (NY)
Adjudicated bankrupt 04/01/1974
Stockholders' equity unlikely

CARIBBEAN SUGAR CO. (CUBA)
Liquidated 02/02/1959
Details not available

CARIBBEAN VENTURE CORP (CO)
Name changed to Ringor International Ltd. 03/13/1989
(See Ringor International Ltd.)

CARIBBEAN VENTURES INC (NV)
Common $0.001 par split (5) for (1) by issuance of (4) additional shares payable 03/15/2000 to holders of record 02/11/2000
Name changed to Internetfinancialcorp.com Inc. 02/23/2000
Internetfinancialcorp.com Inc. recapitalized as APO Health Inc. 06/01/2001 which name changed to Paivis, Corp. 05/19/2006
(See Paivis, Corp.)

CARIBBEAN VILLA CATERING CORP (NV)
Common $0.001 par split (20) for (1) by issuance of (19) additional shares payable 07/14/2009 to holders of record 07/14/2009
Name changed to Globotek Holdings, Inc. 03/05/2010
Globotek Holdings, Inc. name changed to Itoco Mining Corp. 12/01/2015 which name changed to Itoco Inc. 05/08/2018

CARIBE PETES INC (BC)
Recapitalized as Crio Group Developments Inc. 04/06/1989
Each share Common no par exchanged for (0.2) share Common no par
Crio Group Developments Inc. name changed to Tele Pacific International Communications Corp. 10/14/1992

which name changed to Pacific AD-Link Corp. 12/17/1997 which name changed to Pacific E-Link Corp. 07/15/1999
(See Pacific E-Link Corp.)

CARIBGOLD MINERALS INC (ON)
Recapitalized as Ranger Canyon Energy Inc. 04/27/2005
Each share Common no par exchanged for (0.16666666) share Common no par

CARIBGOLD RES INC (ON)
Merged into Unigold Inc. 12/30/2002
Each share Common no par exchanged for (0.5) share Common no par and (1) share Caribgold Minerals Inc. Common no par
(See each company's listing)

CARIBINER INTL INC (DE)
Common 1¢ par split (2) for (1) by issuance of (1) additional share payable 06/20/1997 to holders of record 05/30/1997 Ex date - 06/23/1997
Name changed to Audio Visual Services Corp. 06/29/2000
(See Audio Visual Services Corp.)

CARIBOO BELL COPPER MINES LTD (BC)
Merged into Highland-Crow Resources Ltd. 09/25/1978
Each share Common no par exchanged for (0.11111111) share Capital Stock no par
Highland-Crow Resources Ltd. merged into Noramco Mining Corp. 01/01/1988 which name changed to Quest Capital Corp. 01/03/1995 which name changed to Quest Oil & Gas Inc. 11/15/1996 which merged into EnerMark Income Fund 04/18/1997 which merged into Enerplus Resources Fund 06/22/2001 which reorganized as Enerplus Corp. 01/03/2011

CARIBOO DIATOMITE CONSOLIDATED 1960 LTD. (BC)
Name changed 10/28/1977
Name changed from Cariboo Diatomite Ltd. to Cariboo Diatomite Consolidated 1960 Ltd. 10/28/1977
Struck off register and declared dissolved for failure to file returns 05/23/1986

CARIBOO GOLD FIELDS LTD (BC)
Delisted from Toronto Venture Stock Exchange 12/23/2005

CARIBOO GOLD QUARTZ MNG LTD (BC)
Merged into Coseka Resources Ltd. 06/16/1972
Each share Capital Stock $1 par exchanged for (0.555555) share Common no par
(See Coseka Resources Ltd.)

CARIBOO HUDSON GOLD MINES (1946) LTD. (BC)
Struck off register and declared dissolved for failure to file reports 12/02/1971

CARIBOO-HUDSON GOLD MINES LTD. (BC)
Acquired by Cariboo Hudson Gold Mines 00/00/1946
Each share Capital Stock exchanged for (0.25) share Capital Stock
(See Cariboo Hudson Gold Mines (1946) Ltd.)

CARIBOO KING GOLD, INC. (WA)
Charter revoked and declared dissolved for non-payment of fees 07/01/1938

CARIBOO SYNDICATE, INC. (NY)
Charter revoked for failure to file reports and pay fees 12/15/1939

CARIBOU COFFEE INC (MN)
Acquired by JAB Beech Inc. 01/24/2013

Each share Common 1¢ par exchanged for $16 cash

CARIBOU COPPER RES LTD (ON)
Reincorporated under the laws of British Columbia as Caribou King Resources Ltd. 12/20/2011
Caribou King Resources Ltd. name changed to CKR Carbon Corp. (BC) 11/09/2015 which reincorporated in Ontario 01/01/2017 which name changed to Gratomic Inc. 12/22/2017

CARIBOU ENERGY INC (CO)
Recapitalized as Texas Petroleum Corp. 03/13/1987
Each share Common $0.001 par exchanged for (0.01) share Common 1¢ par
Texas Petroleum Corp. name changed to E.T. Network, Inc. 11/18/1993 which recapitalized as E.T. Capital Inc. 02/08/1995 which recapitalized as eCom.com, Inc. (CO) 10/15/1999 which reincorporated in Nevada 06/10/2000 which recapitalized as E.T. Corp. 04/12/2002 which recapitalized as ParaFin Corp. 10/15/2004

CARIBOU KING RES LTD (BC)
Each share old Common no par exchanged for (0.06666666) share new Common no par 11/17/2014
Name changed to CKR Carbon Corp. (BC) 11/09/2015
CKR Carbon Corp. (BC) reincorporated in Ontario 01/01/2017 which name changed to Gratomic Inc. 12/22/2017

CARIBOU MINING CO. (UT)
Merged into Intermountain Petroleum Co. 07/14/1961
Each share Common 10¢ par exchanged for (0.2) share Common 10¢ par
(See Intermountain Petroleum Co.)

CARIBOU OIL MNG CO (CA)
Voluntarily dissolved 12/27/2007
Details not available

CARIBOU RES CORP (AB)
Merged into JED Oil Inc. 07/31/2007
Each share Common no par exchanged for (0.1) share Common no par
(See JED Oil Inc.)

CARILLON CASH RESERVES, INC. (MD)
Voluntarily dissolved 02/02/1994
Details not available

CARILLON INVT TR (MA)
Completed liquidated 10/26/1999
Details not available

CARINA MINERALS RES CORP (CANADA)
Recapitalized as Consolidated Carina Resources Corp. 05/11/1990
Each share Common no par exchanged for (0.33333333) share Common no par
Consolidated Carina Resources Corp. recapitalized as United Carina Resources Corp. 09/22/1995 which name changed to United Uranium Corp. (Canada) 07/25/2007 which reincorporated in Saskatchewan 11/05/2008 which reorganized in British British Columbia as Karoo Exploration Corp. 09/15/2013 which recapitalized as Bruin Point Helium Corp 12/11/2017 which name changed to American Helium Inc. 05/11/2018

CARING PRODS INTL INC (DE)
Each share old Common no par exchanged for (0.16666666) share new Common no par 06/16/1997
Each share new Common no par exchanged for (0.25) share old Common 1¢ par 11/04/1997
Each share old Common 1¢ par

exchanged for (0.01) share new Common 1¢ par 07/16/2001
Name changed to US Global Aerospace, Inc. 09/26/2002
US Global Aerospace, Inc. name changed to US Global Nanospace, Inc. 07/24/2003

CARINOR PORCUPINE GOLD MINES, LTD. (ON)
Charter revoked for failure to file reports and pay taxes 00/00/1949

CARISSA MNG CORP (BC)
Recapitalized as Rockwell Ventures Inc. 10/27/1995
Each share Common no par exchanged for (0.2) share Common no par
Rockwell Ventures Inc. name changed to Rockwell Diamonds Inc. 05/17/2007

CARIUM MINES LTD. (ON)
Completely liquidated
Each share Common received initial distribution of $1.50 cash 11/30/1961
Each share Common received second and final distribution of $0.246 cash 12/24/1962
Note: Certificates were not required to be surrendered and are without value

CARL CAP CORP (BC)
Name changed to Carl Data Solutions Inc. 10/28/2015

CARL CREEK RES LTD (BC)
Reorganized under the laws of Alberta as Tanqueray Resources Ltd. 10/07/1986
Each share Common no par exchanged for (0.25) share Common no par
Tanqueray Resources Ltd. recapitalized as Tanqueray Exploration Ltd. 09/13/2011 which name changed to ImmunoPrecise Antibodies Ltd. 12/29/2016

CARLATERAL INC (NV)
Name changed to Orient Paper, Inc. 01/14/2008
Orient Paper, Inc. name changed to IT Tech Packaging, Inc. 08/01/2018

CARLAW CAP CORP (ON)
Name changed to Nyah Resources Corp. 01/22/2008
Nyah Resources Corp. recapitalized as Forbes & Manhattan Coal Corp. 09/27/2010 which name changed to Buffalo Coal Corp. 07/21/2014

CARLAW CAP II CORP (ON)
Name changed to TrueContext Mobile Solutions Corp. 08/20/2009
TrueContext Mobile Solutions Corp. name changed to ProntoForms Corp. 06/19/2013

CARLAW CAP III CORP (ON)
Recapitalized as Galane Gold Ltd. 09/06/2011
Each share Common no par exchanged for (0.25) share Common no par

CARLAW CAP IV INC (ON)
Recapitalized as OneRoof Energy Group, Inc. 03/13/2014
Each share Common no par exchanged for (0.1) share Common no par

CARLAW CAP V CORP (ON)
Common no par split (2) for (1) by issuance of (1) additional share payable 07/04/2018 to holders of record 06/27/2018
Name changed to Eve & Co Inc. 07/04/2018

CARLETON CORP (MN)
Each share old Common 5¢ par exchanged for (0.2) share new Common 5¢ par 09/15/1998
Merged into Oracle Corp. 01/21/2000

CAR-CAR

Each share new Common 5¢ par exchanged for $2.45 cash

CARLETON ENTERPRISES (MT)
Reincorporated under the laws of Nevada as SCN, Ltd. 11/13/1984
SCN, Ltd. recapitalized as Health Care Centers America Inc. 01/04/1994 which name changed to Hexagon Consolidated Companies of America Inc. 08/31/1999 which name changed to NMC Inc. 09/09/2003

CARLETON RES CORP (AB)
Struck of register for failure to file annual reports 11/01/1999

CARLETON VENTURES CORP (NV)
Name changed to Uranerz Energy Corp. 07/28/2005
Uranerz Energy Corp. merged into Energy Fuels, Inc. 06/19/2015

CARLEY ENTERPRISES INC (DE)
SEC revoked common stock registration 08/04/2011

CARLIN GOLD CO (ON)
Recapitalized as Altair International Gold Inc. 03/08/1994
Each share Common no par exchanged for (0.33333333) share Common no par
Altair International Gold Inc. name changed to Altair International Inc. (ON) 11/06/1996 which reincorporated in Canada 07/02/2002 which name changed to Altair Nanotechnologies Inc. 07/17/2002

CARLIN GOLD CORP (CANADA)
Reincorporated under the laws of British Columbia 08/29/2007

CARLIN RES CORP (CANADA)
Recapitalized as Consolidated Carlin Resources Corp. 06/03/1999
Each share Common no par exchanged for (0.2) share Common no par
Consolidated Carlin Resources Corp. recapitalized as Carlin Gold Corp. (Canada) 05/16/2000 which reincorporated in British Columbia 08/29/2007

CARLING BREWERIES, LTD.
Acquired by Brewing Corp. of Canada Ltd. 00/00/1930
Details not available

CARLING BREWERIES (ALBERTA) LTD. (AB)
Acquired by Canadian Breweries Ltd. 10/29/1963
Details not available

CARLING BREWING CO., INC. (VA)
Merged into Carling National Breweries, Inc. 10/31/1975
Each share Capital Stock $15 par exchanged for $27 cash

CARLING GOLD RES INC (ON)
Name changed 06/22/1984
Name changed from Carling Copper Mines Ltd. to Carling Gold Resources Inc. 06/22/1984
Recapitalized as Jourdan Resources Inc. (ON) 11/04/1994
Each share Common no par exchanged for (0.33333333) share Common no par
Jourdan Resources Inc. (ON) reincorporated in Canada 12/14/1994

CARLING OKEEFE LTD (ON)
Acquired by Elders IXL Ltd. 05/01/1987
Each share Common no par exchanged for $18 cash
$2.20 Preference Ser. A $50 par called for redemption 07/28/1989
$2.65 Preference Ser. B $50 par called for redemption 07/28/1989
Public interest eliminated

CARLISLE CORP (DE)
Common $1 par changed to no par and (1) additional share issued 05/27/1960
Common no par split (2) for (1) by issuance of (1) additional share 10/11/1967
Common no par split (2) for (1) by issuance of (1) additional share 05/10/1979
Common no par changed to $1 par and (1) additional share issued 05/08/1981
Reorganized as Carlisle Companies Inc. 05/30/1986
Each share Common $1 par exchanged for (1) share Common $1 par

CARLISLE ENTERPRISES, INC. (NV)
Name changed to Best Way, Inc. 04/15/1997
Best Way, Inc. recapitalized as Ziasun Technologies Inc. 09/10/1998 which merged into INVESTools Inc. 12/06/2001 which name changed to thinkorswim Group Inc. 06/06/2008 which merged into TD AMERITRADE Holding Corp. 06/11/2009

CARLISLE GOLDFIELDS LTD (ON)
Each share old Common no par exchanged for (0.15384615) share new Common no par 01/28/2015
Merged into Alamos Gold Inc. 01/08/2016
Each share new Common no par exchanged for (0.0942) share Class A Common no par and (0.0942) Common Stock Purchase Warrant expiring 01/07/2019
Note: Unexchanged certificates will be cancelled and become without value 01/08/2022

CARLISLE HLDGS LTD (BELIZE)
Name changed to BB Holdings Ltd. 08/18/2005
(See BB Holdings Ltd.)

CARLISLE PLASTICS INC (DE)
Merged into Tyco International Ltd. (MA) 09/09/1996
Each share Class A Common 1¢ par exchanged for (0.172185) share Common 50¢ par
Tyco International Ltd. (MA) merged into Tyco International Ltd. (Bermuda) 07/29/1997 which reincorporated in Switzerland 03/17/2009 which merged into Johnson Controls International PLC 09/06/2016

CARLMAC GOLD MINES, LTD. (ON)
Charter revoked for failure to file reports and pay taxes 01/00/1957

CARLMAND MINES LTD. (ON)
Charter cancelled 00/00/1969

CARLON PRODUCTS CORP. (OH)
Completely liquidated 12/07/1964
Each share Common no par exchanged for first and final distribution of $6.75 cash

CARLSBAD INC (NV)
Reincorporated under the laws of Wisconsin as Genroco, Inc. 03/31/1990
Genroco, Inc. reorganized as VideoPropulsion Interactive Television, Inc. 05/03/2006

CARLSBAD VENTURES INC (BC)
Recapitalized as Zeus Energy Corp. 08/10/1994
Each share Common no par exchanged for (0.2) share Common no par
Zeus Energy Corp. merged into U.S. Oil & Gas Resources Inc. 11/13/1997 which reorganized as Odyssey Petroleum Corp. 08/25/2005 which recapitalized as Petrichor Energy Inc. 03/03/2011

CARLSBERG CAP CORP (CA)
Stock Dividend - 50% 03/21/1980
Reincorporated under the laws of Delaware as Carlsberg Corp. and Common 25¢ par changed to Common 5¢ par 07/01/1980
Carlsberg Corp. merged into Southmark Corp. 02/25/1986
(See Southmark Corp.)

CARLSBERG CORP (DE)
Merged into Southmark Corp. 02/25/1986
Each share Common 25¢ par exchanged for (0.10178) share Adjustable Rate Preferred Ser. D $2 par and $5.50 cash
(See Southmark Corp.)

CARLSON MINES LTD (QC)
Cease trade order effective 06/01/1988
Stockholders' equity unlikely

CARLTON COMMUNICATIONS PLC (ENGLAND)
ADR agreement terminated 01/30/2004
Each ADR for Ordinary exchanged for $18.9749 cash
Exchangeable Capital Securities called for redemption at $25 plus $0.21 accrued dividends on 04/23/2004
Public interest eliminated

CARLTON CORP. (UT)
Name changed to Safety Technology, Inc. 08/01/1987
Safety Technology, Inc. recapitalized as CHS Electronics, Inc. (UT) 01/00/1994 which reorganized in Florida 03/14/1996
(See CHS Electronics, Inc. (FL))

CARLTON TRAIL LTD PARTNERSHIP (MB)
Each old Class A Common Unit of Ltd. Partnership Int. exchanged for (10) new Class A Common Units of Ltd. Partnership Int. 12/30/2004
Plan of arrangement effective 12/17/2010
Each new Class A Common Unit of Ltd. Partnership Int. exchanged for (1) Calgary Capital Investment Trust Class A Unit, (1) Westcan Investment Trust Class A Unit and $0.143 cash

CARLTONS CLEANING CAROUSELS LTD (BC)
Completely liquidated
Each share Common no par received initial distribution of $0.05 cash 00/00/1978
Each share Common no par received second and final distribution of $0.04 cash 00/00/1985
Note: Certificates were not required to be surrendered and are without value

CARLYLE & CO. JEWELERS (DE)
Acquired by Finlay Enterprises, Inc. 05/19/2005
Details not available

CARLYLE CORP (AB)
Name changed to Azterra Corp. 02/26/1998
(See Azterra Corp.)

CARLYLE EAGLE PETE LTD (AB)
Under plan of merger name changed to Carlyle Energy Ltd. 10/28/1983
(See Carlyle Energy Ltd.)

CARLYLE ENERGY LTD (AB)
Placed in receivership 04/27/1989
No stockholders' equity

CARLYLE GAMING & ENTMT LTD (CO)
SEC revoked common stock registration 03/13/2009

CARLYLE GOLF INC (CO)
Each share old Common $0.001 par exchanged for (0.01) share new Common $0.001 par 08/08/2007

Name changed to HeadsUp Entertainment International, Inc. 10/19/2007

CARLYLE INDS INC (DE)
Merged into Levcor International, Inc. 01/07/2003
Each share Common $1 par exchanged for (0.2) share Common 1¢ par

CARLYLE MINES, LTD. (QC)
Charter cancelled 00/00/1961

CARLYLE MNG CORP (BC)
Name changed to Rugby Mining Ltd. 03/06/2009

CARLYLE SHARE, LTD. (NY)
Liquidation completed
Each share Preferred $5 par exchanged for first and final distribution of $5 cash 10/25/1966
Each share Common $1 par exchanged for initial distribution of $10 cash 11/01/1966
Each share Common $1 par received second and final distribution of $0.3021047 cash 09/27/1967

CARMA CORP (AB)
Merged into Brookfield Properties Corp. 09/20/2000
Each share Common no par exchanged for (0.26666666) share Common no par
Brookfield Properties Corp. name changed to Brookfield Office Properties Inc. 05/09/2011
(See Brookfield Office Properties Inc.)

CARMA DEVELOPERS LTD (AB)
Capital Stock no par reclassified as Conv. Class A Common no par 09/10/1975
Conv. Class A Common no par split (3) for (2) by issuance of (0.5) additional share 09/19/1975
Conv. Class A Common no par and Conv. Class B Common no par split (2) for (1) by issuance of (1) additional share respectively 11/26/1976
Conv. Class A Common no par split (2) for (1) by issuance of (1) additional share 12/15/1978
Conv. Class B Common no par split (2) for (1) by issuance of (1) additional share 12/15/1978
Conv. Class A Common no par split (2) for (1) by issuance of (1) additional share 11/24/1980
Conv. Class B Common no par split (2) for (1) by issuance of (1) additional share 11/24/1980
Under plan of reorganization each share 8.75% Conv. Preferred Ser. A $20 par, Conv. Class A Common no par and Conv. Class B Common no par automatically became (1) share Carma Ltd. 8.75% Conv. Preferred Ser. A $20 par, Conv. Class A Common no par and Conv. Class B Common no par respectively 08/28/1981
Each share 8.75% First Preferred Ser. A $20 par exchanged for (5) shares Carma Ltd. Conv. Class A Common no par 06/30/1984
Carma Ltd. recapitalized as Consolidated Carma Corp. 12/02/1987 which name changed to Carma Corp. 05/15/1996 which merged into Brookfield Properties Corp. 09/20/2000 which name changed to Brookfield Office Properties Inc. 05/09/2011
(See Brookfield Office Properties Inc.)

CARMA FINL SVCS CORP (ON)
Name changed to Synergex Corp. 03/17/2005

CARMA LTD (AB)
Each share 8.75% Conv. Preferred Ser. A $20 par exchanged for (3.5) shares Conv. Class A Common no par 04/04/1984
Conv. Class A Common no par

reclassified as Class A Common no par 03/27/1986
Conv. Class B Common no par reclassified as Class A Common no par 03/27/1986
Recapitalized as Consolidated Carma Corp. 12/02/1987
Each share Class A Common no par exchanged for (0.1) share Class A Common no par
Consolidated Carma Corp. name changed to Carma Corp. 04/19/1996 which merged into Brookfield Properties Corp. 09/20/2000 which name changed to Brookfield Office Properties Inc. 05/09/2011
(See Brookfield Office Properties Inc.)

CARMAC RES LTD (BC)
Common 50¢ par changed to no par 12/22/1980
Recapitalized as Camnor Resources Ltd. 05/15/1992
Each share Common no par exchanged for (0.5) share Common no par
Camnor Resources Ltd. recapitalized as Stornoway Ventures Ltd. 10/30/2000 which merged into Stornoway Diamond Corp. (BC) 07/16/2003 which reincorporated in Canada 10/28/2011

CARMAN & CO., INC. (NY)
Each share Class B no par exchanged for (1) share Common $10 par 00/00/1946
Each share Common $10 par exchanged for (4) shares Common $2.50 par 00/00/1947
Dissolution approved 00/00/1954
Details not available

CARMAN LABORATORIES, INC. (MA)
Name changed to CLI Corp. (MA) 06/06/1967
CLI Corp. (MA) reincorporated in Delaware as Tallman Industries, Inc. 06/02/1972 which merged into Data-Design Laboratories (CA) 04/30/1980 which reincorporated in Delaware as Data-Design Laboratories, Inc. 12/01/1986 which name changed to DDL Electronics, Inc. 12/17/1993 which name changed to SMTEK International, Inc. 10/09/1998 which merged into CTS Corp. 02/01/2005

CARMANAH RES LTD (AB)
Each share old Common no par exchanged for (0.2) share new Common no par 06/12/1995
Cease trade order effective 02/02/2001
Stockholders' equity unlikely

CARMANAH TECHNOLOGIES CORP (AB)
Reincorporated under the laws of British Columbia 08/24/2010

CARMAX EXPL LTD (CANADA)
Recapitalized as Carmax Mining Corp. 09/02/2010
Each share Common no par exchanged for (0.1) share Common no par
Carmax Mining Corp. name changed to District Copper Corp. 07/03/2018

CARMAX MNG CORP (CANADA)
Each share old Common no par exchanged for (0.5) share new Common no par 11/17/2017
Name changed to District Copper Corp. 07/03/2018

CARME INC (NV)
Each share old Common $0.0001 par exchanged for (0.33333333) share new Common $0.0001 par 08/14/1986
Acquired by International Research & Development Corp. 01/18/1990
Each share new Common $0.0001 par exchanged for $5.25 cash

CARMEL BANCORPORATION (CA)
Charter cancelled for failure to file reports and pay taxes 12/01/1992

CARMEL CAP INC (NV)
Charter revoked for failure to file reports and pay fees 07/01/1999

CARMEL CONTAINER SYS LTD (ISRAEL)
Acquired by Hadera Paper Ltd. 10/05/2010
Each share Ordinary ILS 1 par exchanged for $22.50 cash

CARMEL ENERGY INC (DE)
SEC revoked common stock registration 02/08/2011

CARMEL PETROLEUM INC. (DE)
No longer in existence having become inoperative and void for non-payment of taxes 04/01/1961

CARMEL RES LTD (BC)
Cease trade order effective 07/23/2001
Stockholders' equity unlikely

CARMELITA RES LTD (BC)
Name changed 10/16/1996
Name changed from Carmelita Petroleum Ltd. to Carmelita Resources Ltd. 10/16/1996
Recapitalized as Pierre EnTerprises Ltd. 07/05/2000
Each share Common no par exchanged for (0.1) share Common no par
Pierre EnTerprises Ltd. recapitalized as Leeta Gold Corp. 02/01/2011 which name changed to HIVE Blockchain Technologies Ltd. 09/18/2017

CARMEN ENERGY INC (AB)
Name changed to Margaux Resources Ltd. 07/24/2013

CARMER INDUSTRIES, INC. (NJ)
Adjudicated bankrupt 03/27/1965
No stockholders' equity

CARMIKE CINEMAS INC (DE)
Each share Class A Common 3¢ par exchanged for (0.194925) share Common 3¢ par 01/31/2002
Merged into AMC Entertainment Holdings, Inc. 12/21/2016
Each share Common 3¢ par exchanged for $33.06 cash

CARMINA TECHNOLOGIES INC (UT)
Recapitalized as Advanced Integrated Management Services, Inc. 06/29/2004
Each share Common no par exchanged for (0.005) share Common no par
Advanced Integrated Management Services, Inc. reorganized as AIMSI Technologies, Inc. 11/17/2004
(See AIMSI Technologies, Inc.)

CARMINE FOODS INC (VA)
Name changed to Seafood Holding Corp. 06/01/1980
Seafood Holding Corp. assets transferred to Seafood Holding Corp. Liquidating Trust 01/02/1981
(See Seafood Holding Corp. Liquidating Trust)

CARMINE RES INC (AB)
Reincorporated under the laws of Ontario as Beckett Technologies Corp. 05/10/1994
(See Beckett Technologies Corp.)

CARMODY CORP (NY)
5.5% Preferred $100 par called for redemption 00/00/1963
Common 10¢ par split (2) for (1) by issuance of (1) additional share 01/14/1966
Common 10¢ par split (4) for (3) by issuance of (0.33333333) additional share 03/15/1969
Name changed to 2361 Wehrle Drive Liquidating Corp. 11/18/1969

(See 2361 Wehrle Drive Liquidating Corp.)

CARMONT MINES LTD. (ON)
Completely liquidated 07/07/1971
Each share Common $1 par exchanged for first and final distribution of (0.33333333) share Avilla International Explorations Ltd. Capital Stock no par
(See Avilla International Explorations Ltd.)

CARNA INC (DE)
Name changed to Mark Correctional Systems, Inc. 10/15/1992
Mark Correctional Systems, Inc. name changed to Mark Solutions, Inc. 11/10/1993 which name changed to Mark Holdings Inc. 12/26/2001
(See Mark Holdings Inc.)

CARNABY COMMUNICATIONS CORP (MN)
Statutorily dissolved 10/16/1991

CARNABY SHOPS FLA INC (DE)
Charter cancelled and declared inoperative and void for non-payment of taxes 03/01/1984

CARNACO EQUIP CO (DE)
Merged into Carnation Co. 10/30/1970
Each share Common 10¢ par exchanged for (0.064516) share Common $2 par
(See Carnation Co.)

CARNATION CO (DE)
Common $25 par changed to no par 00/00/1929
Common no par changed to $5.50 par and (2) additional shares issued 04/27/1956
3.75% Preferred $100 par called for redemption 12/01/1962
Common $5.50 par changed to $2.75 par and (1) additional share issued 04/30/1965
Common $2.75 par changed to $2 par and (0.5) additional share issued 05/02/1968
Common $2 par split (3) for (2) by issuance of (0.5) additional share 05/07/1971
Common $2 par split (3) for (2) by issuance of (0.5) additional share 01/06/1973
Common $2 par split (2) for (1) by issuance of (1) additional share 06/22/1977
Merged into Nestle S.A. 01/30/1985
Each share Common $2 par exchanged for $83 cash

CARNATION MILK PRODUCTS CO.
Name changed to Carnation Co. 00/00/1929
(See Carnation Co.)

CARNDESSON MINES LTD (ON)
Charter cancelled and declared dissolved for failure to file returns and pay fees 04/09/1975

CARNEGIE BANCORP (NJ)
Stock Dividends - 5% payable 05/15/1996 to holders of record 04/24/1996; 5% payable 03/19/1997 to holders of record 02/12/1997
Merged into Sovereign Bancorp, Inc. 07/31/1998
Each share Common $5 par exchanged for (2.022) shares Common no par
Sovereign Bancorp, Inc. merged into Banco Santander, S.A. 01/30/2009

CARNEGIE BANK, N.A. (PRINCETON, NJ)
Under plan of reorganization each share Common $5 par automatically became (1) share Carnegie Bancorp Common $5 par 04/12/1994
Carnegie Bancorp merged into Sovereign Bancorp, Inc. 07/31/1998 which merged into Banco Santander, S.A. 01/30/2009

CARNEGIE CAP INC (NV)
Name changed to National Building Supply Inc. 11/04/1991
(See National Building Supply Inc.)

CARNEGIE CAPPIELLO TR (OH)
Name changed 11/30/1985
Name changed from Carnegie-Cappiello Growth Trust to Carnegie-Cappiello Trust and Shares of Bene. Int. 10¢ par reclassified as Growth Series Shares of Bene. Int. 10¢ par 11/30/1985
Under plan of reorganization each Growth Series Share of Bene. Int. 10¢ par automatically became (1) share Fortis Growth Fund, Inc. Common 1¢ par 06/05/1992
(See Fortis Growth Fund, Inc.)
Under plan of reorganization each share Total Return Series 10¢ par automatically became (1) share Fortis Advantage Portfolios, Inc. Asset Allocation Portfolio 1¢ par 06/05/1992
(See Fortis Advantage Portfolios, Inc.)

CARNEGIE COOKE & CO (NV)
Name changed to TrackBets International Inc. 01/25/2008
(See TrackBets International Inc.)

CARNEGIE FINL CORP (OH)
Name changed 05/05/1973
Class B Common $1 par reclassified as Class A Common $1 par and (49) additional shares issued 12/21/1972
Class C Common $1 par reclassified as Class A Common $1 par 12/21/1972
Stock Dividend - 150% 02/13/1973
Name changed from Carnegie Financial Co. to Carnegie Financial Corp. 05/05/1973
Charter cancelled for non-payment of taxes 01/04/2007

CARNEGIE FINL CORP (PA)
Merged into Fidelity Bancorp, Inc. 02/22/2002
Each share Common 10¢ par exchanged for (0.68) share Common 1¢ par and $3.0975 cash
Fidelity Bancorp, Inc. merged into WesBanco, Inc. 12/03/2012

CARNEGIE GOVT SECS TR (MA)
Completely liquidated 11/19/1999
Each share Money Market Ser. 10¢ par received first and final distribution of approximately $1 cash

CARNEGIE GROUP INC (DE)
Merged into Logica plc 11/11/1998
Each share Common 1¢ par exchanged for $5 cash

CARNEGIE INDS INC (NY)
Charter cancelled and proclaimed dissolved for failure to pay taxes 09/30/1981

CARNEGIE INTL CORP (CO)
Each share Common no par received distribution of (0.33333333) share Timecast Corp. Common payable 10/29/1997 to holders of record 09/15/1997
SEC revoked common stock registration 07/14/2003

CARNEGIE INTL CORP (IN)
Charter revoked for failure to file annual reports 10/30/1989

CARNEGIE METALS CO.
Properties turned over to Mexican Labor Union 00/00/1940
Details not available

CARNEGIE MINES LTD. (CANADA)
Recapitalized as Carnegie Mining Corp. Ltd. 01/09/1958
Each share Common no par exchanged for (0.166666) share Common no par
(See Carnegie Mining Corp. Ltd.)

CAR-CAR FINANCIAL INFORMATION, INC.

CARNEGIE MNG LTD (CANADA)
Merged into Kam-Kotia Mines Ltd. 01/01/1985
Each share Common no par exchanged for (0.2) shares Common no par
Note: Holdings of (99) shares or fewer exchanged for $0.35 cash per share
(See Kam-Kotia Mines Ltd.)

CARNEGIE TAX FREE INCOME TR (MA)
Completely liquidated 11/12/1999
Each Share of Bene. Int. 10¢ par received net asset value

CARNES CREEK EXPLS LTD (BC)
Recapitalized as Marathon Telecom Corp. 02/06/1991
Each share Common no par exchanged for (0.33333333) share Common no par
(See Marathon Telecom Corp.)

CARNEY CO., INC. (MN)
Dissolved by court order and liquidated for benefit of creditors 02/13/1968
No stockholders' equity

CARNIVAL CORP (PANAMA)
Name changed 04/25/1994
Name changed from Carnival Cruise Lines, Inc. to Carnival Corp. 04/25/1994
Class A Common 1¢ par split (2) for (1) by issuance of (1) additional share 12/14/1994
Class A Common 1¢ par reclassified as Common 1¢ par and (1) additional share issued payable 06/12/1998 to holders of record 05/29/1998 Ex date - 06/15/1998
Common 1¢ par reclassified as Paired Certificates 04/17/2003 (Additional Information in Active)

CARNIVAL RES LTD (BC)
Cease trade order effective 03/18/2002
Stockholders' equity unlikely

CARO CLOTH CORP.
Assets distributed 00/00/1945
Details not available

CAROL INFO SERVICES LTD (INDIA)
GDR agreement terminated 07/11/2012
Each Sponsored GDR for Equity shares exchanged for (1) Equity share
Note: Unexchanged GDR's will be sold and the proceeds, if any, held for claim after 10/08/2012

CAROL WIRE & CABLE CORP (RI)
Class B Common $1 par reclassified as Class A Common $1 par 01/02/1968
Stock Dividend - Class A - 25% 02/27/1967
Name changed to Roosevelt Avenue Corp. 03/08/1968
(See Roosevelt Avenue Corp.)

CAROLANDO CORP (NC)
Completely liquidated 06/27/1980
Each share Common no par exchanged for first and final distribution of $0.03109 cash

CAROLCO PICTURES INC (DE)
Common Stock Purchase Rights declared for Common stockholders of record 07/01/1990 were redeemed at $0.01 per right 11/19/1993 for holders of record 10/19/1993
Plan of reorganization under Chapter 11 Federal Bankruptcy Code effective 06/02/1997
No stockholders' equity

CAROLCO PICTURES INC (FL)
Each share old Common $0.0001 par exchanged for (0.0001) share new Common $0.0001 par 02/23/2017
Name changed to Recall Studios, Inc. 11/29/2017

CAROLET CORP. (MA)
Liquidation completed 02/14/1955
Details not available

CAROLIAN SYS INTL INC (ON)
Name changed to Delrina Corp. 01/18/1990
(See Delrina Corp.)

CAROLIN MINES LTD (BC)
Common 50¢ par changed to no par 11/00/1979
Common no par reclassified as Class A Common no par 02/00/1987
Name changed to Anglo Swiss Mining Corp. and Class A Common no par reclassified as Common no par 02/01/1990
Anglo Swiss Mining Corp. recapitalized as Anglo Swiss Industries Inc. 07/22/1992 which name changed to Anglo Swiss Resources Inc. 11/28/1997 which recapitalized as Gungnir Resources Inc. 06/20/2014

CAROLINA ALLIANCE BK (SPARTANBURG, SC)
Stock Dividends - 10% payable 10/07/2014 to holders of record 09/22/2014 Ex date - 09/18/2014; 5% payable 02/10/2016 to holders of record 01/26/2016 Ex date - 01/22/2016; 5% payable 09/19/2017 to holders of record 09/05/2017 Ex date - 08/31/2017
Reorganized as CAB Financial Corp. 10/23/2017
Each share Common $1 par exchanged for (1) share Common $1 par

CAROLINA BANCORP INC (DE)
Merged into BB&T Financial Corp. 08/20/1990
Each share Common 1¢ par exchanged for (0.816) share Common $2.50 par
BB&T Financial Corp. merged into Southern National Corp. 02/28/1995 which merged into BB&T Corp. 05/19/1997

CAROLINA BK (GREENSBORO, NC)
Stock Dividend - 10% payable 10/02/2000 to holders of record 09/30/2000
Under plan of reorganization each share Common $5 par automatically became (1) share Carolina Bank Holdings, Inc. Common $1 par 11/01/2000
Carolina Bank Holdings, Inc. merged into First Bancorp 03/03/2017

CAROLINA BK HLDGS INC (NC)
Common $1 par split (6) for (5) by issuance of (0.2) additional share payable 04/29/2004 to holders of record 04/20/2004
Common $1 par split (6) for (5) by issuance of (0.2) additional share payable 11/29/2005 to holders of record 11/15/2005 Ex date - 11/10/2005
Common $1 par split (6) for (5) by issuance of (0.2) additional share payable 06/29/2007 to holders of record 06/15/2007 Ex date - 06/13/2007
Stock Dividend - 10% payable 10/22/2001 to holders of record 10/01/2001
Merged into First Bancorp 03/03/2017
Each share Common $1 par exchanged for either (1.002) shares Common no par or $20 cash

CAROLINA CAP CORP (BC)
Name changed to Broadway Gold Mining Ltd. 10/18/2016

CAROLINA CARIBBEAN CORP (NC)
Each share Common $5 par exchanged for (1.5) shares Common $3.33333333 par 08/27/1968
Common $3.33333333 par changed to $0.83333333 par and (3) additional shares issued 07/11/1969
Plan of reorganization under Chapter X Bankruptcy Act confirmed 07/07/1981
No stockholders' equity

CAROLINA CAS INS CO (FL)
Stock Dividends - 10% 03/01/1980; 20% 02/20/1981; 10% 03/01/1982
Merged into Berkley (W. R.) Corp. 01/30/1985
Each share Common $1 par exchanged for (0.25) share Common 20¢ par

CAROLINA CASUALTY INSURANCE CO. (NC)
Stock Dividends - 10% 11/02/1953; 17.04% 06/26/1961
Merged into Carolina Casualty Insurance Co. (FL) 03/31/1966
Each share Class A Common $1 par or Class B Common $1 par exchanged for (0.736) share Common $1 par
Carolina Casualty Insurance Co. (FL) merged into Berkley (W. R.) Corp. 01/30/1985

CAROLINA CLINCHFIELD & OHIO RY (VA)
Acquired by CSX Corp. 08/25/1982
Each share Common $100 par exchanged for (1) share $7 Conv. Preferred Ser. A no par
(See CSX Corp.)

CAROLINA CO AT PINEHURST INC (WY)
Placed in receivership 02/16/2006
Distributions will be made on a pro rata basis to holders who filed an Allowed Claim prior to 10/05/2007

CAROLINA CMNTY BANCSHARES INC (SC)
Merged into First Bancorp 01/15/2003
Each share Common $1 par exchanged for (0.08) share Common $5 par and $20 cash

CAROLINA DYEING & WINDING INC.
Dissolved 00/00/1940
Details not available

CAROLINA ENERGIES INC (DE)
Common $1 par split (5) for (4) by issuance of (0.25) additional share 09/01/1979
Merged into South Carolina Electric & Gas Co. 04/28/1982
Each share Common $1 par exchanged for (1.714) shares Common $4.50 par
South Carolina Electric & Gas Co. reorganized as SCANA Corp. (Old) 12/31/1984 which merged into SCANA Corp. (New) 02/10/2000

CAROLINA FMRS COOP WHSE (NC)
Called for redemption at $500 plus $40 accrued dividends on 03/31/2000

CAROLINA FGHT CARRIERS CORP (NC)
Common $1 par changed to 50¢ par and (1) additional share issued 05/17/1971
Under plan of reorganization each share 4% Preferred $100 par and Common 50¢ par automatically became (1) share Carolina Freight Corp. 4% Preferred $100 par and Common 50¢ par respectively 12/31/1982
Carolina Freight Corp. name changed to Worldway Corp. 06/14/1995
(See Worldway Corp.)

CAROLINA FGHT CORP (NC)
Common 50¢ par split (2) for (1) by issuance of (1) additional share 06/09/1983
Name changed to Worldway Corp. 06/14/1995
(See Worldway Corp.)

CAROLINA FINL CORP OLD (DE)
Stock Dividend - 10% 01/02/1992
Acquired by SouthTrust Corp. 10/23/1992
Each share Common 1¢ par exchanged for (0.9546) share Common $2.50 par
SouthTrust Corp. merged into Wachovia Corp. (Ctfs. dated after 09/01/2001) 11/01/2004 which merged into Wells Fargo & Co. (New) 12/31/2008

CAROLINA FINCORP INC (NC)
Merged into FNB Corp. 04/11/2000
Each share Common no par exchanged for (0.79) share Common $2.50 par
FNB Corp. name changed to FNB United Corp. 04/28/2006 which name changed to CommunityOne Bancorp 07/01/2013 which merged into Capital Bank Financial Corp. 10/26/2016

CAROLINA FIRST BANCSHARES INC (NC)
Common $2.50 par split (5) for (4) by issuance of (0.25) additional share payable 08/23/1996 to holders of record 08/09/1996
Common $2.50 par split (2) for (1) by issuance of (1) additional share payable 08/22/1997 to holders of record 08/08/1997
Stock Dividends - 10% 12/29/1993; 5% payable 12/22/1995 to holders of record 12/08/1995; 10% payable 07/23/1999 to holders of record 07/09/1999
Merged into First Charter Corp. 04/04/2000
Each share Common $2.50 par exchanged for (2.267) shares Common no par
First Charter Corp. merged into Fifth Third Bancorp 06/06/2008

CAROLINA FIRST CORP (SC)
Conv. Preferred Ser. 1992 no par called for redemption 12/31/1993
$1.88 Conv. Preferred Ser. 1993 no par called for redemption 02/05/1996
7.32% Conv. Preferred Ser. 1994 no par called for redemption 02/29/1996
Stock Dividend - 20% payable 01/30/1997 to holders of record 01/15/1997
Name changed to South Financial Group, Inc. 04/24/2000
South Financial Group, Inc. merged into Toronto-Dominion Bank (Toronto, ON) 09/30/2010

CAROLINA FIRST MTG LN TR (SC)
144A Floating Rate Preferred Ser. 2000B called for redemption at $100,000 on 04/30/2007

CAROLINA FIRST NATL BK (LINCOLNTON, NC)
Merged into NCNB Corp. 12/31/1981
Each share Capital Stock $5 par exchanged for (2.2) shares Common $2.50 par
NCNB Corp. name changed to NationsBank Corp. 12/31/1991 which reincorporated in Delaware as BankAmerica Corp. (Old) 09/25/1998 which merged into BankAmerica Corp. (New) 09/30/1998 which name changed to Bank of America Corp. 04/28/1999

CAROLINA FUND, INC. (SC)
Involuntarily dissolved for failure to pay taxes 01/30/2008

CAROLINA GEORGIA SERVICE
Properties sold to Colonial Ice Co. 00/00/1932
No stockholders' equity

CAROLINA GOLD RES LTD (BC)
Recapitalized as Rutherford Ventures Corp. 10/08/1992
Each share Common no par

exchanged for (0.5) share Common no par
Rutherford Ventures Corp. name changed to Diamond Fields Resources Inc. 04/06/1993 which merged into Inco Ltd. 08/21/1996
(See Inco Ltd.)

CAROLINA IN THE PINES INC (CO)
Name changed to Dunhill Holdings, Inc. 05/04/1987
Dunhill Holdings, Inc. recapitalized as Williamson (E.B.) & Co., Inc. 04/28/1989
(See Williamson (E.B.) & Co., Inc.)

CAROLINA INSURANCE CO.
Merged into Home Insurance Co. 00/00/1948
Each share Capital Stock $10 par exchanged for (1.212) shares Common $5 par
(See Home Insurance Co.)

CAROLINA INVT PARTNERS LTD PARTNERSHIP (NC)
Company terminated registration of Units of Ltd. Partnership and is no longer public as of 05/03/2007
Details not available

CAROLINA METAL PRODS CORP (NC)
Completely liquidated 01/25/1980
Each share Common $1 par exchanged for first and final distribution of $0.40 cash

CAROLINA MINES LTD. (BC)
Struck off the Register and dissolved for failure to file returns 10/18/1962

CAROLINA MOUNTAIN TELEPHONE CO.
Merged into Western Carolina Telephone Co. 00/00/1952
Each share Capital Stock $1 par exchanged for (0.1850516) share new Common $10 par
(See Western Carolina Telephone Co.)

CAROLINA MTN HLDG CO (NC)
Acquired by NCNB Corp. 05/18/1990
Each share Common $1 par exchanged for $9 cash

CAROLINA MTN PWR CORP (DE)
In process of liquidation
Each share Capital Stock no par exchanged for initial distribution of $25 cash 07/29/1965
Each share Capital Stock no par received second distribution of $10 cash 01/20/1966
Note: Details on subsequent distributions, if any, are not available

CAROLINA NAT GAS CORP (DE)
Common $2.50 par changed to $1 par 00/00/1953
Merged into Piedmont Natural Gas Co., Inc. 07/31/1968
Each share Common $1 par exchanged for (0.12) share $6 Conv. 2nd Preferred no par
(See Piedmont Natural Gas Co., Inc.)

CAROLINA NATIONAL MORTGAGE INVESTMENT CO., INC. (SC)
Merged into Citizens & Southern Corp. 01/01/1971
Each share 6% Preferred $100 par exchanged for $104 cash

CAROLINA PAC PLYWOOD INC (OR)
Capital Stock no par split (1.4) for (1) by issuance of (0.4) additional share 12/31/1961
Capital Stock no par split (1.4) for (1) by issuance of (0.4) additional share 08/25/1964
Merged into Southwest Forest Industries, Inc. 06/12/1975
Each share Capital Stock no par exchanged for $3.75 cash

CAROLINA PIPELINE CO (DE)
Common $1 par split (3) for (2) by issuance of (0.5) additional share 03/14/1966
Common $1 par split (5) for (4) by issuance of (0.25) additional share 09/14/1971
$6 Conv. Preferred Ser. B no par called for redemption 07/31/1972
Common $1 par split (5) for (4) by issuance of (0.25) additional share 08/01/1974
Stock Dividend - 10% 09/01/1976
Name changed to Carolina Energies, Inc. 11/30/1977
Carolina Energies, Inc. merged into South Carolina Electric & Gas Co. 04/28/1982 which reorganized as SCANA Corp. (Old) 12/31/1984 which merged into SCANA Corp. (New) 02/10/2000

CAROLINA PORTLAND CEMENT CO.
Liquidated 00/00/1949
Details not available

CAROLINA PWR & LT CO (NC)
$6 Preferred called for redemption 06/15/1945
$7 Preferred called for redemption 06/15/1945
Common no par split (2) for (1) by issuance of (1) additional share 06/21/1954
Common no par split (2) for (1) by issuance of (1) additional share 06/12/1964
$14 Serial Preferred no par called for redemption 05/07/1986
$11.16 Preferred no par called for redemption 10/01/1986
$2.675 Preference Ser. A no par called for redemption 04/22/1987
$8.48 Preferred no par called for redemption 10/01/1992
$9.10 Preferred no par called for redemption 10/01/1992
Common no par split (2) for (1) by issuance of (1) additional share 01/30/1993
$7.72 Preferred no par called for redemption at $101 on 07/01/1997
$7.95 Preferred no par called for redemption at $101 on 07/01/1997
Under plan of reorganization each share Common no par automatically became (1) share CP&L Energy, Inc. Common no par 06/19/2000
CP&L Energy, Inc. name changed to Progress Energy, Inc. 12/11/2000 which merged into Duke Energy Corp. 07/02/2012
$4.20 Preferred $100 par called for redemption at $102 plus $0.77 accrued dividends on 03/08/2013
$5 Preferred $100 par called for redemption at $110 plus $0.917 accrued dividends on 03/08/2013
$5.44 Preferred $100 par called for redemption at $101 plus $0.997 accrued dividends on 03/08/2013

CAROLINA PREMIER BK (CHARLOTTE, NC)
Reorganized as Premara Financial, Inc. 07/12/2011
Each Unit exchanged for (5) shares Common 1¢ par
Each share Common $5 par exchanged for (1) share Common 1¢ par
Premara Financial, Inc. merged into Select Bancorp, Inc. (New) 12/15/2017

CAROLINA SVGS BK INC SSB (GREENSBORO, NC)
Name changed to Carolina Bank (Greensboro, NC) 10/01/1997
Carolina Bank (Greensboro, NC) was acquired by Carolina Bank Holdings, Inc. 11/01/2000 which merged into First Bancorp 03/03/2017

CAROLINA SOUTHN BK (SPARTANBURG, SC)
Common $5 par split (3) for (2) by issuance of (0.5) additional share payable 05/17/1996 to holders of record 05/06/1996
Common $5 par split (3) for (2) by issuance of (0.5) additional share payable 12/30/1997 to holders of record 12/19/1997
Stock Dividends - 5% payable 09/16/1996 to holders of record 09/04/1996; 5% payable 08/18/1997 to holders of record 08/06/1997; 3% payable 10/01/1998 to holders of record 09/16/1998; 5% payable 01/10/2000 to holders of record 12/31/1999
Merged into Synovus Financial Corp. 02/16/2001
Each share Common $5 par exchanged for (0.8514) share Common $1 par

CAROLINA SPACE STAS INC (NC)
Liquidated under Chapter 11 Federal Bankruptcy Code 08/05/1986
No stockholders' equity

CAROLINA ST BK (GASTONIA, NC)
Merged into Southern National Bank of North Carolina (Lumberton, NC) 09/30/1979
Each share Capital Stock $5 par exchanged for $14.25 cash

CAROLINA ST BK (SHELBY & KINGS MTN, NC)
Merged into First Charter Corp. 12/22/1997
Each share Common $4.50 par exchanged for (1.023) shares Common $5 par
First Charter Corp. merged into Fifth Third Bancorp 06/06/2008

CAROLINA STL CORP (NC)
Capital Stock $20 par changed to $4 par and (4) additional shares issued 02/27/1967
Capital Stock $4 par changed to $1.33333333 par and (2) additional shares issued 08/16/1974
Merged into CS Holdings Inc. 05/31/1985
Each share Capital Stock $1.33333333 par exchanged for $35.74 cash

CAROLINA TEL & TELEG CO (NC)
Common Capital Stock $100 par changed to $20 par and (4) additional shares issued 10/30/1959
Common Capital Stock $20 par changed to $6.66666666 par and (2) additional shares issued 10/01/1965
Merged into United Utilities, Inc. 03/28/1969
Each share Common Capital Stock $6.66666666 par exchanged for (1) share Conv. 2nd Preferred no par
United Utilities, Inc. name changed to United Telecommunications, Inc. 06/02/1972 which name changed to Sprint Corp. (KS) 02/26/1992 which name changed to Sprint Nextel Corp. 08/12/2005 which merged into Sprint Corp. (DE) 07/10/2013

CAROLINA TR BK (LINCOLNTON, NC)
Common $5 par changed to $2.50 par 05/16/2011
Stock Dividends - 10% payable 12/16/2005 to holders of record 12/01/2005; 10% payable 11/17/2006 to holders of record 11/03/2006; 10% payable 12/10/2007 to holders of record 11/26/2007 Ex date - 11/21/2007
Under plan of reorganization each share Common $2.50 par automatically became (1) share Carolina Trust BancShares Inc. Common $2.50 par 08/16/2016

CAROLINA UTILITIES CO.
Liquidation completed 00/00/1950
Details not available

CAROLINAS CAPITAL CORP. (NC)
Liquidation completed
Each share Common $1 par exchanged for initial distribution of $5 cash 07/06/1967
Each share Common $1 par received second distribution of (0.6) share Scope, Inc. Capital Stock $1 par 08/07/1967
Each share Common $1 par received third distribution of (0.2) share Synalloy Corp. Common $1 par 08/17/1967
Each share Common $1 par received fourth distribution of $1.45 cash 01/31/1968
Each share Common $1 par received fifth and final distribution of $0.1768335327 cash 12/31/1968
(See each company's listing)

CAROLINE SVGS BK (BOWLING GREEN, VA)
Stock Dividend - 5% payable 03/31/1999 to holders of record 02/26/1999
Merged into Virginia Commonwealth Financial Corp. 02/14/2000
Each share Common $4 par exchanged for (0.7959) share Common $2.50 par
Virginia Commonwealth Financial Corp. merged into Virginia Financial Group, Inc. 01/22/2002 which name changed to StellarOne Corp. 02/28/2008 which merged into Union First Market Bankshares Corp. 01/02/2014 which name changed to Union Bankshares Corp. 04/28/2014

CAROLYN BEAN PUBG LTD (DE)
Common 1¢ par split (3) for (2) by issuance of (0.5) additional share 01/17/1986
Each share old Common 1¢ par exchanged for (0.0625) share new Common 1¢ par 08/07/1990
Name changed to Healthy Planet Products, Inc. 08/02/1993
(See Healthy Planet Products, Inc.)

CAROLYN PARK CORP. (NY)
Liquidation completed 00/00/1941
Details not available

CAROM CAP CORP (FL)
Name changed to Jillian's Entertainment Corp. 11/13/1991
(See Jillian's Entertainment Corp.)

CARONI MINERAL CORP (UT)
Merged out of existence 03/04/1988
Details not available

CAROUSEL CAP INC (NV)
Charter revoked for failure to file reports and pay fees 11/01/1989

CAROUSEL FASHIONS INC (DE)
Charter cancelled and declared inoperative and void for non-payment of taxes 03/01/1976

CAROUSEL THEATRE, INC. (MA)
Charter revoked for failure to file reports and pay fees 10/14/1964

CARPATHIAN GOLD INC (CANADA)
Name changed to Euro Sun Mining Inc. 08/26/2016

CARPATSKY PETE INC (AB)
Merged into Cardinal Resources PLC 04/15/2005
Each share Common no par exchanged for (0.5) Ordinary Share

CARPE DIEM ENTERPRISES INC (NV)
Name changed to Esarti Electric Technologies Corp. 07/11/2000
Esarti Electric Technologies Corp. name changed to Evader, Inc. (NV) 08/15/2003 which reincorporated in Wyoming 05/25/2012 which name changed to Critic Clothing, Inc. 12/14/2015 which recapitalized as Deep Green Waste & Recycling, Inc. 09/27/2017

CARPEL CORP. (DE)
Merged into Colonial Food Distributors, Inc. 12/28/1963
Each share Capital Stock no par exchanged for (0.2) share Common $10 par
(See Colonial Food Distributiors, Inc.)

CARPENTER (L.E.) & CO. (NJ)
Stock Dividends - 25% 10/01/1959; 25% 11/10/1960; 25% 09/29/1961
Completely liquidated 08/11/1967
Each share Common $1 par exchanged for first and final distribution of (0.16) share Dayco Corp. (DE) $4.25 Conv. Preferred Ser. A no par
Dayco Corp. (DE) reincorporated in Michigan 08/31/1982 which name changed to Day International Corp. 02/23/1987
(See Day International Corp.)

CARPENTER LAKE RES LTD (BC)
Recapitalized as Wayside Gold Mines Ltd. 02/21/1992
Each share Common no par exchanged for (0.25) share Common no par
Wayside Gold Mines Ltd. recapitalized as International Wayside Gold Mines Ltd. 02/08/1994 which name changed to Barkerville Gold Mines Ltd. 01/21/2010

CARPENTER-MORTON CO. (MA)
Acquired by Oxford Electric Corp. (DE) 10/18/1968
Each share 4.5% Preferred $100 par or 6% Preferred $100 par exchanged for (2) shares Common no par
Each share Common no par exchanged for (1) share Common no par
Oxford Electric Corp. (DE) name changed to Seaport Corp. 09/15/1973
(See Seaport Corp.)

CARPENTER PAPER CO. (DE)
Stock Dividend - 100% 05/23/1952
Acquired by Champion Paper & Fibre Co. on a (1.825) for (1) basis 03/31/1961
Champion & Fibre Co. name changed to Champion Papers Inc. 07/31/1961 which merged into U.S. Plywood-Champion Papers Inc. 02/28/1967 which name changed to Champion International Corp. 05/12/1972 which merged into International Paper Co. 06/20/2000

CARPENTER PAPER CO OF NEB (DE)
Common $1 par split (3) for (2) by issuance of (0.5) additional share 05/07/1976
Common $1 par split (4) for (3) by issuance of (0.33333333) additional share 06/07/1977
Stock Dividends - 100% 06/30/1972; 15% 02/26/1980
Through purchase offer majority acquired by Alco Standard Corp. as of 07/31/1983
Public interest eliminated

CARPENTER STEEL CO. (NJ)
Common $100 par changed to no par 00/00/1933
Each share Common no par exchanged for (5) shares Common $5 par 00/00/1937
Common $5 par split (2) for (1) by issuance of (1) additional share 04/15/1966
Stock Dividends - 10% 08/18/1950; 100% 02/24/1956; 10% 06/28/1963
Stock Distribution - 100% 10/30/1959
Reincorporated under the laws of Delaware as Carpenter Technology Corp. 11/04/1968

CARPENTER W R HLDGS LTD (AUSTRALIA)
Acquired by Griffin East Pty Ltd. 02/15/1984
Details not available

CARPENTIERS GOLDFIELDS, LTD. QC
Charter cancelled 09/00/1950

CARPET CASTLE INC.
Name changed to FECC, Inc. 04/01/1980
FECC, Inc. name changed to Argus Industries, Inc. 01/06/1987
(See Argus Industries, Inc.)

CARPET HLDGS INC (CO)
Name changed to IQ Holdings Inc. (CO) 05/05/1997
IQ Holdings Inc. (CO) reorganized in Texas as Scenario Systems International, Inc. 08/01/2007 which reorganized in Wyoming as Insight ID, Inc. 09/18/2013

CARPET SHOWPLACE USA INC (FL)
Proclaimed dissolved for failure to file reports and pay fees 09/24/1999

CARPETS INTL LTD (ENGLAND)
Name changed to Debron Investments PLC 01/15/1986
(See Debron Investments PLC)

CARPHONE WAREHOUSE (UNITED KINGDOM)
ADR agreement terminated 02/15/2011
Details not available

CARPITA CORP (ON)
Filed an assignment in bankruptcy under the Canada Federal Bankruptcy Statute 06/29/1990
No stockholders' equity

CARR BOYD MINERALS LTD (AUSTRALIA)
Merged into Ashton Gold Ltd. 11/14/1990
Each ADR for Ordinary exchanged for $0.89 cash

CARR-CONSOLIDATED BISCUIT CO. (IL)
Bankrupt 02/18/1955
Stockholders' equity unlikely

CARR FASTENER CORP.
Merged into United-Carr Fastener Corp. (MA) 00/00/1929
Details not available

CARR-GOTTSTEIN FOODS CO (DE)
Merged into Safeway Inc. 04/16/1999
Each share Common 1¢ par exchanged for $12.50 cash

CARR RLTY CORP (MD)
Name changed to CarrAmerica Realty Corp. 05/01/1996
(See CarrAmerica Realty Corp.)

CARRACO OIL CO. (DE)
No longer in existence having become inoperative and void for non-payment of taxes 04/01/1966

CARRAMERICA RLTY CORP (MD)
8.45% Depositary Preferred Ser. D called for redemption at $25 plus $0.246458 accrued dividend on 10/12/2003
8.55% Depositary Preferred Ser. C called for redemption at $25 plus $0.249375 accrued dividend on 10/12/2003
8.57% Preferred Ser. B called for redemption at $25 plus $0.249958 accrued dividend on 10/12/2003
Merged into Nantucket Parent LLC 07/13/2006
Each share 7.50% Preferred Ser. E 1¢ par exchanged for $25.385 cash
Each share Common 1¢ par exchanged for $44.75 cash

CARRARA EXPL CORP (BC)
Recapitalized as PreveCeutical Medical Inc. 07/14/2017
Each share Common no par exchanged for (0.33333333) share Common no par

CARRAVELLE MINES LTD. (ON)
Under plan of merger name changed to Caravelle Mines Ltd. and Common $1 par changed to no par 11/13/1969

CARREKER CORP (DE)
Name changed 06/23/2000
Name changed from Carreker-Antinori, Inc. to Carreker Corp. 06/23/2000
Merged into CheckFree Corp. (New) 04/02/2007
Each share Common 1¢ par exchanged for $8.05 cash

CARRERA CAP CORP (CO)
Name changed to Environetics, Inc. 02/08/1988

CARRERA RES LTD (BC)
Name changed to Desen Computer Industries Inc. 04/25/1986
(See Desen Computer Industries Inc.)

CARRERAS LTD (ENGLAND)
Each share A Ordinary exchanged for (8) shares Class B Ordinary 2s6d par 00/00/1952
ADR's for Class B Ordinary 2s6d par changed to 12-1/2p par per currency change 02/15/1971
Name changed to Rothmans International Ltd. 09/07/1972
(See Rothmans International PLC)

CARRIAGE AUTOMOTIVE GROUP INC (ON)
Each share old Common no par exchanged for (0.1) share new Common no par 09/22/1999
Name changed to Cars4u.com Ltd. 02/14/2000
Cars4u.com Ltd. name changed to Cars4u Ltd. 01/30/2003 which recapitalized as Chesswood Income Fund 05/10/2006 which reorganized as Chesswood Group Ltd. 01/04/2011

CARRIAGE INDS INC (GA)
Merged into Dixie Yarns, Inc. 03/21/1993
Each share Common 2¢ par exchanged for either (1.019) shares Common $3 par or (0.769) share Common $3 par and $3.25 cash
Note: Option to elect to receive stock and cash expired 04/11/1993
Dixie Yarns, Inc. name changed to Dixie Group, Inc. 05/02/1997

CARRIAGE PPTYS INC (PA)
Completely liquidated 05/21/1984
Each share Common $1 par exchanged for first and final distribution of $19.02 cash

CARRIAGE SVCS CAP TR (DE)
7% 144A Term Income Deferrable Equity Securities called for redemption at $50 plus $0.4375 accrued dividends on 04/16/2014
7% Term Income Deferrable Equity Securities called for redemption at $50 plus $0.4375 accrued dividends on 04/16/2014

CARRIAN INVT LTD (HONG KONG)
Company placed in receivership 11/00/1983
No ADR holders' equity

CARRICK GOLD LTD (AUSTRALIA)
Name changed to KalNorth Gold Mines Ltd. 11/08/2012
(See KalNorth Gold Mines Ltd.)

CARRIER ACCESS CORP (DE)
Merged into Turin Networks, Inc. 02/11/2008
Each share Common $0.001 par exchanged for $2.60 cash

CARRIER CORP (DE)
Each share 7% Preferred $100 par exchanged for (5) shares Common no par 00/00/1936
Common no par changed to $1 par 00/00/1938
Common $1 par changed to $10 par 00/00/1944
Common $10 par split (3) for (2) by issuance of (0.5) additional share 04/29/1965
4.8% 2nd Preferred $50 par called for redemption 01/17/1966
Common $10 par changed to $5 par and (1) additional share issued 03/31/1969
4.5% Preferred $50 par reclassified as 4.5% Sr. Preferred $50 par 03/03/1969
Common $5 par changed to $2.50 par and (1) additional share issued 03/31/1969
Common $2.50 par split (3) for (2) by issuance of (0.5) additional share 07/31/1972
4.5% Sr. Preferred $50 par called for redemption 07/03/1979
Stock Dividend - 10% 03/01/1951
Acquired by United Technologies Corp. 07/06/1979
Each share $1.86 Conv. Preferred $2.50 par exchanged for (1.815) shares $2.55 Conv. Preferred $1 par
Each share 4.5% Preferred $100 par exchanged for (1) share $4.50 Preferred $1 par
Each share Common $2.50 par exchanged for (1) share $2.55 Conv. Preferred $1 par

CARRIER ENGINEERING CORP.
Merged into Carrier Corp. 10/31/1930
Details not available

CARRIER J D SHOE LTD (ON)
Completely liquidated 00/00/1979
No stockholders' equity

CARRIER1 INTL S A (LUXEMBOURG)
Declared in bankruptcy by Luxembourg court 02/22/2002
ADR holders' equity unlikely

CARRIERS & GEN CORP (MD)
Common $1 par split (2) for (1) by issuance of (1) additional share 07/01/1971
Merged into Dividend Shares, Inc. 09/15/1981
Each share Common $1 par exchanged for (4.228) shares Capital Stock 25¢ par
Dividend Shares, Inc. name changed to Bullock Dividend Shares, Inc. 01/01/1985 which name changed to Alliance Dividend Shares, Inc. 03/13/1987 which name changed to Alliance Growth & Income Fund, Inc. 10/17/1989 which name changed to AllianceBernstein Growth & Income Fund, Inc. 03/31/2003

CARRIGAN GOLD CORP (UT)
Name changed to Viking Broadcasting Corp. 03/23/1987
Viking Broadcasting Corp. recapitalized as Meditecnic Inc. 04/18/1998

CARRIGAN INDS LTD (BC)
Struck off register and declared dissolved for failure to file returns 12/09/1991

CARRIGAN GEORGE S CO (MA)
Name changed to Gescar Corp. 12/23/1971
(See Gescar Corp.)

CARRINGTON LABS INC (TX)
Name changed to DelSite, Inc. 07/31/2008
(See DelSite, Inc.)

CARRM CONVERTIBLE CAR CORP. (DE)
No longer in existence having become inoperative and void for non-payment of taxes 03/17/1926

CARROLL CNTY BK & TR CO (WESTMINSTER, MD)
Common $10 par split (2) for (1) by issuance of (1) additional share 11/25/1987
Under plan of reorganization each share Capital Stock $10 par automatically became (1) share Mason-Dixon Bancshares, Inc. Common $10 par 03/09/1992

Mason-Dixon Bancshares, Inc. merged into BB&T Corp. 07/14/1999

CARROLL COUNTY NATIONAL BANK (WESTMINSTER, MD)
Stock Dividend - 25% 01/25/1951
Merged into Carroll County Bank & Trust Co. (Westminster, MD) 12/14/1962
Each share Capital Stock $10 par exchanged for (1) share Capital Stock $10 par
Carroll County Bank & Trust Co. (Westminster, MD) reorganized as Mason Dixon Bancshares, Inc. 03/09/1992 which merged into BB&T Corp. 07/14/1999

CARROLL CNTY TR CO (CONWAY, NH)
Merged into Indian Head Banks, Inc. 10/10/1978
Each share Capital Stock $100 par exchanged for (20) shares Common $5 par
Indian Head Banks, Inc. acquired by Fleet/Norstar Financial Group, Inc. 12/21/1988 which name changed to Fleet Financial Group, Inc. (New) 04/15/1992 which name changed to Fleet Boston Corp. 10/01/1999 which name changed to FleetBoston Financial Corp. 04/18/2000 which merged into Bank of America Corp. 04/01/2004

CARROLLTON BANCORP (MD)
Common $10 par split (6) for (5) by issuance of (0.2) additional share 03/10/1995
Common $10 par changed to $1 par and (1) additional share issued payable 07/01/1999 to holders of record 06/18/1999
Stock Dividends - 2% payable 03/08/1976 to holders of record 02/23/1996; 5% payable 03/14/1997 to holders of record 02/21/1997; 5% payable 03/13/1998 to holders of record 02/20/1998; 5% payable 12/03/2002 to holders of record 11/15/2002 Ex date - 11/13/2002
Name changed to Bay Bancorp, Inc. 11/01/2013
Bay Bancorp, Inc. merged into Old Line Bancshares, Inc. 04/13/2018

CARROLLTON BK (BALTIMORE, MD)
Common $10 par split (2) for (1) by issuance of (1) additional share 04/16/1986
Stock Dividends - 10% 10/16/1972; 10.005% 02/27/1974; 10.000182% 02/25/1976; 10% 04/17/1980; 10% 04/15/1982; 20% 04/18/1984; 20.000415% 04/17/1985; 10.00013% 04/15/1987; 10% 04/15/1988
Under plan of reorganization each share Common $10 par automatically became (1) share Carrollton Bancorp Common $10 par 05/22/1990
Carrollton Bancorp name changed to Bay Bancorp, Inc. 11/01/2013 which merged into Old Line Bancshares, Inc. 04/13/2018

CARROLS, INC. (DE)
Completely liquidated 12/01/1965
Each share Common $1 par received first and final distribution of (0.1) share Tastee Freez Industries, Inc. Common 67¢ par
Note: Certificates were not required to be surrendered and are without value
(See Tastee Freez Industries, Inc.)

CARROLS CORP (DE)
Common 10¢ par split (2) for (1) by issuance of (1) additional share 08/26/1983
Acquired by a private company 12/22/1986
Each share Common 10¢ par exchanged for $11.25 cash

CARROLS DEVELOPMENT CORP. (DE)
Common 10¢ par split (3) for (2) by issuance of (0.5) additional share 02/01/1983
Stock Dividend - 10% 12/15/1981
Name changed to Carrols Corp. 07/22/1983
(See Carrols Corp.)

CARROT PATCH INC. (UT)
Name changed to White Oil Co., Inc. 06/01/1981
(See White Oil Co., Inc.)

CARRTONE LABORATORIES, INC. (DE)
Each share old Common 10¢ par exchanged for (0.33333333) share new Common 10¢ par 08/27/1958
New Common 10¢ par changed to 70¢ par 08/16/1965
Name changed to Century Laboratories, Inc. (DE) 09/08/1967
Century Laboratories, Inc. (DE) name changed to Vista Continental Corp. 07/12/2002 which name changed to Wolverine Holding Corp. 11/06/2009

CARRTONE LABORATORIES, INC. (LA)
Name changed to Century Laboratories, Inc. (LA) 08/28/1969
(See Century Laboratories, Inc. (LA))

CARRUS CAP CORP (BC)
Each share old Common no par exchanged for (1) share new Common no par to reflect a (1) for (500) reverse split followed by a (500) for (1) forward split 02/27/2012
Note: Holders of (499) or fewer pre-split shares will receive $0.08034 cash per share
Unexchanged certificates of holders entitled to cash were cancelled and became without value 02/27/2014
Each share new Common no par received distribution of (0.296) share Solutions4CO2 Inc. Common no par payable 03/30/2012 to holders of record 03/27/2012 Ex date - 03/23/2012
Each share new Common no par received distribution of (0.2) share BioAB Strategies Ltd. Common no par, (0.2) share BioDE Ventures Ltd. Common no par and (0.2) share BioHEP Technologies Ltd. Common no par payable 04/11/2014 to holders of record 04/11/2014 Ex date - 04/09/2014
Each share new Common no par (14575B 20 0) exchanged again for (0.14285714) share new Common no par 05/23/2014
Name changed to Global Blockchain Technologies Corp. 10/05/2017

CARRY WALKER INC (NV)
Name changed to Zuma Beach Entertainment, Inc. 07/22/2003

CARS-R-TRUCKS INC (NV)
Name changed to Consolidated Energy & Resources Inc. 11/13/1991
Consolidated Energy & Resources Inc. recapitalized as Hemkat Sports International Corp. 04/12/1994 which name changed to Market Basket Enterprises, Inc. 12/28/1995 which reorganized as J.T.'s Restaurants, Inc. 11/12/1996 which name changed to National Integrated Food Service Corp. 12/10/1998
(See National Integrated Food Service Corp.)

CARSCOR PORCUPINE GOLD MINES, LTD. (ON)
Charter revoked for failure to file reports and pay taxes 01/00/1958

CARS4U LTD (ON)
Name changed 01/30/2003
Name changed from Cars4u.com Ltd. to Cars4u Ltd. 01/30/2003

Each share old Common no par exchanged for (1) share new Common no par to reflect a (1) for (100) reverse split followed by a (100) for (1) forward split 02/23/2004
Note: Holders of (99) or fewer pre-split shares received $0.54 cash per share
Recapitalized as Chesswood Income Fund 05/10/2006
Each share new Common no par exchanged for (0.05455537) Trust Unit no par
Chesswood Income Fund reorganized as Chesswood Group Ltd. 01/04/2011

CARSHAW PORCUPINE GOLD MINES LTD. (ON)
Charter cancelled for failure to file reports and pay fees 08/09/1972

CARSO GLOBAL TELECOM S A DE C V (MEXICO)
Sponsored ADR's for Participation Ordinary split (4) for (1) by issuance of (3) additional ADR's payable 03/17/2000 to holders of record 03/09/2000
Sponsored ADR's for Participation Ordinary received distribution of (1) America Telecom S.A. de C.V. Sponsored ADR for Ordinary payable 05/07/2002 to holders of record 05/06/2002
ADR agreement terminated 09/15/2010
Each Sponsored ADR's for Participation Ordinary exchanged for $8.218971 cash

CARSON DEV CORP (WA)
Charter expired 10/31/2010

CARSON HILL GOLD MINING CORP. (NV)
Dissolved 00/00/1954
Details not available

CARSON INC (DE)
Merged into Cosmair Inc. 08/11/2000
Each share Class A Common 1¢ par exchanged for $5.20 cash

CARSON INDS CORP (WA)
Charter cancelled and proclaimed dissolved for failure to file reports 12/23/1996

CARSON INVT CO (NV)
Name changed to Carson Industries Corp. 04/26/2006

CARSON LABORATORIES, INC. (CT)
Adjudicated bankrupt 07/05/1974
Stockholders' equity unlikely

CARSON OIL & EXPL INC (WA)
Recapitalized as Carson Industries, Corp. 10/28/1985
Each share Common no par exchanged for (0.1) share Common no par
(See Carson Industries, Corp.)

CARSON PIRIE SCOTT & CO (IL)
Merged into Proffitt's, Inc. 01/31/1998
Each share Common 1¢ par exchanged for (1.75) shares Common 10¢ par
Proffitt's, Inc. merged into Saks Inc. 09/17/1998
(See Saks Inc.)

CARSON PIRIE SCOTT & CO NEW (DE)
Merged into Bergner (P.A.) & Co. Holding Co. 07/07/1989
Each share Common 1¢ par exchanged for $27.50 cash

CARSON PIRIE SCOTT & CO OLD (DE)
Reincorporated 12/04/1969
4.5% Preferred $100 par called for redemption 12/13/1965
4.25% Conv. Preferred $100 par called for redemption 12/29/1965
State of incorporation changed from (IL) to (DE) 12/04/1969
Common $5 par split (3) for (2) by issuance of (0.5) additional share 05/12/1978
Common $5 par split (2) for (1) by issuance of (1) additional share 06/24/1985
Merged into Greyhound Corp. 11/27/1987
Each share Common $5 par exchanged for $30.05 cash

CARSTAIRS BROTHERS DISTILLING CO. INC.
Acquired by Distillers Corp.-Seagrams Ltd. 00/00/1937
Details not available

CARSUNLIMITED COM INC (NV)
Recapitalized as Versadial, Inc. 03/02/2007
Each share Common $0.001 par exchanged for (0.02222222) share Common $0.0001 par

CARTA RES LTD (BC)
Name changed to Earthramp.com Communications Inc. (BC) 12/24/1999
Earthramp.com Communications Inc. (BC) reincorporated in Alberta 00/00/2001 which name changed to Champlain Resources Inc. 09/18/2007 which recapitalized as Beacon Resources Inc. 04/20/2012

CARTAN HLDGS INC (NV)
Name changed to Shiner International, Inc. 08/15/2007

CARTAWAY RES CORP (AB)
Name changed 04/24/1996
Name changed from Cartaway Container Corp. to Cartaway Resources Corp. 04/24/1996
Cease trade order effective 09/10/1999
Stockholders' equity unlikely

CARTE BLANCHE CORP (DE)
Merged into Avco Corp. 08/01/1975
Each share Class A $1 par exchanged for $0.25 cash

CARTEL ACQUISITIONS INC (CO)
Name changed to Helix Biomedix Inc. (CO) 06/11/1989
Helix Biomedix Inc. (CO) reincorporated in Delaware 12/29/2000

CARTER & CHURCHILL INC (MD)
Name changed to Profile Sports Corp. 07/27/1970
(See Profile Sports Corp.)

CARTER BLATCHFORD CORP. (DE)
Completely liquidated 12/15/1975
Each share Capital Stock $1 par exchanged for first and final distribution of $0.10 cash

CARTER (J.W.) CO. (DE)
Stock Dividend - 100% 03/24/1948
Merged into Blue Bell, Inc. (DE) 09/30/1967
Each share Capital Stock $1 par exchanged for (0.2) share Common $5 par
(See Blue Bell, Inc. (DE))

CARTER GROUP INC (DE)
Name changed to Utilities & Industries Corp. (DE) 11/20/1974
Each share Common 10¢ par exchanged for (1) share Common 10¢ par
(See Utilities & Industries Corp. (DE))

CARTER HAWLEY HALE STORES INC (DE)
Reincorporated 7/26/84
$2 Conv. Preferred Ser. A $5 par called for redemption 06/14/1984
State of incorporation changed from (CA) to (DE) 07/26/1984
Common $5 par changed to 1¢ par 08/27/1987
Each share Common 1¢ par received distribution of (1) share Neiman-Marcus Group, Inc. Common 1¢ par 09/10/1987
Note: An additional distribution of

stock and cash or $17 cash only was made 10/09/1987
Reorganized 10/09/1992
Each share old Common 1¢ par exchanged for (0.081) share new Common 1¢ par and (0.084) Common Stock Purchase Warrant expiring 10/09/1999
Name changed to Broadway Stores, Inc. 06/17/1994
Broadway Stores, Inc. merged into Federated Department Stores, Inc. 10/11/1995

CARTER JAMES B LTD (MB)
Through purchase offer 99% of Class A no par and 100% of Class B no par acquired by Budd Automotive Co. of Canada Ltd. as of 02/14/1974
Public interest eliminated

CARTER LAMBERT HLDGS INC (NV)
Name changed to Electronic Manufacturing Solutions & Services Inc. 12/01/2000
Electronic Manufacturing Solutions & Services Inc. name changed to Searchlight Solutions Ltd. 06/13/2003

CARTER MOTORS LTD. (ON)
Liquidated 00/00/1956
Details not available

CARTER (MARY) PAINT CO. (DE)
Common $1 par reclassified as Class B Common $1 par 01/06/1965
Name changed to Resorts International, Inc. 06/28/1968
(See Resorts International, Inc.)

CARTER PRODUCTS, INC. (MD)
Common $1 par split (3) for (1) by issuance of (2) additional shares 04/10/1964
Name changed to Carter-Wallace, Inc. (MD) 07/23/1965
Carter-Wallace, Inc. (MD) reincorporated in Delaware 11/29/1968
(See Carter-Wallace, Inc. (DE))

CARTER PRODUCTS CORP. (OH)
Name changed to Carlon Products Corp. 00/00/1950
(See Carlon Products Corp.)

CARTER WALLACE INC (DE)
Reincorporated 11/29/1968
State of incorporation changed from (MD) to (DE) 11/29/1968
Each share Common $1 par received distribution of (1) share Non-transferable Conv. Class B Common $1 par 10/27/1987
Common $1 par split (3) for (1) by issuance of (2) additional shares 05/06/1992
Non-transferable Conv. Class B Common $1 par split (3) for (1) by issuance of (2) additional shares 05/06/1992
Merged into MCC Acquisition Holdings Corp. 09/28/2001
Each share Common $1 par exchanged for $20.44 cash
Each share Non-transferable Conv. Class B Common $1 par exchanged for $20.44 cash

CARTER WILLIAM CO (MA)
1984 Voting Trust Agreement terminated and each VTC for Common 1948 Ser. $100 par exchanged for either (10) VTC's for Common 1968 Ser. $10 par or (10) shares Common $10 par at the certificate holders option 04/25/1968
Common $100 par changed to $10 par and (9) additional shares issued 05/03/1968
VTC's for Common 1968 Ser. $10 par and Common $10 par changed to $5 par and (1) additional share issued respectively 06/09/1972
Common $5 par split (2) for (1) by issuance of (1) additional share 05/14/1982

VTC's for Common 1968 Ser. $5 par split (2) for (1) by issuance of (1) additional certificate 05/14/1982
Common $5 par split (3) for (2) by issuance of (0.5) additional share 05/15/1984
Voting Trust Agreement terminated 04/25/1988
Each VTC for Common 1968 Ser. $5 par automatically became (1) share Common $5 par
Acquired by BW Acquisition Corp. 06/30/1988
Each share Common $5 par exchanged for $70 cash

CARTERET BANCORP INC (DE)
Acquired by Home Group, Inc. 08/08/1988
Each share Common 1¢ par exchanged for $19 cash
$2.25 Conv. Preferred Ser. 1, 1¢ par called for redemption 09/08/1988
Public interest eliminated

CARTERET SAVINGS & LOAN ASSOCIATION, F.A. (USA)
Stock Dividend - 15% 08/14/1985
Name changed to Carteret Savings Bank, F.A. (Morristown, NJ) 01/15/1986
Carteret Savings Bank, F.A. (Carteret, N.J.) reorganized in Delaware as Carteret Bancorp Inc. 08/17/1987
(See Carteret Bancorp Inc. (DE))

CARTERET SVGS BK F A (MORRISTOWN, NJ)
Reorganized under the laws of Delaware as Carteret Bancorp Inc. 08/17/1987
Each share $2.25 Conv. Preferred Ser. 1, 1¢ par exchanged for (1) share $2.25 Conv. Preferred Ser. 1, 1¢ par
Each share Common 1¢ par exchanged for (1) share Common 1¢ par
(See Carteret Bancorp Inc. (DE))

CARTERFONE COMMUNICATIONS CORP (MN)
Merged into Cable & Wireless North America, Inc. 09/20/1979
Each share Common 10¢ par exchanged for $7.52 cash

CARTESIAN INC (DE)
Acquired by Cartesian Holdings, LLC 06/28/2018
Each share Common $0.005 par exchanged for $0.40 cash

CARTHAGE CORP. (OH)
Liquidated 02/15/1956
Details not available

CARTHAGE MLS INC (OH)
Each share 8% Preferred $100 par exchanged for (1) share Class A 6% Preferred $100 par and (1) share Class B Preferred $40 par 00/00/1935
Each share old Common no par exchanged for (1) share new Common no par 00/00/1935
Each share new Common no par exchanged for (4) shares new Common no par 00/00/1946
New Common no par split (2) for (1) by issuance of (1) additional share 01/15/1960
Stock Dividend - 12% 01/18/1956
Merged into Springlawn, Inc. of Ohio 12/24/1973
Each share new Common no par exchanged for $15 cash

CARTHAGE PULP & BOARD CO., INC.
Acquired by bondholders committee 00/00/1934
No stockholders' equity

CARTHAGE SULPHITE PULP & PAPER CO.
Succeeded by Carthage Pulp & Board Co., Inc. 00/00/1926
Details not available

CARTIER-MALARTIC GOLD MINES LTD. (QC)
Acquired by Cartier Quebec Explorations Ltd. 09/23/1958
Each share Capital Stock $1 par exchanged for (0.2) share Capital Stock $1 par
Cartier Quebec Explorations Ltd. recapitalized as Cartier Resources Inc. 10/01/1980 which recapitalized as Rockabee Investments Inc. 09/20/1993 which recapitalized as Root Industries Inc. 12/31/1993 which name changed to Armstrong Corp. 01/26/1999
(See Armstrong Corp.)

CARTIER PARTNERS FINL GROUP INC (AB)
Merged into Dundee Wealth Management Inc. 12/30/2003
Each share Common no par exchanged for (0.021192) share Common no par and $0.54 cash
Dundee Wealth Management Inc. name changed to DundeeWealth Inc. 06/28/2007 which was acquired by Bank of Nova Scotia (Halifax, NS) 03/09/2011

CARTIER RES INC OLD (ON)
Recapitalized 10/01/1980
Capital Stock $1 par changed to no par 06/10/1971
Recapitalized from Cartier Quebec Explorations Ltd. to Cartier Resources Inc. 10/01/1980
Each share Capital Stock no par exchanged for (0.2) share Capital Stock no par
Capital Stock no par split (3) for (1) by issuance of (2) additional shares 02/05/1985
Recapitalized as Rockabee Investments Inc. 09/20/1993
Each share Common no par exchanged for (0.1) share Common no par
Rockabee Investments Inc. recapitalized as Root Industries Inc. 12/31/1993 which name changed to Armstrong Corp. 01/26/1999
(See Armstrong Corp.)

CARTRIDGE TELEVISION INC (DE)
Adjudicated bankrupt 10/31/1974
Stockholders' equity unlikely

CARTWRIGHT CAP LTD (AB)
Name changed to Acer Capital Corp. 05/20/1998

CARULLA VIVERO S A (COLOMBIA)
Name changed 06/12/2001
Name changed from Carulla & Cia S.A. to Carulla Vivero S.A. 06/12/2001
ADR agreement terminated 08/29/2007
Each 144A Sponsored ADR for Class A exchanged for $15.187642 cash

CARUSCAN CORP (ON)
6% Conv. Class A $5 par called for redemption 04/02/1981
Old Common no par reclassified as new Common no par 08/20/1981
Each share new Common no par received distribution of (1) share Class B no par 08/28/1981
New Common no par reclassified as Class A Subordinate no par 06/13/1983
Merged into Crownx Inc. 01/31/1986
Each share Class A Subordinate no par exchanged for (0.11111111) share Class A Non-Vtg. no par
Each share Class B no par exchanged for (0.11111111) share Class A Non-Vtg. no par
Note: U.S. shareholders received $2.40 cash per share in exchange for each share Class A Subordinate Vtg. no par and/or Class B no par
Crownx Inc. name changed to Extendicare Inc. 11/17/1994
(See Extendicare Inc.)

CARUSO FOODS INC (NY)
Each share Common 1¢ par exchanged for (0.33333333) share Common 3¢ par 08/30/1960
Name changed to Rite Industries Inc. 08/26/1971

CARV COM INC (CO)
Recapitalized 12/14/1998
Recapitalized from Carv Industries, Inc. to Carv.com, Inc. 12/14/1998
Each share Common $0.001 par exchanged for (0.04) share Common $0.001 par
Reincorporated under the laws of Nevada as PacificTradingPost.Com, Inc. 02/26/1999
PacificTradingPost.Com, Inc. recapitalized as IDC Technologies Inc. 11/23/2001 which name changed to Jill Kelly Productions Holding, Inc. 08/20/2003 which name changed to eWorldCompanies, Inc. 03/13/2007

CARVEL CORP (DE)
Through purchase offer over 99% reacquired by the company 00/00/1978
Public interest eliminated

CARVELLE CAP INC (AB)
Name changed to Lexoil Inc. 12/19/2002
Lexoil Inc. was acquired by Aquest Explorations Ltd. 11/21/2003 which recapitalized as Aquest Energy Ltd. 02/04/2004 which recapitalized as Anderson Energy Ltd. 09/01/2005 which name changed to Anderson Energy Inc. 01/27/2015 which name changed to InPlay Oil Corp. 11/10/2016

CARVER BANCORP INC (DE)
Conv. Preferred Ser. A 1¢ par called for redemption at $26.97 plus $0.65 accrued dividends on 10/15/2004
Conv. Preferred Ser. B 1¢ par called for redemption at $26.97 plus $0.65 accrued dividends on 10/15/2004
(Additional Information in Active)

CARVER CORP (DE)
Charter cancelled and declared inoperative and void for non-payment of taxes 04/15/1972

CARVER CORP (WA)
Old Common 1¢ par split (5) for (4) by issuance of (0.25) additional share 10/02/1985
Each share old Common 1¢ par exchanged for (0.01) share new Common 1¢ par 05/14/2007
Name changed to Hollund Industrial, Inc. 11/20/2007
Hollund Industrial, Inc. name changed to Hollund Industrial Marine, Inc. 08/18/2008

CARVER FED SVGS BK (NEW YORK, NY)
Under plan of reorganization each share Common 1¢ par automatically became (1) share Carver Bancorp Inc. (DE) Common 1¢ par 10/03/1996

CARWIN CO. (CT)
Acquired by Upjohn Co. (DE) 10/23/1962
Each share Common $2 par exchanged for (0.875) share Common $1 par
Upjohn Co. (DE) merged into Pharmacia & Upjohn Inc. 11/02/1995 which merged into Pharmacia Corp. 03/31/2000 which merged into Pfizer Corp. 04/16/2003

CARY CHEMICALS INC. (DE)
Merged into Tenneco Manufacturing Co. 04/12/1965
Each share Common 10¢ par exchanged for (0.1) share Common $5 par
(See Tenneco Manufacturing Co.)

CARY-TAYLOR CORP. (TX)
Adjudicated bankrupt 04/28/1965
No stockholders' equity

CASA BELLA IMPORTS INC (FL)
Proclaimed dissolved for failure to file reports and pay fees 11/04/1988

CASA DEL SOL CAP LTD (AB)
Name changed to Tiger-Cat Energy Ltd. 11/03/2005
Tiger-Cat Energy Ltd. merged into RMS Systems Inc. 09/29/2008 which merged into PHX Energy Services Corp. 12/02/2013

CASA ELECTRONICS CORP. (CA)
Company's plant and assets sold for federal taxes 00/00/1963
No stockholders' equity

CASA GRANDE ENERGY & MINES LTD (BC)
Name changed to Medical Polymers Technologies, Inc. 05/22/1992
Medical Polymers Technologies, Inc. recapitalized as U.S. Medical Systems, Inc. 12/19/1996 which recapitalized as Sharps Compliance Corp. 07/24/1998

CASA GRANDE MNG CO (CO)
Name changed to Datafusion Corp. 07/11/1984

CASA GRANDE RESOURCES, INC. (UT)
Name changed to MPA Associates, Inc. 02/03/1984
(See MPA Associates, Inc.)

CASA HAVANA INC (NV)
Name changed to Design Marketing Concepts, Inc. 12/09/2009
(See Design Marketing Concepts, Inc.)

CASA INTL CORP (DE)
Each share Common 10¢ par exchanged for (0.2) share Common 50¢ par 02/01/1960
Completely liquidated 07/01/1982
Each share Common 50¢ par exchanged for $0.95 cash

CASA MADERA GOLD MINING SYNDICATE, INC. (NV)
Charter revoked for failure to file reports and pay fees 03/02/1931

CASA MUNRAS HOTELS PARTNERS L P (CA)
Liquidation completed
Each Unit of Ltd. Partnership Int. received initial distribution of approximately $529.30 cash 03/09/2006
Each Unit of Ltd. Partnership Int. received second and final distribution of approximately $529 cash payable 06/30/2006 to holders of record 06/30/2006

CASA OLE RESTAURANTS INC (TX)
Name changed to Mexican Restaurants, Inc. 05/24/1999
(See Mexican Restaurants, Inc.)

CASABLANCA CAP CORP (AB)
Name changed to Purepoint Uranium Group Inc. 05/30/2005

CASABLANCA INDS INC (DE)
Common $1 par split (2) for (1) by issuance of (1) additional share 03/31/1983
Stock Dividend - 10% 01/24/1984
5% Preferred Initial Ser. $25 par called for redemption 05/05/1989
Acquired by Casablanca Holding Co. 06/02/1989
Each share Common $1 par exchanged for $11.125 cash

CASADECOMPUTERS COM INC (NV)
Charter revoked for failure to file reports and pay fees 03/31/2008

CASAKIRK GOLD MINES, LTD. (ON)
Charter cancelled and company declared dissolved for default in filing returns 05/27/1965

CASALE INDS INC (NJ)
Acquired by Casale Acquisition Corp. 07/28/1987
Each share Common 10¢ par exchanged for $22 cash

CASAMIRO RESOURCE CORP (BC)
Cease trade order effective 04/30/2002
Stockholders' equity unlikely

CASAU EXPL LTD (BC)
Struck off register and declared dissolved for failure to file returns 04/16/1992

CASAVAN INDUSTRIES INC. (NJ)
Charter revoked for failure to file reports and pay fees 02/05/1963

CASAVANT FRERES LTEE (QC)
Class B no par 100% acquired by Nadeau Corp. Ltd. at $1.50 per share through purchase offer which expired 11/18/1976
Acquired by Nadeau Corp. Ltd. 03/07/1977
Each share Class A no par exchanged for $3 cash

CASAVANT MNG KIMBERLITE INTL INC (NV)
Common $0.0001 par split (2) for (1) by issuance of (1) additional share payable 09/29/2003 to holders of record 09/12/2003 Ex date - 09/30/2003
Each share Common $0.0001 par received distribution of (1) share Casavant Mining International Corp. Restricted Common payable 10/03/2003 to holders of record 09/19/2003
Name changed to CMKM Diamonds Inc. 02/05/2004
(See CMKM Diamonds, Inc.)

CASCADE BANCORP (OR)
Old Common no par split (2) for (1) by issuance of (1) additional share payable 07/08/1997 to holders of record 07/01/1997
Old Common no par split (3) for (2) by issuance of (0.5) additional share payable 07/06/1998 to holders of record 06/29/1998
Old Common no par split (3) for (2) by issuance of (0.5) additional share payable 05/31/2002 to holders of record 05/24/2002 Ex date - 06/03/2002
Old Common no par split (5) for (4) by issuance of (0.25) additional share payable 04/09/2004 to holders of record 04/02/2004 Ex date - 04/12/2004
Old Common no par split (5) for (4) by issuance of (0.25) additional share payable 11/03/2006 to holders of record 10/27/2006 Ex date - 11/06/2006
Each share old Common no par exchanged for (0.1) share new Common no par 11/22/2010
Stock Dividends - 10% 07/31/1995; 10% payable 07/23/1996 to holders of record 07/15/1996; 10% payable 08/05/1999 to holders of record 07/29/1999; 20% payable 06/22/2001 to holders of record 06/15/2001
Merged into First Interstate BancSystem, Inc. 05/30/2017
Each share new Common no par exchanged for (0.14864) share Class A Common no par and $1.91 cash

CASCADE BUSINESS COLLEGES CORP (WA)
Chapter 11 Federal Bankruptcy Code converted to Chapter 7 on 02/09/1990
No stockholders' equity

CASCADE COACHING CORP (NV)
Common $0.00001 par split (9) for (1) by issuance of (8) additional shares payable 12/05/2007 to holders of record 12/03/2007 Ex date - 12/06/2007
Name changed to Empire Water Corp. 01/03/2008
(See Empire Water Corp.)

CASCADE COMMUNICATIONS CORP (DE)
Common $0.001 par split (2) for (1) by issuance of (1) additional share 06/06/1995
Common $0.001 par split (3) for (2) by issuance of (0.5) additional share payable 02/27/1996 to holders of record 02/12/1996
Common $0.001 par split (5) for (4) by issuance of (0.25) additional share payable 06/10/1996 to holders of record 05/31/1996
Merged into Ascend Communications, Inc. 06/30/1997
Each share Common $0.001 par exchanged for (0.7) share Common $0.001 par
Ascend Communications, Inc. merged into Lucent Technologies Inc. 06/24/1999 which merged into Alcatel-Lucent S.A. 11/30/2006

CASCADE CORP (OR)
Common 50¢ par split (4) for (1) by issuance of (3) additional shares 06/13/1986
Common 50¢ par split (2) for (1) by issuance of (1) additional share 06/14/1988
Common 50¢ par split (2) for (1) by issuance of (1) additional share 03/15/1995
Acquired by Toyota Industries Corp. 03/28/2013
Each share Common 50¢ par exchanged for $65 cash

CASCADE ENERGY INC (NV)
Old Common $0.001 par split (8) for (1) by issuance of (7) additional shares payable 05/06/2005 to holders of record 05/06/2005
Each share old Common $0.001 par exchanged for (0.04) share new Common $0.001 par 04/29/2015
Name changed to Cannabis Strategic Ventures 12/01/2017

CASCADE FERTILIZERS LTD (AB)
Each share Common no par exchanged for (1) share Class A no par and $0.01 cash 01/31/1990
Name changed to Verdant Valley Ventures Inc. 05/25/1990
Verdant Valley Ventures Inc. name changed to Biotechna Environmental Ltd. (AB) 09/13/1996 which reincorporated in British West Indies 05/08/1998 which recapitalized as Biotechna Environmental (2000) Corp. 05/12/2000

CASCADE FINL CORP (WA)
Reincorporated 05/12/2003
Common 1¢ par split (5) for (4) by issuance of (0.25) additional share 06/12/1995
State of incorporation changed from (DE) to (WA) 05/12/2003
Common 1¢ par split (5) for (4) by issuance of (0.25) additional share payable 12/19/2003 to holders of record 12/05/2003 Ex date - 12/22/2003
Common 1¢ par split (5) for (4) by issuance of (0.25) additional share payable 05/19/2006 to holders of record 05/05/2006 Ex date - 05/22/2006
Stock Dividends - 25% payable 06/10/1996 to holders of record 05/31/1996; 25% payable 06/27/1997 to holders of record 05/30/1997; 25% payable 06/19/1998 to holders of record 05/29/1998; 25% payable 06/25/1999 to holders of record 06/04/1999; 10% payable 10/31/2001 to holders of record 10/15/2001
Acquired by Opus Acquisition, Inc. 06/30/2011
Each share Common 1¢ par exchanged for $0.45 cash

CASCADE INDUSTRIES, INC. (OH)
Each share Common no par exchanged for (1) share Common $10 par 11/12/1973
Preferred $100 par called for redemption 09/30/1990
Completely liquidated 04/12/1991
Details not available

CASCADE INDS INC (NJ)
Plan of reorganization under Chapter 11 Federal Bankruptcy proceedings confirmed 02/25/1991
No stockholders' equity

CASCADE INTL INC (UT)
Name changed 07/31/1987
Name changed from Cascade Importers, Inc. to Cascade International, Inc. 07/31/1987
Chapter 11 bankruptcy proceedings converted to Chapter 7 on 02/14/1994
No stockholders' equity

CASCADE LODE MINES LTD. (BC)
Recapitalized as Trans-Ore Mines Ltd. 06/12/1962
Each share Capital Stock no par exchanged for (0.2) share Capital Stock no par
(See Trans-Ore Mines Ltd.)

CASCADE METALS INC (AB)
Reincorporated under the laws of Cayman Islands as American Gold Capital Corp. 10/16/2001
American Gold Capital Corp. merged into Chesapeake Gold Corp. 02/23/2007

CASCADE MICROTECH INC (OR)
Merged into FormFactor, Inc. 06/24/2016
Each share Common 1¢ par exchanged for (0.6534) share Common $0.001 par and $16 cash

CASCADE MINERALS INC (BC)
Name changed to Finavera Renewables Inc. 01/04/2007
Finavera Renewables Inc. recapitalized as Finavera Wind Energy Inc. 02/08/2011 which name changed to Finavera Solar Energy Inc. 07/03/2015 which name changed to Solar Alliance Energy Inc. 02/01/2016

CASCADE MOLYBDENUM MINES LTD (BC)
Name changed to New Cascade Minerals Ltd. 06/17/1975
(See New Cascade Minerals Ltd.)

CASCADE MTN MNG INC (NV)
Recapitalized as National Parking Systems, Inc. 01/07/2005
Each share Common $0.001 par exchanged for (0.00025) share Common $0.001 par
National Parking Systems, Inc. name changed to BioStem, Inc. 11/18/2005 which recapitalized as Joytoto USA, Inc. 10/31/2007 which recapitalized as Pollex, Inc. 10/24/2008 which name changed to eMARINE Global Inc. 09/12/2017

CASCADE NAT GAS CORP (WA)
Common no par changed to $1 par 04/00/1986
7.5% Conv. Jr. Preferred $25 par called for redemption 05/01/1985
Common $1 par split (3) for (2) by issuance of (0.5) additional share 12/20/1993
$0.55 Preferred Ser. A no par called for redemption 11/01/1995
$0.55 Preferred Ser. C no par called for redemption at $10 on 11/01/2000
Merged into MDU Resources Group, Inc. 07/02/2007
Each share Common $1 par exchanged for $26.50 cash

CASCADE OIL, LTD. (ON)
Charter revoked for failure to file reports and pay fees 08/03/1964

CASCADE OIL & GAS LTD (AB)
Name changed to Grey Wolf Exploration, Inc. (Old) 06/11/1998
Grey Wolf Exploration, Inc. (Old) acquired by Abraxas Petroleum Corp. 10/05/2001

CASCADE PAC RES LTD (ON)
Charter cancelled and proclaimed dissolved for failure to pay taxes and file returns 12/29/1986

CASCADE POOLS CORP. (NJ)
Name changed to Cascade Industries, Inc. (NJ) 01/13/1962
(See Cascade Industries, Inc. (NJ))

CASCADE RESEARCH CORP. (CA)
Name changed to Evergreen Western 10/23/1963
Evergreen Western merged into S.O. Systems, Inc. (CA) 11/27/1964 which was acquired by Kalvar Corp. (LA) 04/03/1968 which reincorporated in Delaware 11/12/1981
(See Kalvar Corp. (DE))

CASCADE SVGS BK FSB (EVERETT, WA)
Common $1 par split (5) for (4) by issuance of (0.25) additional share 11/22/1993
Common $1 par split (5) for (4) by issuance of (0.25) additional share 07/15/1994
Under plan of reorganization each share Common $1 par automatically became (1) share Cascade Financial Corp. Common 1¢ par 11/30/1994
Cascade Financial Corp. (DE) reincorporated in Washington 05/12/2003
(See Cascade Financial Corp. (WA))

CASCADE SLED DOG ADVENTURES INC (NV)
Name changed to Sunset Brands, Inc. 11/02/2004
Sunset Brands, Inc. name changed to Sunset Capital Assets, Inc. 02/02/2015

CASCADE SPRINGS LTD (NV)
Name changed to Colorado Gold Mines, Inc. 07/30/2012
Colorado Gold Mines, Inc. recapitalized as Buscar Oil, Inc. 07/18/2014 which name changed to Buscar Co. 06/15/2015

CASCADE STL ROLLING MLS (OR)
Stock Dividend - 10% 10/21/1983
Acquired by Schnitzer Steel Products Co. 10/08/1984
Each share Common no par exchanged for $12 cash

CASCADE TECHNOLOGY CORP (MI)
Assets acquired by Teltronics, Inc. 02/19/1999
Details not available

CASCADE WIND CORP (NV)
Name changed to XZERES Wind Corp. 05/17/2010
XZERES Wind Corp. name changed to XZERES Corp. 05/17/2011
(See XZERES Corp.)

CASCADES INC (QC)
Class A Preferred Ser. I no par called for redemption at $0.31849 on 09/01/1997
(Additional Information in Active)

CASCADES PAPERBOARD INTL INC (CANADA)
Name changed to Paperboard Industries International, Inc. 07/12/1996
Paperboard Industries International, Inc. merged into Cascades Inc. 12/31/2000

CASCADES PLYWOOD CORP. (DE)
Merged into United States Plywood Corp. 02/23/1962
Each share Common $1 par exchanged for (0.7) share Common $1 par
United States Plywood Corp. merged into U.S. Plywood-Champion Papers Inc. 02/28/1967 which name changed to Champion International Corp. 05/12/1972 which merged into International Paper Co. 06/20/2000

CASCADIA BRANDS INC (CANADA)
Merged into 3450163 Canada Inc. 08/12/1998
Each share Common no par exchanged for $8 cash

CASCADIA CAP CORP (NV)
Common $0.0001 par split (3.25) for (1) by issuance of (2.25) additional shares payable 02/18/2002 to holders of record 02/18/2002
Ex date - 02/26/2002
Name changed to Storage Alliance Inc. 11/18/2002
Storage Alliance Inc. recapitalized as ReBuilder Medical, Inc. 11/27/2006 which name changed to Pizza International, Inc. 12/14/2006 which name changed to Look Entertainment, Inc. 05/23/2007 which recapitalized as VTEC, Inc. 07/05/2007 which name changed to United Consortium, Ltd. (Old) 03/10/2008 which reorganized as United Consortium, Ltd. (New) 05/05/2010

CASCADIA CONSUMER ELECTRONICS CORP (BC)
Name changed to Cascadia Blockchain Group Corp. 09/10/2018

CASCADIA INTL RES INC (AB)
Reincorporated 02/27/2004
Each share old Common no par exchanged for (0.25) share new Common no par 04/19/2002
Each share new Common no par exchanged again for (0.5) share new Common no par 02/10/2003
Place of incorporation changed from (BC) to (AB) 02/27/2004
Recapitalized as Cascadia Resources Inc. 02/06/2009
Each share Common no par exchanged for (0.33333333) share Common no par
Cascadia Resources Inc. recapitalized as Kaymus Resources Inc. 07/31/2014

CASCADIA MINES & RES LTD (BC)
Recapitalized as Noble Metal Group Inc. 12/27/1989
Each share Common no par exchanged for (0.2) share Common no par

CASCADIA RESOURCES INC (AB)
Recapitalized as Kaymus Resources Inc. 07/31/2014
Each share Common no par exchanged for (0.2) share Common no par

CASCADIA RESOURCES LTD. (BC)
Name changed to Cascadia Mines & Resources Ltd. 11/24/1980
Cascadia Mines & Resources Ltd. recapitalized as Noble Metal Group Inc. 12/27/1989

CASCADIA TECHNOLOGIES LTD (BC)
Delisted from Vancouver Stock Exchange 03/02/1998

CASCADIAN THERAPEUTICS INC (DE)
Each share old Common $0.0001 par exchanged for (0.16666666) share new Common $0.0001 par 11/29/2016
Acquired by Seattle Genetics, Inc. 03/09/2018

Each share new Common $0.0001 par exchanged for $10 cash

CASCAL N V (NETHERLANDS)
97.66% acquired by Sembcorp Industries Ltd. at $6.75 cash per share through purchase offer which expired 08/09/2010
Note: Remaining holders received $10.13 cash per share through Dutch Court squeeze-out procedure 12/11/2012

CASCO BK & TR CO (PORTLAND, ME)
Capital Stock $25 par changed to $12.50 par and (1) additional share issued 02/26/1962
Stock Dividend - 11% 02/11/1970
99.97% acquired by Casco-Northern Corp. through exchange offer which expired 08/13/1972
Public interest eliminated

CASCO BAY LIGHT & POWER CO.
Name changed 00/00/1942
Name changed from Casco Bay Light & Water Co. to Casco Bay Light & Power Co. 00/00/1942
Acquired by Central Maine Power Co. 00/00/1964
Details not available

CASCO CHEMICAL CORP. (TX)
Charter revoked for non-payment of franchise taxes 06/14/1963

CASCO INTL INC (DE)
Merged into Davis Holdings of North Carolina, Inc. 12/28/2001
Each share Common 1¢ par exchanged for $2.10 cash

CASCO NORTHN CORP (ME)
$7 Conv. Preference no par called for redemption 06/30/1983
Merged into Bank of Boston Corp. 03/30/1984
Each share Common $10 par exchanged for (0.85) share Adjustable Rate Preferred Ser. A no par
Bank of Boston Corp. name changed to BankBoston Corp. 04/25/1997
(See BankBoston Corp.)

CASCO PRODUCTS CORP. (CT)
Stock Dividend - 200% 08/00/1946
Merged into S.K.O. Inc. 03/16/1961
Each share Common no par exchanged for $10.15 cash

CASDIM INTL SYS INC (DE)
Reincorporated 04/25/1997
State of incorporation changed from (CO) to (DE) and Common $0.00001 par changed to 1¢ par 04/25/1997
Each share old Common 1¢ par exchanged for (0.125) share new Common 1¢ par 06/30/1998
Charter cancelled and declared void for failure to pay franchise taxes 03/01/2000

CASE CLOTHES, INC.
Dissolved 00/00/1948
Details not available

CASE CORP (DE)
Name changed 06/24/1994
Name changed from Case Equipment Corp. to Case Corp. 06/24/1994
$4.50 Conv. Preferred Ser. A 1¢ par called for redemption at $51.3594 plus $0.734 accrued dividends or (2.2686) shares Common 07/06/1999
Merged into New Holland N.V. 11/12/1999
Each share Common 1¢ par exchanged for $55 cash

CASE ENERGY INC (UT)
Name changed to Environmental Services, Inc. (UT) 07/28/1987
Environmental Services, Inc. (UT) reincorporated in Delaware as Environmental Services of America, Inc. 07/25/1988

(See Environmental Services of America, Inc.)

CASE FINL INC (DE)
SEC revoked common stock registration 01/17/2014

CASE FOWLER LUMBER CO.
Liquidated 00/00/1935
Details not available

CASE-HOYT CORP. (NY)
Merged into Bell Canada Enterprises Inc. 05/30/1984
Each share Common $1 par exchanged for (0.844) share Common no par
Bell Canada Enterprises Inc. name changed to BCE Inc. 01/04/1988

CASE J I CO (WI)
Each share Common $100 par exchanged for (4) shares Common $25 par 00/00/1943
Each share Common $25 par exchanged for (2) shares Common $12.50 par 00/00/1952
Common $12.50 par changed to $1 par 04/20/1962
Recapitalized 02/19/1965
Each share 7% Preferred $100 par exchanged for $175 principal amount of 5.5% Subord. Debentures due 02/01/1990
Each share 6.5% 2nd Preferred $7 par exchanged for $9.35 principal amount of 5.5% Subord. Debentures due 02/01/1990
Stock Dividends - 10% 12/10/1948; 10% 12/08/1950
Acquired by Tenneco Inc. 08/04/1970
Each share $1.44 2nd Conv. Preferred Ser. A $1 par exchanged for (0.26) share $5.50 Conv. Preferred no par
Each share Common $1 par exchanged for (0.17) share $5.50 Conv. Preference no par
(See Tenneco Inc.)

CASE LOCKWOOD & BRAINARD CO.
Reorganized as Connecticut Printers, Inc. 00/00/1947
Each share Common $100 par exchanged for (10) shares Common $10 par
(See Connecticut Printers, Inc.)

CASE (J.I.) PLOW WORKS, INC.
Liquidated 00/00/1929
Details not available

CASE POMEROY & CO (DE)
Each share Common $5 par exchanged for (1) share Class A Common $5 par 04/03/1986
6% Preferred $10 par called for redemption at $10 on 01/03/2007
10% Preference $10 par called for redemption at $10 on 01/03/2007
Merged into CP Newco, Inc. 01/03/2007
Each share Class A Common $5 par exchanged for $1,855 cash
Each share Class B Common $5 par exchanged for $1,855 cash

CASE RES INC (AB)
Merged into Fairborne Energy Ltd. (Old) 07/29/2004
Each share Common no par exchanged for (0.0909) share Common no par
(See Fairborne Energy Ltd. (Old))

CASE (J.I.) THRESHING MACHINE CO.
Name changed to Case (J.I.) Co. 00/00/1929
Case (J.I.) Co. acquired by Tenneco Inc. 08/04/1970
(See Tenneco Inc.)

CASEY CONTAINER CORP (NV)
Name changed to Snoogoo Corp. 02/24/2015

CASEY JONES, INC.
Acquired by Blue Bell, Inc. (N.C.)
00/00/1944
Details not available

CASEY SUMMIT GOLD MINES LTD.
Acquired by Argosy Gold Mines Ltd.
00/00/1936
Each share Capital Stock exchanged for (0.226) share new Capital Stock
Argosy Gold Mines Ltd. assets transferred to Jason Mines Ltd. 00/00/1938 which recapitalized as New Jason Mines Ltd. 00/00/1948
(See New Jason Mines Ltd.)

CASGORAN MINES LTD. (ON)
Merged into Ver-Million Gold Placer Mining Ltd. share for share 09/27/1960
(See Ver-Million Gold Placer Mining Ltd.)

CASH AMER INTL INC (TX)
Name changed 04/21/1992
Name changed from Cash America Investments, Inc. to Cash America International, Inc. 04/21/1992
Each share Common 10¢ par received distribution of (0.915) share Enova International, Inc. Common $0.00001 par payable 11/13/2014 to holders of record 11/03/2014 Ex date - 11/13/2014
Merged into FirstCash, Inc. 09/02/2016
Each share Common 10¢ par exchanged for (0.84) share Common 1¢ par

CASH CAN INC (DE)
Plan of reorganization under Chapter 11 Federal Bankruptcy Code effective 03/29/2000
Stockholders' equity unlikely

CASH CDA GROUP LTD (AB)
Recapitalized 01/05/1996
Recapitalized from Cash Canada Pawn Corp. to Cash Canada Group Ltd. 01/05/1996
Each share Common no par exchanged for (0.25) share Common no par
Filed an Assignment for the Benefit of Creditors 12/29/2009
No stockholders' equity

CASH EQUIVALENT FD INC (MD)
Reincorporated under the laws of Massachusetts as Cash Equivalent Fund and Common $0.001 par reclassified as Shares of Bene. Int. no par 11/29/1985

CASH 4 PPTYS 247 (NV)
Common $0.0001 par split (10) for (1) by issuance (9) additional shares payable 01/31/2005 to holders of record 01/17/2005 Ex date - 02/01/2005
Name changed to Vegas Equity International Corp. 02/01/2006
(See Vegas Equity International Corp.)

CASH INDS INC (CO)
Chapter 11 bankruptcy proceedings converted to Chapter 7 on 04/03/1985
Stockholders' equity unlikely

CASH INVESTMENT CORP. (UT)
Recapitalized as Adanac Resources, Inc. 03/23/1981
Each share Common 1¢ par exchanged for (5) shares Common $0.002 par

CASH MGMT TR AMER (MA)
Merged into American Funds Money Market Fund 07/10/2009
Details not available

CASH MINERALS LTD (ON)
Reincorporated 06/07/2005
Place of incorporation changed from (BC) to (ON) 06/07/2005
Recapitalized as Pitchblack Resources Ltd. 06/25/2010
Each share Common no par exchanged for (0.05) share Common no par
Pitchblack Resources Ltd. recapitalized as Troilus Gold Corp. 01/03/2018

CASH NOW CORP (NV)
Name changed to Esprit Financial Group, Inc. 04/13/2007
Esprit Financial Group, Inc. recapitalized as Monarc Corp. 02/13/2008 which recapitalized as Flexpower, Inc. 05/12/2014

CASH RES LTD (BC)
Recapitalized as Cash Minerals Ltd. (BC) 05/07/2001
Each share Common no par exchanged for (0.2) share Common no par
Cash Minerals Ltd. (BC) reincorporated in Ontario 06/07/2005 which recapitalized as Pitchblack Resources Ltd. 06/25/2010 which recapitalized as Troilus Gold Corp. 01/03/2018

CASH RESV MGMT INC (MD)
Merged into Shearson Lehman Daily Dividend Inc. 12/02/1988
Details not available

CASH SYS INC (DE)
Merged into Global Cash Access Holdings, Inc. 08/08/2008
Each share Common $0.001 par exchanged for $0.50 cash

CASH TECHNOLOGIES INC (DE)
SEC revoked common stock registration 10/18/2013

CASHAY CORP.
Out of business 00/00/1941
Details not available

CASHBUILDER INC (CO)
Each share old Common no par exchanged for (0.1) share new Common no par 03/07/1998
Each share new Common no par exchanged again for (0.01) share new Common no par 11/20/1995
Name changed to Fanatics Only, Inc. 02/28/1996
(See Fanatics Only, Inc.)

CASHCAN CORP (OH)
Charter forfeited for failure to maintain a registered agent 08/26/1991

CASHCO VENTURE CAP CORP (NV)
Name changed 04/12/2001
Each share old Common $0.001 par exchanged for (0.04) share new Common $0.001 par 03/16/2001
Name changed from Cashco Management, Inc. to Cashco Venture Capital Corp. 04/12/2001
Name changed to GrowthLogic, Inc. 06/11/2001
GrowthLogic, Inc. name changed to Sunburst Alliance, Inc. 01/25/2005
(See Sunburst Alliance, Inc.)

CASHMAN FARRELL VALUE FD INC (DE)
Name changed to Capstone Cashman Farrell Value Fund, Inc. 07/31/1992
(See Capstone Cashman Farrell Value Fund, Inc.)

CASHMERE VY BK WASH OLD (CASHMERE, WA)
Under plan of reorganization each share Common no par automatically became (2) shares Cashmere Valley Financial Corp. Common no par 04/01/2005
Cashmere Valley Financial Corp. reorganized as Cashmere Valley Bank (Cashmere, WA) (New) 06/28/2013

CASHMERE VY FINL CORP (WA)
Under plan of reorganization each share Common no par automatically became (1) share Cashmere Valley Bank (Cashmere, WA) (New)
Common no par 06/28/2013

CASHTEK CORP (DE)
Chapter 11 Federal Bankruptcy proceedings terminated 01/31/2001
No stockholders' equity

CASINO & CR SVCS INC (DE)
Merged into Hospitality Franchise Systems, Inc. 05/11/1995
Each share Common $0.001 par exchanged for (0.294) share Common 1¢ par
Hospitality Franchise Systems, Inc. name changed to HFS Inc. 08/31/1995 which merged into Cendant Corp. 12/17/1997 which reorganized as Avis Budget Group, Inc. 09/01/2006

CASINO AIRLINK INC (NV)
Recapitalized as Cotton & Western Mining, Inc. 02/14/2006
Each share Common 10¢ par exchanged for (0.01333333) share Common 10¢ par

CASINO AMER INC (DE)
Common 1¢ par split (3) for (2) by issuance of (0.5) additional share 06/04/1993
Common 1¢ par split (3) for (2) by issuance of (0.5) additional share 04/19/1994
Name changed to Isle of Capri Casinos, Inc. 10/01/1998
(See Isle of Capri Casinos, Inc.)

CASINO ANTIQUES LTD (DE)
Name changed to TecFin Corp. 04/01/1983

CASINO CO. OF SPRING LAKE, NEW JERSEY (NJ)
In process of liquidation
Each share Capital Stock $50 par exchanged for initial distribution of $250 cash 12/31/1976
Note: Details on subsequent distributions, if any, are not available

CASINO CRUISES CORP
United States District Court, Los Angeles found 00/00/1998 stock was sold in fraudulent scheme
No stockholders' equity

CASINO DATA SYS (NV)
Common no par split (3) for (2) by issuance of (0.5) additional share 10/11/1995
Common no par split (3) for (2) by issuance of (0.5) additional share payable 02/27/1996 to holders of record 02/20/1996
Merged into Aristocrat Leisure Ltd. 07/02/2001
Each share Common no par exchanged for $9.25 cash

CASINO ENTMT TELEVISION INC (DE)
Reorganized as Ouvo, Inc. 05/06/2005
Each share Common $0.0001 par exchanged for (16) shares Common $0.0001 par
Ouvo, Inc. reorganized as Trustcash Holdings, Inc. 06/13/2007

CASINO GAMING SYS INC (MT)
Recapitalized as Allison Industries, Ltd. 10/07/1982
Each share Common 1¢ par exchanged for (0.33333333) share Common 1¢ par
(See Allison Industries, Ltd.)

CASINO IN THE MTNS CORP (NY)
Reincorporated under the laws of Delaware as Liberty Resources Inc. 09/16/1982
Liberty Resources Inc. name changed to Bristol-Sterling Financial Corp. 10/05/1988
(See Bristol-Sterling Financial Corp.)

CASINO JOURNAL PUBG GROUP INC (NV)
Each share old Common $0.001 par received distribution of (0.33333333) share Gaming Venture Corp. U.S.A. Common $0.001 par payable 04/30/2003 to holders of record 04/01/2003 Ex date - 03/28/2003
Each share old Common $0.001 par exchanged for (0.33333333) share new Common $0.001 par 04/01/2004
Recapitalized as TableMAX Corp. 08/19/2008
Each share Common $0.001 par exchanged for (0.16201047) share Common $0.001 par

CASINO MAGIC CORP (MN)
Common 1¢ par split (3) for (1) by issuance of (2) additional shares 06/18/1993
Merged into Hollywood Park, Inc. (New) 10/15/1998
Each share Common 1¢ par exchanged for $2.27 cash

CASINO PIRATA COM LTD (NV)
Name changed to Advantage Technologies, Inc. 11/30/1999
Advantage Technologies, Inc. recapitalized as Expo Holdings Inc. 05/30/2006

CASINO PLAYERS & TRAVEL INTL INC (NV)
Charter permanently revoked 11/01/2010

CASINO PLAYERS INC (NV)
Name changed to Medytox Solutions, Inc. 10/27/2011
Medytox Solutions, Inc. merged into Rennova Health, Inc. 11/03/2015

CASINO RESOURCE CORP (MN)
Each share old Common 1¢ par exchanged for (0.5) share new Common 1¢ par 06/25/1993
Name changed to BounceBackTechnologies.com, Inc. (MN) 01/14/2000
BounceBackTechnologies.com, Inc. (MN) reincorporated in Delaware as Name Dynamics, Inc. 11/05/2010 which name changed to UBL Interactive, Inc. 07/03/2012

CASINO SILVER MINES LTD (BC)
Merged into Pacific Sentinel Gold Corp. 03/04/1993
Each share Common no par exchanged for (0.75) share Common no par and (0.75) Common Stock Purchase Warrant expiring 05/31/1993
Pacific Sentinel Gold Corp. merged into Great Basin Gold Ltd. 12/18/1997
(See Great Basin Gold Ltd.)

CASINO SPORTS VENTURES INC (UT)
Proclaimed dissolved for failure to file annual reports 12/31/1986

CASINO SYS INC (UT)
Name changed to Black Beaver, Inc. and Common 1¢ par changed to $0.005 par 01/02/1981
Black Beaver, Inc. merged into Nevaco Systems, Inc. 10/09/1982

CASINO TECHNOLOGY CORP (DE)
Name changed to Currency Technology Corp. 08/01/1983
(See Currency Technology Corp.)

CASINOBUILDERS COM INC (NV)
Each share old Common $0.001 par exchanged for (0.004) share new Common $0.001 par 04/17/2001
Name changed to Proxity Digital Networks Inc. 10/31/2001
Proxity Digital Networks Inc. name changed to Proxity, Inc. 01/14/2005 which recapitalized as CAVU Resources Inc. 05/06/2009

CASINOS INTL INC (CO)
Name changed to Classic Restaurants International Inc. (CO) 09/29/1995

Classic Restaurants International Inc. (CO) reincorporated in Georgia 04/10/1998 which recapitalized as Creative Recycling Technologies Inc. 04/30/1998 which name changed to Ingen Technologies, Inc. 11/01/2004

CASINOS OF THE WORLD INC (NV)
Name changed to Clean Way Corp. 04/16/1993
Clean Way Corp. name changed to Trader Secrets.com 09/10/1999 which name changed to Voip Technology Inc. 03/13/2000 which recapitalized as Oxford Ventures Inc. 01/30/2002 which recapitalized as ULURU Inc. 04/05/2006

CASINOVATIONS INC (NV)
Name changed to CVI Technology, Inc. 05/02/2000
CVI Technology, Inc. name changed to VendingData Corp. 07/24/2000 which name changed to Elixir Gaming Technologies, Inc. 09/12/2007 which name changed to Entertainment Gaming Asia Inc. 07/26/2010
(See Entertainment Gaming Asia Inc.)

CASITA ENTERPRISES INC (NV)
Name changed to Envision Solar International, Inc. 04/30/2010

CASMONT INDUSTRIES LTD. (CANADA)
Voluntarily dissolved 05/31/1959
Details not available

CASMYN CORP (CO)
Stock Dividends - 2% payable 06/30/1999 to holders of record 06/30/1999; 2% payable 09/30/1999 to holders of record 09/30/1999
Reorganized under the laws of Nevada as Aries Ventures Inc. 04/11/2000
Each share 1st Conv. Preferred 4¢ par exchanged for (5.27) shares Common 1¢ par
Each share Common 4¢ par exchanged for (0.002) share Common 1¢ par
Note: Holders of (49,999) or fewer pre-split shares received $1 cash per share
Note: Unexchanged certificates were cancelled and became without value 04/10/2001
Aries Ventures Inc. (NV) reincorporated in Delaware as Cardium Therapeutics, Inc. 01/23/2006 which name changed to Taxus Cardium Pharmaceuticals Group, Inc. 10/07/2014

CASON GOLD MINES LTD.
Name changed to Coulee Lead & Zinc Mines Ltd. 00/00/1949
Coulee Lead & Zinc Mines Ltd. merged into Wayfair Explorations Ltd. 11/00/1980
(See Wayfair Explorations Ltd.)

CASON WINDSOR EQUITY GROUP INC (DE)
Charter cancelled and declared inoperative and void for non-payment of taxes 12/29/1991

CASPEN OIL INC (NV)
Charter revoked for failure to file reports and pay taxes 04/30/2012

CASPER NATIONAL BANK (CASPER, WY)
Each share Common $100 par exchanged for (5) shares Common $20 par 01/17/1952
Stock Dividend - 12.5% 02/25/1954
Name changed to First National Bank (Casper, WY) 12/02/1957
First National Bank (Casper, WY) merged into Western Bancorporation 07/01/1980 which name changed to First Interstate Bancorp 06/01/1981 which merged into Wells Fargo & Co. (Old) 04/01/1996 which merged into Wells Fargo & Co. (New) 11/02/1998

CASPERS TIN PLATE CO (IL)
Each share Common $100 par exchanged for (80) shares Common $1 par 00/00/1950
Through purchase offer over 99.7% acquired by Ball Corp. as of 00/00/1964
Public interest eliminated

CASPIAN ENERGY INC (BC)
Reincorporated 02/25/2015
Each share old Common no par exchanged for (0.1) share new Common no par 02/21/2014
Place of incorporation changed from (ON) to (BC) 02/25/2015
Each share new Common no par exchanged again for (0.00000001) share new Common no par 09/26/2018
Notes: Holders of (44,999,999) or fewer pre-split shares received $0.01 cash per share
Unexchanged certificates will be cancelled and become without value 09/26/2024

CASPIAN ENERGY INTL INC (NV)
Each (11) shares old Common 1¢ par exchanged for (1) share new Common 1¢ par 03/09/2007
Reincorporated under the laws of Delaware as Cardiac Network, Inc. 05/09/2007

CASPIAN MINERALS PLC (KAZAKHSTAN)
Name changed to Exillon Energy PLC 10/09/2009

CASPIAN OIL TOOLS LTD (BERMUDA)
Cease trade order effective 03/26/2001

CASPIAN RES LTD (BC)
Cease trade order effective 07/10/1981
Stockholders' equity unlikely

CASS BK & TR CO (ST. LOUIS, MO)
Capital Stock $20 par changed to $10 par and (1) additional share issued 01/08/1963
Stock Dividends - 100% 01/18/1966; 100% 07/31/1981; 100% 09/15/1981
Reorganized as Cass Commercial Corp. 03/07/1983
Each share Capital Stock $10 par exchanged for (1) share Common $10 par
Cass Commerical Corp. name changed to Cass Information Systems, Inc. 01/30/2001

CASS COML CORP (MO)
Common $10 par split (2) for (1) by issuance of (1) additional share 10/14/1983
Common $10 par changed to $2.50 par 05/00/1989
Common $2.50 par split (4) for (1) by issuance of (3) additional shares 06/01/1989
Common $2.50 par changed to 50¢ par 04/00/1996
Common 50¢ par split (2) for (1) by issuance of (1) additional share payable 03/15/1997 to holders of record 03/05/1997
Name changed to Cass Information Systems, Inc. 01/30/2001

CASS M L PETE CORP (AB)
Reincorporated 09/22/1994
Place of incorporation changed from (BC) to (AB) 09/22/1994
Delisted from Toronto Stock Exchange 09/14/2001

CASSANDRA RES INC (BC)
Recapitalized as Consolidated Cassandra Resources Inc. (BC) 06/29/1993
Each share Common no par exchanged for (0.33333333) share Common no par
Consolidated Cassandra Resources Inc. (BC) reincorporated in Yukon Territory as Bolivar Goldfields Ltd. 09/27/1993 which name changed to Storage @ccess Technologies Inc. 02/09/2001 which recapitalized as BluePoint Data Storage, Inc. 01/31/2003 which name changed to BluePoint Data, Inc. 07/27/2009
(See BluePoint Data, Inc.)

CASSCO CAP CORP NEW (DE)
Each share Common $0.0001 par exchanged for (0.01428571) share Common $0.00333 par 11/26/1999
Recapitalized as Diversified Technology Group Inc. (DE) 06/23/2000
Each share Common $0.00333 par exchanged for (0.02) share Common $0.001 par
Diversified Technology Group Inc. (DE) reincorporated in Nevada 10/04/2000 which reorganized as Diversified Technologies Group Inc. 11/14/2000 which name changed to X-Change Corp. 07/30/2001 which name changed to Endocan Corp. 11/06/2013

CASSCO CAP CORP OLD (DE)
Name changed to International K.C. Jakes BBQ & Grill, Inc. 07/20/1992
International K.C. Jakes BBQ & Grill, Inc. name changed to Cassco Capital Corp. (New) 07/18/1994 which recapitalized as Diversified Technology Inc. 06/23/2000 which name changed to Diversified Technologies Group, Inc. 11/14/2000 which name changed to X-Change Corp. 07/30/2001 which name changed to Endocan Corp. 11/06/2013

CASSCO CORP (VA)
Each share Capital Stock $1 par exchanged for (0.01) share Capital Stock $100 par 07/15/1969
Last date to exchange Capital Stock $1 par was 07/15/1971 after which shareholder rights were forfeited
Each share Capital Stock $100 par exchanged for (0.1) share Capital Stock $1,000 par 07/20/1972
Last date to exchange Capital Stock $100 par was 07/20/1974 after which shareholder rights were forfeited
Acquired by WLR Foods, Inc. 04/12/1990
Details not available
(See WLR Foods, Inc.)

CASSETE MINES LTD. (ON)
Merged into Summit Explorations & Holdings Ltd. 09/19/1969
Each share Capital Stock no par exchanged for (0.1) share Capital Stock no par
Summit Explorations & Holdings Ltd. name changed to Summit Diversified Ltd. 03/03/1972 which merged into Sumtra Diversfied Inc. 08/30/1978

CASSETTE CARTRIDGE CORP (DE)
Adjudicated bankrupt 02/14/1973
Stockholders' equity unlikely

CASSETTE ED SYS CORP (DE)
Reincorporated under the laws of Nevada as Genatron, Inc. 01/12/1987
(See Genatron, Inc.)

CASSETTE MAGNETICS CORP (NY)
Dissolved by proclamation 12/20/1977

CASSETTE SCIENCES CORP (DE)
Charter cancelled and declared inoperative and void for non-payment of taxes 03/01/1974

CASSIA PETE CORP (BC)
Struck off register and declared dissolved for failure to file returns 09/09/1988

CASSIAR ASBESTOS CORP. LTD. (CANADA)
Name changed to Cassiar Resources Ltd. 08/25/1980
(See Cassiar Resources Ltd.)

CASSIAR CONS MINES LTD (BC)
Recapitalized as Pacific Cassiar Mines Ltd. 10/22/1976
Each share Capital Stock 50¢ par exchanged for (0.2) share Capital Stock no par
Pacific Cassiar Mines Ltd. name changed to Pacific Cassiar Ltd. 11/20/1978
(See Pacific Cassiar Ltd.)

CASSIAR COPPERFIELDS LTD. (BC)
Struck off register and declared dissolved for failure to file reports and pay fees 09/24/1970

CASSIAR MAGNESIUM INC (ON)
Name changed 04/25/2000
Name changed from Cassiar Mines & Metals, Inc. to Cassiar Magnesium Inc. 04/25/2000
Name changed to Cassiar Resources Inc. 07/25/2001
Cassiar Resources Inc. name changed to Troutline Investments Inc. (ON) 06/30/2003 which reorganized in Alberta as Innova Exploration Ltd. 04/16/2004
(See Innova Exploration Ltd.)

CASSIAR MNG CORP (CANADA)
Merged into Princeton Mining Corp. 12/14/1989
Each share Common no par exchanged for (1) share Common no par
(See Princeton Mining Corp.)

CASSIAR RAINBOW GOLD MINES LTD. (ON)
Charter cancelled 04/30/1962

CASSIAR RES INC (ON)
Name changed to Troutline Investments Inc. (ON) 06/30/2003
Troutline Investments Inc. (ON) reorganized in Alberta as Innova Exploration Ltd. 04/16/2004
(See Innova Exploration Ltd.)

CASSIAR RES LTD (CANADA)
Acquired by 96130 Canada Ltd. 12/22/1980
Each share Capital Stock no par exchanged for $16.15 cash

CASSIAR YUKON GOLD MINES, LTD. (BC)
Struck off the British Columbia register and dissolved by default 12/01/1960

CASSIDY GOLD CORP (BC)
Each share old Common no par exchanged for (0.33333333) share new Common no par 09/22/2009
Each share new Common no par exchanged again for (0.00000016) share new Common no par 06/20/2017
Notes: In effect holders received $0.005 cash per share and public interest was eliminated
No distribution will be made to holders entitled to receive less than $1 cash
Unexchanged certificates will be cancelled and become without value 06/20/2019

CASSIDY MEDIA INC (NV)
Common $0.0001 par changed to $0.00001 par and (27.5) additional shares issued payable 05/22/2007 to holders of record 05/08/2007
Ex date - 05/23/2007
Name changed to RussOil Corp. 05/23/2007
(See RussOil Corp.)

CASSIDY RES LTD (BC)
Recapitalized as Massif Minerals Corp. 11/03/1989
Each share Common no par

exchanged for (0.5) share Common no par
Massif Minerals Corp. recapitalized as World Wide Oil & Gas Inc. 06/25/1991
(See World Wide Oil & Gas Inc.)

CASSIDY VENTURES INC (NV)
Common $0.001 par split (20) for (1) by issuance of (19) additional shares payable 03/18/2013 to holders of record 03/18/2013
Ex date - 03/19/2013
Recapitalized as Lash, Inc. 02/14/2017
Each share Common $0.001 par exchanged for (0.01428571) share Common $0.001 par
Lash, Inc. name changed to Artisan Consumer Goods, Inc. 05/09/2018

CASSIDY YELLOWKNIFE MINES, LTD. (ON)
Charter cancelled for failure to pay taxes and file returns 11/06/1979

CASSIDY'S LTD. (CANADA)
Acquired by Caradsco Ltd. 00/00/1952
Each share Common exchanged for $12.25 cash

CASSIDYS LTD (QC)
Each share 6% Preferred $100 par exchanged for (15) shares Capital Stock no par 06/04/1965
Each share Common $1 par exchanged for (18) shares Capital Stock no par 06/04/1965
Capital Stock no par reclassified as Common no par 05/14/1969
Common no par split (2) for (1) by issuance of (1) additional share 06/02/1969
Common no par split (2) for (1) by issuance of (1) additional share 12/29/1986
Placed in receivership 12/20/1999
No stockholders' equity

CASTAGNA ELECTRS CORP (DE)
Reincorporated 06/28/1968
State of incorporation changed from (NY) to (DE) 06/28/1968
Charter cancelled and declared inoperative and void for non-payment of taxes 03/01/1975

CASTALIA BKG CO (OH)
Merged into Citizens Interim Bank (Sandusky, OH) 05/01/1990
Each share Common $12.50 par exchanged for $172.93 cash

CASTECH ALUM GROUP INC (DE)
Merged into Commonwealth Aluminum Corp. 09/20/1996
Each share Common 1¢ par exchanged for $20.50 cash

CASTELLE (CA)
Merged into Captaris, Inc. 07/11/2007
Each share Common no par exchanged for $4.14 cash

CASTELLO CASINO CORP (ON)
Name changed 01/21/1993
Reincorporated 10/16/1995
Recapitalized 03/10/1997
Name changed from Castello Resources Ltd. to Castello Business Systems Ltd. 01/21/1993
Place of incorporation changed from (BC) to (ONT) 10/16/1995
Recapitalized from Castello Business Systems Ltd. to Castello Casino Corp. 03/10/1997
Each share Common no par exchanged for (0.25) share Common no par
Recapitalized as BioForest Pacific Inc. 01/12/2001
Each (14) shares Common no par exchanged for (1) share Common no par
BioForest Pacific Inc. recapitalized as Byron Resources Inc. 04/15/2003 which recapitalized as Byron Global Corp. 08/11/2004 which

recapitalized as Byron Americor Inc. 07/30/2007 which name changed to Ungava Mines Inc. 10/12/2007

CASTER MOBILHOMES CORP (CA)
Name changed to Mission Park Corp. 12/31/1973
(See Mission Park Corp.)

CASTILLIAN RES CORP (ON)
Reincorporated 05/10/2006
Common no par split (2) for (1) by issuance of (1) additional share payable 12/31/2003 to holders of record 12/19/2003
Place of incorporation changed from (BC) to (ON) 05/10/2006
Each share old Common no par exchanged for (0.2) share new Common no par 02/19/2013
Name changed to Coastal Gold Corp. 06/28/2013
Coastal Gold Corp. merged into First Mining Finance Corp. 07/10/2015 which name changed to First Mining Gold Corp. 01/11/2018

CASTILLO INC (DE)
Reincorporated 10/08/2009
State of incorporation changed from (NV) to (DE) 10/08/2009
Name changed to TechniScan, Inc. 10/19/2009

CASTLE & COOKE, LTD. (HI)
Each share Common $100 par exchanged for (5) shares Common $20 par 00/00/1944
Common $20 par changed to $10 par and (1) additional share issued 10/07/1957
Under plan of merger name changed to Castle & Cooke, Inc. (Old) and (0.5) share Capital Stock $10 par distributed 05/29/1958
Castle & Cooke, Inc. (Old) name changed to Dole Food Co., Inc. (HI) 07/30/1991 which reincorporated in Delaware 07/01/2001
(See Dole Food Co., Inc. (Old) (DE))

CASTLE & COOKE HOMES INC (HI)
Merged into Dole Acquisition Corp. 01/03/1995
Each share Common no par exchanged for $15.75 cash

CASTLE & COOKE INC NEW (HI)
Merged into Flexi-Van Leasing, Inc. 09/06/2000
Each share Common no par exchanged for $19.25 cash

CASTLE & COOKE INC OLD (HI)
Capital Stock $10 par split (3) for (2) by issuance of (0.5) additional share 03/01/1966
Capital Stock $10 par reclassified as Common $10 par 08/09/1966
Common $10 par split (2) for (1) by issuance of (1) additional share 11/01/1968
Common $10 par changed to no par 05/04/1979
$6.60 Conv. Preferred Ser. A no par called for redemption 08/20/1986
$12.50 Conv. Exchangeable Preferred no par called for redemption 08/22/1986
$12.50 Depositary Receipts called for redemption 08/22/1986
90¢ Conv. Preferred no par called for redemption 09/15/1988
Stock Dividends - 10% 04/30/1965; 10% 02/28/1975; 10% 03/08/1976; 10% 03/14/1977; 10% 03/13/1978; 10% 03/19/1979; In 90¢ Conv. Preferred to to holders of Common - 11.1% 07/22/1985
Name changed to Dole Food Co., Inc. (HI) 07/30/1991
Dole Food Co., Inc. (HI) reincorporated in Delaware 07/01/2001
(See Dole Food Co., Inc. (Old) (DE))

CASTLE & MORGAN HLDGS INC (DE)
Each share old Common $0.0001 par

exchanged for (0.33333333) share new Common $0.0001 par 04/13/2006
Name changed to Osteologix, Inc. (DE) 06/05/2006
Osteologix, Inc. (DE) reincorporated in Ireland as Osteologix Holdings PLC 07/28/2011

CASTLE A M & CO (DE)
Reincorporated 04/26/1967
Each share old Capital Stock $10 par exchanged for (2) shares new Capital Stock $10 par 00/00/1937
State of incorporation changed from (IL) to (DE) 04/26/1967
Common $10 par changed to $5 par and (1) additional share issued 11/25/1974
Common $5 par changed to no par 04/30/1982
Common no par split (5) for (4) by issuance of (0.25) additional share 06/29/1984
Common no par split (5) for (4) by issuance of (0.25) additional share 06/10/1988
Common no par split (3) for (2) by issuance of (0.5) additional share 05/24/1989
Common no par split (3) for (2) by issuance of (0.5) additional share 08/26/1994
Stock Dividends - 100% 11/24/1950; 20% 06/29/1978; 20% 06/04/1979; 20% 06/30/1980; 20% 06/29/1981; 20% 06/28/1985
Reincorporated under the laws of Maryland and Common no par changed to 1¢ par 06/05/2001

CASTLE BANCGROUP INC (DE)
Common 33¢ par split (2) for (1) by issuance of (1) additional share payable 05/20/1999 to holders of record 05/10/1999
Merged into First National of Illinois, Inc. 02/01/2002
Each share Common 33¢ par exchanged for $18 cash

CASTLE BAY ENTERPRISES LTD (BC)
Recapitalized as Radiant Communications Corp. 05/14/2002
Each share Common no par exchanged for (0.05555555) share Common no par
(See Radiant Communications Corp.)

CASTLE BRANDS INC (DE)
Reincorporated under the laws of Florida 02/09/2010

CASTLE CAP CORP (NY)
Merged into Penn-Dixie Industries, Inc. 12/18/1979
Each share Common 10¢ par exchanged for $1.75 cash

CASTLE CAP CORP NEW (AB)
Recapitalized as Hewlyn Corp. 06/12/1989
Each share Common no par exchanged for (0.28571428) share Common no par
(See Hewlyn Corp.)

CASTLE CAP INC (ON)
Reorganized under the laws of Nova Scotia as EnerVision Inc. 08/12/1998
Each share Common no par exchanged for (0.25) share Common no par
EnerVision Inc. name changed to Helical Corp. Inc. 09/29/2004

CASTLE DENTAL CTRS INC (DE)
Common $0.001 par changed to $0.000001 par 01/29/2003
Merged into Bright Now! Dental, Inc. 06/14/2004
Each share Common $0.000001 par exchanged for $0.1572 cash

CASTLE ENERGY CORP (DE)
Each share Common 5¢ par

exchanged for (0.1) share Common 50¢ par 06/01/1987
Each share old Common 50¢ par exchanged for (0.5) share new Common 50¢ par 11/12/1993
New Common 50¢ par split (3) for (1) by issuance of (2) additional shares payable 01/31/2000 to holders of record 01/12/2000
Merged into Delta Petroleum Corp. 05/01/2006
Each share new Common 50¢ par exchanged for (1.16388662) shares Common 1¢ par
(See Delta Petroleum Corp.)

CASTLE ENTMT INC (CA)
Merged into Malibu Grand Prix Corp. 04/13/1984
Each share Common no par exchanged for (1) share Common 1¢ par
(See Malibu Grand Prix Corp.)

CASTLE GOLD CORP (CANADA)
Acquired by Argonaut Gold Inc. 01/20/2010
Each share Common no par exchanged for $1.29 cash

CASTLE GROUP INC (DE)
Charter cancelled and declared inoperative and void for non-payment of taxes 06/25/1987

CASTLE HLDG CORP (NV)
Common $0.0025 par split (2) for (1) by issuance of (1) additional share payable 12/28/1998 to holders of record 12/22/1998
Common $0.0025 par split (4) for (1) by issuance of (3) additional shares payable 06/25/1999 to holders of record 06/18/1999
Each share Common $0.0025 par received distribution of (1) share Castle Advisors, Inc. Restricted Common payable 11/17/2014 to holders of record 11/10/2014
Name changed to Enerkon Solar International, Inc. 11/03/2017

CASTLE INDS INC (TX)
Plan of reorganization under Chapter 11 Federal Bankruptcy proceedings confirmed 11/25/1987
No stockholders' equity

CASTLE METALS CORP (BC)
Recapitalized as Castillian Resources Corp. (BC) 07/29/2002
Each share Common no par exchanged for (0.1) share Common no par
Castillian Resources Corp. (BC) reincorporated in Ontario 05/10/2006 which name changed to Coastal Gold Corp. 06/28/2013 which merged into First Mining Finance Corp. 07/10/2015 which name changed to First Mining Gold Corp. 01/11/2018

CASTLE MINERALS INC (BC)
Recapitalized as Castle Rock Exploration Corp. 01/27/1995
Each share Common no par exchanged for (0.5) share Common no par
Castle Rock Exploration Corp. recapitalized as Castle Metals Corp. 08/24/1998 which recapitalized as Castillian Resources Corp. (BC) 07/29/2002 which reincorporated in Ontario 05/10/2006 which name changed to Coastal Gold Corp. 06/28/2013 which merged into First Mining Finance Corp. 07/10/2015 which name changed to First Mining Gold Corp. 01/11/2018

CASTLE MTN MNG CO (ON)
Name changed to NewCastle Gold Ltd. 06/30/2015
NewCastle Gold Ltd. merged into Equinox Gold Corp. 12/22/2017

CASTLE OIL & GAS LTD (AB)
Each share old Capital Stock no par

exchanged for (0.00002) share new Capital Stock no par 12/09/1983
Note: In effect holders received $5.143 cash per share and public interest was eliminated
For holdings of (50,000) shares or more option to receive stock expired 02/28/1984

CASTLE RES INC (ON)
Reincorporated 08/12/2011
Place of incorporation changed from (AB) to (ON) 08/12/2011
Each share old Common no par exchanged for (0.33333333) share new Common no par 10/20/2015
Each share new Common no par exchanged again for (0.1) share new Common no par 07/08/2016
Each (7,721,166) shares new Common no par exchanged again for (1) share new Common no par 01/05/2018
Notes: In effect holders received $0.20 cash per share and public interest was eliminated
No distribution will be made to holders entitled to less than $10
Unexchanged certificates will be cancelled and become without value 01/05/2021

CASTLE ROCK EXPL CORP (BC)
Recapitalized as Castle Metals Corp. 08/24/1998
Each share Common no par exchanged for (0.2) share Common no par
Castle Metals Corp. recapitalized as Castillian Resources Corp. (BC) 07/29/2002 which reincorporated in Ontario 05/10/2006 which name changed to Coastal Gold Corp. 06/28/2013 which merged into First Mining Finance Corp. 07/10/2015 which name changed to First Mining Gold Corp. 01/11/2018

CASTLE ROCK PETE LTD (AB)
Merged into Arrow Energy Ltd. 10/04/2007
Each share Class A no par exchanged for (0.2) share Common no par
Each share Class B no par exchanged for (2) shares Common no par
Arrow Energy Ltd. recapitalized as Kallisto Energy Corp. 11/02/2009 which name changed to Toro Oil & Gas Ltd. 11/25/2014
(See Toro Oil & Gas Ltd.)

CASTLE SILVER RES INC (CANADA)
Name changed to Canada Cobalt Works Inc. 02/23/2018

CASTLE TECHNOLOGIES INC (WY)
Each share old Common $0.001 par exchanged for (0.01) share new Common $0.001 par 09/12/2008
Recapitalized as Hawaiian Hospitality Group, Inc. 08/14/2009
Each share Common $0.001 par exchanged for (0.005) share Common $0.001 par

CASTLE TIN MINES LTD. (ON)
Merged into Pacific Asbestos Ltd. 06/24/1968
Each share Common $1 par exchanged for (0.452684) share Capital Stock no par
Pacific Asbestos Ltd. name changed to Woodsreef Minerals Ltd. 07/26/1972 which recapitalized as Transpacific Asbestos, Inc. 04/30/1981 which name changed to Transpacific Resources Inc. 09/06/1984
(See Transpacific Resources Inc.)

CASTLE-TRETHEWEY MINES, LTD. (ON)
Assets sold to McIntyre Porcupine Mines Ltd. 12/16/1959
Each share Capital Stock $1 par exchanged for (0.01282) share Common $5 par and $4.93 cash
McIntyre Porcupine Mines Ltd. name changed to McIntyre Mines Ltd. 05/31/1974 which merged into Falconbridge Ltd. 01/24/1989
(See Falconbridge Ltd.)

CASTLE U S CORP (VA)
Charter dissolved 00/00/1990

CASTLE VENTURES CORP (FL)
Name changed to Admar Group Inc. 09/29/1986
(See Admar Group Inc.)

CASTLE VIEW EQUINE CTR INC (CA)
Charter suspended for failure to file reports and pay fees 02/01/1990

CASTLEBAR SILVER & COBALT MINES LTD (ON)
Merged into Canhorn Mining Corp. 01/09/1986
Each share Common $1 par exchanged for (0.03039513) share Common no par
Canhorn Mining Corp. merged into Canhorn Chemical Corp. 04/26/1995 which merged into Nayarit Gold Inc. 05/02/2005 which merged into Capital Gold Corp. 08/02/2010 which merged into Gammon Gold Inc. (QC) 04/08/2011 which reincorporated in Ontario as AuRico Gold Inc. 06/14/2011 which merged into Alamos Gold Inc. (New) 07/06/2015

CASTLEGUARD ENERGY INC (FL)
SEC revoked common stock registration 11/02/2010

CASTLEPOINT HLDGS LTD (BERMUDA)
Merged into Tower Group, Inc. 02/05/2009
Each share Common 1¢ par exchanged for (0.47) share Common 1¢ par and $1.83 cash
Tower Group, Inc. merged into Tower Group International, Ltd. 03/14/2013
(See Tower Group International, Ltd.)

CASTLEROCK CAP INC (AB)
Name changed to CastleRock Resources Inc. 03/14/2003
CastleRock Resources Inc. recapitalized as Andina Minerals Inc. 12/31/2004
(See Andina Minerals Inc.)

CASTLEROCK RES INC (AB)
Recapitalized as Andina Minerals Inc. 12/31/2004
Each share Common no par exchanged for (0.2) share Common no par
(See Andina Minerals Inc.)

CASTLESTAR CAP DEVS CORP (ON)
Recapitalized as Southern Frontier Resources Inc. 11/11/1993
Each share Common no par exchanged for (0.2) share Common no par
(See Southern Frontier Resources Inc.)

CASTLETON INDS INC (DE)
Merged into Racing Corp. of America 05/31/1978
Each share Common $1 par exchanged for $4.25 cash

CASTLETON INVS CORP (FL)
Name changed to Southern Gourmet Products, Inc. 01/11/1990
(See Southern Gourmet Products, Inc.)

CASTLEWOOD INTL CORP (FL)
Name changed to Big Daddy's Lounges, Inc. 01/26/1976
Big Daddy's Lounges, Inc. name changed to Flanigan's Enterprises Inc. 01/03/1978

CASTLEWORTH VENTURES INC (BC)
Name changed to Pan-Nevada Gold Corp. 01/20/2006
Pan-Nevada Gold Corp. merged into Midway Gold Corp. 04/13/2007
(See Midway Gold Corp.)

CASTMOR RES LTD (NV)
Each share old Common $0.0001 par exchanged for (0.2) share new Common $0.0001 par 09/17/2010
Name changed to Red Giant Entertainment, Inc. (NV) 07/19/2012
Red Giant Entertainment, Inc. (NV) reincorporated in Florida 03/06/2017

CASTPRO COM INC (NV)
Each share old Common $0.001 par exchanged for (3) shares new Common $0.001 par 07/21/2000
Name changed to Thaon Communications, Inc. 11/27/2000
Thaon Communications, Inc. recapitalized as PracticeXpert, Inc. 07/21/2003
(See PracticeXpert, Inc.)

CASTWELL PRECAST CORP (NV)
Recapitalized as Summer Energy Holdings, Inc. 03/28/2012
Each share Common $0.001 par exchanged for (0.25) share Common $0.001 par

CASTYPE CORP OF AMERICA (DE)
Charter cancelled and declared inoperative and void for non-payment of taxes 00/00/1941

CASUAL MALE CORP (DE)
Plan of reorganization under Chapter 11 Federal Bankruptcy proceedings confirmed 02/02/1991
Holders had option to elect to receive: (A) A pro rata share of 10% of the consolidated net earnings of TCM Apparel, Inc. for seven fiscal years beginning 02/03/1991 and ending 01/30/1998, the aggregate payment not to exceed $5,000,000 or (B) $0.25 cash per share subject to a maximum payment of $1,000 regardless of the number of shares held
Note: Option to elect to receive (A) expired 03/12/1991
Unexchanged certificates were cancelled and became without value 02/03/1996

CASUAL MALE CORP (MA)
Plan of reorganization under Chapter 11 Federal Bankruptcy Code effective 12/10/2003
No stockholders' equity

CASUAL MALE RETAIL GROUP INC (NV)
Old Common 1¢ par reclassified as new Common 1¢ par 08/27/2009
Name changed to Destination XL Group, Inc. 02/25/2013

CASUALTY INS CO (IL)
Reorganized under the laws of Nevada as CIC Financial Corp. 08/31/1969
Each share Common $3 par exchanged for (1) share Common $1 par
(See CIC Financial Corp.)

CASURINA PERFORMANCE FD (ON)
Name changed to Front Street Performance Fund 07/30/2004
Front Street Performance Fund merged into Front Street Performance Fund II 09/01/2006 which merged into Front Street Mutual Funds Ltd. 03/02/2009

CASWAN ENVIRONMENTAL SVCS INC (AB)
Cease trade order effective 04/23/2002
Stockholders' equity unlikely

CASYNDEKAN INC (CO)
Adjudicated bankrupt 03/13/1973
Stockholders' equity unknown

CAT LAKE MINES LTD (ON)
Merged into Fundy Chemical International Ltd. 03/16/1973
Each share Common no par exchanged for (0.307692) share Common no par
(See Fundy Chemical International Ltd.)

CATACA RES INC (NV)
Name changed to Flitways Technology Inc. 11/10/2016

CATADYNE CORP (FL)
Each share old Common no par exchanged for (0.001) share new Common no par 08/26/1997
Each share new Common no par exchanged again for (0.2) share new Common no par 02/27/2004
Name changed to Northeast Auto Acceptance Corp. (FL) 03/19/2004
Northeast Auto Acceptance Corp. (FL) reincorporated in Nevada as Northeast Automotive Holdings, Inc. 03/10/2008 which name changed to Kogeto, Inc. 03/11/2014
(See Kogeto, Inc.)

CATALIN CORP. (DE)
Acquired by Ashland Oil & Refining Co. 02/03/1966
Each share Capital Stock $1 par exchanged for (0.13333333) share $2.40 Conv. Preferred no par
Ashland Oil & Refining Co. name changed to Ashland Oil, Inc. 02/02/1970 which name changed to Ashland Inc. (Old) 01/27/1995
(See Ashland Inc. (Old))

CATALIN CORP. OF AMERICA (DE)
Capital Stock no par changed to $1 par 00/00/1932
$1.20 Preferred $1 par called for redemption 02/16/1959
Name changed to Catalin Corp. 04/16/1965
Catalin Corp. acquired by Ashland Oil & Refining Co. 02/03/1966 which name changed to Ashland Oil, Inc. 02/02/1970 which name changed to Ashland Inc. (Old) 01/27/1995
(See Ashland Inc. (Old))

CATALINA CAP CORP (DE)
Name changed to Instant Video Technologies Inc. 08/19/1992
Instant Video Technologies Inc. name changed to Burst.com, Inc. 01/27/2000 which name changed to Democrasoft, Inc. 04/27/2010 which name changed to Democrasoft Holdings, Inc. 04/22/2013

CATALINA CAP CORP (NV)
Name changed to Ad-Care, Inc. 11/19/1987
Ad-Care, Inc. name changed to Care Visions Corp. 01/08/1990
(See Care Visions Corp.)

CATALINA ENERGY & RES LTD (BC)
Name changed to Alaska Apollo Gold Mines Ltd. 12/14/1981
Alaska Apollo Gold Mines Ltd. recapitalized as Alaska Apollo Resources Inc. 10/14/1992 which recapitalized as Daugherty Resources, Inc. 06/29/1998 which name changed to NGAS Resources Inc. 07/05/2004 which merged into Magnum Hunter Resources Corp. 04/13/2011
(See Magnum Hunter Resources Corp.)

CATALINA ENERGY CORP (BC)
Each share old Common no par exchanged for (0.5) share new Common no par 11/13/2007
Recapitalized as Catalina Metals Corp. 02/14/2011
Each share new Common no par exchanged for (0.33333333) share Common no par
Catalina Metals Corp. name changed

to True Grit Resources Ltd. 06/28/2012

CATALINA LTG INC (FL)
Each share old Common 1¢ par exchanged for (0.2) share new Common 1¢ par 04/08/2002
Assets sold for the benefit of creditors 04/13/2010
No stockholders' equity

CATALINA MARKETING CORP (DE)
Common 1¢ par split (2) for (1) by issuance of (1) additional share payable 07/15/1996 to holders of record 06/24/1996 Ex date - 07/16/1996
Common 1¢ par split (3) for (1) by issuance of (2) additional shares payable 08/17/2000 to holders of record 07/26/2000 Ex date - 08/18/2000
Merged into Checkout Holding Corp. 10/01/2007
Each share Common 1¢ par exchanged for $32.50 cash

CATALINA METALS CORP (BC)
Name changed to True Grit Resources Ltd. 06/28/2012

CATALINA SVGS & LN ASSN (AZ)
Under plan of acquisition each share Perm. Res. Guarantee $1 par exchanged for $25.94 cash 03/24/1981

CATALYST COMMUNICATIONS CORP (UT)
Recapitalized as ComCentral Corp. 07/16/1991
Each share Common $0.001 par exchanged for (0.05) share Common $0.001 par
ComCentral Corp. name changed to Tianrong Building Material Holdings, Ltd. 08/21/1995
(See Tianrong Building Material Holdings, Ltd.)

CATALYST COMMUNICATIONS INC (UT)
Each share Common $0.001 par received distribution of (0.1) share Global Resources Group, Inc. Common payable 05/21/1998 to holders of record 03/09/1998
Name changed to DNAPrint Genomics, Inc. 07/07/2000
(See DNAPrint Genomics, Inc.)

CATALYST COPPER CORP (BC)
Each share old Common no par exchanged for (0.1) share new Common no par 12/31/2013
Each share new Common no par exchanged again for (0.33333333) share new Common no par 06/06/2014
Merged into NewCastle Gold Ltd. 05/27/2016
Each share new Common no par exchanged for (1) share Common no par
Note: Unexchanged certificates will be cancelled and become without value 05/26/2019
NewCastle Gold Ltd. merged into Equinox Gold Corp. 12/22/2017

CATALYST ENERGY CORP (LA)
Name changed 05/08/1987
Reincorporated 12/23/1987
Stock Dividend - 20% 01/03/1986
Name changed from Catalyst Energy Development Corp. to Catalyst Energy Corp. 05/08/1987
State of incorporation changed from (DE) to (LA) 12/23/1987
Merged into Merrimac Corp. 11/15/1988
Each share Common 10¢ par exchanged for $11.25 cash

CATALYST ENERGY SVCS INC (DE)
Merged into CDI Holdings Inc. 05/23/1997
Each share Common 1¢ par exchanged for $0.70 cash

Starstream Communications Group, Inc.

CATALYST EQUITY CORP (NM)
Merged out of existence 02/22/1999
Details not available

CATALYST HEALTH SOLUTIONS INC (DE)
Merged into SXC Health Solutions Corp. 07/03/2012
Each share Common 1¢ par exchanged for (0.6606) share Common no par and $28 cash
SXC Health Solutions Corp. name changed to Catamaran Corp. 07/11/2012
(See Catamaran Corp.)

CATALYST INTL INC (DE)
Merged into ComVest Investment Partners II LLC 09/09/2004
Each share Common 10¢ par exchanged for $2.50 cash

CATALYST LTG GROUP INC (DE)
Each share Common 1¢ par exchanged for (0.1) share Common $0.0001 par 09/25/2007
Name changed to Phototron Holdings, Inc. 03/09/2011
Phototron Holdings, Inc. name changed to Growlife, Inc. 08/08/2012

CATALYST MEDIA GROUP PLC (UNITED KINGDOM)
ADR agreement terminated 02/21/2008
No ADR's remain outstanding

CATALYST PAPER CORP NEW (CANADA)
Shares reacquired 01/25/2017
Each share Common no par exchanged for $0.50 cash

CATALYST PAPER CORP OLD (CANADA)
Plan of reorganization under Companies' Creditors Arrangement Act effective 09/13/2012
No stockholders' equity

CATALYST PHARMACEUTICAL PARTNERS INC (DE)
Name changed to Catalyst Pharmaceuticals, Inc. 05/29/2015

CATALYST RESH CORP (MD)
Merged into Mine Safety Appliances Co. 03/01/1974
Each share Common 32¢ par exchanged for $1 cash

CATALYST RESOURCE GROUP INC (FL)
SEC revoked common stock registration 04/05/2016

CATALYST SEMICONDUCTOR INC (DE)
Merged into ON Semiconductor Corp. 10/10/2008
Each share Common $0.001 par exchanged for (0.706) share Common 1¢ par

CATALYST THERMAL ENERGY CORP (DE)
Name changed to United Thermal Corp. 04/01/1990
(See United Thermal Corp.)

CATALYST VENTURES CORP (BC)
Recapitalized as International Catalyst Ventures Inc. (BC) 02/23/2000
Each share Common no par exchanged for (0.16666666) share Common no par
International Catalyst Ventures Inc. (BC) reincorporated in Yukon 09/08/2000 which recapitalized as Aberdeen International Inc. 11/23/2001 which reincorporated in Ontario 07/04/2006

CATALYST VENTURES INC (FL)
Name changed to WorldVest, Inc. 07/23/2009

WorldVest, Inc. name changed to Iron Mining Group, Inc. 11/10/2010
(See Iron Mining Group, Inc.)

CATALYSTS & CHEMICALS, INC. (DE)
Name changed to United Catalysts Inc. 11/28/1977

CATALYTIC SOLUTIONS INC (CA)
Merged into Clean Diesel Technologies, Inc. 10/18/2010
Each share Common no par exchanged for (0.007888) share new Common 1¢ par and (1) Common Stock Purchase Warrant expiring 10/13/2013
Clean Diesel Technologies, Inc. name changed to CDTi Advanced Materials, Inc. 03/15/2018

CATALYTICA ENERGY SYS INC (DE)
Merged into Renegy Holdings, Inc. 10/01/2007
Each share Common $0.0005 par exchanged for (0.14285714) share Common $0.001 par
(See Renegy Holdings, Inc.)

CATALYTICA INC (DE)
Common $0.001 par received distribution of (0.16547) share Catalyst Energy Systems, Inc. Common $0.0005 par payable 12/15/2000 to holders of record 12/15/2000 Ex date - 12/18/2000
Merged into DSM N.V. 12/15/2000
Each share Common $0.001 par exchanged for $10.141 cash

CATAMARAN CORP (YT)
Common no par split (2) for (1) by issuance of (1) additional share payable 10/01/2012 to holders of record 09/20/2012 Ex date - 10/02/2012
Acquired by UnitedHealth Group Inc. 07/27/2015
Each share Common no par exchanged for USD$61.50 cash

CATANIA BROS FOODS INC (DE)
Name changed to Joedot Holdings, Inc. 12/10/1993
(See Joedot Holdings, Inc.)

CATAPULT COMMUNICATIONS CORP (NV)
Acquired by Ixia 06/23/2009
Each share Common $0.001 par exchanged for $9.25 cash

CATAPULT ENERGY LTD PARTNERSHIP I (AB)
Completely liquidated
Each Unit of Ltd. Partnership received first and final distribution of $4.76 cash payable 03/31/2008 to holders of record 03/31/2008

CATARACT MINING CORP. (AZ)
Reorganized under the laws of Nevada as Alaska International Corp. 10/19/1959
Each share Common 5¢ par exchanged for (0.1) share Common 3¢ par
Alaska International Corp. recapitalized as C/W Industries Group, Inc. 03/29/1978
(See C/W Industries Group, Inc.)

CATARACT URANIUM MINING & EXPLORATION CORP. (AZ)
Name changed to Cataract Mining Corp. (AZ) 05/28/1956
Cataract Mining Corp. (AZ) reorganized in Nevada as Alaska International Corp. 10/19/1959 which recapitalized as C/W Industries Group, Inc. 03/29/1978
(See C/W Industries Group, Inc.)

CATARAQUI GOLD MINES, LTD. (ON)
Charter revoked for failure to file reports and pay taxes 00/00/1950

CATAWBA VY BANCSHARES INC (NC)
Stock Dividends - 10% payable 11/22/1999 to holders of record 11/01/1999; 10% payable 03/15/2001 to holders of record 02/28/2001
Under plan of merger name changed to United Community Bancorp 01/03/2002
United Community Bancorp name changed to Integrity Financial Corp. 05/30/2003 which merged into FNB United Corp. 04/28/2006 which name changed to CommunityOne Bancorp 07/01/2013

CATAWBA VY BK (HICKORY, NC)
Common $5 par split (6) for (5) by issuance of (0.2) additional share payable 12/01/1997 to holders of record 11/01/1997
Common $5 par split (5) for (4) by issuance of (0.25) additional share payable 08/28/1998 to holders of record 08/14/1998
Under plan of reorganization each share Common $5 par automatically became (1) share Catawba Valley Bancshares, Inc. Common $1 par 07/01/1999
Catawba Valley Bancshares, Inc. name changed to United Community Bancorp 01/03/2002 which name changed to Integrity Financial Corp. 05/30/2003 which merged into FNB United Corp. 04/28/2006 which name changed to CommunityOne Bancorp 07/01/2013

CATAWISSA RAILROAD CO. (PA)
Merged into Reading Co. 06/30/1953
Each share 5% Preferred $50 par exchanged for (1) share 4% 1st Preferred $50 par
Each share Common $50 par exchanged for (0.03333333) share Common $50 par
Reading Co. merged into Reading Entertainment Inc. (DE) 10/15/1996 which reincorporated in Nevada 12/29/1999 which merged into Reading International, Inc. 12/31/2001

CATCH A RISING STAR INC (DE)
Chapter 11 bankruptcy proceedings converted to Chapter 7 on 11/26/1993
Stockholders' equity unlikely

CATCH BY GENE (NV)
Charter revoked for failure to file reports and pay taxes 07/31/2012

CATCH THE WIND LTD (CAYMAN ISLANDS)
Recapitalized as BlueScout Technologies Ltd. 11/07/2012
Each share Common USD $0.0001 par exchanged for (0.05) share Common USD $0.0001 par

CATCH THE WIND LTD (DE)
Reincorporated under the laws of Cayman Islands 06/28/2010
Catch the Wind Ltd. (Cayman Islands) recapitalized as BlueScout Technologies Ltd. 11/07/2012
(See BlueScout Technologies Ltd.)

CATCHER HLDGS INC (DE)
SEC revoked common stock registration 02/22/2012

CATEAR RES LTD (BC)
Struck from the register and dissolved 04/08/1994

CATEGORY 5 TECHNOLOGIES INC (NV)
Merged into Avalon Digital Marketing Systems, Inc. 10/01/2002
Each share Common $0.001 par exchanged for (0.23) share Common $0.0001 par and (0.5) Common Stock Purchase Warrant

CATELLUS DEV CORP NEW (DE)
Merged into ProLogis 09/15/2005
Each share Common 1¢ par exchanged for $33.81 cash

CATELLUS DEV CORP OLD (DE)
$3.75 Conv. Preferred Ser. A 1¢ par called for redemption at $52.25 on 05/01/1997
$3.625 144A Conv. Exchangeable Preferred Ser. B 1¢ par called for redemption at $52.5375 plus $0.4933 accrued dividends on 06/19/1997
Reorganized as Catellus Development Corp. (New) 12/01/2003
Each share Common 1¢ par exchanged for (1) share Common 1¢ par
(See Catellus Development Corp. (New))

CATER BARNARD PLC (UNITED KINGDOM)
ADR agreement terminated 08/09/2007
No ADR's remain outstanding

CATER ENERGY INC (BC)
Recapitalized as Houston Metals Corp. 10/27/1986
Each share Common no par exchanged for (0.5) share Common no par
Houston Metals Corp. recapitalized as Pacific Houston Resources, Inc. 03/30/1989
(See Pacific Houston Resources, Inc.)

CATERPILLAR TRACTOR CO. (CA)
Each share Common $25 par exchanged for (5) shares Common no par 00/00/1926
Each share Common no par exchanged for (2) shares Common $10 par 00/00/1949
Common $10 par split (2) for (1) by issuance of (1) additional share 05/16/1955
Common $10 par changed to no par and (2) additional shares issued 09/11/1959
4.2% Preferred $100 par called for redemption 11/09/1962
Common no par split (2) for (1) by issuance of (1) additional share 07/03/1964
Common no par split (3) for (2) by issuance of (0.5) additional share 07/23/1976
Reincorporated under the laws of Delaware as Caterpillar Inc. and Common no par changed to $1 par 05/22/1986

CATHAY BANCORP INC (DE)
Common 1¢ par split (6) for (5) by issuance of (0.2) additional share 05/15/1992
Common 1¢ par split (2) for (1) by issuance of (1) additional share payable 05/09/2002 to holders of record 04/19/2002 Ex date - 05/10/2002
Under plan of merger name changed to Cathay General Bancorp 10/20/2003

CATHAY BK (LOS ANGELES, CA)
Common $10 par changed to $5 par and (1) additional share issued 08/01/1973
Common $5 par changed to no par 05/18/1982
Common no par split (5) for (1) by issuance of (4) additional shares 07/29/1983
Common no par split (6) for (5) by issuance of (0.2) additional share 01/31/1990
Stock Dividends - 10% 09/25/1987; 10% 09/12/1988
Reorganized under the laws of Delaware as Cathay Bancorp Inc. and Common no par changed to 1¢ par 12/10/1990
Cathay Bancorp Inc. name changed to Cathay General Bancorp 10/20/2003

CATHAY FST PRODS CORP (CANADA)
Dissolved for non-compliance 07/22/2018

CATHAY INTL HLDGS INC (ID)
Recapitalized as Cyber Operations Inc. 11/21/2006
Each share Common 1¢ par exchanged for (0.11781615) share Common 1¢ par

CATHAY MERCHANT GROUP INC (DE)
Name changed to Mansfelder Metals Ltd. 02/21/2008

CATHAY OVERSEAS INC (AB)
Delisted from Alberta Stock Exchange 05/05/1998

CATHAYONE INC (DE)
Chapter 11 bankruptcy proceedings converted to Chapter 7 on 03/13/2002
Stockholders' equity unlikely

CATHEDRAL ENERGY SVC INCOME TR (AB)
Reorganized as Cathedral Energy Services Ltd. (New) 12/18/2009
Each Trust Unit exchanged for (1) share Common no par
Note: Unexchanged certificates were cancelled and became without value 12/18/2015

CATHEDRAL ENERGY SVCS LTD OLD (AB)
Recapitalized as Cathedral Energy Service Income Trust 07/30/2002
Each share Common no par exchanged for (1) Trust Unit no par
Cathedral Energy Service Income Trust reorganized as Cathedral Energy Services Ltd. (New) 12/18/2009

CATHEDRAL GOLD CORP (ON)
Reorganized under the laws of Alberta as Cathedral Energy Services Ltd. (Old) 11/14/2000
Each share Common no par exchanged for (0.2) share Common no par
Cathedral Energy Services Ltd. (Old) recapitalized as Cathedral Energy Service Income Trust 07/30/2002 which reorganized as Cathedral Energy Services Ltd. (New) 12/18/2009

CATHEDRAL MINERALS LTD (BC)
Merged into Mintek Resources Ltd. 01/04/1983
Each share Common no par exchanged for (0.33333333) share Common no par
Mintek Resources Ltd. recapitalized as Coast Diamond Ventures Ltd. 10/19/1992 which recapitalized as Avcan Global Systems Inc. 07/04/1994 which recapitalized as ASC Avcan Systems Corp. 04/21/1999 which recapitalized as Avcan Systems Inc. (BC) 09/07/2001 which reincorporated in Canada as Optimal Geomatics Inc. 10/09/2003 which merged into Aeroquest International Ltd. 09/30/2009
(See Aeroquest International Ltd.)

CATHEL PARTNERS LTD (DE)
HITK Corp. owned 87.6% as of 06/30/2000
Public interest eliminated

CATHERINES STORES CORP (TN)
State of incorporation changed from (DE) to (TN) 01/29/1995
Merged into Charming Shoppes, Inc. 01/11/2000
Each share Common 1¢ par exchanged for $21 cash

CATHETER CORP AMER (DE)
Name changed to CCA Industries, Inc. 12/18/1984

CATHROY LARDER MINES LTD (ON)
Dissolved 00/00/1976
Details not available

CATLIN GROUP LTD (BERMUDA)
Acquired by XL Group PLC 05/27/2015
Each Sponsored ADR for Common exchanged for $21.70629 cash

CATLOW RES LTD (BC)
Delisted from Vancouver Stock Exchange 03/02/1988

CATO CORP OLD (DE)
Through purchase offer reverted to a private company 04/00/1980
Public interest eliminated

CATO STORES INC (DE)
Name changed to Cato Corp. (Old) (DE) 06/01/1970
(See Cato Corp. (Old) (DE))

CATS EYE CAP CORP (BC)
Name changed to Lakeland Resources Inc. 08/19/2010
Lakeland Resources Inc. recapitalized as ALX Uranium Corp. 09/25/2015

CATSKILL FINL CORP (DE)
Merged into Troy Financial Corp. 11/13/2000
Each share Common 1¢ par exchanged for $23 cash

CATTHAI CORP (NV)
SEC revoked common stock registration 10/14/2009

CATTLEGUARD INC (TX)
Proclaimed dissolved for failure to file reports and pay fees 10/14/1991

CATTLEMANS INC (DE)
Recapitalized as Omoplata Inc. 09/24/2010
Each share Common $0.001 par exchanged for (0.01) share Common $0.001 par
Omoplata Inc. name changed to Jet Neko, Inc. 05/27/2011
(See Jet Neko, Inc.)

CATTLEMEN'S FINANCIAL SERVICES, INC. (TX)
Merged into Victoria Bankshares, Inc. 08/24/1995
Each share Common $8 par exchanged for $8 cash

CATTLEMEN'S LIFE INSURANCE CO. (TX)
Receivership closed 08/25/1982
No stockholders' equity

CATTLEMENS FNDTN INC (KS)
Completely liquidated 02/11/1972
Each share Common 10¢ par received first and final distribution of (1.2737) shares Twin Americas Agricultural & Industrial Developers, Inc. Common 10¢ par
Notes: Certificates were not required to be surrendered and are without value
Twin Americas Agricultural & Industrial Developers, Inc. is a Panamanian company

CATTLEMENS INVT CO (OK)
Merged into Roosevelt National Investment Co. (IL) 07/26/1976
Each share Capital Stock 10¢ par exchanged for (0.2) share Class A Common $1 par and $0.26 cash
Roosevelt National Investment Co. (IL) reorganized in Delaware as Universal Guaranty Investment Co. 06/14/1990
(See Universal Guaranty Investment Co.)

CATTLESALE CO (DE)
Charter cancelled and declared inoperative and void for non-payment of taxes 03/01/2005

CATUITY INC (DE)
Each share old Common $0.001 par exchanged for (0.06666666) share new Common $0.001 par 11/12/2004
Company ceased operations 10/31/2007
Stockholders' equity unlikely

CAULFIELD RES LTD (BC)
Delisted from Vancouver Stock Exchange 03/02/1989

CAULFIELDS DAIRY LTD.
Acquired by Borden Co. 00/00/1929
Details not available

CAUSEWAY ENERGY CORP (AB)
Merged into Bushmills Energy Corp. 08/29/2001
Each share Common no par exchanged for (0.2) share Common no par and $2.58 cash
Bushmills Energy Corp. merged into Brooklyn Energy Corp. 02/03/2003
(See Brooklyn Energy Corp.)

CAUSEWAY ENTMT CO (NV)
Recapitalized as United Bullion Exchange Inc. 05/10/2011
Each share Common $0.00001 par exchanged for (0.00333333) share Common $0.0001 par

CAUSSA CAP CORP (ON)
Recapitalized as Rainbow Gold Ltd. 01/20/2003
Each share Common no par exchanged for (0.1) share Common no par
Rainbow Gold Inc. recapitalized as Jaguar Mining Inc. 10/16/2003

CAVA RES INC (ON)
Each share old Common no par exchanged for (0.1) share new Common no par 01/26/2016
Name changed to Gold Rush Cariboo Corp. 06/21/2018

CAVALCADE SPORTS MEDIA INC (NV)
Each share old Common $0.001 par exchanged for (0.03333333) share new Common $0.001 par 09/04/2003
Name changed to Pacificap Entertainment Holdings, Inc. 12/10/2003
(See Pacificap Entertainment Holdings, Inc.)

CAVALCADE SPORTS NETWORK INC (NV)
Name changed to Thin Express Inc. 09/12/2001
Thin Express Inc. recapitalized as CyberKey Corp. 02/18/2003 which name changed to CyberKey Solutions, Inc. 04/24/2006
(See CyberKey Solutions, Inc.)

CAVALIER APARTMENTS CORP. (DE)
Voting Trust Agreement terminated 11/27/1954
Each VTC for Capital Stock no par exchanged for (1) share Capital Stock 5¢ par
Liquidation completed
Each share Capital Stock 5¢ par exchanged for initial distribution of $44 cash 05/12/1964
Each share Capital Stock 5¢ par received second distribution of $2 cash 10/28/1964
Each share Capital Stock 5¢ par received third distribution of $1.50 cash 12/09/1964
Each share Capital Stock 5¢ par received fourth and final distribution of $0.85 cash 11/01/1967

CAVALIER CAP CORP (UT)
Recapitalized as Los Angeles Securities Group 05/01/1986
Each share Common $0.001 par exchanged for (0.02) share Common 5¢ par
Los Angeles Securities Group name changed to Above Technologies, Inc. 04/20/1990

CAVALIER CENTRAL BANK & TRUST CO. (HOPEWELL, VA)
Merged into Central National Corp. (VA) 12/31/1975
Each share Common $50 par exchanged for (12) shares Common $5 par
Central National Corp. (VA) merged into Commonwealth Banks, Inc. 12/31/1978 which name changed to Central Fidelity Banks, Inc. 06/01/1979 which merged into Wachovia Corp. (New) (Ctfs. dated between 05/20/1991 and 09/01/2001) 12/15/1997 which merged into Wachovia Corp. (Ctfs. dated after 09/01/2001) 09/01/2001 which merged into Wells Fargo & Co. (New) 12/31/2008

CAVALIER CORP. (MN)
Name changed to Philmon & Hart Laboratories, Inc. 03/05/1975
Philmon & Hart Laboratories, Inc. name changed to Spearhead Industries, Inc. 10/07/1980
(See Spearhead Industries, Inc.)

CAVALIER CORP (NEW ZEALAND)
ADR agreement terminated 03/13/2018
No ADR's remain outstanding

CAVALIER ENERGY LTD (AB)
Reincorporated 02/07/1978
Name and place of incorporation changed from Cavalier Energy Inc. (ON) to Cavalier Energy Ltd. (AB) 02/07/1978
Acquired by Cavalier Capital Corp. 04/00/1988
Each share Common no par exchanged for $9.25 cash

CAVALIER GROUP (WY)
Name changed to China Health Care Corp. 05/16/2008

CAVALIER HOMES INC (DE)
Common 10¢ par split (5) for (4) by issuance of (0.25) additional share 11/16/1992
Common 10¢ par split (5) for (4) by issuance of (0.25) additional share 11/15/1993
Common 10¢ par split (5) for (4) by issuance of (0.25) additional share 08/15/1995
Common 10¢ par split (3) for (2) by issuance of (0.5) additional share payable 02/14/1996 to holders of record 01/31/1996 Ex date - 02/15/1996
Common 10¢ par split (5) for (4) by issuance of (0.25) additional share payable 11/14/1996 to holders of record 10/31/1996 Ex date - 11/15/1996
Merged into Southern Energy Homes, Inc. 09/01/2009
Each share Common 10¢ par exchanged for $2.75 cash

CAVALIER HOTEL CORP.
In process of liquidation 00/00/1945
Details not available

CAVALIER MFG INC (AZ)
Name changed to Cavco Industries Inc. 01/04/1974
(See Cavco Industries Inc.)

CAVALIER MINING CORP. LTD. (ON)
Charter cancelled 09/18/1961

CAVALIER RADIO & ELECTRONICS CORP. (NY)
Adjudicated bankrupt 03/01/1963
No stockholders' equity

CAVALIER RESOURCES CORP. (UT)
Recapitalized as Saker One Corp. (UT) 09/06/1983
Each share Common $0.001 par exchanged for (0.05) share Common 1¢ par
Saker One Corp. (UT) reorganized in Nevada as Triad Compressor Inc. 01/07/1999 which name changed to Triad Innovations, Inc. 09/10/1999

CAVALRY BANCORP INC (TN)
Merged into Pinnacle Financial Partners, Inc. 03/15/2006
Each share Common no par exchanged for (0.95) share Common $1 par

CAVAN VENTURES INC (BC)
Each share old Common no par exchanged for (0.2) share new Common no par 02/07/2017
Name changed to Vertical Exploration Inc. 01/10/2018

CAVAN YELLOWKNIFE MINES, LTD. (ON)
Charter revoked for failure to file reports and pay taxes 11/07/1955

CAVANAGH CMNTYS CORP (DE)
Name changed to Royale Group Ltd. 02/29/1984
(See Royale Group Ltd.)

CAVANAGH LEASING CORP (DE)
Common 1¢ par split (3) for (2) by issuance of (0.5) additional share 06/30/1969
Name changed to Cavanagh Communities Corp. 07/10/1970
Cavanagh Communities Corp. name changed to Royale Group Ltd. 02/29/1984
(See Royale Group Ltd.)

CAVANAUGH-DOBBS, INC.
Acquired by Hat Corp. of America 00/00/1932
Details not available

CAVANAUGHS HOSPITALITY CORP (WA)
Name changed to WestCoast Hospitality Corp. 03/01/2000
WestCoast Hospitality Corp. name changed to Red Lion Hotels Corp. 09/19/2005

CAVCO INDS INC (AZ)
Common no par split (5) for (4) by issuance of (0.25) additional share 12/15/1978
Common no par split (3) for (2) by issuance of (0.5) additional share 09/22/1983
Common no par changed to 10¢ par 02/24/1988
Common 10¢ par changed to 5¢ par and (1) additional share issued 04/08/1992
Common 5¢ par split (3) for (2) by issuance of (0.5) additional share 12/15/1994
Merged into MFH Acquisition Co. 03/27/1997
Each share Common 5¢ par exchanged for $26.75 cash

CAVELL ENERGY CORP (AB)
Merged into Paramount Energy Trust 07/19/2004
Each share Common no par exchanged for (0.13868055) share Common no par and $0.8259757 cash
Paramount Energy Trust reorganized as Perpetual Energy Inc. 07/06/2010

CAVENDISH CAP CORP (DE)
Name changed to Screen Television & Media Publishing, Inc. 06/08/1989
(See Screen Television & Media Publishing, Inc.)

CAVENDISH URANIUM MINES CORP. (DE)
No longer in existence having become inoperative and void for non-payment of taxes 04/01/1962

CAVENHAM FOREST INDS INC (DE)
Merged into GOSL Acquisition Corp. 01/31/1991
Each share Common no par exchanged for $96.53 cash

CAVERN RES LTD (BC)
Name changed to Southwest Technologies Inc. 07/20/1984
(See Southwest Technologies Inc.)

CAVICO CORP (DE)
Each share old Common $0.001 par exchanged for (0.025) share new Common $0.001 par 08/19/2009
SEC revoked common stock registration 08/12/2013

CAVIO INTL CORP (NV)
Each share old Common $0.001 par exchanged for (0.1) share new Common $0.001 par 03/03/2003
Name changed to Allied Energy Inc. 09/18/2003
Allied Energy Inc. name changed to FloodSmart, Inc. 09/29/2005 which name changed to Axis Energy Corp. 08/01/2006

CAVION TECHNOLOGIES INC (CO)
Recapitalized as Concord Ventures, Inc. (CO) 11/10/2006
Each share Common $0.0001 par exchanged for (0.1) share Common $0.0001 par
Concord Ventures, Inc. (CO) reincorporated in Delaware as Golden Dragon Holding Co. 05/13/2011 which name changed to CannaPharmaRx, Inc. 03/23/2015

CAVIT SCIENCES INC (FL)
SEC revoked common stock registration 10/05/2011

CAVITRON CORP (DE)
Reincorporated 05/31/1973
Name changed to Cavitron Ultrasonics Inc. 09/29/1961 which name changed back to Cavitron Corp. 02/28/1967
6% 1st Preferred $100 par called for redemption 11/09/1967
$1.50 Preferred $25 par called for redemption 11/09/1967
Non-Cum. Preferred $100 par called for redemption 12/09/1967
State of incorporation changed from (NY) to (DE) 05/31/1973
Merged into Cooper Laboratories, Inc. 05/22/1981
Each share Common 10¢ par exchanged for $36.50 cash

CAVITRON ULTRASONICS INC. (NY)
Voting Trust Agreement terminated 07/17/1962
Each VTC for Common 10¢ par exchanged for (1) share Common 10¢ par
Name changed to Cavitron Corp. (NY) 02/28/1967
Cavitron Corp. (NY) reincorporated in Delaware 05/31/1973
(See Cavitron Corp. (DE))

CAVIUM INC (DE)
Merged into Marvell Technology Group Ltd. 07/06/2018
Each share Common $0.001 par exchanged for (2.1757) shares Common $0.002 par and $40 cash

CAVIUM NETWORKS INC (DE)
Name changed to Cavium, Inc. 06/17/2011
(See Cavium, Inc.)

CAXTON GROUP INC (ON)
Name changed to Pareto Corp. 07/23/2002
(See Pareto Corp.)

CAYCUSE COPPER CO. LTD. (BC)
Struck off register and declared dissolved for failure to file reports 05/15/1969

CAYDEN RES INC (BC)
Common no par split (3) for (1) by issuance of (2) additional shares payable 11/19/2010 to holders of record 11/19/2010 Ex date - 11/17/2010
Merged into Agnico Eagle Mines Ltd. 11/28/2014
Each share Common no par exchanged for for (0.09) share Common no par and $0.01 cash
Note: Unexchanged certificates will be cancelled and become without value 11/28/2020

CAYE CHAPEL INC (NV)
Each share old Common $0.001 par exchanged for (0.05) share new Common $0.001 par 02/15/2002
Recapitalized as OncBio Inc. 07/08/2004
Each share new Common $0.001 par exchanged for (0.5) share Common $0.001 par
OncBio Inc. recapitalized as Stem Cell Ventures, Inc. 12/05/2005 which recapitalized as Pipejoin Technologies, Inc. 09/11/2007

CAYENNE SOFTWARE INC (MA)
Merged into Sterling Software Inc. 10/26/1998
Each share Common 1¢ par exchanged for $0.375 cash

CAYMAN ACQUISITIONS INC (CO)
Recapitalized as Omicron Holdings, Inc. 11/30/1990
Each share Common no par exchanged for (0.05) share Common no par

CAYMAN CORP (DE)
Reorganized under the laws of Oklahoma as Cayman Resources Corp. 04/20/1982
Each share Common 10¢ par exchanged for (1) share Common 10¢ par
Cayman Resources Corp. name changed to Oklahoma Energy Corp. 09/02/1997
(See Oklahoma Energy Corp.)

CAYMAN PURCHASING & SUPPLY INC (FL)
Name changed to Patagonia Gold Corp. (FL) 11/12/1997
Patagonia Gold Corp. (FL) reorganized in British Virgin Islands as Patagonia Gold Ltd. 11/29/2002

CAYMAN RES CORP (OK)
Name changed to Oklahoma Energy Corp. 09/02/1997
(See Oklahoma Energy Corp.)

CAYMAN WTR CO LTD (CAYMAN ISLANDS)
Name changed to Consolidated Water Co. Ltd. 12/03/1998

CAYMUS RES INC (BC)
Completely liquidated 03/31/2014
Each share Common no par received pro rata distribution of Tasman Metals Ltd. Units consisting of (1) share Common no par and (1) Common Stock Purchase Warrant expiring 02/11/2017

CAYMUS VENTURES CORP (BC)
Name changed to West Dynamic Toll Road Ltd. (BC) 07/08/1996
West Dynamic Toll Road Ltd. (BC) reincorporated in Bermuda 04/04/1997
(See West Dynamic Toll Road Ltd.)

CAYO RES CORP (AB)
Merged into Pure Gold Minerals Inc. 11/20/1997
Each share Common no par exchanged for (0.6) share Common no par
Pure Gold Minerals Inc. recapitalized as Pure Diamonds Exploration Inc. 12/05/2006 which recapitalized as Burnstone Ventures Inc. 08/14/2009

CAYUGA LAKE NATIONAL BANK (UNION SPRINGS, NY)
Common $50 par changed to $10 par and (4) additional shares issued 03/25/1978
Reorganized as Cayuga Lake Bank Corp. 03/31/1988
Each share Common $10 par exchanged for (1) share Common $10 par

CAYUGA SVGS BK (AUBURN, NY)
Under plan of reorganization each

share Floating Rate Preferred Ser. A $1 par and Common $1 par automatically became (1) share Iroquois Bancorp, Inc. Floating Rate Preferred Ser. A $1 par or Common $1 par respectively 03/01/1990
(See Iroquois Bancorp Inc.)

CAYUGA STEAMSHIP CO. LTD. (ON)
Assets sold for the benefit of creditors 12/02/1969
No stockholders' equity

CAYZOR ATHABASKA MINES LTD. (ON)
Name changed to New Cayzor Athabaska Mines Ltd. 04/03/1967
(See New Cayzor Athabaska Mines Ltd.)

CAZA GOLD CORP (BC)
Each share old Common no par exchanged for (0.33333333) share new Common no par 12/13/2013
Acquired by Royal Road Minerals Ltd. 05/23/2017
Each share new Common no par exchanged for (0.16) share Ordinary no par

CAZA OIL & GAS INC (BC)
Each (560,000,000) shares old Common no par exchanged for (1) share new Common no par 05/16/2016
Note: In effect holders received USD$0.00481 cash per share and public interest was eliminated
Unexchanged certificates will be cancelled and become without value 05/16/2021

CAZADOR ACQUISITION CORP LTD (CAYMAN ISLANDS)
Units separated 09/27/2012
Reorganized under the laws of Delaware as Net Element International, Inc. 10/03/2012
Each share Ordinary $0.0001 par exchanged for (1) share Common $0.0001 par
Net Element International, Inc. name changed to Net Element, Inc. (New) 12/09/2013

CAZADOR EXPLS LTD (BC)
Merged into Granduc Mining Corp. 11/08/1993
Each share Common no par exchanged for (0.6) share Common no par
Granduc Mining Corp. merged into Black Hawk Mining Inc.-Compagnie Miniere Black Hawk Inc. 07/01/1996 which merged into Glencairn Gold Corp. 10/20/2003 which recapitalized as Central Sun Mining Inc. 12/05/2007 which was acquired by B2Gold Corp. 03/31/2009

CB & T BANCSHARES INC (GA)
Common $2.50 par split (2) for (1) by issuance of (1) additional share 01/03/1984
Common $2.50 par split (3) for (2) by issuance of (0.5) additional share 04/01/1985
Common $2.50 par changed to $1 par 04/29/1985
Common $1 par split (3) for (2) by issuance of (0.5) additional share 10/01/1986
Common $1 par split (3) for (2) by issuance of (0.5) additional share 10/03/1988
Stock Dividend - 100% 07/01/1977
Name changed to Synovus Financial Corp. 08/21/1989

CB BANCORP INC (DE)
Common 1¢ par split (2) for (1) by issuance of (1) additional share 02/23/1994
Merged into Pinnacle Financial Services, Inc. 08/01/1997
Each share Common 1¢ par exchanged for (1.2095) shares Common no par
Pinnacle Financial Services, Inc.

merged into CNB Bancshares Inc. 04/17/1998 which merged into Fifth Third Bancorp 10/29/1999

CB BANCSHARES, INC. (IN)
Name changed to CommerceAmerica Corp. 04/22/1985
CommerceAmerica Corp. merged into Indiana National Corp. 08/29/1986 which name changed to INB Financial Corp. 04/26/1989 which merged into NBD Bancorp, Inc. 10/15/1992 which name changed to First Chicago NBD Corp. 12/01/1995 which merged into Bank One Corp. 10/02/1998 which merged into J.P. Morgan Chase & Co. 12/31/2000 which name changed to JPMorgan Chase & Co. 07/20/2004

CB BANCSHARES INC (HI)
Stock Dividends - 10% payable 06/28/2001 to holders of record 06/15/2001 Ex date - 06/13/2001; 10% payable 06/27/2002 to holders of record 06/14/2002 Ex date - 06/12/2002; 10% payable 06/27/2003 to holders of record 06/16/2003 Ex date - 06/12/2003
Merged into Central Pacific Financial Corp. 09/15/2004
Each share Common $1 par exchanged for (1.98720946) shares Common no par and $39.33974069 cash

CB COML HLDGS INC (DE)
Name changed to CB Commercial Real Estate Services Group Inc. 12/02/1996
CB Commercial Real Estate Services Group Inc. name changed to CB Richard Ellis Services Inc. 05/19/1998
(See CB Richard Ellis Services Inc.)

CB COML REAL ESTATE SVCS GROUP INC (DE)
Name changed to CB Richard Ellis Services Inc. 05/19/1998
(See CB Richard Ellis Services Inc.)

CB CREST INC (UT)
Proclaimed dissolved for failure to pay taxes 06/01/1994

CB FINL CORP (MI)
Common $7.50 par split (3) for (2) by issuance of (0.5) additional share 01/15/1986
Common $7.50 par split (2) for (1) by issuance of (1) additional share 11/17/1989
Merged into Citizens Banking Corp. 07/01/1997
Each share Common $7.50 par exchanged for (1.489) shares Common $10 par
Citizens Banking Corp. name changed to Citizens Republic Bancorp, Inc. 04/26/2007 which merged into FirstMerit Corp. 04/12/2013 which merged into Huntington Bancshares Inc. 08/16/2016

CB FINL CORP (NC)
Reclassification effective 03/17/2008
Old Common reverse split (1) for (132) followed by a (132) for (1) forward split
Holders of between (264) to (791) post-split shares reclassified as Ser. A Preferred no par
Holders of (263) or fewer post-split shares reclassified as Ser. B Preferred no par
Holders of (792) or more post-split shares retained their interests
Holders of (131) or fewer pre-split shares received $20 cash
Ser. A Preferred no par reclassified as new Common no par 05/28/2015
Ser. B Preferred no par reclassified as new Common no par 05/28/2015
Stock Dividends - 5% payable 08/26/2005 to holders of record 06/28/2005; 5% payable 04/30/2008

to holders of record 03/31/2008 Ex date - 03/27/2008
Acquired by PB Financial Corp. 04/03/2018
Each share new Common no par exchanged for $0.235 cash

CB GOLD INC (BC)
Name changed to Red Eagle Exploration Ltd. 03/06/2017
Red Eagle Exploration Ltd. merged into Red Eagle Mining Corp. 04/25/2018

CB PAK INC (CANADA)
Merged into Stone Consolidated Inc. 12/13/1989
Each share Common no par exchanged for $11.25 cash

CB PHARMA ACQUISITION CORP (CAYMAN ISLANDS)
Name changed to Origo Acquisition Corp. 06/23/2016
(See Origo Acquisition Corp.)

CB RES LTD (BC)
Recapitalized as Next Gen Metals Inc. 08/18/2009
Each share Common no par exchanged for (0.13333333) share Common no par
Next Gen Metals Inc. recapitalized as Namaste Technologies Inc. 03/02/2016

CB RICHARD ELLIS GROUP INC (DE)
Class A Common 1¢ par split (3) for (1) by issuance of (2) additional shares payable 06/01/2006 to holders of record 05/15/2006 Ex date - 06/02/2006
Name changed to CBRE Group, Inc. 10/05/2011

CB RICHARD ELLIS SVCS INC (DE)
Merged into Blum CB Corp. 07/20/2001
Each share Common 1¢ par exchanged for $16 cash

CB&T FINL CORP (WV)
Common $1 par split (2) for (1) by issuance of (1) additional share 07/31/1986
Common $1 par split (3) for (2) by issuance of (0.5) additional share 04/15/1990
Stock Dividend - 10% 03/25/1988
Acquired by Huntington Bancshares Inc. 06/25/1993
Each share Common $1 par exchanged for (1.2892) shares Common no par

CBB CAP LTD (CANADA)
Recapitalized as PIC Capital Inc. 03/05/1990
Each share Class A Common no par exchanged for (0.2) share Class A Common par
PIC Capital Inc. name changed to Pioneer Geophysical Services Inc. 10/11/1994 which recapitalized as Xplore Technologies Corp. (Canada) 03/24/1997 which reincorporated in Delaware 06/20/2007
(See Xplore Technologies Corp.)

CBBC BANCORP (CA)
Merged into Suncrest Bank (Visalia, CA) 05/21/2018
Each share Common no par exchanged for $23.75 cash

CBC BANCORP INC (CT)
Each share Common $2.50 par exchanged for (0.33333333) share Common 1¢ par 08/09/1994
Completely liquidated 11/30/1997
No stockholders' equity
Note: Holders were given the opportunity to purchase (1) share of Connecticut Bank Commerce (Stamford, CT) Common 1¢ par for each share held until 07/31/1998

CBCI TELECOM INC (ON)
Acquired by Tandberg ASA 06/12/1997
Each share Common no par exchanged for $6.60 cash

CBCOM INC (DE)
SEC revoked common stock registration 05/31/2011

CBCT BANCSHARES INC (MD)
Merged into Bastrop Bancshares, Inc. 07/27/2002
Each share Common 1¢ par exchanged for $25.01 cash

CBD ENERGY LTD (AUSTRALIA)
Name changed to BlueNRGY Group Ltd. 05/26/2015

CBES BANCORP INC (DE)
Merged into NASB Financial, Inc. 12/19/2002
Each share Common 1¢ par exchanged for $17.50 cash

CBEYOND INC (DE)
Name changed 06/28/2006
Name changed from Cbeyond Communications Inc. to Cbeyond, Inc. 06/28/2006
Acquired by Birch Communications, Inc. 07/18/2014
Each share Common 1¢ par exchanged for $10 cash

CBI DISTRIBUTION TRUST (DE)
In process of liquidation
Each Unit of Bene. Int. received initial distribution of $0.72 cash payable 03/01/2000 to holders of record 04/12/1999
Note: Details on subsequent distribution(s), if any, are not available

CBI INDS INC (DE)
Recapitalized 10/31/1988
Each share $3.50 Conv. Exchangeable Preferred Ser. B $1 par exchanged for $50 principal amount of 7% Conv. Subordinated Debentures due 10/30/2011
Common $2.50 par split (3) for (2) by issuance of (0.5) additional share 06/21/1991
Merged into Praxair, Inc. 03/13/1996
Each share 6.75% Preferred Ser. E 1¢ par exchanged for (1) share 6.75% Preferred Ser. B 1¢ par
Each share 7.48% Preferred Ser. D 1¢ par exchanged for (1) share 7.48% Preferred Ser. A 1¢ par
Each share Common $2.50 par exchanged for $33 cash

CBK AGRONOMICS INC (DE)
Name changed to General Energy Corp. (DE) 10/10/1972
General Energy Corp. (DE) merged into Kirby Exploration Co. 07/15/1983 which reorganized as Kirby Exploration Co. Inc. 08/01/1984 which name changed to Kirby Corp. 05/01/1990

CBK INDS INC (DE)
Name changed to CBK Agronomics, Inc. 04/24/1969
CBK Agronomics, Inc. name changed to General Energy Corp. (DE) 10/10/1972 which merged into Kirby Exploration Co. 07/15/1983 which reorganized as Kirby Exploration Co. Inc. 08/01/1984 which name changed to Kirby Corp. 05/01/1990

CBL & ASSOC PPTYS INC (DE)
9% Preferred Ser. A 1¢ par called for redemption at $25 on 11/28/2003
8.75% Preferred Ser. B 1¢ par called for redemption at $50 plus $1.069437 accrued dividends on 06/28/2007
7.75% Depositary Preferred Ser C called for redemption at $25 plus $0.19375 accrued dividends on 11/05/2012
(Additional Information in Active)

CBL MED INC (DE)
Charter forfeited for failure to maintain a registered agent 02/25/1998

CBLX HLDGS INC (CO)
Recapitalized as Evans Environmental Corp. 05/03/1993
Each share Common $0.001 par exchanged for (0.33333333) share Common $0.001 par
Evans Environmental Corp. name changed to ECOS Group, Inc. (CO) 11/01/1996 which reincorporated in Florida 02/22/2000 which recapitalized as Third Millennium Telecommunications, Inc. (FL) 10/01/2001 which reincorporated in Delaware as TMTM Merger Co. 09/04/2009 which recapitalized as Green Processing Technologies, Inc. 06/16/2010 which recapitalized as Umbra Applied Technologies Group, Inc. 01/13/2014

CBM INC (DE)
Chapter 11 bankruptcy proceedings converted to Chapter 7 on 03/09/1983
No stockholders' equity

CBNI DEV INC (DE)
Each share old Common 1¢ par exchanged for (0.1) share new Common 1¢ par 02/14/1994
Name changed to Affinity Teleproductions Inc. 02/28/1994
Affinity Teleproductions Inc. name changed to Affinity Entertainment, Inc. 07/03/1996 which name changed to Tour CFG Inc. 11/04/1997
(See Tour CFG Inc.)

CBNY INVT SVCS CORP (NY)
Acquired by private investors 05/20/2002
Each share Common $1 par exchanged for $10.15 cash

CBO RES CORP (BC)
Struck off register and declared dissolved for failure to file returns 09/25/1998

CBOC CONTINENTAL INC (CANADA)
Reorganized as Coastal Group Inc. 04/17/2001
Each share Common no par exchanged for (1) Dividend Share, (1) Multiple Share and (1) Subordinate Share
Coastal Group Inc. merged into Continental (CBOC) Corp. 08/30/2002 which name changed to Stonington Capital Corp. 06/22/2004 which merged into Pyxis Capital Inc. 02/27/2006
(See Pyxis Capital Inc.)

CBOE HLDGS INC (DE)
Name changed to Cboe Global Markets, Inc. 10/18/2017

CBOT HLDGS INC (DE)
Merged into CME Group Inc. 07/12/2007
Each share Class A Common $0.001 par exchanged for (0.375) share Common 1¢ par

CBP CARBON GREEN INC (NV)
Name changed to Millennium Energy Corp. 03/26/2008
(See Millennium Energy Corp.)

CBP CARBON INDS INC (NV)
Reorganized under the laws of British Virgin Islands 02/14/2012
Each share Common $0.001 par exchanged for (0.001) share Common $0.001 par

CBQ INC (CO)
Reincorporated under the laws of Florida as China Direct Trading Corp. 05/17/2004
China Direct Trading Corp. name changed to CHDT Corp. 07/16/2007 which name changed to Capstone Companies, Inc. 07/06/2012

CBR BREWING INC (FL)
Reincorporated under the laws of British Virgin Islands 03/14/2003

CBR CAP TR I (DE)
144A Floating Rate Capital Securities called for redemption at $52,500 on 02/23/2006

CBR GOLD CORP (AB)
Each share Common 1¢ par received distribution of (1) share North Country Gold Corp. Common 1¢ par payable 04/15/2010 to holders of record 04/09/2010
Name changed to Niblack Mineral Development Inc. 04/15/2010
Niblack Mineral Development Inc. merged into Heatherdale Resources Ltd. 01/23/2012

CBR INTL BIOTECHNOLOGIES CORP (BC)
Recapitalized as Newen Enterprises Inc. 03/30/1993
Each share Common no par exchanged for (0.16666666) share Common no par
Newen Enterprises Inc. recapitalized as Consolidated Newen Enterprises Inc. 11/02/1998 which recapitalized as North American Gold Inc. 04/07/2003 which name changed to Northland Resources Inc. (BC) 09/07/2005 which reincorporated in Luxembourg as Northland Resources S.A. 06/14/2010

CBRE RLTY FIN INC (MD)
Name changed to Realty Finance Corp. 02/03/2009
Realty Finance Corp. name changed to CV Holdings, Inc. 11/07/2013

CBRL GROUP INC (TN)
Name changed to Cracker Barrel Old Country Store, Inc. 12/08/2008

CBS CORP (PA)
Merged into Viacom Inc. (Old) 05/04/2000
Each share Common $1 par exchanged for (1.085) shares Class B Common 1¢ par
(See Viacom Inc. (Old))

CBS INC (NY)
$1 Conv. Preference Ser. A $1 par called for redemption 01/31/1992
Common $2.50 par split (5) for (1) by issuance of (4) additional shares 10/18/1994
Merged into Westinghouse Electric Corp. 11/24/1995
Each share Common $2.50 par exchanged for $82.065 cash

CBS OUTDOOR AMERS INC (MD)
Name changed to OUTFRONT Media Inc. 11/20/2014

CBT CORP (CT)
Under plan of reorganization each share Common $10 par received an additional (0.2) share Common $10 par 03/07/1970
Stock Dividends - 50% 10/20/1978; 20% 10/16/1980; 50% 07/16/1981
Merged into Bank of New England Corp. 06/14/1985
Each share Common $10 par exchanged for (1) share Common $5 par
(See Bank of New England Corp.)

CBT CORP (KY)
Common no par split (3) for (2) by issuance of (0.5) additional share 05/29/1992
Common no par split (2) for (1) by issuance of (1) additional share 10/25/1994
Merged into Mercantile Bancorporation, Inc. 07/01/1998
Each share Common no par exchanged for (0.6513) share Common 1¢ par
Mercantile Bancorporation, Inc. merged into Firstar Corp. (New) 09/20/1999 which merged into U.S. Bancorp (New) 02/27/2001

CBT FINL CORP (PA)
Common no par split (2) for (1) by issuance of (1) additional share payable 08/31/2003 to holders of record 08/10/2003 Ex date - 09/02/2003
Merged into Riverview Financial Corp. (New) 10/02/2017
Each share Common no par exchanged for (2.86) shares Common no par

CBT GROUP PUB LTD (IRELAND)
Restricted Sponsored ADR's for Ordinary split (2) for (1) by issuance of (1) additional ADR payable 05/20/1996 to holders of record 05/15/1996
Old Sponsored ADR's for Ordinary split (2) for (1) by issuance of (1) additional ADR payable 05/20/1996 to holders of record 05/15/1996
Old Sponsored ADR's for Ordinary split (2) for (1) by issuance of (1) additional ADR payable 03/09/1998 to holders of record 03/02/1998 Ex date - 03/10/1998
Each old Sponsored ADR for Ordinary exchanged for (1) new Sponsored ADR for 05/22/1998
Name changed to SmartForce PLC 02/15/2000
SmartForce PLC name changed to SkillSoft PLC 11/19/2002
(See SkillSoft PLC)

CBWL HAYDEN STONE INC (DE)
Name changed to Hayden Stone Inc. 10/03/1972
Hayden Stone Inc. name changed to Shearson Hayden Stone Inc. 09/26/1974 which name changed to Shearson Loeb Rhodes, Inc. 12/19/1979 which merged into American Express Co. 06/29/1981

CBX VENTURES INC (BC)
Reorganized as Alma Resources Ltd. 12/05/2005
Each share Common no par exchanged for (3) shares Common no par
Alma Resources Ltd. name changed to Remstar Resources Ltd. 05/15/2008 which name changed to Avarone Metals Inc. 02/03/2014

CC ASSETS DISTRIBUTION CORP. (DE)
Liquidation completed
Each share Capital Stock $100 par received initial distribution of $2,125 cash 03/28/1982
Each share Capital Stock $100 par received second and final distribution of $95.65 cash 02/13/1985
Note: Certificates were not required to be surrendered and are without value

CC MEDIA HLDGS INC (DE)
Name changed to iHeartMedia, Inc. 09/17/2014

CCA COS INC (DE)
Recapitalized as Lottery & Wagering Solutions Inc. 10/01/2001
Each share Common $0.001 par exchanged for (0.05) share Common $0.001 par

CCA PRISON RLTY TR (MD)
Merged into Prison Realty Corp. 12/31/1998
Each share 8% Preferred Ser. A 1¢ par exchanged for (1) share 8% Preferred Ser. A 1¢ par
Each share Common 1¢ par exchanged for (1) share Common 1¢ par
Prison Realty Corp. name changed to Prison Realty Trust Inc. 05/11/1999 which name changed to Corrections Corp. of America 10/01/2000 which name changed to CoreCivic, Inc. 11/09/2016

CCAIR INC (DE)
Merged into Mesa Air Group, Inc. 06/10/1999
Each share Common 1¢ par exchanged for (0.6214) share Common no par
(See Mesa Air Group, Inc.)

CCB BANCORP INC (PA)
Merged into Mellon National Corp. 09/14/1983
Each share Common $5 par exchanged for (1) share $2.80 Preferred Ser. A $1 par and (0.5) share Common 50¢ par
Mellon National Corp. name changed to Mellon Bank Corp. 09/30/1984 which name changed to Mellon Financial Corp. 10/17/1999 which merged into Bank of New York Mellon Corp. 07/01/2007

CCB BANKSHARES INC (VA)
Merged into Bank of McKenney (McKenney, VA) 11/10/2017
Each share Common $5 par exchanged for (0.935) share Common $2 par
Bank of McKenney (McKenney, VA) name changed to Touchstone Bank (McKenney, VA) 11/28/2017

CCB FINL CORP (NC)
Common $5 par split (2) for (1) by issuance of (1) additional share 07/25/1984
Common $5 par split (3) for (2) by issuance of (0.5) additional share 10/01/1992
Common $5 par split (2) for (1) by issuance of (1) additional share payable 10/01/1998 to holders of record 09/15/1998 Ex date - 10/02/1998
Merged into National Commerce Bancorporation 07/05/2000
Each share Common $5 par exchanged for (2.45) shares Common $2 par
National Commerce Bancorporation name changed to National Commerce Financial Corp. 04/25/2001 which merged into SunTrust Banks, Inc. 10/01/2004

CCBT BANCORP INC (MA)
Name changed to CCBT Financial Companies Inc. 09/23/1999
CCBT Bancorp Inc. merged into Banknorth Group, Inc. (ME) 04/30/2004 which merged into TD Banknorth Inc. 03/01/2005
(See TD Banknorth Inc.)

CCBT FINL COS INC (MA)
Merged into Banknorth Group, Inc. 04/30/2004
Each share Common $2.50 par exchanged for (1.084) shares Common 1¢ par

CCC, INC. (DE)
Completely liquidated 05/01/1971
Each share Common 1¢ par exchanged for first and final distribution of $0.01 cash

CCC FRANCHISING CORP (NY)
Name changed to Primedex Health Systems, Inc. 11/24/1992
Primedex Health Systems, Inc. recapitalized as RadNet, Inc. (NY) 11/28/2006 which reincorporated in Delaware 09/03/2008

CCC GLOBALCOM CORP (NV)
Common $0.001 par changed to $0.0001 par 06/18/2008
Name changed to Bakken Water Transfer Services, Inc. 08/13/2015

CCC INFORMATION SVCS GROUP INC (DE)
Merged into Cougar Holdings, Inc. 02/10/2006
Each share Common 10¢ par exchanged for $26.50 cash

CCC INFORMATION SVCS INC (DE)
Acquired by Financial Protection Services Inc. 01/26/1988
Each share Common 1¢ par exchanged for $9 cash

CCC INTL TRADE INC (AB)
Recapitalized as Canin Industrial Group Inc. 04/06/1990
Each share Common no par exchanged for (0.5) share Common no par
(See Canin Industrial Group Inc.)

CCC INTERNET SOLUTIONS INC (BC)
Name changed to Armada Data Corp. 01/26/2004

CCE SPINCO INC (DE)
Name changed to Live Nation, Inc. 01/06/2006
Live Nation, Inc. name changed to Live Nation Entertainment, Inc. 01/27/2010

CCG CAP CORP (DE)
Each share old Common $0.025 par exchanged for (0.06666666) share new Common $0.025 par 08/03/1992
Recapitalized as Interaxx Technologies Inc. 10/16/1997
Each share new Common $0.025 par exchanged for (0.06666666) share Common $0.025 par
(See Interaxx Technologies Inc.)

CCH INC (DE)
Merged into Wolters Kluwer N.V. 01/10/1996
Each share Class A Common $1 par exchanged for $55.50 cash
Each share Non-Vtg. Class B Common $1 par exchanged for $55.50 cash

CCI CODED COMMUNICATIONS INC (BC)
Reincorporated under the laws of Delaware as Coded Communications Corp. 08/27/1993
(See Coded Communications Corp.)

CCI CORP (DE)
Under plan of merger name changed to CCI Marquardt Corp. 06/12/1968 which name changed back to CCI Corp. 09/26/1969
Each share $1.25 Conv. Preferred Ser. A $1 par exchanged for (4) shares Common 50¢ par and (1) share CCI Life Systems, Inc. Common 10¢ par 01/28/1974
Under plan of merger each share Common 50¢ par exchanged for $16 cash 01/20/1983

CCI GROUP INC (UT)
Chapter 11 bankruptcy proceedings converted to Chapter 7 on 01/10/2008
Stockholders' equity unlikely

CCI HOLDING CORP. (NY)
Administratively dissolved 12/24/1991

CCI LIFE SYS INC (DE)
Merged into Dialco Inc. 09/18/1978
Each share Common 10¢ par exchanged for $3.25 cash

CCI LIQUIDATING CORP. (IN)
Liquidation completed
Each share Common $1 par received second and final distribution of $0.14618877 cash 12/31/1990
(See Crime Control, Inc. for previous distribution)

CCI MARQUARDT CORP (DE)
Name changed to CCI Corp. 09/26/1969
(See CCI Corp.)

CCM MFG TECHNOLOGIES INC (DE)
SEC revoked common stock registration 05/30/2008

CCNB CORP (PA)
Common $1 par split (3) for (1) by issuance of (2) additional shares 08/15/1986
Merged into PNC Financial Corp. 10/23/1992
Each share Common $1 par exchanged for (1.32) share Common $5 par
PNC Financial Corp. name changed to PNC Bank Corp. 02/08/1993 which name changed to PNC Financial Services Group, Inc. 03/15/2000

CCP INS INC (IN)
Merged into Conseco Inc. 08/31/1995
Each share Common no par exchanged for $23.25 cash

CCP WORLDWIDE INC (DE)
Name changed to Dyadic International, Inc. 11/05/2004

CCR INC (UT)
Each share Common $0.0001 par exchanged for (0.1) share Common $0.001 par 06/29/1990
Each share old Common $0.001 par exchanged for (0.33333333) share new Common $0.001 par 10/01/1991
Each share Common $0.001 par exchanged for (0.33333333) share Common $0.0001 par 12/27/1993
Reincorporated under the laws of Nevada as Quantum Learning Systems, Inc. 04/28/1994
Quantum Learning Systems, Inc. name changed to Costa Rica International, Inc. 08/28/1996 which name changed to Rica Foods, Inc. 08/24/1998
(See Rica Foods, Inc.)

CCR TECHNOLOGIES LTD (AB)
Petition under Bankruptcy and Insolvency Act effective 03/01/2011
No stockholders' equity

CCS CAP INC (BC)
Reincorporated under the laws of Cayman Islands as China Health Labs & Diagnostics Ltd. and Common no par changed to USD$0.00005 par 10/25/2010
(See China Health Labs & Diagnostics Ltd.)

CCS INC (AB)
Merged into Red Sky Acquisition Corp. 11/15/2007
Each Ser. A Exchangeable Share no par exchanged for $128.55666 cash

CCS INCOME TR (AB)
Trust Units split (2) for (1) by issuance of (1) additional Unit payable 03/03/2005 to holders of record 02/28/2005
Merged into Red Sky Acquisition Corp. 11/15/2007
Each Trust Unit exchanged for $46 cash

CCT CAP LTD (BC)
Each share old Common no par exchanged for (0.16666666) share new Common no par 01/30/2014
Name changed to Mezzi Holdings Inc. 10/29/2014
Mezzi Holdings Inc. name changed to Omni Commerce Corp. 04/13/2018

CCX INC (DE)
Prepackaged plan of reorganization under Chapter 11 Federal Bankruptcy Code filed 03/24/1994
No stockholders' equity

CCX NETWORK INC (DE)
Common 10¢ par split (3) for (2) by issuance of (0.5) additional share 03/21/1986
Name changed to Acxiom Corp. 07/20/1988
Acxiom Corp. reorganized as Acxiom Holdings, Inc. 09/21/2018 which name changed to LiveRamp Holdings, Inc. 10/02/2018

CD MAX INC (DE)
Name changed to IMARK Technologies, Inc. 12/31/1997
IMARK Technologies, Inc. recapitalized as Pharm Control Ltd. 11/08/2006

CD PLUS COM LTD (ON)
Filed for protection under Companies' Creditors Arrangement Act 02/07/2001
No stockholders' equity

CD RADIO INC (DE)
Name changed to Sirius Satellite Radio Inc. 11/19/1999
Sirius Satellite Radio Inc. name changed to Sirius XM Radio, Inc. 08/06/2008 which name changed to Sirius XM Holdings Inc. 11/15/2013

CD ROM NETWORK CORP (ON)
Cease trade order effective 09/22/2003
Stockholders' equity unlikely

CD-ROM YEARBOOK INC (OK)
Name changed to 2Themart.com, Inc. 01/19/1999
(See 2Themart.com, Inc.)

CD TRADING CARDS INC (FL)
Name changed to NEX2U, Inc 07/06/2005
NEX2U, Inc. name changed to KMA Capital Partners, Inc. 06/09/2006

CD WHSE INC (DE)
Chapter 11 bankruptcy proceedings converted to Chapter 7 on 12/18/2003
Stockholders' equity unlikely

CD&L INC (DE)
Merged into Velocity Express Corp. 08/18/2006
Each share Common $0.001 par exchanged for $3 cash

CDBEAT COM INC (DE)
Name changed to Spinrocket.com, Inc. 04/19/2000
Spinrocket.com, Inc. name changed to Connectivcorp 09/11/2000 which name changed to Majesco Holdings Inc. 04/14/2004 which name changed to Majesco Entertainment Co. 04/11/2005 which name changed to PolarityTE, Inc. 01/11/2017

CDC CAP CORP (DE)
Charter cancelled and declared inoperative and void for non-payment of taxes 06/27/1980

CDC CORP (CAYMAN ISLANDS)
Each share old Class A Common $0.00025 par exchanged for (0.33333333) share new Class A Common $0.00025 par 08/23/2010
Plan of reorganization under Chapter 11 Federal Bankruptcy proceedings effective 12/19/2012
Assets transferred to CDC Liquidation Trust and Class A Common $0.00025 par reclassified as Shares of Bene. Int.
Each Share of Bene. Int. received initial distribution of $3.30 cash payable 12/24/2012 to holders of record 12/19/2012
Each Share of Bene. Int. received second distribution of $1.39 cash payable 07/29/2013 to holders of record 12/19/2012
Each Share of Bene. Int. received third distribution of $0.60 cash payable 05/21/2014 to holders of record 12/19/2012
Each Share of Bene. Int. received fourth distribution of $0.40 cash payable 12/21/2015 to holders of record 12/19/2012
Each Share of Bene. Int. received fifth and final distribution of $0.05 cash payable 12/15/2017 to holders of record 12/19/2012

CDC LIFE SCIENCES INC (CANADA)
Common no par split (2) for (1) by issuance of (1) additional share 07/10/1986
Name changed to Connaught Biosciences Inc. 07/04/1988
(See Connaught Biosciences Inc.)

CDC NVEST CASH MGMT TR (MA)
Name changed to Ixis Advisor Cash Management Trust 04/05/2005
Ixis Advisor Cash Management Trust name changed to Natixis Cash Management Trust 06/20/2007
(See Natixis Cash Management Trust)

CDC NVEST FDS TR I (MA)
Reorganized as IXIS Advisors Funds Trust I 04/29/2005
Details not available

CDC NVEST FDS TR II (MA)
Short Term Bond Fund Class Y completely liquidated 02/28/2003
Details not available
Reorganized as IXIS Advisor Funds Trust II 05/01/2005
Details not available

CDC NVEST TAX EXEMPT MONEY MKT TR (MA)
Completely liquidated 11/14/2003
Each share Class A $1 par received $1 cash

CDC SOFTWARE CORP (CAYMAN ISLANDS)
Each Sponsored ADR for Class A Ordinary exchanged for $10.45 cash 04/12/2012

CDG INVTS INC (AB)
Each share Common no par received distribution of (0.33333333) share Tyler Resources Inc. Common no par and $0.07 cash payable 05/12/2006 to holders of record 04/28/2006 Ex date - 04/26/2006
Recapitalized as Preo Software Inc. (Old) 07/24/2008
Each share Common no par exchanged for (0.25) share Common no par
Note: Holders of (3,999) shares or fewer received $0.021484 cash per share
Preo Software Inc. (Old) merged into Preo Software Inc. (New) 08/03/2010
(See Preo Software Inc. (New))

CDI ED CORP (ON)
Acquired by Corinthian Colleges, Inc. 10/08/2003
Each share Common no par exchanged for $4.33 cash

CDIS SOFTWARE INC (BC)
Recapitalized as International CDIS Software Inc. 03/06/1989
Each share Conv. Class A Preferred $4 par exchanged for (0.125) share Common no par
Each share Common no par exchanged for (0.125) share Common no par
International CDIS Software Inc. name changed to A.T.H. Fund Inc. 07/24/1990
(See A.T.H. Fund Inc.)

CDK SVCS LTD (AB)
Name changed to EcoMax Energy Services Ltd. (AB) 07/05/2005
EcoMax Energy Services Ltd. (AB) reincorporated in British Columbia as Tasca Resources Ltd. 10/19/2011

CDKNET COM INC (DE)
Each share old Common $0.0001 par exchanged for (0.02) share new Common $0.0001 par 11/21/2003
Name changed to Arkados Group, Inc. 09/06/2006
Arkados Group, Inc. name changed to Solbright Group, Inc. 11/07/2017

CDL HOTELS INTL LTD (HONG KONG)
Sponsored ADR's for Ordinary split

(3.6175) for (1) by issuance of (2.6175) additional ADR's payable 09/01/2000 to holders of record 08/16/2000 Ex date - 08/16/2000
Name changed to City e-Solutions Ltd. 09/05/2000
(See City e-Solutions Ltd.)

CDM, INC. (DE)
Liquidation completed
Each share Common $1 par exchanged for initial distribution of (0.091149) share Sanders Associates, Inc. (DE) Common $1 par 12/21/1965
Each share Common $1 par received second and final distribution of (0.014137) share Sanders Associates, Inc. (DE) 08/19/1966
(See Sanders Associates, Inc. (DE))

CDM CAP CORP (AB)
Name changed to CDK Services Ltd. 07/28/1999
CDK Services Ltd. name changed to EcoMax Energy Services Ltd. (AB) 07/05/2005 which reincorporated in British Columbia as Tasca Resources Ltd. 10/19/2011

CDM LIQ CO (UT)
Completely liquidated 03/10/1980
Each share Capital Stock 50¢ par exchanged for first and final distribution of $2.8176 cash

CDMI PRODUCTIONS INC (NY)
Reincorporated under the laws of Delaware as Gener8Xion Entertainment, Inc. 01/14/2005
(See Gener8Xion Entertainment, Inc.)

CDNET CANADA INC (ON)
Delisted from Toronto Venture Stock Exchange 06/05/2002

CDNOW INC (DE)
Merged into Bertlsmann Inc. 09/01/2000
Each share Common no par exchanged for $3 cash

CDNOW INC (PA)
Under plan of merger each share Common no par automatically became (1) share CDnow, Inc. (DE) Common no par 03/17/1999
(See CDnow, Inc. (DE))

CDOOR CORP (DE)
Reorganized as Sinobiomed Inc. 03/02/2007
Each share Common $0.0001 par exchanged for (40) shares Common $0.0001 par
Sinobiomed Inc. recapitalized as Sitoa Global Inc. 08/04/2011 which recapitalized as Seratosa Inc. 12/17/2013 which recapitalized as Weyland Tech, Inc. 09/01/2015

CDP COMPUTER DATA PROCESSORS LTD (AB)
Merged into Digitech Ltd. 10/15/1973
Each share Common $1 par exchanged for (1) share Common no par
Digitech Ltd. recapitalized as Colin Energy Corp. 11/17/1987 which recapitalized as International Colin Energy Corp. 06/06/1990 which merged into Morgan Hydrocarbons Inc. 07/01/1996 which was acquired by Stampeder Exploration Ltd. 10/15/96 which was acquired by Gulf Canada Resources Ltd. 09/10/1997
(See Gulf Canada Resources Ltd.)

CDP CONTROL CORP. (VA)
Reincorporated under the laws of Delaware as Professional Associates, Inc. 05/15/1974
(See Professional Associates, Inc.)

CDP TECHNOLOGIES INC (DE)
Name changed to Ovid Technologies, Inc. 05/01/1995
Ovid Technologies, Inc. merged into Wolters Kluwer N.V. 11/09/1998

CDR RES INC (BC)
Struck off register and declared dissolved for failure to file returns 02/08/1991

CDRH LTD (CANADA)
Name changed to Foodex Systems Ltd. 05/09/1972
Foodex Systems Ltd. merged into Foodex Inc. 06/30/1978 which merged into Dexleigh Corp. 06/30/1984
(See Dexleigh Corp.)

CDSI HLDGS INC (DE)
Name changed to SG Blocks, Inc. 11/09/2011

CDSS WIND DOWN INC (DE)
Under plan of partial liquidation each share Common 1¢ par received distribution of $0.50 cash payable 01/05/2007 to holders of record 01/02/2007
Recapitalized as Green Energy Management Services Holdings, Inc. 09/22/2010
Each share Common 1¢ par exchanged for (1/3) share Common $0.0001 par

CDT VENTURES INC (UT)
Involuntarily dissolved 06/01/1991

CDW COMPUTERS CTRS INC (IL)
Common 1¢ par split (2) for (1) by issuance of (1) additional share 05/06/1994
Common 1¢ par split (3) for (2) by issuance of (0.5) additional share payable 07/15/1996 to holders of record 07/05/1996
Common 1¢ par split (2) for (1) by issuance of (1) additional share payable 05/19/1999 to holders of record 05/05/1999
Common 1¢ par split (2) for (1) by issuance of (1) additional share payable 06/21/2000 to holders of record 06/14/2000
Name changed to CDW Corp. 06/17/2003
(See CDW Corp.)

CDX COM INC (CO)
Name changed 01/08/2001
Each share old Common 1¢ par exchanged for (0.16666666) share new Common 1¢ par 06/21/1985
Name changed from CDX Corp. to CDX.Com, Inc. 01/08/2001
Common 1¢ par split (3.33) for (1) by issuance of (2.33) additional shares payable 01/24/2001 to holders of record 01/23/2001 Ex date - 01/25/2001
Reorganized under the laws of Oklahoma as Airguide, Inc. 08/29/2005
Each share Common 1¢ par exchanged for (0.001) share Common $0.001 par
Note: Holders of (100,000) or fewer pre-split shares received (100) shares
Airguide, Inc. name changed to Amerex Group, Inc. 03/01/2007
(See Amerex Group, Inc.)

CE CO MANUFACTURING CO., INC.
Acquired by Gold Seal Electrical Co. 00/00/1932
Details not available

CE COMPUTER EQUIP AG (GERMANY)
Name changed to Ceyoniq AG 03/02/2001
(See Ceyoniq AG)

CE FRANKLIN LTD (AB)
Acquired by National Oilwell Varco, Inc. 07/19/2012
Each share Common no par exchanged for $12.75 cash

CE SOFTWARE HLDGS INC (DE)
Each share Common 2¢ par exchanged for (0.2) share Common 10¢ par 06/30/1997

Name changed to Lightning Rod Software, Inc. 05/02/2000
(See Lightning Rod Software, Inc.)

CEA ACQUISITION CORP (DE)
Name changed to etrials Worldwide, Inc. 02/10/2006 etrials Worldwide, Inc. merged into Merge Healthcare Inc. 07/20/2009
(See Merge Healthcare Inc.)

CEA LAB INC (KS)
Reincorporated 10/16/1995
Each share old Common no par exchanged for (0.01) share new Common no par 04/28/1989
State of incorporation changed from (CO) to (KS) 10/16/1995
Each share new Common no par exchanged for (0.1) share Common $0.001 par 11/30/1995
Each share Common $0.001 par received distribution of (1) share Gourmet's Choice Coffee Co., Inc. Common 1¢ par payable 03/31/1997 to holders of record 03/14/1997
Name changed to Courtleigh Capital Inc. (KS) 09/29/1997
Courtleigh Capital Inc. (KS) recapitalized in Nevada as Stockup.Com Inc. 02/22/1999 which reorganized as Preference Technologies Inc. 02/23/2000
(See Preference Technologies Inc.)

CEANIC CORP (LA)
Merged into CC Acquisition Corp. 08/17/1998
Each share Common no par exchanged for $20 cash

CEAPRO INC (AB)
Reincorporated under the laws of Canada 08/28/2002

CEASAR RES LTD (BC)
Name changed to Audre Recognition Systems Inc. 04/07/1987
Audre Recognition Systems Inc. reorganized as eXtr@ct, Inc. 04/17/2000
(See eXtr@ct, Inc.)

CEASE FIRE CORP (DE)
Reverted to private company 00/00/1992
Details not available

CEATECH USA INC (CO)
Each share Common no par received distribution of (1) share Ceatech Enterprises Restricted Common payable 03/16/2007 to holders of record 02/28/2007
Chapter 11 bankruptcy proceedings terminated 05/02/2007
Stockholders' equity unlikely

CEB INC (DE)
Merged into Gartner, Inc. 04/05/2017
Each share Common 1¢ par exchanged for (0.2284) share Common $0.0005 par and $54 cash

CEBCO INC (DE)
Stock Dividend - 1900% 03/01/1976
Name changed to Redmond Capital Corp. 04/17/1985
Redmond Capital Corp. name changed to Dominion Capital Corp. 08/12/1985
(See Dominon Capital Corp.)

CEBETON INDS (UT)
Proclaimed dissolved for failure to pay taxes 11/09/1974

CEBU SUGAR CO., INC. (PHILIPPINES)
Each (2) shares Capital Stock 10 Pesos par exchanged for (2) shares Capital Stock 1 Peso par, (1) share Bogo-Medellin Milling Co. and 3 Pesos cash 00/00/1949
Out of business 07/20/1955
Details not available

CEC CORP (FL)
Each share Common 1¢ par exchanged for (0.33333333) share Common 3¢ par 08/03/1971

Name changed to Douglass Industries, Inc. 07/18/1972
(See Douglass Industries, Inc.)

CEC ENTMT INC (KS)
Common 10¢ par split (3) for (2) by issuance of (0.5) additional share payable 07/23/1999 to holders of record 07/01/1999 Ex date - 07/26/1999
Variable Dividend Preferred Class A called for redemption at $60 on 10/31/2003
Common 10¢ par split (3) for (2) by issuance of (0.5) additional share payable 03/15/2004 to holders of record 02/25/2004 Ex date - 03/16/2004
Acquired by Apollo Global Management, LLC 02/14/2014
Each share Common 10¢ par exchanged for $54 cash

CEC PPTYS INC (DE)
Charter cancelled and declared void for failure to pay franchise taxes 03/01/2001

CEC RES LTD (AB)
99.6% acquired by Carbon Energy Corp. through purchase offer which expired 02/26/2001
Public interest eliminated

CECIL BANCORP INC (MD)
Common 1¢ par split (2) for (1) by issuance of (1) additional share payable 03/31/2004 to holders of record 03/15/2004
Common 1¢ par split (2) for (1) by issuance of (1) additional share payable 05/16/2007 to holders of record 05/02/2007 Ex date - 05/17/2007
Common 1¢ par split (2) for (1) by issuance of (1) additional share payable 06/07/2011 to holders of record 05/31/2011 Ex date - 06/08/2011
Stock Dividends - 1% payable 01/12/2006 to holders of record 12/26/2005 Ex date - 12/21/2005; 1% payable 04/26/2006 to holders of record 04/05/2006 Ex date - 04/05/2006; 1% payable 10/26/2006 to holders of record 10/12/2006 Ex date - 10/10/2006
Plan of reorganization under Chapter 11 Federal Bankruptcy proceedings effective 10/27/2017
No stockholders' equity

CECIL FOODS, INC. (IN)
Assets sold for benefit of creditors in 04/00/1971
No stockholders' equity

CECO CORP (DE)
Common $10 par split (4) for (3) by issuance of (1/3) additional share 12/31/1964
Common $10 par changed to no par 07/31/1967
Common no par split (2) for (1) by issuance of (1) additional share 09/30/1967
Common no par split (3) for (2) by issuance of (0.5) additional share 01/03/1984
Under plan of reorganization each share Common no par automatically became (1) share Ceco Industries, Inc. Common no par 08/01/1984
(See Ceco Industries, Inc.)

CECO ENVIRONMENTAL CORP (NY)
Reincorporated under the laws of Delaware 01/11/2002

CECO INDUSTRIES, INC. (NY)
Recapitalized as F & B/Ceco Industries, Inc. 10/30/1964
Each share Common 25¢ par exchanged for (0.25) share Common 25¢ par
(See F & B/Ceco Industries, Inc.)

CECO INDS INC (DE)
$3.85 Conv. Preferred Ser. A no par called for redemption 08/16/1985
$5 Conv. Preferred Ser. B no par called for redemption 08/16/1985
Merged into M C Co. 12/09/1986
Each share Common no par exchanged for $15 principal amount of Discount Subord. Debentures due 11/30/2000 and $35.50 cash

CECO STEEL PRODUCTS CORP. (DE)
Name changed to Ceco Corp. 12/18/1964
Ceco Corp. reorganized as Ceco Industries, Inc. 08/01/1984
(See Ceco Industries, Inc.)

CECO SYS INC (DE)
Merged into Consolidated Brands, Inc. 12/04/1985
Each share Common 20¢ par exchanged for $1.10 cash

CECS CORP (DE)
Charter cancelled and declared inoperative and void for non-payment of taxes 03/01/2003

CED-OR CORP (QC)
Delisted from Toronto Venture Stock Exchange 06/22/2006

CEDAR CAP CORP (AB)
Recapitalized as Vancan Capital Corp. 02/27/2002
Each share Common no par exchanged for (0.25) share Common no par
Vancan Capital Corp. name changed to Max Resources Corp. 05/14/2004

CEDAR CITY MINES LTD (BC)
Struck off register and declared dissolved for failure to file returns 01/02/1979

CEDAR CORP (AB)
Struck off register for failure to file annual returns 10/22/1998

CEDAR GROUP INC (DE)
Common $0.001 par split (4) for (3) by issuance of (0.33333333) additional share 02/06/1990
Each share old Common $0.001 par exchanged for (0.0696007) share new Common $0.001 par 09/30/1993
Name changed to Dominion Bridge Corp. 08/01/1996
(See Dominion Bridge Corp.)

CEDAR INCOME FD LTD OLD (MD)
Name changed 10/01/1989
Reincorporated 06/26/1998
Name changed from Cedar Income Fund I Ltd. to Cedar Income Fund Ltd. (Old) (IA) 10/01/1989
State of incorporation changed from (IA) to (MD) 06/26/1998
Name changed to Uni-Invest (U.S.A.), Ltd. 02/29/2000
Uni-Invest (U.S.A.), Ltd. name changed to Cedar Income Fund Ltd. (New) 08/03/2000 which name changed to Cedar Shopping Centers Inc. 08/05/2003 which name changed to Cedar Realty Trust, Inc. 11/10/2011

CEDAR INCOME FUND LTD NEW (MD)
Common 1¢ par split (2) for (1) by issuance of (1) additional share payable 07/14/2003 to holders of record 07/07/2003 Ex date - 07/15/2003
Name changed to Cedar Shopping Centers Inc. 08/05/2003
Cedar Shopping Centers Inc. name changed to Cedar Realty Trust, Inc. 11/10/2011

CEDAR MTN DISTRS INC (NV)
Each share old Common $0.001 par exchanged for (0.33333333) share new Common $0.001 par 06/03/2005
Name changed to iCurie, Inc. 07/14/2005
iCurie, Inc. name changed to Celsia Technologies, Inc. 10/09/2006
(See Celsia Technologies, Inc.)

CEDAR MTN EXPL INC (AB)
Name changed to Graphite One Resources Inc. (AB) 03/23/2012
Graphite One Resources Inc. (AB) reincorporated in British Columbia 09/12/2014

CEDAR OILS LTD (AB)
Name changed to Seneca Metal Products Ltd. 01/26/1990
Seneca Metal Products Ltd. recapitalized as Cedar Corp. 05/18/1994
(See Cedar Corp.)

CEDAR POINT FIELD TR
Completely liquidated 01/11/1991
Each Ctf. of Bene. Int. no par received first and final distribution of $0.1109 cash
Note: Certificates were not required to be surrendered and are without value

CEDAR POINT INC (OH)
Preferred $100 par called for redemption 04/01/1973
Stock Dividend - 100% 07/20/1971
Acquired by a private investor group 07/29/1983
Each share Common $1 par exchanged for $40 cash

CEDAR RAPIDS CADDOO, INC. (IA)
Name changed to Cock-A-Doodle Doo of Iowa, Inc. 05/01/1963
(See Cock-A-Doodle Doo of Iowa, Inc.)

CEDAR RLTY TR INC (MD)
Name changed 11/10/2011
Each share Common 1¢ par exchanged for (0.16666666) share Common 6¢ par 10/20/2003
Name changed from Cedar Shopping Centers, Inc. to Cedar Realty Trust, Inc. 11/10/2011
8.875% Preferred Ser. A 1¢ par called for redemption at $25 plus $0.1171 accrued dividends on 03/11/2013
(Additional Information in Active)

CEDAR RIDGE INTL INC (UT)
Name changed 07/23/1997
Each share old Common $0.001 par exchanged for (0.01) share new Common $0.001 par 01/21/1997
Name changed from to Cedar Ridge Oil & Gas, Inc. to Cedar Ridge International, Inc. 07/23/1997
Charter expired 07/11/2001

CEDAR TALISMAN CONSOLIDATED MINES CO. (UT)
Bankrupt 00/00/1954
Details not available

CEDARA SOFTWARE CORP (ON)
Merged into Merge Technologies Inc. 06/01/2005
Each share Common no par exchanged for either (0.587) share Common no par or (0.587) share Merge Cedara ExchangeCo Ltd. Non-Vtg. Exchangeable Share no par
Note: Non-electing Canadian holders received Exchangeable shares
(See Merge Cedara ExchangeCo Ltd.)
Merge Technologies Inc. name changed to Merge Healthcare Inc. (WI) 02/22/2008 which reincorporated in Delaware 12/05/2008
(See Merge Healthcare Inc.)

CEDARMINE RES INC (AB)
Delisted from Alberta Stock Exchange 05/17/1994

CEDARVALE MINES LTD (QC)
Charter annulled for failure to file reports or pay fees 00/00/1985

CEDINO (CANADA) LTD. (CANADA)
Deemed to no longer be a subsisting company 00/00/1954
No stockholders' equity

CEDRIC KUSHNER PROMOTIONS INC (DE)
Each share Class A Common 1¢ par exchanged for (1) share Common 1¢ par 12/16/2004
Name changed to Ckrush, Inc. 12/27/2005
(See Ckrush, Inc.)

CEDUNA CAP CORP (YT)
Reorganized under the laws of British Columbia as Titan Uranium Exploration Inc. 06/03/2005
Each share Common no par exchanged for (0.5) share Common no par
Titan Uranium Exploration Inc. name changed to Titan Uranium Inc. (BC) 06/27/2005 which reincorporated in Canada 02/19/2009 which merged into Energy Fuels Inc. 02/24/2012

CEDYCO CORP (DE)
Company believed out of business as of 11/00/2008
Stockholders' equity unlikely

CEDYNA FINL CORP (JAPAN)
ADR agreement terminated 05/24/2017
No ADR's remain outstanding

CEEE GROUP CORP (CO)
Reorganized under the laws of Delaware as Atlantic International Entertainment, Ltd. 11/26/1996
Each share Common $0.001 par exchanged for (0.33333333) share Common $0.001 par
Atlantic International Entertainment, Ltd. name changed to Online Gaming Systems, Ltd. 10/01/1999 which name changed to Advanced Resources Group Ltd. 02/15/2007

CEIBA ENERGY SVCS INC (AB)
Merged into Secure Energy Services Inc. 08/09/2017
Each share Common no par exchanged for $0.205 cash
Note: Unexchanged certificates will be cancelled and become without value 08/01/2020

CEIL CHAPMAN INC (DE)
Charter cancelled and declared inoperative and void for non-payment of taxes 03/01/1975

CEL COMMUNICATIONS INC (NY)
Each share old Common 1¢ par exchanged for (0.14400969) share new Common 1¢ par 04/27/1990
Filed a petition under Chapter 11 Federal Bankruptcy Code 08/18/1994
Stockholders' equity unlikely

CELANESE AG (GERMANY)
Squeeze-out merger effective 02/01/2007
Each share Ordinary no par exchanged for $86.343411 cash

CELANESE CDA INC (CANADA)
Name changed 01/08/1980
Name changed from Celanese Canada Ltd.- Celanese Canada Ltee. to Celanese Canada Inc. 01/08/1980
$1 Preferred $25 par reclassified as $1.24 Preferred Ser. 2 $25 par 10/28/1986
$1.75 Preferred $25 par reclassified as $2.16 Preferred Ser. 1 $25 par 10/28/1986
$1.24 Preferred Ser. 2 $25 par called for redemption 03/31/1993
$2.16 Preferred Ser. 1 $25 par called for redemption 03/31/1993
Common no par split (3) for (1) by issuance of (2) additional shares 05/30/1994
Merged into HNA Acquisition 08/23/1999

Each share Common no par exchanged for $27.25 cash

CELANESE CORP. OF AMERICA (DE)
Each share old Common no par exchanged for (4) shares new Common no par 05/00/1927
Each share 1st Preferred $100 par exchanged for (1) share 7% 2nd Preferred $100 par and (1.5) shares new Common no par 12/05/1941
New Common no par split (5) for (2) by issuance of (3) additional shares 09/25/1946
Stock Dividend - 25% 07/15/1959
Name changed to Celanese Corp. 04/13/1966
(See Celanese Corp.)

CELANESE CORP (DE)
Certificates dated after 01/25/2005
4.25% Conv. Perpetual Preferred 1¢ par called for redemption at (0.8525) share Ser. A Common $0.0001 par 02/22/2010
(Additional Information in Active)

CELANESE CORP (DE)
Certificates dated prior to 02/27/1987
Merged into American Hoechst Corp. 02/27/1987
Each share Conv. Preference no par exchanged for $172.40 cash
Each share 7% 2nd Preferred $100 par exchanged for $102 cash
Each share Common no par exchanged for $245 cash
4.5% Preferred Ser. A $100 par called for redemption 03/30/1987
Public interest eliminated

CELATOR PHARMACEUTICALS INC (DE)
Acquired by Jazz Pharmaceuticals PLC 07/12/2016
Each share Common $0.001 par exchanged for $30.25 cash

CELCOR INC (DE)
Each share old Common $0.001 par exchanged for (0.2) share new Common $0.001 par 11/10/1993
Name changed to Northeast (USA) Corp. 10/25/1996
Northeast (USA) Corp. name changed to Buy It Cheap.com, Inc. 12/13/1999 which recapitalized as Advanced Battery Technologies, Inc. 07/12/2004
(See Advanced Battery Technologies, Inc.)

CELEBDIRECT INC (DE)
Name changed to Muscle Flex, Inc. 10/01/2008
Muscle Flex, Inc. name changed to Bravada International, Ltd. 07/19/2010

CELEBRATE EXPRESS INC (WA)
Merged into Liberty Media Corp. 08/29/2008
Each share Common $0.001 par exchanged for $3.90 cash

CELEBRATION CELLARS LTD (AB)
Name changed to WNS Inc. 07/03/2001
WNS Inc. name changed to WNS Emergent Inc. 05/01/2002 which name changed to CriticalControl Solutions Corp. 06/14/2004 which name changed to Critical Control Energy Services Corp. 07/03/2015

CELEBRITY ENERGY CORP (BC)
Recapitalized as Polar Bear Development Corp. 02/27/1995
Each share Common no par exchanged for (0.25) share Common no par
(See Polar Bear Development Corp.)

CELEBRITY ENTMT GROUP INC (WY)
Reincorporated 01/11/1996
State of incorporation changed from (NV) to (WY) 01/11/1996
Each share old Common $0.001 par

exchanged for (0.1) share new
Common $0.001 par 12/18/1997
Reincorporated under the laws of
Delaware as Sharp Holding Corp.
04/19/2001
Sharp Holding Corp. recapitalized as
Cooper Holding Corp. 10/28/2010
which recapitalized as Crednology
Holding Corp. 05/03/2013

CELEBRITY ENTMT INC (DE)
Each share old Common $0.0001 par
exchanged for (0.2) share new
Common $0.0001 par 08/03/1995
Each share new Common $0.0001
par exchanged again for (0.02)
share new Common $0.0001 par
03/12/1997
Name changed to Injectomatic
Systems International Inc.
04/23/2003
Injectomatic Systems International
Inc. name changed to Galton
Biometrics Inc. 10/26/2004
(See Galton Biometrics Inc.)

CELEBRITY INC (TX)
Each share old Common 1¢ par
exchanged for (0.25) share new
Common 1¢ par 03/01/1999
Merged into KRG Capital Partners,
LLC 08/19/2003
Each share new Common 1¢ par
exchanged for $5.6811439 cash
Note: Each share new Common 1¢
par received an initial distribution of
$0.37795742 cash from escrow
04/13/2006
Each share new Common 1¢ par
received a second distribution of
$0.04935173 cash from escrow
04/25/2006

CELEBRITY NETWORK INC (NV)
Recapitalized as Laforza Automobiles
Inc. 08/26/1997
Each share Common $0.001 par
exchanged for (0.05) share Common
$0.001 par
Laforza Automobiles Inc. name
changed to U.S. Sustainable Energy
Corp. 11/01/2006 which
recapitalized as Zeons Corp.
02/26/2010

CELEBRITY RESORTS INC (DE)
Common $0.0001 par split (2) for (1)
by issuance of (1) additional share
06/14/1991
Recapitalized as Celebrity
Entertainment Inc. 09/20/1993
Each share Common $0.0001 par
exchanged for (0.2) share Common
$0.0001 par
Celebrity Entertainment Inc. name
changed to Injectomatic Systems
International Inc. 04/23/2003 which
name changed to Galton Biometrics
Inc. 10/26/2004
(See Galton Biometrics Inc.)

CELEBRITY RESORTS INC (NV)
Reorganized as Sandculture.com, Inc.
11/07/2000
Each share Common $0.001 par
exchanged for (6) shares Common
$0.001 par
Sandculture.com, Inc. name changed
to Dinozine Ventures Inc.
10/15/2001 which name changed to
Zamage Digital Art Imaging, Inc.
04/05/2004

CELEBRITY SPORTS NETWORK INC (CO)
Common $0.001 par split (40) for (1)
by issuance of (39) additional
shares payable 09/20/2001 to
holders of record 09/19/2001
Ex date - 09/21/2001
Name changed to Powder River
Basin Gas Corp. (CO) 12/07/2001
Powder River Basin Gas Corp. (CO)
reincorporated in Oklahoma as
Powder River Petroleum
International, Inc. 12/13/2007
(See Powder River Petroleum
International, Inc.)

CELERA CORP (DE)
Acquired by Quest Diagnostics Inc.
05/17/2011
Each share Common 1¢ par
exchanged for $8 cash

CELEREX CORP (WA)
Chapter 11 bankruptcy proceedings
terminated 12/20/1996
Details not available

CELERIS CORP (MN)
Each share old Common 1¢ par
exchanged for (0.33333333) share
new Common 1¢ par 07/30/1999
Completely liquidated 12/03/2002
Each share new Common 1¢ par
exchanged for first and final
distribution of $0.25 cash

CELERITEK INC (CA)
Under plan of partial liquidation each
share Common no par received
initial distribution of $0.62 cash
payable 06/24/2005 to holders of
record 06/10/2005
Each share Common no par received
second distribution of $0.12 cash
payable 12/22/2005 to holders of
record 07/22/2005
Recapitalized as Strasbaugh
05/25/2007
Each share Common no par
exchanged for (0.03225806) share
Common no par
Note: Corporate name changed to
CTK Windup Corp. 07/11/2005

CELERITY COMPUTING (CA)
Completely liquidated 03/22/1990
Each share Common no par
exchanged for first and final
distribution of $0.0012959 cash

CELERITY SOLUTIONS INC (DE)
Company terminated registration of
common stock and is no longer
public as of 11/22/2002
Details not available

CELERITY SYS INC (DE)
Each share old Common $0.001 par
exchanged for (0.05) share new
Common $0.001 par 04/24/2002
Name changed to Homeland Security
Capital Corp. 02/02/2006
Homeland Security Capital Corp.
recapitalized as Timios National
Corp. 08/29/2012
(See Timios National Corp.)

CELERON CORP (LA)
Merged into Goodyear Tire & Rubber
Co. 06/21/1983
Each share Common no par
exchanged for (1.15) shares
Common no par

CELESIO AG (GERMANY)
Name changed to McKesson Europe
AG 09/26/2017

CELEST MEDICHEM INC (YT)
Name changed to Kronofusion
Technologies Inc. 12/12/2001
Kronofusion Technologies Inc.
recapitalized as Consolidated
Kronofusion Technologies Inc.
08/13/2003 which recapitalized as
JER Envirotech International Corp.
(YT) 09/22/2004 which
reincorporated in British Columbia
02/13/2009
(See JER Envirotech International
Corp.)

CELESTA CORP (CO)
Name changed to Innovative Holdings
& Technologies Inc. 02/27/1998
(See Innovative Holdings &
Technologies Inc.)

CELESTA II CORP (CO)
Recapitalized as Spectrum
Resources, Inc. (CO) 07/14/1989
Each share Common $0.0001 par
exchanged for (0.04) share Common
$0.0001 par
Spectrum Resources, Inc. (CO) name
changed to Spectrum Datatech, Inc.

07/24/1989 which name changed to
Spindle Oil & Gas, Inc. 06/07/1991
(See Spindle Oil & Gas, Inc.)

CELESTAR EXPL LTD (AB)
Recapitalized as CanScot Resources
Ltd. 05/26/1999
Each share Common no par
exchanged for (0.2) share Common
no par
(See CanScot Resources Ltd.)

CELESTE, INC. (CT)
Name changed to Celeste Industries
Corp. 04/17/1969
(See Celeste Industries Corp.)

CELESTE COPPER CORP (AB)
Name changed to Celeste Mining
Corp. 11/29/2012

CELESTE INDUSTRIES CORP. (CT)
Each share old Common no par
exchanged for (0.00066666) share
new Common no par 03/31/1978
Note: In effect holders received $2.50
cash per share and public interest
was eliminated

CELESTE RES INC (BC)
Delisted from Vancouver Stock
Exchange 11/13/1987

CELESTIAL DELIGHTS USA CORP (NV)
Common $0.00001 par split (8) for (1)
by issuance of (7) additional shares
payable 06/09/2009 to holders of
record 06/08/2009 Ex date -
06/10/2009
Name changed to Far East Wind
Power Corp. 02/09/2010

CELESTIAL ENERGY INC (AB)
Name changed to Primera Energy
Resources Ltd. 07/12/2007
Primera Energy Resources Ltd.
merged into Touchstone Exploration
Inc. (BC) 12/05/2012 which merged
into Touchstone Exploration Inc.
(AB) 05/20/2014

CELESTIAL SEASONINGS INC (DE)
Common 1¢ par split (2) for (1) by
issuance of (1) additional share
payable 09/25/1998 to holders of
record 09/11/1998
Merged into Hain Celestial Group,
Inc. 05/30/2000
Each share Common 1¢ par
exchanged for (1.265) shares
Common 1¢ par

CELESTIAL VENTURES CORP (NV)
Each share old Common $0.0001 par
exchanged for (0.0142857) share
new Common $0.0001 par
02/24/1993
Each share new Common $0.0001
par exchanged for (0.06666666)
share Common $0.001 par
05/03/1996
Charter revoked for failure to file
reports and pay fees 02/01/2003

CELEX GROUP INC (MN)
Common 1¢ par split (3) for (2) by
issuance of (0.5) additional share
04/12/1994
Name changed to Successories Inc.
09/16/1996
(See Successories Inc.)

CELEXX CORP (NV)
SEC revoked common stock
registration 02/08/2011

CELICO RES LTD (BC)
Struck off register and declared
dissolved for failure to file returns
06/05/1992

CELINA FINL CORP (OH)
Class A Common $1 par changed to
50¢ par and (1) additional share
issued 09/18/1978
Acquired by CFC Acquisition, LLC
12/31/2004
Each share Class A Common 50¢ par
exchanged for $5.80 cash

CELITE CO.
Acquired by Johns-Manville Corp.
(NY) 00/00/1928
Details not available

CELL BIO SYS INC (NV)
Name changed to Tulip BioMed, Inc.
(NV) 06/02/2006
Tulip BioMed, Inc. (NV) reorganized
in Florida as Bitcoin Services, Inc.
03/21/2016

CELL BIO-SYSTEMS INC (NY)
Name changed to Franklin Scientific,
Inc. 04/27/2004
(See Franklin Scientific, Inc.)

CELL GENESYS INC (DE)
Merged into BioSante
Pharmaceuticals, Inc. 10/14/2009
Each share Common $0.001 par
exchanged for (0.1828) share
Common no par
BioSante Pharmaceuticals, Inc.
recapitalized as ANI
Pharmaceuticals, Inc. 07/18/2013

CELL LIFE (CA)
Each share old Common no par
exchanged for (0.05) share new
Common no par 12/04/1982
Charter cancelled for failure to file
reports and pay taxes 10/01/1984

CELL-LOC INC (AB)
Plan of arrangement effective
12/03/2003
Each share Common no par
exchanged for (0.5) share Capitol
Energy Resources Ltd. Common no
par and (1) share Cell-Loc Location
Technologies Inc. Common no par
(See each company's listing)

CELL-LOC LOCATION TECHNOLOGIES INC (AB)
Each share old Common no par
exchanged for (0.2) share new
Common no par 05/21/2008
Reorganized as Times Three Wireless
Inc. 12/05/2011
Each share new Common no par
exchanged for (1) share Common
no par
Note: Unexchanged certificates were
cancelled and became without value
12/05/2017
(See Times Three Wireless Inc.)

CELL PATHWAYS INC NEW (DE)
Merged into OSI Pharmaceuticals,
Inc. 06/12/2003
Each share Common 1¢ par
exchanged for (0.0567) share
Common 1¢ par
(See OSI Pharmaceuticals, Inc.)

CELL PATHWAYS INC OLD (DE)
Merged into Cell Pathways, Inc.
(New) 11/04/1998
Each share Common no par
exchanged for (1) share Common
no par
Cell Pathways, Inc. (New) merged
into OSI Pharmaceuticals, Inc.
06/12/2003
(See OSI Pharmaceuticals, Inc.)

CELL PWR TECHNOLOGIES INC (FL)
Each share old Common no par
exchanged for (0.16666666) share
new Common no par 04/11/2006
SEC revoked common stock
registration 11/10/2010

CELL PRODS INC (NJ)
Assets sold for benefit of creditors
10/00/1974
No stockholders' equity

CELL ROBOTICS INTL INC (CO)
Each share Conv. Ser. A Preferred
exchanged for (4) shares Common
$0.0001 par 02/15/1999
SEC revoked common stock
registration 11/02/2010

CELL TECH INTL INC (DE)
Company terminated registration of
common stock and is no longer
public as of 12/29/2004

CELL TECHNOLOGY INC (DE)
Name changed to Air Methods Corp. 11/13/1991
(See Air Methods Corp.)

CELL THERAPEUTICS INC (WA)
Each share old Common no par exchanged for (0.25) share new Common no par 04/16/2007
Each share new Common no par exchanged again for (0.1) share new Common no par 09/02/2008
Each share new Common no par exchanged again for (0.16666666) share new Common no par 05/16/2011
Each share new Common no par exchanged again for (0.2) share new Common no par 09/04/2012
Each share Preferred Ser. 17 no par exchanged for (714.2857142) shares new Common no par 11/10/2012
Name changed to CTI BioPharma Corp. (WA) 06/02/2014
CTI BioPharma Corp. (WA) reincorporated in Delaware 01/29/2018

CELL WIRELESS CORP (NV)
SEC revoked common stock registration 10/29/2010

CELLADON CORP (DE)
Recapitalized as Eiger BioPharmaceuticals, Inc. 03/23/2016
Each share Common $0.001 par exchanged for (0.06666666) share Common $0.001 par

CELLARDOR MINES LTD (BC)
Struck off register and declared dissolved for failure to file returns 08/30/1976

CELLCEUTIX CORP (NV)
Name changed to Innovation Pharmaceuticals Inc. 06/09/2017

CELLCOM 1 CORP (DE)
Each share old Common $0.001 par exchanged for (0.33333333) share new Common $0.001 par 06/07/1989
Name changed from Cellcom Corp. to Cellcom 1 Corp. 06/02/2005
SEC revoked common stock registration 11/02/2010

CELLCOR INC (DE)
Merged into Cytogen Corp. 10/16/1995
Each share Common 1¢ par exchanged for (0.6) share Common 1¢ par
(See Cytogen Corp.)

CELLDONATE INC (NV)
Common $0.001 par split (10) for (1) by issuance of (9) additional shares payable 10/31/2010 to holders of record 10/29/2010 Ex date - 11/01/2010
Recapitalized as Gold Torrent, Inc. (NV) 03/21/2014
Each share Common $0.001 par exchanged for (0.2) share Common no par
Gold Torrent, Inc. (NV) reincorporated in British Columbia as Gold Torrent (Canada) Inc. 03/01/2018

CELLEGY PHARMACEUTICALS INC (DE)
Reincorporated 09/02/2004
State of incorporation changed from (CA) to (DE) and Common no par changed to $0.0001 par 09/02/2004
Recapitalized as Adamis Pharmaceuticals Corp. 04/22/2009
Each share Common $0.0001 par exchanged for (0.10071446) share Common $0.0001 par

CELLEX BIOSCIENCES INC (MN)
Each share old Common no par exchanged for (0.05) share new Common no par 12/19/1995
Plan of reorganization under Chapter 11 Federal Bankruptcy proceedings effective 07/31/1999
No stockholders' equity
Reincorporated under the laws of Delaware as Biovest International, Inc. and new Common no par changed to 1¢ par 05/07/2001
(See Biovest International, Inc.)

CELLMETRIX INC (NY)
Charter cancelled and proclaimed dissolved for failure to pay taxes 12/24/2002

CELLNET DATA SYS INC (DE)
Plan of reorganization under Chapter 11 Federal Bankruptcy Code effective 09/12/2000
No stockholders' equity

CELLNET FDG LLC (DE)
Plan of reorganization under Chapter 11 Federal Bankruptcy Code effective 09/12/2000
No stockholders' equity

CELLPOINT INC (NV)
Chapter 11 bankruptcy proceedings dismissed 09/03/2003
No stockholders' equity

CELLPRO INC (DE)
Name changed to CPX Corp. 06/01/1999
CPX Corp. name changed to Steel Partners, Ltd. 07/03/2002
(See Steel Partners, Ltd.)

CELLSTAR CORP (DE)
Old Common 1¢ par split (3) for (2) by issuance of (0.5) additional share payable 06/17/1997 to holders of record 06/02/1997 Ex date - 06/18/1997
Old Common 1¢ par split (2) for (1) by issuance of (1) additional share payable 06/23/1998 to holders of record 06/05/1998 Ex date - 06/24/1998
Each share old Common 1¢ par exchanged for (0.2) share new Common 1¢ par 02/22/2002
Name changed to CLST Holdings, Inc. 05/31/2007

CELLTECH GROUP PLC (UNITED KINGDOM)
ADR agreement terminated 10/07/2004
Each Sponsored ADR for Ordinary exchanged for $19.6961 cash

CELLTECH MEDIA INC (ON)
Recapitalized as Smartel Communications Corp. 06/21/1995
Each share Class A Subordinate no par exchanged for (0.2) share Common no par
Smartel Communications Corp. name changed to Intasys Corp. 07/29/1996 which name changed to Mamma.com Inc. 01/12/2004 which name changed to Copernic Inc. 06/21/2007 which merged into Comamtech. (ON) 11/04/2010 which reincorporated in Delaware as DecisionPoint Systems, Inc. (New) 06/22/2011

CELLTECK INC (NV)
Recapitalized as Eos Petro, Inc. 05/21/2013
Each share Common $0.0001 par exchanged for (0.00125) share Common $0.0001 par
Note: No holder of (2,000) or more shares will receiver fewer than (100) shares
Holders of (1,999) or fewer shares received $0.025 cash per share

CELLTRONICS INC (NV)
Each share Common $0.001 par exchanged for (0.1) share Common 1¢ par 04/17/1987
Name changed to RF Industries, Ltd. 11/01/1990

CELLU CRAFT INC (DE)
Reincorporated 01/14/1971
Common $1 par split (2) for (1) by issuance of (1) additional share 06/07/1968
State of incorporation changed from (NY) to (DE) 01/14/1971
Common $1 par split (2) for (1) by issuance of (1) additional share 04/14/1983
Acquired by a group of investors 03/23/1984
Each share Common $1 par exchanged for $9 cash

CELLU TISSUE HLDGS INC (DE)
Acquired by Clearwater Paper Corp. 12/27/2010
Each share Common 1¢ par exchanged for $12 cash

CELLUFONE CORP (DE)
Name changed to Celcor, Inc. 05/02/1986
Celcor, Inc. name changed to Northeast (USA) Corp. 10/25/1996 which name changed to Buy It Cheap.com, Inc. 12/13/1999 which recapitalized as Advanced Battery Technologies, Inc. 07/12/2004
(See Advanced Battery Technologies, Inc.)

CELLULAR AMER INC (NJ)
Each share Common no par exchanged for initial distribution of (0.01486206664) share of Alltel Corp. Common $1 par 12/08/1988
Assets transferred to Cellular America Trust and Common no par reclassified as Shares of Bene. Int. no par 09/21/1989
(See Cellular America Trust)

CELLULAR AMERICA TRUST (NJ)
In process of liquidation
Details not available

CELLULAR COMMUNICATIONS INC NEW (DE)
Redeemable Common Ser. A 1¢ par split (3) for (2) by issuance of (0.5) additional share 05/13/1994
Merged into Airtouch Communications, Inc. 08/16/1996
Each share Conv. Preferred 1¢ par exchanged for (0.9) share 6% Conv. Class B Mandatorily Preferred 1¢ par and (0.578) share 4.25% Conv. Class C Preferred 1¢ par
Each share Ser. A Common 1¢ par exchanged for (0.9) share 6% Conv. Class B Mandatorily Preferred 1¢ par and (0.578) share 4.25% Conv. Class C Preferred 1¢ par

CELLULAR COMMUNICATIONS INC OLD (DE)
Common 1¢ par split (5) for (4) by issuance of (0.25) additional share 02/23/1987
Common 1¢ par split (3) for (2) by issuance of (0.5) additional share 10/06/1987
Common 1¢ par split (4) for (3) by issuance of (0.33333333) additional share 07/06/1988
Merged into Cellular Communications, Inc. (New) 07/31/1991
Each share Common 1¢ par exchanged for (1) share Conv. Part. Preferred 1¢ par
Cellular Communications, Inc. (New) merged into Airtouch Communications, Inc. 08/16/1996 which merged into Vodafone Airtouch PLC 06/30/1999 which name changed to Vodafone Group PLC (New) 06/28/2000

CELLULAR COMMUNICATIONS INTL INC (DE)
Common 1¢ par split (3) for (2) by issuance of (0.5) additional share 05/13/1994
Common 1¢ par split (3) for (2) by issuance of (0.5) additional share payable 04/14/1998 to holders of record 04/01/1998
Merged into Mannesmann A.G. 03/25/1999
Each share Common 1¢ par exchanged for $80 cash

CELLULAR COMMUNICATIONS P R INC NEW (DE)
Merged into SBC Communications, Inc. 08/24/1999
Each share Common 1¢ par exchanged for $29.50 cash

CELLULAR COMMUNICATIONS P R INC OLD (DE)
Common 1¢ par split (5) for (4) by issuance of (0.25) additional share 10/06/1992
Name changed to CoreComm Inc. 02/03/1997
CoreComm Inc. name changed to Cellular Communications of Puerto Rico, Inc. (New) 09/02/1998
(See Cellular Communications of Puerto Rico, Inc. (New))

CELLULAR CONCRETE PRODUCTS OF COLORADO, INC. (CO)
Charter revoked for failure to file reports and pay fees 10/18/1966

CELLULAR DYNAMICS INTL INC (WI)
Acquired by FUJIFILM Holdings Corp. 05/01/2015
Each share Common $0.0001 par exchanged for $16.50 cash

CELLULAR GROUP INC (NV)
Name changed to Wireless Advantage, Inc. 07/14/1994

CELLULAR INC (CO)
Name changed to Commnet Cellular Inc. 03/01/1994
(See Commnet Cellular Inc.)

CELLULAR INFORMATION SYS INC (DE)
Merged into PriceCellular Wireless Corp. 06/20/1997
Each share Class A Common 1¢ par exchanged for $1 cash

CELLULAR PRODS INC (NY)
SEC revoked common stock registration 11/10/2010

CELLULAR RADIO SYS INC (CO)
Recapitalized as Silverthorne Production Companies 05/31/1988
Each share Common $0.001 par exchanged for (0.05) share Common $0.001 par
Silverthorne Production Companies name changed to Cognigen Networks, Inc. (CO) 07/12/2000 which reorganized in Delaware as BayHill Capital Corp. 04/23/2008 which name changed to Agricon Global Corp. 06/01/2012 which recapitalized as StrategaBiz, Inc. 12/16/2014 which name changed to CryptoSign, Inc. 07/06/2015 which name changed to NABUfit Global, Inc. 12/10/2015 which name changed to NewBridge Global Ventures, Inc. 12/12/2017

CELLULAR TECHNICAL SVCS INC (DE)
Common $0.001 par split (2) for (1) by issuance of (1) additional share 02/15/1994
Common $0.001 par split (2) for (1) by issuance of (1) additional share payable 06/27/1996 to holders of record 06/24/1996
Each share old Common $0.001 par exchanged for (0.1) share new Common $0.001 par 01/05/1999
Name changed to SafeStitch Medical, Inc. 02/11/2008
SafeStitch Medical, Inc. name changed to TransEnterix, Inc. 12/09/2013

CELLULAR TECHNOLOGY INC (DE)
Name changed to Infopage, Inc. 11/06/1986

Infopage, Inc. recapitalized as Tamija Gold & Diamond Exploration, Inc. 07/31/2006
(See Tamija Gold & Diamond Exploration, Inc.)

CELLULAR TEL ENTERPRISES INC (DE)
Charter cancelled and declared inoperative and void for non-payment of taxes 03/01/1995

CELLULAR TELECOMMUNICATIONS & TECHNOLOGIES INC (UT)
Recapitalized as China Biomedical Group Inc. 04/03/1995
Each share Common no par exchanged for (0.5) share Common no par
China Biomedical Group Inc. name changed to Internet Holdings Ltd. 06/30/1996 which name changed to HTTP Technology, Inc. (UT) 11/28/2000 which reincorporated in Delaware 12/19/2000 which name changed to Medicsight, Inc. 10/28/2002 which name changed to MGT Capital Investments, Inc. 01/24/2007

CELLULARVISION USA INC (DE)
Name changed to SpeedUs.com, Inc. 01/06/1999
SpeedUs.com, Inc. name changed to Speedus Corp. 06/06/2002

CELLULOID CO.
Merged into Celluloid Corp. 00/00/1927
Details not available

CELLULOID CORP.
Merged into Celanese Corp. of America 12/05/1941
Each share 7% 1st Preferred exchanged for (1.25) shares 5% Prior Preferred $100 par
Each share $7 Preferred exchanged for either (0.5) share 5% Prior Preferred $100 par or (2) shares Common no par
Each share Common exchanged for (0.25) share Common no par
Celanese Corp. of America name changed to Celanese Corp. 04/13/1966
(See Celanese Corp.)

CELLWAY VENTURES INC (NV)
Name changed to AcronGenomics Inc. 03/05/2004
(See AcronGenomics Inc.)

CELLYNX GROUP INC (NV)
SEC revoked common stock registration 05/04/2016

CELOTEX CO. (DE)
Reorganized as Celotex Corp. 00/00/1935
Each share Preferred $100 par exchanged for (0.51) share Preferred $100 par
Each share Common no par exchanged for (0.33333333) share Common no par
Celotex Corp. merged into Walter (Jim) Corp. 08/31/1964

CELOTEX CORP. (DE)
Each share Preferred $100 par exchanged for (5) shares Preferred $20 par 00/00/1943
Common no par changed to $1 par 02/23/1956
Merged into Walter (Jim) Corp. 08/31/1964
5% Preferred $20 par exchanged share for share
Each share Common $1 par exchanged for (1.1) shares Common $0.16666666 par
(See Walter (Jim) Corp.)

CELOX LABS INC (MN)
Name changed 05/18/1995
Name changed from Celox Corp. to Celox Laboratories, Inc. 05/18/1995
Name changed to Protide Pharmaceuticals, Inc. 01/10/2001
(See Protide Pharmaceuticals, Inc.)

CELSIA TECHNOLOGIES INC (NV)
Each share Common $0.001 par exchanged for (0.1) share new Common $0.001 par 01/26/2009
Voluntarily dissolved 04/30/2012
Details not available

CELSION CORP (MD)
Reincorporated under the laws of Delaware 08/18/2000

CELSUS THERAPEUTICS PLC (ENGLAND & WALES)
Each old Sponsored ADR for Ordinary exchanged for (0.2) new Sponsored ADR for Ordinary 01/03/2014
Basis changed from (1:2) to (1:10) 01/03/2014
Each new Sponsored ADR for Ordinary exchanged for (0.1) new Sponsored ADR for for Ordinary 09/17/2015
Basis changed from (1:10) to (1:100) 09/17/2015
Name changed to Akari Therapeutics PLC 09/18/2015

CELTA DEVELOPMENT & MINING CO. LTD. (CANADA)
Recapitalized as Dablon Mining Corp. Ltd. 01/04/1957
Each share Capital Stock no par exchanged for (0.33333333) share Capital Stock no par
(See Dablon Mining Corp. Ltd.)

CELTIC CROSS LTD (NV)
Reorganized as eSavingsStore.com, Inc. 07/27/2006
Each share Common $0.001 par exchanged for (30) shares Common $0.001 par
eSavingsStore.com, Inc. name changed to Immureboost, Inc. 07/19/2007 which name changed to Fountain Healthy Aging, Inc. 10/09/2008
(See Fountain Healthy Aging, Inc.)

CELTIC EXPL LTD (AB)
Common no par split (2) for (1) by issuance of (1) additional share payable 05/10/2010 to holders of record 05/06/2010 Ex date - 05/04/2010
Merged into Kelt Exploration Ltd. 02/26/2013
Each share Common no par exchanged for (0.5) share Common no par and $24.50 cash

CELTIC INVT INC (IL)
Reincorporated 02/23/1998
State of incorporation changed from (DE) to (IL) 02/23/1998
Each share old Common $0.001 par exchanged for (0.00002) share new Common $0.001 par 03/10/2006
Note: Holders of (49,999) or fewer pre-split shares received scrip which was cancelled and became without value 12/31/2006

CELTIC MINERALS LTD (BC)
Recapitalized as Citlec Minerals Ltd. 07/22/1975
Each share Common 50¢ par exchanged for (0.25) share Common no par
Citlec Minerals Ltd. merged into Acheron Resources Ltd. 10/01/1982 which recapitalized as Abaddon Resources Inc. 09/12/1994 which recapitalized as Consolidated Abaddon Resources Inc. 01/31/2001 which name changed to Aben Resources Ltd. 01/13/2011

CELTIC RES HLDGS PLC (BC)
Company advised no GDR's remain outstanding as of 11/14/2007

CELTIC RES LTD (BC)
Name changed to U.R. Flowers Corp. 02/11/1992
U.R. Flowers Corp. recapitalized as Redstar Resources Corp. 04/19/1996 which recapitalized as Redstar Gold Corp. 04/26/2002

CELTOR CHEMICAL CORP. (CA)
Assets liquidated for benefit of creditors 10/06/1964
No stockholders' equity

CELTRIX PHARMACEUTICALS INC (DE)
Name changed 12/12/1991
Name changed from Celtrix Laboratories, Inc. to Celtrix Pharmaceuticals Inc. 12/12/1991
Merged into Insmed Inc. 05/31/2000
Each share Common 1¢ par exchanged for (1) share Common 1¢ par

CELTRON INTL INC (NV)
Name changed to Satellite Security Corp. 05/31/2006
Satellite Security Corp. name changed to Mobicom Corp. 05/22/2008
(See Mobicom Corp.)

CELUTEL INC (DE)
Reincorporated 06/06/1988
Common 1¢ par reclassified as Class A Common 1¢ par 12/31/1987
State of incorporation changed from (AZ) to (DE) 06/06/1988
Each share Class A Common 1¢ par exchanged for (0.05) share Class A Common 20¢ par 05/25/1990
Merged into Century Telephone Enterprises, Inc. 02/10/1994
Each share Class A Common 20¢ par exchanged for (0.149) share Common $1 par and $3.699 cash
Century Telephone Enterprises, Inc. name changed to CenturyTel, Inc. 05/10/1999 which name changed to CenturyLink, Inc. 06/01/2010

CEM CORP (NC)
Merged into MJC Acquisition Corp. 05/31/2000
Each share Common 5¢ par exchanged for $11.15 cash

CEMARA HEALTH INC (MN)
Reincorporated under the laws of Oklahoma as Cemara Inc. 06/15/1999
(See Cemara Inc.)

CEMARA INC (OK)
Completely liquidated 11/01/2000
Each share Common 1¢ par exchanged for first and final distribution of $0.2335 cash

CEMENT INTERNATIONAL CORP. (FL)
Name changed to Comp-Tronics, Inc. 09/09/1969
Comp-Tronics, Inc. name changed to Silvatex, Inc. 01/07/1980 which name changed to Grandma's Inc. 07/30/1982
(See Grandma's Inc.)

CEMENT NATL BK (NORTHAMPTON, PA)
Merged into Northeastern Bancorp, Inc. 09/01/1983
Each share Common $2.50 par exchanged for (1) share $2.60 Preferred Ser. A $10 par, (0.75) share Common $10 par and (1) Common Stock Purchase Warrant expiring 08/31/1993
Northeastern Bancorp, Inc. merged into PNC Financial Corp 01/30/1985 which name changed to PNC Bank Corp. 02/08/1993 which name changed to PNC Financial Services Group, Inc. 03/15/2000

CEMENTITIOUS MATLS INC (NV)
Name changed to NaturalNano, Inc. 12/02/2005
NaturalNano, Inc. name changed to Omni Shrimp, Inc. 05/03/2017

CEMENTOS DIAMANTE S A (COLOMBIA)
ADR agreement terminated 03/24/2002
Each 144A Sponsored ADR for Class B exchanged for $3.60 cash

CEMENTOS LIMA S A (PERU)
Stock Dividends - In Sponsored ADR's to holders of Sponsored ADR's 20.70511% payable 06/05/1996 to holders of record 04/23/1996; 4.9999% payable 05/21/1998 to holders of record 05/11/1998; 6.4999% payable 06/03/1999 to holders of record 05/13/1999 Ex date - 05/11/1999; 5.5% payable 06/05/2000 to holders of record 05/15/2000 Ex date - 05/11/2000; 3.7999% payable 07/18/2001 to holders of record 06/22/2001 Ex date - 06/20/2001; 2.3418% payable 10/11/2002 to holders of record 09/20/2002 Ex date - 09/18/2002; 105% payable 06/27/2008 to holders of record 06/10/2008 Ex date - 06/30/2008; 38.7156% payable 05/13/2011 to holders of record 04/18/2011 Ex date - 05/16/2011
In 144A Sponsored ADR's to holders of 144A Sponsored ADR's 20.70511% payable 06/05/1996 to holders of record 04/23/1996; 4.9999% payable 05/21/1998 to holders of record 05/11/1998; 6.4999% payable 06/03/1999 to holders of record 05/13/1999 Ex date - 05/11/1999; 5.5% payable 06/05/2000 to holders of record 05/15/2000 Ex date - 05/11/2000; 3.7999% payable 07/18/2001 to holders of record 06/22/2001 Ex date - 06/20/2001; 2.3418% payable 10/11/2002 to holders of record 09/20/2002 Ex date - 09/18/2002; 105% payable 06/27/2008 to holders of record 06/10/2008 Ex date - 06/06/2008
Name changed to Union Andina de Cementos S.A.A. 08/28/2012
(See Union Andina de Cementos S.A.A.)

CEMENTOS PAZ DEL RIO S A (COLOMBIA)
ADR agreement terminated 10/31/2005
Each Sponsored 144 ADR for Ordinary exchanged for $60.48381 cash

CEMETERY CARE INVT FD INC (MD)
Liquidation completed
Each share Common $1 par received initial distribution of $10 cash 10/01/1969
Each share Common $1 par received second and final distribution of $0.468 cash 12/23/1969
Note: Certificates were not required to be surrendered and are without value

CEMETERY SVCS INTL INC (DE)
Name changed to Morlan International Inc. 05/01/1974
Morlan International Inc. merged into Service Corp. International 11/06/1987

CEMEX S A (MEXICO)
ADR agreement terminated 03/14/2000
Each Sponsored ADR for Ordinary exchanged for $9.8523847 cash
Basis changed from (1:5) to (1:10) 06/29/2005
Sponsored ADR's for Ordinary Participation Certificates split (2) for (1) by issuance of (1) additional ADR payable 07/21/2006 to holders of record 07/14/2006 Ex date - 07/24/2006
Name changed to CEMEX, S.A.B. de C.V. 08/15/2006

CEMPRA INC (DE)
Recapitalized as Melinta Therapeutics, Inc. 11/06/2017
Each share Common $0.001 par exchanged for (0.2) share Common $0.001 par

CEN-COM, INC. (FL)
Proclaimed dissolved for failure to file reports and pay fees 12/01/1977

CENALTA ENERGY SVCS INC (AB)
Acquired by Precision Drilling Corp. 10/18/2000
Each share Common no par exchanged for (0.1432) share Common no par
(See Precision Drilling Corp.)

CENCALL COMMUNICATIONS CORP (DE)
Name changed to OneComm Corp. 05/27/1994
Onecomm Corp. acquired by Nextel Communications, Inc. 07/31/1995 which merged into Sprint Nextel Corp. 08/12/2005 which merged into Sprint Corp. (DE) 07/10/2013

CENCO CORP. (DE)
Name changed to Cenco Instruments Corp. 11/26/1957
Cenco Instruments Corp. name changed to Cenco Inc. 10/06/1972
(See Cenco Inc.)

CENCO HOSP & CONVALESCENT HOMES CORP (DE)
Merged into Cenco, Inc. 11/30/1972
Each share Common $1 par exchanged for $11.25 cash

CENCO INC (DE)
Merged into Manor Care, Inc. 07/22/1982
Each share Common $1 par exchanged for $16.50 principal amount of 15.5% Subordinated Debentures due 01/01/2002
$3 Conv. Preferred $5 par called for redemption 09/01/1982
Public interest eliminated

CENCO INSTRUMENTS CORP. (DE)
Common $1 par split (2) for (1) by issuance of (1) additional share 01/25/1965
Common $1 par split (2) for (1) by issuance of (1) additional share 06/27/1972
Name changed to Cenco Inc. 10/06/1972
(See Cenco Inc.)

CENCO PETE LTD (BC)
Reorganized as IGC Internet Gaming Corp. 08/07/1996
Each share Common no par exchanged for (1.5) shares Common no par
IGC Internet Gaming Corp. name changed to IGN Internet Global Network Inc. 11/20/1996 which recapitalized as AssistGlobal Technologies Corp. 09/23/2003 which recapitalized as Bassett Ventures Inc. 07/08/2005 which name changed to Arris Resources Inc. 06/25/2007 which name changed to RTN Stealth Software Inc. 01/08/2010 which name changed to Quantitative Alpha Trading Inc. 04/29/2011 which reincorporated in Ontario 12/09/2011
(See Quantitative Alpha Trading Inc.)

CENCOM INC (NV)
Common $1 par split (3) for (2) by issuance of (0.5) additional share 09/30/1982
Stock Dividends - 10% 06/30/1976; 10% 12/20/1977; 10% 12/15/1978
Merged into Pacific Telecom, Inc. 03/31/1983
Each share Common $1 par exchanged for (0.8) share Common $1 par
Pacific Telecom, Inc. merged into Pacificorp Holdings Corp. 09/27/1995

CENCOR INC (DE)
Common $1 par reclassified as Preferred $1 par 12/21/1978
Preferred $1 par called for redemption 06/01/1987
Old Regular Common $1 par split (3) for (2) by issuance of (0.5) additional share 04/23/1986
Each share old Regular Common $1 par exchanged for (0.2) share new Regular Common $1 par 08/31/1990
Stock Dividends - 100% 06/06/1972; 200% 05/15/1985
Liquidation completed
Each share new Regular Common $1 par received initial distribution of $5.35 cash payable 03/09/1998 to holders of record 02/16/1998
Each share new Regular Common $1 par received second distribution of $4.25 cash 06/07/1999
Each share new Regular Common $1 par received third and final distribution of $3.312 cash payable 12/17/1999 to holders of record 12/06/1999 Ex date - 12/20/1999
Note: Certificates were not required to be surrendered and are without value

CENCOSUD S A (CHILE)
Sponsored Reg. S ADR's for Common split (5) for (1) by issuance of (4) additional ADR's payable 04/03/2012 to holders of record 04/02/2012 Ex date - 04/04/2012
Sponsored 144A ADR's for Common split (5) for (1) by issuance of (4) additional ADR's payable 04/03/2012 to holders of record 04/02/2012 Ex date - 04/04/2012
ADR agreement terminated 04/26/2012
Each Sponsored 144A ADR for Common exchanged for $15.755097 cash
Each Sponsored Reg. S ADR for Common exchanged for (1) Sponsored ADS for Common 06/22/2012
Each Temporary Sponsored ADR for Common exchanged for (1) Sponsored ADR for Common 07/23/2012
ADR agreement terminated 06/29/2017
Each Sponsored ADR for Common exchanged for $8.691157 cash

CENCOTECH INC (ON)
Reincorporated 10/13/1999
Name changed 07/01/2000
Place of incorporation changed from (AB) to (ON) 10/13/1999
Name changed from Cenco Technologies Corp. to CencoTech Inc. 07/01/2000
Name changed to NamSys Inc. 11/01/2016

CENDANT CAP I (DE)
6.45% Trust Originated Preferred Securities called for redemption 03/01/2001

CENDANT CORP (DE)
Common 1¢ par reclassified as CD Common 1¢ par 03/21/2000
Each Income Preferred Redeemable Increased Dividend Equity Security received approximately (1.35) shares Common 1¢ par 02/16/2001
Each Growth Preferred Redeemable Increased Dividend Equity Security received approximately (1.35) shares Common 1¢ par 02/16/2001
Each Upper DECS received (2.2027) shares CD stock 1¢ par 08/17/2004
Each share CD Common 1¢ par received distribution of (0.05) share PHH Common 1¢ par payable 01/31/2005 to holders of record 01/19/2005 Ex date - 02/01/2005
Each share CD Common 1¢ par received distribution of (0.25) share Realogy Corp. Common 1¢ par payable 07/31/2006 to holders of record 07/21/2006 Ex date - 08/01/2006
Each share CD Common 1¢ par received distribution of (0.2) share Wyndham Worldwide Corp. Common 1¢ par payable 07/31/2006 to holders of record 07/21/2006 Ex date - 08/01/2006
Reorganized as Avis Budget Group, Inc. 09/01/2006
Each share CD Common 1¢ par exchanged for (0.1) share Common 1¢ par

CENERGY CORP (NV)
Acquired by Conquest Exploration Co. 09/25/1987
Each share Common 25¢ par exchanged for (1.5625) shares Common 20¢ par and $3 cash
Conquest Exploration Co. merged into American Exploration Co. 02/11/1991 which merged into Louis Dreyfus Natural Gas Corp. 10/14/1997 which merged into Dominion Resources, Inc. (New) 11/01/2001 which name changed to Dominion Energy, Inc. 05/11/2017

CENEX HARVEST STS COOPS (MN)
Name changed to CHS Inc. 08/05/2003

CENEX LTD (ON)
Receiver appointed 09/19/1979
Assets subsequently liquidated
No stockholders' equity

CENFED FINL CORP (DE)
Common 1¢ par split (3) for (2) by issuance of (0.5) additional share 05/07/1993
Stock Dividends - 10% payable 05/10/1996 to holders of record 04/19/1996; 10% payable 05/02/1997 to holders of record 04/17/1997
Merged into Golden State Bancorp Inc. 04/21/1998
Each share Common 1¢ par exchanged for (1.2) shares Common $1 par
(See Golden State Bancorp Inc.)

CENIT BANCORP INC (DE)
Common 1¢ par split (3) for (1) by issuance of (2) additional shares payable 04/24/1998 to holders of record 04/08/1998
Merged into SouthTrust Corp. 08/03/2001
Each share Common 1¢ par exchanged for (1.14) shares Common $2.50 par
SouthTrust Corp. merged into Wachovia Corp. (Ctfs. dated after 09/01/2001) 11/01/2004 which merged into Wells Fargo & Co. (New) 12/31/2008

CENIT CORP (ON)
Name changed to Superior Copper Corp. 01/24/2012
Superior Copper Corp. merged into Nighthawk Gold Corp. 05/30/2016

CENLAR FED SVGS BK (PRINCETON, NJ)
11.5% Exchangeable Sr. Preferred Ser. A no par called for redemption at $25 on 06/05/1998

CENNA COMMUNICATIONS GROUP INC (DE)
Each share old Common 1¢ par exchanged for (0.14285714) share new Common 1¢ par 09/18/1996
Name changed to First Equities Corp. 09/23/1996

CENO ENERGY LTD (AB)
Name changed to Vital Energy Inc. 10/10/2014

CENOL CO (IL)
Recapitalized 00/00/1952
Class A reclassified as Common no par
Each share Class B exchanged for (0.25) share Common no par
Merged into Burgess Vibrocrafters, Inc. 12/31/1969
Each share Common no par exchanged for (0.4) share Common $3 par
(See Burgess Vibrocrafters, Inc.)

CENPRO TECHNOLOGIES INC (AB)
Cease trade order effective 12/09/2004

CENT RAM DEV CORP (BC)
Name changed to I.S.L. Industries Ltd. 01/07/1983
(See I.S.L. Industries Ltd.)

CENTACOM TECHNOLOGIES INC (DE)
Recapitalized as Insight Medical Group, Inc. 04/10/2008
Each share Common $0.001 par exchanged for (0.05) share Common $0.001 par
(See Insight Medical Group, Inc.)

CENTALE INC (NY)
Each share old Common 1¢ par exchanged for (0.02857142) share new Common 1¢ par 03/05/2008
Recapitalized as NexxNow, Inc. 06/09/2008
Each share Common 1¢ par exchanged for (0.25) share Common 1¢ par
NexxNow, Inc. name changed to InoLife Technologies, Inc. 01/20/2010

CENTAMIN EGYPT LTD (AUSTRALIA)
Reincorporated under the laws of Jersey as Centamin PLC 12/30/2011

CENTAUR BIORESEARCH INC (NV)
Recapitalized as Advanced Global Industries Corp. 07/11/2002
Each share Common $0.001 par exchanged for (0.01) share Common $0.001 par
Advanced Global Industries Corp. name changed to Synova Healthcare Group, Inc. 02/10/2005
(See Synova Healthcare Group, Inc.)

CENTAUR MINI COMPUTER DEVICES, INC. (NY)
Name changed to Centaur Mini Devices, Inc.12/00/1969
Centaur Mini Devices, Inc. (NY) reincorporated in Delaware as Dyna-Jet Corp. 12/02/1971
(See Dyna-Jet Corp.)

CENTAUR MINI DEVICES INC (NY)
Reincorporated under the laws of Delaware as Dyna-Jet Corp. 12/02/1971
(See Dyna-Jet Corp.)

CENTAUR MNG & EXPL LTD (AUSTRALIA)
Each old Sponsored ADR for Ordinary exchanged for (0.6) new Sponsored ADR for Ordinary 02/22/1997
Each new Sponsored ADR for Ordinary exchanged for (0.125) Sponsored ADR for Ordinary 12/09/1999
Each Sponsored ADR for Ordinary exchanged for (0.1) new Sponsored ADR for Ordinary 08/23/2000
Delisted due to failure to pay annual listing fee 08/30/2002
No ADR holders' equity

CENTAUR RES LTD (BC)
Name changed to Technologia Systems Corp. and (1) additional share issued 06/07/1990
Technologia Systems Corp. recapitalized as Master Player Home Entertainment Corp. 02/11/1994 which recapitalized as International Player Enterprises Inc. 03/17/1997

CENTAUR SCIENCES INC (DE)
Charter cancelled and declared inoperative and void for non-payment of taxes 03/01/1995

CENTAUR TECHNOLOGIES INC (NV)
Name changed to Traderalert.Com, Inc. 05/06/1999
Traderalert.Com, Inc. name changed to Equityalert.Com, Inc. 06/02/1999 which recapitalized as InnoTech Corp. 07/31/2001

CENTAURI COMMUNICATIONS INC (UT)
Each share old Common no par exchanged for (0.1) share new Common no par 11/01/1984
Involuntarily dissolved 09/30/1986

CENTAURUS RES CORP (DE)
Name changed to Kahzam, Inc. 07/08/2009
Kahzam, Inc. name changed to Madison Ave. Media, Inc. 06/17/2010

CENTEL CABLE TELEVISION CO (DE)
Acquired by a subsidiary company 08/24/1989
Each share Class A Common 1¢ par exchanged for $45.625 cash

CENTEL CORP (KS)
Common $2.50 par split (3) for (2) by issuance of (0.5) additional share 10/30/1987
Common $2.50 par split (3) for (2) by issuance of (0.5) additional share 04/27/1989
Common $2.50 par split (3) for (2) by issuance of (0.5) additional share 02/21/1990
$2.55 Preferred no par called for redemption 07/31/1992
4.72% Preferred 1st Ser. $50 par called for redemption 07/31/1992
4.72% Preferred 2nd Ser. $50 par called for redemption 07/31/1992
4.75% Preferred Ser. A $50 par called for redemption 07/31/1992
4.75% Preferred Ser. B $50 par called for redemption 07/31/1992
5% Preferred $25 par called for redemption 07/31/1992
Acquired by Sprint Corp. (KS) 03/09/1993
Each share Common $2.50 par exchanged for (1.37) shares Common $2.50 par
Sprint Corp. (KS) name changed to Sprint Nextel Corp. 08/12/2005 which merged into Sprint Corp. (DE) 07/10/2013

CENTENARIO COPPER CORP (BC)
Merged into Quadra Mining Ltd. 04/09/2009
Each share Common no par exchanged for (0.28) share Common no par
Quadra Mining Ltd. name changed to Quadra FNX Mining Ltd. 05/27/2010
(See Quadra FNX Mining Ltd.)

CENTENNIAL ACQUISITIONS INC (CO)
Charter suspended for failure to file annual reports 09/30/1989

CENTENNIAL APPRECIATION PORTFOLIO (NY)
Registration terminated 07/20/1994
Details not available

CENTENNIAL AVIATION INC (DE)
Charter cancelled and declared inoperative and void for non-payment of taxes 03/01/1999

CENTENNIAL BANC SH CORP (CO)
Name changed to Easyqual.com Inc. 06/20/2000
Easyqual.com Inc. name changed to Entrust Financial Services, Inc. (CO) 04/09/2001 which reincorporated in Delaware as Enthrust Financial Services, Inc. 01/11/2007 which name changed to Rodman & Renshaw Capital Group, Inc. 08/31/2007 which name changed to Direct Markets Holdings Corp. 06/01/2012
(See Direct Markets Holdings Corp.)

CENTENNIAL BANCORP (OR)
Common $2 par split (2) for (1) by issuance of (1) additional share payable 02/20/1998 to holders of record 01/30/1998
Common $2 par changed to no par 05/00/1998
Stock Dividends - 10% 02/21/1991; 10% 02/21/1992; 10% 02/22/1993; 10% 03/11/1994; 10% 02/21/1995; 10% payable 02/21/1996 to holders of record 01/31/1996; 5% payable 08/15/1996 to holders of record 07/31/1996; 10% payable 02/21/1997 to holders of record 01/31/1997; 10% payable 08/22/1997 to holders of record 07/31/1997; 5% payable 08/21/1998 to holders of record 07/31/1998; 10% payable 02/19/1999 to holders of record 01/29/1999; 5% payable 08/20/1999 to holders of record 07/30/1999; 10% payable 03/03/2000 to holders of record 02/11/2000; 5% payable 08/18/2000 to holders of record 07/31/2000; 10% payable 02/23/2001 to holders of record 02/02/2001 Ex date - 01/31/2001; 5% payable 08/15/2001 to holders of record 07/31/2001 Ex date - 07/27/2001; 5% payable 02/22/2002 to holders of record 02/01/2002 Ex date - 01/30/2002
Merged into Umpqua Holdings Corp. 11/18/2002
Each share Common no par exchanged for (0.5343) share Common no par
Note: Holders of (100) shares or fewer received $9.35 cash per share

CENTENNIAL BANK (OLYMPIA, WA)
Merged into West Coast Bancorp (New) 02/28/1998
Details not available

CENTENNIAL BK (PHILADELPHIA, PA)
Ordered closed and declared insolvent 10/20/1976
No stockholders' equity

CENTENNIAL BK (SOUTHERN PINES, NC)
Merged into Crescent Financial Corp. 09/02/2003
Each share Common $3.50 par exchanged for $10.11 cash

CENTENNIAL BK HLDGS INC (DE)
Name changed to Guaranty Bancorp 05/12/2008

CENTENNIAL BANKSHARES INC (UT)
Company's principal asset placed in receivership 03/05/2010
Stockholders' equity unlikely

CENTENNIAL BEN CORP (CA)
Common no par split (3) for (2) by issuance of (0.5) additional share 04/02/1984
Name changed to West Coast Bancorp (New) 06/22/1989
West Coast Bancorp (New) merged into Sunwest Bank (New) (Tustin, CA) 02/04/2002
(See Sunwest Bank (New) (Tustin, CA))

CENTENNIAL CAP APPRECIATION FD INC (MD)
Merged into Oppenheimer Variable Account Funds 08/15/1986
Details not available

CENTENNIAL COMMUNICATIONS CORP (DE)
Name changed 02/29/2000
Under plan of merger each share old Class A Common 1¢ par exchanged for either (0.0932602) share new Class A Common 1¢ par and $37.629701 cash or $41.50 cash 01/07/1999
Note: Non-electors received cash only
New Class A Common 1¢ par split (3) for (1) by issuance of (2) additional shares payable 01/13/1999 to holders of record 01/08/1999
New Class A Common 1¢ par split (3) for (1) by issuance of (2) additional shares payable 01/20/2000 to holders of record 01/10/2000
Name changed from Centennial Cellular Corp. to Centennial Communications Corp. 02/29/2000
Acquired by AT&T Inc. 11/06/2009
Each share new Class A Common 1¢ par exchanged for $8.50 cash

CENTENNIAL CORP (DE)
Name changed to Foremost Corp. of America (DE) 10/25/1978
Foremost Corp. of America (DE) reincorporated in Michigan 06/30/1998
(See Foremost Corp. of America)

CENTENNIAL DEVELOPMENT FUND V (CA)
Merged into Centennial Group, Inc. 06/25/1987
Each Unit of Ltd. Partnership exchanged for (85) shares Common no par
(See Centennial Group, Inc.)

CENTENNIAL EQUITY INCOME FD INC (MD)
Name changed to Oppenheimer Equity Income Fund, Inc. (MD) 03/31/1983
Oppenheimer Equity Income Fund, Inc. (MD) reincorporated in Massachusetts as Oppenheimer Equity Income Fund 11/01/1986 which name changed to Oppenheimer Capital Income Fund 03/03/1999

CENTENNIAL FINL CORP (DE)
Name changed to Glenway Financial Corp. 08/20/1993
Glenway Financial Corp. merged into Fidelity Financial of Ohio, Inc. 03/19/1999 which merged into Provident Financial Group, Inc. 02/04/2000 which merged into National City Corp. 07/01/2004 which was acquired by PNC Financial Services Group, Inc. 12/31/2008

CENTENNIAL FIRST FINL SVCS (CA)
Stock Dividends - 5% payable 01/21/2000 to holders of record 01/10/2000; 5% payable 04/01/2002 to holders of record 03/01/2002 Ex date - 02/27/2002; 5% payable 03/07/2003 to holders of record 02/07/2003 Ex date - 02/05/2003
Name changed to 1st Centennial Bancorp 03/03/2003

CENTENNIAL FLOURING MILLS CO. (WA)
Each share Capital Stock $100 par exchanged for (5) shares Capital Stock $20 par 00/00/1937
Name changed to Centennial Mills, Inc. 09/22/1955
Centennial Mills, Inc. merged into United Pacific Corp. 06/30/1960 which merged into VWR United Corp. 11/30/1966 which name changed to Univar Corp. (DE) 03/01/1974 which reincorporated in Washington 03/01/1996
(See Univar Corp. (WA))

CENTENNIAL FUND, INC. (DE)
Completely liquidated 08/30/1968
Each share Common $1 par exchanged for first and final distribution of (0.664856) share Gryphon Fund, Inc. Capital Stock $1 par
Gryphon Fund, Inc. name changed to Founders Growth Fund, Inc. 11/09/1970
(See Founders Growth Fund, Inc.)

CENTENNIAL FUND II, INC. (MD)
Name changed to Second Centennial Fund, Inc. 06/20/1961
Second Centennial Fund, Inc. liquidated for Gryphon Fund, Inc. 08/30/1968 which name changed to Founders Growth Fund, Inc. 11/09/1970
(See Founders Growth Fund, Inc.)

CENTENNIAL GOVT TR (MA)
Completely liquidated 11/22/2009
Each Share of Bene. Int. no par received net asset value

CENTENNIAL GROUP INC (DE)
Certificates dated prior to 12/31/1986
Each share Common 10¢ par exchanged for (0.2) share Common 50¢ par 08/15/1985
Note: Holdings of (499) shares or fewer exchanged for $1.21 cash per share
Acquired by Investors Savings Bank (Richmond, VA) 12/31/1986
Each share Preferred $3 par exchanged for $1.50 cash
Each share Common 50¢ par exchanged for (0.13553) share 8.5% Conv. Preferred Ser. B $10 par and $1.112 cash
(See Investors Savings Bank (Richmond, VA))

CENTENNIAL GROUP INC NEW (DE)
Incorporated 02/17/1987
Plan of reorganization under Chapter 11 Federal Bankruptcy proceedings confirmed 02/23/1994
Stockholders' equity unlikely

CENTENNIAL HEALTHCARE CORP (GA)
Merged into Warburg Pincus Equity Partners, L.P. 06/14/2000
Each share Common 1¢ par exchanged for $5.50 cash

CENTENNIAL LIFE INSURANCE CO. (OR)
Merged into Transpacific Life Insurance Co. 12/31/1965
Each share Capital Stock 50¢ par exchanged for (1) share Common 30¢ par
Transpacific Life Insurance Co. merged into American Guaranty Life Insurance Co. (OR) 10/04/1967 which reorganized as American Guaranty Corp. (OR) 07/01/1969 which name changed to American Guaranty Financial Corp. 12/04/1970 which name changed to Encore Group Inc. 07/18/1990
(See Encore Group Inc.)

CENTENNIAL LIFE INS CO (KS)
Stock Dividends - 10% 01/15/1968; 10% 03/16/1970
Merged into ERC Corp. 05/23/1974
Each share Common $1 par exchanged for (0.25) share Common $2.50 par
(See ERC Corp.)

CENTENNIAL MILL CO. (WA)
Name changed to Centennial Flouring Mills Co. 00/00/1932
Centennial Flouring Mills Co. name changed to Centennial Mills, Inc. 09/22/1955 which merged into United Pacific Corp. 06/30/1960 which merged into VWR United Corp. 11/30/1966 which name changed to Univar Corp. (DE) 03/01/1974 which reincorporated in Washington 03/01/1996
(See Univar Corp. (WA))

CENTENNIAL MILLS INC (WA)
Merged into United Pacific Corp. 06/30/1960
Each share Capital Stock $20 par exchanged for (1.35) shares Common $1 par

United Pacific Corp. merged into VWR United Corp. 11/30/1966 which name changed to Univar Corp. (DE) 03/01/1974 which reincorporated in Washington 03/01/1996
(See Univar Corp. (WA))

CENTENNIAL MINERALS LTD (BC)
Acquired by Pegasus Gold Inc. 03/26/1986
Each (100) shares Common no par exchanged for (30) shares Common no par and (100) Common Stock Purchase Warrants expiring 10/03/1988
(See Pegusus Gold Inc.)

CENTENNIAL MINES LTD. (BC)
Merged into Magnum Consolidated Mining Co. Ltd. 01/00/1962
Each share Capital Stock no par exchanged for (0.25) share Capital Stock no par
Magnum Consolidated Mining Co. Ltd. liquidated for Brameda Resources Ltd. 03/11/1970 which merged into Teck Corp. 02/08/1979 which name changed to Teck Cominco Ltd. 09/12/2001 which name changed to Teck Resources Ltd. 04/27/2009

CENTENNIAL MINES LTD (NB)
Charter surrendered 11/15/1972
No stockholders' equity

CENTENNIAL MTG INCOME FD L P (CA)
Completely liquidated
Each Unit of Ltd. Partnership Int. received first and final distribution of $21.17 cash payable 12/04/2001 to holders of record 11/15/2001
Each Unit of Ltd. Partnership Int. II received first and final distribution of $26.82 cash payable 12/01/2003 to holders of record 11/15/2003

CENTENNIAL MTG LTD (BC)
60¢ Preference $10 par reclassified as 6% Preference Ser. A $10 par 12/03/1964
Assets assigned for the benefit of creditors 01/02/1969
No stockholders' equity

CENTENNIAL PETE INC (CO)
Charter suspended for failure to file annual reports 01/01/1992

CENTENNIAL REAL ESTATE INVT TR (MA)
Name changed to CPL Real Estate Investment Trust 08/13/1986
(See CPL Real Estate Investment Trust)

CENTENNIAL SVGS BK F S B (DURANGO, CO)
Common $1 par split (2) for (1) by issuance of (1) additional share 05/01/1986
Acquired by Aspen Bancshares, Inc. 10/06/1993
Each share Common $1 par exchanged for $23.45 cash

CENTENNIAL STATE LIFE INSURANCE CO. (CO)
Merged into Allservice Life Insurance Co. 00/00/1960
Each share Common $1 par exchanged for (0.27789) share Common 20¢ par
Allservice Life Insurance Co. merged into Western Empire Life Insurance Co. 09/24/1963 which merged into Bankers Union Life Insurance Co. 03/12/1973 which merged into I.C.H. Corp. 10/14/1982 which name changed to Southwestern Life Corp. (New) 06/15/1994 which name changed to I.C.H. Corp. (New) 10/10/1995
(See I.C.H. Corp. (New))

CENTENNIAL TAX EXEMPT CASH FD INC (MD)
Name changed to Daily Cash Tax Exempt Fund Inc. (MD) 05/27/1982

Daily Cash Tax Exempt Fund Inc. (MD) reorganized in Massachusetts as Centennial Tax Exempt Trust 09/27/1985
(See Centennial Tax Exempt Trust)

CENTENNIAL TAX EXEMPT TR (MA)
Completely liquidated 02/13/2009
Each Share of Bene. Int. no par received net asset value

CENTENNIAL TECHNOLOGIES INC (DE)
Old Common 1¢ par split (3) for (2) by issuance of (0.5) additional share 08/30/1995
Old Common 1¢ par split (2) for (1) by issuance of (1) additional share payable 11/25/1996 to holders of record 11/18/1996 Ex date - 11/26/1996
Each share old Common 1¢ par exchanged for (0.125) share new Common 1¢ par 07/22/1999
Merged into Solectron Corp. 05/01/2001
Each share new Common 1¢ par exchanged for (0.542) share Common $0.001 par
Solectron Corp. merged into Flextronics International Ltd. 10/01/2007 which name changed to Flex Ltd. 09/28/2016

CENTENNIAL TURF CLUB INC (CO)
Merged into D.S. Acquisitions, Inc. 02/07/1984
Each share Common $5 par exchanged for $44.26 cash

CENTENNIAL VILLAS INC (WA)
Acquired by Brown Acquisition Co. 06/10/1980
For holdings of (4,999) or fewer each share Common no par exchanged for $1.85 cash
For holdings of (5,000) or more each share Common no par exchanged for $0.50 cash

CENTER BANCORP INC (NJ)
Common $5 par changed to no par and (1) additional share issued 04/01/1988
Common no par split (2) for (1) by issuance of (1) additional share 07/01/1993
Common no par split (3) for (2) by issuance of (0.5) additional share payable 05/29/1998 to holders of record 05/01/1998
Common no par split (2) for (1) by issuance of (1) additional share payable 06/02/2003 to holders of record 05/19/2003 Ex date - 06/03/2003
Stock Dividends - 5% payable 05/31/1997 to holders of record 05/18/1997; 5% payable 06/01/1999 to holders of record 05/18/1999; 5% payable 06/01/2001 to holders of record 05/18/2001 Ex date - 05/16/2001; 5% payable 06/01/2002 to holders of record 05/17/2002 Ex date - 05/15/2002; 5% payable 06/01/2004 to holders of record 05/18/2004; 5% payable 06/15/2005 to holders of record 05/31/2005 Ex date - 05/26/2005; 5% payable 06/01/2007 to holders of record 05/01/2007 Ex date - 04/27/2007
Under plan of merger name changed to ConnectOne Bancorp, Inc. (New) 07/01/2014

CENTER BKS INC (DE)
Name changed to Skaneateles Bancorp, Inc. 04/16/1997
Skaeneateles Bancorp, Inc. merged into BSB Bancorp, Inc. 07/01/1999 which merged into Partners Trust Financial Group, Inc. (DE) 07/14/2004 which merged into M&T Bank Corp. 11/30/2007

CENTER FINL CORP (CA)
Common no par split (2) for (1) by issuance of (1) additional share payable 03/05/2004 to holders of record 02/17/2004 Ex date - 03/08/2004
Stock Dividend - 8% payable 03/28/2003 to holders of record 03/14/2003 Ex date - 03/12/2003
Merged into BBCN Bancorp, Inc. 12/01/2011
Each share Common no par exchanged for (0.7805) share Common $0.001 par
BBCN Bancorp, Inc. name changed to Hope Bancorp, Inc. 08/01/2016

CENTER FINL CORP (CT)
Merged into First Union Corp. 11/13/1996
Each share Common $1 par exchanged for (0.3539) share Common $3.33333333 par
First Union Corp. name changed to Wachovia Corp. (Ctfs. dated after 09/01/2001) 09/01/2001 which merged into Wells Fargo & Co. (New) 12/31/2008

CENTER FOR WOUND HEALING INC (NV)
Acquired by Sverica International 12/23/2010
Each share Common $0.001 par exchanged for $0.567522 cash
Note: An additional distribution of $0.00870495 cash per share was paid from escrow 06/15/2012

CENTER INCOME PPYTS (MN)
Partnership inactive as of 00/00/2007
Details not available

CENTER LAB MEDICINE INC (DE)
Merged into Damon Corp. 06/01/1977
Each share Capital Stock $0.0167 par exchanged for (0.3736) share Common 25¢ par
(See Damon Corp.)

CENTER LABS INC (NY)
Merged into Alcon Laboratories, Inc. 05/01/1970
Each share Common 10¢ par exchanged for $12 cash

CENTER ST BK (DENVER, CO)
Name changed to Century Bank (Denver, CO) 01/01/1973
(See Century Bank (Denver, CO))

CENTER ST BK (MODESTO, CA)
Acquired by Union Safe Deposit Bank (Stockton, CA) 11/13/1987
Details not available

CENTER STAR GOLD MINES INC (NV)
Each share old Common 10¢ par exchanged for (0.25) share new Common 10¢ par 08/12/1998
Recapitalized as Link.Com Inc. 03/13/2000
Each share new Common 10¢ par exchanged for (0.22222222) share Common 10¢ par
Link.Com Inc. name changed to eClickMD, Inc. 07/25/2000 which reorganized as SecureCARE Technologies, Inc. 12/15/2003 which name changed to Scrypt, Inc. 03/11/2014

CENTER TR INC (MD)
Merged into Pan Pacific Retail Properties, Inc. 01/17/2003
Each share Common 1¢ par exchanged for (0.218) share Common 1¢ par
Pan Pacific Retail Properties, Inc. merged into Kimco Realty Corp. 10/31/2006

CENTERBANC SVGS ASSN ST PETERSBURG (FL)
Acquired by Kinder-Care Learning Centers, Inc. 05/22/1986
Each share Common $2 par exchanged for $35 cash

CENTERBANK (WATERBURY, CT)
Under plan of reorganization each share Common $1 par automatically became (1) share Center Financial Corp. Common $1 par 07/07/1995
Center Financial Corp. merged into First Union Corp. 11/13/1996 which name changed to Wachovia Corp. (Ctfs. dated after 09/01/2001) 09/01/2001 which merged into Wells Fargo & Co. (New) 12/31/2008

CENTERCORE INC (DE)
Name changed to Core Technologies of Pennsylvania, Inc. 08/25/1995
(See Core Technologies of Pennsylvania, Inc.)

CENTERIOR ENERGY CORP (OH)
Merged into FirstEnergy Corp. 11/08/1997
Each share Common no par exchanged for (0.525) share Common 10¢ par

CENTERLINE HLDG CO (DE)
Each share 11% Conv. Ser. A Preferred no par exchanged for (0.481995) Special Ser. Ser. A Share no par 03/05/2010
Each Special Ser. A Share no par automatically became (15) Common Shares of Bene. Int. no par 10/06/2010
Each old Common Share of Bene. Int. no par exchanged for (0.0002) new Common Share of Bene. Int. no par 03/14/2013
Note: Holders of (4,999) or fewer pre-split shares received $0.07 cash per share
New Common Shares of Bene. Int. no par split (35) for (1) by issuance of (34) additional shares payable 03/14/2013 to holders of record 03/14/2013
Acquired by Hunt Capital Partners, LLC 11/14/2013
Each new Common Share of Bene. Int. no par exchanged for $39.89 cash

CENTERPLATE INC (DE)
Merged into KPLT Holdings, Inc. 01/28/2009
Each Income Deposit Security 1¢ par received $5.70 principal amount of 13.5% Subordinated Notes due 12/10/2013 and $0.01 cash
Each share Common 1¢ par exchanged for $0.01 cash

CENTERPOINT BK (BEDFORD, NH)
$8 Exchangeable Preferred Ser. A $1 par called for redemption 02/01/1994
Merged into Community Bankshares Inc. 03/20/1996
Each share Common $1 par exchanged for (1.073) shares Common $1 par
Community Bankshares Inc. merged into CFX Corp. 08/29/1997 which merged into Peoples Heritage Financial Group, Inc. 04/10/1998 which name changed to Banknorth Group, Inc. (ME) 05/10/2000 which merged into TD Banknorth Inc. 03/01/2005
(See TD Banknorth Inc.)

CENTERPOINT CORP (DE)
Company terminated registration of common stock and is no longer public as of 02/10/2003
Details not available

CENTERPOINT PPTYS TR (MD)
Name changed 10/15/1997
Name changed from Centerpoint Properties Corp. to Centerpoint Properties Trust 10/15/1997
8.48% Preferred Shares of Bene. Int. Ser. A $0.001 par called for redemption at $25 plus $0.0353 accrued dividends on 05/06/2003
Common Shares of Bene. Int. $0.001 par split (2) for (1) by issuance of (1) additional share payable 06/30/2004 to holders of record 06/01/2004 Ex date - 07/01/2004

Merged into CalEast Solstice, LLC 03/08/2006
Each Common Share of Bene. Int. $0.001 par exchanged for $50 cash
7.5% Conv. Preferred Shares of Bene. Int. Ser. B $0.001 par called for redemption at $50 on 04/12/2006
Flexible Preferred Shares of Bene. Int. Ser. D $0.001 par called for redemption at $1,000 plus $11.18 accrued dividends on 12/19/2014
Public interest eliminated

CENTERPOINTE CMNTY BK (HOOD RIV, OR)
Merged into Northwest Bancorporation, Inc. 07/14/2017
Each share Common exchanged for (1.006201) shares Common no par and $0.273618 cash
Northwest Bancorporation, Inc. merged into First Interstate BancSystem, Inc. 08/16/2018

CENTERPULSE LTD (SWITZERLAND)
Acquired by Zimmer Holdings, Inc. 10/02/2003
Each Sponsored ADR for Ordinary exchanged for (0.368) share Common 1¢ par and $9.31 cash
Zimmer Holdings, Inc. name changed to Zimmer Biomet Holdings, Inc. 06/29/2015

CENTERRE BANCORPORATION (MO)
Acquired by Boatmen's Bancshares, Inc. 12/09/1988
Each share Common $10 par exchanged for (1.826) shares Common $10 par
Boatmen's Bancshares, Inc. merged into NationsBank Corp. 01/07/1997 which reincorporated in Delaware as BankAmerica Corp. (Old) 09/25/1998 which merged into BankAmerica Corp. (New) 09/30/1998 which name changed to Bank of America Corp. 04/28/1999

CENTERRE BANK OF KANSAS CITY, N.A. (KANSAS CITY, MO)
6% Preferred Class A $36 par called for redemption 02/28/1989
6% Preferred Class B $85 par called for redemption 02/28/1989
Public interest eliminated

CENTERRE TRUST CO. (ST. LOUIS, MO)
Name changed to Boatmen's Trust Co. (St. Louis, MO) 12/09/1988
(See Boatmen's Trust Co. (St. Louis, MO))

CENTERSCOPE INC (CO)
Recapitalized as CWE Inc. 09/23/1991
Each share Common $0.0001 par exchanged for (0.2) share Common $0.0001 par
(See CWE Inc.)

CENTERSPAN COMMUNICATIONS CORP (OR)
Reorganized under the laws of Nevada as Suvanza 03/19/2010
Each share Common no par exchanged for (0.01) share Common $0.001 par

CENTERSTAGING CORP (DE)
Charter cancelled and declared inoperative and void for non-payment of taxes 03/01/2009

CENTERSTATE BK FLA (WINTER HAVEN, FL)
Merged into CenterState Banks of Florida, Inc. 12/31/2002
Each share Common 1¢ par exchanged for (0.53631) share Common 1¢ par and $2.40 cash
CenterState Banks of Florida, Inc. name changed to Centerstate Banks, Inc. 06/17/2009 which changed to CenterState Bank Corp. 09/08/2017

CENTERSTATE BKS INC (FL)
Name changed 06/17/2009
Common 1¢ par split (2) for (1) by issuance of (1) additional share payable 05/22/2006 to holders of record 05/08/2006 Ex date - 05/23/2006
Name changed from Centerstate Banks of Florida, Inc. to Centerstate Banks, Inc. 06/17/2009
Name changed to CenterState Bank Corp. 09/08/2017

CENTERTRUST RETAIL PPYTS INC (MD)
Name changed to Center Trust, Inc. 07/21/1999
Center Trust, Inc. merged into Pan Pacific Retail Properties, Inc. 01/17/2003 which merged into Kimco Realty Corp. 10/31/2006

CENTEX CONSTR PRODS INC (DE)
Name changed to Eagle Materials, Inc. 01/30/2004

CENTEX CORP (NV)
Common 50¢ par changed to 25¢ par and (1) additional share issued 05/06/1970
Common 25¢ par split (3) for (2) by issuance of (0.5) additional share 06/24/1983
Common 25¢ par split (2) for (1) by issuance of (1) additional share 08/31/1992
Common 25¢ par split (2) for (1) by issuance of (1) additional share payable 02/27/1998 to holders of record 02/13/1998 Ex date - 03/02/1998
Each share Common 25¢ par received distribution of (0.05) share Cavco Industries, Inc. Common 1¢ par payable 06/30/2003 to holders of record 06/12/2003 Ex date - 07/01/2003
Each share Common 25¢ par received distribution of (0.044322) share Eagle Materials Inc. Common 1¢ par payable 01/30/2004 to holders of record 01/14/2004 Ex date - 02/02/2004
Each share Common 25¢ par received distribution of (0.149019) share Eagle Materials Inc. Class B Common 1¢ par payable 01/30/2004 to holders of record 01/14/2004 Ex date - 02/02/2004
Common 25¢ par split (2) for (1) by issuance of (1) additional share payable 03/12/2004 to holders of record 02/29/2004 Ex date - 03/15/2004
Stock Dividend - 100% 03/26/1971
Merged into Pulte Homes, Inc. 08/18/2009
Each share Common 25¢ par exchanged for (0.975) share Common 1¢ par
Pulte Homes, Inc. name changed to PulteGroup, Inc. 03/22/2010

CENTEX TELEMANAGEMENT INC (DE)
Common 1¢ par split (2) for (1) by issuance of (1) additional share 06/04/1991
Merged into MFS Acquisition Co. No. 1, Inc. 06/20/1994
Each share Common 1¢ par exchanged for $11 cash

CENTIGRAM COMMUNICATIONS CORP (DE)
Merged into ADC Telecommunications, Inc. 07/27/2000
Each share Common $0.001 par exchanged for $24.12 cash
Note: An additional payment of $2.33 cash per share was made 09/01/2000

CENTILLION INDS INC (AB)
Name changed to Palo Duro Energy Inc. (AB) 05/29/2007

Palo Duro Energy Inc. (AB) reincorporated in British Columbia 12/19/2014 which recapitalized as CarbonOne Technologies Inc. 07/28/2015 which name changed to TekModo Industries Inc. 10/12/2016 which recapitalized as Lincoln Ventures Ltd. 07/16/2018

CENTILLIUM COMMUNICATIONS INC (DE)
Merged into TranSwitch Corp. 10/27/2008
Each share Common $0.001 par exchanged for (0.5981) share Common $0.001 par and $0.36 cash

CENTINELA BK (INGLEWOOD, CA)
Each share Common $10 par exchanged for (2) shares Common $5 par 07/21/1972
Merged into Tokai Bank of California (Los Angeles, CA) 08/15/1975
Each share Common $5 par exchanged for $5 principal amount of 9% Subord. Capital Notes due 08/15/1982 and $10 cash

CENTINELA VALLEY BK (INGLEWOOD, CA)
Name changed to Centinela Bank (Inglewood, CA) 02/20/1969
(See Centinela Bank (Inglewood, CA))

CENTIRE INTL INC (NV)
Reincorporated under the laws of Florida as Jericho Energy Co., Inc. 07/18/2008

CENTIV INC (DE)
Reincorporated 06/12/2002
State of incorporation changed from (GA) to (DE) 06/12/2002
Each share old Common $0.001 par exchanged for (1/3) share new Common $0.001 par 06/16/2003
Reorganized under the laws of Nevada as CNTV Entertainment Group, Inc. 11/19/2004
Each share Common $0.001 par exchanged for (0.1) share Common $0.001 par
CNTV Entertainment Group, Inc. recapitalized as Degama Software Solutions, Inc. 05/29/2008

CENTIVA CAP INC (CANADA)
Each share Common no par received distribution of (1) share Aylen Capital Inc. Common no par payable 09/30/2011 to holders of record 07/05/2011
Name changed to Spackman Equities Group Inc. 09/30/2011

CENTLIVRE BREWING CORP. (IN)
Under plan of merger name changed to Baldwin-Montrose Chemical Co., Inc. 06/26/1961
Baldwin-Montrose Chemical Co., Inc. merged into Chris-Craft Industries, Inc. 06/19/1968 which merged into News Corp., Ltd. 07/31/2001 which reorganized as News Corp. (Old) 11/03/2004 which name changed to Twenty-First Century Fox, Inc. 07/01/2013

CENTOCOR INC (PA)
Common 1¢ par split (2) for (1) by issuance of (1) additional share 05/24/1991
Merged into Johnson & Johnson 10/07/1999
Each share Common 1¢ par exchanged for (0.639) share Common $1 par

CENTOR INC (NV)
Common $0.001 par split (6) for (1) by issuance of (5) additional shares payable 03/20/2013 to holders of record 03/20/2013
Name changed to Centor Energy, Inc. 12/31/2013

CENTPAC DEV INC (BC)
Name changed to Tracer Resources Corp. 06/19/1979

(See Tracer Resources Corp.)

CENTRA CAP CORP (NV)
Reincorporated 04/24/1996
Reincorporated 07/02/1998
State of incorporation changed from (CO) to (DE) 04/24/1996
State of incorporation changed from (DE) to (NV) 07/02/1998
Charter revoked for failure to file reports and pay fees 04/00/2004

CENTRA CORP (NV)
Recapitalized as Greenway Environmental Systems, Inc. 05/10/1991
Each share Common $0.001 par exchanged for (0.25) share Common $0.001 par
Greenway Environmental Systems, Inc. recapitalized as Travel Dynamics, Inc. 01/13/1999 which name changed to TRU Dynamics International, Inc. 02/14/2001
(See TRU Dynamics International, Inc.)

CENTRA FINL HLDGS INC (WV)
Merged into United Bankshares, Inc. 07/08/2011
Each share Common $1 par exchanged for (0.7676) share Common $2.50 par

CENTRA FINL INC (WI)
Merged into Associated Banc-Corp 02/21/1997
Each share Common $20 par exchanged for (2) shares Common 1¢ par

CENTRA GAS MANITOBA INC. (MB)
Acquired by Manitoba Hydro-Electric Board 07/30/1999
Details not available

CENTRA GAS ONT INC (ON)
$2.60 1st Preference 1st Ser. $50 par called for redemption at $50.50 on 09/01/1997
$2.70 1st Preference 2nd Ser. $50 par called for redemption at $50.50 on 09/15/1997
7.85% 2nd Preference Ser. A $25 par called for redemption at $25 on 09/15/1997

CENTRA SOFTWARE INC (DE)
Merged into Saba Software, Inc. 01/31/2006
Each share Common $0.001 par exchanged for (0.354) share new Common $0.001 par and $0.663 cash
(See Saba Software, Inc.)

CENTRAC ASSOC INC (WA)
Plan of reorganization under Chapter 11 Federal Bankruptcy proceedings confirmed 08/08/1988
No stockholders' equity

CENTRACAN INC (FL)
Each share old Common $0.0001 par exchanged for (0.04347826) share new Common $0.0001 par 08/22/2003
Name changed to EcoReady Corp. 12/23/2010

CENTRACK INTL INC (DE)
Charter forfeited for failure to maintain a registered agent 08/07/2002

CENTRACORE PPTYS TR (MD)
Merged into GEO Group, Inc. (Old) 01/24/2007
Each share Common $0.001 par exchanged for $32 cash

CENTRAFARM GROUP N V (NETHERLANDS)
Common 3.33 Gldrs. par split (3) for (2) by issuance of (0.5) additional share 04/15/1987
Completely liquidated 05/16/1988
Each share Common 3.33 Gldrs. par exchanged for first and final distribution of $12.50 cash

CENTRAIS ELETRICAS DE SANTA CATARINA S/A (BRAZIL)
Sponsored GDR's for Reg. S Preferred B reclassified as Sponsored ADR's for Preferred Ser. B 02/03/2003
Basis changed from (1:100) to (1:1) 10/05/2006
Sponsored ADR's for Preferred Ser. B reclassified as Sponsored ADR's for Preferred 02/24/2012
Stock Dividend - 400% payable 10/05/2006 to holders of record 10/04/2006 Ex date - 10/06/2006
ADR agreement terminated 08/25/2017
Each Sponsored ADR for Preferred exchanged for $7.06304 cash

CENTRAIS GERADORAS DO SUL DO BRASIL S A- GERASUL (BRAZIL)
Name changed to Tractebel Energia S.A. 03/05/2002
Tractebel Energia S.A. name changed to Engie Brasil Energia S.A. 10/05/2016

CENTRAL & EASTERN CANADA MINES (1958) LTD. (ON)
Charter cancelled and company declared dissolved for default in filing returns 12/30/1970

CENTRAL & EASTN TR CO (MONCTON, NB)
Under plan of merger each share Conv. Class A $4 par and Conv. Class B $4 par automatically became (1) share Central Trust Co. (Moncton, NB) Common $4 par respectively 03/01/1981

CENTRAL & NOVA SCOTIA TR CO (HALIFAX, NS)
Merged into Central & Eastern Trust Co. (Moncton, NB) 07/02/1976
Each share Common $1 par exchanged for (1) share Conv. Class A $4 par
Central & Eastern Trust Co. (Moncton, NB) merged into Central Trust Co. (Moncton, NB) 03/01/1981

CENTRAL & SOUTH AMERICAN ACCEPTANCE CORP. (DE)
Name changed to Casa International Corp. 05/12/1958
(See Casa International Corp.)

CENTRAL & SOUTH WEST CORP (DE)
Common $5 par changed to $2.50 par and (1) additional share issued 01/15/1960
Common $2.50 par changed to $7 par 04/16/1969
Common $7 par changed to $3.50 par and (1) additional share issued 05/15/1973
Common $3.50 par split (2) for (1) by issuance of (1) additional share 03/06/1992
Merged into American Electric Power Co., Inc. 06/15/2000
Each share Common $3.50 par exchanged for (0.6) share Common $6.50 par

CENTRAL & SOUTH WEST UTILITIES CO.
Merged into Central & South West Corp. 00/00/1947
Each share $7 Prior Lien Preferred no par exchanged for (10) shares new Common $5 par and $1.5166 cash
Each share $7 Preferred no par exchanged for (18.5847) shares new Common $5 par
Each share Common 50¢ par exchanged for (0.8095) share new Common $5 par

CENTRAL & SOUTHN HLDG CO (FL)
Proclaimed dissolved for failure to file reports and pay fees 11/09/1990

CENTRAL & SOUTHN HLDG CO MILLEDGEVILLE (GA)
Common $1 par split (5) for (4) by issuance of (0.25) additional share 01/23/1989
Merged into Premier Bancshares Inc. (New) 06/23/1997
Each share Common $1 par exchanged for (1) share Common $5 par
Premier Bancshares Inc. (New) merged into BB&T Corp. 01/13/2000

CENTRAL & ST NATL CORP ALA (DE)
Stock Dividend - 100% 01/31/1973
Name changed to Central Bancshares of the South Inc. 01/23/1973
Central Bancshares of the South, Inc. name changed to Compass Bancshares, Inc. 11/08/1993 which merged into Banco Bilbao Vizcaya Argentaria, S.A. 09/07/2007

CENTRAL AGUIRRE ASSOCIATES
Name changed to Central Aguirre Sugar Co. (MA) and Common no par changed to $5 par 00/00/1947
Central Aguirre Sugar Co. (MA) name changed to Aguirre Co. 11/14/1968
(See Aguirre Co.)

CENTRAL AGUIRRE SUGAR CO. (MA)
Name changed to Aguirre Co. 11/14/1968
(See Aguirre Co.)

CENTRAL AGUIRRE SUGAR CO. (PR)
Name changed to Aguirre Corp. 12/14/1978
(See Aguirre Corp.)

CENTRAL AIRLINES, INC. (NV)
Each share Common 25¢ par exchanged for (2) shares Common $0.125 par 07/10/1963
Stock Dividend - 20% 02/26/1962
Merged into Frontier Airlines, Inc. 10/01/1967
Each share Common $0.125 par exchanged for (0.571428) share Common 50¢ par
Frontier Airlines, Inc. reorganized as Frontier Holdings, Inc. 05/06/1982
(See Frontier Holdings, Inc.)

CENTRAL ALBERTA WELL SVCS CORP (AB)
Old Common no par reclassified as old Class A Common no par 05/31/2007
Each share old Class A Common no par exchanged for (0.25) share new Class A Common no par 07/12/2007
Each share old Non-Vtg. Class B Common no par exchanged for (0.25) share new Non-Vtg. Class B Common no par 07/12/2007
Each share new Class A Common no par exchanged for (1) share new Common no par 09/14/2009
Each share new Non-Vtg. Class B Common no par exchanged for (1) share new Common no par 09/14/2009
Name changed to CWC Well Services Corp. 07/12/2011
CWC Well Services Corp. name changed to CWC Energy Services Corp. 05/22/2014

CENTRAL ALLOY STEEL CORP.
Assets acquired by Republic Steel Corp. 00/00/1930
Details not available

CENTRAL AMERN EQUITIES CORP (FL)
Each share old Common $0.001 par exchanged for (0.1) share new Common $0.001 par 06/07/2005
Recapitalized as China Aoxing Pharmaceutical Co., Inc. 07/07/2006
Each share new Common $0.001 par exchanged for (0.25) share Common $0.001 par
China Aoxing Pharmaceutical Co., Inc. recapitalized as Aoxing Pharmaceutical Co., Inc. 03/29/2010

CENTRAL AMERICAN LIFE INSURANCE CO. (TX)
Merged into South Coast Life Insurance Co. 06/30/1964
Each share Capital Stock $1 par exchanged for (1) share Capital Stock $1 par
South Coast Life Insurance Co. acquired by USLIFE Holding Corp. 07/25/1967 which name changed to USLIFE Corp. 05/22/1970 which merged into American General Corp. 06/17/1997 which merged into American International Group, Inc. 08/29/2001

CENTRAL AMERICAN PETROLEUM CO. (DE)
Acquired by Petrosur Oil Corp. 02/24/1958
Each share Common exchanged for (0.5) share Common 10¢ par
Petrosur Oil Corp. merged into Techtro-Matic Corp. 08/24/1961
(See Techtro-Matic Corp.)

CENTRAL AMERICAN PLANTATIONS CORP.
In process of liquidation 00/00/1943
Details not available

CENTRAL ARGENTINE RAILWAY LTD.
Acquired by Argentine Government 00/00/1948
Details not available

CENTRAL ARIZONA LIGHT & POWER CO.
Under plan of merger name changed to Arizona Public Service Co. 00/00/1952

CENTRAL ARKANSAS PUBLIC SERVICE CORP.
Liquidated 00/00/1943
Details not available

CENTRAL ARKANSAS RAILWAY & LIGHT CORP.
Name changed to Central Arkansas Public Service Corp. 00/00/1928
(See Central Arkansas Public Service Corp.)

CENTRAL ASBESTOS MINES LTD (QC)
Charter cancelled 01/00/1974

CENTRAL ASIA DEV & CONSTR CO LTD (ON)
Reincorporated under the laws of Wyoming as Amerossi Energy Corp. 11/12/2004
Amerossi Energy Corp. name changed to Nadir Energy & Mining Corp. 06/11/2008
(See Nadir Energy & Mining Corp.)

CENTRAL ASIA GOLD LTD (AUSTRALIA)
Name changed to CGA Mining Ltd. 12/19/2006
CGA Mining Ltd. merged into B2Gold Corp. 01/31/2013

CENTRAL ASIA GOLDFIELDS CORP (ON)
Delisted from Montreal Stock Exchange 06/30/1999

CENTRAL ASSET FD INC (MD)
Auction Market Preferred 144A Ser. A called for redemption at $100,000 on 11/27/1998
Auction Market Preferred 144A Ser. B called for redemption at $100,000 on 12/10/1998

CENTRAL ATLANTIC STATES SERVICE CORP.
Reorganized as Cassco Corp. 00/00/1934
Details not available

CENTRAL AZUCARERA DE BAIS, INC. (PHILIPPINES)
9% Preferred P10 par called for redemption 06/30/1974
Registration of securities voluntarily revoked 03/14/2006

CENTRAL B C EXPLS LTD (BC)
Struck off register and declared dissolved for failure to file returns 05/10/1985

CENTRAL BANCOMPANY (MO)
Under plan of merger each share Common $10 par exchanged for $230 cash 05/12/2005
Under plan of merger each share Non-Vtg. Class B $10 par exchanged for $230 cash 05/12/2005
Note: Holders of (1,000) or more shares retained their interests

CENTRAL BANCORP INC (FL)
In process of liquidation
Each share Common $5 par exchanged for initial distribution of $29 cash 07/02/1984
Each share Common $5 par received second distribution of $1 cash 01/18/1985
Each share Common $5 par received third distribution of $0.75 cash 10/23/1985
Note: Details on subsequent distributions, if any, are not available

CENTRAL BANCORP INC (MA)
Merged into Independent Bank Corp. 11/10/2012
Each share Common $1 par exchanged for (1.0533) shares Common 1¢ par

CENTRAL BANCORPORATION, INC. (CO)
Merged into CBI Acquisition Corp. 12/02/1988
Each share Common $1 par exchanged for $12.57 cash

CENTRAL BANCORPORATION (WA)
Common $5 par changed to $1.67 par and (2) additional shares issued 00/00/1987
Merged into Interwest Bancorp, Inc. 08/31/1996
Each share Common $1.67 par exchanged for (1.41) shares Common 20¢ par
Interwest Bancorp, Inc. name changed to Pacific Northwest Bancorp 09/01/2000 which merged into Wells Fargo & Co. (New) 11/03/2003

CENTRAL BANCORPORATION INC (DE)
Common $10 par changed to $5 par and (1) additional share issued 03/23/1970
Ser. A Preferred $100 par called for redemption 10/15/1973
Common $5 par split (3) for (2) by issuance of (0.5) additional share 01/07/1986
Common $5 par split (3) for (2) by issuance of (0.5) additional share 01/06/1987
Stock Dividend - 10% 02/28/1975
Merged into PNC Financial Corp 02/29/1988
Each share Common $5 par exchanged for (1.067) shares Common $5 par
PNC Financial Corp name changed to PNC Bank Corp. 02/08/1993 which name changed to PNC Financial Services Group, Inc. 03/15/2000

CENTRAL BANCORPORATION INC (TX)
Merged into Norwest Corp. 01/28/1997
Each share Common no par exchanged for (1.7745) shares Common $1.66666666 par
Norwest Corp. name changed to Wells Fargo & Co. (New) 11/02/1998

CENTRAL BANCSHARES INC (TX)
Each share old Common $1 par exchanged for (0.01) share new Common $1 par 06/04/2007
Under plan of merger each share new Common $1 par exchanged for $7,975 cash

CENTRAL BANCSHARES SOUTH INC (DE)
Common $2 par split (2) for (1) by issuance of (1) additional share 10/02/1985
Common $2 par split (3) for (2) by issuance of (0.5) additional share 10/02/1986
Common $2 par split (3) for (2) by issuance of (0.5) additional share 07/02/1992
Name changed to Compass Bancshares, Inc. 11/08/1993
Compass Bancshares, Inc. merged into Banco Bilbao Vizcaya Argentaria, S.A. 09/07/2007

CENTRAL BK & TR (LANDER, WY)
Each (4,500) shares old Common exchanged for (1) share new Common 10/12/2000
Note: In effect holders received $17.68 cash per share and public interest was eliminated

CENTRAL BANK & TRUST (MARSHFIELD, WI)
Name changed to M&I Central Bank & Trust (Marshfield, WI) 01/23/1984
(See M&I Central Bank & Trust (Marshfield, WI))

CENTRAL BANK & TRUST CO. (DENVER, CO)
Each share Common Capital Stock $100 par exchanged for (15) shares Common Capital Stock $10 par to effect a (10) for (1) split and 50% stock dividend 00/00/1953
Stock Dividends - 40% 00/00/1945; 42.8% 00/00/1946; 42.8% 00/00/1949; 10% 01/24/1958
Name changed to Central Bank (Denver, CO) 05/01/1975
Central Bank (Denver, CO) reorganized as Central Bancorporation, Inc. 12/31/1980
(See Central Bancorporation, Inc.)

CENTRAL BANK & TRUST CO. NEW YORK, N.A. (BROOKLYN, NY)
Name changed to Central National Bank of New York (Brooklyn, NY) 04/07/1981
(See Central National Bank of New York (Brooklyn, NY))

CENTRAL BK & TR CO (JONESBORO, GA)
Merged into Trust Co. of Georgia 04/00/1977
Details not available

CENTRAL BK & TR CO (MIAMI, FL)
Each share Capital Stock $100 par exchanged for (5) shares Capital Stock $20 par 03/08/1951
Each share Capital Stock $20 par exchanged for (2) shares Capital Stock $10 par 12/15/1955
Stock Dividends - 20% 03/08/1951; 25% 12/31/1951; 17.6% 12/31/1954; 25% 02/19/1960; 20% 12/28/1961; 14.3% 12/31/1962
98.93% by Central Bancorp, Inc. through exchange offer which expired 07/31/1969
Public interest eliminated

CENTRAL BANK & TRUST OF TULSA (TULSA, OK)
Bank failed 09/11/1986
No stockholders' equity

CENTRAL BANK (DENVER, CO)
Under plan of reorganization each share Common Capital $10 par automatically became (1) share Central Bancorporation, Inc. Common $1 par 12/31/1980
(See Central Bancorporation, Inc.)

CENTRAL BK (GLENDALE, CA)
Name changed to OneCentral Bank (Glendale, CA) 07/12/1985
OneCentral Bank (Glendale, CA) merged into Glendale Federal Bank, FSB (Glendale, CA) 01/31/1997

CENTRAL BK (GRAND RAPIDS, MI)
Common $20 par changed to $10 par and (1) additional share issued plus a 20% stock dividend paid 06/01/1969
Stock Dividends - 100% 02/00/1956; 20% 05/00/1966; 10% 03/01/1968; 26.26% 03/01/1971
Name changed to Central Bank, N.A. (Grand Rapids, MI) 11/11/1972
Central Bank, N.A. (Grand Rapids, MI) merged into Michigan National Corp.(DE) 12/09/1974 which reincorporated in Michigan 04/20/1983
(See Michigan National Corp. (MI))

CENTRAL BANK (HOUSTON, TX)
Under plan of reorganization each share Common $10 par automatically became (1) share Central Bancshares Inc. Common $1 par 02/16/1982
(See Central Bancshares Inc.)

CENTRAL BK (MIAMI, FL)
Merged into BankUnited Financial Corp. 06/19/1998
Each share Common exchanged for (3.37) shares Class A Common 1¢ par
(See BankUnited Financial Corp.)

CENTRAL BK (MONROE, LA)
Stock Dividends - 11.11111111% 11/02/1970; 10% 11/18/1976; 10% 10/19/1977; 20% 11/15/1978; 20% 04/22/1981
Under plan of reorganization each share Common $12.50 par automatically became (1) share Central Corp. Common $12.50 par 04/30/1982
Central Corp. merged into First Commerce Corp. 10/20/1995 which merged into Banc One Corp. 06/12/1998 which merged into Bank One Corp. 10/02/1998 which merged into J.P. Morgan Chase & Co. 12/31/2000 which name changed to JPMorgan Chase & Co. 07/20/2004

CENTRAL BK (TAMPA, FL)
Merged into South Financial Group, Inc. 12/31/2002
Each share Common exchanged for (9.85) shares Common $1 par
South Financial Group, Inc. merged into Toronto-Dominion Bank (Toronto, ON) 09/30/2010

CENTRAL BK (WEST ALLIS, WI)
Under plan of reorganization each share Common $20 par automatically became (1) share Centra Financial, Inc. Common 1¢ par 03/17/1986
Centra Financial, Inc. merged into Associated Banc-Corp 02/21/1997

CENTRAL BANK CO. (LORAIN, OH)
Common $25 par changed to $10 par and (1.5) additional shares issued plus a 20% stock dividend paid 05/25/1960
Stock Dividends - 33.33333333% 09/22/1955; 25% 06/03/1957
Name changed to Central Security National Bank of Lorain County (Lorain, OH) 12/29/1964
Central Security National Bank of Lorain County (Lorain, OH) merged into Central Bancorporation, Inc. 02/15/1978 which merged into PNC Financial Corp 02/29/1988 which name changed to PNC Bank Corp. 02/08/1993 which name changed to PNC Financial Services Group, Inc. 03/15/2000

CENTRAL BK FOR SVGS (MERIDEN, CT)
Under plan of reorganization each share Common $1 par automatically became (1) share Cenvest, Inc. and Common 1¢ par 09/22/1987
(See Cenvest, Inc.)

CENTRAL BK N A (GRAND RAPIDS, MI)
Merged into Michigan National Corp. (DE) 12/09/1974
Each share Common $10 par exchanged for (0.809433) share Common $10 par
Michigan National Corp. (DE) reincorporated in Michigan 04/20/1983
(See Michigan National Corp. (MI))

CENTRAL BK N A (OAKLAND, CA)
Each share Common $5 par exchanged for (0.05) share Common $100 par 04/06/1973
Note: In effect holders received $47.50 cash per share and public interest was eliminated

CENTRAL BANK OF ALABAMA, N.A. (DECATUR, AL)
Through exchange offer 99.99% acquired by Central & State National Corp. 00/00/1972
Public interest eliminated

CENTRAL BANK OF GEORGIA (MACON, GA)
Merged into SBT Corp. 02/01/1983
Each share Common $2 par exchanged for (1.2941) shares Common $5 par
SBT Corp. merged into First Railroad & Banking Co. of Georgia 05/07/1984 which was acquired by First Union Corp. 11/01/1986 which name changed to Wachovia Corp. (Ctfs. dated after 09/01/2001) 09/01/2001 which merged into Wells Fargo & Co. (New) 12/31/2008

CENTRAL BANK OF PALM BEACH COUNTY (WEST PALM BEACH, FL)
99% acquired by Pan American Banks Inc. through purchase offer which expired 00/00/1979
Public interest eliminated

CENTRAL BANKSHARES INC (GA)
Merged into ABC Bancorp 07/31/1996
Each share Common no par exchanged for (2.2284) shares Common no par
ABC Bancorp name changed to Ameris Bancorp 12/01/2005

CENTRAL BARGE CO.
Merged into Mississippi Valley Barge Line Co. 06/30/1952
Each share Particapating Stock $10 par exchanged for $20 principal amount of 5% Debentures
Each share Common $5 par exchanged for (2.875) shares Common $1 par
Mississippi Valley Barge Line Co. merged into Chromalloy American Corp. (NY) 06/04/1968 which reincorporated in Delaware 10/31/1968 which merged into Sun Chemical Corp. 12/23/1986 which name changed to Sequa Corp. 05/08/1987
(See Sequa Corp.)

CENTRAL BKG SYS INC (DE)
Capital Stock $5 par changed to $2.50 par and (1) additional share issued 07/30/1971
Stock Dividends - 25% 01/15/1986; 10% 10/20/1987
Charter cancelled and declared inoperative and void for non-payment of taxes 06/26/1990

CENTRAL BORE NL (AUSTRALIA)
Name changed to Central Exchange Ltd. 12/21/1999
Central Exchange Ltd. name changed to Orion Equities Ltd. 12/13/2005

CENTRAL BRASS & FIXTURE CO.
Acquired by Electric Auto-Lite Co. 00/00/1935
Details not available

CENTRAL BREVARD NATL BK (COCOA, FL)
Stock Dividends - 20% 02/23/1961; 25% 02/11/1966; 20% 02/10/1967
Name changed to Sun Bank of Cocoa, N.A. (Cocoa, FL) 03/01/1973
(See Sun Bank of Cocoa, N.A. (Cocoa, FL))

CENTRAL BROADCASTING CORP. (IN)
Voluntarily dissolved 11/30/1989
Details not available

CENTRAL BUILDING TRUST
Liquidation completed 00/00/1949
Details not available

CENTRAL BUSINESS PROPERTIES, INC. (CA)
Capital Stock $100 par changed to $20 par 00/00/1953
Liquidation completed 07/28/1955
Details not available

CENTRAL BUSINESS REDEVELOPMENT CORP. (GA)
Shares reacquired 07/01/1982
Each share Common $10 par exchanged for $10.7829 cash

CENTRAL CALIF BK (SONORA, CA)
Merged into Western Sierra Bancorp 04/01/2002
Each share Common no par exchanged for either (0.711) share Common no par or $14.10 cash
Note: Option to receive stock expired 05/10/2002
Western Sierra Bancorp merged into Umpqua Holdings Corp. 06/05/2006

CENTRAL CALIFORNIA TITLE CO. (CA)
Name changed to First American Title Co. of Central California 01/05/1962
(See First American Title Co. of Central California)

CENTRAL CDA FOODS CORP (QC)
Name changed to Central Industries Corp. Inc. 06/05/2007

CENTRAL CANADA INVESTMENTS LTD. (ON)
Liquidation completed 06/27/1960
Details not available

CENTRAL CAP CORP (CANADA)
Common no par split (3) for (2) by issuance of (0.5) additional share 05/11/1987
Class A Subordinate no par split (3) for (2) by issuance of (0.5) additional share 05/11/1987
Each share old Common no par exchanged for (0.0158531) share new Common no par 01/04/1993
Each share Class A Subordinate no par exchanged for (0.0158531) share new Common no par 01/04/1993
Each share 7.625% Retractable Sr. Preferred Ser. B no par exchanged for (0.1319261) share new Common no par 01/04/1993
Each share 7.625% Retractable Sr. Preferred Ser. C no par exchanged for (0.1319261) share new Common no par 01/04/1993
Recapitalized as YMG Capital Management Inc. 02/20/1998
Each share new Common no par exchanged for (0.2) share Common no par
(See YMG Capital Management Inc.)

CENTRAL CAP VENTURE CORP (NV)
SEC revoked common stock registration 06/04/2012

CENTRAL CAROLINA BK & TR CO (DURHAM, NC)
Common $25 par changed to $5 par and (4) additional shares issued 12/29/1964

Stock Dividends - 100% 09/01/1972; 100% 02/15/1980
Reorganized as CCB Financial Corp. 07/01/1983
Each share Common $5 par exchanged for (1) share Common $5 par
CCB Financial Corp. merged into National Commerce Bancorporation 07/05/2000 which name changed to National Commerce Financial Corp. 04/25/2001 which merged into SunTrust Banks, Inc. 10/01/2004

CENTRAL CEMETERY CO ILL (IL)
Merged into Service Corp. International 10/03/1996
Each share Common $10 par exchanged for $515.63 cash
Note: Approximately $44.10 per share will be placed in escrow for possible future distribution

CENTRAL CHARGE SVC INC (DE)
Common 10¢ par changed to $1 par and (1) additional share issued 06/20/1961
Merged into Riggs National Bank (Washington, DC) 08/31/1969
Each share Common $1 par exchanged for (0.2) share $4 Conv. Preferred $10 par
(See Riggs National Bank (Washington, DC))

CENTRAL CHEAM COPPER MINES LTD. (BC)
Struck off register and declared dissolved for failure to file reports and pay fees 05/07/1970

CENTRAL CHEM CORP (MD)
Each share 6% Non-Cumulative Preferred $10 par exchanged for (0.2) share 6% Preferred $10 par; $6.50 principal amount of 6% 12-year Registered Bonds and $1.50 cash 11/16/1961
6% Preferred $10 par called for redemption 06/30/1977

CENTRAL CHIBOUGAMAU MINES (QC)
Name changed to Brunswick-Quebec Development Ltd. 00/00/1953
Brunswick-Quebec Development Ltd. name changed to Abadex Mines Ltd. 00/00/1957
(See Abadex Mines Ltd.)

CENTRAL CITY HOLDING CO.
Property sold 00/00/1944
No stockholders' equity

CENTRAL CO OPERATIVE BK (SOMERVILLE, MA)
Merged into Central Bancorp, Inc. 01/08/1999
Each share Common $1 par exchanged for (1) share Common $1 par
Central Bancorp, Inc. merged into Independent Bank Corp. 11/10/2012

CENTRAL COAL & COKE CO.
Reorganized as Central Coal & Coke Corp. and each share Preferred and/or Common exchanged for (1) share new Common no par 00/00/1936
Central Coal & Coke Corp. name changed to Central Natural Resources, Inc. 12/26/2000

CENTRAL COAL & COKE CORP (DE)
Common $1 par split (2) for (1) by issuance of (1) additional share 05/22/1968
Stock Dividend - 100% 03/21/1962
Name changed to Central Natural Resources, Inc. 12/26/2000

CENTRAL COAST BANCORP (CA)
Common no par split (5) for (4) by issuance of (0.25) additional share payable 02/26/1999 to holders of record 02/08/1999
Common no par split (5) for (4) by issuance of (0.25) additional share payable 02/28/2002 to holders of record 02/14/2002 Ex date - 03/01/2002
Common no par split (5) for (4) by issuance of (0.25) additional share payable 02/28/2005 to holders of record 02/14/2005 Ex date - 03/01/2005
Stock Dividends - 10% payable 08/15/1996 to holders of record 07/08/1996; 10% payable 02/28/2000 to holders of record 02/14/2000; 10% payable 02/28/2001 to holders of record 02/14/2001 Ex date - 02/12/2001; 10% payable 02/28/2003 to holders of record 02/14/2003 Ex date - 2/12/2003; 10% payable 02/27/2004 to holders of record 02/12/2004
Merged into VIB Corp. 01/31/2006
Each share Common no par exchanged for $25 cash

CENTRAL COAST NATL BK (ARROYO GRANDE, CA)
Merged into Santa Lucia National Bank (Atascadero, CA) 07/10/1995
Each share Common no par exchanged for (0.188) share Common $5 par
Santa Lucia National Bank (Atascadero, CA) reorganized as Santa Lucia Bancorp 04/03/2006
(See Santa Lucia Bancorp)

CENTRAL COLD STORAGE CO (IL)
Name changed to Central Enterprises, Inc. 07/30/1974
(See Central Enterprises, Inc.)

CENTRAL COLO BANCORP INC (CO)
99.9% acquired by Baldwin (D.H.) Co. through exchange offer which expired 06/19/1974
Public interest eliminated

CENTRAL COMMONWEALTH SERVICE CORP. (DE)
Incorporated 05/02/1933
No longer in existence having become inoperative and void for non-payment of taxes 04/01/1939

CENTRAL COMMUNICATIONS CORP (WI)
Reincorporated under the laws of Nevada as Cencom Inc. 06/01/1974
Cencom Inc. merged into Pacific Telecom, Inc. 03/31/1983
(See Pacific Telecom, Inc.)

CENTRAL COMMUNITY TELEPHONE CO. LTD. (ON)
Merged into Community Telephone Co. of Ontario Ltd. 06/28/1971
Each share Preference Ser. A $25 par exchanged for (25) shares 1st Preference Ser. C $1 par

CENTRAL COMPUTER CORP. (CA)
Adjudicated bankrupt 06/23/1971
Stockholders' equity unlikely

CENTRAL COMPUTING INC (KS)
Name changed to Capital And Services, Inc. 08/16/1991
(See Capital And Services, Inc.)

CENTRAL CONDITIONING CORP.
Liquidated 00/00/1950
Details not available

CENTRAL CONNECTICUT POWER & LIGHT CO.
Merged into Connecticut Light & Power Co. 00/00/1932
Details not available

CENTRAL COOPERATIVES, INC. (WI)
Merged into Midland Cooperatives, Inc. 12/01/1963
Each share 5% Preferred $25 par exchanged for 5% Preferred Ser. A $100 par on a dollar for dollar basis or for cash in the form of a Demand Note

CENTRAL CORP. (DE)
inoperative and void for non-payment of taxes 04/01/1960

CENTRAL CORP (GA)
Reorganized under Chapter 11 Federal Bankruptcy Code as Resurgens Communications Group, Inc. 05/16/1989
Each share Common 1¢ par exchanged for (0.1) share Common 1¢ par and (0.1) Common Stock Purchase Warrant expiring 05/16/1994
Resurgens Communications Group, Inc. name changed to LDDS Communications, Inc. 09/15/1993 which name changed to Worldcom, Inc. 05/26/1995 which name changed to WorldCom Inc. (New) 05/01/2000
(See WorldCom Inc. (New))

CENTRAL CORP (LA)
Common $12.50 par split (5) for (4) by issuance of (0.25) additional share 05/22/1985
Common $12.50 par split (5) for (4) by issuance of (0.25) additional share 02/19/1992
Common $12.50 par split (3) for (1) by issuance of (2) additional shares 05/26/1993
Common $12.50 par split (3) for (2) by issuance of (0.5) additional share 05/25/1994
Stock Dividend - 25% 06/22/1983
Merged into First Commerce Corp. 10/20/1995
Each share Common $12.50 par exchanged for (1.67) shares Common $5 par
First Commerce Corp. merged into Banc One Corp. 06/12/1998 which merged into Bank One Corp. 10/02/1998 which merged into J.P. Morgan Chase & Co. 12/31/2000 which name changed to JPMorgan Chase & Co. 07/20/2004

CENTRAL CORPORATE REPORTS SVC INC (DE)
Each share Common 1¢ par exchanged for (0.4) share Common $0.025 par 12/01/1981
Name changed to Corporate Capital Resources, Inc. 07/18/1983
(See Corporate Capital Resources, Inc.)

CENTRAL CORPORATE REPORTS SVC INC NEW (DE)
Name changed to Combined Assets Inc. 06/06/1990
Combined Assets Inc. name changed to Environmental Products & Technologies Corp. 01/13/1995
(See Environmental Products & Technologies Corp.)

CENTRAL CNTYS BK (STATE COLLEGE, PA)
Common $20 par changed to $5 par and (3) additional shares issued 12/31/1974
Reorganized as CCB Bancorp, Inc. 07/01/1982
Each share Common $5 par exchanged for (1) share Common $5 par
CCB Bancorp, Inc. merged into Mellon National Corp. 09/14/1983 which name changed to Mellon Bank Corp. 09/30/1984 which name changed to Mellon Financial Corp. 10/17/1999 which merged into Bank of New York Mellon Corp. 07/01/2007

CENTRAL COUNTIES GAS CO.
Acquired by Southern California Gas Co. 00/00/1927
Details not available

CENTRAL CRUDE LTD (ON)
Reincorporated 07/02/1991
Place of incorporation changed from (BC) to (ON) 07/02/1991
Name changed to River Gold Mines Ltd. 07/27/1994
River Gold Mines Ltd. merged into Wesdome Gold Mines Ltd. 02/01/2006

CENTRAL DATA SYS INC (OH)
Merged into Itel Corp. 09/23/1975
Each share Common no par exchanged for $7.64 cash

CENTRAL DEL RIO OILS LTD (AB)
Capital Stock no par changed to $1 par 10/01/1969
Name changed to PanCanadian Petroleum Ltd. 11/24/1971
PanCanadian Petroleum Ltd. name changed to PanCanadian Energy Corp. 10/01/2001
PanCanadian Energy Corp. name changed to EnCana Corp. 04/05/2002

CENTRAL DETROIT WHSE CO (MI)
Stock Dividend - 10% 05/10/1947
Merged into CDE Acquisition Corp. 07/20/1999
Each share Common $1 par exchanged for $5.43 cash

CENTRAL DISTRIBUTING CO. (DE)
Dissolved 07/24/1944
Details not available

CENTRAL DISTRIBUTORS, INC.
Acquired by Borden Co. 00/00/1929
Details not available

CENTRAL DUPARQUET MINES LTD (QC)
Charter cancelled 06/06/1981

CENTRAL DYNAMICS LTD (CANADA)
Common no par split (4) for (1) by issuance of (3) additional shares 06/18/1968
Recapitalized as International Datacasting Corp. 02/03/1988
Each share Common no par exchanged for (0.1) share Common no par
International Datacasting Corp. merged into Novra Technologies Inc. 06/21/2016

CENTRAL ELECTRIC & GAS CO. (DE)
Common $1 par changed to $3.50 par 00/00/1947
Common $3.50 par changed to $5 par 00/00/1959
Under plan of merger name changed to Western Power & Gas Co. 05/01/1961
Western Power & Gas Co. name changed to Western Power & Gas Co. 07/01/1965 which name changed to Central Telephone & Utilities Corp. 06/05/1968 which name changed to Centel Corp. 04/30/1982 which was acquired by Sprint Corp. (KS) 03/09/1993 which name changed to Sprint Nextel Corp. 08/12/2005 which merged into Sprint Corp. (DE) 07/10/2013

CENTRAL ELECTRIC & TELEPHONE CO.
Name changed to Central Electric & Gas Co. 00/00/1944
Central Electric & Gas Co. name changed to Western Power & Gas Co. 05/01/1961 which name changed to Western Power & Gas Co., Inc. 07/01/1965 which name changed to Central Telephone & Utilities Corp. 06/05/1968 which name changed to Centel Corp. 04/30/1982 which was acquired by Sprint Corp. (KS) 03/09/1993 which name changed to Sprint Nextel Corp. 08/12/2005 which merged into Sprint Corp. (DE) 07/10/2013

CENTRAL ENERGY CORP (TX)
Liquidation completed
Each share Common 1¢ par exchanged for initial distribution of $0.20 cash 11/30/1972
Each share Common 1¢ par received second and final distribution of $0.15 cash 12/28/1972

CENTRAL ENTERPRISES INC (IL)
Liquidation completed
Each share Capital Stock $20 par received initial distribution of $346.6540349 principal amount of Oxford Properties, Inc. 6% Evidence of Obligation due 03/01/1983 and $10 cash 01/01/1982
Each share Capital Stock $20 par received second distribution of $10 cash 03/00/1983
Each share Capital Stock $20 par received third distribution of $0.30 cash 02/00/1984
Each share Capital Stock $20 par received fourth distribution of $0.23 cash 02/27/1985
Each share Capital Stock $20 par received fifth and final distribution of $3.66 cash 07/19/1985
Note: Certificates were not required to be surrendered and are without value

CENTRAL EQUITY TR (NY)
Completely liquidated 12/01/2003
Details not available

CENTRAL EUREKA CORP. (CA)
Name changed to Pacific Industries, Inc. (CA) 09/21/1956
Pacific Industries, Inc. (CA) reincorporated in Delaware as Frye Industries, Inc. 12/31/1970 which merged into Wheelabrator-Frye Inc. 11/04/1971 which merged into Signal Companies, Inc. 02/01/1983 which merged into Allied-Signal Inc. 09/19/1985 which name changed to AlliedSignal Inc. 04/26/1993 which name changed to Honeywell International Inc. 12/01/1999

CENTRAL EUREKA MINING CO. (CA)
Name changed to Central Eureka Corp. 00/00/1953
Central Eureka Corp. name changed to Pacific Industries, Inc. (CA) 09/21/1956 which reincorporated in Delaware as Frye Industries, Inc. 12/31/1970 which merged into Wheelabrator-Frye Inc. 11/04/1971 which merged into Signal Companies, Inc. 02/01/1983 which merged into Allied-Signal Inc. 09/19/1985 which name changed to AlliedSignal Inc. 04/26/1993 which name changed to Honeywell International Inc. 12/01/1999

CENTRAL EUROPE RUSSIA & TURKEY FD INC (MD)
Name changed 06/25/2003
Name changed 04/29/2013
Name changed from Central European Equity Fund, Inc. to Central Europe & Russia Fund, Inc. 06/25/2003
Name changed from Central Europe & Russia Fund, Inc. to Central Europe, Russia & Turkey Fund, Inc. 04/29/2013
Name changed to Central & Eastern Europe Fund Inc. 08/01/2017

CENTRAL EUROPEAN DISTR CORP (DE)
Common 1¢ par split (3) for (2) by issuance of (0.5) additional share payable 05/30/2003 to holders of record 05/19/2003 Ex date - 06/02/2003
Common 1¢ par split (3) for (2) by issuance of (0.5) additional share payable 05/28/2004 to holders of record 05/17/2004
Common 1¢ par split (3) for (2) by issuance of (0.5) additional share payable 06/12/2006 to holders of record 05/29/2006 Ex date - 06/13/2006
Plan of reorganization under Chapter 11 Federal Bankruptcy proceedings effective 06/05/2013
No stockholders' equity

CENTRAL EUROPEAN GROWTH FD PLC (HUNGARY)
Reported in process of liquidation 00/00/2000
Details not available

CENTRAL EUROPEAN VALUE FD INC (MD)
Name changed to Cornerstone Strategic Return Fund, Inc. 07/06/2000
Cornerstone Strategic Return Fund, Inc. merged into Cornerstone Total Return Fund, Inc. 10/30/2002

CENTRAL EXCHANGE LTD (AUSTRALIA)
Ordinary split (2) for (1) by issuance of (1) additional share payable 06/11/2004 to holders of record 06/11/2004
Name changed to Orion Equities Ltd. 12/13/2005

CENTRAL EXPLORERS, LTD. (ON)
Capital Stock no par changed to $1 par 05/07/1953
Assets transferred to Central Hadley Corp. 01/28/1958
Central Hadley Corp. name changed to United States Filter Corp. (Old) 04/23/1965
(See United States Filter Corp. (Old))

CENTRAL EXPLORERS INC (AB)
Acquired by Poco Petroleums Ltd. 01/01/1992
Each share Common no par exchanged for $0.35 cash

CENTRAL FD CDA LTD (AB)
Reincorporated 04/06/1990
Place of incorporation changed from (ON) to (AB) 04/06/1990
Reorganized under the laws of Ontario as Sprott Physical Gold & Silver Trust 01/16/2018
Each share Non-Vtg. Class A no par exchanged for (1) Trust Unit
Each share Common no par exchanged for $500 cash
Note: Unexchanged certificates will be cancelled and become without value 01/15/2021

CENTRAL FDRY CO (ME)
5% Preferred $100 par called for redemption 09/05/1959
Name changed to Gable Industries, Inc. 06/30/1971
Gable Industries, Inc. name changed to Hajoca Corp. 12/29/1978
(See Hajoca Corp.)

CENTRAL FGHT LINES INC (NV)
Merged into North American Truck Lines, LLC 11/28/2006
Each share Common $0.001 par exchanged for $2.25 cash

CENTRAL FGHT LINES INC (TX)
Merged into Roadway Services, Inc. 04/06/1993
Each share Common $10 par exchanged for $104.50 cash

CENTRAL FIBRE PRODUCTS CO. (DE)
Name changed 01/01/1955
Each share Preferred $100 par exchanged for (4) shares 6% Preferred $25 par 00/00/1940
Each share Common or Non-Vtg. Common $5 par exchanged for (2) shares Common or Non-Vtg. Common $2.50 par respectively 07/00/1953
Name changed from Central Fibre Products Co., Inc. to Central Fibre Products Co. 01/01/1955
Merged into Packaging Corp. of America 07/31/1959
Each share Common or Non-Vtg. Common $2.50 par exchanged for (1.25) shares Common $5 par
Packaging Corp. of America acquired by Tennessee Gas Transmission Co. 06/08/1965 which name changed to Tenneco Inc. 04/11/1966 which merged into El Paso Natural Gas Co. 12/12/1996 which reorganized as El Paso Energy Corp. 08/01/1998 which name changed to El Paso 02/05/2001

CENTRAL FID BKS INC (VA)
Common $5 par split (3) for (2) by issuance of (0.5) additional share 09/20/1983
Common $5 par split (3) for (2) by issuance of (0.5) additional share 05/31/1985
$6 Conv. Preferred Ser. A $100 par called for redemption 03/24/1986
Common $5 par split (3) for (2) by issuance of (0.5) additional share 07/01/1991
Common $5 par split (3) for (2) by issuance of (0.5) additional share 02/22/1993
Common $5 par split (3) for (2) by issuance of (0.5) additional share payable 06/14/1996 to holders of record 05/20/1996
Merged into Wachovia Corp. (New) (Ctfs. dated between 05/20/1991 and 09/01/2001) 12/15/1997
Each share Common $5 par exchanged for (0.63) share Common $5 par
Wachovia Corp. (New) (Ctfs. dated between 05/20/1991 and 09/01/2001) merged into Wachovia Corp. (Ctfs. dated after 09/01/2001) 09/01/2001 which merged into Wells Fargo & Co. (New) 12/31/2008

CENTRAL FINL ACCEP CORP (DE)
Completely liquidated 02/28/2001
Each share Common 1¢ par exchanged for first and final distribution of (1) share Banner Central Finance Co. Common 1¢ par and Hispanic Express Inc. Common 1¢ par
(See each company's listing)

CENTRAL FINL CORP (MI)
Acquired by Susquehanna Bancshares, Inc. 09/01/1993
Each share Common $1 par exchanged for (1.57) shares Common $2 par
Susquehanna Bancshares, Inc. merged into BB&T Corp. 08/01/2015

CENTRAL FINL CORP (VT)
Merged into New Hampshire Thrift Bancshares, Inc. 10/25/2013
Each share Common $2 par exchanged for (8.699) shares Common 1¢ par
New Hampshire Thrift Bancshares, Inc. name changed to Lake Sunapee Bank Group 06/01/2015 which merged into Bar Harbor Bankshares 01/13/2017

CENTRAL FIRE INSURANCE CO. OF BALTIMORE
Name changed to Central Insurance Co. of Baltimore 00/00/1938
(See Central Insurance Co. of Baltimore)

CENTRAL FIRST NATIONAL BANK (CORAL GABLES, FL)
Name changed back to Coral Gables First National Bank (Coral Gables, FL) 02/07/1966
Coral Gables First National Bank (Coral Gables, FL) name changed to First National Bank (Coral Gables, FL) 11/08/1974 which merged into Flagship First National Bank (Miami Beach, FL) 05/01/1978 which location was changed to (Miami, FL) 03/18/1980 which name changed to Sun Bank/Miami, N.A. (Miami, FL) 04/01/1985 which name changed to SunTrust Bank, Miami, N.A. (Miami, FL) 10/06/1995
(See SunTrust Bank, Miami, N.A. (Miami, FL))

CENTRAL FLA ST BK (BELLEVIEW, FL)
Bank closed and FDIC appointed receiver 01/20/2012
Stockholders' equity unlikely

CENTRAL FRANKLIN PROCESS CO. (DE)
Common no par exchanged (10) for (1) 00/00/1946
Completely liquidated 12/31/1956
Each share Common no par exchanged for (0.5) share Franklin Process Co. Common no par
(See Franklin Process Co.)

CENTRAL GA RY CO (GA)
Reorganized 01/01/1948
No equity for holders of record prior to this date; certificates are valueless
(Ctfs. dated after 01/01/1948 - see below)
Merged into Southern Railway Co. 06/01/1971
Each share Preferred Ser. A $100 par or Preferred Ser. B $100 par exchanged for $84 cash
Each share Common no par exchanged for $47.40 cash

CENTRAL GAS & ELECTRIC CO.
Reorganized under the laws of Delaware as Central Public Utility Corp. (Old) 00/00/1935
Details not available

CENTRAL GAS UTILITIES LTD. (AB)
Struck off register and deemed to be dissolved 11/15/1967

CENTRAL GOLDTRUST (ON)
Name changed 01/16/2009
Name changed from Central Gold-Trust to Central GoldTrust 01/16/2009
Merged into Sprott Physical Gold Trust 01/19/2016
Each Trust Unit exchanged for (4.4108) Units

CENTRAL GTY TRUSTCO LTD (ON)
Common no par split (2) for (1) by issuance of (1) additional share 07/18/1989
Completely liquidated 00/00/1999
No stockholders' equity

CENTRAL HADLEY CORP. (DE)
Common $1 par changed to no par 08/24/1964
Name changed to United States Filter Corp. (Old) 04/23/1965
(See United States Filter Corp. (Old))

CENTRAL HANOVER BANK & TRUST CO. (NEW YORK, NY)
Name changed to Hanover Bank (New York, NY) 00/00/1951
Hanover Bank (New York, NY) merged into Manufacturers Hanover Trust Co. (New York, NY) 09/08/1961 which reorganized in Delaware as Manufacturers Hanover Corp. 04/28/1969 which merged into Chemical Banking Corp. 12/31/1991 which name changed to Chase Manhattan Corp. (New) 03/31/1996 which name changed to J.P. Morgan Chase & Co. 12/31/2000 which name changed to JPMorgan Chase & Co. 07/20/2004

CENTRAL HISPANO CAPITAL LTD (SPAIN)
Name changed to BCH Capital Ltd. 06/15/1998
(See BCH Capital Ltd.)

CENTRAL HISPANO INTL INC (SPAIN)
Name changed to BCH International Puerto Rico, Inc. 06/23/1998
(See BCH International Puerto Rico, Inc.)

CENTRAL HLDG CO (MI)
Acquired by Standard Federal Bank (Troy, MI) 04/08/1994

Each share Common no par exchanged for $5.50 cash

CENTRAL HOME SECURITIES CORP.
Dissolved 00/00/1936
Details not available

CENTRAL HOME TR CO (ELIZABETH, NJ)
Capital Stock $20 par changed to $10 par and (1) additional share issued 03/15/1965
Reorganized as United Jersey Banks 10/01/1970
Each share Capital Stock $10 par exchanged for (1.33333333) shares Common $5 par
United Jersey Banks name changed to UJB Financial Corp. 06/30/1989 which name changed to Summit Bancorp 03/01/1996 which merged into FleetBoston Financial Corp. 03/01/2001 which merged into Bank of America Corp. 04/01/2004

CENTRAL HUDSON GAS & ELEC CORP (NY)
Each share old Common no par exchanged for (3.5) shares new Common no par 00/00/1929
5.25% Preferred $100 par called for redemption 12/03/1954
Common no par changed to $5 par 02/28/1989
Adjustable Rate Depository Preferred Ser. A called for redemption 12/03/1993
8.4% Preferred $100 par called for redemption 12/03/1993
7.44% Preferred Ser. G $100 par called for redemption 10/01/1995
7.72% Preferred $100 par called for redemption 01/01/1996
Under plan of reorganization each share Common $5 par automatically became (1) share CH Energy Group, Inc. Common 10¢ par 12/15/1999
(See CH Energy Group, Inc.)
4.35% Preferred Ser. D $100 par called for redemption at $101 on 05/18/2012
4.96% Preferred Ser. E $100 par called for redemption at $101 on 05/18/2012
4.5% Preferred $100 par called for redemption at $107 plus $1 accrued dividends on 03/21/2013
4.75% Preferred $100 par called for redemption at $106.75 plus $1.056 accrued dividends on 03/21/2013

CENTRAL ILL BANC SHS INC (IL)
Merged into Magna Group, Inc. 10/25/1984
Each share Common $1 par exchanged for (0.252) share Common $2 par
Magna Group, Inc. merged into Union Planters Corp. 07/01/1998 which merged into Regions Financial Corp. (New) 07/01/2004

CENTRAL ILL ELEC & GAS CO (IL)
Common no par changed to $15 par 00/00/1944
Common $15 par changed to $10 par and (0.5) additional share issued 08/01/1955
Common $10 par changed to $8 par and (0.25) additional share issued 12/09/1958
Common $8 par changed to $4 par and (1) additional share issued 08/11/1961
Common $4 par split (4) for (3) by issuance of (0.33333333) additional share 10/20/1964
Merged into Commonwealth Edison Co. 12/09/1966
Each share Common $4 par exchanged for (1) share $1.425 Conv. Preferred no par

CENTRAL ILL FINL CORP (DE)
Under plan of reorganization each share Common $1 par automatically became (1) share Central Illinois Financial Co., Inc. Common 1¢ par 10/20/1995
Central Illinois Financial Co., Inc. name changed to BankIllinois Financial Corp. 02/27/1998 which merged into Main Street Trust, Inc. 03/23/2000 which merged into First Busey Corp. 08/01/2007

CENTRAL ILL FINL INC (DE)
Stock Dividend - 5% payable 05/15/1996 to holders of record 05/01/1996
Name changed to BankIllinois Financial Corp. 02/27/1998
BankIllinois Financial Corp. merged into Main Street Trust, Inc. 03/23/2000 which merged into First Busey Corp. 08/01/2007

CENTRAL ILL INC (DE)
Common $5 par split (7) for (5) by issuance of (0.4) additional share 09/30/1986
Acquired by AMCORE Financial, Inc. 04/09/1990
Each share Common $5 par exchanged for (3.33) shares Common 50¢ par
(See AMCORE Financial, Inc.)

CENTRAL ILL LT CO (IL)
Common no par split (2) for (1) by issuance of (1) additional share 04/21/1958
Common no par split (2) for (1) by issuance of (1) additional share 04/08/1965
$2.625 Class A Preferred no par called for redemption 07/02/1984
$2.875 Class A Preferred no par called for redemption 01/02/1985
Under plan of reorganization each share Common no par automatically became (1) share CILCORP Inc. Common no par 05/07/1985
7.56% Preferred $100 par called for redemption 07/08/1993
7.72% Preferred $100 par called for redemption 08/27/1993
8.28% Preferred $100 par called for redemption 08/27/1993
Auction Market Preferred no par called for redemption at $100,000 on 07/03/2000
5.85% Class A Preferred $100 par called for redemption at $100 on 07/01/2008
4.50% Preferred $100 par called for redemption at $110 on 08/02/2010
4.64% Preferred $100 par called for redemption at $102 on 08/02/2010

CENTRAL ILL PUB SVC CO (IL)
Common no par changed to $40 par 00/00/1933
Each share Common $40 par exchanged for (4) shares Common $10 par 00/00/1946
6% Preferred $100 par called for redemption 12/27/1946
$6 Preferred no par called for redemption 12/27/1946
5.25% Preferred $100 par called for redemption 06/30/1954
Common $10 par changed to no par and (2) additional shares issued 05/08/1962
9.25% Preferred $100 par called for redemption 09/30/1980
10% Preferred $100 par called for redemption 03/31/1986
10.25% Preferred $100 par called for redemption 09/30/1986
Under plan of reorganization each share Common no par automatically became (1) share CIPSCO Inc. Common no par 10/01/1990
(See CIPSCO Inc.)
8% Preferred $100 par called for redemption 07/03/1992
7.48% Preferred $100 par called for redemption 06/03/1993
8.08% Preferred $100 par called for redemption 11/15/1993
Auction Preferred Ser. A called for redemption at $100 on 12/31/2003
Under plan of merger name changed to Ameren Illinois Co. 10/01/2010

CENTRAL ILLINOIS SECURITIES CORP. (DE)
Common no par changed to $1 par 00/00/1932
Stock Dividends - 10% 01/16/1956; 10% 01/15/1957
Name changed to Central Securities Corp. (DE) 02/25/1959

CENTRAL IND BANCORP (IN)
Common no par split (4) for (3) by issuance of (0.33333333) additional share 05/18/1993
Merged into National City Corp. 01/01/1995
Each share Common no par exchanged for (1.08) shares Common $4 par
National City Corp. acquired by PNC Financial Services Group, Inc. 12/31/2008

CENTRAL IND GAS CO (IN)
Stock Dividends - 10% 05/06/1955; 10% 01/29/1963
Completely liquidated 01/10/1967
Each share Common $5 par exchanged for first and final distribution of (0.6026) share American Natural Gas Co. (DE) Common $10 par
American Natural Gas Co. (DE) reincorporated in Michigan 06/30/1975 which name changed to American Natural Resources Co. (MI) 05/10/1976 which reincorporated in Delaware 06/30/1983
(See American Natural Resources Co. (DE))

CENTRAL INDIANA POWER CO.
Merged into Public Service Co. of Indiana, Inc. 09/06/1941
Each share 6% or 7% Preferred exchanged for (1) share 5% Preferred $100 par, (2) shares Common no par and $12.58 cash
(See Public Service Co. of Indiana, Inc.)

CENTRAL INSTRUMENT CORP. (NY)
Defunct in October 1963
No stockholders' equity

CENTRAL INSURANCE CO. OF BALTIMORE
In process of liquidation 00/00/1946
Details not available

CENTRAL INVESTMENT CORP. (AZ)
Merged into Financial Corp. of Arizona (AZ) 10/17/1962
Each share Common $1 par exchanged for (0.444444) share Capital Stock $5 par
Financial Corp. of Arizona (AZ) reincorporated in Delaware 06/01/1970 which name changed to FCA Industries, Inc. 04/24/1975
(See FCA Industries, Inc.)

CENTRAL INVT CORP (OH)
Merged into CIC Acquisition Inc. 10/15/1996
Each share Common no par exchanged for $460 cash

CENTRAL INVT CORP DENVER (CO)
Completely liquidated 12/31/1968
Each share Common $2.50 par exchanged for first and final distribution of (0.350877) share Dillon Companies, Inc. Common $1.25 par
Dillon Companies, Inc. merged into Kroger Co. 01/25/1983

CENTRAL INVT FD INC (MD)
144A Auction Market Preferred Ser. B called for redemption at $100,000 on 10/28/1998
144A Auction Market Preferred Ser. A called for redemption at $100,000 on 12/03/1998

CENTRAL INVESTORS CORP.
Acquired by Boston Fund, Inc. 00/00/1940
Details not available

CENTRAL INVESTORS LIFE INSURANCE CO. (AR)
Placed into rehabilitation by Court Order 12/06/1983
No stockholders' equity

CENTRAL INVESTORS LIFE INSURANCE CO. (KY)
Merged into Citizens Security Life Insurance Co. 09/15/1971
Each share Common $1 par exchanged for (0.75) share Common $1 par
Citizens Security Life Insurance Co. reorganized as Citizens Financial Corp. 02/04/1991

CENTRAL IOWA POWER & LIGHT CO.
Merged into Iowa Public Service Co. 00/00/1927
Details not available

CENTRAL IRON & STEEL CO.
Merged into Barium Steel Corp. (DE) 00/00/1946
Each share Capital Stock $10 par exchanged for (1.25) shares Capital Stock $1 par
Barium Steel Corp. (DE) name changed to Phoenix Steel Corp. 05/04/1959
(See Phoenix Steel Corp.)

CENTRAL JERSEY BANCORP (NJ)
Ctfs. dtd. after 01/01/2005
Common 1¢ par split (2) for (1) by issuance of (1) additional share payable 07/01/2005 to holders of record 06/15/2005 Ex date - 07/05/2005
Stock Dividends - 5% payable 07/01/2006 to holders of record 06/15/2006 Ex date - 06/13/2006; 5% payable 07/02/2007 to holders of record 06/15/2007 Ex date - 06/14/2007; 5% payable 07/01/2008 to holders of record 06/13/2008 Ex date - 06/11/2008
Acquired by Kearny Financial Corp. 11/30/2010
Each share Common 1¢ par exchanged for $7.50 cash

CENTRAL JERSEY BANCORP (NJ)
Ctfs. dtd. prior to 01/14/1995
Common $2.50 par split (2) for (1) by issuance of (1) additional share 07/01/1988
Merged into National Westminster Bank PLC (London, England) 01/14/1995
Each share Common $2.50 par exchanged for either (0.7243) ADR for Ordinary £1 par or $33.50 cash
Note: Option to elect to receive cash expired 02/06/1995

CENTRAL JERSEY BK & TR CO (FREEHOLD, NJ)
Capital Stock $5 par changed to $2.50 par and (1) additional share issued 05/17/1963
Reorganized as Central Jersey Bancorp (Ctfs. dtd. prior to 01/14/1995) 05/31/1985
Each share Capital Stock $2.50 par exchanged for (1) share Common $2.50 par
Central Jersey Bancorp (Ctfs. dtd. prior to 01/14/1995 merged into National Westminster Bank PLC (London, England) 01/14/1995

CENTRAL JERSEY FINL CORP (NJ)
Common no par split (5) for (4) by issuance of (0.25) additional share 10/22/1993
Stock Dividends - 10% 10/01/1992; 10% 09/02/1994
Merged into Summit Bancorp 12/07/1996
Each share Common no par

exchanged for (0.875) share Common $1.20 par
Summit Bancorp merged into FleetBoston Financial Corp. 03/01/2001 which merged into Bank of America Corp. 04/01/2004

CENTRAL JERSEY INDS INC (NJ)
Reincorporated under the laws of Delaware as CJI Industries, Inc. and Common $1 par reclassified as Class A $1 par 07/30/1986
CJI Industries, Inc. name changed to Triangle Industries, Inc. (New) 07/07/1988
(See Triangle Industries, Inc. (New))

CENTRAL JERSEY SAVINGS & LOAN ASSOCIATION (NJ)
Common $1 par split (3) for (2) by issuance of (0.5) additional share 09/01/1987
Name changed to Central Jersey Savings Bank S.L.A. (East Brunswick, NJ) 07/11/1988
Central Jersey Savings Bank S.L.A. (East Brunswick, NJ) reorganized as Central Jersey Financial Corp. 12/12/1989 which merged into Summit Bancorp 12/07/1996 which merged into FleetBoston Financial Corp. 03/01/2001 which merged into Bank of America Corp. 04/01/2004

CENTRAL JERSEY SVGS BK S L A (EAST BRUNSWICK, NJ)
Under plan of reorganization each share Common $1 par automatically became (1) share Central Jersey Financial Corp. Common no par 12/12/1989
Central Jersey Financial Corp. merged into Summit Bancorp 12/07/1996 which merged into FleetBoston Financial Corp. 03/01/2001 which merged into Bank of America Corp. 04/01/2004

CENTRAL KANSAS POWER CO. (KS)
4.75% Preferred $100 par called for redemption 03/31/1966
Merged into United Utilities, Inc. 05/26/1967
Each share Common $9 par exchanged for (0.33333333) shares Common $2.50 par
United Utilities, Inc. name changed to United Telecommunications, Inc. 06/02/1972 which name changed to Sprint Corp. (KS) 02/26/1992 which name changed to Sprint Nextel Corp. 08/12/2005 which merged into Sprint Corp. (DE) 07/10/2013

CENTRAL KANSAS TELEPHONE CO.
In process of liquidation 00/00/1946
Details not available

CENTRAL KENTUCKY NATURAL GAS CO.
Acquired by Columbia Gas & Electric Corp. 00/00/1927
Details not available

CENTRAL LA ELEC INC (LA)
Each share Common $10 par exchanged for (2) shares Common $5 par 00/00/1953
Common $5 par split (2) for (1) by issuance of (1) additional share 10/12/1960
Common $5 par changed to $4 par and (1) additional share issued 02/15/1966
5.04% Conv. Preferred $100 par called for redemption 05/02/1978
Under plan of reorganization each share old Common $4 par automatically became (1) share Central Louisiana Energy Corp. Common no par 08/02/1978
(See Central Louisiana Energy Corp. - in Obsolete)
$4.18 Preferred 1982 Ser. $25 par called for redemption 09/01/1987

8.95% Preferred $100 par called for redemption 09/01/1987
New Common $4 par changed to $2 par and (1) additional share issued 05/22/1992
Name changed to Cleco Corp. 04/27/1998
Cleco Corp. name changed to Cleco Utilities Group Inc. 05/14/1999
4.50% Preferred 1955 Ser. $10 par called for redemption at $102 on 06/30/1999

CENTRAL LA ENERGY CORP (LA)
Common no par split (2) for (1) by issuance of (1) additional share 05/15/1980
Name changed to Celeron Corp. 07/01/1982
Celeron Corp. merged into Goodyear Tire & Rubber Co. 06/21/1983

CENTRAL-LEDUC OILS LTD. (AB)
Name changed to Central-Del Rio Oils Ltd. 04/15/1957
Central-Del Rio Oils Ltd. name changed to PanCanadian Petroleum Ltd. 11/24/1971 which name changed to PanCanadian Energy Corp. 10/01/2001 which name changed to EnCana Corp. 04/05/2002

CENTRAL LIFE INSURANCE CO. OF ILLINOIS (IL)
Name changed to Central Standard Life Insurance Co. 04/30/1951
Central Standard Life Insurance Co. name changed to Reliance Standard Life Insurance Co. 08/09/1965
(See Reliance Standard Life Insurance Co.)

CENTRAL MANHATTAN PPTYS INC (NY)
Reorganized 00/00/1941
No equity for old Class A or B Stock
Each share Common 10¢ par exchanged for (0.04) share Common $1 par 00/00/1952
Merged into Southwest Holdings Co. 04/02/1968
Each share Common $1 par exchanged for (1) share Class A Preferred $1 par
(See Southwest Holdings Co.)

CENTRAL MANITOBA MINES LTD. (MB)
Recapitalized as Consolidated Manitoba 09/04/1964
Each share Common exchanged for (0.2) share Common
(See Consolidated Manitoba Mines Ltd.)

CENTRAL MASSACHUSETTS LIGHT & POWER CO.
Liquidated 00/00/1938
Details not available

CENTRAL MATACHEWAN MINING CORP. LTD.
Recapitalized as Richore Gold Mines Ltd. 00/00/1953
Each share Capital Stock $1 par exchanged for (0.66666666) share Capital Stock $1 par
Richore Gold Mines Ltd. liquidated for Avilla International Explorations Ltd. 07/07/1971
(See Avilla International Explorations Ltd.)

CENTRAL ME PWR CO (ME)
Common no par changed to $10 par 00/00/1942
Common $10 par changed to $5 par and (1) additional share issued 12/04/1963
5% Preferred $50 par called for redemption 07/01/1946
6% Preferred $100 par called for redemption 07/01/1946
7% Preferred $100 par called for redemption 07/01/1946
4.6% Conv. Preferred $100 par called for redemption 07/10/1964

$11.25 Preferred $100 par called for redemption 12/10/1986
11.75% Preferred $100 par called for redemption 12/10/1986
12.75% Preferred $100 par called for redemption 01/02/1990
8.4% Preferred $100 par called for redemption 03/26/1993
7.875% Preferred $100 par called for redemption at $100 on 04/01/1998
8.875% Preferred $100 par called for redemption at $100 on 07/01/1998
Under plan of reorganization each share Common $5 par automatically became (1) share CMP Group, Inc. Common $5 par 09/01/1998
(See CMP Group, Inc.)
Flexible Money Market Preferred Ser. A $100 par called for redemption at $100 on 10/21/2000
3.5% Preferred $100 par called for redemption at $101 on 06/10/2005
4.6% Preferred $100 par called for redemption at $101 on 06/22/2012
4.75% Preferred $100 par called for redemption at $101 on 06/22/2012
(Additional Information in Active)

CENTRAL MENDOCINO COUNTY POWER CO.
Assets sold 00/00/1941
Details not available

CENTRAL METAL MINES LTD. (QC)
Charter annulled for failure to file reports and pay fees 11/27/1976

CENTRAL MEXICAN OIL CO. (DE)
Charter cancelled and declared inoperative and void for non-payment of taxes 04/01/1930

CENTRAL MIDLAND COAL CO., INC. (WV)
Acquired by Eastern Gas & Fuel Associates 05/20/1966
Each share Common 20¢ par exchanged for (4) shares Common $10 par
Eastern Gas & Fuel Associates name changed to Eastern Enterprises 04/28/1989
(See Eastern Enterprises)

CENTRAL MINERA CORP (YT)
Cease trade order effective 11/26/2001

CENTRAL MINERALS CO., INC. (UT)
Name changed to Combined Production Associates, Ltd. 12/08/1959
Combined Production Associates, Ltd. acquired by Intergeneral Industries, Inc. 05/21/1969
(See Intergeneral Industries, Inc.)

CENTRAL MINING & DEVELOPMENT CO. (AZ)
Charter revoked for failure to file reports and pay fees 08/23/1927

CENTRAL MINING & INVESTMENT CORP. LTD. (ENGLAND)
Merged into Charter Consolidated Ltd. 05/05/1965
Each ADR for Ordinary £1 par exchanged for (2.875) ADR's for Ordinary 5s par

CENTRAL MINING CORP. (QC)
Acquired by Pan American Mines Ltd. 05/28/1971
Each share Capital Stock $1 par exchanged for (1.5) shares Capital Stock no par
(See Pan American Mines Ltd.)

CENTRAL MNG CORP (CO)
Each share Common 10¢ par exchanged for (10) shares Common 1¢ par 06/08/1970
Declared defunct and inoperative for failure to pay taxes and file annual reports 01/31/1977

CENTRAL MISSISSIPPI VALLEY ELECTRIC PROPERTIES
Dissolved 00/00/1937
Details not available

CENTRAL MO TR CO (JEFFERSON CITY, MO)
Stock Dividends - 100% 11/01/1947; 100% 11/05/1951
Name changed to Central Trust Bank (Jefferson City, MO) 06/01/1969
Central Trust Bank (Jefferson City, MO) reorganized as Central Bancompany 12/31/1971
(See Central Bancompany)

CENTRAL MORTGAGE & INVESTMENT CORP. (FL)
Name changed to Lehigh Building & Development Co. 01/31/1962
(See Lehigh Building & Development Co.)

CENTRAL MTG & RLTY TR (MA)
Merged into Central Realty Investors, Inc. 05/01/1986
Each Share of Bene. Int. $1 par exchanged for (1) share Common 10¢ par
(See Central Realty Investors, Inc.)

CENTRAL MTG BANCSHARES INC (MO)
Merged into Mercantile Bancorporation, Inc. 05/01/1995
Each share Common $1 par exchanged for (0.597) share Common $5 par
Mercantile Bancorporation, Inc. merged into Firstar Corp. (New) 09/20/1999 which merged into U.S. Bancorp (DE) 02/27/2001

CENTRAL MUT FD INC (MD)
Name changed to Basic Growth Fund Inc. 11/26/1976
(See Basic Browth Fund Inc.)

CENTRAL MUT TEL INC (VA)
Stock Dividend - 10% 01/25/1963
Recapitalized as Commonwealth Telephone Co. of Virginia 07/01/1968
Each share Common $10 par exchanged for (1.5) shares Common $10 par
Commonwealth Telephone Co. of Virginia merged into Continental Telephone Corp. 07/15/1971 which name changed to Continental Telecom Inc. 05/06/1982 which name changed to Contel Corp. 05/01/1986 which merged into GTE Corp. 03/14/1991 which merged into Verizon Communications Inc. 06/30/2000

CENTRAL N Y PWR CORP (NY)
Merged into Niagara Mohawk Power Corp. 01/05/1950
Each share 3.4% Preferred $100 par exchanged for (1) share 3.4% Preferred $100 par

CENTRAL NATL BANCSHARES INC (IA)
Common $1 par split (2.375) for (1) by issuance of (1.375) additional shares 08/15/1977
Stock Dividend - 100% 07/15/1975
Name changed to United Central Bancshares Inc. 04/16/1981
United Central Bancshares Inc. name changed to First Interstate of Iowa, Inc. 06/24/1985 which merged into Boatmen's Bancshares, Inc. 04/01/1992 which merged into NationsBank Corp. 01/07/1997 which reincorporated in Delaware as BankAmerica Corp. (Old) 09/25/1998 which merged into BankAmerica Corp. (New) 09/30/1998 which name changed to Bank of America Corp. 04/28/1999

CENTRAL NATL BK & TR CO (DES MOINES, IA)
Each share Common $100 par exchanged for (20) shares Common $10 par to effect a (10) for (1) split and 100% stock dividend 04/13/1964
Stock Dividends - 20% 12/11/1940;

51.5% 12/26/1941; 25% 12/27/1945; 100% 01/10/1956; 10% 09/15/1967
Name changed to United Central Bank of Des Moines N.A. (Des Moines, IA) 04/16/1981
(See United Central Bank of Des Moines N.A. (Des Moines, IA))

CENTRAL NATL BK (CANAJOHARIE, NY)
Capital Stock $10 par split (2) for (1) by issuance of (1) additional share 06/10/1986
Capital Stock $10 par changed to $5 par and (1) additional share issued 04/16/1988
Stock Dividends - 10% 10/26/1956; 10% 07/17/1959; 10% 02/28/1967; 10% 03/24/1969; 10% 07/05/1972; 100% 04/15/1980
Under plan of reorganization each share Common $5 par automatically became (1) share CNB Financial Corp. Common $5 par 01/05/1993
CNB Financial Corp. merged into NBT Bancorp Inc. 11/09/2001

CENTRAL NATL BK (CHICAGO, IL)
Stock Dividends - 20% 12/01/1944; 14.28571428% 12/30/1946; (3) for (13) 03/06/1951; 25% 01/27/1954; 25% 12/09/1963
Reorganized under the laws of Delaware as Central National Chicago Corp. 02/11/1969
Each share Capital Stock $10 par exchanged for (1) share Common $10 par
Central National Chicago Corp. merged into Exchange International Corp. 08/21/1982 which name changed to Exchange Bancorp, Inc. 05/17/1988
(See Exchange Bancorp, Inc.)

CENTRAL NATL BK (CLEVELAND, OH)
Common $20 par changed to $16 par 00/00/1951
Common $16 par changed to $12 par and (0.33333333) additional share issued plus a 16.66666666% stock dividend paid 03/17/1966
Common $12 par changed to $8 par and (0.5) additional share issued 05/01/1970
Stock Dividends - 10% 12/30/1949; 10% 02/23/1951; 10% 02/26/1963; 10% 03/01/1968
Under plan of reorganization each share Common $8 par automatically became (1) share Centran Bancshares Corp. Common $8 par 12/31/1971
Centran Bancshares Corp. name changed to Centran Corp. 04/05/1974
(See Centran Corp.)

CENTRAL NATL BK (HOUSTON, TX)
Name changed to Central Bank (Houston, TX) 08/01/1979
Central Bank (Houston, TX) reorganized as Central Bancshares Inc. 02/16/1982
(See Central Bancshares Inc.)

CENTRAL NATL BK (LYNCHBURG, VA)
Stock Dividends - 10% payable 07/31/2000 to holders of record 06/30/2000 Ex date - 08/21/2000; 10% payable 07/31/2001 to holders of record 06/30/2001; 10% payable 07/31/2002 to holders of record 06/28/2002 Ex date - 07/29/2002; 10% payable 0/31/2003 to holders of record 09/30/2003 Ex date - 11/03/2003
Merged into Carter Bank & Trust (Martinsville, VA) 12/29/2006
Each share Common $5 par exchanged for (5.47) shares Common

CENTRAL NATL BK (MIAMI, FL)
Name changed to Eagle National Bank (Miami, FL) 11/02/1981

CENTRAL NATL BK (RICHMOND, VA)
Capital Stock $20 par changed to $7.50 par and (2) additional shares issued 09/14/1962
Stock Dividends - 25% 02/01/1950; 20% 10/17/1951; 16.66666666% 08/25/1953; 14.28571428% 04/20/1955; 12.5% 06/15/1956; 16% 07/01/1958; 16.66666666% 07/05/1960; 14.28571428% 10/11/1961; 10% 10/27/1964; 16.66666666% 06/09/1967
Reorganized as Central National Corp. (VA) 12/31/1968
Each share Capital Stock $7.50 par exchanged for (1) share Common $7.50 par
Central National Corp. (VA) merged into Commonwealth Banks, Inc. 12/31/1978 which name changed to Central Fidelity Banks, Inc. 06/01/1979 which merged into Wachovia Corp. (New) (Ctfs. dated between 05/20/1991 and 09/01/2001) 12/15/1997 which merged into Wachovia Corp. (Ctfs. dated after 09/01/2001) 09/01/2001 which merged into Wells Fargo & Co. (New) 12/31/2008

CENTRAL NATL BK (SAN ANGELO, TX)
Common $75 par changed to $7.50 par and (9) additional shares issued 01/30/1962
Stock Dividends - 20% 04/17/1961; 50% 10/01/1962; 10% 01/31/1966; 10% 07/12/1968; 20% 08/01/1974
Bank closed 03/22/1990
Stockholders' equity unlikely

CENTRAL NATL BK (STERLING, IL)
Reorganized as Central of Illinois, Inc. 07/01/1982
Each share Common $5 par exchanged for (1) share Common $5 par
Central of Illinois, Inc. acquired by AMCORE Financial, Inc. 04/09/1990
(See AMCORE Financial, Inc.)

CENTRAL NATL BK (WAUSAU, WI)
Acquired by M&I First American National Bank (Wausau, WI) 08/01/1990
Each share Capital Stock $5 par exchanged for $78.13 cash

CENTRAL NATL BK MD (SILVER SPRING, MD)
Common $10 par changed to $5 par and (1) additional share issued 01/15/1983
Stock Dividend - 30% 03/01/1971
Merged into Citizens Bancorp 03/21/1986
Each share Common $5 par exchanged for (0.38095238) share Common $10 par
Citizens Bancorp merged into Crestar Financial Corp. 12/31/1996 which merged into SunTrust Banks, Inc. 12/31/1998

CENTRAL NATL BK NEW YORK (BROOKLYN, NY)
Each share Capital Stock $2.50 par exchanged for (0.05) share Capital Stock $50 par 12/31/1984
Declared insolvent and taken over by FDIC 09/01/1987
Stockholders' equity undetermined

CENTRAL NATL CHICAGO CORP (DE)
Common $10 par changed to $1 par 05/01/1981
Stock Dividends - 10% 02/16/1970; 10% 03/31/1974
Merged into Exchange International Corp. 08/21/1982
Each share Common $1 par exchanged for (1/3) share 8% Conv. Preferred Ser. B $18 par
(See Exchange International Corp.)

CENTRAL NATL CORP (VA)
Common $7.50 par changed to $6 par and (0.25) additional shares issued 05/15/1970
Common $6 par changed to $5 par and (0.2) additional shares issued 09/11/1972
Merged into Commonwealth Banks, Inc. 12/31/1978
Each share Common $5 par exchanged for (1.25) shares Common $5 par
Commonwealth Banks, Inc. name changed to Central Fidelity Banks, Inc. 06/01/1979 which merged into Wachovia Corp. (New) (Ctfs. dated between 05/20/1991 and 09/01/2001) 12/15/1997 which merged into Wachovia Corp. (Ctfs. dated after 09/01/2001) 09/01/2001 which merged into Wells Fargo & Co. (New) 12/31/2008

CENTRAL NATL FINL CORP (DE)
Merged into Deere & Co. 02/22/1982
Each share Common $1 par exchanged for $36 cash
$7 Preferred Ser. A no par called for redemption 03/31/1982
Public interest eliminated

CENTRAL NATL LIFE INS CO (IL)
Common $1.50 par changed to $1 par and (0.5) additional share issued 05/30/1970
Merged into Central-National Financial Corp. 06/30/1970
Each share Common $1 par exchanged for (1) share Common $1 par
(See Central-National Financial Corp.)

CENTRAL NETWORK COMMUNICATIONS INC (DE)
Each share old Common $0.0001 par exchanged for (0.01) share new Common $0.0001 par 12/29/2005
Name changed to JATI Technologies, Inc. 09/14/2006
JATI Technologies, Inc. recapitalized as Merco Sud Agro-Financial Equities Corp. 03/25/2009

CENTRAL NEW ENGLAND RAILWAY
Merged into New York, New Haven & Hartford Railroad Co. 00/00/1927
Details not available

CENTRAL NEW HAMPSHIRE TELEPHONE CO.
Acquired by New England Telephone & Telegraph Co. 00/00/1930
Details not available

CENTRAL NEW YORK MORTGAGE & HOMEBUILDING CO., INC.
Name changed to Central New York Mortgage Corp. 00/00/1930
(See Central New York Mortgage Corp.)

CENTRAL NEW YORK MORTGAGE & TITLE CO.
Liquidated 00/00/1935
Details not available

CENTRAL NEW YORK MORTGAGE CORP.
Bankrupt 00/00/1937
Details not available

CENTRAL NEWSPAPERS INC (IN)
Merged into Gannett Co., Inc. (Old) 08/04/2000
Each share Class A Common no par exchanged for $64 cash
Each share Class B Common no par exchanged for $6.40 cash

CENTRAL NORSEMAN CORP N L (AUSTRALIA)
Stock Dividends - 700% 06/08/1987; 0.047% payable 02/13/1998 to holders of record 01/06/1998
ADR agreement terminated 02/27/2002
Each ADR for Ordinary exchanged for $0.229 cash
Note: Due to ADR's being unsponsored exchange rate may vary dependent upon depositary agent

CENTRAL NORTHERN AIRWAYS LTD. (CANADA)
Name changed to Transair Ltd. 05/09/1956
(See Transair Ltd.)

CENTRAL OHIO LIGHT & POWER CO. (OH)
Acquired by Ohio Power Co. 02/00/1955
Each share Common $10 par received $50 cash
Note: Certificates were not required to be exchanged and are without value

CENTRAL OHIO STEEL PRODUCTS CO. (OH)
Each share Common no par exchanged for (4) shares Common $1 par 00/00/1936
Stock Dividend - 33.33333333% 12/25/1946
Merged into Hercules Galion Products, Inc. 08/31/1955
Each share Common $1 par exchanged for (2) shares Common 10¢ par
Hercules Galion Products, Inc. name changed to Peabody Galion Corp. 12/11/1969 which name changed to Peabody International Corp. 11/19/1976 which merged into Pullman-Peabody Co. 10/24/1985 which name changed back to Pullman Co. 02/12/1987
(See Pullman Co.)

CENTRAL OIL CO. (MS)
Acquired by Amax Inc. 07/31/1975
Each share Common $1 par exchanged for (91.740994) shares Common $1 par
Amax Inc. merged into Cyprus Amax Minerals Co. 11/15/1993 which merged into Phelps Dodge Corp. 12/02/1999 which merged into Freeport-McMoRan Copper & Gold Inc. 03/19/2007 which name changed to Freeport-McMoRan Inc. 07/14/2014

CENTRAL OIL CORP (CO)
Name changed to Netgain Development, Inc. 11/12/1999
(See Netgain Development, Inc.)

CENTRAL OKLA OIL CORP (DE)
Charter cancelled and declared inoperative and void for non-payment of taxes 03/01/1975

CENTRAL OKLAHOMA SERVICE CO.
Reorganized as Central Dairy Products Co. 12/01/1936
No stockholders' equity

CENTRAL ONT SVGS & LN CORP (ON)
Merged into Ontario Trust Co. 12/31/1971
Each share Common $5 par exchanged for (1.2969) shares Common $5 par
Ontario Trust Co. merged into Canada Trust Co.-La Societe Canada Trust (London, ON) 12/31/1976

CENTRAL OUTDOOR ADVERTISING CO., INC. (NJ)
Name changed to Packer Corp. (NJ) 04/04/1960
(See Packer Corp. (NJ))

CENTRAL PA FINL CORP (PA)
Acquired by Fulton Financial Corp. 09/30/1994
Each share Common $1 par exchanged for $23 cash

CENTRAL PA GAS CO (PA)
Acquired by Columbia Gas System, Inc. 05/31/1966
Each share $6 Preferred no par exchanged for (4.496) shares Common $10 par
Each share Common no par exchanged for (0.4) share Common $10 par

CENTRAL PA SVGS ASSN SHAMOKIN (PA)
Common $1 par split (3) for (2) by issuance of (0.5) additional share 11/18/1985
Name changed to Central Pennsylvania Financial Corp. 06/16/1986
Central Pennsylvania Financial Corp. acquired by Fulton Financial Corp. 09/30/1994

CENTRAL PAC BK (HONOLULU, HI)
Common $20 par changed to $5 par and (3) additional shares issued 02/09/1966
Reorganized as CPB Inc. 11/12/1982
Each share Common $5 par exchanged for (1) share Common $5 par
CPB Inc. name changed to Central Pacific Financial Corp. 04/23/2003

CENTRAL PAC CORP (CA)
Stock Dividend - 50% 03/01/1982
Acquired by Wells Fargo & Co. (Old) 03/31/1990
Each share Common no par exchanged for (0.3969) share Common $5 par
Wells Fargo & Co. (Old) merged into Wells Fargo & Co. (New) 11/02/1998

CENTRAL PAC MINERALS N L (AUSTRALIA)
Each old ADR for Ordinary exchanged for (5) new ADR's for Ordinary 03/12/1980
Acquired by Southern Pacific Petroleum N.L. 03/01/2002
Each new ADR for Ordinary exchanged for (0.1332) Sponsored ADR for Ordinary
Southern Pacific Petroleum N.L. name changed to Laguna Resources NL 02/12/2010
(See Laguna Resources NL)

CENTRAL PAPER CO., INC. (MI)
Reorganized 00/00/1935
Each share 7% Preferred exchanged for (1) share new Common $1 par
Each share 8% Preferred exchanged for (1.125) shares new Common $1 par
Each share old Common exchanged for (0.04666666) share new Common $1 par
Merged into Warren (S.D.) Co. 00/00/1953
Each share new Common $1 par exchanged for (0.5) share Common no par
Warren (S.D.) Co. merged into Scott Paper Co. 05/17/1967 which merged into Kimberly-Clark Corp. 12/12/1995

CENTRAL PARK VIEW OPERATING CORP.
Liquidated 00/00/1940
Details not available

CENTRAL PATRICIA GOLD MINES LTD (ON)
Capital Stock $1 par reclassified as Common no par 06/30/1978
Under plan of merger name changed to Central Patricia Ltd. 06/19/1980
Central Patricia Ltd. merged into Conwest Exploration Co. Ltd. (Old) (ON) 08/27/1982 which merged into Conwest Exploration Co. Ltd. (New) (AB) 09/01/1993 which merged into Alberta Energy Co. Ltd. 01/31/1996 which merged into EnCana Corp. 01/03/2003

CENTRAL PATRICIA LTD (ON)
6% Non-Vtg. Non-Cum. Retractable Preference $8 par called for redemption 06/21/1982
Merged into Conwest Exploration Co. Ltd. (Old) (ON) 08/27/1982
Each share Common no par exchanged for (1.1) shares Class B no par
Conwest Exploration Co. Ltd. (Old) (ON) merged into Conwest Exploration Co. Ltd. (New) (AB) 09/01/1993 which merged into Alberta Energy Co. Ltd. 01/31/1996 which merged into EnCana Corp. 01/03/2003

CENTRAL PATRICIA MINES LTD.
Reorganized as Central Patricia Gold Mines Ltd. 00/00/1931
Each share Capital Stock $1 par exchanged for (0.25) share Capital Stock $1 par
Central Patricia Gold Mines Ltd. name changed to Central Patricia Ltd. 06/19/1980 which merged into Conwest Exploration Co. Ltd. (Old) (ON) 08/27/1982 which merged into Conwest Exploration Co. Ltd. (New) (AB) 09/01/1993 which merged into Alberta Energy Co. Ltd. 01/31/1996 which merged into EnCana Corp. 01/03/2003

CENTRAL PENN NATL BK (PHILADELPHIA, PA)
Stock Dividend - 10% 02/09/1960
Reorganized as CP Financial Corp. 10/01/1969
Each share Capital Stock $10 par exchanged for (3) shares Common $1 par
CP Financial Corp. name changed to Central Penn National Corp. 05/06/1976 which merged into Meridian Bancorp, Inc. 06/30/1983 which merged into CoreStates Financial Corp 04/09/1996 which merged into First Union Corp. 04/28/1998 which name changed to Wachovia Corp. (Ctfs. dated after 09/01/2001) 09/01/2001 which merged into Wells Fargo & Co. (New) 12/31/2008

CENTRAL PENN NATL CORP (PA)
Merged into Meridian Bancorp, Inc. 06/30/1983
Each share Common $1 par exchanged for (0.875) share Common $5 par
Meridian Bancorp, Inc. merged into CoreStates Financial Corp 04/09/1996 which merged into First Union Corp. 04/28/1998 which name changed to Wachovia Corp. (Ctfs. dated after 09/01/2001) 09/01/2001 which merged into Wells Fargo & Co. (New) 12/31/2008

CENTRAL PKG CORP (TN)
Common 1¢ par split (3) for (2) by issuance of (0.5) additional share payable 03/19/1996 to holders of record 03/04/1996 Ex date - 03/20/1996
Common 1¢ par split (3) for (2) by issuance of (0.5) additional share payable 12/12/1997 to holders of record 12/05/1997 Ex date - 12/15/1997
Merged into KCPC Holdings, Inc. 05/22/2007
Each share Common 1¢ par exchanged for $22.53 cash

CENTRAL PLAZA BK & TR CO (ST. PETERSBURG, FL)
Merged into Rutland Bank (St. Petersburg, FL) 05/01/1981
Each share Common $4 par exchanged for (17.7355) shares Common $1 par
(See Rutland Bank (St. Petersburg, FL))

CENTRAL PLAZA HOTEL, INC. (IL)
Voluntarily dissolved 04/10/1950
Details not available

CENTRAL PORCUPINE MINES LTD. (ON)
Recapitalized as United Porcupine Mines Ltd. 05/04/1964
Each share Captial Stock $1 par exchanged for (0.25) share Common $1 par
United Porcupine Mines Ltd. merged into Dynacore Explorations Ltd. 07/15/1967 which recapitalized as Dynaco Resources Ltd. 02/09/1971
(See Dynaco Resources Ltd.)

CENTRAL PWR & LT CO (TX)
10.10% Preferred $100 par called for redemption 05/30/1986
7.12% Preferred $100 par called for redemption 04/10/1997
8.72% Preferred $100 par called for redemption 04/10/1997
Auction Preferred Ser. B called for redemption at $100,000 on 11/10/1999
Money Market Preferred $100 par called for redemption at $500,000 on 11/23/1999
Name changed to AEP Texas Central Co. 02/24/2003
(See AEP Texas Central Co.)

CENTRAL POWER CO.
Dissolved 00/00/1941
Details not available

CENTRAL PROPERTIES CO.
Bankrupt 00/00/1933
Stockholders' equity unlikely

CENTRAL PUBLIC SERVICE CORP. (MD)
Reorganized under the laws of Delaware as Central Public Utility Corp. (Old) 00/00/1935
Details not available

CENTRAL PUBLIC UTILITY CORP. NEW (DE)
Merged into Consolidated Electronics Industries Corp. 10/16/1959
Each share Capital Stock $6 par exchanged for (1) share Common $5 par
Consolidated Electronics Industries Corp. name changed to North American Philips Corp. 02/14/1969
(See North American Philips Corp.)

CENTRAL PUBLIC UTILITY CORP. OLD (DE)
Reorganized as Central Public Utility Corp. (New) 00/00/1952
No stockholders' equity

CENTRAL PUERTO S A (ARGENTINA)
ADR agreement terminated 04/29/2002
Each ADR for 144A Class B exchanged for $2.05625983 cash
(Additional Information in Active)

CENTRAL RAILWAY OF ARKANSAS
Road abandoned 00/00/1932
Details not available

CENTRAL RAILWAY SIGNAL CO., INC.
Assets sold 00/00/1949
Details not available

CENTRAL REAL ESTATE CO., INC. (RI)
Ceased operations 00/00/1984
Details not available

CENTRAL RLTY INVS INC (DE)
Charter cancelled and declared inoperative and void for non-payment of taxes 03/01/1992

CENTRAL RECORDS CORP. (NY)
Name changed to Electronic Micro-Ledger Accounting Corp. 08/04/1952
(See Micro-Ledger Accounting Corp.)

CENTRAL REPUBLIC CO. (DE)
Capital Stock $10 par changed to $5 par 00/00/1938
Stock Dividend - 10% 07/15/1946
Name changed to C.R. Liquidating Co. 09/16/1957
(See C.R. Liquidating Co.)

CENTRAL RES CORP (BC)
Each share old Common no par exchanged for (0.33333333) share new Common no par 07/12/2013
Each share new Common no par exchanged again for (0.33333333) share new Common no par 07/25/2014
Name changed to Uranium Standard Resources Ltd. 10/02/2014
Uranium Standard Resources Ltd. recapitalized as Palisades Ventures Inc. 12/01/2015 which recapitalized as Fremont Gold Ltd. 07/07/2017

CENTRAL RESV LIFE CORP (OH)
Common no par split (3) for (2) by issuance of (0.5) additional share 07/10/1985
Name changed to Ceres Group Inc. 12/08/1998
(See Ceres Group Inc.)

CENTRAL RR CO N J (NJ)
Each share Common $100 par exchanged for (1) share Class B $50 par 00/00/1949
Class A $50 par and Class B $50 par reclassified as Common $50 par 10/03/1955
Under plan of reorganization each share Common $50 par exchanged for (1) Central Jersey Industries, Inc. Non-Transferable Ctf. of Contingent Int. 08/15/1979
Note: Unexchanged certificates were cancelled and became without value 09/14/1984

CENTRAL SVGS BK & TR CO (MONROE, LA)
Each share Common $100 par exchanged for (4.4) shares Common $25 par to effect a (4) for (1) split and a 10% stock dividend 01/26/1960
Each share Common $25 par exchanged for (2.2) shares Common $12.50 par to effect a (2) for (1) split and a 10% stock dividend 01/28/1964
Stock Dividends - 100% 01/22/1952; 10% 01/24/1961; 12.5% 08/01/1969
Name changed to Central Bank (Monroe, LA) 03/11/1970
Central Bank (Monroe, LA) reorganized as Central Corp. 04/30/1982 which merged into First Commerce Corp. 10/20/1995 which merged into Banc One Corp. 06/12/1998 which merged into Bank One Corp. 10/02/1998 which merged into J.P. Morgan Chase & Co. 12/31/2000 which name changed to JPMorgan Chase & Co. 07/20/2004

CENTRAL SCOTT TEL CO
Merged into Brightom Communications Corp. 07/15/1999
Each share Common exchanged for $396.95 cash

CENTRAL SEC NATL BK LORAIN CNTY (LORAIN, OH)
Common $10 par changed to $7.50 par and (0.33333333) additional share issued 02/20/1969
Merged into Central Bancorporation, Inc. 02/15/1978
Each share Common $7.50 par exchanged for (1.4175) shares Common $5 par
Central Bancorporation, Inc. merged into PNC Financial Corp 02/29/1988 which name changed to PNC Bank Corp. 02/08/1993 which name changed to PNC Financial Services Group, Inc. 03/15/2000

CEN-CEN   FINANCIAL INFORMATION, INC.

CENTRAL SECS CORP (DE)
$1.40 Preference Ser. A no par called for redemption 11/01/1961
$1.50 Conv. Preference no par called for redemption 08/01/1963
$1.40 Conv Preference Ser. B no par called for redemption 11/01/1968
$1.25 Conv. Preference Ser. C no par called for redemption 12/01/1984
$2 Conv. Preference Ser. D no par called for redemption at $27.50 on 08/01/1999
(Additional Information in Active)

CENTRAL SVC INDS INC (DE)
Acquired by Jessica Equities, Inc. 12/14/1983
Each share Common 1¢ par exchanged for $0.65 cash

CENTRAL SIERRA BK (SAN ANDREAS, CA)
Stock Dividends - 6% payable 05/03/1996 to holders of record 04/09/1996; 5% payable 01/22/2003 to holders of record 01/14/2003 Ex date - 01/22/2003
Merged into Western Sierra Bancorp 07/11/2003
Each share Common no par exchanged for either (0.7821337) share Common no par or $24.7441 cash
Note: Option to receive stock expired 08/19/2003
Western Sierra Bancorp merged into Umpqua Holdings Corp. 06/05/2006

CENTRAL SOUTH BANCORP, INC. (TN)
Merged into Commerce Union Corp. 09/22/1986
Each share Common $5 par exchanged for (2.1967) shares Common $6.66666666 par
Commerce Union Corp. merged into Sovran Financial Corp. 11/01/1987 which merged into C&S/Sovran Corp. 09/01/1990 which merged into NationsBank Corp. 12/31/1991 which reincorporated in Delaware as BankAmerica Corp. (Old) 09/25/1998 which merged into BankAmerica Corp. (New) 09/30/1998 which name changed to Bank of America Corp. 04/28/1999

CENTRAL SOYA INC (IN)
Common no par split (2) for (1) by issuance of (1) additional share 11/23/1959
Common no par split (2) for (1) by issuance of (1) additional share 10/12/1966
Common no par split (2) for (1) by issuance of (1) additional share 02/05/1974
Stock Dividends - 20% 12/31/1945; 150% 08/29/1946; 50% 12/15/1950
Merged into Shamrock Holdings Inc. 07/19/1985
Each share Common no par exchanged for $24.25 cash

CENTRAL SPECIALTY CO.
Liquidation completed 12/01/1945
Details not available

CENTRAL SPRINKLER CORP (PA)
Common 1¢ par split (3) for (2) by issuance of (0.5) additional share 04/15/1986
Common 1¢ par split (5) for (4) by issuance of (0.25) additional share 04/16/1990
Merged into Tyco International Ltd. (New) 08/26/1999
Each share Common 1¢ par exchanged for $30 cash

CENTRAL ST BK (BROOKLYN, NY)
Capital Stock $5 par changed to $2.50 par and (1) additional share issued 08/23/1963
Name changed to Central Bank & Trust Co. New York, N.A. (Brooklyn, NY) 01/20/1981
Central Bank & Trust Co. New York, N.A. (Brooklyn, NY) name changed to Central National Bank of New York (Brooklyn, NY) 04/07/1981
(See Central National Bank of New York (Brooklyn, NY))

CENTRAL ST BK (CONNERSVILLE, IN)
Under plan of reorganization each share Common $10 par automatically became (1) share C.S. Bancshares, Inc. Common $10 par 11/01/1984
C.S. Bancshares, Inc. merged into Fifth Third Bancorp 08/25/1989

CENTRAL ST BK (MARSHFIELD, WI)
Name changed to Central Bank & Trust (Marshfield, WI) 01/09/1979
Central Bank & Trust (Marshfield, WI) name changed to M&I Central Bank & Trust (Marshfield, WI) 01/23/1984
(See M&I Central Bank & Trust (Marshfield, WI))

CENTRAL STAMPING CO. (NY)
Name changed to Savory Inc. 00/00/1943
Savory Inc. name changed to Lisk Savory Corp. 00/00/1944
(See Lisk Savory Corp.)

CENTRAL STANDARD LIFE INSURANCE CO. (IL)
Each share Common $20 par exchanged for (20) shares Common $1 par 03/30/1960
Stock Dividends - 10% 12/27/1961; 10% 12/28/1962
Name changed to Reliance Standard Life Insurance Co. 08/09/1965
(See Reliance Standard Life Insurance Co.)

CENTRAL STATE BANK (DES MOINES, IA)
Name changed to Central National Bank & Trust Co. (Des Moines, IA) 05/15/1929
Central National Bank & Trust Co. (Des Moines, IA) name changed to United Central Bank of Des Moines N.A. (Des Moines, IA) 04/16/1981

CENTRAL STATES EDISON, INC. (DE)
Liquidation completed 00/00/1950
Details not available

CENTRAL STATES EDISON CO.
Reorganized as Central States Edison, Inc. 00/00/1935
Details not available

CENTRAL STATES ELECTRIC CO.
Merged into Iowa Electric Light & Power Co. 08/16/1951
Each share 7% Preferred A $25 par exchanged for (0.5) share 4.80% Preferred $50 par and $15.75 in cash
Each share 6% Preferred B $25 par exchanged for (0.5) share 4.80% Preferred $50 par and $13.50 in cash
Each share 6% Preferred C $25 par exchanged for (0.5) share 4.80% Preferred $50 par and $13.50 in cash
Each share Class A Common $25 par exchanged for (2) shares Common $5 par
Each share Class B Common $25 par exchanged for (2) shares Common $5 par
(See Iowa Electric Light & Power Co.)

CENTRAL STATES LIFE INSURANCE CO. (MO)
Assets sold 00/00/1941
Charter forfeited for non-compliance with corporation laws 01/01/1942

CENTRAL STATES POWER & LIGHT CORP.
Liquidated 00/00/1948
Details not available

CENTRAL STS RES INC (UT)
Charter cancelled for non-payment of taxes 03/23/1973

CENTRAL STATES UTILITIES CORP.
Liquidated 00/00/1948
No stockholders' equity

CENTRAL STD CONS MINES (UT)
Charter expired 10/29/2003

CENTRAL STL & WIRE CO (DE)
Reincorporated 11/19/1958
Stock Dividend - 25% 12/20/1950
State of incorporation changed from (IL) to (DE) 11/19/1958
Acquired by Ryerson Holding Corp. 07/02/2018
Each share Common $5 par exchanged for $616.32 cash

CENTRAL STS ELEC CORP (VA)
Liquidation completed
Each share 7% Preferred $100 par stamped to indicate initial distribution of (17.21) shares Blue Ridge Mutual Fund, Inc. Common $1 par 06/28/1951
Each share Stamped 7% Preferred $100 par stamped to indicate second distribution of $10 cash 01/26/1954
Each share Stamped 7% Preferred $100 par stamped to indicate third distribution of $6 cash 11/30/1955
Each share Stamped 7% Preferred $100 par stamped to indicate fourth distribution of (0.147836) share Blue Ridge Mutual Fund, Inc. Common $1 par and $3.05 cash 11/14/1957
(See Blue Ridge Mutual Fund, Inc.)
Each share Stamped 7% Preferred $100 par exchanged for fifth distribution of $3.25 cash and a Non-transferable Receipt entitling holder to further distributions 07/01/1972
Each Non-transferable Receipt exchanged for sixth and final distribution of $15 cash 11/11/1977
No stockholders' equity for 6% Preferred $100 par, Optional Preferred Ser. 1929 $100 par, Optional Preferred Dividend Ser. $100 par or Common $1 par

CENTRAL STS LIFE INS CO (TX)
Merged into Alamo Life Insurance Co. 05/31/1967
Each share Common no par exchanged for (1) share Common no par
Alamo Life Insurance Co. merged into First Continental Life & Accident Insurance Co. 05/31/1972 which merged into First Continental Life Group, Inc. 12/31/1973
(See First Continental Life Group, Inc.)

CENTRAL SUDBURY LEAD-ZINC MINES LTD. (ON)
Name changed to Stackpool Mining Co. Ltd. 03/17/1957
Stackpool Mining Co. Ltd. recapitalized as Stackpool Mining & Holding Corp. Ltd. 09/19/1962 which liquidated for Stackpool Enterprises Ltd. 07/30/1971 which name changed to Geneva Capital Ventures Inc.- Enterprises de Placements Geneve Inc. 04/25/1973
(See Geneva Capital Ventures Inc.- Enterprises de Placements Geneve Inc.)

CENTRAL SUN MNG INC (CANADA)
Acquired by B2Gold Corp. 03/31/2009
Each share Common no par exchanged for (1.28) shares Common no par

CENTRAL TEL & UTILS CORP (KS)
Name changed to Centel Corp. 04/30/1982
Centel Corp. acquired by Sprint Corp. (KS) 03/09/1993 which name changed to Sprint Nextel Corp. 08/12/2005 which merged into Sprint Corp. (DE) 07/10/2013

CENTRAL TEL CO ILL (IL)
Ctfs. dated prior to 12/01/1971
Common $10 par changed to $5 par and (1) additional share issued 05/29/1967
Merged into Central Telephone Co. (New) 12/01/1971
Each share 6% Preference $100 par exchanged for (1) share $6 Preferred Ser. 1 no par
Each share 5.65% Preferred Ser. D $20 par exchanged for (1) share $1.13 Preferred no par
Each share 5% Preferred Ser. C $20 par exchanged for $1 Preferred no par
Each share Common $5 par exchanged for (0.5) share Conv. Jr. Preferred no par
(See Central Telephone Co. (New))

CENTRAL TEL CO NEW (DE)
$1.50 Preferred no par called for redemption 00/00/1984
$1 Preferred no par called for redemption 10/01/1991
$1.13 Preferred no par called for redemption 10/01/1991
$6 Preferred Ser. 1 no par called for redemption 10/01/1991
$6 Preferred Ser. 2 no par called for redemption 10/01/1991
$2 Jr. Conv. Preferred no par called for redemption 01/16/1996
$1.24 Preferred no par called for redemption 12/09/1996
$5 Preferred no par called for redemption 12/09/1996

CENTRAL TEL CO OLD (DE)
Certificates dated prior to 12/01/1971
Common $10 par split (11) for (10) by issuance of (0.1) additional share 01/02/1957
Common $10 par split (1.3) for (1) by issuance of (0.3) additional share 12/04/1959
5.5% Preferred no par called for redemption 10/15/1962
5.44% Preferred $25 par called for redemption 12/31/1963
5.48% Conv. Preferred $25 par called for redemption 12/31/1963
$1.35 Preferred no par called for redemption 08/03/1964
Common $10 par split (3) for (2) by issuance of (0.5) additional share 06/09/1967
Merged into Central Telephone Co. (New) 12/01/1971
Each share $2.50 Preferred Ser. A. no par exchanged for (1) share $2.50 Preferred no par
Each share $2.50 Preferred Ser. C no par exchanged for (1) share $2.50 Preferred no par
Each share $4.70 Preferred no par exchanged for (1) share $4.70 Preferred no par
Each share 4.96% Preferred $25 par exchanged for (1) share $1.24 Preferred no par
Each share $5 Preferred no par exchanged for (1) share $5 Preferred no par
Each share 6% Preferred $25 par exchanged for (1) share $1.50 Preferred no par
Each share Common $10 par exchanged for (1) share Conv. Jr. Preferred no par
(See Central Telephone Co. (New))

CENTRAL TELECOMMUNICATION CO JOINT-STOCK (RUSSIA)
Sponsored ADR's for Ordinary split (4) for (1) by issuance of (3) additional ADR's payable 07/31/2008 to holders of record 07/24/2008 Ex date - 08/01/2008
Merged into Rostelecom OJSC 04/13/2011

Each Sponsored ADR for Ordinary exchanged for $35.981084 cash

CENTRAL TERESA SUGAR CO. (MD)
Charter revoked for failure to file reports and pay fees 04/27/1930

CENTRAL TEX BANCORP INC (TX)
Merged into Compass Bancshares, Inc. 07/14/1997
Each share Common $10 par exchanged for (3.84375) shares Common $2 par
Compass Bancshares, Inc. merged into Banco Bilbao Vizcaya Argentaria, S.A. 09/07/2007

CENTRAL TITLE & TRUST CO. (AZ)
Proclaimed dissolved 09/27/1976

CENTRAL TRACTION CO.
Merged into Pittsburgh Railways Co. 09/30/1950
Each share Common $50 par exchanged for (2.5) shares Common no par and $3 cash
Pittsburgh Railways Co. name changed to Pittway Corp. (PA) 11/28/1967 which merged into Pittway Corp. (DE) 12/28/1989
(See Pittway Corp. (DE))

CENTRAL TRACTOR FARM & CTRY INC (DE)
Merged into J.W. Childs Equity Partners L.P. 03/27/1997
Each share Common 1¢ par exchanged for $14.25 cash

CENTRAL TRANS RENT GROUP PLC (UNITED KINGDOM)
Acquired by GE Capital 11/24/1997
Each Sponsored ADR for Ordinary exchanged for the U.S. dollar equivalent of 48 pence

CENTRAL TRANSFORMER CORP (AR)
5% 1st Preferred $100 par called for redemption 11/04/1968
Stock Dividends - 80% 12/15/1957; 50% 09/03/1959; 100% 12/15/1967
Merged into Colt Industries Inc. (DE) 11/04/1968
Each share 5% 2nd Preferred $55 par exchanged for (1) share $2.75 Preferred Ser. E. $1 par
Each share Common $1 par exchanged for (0.76923) share Common $1 par
Colt Industries Inc. (DE) reincorporated in Pennsylvania 05/06/1976
(See Colt Industries Inc. (PA))

CENTRAL TR BK (JEFFERSON CITY, MO)
Reorganized as Central Bancompany, Inc. 12/31/1971
Each share Capital Stock $100 par exchanged for (10) shares Common $10 par
(See Central Bancompany, Inc.)

CENTRAL TRUST CAPITAL BANK (HARRISBURG, PA)
Merged into National Bank & Trust Co. of Central Pennsylvania (York, PA) 10/13/1961
Each share Capital Stock $10 par exchanged for (1) share Capital Stock $10 par
National Bank & Trust Co. of Central Pennsylvania (York, PA) merged into National Central Bank (Lancaster, PA) 12/07/1970 which reorganized as National Central Financial Corp. 12/31/1972 which merged into CoreStates Financial Corp 05/02/1983 which merged into First Union Corp. 04/28/1998 which name changed to Wachovia Corp. (Ctfs. dated after 09/01/2001) 09/01/2001 which merged into Wells Fargo & Co. (New) 12/31/2008

CENTRAL TRUST CO. (HARRISBURG, PA)
Merged into Central Trust Capital Bank (Harrisburg, PA) 07/03/1958 Each share Capital Stock exchanged for (1) share Capital Stock $10 par
Central Trust Capital Bank (Harrisburg, PA) merged into National Bank & Trust Co. of Central Pennsylvania (York, PA) 10/13/1961 which merged into National Central Bank (Lancaster, PA) 12/07/1970 which reorganized as National Central Financial Corp. 12/31/1972 which merged into Corestates Financial Corp 05/02/1983 which merged into First Union Corp. 04/28/1998 which name changed to Wachovia Corp. (Ctfs. dated after 09/01/2001) 09/01/2001 which merged into Wells Fargo & Co. (New) 12/31/2008

CENTRAL TR CO (CINCINNATI, OH)
Each share Capital Stock $100 par exchanged for (4) shares Capital Stock $25 par 00/00/1951
Capital Stock $25 par changed to $10 par and (1.7) additional shares issued 01/23/1962
Stock Dividends - 12% 01/20/1955; 10% 07/08/1960; 10% 01/23/1963; 10% 01/27/1965
95% acquired by Central Bancorporation, Inc. through exchange offer which expired 07/30/1969
Public interest eliminated

CENTRAL TR CO (ROCHESTER, NY)
Common $10 par changed to $20 par 00/00/1946
Common $20 par changed to $10 par and (1) additional share issued 03/15/1966
Common $10 par changed to $15 par 02/24/1970
Stock Dividend - 10% 02/02/1959
Acquired by Charter New York Corp. 06/01/1970
Each share Common $15 par exchanged for (0.75) share $4 Conv. Preferred $1 par
Charter New York Corp. name changed to Irving Bank Corp. 10/17/1979 which merged into Bank of New York Co., Inc. 12/30/1988 which merged into Bank of New York Mellon Corp. 07/01/2007

CENTRAL TR CO CDA (MONCTON, NB)
Each share Common $100 par exchanged for (10) shares Common $10 par 04/28/1956
Each share Common $10 par exchanged for (2) shares Common $5 par 08/01/1958
Common $5 par changed to $1 par and (4) additional shares issued 05/01/1970
Merged into Central & Nova Scotia Trust Co. (Halifax, NS) 01/01/1974
Each share Common $1 par exchanged for (1) share Common $1 par
Central & Nova Scotia Trust Co. (Halifax, NS) merged into Central & Eastern Trust Co. (Moncton, NB) 07/02/1976 which merged into Central Trust Co. (Moncton, NB) 03/01/1981

CENTRAL TUBE CO.
Liquidated 00/00/1940
Details not available

CENTRAL UNION DEPOT & RAILWAY CO. OF CINCINNATI
Dissolved 00/00/1935
Details not available

CENTRAL UTD CORP (IA)
Merged into LOA Merger Corp. 07/30/1993
Each share Common $1 par exchanged for $6.06 cash

CENTRAL UNITED LIFE INSURANCE CO. (IA)
Each share Common 35¢ par exchanged for (0.1) share Common $3.50 par 09/10/1973
Merged into Central United Corp. 03/31/1975
Each share Common $3.50 par exchanged for (10.4) shares Common $1 par
(See Central United Corp.)

CENTRAL URANIUM & MILLING CORP. (DE)
Name changed to Montana Chemical & Milling Corp. 00/00/1956
(See Montana Chemical & Milling Corp.)

CENTRAL UTILS PRODTN CORP (NV)
Plan of reorganization under Chapter 11 Federal Bankruptcy Code effective 02/26/2007
No stockholders' equity

CENTRAL VA BANKSHARES INC (VA)
Common $2.50 changed to $1.25 par and (1) additional share issued payable 08/14/1998 to holders of record 07/31/1998
Stock Dividends - 5% payable 12/13/2002 to holders of record 11/15/2002 Ex date - 11/13/2002; 5% payable 06/15/2004 to holders of record 05/21/2004; 5% payable 06/15/2006 to holders of record 05/31/2006 Ex date - 05/26/2006; 5% payable 06/13/2008 to holders of record 05/30/2008 Ex date - 05/28/2008
Acquired by C&F Financial Corp. 10/01/2013
Each share Common $1.25 par exchanged for $0.32 cash

CENTRAL VY BANCORP (CA)
Merged into 1867 Western Financial Corp. 11/18/2003
Each share Common no par exchanged for $26 cash

CENTRAL VALLEY BANK OF CALIFORNIA (RICHMOND, CA)
Each share Common $25 par exchanged for (2.5) shares Common $10 par 02/15/1956
Name changed to Central Valley National Bank (Oakland, CA) 03/01/1956
Central Valley National Bank (Oakland, CA) name changed to Central Bank, N.A. (Oakland, CA) 03/01/1971
(See Central Bank, N.A. (Oakland, CA))

CENTRAL VALLEY NATL BK (CENTRAL VALLEY, NY)
Merged into First National City Corp. 03/06/1973
Each share Capital Stock $10 par exchanged for (0.75) share Common $6.75 par
First National City Corp. name changed to Citicorp 03/26/1974 which merged into Citigroup Inc. 10/08/1998

CENTRAL VALLEY NATL BK (OAKLAND, CA)
Common $10 par changed to $5 par and (1) additional share issued 09/08/1967
Name changed to Central Bank, N.A. (Oakland, CA) 03/01/1971
(See Central Bank, N.A. (Oakland, CA)

CENTRAL VERMONT RAILWAY CO.
Sold under foreclosure 00/00/1929
Details not available

CENTRAL VT PUB SVC CORP (VT)
Common no par reduced by 10% of stated face value 00/00/1948
Common no par changed to $6 par 00/00/1952
Common $6 par split (4) for (3) by issuance of (0.33333333) additional share 10/13/1983
13.5% Preferred $100 par called for redemption 04/01/1984
5.44% 2nd Conv. Preferred Ser. A $50 par called for redemption 02/27/1987
Common $6 par split (3) for (2) by issuance of (0.5) additional share 02/11/1993
9% Preferred $25 par called for redemption 01/24/1994
4.15% Preferred $100 par called for redemption at $105.50 plus $0.921612 accrued dividends on 06/22/2012
4.65% Preferred $100 par called for redemption at $105 plus $1.037951 accrued dividends on 06/22/2012
4.75% Preferred $100 par called for redemption at $101 plus $1.065219 accrued dividends on 06/22/2012
5.375% Preferred $100 par called for redemption at $105 plus $1.196892 accrued dividends on 06/22/2012
Acquired by Gaz Metro L.P. 06/27/2012
Each share Common $6 par exchanged for $35.25 cash

CENTRAL WAREHOUSE & REFRIGERATION CO.
Liquidation completed 00/00/1948
Details not available

CENTRAL WEST CO (DE)
Capital Stock $5 par changed to $1 par 00/00/1938
Completely liquidated 02/06/1976
Each share Capital Stock $1 par exchanged for first and final distribution of $12 cash

CENTRAL WEST END BK (ST. LOUIS, MO)
Merged into City Bank (St. Louis, MO) 06/30/1974
Each share Capital Stock $20 par exchanged for $99 cash

CENTRAL WEST END SVGS & LN ASSN (ST. LOUIS, MO)
Under plan of reorganization each share Common $1 par automatically became (1) share CWE Bancorp Inc. Common $1 par 01/15/2003
(See CWE Bancorp Inc.)

CENTRAL WEST POWER CO.
Acquired by Southeastern Indiana Corp. 00/00/1935
Details not available

CENTRAL WEST PUBLIC SERVICE CO.
Reorganized as Central Electric & Telephone Co. 00/00/1936
Each share Ser. A. Preferred $100 par or Ser. B Preferred $100 par exchanged for (0.33333333) shares Common $1 par
Class A Common and Class B Common had no equity
Central Electric & Telephone Co. name changed to Central Electric & Gas Co. 00/00/1944 which name changed to Western Power & Gas Co. 05/01/1961 which name changed to Western Power & Gas Co., Inc. 07/01/1965 which name changed to Central Telephone & Utilities Corp. 06/05/1968 which name changed to Centel Corp. 04/30/1982 which was acquired by Sprint Corp. (KS) 03/09/1993 which name changed to Sprint Nextel Corp. 08/12/2005 which merged into Sprint Corp. (DE) 07/10/2013

CENTRAL WEST VIRGINIA & SOUTHERN RAILROAD CO.
Out of business 00/00/1930
Details not available

CENTRAL WHARF & WET DOCK CORP.
Liquidation completed 00/00/1950
Details not available

CENTRAL WIS BANKSHARES INC (WI)
Common $10 par changed to $5 par and (1) additional share issued 09/28/1978
Common $5 par changed to $2.50 par 05/15/1984
Common $2.50 par split (2) for (1) by issuance of (1) additional share 02/28/1986
Stock Dividends - 10% 08/09/1977; 10% 03/29/1979; 10% 01/01/1983; 10% 01/01/1984; 10% 01/01/1985; 10% 01/01/1986; 10% 01/01/1987
Merged into Marshall & Ilsley Corp. (Old) 02/29/1988
Each share Common $2.50 par exchanged for (0.77) share Common $1 par
(See Marshall & Ilsley Corp. (Old))

CENTRAL WISCONSIN MOTOR TRANSPORT CO. (IL)
6% Conv. Preferred $100 par called for redemption 10/31/1964
Stock Dividend - 40% 07/09/1965
Reincorporated under the laws of Delaware as C W Transport, Inc. 12/31/1966
C W Transport, Inc. (DE) merged into Gerber Products Co. 08/24/1979
(See Gerber Products Co.)

CENTRAL WYOMING OIL & URANIUM CORP. (DE)
No longer in existence having become inoperative and void for non-payment of taxes 04/01/1961

CENTRAL ZEBALLOS GOLD MINES LTD.
Completely liquidated 03/00/1957
Each share Common received first and final distribution of $0.333 cash

CENTRAL ZONE PROPERTY CORP. (NY)
Liquidation completed 08/18/1959
Details not available

CENTRALARM INTL INC (UT)
Each share Common 1¢ par exchanged for (5) shares Common $0.002 par 06/17/1977
Voluntarily dissolved 12/29/1988
Details not available

CENTRALIA & CENTRAL CITY TRACTION
Discontinued operation 00/00/1930
Details not available

CENTRAM EXPL LTD (AB)
Reincorporated under the laws of Canada as Pancontinental Uranium Corp. 09/10/2007
Pancontinental Uranium Corp. name changed to Pancontinental Uranium Corp. 07/29/2016 which name changed to Pancontinental Resources Corp. 07/13/2018

CENTRAN BANCSHARES CORP. (DE)
Name changed to Centran Corp. 04/05/1974
(See Centran Corp.)

CENTRAN BANK (AKRON, OH)
99.6% held by Centran Corp. as of 05/15/1982
Public interest eliminated

CENTRAN CORP (DE)
Merged into Society Corp. 09/03/1985
Each share Common $8 par exchanged for $36 cash

CENTRAPLEX CORP (CO)
Name changed to RJO Biologicals Inc. 05/15/1991
(See RJO Biologicals Inc.)

CENTRASIA MNG CORP (BC)
Name changed to Kola Mining Corp. 03/27/2008
Kola Mining Corp. name changed to Mitchell Resources Ltd. 05/27/2015 which name changed to Hannan Metals Ltd. 01/10/2017

CENTRE CAP CORP (NV)
Each share old Common $0.001 par exchanged for (0.33333333) share new Common $0.001 par 03/22/1999
Each share new Common $0.001 par exchanged again for (150) shares new Common $0.001 par 05/15/2003
Name changed to Golden Health Holdings, Inc. 04/15/2004
(See Golden Health Holdings, Inc.)

CENTRE CIRCUITS, INC. (PA)
Name changed to Chemcut Corp. 04/08/1965
(See Chemcut Corp.)

CENTRE HILL MINES LTD. (ON)
Recapitalized as Munro Copper Mines Ltd. 02/28/1966
Each share Capital Stock $1 par exchanged for (0.5) share Capital Stock $1 par
(See Munro Copper Mines Ltd.)

CENTRE LAKE URANIUM MINES LTD. (ON)
Merged into Bicroft Uranium Mines Ltd. 05/02/1955
Each share Capital Stock $1 par exchanged for (0.5) share Capital Stock $1 par and (0.1) share Paudash Lake Uranium Mines Ltd. Capital Stock $1 par
(See each company's listing)

CENTRE TOWNSHIP BUILDING CORP. (IN)
Under plan of reorganization each share Common $10 par exchanged for $10 cash 07/22/1974

CENTRE VIDEO CORP. (PA)
Merged into Tele-Communications, Inc. (Old) 02/16/1971
Each share Capital Stock no par exchanged for (2.13) shares Common $1 par
Tele-Communications, Inc. (Old) merged into Tele-Communications, Inc. (New) 08/05/1994 which merged into AT&T Corp. 03/09/1999 which merged into AT&T Inc. 11/18/2005

CENTREE CORP (DE)
Name changed to Air Florida System, Inc. 12/26/1973
Air Florida System, Inc. name changed to Jet Florida System, Inc. 08/15/1985
(See Jet Florida Systems, Inc.)

CENTREFIELD PETROLEUMS LTD. (ON)
Acquired by Ellesmere Oil & Development Ltd. 00/00/1952
Each share Capital Stock no par exchanged for (0.05) share Capital Stock no par
Ellesmere Oil & Development Ltd. merged into New Concord Development Corp. Ltd. 00/00/1952
(See New Concord Development Corp. Ltd.)

CENTREFUND RLTY CORP (ON)
Name changed to First Capital Realty Inc. 09/07/2001

CENTREMAQUE GOLD MINES LTD. (QC)
Recapitalized as Norsyncomaque Mining Ltd. 08/07/1956
Each share Capital Stock $1 par exchanged for (0.25) share Capital Stock $1 par
Norsyncomaque Mining Ltd. recapitalized as Silvermaque Mining Ltd. 07/04/1961 which recapitalized as Geomaque Explorations Ltd./Explorations Geomaque Ltee. 09/19/1986 which merged into Defiance Mining Corp. 06/25/2003 which merged into Rio Narcea Gold Mines, Ltd. 09/03/2004
(See Rio Narcea Gold Mines, Ltd.)

CENTRENERGO ST JT STK ENERGY CO (UKRAINE)
Reg. S GDR's for Ordinary split (5) for (1) by issuance of (4) additional GDR's payable 02/22/2005 to holders of record 02/18/2005 Ex date - 02/23/2005
Basis changed from (1:50) to (1:10) 02/23/2005
GDR agreement terminated 07/06/2018
Each Reg. S GDR for Ordinary exchanged for (10) shares Ordinary
Note: Unexchanged GDR's will be sold and the proceeds, if any, held for claim after 01/07/2019

CENTREVILLE NATL BK (CENTREVILLE, MD)
Merged into Shore Bancshares, Inc. 07/01/1996
Each share Common $10 par exchanged for (2) shares Common 1¢ par

CENTREX CORP (OH)
Merged into Centex Merger Corp. 09/20/2001
Each share Common no par exchanged for $10 cash

CENTREX INC (OK)
Each share old Common $0.001 par exchanged for (0.005) share new Common $0.001 par 12/19/2005
Name changed to Microholdings US, Inc. 01/17/2007

CENTRIC ENERGY CORP (BC)
Merged into Africa Oil Corp. 02/22/2011
Each share Common no par exchanged for (0.3077) share Common no par and $0.0001 cash

CENTRIFORCE TECHNOLOGY CORP (NJ)
Recapitalized as ADB International Group, Inc. (NJ) 05/20/2010
Each share Common $0.001 par exchanged for (0.01) share Common $0.0001 par
ADB International Group, Inc. (NJ) reorganized in Delaware 08/04/2014 which name changed to E- Qure Corp. 10/09/2014

CENTRIFUGAL PIPE CORP.
Liquidation completed 00/00/1954
Details not available

CENTRINITY INC (CANADA)
Merged into Open Text Corp. 11/01/2002
Each share Class A Common no par exchanged for $1.26 cash

CENTRIS GROUP INC (DE)
Common 1¢ par split (2) for (1) by issuance of (1) additional share payable 02/27/1998 to holders of record 02/18/1998 Ex date - 03/02/1998
Merged into HCC Insurance Holdings, Inc. 12/20/1999
Each share Common 1¢ par exchanged for $12.50 cash

CENTRIX BK & TR (BEDFORD, NH)
Common $1 par split (3) for (2) by issuance of (0.5) additional share payable 09/12/2003 to holders of record 08/06/2003
Common $1 par split (3) for (2) by issuance of (0.5) additional share payable 02/03/2006 to holders of record 12/30/2005 Ex date - 02/06/2006
Acquired by Eastern Bank Corp. 10/24/2014
Each share Common $1 par exchanged for $41 cash

CENTRIX YELLOWKNIFE MINES, LTD. (ON)
Charter revoked for failure to file reports and pay taxes 00/00/1955

CENTROCK INC (NV)
Name changed to Huading Financial Networks Inc. 05/19/2000
(See Huading Financial Networks Inc.)

CENTROCOM CORP (NV)
Reorganized under the laws of Delaware as JMI Telecom Corp. 08/06/2007
Each share Common $0.0005 par exchanged for (0.005) share Common $0.0005 par
JMI Telecom Corp. name changed to UA Multimedia Inc. 06/05/2012

CENTROID CONS MINES CO (NV)
Each (15) shares old Common $0.001 par exchanged for (1) share new Common $0.001 par 09/20/1999
Name changed to eGene, Inc. 07/12/2004
eGene, Inc. merged into Qiagen N.V. 07/09/2007

CENTRON EQUITY CORP. LTD. (AB)
Struck off register for failure to file annual returns 07/15/1978

CENTRONICS CORP (DE)
Name changed to Ekco Group, Inc. 04/29/1988
(See Ekco Group, Inc.)

CENTRONICS DATA COMPUTER CORP. (DE)
Common 1¢ par split (3) for (1) by issuance of (2) additional shares 02/28/1972
Common 1¢ par split (2) for (1) by issuance of (1) additional share 11/08/1972
Common 1¢ par split (5) for (4) by issuance of (0.25) additional share 10/03/1977
Name changed to Centronics Corp. 02/17/1987
Centronics Corp. name changed to Ekco Group, Inc. 04/29/1988
(See Ekco Group, Inc.)

CENTRUE FINL CORP NEW (DE)
Each share old Common $1 par exchanged for (0.03333333) share new Common $1 par 05/29/2015
Merged into Midland States Bancorp, Inc. 06/09/2017
Each share new Common $1 par exchanged for (0.7604) share Common 1¢ par

CENTRUE FINL CORP OLD (DE)
Common 1¢ par split (2) for (1) by issuance of (1) additional share payable 10/31/2003 to holders of record 10/20/2003
Merged into Centrue Financial Corp. (New) 11/13/2006
Each share old Common 1¢ par exchanged for (1.2) shares Common 1¢ par
Centrue Financial Corp. (New) merged into Midland States Bancorp, Inc. 06/09/2017

CENTRUM BUSINESS SYS INC (NC)
Reincorporated 11/19/1987
State of incorporation changed from (CA) to (NC) 11/19/1987
Administratively dissolved 12/08/1993

CENTRUM INDS INC (DE)
Reincorporated 11/00/1990
State of incorporation changed from (ND) to (DE) 11/00/1990
Company's only asset's petition under Chapter 11 Federal Bankruptcy Code confirmed 02/05/2003
Stockholders' equity unlikely

CENTRUS VENTURES INC (NV)
Old Common $0.001 par split (3) for (1) by issuance of (2) additional shares payable 06/08/2007 to holders of record 06/08/2007
Name changed to Royal Mines & Minerals Corp. 10/08/2007

FINANCIAL INFORMATION, INC.

CEN-CEN

CENTRUST BK (MIAMI, FL)
Name changed 06/01/1989
Each share old Common 1¢ par exchanged for (0.5) share Conv. Adjustable Rate Part. Preferred Ser. 1, 1¢ par and (0.5) share new Common 1¢ par 03/20/1987
Name changed from CenTrust Savings Bank (Miami, FL) to CenTrust Bank (Miami, FL) 06/01/1989
Placed in receivership 03/09/1990
No stockholders' equity

CENTRUST CAP CORP (DE)
Adjustable Rate Preferred $1 par called for redemption 01/31/1992
Public interest eliminated

CENTRUST FIN CORP (DE)
Dutch Auction Rate Transferable Securities Preferred $1 par called for redemption 12/13/1989
Public interest eliminated

CENTRUST FIN CORP II (DE)
Exchangeable Remarketed Preferred no par called for redemption 11/21/1989
Exchangeable Remarketed Preferred Ser. D no par called for redemption 11/21/1989
Exchangeable Remarketed Preferred Ser. E no par called for redemption 11/29/1989
Exchangeable Remarketed Preferred Ser. F no par called for redemption 12/06/1989
Exchangeable Remarketed Preferred Ser. G no par called for redemption 12/13/1989
Exchangeable Remarketed Preferred Ser. A no par called for redemption 12/20/1989
Exchangeable Remarketed Preferred Ser. B no par called for redemption 12/28/1989
Exchangeable Remarketed Preferred Ser. C no par called for redemption 01/04/1990
Public interest eliminated

CENTRUST TR (MA)
Trust terminated 06/08/2000
Details not available

CENTURA BKS INC (NC)
Merged into Royal Bank of Canada (Montreal, QC) 06/05/2001
Each share Common no par exchanged for (1.684) shares Common no par

CENTURA ENERGY CORP (MN)
Merged into Minden Oil & Gas Inc. 02/11/1983
Each share Common 5¢ par exchanged for (1) share Common 5¢ par
Minden Oil & Gas Inc. name changed to Castle Energy Corp. 11/16/1986 which merged into Delta Petroleum Corp. 05/01/2006
(See Delta Petroleum Corp.)

CENTURA PETE CORP (MN)
Completely liquidated 08/31/1979
Each share Common 5¢ par exchanged for first and final distribution of (1) share Centura Energy Corp. Common 5¢ par
Centura Energy Corp. merged into Minden Oil & Gas Inc. 02/11/1983 which name changed to Castle Energy Corp. 11/16/1986 which merged into Delta Petroleum Corp. 05/01/2006
(See Delta Petroleum Corp.)

CENTURA RES INC (BC)
Recapitalized as Polar Resources Corp. 02/14/2005
Each share Common no par exchanged for (0.5) share Common no par

CENTURA SOFTWARE CORP (DE)
Reincorporated 02/16/1999
State of incorporation changed from (CA) to (DE) 02/16/1999
Plan of reorganization under Chapter 11 Federal Bankruptcy proceedings effective 08/10/2004
No stockholders' equity

CENTURI INC (FL)
Proclaimed dissolved for failure to file reports and pay fees 10/11/1991

CENTURION BANCORP INC (WV)
Capital Stock $10 par split (2) for (1) by issuance of (1) additional share 06/13/1984
Merged into Key Centurion Bancshares, Inc. 11/30/1985
Each share Capital Stock $10 par exchanged for (1) share Common $3 par
Key Centurion Bancshares, Inc. merged into Banc One Corp. 05/03/1993 which merged into Bank One Corp. 10/02/1998 which merged J.P. Morgan Chase & Co. 12/31/2000 which name changed to JPMorgan Chase & Co. 07/20/2004

CENTURION BK LTD (INDIA)
Merged into HDFC Bank Ltd. 05/23/2008
Each Sponsored GDR for Equity Shares exchanged for (0.03448275) ADR for Equity Shares

CENTURION CORP (NV)
Charter revoked for failure to file reports and pay fees 03/03/1980

CENTURION ENERGY INTL INC (AB)
Merged into Dana Gas PJSC 01/09/2007
Each share Common no par exchanged for $12 cash

CENTURION EQUITIES CORP (ON)
Name changed to Amcan Industries Corp. 08/17/1979
(See Amcan Industries Corp.)

CENTURION EQUITIES LTD (AB)
Name changed to Fire Boss Services Ltd. 12/21/1990
First Boss Services Ltd. name changed to Boss Energy Ltd. 03/03/1994 which merged into Canadian Leader Energy Inc. 11/02/1995 which merged into Centurion Energy International Inc. 05/20/1997
(See Centurion Energy International Inc.)

CENTURION EXPLORATION INC. (UT)
Recapitalized as Prosaca Inc. 10/27/1983
Each share Common $0.001 par exchanged for (0.1) share Common 1¢ par
(See Prosaca Inc.)

CENTURION EXPL INC NEW (BC)
Merged 12/28/1982
Merged from Centurion Exploration Inc. (Old) to Centurion Exploration Inc. (New) 12/28/1982
Each share Common no par exchanged for (1) share Common no par
Merged into Beaver Resources Inc. (New) 06/13/1983
Each share Common no par exchanged for (1) share Common no par
(See Beaver Resources Inc. (New))

CENTURION FD INC (MD)
Merged into Bayrock Growth Fund, Inc. 07/06/1973
Each share Common $1 par exchanged for (2.43) shares Common 10¢ par
Bayrock Growth Fund, Inc. acquired by Affiliated Fund, Inc. (DE) 09/03/1975 which reincorporated in Maryland 11/26/1975 which name changed to Lord Abbett Affiliated Fund, Inc. 03/01/1996

CENTURION FINL INC (DE)
Common $1 par split (2) for (1) by issuance of (1) additional share 04/14/1981
Merged into Ohio Mutual Insurance Association 12/28/1983
Each share Common $1 par exchanged for $16 cash

CENTURION GOLD HLDGS INC (FL)
Common $0.0001 par split (3) for (1) by issuance of (2) additional shares payable 07/28/2003 to holders of record 07/18/2003 Ex date - 07/29/2003
SEC revoked common stock registration 08/25/2011

CENTURION GOLD LTD (BC)
Merged into Siskon Gold Corp. 08/23/1991
Each share Common no par exchanged for (1) share Common $0.001 par
(See Siskon Gold Corp.)

CENTURION GROWTH FD INC (DE)
Fund terminated 05/10/1995
Details not available

CENTURION MINERALS LTD (BC)
Incorporated 00/00/1972
Common no par split (3) for (1) by issuance of (2) additional shares 06/08/1987
Merged into Centurion Gold Ltd. 06/06/1988
Each share Common no par exchanged for (1) share Common no par
Centurion Gold Ltd. merged into Siskon Gold Corp. 08/23/1991
(See Siskon Gold Corp.)

CENTURION MINES CORP (UT)
Recapitalized as Grand Central Silver Mines Inc. 02/04/1998
Each share Common $0.001 par exchanged for (0.1) share Common $0.001 par
(See Grand Central Silver Mines Inc.)

CENTURION MINES LTD. (ON)
Merged into Caravelle Mines Ltd. 11/13/1969
Each share Capital Stock $1 par exchanged for (0.5) share Common no par
(See Caravelle Mines Ltd.)

CENTURION OIL & MINERALS CO (TX)
Name changed to Comco Centurion Oil & Minerals Co. 05/07/1979
(See Comco Centurion Oil & Minerals Co.)

CENTURION SAVINGS & LOAN ASSOCIATION (CA)
Acquired by Atlantic Financial Federal 08/14/1987
Each share Guarantee Stock $8 par exchanged for $24 cash

CENTURION III CORP (CO)
Name changed to WealthBuilders Financial Corp. 07/10/1989

CENTURY ACCEP CORP (DE)
Old Class A Common $1 par reclassified as Common $1 par 00/00/1954
New Class A Common $1 par called for redemption 03/17/1960
70¢ Preferred $5 par called for redemption 07/01/1984
Each share Common $1 par exchanged for (0.00294117) share Common $340 par 12/27/1989
Note: In effect holders received $27.84 cash per share and public interest was eliminated

CENTURY ALUMINUM CORP. (IN)
Charter revoked for failure to file annual reports 06/01/1970

CENTURY BANCORP CAP TR (DE)
8.3% Trust Preferred Securities called for redemption at $10 on 01/10/2005

CENTURY BANCORP INC (NC)
Common no par split (3) for (1) by issuance of (2) additional shares payable 04/06/1998 to holders of record 03/27/1998
Merged into First Bancorp 05/17/2001
Each share Common no par exchanged for either (0.55482612) share Common no par and $11.6774 cash or $20 cash
Note: Option to receive stock and cash expired 06/22/2001

CENTURY BANCORP LTD (OK)
Reincorporated under the laws of Nevada as Century Group, Inc. 05/08/2006

CENTURY BANCSHARES INC (DE)
$0.60 Conv. Preferred Ser. A $1 par called for redemption 12/10/1995
Stock Dividends - 5% payable 05/23/1997 to holders of record 05/07/1997; 5% payable 06/29/1998 to holders of record 05/29/1998; 5% payable 05/28/1999 to holders of record 04/28/1999; 5% payable 04/17/2000 to holders of record 03/15/2000; 5% payable 06/29/2001 to holders of record 05/31/2001 Ex date - 05/29/2001
Merged into United Bankshares, Inc. 12/10/2001
Each share Common $1 par exchanged for (0.45) share Common $2.50 par and $3.43 cash

CENTURY BK & TR (COLDWATER, MI)
Reorganized as Century Financial Corp. (MI) 12/13/1989
Each share Common $10 par exchanged for (1) share Common $1 par

CENTURY BANK (DENVER, CO)
Acquired by Key Bank of Colorado (Fort Collins, CO) 03/25/1994
Details not available

CENTURY BK (LOS ANGELES, CA)
Common $5 par split (3) for (1) by issuance of (2) additional shares 05/18/1962
Merged into Century Holding Corp. 09/03/1981
Each share Common $5 par exchanged for $34.60 cash

CENTURY BANK (NEW ORLEANS, LA)
Acquired by First National Bank (Covington, LA) 12/31/1987
Details not available

CENTURY BK (PHOENIX, AZ)
Declared insolvent by Superintendent of Banks 10/19/1989
Stockholders' equity unlikely

CENTURY BKS INC (FL)
Stock Dividend - 10% 03/10/1979
Merged into Sun Banks of Florida, Inc. 07/01/1982
Each share Common $1 par exchanged for (0.9) share Common $2.50 par
Sun Banks of Florida, Inc. name changed to Sun Banks, Inc. 05/02/1983 which merged into SunTrust Banks, Inc. 07/01/1985

CENTURY BLDRS GROUP INC (FL)
Merged into New Century Homebuilders, Inc. 05/07/2002
Each share Common $0.001 par exchanged for $0.90 cash

CENTURY BLVD CORP (NV)
In process of liquidation
Each share Common $1 par received initial distribution of $10 cash 06/21/1971
Each share Common $1 par exchanged for second distribution of $6 cash 07/30/1971

Each share Common $1 par received third distribution of $27 cash 07/14/1972
Each share Common $1 par received fourth distribution of $1 cash 10/26/1973
Note: Details on subsequent distributions, if any, are not available

CENTURY BUILDING CORP.
Liquidation completed 00/00/1950
Details not available

CENTURY BUSINESS CR CORP (NY)
Acquired by CBC Acquisition Corp. 08/17/1987
Each share Common $3.84 par exchanged for $24.40 cash

CENTURY BUSINESS SVCS INC (DE)
Name changed to CBIZ, Inc. 08/01/2005

CENTURY CAMERA INC (MN)
Statutorily dissolved 11/12/1991

CENTURY CELLULAR CORP (DE)
Name changed to Centennial Cellular Corp. 02/07/1992
Centennial Cellular Corp. name changed to Centennial Communications Corp. 02/29/2000
(See Centennial Communications Corp.)

CENTURY CHEMICAL CORP. (DE)
Incorporated 10/07/1918
No longer in existence having become inoperative and void for non-payment of taxes 03/21/1923

CENTURY CHEMICAL CORP. (DE)
Incorporated 09/05/1958
No longer in existence having become inoperative and void for non-payment of taxes 04/01/1963

CENTURY CINEMA CORP (NY)
Recapitalized as Diagnostic Medical Equipment Corp. 05/25/1974
Each share Common 5¢ par exchanged for (0.33333333) share Common 1¢ par
Diagnostic Medical Equipment Corp. name changed to Universal Medical Equipment Corp. 06/13/1983
(See Universal Medical Equipment Corp.)

CENTURY CIRCUIT INC (DE)
8% Preferred $100 par called for redemption 05/15/1969
Common $5 par changed to no par and (3) additional shares issued 06/02/1969
Merged into ACT Acquisition Corp. 04/23/1981
Each share Common no par exchanged for $35 cash

CENTURY CIRCUITS LTD (ON)
Name changed to Canadian Financial Holdings Corp. 01/13/1998
Canadian Financial Holdings Corp. recapitalized as Calderone Corp. 07/10/1998 which name changed to Cardinal Factor Corp. 07/21/2000
(See Cardinal Factor Corp.)

CENTURY CO.
Merged into Appleton (D)- Century Co., Inc. 00/00/1933
Details not available

CENTURY COMMUNICATIONS CORP (NJ)
Class A Common 1¢ par split (3) for (2) by issuance of (0.5) additional share 05/18/1987
Class A Common 1¢ par split (3) for (2) by issuance of (0.5) additional share 12/01/1988
Class A Common 1¢ par split (3) for (2) by issuance of (0.5) additional share 09/15/1989
Merged into Adelphia Communications Corp. 10/01/1999
Each share Class A Common 1¢ par exchanged for (0.77269147) share Class A Common 1¢ par
Each share Class B Common 1¢ par exchanged for (0.84271335) share Class A Common 1¢ par
(See Adelphia Communications Corp.)

CENTURY COMPUTER CORP (NV)
Charter revoked for failure to file reports and pay fees 01/01/1986

CENTURY CONTROLS CORP. (DE)
Charter cancelled for non-payment of taxes 04/01/1959

CENTURY CONVALESCENT CTRS INC (DE)
Name changed to National Health Services, Inc. 11/10/1971
National Health Services, Inc. name changed to Carex International, Inc. 04/01/1974 which name changed to Medica USA, Inc. 09/13/1980 which name changed to Pacific Realm, Inc. 07/06/1984 which name changed to aeroTelesis, Inc. 10/22/2003
(See aeroTelesis, Inc.)

CENTURY CTRLS INTL INC (UT)
Name changed to Blue Earth Resources, Inc. 09/27/2010

CENTURY DEV CORP (UT)
Name changed to Cendeco, Inc. 10/20/1972

CENTURY ELEC CO (MO)
Each share Capital Stock $100 par exchanged for (10) shares Capital Stock $10 par 00/00/1937
Merged into Gould Inc. 06/02/1972
Each share Capital Stock $10 par exchanged for (1.35) shares Common $4 par
(See Gould Inc.)

CENTURY ELECTRONICS CO., INC. (NY)
Name changed to Mercury Electronics Corp. 06/06/1960
Mercury Electronics Corp. name changed to Airnado, Inc. 11/28/1983
(See Airnado, Inc.)

CENTURY ENERGY CORP (ON)
Name changed to Senternet Technologies Inc. 04/08/1997
Senternet Technologies Inc. name changed to Senternet Phi Gamma Inc. 01/22/2014

CENTURY ENERGY LTD (AB)
Each share old Common no par exchanged for (0.1) share new Common no par 10/15/2014
Reincorporated under the laws of British Columbia 10/20/2016

CENTURY ENGINEERS, INC. (CA)
Name changed to Royal Industries, Inc. 10/08/1957
Royal Industries, Inc. name changed to Royal Industries (CA) which reincorporated in Delaware as Royal Industries, Inc. 11/25/1968
(See Royal Industries, Inc. (DE))

CENTURY FACTORS INC (NY)
Stock Dividend - 20% 09/15/1982
Name changed to Century Business Credit Corp. 05/22/1985
(See Century Business Credit Corp.)

CENTURY FED SVGS & LN ASSN SANTA FE N MEX (USA)
Acquired by Gerald Peters & Century Financial Services 09/29/1989
Each share Common $1 par exchanged for $28.29 cash

CENTURY FINL CAP GROUP INC (ON)
Each share old Common no par exchanged for (0.1) share new Common no par 04/28/2014
Stock Dividend - 100% payable 03/16/2018 to holders of record 03/05/2018
Name changed to FSD Pharma Inc. and new Common no par reclassified as Class B Subordinate no par 05/29/2018

CENTURY FINL CORP (PA)
Common $0.835 par split (3) for (2) by issuance of (0.5) additional share payable 05/30/1997 to holders of record 05/14/1997
Merged into Citizens Bancshares, Inc. 05/12/1998
Each share Common $0.835 par exchanged for (0.7926) share Common no par
Note: Rate is post Citizens Bancshares (2) for (1) split paid 06/01/1998 to holders of record 05/12/1998
Citizens Bancshares, Inc. name changed to Sky Financial Group, Inc. 10/02/1998 which merged into Huntington Bancshares Inc. 07/02/2007

CENTURY FINL CORP OF MICH (DE)
Common $12.50 par split (5) for (4) by issuance of (0.25) additional share 07/01/1974
Name changed to Second National Corp. (DE) 04/13/1977
Second National Corp. (DE) merged into Citizens Banking Corp. 12/18/1985 which name changed to Citizens Republic Bancorp, Inc. 04/26/2007 which merged into FirstMerit Corp. 04/12/2013 which merged into Huntington Bancshares Inc. 08/16/2016

CENTURY FOOD MARKETS CO. (OH)
Each share Common $2.50 par exchanged for (2) shares Common $1 par 00/00/1956
Stock Dividend - 10% 12/10/1955
Name changed to C-F-M Co. 06/12/1961
(See C-F-M Co.)

CENTURY GEN CORP (DE)
Common 10¢ par split (3) for (2) by issuance of (0.5) additional share 04/21/1980
Recapitalized as Prism Software Corp. 09/29/1992
Each share Common 10¢ par exchanged for (0.1) share Common 10¢ par

CENTURY GEOPHYSICAL CORP (DE)
Under plan of reorganization each share old Common no par received (0.05) share new Common $1 par
Each share 5% Conv. Preferred $4 par automatically became (1) share new Common $1 par 06/30/1976
Stock Dividend - 33.33333333% 07/20/1973
Merged into CGC Acquisition Corp. 06/15/1990
Each share new Common $1 par exchanged for $9 cash

CENTURY GLOBAL COMMODITIES CORP (BC)
Reincorporated under the laws of Cayman Islands and Common no par reclassified as Ordinary CAD $0.001 par 03/10/2016

CENTURY GOLD CORP (CANADA)
Name changed to Novra Technologies Inc. 07/06/2001

CENTURY GOLD VENTURES INC (NV)
Each share old Common $0.001 par exchanged for (0.00222222) share new Common $0.001 par 07/19/2013
Name changed to Hub Deals Corp. 05/24/2018

CENTURY GREETINGS INC (DE)
Liquidation completed
Each share Common 1¢ par received initial distribution of $1.70 cash 08/01/1977
Each share Common 1¢ par received second and final distribution of $0.895 cash 02/01/1978
Note: Certificates were not required to be surrendered and are without value

CENTURY INDUSTRIES, INC. (DE)
Recapitalized as 20th Century Industries, Inc. 10/11/1961
Each share Common 5¢ par exchanged for (0.1) share Common 50¢ par
(See 20th Century Industries, Inc.)

CENTURY INDS INC (NV)
Reorganized 02/16/2000
Each share old Common 1¢ par exchanged for (0.33333333) share new Common 1¢ par 03/21/1994
Class B Common 1¢ par reclassified as Class A Common 1¢ par 12/30/1999
Reorganized from (DC) to under the laws of Nevada 02/16/2000
Each share old Class A Common 1¢ par exchanged for (0.1) share new Class A Common 1¢ par
Charter permanently revoked 02/28/2002

CENTURY INDS INC (NY)
Common no par changed to $6 par and (0.66666666) additional share issued 04/02/1965
Common $6 par changed to $4.80 par and (0.25) additional share issued 05/20/1966
Common $4.80 par changed to $3.84 par and (0.25) additional share issued 05/20/1969
Stock Dividends - 10% 12/28/1956; 10% 12/30/1957; 10% 12/30/1960; 10% 12/29/1961
Name changed to Century Factors, Inc. 06/02/1975
Century Factors, Inc. name changed to Century Business Credit Corp. 05/22/1985
(See Century Business Credit Corp.)

CENTURY INTERPLEX CORP (BC)
Struck off register and declared dissolved for failure to file returns 06/27/1977

CENTURY INVESTMENT CORP. (IN)
Completely liquidated 07/15/1974
Each share Common no par exchanged for first and final distribution of $178 cash

CENTURY INVESTORS, INC. (DE)
Merged into American Manufacturing Co., Inc. 12/20/1960
Each share Common $2 par exchanged for (1.27) shares Common $12.50 par and (0.03073) share Common represented by an Interim Certificate
American Manufacturing Co., Inc. assets transferred to American Manufacturing Co., Ltd. Liquidating Trust 05/20/1980
(See American Manufacturing Co., Inc. Liquidating Trust)

CENTURY IRON MINES CORP (BC)
Reincorporated 10/17/2014
Place of incorporation changed from (Canada) to (BC) 10/17/2014
Name changed to Century Global Commodities Corp. (BC) 11/16/2015
Century Global Commodities Corp. (BC) reincorporated in Cayman Islands 03/10/2016

CENTURY LABORATORIES, INC. (LA)
Charter revoked for failure to file annual reports 05/13/1982

CENTURY LABS INC (DE)
Each share old Common 70¢ par exchanged for (0.05) share new Common 70¢ par 11/30/2000
Name changed to Vista Continental Corp. 07/12/2002
Vista Continental Corp. name changed to Wolverine Holding Corp. 11/06/2009

CENTURY LIFE DIVERSIFIED INC (TX)
Placed in receivership 10/01/1969
No stockholders' equity

CENTURY LIFE INS CO (TX)
Reorganized as Century Life Diversified, Inc. 12/27/1966
Each share Common $1 par exchanged for (1) share Common $1 par
(See Century Life Diversified, Inc.)

CENTURY MED INC (NV)
Common $1 par changed to 10¢ par 02/07/1969
Each share Common 10¢ par exchanged for (0.2) share Common 50¢ par 08/25/1972
Charter revoked for failure to file reports and pay fees 03/06/1978

CENTURY MEDICORP (CA)
Each share old Common no par exchanged for (0.2) share new Common no par 05/11/1990
Merged into Foundation Health Corp. 10/15/1992
Each share new Common no par exchanged for (0.8) share Common 1¢ par
Foundation Health Corp. merged into Foundation Health Systems, Inc. 04/01/1997 which name changed to Health Net, Inc. 11/06/2000

CENTURY MILESTONE S & T CO LTD (CO)
Recapitalized as Sino Real Property Development Corp. 10/21/2003
Each share Common $0.0001 par exchanged for (0.01) share Common $0.0001 par

CENTURY MINING & DEVELOPMENT CORP. (DE)
Name changed to Century Industries, Inc. 12/17/1959
Century Industries, Inc. recapitalized as 20th Century Industries, Inc. 10/11/1961
(See 20th Century Industries, Inc.)

CENTURY MNG CORP (CANADA)
Reincorporated 07/22/2004
Place of incorporation changed from (YT) to (Canada) 07/22/2004
Merged into White Tiger Gold Ltd. 10/20/2011
Each share Common no par exchanged for (0.4) share Common no par
Note: Unexchanged certificates were cancelled and became without value 10/20/2017
White Tiger Gold Ltd. name changed to Mangazeya Mining Ltd. 09/23/2013

CENTURY MINING CORP LTD (QC)
Charter cancelled 02/00/1974

CENTURY NATL BK & TR (NEW YORK, NY)
Stock Dividend - 10% 03/04/1968
Merged into Banco Exterior de Espana 07/01/1980
Each share Common Capital Stock $10 par exchanged for $44.75 cash

CENTURY NATIONAL BANK & TRUST CO. (ROCHESTER, PA)
Common $10 par changed to $5 par and (1) additional share issued plus a 50% stock dividend paid 04/01/1981
Stock Dividend - 25% 12/09/1985
Under plan of reorganization each share Common $5 par automatically became (1) share Century Financial Corp. Common $0.835 par 06/01/1988
Century Financial Corp. merged into Citizens Bancshares, Inc. 05/12/1998 which name changed to Sky Financial Group, Inc. 10/02/1998 which merged into Huntington Bancshares Inc. 07/02/2007

CENTURY NATIONAL BANK (NEW ORLEANS, LA)
Name changed to Century Bank (New Orleans, LA) 09/25/1980
(See Century Bank (New Orleans, LA))

CENTURY NATL BK (ORLANDO, FL)
Merged into Seacoast Banking Corp of Florida 04/29/2005
Each share Common 10¢ par exchanged for (1.41537) shares Common 10¢ par

CENTURY NATIONAL BANK (WASHINGTON, DC)
Acquired by United Bank (Fairfax, VA) 12/08/2001
Details not available

CENTURY NATURAL GAS & OIL CORP. (DE)
Each share Common 10¢ par exchanged for (0.2) share Common 50¢ par 12/01/1955
Name changed to Century-Special Corp. 07/12/1961
Century-Special Corp. acquired by International Controls Corp. 10/16/1967
(See International Controls Corp.)

CENTURY NUCLEAR INC (WY)
Merged into Western States Mining, Inc. 01/25/1972
Each share Common 1¢ par exchanged for (0.125) share Common 1¢ par
Western States Mining, Inc. name changed to U.S. Energy Corp. 02/22/1973

CENTURY OIL & GAS CORP (CO)
Reincorporated under the laws of Delaware and Common 1¢ par reclassified as Class A 1¢ par 10/07/1975
Century Oil & Gas Corp. (DE) (Old) merged into Century Oil & Gas Corp. (DE) (New) 05/12/1978
(See Century Oil & Gas Corp. (DE) (New))

CENTURY OIL & GAS CORP NEW (DE)
Reorganized 05/12/1978
Reorganized from Century Oil & Gas Corp. (Old) (DE) to Century Oil & Gas Corp. (New) (DE) 05/12/1978
Each share Class A 1¢ par exchanged for (0.1) share Class A 2¢ par
Charter cancelled and declared inoperative and void for non-payment of taxes 03/01/1987

CENTURY OILS LTD. (MB)
Acquired by Oregon Natural Gas Reserves Ltd. on a (1) for (7.5) basis 05/09/1960
(See Oregon Natural Gas Reserves Ltd.)

CENTURY PAC FINL CORP (DE)
Name changed 09/29/1998
Name changed from Century Pacific Corp. to Century Pacific Financial Corp. 09/29/1998
Each share old Common 4¢ par exchanged for (0.14285714) share new Common 4¢ par 07/17/2002
Each share new Common 4¢ par exchanged exchanged again for (0.4) share new Common 4¢ par 08/12/2003
New Common 4¢ par changed to $0.001 par 06/28/2009
Recapitalized as People's Liberation, Inc. 01/06/2006
Each share Common $0.001 par exchanged for (0.1081081) share Common $0.001 par
People's Liberation, Inc. name changed to Sequential Brands Group, Inc. (Old) 03/26/2012 which reorganized as Sequential Brands Group, Inc. (New) 12/07/2015

CENTURY PAPERS INC (TX)
Common $1 par split (3) for (2) by issuance of (0.5) additional share 07/13/1984
Stock Dividends - 10% 08/09/1974; 10% 08/12/1975; 10% 10/06/1976
Acquired by National Sanitary Supply Co. 09/30/1988
Each share Common $1 par exchanged for $19 cash
Note: Each share Common $1 par received initial escrow payment of $1 cash 00/00/1989
Each share Common $1 par received second and final escrow payment of $1.17 cash 06/06/1991

CENTURY PK PICTURES CORP (MN)
Each share old Common $0.001 par exchanged for (0.05) share new Common $0.001 par 06/30/1988
Recapitalized as IsoRay, Inc. 08/17/2005
Each share new Common $0.001 par exchanged for (0.03333333) share Common $0.001 par

CENTURY PPTYS (CA)
Stock Dividend - 10% 08/16/1976
Liquidation completed
Each share Common $1 par exchanged for initial distribution of $45.19 cash 02/10/1981
Each share Common $1 par received second distribution of $16.658 cash 12/23/1981
Each share Common $1 par received third and final distribution of $1.2532 cash 02/15/1985

CENTURY REALTY CO. (OH)
Liquidation completed 05/20/1960
Details not available

CENTURY RLTY TR (IN)
Liquidation completed
Each Share of Bene. Int. no par received initial distribution of $18.25 cash payable 11/20/2006 to holders of record 11/10/2006 Ex date - 11/21/2006
Each Share of Bene. Int. no par received second and final distribution of $1.66 cash payable 12/28/2006 to holders of record 11/10/2006 Ex date - 12/29/2006
Note: Certificates were not required to be surrendered and are without value

CENTURY RIBBON MILLS, INC. (NY)
Name changed to Century Industries Co., Inc. 11/30/1956
Century Industries Co., Inc. name changed to Century Factors, Inc. 06/02/1975 which name changed to Century Business Credit Corp. 05/22/1985
(See Century Business Credit Corp.)

CENTURY SAVINGS & LOAN ASSOCIATION, INC. (NC)
Merged into Scottish Savings & Loan Association, Inc. (New) 04/01/1981
Each share Common $10 par exchanged for (1.2813) shares Common $1 par
Scottish Savings & Loan Association, Inc. (New) merged into Southeastern Savings & Loan Co. 01/17/1984 which name changed to Southeastern Savings Bank, Inc. 07/13/1988
(See Southeastern Savings Bank, Inc.)

CENTURY SVGS ASSN KANS (KS)
Declared insolvent and receiver appointed 06/25/1985
No stockholders' equity

CENTURY SEC BK (DULUTH, GA)
Bank closed and FDIC appointed receiver 03/19/2010
Stockholders' equity unlikely

CENTURY SHS TR (MA)
Shares of Bene. Int. no par changed to $1 par 00/00/1937
Shares of Bene. Int. $1 par split (3) for (1) by issuance of (2) additional shares 03/16/1959
Stock Dividend - 200% 05/06/1952
Merged into Century Capital Management Trust 07/31/2001
Each Share of Bene. Int. $1 par received (1) Century Shares Trust Investor Share

CENTURY SILVER MINES INC (ID)
Each share old Common 10¢ par exchanged for (0.12919896) share new Common 10¢ par 01/22/1999
Reincorporated under the laws of Florida as Sense Holdings, Inc. 08/20/1999
Sense Holdings, Inc. name changed to China America Holdings, Inc. 11/27/2007 which recapitalized as Ziyang Ceramics Corp. 01/27/2012
(See Ziyang Ceramics Corp.)

CENTURY SOUTH BKS INC (GA)
Merged into BB&T Corp. 06/07/2001
Each share Common $1 par exchanged for (0.93) share Common $5 par

CENTURY-SPECIAL CORP. (DE)
Common 50¢ par changed to 5¢ par 07/12/1961
Completely liquidated 10/16/1967
Each share Common 5¢ par exchanged for first and final distribution of (0.1) share International Controls Corp. Common 10¢ par
(See International Controls Corp.)

CENTURY TECHNOLOGIES INC (CO)
SEC revoked common stock registration 01/21/2011

CENTURY TECHNOLOGIES INC (ON)
Delisted from Canadian Dealer Network 01/03/1995

CENTURY TEL ENTERPRISES INC (LA)
Common $1 par split (3) for (2) by issuance of (0.5) additional share 08/01/1988
Common $1 par split (3) for (2) by issuance of (0.5) additional share 03/24/1989
Common $1 par split (3) for (2) by issuance of (0.5) additional share 12/31/1992
Each share 5% Conv. Preferred Ser. K $25 par exchanged for (0.986972) share Common $1 par 07/02/1997
Common $1 par split (3) for (2) by issuance of (0.5) additional share payable 03/31/1998 to holders of record 03/10/1998 Ex date - 04/01/1998
Common $1 par split (3) for (2) by issuance of (0.5) additional share payable 03/31/1999 to holders of record 03/10/1999 Ex date - 04/01/1999
Name changed to CenturyTel, Inc. 05/10/1999
CenturyTel, Inc. name changed to CenturyLink, Inc. 06/01/2010

CENTURY TERMINALS, INC. (CA)
Charter suspended for failure to file reports and pay fees 07/01/1988

CENTURY TEXTILES & INDS LTD (INDIA)
Stock Dividend - 100% payable 01/21/1998 to holders of record 09/25/1997
ADR agreement terminated 01/12/2015
Each 144A GDR for Equity Shares exchanged for $5.187616 cash

CENTURY TRUST CO. (TX)
Charter revoked for failure to file reports and pay fees 09/20/1966

CENTURY 21 MNG INC (UT)
Each share old Common $0.005 par exchanged for (0.05) share new Common $0.005 par 09/01/1982
Controlling interest acquired by TV

Communications Network, Inc. 12/00/1989
Public interest eliminated

CENTURY 21 REAL ESTATE CORP (CA)
Stock Dividend - 25% 06/22/1979
Merged into Trans World Corp. (DE) 10/31/1979
Each share Common 1¢ par exchanged for (0.99) share $2.66 Conv. Preferred Ser. C no par
Trans World Corp. (DE) name changed to Transworld Corp. (DE) 04/25/1984 which assets were transferred to Transworld Corp. Liquidating Trust 12/31/1986
(See Transworld Corp. Liquidating Trust)

CENTURY II HLDGS INC (ON)
Acquired by TransForce Income Fund 11/02/2007
Each share Common no par exchanged for $10.20 cash

CENTURY URANIUM CORP. (DE)
Recapitalized as Century Mining & Development Corp. 07/09/1956
Each share Common $1 par exchanged for (0.5) share Common $1 par
Century Mining & Development Corp. name changed to Century Industries, Inc. 12/17/1959 which recapitalized as 20th Century Industries, Inc. 10/11/1961
(See 20th Century Industries, Inc.)

CENTURYTEL INC (LA)
Each Corporate Unit received (0.8088) share Common $1 par 05/13/2005
5% Conv. Preferred Ser. K $1 par called for redemption on 07/02/1997
Name changed to CenturyLink, Inc. 06/01/2010

CENUCO INC (DE)
Name changed to Ascendia Brands, Inc. 05/12/2006
(See Ascendia Brands, Inc.)

CENVEO INC (CO)
Each share old Common no par exchanged for (0.125) share new Common no par 07/14/2016
Plan of reorganization under Chapter 11 Federal Bankruptcy proceedings effective 09/07/2018
No stockholders' equity

CENVEST INC (DE)
Charter cancelled and declared inoperative and void for non-payment of taxes 06/17/1993

CENVILL CMNTYS INC (DE)
Common 1¢ par split (3) for (2) by issuance of (0.5) additional share 01/01/1978
Stock Dividends - 50% 02/19/1973; 10% 07/01/1977
Under plan of reorganization each share Common 1¢ par exchanged for (1) Non-Separable Unit consisting of (1) share Cenvill Investors, Inc. Common 1¢ par and (1) share Cenvill Development Corp. Common 1¢ par 07/31/1981
Cenvill Investors, Inc. name changed to CV Reit, Inc. 05/10/1990 which merged into Kramont Realty Trust 06/16/2000
(See Kramont Realty Trust)

CENVILL DEV CORP NEW (DE)
Liquidating Plan of Reorganization under Chapter 11 Federal Bankruptcy proceedings confirmed 01/26/1994
No stockholders' equity

CENVILL INVS INC (DE)
Paired certificates terminated 12/28/1981
Each Unit (issued as Non-Separable Unit consisting of (1) share of Cenvill Investors, Inc. Common 1¢ par and (1) share Cenvill Development Corp. Common 1¢ par) exchanged for (1) share Cenvill Investors, Inc. Common 1¢ par and (1) share Cenvill Development Corp. Common 1¢ par
Common 1¢ par split (2) for (1) by issuance of (1) additional share 05/16/1983
Name changed to CV Reit, Inc. 05/10/1990
CV Reit, Inc. merged into Kramont Realty Trust 06/16/2000
(See Kramont Realty Trust)

CEO CR INC (NV)
Name changed to Media Awareness International, Inc. (Old) 04/17/2008
Media Awareness International, Inc. (Old) reorganized as Golfsmart Media, Inc. 06/02/2008 which name changed to Media Awareness International, Inc. (New) 08/29/2008 which recapitalized as Cloud Technologies, Inc. 06/17/2009

CEP INDS INC (UT)
Proclaimed dissolved for failure to file annual reports 06/01/1989

CEPEDA MINERALS INC (BC)
Cease trade order effective 10/26/2001
Stockholders' equity unlikely

CEPHALON INC (DE)
Conv. Exchangeable Preferred called for redemption at $52.90 on 10/01/2001
Acquired by Teva Pharmaceutical Industries Ltd. 10/14/2011
Each share Common 1¢ par exchanged for $81.50 cash

CEPHALON RESOURCE CORP (AB)
Delisted from Alberta Stock Exchange 12/24/1998

CEPHAS HLDG CORP (DE)
Each share old Common $0.001 par exchanged for (0.004) share new Common $0.001 par 01/24/2012
SEC revoked common stock registration 07/13/2015

CEPHEID (CA)
Acquired by Danaher Corp. 11/07/2016
Each share Common no par exchanged for $53 cash

CEPTOR CORP (DE)
SEC revoked common stock registration 11/10/2010

CEQUEL ENERGY INC (AB)
Merged into Progress Energy Trust 07/02/2004
Each share Common no par exchanged for (0.695) Trust Unit no par, (0.139) share ProEx Energy Ltd. Common no par and (0.139) Cyries Energy Inc. Common no par
(See each company's listing)

CERADYNE CORP (DE)
Reincorporated 06/00/1987
State of incorporation changed from (CA) to (DE) and Common 10¢ par changed to 1¢ par 06/00/1987
Common 1¢ par split (3) for (2) by issuance of (0.5) additional share payable 04/07/2004 to holders of record 03/30/2004 Ex date - 04/08/2004
Common 1¢ par split (3) for (2) by issuance of (0.5) additional share payable 01/18/2005 to holders of record 01/10/2005 Ex date - 01/19/2005
Acquired by 3M Co. 11/29/2012
Each share Common 1¢ par exchanged for $35 cash

CERADYNE INC (DE)
Ctfs. dtd. prior to 05/03/1974
Merged into TRE Corp. 05/03/1974
Each share Class A Common 1¢ par exchanged for (0.052775) share Common $1 par
Each share Class B Common 10¢ par exchanged for (0.052775) share Common $1 par
(See TRE Corp.)

CERAGENIX PHARMACEUTICALS INC (DE)
Chapter 7 bankruptcy proceedings terminated 02/06/2017
Stockholders' equity unlikely

CERAMETAL INDUSTRIES LTD. (ON)
Assets liquidated for the benefit of creditors 06/24/1963
No stockholders' equity

CERAMIC PROTN CORP (AB)
Reincorporated under the laws of Delaware as Protective Products of America, Inc. 08/08/2008
(See Protective Products of America, Inc.)

CERAMIC TECHNOLOGY INC (CO)
Charter suspended for failure to file annual reports 06/01/1995

CERAMICA CARABOBO C A (VENEZUELA)
Sponsored ADR's for Ordinary split (4) for (3) by issuance of (1/3) additional ADR 02/01/1994
Sponsored ADR for Ser. B split (4) for (3) by issuance of (0.33333333) additional ADR 02/01/1994
Each Sponsored ADR for Ordinary exchanged for (0.1) Sponsored ADR for Ser. A 01/02/1998
Each old Sponsored ADR for Ser. B exchanged for (0.1) new Sponsored ADR for Ser. B 01/02/1998
Sponsored ADR's for Ser. A reclassified as Sponsored ADR's for Common 08/23/2002
Sponsored ADR's for Ser. B reclassified as Sponsored ADR's for Common 08/23/2002
Each old Sponsored ADR for Common exchanged for (0.01) new Sponsored ADR for Common 06/17/2008
Stock Dividends - 10% payable 04/01/1996 to holders of record 03/22/1996; 10% payable 02/23/1998 to holders of record 02/17/1998; 5% payable 08/04/2005 to holders of record 07/21/2005 Ex date - 07/19/2005
ADR agreement terminated 12/08/2017
Each new Sponsored ADR for Common exchanged for (10) shares Common
Note: Unexchanged ADR's will be sold and the proceeds, if any, held for claim after 12/13/2018

CERAMICS PROCESS SYS CORP (DE)
Name changed to CPS Technologies Corp. 03/23/2007

CERAMICUS INC (NY)
Merged out of existence 01/31/2002
Details not available

CERASEAL CHEMICAL CORP. (DE)
No longer in existence having become inoperative and void for non-payment of taxes 04/01/1961

CERBCO INC (DE)
Name changed 02/29/1988
Class A Common 10¢ par split (5) for (4) by issuance of (0.25) additional share 11/17/1983
Class B Common 10¢ par split (5) for (4) by issuance of (0.25) additional share 11/17/1983
Name changed from Cerberonics, Inc. to CERBCO, Inc., Class A Common 10¢ par and Class B Common reclassified as Common 10¢ par and Conv. Class B Common 10¢ par respectively 02/29/1988
Liquidation completed
Each share Common 10¢ par received initial distribution of $9 cash payable 08/01/2005 to holders of record 07/15/2005 Ex date - 08/02/2005
Each share Conv. Class B Common 10¢ par received initial distribution of $9 cash payable 08/01/2005 to holders of record 07/15/2005 Ex date - 08/02/2005
Each share Conv. Class B Common 10¢ par received second distribution of $0.50 cash payable 01/17/2006 to holders of record 01/03/2006 Ex date - 01/18/2006
Each share Conv. Class B Common 10¢ par received second distribution of $0.50 cash payable 01/17/2006 to holders of record 01/03/2006 Ex date - 01/18/2006
Each share Conv. Class B Common 10¢ par received third distribution of $0.50 cash payable 10/31/2006 to holders of record 10/13/2006 Ex date - 11/01/2006
Each share Conv. Class B Common 10¢ par received third distribution of $0.50 cash payable 10/31/2006 to holders of record 10/13/2006 Ex date - 11/01/2006
Each share Common 10¢ par received fourth and final distribution of $0.35 cash payable 06/29/2007 to holders of record 06/14/2007 Ex date - 07/02/2007
Each share Conv. Class B Common 10¢ par received fourth and final distribution of $0.35 cash payable 06/29/2007 to holders of record 06/14/2007 Ex date - 07/02/2007
Note: Certificates were not required to be surrendered and are without value

CERCAL MINERALS CORP (ON)
Delisted from Alberta Stock Exchange 09/18/1995

CERENT CORP (DE)
Merged into Cisco Systems, Inc. 11/01/1999
Each share Common $0.001 par exchanged for (1.367) shares Common no par
Note: An additional (0.071954223) share is being held in escrow for future distribution

CERES CAP CORP (AB)
Name changed to Reliable Energy Ltd. 09/30/2009
Reliable Energy Ltd. merged into Crescent Point Energy Corp. 05/01/2012

CERES GROUP INC (OH)
Merged into Great American Financial Resources, Inc. 08/07/2006
Each share Common no par exchanged for $6.13 cash

CERES INC (DE)
Each share old Common 1¢ par exchanged for (0.125) share new Common 1¢ par 04/09/2015
Acquired by Land O'Lakes, Inc. 08/01/2016
Each share new Common 1¢ par exchanged for $0.40 cash

CERES RES LTD (CANADA)
Merged into Talcorp Ltd. 02/11/1983
Each share Common no par exchanged for (1) share $3 Conv. Preference no par and (0.5) share Common no par
Talcorp Ltd. reorganized as Consolidated Talcorp Ltd. 08/07/1986 which name changed to Sound Insight Enterprises Ltd. 12/07/1990 which merged into CamVec Corp. 09/11/1992 which name changed to AMJ Campbell Inc. 08/14/2001
(See AMJ Campbell Inc.)

CEREUS TECHNOLOGY PARTNERS INC (DE)
Merged into Verso Technologies, Inc. 10/02/2000
Each share Common 1¢ par

exchanged for (1.75) shares Common 1¢ par

CEREX ENTMT CORP (NV)
Name changed to CERX Entertainment Corp. 03/19/1997
CERX Entertainment Corp. name changed to CERX Venture Corp. 03/23/1998 which name changed to Ebonlineinc.com 07/12/1999 which name changed to MoneyZone.com (NV) 12/16/1999 which reincorporated in Delaware as MoneyZone.com, Inc. 06/12/2001 which name changed to QT 5, Inc. 01/08/2003 which recapitalized as Addison-Davis Diagnostics, Inc. 11/18/2004
(See Addison-Davis Diagnostics, Inc.)

CERF INC (AB)
Name changed to Canadian Equipment Rentals Corp. 06/27/2016
Canadian Equipment Rentals Corp. name changed to Zedcor Energy Inc. 06/30/2017

CERIDIAN CORP NEW (DE)
Merged into Foundation Holdings, Inc. 11/09/2007
Each share Common 1¢ par exchanged for $36 cash

CERIDIAN CORP OLD (DE)
4.5% Preferred $100 par called for redemption 08/13/1992
5.5% Depositary Preferred called for redemption 12/31/1996
Common 50¢ par split (2) for (1) by issuance of (1) additional share payable 02/26/1999 to holders of record 02/10/1999 Ex date - 03/01/1999
Each share Common 50¢ par received distribution of (1) share Ceridian Corp. (New) Common 1¢ par payable 03/30/2001 to holders of record 03/16/2001
Recapitalized as Arbitron Inc. 03/30/2001
Each share Common 50¢ par exchanged for (0.2) share Common 50¢ par
(See each company's listing)

CERIND CORP. (DE)
Liquidation completed 12/31/1964
Details not available

CERION TECHNOLOGIES INC (DE)
Assets transferred to Cerion Technologies Liquidating Trust 12/31/1998
In process of liquidation
Each share Common 1¢ par exchanged for initial distribution of $0.56 cash 07/15/2009
Each share Common 1¢ par received second and final distribution of $0.04 cash payable 08/13/2010 to holders of record 07/15/2009

CERISTAR INC (DE)
Recapitalized as Endavo Media & Communications, Inc. 09/24/2004
Each share Common $0.001 par exchanged for (0.0625) share Common $0.001 par
Endavo Media & Communications, Inc. name changed to Integrated Media Holdings, Inc. (DE) 04/21/2006 which reorganized in Nevada as Arrayit Corp. 03/19/2009

CERLIST DIESEL, INC. (NC)
Assets sold 06/25/1963
No stockholders' equity

CERMAQ ASA (NORWAY)
ADR agreement terminated 12/03/2014
Each ADR for Ordinary exchanged for $14.062655 cash

CERNA COPPER MINES LTD (BC)
Completely liquidated 00/00/1969
Each share Capital Stock no par received first and final distribution of (0.25) share Dison International Ltd. Common no par
(See Dison International Ltd.)

CERON RES CORP (DE)
Merged into Wasatch Pharmaceutical Inc. 01/24/1996
Each share Common 1¢ par exchanged for (0.43408761) share Common 1¢ par
(See Wasatch Pharmaceutical Inc.)

CEROTEX HLDGS INC (CO)
Name changed to Showstar Entertainment Corp. (CO) 05/22/1998
Showstar Entertainment Corp. (CO) name changed to Showstar Online.Com, Inc. (CO) 06/25/1999 which reincorporated in Washington 09/15/2000 which recapitalized as Sonoran Energy Inc. 06/03/2002

CERPLEX GROUP INC (DE)
Under plan of merger each share old Common $0.001 par exchanged for (1.070167) shares new Common $0.001 par 04/30/1998
Each share new Common $0.001 par exchanged again for (0.1) share new Common $0.001 par 10/06/1998
Chapter 11 bankruptcy proceedings converted to Chapter 7 Federal Bankruptcy on 02/06/2001
No stockholders' equity

CERPROBE CORP (CA)
Merged into Kulicke & Soffa Industries, Inc. 11/24/2000
Each share Common 5¢ par exchanged for $20 cash

CERRITOS HLDGS INC (NV)
Name changed to Tradamax (Asia) Group 11/20/2000
Tradamax (Asia) Group recapitalized as Tradamax Group 01/16/2001
(See Tradamax Group)

CERRITOS VY BANCORP (CA)
Each share old Common no par exchanged for (0.5271) share new Common no par and $13.4871 cash 09/13/1999
Merged into Bank of Orange County (Orange, CA) 08/15/2002
Each share new Common no par exchanged for $9.79 cash

CERRITOS VY BK (NORWALK, CA)
Common $6 par changed to $3 par and (1) additional share issued 08/20/1980
Merged into Cerritos Merger Co. 09/13/1999
Each share Common $3 par exchanged for (0.5271) share Common $3 par and $13.4871 cash

CERRO CORP (NY)
Common $5 par changed to $3.33333333 par and (0.5) additional share issued 12/04/1964
Merged into Cerro-Marmon Corp. 02/24/1976
Each share Common $3.333333 par exchanged for (1) share $2.25 Preferred Ser. A $1 par
Cerro-Marmon Corp. name changed to Marmon Group, Inc. 06/03/1977
(See Marmon Group, Inc.)

CERRO DE PASCO COPPER CORP.
Name changed to Cerro De Pasco Corp. 00/00/1951
Cerro De Pasco Corp. name changed to Cerro Corp. 01/01/1961 which merged into Cerro-Marmon Corp. 02/24/1976 which name changed to Marmon Group, Inc. 06/03/1977
(See Marmon Group, Inc.)

CERRO DE PASCO CORP. (NY)
Capital Stock $5 par reclassified as Common $5 par 06/24/1955
Stock Dividend - 10% 02/10/1956
Name changed to Cerro Corp. 01/01/1961
Cerro Corp. merged into Cerro-Marmon Corp. 02/24/1976 which name changed to Marmon Group, Inc. 06/03/1977
(See Marmon Group, Inc.)

CERRO DORADO INC (NV)
Reincorporated 07/14/1999
State of incorporation changed from (FL) to (NV) 07/14/1999
Recapitalized as AURYN Mining Corp. 08/14/2018
Each share Common $0.001 par exchanged for (0.01) share Common $0.001 par

CERRO GORDO MINES CO.
Company in hands of Federal Receivers 00/00/1934
Stockholders' equity unlikely

CERRO MARMON CORP (DE)
Name changed to Marmon Group, Inc. 06/03/1977
(See Marmon Group, Inc.)

CERRO MNG CORP (NV)
Name changed to Maxxon Inc. 05/15/1997
Maxxon Inc. recapitalized as Revolutions Medical Corp. 01/18/2007

CERRO MINING LTD. (BC)
Name changed to Crownex International Ltd. 08/13/1969
Crownex International Ltd. recapitalized as Dison International Ltd. 12/10/1971
(See Dison International Ltd.)

CERRO RESOURCES NL (AUSTRALIA)
Plan of arrangement effective 06/04/2013
Each share Ordinary exchanged for (0.023) share Primero Mining Corp. Common no par and (0.1) share Santana Minerals Ltd. Ordinary
Note: Holders entitled to (100) or fewer Primero Mining Corp. shares will receive cash
(See each company's listing)

CERTAIN TEED CORP (MD)
Name changed 05/28/1976
Common no par changed to $1 par 00/00/1936
Common $1 par split (2) for (1) by issuance of (1) additional share 08/01/1972
Conv. Preferred Ser. A $1 par called for redemption 12/31/1973
Stock Dividend - 25% 12/15/1961
Name changed from Certain-Teed Products Corp. to Certain-Teed Corp. 05/28/1976
Merged into Saint-Gobain Investments Inc. 05/31/1988
Each share Common $1 par exchanged for $47.50 cash

CERTEGY INC (GA)
Name changed to Fidelity National Information Services, Inc. 02/01/2006

CERTICOM CORP (CANADA)
Reincorporated 01/14/1998
Reincorporated 01/13/2003
Place of incorporation changed from (ON) to (Yukon) 01/14/1998
Common no par split (2) for (1) by issuance of (1) additional share payable 07/12/2000 to holders of record 07/05/2000
Place of incorporation changed from (Yukon) to (Canada) 01/13/2003
Merged into Research In Motion Ltd. 03/23/2009
Each share Common no par exchanged for $3 cash

CERTIFIED COLL CORP (DE)
Common 1¢ par split (3) for (2) by issuance of (0.5) additional share 02/07/1986
Common 1¢ par split (3) for (2) by issuance of (0.5) additional share 08/04/1986
Name changed to CCC Information Services Inc. 05/12/1987 which name changed to Marmon Group, Inc. 06/03/1977
(See Marmon Group, Inc.)
(See CCC Information Services Inc.)

CERTIFIED CONSUMER SVC CORP (NY)
Filed certificate of voluntary dissolution 02/06/2002
Details not available

CERTIFIED CORP (DE)
Stock Dividend - 10% 01/02/1974
Merged into Plainville Manufacturing Co. 09/28/1979
Each share Common 10¢ par exchanged for $8 cash

CERTIFIED CR CORP LA INC (LA)
Charter revoked for failure to file annual reports 05/13/1982

CERTIFIED CREATIONS INC (NY)
Charter cancelled and proclaimed dissolved for failure to pay taxes 11/19/2003

CERTIFIED CREDIT & THRIFT CORP. (OH)
Recapitalized as Capitol Center Corp. 07/07/1964
Each share Class A $10 par exchanged for (100/101) share Common $1 par
Each share Class B 20¢ par exchanged for (1/101) share Common $1 par
(See Capitol Center Corp.)

CERTIFIED CREDIT CORP. (OH)
Adjudicated bankrupt 06/00/1965
No stockholders' equity

CERTIFIED DIABETIC SVCS INC (DE)
Plan of reorganization under Chapter 11 bankruptcy proceedings effective 09/21/2010
No stockholders' equity

CERTIFIED DIABETIC SUPPLIES INC (FL)
Reincorporated under the laws of Delaware as Certified Diabetic Services, Inc. and Common $0.001 par changed to 1¢ par 09/02/1997
(See Certified Diabetic Services, Inc.)

CERTIFIED ENVIRONMENTAL GROUP INC (DE)
Company terminated common stock registration and is no longer public as of 12/20/1999

CERTIFIED FIN INC (NY)
Name changed to Certified Consumer Service Corp. 10/01/1974
(See Certified Consumer Service Corp.)

CERTIFIED FINL INC (CA)
Completely liquidated 05/19/1969
Each share Common $1 par exchanged for first and final distribution of (0.5) share Voss Corp. Common 10¢ par
(See Voss Corp.)

CERTIFIED INDUSTRIES, INC. (DE)
Name changed to Cerind Corp. 04/30/1964
(See Cerind Corp.)

CERTIFIED MFG INC (WA)
Merged into NEA, Inc. 12/30/1977
Each share Common $1 par exchanged for $1.62 cash

CERTIFIED PHARMACAL CORP (DE)
Name changed to Certified Corp. 10/24/1968
(See Certified Corp.)

CERTIFIED SVCS INC (NV)
Plan of reorganization under Chapter 11 Federal Bankruptcy proceedings confirmed 01/16/2008
Stockholders' equity unlikely

CERTIFIED TECHNOLOGIES CORP (MN)
Each share old Common no par exchanged for (0.25) share new Common no par 09/30/1993
Reorganized under the laws of Nevada 03/28/2008
Each share Common no par

exchanged for (0.16666666) share Common $0.001 par
Certified Technologies Corp. (NV) name changed to Zhaoheng Hydropower Co. (NV) 07/30/2008 which reincorporated in British Virgin Islands as Zhaoheng Hydropower Ltd. 09/30/2009

CERTIFIED TECHNOLOGIES CORP (NV)
Name changed to Zhaoheng Hydropower Co. (NV) 07/30/2008
Zhaoheng Hydropower Co. (NV) reincorporated in British Virgin Islands as Zhaoheng Hydropower Ltd. 09/30/2009

CERTIGUE MINING & DREDGING CO. (SD)
Charter expired by time limitation 06/20/1925

CERTLESS COMPUTER CORP (NY)
Name changed to 3C General Corp. 08/17/1971
(See 3C General Corp.)

CERTO CORP.
Acquired by Postum Co., Inc. 04/30/1929
Details not available
Postum Co., Inc. name changed to General Foods Corp. 07/24/1929
(See General Foods Corp.)

CERTRON CORP (CA)
Common no par split (3) for (2) by issuance of (0.5) additional share 11/12/1969
Name changed to Cybrdi, Inc. 04/02/2005

CERULEAN FIRMAMENT CORP. (DE)
Charter cancelled and declared inoperative and void for non-payment of taxes 04/15/1973

CERULEAN GROUP INC (NV)
Reincorporated under the laws of Delaware as Enumeral Biomedical Holdings, Inc. 07/21/2014
(See Enumeral Biomedical Holdings, Inc.)

CERULEAN PHARMA INC (DE)
Recapitalized as Dare Bioscience, Inc. 07/20/2017
Each share Common $0.0001 par exchanged for (0.1) share Common $0.0001 par

CERVECERIA CORONA INC (DE)
Plan of reorganization under Chapter 11 Federal Bankruptcy proceedings confirmed 08/03/1987
No stockholders' equity

CERVECERIA NACIONAL S A (PANAMA)
ADR agreement terminated 11/13/2009
No ADR's remain outstanding

CERVIN CAP CORP (CANADA)
Name changed to R.A.N.K.I.N. Technologies Inc. 06/11/1999
R.A.N.K.I.N. Technologies Inc. name changed to Boomerang Tracking Inc. 12/04/2000
(See Boomerang Tracking Inc.)

CERVUS CORP (AB)
Each share Common no par received distribution of (1) Cervus LP Unit payable 05/22/2003 to holders of record 03/19/2003
Reorganized as Proventure Income Fund 12/31/2005
Each share Common no par exchanged for (1) Trust Unit
Note: Unexchanged certificates were cancelled and became without value 12/31/2006
Proventure Income Fund name changed to Summit Industrial Income REIT 10/05/2012

CERVUS FINL GROUP INC (AB)
Liquidation completed
Each share Common no par received first and final distribution of $0.09307 cash payable 04/27/2007 to holders of record 04/19/2007
Note: Certificates were not required to be surrendered and are without value

CERVUS INTL INC (AB)
Recapitalized as Cervus Corp. 04/11/2000
Each share Common $0.001 par exchanged for (0.5) share Common $0.001 par
Cervus Corp. reorganized as Proventure Income Fund 12/31/2005 which name changed to Summit Industrial Income REIT 10/05/2012

CERVUS L P (AB)
Merged into Cervus Equipment Corp. 10/27/2009
Each Unit no par exchanged for (1.5) shares Common no par

CERX VENTURE CORP (NV)
Name changed 03/23/1998
Name changed from CERX Entertainment Corp. to CERX Venture Corp. 03/23/1998
Each share old Common $0.001 par exchanged for (0.35) share new Common $0.001 par 06/28/1999
Name changed to Ebonlineinc.com 07/12/1999
Ebonlineinc.com name changed to MoneyZone.com (NV) 12/16/1999 which reincorporated in Delaware as MoneyZone.com, Inc. 06/12/2001 which name changed to QT 5, Inc. 01/08/2003 which recapitalized as Addison-Davis Diagnostics, Inc. 11/18/2004
(See Addison-Davis Diagnostics, Inc.)

CERXNET INC (NV)
Name changed 05/10/1999
Name changed from Cerx Entertainment Corp. to Cerxnet Inc. 05/10/1999
Name changed to GlobalNet Equities, Inc. 01/12/2001
GlobalNet Equities, Inc. recapitalized as Global Net Energy Corp. 10/10/2001 which name changed to Auction Floor, Inc. 01/11/2007
(See Auction Floor, Inc.)

CES INTL INC (NV)
Charter permanently revoked 01/31/2011

CES SOFTWARE PLC (ENGLAND & WALES)
Name changed to FUN Technologies PLC 02/04/2005
FUN Technologies PLC reorganized as Fun Technologies Inc. 03/13/2006
(See Fun Technologies Inc.)

CESCO INC (TX)
Merged into Browning-Ferris Industries, Inc. 07/06/1972
Each share Common 1¢ par exchanged for (0.8) share Common $0.16666666 par
(See Browning-Ferris Industries, Inc.)

CESKA SPORITELNA A S (CZECH REPUBLIC)
Acquired by Anteilsverwaltungssparkasse 09/10/2002
Each Reg. S GDR for Ordinary exchanged for $14.0085 cash

CESKE RADIOKOMUNIKACE A S (CZECH REPUBLIC)
GDR agreement terminated 01/17/2005
Each 144A Sponsored GDR for Ordinary exchanged for $19.7203 cash
Each Reg. S Sponsored GDR for Ordinary exchanged for $19.7203 cash

CESKY TELECOM A S (CZECH REPUBLIC)
Name changed to Telefonica O2 Czech Republic, A.S. 07/27/2006
Telefonica O2 Czech Republic, A.S. name changed to Telefonica Czech Republic, A.S. 06/10/2011
(See Telefonica Czech Republic, A.S.)

CESSLAND GAS & OIL CORP. LTD. (ON)
Merged into Cessland Corp. Ltd. 03/15/1962
Each share Capital Stock $1 par exchanged for (0.5) share Capital Stock no par
(See Cessland Corp. Ltd.)

CESSLAND LTD (ON)
Capital Stock no par split (2) for (1) by issuance of (1) additional share 02/24/1967
Delisted from Canadian Dealer Network 01/03/1995

CESSNA AIRCRAFT CO (KS)
Each share Common no par exchanged for (2) shares Common $1 par 02/15/1937
Common $1 par split (3) for (1) by issuance of (2) additional shares 03/04/1961
Common $1 par split (2) for (1) by issuance of (1) additional share 03/04/1969
Common $1 par split (2) for (1) by issuance of (1) additional share 11/14/1978
Stock Dividends - 100% 06/30/1944; 10% 12/15/1958
Acquired by General Dynamics Corp. 03/03/1986
Each share Common $1 par exchanged for $30 cash

CET SVCS INC (CA)
Name changed 08/07/2003
Name changed from CET Environmental Services, Inc. to CET Services, Inc. 08/07/2003
Reorganized under the laws of Colorado as BioMedical Technology Solutions Holdings, Inc. 09/03/2008
Each share Common no par exchanged for (0.33333333) share Common no par

CETACEAN INDS INC (NV)
Recapitalized as Trinon Inc. 02/17/1998
Each share Common $0.001 par exchanged for (0.25) share Common $0.001 par
Trinon Inc. name changed to Lexico Resources International Corp. 10/22/1998
(See Lexico Resources International Corp.)

CETACEAN INDS INC (UT)
Reincorporated under the laws of Nevada 08/26/1997
Cetacean Industries Inc. recapitalized as Trinon Inc. 02/17/1998 which name changed to Lexico Resources International Corp. 10/22/1998
(See Lexico Resources International Corp.)

CETALON CORP (NV)
Plan of reorganization under Chapter 11 Federal Bankruptcy proceedings effective 06/08/2004
Stockholders' equity unlikely

CETEC CORP (DE)
Reincorporated 05/12/1986
State of incorporation changed from (CA) to (DE) 05/12/1986
Merged into Mark IV Industries, Inc. 07/14/1988
Each share Common no par exchanged for $11 cash

CETEC ENGR INC (BC)
Recapitalized as International Cetec Investments Inc. 12/22/1995
Each share Common no par exchanged for (3) shares Preferred no par and (0.33333333) share Common no par
(See International Cetec Investments Inc.)

CETECO HLDG N V (NETHERLANDS)
ADR agreement terminated 12/29/2008
Each Sponsored ADR for Ordinary exchanged for $0.06695 cash

CETEK TECHNOLOGIES INC (NV)
Reincorporated 04/11/2006
Each share old Common $0.001 par exchanged for (0.00666666) share new Common $0.001 par 12/23/2002
State of incorporation changed from (DE) to (NV) 04/11/2006
Each share new Common $0.001 par exchanged again for (0.00016666) share new Common $0.001 par 04/21/2014
Name changed to High Velocity Enterprises, Inc. and new Common $0.001 par changed to $0.0001 par 06/24/2014
High Velocity Enterprises, Inc. reorganized as NanoTech Gaming, Inc. 04/23/2015

CETRON ELECTR CORP (DE)
Capital Stock $1 par changed to no par 10/07/1964
Capital Stock no par changed to 25¢ par 04/22/1968
Stock Dividend - 25% 11/15/1960
Merged into Rich-Cet Co. 12/07/1981
To holdings of (100) or fewer shares: Each share exchanged for $4 cash
To holdings of (101) or more shares: Each share exchanged for $4.68 principal amount of 9% Subordinated Installment Debentures due 1982 - 1987 and $0.82 cash

CETRONE ENERGY CO (NV)
Common $0.001 par split (200) for (1) by issuance of (199) additional shares payable 08/12/2010 to holders of record 08/12/2010
Ex date - 08/13/2010
Name changed to Fresh Start Private Management Inc. 08/18/2010
Fresh Start Private Management Inc. name changed to BioCorRx Inc. 02/20/2014

CETUS CORP (DE)
Merged into Chiron Corp. 12/12/1991
Each share Common 1¢ par exchanged for (0.3) share Common 1¢ par
(See Chiron Corp.)

CETUS HEALTHCARE LTD PARTNERSHIP II (CA)
Limited Partnership dissolved 12/28/1990
Details not available

CEVAL ALIMENTOS S A (BRAZIL)
ADR agreement terminated 3/5/2002
Each Sponsored ADR for Preference no par exchanged for $2.225033 cash

CEYONIQ AG (GERMANY)
ADR agreement terminated 10/31/2008
No ADR holders' equity

CEZAR INDS LTD (DE)
Each share old Common 15¢ par exchanged for (0.05) share new Common 15¢ par 05/01/1992
Charter cancelled and declared inoperative and void for non-payment of taxes 05/24/1994

CF & I STL CORP (CO)
5.5% Preferred Ser. B $50 par called for redemption 03/31/1967
Plan of reorganization under Chapter 11 Federal Bankruptcy Code effective 03/03/1993
No stockholders' equity

CF BANCORP INC (DE)
Stock Dividend - 10% 07/30/1993
Merged into First Midwest Bancorp, Inc. 12/29/1995
Each share Common 1¢ par exchanged for (1.4545) shares Common 1¢ par

CF CORP (CAYMAN ISLANDS)
Units separated 12/01/2017
Name changed to FGL Holdings and Class A Ordinary $0.0001 par reclassified as Ordinary $0.0001 par 12/01/2017

CF INCOME PARTNERS L P (DE)
Completely liquidated 03/17/1994
Each Depositary Unit exchanged for first and final distribution of $1 cash

CFB BANCORP INC (FL)
Merged into Compass Bancshares, Inc. 08/23/1996
Each share Common 1¢ par exchanged for (0.61106) share Common $2 par
Compass Bancshares, Inc. merged into Banco Bilbao Vizcaya Argentaria, S.A. 09/07/2007

CFB CAP I (DE)
Capital Securities called for redemption at $25 on 05/01/2002

CFB CAP II (DE)
8.20% Capital Securities called for redemption at $25 on 04/04/2003

CFB CAP III (DE)
8.125% Capital Securities called for redemption at $25 on 04/15/2007

CFB CAP IV (DE)
7.60% Capital Securities called for redemption at $25 on 03/15/2008

CFC FINL CORP (CA)
Name changed to Madison & Burke Capital 01/01/1973
(See Madison & Burke Capital)

CFC INDS INC (NY)
Completely liquidated 11/22/1967
Each share Common 10¢ par exchanged for first and final distribution of $0.791 cash

CFC INTL INC (DE)
Merged into Illinois Tool Works Inc. 09/06/2006
Each share Common 1¢ par exchanged for $16.75 cash

CFC PFD TR (DE)
9.375% Trust Preferred Securities called for redemption at $25 on 12/31/2002

CFCF INC (CANADA)
Acquired by Videotron Group Ltd. 03/31/1997
Each Subordinate Share no par exchanged for $21.50 cash

CFCN COMMUNICATIONS LTD (ON)
Acquired by Maclean-Hunter Ltd. 07/01/1977
Each share Common no par exchanged for $14 cash

CFE ENTERPRISES INC (NV)
Each share old Common $0.001 par exchanged for (0.002) share new Common $0.001 par 09/12/2005
Note: No holder will receive fewer than (20) shares
Name changed to Nutech, Inc. 04/17/2006

CFE INDS INC (AB)
Recapitalized as Commercial Solutions Inc. 10/01/2002
Each share Common no par exchanged for (0.2) share Common no par
(See Commercial Solutions Inc.)

CFI INC (GA)
Recapitalized as Fletcher-Flora Health Care Systems, Inc. 06/06/2005
Each share Common no par exchanged for (0.11111111) share Common no par
(See Fletcher-Flora Health Care Systems, Inc.)

CFI INDS INC (DE)
Merged into Ivex Packaging Corp. 08/16/1996
Each share Common $1 par exchanged for $6.22 cash

CFI MTG INC (DE)
SEC revoked common stock registration 11/24/2009

CFI PROSERVICES INC (OR)
Name changed to Concentrex Inc. 05/19/2000
(See Concentrex Inc.)

CFM INC (ON)
Name changed 03/18/1996
Name changed 02/12/2002
Name changed from CFM International Inc. to CFM Majestic Inc. 03/18/1996
Common no par split (2) for (1) by issuance of (1) additional share payable 03/12/1998 to holders of record 03/05/1998
Name changed from CFM Majestic Inc. to CFM Inc. 02/12/2002
Merged into Ontario Teachers' Pension Plan Board 04/12/2005
Each share Common no par exchanged for $1.50 cash

CFM TECHNOLOGIES INC (PA)
Merged into Mattson Technology, Inc. 12/29/2000
Each share Common no par exchanged for (0.5223) share Common $0.001 par
(See Mattson Technology, Inc.)

CFO CONSULTANTS INC (NV)
Recapitalized as Kaibo Foods Co. Ltd. (NV) 03/24/2011
Each share Common $0.001 par exchanged for (0.0621504) share Common $0.001 par
Kaibo Foods Co. Ltd. (NV) reincorporated in Delaware 09/06/2017 which recapitalized as C-Cube Genetics, Inc. 07/30/2018

CFR PHARMACEUTICALS S A (CHILE)
Acquired by Abbott Laboratories 09/26/2014
Each 144A Sponsored ADR for Ordinary exchanged for $34.65 cash
Each Reg. S Sponsored ADR for Ordinary exchanged for $34.65 cash

CFS BANCORP INC (IN)
Reincorporated 06/30/2005
State of incorporation changed from (DE) to (IN) 06/30/2005
Merged into First Merchants Corp. 11/12/2013
Each share Common 1¢ par exchanged for (0.65) share Common no par

CFS BANCSHARES INC (DE)
Merged into Citizens Trust Bank (Atlanta, GA) 02/28/2003
Each share Common 1¢ par exchanged for $65.04 cash

CFS CONTL INC (DE)
Common $1 par split (3) for (2) by issuance of (0.5) additional share 12/14/1983
Stock Dividend - 100% 03/01/1973
Merged into Staley (A.E.) Manufacturing Co. 11/30/1984
Each share Common $1 par exchanged for $38 cash

CFS CORP (CT)
Placed in receivership 04/12/1990
No stockholders' equity

CFS FINL CORP (VA)
Merged into Crestar Financial Corp. 05/14/1993
Each share Common $1 par exchanged for (0.524) share Common $5 par
Crestar Financial Corp. merged into SunTrust Banks, Inc. 12/31/1998

CFS GROUP INC (CANADA)
Name changed 06/22/1987
Name changed from CFS Refractories Inc. to CFS Group Inc. 06/22/1987
Acquired by Ajawak Investments Ltd. 09/01/2000
Each share Common no par exchanged for $3 cash

CFS INTL INC (AB)
Merged into Ports International Enterprises Ltd. 01/01/2006
Each share Common no par exchanged for $3.75 cash

CFS INVT TR (MA)
Kalliston Preferred Plus Fund no par completely liquidated 08/31/1990
Details not available
Calamos Small/Mid Cap Convertible Fund no par reclassified as Calamos Growth & Income Fund 04/29/1994
Name changed to Calamos Investment Trust (New) 06/23/1997

CFSB BANCORP INC (DE)
Common 1¢ par split (4) for (3) by issuance of (0.33333333) additional share 07/20/1992
Common 1¢ par split (4) for (3) by issuance of (0.33333333) additional share 09/15/1993
Common 1¢ par split (3) for (2) by issuance of (0.5) additional share payable 12/18/1997 to holders of record 12/01/1997
Stock Dividends - 10% 12/22/1994; 10% 10/13/1995; 10% payable 09/12/1996 to holders of record 08/30/1996; 10% payable 06/16/1997 to holders of record 05/30/1997; 10% payable 06/12/1998 to holders of record 05/29/1998; 10% payable 06/14/1999 to holders of record 05/28/1999
Merged into Old Kent Financial Corp. 07/09/1999
Each share Common 1¢ par exchanged for (0.5939) share Common $1 par
Old Kent Financial Corp. merged into Fifth Third Bancorp 04/02/2001

CFW COMMUNICATIONS CO (VA)
Common no par split (2) for (1) by issuance of (1) additional share 05/23/1990
Common no par split (2) for (1) by issuance of (1) additional share 05/21/1993
Name changed to NTelos Inc. 12/06/2000
(See NTelos Inc.)

CFX CORP (NH)
Each share $1.3875 Conv. Preferred Ser. A $1 par exchanged for (1.1025) shares Common $1 par 04/30/1995
Common $1 par changed to $0.66666666 par and (0.5) additional share issued 07/21/1995
Stock Dividends - 5% payable 01/19/1996 to holders of record 12/22/1995; 5% payable 01/17/1997 to holders of record 12/20/1996
Ex date - 12/18/1996
Merged into Peoples Heritage Financial Group, Inc. 04/10/1998
Each share Common $0.66666666 par exchanged for (0.667) share Common 1¢ par
Peoples Heritage Financial Group, Inc. name changed to Banknorth Group, Inc. (ME) 05/10/2000 which merged into TD Banknorth Inc. 03/01/2005
(See TD Banknorth Inc.)

CGA COMPUTER ASSOC INC (DE)
Stock Dividends - 10% 05/25/1979; 100% 02/01/1980; 50% 11/24/1980
Name changed to CGA Computer, Inc. 10/27/1983
(See CGA Computer, Inc.)

CGA COMPUTER ASSOC INC (NY)
Name changed to TMD Management Co. 06/14/1974
(See TMD Management Co.)

CGA COMPUTER INC (DE)
Merged into a private company 11/02/1984
Each share Common 10¢ par exchanged for $13 cash

CGA MNG LTD (AUSTRALIA)
Merged into B2Gold Corp. 01/31/2013
Each share Ordinary exchanged for (0.74) share Common no par

CGB&L FINL GROUP INC (DE)
Merged into Bement Bancshares Inc. 10/18/2002
Each share Common 1¢ par exchanged for $20.50 cash

CGC INC (CANADA)
Common no par split (2) for (1) by issuance of (1) additional share 12/04/1987
Under plan of merger each share Common no par exchanged for $11 cash 01/09/1997

CGC MINES LTD (ON)
Charter cancelled for failure to pay taxes and file returns 05/09/1977

CGF MUTUAL FUNDS CORP.
Fund terminated 01/29/2010
Each share Income & Equity Class A received first and final distribution of $1.54 cash

CGF RESOURCE 2008 FLOW THRU LTD PARTNERSHIP (AB)
Merged into Energy Income Fund 10/04/2010
Each Unit no par automatically became (3.0177) Trust Units no par

CGI COMMUNICATIONS SVCS INC (DE)
Recapitalized as Axxess Pharma, Inc. (DE) 07/30/2008
Each share Common $0.0001 par exchanged for (0.2) share Common $0.0001 par
Axxess Pharma, Inc. (DE) reincorporated in Nevada 12/06/2012 which recapitalized as Allstar Health Brands, Inc. 06/27/2017

CGI HLDG CORP (NV)
Name changed to Think Partnership, Inc. 03/14/2006
Think Partnership, Inc. name changed to Kowabunga! Inc. 10/01/2008 which name changed to Inuvo, Inc. 07/30/2009

CGM CAP DEV FD (MA)
Merged into CGM Trust 06/27/2008
Each share Common $1 par received Focus Fund no par at net asset value

CGS LABORATORIES INC. (CT)
Name changed to Trak Electronics Co., Inc. 01/23/1961
Trak Electronics Co., Inc. name changed to Wiltek, Inc. 05/17/1967 which name changed to E-Sync Networks Inc. 07/28/1999
(See E-Sync Networks Inc.)

CGT RES INC (NV)
Name changed to HealthSonix, Inc. 05/08/2006
(See HealthSonix, Inc.)

CH ENERGY GROUP INC (NY)
Acquired by FortisUS, Inc. 06/27/2013
Each share Common 10¢ par exchanged for $65 cash

CH FINL CORP (BC)
Struck off register and declared dissolved for failure to file returns 07/03/1992

CH LTG INTL CORP (DE)
SEC revoked common stock registration 01/17/2013

CHABELA MINERALS INC (CANADA)
Recapitalized as Amseco Exploration Ltd. 12/15/2005
Each share Common no par exchanged for (0.1) share Common no par

CHABLIS RES LTD (BC)
Common no par split (3) for (1) by issuance of (2) additional shares 05/18/1988
Name changed to Westhill Resources Ltd. 09/07/1988
Westhill Resources Ltd. recapitalized as Breckenridge Resources Ltd. 03/03/1992 which recapitalized as GTO Resources Inc. 08/07/2003 which recapitalized as Ram Power, Corp. 10/20/2009 which recapitalized as Polaris Infrastructure Inc. 05/15/2015

CHACE OIL INC (NM)
Merged into Cobb Nuclear Corp. 01/14/1980
Each share Common 1¢ par exchanged for (0.33333333) share Common 1¢ par
Cobb Nuclear Corp. name changed to Cobb Resources Corp. 01/02/1981 which name changed to Family Room Entertainment Corp. 04/26/2000

CHAD THERAPEUTICS INC (CA)
Common 1¢ par split (2) for (1) by issuance of (1) additional share 10/15/1993
Stock Dividend - 3% payable 10/15/1996 to holders of record 10/01/1996 Ex date - 09/27/1996
Chapter 7 bankruptcy proceedings terminated 08/30/2018
Stockholders' equity unlikely

CHADBOURN GOTHAM INC (NC)
5% Conv. Preferred $20 par called for redemption 07/19/1968
4.5% Conv. Preferred $50 par called for redemption 09/26/1968
Name changed to Chadbourn Inc. 01/31/1969
Chadbourn Inc. reorganized as Stanwood Corp. 06/12/1975 which was acquired by Delta Woodside Industries, Inc. (DE) 09/07/1988 which merged into Delta Woodside Industries, Inc. (SC) 11/15/1989
(See Delta Woodside Industries, Inc. (SC))

CHADBOURN HOSIERY MILLS, INC. (NC)
Merged into Chadbourn Gotham, Inc. 09/30/1955
Each share Preferred $50 par exchanged for (1) share 4.5% Preferred $50 par
Each share Common $1 par exchanged for (3) shares Common $1 par
Chadbourn Gotham, Inc. name changed to Chadbourn Inc. 01/31/1969 which reorganized as Stanwood Corp. 06/12/1975 which was acquired by Delta Woodside Industries, Inc. (DE) 09/07/1988 which merged into Delta Woodside Industries, Inc. (SC) 11/15/1989
(See Delta Woodside Industries, Inc. (SC))

CHADBOURN INC (NC)
Reorganized as Stanwood Corp. 06/12/1975
Each share 6% Preferred $50 par automatically became (1) share 6% Preferred $50 par
Each share $0.46666666 Conv. Jr. Preferred Ser. A $10 par exchanged for (1.3) shares Common $1 par
Each share Common $1 par exchanged for (0.2) share Common $1 par
Stanwood Corp. acquired by Delta Woodside Industries, Inc. (DE) 09/07/1988 which merged into Delta Woodside Industries, Inc. (SC) 11/15/1989
(See Delta Woodside Industries, Inc. (SC))

CHADMOORE WIRELESS GROUP INC (CO)
Liquidation completed
Each share Common $0.001 par received initial distribution of $0.3323 cash payable 07/12/2002 to holders of record 02/22/2002 Ex date - 07/15/2002
Each share Common $0.001 par received second distribution of $0.061967 cash payable 02/28/2003 to holders of record 02/22/2002 Ex date - 03/17/2003
Each share Common $0.001 par received third distribution of $0.10146414 cash payable 12/09/2003 to holders of record 02/22/2002 Ex date - 12/12/2003
Each share Common $0.001 par received fourth distribution of $0.172617 cash payable 10/16/2006 to holders of record 02/22/2002
Each share Common $0.001 par received fifth and final distribution of $0.00211 cash payable 04/30/2008 to holders of record 02/22/2002
Note: Certificates were not required to be surrendered and are without value

CHADO OIL & GAS INC (TX)
Name changed to Mineral Development, Inc. 12/12/1977
Mineral Development, Inc. recapitalized as Exco Resources Inc. 07/18/1996
(See Exco Resources Inc.)

CHADWICK-HOSKINS CO.
Merged into Textron Inc. (RI) 00/00/1946
Details not available

CHADWICK MILLER INC (MA)
Merged into Chadcliff Corp. 10/03/1984
Each share Common $1 par exchanged for $25 cash

CHAI CHA NA MNG INC (CANADA)
Dissolved for non-compliance 12/16/2016

CHAI NA TA CORP (CANADA)
Name changed 04/28/1994
Common no par split (3) for (2) by issuance of (0.5) additional share 09/09/1991
Name changed from Chai-Na-Ta Ginseng Products Ltd. to Chai-Na-Ta Corp. 04/28/1994
Each share old Common no par exchanged for (0.25) share new Common no par 10/18/1996
Stock Dividend - 2.5% payable 05/22/1997 to holders of record 05/08/1997
Completely liquidated 08/03/2012
Each share new Common no par exchanged for first and final distribution of $0.293 cash

CHAICHEM HLDGS INC (NV)
Name changed to Excelsior Biotechnology, Inc. 05/16/2005
Excelsior Biotechnology, Inc. name changed to Targetviewz, Inc. 03/03/2006 which recapitalized as Greenway Energy 11/15/2007 which name changed to Greenway Technology 09/19/2008

CHAIN & GENERAL EQUITIES, INC.
Merged into Equity Corp. 00/00/1935
Details not available

CHAIN BELT CO (WI)
Capital Stock $100 par changed to Capital Stock no par 00/00/1928
Each share old Capital Stock no par exchanged for (3) shares new Capital Stock no par 00/00/1937
New Capital Stock no par changed to $10 par 00/00/1952
Stock Dividend - 50% 02/25/1959
Name changed to Rex Chainbelt Inc. 01/23/1964
Rex Chainbelt Inc. name changed to Rexnord Inc. 01/26/1973
(See Rexnord Inc.)

CHAIN ENERGY CORP (AB)
Acquired by Argonauts Group Ltd. 03/31/2002
Each share Common no par exchanged for either (0.44) share Common no par or $1 cash
Note: Option to receive stock expired 05/27/2002
Argonauts Group Ltd. name changed to Cequel Energy Inc. 06/07/2002
(See Cequel Energy Inc.)

CHAIN LAKES RESH CORP (MI)
Adjudicated bankrupt 03/19/1973
No stockholders' equity

CHAIN REALTY TRUST
Dissolved 00/00/1929
Details not available

CHAIN STORE FUND, INC.
Liquidated 00/00/1933
Details not available

CHAIN STORE INVESTMENT CORP. (DE)
Name changed to Special Investments & Securities, Inc. 00/00/1952
(See Special Investments & Securities, Inc.)

CHAIN STORE INVESTORS TRUST
Liquidated 00/00/1942
Details not available

CHAIN STORE REAL ESTATE TRUST (MA)
Completely liquidated 04/07/1965
Details not available

CHAIN STORE SHAREOWNERS, INC.
Liquidated 00/00/1931
Details not available

CHAIN STORE STOCKS, INC.
Liquidated 00/00/1933
Details not available

CHAIR E YACHT INC (WY)
Name changed to Nitram, Inc. 07/17/1978
Nitram, Inc. recapitalized as Diversified Resources, Inc. 02/22/1984 which recapitalized as Techtower Group, Inc. 07/20/1984
(See Techtower Group, Inc.)

CHAIRMAN CAP CORP (ON)
Reorganized under the laws of Channel Islands as Longreach Oil & Gas Ltd. 10/04/2010
Each share Common no par exchanged for (0.2) share Common no par
Longreach Oil & Gas Ltd. name changed to PetroMaroc Corp. PLC 07/14/2014

CHAKWAL CEM LTD (PAKISTAN)
Name changed to Pakistan Cement Co. Ltd. 08/31/2005
Pakistan Cement Co. Ltd. name changed to Lafarge Pakistan Cement Ltd. 03/20/2009

CHAL BERT DRILLING WESTN LTD (AB)
Struck off register for failure to file annual returns 12/23/1983

CHALCO ENGR CORP (DE)
Name changed to Chalco Industries Inc. 08/24/1970
(See Chalco Industries Inc.)

CHALCO INDS INC (DE)
Charter cancelled and declared inoperative and void for non-payment of taxes 03/01/1996

CHALET GOURMET CORP (CA)
Proclaimed dissolved 07/03/1998

CHALEUR METALS LTD. (NB)
Charter forfeited for failure to file reports 11/16/1977

CHALICE DIAMOND CORP (BC)
Each share old Common no par exchanged for (0.1) share new Common no par 10/22/2010
Name changed to La Ronge Gold Corp. 06/30/2011
La Ronge Gold Corp. name changed to Select Sands Corp. 11/14/2014

CHALICE MNG INC (BC)
Recapitalized as International Chalice Resources Inc. 01/27/1999
Each share Common no par exchanged for (0.2) share Common no par
International Chalice Resources Inc. recapitalized as Golden Chalice Resources Inc. 08/15/2003 which recapitalized as Rogue Resources Inc. (Old) 10/15/2010 which name changed to Rogue Iron Ore Corp. 01/23/2012 which reorganized as Rogue Resources Inc. (New) 12/24/2013

CHALK MEDIA CORP (BC)
Merged into Research in Motion Ltd. 01/30/2009
Each share Common no par exchanged for $0.142 cash

CHALLENGE INC (UT)
Merged into Argosy Energy Inc. 08/11/1986
Each share Common $0.0025 par exchanged for (2.75) shares Common $0.001 par
Argosy Energy Inc. acquired by Garnet Resources Corp. 09/22/1988 which merged into Aviva Petroleum Inc. 10/28/1998
(See Aviva Petroleum Inc.)

CHALLENGE OIL & GAS CO (CO)
Merged into Berry Industries Corp. (New) 07/01/1979
Each share Capital Stock 1¢ par exchanged for (0.1) share Common $1 par
Berry Industries Corp. (New) name changed to Strata Search, Inc. 12/23/1987
(See Strata Search, Inc.)

CHALLENGER AIRLINES CO.
Merged into Frontier Airlines, Inc. on a share for share basis 00/00/1950
Frontier Airlines, Inc. reorganized as Frontier Holdings, Inc. 05/06/1982
(See Frontier Holdings, Inc.)

CHALLENGER DEEP RES CORP (AB)
Name changed to DeepMarkit Corp. 11/02/2015

CHALLENGER DEV CORP (BC)
Recapitalized as DGS Minerals Inc. 04/12/2013
Each share Common no par exchanged for (0.1) share Common no par
DGS Minerals Inc. name changed to Dragon Legend Entertainment (Canada) Inc. 02/13/2017

CHALLENGER ENERGY CORP (CANADA)
Merged into Canadian Superior Energy Inc. 09/24/2009
Each share Common no par exchanged for (0.51) share Common no par
Canadian Superior Energy Inc. recapitalized as Sonde Resources Corp. 06/08/2010
(See Sonde Resources Corp.)

CHALLENGER EXPL LTD (BC)
Struck off register and declared dissolved for failure to file returns 10/21/1983

CHALLENGER FINL SVCS GROUP LTD (AUSTRALIA)
Name changed to Challenger Ltd. 12/31/2010

CHALLENGER INTL LTD (BERMUDA)
Each share Common 1¢ par reclassified as (1) share Special Restricted Stock 1¢ par 07/13/1992
Each share Class A Common 1¢ par reclassified as (1) share Special Restricted Stock 1¢ par 07/13/1992
Note: Class A Common 1¢ par issued to non-U.S. citizens and residents only
Name changed to Intelect Communications Systems Ltd. (Bermuda) 12/15/1995
Intelect Communications Systems Ltd. (Bermuda) reincorporated in Delaware as Intelect Communications Inc. 12/05/1997 which name changed to TeraForce Technology Corp. 01/31/2001
(See TeraForce Technology Corp.)

CHALLENGER INTL SVCS LTD (ON)
99% of Class B Common no par acquired by Turbo Resources Ltd. as of 12/05/1979
Each share $2.50 Special Class A no par exchanged for $2 cash 12/15/1984
Public interest eliminated

CHALLENGER INVT FD INC (MD)
Name changed to Farm Bureau Growth Fund, Inc. 07/31/1978
Farm Bureau Growth Fund, Inc. name changed to FBL Series Fund, Inc. 12/01/1987 which name changed to EquiTrust Series Fund, Inc. 05/01/1998

CHALLENGER MINERALS LTD (BC)
Recapitalized as Challenger Development Corp. 02/02/2005
Each share Common no par exchanged for (0.25) share Common no par
Challenger Development Corp. recapitalized as DGS Minerals Inc. 04/12/2013 which name changed to Dragon Legend Entertainment (Canada) Inc. 02/13/2017

CHALLENGER MINES LTD. (BC)
Struck off register and declared dissolved for failure to file returns 07/11/1977

CHALLENGER POWERBOATS INC (NV)
Each share old Common $0.001 par exchanged for (0.05) share new Common $0.001 par 10/31/2007
Plan of liquidation under Chapter 7 Federal Bankruptcy Code effective 12/24/2008
No stockholders' equity

CHALLENGER PRODS INC (PA)
Adjudicated bankrupt 04/17/1967
No stockholders' equity

CHALLIS ENTERPRISES INC (DE)
Recapitalized as Pro-Tec Sports International, Inc. 09/12/1988
Each share Common $0.0001 par exchanged for (0.1) share Common $0.001 par
(See Pro-Tec Sports International, Inc.)

CHALMERS OIL & GAS CO. (DE)
Common $5 par changed to $1 par 00/00/1928
Completely liquidated
Holders of Preferred $5 par record 05/17/1960 received first and final distribution of $14 cash
Common $1 par holders have no equity; certificates are valueless

CHALONE WINE GROUP LTD (CA)
Name changed 05/16/1991
Name changed from Chalone Inc. to Chalone Wine Group, Ltd. 05/16/1991
Merged into Diageo PLC 02/08/2005

Each share Common no par exchanged for $14.25 cash

CHAMAELO ENERGY INC (AB)
Plan of arrangement effective 06/27/2005
Each share Common no par exchanged for (0.5) share Chamaelo Exploration Ltd. Common no par and (0.5) Vault Energy Trust, Trust Unit no par
(See each company's lising)

CHAMAELO EXPL LTD (AB)
Merged into Kereco Energy Ltd. 10/22/2006
Each share Common no par exchanged for (0.51) share Common no par
Kereco Energy Ltd. name changed to Cadence Energy Inc. 05/14/2008
(See Cadence Energy Inc.)

CHAMBERLAIN MFG CORP (IA)
Name changed 03/10/1967
Name changed from Chamberlain Corp. to Chamberlain Manufacturing Corp. 03/10/1967
Merged into Thrall Car Manufacturing Co. 01/30/1980
Each share Common $2.50 par exchanged for $30 cash

CHAMBERLAIN OIL & GAS LTD. (AB)
Capital Stock $1 par changed to no par 00/00/1954
Recapitalized as New Chamberlain Petroleums Ltd. 05/23/1956
Each share Capital Stock no par exchanged (0.25) share Common 50¢ par
New Chamberlain Petroleums Ltd. name changed to Sarcee Petroleums Ltd. 03/09/1959
(See Sarcee Petroleums Ltd.)

CHAMBERLIN CO AMER (DE)
Reincorporated 09/30/1957
Each share Common $5 par exchanged for (3) shares Common $2.50 par 00/00/1947
State of incorporation changed from (MI) to (DE) 09/30/1957
Under plan of merger each share old Common $2.50 par exchanged for (1) share new Common $2.50 par and $0.8244 cash 10/01/1959
5% Preferred $25 par called for redemption 03/01/1974
Liquidation completed
Each share Common $2.50 par exchanged for initial distribution of $6 cash 12/18/1974
Each share Common $2.50 par received second distribution of $5 cash 07/01/1975
Each share Common $2.50 par received third and final distribution of $2.75 cash 12/09/1975

CHAMBERLIN METAL WEATHERSTRIP CO.
Name changed to Chamberlin Co. of America (MI) 00/00/1944
Chamberlin Co. of America (MI) reincorporated in Delaware 09/30/1957
(See Chamberlin Co. of America (DE))

CHAMBERS DEV INC (DE)
Common $1 par changed to 50¢ par 04/04/1986
Class A Common $1 par split (2) for (1) by issuance of (1) additional share 08/03/1988
Common 50¢ par split (2) for (1) by issuance of (1) additional share 08/03/1988
Class A Common 50¢ par split (2) for (1) by issuance of (1) additional share 05/14/1990
Common 50¢ par split (2) for (1) by issuance of (1) additional share 05/14/1990
Stock Dividend - in Class A Common to holders of Common 100% 04/16/1986

Merged into USA Waste Services, Inc. 06/30/1995
Each share Class A Common 50¢ par exchanged for (0.41667) share Common 1¢ par
Each share Common 50¢ par exchanged for (0.41667) share Common 1¢ par
USA Waste Services, Inc. merged into Waste Management, Inc. 07/16/1998

CHAMBERS STR PPTYS (MD)
Under plan of merger name changed to Gramercy Property Trust 12/17/2015
(See Gramercy Property Trust)

CHAMBERSBURG TR CO (CHAMBERSBURG, PA)
Stock Dividends - 10% 06/15/1976; 20% 12/01/1983
Merged into Financial Trans Corp. 07/20/1984
Each share Capital Stock $10 par exchanged for (4.4) shares Common $5 par
Financial Trans Corp. name changed to Financial Trust Corp. 05/16/1985 which merged into Keystone Financial, Inc. 05/30/1997 which merged into M&T Bank Corp. 10/06/2000

CHAMP AUTOMOTIVE INTL CORP (UT)
Involuntarily dissolved 10/01/1988

CHAMP CLARK BRIDGE CO.
Sold to Pike County, MO 00/00/1941
Details not available

CHAMPAGNE CAP CORP (AB)
Struck off register for failure to file annual returns 08/01/1992

CHAMPAGNE RES LTD (BC)
Recapitalized as Pass Lake Resources Ltd. 01/27/1988
Each share Common no par exchanged for (0.5) share Common no par
Pass Lake Resources Ltd. recapitalized as Arlington Ventures Ltd. Canada (BC) 11/13/1992 which reincorporated in Yukon as Arlington Oil & Gas Ltd. 06/27/2001 which recapitalized as Cypress Hills Resource Corp. (Yukon) 03/12/2003 which reincorporated in Alberta 07/26/2005

CHAMPAIGN BANCORP, INC. (DE)
Merged into Midwest Financial Group, Inc. 02/08/1983
Each share Common $25 par exchanged for (4.32) shares Common $5 par
Midwest Financial Group, Inc. merged into First of America Bank Corp. 11/01/1989 which merged into National City Corp. 03/31/1998 which was acquired by PNC Financial Services Group, Inc. 12/31/2008

CHAMPAIGN NATL BK (CHAMPAIGN, IL)
Reorganized as Central Illinois Financial Corp. 09/13/1984
Each share Capital Stock $20 par exchanged for (1) share Common $1 par
Central Illinois Financial Corp. reorganized as Central Illinois Financial Co., Inc. 10/20/1995 which name changed to BankIllinois Financial Corp. 02/27/1998 which merged into Main Street Trust, Inc. 03/23/2000 which merged into First Busey Corp. 08/01/2007

CHAMPAIGN NATL BK (URBANA, OH)
Name changed 04/20/1992
Name changed from Champaign National Bank (Urbana, OH) to Champaign National Bank & Trust (Urbana, OH) 04/20/1992

Reorganized as Futura Banc Corp. 07/01/1994
Each share Common $100 par exchanged for (2) shares Common no par
Futura Banc Corp. merged into First Citizens Banc Corp. 12/17/2007 which name changed to Civista Bancshares, Inc. 05/04/2015

CHAMPAY CO. OF ST. LOUIS
Bankrupt 00/00/1948
Stockholders' equity unlikely

CHAMPBURGER CORP (DE)
Charter cancelled and declared inoperative and void for non-payment of taxes 04/15/1972

CHAMPION COATED PAPER CO.
Recapitalized as Champion Paper & Fibre Co. 00/00/1935
Details not available

CHAMPION COMMUNICATIONS SVCS INC (DE)
Voluntarily dissolved 09/29/2011
Details not available

CHAMPION COMPUTER RENTALS INC (CO)
Each share old Common no par exchanged for (0.01) share new Common no par 02/10/1994
Name changed to ISO Block Products USA, Inc. 09/20/1994
ISO Block Products USA, Inc. recapitalized as Cryocon Inc. 09/21/2000
(See Cryocon Inc.)

CHAMPION COPPER CO. (ME)
Charter revoked for failure to file reports and pay fees 12/14/1918

CHAMPION ENERGY CORP (UT)
Recapitalized as Champion Financial Corp. (UT) 11/15/1989
Each share Common $0.001 par exchanged for (0.04) share Common $0.001 par
Champion Financial Corp. (UT) reorganized in Delaware as HealthStar Corp. 11/16/1998 which name changed to BlueStone Holding Corp. 09/05/2001
(See BlueStone Holding Corp.)

CHAMPION ENTERPRISES INC (MI)
Common $1 par split (2) for (1) by issuance of (1) additional share 05/30/1995
Common $1 par split (2) for (1) by issuance of (1) additional share payable 05/31/1996 to holders of record 05/16/1996 Ex date - 06/03/1996
Plan of reorganization under Chapter 11 Federal Bankruptcy proceedings effective 05/23/2011
No stockholders' equity

CHAMPION FINL CORP (UT)
Each share old Common $0.001 par exchanged for (0.1) share new Common $0.001 par 08/27/1993
Reorganized under the laws of Delaware as HealthStar Corp. 11/16/1998
Each share new Common $0.001 par exchanged for (0.5) share Common $0.001 par
HealthStar Corp. name changed to BlueStone Holding Corp. 09/05/2001
(See BlueStone Holding Corp.)

CHAMPION GOLD, INC.
Reorganized as Champion Mines Co. 00/00/1935
Details not available

CHAMPION GOLD & SILVER INC (ID)
Recapitalized as Western Continental, Inc. 06/17/1993
Each share Common 10¢ par exchanged for (0.05) share Common 10¢ par
(See Western Continental, Inc.)

CHAMPION GOLD RES INC (ON)
Recapitalized as Champion Natural Health.com Inc. 07/21/2000
Each share Common no par exchanged for (0.008) share Subordinate no par
Each share Subordinate no par exchanged for (0.2) share Subordinate no par
Each share Multiple no par exchanged for (0.2) share Multiple no par
Champion Natural Health.com Inc. reorganized as Champion Minerals Inc. 10/13/2006 which name changed to Champion Iron Mines Ltd. 08/30/2012 which merged into Champion Iron Ltd. 03/31/2014

CHAMPION HEALTHCARE CORP (DE)
Merged into Paracelsus Healthcare Corp. 08/16/1996
Each share Common 1¢ par exchanged for (1) share Common no par
(See Paracelsus Healthcare Corp.)

CHAMPION HOME BLDRS CO (MI)
Common $1 par split (2) for (1) by issuance of (1) additional share 07/05/1968
Common $1 par split (2) for (1) by issuance of (1) additional share 03/26/1969
Common $1 par split (2) for (1) by issuance of (1) additional share 05/28/1971
Common $1 par split (5) for (1) by issuance of (4) additional shares 07/28/1972
Reorganized as Champion Enterprises, Inc. 06/27/1987
Each share Common $1 par exchanged for (0.2) share Common $1 par
(See Champion Enterprises, Inc.)

CHAMPION INC (DE)
Charter cancelled and declared inoperative and void for non-payment of taxes 03/01/1983

CHAMPION INDUSTRIES, INC. (DE)
No longer in existence having become inoperative and void for non-payment of taxes 04/01/1966

CHAMPION INDUSTRIES, INC. (MO)
Liquidation completed
Each share 5% Preferred $50 par exchanged for first and final distribution of $50 cash 05/23/1958
Each share Common $1 par exchanged for initial distribution of $2 cash 05/23/1958
Each share Common $1 par received second distribution of $0.50 cash 07/25/1958
Each share Common $1 par received third and final distribution of $0.21 cash 09/14/1959

CHAMPION INTL CORP (NY)
$5.50 Preferred no par called for redemption 04/01/1977
$1.20 Conv. Preference $1 par called for redemption 04/14/1986
$4.60 Conv. Preference $1 par called for redemption 05/27/1986
Preferred Stock Purchase Rights declared for Common stockholders of record 04/01/1986 were redeemed at $0.05 per right 02/20/1991 for holders of record 02/01/1991
Merged into International Paper Co. 06/20/2000
Each share Common 50¢ par exchanged for (0.7073) share Common $1 par and $50 cash

CHAMPION IRON MINES LTD (ON)
Merged into Champion Iron Ltd. 03/31/2014
Each share Common no par exchanged for (0.7333333) share Ordinary

CHAMPION LIFE INSURANCE CO. (IL)
Name changed to American Security Life Insurance Co. (IL) 07/08/1966
(See American Security Life Insurance Co. (IL))

CHAMPION MINERALS INC (ON)
Name changed to Champion Iron Mines Ltd. 08/30/2012
Champion Iron Mines Ltd. merged into Champion Iron Ltd. 03/31/2014

CHAMPION MINES CO. (CO)
Each share Common 1¢ par exchanged for (0.1) share Common 10¢ par 01/15/1956
Name changed to Trans World Corp. (CO) 02/20/1968
Trans World Corp. (CO) recapitalized as International Recreation & Sports, Inc. 11/08/1968
(See International Recreation & Sports, Inc.)

CHAMPION MOTORS CO. (MN)
Name changed to Airmotive Machining & Engineering Corp. 03/26/1958
Airmotive Machining & Engineering Corp. name changed to Airmac Corp. 02/15/1967 which merged into Apache Corp. 03/03/1969

CHAMPION MUT FD CDA LTD (CANADA)
Name changed to Prevest Mutual Fund Ltd. 06/05/1972
(See Prevest Mutual Fund Ltd.)

CHAMPION NAT HEALTH COM INC (ON)
Reorganized as Champion Minerals Inc. 10/13/2006
Each Subordinate Share no par exchanged for (0.16666666) share Common no par
Each Multiple Share no par exchanged for (0.16666666) share Common no par
Champion Minerals Inc. name changed to Champion Iron Mines Ltd. 08/30/2012 which merged into Champion Iron Ltd. 03/31/2014

CHAMPION OIL & GAS CORP (BC)
Recapitalized as Winkelmann Countermeasures Inc. 10/25/1985
Each share Common no par exchanged for (0.25) share Common no par
(See Winkelmann Countermeasures Inc.)

CHAMPION OIL & MNG CO (NV)
Charter revoked for failure to file reports and pay fees 07/01/1992

CHAMPION PAPER & FIBER CO (OH)
Common no par split (2) for (1) by issuance of (1) additional share 07/31/1956
Stock Dividends - 100% 10/09/1946; 100% 08/01/1951
Name changed to Champion Papers Inc. 07/31/1961
Champion Papers Inc. merged into U.S. Plywood-Champion Papers Inc. 02/28/1967 which name changed to Champion International Corp. 05/12/1972 which merged into International Paper Co. 06/20/2000

CHAMPION PAPERS INC. (OH)
Merged into U.S. Plywood-Champion Papers Inc. 02/28/1967
Each share $4.50 Preferred no par exchanged for (1) share $5.50 Preferred no par
Each share Common no par exchanged for (1) share $1.20 Conv. Preference $1 par and (0.4) share Common $1 par
U.S. Plywood-Champion Papers Inc. name changed to Champion International Corp. 05/12/1972 which merged into International Paper Co. 06/20/2000

CHAMPION PARTS INC (IL)
Name changed 05/27/1988
Common 10¢ par split (4) for (3) by issuance of (0.33333333) additional share 12/23/1969
Common 10¢ par split (5) for (4) by issuance of (0.25) additional share 08/22/1972
Common 10¢ par split (5) for (4) by issuance of (0.25) additional share 09/18/1986
Stock Dividends - 20% 06/20/1967; 25% 12/21/1970
Name changed from Champion Parts Rebuilders, Inc. to Champion Parts, Inc. 05/27/1988
Chapter 11 bankruptcy proceedings converted to Chapter 7 on 01/25/2008
Stockholders' equity unlikely

CHAMPION PNEUMATIC MACHINERY CO., INC. (NY)
Merged into American Visionic, Inc. 08/16/1963
Each share Common $1 par exchanged for $2 cash

CHAMPION PRODS INC (NY)
Common $1 par split (3) for (2) by issuance of (0.5) additional share 05/28/1980
Common $1 par split (2) for (1) by issuance of (1) additional share 04/24/1987
Merged into Sara Lee Corp. 04/28/1989
Each share Common $1 par exchanged for $77 cash

CHAMPION RD MACHY LTD (CANADA)
Merged into Volvo AB 03/26/1997
Each share Common no par exchanged for $15 cash

CHAMPION RES INC (BC)
Each share old Common no par exchanged for (0.1) share new Common no par 01/25/2002
Reorganized under the laws of Canada as Red Back Mining Inc. 04/27/2004
Each share Common no par exchanged for (1/3) share Common no par
Red Back Mining Inc. merged into Kinross Gold Corp. 09/22/2010

CHAMPION SHOE MACHINERY CO. (MO)
Reorganized 00/00/1941
Each share 7% Preferred $100 par exchanged for (0.4) share 5% Preferred $50 par and (10) shares Common $1 par
Each share 5% Jr. Preferred exchanged for (15) shares Common $1 par
Each share old Common exchanged for (0.1) share new Common $1 par
Name changed to Champion Industries, Inc. (MO) 00/00/1954
(See Champion Industries, Inc. (MO))

CHAMPION SILVER MNG CO (MT)
Name changed to Western Geothermal & Power Corp. 09/01/1974
(See Western Geothermal & Power Corp.)

CHAMPION SPARK PLUG CO (DE)
Each share Common $10 par exchanged for (6) shares Common $1.66666666 par 08/20/1958
Common $1.66666666 par changed to $0.83333333 par and (1) additional share issued 05/14/1968
Common $0.83333333 par changed to 30¢ par and (2) additional shares issued 05/14/1973
Merged into Cooper Industries, Inc. 07/24/1989
Each share Common 30¢ par exchanged for $21 cash

CHAMPION TECHNOLOGY HLDGS LTD (HONG KONG)
Old Sponsored ADR's for Ordinary split (2) for (1) by issuance of (1) additional ADR payable 07/06/1998 to holders of record 04/16/1998
Each old Sponsored ADR for Ordinary exchanged for (0.04) new Sponsored ADR for Ordinary 06/12/2002
Stock Dividend - 100% payable 12/31/2001 to holders of record 11/30/2001 Ex date - 11/30/2001
ADR agreement terminated 12/31/2003
Each new Sponsored ADR for Ordinary exchanged for $0.71031917 cash
Each new Sponsored ADR for Ordinary received distribution of $0.060548 cash payable 08/13/2004 to holders of record 01/26/2004
ADR agreement terminated 01/24/2018
No ADR's remain outstanding

CHAMPION VENTURES INC. (CO)
Reincorporated under the laws of Nevada 12/31/1970
Champion Ventures, Inc. (NV) name changed to Internet Golf Association, Inc. 05/18/1999 which name changed to American Oriental Bioengineering Inc. 01/03/2002

CHAMPION VENTURES INC (NV)
Name changed to Internet Golf Association, Inc. 05/18/1999
Internet Golf Association, Inc. name changed to American Oriental Bioengineering Inc. 01/03/2002

CHAMPIONLYTE HLDGS INC (FL)
Name changed 03/26/2003
Name changed from ChampionLyte Products, Inc. to Championlyte Holdings, Inc. 03/26/2003
Name changed to Cargo Connection Logistics Holding, Inc. 05/26/2005

CHAMPIONS BIOTECHNOLOGY INC (DE)
Name changed 02/02/2007
Each share Common $0.00001 par exchanged for (0.01) share Common $0.001 par 11/01/2001
Each share 12% Conv. Preferred Ser. A $10 par exchanged for (15) shares Common $0.001 par 11/11/2003
Name changed from Champions Sports Inc. to Champions Biotechnology, Inc. 02/02/2007
Name changed to Champions Oncology, Inc. 04/20/2011

CHAMPIONSHIP AUTO RACING TEAMS INC (DE)
Liquidation completed
Each share Common 1¢ par exchanged for initial distribution of $0.29 cash 12/29/2005
Each share Common 1¢ par received second and final distribution of $0.03 cash payable 02/18/2009 to holders of record 12/29/2005

CHAMPLAIN FOREST PRODUCTS LTD. (ON)
Declared bankrupt 00/00/1975
No stockholders' equity

CHAMPLAIN LTEE. LA MINE D'OR
Name changed to Wasa Lake Gold Mines Ltd. 00/00/1944
Wasa Lake Gold Mines Ltd. recapitalized as Lake Wasa Mining Corp. 01/00/1947 which recapitalized as Wasamac Mines Ltd. 10/07/1960 which was acquired by Wright-Hargreaves Mines, Ltd. 01/03/1969 which merged into LAC Minerals Ltd. (New) 07/29/1985 which was acquired by American Barrick Resources Corp. 10/17/1994 which name changed to Barrick Gold Corp. 01/18/1995

CHAMPLAIN NATL CORP (NY)
Merged into International Industries, Inc. (DE) 03/27/1969
Each share Capital Stock no par exchanged for (1) share $1.70 Conv. Preference Ser. A $1 par
International Industries, Inc. (DE) merged into IHOP Corp. 09/17/1976
(See IHOP Corp.)

CHAMPLAIN RES INC (AB)
Recapitalized as Beacon Resources Inc. 04/20/2012
Each share Common no par exchanged for (0.1) share Common no par

CHAMPLIN OIL & REFINING CO. (DE)
Merged into Celanese Corp. of America 10/29/1964
Each share Preferred no par exchanged for (1) share Conv. Preferred no par
Each share Common $1 par exchanged for (0.66666666) share Common no par
Celanese Corp. of America name changed to Celanese Corp. 04/13/1966
(See Celanese Corp.)

CHAMPPS ENTMT INC (DE)
Merged into F&H Acquisition Corp. 10/22/2007
Each share Common 1¢ par exchanged for $5.60 cash

CHAMPPS ENTMT INC (MN)
Merged into DAKA International, Inc. 02/21/1996
Each share Common 1¢ par exchanged for (0.43) share new Common 1¢ par
(See DAKA International, Inc.)

CHANARAL RES INC (FL)
Name changed to Alkane, Inc. 04/03/2009

CHANCE A B CO (MO)
Common $5 par changed to $2.50 par and (1) additional share issued 12/31/1964
Common $2.50 par changed to $1.25 par and (1) additional share issued 12/31/1973
Merged into Emerson Electric Co. 05/15/1975
Each share Common $1.25 par exchanged for (0.74) share Common $1 par

CHANCE MNG & EXPL LTD (ON)
Name changed to East Indies Mining Corp. 06/20/1996
East Indies Mining Corp. merged into Falcon Well Services, Ltd. 02/13/1998
(See Falcon Well Services, Ltd.)

CHANCE VOUGHT AIRCRAFT, INC. (DE)
Name changed to Chance Vought Corp. 12/31/1960
(See Chance Vought Corp.)

CHANCE VOUGHT CORP. (DE)
Completely liquidated 08/16/1961
Each share Common $1 par exchanged for first and final distribution of $43.50 principal amount of 5.5% Conv. Debentures due 09/01/1976, (0.2) $30 Stock Purchase Warrant and (0.2) $40 Stock Purchase Warrant of Ling-Temco-Vought, Inc.
Note: Holders will receive cash only after 02/29/1968

CHANCELLOR BROADCASTING CO (DE)
Merged into Chancellor Media Corp. 09/05/1997
Each share Class A Common 1¢ par exchanged for (0.9091) share Common 1¢ par
Chancellor Media Corp. name changed to AMFM, Inc. 07/13/1999 which merged into Clear Channel Communications, Inc. 08/30/2000
(See Clear Channel Communications, Inc.)

CHANCELLOR CORP (MA)
Proclaimed dissolved for failure to file reports and pay taxes 05/31/2007

CHANCELLOR CORP (NV)
Name changed to Topaz Group, Inc. 12/02/1998
(See Topaz Group, Inc.)

CHANCELLOR ENERGY RES INC (ON)
Merged into HCO Energy Ltd. 04/02/1996
Each share Common no par exchanged for (0.32) share Common no par
HCO Energy Ltd. merged into Pinnacle Resources Ltd. (New) 10/20/1997 which merged into Renaissance Energy Ltd. 07/16/1998 which merged into Husky Energy Inc. 08/25/2000

CHANCELLOR ENTERPRISES HLDGS INC (ON)
Merged into Dynamic Fuel Systems Inc. 01/01/2004
Each share Common no par exchanged for (1) share Common no par
Dynamic Fuel Systems Inc. name changed to DynaCERT Inc. 12/31/2012

CHANCELLOR FDS INC (MD)
Dissolved 00/00/1997
Details not available

CHANCELLOR GROUP LTD (CANADA)
Declared bankruptcy 06/15/1992
Details not available

CHANCELLOR HALL, INC.
Bankrupt 00/00/1943
Stockholders' equity unlikely

CHANCELLOR HIGH YIELD FD INC (MD)
Name changed to Prudential-Bache High Yield Fund, Inc. 04/22/1983
Prudential-Bache High Yield Fund, Inc. name changed to Prudential High Yield Fund, Inc. 06/03/1992 which name changed to Dryden High Yield Fund, Inc. 09/15/2003

CHANCELLOR MEDIA CORP (DE)
Common 1¢ par split (2) for (1) by issuance of (1) additional share payable 01/12/1998 to holders of record 12/29/1997
Name changed to AMFM, Inc. 07/13/1999
AMFM, Inc. merged into Clear Channel Communications, Inc. 08/30/2000
(See Clear Channel Communications, Inc.)

CHANCELLOR NEW DECADE GROWTH FD INC (MD)
Common 1¢ par split (3) for (2) by issuance of (0.5) additional share 08/05/1983
Name changed to Prudential-Bache New Decade Growth Fund, Inc. 01/19/1984
Prudential-Bache New Decade Growth Fund, Inc. name changed to Prudential-Bache Growth Opportunity Fund, Inc. 06/00/1985 which name changed to Prudential Growth Opportunity Fund Inc. 03/15/1991 which name changed to Prudential Small Companies Fund, Inc. 05/30/1996 which name changed to Jennison Small Company Fund, Inc. 11/25/2003

CHANCERY RES INC (NV)
Each share old Common $0.00001 par exchanged for (25) shares new Common $0.00001 par 02/04/2008

Name changed to AirTrona International, Inc. 11/26/2013

CHANCO MED & ELECTR INDS (CA)
Capital Stock $1 par changed to 80¢ par and (0.25) additional share issued 09/23/1969
Capital Stock 80¢ par changed to 64¢ par and (0.25) additional share issued 04/22/1970
Capital Stock 64¢ par changed to $0.576 par and (0.1) additional share issued 08/10/1970
Name changed to Chanco Medical Industries 09/14/1970
Chanco Medical Industries merged into American Medical International, Inc. (CA) 08/31/1972 which reincorporated in Delaware 08/31/1976 which merged into American Medical Holdings, Inc. 01/12/1990 which merged into National Medical Enterprises, Inc. 02/28/1995 which name changed to Tenet Healthcare Corp. 06/23/1995

CHANCO MED INDS (CA)
Common $0.576 par changed to no par and (0.5) additional share issued 01/11/1971
Merged into American Medical International, Inc. (CA) 08/31/1972
Each share Common no par exchanged for (0.25) share Common no par
American Medical International, Inc. (CA) reincorporated in Delaware 08/31/1976 which merged into American Medical Holdings, Inc. 04/12/1990 which merged into National Medical Enterprises, Inc. 02/28/1995 which name changed to Tenet Healthcare Corp. 06/23/1995

CHANDALAR RES LTD (BC)
Merged into International Park West Financial Corp. 06/20/1978
Each share Capital Stock no par exchanged for (1) share Common no par
(See International Park West Financial Corp.)

CHANDEL ENTERPRISES INC (CA)
Common $1 par changed to 25¢ par and (3) additional shares issued 10/06/1975
Charter cancelled for failure to file reports and pay fees 11/02/1987

CHANDELEUR BAY PRODTN LTD (BC)
Recapitalized as Golden Raven Resources Ltd. 12/11/1999
Each share Common no par exchanged for (0.14285714) share Common no par

CHANDELIER BUSINESS SVCS INC (NV)
Name changed to Internet Marketing, Inc. 03/00/1999
(See Internet Marketing, Inc.)

CHANDLER-CLEVELAND MOTORS CORP.
Acquired by Hupp Motor Car Corp. 00/00/1929
Details not available

CHANDLER FD INC (DE)
In process of liquidation
Each share Common $1 par exchanged for initial distribution of $2.10 cash 01/24/1984
Note: Details on subsequent distributions, if any, are not available

CHANDLER INS LTD (CAYMAN ISLANDS)
Stock Dividend - 25% 06/08/1989
Each (1,000,000) shares old Common $1.67 par exchanged for (1) share new Common $1.67 par 03/28/2001
Note: In effect holders received $10 cash per share and public interest was eliminated

CHANDLER LEASING CORP. (MA)
Common $1 par split (2) for (1) by issuance of (1) additional share 03/08/1967
Merged into PepsiCo, Inc. (DE) 06/28/1968
Each share Common $1 par exchanged for (0.58824) share Capital Stock $0.16666666 par
PepsiCo, Inc. (DE) reincorporated in North Carolina 12/04/1986

CHANDLER OIL & GAS CO (UT)
Recapitalized as Pana Petrol Corp. 12/30/1985
Each share Common $0.005 par exchanged for (0.1) share Common $0.005 par

CHANDLER-WASHINGTON, INC. (DE)
Liquidation completed 09/12/1952
Details not available

CHANEY MANUFACTURING CO., INC. (OH)
Name changed to Thermometer Corp.of America 00/00/1954
Thermometer Corp. of America name changed to Springfield Greene Industries, Inc. 09/25/1959 which name changed to Mid-Continent Manufacturing Co. (OH) 08/18/1964 which reincorporated in Delaware as Mid-Con Inc. 10/31/1968 which merged into A-T-O Inc. 10/29/1969 which name changed to Figgie International Inc. (OH) 06/01/1981 which reorganized in Delaware as Figgie International Holdings Inc. 07/18/1983 which name changed to Figgie International Inc. 12/31/1986 which name changed to Scott Technologies, Inc. 05/20/1998 which merged into Tyco International Ltd. (Bermuda) 05/03/2001 which reincorporated in Switzerland 03/17/2009 which merged into Johnson Controls International PLC 09/06/2016

CHANGE TECHNOLOGY PARTNERS INC (DE)
Name changed to Neurologix, Inc. and Common 1¢ par changed to $0.001 par 02/12/2004
(See Neurologix, Inc.)

CHANGEPOINT CORP (ON)
Acquired by Compuware Corp. 05/04/2004
Details not available

CHANIN DEV CORP (NV)
Name changed to Regency Development Corp. 02/05/1974
(See Regency Development Corp.)

CHANNEL AMER BROADCASTING INC (FL)
Recapitalized as DTG Industries, Inc. 03/22/2004
Each share Common no par exchanged for (0.00111111) share Common no par
DTG Industries, Inc. name changed to DTG Multimedia, Inc. (FL) 06/04/2004 which reorganized in Nevada as Amazing Technologies Corp. 12/23/2004 which name changed to Mvive, Inc. 08/24/2007
(See Mvive Inc.)

CHANNEL AMER TELEVISION NETWORK INC (DE)
Name changed 04/25/1994
Name changed from Channel America LPTV Holdings, Inc. to Channel America Television Network, Inc. 04/25/1994
Each share old Common 1¢ par exchanged for (0.02) share new Common 1¢ par 05/09/1994
SEC revoked common stock registration 07/26/2010

CHANNEL COPPER MINES LTD (BC)
Dissolved 10/07/1983
Details not available

CHANNEL COS INC (DE)
Common $1 par split (3) for (2) by

CHANNEL GOLD MINES LTD. (DE)
issuance of (0.5) additional share 04/19/1972
Merged into Grace (W.R.) & Co. 02/25/1977
Each share Common $1 par exchanged for $17 cash

CHANNEL GOLD MINES LTD. (DE)
Charter cancelled and declared inoperative and void for non-payment of taxes 04/01/1938

CHANNEL GOLD RES CORP (BC)
Recapitalized as St. Elias Exploration Corp. 04/17/1979
Each share Common no par exchanged for (0.2) share Common no par
St. Elias Exploration Corp. name changed to Bigstone Minerals Ltd. 01/19/1984 which recapitalized as Adamas Resources Corp. 08/30/1993 which recapitalized as Britannica Resources Corp. 08/27/2002 which name changed to Trinity Valley Energy Corp. 10/08/2013 which recapitalized as Smooth Rock Ventures Corp. 11/15/2017

CHANNEL INDS LTD (DE)
Charter cancelled and declared inoperative and void for non-payment of taxes 03/01/1988

CHANNEL IS NATL BK (OXNARD, CA)
Merged into Americorp 12/31/1998
Each share Common $10 par exchanged for (0.7282) share Common $1 par
(See Americorp)

CHANNEL ONE, INC. (NV)
Name changed to Grease 'N Go International, Inc. 06/12/1989
Grease 'N Go International, Inc. name changed to Autocare Corp. 10/15/1991
(See Autocare Corp.)

CHANNEL I CDA INC (ON)
Recapitalized as Zaurak Capital Corp. 12/01/1999
Each share Common no par exchanged for (0.083333331) share Common no par
(See Zaurak Capital Corp.)

CHANNEL I INC (NV)
Name changed 03/02/1995
Name changed from Channel I Ltd. to Channel I Inc. 03/02/1995
Name changed to WaveRider Communications Inc. 05/27/1997
WaveRider Communications Inc. merged into Wave Wireless Corp. 03/30/2006
(See Wave Wireless Corp.)

CHANNEL RES LTD NEW (BC)
Merged into West African Resources Ltd. 01/17/2014
Each share Common exchanged for (0.25) share Ordinary and 0.125) Ordinary Stock Purchase Warrant expiring 12/17/2017
Note: Unexchanged certificates will be cancelled and become without value 01/17/2020

CHANNEL RES LTD OLD (BC)
Under plan of merger name changed to Channel Resources Ltd. (New) 10/31/1989
Channel Resources Ltd. (New) merged into West African Resources Ltd. 01/17/2014

CHANNELINX COM INC
Plan of reorganization under Chapter 11 Federal Bankruptcy Code effective 07/31/2003
No stockholders' equity

CHANNING BD FD INC (MD)
Common $10 par changed to $1 par 11/11/1971
Name changed to American General Capital Bond Fund, Inc. 11/21/1975
American General Capital Bond Fund, Inc. name changed to American Capital Corporate Bond Fund, Inc. (MD) 09/09/1983 which reincorporated in Delaware as Van Kampen American Capital Corporate Bond Fund 08/05/1995 which name changed to Van Kampen Corporate Bond Fund 07/14/1998

CHANNING CORP. (DE)
Common $5 par changed to $1.50 par and (1) additional share issued 06/30/1959
Merged into Channing Financial Corp. 12/31/1963
Each share Common $1.50 par exchanged for (1.7) share Common $1 par
Channing Financial Corp. acquired by American General Insurance Co. 03/28/1969 which reorganized as American General Corp. 07/01/1980 which merged into American International Group, Inc. 08/29/2001

CHANNING FINL CORP (DE)
Acquired by American General Insurance Co. 03/28/1969
Each share 80¢ Conv. Preferred $1 par exchanged for (0.12) share $1.80 Conv. Preferred $1.50 par and (0.96) share Common $1.50 par
Each share Common $1 par exchanged for (0.1) share $1.80 Conv. Preferred $1.50 par and (0.8) share Common $1.50 par
American General Insurance Co. reorganized as American General Corp. 07/01/1980 which merged into American International Group, Inc. 08/29/2001

CHANNING INCOME FD INC (MD)
Merged into American General Shares, Inc. 09/02/1975
Each share Common 1¢ par exchanged for (1) share Income Fund 1¢ par
American General Shares, Inc. merged into American General Enterprise Fund, Inc. 08/31/1979 which name changed to American Capital Enterprise Fund, Inc. (MD) 09/09/1983 which reincorporated in Delaware as Van Kampen American Capital Enterprise Fund 08/03/1995 which name changed to Van Kampen Enterprise Fund 08/31/1998

CHANNING INTERNATIONAL GROWTH FUND, INC. (MD)
Acquired by Channing Shares, Inc. (DE) 08/30/1966
Each share Common 1¢ par exchanged for (0.52937) Growth Fund Share 1¢ par
Channing Shares, Inc. (DE) reincorporated in Maryland 10/09/1973 which merged into American General Shares, Inc. 09/02/1975 which merged into American General Enterprise Fund, Inc. 08/31/1979 which name changed to American Capital Enterprise Fund, Inc. (MD) 09/09/1983 which reincorporated in Delaware as Van Kampen American Capital Enterprise Fund 08/03/1995 which name changed to Van Kampen Enterprise Fund 08/31/1998

CHANNING INVESTMENT FUNDS, INC. (DE)
Name changed to Channing Securities, Inc. (DE) 04/01/1965
Channing Securities, Inc. (DE) reincorporated in Maryland 10/09/1973 which merged into American General Shares, Inc. 09/02/1975 which merged into American General Enterprise Fund, Inc. 08/31/1979 which name changed to American Capital Enterprise Fund, Inc. (MD) 09/09/1983 which reincorporated in Delaware as Van Kampen American Capital Enterprise Fund 08/03/1995 which name changed to Van Kampen Enterprise Fund 08/31/1998

CHANNING SECS INC (MD)
Reincorporated 10/09/1973
State of incorporation changed from (DE) to (MD) 10/09/1973
Common Stock Fund Shares 1¢ par reclassified as American Fund Shares 1¢ par 12/31/1973
Merged into American General Shares, Inc. 09/02/1975
Each American Fund Share 1¢ par exchanged for (0.1842509606) share Income Fund 1¢ par
Each Special Fund Share 1¢ par exchanged for (0.3761179060) share Capital Growth Fund 1¢ par
American General Shares, Inc. merged into American General Enterprise Fund, Inc. 08/31/1979 which name changed to American Capital Enterprise Fund, Inc. (MD) 09/09/1983 which reincorporated in Delaware as Van Kampen American Capital Enterprise Fund 08/03/1995 which name changed to Van Kampen Enterprise Fund 08/31/1998

CHANNING SHS INC (MD)
Reincorporated 10/09/1973
Growth Fund Shares 1¢ par split (2) for (1) by issuance of (1) additional share 08/16/1968
State of incorporation changed from (DE) to (MD) 10/09/1973
Merged into American General Shares, Inc. 09/02/1975
Each Balanced Fund Share 1¢ par exchanged for (1.423575580) shares Income Fund 1¢ par
Each Growth Fund Share 1¢ par exchanged for (1) share Capital Growth Fund 1¢ par
American General Shares, Inc. merged into American General Enterprise Fund, Inc. 08/31/1979 which name changed to American Capital Enterprise Fund, Inc. (MD) 09/09/1983 which reincorporated in Delaware as Van Kampen American Capital Enterprise Fund 08/03/1995 which name changed to Van Kampen Enterprise Fund 08/31/1998

CHANNING VENTURE FD INC (MD)
Reincorporated 09/19/1973
State of incorporation changed from (DE) to (MD) 09/19/1973
Name changed to American General Venture Fund, Inc. 11/21/1975
American General Venture Fund, Inc. name changed to American Capital Venture Fund, Inc. 09/09/1983 which name changed to American Capital Emerging Growth Fund, Inc. 07/24/1990
(See American Capital Emerging Growth Fund, Inc.)

CHANNON (H.) CO.
Acquired by Hibbard, Spencer, Bartlett & Co. 00/00/1939
Details not available

CHANSLOR & LYON-PALACE CORP.
Name changed to Channing Corp. 00/00/1952
Channing Corp. merged into Channing Financial Corp. 12/31/1963 which was acquired by American General Insurance Co. 03/28/1969 which reorganized as American General Corp. 07/01/1980 which merged into American International Group, Inc. 08/29/2001

CHANTAL PHARMACEUTICAL CORP (NV)
Reincorporated under the laws of Delaware 01/16/1985
(See Chantal Pharmaceutical Corp. (DE))

CHANTAL PHARMACEUTICAL CORP NEW (DE)
Each share old Common 1¢ par exchanged for (0.5) share new Common 1¢ par 04/30/1992
Chapter 7 bankruptcy case closed 12/26/2006
No stockholders' equity

CHANTAL SKIN CARE CORP (DE)
Recapitalized as Utix Group, Inc. 11/21/2003
Each share Common 1¢ par exchanged for (0.05) share Common $0.001 par
(See Utix Group, Inc.)

CHAOLEI MARKETING & FIN CO (FL)
Administratively dissolved 09/23/2011

CHAOS GROUP INC (NV)
Name changed to Luminart Corp. (NV) 04/23/1998
Luminart Corp. (NV) reincorporated in Wyoming 05/27/2009
(See Luminart Corp.)

CHAP MERCANTILE INC (AB)
Reorganized under the laws of Ontario as Silver Wheaton Corp. 12/21/2004
Each share Common no par exchanged for (0.2) share Common no par
Silver Wheaton Corp. name changed to Wheaton Precious Metals Corp. 05/16/2017

CHAPARRAL GOLD CORP (BC)
Acquired by Waterton Precious Metals Fund II Cayman, L.P. 02/20/2015
Each share Common no par exchanged for $0.61 cash
Note: Unexchanged certificates will be cancelled and become without value 02/19/2021

CHAPARRAL RES INC (DE)
Reincorporated 04/21/1999
Each share Common 1¢ par exchanged for (0.1) share Common 10¢ par 10/02/1978
Common 10¢ par split (4) for (1) by issuance of (3) additional shares 01/26/1981
Common 10¢ par split (2) for (1) by issuance of (1) additional share 05/22/1981
State of incorporation changed from (CO) to (DE) 04/21/1999
Each share Common 10¢ par exchanged for (0.01666666) share Common $0.0001 par
Merged into LUKOIL Overseas Holding 09/29/2006
Each share Common $0.0001 par exchanged for $5.80 cash

CHAPARRAL STL CO NEW (DE)
Common 1¢ par split (2) for (1) by issuance of (1) additional share payable 09/01/2006 to holders of record 08/15/2006 Ex date - 09/05/2006
Merged into Gerdau Ameristeel Corp. 09/14/2007
Each share Common 1¢ par exchanged for $86 cash

CHAPARRAL STL CO OLD (DE)
Merged into Texas Industries, Inc. 12/31/1997
Each share Common 10¢ par exchanged for $15.50 cash

CHAPEAU INC (UT)
Each share old Common $0.001 par exchanged for (0.06666666) share new Common $0.001 par 06/12/1998
Chapter 11 bankruptcy proceedings converted to Chapter 7 on 12/02/2008
Stockholders' equity unlikely

CHAPEL MTN INDS INC (TX)
Charter forfeited for failure to pay taxes 01/21/1985

CHAPEL RES INC (BC)
Name changed to Broadway Beverages Ltd. 09/03/1987
(See Broadway Beverages Ltd.)

CHAPIN-SACKS, INC.
Dissolution approved 00/00/1935
Details not available

CHAPLEAU RES LTD (BC)
Merged into Magellan Minerals Ltd. 09/01/2009
Each share Common no par exchanged for (0.267) share Common no par
Magellan Minerals Ltd. merged into Anfield Nickel Corp. 05/06/2016 which name changed to Anfield Gold Corp. 05/11/2016 which merged into Equinox Gold Corp. 12/22/2017

CHAPMAN CAP MGMT HLDGS INC (DC)
Merged into eChapman.com, Inc. 06/20/2000
Each share Common $0.001 par exchanged for (2.23363) shares Common $0.001 par
eChapman.com, Inc. name changed to eChapman, Inc. 01/22/2002
(See eChapman, Inc.)

CHAPMAN ENERGY INC (DE)
Each share $1.20 Conv. Preferred $1 par exchanged for (3) shares Common $0.001 par 06/25/1987
Each share Common $0.001 par exchanged for (0.05) share Common 2¢ par 05/30/1989
Name changed to Coda Energy, Inc. 10/10/1989
(See Coda Energy, Inc.)

CHAPMAN HLDGS INC (MD)
Merged into eChapman.com, Inc. 06/20/2000
Each share Common $0.001 par exchanged for (1.93295) shares Common $0.001 par
eChapman.com, Inc. name changed to eChapman, Inc. 01/22/2002
(See eChapman, Inc.)

CHAPMAN VALVE MANUFACTURING CO. (MA)
Each share Common $100 par exchanged for (4) shares Common $25 par 00/00/1931
Stock Dividends - 25% 11/10/1948; 20% 06/01/1953
Preferred $100 par completely liquidated 10/01/1959
Name changed to C.V.M. Corp. 09/30/1959
(See C.V.M. Corp.)

CHAPPARAL MINES LTD (BC)
Name changed to Chapparal Petroleums Ltd. 09/27/1973
Chapparal Petroleums Ltd. recapitalized as Richdale Petroleums Ltd. 07/15/1974
(See Richdale Petroleums Ltd.)

CHAPPARAL PETROLEUMS LTD. (BC)
Recapitalized as Richdale Petroleums Ltd. 07/15/1974
Each share Capital Stock no par exchanged for (0.2) share Capital Stock no par
(See Richdale Petroleums Ltd.)

CHAPPELL OIL CO. (WY)
Completely liquidated 01/02/1964
Details not available

CHAPPELL SECS CORP (IN)
Ceased operations 00/00/1967
Stockholders' equity unlikely

CHAPTERS INC (ON)
Name changed to Indigo Books & Music Inc. 08/14/2001

CHAPTERS ONLINE INC (NB)
Acquired by Indigo Books & Music Inc. 11/13/2001
Each share Common no par exchanged for (0.14005602) share Common no par

CHAPUT COPPER MINES, LTD. (ON)
Charter revoked for failure to file reports and pay taxes 00/00/1957

CHAPUT HUGHES MINES LTD.
Completely liquidated 00/00/1929
Each share Capital Stock $1 par received first and final distribution of (0.1) share Kirkland Lake Gold Mining Capital Stock $1 par
Kirkland Lake Gold Mining Co. Ltd. recapitalized as Kirkland Minerals Corp. Ltd. 05/03/1956 which was acquired by Groundstar Resources Ltd. (BC) 08/31/1973 which reincorporated in Alberta 10/28/2005

CHARAN INDS INC (DE)
Acquired by private investors 09/21/1984
Each share Common 50¢ par exchanged for $5 cash

CHARAN INDS INC N Y (NJ)
Merged into CHV Industries, Inc. 08/04/1977
Each share Common 40¢ par exchanged for $4.50 cash

CHARCOAL IRON CO. OF AMERICA
Succeeded by Newberry Lumber & Chemical Co. 00/00/1929
Details not available

CHARCOALS HLDG CORP (FL)
Administratively dissolved 11/08/1994

CHARDAN CHINA ACQUISITION CORP (DE)
Reincorporated under the laws of British Virgin Islands as Origin Agritech Ltd. 11/09/2005

CHARDAN NORTH CHINA ACQUISITION CORP (DE)
Reincorporated under the laws of British Virgin Islands as HLS Systems International, Ltd. 09/24/2007
HLS Systems International, Ltd. name changed to Hollysys Automation Technologies, Ltd. 07/17/2009

CHARDAN SOUTH CHINA ACQUISITION CORP (DE)
Reincorporated under the laws of British Virgin Islands as A-Power Energy Generation Systems, Ltd. 01/18/2009
(See A-Power Energy Generation Systems, Ltd.)

CHARDAN 2008 CHINA ACQUISITION CORP (BRITISH VIRGIN ISLANDS)
Name changed to DJSP Enterprises, Inc. 01/19/2010

CHARDON SVGS BK CO (CHARDON, OH)
Stock Dividend - 20% 09/08/1970
Acquired by Banc One Corp. (DE) 12/22/1982
Each share Common $10 par exchanged for (3.40898) shares Common no par
Escrowed shares distributed 06/00/1985
Exact Rate not available
Banc One Corp. (DE) reincorporated in Ohio 05/01/1989 which merged into Bank One Corp. 10/02/1998 which merged into J.P. Morgan Chase & Co. 12/31/2000 which name changed to JPMorgan Chase & Co. 07/20/2004

CHARG IT FLA INC (FL)
Liquidation completed
Each share Common 25¢ par stamped to indicate initial distribution of $5.10 cash 06/05/1974
Each share Stamped Common 25¢ par exchanged for second and final distribution of $0.07 cash 02/07/1977

CHARG-IT OF BALTIMORE, INC. (MD)
Stock Dividend - 10% 05/01/1964
Name changed to C.I.B., Inc. 05/01/1967
(See C.I.B., Inc.)

CHARGER ENERGY CORP (AB)
Acquired by Spyglass Resources Corp. 04/04/2013
Each share Class A no par exchanged for (0.18) share Common no par

CHARGER ENERGY INC (AB)
Name changed 08/23/1999
Name changed from Charger Petroleums Inc. to Charger Energy Inc. 08/23/1999
Recapitalized as Arapahoe Energy Corp. (Old) 04/15/2003
Each share Common no par exchanged for (0.1) share Common no par
Arapahoe Energy Corp. (Old) reorganized as Arapahoe Energy Corp. (New) 02/06/2004 which name changed to Canadian Phoenix Resources Corp. 01/07/2008 which recapitalized as Knol Resources Corp. 03/11/2013

CHARGER PETROLEUMS LTD.
Name changed to Hy-Charger Petroleums Ltd. and Capital Stock $0.25 par changed to $1 par 00/00/1951
Hy-Charger Petroleums Ltd. recapitalized as Vandoo Consolidated Explorations Ltd. 03/16/1956
(See Vandoo Consolidated Explorations Ltd.)

CHARGER RES LTD (BC)
Recapitalized as Tantalus Resources Ltd. 12/21/1984
Each share Common no par exchanged for (0.2) share Common no par
Tantalus Resources Ltd. recapitalized as Tapango Resources Ltd. 11/22/1996 which merged into CarbonOne Technologies Inc. 07/27/2015 which name changed to TekModo Industries Inc. 10/12/2016 which recapitalized as Lincoln Ventures Ltd. 07/16/2018

CHARGER VENTURES INC (NV)
Name changed to Global Industrial Services Inc. 03/30/2000
(See Global Industrial Services Inc.)

CHARGIT INC (NY)
Chapter 11 Federal Bankruptcy Code converted to Chapter 7 on 04/10/1987
Stockholders' equity unlikely

CHARGOLD RES LTD (BC)
Recapitalized as International Chargold Resources Ltd. 05/02/1996
Each share Common no par exchanged for (0.5) share Common no par
International Chargold Resources Ltd. recapitalized as Odessa Gold Corp. 05/23/2002 which recapitalized as Emerson Exploration Inc. 04/20/2005 which name changed to GBS Gold International, Inc. 09/19/2005

CHARIOT ENTMT INC (NV)
Each share old Common 10¢ par exchanged for (0.33333333) share new Common 10¢ par 08/16/1994
Name changed to AutoCorp Equities Inc. 09/23/1994
AutoCorp Equities Inc. name changed to Homeland Security Network, Inc. 03/16/2005 which name changed to Global Ecology Corp. 01/05/2010

CHARIOT GROUP INC (DE)
Stock Dividend - 10% 06/26/1987
Merged into Summit Metals, Inc. 08/07/1995
Each share Common 10¢ par exchanged for $4 principal amount of 8% Promissory Notes due 07/31/2005

CHARIOT INTL HLDGS LTD (DE)
Charter cancelled and declared inoperative and void for non-payment of taxes 03/01/2000

CHARIOT RES LTD (BC)
Reincorporated 10/28/2004
Place of incorporation changed from (YT) to (BC) 10/28/2004
Acquired by China Sci-Tech Holdings Ltd. 06/14/2010
Each share Common no par exchanged for $0.67 cash

CHARIOT SEVEN PRODUCTIONS (NV)
Recapitalized as Upscale Trends Inc. 10/16/1994
Each share Common $0.001 par exchanged for (0.05) share Common $0.001 par
Upscale Trends Inc. name changed to Electric Entertainment International Inc. 03/07/1997 which recapitalized as Private Media Group Ltd. 12/16/1997
(See Private Media Group Ltd.)

CHARIS CORP. (NY)
Capital Stock no par changed to $10 par 00/00/1934
Name changed to Taylor International Corp. (NY) 05/25/1959
Taylor International Corp. (NY) reincorporated in Nevada 06/27/1969
(See Taylor International Corp. (NV))

CHARISTA GLOBAL CORP (UT)
Each share old Common $0.001 par exchanged for (0.001) share new Common $0.001 par 11/22/2010
Name changed to UBK Resources Co. 09/12/2011

CHARITYVILLE COM INTL INC (CANADA)
Name changed to eNblast productions inc. 06/14/2000
(See eNblast productions inc.)

CHARLEBOISE LAKE URANIUM LTD. (ON)
Acquired by Consolidated Ranwick Uranium Mines Ltd. 12/00/1953
Each share Capital Stock exchanged for (0.25) share Capital Stock $1 par
Consolidated Ranwick Uranium Mines Ltd. name changed to International Ranwick Ltd. 06/29/1955 which name changed to International Molybdenum Mines Ltd. 08/00/1959 which merged into Pax International Mines Ltd. 01/31/1962 which recapitalized as Geo-Pax Mines Ltd. 09/00/1968
(See Geo-Pax Mines Ltd.)

CHARLEMAGNE RES LTD (BC)
Name changed 02/22/1984
Name changed from Charlemagne Oil & Gas Ltd. to Charlemagne Resources Ltd. 02/22/1984
Struck off register and declared dissolved for failure to file returns 07/22/1994

CHARLES CORP.
Liquidation completed 00/00/1950
Details not available

CHARLES JW FINL SVCS INC (FL)
Common $0.001 par split (3) for (2) by issuance of (0.5) additional share payable 02/07/1997 to holders of record 01/24/1997
Merged into JWGenesis Financial Corp. 06/12/1998
Each share Common $0.001 par exchanged for (1) share Common $0.001 par

CHA-CHA

(See JWGenesis Financial Corp.)

CHARLES OF THE RITZ, INC. (DE)
Merged into Lanvin-Charles of the Ritz, Inc. 01/21/1964
Each share Common $1 par exchanged for (1.3) shares Common $1 par
Lanvin-Charles of the Ritz, Inc. merged into Squibb Corp. 04/30/1971 which merged into Bristol-Myers Squibb Co. 10/04/1989

CHARLES RIV ASSOCS INC (MA)
Name changed to CRA International, Inc. 05/06/2005

CHARLES RIV LABORATORIES HLDGS INC (DE)
Name changed to Charles River Laboratories International Inc. 05/18/2000

CHARLES RIVER BREEDING LABS INC (DE)
Common $1 par split (5) for (4) by issuance of (0.25) additional share 03/07/1972
Common $1 par split (3) for (2) by issuance of (0.5) additional share 01/10/1973
Common $1 par split (3) for (2) by issuance of (0.5) additional share 10/17/1980
Merged into Bausch & Lomb Inc. 02/16/1984
Each share Common $1 par exchanged for (1.75) shares Common 40¢ par
(See Bausch & Lomb Inc.)

CHARLES STR GARAGE CO (MA)
Voluntarily dissolved 02/10/1981
Details not available

CHARLES TOWN RACING ASSN INC (WV)
Each VTC for Common 10¢ par exchanged for (0.2) VTC for Common 50¢ par 11/08/1962
Voting Trust Agreement terminated 07/22/1968
Each VTC for Common 50¢ par exchanged for (1) share Common 50¢ par
Name changed to Shenandoah Corp. (WV) 06/01/1970
(See Shenandoah Corp. (WV))

CHARLESBANK TR CO (CAMBRIDGE, MA)
Merged into UST Corp. 01/03/1983
Each share Common Capital Stock $5 par exchanged for $38 cash

CHARLESTON BASICS INC (DE)
Name changed to Paneltech International Holdings, Inc. 02/08/2010

CHARLESTON INTERURBAN R.R.
Acquired by Charleston Transit Co. 00/00/1935
Details not available

CHARLESTON NATL BK (CHARLESTON, WV)
Each share Capital Stock $25 par exchanged for (3.125) shares Capital Stock $10 par to effect a (5) for (2) split and a 25% stock dividend 02/15/1969
Stock Dividends - 41.17% 11/06/1945; 100% 03/18/1955; 33.33333333% 01/31/1963
Reorganized as Centurion Bancorp Inc. 05/20/1982
Each share Capital Stock $10 par exchanged for (1) share Capital Stock $10 par
Centurion Bancorp Inc. merged into Key Centurion Bancshares, Inc. 11/30/1985 which merged into Banc One Corp. 05/03/1993 which merged into Bank One Corp. 10/02/1998 which merged into J.P. Morgan Chase & Co. 12/31/2000 which name changed to JPMorgan Chase & Co. 07/20/2004

CHARLESTON RES LTD (BC)
Recapitalized as Envipco Canada Western Inc. 01/06/1988
Each share Common no par exchanged for (0.25) share Common no par
Envipco Canada Western Inc. name changed to Automated Recycling Inc. 08/20/1999 which name changed to Oceanlake Commerce Inc. 03/01/2001

CHARLESTON RUBR CO (OH)
Common $5 par changed to $2.50 par and (1) additional share issued 04/11/1966
Stock Dividends - 10% 01/21/1963; 10% 01/20/1968
Name changed to CRC Liquidating Corp. 02/25/1975
CRC Liquidating Corp. liquidated for Norton Co. 10/00/1976
(See Norton Co.)

CHARLESTON TRAN CO (WV)
Liquidation completed
Each share Common no par exchanged for initial distribution of $80.07 cash 12/27/1973
Each share Common no par received second distribution of $110 cash 03/22/1974
Each share Common no par received third and final distribution of $7 cash 11/04/1974

CHARLESTOWN GAS & ELECTRIC CO.
Stock purchased by Eastern Gas & Fuel Associates 00/00/1930
Details not available

CHARLIE CHAN RESTAURANTS INC (DE)
Charter cancelled for failure to file reports 04/19/1988

CHARLIE GPS INC (NV)
Name changed to Live Event Media, Inc. 12/04/2012
Live Event Media, Inc. name changed to Eventure Interactive, Inc. 03/14/2013

CHARLIE O BEVERAGES LTD (MB)
Reincorporated under the laws of Oklahoma as Charlie O Co., Inc. 02/13/1990
Charlie O Co., Inc. recapitalized as Sooner Holdings Inc. 10/24/1995 which recapitalized as FlyingEagle PU Technical Corp. 01/30/2012

CHARLIE O CO INC (OK)
Recapitalized as Sooner Holdings Inc. 10/24/1995
Each share Common no par exchanged for (0.05) share Common $0.001 par
Sooner Holdings Inc. recapitalized as FlyingEagle PU Technical Corp. 01/30/2012

CHARLIM EXPLS LTD (CANADA)
Merged into Corporation Lithos 10/26/1994
Each share Common no par exchanged for (0.38461538) share Common no par
Corporation Lithos name changed to Limtech Lithium Metal Technologies Inc. 08/25/1999 which recapitalized as Limtech Lithium Industries Inc. 12/16/2002
(See Limtech Lithium Industries Inc.)

CHARLOR EXPLS LTD (ON)
Name changed to Canadian Oriental Holdings Ltd. 05/30/1973
Canadian Oriental Holdings Ltd. name changed to Canalite Ltd. 12/20/1974
(See Canalite Ltd.)

CHARLOTTE CHARLES INC (DE)
Name changed to MSR Foods, Inc. 03/26/1990
(See MSR Foods, Inc.)

CHARLOTTE MINES LTD. (ON)
Charter cancelled for failure to pay taxes and file returns 10/31/1973

CHARLOTTE MTR SPEEDWAY INC (NC)
Under plan of reorganization each share Common $1 par exchanged for (1) share Common no par 04/19/1963
Each share old Common no par exchanged for (0.01) share new Common no par 03/21/1983
Merged into CMS Holding Co., Inc. 09/27/1985
Each share new Common no par exchanged for $300 cash

CHARLOTTE RES LTD (BC)
Incorporated 00/00/1980
Recapitalized as New Pioneer Explorations Ltd. 01/04/1984
Each share Common no par exchanged for (0.33333333) share Common no par
(See New Pioneer Explorations Ltd.)

CHARLOTTE RUSSE HLDG INC (DE)
Merged into Advent CR Holdings, Inc. 10/14/2009
Each share Common 1¢ par exchanged for $17.50 cash

CHARLOTTE-SHELDON, INC. (NY)
Name changed to Data Cablevision, Inc. 08/13/1982
Data Cablevision, Inc. name changed to T.C.C., Inc. 07/22/1983
(See T.C.C., Inc.)

CHARLOTTESVILLE WOOLEN MILLS (VA)
Dissolved 01/00/1966
No stockholders' equity

CHARLTON MILLS
Liquidated 00/00/1938
Details not available

CHARM COMMUNICATIONS INC (CAYMAN ISLANDS)
Acquired by Engadin Parent Ltd. 09/25/2014
Each ADR for Class A Ordinary exchanged for $4.65 cash

CHARM YELLOWKNIFE GOLD MINES, LTD. (ON)
Charter revoked for failure to file reports and pay taxes 00/00/1956

CHARME PPTYS INC (DE)
Reorganized 06/01/1983
Reorganized from Charmec Group, Inc. to Charme Properties Inc. 06/01/1983
Each share Common 1¢ par exchanged for (0.05) share Common 1¢ par
Charter forfeited for failure to maintain a registered agent 09/24/1985

CHARMED HOMES INC (NV)
Recapitalized as Iveda Corp. 10/12/2009
Each share Common $0.00001 par exchanged for (0.5) share Common $0.00001 par
Iveda Corp. name changed to Iveda Solutions, Inc. 04/25/2011

CHARMIN PAPER MILLS, INC. (WI)
Each share Common $5 par exchanged for (2) shares Common $2.50 par 07/01/1955
Merged into Procter & Gamble Co. 01/17/1957
Each share Common $2.50 par exchanged for (0.5) share Common $2 par

CHARMING SHOPPES INC (PA)
Common 10¢ par split (2) for (1) by issuance of (1) additional share 02/24/1978
Common 10¢ par split (2) for (1) by issuance of (1) additional share 08/24/1978
Common 10¢ par split (4) for (3) by issuance of (1/3) additional share 01/06/1983

Common 10¢ par split (3) for (2) by issuance of (0.5) additional share 10/09/1984
Common 10¢ par split (3) for (2) by issuance of (0.5) additional share 04/25/1986
Common 10¢ par split (3) for (2) by issuance of (0.5) additional share 11/28/1986
Common 10¢ par split (2) for (1) by issuance of (1) additional share 12/07/1992
Stock Dividends - 20% 01/15/1977; 50% 09/15/1977; 25% 06/15/1981
Acquired by Ascena Retail Group, Inc. 06/18/2012
Each share Common 10¢ par exchanged for $7.35 cash

CHARMS CO (DE)
Acquired by Tootsie Roll Industries, Inc. 09/22/1988
Each share Non-Vtg. Common no par exchanged for $950.71 cash

CHARNITA INC (PA)
Adjudicated bankrupt 10/08/1974
Stockholders' equity unlikely

CHARO RES INC (TX)
Charter forfeited for failure to pay taxes 02/02/1993

CHAROEN POKPHAND FEEDMILL LTD (THAILAND)
Stock Dividends - 10% payable 06/04/1999 to holders of record 05/10/1999 Ex date - 05/06/1999; 10% payable 01/08/2000 to holders of record 11/24/1999; 83% payable 05/05/2000 to holders of record 04/04/2000
Name changed to Charoen Pokphand Foods Public Co., Ltd. 04/20/2000

CHARRINGTON BUSINESS CONSULTANTS INC (ON)
Reorganized as Digital Duplication Inc. 11/15/2000
Each share Common no par exchanged for (3) shares Common no par
(See Digital Duplication Inc.)

CHARRIOT RES LTD (ON)
Charter cancelled for failure to file reports and pay taxes 09/12/1988

CHARRON WILLIAMS SYS INC (FL)
Reported out of business 00/00/1986
No stockholders' equity

CHART ACQUISITION CORP (DE)
Units separated 08/04/2015
Name changed to Tempus Applied Solutions Holdings, Inc. 08/04/2015

CHART HOUSE ENTERPRISES (CA)
Merged into Self Service Restaurants, Inc. 04/30/1974
Each share Common 10¢ par exchanged for (0.345978) share Common no par
Self Service Restaurants, Inc. name changed to Chart House Inc. 05/28/1974 which merged into Diversifoods Inc. 12/28/1983
(See Diversifoods Inc.)

CHART HOUSE ENTERPRISES INC (DE)
Each share old Common 1¢ par exchanged for (0.16666666) share new Common 1¢ par 02/22/2002
Name changed to Angelo & Maxie's Inc. 08/02/2002
Angelo & Maxie's Inc. name changed to AM-CH, Inc. 02/07/2005
(See AM-CH, Inc.)

CHART HOUSE INC (LA)
Common no par split (2) for (1) by issuance of (1) additional share 08/29/1975
Common no par split (2) for (1) by issuance of (1) additional share 07/15/1981
Common no par split (3) for (2) by issuance of (0.5) additional share 10/17/1983

Merged into Diversifoods Inc. 12/28/1983
Each share Common no par exchanged for (1.17) shares Common 1¢ par
(See Diversifoods Inc.)

CHART INDS INC (DE)
Old Common 1¢ par split (3) for (2) by issuance of (0.5) additional share payable 06/30/1997 to holders of record 06/16/1997 Ex date - 07/01/1997
Old Common 1¢ par split (3) for (2) by issuance of (0.5) additional share payable 06/30/1998 to holders of record 06/16/1998 Ex date - 07/01/1998
Each share old Common 1¢ par exchanged for approximately (0.01035747) share new Common 1¢ par and (0.0109026) Common Stock Purchase Warrant expiring 09/12/2010
Note: Unexchanged certificates were cancelled and became without value 09/15/2004
Merged into First Reserve Corp. 10/17/2005
Each share new Common 1¢ par exchanged $64.75 cash
(Additional Information in Active)

CHART-PAK, INC. (CT)
Acquired by Avery Products Corp. 11/30/1966
Each share Common $1 par exchanged for (0.75) share Common $1 par
Avery Products Corp. name changed to Avery International Corp. (CA) 03/31/1976 which reincorporated in Delaware 04/01/1977 which name changed to Avery Dennison Corp. 10/16/1990

CHART SVC INST INC (FL)
Reorganized as Infinity Petroleum Corp. 01/19/1982
Each share Common 1¢ par exchanged for (2.5) shares Common 1¢ par
(See Infinity Petroleum Corp.)

CHARTA MINES LTD NEW (BC)
Name changed 01/31/1972
Under plan of merger name changed from Charta Mines Ltd. (Old) to Charta Mines Ltd. (New) and each share Common 50¢ par exchanged for (2) shares Common 50¢ par 01/31/1972
Recapitalized as Windmill Enterprises Ltd. 05/30/1977
Each share Common 50¢ par exchanged for (0.25) share Common no par
Windmill Enterprises Ltd. recapitalized as Todwind Development Corp. 07/20/1984
(See Todwind Development Corp.)

CHARTER BANCORP (CA)
Completely liquidated 09/05/1973
Each share Common 10¢ par exchanged for first and final distribution of (0.318572) share Charter Bank (Culver City, CA) Common $10 par
(See Charter Bank (Culver City, CA))

CHARTER BANCSHARES INC (TX)
Common $1 par split (3) for (2) by issuance of (0.5) additional share 06/30/1983
Common $1 par split (5) for (3) by issuance of (0.66666666) additional share 03/02/1984
Stock Dividend - 10% 06/30/1982
8% Preferred $50 par called for redemption 03/31/1996
Merged into NationsBank Corp. (NC) 05/24/1996
Each share Common $1 par exchanged for (0.385) share Common no par
NationsBank Corp. (NC) reincorporated in Delaware as BankAmerica Corp. (Old) 09/25/1998 which merged into BankAmerica Corp. (New) 09/30/1998 which name changed to Bank of America Corp. 04/28/1999

CHARTER BK & TR CO (MARIETTA, GA)
Merged into Merit Holding Corp. 02/14/1995
Each share Common $3.33333333 par exchanged for (1.61) shares Common $2.50 par
Merit Holding Corp. merged into Synovus Financial Corp. 10/01/1999

CHARTER BANK (BELLEVUE, WA)
Stock Dividends - 20% payable 08/10/1999 to holders of record 07/31/1999; 20% payable 08/14/2000 to holders of record 07/31/2000 Ex date - 08/14/2000
Reorganized as Charter Financial Corp. 01/08/2001
Each share Common no par exchanged for (1) share Common no par
Charter Financial Corp. merged into Boston Private Financial Holdings, Inc. 07/02/2007

CHARTER BK (CULVER CITY, CA)
Liquidation completed
Each share Common $10 par exchanged for initial distribution of $28.89105 cash 12/31/1973
Each share Common $10 par received second and final distribution of $0.3023147 cash 09/16/1974

CHARTER BK GROUP INC (DE)
Acquired by NBD Bancorp, Inc. 08/31/1988
Each share Common $1 par exchanged for (0.87) share Common $1 par
NBD Bancorp, Inc. name changed to First Chicago NBD Corp. 12/01/1995 which merged into Bank One Corp. 10/02/1998 which merged into J.P. Morgan Chase & Co. 12/31/2000 which name changed to JPMorgan Chase & Co. 07/20/2004

CHARTER BANKSHARES CORP (FL)
Each share Common $1 par exchanged for (1/3) share Common $3 par 05/15/1972
Merged into Century Banks, Inc. 04/08/1976
Each share Common $3 par exchanged for (1) share Common $1 par
Century Banks, Inc. merged into Sun Banks of Florida, Inc. 07/01/1982 which name changed to Sun Banks, Inc. 05/02/1983 which merged into SunTrust Banks, Inc. 07/01/1985

CHARTER CO (FL)
$1.75 Conv. Preferred Ser. E $1 par called for redemption 07/01/1974
Common $1 par split (5) for (1) by issuance of (4) additional shares 07/16/1975
Reorganized under Chapter 11 Federal Bankruptcy Code 03/31/1987
Each share Conv. Depositary Preferred exchanged for (1) share Common 10¢ par
Common $1 par changed to 10¢ par
Name changed to Spelling Entertainment Group Inc. (FL) 10/14/1992
Spelling Entertainment Group Inc. (FL) reincorporated in Delaware 05/30/1995
(See Spelling Entertainment Group Inc.)

CHARTER COMMUNICATIONS INC (NY)
Merged into Grosset & Dunlop 04/08/1976
Each share Common $1 par exchanged for $0.60 cash

CHARTER COMMUNICATIONS INC OLD (DE)
Plan of reorganization under Chapter 11 Federal Bankruptcy proceedings effective 11/30/2009
No old Class A Common stockholders' equity
Under plan of reorganization each share new Class A Common $0.001 par automatically became (0.9042) share Charter Communications, Inc. (New) Class A Common $0.001 par 05/18/2016

CHARTER COMMUNICATIONS INTL INC (NV)
Name changed to Pointe Communications Corp. 09/09/1998
Pointe Communications Corp. merged into Telscape International Inc. (New) 06/02/2000
(See Telscape International Inc. (New))

CHARTER CONS LTD (ENGLAND)
Merged into Charter PLC 08/23/1993
Each ADR for Ordinary exchanged for approximately $10.66 cash

CHARTER CREDIT CORP. (NY)
Merged into Cabot Knitting Mills, Inc. 02/15/1966
Each share Common 10¢ par exchanged for (1) share Common 1¢ par
(See Cabot Knitting Mills, Inc.)

CHARTER CRELLIN INC (DE)
Merged into GTC/NFJ Plastics Holding Corp. 05/18/1989
Each share Common 1¢ par exchanged for $27 cash

CHARTER DESIGN & MFG CORP (MN)
Completely liquidated 04/23/1981
Each share Common 10¢ par exchanged for first and final distribution of $0.30 cash

CHARTER EQUITIES INC (AZ)
Reincorporated 01/23/2008
State of incorporation changed from (WA) to (AZ) 01/23/2008
Reorganized under the laws of Nevada as Global Recycle Energy, Inc. 04/15/2008
Each share Common $0.001 par exchanged for (0.02) share Common $0.001 par
Global Recycle Energy, Inc. name changed to ATI Modular Technology Corp. 06/13/2017 which recapitalized as AmericaTowne Holdings, Inc. 03/08/2018

CHARTER FEDERAL SAVINGS & LOAN ASSOCIATION (USA)
Common 1¢ par split (3) for (1) by issuance of (2) additional shares 05/09/1986
Name changed to Charter Federal Savings Bank (Bristol, VA) 10/13/1988
Charter Federal Savings Bank (Bristol, VA) merged into First American Corp. (TN) 12/01/1995 which merged into AmSouth Bancorporation 10/01/1999 which merged into Regions Financial Corp. 11/04/2006

CHARTER FED SVGS BK (BRISTOL, VA)
Each share old Common 1¢ par exchanged for (0.2) share new Common 1¢ par 12/20/1993
Merged into First American Corp. (TN) 12/01/1995
Each share new Common 1¢ par exchanged for (0.3398) share Common $5 par
First American Corp. (TN) merged into AmSouth Bancorporation 10/01/1999 which merged into Regions Financial Corp. 11/04/2006

CHARTER FED SVGS BK (RANDOLPH, NJ)
Under plan of reorganization each share Common 1¢ par automatically became (1) share Charter One Bancorp, Inc. (DE) Common 1¢ par 09/17/1990
Charter One Bancorp, Inc. (DE) name changed to Charter FSB Bancorp, Inc. 01/28/1991 which merged into Sovereign Bancorp, Inc. 11/01/1994 which merged into Banco Santander, S.A. 01/30/2009

CHARTER FINANCIAL CORP. OF ILLINOIS (DE)
$2 Preferred $50 par called for redemption 02/28/1985
Reorganized as Charter Bank Group, Inc. 12/31/1986
Each share Common $7.50 par exchanged for (17.722) shares Common $1 par
Charter Bank Group, Inc. acquired by NBD Bancorp, Inc. 08/31/1988 which name changed to First Chicago NBD Corp. 12/01/1995 which merged into Bank One Corp. 10/02/1998 which merged into J.P. Morgan Chase & Co. 12/31/2000 which name changed to JPMorgan Chase & Co. 07/20/2004

CHARTER FINL CORP (MA)
Merged into Hartford National Corp. 11/19/1986
Each share Common $2 par exchanged for (1.66) shares Common $6.25 par
Hartford National Corp. merged into Shawmut National Corp. 02/29/1988 which merged into Fleet Financial Group Inc. (New) 11/30/1995 which name changed to Fleet Boston Corp. 10/01/1999 which name changed to FleetBoston Financial Corp. 04/18/2000 which merged into Bank of America Corp. 04/01/2004

CHARTER FINL CORP (USA)
Merged into CenterState Bank Corp. 09/04/2018
Each share Common 1¢ par exchanged for (0.738) share Common 1¢ par and $2.30 cash

CHARTER FINL CORP (WA)
Stock Dividends - 20% payable 08/22/2001 to holders of record 07/31/2001 Ex date - 08/23/2001; 20% payable 08/21/2002 to holders of record 07/31/2002 Ex date - 07/29/2002; 20% payable 08/21/2003 to holders of record 07/31/2003 Ex date - 07/29/2003
Merged into Boston Private Financial Holdings, Inc. 07/02/2007
Each share Common no par exchanged for either (1.5951) shares Common $1 par or $45.70 cash

CHARTER FINL INC (IL)
Merged into Magna Group, Inc. 05/01/1998
Each share Common 10¢ par exchanged for (0.5751) share Common $2 par
Magna Group, Inc. merged into Union Planters Corp. 07/01/1998 which merged into Regions Financial Corp. (New) 07/01/2004

CHARTER FINL NETWORK INC (NJ)
Name changed to Imagine America, Inc. (New) 08/10/1995

CHARTER FSB BANCORP INC (DE)
Common 1¢ par split (3) for (2) by issuance of (0.5) additional share 08/07/1992
Merged into Sovereign Bancorp, Inc. 11/01/1994
Each share Common 1¢ par exchanged for (3.4) shares Common no par
Sovereign Bancorp, Inc. merged into Banco Santander, S.A. 01/30/2009

CHARTER GOLF INC (DE)
Name changed to Ashworth, Inc. 04/06/1994
(See Ashworth, Inc.)

CHARTER GROUP INC (DE)
Name changed 08/16/1973
Name changed from Charter Funding Corp. to Charter Group, Inc. 08/16/1973
Voluntarily dissolved 12/27/1988
Details not available

CHARTER GROUP INTL INC (NV)
Name changed to Signature Brands, Inc. 09/05/1997
(See Signature Brands, Inc.)

CHARTER INDS INC (DE)
Charter cancelled and declared inoperative and void for non-payment of taxes 03/01/1979

CHARTER INDS LTD NEW (CANADA)
Name changed 08/18/1986
Name changed from Charter Industries (1982) Ltd. to Charter Industries Ltd. (New) 08/18/1986
Acquired by International Factors Corp. 02/15/1994
Each share Common no par exchanged for $15.60 cash

CHARTER INDS LTD OLD (QC)
Merged into Charter Industries (1982) Ltd. 11/19/1982
Each share Common $1 par exchanged for (1) share Common no par
Charter Industries (1982) Ltd. name changed to Charter Industries Ltd. (New) 08/18/1986
(See Charter Industries Ltd. (New))

CHARTER INTL PLC (JERSEY)
Acquired by Colfax Corp. 01/13/2012
Each ADR for Common exchanged for $15.68852 cash

CHARTER INV RELATIONS NORTH AMER INC (FL)
Reorganized under the laws of Nevada as Millionaire.Com 11/24/1998
Each share Common $0.001 par exchanged for (3) shares Common $0.001 par
(See Millionaire.Com)

CHARTER MED CORP (DE)
Old Common 25¢ par split (3) for (2) by issuance of (0.5) additional share 12/28/1978
Old Common 25¢ par split (3) for (2) by issuance of (0.5) additional share 03/03/1980
Old Common 25¢ par split (3) for (2) by issuance of (0.5) additional share 11/03/1980
Old Common 25¢ par split (2) for (1) by issuance of (1) additional share 05/29/1981
Old Common 25¢ par reclassified as Class B Common 25¢ par 10/28/1981
Class A Common 25¢ par split (3) for (2) by issuance of (0.5) additional share 09/30/1982
Class B Common 25¢ par split (3) for (2) by issuance of (0.5) additional share 09/30/1982
Class A Common 25¢ par split (3) for (2) by issuance of (0.5) additional share 09/01/1983
Class B Common 25¢ par split (3) for (2) by issuance of (0.5) additional share 09/01/1983
Class A Common 25¢ par split (3) for (2) by issuance of (0.5) additional share 04/15/1985
Class B Common 25¢ par split (3) for (2) by issuance of (0.5) additional share 04/15/1985
$0.75 Ser. A Preferred no par called for redemption 09/01/1985
$0.80 Ser. B Preferred no par called for redemption 09/01/1985
Merged into WAF Acquisition Corp. 09/01/1988
Each share Class A Common 25¢ par exchanged for $7 principal amount of 15.87% Jr. Subordinated Debentures due 08/15/2008 and $30.35 cash
Each share Class B Common 25¢ par exchanged for $7 principal amount of 15.85% Jr. Subordinated Debentures due 08/15/2008 and $30.25 cash
Plan of reorganization under Chapter 11 Federal Bankruptcy Code effective 07/21/1992
Each share Adjustable Rate Exchangeable Ser. A Preferred no par exchanged for (0.357) share new Common 25¢ par and (0.165) Common Stock Purchase Warrant expiring 06/30/2002
Name changed to Magellan Health Services, Inc. 12/22/1995
Magellan Health Services, Inc. name changed to Magellan Health, Inc. 06/13/2014

CHARTER MINERALS INC (BC)
Recapitalized as New Charter Minerals Inc. 05/21/1991
Each share Common no par exchanged for (0.5) share Common no par
New Charter Minerals Inc. name changed to Cambridge BioChemics Inc. 04/23/1992 which name changed to Cambridge Softek Inc. 06/23/1993 which recapitalized as Alantra Venture Corp. 11/21/1994
(See Alantra Venture Corp.)

CHARTER MNG N L (AUSTRALIA)
ADR agreement terminated 02/27/2009
No ADR holders' equity

CHARTER MORTGAGE & INVESTMENT CO. (FL)
Name changed to Charter Co. 07/01/1963
Charter Co. name changed to Spelling Entertainment Group Inc. (FL) 10/14/1992 which reincorporated in Delaware 05/30/1995
(See Spelling Entertainment Group Inc.)

CHARTER MUN MTG ACCEP CO (DE)
Name changed to CharterMac 11/17/2003
CharterMac name changed to Centerline Holding Co. 04/02/2007
(See Centerline Holding Co.)

CHARTER N Y CORP (NY)
Name changed to Irving Bank Corp. 10/17/1979
Irving Bank Corp. merged into Bank of New York Co., Inc. 12/30/1988 which merged into Bank of New York Mellon Corp. 07/01/2007

CHARTER NATIONAL BANCORP (CA)
Merged into InBancshares 04/01/1988
Each share Common no par exchanged for $13.25 cash

CHARTER OAK BK & TR CO (HARTFORD, CT)
Stock Dividend - 25% 01/29/1974
Merged into Colonial Bancorp, Inc. 09/01/1983
Each share Common $6.25 par exchanged for $35 cash

CHARTER OAK BK (NAPA, CA)
Bank closed and FDIC appointed receiver 02/18/2011
Stockholders' equity unlikely

CHARTER OAK LIFE INS CO (AZ)
Each share Class A Common 20¢ par exchanged for (2) shares Class A Common 5¢ par 03/30/1964
Each share Common $1 par exchanged for (2) shares Class B Common 25¢ par 03/30/1964
Class A Common 5¢ par changed to 20¢ par 05/15/1969
Class B Common 25¢ par changed to 20¢ par 05/15/1969
Acquired by Security National Life Insurance Co. (UT) 12/00/1970
Each share Class A Common 20¢ par exchanged for (1.333333) shares Class A Common $1 par
Each share Class B Common 20¢ par exchanged for (1.333333) shares Class A Common $1 par
Security National Life Insurance Co. (UT) merged into S.N.L. Financial Corp. 03/24/1980 which name changed to Security National Financial Corp. 12/27/1990

CHARTER OIL LTD (BC)
Common no par changed to $1 par 00/00/1952
Common $1 par changed to no par 12/28/1984
Recapitalized as Trans-Dominion Energy Corp. 09/11/1985
Each share Common no par exchanged for (0.33333333) share Common no par
Trans-Dominion Energy Corp. recapitalized as Madison Oil Co. Inc. (BC) 05/25/2000 which reincorporated in Delaware 07/12/2000 which merged into Torreador Resources Corp. 12/31/2001 which merged into ZaZa Energy Corp. 02/22/2012

CHARTER ONE BANCORP INC (DE)
Name changed to Charter FSB Bancorp, Inc. 01/28/1991
Charter FSB Bancorp, Inc. merged into Sovereign Bancorp, Inc. 11/01/1994 which merged into Banco Santander, S.A. 01/30/2009

CHARTER ONE FINL INC (DE)
Common 1¢ par split (3) for (2) by issuance of (0.5) additional share 05/27/1992
Common 1¢ par split (3) for (2) by issuance of (0.5) additional share 11/19/1993
Common 1¢ par split (2) for (1) by issuance of (1) additional share payable 05/20/1998 to holders of record 05/06/1998
Stock Dividends - 5% payable 09/30/1996 to holders of record 09/13/1996; 5% payable 10/31/1997 to holders of record 10/17/1997; 5% payable 09/30/1998 to holders of record 09/14/1998; 5% payable 09/30/1999 to holders of record 09/14/1999; 5% payable 09/30/2000 to holders of record 09/14/2000; 5% payable 09/28/2001 to holders of record 09/14/2001; 5% payable 09/30/2002 to holders of record 09/13/2002
Merged into Royal Bank of Scotland Group PLC 08/31/2004
Each share Common 1¢ par exchanged for $44.50 cash

CHARTER PAC BK (AGOURA, CA)
Common no par split (9) for (5) by issuance of (0.8) additional share 11/01/1989
Common no par split (18) for (5) by issuance of (2.6) additional share 07/24/1991
Merged into First Banks America, Inc. 10/17/2001
Each share Common no par exchanged for $3.70 cash

CHARTER PWR SYS INC (DE)
Name changed to C&D Technologies, Inc. 07/03/1997
(See C&D Technologies, Inc.)

CHARTER REAL ESTATE INVT TR (ON)
Name changed to Partners Real Estate Investment Trust 11/03/2010

CHARTER RLTY HLDGS LTD (AB)
Reorganized under the laws of Ontario as Charter Real Estate Investment Trust 05/14/2007
Each share Common no par exchanged for (0.1) Trust Unit
Charter Real Estate Investment Trust name changed to Partners Real Estate Investment Trust 11/03/2010

CHARTER RES INC (NV)
Reincorporated 01/18/1994
Each share Common $0.001 par exchanged for (0.05) share new Common 2¢ par 04/19/1991
State of incorporation changed from Utah to Nevada 01/18/1994
Each share new Common 2¢ par exchanged for (0.2) share Common 10¢ par 02/22/1994
Recapitalized as Synfuel Technology Inc. 05/03/1995
Each share Common 10¢ par exchanged for (0.01333333) share Common 10¢ par
Synfuel Technology Inc. recapitalized as Rigid Airship USA Inc. 11/10/1998
(See Rigid Airship USA Inc.)

CHARTER SAVINGS BANK (HUNTINGTON BEACH, CA)
Declared insolvent and taken over by the Resolution Trust Corp. 12/07/1990
Stockholders' equity unlikely

CHARTER 17 BANCORP INC (IN)
Common $10 par changed to $5 par and (1) additional share issued 05/15/1984
Merged into Banc One Corp. (DE) 08/31/1987
Each share Common $5 par exchanged for (1.4611) shares Common no par
Banc One Corp. (DE) reincorporated in Ohio 05/01/1989 which merged into Bank One Corp. 10/02/1998 which merged into J.P. Morgan Chase & Co. 12/31/2000 which name changed to JPMorgan Chase & Co. 07/20/2004

CHARTER VENTURES INC (DE)
Recapitalized as Finca Consulting Inc. 07/22/1991
Each share Common 1¢ par exchanged for (0.002) share Common 1¢ par
(See Finca Consulting Inc.)

CHARTER WEST CORP (DE)
Name changed to Sellinger Pharmaceuticals Inc. and Common 10¢ par changed to $0.001 par 06/22/1983
Sellinger Pharmaceuticals Inc. name changed to Promedica Inc. 06/28/1988 which name changed to Zhou Lin International Inc. 11/28/1994 which name changed to Renu-U-International Inc. 12/24/1996 which name changed to Colormax Technologies, Inc. 09/07/1999
(See Colormax Technologies, Inc.)

CHARTERBANK INC (MA)
Common $10 par split (2) for (1) by issuance of (1) additional share 09/03/1982
Merged into Conifer/Essex Group, Inc. 06/30/1984
Each share Common $1 par exchanged for (2.6) shares Common $1 par or $101 cash or a combination of stock and cash
Note: Option expired 08/13/1984 after which holders received stock only
Conifer/Essex Group, Inc. name changed back to Conifer Group Inc. (New) 01/01/1985 which merged into Bank of New England Corp. 04/22/1987
(See Bank of New England Corp.)

CHARTERCORP (MO)
Common $6.25 par changed to $3 par and (1) additional share issued 06/01/1984

Merged into Boatmen's Bancshares, Inc. 01/28/1985
Each share Common $3 par exchanged for (0.9) share Common $10 par and $5 cash
Boatmen's Bancshares, Inc. merged into NationsBank Corp. (NC) 01/07/1997 which reincorporated in Delaware as BankAmerica Corp. (Old) 09/25/1998 which merged into BankAmerica Corp. (New) 09/30/1998 which name changed to Bank of America Corp. 04/28/1999

CHARTERED INVESTORS, INC.
Dissolved 00/00/1941
Details not available

CHARTERED SEMICONDUCTOR MFG LTD (SINGAPORE)
Each old Sponsored ADR for Ordinary exchanged for (0.1) new Sponsored ADR for Ordinary 05/21/2009
Acquired by ATIC International Investment Co. LLC 12/18/2009
Each new Sponsored ADR for Ordinary exchanged for $18.994912 cash

CHARTERED TRUST & EXECUTOR CO. (ON)
Recapitalized as Chartered Trust Co. (Toronto, ON) 07/01/1949
Each share Capital Stock $100 par exchanged for (5) shares Capital Stock $20 par
Chartered Trust Co. (Toronto, ON) merged into Eastern & Chartered Trust Co. (Toronto, ON) 11/30/1963 which merged into Canada Permanent Mortgage Corp. 12/01/1967 which merged into Canada Trustco Mortgage Co. 12/31/1985
(See Canada Trustco Mortgage Co.)

CHARTERED TRUST CO. (TORONTO, ON)
Each share Capital Stock $20 par exchanged for (2) shares Capital Stock $10 par 05/22/1963
Merged into Eastern & Chartered Trust Co. (Toronto, ON) 11/30/1963
Each share Capital Stock $10 par exchanged for (1.1) shares Capital Stock $10 par
Eastern & Chartered Trust Co. (Toronto, ON) merged into Canada Permanent Mortgage Corp. 12/01/1967 which merged into Canada Trustco Mortgage Co. 12/31/1985
(See Canada Trustco Mortgage Co.)

CHARTERHALL OIL CDA LTD (AB)
Acquired by Charterhall North America PLC 10/31/1985
For holdings of (449) shares or fewer each share Common no par exchanged for $0.75 cash
For holdings of (450) shares or more each (4.5) shares Common no par exchanged for (1) share Ordinary 10p par or $0.75 cash
Note: Option to receive stock expired 12/16/1985

CHARTERHOUSE PFD SH INDEX CORP (ON)
Merged into Jov Leon Frazer Preferred Equity Fund 01/30/2009
Each PSI Preferred Share no par received (1.70389) Class A Units no par

CHARTERMAC (DE)
Name changed to Centerline Holding Co. 04/02/2007
(See Centerline Holding Co.)

CHARTERS TOWERS GOLD MINES LTD (AUSTRALIA)
Name changed 01/12/2001
Name changed from Charters Towers Gold Mines NL to Charters Towers Gold Mines Ltd. 01/12/2001
Name changed to Citigold Corp. Ltd. 12/19/2003

(See Citigold Corp. Ltd.)

CHARTIERS VALLEY WATER CO.
Merged into South Pittsburgh Water Co. 00/00/1939
Details not available

CHARTWELL CABLE FD INC (CO)
Each share Common $0.0001 par exchanged for (0.001) share Common 10¢ par 05/02/1990
Name changed to Siemann Educational Systems, Inc. 09/18/1997

CHARTWELL CAP CORP (CO)
Administratively dissolved 03/01/2000

CHARTWELL DIVID & INCOME FD INC (MD)
Name changed to Dividend & Income Fund, Inc. (MD) 02/14/2011
Dividend & Income Fund, Inc. (MD) reorganized in Delaware as Dividend & Income Fund 05/14/2012

CHARTWELL GROUP LTD (DE)
Common 10¢ par split (2) for (1) by issuance of (1) additional share 03/18/1987
Reorganized as IL International Inc. 11/27/1991
Each share Common 10¢ par exchanged for (0.6366) share Common 1¢ par
(See IL International Inc.)

CHARTWELL LEISURE INC (DE)
Merged into Whitehall Street Real Estate Limited Partnership IX 03/16/1998
Each share Common 1¢ par exchanged for $17.25 cash

CHARTWELL PARTNERS L P (KS)
Charter forfeited for failure to file annual report 07/15/1997

CHARTWELL PUBG INC (NV)
Name changed to Chartwell International, Inc. 06/28/1993

CHARTWELL RE CORP (DE)
Merged into Trenwick Group Inc. 10/27/1999
Each share Common 1¢ par exchanged for (0.825) share Common 10¢ par
Trenwick Group Inc. merged into Trenwick Group Ltd. 09/27/2000
(See Trenwick Group Ltd.)

CHARTWELL RES INC (DE)
Name changed to International Imaging Technologies, Inc. 09/18/1984
(See International Imaging Technologies, Inc.)

CHARTWELL SENIORS HSG REAL ESTATE TR (ON)
Name changed to Chartwell Retirement Residences 01/15/2013

CHARTWELL TECHNOLOGY INC (AB)
Merged into Amaya Gaming Group Inc. 07/18/2011
Each share Common no par exchanged for (0.125) share Common no par and $0.875 cash
Amaya Gaming Group Inc. name changed to Amaya Inc. (QC) 12/04/2014 which reincorporated in Ontario as Stars Group Inc. 08/01/2017

CHARTWELL VENTURES LTD (AB)
Reincorporated 01/17/1996
Place of incorporation changed from (BC) to (AB) 01/17/1996
Name changed to Chartwell Technology, Inc. 12/08/1998
Chartwell Technology, Inc. merged into Amaya Gaming Group Inc. 07/18/2011 which name changed to Amaya Inc. (QC) 12/04/2014 which reincorporated in Ontario as Stars Group Inc. 08/01/2017

CHARVET JACKSON & CO INC (OR)
Charter cancelled for failure to file reports and pay fees 10/18/1973

CHARVOZ CARSEN CORP (DE)
Common 10¢ par reclassified as Conv. Class B Common 10¢ par 08/06/1986
Stock Dividends - 10% 04/11/1980; 25% 12/30/1985
Name changed to Stendig Industries, Inc. 12/18/1986
Stendig Industries, Inc. name changed to Cantel Industries, Inc. 04/17/1989 which name changed to Cantel Medical Corp. 04/07/2000

CHARYS HLDG CO INC (DE)
Plan of reorganization under Chapter 11 Federal Bankruptcy Code effective 03/12/2009
Stockholders' equity unlikely

CHASE AMER CORP (NV)
Charter revoked for failure to file reports and pay fees 10/01/1998

CHASE BAG CO (DE)
Each share old Common no par exchanged for (2) shares new Common no par 00/00/1951
Name changed to Chase Packaging Corp. 10/01/1987
(See Chase Packaging Corp.)

CHASE BRASS INDS INC (DE)
Name changed to Chase Industries Inc. 05/14/1997
Chase Industries Inc. merged into Olin Corp. 09/27/2002

CHASE CANDY CO. (MO)
Stock Dividend - 100% 10/03/1946
Name changed to Bunte Brothers Chase Candy Co. 00/00/1954
Bunte Brothers Chase Candy Co. name changed to Chase General Corp. 03/26/1962

CHASE CAP CORP (CA)
Charter cancelled for failure to file reports and pay taxes 05/01/1984

CHASE CAP FD BOSTON INC (MA)
Completely liquidated
Each share Common $1 par exchanged for first and final distribution of (1.07089) shares Chase Frontier Capital Fund of Boston, Inc. Common $1 par 12/01/1971
Chase Frontier Capital Fund of Boston, Inc. reorganized as Phoenix-Chase Series Fund 02/27/1981 which name changed to Phoenix Series Fund 10/12/1982
(See Phoenix Series Fund)

CHASE CAP V (DE)
7.03 Capital Securities Ser. E called for redemption at $25 on 11/01/2004

CHASE CAPITAL FUND, INC. (MA)
Name changed to Chase Capital Fund of Boston, Inc. 06/25/1970
Chase Capital Fund of Boston, Inc. liquidated for Chase Frontier Capital Fund of Boston, Inc. 12/01/1971 which reorganized as Phoenix-Chase Series Fund 02/27/1981 which name changed to Phoenix Series Fund 10/12/1982
(See Phoenix Series Fund)

CHASE CAP VII (DE)
7% Guaranteed Capital Securities Ser. G called for redemption at $25 on 11/01/2004

CHASE CAP VIII (DE)
Capital Securities Ser. H called for redemption at $25 on 07/31/2005

CHASE CONV FD BOSTON INC (MA)
Reorganized as Phoenix-Chase Series Fund and Common $1 par reclassified as Convertible Fund Series, Shares of Bene. Int. $1 par 03/19/1972
Phoenix-Chase Series Fund name changed to Phoenix Series Fund 10/12/1982

(See Phoenix Series Fund)

CHASE CORP.
Name changed to Amerex Holding Corp. 00/00/1934
Amerex Holding Corp. liquidated for American Express Co. 12/04/1950

CHASE DEV CORP (DE)
Each share Common 1¢ par exchanged for (0.1) share Common 10¢ par 11/03/1980
Merged into CDC Corp. 05/16/1985
Each share Common 10¢ par exchanged for $10 cash

CHASE ENGINE CO. (ME)
Charter suspended for non-payment of taxes 00/00/1911

CHASE FD BOSTON (MA)
Shares of Bene. Int. $1 par split (2) for (1) by issuance of (1) additional share 04/27/1961
Reorganized as Phoenix-Chase Series Fund 07/28/1980
Each Share of Bene. Int. $1 par exchanged for (1) Growth Fund Series Share of Bene. Int. $1 par
Phoenix-Chase Series Fund name changed to Phoenix Series Fund 10/12/1982
(See Phoenix Series Fund)

CHASE FED SVGS BK (MIAMI, FL)
Merged into NationsBank Corp. 08/13/1996
Each share Common 1¢ par exchanged for $5.24 cash

CHASE FRONTIER CAP FD BOSTON INC (MA)
Stock Dividend - 1100% 12/01/1971
Reorganized as Phoenix-Chase Series Fund 02/27/1981
Each share Common $1 par exchanged for (1) Stock Fund Series Share of Bene. Int. $1 par
Phoenix-Chase Series Fund name changed to Phoenix Series Fund 10/12/1982
(See Phoenix Series Fund)

CHASE FRONTIER FD INC (MA)
Name changed to Chase Frontier Fund of Boston, Inc. 05/20/1970
Chase Frontier Fund of Boston, Inc. name changed to Chase Frontier Capital Fund of Boston, Inc. 12/01/1971 which reorganized as Phoenix-Chase Series Fund 02/27/1981 which name changed to Phoenix Series Fund 10/12/1982
(See Phoenix Series Fund)

CHASE FRONTIER FUND OF BOSTON, INC. (MA)
Name changed to Chase Frontier Capital Fund of Boston, Inc. 12/01/1971
Chase Frontier Capital Fund of Boston, Inc. reorganized as Phoenix-Chase Series Fund 02/27/1981 which name changed to Phoenix Series Fund 10/12/1982
(See Phoenix Series Fund)

CHASE HANOVER CORP (UT)
Each share Capital Stock 1¢ par exchanged for (0.2) share Capital Stock $1 par 10/28/1983
Proclaimed dissolved for failure to pay taxes 12/31/1985

CHASE HOTEL, INC. (MO)
Minority shares sold by Voting Trustees 00/00/1947
Details not available

CHASE INDS INC (DE)
Common 1¢ par split (3) for (2) by issuance of (0.5) additional share payable 06/26/1998 to holders of record 06/06/1998 Ex date - 06/29/1998
Merged into Olin Corp. 09/27/2002
Each share Common 1¢ par exchanged for (0.64) share Common $1 par

CHASE MANHATTAN BK (NEW YORK, NY)
Stock Dividend - 50% 03/06/1964
Name changed to Chase Manhattan Bank (N.A.), (New York, NY) 09/23/1965
Chase Manhattan Bank (N.A.), (New York, NY) reorganized as Chase Manhattan Corp. (Old) 06/04/1969 which merged into Chase Manhattan Corp. (New) 03/31/1996 which name changed to J.P. Morgan Chase & Co. 12/31/2000 which name changed to JPMorgan Chase & Co. 07/20/2004 01/30/1959) (West Indies Bank & Trust Co.

CHASE MANHATTAN BK N A (NEW YORK, NY)
Capital Stock $12.50 par split (3) for (2) by issuance of (0.5) additional share 04/15/1969
Reorganized as Chase Manhattan Corp. 06/04/1969
Each share Capital Stock $12.50 par exchanged for (1) share Common $12.50 par

CHASE MANHATTAN CORP (DE)
Common $12.50 par split (2) for (1) by issuance of (1) additional share 02/13/1986
10.5% Preferred Ser. D no par called for redemption 08/17/1992
Floating Rate Preferred Ser. E no par called for redemption 09/20/1993
6.75% Preferred Ser. B no par called for redemption 09/24/1993
7.6% Preferred Ser. C no par called for redemption 09/24/1993
Floating Rate Preferred Ser. F no par called for redemption 07/15/1994
Merged into Chase Manhattan Corp. (New) 03/31/1996
Each share Adjustable Rate Preferred Ser. N no par exchanged for (1) share Adjustable Rate Preferred Ser. N $1 par
Each share 8.32% Preferred Ser. L no par exchanged for (1) share 8.32% Preferred Ser. L $1 par
Each share 8.4% Preferred Ser. M no par exchanged for (1) share 8.4% Preferred $1 par
Each share 8.5% Preferred Ser. K no par exchanged for (1) share 8.5% Preferred $1 par
Each share 9.08% Preferred Ser. J no par exchanged for (1) share 9.08% Preferred $1 par
Each share 9.76% Preferred Ser. H no par exchanged for (1) share 9.76% Preferred $1 par
Each share 10.5% Preferred Ser. G no par exchanged for (1) share 10.5% Preferred $1 par
Each share 10.84% Preferred Ser. I no par exchanged for (1) share 10.84% Preferred $1 par
Each share Common $2 par exchanged for (1.04) shares Common $1 par
Chase Manhattan Corp. (New) name changed to J.P. Morgan Chase & Co. 12/31/2000 which name changed to JPMorgan Chase & Co. 07/20/2004

CHASE MANHATTAN CORP NEW (DE)
9.08% Preferred $1 par called for redemption 03/31/1997
8.375% Preferred $1 par called for redemption at $25 par on 06/30/1997
8.5% Preferred $1 par called for redemption at $25 on 06/30/1997
8.32% Preferred $1 par called for redemption at $25 on 09/30/1997
7.92% Depositary Preferred called for redemption at $25 on 03/06/1998
8.4% Preferred $1 par called for redemption at $25 on 03/31/1998
7.58% Depositary Preferred called for redemption at $25 on 04/01/1998
Common $1 par split (2) for (1) by issuance of (1) additional share payable 06/12/1998 to holders of record 05/20/1998 Ex date - 06/15/1998
7.5% Depositary Preferred called for redemption at $25 on 06/30/1998
10.5% Preferred $1 par called for redemption at $25 on 09/30/1998
9.76% Preferred $1 par called for redemption at $25 on 09/30/1999
Common $1 par split (3) for (2) by issuance of (0.5) additional share payable 06/09/2000 to holders of record 05/17/2000 Ex date - 06/12/2000
10.96% Preferred $1 par called for redemption at $25 on 06/30/2000
Under plan of merger name changed to J.P. Morgan Chase & Co. 12/31/2000
J.P. Morgan Chase & Co. name changed to JPMorgan Chase & Co. 07/20/2004

CHASE MANHATTAN MTG & RLTY TR (MA)
Shares of Bene. Int. $1 par reclassified as Common $1 par 09/27/1974
Name changed to Triton Group 06/02/1980
Triton Group (MA) reorganized in Delaware as Triton Group Ltd. 01/30/1981 which merged into Intermark, Inc. 08/30/1990 which reorganized as Triton Group Ltd. (New) 06/25/1993 which name changed to Alarmguard Holdings, Inc. 04/16/1997

CHASE MED GROUP INC (DE)
Recapitalized as Red Branch Technologies, Inc. 05/23/2007
Each share Common 1¢ par exchanged for (0.01) share Common 1¢ par

CHASE NATIONAL BANK (NEW YORK, NY)
Capital Stock $13.55 par changed to $15 par 00/00/1944
Merged into Chase Manhattan Bank (New York, NY) 03/31/1955
Each share Capital Stock $15 par exchanged for (1.25) shares Capital Stock $12.50 par
Chase Manhattan Bank (New York, NY) name changed to Chase Manhattan Bank (N.A.) (New York, NY) 09/23/1965 which reorganized as Chase Manhattan Corp. (Old) 06/04/1969 which merged into Chase Manhattan Corp. (New) 03/31/1996 which name changed to J.P. Morgan Chase & Co. 12/31/2000 which name changed to JPMorgan Chase & Co. 07/20/2004

CHASE NATIONAL INVESTMENT CO. (MO)
Completely liquidated 01/19/1966
Each share Common $1 par exchanged for first and final distribution of (0.285714) share Chase National Life Insurance Co. Common $1 par
Chase National Life Insurance Co. merged into I.C.H. Corp. 10/28/1982 which name changed to Southwestern Life Corp. (New) 06/15/1994 which name changed to I.C.H. Corp. (New) 10/10/1995
(See I.C.H. Corp. (New))

CHASE NATL LIFE INS CO (MO)
Common $1 par changed to $1.25 par 03/16/1971
Common $1.25 par changed to $2 par 09/17/1974
Merged into I.C.H. Corp. 10/28/1982
Each share Common $2 par exchanged for (1.5964) shares Common $1 par
I.C.H. Corp. name changed to Southwestern Life Corp. (New) 06/15/1994 which name changed to I.C.H. Corp. (New) 10/10/1995
(See I.C.H. Corp. (New))

CHASE OILS & MINERALS CORP. (OK)
Recapitalized as Hemisphere Minerals Inc. 06/05/1969
Each share Common 2¢ par exchanged for (0.25) share Common 8¢ par
(See Hemisphere Minerals Inc.)

CHASE PACKAGING CORP (DE)
Merged into Union Camp Corp. 12/28/1990
Each share Common no par exchanged for $330.18 cash

CHASE PFD CAP CORP (DE)
8.1% Preferred Ser. A $25 par called for redemption at $25 on 02/28/2002

CHASE RESOURCE CORP NEW (BC)
Cease trade order effective 08/28/2001

CHASE RESOURCE CORP OLD (BC)
Merged into Chase Resource Corp. (New) 05/30/1997
Each share Common no par exchanged for (1) share Common no par
(See Chase Resource Corp. (New))

CHASE REVEL INC (NV)
Name changed to Entrepreneur Group, Inc. 11/06/1984
(See Entrepreneur Group, Inc.)

CHASE SECURITIES CORP.
Name changed to Chase Corp. 00/00/1933
Chase Corp. name changed to Amerex Holding Corp. 00/00/1934 which liquidated for American Express Co. 12/04/1950

CHASE SPL FD BOSTON INC (MA)
Reorganized as Phoenix-Chase Series Fund 02/27/1981
Each share Common $1 par exchanged for (1.4273) Stock Fund Series Shares of Bene. Int. $1 par
Phoenix-Chase Series Fund name changed to Phoenix Series Fund 10/12/1982
(See Phoenix Series Fund)

CHASE SPL FD INC (MA)
Name changed to Chase Special Fund of Boston, Inc. 05/29/1970
Chase Special Fund of Boston, Inc. reorganized as Phoenix-Chase Series Fund 02/27/1981 which name changed to Phoenix Series Fund 10/12/1982
(See Phoenix Series Fund)

CHASENS INTL CORP (DE)
Name changed to Tril-Medianet.Com, Inc. 07/21/1999
Tril-Medianet.Com, Inc. name changed to Tec Factory, Inc. 11/28/2000 which name changed to HeartSTAT Technology, Inc. 02/26/2004 which name changed to Verdant Technology Corp. 03/01/2006
(See Verdant Technology Corp.)

CHASERS, INC.
Merged into Brown-Allen Chemicals, Inc. 00/00/1952
Each share Common exchanged for (1) share Common $1 par
Brown-Allen Chemicals, Inc. name changed to Standard Magnesium Corp. 11/13/1961 which recapitalized in Delaware as Standard Magnesium & Chemical Co. 05/31/1963
(See Standard Magnesium & Chemical Co.)

CHASKO, INC. (UT)
Name changed to American Technology Corp. (UT) 03/23/1982
American Technology Corp. (UT) reorganized in Delaware 07/14/1992 which name changed to LRAD Corp. 03/25/2010
(See I.C.H. Corp. (New))

CHASTAIN CAP CORP (GA)
Liquidation completed
Each share Common 1¢ par received initial distribution of $7.45 cash payable 11/29/1999 to holders of record 11/19/1999
Each share Common 1¢ par received second and final distribution of $0.53 cash payable 09/25/2000 to holders of record 09/25/2000

CHATAWAY EXPL LTD (BC)
Recapitalized as Chatex Industries Ltd. 08/20/1973
Each share Capital Stock no par exchanged for (0.25) share Capital Stock no par
Chatex Industries Ltd. recapitalized as Rhodes Resources Inc. 02/02/1978 which recapitalized as International Rhodes Resources Ltd. 09/27/1982 which recapitalized as Consolidated Rhodes Resources Ltd. 02/16/1989 which which recapitalized as Fairhaven Resources Ltd. 03/04/1992 which recapitalized as International Fairhaven Resources Ltd. 05/29/2002
(See International Fairhaven Resources Ltd.)

CHATCO STEEL PRODUCTS LTD. (ON)
Bankrupt 09/23/1957
Stockholders' equity unlikely

CHATCOM INC (CA)
Recapitalized as Southern Energy Co. Inc. (CA) 11/19/2007
Each share Common no par exchanged for (0.0025) share Common no par
Southern Energy Co. Inc. (CA) reincorporated in Nevada 12/13/2007
(See Southern Energy Co. Inc.)

CHATEAU CMNTYS INC (MD)
Merged into Hometown America, L.L.C. 10/16/2003
Each share Common 1¢ par exchanged for $29.25 cash

CHATEAU DE VILLE INC (DE)
Merged into CDV Acquisition Corp. 11/09/1984
Each share Common 10¢ par exchanged for $2.50 cash

CHATEAU GAI WINES LTD (CANADA)
Capital Stock no par split (3) for (1) by issuance of (2) additional shares 07/24/1962
Acquired by Labatt (John) Ltd. 08/27/1973
Each share Capital Stock no par exchanged for $44.75 cash

CHATEAU PPTYS INC (MD)
Each share Common 1¢ par received a special dividend of (0.069) additional share payable 02/21/1997 to holders of record 01/30/1997
Name changed to Chateau Communities, Inc. 05/22/1997
(See Chateau Communities, Inc.)

CHATEAU STORES CDA LTD (CANADA)
Name changed to Le Chateau Inc. 09/18/2000

CHATEAUGAY ORE & IRON CO.
Dissolved 00/00/1944
Details not available

CHATEX INDS LTD (BC)
Recapitalized as Rhodes Resources Inc. 02/02/1978
Each share Capital Stock no par exchanged for (0.33333333) share Capital Stock no par
Rhodes Resources Inc. recapitalized as International Rhodes Resources Ltd. 09/27/1982 which recapitalized as Consolidated Rhodes Resources Ltd. 02/16/1989 which recapitalized as Fairhaven Resources Ltd.

03/04/1992 which recapitalized as International Fairhaven Resources Ltd. 05/29/2002
(See International Fairhaven Resources Ltd.)

CHATHAM BUILDING CORP. (IL)
Liquidation completed 08/20/1959
Details not available

CHATHAM CORP (DE)
5% Conv. Preferred $10 par called for redemption 04/20/1966
(Additional Information in Active)

CHATHAM CORP (THE) (FL)
Voluntarily dissolved 04/17/1984
Details not available

CHATHAM ENERGY CORP (NV)
Name changed to World Technologies & Trading Co. 05/30/1983
World Technologies & Trading Co. recapitalized as Gaensel Gold Mines Inc. 08/06/1984 which name changed to Best Medical Treatment Group Inc. 12/19/1997 which name changed to Jenson International Inc. 06/12/1998
(See Jenson International Inc.)

CHATHAM HI TECH GROUP (NV)
Name changed to Medicade, Inc. 08/02/1984
Medicade, Inc. name changed to Sassoon International, Inc. 02/20/1986
(See Sassoon International, Inc.)

CHATHAM INTL INC (FL)
Name changed to Art, Music & Entertainment, Inc. 07/18/1996
(See Art, Music & Entertainment, Inc.)

CHATHAM MFG CO (NC)
Each share Common $100 par exchanged for (100) shares Common $1 par 00/00/1941
Each share Common $1 par exchanged for (0.006) share 4% Preferred $100 par, (0.2) share Class A Common $1 par and (0.2) share Class B Common $1 par 00/00/1948
Class A Common $1 par and Class B Common $1 par reclassified as Common $1 par 05/18/1974
Merged into Northern Feather Ltd. 06/10/1988
Each share Common $1 par exchanged for $56 cash

CHATHAM PHENIX ALLIED CORP.
Name changed to Securities-Allied Corp. 00/00/1931
(See Securities-Allied Corp.)

CHATHAM RAILROAD CO.
Road abandoned 00/00/1937
Details not available

CHATHAM RES LTD (BC)
Recapitalized as Westmount Resources Ltd. (Old) 07/25/1977
Each share Capital Stock no par exchanged for (0.25) share Capital Stock no par
(See Westmount Resources Ltd. (Old))

CHATHAM SECURITIES INC. (IL)
Liquidation completed
Each share Common $1 par exchanged for initial distribution of $0.64 cash 08/24/1972
Each share Common $1 par received second and final distribution of $0.1685 cash 11/22/1972

CHATHAM TR CO (CHATHAM, NJ)
Capital Stock $100 par changed to $25 par and (3) additional shares issued plus a 25% stock dividend paid 01/08/1957
Capital Stock $25 par changed to $5 par and (4) additional shares issued 01/23/1968
Stock Dividends - 10% 12/29/1969; 10% 12/29/1971; 15% 12/28/1972
Acquired by Summit Bancorporation 07/01/1979

Each share Capital Stock $5 par exchanged for (1.2) shares Common no par
Summit Bancorporation merged into Summit Bancorp 03/01/1996 which merged into FleetBoston Financial Corp. 03/01/2001 which merged into Bank of America Corp. 04/01/2004

CHATSWORTH APARTMENTS (MI)
Liquidation for cash completed 03/03/1964
Details not available

CHATSWORTH ENTERPRISES INC (FL)
Proclaimed dissolved for failure to file reports and pay fees 06/22/1988

CHATTAHOOCHEE & GULF R.R. CO.
Liquidated 00/00/1948
Details not available

CHATTAHOOCHEE BANCORP INC (GA)
Merged into Bank South Corp. 03/15/1994
Each share Common $1 par exchanged for (0.6988) share Common $5 par
Bank South Corp. merged into NationsBank Corp. (NC) 01/09/1996 which reincorporated in Delaware as BankAmerica Corp. (Old) 09/25/1998 which merged into BankAmerica Corp. (New) 09/30/1998 which name changed to Bank of America Corp. 04/28/1999

CHATTANOOGA GAS CO (TN)
Merged into Jupiter Industries, Inc. 11/12/1971
Each share Common $1 par exchanged for $13.50 cash
Note: Unexchanged certificates were cancelled and became without value 11/12/1977

CHATTANOOGA NEWSPAPER CORP. (TN)
Charter revoked for failure to file reports and pay fees 01/02/1942

CHATTEM INC (TN)
Name changed 10/02/1978
Name changed from Chattem Drug & Chemical Co. to Chattem Inc. 10/02/1978
Each share Preferred Ser. A no par converted into (4) shares Common no par 00/00/1989
(Additional Information in Active)

CHATTER BOX CALL CTR LTD (DE)
SEC revoked common stock registration 06/10/2015

CHATTOWN COM NETWORK INC (DE)
Name changed to eLocity Networks Corp. 12/19/2000
eLocity Networks Corp. name changed to Diversified Financial Resources Corp. (DE) 08/23/2002 which reincorporated in Nevada 05/12/2006 which name changed to China Fruits Corp. 09/08/2006

CHATWINS GROUP INC (DE)
Merged into Reunion Industries, Inc. 03/16/2000
Details not available

CHATWOOD RES LTD (BC)
Recapitalized as Logicon Products Ltd. 11/10/1988
Each share Common no par exchanged for (0.33333333) share Common no par
(See Logicon Products Ltd.)

CHATWORTH RES INC (BC)
Merged into ComWest Enterprise Corp. 12/12/2005
Each share Common no par exchanged for (0.3728) share Non-Vtg. Class A no par and (0.3728) share Class B no par
ComWest Enterprise Corp. name changed to Unisync Corp. 08/01/2014

CHAUNCEY ENTERPRISES INC (NJ)
Reincorporated under the laws of Delaware as American Recreation Services Inc. 06/24/1971
(See American Recreation Services Inc.)

CHAUS BERNARD INC (NY)
Each share old Common 1¢ par exchanged for (0.1) share new Common 1¢ par 12/09/1997
Acquired by Camuto Group 07/10/2012
Each share new Common 1¢ par exchanged for $0.21 cash

CHAUVCO RES INTL LTD (BERMUDA)
Placed in bankruptcy by Alberta Court of Queen's Bench 01/26/1999
Stockholders' equity unlikely

CHAUVCO RES LTD (AB)
Class A Common no par split (2) for (1) by issuance of (1) additional share 08/14/1985
Each share Class B Common no par exchanged for (21.73) shares Class A Common no par 10/26/1986
Class A Common no par reclassified as Common no par 05/03/1990
Common no par split (2) for (1) by issuance of (1) additional share 06/22/1992
Each share Class A Common no par received distribution of (1) share Chauvco Resources International Ltd. Common no par 12/22/1997
Plan of arrangement effective 12/18/1997
Each share Class A Common no par exchanged for either (0.493827) share of Pioneer Natural Resources Co. Common no par or Exchangeable Share no par
Note: Shares held by Non-Canadians or non-electors will receive Common

CHAVA RES LTD (BC)
Common no par split (2) for (1) by issuance of (1) additional share payable 06/18/2009 to holders of record 06/18/2009
Name changed to Minaurum Gold Inc. 11/20/2009

CHAVANNES INTL CORP (DE)
Name changed 07/15/1968
Name changed from Chavannes Industrial Synthetics Inc. to Chavannes International Corp. 07/15/1968
Charter cancelled and declared inoperative and void for non-payment of taxes 06/08/1987

CHAVIN CDA LTD (BC)
Reincorporated 08/31/1982
Place of incorporation changed from (ON) to (BC) 08/31/1982
Merged into Dominion Explorers Inc. (Old) 07/25/1986
Each share Class B no par exchanged for (0.125) share Subordinate no par
Each share Common no par exchanged for (0.125) share Subordinate no par
Dominion Explorers Inc. (Old) merged into Dominion Explorers Inc. (New) 12/31/1994 which merged into Neutrino Resources Inc. 02/28/1997
(See Neutrino Resources Inc.)

CHAY ENTERPRISES INC (CO)
Each share old Common no par exchanged for (0.28571428) share new Common no par 08/01/2008
Reincorporated under the laws of Delaware as Ampio Pharmaceuticals, Inc. and Common no par changed to $0.0001 par 03/31/2010

CHC CORP (MD)
Stock Dividends - 10% 03/31/1975; 10% 01/15/1976; 10% 01/31/1977
In process of liquidation
Each share Common 50¢ par exchanged for initial distribution of $6 cash 11/07/1977
Each share Common 50¢ par received second distribution of $2.50 cash 03/21/1978
Each share Common 50¢ par received third distribution of $0.75 cash 12/20/1979
Further details not available

CHC GROUP LTD (CAYMAN ISLANDS)
Each share old Ordinary $0.0001 par exchanged for (0.03333333) share new Ordinary $0.0001 par 12/11/2015
Plan of reorganization under Chapter 11 Federal Bankruptcy proceedings effective 03/24/2017
No stockholders' equity

CHC HELICOPTER CORP (CANADA)
Each share Common no par exchanged for (0.5) share Subordinate Class A no par and (0.5) share Multiple Class B no par 09/27/1991
Subordinate Class A no par split (2) for (1) by issuance of (1) additional share payable 04/18/2005 to holders of record 04/14/2005 Ex date - 04/19/2005
Multiple Class B no par split (2) for (1) by issuance of (1) additional share payable 04/20/2005 to holders of record 04/14/2005 Ex date - 04/12/2005
Merged into First Reserve Corp. 09/16/2008
Each share Subordinate Class A no par exchanged for $32.68 cash
Each share Multiple Class B no par exchanged for $32.68 cash

CHC RLTY CAP CORP (ON)
Recapitalized as CHC Student Housing Corp. 02/20/2015
Each share Common no par exchanged for (0.0117647) share Common no par

CHDT CORP (FL)
Name changed to Capstone Companies, Inc. 07/06/2012

CHEAP TICKETS INC (DE)
Merged into Cendant Corp. 10/09/2001
Each share Common $0.001 par exchanged for $16.50 cash

CHECCHI & CO (DE)
5.5% Conv. Preferred $8 par called for redemption 06/14/1971
Company became private 00/00/1981
Details not available

CHECK EXPRESS INC (FL)
Each share old Common $0.0002 par exchanged for (0.1) share new Common $0.0002 par 09/25/1989
Each share new Common $0.0002 par exchanged for (0.5) share Common $0.004 par 09/28/1992
Merged into ACE Cash Express, Inc. 02/01/1996
Each share Common $0.004 par exchanged for $1.20 cash

CHECK RITE INTL INC (UT)
Merged into Broadcast International, Inc. (Old) 12/03/1990
Each share Common 1¢ par exchanged for (0.03721844) share new Common 10¢ par
Broadcast International, Inc. merged into Data Broadcasting Corp. 06/30/1995 which name changed to Interactive Data Corp. 06/20/2001
(See Interactive Data Corp.)

CHECK TECHNOLOGY CORP (MN)
Name changed to Delphax Technologies Inc. 04/01/2002

CHECKER CAB MANUFACTURING CORP. (NJ)
Each share Common no par exchanged for (0.25) share Common $5 par 00/00/1932

Each share Common $5 par exchanged for (4) shares Common $1.25 par 00/00/1946
Name changed to Checker Motors Corp. 03/14/1958
(See Checker Motors Corp.)

CHECKER MTRS CORP (NJ)
Stock Dividend - 10% 01/02/1979
$1.60 Conv. Preferred $40 par called for redemption 03/06/1985
Merged into Checker Holding Corp. 03/04/1986
For holdings of (9) shares or fewer each share Common $1.25 par exchanged for $58.95 cash
For holdings of (10) shares or more each share Common $1.25 par exchanged for $11 principal amount of Subord. Debentures due 04/15/1992 and $51 cash

CHECKERS DRIVE-IN RESTAURANTS INC (DE)
Common $0.001 par split (3) for (2) by issuance of (0.5) additional share 02/20/1992
Common $0.001 par split (2) for (1) by issuance of (1) additional share 09/03/1992
Common $0.001 par split (3) for (2) by issuance of (0.5) additional share 06/30/1993
Each share old Common $0.001 par exchanged for (0.08333333) share new Common $0.001 par 08/09/1999
Merged into Taxi Holdings Corp. 06/20/2006
Each share Common $0.001 par exchanged for $15 cash

CHECKERS RESTAURANT GROUP INC (DE)
Chapter 11 bankruptcy proceedings converted to Chapter 7 on 02/15/1991
No stockholders' equity

CHECKFREE CORP NEW (DE)
Merged into Fiserv, Inc. 12/03/2007
Each share Common 1¢ par exchanged for $48 cash

CHECKFREE CORP OLD (DE)
Under plan of reorganization each share Common 1¢ par automatically became (1) share CheckFree Holdings Corp. Common 1¢ par 12/23/1997
CheckFree Holdings Corp. name changed to CheckFree Corp. (New) 08/03/2000
(See CheckFree Corp. (New))

CHECKFREE HLDGS CORP (DE)
Name changed to CheckFree Corp. (New) 08/03/2000
(See CheckFree Corp. (New))

CHECKMATE ELECTRS INC (GA)
Reorganized 06/24/1993
Reorganized from Nevada to under the laws of Georgia 06/24/1993
Each share old Common 1¢ par exchanged for (0.2) share new Common 1¢ par
Merged into IVI Checkmate Corp. 06/25/1998
Each share new Common 1¢ par exchanged for (1.2775) shares Common 1¢ par
(See IVI Checkmate Corp.)

CHECKMATE RES LTD (BC)
Delisted from Vancouver Stock Exchange 04/07/1986

CHECKPOINT GENETICS PHARMACEUTICALS INC (NV)
Common $0.001 par split (2) for (1) by issuance of (1) additional share payable 03/15/2001 to holders of record 03/05/2001 Ex date - 03/16/2001
Recapitalized as InterNatural Pharmaceuticals, Inc. 07/13/2001
Each share Common $0.001 par exchanged for (0.1) share Common $0.001 par

CHECKPOINT SYS INC (PA)
Common 10¢ par split (2) for (1) by issuance of (1) additional share 07/01/1983
Common 10¢ par split (2) for (1) by issuance of (1) additional share 05/27/1986
Common 10¢ par split (2) for (1) by issuance of (1) additional share payable 02/22/1996 to holders of record 01/18/1996 Ex date - 02/23/1996
Preferred Stock Purchase Rights declared for Common stockholders of record 12/00/1988 were redeemed at $0.005 per right 04/08/1997 for holders of record 03/24/1997
Stock Dividends - 100% 08/22/1980; 50% 07/13/1981
Acquired by CCL Industries Inc. 05/13/2016
Each share Common 10¢ par exchanged for $10.15 cash

CHECKROBOT INC (DE)
Merged into Uniquest, Inc. 09/02/1992
Each share Common 1¢ par exchanged for (0.34675) share Common 1¢ par
(See Uniquest, Inc.)

CHEDABUCTO MINING CORP. LTD. (ON)
Charter cancelled 00/00/1960

CHEERS INTL TELEMARKETING LTD (BC)
Recapitalized as American Highland Mining Corp. 01/04/1990
Each share Common no par exchanged for (0.5) share Common no par
American Highland Mining Corp. name changed to Cryocon Containers Inc. 02/26/1992 which recapitalized as Cryocon-Pacific Containers Inc. 06/17/1993 which recapitalized as Alda Industries Corp. 05/06/1996 which recapitalized as Crux Industries Inc. 07/14/1999 which name changed to Mont Blanc Resources Inc. 11/18/2005 which name changed to Sonora Gold & Silver Corp. 07/17/2008

CHEETAH CONSULTING INC (FL)
Name changed to Vision Industries Corp. 02/18/2009
(See Vision Industries Corp.)

CHEETAH ENTERPRISES INC (NV)
Name changed to Wari, Inc. 09/10/2018

CHEETAH VENTURES LTD (BC)
Common no par split (2) for (1) by issuance of (1) additional share payable 09/29/2010 to holders of record 09/15/2010 Ex date - 09/13/2010
Name changed to Emperor Minerals Ltd. 10/21/2010
Emperor Minerals Ltd. name changed to Emperor Oil Ltd. 08/24/2012

CHEEZEM DEV CORP (FL)
Common 1¢ par split (5) for (4) by issuance of (0.25) additional share 07/27/1979
Stock Dividends - 50% 07/20/1973; 10% 08/11/1980; 10% 04/15/1981; 10% 07/30/1982; 10% 08/02/1983; 10% 08/27/1984; 10% 09/11/1985
Name changed to Justice Investment Corp. 09/16/1985
Justice Investment Corp. name changed to American Community Development Group, Inc. 09/30/1986
(See American Community Development Corp.)

CHEF PIERRE INC (DE)
Acquired by Consolidated Foods Corp. 05/12/1978
Each share Common 50¢ par exchanged for (1.269) shares Common $1.33333333 par
Consolidated Foods Corp. name changed to Sara Lee Corp. 04/02/1985 which recapitalized as Hillshire Brands Co. 06/29/2012
(See Hillshire Brands Co.)

CHEF SELECTIONS INC (CO)
Common $0.0001 par split (2) for (1) by issuance of (1) additional share payable 07/03/2006 to holders of record 06/30/2006 Ex date - 07/05/2006
Recapitalized as Talisman Holdings, Inc. 04/14/2010
Each share Common $0.0001 par exchanged for (0.01) share Common $0.0001 par
Talisman Holdings, Inc. recapitalized as Fidelity Holding Corp. 08/20/2014

CHEFLIVE INC (NV)
Old Common $0.001 par split (2) for (1) by issuance of (1) additional share payable 07/02/2007 to holders of record 07/02/2007
Name changed to Naturally Iowa, Inc. 08/06/2007
Naturally Iowa, Inc. name changed to Totally Green, Inc. 11/04/2010

CHEFS INTL INC (DE)
Each share old Common 1¢ par exchanged for (0.33333333) share new Common 1¢ par 06/07/1993
Each share new Common 1¢ par exchanged again for (0.33333333) share new Common 1¢ par 11/22/1996
Merged into Lombardi Restaurant Group, Inc. 06/03/2005
Each share new Common 1¢ par exchanged for $3.12 cash

CHELAN RES INC (BC)
Struck off register and declared dissolved for failure to file returns 08/13/1993

CHELIK RES INC (BC)
Name changed to High Desert Mineral Resources Inc. 03/07/1989
(See High Desert Mineral Resources Inc.)

CHELL GROUP CORP (NY)
SEC revoked common stock registration 03/03/2011

CHELLEW GOLD MINES LTD. (ON)
Name changed to Chellew Mines Ltd. 08/17/1955
(See Chellew Mines Ltd.)

CHELLEW MINES LTD. (ON)
Charter revoked for failure to file reports and pay fees 06/30/1969

CHELSEA ACQUISITION CORP (AB)
Reorganized under the laws of Canada as Pediapharm Inc. 12/27/2013
Each share Common no par exchanged for (0.33333333) share Common no par

CHELSEA ATWATER INC (NV)
Name changed to CEREX Entertainment Corp. 01/29/1997
CEREX Entertainment Corp. name changed to CERX Entertainment Corp. 03/19/1997 which name changed to CERX Venture Corp. 03/23/1998 which name changed to Ebonlineinc.com 07/08/1999 which name changed to MoneyZone.com (NV) 12/17/1999 which reincorporated in Delaware as MoneyZone.com, Inc. 06/12/2001 which name changed to QT 5, Inc. 01/08/2003 which recapitalized as Addison-Davis Diagnostics, Inc. 11/18/2004
(See Addison-Davis Diagnostics, Inc.)

CHELSEA COLLECTION INC (NV)
Common $0.001 par split (15) for (1) by issuance of (14) additional shares payable 08/10/2006 to holders of record 08/09/2006 Ex date - 08/11/2006
Recapitalized as G-H-3 International, Inc. 10/30/2006
Each share Common $0.001 par exchanged for (0.05) share Common $0.001 par

CHELSEA EXCHANGE CORP.
Liquidated 00/00/1939
Details not available

CHELSEA GCA RLTY INC (MD)
Name changed to Chelsea Property Group, Inc. 01/01/2001
Chelsea Property Group, Inc. merged into Simon Property Group, Inc. 10/14/2004

CHELSEA HOTEL CO. (IL)
Completely liquidated 07/22/1966
Each share Capital Stock $5 par exchanged for first and final distribution of $7.60 cash

CHELSEA INDS INC (MA)
Reincorporated 03/31/1977
Common $1 par split (3) for (2) by issuance of (0.5) additional share 02/29/1968
Common $1 par split (3) for (2) by issuance of (0.5) additional share 02/28/1969
State of incorporation changed from (DE) to (MA) 03/31/1977
Stock Dividend - 10% 03/30/1979
Acquired by CI Acquisition Corp. 10/06/1989
Each share Common $1 par exchanged for $29.50 cash

CHELSEA MGMT GROUP INC (NV)
Name changed to Great Lakes Biogas Technologies Inc. 07/02/2008
Great Lakes Biogas Technologies Inc. merged into American Great Lakes Corp. 05/01/2009 which recapitalized as Unique Transportation Solutions, Inc. 12/02/2009
(See Unique Transportation Solutions, Inc.)

CHELSEA MINERALS CORP (BC)
Merged into Sennen Resources Ltd. 05/13/2011
Each share Common no par exchanged for (0.4) share Common no par
Note: Unexchanged certificates were be cancelled and became without value 05/13/2017
Sennen Resources Ltd. name changed to Sennen Potash Corp. 04/15/2013

CHELSEA NATL BK (NEW YORK, NY)
Capital Stock $10 par changed to $5 par and (1) additional share issued 04/27/1970
In process of liquidation
Each share Capital Stock $5 par received initial distribution of $1 cash 02/29/1980
Each share Capital Stock $5 par received second distribution of $0.30 cash 07/01/1984
Details on additional distributions, if any, are not available

CHELSEA PPTY GROUP INC (MD)
Common 1¢ par split (2) for (1) by issuance of (1) additional share payable 05/28/2002 to holders of record 05/14/2002 Ex date - 05/29/2002
Merged into Simon Property Group, Inc. 10/14/2004
Each share 8.375% Preferred Ser. A 1¢ par exchanged for (1) share 8.375% Preferred Ser. A
Each share Common 1¢ par exchanged for (0.3) share 6% Conv. Perpetual Conv. Preferred Ser. I,

(0.2936) share Common 1¢ par and $36 cash

CHELSEA RES & DEVS LTD (ON)
Charter cancelled and proclaimed dissolved for failure to pay taxes and file returns 06/05/1992

CHELSEA SCREW CO. OF CHELSEA, MICHIGAN
Acquired by Federal Screw Works 00/00/1928
Details not available

CHELSEA STR FINL HLDG CORP (UT)
Name changed to Wexford Technology Inc. 12/03/1993
Wexford Technology Inc. name changed to sureBET Casinos, Inc. 06/24/1999
(See sureBET Casinos, Inc.)

CHELSEA THERAPEUTICS INTL LTD (DE)
Acquired by H. Lundbeck A/S 06/24/2014
Each share Common $0.0001 par exchanged for $6.44 cash and (1) Non-transferable Contingent Value Right

CHELSEA TITLE & GTY CO (NJ)
Common $25 par split (5) for (4) by issuance of (0.5) additional share 06/15/1972
Merged into Chicago Title Corp. 00/00/1986
Details not available

CHELSEA TOWNE LTD (NY)
Dissolved by proclamation 12/24/1991

CHELSEY VENTURES LTD (CO)
Name changed to PHS Industries, Inc. 05/08/1989

CHELTEN AVENUE BUILDING CORP. (PA)
Dissolved 06/30/1961
Details not available

CHELTEN CORP.
In process of liquidation 00/00/1945
Details not available

CHELTENHAM BK (CHELTENHAM, PA)
Capital Stock $5 par changed to $2.50 par and (1) additional share issued 12/01/1978
Under plan of reorganization each share Common $2.50 par automatically became (1) share Cheltenham Corp. Common $1 par 07/01/1982
Cheltenham Corp. merged into Independence Bancorp, Inc. (PA) 09/01/1983 which merged into CoreStates Financial Corp 06/27/1994 which merged into First Union Corp. 04/28/1998 which name changed to Wachovia Corp. (Ctfs. dated after 09/01/2001) 09/01/2001 which merged into Wells Fargo & Co. (New) 12/31/2008

CHELTENHAM CORP (PA)
Merged into Independence Bancorp, Inc. (PA) 09/01/1983
Each share Common $1 par exchanged for (2.5) shares Common $2.50 par
Independence Bancorp, Inc. (PA) merged into CoreStates Financial Corp 06/27/1994 which merged into First Union Corp. 04/28/1998 which name changed to Wachovia Corp. (Ctfs. dated after 09/01/2001) 09/01/2001 which merged into Wells Fargo & Co. (New) 12/31/2008

CHELTENHAM NATIONAL BANK (CHELTENHAM, PA)
Capital Stock $10 par changed to $5 par and (1) additional share issued 05/27/1964
Stock Dividend - 10% 02/01/1962
Name changed to Cheltenham Bank (Cheltenham, PA) 03/19/1973
Cheltenham Bank (Cheltenham, PA) reorganized as Cheltenham Corp. 07/01/1982 which merged into Independence Bancorp, Inc. (PA) 09/01/1983 which merged into CoreStates Financial Corp 06/27/1994 which merged into First Union Corp. 04/28/1998 which name changed to Wachovia Corp. (Ctfs. dated after 09/01/2001) 09/01/2001 which merged into Wells Fargo & Co. (New) 12/31/2008

CHELYABINSK SVYAZINFORM (RUSSIA)
ADR agreement terminated 12/19/2002
Each Sponsored ADR for Ordinary exchanged for $3.52027 cash

CHELYABINSK ZINC PLT PJSC (RUSSIA)
Name changed 08/18/2016
Basis changed from (1:0.1) to (1:1) 10/02/2007
Name changed from Chelyabinsk Zinc Plant JSC to Chelyabinsk Zinc Plant PJSC 08/18/2016
GDR agreement terminated 08/22/2018
Each 144A Sponsored GDR for Ordinary exchanged for $9.247942 cash
Each Reg. S Sponsored GDR for Ordinary exchanged for $9.247942 cash (1st Ent. 01/08/2007 - TA adv.)

CHEM AERO INC (CA)
Capital Stock 50¢ par changed to 25¢ par and (1) additional share issued 04/15/1971
Charter suspended for failure to file reports and pay fees 01/02/1981

CHEM-AG PRODUCTS, INC. (CO)
Charter revoked for failure to file reports and pay fees 10/17/1967

CHEM INTL INC (DE)
Each share old Common $0.002 par exchanged for (0.25) share new Common $0.002 par 07/02/1996
Name changed to Integrated Health Technologies Inc. 01/05/2001
Integrated Health Technologies Inc. name changed to Integrated BioPharma, Inc. 04/15/2003

CHEM-LAWN CORP. (OH)
Common no par split (3) for (2) by issuance of (0.5) additional share 12/15/1979
Common no par split (3) for (2) by issuance of (0.5) additional share 11/12/1980
Name changed to ChemLawn Corp. 04/21/1983
(See ChemLawn Corp.)

CHEM NUCLEAR SYS INC (WA)
Common 10¢ par split (3) for (2) by issuance of (0.5) additional share 12/01/1980
Common 10¢ par changed to 5¢ par and (1) additional share issued 01/29/1982
Merged into Waste Management, Inc. (Old) 10/28/1982
Each share Common 5¢ par exchanged for (0.3657) share Common $1 par
Waste Management, Inc. (Old) name changed to WMX Technologies Inc. 05/14/1993 which name changed to Waste Management, Inc. (New) 05/12/1997

CHEM-ORE MINES, LTD. (ON)
Charter revoked for failure to file reports and pay taxes 00/00/1952

CHEM RX CORP (DE)
Plan of reorganization under Chapter 11 Federal Bankruptcy proceedings effective 04/29/2011
No stockholders' equity

CHEM-SEARCH, INC. (MN)
Name changed to T.K. Products, Inc. 12/19/1963
(See T.K. Products, Inc.)

CHEM TECHNICS INC (DE)
Chapter 11 Federal Bankruptcy proceedings converted to Chapter 7 on 12/12/1985
Stockholders' equity unlikely

CHEM TRONICS INC (CA)
Common no par split (3) for (2) by issuance of (0.5) additional share 05/02/1983
Acquired by Interlake, Inc. 12/04/1984
Each share Common no par exchanged for $23.50 cash

CHEMAIR CORP AMER (FL)
Stock Dividend - 200% 02/05/1971
Name changed to Beauty Brands Group, Inc. 03/10/1983
(See Beauty Brands Group, Inc.)

CHEMALLOY MINERALS LTD (ON)
Recapitalized as International Chemalloy Corp. 11/21/1974
Each share Capital Stock $1 par exchanged for (0.33333333) share Capital Stock no par
International Chemalloy Corp. recapitalized as Denbridge Capital Corp. (ON) 01/20/1986 which reincorporated in Canada 02/24/1994 which recapitalized as Atlantis Systems Corp. 06/11/2001
(See Atlantis Systems Corp.)

CHEMANOX INC (DE)
Assets sold for benefit of creditors 00/00/1973
No stockholders' equity

CHEMAPHOR INC (CANADA)
Name changed to Avivagen Inc. 05/30/2012

CHEMATOMICS, INC. (DE)
No longer in existence having become inoperative and void for non-payment of taxes 04/01/1963

CHEMBOND LTD (ON)
Acquired by Mapei Acquisition Inc. 12/06/2001
Each share Common no par exchanged for $0.10 cash

CHEMCELL (1963) LTD. (CANADA)
Name changed to Chemcell Ltd.-Chemcell Ltee. 06/01/1966
Chemcell Ltd.-Chemcell Ltee. name changed to Celanese Canada Ltd.-Celanese Canada Ltee. 01/07/1972 which name changed to Celanese Canada Inc. 01/08/1980
(See Calanese Canada Inc.)

CHEMCELL LTD CHEMCELL LTEE (CANADA)
Name changed to Celanese Canada Ltd.- Celanese Canada Ltee. 01/07/1972
Celanese Canada Ltd.-Celanese Canada Ltee. name changed to Celanese Canada Inc. 01/08/1980
(See Celanese Canada Inc.)

CHEMCLEAR INC (PA)
Common 10¢ par split (2) for (1) by issuance of (1) additional share 06/18/1986
Merged into Clean Harbors, Inc. 01/26/1989
Each share Common 10¢ par exchanged for (0.16402) share Common 1¢ par and $2.1986 cash

CHEMCUT CORP (PA)
Common $1 par split (2) for (1) by issuance of (1) additional share 03/18/1966
Merged into Schering AG 02/20/1980
Each share Common $1 par exchanged for $56 cash

CHEMDESIGN CORP (MA)
Merged into Zeto Acquisition Corp. 07/15/1994
Each share Common 1¢ par exchanged for $8.50 cash

CHEMDEX CORP (DE)
Name changed to Ventro Corp. 03/01/2000
Ventro Corp. name changed to NexPrise, Inc. 01/15/2002

CHEMECON CORP. (DE)
Merged into Larsen Industries, Inc. on a (0.7) for (1) basis 12/28/1960
Larsen Industries, Inc. name changed to United Technical Industries, Inc. 03/22/1961 which was liquidated for for Stickelber & Sons, Inc. 12/02/1964 which merged into Marion Corp. 02/01/1965
(See Marion Corp.)

CHEMED CORP (DE)
Capital Stock $1 par split (2) for (1) by issuance of (1) additional share 11/10/1981
Name changed to Roto-Rooter, Inc. (New) 05/19/2003
Roto-Rooter, Inc. (New) name changed to Chemed Corp. 05/17/2004

CHEMELEX, INC. (NY)
Acquired by Raychem Corp. (CA) 07/00/1969
Details not available

CHEMETRON CORP (DE)
4.75% Preferred $100 par called for redemption 08/30/1968
4.25% Preferred $100 par called for redemption 10/27/1969
Merged into Allegheny Ludlum Industries, Inc. 11/30/1977
Each share Common $1 par exchanged for (2.2) shares $2.19 Preferred no par
Allegheny Ludlum Industries, Inc. name changed to Allegheny International Inc. 04/29/1981
(See Allegheny International Inc.)

CHEMEX CORP (WY)
Name changed to Chemex Pharmaceuticals, Inc. (WY) 10/16/1983
Chemex Pharmaceuticals, Inc. (WY) reincorporated in Delaware 06/30/1989 which name changed to Access Pharmaceuticals, Inc. 01/25/1996 which recapitalized as PlasmaTech Biopharmaceuticals, Inc. 10/24/2014 which name changed to Abeona Therapeutics Inc. 06/22/2015

CHEMEX INDS INC (FL)
Involuntarily dissolved 11/04/1988

CHEMEX PHARMACEUTICALS INC (DE)
Reincorporated 06/30/1989
State of incorporation changed from (WY) to (DE) 06/30/1989
Each share Common 1¢ par exchanged for (0.5) share Common 4¢ par to reflect a (1) for (4) reverse split followed by a (2) for (1) forward split 04/15/1992
Name changed to Access Pharmaceuticals, Inc. 01/25/1996
Access Pharmaceuticals, Inc. recapitalized as PlasmaTech Biopharmaceuticals, Inc. 10/24/2014 which name changed to Abeona Therapeutics Inc. 06/22/2015

CHEMFAB CORP (DE)
Merged into Compagnie de Saint-Gobain 09/05/2000
Each share Common 10¢ par exchanged for $18.25 cash

CHEMFIRST CORP (NJ)
Charter revoked for failure to file reports and pay fees 08/05/1995

CHEMFIRST INC (MS)
Merged into Du Pont (E.I.) de Nemours & Co. 11/06/2002
Each share Common $1 par exchanged for $29.20 cash

CHEMFIX TECHNOLOGIES INC (DE)
Common 1¢ par split (3) for (1) by issuance of (2) additional shares 07/29/1983
Each share old Common 1¢ par

exchanged for (0.1) share new Common 1¢ par 01/15/1997
Recapitalized as Fowler Oil & Gas Corp. 02/10/2005
Each share Common 1¢ par exchanged for (0.00333333) share Common 1¢ par
(See Fowler Oil & Gas Corp.)

CHEMGENEX PHARMACEUTICALS LTD (AUSTRALIA)
Basis changed from (1:10) to (1:15) 06/24/2005
Each Sponsored ADR for Ordinary received distribution of $0.106919 cash payable 11/27/2009 to holders of record 11/16/2009 Ex date - 11/12/2009
Acquired by Cephalon, Inc. 07/21/2011
Each Sponsored ADR for Ordinary exchanged for $10.765111 cash

CHEMGRAPHICS INC (MN)
Reincorporated under the laws of Nevada as Flagship International Holding, Ltd. 11/22/1999

CHEMI TECH LABS INC (DE)
Charter cancelled and declared inoperative and void for non-payment of taxes 03/01/1987

CHEMI TROL CHEM CO (OH)
Common no par split (6) for (5) by issuance of (0.2) additional share 11/30/1992
Stock Dividends - 10% 03/15/1994; 10% 03/15/1995
Merged into Harsco Corp. 06/17/1998
Each share Common no par exchanged for $23 cash

CHEMICAL & AEROSPACE PRODS INC (CA)
Name changed to Chem Aero, Inc. 10/15/1970
(See Chem Aero, Inc.)

CHEMICAL & METALLURGICAL ENTERPRISES INC (UT)
Charter suspended for failure to pay taxes 03/31/1961

CHEMICAL & POLLUTION SCIENCES INC (NJ)
Name changed to CPS Chemical Co., Inc. 12/20/1979
(See CPS Chemical Co., Inc.)

CHEMICAL BANK & TRUST CO. (NEW YORK, NY)
Stock Dividends - 25% 11/24/1945; 10% 12/09/1953
Under plan of merger name changed to Chemical Corn Exchange Bank (New York, NY) 10/18/1954
Chemical Corn Exchange Bank (New York, NY) merged into Chemical Bank New York Trust Co. (New York, NY) 09/08/1959 which reorganized as Chemical New York Corp. 02/17/1969 which name changed to Chemical Banking Corp. 04/29/1988 which name changed to Chase Manhattan Corp. (New) 03/31/1996 which name changed to J.P. Morgan Chase & Co. 12/31/2000 which name changed to JPMorgan Chase & Co. 07/20/2004

CHEMICAL BK & TR CO (MIDLAND, MI)
Stock Dividends - 33.33333333% 02/06/1967; 25% 02/16/1970
Reorganized as Chemical Financial Corp. 07/01/1974
Each share Capital Stock $20 par exchanged for (2) shares Common $10 par

CHEMICAL BK & TR CO (SOUTH CHARLESTON, WV)
Common $25 par split (2) for (1) by issuance of (1) additional share 03/18/1976
Merged into National Banc of Commerce Co. 01/20/1987
Each share Common $25 par exchanged for (5.6) shares Common $1.25 par
National Banc of Commerce Co. name changed to Commerce Banc Corp. 04/21/1992 which merged into Huntington Bancshares Inc. 09/24/1993

CHEMICAL BANK-EASTERN, N.A. (GREENWICH, NY)
Acquired by Chemical New York Corp. 09/29/1978
Each share Capital Stock $100 par exchanged for (56.34) shares Common $12 par
Chemical New York Corp. name changed to Chemical Banking Corp. 04/29/1988 which name changed to Chase Manhattan Corp. (New) 03/31/1996 which name changed to J.P. Morgan Chase & Co. 12/31/2000 which name changed to JPMorgan Chase & Co. 07/20/2004

CHEMICAL BK NEW YORK TR CO (NEW YORK, NY)
Stock Dividend - 50% 03/11/1965
Reorganized under the laws of Delaware as Chemical New York Corp. 02/17/1969
Each share Capital Stock $12 par exchanged for (1) share Common $12 par
Chemical New York Corp. name changed to Chemical Banking Corp. 04/29/1988 which name changed to Chase Manhattan Corp. (New) 03/31/1996 which name changed to J.P. Morgan Chase & Co. 12/31/2000 which name changed to JPMorgan Chase & Co. 07/20/2004

CHEMICAL BKG CORP (DE)
Each share Conv. Class B Common no par exchanged for (0.03) share Common $1 par 03/27/1992
Adjustable Rate Preferred no par called for redemption 08/25/1992
Adjustable Rate Preferred Ser. B no par called for redemption 09/30/1992
Adjustable Dividend Preferred Ser. E no par called for redemption 04/30/1993
Adjustable Dividend Preferred Ser. F no par called for redemption 06/22/1993
Depositary Shares called for redemption 12/31/1993
10.75% Preferred no par called for redemption 12/31/1993
Adjustable Rate Preferred Ser. C no par called for redemption 07/15/1994
10% Conv. Preferred no par called for redemption 05/31/1995
Name changed to Chase Manhattan Corp. (New) 03/31/1996
Chase Manhattan Corp. (New) name changed to J.P. Morgan Chase & Co. 12/31/2000 which name changed to JPMorgan Chase & Co. 07/20/2004

CHEMICAL CONSORTIUM HLDGS INC (DE)
Each share old Common $0.0001 par exchanged for (0.1) share new Common $0.0001 par 08/29/2005
Name changed to New NRG, Inc. 05/21/2007
(See New NRG, Inc.)

CHEMICAL CONTOUR CORP. (CA)
Merged into Automation Industries, Inc. (CA) 08/31/1965
Each share Common no par exchanged for (0.32) share Conv. Preferred Ser. A $3 par
(See Automation Industries, Inc. (CA))

CHEMICAL CORN EXCHANGE BANK (NEW YORK, NY)
Stock Dividend - 10% 09/30/1955
Merged into Chemical Bank New York Trust Co. (New York, NY) 09/08/1959

Each share Capital Stock $10 par exchanged for (1) share Capital Stock $12 par
Chemical Bank New York Trust Co. (New York, NY) reorganized as Chemical New York Corp. 02/17/1969 which name changed to Chemical Banking Corp. 04/29/1988 which name changed to Chase Manhattan Corp. (New) 03/31/1996 which name changed to J.P. Morgan Chase & Co. 12/31/2000 which name changed to JPMorgan Chase & Co. 07/20/2004

CHEMICAL DEPENDENCY HEALTHCARE INC (CA)
Recapitalized as La Jolla Diagnostics, Inc. 04/17/1995
Each share Common no par exchanged for (0.1) share Common no par
La Jolla Diagnostics, Inc. name changed to NatureWell, Inc. (CA) 01/04/2001 which reincorporated in Delaware 10/25/2001 which recapitalized as Brazil Interactive Media, Inc. 05/30/2013 which name changed to American Cannabis Co., Inc. 10/10/2014

CHEMICAL ENTERPRISES, INC. (DE)
Liquidation completed
Each share Common 25¢ par exchanged for initial distribution of $7.75 cash 11/30/1966
Each share Common 25¢ par received second distribution of $0.15 cash 03/09/1967
Each share Common 25¢ par received third and final distribution of $0.189 cash 08/11/1969

CHEMICAL EXPRESS CO (TX)
Merged into CX Transportation Inc. 09/29/1977
Each share Common 50¢ par exchanged for $5 cash

CHEMICAL FABRICS CORP (DE)
Name changed to Chemfab Corp. 11/06/1991
(See Chemfab Corp.)

CHEMICAL FD INC (MD)
Reincorporated 04/01/1987
Common $1 par changed to 50¢ par and (1) additional share issued 07/15/1955
Common 50¢ par changed to 25¢ par and (1) additional share issued 04/15/1959
Common 25¢ par changed to $0.125 par and (1) additional share issued 03/17/1972
State of incorporation changed from (DE) to (MD) 02/08/1979
Name changed to Alliance Fund, Inc. 04/01/1987
Alliance Fund, Inc. name changed to Alliance Mid-Cap Growth Fund Inc. 02/01/2002 which name changed to AllianceBernstein Mid-Cap Growth Fund, Inc. 03/31/2003

CHEMICAL FIRE & CASUALTY INSURANCE CO. (TN)
Liquidated 12/13/1959
No stockholders' equity

CHEMICAL INVS INC (IN)
Common no par split (3) for (2) by issuance of (0.5) additional share 09/25/1981
Common no par split (2) for (1) by issuance of (1) additional share 05/03/1982
Chapter 11 bankruptcy proceedings dismissed 06/26/1986
No stockholders' equity

CHEMICAL LEAMAN CORP (PA)
Each share old Common $2.50 par exchanged for (0.005) share new Common $2.50 par 09/15/1994
Merged into CLC Merger Corp. 03/25/1996
Each share new Common $2.50 par exchanged for $6,000 cash

CHEMICAL LEAMAN TANK LINES INC (DE)
Merged into Chemical Leaman Corp. 07/07/1977
Each share Common $2.50 par exchanged for (1) share Common $2.50 par
(See Chemical Leaman Corp.)

CHEMICAL LIME CO.
Acquired by National Gypsum Co. 00/00/1940
Each share Preferred exchanged for (0.075) share Preferred no par
No Common stockholders' equity
(See National Gypsum Co.)

CHEMICAL MLG INTL CORP (CA)
Stock Dividend - 100% 06/24/1968
Name changed to C M Industries 10/15/1970
(See C M Industries)

CHEMICAL NAT RES INC (DE)
Charter cancelled and declared inoperative and void for non-payment of taxes 03/01/1979

CHEMICAL NEW YORK CORP (DE)
$1.875 Conv. Preferred no par called for redemption 03/01/1987
Stock Dividends - 50% 04/15/1982; 50% 04/13/1984
Name changed to Chemical Banking Corp. 04/29/1988
Chemical Banking Corp. name changed to Chase Manhattan Corp. (New) 03/31/1996 which name changed to J.P. Morgan Chase & Co. 12/31/2000 which name changed to JPMorgan Chase & Co. 07/20/2004

CHEMICAL PAPER MANUFACTURING CO. (MA)
Each share Common $100 par exchanged for (4) shares Common $25 par 00/00/1953
Stock Dividend - 50% 06/25/1953
Merged into Chemical Paper Manufacturing Corp. on a (1) for (4.5) basis 06/17/1957

CHEMICAL PROCESS CO. (NV)
Liquidation completed 01/02/1962
Details not available

CHEMICAL PROCESS CO. (OH)
Liquidation completed
Each share Common $2.50 par exchanged for initial distribution of (0.37666) share Borg-Warner Corp. (IL) Common $5 par 10/16/1956
Each share Common $2.50 par received second and final distribution of (0.04) share Borg-Warner Corp. (IL) Common $5 par 10/21/1957
Borg-Warner Corp. (IL) reincorporated in Delaware 10/31/1967
(See Borg-Warner Corp. (DE))

CHEMICAL PRODS CORP (RI)
Name changed to CPL Corp. 06/13/1973
(See CPL Corp.)

CHEMICAL PRODUCTS CORP. (NV)
Charter revoked for failure to file reports and pay fees 03/04/1963

CHEMICAL RESEARCH (DE)
Capital Stock no par changed to $1 par 00/00/1935
Capital Stock $1 par changed to 50¢ par 00/00/1948
Recapitalized as Florida Canada Corp. 12/20/1956
Each share Capital Stock 50¢ par exchanged for (0.5) share Capital Stock $1 par
Florida Canada Corp. name changed to General Development Corp. 04/28/1958 which name changed to GDV Inc. 05/23/1977
(See GDV, Inc.)

CHEMICAL SEPARATIONS CORP. (TN)
Adjudicated bankrupt 06/27/1984

Stockholders' equity unlikely

CHEMICAL STATE SAVINGS BANK (MIDLAND, MI)
Each share Capital Stock $100 par exchanged for (5) shares Capital Stock $20 par 10/20/1953
Stock Dividends - 20% 11/30/1955; 25% 11/25/1957
Name changed to Chemical Bank & Trust Co. (Midland, MI) 10/06/1964
Chemical Bank & Trust Co. (Midland, MI) reorganized as Chemical Financial Corp. 07/01/1974

CHEMICAL VENTURES SYNDICATE, LTD. (DE)
No longer in existence having become inoperative and void for non-payment of taxes 04/01/1961

CHEMICAL WASTE MGMT INC (DE)
Common 1¢ par split (2) for (1) by issuance of (1) additional share 10/05/1989
Merged into WMX Technologies Inc. 01/24/1995
For holdings of (82) shares or more each share Common 1¢ par exchanged for $1.2330456 principal amount of Conv. Subordinated Notes due 01/24/2005
For holdings of (81) shares or fewer each share Common 1¢ par exchanged for $9.725 cash

CHEMINEER INC (OH)
Stock Dividends - 200% 12/01/1975; 50% 09/15/1977
Merged into Interpace Corp. 02/08/1983
Each share Common no par exchanged for $21 cash

CHEMINIS GOLD MINES LTD.
Acquired by Amalgamated Larder Mines Ltd. 00/00/1942
Each share Capital Stock $1 par exchanged for (0.2) share Capital Stock $1 par
Amalgamated Larder Mines Ltd. recapitalized as Larder Resources Inc. 09/08/1980 which merged into International Larder Minerals Inc. 05/01/1986 which merged into Explorers Alliance Corp. 10/13/2000
(See Explorers Alliance Corp.)

CHEMIONICS ENGINEERING LABORATORIES, INC. (NC)
Bankrupt 07/02/1962
No stockholders' equity

CHEMIRAD CORP (DE)
Charter cancelled and declared inoperative and void for non-payment of taxes 03/01/1976

CHEMLAWN CORP (OH)
Common no par split (3) for (2) by issuance of (0.5) additional share 01/16/1984
Merged into EcoLab Inc. 05/04/1987
Each share Common no par exchanged for $36.50 cash

CHEMO-VIVE PROCESSES, INC. (DE)
Name changed to Visual Environments, Inc. and Class A Common 10¢ par reclassified as Common 10¢ par 10/03/1969
(See Visual Environments, Inc.)

CHEMOIL INDUSTRIES, INC. (DE)
Merged into Szabo Food Service, Inc. 02/27/1962
Each share Common $1 par exchanged for (0.5) share Common $1 par and (0.05) share 5% Conv. Preferred $10 par
Szabo Food Service, Inc. name changed to Oakbrook Consolidated, Inc. 08/19/1975
(See Oakbrook Consolidated, Inc.)

CHEMOKINE THERAPEUTICS CORP (DE)
SEC revoked common stock registration 04/24/2012

CHEMOLA CORP (DE)
Merged into Hi-Port Industries, Inc. 04/29/1974
Each share Common 1¢ par exchanged for (0.2) share Common 5¢ par
(See Hi-Port Industries, Inc.)

CHEMOLD CORP (NY)
Each share old Class A 5¢ par exchanged for (0.1) share new Common Class A 5¢ par 05/19/1980
Merged into Great American Industries, Inc. 10/19/1984
Each share new Class A 5¢ par exchanged for $7.25 cash

CHEMOLENE INDS INC (DE)
Acquired by Magic Marker Corp. (NY) 10/29/1971
Each share Common 10¢ par exchanged for (1) share Common 50¢ par
Magic Marker Corp. (NY) reincorporated in Delaware 09/00/1975
(See Magic Marker Corp. (DE))

CHEMONICS CORP. (DE)
Out of business 00/00/1963
No stockholders' equity

CHEMPLAST INC (NJ)
Merged into Norton Co. 02/09/1982
Each share Common 25¢ par exchanged for (0.383) share Common $5 par
(See Norton Co.)

CHEMPLATE CORP (CA)
Each share Common $1 par exchanged for (2) shares Common 50¢ par 05/31/1968
Stock Dividends - 100% 03/07/1969; 100% 03/31/1971; 50% 05/01/1972; 50% 05/01/1973; 100% 01/28/1985
Plan of reorganization under Chapter 11 Federal Bankruptcy proceedings confirmed 00/00/1986
No stockholders' equity

CHEMPOWER INC (OH)
Merged into American Eco Corp. 03/03/1997
Each share Common 10¢ par exchanged for $6.20 cash

CHEMPROX CORP. (MD)
Charter revoked for failure to file reports and pay fees 10/30/1969

CHEMSEP CORP (UT)
Involuntarily dissolved 03/31/1983

CHEMSOL, INC. (NJ)
Merged into Cenco Instruments Corp. 09/30/1965
Each share Common 50¢ par exchanged for (0.1424) share Common $1 par
Cenco Instruments Corp. name changed to Cenco Inc. 10/06/1972
(See Cenco Inc.)

CHEMSPEC INTL LTD (CAYMAN ISLANDS)
Acquired by Halogen Ltd. 08/19/2011
Each ADR for Ordinary exchanged for $8.10 cash

CHEMSTAT CORP (DE)
Dissolved 00/00/1995
Details not available

CHEMTECH INDS INC (TX)
Name changed to Waste Resources Corp. 05/03/1972
Waste Resources Corp. merged into Warner Co. 07/06/1977
(See Warner Co.)

CHEMTRAK INC OLD (DE)
Each share old Common $0.001 par exchanged for (0.2) share new Common $0.001 par 07/31/1998
Recapitalized as Medivisor Marketing, Inc. 05/16/2006
Each share new Common $0.001 par exchanged for (0.01) share Common $0.001 par
Medivisor Marketing, Inc. name changed to ChemTrak, Inc. (New) 08/30/2006

CHEMTREE CORP (DE)
Name changed to Fastcrete Corp. 01/14/1985
(See Fastcrete Corp.)

CHEMTRONIC CORP. (TN)
Name changed to Nashville Electronics Inc. 05/03/1961
Nashville Electronics Inc. name changed to Whale Electronics, Inc. 06/30/1967 which name changed to Whale, Inc. 01/31/1969
(See Whale, Inc.)

CHEMTRONICS RESEARCH INC. (MN)
Name changed to Tronchemics Research Inc. 05/02/1962
(See Tronchemics Research Inc.)

CHEMTRUST INDS CORP (DE)
Assets sold by Court Order 08/14/1981
No stockholders' equity

CHEMTURA CORP (DE)
Plan of reorganization under Chapter 11 Federal Bankruptcy proceedings effective 11/10/2010
Each share old Common 1¢ par exchanged for (0.0150644) share new Common 1¢ par
Each share old Common 1¢ par received an initial additional distribution of (0.000861) share new Common 1¢ par and $0.0018883 cash payable 02/25/2011 to holders of record 11/10/2010
Each share old Common 1¢ par received a second additional distribution of (0.0061892) share new Common 1¢ par and $0.0135773 cash payable 03/16/2012 to holders of record 11/10/2010
Each share old Common 1¢ par received a third and final additional distribution of (0.0008539) share new Common 1¢ par and $0.0002901 cash payable 07/09/2012 to holders of record 11/10/2010
Acquired by Lanxess Deutschland GmbH 04/21/2017
Each share new Common 1¢ par exchanged for $33.50 cash

CHEMUNG CANAL TR CO (ELMIRA, NY)
Each share Capital Stock $20 par exchanged for (5) shares Capital Stock $5 par to effect a (4) for (1) split and 25% stock dividend 00/00/1951
Capital Stock $5 par changed to $12.50 par 02/14/1967
Capital Stock $12.50 par changed to $20 par 03/19/1970
Capital Stock $20 par changed to $25 par 05/24/1979
Capital Stock $25 par changed to $15 par and (1) additional share issued 04/17/1984
Under plan of reorganization each share Capital Stock $5 par automatically became (1) share Chemung Financial Corp. Common $15 par 07/01/1985

CHEMUNG TELEPHONE CO.
Acquired by Pennsylvania Telephone Corp. 00/00/1930
Details not available

CHEMWAY CORP (DE)
Completely liquidated 04/30/1971
Each share Capital Stock $1 par exchanged (0.2) share Cooper Laboratories, Inc. Common 10¢ par, $4 principal amount of 7.5% Conv. Subord. Debentures due 01/01/1991 and $2 cash
(See Cooper Laboratories, Inc.)

CHEMWELL INDS INC (CA)
Capital Stock $1 par changed to 25¢ par and (1) additional share issued 09/14/1971
Name changed to Capital Star Petroleum 12/21/1981
(See Capital Star Petroleum)

CHEMWORTH CORP (DE)
Charter cancelled and declared inoperative and void for non-payment of taxes 06/26/1990

CHEN HSONG HLDGS LTD (HONG KONG)
ADR agreement terminated 11/01/1999
Each Sponsored ADR for Ordinary exchanged for $1.60 cash

CHENANGO & UNADILLA TELEPHONE CORP. (NY)
Each share 6.5% Preferred Ser. A $100 par or 6% Preferred Ser. B $100 par and 7% Preferred $100 par exchanged for (1) share 6% Preferred $100 par 00/00/1941
6% Preferred $100 par reclassified as 4.52% Class A Preferred $100 par 00/00/1949
Each share Common $100 par exchanged for (5) shares Common $20 par 00/00/1952
Each share Common $20 par exchanged for (2) shares Common $10 par 06/08/1964
Name changed to C & U Communications Corp. 01/19/1966
C & U Communications Corp. acquired by Continental Telephone Corp. 01/18/1968 which name changed to Continental Telecom Inc. 05/06/1982 which name changed to Contel Corp. 05/01/1986 which merged into GTE Corp. 03/14/1991 which merged into Verizon Communications Inc. 06/30/2000

CHENANGO GRAPHICS, INC. (NY)
Name changed to Chenango Industries, Inc. 02/25/1971

CHENEY BIGELOW WIRE WORKS, INC. (MA)
Preferred $50 par changed to $25 par 00/00/1934
Common no par changed to $10 par 12/08/1955
Preferred $25 par called for redemption 02/01/1962
Acquired by National Standard Co. (DE) 09/11/1962
Each share Prior Preferred $25 par exchanged for (0.9) share Common $10 par
Common exchanged on a (3) for (1) basis
National-Standard Co. (DE) reincorporated in Indiana 01/31/1994
(See National-Standard Co.)

CHENEY RES INC (WA)
Name changed to Time Management Software, Inc. (WA) and Common 5¢ par changed to 1¢ par 09/11/1984
Time Management Software, Inc. (WA) reincorporated in Oklahoma as TMS, Inc. 06/01/1990
(See TMS, Inc.)

CHENGHUI RLTY HLDG CO (CO)
Name changed to Social Detention, Inc. 11/14/2016

CHENI GOLD MINES INC (CANADA)
Plan of arrangement effective 12/30/1994
Each share Common no par exchanged for (1) share Cheni Resources Inc. Common no par and (0.2) share Meota Resources Corp. Class A Common no par
(See each company's listing)

CHENI RES INC (ON)
Reincorporated 10/23/2000
Place of incorporation changed from (Canada) to (ON) 10/23/2000
Acquired by Rodin Communications Corp. 10/31/2000

Each share Common no par exchanged for (1) share Common no par

CHENIERE ENERGY PARTNERS LP HLDGS LLC (DE)
Merged into Cheniere Energy, Inc. 09/20/2018
Each Common Share exchanged for (0.475) share new Common 1¢ par

CHENNAULT GOLD MINES, LTD. (ON)
Charter revoked for failure to file reports and pay taxes 00/00/1952

CHEQ-IT LTD (AB)
Acquired by Tuscany International Drilling Inc. 04/16/2010
Each share Common no par exchanged for (0.0265) share Common no par
Note: Unexchanged certificates were cancelled and became without value 04/16/2014
(See Tuscany International Drilling Inc.)

CHEQUE ALERT INC (DE)
Name changed to Thunder Oil & Gas, Inc. 10/19/1995
Thunder Oil & Gas, Inc. recapitalized as Command Entertainment Inc. 12/14/1995 which recapitalized as International Industries Inc. 01/21/1998 which name changed to International Internet Inc. 02/25/1999 which name changed to Evolve One, Inc. 11/30/2000 which name changed to China Direct, Inc. (DE) 09/19/2006 which reincorporated in Florida 06/21/2007 which name changed to China Direct Industries, Inc. 05/29/2009 which name changed to CD International Enterprises, Inc. 02/29/2012

CHEQUEMATE INTL INC (UT)
Each share old Common 1¢ par exchanged for (0.25) share new Common 1¢ par 02/02/2000
Name changed to C-3D Digital, Inc. 01/08/2002
(See C-3D Digital, Inc.)

CHER-O-KEE PHOTOFINISHERS, INC. (TN)
Acquired by Crown-Bremson Industries, Inc. 10/04/1961
Each share Class A and/or B Common 40¢ par exchanged for (0.33333333) share Common $1 par
Crown-Bremson Industries, Inc. acquired by Berkey Photo, Inc. 01/28/1965 which name changed to Berkey, Inc. 09/20/1985
(See Berkey, Inc.)

CHERAMI NAT PET FOODS INC (NY)
Charter cancelled and proclaimed dissolved for failure to pay taxes 12/24/1991

CHERENSON CARROLL & HOLZER (NJ)
Each share old Common no par exchanged for (0.0001) share new Common no par 01/26/2004
Note: In effect holders received $1.50 cash per share and public interest was eliminated

CHERNE MED INC (MN)
Name changed 04/20/1978
Reorganized 06/30/1987
Name changed 12/29/1989
Name changed from Cherne Industrial, Inc. to Cherne Industries, Inc. 04/20/1978
Common 10¢ par split (6) for (1) by issuance of (5) additional shares 08/17/1983
Common 10¢ par changed to no par and (2) additional shares issued 07/01/1986
Stock Dividend - 100% 12/16/1985
Under plan of reorganization each share Cherne Industries, Inc. Common no par automatically became (1) share Cherne Enterprises, Inc. Common no par 06/30/1987
Name changed from Cherne Enterprises, Inc. to Cherne Medical, Inc. 12/29/1989
Name changed to Vital Heart Systems, Inc. 06/01/1992
Vital Heart Systems, Inc. recapitalized as Vital Health Technologies, Inc. 10/02/2000 which name changed to Caribbean American Health Resorts, Inc. 03/31/2003
(See Caribbean American Health Resorts, Inc.)

CHERNIGOVSKOE KHIMVOLOKNO OPEN JT STK CO (UKRAINE)
GDR agreement terminated 03/30/2015
GDR holders' equity unlikely

CHEROKEE BKG CO (GA)
Plan of reorganization effective 11/03/2005
Each share Common no par held by holders of (1,099) or fewer shares exchanged for $17.75 cash
Stock Dividend - 10% payable 10/21/2003 to holders of record 10/7/2003 Ex date - 10/10/2003
Acquired by Hamilton State Bancshares, Inc. 02/17/2014
Each share Common no par exchanged for $4 cash

CHEROKEE COUNTY OIL CO. (TX)
Charter forfeited for failure to pay taxes 03/30/1950

CHEROKEE CR LIFE INS CO (GA)
Name changed to Cherokee National Life Insurance Co. 12/17/1970
Cherokee National Life Insurance Co. acquired by CNL Financial Corp. 00/00/1984
(See CNL Financial Corp.)

CHEROKEE DEVS LTD (BC)
Recapitalized as International Cherokee Developments Ltd. 11/05/1982
Each share Common no par exchanged for (0.33333333) share Common no par
International Cherokee Developments Ltd. recapitalized as GLS Global Listing Service Ltd. 11/30/1989 which name changed to GLS Global Assets Ltd. 08/27/1992 which name changed to Mobile Lottery Solutions Inc. 02/20/2006 which name changed to NuMedia Games Inc. 09/27/2007 which recapitalized as Brandgamz Marketing Inc. 06/04/2008

CHEROKEE FED BK FSB (CANTON, GA)
Name changed 06/12/1991
Name changed from Cherokee Federal Savings Bank (Canton, GA) to Cherokee Federal Bank, FSB (Canton, GA) 06/12/1991
Acquired by Community Bank Capital Corp. 01/12/1993
Each share Common $1 par exchanged for $12 cash

CHEROKEE GOLD MINES, LTD. (ON)
Charter cancelled 07/27/1959

CHEROKEE GROUP (CA)
Common no par split (2) for (1) by issuance of (1) additional share 04/30/1986
Common no par split (2) for (1) by issuance of (1) additional share 02/26/1987
Merged into Green Acquisition Co. 05/10/1989
Each share Common no par exchanged for $2.66 principal amount of Sr. Subordinated Debentures due 04/15/2001 and $12.03 cash

CHEROKEE INC NEW (DE)
Ctfs. dated prior to 12/23/1994
Reorganized as Cherokee Inc. (New) 12/23/1994
Each share Common 1¢ par exchanged for (0.019935) share Common 2¢ par

CHEROKEE INC OLD (DE)
Reorganized as Cherokee Inc. (New) (Ctfs. dated prior to 12/22/1994) 05/28/1993
Each share Common 1¢ par exchanged for (0.0458) share Common 1¢ par, (0.0286) Common Stock Purchase Warrant Ser. A expiring 11/01/1999, (0.0358) Common Stock Purchase Warrant Ser. B expiring 11/01/1999 and (0.1073) Common Stock Purchase Warrant Ser. C expiring 11/01/1999
Each share Class B Common 1¢ par exchanged for (0.0458) share Common 1¢ par, (0.0286) Common Stock Purchase Warrant Ser. A expiring 11/01/1999, (0.0358) Common Stock Purchase Warrant Ser. B expiring 11/01/1999 and (0.1073) Common Stock Purchase Warrant Ser. C expiring 11/01/1999
Cherokee Inc. (New) (Ctfs. dated prior to 12/22/1994) reorganized as Cherokee Inc. (New) (Ctfs. dated after 12/23/1994) 12/23/1994

CHEROKEE INS CO (TN)
Stock Dividend - 33.33333333% 05/30/1966
Merged into Cherokee Equity Corp. 12/02/1968
Each share Capital Stock $5 par exchanged for (1) share Common no par

CHEROKEE INTL CORP (DE)
Merged into Lineage Power Holdings, Inc. 11/21/2008
Each share Common $0.001 par exchanged for $3.20 cash

CHEROKEE MINERALS & OIL INC (NV)
Each share old Common 1¢ par exchanged for (0.02) share new Common 1¢ par 02/27/1996
Name changed to HydroMaid International, Inc. 01/20/1999
(See HydroMaid International, Inc.)

CHEROKEE NATL LIFE INS CO (GA)
100% acquired by CNL Financial Corp. through exchange offer which expired 00/00/1984
Public interest eliminated

CHEROKEE RES CORP (NY)
Charter cancelled and proclaimed dissolved for failure to pay taxes 06/27/2001

CHEROKEE RES LTD (AB)
Merged into Bonanza Resources Ltd. 10/07/1983
Each share Common no par exchanged for (1.425) shares Common no par and Common Stock Purchase Warrants expiring 12/31/1984
Bonanza Resources Ltd. recapitalized as CanCapital Corp. (AB) 02/09/1987 which reincorporated in British Columbia 05/12/1993 which recapitalized as Prada Holdings Ltd. (BC) 07/14/1994 which reincorporated in Yukon 07/26/1996
(See Prada Holdings Ltd.)

CHEROKEE SPINNING CO.
Name changed to Cherokee Textile Mills 00/00/1945
Cherokee Textile Mills name changed to New Cherokee Corp. 05/20/1989
(See New Cherokee Corp.)

CHEROKEE TEXTILE MLS (TN)
Stock Dividend - 200% 03/10/1953
Name changed to New Cherokee Corp. 05/20/1989
(See New Cherokee Corp.)

CHEROKEE URANIUM MINING CORP. (DE)
Name changed to Orion Food Systems, Inc. 08/19/1970
Orion Food Systems, Inc. merged into Munzig International, Inc. 09/08/1972
(See Munzig International, Inc.)

CHEROKEE-UTAH URANIUM CORP. (UT)
Merged into Beaver Mesa Uranium, Inc. 08/22/1955
Each share Capital Stock $1 par exchanged for (0.1) share Capital Stock 25¢ par
Beaver Mesa Uranium, Inc. name changed to Beaver Mesa Exploration Co. 03/10/1970
(See Beaver Mesa Exploration Co.)

CHEROKEE-WARREN OIL & GAS CO. (OK)
Voluntarily dissolved 11/29/1941
Details not available

CHERRY BURRELL CORP (DE)
Each share Common no par exchanged for (3) shares Common $5 par 00/00/1937
5% Preferred $100 par called for redemption 04/30/1946
4% Preferred 1947 Ser. $100 par called for redemption 11/00/1967
Common $5 par split (2) for (1) by issuance of (1) additional share 04/21/1972
Name changed to Paxall, Inc. 07/31/1974
Paxall, Inc. name changed to Paxall Group, Inc. 04/04/1983
(See Paxall Group, Inc.)

CHERRY CORP (DE)
Merged into CABO Acquisition Corp. 07/17/2000
Each share new Common $1 par exchanged for $26.40 cash

CHERRY CREEK BANK (DENVER, CO)
Stock Dividends - 25% 02/02/1960; 10% 03/06/1961
Name changed to Cherry Creek National Bank (Denver, CO) 10/02/1961
(See Cherry Creek National Bank (Denver, CO))

CHERRY CREEK GOLD CORP (UT)
Name changed to Toner Systems International, Inc. (UT) 12/30/1994
Toner Systems International, Inc. (UT) reincorporated in Nevada 02/09/1998 which reorganized as Trident Systems International, Inc. 01/25/2001 which name changed to AAMPRO Group, Inc. 01/07/2003
(See AAMPRO Group, Inc.)

CHERRY CREEK NATL BK (DENVER, CO)
Stock Dividend - 25% 03/15/1964
Through voluntary exchange offer 100% acquired by Mountain Banks Ltd. as of 04/17/1972
Public interest eliminated

CHERRY ELECTRICAL PRODS CORP (DE)
Name changed to Cherry Corp. 07/02/1986
(See Cherry Corp)

CHERRY HILL FOODS INC (DE)
Charter cancelled and declared inoperative and void for non-payment of 03/01/1979

CHERRY HILL NATL BK (MEDFORD, NJ)
Merged into Meridian Bancorp, Inc. 04/16/1993
Each share Common $5 par exchanged for (0.1652) share Common $5 par
Meridian Bancorp, Inc. merged into CoreStates Financial Corp 04/09/1996 which merged into First Union Corp. 04/28/1998 which name

changed to Wachovia Corp. (Ctfs. dated after 09/01/2001) 09/01/2001 which merged into Wells Fargo & Co. (New) 12/31/2008

CHERRY LAKE MINES, LTD.
Name changed to Norzinc Mines Ltd. 04/00/1951
(See Norzinc Mines Ltd.)

CHERRY LANE FASHION GROUP NORTH AMER LTD (BC)
Name changed to Maracote International Resources, Inc. 07/08/1998
Maracote International Resources, Inc. recapitalized as Lund Ventures Ltd. 05/28/2001 which recapitalized as Lund Gold Ltd. 07/10/2003 which recapitalized as Lund Enterprises Corp. 12/19/2013

CHERRY RIVET CO.
Merged into Townsend Co. 00/00/1951
Each share Capital Stock $1 par exchanged (0.15384615) share Common $12.50 par
(See Townsend Co.)

CHERRY TANKERS INC (DE)
Name changed to Genesis Fluid Solutions Holdings, Inc. (DE) and Common $0.0001 par changed to $0.001 par 11/23/2009
Genesis Fluid Solutions Holdings, Inc. (DE) reincorporated in Nevada as Blue Earth, Inc. 10/29/2010
(See Blue Earth, Inc.)

CHERRY TREE CAP CORP (NV)
Name changed to VisualMED Clinical Systems Corp. 05/10/2000
VisualMED Clinical Systems Corp. name changed to Visual Healthcare Corp. 12/20/2004

CHERRYHILL RES INC (AB)
Reorganized as Daedalian eSolutions Inc. 12/01/2000
Each share Common no par exchanged for (3) shares Common no par
Daedalian eSolutions Inc. acquired by Telus Corp. 07/26/2001

CHERRYVILLE NATL BK (CHERRYVILLE, NC)
Merged into Southern National Corp. 03/31/1984
Each share Common $25 par exchanged for (4.5) shares Common $5 par
Southern National Corp. merged into BB&T Corp. 05/19/1997

CHERYL & CO
8.50% Preferred Ser. A called for redemption at $10 on 08/01/1998
9.50% Preferred Ser. E called for redemption at $10 on 12/29/2000

CHERYL RES INC (BC)
Merged into Tymar Resources Inc. 10/31/1989
Each share Common no par exchanged for (0.45454545) share Common no par
Tymar Resources Inc. recapitalized as Baja Gold, Inc. 01/25/1993 which merged into Viceroy Resource Corp. 05/30/1996 which merged into Quest Capital Corp. (BC) 06/30/2003 which reincorporated in Canada 05/27/2008 which name changed to Sprott Resource Lending Corp. 09/10/2010 which merged into Sprott Inc. 07/24/2013

CHESA INTL LTD (DE)
Charter cancelled and declared inoperative and void for non-payment of taxes 03/01/1984

CHESAPEAKE & COLORADO CORP. (DE)
Reorganized under the laws of Nevada 12/02/1957
Each share Common 5¢ par exchanged for (0.02) share Common $2.50 par
Chesapeake & Colorado Corp. (NV) merged into Radorock Resources, Inc. 04/30/1959 which merged into Federal Resources Corp. 05/02/1960
(See Federal Resources Corp.)

CHESAPEAKE & COLORADO CORP. (NV)
Merged into Radorock Resources, Inc. 04/30/1959
Radorock Resources, Inc. merged into Federal Resources Corp. 05/02/1960
(See Federal Resources Corp.)

CHESAPEAKE & COLORADO URANIUM CORP. (DE)
Name changed to Chesapeake & Colorado Corp. (DE) 03/06/1956
Chesapeake & Colorado Corp. (DE) reorganized in Nevada 12/02/1957 which merged into Radorock Resources, Inc. 04/30/1959 which merged into Federal Resources Corp. 05/02/1960
(See Federal Resources Corp.)

CHESAPEAKE & OHIO RY CO (VA)
Each share Common $100 par exchanged for (4) shares Common $25 par 00/00/1929
3.5% Conv. Preferred $100 par called for redemption 02/01/1966
Under plan of reorganization each share Common $25 par automatically became (1) share Chessie System, Inc. Common $25 par 06/15/1973
Chessie System, Inc. merged into CSX Corp. 11/01/1980

CHESAPEAKE BK CORP (VA)
Merged into Jefferson Bankshares, Inc. 09/01/1989
Each share Common $5 par exchanged for (1.1333) shares Common $2.50 par
Jefferson Bankshares, Inc. merged into Wachovia Corp. (New) (Ctfs. dated between 05/20/1991 and 09/01/1997) 10/31/1997 which merged into Wachovia Corp. (Ctfs. dated after 09/01/2001) 09/01/2001 which merged into Wells Fargo & Co. (New) 12/31/2008

CHESAPEAKE BIOLOGICAL LABS INC (MD)
Merged into Cangene Corp. 02/09/2001
Each share Class A Common 1¢ par exchanged for $4.60 cash

CHESAPEAKE-CAMP CORP.
Name changed to Camp Manufacturing Co., Inc. 00/00/1945
Camp Manufacturing Co., Inc. merged into Union Bag-Camp Paper Corp. 07/12/1956 which name changed to Union Camp Corp. 04/27/1966 which merged into International Paper Co. 04/30/1999

CHESAPEAKE COMPUTER SYS INC (BC)
Struck off register and declared dissolved for failure to file returns 11/01/1991

CHESAPEAKE CORP. (MD)
Dissolution completed 00/00/1942
Details not available

CHESAPEAKE CORP (VA)
Reorganized 00/00/1941
Name changed 04/27/1984
Reorganized from Chesapeake Corp. to Chesapeake Corp. of Virginia 00/00/1941
Each share Common $25 par exchanged for (5) shares Common $5 par
Common $5 par split (2) for (1) by issuance of (1) additional share 04/06/1956
Common $5 par split (4) for (3) by issuance of (0.33333333) additional share 12/14/1965
Common $5 par split (3) for (2) by issuance of (0.5) additional share 05/14/1976
Common $5 par split (2) for (1) by issuance of (1) additional share 09/17/1979
Name changed from Chesapeake Corp. of Virginia back to Chesapeake Corp. and Common $5 par changed to $1 par 04/27/1984
Common $1 par split (3) for (2) by issuance of (1) additional share 09/29/1987
Stock Dividend - 25% 10/20/1950
Plan of reorganization under Chapter 11 Federal Bankruptcy proceedings effective 04/18/2011
No stockholders' equity

CHESAPEAKE ENERGY CORP (OK)
Reincorporated 12/31/1996
Common 1¢ par changed to $0.005 par and (1) additional share issued 12/16/1994
Common $0.005 par changed to 15¢ par 12/15/1995
Common 15¢ par changed to 10¢ par and (0.5) additional share issued payable 12/28/1995 to holders of record 12/15/1995 Ex date - 12/29/1995
Common 10¢ par split (3) for (2) by issuance of (0.5) additional share payable 06/28/1996 to holders of record 05/28/1996 Ex date - 07/01/1996
State of incorporation changed from (DE) to (OK) and Common 10¢ par changed to 1¢ par 12/31/1996
7% 144A Conv. Preferred called for redemption at $2.45 plus $0.875 accrued dividends and (5) shares Common 1¢ par on 05/01/2001
7% Conv. Preferred called for redemption at $2.45 plus $0.875 accrued dividends and (5) shares Common 1¢ par on 05/01/2001
Each share 6.75% Conv. Preferred 1¢ par exchanged for (6.4935) shares Common 1¢ par 11/22/2004
Each share 6% 144A Conv. Preferred 1¢ par exchanged for (4.8605) shares Common 1¢ par 03/20/2006
Each share 6% Conv. Preferred 1¢ par exchanged for (4.8605) shares Common 1¢ par 03/20/2006
Each share 5% Conv. Preferred Ser. 2003 1¢ par exchanged for (6.0962) shares Common 1¢ par 11/20/2006
Each share 4.125% 144A Conv. Preferred 1¢ par exchanged for (60.299) shares Common 1¢ par 03/31/2009
Each share 4.125% Conv. Preferred 1¢ par exchanged for (60.299) shares Common 1¢ par 03/31/2009
Each share 6.25% Conv. Preferred 1¢ par exchanged for (8.6218) shares Common 1¢ par 06/15/2009
Each share 5% Conv. Preferred Ser. 2005 1¢ par automatically became (4.1548) shares Common 1¢ par 05/03/2010
Each share 5% 144A Conv. Preferred Ser. 2005 1¢ par automatically became (4.1548) shares Common 1¢ par 05/03/2010
(Additional Information in Active)

CHESAPEAKE GOLD CORP (BC)
Each share Class A Ser. 1 no par automatically became (10) shares Common no par 02/13/2008
(Additional Information in Active)

CHESAPEAKE INDUSTRIES, INC. (OH)
4% Preferred $100 par reclassified as $4 Preferred $10 par 00/00/1954
Name changed to America Corp. (OH) 08/10/1959
America Corp. (OH) reorganized in Delaware 12/31/1963 which name changed to Pathe Industries, Inc. (DE) 11/20/1964
(See Pathe Industries, Inc. (DE))

CHESAPEAKE INDS INC (MD)
Stock Dividends - 10% 09/15/1977; 10% 07/01/1978; 10% 03/15/1979; 20% 09/19/1980; 10% 03/12/1982; 10% 12/14/1984; 10% 06/06/1986
Plan of reorganization under Chapter 11 Federal Bankruptcy proceedings confirmed 04/01/1997
No stockholders' equity

CHESAPEAKE INSTR CORP (MD)
Merged into Gould Inc. 06/05/1975
Each share Common $1 par exchanged for (0.23) share Common $4 par
(See Gould Inc.)

CHESAPEAKE INVS INC (MD)
Completely liquidated 02/28/2005
Each share Common 50¢ par exchanged for first and final distribution of $4.161176 cash

CHESAPEAKE LIFE INS CO (OK)
Recapitalized 09/27/1993
Class A $10 par and Class B $10 par changed to $2 par and (4) additional shares issued respectively 04/03/1961
Class A $2 par and Class B $2 par changed to $1 par and (1) additional share issued respectively 04/30/1963
Class A $1 par and Class B $1 par split (6) for (5) by issuance of (0.2) additional share respectively 06/15/1969
Class A $1 par and Class B $1 par changed to $1.50 par 05/05/1975
Class A $1.50 par and Class B $1.50 par changed to $1.60 par 09/10/1984
Stock Dividend - Class A & B - 10% 04/03/1967
Recapitalized from (MD) to under the laws of (OK) 09/27/1993
Each share Class A $1.60 par exchanged for (0.02) share new Class A $140 par
Each share Class B $1.60 par exchanged for (0.02) share new Class B $140 par
Note: In effect holders received $11.90 cash per share and majority interest was eliminated
Each share new Class A $140 par exchanged again for (0.00333333) share new Class A $140 par 12/10/1998
Each share new Class B $140 par exchanged again for (0.00333333) share new Class B $140 par 12/10/1998
Note: In effect holders received $1,501.37 cash per share and public interest was eliminated

CHESAPEAKE LODGING TR (MD)
7.75% Preferred Shares of Bene. Int. Ser. A 1¢ par called for redemption at $25 on 07/17/2017
(Additional Information in Active)

CHESAPEAKE MIDSTREAM PARTNERS LP (DE)
Name changed to Access Midstream Partners, L.P. 07/24/2012
Access Midstream Partners, L.P. name changed to Williams Partners L.P. (New) 02/02/2015 which merged into Williams Companies, Inc. 08/10/2018

CHESAPEAKE NATL BK (TOWSON, MD)
Merged into First American Bank of Maryland (Silver Spring, MD) 12/31/1978
Each share Common $10 par exchanged for (1.5) shares Common $10 par
(See First American Bank of Maryland (Silver Spring, MD))

CHESAPEAKE PAPERBOARD CO (MD)
Acquired by Caraustar Industries, Inc. 00/00/1998
Details not available

CHESAPEAKE SYS CORP (MD)
Common $1 par changed to $0.33333333 par and (2) additional shares issued 07/21/1967
Liquidation completed
Each share Common $0.33333333 par exchanged for initial distribution of $0.40 cash 02/27/1974
Each share Common $0.33333333 par received second and final distribution of $0.185 cash 08/15/1974

CHESAPEAKE TRUST
Trust terminated 00/00/1942
Details not available

CHESBAR CHIBOUGAMAU MINES LTD. (QC)
Recapitalized as Chesbar Iron Powder Ltd. 08/08/1969
Each share Common $1 par exchanged for (0.2) share Common no par
Chesbar Iron Powder Ltd. name changed to Chesbar Resources Inc. - Ressources Chesbar Inc. 03/28/1973 which name changed to Jaguar Nickel Inc. 06/26/2003 which name changed to Jaguar Financial Inc. (QC) 08/01/2007 which reincorporated in Ontario as Jaguar Financial Corp. 07/08/2008

CHESBAR RES INC (QC)
Name changed 03/28/1973
Name changed from Chesbar Iron Powder Ltd. to Chesbar Resources Inc.- Ressources Chesbar Inc. 03/28/1973
Name changed to Jaguar Nickel Inc. 06/26/2003
Jaguar Nickel Inc. name changed to Jaguar Financial Inc. (QC) 08/01/2007 which reincorporated in Ontario as Jaguar Financial Corp. 07/08/2008

CHESEBROUGH MANUFACTURING CO. CONSOLIDATED (NY)
Each share Common $100 par exchanged for (4) shares Common $25 par 00/00/1934
Each share Common $25 par exchanged for (2.5) shares Common $10 par 00/00/1946
Under plan of merger name changed to Chesebrough-Pond's, Inc. 06/30/1955
(See Chesebrough-Pond's, Inc.)

CHESEBROUGH PONDS INC (NY)
Capital Stock $10 par changed to $2 par and (4) additional shares issued 05/20/1960
Capital Stock $2 par changed to $1 par and (2) additional shares issued 11/25/1964
Capital Stock $1 par reclassified as Common $1 par 05/10/1966
Common $1 par split (2) for (1) by issuance of (1) additional share 06/25/1976
Merged into Unilever Acquisition Corp. 02/10/1987
Each share Common $1 par exchanged for $72.50 cash

CHESGO MINES, LTD. (ON)
Charter cancelled and company declared dissolved for failure to file returns 06/03/1965

CHESHIRE DISTRS INC (DE)
Recapitalized as LMIC, Inc. 07/21/2003
Each share Common $0.001 par exchanged for approximately (0.01500715) share Common $0.001 par
LMIC, Inc. name changed to Z Holdings Group, Inc. 10/15/2012

which name changed to Ariel Clean Energy, Inc. 08/20/2015

CHESHIRE FINL CORP (KEENE, NH)
Name changed to CFX Corp. 04/20/1994
CFX Corp. merged into Peoples Heritage Financial Group, Inc. 04/10/1998 which name changed to Banknorth Group, Inc. (ME) 05/10/2000 which merged into TD Banknorth Inc. 03/01/2005
(See TD Banknorth Inc.)

CHESKIRK MINES LTD. (ON)
Recapitalized as Green Point Mines Ltd. 12/10/1965
Each share Capital Stock $1 par exchanged for (0.2) share Capital Stock $1 par
(See Green Point Mines Ltd.)

CHESNEE MILLS
Acquired by Saxon Mills 00/00/1936
Details not available

CHESS & WYMOND
Dissolved 00/00/1951
Details not available

CHESS MARY INC (DE)
Acquired by Del Laboratories, Inc. 01/00/1968
Details not available

CHESS MNG CORP (QC)
Charter cancelled for failure to file reports 08/20/1966

CHESS SUPERSITE CORP (DE)
Each share old Common $0.0001 par exchanged for (0.001) share new Common $0.0001 par 11/01/2017
Name changed to Target Group Inc. 07/03/2018

CHESS URANIUM CORP. (QC)
Name changed to Chess Mining Corp. 04/16/1958
(See Chess Mining Corp.)

CHESSCO INDS INC (DE)
Stock Dividends - 10% 04/15/1977; 10% 12/01/1977; 10% 12/01/1978
Acquired by a group of investors 05/28/1986
Each share Common 10¢ par exchanged for $5.50 cash

CHESSIE SYS INC (VA)
Common $25 par changed to $12.50 par and (1) additional share issued 12/27/1974
Merged into CSX Corp. 11/01/1980
Each share Common $12.50 par exchanged for (1) share Common $1 par

CHESSMINSTER GROUP LTD (CANADA)
Name changed to Pyrok Group PLC 11/08/1989
(See Pyrok Group PLC)

CHESSTOWN CAP INC (ON)
Name changed to Falcon Gold Corp. 08/09/2011

CHESSWOOD INCOME FD (ON)
Reorganized as Chesswood Group Ltd. 01/04/2011
Each Trust Unit no par exchanged for (1) share Common no par
Note: Holders of (99) or fewer Trust Units will receive $6.05 cash per Unit
Holders receiving Common stock must exchange certificates prior to 01/04/2016
Holders receiving cash must exchange certificates prior to 01/04/2017

CHESTATEE BANCSHARES INC (GA)
Reclassification effective 03/24/2008
Common holders of between (441) and (2,200) shares reclassified as Class A Preferred no par
Common holders of (440) shares or fewer reclassified as Class B Preferred no par
Stock Dividend - 10% payable

09/09/2005 to holders of record 08/20/2005 Ex date - 09/13/2005
Administratively dissolved 12/31/2015

CHESTER & MEDIA ELECTRIC RAILWAY CO.
Dissolved 00/00/1936
Details not available

CHESTER BANCORP INC (DE)
Company terminated registration of common stock and is no longer public as of 05/00/2003

CHESTER-CAMBRIDGE BANK & TRUST CO. (CHESTER, PA)
Merged into Philadelphia National Bank (Philadelphia, PA) 02/20/1954
Each share Capital Stock $20 par exchanged for (2/3) share Capital Stock $20 par
Philadelphia National Bank (Philadelphia, PA) reorganized as PNB Corp. 11/01/1969 which name changed to Philadelphia National Corp. 04/23/1973 which merged into Corestates Financial Corp 05/02/1983 which merged into First Union Corp. 04/28/1998 which name changed to Wachovia Corp. (Ctfs. dated after 09/01/2001) 09/01/2001 which merged into Wells Fargo & Co. (New) 12/31/2008

CHESTER CO-OPERATIVE TELEPHONE EXCHANGE (IA)
Voluntarily dissolved 08/24/1962
Details not available

CHESTER CNTY BANCSHARES INC (PA)
Merged into State Bancshares, Inc. 03/29/1994
Each share Common $1 par exchanged for (0.25) share Common $1 par
State Bancshares, Inc. name changed to JeffBanks, Inc. 05/22/1995 which merged into Hudson United Bancorp 11/30/1999 which merged into TD Banknorth Inc. 01/31/2006
(See TD Banknorth Inc.)

CHESTER CNTY SEC FD INC (PA)
Recapitalized as Net Lnnx Inc. 01/19/1996
Each share Common no par exchanged for (0.05) share Common no par
Net Lnnx Inc. name changed to Printonthenet.com, Inc. 08/27/1999 which name changed to NexPub, Inc. 12/19/2000
(See NexPub, Inc.)

CHESTER ELECTR LABS INC (CT)
Common no par split (2) for (1) by issuance of (1) additional share 05/03/1968
Merged into General Telephone & Electronics Corp. 10/03/1969
Each share Common no par exchanged for (0.5) share 4% Conv. Preferred $50 par
General Telephone & Electronics Corp. name changed to GTE Corp. 07/01/1982 which merged into Verizon Communications Inc. 06/30/2000

CHESTER HLDGS LTD (CO)
Each share old Common $0.001 par exchanged for (0.2) share new Common $0.001 par 12/20/1993
Recapitalized as First Light Resources Inc. 11/09/2005
Each share new Common $0.001 par exchanged for (0.001) share Common $0.001 par
First Light Resources Inc. name changed to Invercoal, Inc. 06/28/2006 which recapitalized as Core International Ltd. 04/02/2007 which recapitalized as Therma-Med, Inc. 12/31/2008

CHESTER LITHO INC. (NY)
Name changed to Kellogg-American, Inc. 04/09/1963
(See Kellogg-American, Inc.)

CHESTER NATL BK (CHESTER, NY)
$1.25 Preferred $25 par called for redemption 12/31/1976
Merged into First Commercial Banks, Inc. 12/31/1976
Each share Common $5 par exchanged for $27 cash

CHESTER PURE SILK HOSIERY CO.
Liquidated 00/00/1943
Details not available

CHESTER STREET RAILWAY
In process of dissolution 00/00/1936
Details not available

CHESTER VY BANCORP INC (PA)
Common $1 par split (5) for (4) by issuance of (0.25) additional share 12/17/1993
Common $1 par split (5) for (4) by issuance of (0.25) additional share payable 03/19/1997 to holders of record 03/05/1997
Common $1 par split (3) for (2) by issuance of (0.5) additional share payable 12/18/1998 to holders of record 12/04/1998
Stock Dividends - 5% payable 09/18/1996 to holders of record 09/04/1996; 5% payable 09/18/1997 to holders of record 09/04/1997; 5% payable 09/18/1998 to holders of record 09/04/1998; 5% payable 09/17/1999 to holders of record 09/03/1999; 5% payable 09/15/2000 to holders of record 09/01/2000; 5% payable 09/14/2001 to holders of record 09/01/2001; 5% payable 09/16/2002 to holders of record 09/02/2002 Ex date - 08/28/2002; 5% payable 09/15/2003 to holders of record 09/02/2003 Ex date - 08/28/2003; 5% payable 09/30/2004 to holders of record 09/17/2004
Merged into Willow Grove Bancorp, Inc. (New) 08/31/2005
Each share Common $1 par exchanged for either (1.4823) shares Common 1¢ par or $27.90 cash
Note: Option to receive stock expired 09/09/2005
Willow Grove Bancorp, Inc. (New) name changed to Willow Financial Bancorp, Inc. 09/22/2006 which merged into Harleysville National Corp. 12/08/2008 which merged into First Niagara Financial Group, Inc. (New) 04/09/2010 which merged into KeyCorp (New) 08/01/2016

CHESTER WATER SERVICE CO.
Sold to the City of Chester, PA 00/00/1939
Details not available

CHESTERFIELD FINL CORP (DE)
Merged into MAF Bancorp, Inc. 11/01/2004
Each share Common 1¢ par exchanged for (0.2536) share Common 1¢ par and $20.48 cash
MAF Bancorp, Inc. merged into National City Corp. 09/01/2007 which was acquired by PNC Financial Services Group, Inc. 12/31/2008

CHESTERVILLE LARDER LAKE GOLD MINING CO., LTD. (ON)
Name changed to Chesterville Mines Ltd. 06/19/1946
(See Chesterville Mines Ltd.)

CHESTERVILLE MINES LTD (ON)
Charter cancelled and declared dissolved for failure to file returns and pay fees 11/09/1976

CHESTNUT & SMITH CORP.
Liquidated 00/00/1935
Details not available

CHESTNUT FARMS DAIRY, INC.
Acquired by National Dairy Products Corp. 00/00/1929
Details not available

CHESTNUT HILL BK & TR CO (BOSTON, MA)
Merged into Atlantic Bank & Trust Co. (Boston, MA) 05/10/1995
Each share Common par exchanged for (0.275) share Common $1 par
Atlantic Bank & Trust Co. (Boston, MA) name changed to Capital Crossing Bank (Boston, MA) 09/02/1999
(See Capital Crossing Bank (Boston, MA))

CHESTNUT HILL NATL BK (PHILADELPHIA, PA)
Under plan of reorganization each share Common $10 par automatically became (1) share Community Financial Bancorp, Inc. 01/03/1991
(See Community Financial Bancorp, Inc.)

CHESTNUT STR CASH FD INC (MD)
Completely liquidated 05/01/1992
Details not available

CHESTNUT STR CORP (IL)
Liquidation completed
Each share Common no par exchanged for initial distribution of $27 cash 04/28/1980
Each share Common no par received second and final distribution of $1.84 cash 12/12/1980

CHEUNG KONG HLDGS LTD (HONG KONG)
Each ADR for Ordinary received distribution of (3) additional ADR's to effect a (4) for (1) split and 25% stock dividend 07/02/1987
Stock Dividend - 30% 07/22/1981
Merged into CK Hutchison Holdings Ltd. 04/10/2015
Each ADR for Ordinary exchanged for (1) ADR for Ordinary

CHEUNG KONG INFRASTRUCTURE HLDGS LTD (BERMUDA)
Name changed to CK Infrastructure Holdings Ltd. 06/19/2017

CHEUNG LABS INC (MD)
Name changed to Celsion Corp. (MD) 05/01/1998
Celsion Corp. (MD) reincorporated in Delaware 08/18/2000

CHEVALIER INTL HLDGS LTD (BERMUDA)
ADR agreement terminated 08/10/2017
No ADR's remain outstanding

CHEVALIER PAC HLDGS LTD (BERMUDA)
Name changed 11/05/1999
Name changed 06/11/2007
Name changed from Chevalier (OA) International Ltd. to Chevalier iTech Holdings Ltd. 11/05/1999
Name changed from Chevalier iTech Holdings Ltd. to Chevalier Pacific Holdings Ltd. 06/11/2007
Name changed to Dingyi Group Investment Ltd. 12/24/2012
(See Dingyi Group Investment Ltd.)

CHEVANING MNG & EXPL LTD (NY)
Each share Common 5¢ par exchanged for (0.14) share Common 75¢ par 01/02/1985
Merged into Omni Natural Resources Ltd. 05/04/1987
Each share Common 75¢ par held by U.S. Residents exchanged for $1.50 cash
Each share Common 75¢ par held by Non-U.S. Residents exchanged for (1) share Ordinary Stock 50p par

CHEVIOT FINL CORP (MD)
Merged into MainSource Financial Group, Inc. 05/23/2016

Each share Common 1¢ par exchanged for (0.6916) share Common no par
MainSource Financial Group, Inc. merged into First Financial Bancorp 04/02/2018

CHEVIOT FINL CORP (USA)
Reorganized under the laws of Maryland 01/18/2012
Each share Common 1¢ par exchanged for (0.857) share Common 1¢ par
Cheviot Financial Corp. (MD) merged into MainSource Financial Group, Inc. 05/23/2016 which merged into First Financial Bancorp 04/02/2018

CHEVRON CORP (DE)
Common $3 par changed to $1.50 par and (1) additional share issued 06/10/1994
Common $1.50 par changed to 75¢ par 04/26/2000
Under plan of merger name changed to ChevronTexaco Corp. 10/09/2001
ChevronTexaco Corp. name changed to Chevron Corp. 05/09/2005

CHEVRONTEXACO CORP (DE)
Common 75¢ par split (2) for (1) by issuance of (1) additional share payable 09/10/2004 to holders of record 08/19/2004 Ex date - 09/13/2004
Name changed to Chevron Corp. 05/09/2005

CHEVWAY CORP (DE)
Name changed to Genway Corp. 05/25/1970
(See Genway Corp.)

CHEVY CHASE BK & TR CO (CHEVY CHASE, MD)
Merged into Citizens Bank & Trust Co. of Maryland (Riverdale, MD) 09/24/1977
Each share Common $10 par exchanged for (1) share Capital Stock $10 par
Citizens Bank & Trust Co. of Maryland (Riverdale, MD) reorganized as Citizens Bancorp 05/19/1982 which merged into Crestar Financial Corp. 12/31/1996 which merged into SunTrust Banks, Inc. 12/31/1998

CHEVY CHASE BK F S B (CHEVY CHASE, MD)
13% Perpetual Preferred Ser. A 1¢ par called for redemption at $27.25 on 10/31/2003

CHEVY CHASE BK FSB (BETHESDA, MD)
8% Preferred Ser. C 1¢ par called for redemption at $25 on 03/30/2009

CHEVY CHASE DAIRY
Acquired by National Dairy Products Corp. 00/00/1930
Details not available

CHEVY CHASE PFD CAP CORP (MD)
10.375% Exchangeable Preferred Ser. A $5 par called for redemption at $50 on 03/30/2009

CHEVY DEV CORP (BC)
Name changed 07/02/1985
Name changed from Chevy Oil Corp. to Chevy Development Corp. 07/02/1985
Common no par split (4) for (1) by issuance of (3) additional shares 09/23/1986
Name changed to International Cargocare Corp. 09/02/1992
International Cargocare Corp. recapitalized as CVAC Industries Inc. 12/14/1993 which recapitalized as Saddlerock Resources Inc. 11/27/1995 which name changed to MDX Medical Inc. 07/07/2000 which name changed to Urodynamix Technologies Ltd. 06/21/2006 which recapitalized as Venturi Ventures Inc. 08/29/2011

(See Venturi Ventures Inc.)

CHEWIE NEWGETT INC (NV)
Charter revoked for failure to file reports and pay fees 09/01/1990

CHEYENNE ENERGY INC (AB)
Placed in receivership 02/11/2008
Stockholders' equity unlikely

CHEYENNE OIL CO. (DE)
Charter cancelled and declared inoperative and void for non-payment of taxes 04/01/1930

CHEYENNE OIL VENTURES, INC. (DE)
Merged into Fremont Uranium Corp. (CO) 09/21/1955
Each share Common exchanged for (2) shares Common
Fremont Uranium Corp. (CO) merged into King Oil, Inc. 09/05/1956 which recapitalized as Lane Wood, Inc. 08/10/1964
(See Lane Wood, Inc.)

CHEYENNE PETE CORP (BC)
Delisted from Vancouver Stock Exchange 03/02/1990

CHEYENNE RES INC (WY)
Recapitalized as Paradigm Holdings, Inc. (WY) 09/14/2004
Each share Common 1¢ par exchanged for (0.0117647) share Common 1¢ par
Paradigm Holdings, Inc. (WY) reincorporated in Nevada 12/14/2010
(See Paradigm Holdings, Inc. (NV))

CHEYENNE SOFTWARE INC (DE)
Common 1¢ par split (5) for (2) by issuance of (1.5) additional shares 07/17/1987
Common 1¢ par split (3) for (2) by issuance of (0.5) additional share 03/25/1992
Common 1¢ par split (3) for (2) by issuance of (0.5) additional share 04/08/1993
Common 1¢ par split (3) for (2) by issuance of (0.5) additional share 03/29/1994
Merged into Computer Associates International, Inc. 12/02/1996
Each share Common 1¢ par exchanged for $30.50 cash

CH4 ENERGY INC (NV)
Each share old Common $0.001 par exchanged for (0.04) share new Common $0.001 par 06/30/2008
Recapitalized as High Sierra Acquisitions Inc. 04/17/2014
Each share new Common $0.001 par exchanged for (0.04) share Common $0.001 par
High Sierra Acquisitions, Inc. name changed to Anaszi Energy Corp. 11/20/2014 which name changed to Solar Quartz Technologies, Inc. 12/19/2016

CHI-CHIS INC (MN)
Common 1¢ par split (2) for (1) by issuance of (1) additional share 10/25/1979
Common 1¢ par split (3) for (2) by issuance of (0.5) additional share 06/01/1981
Common 1¢ par split (3) for (2) by issuance of (0.5) additional share 06/25/1982
Common 1¢ par split (3) for (2) by issuance of (0.5) additional share 12/17/1982
Common 1¢ par split (3) for (2) by issuance of (0.5) additional share 09/27/1983
Merged into F.M. Acquisition Corp. 04/13/1988
Each share Common 1¢ par exchanged for $10.15 cash

CHI ENERGY INC (DE)
Acquired by Enel S.p.A. 12/12/2000
Each share Ser. A Common $0.001 par exchanged for $16.01 cash

Each share Ser. B Common $0.001 par exchanged for $16.01 cash

CHI MEI OPTOELECTRONICS CORP (TAIWAN)
Stock Dividends - 10.181128611% payable 09/09/2004 to holders of record 08/05/2004 Ex date - 08/03/2004; 13.43541% payable 09/08/2005 to holders of record 08/05/2005 Ex date - 08/03/2005; 4.55597% payable 09/13/2006 to holders of record 08/01/2006; 4% payable 08/07/2007 to holders of record 07/05/2007; 5% payable 08/18/2008 to holders of record 07/14/2008
GDR agreement terminated 02/08/2010
Each Reg. S Sponsored GDR for Ordinary exchanged for $7.507185 cash
Each 144A Sponsored GDR for Ordinary exchanged for $7.507185 cash

CHI RESH INC (DE)
Charter cancelled and declared inoperative and void for non-payment of taxes 03/01/2009

CHIA HSIN CEMENT CORP (TAIWAN)
Stock Dividends - 2% payable 10/08/1999 to holders of record 07/29/1999; 8.78846% payable 10/02/2008 to holders of record 08/12/2008 Ex date - 08/08/2008
GDR agreement terminated 07/27/2009
Each Sponsored GDR for Common exchanged for $4.65829 cash

CHIB KAYRAND COPPER MINES LTD (ON)
Capital Stock $1 par changed to no par 07/08/1975
Merged into Cinequity Corp. (New) 11/24/1981
Each share Capital Stock no par exchanged for (0.2) share Common no par
(See Cinequity Corp. (New))

CHIBEX LTD (QC)
Charter cancelled for failure to file reports 01/25/1986

CHIBEX MNG CORP (QC)
Name changed to Chibex Ltd.-Chibex Ltee. and Capital Stock $1 par changed to no par 12/19/1972
(See Chibex Ltd.-Chibex Ltee.)

CHIBLOW MINES LTD. (ON)
Merged into Alchib Developments Ltd. 07/10/1969
Each share Capital Stock $1 par exchanged for (0.31) share Capital Stock no par
Alchib Developments Ltd. merged into Kalrock Developments Ltd. 10/23/1978 which merged into Kalrock Resources Ltd. 08/08/1990 which merged into Cercal Minerals Corp. 07/09/1993
(See Cercal Minerals Corp.)

CHIBMAC MINES LTD. (QC)
Acquired by Sulphur Converting Corp. 00/00/1952
Each share Capital Stock $1 par exchanged for (0.06666666) share Capital Stock $1 par
(See Sulphur Converting Corp.)

CHIBOUG COPPER LTD (QC)
Recapitalized as Guyana Goldfields Inc. (QC) 01/24/1995
Each share Common $1 par exchanged for (0.25) share Common no par
Guyana Goldfields Inc. (QC) reorganized in Canada 05/26/2005

CHIBOUGAMAU BRUNSWICK MINERALS LTD. (NB)
Charter forfeited 12/09/1959

CHIBOUGAMAU EXPLORERS LTD. (QC)
Acquired by Anacon Lead Mines Ltd. 00/00/1955
Each share Capital Stock no par exchanged for (0.33333333) share Capital Stock no par
Anacon Lead Mines was recapitalized as Key Anacon Mines Ltd. 02/14/1964
(See Key Anacon Mines Ltd.)

CHIBOUGAMAU JACULET MINES LTD. (ON)
Acquired by Copper Rand Chibougamau Mines Ltd. 08/29/1960
Each share Capital Stock 75¢ par exchanged for (0.2) Capital Stock $1 par
Copper Rand Chibougamau Mines Ltd. merged into Patino Mining Corp. 11/26/1962 which reorganized as Patino N.V. 12/20/1971
(See Patino N.V.)

CHIBOUGAMAU MNG & SMLT INC (QC)
Name changed to C.M. & S. Mines Inc.-Les Mines C.M. & S. Inc. 01/23/1980
C.M. & S. Mines Inc.-Les Mines C.M. & S. Inc. recapitalized as Camchib Resources Inc.-Les Ressources Camchib Inc. 10/31/1980 which merged into Campbell Resources Inc. (New) 06/08/1983
(See Campbell Resources Inc. (New))

CHIBOUGAMAU PROSPECTORS LTD.
Dissolved and each (100) shares Capital Stock received (20) shares Capital Stock of Consolidated Chibougamau Goldfields Ltd. and (2) shares Capital Stock of Northern Chibougamau Mines Ltd. 00/00/1936

CHIBTOWN COPPER CORP. (QC)
Name changed to Rainbow Mines Ltd. (QC) 03/24/1969
Rainbow Mines Ltd. (QC) name changed to Lederic Mines Ltd. 05/29/1970 which recapitalized as Lederic Group Inc. 12/01/1972
(See Lederic Group Inc.)

CHIC BY H I S INC (DE)
Name changed to Durango Apparel Inc. 06/05/2000
(See Durango Apparel Inc.)

CHICAGO, AURORA & ELGIN CORP.
Bankrupt 00/00/1945
Stockholders' equity unlikely

CHICAGO, AURORA & ELGIN RAILROAD CO.
Reorganized 00/00/1947
No stockholders' equity

CHICAGO, AURORA & ELGIN RAILWAY CO. (IL)
Reorganized as Aurora Corp. of Illinois 10/01/1959
Each share Common $1 par exchanged for (1) share Common $1 par
(See Aurora Corp. of Illinois)

CHICAGO, AURORA & ELGIN REAL ESTATE LIQUIDATING CORP. (IL)
Liquidation completed
Each share Common 30¢ par exchanged for initial distribution of $0.30 cash 07/07/1950
Each share Common 30¢ par received second and final distribution of $0.20 cash 09/10/1953

CHICAGO, AURORA & ELGIN TRUST (IL)
Reorganized 10/31/1949
Each Part. Ctf. Ser. A $1 par exchanged for (1) share Chicago, Aurora & Elgin Railway Co. Common $1 par
Each Part. Ctf. Ser. B 30¢ par exchanged for (1) share Chicago, Aurora & Elgin Real Estate Liquidating Corp. Common 30¢ par
(See each company's listing)

CHICAGO, DULUTH & GEORGIAN BAY TRANSIT CO. (IN)
7% Preferred $100 par changed to $75 par and $25 cash distributed 11/28/1962
Each share 7% Preferred $75 par exchanged for (1) share 7% Preferred $55 par and $20 cash 11/20/1963
Liquidation completed
Each share 7% Preferred $55 par received first and final distribution of $172 cash 02/09/1968
Note: Certificates were not required to be surrendered and are without value
Each share Common $5 par received initial distribution of $50 cash 02/09/1968
Each share Common $5 par received second distribution of $20 cash 02/20/1969
Each share Common $5 par received third distribution of $15 cash 11/21/1969
Each share Common $5 par received fourth distribution of $15 cash 01/23/1970
Common $5 par changed to $1 par 01/18/1971
Each share Common $1 par received fifth distribution of $4 cash 02/11/1971
Each share Common $1 par received sixth distribution of $3.30 cash 11/23/1971
Each share Common $1 par received seventh distribution of $2.15 cash 10/11/1972
Each share Common $1 par received eighth distribution of $3.276 cash 01/11/1974
Each share Common $1 par received ninth and final distribution of $1.50 cash 04/15/1974
Note: Certificates were not required to be surrendered and are without value

CHICAGO, ROCK ISLAND & PACIFIC RAILWAY CO. (IL & IA)
Reorganized as Chicago, Rock Island & Pacific Railroad Co. 00/00/1948
No stockholders' equity

CHICAGO, SOUTH BEND & NORTHERN INDIANA RAILWAY CO.
Acquired by Northern Indiana Railway, Inc. 00/00/1930
Details not available

CHICAGO & ALTON RAILROAD CO. (IL)
Acquired by Baltimore & Ohio Railroad Co. 00/00/1931
Details not available

CHICAGO & EASTERN ILLINOIS RAILWAY CO.
Reorganized as Chicago & Eastern Illinois Railroad Co. 00/00/1941
No stockholders' equity

CHICAGO & EASTN ILL RR CO (IN)
Class A $40 par called for redemption 10/29/1965
Common no par split (2) for (1) by issuance of (1) additional share 02/24/1966
Merged into Missouri Pacific Railroad Co. 10/15/1976
Each share Common no par exchanged for (1.1) shares Common no par
Missouri Pacific Railroad Co. merged into Missouri Pacific Corp. 11/01/1978 which merged into Union Pacific Corp. 12/22/1982

CHICAGO & NORTH WESTERN RAILWAY CO. (WI)
Certificates dated prior to 06/01/1944
Reorganized 06/01/1944
No stockholders' equity

CHICAGO & NORTH WESTN RY CO (WI)
Ctfs. dated after 06/01/1944
Name changed to Northwest Chemco, Inc. 06/05/1972
(See Northwest Chemco, Inc.)

CHICAGO & NORTH WESTN TRANS CO (DE)
Certificates dated after 05/09/1994
Name changed 05/09/1994
Exchangeable Preferred 1¢ par called for redemption 05/08/1992
Each Common Trust Receipt 1¢ par exchanged for (1) share Common 1¢ par 05/08/1992
Name changed from Chicago & North Western Holdings Corp. to Chicago & North Western Transportation Co. 05/09/1994
Merged into Union Pacific Corp. 06/23/1995
Each share Common 1¢ par exchanged for $35 cash

CHICAGO & NORTH WESTN TRANSN CO (DE)
Certificates dated prior to 06/21/1985
Class A Common $0.83333333 par changed to 28¢ par and (2) additional shares issued 08/28/1981
Under plan of reorganization each share Class A Common 28¢ par automatically became (1) share CNW Corp. Common $1 par 06/21/1985
CNW Corp. merged into Chicago & North Western Holdings Corp. 10/26/1989 which name changed to Chicago & North Western Transportation Co. 05/09/1994
(See Chicago & North Western Transportation Co. (Ctfs. dated after 05/09/1994))

CHICAGO & SOUTHERN AIR LINES, INC. (DE)
Merged into Delta Air Lines, Inc. 00/00/1953
Each share Common no par exchanged for $21 principal amount of 5.5% Conv. Debentures

CHICAGO & ST. PAUL TELEGRAPH CO. (WI)
Dissolved 08/23/1954
Details not available

CHICAGO & WEST TOWNS RAILWAYS, INC. (IL)
Reorganized 00/00/1954
No stockholders' equity

CHICAGO & WEST TOWNS RWY. CO.
Acquired at foreclosure by Chicago & West Towns Railways, Inc. 00/00/1932
Details not available

CHICAGO AERIAL INDS INC (DE)
Merged into Bourns, Inc. 07/31/1969
Each share Common $2 par exchanged for (1) share Common 50¢ par
(See Bourns, Inc.)

CHICAGO ALLERTON HOTEL CO (IL)
Liquidation completed
Each share Common no par stamped to indicate initial distribution of $28 cash 04/08/1974
Each share Stamped Common no par exchanged for second and final distribution of $3.02 cash 03/21/1975

CHICAGO APPARATUS CO. (IL)
Merged into Matheson Co., Inc. 12/31/1963
Details not available

CHICAGO ARTIFICIAL ICE CO. (DE)
Dissolution completed 12/08/1956
Details not available

CHICAGO BK COMM (CHICAGO, IL)
Name changed to Associated Bank Chicago (Chicago, IL) 10/17/1988
(See Associated Bank Chicago (Chicago, IL))

CHICAGO BEACH HOTEL, INC.
Property sold to the U.S. Government 00/00/1944
No stockholders' equity

CHICAGO BLDRS BLDG CO (IL)
In process of liquidation
Each share Common no par received initial distribution of $140 cash 02/20/1979
Each share Common no par exchanged for second distribution of $18.50 cash 09/17/1979
Note: Details on subsequent distributions, if any, are not available

CHICAGO BOX & CRATING CO.
Property sold at foreclosure 00/00/1929
Stockholders' equity unlikely

CHICAGO BRDG & IRON CO (IL)
Common $20 par changed to $6.66666666 par and (2) additional shares issued 04/30/1965
Common $6.66666666 par changed to $5 par and (3) additional shares issued 06/15/1972
Reincorporated under the laws of Delaware as CBI Industries, Inc. and Common $5 par changed to $2.50 par 08/22/1979
(See CBI Industries, Inc.)

CHICAGO BRDG & IRON CO N V (NETHERLANDS)
Common EUR 0.01 par split (2) for (1) by issuance of (1) additional share payable 02/10/2003 to holders of record 02/03/2003 Ex date - 02/11/2003
Common EUR 0.01 par split (2) for (1) by issuance of (1) additional share payable 03/31/2005 to holders of record 03/21/2005 Ex date - 04/01/2005
Merged into McDermott International, Inc. 05/10/2018
Each share Common EUR 0.01 par exchanged for (0.82407) share new Common $1 par

CHICAGO BROADWAY PROPERTIES TRUST
Trust terminated 00/00/1949
Details not available

CHICAGO BUILDERS BUILDING CORP.
Reorganized as Chicago Builders Building Co. 00/00/1936
Stockholders' equity unlikely

CHICAGO BURLINGTON & QUINCY RR CO (IL)
Merged into Burlington Northern Inc. 03/02/1970
Each share Capital Stock $100 par exchanged for (3.25) shares Common no par
Burlington Northern Inc. name changed to Burlington Northern Santa Fe Corp. 09/22/1995
(See Burlington Northern Santa Fe Corp.)

CHICAGO CEMETERY ASSN (IL)
Name changed to Chicago Cemetery Corp. 12/06/1972
(See Chicago Cemetery Corp.)

CHICAGO CEMETERY CORP (IL)
Merged into CCC Acquisition Corp. 11/08/1996
Each share Common $10 par exchanged for $600 cash
Note: An additional undisclosed sum is being held in escrow for distribution on or about 11/04/1999

CHICAGO CITY & CONNECTING RWYS.
Sold to City of Chicago 00/00/1947

No stockholders' equity

CHICAGO CITY BK & TR CO (CHICAGO, IL)
Each share Capital Stock $50 par exchanged for (10) shares Capital Stock $5 par 01/20/1970
Stock Dividends - 25% 12/15/1943; 25% 10/16/1953; 100% 07/14/1960; 20% 12/27/1962
Each share Capital Stock $5 par exchanged for (0.00001) share Capital Stock $5 par 06/22/1989
Note: In effect holders received $23.50 cash per share and public interest was eliminated

CHICAGO CITY RAILWAY CO.
Sold to City of Chicago 00/00/1947
No stockholders' equity

CHICAGO COLD STORAGE WAREHOUSE CO.
Acquired by Beatrice Creamery Co. 00/00/1931
Details not available

CHICAGO CONSUMERS COOPERATIVE, INC. (DC)
Assets reported sold for benefit of creditors 00/00/1953
No stockholders' equity

CHICAGO CORP. (DE)
Name changed to Champlin Oil & Refining Co. 12/31/1956
Champlin Oil & Refining Co. merged into Celanese Corp. of America 10/29/1964
Celanese Corp. of America name changed to Celanese Corp. 04/13/1966
(See Celanese Corp.)

CHICAGO DAILY NEWS, INC. (IL)
Common no par changed to $1 par 00/00/1947
Merged into Field Enterprises, Inc. 07/27/1959
Each share Common $1 par exchanged for (1) 5% 5-yr. Debenture

CHICAGO DOCK & CANAL TR (IL)
Shares of Bene. Int. $100 par changed to no par and (199) additional shares issued 09/30/1986
Merged into CityFront Center, L.L.C. 04/18/1997
Each Share of Bene. Int. no par exchanged for $25 cash

CHICAGO FIRE & MARINE INSURANCE CO. OF CHICAGO
Merged into Lincoln Fire Insurance Co. of New York 00/00/1931
Details not available

CHICAGO FLEXIBLE SHAFT CO.
Name changed to Sunbeam Corp. (IL) 00/00/1946
Sunbeam Corp. (IL) reincorporated in Delaware 07/18/1969 which merged into Allegheny International Inc. 01/02/1982
(See Allegheny International Inc.)

CHICAGO FUSE MANUFACTURING CO. (IL)
Merged into Chicago-Jefferson Fuse & Electric Co. 02/21/1928
Details not available

CHICAGO GREAT WESTERN RAILROAD CO. (IL)
Reorganized as Chicago Great Western Railway Co. (IL) 02/19/1941
Each share 4% Preferred exchanged for (0.5) share Common $50 par
Common stockholders had no equity
Chicago Great Western Railway Co. (IL) reincorporated in Delaware 12/31/1955 which merged into Chicago & North Western Railway Co. 07/01/1968 which name changed to Northwest Chemco, Inc. 06/05/1972
(See Northwest Chemco, Inc.)

CHICAGO GREAT WESTERN RAILWAY CO. (IL)
Reincorporated under the laws of Delaware 12/31/1955
Chicago Great Western Railway Co. (DE) merged into Chicago & North Western Railway Co. 07/01/1968 which name changed to Northwest Chemco, Inc. 06/05/1972
(See Northwest Chemco, Inc.)

CHICAGO GREAT WESTN RY CO (DE)
Common $50 par changed to $10 par 09/17/1959
Each Ctf. of Deposit for Preferred $50 par exchanged for (0.75) share Northwest Industries, Inc. 5% Conv. Preferred Ser. A $100 par 07/01/1968
Each Ctf. of Deposit for Common $10 par exchanged for (0.7) share Northwest Industries, Inc. Common no par 07/01/1968
Merged into Chicago & North Western Railway Co. 07/01/1968
Each share Preferred $50 par exchanged for (0.75) share 5% Preferred Ser. A $100 par
Each share Common $10 par exchanged for (0.7) share Common no par
Chicago & North Western Railway Co. name changed to Northwest Chemco, Inc. 06/05/1972
(See Northwest Chemco, Inc.)

CHICAGO HEIGHTS NATL BK (CHICAGO HEIGHTS, IL)
Stock Dividends - 20% 12/31/1952; 14% 12/07/1953; 11% 10/22/1954; 50% 06/20/1958; 50% 12/04/1962; 11% 02/15/1968; 50% 03/10/1973
Name changed to Bank Calumet, N.A. (Chicago Heights, IL) 10/10/1996
(See Bank Calumet, N.A. (Chicago Heights, IL))

CHICAGO HELICOPTER AWYS INC (DE)
Common $1 par split (2) for (1) by issuance of (1) additional share 06/10/1960
Trust Agreement expired and each VTC for Common $1 par exchanged for (1) share Common $1 par 05/25/1965
Name changed to Chicago Helicopter Industries, Inc. 05/12/1969
Chicago Helicopter Industries, Inc. name changed to D.M. Holdings, Inc. 10/20/1981
(See D.M. Holdings, Inc.)

CHICAGO HELICOPTER INDS INC (DE)
Name changed to D.M. Holdings, Inc. 10/20/1981
(See D.M. Holdings, Inc.)

CHICAGO HOLDING CORP. (DE)
Liquidated 01/15/1968
Each share Common $5 par exchanged for initial distribution of $60 cash
Note: Attorneys for company advised all holders have complied with requirements for payments of liquidating distributions and will not furnish further information for dissemination

CHICAGO INDIANAPOLIS & LOUISVILLE RY CO (IN)
Reorganized 04/24/1946 with no stockholders' equity
Certificates prior dated are valueless
Name of the new Chicago, Indianapolis & Louisville Railway Co. changed to Monon Railroad and Stock Trust terminated 01/10/1956
Monon Railroad merged into Louisville & Nashville Railroad Co. 07/31/1971 which merged into Seaboard Coast Line Industries, Inc. 11/10/1972 which merged CSX Corp. 11/01/1980

CHICAGO INSULATED WIRE & MANUFACTURING CO.
Merged into Inland Wire & Cable Co. 00/00/1927
Details not available

CHICAGO INVESTORS, INC.
Merged into Chicago Corp. 00/00/1932
Details not available

CHICAGO-JEFFERSON FUSE & ELECTRIC CO. (IL)
Name changed to Jefferson Electric Co. (IL) 02/15/1929
Jefferson Electric Co. (IL) reincorporated in Delaware 02/10/1960 which was acquired by Litton Industries, Inc. 02/23/1967
(See Litton Industries, Inc.)

CHICAGO MAIL ORDER CO.
Name changed to Aldens, Inc. 03/27/1946
Aldens, Inc. merged into Gamble-Skogmo, Inc. 12/31/1964 which merged into Wickes Companies, Inc. 01/26/1985 which name changed to Collins & Aikman Group Inc. 07/17/1992
(See Collins & Aikman Group Inc.)

CHICAGO MEDICAL ARTS BUILDING CORP. (IL)
Each share Capital Stock $50 par exchanged for (5) shares Capital Stock $1 par 00/00/1948
Liquidation completed 11/03/1960
Details not available

CHICAGO MERCANTILE EXCHANGE HLDGS INC (DE)
Under plan of merger name changed to CME Group Inc. 07/12/2007

CHICAGO MILL & LUMBER CO. (DE)
Class A and C no par changed to Capital Stock no par 00/00/1939
Capital Stock no par exchanged (5) for (1) 00/00/1941
Capital Stock no par changed to $10 par and (1) additional share issued 03/22/1954
Completely liquidated 06/29/1965
Details not available

CHICAGO MILL TIMBER CORP. (DE)
Name changed to Chicago Mill & Lumber Co. 00/00/1936
(See Chicago Mill & Lumber Co.)

CHICAGO MILWAUKEE CORP (DE)
Reincorporated 01/01/1994
Each share Common $1 par received distribution of (1) Heartland Partners, L.P. Class A Unit of Ltd. Partnership 06/30/1990
(See Heartland Partners, L.P.)
$5 Prior Preferred no par called for redemption 06/16/1993
State of incorporation changed from (DE) to (MD) 01/01/1994
Liquidation completed
Each share Common $1 par received initial distribution of $133.92 cash 05/00/1995
Each share Common $1 par received second and final distribution of $1.65 cash payable 10/25/1996 to holders of record 05/22/1995
Note: Certificates were not required to be surrendered and are without value

CHICAGO MILWAUKEE ST PAUL & PAC RR CO (WI)
Reorganized 00/00/1945
No stockholders' equity
Preferred and Common Voting Trust Agreements terminated 00/00/1950
Voluntary Exchange Offer withdrawn 02/25/1970
Each Ctf. of Deposit for 5% Preferred Ser. A $100 par exchanged for (1) share 5% Preferred Ser. A $100 par
Each Ctf. of Deposit for Common no par exchanged for (1) share Common no par

Name changed to CMC Real Estate Corp. 11/25/1985
(See CMC Real Estate Corp.)

CHICAGO MINIATURE LAMP INC (OK)
Common 1¢ par split (3) for (2) by issuance of (0.5) additional share payable 08/27/1996 to holders of record 08/16/1996
Common 1¢ par split (3) for (2) by issuance of (0.5) additional share payable 03/06/1998 to holders of record 02/23/1998 Ex date - 03/09/1998
Name changed to SLI, Inc. 04/27/1998
(See SLI, Inc.)

CHICAGO MOLDED PRODS CORP (DE)
Reincorporated 05/12/1961
Each share Common no par exchanged for (58) shares Common $1 par 00/00/1939
Stock Dividends - 50% 01/26/1951; 33.33333333% 01/25/1952; 10% 07/20/1956
State of incorporation changed from (IL) to (DE) 05/12/1961
Company reported out of business 00/00/1989
Details not available

CHICAGO MUSICAL INSTR CO (DE)
Reincorporated 10/18/1962
Common $1 par split (2) for (1) by issuance of (1) additional share 06/07/1962
Under plan of merger state of incorporation changed from (IL) to (DE) 10/18/1962
Merged into Norlin Corp. 10/31/1973
Each share Common $1 par exchanged for $26.50 cash

CHICAGO NATL LEAGUE BALL CLUB INC (DE)
Name changed to CC Assets Distribution Corp. 09/01/1981
(See CC Assets Distribution Corp.)

CHICAGO NATIONAL LIFE INSURANCE CO. (IL)
Merged into All American Life & Casualty Co. 06/28/1966
Each share Common $1 par exchanged for (0.470588) share Common $1 par
All American Life & Casualty Co. acquired by All American Life & Financial Corp. 03/18/1968
(See All American Life & Financial Corp.)

CHICAGO-NEW YORK ELECTRIC AIR LINE RAILROAD CO. (ME)
Out of business 04/20/1915
Details not available

CHICAGO NIPPLE MFG CO (DE)
Recapitalized 09/13/1923
Each share Class A $10 par exchanged for (0.2) share Class A $50 par
Each share Class B $10 par exchanged for (0.2) share Class B $50 par
Recapitalized 08/26/1935
Each share Class A $50 par exchanged for (1) share Common $5 par
Each share Class B $50 par exchanged for (0.5) share Common $5 par
Completely liquidated 04/01/1969
Each share Common $5 par exchanged for first and final distribution of $19 cash

CHICAGO NORTH SHORE & MILWAUKEE RAILROAD CO.
Reorganized as Chicago North Shore & Milwaukee Railway Co. 00/00/1946
No stockholders' equity

CHICAGO NORTH SHORE & MILWAUKEE RAILWAY CO.
Reorganized as Chicago North Shore System, Inc. (DE) 00/00/1953
Each share Common no par exchanged for (1) share Capital Stock $1 par
Chicago North Shore System, Inc. name changed to Susquehanna Corp. 06/01/1956
(See Susquehanna Corp.)

CHICAGO NORTH SHORE SYSTEM, INC. (DE)
Name changed to Susquehanna Corp. 06/01/1956
(See Susquehanna Corp.)

CHICAGO NUT MANUFACTURING CO.
Merged into United Screw & Bolt Corp. 00/00/1930
Details not available

CHICAGO PAC CORP (DE)
Common 1¢ par split (3) for (1) by issuance of (2) additional shares 05/31/1985
Common 1¢ par split (3) for (2) by issuance of (0.5) additional share 09/01/1988
Merged into Maytag Corp. 01/26/1989
Each share Common 1¢ par exchanged for (2.7272) shares Common $1.25 par
Maytag Corp. merged into Whirlpool Corp. 03/31/2006

CHICAGO PIZZA & BREWERY INC (CA)
Name changed to BJ's Restaurants Inc. 08/16/2004

CHICAGO PNEUMATIC TOOL CO (NJ)
Each share Capital Stock $100 par exchanged for (2) shares $3.50 Preference no par and (2) shares Common no par 00/00/1928
Each share $3.50 Preference no par exchanged for (1) share $3 Preference no par and (0.75) share Common no par 00/00/1937
$2.50 Preferred no par called for redemption 11/01/1947
Common no par changed to $5 par and (1) additional share issued 00/00/1954
$3 Preference no par called for redemption 05/31/1956
Common $5 par changed to $8 par and (2) additional shares issued 04/12/1957
Stock Dividends - 10% 04/02/1956; 10% 01/20/1967
Acquired by Danaher Corp. 12/30/1986
Each share Common $8 par exchanged for $38 cash

CHICAGO PRODUCE DISTRICT TRUST
Liquidation completed 00/00/1953
Details not available

CHICAGO PUBLISHING & MEDIA CO., INC. (DE)
Charter forfeited for failure to maintain a registered agent 02/25/1999

CHICAGO RAILWAYS CO.
Sold to City of Chicago 00/00/1947
No stockholders' equity

CHICAGO RAPID TRANSIT CO.
Sold to City of Chicago 00/00/1947
No stockholders' equity

CHICAGO ROCK IS & PAC RR CO (DE)
Common no par split (2) for (1) by issuance of (1) additional share 01/20/1956
Each Union Pacific Railroad Co. Ctf. of Dep. Ser. A no par or Union Pacific Railroad Co. Ctf. of Dep. Ser. B no par exchanged for (1) share Common no par 11/15/1974
Under plan of reorganization name changed to Chicago Pacific Corp. and Common no par changed to 1¢ par 06/01/1984
Chicago Pacific Corp. merged into Maytag Corp. 01/26/1989 which merged into Whirlpool Corp. 03/31/2006

CHICAGO RY EQUIP CO (IL)
Under plan of merger each share Common received (0.45) share American Seal-Kap Corp. of Delaware 5% Preferred 4th Ser. $100 par 05/31/1961
(See American Seal-Kap Corp. of Delaware)

CHICAGO SOUTH SHORE & SOUTH BEND RR (IN)
Each share Class A Preferred no par exchanged for (1) share 2nd Preferred $100 par 00/00/1938
Each share Class B Preferred no par exchanged for (1) share Common no par 00/00/1938
Each share 1st Preferred $100 par exchanged for (1.3574) shares new Common $50 par 00/00/1942
Each share 2nd Preferred $100 par exchanged for (1) share Common $50 par 00/00/1942
Each share Common $50 par exchanged for (4) shares Common $12.50 par 00/00/1944
Through voluntary purchase offer Chesapeake & Ohio Railway Co. acquired over 94% of Common as of 02/01/1967
Public interest eliminated

CHICAGO ST PAUL MINNEAPOLIS & OMAHA RY CO (WI)
Name changed to Omaha Properties Co. 08/08/1972
(See Omaha Properties Co.)

CHICAGO THOROUGHBRED ENTERPRISES INC (DE)
Merged into Madison Square Garden Corp. (MI) 02/04/1972
Each share 5.5% Preferred $100 par exchanged for (22.08) shares Common $1 par
Each share Common no par exchanged for (2,337.66) shares Common $1 par
(See Madison Square Garden Corp. (MI))

CHICAGO TITLE & TRUST CO. (IL)
Each share Common $100 par exchanged for (5) shares Common $20 par 00/00/1946
Common $20 par changed to $6.66666666 par and (2) additional shares issued 12/15/1963
Through voluntary exchange offer Lincoln National Corp. acquired 99.6% of Common as of 11/14/1969
Each share Common $6.66666666 par exchanged for (0.001667) share Common $4,000 par 02/24/1971
Public interest eliminated

CHICAGO TITLE CORP (DE)
Merged into Fidelity National Financial, Inc. 03/20/2000
Each share Common $1 par exchanged for either (2.706) shares Common $0.0001 par and $13.6304 cash, or $49.2879 cash
Note: Option to receive stock and cash expired 03/20/2000
Fidelity National Financial, Inc. merged into Fidelity National Information Services, Inc. 11/09/2006

CHICAGO TOWEL CO. (IL)
Name changed to Means (F.W.) & Co. 05/02/1960
Means (F.W.) & Co. name changed to Means Services, Inc. 07/02/1979
(See Means Services, Inc.)

CHICAGO TRANSFER & CLEARING CO.
Name changed to Clearing Industrial District, Inc. 00/00/1934
(See Clearing Industrial District, Inc.)

CHICAGO YELLOW CAB INC (NY)
Merged into Checker Motors Corp. 05/01/1969
Each share Capital Stock no par exchanged for (1) share $1.60 Conv. Preferred $40 par
(See Checker Motors Corp.)

CHICHIBU ONODA CEM CORP (JAPAN)
Name changed to Taiheiyo Cement Corp. 10/01/1998

CHICKASHA COTTON OIL CO (DE)
Each share Capital Stock $10 par exchanged for (2) shares Capital Stock $5 par 10/16/1956
Acquired by Toyo Menka Kaisha, Ltd. 06/04/1981
Each share Capital Stock $5 par exchanged for $133.41 cash

CHICKEN CHEF SYS INC (MS)
Merged into Cal-Maine Foods, Inc. 06/24/1970
Each share Common $1 par exchanged for (0.384615) share Common 1¢ par

CHICKEN HAWK INC (DE)
Name changed to Plaza Group, Inc. 02/18/1987
Plaza Group, Inc. name changed to Union 69, Ltd. 04/02/1996 which name changed to Save on Meds.Com, Inc. 03/02/2000 which name changed to My Meds Express.Com, Inc. 07/26/2000
(See My Meds Express.Com, Inc.)

CHICKEN HOLIDAY INC (DE)
Charter cancelled and declared inoperative and void for non-payment of taxes 03/01/1974

CHICKEN KITCHEN CORP (FL)
Name changed to Claremont Enterprises Inc. 01/11/2002
Claremont Enterprises Inc. recapitalized as OSF, Inc. (FL) 05/12/2003 which reincorporated in Delaware 07/25/2003 which recapitalized as Tensas Inc. 04/01/2005 which name changed to PGI Energy, Inc. 02/28/2011

CHICKEN UNLIMITED ENTERPRISES INC (DE)
Stock Dividends - 10% 02/05/1971; 15% 01/17/1972; 10% 04/19/1974
Name changed to CUE Industries, Inc. 08/26/1982
(See CUE Industries, Inc.)

CHICOBI LAKE MINES LTD. (ON)
Charter cancelled and proclaimed dissolved for failure to file returns and pay taxes 07/19/1982

CHICOPEE BANCORP INC (MA)
Merged into Western New England Bancorp, Inc. 10/24/2016
Each share Common no par exchanged for (2.425) shares Common 1¢ par

CHICOPEE BK & TR CO (CHICOPEE, MA)
Declared insolvent 05/09/1975
Stockholders' equity unlikely

CHICOS PIZZA FRANCHISES INC (OR)
Merged into P&P Pizzas, Inc. 04/29/1980
Each share Common 1¢ par exchanged for $2.30 cash

CHIEF AUTOMOTIVE SYS INC (DE)
Common 10¢ par split (3) for (2) by issuance of (0.5) additional share 03/04/1986
Common 10¢ par split (3) for (2) by issuance of (0.5) additional share 11/03/1986
Merged into Dover Corp. 08/05/1988
Each share Common 10¢ par exchanged for $15 cash

CHIEF CONS MNG CO (AZ)
Common $1 par changed to 50¢ par 12/04/1967
Common 50¢ par changed to 1¢ par 03/12/2008
SEC revoked preferred and common stock registration 04/08/2011

CHIEF REDWATER OILS LTD.
Assets acquired by West Plains Oil Resources Ltd. 00/00/1952
Details not available

CHIEF UTE URANIUM, INC. (UT)
Merged into Uranium Corp. of America 04/05/1955
Each share Capital Stock exchanged for (0.05) share Capital Stock 20¢ par
Uranium Corp. of America (UT) merged into Chemical & Metallurgical Enterprises, Inc. 11/05/1956
(See Chemical & Metallurgical Enterprises, Inc.)

CHIEFTAIN DEV LTD (AB)
Common 50¢ par changed to no par and (1) additional share issued 06/22/1979
Common no par split (3) for (2) by issuance of (0.5) additional share 07/11/1980
9% Conv. 2nd Preferred 1976 Ser. $50 par called for redemption 11/30/1982
Common no par split (3) for (2) by issuance of (0.5) additional share 11/10/1983
$4 Conv. 2nd Preferred 1983 Ser. $50 par reclassified as $4 Conv. Class A Preferred 1983 Ser. no par 06/09/1985
9.5% Conv. 2nd Preferred 1981 Ser. $50 par reclassified as $4.75 Conv. Class A Preferred 1981 Ser. no par 06/09/1985
$4 Conv. Class A Preferred 1983 Ser. no par called for redemption 08/26/1988
$4.75 Conv. Class A Preferred 1981 Ser. no par called for redemption 08/26/1988
Merged into Alberta Energy Co. Ltd. 09/01/1988
Each share Common no par exchanged for $14 cash

CHIEFTAIN INTL FDG CORP (NV)
$1.8125 Conv. Preferred $25 par called for redemption at $25.2014 plus $0.292 accrued dividends on 08/28/2001

CHIEFTAIN INTL INC (AB)
Acquired by Hunt Oil Co. 08/07/2001
Each share Common no par exchanged for $29 cash

CHIEFTAIN METALS INC (ON)
Merged into Chieftain Metals Corp. 05/22/2013
Each share Common no par exchanged for (1) share Common no par

CHIEFTAIN OIL & MINING CORP. (UT)
Name changed to Drexel Industries, Inc. 08/28/1961
(See Drexel Industries, Inc.)

CHIEFTAIN URANIUM MINES, INC. (UT)
Name changed to Chieftain Oil & Mining Corp. 11/27/1956
Chieftain Oil & Mining Corp. name changed to Drexel Industries, Inc. 08/28/1961
(See Drexel Industries, Inc.)

CHILCO RES LTD (BC)
Merged into Bonanza Oil & Gas Ltd. (Old) 10/08/1980
Each share Common no par exchanged for $3.40 cash

CHILCO RIV HLDGS INC (NV)
Each share old Common $0.001 par

FINANCIAL INFORMATION, INC.   CHI-CHI

exchanged for (2) shares new Common $0.001 par 07/10/2006
Charter revoked for failure to file reports and pay fees 06/30/2009

CHILCOTT PORTFOLIO MANAGEMENT, INC. (CO)
Charter suspended for failure to file annual reports 09/30/1982

CHILD CARE CTRS NORTH AMER INC (CO)
Chapter 11 bankruptcy proceedings converted to Chapter 7 on 03/03/1995
Stockholders' equity unlikely

CHILD GUARD CORP (MN)
Name changed to Tollycraft Yacht Corp. (MN) 01/30/1996
Tollycraft Yacht Corp. (MN) reorganized in Nevada 12/29/1996 which name changed to Childguard Corp. 03/27/2002 which name changed to EWAN 1 Inc. 04/17/2002 which name changed to Advanced Technetix, Inc. 09/26/2006 which name changed to AccessKey IP, Inc. 03/26/2007

CHILD VISION INC (DE)
Reorganized as Shanghai Yutong Pharma, Inc. 07/15/2005
Each share Common 1¢ par exchanged for (5) shares Common $0.001 par
Shanghai Yutong Pharma, Inc. name changed to ANBC, Inc. 08/23/2016

CHILD WORLD INC (MA)
Ctfs. dated prior to 01/20/1981
Common 10¢ par split (3) for (2) by issuance of (0.5) additional share 06/30/1972
Merged into Cole National Corp. 01/20/1981
Each share Common 10¢ par exchanged for $16.75 cash

CHILD WORLD INC NEW (MA)
Certificates dated after 08/23/1985
Filed a petition under Chapter 11 Federal Bankruptcy Code 05/07/1992
Stockholders' equity unlikely

CHILD WRIT & CO INC (TX)
Reincorporated 03/00/1992
State of incorporation changed from (DE) to (TX) 03/00/1992
Reorganized as American Cascade Energy, Inc. 06/15/1992
Each share Common $0.001 par exchanged for (0.25) share Common $0.001 par
(See American Cascade Energy, Inc.)

CHILDCRAFT ED CORP (NY)
Stock Dividends - 10% 06/30/1980; 10% 08/14/1981; 10% 07/02/1982
Merged into CEC Holdings Corp. 05/02/1984
Each share Common 25¢ par exchanged for $2 principal amount of Childcraft Education Corp. Subordinated Notes due 05/01/1991, (0.15) Childcraft Education Corp. Common Stock Purchase Warrant due 05/01/1986 and $4 cash

CHILDCRAFT EQUIP INC (NY)
Name changed to Childcraft Education Corp. 06/25/1969
(See Childcraft Education Corp.)

CHILDGUARD CORP (NV)
Name changed to Ewan 1 Inc. 04/17/2002
Ewan 1 Inc. name changed to Advanced Technetix, Inc. 09/26/2006 which name changed to AccessKey IP, Inc. 03/26/2007
(See AccessKey IP, Inc.)

CHILDHOOD PRODUCTIONS INC (NY)
Name changed to Cinecom Corp. 04/14/1969
(See Cinecom Corp.)

CHILDREN S INTERNET INC (NV)
Old Common $0.001 par split (2) for (1) by issuance of (1) additional share payable 03/10/2005 to holders of record 03/07/2005 Ex date - 03/11/2005
Each share old Common $0.001 par exchanged for (0.004) share new Common $0.001 par 10/15/2010
Each share new Common $0.001 par exchanged again for (0.0002) share new Common $0.001 par 04/15/2011
Reorganized under the laws of Wyoming as FlashZero Corp. 03/11/2015
Each share new Common $0.001 par exchanged for (0.04) share Common $0.00001 par

CHILDREN'S WONDERLAND INC (CA)
SEC revoked common stock registration 12/05/2012

CHILDRENS BEVERAGE GROUP INC (DE)
Charter cancelled and declared inoperative and void for non-payment of taxes 03/01/2001

CHILDRENS BROADCASTING CORP (MN)
Each share Common $0.001 par exchanged for (0.5) share Common 2¢ par 01/23/1996
Name changed to INTELEFILM Corp. 10/07/1999
(See INTELEFILM Corp.)

CHILDRENS COMPREHENSIVE SVCS INC (TN)
Each share old Common 1¢ par exchanged for (0.5) share new Common 1¢ par 03/21/1996
Merged into Kids Holdings, Inc. 01/04/2002
Each share new Common 1¢ par exchanged for $6 cash

CHILDRENS CREATIVE WORKSHOP LTD (NV)
Name changed to Kent Holdings Ltd. 07/16/1991
(See Kent Holdings Ltd.)

CHILDRENS DISCOVERY CTRS AMER INC (DE)
Each share old Class A Common 1¢ par exchanged for (0.125) share new Class A Common 1¢ par 10/10/1997
Merged into KBI Acquisition Corp. 05/08/1998
Each share new Common 1¢ par exchanged for $12.25 cash

CHILDRENS PL INC (DE)
Merged into Federated Department Stores, Inc. 03/12/1982
Each share Common 1¢ par exchanged for $30.50 cash

CHILDRENS PL RETAIL STORES INC (DE)
Name changed to Children's Place, Inc. 06/18/2014

CHILDRENS WORLD INC (DE)
Merged into GrandMet USA, Inc. 09/07/1983
Each share Common 10¢ par exchanged for $13 cash

CHILDROBICS INC (NY)
Chapter 7 bankruptcy proceedings terminated 09/30/2003
No stockholders' equity

CHILDS CO. (NY)
Reorganized 00/00/1948
Each share 7% Preferred $100 par exchanged for (1) share 5.5% Preferred $100 par and (12) shares Common $1 par
Each share Common no par exchanged for (1) share Common $1 par
Each share 5.5% Preferred $100 par exchanged for (4.4) shares 5% Preferred $25 par 00/00/1951
Name changed to Hotel Corp. of America 02/23/1956
Hotel Corp. of America name changed to Sonesta International Hotels Corp. 06/01/1970
(See Sonesta International Hotels Corp.)

CHILDS GOLD MINES, LTD.
Recapitalized as Childs Red Lake Gold Mines, Ltd. 00/00/1945
Each share Capital Stock $10 par exchanged for (0.00487804) share Capital Stock $1 par
(See Childs Red Lake Gold Mines Ltd.)

CHILDS RED LAKE GOLD MINES, LTD. (ON)
Charter cancelled 11/00/1959

CHILDTIME LEARNING CTRS INC (MI)
Name changed to Learning Care Group, Inc. 08/17/2004
(See Learning Care Group, Inc.)

CHILE COPPER CO (DE)
Completely liquidated 03/15/1984
Each share Common $25 par received first and final distribution of $1.88 cash
Note: Certificates were not required to be surrendered and are without value

CHILE FD INC (MD)
Common $0.001 par split (2) for (1) by issuance of (1) additional share 07/14/1995
Name changed to Aberdeen Chile Fund, Inc. 03/26/2010
Aberdeen Chile Fund, Inc. name changed to Aberdeen Emerging Markets Equity Income Fund, Inc. 04/30/2018

CHILEAN GOLD LTD (BC)
Name changed to Earth Star Diamonds Ltd. 05/23/2002
Earth Star Diamonds Ltd. merged into Nordic Diamonds Ltd. 11/24/2003 which recapitalized as Western Standard Metals Ltd. 06/12/2009 which merged into Terraco Gold Corp. (AB) 01/25/2011 which reincorporated in British Columbia 06/08/2011

CHILECTRA S A (CHILE)
ADR agreement terminated 02/01/2002
Each Sponsored ADR for Ordinary exchanged for $10.45408 cash

CHILES OFFSHORE CORP (DE)
Merged into Noble Drilling Corp. (DE) 09/16/1994
Each share $1.50 Conv. Preferred $1 par exchanged for (1) share $1.50 Conv. Preferred $1 par
Each share Common 1¢ par exchanged for (0.75) share Common 10¢ par
Noble Drilling Corp. (DE) reincorporated in Cayman Islands as Noble Corp. 04/30/2002

CHILES OFFSHORE INC (DE)
Merged into ENSCO International Inc. (DE) 08/07/2002
Each share Common 1¢ par exchanged for (0.6575) share Common 10¢ par and $5.25 cash
ENSCO International Inc. (DE) reorganized in England & Wales as Ensco International PLC 12/23/2009 which name changed to Ensco PLC 03/31/2010

CHILESAT CORP S A (CHILE)
ADR agreement terminated 02/18/2005
Each Sponsored ADR for Ordinary exchanged for $2.5867 cash

CHILGENER S A (CHILE)
Name changed to Gener S.A. 04/03/1998
(See Gener S.A.)

CHILIS INC (DE)
Common 10¢ par split (3) for (2) by issuance of (0.5) additional share 06/16/1989
Common 10¢ par split (3) for (2) by issuance of (0.5) additional share 03/14/1991
Name changed to Brinker International, Inc. 05/09/1991

CHILL CAN INDS INC (FL)
Each share Common $1 par exchanged for (5) shares Common 20¢ par 08/17/1970
Proclaimed dissolved for failure to file reports and pay fees 09/03/1976

CHILL TECH INDS INC (NV)
Charter expired 10/17/2007

CHILLICOTHE PAPER CO. (OH)
Each share Common $100 par exchanged for (10) shares Common $10 par 00/00/1952
Merged into Mead Corp. 11/25/1955
Each share Common $10 par exchanged for (1.5) shares Common $25 par
Mead Corp. merged into MeadWestvaco Corp. 01/29/2002 which merged into WestRock Co. 07/01/2015

CHILLICOTHE TEL CO (OH)
Under plan of reorganization each share Common no par automatically became (1) share Horizon Telcom, Inc. Common no par 01/01/1996
(See Horizon Telcom, Inc)

CHILLICOTHE WATER CO.
Acquired by the City of Chillicothe, MO 00/00/1937
Details not available

CHILMARK ENTMT GROUP INC (NV)
Old Common $0.001 par split (2) for (1) by issuance of (1) additional share payable 11/14/2003 to holders of record 11/11/2003 Ex date - 11/17/2003
Each share old Common $0.001 par exchanged for (0.1) share new Common $0.001 par 01/17/2006
Recapitalized as Integrated Bio Energy Resources, Inc. 03/13/2007
Each share new Common $0.001 par exchanged for (0.01) share Common $0.001 par
Integrated Bio Energy Resources, Inc. name changed to Onslow Holdings, Inc. 01/30/2014

CHILQUINTA S A (CHILE)
Basis changed from (1:1) to (1:3) 01/22/1999
Name changed to Almendral S.A. 06/20/2001
(See Almendral S.A.)

CHILTON CO (DE)
Each share Preferred $100 par exchanged for (10) shares Common $10 par 00/00/1936
Merged into Ambroad, Inc. 08/02/1979
Each share Common $10 par exchanged for $86 cash

CHILTON CORP (TX)
Common $1 par changed to 50¢ par and (1) additional share issued 09/01/1969
Common 50¢ par split (3) for (2) by issuance of (0.5) additional share 08/31/1983
Common 50¢ par split (3) for (2) by issuance of (0.5) additional share 11/30/1984
Stock Dividend - 100% 11/30/1982
Merged into Borg-Warner Corp. 03/17/1986
Each share Common 50¢ par exchanged for $33 cash

CHILTON PPTYS INC (NY)
Reorganized under the laws of Colorado as HSC Services, Inc. 02/01/1971
Each share Common $1 par exchanged for (7) shares Common 10¢ par
(See HSC Services, Inc.)

CHIME COMMUNICATIONS PLC (UNITED KINGDOM)
ADR agreement terminated 08/22/2016
No ADR's remain outstanding

CHIMEI INNOLUX CORP (TAIWAN)
Name changed to Innolux Corp. 01/02/2013
(See Innolux Corp.)

CHIMERA RES LTD (BC)
Common no par split (4) for (1) by issuance of (3) additional shares 04/09/1984
Recapitalized as E.S.I. Industries Corp. 08/09/1985
Each share Common no par exchanged for (0.33333333) share Common no par
(See E.S.I. Industries Corp.)

CHIMERA TECHNOLOGY CORP (NV)
Each share old Common no par exchanged for (0.00125) share new Common no par 05/15/2003
Each share new Common no par exchanged for (5) shares Common $0.001 par 11/06/2003
Recapitalized as Oriens Travel & Hotel Management Corp. 08/21/2007
Each share Common $0.001 par exchanged for (0.005) share Common $0.001 par
Oriens Travel & Hotel Management Corp. recapitalized as Pure Hospitality Solutions, Inc. 11/12/2014

CHIMNEY CREEK-FRASER PLACER MINES, LTD. (ON)
Charter revoked for failure to file reports and pay taxes 00/00/1956

CHIMO GOLD MINES LTD (ON)
Merged into Conwest Exploration Co., Ltd. (Old) (ON) 08/27/1982
Each share Capital Stock $1 par exchanged for (0.3) share Class B no par
Conwest Exploration Co., Ltd. (Old) (ON) merged into Conwest Exploration Co. Ltd. (New) (AB) 09/01/1993 which merged into Alberta Energy Co. Ltd. 01/31/1996 which merged into EnCana Corp. 01/03/2003

CHINA ADNET ENTERPRISES INC (CA)
Charter suspended for failure to file reports and pay fees 10/01/2008

CHINA ADVANCED CONSTR MATLS GROUP INC (DE)
Reorganized under the laws of Nevada 08/02/2013
Each share Common $0.001 par exchanged for (0.08333333) share Common $0.001 par 08/02/2013

CHINA ADVANCED TECHNOLOGY (NV)
Name changed to Goliath Film & Media Holdings 01/20/2012

CHINA AEROSPACE INTL HLDGS LTD (HONG KONG)
ADR agreement terminated 12/01/2005
Each Unsponsored ADR for Ordinary exchanged for $0.39614 cash

CHINA AGRO SCIENCES CORP (FL)
Name changed to China HGS Real Estate Inc. 11/24/2009

CHINA AGRO TECHNOLOGY HLDGS LTD (BELIZE)
Each share old Common $0.001 par exchanged for (0.0005) share new Common $0.001 par 06/22/2011
Note: No holder will receive fewer than (100) shares
SEC revoked common stock registration 04/09/2012

CHINA AMER HLDGS INC (FL)
Recapitalized as Ziyang Ceramics Corp. 01/27/2012
Each share Common $0.001 par exchanged for (0.0025) share Common $0.001 par
(See Ziyang Ceramics Corp.)

CHINA AOXING PHARMACEUTICAL CO INC (FL)
Recapitalized as Aoxing Pharmaceutical Co., Inc. 03/29/2010
Each share Common $0.001 par exchanged for (0.5) share Common $0.001 par

CHINA ARCHITECTURAL ENGR INC (DE)
Each share old Common $0.001 par exchanged for (0.25) share new Common $0.001 par 12/21/2010
Name changed to China CGame, Inc. 03/28/2011

CHINA ARMCO METALS INC (NV)
Name changed to Armco Metals Holdings, Inc. 07/18/2013

CHINA ARTISTS AGY INC (NV)
Name changed to China Entertainment Group, Inc. 08/22/2005
China Entertainment Group, Inc. name changed to Safe & Secure TV Channel, Inc. 08/12/2010 which name changed to Cosmos Group Holdings Inc. 03/31/2016

CHINA BAICAOTANG MEDICINE LTD (DE)
Name changed to China BCT Pharmacy Group, Inc. 07/22/2010

CHINA BAK BATTERY INC (NV)
Each share old Common $0.001 par exchanged for (0.2) share new Common $0.001 par 10/26/2012
Name changed to CBAK Energy Technology, Inc. 01/17/2017

CHINA BASIC INDS INC (UT)
Proclaimed dissolved for failure to pay taxes 10/01/1997

CHINA BILINGUAL TECHNOLOGY & ED GROUP INC (NV)
Name changed to Capstone Technologies Group, Inc. 05/19/2017

CHINA BIO ENERGY CORP (DE)
Name changed to Wave Sync Corp. 10/05/2015

CHINA BIO ENERGY HLDG GROUP CO LTD (DE)
Name changed to China Integrated Energy, Inc. 09/18/2009
(See China Integrated Energy, Inc.)

CHINA BIO HEALTH GROUP INC (NV)
Name changed to Emerging Media Holdings Inc. 07/18/2006
Emerging Media Holdings Inc. name changed to Lifestyle Medical Network Inc. 07/31/2012

CHINA BIOLIFE ENTERPRISES INC (NV)
Recapitalized as Asia Pacific Energy Inc. 12/07/2007
Each share Common $0.002 par exchanged for (0.005) share Common $0.002 par

CHINA BIOLOGIC PRODS INC (TX)
Reincorporated under the laws of Cayman Islands as China Biologic Products Holdings, Inc. and Common $0.0001 par reclassified as Ordinary $0.0001 par 07/24/2017

CHINA BIOMEDICAL GROUP INC (UT)
Each share old Common no par exchanged for (0.2) share new Common no par 01/31/1996
Name changed to Internet Holdings Ltd. 06/30/1996
Internet Holdings Ltd. name changed to HTTP Technology, Inc. (UT) 11/28/2000 which reincorporated in Delaware 12/19/2000 which name changed to Medicsight, Inc. 10/28/2002 which name changed to MGT Capital Investments, Inc. 01/24/2007

CHINA BIONANOMETER INDS CORP (NV)
SEC revoked common stock registration 09/04/2013

CHINA BIOPHARMACEUTICALS HLDGS INC (DE)
Merged into NeoStem, Inc. 10/30/2009
Each share Common 1¢ par exchanged for (0.1921665) share Common $0.001 [ar

CHINA BROADBAND CORP (NV)
Name changed to China Energy Ventures Corp. 12/30/2003
China Energy Ventures Corp. name changed to Big Sky Energy Corp. 12/15/2004
(See Big Sky Energy Corp.)

CHINA BROADBAND INC (NV)
Name changed to YOU On Demand Holdings, Inc. 04/05/2011
YOU On Demand Holdings, Inc. name changed to Wecast Network, Inc. 11/14/2016 which name changed to Seven Stars Cloud Group, Inc. 07/17/2017

CHINA CABLECOM HOLDINGS LTD (BRITISH VIRGIN ISLANDS)
Each old Unit exchanged for (0.33333333) new Unit 03/02/2010
Each share Ordinary $0.0005 par exchanged for (0.33333333) share Ordinary $0.0015 par 03/02/2010
Units separated 04/05/2010
SEC revoked ordinary stock registration 02/13/2014

CHINA CAP HLDGS CORP (NV)
Charter permanently revoked 06/30/2011

CHINA CAREER BLDR CORP (DE)
Recapitalized as iMing Corp. 06/08/2012
Each share Common $0.001 par exchanged for (0.002) share Common $0.001 par

CHINA CEETOP COM INC (OR)
Name changed to Ceetop Inc. 09/19/2013

CHINA CELLULAR COMMUNICATIONS CORP (BC)
Name changed to China Jinrong Corp. 12/09/1993
China Jinrong Corp. recapitalized as Rystar Development Ltd. (BC) 06/25/1996 which reincorporated in Canada as Rystar Communications Ltd. 03/31/1998
(See Rystar Communications Ltd.)

CHINA CENTY DRAGON MEDIA INC (DE)
SEC revoked common stock registration 01/16/2014

CHINA CLIPPER GOLD MINES LTD (ON)
Recapitalized as Kinloch Resources Inc. 05/07/2001
Each share Common no par exchanged for (0.07692307) share Common no par
Kinloch Resources Inc. recapitalized as Stylus Energy Inc. 03/01/2005
(See Stylus Energy Inc.)

CHINA CONTAINER HLDGS LTD (NV)
Reincorporated under the laws of Delaware as Asiana Dragons, Inc. 12/22/2009
Asiana Dragons, Inc. recapitalized as Annabidiol Corp. 01/08/2018

CHINA CONTL INC (NV)
Reincorporated 01/11/2002
State of incorporation changed from (UT) to (NV) 01/11/2002
SEC revoked common stock registration 11/03/2006

CHINA CONVERGENT CORP LTD (AUSTRALIA)
Name changed 12/21/2000
Name changed from China Broadband Corp. Ltd. to China Convergent Corp. Ltd. 12/21/2000
Each old Sponsored ADR for Class A exchanged for (0.2) new Sponsored ADR for Class A 05/22/2001
Basis changed from (1:20) to (1:100) 05/22/2001
ADR agreement terminated 05/04/2009
No ADR holders' equity

CHINA CORD BLOOD CORP. (CAYMAN ISLANDS)
Name changed to Global Cord Blood Corp. 03/22/2018

CHINA COSCO HLDGS CO LTD (CHINA)
Name changed to COSCO SHIPPING Holdings Co., Ltd. 11/21/2016

CHINA CR HLDGS LTD (HONG KONG)
Name changed to Xpress Group Ltd. 06/13/2007
Xpress Group Ltd. name changed to Heng Fai Enterprises Ltd. 10/22/2013
(See Heng Fai Enterprises Ltd.)

CHINA DATACOM CORP (NV)
Name changed to Digital Paint International Holding Co. Ltd. 02/15/2008
Digital Paint International Holding Co. Ltd. recapitalized as Direct Coating, Inc. 07/06/2009
(See Direct Coating, Inc.)

CHINA DIAMOND CORP (YT)
Delisted from Toronto Venture Stock Exchange 05/23/2007

CHINA DIGITAL ANIMATION DEV INC (NY)
SEC revoked common stock registration 08/04/2014

CHINA DIGITAL COMMUNICATION GROUP (NV)
Each share old Common $0.001 par exchanged for (0.1) share new Common $0.001 par 07/13/2009
Name changed to New Energy Systems Group 11/18/2009

CHINA DIGITAL MEDIA CORP (NV)
SEC revoked common stock registration 02/10/2011

CHINA DIGITAL VENTURES CORP (NV)
Reorganized as Paradigm Resource Management Corp. 06/25/2012
Each share Common $0.001 par exchanged for (100) shares Common $0.001 par
Paradigm Resource Management Corp. recapitalized as Alternative Investment Corp. 02/25/2016

CHINA DIGITAL WIRELESS INC (NV)
Name changed to China Recycling Energy Corp. 03/08/2007

CHINA DING CHENG SCIENCE HLDGS CO LTD (NV)
Name changed to China Transportation International Holdings Group Ltd. 04/23/2010
(See China Transportation International Holdings Group Ltd.)

CHINA DIRECT INDS INC (FL)
Reincorporated 06/21/2007
Name changed 05/29/2009
State of incorporation changed from (DE) to (FL) 06/21/2007

Each share old Common $0.0001 par exchanged for (1) share new Common $0.0001 par to reflect a (1) for (100) reverse split followed by a (100) for (1) forward split 09/22/2008
Note: Holders of (99) or fewer pre-split shares received $5.07 cash per share
Name changed from China Direct, Inc. to China Direct Industries, Inc. 05/29/2009
Name changed to CD International Enterprises, Inc. 02/29/2012

CHINA DIRECT TRADING CORP (FL)
Name changed to CHDT Corp. 07/16/2007
CHDT Corp. name changed to Capstone Companies, Inc. 07/06/2012

CHINA DISCOVERY ACQUISITION CORP (CAYMAN ISLANDS)
Name changed to Si Mei Te Food Ltd. 08/30/2010
(See Si Mei Te Food Ltd.)

CHINA DRILL CORP (BC)
Name changed to Yalian Steel Corp. 12/08/2008
(See Yalian Steel Corp.)

CHINA ED TECHNOLOGY INC (NV)
Recapitalized as Valentine Beauty, Inc. 12/11/2013
Each share Common $0.0001 par exchanged for (0.004) share Common $0.0001 par

CHINA 88 CAP CORP (AB)
Recapitalized as GeoVenCap Inc. 11/24/2011
Each share Common no par exchanged for (0.2) share Common no par
(See GeoVenCap Inc.)

CHINA ELEC MTR INC (DE)
SEC revoked common stock registration 08/13/2014

CHINA ENERGY & CARBON BLACK HLDGS INC (NV)
Recapitalized as CO2 Tech Ltd. 01/09/2007
Each share Common 2¢ par exchanged for (0.0005) share Common 2¢ par

CHINA ENERGY CORP (NV)
Each share old Common $0.001 par exchanged for (0.00000008) share new Common $0.001 par 09/18/2013
Note: In effect holders received $0.14 cash per share and public interest was eliminated

CHINA ENERGY SVGS TECHNOLOGY INC (NV)
SEC revoked common stock registration 12/06/2006

CHINA ENERGY VENTURES CORP (NV)
Name changed to Big Sky Energy Corp. 12/15/2004
Each share Common $0.001 par exchanged for (1) share Common $0.001 par
(See Big Sky Energy Corp.)

CHINA ENTMT GROUP INC (NV)
Name changed to Safe & Secure TV Channel, Inc. 08/12/2010
Safe & Secure TV Channel, Inc. name changed to Cosmos Group Holdings Inc. 03/31/2016

CHINA EVERGREEN ENVIRONMENTAL CORP (NV)
Name changed to China Water Group, Inc. 11/14/2006

CHINA EXECUTIVE ED CORP (NV)
Acquired by Beyond Extreme Training Corp. 07/08/2013
Each share Common $0.001 par exchanged for $0.324 cash

CHINA EXPERT TECHNOLOGY INC (NV)
SEC revoked common stock registration 03/24/2011

CHINA FIRE & SEC GROUP INC (FL)
Acquired by Amber Parent Ltd. 11/04/2011
Each share Common $0.001 par exchanged for $9 cash

CHINA FIRST CAP CORP (BC)
Merged into Black Hawk Mining Inc.-Compagnie Miniere Black Hawk Inc. 07/16/1990
Each share Common no par exchanged for (0.4) share Common no par
Black Hawk Mining Inc.-Compagnie Miniere Black Hawk Inc. merged into Glencairn Gold Corp. 10/20/2003 which recapitalized as Central Sun Mining Inc. 12/05/2007 which was acquired by B2Gold Corp. 03/31/2009

CHINA FISHERY GROUP LTD (CAYMAN ISLANDS)
ADR agreement terminated 10/15/2018
Each ADR for Ordinary exchanged for (10) shares Ordinary
Note: Unexchanged ADR's will be sold and the proceeds, if any, held for claim after 01/16/2019

CHINA FOOD SVCS CORP (FL)
Reorganized under the laws of Nevada as California Grapes International, Inc. 11/09/2012
Each share Common $0.001 par exchanged for (0.1) share Common $0.001 par

CHINA FORESTRY INC (NV)
Each share old Common $0.001 par exchanged for (0.1) share new Common $0.001 par 06/15/2012
Name changed to China Senior Living Industry International Holding Corp. 09/28/2015

CHINA FORESTRY IND GROUP INC (NV)
Name changed to Silvan Industries, Inc. 12/20/2011
(See Silvan Industries, Inc.)

CHINA FORTUNE ACQUISITION CORP (CAYMAN ISLANDS)
Completely liquidated 08/27/2009
Each Unit exchanged for first and final distribution of $7.976735 cash
Each share Ordinary $0.0001 par exchanged for first and final distribution of $7.976735 cash

CHINA FST ENERGY CORP (NV)
Reorganized as Narnia Corp. 01/25/2012
Each share Common $0.00001 par exchanged for (9) shares Common $0.00001 par
Narnia Corp. name changed to Neologic Animation Inc. 05/11/2012
(See Neologic Animation Inc.)

CHINA FUNDAMENTAL ACQUISITION CORP (CAYMAN ISLANDS)
Name changed to Wowjoint Holdings Ltd. 04/09/2010

CHINA GAS HLDGS LTD (HONG KONG)
ADR agreement terminated 11/30/2007
Each Sponsored ADR for Ordinary exchanged for $50.118322 cash

CHINA GATEWAY HLDGS INC (DE)
Name changed to Chemical Consortium Holdings Inc. 10/12/2001
Chemical Consortium Holdings Inc. name changed to New NRG, Inc. 05/21/2007
(See New NRG, Inc.)

CHINA GLOBAL DEV INC (NV)
Recapitalized as Arizona Ventures, Inc. 11/18/2002
Each share Common $0.001 par exchanged for (0.1) share Common $0.001 par
Arizona Ventures, Inc. name changed to Fox River Holdings, Inc. 10/13/2003 which name changed to Zynex Medical Holdings, Inc. 12/23/2003 which name changed to Zynex, Inc. 07/08/2008

CHINA GLOBAL DISTR CORP (NV)
Name changed to Rodedawg International Industries, Inc. 07/26/2005

CHINA GLOBAL MEDIA INC (NV)
SEC revoked common stock registration 08/26/2016

CHINA GOGREEN ASSETS INVT LTD (BERMUDA)
ADR agreement terminated 03/29/2013
No ADR's remain outstanding

CHINA GOLD CORP (NV)
Common no par split (5) for (1) by issuance of (4) additional shares payable 05/15/2006 to holders of record 05/12/2006 Ex date - 05/16/2006
Charter revoked for failure to file reports and pay fees 01/01/2008

CHINA GOLD RESOURCE INC (NV)
Name changed to WiseMobi, Inc. 05/13/2008
WiseMobi, Inc. recapitalized as New Infinity Holdings, Ltd. 02/23/2015

CHINA GOOD ELEC INC (NV)
Old Common $0.001 par split (10) for (1) by issuance of (9) additional shares payable 08/01/2008 to holders of record 08/01/2008
Each share new Common $0.001 par exchanged for (0.03333333) share new Common $0.001 par 05/18/2010
Name changed to Victory Marine Holdings Corp. 05/07/2018

CHINA GRANITE CORP (NV)
Name changed to Strategic Rare Earth Metals, Inc. 06/30/2006
Strategic Rare Earth Metals, Inc. name changed to Affinity Beverage Group, Inc. 04/13/2016

CHINA GREEN CREATIVE INC (NV)
Each share old Common $0.001 par exchanged for (0.01666666) share new Common $0.001 par 07/23/2012
Name changed to China Shianyun Group Corp., Ltd. 08/30/2013

CHINA GREEN ENERGY INDS INC (NV)
Recapitalized as Reelcause, Inc. 12/24/2014
Each share Common $0.0001 par exchanged for (0.02) share Common $0.001 par

CHINA GREEN LTG LTD (CO)
SEC revoked common stock registration 08/01/2014

CHINA GREEN STAR AGRIC CORP (ON)
Name changed to GreenStar Agricultural Corp. 07/05/2013

CHINA GRENTECH CORP LTD (CAYMAN ISLANDS)
Acquired by Talenthome Management Ltd. 04/17/2012
Each ADR for Ordinary exchanged for $3.10 cash

CHINA GROVE COTTON MLS (NC)
Each share Common $100 par exchanged for (5) shares Common $25 par to effect a (4) for (1) split and a 25% stock dividend 00/00/1951
Common $25 par changed to $12.50 par and (2) additional shares issued to effect a (2) for (1) split and a 50% stock dividend 04/26/1973
Stock Dividend - 25% 12/15/1976
Acquired by Dixie Yarns, Inc. 08/00/1986
Each share Common $12.50 par exchanged for $60 cash

CHINA GROWTH ENTERPRISES CORP (BC)
Reincorporated under the laws of Ontario as T S Telecom Ltd. 02/27/1996
T S Telecom Ltd. (ONT) reorganized in British Columbia as Quanta Resources Inc. 03/09/2009

CHINA GROWTH EQUITY INVESTMENT LTD (CAYMAN ISLANDS)
Units separated 02/26/2013
Name changed to Pingtan Marine Enterprise Ltd. 02/26/2013

CHINA HEALTH HLDG INC (NV)
Stock Dividend - 25% payable 03/17/2006 to holders of record 02/28/2006 Ex date - 03/20/2006
Name changed to China Holdings, Inc. 05/11/2007

CHINA HEALTH LABS & DIAGNOSTICS LTD. (CAYMAN ISLANDS)
Each share Common USD$0.00005 par exchanged for (0.00000002) share Common USD$2,350 par 01/13/2014
Note: In effect holders received CAD$0.62 cash per share and public interest was eliminated
Unexchanged certificates will be cancelled and become without value 01/13/2020

CHINA HEALTH MGMT CORP (NV)
Each share old Common $0.001 par exchanged for (0.1) share new Common $0.001 par 10/30/2006
Charter permanently revoked 03/31/2009

CHINA HEALTHCARE ACQUISITION CORP (DE)
Each Unit received distribution of $5.89 cash payable 03/10/2009 to holders of record 03/05/2009 Ex date - 03/11/2009
Each share Common $0.0001 par received distribution of $5.89 cash payable 03/10/2009 to holders of record 03/05/2009 Ex date - 03/11/2009
Company terminated common stock registration and is no longer public as of 08/13/2009

CHINA HELI RESOURCE RENEWABLE INC (BRITISH VIRGIN ISLANDS)
Recapitalized 11/07/2008
Recapitalized from China Pharmaceuticals International Corp. to China Heli Resource Renewable Inc. 11/07/2008
Each share Common no par exchanged for (0.01) share Common no par
SEC revoked common stock registration 08/26/2016

CHINA HLDGS ACQUISITION CORP (DE)
Reincorporated under the laws of British Virgin Islands as China Ceramics Co., Ltd. 01/22/2010

CHINA HUAREN ORGANIC PRODS INC (DE)
SEC revoked common stock registration 03/06/2017

CHINA HYDROELECTRIC CORP (CAYMAN ISLANDS)
Acquired by CPT Wyndham Holdings Ltd. 07/09/2014
Each Sponsored ADR for Ordinary exchanged for $3.46 cash

CHINA INDL GROUP INC (CO)
Administratively dissolved 12/01/1999

CHINA INFORMATION SEC TECHNOLOGY INC (NV)
Name changed to China Information Technology, Inc. (NV) 08/26/2010
China Information Technology, Inc. (NV) reorganized in British Virgin Islands 11/01/2012 which name changed to Taoping Inc. 06/04/2018

CHINA INFORMATION TECHNOLOGY INC (BRITISH VIRGIN ISLANDS)
Name changed to Taoping Inc. 06/04/2018

CHINA INFORMATION TECHNOLOGY INC (NV)
Each share old Common 1¢ par exchanged for (0.5) share new Common 1¢ par 03/02/2012
Reorganized under the laws of British Virgin Islands 11/01/2012
Each share new Common 1¢ par exchanged for (1) share Ordinary 1¢ par
China Information Technology, Inc. (British Virgin Islands) name changed to Taoping Inc. 06/04/2018

CHINA INSONLINE CORP (DE)
Recapitalized as China Bio-Energy Corp. 02/03/2011
Each share Common $0.001 par exchanged for (0.025) share Common $0.001 par
China Bio-Energy Corp. name changed to Wave Sync Corp. 10/05/2015

CHINA INS INTL HLDGS CO LTD (HONG KONG)
Name changed to China Taiping Insurance Holdings Co., Ltd. 08/31/2009

CHINA INTEGRATED ENERGY INC (DE)
SEC revoked common stock registration 12/23/2014

CHINA INTELLIGENT LTG & ELECTRONICS INC (DE)
Each share old Common $0.0001 par exchanged for (0.5) share new Common $0.0001 par 05/12/2010
SEC revoked common stock registration 09/16/2013

CHINA INTL ENTERPRISES INC (CANADA)
Reincoporated under the laws of Delaware as China Software Technology Group Co., Ltd. and Common no par changed to $0.001 par 11/16/2006
China Software Technology Group Co., Ltd. recapitalized as American Wenshen Steel Group, Inc. 10/12/2007
(See American Wenshen Steel Group, Inc.)

CHINA INTL TOURISM HLDGS LTD (NV)
Each share old Common $0.0001 par exchanged for (0.005) share new Common $0.0001 par 04/03/2009
Name changed to China Logistics, Inc. (NV) 08/10/2009
China Logistics, Inc. (NV) reorganized in British Virgin Islands as Hutech21 Co., Ltd. 03/21/2011

CHINA INTERNET GLOBAL ALLIANCE LTD (HONG KONG)
Name changed to China Strategic Holdings Ltd. (New) 12/15/2000
(See China Strategic Holdings Ltd. (New))

CHINA IVY SCH INC (NV)
Each share old Common $0.001 par exchanged for (0.05) share new Common $0.001 par 01/14/2009
Reincorporated under the laws of Wyoming as Resources Global Services Group 10/05/2018

CHINA JIANGSU GOLDEN HORSE STL BALL INC (NV)
Recapitalized as Santana Mining Inc. 12/24/2008
Each share Common $0.001 par exchanged for (0.002) share Common $0.001 par
(See Santana Mining Inc.)

CHINA JIANYE FUEL INC (DE)
SEC revoked common stock registration 10/24/2014

CHINA JINRONG CORP (BC)
Recapitalized as Rystar Development Ltd. (BC) 06/25/1996
Each share Common no par exchanged for (0.25) share Common no par
Rystar Development Ltd. (BC) reincorporated in Canada as Rystar Communications Ltd. 03/31/1998
(See Rystar Communications Ltd.)

CHINA JIUHAO HEALTH IND CORP LTD (CAYMAN ISLANDS)
ADR agreement terminated 02/12/2015
No ADR's remain outstanding

CHINA KANGHUI HLDGS (CAYMAN ISLANDS)
Acquired by Medtronic, Inc. 11/01/2012
Each Sponsored ADR for Ordinary exchanged for $30.75 cash

CHINA LITHIUM TECHNOLOGIES INC (NV)
SEC revoked common stock registration 09/20/2013

CHINA LODGING GROUP LTD (CAYMAN ISLANDS)
Sponsored ADR's for Ordinary split (4) for (1) by issuance of (3) additional ADR's payable 05/24/2018 to holders of record 05/21/2018 Ex date - 05/25/2018
Basis changed from (1:4) to (1:1) 05/25/2018
Name changed to Huazhu Group Ltd. 06/15/2018

CHINA LOGISTICS INC (NV)
Reorganized under the laws of British Virgin Islands as Hutech21 Co., Ltd. 03/21/2011
Each share Common $0.0001 par exchanged for (0.01) share Common $0.0001 par

CHINA LT & PWR LTD (HONG KONG)
Each Unsponsored ADR for Ordinary exchanged for (1) Sponsored ADR for Ordinary 11/17/1997
Stock Dividends - 25% 01/27/1984; 33.33333333% 01/18/1985; 20% 01/24/1986; 20% 12/31/1987; 20% 12/29/1988; 20% 01/05/1990; 20% 01/05/1994
Name changed to CLP Holdings Ltd. 01/06/1998

CHINA MARKETING MEDIA HLDGS INC (TX)
SEC revoked common stock registration 08/20/2015

CHINA MASS MEDIA CORP (CAYMAN ISLANDS)
Name changed 04/16/2009
Name changed from China Mass Media International Advertising Corp. to China Media Corp. 04/16/2009
Each old Sponsored ADR for Ordinary exchanged for (0.1) new Sponsored ADR for Ordinary 11/28/2011
Basis changed from (1:30) to (1:300) 11/28/2011
Stock Dividend - 10% payable 01/18/2011 to holders of record 06/16/2010 Ex date - 06/14/2010
Acquired by China Mass Media Holdings Ltd. 11/06/2012
Each new Sponsored ADR for Ordinary exchanged for $4.95 cash

CHINA MED & HEALTHCARE GROUP LTD (BERMUDA)
ADR agreement terminated 11/29/2017
Each Sponsored ADR for Common exchanged for (10) shares Common
Note: Unexchanged ADR's will be sold and the proceeds, if any, held for claim after 12/03/2018

CHINA MEDIA GROUP CORP (TX)
Name changed to Median Group Inc. 05/25/2016

CHINA MEDIA NETWORKS INTL INC (NV)
Name changed to Medical Solutions Management Inc. 08/04/2006
(See Medical Solutions Management Inc.)

CHINA MEDIAEXPRESS HLDGS INC (DE)
SEC revoked common stock registration 08/28/2012

CHINA MEDIA1 CORP (NV)
SEC revoked common stock registration 03/01/2011

CHINA MEDICINE CORP (DE)
Reincorporated under the laws of Nevada 06/10/2009

CHINA MERCHANTS HLDGS INTL CO LTD (HONG KONG)
Name changed to China Merchants Port Holdings Co. Ltd. 08/29/2016

CHINA METRO-RURAL HLDGS LTD (BRITISH VIRGIN ISLANDS)
Each share Ordinary $0.001 par received distribution of (7.7) shares Man Sang International Ltd. Ordinary payable 08/23/2010 to holders of record 08/09/2010 Ex date - 08/24/2010
Acquired by CMR Merger Sub Ltd. 08/18/2016
Each share Ordinary $0.001 par exchanged for $1.03 cash

CHINA MINERAL ACQUISITION CORP (DE)
Completely liquidated 12/22/2006
Each share Common $0.0001 par exchanged for first and final distribution of $5.452481 cash

CHINA MINERALS MNG CORP (BC)
Each share old Common no par exchanged for (0.04) share new Common no par 09/13/2017
Name changed to Wildsky Resources Inc. 08/22/2018

CHINA MINERALS TECHNOLOGIES INC (NV)
Name changed to China GengSheng Minerals, Inc. 07/30/2007

CHINA MING YANG WIND PWR GROUP LTD (CAYMAN ISLANDS)
Acquired by Zhongshan Ruisheng Antai Investment Co., Ltd. 06/23/2016
Each Sponsored ADR for Ordinary exchanged for $2.46 cash

CHINA MOBILE GAMES & ENTMT GROUP LTD (CAYMAN ISLANDS)
ADR agreement terminated 08/13/2015
Each Sponsored ADR for Class A Ordinary exchanged for $21.93 cash

CHINA MOBILE HONG KONG LTD (HONG KONG)
Sponsored ADR's for Ordinary split (4) for (1) by issuance of (3) additional ADR's payable 07/05/2000 to holders of record 07/03/2000
Name changed to China Mobile Ltd. 05/29/2006

CHINA MOBILE MEDIA TECHNOLOGY INC (NV)
SEC revoked common stock registration 10/04/2012

CHINA MOBILITY SOLUTIONS INC (FL)
Recapitalized as Global Peopleline Telecom Inc. 08/06/2008
Each share Common $0.001 par exchanged for (0.01) share Common $0.001 par
(See Global Peopleline Telecom Inc.)

CHINA MOTOR CORP. (DE)
No longer in existence having become inoperative and void for non-payment of taxes 04/01/1951

CHINA NATL MATLS CO LTD (CHINA)
ADR agreement terminated 05/29/2018
Each ADR for H Shares issued by Bank of New York exchanged for $18.862935 cash

CHINA NEPSTAR CHAIN DRUGSTORE LTD (CAYMAN ISLANDS)
ADR agreement terminated 09/02/2015
Each Sponsored ADR for Ordinary exchanged for $2.57 cash

CHINA NETCOM GROUP CORP (HONG KONG) LTD (HONG KONG)
Merged into China Unicom (Hong Kong) Ltd. 10/15/2008
Each Sponsored ADR for Ordinary exchanged for (3.016) Sponsored ADR's for Ordinary

CHINA NETTV HLDGS INC (NV)
Each share old Common $0.001 par exchanged for (2.5) shares new Common $0.001 par 12/18/2001
Name changed to Great China Mining, Inc. 01/20/2006
Great China Mining, Inc. merged into Continental Minerals Corp. (Incorporated 02/07/1962) 12/15/2006
(See Continental Minerals Corp. (Incorporated 02/07/1962))

CHINA NEW MEDIA CORP (DE)
Name changed to V Media Corp. 07/24/2012
(See V Media Corp.)

CHINA 9D CONSTR GROUP (NV)
SEC revoked common stock registration 03/24/2011

CHINA NORTH EAST PETE HLDGS LTD (NV)
SEC revoked common stock registration 04/05/2013

CHINA NORTHN MED DEVICE INC (NV)
Name changed to HCi VioCare 03/21/2014
HCi VioCare recapitalized as Rafina Innovations Inc. 07/09/2018

CHINA NORTHWEST BIOTECH CORP (NV)
Recapitalized as LGM Biopharma, Inc. 06/29/2007
Each share Common $0.001 par exchanged for (0.02) share Common $0.001 par
LGM Biopharma, Inc. name changed to Syncronys International, Inc. 12/11/2007 which name changed to Seeker Tec International, Inc. 04/24/2013

CHINA NOW INC (FL)
Administratively dissolved 09/23/2011

CHINA NUOKANG BIO-PHARMACEUTICAL INC (CAYMAN ISLANDS)
ADR agreement terminated 03/11/2013
Each Sponsored ADS for Ordinary exchanged for $5.75 cash

CHINA NUVO SOLAR ENERGY INC (NV)
Name changed to SurgLine International, Inc. 01/27/2012

CHINA OIL & METHANOL GROUP INC (NV)
Common $0.001 par split (10) for (1) by issuance of (9) additional shares payable 07/27/2007 to holders of record 07/19/2007 Ex date - 07/30/2007
Charter revoked for failure to file reports and pay taxes 04/30/2009

CHINA ONE CORP (CAYMAN ISLANDS)
Reincorporated 12/02/2008
Place of incorporation changed from (Canada) to (Cayman Islands) 12/02/2008
Each share old Common no par exchanged for (0.36358347) share new Common no par 12/18/2008
Name changed to IND DairyTech Ltd. 08/17/2009
(See IND DairyTech Ltd.)

CHINA ONLINE BERMUDA LTD (BERMUDA)
Each old Sponsored ADR for Ordinary exchanged for (0.04) new Sponsored ADR for Ordinary 08/29/2003
Name changed to COL Capital Ltd. 07/09/2004
COL Capital Ltd. name changed to China Medical & HealthCare Group Ltd. 03/11/2016
(See China Medical & HealthCare Group Ltd.)

CHINA OPPORTUNITIES FD INC (ON)
Called for redemption at $15.92 on 04/26/1999

CHINA OPPORTUNITY ACQUISITION CORP (DE)
Reincorporated under the laws of British Virgin Islands as Golden Green Enterprises Ltd. and Common $0.0001 par reclassified as Ordinary no par 03/17/2009
Golden Green Enterprises Ltd. name changed to China Gerui Advanced Materials Group Ltd. 12/14/2009

CHINA OPPORTUNITY INC (ON)
Name changed to Gondwana Gold Inc. 06/29/2011
Gondwana Gold Inc. name changed to Pan African Oil Ltd. 06/18/2013 which merged into Eco (Atlantic) Oil & Gas Ltd. 01/28/2015

CHINA ORGANIC AGRICULTURE INC (FL)
Administratively dissolved 09/28/2012

CHINA ORGANIC FERTILIZER INC (NV)
SEC revoked common stock registration 08/19/2015

CHINA OVERSEAS LD & INVT LTD (HONG KONG)
ADR agreement terminated 10/08/2002
Each Sponsored ADR for Common exchanged for $3.877506 cash (Additional Information in Active)

CHINA PAC INC (NV)
Each share old Common $0.001 par exchanged for (0.25) share new Common $0.001 par 07/09/1996
Each share new Common $0.001 par exchanged again for (0.2) share new Common $0.001 par 09/28/1998
Chapter 11 bankruptcy proceedings terminated 06/13/2001
Stockholders' equity unlikely

CHINA PACKAGING GROUP INC (NV)
Name changed to China Shengda Packaging Group, Inc. 12/09/2010
(See China Shengda Packaging Group, Inc.)

CHINA PET PHARMACY INC (FL)
Name changed to China M161 Network Co. 02/11/2008

CHINA PHARMA HLDGS INC (DE)
Reincorporated under the laws of Nevada 12/27/2012

CHINA PHARMACEUTICAL GROUP LTD (HONG KONG)
Name changed 06/04/2003
Name changed from China Pharmaceutical Enterprise & Investment Corp. Ltd. to China Pharmaceutical Group Ltd. 06/04/2003
Name changed to CSPC Pharmaceutical Group Ltd. 02/25/2013
(See CSPC Pharmaceutical Group Ltd.)

CHINA PHARMACEUTICALS CORP (DE)
Each share Common $0.0001 par received distribution of (1) share E-Trend Networks Inc. (NV) Restricted Common payable 04/30/2004 to holders of record 04/22/2004 Ex date - 04/20/2004
Reincorporated under the laws of British Virgin Islands as China Pharmaceuticals International Corp. and Common $0.0001 par changed to no par 08/26/2004
China Pharmaceuticals International Corp. recapitalized as China Heli Resource Renewable Inc. 11/07/2008
(See China Heli Resource Renewable Inc.)

CHINA PPTYS DEVS INC (CO)
SEC revoked common stock registration 07/08/2013

CHINA PREM FOOD CORP (DE)
Name changed 01/31/2000
Name changed from China Peregrine Food Corp. to China Premium Food Corp. 01/31/2000
Name changed to Bravo! Foods International Corp. 03/27/2001
Bravo! Foods International Corp. name changed to Bravo! Brands, Inc. 04/09/2007
(See Bravo! Brands, Inc.)

CHINA PREM LIFESTYLE ENTERPRISE INC (NV)
Each share Common $0.001 par exchanged for (0.2) share Common $0.005 par 12/10/2007
Acquired by Auto Italia Holdings Ltd. 09/24/2014
Each share Common $0.005 par exchanged for $0.085 cash

CHINA PROSPERITY INTL HLDGS LTD (AUSTRALIA)
Name changed to China Broadband Corp. Ltd. 06/29/2000
China Broadband Corp. Ltd. name changed to China Convergent Corp. Ltd. 12/21/2000
(See China Convergent Corp. Ltd.)

CHINA PRTG & PACKAGING INC (NV)
Common $0.001 par split (5) for (2) by issuance of (1.5) additional shares payable 06/17/2011 to holders of record 06/15/2011 Ex date - 06/20/2011
SEC revoked common stock registration 01/19/2016

CHINA PRTG INC (NV)
Each share old Common $0.001 par exchanged for (0.03333333) share new Common $0.001 par 05/17/2005
Name changed to CYIOS Corp. 11/07/2005

CHINA PUB SEC TECHNOLOGY INC (FL)
Reincorporated under the laws of Nevada as China Information Security Technology, Inc. 04/07/2008
China Information Security Technology, Inc. (NV) name changed to China Information Technology, Inc. 08/26/2010 which reorganized in British Virgin Islands 11/01/2012 which name changed to Taoping Inc. 06/04/2018

CHINA REAL ESTATE INFORMATION CORP (CAYMAN ISLANDS)
Merged into E-House (China) Holdings Ltd. 04/23/2012
Each ADR for Ordinary exchanged for (0.6) ADR for Ordinary and $1.70 cash

CHINA RENEWABLE ENERGY HLDGS INC (FL)
Name changed to Green Global Investments, Inc. 02/13/2012
Green Global Investments, Inc. name changed to LivingVentures, Inc. 02/06/2013

CHINA RES DEV INC (NV)
Each share old Common $0.001 par exchanged for (0.1) share new Common $0.001 par 01/16/1997
Each share new Common $0.001 par exchanged again for (0.1) share new Common $0.001 par 06/11/1999
Reincorporated under the laws of British Virgin Islands as China Natural Resources, Inc. and new Common $0.001 par changed to no par 11/24/2004

CHINA RES ENTERPRISE LTD (HONG KONG)
Sponsored ADR's for Ordinary split (10) for (1) by issuance of (9) additional ADR's payable 12/30/1997 to holders of record 12/26/1997
Each Sponsored ADR for Ordinary received distribution of $0.0505 cash payable 08/28/2003 to holders of record 08/18/2013
Name changed to China Resources Beer (Holdings) Co. Ltd. 11/05/2015

CHINA RICH HLDGS LTD (HONG KONG)
Name changed to Yueshou Environmental Holdings Ltd. 02/20/2008
(See Yueshou Environmental Holdings Ltd.)

CHINA RONGSHENG HEAVY INDS GROUP HLDGS LTD (CAYMAN ISLANDS)
ADR agreement terminated 12/26/2017
No ADR's remain outstanding

CHINA RUITAI INTL HLDGS CO LTD (DE)
SEC revoked common stock registration 01/16/2014

CHINA SEAS RES CORP (BC)
Struck off register and declared dissolved for failure to file returns 04/16/1993

CHINA SEC & SURVEILLANCE TECHNOLOGY INC (BRITISH VIRGIN ISLANDS)
Reincorporated under the laws of Delaware and Common 1¢ par changed to $0.0001 par 11/24/2006
(See China Security & Surveillance Technology, Inc. (DE))

CHINA SEC & SURVEILLANCE TECHNOLOGY INC (DE)
Acquired by Rightmark Holdings Ltd. 09/16/2011
Each share Common $0.0001 par exchanged for $6.50 cash

CHINA SELECT CAP PARTNERS CORP (BC)
Name changed to Urban Select Capital Corp. 10/19/2011

CHINA SHANDONG INDS INC (DE)
Old Common $0.0001 par split (15) for (1) by issuance of (14) additional shares payable 01/04/2010 to holders of record 01/04/2010
Each share old Common $0.0001 par exchanged for (0.5) share new Common $0.0001 par 08/18/2010
Each share new Common $0.0001 par exchanged again for (0.66666666) share new Common $0.0001 par 01/18/2011
New Common $0.0001 par split (5) for (1) by issuance of (4) additional shares payable 04/12/2011 to holders of record 04/12/2011
Acquired by CAOPU Holdco, Inc. 09/03/2013
Each share new Common $0.0001 par exchanged for $0.60 cash

CHINA SHENGDA PACKAGING GROUP INC (NV)
Each share old Common $0.001 par exchanged for (0.2) share new Common $0.001 par 05/19/2015
Acquired by Yida International Holdings Ltd. 09/15/2015
Each share new Common $0.001 par exchanged for $7.25 cash

CHINA SHENGHUO PHARMACEUTICAL HLDGS INC (DE)
Each share old Common $0.0001 par exchanged for (0.00000263) share new Common $0.0001 par 05/17/2013
Note: In effect holders received $0.16 cash per share and public interest was eliminated

CHINA SHIPPING CONTAINER LINES CO LTD (CHINA)
Name changed to COSCO SHIPPING Development Co., Ltd. 01/10/2017

CHINA SHIPPING DEV LTD (CHINA)
Name changed to COSCO SHIPPING Energy Transportation Co., Ltd. 12/23/2016
(See COSCO SHIPPING Energy Transportation Co., Ltd.)

CHINA SHOUGUAN MNG CORP (NV)
Recapitalized as China Shouguan Investment Holding Group Corp. 03/14/2017
Each share Common $0.0001 par exchanged for (0.25) share Common $0.0001 par

CHINA SHUANGJI CEM CORP (DE)
Recapitalized as Citisource, Inc. (New) 10/02/2007
Each share Common 1¢ par exchanged for (0.01) share Common 1¢ par
Note: Holders of between (100) and (9,999) shares received (100) shares
Holders of (99) shares or fewer were not affected
Citisource, Inc. (New) name changed to Cannon Exploration, Inc. 04/08/2008

CHINA SHUANGJI CEM LTD (DE)
SEC revoked common stock registration 06/27/2013

CHINA SOARING INC (NV)
Name changed to Sino Payments, Inc. 12/17/2008
Sino Payments, Inc. name changed to Value Exchange International, Inc. 10/05/2014

CHINA SOFTWARE TECHNOLOGY GROUP CO LTD (DE)
Recapitalized as American Wenshen Steel Group, Inc. 10/12/2007
Each share Common $0.001 par exchanged for (0.02222222) share Common $0.001 par
(See American Wenshen Steel Group, Inc.)

CHINA SOLAR ENERGY HLDGS LTD (HONG KONG)
Each old Sponsored ADR for Ordinary exchanged for (0.1) new Sponsored ADR for Ordinary 05/16/2013
ADR agreement terminated 01/07/2016
Each new Sponsored ADR for

CHINA SOUTH LOCOMOTIVE & ROLLING STK CORP LTD (CHINA)
Ordinary exchanged for (20) shares Ordinary
Note: Unexchanged ADR's will be sold and the proceeds, if any, held for claim after 05/09/2016

CHINA SOUTH LOCOMOTIVE & ROLLING STK CORP LTD (CHINA)
Name changed to CSR Corp. Ltd. 10/12/2010
(See CSR Corp. Ltd.)

CHINA STATIONERY & OFFICE SUPPLY INC (DE)
Recapitalized as Global Arena Holding, Inc. 05/27/2011
Each share Common $0.001 par exchanged for (0.05) share Common $0.001 par

CHINA STRATEGIC HLDGS LTD NEW (HONG KONG)
Each Sponsored ADR for Ordinary exchanged for (0.1) old Sponsored ADR for Ordinary 10/05/2001
Each old Sponsored ADR for Ordinary exchanged for (0.5) new Sponsored ADR for Ordinary 06/07/2006
Each new Sponsored ADR for Ordinary received distribution of $1.60097 cash payable 08/24/2007 to holders of record 08/17/2007
ADR agreement terminated 11/30/2017
Each new Sponsored ADR for Ordinary exchanged for (10) shares Ordinary

CHINA STRATEGIC HLDGS LTD OLD (HONG KONG)
Name changed 07/12/1994
Name changed from China Strategic Investment Ltd. to China Strategic Holdings Ltd. (Old) 07/12/1994
Sponsored ADR's for Ordinary split (5) for (1) by issuance of (4) additional ADR's payable 11/14/1997 to holders of record 11/07/1997
Name changed to China Internet Global Alliance Ltd. 07/19/2000
China Internet Global Alliance Ltd. name changed to China Strategic Holdings Ltd. (New) 12/15/2000
(See China Strategic Holdings Ltd. (New))

CHINA SWINE GENETICS INC (DE)
Name changed to Sen Yu International Holdings, Inc. 08/25/2010
(See Sen Yu International Holdings, Inc.)

CHINA SXAN BIOTECH INC (NV)
Each share Common $0.001 par received distribution of (1) share Infrared Systems International Common $0.001 par payable 12/29/2008 to holders of record 12/22/2008 Ex date - 01/02/2009
Recapitalized as China Organic Fertilizer, Inc. 04/21/2010
Each share Common $0.001 par exchanged for (0.1) share Common $0.001 par
(See China Organic Fertilizer, Inc.)

CHINA TECHNICAL SVCS CORP (NY)
Dissolved by proclamation 06/24/1992

CHINA TECHNOLOGY DEVELOPMENT GROUP CORP (BRITISH VIRGIN ISLANDS)
Recapitalized as Renewable Energy Trade Board Corp. (British Virgin Islands) 10/25/2012
Each share Common 1¢ par exchanged for (0.1) share Common 10¢ par
Renewable Energy Trade Board Corp. (British Virgin Islands) reincorporated in Cayman Islands as New Energy Exchange Ltd. 08/12/2015

CHINA TECHNOLOGY GLOBAL CORP (BRITISH VIRGIN ISLANDS)
SEC revoked common stock registration 06/17/2010

CHINA TEL GROUP INC (NV)
Name changed to VelaTel Global Communications, Inc. 07/25/2011
(See VelaTel Global Communications, Inc.)

CHINA TELECOM HONG KONG LTD (HONG KONG)
Name changed to China Mobile (Hong Kong) Ltd. 07/05/2000
China Mobile (Hong Kong) Ltd. name changed to China Mobile Ltd. 05/29/2006

CHINA 3C GROUP (NV)
Recapitalized as Yosen Group, Inc. 12/31/2012
Each share Common $0.001 par exchanged for (0.2) share Common $0.001 par

CHINA TIRE E-COMMERCE COM LTD (BERMUDA)
Name changed 09/13/2000
Name changed from China Tire Holdings Ltd. to China Tire e-Commerce.com Ltd. 09/13/2000
Name changed to China Enterprises Ltd. 07/04/2001

CHINA TITANIUM & CHEM CORP (NV)
Name changed to Far Vista Interactive Corp. 09/19/2008
Far Vista Interactive Corp. name changed to Far Vista Petroleum Corp. 05/30/2013

CHINA TRACTOR HLDGS INC (DE)
SEC revoked common stock registration 12/18/2013

CHINA TRADE CORP (MD)
Name changed to International Capital & Technology Corp. 12/20/1982
(See International Capital & Technology Corp.)

CHINA TRANSINFO TECHNOLOGY CORP (NV)
Acquired by TransCloud Co., Ltd. 11/01/2012
Each share Common $0.001 par exchanged for $5.80 cash

CHINA TRANSN INTL HLDGS GROUP LTD (NV)
SEC revoked common stock registration 12/24/2014

CHINA TREASURE INC (NV)
Name changed to China Pacific, Inc. 01/25/1996
(See China Pacific, Inc.)

CHINA UNICOM LTD (CHINA)
Under plan of merger name changed to China Unicom (Hong Kong) Ltd. 10/15/2008

CHINA UNISTONE ACQUISITION CORP (DE)
Reincorporated under the laws of British Virgin Islands as Yucheng Technologies Ltd. 11/28/2006
(See Yucheng Technologies Ltd.)

CHINA UNITECH GROUP INC (NV)
Name changed to China Internet Cafe Holdings Group, Inc. 02/01/2011

CHINA VANTAGEPOINT ACQUISITION CO (CAYMAN ISLANDS)
Each Unit exchanged for (0.01) share Ordinary $0.001 par and $5.98378254 cash 02/25/2013
Note: Holders of (99) or fewer Units received cash portion only
SEC revoked common stock registration 08/26/2016

CHINA VENTURES INC (BC)
Recapitalized as China Education Resources, Inc. 12/16/2004
Each share Common no par exchanged for (0.2) share Common no par

CHINA VITUP HEALTH CARE HLDGS INC (NV)
Recapitalized as Emergency Pest Services, Inc. 05/28/2015
Each share Common $0.0001 par exchanged for (0.03333333) share Common $0.001 par

CHINA VOICE HLDG CORP (NV)
Reincorporated 07/22/2008
State of incorporation changed from (NY) to (NV) 07/22/2008
SEC revoked common stock registration 02/11/2013

CHINA VOIP & DIGITAL TELECOM INC (NV)
Name changed to China Intelligence Information Systems, Inc. 11/24/2010

CHINA WEST COAL ENERGY INC (NV)
Name changed to Sino Clean Energy, Inc. 08/20/2007

CHINA WEST INTL INC (NV)
Name changed to Intergold Corp. 08/27/1997
Intergold Corp. name changed to Lexington Resources, Inc. 11/20/2003
(See Lexington Resources, Inc.)

CHINA WI MAX COMMUNICATIONS INC (NV)
SEC revoked common stock registration 09/20/2013

CHINA WIND ENERGY INC (NV)
SEC revoked common stock registration 03/16/2012

CHINA WIND PWR INTL CORP (ON)
Completely liquidated 11/08/2017
Each share Common no par received first and final distribution of $0.1314 cash

CHINA WIND SYS INC (DE)
Each share old Common $0.001 par exchanged for (0.33333333) share new Common $0.001 par 10/13/2009
Name changed to Cleantech Solutions International, Inc. (DE) 06/16/2011
Cleantech Solutions International, Inc. (DE) reincorporated in Nevada 08/10/2012 which name changed to Sharing Economy International Inc. 01/08/2018

CHINA WIRELESS COMMUNICATIONS INC (NV)
Recapitalized as Media Exchange Group, Inc. 05/06/2011
Each share Common $0.001 par exchanged for (0.002) share Common $0.001 par
Media Exchange Group, Inc. name changed to Intellicell Biosciences, Inc. 07/07/2011
(See Intellicell Biosciences, Inc.)

CHINA WIRELESS TECHNOLOGIES LTD (CAYMAN ISLANDS)
Name changed to Coolpad Group Ltd. 01/10/2014

CHINA WORLD TRADE CORP (NV)
Each share old Common $0.001 par exchanged for (0.03333333) share new Common $0.001 par 09/03/2002
Name changed to Uonlive Corp. 09/05/2008

CHINA WTR & DRINKS INC (NV)
Merged into Heckmann Corp. 10/30/2008
Each share Common $0.001 par exchanged for (0.8) share Common $0.001 par
Heckmann Corp. name changed to Nuverra Environmental Solutions, Inc. 05/20/2013
(See Nuverra Environmental Solutions, Inc.)

CHINA XIBOLUN TECHNOLOGY HLDGS CORP (NV)
Name changed to Borneo Industrial Fishery Corp. Inc. 07/30/2015
Borneo Industrial Fishery Corp. Inc. name changed to Shenzhen Yidian Double Way of Innovation Culture Media Corp. 04/26/2017

CHINA XIN NETWORK MEDIA CORP (FL)
Name changed to Bio-Tracking Security Inc. 06/22/2004
Bio-Tracking Security Inc. recapitalized as Nord Oil International Inc. 10/25/2005 which name changed to North West Oil Group, Inc. 11/16/2006

CHINA XINIYA FASHION LTD (CAYMAN ISLANDS)
Each old Sponsored ADR for Ordinary exchanged for (0.25) new Sponsored ADR for Ordinary 12/17/2014
Basis changed from (1:4) to (1:16) 12/17/2014
Each new Sponsored ADR for Ordinary exchanged again for (0.33333333) new Sponsored ADR for Ordinary 12/28/2017
Basis changed from (1:16) to (1:48) 12/28/2017
Name changed to Dunxin Financial Holdings Ltd. 03/05/2018

CHINA YCT INTL GROUP INC (DE)
Name changed to Spring Pharmaceutical Group, Inc. 08/31/2018

CHINA YIDA HLDG CO (NV)
Reincorporated 11/19/2012
Each share old Common $0.001 par exchanged for (0.25) share new Common $0.001 par 06/16/2009
State of incorporation changed from (DE) to (NV) 11/19/2012
Each share new Common $0.001 par exchanged for (0.2) share new Common $0.001 par
Acquired by China Yida Holding Acquisition Co. 07/08/2016
Each share new Common $0.001 par exchanged for $3.32 cash

CHINA YILI PETE CO (NV)
Each share Common $0.001 par received distribution of (0.395) share ASAP Expo, Inc. Common $0.001 par payable 01/14/2009 to holders of record 12/31/2008 Ex date - 12/29/2008
SEC revoked common stock registration

CHINA YINGXIA INTL INC (FL)
SEC revoked common stock registration 03/07/2012

CHINA YOUTH MEDIA INC (DE)
Recapitalized as Midwest Energy Emissions Corp. 10/07/2011
Each share Common $0.001 par exchanged for (0.0090909) share Common $0.001 par

CHINA YOUTV CORP (NV)
Recapitalized as Microelectronics Technology Co. 10/06/2009
Each share Common $0.00001 par exchanged for (0.001) share Common $0.00001 par

CHINA ZIRCONIUM LTD (CAYMAN ISLANDS)
Ceased to be a reporting issuer 10/22/2009

CHINAB2BSOURCING COM INC (DE)
Name changed to International Smart Sourcing, Inc. (New) 08/15/2001
International Smart Sourcing, Inc. (New) name changed to Network 1 Financial Group, Inc. 08/12/2009

CHINACAST COMMUNICATION HLDGS LTD (BERMUDA)
ADR agreement terminated 01/11/2011

Each Sponsored ADR for Ordinary exchanged for $7.640994 cash

CHINACOM TECHNOLOGIES INC (BC)
Merged into VendTek Systems Inc. 04/26/2002
Each share Common no par exchanged for (0.5) share Common no par
(See VendTek Systems Inc.)

CHINADOTCOM CORP. (CAYMAN ISLANDS)
Name changed 05/08/2000
Class A $0.001 par split (2) for (1) by issuance of (1) additional share payable 12/13/1999 to holders of record 12/06/1999
Name changed from China.com Corp. to chinadotcom corp., Class A $0.001 par changed to $0.00025 par and (1) additional share issued 05/08/2000
Name changed to CDC Corp. 04/27/2005
(See CDC Corp.)

CHINAEDU CORP (CAYMAN ISLANDS)
Acquired by ChinaEdu Holdings Ltd. 04/23/2014
Each Sponsored ADR for Ordinary exchanged for $7 cash

CHINAGROWTH NORTH ACQUISITION CORP (CAYMAN ISLANDS)
Name changed to UIB Group Ltd. 01/27/2009

CHINAGROWTH SOUTH ACQUISITION CORP (CAYMAN ISLANDS)
Name changed to China TopReach Inc. 01/27/2009

CHINAMALLUSA COM INC (UT)
Charter expired 07/11/2001

CHINATEK INC (WA)
Each share old Common $0.001 par exchanged for (0.4) share new Common $0.001 par 05/16/1994
Charter cancelled and proclaimed dissolved for failure to pay fees 10/23/1995

CHINATRUST FINL HLDG CO LTD (TAIWAN)
Stock Dividends - 7.43283% payable 10/05/2005 to holders of record 08/24/2005; 10.9814% payable 12/02/2005 to holders of record 10/31/2005; 10.987% payable 10/06/2006 to holders of record 08/09/2006; 7.528% payable 10/28/2008 to holders of record 08/29/2008; 3.17741% payable 10/22/2009 to holders of record 09/04/2009; 6.4% payable 10/15/2010 to holders of record 08/31/2010; 6.43459% payable 11/04/2011 to holders of record 09/13/2011; 7.7261% payable 10/30/2012 to holders of record 09/18/2012
Name changed to CTBC Financial Holding Co., Ltd. 07/03/2013
(See CTBC Financial Holding Co., Ltd.)

CHINDEX INTL INC (DE)
Common 1¢ par split (2) for (1) by issuance of (1) additional share payable 09/02/2003 to holders of record 08/18/2003 Ex date - 09/03/2003
Common 1¢ par split (2) for (1) by issuance of (1) additional share payable 01/26/2004 to holders of record 01/10/2004 Ex date - 01/27/2004
Common 1¢ par split (3) for (2) by issuance of (0.5) additional share payable 04/16/2008 to holders of record 04/01/2008 Ex date - 04/17/2008
Acquired by Healthy Harmony Holdings, L.P. 09/29/2014
Each share Common 1¢ par exchanged for $24 cash

CHING CHING INC (DE)
Charter cancelled and declared inoperative and void for non-payment of taxes 03/01/1991

CHINO COML BK N A (CHINO, CA)
Common $5 par split (3) for (2) by issuance of (0.5) additional share payable 06/17/2004 to holders of record 05/20/2004 Ex date - 06/18/2004
Under plan of reorganization each share Common $5 par automatically became (1) share Chino Commercial Bancorp Common no par 06/30/2006

CHINOOK CAP CORP (BC)
Merged into Terrace Resources Inc. (New) 06/02/2009
Each share Common no par exchanged for (0.56481) share Common no par
Terrace Resources Inc. (New) name changed to Terrace Energy Corp. 06/24/2011

CHINOOK ENERGY INC OLD (AB)
Plan of arrangement effective 12/16/2016
Each share Common no par exchanged for (1) share Chinook Energy Inc. (New) Common no par and (0.70343) share Craft Oil Ltd. Common no par
Note: Unexchanged certificates will be cancelled and become without value 12/16/2019

CHINOOK ENERGY SVCS INC (AB)
Name changed to Deep Resources Ltd. 11/08/2002
Deep Resources Ltd. merged into Choice Resources Corp. 08/01/2006 which merged into Buffalo Resources Corp. 08/03/2007 which merged into Twin Butte Energy Ltd. 10/15/2009

CHINOOK TESTING INC (AB)
Recapitalized as Chinook Energy Services Inc. 10/22/2001
Each share Common no par exchanged for (0.2) share Common no par
Chinook Energy Services Inc. name changed to Deep Resources Ltd. 11/08/2002 which merged into Choice Resources Corp. 08/01/2006 which merged into Buffalo Resources Corp. 08/03/2007 which merged into Twin Butte Energy Ltd. 10/15/2009

CHIPCOM CORP (DE)
Common 2¢ par split (3) for (2) by issuance of (0.5) additional share 11/14/1994
Merged into 3Com Corp. (CA) 10/13/1995
Each share Common 2¢ par exchanged for (1.06) shares Common no par
3Com Corp. (CA) reincorporated in Delaware 06/11/1997
(See 3Com Corp.)

CHIPMAN ENERGY LTD (QC)
Recapitalized as Avatar Energy Inc. 05/15/1996
Each share Common no par exchanged for (0.22222222) share Common no par
Avatar Energy Inc. merged into Neutrino Resources Inc. 11/26/1996
(See Neutrino Resources Inc.)

CHIPMAN LAKE MINES LTD (ON)
Completely liquidated 02/25/1971
Each share Common $1 par exchanged for first and final distribution of (0.142857) share Chipman Mining & Energy Corp. Ltd. Common no par
Chipman Mining & Energy Corp. Ltd. name changed to Chipman Energy Ltd. 08/12/1994 which recapitalized as Avatar Energy Inc. 05/15/1996 which merged into Neutrino Resources Inc. 11/26/1996
(See Neutrino Resources Inc.)

CHIPMAN LAKE URANIUM MINES LTD. (ON)
Name changed to Chipman Lake Mines Ltd. 00/00/1951
Chipman Lake Mines Ltd. liquidated for Chipman Mining & Energy Corp. Ltd. 02/25/1971 which name changed to Chipman Energy Ltd. 08/12/1994 which recapitalized as Avatar Energy Inc. 05/15/1996 which merged into Neutrino Resources Inc. 11/26/1996
(See Neutrino Resources Inc.)

CHIPMAN MNG & ENERGY LTD (QC)
Name changed to Chipman Energy Ltd. 08/12/1994
Chipman Energy Ltd. recapitalized as Avatar Energy Inc. 05/15/1996 which merged into Neutrino Resources Inc. 11/26/1996
(See Neutrino Resources Inc.)

CHIPMOS TECHNOLOGIES (BERMUDA) LTD (BERMUDA)
Each share Common USD $0.01 par exchanged for (0.25) share Common USD $0.04 par 01/24/2011
Merged into ChipMOS TECHNOLOGIES INC. 11/01/2016
Each share Common USD $0.04 par exchanged for (0.9355) Sponsored ADR for Common and $3.71 cash

CHIPOLA OIL CORP (CO)
Reincorporated under the laws of Delaware as Terrapet Energy Corp. and Common no par changed to 1¢ par 11/01/1982
(See Terrapet Energy Corp.)

CHIPPAC INC (DE)
Merged into STATS ChipPAC Ltd. 08/04/2004
Each share Class A Common 1¢ par exchanged for (0.87) 144A Sponsored ADR for Ordinary S$0.25 par
(See STATS ChipPAC Ltd.)

CHIPPEWA-KIRKLAND MINES LTD.
Acquired by Mid-Kirk Gold Mines Ltd. 00/00/1936
Each share Capital Stock exchanged for (0.17) share Capital Stock
(See Mid-Kirk Gold Mines Ltd.)

CHIPPEWA PLASTICS, INC. (WI)
Merged into Rexall Drug Co. 03/31/1959
Each share 6% Preferred Ser. A $10 par exchanged for (0.75) share Capital Stock $2.50 par
Each share Common $1 par exchanged for (0.5) share Capital Stock $2.50 par
Rexall Drug Co. name changed to Rexall Drug & Chemical Co. 04/24/1959 which name changed to Dart Industries, Inc. 04/22/1969 which reorganized as Dart & Kraft, Inc. 09/25/1980 which name changed to Kraft, Inc. (New) 11/21/1986
(See Kraft, Inc. (New))

CHIPPEWA RES CORP (CO)
Recapitalized as Underwriters Financial Group, Inc. 11/12/1992
Each share Common $0.001 par exchanged for (0.1) share Common $0.001 par
(See Underwriters Financial Group, Inc.)

CHIPPEWA VY BK (RITTMAN, OH)
Merged into Wayne Bancorp, Inc. (OH) 03/31/1998
Each share Common no par exchanged for (2.1916) shares Common $1 par
(See Wayne Bancorp, Inc. (OH))

CHIPS & TECHNOLOGIES INC (DE)
Merged into Intel Corp. 01/30/1998
Each share Common 1¢ par exchanged for $17.50 cash

CHIPS WORLDWIDE NETWORK INC (DE)
Charter cancelled and declared inoperative and void for non-payment of taxes 03/01/1990

CHIPSOFT INC (DE)
Merged into Intuit Inc. 12/12/1993
Each share Class A Common 1¢ par exchanged for (0.446) share Common 1¢ par

CHIPWICH INC (NY)
Plan of reorganization under Chapter 11 Federal Bankruptcy Code effective 08/20/1994
No stockholders' equity

CHIQUITA BRANDS INTL INC (NJ)
Each $1.32 Depositary Preferred Ser. C exchanged for (1) share Common 33¢ par 09/07/1995
Plan of reorganization under Chapter 11 Federal Bankruptcy Code effective 03/19/2002
Each share $2.75 Ser. A Preferred $1 par received distribution of (0.075422) share Common 1¢ par and (1.25703) Common Stock Purchase Warrants expiring 03/19/2009
Each share $3.75 Conv. Preferred Ser. B $1 par received distribution of (0.09527) share Common 1¢ par and (1.587827) Common Stock Purchase Warrants expiring 03/19/2009
Each share $2.50 Conv. Preference Ser. C $1 par received distribution of (0.07488434) share Common 1¢ par and (1.24811633) Common Stock Purchase Warrants expiring 03/19/2009
Each share Common 33¢ par exchanged for (0.007132) share Common 1¢ par and (0.118868) Common Stock Purchase Warrant expiring 03/19/2009
Note: Preferred and Preference not required to be surrendered and are without value
Acquired by Cavendish Global Ltd. 01/06/2015
Each share Common 1¢ par exchanged for $14.50 cash

CHIRAL QUEST INC (MN)
Name changed to VioQuest Pharmaceuticals, Inc. (MN) 08/27/2004
VioQuest Pharmaceuticals, Inc. (MN) reincorporated in Delaware 10/06/2005

CHIREX INC (DE)
Merged into RHODIA 09/06/2000
Each share Common 1¢ par exchanged for $31.25 cash

CHIRON CORP (DE)
Reincorporated 02/06/1987
State of incorporation changed from (CA) to (DE) and Common no par changed to 1¢ par 02/06/1987
Common 1¢ par split (4) for (1) by issuance of (3) additional shares payable 08/02/1996 to holders of record 07/19/1996 Ex date - 08/05/1996
Merged into Novartis AG 04/20/2006
Each share Common 1¢ par exchanged for $48 cash

CHIROPRACTIC 21 INTL INC (NV)
Each share old Common $0.004 par exchanged for (0.1) share new Common $0.004 par 04/12/2000
Each share new Common $0.004 par exchanged for (0.33333333) share Common $0.001 par 12/08/2003
Name changed to visionGATEWAY, Inc. 03/10/2004

(See visionGATEWAY, Inc.)

CHIRRIPO RES INC (CANADA)
Acquired by Milagro Energy Inc. 03/07/2006
Each share Common no par exchanged for (0.5) share Common no par and $0.50 cash
Milagro Energy Inc. acquired by Second Wave Petroleum Inc. 08/29/2008
(See Second Wave Petroleum Inc.)

CHISEN ELEC CORP (NV)
Common $0.001 par split (10) for (1) by issuance of (9) additional shares payable 11/22/2011 to holders of record 11/22/2011
Recapitalized as Digital Day Agency, Inc. 09/26/2017
Each share Common $0.001 par exchanged for (0.0001) share Common $0.001 par

CHISHOLM RES INC (BC)
Charter cancelled 08/25/1989

CHISHOLM RES INC (NV)
Charter permanently revoked 04/30/2002

CHISTE CORP (NV)
Recapitalized as HydroGen Corp. 08/19/2005
Each share Common $0.001 par exchanged for (0.04) share Common $0.001 par
Note: Holders of between (100) and (2,499) shares will receive (100) shares
Holders of (99) or fewer shares were not affected by the reverse split
(See HydroGen Corp.)

CHISUM ENTERPRISES INC (UT)
Name changed to Collision Centers International, Inc. 04/11/1988
(See Collision Centers International, Inc.)

CHITALY HLDGS LTD (CAYMAN ISLANDS)
Name changed to Royale Furniture Holdings Ltd. 11/16/2007
(See Royale Furniture Holdings Ltd.)

CHITTENDEN CAP TR I (DE)
8% Guaranteed Capital Securities called for redemption at $25 on 07/01/2007

CHITTENDEN CORP (VT)
Common $10 par changed to $1 par and (1) additional share issued 07/01/1987
Common $1 par split (5) for (4) by issuance of (0.25) additional share 09/24/1993
Common $1 par split (5) for (4) by issuance of (0.25) additional share 05/26/1995
Common $1 par split (5) for (4) by issuance of (0.25) additional share 05/24/1996
Common $1 par split (5) for (4) by issuance of (0.25) additional share payable 12/12/1997 to holders of record 11/28/1997
Common $1 par split (5) for (4) by issuance of (0.25) additional share payable 09/14/2001 to holders of record 08/31/2001 Ex date - 09/17/2001
Common $1 par split (5) for (4) by issuance of (0.25) additional share payable 09/10/2004 to holders of record 08/27/2004 Ex date - 09/13/2004
Merged into People's United Financial, Inc. 01/01/2008
Each share Common $1 par exchanged for $35.636 cash

CHITTENDEN TR CO (BURLINGTON, VT)
Each share Common $100 par exchanged for (5) shares Common $20 par 00/00/1945
Common $20 par changed to $10 par and (1) additional share issued 06/05/1970
Stock Dividend - 50% 10/15/1973
99.7% acquired by Chittenden Corp. through exchange offer which expired 11/14/1974
Public interest eliminated

CHIVOR EMERALD CORP. (DE)
Charter cancelled and declared inoperative and void for non-payment of taxes 10/01/1960

CHIVOR EMERALD MINES INC (BRITISH VIRGIN ISLANDS)
Company ceased operations 00/00/1999
Details not available

CHK WIRELESS TECHNOLOGIES INC (BC)
Name changed to GridSense Systems Inc. 07/25/2003
GridSense Systems Inc. recapitalized as Viridis Energy Inc. 07/17/2009 which name changed to Viridis Holdings Corp. 08/14/2018

CHLORIDE CONNREX CORP (DE)
Merged into Chloride Inc. 12/27/1974
Each share Common $5 par exchanged for $10 cash

CHLORIDE GROUP PLC (UNITED KINGDOM)
Acquired by Emerson Electric Co. 09/03/2010
Each ADR for Ordinary exchanged for $29.644 cash

CHLORMET TECHNOLOGIES INC (BC)
Name changed to PUF Ventures Inc. 11/13/2015

CHLOROPHYLL CHEMICAL CORP. (DE)
No longer in existence having become inoperative and void for non-payment of taxes 04/01/1955

CHO HUNG BK (KOREA)
GDR agreement terminated 10/27/2004
Each new Sponsored GDR for Common exchanged for $1.8642 cash

CHOCK FULL O NUTS CORP (NY)
Common $1 par changed to 25¢ par and (3) additional shares issued 11/30/1960
Merged into Sara Lee Corp. 10/15/1999
Each share Common 25¢ par exchanged for (0.4707) share Common 1¢ par
Sara Lee Corp. recapitalized as Hillshire Brands Co. 06/29/2012
(See Hillshire Brands Co.)

CHOCOLATE CANDY CREATIONS INC (DE)
SEC revoked common stock registration 03/22/2013

CHOICE BK (OSHKOSH, WI)
Reorganized as Choice Bancorp, Inc. 03/18/2011
Each share Common $1 par exchanged for (1) share Common $1 par

CHOICE DRUG SYS INC (NY)
Name changed to Capstone Pharmacy Services Inc. (NY) 08/29/1995
Capstone Pharmacy Services Inc. (NY) reincorporated in Delaware 10/02/1995 which name changed to PharMerica, Inc. 12/08/1997 which name changed to Bergen Brunswig Corp. 04/26/1999 which merged into AmeriSourceBergen Corp. 08/29/2001

CHOICE FOODS CORP (AB)
Recapitalized as White Swan Resources Inc. 01/19/1995
Each share Common no par exchanged for (0.1) share Common no par
White Swan Resources Inc. recapitalized as Africa Diamond Holdings Ltd. (AB) 01/19/1999 which reincorporated in Bermuda as Sierra Leone Diamond Co. Ltd. 01/06/2004 which name changed to African Minerals Ltd. 08/15/2007

CHOICE GOLD CORP (BC)
Recapitalized as Copperbank Resources Corp. 10/22/2014
Each share Common no par exchanged for (0.2) share Common no par
Note: Unexchanged certificates were cancelled and became without value 10/22/2017

CHOICE HOTELS INTL INC OLD (DE)
Name changed 11/01/1996
Name changed from Choice Hotels Holdings, Inc. to Choice Hotels International, Inc. (Old) 11/01/1996
Each share Common 1¢ par received distribution of (1) share Choice Hotels International, Inc. (New) Common 1¢ par payable 10/15/1997 to holders of record 10/07/1997
Recapitalized as Sunburst Hospitality Corp. 10/15/1997
Each share Common 1¢ par exchanged for (0.33333333) share Common 1¢ par
(See Sunburst Hospitality Corp.)

CHOICE ONE COMMUNICATIONS INC (DE)
Plan of reorganization under Chapter 11 Federal Bankruptcy Code effective 11/18/2004
No stockholders' equity

CHOICE RES CORP (AB)
Reincorporated 09/29/2004
Place of incorporation changed from (BC) to (AB) 09/29/2004
Merged into Buffalo Resources Corp. 08/03/2007
Each share Common no par exchanged for (0.474) share Common no par
Buffalo Resources Corp. merged into Twin Butte Energy Ltd. 10/15/2009

CHOICE SOFTWARE SYS LTD (AB)
Recapitalized as Timbuktu Gold Corp. 12/29/1995
Each share Common no par exchanged for (0.21929824) share Common no par
Timbuktu Gold Corp. name changed to Marchmont Gold Corp. 06/11/1997 which recapitalized as Adulis Minerals Corp. 05/18/2000 which recapitalized as Adulis Resources Inc. 05/01/2001 which name changed to Solana Resources Ltd. 10/18/2005 which merged into Gran Tierra Energy Inc. (NV) 11/17/2008 which reincorporated in Delaware 10/31/2016

CHOICE SPORTS NETWORK INC (DE)
Name changed to Sports Entertainment & Learning Network Inc. 09/15/2000

CHOICECARE CORP (OH)
Merged into Humana Inc. 10/17/1997
Each share Common no par exchanged for $16.38 cash

CHOICELAND IRON MINES LTD (ON)
Recapitalized as Atlantic Goldfields Inc. 08/05/1987
Each share Common no par exchanged for (0.1) share Common no par
Atlantic Goldfields Inc. recapitalized as Dexus Inc. 06/22/1990 which was acquired by Trimin Enterprises Inc. (BC) 06/30/1993 which reorganized as Trimin Enterprises Inc. (Canada) 07/27/1998
(See Trimin Enterprises Inc.)

CHOICEPOINT INC (GA)
Common 10¢ par split (2) for (1) by issuance of (1) additional share payable 11/24/1999 to holders of record 11/10/1999 Ex date - 11/26/1999
Common 10¢ par split (3) for (2) by issuance of (0.5) additional share payable 03/07/2001 to holders of record 02/16/2001
Common 10¢ par split (4) for (3) by issuance of (0.33333333) additional share payable 06/06/2002 to holders of record 05/16/2002 Ex date - 06/07/2002
Merged into Reed Elsevier PLC 09/19/2008
Each share Common 10¢ par exchanged for $50 cash

CHOICEPOKER COM INC (TX)
Name changed to Viva World Trade, Inc. 09/11/2006

CHOICES ENTMT CORP (DE)
Name changed to CECS Corp. 08/09/2000
(See CECS Corp.)

CHOICETEL COMMUNICATIONS INC (MN)
Name changed to Sontra Medical Corp. 06/24/2002
Sontra Medical Corp. name changed to Echo Therapeutics, Inc. (MN) 10/08/2007 which reincorporated in Delaware 06/09/2008

CHOLESTECH CORP (CA)
Merged into Inverness Medical Innovations, Inc. 09/12/2007
Each share Common no par exchanged for (0.43642) share Common $0.001 par
Inverness Medical Innovations, Inc. name changed to Alere Inc. 07/14/2010
(See Alere Inc.)

CHOLLAR GOLD & SILVER MINING CO.
Merged into Consolidated Chollar Gould & Savage Mining Co. 00/00/1933
Details not available

CHOMERICS INC (DE)
Common 10¢ par split (3) for (2) by issuance of (0.5) additional share 06/20/1980
Merged into Grace (W.R.) & Co. (CT) 07/25/1985
Each share Common 10¢ par exchanged for (0.780487) share Common $1 par
Grace (W.R.) & Co. (CT) reincorporated in New York 05/19/1988
(See Grace (W.R.) & Co.)

CHONDROGENE LTD (ON)
Name changed to GeneNews Ltd. 10/26/2006

CHOOSE RAIN INC (NV)
Name changed to Rooshine Inc. 09/21/2017

CHOPP COMPUTER CORP (DE)
Each share old Common $0.0002 par exchanged for (0.05) share new Common $0.0002 par 06/20/1996
Name changed to ANTs software.com 02/18/1999
ANTs software.com name changed to ANTs software, inc. 04/05/2001
(See ANTs software inc.)

CHOPP COMPUTER INC (BC)
Common no par split (3) for (1) by issuance of (2) additional shares 08/28/1985
Common no par split (2) for (1) by issuance of (1) additional share 01/24/1986
Through exchange offer over 95% acquired by Sullivan Computer Corp. as of 11/14/1986
Public interest eliminated

CHOPPER MINES LTD (BC)
Recapitalized as Dragoon Resources Ltd. 11/09/1984
Each share Common no par exchanged for (0.2) share Common no par
Dragoon Resources Ltd. recapitalized as Seabridge Resources Inc. 05/20/1998 which name changed to Seabridge Gold Inc. (BC) 06/20/2002 which reincorporated in Canada 10/21/2002

CHORDIANT SOFTWARE INC (DE)
Each share old Common $0.001 par exchanged for (0.4) share new Common $0.001 par 02/20/2007
Merged into Pegasystems Inc. 04/22/2010
Each share new Common $0.001 par exchanged for $5 cash

CHORUS COMMUNICATIONS GROUP LTD (WI)
Common $3.33333333 par split (2) for (1) by issuance of (1) additional share payable 04/15/1998 to holders of record 04/01/1998
Merged into Telephone & Data Systems, Inc. 09/04/2001
Each share Common $3.33333333 par exchanged for $36.07 cash

CHOWAN RIV LMBR INC (NC)
Charter suspended for failure to file reports 03/01/1972

CHOY FOODS CORP (DE)
Name changed to International Fine Foods, Inc. 02/01/1983
International Fine Foods, Inc. name changed to Fresh Maid, Inc. 02/16/1989
(See Fresh Maid, Inc.)

CHRIS CRAFT INDS INC (DE)
$2 Conv. Preferred 1969 Ser. $1 par called for redemption 12/08/1977
$1 Prior Preferred no par called for redemption at $25 plus $0.25 accrued dividends on 09/14/2000
Capital Stock $1 par reclassified as Common $1 par 04/26/1966
Common $1 par changed to 50¢ par and (1) additional share issued 05/19/1969
Common 50¢ par split (3) for (1) by issuance of (2) additional shares 02/10/1983
Each share Common 50¢ par received distribution of (2) shares Conv. Class B Common 50¢ par 11/17/1986
Stock Dividends - in Common to holders of Common 3% payable 04/02/1996 to holders of record 03/20/1996; 3% payable 04/02/1997 to holders of record 03/20/1997; Ex date - 03/18/1997; 3% payable 04/02/1998 to holders of record 03/20/1998 Ex date - 03/18/1998; 3% payable 04/01/1999 to holders of record 03/18/1999; 3% payable 04/14/2000 to holders of record 03/31/2000; in Class B Common to holders of Class B Common 3% payable 04/02/1996 to holders of record 03/20/1996; 3% payable 04/02/1998 to holders of record 03/20/1998; in $1.40 Preferred to holders of $1.40 Preferred 3% payable 04/14/2000 to holders of record 03/31/2000
Merged into News Corp., Ltd. 07/31/2001
Each share $1.40 Conv. Preferred $1 par exchanged for (81.68) Sponsored ADR's for Ltd. Vtg. Preferred
Each share Class B Common 50¢ par exchanged for either (1.1591) Sponsored ADR's for Ltd. Vtg. Preferred and $34 cash (Mixed election) or (0.5680) ADR for Ltd. Vtg. Preferred and $50.03 cash (Cash election)
Each share Common 50¢ par exchanged for (1.1591) Sponsored ADR's for Ltd. Vtg. Preferred and $34 cash (Mixed election) or (0.5680) ADR for Ltd. Vtg. Preferred and $50.03 cash (Cash election)
Note: All stock or Non-electors received (2.2735) ADR's per share News Corp., Ltd. reorganized as News Corp. 11/03/2004

CHRIS DE KAR, INC. (DE)
Recapitalized as Silverton Industries 07/01/1987
Each share Common $0.001 par exchanged for (0.01) share Common 1¢ par
Silverton Industries, Inc. name changed to Consolidated Media Corp. 07/18/1988
(See Consolidated Media Corp.)

CHRISKEN PARTNERS CASH INCOME FD L P (DE)
Completely liquidated 12/28/2005
Details not available

CHRISLIN PHOTO INDUSTRIES CORP. (NY)
Merged into Camera Corp. of America 01/12/1965
Each share Class A 5¢ par exchanged for (4) shares Common 10¢ par
(See Camera Corp. of America)

CHRISTENSEN INC (UT)
Merged into Norton Co. 03/03/1977
Each share Common no par exchanged for (0.56) share Common $10 par
(See Norton Co.)

CHRISTIAN DIOR S A (FRANCE)
Each ADR for Ordinary received distribution of $3.67023 cash payable 02/24/2015 to holders of record 01/23/2015 Ex date - 01/21/2015
Each ADR for Ordinary received distribution of $1.274558 cash payable 02/25/2015 to holders of record 01/23/2015 Ex date - 01/21/2015
Name changed to Christian Dior S.E. 07/28/2017

CHRISTIAN EMPIRE GROUP (AZ)
Charter revoked for failure to file reports or pay fees 12/20/1971

CHRISTIAN FID LIFE INS CO (TX)
Common $3.65 par changed to $7.23 par 04/22/1975
Common $7.23 par changed to $10 par 04/24/1979
Merged into Oxford Life Insurance Co. 10/30/2000
Each share Common $10 par exchanged for $313.2216 cash

CHRISTIAN FNDTN LIFE INS CO (AR)
Merged into American Pyramid Companies Inc. 01/21/1969
Each share Common no par exchanged for (1.6) shares Common no par
American Pyramid Companies Inc. merged into American Consolidated Corp. 02/28/1977 which merged into I.C.H. Corp. 04/18/1985 which name changed to Southwestern Life Corp. (New) 06/15/1994 which name changed to I.C.H. Corp. (New) 10/10/1995
(See I.C.H. Corp. (New))

CHRISTIAN PETROLEUM CORP. (BC)
Merged into Nexus Resource Corp. 10/25/1982
Each share Common no par exchanged for (0.25) share Common no par
Nexus Resource Corp. recapitalized as Pacific Gold Corp. (BC) 07/05/1990 which reincorporated in Alberta 05/12/1994 which reincorporated in Ontario 06/27/1995 which name changed to Worldtek (Canada) Ltd. 07/04/1996
(See Worldtek (Canada) Ltd.)

CHRISTIAN PURCHASING NETWORK INC (FL)
Common $0.001 par split (5) for (2) by issuance of (1.5) additional shares 06/28/1991
Name changed to Jordan American Holdings, Inc. 06/01/1993
Jordan American Holdings, Inc. name changed to Gundaker/Jordan American Holdings, Inc. 09/15/2003
(See Gundaker/Jordan American Holdings, Inc.)

CHRISTIAN SALVESEN PLC (UNITED KINGDOM)
Each Sponsored ADR for Ordinary exchanged for (0.888) Sponsored ADR for Ordinary 04/30/1997
Acquired by Groupe Norbert Dentressangle 12/14/2007
Details not available

CHRISTIAN UNVL LIFE INS CO (IL)
Each share Common 5¢ par exchanged for (0.05) share Common $1 par 11/19/1968
Merged into Central-National Financial Corp. 12/31/1970
Each share Common $1 par exchanged for (1) share Common $1 par
(See Central-National Financial Corp.)

CHRISTIANA & COATESVILLE ST. RWY.
Merged into Conestoga Transportation Co. 00/00/1931
Details not available

CHRISTIANA BK & TR CO (GREENVILLE, DE)
Stock Dividends - 3% payable 07/02/2001 to holders of record 06/01/2001 Ex date - 06/14/2001; 3% payable 03/15/2004 to holders of record 03/01/2004 Ex date - 02/26/2004; 5% payable 11/30/2005 to holders of record 11/15/2005 Ex date - 11/10/2005; 5% payable 08/31/2006 to holders of record 08/16/2006 Ex date - 08/14/2006; 5% payable 11/30/2006 to holders of record 11/15/2006 Ex date - 11/13/2006
Merged into National Penn Bancshares, Inc. 01/07/2008
Each share Common $1 par exchanged for (2.241) shares Common no par
National Penn Bancshares, Inc. merged into BB&T Corp. 04/01/2016

CHRISTIANA COS INC (WI)
Reincorporated 10/31/1992
State of incorporation changed from (DE) to (WI) 10/31/1992
Merged into Weatherford International Inc. (New) (DE) 02/08/1999
Each share Common $1 par exchanged for (0.85443) share Common $1 par or $3.50 cash
Weatherford International Inc. (New) (DE) reincorporated in Bermuda as Weatherford International Ltd. 06/26/2002 which reincorporated in Switzerland 02/25/2009 which reincorporated in Ireland as Weatherford International PLC 06/18/2014

CHRISTIANA OIL CORP (DE)
Under plan of merger each share Common $3 par exchanged for (4) shares Common $1 par 03/26/1956
Name changed to Christiana Companies, Inc. (DE) 12/01/1970
Christiana Companies, Inc. (DE) reincorporated in Wisconsin 10/31/1992 which merged into Weatherford International Inc. (New) (DE) 02/08/1999 which reincorporated in Bermuda as Weatherford International Ltd. 06/26/2002 which reincorporated in Switzerland 02/25/2009 which reincorporated in Ireland as Weatherford International PLC 06/18/2014

CHRISTIANA SECS CO (DE)
Common $100 par changed to $1.25 par and (79) additional shares issued 03/14/1961
Merged into Du Pont (E.I.) de Nemours & Co. 10/17/1977
Each share 7% Preferred $100 par exchanged for (1.0881) shares Common $5 par and 33¢ cash
Each share Common $1.25 par exchanged for (1.1289) shares Common $5 par
Du Pont (E.I.) de Nemours & Co. merged into DowDuPont Inc. 09/01/2017

CHRISTIE BROWN & CO., LTD.
Acquired by National Biscuit Co. 00/00/1928
Details not available

CHRISTIE LAKE MINES LTD. (ON)
Charter cancelled and company declared dissolved for default in filing returns 05/27/1965

CHRISTIES INTL PLC (ENGLAND)
Each Unsponsored ADR for Ordinary exchanged for (4) Unsponsored ADR's for Ordinary 06/05/1989
Each Unsponsored ADR for Ordinary exchanged for (0.1) Sponsored ADR for Ordinary 12/09/1992
Merged into Swiss Bank Corp. 10/07/1998
Each Sponsored ADR for Ordinary exchanged for $67.2224 cash

CHRISTINA CAP CORP (NY)
Dissolved by proclamation 12/20/1977

CHRISTINA EXPLS LTD (BC)
Name changed to I.E.S. Technologies Corp. 08/03/1990
(See I.E.S. Technologies Corp.)

CHRISTINA GOLD RES LTD (BC)
Recapitalized as PowerHouse Energy Corp. 12/11/1998
Each share Common no par exchanged for (0.5) share Common no par
PowerHouse Energy Corp. recapitalized as International Powerhouse Energy Corp. 09/18/2001 which name changed to Sea Breeze Power Corp. 07/30/2003

CHRISTINES PRECIOUS PETALS INC (NV)
Name changed to Global Business Markets, Inc. 09/05/2003
Global Business Markets, Inc. name changed to GREM USA 03/03/2005

CHRISTMAS CLUB, A CORP. (NY)
Merged into Christmas Club A Corp. (DE) 01/02/1968
Each share Common $1 par exchanged for $241.94 cash

CHRISTMAS CLUB A CORP. (DE)
99% acquired by Osceola Operating Corp. through purchase offer as of 05/09/1967
Public interest eliminated

CHRISTMAS GUILD INC (NV)
Each share old Common $0.001 par exchanged for (0.00133333) share new Common $0.001 par 08/16/1995
Name changed to Cypress Financial Services, Inc. 12/04/1995
Cypress Financial Services, Inc. name changed to RevCare, Inc. 08/09/2000
(See RevCare, Inc.)

CHRISTO QUEBEC GOLD MINES, LTD. (ON)
Merged into Pardee Amalgamated Mines Ltd. 12/00/1954
Each share Common exchanged for (0.00133333) share Common $1 par

Pardee Amalgamated Mines Ltd. liquidated for Rio Algom Mines Ltd. 11/09/1961 which name changed to Rio Algom Ltd. 04/30/1975
(See Rio Algom Ltd.)

CHRISTOPHER & TENTH ST. R.R. CO.
Acquired by New York Railways Corp. 00/00/1935
Details not available

CHRISTOPHER ACQUISITIONS INC (CO)
Name changed to Hotwire Action Graphics International, Inc. 10/23/1989

CHRISTOPHER JAMES GOLD CORP (BC)
Recapitalized as Gunpoint Exploration Ltd. 11/16/2010
Each share Common no par exchanged for (0.1) share Common no par

CHRISTOPHER SILVER MINES LTD. (ON)
Merged into Agnico Mines Ltd. 00/00/1959
Each share Common no par exchanged for (0.2) share Capital Stock $1 par
Agnico Mines Ltd. merged into Agnico-Eagle Mines Ltd. 06/01/1972 which name changed to Agnico Eagle Mines Ltd. 04/30/2013

CHRISTOS TR (OR)
Involuntarily dissolved 05/24/1991

CHROMALINE CORP (MN)
Name changed 03/16/1982
Common 50¢ par changed to 10¢ par and (1) additional share issued 12/11/1978
Name changed from Chroma-Glo, Inc. to Chromaline Corp. 03/16/1982
Common 10¢ par split (2) for (1) by issuance of (1) additional share 05/13/1988
Name changed to Ikonics Corp. 12/16/2002

CHROMALLOY AMERN CORP (DE)
Reincorporated 10/31/1968
Common 10¢ par split (3) for (2) by issuance of (0.5) additional share 10/02/1967
State of incorporation changed from (NY) to (DE) 10/31/1968
$5 Conv. Preferred Ser. A $1 par reclassified as $5 Conv. Preferred $1 par 10/31/1968
Common 10¢ par changed to $1 par and (0.5) additional share issued 11/20/1968
Merged into Sun Chemical Corp. 12/23/1986
Each share $5 Conv. Preferred $1 par exchanged for (1) share $5 Conv. Preferred no par
Each share Common $1 par exchanged for (0.34) share Class A Common no par
Sun Chemical Corp. name changed to Sequa Corp. 05/08/1987
(See Sequa Corp.)

CHROMALLOY CORP. (NY)
Under plan of merger name changed to Chromalloy American Corp. (NY) 03/01/1966
Chromalloy American Corp. (NY) reincorporated in Delaware 10/31/1968 which merged into Sun Chemical Corp. 12/23/1986 which name changed to Sequa Corp. 05/08/1987
(See Sequa Corp.)

CHROMALUX CORP (FL)
Each share old Common $0.0001 par exchanged for (100) shares new Common $0.0001 par 07/08/1988
Note: Upon exchange each share new Common received distribution of (1) Common Stock Purchase Warrant expiring 03/31/1989

Administratively dissolved 08/13/1993

CHROMASCO CORP. LTD. (ON)
Merged into Chromasco Ltd. (ON) 07/15/1974
Each share Common no par exchanged for (8) shares Common no par
Chromasco Ltd. (ON) reincorporated in Canada 07/23/1980 which name changed to Timminco Ltd.-Timminco Ltee. 02/09/1984

CHROMASCO LTD NEW (CANADA)
Reincorporated 07/23/1980
Place of incorporation changed from (ON) to (Canada) 07/23/1980
Name changed to Timminco Ltd.-Timminco Ltee. 02/09/1984

CHROMATICS COLOR SCIENCES INTL INC (NY)
Each share old Common $0.001 par exchanged for (1.5) shares new Common $0.001 par 02/17/1998
SEC revoked common stock registration 12/05/2012

CHROMAVISION MED SYS INC (DE)
Name changed to Clarient, Inc. 03/15/2005
(See Clarient, Inc.)

CHROMCRAFT REVINGTON INC (DE)
Common 1¢ par split (2) for (1) by issuance of (1) additional share payable 06/10/1998 to holders of record 05/27/1998 Ex date - 06/11/1998
Merged into Sport-Haley Holdings, Inc. 11/08/2013
Each share Common 1¢ par exchanged for $0.44083 cash
Note: $0.12245 cash per share will be held in escrow for possible future distribution

CHROME CAP INC (AB)
Name changed to Blacksteel Energy Inc. 01/12/2010

CHROMEDX CORP (ON)
Name changed to Relay Medical Corp. 07/09/2018

CHROMEX NICKEL MINES LTD (CANADA)
Merged into Maiden Creek Mining Co., Inc. 09/01/1994
Each share Common 10¢ par exchanged for (1) share Common no par
(See Maiden Creek Mining Co., Inc.)

CHROMITE WESTERN INC. (BC)
100% acquired by Interstrat Resources Inc. through exchange offer which expired 00/00/1984
Public interest eliminated

CHROMIUM MNG & SMLT LTD (ON)
Capital Stock no par exchanged (1) for (10) 00/00/1941
Capital Stock no par reclassified as Common no par 12/20/1965
Merged into Chromasco Ltd. (ON) 07/15/1974
Each share Common no par exchanged for (1) share Common no par
Chromasco Ltd. (ON) reincorporated in Canada 07/23/1980 which name changed to Timminco Ltd.-Timminco Ltee. 02/09/1984

CHROMOS MOLECULAR SYS INC (BC)
Merged into Calyx Bio-Ventures Inc. 09/18/2008
Each share Common no par exchanged for (0.1) share Common no par and (0.1) share CHR Investment Corp. Class A Preferred
Calyx Bio-Ventures Inc. name changed to Calyx Ventures Inc. 02/05/2018

CHRON ORGANIZATION INC (NV)
Name changed to Zenergy Brands, Inc. 12/01/2017

CHRONAR CORP (NJ)
Common no par split (3) for (1) by issuance of (2) additional shares 09/12/1983
Stock Dividends - 10% 08/06/1987; 10% 10/03/1988
Liquidating Plan of Reorganization under Chapter 11 Federal Bankruptcy proceedings confirmed 11/30/1992
No stockholders' equity

CHRONETICS INC (NY)
Dissolved by proclamation 01/25/2012

CHRONICLE COMMUNICATIONS INC (GA)
Each share old Common no par exchanged for (0.05) share new Common no par 12/15/1997
Each share new Common no par exchanged again for (0.25) share new Common no par 07/01/1998
Reincorporated under the laws of Florida as Stampede Worldwide Inc. 04/20/2000

CHRONIMED INC (MN)
Common 1¢ par split (3) for (2) by issuance of (0.5) additional share 02/21/1994
Merged into BioScrip, Inc. 03/12/2005
Each share Common 1¢ par exchanged for (1.12) shares Common $0.0001 par

CHRONODYNAMICS LTD (DE)
Each share Common $0.0001 par exchanged for (0.01) share Common $0.001 par 07/24/1989
Charter cancelled and declared inoperative and void for non-payment of taxes 03/01/1991

CHRONOLOGICS INC (NY)
Completely liquidated 03/03/1971
Each share Common 5¢ par exchanged for first and final distribution of (0.33333333) share Meson Electronics Co., Inc. Common 5¢ par
Meson Electronics Co., Inc. name changed to Stellex Industries, Inc. 11/04/1974
(See Stellex Industries, Inc.)

CHRYSALIS CAP CORP (ON)
Name changed to PharmEng International Inc. 06/17/2005
(See PharmEng International Inc.)

CHRYSALIS CAP II CORP (ON)
Reorganized under the laws of Canada as Tangarine Payment Solutions Corp. 08/15/2006
Each share Common no par exchanged for (0.33333333) share Common no par
(See Tangarine Payment Solutions Corp.)

CHRYSALIS CAP III CORP (CANADA)
Name changed to U.S. Silver Corp. 03/05/2007
U.S. Silver Corp. merged into U.S. Silver & Gold Inc. 08/13/2012 which merged into Scorpio Mining Corp. 12/31/2014 which name changed to Americas Silver Corp. 05/27/2015

CHRYSALIS CAP IV CORP (CANADA)
Recapitalized as Homeland Energy Group Ltd. (Canada) 03/05/2008
Each share Common no par exchanged for (0.5) share Common no par
Homeland Energy Group Ltd. (Canada) reorganized in British Columbia as Sixonine Ventures Corp. 03/22/2017

CHRYSALIS CAP V CORP (CANADA)
Name changed to Enssolutions Group Inc. 11/18/2009

CHRYSALIS CAP VI CORP (CANADA)
Name changed to Exclamation Investments Corp. 07/20/2010

CHRYSALIS CAP VII CORP (CANADA)
Name changed to Alexander Nubia International Inc. (Canada) 10/05/2010
Alexander Nubia International Inc. (Canada) reincorporated in British Columbia as Aton Resources Inc. 06/27/2016

CHRYSALIS CAP VIII CORP (CANADA)
Recapitalized as Spectra7 Microsystems Inc. 02/19/2013
Each share Common no par exchanged for (0.25882328) share Common no par

CHRYSALIS CAP IX CORP (CANADA)
Recapitalized as Inspira Financial Inc. 07/14/2015
Each share Common no par exchanged for (0.56657223) share Common no par

CHRYSALIS HOTELS & RESORTS CORP (FL)
Name changed to Cyberecord, Inc. 04/20/1999
(See Cyberecord, Inc.)

CHRYSALIS HOTELS & RESORTS CORP (NV)
Charter permanently revoked 07/01/2004

CHRYSALIS INTL CORP (DE)
Merged into Phoenix International Life Sciences Inc. 04/30/1999
Each share Common 1¢ par exchanged for (0.08527) share Common no par
Phoenix International Life Sciences Inc. merged into MDS Inc. 05/15/2000 which name changed to Nordion Inc. 11/01/2010
(See Nordion Inc.)

CHRYSLER CORP (DE)
Common no par changed to $5 par 10/28/1932
Each share Common $5 par exchanged for (2) shares Common $2.50 par 07/11/1947
Common $2.50 par changed to $25 par 04/25/1949
Common $25 par changed to $12.50 par and (1) additional share issued 05/10/1963
Common $12.50 par changed to $6.25 par and (1) additional share issued 01/10/1964
Common $6.25 par changed to no par 06/04/1981
$2.75 Preferred no par called for redemption 10/31/1984
Common no par split (3) for (2) by issuance of (0.5) additional share 03/05/1986
Common no par changed to $1 par 06/01/1986
Common $1 par split (3) for (2) by issuance of (0.5) additional share 04/13/1987
$2.375 Conv. Preferred 1¢ par called for redemption 08/31/1989
Common $1 par split (2) for (1) by issuance of (1) additional share payable 07/15/1996 to holders of record 06/15/1996 Ex date - 07/16/1996
$4.625 144A Depositary Preferred called for redemption at $51.85 on 07/24/1998
Merged into DaimlerChrysler AG 11/12/1998
Each share Common $1 par exchanged for (0.6235) share Ordinary no par

CHRYSOS CAP CORP (CANADA)
Name changed to Frontline Gold Corp. 03/08/2010

CHS ELECTRONICS INC (FL)
Reorganized 03/14/1996
Reorganized from (UT) to under the laws of Florida 03/14/1996
Each share Common $0.001 par exchanged for (0.5) share Common $0.001 par
Common $0.001 par split (3) for (2) by issuance of (0.5) additional share payable 09/15/1997 to holders of record 09/02/1997
Plan of reorganization under Chapter 11 Federal Bankruptcy proceedings confirmed 07/26/2000
No stockholders' equity

CHUAN HUP CDA LTD (BC)
Recapitalized as IGT International Growth Technologies Inc. 09/25/1992
Each share Common no par exchanged for (0.25) share Common no par
IGT International Growth Technologies Inc. name changed to IGT Pharma, Inc. (BC) 02/27/1997 which reincorporated in Canada as Prescient Neuropharma Inc. 02/19/2001 which reincorporated in British Columbia 12/21/2007 which name changed to PNO Resources Ltd. 02/09/2012 which merged into Sandspring Resources Ltd. 09/15/2015

CHUAN-LO ENTERPRISES, INC. (MN)
Acquired by Margolis & Co., Inc. 03/02/1972
Each share Common 10¢ par exchanged for (0.5) share Common 1¢ par
(See Margolis & Co., Inc.)

CHUANGS HLDS LTD (HONG KONG)
ADR agreement terminated 04/09/1991
Details not available

CHUBASCO RESOURCES CORP (NV)
Name changed to Relationserve Media, Inc. (NV) 06/24/2005
Relationserve Media, Inc. (NV) reincorporated in Delaware 08/29/2005 which name changed to SendTec, Inc. 07/26/2006

CHUBB CORP (NJ)
Capital Stock $1 par reclassified as Common $1 par 04/14/1970
Common $1 par split (3) for (2) by issuance of (0.5) additional share 05/25/1970
Common $1 par split (3) for (2) by issuance of (0.5) additional share 06/01/1972
Common $1 par split (3) for (2) by issuance of (0.5) additional share 05/30/1984
Common $1 par split (3) for (2) by issuance of (0.5) additional share 10/24/1985
$4.25 Conv. Exchangeable Preferred $1 par called for redemption 04/28/1986
Common $1 par split (2) for (1) by issuance of (1) additional share 05/30/1990
Common $1 par split (2) for (1) by issuance of (1) additional share payable 05/03/1996 to holders of record 04/19/1996 Ex date - 05/06/1996
Each Corporate Unit received (0.3618) share Common $1 par 11/16/2005
Common $1 par split (2) for (1) by issuance of (1) additional share payable 04/18/2006 to holders of record 03/31/2006 Ex date - 04/19/2006
Each 7% Corporate Unit received (0.7002) share Common $1 par 08/16/2006
Merged into Chubb Ltd. 01/15/2016
Each share Common $1 par exchanged for (0.6019) share Common CHF 24.15 par and $62.93 cash

CHUBB INVT FDS INC (MD)
Name changed to Van Eck/Chubb Funds, Inc. and Growth Fund 1¢ par reclassified as Growth & Income Fund Class A 1¢ par 10/01/1997
Van Eck/Chubb Funds, Inc. name changed to Van Eck Funds, Inc. 01/01/2002

CHUCO GOLD MINES, LTD. (ON)
Charter cancelled by the Province of Ontario for default 05/11/1957

CHUCO PROSPECTING SYNDICATE
Succeeded by Chuco Gold Mines, Ltd. 00/00/1948
Details not available

CHUDLEIGH VENTURE INC (ON)
Name changed to Xylitol Canada Inc. 08/18/2010
Xylitol Canada Inc. name changed to Sweet Natural Trading Co. 12/12/2017

CHUKUNI RES INC (ON)
Recapitalized 10/02/1985
Recapitalized from Chukuni Gold Mines Ltd. to Chukuni Resources Inc. 10/02/1985
Each share Common no par exchanged for (0.1) share Common no par
Delisted from Canadian Dealer Network 01/03/1995

CHUM LTD (ON)
Conv. Class A $10 par called for redemption 11/10/1969
Each share old Common no par exchanged for (1) share Class B no par and (2) shares new Common no par 12/31/1969
Class B no par split (3) for (1) by issuance of (2) additional shares 09/22/1986
New Common no par split (3) for (1) by issuance of (2) additional shares 09/22/1986
Class B no par split (2) for (1) by issuance of (1) additional share payable 01/15/2004 to holders of record 01/09/2004 Ex date - 01/07/2004
New Common no par split (2) for (1) by issuance of (1) additional share payable 01/15/2004 to holders of record 01/09/2004 Ex date - 01/07/2004
Acquired by Bell Globemedia Acquisition Corp. 10/24/2006
Each share new Common no par exchanged for $47.25 cash
Each share Class B Common no par exchanged for $47.25 cash

CHUN CAN INTL GROUP (NV)
Name changed to Yutudao Marine Biotechnology Inc. 03/27/2018

CHUO MITSUI TR HLDGS INC (JAPAN)
Merged into Sumitomo Mitsui Trust Holdings Inc. 04/01/2011
Each ADR for Common exchanged for (2) Sponsored ADR's for Common

CHURCH-PLUMMER ENGINEERING CO. LTD.
Bankrupt 00/00/1943
Stockholders' equity unlikely

CHURCHILL APARTMENTS TRUST
Acquired by Churchill Building Corp. 08/12/1946
Each Certificate of Participation no par exchanged for (1) share Common no par
(See Churchill Building Corp.)

CHURCHILL BUILDING CORP. (IL)
Liquidation completed 10/07/1948
Details not available

CHURCHILL COPPER LTD (BC)
Recapitalized as Consolidated Churchill Copper Corp. Ltd. 07/20/1972
Each share Common no par exchanged for (0.1) share Common no par
(See Consolidated Churchill Copper Corp. Ltd.)

CHURCHILL CORP. (DE)
Liquidated 00/00/1955
Details not available

CHURCHILL CORP (AB)
Name changed to Stuart Olson Inc. 05/27/2014

CHURCHILL COS INC (WA)
Each share old Common no par exchanged for (0.03333333) share new Common no par 05/11/1992
Chapter 7 bankruptcy case closed 10/07/1999
No stockholders' equity

CHURCHILL ENERGY INC (AB)
Reincorporated 06/29/2006
Place of incorporation changed from (SK) to (AB) 06/29/2006
Merged into Zargon Energy Trust 09/23/2009
Each share Class A Common no par exchanged for (0.01363) Trust Unit no par
Zargon Energy Trust reorganized as Zargon Oil & Gas Ltd. (New) 01/07/2011

CHURCHILL ENERGY INC (BC)
Recapitalized as Consolidated Churchill Enterprises Inc. 03/06/1986
Each share Common no par exchanged for (0.54945054) share Common no par
Consolidated Churchill Enterprises Inc. recapitalized as Samia Ventures Inc. 10/05/1992
(See Samia Ventures Inc.)

CHURCHILL EXPLORATION CO. (NV)
Merged into Apex Minerals Corp. 04/14/1961
Each share Capital Stock exchanged for (1) share Capital Stock $1 par
Apex Minerals Corp. recapitalized as Limotran Corp. 08/01/1972

CHURCHILL FD INC (DE)
Name changed to Beacon Income Fund, Inc. 05/24/1978
(See Beacon Income Fund, Inc.)

CHURCHILL GROUP (CA)
Merged into Waterloo Management Co. 12/29/1978
Each share Common 10¢ par exchanged for $8.38 cash

CHURCHILL GROWTH AA INDL COMMUNICATIONS INC (ON)
Recapitalized as Telecommerce Corp. 06/23/1987
Each share Common no par exchanged for (0.1) share Common no par
Telecommerce Corp. recapitalized as E Ventures Inc. 02/25/1999
(See E Ventures Inc.)

CHURCHILL PETES INC (BC)
Name changed to Packard Resources Ltd. 01/31/1983
Packard Resources Ltd. recapitalized as Conpac Resources Ltd. (BC) 09/09/1986 which reincorporated in Canada as ConPak Seafoods Inc. 04/10/1987
(See ConPak Seafoods Inc.)

CHURCHILL RES LTD (BC)
Merged into Greystar Resources Ltd. (New) 08/15/1997
Each share Common no par exchanged for (1.3) shares Common no par
Greystar Resources Ltd. (New) name changed to Eco Oro Minerals Corp. 08/19/2011

CHURCHILL SBEC LTD (AB)
Merged into Churchill Corp. 11/30/1987
Each share Common no par exchanged for (3.3) shares Class A Common no par
Churchill Corp. name changed to Stuart Olson Inc. 05/27/2014

CHURCHILL STEREO CORP (DE)
Name changed to C.P. Liquidating Corp. 12/19/1972
(See C.P. Liquidating Corp.)

CHURCHILL TAX FREE FD KY (MA)
Name changed to Churchill Tax-Free Trust 06/00/1988

CHURCHILL TECHNOLOGY INC (CO)
Each share Common $0.001 par exchanged exchanged for (0.05) share Common 2¢ par 05/22/1992
Chapter 11 bankruptcy proceedings converted to Chapter 7 on 08/02/2000
Stockholders' equity unlikely

CHURCHILL VENTURES LTD (DE)
Liquidation completed
Each share Common $0.001 par exchanged for initial distribution of $8.08480434 cash 12/22/2008
Each share Common $0.001 par received second and final distribution of $0.15086285 cash payable 02/22/2010 to holders of record 12/22/2008

CHURCHMEN'S FINANCIAL CORP. (SC)
Voluntarily dissolved 12/11/1969
Details not available

CHURCHS FRIED CHICKEN INC (TX)
Common 25¢ par changed to $0.16666666 par and (0.5) additional share issued 04/20/1970
Common $0.16666666 par changed to 12¢ par and (0.5) additional share issued 04/14/1972
7% Conv. Preferred $100 par called for redemption 12/29/1974
Common 12¢ par changed to 8¢ par and (0.5) additional share issued 05/13/1977
Common 8¢ par changed to 4¢ par and (1) additional share issued 09/22/1978
Common 4¢ par split (3) for (2) by issuance of (0.5) additional share 05/13/1983
Common 4¢ par split (2) for (1) by issuance of (1) additional share 04/12/1985
Acquired by Copeland (AI) Enterprises, Inc. 09/21/1989
Each share Common 4¢ par exchanged for (0.44) share 17.5% Exchangeable Preferred $0.001 par
(See Copeland (AI) Enterprises, Inc.)

CHURNGOLD CORP. (DE)
Dissolved 06/30/1957
Details not available

CHUSKA RES CORP (BC)
Merged into Harken Energy Corp. 02/15/1993
Each share Common no par exchanged for (1.2618) shares Common 1¢ par
Harken Energy Corp. recapitalized as HKN, Inc. 06/06/2007

CHUTE CANYON URANIUM CO. (UT)
Liquidation completed 08/31/1962
Details not available

CHUTINE RES LTD (ON)
Reincorporated 00/00/1988
Place of incorporation changed from (BC) to (ON) 00/00/1988
Recapitalized as International CHS Resource Corp. 03/15/1995
Each share Common no par exchanged for (0.1) share Common no par
International CHS Resource Corp. recapitalized as CHS Resources Inc. 12/10/2010

CHYF MEDIA GROUP HLDG CO (NV)
Name changed to HYQC Investment Holding Co. 09/24/2015

CHYKA MINES LTD. (ON)
Declared dissolved 09/28/1964
No stockholders' equity

CHYRON CORP (NY)
Old Common 1¢ par split (4) for (3) by issuance of (0.33333333) additional share 10/23/1978
Old Common 1¢ par split (4) for (3) by issuance of (0.33333333) additional share 01/18/1980
Old Common 1¢ par split (3) for (2) by issuance of (0.5) additional share 02/16/1981
Old Common 1¢ par split (3) for (2) by issuance of (0.5) additional share 02/04/1983
Old Common 1¢ par split (3) for (2) by issuance of (0.5) additional share 11/30/1983
Old Common 1¢ par split (3) for (2) by issuance of (0.5) additional share 08/20/1984
Each share old Common 1¢ par exchanged for (0.33333333) share new Common 1¢ par 02/07/1997
Each share new Common 1¢ par exchanged again for (0.33333333) share new Common 1¢ par 09/20/2007
Stock Dividend - 10% 08/15/1985
Name changed to ChyronHego Corp. 05/23/2013
(See ChyronHego Corp.)

CHYRONHEGO CORP (NY)
Acquired by Vector CH Holdings (Cayman), L.P. 03/09/2015
Each share Common 1¢ par exchanged for $2.82 cash

CI FINL INC (ON)
Reorganized as CI Financial Income Fund 06/30/2006
Each share Common no par exchanged for (1) Trust Unit no par
Note: Option to receive (1) Special Unit and (1) Canadian International LP Class B Unit expired 06/20/2006
CI Financial Income Fund reorganized as CI Financial Corp. 01/01/2009

CI FINL INCOME FD (ON)
Plan of arrangement effective 01/01/2009
Each Unit no par exchanged for (1) share CI Financial Corp. Common no par

CI GLOBAL OPPORTUNITIES II FD (ON)
Completely liquidated
Each Unit no par received first and final distribution of $8.4756 cash payable 07/13/2007 to holders of record 06/29/2007

CI MASTER LTD PARTNERSHIP (ON)
Completely liquidated
Each Unit of Ltd. Partnership received first and final distribution of $0.015 cash payable 05/02/2014 to holders of record 04/30/2014

CI RES INTL LTD (BC)
Cease trade order effective 04/04/1985

CIAO CUCINA CORP (OH)
Filed a petition under Chapter 11 Federal Bankruptcy Code 12/00/1998
No stockholders' equity

CIATTIS INC (DE)
Reorganized under the laws of Minnesota 02/22/1993
Each share Common 1¢ par exchanged for (0.25) share Common 1¢ par
Ciatti's Inc. (MN) name changed to Premium Restaurant Co. 11/19/1997
(See Premium Restaurant Co.)

CIATTIS INC (MN)
Name changed to Premium Restaurant Co. 11/19/1997
(See Premium Restaurant Co.)

CIBA GEIGY A G (SWITZERLAND)
Sponsored ADR's for Ordinary split (2) for (1) by issuance of (1) additional ADR 07/03/1992
Merged into Novartis AG 12/23/1996
Each Sponsored ADR for Ordinary exchanged for (1.0666666) Sponsored ADR's for Ordinary

CIBA HOLDING AG (SWITZERLAND)
Name changed 10/08/2008
ADR agreement terminated 09/05/2000
Each 144A Sponsored ADR for Ordinary exchanged for $29.287461 cash
Note: Holders had until 03/06/2001 to surrender their 144A ADR's for new ADR's
Name changed from Ciba Specialty Chemicals Holding Inc. to Ciba Holding AG 10/08/2008
Acquired by BASF SE 06/23/2009
Each Sponsored ADR for Ordinary exchanged for $22.915277 cash

CIBER INC (DE)
Common 1¢ par split (2) for (1) by issuance of (1) additional share payable 06/14/1996 to holders of record 05/31/1996
Common 1¢ par split (2) for (1) by issuance of (1) additional share payable 03/31/1998 to holders of record 03/18/1998 Ex date - 04/01/1998
Name changed to CMTSU Liquidation, Inc. 12/22/2017

CIBOLA ENERGY CORP (NM)
Each share old Common 1¢ par exchanged for (0.01) share new Common 1¢ par 12/29/1992
Shares reacquired 03/29/1996
Each share new Common 1¢ par exchanged for $26.60 cash

CIBOLA LIFE INSURANCE CO. (NM)
Company placed in receivership 00/00/1980
Stockholders' equity unlikely

CIBONEY GROUP LTD (JAMAICA)
ADR agreement terminated 06/18/2011
Each Sponsored ADR for Ordinary exchanged for $0.001931 cash

CIC CANOLA INDS CDA INC (AB)
Reincorporated under the laws of Canada as Canadian Agra Foods Inc. 11/06/1996
(See Canadian Agra Foods Inc.)

CIC CAP LTD (BC)
Reincorporated 11/23/2013
Place of incorporation changed from (Canada) to (BC) 11/23/2013
Note: Company trades on AIM Market only

CIC CORP (DE)
Name changed to Firstmark Corp. 05/07/1973
(See Firstmark Corp.)

CIC COSMETICS INTL CORP (TX)
Name changed to American Cosmetics Laboratories, Inc. 12/13/1983
(See American Cosmetics Laboratories, Inc.)

CIC ENERGY CORP (BRITISH VIRGIN ISLANDS)
Acquired by Jindal Steel & Power Ltd. 09/10/2012
Each share Common no par exchanged for $2 cash

CIC FINL CORP (NV)
Stock Dividends - 50% 02/01/1971; 50% 02/10/1972; 25% 01/26/1973; 25% 12/28/1977; 25% 12/27/1978; 15% 12/27/1979; 25% 12/30/1980; 25% 12/28/1981
Merged into Continental Corp. (NY) 09/14/1982
Each share Common $1 par exchanged for $25 cash

CIC HLDG CO INC (DE)
Recapitalized as Global Wear Ltd. 01/10/2008
Each share Common $0.0001 par exchanged for (0.2) share Common $0.0001 par
Global Wear Ltd. recapitalized as Sovereign Wealth Corp. 03/12/2008 which name changed to Lenco Mobile Inc. 02/25/2009
(See Lenco Mobile Inc.)

CIC LEASING CORP (DE)
Name changed to CIC Corp. 05/01/1972
CIC Corp. name changed to Firstmark Corp. 05/07/1973
(See Firstmark Corp.)

CIC MNG RES LTD (CANADA)
Name changed to CIC Capital Ltd. (Canada) 05/31/2013
CIC Capital Ltd. (Canada) reincorporated in British Columbia 11/23/2013
(See CIC Capital Ltd.)

CICADA MINES LTD (BC)
Struck off register and declared dissolved for failure to file returns 04/14/1975

CICERO RES CORP NEW (BC)
Reincorporated 05/20/2009
Place of incorporation changed from (NV) to (BC) 05/20/2009
Name changed to Intelimax Media Inc. 07/01/2009
Intelimax Media Inc. recapitalized as DraftTeam Fantasy Sports Inc. 01/31/2014 which merged into DraftTeam Daily Fantasy Sports Corp. 03/13/2015 which name changed to Fantasy Aces Daily Fantasy Sports Corp. 10/06/2015

CICERO RES CORP OLD (NV)
Each share Common $0.00001 par exchanged for (0.01) share Cicero Resources Corp. (New) (NV) Common $0.00001 par 05/15/2009
Cicero Resources Corp. (New) (NV) reincorporated in British Columbia 05/20/2009 which name changed to Intelimax Media Inc. 07/01/2009 which recapitalized as DraftTeam Fantasy Sports Inc. 01/31/2014 which merged into DraftTeam Daily Fantasy which name changed to Fantasy Aces Daily Fantasy Sports Corp. 10/06/2015

CICERO ST BK (CICERO, IL)
Liquidation completed
Each share Common received initial distribution of $20 cash 12/10/1996
Each share Common received second and final distribution of $1.415 cash payable 06/18/1997 to holders of record 06/12/1997
Note: Certificates were not required to be exchanged and are without value

CICLO CAP CORP (ON)
Reincorporated 06/28/1999
Place of incorporation changed from (Canada) to (ON) 06/28/1999
Plan of arrangement effective 07/22/1999
Each share Common no par exchanged for (1) share Patent Enforcement & Royalties Ltd. Common no par
Patent Enforcement & Royalties Ltd. name changed to Blue Pearl Mining Ltd. 04/15/2005 which name changed to Thompson Creek Metals Co., Inc. (ON) 05/15/2007 which reincorporated in British Columbia 07/29/2008 which merged into Centerra Gold Inc. 10/21/2016

CIDCO GROUP INC (KS)
Each share old Common no par exchanged for (0.1) share new Common no par 06/07/1988
Charter forfeited for failure to file reports 02/15/1990

CIDCO INC (DE)
Merged into EarthLink, Inc. 02/06/2002
Each share Common 1¢ par exchanged for $0.36 cash

CIE-NERGY PLY-FOIL CDA INC (CANADA)
Dissolved for non-compliance 09/08/2013

CIELO GOLD CORP (BC)
Name changed to Cielo Waste Solutions Inc. 08/14/2013

CIENEGA BASIN OIL & GAS CO. (AZ)
Charter revoked for failure to file reports or pay fees 12/08/1958

CIENEGA CREEK HLDGS INC (NV)
Recapitalized as China Domestica Bio-technology Holdings, Inc. 07/08/2010
Each share Common $0.001 par exchanged for (0.02173913) share Common $0.001 par

CIERRA PAC VENTURES LTD (BC)
Recapitalized as Alange Energy Corp. 07/15/2009
Each share Common no par exchanged for (0.33333333) share Common no par
Alange Energy Corp. recapitalized as PetroMagdalena Energy Corp. 07/19/2011
(See PetroMagdalena Energy Corp.)

CIESTA GOLD EXPL CORP (BC)
Name changed to Rough River Petroleum Corp. 07/18/1985
(See Rough River Petroleum Corp.)

CIFC DEERFIELD CORP (DE)
Name changed to CIFC Corp. 07/19/2011
CIFC Corp. reorganized as CIFC LLC 01/04/2016
(See CIFC LLC)

CIFC LLC (DE)
Reorganized 01/04/2016
Under plan of reorganization each share CIFC Corp. Common $0.001 par automatically became (1) CIFC LLC Common Share 01/04/2016
Acquired by F.A.B. Holdings I L.P. 11/21/2016
Each Common Share exchanged for $11.36 cash

CI4NET COM INC (DE)
Charter cancelled and declared inoperative and void for non-payment of taxes 03/01/2002

CIFRA S A DE C V (MEXICO)
Unsponsored ADR's for Ser. B split (2) for (1) by issuance of (1) additional ADR 11/05/1990
Each Unsponsored ADR for Ser. B exchanged for (1) Sponsored ADR for Ser. V 12/24/1997
Stock Dividends - 200% 08/13/1987; 100% 08/23/1988; 52.311% 12/29/1989; 11.645505% payable 01/26/1998 to holders of record 01/20/1998
Name changed to Wal-Mart de Mexico, S.A. de C.V. 03/09/2000
Wal-Mart de Mexico, S.A. de C.V. name changed to Wal-Mart de Mexico, S.A.B. de C.V. 03/09/2007
(See Wal-Mart de Mexico, S.A. de C.V.)

CIG WIRELESS CORP (NV)
Acquired by Vertical Bridge Acquisitions, LLC 05/15/2015
No stockholders' equity

CIGAR KING CORP (NV)
Name changed to Starberrys Corp. 09/13/2002
Starberrys Corp. name changed to Visualant Inc. 08/18/2004 which

name changed to Know Labs, Inc. 05/25/2018

CIGAR OIL & GAS LTD (AB)
Merged into Pivotal Energy Ltd. 01/10/2003
Each share Common no par exchanged for (0.471429) share Common no par
Pivotal Energy Ltd. merged into Fairborne Energy Ltd. (Old) 07/08/2003
(See Fairborne Energy Ltd. (Old))

CIGARS MFOV INC (OK)
Name changed to Fernhill Beverage, Inc. 12/09/2015

CIGLARETTE INC (NV)
Name changed to Kirin International Holding, Inc. 03/23/2011
Kirin International Holding, Inc. name changed to Yangtze River Development Ltd. 01/22/2016 which name changed to Yangtze River Port & Logistics Ltd. 02/14/2018

CIGMA METALS CORP (FL)
Name changed 02/23/1999
Name changed from Cigma Ventures Corp. to Cigma Metals Corp. 02/23/1999
Each share old Common $0.0001 par exchanged for (2) shares new Common $0.0001 par 05/22/2006
SEC revoked common stock registration 08/20/2015

CIGNA AGGRESSIVE GROWTH FD INC (MD)
Reorganized under the laws of Massachusetts as CIGNA Funds Group Aggressive Growth Fund and Common 1¢ par changed to no par 04/30/1985
CIGNA Funds Group reincorporated in Delaware as AIM Funds Group 06/30/1992

CIGNA CASH FD INC (MD)
Under plan of reorganization each share Common $0.001 par automatically became (1) share CIGNA Funds Group (MA) Cash Fund no par 04/30/1985
CIGNA Funds Group (MA) reincorporated in Delaware as AIM Funds Group 06/30/1992

CIGNA CORP (DE)
$2.75 Conv. Preferred Ser. A $1 par called for redemption 07/13/1987
Recapitalized 07/10/1988
Each share $4.10 Conv. Exchangeable Preferred Ser. C $1 par exchanged for $50 principal amount of 8.20% Conv. Subordinated Debentures due 07/10/2010
(Additional Information in Active)

CIGNA FDS GROUP (MA)
Reincorporated under the laws of Delaware as AIM Funds Group 06/30/1992

CIGNA GROWTH FD INC (MD)
Reorganized under the laws of Massachusetts as CIGNA Funds Group Growth Fund and Common $1 par changed to no par 04/30/1985
CIGNA Funds Group (MA) reincorporated in Delaware as Aim Funds Group 06/30/1992

CIGNA HIGH INCOME SHS (MA)
Name changed to BlackRock High Income Shares 03/15/2005
BlackRock High Income Shares merged into BlackRock Corporate High Yield Fund VI, Inc. 11/18/2013

CIGNA HIGH YIELD FD INC (MD)
Under plan of reorganization each share Common 1¢ par automatically became (1) share CIGNA Funds Group (MA) High Yield Fund no par 04/30/1985
CIGNA Funds Group (MA) reincorporated in Delaware as AIM Funds Group 06/30/1992

CIGNA INCOME FD INC (MD)
Under plan of reorganization each share Common 1¢ par automatically became (1) share CIGNA Funds Group (MA) Income Fund no par 04/30/1985
CIGNA Funds Group (MA) reincorporated in Delaware as AIM Funds Group 06/30/1992

CIGNA INCOME REALTY-I LIMITED PARTNERSHIP (DE)
Completely liquidated 06/30/1997
Details not available

CIGNA MONEY MKT FD INC (MD)
Under plan of reorganization each share Common 1¢ par automatically became (1) CIGNA Funds Group (MA) Money Market Fund no par 04/30/1985
CIGNA Funds Group (MA) reincorporated in Delaware as AIM Funds Group 06/30/1992

CIGNA MUN BD FD INC (MD)
Under plan of reorganization each share Common 1¢ par automatically became (1) share CIGNA Funds Group (MA) Municipal Bond Fund no par 04/30/1985
CIGNA Funds Group (MA) reincorporated in Delaware as AIM Funds Group 06/30/1992

CIGNA TAX EXEMPT CASH FD INC (MD)
Under plan of reorganization each share Common 1¢ par automatically became (1) share CIGNA Funds Group (MA) Tax-Exempt Cash Fund no par 04/30/1985
CIGNA Funds Group (MA) reincorporated in Delaware as AIM Funds Group 06/30/1992

CIGNA VALUE FD INC (MD)
Under plan of reorganization each share Common 1¢ par automatically became (1) share CIGNA Funds Group (MA) Value Fund no par 04/30/1985
CIGNA Funds Group (MA) reincorporated in Delaware as AIM Funds Group 06/30/1992

CIGNAL OIL CO (UT)
Each share old Common $0.001 par exchanged for (0.2) share new Common $0.001 par 04/02/1996
Name changed to Roatan Medical Technologies, Inc. (UT) 04/15/1996
Roatan Medical Technologies, Inc. (UT) reincorporated in Nevada 07/00/1996 which name changed to Technology Acquisition Corp. 11/01/2001 which name changed to Minrad International, Inc. (NV) 12/21/2004 which reincorporated in Delaware 04/25/2005
(See Minrad International, Inc.)

CIGNUS VENTURES INC (NV)
Reorganized as Smartlinx Inc. 10/14/2009
Each share Common $0.001 par exchanged for (2.7) shares Common $0.001 par

CII FINL INC (CA)
Merged into Sierra Health Services, Inc. 10/31/1995
Each share Common no par exchanged for (0.37) share Common 1¢ par
(See Sierra Health Services, Inc.)

CII INVT CORP (OH)
Completely liquidated 06/26/1979
Each share Common no par exchanged for first and final distribution of $110.48 cash

CIIT INC (CANADA)
Common no par split (5) for (1) by issuance of (4) additional shares 07/07/1980
Acquired by CIIT Acquisition Inc. 01/17/1992
Each share 5% Preferred $100 par exchanged for $105 cash
Each share Common no par exchanged for $16.15 cash

CILCORP INC (IL)
Merged into AES Corp. 10/18/1999
Each share Common no par exchanged for $65 cash

CIM HIGH YIELD SECS (MA)
Liquidation completed
Each Share of Bene. Int. 1¢ par received initial distribution of approximately $4.26 cash payable 02/24/2006 to holders of record 02/03/2006
Each Share of Bene. Int. 1¢ par received second and final distribution of $0.014 cash payable 04/28/2006 to holders of record 02/03/2006

CIMA LABS INC (DE)
Merged into Cephalon, Inc. 08/12/2004
Each share Common 1¢ par exchanged for $34 cash

CIMA RES LTD (BC)
Recapitalized as Consolidated Cima Resources Ltd. (BC) 08/23/1984
Each share Common no par exchanged for (0.25) share Common no par
Consolidated Cima Resources Ltd. (BC) reincorporated in Canada as Hankin Atlas Industries Ltd. 08/15/1989 which name changed to Hankin Water Technologies Ltd. 03/26/1999
(See Hankin Water Technologies Ltd.)

CIMARRON CONS MNG & OIL INC (ID)
Charter forfeited for failure to file reports 12/01/1993

CIMARRON CORP (DE)
Stock Dividend - 400% 05/20/1980
Charter cancelled and declared inoperative and void for non-payment of taxes 03/01/1998

CIMARRON CORP (UT)
Name changed to Mariah International Inc. 06/17/1987
Mariah International Inc. merged into MG Gold Corp. 05/15/1997 which name changed to MG Natural Resources Corp. 10/12/1998 which name changed to Xenolix Technologies Inc. 06/14/2000 which name changed to Pershing Resources Co., Inc. 04/27/2004

CIMARRON GRANDVIEW GROUP INC (WA)
Name changed 07/25/1990
Name changed from Cimarron Gas & Oil Inc. of Washington to Cimarron-Grandview Group, Inc. 07/25/1990
Recapitalized as Full Moon Universe, Inc. 01/04/2001
Each share Common no par exchanged for (0.2) share Common no par
(See Full Moon Universe, Inc.)

CIMARRON INVT INC (KS)
Merged into AFC Acquisition Co. 08/20/1990
Each share Common 50¢ par exchanged for $11.37 cash

CIMARRON MED INC (UT)
Name changed 06/16/2015
Name changed from Cimarron Software, Inc. to Cimarron Medical, Inc. 06/16/2015
Name changed to Sun BioPharma, Inc. (UT) and Common no par changed to $0.001 par 09/09/2015
Sun BioPharma, Inc. (UT) reincorporated in Delaware 05/25/2016

CIMARRON MINERALS LTD (BC)
Reorganized under the laws of Canada as DiscFactories Corp. 05/01/2000
Each share Common no par exchanged for (0.5) share Common no par
DiscFactories Corp. name changed to Excalibur Resources Ltd. 02/20/2007 which recapitalized as Metalla Royalty & Streaming Ltd. (Canada) 12/07/2016 which reincorporated in British Columbia 11/16/2017

CIMARRON MINING CORP. (UT)
Recapitalized as Cimarron Corp. (UT) 11/15/1979
Each share Capital Stock $0.005 par exchanged for (0.1) share Capital Stock 5¢ par
Cimarron Corp. (UT) name changed to Mariah International Inc. 06/17/1987 which merged into MG Gold Corp. 05/15/1997 which name changed to MG Natural Resources Corp. 10/12/1998 which name changed to Xenolix Technologies Inc. 06/14/2000 which name changed to Pershing Resources Co., Inc. 04/27/2004

CIMARRON OILS, INC. (DE)
No longer in existence having become inoperative and void for non-payment of taxes 04/15/1968

CIMARRON PETE LTD (AB)
Merged into Newport Petroleum Corp. 04/09/1997
Each share Common no par exchanged for (2.7) shares Common no par
(See Newport Petroleum Corp.)

CIMATRON LTD (ISRAEL)
Merged into 3D Systems Corp. 02/09/2015
Each share Ordinary ILS 0.10 par exchanged for $8.97 cash

CIMBIX CORP (WA)
Each share old Common $0.0001 par exchanged for (0.005) share new Common $0.0001 par 10/08/2004
New Common $0.0001 par split (4) for (1) by issuance of (3) additional shares payable 07/08/2005 to holders of record 07/06/2005
Ex date - 07/11/2005
Name changed to Wataire International, Inc. 10/17/2006
Wataire International, Inc. name changed to Watair Inc. 10/08/2010 which recapitalized Cabo Verde Capital Inc. (WA) 05/22/2014 which reincorporated in Delaware 07/23/2014 which reincorporated in Nevada 11/05/2015

CIMCO INC (DE)
Name changed 08/21/1987
Name and state of incorporation changed from CIMCO (CA) to CIMCO, Inc. (DE) 08/21/1987
Common 1¢ par split (5) for (4) by issuance of (0.25) additional share 05/02/1989
Merged into Hanna (M.A.) Co. (New) 04/23/1996
Each share Common 1¢ par exchanged for $10.50 cash

CIMCO LTD (CANADA)
98.13% of Class A Non-Redm. Part. Preference and 99.94% of Common held by Toromont Industrial Holdings Ltd. as of 00/00/1976 and 00/00/1973 respectively
Public interest eliminated

CIMED INTL INC (UT)
Name changed to Questar International Inc. 03/05/1997
Questar International Inc. name changed to DNA Medical Technologies Inc. 08/27/1998

CIMEMTOS DE PORTUGAL S A (PORTUGAL)
ADR agreement terminated 04/06/2003
Each 144A Sponsored ADR for Ordinary exchanged for $8.0631076 cash

CIMENTS FRANCAIS (FRANCE)
ADR agreement terminated 12/28/2011
Each Sponsored ADR for Class A Common exchanged for $28.910395 cash
Each ADR for Common exchanged for $26.526849 cash 08/22/2014

CIMFLEX TEKNOWLEDGE CORP (DE)
Name changed to Teknowledge Corp. 06/30/1994
(See Teknowledge Corp.)

CIMNET INC (DE)
Merged into Invensys Systems, Inc. 07/02/2007
Each share Common no par exchanged for $2.43 cash

CIMOTA ENTERPRISES, INC. (ID)
Recapitalized as Priority Air Enterprises, Inc. 06/21/1971
Each share Common 10¢ par exchanged for (0.1) share Common 1¢ par
(See Priority Air Enterprises, Inc.)

CIMTEK INTEGRATED MFG TECHNOLOGIES INC (BC)
Recapitalized as Jakarta Development Corp. 01/17/1997
Each share Common no par exchanged for (0.2) share Common no par
Jakarta Development Corp. name changed to P.P.M. Development Corp. 07/10/1998 which recapitalized as Consolidated P.P.M. Development Corp. 04/27/1999 which name changed to Consolidated Global Diamond Corp. 04/23/2004 which name changed to Gem International Resources Inc. 10/30/2009

CINAPORT ACQUISITION CORP (ON)
Recapitalized as Mettrum Health Corp. 10/02/2014
Each share Common no par exchanged for (0.06866952) share Common no par
Mettrum Health Corp. merged into Canopy Growth Corp. 02/02/2017

CINAR CORP (CANADA)
Name changed 12/10/1998
Each share Common no par exchanged for (0.5) share Class A Multiple no par and (0.5) share Class B Subordinate no par 04/04/1995
Class A Multiple no par split (2) for (1) by issuance of (1) additional share payable 05/04/1998 to holders of record 03/18/1998
Class B Subordinate no par split (2) for (1) by issuance of (1) additional share payable 05/04/1998 to holders of record 03/18/1998
Name changed from Cinar Films Inc. to Cinar Corp. 12/10/1998
Acquired by an investor group 03/01/2004
Each share Class A Multiple no par exchanged for $3.60 cash
Each share Class B Subordinate no par exchanged for $3.60 cash

CINATONE PUBLISHING & RECORDING CO., INC. (TN)
Charter revoked for non-payment of taxes 01/08/1959

CINCH ENERGY CORP (AB)
Merged into Tourmaline Oil Corp. 07/12/2011
Each share Common no par exchanged for (0.06366) share Common no par

Note: Unexchanged certificates were cancelled and became without value 07/14/2016

CINCH LAKE URANIUM MINES, LTD. (ON)
Name changed to Lake Cinch Mines Ltd. 00/00/1954
Lake Cinch Mines Ltd. merged into Dickenson Mines Ltd. (Old) 10/14/1960 which merged into Dickenson Mines Ltd. (New) 10/31/1980 which merged into Goldcorp Inc. (New) 03/31/1994

CINCINNATI, HAMILTON & DAYTON RAILWAY CO.
Name changed to Cincinnati & Lake Erie Railroad Co. 00/00/1930
(See Cincinnati & Lake Erie Railroad Co.)

CINCINNATI, SANDUSKY & CLEVELAND RAILROAD CO.
Merged into Cleveland, Cincinnati, Chicago & St. Louis Railway Co. 00/00/1938
Details not available

CINCINNATI & LAKE ERIE RAILROAD CO.
Reorganized as Cincinnati & Lake Erie Transportation Co. 00/00/1941
No stockholders' equity

CINCINNATI & SUBN BELL TEL CO (OH)
Common $50 par changed to $25 par and (1) additional share issued 12/15/1965
Name changed to Cincinnati Bell Inc. (Old) 03/16/1970
Cincinnati Bell Inc. (Old) reorganized as Cincinnati Bell Inc. (New) 07/01/1983 which name changed to Broadwing Inc. 11/15/1999 which name changed back to Cincinnati Bell Inc. (New) 05/16/2003

CINCINNATI BALL CRANK CO. (OH)
Name changed to Balcrank, Inc. 00/00/1943
Balcrank, Inc. name changed to Disney Street Corp. 11/30/1962
(See Disney Street Corp.)

CINCINNATI BELL INC. (OLD) (OH)
Common $25 par changed to $12.50 par and (1) additional share issued 04/15/1971
Name changed to Broadwing Inc. 11/15/1999
Broadwing Inc. name changed to Cincinnati Bell Inc. (New) 05/16/2003

CINCINNATI BELL INC NEW (OH)
Common $12.50 par changed to $1 par and (1) additional share issued 05/21/1986
Common $1 par split (2) for (1) by issuance of (1) additional share 05/20/1987
Common $1 par split (2) for (1) by issuance of (1) additional share 05/22/1989
Common $1 par split (2) for (1) by issuance of (1) additional share payable 05/30/1997 to holders of record 05/02/1997 Ex date - 06/02/1997
Each share Common $1 par received distribution of (1) share Convergys Corp. Common no par payable 12/31/1998 to holders of record 12/01/1998 Ex date - 01/04/1999
Common $1 par changed to 1¢ par 04/26/1999
Name changed to BroadWing Inc. 11/15/1999
BroadWing Inc. name changed back to Cincinnati Bell Inc. (New) 05/16/2003

CINCINNATI CAR CO.
Merged into Cincinnati Car Corp 00/00/1928
Details not available

CINCINNATI CAR CORP.
Corporation dissolved and charter surrendered 00/00/1937

CINCINNATI ECONOMY DRUG CO (OH)
Over 95% acquired by Williamsburg Financial Corp. through purchase offer as of 06/01/1979
Public interest eliminated

CINCINNATI ENERGY CORP (ON)
Charter cancelled and declared dissolved 06/11/1994

CINCINNATI ENQUIRER INC (OH)
Common $10 par and VTC's for Common $10 par changed to no par respectively and (1) additional share issued 05/07/1962
Voting Trust Agreement terminated 07/31/1971
Each VTC for Common no par exchanged for (1) share Common no par
Merged into American Financial Corp. 12/28/1972
Each share Common no par exchanged for (3.33333333) shares Common no par
(See American Financial Corp.)

CINCINNATI EQUITABLE INS CO (OH)
Merged into CEA Corp. 12/30/1985
Each share Common $1 par exchanged for $47 cash

CINCINNATI FINL CORP (DE)
Common $2 par split (3) for (2) by issuance of (0.5) additional share 04/21/1972
Common $2 par split (2) for (1) by issuance of (1) additional share 04/30/85 04/30/1985
Stock Dividends - 10% 4/30/1975; 10% 04/30/1979; 10% 04/30/1980; 10% 04/15/1982
Reincorporated under the laws of Ohio 04/09/1992

CINCINNATI FUND, INC. (OH)
Liquidation completed 00/00/1954
Details not avialable

CINCINNATI GAS & ELEC CO (OH)
5% Preferred $100 par called for redemption 01/01/1946
Common $8.50 par changed to $17 par 00/00/1952
Common $17 par changed to $8.50 par and (1) additional share distributed 00/00/1953
Common $8.50 par split (2) for (1) by issuance of (1) additional share 05/29/1963
12.52% Preferred $100 par called for redemption 07/01/1986
10.20% Preferred $100 par called for redemption 01/31/1992
9.30% Preferred $100 par called for redemption 10/01/1992
9.52% Preferred $100 par called for redemption 10/01/1992
Common $8.50 par split (3) for (2) by issuance of (0.5) additional share 12/02/1992
9.28% Preferred $100 par called for redemption 04/01/1994
Merged into Cinergy Corp. 10/24/1994
Each share Common $8.50 par exchanged for (1) share Common 1¢ par
Cinergy Corp. merged into Duke Energy Corp. (DE) 04/03/2006
7.44% Preferred $100 par called for redemption 07/01/1995
9.15% Preferred $100 par called for redemption 07/01/1995
4% Preferred $100 par called for redemption at $108 on 03/10/2006
4.75% Preferred $100 par called for redemption at $101 on 03/10/2006
7.875% Preferred $100 par called for redemption 09/18/1996

CINCINNATI INDS INC (OH)
Name changed to CII Investment Corp. 04/01/1974
(See CII Investment Corp.)

CINCINNATI INS CO (OH)
Common $20 par changed to $5 par and (3) additional shares issued 11/04/1966
Stock Dividends - 10% 04/10/1965; 10% 04/10/1966; 10% 04/10/1967; 10% 04/10/1968
99.97% acquired by Cincinnati Financial Corp. through voluntary exchange offer which expired 08/04/1969
Public interest eliminated

CINCINNATI INTER TERM RR CO (OH)
1st Preferred called for redemption at $105 on 08/15/2008

CINCINNATI MICROWAVE INC (OH)
Common no par split (3) for (2) by issuance of (0.5) additional share 06/28/1985
Liquidating Plan of Reorganization under Chapter 11 Federal Bankruptcy proceedings confirmed 01/12/1998
No stockholders' equity

CINCINNATI MILACRON INC (DE)
Reincorporated 04/27/1983
Common $10 par split (2) for (1) by issuance of (1) additional share 01/10/1978
Common $10 par changed to $5 par and (1) additional share issued 07/06/1979
Common $5 par changed to $1 par and (0.5) additional share issued 01/16/1981
State of incorporation changed from (OH) to (DE) 04/27/1983
Name changed to Milacron Inc. 10/05/1998
(See Milacron Inc.)

CINCINNATI MLG MACH CO (OH)
Each share Common $25 par exchanged for (0.6) share 4% Preferred $100 par and (9) shares Common $10 par 00/00/1945
Common $10 par split (2) for (1) by issuance of (1) additional share 12/29/1955
Common $10 par split (2) for (1) by issuance of (1) additional share 08/03/1966
Name changed to Cincinnati Milacron Inc. (OH) 05/01/1970
Cincinnati Milacron Inc. (OH) reincorporated in Delaware 04/27/1983 which name changed to Milacron Inc. 10/05/1998
(See Milacron Inc.)

CINCINNATI NEW ORLEANS & TEX PAC RY CO (OH)
Each share Common $100 par exchanged for (5) shares Common $20 par 00/00/1939
Merged into Southern Railway Co. 04/01/1970
Each share Preferred $100 par exchanged for 5% Preferred $20 par and (0.333333) share Common no par
Each share Common $20 par exchanged for (2.666666) shares Common no par
Southern Railway Co. merged into Norfolk Southern Corp. 06/01/1982

CINCINNATI NORTHERN RAILROAD CO.
Merged into Cleveland, Cincinnati, Chicago & St. Louis Railway Co. 00/00/1938
Details not available

CINCINNATI PLANER CO.
Dissolved 00/00/1950
Details not available

CINCINNATI-PORCUPINE MINES LTD. (ON)
Name changed to Cincinnati Resources Inc. and Capital Stock $1 par changed to no par 12/11/1980
Cincinnati Resources Inc. recapitalized as Cincinnati Energy Corp. 01/20/1983
(See Cincinnati Energy Corp.)

CINCINNATI RES INC (ON)
Recapitalized as Cincinnati Energy Corp. 01/20/1983
Each share Capital Stock no par exchanged for (0.2) share Common no par
(See Cincinnati Energy Corp.)

CINCINNATI RUBBER MANUFACTURING CO.
Each share Common no par exchanged for (4) shares Common $5 par 00/00/1941
Acquired by Thor Power Tool Co. 12/22/1955
Each share Preferred exchanged for approximately $104 cash
Each share Common $5 par exchanged for approximately $20.25 cash

CINCINNATI STREET RAILWAY CO.
Recapitalized as Cincinnati Transit Co. 00/00/1952
Each share Common $25 par exchanged for (1) share Common $12.50 par and $12.50 principal amount of Debentures
Cincinnati Transit Co. recapitalized as American Controlled Industries, Inc. 01/10/1969
(See American Controlled Industries, Inc.)

CINCINNATI TERM WHSE INC (OH)
Recapitalized 00/00/1945
Each share 6% Preferred $50 par exchanged for $62.50 principal amount of 2nd Mortgage Income Bonds
Each share Common no par exchanged for (1) share Common $1 par
Became private 00/00/1976
Details not available

CINCINNATI TRACTION BUILDING CO. (OH)
Liquidated 00/00/1954
Details not available

CINCINNATI TRAN CO (OH)
Recapitalized as American Controlled Industries, Inc. 01/10/1969
Each share Common $12.50 par exchanged for (3) shares Common no par
(See American Controlled Industries, Inc.)

CINCINNATI UN GROUP INC (OH)
Name changed 09/21/1990
Each share Capital Stock $100 par exchanged for (5) shares Common Capital Stock no par 00/00/1928
Name changed from Cincinnati Union Stock Yards Co. to Cincinnati Union Group, Inc. 09/21/1990
Charter cancelled for failure to file reports and pay fees 01/04/2007

CINCO INC (NV)
Reorganized as Alynx, Co. (NV) 09/21/2006
Each share Common 1¢ par exchanged for (10) shares Common $0.001 par
Alynx, Co. (NV) reorganized in Florida as MiMedx Group, Inc. 04/02/2008

CINCORO CAP CORP (BC)
Recapitalized as Scorpio Gold Corp. 06/15/2009
Each share Common no par exchanged for for (0.33333333) share Common no par

CINDERELLA CLOTHING INDS INC (PA)
Chapter 7 bankruptcy proceedings terminated 01/26/2010
No stockholders' equity

CINDERELLA GOLD MINES, LTD. (ON)
Charter cancelled and company declared dissolved for default in filing returns 05/27/1965

CINDY MINES LTD. (BC)
Struck off register and declared dissolved for failure to file returns 10/21/1974

CINDYS INC (DE)
Reincorporated 03/05/1982
Stock Dividend - 10% 10/25/1977
State of incorporation changed from (GA) to (DE) 03/05/1982
Merged into Prime Motor Inns Inc. 03/06/1984
Each share Common 10¢ par exchanged for (0.17) share Common 5¢ par
Prime Motor Inns Inc. reorganized as Prime Hospitality Corp. 07/31/1992
(See Prime Hospitality Corp.)

CINE CHROME LABS INC (CO)
Name changed to Medco Health Care Services, Inc. 05/21/1984
Medco Health Care Services, Inc. name changed to Cine-Chrome Video Corp. 10/21/1985 which name changed to Network 4, Inc. 06/25/1986 which recapitalized as CEEE Group Corp. (CO) 05/00/1987 which reorganized in Delaware as Atlantic International Entertainment, Ltd. 11/26/1996 which name changed to Online Gaming Systems, Ltd. 10/01/1999 which name changed to Advanced Resources Group Ltd. 02/15/2007

CINE-CHROME VIDEO CORP. (CO)
Name changed to Network 4, Inc. 06/25/1986
Network 4, Inc. recapitalized as CEEE Group Corp. (CO) 05/00/1987 which reorganized in Delaware as Atlantic International Entertainment, Ltd. 11/26/1996 which name changed to Online Gaming Systems, Ltd. 10/01/1999 which name changed to Advanced Resources Group Ltd. 02/15/2007

CINE-MAX CINEMAS INC (UT)
Each share old Common $0.001 par exchanged for (0.2) share new Common $0.001 par 02/13/1996
Name changed to Phone Time Resources, Inc. 02/07/1997
Phone Time Resources, Inc. recapitalized as Global Access Pagers Inc. 04/21/1998 which name changed to Integrated Communication Networks Inc. 01/29/1999
(See Integrated Communication Networks Inc.)

CINE PRIME CORP (NY)
Charter cancelled and proclaimed dissolved for failure to pay taxes and file reports 12/15/1975

CINE-SOURCE INC (CO)
Each share old Common no par exchanged for (0.01) share new Common no par 01/11/1990
Reorganized under the laws of Nevada as First Quantum Ventures, Inc. 05/21/2004
Each share new Common no par exchanged for (0.005) share Common $0.001 par
First Quantum Ventures, Inc. name changed to DiMi Telematics International, Inc. 03/16/2012 which name changed to Bespoke Extracts, Inc. 03/10/2017

CINECOLOR, INC.
Reorganized as Cinecolor Corp. 00/00/1944
Stockholders received nothing but rights to subscribe to new Debentures accompanied by Common Stock
(See Cinecolor Corp.)

CINECOLOR CORP. (CA)
Name changed to Color Corp. of America 00/00/1953
Color Corp. of America name changed to Houston Fearless Corp. 06/01/1957 which merged into Image Systems, Inc. (CA) 04/20/1970 which reincorporated in Delaware 08/29/1974
(See Image Systems, Inc. (DE))

CINECOM CORP (NY)
Common 1¢ par split (2) for (1) by issuance of (1) additional share 05/01/1969
Adjudicated bankrupt 07/26/1973
Stockholders' equity unlikely

CINEDIGM DIGITAL CINEMA CORP (DE)
Name changed to Cinedigm Corp. 10/09/2013

CINEMA FEATURES INC (UT)
Recapitalized as Focal Corp. 06/18/1993
Each share Common 5¢ par exchanged for (0.1) share Common 5¢ par
Focal Corp. name changed to Indigenous Global Development Corp. 07/02/2002
(See Indigenous Global Development Corp.)

CINEMA 5 LTD (NY)
Merged into Nationwide Theatres Corp. 09/27/1979
Each share Common $1 par exchanged for $5 cash

CINEMA V LTD (NY)
Name changed 02/10/1970
Name changed from Cinema V Distributing, Inc. to Cinema 5 Ltd. 02/10/1970
Merged into Nationwide Theatres Corp. 09/27/1979
Each share Common $1 par exchanged for $5 cash

CINEMA INTERNET NETWORKS INC (CANADA)
Reorganized under the laws of British Columbia as Quentin Ventures Ltd. 06/27/2014
Each share Common no par exchanged for for (0.05) share Common no par
Quentin Ventures Ltd. name changed to Identillect Technologies Corp. 05/25/2016

CINEMA LABORATORIES, INC.
Acquired by Pathe Laboratories, Inc. 00/00/1939
Details not available

CINEMA MAGAZINE, INC.
Bankrupt 00/00/1938
Stockholders' equity unlikely

CINEMA RIDE INC (DE)
Each share Common 1¢ par exchanged for (0.125) share Common 8¢ par 05/29/1998
Name changed to Tix Corp. 03/03/2005

CINEMA STAR CORP (NV)
Name changed to Impact Resources, Inc. 12/29/1983
Impact Resources, Inc. recapitalized as Dyna-Seal Corp. 09/11/1989 which name changed to Interactive Buyers Network International Ltd. 07/21/1995 which name changed to Vsource, Inc. (NV) 12/03/1999 which reincorporated in Delaware 11/08/2000 which name changed to Tri-Isthmus Group, Inc. 12/30/2005 which name changed to First Physicians Capital Group, Inc. 01/08/2010

CINEMA TELEVISION LTD. (ENGLAND)
Recapitalized as Rank Cintel Ltd. 03/18/1958
Each share Ordinary 6d par exchanged for (0.2) share Ordinary 5s par
Rank Cintel Ltd. name changed to Bush & Rank Cintel Ltd. 10/06/1960 which name changed to Rank Radio & Television Ltd. 12/03/1962
(See Rank Radio & Television Ltd.)

CINEMAELECTRIC INC (UT)
Charter expired 08/24/2006

CINEMAGE CORP (AB)
Name changed 08/16/2002
Name changed from Cinemage Capital Corp. to Cinemage Corp. 08/16/2002
Recapitalized as Fibresources Corp. 12/08/2008
Each share Common no par exchanged for (0.2) share Common no par

CINEMAISON 3D INC (QC)
Name changed to SENSIO Technologies Inc. 06/05/2006
(See SENSIO Technologies Inc.)

CINEMAS UNIS LTEE. (QC)
Shares redeemed 00/00/1981
Details not available

CINEMASTAR LUXURY THEATERS INC (DE)
Reorganized 12/01/1998
State of incorporation changed from (CA) to (DE) 12/01/1998
Each share Common no par exchanged for (0.14285714) share Common no par
Plan of reorganization under Chapter 11 Federal Bankruptcy proceedings confirmed 10/05/2001
Holders who made a capital contribution received new Common on a share for share basis
Holders who did not make a capital contribution received interest free promissory notes
Certificates were not required to be exchanged and are without value

CINEMASTERS GROUP INC (NY)
Reincorporated under the laws of Delaware as Avenue Entertainment Group, Inc. 04/14/1997
Avenue Entertainment Group, Inc. name changed to alpha-En Corp. 07/22/2008

CINEMATION INDS INC (NY)
Charter cancelled and proclaimed dissolved for failure to pay taxes 03/26/1980

CINEMATRONICS INC (DE)
Charter cancelled and declared inoperative and void for non-payment of taxes 03/01/1989

CINEMAX PICTURES & PRODTN CO INTL INC (WA)
Name changed to Circa Pictures & Production Company International, Inc. 04/03/2008

CINEMAYA MEDIA GROUP INC (DE)
Common $0.0001 par split (2) for (1) by issuance of (1) additional share payable 07/10/2007 to holders of record 07/02/2007 Ex date - 07/11/2007
Recapitalized as SNM Global Holdings 11/14/2008
Each share Common $0.0001 par exchanged for (0.005) share Common $0.0001 par

CINEPLEX GALAXY INCOME FD (ON)
Under plan of reorganization each Trust Unit no par automatically

became (1) share Cineplex Inc. Common no par 01/04/2011

CINEPLEX ODEON CORP (ON)
Name changed 07/09/1985
Name changed from Cineplex Corp. to Cineplex Odeon Corp. 07/09/1985
Retractable Conv. Preference no par called for redemption 11/30/1987
Merged into Loews Cineplex Entertainment Corp. 05/14/1998
Each share Common no par exchanged for (0.1) share Common 1¢ par
(See Loews Cineplex Entertainment Corp.)

CINEQUITY CORP NEW (ON)
Charter cancelled for failure to file reports and pay taxes 07/09/1994

CINEQUITY CORP OLD (ON)
Merged into Cinequity Corp. (New) 11/24/1981
Each share Class A no par exchanged for (5) shares Common no par
Each share Common no par exchanged for (5) shares Common no par
(See Cinequity Corp. (New))

CINERAMA INC (NY)
Conv. Preference Ser. A $1 par called for redemption 09/09/1969
Each share Common 1¢ par exchanged for (0.2) share Common 5¢ par 10/17/1974
Merged into Forkel Enterprises, Inc. 08/29/1978
Each share Common 5¢ par exchanged for $5 cash

CINERAMA PRODUCTIONS CORP. (NY)
Each share Common 5¢ par exchanged for (2) shares Common 1¢ par 00/00/1953
Reincorporated under the laws of Delaware as Amedco, Inc. 09/30/1960 which recapitalized as Gulf States Industries, Inc. 05/15/1962
(See Gulf States Industries, Inc.)

CINERGI PICTURES ENTMT INC (DE)
Issue Information - 3,000,000 shares COM offered at $9 per share on 06/17/1994
Merged into Valdina Corp. N.V. 12/30/97
Each share Common 1¢ par exchanged for $2.52 cash

CINERGY CORP (DE)
Each Income Preferred Redeemable Increased Dividend Equity Security received (1.4536) shares Common 1¢ par 02/16/2005
Merged into Duke Energy Corp. (DE) 04/03/2006
Each share Common 1¢ par exchanged for (1.56) shares Common $0.001 par

CINETEX INDS LTD (NY)
Name changed to Videovision Inc. 11/30/1978
Videovision Inc. name changed to Vision Communications Corp. 05/25/1984
(See Vision Communications Corp.)

CINETRON CORP (NY)
Dissolved by proclamation 09/29/1993

CINEVIDEO INTERNATIONAL CORP. (DE)
Reincorporated 06/30/1976
State of incorporation changed from (MN) to (DE) 06/30/1976
Each share Common 1¢ par exchanged for (2) shares Common 1¢ par
Name changed to C V International Corp. 07/10/1979
(See C V International Corp.)

CINEVISION LTEE (QC)
Adjudicated bankrupt 04/26/1976

Stockholders' equity unlikely

CINJET INC (NV)
Name changed to Solis Tek Inc. 09/02/2015
Solis Tek Inc. name changed to Generation Alpha, Inc. 09/27/2018

CINNABAR ENTERPRISES INC (CO)
Each share old Common no par exchanged for (0.04) share new Common no par 09/11/1997
Reincorporated under the laws of Nevada as All Line, Inc. 08/20/2007
(See All Line, Inc.)

CINNABAR MINING CO. (WY)
Charter forfeited for failure to pay taxes 07/19/1927

CINNABAR PEAK MINES LTD (AB)
Name changed to Sierra Capital Corp. 09/19/1994

CINNABAR RES LTD (AB)
Delisted from Vancouver Stock Exchange 11/16/1990

CINNABAR VENTURES INC (NV)
Common $0.001 par split (3) for (1) by issuance of (2) additional shares payable 11/16/2009 to holders of record 11/05/2009 Ex date - 11/17/2009
Name changed to Yippy, Inc. 05/28/2010

CINOLA MINES LTD (BC)
Recapitalized as Consolidated Cinola Mines Ltd. 01/10/1973
Each share Common no par exchanged for (0.5) share Common no par
Consolidated Cinola Mines Ltd. name changed to City Resources (Canada) Ltd. 12/09/1986 which name changed to Misty Mountain Gold Ltd. 04/22/1994 which recapitalized as Misty Mountain Gold Inc. 11/10/1995 which name changed to Continental Minerals Corp. (Incorporated 02/07/1962) 10/18/2001
(See Continental Minerals Corp. (Incorporated 02/07/1962))

CINRAM INTL INC (CANADA)
Name changed 06/12/1997
Common no par split (3) for (1) by issuance of (2) additional shares 07/16/1987
Common no par split (2) for (1) by issuance of (1) additional share 06/24/1993
Name changed from Cinram Ltd. to Cinram International Inc. 06/12/1997
Common no par split (2) for (1) by issuance of (1) additional share payable 03/04/1998 to holders of record 02/27/1998
Reorganized as Cinram International Income Fund 05/08/2006
Each share Common no par exchanged for (1) Trust Unit no par

CINS HLDG CORP (CAYMAN ISLANDS)
Name changed to Sino Rise Group Holding Corp. 01/29/2016

CINTAS CORP (OH)
Reincorporated under the laws of Washington 11/13/1986

CINTECH SOLUTIONS INC (OH)
Name changed 10/25/2000
Name changed from Cinetech Tele-Management Systems Inc. to Cinetech Solutions Inc. 10/25/2000
Chapter 11 bankruptcy petition dismissed 12/30/2003
No stockholders' equity

CINTEL CORP (NV)
Recapitalized as Chun Can Capital Group 03/16/2017
Each share Common $0.001 par exchanged for (0.00025) share Common $0.001 par

CINTRA CONCESIONES DE INFRAESTRUCTURAS (SPAIN)
Name changed to Ferrovial S.A. 01/29/2010

CINZANO, LTD. (CANADA)
Class A Ordinary 5s par and Class B Ordinary 5s par changed to no par 00/00/1944
5.5% Preference £1 par called for redemption 01/31/1961
Each share Class A Ordinary £1 par acquired by Instituto Finanziaro Industrial of Turin for £1 11p 6s cash 01/31/1961

CIP, INC. (DE)
Liquidation completed
Each share Capital Stock 10¢ par received third and final distribution of $2.30 cash 03/29/1971
Note: Initial and second distributions were paid under former name, Investors Planning Corp. of America

CIP HLDGS INC (FL)
Recapitalized as Pan-International Holdings, Inc. 4/11/89
Each share Common $0.000001 par exchanged for (0.01) share Common $0.0001 par
Pan-International Holdings, Inc. recapitalized as Curtin International Productions (New), Inc. 9/15/89 which name changed to First Response Medical, Inc. 11/23/89 which recapitalized as RMS Titanic, Inc. 5/19/93 which name changed to Premier Exhibitions, Inc. 10/18/2004

CIPHER DATA PRODS INC (CA)
Common $1 par split (2) for (1) by issuance of (1) additional share 5/24/83
Merged into Archive Corp. 4/24/90
Each share Common $1 par exchanged for $8.25 cash

CIPHER HLDGS CORP (DE)
Name changed to Imagin Molecular Corp. 07/05/2005
(See Imagin Molecular Corp.)

CIPHER VOICE INC (NV)
Each share Common $0.001 par exchanged for (0.14285714) share Common $0.007 par 10/30/1996
Name changed to Galaxy Enterprises Inc. 12/23/1996
Galaxy Enterprises Inc. merged into Netgateway, Inc. 06/26/2000 which recapitalized as iMergent, Inc. 07/02/2002 which name changed to Crexendo, Inc. (DE) 05/23/2011 which reincorporated in Nevada 12/13/2016

CIPHERGEN BIOSYSTEMS INC (DE)
Issue Information - 5,500,000 shares COM offered at $16 per share on 09/28/2000
Name changed to Vermillion, Inc. 08/27/2007

CIPHERPASS CORP (NV)
Recapitalized as Javalon Technology Group, Inc. (NV) 09/06/2007
Each share Common $0.001 par exchanged for (0.02) share Common $0.001
Note: Holders of (499) or fewer pre-split shares received $0.08 cash per share
Javalon Technology Group, Inc. (NV) reincorporated in British Virgin Islands as WorldVest Equity, Inc. 11/13/2008

CIPRICO INC (DE)
Reincorporated 01/27/1988
Stock Dividends - 10% 12/17/1984; 10% 01/17/1986
State of incorporation changed from (MN) to (DE) 01/27/1988
Common 1¢ par split (3) for (2) by issuance of (0.5) additional share payable 04/12/1996 to holders of record 03/27/1996
Chapter 11 bankruptcy proceedings

converted to Chapter 7 on 05/07/2009
No stockholders' equity

CIPSCO INC (IL)
Merged into Ameren Corp. 12/31/1997
Each share Common no par exchanged for (1.03) shares Common 1¢ par

CIPWAY GOLD MINES LTD. (ON)
Charter revoked for failure to file reports and pay taxes in 00/00/1957

CIR TECH INC (MN)
Merged into Data-Design Laboratories 07/16/1979
Each share Common 5¢ par exchanged for $0.05 cash

CIRCA PHARMACEUTICALS INC (NY)
Merged into Watson Pharmaceuticals, Inc. 07/17/1995
Each share Common 1¢ par exchanged for (0.86) share Common $0.0033 par
Watson Pharmaceuticals, Inc. name changed to Actavis, Inc. (NV) 01/24/2013 which reorganized in Ireland as Actavis PLC 10/01/2013 which name changed to Allergan PLC 06/15/2015

CIRCA TELECOMMUNICATIONS INC (AB)
Name changed to Circa Enterprises Inc. 11/02/1994

CIRCADIAN INC (CA)
Charter forfeited and declared void for failure to pay franchise taxes 03/18/1987

CIRCADIAN SYSTEMS, INC. (DE)
Name changed to Harbour Intermodal, Ltd. 03/03/1993
(See Harbour Intermodal, Ltd.)

CIRCADIAN TECHNOLOGIES LTD (AUSTRALIA)
Name changed to Opthea Ltd. 12/22/2015

CIRCLE-BAR KNITTING CO., LTD. (CANADA)
Each share Common $100 par exchanged for (22) shares Common no par 00/00/1944
Each share Common no par exchanged for (1) share new Common no par and (1) share Class A no par 00/00/1947
Recapitalized as Bell Knit Industries Ltd. 08/12/1964
Each share Class A Preference no par exchanged for (5) shares Common no par
Each share Common no par exchanged for (0.5) share Common no par
(See Bell Knit Industries Ltd.)

CIRCLE BLDRS CORP (BC)
Name changed to Miromit Solar Corp. 09/09/1977
Each share Common no par exchanged for (1) share Common no par

CIRCLE CLIFFS MNG INDS INC (UT)
Recapitalized as Consolidated Equities & Management, Inc. 06/28/1971
Each share Common 2¢ par exchanged for (0.05) share Capital Stock 2¢ par
(See Consolidated Equities & Management, Inc.)

CIRCLE CLIFFS URANIUM CO. (UT)
Name changed to Circle Cliffs Mining Industries, Inc. 02/12/1969
Circle Cliffs Mining Industries, Inc. recapitalized as Consolidated Equities & Management, Inc. 06/28/1971
(See Consolidated Equities & Management, Inc.)

CIRCLE CTLS CORP (NJ)
Company liquidated 00/00/1991
No stockholders' equity

CIRCLE ENERGY INC (BC)
Acquired by Rider Resources Inc. 11/22/2001
Each share Common no par exchanged for either (0.42) share Common no par or $0.48 cash
Note: Option to receive cash expired 01/21/2002
Rider Resources Inc. merged into Rider Resources Ltd. 02/21/2003 which merged into NuVista Energy Ltd. 03/04/2008

CIRCLE ENERGY INC (CO)
Reorganized under the laws of Delaware as Circle Corp. 04/22/1987
Each share Common 1¢ par exchanged for (0.02) share Common $0.001 par

CIRCLE EXPRESS INC (IN)
Common no par split (3) for (2) by issuance of (0.5) additional share 05/16/1986
Reorganized as Intrenet, Inc. 01/15/1991
Each share Common no par exchanged for (0.04) share Common no par
Note: Unexchanged certificates were cancelled and became without value 01/16/1992
(See Intrenet, Inc.)

CIRCLE F INDS INC (DE)
Name changed to Cirfico Holdings Corp. 12/14/1979
(See Cirfico Holdings Corp.)

CIRCLE FINL CORP (OH)
Merged into Fidelity Financial of Ohio, Inc. 10/11/1996
Each share Common $1 par exchanged for either (3.85) shares Common 10¢ par, $38 cash, or a combination thereof
Note: Option to elect to receive stock expired 11/20/1996
Fidelity Financial of Ohio, Inc. merged into Provident Financial Group, Inc. 02/04/2000 which merged into National City Corp. 07/01/2004 which was acquired by PNC Financial Services Group, Inc. 12/31/2008

CIRCLE FINE ART CORP (DE)
Each share Common 10¢ par exchanged for (0.33333333) share Common 1¢ par 12/13/1994
Plan of reorganization under Chapter 11 Federal Bankruptcy proceedings confirmed 09/28/2001
Stockholders' equity unlikely

CIRCLE 5 CONTESTS INC (NY)
Name changed to Aerocon, Inc. and Common 5¢ par changed to 1¢ par 07/23/1970
Aerocon, Inc. merged into Alphanumeric, Inc. 01/28/1972
(See Alphanumeric, Inc.)

CIRCLE GROUP HLDGS INC (IL)
Name changed 01/10/2003
Common $0.0001 par changed to $0.00005 par and (1) additional share issued payable 08/06/1999 to holders of record 07/22/1999
Name changed from Circle Group Internet, Inc. to Circle Group Holdings Inc. 01/10/2003
Name changed to Z-Trim Holdings, Inc. (IL) 06/22/2006
Z-Trim Holdings, Inc. (IL) reincorporated in Nevada as Agritech Worldwide, Inc. 04/04/2016

CIRCLE INCOME SHS INC (IN)
Merged into One Group 01/22/2001
Each share Common $1 par exchanged for Income Bond Fund Class A on a net asset basis
(See One Group)

CIRCLE INTL GROUP INC (DE)
Merged into EGL, Inc. 10/02/2000
Each share Common no par exchanged for (1) share Common $0.001 par

CIRCLE K CORP (DE)
Merged into Tosco Corp. 05/30/1996
Each share Common 1¢ par exchanged for (0.6162) share Common 75¢ par
Tosco Corp. merged into Phillips Petroleum Co. 09/14/2001 which name changed to ConocoPhillips 08/30/2002

CIRCLE K CORP (TX)
Common $1 par split (2) for (1) by issuance of (1) additional share 02/24/1966
Common $1 par split (3) for (2) by issuance of (0.5) additional share 03/15/1968
Common $1 par split (3) for (2) by issuance of (0.5) additional share 12/30/1968
Common $1 par split (3) for (2) by issuance of (0.5) additional share 04/05/1971
Common $1 par split (3) for (2) by issuance of (0.5) additional share 01/07/1972
Common $1 par split (2) for (1) by issuance of (1) additional share 01/30/1980
Common $1 par split (3) for (2) by issuance of (0.5) additional share 10/15/1985
Common $1 par split (2) for (1) by issuance of (1) additional share 09/15/1986
Plan of reorganization under Chapter 11 Federal Bankruptcy Code effective 07/27/1993
No stockholders' equity

CIRCLE K FOOD STORES, INC. (TX)
Name changed to Circle K Corp. 09/08/1964
(See Circle K Corp.)

CIRCLE K SUNKUS CO LTD (JAPAN)
ADR agreement terminated 10/04/2012
Each ADR for Common exchanged for $44.979083 cash

CIRCLE KEY LIFE INS CO (IA)
Name changed to Central United Life Insurance Co. 04/30/1971
Central United Life Insurance Co. merged into Central United Corp. 03/31/1975
(See Central United Corp.)

CIRCLE RUBR CO (MN)
Stock Dividends - 25% 08/31/1977; 10% 09/01/1978
Merged into Fluorocarbon Co. 03/27/1979
Each share Common 10¢ par exchanged for (0.85) share Common 20¢ par
Fluorocarbon Co. name changed to Furon Co. 01/31/1990
(See Furon Co.)

CIRCLE SEAL CORP (CA)
Merged into Brunswick Corp. 01/20/1977
Each share Common no par exchanged for $17.354 cash

CIRCLE SEVEN OIL & GAS INC (CO)
Completely liquidated 07/21/1989
Each share Common $0.001 par exchanged for first and final distribution of $0.004 cash

CIRCLE SYS INC (FL)
Recapitalized as Trio Industries Group, Inc. 04/12/2004
Each share Common $0.001 par exchanged for (0.025) share Common $0.001 par
(See Trio Industries Group, Inc.)

CIRCLE THEATRE CO (IN)
In process of liquidation
Each share Common no par received initial distribution of $1 cash 12/16/1968
Each share Common no par received second distribution of $14 cash 03/14/1969
Each share Common no par received third distribution of $38 cash 04/01/1969
Note: Details on subsequent distributions, if any, are not available

CIRCLE WIRE & CABLE CORP. (NY)
Name changed to C.W.C. Liquidating Corp. 12/02/1955
(See C.W.C. Liquidating Corp.)

CIRCLE YELLOWKNIFE MINES LTD. (ON)
Charter cancelled and declared dissolved for failure to pay taxes and file returns 12/07/1977

CIRCLETRONICS INC (CANADA)
Reincorporated under the laws of Nevada as ColorStars Group and Common no par changed to $0.001 par 11/03/2005

CIRCO CRAFT INC (QC)
Merged into HMTF Canada Acquisition Inc. 10/04/1996
Each share Common no par exchanged for $11 cash

CIRCON CORP (DE)
Reincorporated 11/06/1987
State of incorporation changed from (CA) to (DE) 11/06/1987
Merged into Maxxim Medical, Inc. 01/08/1999
Each share Common 1¢ par exchanged for $15 cash

CIRCUIT BRD ONE INC (MN)
Ceased operations 10/08/1992
Stockholders' equity unlikely

CIRCUIT CITY STORES INC (VA)
Preferred Ser. D $20 par called for redemption 06/25/1986
Common $1 par split (2) for (1) by issuance of (1) additional share 07/14/1989
Issue Information - 21,860,000 shares CARMAX GROUP COM offered at $20 per share on 02/04/1997
Each share Carmax Group Common 50¢ par exchanged for (1) share CarMax Inc. Common 50¢ par 10/01/2002
(See CarMax Inc.)
Preferred Stock Purchase Rights declared for Common stockholders of record 04/29/1998 were redeemed at $0.01 per right 05/15/2005 for holders of record 05/01/2005
Common $1 par split (2) for (1) by issuance of (1) additional share 05/23/1986
Common $1 par split (2) for (1) by issuance of (1) additional share 07/14/1989
Common $1 par changed to 50¢ par and (1) additional share issued 03/18/1993
Common 50¢ par reclassified as Circuit City Group Common 50¢ par 02/04/1997
Circuit City Group Common 50¢ par split (2) for (1) by issuance of (1) additional share payable 07/15/1999 to holders of record 06/30/1999 Ex date - 07/16/1999
Each share Circuit City Group Common 50¢ par received distribution of (0.314) share CarMax Inc. Common 50¢ par payable 09/30/2002 to holders of record 09/16/2002 Ex date - 10/01/2002
Circuit City Group Common 50¢ par reclassified as Common 50¢ par 10/01/2002
Plan of reorganization under Chapter 11 Federal Bankruptcy proceedings effective 11/01/2010
No stockholders' equity

CIRCUIT FOIL CORP (NJ)
Common 25¢ par split (5) for (4) by issuance of (0.25) additional share 04/15/1965
Common 25¢ par split (3) for (2) by issuance of (0.5) additional share 11/12/1968
Name changed to Yates Industries, Inc. 06/25/1970
(See Yates Industries, Inc.)

CIRCUIT RESH LABS INC (AZ)
Each share Common no par exchanged for (0.125) share Common 10¢ par 09/11/1992
Common 10¢ par split (2) for (1) by issuance of (1) additional share payable 08/15/2000 to holders of record 07/31/2000
Ceased operations 03/05/2009
Stockholders' equity unlikely

CIRCUIT SCIENCE INC (MN)
Stock Dividend - 50% 07/15/1971
Name changed to Prestige Electronics, Inc. 05/31/1977
Prestige Electronics, Inc. name changed to Multaplex Corp. 03/26/1984
(See Multaplex Corp.)

CIRCUIT SOURCE INTL INC (NV)
Name changed to CSI Technologies, Inc. 07/24/2003
(See CSI Technologies, Inc.)

CIRCUIT SYS INC (IL)
Chapter 11 bankruptcy case closed 12/22/2006
Stockholders' equity unlikely

CIRCUIT TECHNOLOGY INC (NY)
Merged into General Electric Co. Ltd. (New) 01/09/1981
Each share Common 20¢ par exchanged for $13.50 cash

CIRCUIT WORLD CORP (CANADA)
Each share old Common no par exchanged for (0.025) share new Common no par 12/29/1998
Name changed to Firan Technology Group Corp. 05/18/2004

CIRCUITRONICS, INC. (DE)
Reorganized as National System Analysts, Inc. 07/07/1973
Each share Class A Common 1¢ par exchanged for (3) shares Common 1¢ par
National System Analysts, Inc. name changed to NSA, Inc. 01/30/1975
(See NSA, Inc.)

CIRCULAR LOGIC SYS INC (FL)
Name changed to Dynamic Media, Inc. (New) 11/18/2005
(See Dynamic Media, Inc. (New))

CIRCULATION MARKETING INC (UT)
Recapitalized as Intermountain Energy Corp. 09/27/1999
Each share Common $0.005 par exchanged for (0.5) share Common $0.005 par
(See Intermountain Energy Corp.)

CIRCUMPACIFIC ENERGY CORP (BC)
Reincorporated 06/16/1997
Reincorporated 00/00/2006
Place of incorporation changed from (BC) to (YT) 06/16/1997
Place of incorporation changed from (YT) to (BC) 00/00/2006
Acquired by Western Petroleum Commodities Inc. 11/25/2010
Each share Common no par exchanged for $0.18 cash

CIRCUS CIRCUS ENTERPRISES INC (NV)
Common 10¢ par changed to 5¢ par and (1) additional share issued 07/15/1986
Common 5¢ par split (2) for (1) by issuance of (1) additional share 07/26/1991
Common 5¢ par split (3) for (2) by

issuance of (0.5) additional share 07/23/1993
Name changed to Mandalay Resort Group 06/18/1999
(See Mandalay Resort Group)

CIRCUS CORP (DE)
Name changed to Evergood Products Corp. 11/13/1970
(See Evergood Products Corp.)

CIRCUS FOODS, INC. (CA)
Assets sold 08/07/1959
Each share Capital Stock $1 par received approximately $1.75 cash

CIRCUS HALL OF FAME, INC. (FL)
Liquidation completed
Each share Capital Stock $100 par exchanged for initial distribution of $70 cash 07/10/1980
Each share Capital Stock $100 par received second distribution of $127 cash 01/07/1981
Each share Capital Stock $100 par received third distribution of $25 cash 06/24/1981
Each share Capital Stock $100 par received fourth and final distribution of $4.18 cash 12/29/1981

CIRCUTEK INC (NJ)
Adjudicated bankrupt 11/04/1970
No stockholders' equity

CIRFICO HLDGS CORP (DE)
Liquidation completed
Each share Common $1 par received initial distribution of $7 cash 06/18/1984
Each share Common $1 par exchanged for second and final distribution of $2.50 cash 05/05/1985

CIRILIUM HLDGS INC (FL)
Reorganized 01/09/2007
Reorganized from (DE) to under the laws of Florida 01/09/2007
Each share Common $0.001 par exchanged for (0.01) share Common $0.001 par
Name changed to Cambridge Park Limited, Inc. 02/22/2007
Cambridge Park Limited, Inc. recapitalized as Family Entertainment Corp. 11/30/2007 which recapitalized as Airborne Security & Protective Services, Inc. (Ctfs. dated prior to 09/30/2009) 09/16/2008 which name changed to Harbor Brewing Co., Inc. 09/30/2009 which name changed to CTGX Mining, Inc. 02/28/2013

CIRO INC (DE)
Charter cancelled and declared inoperative and void for non-payment of taxes 03/01/1996

CIRO INTL INC (NV)
Each share old Common $0.001 par exchanged for (0.28571428) share new Common $0.001 par 06/10/2003
Name changed to Advanced Bio/Chem, Inc. 06/30/2003
Advanced Bio/Chem, Inc. name changed to Industrial Enterprises of America, Inc. 12/09/2004
(See Industrial Enterprises of America, Inc.)

CIROND CORP (NV)
Common $0.001 par split (16) for (1) by issuance of (15) additional shares payable 10/16/2003 to holders of record 10/16/2003 Ex date - 10/17/2003
Recapitalized as Amarium Technologies, Inc. 08/31/2006
Each share Common $0.001 par exchanged for (0.01538461) share Common $0.001 par
Amarium Technologies, Inc. recapitalized as Calissio Resources Group, Inc. 10/06/2014

CIROND TECHNOLOGIES INC (CO)
Name changed to Seaside Holdings Inc. 03/17/2003

CIRQUE ENERGY CORP (AB)
Reincorporated 01/05/1994
Recapitalized 05/11/1998
Place of incorporation changed from (ON) to (AB) 01/05/1994
Recapitalized from Cirque Energy Ltd. to Cirque Energy Corp. 05/11/1998
Each share old Common no par exchanged for (0.25) share new Common no par
Merged into Tikal Resources Corp. 05/31/1999
Each share new Common no par exchanged for (1) share Common no par
Tikal Resources Corp. was acquired by BelAir Energy Corp. 12/14/2001 which merged into Purcell Energy Ltd. (New) 09/04/2003
(See Purcell Energy Ltd. (New))

CIRRUS ENERGY CORP (AB)
Acquired by Oranje-Nassau Energie B.V. 04/14/2011
Each share Common no par exchanged for $1.15 cash

CIRRUS LOGIC INC (CA)
Common no par split (2) for (1) by issuance of (1) additional share 7/17/95
Reincorporated under the laws of Delaware and Common no par changed to $0.001 par 2/18/99

CIRUS TELECOM INC (DE)
Common $0.0001 par split (4) for (1) by issuance of (3) additional shares payable 04/11/2001 to holders of record 04/06/2001 Ex date - 04/12/2001
Recapitalized as THC Communications Inc. 03/08/2002
Each share Common $0.0001 par exchanged for (0.2) share Common $0.0001 par
(See THC Communications Inc.)

CIS ACQUISITION LTD (BRITISH VIRGIN ISLANDS)
Units separated 10/02/2014
Class A Shares $0.0001 par reclassified as Ordinary $0.0001 par 10/02/2014
Note: Unconverted Class A Shares received $10.40 cash per share from the termination of the trust account
Name changed to Delta Technology Holdings Ltd. 06/01/2015

CIS CAP EQUIP FD LTD (FL)
Registration terminated 12/20/95
Unit of Ltd. Partnership 1 details not available
Registration terminated 1/6/97
Unit of Ltd. Partnership 2 details not available

CIS COM INC (FL)
Name changed to InterAmerican Resources, Inc. 08/13/2001
InterAmerican Resources, Inc. name changed to Allixon Corp. 06/04/2004 which recapitalized as Simcoe Mining Resources Corp. 01/16/2008

CIS TECHNOLOGIES INC (DE)
Reincorporated 5/3/89
Place of incorporation changed from (BC) to (DE) 5/3/89
Merged into National Data Corp. 5/31/96
Each share Common no par exchanged for (0.08682) share Common $0.125 par
National Data Corp. name changed to NDCHealth Corp. 10/25/2001 which merged into Per-Se Technologies, Inc. 1/6/2006
(See Per-Se Technologies, Inc.)

CIS-TEX, INC. (TX)
Charter forfeited for failure to pay taxes 1/13/67

CISCO DOME RES INC (UT)
Reorganized 05/10/1983
Each share Common $0.001 par exchanged for (0.05) share Common no par 05/03/1982
Reorganized from Cisco Dome Oil & Gas Corp. to Cisco Dome Resources, Inc. 05/10/1983
Each share Common no par exchanged for (5) shares Common no par
Involuntarily dissolved 03/31/1985

CISCO GROUP, INC. (CO)
Adjudicated bankrupt 07/14/1966
No stockholders' equity

CISCO RES LTD (BC)
Recapitalized as Consolidated Cisco Resources Ltd. 8/9/88
Each share Common no par exchanged for (0.5) share Common no par
Consolidated Cisco Resources Ltd. name changed to Inca Gold Ltd. 9/5/91 which name changed to Airpro Industries Inc. 12/10/92 which recapitalized as Camelot Industries Inc. 5/8/95 which merged into DC Diagnosticare, Inc. 7/15/96
(See DC Diagnosticare, Inc.)

CISTRON BIOTECHNOLOGY INC (DE)
Merged into Celltech Group PLC 11/07/2000
Each share Common 1¢ par exchanged for (0.0202) Sponsored ADR for Ordinary
(See Celltech Group PLC)

CIT GROUP INC NEW (DE)
Plan of reorganization under Chapter 11 Federal Bankruptcy proceedings effective 12/10/2009
Preferred holders are expected to receive an undetermined amount of contingent value rights
Each Corporate Unit received $1.7778785 principal amount of 7% Notes due 05/01/2013, $2.6668177 principal amount of 7% Notes due 05/01/2014, $2.6668177 principal amount of 7% Notes due 05/01/2015, $4.4446962 principal amount of 7% Notes due 05/01/2016, $6.2225747 principal amount of 7% Notes due 05/01/2017 and (0.1530357) share new Common 1¢ par
No stockholders' equity for old Common
(Additional Information in Active)

CIT GROUP INC OLD (DE)
Merged into Tyco International Ltd. (Bermuda) 06/01/2001
Each share Class A Common 1¢ par exchanged for (0.6907) share Common 20¢ par
Tyco International Ltd. (Bermuda) reincorporated in Switzerland 03/17/2009 which merged into Johnson Controls International PLC 09/06/2016

CITA BIOMEDICAL INC (DE)
Reincorporated 05/29/2002
State of incorporation changed from (CO) to (DE) 05/29/2002
Recapitalized as Xino Corp. 01/07/2005
Each share Common 1¢ par exchanged for (0.04) share Common 1¢ par
Xino Corp. reorganized as AsherXino Corp. 08/19/2009
(See AsherXino Corp.)

CITADEL ASSET MGMT LTD (CO)
Name changed to Citadel Environmental Group, Inc. 08/12/1996
Citadel Environmental Group, Inc. recapitalized as SAN Holdings, Inc. 03/02/2000
(See SAN Holdings, Inc.)

CITADEL BROADCASTING CO (NV)
13.25% Exchangeable Preferred Ser. A 144A called for redemption at $113.25 on 08/02/1999
99.96% of 13.25% Exchangeable Preferred Ser. B no par acquired at $121.063 per share through purchase offer which expired 06/26/2001
13.25% Exchangeable Preferred Ser. B no par called for redemption at $107.73 on 07/01/2002

CITADEL BROADCASTING CORP (DE)
Each share Common 1¢ par received distribution of $2.46 cash payable 06/12/2007 to holders of record 06/08/2007 Ex date - 06/13/2007
Plan of reorganization under Chapter 11 Federal Bankruptcy proceedings effective 06/03/2010
No Common stockholders' equity
Merged into Cumulus Media Inc. 09/16/2011
Each share Class A Common $0.001 par exchanged for (1.521) shares Class A Common 1¢ par and $30.40 cash
Each share Class B Common $0.001 par exchanged for (1.521) shares Class A Common 1¢ par and $30.40 cash

CITADEL CAP CORP (ON)
Retractable 1st Preferred Ser. A no par called for redemption at $25 on 12/23/1992

CITADEL COMMUNICATIONS CORP (NV)
Merged into FLCC Holdings, Inc. 06/27/2001
Each share Class A Common exchanged for $26 cash
Each share Common $0.001 par exchanged for $26 cash

CITADEL COMPUTER SYS INC (DE)
Name changed to Citadel Technology Inc. 02/27/1998
Citadel Technology Inc. name changed to CT Holdings, Inc. 11/30/1999 which recapitalized as CT Holdings Enterprises, Inc. 02/28/2007 which recapitalized as Xcorporeal, Inc. 10/15/2007

CITADEL DIVERSIFIED INVT TR (ON)
Each Installment Receipt no par exchanged for (1) Trust Unit no par 09/16/1998
Name changed to Blue Ribbon Income Fund 11/20/2009

CITADEL ENVIRONMENTAL GROUP INC (CO)
Recapitalized as SAN Holdings, Inc. 03/02/2000
Each (36) shares Common no par exchanged for (1) share Common no par
(See SAN Holdings, Inc.)

CITADEL FUND, INC. (FL)
Reincorporated under the laws of Maryland as American National Growth Fund, Inc. 08/01/1968
American National Growth Fund, Inc. name changed to SM&R Growth Fund, Inc. 01/01/1999
(See SM&R Growth Fund, Inc.)

CITADEL GOLD MINES INC (ON)
Recapitalized as Anconia Resources Corp. 06/20/2011
Each share Common no par exchanged for (0.2) share Common no par

CITADEL HLDG CORP (NV)
Reincorporated 01/05/2000
Reorganized from under the laws of (DE) to (NV) 01/05/2000
Each share Common 1¢ par exchanged for (0.8) share Non-Vtg. Class A Common 1¢ par and (0.2) share Class B Common 1¢ par
Under plan of merger name changed

to Reading International, Inc. 12/31/2001

CITADEL HYTES FD (AB)
Trust Units no par split (2) for (1) by issuance of (1) additional Unit payable 11/15/2005 to holders of record 11/15/2005 Ex date - 11/10/2005
Under plan of merger each Trust Unit no par automatically became (1.7545) Citadel Income Fund Trust Units no par 12/02/2009

CITADEL INCOME & GROWTH FD (AB)
Merged into Citadel Premium Income Fund 07/20/2006
Each Trust Unit no par exchanged for (0.945) Trust Unit no par
Citadel Premium Income Fund merged into Citadel Income Fund 12/02/2009

CITADEL INDS INC (DE)
Reincorporated 08/17/1966
State of incorporation changed from (NY) to (DE) 08/17/1966
Plan of Participation Fund completed
Bearer Ctfs. of Participation no par stamped to indicate initial distribution of $1.50 cash per share 07/16/1968
Bearer Ctfs. of Participation no par stamped to indicate second distribution of $2.50 cash per share 01/29/1969
Bearer Ctfs. of Participation no par stamped to indicate third distribution of 30¢ cash per share 07/05/1972
Bearer Ctfs. of Participation no par stamped to indicate fourth distribution of $1.25 cash per share 03/17/1975
Each Bearer Ctf. of Participation no par exchanged for fifth and final distribution of $0.366 cash per share 08/02/1976
Stock Dividend - 100% 08/31/1966
Liquidation completed
Each share Common $1 par received initial distribution of $11 cash 05/31/1973
Each share Common $1 par received second distribution of $1.50 cash 03/07/1974
Each share Common $1 par received third distribution of $1.50 cash 03/19/1975
Each share Common $1 par received fourth distribution of $1.50 cash 05/18/1976
Each share Common $1 par exchanged for fifth and final distribution of $4.5006 cash 11/26/1976

CITADEL INVT SYS INC (CO)
Name changed to Sangui BioTech International, Inc. 10/20/1997

CITADEL LIFE INS CO N Y (NY)
Voting Trust Agreement terminated 09/09/1965
Each VTC for Common $10 par exchanged for (1) share Common $10 par
Common $10 par changed to $5 par 12/31/1966
Common $5 par changed to $2.50 par 05/17/1968
Common $2.50 par changed to $1.40 par 09/04/1970
Common $1.40 par changed to $1 par 09/20/1972
Merged into American General Life Insurance Co. of New York 04/01/1977
Each share Common $1 par exchanged for $8 cash

CITADEL MULTI-SECTOR INCOME FD (AB)
Merged into Citadel Premium Income Fund 07/20/2006
Each Trust Unit no par exchanged for (0.976) Trust Unit no par

Citadel Premium Income Fund merged into Citadel Income Fund 12/02/2009

CITADEL PREM INCOME FD (AB)
Under plan of merger each Trust Unit no par automatically became (1.1581) Citadel Income Fund Trust Units no par 12/02/2009

CITADEL S-1 INCOME TR FD (AB)
Trust Units no par split (2) for (1) by issuance of (1) additional Unit payable 11/15/2005 to holders of record 11/15/2005 Ex date - 11/10/2005
Under plan of merger each Trust Unit no par automatically became (1.8629) Citadel Income Fund Trust Units no par 12/02/2009

CITADEL SEC SOFTWARE INC (DE)
Assets transferred to CDSS Wind Down Inc. 12/19/2006
CDSS Wind Down Inc. recapitalized as Green Energy Management Services Holdings, Inc. 09/22/2010

CITADEL SMART FD (AB)
Merged into Energy Income Fund 03/27/2012
Each Trust Unit exchanged for (3.074) Trust Units

CITADEL STABLE S-1 INCOME FD (AB)
Under plan of merger each Unit no par automatically became (1.0765) Citadel Income Fund Trust Units no par 12/02/2009

CITADEL TECHNOLOGY INC (DE)
Name changed to CT Holdings, Inc. 11/30/1999
CT Holdings, Inc. recapitalized as CT Holdings Enterprises, Inc. 02/28/2007 which recapitalized as Xcorporeal, Inc. 10/15/2007

CITATION COMPUTER SYS INC (MO)
Merged into Cerner Corp. 08/22/2000
Each share Common 10¢ par exchanged for (0.1526) share Common 1¢ par and $0.51 cash

CITATION CORP (DE)
Merged into Kelso & Co. 12/01/1999
Each share Common 1¢ par exchanged for $17 cash

CITATION CORP (MN)
Statutorily dissolved 10/07/1991

CITATION COS INC (MI)
Reincorporated 05/31/1977
State of incorporation changed from (DE) to (MI) 05/31/1977
Stock Dividends - 10% 12/01/1976; 10% 09/01/1977
Acquired by Citation Walther Co. 12/11/1980
Each share Common $1 par exchanged for $15 cash

CITATION GOLD CORP (BC)
Name changed to Cogenix Power Corp. 09/11/1992
Cogenix Power Corp. recapitalized as Global Cogenix Industrial Corp. 07/25/1996 which recapitalized as Highwater Power Corp. 07/11/2006
(See Highwater Power Corp.)

CITATION INS GROUP (CA)
Under plan of merger name changed to PICO Holdings Inc. (CA) 11/20/1996
PICO Holdings Inc. (CA) reincorporated in Delaware 05/31/2017

CITATION MFG INC (AR)
Adjudicated bankrupt 03/05/1979
Stockholders' equity unlikely

CITATION MINES LTD. (BC)
Struck off register for failure to file returns 00/00/1965

CITATION OILS LTD. (ON)
Merged into Consolidated East Crest Oil Co. Ltd. 01/20/1956
Each share Capital Stock $1 par exchanged for (0.25) share Capital Stock no par
Consolidated East Crest Oil Co. Ltd. liquidated for Pan Ocean Oil Corp. 01/01/1972
(See Pan Ocean Oil Corp.)

CITATION RES INC (BC)
Recapitalized as Macarthur Diamonds Ltd. (BC) 10/24/2002
Each share Common no par exchanged for (0.4) share Common no par
Macarthur Diamonds Ltd. (BC) reincorporated in Australia 12/02/2002 which recapitalized as Macarthur Minerals Ltd. 07/07/2005

CITATION RES INC (ON)
Merged into Inlet Resources Ltd. 07/08/2014
Each share Common no par exchanged for (0.5) share Common no par
Note: Unexchanged certificates will be cancelled and become without value 07/08/2020
Inlet Resources Ltd. name changed to Guerrero Ventures Inc. 08/19/2014

CITATION SILVER MINES LTD (BC)
Struck off register and declared dissolved for failure to file returns 10/21/1974

CITCO GROWTH INVTS LTD (BC)
Reincorporated 05/31/1989
Place of incorporation changed from (Canada) to (BC) 05/31/1989
Each share old 6% Preferred no par exchanged for (0.001) share new 6% Preferred no par 05/08/1990
Name changed to First Global Investments Inc. 07/28/2005

CITEL INC (CA)
Plan of reorganization under Chapter 11 Federal Bankruptcy proceedings confirmed 12/12/1985
No stockholders' equity

CITEX MINES LTD (BC)
Recapitalized as Consolidated Citex Resources Inc. 07/18/1975
Each share Common 50¢ par exchanged for (0.2) share Common no par
Consolidated Citex Resources Inc. recapitalized as Pacific Foam Form, Inc. 12/17/1979
(See Pacific Foam Form, Inc.)

CITFED BANCORP INC (DE)
Common 1¢ par split (3) for (2) by issuance of (0.5) additional share payable 11/29/1996 to holders of record 11/15/1996
Common 1¢ par split (3) for (2) by issuance of (0.5) additional share payable 11/28/1997 to holders of record 11/14/1997
Merged into Fifth Third Bancorp 06/26/1998
Each share Common 1¢ par exchanged for (1.005) shares Common no par

CITI BANCSHARES INC (FL)
Each share old Common 10¢ par exchanged for (10) shares new Common 1¢ par 03/09/1989
Merged into Huntington Bancshares Inc. 02/28/1997
Each share Common 1¢ par exchanged for either (0.9983) share Common no par, (0.5990) share Common no par and $12 cash, or $30 cash
Note: Option for holders of (100) or more shares to receive cash and stock or cash only expired 03/31/1997
Holdings of (99) shares or fewer received cash

CITIBANK N A (NY)
Fixed Adjustable Rate Preferred Ser. A called for redemption at $100 plus $0.246556 accrued dividends on 12/29/2005
Fixed Adjustable Rate Preferred Ser. B called for redemption at $100 plus $0.253167 accrued dividends on 12/29/2005

CITIBANK WEST FSB (SAN FRANCISCO, CA)
U.S. Supreme Court denied petition for a writ of certiorari in California Federal Bank v. United States 10/05/2005
As a consequence holders of Contingent Litigation Recovery Participation Interests will not receive any payment as expenses exceeded judgment amount

CITIC PAC LTD (HONG KONG)
Name changed to CITIC Ltd. 10/23/2014

CITICASTERS INC (FL)
Class A Common 1¢ par split (3) for (2) by issuance of (0.5) additional share 05/04/1995
Class A Common 1¢ par split (3) for (2) by issuance of (0.5) additional share 11/30/1995
Merged into Jacor Communications, Inc. 09/18/1996
Each share Class A Common 1¢ par exchanged for $29.50 cash

CITICORP (DE)
Money Market Preferred Ser. 5A no par split (5) for (1) by issuance of (4) additional shares 04/24/1987
Money Market Preferred Ser. 5B no par split (5) for (1) by issuance of (4) additional shares 04/24/1987
Money Market Preferred Ser. 5C no par split (5) for (1) by issuance of (4) additional shares 04/24/1987
Money Market Preferred Ser. 5D no par split (5) for (1) by issuance of (4) additional shares 04/24/1987
Money Market Preferred Ser. 5E no par split (5) for (1) by issuance of (4) additional shares 04/24/1987
Money Market Preferred Ser. 5F no par split (5) for (1) by issuance of (4) additional shares 04/24/1987
Money Market Preferred Ser. 5G no par split (5) for (1) by issuance of (4) additional shares 04/24/1987
Common $4 par changed to $1 par 04/21/1987
Common $1 par split (2) for (1) by issuance of (1) additional share 11/09/1987
Price Adjustable Rate Preferred 4th Ser. no par called for redemption 09/01/1994
9.12% Preferred Ser. 9 no par called for redemption 07/21/1995
Conv. Depository Preferred Ser. 13 called for redemption 02/20/1996
Conv. Preferred Ser. 13 no par called for redemption 02/20/1996
9.08% Depositary Preferred Ser. 14 called for redemption 03/17/1997
9.08% Preferred Ser. 14 no par called for redemption 03/17/1997
Adjustable Rate Preferred 2nd Ser. no par called for redemption at $100 on 02/28/1998
Adjustable Rate Preferred 3rd Ser. no par called for redemption at $100 on 02/28/1998
8% Depositary Preferred Ser. 16 called for redemption at $25 on 06/01/1998
Graduated Rate Preferred Ser. 8A no par called for redemption at $100 on 08/15/1998
7.5% Depositary Preferred 17 called for redemption 09/01/1998
Merged into Citigroup Inc. 10/08/1998
Each share Common $1 par exchanged for (2.5) shares Common 1¢ par
Under plan of merger name changed to Citigroup Inc. and Adjustable Depositary Preferred Ser. 18 $1 par,

Adjustable Depositary Preferred Ser. 19 $1 par, 8.30% Depositary Preferred Ser. 20 $1 par, 8.50% Depositary Preferred Ser. 21 $1 par, 7.75% Depositary Preferred Ser. 22 $1 par, Adjustable Depositary Preferred Ser. 23 $1 par, Graduated Rate Preferred Ser. 8B $1 par, 7.50% Preferred Ser. 17 $1 par, Adjustable Dividend Preferred Ser. 18 $1 par, Adjustable Dividend Preferred Ser. 19 $1 par, 8.30% Preferred Ser. 20 $1 par, 8.50% Preferred Ser. 21 $1 par, and 7.75% Preferred Ser. 22 $1 par, reclassified as Adjustable Depositary Preferred Ser. Q $1 par, Adjustable Preferred Ser. R $1 par, 8.30% Depositary Preferred Ser. S $1 par, 8.50% Depositary Preferred Ser. T $1 par, 7.75% Depositary Preferred Ser. U $1 par, 6.365% Preferred Ser. F $1 par, Graduated Rate Preferred Ser. O $1 par, 6.365% Preferred Ser. F $1 par, Adjustable Rate Preferred Ser. Q $1 par, Adjustable Rate Preferred Ser. R $1 par, 8.3% Preferred Ser. S $1 par, 6.365% Preferred Ser. F $1 par and 7.75% Preferred Ser. U $1 par respectively 10/08/1998

CITICORP CAP III (DE)
7.1% Capital Securities Preferred called for redemption at $25 on 10/03/2003 06/19/1998

CITIES SVC CO (DE)
Each share Common $20 par exchanged for (4) shares Common no par 00/00/1929

Each share Common no par exchanged for (0.1) share Common $10 par 00/00/1938

Common $10 par split (5) for (2) by issuance of (1.5) additional shares 03/07/1955

Common $10 par changed to $5 par and (1) additional share issued 10/27/1965

$2.25 Conv. Preference no par called for redemption 11/02/1970

$4.40 Conv. Preferred no par called for redemption 11/02/1970

Common $5 par changed to $2 par and (2) additional shares issued 06/09/1980

Merged into Occidental Petroleum Corp. (CA) 12/03/1982

Each share Common $2 par exchanged for $3.32 principal amount of Zero Coupon Guaranteed Notes due 12/03/1985, $3.98 principal amount of Zero Coupon Guaranteed Notes due 12/03/1986, $4.42 principal amount of Zero Coupon Guaranteed Notes due 12/03/1987, $5.97 principal amount of Zero Coupon Guaranteed Notes due 12/03/1988, $7.63 principal amount of Zero Coupon Guaranteed Notes due 12/03/1989 of Cities Service Co. and (0.41) share Occidental Petroleum Corp. $15.50 Preferred $1 par

(See Occidental Petroleum Corp. (CA))

CITIES SERVICE POWER & LIGHT CO.
Liquidated 00/00/1944
Details not available

CITIES SERVICE REFINING CO. (MA)
Reorganized 00/00/1936
No stockholders' equity

CITIES SERVICE SUPPLY CORP.
Name changed to Southern Cities Supply Co. 00/00/1927
(See Southern Cities Supply Co.)

CITIFUNDS TAX FREE RESVS (MA)
Name changed to Citi Tax Free Reserves 12/28/2000

CITIGOLD CORP LTD (AUSTRALIA)
ADR agreement terminated 03/07/2016
Each Sponsored ADR for Ordinary exchanged for $0.161912 cash

CITIGROUP CAP I (DE)
8% Trust Preferred Securities called for redemption at $25 on 01/07/2002

CITIGROUP CAP IV (DE)
6.85% Guaranteed Preferred Trust Securities called for redemption at $25 on 03/03/2003

CITIGROUP CAP V (DE)
7% Guaranteed Trust Preferred Securities called for redemption at $25 on 11/15/2003

CITIGROUP CAP VI (DE)
6.875% Trust Preferred Securities called for redemption at $25 on 10/14/2004

CITIGROUP CAP VII (DE)
7.125% Capital Securities called for redemption at $25 plus $0.301823 accrued dividends on 04/16/2013

CITIGROUP CAP VIII (DE)
6.95% Capital Securities called for redemption at $25 plus $0.149618 accrued dividends on 04/16/2013

CITIGROUP CAP IX (DE)
6% Trust Preferred Securities called for redemption at $25 plus $0.3125 accrued dividends on 04/28/2014

CITIGROUP CAP X (DE)
6.1% Trust Preferred Securities called for redemption at $25 plus $0.38125 accrued dividends on 10/01/2013

CITIGROUP CAP XI (DE)
6% Trust Preferred Securities called for redemption at $25 plus $0.12917 accrued dividends on 04/28/2014

CITIGROUP CAP XII (DE)
8.5% Fixed Rate/Floating Rate Trust Preferred Securities called for redemption at $25 plus $0.53125 accrued dividends on 07/18/2012

CITIGROUP CAP XIV (DE)
6.875% Enhanced Trust Preferred Securities called for redemption at $25 plus $0.076389 accrued dividends on 04/16/2013

CITIGROUP CAP XV (DE)
6.5% Enhanced Trust Preferred Securities called for redemption at $25 plus $0.139931 accrued dividends on 04/16/2013

CITIGROUP CAP XVI (DE)
6.45% Enhanced Trust Preferred Securities called for redemption at $25 plus $0.067188 accrued dividends on 07/15/2013

CITIGROUP CAP XVII (DE)
6.35% Enhanced Trust Preferred Securities called for redemption at $25 plus $0.18962 accrued dividends on 04/28/2014

CITIGROUP CAP XIX (DE)
7.25% Enhanced Trust Preferred Securities called for redemption at $25 plus $0.3021 accrued dividends on 08/15/2012

CITIGROUP CAP XX (DE)
7.875% Enhanced Trust Preferred Securities called for redemption at $25 plus $0.503125 accrued dividends on 12/17/2012

CITIGROUP FDG INC (DE)
Premium Mandatory Callable Equity Linked Securities based on Petrochina Co., Ltd. called for redemption at $11.45 on 11/09/2006
Premium Mandatory Callable Equity Linked Securities based on Valero Energy Corp. called for redemption at $11.30 on 04/27/2007
Premium Mandatory Callable Equity Linked Securities based on Cemex, S.A.B. de C.V. called for redemption at $10.50 plus $0.17889 accrued dividends on 05/01/2007
Each Equity Linked Security based on Toll Brothers, Inc. exchanged for (0.33979) share Common 1¢ par 11/05/2007

CITIGROUP GLOBAL MKTS HLDGS INC (NY)
Premium Mandatory Callable Equity-Linked Securities based upon JPMorgan Chase & Co. Common called for redemption at $10.90 on 12/12/2005

CITIGROUP INC (DE)
8.08% Depositary Preferred Ser. J called for redemption at $25 plus $0.230056 accrued dividends on 02/11/1999
Graduated Rate Preferred Ser. O $1 par called for redemption at $100 on 08/15/1999
8.3% Depositary Preferred Ser. S called for redemption at $25 on 11/15/1999
8.5% Depositary Preferred Ser. T called for redemption at $25 on 02/15/2000
8.4% Depositary Preferred Ser. K called for redemption at $25 plus $0.2975 accrued dividends on 11/21/2001
7.75% Depositary Preferred Ser. U called for redemption at $25 on 01/07/2002
Adjustable Rate Preferred Ser. Q $1 par called for redemption at $25 on 03/03/2003
Adjustable Depositary Preferred Ser. QQ $1 par called for redemption at $25 on 03/03/2003
Adjustable Rate Preferred Ser. R $1 par called for redemption at $25 on 03/03/2003
Adjustable Depositary Preferred Ser. RR called for redemption at $25 on 03/03/2003
Fixed Adjustable Depositary Preferred Ser. V called for redemption at $50 on 02/15/2006
6.365% Depositary Preferred Ser. F called for redemption at $50 plus $0.795625 accrued dividends on 06/18/2007
6.213% Depositary Preferred Ser. G called for redemption at $50 plus $0.353793 accrued dividends on 07/11/2007
6.213% Depositary Preferred Ser. H called for redemption at $50 plus $0.510591 accrued dividends on 09/10/2007
5.864% Depositary Preferred Ser. M called for redemption at $50 plus $0.5538 accrued dividends on 10/09/2007
6.5% Depositary Preferred Ser. T called for redemption at $50 plus $0.28889 accrued dividends on 06/17/2013
8.5% Depositary Preferred Ser. F called for redemption at $25 on 06/17/2013
8.125% Depositary Preferred Ser. AA called for redemption at $25 on 02/15/2018
5.8% Depositary Preferred Ser. C called for redemption at $25 on 10/22/2018
(Additional Information in Active)

CITIGROUP INVTS CORPORATE LN FD INC (MD)
Name changed to LMP Corporate Loan Fund Inc. 10/09/2006
LMP Corporate Loan Fund Inc. name changed to Western Asset Corporate Loan Fund Inc. 04/04/2016

CITINATIONAL DEV TR (CA)
Liquidation completed
Each Share of Bene. Int. $1 par received initial distribution of $2.50 cash 09/28/1984
Each Share of Bene. Int. $1 par received second distribution of $3 cash 02/28/1986
Each Share of Bene. Int. $1 par received third distribution of $4.75 cash 09/15/1987
Each Share of Bene. Int. $1 par received fourth and final distribution of $3.03 cash 07/12/1993

CITIPOSTAL INC (DE)
Common 1¢ par split (2) for (1) by issuance of (1) additional share 9/3/84
Each share Common 1¢ par exchanged for (0.25) share Common 4¢ par 2/4/87
Filed a petition under Chapter 11 Federal Bankruptcy Code 9/28/98
Details not available

CITIRAYA INDS LTD (SINGAPORE)
ADR agreement terminated 03/15/2007
No ADR's remain outstanding

CITISAVE FINL CORP (LA)
Merged into Deposit Guaranty Corp. 07/31/1997
Each share Common 1¢ par exchanged for $20.50 cash

CITISOURCE INC NEW (DE)
Name changed to Cannon Exploration, Inc. 04/08/2008

CITISOURCE INC OLD (DE)
Recapitalized as China Shuangji Cement Corp. 06/28/2006
Each (5.8) shares Common 1¢ par exchanged for (1) share Common 1¢ par
China Shuangji Cement Corp. recapitalized as Citisource, Inc. (New) 10/02/2007 which name changed to Cannon Exploration, Inc. 04/08/2008

CITIWIDE CAP CORP (DE)
Charter cancelled and declared inoperative and void for non-payment of taxes 03/01/1987

CITIZEN HLDGS CO LTD (JAPAN)
Name changed to Citizen Watch Co., Ltd. 10/03/2016

CITIZENS & FMRS BK (WEST POINT, VA)
Under plan of reorganization each share Common $1 par automatically became (1) share C&F Financial Corp. Common $1 par 03/07/1994

CITIZENS & MANUFACTURERS NATIONAL BANK (WATERBURY, CT)
Each share Capital Stock $100 par exchanged for (4) shares Capital Stock $25 par 00/00/1948
Stock Dividend - 33.33333333% 01/18/1956
Merged into Colonial Bank & Trust Co. (Waterbury, CT) 06/30/1959
Each share Capital Stock $25 par exchanged for (2) shares Capital Stock $10 par
Colonial Bank & Trust Co. (Waterbury, CT) reorganized as Colonial Bancorp, Inc. (CT) 06/01/1970 which merged into Bank of Boston Corp. 06/20/1985 which name changed to BankBoston Corp. 04/25/1997 which merged into Fleet Boston Corp. 10/01/1999 which name changed to FleetBoston Financial Corp. 04/18/2000 which merged into Bank of America Corp. 04/01/2004

CITIZENS & NORTHERN BANK (WELLSBORO, PA)
Reorganized as Citizens & Northern Corp. 06/01/1987
Each share Common $5 par exchanged for (4) shares Common $1 par

CITIZENS & SOUTHERN BANK (TUCKER, GA)
Acquired by Citizens & Southern

National Bank (Savannah, GA) 01/02/1976
Each share Capital Stock $10 par exchanged for (23.7) shares Capital Stock $2.50 par

CITIZENS & SOUTHERN BANK OF CLAYTON COUNTY (FOREST PARK, GA)
Merged into Citizens & Southern Georgia Corp. 12/31/1981
Each share Common Capital Stock $1 par exchanged for $123.35 cash

CITIZENS & SOUTHERN BANK OF EFFINGHAM COUNTY (SPRINGFIELD, GA)
Merged into Citizens & Southern Georgia Corp. 09/01/1984
Each share Capital Stock $10 par exchanged for (5.4118583) shares Common $2.50 par
Citizens & Southern Georgia Corp. name changed to Citizens & Southern Corp. 05/20/1986 which merged into C&S/Sovran Corp. 09/01/1990 which merged into NationsBank Corp. (NC) 12/31/1991 which reincorporated in Delaware as BankAmerica Corp. (Old) 09/25/1998 which merged into BankAmerica Corp. (New) 09/30/1998 which name changed to Bank of America Corp. 04/28/1999

CITIZENS & SOUTHERN BANK OF HOUSTON COUNTY (WARNER ROBINS, GA)
Acquired by Citizens & Southern Georgia Corp. 05/31/1982
Each share Common $5 par exchanged for $46 principal amount of 14% Notes due 05/31/1987 and $20 cash

CITIZENS & SOUTHERN BANK OF NORTH FULTON (ROSWELL, GA)
Acquired by Citizens & Southern National Bank (Savannah, GA) 10/31/1975
Each share Capital Stock $10 par exchanged for (10) shares Capital Stock $2.50 par
Citizens & Southern National Bank (Savannah, GA) reorganized as Citizens & Southern Georgia Corp. 12/31/1980 which name changed to Citizens & Southern Corp. 05/20/1986 which merged into C&S/Sovran Corp. 09/01/1990 which merged into NationsBank Corp. (NC) 12/31/1991 which reincorporated in Delaware as BankAmerica Corp. (Old) 09/25/1998 which merged into BankAmerica Corp. (New) 09/30/1998 which name changed to Bank of America Corp. 04/28/1999

CITIZENS & SOUTHERN BANK OF SANDY SPRINGS (ATLANTA, GA)
Acquired by Citizens & Southern National Bank (Savannah, GA) 10/31/1975
Each share Capital Stock $10 par exchanged for (20.51) shares Capital Stock $2.50 par
Citizens & Southern National Bank (Savannah, GA) reorganized as Citizens & Southern Georgia Corp. 12/31/1980 which name changed to Citizens & Southern Corp. 05/20/1986 which merged into C&S/Sovran Corp. 09/01/1990 which merged into NationsBank Corp. (NC) 12/31/1991 which reincorporated in Delaware as BankAmerica Corp. (Old) 09/25/1998 which merged into BankAmerica Corp. (New) 09/30/1998 which name changed to Bank of America Corp. 04/28/1999

CITIZENS & SOUTHERN BANK OF WEST GEORGIA (LA GRANGE, GA)
Acquired by Citizens & Southern National Bank of Georgia (Atlanta, GA) 12/31/1985
Details not available

CITIZENS & SOUTHERN GEORGIA CORP. (GA)
Name changed to Citizens & Southern Corp. 05/20/1986
Citizens & Southern Corp. merged into C&S/Sovran Corp. 09/01/1990 which merged into NationsBank Corp. (NC) 12/31/1991 which reincorporated in Delaware as BankAmerica Corp. (Old) 09/25/1998 which merged into BankAmerica Corp. (New) 09/30/1998 which name changed to Bank of America Corp. 04/28/1999

CITIZENS & SOUTHERN NATIONAL BANK OF GEORGIA (SAVANNAH, GA)
Stock Dividend - 10% 02/01/1968
Name changed back to Citizens & Southern National Bank (Savannah, GA) 02/01/1969
Citizens & Southern National Bank (Savannah, GA) reorganized as Citizens & Southern Georgia Corp. 12/31/1980 which name changed to Citizens & Southern Corp. 05/20/1986 which merged into C&S/Sovran Corp. 09/01/1990 which merged into NationsBank Corp. (NC) 12/31/1991 which reincorporated in Delaware as BankAmerica Corp. (Old) 09/25/1998 which merged into BankAmerica Corp. (New) 09/30/1998 which name changed to Bank of America Corp. 04/28/1999

CITIZENS & SOUTHERN NATIONAL BANK OF SANDY SPRINGS (ATLANTA, GA)
Name changed to Citizens & Southern Bank of Sandy Springs (Atlanta, GA) 10/01/1969
Citizens & Southern Bank of Sandy Springs (Atlanta, GA) acquired by Citizens & Southern National Bank (Savannah, GA) 10/31/1975 which reorganized as Citizens & Southern Georgia Corp. 12/31/1980 which name changed to Citizens & Southern Corp. 05/20/1986 which merged into C&S/Sovran Corp. 09/01/1990 which merged into NationsBank Corp. (NC) 12/31/1991 which reincorporated in Delaware as BankAmerica Corp. (Old) 09/25/1998 which merged into BankAmerica Corp. (New) 09/30/1998 which name changed to Bank of America Corp. 04/28/1999

CITIZENS & SOUTHERN PARK NATIONAL BANK (ATLANTA, GA)
Acquired by Citizens & Southern National Bank (Savannah, GA) 10/31/1975
Each share Common $10 par exchanged for (6.4) shares Capital Stock $2.50 par

CITIZENS & SOUTHERN SOUTH DEKALB BANK (DECATUR, GA)
Acquired by Citizens & Southern National Bank (Savannah, GA) 10/31/1975
Each share Common Capital Stock $10 par exchanged for (5.09) shares Capital Stock $2.50 par

CITIZENS & SOUTHN BK (ALBANY, GA)
Acquired by Citizens & Southern National Bank of Georgia (Atlanta, GA) 12/31/1985
Details not available

CITIZENS & SOUTHN BK (LA GRANGE, GA)
Name changed to Citizens & Southern Bank of West Georgia (La Grange, GA) 07/05/1972
(See Citizens & Southern Bank of West Georgia (La Grange, GA))

CITIZENS & SOUTHN CAP CORP (GA)
Completely liquidated 05/30/1973
Each share Common $1 par exchanged for first and final distribution of (0.5757) share Citizens & Southern National Bank (Savannah, GA) Capital Stock $2.50 par
Citizens & Southern National Bank (Savannah, GA) reorganized as Citizens & Southern Georgia Corp. 12/31/1980 which name changed to Citizens & Southern Corp. 05/20/1986 which merged into C&S/Sovran Corp. 09/01/1990 which merged into NationsBank Corp. (NC) 12/31/1991 which reincorporated in Delaware as BankAmerica Corp. (Old) 09/25/1998 which merged into BankAmerica Corp. (New) 09/30/1998 which name changed to Bank of America Corp. 04/28/1999

CITIZENS & SOUTHN CORP (DE)
Common $5 par changed to $2.50 par and (1) additional share issued 04/15/1973
Common $2.50 par split (2) for (1) by issuance of (1) additional share 08/15/1983
Stock Dividend - 10% 10/02/1978
Acquired by Citizens & Southern Georgia Corp. 03/31/1986
Each share Common $2.50 par exchanged for $55 cash

CITIZENS & SOUTHN CORP (GA)
Merged into C&S/Sovran Corp. 09/01/1990
Each share Money Market Preferred Ser. A no par exchanged for (1) share Common $1 par
Each share Money Market Preferred Ser. B no par exchanged for (1) share Common $1 par
Each share Common $2.50 par exchanged for (1) share Common $1 par
C&S/Sovran Corp. merged into NationsBank Corp. (NC) 12/31/1991 which reincorporated in Delaware as BankAmerica Corp. (Old) 09/25/1998 which merged into BankAmerica Corp. (New) 09/30/1998 which name changed to Bank of America Corp. 04/28/1999

CITIZENS & SOUTHN NATL BK (SAVANNAH, GA)
Capital Stock $10 par changed to $5 par and (1) additional share issued plus a 10% stock dividend paid 01/22/1965
Name changed to Citizens & Southern National Bank of Georgia (Savannah, GA) 01/29/1968 which name changed back to Citizens & Southern National Bank (Savannah, GA) 02/01/1969
Capital Stock $5 par changed to $2.50 par and (1) additional share issued 01/07/1970
Capital Stock $2.50 par changed to $5 par 02/12/1971
Capital Stock $5 par changed to $2.50 par and (1) additional share issued 02/28/1973
Stock Dividends - 10% 01/21/1966; 10% 02/08/1967; 10% 02/01/1969
Under plan of reorganization each share Capital Stock $2.50 par automatically became (1) share Citizens & Southern Georgia Corp. Common $2.50 par 12/31/1980
Citizens & Southern Georgia Corp. name changed to Citizens & Southern Corp. 05/20/1986 which merged into C&S/Sovran Corp. 09/01/1990 which merged into NationsBank Corp. (NC) 12/31/1991 which reincorporated in Delaware as BankAmerica Corp. (Old) 09/25/1998 which merged into BankAmerica Corp. (New) 09/30/1998 which name changed to Bank of America Corp. 04/28/1999

CITIZENS & SOUTHN NATL BK S C (CHARLESTON, SC)
Common $10 par changed to $5 par and (1) additional share issued plus a 10% stock dividend paid 02/09/1968
Stock Dividends - 10% 04/27/1959; 10% 01/26/1961; 10% 01/31/1964; 25% 10/08/1965; 10% 07/29/1966
Reorganized as Citizens & Southern Corp. 06/30/1969
Each share Common $5 par exchanged for (1) share Common $5 par
(See Citizens & Southern Corp.)

CITIZENS & SOUTHN RLTY INVS (MD)
Name changed to Southmark Properties and Shares of Bene. Int. $1 par reclassified as Common Shares of Bene. Int. $1 par 01/31/1980
Southmark Properties reorganized as Southmark Corp. 05/01/1982

CITIZENS BANCGROUP INC (AL)
Merged into Charter Federal Savings & Loan 08/18/1999
Each share Common exchanged for $6.2043 cash

CITIZENS BANCORP (CA)
Stock Dividends - 5% payable 06/13/2005 to holders of record 05/30/2005 Ex date - 06/03/2005; 5% payable 06/14/2006 to holders of record 05/31/2006 Ex date - 05/26/2006; 5% payable 06/05/2007 to holders of record 05/22/2007 Ex date - 05/18/2007; 5% payable 06/19/2008 to holders of record 06/05/2008 Ex date - 06/03/2008
Principal asset placed in receivership 09/23/2011
Stockholders' equity unlikely

CITIZENS BANCORP (IN)
Merged into Lincoln Bancorp 09/26/2000
Each share Common no par exchanged for (0.9375) share Common no par and $9.375 cash
Lincoln Bancorp acquired by First Merchants Corp. 12/31/2008

CITIZENS BANCORP (MD)
Common $10 par changed to $2.50 par and (3) additional shares issued 04/15/1988
Merged into Crestar Financial Corp. 12/31/1996
Each share Common $2.50 par exchanged for (0.835) share Common $5 par
Crestar Financial Corp. merged into SunTrust Banks, Inc. 12/31/1998

CITIZENS BANCORP (NJ)
Liquidation completed
Each share Capital Stock no par exchanged for initial distribution of $18.75 cash 02/21/1985
Each share Capital Stock no par received second and final distribution of $0.3325 cash 05/09/1985

CITIZENS BANCORP INC (KY)
Merged into Farmers Capital Bank Corp. 12/06/2005
Each share Common no par exchanged for $72.054 cash

CITIZENS BANCORP INC (PA)
Common no par split (3) for (1) by issuance of (2) additional shares payable 05/15/1998 to holders of record 05/15/1998
Stock Dividends - 1% payable 01/19/1999 to holders of record 01/11/1999; 1% payable 01/18/2000 to holders of record 01/10/2000; 1% payable 01/19/2001 to holders of record 01/08/2001 Ex date -

01/23/2001; 1% payable 01/18/2002 to holders of record 01/07/2002
Merged into Citizens & Northern Corp. 04/30/2007
Each share Common no par exchanged for (0.6587463) share Common $1 par and $14.059297 cash

CITIZENS BANCORPORATION (WI)
Stock Dividends - 100% 06/01/1972; 10% 01/01/1977; 10% 07/01/1978; 100% 06/01/1981; 10% 05/16/1983
Name changed to First Interstate Corp. of Wisconsin 08/14/1984
First Interstate Corp. of Wisconsin acquired by Norwest Corp. 04/30/1990 which name changed to Wells Fargo & Co. (New) 11/02/1998

CITIZENS BANCORPORATION INC (FL)
Merged into SunTrust Banks, Inc. 10/01/1998
Details not available

CITIZENS BANCSHARES, INC. (TN)
Charter revoked for non-payment of taxes 01/21/1982

CITIZENS BANCSHARES FLA INC (FL)
Merged into Atlantic Bancorporation (FL) 09/30/1973
Each share Common $5 par exchanged for (1) share Common $1 par
Atlantic Bancorporation (FL) acquired by First Union Corp. 11/15/1985 which name changed to Wachovia Corp. (Ctfs. dated after 09/01/2001) 09/01/2001 which merged into Wells Fargo & Co. (New) 12/31/2008

CITIZENS BANCSHARES INC (OH)
Common no par split (3) for (2) by issuance of (0.5) additional share payable 01/12/1996 to holders of record 12/31/1995
Common no par split (2) for (1) by issuance of (1) additional share payable 06/01/1998 to holders of record 05/12/1998
Under plan of merger name changed to Sky Financial Group, Inc. 10/02/1998
Sky Financial Group, Inc. merged into Huntington Bancshares Inc. 07/02/2007

CITIZENS BANK & TRUST CO. (WARTBURG, TN)
Merged into Union Planters Corp. 11/30/1989
Each share Common no par exchanged for (173.400836) shares Common $5 par
Union Planters Corp. merged into Regions Financial Corp. (New) 07/01/2004

CITIZENS BK & TR CO (BLACKSTONE, VA)
Reorganized as Citizens Bancorp of Virginia, Inc. 12/18/2003
Each share Common 50¢ par exchanged for (1) share Common 50¢ par

CITIZENS BK & TR CO (GLASTONBURY, CT)
Merged into Bank of New England Corp. 09/30/1985
Each share Common $5 par exchanged for (1.65) shares Common $5 par
(See Bank of New England Corp)

CITIZENS BK & TR CO (MARKS, MS)
Under plan of reorganization each share Common $10 par automatically became (1) share CB&T Bancshares Corp. Common $10 par 10/01/1997

CITIZENS BK & TR CO (PALMERTON, PA)
Merged into Harleysville National Corp. 04/28/2000
Each share Common $50 par exchanged for (166) shares Common $1 par
Harleysville National Corp. merged into First Niagara Financial Group, Inc. (New) 04/09/2010 which merged into KeyCorp (New) 08/01/2016

CITIZENS BK & TR CO (SARASOTA, FL)
Capital Stock $25 par changed to $10 par and (1.5) additional shares issued 11/30/1960
Stock Dividend - 58.73% 03/15/1970
Name changed to Pan American Bank (Sarasota, FL) 05/30/1972
(See Pan American Bank (Sarasota, FL))

CITIZENS BK & TR CO MD (RIVERDALE, MD)
Stock Dividends - 10% 04/12/1971; 10.276% 04/05/1973
Under plan of reorganization each share Capital Stock $10 par automatically became (1) share Citizens Bancorp Common $10 par 05/19/1982
Citizens Bancorp merged into Crestar Financial Corp. 12/31/1996 which merged into SunTrust Banks, Inc. 12/31/1998

CITIZENS BK (CORVALLIS, OR)
Common $5 par split (2) for (1) by issuance of (1) additional share payable 10/05/1996 to holders of record 09/17/1996
Stock Dividends - 100% 03/01/1973; 10% 04/15/1977; 10% 06/15/1979; 100% 00/00/1985; 10% 00/00/1986; 10% 00/00/1987; 10% 00/00/1989; 10% 00/00/1990; 10% 00/00/1992
Under plan of reorganization each share Common $5 par automatically became (1) share Citizens Bancorp Common $5 par 07/01/1997

CITIZENS BK (COSTA MESA, CA)
Capital Stock $3 par changed to no par and (0.5) additional share issued 06/30/1980
Stock Dividend - 10% 06/29/1981
Each share Capital Stock no par exchanged for (0.0002) share Capital Stock no par 12/09/1987
Note: In effect holders received $12.50 cash per share and public interest was eliminated

CITIZENS BK (FREDERICKSBURG, OH)
Merged into Wayne Bancorp, Inc. 12/15/1986
Details not available

CITIZENS BK (HAMILTON, OH)
Capital Stock $10 par split (2) for (1) by issuance of (1) additional share 11/06/1974
Stock Dividends - 50% 05/01/1969; 11.11111111% 06/09/1972
Acquired by Society Corp. 01/06/1982
Each share Capital Stock $10 par exchanged for $53.50 cash

CITIZENS BK (HOUSTON, TX)
Capital Stock $100 par changed to $5 par and (19) additional shares issued 09/03/1969
Merged into Houston-Citizens Bank & Trust Co. (Houston, TX) 11/01/1970
Each share Capital Stock $5 par exchanged for (1) share Common $10 par
Houston-Citizens Bank & Trust Co. (Houston, TX) reorganized as First International Bancshares, Inc. 12/31/1972 which name changed to InterFirst Corp. 12/31/1981 which merged into First RepublicBank Corp. 06/06/1987
(See First RepublicBank Corp.)

CITIZENS BK (MICHIGAN CITY, IN)
Under plan of reorganization each share Common $10 par automatically became (1) share Citizens Michiana Financial Corp. Common $10 par 12/09/1982
Citizens Michiana Financial Corp. merged into Horizon Bancorp 10/01/1986 which name changed to Horizon Bancorp, Inc. 05/08/2018

CITIZENS BK (MURPHY, NC)
Stock Dividends - 10% 02/13/1987; 10% 03/21/1988
Merged into Union County Bank (Blairsville, GA) 03/14/1990
Each share Common $2.50 par exchanged for $10 cash

CITIZENS BK (PHILADELPHIA, PA)
Common $5 par changed to $2.50 par and (1) additional share issued 10/18/1968
Name changed to Centennial Bank (Philadelphia, PA) 01/07/1972
(See Centennial Bank (Philadelphia, PA))

CITIZENS BK (PIKEVILLE, KY)
Merged into Trans Financial Bancorp, Inc. 08/02/1993
Details not available

CITIZENS BK (SALINE, MI)
Common $20 par changed to $10 par and (1) additional share issued 05/17/1978
Stock Dividend - 33.33333333% 06/01/1973
Merged into Citizens Trust (Ann Arbor, MI) 12/31/1983
Each share Common $10 par exchanged for (1.4) shares Common $10 par
Citizens Trust (Ann Arbor, MI) reorganized as Citizens Trust Bancorp, Inc. 07/01/1986 which merged into Trustcorp, Inc. 09/30/1987 which was acquired by Society Corp. 01/05/1990 which merged into Keycorp (New) 03/01/1994

CITIZENS BK (SHEBOYGAN, WI)
Capital Stock $100 par changed to $10 par plus a 80% stock dividend paid 01/10/1956
Stock Dividends - 53.8% 01/02/1964; 25% 02/15/1968
Through voluntary exchange offer over 99% acquired by Citizens Bancorporation 00/00/1971
Public interest eliminated

CITIZENS BK HLDG CO (ID)
Acquired by Glacier Bancorp, Inc. 04/01/2005
Each share Common $5 par exchanged for either approximately (1.171) shares Common 1¢ par, $37.47 cash, or a combination thereof
Note: Holders of (99) or fewer shares received cash

CITIZENS BK MD (RIVERDALE, MD)
Stock Dividends - 100% 05/12/1964; 10% 01/20/1965; 10% 04/01/1966
Name changed to Citizens Bank & Trust Co. of Maryland (Riverdale, MD) 09/23/1968
Citizens Bank & Trust Co. of Maryland (Riverdale, MD) reorganized as Citizens Bancorp 05/19/1982 which merged into Crestar Financial Corp. 12/31/1996 which merged into SunTrust Banks, Inc. 12/31/1998

CITIZENS BK NEV CNTY (NEVADA CITY, CA)
Common $10 par split (2) for (1) by issuance of (1) additional share payable 05/28/1999 to holders of record 05/14/1999
Common $10 par split (5) for (4) by issuance of (0.25) additional share payable 04/23/2001 to holders of record 04/10/2001 Ex date - 04/24/2001
Under plan of reorganization each share Common $10 par automatically became (1) share Citizens Bancorp Common no par 06/01/2003
(See Citizens Bancorp)

CITIZENS BK PALM BEACH CNTY (WEST PALM BEACH, FL)
96.66% acquired by First Bancshares of Florida, Inc. through voluntary exchange offer which expired 11/15/1970
Public interest eliminated

CITIZENS BK PASO ROBLES N A (PASO ROBLES, CA)
Merged into Bank of Santa Maria (Santa Maria, CA) 05/03/1996
Each share Common no par exchanged for $16.94 cash

CITIZENS BANKSHARES INC (NM)
Company went private 12/29/2000
Each share Common $1 par exchanged for $50 cash

CITIZENS BKG CO (SANDUSKY, OH)
Reorganized as First Citizens Banc Corp. 08/31/1987
Each share Capital Stock $20 par exchanged for (1) share Common no par
First Citizens Banc Corp. name changed to Civista Bancshares, Inc. 05/04/2015

CITIZENS CABLE COMMUNICATIONS INC (IN)
Acquired by Comcast Corp. (Old) 04/11/1986
Each share Common no par exchanged for $14.37 cash

CITIZENS CAS CO N Y (NY)
$1.25 Prior Preferred $2.50 par changed to $7.50 par 00/00/1949
$1.25 Prior Preferred $7.50 par changed to $25 par 00/00/1950
$1.25 Prior Preferred $25 par called for redemption 00/00/1955
Common $2 par changed to $1.20 par 00/00/1941
Common $1.20 par changed to $1.30 par 00/00/1946
Common $1.30 par changed to $1 par and then changed to $1.35 par 00/00/1947
Common $1.35 par changed to $1.50 par 00/00/1950
Common $1.50 par changed to $2 par 00/00/1953
$1.50 Preferred called for redemption 07/29/1957
Common $2 par reclassified as Class A Common $2 par 11/30/1959
Stock Dividends - 25% 05/01/1953; 10% 05/25/1955; 11-1/9% 07/29/1957; 10% 10/13/1959
Ordered dissolved 06/17/1971
No stockholders' equity

CITIZENS COMM NATL BK (VERSAILLES, KY)
Under plan of reorganization each share Common $12 par automatically became (1) share Citizens Commerce Bancshares, Inc. Common $12 par 08/14/1998

CITIZENS COML & SVGS BK (FLINT, MI)
Common $20 par changed to $10 par and (1) additional share issued 04/25/1966
Stock Dividends - 50% 08/31/1944; 25% 01/14/1947; 20% 02/01/1950; 10% 01/00/1952; 20% 02/19/1954; 12.5% 03/02/1955; 50% 02/04/1957; 12.5% 03/01/1960; 10% 02/15/1965; 10% 06/15/1968; 20% 06/01/1970; 10% 06/30/1973; 11.11111111% 06/30/1975; 10% 06/18/1979
Reorganized as Citizens Banking Corp. 01/01/1982
Each share Common $10 par exchanged for (1) share Common $10 par
Citizens Banking Corp. name changed to Citizens Republic Bancorp, Inc. 04/26/2007 which merged into FirstMerit Corp.

04/12/2013 which merged into Huntington Bancshares Inc. 08/16/2016

CITIZENS COML TR & SVGS BK (PASADENA, CA)
Merged into CVB Financial Corp. 03/29/1996
Each share Common no par exchanged for $2,035.78 cash

CITIZENS COMMUNICATIONS, INC. (IN)
5% Preferred 1955 Ser. $100 par called for redemption 10/31/1967
Merged into United Utilities, Inc. 02/19/1968
Each share Common no par exchanged for (2.4) shares Common $2.50 par
United Utilities, Inc. name changed to United Telecommunications, Inc. 06/02/1972 which name changed to Sprint Corp. (KS) 02/26/1992 which name changed to Sprint Nextel Corp. 08/12/2005 which merged into Sprint Corp. (DE) 07/10/2013

CITIZENS COMMUNICATIONS CO (DE)
Each Equity Unit received (1.7475) shares Common 25¢ par 08/17/2004
Name changed to Frontier Communications Corp. 07/31/2008

CITIZENS CMNTY BANCORP (USA)
Reorganized under the laws of Maryland as Citizens Community Bancorp, Inc. 11/01/2006
Each share Common 1¢ par exchanged for (1.91067) shares Common 1¢ par

CITIZENS CMNTY BANCORP INC (FL)
Common 1¢ par split (2) for (1) by issuance of (1) additional share payable 12/15/1997 to holders of record 11/28/1997
Stock Dividend - 8% payable 01/19/1999 to holders of record 12/31/1998
Merged into F.N.B. Corp. (PA) 04/30/2001
Each share Common 1¢ par exchanged for (0.524) share Common $2 par
F.N.B. Corp. (PA) reincorporated in Florida 06/13/2001

CITIZENS CMNTY BK (POCATELLO, ID)
Under plan of reorganization each share Common $5 par automatically became (1) share Citizens Bank Holding Co. Common $5 par 07/01/2002
Citizens Bank Holding Co. acquired by Glacier Bancorp, Inc. 04/01/2005

CITIZENS CMNTY BK (RIDGEWOOD, NJ)
Placed in receivership with FDIC 05/01/2009
Stockholders' equity unlikely

CITIZENS CMNTY BK (SOUTH HILL, VA)
Stock Dividend - 10% payable 07/22/2011 to holders of record 06/15/2011 Ex date - 06/13/2011
Under plan of reorganization each share Common $5 par automatically became (1) share CCB Bankshares, Inc. Common $5 par 12/31/2015
CCB Bankshares, Inc. merged into Bank of McKenney (McKenney, VA) 11/10/2017 which name changed to Touchstone Bank (McKenney, VA) 11/28/2017

CITIZENS CORP (DE)
Merged into Allmerica Financial Corp. 12/14/1998
Each share Common 1¢ par exchanged for $33.25 cash

CITIZENS CREDIT CORP. (DE)
Liquidation completed
Each share Class A Common $1 par exchanged for initial distribution of $0.50 cash 10/07/1968
Each share Class B Common 25¢ par exchanged for initial distribution of $0.125 cash 10/07/1968
Each share Class A Common $1 par received second and final distribution of $0.50 cash 05/11/1970
Each share Class B Common 25¢ par received second and final distribution of $0.125 cash 05/11/1970

CITIZENS EXPRESS CO. (GA)
Merged into Bank South Corp. 07/27/1994
Each share Common $2 par exchanged for (2.125) shares Common no par
Bank South Corp. merged into NationsBank Corp. (NC) 01/09/1996 which reincorporated in Delaware as BankAmerica Corp. (Old) 09/25/1998 which merged into BankAmerica Corp. (New) 09/30/1998 which name changed to Bank of America Corp. 04/28/1999

CITIZENS FED BK A FED SVGS BK (MIAMI, FL)
Name changed to NationsBank N.A. (South Atlanta, GA) 01/10/1996
(See NationsBank N.A. (South Atlanta, GA))

CITIZENS FED SVGS & LN ASSN BERLIN (NJ)
Acquired by Howard Savings Bank (Newark, NJ) 04/10/1984
Each share Common 1¢ par exchanged for $13 cash

CITIZENS FED SVGS & LN ASSN MIAMI FLA (USA)
Acquired by Citizens Savings Financial Corp. 07/15/1980
Each share Common 1¢ par exchanged for (1) share Common 1¢ par
Citizens Savings Financial Corp. name changed to CSF Holdings, Inc. 05/01/1991
(See CSF Holdings, Inc.)

CITIZENS FED SVGS BK PORT ST JOE (PORT ST. JOE, FL)
Acquired by Banc Corp. 02/15/2002
Details not available

CITIZENS FID BK & TR CO (LOUISVILLE, KY)
Each share Capital Stock $100 par exchanged for (4) shares Capital Stock $25 par 00/00/1948
Each share Capital Stock $25 par exchanged for (2.5) shares Capital Stock $10 par 05/21/1957
Stock Dividends - 14-2/7% 12/15/1954; 12-1/2% 12/17/1956; 11-1/9% 05/21/1957; 33-1/3% 12/24/1968; 25% 09/11/1970; 100% 09/20/1972
Reorganized as Citizens Fidelity Corp. 02/15/1974
Each share Capital Stock $10 par exchanged for (1) share Common $10 par
Citizens Fidelity Corp. merged into PNC Financial Corp 02/27/1987 which name changed to PNC Bank Corp. 02/08/1993 which name changed to PNC Financial Services Group, Inc. 03/15/2000

CITIZENS FID CORP (KY)
Common $10 par changed to $5 par and (1) additional share issued 03/06/1981
Common $5 par split (3) for (2) by issuance of (0.5) additional share 05/24/1984
Common $5 par split (3) for (2) by issuance of (0.5) additional share 02/19/1986
Stock Dividends - 25% 12/15/1976; 50% 05/24/1978
Merged into PNC Financial Corp 02/27/1987
Each share Common $5 par exchanged for (0.77) share Common $5 par
PNC Financial Corp name changed to PNC Bank Corp. 02/08/1993 which name changed to PNC Financial Services Group, Inc. 03/15/2000

CITIZENS FINL CORP (OH)
Common no par split (3) for (2) by issuance of (0.5) additional share 06/14/1971
Common no par split (3) for (2) by issuance of (0.5) additional share 03/24/1972
Stock Dividend - 40% 09/15/1967
Merged into FIserv, Inc. 05/11/1988
Each share Common no par exchanged for $7.35 cash
$2 Conv. Preferred no par merged out of existence 02/01/1996
Details not available

CITIZENS FINL GROUP INC OLD (DE)
Common $1 par split (2) for (1) by issuance of (1) additional share 05/15/1987
Acquired by Royal Bank of Scotland Group PLC 12/16/1988
Each share Common $1 par exchanged for $30.60 cash

CITIZENS FIRST BANCORP INC (DE)
Principal asset placed in receivership 04/30/2010

CITIZENS FIRST BANCORP INC (KY)
Merged into Liberty United Bancorp, Inc. 03/29/1985
Each share Common no par exchanged for $76.12 cash

CITIZENS FIRST BANCORP INC (NJ)
Common no par split (2) for (1) by issuance of (1) additional share 07/19/1983
Common no par split (2) for (1) by issuance of (1) additional share 06/09/1986
Common no par split (6) for (5) by issuance of (0.2) additional share 02/01/1987
Common no par split (6) for (5) by issuance of (0.2) additional share 02/01/1988
Common no par split (6) for (5) by issuance of (0.2) additional share 02/01/1989
$2.50 Preferred Ser. A no par called for redemption 07/14/1994
Stock Dividends - 10% 02/01/1983; 10% 02/01/1984; 15% 02/01/1985; 15% 02/01/1986
Merged into National Westminster Bank PLC 10/01/1994
Each share Common no par exchanged for either (0.22034) ADR for Ordinary, $9.75 cash or a combination thereof
Note: Option to receive ADR's or combination expired 10/24/1994

CITIZENS FIRST BANCSHARES INC (FL)
Merged into Citi-Bancshares, Inc. 04/19/1996
Each share Common 1¢ par exchanged for (1.317911) shares Common 1¢ par

CITIZENS FIRST FINL CORP (DE)
Merged into Main Street Trust, Inc. 04/01/2005
Each share Common 1¢ par exchanged for (0.38787) share Common 1¢ par and $22.71574 cash
Main Street Trust, Inc. merged into First Busey Corp. 08/01/2007

CITIZENS 1ST NATL BK (TYLER, TX)
Common $10 par changed to $5 par and (1) additional share issued 04/14/1977
Stock Dividends - 10% 01/17/1967; 100% 04/10/1975; 25% 04/09/1979
Merged into First City Bancorporation of Texas, Inc. (TX) 09/01/1982
Each share Common $5 par exchanged for (2) shares Common $3.25 par
(See First City Bancorporation of Texas, Inc. (TX))

CITIZENS FIRST NATIONAL BANK & TRUST CO. (RIDGEWOOD, NJ)
Capital Stock $25 par changed to $30 par 00/00/1944
Capital Stock $30 par changed to $36 par 00/00/1952
Capital Stock $36 par changed to $18 par and (1) additional share issued 06/18/1959
Name changed to Citizens First National Bank (Ridgewood, NJ) and Capital Stock $18 par changed to $30 par 03/30/1962
Citizens First National Bank (Ridgewood, NJ) merged into Citizens First National Bank of New Jersey (Ridgewood, NJ) 11/30/1973 which reorganized as Citizens First Bancorp, Inc. 10/01/1982 which merged into National Westminster Bank PLC 10/01/1994

CITIZENS FIRST NATIONAL BANK (BLOOMINGTON, IN)
Name changed to First National Bank (Bloomington, IN) 03/01/1966
First National Bank (Bloomington, IN) reorganized as First National Corp. (IN) 05/14/1985 which was acquired by BancOne Corp. (DE) 06/01/1987 which reincorporated in Ohio 05/01/1989 which merged into Bank One Corp. 10/02/1998 which merged into J.P. Morgan Chase & Co. 12/31/2000 which name changed to JPMorgan Chase & Co. 07/20/2004

CITIZENS FIRST NATL BK (CRESCENT CITY, FL)
Merged into Carolina First Corp. 04/23/1999
Each share Common no par exchanged for (4.6224) shares Common $1 par
Carolina First Corp. name changed to South Financial Group, Inc. 04/24/2000 which merged into Toronto-Dominion Bank (Toronto, ON) 09/30/2010

CITIZENS FIRST NATIONAL BANK (PRINCETON, IL)
Reorganized as Princeton National Bancorp, Inc. 12/29/1982
Each share Common $10 par exchanged for (2) shares Common $5 par
(See Princeton National Bancorp, Inc.)

CITIZENS FIRST NATL BK N J (RIDGEWOOD, NJ)
Reorganized as Citizens First Bancorp, Inc. 10/01/1982
Each share Common $5 par exchanged for (1) share Common no par
Citizens First Bancorp, Inc. merged into National Westminster Bank PLC 10/01/1994

CITIZENS 1ST NATL BK (RIDGEWOOD, NJ)
Capital Stock $30 par changed to $7.50 par and (3) additional shares issued 03/01/1966
Capital Stock $7.50 par changed to $5 par and (2) additional shares issued 10/15/1969
Under plan of merger name changed to Citizens First National Bank of New Jersey (Ridgewood, NJ) 11/30/1973
Citizens First National Bank of New Jersey (Ridgewood, NJ) reorganized as Citizens First Bancorp, Inc. 10/01/1982 which merged into

National Westminster Bank PLC 10/01/1994

CITIZENS GAS, ELECTRIC & POWER CO. OF NANTUCKET
Name changed to Nantucket Gas & Electric Co. 00/00/1931
Nantucket Gas & Electric Co. name changed to Nantucket Electric Co. 05/17/1973 which merged into New England Electric System 03/26/1996
(See New England Electric System)

CITIZENS GAS FUEL CO. OLD (MI)
Merged into Adrian Gas & Fuel Co. share for share 00/00/1951
Adrian Gas & Fuel Co. name changed to Citizens Gas Fuel Co. (New) 00/00/1951 which was acquired by MCN Corp. 07/31/1990 which name changed to MCN Energy Group Inc. 04/28/1997 which merged into DTE Energy Co. 05/31/2001

CITIZENS GAS FUEL CO NEW (MI)
Each share Common $5 par exchanged for (3) shares Common $3 par 07/12/1955
Stock Dividends - 15% 07/24/1974; 15% 09/15/1976; 15% 07/26/1977; 20% 07/26/1979; 20% 07/29/1981; 20% 01/27/1984
Acquired by MCN Corp. 07/31/1990
Each share Common $3 par exchanged for (0.9142) share Common 1¢ par
MCN Corp. name changed to MCN Energy Group Inc. 04/28/1997

CITIZENS GROWTH PPTYS (OH)
Completely liquidated
Each Share of Bene. Int. $1 par received first and final distribution of $2.70 cash payable 11/12/2002 to holders of record 10/24/2002 Ex date - 11/19/2002
Note: Certificates were not required to be surrendered and are now valueless

CITIZENS GWINNETT BANKSHARES INC (GA)
Merged into Premier Bancshares Inc. (New) 12/12/1997
Each share Common exchanged for (8) shares Common $5 par
Premier Bancshares Inc. (New) merged into BB&T Corp. 01/13/2000

CITIZENS HOLDING CO. (FL)
Completely liquidated 08/01/1969
Each share Common $5 par exchanged for (0.3) share Barnett National Securities Corp. Common $4 par
Barnett National Securities Corp. name changed to Barnett Banks of Florida, Inc. 10/03/1969 which name changed to Barnett Banks, Inc. 04/24/1987 which merged into NationsBank Corp. (NC) 01/09/1998 which reincorporated in Delaware as BankAmerica Corp. (Old) 09/25/1998 which merged into BankAmerica Corp. (New) 09/30/1998 which name changed to Bank of America Corp. 04/28/1999

CITIZENS HOLDING CO. (OH)
Name changed to United Magazine Co. 12/29/89
(See United Magazine Co.)

CITIZENS HLDG CORP (FL)
Merged into F.N.B Corp. 08/31/1998
Each share Common 10¢ par exchanged for (1.743) shares Common $2 par
F.N.B. Corp. (PA) reincorporated in Florida 06/13/2001

CITIZENS HOME INSURANCE CO. (SC)
Liquidation completed
Each share Common $2 par received initial distribution of $0.51 cash 10/13/1969
Each share Common $2 par received second and final distribution of $0.12172 cash 04/24/1970
Note: Certificates were not required to be surrendered and are without value

CITIZENS HOTEL CO (TX)
Dissolved 04/23/1968
No stockholders' equity

CITIZENS INDPT BANCORP (AL)
Merged into First Commercial Bancshares, Inc. 03/04/1991
Each share Common 10¢ par exchanged for (0.9) share Common $1 par
First Commercial Bancshares, Inc. merged into Synovus Financial Corp. 12/31/1992

CITIZENS INSURANCE CO. OF MISSOURI
Liquidated 00/00/1930
Details not available

CITIZENS INS CO AMER (TX)
Common $1 par reclassified as Class A Common $1 par 12/20/1978
Stock Dividend - 10% 10/20/1980
Merged into Citizens, Inc. 12/01/1988
Each share Class A Common $1 par exchanged for (11.2918) shares Class A Common $1 par

CITIZENS INVTS INC (NJ)
Name changed to Sun Bancorp Inc. 04/18/1995
Sun Bancorp Inc. merged into OceanFirst Financial Corp. 01/31/2018

CITIZENS LIFE INS CO N Y (NY)
Each share Common $4 par exchanged for (2) shares Common $2 par 09/24/1958
Stock Dividends - 12.5% 12/10/1963; 11.11111111% 05/29/1964; 10% 05/20/1966
Name changed to Executive Life Insurance Co. of New York 09/11/1969
(See Executive Life Insurance Co. of New York)

CITIZENS MARINE JEFFERSON BANK (NEWPORT NEWS, VA)
Through voluntary exchange offer all but directors qualifying shares acquired by United Virginia Bankshares, Inc. as of 03/13/1963
Public interest eliminated

CITIZENS MICHIANA FINL CORP (IN)
Common $10 par split (2) for (1) by issuance of (1) additional share 07/12/1985
Merged into Horizon Bancorp 10/01/1986
Each share Common $10 par exchanged for (1) share Common no par
Horizon Bancorp name changed to Horizon Bancorp, Inc. 05/08/2018

CITIZENS MORRIS PLAN CO.
Liquidated 00/00/1944
Details not available

CITIZENS MTG INVT TR (MA)
Reorganized under Chapter X Bankruptcy Act 03/25/1982
No equity to old Shares of Bene. $1 par
Reincorporated under the laws of Georgia as Citizens Properties, Inc. and new Shares of Bene. Int. $1 par reclassified as Common $1 par 02/22/1989
Citizens Properties, Inc. merged into Realmark Holdings Corp. 06/30/1995 which was acquired by Realmark Acquisitions LLC 04/13/2005 which name changed to Realmark Acquisitions II LLC 07/12/2005

CITIZENS NATL BANCORP INC (DE)
Stock Dividends - 7.5% payable 01/07/2000 to holders of record 12/17/1999; 7.5% payable 01/05/2001 to holders of record 12/21/2000 Ex date - 12/27/2000; 6% payable 01/07/2002 to holders of record 12/12/2001 Ex date - 12/21/2001; 6% payable 01/10/2003 to holders of record 12/18/2002 Ex date - 12/20/2002; 7.5% payable 01/12/2004 to holders of record 12/16/2003 Ex date - 12/12/2003; 8% payable 01/14/2005 to holders of record 12/27/2004 Ex date - 12/22/2004; 8% payable 01/16/2006 to holders of record 12/26/2005 Ex date - 12/21/2005; 8% payable 01/12/2007 to holders of record 12/27/2006 Ex date - 12/22/2006; 2% payable 01/14/2008 to holders of record 12/28/2007 Ex date - 12/26/2007
Acquired by ESB Bancorp, Inc. 07/01/2015
Each share Common 1¢ par exchanged for $67.50 cash

CITIZENS NATIONAL BANK & TRUST CO. (MANSFIELD, OH)
Merged into First National Bank (Mansfield, OH) 04/01/1953
Each share Capital Stock $25 par exchanged for (1.175) shares Capital Stock $25 par
First National Bank (Mansfield, OH) name changed to First Buckeye Bank, N.A. (Mansfield, OH) 03/12/1980 which merged into Toledo Trustcorp, Inc. 12/30/1982 which name changed to TrustCorp, Inc. 04/10/1986 which was acquired by Society Corp. 01/05/1990 which was merged into KeyCorp (New) 03/01/1994

CITIZENS NATL BK & TR CO (HOUMA, LA)
Capital Stock $25 par changed to $5 par and (4) additional shares issued plus a 20% stock dividend paid 02/24/1970
Stock Dividends - 100% 01/18/1945; 100% 01/24/1956; 33.33333333% 01/25/1961; 25% 02/11/1963; 10% 02/08/1965
Name changed to First National Bank (Houma, LA) 01/02/1973
First National Bank (Houma, LA) reorganized as First National Bankshares, Inc. 07/31/1982 which merged into Whitney Holding Corp. 02/28/1997 which merged into Hancock Holding Co. 06/04/2011 which name changed to Hancock Whitney Corp. 05/25/2018

CITIZENS NATL BK & TR CO (MARSHFIELD, WI)
Reorganized as Dairyland Bancshares, Inc. 02/15/1984
Each share Common Capital Stock $5 par owned by Wisconsin residents exchanged for (1) share Common $10 par
Each share Common Capital Stock $5 par owned by non-residents of Wisconsin exchanged for $60 cash
(See Dairyland Bancshares, Inc.)

CITIZENS NATL BK & TR CO (PORT RICHEY, FL)
Merged into Gulf West Banks, Inc. 01/16/1998
Each share Common $1 par exchanged for (3.2337) shares Common $1 par
Gulf West Banks, Inc. merged into South Financial Group, Inc. 08/31/2002

CITIZENS NATL BK & TR CO (WELLSVILLE, NY)
Common $25 par changed to $10 par and (1.5) additional shares issued 12/31/1969
Merged into Key Banks Inc. 11/07/1980
Each share Common $10 par exchanged for (2.75) shares Common $5 par
Key Banks Inc. name changed to KeyCorp (NY) 08/28/1985 which merged into KeyCorp (New) (OH) 03/01/1994

CITIZENS NATL BK (ABILENE, TX)
Capital Stock $20 par changed to $10 par and (1) additional share issued 01/25/1966
Stock Dividends - 12.5% 02/01/1971
Merged into First International Bancshares, Inc. 11/15/1973
Each share Capital Stock $10 par exchanged for (1.4) shares Common $5 par
First International Bancshares, Inc. name changed to InterFirst Corp. 12/31/1981 which merged into First RepublicBank Corp. 06/06/1987
(See First RepublicBank Corp.)

CITIZENS NATL BK (ASHLAND, PA)
Merged into Community Banks, Inc. 01/12/1996
Each share Common $20 par exchanged for (28.912) shares Common $5 par
Community Banks, Inc. merged into Susquehanna Bancshares, Inc. 11/16/2007 which merged into BB&T Corp. 08/01/2015

CITIZENS NATL BK (BERKELEY SPRINGS, WV)
Merged into CNB Financial Services Inc. 08/31/2000
Each share Common exchanged for (2) shares Common $1 par

CITIZENS NATL BK (BOCA RATON, FL)
Name changed to Colonial National Bank (Boca Raton, FL) 04/01/1982
Colonial National Bank (Boca Raton, FL) name changed to Colonial Trust Co., N.A. (Palm Beach, FL) 01/01/1983 which reorganized as Colonial Trust National Bank (Palm Beach, FL) 10/28/1986 which name changed to Palm Beach National Bank & Trust Co. (Boca Raton, FL) 06/22/1990 which reorganized as Palm National Holding Co. 05/01/1997 which merged into Colonial BancGroup, Inc. 09/03/2002
(See Colonial BancGroup, Inc.)

CITIZENS NATL BK (BOWLING GREEN, KY)
Stock Dividends - 25% 02/21/1958; 100% 05/01/1981
Reorganized as Kentucky Southern Bancorp Inc. 10/00/1984
Each share Common $10 par exchanged for (1) share Common $10 par
Kentucky Southern Bancorp Inc. name changed to Trans Financial Bancorp, Inc. 09/24/1985 which name changed to Trans Financial, Inc. 04/24/1995 which merged into Star Banc Corp. 08/21/1998 which merged into Firstar Corp. (New) 11/20/1998 which merged into U.S. Bancorp (DE) 02/27/2001

CITIZENS NATL BK (CHEBOYGAN, MI)
Stock Dividend - 50% 03/15/1982
Under plan of reorganization each share Common $5 par automatically became (1) share CNB Corp. Common $5 par 12/31/1985

CITIZENS NATIONAL BANK (CHILLICOTHE, MO)
Merged into Citizens Bancshares Co. 05/01/1970
Each share Capital Stock $25 par exchanged for (1) share Common $2.50 par

CITIZENS NATL BK (CHILLICOTHE, OH)
Reorganized as First Capital Bancshares, Inc. 03/31/1998
Each share Common no par

exchanged for (10) shares Common no par
First Capital Bancshares, Inc. merged into LCNB Corp. 01/11/2013

CITIZENS NATIONAL BANK (CONCORD, NC)
Merged into First Charter Corp. 10/00/1984
Details not available

CITIZENS NATL BK (DANVILLE, KY)
Under plan of reorganization each share Common Capital Stock $10 par automatically became (1) share Danville Bancorp, Inc. Common $10 par 09/05/1983
(See Danville Bancorp, Inc.)

CITIZENS NATL BK (DECATUR, IL)
Capital Stock $62.50 par changed to $100 par 00/00/1946
Capital Stock $100 par changed to $25 par and (3) additional shares issued 04/12/1966
Stock Dividends - 50% 01/14/1955; 66.66666666% 01/22/1962
Merged into Midwest Financial Group, Inc. 12/30/1983
Each share Capital Stock $25 par exchanged for (6.75) shares Common $5 par
Midwest Financial Group, Inc. merged into First of America Bank Corp. 11/01/1989 which merged into National City Corp. 03/31/1998 which was acquired by PNC Financial Services Group, Inc. 12/31/2008

CITIZENS NATL BK (DENISON, TX)
Acquired by Texas American Bancshares Inc. 05/15/1979
Each share Common $20 par exchanged for (1.07) shares Common $5 par
(See Texas American Bancshares Inc.)

CITIZENS NATL BK (ENGLEWOOD, NJ)
Capital Stock $60 par changed to $20 par and (2) additional shares issued plus a 10% stock dividend paid 01/25/1957
Capital Stock $20 par changed to $10 par and (1) additional shares issued 01/20/1960
Capital Stock $10 par changed to $5 par and (1) additional shares issued 01/25/1965
Merged into Midlantic Banks Inc. 06/30/1972
Each share Capital Stock $5 par exchanged for (1) share $2 Conv. Preferred no par and (1) Common Stock Purchase Warrant expiring 09/28/1977
Midlantic Banks Inc. merged into Midlantic Corp. 01/30/1987 which merged into PNC Bank Corp. 12/31/1995 which name changed to PNC Financial Services Group, Inc. 03/15/2000

CITIZENS NATL BK (EVANSVILLE, IL)
Each share Capital Stock $100 par exchanged for (4) shares Capital Stock $25 par 00/00/1948
Each share Capital Stock $25 par exchanged for (2) shares Capital Stock $12.50 par 04/10/1958
Capital Stock $12.50 par changed to $10 par and (0.25) additional share issued plus a 60% stock dividend paid 08/01/1974
Stock Dividends - 25% 00/00/1948; 20% 01/27/1961; 16.66666666% 01/25/1965; 14.5% 02/15/1968; 12.5% 02/20/1970; 11.11111111% 03/19/1973
Under plan of reorganization each share Capital Stock $10 par automatically became (1) share CNB Bancshares Inc. Common no par 01/03/1984

CNB Bancshares Inc. merged into Fifth Third Bancorp 10/29/1999

CITIZENS NATIONAL BANK (FAIRFIELD, CT)
Merged into South Norwalk Savings Bank (Norwalk, CT) 11/07/1983
Each share Common $6.25 par exchanged for $15.50 cash

CITIZENS NATL BK (GASTONIA, NC)
Each share Common $20 par exchanged for (2.6) shares Common $10 par to effect a (2) for (1) split and a 30% stock dividend 10/02/1957
Common $10 par changed to $5 par and (1) additional share issued 02/12/1970
Common $5 par changed to $2.50 par and (1) additional share issued 03/01/1973
Stock Dividends - 33.33333333% 02/02/1961; 20% 02/15/1966
Under plan of merger name changed to Independence National Bank (Gastonia, NC) 06/01/1976
Independence National Bank (Gastonia, NC) merged into Branch Corp. 10/05/1981 which name changed to BB&T Financial Corp. 05/10/1988 which merged into Southern National Corp. 02/28/1995 which merged into BB&T Corp. 05/19/1997

CITIZENS NATL BK (GREENCASTLE, PA)
Common $10 par changed to $5 par and (1) additional share issued 04/01/1978
Merged into Susquehanna Bancshares, Inc. 10/01/1985
Each share Common $5 par exchanged for (1.4) shares Common $5 par
Susquehanna Bancshares, Inc. merged into BB&T Corp. 08/01/2015

CITIZENS NATL BK (HANFORD, CA)
Common Capital Stock $10 par changed to $5 par and (1) additional share issued 05/01/1980
Merged into Mineral King National Bank (Visalia, CA) 12/28/1990
Each share Common Capital Stock $5 par exchanged for $25.4434 cash

CITIZENS NATL BK (HOLLYWOOD, FL)
Through voluntary exchange offer Citizens Bancshares of Florida, Inc. held 98.28% as of 00/00/1973
Public interest eliminated

CITIZENS NATL BK (LANSFORD, PA)
Acquired by Harleysville National Corp. 02/13/1991
Each share Common $100 par exchanged for (301) shares Common $1 par
Harleysville National Corp. merged into First Niagara Financial Group, Inc. (New) 04/09/2010 which merged into KeyCorp (New) 08/01/2016

CITIZENS NATL BK (LAUREL, MD)
Acquired by Mercantile Bankshares Corp. 12/13/1973
Each share Common exchanged for (3.875) shares Common $2 par
Mercantile Bankshares Corp. merged into PNC Financial Services Group, Inc. 03/02/2007

CITIZENS NATL BK (LEESBURG, FL)
Reorganized as Citi-Bancshares, Inc. 10/01/1983
Each share Capital Stock $10 par exchanged for (1) share Common 10¢ par
Citi-Bancshares, Inc. merged into Huntington Bancshares Inc. 02/28/1997

CITIZENS NATIONAL BANK (LOS ANGELES, CA)
Stock Dividends - 50% 07/09/1959; 10% 02/10/1962
Merged into Crocker-Citizens National Bank (San Francisco, CA) 11/01/1963
Each share Capital Stock $10 par exchanged for (1.9) shares Common Capital Stock $10 par
Crocker-Citizens National Bank (San Francisco, CA) reorganized in Delaware as Crocker National Corp. 04/21/1969
(See Crocker National Corp.)

CITIZENS NATL BK (LUBBOCK, TX)
Each share Capital Stock $100 par exchanged for (5) shares Capital Stock $20 par plus a 100% stock dividend paid 00/00/1948
Stock Dividends - 50% 11/16/1949; 10% 12/27/1951; 11.11111111% 10/19/1953; 14.28571428% 12/21/1962
Through purchase offer 99.982% acquired by Texas Commerce Bancshares, Inc. as of 01/11/1973
Public interest eliminated

CITIZENS NATL BK (MALONE, NY)
Merged into Community Bank System, Inc. 01/26/2001
Each share Common $6.25 exchanged for (1.7) shares Common no par

CITIZENS NATL BK (MARTINSBURG, WV)
Acquired by One Valley Bancorp of West Virginia, Inc. 01/12/1984
Each share Common $10 par exchanged for $137.54 cash

CITIZENS NATL BK (MERIDIAN, MS)
Shares reacquired 06/02/2000
Each share Common exchanged for $435 cash

CITIZENS NATL BK (MEYERSDALE, PA)
Merged into Riverview Financial Corp. (New) 12/31/2015
Each share Common $1 par exchanged for (2.9586) shares Common no par

CITIZENS NATL BK (NAPLES, FL)
Capital Stock $2.50 par changed to $1.25 par and (1) additional shares issued 03/05/1973
Stock Dividend - 25% 01/18/1980
Acquired by Flagship Banks Inc. 08/06/1982
Each share Capital Stock $1.25 par exchanged for (1) share Common $1 par
Flagship Banks Inc. merged into Sun Banks, Inc. 01/01/1984 which merged into SunTrust Banks, Inc. 07/01/1985

CITIZENS NATL BK (NEW CASTLE, PA)
Each share Common $100 par exchanged for (5) shares Common $20 par plus a 200% stock dividend paid 00/00/1950
Common $20 par changed to $10 par and (1) additional shares issued 07/14/1965
Common $10 par changed to $5 par and (1) additional shares issued 03/31/1978
Merged into Mellon Bank Corp. 01/07/1985
Each share Common $5 par exchanged for $60 cash

CITIZENS NATL BK (ORLANDO, FL)
Capital Stock $10 par changed to $5 par and (1) additional share issued plus a 10% stock dividend paid 02/15/1970
Name changed to Pan American Bank of Orlando, N.A. (Orlando, FL) 04/12/1974
(See Pan American Bank of Orlando, N.A. (Orlando, FL))

CITIZENS NATL BK (SAN ANTONIO, TX)
Merged into Frostbank Corp. 05/01/1973
Each share Common $5 par exchanged for (0.685) share Common $10 par
Frostbank Corp. merged into Cullen/Frost Bankers, Inc. 07/07/1977

CITIZENS NATL BK (ST PETERSBURG, FL)
Stock Dividend - 12.5% 02/02/1960
Name changed to Barnett National Bank (St. Petersburg, FL) 01/01/1970
(See Barnett National Bank (St. Petersburg, FL))

CITIZENS NATL BK (TELL CITY, IN)
Merged into Old National Bancorp 04/28/1995
Each share Common $10 par exchanged for (2.909) shares Common no par

CITIZENS NATIONAL BANK (TYLER, TX)
Name changed to Citizens First National Bank (Tyler, TX) 12/31/1955
Citizens First National Bank (Tyler, TX) merged into First City Bancorporation of Texas, Inc. (TX) 09/01/1982
(See First City Bancorporation of Texas, Inc. (TX))

CITIZENS NATL BK (VICTORIA, TX)
Merged into Texas Financial Bancshares Inc. 10/31/1997
Each share Common no par exchanged for $35 cash

CITIZENS NATL BK (WACO, TX)
Merged into RepublicBank Corp. 09/01/1982
Each share Capital Stock $10 par exchanged for (2.4) shares Common $5 par
RepublicBank Corp. name changed to First RepublicBank Corp. 06/06/1987
(See First RepublicBank Corp.)

CITIZENS NATL BK (WELLSVILLE, NY)
Name changed to Citizens National Bank & Trust Co. (Wellsville, NY) 02/27/1968
Citizens National Bank & Trust Co. (Wellsville, NY) merged into Key Banks Inc. 11/07/1980 which name changed to KeyCorp (NY) 08/28/1985 which merged into KeyCorp (New) (OH) 03/01/1994

CITIZENS NATIONAL BANK (WINSTON-SALEM, NC)
Merged into Peoples Bancorporation 01/22/1988
Each share Common $5 par exchanged for $16.72 cash

CITIZENS NATIONAL BANK OF SOUTH JERSEY (WOODBINE, NJ)
Common $100 par changed to $10 par 11/05/1970
Stock Dividend - 100% 11/13/1970
Merged into Citizens National Bank of South Jersey (Bridgeton, NJ) 01/26/1972
Each share Common $10 par exchanged for (2.666666) shares Common $3 par
Citizens National Bank of South Jersey (Bridgeton, NJ) acquired by Citizens Bancorp (NJ) 11/02/1972
(See Citizens Bancorp. (NJ))

CITIZENS NATL BK SOUTH JERSEY (BRIDGETON, NJ)
Acquired by Citizens Bancorp (NJ) 11/02/1972
Each share Common $3 par exchanged for (1.5) shares Capital Stock no par
(See Citizens Bancorp (NJ))

CITIZENS NATL BK SOUTHINGTON (PLANTSVILLE, CT)
Merged into Northeast Bancorp, Inc. 11/30/1984
Each share Common $5 par exchanged for (1.25633) shares Common $5 par and $20.31 cash
Northeast Bancorp, Inc. merged into First Fidelity Bancorporation (New) 05/03/1993 which merged into First Union Corp. 01/01/1996 which name changed to Wachovia Corp. (Ctfs. dated after 09/01/2001) 09/01/2001 which merged into Wells Fargo & Co. (New) 12/31/2008

CITIZENS NATL BK SOUTHN MD (LEXINGTON PARK, MD)
Name changed to Maryland Bank & Trust Co. (Lexington Park, MD) 08/16/1971
(See Maryland Bank & Trust Co. (Lexington Park, MD))

CITIZENS NATL BK TEX (BELLAIRE, TX)
Reorganized as CNBT Bancshares, Inc. 07/08/1998
Each share Common $1 par exchanged for (1) share Common $1 par
(See CNBT Bancshares, Inc.)

CITIZENS NATL BK WEST HOLLYWOOD (HOLLYWOOD, FL)
Acquired by Citizens Bancshares of Florida, Inc. 02/23/1971
Details not available

CITIZENS NATL CORP (FL)
Common $2.50 par split (2) for (1) by issuance of (1) additional share 03/01/1993
Merged into AmSouth Bancorporation 04/04/1994
Each share Common $2.50 par exchanged for (0.3609) share Common $1 par
AmSouth Bancorporation merged into Regions Financial Corp. 11/04/2006

CITIZENS NATIONAL LIFE INSURANCE CO. (IN)
Stock Dividends - 12.5% 05/15/1958; 10% 04/15/1959; 10% 08/31/1960; 10% 11/01/1962
Merged into Great Northern Life Insurance Co. 12/27/1963
Each share Common exchanged for (1) share Common $1 par
Great Northern Life Insurance Co. was acquired by Midwestern United Life Insurance Co. 07/26/1965
(See Midwestern United Life Insurance Co.)

CITIZENS PASSENGER RAILWAY CO. OF PHILADELPHIA
Acquired by Philadelphia Transportation Co. 00/00/1940
Each share Common exchanged for $100.85 principal amount of 3%-6% Consolidated Mortgage Bonds and (0.845) share $1 Part. Preferred $20 par
(See Philadelphia Transportation Co.)

CITIZENS PPTYS INC (GA)
Merged into Realmark Holdings Corp. 06/30/1995
Each share Common $1 par exchanged for (1.09) shares new Common no par $1.20 Preferred called for redemption at $1 on 09/15/2000
Realmark Holdings Corp. acquired by Realmark Acquisitions LLC 04/13/2005 which name changed to Realmark Acquisitions II LLC 07/12/2005

CITIZENS REP BANCORP INC (MI)
Name changed 04/26/2007
Common $10 par split (3) for (2) by issuance of (0.5) additional shares 08/11/1986
Common $10 par split (2) for (1) by issuance of (1) additional share 05/12/1993
Common $10 par changed to no par and (0.5) additional share issued payable 11/18/1997 to holders of record 10/27/1997
Stock Dividend - 100% 05/14/1985
Name changed from Citizens Banking Corp. to Citizens Republic Bancorp, Inc. 04/26/2007
Each share Conv. Contingent Perpetual Preferred Ser. A no par exchanged for (12.5) shares old Common no par 09/26/2008
Each share old Common no par exchanged for (0.1) share new Common no par 07/05/2011
Merged into FirstMerit Corp. 04/12/2013
Each share new Common no par exchanged for (1.37) shares Common no par
FirstMerit Corp. merged into Huntington Bancshares Inc. 08/16/2016

CITIZENS SAVINGS & INVESTMENT CO. (DE)
Charter cancelled and declared inoperative and void for non-payment of taxes 00/00/1922

CITIZENS SVGS & LN ASSN (CA)
Merged into United Financial Corp. of California 03/16/1973
Each share Guarantee Stock no par exchanged for (2.25) shares Capital Stock $1 par
(See United Financial Corp. of California)

CITIZENS SVGS & LN ASSN ROCKY MT (NC)
Name changed to Citizens Savings Bank Inc. 09/11/1989
(See Citizens Savings Bank Inc.)

CITIZENS SAVINGS & LOAN CO. (OH)
Merged into Continental Federal Savings & Loan Association 12/31/1979
Each share Capital Stock 25¢ par exchanged for $6.5088 cash

CITIZENS SVGS & LN CORP (CHATTANOOGA, TN)
Each share old Common $10 par exchanged for (0.001) share new Common $10 par 09/11/2001
Note: In effect holders received $160 cash per share and public interest was eliminated

CITIZENS SVGS ASSN (OH)
Name changed to Citizens Savings Bank (Canton, OH) 05/17/1983
Citizens Savings Bank (Canton, OH) merged into Civista Corp. 08/14/1988 which merged into FirstMerit Corp. 01/31/1995 which merged into Huntington Bancshares Inc. 08/16/2016

CITIZENS SVGS BK & TR CO (ST JOHNSBURY, VT)
Merged into Union Bankshares, Inc. 11/30/1999
Each share Common $1 par exchanged for (6.5217) shares Common $2 par

CITIZENS SVGS BK (CANTON, OH)
Merged into Civista Corp. 08/14/1988
Each share Common $5 par exchanged for (1) share Common $5 par
Civista Corp. merged into FirstMerit Corp. 01/31/1995 which merged into Huntington Bancshares Inc. 08/16/2016

CITIZENS SAVINGS BANK (DENVER, CO)
Stock Dividend - 100% 06/00/1957
Merged into Colorado State Bank (Denver, CO) 10/15/1965
Details not available

CITIZENS SVGS BK (MARTINS FERRY, OH)
Reorganized as United Bancorp, Inc. 01/02/1984
Each share Common $20 par exchanged for (4) shares Common $10 par

CITIZENS SVGS BK CO (PEMBERVILLE, OH)
Merged into Rurban Financial Corp. 10/03/1994
Each share Common no par exchanged for (3.914) shares Common no par
Rurban Financial Corp. name changed to SB Financial Group, Inc. 04/25/2013

CITIZENS SVGS BK F S B (ITHACA, NY)
Stock Dividend - 10% 10/15/1988
Reorganized as Ithaca Bancorp, Inc. 09/17/1990
Each share Common $1 par exchanged for (1) share Common 1¢ par
Ithaca Bancorp, Inc. acquired by First Empire State Corp. 12/01/1994 which name changed to M&T Bank Corp. 06/01/1998

CITIZENS SVGS BK F S B (SILVER SPRINGS, MD)
Under plan of reorganiation each share Common 1¢ par automatically became (1) share First Citizens Financial Corp. Common 1¢ par 08/02/1989
First Citizens Financial Corp. merged into Provident Bankshares Corp. 08/22/1997 which was acquired by M&T Bank Corp. 05/26/2009

CITIZENS SVGS BK INC (NC)
Merged into Southern Bancshares Inc. 07/09/1993
Each share Common $1 par exchanged for $6.33 cash

CITIZENS SVGS FINL CORP (FL)
Common 1¢ par split (2) for (1) by issuance of (1) additional share 05/18/1983
Common 1¢ par reclassified as Class A Common 1¢ par 05/19/1983
Class A Common 1¢ par split (3) for (2) by issuance of (0.5) additional share 07/08/1987
Class A Common 1¢ par reclassified as Class B Common 1¢ par 04/29/1988
Stock Dividend - 20% 07/26/1985
Name changed to CSF Holdings, Inc. 05/01/1991
(See CSF Holdings, Inc.)

CITIZENS SEC GROUP INC (MN)
Merged into Meridian Insurance Group, Inc. 7/31/96
Each share Common 1¢ par exchanged for $12.50 cash

CITIZENS SEC LIFE INS CO (KY)
Under plan of reorganization each share Common $1 par automatically became (1) share Citizens Financial Corp. Class A no par 2/4/91

CITIZENS SOUTH BKG CORP (DE)
Stock Dividend - 5% payable 11/15/2010 to holders of record 11/01/2010 Ex date - 10/28/2010
Merged into Park Sterling Corp. 10/01/2012
Each share Common $1 par exchanged for (0.156721) share Common $1 par and $6.26 cash

CITIZENS SOUTH BKG CORP (USA)
Reorganized as Citizens South Banking Corp. (DE) 10/01/2002
Each share Common $1 par exchanged for (2.1408) shares Common $1 par
Citizens South Banking Corp. (DE) merged into Park Sterling Corp. 10/01/2012 which merged into South State Corp. 11/30/2017

CITIZENS SOUTHN BK INC (BECKLEY, WV)
Merged into First Community Bancshares Inc. (NV) 10/31/2000
Each share Common no par exchanged for (1.74) shares Common $1 par
First Community Bancshares, Inc. (NV) reincorporated in Virginia 10/09/2018

CITIZENS ST BK (CORPUS CHRISTI, TX)
Reorganized as Corpus Christi Bancshares, Inc. 3/1/85
Each share Common $5 par exchanged for (1) share Common $5 par
(See Corpus Christi Bancshares, Inc.)

CITIZENS ST BK (OWENSBORO, KY)
Reorganized as Citizens First Bancorp, Inc. (KY) 8/5/82
Each share Common $5 par exchanged for (1) share Common no par
(See Citizens First Bancorp, Inc. (KY))

CITIZENS ST BK (SANTA PAULA, CA)
Merged into Santa Barbara Bancorp 09/30/1997
Each share Common $25 par exchanged for $1,925 cash

CITIZENS ST BK (VINELAND, NJ)
Reorganized as Citizens Bancorp (NJ) 2/14/72
Each share Common $10 par exchanged for (1) share Capital Stock no par
(See Citizens Bancorp (NJ))

CITIZENS STATE BANK (HOUSTON, TX)
Name changed to Citizens Bank (Houston, Tex.) 6/19/68
Citizens Bank (Houston, Tex.) merged into Houston-Citizens Bank & Trust Co. (Houston, Tex.) 11/1/70 which reorganized as First International Bancshares, Inc. 12/31/72 which name changed to InterFirst Corp. 12/31/81 which merged into First RepublicBank Corp. 6/6/87
(See First RepublicBank Corp.)

CITIZENS STATE BANK OF NEW JERSEY (LACEY TOWNSHIP, NJ)
Capital Stock $5 par changed to $3.33 par and (0.5) additional share issued 08/01/1977
Capital Stock $3.33 par changed to $2.67 par and (0.25) additional share issued 05/18/1979
Capital Stock $2.67 par changed to $2 par 04/28/1987
6% Conv. Preferred $14 par called for redemption 12/31/1988
Acquired by Commerce Bancorp, Inc. 12/31/1988
Each share Capital Stock $2 par exchanged for (4.585) shares Common $1.5625 par and $4 cash
Commerce Bancorp, Inc. merged into Toronto-Dominion Bank (Toronto, ONT) 03/31/2008

CITIZENS STD LIFE INS CO (TX)
Common no par changed to $1 par 4/15/69
Stock Dividend - 10% 2/15/74
Name changed to Citizens Insurance Co. of America 2/3/78
Citizens Insurance Co. of America merged into Citizens, Inc. 12/1/88

CITIZENS TELEPHONE CO. (IN)
Each share Common $10 par exchanged for (0.3) share old Common no par 00/00/1927
Each share old Common no par exchanged for (2) shares new Common no par 00/00/1957
Name changed to Citizens Communications, Inc. 12/31/1966
Citizens Communications, Inc.

merged into United Utilities, Inc. 02/19/1968 which name changed to United Telecommunications, Inc. 06/02/1972 which name changed to Sprint Corp. (KS) 02/26/1992 which name changed to Sprint Nextel Corp. 08/12/2005 which merged into Sprint Corp. (DE) 07/10/2013

CITIZENS TRACTION CO.
Merged into Pittsburgh Railways Co. 9/30/50
Each share Common $50 par exchanged for (4.2) shares Common no par and $5 cash
Pittsburgh Railways Co. name changed to Pittway Corp. (PA) 11/28/67 which merged into Pittway Corp. (DE) 12/28/89
(See Pittway Corp. (DE))

CITIZENS TR & SVGS BK (SOUTH HAVEN, MI)
Each share Common $20 par received distribution of (4) shares Common $5 par 06/15/1984
Note: Common $20 par certificates are now valueless
Stock Dividends - 33.33333333% 01/23/1965; 33.33333333% 02/11/1970
Merged into Shoreline Financial Corp. 12/24/1987
Each share Common $5 par exchanged for (1.398884) shares Common $1 par
Shoreline Financial Corp. merged into Chemical Financial Corp. 01/09/2001

CITIZENS TR (ANN ARBOR, MI)
Reorganized as Citizens Trust Bancorp, Inc. 07/01/1986
Each share Common $10 par exchanged for (2) shares Common $5 par
Citizens Trust Bancorp, Inc. merged into Trustcorp, Inc. 09/30/1987 which was acquired by Society Corp. 01/05/1990 which merged into KeyCorp (New) 03/01/1994

CITIZENS TR BANCORP INC (MI)
Merged into Trustcorp, Inc. 09/30/1987
Each share Common $5 par exchanged for (2.5) shares Common $20 par
Trustcorp, Inc. acquired by Society Corp. 01/05/1990 which merged into KeyCorp (New) 03/01/1994

CITIZENS TR BK (PORTSMOUTH, VA)
Common $12 par changed to $4 par and (2) additional shares issued 7/15/73
Under plan of reorganization each share Common $4 par automatically became (1) share Citizens Trust Co. (Portsmouth, VA) Common $4 par 10/1/83
(See Citizens Trust Co. (Portsmouth, VA))

CITIZENS TRUST CO. (SCHENECTADY, NY)
Each share Common $100 par exchanged for (4) shares Common $25 par and 33-1/3% stock dividend paid in 1945
Each share Common $25 par exchanged for (2-7/9) shares Common $10 par 1/17/61
Stock Dividends - 25% 1950; 20% 1953; 16-2/3% 8/1/56; 12-1/2% 1/23/59
Merged into National Commercial Bank & Trust Co. (Albany, NY) 6/25/65
Each share Common $10 par exchanged for (1.75) shares Common $7.50 par
National Commercial Bank & Trust Co. (Albany, NY) reorganized as First Commercial Banks Inc. 12/31/71 which name changed to

Key Banks Inc. 4/23/79 which name changed to KeyCorp (NY) 8/28/85 which merged into KeyCorp (New) (OH) 3/1/94

CITIZENS TR CO (PROVIDENCE, RI)
Stock Dividend - 66-2/3% 12/31/48
Acquired by Citizens Bank of Rhode Island (Providence, RI) 3/1/97
Details not available

CITIZENS TR CO NEW (PORTSMOUTH, VA)
Common $10 par changed to $3.33-1/3 par and (2) additional shares issued 1/30/70
Stock Dividends - 10% 12/15/70; 10% 12/15/71; 15% 12/29/72
Name changed to Citizens Trust Bank (Portsmouth, VA) and Common $3.33-1/3 par changed to $12 par 1/16/73 which reorganized back as Citizens Trust Co. (Portsmouth, VA) 10/1/83
Merged into Bank of Virginia Co. 4/1/85
Each share Common $4 par exchanged for $48.50 cash

CITIZENS UN NATL BK & TR CO (LEXINGTON, KY)
Stock Dividends - 20% 01/21/1964; 25% 03/05/1969; 33.33333333% 03/06/1974; 25% 03/10/1977; 100% 05/15/1981
Acquired by KYNB Bancshares Inc. 03/28/1983
Details not available

CITIZENS UNDERWRITERS CORP. (CA)
Charter suspended for failure to pay taxes 05/18/1950

CITIZENS UTILS CO (DE)
Common $1 par changed to $0.33333333 par and (2) additional shares issued 00/00/1952
5% 1st Ser. Preferred no par called for redemption 10/15/1953
Ser. B $0.33333333 par reclassified as Ser. B Common $0.33333333 par 01/30/1956
Conv. Ser. A Common $0.33333333 par changed to $0.16666666 par and (1) additional share issued 05/14/1959
Ser. B Common $0.33333333 par changed to $0.16666666 par and (1) additional share issued 05/14/1959
Conv. Ser. A Common $0.16666666 par changed to $1 par 06/08/1962
Ser. B Common $0.16666666 par changed to $1 par 06/08/1962
Conv. Ser. A Common $1 par split (3) for (2) by issuance of (0.5) additional share 05/24/1966
Ser. B Common $1 par split (3) for (2) by issuance of (0.5) additional share 05/24/1966
Conv. Ser. A Common $1 par changed to 50¢ par and (1) additional share issued 12/31/1982
Ser. B Common $1 par changed to 50¢ par and (1) additional share issued 12/31/1982
Conv. Ser. A Common 50¢ par changed to 25¢ par and (1) additional share issued 07/31/1986
Ser. B Common 50¢ par changed to 25¢ par and (1) additional share issued 07/31/1986
Conv. Ser. A Common 25¢ par split (3) for (2) by issuance of (0.5) additional share 07/24/1992
Ser. B Common 25¢ par split (3) for (2) by issuance of (0.5) additional share 07/24/1992
Conv. Ser. A Common 25¢ par split (2) for (1) by issuance of (1) additional share 08/31/1993
Ser. B Common 25¢ par split (2) for (1) by issuance of (1) additional share 08/31/1993
Conv. Ser. A Common 25¢ par converted into Ser. B Common 25¢ par 08/25/1997

Stock Dividends - 1.6% payable 03/31/1996 to holders of record 03/01/1996; 1.6% payable 06/30/1996 to holders of record 06/03/1996; 1.6% payable 09/30/1996 to holders of record 09/03/1996; 1.6% payable 03/31/1997 to holders of record 03/01/1997; 1.6% payable 06/30/1997 to holders of record 06/02/1997; 1% payable 12/31/1997 to holders of record 12/01/1997; 0.75% payable 03/31/1998 to holders of record 03/01/1998; 0.75% payable 09/30/1998 to holders of record 09/01/1998; 0.75% payable 12/31/1998 to holders of record 12/01/1998
Name changed to Citizens Communications Co. 05/18/2000
Citizens Communications Co. name changed to Frontier Communications Corp. 07/31/2008

CITIZENS UTILS TR (DE)
5% Conv. Equity Preferred Income Securities called for redemption at $50 on 12/15/2008

CITIZENS VY BK (ALBANY, OR)
Stock Dividends - 10% 12/18/1970; 10% 05/15/1973; 100% 04/20/1978
Reorganized as Northwest Bancorp 12/31/1981
Each share Common $5 par exchanged for (1) share Common $1 par
Northwest Bancorp merged into KeyCorp (NY) 11/10/1986 which merged into KeyCorp (New) (OH) 03/01/1994

CITIZENS WATER CO. OF BURLINGTON, IOWA
Acquired by the City of Burlington, Iowa 00/00/1943
Details not available

CITIZENS WESTERN CORP (CA)
Reorganized 04/01/1985
Under plan of reorganization name changed from Citizens Western Bank (San Diego, CA) to Citizens Western Corp. 04/01/1985
Liquidation completed
Each share Common no par received initial distribution of $1 cash per share 06/00/1992
Each share Common no par received second and final distribution of $0.89 cash per share 06/00/1993
Note: Certificates were not required to be surrendered and are without value

CITIZENS WHOLESALE SUPPLY CO.
Dissolved 00/00/1948
Details not available

CITLEC MINERALS LTD (BC)
Merged into Acheron Resources Ltd. 10/01/1982
Each share Common no par exchanged for (0.5) share Common no par
Acheron Resources Ltd. recapitalized as Abaddon Resources Inc. 09/12/1994 which recapitalized as Consolidated Abaddon Resources Inc. 01/31/2001 which name changed to Aben Resources Ltd. 01/13/2011

CITNAT BANCORP INC (OH)
Merged into Security Banc Corp. 09/30/1996
Each share Common $5 par exchanged for (2.1842437) shares Common $6.25 par
Security Banc Corp. merged into Park National Corp. 03/23/2001

CITOTECH SYS INC (CANADA)
Recapitalized as SmartCool Systems Inc. 07/21/2004
Each share Common no par exchanged for (0.33333333) share Common no par

CITRA-LARTIC MINES LTD. (ON)
Recapitalized as Consolidated Thor Mines Ltd. 09/30/1955
Each share Capital Stock exchanged for (0.2) share Capital Stock
Consolidated Thor Mines Ltd. name changed to Nealon Mines Ltd. 01/18/1957
(See Nealon Mines Ltd.)

CITRALAM MALARTIC MINES LTD.
Recapitalized as Citra-Lartic Mines Ltd. 00/00/1950
Each share Capital Stock exchanged for (0.25) share Capital Stock
Citra-Lartic Mines Ltd. recapitalized as Consolidated Thor Mines Ltd. 09/30/1955 which name was changed to Nealon Mines Ltd. 01/18/1957
(See Nealon Mines Ltd.)

CITRUS BK (KISSIMMEE, FL)
Merged into Carolina First Corp. 07/01/1999
Each share Common $4 par exchanged for (1.493) shares Common $1 par
Carolina First Corp. name changed to South Financial Group, Inc. 04/24/2000 which merged into Toronto-Dominion Bank (Toronto, ON) 09/30/2010

CITRUS CANDY CO., INC. (NY)
Dissolved 12/16/1935
Details not available

CITRUS CHEMICAL CORP. (FL)
Dissolved 11/23/1936
Details not available

CITRUS CNTY LD BUR INC (NEW) (FL)
Name changed 07/31/1981
Under plan of merger name changed from Citrus County Land Bureau, Inc. (Old) to Citrus County Land Bureau, Inc. (New) and each share Common 10¢ par exchanged for (1) share Common 10¢ par or $3 cash 07/31/1981
Merged into Sun Equities Corp. 06/18/1986
Each share Common 10¢ par exchanged for (1) share Common 1¢ par
(See Sun Equities Corp.)

CITRUS FINL SVCS INC (FL)
Stock Dividend - 10% payable 05/31/1998 to holders of record 05/08/1998
Merged into CIB Marine Bancshares, Inc. 09/17/2001
Each share Common no par exchanged for (0.4634) share Common $1 par
(See CIB Marine Bancshares, Inc.)

CITRUS NATL BK (WEST COVINA, CA)
Common $10 par changed to $5 par and (1) additional share issued 04/10/1970
Merged into Golden State Bancorporation 10/30/1970
Each share Common $5 par exchanged for (1.9) shares Common $2.50 par
(See Golden State Bancorporation)

CITRUS STATE BANK (COVINA, CA)
Under plan of merger name changed to California State Bank (Covina, CA) 11/19/1985
California State Bank (Covina, CA) merged into First Security Corp. 05/30/1998 which merged into Wells Fargo & Co. (New) 10/26/2000

CITY & COUNTY BANK OF WASHINGTON COUNTY (JOHNSON CITY, TN)
Name changed to First Peoples Bank of Washington County (Johnson City, TN) 07/25/1983
(See First Peoples Bank of

Washington County (Johnson City, TN))

CITY & SUBURBAN HOMES CO. (NY)
Capital Stock $10 par changed to $1 par and $14 cash distributed 00/00/1950
Merged into Diversified Management Corp. 04/07/1961
Each share Capital Stock $1 par exchanged for $50.25 cash

CITY AUTO RES SVCS INC (DE)
Name changed to CyPro International, Inc. 08/15/1998

CITY AUTO STAMPING CO. (OH)
Capital Stock no par changed to $5 par 00/00/1945
Capital Stock $5 par split (2) for (1) by issuance of (1) additional share 02/10/1956
Name changed to Globe-Wernicke Industries, Inc. 07/01/1957
Globe-Wernicke Industries, Inc. merged into Sheller-Globe Corp. 12/30/1966
(See Sheller-Globe Corp.)

CITY BANCORP OF NORMAN, INC. (OK)
Acquired by First Fidelity Bancorp, Inc. (OK) 09/08/1992
Details not available

CITY BANK & TRUST CO. (JACKSON, MI)
Common $20 par changed to $10 par and (1) additional share issued 01/07/1964
Name changed to City Bank & Trust Co., (N.A.) (Jackson, MI) 08/04/1964
City Bank & Trust Co., (N.A.) (Jackson, MI) reorganized as CB Financial Corp. 08/06/1981 which merged into Citizens Banking Corp. 07/01/1997 which name changed to Citizens Republic Bancorp, Inc. 04/26/2007 which merged into FirstMerit Corp. 04/12/2013 which merged into Huntington Bancshares Inc. 08/16/2016

CITY BANK & TRUST CO. (READING, PA)
Stock Dividend - 50% 01/02/1959
Merged into Peoples Trust City Bank (Reading, PA) 08/01/1960
Each share Capital Stock $10 par exchanged for (1.7) shares Common $5 par
Peoples Trust City Bank (Reading, PA) name changed to Bank of Pennsylvania (Reading, PA) 07/01/1968 which reorganized as B O P Corp. 08/12/1969 which name changed to Bancorp of Pennsylvania 03/25/1981
(See Bancorp of Pennsylvania)

CITY BK & TR CO (BOSTON, MA)
In process in liquidation
Each share Capital Stock $5 par exchanged for initial distribution of $31.50 cash 11/15/1980
Note: Details on subsequent distributions, if any, are not available

CITY BK & TR CO (KANSAS CITY, MO)
100% acquired by City Bancshares, Inc. through exchange offer which expired 12/08/1978
Public interest eliminated

CITY BK & TR CO (ST PETERSBURG, FL)
Capital Stock $20 par changed to $10 par and (1) additional share issued plus a 20% stock dividend paid 02/17/1969
Stock Dividend - 25% 02/24/1971
Through voluntary exchange offer First at Orlando Corp. acquired 100% of Capital Stock as of 02/12/1972
Public interest eliminated

CITY BK & TR CO (TULSA, OK)
Name changed to Bank of Oklahoma, City Plaza (Tulsa, OK) 03/23/1984
(See Bank of Oklahoma, City Plaza (Tulsa, OK))

CITY BK & TR CO N A (JACKSON, MI)
Common $10 par changed to $7.50 par and (0.65) additional share issued to provide for a (3) for (2) split and a 10% stock dividend 05/15/1981
Stock Dividends - 10% 02/25/1966; 10% 03/15/1967; 10% 03/19/1968; 10% 04/06/1970; 16.53% 04/20/1973; 10.86474% 04/15/1977; 10% 05/01/1979
Reorganized as CB Financial Corp. 08/06/1981
Each share Common $7.50 par exchanged for (1) share Common $7.50 par
CB Financial Corp. merged into Citizens Banking Corp. 07/01/1997 which name changed to Citizens Republic Bancorp, Inc. 04/26/2007 which merged into FirstMerit Corp. 04/12/2013 which merged into Huntington Bancshares Inc. 08/16/2016

CITY BANK (ANCHORAGE, AK)
Name changed to City National Bank (Anchorage, AK) 09/29/1953
City National Bank (Anchorage, AK) name changed to Alaska Statebank (Anchorage, AK) 09/01/1962
(See Alaska Statebank (Anchorage, AK))

CITY BK (LYNNWOOD, WA)
Common $1 par split (3) for (1) by issuance of (2) additional shares payable 05/15/1998 to holders of record 04/20/1998
Common $1 par split (3) for (2) by issuance of (0.5) additional share payable 12/22/2006 to holders of record 12/08/2006 Ex date - 12/26/2006
Stock Dividends - 20% 02/10/1993; 20% 02/10/1994; 20% 02/10/1995; 30% payable 01/31/1996 to holders of record 01/17/1996; 25% payable 01/31/1997 to holders of record 01/17/1997; 20% payable 01/30/1998 to holders of record 01/16/1998; 20% payable 01/29/1999 to holders of record 01/15/1999; 20% payable 01/28/2000 to holders of record 01/14/2000
Closed and placed in receivership 04/16/2010
Stockholders' equity unlikely

CITY BK CO (LORAIN, OH)
Each share Common $20 par exchanged for (2) shares Common $10 par 01/25/1972
Stock Dividends - 10% 01/22/1974; 10% 04/25/1978; 10% 03/28/1980
Merged into Central Trust Co. of Northern Ohio, N.A. (Cincinnati, OH) 07/14/1984
Each share Common $10 par exchanged for $30 cash

CITY BK HONOLULU (HONOLULU, HI)
Capital Stock $20 par changed to $10 par and (1) additional share issued 09/04/1962
Capital Stock $10 par changed to $5 par and (1) additional share issued 03/05/1970
Reorganized as CB Bancshares, Inc. 10/14/1980
Each share Capital Stock $5 par exchanged for (1) share Common $1 par
CB Bancshares, Inc. merged into Central Pacific Financial Corp. 09/15/2004

CITY BK KENT (KENT, OH)
Acquired by CleveTrust Corp. 08/26/1975
Each share Common $4.50 par exchanged for $24 cash
Note: An initial additional distribution of $0.40 cash per share was made 07/08/1977
Second and final additional distribution of $1.055 cash per share was made 12/31/1977

CITY BK LAUDERHILL (LAUDERHILL, FL)
Name changed to City National Bank (Lauderhill, FL) 03/01/1976
City National Bank (Lauderhill, FL) recapitalized as Union Bank of Florida (Lauderhill, FL) 06/02/1980
(See Union Bank of Florida (Lauderhill, FL))

CITY BANK OF WASHINGTON (WASHINGTON, DC)
Completely liquidated 05/29/1959
Each share Capital Stock $20 par exchanged for first and final distribution of $325 cash

CITY BK PHILADELPHIA (PHILADELPHIA, PA)
Completely liquidated 12/22/1989
Each share Capital Stock $5 par received first and final distribution of $2.34 cash

CITY BK SAN DIEGO (SAN DIEGO, CA)
Completely liquidated 05/29/1969
Each share Common $10 par exchanged for first and final distribution of $33.80 cash

CITY BK ST LOUIS (ST. LOUIS, MO)
Common $10 par changed to $5 par and (1) additional share issued 11/08/1977
Merged into CharterCorp 03/07/1983
Each share Common $5 par exchanged for (1.03) shares Common $6.25 par
CharterCorp merged into Boatmen's Bancshares, Inc. 01/28/1985 which merged into NationsBank Corp. (NC) 01/07/1997 which reincorporated in Delaware as BankAmerica Corp. (Old) 09/25/1998 which merged into BankAmerica Corp. (New) 09/30/1998 which name changed to Bank Bank of America Corp. 04/28/1999

CITY BOND & MORTGAGE CORP.
In process of liquidation 00/00/1943
Details not available

CITY CERTIFICATES CORP.
Dissolved 00/00/1939
Details not available

CITY COACH LINES (DE)
Reincorporated 04/09/1959
Each share Common $5 par exchanged for (2) shares Common $2.50 par 07/30/1956
State of incorporation changed from (MI) to (DE) 04/09/1959
Charter cancelled and declared inoperative and void for non-payment of taxes 10/23/1989

CITY COMM BK (SANTA BARBARA, CA)
Stock Dividend - 10% payable 11/27/1998 to holders of record 10/30/1998
Merged into Mid-State Bancshares 08/31/1999
Each share Common no par exchanged for (0.6775) share Common no par
(See Mid-State Bancshares)

CITY COMM CORP (AK)
Name changed to Alaska Bancshares, Inc. 07/28/1970
Alaska Bancshares, Inc. acquired by Alaska Bancorporation 02/07/1979
(See Alaska Bancorporation)

CITY COMPANY OF HARTFORD, INC.
Merged into Connecticut Investment Management Corp. 00/00/1931
Details not available

CITY E SOLUTIONS LTD (HONG KONG)
Each old Sponsored ADR for Ordinary exchanged for (0.05) new Sponsored ADR for Ordinary 10/13/2000
ADR agreement terminated 08/28/2015
Each new Sponsored ADR for Ordinary exchanged for $3.594699 cash

CITY FED SVGS BK BEDMINSTER N J (USA)
Common 1¢ par split (2) for (1) by issuance of (1) additional share 11/19/1982
Common 1¢ par split (2) for (1) by issuance of (1) additional share 05/20/1983
Reorganized under the laws of Delaware as CityFed Financial Corp. 12/19/1984
Each share $2.10 Conv. Preferred Ser. B $25 par exchanged for (1) share $2.10 Conv. Preferred Ser. B $25 par
Each share $2.20 Conv. Preferred $25 par exchanged for $2.20 Conv. Preferred $25 par
Each share Common 1¢ par exchanged for (1) share Common 1¢ par
(See CityFed Financial Corp.)

CITY FIN INC (MD)
Merged into USLIFE Holding Corp. 04/18/1969
Each share Common no par exchanged for (0.05883) share $5 Conv. Preferred Ser. B no par and (0.17778) share Common $2 par
USLIFE Holding Corp. name changed to USLIFE Corp. 05/22/1970 which merged into American General Corp. 06/17/1997 which merged into American International Group, Inc. 08/29/2001

CITY FINANCE CO. (TN)
Merged into Talcott (James), Inc. 01/13/1966
Each share Common $5 par exchanged for (0.25) share 4.5% Conv. Preferred Ser. I-F $50 par
(See Talcott (James), Inc.)

CITY GAS CO. OF NORFOLK, VA
Merged into Virginia Electric & Power Co. 00/00/1930
Details not available

CITY GAS CO FLA (FL)
Common $1 par changed to 1¢ par and (2) additional shares issued 08/17/1987
Merged into NUI Corp. (Old) 07/29/1988
Each share Common 1¢ par exchanged for $15.67 value of Common $7 par, $15.67 cash or a combination thereof
NUI Corp. (Old) reorganized as NUI Corp. (New) 03/01/2001
(See NUI Corp. (New))

CITY GOLD CORP (CANADA)
Name changed to Extracare Corp. 09/28/1988
Extracare Corp. name changed to South Pacific Resources Inc. 06/17/1994 which name changed to South Pacific Resources Corp. 10/24/1994 which recapitalized as Lexacal Investment Corp. 07/24/1998 which name changed to New West Energy Services Inc. 10/26/2007

CITY HLDG CAP TR II (DE)
9.125% Capital Securities called for redemption at $25 plus $0.044357 accrued dividends on 11/07/2003

CITY ICE & COAL CO.
Dissolved 00/00/1928
Details not available

CITY ICE & FUEL CO. (OH)
Name changed to City Products Corp. 04/21/1949
(See City Products Corp.)

CITY INSURANCE CO. OF PENN.
Merged into Allemannia Fire Insurance Co. 00/00/1930
Details not available

CITY INVESTING CO. (NY)
Each share 7% Preferred $100 par exchanged for (1.3) shares 5.5% Preferred $100 par 00/00/1944
Each share Common $100 par exchanged for (0.15) share 5.5% Preferred $100 par and (2) shares Common no par 00/00/1944
Each share Common no par exchanged for (6) shares Common $5 par 00/00/1946
5.5% Preferred $100 par called for redemption 01/01/1965
Stock Dividends - 10% 10/31/1952; 15% 09/25/1953
Reincorporated under the laws of Delaware 02/09/1968
(See City Investing Co. (DE))

CITY INVESTING CO (DE)
Common $5 par changed to $2.50 par and (1) additional share issued 03/08/1968
Common $2.50 par changed to $1.25 par and (1) additional share issued 03/20/1969
Each Certificate of Contingent Interest (issued on merger of Hayes Holding Co.) exchanged for (0.346513) share City Investing Co. Common $1.25 par 12/08/1971
In process of liquidation
Each share $1.31 Conv. Preference Ser. A $1 par exchanged for first and final distribution of $14.9074 cash 06/28/1985
Each share $2 Conv. Preference Ser. B $1 par exchanged for first and final distribution of $40.3167 cash 06/28/1985
Each share $2.875 Conv. Exchangeable Preference Ser. E $1 par exchanged for first and final distribution of $25.4552 cash 06/28/1985
Each share Common $1.25 par received initial distribution of $7.50 cash 07/16/1985
Each share Common $1.25 par received second distribution of $4 cash 09/25/1985
Assets transferred to City Investing Co. Liquidating Trust and Common $1.25 par reclassified as Units of Bene. Int. no par 09/25/1985
(See City Investing Co. Liquidating Trust)

CITY INVESTING CO LIQ TR (DE)
Liquidation completed
Each Unit of Bene. Int. no par received initial distribution of $0.25 cash 04/11/1986
Each (113) Units of Bene. Int. no par received second distribution of (10) shares General Development Corp. (New) Common $1 par 07/03/1986
Each Unit of Bene. Int. no par received third distribution of $0.25 cash 04/10/1987
Each Unit of Bene. Int. no par received fourth distribution of $0.75 cash 06/12/1987
Each Unit of Bene. Int. no par received fifth distribution of $0.025 cash 04/11/1988
Each Unit of Bene. Int. no par received sixth distribution of $2 cash 05/11/1988
Each Unit of Bene. Int. no par received seventh distribution of $1 cash 11/15/1988
Each Unit of Bene. Int. no par received eighth distribution of $1 cash 05/12/1990
Each Unit of Bene. Int. no par received ninth distribution of $2 cash payable 08/15/2005 to holders of record 08/08/2005
Each Unit of Bene. Int. no par received tenth and final distribution of $0.116 cash payable 04/18/2006 to holders of record 03/31/2006
Ex date - 04/19/2006
Note: Certificates were not required to be surrendered and are without value

CITY INVESTING MTG GROUP (MA)
Name changed to C.I. Mortgage Group 01/27/1971
C.I. Mortgage Group name changed to Enterprise Development Group 05/29/1981
(See Enterprise Development Group)

CITY LANGUAGE EXCHANGE INC (DE)
Common $0.000001 par changed to $0.0001 par and (4) additional shares issued payable 07/01/2008 to holders of record 06/23/2008
Ex date - 07/02/2008
Name changed to Game Trading Technologies, Inc. 02/26/2010
(See Game Trading Technologies, Inc.)

CITY LN INC (DE)
Reorganized under the laws of Nevada 09/17/2008
Each share Common $0.001 par exchanged for (0.14285714) share Common $0.001 par

CITY MACHINE & TOOL CO.
Merged into City Auto Stamping Co. 00/00/1931
Details not available

CITY MEDIA INC (UT)
Name changed to THC Farmaceuticals, Inc. 04/08/2015

CITY NATL BANCSHARES INC (LA)
Common $10 par split (2) for (1) by issuance of (1) additional share 11/15/83
Merged into First Commerce Corp. 7/1/85
Each share Common $10 par exchanged for (2.25) shares Common $5 par
First Commerce Corp. merged into Banc One Corp. 6/12/98 which merged into Bank One Corp. 10/2/98 which merged into J.P. Morgan Chase & Co. 12/31/2000 which name changed to JPMorgan Chase & Co. 7/20/2004

CITY NATIONAL BANK & TRUST CO. (CHICAGO, IL)
Each share Capital Stock $100 par exchanged for (4) shares Capital Stock $25 par 00/00/1952
Stock Dividends - 25% 08/8/1950; 12-2/3% 02/03/1954; 25% 01/11/1957; 14-2/7% 01/21/1959; 12-1/2% 01/20/1960
Merged into Continental Illinois National Bank & Trust Co. (Chicago, IL) 09/01/1961
Each share Capital Stock $25 par exchanged for (1.05) shares Capital Stock $33-1/3 par
Continental Illinois National Bank & Trust Co. (Chicago, IL) reorganized in Delaware as Conill Corp. 03/31/1969 which name changed to Continental Illinois Corp. 03/27/1972 which reorganized as Continental Illinois Holding Corp. 09/27/1984
(See Continental Illinois Holding Corp.)

CITY NATIONAL BANK & TRUST CO. (OKLAHOMA CITY, OK)
Capital Stock $100 par changed to $10 par and (9) additional shares issued 7/15/69
Stock Dividends - 150% 1/5/46; 50% 1/26/50; 33-1/3% 2/1/57; 25% 9/27/62; 50% 9/2/69
Name changed to First City Bank, N.A. (Oklahoma City, OK) 4/21/81
(See First City Bank, N.A. (Oklahoma City, OK))

CITY NATL BK & TR CO (COLUMBUS, OH)
Stock Dividends - 25% 06/30/1941; 33-1/3% 01/17/1997; 25% 01/18/1954; 20% 01/16/1956; 33-1/3% 01/17/1958; 33-1/3% 05/17/1962; 14-2/7% 01/30/1964; 12-1/2% 01/28/1966; 11-1/9% 03/15/1968
Through voluntary exchange offer 99.94% held by First Banc Group of Ohio, Inc. as of 12/06/1968
Public interest eliminated

CITY NATL BK & TR CO (GLOVERSVILLE, NY)
Common Capital Stock $20 par changed to $10 par and (1) additional share issued 2/1/65
Common Capital Stock $10 par changed to $5 par and (1) additional share issued 3/9/70
Stock Dividends - 100% 3/1/74; 100% 5/2/88
Under plan of reorganization each share Common Capital Stock $5 par automatically became (1) share CNB Bancorp, Inc. Common $5 par 1/3/89
(See CNB Bancorp, Inc.)

CITY NATL BK & TR CO (HACKENSACK, NJ)
Name changed to City National Bank (Hackensack, NJ) 12/31/66
(See City National Bank (Hackensack, NJ))

CITY NATL BK & TR CO (KANSAS CITY, MO)
Each share Capital Stock $100 par exchanged for (8) shares Capital Stock $25 par to effect a (4) for (1) split and a 100% stock dividend 12/12/50
Stock Dividends - 66-2/3% 12/3/41; 100% 2/11/48; 25% 2/10/55; 100% 2/6/59
Reorganized as Missouri Bancshares, Inc. 12/19/69
Each share Capital Stock $25 par exchanged for (2) shares Common $12.50 par
Missouri Bancshares, Inc. name changed to United Missouri Bancshares, Inc. 9/1/71 which name changed to UMB Financial Corp. 4/22/94

CITY NATL BK & TR CO (NORMAN, OK)
Reorganized as City Bancorp of Norman, Inc. 11/01/1982
Each share Common $1 par exchanged for (5) shares Common $1 par
(See City Bancorp of Norman, Inc.)

CITY NATIONAL BANK (ANCHORAGE, AK)
Name changed to Alaska Statebank (Anchorage, AK) 09/01/1962
(See Alaska Statebank (Anchorage, AK))

CITY NATL BK (AUSTIN, TX)
Capital Stock $20 par changed to $10 par and (1) additional share issued 11/11/1964
Acquired by First City Bancorporation of Texas, Inc. (TX) 07/28/1977
Each share Capital Stock $10 par exchanged for (1.8669) shares Common $6.50 par
(See First City Bancorporation of Texas, Inc. (TX))

CITY NATL BK (BATON ROUGE, LA)
Stock Dividends - 66.66666666% 10/01/1942; 100% 01/18/1955; 10% 12/19/1957; 12.5% 09/23/1960; 11.11111111% 08/11/1961; 20% 04/02/1974; 16.66666666% 05/17/1976; (1) for (7) 05/19/1978; 25% 05/01/1981
Under plan of reorganization each share Capital Stock $10 par automatically became (1) share City National Bancshares, Inc. Common $10 par 09/01/1982
City National Bancshares, Inc. merged into First Commerce Corp. 07/01/1985 which merged into Banc One Corp. 06/12/1998 which merged into Bank One Corp. 10/02/1998 which merged into J.P. Morgan Chase & Co. 12/31/2000 which name changed to JPMorgan Chase & Co. 07/20/2004

CITY NATL BK (BEVERLY HILLS, CA)
Each share Common $10 par exchanged for (3) shares Common $5 par to effect a (2) for (1) split and a 50% stock dividend 11/10/1960
Each share Common $5 par exchanged for (0.05) share Common $100 par 06/30/1970
Through voluntary exchange offer 99.5% held by City National Corp. 11/00/1971
Public interest eliminated

CITY NATL BK (BIRMINGHAM, AL)
Stock Dividends - 10% 01/30/1970; 10% 02/23/1973
Merged into Southland Bancorporation 02/28/1975
Each share Common $5 par exchanged for (1.45) shares Common $2.50 par
Southland Bancorporation name changed to Colonial BancGroup, Inc. 12/31/1981
(See Colonial BancGroup, Inc.)

CITY NATL BK (CHARLESTON, WV)
Common $10 par changed to $5 par and (1) additional share issued 09/02/1980
Reorganized as City Holding Co. 03/07/1984
Each share Common $5 par exchanged for (1) share Common $5 par

CITY NATL BK (CHARLOTTE, NC)
Merged into Branch Corp. 06/06/1983
Each share Capital Stock $100 par exchanged for (30) shares Common $2.50 par
Branch Corp. name changed to BB&T Financial Corp. 05/10/1988 which merged into Southern National Corp. 02/28/1995 which merged into BB&T Corp. 05/19/1997

CITY NATIONAL BANK (CLINTON, IA)
Stock Dividends - 25% 08/00/1955; 20% 10/16/1959
Name changed to First National Bank (Clinton, IA) 04/01/1966
(See First National Bank (Clinton, IA))

CITY NATIONAL BANK (COCOA, FL)
99% held by Southeast Banking Corp. as of 07/31/1974
Public interest eliminated

CITY NATL BK (CORAL GABLES, FL)
Completely liquidated 01/01/1977
Each share Capital Stock $10 par exchanged for first and final distribution of $20.43 cash

CITY NATL BK (DETROIT, MI)
Stock Dividends - 10% 02/03/1964; 75% 09/15/1969
Under plan of reorganization each share Common $10 par automatically became (1) share Northern States Financial Corp. Common $10 par 10/31/1972
Northern States Financial Corp. name changed to Northern States Bancorporation, Inc. 03/27/1973 which merged into First American Bank Corp. 10/09/1981 which name

CIT-CIT FINANCIAL INFORMATION, INC.

changed to First of America Bank Corp. 01/14/1983
(See First of America Bank Corp.)

CITY NATL BK (FAIRMONT, WV)
Merged into Mountaineer Bankshares of W. Va., Inc. 03/31/1986
Each share Capital Stock $25 par exchanged for (1) share Common $2.50 par
Mountaineer Bankshares of W. Va., Inc. merged into One Valley Bancorp of West Virginia, Inc. 01/28/1994 which name changed to One Valley Bancorp Inc. 04/30/1996 which merged into BB&T Corp. 07/06/2000

CITY NATL BK (FORT SMITH, AR)
Common $10 par changed to $5 par and (1) additional share issued plus a 13.63% stock dividend paid 12/31/1970
Stock Dividends - 14.3% 07/01/1963; 11.5% 07/01/1965; 10% 07/01/1968; 200% 02/28/1978
Reorganized as First City Corp. 12/15/1980
Each share Common $5 par exchanged for (0.55) share Preferred $6 par and (0.55) share Common $2 par
(See First City Corp.)

CITY NATIONAL BANK (GALVESTON, TX)
Stock Dividends - 100% 01/24/1947; 25% 01/18/1951
Name changed to Moody National Bank (Galveston, TX) 03/01/1953

CITY NATIONAL BANK (HACKENSACK, NJ)
Merged into First National State Bancorporation 12/21/1970
Each share Capital Stock $12.50 par exchanged for $187.50 cash

CITY NATIONAL BANK (HALLANDALE, FL)
Name changed to City National Bank of Florida (Hallandale, FL) 07/07/1983

CITY NATIONAL BANK (LAUDERHILL, FL)
Recapitalized as Union Bank of Florida (Lauderhill, FL) 06/02/1980
Each share Capital Stock $10 par exchanged for (0.16666666) share Common $5 par
(See Union Bank of Florida (Lauderhill, FL))

CITY NATL BK (MIAMI, FL)
5% Preferred $100 par called for redemption 12/31/1965
Through voluntary exchange offer by City National Bank Corp. all but Directors Qualifying Shares acquired by 12/31/1970
Public interest eliminated

CITY NATL BK (MIAMI BEACH, FL)
Completely liquidated 01/01/1977
Each share Capital Stock $10 par exchanged for first and final distribution of $34.80 cash

CITY NATL BK (MILLVILLE, NJ)
Acquired by United Jersey Banks 05/01/1972
Each share Common $10 par exchanged for (2.25) shares Common $5 par
United Jersey Banks name changed to UJB Financial Corp. 06/30/1989 which name changed to Summit Bancorp 03/01/1996 which merged into FleetBoston Financial Corp. 03/01/2001 which merged into Bank of America Corp. 04/01/2004

CITY NATL BK (TULSA, OK)
Name changed to City Bank & Trust Co. (Tulsa, OK) 01/02/1970
City Bank & Trust Co. (Tulsa, OK) name changed to Bank of Oklahoma, City Plaza (Tulsa, OK) 03/23/1984

(See Bank of Oklahoma, City Plaza (Tulsa, OK))

CITY NATL BK (TUSCALOOSA, AL)
Stock Dividends - 33.33333333% 02/05/1944; 50% 07/14/1947; 25% 01/16/1951; 10% 06/03/1968
Merged into First Alabama Bancshares, Inc. 12/31/1973
Each share Capital Stock $100 par exchanged for (1.35) shares Common $2.50 par
First Alabama Bancshares, Inc. name changed to Regions Financial Corp. (Old) 05/02/1994 which merged into Regions Financial Corp. (New) 07/01/2004

CITY NATL BK (WICHITA FALLS, TX)
Each share Common $25 par exchanged for (2.5) shares Common $10 par 01/12/1955
Stock Dividends - 10% 06/20/1956; 10% 12/20/1956; 10% 12/19/1958; 10% 12/01/1965; 20% 02/10/1976
Acquired by First International Bancshares, Inc. 04/14/1978
Each share Common $10 par exchanged for (2.25) shares Common $5 par
First International Bancshares, Inc. name changed to InterFirst Corp. 12/31/1981 which merged into First RepublicBank Corp. 06/06/1987
(See First RepublicBank Corp.)

CITY NATL BK NEW JERSEY (NEWARK, NJ)
Under plan of reorganization each share Common $25 par automatically became (1) share City National Bancshares Corp. Common $10 par 01/03/1984

CITY NATIONAL BANK OF FLORIDA (MIAMI, FL)
83% acquired by Caja Madrid 04/14/2008
Public interest eliminated

CITY NATL CORP (DE)
Common $5 par changed to $1 par 06/24/1981
Common $1 par split (2) for (1) by issuance of (1) additional share 07/15/1986
Common $1 par split (5) for (4) by issuance of (0.25) additional share 10/16/1989
Stock Dividends - 100% 07/14/1978; 100% 10/15/1980; 10% 10/15/1982; 10% 10/16/1984; 10% 10/16/1985; 10% 01/15/1988; 20% 10/17/1988
Merged into Royal Bank of Canada (Montreal, QC) 11/02/2015
Each share 5.5% Depositary Preferred Ser. C exchanged for (1) share 5.5% Depositary Preferred Ser. C
Each share 6.75% Depositary Preferred Ser. D exchanged for (1) share 6.75% Depositary Preferred Ser. D
Each share Common $1 par exchanged for (0.2282094) share Common no par and $77.01234494 cash

CITY NETWORK INC (NV)
SEC revoked common stock registration 06/27/2011

CITY NEWS PRTG CORP (NY)
Merged into Blair (John) & Co. 11/03/1969
Each share Class B $1 par or Common $1 par exchanged for (0.4865) share Common $1 par
(See Blair (John) & Co.)

CITY OF NEW YORK INSURANCE CO.
Merged into Home Insurance Co. 00/00/1948
Each share Capital Stock $10 exchanged for (0.846) share Common $5 par
(See Home Insurance Co.)

CITY PHARMACY (FREEPORT) LTD. (BAHAMAS)
Name changed to City Associated Enterprises, Ltd. 00/00/1969

CITY PRODS CORP (OH)
Common no par split (2) for (1) by issuance of (1) additional share 05/29/1961
Each share Common no par exchanged for (0.5) share $3.20 Preferred no par 04/30/1968
$3.20 Preferred no par called for redemption 06/30/1968
Public interest eliminated

CITY RADIO STORES, INC.
Merged into Atlas Stores Corp. 00/00/1929
Details not available

CITY RAILWAY CO. (OH)
Recapitalized 00/00/1953
Each share Preferred $100 par exchanged for (4) shares Preferred $25 par
Each share Common $100 par exchanged for (4) shares Common $25 par
Name changed to Midwest Securities, Inc. (OH) 04/02/1956
Midwest Securities, Inc. (OH) reincorporated in Delaware as Midwest Securities Investment, Inc. 06/15/1959
(See Midwest Securities Investment, Inc.)

CITY RES CDA LTD (BC)
Name changed to Misty Mountain Gold Ltd. 04/22/1994
Misty Mountain Gold Ltd. recapitalized as Misty Mountain Gold Inc. 11/10/1995 which name changed to Continental Minerals Corp. (Incorporated 02/07/1962) 10/18/2001
(See Continental Minerals Corp. (Incorporated 02/07/1962))

CITY RES LTD (AUSTRALIA)
Each Unsponsored ADR for Ordinary exchanged for (0.1) Sponsored ADR for Ordinary 09/30/1988
Liquidator declared Ordinary shares worthless 10/02/1991
No ADR holders' equity

CITY SVGS & LN ASSN (CA)
Name changed to Gibraltar Savings & Loan Assn. of Northern California 12/11/1969
(See Gibraltar Savings & Loan Assn. of Northern California)

CITY SAVINGS & TRUST CO. (EDMONTON, AB)
Each share Common $10 par exchanged for (5) shares Common $2 par 06/30/1967
Location changed to Calgary, AB 08/00/1977
City Savings & Trust Co. (Calgary, AB) name changed to First City Trust Co. (Calgary, AB) 10/30/1978
(See First City Trust Co. (Calgary, AB))

CITY SVGS & TR CO (CALGARY, AB)
Name changed to First City Trust Co. (Calgary, AB) 10/30/1978
(See First City Trust Co. (Calgary, AB))

CITY SVGS BK (MERIDEN, CT)
Acquired by Dime Financial Corp. (CT) 12/02/1988
Each share Common $1 par exchanged for $16 cash

CITY SVGS FINL CORP (IN)
Merged into LaPorte Bancorp, Inc. (USA) 10/16/2007
Each share Common no par exchanged for (3.4) shares Common 1¢ par
LaPorte Bancorp, Inc. (USA) reorganized in Maryland 10/05/2012 which merged into Horizon Bancorp

07/18/2016 which name changed to Horizon Bancorp, Inc. 05/08/2018

CITY SHAREHOLDERS, INC.
Liquidated 00/00/1931
No stockholders' equity

CITY SHARES, INC. (NY)
Name changed to City Union Corp. 00/00/1931
(See City Union Corp.)

CITY SPECIALTY STORES, INC. (NY)
4.5% Preferred $50 par called for redemption 11/30/1960
Merged into City Stores Co. 01/28/1961
Each share Common $1 par exchanged for (0.66666666) share Common $5 par
City Stores Co. name changed to CSS Industries, Inc. 09/24/1985

CITY STORES CO (DE)
Each share Class B no par exchanged for (4) shares Common no par 00/00/1929
Each share Class A no par exchanged for (1) share Common $5 par 00/00/1935
Each share Common no par exchanged for (0.83333333) share Common $5 par 00/00/1935
4.5% Preferred $100 par called for redemption 01/30/1959
Common $5 par changed to 10¢ par 08/05/1981
Name changed to CSS Industries, Inc. 09/24/1985

CITY TELECOM H K LTD (HONG KONG)
Name changed to Hong Kong Television Network Ltd. 01/28/2013

CITY TITLE INS CO (NY)
Each share Capital Stock $5 par exchanged for (2.4) shares Capital Stock $2.50 par 00/00/1951
Capital Stock $2.50 par changed to $5 par 06/05/1978
Name changed to National Attorneys' Title Insurance Co. 12/01/1982
National Attorneys' Title Insurance Co. name changed to New York TRW Title Insurance Co. 07/12/1990
(See New York TRW Title Insurance Co.)

CITY TR CO (BRIDGEPORT, CT)
Common $10 par changed to $5 par and (1) additional share issued plus a 25% stock dividend paid 04/07/1969
Under plan of reorganization each share Common $5 par automatically became (1) share Connecticut Financial Services Corp. Common $5 par 01/02/1970
Connecticut Financial Services Corp. name changed to Citytrust Bancorp, Inc. 04/12/1978
(See Citytrust Bancorp, Inc.)

CITY UNION CORP. (NY)
Common $10 par changed to $1 par 00/00/1934
Completely liquidated 05/12/1967
Each share Common $1 par exchanged for first and final distribution of $0.29 cash

CITY WTR CO CHATTANOOGA (TN)
Name changed to Tennessee-American Water Co. 08/31/1973
(See Tennessee-American Water Co.)

CITYFED FINL CORP (DE)
Stock Dividend - 59.2% 08/28/1985
$2.20 Conv. Preferred $25 par called for redemption 05/30/1986
SEC revoked common stock registration 09/03/2010

CITYHOME CORP (DE)
Name changed to Home Group, Inc. 06/16/1978
Home Group, Inc. name changed to AmBase Corp. 05/19/1989

CITYSCAPE FINL CORP (DE)
Stock Dividend - 100% payable 07/01/1996 to holders of record 06/24/1996
Plan of reorganization under Chapter 11 Federal Bankruptcy Code effective 07/01/1999
No stockholders' equity

CITYSCAPE FINL CORP NEW (DE)
Name changed to AMC Financial, Inc. 07/01/1999
AMC Financial, Inc. name changed to AMC Financial Holdings, Inc. 04/13/2004

CITYSIDE TICKETS INC (NV)
Name changed to Causeway Entertainment Co. and Common $0.001 par changed to $0.00001 par 10/11/2010
Causeway Entertainment Co. recapitalized as United Bullion Exchange Inc. 05/10/2011

CITYTRUST BANCORP INC (CT)
Common $5 par changed to $2.50 par and (1) additional share issued 11/01/1983
Declared insolvent by the Connecticut State Banking Department 07/09/1991
Stockholders' equity unlikely

CITYVIEW CORPORATION LTD NEW (AUSTRALIA)
Name changed to CVI Energy Corporation Ltd. 12/03/2010

CITYVIEW CORPORATION LTD OLD (AUSTRALIA)
Each share old Ordinary exchanged for (0.2) share new Ordinary 04/14/1997
Name changed to CityView Energy Corporation Ltd. 05/19/1997
CityView Energy Corporation Ltd. name changed to CityView Corporation Ltd. (New) 08/31/2000 which name changed to CVI Energy Corporation Ltd. 12/03/2010
(See CVI Energy Corporation.Ltd.)

CITYVIEW ENERGY CORPORATION LTD (AUSTRALIA)
Name changed to CityView Corporation Ltd. (New) 08/31/2000
CityView Corporation Ltd. (New) name changed to CVI Energy Corporation Ltd. 12/03/2010
(See CVI Energy Corporation Ltd.)

CITYVIEW INVESTMENTS LTD (AUSTRALIA)
Name changed to CityView Corporation Ltd. (Old) 08/09/1996
CityView Corporation Ltd. (Old) name changed to CityView Energy Corporation Ltd. 05/19/1997 which name changed to CityView Corporation Ltd. (New) 08/31/2000 which name changed to CVI Energy Corporation Ltd. 12/03/2010
(See CVI Energy Corporation Ltd.)

CITYXPRESS CORP (FL)
Name changed 06/17/2002
Name changed from CityXpress.com Corp. to CityXpress Corp. 06/17/2002
Reorganized under the laws of Oklahoma as Cigars MFOV, Inc. 07/09/2015
Each share Common $0.001 par exchanged for (0.001) share Common $0.001 par
Cigars MFOV, Inc. name changed to Fernhill Beverage, Inc. 12/09/2015

CIVEO CORP (DE)
Reincorporated under the laws of British Columbia and Common 1¢ par changed to no par 07/17/2015

CIVIC BANCORP (CA)
Stock Dividends - 5% payable 11/10/1997 to holders of record 10/29/1997; 5% payable 05/14/1999 to holders of record 04/30/1999; 5% payable 04/12/2000 to holders of record 03/29/2000; 5% payable 05/16/2001 to holders of record 05/02/2001
Acquired by City National Corp. 02/28/2002
Each share Common no par exchanged for $20.25 cash

CIVIC CTR BK & TR CO (CHICAGO, IL)
Under plan of merger name changed to Chicago Bank of Commerce (Chicago, IL) 01/03/1972
Chicago Bank of Commerce (Chicago, IL) name changed to Associated Bank Chicago (Chicago, IL) 10/17/1988
(See Associated Bank Chicago (Chicago, IL))

CIVIC ENTERPRISES INC (DE)
Merged into Aetna Life & Casualty Co. 07/31/1969
Each share $1.10 Conv. Preference $15 par exchanged for (1.1538) shares $2 Conv. Preferred no par
Each share Common $2 par exchanged for (0.5) share $2 Conv. Preferred no par
Aetna Life & Casualty Co. name changed to Aetna, Inc. (CT) 07/19/1996 which merged into ING Groep N.V. 12/13/2000

CIVIC EQUITIES CORP (DE)
Name changed to Global Agricultural Holdings, Inc. 10/21/2008

CIVIC FEDERAL SAVINGS & LOAN ASSOCIATION (USA)
Merged into Southern California Savings & Loan Association 12/31/1980
Each share Capital Stock no par exchanged for $31 cash

CIVIC FIN CORP (WI)
Each share Common $4 par exchanged for (2) shares Common $2 par 05/22/1959
5.6% Preferred no par called for redemption 06/01/1959
Common $2 par split (3) for (2) by issuance of (0.5) additional share 02/01/1968
Merged into Aetna Life & Casualty Co. 07/31/1969
Each share $1.10 Conv. Preference $15 par exchanged for (1.1538) shares $2 Conv. Preferred no par
Each share Common $2 par exchanged for (0.5) share $2 Conv. Preferred no par
Aetna Life & Casualty Co. name changed to Aetna, Inc. (CT) 07/19/1996 which merged into ING Groep N.V. 12/13/2000

CIVIC UTILITIES CORP.
Out of business 00/00/1935
Details not available

CIVIL SVC EMPLOYEES INS CO (CA)
Capital Stock $10 par changed to $5 par and (1) additional share issued 09/30/1960
Capital Stock $5 par changed to $2.50 par 09/19/1961
Stock Dividends - 16.66666666% 02/16/1959; 10% 03/21/1960; 10% 03/15/1961; 10% 03/22/1965; 10% 03/22/1966; 10% 03/31/1967; 10% 03/20/1968; 10% 02/28/1969
Each share Capital Stock $2.50 par exchanged for (0.001) share Capital Stock $2,500 par 12/15/1972
Note: In effect holders received $23.46 cash per share and public interest was eliminated

CIVISTA CORP (OH)
Common $5 par split (4) for (1) by issuance of (3) additional shares 02/21/1992
Common $5 par split (2) for (1) by issuance of (1) additional share 11/22/1993
Merged into FirstMerit Corp. 01/31/1995
Each share Common $5 par exchanged for (1.723) shares Common no par
FirstMerit Corp. merged into Huntington Bancshares Inc. 08/16/2016

CIVITAS BANKGROUP INC (TN)
Stock Dividends - 0.25% payable 11/15/2004 to holders of record 10/29/2004 Ex date - 10/27/2004; 0.25% payable 08/26/2005 to holders of record 08/05/2005 Ex date - 08/03/2005; 0.25% payable 11/18/2005 to holders of record 11/04/2005 Ex date - 11/02/2005; 0.25% payable 02/17/2006 to holders of record 02/03/2006 Ex date - 02/01/2006
Merged into Green Bankshares, Inc. 05/18/2007
Each share Common 50¢ par exchanged for either (0.2674) share Common $2 par or (0.15880886) share Common $2 par and $4.162525 cash
Note: Option to receive stock and cash expired 06/04/2007
Green Bankshares, Inc. merged into Capital Bank Financial Corp. 09/20/2012 which merged into Capital Bank Financial Corp. 11/30/2017

CIX SPLIT CORP (ON)
Class A Shares called for redemption at $7.1437 on 01/31/2011
Priority Shares called for redemption at $10 on 01/31/2011

CJA INDS INC (NY)
Charter cancelled and proclaimed dissolved for failure to pay taxes 12/16/1974

CJHC CAP LTD (AB)
Name changed to Dragon-Tex (Group) Ltd. (AB) 01/21/2004
Dragon-Tex (Group) Ltd. (AB) reorganized in British Columbia as Med BioGene Inc. 04/28/2006

CJI INDS INC (DE)
Under plan of merger name changed to Triangle Industries, Inc. (New) 07/07/1988
(See Triangle Industries, Inc. (New))

CJM TEAM CORP (CO)
Recapitalized as Teleplus Consumer Services, Inc. (CO) 11/22/2002
Each share Common $0.001 par exchanged for (0.00666666) share Common $0.001 par
Note: Holders of between (101) and (15,000) shares received (100) shares only
Holders of (99) shares or fewer will not be affected by the reverse split
Teleplus Consumer Services, Inc. (CO) reincorporated in Nevada 04/10/2003 which recapitalized as Scrip Advantage, Inc. 01/05/2005
(See Scrip Advantage, Inc.)

CJS HLDGS INC (DE)
Charter cancelled and declared void for failure to pay franchise taxes 03/01/1996

CJT FINL INC (NV)
Each share old Common $0.001 par exchanged for (0.1) share new Common $0.001 par 08/16/2010
Name changed to Gold & Silver Mining of Nevada, Inc. 09/20/2013
Gold & Silver Mining of Nevada, Inc. recapitalized as Rainmaker Worldwide Inc. 06/15/2017

CK FED SVGS BK (CONCORD, NC)
Acquired by SouthTrust Corp. 12/11/1992
Each share Common $1 par exchanged for (0.95) share Common $2.50 par
SouthTrust Corp. merged into Wachovia Corp. (Ctfs. dated after 09/01/2001) 11/01/2004 which merged into Wells Fargo & Co. (New) 12/31/2008

CK WITCO CORP (DE)
Name changed to Crompton Corp. 04/27/2000
Crompton Corp. name changed to Chemtura Corp. 07/01/2005
(See Chemtura Corp.)

CKC LIQUIDATING CO. (CT)
Liquidation completed
Each share Common $2.50 par exchanged for initial distribution of (0.58) share LeaRonal, Inc. Common $1 par and $18 cash 10/21/1983
Each share Common $2.50 par received second distribution of $2 cash 12/17/1984
Each share Common $2.50 par received third distribution of $1.50 cash 02/14/1985
Each share Common $2.50 par received fourth distribution of $2.50 cash 07/31/1986
Each share Common $2.50 par received fifth and final distribution of $0.55 cash 07/25/1988
(See LeoRonal, Inc.)

CKD VENTURES LTD (BC)
Recapitalized as Alchemy Ventures Ltd. (BC) 05/14/1999
Each share Common no par exchanged for (0.1) share Common no par
Alchemy Ventures Ltd. (BC) reincorporated in Canada as i-minerals inc. 01/22/2004 which name changed to I-Minerals Inc. 12/15/2011

CKE RESTAURANTS INC (DE)
Common 1¢ par split (3) for (2) by issuance of (0.5) additional share payable 01/22/1997 to holders of record 01/02/1997 Ex date - 01/23/1997
Stock Dividends - 10% payable 02/04/1998 to holders of record 01/20/1998; 10% payable 01/11/1999 to holders of record 12/28/1998
Merged into Columbia Lake Acquisition Holdings, Inc. 07/12/2010
Each share Common 1¢ par exchanged for $12.55 cash

CKF BANCORP INC (DE)
Common 1¢ par split (2) for (1) by issuance of (1) additional share payable 12/11/2003 to holders of record 11/26/2003 Ex date - 12/12/2003
Merged into Kentucky First Federal Bancorp 12/31/2012
Each share Common 1¢ par exchanged for (1.1743) shares Common 1¢ par

CKR CARBON CORP (ON)
Reincorporated 01/01/2017
Place of incorporation changed from (BC) to (ON) 01/01/2017
Name changed to Gratomic Inc. 12/22/2017

CKRUSH INC (DE)
Each share old Common 1¢ par exchanged for (0.1) share new Common 1¢ par 10/10/2007
SEC revoked common stock registration 06/13/2012

CKS GROUP INC (DE)
Merged into USWeb Corp. 12/17/1998
Each share Common $0.001 par exchanged for (1.5) shares Common $0.001 par
USWeb Corp. merged into Whitmann-Hart, Inc. 03/01/2000 which name changed to Marchfirst Inc. 03/23/2000
(See Marchfirst Inc.)

CKX INC (DE)
Each share Common 1¢ par received distribution of (0.2) share FX Real Estate & Entertainment Inc. Common 1¢ par payable 01/10/2008 to holders of record 12/31/2007
Acquired by Colonel Holdings, Inc. 06/22/2011
Each share Common 1¢ par exchanged for $5.50 cash

CL ASSETS INC (MD)
Completely liquidated 12/22/1986
Each share $2.10 Preference Ser. A $1 par received first and final distribution of $40 cash
Each share Common $1 par received first and final distribution of $8.04 cash
Note: Certificates were not required to be surrendered and are now valueless

CL&P CAP L P
9.30% Monthly Income Preferred Securities Ser. A called for redemption at $25 on 04/30/2001

CLABIR CORP (DE)
Reincorporated 07/01/1977
State of incorporation changed from (FL) to (DE) 07/01/1977
Common 10¢ par split (3) for (2) by issuance of (0.5) additional share 03/16/1981
Common 10¢ par reclassified as Class A Common 10¢ par 07/29/1986
Stock Dividend - 10% 04/14/1983
Merged into Empire of Carolina, Inc. 12/29/1989
Each share $3.3125 Preferred $1 par exchanged for (0.2) share Common 10¢ par
Each share Class A Common 10¢ par exchanged for (0.1) share Common 10¢ par
Each share Class B Common 10¢ par exchanged for (0.1) share Common 10¢ par
(See Empire of Carolina, Inc.)

CLADDAGH GOLD LTD (CANADA)
Recapitalized as Resorts Unlimited Management Inc. 09/01/2000
Each share Common no par exchanged for (0.25) share Common no par
(See Resorts Unlimited Management Inc.)

CLAFLINS, INC.
Liquidated 00/00/1926
Details not available

CLAGGETT SHARES CORP.
Out of business 00/00/1933
Details not available

CLAIBORNE INDS LTD (AB)
Common no par reclassified as Class A no par 11/30/1979
Acquired by 172071 Canada Inc. 05/08/1990
Each share Class A no par exchanged for $12 cash

CLAIM LAKE RES INC (ON)
Recapitalized as Fort Chimo Minerals Inc. 04/14/2005
Each share Common no par exchanged for (0.5) share Common no par
Fort Chimo Minerals Inc. recapitalized as Mag Copper Ltd. 06/15/2011 which recapitalized as Integra Resources Corp. 08/22/2017

CLAIMER RES INC (BC)
Reorganized as Canadian Strategic Holdings Ltd. 04/11/1989
Each share Common no par exchanged for (1) share Common no par
(See Canadian Strategic Holdings Ltd.)

CLAIMSNET COM INC (DE)
Recapitalized as TransCoastal Corp. 07/31/2013
Each share Common $0.001 par exchanged for (0.005) share Common $0.001 par

CLAIMSTAKER RES LTD (BC)
Name changed to J-Pacific Gold Inc. 09/05/2001
J-Pacific Gold Inc. recapitalized as Sona Resources Corp. 01/27/2010 which merged into Skeena Resources Ltd. 09/16/2016

CLAIRE TECHNOLOGIES INC (NV)
Each share old Common $0.001 par exchanged for (0.25) share new Common $0.001 par 10/01/1997
Charter permanently revoked for failure to file reports and pay fees 02/01/2005

CLAIRES STORES INC (FL)
Reincorporated 6/30/2000
Common 5¢ par split (3) for (2) by issuance of (0.5) additional share 04/16/1984
Common 5¢ par split (3) for (2) by issuance of (0.5) additional share 07/24/1984
Common 5¢ par split (2) for (1) by issuance of (1) additional share 02/01/1985
Common 5¢ par split (3) for (2) by issuance of (0.5) additional share 10/04/1985
Common 5¢ par split (3) for (2) by issuance of (0.5) additional share payable 02/21/1996 to holders of record 02/07/1996 Ex date - 02/26/1996
Non-transferable Conv. Class A Common 5¢ par split (3) for (2) by issuance of (0.5) additional share payable 02/21/1996 to holders of record 02/07/1996
Common 5¢ par split (3) for (2) by issuance of (0.5) additional share payable 09/12/1996 to holders of record 08/29/1996 Ex date - 09/13/1996
State of incorporation changed from (DE) to (FL) 06/30/2000
Common 5¢ par split (2) for (1) by issuance of (1) additional share payable 12/19/2003 to holders of record 12/05/2003 Ex date - 12/22/2003
Stock Dividend - In Non-transferable Conv. Class A Common to holders of Common 25% 07/17/1987
Merged into Bauble Holdings Corp. 05/29/2007
Each share Common 5¢ par exchanged for $33 cash
Each share Class A Common 5¢ par exchanged for $33 cash

CLAIRETON COURT BUILDING CORP. (IL)
Liquidation completed 00/00/1949
Details not available

CLAIRSON INTL CORP (FL)
Merged into C-Corp. Acquisition, Inc. 03/09/1990
Each share Common 1¢ par exchanged for $8.79 cash
Note: An additional $0.71 cash per share was paid 03/00/1993

CLAIRTONE SOUND LTD (ON)
Capital Stock no par reclassified as Common no par 03/03/1966
6.75% 1st Preferred Ser. A $10 par and 6.75% 1st Preferred Ser. B $10 par reclassified as Common no par 12/23/1968
Charter cancelled and declared dissolved for failure to file returns and pay fees 03/16/1976

CLAMSHELL ENTERPRISES INC (NV)
Name changed to MediaNet Group Technologies, Inc. 05/22/2003
MediaNet Group Technologies, Inc. name changed to DubLi, Inc. 09/27/2012 which name changed to Ominto, Inc. 07/01/2015

CLAN RES LTD (BC)
Name changed to Energy Metals Corp. 12/20/2004
Each share Common no par exchanged for (1) share Common no par
Energy Metals Corp. merged into Uranium One Inc. 08/10/2007
(See Uranium One Inc.)

CLANCY MULDOON ICE CREAM INC (NV)
Charter cancelled for failure to pay taxes 09/01/1988

CLARAGE FAN CO (MI)
Common $1 par changed to $10 par in 1950
Merged into Zurn Industries, Inc. 3/7/69
Each share Common $10 par exchanged for (2) shares $1 Conv. Preferred $1 par
(See Zurn Industries, Inc.)

CLARCAN PETE CORP (TX)
Merged into Utah International Inc. 03/29/1974
Each share Common no par exchanged for (0.125) share Common $2 par
Utah International Inc. merged into General Electric Co. 12/20/1976

CLARCO, INC. (FL)
Incorporated in 1968
Name changed to D & R International Corp. 4/2/74
D & R International Corp. name changed to Compu-Tech International Inc. 12/19/77
(See Compu-Tech International Inc.)

CLARCO, INC. (FL)
Incorporated in 1975
Proclaimed dissolved for failure to file annual reports and pay fees 10/11/91

CLARCOR INC (DE)
Common $1 par split (3) for (2) by issuance of (0.5) additional share 01/12/1990
Common $1 par split (3) for (2) by issuance of (0.5) additional share 02/14/1992
Common $1 par split (3) for (2) by issuance of (0.5) additional share payable 04/24/1998 to holders of record 04/10/1998 Ex date - 04/27/1998
Common $1 par split (2) for (1) by issuance of (1) additional share payable 04/29/2005 to holders of record 04/15/2005 Ex date - 05/02/2005
Acquired by Parker-Hannifin Corp. 02/28/2017
Each share Common $1 par exchanged for $83 cash

CLARE INC (MA)
Merged into IXYS Corp. 06/10/2002
Each share Common 1¢ par exchanged for (0.49147) share Common 1¢ par
(See IXYS Corp.)

CLAREMONT CAP CORP (DE)
Name changed to Bergstrom Capital Corp. 11/08/1988
(See Bergstrom Capital Corp.)

CLAREMONT ENTERPRISES INC (FL)
Recapitalized as OSF, Inc. (FL) 05/12/2003
Each share Common $0.0005 par exchanged for (0.01) share Common $0.0005 par
OSF, Inc. (FL) reincorporated in Delaware 07/25/2003 which recapitalized as Tensas Inc. 04/01/2005 which name changed to PGI Energy, Inc. 02/28/2011

CLAREMONT INDS INC (ON)
Delisted from Canadian Dealer Network 01/03/1995

CLAREMONT MINES LTD. (QC)
Charter annulled for failure to file reports or pay fees 11/11/1972

CLAREMONT MINES LTD (ON)
Name changed to Claremont Industries Inc. 02/19/1987
(See Claremont Industries Inc.)

CLAREMONT OIL CO. (CA)
Completely liquidated 11/02/1965
Details not available

CLAREMONT TECHNOLOGIES CORP (NV)
Old Common $0.001 par split (3.2) for (1) by issuance of (2.2) additional shares payable 07/30/2003 to holders of record 07/28/2003 Ex date - 07/31/2003
Each share old Common $0.001 par exchanged for (0.01) share new Common $0.001 par 10/12/2006
Name changed to China Ivy School, Inc. (NV) 01/09/2007
China Ivy School, Inc. (NV) reincorporated in Wyoming as Resources Global Services Group 10/05/2018

CLAREMONT TECHNOLOGY GROUP INC (OR)
Merged into Complete Business Solutions, Inc. 07/24/1998
Each share Common no par exchanged for (0.7755055) share Common no par
Complete Business Solutions, Inc name changed to Covansys Corp. 06/07/2001
(See Covansys Corp.)

CLARENDON BK & TR (ARLINGTON, VA)
Capital Stock $20 par changed to $10 par and (1) additional share issued 10/16/1972
Merged into First American Bank of Virginia (McLean, VA) 03/31/1978
Each share Capital Stock $10 par exchanged for (1.25) shares Common $10 par
(See First American Bank of Virginia (McLean, VA))

CLARENDON GOLD MINES LTD. (ON)
Charter revoked for failure to file reports and pay taxes 00/00/1957

CLARENDON TR CO (ARLINGTON, VA)
Name changed to Clarendon Bank & Trust (Arlington, VA) 08/03/1972
Clarendon Bank & Trust (Arlington, VA) merged into First American Bank of Virginia (McLean, VA) 03/31/1978
(See First American Bank of Virginia (McLean, VA))

CLARENT CORP (DE)
Plan of reorganization under Chapter 11 Federal Bankruptcy Code effective 04/01/2004
Holders are expected to receive an Interest Holder Claim equal to $0.80 per share. If adequate proceeds are available, they will receive their pro rata share of cash.

CLARENT HOSP CORP (DE)
In process of liquidation
Each share Common 1¢ par received initial distribution of $1.50 cash payable 02/14/2003 to holders of record 01/24/2003 Ex date - 02/18/2003
Each share Common 1¢ par received second distribution of $1.25 cash payable 02/12/2004 to holders of record 02/05/2004 Ex date - 02/13/2004
Each share Common 1¢ par received third distribution of $0.50 cash payable 12/15/2004 to holders of record 12/01/2004 Ex date - 12/16/2004
Each share Common 1¢ par received

fourth distribution of $1 cash payable 04/27/2006 to holders of record 04/20/2006 Ex date - 04/28/2006
Each share Common 1¢ par received fifth distribution of $0.50 cash payable 02/17/2007 to holders of record 02/01/2007 Ex date - 02/16/2007
Each share Common 1¢ par received sixth distribution of $0.25 cash payable 10/31/2007 to holders of record 10/24/2007 Ex date - 11/01/2007
Each share Common 1¢ par received seventh distribution of $0.10 cash payable 10/31/2008 to holders of record 10/25/2008 Ex date - 11/03/2008
Assets transferred to Clarent Hospital Corp. Liquidating Trust and Common 1¢ par reclassified as Shares of Bene Int. 12/20/2008
Note: Details on additional distributions, if any, are not available

CLAREPINE DEVS LTD (AB)
Name changed 04/14/1970
Name changed from Clarepine Oil & Gas Ltd. to Clarepine Develpoments Ltd. 04/14/1970
Struck off register and declared dissolved for failure to file returns 12/01/1993

CLAREPINE INDS INC (AB)
Struck from the register 11/01/1993

CLARICA LIFE INS CO (ON)
Merged into Sun Life Financial Services of Canada Inc. 05/31/2002
Each share Common no par exchanged for (1.5135) shares Common no par
Sun Life Financial Services of Canada Inc. name changed to Sun Life Financial Inc. 07/02/2003

CLARIDGE HOTEL & CASINO CORP (NY)
Plan of reorganization under Chapter 11 Federal Bankruptcy proceedings effective 06/04/2001
No stockholders' equity

CLARIDGE VENTURES INC (NV)
Common $0.001 par split (35) for (1) by issuance of (34) additional shares payable 10/05/2012 to holders of record 10/05/2012
Recapitalized as Indo Global Exchange(s) Pte. Ltd. 08/06/2013
Each share Common $0.001 par exchanged for (0.25) share Common $0.001 par

CLARIENT INC (DE)
Merged into General Electric Co. 12/22/2010
Each share Common 1¢ par exchanged for $5 cash

CLARIFY INC (DE)
Common $0.0001 par split (2) for (1) by issuance of (1) additional share payable 10/11/1996 to holders of record 09/30/1996
Merged into Nortel Networks Corp. (Old) 03/17/2000
Each share Common $0.0001 par exchanged for (1.3) shares Common no par
Nortel Networks Corp. (Old) reorganized as Nortel Networks Corp. (New) 05/01/2000
(See Nortel Networks Corp. (New))

CLARINET RES LTD (AB)
Recapitalized as Symmetry Resources Inc. 08/16/1996
Each share Common no par exchanged for (0.25) share Common no par
Symmetry Resources Inc. merged into Berkley Petroleum Corp. 01/31/2000
(See Berkley Petroleum Corp.)

CLARINGTON CORP (ON)
Acquired by Industrial Alliance Insurance & Financial Services Inc. 01/13/2006
Each share Common no par exchanged for $15 cash

CLARINGTON DIVERSIFIED INCOME & GROWTH FD (ON)
Under plan of merger each Unit automatically became IA Clarington Tactical Income Fund Ser. X Units on a net asset basis 06/26/2009

CLARINS S A (FRANCE)
Sponsored ADR's for Ordinary split (7) for (1) by issuance of (6) additional ADR's 11/26/1991
Each 144A Sponsored ADR for Ordinary exchanged for (1) Sponsored ADR for Ordinary 11/13/1998
Stock Dividends - 12.5% 09/25/1992; 11.1111111% payable 01/28/1998 to holders of record 10/30/1997; 16.66666666% payable 11/01/1999 to holders of record 10/26/1999; 14.29% payable 12/08/2000 to holders of record 11/28/2000; 12.5% payable 11/19/2001 to holders of record 10/26/2001 Ex date - 10/24/2001; 11.11111111% payable 11/14/2003 to holders of record 10/28/2003 Ex date - 10/29/2003; 20% payable 11/04/2004 to holders of record 10/29/2004 Ex date - 10/27/2004; 16.66666666% payable 11/09/2005 to holders of record 10/31/2005 Ex date - 10/27/2005
Acquired by Societe Financiere FC 09/23/2008
Each Sponsored ADR for Ordinary exchanged for $15.16472 cash

CLARION CAP CORP (DE)
Each share old Common $1 par exchanged for (0.01) share new Common $1 par 02/20/1990
Note: In effect holders received an undisclosed amount of cash per share and public interest was eliminated

CLARION COML HLDGS INC (MD)
Liquidation completed
Each share Class A Common $0.001 par received initial distribution of $4 cash payable 10/26/2001 to holders of record 10/19/2001 Ex date - 10/29/2001
Each share Class A Common $0.001 par received second distribution of $2 cash payable 12/19/2001 to holders of record 12/12/2001
Each share Class A Common $0.001 par received third distribution of $3.11 cash payable 03/08/2002 to holders of record 03/01/2002
Each share Class A Common $0.001 par received fourth and final distribution of $0.0735 cash payable 06/30/2005 to holders of record 06/24/2005 Ex date - 07/08/2005
Note: Certificates were not required to be surrendered and are without value

CLARION ENVIRONMENTAL TECHNOLOGIES INC (BC)
Name changed to Clarion Resources Ltd. 12/05/1997
(See Clarion Resources Ltd.)

CLARION HOUSE INC (NV)
Each share old Common $0.001 par exchanged for (0.1) share new Common $0.001 par 10/21/1993
Each share new Common $0.001 par exchanged for (0.2) share Common 1¢ par 04/27/1996
Reincorporated under the laws of Delaware as Clarion Technologies, Inc. and Common 1¢ par changed to $0.001 par 10/02/1998
(See Clarion Technologies, Inc.)

CLARION PETES LTD (AB)
Merged into Roxy Petroleum Ltd. 12/10/1981
Each share Common no par exchanged for (1) share Common no par and (0.5) Common Stock Purchase Warrant expiring 12/15/1983
Roxy Petroleum Ltd. recapitalized as Canadian Roxy Petroleum Ltd. 06/20/1985 which merged into Numac Energy Inc. 04/01/1994
(See Numac Energy Inc.)

CLARION RES LTD (BC)
Delisted from Canadian Dealer Network 05/31/2001

CLARION RIVER POWER CO.
Acquired by Pennsylvania Electric Co. by payment of $10 per share of Participating Capital Stock in 1944

CLARION TECHNOLOGIES INC (DE)
Each share old Common $0.001 par exchanged for (0.00000025) share new Common $0.001 par 05/31/2016
Note: In effect holders received $1 cash per holdings and public interest was eliminated

CLARISE SPORTSWEAR INC (NY)
Reincorporated under the laws of Delaware as Acmatic Industries, Inc. 11/24/1969
Acmatic Industries, Inc. name changed to National Medical Products, Inc. 12/23/1970
(See National Medical Products, Inc.)

CLARITI TELECOMMUNICATIONS INTL LTD (DE)
Each share old Common no par exchanged for (0.25) share new Common no par 07/03/2000
Reorganized under Chapter 11 Federal Bankruptcy Code as Integrated Data Corp. 11/12/2002
Each share new Common no par exchanged for (0.01) share Common $0.001 par

CLARITY TELECOM NETWORKING INC (AB)
Name changed to NTG Clarity Networks Inc. 03/06/2001

CLARK / BARDES INC (DE)
Name changed 06/06/2001
Name changed from Clark/Bardes Holdings, Inc. to Clark/Bardes, Inc. 06/06/2001
Name changed to Clark, Inc. 05/11/2003
(See Clark, Inc.)

CLARK & WILLOW STREETS CORP.
Dissolved 00/00/1938
Details not available

CLARK ANTHONY INTL INS BROKERS LTD (AB)
Name changed to ACL International Ltd. 05/01/2014
ACL International Ltd. name changed to Bow Energy Ltd. 02/15/2017 which merged into Petrolia Energy Corp. 03/07/2018

CLARK AUTOMOTIVE PRODS CORP (MI)
Name changed to CAPCO Automotive Products Corp. 08/10/1994
(See CAPCO Automotive Products Corp.)

CLARK CABLE CORP (OH)
Name changed to Clark Consolidated Industries, Inc. 06/11/1973
(See Clark Consolidated Industries, Inc.)

CLARK CDN EXPL CO (TX)
Recapitalized as Clarcan Petroleum Corp. 01/24/1973
Each share Common no par exchanged for (0.222) share Common no par
Clarcan Petroleum Corp. merged into Utah International Inc. 03/29/1974

which merged into General Electric Co. 12/20/1976

CLARK (D.L.) CO. (PA)
Merged into Beatrice Foods Co. 10/21/1955
Each share Common no par exchanged for (0.28571428) share Common $12.50 par
Beatrice Foods Co. name changed to Beatrice Companies, Inc. 06/05/1984
(See Beatrice Companies, Inc.)

CLARK CONS INDS INC (OH)
6% Conv. Preferred Ser. A no par called for redemption 11/25/1988
Acquired by Willcox & Gibbs, Inc. 01/18/1989
Each share Common 10¢ par exchanged for $24 cash

CLARK CONTROLLER CO. (OH)
Each share Common no par exchanged for (3) shares Common $1 par 00/00/1936
Stock Dividends - 100% 05/15/1953; 10% 12/14/1956
Merged into Smith (A. O.) Corp. 12/20/1965
Each share Common $1 par exchanged for $20 cash

CLARK COPY INTL CORP (DE)
Each share old Common 10¢ par exchanged for (0.001) share new Common 10¢ par 11/23/1989
Merged into White Business Machines, Inc. 04/07/1990
Each share new Common 10¢ par exchanged for (1) share Common no par

CLARK CNTY BANCORPORATION (WA)
Company's sole asset placed in receivership 01/16/2009
Stockholders' equity unlikely

CLARK CNTY ST BK (JEFFERSONVILLE, IN)
Under plan of reorganization each share Capital Stock $10 par automatically became (1) share Clark Financial Corp. Common no par 04/29/1983
Clark Financial Corp. merged into CB Bancshares, Inc. 12/01/1984 which merged into Central Pacific Financial Corp. 09/15/2004

CLARK DICK PRODTNS INC (DE)
Stock Dividends - 5% payable 05/15/1998 to holders of record 05/04/1998; 5% payable 06/11/1999 to holders of record 05/12/1999; 10% payable 06/23/2000 to holders of record 05/25/2000
Merged into DCPI Investco, Inc. 07/25/2002
Each share Common 1¢ par exchanged for $14.50 cash

CLARK EQUIP CO (DE)
Reincorporated 07/01/1968
Each share Common $100 par exchanged for (5) shares Common no par 00/00/1927
Each share Common no par exchanged for (2) shares Common $20 par 00/00/1947
Each share Common $20 par exchanged for (2) shares Common $15 par 05/15/1956
5% Preferred called for redemption 06/15/1959
Common $15 par changed to $10 par and (1) additional share issued 05/13/1960
Common $10 par changed to $7.50 par and (1) additional share issued 05/16/1966
Stock Dividends - 16.66666666% 04/15/1929; 10% 12/15/1948; 25% 04/02/1951; 50% 12/15/1952
State of incorporation changed from (MI) to (DE) 07/01/1968
Merged into Ingersoll-Rand Co. (NJ) 05/31/1995

Each share Common $7.50 par exchanged for $86 cash

CLARK FINANCIAL CORP. (IN)
Merged into CB Bancshares, Inc. 12/01/1984
Each share Common no par exchanged for (2.3) shares Common $5 par
CB Bancshares, Inc. merged into Central Pacific Financial Corp. 09/15/2004

CLARK GOLD MINES LTD (QC)
Charter cancelled 10/16/1982
No stockholders' equity

CLARK HLDGS INC (DE)
Acquired by Gores Logistics Holdings, L.L.C. 11/04/2011
Each share Common $0.0001 par exchanged for $0.46 cash

CLARK INC (DE)
Acquired by AEGON N.V. 03/12/2007
Each share Common 1¢ par exchanged for $17.21 cash

CLARK J L MFG CO (DE)
Reincorporated 03/31/1969
State of incorporation changed from (IL) to (DE) 03/31/1969
Common $1 par split (3) for (2) by issuance of (0.5) additional share 05/14/1971
Common $1 par split (3) for (2) by issuance of (0.5) additional share 08/11/1978
Common $1 par split (2) for (1) by issuance of (1) additional share 04/13/1983
Stock Dividends - 50% 05/14/1976; 50% 05/13/1977
Name changed to Clarcor 10/01/1987
(See Clarcor)

CLARK LIGHTER CO., INC.
Liquidated 00/00/1932
No stockholders' equity

CLARK MFG CO (MO)
Adjudicated bankrupt 07/24/1974
Stockholders' equity unlikely

CLARK MATL HANDLING CO (DE)
Plan of reorganization under Chapter 11 Federal Bankruptcy Code effective 08/18/2004
No stockholders' equity

CLARK MED TECHNOLOGY INC (WA)
Charter forfeited for failure to file reports and pay fees 06/01/1992

CLARK MELVIN SECS CORP (DE)
Assets taken over by the Securities Investor Protection Corp. 10/17/2001
Stockholders' equity unlikely

CLARK NATIONAL LIFE INSURANCE CO. (IN)
Merged into First United Life Insurance Co. 11/15/1965
Each share Capital Stock $1 par exchanged for (0.4) share Capital Stock $1 par
First United Life Insurance Co. reorganized as First United, Inc. 02/25/1970
(See First United, Inc.)

CLARK OIL & REFNG CORP (WI)
$1.20 Preferred Ser. A $20 par called for redemption 06/30/1956
$1.20 Preferred Ser. B $20 par called for redemption 12/31/1956
Common $1 par split (2) for (1) by issuance of (1) additional share 04/07/1966
Common $1 par split (2) for (1) by issuance of (1) additional share 11/29/1968
Common $1 par split (2) for (1) by issuance of (1) additional share 12/29/1980
Acquired by Apex Oil Co. 10/30/1981
Each share Common $1 par exchanged for $37 cash

CLARK OIL CO. (CA)
In process of liquidation
Each share Common $1 par received initial distribution of $9 cash 01/06/1975
Each share Common $1 par received second distribution of $1.60 cash 01/21/1977
Note: Details on subsequent distributions, if any, are not available

CLARK PHARMACEUTICAL LABS LTD (ON)
Recapitalized as Dimethaid Research Inc. 11/14/1990
Each share Common no par exchanged for (0.25) share Common no par
Each share Class A Common no par exchanged for (0.08333333) share Common no par
Dimethaid Research Inc. name changed to Nuvo Research Inc. 10/31/2005 which name changed to Nuvo Pharmaceuticals Inc. 03/07/2016

CLARK'S SPAS, INC.
Out of business 00/00/1935
Details not available

CLARKE CAN INC (PA)
Name changed to Clarke Corp. 11/05/1969
(See Clarke Corp.)

CLARKE CORP (PA)
Believed out of business 00/00/1988
Details not available

CLARKE-GRAVELY CORP (DE)
Merged into Studebaker-Worthington, Inc. 08/12/1976
Each share Common $1 par exchanged for $14.75 cash

CLARKSBURG-COLUMBUS SHORT ROUTE BRIDGE CO.
Property sold to State of West Virginia 00/00/1937
No stockholders' equity

CLARKSON INDS INC (NY)
Merged into Thomas Tilling Ltd. 03/02/1978
Each share Common $1 par exchanged for $22 cash

CLARKSON LABORATORIES, INC. (DE)
Completely liquidated 03/18/1968
Each share Common 1¢ par exchanged for first and final distribution of (0.35) share Universal Container Corp. Class A Common 10¢ par
(See Universal Container Corp.)

CLARNOR MALARTIC MINES LTD. (ON)
Charter cancelled 00/00/1960

CLARON VENTURES INC (NV)
Each share old Common $0.001 par exchanged for (26) shares new Common $0.001 par 11/10/2006
Name changed to Outback Energy Corp. 01/29/2007
Outback Energy Corp. recapitalized as PetroNational Corp. 07/08/2008 which name changed to Custom Restaurant & Hospitality Group, Inc. 11/20/2008

CLAROSTAT MFG INC (NY)
Stock Dividend - 10% 06/01/1947
Acquired by Hawker Siddeley Group PLC 04/13/1987
Each share Common $1 par exchanged for $74 cash

CLARRY GOLD MINES, LTD. (ON)
Dissolved 01/12/1959
Details not available

CLARUS CORP (ON)
Discharged from receivership 12/00/1997
No stockholders' equity

CLARUS CORP OLD (DE)
Name changed to Black Diamond, Inc. 01/20/2011
Black Diamond, Inc. name changed back to Clarus Corp. 08/14/2017

CLARY CORP (DE)
Acquired by Addmaster Corp. 02/13/2003
Each share 5.50% Conv. Preferred $5 par exchanged for $5.50 cash
Each share Common $1 par exchanged for $2 cash

CLARY MULTIPLIER CORP. (CA)
Name changed to Clary Corp. 00/00/1955
(See Clary Corp.)

CLASCO INC (MD)
Each share Common 1¢ par exchanged for (0.4) share Common $0.025 par 12/18/1972
Merged into MCD Holdings, Inc. 10/01/1973
Each share Common $0.025 par exchanged for (1) share Common 50¢ par
MCD Holdings, Inc. name changed to Chesapeake Investors, Inc. 08/14/1980
(See Chesapeake Investors, Inc.)

CLASS INC (DE)
Recapitalized as Avery Communications, Inc. 12/12/1994
Each share Common 1¢ par exchanged for (0.25) share Common 1¢ par
(See Avery Communications, Inc.)

CLASS INTL CORP (MD)
Out of business 01/00/1978
No stockholders' equity

CLASS-IQUE TALENT AGY INC (NV)
Reorganized as PhaserTek Medical, Inc. (NV) 01/10/2002
Each share Common $0.001 par exchanged for (2.564) shares Common $0.001 par
PhaserTek Medical, Inc. (NV) reincorporated in Delaware as Union Equity, Inc. 11/23/2004 which recapitalized as Kona Gold Solutions, Inc. 08/13/2015

CLASS STUDENT SVCS INC (MD)
Name changed to Class International Corp. 07/02/1970
(See Class International Corp.)

CLASSIC AUTO ACCESSORIES (CA)
Name changed to FCR Automotive Group, Inc. (CA) 07/27/1988
FCR Automotive Group, Inc. (CA) reorganized in Delaware as Simco America Inc. 10/28/2005 which name changed to Leo Motors, Inc. 11/05/2007

CLASSIC BANCSHARES INC (DE)
Stock Dividend - 10% payable 11/17/2003 to holders of record 11/03/2003 Ex date - 10/30/2003
Merged into City Holding Co. 05/20/2005
Each share Common 1¢ par exchanged for (0.9624) share Common $2.50 par and $11.08 cash

CLASSIC COMMUNICATIONS INC (DE)
Plan of reorganization under Chapter 11 Federal Bankruptcy Code effective 01/16/2001
No stockholders' equity

CLASSIC CORP (MD)
Acquired by Maryland Mattress Corp. 03/12/1991
Each share Common 1¢ par exchanged for $0.20 cash

CLASSIC COSTUME CO INC (DE)
Common $0.001 par split (7) for (1) by issuance of (6) additional shares payable 07/01/2009 to holders of record 05/15/2009 Ex date - 07/02/2009

Name changed to Electric Car Co., Inc. 10/23/2009

CLASSIC FINANCIAL CORP. (ID)
Name changed to Gourmet General Corp. 10/19/1979
Gourmet General Corp. merged into American General Industries 07/15/1984 which name changed to Pagers Plus 11/18/1987 which name changed to PagePrompt USA 03/09/1994
(See PagePrompt USA)

CLASSIC GOLD RES LTD (BC)
Delisted from Toronto Stock Venture Exchange 06/20/2003

CLASSIC GOLF CARS INC (NV)
Charter revoked for failure to file reports and pay fees 11/01/1989

CLASSIC GOLF CORP (NV)
Recapitalized as Indexonly Technologies Inc. 09/14/1999
Each share Common $0.001 par exchanged for (0.04) share Common $0.001 par
Indexonly Technologies Inc. name changed to Nutrifeeds Technologies Inc. 05/05/2003 which name changed to Advanced Solutions & Technologies, Inc. 01/16/2004
(See Advanced Solutions & Technologies, Inc.)

CLASSIC MED GROUP INC (MN)
Acquired by Tyco International Ltd. 12/07/1993
Each share Common 1¢ par exchanged for $0.7345 cash

CLASSIC MNG CORP (UT)
Involuntarily dissolved 10/01/1991

CLASSIC RESTAURANTS INTL INC (FL)
Proclaimed dissolved for failure to file reports and pay fees 09/24/1999

CLASSIC RESTAURANTS INTL INC (GA)
Reincorporated 04/10/1998
State of incorporation changed from (CO) to (GA) 04/10/1998
Recapitalized as Creative Recycling Technologies, Inc. 04/14/1998
Each share Common no par exchanged for (0.05) share Common no par
Creative Recycling Technologies, Inc. name changed to Ingen Technologies, Inc. 11/01/2004
(See Ingen Technologies, Inc.)

CLASSIC RULES JUDO CHAMPIONSHIPS INC (DE)
Name changed to Judo Capital Corp. 03/21/2017

CLASSIC VACATION GROUP LIQUIDATING TR (NY)
Name changed 03/22/2002
Name changed from Classic Vacation Group Inc. to Classic Vacation Group Liquidating Trust 03/22/2002
Liquidation completed
Each share Common 1¢ par received initial distribution of $0.26 cash payable 04/08/2002 to holders of record 03/21/2002
Each share Common 1¢ par received second and final distribution of $0.3036 cash payable 05/09/2003 to holders of record 03/21/2002

CLASSIC VENTURES INC (DE)
Each share Common $0.00001 par exchanged for (0.05) share Common $0.0002 par 10/13/1987
Charter cancelled and declared inoperative and void for non-payment of taxes 03/01/1992

CLASSIC VIDEO THEATRE INC (DE)
Recapitalized as Seaton Group Inc. 05/10/1996
Each share Common $0.001 par exchanged for (0.05) share Common $0.001 par
Seaton Group Inc. name changed to

United Information Systems Inc.
12/05/1997
(See United Information Systems Inc.)

CLASSICA GROUP INC (NY)
Each share old Common $0.001 par exchanged for (0.2) share new Common $0.001 par 10/06/1999
Chapter 7 bankruptcy proceedings terminated 06/23/2009
No stockholders' equity

CLASSICS INTL ENTMT INC (DE)
Recapitalized as Piranha Inc. 02/28/2000
Each share Common $0.001 par exchanged for (0.28653295) share Common $0.001 par
(See Piranha Inc.)

CLASSICVISION ENTMT INC (DE)
Stock Dividend - 200% payable 06/28/1996 to holders of record 06/17/1996
Recapitalized as Allixion International Corp. 07/20/2005
Each share Common 10¢ par exchanged for (0.00133333) share Common 10¢ par
Note: No holder will receive fewer than (100) post split shares

CLASSIFIED FINL CORP (WI)
Reincorporated 02/02/1979
Stock Dividend - 100% 06/30/1972
State of incorporation changed from (DE) to (WI) 02/09/1979
Common $3 par changed to 10¢ par 04/28/1983
Merged into Rathbone, King & Seeley, Inc. 10/01/1990
Each share Common 10¢ par exchanged for (0.16725) share Common 10¢ par and $0.222 cash
Note: Rathbone, King & Seeley, Inc. is privately held

CLASSIFIED INSURANCE CORP. (WI)
Merged into Classified Financial Corp. 12/00/1969
Each share Common $3 par exchanged for (1) share Common $3 par
(See Classified Financial Corp.)

CLASSIFIED ONLINE COM (NV)
Name changed to X-Ramp.com, Inc. 05/26/2000
(See X-Ramp.com, Inc.)

CLASSIFIED RISK INSURANCE CORP. (WI)
Name changed to Classified Insurance Corp. 10/29/1965
Classified Insurance Corp. merged into Classified Financial Corp. 12/00/1969
(See Classified Financial Corp.)

CLAUDE LAKE MINES, LTD. (QC)
Declared dissolved for failure to file reports and pay fees 00/00/1961

CLAUDE NEON, INC. (NY)
Name changed to Dynamics Corp. of America (NY) 05/03/1955
Dynamics Corp. of America (NY) merged into CTS Corp. 10/16/1997

CLAUDE NEON ADVERTISING LTD. (CANADA)
Name changed 08/05/1965
Each share 7% Preferred $100 par exchanged for (1) share Non-Cum. Preferred $49 par, (10) shares Class B no par and $50 principal amount of 5% Notes 00/00/1949
Each share Common no par exchanged for (0.1) share Class A 10¢ par 00/00/1949
Name changed from Claude Neon General Advertising Ltd. to Claude Neon Advertising Ltd. 08/05/1965
Acquired by Mediacom Inc. 02/01/1979
Details not available

CLAUDE NEON ELECTRICAL PRODUCTS, INC.
Succeeded by Claude Neon Electrical Products Corp., Ltd. 00/00/1929
Details not available

CLAUDE NEON ELECTRICAL PRODUCTS CORP. LTD.
Merged into Electrical Products Corp. 00/00/1938
Details not available

CLAUDE NEON LIGHTS, INC.
Name changed to Claude Neon, Inc. 00/00/1946
Claude Neon, Inc. name changed to Dynamics Corp. of America (NY) 05/03/1955 which merged into CTS Corp. 10/16/1997

CLAUDE NEON LIGHTS OF MARYLAND, INC. (MD)
Charter forfeited for failure to file reports and pay fees 10/27/1944

CLAUDE NEON SOUTHERN CORP. (FL)
Charter cancelled and proclaimed dissolved for non-payment of taxes 07/07/1942

CLAUDE RES INC (CANADA)
Merged into Silver Standard Resources Inc. 06/06/2016
Each share Common no par exchanged for (0.185) share Common no par and $0.001 cash
Note: Unexchanged certificates will be cancelled and become without value 06/06/2022
Silver Standard Resources Inc. name changed to SSR Mining Inc. 08/03/2017

CLAUDE SOUTHERN CORP. (FL)
Stock Dividend - 10% 05/02/1966
Name changed to Plastic Dynamics Corp. 01/17/1968
Plastic Dynamics Corp. name changed to Jerry's, Inc. (FL) 08/18/1969 which reincorporated in Nevada 03/16/2004 which recapitalized as Diamond Ranch Foods, Ltd. 05/10/2004 which name changed to Plandai Biotechnology, Inc. 01/05/2012

CLAUDIOS RESTAURANT GROUP INC (AB)
Reincorporated 10/01/1989
Place of incorporation changed from (ON) to (AB) 10/01/1989
Dissolved 04/02/2001
Details not available

CLAUSING CORP (DE)
Common $1 par split (3) for (2) by issuance of (0.5) additional share 04/27/1979
Common $1 par split (3) for (2) by issuance of (0.5) additional share 04/28/1980
Common $1 par split (2) for (1) by issuance of (1) additional share 08/05/1983
Merged into Rexnord Inc. 06/28/1984
Each share Common $1 par exchanged for $13.50 cash

CLAUSS CUTLERY CO. (OH)
Merged into Alco Standard Corp. 10/13/1967
Each share $6 Preferred no par exchanged for (1.5) shares $1 Conv. Preference no par
Each share Common no par exchanged for (0.6284) share $1 Conv. Preference no par
Alco Standard Corp. name changed to IKON Office Solutions, Inc. 01/24/1997
(See IKON Office Solutions, Inc.)

CLAUSSENS BAKERIES INC (GA)
Each (3) shares Class A or B Common $1 par exchanged for (1) share Common $1 par and $10 principal amount of 6% Debentures 00/00/1956
Acquired by Claussens, Inc. 10/01/1963
Each share Common $1 par exchanged for of $4 principal amount of Fuqua Industries, Inc. 6% Debentures

CLAUSSNER HOSIERY CO. (KY)
Common $5 par changed to $10 par 04/27/1959
Name changed to Avondale Corp. 04/29/1963
(See Avondale Corp.)

CLAVERNY RES INC (QC)
Merged into Acabit Explorations Inc. 02/15/1990
Each share Common no par exchanged for (1.30825) shares Common no par
Acabit Explorations Inc. name changed to Western Pacific Mining Exploration Inc. 10/17/1996 which recapitalized as Sierra Minerals Inc. 12/05/2002 which recapitalized as Goldgroup Mining Inc. 05/07/2010

CLAVIER CORP (NY)
Each share Common 5¢ par exchanged for (0.1) share Common 50¢ par 07/19/1966
Merged into Dero Research & Development Corp. 09/24/1969
Each share Common 50¢ par exchanged for (0.05) share Common 5¢ par
Dero Research & Development Corp. name changed to Dero Industries Inc. 02/10/1971
(See Dero Industries Inc.)

CLAVIS TECHNOLOGIES INTL CO LTD (NV)
SEC revoked common stock registration 11/24/2014

CLAVOS ENTERPRISES INC (ON)
Recapitalized 01/29/1997
Recapitalized from Clavos Porcupine Mines, Ltd. to Clavos Enterprises Inc. 01/29/1997
Each share old Common no par exchanged for (0.5) share new Common no par
Merged into Magnesium Alloy Corp. 10/23/1997
Each share new Common no par exchanged for (0.5) share Common no par
Magnesium Alloy Corp. name changed to MagIndustries Corp. (ON) 02/04/2005 which reincorporated in Canada 01/10/2006

CLAW LAKE GOLD MINES, LTD. (ON)
Dissolved 04/14/1958

CLAW LAKE MOLYBDENUM MINES LTD (ON)
Charter cancelled for failure to pay taxes and file returns 03/16/1976

CLAW RES LTD (BC)
Struck off register and declared dissolved for failure to file returns 08/05/1994

CLAWSON (F.W.) LAND CO.
Liquidation completed 00/00/1941
Details not available

CLAXSON INTERACTIVE GROUP INC (BRITISH VIRGIN ISLANDS)
Merged into Remainco Inc. 07/14/2008
Each share Class A Common 1¢ par exchanged for $13.75 cash

CLAY COUNTY STATE BANK (EXCELSIOR SPRINGS, MO)
100% acquired by Commerce Bancshares, Inc. through exchange offer which expired 03/10/1972
Public interest eliminated

CLAY ML TECHNICAL SYS INC (ON)
Declared bankrupt 01/12/1990
No stockholders' equity

CLAY-TECH INDS INC (AB)
Wound up 02/02/2004
Each share Common no par received approximately $0.09 cash

CLAY TOWNSHIP BUILDING CORP. (IN)
Completely liquidated 07/01/1973
Each share Common $10 par exchanged for first and final distribution of $10 cash

CLAYBAR URANIUM & OIL LTD. (ON)
Recapitalized as Canbridge Oil Exploration Ltd. 01/21/1965
Each share Capital Stock $1 par exchanged for (1) share Capital Stock 90¢ par
Canbridge Oil Exploration Ltd. merged into Thomson Drilling Co. Ltd. 12/31/1970 which name changed to Thomson Industries Ltd. 07/01/1973
(See Thomson Industries Ltd.)

CLAYCO PETE CORP (DE)
Charter cancelled and declared inoperative and void for non-payment of taxes 03/01/1990

CLAYLOON MINING & FERTILIZER CO. (WA)
Each share Common 5¢ par exchanged for (0.25) share Common 20¢ par 10/21/1966
Merged into Ships Stores, Inc. 08/19/1971
Each share Common 20¢ par exchanged for (1) share Common 10¢ par
(See Ships Stores, Inc.)

CLAYLOON URANIUM CO., INC. (WA)
Name changed to Clayloon Mining & Fertilizer Co. 05/04/1964
Clayloon Mining & Fertilizer Co. merged into Ships Stores, Inc. 08/19/1971
(See Ships Stores, Inc.)

CLAYMAC MINES LTD. (ON)
Name changed to Texcan Energy & Resources, Inc. 02/12/1980
Texcan Energy & Resources, Inc. name changed to Geovex Petroleum Corp. 10/29/1981 which merged into Flying Cross Resources Ltd. 12/04/1985 which merged into International Larder Minerals Inc. 05/01/1986 which merged into Explorers Alliance Corp. 10/13/2000
(See Explorers Alliance Corp.)

CLAYMONT STL HLDGS INC (DE)
Merged into Evraz Group S.A. 01/25/2008
Each share Common $0.001 par exchanged for $23.50 cash

CLAYMORE ADVANTAGED CDN BD ETF (ON)
Name changed to iShares Advantaged Canadian Bond Index Fund 03/29/2012
iShares Advantaged Canadian Bond Index Fund name changed to iShares High Quality Canadian Bond Index ETF 11/20/2013 which name changed to iShares Core High Quality Canadian Bond Index ETF 07/21/2014 which name changed to iShares High Quality Canadian Bond Index ETF 06/15/2017

CLAYMORE ADVANTAGED CONV BD ETF (ON)
Name changed to iShares Advantaged Convertible Bond Index Fund 03/29/2012
iShares Advantaged Convertible Bond Index Fund name changed to iShares Convertible Bond Index ETF 11/26/2013

CLAYMORE ADVANTAGED HIGH YIELD BD ETF (ON)
Name changed to iShares Advantaged U.S. High Yield Bond

Index Fund (CAD-Hedged) 03/29/2012
iShares Advantaged U.S. High Yield Bond Index Fund (CAD-Hedged) name changed to iShares Advantaged U.S. High Yield Bond Index ETF (CAD-Hedged) 11/26/2013

CLAYMORE ADVANTAGED SHORT DURATION HIGH INCOME ETF (ON)
Name changed to iShares Advantaged Short Duration High Income Fund 03/29/2012
iShares Advantaged Short Duration High Income Fund name changed to iShares Advantaged Short Duration High Income ETF 10/18/2013 which name changed to iShares Advantaged Short Duration High Income ETF (CAD-Hedged) 11/04/2014 which name changed to iShares Short Duration High Income ETF (CAD-Hedged) 02/29/2016

CLAYMORE BALANCED GROWTH COREPORTFOLIO ETF (ON)
Name changed to iShares Balanced Growth CorePortfolio Fund 03/29/2012
iShares Balanced Growth CorePortfolio Fund name changed to iShares Balanced Growth CorePortfolio ETF 06/04/2014

CLAYMORE BALANCED INCOME COREPORTFOLIO ETF (ON)
Name changed to iShares Balanced Income CorePortfolio Fund 03/29/2012
iShares Balanced Income CorePortfolio Fund name changed to iShares Balanced Income CorePortfolio ETF 06/04/2014

CLAYMORE BRIC ETF (ON)
Name changed to iShares BRIC Index Fund 03/29/2012
iShares BRIC Index Fund name changed to iShares BRIC Index ETF 06/04/2014

CLAYMORE BROAD COMMODITY ETF (AB)
Name changed to iShares Broad Commodity Index Fund (CAD-Hedged) 03/29/2012
iShares Broad Commodity Index Fund (CAD-Hedged) name changed to iShares Broad Commodity Index ETF (CAD-Hedged) 10/18/2013
(See iShares Broad Commodity Index ETF (CAD-Hedged))

CLAYMORE BROAD EMERGING MKTS ETF (ON)
Name changed to iShares Broad Emerging Markets Fund 03/29/2012
iShares Broad Emerging Markets Fund name changed to iShares Emerging Markets Fundamental Index ETF 05/28/2013

CLAYMORE CDN DIVID & INCOME ACHIEVERS ETF (ON)
Name changed to Claymore S&P/TSX Canadian Dividend ETF 07/09/2009
Claymore S&P/TSX Canadian Dividend ETF name changed to iShares S&P/TSX Canadian Dividend Aristocrats Index Fund 03/29/2012 which name changed to iShares S&P/TSX Canadian Dividend Aristocrats Index ETF 06/04/2014

CLAYMORE CDN FINL MONTHLY INCOME ETF (ON)
Units no par reclassified as Advisor Class Units 08/17/2009
Name changed to iShares Canadian Financial Monthly Income Fund 03/29/2012
iShares Canadian Financial Monthly Income Fund name changed to iShares Canadian Financial Monthly Income ETF 10/18/2013

CLAYMORE CANADIAN FUNDAMENTAL INDEX ETF (CANADA)
Name changed to iShares Canadian Fundamental Index Fund 03/29/2012
iShares Canadian Fundamental Index Fund name changed to iShares Canadian Fundamental Index ETF 06/04/2014

CLAYMORE CDN FUNDAMENTAL 100 MONTHLY INCOME ETF (ON)
Merged into Claymore Canadian Fundamental Index ETF 10/01/2007
Each Unit no par received (0.8615) Common Unit no par
Claymore Canadian Fundamental Index ETF name changed to iShares Canadian Fundamental Index Fund 03/29/2012 which name changed to iShares Canadian Fundamental Index ETF 06/04/2014

CLAYMORE CHINA ETF (ON)
Name changed to iShares China All-Cap Index Fund 03/29/2012
iShares China All-Cap Index Fund name changed to iShares China All-Cap Index ETF 06/04/2014
(See iShares China All-Cap Index ETF)

CLAYMORE DIVID & INCOME FD (DE)
Auction Market Preferred Ser. T28 1¢ par called for redemption at $25,000 on 08/12/2009
Auction Market Preferred Ser. TH28 1¢ par called for redemption at $25,000 on 08/28/2009
Auction Market Preferred Ser. F7 1¢ par called for redemption at $25,000 on 02/01/2010
Auction Market Preferred Ser. M7 1¢ par called for redemption at $25,000 on 02/02/2010
Auction Market Preferred Ser. W7 1¢ par called for redemption at $25,000 on 02/04/2010
Name changed to Guggenheim Enhanced Equity Strategy Fund 05/16/2011
Guggenheim Enhanced Equity Strategy Fund merged into Guggenheim Enhanced Equity Income Fund 03/20/2017

CLAYMORE EQUAL WEIGHT BANC & LIFECO ETF (ON)
Name changed 02/06/2008
Name changed from Claymore Equal Weight Banc & Lifeco Trust to Claymore Equal Weight Banc & Lifeco ETF and Trust Units reclassified as Advisor Class Units 02/06/2008
Name changed to iShares Equal Weight Banc & Lifeco Fund 03/29/2012
iShares Equal Weight Banc & Lifeco Fund name changed to iShares Equal Weight Banc & Lifeco ETF 10/18/2013

CLAYMORE EXCHANGE-TRADED FD TR (DE)
Trust terminated 02/29/2008
Each share Claymore/BIR Leaders 50 ETF no par received $22.5085 cash
Each share Claymore/BIR Leaders Mid-Cap Value ETF no par received $21.611 cash
Each share Claymore/BIR Leaders Small-Cap Core ETF no par received $22.029 cash
Each share Claymore Clear Mid-Cap Growth Index ETF no par received $22.7728 cash
Each share Claymore/IndexIQ Small-Cap Value ETF no par received $19.3406 cash
Each share Claymore/KLD Sudan Free Large-Cap Core ETF no par received $22.1005 cash
Each share Claymore/Robeco Boston Partners Large-Cap Value ETF no par received $21.5725 cash
Each share Claymore/LGA Green ETF no par received $23.7413 cash
Each share Claymore/Zacks Growth & Income Index ETF no par received $22.7174 cash
Claymore/Clear Spin-Off ETF no par reclassified as Claymore/Beacon Spin-Off ETF no par 06/15/2009
Claymore/Great Companies Large-Cap Growth Index ETF no par reclassified as Claymore/BNY Mellon International Small Cap LDRs ETF no par 07/27/2009
Trust terminated 12/18/2009
Each share Claymore/Morningstar Information Super Sector Index ETF no par received $21.7165 cash
Each share Claymore/Morningstar Services Super Sector Index ETF no par received $17.7965 cash
Each share Claymore U.S.-1 - The Capital Markets Index ETF no par received $46.7798 cash
Trust terminated 12/21/2009
Each share Claymore/Morningstar Manufacturing Super Sector Index ETF no par received $20.5123 cash
Sabrient Stealth Portfolio ETF no par reclassified as Wilshire Micro-Cap ETF no par 08/20/2010
Trust terminated 09/17/2010
Each share Claymore/Zacks Dividend Rotation ETF no par received $19.9309 cash
Claymore/BNY Mellon International Small Cap LDRs ETF no par reclassified as Guggenheim International Small Cap LDRs ETF no par 09/27/2010
Claymore/Beacon Spin-Off ETF no par reclassified as Guggenheim Spin-Off ETF no par 09/27/2010
Claymore/BNY Mellon BRIC ETF no par reclassified as Guggenheim BRIC ETF no par 09/27/2010
Claymore BulletShares 2011 Corporate Bond ETF no par reclassified as Guggenheim BulletShares 2011 Corporate Bond ETF no par 09/27/2010
Claymore BulletShares 2012 Corporate Bond ETF no par reclassified as Guggenheim BulletShares 2012 Corporate Bond ETF no par 09/27/2010
Claymore BulletShares 2013 Corporate Bond ETF no par reclassified as Guggenheim BulletShares 2013 Corporate Bond ETF no par 09/27/2010
Claymore BulletShares 2014 Corporate Bond ETF no par reclassified as Guggenheim BulletShares 2014 Corporate Bond ETF no par 09/27/2010
Claymore BulletShares 2015 Corporate Bond ETF no par reclassified as Guggenheim BulletShares 2015 Corporate Bond ETF no par 09/27/2010
Claymore BulletShares 2016 Corporate Bond ETF no par reclassified as Guggenheim BulletShares 2016 Corporate Bond ETF no par 09/27/2010
Claymore BulletShares 2017 Corporate Bond ETF no par reclassified as Guggenheim BulletShares 2017 Corporate Bond ETF no par 09/27/2010
Claymore/MAC Global Solar Energy Index ETF no par reclassified as Guggenheim Solar ETF no par 09/27/2010
Claymore/Ocean Tomo Growth Index ETF no par reclassified as Guggenheim Ocean Tomo Growth Index ETF no par 09/27/2010
Claymore/Ocean Tomo Patent ETF no par reclassified as Guggenheim Ocean Tomo Patent ETF no par 09/27/2010
Claymore/Raymond James SB-1 Equity ETF no par reclassified as Guggenheim Raymond James SB-1 Equity ETF no par 09/27/2010
Claymore/S&P Global Dividend Opportunities Index ETF no par reclassified as Guggenheim S&P Global Dividend Opportunities Index ETF no par 09/27/2010
Claymore/Sabrient Defensive Equity Index ETF no par reclassified as Guggenheim Defensive Equity ETF no par 09/27/2010
Claymore/Sabrient Insider ETF no par reclassified as Guggenheim Insider Sentiment ETF no par 09/27/2010
Claymore/Zacks Mid-Cap Core ETF no par reclassified as Guggenheim Mid-Cap Core ETF no par 09/27/2010
Claymore/Zacks Multi-Asset Income Index ETF no par reclassified as Guggenheim Multi-Asset Income ETF no par 09/27/2010
Claymore/Zacks Sector Rotation ETF no par reclassified as Guggenheim Sector Rotation ETF no par 09/27/2010
Claymore U.S. Capital Markets Bond ETF no par reclassified as Guggenheim Enhanced Core Bond ETF no par 06/01/2011
Claymore U.S. Capital Markets Micro-Term Fixed Income ETF no par reclassified as Guggenheim Enhanced Ultra-Short Bond ETF no par 06/01/2011
Guggenheim Enhanced Ultra-Short Bond ETF no par reclassified as Guggenheim Enhanced Short Duration Bond ETF no par 12/05/2011
Trust terminated 12/30/2011
Each share Guggenheim BulletShares 2011 Corporate Bond ETF no par received $20.1199 cash
Each share Guggenheim Solar ETF no par automatically became (0.1) share Claymore Exchange-Traded Fund Trust 2 Guggenheim Solar ETF no par 02/15/2012
Trust terminated 03/23/2012
Each share Guggenheim International Small Cap LDRs ETF no par received $18.44 cash
Each share Guggenheim Ocean Tomo Growth Growth Index ETF no par received $32.52 cash
Each share Guggenheim Ocean Tomo Patent ETF no par received $27.78 cash
Each share Guggenheim Sector Rotation ETF no par received $27.05 cash
Trust terminated 03/22/2013
Each share Wilshire 4500 Completion ETF no par received $36.844581 cash
Each share Wilshire 5000 Total Market ETF no par received $34.818612 cash
Guggenheim Enhanced Short Duration Bond ETF no par reclassified as Guggenheim Enhanced Short Duration ETF no par 09/30/2013
Trust terminated 12/31/2013
Each share Guggenheim BulletShares 2012 Corporate Bond ETF no par received $20.4578 cash
Each share Guggenheim BulletShares 2012 High Yield Corporate Bond ETF no par received $25.419 cash
Each share Guggenheim BulletShares 2013 Corporate Bond ETF no par received $20.76709 cash
Each share Guggenheim BulletShares 2013 High Yield Corporate Bond ETF no par received $25.56137 cash
Trust terminated 03/10/2014
Each share Guggenheim Enhanced

Core Bond ETF no par received $50.01 cash

Trust terminated 12/31/2014

Each share Guggenheim BulletShares 2014 Corporate Bond ETF no par received $21.15144 cash

Each share Guggenheim BulletShares 2014 High Yield Corporate Bond ETF no par received $26.25136 cash

Trust terminated 12/31/2015

Each share Guggenheim BulletShares 2015 Corporate Bond ETF no par received $21.67973 cash

Each share Guggenheim BulletShares 2015 High Yield Corporate Bond ETF no par received $25.74107 cash

Guggenheim Spin-Off ETF no par reclassified as Guggenheim S&P Spin-Off ETF no par 05/20/2016

Trust terminated 12/29/2016

Each share Guggenheim BulletShares 2016 Corporate Bond ETF no par received $22.0836 cash

Each share Guggenheim BulletShares 2016 High Yield Corporate Bond ETF no par received $25.81559 cash

Guggenheim Enhanced Short Duration ETF no par reclassified as Guggenheim Ultra Short Duration ETF no par 06/30/2017

Trust terminated 12/22/2017

Each share Guggenheim Large Cap Optimized Diversification ETF no par received $29.7795 cash

Trust terminated 12/29/2017

Each share Guggenheim BulletShares 2017 Corporate Bond ETF no par received $22.629 cash

Each share Guggenheim BulletShares 2017 High Yield Corporate Bond ETF no par received $25.723 cash

Under plan of reorganization each share Guggenheim BulletShares 2018 Corporate Bond ETF no par, Guggenheim BulletShares 2019 Corporate Bond ETF no par, Guggenheim BulletShares 2020 Corporate Bond ETF no par, Guggenheim BulletShares 2021 Corporate Bond ETF no par, Guggenheim BulletShares 2022 Corporate Bond ETF no par, Guggenheim BulletShares 2023 Corporate Bond ETF no par, Guggenheim BulletShares 2024 Corporate Bond ETF no par, Guggenheim BulletShares 2025 Corporate Bond ETF no par, Guggenheim BulletShares 2026 Corporate Bond ETF no par, Guggenheim BulletShares 2027 Corporate Bond ETF no par, Guggenheim BulletShares 2018 High Yield Corporate Bond ETF no par, Guggenheim BulletShares 2019 High Yield Corporate Bond ETF no par, Guggenheim BulletShares 2020 High Yield Corporate Bond ETF no par, Guggenheim BulletShares 2021 High Yield Corporate Bond ETF no par, Guggenheim BulletShares 2022 High Yield Corporate Bond ETF no par, Guggenheim BulletShares 2023 High Yield Corporate Bond ETF no par, Guggenheim BulletShares 2024 High Yield Corporate Bond ETF no par and Guggenheim Defensive Equity ETF no par automatically became (1) share PowerShares Exchange-Traded Self-Indexed Fund Trust BulletShares 2018 Corporate Bond Portfolio 1¢ par, BulletShares 2019 Corporate Bond Portfolio 1¢ par, BulletShares 2020 Corporate Bond Portfolio 1¢ par, BulletShares 2021 Corporate Bond Portfolio 1¢ par, BulletShares 2022 Corporate Bond Portfolio 1¢ par, BulletShares 2023 Corporate Bond Portfolio 1¢ par, BulletShares 2024 Corporate Bond Portfolio 1¢ par, BulletShares 2025 Corporate Bond Portfolio 1¢ par, BulletShares 2026 Corporate Bond Portfolio 1¢ par, BulletShares 2027 Corporate Bond Portfolio 1¢ par, BulletShares 2018 High Yield Corporate Bond Portfolio 1¢ par, BulletShares 2019 High Yield Corporate Bond Portfolio 1¢ par, BulletShares 2020 High Yield Corporate Bond Portfolio 1¢ par, BulletShares 2021 High Yield Corporate Bond Portfolio 1¢ par, BulletShares 2022 High Yield Corporate Bond Portfolio 1¢ par, BulletShares 2023 High Yield Corporate Bond Portfolio 1¢ par, BulletShares 2024 High Yield Corporate Bond Portfolio 1¢ par or Defensive Equity Portfolio 1¢ par respectively 04/06/2018

(See PowerShares Exchange-Traded Self-Indexed Fund Trust)

Under plan of reorganization each share Guggenheim Dow Jones Industrial Average Dividend ETF no par, Guggenheim Insider Sentiment ETF no par, Guggenheim Mid-Cap Core ETF no par, Guggenheim Multi-Asset Income ETF no par, Guggenheim S&P Spin-Off ETF no par and Wilshire Micro-Cap ETF no par automatically became (1) share PowerShares Exchange-Traded Fund Trust Dow Jones Industrial Average Dividend Portfolio 1¢ par, Insider Sentiment Portfolio 1¢ par, Zacks Mid-Cap Portfolio 1¢ par, Zacks Multi-Asset Income Portfolio 1¢ par, S&P Spin-Off Portfolio 1¢ par or Wilshire Micro-Cap Portfolio 1¢ par respectively 04/06/2018

(See PowerShares Exchange-Traded Fund Trust)

Under plan of reorganization each share Guggenheim S&P Global Dividend Opportunities Index ETF no par automatically became (1) share PowerShares Exchange-Traded Fund Trust II S&P Global Dividend Opportunities Index Portfolio 1¢ par 04/06/2018

(See PowerShares Exchange-Traded Fund Trust II)

Under plan of reorganization each share Guggenheim Ultra Short Duration ETF no par automatically became (1) share PowerShares Actively Managed Exchange-Traded Fund Trust Ultra Short Duration Portfolio 1¢ par 04/06/2018

(See PowerShares Actively Managed Exchange-Traded Fund Trust)

Under plan of reorganization each share Guggenheim BulletShares 2025 High Yield Corporate Bond ETF no par automatically became (1) share PowerShares Exchange-Traded Self-Indexed Fund Trust BulletShares 2025 High Yield Corporate Bond Portfolio 1¢ par 05/18/2018

(See PowerShares Exchange-Traded Self-Indexed Fund Trust)

Under plan of reorganization each share Guggenheim Brazil Russia India & China ETF no par, Guggenheim Raymond James SB-1 Equity ETF no par or Wilshire US REIT ETF no par automatically became (1) share PowerShares Exchange-Traded Fund Trust BRIC Portfolio 1¢ par, Raymond James SB-1 Equity Portfolio 1¢ par or Wilshire US REIT Portfolio 1¢ par respectively 05/18/2018

(See PowerShares Exchange-Traded Fund Trust)

CLAYMORE EXCHANGE TRADED FD TR 2 (DE)

Trust terminated 02/29/2008

Each share Claymore/Clear Global Vaccine Index ETF no par received $21.3471 cash

Each share Claymore/Robeco Developed World Equity ETF no par received $22.6951 cash

Trust terminated 09/17/2010

Each share Claymore/Beacon Global Exchanges, Brokers & Asset Managers Index ETF no par received $12.23 cash

Each share Claymore/Robb Report Global Luxury Index ETF no par received $19.7747 cash

Each share Claymore/Zacks Country Rotation ETF no par received $15.9739 cash

Claymore/AlphaShares China All-Cap ETF no par reclassified as Guggenheim China All-Cap ETF no par 09/27/2010

Claymore/AlphaShares China Real Estate ETF no par reclassified as Guggenheim China Real Estate ETF no par 09/27/2010

Claymore/AlphaShares China Small Cap Index ETF no par reclassified as Guggenheim China Small Cap ETF no par 09/27/2010

Claymore/BNY Mellon EW Euro-Pacific LDRs ETF no par reclassified as Guggenheim EW Euro-Pacific LDRs ETF no par 09/27/2010

Claymore/BNY Mellon Frontier Markets ETF no par reclassified as Guggenheim Frontier Markets ETF no par 09/27/2010

Claymore/Beacon Global Timber Index ETF no par reclassified as Guggenheim Timber ETF no par 09/27/2010

Claymore China Technology ETF no par reclassified as Guggenheim China Technology ETF no par 09/27/2010

Claymore/NYSE Arca Airline ETF no par reclassified as Guggenheim Airline ETF no par 09/27/2010

Claymore S&P Global Water Index ETF no par reclassified as Guggenheim S&P Global Water Index ETF no par 09/27/2010

Claymore/SWM Canadian Energy Income Index ETF no par reclassified as Guggenheim Canadian Energy Income ETF no par 09/27/2010

Claymore Shipping ETF no par reclassified as Guggenheim Shipping ETF no par 09/27/2010

Claymore/Zacks International Multi-Asset Income Index ETF no par reclassified as Guggenheim International Multi-Asset Income ETF no par 09/27/2010

Trust terminated 03/23/2012

Each share Guggenheim EW Euro-Pacific LDRs ETF no par received $18.44 cash

Trust terminated 03/22/2013

Each share Guggenheim ABC High Dividend ETF no par received $19.395144 cash

Each share Guggenheim Airline ETF no par received $42.986572 cash

Trust terminated 06/21/2013

Each share Guggenheim China Yuan Bond ETF no par received $25.91 cash

Guggenheim Timber ETF no par reclassified as Guggenheim MSCI Global Timber ETF no par 05/20/2016

Trust terminated 09/26/2016

Each share Guggenheim Emerging Markets Real Estate ETF no par received $23.10 cash

Under plan of reorganization each share Guggenheim China All-Cap ETF no par, Guggenheim China Real Estate ETF no par, Guggenheim Frontier Markets ETF no par, Guggenheim International Multi-Asset Income ETF no par, Guggenheim MSCI Global Timber ETF no par, Guggenheim S&P Global Water Index ETF no par and Guggenheim Shipping ETF no par automatically became (1) share PowerShares Exchange-Traded Fund Trust II China All-Cap Portfolio 1¢ par, China Real Estate Portfolio 1¢ par, Frontier Markets Portfolio 1¢ par, Zacks International Multi-Asset Income Portfolio 1¢ par, MSCI Global Timber Portfolio 1¢ par, S&P Global Water Index Portfolio 1¢ par or Shipping Portfolio 1¢ par respectively 04/06/2018

Under plan of reorganization each share Guggenheim Total Return Bond ETF no par automatically became (1) share PowerShares Actively Managed Exchange-Traded Fund Trust Total Return Bond Portfolio 1¢ par 04/06/2018

(See PowerShares Actively Managed Exchange-Traded Fund Trust)

Under plan of reorganization each share Guggenheim U.S. Large Cap Optimized Volatility ETF no par automatically became (1) share PowerShares Exchange-Traded Self-Indexed Fund Trust U.S. Large Cap Optimized Volatility Portfolio 1¢ par 04/06/2018

(See PowerShares Exchange-Traded Self-Indexed Fund Trust)

Under plan of reorganization each share Guggenheim Canadian Energy Income ETF no par, Guggenheim China Small Cap ETF no par, Guggenheim China Technology ETF no par, Guggenheim S&P High Income Infrastructure ETF no par and Guggenheim Solar ETF no par automatically became (1) share PowerShares Exchange-Traded Fund Trust II Canadian Energy Income Portfolio 1¢ par, China Small Cap Portfolio no par, China Technology Portfolio no par, S&P High Income Infrastructure Portfolio no par or Solar Portfolio no par respectively 05/18/2018

CLAYMORE GLOBAL AGRICULTURE ETF (ON)

Name changed to iShares Global Agriculture Index Fund 03/29/2012

iShares Global Agriculture Index Fund name changed to iShares Global Agriculture Index ETF 06/04/2014

CLAYMORE GLOBAL BALANCED GROWTH ETF (ON)

Name changed to Claymore Balanced Growth CorePortfolio ETF 11/21/2008

Claymore Balanced Growth CorePortfolio ETF name changed to iShares Balanced Growth CorePortfolio Fund 03/29/2012 which name changed to iShares Balanced Growth CorePortfolio ETF 06/04/2014

CLAYMORE GLOBAL BALANCED INCOME ETF (ON)

Name changed to Claymore Balanced Income CorePortfolio ETF 11/21/2008

Claymore Balanced Income CorePortfolio ETF name changed to iShares Balanced Income CorePortfolio Fund 03/29/2012 which name changed to iShares Balanced Income CorePortfolio ETF 06/04/2014

CLAYMORE GLOBAL INFRASTRUCTURE ETF (ON)

Name changed to iShares Global Infrastructure Index Fund 03/29/2012

iShares Global Infrastructure Index Fund name changed to iShares

Global Infrastructure Index ETF 06/04/2014

CLAYMORE GLOBAL MONTHLY ADVANTAGE DIVIDEND ETF (ON)
Name changed 04/30/2008
Name changed from Claymore Global Monthly Yield Hog ETF to Claymore Global Monthly Advantaged Dividend ETF 04/30/2008
Name changed to iShares Global Monthly Advantaged Dividend Index Fund 03/29/2012
iShares Global Monthly Advantaged Dividend Index Fund name changed to iShares Global Monthly Dividend Index ETF 11/20/2013 which name changed to iShares Global Monthly Dividend Index ETF (CAD-Hedged) 06/04/2014

CLAYMORE GLOBAL REIT ETF (ON)
Name changed to iShares Global Real Estate Index Fund 03/29/2012
iShares Global Real Estate Index Fund name changed to iShares Global Real Estate Index ETF 06/04/2014

CLAYMORE GOLD BULLION ETF (ON)
Name changed to iShares Gold Bullion Fund 03/29/2012
iShares Gold Bullion Fund name changed to iShares Gold Bullion ETF 10/30/2013

CLAYMORE GOLD BULLION TR (ON)
Name changed to Claymore Gold Bullion ETF and Trust Units no par reclassified as Hedged Common Units 02/16/2010
Claymore Gold Bullion ETF name changed to iShares Gold Bullion Fund 03/29/2012 which name changed to iShares Gold Bullion ETF 10/30/2013

CLAYMORE/GUGGENHEIM STRATEGIC OPPORTUNITIES FD (DE)
Issue Information - 9,100,000 COM SHS OF BEN INT offered at $20 per share on 07/26/2007
Name changed to Guggenheim Strategic Opportunities Fund 03/25/2011

CLAYMORE INTL FUNDAMENTAL INDEX ETF (ON)
Name changed to iShares International Fundamental Index Fund 03/29/2012
iShares International Fundamental Index Fund name changed to iShares International Fundamental Index ETF 06/04/2014

CLAYMORE INVERSE 10 YR GOVT BD ETF (ON)
Completely liquidated
Each Common Unit received first and final distribution of $16.9611 cash payable 06/22/2012 to holders of record 06/22/2012

CLAYMORE JAPAN FUNDAMENTAL INDEX ETF CDN $ HEDGED (ON)
Name changed to iShares Japan Fundamental Index Fund (CAD-Hedged) 03/29/2012
iShares Japan Fundamental Index Fund (CAD-Hedged) name changed to iShares Japan Fundamental Index ETF (CAD-Hedged) 06/04/2014

CLAYMORE MACROSHARES OIL DOWN TRADEABLE TR (NY)
Shares $60 par changed to $20 par and (2) additional shares issued payable 10/22/2007 to holders of record 10/19/2007
Name changed to MACROshares Oil Down Tradeable Trust 11/14/2007
(See MACROshares Oil Down Tradeable Trust)

CLAYMORE MACROSHARES OIL UP TRADEABLE TR (NY)
Shares $60 par changed to $20 par and (2) additional shares issued payable 10/22/2007 to holders of record 10/19/2007
Name changed to MACROshares Oil Up Tradeable Trust 11/14/2007
(See MACROshares Oil Up Tradeable Trust)

CLAYMORE MANAGED FUTURES ETF (ON)
Name changed to iShares Managed Futures Index Fund 03/29/2012
iShares Managed Futures Index Fund name changed to iShares Managed Futures Index ETF 10/18/2013

CLAYMORE NAT GAS COMMODITY ETF (AB)
Each old Common Unit automatically became (0.1) new Common Unit no par 05/10/2011
Name changed to iShares Natural Gas Commodity Index Fund 03/29/2012
iShares Natural Gas Commodity Index Fund merged into iShares Broad Commodity Index Fund (CAD-Hedged) 11/30/2012 which name changed to iShares Broad Commodity Index ETF (CAD-Hedged) 10/18/2013
(See iShares Broad Commodity Index ETF (CAD-Hedged))

CLAYMORE OIL SANDS SECTOR ETF (ON)
Name changed to iShares Oil Sands Index Fund 03/29/2012
iShares Oil Sands Index Fund name changed to iShares Oil Sands Index ETF 06/04/2014
(See iShares Oil Sands Index ETF)

CLAYMORE 1-5 YR LADDERED CORP BD ETF (ON)
Name changed to iShares 1-5 Year Laddered Corporate Bond Index Fund 03/29/2012
iShares 1-5 Year Laddered Corporate Bond Index Fund name changed to iShares 1-5 Year Laddered Corporate Bond Index ETF 06/04/2014

CLAYMORE 1-5 YR LADDERED GOVT BD ETF (ON)
Name changed to iShares 1-5 Year Laddered Government Bond Index Fund 03/29/2012
iShares 1-5 Year Laddered Government Bond Index Fund name changed to iShares 1-5 Year Laddered Government Bond Index ETF 06/04/2014

CLAYMORE 1-10 YR LADDERED CORPORATE BD ETF (ON)
Name changed to iShares 1-10 Year Laddered Corporate Bond Index Fund 03/29/2012
iShares 1-10 Year Laddered Corporate Bond Index Fund name changed to iShares 1-10 Year Laddered Corporate Bond Index ETF 06/04/2014

CLAYMORE 1-10 YR LADDERED GOVT BD ETF (ON)
Name changed to iShares 1-10 Year Laddered Goverment Bond Index Fund 03/29/2012
iShares 1-10 Year Laddered Goverment Bond Index Fund name changed to iShares 1-10 Year Laddered Government Bond Index ETF 06/04/2014

CLAYMORE PREM MONEY MKT ETF (ON)
Name changed to iShares Premium Money Market Fund 04/02/2012
iShares Premium Money Market Fund name changed to iShares Premium Money Market ETF 10/18/2013

CLAYMORE/RAYMOND JAMES SB-1 EQUITY FD (DE)
Merged into Claymore Exchange-Traded Fund Trust 09/03/2008
Each share Common 1¢ par exchanged for (1) share Claymore/Raymond James SB-1 Equity Fund

CLAYMORE RES LTD (BC)
Recapitalized as New Claymore Resources Ltd. (BC) 04/19/1989
Each share Common no par exchanged for (0.25) share Common no par
New Claymore Resources Ltd. (BC) reincorporated in Alberta as Brazalta Resources Corp. 11/26/2004 which name changed to Canacol Energy Ltd. 02/13/2009

CLAYMORE S&P / TSX GLOBAL MNG ETF (ON)
Name changed to iShares S&P/TSX Global Mining Index Fund 03/29/2012
iShares S&P/TSX Global Mining Index Fund name changed to iShares S&P/TSX Global Mining Index ETF 06/04/2014
(See iShares S&P/TSX Global Mining Index ETF)

CLAYMORE S&P GLOBAL WTR ETF (ON)
Name changed to iShares S&P Global Water Index Fund 03/29/2012
iShares S&P Global Water Index Fund name changed to iShares Global Water Index ETF 06/04/2014

CLAYMORE S&P/TSX CDN DIVID ETF (ON)
Name changed to iShares S&P/TSX Canadian Dividend Aristocrats Index Fund 03/29/2012
iShares S&P/TSX Canadian Dividend Aristocrats Index Fund name changed to iShares S&P/TSX Canadian Dividend Aristocrats Index ETF 06/04/2014

CLAYMORE S&P/TSX CDN PFD SH ETF (ON)
Name changed to iShares S&P/TSX Canadian Preferred Share Index Fund 03/29/2012
iShares S&P/TSX Canadian Preferred Share Index Fund name changed to iShares S&P/TSX Canadian Preferred Share Index ETF 06/04/2014

CLAYMORE S&P US DIVID GROWERS ETF (ON)
Name changed to iShares S&P US Dividend Growers Index Fund (CAD-Hedged) 03/29/2012
iShares S&P US Dividend Growers Index Fund (CAD-Hedged) name changed to iShares US Dividend Growers Index ETF (CAD-Hedged) 06/04/2014

CLAYMORE SHORT DURATION HIGH INCOME ETF (ON)
Name changed to Claymore Advantaged Short Duration High Income ETF 05/19/2011
Claymore Advantaged Short Duration High Income ETF name changed to iShares Advantaged Short Duration High Income Fund 03/29/2012 which name changed to iShares Advantaged Short Duration High Income ETF 10/18/2013 which name changed to iShares Advantaged Short Duration High Income ETF (CAD-Hedged) 11/04/2014 which name changed to iShares Short Duration High Income ETF (CAD-Hedged) 02/29/2016

CLAYMORE SILVER BULLION TR (ON)
Name changed to BlackRock Silver Bullion Trust 03/29/2012
BlackRock Silver Bullion Trust name changed to iShares Silver Bullion Fund 11/05/2012 which name changed to iShares Silver Bullion ETF 10/30/2013

CLAYMORE US FUNDAMENTAL INDEX ETF (ON)
Name changed to iShares US Fundamental Index Fund 03/29/2012
iShares US Fundamental Index Fund name changed to iShares US Fundamental Index ETF 06/04/2014

CLAYMORE US FUNDAMENTAL INDEX ETF CDN $ HEDGED (ON)
Name changed to Claymore US Fundamental Index ETF 04/07/2009
Claymore US Fundamental Index ETF name changed to iShares US Fundamental Index Fund 03/29/2012 which name changed to iShares US Fundamental Index ETF 06/04/2014

CLAYMORETFS FTSE RAFI CDN INDEX FD (CANADA)
Name changed to Claymore Canadian Fundamental Index ETF 08/15/2006
Claymore Canadian Fundamental Index ETF name changed to iShares Canadian Fundamental Index Fund 03/29/2012 which name changed to iShares Canadian Fundamental Index ETF 06/04/2014

CLAYOQUOT RES LTD (AB)
Name changed to Bakrie Minarak Energy Inc. 12/12/1997
Bakrie Minarak Energy Inc. name changed to Pertacal Energy Inc. 05/24/2000

CLAYTON BANCSHARES CORP (MO)
Merged into Metro Bancholding Corp. 09/02/1980
Each share Common $1 par exchanged for (1) share Common $1 par
(See Metro Bancholding Corp.)

CLAYTON CORP. OF DELAWARE (DE)
Name changed to Clayton Corp. 04/20/1967
(See Clayton Corp.)

CLAYTON CORP (DE)
Name changed to Clayton Corp. of Delaware 07/15/1956 which name changed back to Clayton Corp. 04/20/1967
Recapitalized 03/29/1985
For holdings of (199) shares or fewer each share Common 1¢ par exchanged for $0.390625 cash
Note: Holders had the option to remain holders of Common 1¢ par. Such option expired 05/06/1985
Holdings of (200) shares or more were not affected
Merged into Clayton Merger Co. 09/14/1987
Each share Common 1¢ par exchanged for $1.13 cash

CLAYTON DUNNING GROUP INC (NV)
Recapitalized as Carlton Companies, Inc. 07/09/2008
Each share Common $0.001 par exchanged for (0.02) share Common $0.001 par

CLAYTON HLDGS INC (DE)
Merged into Cobra Green LLC 07/02/2008
Each share Common 1¢ par exchanged for $6 cash

CLAYTON HOMES INC (DE)
Reincorporated 12/31/1996
Common 10¢ par split (5) for (4) by

FINANCIAL INFORMATION, INC.

CLA-CLE

issuance of (0.25) additional share 09/17/1985
Common 10¢ par split (5) for (4) by issuance of (0.25) additional share 06/11/1986
Common 10¢ par split (5) for (4) by issuance of (0.25) additional share 04/28/1987
Common 10¢ par split (5) for (4) by issuance of (0.25) additional share 09/28/1988
Common 10¢ par split (5) for (4) by issuance of (0.25) additional share 12/12/1990
Common 10¢ par split (5) for (4) by issuance of (0.25) additional share 12/10/1991
Common 10¢ par split (5) for (4) by issuance of (0.25) additional share 12/09/1992
Common 10¢ par split (5) for (4) by issuance of (0.25) additional share 12/08/1993
Common 10¢ par split (5) for (4) by issuance of (0.25) additional share 12/05/1994
Common 10¢ par split (5) for (4) by issuance of (0.25) additional share 12/13/1995
Common 10¢ par split (5) for (4) by issuance of (0.25) additional share payable 12/11/1996 to holders of record 11/27/1996 Ex date - 12/12/1996
Stock Dividend - 25% 10/18/1984
State of incorporation changed from (TN) to (DE) 12/31/1996
Common 10¢ par split (5) for (4) by issuance of (0.25) additional share payable 12/09/1998 to holders of record 11/25/1998 Ex date - 12/10/1998
Merged into Berkshire Hathaway Inc. 08/07/2003
Each share Common 10¢ par exchanged for $12.50 cash

CLAYTON MARK & CO (DE)
Common $5 par changed to $1 par 04/17/1970
Name changed to Mark Controls Corp. 04/16/1971
(See Mark Controls Corp.)

CLAYTON SILVER MINES (AZ)
Common $1 par changed to 10¢ par 00/00/1945
Completely liquidated 08/15/1994
Each share Common 10¢ par exchanged for first and final distribution of (0.05) share Southern Star Consolidated Corp. Common $0.001 par

CLAYTRON ENERGY CORP (BC)
Merged into International Interlake Industries Inc. 12/31/1986
Each share Common no par exchanged for (0.04347826) share Common no par
(See International Interlake Industries Inc.)

CLAYVILLE KNITTING CO.
Acquired by Utica Knitting Co. 00/00/1937
Details not available

CLC AMER INC (DE)
Reorganized under Chapter 11 Federal Bankruptcy Code 12/09/1987
Each share Common 50¢ par exchanged for (0.251327) share Common 1¢ par
Merged into Archer-Daniels-Midland Co. 08/25/1988
Each share Common 1¢ par exchanged for (0.31976) shares Common no par and cash
Each share Common 1¢ par received initial additional payment of $1.16487 cash 09/03/1988
Each share Common 1¢ par received second additional payment of $0.62528 cash 12/02/1988
Note: An additional cash amount is being held in escrow for possible future distribution

CLC HEALTHCARE INC (NV)
Merged into Center Healthcare, Inc. 11/12/2003
Each share Common 1¢ par exchanged for $1 cash

CLE WARE INDS INC (OH)
Name changed to Rayco International Inc. 11/20/1972
Rayco International Inc. merged into FDI, Inc. 10/15/1974 which recapitalized as Interlee, Inc. 12/18/1981
(See Interlee, Inc.)

CLEAN AIR CTLS INC (NY)
Adjudicated bankrupt 10/25/1973
Stockholders' equity unlikely

CLEAN DIESEL TECHNOLOGIES INC (DE)
Each share Common 5¢ par exchanged for (0.2) share old Common 1¢ par 06/19/2007
Each share old Common 1¢ par exchanged for (0.16666666) share new Common 1¢ par 10/18/2010
Each share new Common 1¢ par exchanged exchanged again for (0.2) share new Common 1¢ par 07/25/2016
Name changed to CDTi Advanced Materials, Inc. 03/15/2018

CLEAN ENERGY & PWR INC (NV)
Each share old Common $0.001 par exchanged for (0.001) share new Common $0.001 par 04/26/2010
SEC revoked common stock registration 05/20/2011

CLEAN ENERGY COMBUSTION SYS INC (DE)
Each share old Common $0.0001 par exchanged for (0.33333333) share new Common $0.0001 par 04/28/2004
SEC revoked common stock registration 04/25/2011

CLEAN ENERGY INC (NV)
SEC revoked common stock registration 09/18/2008

CLEAN ENVIRO TECH CORP (NV)
Recapitalized as Cyber Apps World Inc. 04/30/2015
Each share Common $0.001 par exchanged for (0.2) share Common $0.001 par

CLEAN HBRS INC (MA)
Each share Conv. Preferred Ser. B 1¢ par received distribution of (5.82882) shares Common 1¢ par payable 07/15/1999 to holders of record 07/01/1999
Each share Conv. Preferred Ser. B 1¢ par received distribution of (0.686719) share Common 1¢ par payable 10/15/1999 to holders of record 10/01/1999
Each share Conv. Preferred Ser. B 1¢ par received distribution of (0.82902) share Common 1¢ par payable 01/15/2000 to holders of record 01/01/2000
Each share Conv. Preferred Ser. B 1¢ par received distribution of (0.349705) share Common 1¢ par payable 04/15/2000 to holders of record 04/01/2000
Each share Conv. Preferred Ser. B 1¢ par received distribution of (0.49382352) share Common 1¢ par payable 07/15/2000 to holders of record 07/01/2000
Each share Conv. Preferred Ser. B 1¢ par received distribution of (0.3532) share Common 1¢ par payable 10/05/2000 to holders of record 10/01/2000
Each share Conv. Preferred Ser. B 1¢ par received distribution of (0.530694) share Common 1¢ par payable 01/15/2001 to holders of record 01/01/2001
Each share Conv. Preferred Ser. B 1¢ par received distribution of (0.407117) share Common 1¢ par payable 04/15/2001 to holders of record 04/01/2001
Each share Conv. Preferred Ser. B 1¢ par received distribution of (0.10340178) share Common 1¢ par payable 07/15/2003 to holders of record 07/01/2003
Each share Conv. Preferred Ser. B 1¢ par received distribution of (0.20859821) share Common 1¢ par payable 10/15/2003 to holders of record 10/01/2003
Each share Conv. Preferred Ser. B 1¢ par received distribution of (0.11188392) share Common 1¢ par payable 01/15/2004 to holders of record 01/01/2004
Each share Conv. Preferred Ser. B 1¢ par received distribution of approximately (0.2) share Common 1¢ par payable 04/15/2004 to holders of record 04/01/2004 Ex date - 03/31/2004
Conv. Preferred Ser. B 1¢ par called for redemption at $50 plus $0.8438 accrued dividends on 12/31/2007
(Additional Information in Active)

CLEAN HYDROGEN PRODUCERS LTD (NV)
Name changed to Golden Developing Solutions, Inc. 09/27/2017

CLEAN PWR INCOME FD (ON)
Acquired by Macquarie Power & Infrastructure Income Fund (ON) 06/26/2007
Each Trust Unit no par received (0.5581) Trust Unit no par and (1) Contingency Value Receipt
Macquarie Power & Infrastructure Income Fund (ON) reorganized in British Columbia as Macquarie Power & Infrastructure Corp. 01/10/2011 which name changed to Capstone Infrastructure Corp. 04/21/2011
(See Capstone Infrastructure Corp.)

CLEAN SYS TECHNOLOGY GROUP LTD (NY)
SEC revoked common stock registration 08/05/2008

CLEAN WATER TECHNOLOGIES INC (DE)
Each share old Common $0.001 par exchanged for (0.13513513) share new Common $0.001 par 03/22/2006
Name changed to SheerVision, Inc. 06/19/2006

CLEAN WAY CORP (NV)
Common $0.001 par split (4) for (1) by issuance of (3) additional shares 04/21/1993
Each share old Common $0.001 par exchanged for (0.00166666) share new Common $0.001 par 07/09/1998
Name changed to Trader Secrets.com 09/10/1999
Trader Secrets.com name changed to Voip Technology Inc. 03/13/2000 which recapitalized as Oxford Ventures Inc. 01/30/2002 which recapitalized as ULURU Inc. 04/05/2006

CLEAN WIND ENERGY TOWER INC (NV)
Name changed to Solar Wind Energy Tower, Inc. 03/11/2013

CLEAN X-PRESS INC (CO)
Recapitalized as Carlyle Gaming & Entertainment Ltd. 06/20/2008
Each share Common $0.001 par exchanged for (0.06666666) share Common $0.001 par
(See Carlyle Gaming & Entertainment Ltd.)

CLEANER YOGA MAT INC (FL)
Reincorporated under the laws of Delaware as Valeritas Holdings, Inc. and Common no par changed to $0.001 par 04/29/2016

CLEANFIELD ALTERNATIVE ENERGY INC (BC)
Event of default triggered 02/22/2013
Stockholders' equity unlikely

CLEANTECH CAP INC (ON)
Name changed to Char Technologies Ltd. 04/08/2016

CLEANTECH INNOVATIONS INC (NV)
Each share old Common $0.00001 par exchanged for (0.33333333) share new Common $0.00001 par 07/14/2014
Each share new Common $0.00001 par exchanged again for (0.4347826) share new Common $0.00001 par 09/25/2014
Reincorporated under the laws of Delaware as 6D Global Technologies, Inc. 09/29/2014

CLEANTECH SOLUTIONS INTL INC (NV)
Reincorporated 08/10/2012
Each share old Common $0.001 par exchanged for (0.1) share new Common $0.001 par 03/06/2012
State of incorporation changed from (DE) to (NV) 08/10/2012
Each share old Common $0.001 par exchanged for (0.25) share new Common $0.001 par 03/20/2017
Name changed to Sharing Economy International Inc. 01/08/2018

CLEANTECH TRAN INC (NV)
Common $0.001 par split (3) for (1) by issuance of (2) additional shares payable 10/13/2010 to holders of record 10/13/2010 Ex date - 10/14/2010
Name changed to EQCO2, Inc. 07/30/2013
(See EQCO2, Inc.)

CLEAR AIR INC (UT)
Each share Common 2¢ par exchanged for (0.0133333) share Common $0.001 par 10/12/2000
Name changed to Immunoclin International Inc. 10/30/2000
Immunoclin International Inc. name changed to Pacific Health Care Organization, Inc. 01/31/2001

CLEAR CHANNEL COMMUNICATIONS INC (TX)
Common 10¢ par split (6) for (5) by issuance of (0.2) additional share 04/21/1988
Common 10¢ par split (3) for (2) by issuance of (0.5) additional share 05/31/1990
Common 10¢ par split (5) for (4) by issuance of (0.25) additional share 03/31/1992
Common 10¢ par split (5) for (4) by issuance of (0.25) additional share 02/19/1993
Common 10¢ par split (5) for (4) by issuance of (0.25) additional share 02/22/1994
Common 10¢ par split (2) for (1) by issuance of (1) additional share 11/30/1995
Common 10¢ par split (2) for (1) by issuance of (1) additional share payable 12/02/1996 to holders of record 11/13/1996 Ex date - 12/03/1996
Common 10¢ par split (2) for (1) by issuance of (1) additional share payable 07/28/1998 to holders of record 07/21/1998 Ex date - 07/29/1998
Each share Common 10¢ par received distribution of (0.125) share CCE Spinco, Inc. Common 1¢ par payable 12/21/2005 to holders of record 12/14/2005 Ex date - 12/22/2005

Stock Dividend - 10% 05/29/1987
Merged into CC Media Holdings, Inc. 07/30/2008
Each share Common 10¢ par exchanged for $36 cash

CLEAR CHOICE FINL INC (NV)
SEC revoked common stock registration 08/31/2012

CLEAR CREEK CONSOLIDATED MINING CO. (CO)
Succeeded by Clear Creek Corp. 00/00/1939
Details not available

CLEAR CREEK CORP (DE)
Each share old Capital Stock 10¢ par exchanged for (0.1) share new Capital Stock 10¢ par 00/00/1944
Charter cancelled and declared inoperative and void for non-payment of taxes 03/01/1989

CLEAR CREEK RES LTD (BC)
Reorganized under the laws of Yukon as Olympus Stone Inc. 01/10/2000
Each share Common no par exchanged for (0.33333333) share Common no par
Olympus Stone Inc. recapitalized as Gobi Gold Inc. (YT) 10/12/2004 which reincorporated in British Columbia 09/26/2005 which reorganized as East Energy Corp. 08/29/2006 which name changed to Rare Earth Metals Inc. 12/16/2009 which name changed to Canada Rare Earth Corp. 02/08/2013

CLEAR CUT FILM & TECHNOLOGY STUDIOS INC (NV)
Recapitalized as Trans-Global Capital Management, Inc. 02/13/2007
Each share Common $0.005 par exchanged for (0.1) share Common $0.001 par

CLEAR ENERGY INC (AB)
Plan of arrangement effective 08/14/2006
Each share Common no par exchanged for (0.5) share Sure Energy Inc. Common no par, (0.0425) Common Stock Purchase Warrant expiring 09/13/2006 and (0.1667) Sound Energy Trust, Trust Unit
(See each company's listing)

CLEAR LAKE NATL BK (CLEARLAKE, CA)
Name changed to First Counties Bank (Clearlake, CA) 01/28/1998
First Counties Bank (Clearlake, CA) merged into Westamerica Bancorporation 08/17/2000

CLEAR LAKE WTR CO (CA)
Liquidated 10/29/1968
Details not available

CLEAR-LITE HLDGS INC (NV)
SEC revoked common stock registration 10/07/2014

CLEAR MINES LTD (BC)
Recapitalized as Redwood Resources Inc. 08/16/1985
Each share Common no par exchanged for (0.25641025) share Common no par
Redwood Resources Inc. recapitalized as Trooper Explorations Ltd. 06/01/1992 which name changed to Trooper Technologies Inc. 01/27/1995 which name changed to Stream Communications Network, Inc. 10/19/2001 which name changed to Stream Communications Network & Media Inc. 08/17/2004
(See Stream Communications Network & Media Inc.)

CLEAR MTN RES CORP (BC)
Each share old Common no par exchanged for (0.05) share new Common no par 05/18/2016

Name changed to Patriot One Technologies Inc. 08/24/2016

CLEAR PETROLEUMS LTD. (AB)
Struck off register and declared dissolved for failure to file reports or pay fees 00/00/1964

CLEAR SKIES SOLAR INC (DE)
Name changed 01/27/2008
Name changed from Clear Skies Holdings, Inc. to Clear Skies Solar, Inc. 01/27/2008
SEC revoked common stock registration 07/08/2014

CLEAR SYS RECYCLING INC (NV)
Common $0.001 par split (12.5) for (1) by issuance of (11.5) additional shares payable 07/05/2012 to holders of record 06/28/2012
Ex date - 07/06/2012
Name changed to Experience Art & Design, Inc. 05/08/2013

CLEAR VIEW VENTURES INC (BC)
Name changed to Turbodyne Technologies Inc. (BC) 04/21/1994
Turbodyne Technologies Inc. (BC) reincorporated in Canada 12/03/1996 which reincorporated in Delaware in 07/24/1998 which reincorporated in Nevada 09/12/2002

CLEAR WTR MNG INC (NV)
Name changed to e-Casino Gaming Corp. 03/05/1999
e-Casino Gaming Corp. name changed to e-Vegas.com, Inc. 08/02/1999 which name changed to 1st Genx.com, Inc. 07/20/2000 which name changed to 1st Genx, Inc. 03/06/2001 which recapitalized as Oasis Information Systems, Inc. 10/31/2001 which recapitalized as 777 Sports Entertainment, Corp. 02/07/2005 which recapitalized as NT Mining Corp. 11/04/2008 which recapitalized as Sanwire Corp. (NV) 03/07/2013 which reincorporated in Wyoming 07/07/2015

CLEARANCE CORP. (DE)
Dissolved 00/00/1956
Details not available

CLEARANT INC (DE)
Each share old Common $0.001 par exchanged for (0.07142857) share new Common $0.001 par 09/06/2007
SEC revoked common stock registration 08/09/2012

CLEARFIELD & MAHONING RY CO (PA)
Merged into Corman Merger Corp. 11/02/2001
Each share 6% Guaranteed Stock $50 par exchanged for $21.61 cash

CLEARFIELD BK & TR CO (CLEARFIELD, PA)
Capital Stock $12.50 par changed to $6.25 par and (1) additional share issued 02/28/1978
Capital Stock $6.25 par changed to $1.5625 par and (3) additional shares issued 02/28/1986
Under plan of reorganization each share Common $1.5625 par automatically became (1) share CBT Financial Corp. Common no par 02/28/2003
CBT Financial Corp. merged into Riverview Financial Corp. (New) 10/02/2017

CLEARFORD INDS INC (CANADA)
Name changed to Clearford Water Systems Inc. 06/27/2014

CLEARFRAME SOLUTIONS CORP (BC)
Name changed to Clear Gold Resources Inc. 02/25/2013

CLEARFRAME SOLUTIONS INC (BC)
Recapitalized as ClearFrame Solutions Corp. 05/02/2005

Each share Common no par exchanged for (0.05) share Common no par
ClearFrame Solutions Corp. name changed to Clear Gold Resources Inc. 02/25/2013

CLEARING INDL DIST INC (DE)
Through purchase offer Curto Reynolds Oelerich acquired 100% as of 07/14/1971
Public interest eliminated

CLEARING MACHINE CORP. (IL)
Each share Common $1 par exchanged for (1-1/4) shares Common $5 par in 1947
Stock Dividend - 100% 9/5/46
Name changed to R.W.G. Corp. 10/18/54
(See R.W.G. Corp.)

CLEARLINK CAP CORP (ON)
Name changed to Renasant Financial Partners Ltd. 04/03/2006
(See Renasant Financial Partners Ltd.)

CLEARLY CDN BEVERAGE CORP (BC)
Each share old Common no par exchanged for (0.23529411) share new Common no par 02/24/1999
Each share new Common no par exchanged again for (0.1) share new Common no par 05/05/2005
New Common no par reclassified as Ltd. Vtg. Shares no par 03/16/2006
Proposal under Bankruptcy and Insolvency Act effective 05/26/2010
No stockholders' equity

CLEARNET COMMUNICATIONS INC (CANADA)
Acquired by Telus Corp. 01/12/2001
Each share Non-Vtg. Class A no par exchanged for (0.818) Non-Vtg. Share no par and $35 cash

CLEARONE COMMUNICATIONS INC (UT)
Name changed to ClearOne, Inc. 12/13/2012

CLEARPORT PETES LTD (AB)
Merged into Eurogas Corp. 06/30/1995
Each share Common no par exchanged for (0.63) share Common no par
Eurogas Corp. name changed to Dundee Energy Ltd. 06/22/2011

CLEARVIEW ACQUISITIONS INC (NV)
Name changed to Helix Wind, Corp. 04/24/2009

CLEARVIEW CINEMA GROUP INC (DE)
Merged into Cablevision Systems Corp. 12/02/1998
Each share Common 1¢ par exchanged for either (0.5209) share Common 1¢ par, $24.25 cash, or a combination thereof
Note: Option to receive stock and cash or cash only expired 11/30/1998
(See Cablevision Systems Corp.)

CLEARVIEW MINERAL RES CORP (BC)
Recapitalized as Mineral Hill Industries Ltd. 10/22/2004
Each share Common no par exchanged for (0.1) share Common no par

CLEARWATER INC (NV)
Recapitalized as Cinco Inc. 12/01/1998
Each share Common 1¢ par exchanged for (0.04) share Common 1¢ par
Cinco Inc. reorganized as Alynx, Co. (NV) 09/21/2006 which reorganized in Florida as MiMedx Group, Inc. 04/02/2008

CLEARWATER SEAFOODS INCOME FD (ON)
Under plan of reorganization each Trust Unit automatically became (1) share Clearwater Seafoods Inc. (Canada) Common no par 10/03/2011

CLEARWATER TECHNOLOGIES INC (CANADA)
Reincorporated 12/01/2002
Place of incorporation changed from (BC) to (Canada) 12/01/2002
Voluntarily dissolved 06/01/2010
Details not available

CLEARWIRE CORP NEW (DE)
Acquired by Sprint Nextel Corp. 07/09/2013
Each share Class A Common $0.0001 par exchanged for $5 cash

CLEARWIRE CORP OLD (DE)
Merged into Clearwire Corp. (New) 11/28/2008
Each share Class A Common $0.0001 par exchanged for (1) share Class A Common $0.0001 par
(See Clearwire Corp. (New))

CLEARWORKS NET INC (FL)
Merged into Eagle Wireless International, Inc. 02/05/2001
Each share Common $0.001 par exchanged for (0.8) share Common $0.001 par
Eagle Wireless International, Inc. name changed to Eagle Broadband, Inc. 03/04/2002
(See Eagle Broadband, Inc.)

CLEARWORKS TECHNOLOGIES INC (FL)
Name changed to Clearworks.Net Inc. 04/29/1999
Clearworks.Net Inc. merged into Eagle Wireless International, Inc. 02/05/2001 which name changed to Eagle Broadband, Inc. 03/04/2002
(See Eagle Broadband, Inc.)

CLEARY (T.L.) DRILLING CO. LTD. (AB)
Adjudicated bankrupt 06/18/1957
No stockholders' equity

CLEARY (W.B.), INC. (OK)
Merged into Cleary Petroleum, Inc. 02/19/1960
Each share Common no par exchanged for (1) share Common no par
Cleary Petroleum, Inc. merged into Cleary Petroleum Corp. 11/29/1968 which merged into Grace (W.R.) & Co. (CT) 11/01/1973 which reincorporated in New York 05/19/1988
(See Grace (W.R.) & Co.)

CLEARY OIL CO. LTD. (AB)
Recapitalized as Fosca Oil Co. Ltd. 06/12/1957
Each share Capital Stock $10 par exchanged for (5) shares Capital Stock $2 par
(See Fosca Oil Co. Ltd.)

CLEARY PETE CORP (DE)
Merged into Grace (W.R.) & Co. (CT) 11/01/1973
Each share Common $1 par exchanged for (0.377358) share Common $1 par
Grace (W.R.) & Co. (CT) reincorporated in New York 05/19/1988
(See Grace (W.R.) & Co.)

CLEARY PETROLEUM, INC. (DE)
Merged into Cleary Petroleum Corp. 11/29/1968
Each share Common no par exchanged for (0.3931) share Common $1 par
Cleary Petroleum Corp. merged into Grace (W.R.) & Co. 11/01/1973 (CT) which reincorporated in New York 05/19/1988
(See Grace (W.R.) & Co.)

CLEAVER LAKE MINES LTD (BC)
Recapitalized as Lawrence Mining Corp. 08/21/1980
Each share Capital Stock 50¢ par exchanged for (0.2) share Common no par
(See Lawrence Mining Corp.)

CLEBURNE ST BK (CLEBURNE, TX)
Acquired by First Financial Bankshares, Inc. 12/16/1998
Each share Common exchanged for (2.1073) shares Common $10 par
Preferred called for redemption at $15 on 02/25/1999
Public interest eliminated

CLEC HLDG CORP (NJ)
Name changed to Access One Communications, Corp. 05/27/1998
Access One Communications, Corp. merged into TALK.com Inc. 08/10/2000 which name changed to Talk America Holdings Inc. 04/10/2001
(See Talk America Holdings Inc.)

CLECO CORP NEW (LA)
Common $2 par changed to $1 par and (1) additional share issued payable 05/21/2001 to holders of record 05/07/2001 Ex date - 05/22/2001
Each share Adjustable Rate Preferred $100 par exchanged for (9.6) shares Common $1 par 03/00/2007
4.5% Preferred 1951 Ser. $100 par called for redemption at $101 plus $0.296 accrued dividends on 06/24/2011
Acquired by Como 1 L.P. 04/13/2016
Each share Common $1 par exchanged for $55.37 cash

CLECO UTIL GROUP INC (LA)
Name changed 05/14/1999
Name changed from Cleco Corp. to Cleco Utilities Group Inc. 05/14/1999
4.5% Preferred 1955 Ser. called for redemption at $102 plus accrued dividends on 06/30/1999
4.65% Preferred $100 par called for redemption at $102 on 06/30/1999
4.75% Preferred 1965 Ser. $100 par called for redemption at $100 on 06/30/1999
Under plan of reorganization each share Adjustable Rate Preferred $100 par, 4.5% Preferred Ser. 1951 $100 par, and Common $2 par automatically became (1) share Cleco Corp. (New) Adjustable Rate Preferred $100 par, 4.50% Preferred Ser. 1951 $100 par, and Common $2 par respectively 07/01/1999
(See Cleco Corp. (New))

CLEF COMMUNICATIONS INC (UT)
Reorganized under the laws of Delaware as Galaxy Ventures Inc. 01/13/1997
Each share Common $0.001 par exchanged for (0.1) share Common $0.001 par
Galaxy Ventures Inc. recapitalized as Minimally Invasive Surgery Corp. 06/23/1998 which name changed to eCare Solutions Inc. 03/23/2000

CLEMENCEAU MINING CORP.
Liquidation completed
Each share Capital Stock 25¢ par received initial distribution of 20¢ cash 01/14/1942
Each share Capital Stock 25¢ par received second distribution of 25¢ cash 03/12/1947
Each share Capital Stock 25¢ par received third distribution of $0.106 cash 03/01/1948
Note: Certificates were not required to be surrendered and are without value

CLEMENTE STRATEGIC VALUE FD INC (MD)
Name changed 05/26/1999
Name changed from Clemente Global Growth Fund, Inc. to Clemente Strategic Value Fund Inc. 05/26/1999
Name changed to Cornerstone Strategic Value Fund, Inc. 04/23/2001
(See Cornerstone Strategic Value Fund, Inc.)

CLEMENTS GOLDEN PHOENIX ENTERPRISES INC (FL)
Common $0.001 par split (2) for (1) by issuance of (1) additional share payable 08/31/2000 to holders of record 08/25/2000 Ex date - 09/01/2000
Common $0.001 par split (2) for (1) by issuance of (1) additional share payable 10/06/2000 to holders of record 09/29/2000
Each share Common $0.001 par exchanged for (0.25) share Common $0.0001 par 03/02/2001
Name changed to Atlas Resources International, Inc. 05/19/2003
(See Atlas Resources International, Inc.)

CLEMEX TECHNOLOGIES INC (QC)
Acquired by 9804064 Canada Inc. 12/29/2016
Each share Class A Common no par exchanged for $0.20 cash
Note: Unexchanged certificates will be cancelled and become without value 12/29/2022

CLEMSON RES CORP (BC)
Reincorporated 10/22/2012
Place of incorporation changed from (Canada) to (BC) 10/22/2012
Name changed to Oyster Oil & Gas Ltd. 04/16/2013

CLEOPATRA COSMETICS CORP. (NY)
Name changed to Academic Development Corp. 04/03/1969
(See Academic Development Corp.)

CLEOPATRA KOHLIQUE INC (DE)
Reincorporated 01/13/1988
State of incorporation changed from (NY) to (DE) 01/13/1988
Charter cancelled and declared inoperative and void for non-payment of taxes 03/01/1991

CLEOPATRA WIG CREATIONS INC (NY)
Assets sold for benefit of creditors 01/08/1974
No stockholders' equity

CLERANDA COPPER MINES LTD (ON)
Charter cancelled and declared dissolved for failure to file returns and pay fees 05/15/1974

CLERICY CONSOLIDATED MINES LTD. (CANADA)
Declared dissolved for failure to file reports and pay fees 12/16/1980

CLERICY MINES LTD.
Reorganized as Clericy Consolidated Mines Ltd. 00/00/1927
Each share Capital Stock exchanged for (2) shares Capital Stock
(See Clericy Consolidated Mines Ltd.)

CLERMONT CAP INC (BC)
Recapitalized as NexGen Energy Ltd. 04/19/2013
Each share Common no par exchanged for (0.42553191) share Common no par

CLERMONT INDL PKS (OH)
Name changed to Community Improvement Programs, Inc. 05/01/1970
Community Improvement Programs, Inc. name changed to CIP Corp. 04/25/1972
(See CIP Corp.)

CLERNO MINES LTD. (CANADA)
Completely liquidated 11/15/1960
Each share Common received first and final distribution of $0.0132151 cash

CLERO MINES LTD. (QC)
Charter cancelled 02/07/1981

CLETRAC CORP. (DE)
Common $1 par changed to 50¢ par 07/28/1961
Under plan of merger name changed to Hess Oil & Chemical Corp. 05/23/1962
Hess Oil & Chemical Corp. merged into Amerada Hess Corp. 06/20/1969 which name changed to Hess Corp. 05/03/2006

CLEVELAND & BUFFALO TRANSIT CO.
Liquidation approved 00/00/1939
Details not available

CLEVELAND & CINCINNATI TELEGRAPH CO. (OH)
Dissolved 10/05/1954
Details not available

CLEVELAND & PITTSBURGH RR CO (OH & PA)
Merged into Penn Central Corp. 10/24/1978
Each share 4% Special Guaranteed Betterment Stock $50 par exchanged for (1.45) shares Conv. Preference Ser. B $20 par, (0.65) share Common $1 par, $25.08 principal amount of 7% General Mortgage Bonds Ser. A due 12/31/1987 and $6.97 cash
Each share 7% Capital Guaranteed Stock $50 par exchanged for (1.45) shares Conv. Preference Ser. B $20 par, (0.65) share Common $1 par, $31.38 principal amount of 7% General Mortgage Bonds Ser. A due 12/31/1987 and $12.19 cash
Note: a) Distribution is certain only for certificates surrendered prior to 05/01/1985 b) Distribution may also made for certificates surrendered between 05/01/1985 and 12/31/1986 c) No distribution will be made for certificates surrendered after 12/31/1986
Penn Central Corp. name changed to American Premier Underwriters, Inc. 03/25/1994 which merged into American Premier Group, Inc. 04/03/1995 which name changed to American Financial Group, Inc. 06/09/1995 which merged into American Financial Group, Inc. (Holding Co.) 12/02/1997

CLEVELAND & SANDUSKY BREWING CO.
Reorganized as Cleveland-Sandusky Brewing Corp. 00/00/1936
Stockholders received only rights which expired 01/01/1939

CLEVELAND-ALLERTON HOTEL, INC. (OH)
In process of liquidation 00/00/1954
Details not available

CLEVELAND BUILDERS REALTY CO.
Merged into Cleveland Builders Supply Co. 00/00/1943
Details not available

CLEVELAND BUILDERS SUPPLY & BRICK CO.
Name changed to Cleveland Builders Supply Co. 00/00/1928

CLEVELAND CALENDERING & COATING CORP (NY)
Common 50¢ par changed to 10¢ par 10/21/1980
Assets sold at auction 00/00/1985
No stockholders' equity

CLEVELAND CINCINNATI CHICAGO & ST LOUIS RY CO (IN & OH)
Merged into Penn Central Corp. 10/24/1978
Each share 5% Preferred $100 par exchanged for (0.91) share Common $1 par and $26.25 principal amount of non-interest bearing Certificates of Bene. Int. no par
Each share Common $100 par exchanged for (0.73) share Common $1 par and $53.24 principal amount of non-interest bearing Certificates of Bene. Int. no par
Note: a) Distribution is certain only for certificates surrendered prior to 05/01/1985 b) Distribution may also be made for certificates surrendered between 05/01/1985 and 12/31/1986 c) No Distribution will be made for certificates surrendered after 12/31/1986
Penn Central Corp. name changed to American Premier Underwriters, Inc. 03/25/1994 which merged into American Premier Group, Inc. 04/03/1995 which name changed to American Financial Group, Inc. 06/09/1995 which merged into American Financial Group, Inc. (Holding Co.) 12/02/1997

CLEVELAND CLIFFS INC OLD (OH)
$2 Conv. Exchangeable Class A Preferred no par called for redemption 12/15/1988
Common $1 par changed to 50¢ par and (1) additional share issued payable 12/31/2004 to holders of record 12/15/2004 Ex date - 01/03/2005
Common 50¢ par changed to 25¢ par and (1) additional share issued payable 06/30/2006 to holders of record 06/15/2006 Ex date - 07/03/2006
Common 25¢ par changed to $0.125 par and (1) additional share issued payable 05/15/2008 to holders of record 05/01/2008 Ex date - 05/16/2008
Name changed to Cliffs Natural Resources Inc. 10/15/2008
Cliffs Natural Resources Inc. name changed to Cleveland-Cliffs Inc. (New) 08/25/2017

CLEVELAND CLIFFS IRON CO (OH)
Each share $5 Preferred no par exchanged for (1) share $4.50 Preferred $100 par and (1) share Common $1 par 00/00/1947
Common $1 par split (2) for (1) by issuance of (1) additional share 05/21/1968
$4.50 Preferred $100 par called for redemption 10/15/1975
Common $1 par split (2) for (1) by issuance of (1) additional share 12/15/1975
Common $1 par split (2) for (1) by issuance of (1) additional share 09/15/1978
Under plan of reorganization each share Common $1 par automatically became (1) share Cleveland-Cliffs Inc. (Old) Common $1 par 07/01/1985
Cleveland-Cliffs Inc. (Old) name changed to Cliffs Natural Resources Inc. 10/15/2008 which name changed to Cleveland-Cliffs Inc. (New) 08/25/2017

CLEVELAND CO-OPERATIVE STOVE CO.
Name changed to Grand Industries, Inc. 00/00/1948
Grand Industries, Inc. merged into Cleveland Hobbing Machine Co. 00/00/1952 which was acquired by Fanner Manufacturing Co. 08/20/1956 which merged into Textron Inc. (RI) 01/24/1958 which reincorporated in Delaware 01/02/1968

CLEVELAND COMMUNITY SAVINGS CO. (OH)
Charter cancelled by order of the superintendent of the Division of

Savings & Loan Association 11/04/1983

CLEVELAND COPPER CORP. (QC)
Recapitalized as Delta Minerals Corp. 01/20/1965
Each share Common exchanged for (0.25) Common
(See Delta Minerals Corp.)

CLEVELAND DISCOUNT CO. (DE)
Charter cancelled and declared inoperative and void for non-payment of taxes 00/00/1928

CLEVELAND ELEC ILLUM CO (OH)
Common $100 par changed to no par 00/00/1928
Each share Preferred no par exchanged for (5) shares Common no par 00/00/1929
Each share Common no par exchanged for (10) shares Common no par 00/00/1929
Each share Common no par exchanged for (0.91) share Common no par and (0.04) share $4.50 Preferred no par 00/00/1935
Common no par changed to $15 par and (1) additional share issued 05/27/1955
Common $15 par changed to no par and (1) additional share issued 06/12/1963
$4.50 Preferred no par called for redemption 10/01/1963
Common no par split (3) for (2) by issuance of (0.5) additional share 01/09/1978
$12 Preferred Ser. D no par called for redemption 06/16/1978
Merged into Centerior Energy Corp. 04/29/1986
Each share Common no par exchanged for (1.11) shares Common no par
Remarketed Serial Pfd. Ser. P no par called for redemption 08/31/1993
Adjustable Rate Preferred Ser. M no par called for redemption 11/01/1995
$9.125 Preferred Ser. N no par called for redemption at $100 on 02/01/1997
Centerior Energy Corp. merged into FirstEnergy Corp. 11/08/1997
$88 Preferred Ser. R no par called for redemption at $1,000 on 12/01/2001
8.48% Depositary Preferred Ser. T called for redemption at $25 on 02/01/2002
$7.56 Preferred Ser. B no par called for redemption at $102.26 on 07/01/2002
$90 Preferred Ser. S no par called for redemption at $1,000 on 11/01/2002
Adjustable Rate Preferred Ser. L no par called for redemption at $100 on 03/14/2005
$7.40 Preferred Ser. A no par called for redemption at $101 on 03/14/2005
$7.35 Preferred Ser. C no par called for redemption at $101 plus $0.6125 accrued dividends on 06/01/2005
(Additional Information in Active)

CLEVELAND ELEC FING TR I (DE)
9% Trust Preferred Securities called for redemption at $25 plus $0.46875 accrued dividends on 06/01/2007

CLEVELAND FEDERAL SAVINGS & LOAN ASSOCIATION (USA)
Merged into Centura Banks, Inc. 03/29/1995
Each share Common $1 par exchanged for (3.381) shares Common no par
Centura Banks, Inc. merged into Royal Bank of Canada (Montreal, QC) 06/05/2001

CLEVELAND GRAPHITE BRONZE CO. (OH)
Name changed to Clevite Corp. 00/00/1952

Clevite Corp. merged into Gould Inc. 07/31/1969
(See Gould Inc.)

CLEVELAND HARDWARE & FORGING CO. (OH)
Each share Common $20 par exchanged for (4) shares Common $5 par 00/00/1947
Acquired by Porter (H.K.) Co., Inc. (PA) 07/31/1975
Details not available

CLEVELAND HARDWARE CO.
Reorganized as Cleveland Hardware & Forging Co. 00/00/1933
Details not available

CLEVELAND HOBBING MACHINE CO. (OH)
Each share Common no par exchanged for (25) shares Common $4 par 00/00/1936
Each share Common $4 par exchanged for (2.2) shares Common $1 par
Acquired by Fanner Manufacturing Co. 08/20/1956
Each share Common $1 par exchanged for (1) share Common $1 par
Fanner Manufacturing Co. merged into Textron Inc. (RI) 01/24/1958 which reincorporated in Delaware 01/02/1968

CLEVELAND INDIANS BASEBALL INC (OH)
Merged into CIBC Merger Co. 02/15/2000
Each share Class A Common no par exchanged for $22.6612 cash

CLEVELAND MINING & SMELTING CO. LTD. (BC)
Recapitalized as Consolidated Cleveland Resources Ltd. 03/22/1972
Each share Capital Stock no par exchanged for (0.166666) share Capital Stock no par
(See Consolidated Cleveland Resources Ltd.)

CLEVELAND MTG CO (OH)
5% Preferred $100 par called for redemption 04/30/1985
Voluntarily dissolved 11/12/1985
Details not available

CLEVELAND PROFESSIONAL BASKETBALL CO (OH)
Merged into Nationwide Advertising Service, Inc. 09/28/1984
Each share Common no par exchanged for a non-transferable credit for $3 per share applicable to the purchase of tickets or ticket packages for the 1984-85 home regular season basketball games of the Cleveland Cavaliers or $1.25 cash
Note: Option to receive the credit expired 11/15/1984

CLEVELAND QUARRIES CO. (OH)
Common no par changed to $5 par and (4) additional shares issued 08/19/1955
Stock Dividend - 10% 06/10/1955
Name changed to Cleveland Stone Co. 03/27/1964
(See Cleveland Stone Co.)

CLEVELAND RAILWAY CO.
Sold to the City of Cleveland 00/00/1942
Details not available

CLEVELAND REALTY CORP.
Liquidation completed 00/00/1943
Details not available

CLEVELAND SANDUSKY BREWING CORP (OH)
Common no par changed to $1 par 00/00/1945
Stock Dividend - 300% 03/25/1947
Formally dissolved 11/16/1970
No stockholders' equity

CLEVELAND SECS CORP (DE)
Prior Lien Stock $10 par changed to no par 00/00/1929
Each share Prior Lien Stock no par exchanged for (0.1) share Common $5 par 03/14/1956
Each share Common no par exchanged for (0.0005) share Common $5 par 03/14/1956
Under plan of merger each share Common $5 par exchanged for (0.2) share Common $25 par 11/27/1964
Each share old Common $25 par exchanged for (0.25) share new Common $25 par 02/24/1974
Stock Dividend - 300% 07/01/1977
Discontinued operations 12/31/1991
Details not available

CLEVELAND STONE CO (OH)
Liquidation completed
Each share Common $5 par received initial distribution of $25 cash 05/22/1968
Each share Common $5 par received second and final distribution of $7.41 cash 02/22/1969
Note: Certificates were not required to be surrendered and are without value

CLEVELAND STORAGE CO., INC. (OH)
Liquidated 12/31/1954
Details not available

CLEVELAND TERMINALS BLDG. CO.
Acquired by Cleveland Terminal Properties, Inc. 00/00/1951
Each share Common exchanged for $27 cash

CLEVELAND TRACTOR CO.
Merged into Oliver Corp. 00/00/1944
Each share Capital Stock exchanged for (0.66666666) share Common no par
Oliver Corp. name changed to Cletrac Corp. 10/31/1960 which merged into Hess Oil & Chemical Corp. 05/23/1962 which merged into Amerada Hess Corp. 06/20/1969 which name changed to Hess Corp. 05/03/2006

CLEVELAND TRENCHER CO (OH)
Merged into American Hoist & Derrick Co. 10/31/1978
Each share Common $5 par exchanged for (0.2222) share $4.75 Conv. Preferred Ser. B $100 par
American Hoist & Derrick Co. name changed to Amdura Corp. 02/13/1989
(See Amdura Corp.)

CLEVELAND TR CO (CLEVELAND, OH)
Each share Capital Stock $100 par exchanged for (2) shares Capital Stock $50 par 04/01/1953
Capital Stock $50 par changed to $20 par and (1.5) additional shares issued 02/18/1964
Capital Stock $20 par changed to $10 par and (1) additional share issued 05/17/1974
Stock Dividends - 16.66666666% 02/15/1952; 14.28571428% 02/15/1957; 12.5% 02/18/1959; 11.11111111% 02/17/1961; 10% 02/25/1963; 33.33333333% 05/12/1967; 25% 05/09/1969; 20% 05/10/1971
Under plan of reorganization each share Capital Stock $10 par automatically became (1) share Clevetrust Corp. Common $10 par 06/14/1974
Clevetrust Corp. name changed to Ameritrust Corp. 11/13/1979 which merged into Society Corp. 03/16/1992 which merged into KeyCorp (New) 03/01/1994

CLEVELAND TWIST DRILL CO. (OH)
Common $10 par changed to $1 par and (1) additional share issued 06/25/1965
Merged into Acme-Cleveland Corp. 10/25/1968
Each share Common $1 par exchanged for (4) shares Common $1 par
(See Acme-Cleveland Corp.)

CLEVELAND UN STK YDS CO (OH)
Each share Common $100 par exchanged for (4) shares Common no par 00/00/1928
Merged into Mercury Aviation Corp. 12/02/1968
Each share Common no par exchanged for (1) share Common no par
Mercury Aviation Corp. name changed to Mercury Aviation Companies 02/05/1973
(See Mercury Aviation Companies)

CLEVELAND WORSTED MILLS CO. (OH)
Liquidation completed 03/30/1961
Details not available

CLEVELAND WROUGHT PRODUCTS CO.
Merged into United Screw & Bolt Corp. 00/00/1930
Details not available

CLEVEPAK CORP (DE)
Stock Dividend - 100% 04/30/1976
Merged into Madison Management Group Inc. 04/02/1986
Each share $1.84 Conv. Preferred Ser. B no par exchanged for $5.375 principal amount of Great American Management & Investment, Inc. 14% Subord. Notes due 04/01/1992 and $5.375 cash
Each share $2.23 Preferred Ser. A no par exchanged for $6.265 principal amount of Great American Management & Investment, Inc. 14% Subord. Notes due 04/01/1992 and $6.265 cash
Each share Common $1 par exchanged for $5.055 principal amount of Great American Management & Investment, Inc. 14% Subord. Notes due 04/01/1992 and $5.055 cash

CLEVETRUST CORP (DE)
Common $10 par changed to $6.66666666 par and (0.5) additional share issued 06/06/1977
Name changed to Ameritrust Corp. 11/13/1979
Ameritrust Corp. merged into Society Corp. 03/16/1992 which merged into KeyCorp (New) 03/01/1994

CLEVETRUST RLTY INVS (MA)
Each Share of Bene. Int. $1 par received initial distribution of $2.50 cash payable 05/16/1997 to holders of record 05/09/1997
Each Share of Bene. Int. $1 par received second distribution of $1.10 cash payable 06/19/1997 to holders of record 06/12/1997
Each Share of Bene. Int. $1 par received third distribution of $2.10 cash payable 08/18/1997 to holders of record 08/11/1997
Each Share of Bene. Int. $1 par received fourth distribution of $0.70 cash payable 01/19/1998 to holders of record 01/12/1998
Each Share of Bene. Int. $1 par received fifth distribution of $0.785 cash payable 09/15/1998 to holders of record 09/08/1998
Each Share of Bene. Int. $1 par received sixth and final distribution of $0.008 cash payable 12/30/1998 to holders of record 12/23/1998

CLEVITE CORP (OH)
Common $1 par split (2) for (1) by issuance of (1) additional share 00/00/1953

4.5% Preferred $100 par called for redemption 06/17/1965
Merged into Gould Inc. 07/31/1969
Each share $2.50 Conv. Preference Ser. A no par exchanged for (1.71) shares Common $4 par and (1) Common Stock Purchase Warrant expiring 06/30/1976
Each share Common $1 par exchanged for (1.67) shares Common $4 par and (1) Common Stock Purchase Warrant expiring 06/30/1976
(See Gould Inc.)

CLEVITE INDS INC (DE)
Acquired by Pullman Co. 06/26/1987
Each share Common 1¢ par exchanged for $17.50 cash

CLEWISTON CO.
Reorganized as United States Sugar Corp. 00/00/1931
Details not available

CLEWISTON REALTY & DEVELOPMENT CORP.
Dissolved 00/00/1944
Details not available

CLEYO RES INC (ON)
Recapitalized as Eloro Resources Ltd. 07/04/1997
Each share Common no par exchanged for (0.666) share Common no par

CLI RES (BC)
Name changed to Choice Gold Corp. 03/21/2011
Choice Gold Corp. recapitalized as Copperbank Resources Corp. 10/22/2014

CLICA INDS (AZ)
Name changed to Carefree Life Insurance Corp. of America 07/01/1977
Carefree Life Insurance Corp. of America name changed to National Annuity Life Insurance Co. 05/19/1982
(See National Annuity Life Insurance Co.)

CLICK COMM INC (DE)
Each share old Common $0.001 par exchanged for (0.2) share new Common $0.001 par 09/04/2002
Merged into Illinois Tool Works Inc. 10/26/2006
Each share new Common $0.001 par exchanged for $22.75 cash

CLICKABLE ENTERPRISES INC (DE)
SEC revoked common stock registration 06/13/2012

CLICKACTION INC (DE)
Common $0.001 par split (2) for (1) by issuance of (1) additional share payable 04/20/2000 to holders of record 04/05/2000
Merged into infoUSA Inc. 12/03/2002
Each share Common $0.001 par exchanged for $0.15 cash
Note: Each share Common held by eligible record holders received an additional distribution of $0.05 cash 03/23/2003

CLICKER INC (NV)
Each share old Common $0.001 par exchanged for (0.00333333) share new Common $0.001 par 04/01/2010
Each share new Common $0.001 par exchanged again for (0.00333333) share new Common $0.001 par 02/27/2012
SEC revoked common stock registration 04/22/2016

CLICKER RED LAKE MINES LTD (ON)
Merged into Goldquest Exploration Inc. 08/09/1982
Each share Capital Stock $1 par exchanged for (0.05485463) share Common no par

Goldquest Exploration Inc. merged into Goldcorp Inc. (New) 03/31/1994

CLICKESE COM INC (NV)
Name changed to Solutions Technology Inc. 5/8/2001
Solutions Technology Inc. merged into International Mercantile Corp. 1/12/2002 which name changed to T & G2 3/1/2002 which name changed to Softnet Technology Corp. 8/4/2004

CLICKHOUSE COM ONLINE INC (BC)
Recapitalized as Windridge Technology Corp. 09/19/2002
Each share Common no par exchanged for (0.2) share Common no par
Windridge Technology Corp. name changed to Dajin Resources Corp. 01/19/2005

CLICKNSETTLE COM INC (DE)
Each share old Common $0.001 par exchanged for (0.33333333) share new Common $0.001 par 08/23/2001
New Common $0.001 par split (6) for (1) by issuance of (5) additional shares payable 01/05/2004 to holders of record 12/22/2003 Ex date - 01/06/2004
Each share new Common $0.001 par exchanged again for (0.1) share new Common $0.001 par 03/14/2008
Name changed to Cardo Medical, Inc. 11/26/2008
Cardo Medical, Inc. name changed to Tiger X Medical, Inc. 07/13/2011 which name changed to BioCardia, Inc. 10/26/2016

CLICKPAY SOLUTIONS INC (CA)
Reincorporated under the laws of Nevada and Common no par changed to $0.001 par 04/06/2006

CLICKSOFTWARE TECHNOLOGIES LTD (ISRAEL)
Acquired by Optimizer TopCo SARL 07/13/2015
Each share Ordinary ILS 0.02 par exchanged for $12.65 cash

CLICK2LEARN INC (DE)
Name changed 05/30/2001
Name changed from Click2learn.com, Inc. to Click2learn, Inc. 05/30/2001
Merged into SumTotal Systems, Inc. 03/19/2004
Each share Common 1¢ par exchanged for (0.3188) share Common $0.001 par
(See SumTotal Systems, Inc.)

CLIENT TRACK CORP (DE)
Reincorporated 06/01/2006
Each share old Common $0.0001 par exchanged for (0.05882352) share new Common $0.0001 par 04/21/2006
Place of incorporation changed from (TX) to (DE) 06/01/2006
Name changed to CLTC Ventures Corp. 05/29/2007
CLTC Ventures Corp. name changed to Dreamfly Productions Corp. 08/26/2009

CLIFF ENGLE LTD (NY)
Each share old Common $0.001 par exchanged for (0.5) share new Common $0.001 par 02/26/1986
New Common $0.001 par split (3) for (2) by issuance of (0.5) additional share 07/01/1987
Charter cancelled and proclaimed dissolved for failure to pay taxes 12/27/1995

CLIFF GRAPHICS INTL INC (UT)
Name changed to Global Golf Holdings, Inc. 05/08/1995
Global Golf Holdings, Inc. recapitalized as Dino Minichiello Fashions Inc. 11/20/1997 which name changed to Resort World Enterprises, Inc. 06/15/1998 which name changed to Remedent USA, Inc. 10/22/1998 which recapitalized as Remedent, Inc. 06/06/2005

CLIFF MINING CO. (MI)
Liquidation completed 11/30/1955
Details not available

CLIFF RES CORP (ON)
Name changed 00/00/1986
Name changed from Cliff Creek Resources Ltd. to Cliff Resources Corp. 00/00/1986
Name changed to Mineral Resources Corp. 09/13/1995
Mineral Resources Corp. name changed to Minroc Mines Inc. 06/10/1998 which name changed to Cassiar Mines & Metals, Inc. 06/10/1999 which name changed to Cassiar Magnesium Inc. 04/25/2000 which name changed to Cassiar Resources Inc. 07/25/2001 which name changed to Troutline Investments Inc. (ONT) 06/30/2003 which reorganized in Alberta as Innova Exploration Ltd. 04/16/2004
(See Innova Exploration Ltd.)

CLIFF ROCK RES CORP (NV)
Common $0.001 par split (3) for (1) by issuance of (2) additional shares payable 04/29/2009 to holders of record 04/21/2009 Ex date - 04/30/2009
Name changed to Virtual Medical Centre, Inc. 07/06/2010

CLIFFORD CHINA ESTATES INC (NV)
Name changed to Asian Trends Media Holdings, Inc. 08/17/2009
Asian Trends Media Holdings, Inc. recapitalized as YUS International Group Ltd. 05/20/2013

CLIFFS CORP.
Merged into Cleveland-Cliffs Iron Co. 00/00/1947
Each share Common $5 par exchanged for (2.25) shares Common $1 par
Cleveland-Cliffs Iron Co. reorganized as Cleveland-Cliffs Inc. (Old) 07/01/1985 which name changed to Cliffs Natural Resources Inc. 10/15/2008 which name changed to Cleveland-Cliffs Inc. (New) 08/25/2017

CLIFFS DRILLING CO (DE)
$2.3125 Conv. Exchangeable Preferred no par called for redemption 01/17/1996
Common 1¢ par split (2) for (1) by issuance of (1) additional share payable 06/09/1997 to holders of record 05/22/1997 Ex date - 06/10/1997
Merged into R&B Falcon Corp. 11/30/1998
Each share Common 1¢ par exchanged for (1.7) shares Common 1¢ par
R&B Falcon Corp. merged into Transocean Sedco Forex Inc. 01/31/2001 which name changed to Transocean Inc. (Old) 05/09/2002 which merged into Transocean Inc. (New) (Cayman Islands) 11/27/2007 which reorganized in Switzerland as Transocean Ltd. 12/18/2008

CLIFFS NAT RES INC (OH)
Common Stock Purchase Rights declared for Common stockholders of record 10/29/2008 were redeemed at $0.001 per right 06/01/2010 for holders of record 05/14/2010
Each share 3.25% Conv. Perpetual Preferred no par exchanged for (133.0646) shares Common $0.125 par 02/11/2009
Each share 7% Ser. A Mandatory Conv. Depositary Preferred Class A automatically became (0.9052) share Common $0.125 par 02/01/2016

Name changed to Cleveland-Cliffs Inc. (New) 08/25/2017

CLIFFS-ST CLAIR CORP (MI)
Completely liquidated 03/15/1972
Each share Common $1 par exchanged for first and final distribution of (0.3523) share Cleveland-Cliffs Iron Co. Common $1 par
Cleveland-Cliffs Iron Co. reorganized as Cleveland-Cliffs Inc. (Old) 07/01/1985 which name changed to Cliffs Natural Resources Inc. 10/15/2008 which name changed to Cleveland-Cliffs Inc. (New) 08/25/2017

CLIFFSIDE MILLS
Merged into Proximity Manufacturing Co. on a (1.67) for (1) basis in 1945
Proximity Manufacturing Co. merged into Cone Mills Corp. in 1948
(See Cone Mills Corp.)

CLIFTON BANCORP INC (MD)
Merged into Kearny Financial Corp. 04/02/2018
Each share Common 1¢ par exchanged for (1.191) shares Common 1¢ par

CLIFTON CO., LTD.
Liquidated 00/00/1935
Details not available

CLIFTON CONSOLIDATED MINES, LTD. (ON)
Charter cancelled by Province of Ontario for default 00/00/1957

CLIFTON FORGE WAYNESBORO TEL CO (VA)
Each share Common $100 par exchanged for (5) shares Common $20 par in 1950
Common $20 par changed to $10 par and (1) additional share issued 12/12/66
Common $10 par changed to $3 par and (2) additional shares issued 5/1/86
Stock Dividends - 10% 10/31/56; 10% 4/30/60; 10% 7/31/62; 10% 4/30/65
Under plan of reorganization each share Common $3 par automatically became (1) share CFW Communications Co. Common no par 4/22/88
Each share Common $3 par received distribution of (1) additional share Common no par 5/16/88
CFW Communications Co. name changed to NTelos Inc. 12/6/2000
(See NTelos Inc.)

CLIFTON MANUFACTURING CO. (SC)
Each share Capital Stock $100 par exchanged for (5) shares Capital Stock $20 par in 1947
Name changed to Dexter Corp. 9/8/65
(See Dexter Corp.)

CLIFTON OIL & GAS CO.
Dissolved 00/00/1948
Details not available

CLIFTON PORCUPINE MINES LTD.
Succeeded by Clifton Consolidated Mines Ltd. on a (1) for (2) basis in 1942
(See Clifton Consolidated Mines Ltd.)

CLIFTON PRECISION PRODUCTS CO. INC. (DE)
Liquidated 12/10/63
Each share Common $1 par exchanged for $24.75 of Litton Industries, Inc. Common $1 par (based on $79.35 per share) or, at stockholders option, $20 of Litton Industries, Inc. Common $1 par and $7.20 Litton Note
(See Litton Industries, Inc.)

CLIFTON RES LTD (BC)
Recapitalized as Consolidated Clifton Resources Ltd. 01/31/1990
Each share Common no par

exchanged for (0.2) share Common no par
Consolidated Clifton Resources Ltd. name changed to Taina Developments Corp. 09/27/1990 which name changed to Double Eagle Entertainment Corp. 01/06/1994
(See Double Eagle Entertainment Corp.)

CLIFTON SVGS BANCORP INC (USA)
Reorganized under the laws of Maryland as Clifton Bancorp Inc. 04/02/2014
Each share Common 1¢ par exchanged for (0.9791) share Common 1¢ par
Clifton Bancorp Inc. merged into Kearny Financial Corp. 04/02/2018

CLIFTON STAR RES INC (CANADA)
Reincorporated 03/01/2010
Place of incorporation changed from (BC) to (Canada) 03/01/2010
Merged into First Mining Finance Corp. 04/11/2016
Each share Common no par exchanged for (1) share Common no par
Note: Unexchanged certificates will be cancelled and become without value 04/11/2022
First Mining Finance Corp. name changed to First Mining Gold Corp. 01/11/2018

CLIFTON TR BK (BALTIMORE, MD)
Location changed to Clifton Trust Bank (Reisterstown, MD) 6/11/73
Clifton Trust Bank (Reisterstown, MD) merged into First Virginia Banks, Inc. 3/29/90 which merged into BB&T Corp. 7/1/2003

CLIFTON TRUST BANK (REISTERSTOWN, MD)
Stock Dividend - 30% 11/7/86
Merged into First Virginia Banks, Inc. 3/29/90
Each share Capital Stock $10 par exchanged for (1.25) shares Common $1 par
First Virginia Banks, Inc. merged into BB&T Corp. 7/1/2003

CLIMATE ENGR CORP (DE)
Charter cancelled and declared inoperative and void for non-payment of taxes 3/1/75

CLIMATE EXCHANGE PLC (UNITED KINGDOM)
Acquired by IntercontinentalExchange, Inc. 07/08/2010
Each ADR for Ordinary exchanged for $5.709375 cash

CLIMAX MOLYBDENUM CO. (DE)
Each share old Capital Stock no par exchanged for (3) shares new Capital Stock no par 00/00/1935
Merged into American Metal Climax, Inc. 12/31/1957
Each share new Capital Stock no par exchanged for (3) shares Common $1 par
American Metal Climax, Inc. name changed to Amax Inc. 07/01/1974 which merged into Cyprus Amax Minerals Co. 11/15/1993 which merged into Phelps Dodge Corp. 12/02/1999 which merged into Freeport-McMoRan Copper & Gold Inc. 03/19/2007 which name changed to Freeport-McMoRan Inc. 07/14/2014

CLIMAX PETROLEUM CORP. (CO)
Charter revoked for failure to pay franchise taxes 10/11/61

CLIMAX SPINNING CO (NC)
Merged into Belmont Heritage Corp. 09/29/1972
Each share Common $50 par exchanged for (10) shares Common $5 par
(See Belmont Heritage Corp.)

CLINCHFIELD COAL CORP. (VA)
Each share Common $100 par exchanged for (5) shares Common $20 par in 1947
Merged into Pittston Co. (DE & VA) 12/28/56
Each share Common $20 par exchanged for $3.50 Preferred $75 par
Pittston Co. (DE & VA) Delaware incorporation rescinded 5/14/86 which name changed to Brink's Co. 5/5/2003

CLINE DEV CORP (BC)
Recapitalized as Consolidated Cline Development Corp. 09/03/1993
Each share Common no par exchanged for (0.2) share Common no par
Consolidated Cline Development Corp. name changed to Cline Mining Corp. 11/29/1996
(See Cline Mining Corp.)

CLINE LAKE GOLD MINES, LTD.
In process of liquidation 00/00/1943
Details not available

CLINE MNG CORP (BC)
Plan of arrangement under Companies' Creditors Arrangement Act effective 07/08/2015
No stockholders' equity

CLINGER GOLD MINES LTD (ON)
Charter cancelled and dissolved for failure to file returns and pay fees 05/18/1976

CLINI THERM CORP (TX)
Filed a petition under Chapter 11 Federal Bankruptcy Code in January 1991
Stockholders' equity unlikely

CLINIC PROPERTIES ASSOCIATION, INC. (DE)
Liquidation completed
Each share Class A Common $10 par exchanged for initial distribution of $30 cash 7/31/65
Each share Class A Common $10 par received second and final distribution of $1.03 cash 4/4/66

CLINICAL AESTHETICS CENTRE INC (MN)
Reincorporated under the laws of Nevada as Tricom Technology Group, Inc. 07/30/1998
Tricom Technology Group, Inc. name changed to Omninet Media.com Inc. 02/18/2000 which name changed to Omninet Media Corp. 06/01/2001 which name changed to Aquagold International, Inc. 03/28/2008

CLINICAL DATA INC NEW (DE)
Common 1¢ par split (3) for (2) by issuance of (0.5) additional share payable 10/01/2007 to holders of record 09/24/2007 Ex date - 10/02/2007
Merged into Forest Laboratories, Inc. 04/13/2011
Each share Common 1¢ par exchanged for $30 cash and (1) Contingent Value Right
Note: Contingent Value Rights expired 04/13/2018

CLINICAL DATA INC OLD (DE)
Common 1¢ par split (3) for (2) by issuance of (0.5) additional share 01/07/1993
Name changed to Novitron International Inc. 04/12/1994
Novitron International Inc. name changed to Clinical Data, Inc. (New) 10/07/2003
(See Clinical Data, Inc. (New))

CLINICAL DEVELOPMENT CORP. (OK)
Name changed to Oceanography International Corp. 07/09/1969
Oceanography International Corp. name changed to O.I. Corp. 08/08/1980
(See O.I. Corp.)

CLINICAL DIAGNOSTICS INC (CO)
Reorganized under the laws of Delaware as American CDI Corp. 02/14/1992
Each share Common $0.001 par exchanged for (0.01) share Common $0.001 par
American CDI Corp. merged into PolyMedica Industries, Inc. 09/15/1992 which name changed to PolyMedica Corp. 09/19/1997
(See PolyMedica Corp.)

CLINICAL ELECTRS MFG CORP (NJ)
Charter declared void for non-payment of taxes 04/24/1978

CLINICAL HOMECARE LTD (NY)
Merged into Curaflex Health Services, Inc. 3/5/93
Each share Common $0.001 par exchanged for (0.43) share Common $0.001 par
Curaflex Health Services, Inc. merged into Coram Healthcare Corp. 7/8/94
(See Coram Healthcare Corp.)

CLINICAL SCIENCES INC (DE)
Common 1¢ par split (2) for (1) by issuance of (1) additional share 2/22/73
Merged into Incstar Corp. 12/13/89
Each share Common 1¢ par exchanged for (0.8772) share Common 1¢ par
(See Incstar Corp.)

CLINICAL TECHNOLOGIES ASSOC INC (DE)
Name changed to Emisphere Technologies, Inc. 01/27/1992

CLINICAL TRIALS AMERS INC (NV)
Name changed to Next Fuel, Inc. 06/25/2009

CLINICAL TRIALS ASSISTANCE CORP (NV)
Common $0.001 par split (3) for (1) by issuance of (2) additional shares payable 03/12/2004 to holders of record 03/12/2004 Ex date - 03/15/2004
Name changed to IT&E International Group (NV) 06/23/2004
IT&E International Group (NV) reincorporated in Delaware 03/02/2006 which name changed to Averion International Corp. 09/22/2006
(See Averion International Corp.)

CLINICARES INC (NV)
Recapitalized as Catch By Gene, Inc. 04/09/2010
Each share Common $0.001 par exchanged for (0.01) share Common $0.001 par
(See Catch By Gene, Inc.)

CLINICHEM DEV INC (CANADA)
Acquired by BioChem Pharma Inc. 12/15/2000
Each share Common no par exchanged for $18.43 cash

CLINICOM INC (DE)
Common $0.001 par split (2) for (1) by issuance of (1) additional share 09/03/1993
Merged into HBO & Co. 10/02/1995
Each share Common $0.001 par exchanged for (0.4) share Common 5¢ par
HBO & Co. merged into McKesson HBOC Inc. 01/12/1999 which name changed to McKesson Corp. 07/30/2001

CLINICOR INC (NV)
Ceased operations 09/08/2000

Stockholders' equity unlikely

CLINICORP INC (DE)
Common 1¢ par split (3) for (1) by issuance of (2) additional shares 01/27/1993
Each share old Common 1¢ par exchanged for (0.05) share new Common 1¢ par 12/30/1994
Plan of reorganization under Chapter 11 Federal Bankruptcy proceedings confirmed 06/06/1997
No stockholders' equity

CLINTON APPALACHIAN VIII, LIMITED PARTNERSHIP (OH)
Partnership terminated 01/19/1996
Details not available

CLINTON APPALACHIAN IX, LIMITED PARTNERSHIP (OH)
Partnership terminated 04/10/1996
Details not available

CLINTON BK & TR CO (ST JOHNS, MI)
Stock Dividend - 10% 05/15/1981
Merged into CB Financial Corp. 12/31/1983
Each share Common $5 par exchanged for (0.4) share Common $7.50 par
CB Financial Corp. merged into Citizens Banking Corp. 07/01/1997 which name name changed to Citizens Republic Bancorp, Inc. 04/26/2007 which merged into FirstMerit Corp. 04/12/2013 which merged into Huntington Bancshares Inc. 08/16/2016 which merged into Huntington Bancshares Inc. 08/16/2016

CLINTON ENGINES CORP (MI)
Each share old Common no par exchanged for (0.1) share new Common no par 09/09/1974
Merged into Lomart Acquisition Corp. 07/27/1984
Each share new Common no par exchanged for $3.75 cash

CLINTON FOODS INC. (DE)
In process of liquidation
Each share Common $1 par received initial distribution of $43 cash 04/26/1956
Name changed to C.N.I. Liquidating Co. 04/30/1956
(See C.N.I. Liquidating Co.)

CLINTON GAS SYS INC (OH)
Merged into Jenco Development 09/04/1996
Each share Common no par exchanged for $6.75 cash

CLINTON INDUSTRIES, INC. (DE)
Name changed to Clinton Foods, Inc. 00/00/1949
Clinton Foods, Inc. name changed to C.N.I. Liquidating Co. 04/30/1956
(See C.N.I. Liquidating Co.)

CLINTON MACHINE CO. (MI)
Stock Dividend - 10% 05/31/1957
Name changed to Clinton Engines Corp. 02/28/1958
(See Clinton Engines Corp.)

CLINTON MERCHANDISING INC (NY)
Common $1 par changed to 80¢ par and (0.25) additional share issued 01/08/1971
Common 80¢ par split (5) for (4) by issuance of (0.25) additional share 05/19/1972
Acquired by Melville Shoe Corp. 12/20/1972
Each share Common 80¢ par exchanged for (0.438) share Common $1 par
Melville Shoe Corp. name changed to Melville Corp. (NY) 04/14/1976 which reorganized in Delaware as CVS Corp. 11/20/1996 which name changed to CVS/Caremark Corp. 03/22/2007 which name changed to CVS Caremark Corp. 05/10/2007

which name changed to CVS Health Corp. 09/04/2014

CLINTON NATL BK & TR CO (ST. JOHNS, MI)
Common $20 par changed to $5 par 04/01/1974
Stock Dividend - 60% 03/26/1970
Name changed to Clinton Bank & Trust Co. (St. Johns, MI) 08/06/1979
Clinton Bank & Trust Co. (St. Johns, MI) merged into CB Financial Corp. 12/31/1983 which merged into Citizens Banking Corp. 07/01/1997 which name changed to Citizens Republic Bancorp, Inc. 04/26/2007 which merged into FirstMerit Corp. 04/12/2013 which merged into Huntington Bancshares Bancshares Inc. 08/16/2016

CLINTON NATL BK (CLINTON, CT)
Merged into CBT Corp. 05/15/1974
Each share Common $10 par exchanged for (1.5) shares Common $10 par
CBT Corp. merged into Bank of New England Corp. 06/14/1985
(See Bank of New England Corp.)

CLINTON OIL CO (DE)
Common 10¢ par changed to $0.03333333 par and (2) additional shares issued 07/22/1969
Name changed to Energy Reserves Group, Inc. 02/10/1976
(See Energy Reserves Group, Inc.)

CLINTON TITLE & MORTGAGE GUARANTY CO.
Name changed to Lawyers-Clinton Title Insurance Co. of New Jersey 00/00/1949
(See Lawyers-Clinton Title Insurance Co. of New Jersey)

CLINTON TRUST CO. (NEW YORK, NY)
Each share Capital Stock $50 par exchanged for (2.5) shares Capital Stock $20 par 00/00/1946
Each share Capital Stock $20 par exchanged for (2.2) shares Capital Stock $10 par to effect a (2) for (1) split and 10% stock dividend 00/00/1953
Stock Dividend - 12.5% 02/01/1951
Merged into Chase Manhattan Bank (New York, NY) 01/30/1959
Each share Capital Stock $10 par exchanged for (0.55) share Capital Stock $12.50 par
Chase Manhattan Bank (New York, NY) name changed to Chase Manhattan Bank (N.A.) (New York, NY) 09/23/1965 which reorganized as Chase Manhattan Corp. (Old) 06/04/1969 which merged into Chase Manhattan Corp. (New) 03/31/1996 which name changed to J.P. Morgan Chase & Co. 12/31/2000 which name changed to JPMorgan Chase & Co. 07/20/2004

CLINTRIALS RESH INC (DE)
Name changed 02/11/1994
Name changed from Clintrials Inc. to Clintrials Research Inc. 02/11/1994
Common 1¢ par split (3) for (2) by issuance of (0.5) additional share payable 11/25/1996 to holders of record 11/11/1996
Merged into Inveresk Research Group Ltd. 04/02/2001
Each share Common 1¢ par exchanged for $6 cash

CLIP N PIERCE FASHIONS INC (DE)
Name changed to Ocean Resources, Inc. 06/06/2002
(See Ocean Resources, Inc.)

CLIPCLOP COM ENTERPRISES INC (BC)
Recapitalized as Worldwide Technologies Inc. 09/10/2001
Each share Common no par exchanged for (0.14285714) share Common no par
(See Worldwide Technologies Inc.)

CLIPPER BELT LACER CO (MI)
Merged into Belt Fastner Technology, Inc. 01/11/1985
Each share Common $10 par exchanged for $50 cash

CLIPPER MINERALS LTD (BC)
Recapitalized as Stormin Resources Inc. 12/09/1991
Each share Common no par exchanged for (0.37037037) share Common no par
Stormin Resources Inc. name changed to Biocoll Medical Corp. 12/22/1992 which merged into GenSci Regeneration Sciences Inc. 08/12/1997
(See GenSci Regeneration Sciences Inc.)

CLIX ATHABASCA URANIUM MINES LTD. (ON)
Recapitalized as Tinex Development & Exploration Ltd. 12/26/1962
Each share Capital Stock $1 par exchanged for (0.266666) share Capital Stock $1 par
Tinex Development & Exploration Ltd. merged into Can-Con Enterprises & Explorations Ltd. 11/30/1970 which name changed to Aubet Resources Inc. 09/08/1981 which recapitalized as Aubet Explorations Ltd. 09/30/1998 which name changed to Visa Gold Explorations Inc. 08/25/1999
(See Visa Gold Explorations Inc.)

CLIX GROUP INC (NV)
Name changed 08/23/2000
Name changed from Clixhealth.com Inc. to Clix Group Inc. 08/23/2000
Reorganized under the laws of Colorado as RCC Holdings Corp. 04/09/2003
Each share Common $0.001 par exchanged for (0.002) share Common $0.001 par

CLIXTIX INC (NY)
Name changed to Medeorex, Inc. 09/23/2004
Medeorex, Inc. name changed to Karver International, Inc. 11/15/2005
(See Karver International, Inc.)

CLOISONETTE PRODUCTS CORP.
Out of business 00/00/1934
Details not available

CLONUS CORP (CANADA)
Name changed to San-Mar Environmental Corp. 09/22/1997
San-Mar Environmental Corp. recapitalized as Pure Zinc Technologies, Inc. 08/21/1998 which name changed to Charityville.com International Inc. 08/27/1999 which name changed to eNblast productions inc. 06/14/2000
(See eNblast productions inc.)

CLOPAY CORP (MD)
Common $1 par split (5) for (4) by issuance of (0.25) additional share 06/15/1985
Merged into Instrument Systems Corp. 10/23/1986
Each share Common $1 par exchanged for $22.70 cash

CLOPIN SALES CORP.
Out of business 00/00/1932
Details not available

CLOROX CHEMICAL CO. (DE)
Class A and B no par changed to Capital Stock no par 00/00/1931
Capital Stock no par changed to $10 par 00/00/1936
Each share Capital Stock $10 par exchanged for (3) shares Capital Stock 00/00/1944
Stock Dividends - 10% 05/05/1955; 100% 04/20/1956
Merged into Procter & Gamble Co. 08/01/1957
Each share Capital Stock $3.33333333 par exchanged for (0.85) share Common $2 par

CLOROX CO (CA)
Reincorporated 03/12/1973
Common no par split (2) for (1) by issuance of (1) additional share 11/15/1972
State of incorporation changed from (OH) to (CA) and Common no par changed to $1 par 03/12/1973
Reincorporated under the laws of Delaware 10/22/1986

CLOSTER PARK ESTATES, INC.
Out of business 00/00/1935
Details not available

CLOSURE MED CORP (DE)
Merged into Johnson & Johnson 06/03/2005
Each share Common 1¢ par exchanged for $27 cash

CLOTHESTIME INC (DE)
Reincorporated 06/20/1991
Common 1¢ par split (3) for (2) by issuance of (0.5) additional share 08/15/1985
Common 1¢ par split (2) for (1) by issuance of (1) additional share 04/11/1986
State of incorporation changed from (CA) to (DE) 06/20/1991
Plan of reorganization under Chapter 11 Federal Bankruptcy proceedings confirmed 09/10/1997
No stockholders' equity

CLOUD CENTRIC SYS INC (FL)
Reorganized as Cloud Centric, Inc. 08/15/2011
Each share Common $0.001 par exchanged for (1.03) shares Common $0.001 par

CLOUD NINE, INC. (CO)
Charter revoked for failure to file reports and pay fees 10/10/1962

CLOUD SEC CORP (NV)
Each share old Common $0.001 par exchanged for (0.01) share new Common $0.001 par 01/22/2015
Name changed to US-China Biomedical Technology, Inc. 02/09/2018

CLOUD STAR CORP (NV)
Name changed to Cloud Security Corp. 06/03/2013
Cloud Security Corp. name changed to US-China Biomedical Technology, Inc. 02/09/2018

CLOUDBENCH APPLICATIONS INC (BC)
Name changed to BasicGov Systems, Inc. 12/24/2009
BasicGov Systems, Inc. name changed to Pedro Resources Ltd. 09/30/2010

CLOUDBREAK RES LTD (BC)
Reorganized 04/26/2010
Reorganized from Canada to under the laws of British Columbia 04/26/2010
Each share Common no par exchanged for (0.1) share Common no par
Name changed to Petro One Energy Corp. 12/14/2010
Petro One Energy Corp. merged into Goldstrike Resources Ltd. 02/29/2016

CLOUDMONT MINES LTD. (ON)
Charter cancelled for failure to pay taxes and file returns 03/07/1979

CLOUDTECH SENSORS INC (DE)
SEC revoked common stock registration 03/10/2008

CLOUGH GLOBAL ALLOCATION FD (DE)
Auction Market Preferred Ser. W28 called for redemption at $25,000 on 05/22/2008
Name changed to Clough Global Dividend & Income Fund 08/01/2016

CLOUGH GLOBAL EQUITY FD (DE)
Preferred Ser. F7 called for redemption at $25,000 on 04/25/2008
Preferred Ser. M28 called for redemption at $25,000 on 04/29/2008
(Additional Information in Active)

CLOUGH GLOBAL OPPORTUNITIES FD (DE)
Auction Market Preferred Ser. M7 called for redemption at $25,000 on 04/29/2008
Auction Market Preferred Ser. W7 called for redemption at $25,000 on 05/01/2008
Auction Market Preferred Ser. F7 called for redemption at $25,000 on 05/05/2008
Auction Market Preferred Ser. T28 called for redemption at $25,000 on 05/07/2008
Auction Market Preferred Ser. TH28 called for redemption at $25,000 on 05/23/2008
(Additional Information in Active)

CLOVER APPRECIATION PPTYS I LP (DE)
Partnership dissolved 06/27/1997
Each Unit of Limited Partnership received $100 cash

CLOVER CMNTY BK (CLOVER, SC)
Under plan of reorganization each share Common 1¢ par automatically became (1) share Clover Community Bancshares, Inc. Common 1¢ par 06/05/1998

CLOVER LEAF FINL CORP (DE)
Merged into First Clover Leaf Financial Corp. 07/10/2006
Each share Common 10¢ par exchanged for $41.56 cash

CLOVER LUNCH, INC.
Out of business 00/00/1930
Details not available

CLOVER SPLINT COAL CO., INC.
Acquired by Pittsburgh Coal Co. 00/00/1944
Details not available

CLOVERDALE RESOURCES LTD. (BC)
Struck off register and declared dissolved for failure to file returns 02/25/1983

CLOVERDALE SPRING CO., INC. (MD)
Acquired by Allegheny Pepsi-Cola Bottling Co. 09/08/1960
Details not available

CLOVERLEAF FREELAND CORP. (PA)
Bankrupt 02/00/1962
No stockholders' equity

CLOVIS CMNTY BK (CLOVIS, CA)
Under plan of reorganization each share Common no par automatically became (1) share Central Valley Community Bancorp Common no par 11/15/2000

CLOW (JAMES B.) & SONS, INC. (DE)
Name changed to Clow Corp. 05/01/1967
(See Clow Corp.)

CLOW CORP (DE)
Common $6.25 par split (2) for (1) by issuance of (1) additional share 05/15/1969
Merged into McWane, Inc. 06/27/1985
Each share $6 Conv. Preferred Ser. A $1 par exchanged for $100 cash
Each share 7% Preferred $100 par exchanged for $175 cash
Each share Common $6.25 par exchanged for $15 cash

CLTC VENTURES CORP (DE)
Name changed to Dreamfly Productions Corp. 08/26/2009

CLUB ALUMINUM DEVELOPMENT CO.
Name changed to Club Aluminum Utensil Co. 00/00/1927
Club Aluminum Utensil Co. merged into Club Aluminum Products Co. (IL) 00/00/1946 which was acquired by Standard International Corp. 01/02/1968 which name changed to Standex International Corp. (OH) 07/24/1973 which reincorporated in Delaware 06/30/1975

CLUB ALUMINUM PRODUCTS CO. (DE)
Merged into Club Aluminum Products Co. (IL) 00/00/1946
Details not available

CLUB ALUMINUM PRODUCTS CO. (IL)
Completely liquidated 01/02/1968
Each share Common no par exchanged for first and final distribution of (0.33931) share Standard International Corp. Common no par
Standard International Corp. name changed to Standex International Corp. (OH) 07/24/1973 which reincorporated in Delaware 06/30/1975

CLUB ALUMINUM UTENSIL CO.
Merged into Club Aluminum Products Co. (IL) 00/00/1946
Each share Common exchanged for (1) exchanged for (1) share Common no par
Club Aluminum Products Co. (IL) acquired by Standard International Corp. 01/02/1968 which name changed to Standex International Corp. (OH) 07/24/1973 which reincorporated in Delaware 06/30/1975

CLUB AMER INC (CO)
Recapitalized as Plancapital U S A Inc. 01/15/1992
Each share Common $0.001 par exchanged for (0.25) share Common $0.001 par
Plancapital U S A Inc. recapitalized as Continental Capital Corp. 01/31/1995 which recapitalized as RFID Ltd. 06/21/2005 which name changed to OptimizeRx Corp. (CO) 04/30/2008 which reincorporated in Nevada 09/04/2008

CLUB AQUARIUS INC (UT)
Involuntarily dissolved 04/01/1991

CLUB CAR INC (DE)
Merged into Clark Equipment Co. 03/17/1995
Each share Common 1¢ par exchanged for $25 cash

CLUB DE SPORT INC (CO)
Recapitalized as Dominion International Resources Corp. 04/22/1993
Each share Common $0.001 par exchanged for (0.04) share Common $0.001 par
(See Dominion International Resources Corp.)

CLUB MATE HLDGS LTD (BC)
Recapitalized as International Millennium Mining Corp. 07/04/1997
Each share Common no par exchanged for (0.2) share Common no par

CLUB MED INC (CAYMAN ISLANDS)
Acquired by Club Mediterranee 08/01/1995
Each share Common $1 par exchanged for $32 cash

CLUB MEDITERRANEE (FRANCE)
Each ADR for Ordinary exchanged for (2.2) ADR's for Ordinary 06/20/1985

Acquired by Gaillon Invest II 04/27/2015
Each ADR for Ordinary exchanged for $5.270980 cash
Note: Due to ADR's being unsponsored exchange rate may vary

CLUB MONACO INC (ON)
Acquired by Polo Ralph Lauren Corp. 04/01/1999
Each share Common no par exchanged for $13 cash

CLUB-THEATRE NETWORK INC (FL)
Name changed to HI-DEF Enterprises, Inc. 06/01/1993
(See HI-DEF Enterprises, Inc.)

CLUB USPN INC (NV)
Name changed to XL Corp. 03/11/1994
XL Corp. recapitalized as Commercial Labor Management, Inc. 03/20/1995 which name changed to Zeros & Ones, Inc. 07/01/1999 which name changed to Voyant International Corp. 04/30/2007
(See Voyant International Corp.)

CLUB VIVANET INC (OR)
Each share old Common 1¢ par exchanged for (0.05) share new Common 1¢ par 08/26/2008
Name changed to Medical Marijuana, Inc. 04/28/2009

CLUBCHARLIE COM INC (NV)
Name changed to ViaStar Holdings, Inc. 01/22/2001
ViaStar Holdings, Inc. name changed to Viastar Media Corp. 01/23/2004 which name changed to Pop3 Media Corp. 01/21/2005
(See Pop3 Media Corp.)

CLUBCORP HLDGS INC (NV)
Acquired by Constellation Club Parent, Inc. 09/18/2017
Each share Common 1¢ par exchanged for $17.12 cash

CLUBHOUSE VIDEOS INC (FL)
Voluntarily dissolved 08/28/2008
Details not available

CLUBLINK CORP (ON)
Each share old Common no par exchanged for (0.1) share new Common no par 06/12/1996
Each share new Common no par exchanged again for (1) share new Common no par to reflect a (1) for (100) reverse split followed by a (100) for (1) forward split 06/21/2004
Note: Holders of (99) or fewer pre-split shares received $8.16 cash per share
Merged into ClubLink Enterprises Ltd. 07/30/2009
Each share Common no par exchanged for (1.1) shares Common no par

CLUBLINK ENTERPRISES LTD (CANADA)
Name changed to TWC Enterprises Ltd. 06/25/2014

CLUBMART OF AMER INC (DE)
Name changed to Retail Services, Inc. 09/24/1985
(See Retail Services, Inc.)

CLUCAS BOOKER GOLD MINING CO. LTD. (ON)
Charter cancelled for failure to pay taxes and file returns 03/14/1978

CLUCKCORP INTL INC (TX)
Name changed to Harvest Restaurant Group, Inc. 10/01/1997
Harvest Restaurant Group, Inc. name changed to Tanner's Restaurant Group, Inc. 03/12/1999 which changed to Corzon Inc. 09/18/2000 which recapitalized as LecStar Corp. 03/29/2001
(See LecStar Corp.)

CLUCKERS WOOD ROASTED CHICKEN INC (FL)
Name changed to Foodquest, Inc. 10/24/1995
(See Foodquest, Inc.)

CLUETT AMERN CORP (DE)
Stock Dividends - 6.25% payable 11/15/2002 to holders of record 11/01/2002; 6.25% payable 05/15/2003 to holders of record 05/01/2003
12.5% Sr. Exchangeable Preferred Ser. B called for redemption at $102.50 on 11/29/2006
12.5% 144A Sr. Exchangeable Preferred Ser. B called for redemption at $102.50 on 11/29/2006

CLUETT PEABODY & CO INC (NY)
Each share old Common no par exchanged for (3) shares new Common no par 00/00/1937
New Common no par changed to $3.25 par and (1) additional share issued 04/27/1962
4% 2nd Preferred $100 par called for redemption 10/01/1964
Common $3.25 par changed to $1.08333333 par and (2) additional shares issued 05/19/1966
7% Preferred $100 par called for redemption 12/31/1974
Merged into West Point-Pepperell, Inc. 01/15/1986
Each share $1 Conv. Preferred $1 par exchanged for (0.587) share Common $5 par
Each share Common $1.08333333 par exchanged for (0.931) share Common $5 par
(See West Point-Pepperell, Inc.)

CLUFF GOLD PLC (ENGLAND & WALES)
Name changed to Amara Mining PLC 10/03/2012
(See Amara Mining PLC)

CLUFF RES PLC (UNITED KINGDOM)
Acquired by Ashanti Goldfields Ltd. 00/00/1996
Details not available

CLUNY GOLD MINES, LTD. (ON)
Charter revoked for failure to file reports and pay taxes 06/00/1953

CLUSTER TECHNOLOGY CORP (DE)
Each share old Common 1¢ par exchanged for (0.1) share new Common 1¢ par 09/30/1994
SEC revoked common stock registration 09/08/2008

CLUTE CORP (CO)
Petition for reorganization under Chapter X bankruptcy filed 11/05/1962
On 04/08/1970 U.S. Tax court released a decision that debentures were worthless for tax purposes 00/00/1962
It would appear same would be applicable to Conv. Preferred and Common Stocks
Adjudicated bankrupt 04/03/1972
No stockholders' equity

CLUTE FRANCIS H & SON INC (CO)
Proclaimed defunct and inoperative for failure to pay taxes 10/11/1968

CLUTE INTL CORP (CA)
Charter cancelled for failure to file reports and pay taxes 03/02/1992

CLUTTERBUG MOVE MGMT INC (NV)
Name changed to iNeedMD Holdings, Inc. 02/27/2015

CLX MED INC (CO)
Recapitalized 04/09/1993
Name changed 09/02/2004
Name changed 04/30/2008
Recapitalized from CLX Exploration Inc. to CLX Energy Inc. 04/09/1993

Each share Common 1¢ par exchanged for (0.1) share Common 1¢ par
Each share old Common 1¢ par exchanged for (0.25) share new Common 1¢ par to reflect a (1) for (100) reverse split followed by a (25) for (1) forward split 04/02/2001
Note: Holders of (99) or fewer pre-split shares received $0.156 cash per share
Name changed from CLX Energy Inc. to CLX Investment Co., Inc. 09/02/2004
Common 1¢ par split (4) for (3) by issuance of (1/3) additional share payable 10/21/2005 to holders of record 09/30/2005
Name changed from CLX Investment Co., Inc. to CLX Medical, Inc. 04/30/2008
Each share old Common 1¢ par exchanged for (0.0005) share new Common 1¢ par 02/18/2009
SEC revoked common stock registration 04/02/2012

CLYDE AIRCRAFT MANUFACTURING CO., LTD. (ON)
Liquidation completed
Each share Common received initial distribution of $1.485 cash 00/00/1946
Each share Common received second and final distribution of $0.77 cash 03/15/1949

CLYDE-CALLAHAN OIL CO. (TX)
Charter forfeited for failure to pay taxes 04/04/1950

CLYDE FINL CORP (DE)
Exchangeable Auction Market Preferred no par called for redemption 11/29/1989
Public interest eliminated

CLYDE INDS LTD (AUSTRALIA)
Acquired by Edico Pty Ltd. 10/16/1996
Details not available

CLYDE PORCELAIN STEEL CORP.
Merged into Whirlpool Corp. (NY) 00/00/1952
Each share Common 10¢ par exchanged for (0.2) share new 5.5% Preferred $20 par
Whirlpool Corp. (NY) merged into Whirlpool-Seeger Corp. 09/15/1955 which name changed to Whirlpool Corp. (DE) 04/01/1957

CLYDE RES INC (BC)
Struck off register and declared dissolved for failure to file returns 11/10/1994

CLYDESDALE CAP CORP (AB)
Reincorporated under the laws of Ontario as Dundee Realty Corp. 11/21/1996
Dundee Realty Corp. reorganized as Dundee Real Estate Investment Trust 06/30/2003 which name changed to Dream Office Real Estate Investment Trust 05/08/2014

CLYVIA INC (NV)
SEC revoked common stock registration 08/29/2012

CM & S MINES LTD (QC)
Recapitalized as Camchib Resources Inc.-Les Ressources Camchib Inc. 10/31/1980
Each share Capital Stock $1 par exchanged for (0.2) share Capital Stock no par
Camchib Resources Inc.-Les Ressources Camchib Inc. merged into Campbell Resources Inc. (New) 06/08/1983
(See Campbell Resources Inc. (New))

CM BK HLDG CO (LA)
Merged into Hibernia Corp. 08/26/1996
Each share Class A Common $10 par exchanged for $193.524599 cash

Each share Class B Common $10 par exchanged for $96.76229999 cash

CM COMMUNICATIONS INC (DE)
Filed a petition under Chapter 7 Federal Bankruptcy Code 04/00/1991
Stockholders' equity unlikely

CM NT EQUITY CORP (CANADA)
Capital Shares no par called for redemption 03/31/1993
Public interest eliminated

CM PREF CORP (ON)
Adjustable Rate Preferred no par called for redemption 03/31/1993
Public interest eliminated

CMA CAP CORP (CANADA)
Reincorporated 05/05/1995
Place of incorporation changed from (AB) to (Canada) 05/05/1995
Struck from the register and dissolved 11/01/1997

CMA CORP LTD (AUSTRALIA)
Basis changed from (1:20) to (1:0.5) 09/19/2011
ADR agreement terminated 07/27/2015
Each Sponsored ADR for Ordinary exchanged for (0.5) share Ordinary
Note: Unexchanged ADR's will be sold and the proceeds, if any, held for claim after 07/29/2016

CMA MONEY FD (MA)
Name changed to CMA Money Fund 07/30/1981

CMAC COMPUTER SYS LTD (BC)
Delisted from Vancouver Stock Exchange 10/25/1988

CMAC INVT CORP (DE)
Under plan of merger name changed to Radian Group Inc. 06/09/1999

CMC FINANCE GROUP, INC. (NC)
Name changed to CMC Group, Inc. 09/19/1972
(See CMC Group, Inc.)

CMC GROUP INC (NC)
Each share Class A Common $1 par received distribution of (1) share Thunderbird Homes, Inc. Common 10¢ par 08/02/1974
Merged into First Railroad & Banking Co. of Georgia 08/05/1974
Each share Class A Common $1 par exchanged for either (1.4597) shares Conv. Preferred 66-2/3¢ par or $13 cash
Note: Option to receive Preferred expired 04/18/1974
(See First Railroad & Banking Co. of Georgia)

CMC INDS INC (DE)
Merged into Act Manufacturing, Inc. 07/29/1999
Each share Common 1¢ par exchanged for (0.5) share Common 1¢ par
(See Act Manufacturing, Inc.)

CMC INTL INC (WA)
Name changed to Votrax International, Inc. (WA) 01/17/1986
Votrax International, Inc. (WA) reincorporated in Delaware 11/01/1985 which recapitalized as Votrax, Inc. 11/05/1987
(See Votrax, Inc.)

CMC MAGNETICS CORP (TAIWAN)
GDR agreement terminated 01/25/2013
Each Reg. S GDR for Common exchanged for $3.484526 cash

CMC REAL ESTATE CORP (WI)
5% Preferred Ser. A $100 par called for redemption 03/13/1986
Merged into CMCRE Merger Corp. 12/29/1986
Each share Common no par exchanged for $120 cash and (1) Deferred Cash Consideration Right to receive $33.43 cash

CME CAP INC (ON)
Name changed 10/15/1986
Name changed from CME Resources Inc. to CME Capital Inc. and Capital Stock no par reclassified as Participating Class A no par 10/15/1986
Delisted from Canadian Dealer Network 05/31/1996
Details not available

CME MANUFACTURING CO. (CA)
Name changed to Aeromarine Electronics, Inc. 02/24/1964
(See Aeromarine Electronics, Inc.)

CME RLTY INC (NV)
Common $0.001 par split (5) for (1) by issuance of (4) additional shares payable 03/16/2015 to holders of record 03/09/2015 Ex date - 03/17/2015
Name changed to South Beach Spirits, Inc. 09/09/2015

CME SAT INC (MA)
Reincorporated under the laws of Delaware as Medicom International, Inc. 11/05/1987
(See Medicom International, Inc.)

CME TELEMETRIX INC (ON)
Name changed to NIR Diagnostics Inc. 08/23/2004
(See NIR Diagnostics Inc.)

CMERUN INC (FL)
Reorganized under the laws of Delaware as Fundae Acquisition Corp. 01/25/2000
Each share Common $0.001 par exchanged for (5) shares Common $0.001 par
Fundae Acquisition Corp. name changed to C Me Run Corp. 02/02/2000
(See C Me Run Corp.)

CMG HLDGS INC (NV)
Name changed to CMG Holdings Group, Inc. 02/22/2013

CMGI INC (DE)
Name changed 12/17/1998
Common 1¢ par split (3) for (2) by issuance of (0.5) additional share 03/31/1995
Common 1¢ par split (2) for (1) by issuance of (1) additional share payable 02/02/1996 to holders of record 01/19/1996
Each share Common 1¢ par received distribution of (0.0625) share Lycos Inc. Common 1¢ par payable 07/31/1997 to holders of record 06/05/1997
Common 1¢ par split (2) for (1) by issuance of (1) additional share payable 05/11/1998 to holders of record 04/27/1998
Name changed from CMG Information Services, Inc. to CMGI Inc. 12/17/1998
Old Common 1¢ par split (2) for (1) by issuance of (1) additional share payable 01/11/1999 to holders of record 12/28/1998
Old Common 1¢ par split (2) for (1) by issuance of (1) additional share payable 05/27/1999 to holders of record 05/13/1999
Old Common 1¢ par split (2) for (1) by issuance of (1) additional share payable 01/11/2000 to holders of record 12/28/1999
Each share old Common 1¢ par exchanged for (0.1) share new Common 1¢ par 11/01/2007
Name changed to ModusLink Global Solutions, Inc. 09/30/2008
ModusLink Global Solutions, Inc. name changed to Steel Connect, Inc. 02/27/2018

CMI CORP (OK)
Common 10¢ par split (2) for (1) by issuance of (1) additional share 01/30/1970
Each share old Common 10¢ par exchanged for (0.0005) share new Common 10¢ par 02/14/1992
Each share new Common 10¢ par received distribution of (1,999) shares Class A Common 10¢ par 02/14/1992
Note: Holders of fewer than (2,000) old Common 10¢ par will receive a like amount of Class A Common 10¢ par and will not receive any additional new Common 10¢ par
Merged into Terex Corp. 10/01/2001
Each share new Common 10¢ par exchanged for (0.16) share Common 1¢ par
Each share Class A Common 10¢ par exchanged for (0.16) share Common 10¢ par

CMI HLDGS GROUP INC (NV)
Recapitalized as RFMR Acquisition Corp. 04/02/2004
Each share Common $0.001 par exchanged for (0.001) share Common $0.001 par
RFMR Acquisition Corp. name changed to Great Northern Oilsands, Inc. (NV) 11/14/2006 which reorganized in Florida as New Asia Gold Corp. 06/05/2008 which recapitalized as New World Gold Corp. 05/08/2009

CMI INVT CORP (DE)
Common $2.50 par split (3) for (2) by issuance of (0.5) additional share 04/11/1977
Name changed to Verex Corp. 12/30/1977
(See Verex Corp.)

CMJ CAP INC (QC)
Name changed to Power Tech Corporation Inc. 02/11/2005
(See Power Tech Corporation Inc.)

CMKM DIAMONDS INC (NV)
Each share Common $0.0001 par received distribution of (0.00000962) share U.S. Canadian Minerals, Inc. Common $0.001 par payable 10/06/2004 to holders of record 08/20/2004
Each share Common $0.0001 par received distribution of (0.0256) share Casavant International Mining Corp. Restricted Common payable 10/18/2004 to holders of record 08/23/2004
Each share Common $0.0001 par received distribution of (0.00012267) share Juina Mining Corp. Restricted Common 2-1/2¢ par payable 12/10/2004 to holders of record 10/01/2004
SEC revoked common stock registration 10/28/2005

CML GROUP INC (DE)
Common 1¢ par split (2) for (1) by issuance of (1) additional share 08/15/1991
Common 1¢ par split (2) for (1) by issuance of (1) additional share 08/17/1992
Common 1¢ par split (3) for (2) by issuance of (0.5) additional share 08/16/1993
Chapter 11 bankruptcy proceedings dismissed 07/19/2002
Stockholders' equity unlikely

CML HEALTHCARE INC NEW (ON)
Acquired by LifeLabs Ontario Inc. 10/02/2013
Each share Common no par exchanged for $10.75 cash

CML HEALTHCARE INC OLD (ON)
Plan of arrangement effective 02/23/2004
Each share Common no par exchanged for (4) CML HealthCare Income Fund Units no par, (1) share Cipher Pharmaceuticals Inc. Common no par and $7 cash
(See each company's listing)

CML HEALTHCARE INCOME FD (ON)
Under plan of reorganization each Unit automatically became (1) share CML HealthCare Inc. (New) Common no par 01/04/2011
(See CML Healthcare Inc. (New))

CML INDS LTD (ON)
Merged into Supremex Inc. 07/31/2000
Each share Common no par exchanged for $6 cash

CML MICROSYSTEMS PLC (UNITED KINGDOM)
ADR agreement terminated 10/13/2004
Each Sponsored ADR for Ordinary exchanged for $10.54045 cash

CMORE MED SOLUTIONS INC (MN)
Name changed to ProVation Medical, Inc. 04/02/2002

CMP GOLD TR (ON)
Name changed to Goodman Gold Trust 01/15/2013
(See Goodman Gold Trust)

CMP GROUP INC (ME)
Merged into Energy East Corp. 09/01/2000
Each share Common $5 par exchanged for $29.50 cash

CMP INDS INC (NY)
Each share Capital Stock $25 par exchanged for (5) shares Capital Stock $5 par 09/14/1959
20% partial liquidation approved and each share Capital Stock $5 par received $12.50 in cash 10/15/1959
Company went private 01/01/2002
Each share Common $5 par exchanged for $59.24 cash

CMP MEDIA INC (DE)
Merged into MFW Acquisition Holdings Corp. 06/09/1999
Each share Class A Common 1¢ par exchanged for $39 cash

CMP 1988 OIL & GAS DEV L P (AB)
Acquired by Clearport Petroleums Ltd. 01/14/1994
Each Unit of Ltd. Partnership Ser. A exchanged for (2.56613) shares Common no par
Clearport Petroleums Ltd. merged into Eurogas Corp. 06/30/1995 which name changed to Dundee Energy Ltd. 06/22/2011

CMP 1988 OIL & GAS DEV TR (AB)
Acquired by Clearport Petroleums Ltd. 01/14/1994
Each Trust Unit Ser. A exchanged for (2.21081) shares Common no par
Clearport Petroleums Ltd. merged into Eurogas Corp. 06/30/1995 which name changed to Dundee Energy Ltd. 06/22/2011

CMP 1989 OIL & GAS DEV LTD PARTNERSHIP (AB)
Acquired by Clearport Petroleums Ltd. 01/14/1994
Each Unit of Ltd. Partnership exchanged for (1.61863) shares Common no par
Clearport Petroleums Ltd. merged into Eurogas Corp. 06/30/1995 which name changed to Dundee Energy Ltd. 06/22/2011

CMP RES LTD (BC)
Merged into Kinross Gold Corp. 05/31/1993
Each share Common no par exchanged for (2.1) shares Common no par

CMP SUSQUEHANNA RADIO HLDGS CORP (DE)
144A Preferred called for redemption at $10 on 09/16/2011

CMP 2005 RESOURCE LTD PARTNERSHIP (ON)
Under plan of reorganization each Unit of Ltd. Partnership no par

automatically became (46.8799) shares Dynamic Managed Portfolios Ltd. DMP Resource Class no par 02/06/2007

CMQ RES INC (AB)
Each share old Common no par exchanged for (0.1) share new Common no par 08/25/2008
Each (21.000,000) shares new Common no par exchanged again for (1) share new Common no par 07/25/2014
Note: In effect holders received $0.02 cash per share and public interest was eliminated

CMS ADVERTISING INC (DE)
Common 1¢ par split (3) for (2) by issuance of (0.5) additional share 12/08/1986
Common 1¢ par split (3) for (2) by issuance of (0.5) additional share 03/30/1987
Name changed to Unico, Inc. (DE) 09/29/1989
Unico, Inc. (DE) recapitalized as ABSS Corp. (DE) 04/25/2002 which reorganized in Nevada as NT Holding Corp. 08/04/2004 which recapitalized as HST Global, Inc. 07/07/2008

CMS BANCORP INC (DE)
Acquired by Putnam County Acquisition Corp. 04/28/2015
Each share Common 1¢ par exchanged for $13.25 cash

CMS/DATA CORP (FL)
Merged into Quartex Corp. 04/11/1994
Each share Common 1¢ par exchanged for (1.4) shares Common no par
Quartex Corp. name changed to PC Docs Group International Inc. 06/29/1994
(See PC Docs Group International Inc.)

CMS ENERGY CORP (MI)
Issue Information - 7,000,000 shares COM CL G offered at $17.75 per share on 07/21/1995
Each share Class G Common 1¢ par exchanged for (0.7041) shares Common 1¢ par 10/25/1999
Each Adjustable Conv. Trust Security Normal Unit converted into (1.2121) shares Common 1¢ par 07/01/2002
Each Premium Equity Participating Security Unit converted into (1.8913) shares Common 1¢ par 08/18/2003
Each share 4.50% Conv. Preferred Ser. B 1¢ par automatically became (2.9025696) shares Common 1¢ par and $50 cash 09/30/2010
(Additional Information in Active)

CMS ENERGY TR I (DE)
7.75% Quarterly Income Preferred Securities called for redemption at $50 on 02/29/2012

CMS ENHANCEMENTS INC (DE)
Reincorporated 06/01/1987
State of incorporation changed from (CO) to (DE) and each share Common $0.001 par exchanged for (0.14285714) share old Common 1¢ par 06/01/1987
Each share old Common 1¢ par exchanged for (0.25) share new Common 1¢ par 12/06/1989
Name changed to AmeriQuest Technologies, Inc. 03/31/1994
(See AmeriQuest Technologies, Inc.)

CMSF CORP (DE)
Recapitalized as Plures Technologies, Inc. 09/27/2011
Each share Common $0.000001 par exchanged for (0.0025) share Common $0.001 par
Note: No holder will receive fewer than (1) share
(See Plures Technologies, Inc.)

CMT INDS INC (NJ)
Name changed to Matrix Corp. (NJ) 01/12/1979
Matrix Corp. (NJ) reincorporated in Delaware 04/19/1988
(See Matrix Corp. (DE))

CMT INVT CO (CA)
Name changed to Avalon Energy Corp. 10/01/1984
Avalon Energy Corp. merged into Avalon Corp. 04/15/1985
(See Avalon Corp.)

CMT INVESTMENT TRUST (CA)
Under plan of reorganization each Preferred Share of Bene. Int. $7.50 par and Share of Bene. Int. $1 par automatically became (1) share CMT Investment Co. Preferred $7.50 par or (1) share Common $1 par respectively 11/07/1980
CMT Investment Co. name changed to Avalon Energy Corp. 10/01/1984 which merged into Avalon Corp. 04/15/1985
(See Avalon Corp.)

CMX CORP (AL)
Acquired by Chyron Corp. 01/31/1989
Each share Common no par exchanged for (0.21052631) share Common 1¢ par
Chyron Corp. name changed to ChyronHego Corp. 05/23/2013
(See ChyronHego Corp.)

CMYK CAP INC (BC)
Recapitalized as Paget Minerals Corp. 08/18/2009
Each share Common no par exchanged for (0.5) share Common no par
Paget Minerals Corp. recapitalized as Ascent Industries Corp. 08/10/2018

CN BANCORP INC (MD)
Issue Information - 344,828 shares COM offered at $14.50 per share on 01/24/2004
Merged into Sandy Spring Bancorp, Inc. 06/01/2007
Each share Common $10 par exchanged for (0.5871474) share Common $1 par and $2.95 cash

CN BIOSCIENCES INC (DE)
Merged into EM Industries, Inc. 12/30/1998
Each share Common 1¢ par exchanged for $25 cash

CNA FINL CORP (DE)
$1.10 Conv. Preferred Ser. A no par called for redemption 12/29/1983
Money Market Preferred Ser. F no par called for redemption at $100,000 on 04/03/2000
Money Market Preferred Ser. E no par called for redemption at $100,000 on 04/24/2000
(Additional Information in Active)

CNA INCOME SHS INC (MD)
Name changed to Prospect Street Income Shares, Inc. 08/01/2001
Prospect Street Income Shares, Inc. merged into Highland Credit Strategies Fund 07/18/2008 which name changed to Pyxis Credit Strategies Fund 01/11/2012 which name changed to NexPoint Credit Strategies Fund 06/25/2012 which name changed to NexPoint Strategic Opportunities Fund 03/19/2018

CNA LARWIN INVT CO (MD)
Name changed to CL Assets, Inc. 08/06/1976
(See CL Assets, Inc.)

CNA SURETY CORP (DE)
Acquired by CNA Financial Corp. 06/10/2011
Each share Common 1¢ par exchanged for $26.55 cash

CNB BANCORP INC (NY)
Common $5 par split (2) for (1) by issuance of (1) additional share 01/18/1994
Common $5 par changed to $2.50 par and (1) additional share issued payable 02/18/1997 to holders of record 02/10/1997
Common $2.50 par split (3) for (2) by issuance of (0.5) additional share payable 09/01/1999 to holders of record 08/26/1999
Merged into NBT Bancorp Inc. 02/13/2006
Each share Common $2.50 par exchanged for $38 cash

CNB BANCORP INC (VA)
Merged into Citizens National Bank (Windsor, VA) 02/15/2012
Each share Common 1¢ par exchanged for (1) share Common 1¢ par
Note: Company is now private

CNB BANCSHARES INC (IN)
Common no par split (2) for (1) by issuance of (1) additional share 09/03/1985
Common no par split (2) for (1) by issuance of (1) additional share 08/15/1986
Stock Dividends - 12.5% 08/01/1984; 10% 08/15/1987; 10% 01/20/1993; 10% 12/09/1994; 5% payable 10/11/1996 to holders of record 09/20/1996; 5% payable 09/18/1997 to holders of record 08/21/1997; 5% payable 09/18/1998 to holders of record 08/28/1998
Merged into Fifth Third Bancorp 10/29/1999
Each share Common no par exchanged for (0.8825) share Common no par

CNB CAP TR I (DE)
6% Guaranteed Trust Conv. Preferred Securities called for redemption at $25 on 12/31/2001

CNB FINL CORP (KS)
Common $1 par split (2) for (1) by issuance of (1) additional share 04/24/1989
Merged into UMB Financial Corp. 06/25/1993
Each share Common $1 par exchanged for (1.571) shares Common $1 par

CNB FINL CORP (MA)
Merged into United Financial Bancorp, Inc. (MD) 12/04/2009
Each share Common $1 par exchanged for (0.8257) share Common 1¢ par
United Financial Bancorp, Inc. (MD) merged into United Financial Bancorp, Inc. (CT) 05/01/2014

CNB FINL CORP (NY)
Common $5 par changed to $2.50 par and (1) additional share issued 11/10/1994
Common $2.50 par split (3) for (2) by issuance of (0.5) additional share payable 01/15/1997 to holders of record 12/31/1996
Common $2.50 par changed to $1.25 par and (1) additional share issued payable 06/30/1998 to holders of record 06/15/1998
Merged into NBT Bancorp Inc. 11/09/2001
Each share Common $1.25 par exchanged for (1.2) shares Common 1¢ par

CNB FLA BANCSHARES INC (FL)
Merged into South Financial Group, Inc. 07/16/2004
Each share Common 1¢ par exchanged for (0.84) share Common $1 par
South Financial Group, Inc. merged into Toronto-Dominion Bank (Toronto, ON) 09/30/2010

CNB HLDGS INC (GA)
Name changed to First Capital Bancorp, Inc. 12/31/2004
First Capital Bancorp, Inc. merged into Flag Financial Corp. 11/22/2005
(See Flag Financial Corp.)

CNB HLDG CO (FL)
Merged into Colonial BancGroup, Inc. 08/12/1998
Each share Common $1 par exchanged for (5.9742) shares Common $2.50 par
(See Colonial BancGroup, Inc.)

CNB INC (FL)
Name changed to CNB Florida Bancshares Inc. 06/30/1999
CNB Florida Bancshares Inc. merged into South Financial Group, Inc. 07/16/2004 which merged into Toronto-Dominion Bank (Toronto, ON) 09/30/2010

CNBC BANCORP (OH)
Common $5 par split (2) for (1) by issuance of (1) additional share payable 02/17/1998 to holders of record 01/31/1998
Common $5 par split (3) for (2) by issuance of (0.5) additional share payable 05/10/2001 to holders of record 05/03/2001 Ex date - 05/11/2001
Merged into First Merchants Corp. 03/01/2003
Each share Common $5 par exchanged for (1.01) shares Common no par

CNBC BANCORP INC (DE)
Merged into ABN Amro Holding N.V. 11/01/1996
Each share Common $10 par exchanged for $2,043.605 cash

CNBT BANCSHARES INC (TX)
Merged into BOK Financial Corp. 01/12/2001
Each share Common 1¢ par exchanged for $18.032071 cash
Note: An additional $0.20 cash is being held in escrow for possible future distribution

CNC DEVELOPMENT LTD (BRITISH VIRGIN ISLANDS)
SEC revoked preferred and common stock registration 09/05/2013

CNE GROUP INC (DE)
Name changed to Arrow Resources Development, Inc. 12/20/2005

CNET INC (DE)
Name changed 05/01/1997
Name changed from C-Net, Inc. to CNET Inc. 05/01/1997
Common $0.0001 par split (2) for (1) by issuance of (1) additional share payable 03/08/1999 to holders of record 02/22/1999
Common $0.0001 par split (2) for (1) by issuance of (1) additional share payable 05/28/1999 to holders of record 05/19/1999
Name changed to CNET Networks, Inc. 03/02/2000
(See CNET Networks, Inc.)

CNET NETWORKS INC (DE)
Merged into CBS Corp. 06/30/2008
Each share Common $0.0001 par exchanged for $11.50 cash

CNF INC (DE)
Name changed 12/08/2000
Name changed from CNF Transportation Inc. to CNF Inc. 12/08/2000
Name changed to Con-Way Inc. 04/18/2006
(See Con-Way Inc.)

CNF TECHNOLOGIES INC (DE)
Charter cancelled and declared inoperative and void for non-payment of taxes 03/01/2002

CNF TR I (DE)
Conv. Term Guaranteed Securities

Ser. A called for redemption at $51 on 06/01/2004

CNH GLOBAL N V (NETHERLANDS)
Each share Common EUR 0.45 par exchanged for (0.2) share Common EUR 2.25 par 04/01/2003
Merged into CNH Industrial N.V. 09/29/2013
Each share Common EUR 2.25 par exchanged for (3.828) shares Common EUR 0.01 par

CNH HLDGS CO (NV)
Each share old Common $0.001 par exchanged for (0.1) share new Common $0.001 par 03/28/2003
Name changed to Cistera Networks, Inc. 09/27/2005

CNI COMPUTER NETWORKS INTL LTD (BC)
Delisted from Vancouver Stock Exchange 06/20/1988

CNINSURE INC (CAYMAN ISLANDS)
Name changed to Fanhua Inc. 12/07/2016

CNL AMERN PPTYS FD INC (FL)
Name changed 02/01/1995
Name changed from CNL Investment Fund Inc. to CNL American Properties Fund Inc. 02/01/1995
Name changed to CNL Restaurant Properties, Inc. 06/30/2003
CNL Restaurant Properties, Inc. merged into Trustreet Properties, Inc. 02/25/2005
(See Trustreet Properties, Inc.)

CNL FINL CORP (GA)
Under plan of merger each share Common $1 par held by holders of (500) shares or fewer exchanged for $6 cash 09/30/1994
Merged into American United Life Insurance Co. 12/19/2000
Each share Common $1 par exchanged for (1) Non-Transferable Contingent Value Right and $14.22 cash

CNL HEALTH CARE PPTYS INC (MD)
Name changed to CNL Retirement Properties Inc. 09/05/2000
CNL Retirement Properties Inc. merged into Health Care Property Investors, Inc. 10/05/2006 which name changed to HCP, Inc. 09/07/2007

CNL INCOME FD LTD (FL)
Merged into Trustreet Properties, Inc. 02/25/2005
Each Unit of Ltd. Partnership Int. I received (1.3425) shares Conv. Preferred Ser. A $0.001 par and $161.11 cash
Each Unit of Ltd. Partnership Int. II received (2.0833) shares Conv. Preferred Ser. A $0.001 par and $250 cash
Each Unit of Ltd. Partnership Int. III received (1.8472) shares Conv. Preferred Ser. A $0.001 par and $221.67 cash
Each Unit of Ltd. Partnership Int. IV received (1.9328) shares Conv. Preferred Ser. A $0.001 par and $231.9444 cash
Each Unit of Ltd. Partnership Int. V received (1.8055) shares Conv. Preferred Ser. A $0.001 par and $216.67 cash
Each Unit of Ltd. Partnership Int. VI received (3.611) shares Conv. Preferred Ser. A $0.001 par and $433.33 cash
Each Unit of Ltd. Partnership Int. VII received (0.00706) share Conv. Preferred Ser. A $0.001 par and $0.8472 cash
Each Unit of Ltd. Partnership Int. VIII received (0.007044) share Conv. Preferred Ser. A $0.001 par and $0.8452 cash
Each Unit of Ltd. Partnership Int. IX received (0.05556) share Conv. Preferred Ser. A $0.001 par and $6.6667 cash
Each Unit of Ltd. Partnership Int. X received (0.05998) share Conv. Preferred Ser. A $0.001 par and $7.1979 cash
Each Unit of Ltd. Partnership Int. XI received (0.06944) share Conv. Preferred Ser. A $0.001 par and $8.3333 cash
Each Unit of Ltd. Partnership Int. XII received (0.07052) share Conv. Preferred Ser. A $0.001 par and $8.463 cash
Each Unit of Ltd. Partnership Int. XIII received (0.06684) share Conv. Preferred Ser. A $0.001 par and $8.0208 cash
Each Unit of Ltd. Partnership Int. XIV received (0.07346) share Conv. Preferred Ser. A $0.001 par and $8.8148 cash
Each Unit of Ltd. Partnership Int. XV received (0.06892) share Conv. Preferred Ser. A $0.001 par and $8.2708 cash
Each Unit of Ltd. Partnership Int. XVI received (0.06674) share Conv. Preferred Ser. A $0.001 par and $8.0093 cash
Each Unit of Ltd. Partnership Int. XVII received (0.05995) share Conv. Preferred Ser. A $0.001 par and $7.1944 cash
Each Unit of Ltd. Partnership Int. XVIII received (0.06071) share Conv. Preferred Ser. A $0.001 par and $7.2857 cash
(See Trustreet Properties, Inc.)

CNL LIFESTYLE PPTYS INC (MD)
Name changed 03/26/2008
Name changed from CNL Income Properties, Inc. to CNL Lifestyle Properties, Inc. 03/26/2008
Liquidation completed
Each share Common 1¢ par received initial distribution of (0.027219) EPR Properties Common Share of Bene. Int. 1¢ par and $0.10 cash payable 04/20/2017 to holders of record 03/31/2017
Each share Common 1¢ par received second and final distribution of $0.16 cash payable 12/15/2017 to holders of record 12/08/2017
Ex date - 01/11/2018

CNL RLTY INVS INC (DE)
Name changed to Commercial Net Lease Realty, Inc. (DE) 05/19/1993
Commercial Net Lease Realty, Inc. (DE) reincorporated in Maryland 06/03/1994 which name changed to National Retail Properties, Inc. 05/01/2006

CNL RESTAURANT PPTYS INC (MD)
Merged into Trustreet Properties, Inc. 02/25/2005
Each share Common 1¢ par exchanged for (0.16) share 7.5% Conv. Preferred Ser. C $0.001 par and (0.7742) share Common $0.001 par
(See Trustreet Properties, Inc.)

CNL RETIREMENT PPTYS INC (MD)
Merged into Health Care Property Investors, Inc. 10/05/2006
Each share Common 1¢ par exchanged for (0.0865) share Common $1 par and $11.1293 cash

CNLBANCSHARES INC (FL)
Merged into Valley National Bancorp 12/01/2015
Each share Common 1¢ par exchanged for (0.705) share Common no par

CNPC HONG KONG LTD (HONG KONG)
Name changed to Kunlun Energy Co. Ltd. 04/05/2010

CNR CAP CORP (ON)
Name changed to Argonaut Exploration Inc. 12/12/2008

CNR CORP (DE)
Name changed to Rosen Petroleum Corp. 01/20/1971
Each share Common 50¢ par exchanged for (1) share Common 50¢ par
(See Rosen Petroleum Corp.)

CNRP MNG INC (BC)
Each share old Common no par exchanged for (0.1) share new Common no par 05/02/2017
Name changed to Integrated Cannabis Co., Inc. 06/08/2018

CNS BANCORP INC (DE)
Merged into Exchange National Bancshares, Inc. 06/16/2000
Each share Common 1¢ par exchanged for (0.3) share Common $1 par and $8.80 cash
Exchange National Bancshares, Inc. name changed to Hawthorn Bancshares, Inc. 06/18/2007

CNS INC (DE)
Common 1¢ par split (2) for (1) by issuance of (1) additional share 06/22/1995
Merged into GlaxoSmithKline PLC 12/19/2006
Each share Common 1¢ par exchanged for $37.50 cash

CNS RESPONSE INC (DE)
Each share old Common $0.001 par exchanged for (0.03333333) share new Common $0.001 par 04/03/2012
Name changed to MYnd Analytics, Inc. 01/12/2016

CNTV ENTMT GROUP INC (NV)
Recapitalized as Degama Software Solutions, Inc. 05/29/2008
Each share Common $0.001 par exchanged for (0.00074074) share Common $0.001 par

CNW CORP (DE)
$2.125 Conv. Exchangeable Preferred $1 par called for redemption 10/16/1989
Merged into Chicago & North Western Holdings Corp. 10/26/1989
Each share Common $1 par exchanged for (2) shares Exchangeable Preferred 1¢ par
Chicago & North Western Holdings Corp. name changed to Chicago & North Western Transportation Co. 05/09/1994
(See Chicago & North Western Transportation Co.)

CNX COAL RES LP (DE)
Name changed to CONSOL Coal Resources L.P. 11/29/2017

CNX GAS CORP (DE)
Merged into CONSOL Energy Inc. 05/28/2010
Each share Common 1¢ par exchanged for $38.25 cash

CNY FINL CORP (DE)
Merged into Niagara Bancorp, Inc. 07/07/2000
Each share Common no par exchanged for $18.75 cash

CO BUILD COS INC (VIRGIN ISLANDS)
Adjudicated bankrupt 12/28/1976
Stockholders' equity unlikely

CO COUNSEL INC (TX)
Merged into Olsten Corp. 08/09/1996
Each share Common 1¢ par exchanged for (0.1069) share Conv. Class B Common 10¢ par
Olsten Corp. merged into Adecco S.A. 03/15/2000 which name changed to Adecco Group AG 06/03/2016

CO-ENERCO RES LTD (CANADA)
Class A Common no par reclassified as Common no par 12/18/1992
Acquired by Pennzoil Canada Inc. 07/04/1994
Each share Common no par exchanged for $8.60 cash

CO MAXX ENERGY GROUP INC (AB)
Acquired by NuGas Ltd. 05/01/1995
Each share Common no par exchanged for either (0.5) share Common no par and $1.25 cash or $2.25 cash
Note: U.S. holders received cash only
NuGas Ltd. merged into Q Energy Ltd. 09/16/1997
(See Q Energy Ltd.)

CO-MEDIA INC (NV)
Each share old Common $0.0001 par exchanged for (0.05) share new Common $0.0001 par 11/06/2001
Reorganized as Jarvis Group Inc. 01/18/2002
Each share new Common $0.0001 par exchanged for (3) shares Common $0.0001 par
Jarvis Group Inc. name changed to Cash 4 Homes 247 on 05/21/2003 which name changed to Vegas Equity International Corp. 02/01/2006
(See Vegas Equity International Corp.)

CO-OPERATIVE BK (CONCORD, MA)
Reorganized 05/31/1986
Reorganized 11/02/1988
Common $1 par split (3) for (2) by issuance of (0.5) additional share 04/15/1986
Reorganized from Co-Operative Bank (Concord, MA) to Co-Operative Bancorp 05/31/1986
Each share Common $1 par exchanged for (1) share Common $1 par
Reorganized from Co-Operative Bancorp to Co-Operative Bank of Concord (Concord, MA) 11/02/1988
Each share Common $1 par exchanged for (1) share Common $1 par
Merged into Walden Bancorp Inc. 12/08/1995
Each share Common $1 par exchanged for (1) share Common $1 par
Walden Bancorp Inc. merged into UST Corp. 01/03/1997
(See UST Corp.)

CO-OPERATIVE FRUIT GROWERS FINANCE CO., LTD. (NS)
Struck off register and declared dissolved for failure to file returns 08/16/1974

CO-OPERATORS GEN INS CO (CANADA)
Class E Preference Ser. A called for redemption at $25 plus $0.34375 accrued dividends on 07/02/2007
Class E Preference Ser. D called for redemption at $25 on 06/30/2014
(Additional Information in Active)

CO PUBLIC INC (FL)
Name changed to Greater Northwest Research & Development Group, Inc. 05/03/1993
(See Greater Northwest Research & Development Group, Inc.)

CO SE CO INC (MI)
Automatically dissolved 05/15/1980

CO-SIGNER INC (NV)
Name changed to Cross Click Media Inc. 07/14/2014

CO SPACE INC (DE)
Merged into Internap Network Services Corp. (WA) 06/20/2000
Each share Common 1¢ par exchanged for (0.24488) share Common $0.001 par
Internap Network Services Corp.

(WA) reincorporated in Delaware 09/17/2001 which name changed to Internap Corp. 12/04/2014

CO STL INC (ON)
Additional Offering - 15,000,000 shares COM offered at $3.35 per share on 03/04/2002
Subordinate no par reclassified as Common no par 04/27/1994
Name changed to Gerdau Ameristeel Corp. (ON) 10/23/2002
Gerdau Ameristeel Corp. (ON) reincorporated in Canada 05/24/2006
(See Gerdau Ameristeel Corp.)

COA DEV CORP (DE)
Recapitalized as International Child Care Corp. 12/17/2001
Each share Common no par exchanged for (0.1) share Common no par
International Child Care Corp. recapitalized as World Wide Child Care Corp. 05/21/2007

COACH INC (MD)
Common 1¢ par split (2) for (1) by issuance of (1) additional share payable 07/03/2002 to holders of record 06/19/2002 Ex date - 07/05/2002
Common 1¢ par split (2) for (1) by issuance of (1) additional share payable 10/01/2003 to holders of record 09/17/2003 Ex date - 10/02/2003
Common 1¢ par split (2) for (1) by issuance of (1) additional share payable 04/04/2005 to holders of record 03/21/2005 Ex date - 04/05/2005
Name changed to Tapestry, Inc. 10/31/2017

COACH INDS GROUP INC (DE)
Plan of reorganization under Chapter 11 Federal Bankruptcy proceedings effective 12/17/2008
No stockholders' equity

COACH INVTS INC (UT)
Involuntarily dissolved for failure to file reports and pay fees 12/01/1991

COACH USA INC (DE)
Merged into Stagecoach Holdings PLC 07/26/1999
Each share Common 1¢ par exchanged for $42 cash

COACHES AMER INC (TX)
Name changed to Security Southwest Corp. 06/12/1979
(See Security Southwest Corp.)

COACHES AMER LIFE INS CO (TX)
Completely liquidated 01/19/1970
Each share Common no par exchanged for first and final distribution of (0.44444444) shares Coaches of America, Inc. Common no par
Coaches of America, Inc. name changed to Security Southwest Corp. 06/12/1979
(See Security Southwest Corp.)

COACHLIGHT RES LTD (AB)
Merged into Danoil Energy Ltd. 06/30/1998
Each share Common no par exchanged for (0.375) share Class A Subordinate no par and $0.15 cash
Danoil Energy Trust merged into Acclaim Energy Trust 04/20/2001
(See Acclaim Energy Trust)

COACHMAN INC (DE)
Charter cancelled and declared inoperative and void for non-payment of taxes 03/01/2005

COACHMEN INDS INC (IN)
Common no par split (2) for (1) by issuance of (1) additional share 09/06/1976
Common no par split (2) for (1) by issuance of (1) additional share 06/16/1983
Common no par split (2) for (1) by issuance of (1) additional share payable 08/28/1996 to holders of record 08/07/1996
Name changed to All American Group, Inc. 06/11/2010
(See All American Group, Inc.)

COACTIVE MARKETING GROUP INC (DE)
Name changed to mktg, inc. 09/18/2008
(See mktg, inc.)

COAHUILA LEAD & ZINC CO. (MO)
Charter forfeited for failure to file reports 01/01/1932

COAL AND OIL PRODUCTS CORP. (DE)
Charter cancelled for failure to pay taxes 00/00/1930

COAL CITY CORP (DE)
Merged into MB Financial, Inc. (DE) 02/26/1999
Each share Common 1¢ par exchanged for (83.5) shares Common 1¢ par
MB Financial, Inc. (DE) merged into MB Financial, Inc. (MD) 11/07/2001

COAL CREEK ENERGY INC (BC)
Name changed to Corex Gold Corp. 11/18/2003
Corex Gold Corp. merged into Minera Alamos Inc. 04/18/2018

COAL CREEK MNG & MFG CO (TN)
Each share Capital Stock $100 par exchanged for (2) shares Capital Stock no par 10/16/1970
Name changed to Coal Creek Co. 03/16/2006

COAL CREEK MNG CO (CO)
Recapitalized as Ampac National Corp. 12/24/1974
Each share Common 1¢ par exchanged for (0.04) share Common 25¢ par
Ampac National Corp. recapitalized as IPT Corp. 07/20/1992

COAL INC. (WA)
Ceased operations prior to 01/07/1975
No stockholders' equity

COAL OF AFRICA LTD (AUSTRALIA)
ADR agreement terminated 06/18/2015
No ADR's remain outstanding

COAL OPERATORS CASUALTY CO. (PA)
Name changed to Old Republic Insurance Co. 06/01/1955
(See Old Republic Insurance Co.)

COAL RIVER COLLIERIES (WV)
Adjudicated bankrupt 07/16/1928
No stockholders' equity

COAL RIVER MINING & LUMBER CO. (WV)
Liquidation completed
Each share Capital Stock no par exchanged for initial distribution of $100 cash 05/15/1975
Each share Capital Stock no par received second distribution of $49.75 cash 01/02/1976
Each share Capital Stock no par received third and final distribution of $0.3977 cash 12/01/1976

COAL RUN LAND CO. (VA)
Liquidation completed 06/30/1955
Details not available

COAL TECHNOLOGY CORP (DE)
Charter cancelled and declared inoperative and void for non-payment of taxes 03/01/1987

COALCORP MNG INC (BC)
Each share old Common no par exchanged for (0.14285714) share new Common no par 06/14/2007
Name changed to Melior Resources Inc. 09/29/2011

COALITION CROWN MINING CO. (NV)
Charter revoked for failure to file reports and pay fees 03/03/1924

COALSPUR MINES LTD (AUSTRALIA)
Acquired by KC Euroholdings SARL 06/25/2015
Each share Ordinary exchanged for AUD$0.023 cash
Note: Unexchanged certificates will be cancelled and become without value 06/25/2021

COAP SYS INC (NY)
Reorganized under the laws of Delaware as United Vanguard Homes Inc. 03/30/1993
Each share Common 1¢ par exchanged for (0.030003) share Common 1¢ par
(See United Vanguard Homes Inc.)

COAST BANCORP NEW (CA)
Merged into Sierra Bancorp 07/11/2016
Each share Common no par exchanged for (0.1359) share Common no par

COAST BANCORP OLD (CA)
Common no par split (3) for (2) by issuance of (0.5) additional share payable 06/15/1998 to holders of record 05/15/1998
Common no par split (2) for (1) by issuance of (1) additional share payable 02/25/1999 to holders of record 02/05/1999
Merged into Greater Bay Bancorp 05/18/2000
Each share Common no par exchanged for (0.6338) share Common no par
Greater Bay Bancorp merged into Wells Fargo & Co. (New) 10/01/2007

COAST BK (BRADENTON, FL)
Under plan of reorganization each share Common $5 par automatically became (1) share Coast Financial Holdings, Inc. Common $5 par 10/01/2003
(See Coast Financial Holdings, Inc.)

COAST BREWERIES LTD. (CANADA)
Each share old Capital Stock no par exchanged for (10) shares new Capital Stock no par 00/00/1938
Name changed to Lucky Lager Breweries 1954 Ltd. 05/01/1955
Lucky Lager Breweries 1954 Ltd. name changed to Lucky Lager Breweries Ltd. 11/25/1957 which name changed to Labatt Breweries of British Columbia Ltd. 05/24/1967
(See Labatt Breweries of British Columbia Ltd.)

COAST CAP CORP (NV)
Adjustable Rate Preferred no par called for redemption 06/13/1989
Public interest eliminated

COAST CATAMARAN CORP (CA)
Merged into Coleman Co., Inc. 10/05/1976
Each share Common 10¢ par exchanged for $3.75 cash

COAST COML BK (SANTA CRUZ, CA)
Under plan of reorganization each share Common no par automatically became (1) share Coast Bancorp Common no par 07/25/1995
Coast Bancorp merged into Greater Bay Bancorp 05/18/2000 which merged into Wells Fargo & Co. (New) 10/01/2007

COAST COPPER LTD (BC)
Class A $5 par, Class B $5 par and Ordinary $5 par reclassified as Common $5 par 05/01/1967
Acquired by British American Chemical Co. Ltd. 03/30/1980
Each share Common $5 par exchanged for $1 cash

COAST CR CORP (DE)
Money Market Preferred no par called for redemption 12/29/1987
Public interest eliminated

COAST DENTAL SVCS INC (FL)
Reincorporated 08/30/2002
Each share old Common $0.001 par exchanged for (0.33333333) share new Common $0.001 par 07/17/2001
State of incorporation changed from (DE) to (FL) 08/30/2002
Merged into Intelident Solutions Inc. 07/11/2005
Each share new Common $0.001 par exchanged for $9.25 cash

COAST DIAMOND VENTURES INC (BC)
Recapitalized as Avcan Global Systems Inc. 07/04/1994
Each share Common no par exchanged for (0.33333333) share Common no par
Avcan Global Systems Inc. recapitalized as ASC Avcan Systems Corp. 04/21/1999 which recapitalized as Avcan Systems Inc. (BC) 09/07/2001 which reincorporated in Canada as Optimal Geomatics Inc. 10/09/2003 which merged into Aeroquest International Ltd. 09/30/2009
(See Aeroquest International Ltd.)

COAST DISTR SYS INC (DE)
Reincorporated 05/01/1998
Name and state of incorporation changed from Coast Distribution System (CA) to Coast Distribution System, Inc. (DE) and Common no par changed to $0.001 par 05/01/1998
Acquired by LKQ Corp. 08/19/2015
Each share Common $0.001 par exchanged for $5.50 cash

COAST EXPLORATION CO. (NV)
Liquidation completed
Each share Common $1 par stamped to indicate initial distribution of $1 cash 09/30/1966
Each share Stamped Common $1 par exchanged for second and final distribution of $0.04 cash 12/14/1966

COAST EXPLS LTD (BC)
Struck off register and declared dissolved for failure to file returns 04/14/1975

COAST FALCON RES LTD (BC)
Reorganized under the laws of Yukon as Inside Holdings Inc. 10/06/2000
Each share Common no par exchanged for (0.1) share Common no par to reflect a (1) for (1,000) reverse split followed by a (100) for (1) forward split
Inside Holdings Inc. name changed to SHEP Technologies Inc. 10/07/2002
(See SHEP Technologies Inc.)

COAST FED LITIGATION CONTINGENT PMT RTS TR (DE)
Trust terminated 5/30/2003
No equity for holders of rights certificates

COAST FED SVGS & LN ASSN SARASOTA FLA (USA)
Merged into Palmer Financial Corp. 10/31/1989
Each share Common 1¢ par exchanged for $15 cash

COAST FINL HLDGS INC (FL)
Acquired by First Banks, Inc. 11/30/2007
Each share Common $5 par exchanged for $1.86 cash

COAST GUARANTY CO. (CA)
Liquidated 00/00/1939
Details not available

COAST INDL HI TECH FABRICATING LTD (BC)
Name changed to Maximum Resources Inc. 03/21/1994
Maximum Resources Inc. recapitalized as Maximum Ventures Inc. 05/31/1999 which recapitalized as Whistler Gold Exploration Inc. 10/23/2009

COAST MFG INC (DE)
Common 10¢ par split (2) for (1) by issuance of (1) additional share 11/15/1979
Common 10¢ par split (3) for (2) by issuance of (0.5) additional share 08/01/1980
Common 10¢ par split (3) for (2) by issuance of (0.5) additional share 11/16/1981
Liquidation completed
Each share Common 10¢ par received initial distribution of $4.26 cash 12/30/1986
Each share Common 10¢ par received second distribution of $0.50 cash 09/08/1987
Each share Common 10¢ par received third distribution of $0.40 cash 12/11/1987
Each share Common 10¢ par received fourth and final distribution of $0.3038737 cash 01/07/1991
Note: Certificates were not required to be surrendered and are without value

COAST MTN PWR CORP (BC)
Acquired by NovaGold Resources Inc. (NS) 08/03/2006
Each share Common no par exchanged for (0.1245) share Common no par
NovaGold Resources Inc. (NS) reincorporated in British Columbia 06/12/2013

COAST PHOTO MFG INC (DE)
Name changed to Coast Manufacturing Co., Inc. 05/29/1979
(See Coast Manufacturing Co., Inc.)

COAST R V INC (CA)
Name changed to Coast Distribution System (CA) 06/01/1988
Coast Distribution System (CA) reincorporated in Delaware as Coast Distribution System, Inc. 05/01/1998
(See Coast Distribution System, Inc.)

COAST RANGE RES LTD (BC)
Struck off register and declared dissolved for failure to file returns 02/26/1993

COAST ROTORS CO. (CA)
Dissolved 11/01/1962
No stockholders' equity

COAST SVGS & LN ASSN LOS ANGELES (CA)
Reorganized under the laws of Delaware as Coast Savings Financial Inc. 06/15/1989
Coast Savings Financial Inc. merged into Ahmanson (H.F.) & Co. 02/13/1998 which merged into Washington Mutual, Inc. 10/01/1998
(See Washington Mutual, Inc.)

COAST SVGS FINL INC (DE)
Merged into Ahmanson (H.F.) & Co. 02/13/1998
Each share Common no par exchanged for (0.8082) share Common no par and (1) Coast Federal Litigation Contingent Payment Rights Trust Certificate
(See Coast Federal Litigation Contingent Payment Rights Trust)
Ahmanson (H.F.) & Co. merged into Washington Mutual, Inc. 10/01/1998
(See Washington Mutual, Inc.)

COAST SILVER MINES LTD (BC)
Recapitalized as Consolidated Coast Silver Mines Ltd. 06/02/1972
Each share Common 50¢ par exchanged for (0.142857) share Common no par
Consolidated Coast Silver Mines Ltd. recapitalized as Newcoast Silver Mines Ltd. 05/17/1976 which recapitalized as Southern Silver Exploration Corp. 07/16/2004

COAST TIRE & RUBBER CO. (CA)
Charter revoked for failure to file reports and pay fees 03/05/1937

COAST TO COAST INC (NV)
Charter revoked for failure to file reports and pay fees 03/01/1995

COAST VALLEY GAS & ELECTRIC CO.
Acquired by Pacific Gas & Electric Co. 00/00/1928
Details not available

COAST WHSL APPLIANCES INC (CANADA)
Acquired by CWAL Investments Ltd. 09/02/2014
Each share Common no par exchanged for $4.65 cash

COAST WHSL APPLIANCES INCOME FD (AB)
Under plan of reorganization each Unit automatically became (1) share Coast Wholesale Appliances Inc. (Canada) Common no par 01/06/2011
(See Coast Wholesale Appliances Inc. (Canada))

COASTAL ACCEPTANCE CORP. (NH)
Dissolved 12/29/1970
No stockholders' equity

COASTAL AIRWAYS, INC.
Liquidated 00/00/1930
Details not available

COASTAL BANC SVGS ASSN (TX)
Under plan of reorganization each share Common $0.00017 par automatically became (1) share Coastal Bancorp, Inc. Common $0.00017 par 07/31/1994
9% Preferred Ser. A no par called for redemption at $25 plus $0.185 accrued dividends on 07/15/2002
(See Coastal Bancorp, Inc.)

COASTAL BANCORP (ME)
Merged into Suffield Financial Corp. 04/01/1987
Each share Common $1 par exchanged for (2.25655) shares Common $1 par
Suffield Financial Corp. name changed to First Coastal Corp. 05/15/1992
(See First Coastal Corp.)

COASTAL BANCORP INC (TX)
9.12% Preferred Ser. A no par called for redemption at $25 plus $0.19633 accrued dividends on 07/31/2003
Merged into Hibernia Corp. 05/13/2004
Each share Common $0.00017 par exchanged for $41.50 cash

COASTAL BANCSHARES ACQUISITION CORP (DE)
Completely liquidated 03/16/2007
Each share Common 1¢ par exchanged for first and final distribution of $5.50 cash

COASTAL BANKSHARES INC (GA)
Merged into Ameris Bancorp 06/30/2014
Each share Common no par exchanged for (0.4671) share Common $1 par

COASTAL BKG CO INC (SC)
Stock Dividends - 5% payable 03/26/2004 to holders of record 03/12/2004; 5% payable 12/15/2005 to holders of record 12/01/2005
Ex date - 11/29/2005; 5% payable 12/14/2007 to holders of record 11/30/2007 Ex date - 11/28/2007
Acquired by First Federal Bancorp, Inc. 04/03/2018
Each share Common 1¢ par exchanged for $21.50 cash

COASTAL CAP TR I (DE)
9% Trust Preferred Securities called for redemption at $25 plus $0.5625 accrued dividends on 06/30/2007

COASTAL CARIBBEAN OILS, INC. (PANAMA)
Under plan of reorganization each VTC for Common 10¢ par became (1) VTC for Common 1s par of Coastal Caribbean Oils & Minerals, Ltd. 06/18/1962

COASTAL CHEMICAL CORP. (MS)
Merged into Mississippi Chemical Corp. (New) 06/30/1972
Each share Class A Common $25 par exchanged for (1) share Mixed Ser. IV Common $15 par
Each share Class C Common $25 par or Class D Common $25 par exchanged for (1) share Nitrogen Ser. II Common $15 par
Mississippi Chemical Corp. (New) reorganized as Terra Industries Inc. 12/21/2004 which merged into CF Industries Holdings, Inc. 04/15/2010

COASTAL CMNTY BK (EVERETT, WA)
Stock Dividend - 20% payable 11/26/1999 to holders of record 11/26/1999
Under plan of reorganization each share share Common automatically became (1) share Coastal Financial Corp. (WA) Common 10/01/2003

COASTAL CONTACTS INC (CANADA)
Each share old Common no par exchanged for (0.5) share new Common no par 09/05/2012
Acquired by Essilor International S.A. 05/01/2014
Each share Common no par exchanged for $12.45 cash

COASTAL CORP (DE)
Common $0.33333333 par split (3) for (2) by issuance of (0.5) additional share 06/14/1985
Non-Transferable Conv. Class A Common $0.33333333 par split (3) for (2) by issuance of (0.5) additional share 06/14/1985
Common $0.33333333 par split (3) for (2) by issuance of (0.5) additional share 03/19/1987
Non-Transferable Conv. Class A Common $0.33333333 par split (3) for (2) by issuance of (0.5) additional share 03/19/1987
Variable Rate Preferred Ser. F $0.33333333 par called for redemption 04/06/1987
Increasing Rate Preferred Ser. E $0.33333333 par called for redemption 03/26/1988
$2.1125 Conv. Exchangeable Preferred Ser. G $0.33333333 par called for redemption 11/23/1988
8.5% Preferred Ser. H $0.33333333 par called for redemption at $25 plus $0.182986 accrued dividends on 04/15/1998
Common $0.33333333 par split (2) for (1) by issuance of (1) additional share payable 07/01/1998 to holders of record 05/29/1998 Ex date - 07/02/1998
Non-Transferable Conv. Class A Common $0.33333333 par split (3) for (2) by issuance of (0.5) additional share payable 07/01/1998 to holders of record 05/29/1998 Ex date - 07/02/1998
Merged into El Paso Energy Corp. 01/29/2001
Each share $1.19 Conv. Preferred Ser. A $0.33333333 par exchanged for (9.133) shares Common $3 par
Each share $1.83 Conv. Preferred Ser. B $0.33333333 par exchanged for (9.133) shares Common $3 par
Each share $5 Preferred Ser. C $0.33333333 par exchanged for (17.98) shares Common $3 par
Each share Common $0.33333333 par exchanged for (1.23) shares Common $3 par
Each share Conv. Class A Common $0.333333 par exchanged for (1.23) shares Common $3 par
(See El Paso Corp.)
Name changed to El Paso CPG Co. 01/30/2001
(See El Paso CPG Co.)

COASTAL DRILLING PROGRAM LTD (TX)
Units of Ltd. Partnership Int.-1985 completely liquidated 04/00/1995
Details not available
Units of Ltd. Partnership Int.-1986 completely liquidated 04/03/1996
Details not available
Units of Ltd. Partnership Int.-1987 completely liquidated 04/01/1997
Details not available

COASTAL DYNAMICS CORP (CA)
Class A Common 50¢ par reclassified as Common 50¢ par 11/14/1969
Merged into Chemetron Corp. 07/30/1973
Each share Common 50¢ par exchanged for (0.6916) share Common $1 par
Chemetron Corp. merged into Allegheny Ludlum Industries, Inc. 11/30/1977 which name changed to Allegheny International Inc. 04/29/1981
(See Allegheny International Inc.)

COASTAL ENERGY CO (CAYMAN ISLANDS)
Each share Common USD$0.01 par exchanged for (0.25) share Common USD$0.04 par 11/07/2007
Acquired by Condor Acquisition (Cayman) Ltd. 01/17/2014
Each share Common USD$0.04 par exchanged for CAD$19 cash
Note: Unexchanged certificates will be cancelled and become without value 01/17/2020

COASTAL FED SVGS BK (MYRTLE BEACH, SC)
Under plan of reorganization each share Common $1 par automatically became (1) share Coastal Financial Corp. (DE) Common 1¢ par 11/06/1991
Coastal Financial Corp. (DE) merged into BB&T Corp. 05/01/2007

COASTAL FIN I (DE)
8.375% Trust Originated Preferred Securities called for redemption at $25 on 02/08/2006

COASTAL FINANCE CORP. (DE)
Charter cancelled and declared inoperative and void for non-payment of taxes 04/01/1958

COASTAL FINL CORP (CO)
Recapitalized as BDR Industries Inc. 11/17/1994
Each share Common no par exchanged for (0.004) share Common no par
BDR Industries Inc. name changed to Conectisys Corp. 10/16/1995

COASTAL FINL CORP (DE)
Common 1¢ par split (3) for (2) by issuance of (0.5) additional share 02/26/1993
Common 1¢ par split (3) for (2) by issuance of (0.5) additional share 09/17/1993
Common 1¢ par split (3) for (2) by issuance of (0.5) additional share 02/04/1994

Common 1¢ par split (5) for (4) by issuance of (0.25) additional share payable 02/07/1996 to holders of record 01/23/1996
Common 1¢ par split (5) for (4) by issuance of (0.25) additional share payable 07/12/1996 to holders of record 06/28/1996
Common 1¢ par split (4) for (3) by issuance of (0.33333333) additional share payable 05/23/1997 to holders of record 05/09/1997
Common 1¢ par split (4) for (3) by issuance of (0.33333333) additional share payable 06/03/1998 to holders of record 05/20/1998
Common 1¢ par split (3) for (2) by issuance of (0.5) additional share payable 08/28/2001 to holders of record 08/14/2001 Ex date - 08/29/2001
Stock Dividends - 15% 08/28/1992; 5% payable 06/30/1995 to holders of record 06/16/1995; 5% payable 12/15/1999 to holders of record 12/01/1999; 10% payable 04/11/2000 to holders of record 03/28/2000; 10% payable 06/24/2003 to holders of record 06/10/2003 Ex date - 06/06/2003; 10% payable 09/26/2003 to holders of record 09/12/2003 Ex date - 09/10/2003; 10% payable 03/24/2004 to holders of record 03/10/2004; 10% payable 08/27/2004 to holders of record 08/13/2004; 10% payable 01/20/2005 to holders of record 01/06/2005 Ex date - 01/04/2005; 10% payable 11/25/2005 to holders of record 11/10/2005 Ex date - 11/08/2005; 10% payable 09/29/2006 to holders of record 09/08/2006 Ex date - 09/06/2006
Merged into BB&T Corp. 05/01/2007
Each share Common 1¢ par exchanged for (0.385) share Common $5 par

COASTAL FOODS INC (TX)
Each share old Common 1¢ par exchanged for (0.25) share new Common 1¢ par 08/25/2005
Name changed to Newberry Specialty Bakers, Inc. 01/28/2016

COASTAL GOLD CORP (ON)
Merged into First Mining Finance Corp. 07/10/2015
Each share Common no par exchanged for (0.1625) share Common no par
First Mining Finance Corp. name changed to First Mining Gold Corp. 01/11/2018

COASTAL GROUP INC (CANADA)
Merged into Continental (CBOC) Corp. 08/30/2002
Each Dividend Share no par exchanged for (1) Dividend Share no par
Each Multiple Share no par exchanged for (0.8) Multiple Share no par
Each Subordinate Share no par exchanged for (0.8) Subordinate Share no par
Continental (CBOC) Corp. name changed to Stonington Capital Corp. 06/22/2004 which merged into Pyxis Capital Inc. 02/27/2006
(See Pyxis Capital Inc.)

COASTAL HEALTHCARE GROUP INC (DE)
Reincorporated 06/01/1992
State of incorporation changed from (NC) to (DE) 06/01/1992
Name changed to Coastal Physician Group, Inc. 05/17/1995
Coastal Physician Group, Inc. name changed to Phyamerica Physician Group, Inc. 08/02/1999
(See Phymamerica Physician Group, Inc.)

COASTAL HLDGS INC (NV)
Each share old Common 1¢ par exchanged for (0.00083333) share new Common 1¢ par 11/20/2003
Each share new Common 1¢ par exchanged again for (0.0004) share new Common 1¢ par 10/11/2006
Name changed to Canadian Blue Gold, Inc. 10/18/2007
Canadian Blue Gold, Inc. recapitalized as Boreal Water Collection, Inc. 03/19/2008
(See Boreal Water Collection, Inc.)

COASTAL INCOME CORP (CANADA)
Sr. Retractable Preferred called for redemption at $25.20 plus $0.31071 accrued dividends 03/20/2007

COASTAL INDS INC (OH)
Stock Dividend - 20% 03/15/1974
Chapter 11 Federal Bankruptcy proceedings dismissed 06/22/1987
No stockholders' equity

COASTAL INTEGRATED SVCS INC (WY)
Reorganized 04/01/2014
Reorganized from Nevada to Wyoming 04/01/2014
Each share Common $0.001 par exchanged for (0.0004) share Common $0.001 par
Recapitalized as Simply innovative Products, Inc. 02/07/2017
Each share Common $0.001 par exchanged for (0.0004) share Common $0.001 par
Simply Innovative Products, Inc. name changed to White Label Liquid, Inc. 08/10/2018

COASTAL INTL LTD (BERMUDA)
Name changed to Challenger International, Ltd. 12/06/1985
Challenger International, Ltd. name changed to Intelect Communications Systems Ltd. (Bermuda) 12/15/1995 which reincorporated in Delaware as Intelect Communications Inc. 12/05/1997 which name changed to TeraForce Technology Corp. 01/31/2001
(See TeraForce Technology Corp.)

COASTAL INVT CORP (UT)
Proclaimed dissolved for failure to pay taxes 12/31/1983

COASTAL MEDIA INC (NV)
Name changed to Blugrass Energy, Inc. 10/01/2008
Blugrass Energy, Inc. recapitalized as Nogal Energy, Inc. 08/12/2013 which name changed to Novamex Energy, Inc. 12/23/2014

COASTAL MNG LTD (QC)
Recapitalized as Torcan Explorations Ltd. 03/22/1968
Each share Capital Stock $1 par exchanged for (0.33333333) share Capital Stock $1 par
(See Torcan Explorations Ltd.)

COASTAL 1981 DEVELOPMENT PROGRAM, LTD. (TX)
Program terminated 01/01/1991
Details not available

COASTAL OILS LTD. (AB)
Acquired by Federated Petroleums Ltd. 00/00/1951
Each share Capital Stock no par exchanged for (0.14285714) share Capital Stock no par
Federated Petroleums Ltd. merged into Home Oil Co. Ltd. 00/00/1955
(See Home Oil Co. Ltd.)

COASTAL PHYSICIAN GROUP INC (DE)
Name changed to Phyamerica Physician Group, Inc. 08/02/1999
(See Phyamerica Physician Group, Inc.)

COASTAL PLAIN LIFE INS CO (NC)
Common $5 par changed to $2.50 par and (1) additional share issued 04/15/1960
$1.35 Conv. Preferred $5 par called for redemption 04/10/1970
Merged into United Insurance Co. of America 04/01/1977
Each share Common $2.50 par exchanged for $40.67 cash

COASTAL PLAINS OIL CO. (NV)
Recapitalized as Western Oil Corp. 07/25/1960
Each share Common 10¢ par exchanged for (0.1) share Common $1 par
(See Western Oil Corp.)

COASTAL PLAN MGMT CORP (NY)
Merged out of existence 12/06/1984
Details not available

COASTAL PRODUCTS CORP. (FL)
Adjudicated bankrupt 11/20/1968
No stockholders' equity

COASTAL PUBLICATIONS CORP. (NY)
Assets liquidated for benefit of creditors 03/19/1965
No stockholders' equity

COASTAL SVGS BK (PORTLAND, ME)
Under plan of reorganization each share Class A Common $1 par automatically became (1) share Coastal Bancorp Common $1 par 10/27/1986
Coastal Bancorp merged into Suffield Financial Corp. 04/01/1987 which name changed to First Coastal Corp. 05/15/1992
(See First Coastal Corp.)

COASTAL SEC INVT FD (NV)
Name changed to Hanover Fund 00/00/1968
Hanover Fund name changed to F-D Capital Fund 04/00/1970 which merged into Pine Tree Fund, Inc. 11/27/1972
(See Pine Tree Fund, Inc.)

COASTAL SECURITIES ENTERPRISES CORP. (CA)
Completely liquidated 02/27/1967
Each share Capital Stock $1 par exchanged for first and final distribution of (0.16666666) share General Corp. of Ohio Common $1 par
General Corp. of Ohio name changed to General Capital Corp. (OH) 05/13/1971 which reincorporated in Delaware 10/20/1972
(See General Capital Corp. (DE))

COASTAL SVCS GROUP INC (DE)
Reorganized as Unique Pizza & Subs Corp. 03/13/2006
Each share Common $0.0001 par exchanged for (5) shares Common $0.0001 par
Unique Pizza & Subs Corp. name changed to Unique Foods Corp. 06/28/2018

COASTAL SHIP CORP (DE)
Merged into Donmac Corp. 05/16/1968
Each share Capital Stock $1 par exchanged for $87 cash

COASTAL STS CORP (GA)
Merged into Sun Life Insurance Co. of America 05/18/1978
Each share Common $1 par exchanged for $9.75 cash

COASTAL STS GAS CORP (DE)
Name changed to Coastal Corp. 01/01/1980
Coastal Corp. merged into El Paso Energy Corp. 01/29/2001 which name changed to El Paso Corp. 02/05/2001

COASTAL STS GAS PRODUCING CO (DE)
Common $1 par changed to $0.33333333 par and (2) additional shares issued 12/01/1961
Common $0.33333333 par split (2) for (1) by issuance of (1) additional share 01/15/1969
Stock Dividend - 10% 01/08/1968
Under plan of reorganization name changed to Coastal States Gas Corp. and $1.19 Conv. Preferred Ser. A no par changed to $0.33333333 par 01/02/1973
Coastal States Gas Corp. name changed to Coastal Corp. 01/01/1980 which merged into El Paso Energy Corp. 01/29/2001 which name changed to El Paso Corp. 02/05/2001

COASTAL STS LIFE INS CO (GA)
Common $10 par changed to $5 par and (1) additional share issued 05/02/1956
Under plan of merger Common $5 par changed to $2.50 par and (0.66666666) additional share issued 05/08/1957
Common $2.50 par changed to $1.25 par and (1) additional share issued 04/01/1959
Common $1.25 par changed to $1 par and (0.25) additional share issued plus a 20% stock dividend paid 03/01/1965
Stock Dividends - 25% 04/06/1953; 25% 06/01/1955; 10% 06/01/1956; 10% 07/01/1958; 12.5% 08/25/1959; 10% 05/23/1960; 10% 03/02/1964; 10% 08/01/1966
Reorganized as Coastal States Corp. 10/05/1972
Each share Common $1 par exchanged for (1) share Common $1 par
(See Coastal States Corp.)

COASTAL TECHNOLOGIES INC (CA)
Recapitalized as Cyclone Power Technologies, Inc. 07/02/2007
Each share Common $0.16666666 par exchanged for (0.0001) share Common $0.16666666 par

COASTAL TIMBER LAND & PULP CORP. (FL)
Name changed to Coastal Products Corp. 01/11/1966
(See Coastal Products Corp.)

COASTAL VALUE FD INC (ON)
Sr. Preferred called for redemption at $25.20 plus $0.2125 accrued dividends on 02/21/2007

COASTAL VENTURES INC (CO)
Name changed to Southnet Corp. 03/22/1988

COASTAMERICA CORP (DE)
Merged into American Hoist & Derrick Co. 12/27/1988
Each share Common 1¢ par exchanged for $10.50 cash

COASTCAST CORP (CA)
Name changed to Western Metals Corp. 11/22/2005

COASTECH INC (NV)
Name changed to Tufco International, Inc. 07/09/1990

COASTLAND CORP (FL)
Common 10¢ par split (5) for (4) by issuance of (0.25) additional share 03/21/1980
Common 10¢ par split (5) for (4) by issuance of (0.25) additional share 08/22/1980
Each share Common 10¢ par exchanged for (0.5) share Common 20¢ par 10/21/1982
Each share Common 20¢ par exchanged for (1/3) share Common $0.025 par 11/30/1993
Voluntarily dissolved 05/14/1985
Details not available

COASTLAND ENTERPRISES INC. (FL)
Proclaimed dissolved for failure to file reports and pay fees 05/23/1973

COASTLAND OIL CORP.
Merged into Salt Dome Oil Corp. 00/00/1936
Details not available

COASTLINE CORPORATE SVCS INC (FL)
Reincorporated under the laws of Nevada as Dakota Gold Corp. 11/26/2010
Dakota Gold Corp. name changed to American Magna Corp. 07/02/2013

COASTLINE RES LTD (BC)
Name changed 03/29/1988
Name changed from Coastline Petroleum Ltd. to Coastline Resources Ltd. 03/29/1988
Name changed to Remco Environmental Services Ltd. 04/13/1992
Remco Environmental Services Ltd. name changed to La Plata Gold Corp. 06/30/1994 which name changed to Alphamin Resources Corp. (BC) 10/27/2008 which reincorporated in Mauritius 09/30/2014

COASTORO RES LTD (BC)
Merged into T & H Resources Ltd. (ON) 11/15/1988
Each share Common no par exchanged for (0.5) share Common no par
T & H Resources Ltd. (ON) reorganized in Canada as LAB International Inc. 05/16/2002 which name changed to Akela Pharma Inc. 07/13/2007
(See Akela Pharma Inc.)

COASTPORT CAP INC (BC)
Reincorporated 06/01/2005
Place of incorporation changed from (AB) to (BC) 06/01/2005
Reincorporated under the laws of Alberta as Donnybrook Energy Inc. 08/30/2010
Donnybrook Energy Inc. recapitalized as Stonehaven Exploration Ltd. 10/29/2014 which name changed to Front Range Resources Ltd. 08/11/2016 which recapitalized as Arrow Exploration Corp. 10/05/2018

COASTWAY BANCORP INC (MD)
Acquired by HarborOne Bancorp, Inc. 10/05/2018
Each share Common 1¢ par exchanged for $28.25 cash

COASTWIDE ENERGY SVCS INC (DE)
Merged into Tesoro Petroleum Corp. 02/20/1996
Each share Common 1¢ par exchanged for (0.41) share Common $0.16666666 par and $2.55 cash
Tesoro Petroleum Corp. name changed to Tesoro Corp. 11/08/2004 which name changed to Andeavor 08/01/2017 which merged into Marathon Petroleum Corp. 10/01/2018

COATED SALES INC (NJ)
Filed a petition under Chapter 11 Federal Bankruptcy Code 06/16/1988
No stockholders' equity

COATINGS UNLIMITED INC (MA)
Name changed to America's Productions, Inc. (MA) 09/23/1972
America's Productions, Inc. (MA) reincorporated in Delaware 01/10/1973
(See America's Productions, Inc.)

COATS (J. & P.) LTD. (ENGLAND)
Merged into Coats (J. & P.), Patons & Baldwins Ltd. on a (1.5) for (1) basis 03/20/1961
Coats (J. & P.), Patons & Baldwins Ltd. name changed to Coats Patons Ltd. 06/26/1967
(See Coats Patons Ltd.)

COATS PATONS LTD (ENGLAND)
Name changed 06/26/1967
Name changed from Coats (J. & P.) Patons & Baldwins Ltd. to Coats Patons Ltd. 06/26/1967
ADR's for Ordinary £1 par changed to 5s par 06/19/1969
ADR's for Ordinary 5s par changed to 25p par per currency change 02/15/1971
Acquired by Vantona Viyella PLC 00/00/1986
Details not available

COATS PLC (UNITED KINGDOM)
Name changed 05/24/2001
Name changed from Coats Viyella PLC to Coats PLC 05/24/2001
Acquired by Avenue Acquisition Co. 08/08/2003
Each Sponsored ADR for Ordinary exchanged for $2.69216 cash

COATTEC INDS INC (WA)
Charter expired 05/31/2007

COB-SIL-ORE MINES LTD. (ON)
Name changed to Norbank Explorations Ltd. 01/00/1959
(See Norbank Explorations Ltd.)

COBALIS CORP (NV)
Each share old Common $0.001 par exchanged for (1) share new Common $0.001 par 08/23/2004
Note: Unexchanged certificates were cancelled and became without value 10/12/2004
Chapter 11 bankrutpcy proceedings converted to Chapter 7 on 08/22/2011
Stockholders' equity unlikely

COBALT BADGER SILVER MINES LTD. (ON)
Charter cancelled 05/00/1958

COBALT CENTRAL MINES CO. (ME)
Charter suspended for non-payment of taxes 00/00/1913

COBALT CHEMICAL & REFINERY CO. LTD.
Merged into Cobalt Chemicals Ltd. 00/00/1952
Each share Capital Stock $1 par exchanged for (0.33333333) share Capital Stock no par
Cobalt Chemicals Ltd. merged into Quebec Metallurgical Industries Ltd. 00/00/1954 which recapitalized as Q.M.I. Minerals Ltd. 05/31/1963 which merged into Indusmin Ltd. 11/06/1968
(See Indusmin Ltd.)

COBALT CHEMICALS LTD. (ON)
Merged into Quebec Metallurgical Industries Ltd. 00/00/1954
Each share Common exchanged for (0.2) share Common
Quebec Metallurgical Industries Ltd. recapitalized as Q.M.I. Minerals Ltd. 05/31/1963 which merged into Indusmin Ltd. 11/06/1968
(See Indusmin Ltd.)

COBALT COAL CORP (AB)
Recapitalized as Cobalt Coal Ltd. 07/08/2011
Each share Common no par exchanged for (0.1) share Common no par

COBALT CONSOLIDATED MINING CORP. LTD. (ON)
Recapitalized as Agnico Mines Ltd. 10/25/1957
Each (3.5) shares Capital Stock $1 par exchanged for (1) share Capital Stock $1 par
Agnico Mines Ltd. merged into Agnico-Eagle Mines Ltd. 06/01/1972 which name changed to Agnico Eagle Mines Ltd. 04/30/2013

COBALT CONTACT MINES LTD.
Acquired by York Bousquet Gold Mines Ltd. 00/00/1938
Each share Common exchanged for (0.1) share Common
(See York Bousquet Gold Mines Ltd.)

COBALT CORP (WI)
Merged into WellPoint Health Networks Inc. 09/24/2003
Each share Common no par exchanged for (0.1233) share Common 1¢ par and $10.25 cash
WellPoint Health Networks Inc. merged into WellPoint, Inc. 12/01/2004 which name changed to Anthem, Inc. (New) 12/03/2014

COBALT FRONTENAC MINING CO. LTD. (ON)
Liquidated 00/00/1938
Details not available

COBALT GROUP INC (WA)
Acquired by Warburg Pincus Equity Partners, L.P. 11/13/2001
Each share Common 1¢ par exchanged for $3.50 cash

COBALT INTL ENERGY INC (DE)
Each share old Common 1¢ par exchanged for (0.06666666) share new Common 1¢ par 06/26/2017
Plan of reorganization under Chapter 11 Federal Bankruptcy proceedings effective 04/10/2018
No stockholders' equity

COBALT LODE SILVER MINES LTD. (ON)
Merged into Cobalt Consolidated Mining Corp. Ltd. 00/00/1953
Each share Preference $1 par exchanged for (0.2) share Capital Stock $1 par
Each share Common $1 par exchanged for (0.125) share Capital Stock $1 par
Cobalt Consolidated Mining Corp. Ltd. recapitalized as Agnico Mines Ltd. 10/25/1957 which merged into Agnico-Eagle Mines Ltd. 06/01/1972 which name changed to Agnico Eagle Mines Ltd. 04/30/2013

COBALT NETWORKS INC (DE)
Merged into Sun Microsystems, Inc. 12/07/2000
Each share Common $0.001 par exchanged for (1) share Common $0.00067 par
(See Sun Microsystems, Inc.)

COBALT PRODUCTS LTD. (ON)
Merged into Resource Exploration & Development Co. Ltd. 06/11/1968
Each share Capital Stock no par exchanged for (10.989) shares Capital Stock no par
(See Resource Exploration & Development Co., Ltd.)

COBALT YELLOWKNIFE MINES LTD.
Name changed to Waddington Mining Corp. Ltd. 00/00/1949
Waddington Mining Corp. Ltd. name changed to Cop-Ex Mining Corp. Ltd. 03/28/1968 which name changed to Amalgamated Cop-Ex Resources Ltd. 08/25/1981

COBALTECH MNG INC (BC)
Merged into First Cobalt Corp. (BC) 12/04/2017
Each share Common no par exchanged for (0.2632) share Common no par
Note: Unexchanged certificates will be cancelled and become without value 12/04/2023
First Cobalt Corp. (BC) reincorporated in Canada 09/04/2018

COBALTER INC (FL)
Name changed to Cartis, Inc. 01/27/1999

COBANCO INC (CA)
Merged into Pacific Western Bancshares (CA) 05/18/1987
Each share Common no par exchanged for (2.38) shares Common no par
Pacific Western Banchares (CA) reincorporated in Delaware as Pacific Western Bancshares, Inc. 06/30/1989 which merged into Comerica, Inc. 03/30/1994

COBANCORP INC (OH)
Common $5 par split (4) for (3) by issuance of (0.33333333) additional share 07/23/1993
Common $5 par split (4) for (3) by issuance of (0.33333333) additional share 02/22/1994
Merged into FirstMerit Corp. 05/22/1998
Each share Common $5 par exchanged for Common no par and cash equal to a total of $44.50 payable in 83% stock and 17% cash
FirstMerit Corp. merged into Huntington Bancshares Inc. 08/16/2016

COBANK ACB (DENVER, CO)
7% 144A Perpetual Preferred Ser. B called for redemption at $50 on 10/01/2012
7.814% 144A Perpetual Preferred Ser. A called for redemption at $50 on 10/01/2012
144A Perpetual Preferred Ser. C called for redemption at $50 on 07/01/2013
Non-Cum. Subordinate Perpetual Preferred Ser. D called for redemption at $50 plus $1.375 accrued dividends on 10/01/2014

COBANK FINL CORP (CA)
Merged into ValliCorp Holdings, Inc. 03/23/1996
Each share Common $5 par exchanged for (1.1875) shares Common 1¢ par
ValliCorp Holdings, Inc. merged into Westamerica Bancorporation 04/12/1997

COBATEC INC (ON)
Ceased operations 06/00/2012

COBB, ATKINS, BOYD & EGGLESTON, INC. (AR)
Through purchase offer 100% acquired by officers of the company as of 07/00/1969
Public interest eliminated

COBB RES CORP (NM)
Name changed 01/02/1981
Stock Dividend - 100% 07/22/1978
Name changed from Cobb Nuclear Corp. to Cobb Resources Corp. 01/02/1981
Common 1¢ par split (2) for (1) by issuance of (1) additional share 03/20/1981
Each share old Common 1¢ par exchanged for (0.1) share new Common 1¢ par 02/17/2000
Name changed to Family Room Entertainment Corp. 04/26/2000

COBBLESTONE HLDGS INC (DE)
Merged into Meditrust Corp. 05/29/1998
Each share Common 1¢ par exchanged for (3.867) Paired Certificates
Meditrust Corp. name changed to La Quinta Properties, Inc. 06/20/2001 which reorganized as La Quinta Corp. 01/02/2002
(See La Quinta Corp.)

COBBS INC (FL)
Adjudicated bankrupt 06/05/1973
Stockholders' equity unlikely

COBE LABS INC (CO)
Common no par split (3) for (2) by issuance of (0.5) additional share 10/29/1976
Common no par split (2) for (1) by issuance of (1) additional share 06/10/1983

Common no par split (3) for (2) by issuance of (0.5) additional share 01/22/1986
Merged into Polo Acquisition Corp. 07/02/1990
Each share Common no par exchanged for $37 cash

COBEQUID LIFE SCIENCES INC (CANADA)
Name changed 06/23/1992
Reincorporated 09/23/1992
Name changed from Cobequid Resources Ltd. to Cobequid Life Sciences Inc. 06/23/1992
Place of incorporation changed from (NS) to (Canada) 09/23/1992
Acquired by Novartis Animal Health Inc. 06/21/2000
Each share Common no par exchanged for $4 cash

COBI FOODS INC (ON)
Acquired by Minas Group Ltd. 10/12/1995
Each share Common no par exchanged for $0.37 cash

COBIZ FINANCIAL INC (CO)
Name changed 05/17/2007
Common 1¢ par split (3) for (2) by issuance of (0.5) additional share payable 08/13/2001 to holders of record 07/30/2001 Ex date - 08/14/2001
Common 1¢ par split (3) for (2) by issuance of (0.5) additional share payable 05/03/2004 to holders of record 04/26/2004
Name changed from CoBiz Inc. to CoBiz Financial Inc. 05/17/2007
Merged into BOK Financial Corp. 09/28/2018
Each share Common 1¢ par exchanged for (0.17) share Common $0.00006 par and $5.70 cash

COBLE DAIRY PRODS COOP INC (NC)
6% Class A Preferred $20 par called for redemption 08/31/1966
4-1/2% Class B Preferred $100 par called for redemption 05/01/1969
4% Class C Preferred $100 par called for redemption 05/01/1969
Merged into Mid-American Dairymen, Inc. 12/30/1994
Details not available

COBLE DAIRY PRODUCTS, INC. (NC)
Merged into Coble Dairy Products Cooperative, Inc. 03/28/1955
Each share 5% Preferred $50 par exchanged for (1) share 6% Class A Preferred $50 par and $0.625 cash
(See Coble Dairy Products Cooperative, Inc.)

COBRA ELECTRS CORP (DE)
Acquired by Venom Electronics Holdings, Inc. 10/08/2014
Each share Common $0.33333333 par exchanged for $4.30 cash

COBRA ENTERPRISES LTD (BC)
Recapitalized as MVS Modular Vehicle Systems Ltd. 8/22/94
Each share Common no par exchanged for (0.2) share Common no par
MVS Modular Vehicle Systems Ltd. recapitalized as Cobra Pacific Systems Inc. 3/28/96 which name changed to Marathon Foods Inc. 2/16/98

COBRA GOLF INC (DE)
Common $0.001 par split (2) for (1) by issuance of (1) additional share 10/11/94
Merged into American Brands, Inc. 1/26/96
Each share Common $0.001 par exchanged for $36 cash

COBRA INDS INC (DE)
Plan of reorganization under Chapter 11 Federal Bankruptcy Code effective 12/31/2004
No stockholders' equity

COBRA METALS & MINERALS INC (CANADA)
Recapitalized as Bathurst Base Metals Inc. 02/01/1990
Each share Common no par exchanged for (0.1) share Common no par
Bathurst Base Metals Inc. acquired by Breakwater Resources Ltd. (BC) 09/04/1990 which reincorporated in Canada 05/11/1992
(See Breakwater Resources Ltd.)

COBRA OIL & GAS CO (NV)
Common $0.00001 par split (35) for (1) by issuance of (34) additional shares payable 05/07/2008 to holders of record 05/06/2008
Ex date - 05/08/2008
Name changed to Viper Resources Inc. 11/06/2009
Viper Resources Inc. recapitalized as Rambo Medical Group, Inc. 08/09/2013 which name changed to HK eBus Corp. 09/15/2015

COBRA PAC SYS INC (BC)
Name changed to Marathon Foods Inc. 02/16/1998
(See Marathon Foods Inc.)

COBRA TECHNOLOGIES INC (NV)
Name changed to CeleXx Corp. 10/19/1999
(See CeleXx Corp.)

COBRA VENTURE CORP (AB)
Reincorporated under the laws of British Columbia 07/25/2014

COBRATECH INTL INC (NV)
Recapitalized as MetaSource Group, Inc. 05/28/2002
Each share Common $0.001 par exchanged for (0.53267991) share Common $0.001 par
(See MetaSource Group, Inc.)

COBRE EXPL CORP (BC)
Each share old Common no par exchanged for (0.33333333) share new Common no par 02/03/2010
Name changed to Calico Resources Corp. 01/28/2011
Calico Resources Corp. merged into Paramount Gold Nevada Corp. 07/07/2016

COBRE EXPL LTD (BC)
Name changed to Mountain-West Resources Inc. 02/06/1984
Mountain-West Resources Inc. name changed to Mountainstar Gold Inc. 04/02/2012

COBRE MNG CO INC (BC)
Acquired by Phelps Dodge Corp. 03/06/1998
Each share Common no par exchanged for $3.85 cash

COBRE (ANITA), USA, INC. (AZ)
Charter revoked for failure to file reports and pay fees 05/18/1966

COBRIZA METALS CORP (BC)
Merged into Candente Copper Corp. 09/12/2013
Each share Common no par exchanged for for (0.5) share Common no par
Note: Unexchanged certificates will be cancelled and become without value 09/12/2019

COBURN CORP AMER (NY)
6% Conv. Preferred $20 par called for redemption 04/30/1968
Under plan of merger name changed to Lincoln American Corp. (NY) 05/01/1972
Lincoln American Corp. (NY) merged into American General Corp. 09/01/1980 which merged into American International Group, Inc. 08/29/2001

COBURN CR INC (NY)
Name changed to Coburn Corp. of America 07/27/1966
Coburn Corp. of America name changed to Lincoln American Corp. (NY) 05/01/1972 which merged into American General Corp. 09/01/1980 which merged into American International Group, Inc. 08/29/2001

COBURN INTERNATIONAL CORP. (DE)
Name changed to CIC Leasing Corp. 11/21/1968
CIC Leasing Corp. name changed to CIC Corp. 05/01/1972 which name changed to Firstmark Corp. 05/07/1973
(See Firstmark Corp.)

COBURN OPTICAL INDS INC (DE)
Completely liquidated 08/27/1975
Each share Common $1 par exchanged for first and final distribution of (0.2572) share Revlon, Inc. Common $1 par
(See Revlon, Inc.)

COCA COLA BEVERAGES-CDA (CANADA)
Merged into Enterprises KOC Acquisition Co. Ltd. 09/04/1997
Each share Common no par exchanged for $22 cash

COCA-COLA BOTTLERS JAPAN INC (JAPAN)
Name changed 01/30/2009
Name changed 04/03/2017
Name changed from Coca-Cola West Holdings Co., Ltd. to Coca-Cola West Co., Ltd. 01/30/2009
Name changed from Coca-Cola West Co., Ltd. to Coca-Cola Bottlers Japan, Inc. 04/03/2017
Name changed to Coca-Cola Bottlers Japan Holdings Inc. 01/02/2018

COCA-COLA BOTTLING CO. OF CHICAGO, INC. (DE)
Merged into Coca-Cola Co. 01/31/1961
Each share Common exchanged for (0.33333333) share Common no par

COCA-COLA BOTTLING CO. OF ST. LOUIS (DE)
Each share old Common $1 par exchanged for (4) shares new Common $1 par 00/00/1937
Merged into Associated Coca-Cola Bottling Co., Inc. 05/03/1966
Each share Common $1 par exchanged for (0.4) share Common $1 par
(See Associated Coca-Cola Bottling Co., Inc.)

COCA COLA BOTTLING CO CONS (NC)
Reincorporated under the laws of Delaware 05/14/1980

COCA COLA BOTTLING CO HANNIBAL (MO)
Merged into Hannibal, Missouri Bottling Co. 09/30/1969
Each share Preferred no par exchanged for (1) share $1.25 Conv. Preferred no par
Each share Common $1 par exchanged for (1) share Common no par
(See Hannibal, Missouri Bottling Co.)

COCA COLA BOTTLING CO HARTFORD (DE)
Name changed to Coca-Cola Bottling Co. of Southern New England and Common 1¢ par changed to $6 par 04/14/1970
Coca-Cola Bottling Co. of Southern New England acquired by Coca-Cola Bottling Co. of New York, Inc. 08/24/1973
(See Coca-Cola Bottling Co. of New York, Inc.)

COCA COLA BOTTLING CO LOS ANGELES (CA)
Each share Common $100 par exchanged for (25) shares Common no par 00/00/1939
Common no par split (2) for (1) by issuance of (1) additional share 10/16/1964
Common no par split (2) for (1) by issuance of (1) additional share 02/14/1969
Common no par split (3) for (2) by issuance of (0.5) additional share 05/31/1972
$2 Conv. Preferred Ser. A $5 par called for redemption 07/28/1978
Stock Dividends - 10% 02/21/1964; 50% 12/22/1966
Merged into Northwest Industries, Inc. 08/10/1978
Each share Common no par exchanged for $40 cash

COCA COLA BOTTLING CO MIAMI INC (DE)
Common 10¢ par split (5) for (4) by issuance of (0.25) additional share 05/23/1972
Acquired by Miami Acquisition, Inc. 05/12/1983
Each share Common 10¢ par exchanged for $102 cash

COCA COLA BOTTLING CO MID AMER INC (DE)
Merged into Coca-Cola Bottling Co. of Los Angeles 07/07/1978
Each share Common $1 par exchanged for $27.375 cash

COCA COLA BOTTLING CO MID CAROLINAS (NC)
Name changed to Coca-Cola Bottling Co. Consolidated (NC) 01/09/1973
Coca-Cola Bottling Co. Consolidated (NC) reincorporated in Delaware 05/14/1980

COCA COLA BOTTLING CO N Y INC (DE)
Each share Common no par exchanged for (4) shares Common $1.25 par 09/06/1955
Each share Common $1.25 par exchanged for (2) shares Common $1 par 02/05/1960
Common $1 par changed to 50¢ par and (1) additional share issued 11/17/1970
Common 50¢ par changed to 25¢ par and (1) additional share issued 05/25/1972
Merged into Coca-Cola Co. 08/28/1981
Each share Common 25¢ par exchanged for $10.40 cash

COCA COLA BOTTLING CO SOUTHN NEW ENG (DE)
Acquired by Coca-Cola Bottling Co. of New York, Inc. 08/24/1973
Each share Common $6 par exchanged for (10.501) shares Common 25¢ par
(See Coca-Cola Bottling Co. of New York, Inc.)

COCA COLA BOTTLING MIDWEST INC (MN)
Merged into Twentieth Century-Fox Film Corp. 09/27/1977
Each share Common 50¢ par exchanged for $26 cash

COCA COLA BOTTLING PLTS INC (DE)
Merged into Coca-Cola Bottling Co. of New York, Inc. 06/15/1978
Each share Capital Stock no par exchanged for (12) shares Common 25¢ par
(See Coca-Cola Bottling Co. of New York, Inc.)

COCA COLA CO (DE)
Class A no par called for redemption 00/00/1950

Money Market Preferred Ser. C $1 par called for redemption 11/26/1990
Money Market Preferred Ser. D $1 par called for redemption 12/03/1990
Money Market Preferred Ser. A $1 par called for redemption 12/17/1990
Money Market Preferred Ser. B $1 par called for redemption 02/11/1991
(Additional Information in Active)

COCA-COLA ENTERPRISES INC NEW (DE)
Merged into Coca-Cola European Partners PLC 05/31/2016
Each share Common 1¢ par exchanged for (1) share Ordinary EUR 0.01 par and $14.50 cash

COCA COLA ENTERPRISES INC OLD (DE)
Common $1 par split (3) for (1) by issuance of (2) additional shares payable 05/12/1997 to holders of record 05/01/1997 Ex date - 05/13/1997
Merged into Coca-Cola Enterprises, Inc. (New) 10/02/2010
Each share Common $1 par exchanged for (1) share Common 1¢ par and $10 cash
Coca-Cola Enterprises, Inc. (New) merged into Coca-Cola European Partners PLC 05/31/2016

COCA-COLA FEMSA S A DE C V (MEXICO)
Sponsored ADR's for Ser. L Common 1 New Peso par split (3) for (1) by issuance of (2) additional ADR's payable 01/27/1998 to holders of record 01/22/1998 Ex date - 01/28/1998
Name changed to Coca-Cola FEMSA S.A.B de C.V. 12/05/2006

COCA-COLA HELLENIC BOTTLING CO S A (GREECE)
Sponsored ADR's for Ordinary EUR 0.50 par split (3) for (2) by issuance of (0.5) additional ADR payable 11/20/2007 to holders of record 11/19/2007 Ex date - 11/21/2007
Reincorporated under the laws of Switzerland as Coca-Cola HBC AG 04/24/2013

COCA COLA INTL CORP (DE)
Liquidation completed
Each share Common no par exchanged for initial distribution of (192) shares Coca-Cola Co. Common no par plus $3.50 cash 08/06/1980
Each share Common no par received second and final distribution of $0.269592 cash 12/15/1981

COCA MINES INC (CO)
Merged into Hecla Mining Co. 06/26/1991
Each share Common 1¢ par exchanged for (0.24149) share Common 25¢ par

COCALLEN PORCUPINE GOLD MINES LTD. (ON)
Charter cancelled and declared dissolved for failure to file returns and pay fees 04/14/1956

COCENSYS INC (DE)
Each share old Common $0.001 par exchanged for (0.125) share new Common $0.001 par 04/15/1999
Merged into Purdue Pharma L.P. 09/28/1999
Each share Common $0.001 par exchanged for $1.16 cash

COCHENOUR MARCUS GOLD MINES LTD. (ON)
Name changed to Consolidated Marcus Gold Mines Ltd. 00/00/1956
Consolidated Marcus Gold Mines Ltd. recapitalized as Marcus Energy Inc. 08/26/1988 which recapitalized as Marcus Energy Holdings Inc. 11/27/2000 which name changed to Au Martinique Silver Inc. (ON) 07/21/2005 which reincorporated in Canada as Aura Silver Resources Inc. 08/21/2006

COCHENOUR RED LAKE LTD. (ON)
Recapitalized as Coin Lake Gold Mines, Ltd. 00/00/1936
Each share Capital Stock $1 par exchanged for (0.02127659) share Common $1 par
Coin Lake Gold Mines, Ltd. recapitalized as United Coin Mines Ltd. 12/11/1989 which name changed to Winstaff Ventures Ltd. 06/25/1993 which merged into Romarco Minerals Inc. (ON) 07/11/1995 which reincorporated in British Columbia 06/16/2006 which merged into OceanaGold Corp. 10/01/2015

COCHENOUR WILLANS GOLD MINES LTD (ON)
Capital Stock $1 par changed to no par 07/09/1971
Recapitalized as Wilanour Resources Ltd. 08/22/1979
Each share Capital Stock no par exchanged for (0.2) share Capital Stock no par
Wilanour Resources Ltd. merged into Goldcorp Inc. 02/20/1998

COCHISE ENTERPRISES, INC. (UT)
Merged into Bella Vista Ranches, Inc. 10/08/1975
Each share Capital Stock $1 par exchanged for (1) share Capital Stock no par or $1 cash
(See Bella Vista Ranches, Inc.)

COCHISE RES INC (ON)
Merged into Neatt Corp. 08/01/2001
Each share Class B Preference no par exchanged for (0.05) share Common no par
Each share Common no par exchanged for (0.05) share Common no par
(See Neatt Corp.)

COCHRAN & MCCLUER CO.
Dissolved 00/00/1948
Details not available

COCHRAN EQUIPMENT CO. (CA)
Common $1 par changed to 50¢ par and (1) additional share issued 01/31/1962
Name changed to C. & S. Investment Co. 08/27/1965
(See C. & S. Investment Co.)

COCHRAN FOIL CO. (KY)
Under plan of merger each share 5% Preferred $25 par exchanged for (1) share 5% Cum. Preferred $25 par and each share Common no par exchanged for (1) share Common $5 par 00/00/1950
Common $5 par split (3) for (1) by issuance of (2) additional shares 12/20/1956
Acquired by Anaconda Co. 04/30/1958
Each share Common $5 par exchanged for (0.4) share Common no par
Anaconda Co. merged into Atlantic Richfield Co. (PA) 01/13/1977 which reincorporated in Delaware 05/07/1985 which merged into BP Amoco PLC 04/18/2000 which name changed to BP PLC 05/01/2001

COCHRANE DUNLOP LTD (ON)
Recapitalized 06/18/1975
Stock Dividend - on Preferential Class A - 200% 02/16/1953
Recapitalized from Cochrane-Dunlop Hardware Ltd. to Cochrane-Dunlop Ltd. 06/18/1975
Each share $0.80 Preferential Class A no par exchanged for (4) shares Common no par
Each share Common no par exchanged for (6) shares Common no par
Acquired by Frederick (D.H.) Holdings Ltd. 01/08/1982
Each share Common no par exchanged for $10 cash

COCHRANE FURNITURE INC (NC)
Merged into CRI Acquisition Corp. 11/08/1996
Each share Common no par exchanged for $4.75 cash

COCHRANE OIL & GAS LTD (AB)
Recapitalized as Co-Maxx Energy Group Inc. 02/10/1988
Each share Common no par exchanged for (0.125) share Common no par
Co-Maxx Energy Group Inc. acquired by NuGas Ltd. 05/01/1995 which merged into Q Energy Ltd. 09/16/1997
(See Q Energy Ltd.)

COCK-A-DOODLE DOO OF IOWA, INC. (IA)
Charter cancelled for failure to file reports 11/21/1972

COCKERAM RED LAKE MINES LTD. (ON)
Acquired by Nova-Co. Exploration Ltd. 00/00/1948
Each share Capital Stock $1 par exchanged for (0.33333333) share Capital Stock no par
Nova-Co. Exploration Ltd. recapitalized as Optical Data Corp. 07/17/1987 which recapitalized as AVL Information Systems Inc. 03/20/1992 which recapitalized as AVL Information Systems Ltd. 07/31/1996 which recapitalized as AVL Ventures Inc. 02/17/2003
(See AVL Ventures Inc.)

COCKFIELD, BROWN & CO. LTD. (CANADA)
Name changed to Cockfield Brown Inc. 10/03/1979
(See Cockfield Brown Inc.)

COCKFIELD BROWN INC (CANADA)
Discharged from bankruptcy 07/09/1998
No stockholders' equity

COCKSHUTT FARM EQUIPMENT, LTD. (CANADA)
Name changed to C.K.P. Developments, Ltd. 02/02/1962
C.K.P. Developments, Ltd. name changed to C.K.P. Developments, Inc. 10/22/1962 which name changed to Deltona Corp. 11/12/1963
(See Deltona Corp.)

COCKSHUTT PLOW CO. LTD. (CANADA)
Recapitalized as Cockshutt Farm Equipment Ltd. 00/00/1951
Each share Common no par exchanged for (0.5) share Common no par
Cockshutt Farm Equipment Ltd. name changed to C.K.P. Developments, Ltd. 02/02/1962 which was acquired by C.K.P. Developments, Inc. 10/22/1962 which name changed to Deltona Corp. 11/12/1963
(See Deltona Corp.)

COCO GROVE, INC. (PHILIPPINES)
Charter expired by time limitation 00/00/1985

COCOA BEACH STATE BANK (COCOA BEACH, FL)
Name changed to United National Bank (Cocoa Beach, FL) 05/16/1966
United National Bank (Cocoa Beach, FL) merged into First American Bank & Trust of Palm Beach County (North Palm Beach, FL) 03/21/1983
(See First American Bank & Trust of Palm Beach (North Palm Beach, FL))

COCONINO S M A INC (UT)
Name changed to Veltex Corp. 04/01/1999

COCONNECT INC (NV)
Each share old Common $0.001 par exchanged for (0.05) share new Common $0.001 par 07/13/2007
Each share new Common $0.001 par exchanged again for (0.00008333) share new Common $0.001 par 03/10/2009
Note: No holder will receive fewer than (100) shares
Name changed to Mastermind, Inc. 06/22/2018

COCONUT GROVE BK (MIAMI, FL)
Under plan of reorganization each share Common $10 par automatically became (1) share Coconut Grove Bankshares, Inc. Common 1¢ par 04/14/1999

COCONUT PALM ACQUISITION CORP (DE)
Name changed to Equity Media Holdings Corp. 04/25/2007
(See Equity Media Holdings Corp.)

CODA ENERGY INC (DE)
Acquired by Joint Energy Development Investments L.P. 02/16/1996
Each share Common 2¢ par exchanged for $7.75 cash

CODA GROUP PLC
Acquired by Baan Co. N.V. 05/13/1998
Each share Common exchanged for (0.695) New York Registry Share NLG 0.06 par
(See Baan Co. N.V.)

CODA MUSIC TECHNOLOGY INC (MN)
Name changed to Net4Music Inc. 10/20/2000
Net4Music Inc. name changed to MakeMusic! Inc. 05/22/2002 which name changed to MakeMusic, Inc. 06/09/2006
(See MakeMusic, Inc.)

CODDING BANK (ROHNERT PARK, CA)
Acquired by National Bank of the Redwoods (Santa Rosa, CA) 11/04/1994
Each share Common no par exchanged for $12.12 cash

CODDING ENTERPRISES (CA)
Each share old Common no par exchanged for (0.2) share new Common no par 08/28/1970
New Common no par split (4) for (1) by issuance of (3) additional shares 09/14/1972
New Common no par split (4) for (1) by issuance of (3) additional shares 12/01/1978
Stock Dividends - 10% 07/19/1977; 10% 02/26/1981
Company went private 00/00/1986
Details not available

CODDLE CREEK FINL CORP (NC)
Each share old Common no par exchanged for (0.01) share new Common no par 05/17/2004
Note: Holders of (99) or fewer shares received $38 cash per share
Merged into First Community Bancshares, Inc. (NV) 11/14/2008
Each share Common no par exchanged for (0.9046) share Common $1 par and $19.60 cash
First Community Bancshares, Inc. (NV) reincorporated in Virginia 10/09/2018

CODE-ALARM INC (MI)
Assets sold for the benefit of creditors 03/15/2002
Stockholders' equity unlikely

CODE-CARE INC (DE)
Recapitalized as Netgates Inc. 04/12/1996
Each share Common $0.0001 par exchanged for (0.1) share Common $0.0001 par
Netgates Inc. recapitalized as Netgates Holdings, Inc. 06/29/2006 which name changed to Sustainable Energy Development, Inc. 09/05/2006 which recapitalized as United States Oil & Gas Corp. 04/17/2008

CODE NAVY (WY)
Name changed to Universal Power Industry Corp. 06/02/2016

CODE OIL & GAS LTD. (AB)
Struck off register and declared dissolved for failure to file returns 00/00/1965

CODE PETE LTD (BC)
Struck off register and declared dissolved for failure to file returns 10/25/1985

CODE 2 ACTION INC (DE)
Name changed to AV Therapeutics, Inc. 12/27/2013

CODECA INC (DE)
Adjudicated bankrupt 03/24/1975
Stockholders' equity unlikely

CODED COMMUNICATIONS CORP (DE)
Chapter 11 bankruptcy proceedings converted to Chapter 7 on 02/23/1999
Stockholders' equity unlikely

CODENOLL TECHNOLOGY CORP (DE)
Plan of reorganization under Chapter 11 Federal Bankruptcy proceedings confirmed 01/00/1996
Stockholders' equity unlikely

CODERCARD INC (NV)
Charter revoked for failure to file a list of officers 04/01/1991

CODESCO INC (DE)
Merged into IU International Corp. 12/26/1973
Each share Common 10¢ par exchanged for (0.37) share Common $1.25 par
(See IU International Corp.)

CODESMART HLDGS INC (FL)
Common $0.0001 par split (2) for (1) by issuance of (1) additional share payable 06/14/2013 to holders of record 06/14/2013
Administratively dissolved 09/25/2015

CODESTREAM HLDGS INC (NV)
Chapter 11 bankruptcy proceedings converted to Chapter 7 on 05/10/2001
No stockholders' equity

CODEX CORP (DE)
Merged into Motorola, Inc. 05/25/1977
Each share Common $1 par exchanged for (1.155) shares Common $3 par
Motorola, Inc. recapitalized as Motorola Solutions, Inc. 01/04/2011

CODI CORP (DE)
Charter cancelled for non-payment of taxes 03/01/1991

CODIDO INC (NV)
Name changed to Quad Energy Corp. 09/13/2010

CODIMA INC (NV)
Each share old Common $0.001 par exchanged for (1.1) shares new Common $0.001 par 10/13/2011
SEC revoked common stock registration 11/22/2011

CODINE X INTL HLDGS INC (NV)
Each share old Common $0.00001 par exchanged for (0.002) share new Common $0.00001 par 07/22/2008

Name changed to PEI Worldwide Holdings, Inc. 10/20/2009

CODITRON CORP (NY)
Charter cancelled and proclaimed dissolved for failure to pay taxes and file reports 12/15/1975

CODRINGTON RESOURCE CORP (BC)
Each share old Common no par exchanged for (0.33333333) share new Common no par 01/27/2014
Name changed to NRG Metals Inc. 11/23/2015

CODY CAP CORP (CO)
Name changed to Telco Communications, Inc. 04/11/1989
Telco Communications, Inc. recapitalized as Smartsources.Com Inc. (CO) 11/09/1998 which reincorporated in Washington as Infertek, Inc. 06/15/2001 which name changed to Metarunner, Inc. 06/15/2004
(See Metarunner, Inc.)

CODY HOTEL CO.
Dissolved 00/00/1947
Details not available

CODY INDS INC (UT)
Name changed to EMI Energy Corp. 05/12/1982
EMI Energy Corp. name changed to EMI Inc. 09/11/1985

CODY-RECO MINES LTD. (ON)
Recapitalized as Vespar Mines Ltd. on a (1) for (3) basis 03/23/1960
Vespar Mines Ltd. merged into Parlake Resources Ltd. 06/18/1979 which name changed to Concord Capital Corp. 07/23/1991
(See Concord Capital Corp.)

CODY RES INC (NV)
Common $0.001 par split (11.538461) for (1) by issuance of (10.538461) additional shares payable 03/28/2008 to holders of record 03/28/2008
Reincorporated under the laws of Delaware as ChromaDex Corp. 07/15/2008

CODY VENTURES CORP (NV)
Old Common $0.001 par split (2) for (1) by issuance of (1) additional share payable 12/02/2004 to holders of record 12/02/2004 Ex date - 12/03/2004
Each share old Common $0.001 par exchanged for (0.0005) share new Common $0.001 par 01/09/2008
Recapitalized as Paw4mance Pet Products International, Inc. 07/28/2011
Each share new Common $0.001 par exchanged for (0.002) share Common $0.001 par
Paw4mance Pet Products International, Inc. recapitalized as Fearless Films, Inc. 11/19/2014

COELCO LTD (DE)
Reincorporated 6/15/84
State of incorporation changed from (NV) to (DE) 6/15/84
Charter cancelled and declared inoperative and void for non-payment of taxes 3/1/94

COEN COMPANIES, INC. (NV)
Class A no par and Class B no par changed to 10¢ par respectively 00/00/1942
Completely liquidated 12/09/1955
Each share Class A 10¢ par received first and final distribution of $0.396 cash
Note: Certificates were not required to be surrendered and are without value
No equity for holders of Class B 10¢ par

COEUR D ALENE MINES CORP (ID)
Class A $1 par and Class B $1 par reclassified as Common $1 par 08/21/1967
Common $1 par split (5) for (4) by issuance of (0.25) additional share 01/23/1981
Each share Mandatory Adjustable Redeemable Conv. Securities exchanged for (1.111) shares Common $1 par 03/15/2000
Each share Common $1 par exchanged for (0.1) share Common 1¢ par 05/27/2009
Reincorporated under the laws of Delaware as Coeur Mining, Inc. 05/17/2013

COEUR D ALENES CO (ID)
Capital Stock $1 par reclassified as Class B Capital Stock $1 par 08/00/1971
Class A Capital Stock $1 par reclassified as Common no par 02/02/1993
Class B Capital Stock $1 par reclassified as Common no par 02/02/1993
Each share old Common no par exchanged for (1) share new Common no par to reflect a (1,000) for (1) reverse split followed by a (1,000) for (1) forward split 11/27/2002
Note: Holders of (999) or fewer pre-split shares received $0.25 cash per share
Each share new Common no par exchanged again for (1) share new Common no par to reflect a (1) for (50,000) reverse split followed by a (50,000) for (1) forward split 11/01/2017
Note: Holders of (49,999) or fewer pre-split shares received $3.15 cash per share
Each share new Common no par exchanged again for (1) share new Common no par to reflect a (1) for (70,000) reverse split followed by a (7,000) for (1) forward split 06/11/2018
Note: In effect holders received $3.50 cash per share and public interest was eliminated

COEUR D'ALENE EMPIRE MINING CO. (WA)
No longer in existence having been declared dissolved for non-payment of fees 7/1/23

COEUR D'ALENE SILVER GIANT INC. (ID)
Merged into Silver Bowl, Inc. on a (0.5) for (1) basis 3/22/65
(See Silver Bowl, Inc.)

COEUR D'ALENE SYNDICATE MINING CO. (DE)
Incorporated 8/18/22
Charter cancelled and declared inoperative and void for non-payment of taxes 3/1/89

COEUR D'ALENES LEAD CO. (ID)
Dissolution approved 00/00/1952
Details not available

COEXCO PETE INC (AB)
Merged into Tesco Corp. 12/01/1993
Each share Common no par exchanged for (0.3017501) share Common no par
Tesco Corp. merged into Nabors Industries Ltd. 12/15/2017

COFFARO FAMILY PRODS INC (NV)
Each share old Common $0.001 par exchanged for (0.25) share new Common $0.001 par 09/22/2003
Name changed to E-monee.com, Inc. 07/25/2006
(See E-monee.com, Inc.)

COFFEE MAT CORP (NJ)
Common 1¢ par split (2) for (1) by issuance of (1) additional share 6/11/71
Merged into Flagstaff Corp. 12/15/76
Each share Common 1¢ par exchanged for (1) share Common 10¢ par
Flagstaff Corp. name changed to FSF Industries Inc. 11/27/78 which name changed to Trafalgar Industries, Inc. 12/17/79 which merged into Triangle Industries, Inc. (Old) 5/16/84
(See Triangle Industries, Inc. (Old))

COFFEE PACIFICA INC (NV)
Common $0.001 par split (5) for (4) by issuance of (0.25) additional share payable 03/01/2006 to holders of record 02/28/2006 Ex date - 03/02/2006
Name changed to Growers Direct Coffee Co., Inc. 11/27/2007
(See Growers Direct Coffee Co., Inc.)

COFFEE-PAK, INC. (NY)
Proclaimed dissolved for failure to file reports and pay taxes 12/16/68

COFFEE PEOPLE INC (OR)
Merged into Diedrich Coffee, Inc. 07/07/1999
Each share Common no par exchanged for (0.14) share Common no par and $2.11 cash
(See Diedrich Coffee, Inc.)

COFFEE PRODUCTS OF AMERICA, INC. LTD.
Name changed to Ben-Hur Products, Inc. 00/00/1940
Ben-Hur Products, Inc. merged into McCormick & Co., Inc. 00/00/1954

COFFEE TIME PRODS AMER INC (MA)
Completely liquidated 9/30/75
Each share Class A Common $1 par and Class B Common $1 par received first and final distribution of $0.1488 cash respectively
Certificates were not required to be surrendered and are now valueless

COFFEEWORKS INC (FL)
Recapitalized as Universal Laser, Inc. 6/17/98
Each share Common $0.001 par exchanged for (0.5) share Common $0.001 par

COFIAD INC. (QC)
Charter annulled for failure to file reports and pay fees 08/26/1972

COFIS INTL INC (DE)
Recapitalized as U.S. Bridge Corp. 04/29/1994
Each share Common $0.0001 par exchanged for (0.25) share Common $0.0001 par
U.S. Bridge Corp. name changed to USABG Corp. 01/13/1998
(See USABG Corp.)

COFITRAS ENTMT INC (NV)
Each share old Common $0.001 par exchanged for (0.01666666) share new Common $0.001 par 03/12/1999
Name changed to BingoGold.com Inc. 10/27/1999
BingoGold.com Inc. name changed to Gameweaver.com Inc. 11/26/1999 which name changed to Inform Media Group, Inc. 03/15/2002 which name changed to Actionview International, Inc. 08/20/2003 which recapitalized as AVEW Holdings, Inc. 07/31/2015

COFLEXIP (FRANCE)
ADR agreement terminated 1/31/2002
Each Sponsored ADR for Ordinary 10 Frs. par exchanged for $37.099 cash

COG MINERALS CORP. (DE)
Acquired by Colorado Oil & Gas Corp. 12/31/60
Each share Common $1 par exchanged for $0.15 cash

COGAR CORP (NY)
Common 60¢ par changed to 1¢ par 03/12/1973
Merged into Singer Co. 08/06/1975

Each share Common 1¢ par exchanged for $3.375 cash

COGAS ENERGY LTD (BC)
Acquired by Canadian Pioneer Energy Inc. 12/28/1994
For holdings of (49) shares or fewer each share Common no par exchanged for $5.95 cash
For holdings of (50) shares or more each share Common no par exchanged for (0.544) share new Class A Common no par and $2.975 cash
Canadian Pioneer Energy Inc. was acquired by Cimarron Petroleum Ltd. 12/20/1995 which merged into Newport Petroleum Corp. 04/09/1997
(See Newport Petroleum Corp.)

COGDELL SPENCER INC (MD)
Acquired by Ventas, Inc. 04/02/2012
Each share 8.5% Perpetual Preferred Ser. A 1¢ par exchanged for $25 cash
Each share Common 1¢ par exchanged for $4.25 cash

COGECO CABLE INC (CANADA)
Name changed to Cogeco Communications Inc. 01/26/2016

COGECO INC (QC)
Plan of recapitalization effective 03/09/1993
Each share Class B Preferred Ser. 1 no par exchanged for (0.7) Subordinate Vtg. Share no par, $1 cash and a fixed or adjustable rate Promissory Note due 02/07/1994
Note: Option to receive fixed rate Promissory Note expired 03/04/1993
(Additional Information in Active)

COGENCO INTL INC (CO)
Each share Common $0.001 par exchanged for (0.02) share old Common 1¢ par 02/27/1992
Each share old Common 1¢ par exchanged for (0.1) share new Common 1¢ par 08/16/1993
Name changed to Genesis Solar Corp. 08/04/2010

COGENERATION CORP AMER (DE)
Merged into Calpine East Acquisition Corp. 12/20/99
Each share Common 1¢ par exchanged for $25 cash

COGENIC ENERGY SYS INC (DE)
Name changed to U.S. Envirosystems, Inc. 07/14/1994
U.S. Envirosystems, Inc. name changed to U.S. Energy Systems, Inc. 06/27/1996
(See U.S. Energy Systems, Inc.)

COGENIX PWR CORP (BC)
Recapitalized as Global Cogenix Industrial Corp. 07/25/1996
Each share Common no par exchanged for (0.2) share Common no par
Global Cogenix Industrial Corp. recapitalized as Highwater Power Corp. 07/11/2006
(See Highwater Power Corp.)

COGENT CAP CORP (ON)
Delisted from Canadian Dealer Network 10/13/2000

COGENT COMMUNICATIONS GROUP INC (DE)
Each share old Common $0.001 par exchanged for (0.05) share new Common $0.001 par 03/24/2005
Name changed to Cogent Communications Holdings, Inc. 05/16/2014

COGENT INC (DE)
Acquired by 3M Co. 12/01/2010
Each share Common $0.001 par exchanged for $10.50 cash

COGENT INTEGRATED HEALTHCARE SOLUTIONS CORP (CANADA)
Name changed to Silver Recycling Co., Inc. 01/17/2007
(See Silver Recycling Co., Inc.)

COGENT INTEGRATED SOLUTIONS CORP (CANADA)
Recapitalized as Cogent Integrated Healthcare Solutions Corp. 11/29/2005
Each share Common no par exchanged for (0.2) share Common no par
Cogent Integrated Healthcare Solutions Corp. name changed to Silver Recycling Co., Inc. 01/17/2007
(See Silver Recycling Co., Inc.)

COGENTIX MED INC (DE)
Acquired by LM US Parent, Inc. 04/23/2018
Each share Common 1¢ par exchanged for $3.85 cash

COGESCO MNG RES INC (CANADA)
Recapitalized as Nova-Cogesco Resources Inc./Ressources Nova-Cogesco Inc. 08/17/1987
Each share Common no par exchanged for (0.2) share Common no par
Nova-Cogesco Resources Inc./Ressources Nova-Cogesco Inc. merged into CanGold Resources Inc. (BC) 01/31/1994 which reorganized in Ontario as Amalgamated CanGold Inc. 07/31/1995 which merged into Central Asia Goldfields Corp. 01/08/1996
(See Central Asia Goldfields Corp.)

COGHLIN (B.J.) CO., LTD. (CANADA)
Name changed to Wajax Ltd. 01/20/1966
Wajax Ltd. reorganized as Wajax Income Fund 06/15/2005 which reorganized as Wajax Corp. 01/04/2011

COGIENT CORP (ON)
Under Vesting Order assets surrendered to Trustee 02/14/2007
Stockholders' equity unlikely

COGINT INC (DE)
Each share Common $0.0005 par received distribution of (0.13333333) share of Red Violet, Inc. Common $0.001 par payable 03/26/2018 to holders of record 03/19/2018
Ex date - 03/27/2018
Name changed to Fluent, Inc. 04/16/2018

COGITORE RES INC (ON)
Recapitalized as CR Capital Corp. 03/26/2015
Each share Common no par exchanged for (0.1) share Common no par

COGIVAR CORP (CANADA)
Name changed to Kree Tech International Corp. 03/16/2005
(See Kree Tech International Corp.)

COGNICASE INC (CANADA)
Acquired by Groupe CGI Inc. 01/27/2004
Each share Common no par exchanged for $4.50 cash

COGNIGEN NETWORKS INC (CO)
Each share old Common $0.001 par exchanged for (0.125) share new Common $0.001 par 10/17/2001
Reorganized under the laws of Delaware as BayHill Capital Corp. 04/23/2008
Each share Common $0.001 par exchanged for (0.02) share Common $0.0001 par
BayHill Capital Corp. name changed to Agricon Global Corp. 06/01/2012 which recapitalized as StrategaBiz, Inc. 12/16/2014 which name changed to CryptoSign, Inc. 07/06/2015 which name changed to NABUfit Global, Inc. 12/10/2015 which name changed to NewBridge Global Ventures, Inc. 12/12/2017

COGNITIVE SYS INC (DE)
Charter cancelled and declared inoperative and void for non-payment of taxes 03/01/1996

COGNITRONICS CORP (NY)
Common 20¢ par split (3) for (2) by issuance of (0.5) additional share 07/22/1992
Common 20¢ par split (3) for (2) by issuance of (0.5) additional share payable 08/20/1999 to holders of record 07/30/1999
Reincorporated under the laws of Delaware as ThinkEngine Networks, Inc. and Common 20¢ par changed to $0.001 par 01/04/2007
(See ThinkEnginge Networks, Inc.)

COGNIZANT CORP (DE)
Each share Common 1¢ par received distribution of (1) share IMS Health, Inc. Common 1¢ par payable 07/01/1998 to holders of record 06/25/1998 Ex date - 07/01/1998
Name changed to Nielsen Media Research Inc. 07/01/1998
(See Nielsen Media Research Inc.)

COGNOS INC (CANADA)
Common no par split (3) for (1) by issuance of (2) additional shares payable 05/15/1996 to holders of record 05/08/1996
Common no par split (2) for (1) by issuance of (1) additional share payable 04/27/2000 to holders of record 04/20/2000
Merged into International Business Machines Corp. 01/31/2008
Each share Common no par exchanged for USD$58 cash

COGNOSCENTE SOFTWARE INTL INC (BC)
Delisted from Vancouver Stock Exchange 03/01/1999

COGNOSEC AB (SWEDEN)
Name changed to Cyber Security 1 AB 07/27/2018

COGO GROUP INC (CAYMAN ISLANDS)
Name changed to Viewtran Group, Inc. 11/26/2013

COGO GROUP INC (MD)
Reincorporated under the laws of Cayman Islands and Common 1¢ par reclassified as Ordinary USD $0.01 par 08/03/2011
Cogo Group, Inc. (Cayman Islands) name changed to Viewtran Group, Inc. 11/26/2013

COHASSETT SVGS BK (COHASSET, MA)
Merged into Shawmut National Corp. 09/30/1994
Each share Common 10¢ par exchanged for $16 cash

COHEN & CO INC OLD (MD)
Name changed to Institutional Financial Markets, Inc. 01/24/2011
Institutional Financial Markets, Inc. reorganized as Cohen & Co. Inc. (New) 09/05/2017

COHEN & STEERS ADVANTAGE INCOME RLTY FD INC (MD)
Auction Market Preferred Ser. M $0.001 par called for redemption at $25,000 on 07/21/2009
Auction Market Preferred Ser. T7 $0.001 par called for redemption at $25,000 on 07/22/2009
Auction Market Preferred Ser. W $0.001 par called for redemption at $25,000 on 07/23/2009
Auction Market Preferred Ser. TH $0.001 par called for redemption at $25,000 on 07/24/2009
Auction Market Preferred Ser. F28 $0.001 par called for redemption at $25,000 on 07/24/2009
Merged into Cohen & Steers Quality Income Realty Fund, Inc. 12/18/2009
Each share Common $0.001 par exchanged for (1.020507) shares Common $0.001 par

COHEN & STEERS DIVID MAJORS FD INC (MD)
Merged into Cohen & Steers Total Return Realty Fund, Inc. 06/13/2014
Each share Common $0.001 par exchanged for (1.315505) shares Common $0.001 par

COHEN & STEERS EQUITY INCOME FD INC (MD)
Name changed to Cohen & Steers Equity Income Fund, Inc. (New) 09/30/2004

COHEN & STEERS GLOBAL INCOME BLDR INC (MD)
Auction Market Preferred Ser W7 $0.001 par called for redemption at $25,000 on 07/23/2009
(Additional Information in Obsolete)

COHEN & STEERS PREM INCOME RLTY FD INC (MD)
Auction Market Preferred Ser. F $0.001 par called for redemption at $25,000 on 07/20/2009
Auction Market Preferred Ser. M $0.001 par called for redemption at $25,000 on 07/21/2009
Auction Market Preferred Ser. M28 $0.001 par called for redemption at $25,000 on 07/21/2009
Auction Market Preferred Ser. T $0.001 par called for redemption at $25,000 on 07/22/2009
Auction Market Preferred Ser. W28 $0.001 par called for redemption at $25,000 on 07/23/2009
Auction Market Preferred Ser. TH $0.001 par called for redemption at $25,000 on 07/24/2009
Merged into Cohen & Steers Quality Income Realty Fund, Inc. 12/18/2009
Each share Common $0.001 par exchanged for (0.936552) share Common $0.001 par

COHEN & STEERS QUALITY INCOME RLTY FD INC (MD)
Auction Market Preferred Ser. F $0.001 par called for redemption at $25,000 on 07/20/2009
Auction Market Preferred Ser. M7 $0.001 par called for redemption at $25,000 on 07/21/2009
Auction Market Preferred Ser. T $0.001 par called for redemption at $25,000 on 07/22/2009
Auction Market Preferred Ser. M28 $0.001 par called for redemption at $25,000 on 07/24/2009
Auction Market Preferred Ser. TH $0.001 par called for redemption at $25,000 on 07/24/2009
Auction Market Preferred Ser. W $0.001 par called for redemption at $25,000 on 07/24/2009
(Additional Information in Active)

COHEN & STEERS RLTY INCOME FD INC (MD)
Merged into Cohen & Steers Total Return Realty Fund, Inc. 05/31/2001
Each share Common 1¢ par exchanged for (0.611762) share Common $0.001 par

COHEN & STEERS REIT & PFD INCOME FD INC (MD)
Taxable Auction Market Preferred Ser. F7 $0.001 par called for redemption at $25,000 on 07/20/2009
Taxable Auction Market Preferred Ser. M7 $0.001 par called for redemption at $25,000 on 07/21/2009
Taxable Auction Market Preferred Ser.

T7 $0.001 par called for redemption at $25,000 on 07/22/2009
Taxable Auction Market Preferred Ser. W7 $0.001 par called for redemption at $25,000 on 07/23/2009
Taxable Auction Market Preferred Ser. W28A $0.001 par called for redemption at $25,000 on 07/23/2009
Taxable Auction Market Preferred Ser. TH7 $0.001 par called for redemption at $25,000 on 07/24/2009
Auction Market Preferred Ser. T28 $0.001 par called for redemption at $25,000 on 07/24/2009
Auction Market Preferred Ser. TH28 $0.001 par called for redemption at $25,000 on 07/24/2009
Taxable Auction Market Preferred Ser. W28B $0.001 par called for redemption at $25,000 on 07/24/2009
Taxable Auction Market Preferred Ser. W28C $0.001 par called for redemption at $25,000 on 07/24/2009
(Additional Information in Active)

COHEN & STEERS REIT & UTIL INCOME FD INC (MD)
Auction Rate Preferred Ser. F7 $0.001 par called for redemption at $25,000 on 07/20/2009
Auction Rate Preferred Ser. F28 $0.001 par called for redemption at $25,000 on 07/20/2009
Auction Rate Preferred Ser. M7 $0.001 par called for redemption at $25,000 on 07/21/2009
Auction Rate Preferred Ser. T7 $0.001 par called for redemption at $25,000 on 07/22/2009
Auction Market Preferred Ser. T7-2 $0.001 par called for redemption at $25,000 on 07/22/2009
Auction Rate Preferred Ser. W7 $0.001 par called for redemption at $25,000 on 07/23/2009
Auction Market Preferred Ser. M28 $0.001 par called for redemption at $25,000 on 07/24/2009
Auction Rate Preferred Ser. T28 $0.001 par called for redemption at $25,000 on 07/24/2009
Auction Rate Preferred Ser. TH7 $0.001 par called for redemption at $25,000 on 07/24/2009
Auction Rate Preferred Ser. W28 $0.001 par called for redemption at $25,000 on 07/24/2009
Merged into Cohen & Steers Infrastructure Fund, Inc. 03/12/2010
Each share Common $0.001 par exchanged for (0.73456) share Common $0.001 par

COHEN & STEERS SELECT UTIL FD INC (MD)
Auction Market Preferred Ser. TH7 $0.001 par called for redemption at $25,000 on 07/04/2009
Auction Market Preferred Ser. F7 $0.001 par called for redemption at $25,000 on 07/20/2009
Auction Market Preferred Ser. M7 $0.001 par called for redemption at $25,000 on 07/21/2009
Auction Market Preferred Ser. T7 $0.001 par called for redemption at $25,000 on 07/22/2009
Auction Market Preferred Ser. T7-2 $0.001 par called for redemption at $25,000 on 07/22/2009
Auction Market Preferred Ser. T28 $0.001 par called for redemption at $25,000 on 07/22/2009
Auction Market Preferred Ser. W7 $0.001 par called for redemption at $25,000 on 07/23/2009
Auction Market Preferred Ser. TH28 $0.001 par called for redemption at $25,000 on 07/24/2009
Name changed to Cohen & Steers Infrastructure Fund, Inc. 01/04/2010

COHEN & STEERS WORLDWIDE RLTY INCOME FD INC (MD)
Auction Preferred Ser. M7 $0.001 par called for redemption at $25,000 on 07/21/2009
Auction Preferred Ser. W28 $0.001 par called for redemption at $25,000 on 07/24/2009
Merged into Cohen & Steers Quality Income Realty Fund, Inc. 03/12/2010
Each share Common $0.001 par exchanged for (0.93404) share Common $0.001 par

COHEN (DAN) CO. (OH)
Dissolved 12/15/1965
Details not available

COHEN HATFIELD INDS INC (DE)
Name changed to MacAndrews & Forbes Group, Inc. 06/04/1980
(See MacAndrews & Forbes Group, Inc.)

COHEN (HARRY) MERCHANDISING CORP. (NY)
Name changed to John's Bargain Stores Corp. 10/25/1958
John's Bargain Stores Corp. name changed to Stratton Group, Ltd. 08/18/1970
(See Stratton Group, Ltd.)

COHERENT COMMUNICATIONS SYS CORP (DE)
Common 1¢ par split (2) for (1) by issuance of (1) additional share 06/26/1995
Merged into Tellabs, Inc. 08/03/1998
Each share Common 1¢ par exchanged for (0.72) share Common 1¢ par
(See Tellabs, Inc.)

COHERENT INC (CA)
Common 50¢ par changed to $0.33333333 par and (0.5) additional share issued 04/29/1983
Common $0.33333333 par changed to 22¢ par and (0.5) additional share issued 09/28/1984
Reincorporated under the laws of Delaware 10/01/1990

COHERENT RADIATION (CA)
Name changed to Coherent, Inc. (CA) 02/15/1977
Coherent, Inc. (CA) reincorporated in Delaware 10/01/1990

COHESANT INC (DE)
Each share old Common 1¢ par exchanged for (0.00002) share new Common 1¢ par 01/05/2012
Note: In effect holders received $0.60 cash per share and public interest was eliminated

COHESANT TECHNOLOGIES INC (DE)
Each share Common $0.001 par received distribution of (1) share Cohesant Inc. Common 1¢ par payable 02/27/2008 to holders of record 02/26/2008
Merged into Graco Inc. 02/27/2008
Each share Common $0.001 par exchanged for $9.43 cash

COHESION TECHNOLOGIES INC (DE)
Merged into Angiotech Pharmaceuticals, Inc. 01/31/2003
Each share Common $0.001 par exchanged for (0.11688) share Common no par
(See Angiotech Pharmaceuticals, Inc.)

COHN & ROSENBERGER, INC.
Name changed to Coro, Inc. (NY) 00/00/1943
Coro, Inc. (NY) reincorporated in Delaware 01/07/1970 which name changed to Richton International Corp. 02/27/1970
(See Richton International Corp.)

COHO ENERGY INC (TX)
Each share Common 1¢ par exchanged for (0.025) share new Common 1¢ par 03/31/2000
Plan of reorganization under Chapter 11 Federal Bankruptcy Code effective 02/03/2003
No stockholders' equity

COHO RES INC (NV)
Merged into Coho Energy, Inc. 09/29/1993
Each share Common 1¢ par exchanged for (1) share Common 1¢ par
(See Coho Energy, Inc.)

COHO RES LTD (AB)
Class B Common no par reclassified as Class A Subordinate no par 06/12/1985
12% Conv. Preferred Ser. D $10 par called for redemption 12/31/1988
Class A Subordinate no par reclassified as Common no par 07/27/1989
100% of 9% 1st Preferred Ser. A $10 par acquired through a Purchase Offer which expired 00/00/1989
14% 2nd Conv. Preferred Ser. A $10 par called for redemption 07/22/1992
9% 1st Preferred Ser. B $10 par called for redemption 07/15/1993
9% 1st Preferred Ser. C $10 par called for redemption 07/15/1993
Merged into Coho Energy, Inc. 09/29/1993
Each share Common no par exchanged for (0.25974) share Common 1¢ par
(See Coho Energy, Inc.)

COHOES BANCORP INC (DE)
Merged into Hudson River Bancorp, Inc. 04/20/2001
Each share Common 1¢ par exchanged for $19.50 cash

COHOES POWER & LIGHT CORP.
Merged into New York Power & Light Corp. 00/00/1927
Details not available

COHR INC (DE)
Merged into TCF Acquisition Corp. 03/01/1999
Each share Common 1¢ par exchanged for $6.50 cash

COHU ELECTRS INC (DE)
Each share Class A Common $1 par or Class B Common $1 par exchanged for (1) share Common $1 par 03/21/1958
Name changed to Cohu, Inc. 05/15/1972

COI SOLUTIONS INC (NV)
Each share old Common $0.001 par exchanged for (0.125) share new Common $0.001 par 08/31/2001
Recapitalized as Alternate Energy Corp. 05/20/2003
Each share new Common $0.001 par exchanged for (0.45454545) share Common $0.001 par
Alternate Energy Corp. recapitalized as Treaty Energy Corp. 01/27/2009

COIL WINDERS, INC. (NY)
Acquired by Metropolitan Telecommunications Corp. 07/01/1960
Each share Common exchanged for (0.33333333) share Common Metropolitan Telecommunications Corp. name changed to Grow Corp. 12/29/1961 which name changed to Grow Chemical Corp. 10/19/1964 which name changed to Grow Group, Inc. 04/20/1979
(See Grow Group, Inc.)

COIN BILL VALIDATOR INC (NY)
Name changed to Global Payment Technologies, Inc. 07/02/1997

COIN CANYON MINES LTD. (BC)
Merged into Coseka Resources Ltd. 08/20/1971
Each share Common no par exchanged for (0.5) share Common no par
(See Coseka Resources Ltd.)

COIN EXPLORATIONS LTD. (BC)
Name changed to Matador Developments Ltd. 12/20/1972
Matador Developments Ltd. recapitalized as Betina Resources Inc. 03/12/1975 which recapitalized as Nevcal Resources Ltd. 09/06/1983 which recapitalized as Arapahoe Mining Corp. 12/03/1986 which recapitalized as Salus Resource Corp. 05/06/1996 which name changed to Brandon Gold Corp. 12/04/1996 which recapitalized as Redmond Ventures Corp. 09/16/1999 which recapitalized as Crown Point Ventures Ltd. (BC) 03/12/2002 which reincorporated in Alberta as Crown Point Energy Inc. 07/31/2012

COIN LAKE GOLD MINES LTD (ON)
Capital Stock $1 par changed to no par 12/22/1971
Recapitalized as United Coin Mines Ltd. 12/11/1989
Each share Capital Stock no par exchanged for (0.5) share Common no par
United Coin Mines Ltd. name changed to Winstaff Ventures Ltd. 06/25/1993 which merged into Romarco Minerals Inc. (ON) 07/11/1995 which reincorporated in British Columbia 06/16/2006 which merged into OceanaGold Corp. 10/01/2015

COIN PHONES INC (NY)
Chapter 11 Federal Bankruptcy proceedings converted to Chapter 7 on 07/06/1990
Stockholders' equity unlikely

COIN RADIO CORP.
Out of business 00/00/1933
Details not available

COINLESS SYS INC (NV)
Each share old Common $0.001 par exchanged for (0.01538461) share new Common $0.001 par 07/02/2007
Recapitalized as NHS Health Solutions, Inc. (NV) 07/11/2007
Each share new Common $0.001 par exchanged for (0.2) share Common $0.001 par
NHS Health Solutions, Inc. (NV) reincorporated in Florida 02/28/2012
(See NHS Health Solutions, Inc.)

COINLESS VENDING INC (FL)
Recapitalized as Communicare Corp. 07/01/1998
Each share Common $0.001 par exchanged for (0.1) share Common $0.001 par
Communicare Corp. name changed to Oxford Educational Services, Inc. (FL) 08/06/1999 which reincorporated in Delaware as Aspen Global Corp. 01/02/2008 which name changed to Diversified Mortgage Workout Corp. 08/08/2008 which recapitalized as Arem Pacific Corp. 07/29/2013

COINMACH LAUNDRY CORP (DE)
Acquired by CLC Acquisition Corp. 07/13/2000
Each share Common 1¢ par exchanged for $14.25 cash

COINMACH SVC CORP (DE)
Acquired by Spin Holdco Inc. 11/20/2007
Each share Class A Common 1¢ par exchanged for $13.55 cash

COINSTAR INC (DE)
Name changed to Outerwall Inc. 07/02/2013
(See Outerwall Inc.)

COIT INTL INC (TX)
Stock Dividends - 50% 10/15/1970; 100% 01/15/1971
Common 10¢ par split (2) for (1) by issuance of (1) additional share 11/24/1971
Charter cancelled and declared inoperative and void for non-payment of taxes 01/18/1988

COL CAP LTD (BERMUDA)
Each Sponsored ADR for Ordinary received distribution of $0.479952 cash payable 02/02/2015 to holders of record 01/23/2015 Ex date - 01/21/2015
Sponsored ADR's for Ordinary split (20) for (1) by issuance of (19) additional ADR's payable 06/23/2015 to holders of record 06/15/2015 Ex date - 06/24/2015
Name changed to China Medical & HealthCare Group Ltd. 03/11/2016
(See China Medical & HealthCare Group Ltd.)

COL-U-MEX URANIUM CORP. (NV)
Merged into Petroleum Resources Corp. 06/30/1965
Each share Common 10¢ par exchanged for (0.25) share Common 25¢ par
Petroleum Resources Corp. name changed to PRC Corp. 11/09/1970 which name changed to CorTerra Corp. 11/28/1972 which assets were transferred to CorTerra Liquidating Corp. 10/08/1980
(See CorTerra Corp. Liquidating Corp.)

COLABOR INCOME FD (QC)
Reorganized as Colabor Group Inc. 08/28/2009
Each Unit no par exchanged for (1) share Common no par

COLBA NET TELECOM INC (CANADA)
Each share old Common no par exchanged for (0.00000004) share new Common no par 06/29/2016
Note: In effect holders received $0.10 cash per share and public interest was eliminated

COLBER CORP. (NJ)
Common 20¢ par reclassified as Class A Common 20¢ par 08/07/1962
Completely liquidated 06/23/1965
Each share Class A Common 20¢ par exchanged for (1) share Common 50¢ par and $0.1348 amount of 4% Notes of Union Spring & Manufacturing Co.

COLBERTS SEC SVCS INC (RI)
Completely liquidated 05/11/1982
Each share Common 40¢ par exchanged for first and final distribution of $2.978 cash

COLBY RES CORP (BC)
Name changed 03/06/1980
Name changed from Colby Mines Ltd. to Colby Resources Corp. 03/06/1980
Recapitalized as Canplats Resources Corp. 03/22/2001
Each share Common no par exchanged for (0.2) share Common no par
(See Canplats Resources Corp.)

COLCHESTER MINES LTD. (NL)
Struck off register and declared dissolved for failure to file returns 04/02/1976

COLCHIS RES LTD (BC)
Recapitalized as Northewan Minerals Corp. 03/20/1991
Each share Common no par exchanged for (0.2) share Common no par
Northewan Minerals Corp. name changed to Flotek Industries, Inc. (BC) 12/11/1992 which reincorporated in Alberta 09/15/1995 which reorganized in Delaware 11/05/2001

COLD CAM INC (NV)
Name changed to Magicstem Group Corp. 05/04/2015

COLD GIN CORP (DE)
Reincorporated under the laws of Nevada as Bonanza Gold Corp. 12/29/2010
Bonanza Gold Corp. name changed to Brightlane Corp. 09/23/2015

COLD LAKE PIPE LINE CO. LTD. (AB)
Recapitalized as Worldwide Energy Co. Ltd. (AB) 07/01/1967
Each share Capital Stock no par exchanged for (1.04) shares Common no par to effect a share for share exchange plus a 4% stock dividend
Worldwide Energy Co. Ltd. (AB) reincorporated in Delaware as Weco Development Corp. 07/17/1972 which name changed to Worldwide Energy Corp. 06/14/1977 which merged into Triton Corp. (TX) 11/18/1986 which reincorporated in Delaware 05/12/1995 which merged into Triton Energy Ltd. 03/25/1996
(See Triton Energy Ltd.)

COLD LAKE RES INC (BC)
Name changed to FTI Foodtech International Inc. (BC) 01/21/1986
FTI Foodtech International Inc. (BC) reincorporated in Canada 08/28/2008

COLD METAL PRODS INC (NY)
Chapter 11 Bankruptcy proceedings dismissed 04/09/2004
No stockholders' equity

COLD METAL PRODUCTS CO. (OH)
Acquired by Jones & Laughlin Steel Corp. 7/31/57
Each share Common $1 par exchanged for (0.6925) share Common $10 par
(See Jones & Laughlin Steel Corp.)

COLD SPRING CAP INC (DE)
Completely liquidated
Each share Common $0.001 par received first and final distribution of $5.74 cash payable 5/10/2007 to holders of record 5/4/2007
Note: Certificates were not required to be surrendered and are without value

COLDSPRING RES LTD (BC)
Recapitalized as Isleshaven Capital Corp. 07/14/1989
Each share Common no par exchanged for (0.1) share Common no par
Isleshaven Capital Corp. name changed to Nortel Communications Inc. 06/17/1991 which recapitalized as American Nortel Communications Inc. (BC) 05/11/1992 which reincorporated in Wyoming 02/09/1993 which reincorporated in Nevada 08/03/2007

COLDSTREAM COPPER MINES LTD. (ON)
Recapitalized as North Coldstream Mines Ltd. 8/1/59
Each share Capital Stock $1 par exchanged for (0.25) share Capital Stock no par
North Coldstream Mines Ltd. merged into Coldstream Mines Ltd. 1/13/72
(See Coldstream Mines Ltd.)

COLDSTREAM MINES LTD (ON)
Charter cancelled for failure to pay taxes and file returns 06/23/1980

COLDSWITCH TECHNOLOGIES INC (BC)
Name changed to Photon Control Inc. 08/09/2002

COLDWALL INC (DE)
SEC revoked common stock registration 06/15/2006

COLDWATER CREEK INC (DE)
Old Common 1¢ par split (3) for (2) by issuance of (0.5) additional share payable 08/14/2000 to holders of record 07/24/2000
Old Common 1¢ par split (3) for (2) by issuance of (0.5) additional share payable 01/30/2003 to holders of record 01/08/2003 Ex date - 01/31/2003
Old Common 1¢ par split (3) for (2) by issuance of (0.5) additional share payable 09/08/2003 to holders of record 08/18/2003 Ex date - 09/09/2003
Old Common 1¢ par split (3) for (2) by issuance of (0.5) additional share payable 07/23/2004 to holders of record 07/01/2004 Ex date - 07/26/2004
Old Common 1¢ par split (3) for (2) by issuance of (0.5) additional share payable 03/18/2005 to holders of record 02/25/2005 Ex date - 03/21/2005
Old Common 1¢ par split (3) for (2) by issuance of (0.5) additional share payable 01/13/2006 to holders of record 12/23/2005 Ex date - 01/17/2006
Each share old Common 1¢ par exchanged for (0.25) share new Common 1¢ par 10/04/2012
Plan of reorganization under Chapter 11 Federal Bankruptcy proceedings effective 09/26/2014
No stockholders' equity

COLDWELL BANKER & CO (CA)
Common no par split (2) for (1) by issuance of (1) additional share 6/8/79
Merged into Sears, Roebuck & Co. 12/31/81
Each share Common no par exchanged for (2.463) shares Common 75¢ par
Sears, Roebuck & Co. merged into Sears Holdings Corp. 3/24/2005

COLE COMPUTER CORP (NV)
Each share old Common $0.001 par exchanged for (0.00285714) share new Common $0.001 par 09/22/2005
Note: Holders of between (100) and (34,999) shares will receive (100) shares
Holders of (99) or fewer shares were not affected by the reverse split
Name changed to Wilson Holdings, Inc. (NV) 09/29/2005
Wilson Holdings, Inc. (NV) reincorporated in Texas as Green Builders, Inc. 04/08/2008
(See Green Builders, Inc.)

COLE CONSUMER PRODS INC (DE)
Merged into Shelter Resources Corp. 05/12/1980
Each share Common 1¢ par exchanged for $11.25 cash

COLE CR PPTY TR INC (MD)
Acquired by American Realty Capital Properties, Inc. 05/19/2014
Each share Common 1¢ par exchanged for $7.25 cash

COLE CR PPTY TR III INC (MD)
Name changed to Cole Real Estate Investments, Inc. 06/04/2013
Cole Real Estate Investments, Inc. merged into American Realty Capital Properties, Inc. 02/07/2014 which name changed to VEREIT, Inc. 07/31/2015

COLE DRUG INC (TN)
Common 25¢ par changed to $0.125 par and (1) additional share issued 06/07/1968
Merged into Revco D.S., Inc. 11/12/1970
Each share Common $0.125 par exchanged for (0.9) share Common $1 par
(See Revco D.S., Inc.)

COLE INC (UT)
Name changed to Reflect Scientific, Inc. 12/31/2003

COLE INDS INC (TN)
Name changed to First Federal Energy Corp. and Common 10¢ par changed to 1¢ par 03/21/1980
(See First Federal Energy Corp.)

COLE KENNETH PRODTNS INC (NY)
Class A Common 1¢ par split (2) for (1) by issuance of (1) additional share 11/17/1995
Class A Common 1¢ par split (3) for (2) by issuance of (0.5) additional share payable 03/27/2000 to holders of record 03/06/2000
Acquired by KCP Holdco, Inc. 09/25/2012
Each share Class A Common 1¢ par exchanged for $15.25 cash

COLE LUMBER CO.
Out of business 00/00/1930
Details not available

COLE NATL CORP (OH)
Class A Common 50¢ par reclassified as Common 50¢ par 06/02/1964
Common 50¢ par split (3) for (2) by issuance of (0.5) additional share 10/15/1968
45¢ Conv. Preferred Ser. A no par called for redemption 04/10/1972
Common 50¢ par split (5) for (4) by issuance of (0.25) additional share 07/02/1981
Common 50¢ par split (5) for (4) by issuance of (0.25) additional share 06/23/1982
Common 50¢ par split (3) for (2) by issuance of (0.5) additional share 01/13/1983
Stock Dividends - 10% 01/23/1968; 10% 12/07/1976
Acquired by a group of investors 09/17/1984
Each share Common 50¢ par exchanged for $39 cash

COLE NATL CORP NEW (DE)
Preferred Stock Purchase Rights declared for Common stockholders of record 09/01/1995 were redeemed at $0.01 per right 12/20/1999 for holders of record 12/06/1999
Merged into Luxottica Group S.p.A 10/05/2004
Each share Common $0.001 par exchanged for $27.72 cash

COLE PETROLEUM CO.
Succeeded by Cole Petroleum Corp. 00/00/1940
Details not available

COLE PETROLEUM CORP.
In process of liquidation 00/00/1948
Details not available

COLE REAL ESTATE INVTS INC (MD)
Merged into American Realty Capital Properties, Inc. 02/07/2014
Each share Common 1¢ par exchanged for (1.0929) shares Common 1¢ par
American Realty Capital Properties, Inc. name changed to VEREIT, Inc. 07/31/2015

COLE TAYLOR FINL GROUP INC (DE)
Name changed to Reliance Acceptance Group, Inc. 02/13/1997
(See Reliance Acceptance Group, Inc.)

COL-COL   FINANCIAL INFORMATION, INC.

COLE VENDING INDUSTRIES, INC. (IL)
Adjudicated bankrupt 02/07/1962
No stockholders' equity

COLEBROOKDALE RAILROAD CO.
Merged into Reading Co. 12/31/1945
Each share Common exchanged for (0.04) share Common $50 par
Reading Co. merged into Reading Entertainment Inc. (DE) 10/15/1996 which reincorporated in Nevada 12/29/1999 which merged into Reading International, Inc. 12/31/2001

COLECCIONES DE RAQUEL INC (NV)
Name changed to Raquel, Inc. 10/14/1999
Raquel, Inc. recapitalized as Xynergy Corp. 02/15/2002 which name changed to Xynergy Holdings, Inc. 09/11/2008

COLECO INDS INC (CT)
Common no par changed to $1 par 04/01/1963
Common $1 par split (3) for (2) by issuance of (0.5) additional share 01/17/1969
Common $1 par split (2) for (1) by issuance of (1) additional share 12/29/1969
Common $1 par split (2) for (1) by issuance of (1) additional share 07/17/1972
Common $1 par split (2) for (1) by issuance of (1) additional share 01/28/1983
Stock Dividend - 30% 02/15/1969
Reorganized under Chapter 11 Federal Bankruptcy Code 02/01/1990
Each share Common $1 par received distribution of $0.01123 cash
Note: Certificates were not required to be surrendered and are without value

COLEGROVE OIL CO., INC.
Dissolved 00/00/1948
Details not available

COLEMAN AMERN COS INC (DE)
Stock Dividends - 20% 01/17/1972; 33.33333333% 12/18/1972; 25% 07/15/1975
Plan of reorganization under Chapter 11 Federal Bankruptcy Act confirmed 03/31/1982
No stockholders' equity

COLEMAN CABLE & WIRE CO (DE)
Class A Common $1 par split (2) for (1) by issuance of (1) additional share 08/01/1967
Class A Common $1 par and Class B Common $1 par reclassified as Common $1 par 06/16/1971
Name changed to Groman Corp. 04/20/1977
(See Groman Corp.)

COLEMAN CABLE INC (DE)
Acquired by Southwire Co. 02/11/2014
Each share Accredited Investors Common $0.001 par exchanged for $26.25 cash
Each share Common $0.001 par exchanged for $26.25 cash

COLEMAN COLLIERIES LTD (AB)
Company dissolved 09/25/1986
Details not available

COLEMAN ENGR INC (CA)
Class A Common $1 par reclassified as Common $1 par 00/00/1956
Name changed to Coleman Systems 09/11/1970
(See Coleman Systems)

COLEMAN GAS & OIL CO. (TX)
Name changed to Coleman Gas Co. 00/00/1952

COLEMAN INC (KS)
Common $5 par split (3) for (2) by issuance of (0.5) additional share 06/02/1959
4.25% Preferred $50 par called for redemption 08/12/1963
Common $5 par split (2) for (1) by issuance of (1) additional share 05/26/1964
Common $5 par split (2) for (1) by issuance of (1) additional share 01/17/1969
Common $5 par changed to $1 par 07/01/1969
Common $1 par split (2) for (1) by issuance of (1) additional share 01/16/1970
Acquired by MacAndrews & Forbes Holdings Inc. 08/31/1989
Each share Common $1 par exchanged for $74 cash

COLEMAN INC NEW (DE)
Common 1¢ par split (2) for (1) by issuance of (1) additional share payable 07/15/1996 to holders of record 06/28/1996 Ex date - 07/16/1996
Merged into Sunbeam Corp. (New) 01/06/2000
Each share Common 1¢ par exchanged for (0.5677) share Common 1¢ par, (0.381) Common Stock Purchase Warrant expiring 08/24/2003 and $6.44 cash
(See Sunbeam Corp. (New))

COLEMAN KERSTEIN & LOVE INC (DE)
Name changed to Penn General Agencies, Inc. 06/29/1972
Penn General Agencies, Inc. merged into Penncorp Financial, Inc. 01/28/1980 which merged into American Can Co. 01/11/1983 which name changed to Primerica Corp. (NJ) 04/28/1987 which was acquired by Primerica Corp. (DE) 12/15/1988 which name changed to Travelers Inc. 12/31/1993 which name changed to Travelers Group Inc. 04/16/1995 which name changed to Citigroup Inc. 10/08/1998

COLEMAN LAMP & STOVE CO. (KS)
Reorganized as Coleman Co., Inc. 06/13/1945
Each share Common no par exchanged for (0.2) share 4.25% Preferred $50 par and (4) shares Common $5 par
(See Coleman Co., Inc.)

COLEMAN PETROLEUM CO., INC.
Out of business 00/00/1933
Details not available

COLEMAN SYS (CA)
Filed a petition under Chapter 7 Federal Bankruptcy Code 06/29/1983
No stockholders' equity

COLERAINE ASBESTOS LTD. (QC)
Name changed to Coleraine Quebec Asbestos Ltd. 00/00/1949
(See Coleraine Quebec Asbestos Ltd.)

COLERAINE MNG RES INC (QC)
Recapitalized as Exploration Amex, Inc. 11/20/2001
Each share Common no par exchanged for (0.1) share Common no par

COLERAINE QUEBEC ASBESTOS LTD. (QC)
Charter annulled for failure to file reports and pay fees 12/23/1972

COLES BOOK STORES LTD (ON)
Each share Capital Stock no par exchanged for (0.0001) share Capital Stock no par 12/06/1979
Note: In effect holders received $23 cash per share and public interest eliminated

COLES G J & COY LTD (AUSTRALIA)
Stock Dividend - 10% 10/31/1980
Name changed to Coles Myer Ltd. 02/06/1986
(See Coles Myer Ltd.)

COLES MYER LTD (AUSTRALIA)
Each Unsponsored ADR's for Ordinary exchanged for (1.66666666) Sponsored ADR's for Ordinary 10/14/1987
Each old Sponsored ADR for Ordinary exchanged for (0.84) new Sponsored ADR for Ordinary 01/04/1993
Stock Dividend - 12.5% 01/11/1989
ADR agreement terminated 02/06/2006
Each new Sponsored ADR for Ordinary exchanged for $59.7356 cash

COLEVILLE DEVELOPMENT CO. (SK)
Completely liquidated 09/30/1966
Each share Common no par exchanged for first and final distribution of $0.15 cash

COLEVILLE RES LTD (AB)
Recapitalized 07/21/1994
Recapitalized from Coleville Industries Ltd. to Coleville Resources Ltd. 07/21/1994
Each share Common no par exchanged for (0.2) share Common no par
Delisted from Alberta Stock Exchange 09/30/1999

COLEY PHARMACEUTICAL GROUP INC (DE)
Merged into Pfizer Inc. 01/04/2008
Each share Common 1¢ par exchanged for $8 cash

COLFAX ENERGY LTD (AB)
Recapitalized as Germain Industries Ltd. 06/08/1988
Each share Common no par exchanged for (0.125) share Common no par
Germain Industries Ltd. name changed to Marquis Resource Corp. 08/02/1989 which name changed to Panorama Trading Co. Ltd. 10/22/1992 which name changed to Perfect Fry Corp. 05/21/1993 which name changed to Woodrose Corp. (AB) 09/01/2010 which reincorporated in British Columbia as Woodrose Ventures Corp. 11/07/2016 which recapitalized as Novoheart Holdings Inc. 10/03/2017

COLGATE MGMT CORP (DE)
Adjudicated bankrupt 12/02/1970
Details not available

COLGATE PALMOLIVE CO (DE)
Name changed 10/30/1953
Name changed from Colgate-Palmolive-Peet Co. to Colgate-Palmolive Co. 10/30/1953
$3.50 Preferred no par reclassified as $4.25 Preferred no par 05/17/1983
$3 2nd Conv. Preferred no par called for redemption 10/23/1992
$4.25 Preferred no par called for redemption at $100 plus $1.0625 accrued dividends on 06/30/2003
(Additional Information in Active)

COLIGHT INC (MN)
Name changed to Colwell Industries, Inc. 09/01/1980
(See Colwell Industries, Inc.)

COLIMA MINES, INC. (DE)
No longer in existence having become inoperative and void for non-payment of taxes 04/01/1965

COLIMA RES LTD (BC)
Recapitalized as Procordia Explorations Ltd. 04/27/1990
Each share Common no par exchanged for (0.4) share Common no par
Procordia Explorations Ltd. recapitalized as Earthworks Industries Inc. 09/15/1993

COLIN ENERGY CORP (AB)
Recapitalized as International Colin Energy Corp. 06/06/1990
Each share Common no par exchanged for (0.33333333) share Common no par
International Colin Energy Corp. merged into Morgan Hydrocarbons Inc. 07/01/1996 which was acquired by Stampeder Exploration Ltd. 10/15/1996 which was acquired Gulf Canada Resources Ltd. 09/10/1997
(See Gulf Canada Resources Ltd.)

COLISEUM PPTYS INC (DE)
Adjudicated bankrupt 08/23/1974
No stockholders' equity

COLITE INDS INC (SC)
Merged into BG Holding Co., Inc. 04/15/1981
Each share Common 10¢ par exchanged for $5.24 cash

COLLABORATIVE CLINICAL RESH INC (OH)
Name changed to DATATRAK International, Inc. 04/20/1999

COLLABORATIVE FINL NETWORK GROUP INC (DE)
SEC revoked common stock registration 05/10/2011

COLLABORATIVE RESH INC (MA)
Name changed to Genome Therapeutics Corp. 09/06/1994
Genome Therapeutics Corp. name changed to Oscient Pharmaceuticals Corp. 04/13/2004
(See Oscient Pharmaceuticals Corp.)

COLLABRIUM JAPAN ACQUISITION CORP (BRITISH VIRGIN ISLANDS)
Completely liquidated 02/24/2015
Each Unit exchanged for first and final distribution of $10.52619 cash
Each share Ordinary no par exchanged for first and final distribution of $10.52619 cash

COLLABRX INC (DE)
Recapitalized as Rennova Health, Inc. 11/03/2015
Each share Common 1¢ par exchanged for (0.1) share Common 1¢ par

COLLAGEN AESTHETICS INC (DE)
Name changed 08/18/1998
Common no par split (3) for (2) by issuance of (0.5) additional share 07/25/1986
State of incorporation changed from (CA) to (DE) and Common no par changed to 1¢ par 02/12/1987
Name changed from Collagen Corp. to Collagen Aesthetics Inc. 08/18/1998
Merged into Inamed Corp. 09/02/1999
Each share Common 1¢ par exchanged for $16.25 cash

COLLAGENEX PHARMACEUTICALS INC (DE)
Merged into Galderma Laboratories, Inc. 04/11/2008
Each share Common 1¢ par exchanged for $16.60 cash

COLLART GOLD MINES LTD. (ON)
Reported no property 00/00/1953
Stockholders' equity unlikely

COLLATERAL BANKERS, INC.
Merged into Bankers National Investing Corp. 00/00/1940
Each share Common $1 par exchanged for (64.616875) shares Common $1 par
Bankers National Investing Corp. merged into Beneficial Corp. (Old) 00/00/1945 which was acquired by Beneficial Finance Co. 03/15/1968 which name changed to Beneficial Corp. (New) 05/01/1970 which merged into Household International, Inc. 06/30/1998

COPYRIGHTED MATERIAL   598   NO UNAUTHORIZED REPRODUCTION

FINANCIAL INFORMATION, INC.

COLLATERAL CREDIT SERVICE, INC.
Out of business 00/00/1932
Details not available

COLLATERAL EQUITIES TRUST
Merged into Haydock Fund, Inc. on a valuation basis of $5.5662 for Collateral Equities Trust shares against $15.2408 for Haydock Fund, Inc. shares 00/00/1949
(See Haydock Fund, Inc.)

COLLATERAL INVESTMENT CORP.
Out of business 00/00/1931
Details not available

COLLATERAL LOAN CO. (MA)
Liquidation completed 00/00/1959
Details not available

COLLATERAL THERAPEUTICS INC (DE)
Merged into Schering AG 07/03/2002
Each share Common $0.001 par exchanged for (0.1847) Sponsored ADR for Ordinary
(See Schering AG)

COLLATERAL TRUSTEE SHARES SERIES A
Trust terminated 00/00/1948
Details not available

COLLECTIBLE CONCEPTS GROUP INC (DE)
Each share old Common $0.001 par exchanged for (0.01428571) share new Common $0.001 par 06/21/2002
Each share new Common $0.001 par exchanged for (0.01) share Common $0.00001 par 12/18/2006
SEC revoked common stock registration 04/25/2011

COLLECTIBLES AMER INC (NV)
Recapitalized as BeFirst.com Inc. 06/18/1999
Each share Common $0.001 par exchanged for (0.5) share Common $0.001 par
BeFirst.com Inc. name changed to FindWhat.com (NV) 09/03/1999 which reincorporated in Delaware 09/03/2004 which name changed to MIVA, Inc. 06/13/2005 which name changed to Vertro, Inc. 06/09/2009 which merged into Inuvo, Inc. 03/01/2012

COLLECTIBLES ENTMT INC (DE)
Name changed to Netnation Communications, Inc. 04/14/1999
(See Netnation Communications, Inc.)

COLLECTIVE BANCORP INC (DE)
Reorganized 12/30/1988
Common 1¢ par split (2) for (1) by issuance of (1) additional share 07/15/1985
Common 1¢ par split (2) for (1) by issuance of (1) additional share 07/17/1986
Reorganized from Collective Federal Savings & Loan Association to Collective Bancorp, Inc. 12/30/1988
Each share Common 1¢ par exchanged for (1) share Common 1¢ par
Common 1¢ par split (4) for (3) by issuance of (1/3) additional share 07/24/1992
Common 1¢ par split (3) for (2) by issuance of (0.5) additional share 07/23/1993
Merged into Summit Bancorp 08/01/1997
Each share Common 1¢ par exchanged for (0.895) share Common $1.20 par
Summit Bancorp merged into FleetBoston Financial Corp. 03/01/2001 which merged into Bank of America Corp. 04/01/2004

COLLECTIVE BRANDS INC (DE)
Acquired by WBG-PSS Holdings L.L.C. 10/09/2012

Each share Common 1¢ par exchanged for $21.75 cash

COLLECTORS GUILD INTL INC (NY)
Dissolved by proclamation 12/24/1991

COLLEEN COPPER MINES LTD (ON)
Charter cancelled for failure to pay taxes and file returns 03/16/1976

COLLEGE BOUND INC (DE)
Charter cancelled and declared inoperative and void for non-payment of taxes 03/01/2001

COLLEGE BOUND STUDENT ALLIANCE INC (NV)
Reincorporated 08/28/2000
State of incorporation changed from (CO) to (NV) 08/28/2000
Name changed to College Partnership, Inc. (NV) 06/03/2003
College Partnership, Inc. (NV) reincorporated in Delaware as College Partnership Merger Co. 12/19/2007 which name changed to NPI08, Inc. 02/07/2008 which name changed to BlackStar Energy Group, Inc. 02/09/2010 which name changed to BlackStar Enterprise Group, Inc. 09/30/2016

COLLEGE LIFE INS CO AMER (IN)
Stock Dividends - 78% 05/01/1962; 100% 05/01/1964; 10% 05/28/1965; 10% 07/05/1966; 10% 05/29/1967; 10% 05/27/1968
Acquired by United Fidelity Life Insurance Co. 03/29/1988
Details not available

COLLEGE OAK INVTS INC (NV)
Name changed to Baseline Oil & Gas Corp. 01/19/2006
(See Baseline Oil & Gas Corp.)

COLLEGE PARTNERSHIP MERGER CO (DE)
Reincorporated 12/19/2007
Name and place of incorporation changed from College Partnership, Inc. (NV) to College Partnership Merger Co. (DE) 12/19/2007
Name changed to NPI08, Inc. 02/07/2008
NPI08, Inc. name changed to BlackStar Energy Group, Inc. 02/09/2010 which name changed to BlackStar Enterprise Group, Inc. 09/30/2016

COLLEGE PLANNING SYS INC (DE)
Name changed to CPS-Corporate Planning Services Inc. and Common 1¢ par reclassified as Class A Common 1¢ par 07/14/1987
(See CPS-Corporate Planning Services, Inc.)

COLLEGE PLUMBING SUPPLIES LTD (ON)
Declared bankrupt 10/27/1976
No stockholders' equity

COLLEGE SOFTWARE INC (FL)
Name changed to Victor Ebner Enterprises, Inc. 05/21/2001
(See Victor Ebner Enterprises, Inc.)

COLLEGE TELEVISION NETWORK INC (DE)
Name changed to CTN Media Group Inc. 11/18/1999

COLLEGE TONIGHT INC (DE)
Name changed to CT Holdings, Inc. 09/03/2009

COLLEGE TOWN INC (MA)
Stock Dividend - 10% 05/07/1974
Merged into Interco Inc. (Old) 08/23/1974
Each share Common $1 par exchanged for (0.4545) share Common no par 12/21/1973
(See Interco Inc. (Old))

COLLEGE UNIV HLDG CORP (DE)
Merged out of existence 11/13/1986
No stockholders' equity

COLLEGELINK COM INC (DE)
Name changed to Cytation Corp. (DE) 06/21/2001
Cytation Corp. (DE) reincorporated in Florida as Deer Valley Corp. 07/28/2006

COLLEGIATE DISTRG CORP (DE)
Charter cancelled and declared inoperative and void for non-payment of taxes 03/01/1991

COLLEGIATE FDG SVCS INC (DE)
Merged into JPMorgan Chase & Co. 03/01/2006
Each share Common $0.001 par exchanged for $20 cash

COLLEGIATE PAC INC (DE)
Reincorporated 07/21/1999
State of incorporation changed from (PA) to (DE) 07/21/1999
Each share old Common 1¢ par exchanged for (0.2) share new Common 1¢ par 01/14/2000
Name changed to Sport Supply Group, Inc. (New) 07/02/2007
(See Sport Supply Group, Inc. (New))

COLLETTS INC (UT)
Each share Common $0.001 par exchanged for (0.05) share Common 2¢ par 04/20/1972
Each share Common 2¢ par exchanged for (0.001) share Common $100 par 06/26/1978
Note: In effect holders received $0.40 cash per share and public interest eliminated

COLLEXIS HLDGS INC (NV)
Voluntarily dissolved 05/18/2012
Details not available

COLLEY CORP (DE)
Name changed to Games, Inc. 09/16/2002
Games, Inc. recapitalized as InQBate Corp. 10/06/2004
(See InQBate Corp.)

COLLICUTT ENERGY SVCS LTD (AB)
Name changed 04/24/2003
Name changed from Collicutt Hanover Services Ltd. to Collicutt Energy Services Ltd. 04/24/2003
Acquired by Finning International Inc. 02/27/2008
Each share Common no par exchanged for $9.75 cash

COLLING (H.T.) CO. (OH)
Completely liquidated 03/31/1988
Each share Capital Stock $2.50 par exchanged for first and final distribution of $0.9278 cash

COLLINGWOOD CAP CORP (BC)
Name changed to Rainy River Resources Ltd. and (3) additional shares issued 06/17/2005
Rainy River Resources Ltd. merged into New Gold Inc. 10/16/2013

COLLINGWOOD ENERGY INC (BC)
Recapitalized as Collins Resources Ltd. 10/01/1984
Each share Common no par exchanged for (0.2) share Common no par
Collins Resources Ltd. recapitalized as Madison Enterprises Corp. 06/26/1992 which recapitalized as Madison Minerals Inc. 10/29/2004 which recapitalized as Battle Mountain Gold Inc. 05/14/2014 which merged into Gold Standard Ventures Corp. 06/15/2017

COLLINGWOOD TERMS LTD (ON)
Each share 7% Preferred exchanged for (5) shares Preferred no par 00/00/1934
Name changed to Pemstar Holdings Ltd. 12/21/1973
(See Pemstar Holdings Ltd.)

COLLINS & AIKMAN CO.
Merged into Collins & Aikman Corp. 00/00/1927

Details not available

COLLINS & AIKMAN CORP NEW (DE)
Each share old Common 1¢ par exchanged for (0.4) share new Common 1¢ par 05/28/2002
Plan of reorganization under Chapter 11 Federal Bankruptcy Code effective 10/12/2007
No stockholders' equity

COLLINS & AIKMAN CORP OLD (DE)
Each share 7% Preferred $100 par exchanged for (1) share 5% Preferred $100 par 00/00/1937
5% Preferred $100 par called for redemption 08/12/1946
Common no par split (2) for (1) by issuance of (1) additional share 12/01/1961
Common no par split (2) for (1) by issuance of (1) additional share 08/30/1963
Common no par split (3) for (2) by issuance of (0.5) additional share 06/26/1969
Common no par split (2) for (1) by issuance of (1) additional share 06/23/1971
Common no par split (2) for (1) by issuance of (1) additional share 03/01/1985
Merged into Wickes Companies, Inc. 01/14/1987
Each share Common no par exchanged for $53 cash

COLLINS & AIKMAN GROUP INC (DE)
15.50% Exchangeable Jr. Preferred 10¢ par called for redemption 08/12/1994
$2.50 Preferred Ser. A 10¢ par called for redemption 09/01/1994
Public interest eliminated

COLLINS & AIKMAN HLDGS CORP (DE)
15.5% Exchangeable Preferred 1¢ par called for redemption 08/12/1994
Public interest eliminated

COLLINS CHEMICAL & SUPPLY CO. (FL)
Proclaimed dissolved for non-payment of taxes 05/24/1963

COLLINS CO. (CT)
Liquidation completed
Each share Capital Stock $100 par exchanged for initial distribution of $125 cash 12/01/1966
Each share Capital Stock $100 par received second distibution of $130.58213 cash 07/20/1967
Each share Capital Stock $100 par received third and final distribution of $3.16 cash 06/27/1969

COLLINS FLASHLIGHT CORP.
Out of business 00/00/1934
Details not available

COLLINS FOODS INC (DE)
Name changed to Sizzler International, Inc. 05/06/1991
Sizzler International, Inc. name changed to Worldwide Restaurant Concepts Inc. 09/04/2001
(See Worldwide Restaurant Concepts Inc.)

COLLINS FOODS INTL INC (DE)
Reincorporated 10/31/1980
Common 10¢ par split (3) for (2) by issuance of (0.5) additional share 04/25/1972
State of incorporation changed from (CA) to (DE) 10/31/1980
Common 10¢ par split (4) for (3) by issuance of (0.33333333) additional share 10/23/1981
Common 10¢ par split (4) for (3) by issuance of (0.33333333) additional share 07/16/1982
Common 10¢ par split (3) for (2) by

issuance of (0.5) additional share 06/30/1983
Common 10¢ par split (3) for (2) by issuance of (0.5) additional share 11/16/1984
Common 10¢ par split (3) for (2) by issuance of (0.5) additional share 09/11/1985
Merged into PepsiCo, Inc. 03/18/1991
Each share Common 10¢ par exchanged for (0.21525889) share Capital Stock $0.016666666 par

COLLINS INDS INC (MO)
Old Common 10¢ par split (5) for (4) by issuance of (0.25) additional share 01/07/1991
Each share old Common 10¢ par exchanged for (1) share new Common 10¢ par to reflect a (1) for (300) reverse split followed by a (300) for (1) forward split 03/03/2006
Note: Holders of (299) or fewer pre-split shares received $7.70 cash per share
Merged into Steel Partners II, LP 10/31/2006
Each share new Common 10¢ par exchanged for $12.50 cash

COLLINS KEITH PETE CORP (CO)
Each share Common 1¢ par exchanged for (0.1) share Common 10¢ par 12/21/1981
Name changed to Gerber Energy International, Inc. 06/18/1984
Gerber Energy International, Inc. name changed to Gold King Consolidated, Inc. 06/16/1987
(See Gold King Consolidated, Inc.)

COLLINS-MORRIS SHOE CO.
Name changed to Vardaman Shoe Co. 00/00/1940
(See Vardaman Shoe Co.)

COLLINS PROCESS, INC.
Out of business 00/00/1932
Details not available

COLLINS RADIO CO (IA)
Each share Common $5 par exchanged for (1.5) shares Class A Common $1 par and (1.5) shares Class B Common $1 par 05/03/1955
Class A Common $1 par and Class B Common $1 par reclassified as Common $1 par 04/07/1959
4% Preferred called for redemption 10/17/1960
Stock Dividends - 25% 07/31/1952; 10% 07/31/1953; 15% 07/31/1954
Merged into Rockwell International Corp. (Old) 11/14/1973
Each share Common $1 par exchanged for $25 cash

COLLINS RES LTD (BC)
Recapitalized as Madison Enterprises Corp. 06/26/1992
Each share Common no par exchanged for (0.4) share Common no par
Madison Enterprises Corp. recapitalized as Madison Minerals Inc. 10/29/2004 which recapitalized as Battle Mountain Gold Inc. 05/14/2014 which merged into Gold Standard Ventures Corp. 06/15/2017

COLLISION CTRS INTL INC (UT)
Each share Common $0.001 par exchanged for (0.1) share Common 1¢ par 05/26/1988
Merged out of existence 04/17/2001
Details not available

COLLISION KING INC (NV)
Recapitalized as Great Outdoors, Inc. 02/10/2004
Each share Common $0.013 par exchanged for (0.05) share Common 1¢ par
Great Outdoors, Inc. name changed to Pivotal Technology, Inc. 08/21/2006 which name changed to Somatic Systems, Inc. 08/28/2006

COLLOQUIUM CAP CORP (BC)
Name changed to Imagis Technologies Inc. (BC) 02/25/1999
Imagis Technologies Inc. (BC) reincorporated in Canada as Visiphor Corp. 07/07/2005

COLLYER INSULATED WIRE CO. (RI)
Each share Common $100 par exchanged for (10) shares Common no par 00/00/1929
Stock Dividend - 100% 02/15/1967
Completely liquidated 08/31/1967
Each share Common no par exchanged for first and final distribution of (0.5) share Gulf & Western Industries, Inc. (DE) $5.75 Preferred $2.50 par
Gulf & Western Industries, Inc. (DE) name changed to Gulf + Western Inc. 05/01/1986 which name changed to Paramount Communications Inc. 06/05/1989 which merged into Viacom Inc. (Old) 07/07/1994
(See Viacom Inc. (Old))

COLMAN ALEX INC (CA)
Common $1 par split (5) for (4) by issuance of (0.25) additional share 11/12/1971
Merged into Borden, Inc. 06/05/1973
Each share Common $1 par exchanged for (0.5687) share Common $3.75 par
Borden, Inc. merged into RJR Nabisco Holdings Corp. 03/14/1995 which name changed to Nabisco Group Holdings Corp. 06/15/1999
(See Nabisco Group Holdings Corp.)

COLMENA CORP (DE)
Recapitalized as NetWorth Technologies, Inc. 12/16/2004
Each share Common 1¢ par exchanged for (0.1) share Common 1¢ par
NetWorth Technologies, Inc. recapitalized as Solution Technology International, Inc. 08/22/2006 which recapitalized as Reinsurance Technologies Ltd. 06/01/2009
(See Reinsurance Technologies Ltd.)

COLO-KAN FUEL CORP. (CO)
Merged into Fallon Gas Corp. 00/00/1955
Each share Class A Common $0.005 par exchanged for (0.5) share Common 5¢ par
Each share Class B Common $0.005 par exchanged for (0.05) share Common 5¢ par
Fallon Gas Corp. name changed to Fallon Smith Corp. 01/28/1966 which name changed to Imperial Investment Corp. 08/07/1969
(See Imperial Investment Corp.)

COLOMA RESOURCES LTD. (ON)
Acquired by FirstService Corp. 07/31/1988
Details not available

COLOMAC YELLOWKNIFE MINES LTD. (ON)
Merged into Hydra Explorations Ltd. on a (0.04) for (1) basis 11/16/1959
Hydra Explorations Ltd. name changed to Hydra Capital Corp. 12/30/1992 which name changed to Waterford Capital Management Inc. 11/12/1996 which merged into CPI Plastics Group Ltd. 09/21/1998
(See CPI Plastics Group Ltd.)

COLOMBIA CLEAN PWR & FUELS INC (NV)
Reincorporated under the laws of Delaware as Colombia Energy Resources, Inc. 11/04/2011

COLOMBIA EMERALD DEVELOPMENT CORP. (DE)
Investigation by New York State Attorney General concluded sold as part of a fraud and substantially worthless 09/08/1926

COLOMBIA GOLDFIELDS LTD (DE)
Reincorporated 07/31/2006
State of incorporation changed from (NV) to (DE) 07/31/2006
Merged into Medoro Resources Ltd. 11/02/2009
Each share Common $0.00001 par exchanged for (0.336) share Common no par and (0.0108) Common Stock Purchase Warrant expiring 07/22/2011
Note: Unexchanged certificates were cancelled and became without value 11/02/2015
Medoro Resources Ltd. merged into Gran Colombia Gold Corp. 06/14/2011

COLOMBIA INTERNATIONAL CORP., LTD. (NV)
Charter revoked for failure to file reports and pay fees 03/02/1959

COLOMBIA SYNDICATE
Dissolved 00/00/1934
Details not available

COLOMBIAN HOLDING CORP.
Liquidated 00/00/1937
Details not available

COLOMBIAN MINES CORP (BC)
Name changed to NewRange Gold Corp. 12/02/2016

COLOMBO BK (ROCKVILLE, MD)
Merged into FVCBankcorp, Inc. 10/15/2018
Each share Common 1¢ par exchanged for (0.002217) share Common 1¢ par and $0.053157 cash

COLON DEVELOPMENT CO. LTD. (ENGLAND)
6% Preference called for redemption 12/31/1943
Ordinary 7s par changed to 30s par 05/05/1955
Completely liquidated 03/31/1958
Each share Ordinary 30s par exchanged for (1) share Colon Oil Co. Ltd. Common no par
(See Colon Oil Co. Ltd.)

COLON OIL CO. LTD. (CANADA)
Completely liquidated
Each share Common no par exchanged for first and final distribution of USD$35 cash 12/31/1959

COLON OIL CORP.
Reorganized as Colon Development Co. Ltd. 00/00/1936
Each share Ordinary exchanged for (0.25) share Ordinary 7s par Colon Development Co. Ltd. liquidated for Colon Oil Co. Ltd. 03/31/1958
(See Colon Oil Co. Ltd.)

COLONADE CONSTRUCTION CORP. (NY)
Charter revoked for failure to file reports and pay fees 12/15/1950

COLONELS INTL INC (MI)
Name changed to Sports Resorts International Inc. 03/12/2001
(See Sports Resorts International Inc.)

COLONIA CORP (AB)
Name changed to Colonia Energy Corp. 12/12/2005
Colonia Energy Corp. recapitalized as Renegade Petroleum Ltd. 01/19/2010 which merged into Spartan Energy Corp. 04/01/2014 which merged into Vermillion Energy Inc. 05/31/2018

COLONIA ENERGY CORP (AB)
Recapitalized as Renegade Petroleum Ltd. 01/19/2010
Each share Common no par exchanged for (0.1) share Common no par
Renegade Petroleum Ltd. merged into Spartan Energy Corp.

04/01/2014 which merged into Vermilion Energy Inc. 05/31/2018

COLONIAL ACCEP CORP (DE)
Each share 7% Preferred $100 par exchanged for (24) shares Class A Common 1st Ser. $1 par 00/00/1950
Each share Class A Common $1 par exchanged for (1.2) shares Class A Common 1st Ser. $1 par 00/00/1950
Class A Common 1st Ser. $1 par called for redemption 08/21/1964
Acquired by USLIFE Corp. 07/21/1970
Each share $1.20 Preferred $10 par exchanged for (0.2167) share $5 Conv. Preferred Ser. B $1 par
Each share Common $1 par exchanged for (0.6755) share Common $2 par
USLIFE Corp. merged into American General Corp. 06/17/1997 which merged into American International Group, Inc. 08/29/2001

COLONIAL ADVANCED STRATEGIES GOLD TR (MA)
Merged into Colonial Trust III 06/05/1992
Each Share of Bene. Int. no par exchanged for (1) share Natural Resources Fund Class A
Colonial Trust III name changed to Liberty Funds Trust III 04/01/1999

COLONIAL AIR TRANSPORT, INC.
Acquired by Colonial Airways Co.
Details not available

COLONIAL AIRCRAFT CORP (NY)
Each share old Common 10¢ par exchanged for (0.1) share new Common 10¢ par 04/06/1962
Name changed to Colonial Coastal Corp. 11/27/1972
(See Colonial Coastal Corp.)

COLONIAL AIRLINES, INC. (DE)
Acquired by Eastern Air Lines, Inc. 05/31/1956
Each share Capital Stock $1 par exchanged for (0.5) share Common $1 par
Eastern Air Lines, Inc. merged into Texas Air Corp. 11/25/1986
(See Texas Air Corp.)

COLONIAL AIRWAYS CO.
Acquired by Aviation Corp. 00/00/1929
Details not available

COLONIAL AMERN BK (WEST CONSHOHOCKEN, PA)
Merged into OceanFirst Financial Corp. 07/31/2015
Each share Common $1 par exchanged for (0.3658) share Common 1¢ par

COLONIAL AMERN BANKSHARES CORP (VA)
Stock Dividends - 10% 10/01/1976; 100% 06/02/1978; 10% 11/01/1984; 10% 11/01/1986
Acquired by Crestar Financial Corp. 05/01/1989
Each share Common $5 par exchanged for (1.11) shares Common $5 par
Crestar Financial Corp. merged into SunTrust Banks, Inc. 12/31/1998

COLONIAL AMERICAN LIFE INSURANCE CO. (TX)
Merged into American Capitol Insurance Co. (TX) 01/01/1965
Each share Capital Stock no par exchanged for (1) share Capital Stock no par
American Capitol Insurance Co. (TX) reorganized in Delaware as Acap Corp. 10/31/1985 which merged into UTG, Inc. 11/14/2011

COLONIAL AMERN NATL BK (ROANOKE, VA)
Each share Capital Stock $50 par exchanged for (5) shares Capital Stock $10 par 00/00/1946

Capital Stock $10 par changed to $5 par and (1) additional share issued 04/30/1973
Stock Dividends - 50% 01/30/1957; 16.66666666% 08/22/1960; 10% 07/30/1964; 14.28571428% 07/14/1967
Under plan of reorganization each share Capital Stock $5 par automatically became (1) share Colonial American Bankshares Corp. Common $5 par 10/31/1974
Colonial American Bankshares Corp. acquired by Crestar Financial Corp. 05/01/1989 which merged into SunTrust Banks, Inc. 12/31/1998

COLONIAL ASBESTOS CORP. LTD. (ON)
Acquired by Normalloy Explorations Ltd. 00/00/1958
Each share Common exchanged for (1) share Common Normalloy Explorations Ltd. name changed to Normalloy Explorations & Holdings Ltd. 08/23/1963
(See Normalloy Explorations & Holdings Ltd.)

COLONIAL BANCGROUP INC (DE)
Old Common $2.50 par reclassified as Conv. Class B Common $2.50 par and (1) share Class A Common $2.50 par distributed 05/17/1983
Class A Common $2.50 par reclassified as new Common $2.50 par 02/21/1995
Conv. Class B Common $2.50 par reclassified as new Common $2.50 par 02/21/1995
New Common $2.50 par split (2) for (1) by issuance of (1) additional share payable 02/11/1997 to holders of record 02/04/1997 Ex date - 02/12/1997
New Common $2.50 par split (2) for (1) by issuance of (1) additional share payable 08/14/1998 to holders of record 07/31/1998 Ex date - 08/17/1998
Plan of reorganization under Chapter 11 Federal Bankruptcy proceedings effective 06/03/2011
No stockholders' equity

COLONIAL BANCORP INC (CT)
Stock Dividend - 12.5% 01/16/1974
Merged into Bank of Boston Corp. 06/20/1985
Each share Common $10 par exchanged for (0.73) share Conv. Preferred Ser. B no par
Bank of Boston Corp. name changed to BankBoston Corp. 04/25/1997 which merged into Fleet Boston Corp. 10/01/1999 which name changed to FleetBoston Financial Corp. 04/18/2000 which merged into Bank of America Corp. 04/01/2004

COLONIAL BANCORP INC (PA)
Merged into Dauphin Deposit Corp. 09/01/1987
Each share Common $2.50 par exchanged for (4) shares Common $5 par
Dauphin Deposit Corp. merged into Allied Irish Banks, PLC 07/08/1997
(See Allied Irish Banks, PLC)

COLONIAL BANK & TRUST CO. (ANNAPOLIS, MD)
Merged into Suburban Bancorporation 12/31/1973
Each share Common $10 par exchanged for (0.85) share Common $5 par
Suburban Bancorporation name changed to Suburban Bancorp 12/31/1981 which merged into Sovran Financial Corp. 03/31/1986 which merged into C&S/Sovran Corp. 09/01/1990 which merged into NationsBank Corp. (NC) 12/31/1991 which reincorporated in Delaware as BankAmerica Corp. (Old) 09/25/1998 which merged into BankAmerica Corp. (New) 09/30/1998 which name changed to Bank of America Corp. 04/28/1999

COLONIAL BK & TR CO (CHICAGO, IL)
Stock Dividends - 10% 03/01/1969; 10% 03/01/1970; 10% 02/15/1972
Reorganized as First Colonial Bankshares Corp. 10/25/1978
Each share Common $10 par exchanged for (1) share Ser. A Preferred $57 par and (1) share Common $5 par
First Colonial Bankshares Corp. merged into Firstar Corp. (Old) 01/31/1995 which merged into Firstar Corp. (New) 11/20/1998 which merged into U.S. Bancorp (DE) 02/27/2001

COLONIAL BK & TR CO (WATERBURY, CT)
Capital Stock $10 par changed to $20 par 01/29/1963
Capital Stock $20 par changed to $10 par and (1) additional share issued 02/08/1965
Stock Dividends - 10% 02/18/1964; 10% 05/22/1968
Under plan of reorganization each share Capital Stock $10 par automatically became (1) share Colonial Bancorp, Inc. (CT) Capital Stock $10 par 06/01/1970
Colonial Bancorp, Inc. (CT) merged into Bank of Boston Corp. 06/20/1985 which name changed to BankBoston Corp. 04/25/1997 which merged into Fleet Boston Corp. 10/01/1999 which name changed to FleetBoston Financial Corp. 04/18/2000 which merged into Bank of America Corp. 04/01/2004

COLONIAL BK (NEW ORLEANS, LA)
Closed by the State Banking Department 01/14/1988
Stockholders' equity unlikely

COLONIAL BK GRNTS PASS (GRANTS PASS, OR)
Merged into VRB Bancorp 01/05/1998
Each share Preferred exchanged for $43.36 cash

COLONIAL BK SOUTH CAROLINA INC (SC)
Merged into Carolina First Corp. 10/19/1998
Each share Common $1 par exchanged for (0.8142) share Common $1 par
Carolina First Corp. name changed to South Financial Group, Inc. 04/24/2000 which merged into Toronto-Dominion Bank (Toronto, ON) 09/30/2010

COLONIAL BANKSHARES INC (USA)
Reorganized under the laws of Maryland as Colonial Financial Services, Inc. 07/13/2010
Each share Common 10¢ par exchanged for (0.9399) share Common 10¢ par
Colonial Financial Services, Inc. merged into Cape Bancorp, Inc. 04/01/2015 which merged into OceanFirst Financial Corp. 05/02/2016

COLONIAL BKG CO (OR)
Merged into VRB Bancorp 01/05/1998
Each share Common exchanged for $43.36 cash

COLONIAL BRD CO (CT)
Common $5 par changed to $3.33333333 par and (0.5) additional share issued 12/29/1967
Name changed to Lydall, Inc. (CT) 12/31/1969
Lydall, Inc. (CT) reincorporated in Delaware 09/30/1987

COLONIAL CALIF INSD MUN FD (MA)
Name changed to MFS California Insured Municipal Fund 06/29/2007
MFS California Insured Municipal Fund name changed to MFS California Municipal Fund 10/01/2010

COLONIAL CAP APPRECIATION TR (MA)
Name changed to Colonial Equity Income Trust 05/27/1986
(See Colonial Equity Income Trust)

COLONIAL CAP CORP (DE)
Name changed to Mercado Marketing Corp. 12/30/1990
Mercado Marketing Corp. name changed to COFIS International Corp. 06/05/1991 which recapitalized as U.S. Bridge Corp. 04/29/1994 which name changed to USABG Corp. 01/13/1998
(See USABG Corp.)

COLONIAL CAP TR III (DE)
8.32% Guaranteed Preferred Securities called for redemption at $25 on 06/22/2007

COLONIAL CAP TR IV (DE)
Colonial BancGroup, Inc., Guarantor of Trust, Chapter 11 bankruptcy proceedings effective 06/03/2011
Holders may receive an undetermined amount of cash

COLONIAL CHEM CORP (GA)
Each share Class A Common $5 par and Class B Common $5 par exchanged for (2) shares Class A Common $1 par and Class B Common $1 par respectively 11/21/1963
Liquidation completed
Each share Class A Common $1 par exchanged for initial distribution of $4 cash 05/08/1970
Each share Class B Common $1 par exchanged for initial distribution of $4 cash 05/08/1970
Each share Class A Common $1 par received second and final distribution of $0.83457 cash 12/02/1971
Each share Class B Common $1 par received second and final distribution of $0.83457 cash 12/02/1971

COLONIAL COASTAL CORP (NY)
Merged into Colonial Coastal Corp. (MA) 04/18/1979
Each share Common 10¢ par exchanged for $0.22 cash

COLONIAL COML CORP (NY)
Common 50¢ par split (2) for (1) by issuance of (1) additional share 08/10/1971
Common 50¢ par changed to 1¢ par 12/31/1982
Each share Conv. Preferred 1¢ par exchanged for (0.2) share Conv. Preferred 5¢ par 01/30/1998
Each share Common 1¢ par exchanged for (0.2) share Common 5¢ par 01/20/1998
Stock Dividend - 50% 06/30/1978
Name changed to CCOM Group, Inc. 07/26/2012

COLONIAL CONV & SR SECS INC (MA)
Name changed to Colonial Senior Securities, Inc. 03/29/1978
Colonial Senior Securities, Inc. name changed to Colonial High Yield Securities, Inc. 03/19/1980 which name changed to Colonial High Yield Securities Trust 04/30/1985 which merged into Colonial Trust I 09/13/1991 which name changed to Liberty Funds Trust I 04/01/1999

COLONIAL CONVERTIBLE FUND, INC. (MA)
Name changed to Colonial Convertible & Senior Securities, Inc. 03/20/1974
Colonial Convertible & Senior Securities, Inc. name changed to Colonial Senior Securities, Inc. 03/29/1978 which name changed to Colonial High Yield Securities, Inc. 03/19/1980 which name changed to Colonial High Yield Securities Trust 04/30/1985

COLONIAL CORP. OF AMERICA (NY)
Common $1 par split (3) for (1) by issuance of (2) additional shares 06/13/1960
Common $1 par changed to 50¢ par and (1) additional share issued 10/05/1961
Stock Dividend - 25% 03/09/1962
Merged into Kayser-Roth Corp. 04/01/1966
Each share Common 50¢ par exchanged for (1/3) share Common $1 par
Kayser-Roth Corp. merged into Gulf & Western Industries, Inc. (DE) 10/21/1975 which name changed to Gulf + Western Inc. 05/01/1986 which name changed to Paramount Communications Inc. 06/05/1989 which merged into Viacom Inc. (Old) 07/07/1994
(See Viacom Inc. (Old))

COLONIAL CORP (DE)
In process of liquidation
Each Unit consisting of (1) share 7% Preferred $45 par and (1) share Common no par exchanged for $75 cash plus a Trust Certificate 04/19/1968
Holders of Trust Certificates received second distribution of $5.97 cash 05/22/1969
Note: Details on additional distributions are not available

COLONIAL CORP CASH TR II (MA)
Trust terminated 04/30/1991
Details not available

COLONIAL COS INC (DE)
Merged into UNUM Corp. 03/26/1993
Each share Class A $1 par exchanged for (0.731) share Common 10¢ par
Each share Class B $1 par exchanged for (0.731) share Common 10¢ par

COLONIAL DATA TECHNOLOGIES CORP (DE)
Reincorporated 05/19/1995
State of incorporation changed from (MA) to (DE) 05/19/1995
Merged into InteliData Technologies Corp. 11/07/1996
Each share Common 1¢ par exchanged for (1) share Common $0.001 par
InteliData Technologies Corp. merged into Corillian Corp. 10/06/2005
(See Corillian Corp.)

COLONIAL DOWNS HLDGS INC (VA)
Name changed to Colonial Holdings, Inc. 08/15/2000
(See Colonial Holdings, Inc.)

COLONIAL ENERGY SHARES, INC. (MA)
Name changed to Colonial Growth & Energy Shares, Inc. 06/20/1961
Colonial Growth & Energy Shares, Inc. name changed to Colonial Growth Shares, Inc. 06/20/1967 which reorganized as Colonial Growth Shares Trust 09/02/1986 which reorganized as Colonial Trust III 09/13/1991 which name changed to Liberty Funds Trust III 04/01/1999 which name changed to Columbia Funds Trust III 10/13/2003

COLONIAL ENHANCED MTG TR (MA)
Name changed to Colonial Government Mortgage Trust 06/12/1986

(See Colonial Government Mortgage Trust)

COLONIAL EQUITIES INC (MA)
Common $1 par split (3) for (1) by issuance of (2) additional shares 01/08/1968
Merged into Colonial Growth Shares, Inc. 11/21/1975
Each share Common $1 par exchanged for (0.50258287) share Common $1 par
Colonial Growth Shares, Inc. reorganized as Colonial Growth Shares Trust 09/02/1986 which reorganized as Colonial Trust III 09/13/1991

COLONIAL EQUITY INCOME TR (MA)
Trust terminated 10/31/1989
Details not available

COLONIAL FED SVGS BK (BELLEFONTAINE, OH)
Merged into Mid Am, Inc. 07/06/1993
Each share Common 1¢ par exchanged for either (2.6638) shares Common no par or $56.27 cash
Note: Option to elect to receive cash expired 08/03/1993
Mid Am, Inc. merged into Sky Financial Group, Inc. 10/02/1998 which merged into Huntington Bancshares Inc. 07/02/2007

COLONIAL FINANCE CO. NEW (OH)
4.75% Preferred 1947 Ser. $100 par reclassified as 5% Preferred 1947 Ser. $100 par 02/01/1956
5% Preferred 1947 Ser. $100 par called for redemption 10/01/1962
5% Preferred 1956 Ser. $100 par called for redemption 10/01/1962
Stock Dividends - 20% 07/15/1956; 10% 07/15/1957
Liquidation completed
Each share Common $1 par exchanged for initial distribution of (1) Deposit Receipt for Common $1 par and $15 cash 11/05/1962
Each Deposit Receipt for Common $1 par received second distribution of (0.1) share First National Bank & Trust Co. (Lima, OH) Capital Stock $10 par 01/30/1963
Each Deposit Receipt for Common $1 par received third distribution of $7.50 cash 08/08/1963
Each Deposit Receipt for Common $1 par exchanged for fourth and final distribution of $1.075 cash 01/18/1966
(See First National Bank & Trust Co. (Lima, OH))

COLONIAL FINANCE CO. OLD (OH)
Liquidated 00/00/1942
Details not available

COLONIAL FINL SVCS INC (MD)
Merged into Cape Bancorp, Inc. 04/01/2015
Each share Common 10¢ par exchanged for (1.412) shares Common 1¢ par
Cape Bancorp, Inc. merged into OceanFirst Financial Corp. 05/02/2016

COLONIAL FIRST NATL BK (RED BANK, NJ)
Merged into Fidelity Union Bancorporation 06/28/1974
Each share Common $1 par exchanged for (0.1881) share Common $5 par
Fidelity Union Bancorporation merged into First National State Bancorporation 04/05/1984 which name changed to First Fidelity Bancorporation (Old) 05/01/1985 which merged into First Fidelity Bancorporation (New) 02/29/1988 which merged into First Union Corp. 01/01/1996 which name changed to Wachovia Corp. (Ctfs. dated after 09/01/2001) 09/01/2001 which merged into Wells Fargo & Co. (New) 12/31/2008

COLONIAL FOOD DISTRIBUTORS, INC. (MD)
Charter annulled 10/30/1969

COLONIAL FOODS INC (DE)
Merged into Jobemo Corp. 06/13/1979
Each share Common 10¢ par exchanged for $3 cash

COLONIAL FD INC (MA)
Reorganized 12/22/1986
Under plan of reorganization name changed from Colonial Fund, Inc. to Colonial Fund and Common $1 par reclassified as Shares of Bene. Int. $1 par 12/22/1986
Merged into Colonial Trust III 02/14/1992
Each Share of Bene. Int. no par exchanged for (1) share Colonial Fund Class A
Colonial Trust III name changed to Liberty Funds Trust III 04/01/1999

COLONIAL FUND, INC. (DE)
Common $10 par changed to $1 par 05/00/1954
Common $1 par split (5) for (3) by issuance of (2) additional shares 06/00/1954
Common $1 par split (2) for (1) by issuance of (1) additional share 01/21/1957
Merged into Colonial Fund, Inc. (MA) 08/18/1959
Details not available

COLONIAL GAS CO (MA)
$1.80 Conv. Preferred $1 par called for redemption 08/01/1986
Common $5 par changed to $3.33333333 par and (0.5) additional share issued 07/29/1992
Merged into Eastern Enterprises 08/31/1999
Each share Common $3.33333333 par exchanged for $37.50 cash
(See Eastern Enterprises)

COLONIAL GAS ENERGY SYS (MA)
Merged into Colonial Gas Co. 07/30/1981
Each share $1.80 Conv. Preferred no par exchanged for (1) share $1.80 Conv. Preferred $1 par
Each share Common no par exchanged for (1) share Common $5 par
Colonial Gas Co. merged into Eastern Enterprises 08/31/1999
(See Eastern Enterprises)

COLONIAL GEN LIFE INS CO (IL)
Name changed to United National Life Insurance Co. of America 12/02/1968
(See United National Life Insurance Co. of America)

COLONIAL GOVT MONEY MKT TR (MA)
Name changed to Colonial Money Market Trust (New) 04/27/1990
Colonial Money Market Trust (New) merged into Colonial Trust II 09/13/1991 which name changed to Liberty Funds Trust II 04/01/1999

COLONIAL GOVT MTG TR (MA)
Trust terminated 06/30/1989
Details not available

COLONIAL GROUP INC (MA)
Merged into Liberty Financial Companies, Inc. 03/24/1995
Each share Class A Common 10¢ par exchanged for (1) share Common 1¢ par
(See Liberty Financial Companies, Inc.)

COLONIAL GROWTH & ENERGY SHARES, INC. (MA)
Name changed to Colonial Growth Shares, Inc. 06/20/1967
Colonial Growth Shares, Inc. reorganized as Colonial Growth Shares Trust 09/02/1986 which reorganized as Colonial Trust III 09/13/1991 which name changed to Liberty Funds Trust III 04/01/1999 which name changed to Columbia Funds Trust III 10/13/2003

COLONIAL GROWTH SHS TR (MA)
Reorganized 09/02/1986
Common $1 par split (2) for (1) by issuance of (1) additional share 07/14/1967
Reorganized from Colonial Growth Shares to Colonial Growth Shares Trust and Common $1 par reclassified as Shares of Bene. Int. $1 par 09/02/1986
Reorganized as Colonial Trust III 09/13/1991
Each Share of Bene. Int. $1 par exchanged for (1) Growth Share Fund Class A
Colonial Trust III name changed to Liberty Funds Trust III 04/01/1999 which name changed to Columbia Funds Trust III 10/13/2003

COLONIAL HIGH INCOME MUN TR (MA)
Name changed to MFS High Income Municipal Trust 06/29/2007

COLONIAL HIGH YIELD SECS INC (MA)
Name changed to Colonial High Yield Securities Trust and Common $1 par reclassified as Shares of Bene. Int. no par 04/30/1985
Colonial High Yield Securities Trust merged into Colonial Trust I 09/13/1991 which name changed to Liberty Funds Trust I 04/01/1999

COLONIAL HIGH YIELD SECS TR (MA)
Merged into Colonial Trust I 9/13/91
Each Share of Bene. Int. no par exchanged for (1) share High Yield Securities Fund Class A
Colonial Trust I name changed to Liberty Funds Trust I 4/1/99

COLONIAL HLDGS CORP (VA)
Merged into Gameco, Inc. 02/26/2002
Each share Class A Common 1¢ par exchanged for $1.12 cash
Each share Class B Common 1¢ par exchanged for $1.12 cash

COLONIAL INCOME FD (MA)
Name changed 02/23/1987
Name changed from Colonial Income Fund, Inc to Colonial Income Fund and Common $1 par reclassified as Shares of Bene. Int. $1 par 02/23/1987
Merged into Colonial Trust I 05/01/1992
Each Share of Bene. Int. no par exchanged for (1) share Income Fund Class A
Colonial Trust I name changed to Liberty Funds Trust I 04/01/1999

COLONIAL INDS INC (TX)
Each shares old Common no par exchanged for (0.01333333) share new Common no par 11/11/1998
Chapter 7 bankruptcy proceedings terminated 09/30/2009
Stockholders' equity unlikely

COLONIAL INSD MUN FD (MA)
Municipal Auction Rate Preferred called for redemption at $25 on 05/25/2007
Completely liquidated
Each share Common no par received first and final distribution of $14.64401861 cash payable 05/30/2007 to holders of record 05/25/2007
Note: Certificates were not required to be surrendered and are without value

COLONIAL INTER HIGH INCOME FD (MA)
Name changed to MFS Intermediate High Income Fund 06/29/2007

COLONIAL INTERMARKET INCOME TR I (MA)
Name changed to MFS InterMarket Income Trust I 06/29/2007
(See MFS InterMarket Income Trust I)

COLONIAL INTL EQUITY INDEX TR (MA)
Trust terminated 06/01/1995
Details not available

COLONIAL INTL IMPORT LTD (CO)
Involuntarily dissolved for failure to file annual reports and pay taxes 01/01/1991

COLONIAL INVT GRADE MUN TR (MA)
Name changed to MFS Investment Grade Municipal Trust 06/29/2007

COLONIAL INVESTORS SHARES SERIES A
Out of business 00/00/1936
Details not available

COLONIAL LIFE & ACC INS CO (SC)
Class A Common $1 par split (2) for (1) by issuance of (1) additional share 05/07/1973
Class B Non-Vtg. Common $1 par split (2) for (1) by issuance of (1) additional share 05/07/1973
Class A Common $1 par split (5) for (4) by issuance of (0.25) additional share 05/31/1979
Class B Non-Vtg. Common $1 par split (5) for (4) by issuance of (0.25) additional share 05/31/1979
Class A Common $1 par split (3) for (2) by issuance of (0.5) additional share 04/07/1987
Class B Non-Vtg. Common $1 par split (3) for (2) by issuance of (0.5) additional share 04/07/1987
Class A Common $1 par split (2) for (1) by issuance of (1) additional share 06/12/1989
Class B Non-Vtg. Common $1 par split (2) for (1) by issuance of (1) additional share 06/12/1989
Stock Dividends - Class A & B -25% 05/08/1968; 25% 05/06/1970
Reincorporated under the laws of Delaware as Colonial Companies, Inc. 12/18/1989
Colonial Companies, Inc. merged into UNUM Corp. 03/26/1993

COLONIAL LIFE & CASUALTY CO. (AZ)
Merged into Seaboard Life Insurance Co. of America 06/07/1967
Each share Common $1 par exchanged for (1.6) shares Common $1 par
(See Seaboard Life Insurance Co. of America)

COLONIAL LIFE INS CO AMER (NJ)
Each share Capital Stock $100 par exchanged for (10) shares Capital Stock $10 par 00/00/1952
Stock Dividend - 11.11111111% 05/03/1954
Acquired by Federal Insurance Co. 02/27/1975
Each share Capital Stock $10 par exchanged for $286 cash

COLONIAL MANAGEMENT CO. (IL)
Proclaimed dissolved for failure to pay taxes and file reports 04/01/1985

COLONIAL MARBLE CO., INC.
Out of business 00/00/1936
Details not available

COLONIAL MEDICAL & DEVELOPMENT CO. (DE)
Public offering subsequently rescinded 04/27/1972
Each share Capital Stock 1¢ par exchanged for $3 cash

COLONIAL MILLS, INC. (NY)
Name changed to Robbins Mills, Inc. 01/00/1950
Robbins Mills, Inc. merged into Textron American, Inc. 02/24/1955 which name changed to Textron Inc. (RI) 05/15/1956 which was reincorporated in Delaware 01/02/1968

COLONIAL MONEY MKT TR NEW (MA)
Merged into Colonial Trust II 09/13/1991
Each Share of Bene. Int. no par exchanged for (1) Money Market Fund Class A
Colonial Trust II name changed to Liberty Funds Trust II 04/01/1999

COLONIAL MONEY MKT TR OLD (MA)
Name changed to Colonial Government Money Market Trust 06/05/1987
Colonial Government Money Market Trust name changed to Colonial Money Market Trust (New) 04/27/1990 which merged into Colonial Trust II 09/13/1991 which name changed to Liberty Funds Trust II 04/01/1999

COLONIAL MORTGAGE SERVICE CO. (PA)
Completely liquidated 12/31/1969
Each share Common $1 par exchanged for first and final distribution of $19.06 cash

COLONIAL MUN INCOME TR (MA)
Name changed to MFS High Yield Municipal Trust 06/29/2007

COLONIAL NAT GAS CO (VA)
Merged into Tennessee-Virginia Natural Gas Co. 09/27/1979
Each share Common $2 par exchanged for $8.50 cash

COLONIAL NATIONAL BANK (ALEXANDRIA, VA)
Merged into First Virginia Bankshares Corp. 01/26/1968
Each share Common $10 par exchanged for (1.4) shares 5% Conv. Preferred $10 par and (1.5) shares Common $1 par
First Virginia Bankshares Corp. name changed to First Virginia Banks, Inc. 09/01/1978 which merged into BB&T Corp. 07/01/2003

COLONIAL NATIONAL BANK (BOCA RATON, FL)
Name changed to Colonial Trust Co., N.A. (Palm Beach, FL) 01/01/1983
Colonial Trust Co., N.A. (Palm Beach, FL) reorganized as Colonial Trust National Bank (Palm Beach, FL) 10/28/1986 which name changed to Palm Beach National Bank & Trust Co. (Palm Beach, FL) 06/22/1990 which reorganized as Palm Beach National Holding Co. 05/01/1997 which merged into Colonial BancGroup, Inc. 09/03/2002
(See Colonial BancGroup, Inc.)

COLONIAL NATL BK (HADDONFIELD, NJ)
Stock Dividend - 10% 02/15/1968
Acquired by Midlantic Banks Inc. 08/31/1972
Each share Common $5 par exchanged for (0.7) share Common $10 par
Midlantic Banks Inc. merged into Midlantic Corp. 01/30/1987 which merged into PNC Bank Corp. 12/31/1995 which name changed to PNC Financial Services Group, Inc. 03/15/2000

COLONIAL NATURAL GAS CORP. (DE)
Liquidation completed 10/12/64
Each share Common 50¢ par exchanged for initial distribution of (0.02260089) share North Carolina Natural Gas Corp. Common $2.50 par 6/22/60
Each share Common 50¢ par received second and final distribution of (0.0056502) share North Carolina Natural Gas Corp. Common $2.50 par 10/12/64
North Carolina Natural Gas Corp. merged into Carolina Power & Light Co. 7/15/99

COLONIAL NEW YORK INSD MUN FD (MA)
Municipal Auction Rate Preferred called for redemption at $25,000 on 06/10/2005
Completely liquidated
Each share Common no par received first and final distribution of $15.99965212 cash payable 06/14/2005 to holders of record 06/10/2005
Note: Certificates were not required to be surrendered and are without value

COLONIAL NUCLEAR INDUSTRIES, INC. (DE)
Charter revoked for non-payment of taxes 04/01/1959

COLONIAL OHIO TAX EXEMPT TR (MA)
Merged into Colonial Trust V 08/03/1992
Each Share of Bene. Int. no par exchanged for (1) share Ohio Tax Exempt Fund Class A
Colonial Trust V name changed to Liberty Funds Trust V 04/01/1999

COLONIAL OIL & GAS CORP (DE)
Name changed to Cosmic Venture Corp. 06/09/1986
(See Cosmic Venture Corp.)

COLONIAL OIL & GAS LTD (BC)
Each share 5% Conv. 1st Preferred Ser. B no par exchanged for (10) shares Common no par 07/28/1989
Merged into Cogas Energy Ltd. 02/26/1993
Each share Common no par exchanged for (0.5) share Common no par
Cogas Energy Ltd. acquired by Canadian Pioneer Energy Inc. 12/28/1994 which was acquired by Cimarron Petroleum Ltd. 12/20/1995 which merged into Newport Petroleum Corp. 04/09/1997
(See Newport Petroleum Corp.)

COLONIAL OIL CO. (CO)
Completely liquidated 02/27/1981
Each share Common $1 par received first and final distribution of $0.006825 cash

COLONIAL OPT GROWTH TR (MA)
Name changed to Colonial Capital Appreciation Trust 11/08/1984
Colonial Capital Appreciation Trust name changed to Colonial Equity Income Trust 05/27/1986
(See Colonial Equity Income Trust)

COLONIAL PENN GROUP INC (DE)
Stock Dividends - 100% 04/02/1971; 100% 04/04/1972
Acquired by FPL Group, Inc. 12/31/1985
Each share Common 10¢ par exchanged for $35 cash

COLONIAL PPTYS TR (AL)
Reincorporated 09/27/1995
State of incorporation changed from (MD) to (AL) 09/27/1995
8.75% Preferred Ser. A 1¢ par called for redemption at $25 plus $0.2248 accrued dividends 05/07/2003
9.25% Preferred Ser. C called for redemption at $25 plus $0.578125 accrued dividends on 06/30/2006
7.62% Depositary Preferred Ser. E called for redemption at $25 plus $0.3175 accrued dividends on 05/30/2007
8.125% Depositary Preferred Ser. D called for redemption at $25 plus $0.2257 accrued dividends on 09/10/2010
Merged into Mid-America Apartment Communities, Inc. 10/01/2013
Each Common Share of Bene. Int. 1¢ par exchanged for (0.36) share Common 1¢ par

COLONIAL RTYS CO (DE)
Company dissolved 00/00/1988
Details not available

COLONIAL SAND & STONE INC (NY)
Common $1 par split (2) for (1) by issuance of (1) additional share 04/14/1960
Merged into C.S.S. Sand & Cement Co., Inc. 01/23/1974
Each share Common $1 par exchanged for $12 cash

COLONIAL SAVINGS & LOAN ASSOCIATION (CA)
Guarantee Stock $1 par changed to no par 06/27/1969
Merged into Ahmanson (H.F.) & Co. (CA) 10/29/1971
Each share Guarantee Stock no par exchanged for (0.419239) share Common no par
Ahmanson (H.F.) & Co. (CA) reincorporated in Delaware 05/22/1985 which merged into Washington Mutual, Inc. 10/01/1998
(See Washington Mutual, Inc.)

COLONIAL SVGS & LN ASSN RICHMOND (VA)
Merged into Savings & Loan Association 05/07/1985
Each share Common $1 par exchanged for $1.75 cash

COLONIAL SVGS BK S C INC (SC)
Name changed to Colonial Bank of South Carolina Inc. 02/15/1996
Colonial Bank of South Carolina Inc. merged into Carolina First Corp. 10/19/1998 which name changed to South Financial Group, Inc. 04/24/2000 which merged into Toronto-Dominion Bank (Toronto, ON) 09/30/2010

COLONIAL SVCS CO (DE)
Adjudicated bankrupt 01/13/1972
Stockholders' equity unlikely

COLONIAL SMALL STK INDEX TR (MA)
Trust terminated 06/03/1992
Details not available

COLONIAL SR SECS INC (MA)
Name changed to Colonial High Yield Securities, Inc. 03/19/1980
Colonial High Yield Securities, Inc. name changed to Colonial High Yield Securities Trust 04/30/1985 which merged into Colonial Trust I 09/13/1991 which name changed to Liberty Funds Trust I 04/01/1999

COLONIAL ST BK (FREEHOLD, NJ)
Merged into Sovereign Bancorp, Inc. 11/15/1995
Each share Common no par exchanged for $11.60 cash

COLONIAL STATES FIRE INSURANCE CO.
Merged into American Colony Insurance Co. 03/00/1934
Details not available

COLONIAL STEEL CO.
Merged into Vanadium-Alloys Steel Co. 00/00/1928
Details not available

COLONIAL STORES INC (VA)
Each share Common $5 par exchanged for (2) shares Common $2.50 par 00/00/1946
Common $2.50 par split (2) for (1) by issuance of (1) additional share 04/30/1956
5% Preferred $50 par called for redemption 12/27/1963
Common $2.50 par split (3) for (2) by issuance of (0.5) additional share 03/16/1972
Stock Dividend - 20% 03/27/1953
Under plan of merger each share Common $2.50 par exchanged for $35 cash 11/18/1978
$4 Preferred $50 par called for redemption 12/01/1978
Public interest eliminated

COLONIAL TAX EXEMPT HIGH YIELD TR (MA)
Name changed to Colonial Tax-Exempt Trust 09/27/1984
Colonial Tax-Exempt Trust reorganized as Colonial Trust IV 09/13/1991 which name changed to Liberty Funds Trust IV 04/01/1999

COLONIAL TAX EXEMPT TR (MA)
Reorganized as Colonial Trust IV 09/13/1991
Each share Tax-Exempt Fund exchanged for (1) share Tax-Exempt Fund Class A
Each share Insured Fund exchanged for (1) share Insured Fund Class A
Colonial Trust IV name changed to Liberty Funds Trust IV 04/01/1999

COLONIAL TAX MANAGED TR (MA)
Shares of Bene. Int. 10¢ par split (2) for (1) by issuance of (1) additional share 11/14/1983
Name changed to Colonial Tax-Exempt High Yield Trust 09/18/1984
Colonial Tax-Exempt High Yield Trust name changed to Colonial Tax-Exempt Trust 09/27/1984 which reorganized as Colonial Trust IV 09/13/1991 which name changed to Liberty Funds Trust IV 04/01/1999

COLONIAL TRUST CO., N.A. (PALM BEACH, FL)
Under plan of reorganization each share Capital Stock $10 par automatically became (1) share Colonial Trust National Bank (Palm Beach, FL) Common $5 par 10/28/1986
Colonial Trust National Bank (Palm Beach, FL) name changed to Palm Beach National Bank & Trust Co. (Palm Beach, FL) 06/22/1990 which reorganized as Palm Beach National Holding Co. 05/01/1997 which merged into Colonial BancGroup, Inc. 09/03/2002
(See Colonial BancGroup, Inc.)

COLONIAL TRUST CO. (NEW YORK, NY)
Acquired by Meadow Brook National Bank (West Hempstead, NY) 11/14/1960
Each share Capital Stock $25 par exchanged for (0.3) share Capital Stock $5 par and $132.05 cash
Meadow Brook National Bank (West Hempstead, NY) name changed to National Bank of North America (West Hempstead, NY) 05/08/1967
(See National Bank of North America (West Hempstead, NY))

COLONIAL TRUST CO. (WATERBURY, CT)
Capital Stock $25 par changed to $10 par and (1.5) additional shares issued 07/30/1957
Stock Dividends - 50% 06/01/1951; 25% 02/15/1955
Merged into Colonial Bank & Trust Co. (Waterbury, CT) 06/30/1959
Each share Capital Stock $25 par exchanged for (1) share Capital Stock $10 par
Colonial Bank & Trust Co. (Waterbury, CT) reorganized as Colonial Bancorp, Inc. (CT) 06/01/1970 which merged into Bank of Boston Corp. 06/20/1985 which name changed to

COLONIAL TR CO (AZ)
Each share old Common no par exchanged for (0.1) share new Common no par 11/19/1998
Acquired by Gold Star Trust 09/01/2004
Each share new Common no par exchanged for $4.63 cash
Each share new Common no par received an initial distribution of $0.16 cash from escrow 10/25/2005
Each share new Common no par received second and final distribution of $0.50 cash from escrow 01/18/2011

COLONIAL TRUST NATIONAL BANK (PALM BEACH, FL)
Name changed to Palm Beach National Bank & Trust Co. (Palm Beach, FL) 06/22/1990
Palm Beach National Bank & Trust Co. (Palm Beach, FL) reorganized as Palm Beach National Holding Co. 05/01/1997 which merged into Colonial BancGroup, Inc. 09/03/2002
(See Colonial BancGroup, Inc.)

COLONIAL URANIUM CO. (DE)
Name changed to Colonial Nuclear Industries, Inc. 10/12/1955
(See Colonial Nuclear Industries, Inc.)

COLONIAL UTILITIES, INC.
Reorganized as Colonial Utilities Corp. (DE) 00/00/1942
No stockholders' equity

COLONIAL UTILITIES CORP.
Reorganized as Colonial Utilities, Inc. 00/00/1933
Details not available

COLONIAL UTILS CORP (NH)
Reincorporated 02/16/1965
Common no par changed to $1 par 00/00/1944
State of incorporation changed from (DE) to (NH) 02/16/1965
Merged into Northern Utilities, Inc. (NH) 06/30/1969
Each share Common $1 par exchanged for (1) share 7.2% Preference $10 par
Northern Utilities, Inc. (NH) merged into Bay State Gas Co. (New) 10/30/1979
(See Bay State Gas Co. (New))

COLONIAL VA BK (GLOUCESTER, VA)
Merged into Xenith Bankshares, Inc. (Old) 06/30/2014
Each share Common $5 par exchanged for (2.65) shares Common $1 par
Xenith Bankshares, Inc. (Old) merged into Xenith Bankshares, Inc. (New) 08/01/2016 which merged into Union Bankshares Corp. 01/01/2018

COLONIAL VENTURES INC (MA)
Merged into Colonial Growth Shares, Inc. 11/21/1975
Each share Common $1 par exchanged for (0.44662775) share Common $1 par
Colonial Growth Shares, Inc. reorganized as Colonial Growth Shares Trust 09/02/1986 which reorganized as Colonial Trust III 09/13/1991

COLONIAL WESTERN AIRWAYS, INC.
Acquired by Colonial Airways Co. 00/00/1929
Details not available

COLONIAL X RAY CORP (FL)
Filed petition under Chapter 7 Federal Bankruptcy Code 04/27/1987
Stockholders' equity unlikely

COLONNADE CAP CORP (ON)
Name changed to 3P International Energy Corp. 07/19/2010
3P International Energy Corp. name changed to Cub Energy Inc. (ON) 01/30/2012 which reincorporated in Canada 02/28/2012

COLONY CAP INC OLD (MD)
Name changed 04/02/2015
Name changed from Colony Financial, Inc. to Colony Capital, Inc. (Old) and Common 1¢ par reclassified as Class A Common 1¢ par 04/02/2015
Merged into Colony NorthStar, Inc. 01/10/2017
Each share 7.125% Preferred Ser. C 1¢ par exchanged for (1) share 7.125% Preferred Ser. H 1¢ par
Each share 7.5% Preferred Ser. B 1¢ par exchanged for (1) share 7.5% Preferred Ser. G 1¢ par
Each share 8.5% Preferred Ser. A 1¢ par exchanged for (1) share 8.5% Preferred Ser. F 1¢ par
Each share Class A Common 1¢ par exchanged for (1.4663) shares Class A Common 1¢ par
Colony NorthStar, Inc. name changed to Colony Capital, Inc. (New) 06/25/2018

COLONY CORP (DE)
Merged into Shelter Resources Corp. 12/30/1971
Each share Common 10¢ par exchanged for $0.52 cash

COLONY ENERGY LTD (AB)
Reincorporated 04/11/1996
Place of incorporation changed from (BC) to (AB) 04/11/1996
Name changed to Big Bear Exploration Ltd. 02/28/1998
Big Bear Exploration Ltd. merged into Avid Oil & Gas Ltd. 02/02/2000
(See Avid Oil & Gas Ltd.)

COLONY FOODS INC (CA)
Stock Dividend - 20% 12/13/1976
Merged into Knott Hotels Corp. 06/21/1978
Each share Common 10¢ par exchanged for $6.50 cash

COLONY INTL INC (DE)
Each share old Common $0.0001 par exchanged for (0.02) share new Common $0.0001 par 01/04/1999
Name changed to Mobile Pet Systems, Inc. 01/12/1999
Mobile Pet Systems, Inc. name changed to Molecular Imaging Corp. 05/01/2003
(See Molecular Imaging Corp.)

COLONY INVTS LTD (CO)
Name changed to Extended Product Life, Inc. 02/29/1988
Extended Product Life, Inc. name changed to EPL Technologies Inc. 09/30/1994
(See EPL Technologies Inc.)

COLONY KITCHENS, INC. (CA)
Common 10¢ par split (3) for (2) by issuance of (0.5) additional share 04/18/1972
Name changed to Colony Foods, Inc. 11/19/1974
(See Colony Foods, Inc.)

COLONY NORTHSTAR CR REAL ESTATE INC (MD)
Name changed to Colony Credit Real Estate, Inc. 06/25/2018

COLONY NORTHSTAR INC (MD)
8.5% Preferred Ser. F 1¢ par called for redemption at $25 plus $0.401388 accrued dividends on 06/23/2017
8.75% Preferred Ser. A 1¢ par called for redemption at $25 plus $0.230904 accrued dividends on 06/23/2017
8.875% Perpetual Preferred Ser. C 1¢ par called for redemption at $25 on 10/13/2017
Name changed to Colony Capital, Inc. 06/25/2018
8.5% Preferred Ser. D 1¢ par called for redemption at $25 plus $0.277431 accrued dividends on 07/02/2018

COLONY PAC EXPLS LTD (BC)
Merged into zed.i solutions inc. 03/30/2001
Each share Common no par exchanged for (0.342) share Common no par
zed.i solutions inc. name changed to Zedi Inc. 06/20/2007
(See Zedi Inc.)

COLONY STARWOOD HOMES (MD)
Name changed to Starwood Waypoint Homes 07/31/2017
Starwood Waypoint Homes merged into Invitation Homes Inc. 11/16/2017

COLOR ACCENTS HLDGS INC (NV)
Name changed to Muscato Group Inc. 12/03/2009
(See Muscato Group Inc.)

COLOR CANVAS INC (NJ)
Recapitalized as National Color Corp. 09/20/1977
Each share Common 4¢ par exchanged for (0.1) share Common 4¢ par
National Color Corp. name changed to Studio Color Corp. 10/24/1978

COLOR CINEMA PRODUCTIONS, INC.
Acquired by Color Cinema Co. which forfeited its charter 00/00/1933

COLOR CORP. OF AMERICA (CA)
Name changed to Houston Fearless Corp. 06/01/1957
Houston Fearless Corp. merged into Image Systems, Inc. (CA) 04/20/1970 which reincorporated in Delaware 08/29/1974
(See Image Systems, Inc. (DE))

COLOR-CRAFT PRODUCTS, INC. (MI)
Liquidation completed
Each share Common $1 par exchanged for initial distribution of $8.70 cash 07/14/1965
Each share Common $1 par received second distribution of $1.27 cash 05/02/1966
Each share Common $1 par received third and final distribution of $0.03803 cash 07/15/1968

COLOR IMAGING INC (DE)
Each share old Common 1¢ par exchanged for (1) share new Common 1¢ par to reflect a (1) for (2,500) reverse split followed by a (2,500) for (1) forward split 09/23/2005
Note: Holders of (2,499) or fewer pre-split shares received $1.10 cash per share
Reincorporated under the laws of Georgia 08/31/2010

COLOR KINETICS INC (DE)
Merged into Philips Holdings USA, Inc. 08/24/2007
Each share Common $0.001 par exchanged for $34 cash

COLOR LITHOGRAPHY CORP. (DE)
Adjudicated bankrupt 10/14/1966
No stockholders' equity

COLOR MART PAINT INC (NV)
Reincorporated 08/29/2001
State of incorporation changed from (FL) to (NV) 08/29/2001
Each share old Common $0.0001 par exchanged for (0.005) share new Common $0.0001 par 09/18/2001
Name changed to International Artifacts Inc. 10/23/2001
International Artifacts Inc. name changed to Hawaiian Palisade Homes, Inc. 03/25/2002 which name changed to AAA Manufacturing, Inc. 09/27/2004 which recapitalized as Gulf West Property, Inc. (NV) 03/10/2005 which reincorporated in Colorado as Titan Global Entertainment, Inc. 11/10/2005 which recapitalized as Sunset Island Group, Inc. 05/30/2008

COLOR PICTURES INC.
Dissolved 00/00/1934
Details not available

COLOR REPRODUCTIONS INC (DE)
Name changed to Custom Communications System, Inc. 05/27/1969
Custom Communications System, Inc. name changed to Custom Communications Services Inc. 03/08/1979
(See Custom Communications Services Inc.)

COLOR SCIENCES CORP (NY)
Common 1¢ par split (3) for (1) by issuance of (2) additional shares 03/08/1972
Chapter 11 Federal Bankruptcy proceedings converted to Chapter 7 on 11/01/1990
Stockholders' equity unlikely

COLOR SPECTRUM INC (UT)
Involuntarily dissolved for failure to file reports and pay fees 12/01/1990

COLOR STRATEGIES (NV)
Recapitalized as Infinite Technology Corp. 01/04/2000
Each share Common no par exchanged for (0.07637536) share Common no par
Infinite Technology Corp. recapitalized as Flexxtech Corp. 05/12/2000 which name changed to Network Installation Corp. 07/18/2003 which name changed to Siena Technologies, Inc. 10/30/2006 which recapitalized as XnE, Inc. 07/01/2009
(See XnE, Inc.)

COLOR SYS TECHNOLOGY INC (DE)
Each share Common 10¢ par exchanged for (0.66666666) share Common 15¢ par 06/02/1983
Name changed to CST Entertainment Imaging Inc. 04/30/1992
CST Entertainment Imaging Inc. name changed to CST Entertainment, Inc. 04/24/1995 which recapitalized as Legacy Holding, Inc. 06/11/2007
(See Legacy Holding, Inc.)

COLOR TILE INC (DE)
Common $1 par split (2) for (1) by issuance of (1) additional share 01/02/1980
Merged into General Felt Industries, Inc. 12/23/1986
Each share Common $1 par exchanged for $31.50 cash

COLOR TONE ORIGS INC (NY)
Dissolved by proclamation 12/24/1991

COLOR YOUR WORLD INC (ON)
Merged into Color Tile, Inc. 12/01/1984
Each share Common no par exchanged for $28.66 cash

COLORADO & SOUTHN RY CO (CO)
Merged into Burlington Northern Railroad Co. 01/01/1982
Each share Non-Cum. 1st Preferred $100 par exchanged for $35 cash
Each share Non-Cum. 2nd Preferred $100 par exchanged for $35 cash
Each share Common $100 par exchanged for $300 cash

COLORADO BUSINESS BANKSHARES CAP TR I (DE)
10% Capital Securities called for redemption at $10 on 6/30/2005

COLORADO BUSINESS BANKSHARES INC (CO)
Issue Information - 1,400,000 shares COM offered at $12 per share on 06/18/1998
Under plan of merger name changed to CoBiz Inc. 03/12/2001
CoBiz Inc. name changed to CoBiz Financial Inc. 05/17/2007

COLORADO BUSINESS DEVELOPMENT CORP. (CO)
Voluntarily dissolved in 01/00/1982
No stockholders' equity

COLORADO BY-PRODUCTS CO. (CO)
Acquired by Beatrice Foods Co. 11/29/65
Each share Common $10 par exchanged for (0.3524) share Common no par
Beatrice Foods Co. name changed to Beatrice Companies, Inc. 6/5/84
(See Beatrice Companies, Inc.)

COLORADO CASINO RESORTS INC (TX)
Plan of reorganization under Chapter 11 Federal Bankruptcy Code effective 11/20/2000
No stockholders' equity

COLORADO CATERERS, INC. (MD)
Charter revoked for failure to file reports and pay taxes 12/2/64

COLORADO CENT MINES INC (CO)
Name changed to Earth Sciences, Inc. 06/01/1972
(See Earth Sciences, Inc.)

COLORADO CENTRAL POWER CO. (DE)
Each share Common $10 par exchanged for (2) shares Common $5 par in 1951
Common $5 par changed to $2.50 par and (1) additional share issued 7/20/59
Merged into Public Service Co. of Colorado on a (3/5) for (1) basis 12/29/61
Public Service Co. of Colorado name changed to New Century Energies, Inc. 8/1/97 which merged into Xcel Energy Inc. 8/18/2000

COLORADO CERAMIC TILE INC (CO)
Name changed to Nano Labs Corp. 05/07/2012

COLORADO CNB BANKSHARES INC (CO)
Common no par split (2) for (1) by issuance of (1) additional share 08/18/1969
Name changed to Colorado National Bankshares, Inc. 03/23/1971
Colorado National Bankshares, Inc. merged into First Bank System, Inc. 05/28/1993 which name changed to U.S. Bancorp 08/01/1997

COLORADO CONS MINES CO (UT)
Merged into Eureka Standard Consolidated Mining Co. 04/22/1975
Each share Common 10¢ par exchanged for (0.2) share Capital Stock 10¢ par
Eureka Standard Consolidated Mining Co. merged into South Standard Mining Co. 07/29/1983 which merged into Chief Consolidated Mining Co. 07/01/1996
(See Chief Consolidated Mining Co.)

COLORADO CREDIT LIFE, INC. (CO)
Adjudicated bankrupt 11/2/65
No stockholders' equity

COLORADO DOUBLE TAX EXEMPT FD INC (MD)
Completely liquidated 09/01/1999
Each share Common $0.001 par exchanged for net asset value

COLORADO ENERGY CORP (CO)
Under plan of merger each share Common 1¢ par exchanged for $0.25 cash 12/26/1986
Each share Common 1¢ par received an additional distribution of $0.075 cash from escrow 10/17/1989

COLORADO FUEL & IRON CO.
Reorganized as Colorado Fuel & Iron Corp. in 1936
Stockholders received nothing but warrants which expired in 1950

COLORADO FUEL & IRON CORP (CO)
Common no par exchanged (2) for (1) 00/00/1945
Common no par changed to $5 par 12/17/1959
5% Preferred Ser. A $50 par called for redemption 04/15/1966
Stock Dividend - 25% 11/01/1950
Name changed to CF&I Steel Corp. 08/01/1966
(See CF&I Steel Corp.)

COLORADO GAS & FUEL (CO)
Charter revoked for failure to file reports and pay fees 10/10/33

COLORADO GASAHOL INC (CO)
Charter suspended for failure to file annual reports 09/30/1989

COLORADO GOLD & SILVER INC (CO)
Recapitalized as Dynamic I-T, Inc. 08/31/1999
Each share Common no par exchanged for (0.01) share Common no par
Dynamic I-T, Inc. recapitalized as Artwork & Beyond, Inc. 02/10/2004 which recapitalized as Advance Nanotech, Inc. (CO) 12/02/2004 which reincorporated in Delaware 06/19/2006
(See Advance Nanotech, Inc.)

COLORADO GOLD MINES INC (NV)
Recapitalized as Buscar Oil, Inc. 07/18/2014
Each share Common $0.001 par exchanged for (0.00333333) share Common $0.00001 par
Buscar Oil, Inc. name changed to Buscar Co. 06/15/2015

COLORADO IMPERIAL MINING CO. (CO)
Merged into Intranet Computing Corp. (CO) 1/15/70
Each share Capital Stock $1 par exchanged for (1) share Common 10¢ par
Intranet Computing Corp. (CO) reorganized under the laws of Delaware 3/31/72 which name changed to Intranet Corp. 12/18/73 which was acquired by Interscience Systems, Inc. (CA) 12/28/77 which reincorporated in Nevada 3/31/81
(See Interscience Systems, Inc.)

COLORADO INSTRS INC (CO)
Each share Common no par exchanged for (10) shares Common $1 par 08/05/1968
Merged into Mohawk Data Sciences Corp. 09/30/1971
Each share Common $1 par exchanged for (1/9) share Common 10¢ par
Mohawk Data Sciences Corp. name changed to Qantel Corp. 09/17/1987
(See Qantel Corp.)

COLORADO INSURANCE CO. (CO)
Acquired by Equity General Insurance Co. on a (0.1) for (1) basis in 1958
(See Equity General Insurance Co.)

COLORADO INSURANCE GROUP BUILDING, INC. (CO)
Charter revoked for non-payment of franchise taxes 10/11/63

COLORADO INSURANCE SERVICE CO. (CO)
Stock Dividend - 10% 12/30/1962
Name changed to Cisco Group Inc. 05/13/1964
(See Cisco Group Inc.)

COLORADO INTST CORP (DE)
Under plan of merger each share Common $5 par exchanged for (0.875) share Coastal States Gas Corp. $1.83 Conv. Preferred Ser. B 33-1/3¢ par 1/2/73
Note: Preferred Stocks were not affected by the merger
Name changed back to Colorado Interstate Gas Co. 1/1/76
(See Coastal States Gas Corp.)

COLORADO INTST GAS CO (DE)
Stock Dividends - 40% 06/10/1960; 40% 12/19/1963
Name changed to Colorado Interstate Corp. 09/01/1968 which name changed back to Colorado Interstate Gas Co. 01/01/1976
5% Preferred $100 par called for redemption 06/29/1984
5.35% Preferred $100 par called for redemption 07/01/1989
5.5% Preferred $100 par called for redemption 07/31/1996
Public interest eliminated

COLORADO INVS QUALITY TAX EXEMPT TR
Trust terminated 12/15/1996
Details not available

COLORADO MED INC (CO)
Filed petition under Chapter 7 Federal Bankruptcy Code 08/29/1988
Stockholders' equity unlikely

COLORADO MEDTECH INC (CO)
Merged into CIVCO Holding, Inc. 07/21/2003
Each share Common no par exchanged for $4.75 cash

COLORADO MILLING & ELEVATOR CO. (CO)
Merged into Great Western United Corp. 1/15/68
Each share Common $1 par exchanged for (1) share Common $1 par
Great Western United Corp. reorganized as Hunt International Resources Corp. 2/22/78
(See Hunt International Resources Corp.)

COLORADO MINING CORP. (DE)
No longer in existence having become inoperative and void for non-payment of taxes 04/01/1958

COLORADO NATL BK (DENVER, CO)
Each share Capital Stock $100 par exchanged for (2) shares Capital Stock $50 par plus a 50% stock dividend paid 00/00/1941
Capital Stock $50 par changed to $25 par and (3) additional shares issued 00/00/1955
Stock Dividends - (1) for (7.5) 02/02/1959; (1) for (8) 01/25/1962; 33.33333333% 03/01/1971
Merged into Colorado National Bankshares, Inc. 09/27/1982
Each share Capital Stock $25 par exchanged for (12) shares Common no par
Colorado National Bankshares, Inc. merged into First Bank System, Inc. 05/28/1993 which name changed to U.S. Bancorp 08/01/1997

COLORADO NATL BANKSHARES INC (CO)
Common no par split (3) for (2) by issuance of (0.5) additional share 05/15/1979
Common no par split (4) for (3) by issuance of (1/3) additional share 02/02/1981
Common no par split (4) for (3) by issuance of (1/3) additional share 12/27/1982
Common no par split (5) for (4) by issuance of (0.25) additional share 02/17/1984
Stock Dividend - 15% 02/22/1982
Merged into First Bank System, Inc. 05/28/1993
Each share Common no par exchanged for (1.71206) shares Common $1.25 par
First Bank System, Inc. name changed to U.S. Bancorp 08/01/1997

COLORADO OIL & GAS CORP. (DE)
Completely liquidated 07/01/1964
Each share Common $3 par exchanged for first and final distribution of $13.50 cash
$1.25 Preferrred $25 par called for redemption 07/31/1964
Public interest eliminated

COLORADO PRIME CORP (DE)
Merged into KPC Holdings Corp. 09/29/1989
Each share Common 1¢ par exchanged for $17 cash

COLORADO RARE EARTHS INC (NV)
Name changed to U.S. Rare Earths, Inc. 10/28/2011

COLORADO REAL ESTATE & DEVELOPMENT, INC. (DE)
No longer in existence having become inoperative and void for non-payment of taxes 04/01/1964

COLORADO RECREATIONAL INVESTMENT CORP. (CO)
Each share Common 50¢ par exchanged for (2) shares Common 25¢ par 10/15/1969
Each share Common 25¢ par exchanged for (2.5) shares Common 10¢ par 07/01/1971
Out of business 12/31/1980
No stockholders' equity

COLORADO RES INC (WA)
Charter cancelled and proclaimed dissolved for failure to pay fees 12/19/1994

COLORADO RIV & EAGLE CO (DE)
Charter cancelled and declared inoperative and void for non-payment of taxes 03/01/1985

COLORADO SOLAR CORP (CO)
Recapitalized as Ambient Technology Corp. 01/24/1983
Each share Common no par exchanged for (0.2) share Common no par
(See Ambient Technology Corp.)

COLORADO SPRINGS NATL BK (COLORADO SPRINGS, CO)
Common $100 par changed to $20 par and (5) additional shares issued plus a 66.66666666% stock dividend paid 01/21/1952
Common $20 par changed to $10 par and (1) additional share issued 01/29/1969
Stock Dividends - 16.66666666% 09/21/1955; 100% 03/01/1966; 50% 01/26/1971; 100% 02/15/1976; 50% 03/25/1980
Acquired by United Banks of Colorado, Inc. 09/01/1985
Details not available

COLORADO URANIUM MINES, INC. (DE)
Merged into Consolidated Uranium Mines, Inc. 08/07/1953
Each share Common exchanged for (0.2) share Common $0.075 par
(See Consolidated Uranium Mines, Inc.)

COLORADO VENTURE CAP CORP (CO)
Name changed to Tri-Coast Environmental Corp. 01/15/1988

COLORADO WESTERN FINANCIAL CORP. (CO)
Declared defunct and inoperative for failure to pay taxes and file annual reports 10/01/1993

COLORADO WYO RESV CO (WY)
SEC revoked common stock registration 09/21/2011

COLORCON INC (PA)
Each share Common 20¢ par exchanged for (3) shares Common 10¢ par 04/10/1973
Acquired by Berwind Corp. 06/29/1978
Each share Common 10¢ par exchanged for $40 cash

COLORCRAFT CORP. (NC)
Merged into Fuqua Industries, Inc. (PA) 04/28/1967
Each share Common $1 par exchanged for (0.083333) share $2 Conv. Preferred Ser. B $100 par
Fuqua Industries, Inc. (PA) reincorporated in Delaware 05/06/1968 which name changed to Actava Group Inc. 07/21/1993 which name changed to Metromedia International Group, Inc. 11/01/1995
(See Metromedia International Group, Inc.)

COLORFAX INTL INC (BC)
Struck off register and declared dissolved for failure to file returns 07/29/1994

COLORITE PLASTICS, INC. (DE)
Stock Dividend - 25% 11/15/1963
Completely liquidated 10/30/1964
Each share 6% Preferred $100 par exchanged for (2.023) shares Rexall Drug & Chemical Co. Capital Stock $2.50 par
Each share Common 25¢ par exchanged for (0.13308490) share Rexall Drug & Chemical Co. Capital Stock $2.50 par
Rexall Drug & Chemical Co. name changed to Dart Industries, Inc. 04/22/1969 which reorganized as Dart & Kraft, Inc. 09/25/1980 which name changed to Kraft, Inc. (New) 11/21/1986
(See Kraft, Inc. (New))

COLORMAX TECHNOLOGIES INC (DE)
Each share old Common $0.001 par exchanged for (2) shares new Common $0.001 par 01/07/2000
SEC revoked common stock registration 12/02/2010

COLOROCS CORP (GA)
Name changed 12/13/1995
Common 10¢ par changed to 5¢ par and (1) additional share issued 02/18/1986
Each share old Common 5¢ par exchanged for (0.02) share new Common 5¢ par 12/10/1993
Each share new Common 5¢ par exchanged for (0.05) share Common no par 05/05/1995
Name changed from Coloroacs Corp. to Coloroacs Information Technologies, Inc. 12/13/1995
Completely liquidated
Each share Common no par received first and final distribution of (3.80935) share Stealth MediaLabs, Inc. Restricted Common $0.001 par, 5 year Warrants, and $0.93 cash payable 10/03/2003 to holders of record 07/16/2003 Ex date - 10/07/2003
Note: Certificates were not required to be surrendered and are without value

COLORPLATE ENGRAVING CO. (NY)
Proclaimed dissolved for failure to file reports and pay taxes 12/15/1967

COLORTECH CORP (ON)
Merged into Polyplast Muller Canada Inc. 07/12/1996
Each share Common no par exchanged for $2 cash
Each share Class A no par exchanged for $2 cash

COLORTRAN CORP. (DE)
No longer in existence having become inoperative and void for non-payment of taxes 04/15/1968

COLOSSAL ENERGY INC (BC)
Recapitalized as Consolidated Colossal Energy Inc. 12/23/1987
Each share Common no par exchanged for (0.4) share Common no par
Consolidated Colossal Energy Inc. name changed to Draco Gold Mines Inc. 05/02/1988 which merged into Stanford Energy Corp. 06/29/1990 which recapitalized as Stanford Oil & Gas Ltd. 07/10/1998 which merged into Hilton Petroleum Ltd. (BC) 03/31/1999 which reincorporated in Yukon 04/01/1999 which which name changed to Hilton Resources Ltd. (YT) 03/02/2004 which reincorporated in British Columbia 11/23/2004 which recapitalized as Rochester Resources Ltd. 08/26/2005

COLOSSAL RES CORP (BC)
Reincorporated under the laws of Alberta as Top Strike Resources Corp. 12/13/2012

COLOSSAL RES CORP (BC)
Each share old Common no par exchanged for (0.13333333) share new Common no par 06/19/1998
Name changed to Globetech Ventures Corp. 09/20/2000

COLOSSUS CORP (NV)
Company believed out of business 00/00/1981
Details not available

COLOSSUS NICKEL DEVELOPMENT LTD. (BC)
Name changed to Alamos Mines Ltd. 12/00/1959
(See Alamos Mines Ltd.)

COLOSSUS RESOURCE EQUITIES INC (BC)
Merged into Prime Resources Corp. (BC) 02/01/1989
Each share Common no par exchanged for (0.86956521) share Common no par
Prime Resources Corp. (BC) recapitalized as Prime Resources Group Inc. 01/26/1990 which merged into HomeStake Mining Co. 12/03/1998 which merged into Barrick Gold Corp. 12/14/2001

COLOTAH URANIUM CO., INC. (CO)
Proclaimed defunct and inoperative for non-payment of taxes 10/28/1959

COLOURED US INC (NV)
Each share old Common $0.001 par exchanged for (0.01) share new Common $0.001 par 10/20/2010
Name changed to Imperalis Holding Corp. 03/28/2011

COLRAY RES INC (CANADA)
Recapitalized as American Ethanol (International) Corp. 11/22/1993
Each share Common no par exchanged for (0.1) share Common no par
American Ethanol (International) Corp. name changed to American Agri-Technology Corp. 08/19/1996
(See American Agri-Technology Corp.)

COLSON CO.
Reorganized as Colson Corp. 00/00/1935
Details not available

COLSON CORP. (OH)
Stock Dividend - 100% 05/00/1948
Liquidated 00/00/1953
Details not available

COLSPAN ENVIRONMENTAL SYS INC (CO)
Name changed to Apache Resources Ltd. 05/27/1981
Apache Resources Ltd. recapitalized as Danzar Investment Group, Inc. 01/24/1986 which recapitalized as Alexander Mark Investments (USA), Inc. 12/26/1996 which reorganized as Wincroft, Inc. (CO) 05/18/1998 which reorganized in Nevada 02/12/2008 which name changed to Apollo Solar Energy, Inc. 11/03/2008

COLT CAP CORP (BC)
Reincorporated 05/15/2006
Place of incorporation changed from (AB) to (BC) 05/15/2006
Recapitalized as Colt Resources Inc. (BC) 07/18/2007
Each share Common no par exchanged for (0.2) share Common no par
Colt Resources Inc. (BC) reincorporated in Canada 09/23/2011

COLT ENERGY CORP. (NV)
Charter revoked for failure to file a current list of officers 06/01/2002

COLT ENERGY INC (CANADA)
Merged into KeyWest Energy Corp. 12/17/1998
Each share Common no par exchanged for (0.595238) share Common no par
(See Keywest Energy Corp.)

COLT EXPL 1988 LTD (AB)
Reorganized 05/17/1983
Recapitalized 06/30/1988
Reorganized from Colt Exploration Ltd. (BC) to under the laws of Alberta as Colt Exploration (Western) Ltd. 05/17/1983
Each share Common no par exchanged for (1) share Class A Common no par
Recapitalized from Colt Exploration (Western) Ltd. to Colt Exploration (1988) Ltd. 06/30/1988
Each share Class A Common no par exchanged for (0.33333333) share Class A Common no par
Reorganized as Stampede Oils Inc. 12/29/1988
Each share Class A Common no par exchanged for (1) share Class A Common no par
(See Stampede Oils Inc.)

COLT INDUSTRIES INC. (DE)
Reincorporated under the laws of Pennsylvania 5/6/76
(See Colt Industries Inc. (Pa.))

COLT INDS INC (PA)
Under plan of merger reincorporated under the laws of Delaware and 4.5% Conv. Preferred $100 par reclassified as $4.50 Conv. Preferred Ser. B $1 par, 4.25% Conv. Preferred $100 par reclassified as $4.25 Conv. Preferred Ser. C $1 par, $1.60 Conv. Preferred $40 par reclassified as $1.60 Conv. Preferred Ser. A $1 par and Common $3 par changed to $1 par 10/17/1968
Colt Industries Inc. (DE) state of incorporation changed back to Pennsylvania 05/06/1976
Common $1 par split (3) for (2) by issuance of (0.5) additional share 06/30/1978
$4.25 Conv. Preferred Ser. C $1 par called for redemption 00/00/1980
4.50% Conv. Preferred Ser. B $1 par called for redemption 00/00/1980
$1.60 Conv. Preferred Ser. A $1 par called for redemption 05/08/1981
$4.25 Conv. Preferred Ser. D $1 par called for redemption 05/08/1981
$2.75 Preferred Ser. E $1 par called for redemption 11/27/1981
Common $1 par split (2) for (1) by issuance of (1) additional share 01/07/1982
Each share Common $1 par exchanged for (1) share Common 10¢ par and $85 cash 10/07/1986
Merged into Colt Transition Inc. 06/10/1988

Each share Common 10¢ par exchanged for $17 cash

COLT OIL INC (DE)
Reincorporated 01/00/1978
State of incorporation changed from (CO) to (DE) 01/00/1978
Charter cancelled and declared inoperative and void for non-payment of taxes 03/01/1988

COLT RES INC (BC)
Reincorporated under the laws of Canada 09/23/2011

COLT RES LTD (BC)
Capital Stock 50¢ par changed to no par 9/17/76
Recapitalized as Transcolt Resources Corp. 5/8/78
Each share Capital Stock no par exchanged for (0.2) share Capital Stock no par
Transcolt Resources Corp. merged into New Frontier Petroleum Corp. 1/18/82 which recapitalized as PetroMac Energy Inc. 8/30/85
(See PetroMac Energy Inc.)

COLT TELECOM GROUP PLC (UNITED KINGDOM)
Sponsored ADR's for Ordinary split (4) for (1) by issuance of (3) additional ADR's payable 09/03/1998 to holders of record 09/01/1998
ADR agreement terminated 05/10/2006
Each Sponsored ADR for Ordinary exchanged for $4.37765 cash

COLT'S MANUFACTURING CO. (CT)
Capital Stock $25 par changed to $10 par and (4) additional shares issued in 1953
Merged into Penn-Texas Corp. 12/2/55
Each share Capital Stock $10 par exchanged for (0.3) share $1.60 Conv. Preferred $40 par and (0.4) share Common $10 par
Penn-Texas Corp. name changed to Fairbanks Whitney Corp. 5/29/59 which recapitalized as Colt Industries Inc. (PA) 5/15/64 which reincorporated in Delaware 10/17/68 then reincorporated in Pennsylvania 5/6/76
(See Colt Industries Inc. (PA))

COLT'S PATENT FIRE ARMS MANUFACTURING CO.
Name changed to Colt's Manufacturing Co. in 1947
Colt's Manufacturing Co. merged into Penn-Texas Corp. 12/2/55 which name changed to Fairbanks Whitney Corp. 5/29/59 which recapitalized as Colt Industries Inc. (PA) 5/15/64 which reincorporated in Delaware 10/17/68 then reincorporated in Pennsylvania 5/6/76
(See Colt Industries Inc. (PA))

COLTEC CAP TR (DE)
Term Income Deferrable Equity Securities called for redemption at $50 on 11/28/2005

COLTEC INDS INC (PA)
Merged into Goodrich (B.F.) Co. 07/12/1999
Each share Common 1¢ par exchanged for (0.56) share Common $5 par
Goodrich (B.F.) Co. name changed to Goodrich Corp. 06/01/2001
(See Goodrich Corp.)

COLTON CHEMICAL CO. (OH)
Acquired by Air Reduction Co., Inc. 00/00/1954
Each share Common $1 par exchanged for (0.4) share Common no par
Air Reduction Co., Inc. name changed to Airco, Inc. (NY) 10/01/1971 which reincorporated in Delaware 08/03/1977

(See Airco, Inc. (DE))

COLTRANE TECHNOLOGIES INC (BC)
Name changed to Data Deposit Box Inc. 03/03/2015

COLTSTAR VENTURES INC (BC)
Common no par split (2) for (1) by issuance of (1) additional share payable 01/19/2010 to holders of record 01/19/2010 Ex date - 01/18/2010
Recapitalized as Metallis Resources Inc. 07/11/2013
Each share Common no par exchanged for (0.2) share Common no par

COLUCID PHARMACEUTICALS INC (DE)
Acquired by Lilly (Eli) & Co. 03/01/2017
Each share Common $0.001 par exchanged for $46.50 cash

COLUMBIA ACCIDENT & HEALTH INSURANCE CO. (PA)
Merged into Columbia Life Insurance Co. 00/00/1983
Details not available

COLUMBIA AIRCRAFT INDUSTRIES
Liquidated 00/00/1946
Details not available

COLUMBIA AIRCRAFT PRODUCTS, INC.
Bankrupt 00/00/1949
Stockholders' equity unlikely

COLUMBIA AUTOCAR INC (NV)
Name changed to American Peat Co. 04/22/1982
American Peat Co. name changed to American National Hydrocarbon, Inc. 11/15/1982
(See American National Hydrocarbon, Inc.)

COLUMBIA BAKERIES INC (NV)
Each share old Common $0.001 par exchanged for (0.03333333) share new Common $0.001 par 06/18/2003
Plan of reorganization under Chapter 11 Federal Bankruptcy Code effective 11/28/2006
Each share Common $0.001 par exchanged for an undetermined amount of Municipal Payment Systems Inc. (NV) Common $0.001 par
Municipal Payment Systems Inc. (NV) reorganized in Wyoming as Victura Construction Group, Inc. 07/21/2014

COLUMBIA BAKING CO. (DE)
Recapitalized 00/00/1935
Each share 1st Preferred no par exchanged for (1) share Preferred no par
Each share 2nd Preferred no par exchanged for (0.5) share Preferred no par
Each share old Common no par exchanged for (0.5) share new Common no par
Recapitalized 00/00/1946
Preferred no par exchanged (2) for (1)
Common no par exchanged (2) for (1)
Name changed to Southern Bakeries Co. 04/01/1957
Southern Bakeries Co. reorganized as Southern Daisy Industries, Inc. 03/07/1972
(See Southern Daisy Industries, Inc.)

COLUMBIA BANCORP (MD)
Common 1¢ par split (2) for (1) by issuance of (1) additional share payable 06/19/1998 to holders of record 06/09/1998
Merged into Fulton Financial Corp. 02/01/2006
Each share Common 1¢ par exchanged for (2.325) shares Common $2.50 par

COLUMBIA BANCORP (OR)
Common no par split (3) for (2) by issuance of (0.5) additional share payable 03/31/1998 to holders of record 03/26/1998
Common no par split (2) for (1) by issuance of (1) additional share payable 09/11/1998 to holders of record 09/02/1998
Stock Dividends - 10% payable 05/15/2003 to holders of record 05/01/2003 Ex date - 04/29/2003; 10% payable 01/16/2006 to holders of record 01/02/2006
Company's principal asset placed in receivership 01/22/2010
Stockholders' equity unlikely

COLUMBIA BEN HLDGS LTD (BC)
Completely liquidated 05/01/1973
Each share Class A no par or Class B no par received first and final distribution of (0.3237) share NW Financial Corp. Ltd. Common no par
Note: Certificates were not required to be surrendered and are without value
NW Financial Corp. Ltd. recapitalized as Newco Financial Corp. 01/13/1975
(See Newco Financial Corp.)

COLUMBIA BREWERIES, INC. (WA)
Name changed to Heidelberg Brewing Co. (WA) 00/00/1953
Heidelberg Brewing Co. name changed to Brewery Liquidation Co. 12/31/1958
(See Brewery Liquidation Co.)

COLUMBIA BREWING CO.
Acquired by Falstaff Brewing Corp. (DE) 00/00/1948
Each share Common exchanged for (1) share 4.5% Preferred $16.50 par
(See Falstaff Brewing Corp. (DE))

COLUMBIA BREWING CO. LTD. (BC)
Through purchase offer 100% acquired by Labatt of B.C. Ltd. as of 10/11/1974
Public interest eliminated

COLUMBIA BROADCASTING SYS INC (NY)
Each share Class A no par or Class B no par exchanged for (5) shares Class A $5 par or Class B $5 par 00/00/1934
Each share Class A $5 par or Class B $5 par exchanged for (2) shares Class A $2.50 par or Class B $2.50 par 00/00/1937
Class A $2.50 par and Class B $2.50 par split (3) for (1) by issuance of (2) additional shares respectively 05/20/1955
Class A $2.50 par and Class B $2.50 par reclassified as Common $2.50 par 12/23/1958
Common $2.50 par split (2) for (1) by issuance of (1) additional share 02/14/1964
Name changed to CBS Inc. 04/18/1974
(See CBS Inc.)

COLUMBIA CABLE SYS INC (DE)
Under plan of merger name changed to UA-Columbia Cablevision, Inc. 12/29/1972
(See UA-Columbia Cablevision, Inc.)

COLUMBIA CAP CORP (DE)
Each share old Common $0.001 par exchanged for (0.5) share new Common $0.001 par 09/23/1997
Name changed to Finity Holdings Inc. 09/08/2000
Finity Holdings Inc. recapitalized as Patients & Physicians, Inc. (DE) 08/31/2006 which name changed to Flagship Global Health, Inc. 01/24/2017
(See Flagship Global Health, Inc.)

COLUMBIA CAPITAL CORP. (NV)
Reorganized as Service Holding Corp. 02/22/1988

Each share Common $0.001 par exchanged for (0.8) share Common $0.001 par
Service Holding Corp. recapitalized as Shuangyang U.S. Enterprises, Inc. 04/16/1999 which recapitalized as Polymeric Corp. 01/01/2001 which name changed to Lew Corp. 08/27/2001 which name changed to Vintage Energy & Exploration, Inc. 10/02/2007
(See Vintage Energy & Exploration, Inc.)

COLUMBIA CELLULOSE LTD (BC)
7% Preferred $2 par called for redemption 04/30/1965
Acquired by the Province of British Columbia 07/13/1973
Each share $1.20 Preferred $25 par received (2) shares Canadian Cellulose Co. Ltd. Common no par
Each share Common no par received (1) share Canadian Cellulose Co. Ltd. Common no par
Note: Certificates were not required to be surrendered and are without value
(See Canadian Cellulose Co. Ltd.)

COLUMBIA CHASE CORP (NY)
Stock Dividends - 25% 10/30/1980; 40% 12/09/1981
Reincorporated under the laws of Massachusetts as Chase Corp. 03/18/1988

COLUMBIA COLLIERIES LTD. (BC)
Struck off register and declared dissolved for failure to file returns 00/00/1919

COLUMBIA COML BANCORP (OR)
Common no par split (2) for (1) by issuance of (1) additional share payable 05/02/2006 to holders of record 05/01/2006 Ex date - 05/05/2006
Common no par split (2) for (1) by issuance of (1) additional share payable 07/02/2007 to holders of record 07/01/2007 Ex date - 07/03/2007
Name changed to Premier Commercial Bancorp 08/21/2014
Premier Commercial Bancorp merged into Heritage Financial Corp. 07/02/2018

COLUMBIA COMPUTING SVCS LTD (BC)
Merged into Pergamon ABG Investment Corp. 05/02/1989
Each share Common no par exchanged for $5.75 cash

COLUMBIA COPPER CO LTD (BC)
Reincorporated under the laws of Yukon as Kodiak Oil & Gas Corp. 09/28/2001
Kodiak Oil & Gas Corp. merged into Whiting Petroleum Corp. 12/08/2014

COLUMBIA CORP (WA)
Liquidation completed
Each share Common $1 par received initial distribution of $5 cash 09/01/1976
Each share Common $1 par received second distribution of $3 cash 03/11/1977
Each share Common $1 par exchanged for third and final distribution of $2.50 cash 05/25/1977

COLUMBIA CNTY FMRS NATL BK (ORANGEVILLE, PA)
Reorganized as CCFNB Bancorp, Inc. 03/31/1984
Each share Common $5 par exchanged for (1) share Common $5 par

COLUMBIA DAILY INCOME CO (OR)
Common 1¢ par changed to $0.001 par and (9) additional shares issued 04/01/1976

Common $0.001 par reclassified as Class Z 11/01/2002
Merged into Columbia Funds Series Trust 03/27/2006
Details not available

COLUMBIA DATA PRODS INC (DE)
Chapter 11 bankruptcy proceedings converted to Chapter 7 on 11/26/1985
Stockholders' equity unlikely

COLUMBIA ENERGY CORP (NV)
Each share old Common $0.001 par exchanged for (0.14285714) share new Common $0.001 par 10/20/2011
Name changed to Cornwall Resources, Inc. 04/16/2012

COLUMBIA ENERGY GROUP (DE)
Name changed 01/16/1998
Common no par changed to $10 par 04/28/1958
11.25% Preferred Ser. A $50 par called for redemption 11/01/1979
Adjustable Rate Preferred Ser. D $50 par called for redemption 10/03/1988
10.24% Preferred Ser. C $50 par called for redemption 10/03/1988
10.96% Preferred Ser. B $50 par called for redemption 10/03/1988
5.22% Conv. Preferred Ser. B no par called for redemption 02/26/1996
7.89% Preferred Ser. A no par called for redemption 02/26/1996
Name changed from Columbia Gas System, Inc. to Columbia Energy Group 01/16/1998
Common $10 par split (3) for (2) by issuance of (0.5) additional share payable 06/15/1998 to holders of record 06/01/1998 Ex date - 06/16/1998
Common $10 par changed to 1¢ par 05/19/1999
Merged into NiSource Inc. 11/01/2000
Each share Common 1¢ par exchanged for (1) Unit (consisting of a $2.60 Zero Coupon Debenture and a forward equity contract) and $70 cash

COLUMBIA EQUITIES (CA)
Under plan of partial liquidation each share Common no par received (0.9) share CBK Industries, Inc. Capital Stock $1 par 12/30/1966
(See CBK Industries, Inc.)
Name changed to United States Resources Corp. 07/06/1970
(See United States Resources Corp.)

COLUMBIA EQUITIES INC (CA)
Merged into International Turbo Center Inc. 05/15/1990
Each share Common $1 par exchanged for (1) share Common $1 par

COLUMBIA EQUITY TR INC (MD)
Merged into SSPF/CET Operating Company LLC 03/01/2007
Each share Common $0.001 par exchanged for $19.50 cash

COLUMBIA ETF TR (DE)
Columbia Concentrated Large Cap Value Strategy Fund no par reclassified as Columbia Select Large Cap Value ETF no par 03/01/2013
Columbia Core BD Strategy Fund no par reclassified as Columbia Core Bond ETF no par 03/01/2013
Columbia Intermediate Municipal Bond Strategy Fund no par reclassified as Columbia Intermediate Municipal Bond ETF no par 3/01/2013
Columbia Growth Equity Strategy Fund no par reclassified as Columbia Large Cap Growth ETF no par 03/25/2013
Columbia Large-Cap Growth Equity Strategy Fund no par reclassified as

Columbia Select Large Cap Growth ETF no par 03/01/2013
Trust terminated 02/04/2016
Each share Columbia Large Cap Growth ETF no par received $41.00392 cash
Each share Columbia Select Large Cap Growth ETF no par received $38.69974 cash
Each share Columbia Select Large Cap Value ETF no par received $37.99922 cash
Trust terminated 08/02/2017
Each share Columbia Core Bond ETF no par received $51.74455 cash
Each share Columbia Intermediate Municipal Bond ETF no par received $53.14656 cash

COLUMBIA ETF TR II (DC)
Trust terminated 08/02/2017
Each share Columbia EM Strategic Opportunities ETF received $20.00732 cash
Each share Columbia Emerging Markets Core ETF received $20.20798 cash
 (Additional Information in Active)

COLUMBIA EXPLORATIONS LTD. (BC)
Assets acquired by Imperial Metals & Power Ltd. 10/11/1961
Each share Capital Stock $1 par exchanged for (0.16666666) share Common no par
Imperial Metals & Power Ltd. merged into Imperial Metals Corp. (Old) 12/01/1981 which reorganized as Imperial Metals Corp. (New) 04/30/2002

COLUMBIA FED SVGS BK (WENATCHEE, WA)
Common $1 par split (2) for (1) by issuance of (1) additional share 02/18/1987
Stock Dividend - 10% 08/15/1985
Acquired by Washington Mutual Savings Bank (Seattle, WA) 04/29/1988
Each share Common $1 par exchanged for $17.5324 cash

COLUMBIA FILMS, INC. (SC)
Dissolved by forfeiture for non-payment of taxes 10/01/1968

COLUMBIA FINL CORP (PA)
Common $10 par changed to $2 par and (4) additional shares issued 05/30/1986
Common $2 par split (3) for (2) by issuance of (0.5) additional share 12/15/1998
Common $2 par split (4) for (3) by issuance of (0.33333333) additional share payable 09/23/2003 to holders of record 09/02/2003 Ex date - 09/24/2003
Merged into CCFNB Bancorp, Inc. 07/18/2008
Each share Common $2 par exchanged for (0.72) share Common $1.25 par

COLUMBIA FINL KY INC (OH)
Merged into Camco Financial Corp. 11/16/2001
Each share Common no par exchanged for (0.3681) share Common $1 par and $6.90 cash
(See Camco Financial Corp.)

COLUMBIA FIRST BK, A FED SVGS BK (ARLINGTON, VA)
Name changed 10/26/1989
Name changed from Columbia First Federal Savings & Loan Association to Columbia First Bank, A Federal Savings Bank (Arlington, VA) 10/26/1989
Merged into First Union Corp. 11/03/1995
Each share Common 1¢ par exchanged for (1.1852) shares Common $3.33333333 par
First Union Corp. name changed to Wachovia Corp. (Ctfs. dated after 09/01/2001) 09/01/2001 which merged into Wells Fargo & Co. (New) 12/31/2008

COLUMBIA FIXED INCOME SECS FD INC (OR)
Reincorporated 04/29/1988
State of incorporation changed from (DE) to (OR) 04/29/1988
Common 1¢ par reclassified as Class Z 11/01/2002
Merged into Columbia Funds Series Trust 10/07/2005
Details not available

COLUMBIA FUELS INC (BC)
Acquired by SNS Investments Inc. 01/30/1998
Each share Common no par exchanged for $0.09 cash

COLUMBIA FUND, INC. (DE)
Completely liquidated 05/10/1965
Each share Common $1 par exchanged for first and final distribution of $10.685 cash

COLUMBIA GAS & ELECTRIC CORP.
Name changed to Columbia Gas System, Inc. 00/00/1948
Columbia Gas System, Inc. name changed to Columbia Energy Group 01/16/1998 which merged into NiSource Inc. 11/01/2000

COLUMBIA GAS CO. (WA)
Merged into Washington Water Power Co. 05/20/1974
Each share Common 50¢ par exchanged for (0.06135) share Common no par
Washington Water Power Co. name changed to Avista Corp. 12/02/1998

COLUMBIA GEN CORP (DE)
Reincorporated 03/07/1969
State of incorporation changed from (TX) to (DE) 03/07/1969
Each share Common 20¢ par exchanged for (0.2) share Common 50¢ par 08/06/1973
Acquired by Independent Investors Inc. 08/25/1989
Each share Common 50¢ par exchanged for $11.50 cash

COLUMBIA GENERAL LIFE INSURANCE CO. (TX)
Merged into National Empire Life Insurance Co. 03/02/1962
Each share Common exchanged for (0.2) share Common $1 par
National Empire Life Insurance Co. merged into Empire Life Insurance Co. of America (AL) 06/30/1966
(See Empire Life Insurance Co of America (AL))

COLUMBIA GOLD MINES LTD (BC)
Recapitalized as Pacific Ridge Exploration Ltd. 05/12/1999
Each share Common no par exchanged for (0.33333333) share Common no par

COLUMBIA GORGE MINING CO. (ID)
Name changed to Silver Bowl, Inc. 00/00/1936
(See Silver Bowl, Inc.)

COLUMBIA GRAPHOPHONE CO., LTD.
Merged into Electric & Musical Industries Ltd. 04/20/1931
Details not available

COLUMBIA GRAPHOPHONE MANUFACTURING CO. (DE)
Assets sold for the benefit of creditors 02/00/1924
No stockholders' equity

COLUMBIA GYPSUM CO. LTD. (BC)
Struck off register and dissolved for failure to file returns 06/24/1974

COLUMBIA GYPSUM CO. LTD. (WA)
In process of liquidation 00/00/1957
Details not available

COLUMBIA GYPSUM PRODUCTS, INC. (WA)
Assets acquired by Columbia Gypsum Co. 00/00/1954
Each share Common exchanged for (1) share Common
(See Columbia Gypsum Co. Ltd.)

COLUMBIA/HCA HEALTHCARE CORP (DE)
Common 1¢ par split (3) for (2) by issuance of (0.5) additional share payable 10/15/1996 to holders of record 10/01/1996 Ex date - 10/16/1996
Each share Common 1¢ par received distribution of (0.05263157) share LifePoint Hospitals, Inc. Common 1¢ par and (0.05263157) share Triad Hospitals, Inc. Common 1¢ par payable 05/11/1999 to holders of record 04/30/1999 Ex date - 05/12/1999
Name changed to HCA - The Healthcare Co. 05/25/2000 which name changed to HCA Inc. (Ctfs. dated after 06/29/2001) 06/29/2001
(See HCA Inc. (Ctfs. dated after 06/29/2001))

COLUMBIA HEALTHCARE CORP (DE)
Merged into Columbia/HCA Healthcare Corp. 02/10/1994
Each share Common 1¢ par exchanged for (1) share Common 1¢ par
Columbia/HCA Healthcare Corp. name changed to HCA - The Healthcare Co. 05/25/2000 which name changed to HCA Inc. (Ctfs. dated after 06/29/2001) 06/29/2001
(See HCA Inc. (Ctfs. dated after 06/29/2001))

COLUMBIA HOSP CORP (NV)
Each share old Common 1¢ par exchanged for (0.25) share new Common 1¢ par 01/31/1991
Reincorporated under the laws of Delaware as Columbia Healthcare Corp. 09/01/1993
Columbia Healthcare Corp. merged into Columbia/HCA Healthcare Corp. 02/10/1994 which name changed to HCA - The Healthcare Co. 05/25/2000 which name changed to HCA Inc. (Ctfs. dated after 06/29/2001) 06/29/2001
(See HCA Inc. (Ctfs. dated after 06/29/2001))

COLUMBIA INTL CORP (UT)
Involuntarily dissolved for failure to file annual report 05/01/1990

COLUMBIA INTL STK FD INC (OR)
Common 1¢ par reclassified as Class Z 1¢ par 11/01/2002
Merged into Columbia Funds Series Trust I 10/07/2005
Details not available

COLUMBIA INVESTING CORP.
Dissolved 00/00/1934
Details not available

COLUMBIA INVT CORP (TX)
Liquidation completed 03/02/1970
Each share Capital Stock $1 par received initial distribution of (1.36363) shares Siboney Corp. Common 10¢ par 09/16/1969
Each share Capital Stock $1 par received second distribution of (0.23376) share Siboney Corp. Common $1 par 11/19/1969
Each share Capital Stock $1 par received third and final distribution of (0.03897) share Siboney Corp. Common $1 par 03/02/1970
Note: Certificates were not required to be surrendered and are without value

COLUMBIA LABS INC (DE)
Old Common 1¢ par split (2) for (1) by issuance of (1) additional share 06/09/1989
Each share old Common 1¢ par exchanged for (0.125) share new Common 1¢ par 08/09/2013
Name changed to Juniper Pharmaceuticals, Inc. 04/13/2015
(See Juniper Pharmaceuticals, Inc.)

COLUMBIA LEAD & ZINC MINES LTD. (BC)
Struck from British Columbia Registrar of Companies and proclaimed dissolved 03/12/1964

COLUMBIA LEISURE CORP (BC)
Struck off register and declared dissolved for failure to file returns 11/03/1995

COLUMBIA LIFE INSURANCE CO.
Assets sold to Ohio National Life Insurance Co. and liquidated 00/00/1940
Details not available

COLUMBIA LIFE INSURANCE CO. (PA)
Completely liquidated 10/15/1991
Details not available

COLUMBIA LIFE INS CO FLA (FL)
Name changed to Southern Security Life Insurance Co. 11/17/1978
(See Southern Security Life Insurance Co.)

COLUMBIA MACHINERY & ENGINEERING CORP. (OH)
Merged into Lodge & Shipley Co. 00/00/1953
Each share Common 10¢ par exchanged for (0.5) share Common $1 par
(See Lodge & Shipley Co.)

COLUMBIA METALS CORP LTD (ON)
Name changed to NWM Mining Corp. 07/16/2008
(See NWM Mining Corp.)

COLUMBIA METALS EXPLORATION CO. LTD. (SK)
Name changed to Mid-Can Exploration Ltd. 02/22/1965
Mid-Can Exploration Ltd. name changed to St. John's Petroleum Ltd. 05/17/1982 which merged into Westgrowth Petroleums Ltd. (AB) 07/11/1985 which recapitalized as Canadian Westgrowth Ltd. 10/14/1986 which merged into Ulster Petroleums Ltd. 10/27/1987 which merged into Anderson Exploration Ltd. 05/23/2000
(See Anderson Exploration Ltd.)

COLUMBIA MID CAP GROWTH FD INC (OR)
Name changed 10/10/2003
Common 1¢ par split (3) for (1) by issuance of (2) additional shares 01/31/1992
Common 1¢ par reclassified as Class Z 1¢ par 12/06/2002
Name changed from Columbia Special Fund, Inc. to Columbia Mid Cap Growth Fund, Inc. 10/10/2003
Merged into Columbia Funds Series Trust I 03/27/2006
Details not available

COLUMBIA MINES CORP. (ID)
Charter revoked for failure to file reports and pay fees 11/30/1961

COLUMBIA MLS INC (NY)
Capital Stock $100 par changed to $1 par 00/00/1953
Dissolved by proclamation 01/25/2012

COLUMBIA MUTUAL LUMBER CO., LTD. (BC)
Struck off register and declared dissolved for failure to file returns 07/19/1923

COLUMBIA NATL BK (KANSAS CITY, MO)
Capital Stock $100 par split (4) for (1) by issuance of (3) additional shares 01/29/1963
Stock Dividends - 20% 02/24/1955;

25% 06/12/1957; 33.33333333% 01/19/1960
Merged into Columbia Union National Bank & Trust Co. (Kansas City, MO) 09/12/1969
Each share Capital Stock $100 par exchanged for (1) share 6% Conv. Preferred $85 par and (1.125) shares Common $10 par
(See Columbia Union National Bank & Trust Co. (Kansas City, MO))

COLUMBIA NATL BK (SANTA MONICA, CA)
Common $5 par changed to $4 par and (0.25) additional share issued 06/30/1988
Closed by the FDIC 02/22/1993
Stockholders' equity unlikely

COLUMBIA NATL CORP (OH)
Stock Dividend - 10% 01/02/1970
Acquired by NN Corp. 08/24/1979
Each share Common no par exchanged for $16 cash

COLUMBIA NATURAL GAS LTD. (BC)
Dissolved 09/28/1946
Details not available

COLUMBIA NEWBERRY & LAURENS RR CO (SC)
Merged into Seaboard System Railroad, Inc. 04/30/1984
Each share Common $25 par exchanged for $400 cash

COLUMBIA NYEMATIC SYS INC (WA)
Name changed to Columbia Corp. 04/28/1971
(See Columbia Corp.)

COLUMBIA ORE MUN BD FD INC (OR)
Reincorporated 04/29/1988
Name changed 02/22/2000
State of incorporation changed from (DE) to (OR) 04/29/1988
Name changed from Columbia Municipal Bond Fund, Inc. to Columbia Oregon Municipal Bond Fund, Inc. 02/22/2000
Common 1¢ par reclassified as Class Z 1¢ par 11/01/2002
Merged into Columbia Funds Series Trust I 03/27/2006
Details not available

COLUMBIA PAC BK & TR CO (PORTLAND, OR)
Closed by state superintendent of banks 03/18/1983
No stockholders' equity

COLUMBIA PHONOGRAPH CO., INC.
Acquired by Grigsby-Grunow Co. 00/00/1931
Details not available

COLUMBIA PICTURES CORP (NY)
Common no par changed to $5 par 00/00/1954
Common $5 par split (5) for (4) by issuance of (0.25) additional share 07/29/1955
$4.25 Conv. Preferred no par called for redemption 12/11/1967
Common $5 par changed to $2.50 par and (1) additional share issued 01/18/1968
Stock Dividend - 50% 12/29/1945
Under plan of merger name changed to Columbia Pictures Industries, Inc. (NY) 12/28/1968
Columbia Pictures Industries, Inc. (NY) reincorporated in Delaware 12/27/1969 which merged into Coca-Cola Co. 06/21/1982

COLUMBIA PICTURES ENTMT INC (DE)
Merged into Sony USA Inc. 11/07/1989
Each share Common 10¢ par exchanged for $27 cash

COLUMBIA PICTURES INDS INC (DE)
Reincorporated 12/27/1969
State of incorporation changed from (NY) to (DE) 12/27/1969
Merged into Coca-Cola Co. 06/21/1982
Each share Common 10¢ par exchanged for (2.174) shares Common no par

COLUMBIA PIPELINE GROUP INC (DE)
Acquired by TransCanada Corp. 07/01/2016
Each share Common 1¢ par exchanged for $25.50 cash

COLUMBIA PIPELINE PARTNERS LP (DE)
Acquired by Columbia Pipeline Group, Inc. 02/17/2017
Each Common Unit exchanged for $17.10 cash

COLUMBIA PLACERS LTD. (CANADA)
Recapitalized as Maricana Enterprises Ltd. 10/01/1971
Each share Capital Stock $1 par exchanged for (0.1) share Capital Stock no par no par
(See Maricana Enterprises Ltd.)

COLUMBIA POWER CO.
Merged into Cincinnati Gas & Electric Co. 00/00/1928
Details not available

COLUMBIA PRECISION CORP (MD)
Adjudicated bankrupt 07/13/1973
Stockholders' equity unlikely

COLUMBIA RADIATOR CO.
Merged with Columbia Corp. and name changed to Columbia Foundry Co. 00/00/1948
Details not available

COLUMBIA REAL ESTATE EQUITY FD INC (OR)
Common 1¢ par reclassified as Class Z 1¢ par 11/01/2002
Merged into Columbia Funds Series Trust I 03/27/2006
Details not available

COLUMBIA REAL ESTATE INVTS INC (MD)
Liquidation completed
Each share Common 1¢ par exchanged for initial distribution of $10.40 cash 08/09/1994
Each share Common 1¢ par received second and final distribution of $0.1095 cash 07/23/1997
Note: Stockholders who did not surrender their certificates on or before 08/09/1994 are not entitled to any distributions

COLUMBIA REAL ESTATE TITLE INS CO (DC)
Charter revoked for failure to file reports 09/08/1997

COLUMBIA RLTY TR (DC)
Completely liquidated 01/23/1975
Each Class A Share Bene. Int. no par exchanged for first and final distribution of (0.00625) Columbia Realty Venture Limited Partnership Int.

COLUMBIA RIV RES INC (NV)
Each share old Common $0.001 par exchanged for (0.004) share new Common $0.001 par 02/26/2008
Name changed to Traxxec, Inc. 09/09/2008
Traxxec, Inc. name changed to Stem Cell Assurance, Inc. 08/14/2009 which name changed to BioRestorative Therapies, Inc. (NV) 09/16/2011 which reincorporated in Delaware 01/01/2015

COLUMBIA RIVER LONGVIEW BRIDGE CO.
Reorganized as Longview Bridge Co. 00/00/1936

Details not available

COLUMBIA RIVER MINES LTD (BC)
Recapitalized as Consolidated Columbia River Mines Ltd. 07/18/1973
Each share Common no par exchanged for (0.2) share Common no par
Preference not affected except for change of name
Consolidated Columbia River Mines Ltd. recapitalized as Ruth Vermont Mine Ltd. 11/21/1977
(See Ruth Vermont Mine Ltd.)

COLUMBIA RIVER PACKERS ASSOCIATION, INC. (OR)
Each share old Capital Stock no par exchanged for (5) shares new Capital Stock no par 00/00/1948
New Capital Stock no par changed to $5 par 00/00/1954
Merged into Castle & Cooke, Inc. (Old) 06/01/1961
Each share Capital Stock $5 par exchanged for (0.875) share Capital Stock $10 par
Castle & Cooke, Inc. (Old) name changed to Dole Food Co., Inc. (HI) 07/30/1991 which reincorporated in Delaware 07/01/2001
(See Dole Food Co., Inc. (Old) (DE))

COLUMBIA SAND & GRAVEL CO., INC.
Dissolved 00/00/1932
Details not available

COLUMBIA SVGS & LN ASSN (CA)
Ctfs. dtd. before 05/07/1971
Each share Guarantee Stock 50¢ par exchanged for (0.25) share Guarantee Stock $2 par 10/01/1963
Under plan of merger each share Guarantee Stock $2 par exchanged for (0.8) share Guarantee Stock no par 12/01/1969
Note: Certificates were not requested for exchange until 04/23/1970
Merged into USLIFE Savings & Loan Association 05/07/1971
Each share Guarantee Stock no par exchanged for (1.6) shares Guarantee Stock $1 par
(See USLIFE Savings & Loan Association)

COLUMBIA SVGS & LN ASSN (CA)
Ctfs. dated after 11/29/1976
Guarantee Stock $1 par split (2) for (1) by issuance of (1) additional share 09/14/1978
Stock Dividend - In Conv. Preferred Ser. A to holders of Common 100% 05/05/1986
Placed in receivership by the Office of Thrift Supervision 09/13/1991
Stockholders' equity undetermined

COLUMBIA SCIENTIFIC CORP (DE)
Charter cancelled and declared inoperative and void for non-payment of taxes 04/15/1972

COLUMBIA SCIENTIFIC INDS CORP (TX)
Merged into CSI Acquisition Corp. 04/22/1994
Each share Common no par exchanged for $17.067 cash
Note: An additional escrow payment of $0.43525 cash was made 02/07/1997

COLUMBIA SHORT TERM BD FD INC (OR)
Common 1¢ par reclassified as Class Z 1¢ par 12/06/2002
Merged into Columbia Funds Series Trust 09/23/2005
Details not available

COLUMBIA SILVER MINING CO. (WA)
Charter revoked for failure to file reports and pay fees 07/01/1929

COLUMBIA SMALL CAP GROWTH FD INC (OR)
Name changed 10/13/2003
Name changed from Columbia Small Capital Fund, Inc. to Columbia Small Capital Growth Fund, Inc. 10/13/2003
Merged into Columbia Funds Series Trust I 03/27/2006
Details not available

COLUMBIA STEEL CORP.
Acquired by United States Steel Corp. (NJ) 00/00/1930
Details not available

COLUMBIA STRATEGIC INVS FD INC (OR)
Name changed 10/13/2003
Name changed from Columbia Strategic Value Fund, Inc. to Columbia Strategic Investor Fund, Inc. 10/13/2003
Merged into Columbia Funds Series Trust I 03/27/2006
Details not available

COLUMBIA TECHNICAL CORP (NY)
Common 10¢ par split (3) for (1) by issuance of (2) additional shares 05/22/1967
Name changed to Columbia Chase Corp. (NY) 01/03/1977
Columbia Chase Corp. (NY) reincorporated in Massachusetts as Chase Corp. 03/18/1988

COLUMBIA TELEPHONE CO. (PA)
Acquired by United Utilities, Inc. 07/20/1965
Each share Common $25 par exchanged for (0.25) shares Common $2.50 par
United Utilities, Inc. name changed to United Telecommunications, Inc. 06/02/1972 which name changed to Sprint Corp. (KS) 02/26/1992 which name changed to Sprint Nextel Corp. 08/12/2005 which merged into Sprint Corp. (DE) 07/10/2013

COLUMBIA TERMINALS CO. (DE)
Each share old Common no par exchanged for (5) shares new Common no par 00/00/1952
6% Preferred $25 par called for redemption 02/00/1961
Merged into Ryder System, Inc. 03/15/1962
Details not available

COLUMBIA TITLE INSURANCE CO. OF THE DISTRICT OF COLUMBIA (DC)
Name changed to Columbia Real Estate Title Insurance Co. 01/19/1966
(See Columbia Real Estate Title Insurance Co.)

COLUMBIA TOY PRODUCTS, INC. (MO)
Charter revoked for failure to file reports and pay fees 01/01/1968

COLUMBIA-TROY CORP.
Dissolved 00/00/1938
Details not available

COLUMBIA U S GOVT SECS FD INC (OR)
Reincorporated 04/29/1988
Name changed 04/17/1991
State of incorporation changed from (MD) to (OR) 04/29/1988
Name changed from Columbia U.S. Government Guaranteed Securities Fund, Inc. to Columbia U.S. Government Securities Fund, Inc. 04/17/1991
Name changed to Columbia Short Term Bond Fund, Inc. 09/26/2000
(See Columbia Short Term Bond Fund, Inc.)

COLUMBIA UN NATL BK & TR CO (KANSAS CITY, MO)
6% Conv. Preferred $85 par

reclassified as 6% Conv. Preferred Class B $85 par 11/07/1972
Merged into First Union Bancorporation 11/20/1981
Each share Common $10 par exchanged for (2.913) shares Common $10 par or $71 cash
Note: Option to received stock expired 12/11/1981
Name changed to Centerre Bank of Kansas City, N.A. (Kansas City, MO) 01/04/1982
(See Centerre Bank of Kansas City, N.A. (Kansas City, MO)

COLUMBIA UNVL CORP (NV)
Merged into American Heritage Life Insurance Co. 03/03/1997
Each share Common exchanged for $9.6476 cash

COLUMBIA URANIUM, INC. (WA)
Automatically dissolved for non-payment of corporation license fees 07/01/1961

COLUMBIA WESTN INC (OR)
Plan of reorganization under Chapter 11 Federal Bankruptcy Code effective 12/13/1995
Each share Common 1¢ par received an approximate distribution of (0.070347) Pine Brook Capital Inc. Common Stock Purchase Warrant expiring 12/12/2002 on 09/28/1998
Note: Certificates not surrendered prior to 12/13/1996 were cancelled and are without value

COLUMBIA YACHT CORP. (DE)
Each share Class A 10¢ par exchanged for (0.5) share Class A 20¢ par 10/08/1965
Each share Common 10¢ par exchanged for (0.5) share Common 20¢ par 10/08/1965
Name changed to CYC Corp. 04/13/1967
CYC Corp. acquired by Whittaker Corp. (CA) 04/14/1967 which reincorporated in Delaware 06/16/1986
(See Whittaker Corp. (DE))

COLUMBIA YUKON EXPLORATIONS INC (AB)
Each share old Common no par exchanged for (0.10526315) share new Common no par 02/28/2002
Each share new Common no par exchanged again for (0.1) share new Common no par 12/17/2013
Name changed to BC Moly Ltd. 09/24/2014

COLUMBIA YUKON RES LTD (AB)
Recapitalized as Columbia Yukon Explorations Inc. 10/23/1998
Each share Common no par exchanged for (0.14285714) share Common no par
Columbia Yukon Explorations Inc. name changed to BC Moly Ltd. 09/24/2014

COLUMBIALUM STAFFING LTD (NV)
Recapitalized as Resolve Staffing, Inc. 05/28/2002
Each share Common $0.0001 par exchanged for (0.03333333) share Common $0.0001 par
Resolve Staffing, Inc. recapitalized as Choose Rain, Inc. 02/06/2014 which name changed to Rooshine Inc. 09/21/2017

COLUMBIAN BRONZE CORP. (NY)
Merged into Kidde (Walter) & Co., Inc. (NY) 06/09/1965
Each share Common $1 par exchanged for (0.307692) share Common $2.50 par
Kidde (Walter) & Co., Inc. (NY) reincorporated in Delaware 07/02/1968 which name changed to Kidde, Inc. 04/10/1980 which merged into Hanson Trust p.l.c. 12/31/1987 which name changed to Hanson PLC (Old) 01/29/1988 which reorganized as Hanson PLC (New) 10/15/2003

COLUMBIAN CARBON CO. (DE)
Stock Dividend - 200% 09/21/1945
Merged into Cities Service Co. 01/31/1962
Each share Capital Stock no par exchanged for (0.67) share $4.40 Preferred no par
(See Cities Service Co.)

COLUMBIAN ENERGY CO LTD PARTNERSHIP (KS)
Plan of reorganization under Chapter 11 Federal Bankruptcy Code effective 09/30/1993
Each Unit of Ltd. Partnership Int. received $0.09 cash
Note: Certificates were not required to be surrendered and are without value

COLUMBIAN MAGAZINE PUBLISHING CO. (DE)
No longer in existence having become inoperative and void for non-payment of taxes 03/18/1914

COLUMBIAN NATIONAL LIFE INSURANCE CO. (MA)
Each share Capital Stock $100 par exchanged for (5) shares Capital Stock $20 par 00/00/1948
Stock Dividends - 33.33333333% 12/28/1950; 25% 12/15/1954
Name changed to Hartford Life Insurance Co. 06/27/1960
(See Hartford Life Insurance Co.)

COLUMBIAN PAPER CO.
Acquired by Mead Corp. 00/00/1946
Each share Capital Stock exchanged for (0.5) share $5.50 Preferred Ser. B no par and (1) share Common no par
Mead Corp. merged into MeadWestvaco Corp. 01/29/2002 which merged into WestRock Co. 07/01/2015

COLUMBIAN ROPE CO (DE)
Reincorporated 04/24/1990
State of incorporation changed from (NY) to (DE) and Capital Stock $100 par reclassified as Common $5 par 04/24/1990
Charter cancelled and declared inoperative and void for non-payment of taxes 03/01/2009

COLUMBIERE MINES LTD (ON)
Charter cancelled for failure to pay taxes and file returns 05/18/1976

COLUMBINE CAP CORP (UT)
Proclaimed dissolved for failure to file annual report 11/01/1990

COLUMBINE EXPL CORP (CO)
Filed petition under Chapter 7 Federal Bankruptcy Code 06/21/1989
No stockholders' equity

COLUMBINE FD INC (MD)
Deregistered 00/00/1977
Details not available

COLUMBINE FINL CORP (UT)
Each share old Capital Stock 1¢ par exchanged for (3) shares new Capital Stock 1¢ par 04/15/1979
Name changed to Synthonics Technologies, Inc. (UT) 09/16/1996
Synthonics Technologies, Inc. (UT) reincorporated in Delaware 12/23/1999

COLUMBINE METALS INC (CO)
Name changed to Wynn Industries, Inc. 12/30/1968
(See Wynn Industries, Inc.)

COLUMBINE RECREATIONAL CORP. (CO)
Charter revoked for failure to file reports and pay fees 10/14/1968

COLUMBINE TELENET INC (NY)
Name changed to Metrolink Group Inc. 08/25/1989
(See Metrolink Group Inc.)

COLUMBINE URANIUM, INC. (CO)
Proclaimed defunct and inoperative for failure to pay taxes 11/05/1956

COLUMBIUM CORP. (DE)
No longer in existence having become inoperative and void for non-payment of taxes 04/01/1964

COLUMBUS & SOUTHN OHIO ELEC CO (OH)
Each share Common no par exchanged for (5) shares Common $10 par 00/00/1945
Each share Common $10 par exchanged for (2) shares Common $5 par 00/00/1949
6% Preferred $100 par called for redemption 11/05/1962
Common $5 par changed to no par and (1) additional share issued 05/15/1964
Merged into American Power Electric Co., Inc. 12/31/1980
Each share Common no par exchanged for (1.3) shares Common $6.50 par
10.52% Preferred $100 par called for redemption 08/01/1986
Name changed to Columbus Southern Power Co. 09/09/1987
(See Columbus Southern Power Co.)

COLUMBUS & XENIA R.R. CO.
Merged into Little Miami Railroad Co. on a share for share basis 00/00/1943
(See Little Miami Railroad Co.)

COLUMBUS ACQUISITION CORP (DE)
Completely liquidated 06/15/2009
Each Unit exchanged for first and final distribution of $7.98020171 cash
Each share Common $0.0001 par exchanged for first and final distribution of $7.98020171 cash

COLUMBUS AUTO PTS CO (OH)
Each share old Common no par exchanged for (3) shares new Common no par 04/19/1973
Merged into SLILS Inc. 02/27/1987
Each share new Common no par exchanged for $21.41 cash

COLUMBUS BK & TR CO (COLUMBUS, GA)
Each share Capital Stock $100 par exchanged for (10) shares Capital Stock $10 par and dividend of (3) new shares for each (17) new shares 00/00/1949
Capital Stock $10 par changed to $5 par and (1) additional share issued plus a 50% stock dividend paid 03/01/1967
Reorganized as CB&T Bancshares, Inc. 12/06/1972
Each share Capital Stock $5 par exchanged for (2) shares Common $2.50 par
CB&T Bancshares, Inc. name changed to Synovus Financial Corp. 08/21/1989

COLUMBUS COATED FABRICS CORP. (OH)
Acquired by Borden Co. on a (1) for (1.6338) basis 07/27/1961
Borden Co. name changed to Borden, Inc. 04/17/1968 which merged into RJR Nabisco Holdings Corp. 03/14/1995 which name changed to Nabisco Group Holdings Corp. 06/15/1999
(See Nabisco Group Holdings Corp.)

COLUMBUS COFFIN CO. (OH)
Dissolved 07/28/1956
Details not available

COLUMBUS COPPER CORP (BC)
Each share old Common no par exchanged for (0.1) share new Common no par 12/05/2014
Merged into EnerGulf Resources Inc. 10/05/2015

Each share new Common no par exchanged for (0.4937) share Common no par
Note: Unexchanged certificates will be cancelled and become without value 10/05/2021

COLUMBUS ELECTRIC & POWER CO.
Merged into Georgia Power Co. 00/00/1930
Details not available

COLUMBUS ELECTRONICS CORP. (NY)
Class A Common 10¢ par reclassified as Common 10¢ par 09/11/1961
Adjudicated bankrupt 09/05/1963
No stockholders' equity

COLUMBUS ENERGY CORP (CO)
Common 20¢ par split (5) for (4) by issuance of (0.25) additional share payable 06/16/1997 to holders of record 05/27/1997 Ex date - 06/17/1997
Stock Dividends - 10% 03/17/1994; 10% 03/10/1995; 10% payable 03/09/1998 to holders of record 02/23/1998
Merged into Key Production Co., Inc. 01/02/2001
Each share Common 20¢ par exchanged for (0.355) share Common 25¢ par
Key Production Co., Inc. merged into Cimarex Energy Co. 09/30/2002

COLUMBUS EXPL CORP (BC)
Name changed to Organto Foods Inc. 12/22/2015

COLUMBUS FD INC (OH)
Voluntarily dissolved 12/03/1976
Each share Common no par exchanged for $4.29 cash

COLUMBUS FOODS CORP.
Merged into Stokely-Van Camp, Inc. 00/00/1946
Each share Preferred exchanged for (1.75) shares 5% Prior Preference $20 par
Each share Common exchanged for (1) share 5% Prior Preference $20 par and (0.3) share Common $1 par
(See Stokely-Van Camp, Inc.)

COLUMBUS FOUNDERS SVGS & LN ASSN (CA)
Name changed to Columbus Savings & Loan Association (New) 04/10/1970
Columbus Savings & Loan Association (New) merged into Imperial Corp. of America 03/02/1972
(See Imperial Corp. of America)

COLUMBUS GEOGRAPHIC SYS (NV)
SEC revoked common stock registration 08/17/2011

COLUMBUS ICE HOCKEY CLUB, INC. (OH)
Ceased operations 00/00/1970
No stockholders' equity

COLUMBUS INS HLDG CO (DE)
Charter cancelled and declared inoperative and void for non-payment of taxes 03/01/1986

COLUMBUS MANUFACTURING CO.
Acquired by West Point Manufacturing Co. (AL) 00/00/1947
Details not available

COLUMBUS MLS INC (GA)
Common $1 par split (2) for (1) by issuance of (1) additional share 06/02/1986
Acquired by Carpet Mill Store Inc. 12/30/1986
Each share Common $1 par exchanged for $43 cash

COLUMBUS NATL BK (PROVIDENCE, RI)
Stock Dividend - 41.9% 11/20/1944

Reorganized as National Columbus Bancorp, Inc. 02/27/1970
Each share Common $10 par exchanged for (1) share Common $1 par
(See National Columbus Bancorp, Inc.)

COLUMBUS NATIONAL LIFE INSURANCE CO. (GA)
Merged into Coastal States Life Insurance Co. 05/08/1957
Each share Capital Stock $5 par exchanged for (1) share Common $2.50 par
Coastal States Life Insurance Co. reorganized as Coastal States Corp. 10/05/1972
(See Coastal States Corp.)

COLUMBUS NETWORKS CORP NEW (NV)
SEC revoked common stock registration 05/26/2011

COLUMBUS NETWORKS CORP OLD (NV)
Name changed to Legacy West Ventures Corp. 08/16/2004
Legacy West Ventures Corp. name changed to Columbus Networks Corp. (New) 01/19/2005
(See Columbus Networks Corp. (New))

COLUMBUS PACKING CO.
Liquidated 00/00/1938
Details not available

COLUMBUS PLASTIC PRODUCTS, INC. (OH)
Acquired by Borden Co. 02/10/1966
Each share Common no par exchanged for (0.533087) share Capital Stock $3.75 par
Borden Co. name changed to Borden, Inc. 04/17/1968 which merged into RJR Nabisco Holdings Corp. 03/14/1995 which name changed to Nabsico Group Holdings Corp. 06/15/1999
(See Nabisco Group Holdings Corp.)

COLUMBUS RAILWAY, POWER & LIGHT CO.
Merged into Columbus & Southern Ohio Electric Co. 00/00/1937
Each share Common exchanged for (1) share Common no par
Columbus & Southern Ohio Electric Co. name changed to Columbus Southern Power Co. 09/09/1987
(See Columbus Southern Power Co.)

COLUMBUS RLTY TR (TX)
Merged into Post Properties, Inc. 10/24/1997
Each Share of Bene. Int. 1¢ par exchanged for (0.615) share Common 1¢ par
Post Properties, Inc. merged into Mid-America Apartment Communities, Inc. 12/01/2016

COLUMBUS REXALL CONSOLIDATED MINES CO. (UT)
Name changed to Columbus-Rexall Oil Co. 01/15/1957
(See Columbus-Rexall Oil Co.)

COLUMBUS-REXALL OIL CO. (UT)
Properties sold to Grand Deposit Mining Co. 12/00/1961
Holders of each (200) shares Columbus- Rexall Oil Co. Common $1 par were entitled to receive (1) share Grand Deposit Mining Co. Capital Stock 5¢ par
Columbus-Rexall Oil Co. stock certificates were stamped and returned together with the Grand Deposit certificate
Final date to participate was 12/31/1963 although the Charter of Columbus-Rexall Oil Co. was suspended for failure to pay taxes 04/01/1963
(See Grand Deposit Mining Co.)

COLUMBUS SAVINGS & LOAN ASSOCIATION (OLD) (CA)
Merged into Columbus-Founders Savings & Loan Association 06/30/1965
Each share Guarantee Capital Stock $2.50 par exchanged for (2.5) shares Guarantee Capital Stock $1 par
Columbus-Founders Savings & Loan Association name changed to Columbus Savings & Loan Association (New) 04/10/1970 which merged into Imperial Corp. of America (CA) 03/02/1972 which reincorporated in Delaware 09/21/1987
(See Imperial Corp. of America (DE))

COLUMBUS SVGS & LN ASSN NEW (CA)
Merged into Imperial Corp. of America (CA) 03/02/1972
Each share Guarantee Capital Stock $1 par exchanged for (1.4) shares Common $1 par
Imperial Corp. of America (CA) reincorporated in Delaware 09/21/1987
(See Imperial Corp. of America (DE))

COLUMBUS SILVER CORP (BC)
Recapitalized as Columbus Exploration Corp. 02/26/2013
Each share Common no par exchanged for (0.25) share Common no par
Columbus Exploration Corp. name changed to Organto Foods Inc. 12/22/2015

COLUMBUS SOUTHN PWR CO (OH)
$2.42 Preferred $25 par called for redemption 06/01/1990
$3.45 Preferred $25 par called for redemption 06/01/1990
$3.75 Preferred $25 par called for redemption 06/01/1990
4.25% Preferred $100 par called for redemption 06/01/1990
4.65% Preferred $100 par called for redemption 06/01/1990
7.52% Preferred $100 par called for redemption 06/01/1990
8.52% Preferred $100 par called for redemption 06/01/1990
9.5% Preferred $100 par called for redemption 06/01/1990
10% Preferred $100 par called for redemption 06/01/1990
$15.25 Preference no par (Color Brown) called for redemption 06/01/1990
$15.25 Preference no par (Color Blue) called for redemption 06/01/1990
9.5% Ser. Preferred $100 par called for redemption 02/01/1996
7.875% Preferred $100 par called for redemption 03/01/1997
7% Preferred called for redemption at $100 on 08/01/2002
Public interest eliminated

COLUMBUS TRANSN CO (GA)
Common $1 par changed to $5 par 00/00/1950
Liquidation completed
Each share Common $5 par exchanged for initial distribution of $6 cash 09/01/1967
Each share Common $5 par received second distribution of $1.80 cash 01/31/1968
Each share Common $5 par received third and final distribution of $0.515 cash 08/04/1969

COLUMBUS TR CO (NEWBURG, NY)
Each share Common $100 par exchanged for (5) shares Common $20 par 01/20/1965
Stock Dividends - 100% 03/15/1944; 50% 10/09/1953
Merged into Key Banks Inc. 12/01/1984

Each share Common $20 par exchanged for $80 cash

COLUMBUS VENETIAN STEVENS BUILDINGS, INC. (IL)
Assets sold 01/11/1957
No stockholders' equity

COLUMBUS VENTURES INC (NV)
Each share old Common $0.001 par exchanged for (4) shares new Common $0.001 par 05/06/2008
Name changed to Bald Eagle Energy Inc. 07/21/2008

COLUMINDA METALS CORP. LTD. (ON)
Charter cancelled 09/19/1960

COLUSA BIOMASS ENERGY CORP (NV)
Each share old Common $0.001 par exchanged for (0.01) share new Common $0.001 par 09/12/2005
Each share new Common $0.001 par exchanged again for (8) shares new Common $0.001 par 03/20/2006
Name changed to Alpine Management Systems, Inc. 04/30/2008

COLVEST, INC. (UT)
Recapitalized as Far West Minerals, Inc. 09/20/1991
Each share Capital Stock $0.001 par exchanged for (0.1) share Common $0.001 par
Far West Minerals, Inc. recapitalized as Pacific Minerals & Chemical Inc. 06/24/1994 which recapitalized as Nevada Magic Holdings Inc. 01/07/1997 which name changed to To4c Corp. (UT) 06/29/1999 which reorganized in Nevada as Aplox Corp. 04/27/2001 which name changed to Mirador Inc. 07/25/2001 which recapitalized as VWAY International 07/05/2004 which name changed to WorldWide Cannery & Distribution, Inc. 02/08/2006 which name changed to Global Diamond Exchange Inc. 09/22/2006

COLVILLE LAKE EXPLS LTD (ON)
Each share Capital Stock $5 par exchanged for (5) shares Capital Stock $1 par 10/14/1959
Charter cancelled for failure to pay taxes and file returns 07/27/1976

COLWELL CO (CA)
Common $1 par split (3) for (2) by issuance of (0.5) additional share 08/31/1971
Merged into Baldwin-United Corp. 08/29/1980
Each share Common $1 par exchanged for $25 cash

COLWELL INDS INC (MN)
Under plan of merger each share Common 10¢ par exchanged for $15 cash 12/31/2003

COLWELL MTG TR (CA)
Name changed to CMT Investment Trust 04/25/1979
CMT Investment Trust reorganized as CMT Investment Co. 11/07/1980 which name changed to Avalon Energy Corp. 10/01/1984 which merged into Avalon Corp. 04/15/1985
(See Avalon Corp.)

COLWYN RISK FD INC (NJ)
Deregistered 01/08/1981
Details not available

COM AIR CONTAINERS CDA INC (BC)
Dissolved and struck from register on 06/19/1992

COM CIR TEK INC (NY)
Adjudicated bankrupt 09/05/1978
Stockholders' equity unlikely

COM COMP INC (NY)
Assets assigned for benefit of creditors 00/00/1971
No stockholders' equity

COM DEV INTL LTD (CANADA)
Plan of arangement effective 02/08/2016
Each share Common no par exchanged for (0.19785496) share exactEarth Ltd. Common no par and $5.125 cash
Each share Common no par received an additional distribution of $0.12584108 cash from escrow 02/22/2016
Note: Unexchanged certificates will be cancelled and become without value 02/08/2022

COM NAV ELECTRS INC (WV)
Name changed to Aquarius International Corp. 07/01/1972
(See Aquarius International Corp.)

COM 101 INC (NV)
Each share old Common $0.001 par exchanged for (0.00666666) share new Common $0.001 par 07/16/1998
Name changed to Optimal Analytics.com Inc. 06/18/1999
Optimal Analytics.com Inc. recapitalized as Optimal Ventures Inc. 02/20/2002 which name changed to Greenwind Power Corp. USA 04/08/2004 which recapitalized as HD Retail Solutions Inc. 07/07/2009 which name changed to Greenscape Laboratories, Inc. 06/10/2014 which recapitalized as Ultrack Systems, Inc. 04/11/2016

COM OPTICS INC (DE)
Name changed to Tile Fashions, Inc. 10/01/1982

COM SH INC (MI)
Name changed to Comshare, Inc. 01/08/1976
(See Comshare, Inc.)

COM SH SOUTHN INC (TX)
Reincorporated under the laws of Delaware as Computer Complex, Inc. 03/14/1969
Computer Complex, Inc. name changed to Houston Complex, Inc. 11/24/1972
(See Houston Complex, Inc.)

COM SYS INC (CA)
Merged into Resurgens Communications Group, Inc. 02/04/1992
Each share Common no par exchanged for (1) share Common 1¢ par
Resurgens Communications Group, Inc. name changed to LDDS Communications, Inc. 09/15/1993 which name changed to WorldCom, Inc. 05/26/1995 which name changed to MCI WorldCom, Inc. 09/14/1998 which name changed to WorldCom Inc. (New) 05/01/2000
(See WorldCom Inc. (New))

COM/TECH COMMUNICATIONS TECHNOLOGIES INC (NY)
Charter cancelled and proclaimed dissolved for failure to pay taxes 06/27/2001

COM TECH PRODS CORP (NY)
Dissolved 10/11/1967
No stockholders' equity

COM TEK RES INC (CO)
Name changed to Powerhouse Resources Inc. 08/10/1995
(See Powerhouse Resources Inc.)

COM TEL INC (UT)
Proclaimed dissolved for failure to pay taxes 08/01/1989

COM-TRON SYSTEMS LTD. (ON)
Charter cancelled 03/05/1975

COM-TRONIX, INC. (MA)
Acquired by Ovitron Corp. 04/17/1968
Details not available

COM2000 NET TECHNOLOGY INC (DE)
Name changed to China Financial Group, Inc. 08/22/2005

COM VU CORP (DE)
Charter cancelled and declared inoperative and void for non-payment of taxes 03/01/2006

COMA LAKE MINES LTD. (ON)
Charter cancelled and company declared dissolved for default in filing returns 05/27/1965

COMAC COMMUNICATIONS LTD. (ON)
Acquired by Bell Telephone Co. of CanadaLa Compagnie de Telephone Bell du Canada 01/28/1983
Each share Common no par exchanged for $2.40 cash

COMAC FOOD GROUP INC (CANADA)
Name changed to Canada's Pizza Delivery Corp. and Class B no par reclassified as Common no par 01/22/2004
(See Canada's Pizza Delivery Corp.)

COMAGO SMOKELESS FUEL CO.
Dissolved 00/00/1941
Details not available

COMAIR HLDGS INC (KY)
Reincorporated 11/01/1988
Common no par split (3) for (2) by issuance of (0.5) additional share 03/06/1985
Common no par split (3) for (2) by issuance of (0.5) additional share 08/13/1985
Reincorporated from Comair Inc. (OH) to Comair Holdings, Inc. (KY) 11/01/1988
Common no par split (3) for (2) by issuance of (0.5) additional share 02/19/1992
Common no par split (3) for (2) by issuance of (0.5) additional share 04/23/1993
Common no par split (3) for (2) by issuance of (0.5) additional share 08/10/1995
Common no par split (3) for (2) by issuance of (0.5) additional share payable 05/17/1996 to holders of record 05/09/1996
Common no par split (3) for (2) by issuance of (0.5) additional share payable 11/13/1997 to holders of record 11/03/1997
Common no par split (3) for (2) by issuance of (0.5) additional share payable 06/25/1999 to holders of record 03/15/1999
Merged into Delta Air Lines, Inc. 01/11/2000
Each share Common no par exchanged for $23.50 cash

COMALCO LTD (AUSTRALIA)
ADR agreement terminated 07/21/2000
Each ADR for Ordinary exchanged for approximately $27.80 cash

COMAMTECH INC (ON)
Reincorporated under the laws of Delaware as DecisionPoint Systems, Inc. (New) and Common no par changed to $0.001 par 06/22/2011

COMANCHE ENERGY INC (OK)
Reincorporated 04/00/2001
Each share Common no par received distribution of (1) share Energytec.com, Inc. Restricted Common payable 11/04/1999 to holders of record 07/29/1999
State of incorporation changed from (UT) to (OK) and Common no par changed to $0.0001 par 04/00/2001
Name changed to RoadHouse Foods Inc. (OK) 05/03/2005

RoadHouse Foods Inc. (OK) reincorporated in Delaware 07/00/2005 which name changed to Locan, Inc. 06/09/2008
(See Locan, Inc.)

COMANCHE OIL & GAS CORP (UT)
Reorganized under the laws of Nevada as Uplift Nutrition, Inc. 06/29/2006
Each share Common 4¢ par exchanged for (0.5) share Common $0.001 par

COMANCHE PETES INC (BC)
Recapitalized as Camford Capital Corp. 10/18/1989
Each share Common no par exchanged for (0.2) share Common no par
(See Camford Capital Corp.)

COMANCHE URANIUM INC (UT)
Name changed to Comanche Oil & Gas Corp. (UT) 01/16/1969
Each share Capital Stock 1¢ par exchanged for (0.25) share Capital Stock 4¢ par
Comanche Oil & Gas Corp. (UT) reorganized in Nevada as Uplift Nutrition, Inc. 06/29/2006

COMAPLEX MINERALS CORP (AB)
Merged into Agnico-Eagle Mines Ltd. 07/12/2010
Each share Common no par exchanged for (0.1576) share Common no par and (1) share Geomark Exploration Ltd. Common no par
(See each company's listing)

COMAPLEX RES INTL LTD (AB)
Reincorporated 00/00/1987
Place of incorporation changed from (BC) to (AB) 00/00/1987
Common no par split (2) for (1) by issuance of (1) additional share 08/22/1980
Acquired by Comstate Resources Ltd. 12/08/1993
Each share Common no par exchanged for (0.35) share Common no par and $2.35 cash
(See Comstate Resources Ltd.)

COMARA MINING & MILLING CO. LTD. (ON)
Merged into Columbia Metals Corp. Ltd. 00/00/1949
Each share Capital Stock $1 par exchanged for (0.71428571) share Capital Stock $1 par
Columbia Metals Corp. Ltd. name changed to NWM Mining Corp. 07/16/2008
(See NWM Mining Corp.)

COMARK, INC. (DE)
Name changed to Cybermark Systems, Inc. 10/08/1968
(See Cybermark Systems, Inc.)

COMART ASSOC INC (NY)
Name changed to CCI Holding Corp. 06/01/1985
(See CCI Holding Corp.)

COMAS CIGARETTE MACHINE CO.
Name changed to Comas Machine Co. 00/00/1950
(See Comas Machine Co.)

COMAS MACHINE CO., INC. (VA)
Out of business 05/15/1957
Stockholders' equity unlikely

COMBANC INC (DE)
Merged into First Defiance Financial Corp. 01/24/2005
Each share Common no par exchanged for either (0.45457769) share Common 1¢ par and $5.2202 cash or $17.20 cash
Note: Option to receive stock and cash expired 02/22/2005

COMBANCORP (CA)
Merged into BanPonce Financial Corp. 09/30/1996
Each share Common $5 par exchanged for $17.31 cash

COMBANK/APOPKA (APOPKA, FL)
97.93% held by Combanks Corp. as of 03/30/1973
Public interest eliminated

COMBANK/CASSELBERRY (FERN PARK, FL)
96.5% held by Combanks Corp. through exchange offer which expired 03/30/1973
Public interest eliminated

COMBANK/FAIRVILLA (ORLANDO, FL)
98.15% held by Combanks Corp. as of 03/30/1973
Public interest eliminated

COMBANK/PINE CASTLE (PINE CASTLE, FL)
98.17% held by Combanks Corp. as of 03/30/1973
Public interest eliminated

COMBANK/WINTER PARK (WINTER PARK, FL)
99.6% acquired by Combanks Corp. through purchase offer which expired 02/16/1968
Public interest eliminated

COMBANKS CORP (FL)
Acquired by Freedom Savings & Loan Association 04/01/1983
Details not available

COMBICHEM INC (DE)
Merged into Du Pont (E.I.) De Nemours & Co. 11/15/1999
Each share Common $0.001 par exchanged for $6.75 cash

COMBIMATRIX CORP (DE)
Each share old Common $0.001 par exchanged for (0.1) share new Common $0.001 par 12/05/2012
Each share new Common $0.001 par exchanged again for (0.06666666) share new Common $0.001 par 02/01/2016
Merged into Invitae Corp. 11/14/2017
Each share new Common $0.001 par exchanged for (0.8692) share Common $0.0001 par

COMBINATORX INC (DE)
Name changed to Zalicus Inc. 09/09/2010
Zalicus Inc. recapitalized as EPIRUS Biopharmaceuticals, Inc. 07/16/2014

COMBINE CAMERA STORES INC (NY)
Liquidating plan of reorganization under Chapter 11 Federal Bankruptcy proceedings confirmed 12/26/1990
No stockholders' equity

COMBINE CORP (DE)
SEC revoked common stock registration 03/27/2007

COMBINED ASSETS INC (DE)
Name changed to Environmental Products & Technologies Corp. 01/13/1995
(See Environmental Products & Technologies Corp.)

COMBINED COMMUNICATIONS CORP (AZ)
Common no par split (3) for (2) by issuance of (0.5) additional share 05/31/1978
Merged into Gannett Co., Inc. (Old) 06/07/1979
Each share Common no par exchanged for (0.8) share Common no par
Gannett Co., Inc. (Old) name changed to TEGNA Inc. 06/26/2015

COMBINED COMMUNICATIONS CORP (NV)
Recapitalized as R B Capital & Equities Inc. 11/03/1997
Each share Common $0.001 par exchanged for (0.1) share Common $0.001 par
R B Capital & Equities Inc. merged into Triad Industries, Inc. 03/15/1999 which name changed to Direct Equity International, Inc. 05/12/2006

COMBINED COS INC (NV)
Each share old Common 1¢ par exchanged for (0.001) share new Common 1¢ par 02/24/1998
Name changed to Unisat Inc. 05/29/1998
Unisat Inc. name changed to Blagman Media International Inc. 05/06/1999 which recapitalized as Innovation Holdings, Inc. 03/05/2003 which name changed to Marketing Concepts International 10/20/2006

COMBINED COS INTL CORP (NV)
Stock Dividend - 20% 04/17/1995
Charter revoked for failure to file reports and pay fees 12/01/1997

COMBINED DEVELOPMENTS LTD. (AB)
Acquired by Canadian Scotia Ltd. 00/00/1956
Each share Common exchanged for (0.25) share Common
Canadian Scotia Ltd. acquired by Code Oil & Gas Ltd. 00/00/1958
(See Code Oil & Gas Ltd.)

COMBINED ENGINEERED PRODS LTD (CANADA)
Name changed to Compro Ltd. - Compro Ltee. 02/12/1975
(See Compro Ltd. - Compro Ltee.)

COMBINED ENTERPRISES, INC. (MD)
Merged into Doric Distributors, Inc. 03/05/1969
Each share Common 1¢ par exchanged for (0.4) share Common 10¢ par
(See Doric Distributors, Inc.)

COMBINED ENTERPRISES INC (MN)
Common 5¢ par changed to 1¢ par 06/18/1974
Name changed to Mortgage Brokers Network, Inc. 03/06/1989
Mortgage Brokers Network, Inc. name changed to Plenum Communications Inc. 11/22/1991 which name changed to LION, Inc. (MN) 08/20/1999 which reincorporated in Washington 12/15/2000
(See LION, Inc.)

COMBINED ENTERPRISES LTD. (CANADA)
Each share Common no par exchanged for (3) shares Common no par 00/00/1952
Each share old Common no par exchanged for (2) shares new Common no par 05/31/1955
Name changed to Turnbull Elevator Ltd. 09/04/1962
Turnbull Elevator Ltd. name changed to Combined Engineered Products Ltd. 06/08/1966 which name changed to Compro Ltd. - Compro Ltee. 02/12/1975
(See Compro Ltd. - Compro Ltee.)

COMBINED ENTMT ORGANIZATION INC (NV)
Charter permanently revoked 05/01/2003

COMBINED FINL SVCS INC (FL)
Proclaimed dissolved for failure to file reports and pay fees 10/11/1991

COMBINED INDS INC (DE)
Name changed to Garden State Industries, Inc. 06/02/1971
(See Garden State Industries, Inc.)

COMBINED INS CO AMER (IL)
Stock Dividends - 40% 07/30/1956; 42.85714285% 10/15/1957; 20% 10/15/1958; 25% 10/15/1959; 33.33333333% 10/15/1960; 50% 08/31/1961; 66.66666666%

09/21/1962; 20% 09/25/1963; 16.6666666% 09/23/1964; 21.4% 09/23/1965; 17.65% 09/16/1966; 20% 09/22/1967; 20% 09/20/1968; 20% 09/26/1969; 20% 09/28/1970; 20% 09/24/1971; 10% 09/22/1972
Reincorporated under the laws of Delaware as Combined International Corp. 05/30/1980
Combined International Corp. name changed to Aon Corp. (DE) 04/24/1987 which reorganized in England & Wales as Aon PLC 04/02/2012

COMBINED INTL CORP (DE)
$6 Conv. Preference $1 par called for redemption 12/01/1986
Name changed to Aon Corp. (DE) 04/24/1987
Aon Corp. (DE) reorganized in England & Wales as Aon PLC 04/02/2012

COMBINED INVTS INTL (UT)
Name changed to Allied Artists Entertainment Inc. 12/24/1990
(See Allied Artists Entertainment Inc.)

COMBINED LARDER MINES LTD (ON)
Recapitalized as Buffalo Oil Co. Ltd. (SK) 10/18/1993
Each share Capital Stock $1 par exchanged for (0.2) share Common no par
Buffalo Oil Co. Ltd. (SK) reincorporated in Alberta 06/17/2004 which recapitalized as Buffalo Oil Corp. 01/03/2005 which name changed to Buffalo Resources Corp. 08/03/2007 which merged into Twin Butte Energy Ltd. 10/15/2009

COMBINED LOCKS PAPER CO. (DE)
Preferred $25 par called for redemption 03/01/1961
Name changed to Combined Paper Mills, Inc. 06/09/1966
Combined Paper Mills, Inc. merged into National Cash Register Co. 07/31/1969 which name changed to NCR Corp. 05/10/1974 which merged into American Telephone & Telegraph Co. 09/19/1991 which name changed to AT&T Corp. 04/20/1994 which merged into AT&T Inc. 11/18/2005

COMBINED LOGISTICS INTL LTD (BAHAMAS)
Merged into Wilson Logistics Ltd. 01/05/2000
Each share Common no par exchanged for $0.33 cash

COMBINED MEDIA INC (NY)
Each share old Common 1¢ par exchanged for (0.5) share new Common 1¢ par 11/04/1971
Reincorporated under the laws of Florida as Combined Financial Services, Inc. 05/24/1973
(See Combined Financial Services, Inc.)

COMBINED METAL MINES LTD (ON)
Recapitalized as CME Resources Inc. 11/15/1979
Each share Capital Stock no par exchanged for (0.2) share Capital Stock no par
CME Resources Inc. name changed to CME Capital Inc. 10/15/1986
(See CME Capital Inc.)

COMBINED NETWORK INC (IL)
Name changed to Allnet Communication Services, Inc. 11/01/1983
Allnet Communications Services, Inc. merged into ALC Communications Corp. 12/19/1985 which merged into Frontier Corp. 08/15/1995 which merged into Global Crossing Ltd. 09/28/1999
(See Global Crossing Ltd.)

COMBINED OIL CO (DE)
Completely liquidated 05/24/1974
Each share Capital Stock $1 par exchanged for first and final distribution of $2.12 cash

COMBINED PAPER MLS INC (DE)
Merged into National Cash Register Co. 07/31/1969
Each share Class A Common $1 par exchanged for (0.533) share Common $5 par
Each share Class B Common $1 par exchanged for (0.533) share Common $5 par
National Cash Register Co. name changed to NCR Corp. 05/10/1974 which merged into American Telephone & Telegraph Co. 09/19/1991 which name changed to AT&T Corp. 04/20/1994 which merged into AT&T Inc. 11/18/2005

COMBINED PENNY STK FD INC (CO)
Completely liquidated
Each share Common $0.001 par received first and final distribution of $0.01 cash payable 07/28/2005 to holders of record 04/29/2005
Note: Certificates were not required to be surrendered and are without value

COMBINED PPTYS CORP (DE)
Merged into Comprop, Inc. 12/31/1975
Each share Common 25¢ par exchanged for $10 cash

COMBINED PRODTN ASSOC (UT)
Acquired by Intergeneral Industries, Inc. 05/21/1969
Each share Common 10¢ par exchanged for (0.2) share Common 1¢ par
(See Intergeneral Industries, Inc.)

COMBINED PROFESSIONAL SVCS INC (NV)
Common $0.001 par split (2) for (1) by issuance of (1) additional share payable 11/30/2001 to holders of record 11/27/2001 Ex date - 12/03/2001
Reincorporated under the laws of Delaware as Patron Holdings, Inc. 11/22/2002
Patron Holdings, Inc. name changed to Patron Systems Inc. 03/28/2003
(See Patron Systems Inc.)

COMBINED SHS INC (DE)
Acquired by Massachusetts Investors Trust 06/05/1975
Each share Common $1 par exchanged for (0.839847) Ctf. of Bene. Int. $0.33333333 par 06/05/1975

COMBINED TECHNOLOGIES CORP PLC (ENGLAND)
Name changed to Trimoco PLC 04/23/1987
(See Trimoco PLC)

COMBINED TRUST SHARES OF STANDARD OIL GROUP
Trust terminated 00/00/1949
Details not available

COMBUSTION ENGINEERING CO., INC.
Merged into Combustion Engineering-Superheater, Inc. 12/31/1948
Each share Common $1 par exchanged for (0.33333333) share Capital Stock $1 par
Combustion Engineering-Superheater, Inc. name changed to Combustion Engineering, Inc. 04/15/1953
(See Combustion Engineering, Inc.)

COMBUSTION ENGINEERING-SUPERHEATER, INC. (DE)
Name changed to Combustion Engineering, Inc. 04/15/1953
(See Combustion Engineering, Inc.)

COMBUSTION ENGR INC (DE)
Capital Stock no par changed to $1 par 00/00/1954
Capital Stock $1 par split (3) for (1) by issuance of (2) additional shares 05/11/1956
Capital Stock $1 par reclassified as Common $1 par 04/26/1967
Common $1 par split (2) for (1) by issuance of (1) additional share 06/02/1970
Common $1 par split (3) for (2) by issuance of (0.5) additional share 08/31/1977
$1.70 Conv. Preferred Ser. A no par called for redemption 07/24/1978
Common $1 par split (2) for (1) by issuance of (1) additional share 11/10/1980
Merged into ABB Asea Brown Boveri Ltd. 01/30/1990
Each share Common $1 par exchanged for $40 cash

COMBUSTION EQUIP ASSOC INC (NY)
Common 1¢ par split (2) for (1) by issuance of (1) additional share 05/24/1969
Stock Dividend - 55% 05/06/1977
Under plan of reorganization each share Common 1¢ par received distribution of $0.03 cash 03/30/1984
Note: Certificates were not required to be surrendered and are without value
Note: Holdings of (334) or less shares did not participate in the plan and are deemed worthless

COMBUSTION WASTE SYS INC (UT)
Recapitalized as InterContinental Energy Inc. 09/15/1997
Each share Common $0.001 par exchanged for (0.25) share Common $0.001 par

COMC INC (DE)
Reincorporated 12/27/2000
State of incorporation changed from (IL) to (DE) 12/27/2000
Recapitalized as ICF Corp. 06/27/2005
Each share Common 1¢ par exchanged for (0.1) share Common 1¢ par
(See ICF Corp.)

COMCAM INC (DE)
Each share Common $0.0001 par received distribution of (0.05) share ComCam International, Inc. Common $0.0001 par payable 12/28/2007 to holders of record 12/07/2007 Ex date - 12/31/2007
Recapitalized as Monkey Rock Group, Inc. 05/05/2010
Each share Common $0.0001 par exchanged for (0.01176471) share Common $0.0001 par

COMCAST CABLEVISION PHILADELPHIA INC (PA)
Merged into Comcast Co. of Philadelphia Transaction Corp. 03/21/1994
Each share Common $1 par exchanged for $95 cash

COMCAST CORP OLD (PA)
Class A Common no par changed to $1 par 06/11/1981
Class A Common $1 par split (3) for (2) by issuance of (0.5) additional share 01/05/1983
Class A Common $1 par split (3) for (2) by issuance of (0.5) additional share 09/18/1984
Class A Common $1 par split (3) for (2) by issuance of (0.5) additional share 06/27/1985
Class A Common $1 par split (3) for (2) by issuance of (0.5) additional share 12/18/1986
Class A Common $1 par split (3) for (2) by issuance of (0.5) additional share 04/08/1988
Class A Special Common $1 par split (3) for (2) by issuance of (0.5) additional share 04/08/1988
Class A Common $1 par split (3) for (2) by issuance of (0.5) additional share 10/24/1989
Class A Special Common $1 par split (3) for (2) by issuance of (0.5) additional share 10/24/1989
Class A Special Common $1 par split (3) for (2) by issuance of (0.5) additional share 02/02/1994
Class A Common $1 par split (2) for (1) by issuance of (1) additional share payable 05/05/1999 to holders of record 04/20/1999
Class A Special Common $1 par split (2) for (1) by issuance of (1) additional share payable 05/05/1999 to holders of record 04/20/1999
Stock Dividends - 50% 05/15/1980; 50% 04/10/1981; In Class A Special Common to holders of Class A Common 50% 02/02/1994
Merged into Comcast Corp. (New) 11/18/2002
Each share Class A Common $1 par exchanged for (1) share Class A Common 1¢ par
Each share Class A Special Common $1 par exchanged for (1) share Class A Special Common 1¢ par

COMCAST UK CABLE PARTNERS LTD (BERMUDA)
Acquired by NTL Inc. 05/30/2000
Each share Class A Common 1p par exchanged for (0.375) share Common 1¢ par
NTL Inc. reorganized as NTL Europe, Inc. 01/10/2003
(See NTL Europe, Inc.)

COMCENTRAL CORP (UT)
Each share Common $0.001 par exchanged for (0.04) share Common 2¢ par 10/24/1994
Each share Common 2¢ par exchanged for (0.04) share old Common 50¢ par 02/17/1995
Each share old Common 50¢ par exchanged for (0.06666666) share new Common 50¢ par 05/22/1995
Name changed to Tianrong Building Material Holdings, Ltd. 08/21/1995
(See Tianrong Building Material Holdings, Ltd.)

COMCET INC (MD)
Name changed to Comten, Inc. 06/10/1971
Comten, Inc. merged into NCR Corp. 06/13/1979 which merged into American Telephone & Telegraph Co. 09/19/1991 which name changed to AT&T Corp. 04/20/1994 which merged into AT&T Inc. 11/18/2005

COMCO CENTURION OIL & MINERALS CO. (TX)
Charter forfeited for failure to pay taxes 02/21/1983

COMCO MNG & SMLT CORP (BC)
Name changed to Quaker Resources Canada Ltd. 08/18/1986
Quaker Resources Canada Ltd. name changed to SPI Safety Packaging International Ltd. 04/25/1987
(See SPI Safety Packaging International Ltd.)

COMCOA INC (KS)
Reincorporated under the laws of Delaware as Advantage Companies, Inc. and Common no par changed to 1¢ par 01/05/1995
(See Advantage Companies, Inc. (DE))

COMCORP INC (DE)
Merged into Booth Newspapers, Inc. 07/20/1976
Each share Common 20¢ par exchanged for $7.50 cash

COMCORP VENTURES INC (BC)
Name changed to Wildcat Silver Corp. 05/17/2006
Wildcat Silver Corp. name changed to AZ Mining Inc. 06/05/2015 which name changed to Arizona Mining Inc. 10/28/2015
(See Arizona Mining Inc.)

COMDATA HLDG CORP (DE)
Each share old Common 1¢ par exchanged for (0.33333333) share new Common 1¢ par 11/16/1993
Merged into Ceridian Corp. (Old) 12/12/1995
Each share new Common 1¢ par exchanged for (0.57) share Common 50¢ par
(See Ceridian Corp. (Old))

COMDATA NETWORK INC (MD)
Common 2¢ par split (2) for (1) by issuance of (1) additional share 05/25/1976
Common 2¢ par split (3) for (2) by issuance of (0.5) additional share 08/15/1977
Common 2¢ par split (2) for (1) by issuance of (1) additional share 10/01/1979
Common 2¢ par split (3) for (2) by issuance of (0.5) additional share 11/19/1980
Common 2¢ par split (2) for (1) by issuance of (1) additional share 06/21/1983
Stock Dividend - 50% 10/12/1982
Merged into Comdata Holdings Corp. 09/09/1987
Each share Common 2¢ par exchanged for $16.50 cash

COMDATA SYS INC (DE)
Common 1¢ par split (2) for (1) by issuance of (1) additional share 11/15/1969
Charter revoked and proclaimed inoperative and void for non-payment of taxes 03/01/1975

COMDIAL CORP (DE)
Reincorporated 10/01/1982
State of incorporation changed from (OR) to (DE) 10/01/1982
Each share old Common 1¢ par exchanged for (0.33333333) share new Common 1¢ par 08/07/1995
Each share new Common 1¢ par exchanged again for (0.06666666) share new Common 1¢ par 11/26/2002
Plan of reorganization under Chapter 11 Federal Bankruptcy Code effective 08/23/2007
No stockholders' equity

COMDISCO HLDG CO INC (DE)
Liquidation completed
Each share Common 10¢ par received initial distribution of $73.33 cash payable 05/22/2003 to holders of record 05/12/2003 Ex date - 05/23/2003
Each Contingent Distribution Right received initial distribution of $0.01793 cash payable 05/22/2003 to holders of record 05/12/2003 Ex date - 05/08/2003
Each share Common 10¢ par received second distribution of $14.30 cash payable 06/19/2003 to holders of record 06/09/2003 Ex date - 06/05/2003
Each Contingent Distribution Right received second distribution of $0.01621 cash payable 06/19/2003 to holders of record 06/09/2003 Ex date - 06/05/2003
Each share Common 10¢ par received third distribution of $47.60 cash payable 09/08/2003 to holders of record 08/28/2003 Ex date - 09/09/2003
Each Contingent Distribution Right received third distribution of $0.0878 cash payable 09/08/2003 to holders of record 08/28/2003 Ex date - 08/26/2003
Each share Common 10¢ par received fourth distribution of $12 cash payable 12/11/2003 to holders of record 12/01/2003 Ex date - 11/26/2003
Each Contingent Distribution Right received fourth distribution of $0.0514 cash payable 12/11/2003 to holders of record 12/01/2003 Ex date - 11/26/2003
Each share Common 10¢ par received fifth distribution of $11.50 cash payable 05/06/2004 to holders of record 04/26/2004 Ex date - 05/07/2004
Each Contingent Distribution Right received fifth distribution of $0.0187 cash payable 03/04/2004 to holders of record 02/23/2004 Ex date - 02/19/2004
Each Contingent Distribution Right received sixth distribution of $0.0781 cash payable 05/06/2004 to holders of record 04/26/2004 Ex date - 04/22/2004
Each share Common 10¢ par received sixth distribution of $13 cash payable 03/24/2005 to holders of record 03/14/2005 Ex date - 03/28/2005
Each Contingent Distribution Right received seventh distribution of $0.0982 cash payable 12/10/2004 to holders of record 11/30/2004 Ex date - 11/26/2004
Each share Common 10¢ par received seventh distribution of $5 cash payable 01/06/2006 to holders of record 12/27/2005 Ex date - 01/09/2006
Each Contingent Distribution Right received eighth distribution of $0.1456 cash payable 03/24/2005 to holders of record 03/14/2005 Ex date - 03/28/2005
Each Contingent Distribution Right received ninth distribution of $0.0365 cash payable 01/06/2006 to holders of record 12/27/2005 Ex date - 12/22/2005
Each Contingent Distribution Right received tenth distribution of $0.0247 cash payable 03/16/2006 to holders of record 03/06/2006 Ex date - 03/02/2006
Each share Common 10¢ par received eighth distribution of $6.39 cash payable 12/12/2006 to holders of record 12/01/2006 Ex date - 12/13/2006
Each Contingent Distribution Right received eleventh distribution of $0.045 cash payable 12/12/2006 to holders of record 12/01/2006 Ex date - 11/29/2006
Each Contingent Distribution Right received twelfth distribution of $0.15 cash payable 09/17/2007 to holders of record 09/07/2007 Ex date - 09/18/2007
Each Contingent Distribution Right received thirteenth distribution of $0.02586 cash payable 09/25/2008 to holders of record 09/15/2008 Ex date - 09/11/2008
Each share Common 10¢ par received ninth distribution of $3.1273 cash payable 04/21/2011 to holders of record 04/11/2011 Ex date - 04/25/2011
Each Contingent Distribution Right received fourteenth distribution of $0.04985 cash payable 04/21/2011 to holders of record 04/11/2011 Ex date - 04/25/2011
Each share Common 10¢ par received tenth distribution of $2.3455 cash payable 03/12/2015 to holders of record 03/02/2015 Ex date - 03/13/2015
Each Contingent Distribution Right received fifteenth distribution of $0.03739 cash payable 03/12/2015 to holders of record 03/02/2015 Ex date - 03/13/2015
Each share Common 10¢ par received eleventh and final distribution of $4.5642 cash payable 08/05/2016 to holders of record 07/25/2016 Ex date - 08/08/2016
Each Contingent Distribution Right received sixteenth and final distribution of $0.07707 cash payable 08/05/2016 to holders of record 07/25/2016 Ex date - 08/08/2016

COMDISCO INC (DE)
8.75% Preferred Ser. A 10¢ par called for redemption at $25 on 10/20/1997
8.75% Preferred Ser. B 10¢ par called for redemption 07/13/1998
Common 10¢ par split (3) for (2) by issuance of (0.5) additional share 03/07/1978
Common 10¢ par split (2) for (1) by issuance of (1) additional share 09/08/1978
Common 10¢ par split (3) for (2) by issuance of (0.5) additional share 04/13/1979
Common 10¢ par split (5) for (4) by issuance of (0.25) additional share 03/06/1981
Common 10¢ par split (3) for (2) by issuance of (0.5) additional share 04/14/1982
Common 10¢ par split (2) for (1) by issuance of (1) additional share 03/04/1983
Common 10¢ par split (3) for (2) by issuance of (0.5) additional share 03/10/1986
Common 10¢ par split (3) for (2) by issuance of (0.5) additional share 12/08/1995
Common 10¢ par split (3) for (2) by issuance of (0.5) additional share payable 06/16/1997 to holders of record 05/23/1997 Ex date - 06/17/1997
Common 10¢ par split (2) for (1) by issuance of (1) additional share payable 06/15/1998 to holders of record 05/22/1998 Ex date - 06/16/1998
Stock Dividend - 100% 06/02/1972
Plan of reorganization under Chapter 11 Federal Bankruptcy Code effective 08/12/2002
Each share Common 10¢ par exchanged for (1) Comdisco Holding Co., Inc. Contingent Distribution Right
Note: Unexchanged certificates were cancelled and became valueless 08/12/2003

COMED FING I (DE)
8.48% Trust Originated Preferred Securities called for redemption at $25 on 03/20/2003

COMEDCO INC (NY)
Dissolved by proclamation 09/23/1992

COMEDIA CORP (NV)
Charter permanently revoked 06/30/2010

COMER MINES CO. (OR)
Charter revoked for failure to file reports and pay fees 01/16/1917

COMERICA CAP TR I (DE)
7.6% Trust Preferred Securities called for redemption at $25 on 03/19/2007

COMERICA INC (DE)
Adjustable Rate Preferred Ser. A no par called for redemption 02/28/1989
$4.32 Preferred Ser. B no par called for redemption 12/31/1992
Adjustable Fixed Rate Preferred Ser. E no par called for redemption at $50 on 08/31/2001
(Additional Information in Active)

COMET COALITION CO (NV)
Name changed to Resco International, Inc. 06/22/1982
(See Resco International, Inc.)

COMET COALITION MINES CO. (NV)
Name changed to Comet Coalition Co. 10/07/1981
Comet Coalition Co. name changed to Resco International, Inc. 06/22/1982
(See Resco International, Inc.)

COMET DRILLING LTD. (AB)
Bankrupt 00/00/1953
Stockholders' equity unlikely

COMET ENTMT INC (NV)
Name changed 05/08/1989
Name changed from Comet Enterprises Inc. to Comet Entertainment, Inc. 05/08/1989
Recapitalized as Texoil Inc. (New) 03/16/1993
Each share Common 1¢ par exchanged for (0.0357142) share Common 1¢ par
(See Texoil Inc. (New))

COMET GOLD & COPPER MINING CO., LTD. (ID)
Charter forfeited for failure to file reports 11/30/1923

COMET INTL CORP (FL)
Proclaimed dissolved for failure to file reports and pay fees 11/21/1984

COMET-KRAIN MINING CORP. LTD. (BC)
Name changed to Comet Industries Ltd. 04/26/1971

COMET MINING CORP. LTD. (BC)
Merged into Comet-Krain Mining Corp. Ltd. 03/28/1966
Each share Capital Stock no par exchanged for (1) share Capital Stock no par
Comet-Krain Mining Corp. name changed to Comet Industries Ltd. 04/26/1971

COMET PETROLEUMS LTD. (BC)
Struck off the Register of Companies of the Province of British Columbia and dissolved by default 07/11/1960
No stockholders' equity

COMET RICE MLS INC (TX)
Name changed to Country Cupboard, Inc. (TX) 06/01/1970
Country Cupboard, Inc. (TX) reincorporated in Nevada 12/22/1970
(See Country Cupboard, Inc. (NV))

COMET TECHNOLOGIES INC (NV)
Each share old Common $0.001 par exchanged for (0.125) share new Common $0.001 par 03/09/2006
Name changed to China Sky One Medical, Inc. 07/26/2006

COMET TRANS INC (UT)
Proclaimed dissolved for failure to pay taxes 01/31/1976

COMFAX COMMUNICATIONS INDS INC (NY)
Charter cancelled and proclaimed dissolved for failure to pay taxes 09/30/1981

COMFED BANCORP INC (DE)
Reorganized 04/01/1988
Common 1¢ par split (3) for (2) by issuance of (0.5) additional share 04/14/1986
Common 1¢ par split (2) for (1) by issuance of (1) additional share 03/27/1987
Under plan of reorganization each share Comfed Savings Bank (Lowell, MA) Common 1¢ par automatically became (1) share Comfed Bancorp, Inc. Common 1¢ par 04/01/1988
Taken over by the RTC on 09/13/1991
No stockholders' equity

COMFORCE CORP (DE)
Acquired by CFS Parent Corp. 12/28/2010
Each share Common 1¢ par exchanged for $2.50 cash

COMGEN CORP (NV)
Name changed to Planet 411.com Corp. (NV) 02/11/1999
Planet 411.com Corp. (NV) reincorporated in Delaware as Planet411.com Inc. 10/07/1999 which name changed to Ivany Mining, Inc. 07/27/2007 which name changed to Ivany Nguyen, Inc. 02/16/2010 which name changed to Myriad Interactive Media, Inc. 07/25/2011

COMGEN TECHNOLOGY INC (DE)
Name changed to Fox Technology, Inc. 05/27/1986
(See Fox Technology, Inc.)

COMIESA CORP (ON)
99.7% acquired by Agassiz Resources Ltd. through exchange offer as of 03/15/1983
Public interest eliminated

COMINCO FERTILZERS LTD (CANADA)
Name changed to Agrium Inc. 05/19/1995
Agrium Inc. merged into Nutrien Ltd. 01/02/2018

COMINCO LTD (CANADA)
Capital Stock no par reclassified as Common no par 04/22/1976
Common no par split (3) for (1) by issuance of (2) additional shares 05/11/1984
$3.25 Preferred Ser. D no par called for redemption 06/01/1988
Each share $2 Preferred Ser. A $25 par exchanged for (1) share $2.4375 Preferred Ser. B $25 par 06/01/1988
Floating Rate Preferred Ser. G $25 par called for redemption 03/31/1989
Deferred Preferred Ser. H no par called for redemption on 08/14/1992
Tax Deferred Exchangeable Preferred Ser. A $25 par called for redemption 07/22/1996
Tax Deferred Exchangeable Preferred Ser. B $25 par called for redemption 07/22/1996
$2.4375 Preferred Ser. B $25 par called for redemption 07/22/1997
Merged into Teck Corp. 07/20/2001
Each share Common no par exchanged for (1.8) shares Class B Subordinate no par and $6 cash
Teck Corp. name changed to Teck Cominco Ltd. 09/12/2001 which name changed to Teck Resources Ltd. 04/27/2009

COMINCO RES INTL LTD (CANADA)
Acquired by Cominco Ltd. 07/23/1995
Each share Common no par exchanged for (6.15) shares Common no par
Cominco Ltd. merged into Teck Corp. 07/20/2001 which name changed to Teck Cominco Ltd. 09/12/2001 which name changed to Teck Resources Ltd. 04/27/2009

COMINOL INDUSTRIES, INC. (DE)
Name changed to Shieldtron, Inc. 01/24/1962
Shieldtron, Inc. recapitalized as Ocean Research Equipment, Inc. 03/08/1968
(See Ocean Research Equipment, Inc.)

COMITCO INC (FL)
Merged into Comitgo, Inc. (DE) 06/30/1978
Each share Common 1¢ par exchanged for (1) share Common 1¢ par
Note: Holders of fewer than (100) shares who did not surrender their certificates by 07/30/1978 were entitled to $0.95 cash only for each share held
(See Comitco Inc. (DE))

COMITGO INC (DE)
Charter dissolved 02/13/1995

COMLINK COMMUNICATIONS CO (NV)
Old Common $0.001 par split (3) for (1) by issuance of (2) additional shares payable 11/17/2005 to holders of record 11/16/2005
Ex date - 11/18/2005
Each share old Common $0.001 par exchanged for (2) shares new Common $0.001 par 12/12/2006
Name changed to USA Superior Energy Holdings, Inc. 03/16/2007
USA Superior Energy Holdings, Inc. recapitalized as Xsilent Solutions Inc. 06/23/2014 which name changed to Saxon Capital Group Inc. 06/05/2015

COMMANCHE PPTYS INC (NV)
Name changed to Nevacal, Inc. 10/17/2007

COMMAND AWYS INC (DE)
Acquired by AMR Corp. 09/30/1988
Each share Common 1¢ par exchanged for $17 cash

COMMAND CAP INC (AB)
Name changed to Military International Ltd. 07/23/1998
(See Military International Ltd.)

COMMAND CR CORP (NY)
Each share old Common $0.0001 par exchanged for (0.05) share new Common $0.0001 par 09/23/1992
Recapitalized as Dawcin International Corp. 10/16/1996
Each share new Common $0.0001 par exchanged for (0.005) share Common $0.0001 par
(See Dawcin International Corp.)

COMMAND DRILLING CORP (AB)
Acquired by Nabors Industries, Inc. 11/16/2001
Each share Common no par exchanged for $3.40 cash

COMMAND ENTMT INC (DE)
Recapitalized as International Industries Inc. 01/21/1998
Each share Common $0.00001 par exchanged for (0.002) share Common $0.00001 par
International Industries Inc. name changed to International Internet Inc. 02/25/1999 which name changed to Evolve One, Inc. 11/30/2000 which name changed to China Direct, Inc. (DE) 09/19/2006 which reincorporated in Florida 06/21/2007 which name changed to China Direct Industries, Inc. 05/29/2009 which name changed to CD International Enterprises, Inc. 02/29/2012

COMMAND HELICOPTERS INC (OR)
Merged into Black Industries, Inc. 07/02/1973
Each share Common no par exchanged for (0.33333333) share Common $1 par
(See Black Industries, Inc.)

COMMAND PERFORMANCE NETWORK LTD (AB)
Struck off register for failure to file annual returns 11/21/1998

COMMAND PETE CORP (UT)
Name changed to Biomedical Technologies Inc. (UT) 09/29/1983
Biomedical Technologies Inc. (UT) recapitalized as Southern Cross Ventures Inc. (UT) 08/29/1984 which reorganized in Nevada as Centra Corp. 01/20/1989 which recapitalized as Greenway Environmental Systems, Inc. 05/10/1991 which recapitalized as Travel Dynamics, Inc. 01/13/1999 which name changed to TRU Dynamics International, Inc. 02/14/2001
(See TRU Dynamics International, Inc.)

COMMAND POST & TRANSFER CORP (BC)
Reorganized under the laws of Ontario 06/24/1999
Each share Common no par exchanged for (2.2) shares Common no par
(See Command Post & Transfer Corp. (ON))

COMMAND POST & TRANSFER CORP (ON)
Acquired by Technicolor Creative Services Canada, Inc. 06/04/2004
Each share Common no par exchanged for $0.04 cash

COMMAND RES LTD (BC)
Recapitalized as Cordoba Developments Ltd. 01/29/1975
Each share Common no par exchanged for (0.5) share Common no par
Cordoba Developments Ltd. recapitalized as Gold Cup Resources Ltd. 02/02/1977
(See Gold Cup Resources Ltd.)

COMMAND SYS INC (DE)
Merged into ICICI Infotech Inc. 03/22/2001
Each share Common 1¢ par exchanged for $5 cash

COMMANDER AIRCRAFT CO (VA)
Reincorporated under the laws of Delaware as Aviation General, Inc. 08/05/1998
(See Aviation General, Inc.)

COMMANDER NICKEL COPPER MINES LTD (QC)
Recapitalized as Commander Resources Limited (QC) 11/30/1981
Each share Common $1 par exchanged for (1) share Common $1 par
(See Commander Resources Limited (QC))

COMMANDER RED LAKE MINES LTD. (ON)
Merged into Goldquest Exploration Inc. 08/09/1982
Each share Capital Stock no par exchanged for (0.03244646) share Common no par
Goldquest Exploration Inc. merged into Goldcorp Inc. (New) 03/31/1994

COMMANDER RESOURCES LIMITED (QC)
Declared dissolved for failure to file reports and pay fees 07/25/1992

COMMANDER TECHNOLOGIES CORP (BC)
Name changed 05/15/1992
Name changed from Commander Resources Ltd. to Commander Technologies Corp. 05/15/1992
Recapitalized as SCS Solars Computing Systems Inc. 09/12/1995
Each share Common no par exchanged for (0.5) share Common no par

COMMEDIA PICTURES PRODTNS INC (UT)
Proclaimed dissolved for failure to pay taxes 03/31/1985

COMMERCE & INDUSTRY INSURANCE CO. (NY)
Acquired by American International Group, Inc. 07/10/1970
Each share Capital Stock $1 par exchanged for $5 cash

COMMERCE ACCEPTANCE CO., INC. (KS)
Acquired by Southwestern Investment Co. 10/03/1968
Each share 4.75% Preferred $100 par exchanged for $100 cash
Each share 5.5% Preferred $100 par exchanged for $100 cash
Each share Common exchanged for $15 cash

COMMERCE BANC CORP (WV)
Merged into Huntington Bancshares Inc. 09/24/1993
Each share Common $1 par exchanged for (1.0127) shares Common no par

COMMERCE BANCORP INC (DE)
Liquidation completed 11/17/1986
Each share Common $4 par exchanged for initial distribution of $29 cash
Each share Common $4 par received second and final distribution of $0.3195 cash 04/15/1987

COMMERCE BANCORP INC (IL)
Merged into CBI Acquisition Corp. 02/03/1999
Each share Common no par exchanged for $1,098.4523772 cash

COMMERCE BANCORP INC (MI)
Merged into Security Bancorp, Inc. 10/31/1985
Each share Common no par exchanged for (3-1/3) shares $2.64 Conv. Preferred Ser. A 1¢ par
Security Bancorp, Inc. merged into First of America Bank Corp. 05/01/1992 which merged into National City Corp. 03/31/1998 which was acquired by PNC Financial Services Group, Inc. 12/31/2008

COMMERCE BANCORP INC (NJ)
Common $3.125 par changed to $1.5625 par and (1) additional share issued 08/15/1984
Conv. Preferred Ser. A no par called for redemption 03/23/1987
$1.50 Conv. Preferred Ser. B no par called for redemption 08/19/1994
Common $1.5625 par split (5) for (4) by issuance of (0.25) additional share payable 07/24/1998 to holders of record 07/13/1998 Ex date - 07/27/1998
Common $1.5625 par changed to $1 par and (1) additional share issued payable 12/18/2001 to holders of record 12/03/2001 Ex date - 12/19/2001
Common $1 par split (2) for (1) by issuance of (1) additional share payable 03/07/2005 to holders of record 02/25/2005 Ex date - 03/08/2005
Stock Dividends - 20% 08/15/1985; 5% payable 01/26/1996 to holders of record 01/12/1996; 5% payable 01/21/1997 to holders of record 01/08/1997; 5% payable 01/21/1998 to holders of record record 01/07/1998; 5% payable 01/21/1999 to holders of record 01/07/1999; 5% payable 01/21/2000 to holders of record 01/07/2000
Merged into Toronto-Dominion Bank (Toronto, ONT) 03/31/2008
Each share Common $1 par exchanged for (0.4142) share Common no par and $10.50 cash

COMM BANCORP INC (PA)
Common 33¢ par split (3) for (1) by issuance of (2) additional shares 04/01/1996
Merged into F.N.B. Corp. 01/03/2011
Each share Common 33¢ par exchanged for (3.4545) shares Common 1¢ par and $10 cash

COMMERCE BANCORPORATION (WA)
Merged into BancFirst Corp. 10/25/96
Each share Common $2.50 par exchanged for (6.9335) shares Common $1 par

COMMERCE BANK, N.A. (MARLTON, NJ)
Common $6.25 par changed to

$3.125 par and (1) additional share issued 04/13/1982
Under plan of reorganization each share Common $3.125 par automatically became (1) share Commerce Bancorp, Inc. Common $3.125 par 06/30/1983
Commerce Bancorp, Inc. merged into Toronto-Dominion Bank (Toronto, ONT) 03/31/2008

COMMERCE BK (HARRISBURG, PA)
Common $1 par split (2) for (1) by issuance of (1) additional share 08/07/1995
Stock Dividends - 5% payable 02/28/1996 to holders of record 02/09/1996; 5% payable 02/24/1997 to holders of record 02/10/1997; 5% payable 02/17/1998 to holders of record 01/30/1998; 5% payable 02/19/1999 to holders of record 01/29/1999
Under plan of reorganization each share Common $1 par automatically became (1) share Pennsylvania Commerce Bancorp, Inc. Common $1 par 07/01/1999
Pennsylvania Commerce Bancorp, Inc. name changed to Metro Bancorp, Inc. 06/15/2009 which merged into F.N.B. Corp. 02/12/2016

COMMERCE BANK (KANSAS CITY, MO)
Name changed to Commerce Bank of Kansas City, N.A. (Kansas City, Mo.) 6/30/72

COMMERCE BK (VIRGINIA BEACH, VA)
Merged into BB&T Financial Corp. 1/10/95
Each share Common $2.50 par exchanged for (1.305) shares Common $2.50 par
BB&T Financial Corp. merged into Southern National Corp. 2/28/95 which merged into BB&T Corp. 5/19/97

COMMERCE BK ALA (ALBERTVILLE, AL)
Merged into Banc Corp. 11/06/1998
Each share Common $0.001 par exchanged for (2.335) shares Common $0.001 par
Banc Corp. name changed to Superior Bancorp 05/19/2006
(See Superior Bancorp)

COMMERCE BK CORP (MD)
Merged into MainStreet BankGroup Inc. 12/1/97
Each share Common exchanged for (2.059) shares Common $5 par
MainStreet BankGroup Inc. name changed to MainStreet Financial Corp. 6/1/98 which merged into BB&T Corp. 3/8/99

COMMERCE BANK OF BLUE HILLS (KANSAS CITY, MO)
99.5% acquired by Commerce Bancshares, Inc. through voluntary exchange offer which expired 03/22/1972
Public interest eliminated

COMMERCE BANK OF FLORISSANT (FLORISSANT, MO)
Common $20 par changed to $2.50 par and (7) additional shares issued 03/14/1977
Acquired by Commerce Bank of St. Louis, N.A. (St. Louis, MO) 07/01/1985
Details not available

COMMERCE BANK OF KANSAS CITY, N.A. (KANSAS CITY, MO)
99.5% acquired through voluntary exchange offer which expired 11/30/1979
Public interest eliminated

COMMERCE BANK OF MOUND CITY (ST. LOUIS, MO)
Acquired by Commerce Bank of St. Louis, N.A. (St. Louis, MO) 11/3/84
Details not available

COMMERCE BANK OF NEW JERSEY (MARLTON, NJ)
Common $7.50 par changed to $6.25 par and (0.2) additional share issued 06/01/1976
Name changed to Commerce Bank, N.A. (Marlton, NJ) 09/30/1981
Commerce Bank, N.A. (Marlton, NJ) reorganized as Commerce Bancorp, Inc. 06/30/1983 which merged into Toronto-Dominion Bank (Toronto, ONT) 03/31/2008

COMMERCE BK TEMECULA VY (MURRIETA, CA)
Acquired by Nano Financial Holdings, Inc. 05/01/2018
Each share Common no par exchanged for $14.41 cash

COMMERCE BK VA (RICHMOND, VA)
Merged into Community Bankshares Inc. 07/01/1996
Each share Common no par exchanged for (1.4044) shares Common $3 par
Community Bankshares Inc. merged into SouthTrust Corp. 11/30/2001 which merged into Wachovia Corp. (Ctfs. dated after 09/01/2001) 11/01/2004 which merged into Wells Fargo & Co. (New) 12/31/2008

COMMERCE CAP CORP (WI)
Common $1 par split (5) for (4) by issuance of (0.25) additional share 06/20/1969
Reincorporated under the laws of Delaware as Commerce Group Corp. and Common $1 par changed to 10¢ par 11/05/1971
Commerce Group Corp. (DE) reincorporated in Wisconsin 04/01/1999

COMMERCE CAP LTD (CANADA)
Acquired by Eaton/Bay Financial Services Inc. 03/01/1979
Each share Common no par exchanged for $9 cash

COMMERCE CAP MTG CORP (CANADA)
Name changed to Eaton Bay Mortgage Corp. 09/15/1980
Eaton Bay Mortgage Corp. name changed to Seaway Mortgage Corp.-La Corporation d'Hypotheque Seaway 02/03/1982
(See Seaway Mortgage Corp. -La Corporation d'Hypotheque Seaway)

COMMERCE CAP TR CO (CALGARY, ALTA)
Name changed to Eaton Bay Trust Co. (Calgary, AB) 05/05/1981
Eaton Bay Trust Co. (Calgary, AB) name changed to Eaton Trust Co. (Calgary, AB) 11/13/1985 which merged into Laurentian Bank of Canada (Montreal, QC) 02/04/1988

COMMERCE CAP TR I (DE)
8.75% Capital Securities called for redemption at $25 on 07/01/2002

COMMERCE CAP TR II (DE)
5.95% Conv. Trust Preferred Securities called for redemption at $50 plus $0.74375 accrued dividends on 09/14/2005
5.95% Accredited Investors Trust Preferred Securities called for redemption at $50 plus $0.74375 accrued dividends on 09/14/2005
5.95% Conv. Trust Preferred Securities called for redemption at $50 plus $0.743750 accrued dividends on 09/14/2005

COMMERCE CASUALTY CO.
Merged into Glens Falls Indemnity Co. 00/00/1932
Details not available

COMMERCE CLEARING HOUSE INC (DE)
Each share Common $5 par exchanged for (8) shares Common $1 par 11/02/1961
Common $1 par split (5) for (4) by issuance of (0.25) additional share 04/22/1964
Common $1 par split (3) for (2) by issuance of (0.5) additional share 04/30/1971
Common $1 par split (2) for (1) by issuance of (1) additional share 04/28/1972
Common $1 par split (2) for (1) by issuance of (1) additional share 03/19/1986
Common $1 par reclassified as Class A Common $1 par 04/11/1991
Stock Dividends - 100% 04/24/168; in Non-Vtg. Class B Common to holders of Class A Common 100% 04/26/1991
Name changed to CCH Inc. 01/01/1995
(See CCH Inc.)

COMMERCE CORP (RI)
Proclaimed dissolved for failure to file reports and pay fees 04/01/1987

COMMERCE DEV CORP LTD (DE)
Each share old Common $0.001 par exchanged for (0.00045787) share new Common $0.001 par 04/11/2006
Name changed to MMA Media, Inc. 06/05/2007
MMA Media, Inc. recapitalized as China Energy Recovery, Inc. 02/05/2008

COMMERCE DRUG CO. (DE)
Acquired by Maradel Products, Inc. on a (0.765) for (1) basis 01/28/1963
Maradel Products, Inc. name changed to Del Laboratories, Inc. 04/18/1966
(See Del Laboratories, Inc.)

COMMERCE ENERGY GROUP INC (DE)
Preferred Stock Purchase Rights declared for Common stockholders of record 07/01/2004 were redeemed at $0.001 per right 12/17/2008 for holders of record 12/11/2008
Due to lack of quorum at special meeting to approve liquidation, company suspended operations and sole remaining director and officer resigned 09/04/2009
Stockholders' equity unlikely

COMMERCE FD INC (TX)
Reincorporated 3/30/73
State of incorporation changed from (DE) to (TX) 3/30/73
Name changed to Commerce Income Shares, Inc. (TX) 10/14/77
Commerce Income Shares, Inc. (TX) reorganized in Massachusetts as Commerce Income Shares 8/26/85

COMMERCE FINL CORP
Merged into Cullen/Frost Bankers, Inc. 05/20/1999
Each share Common no par exchanged for $229.51 cash

COMMERCE GROUP CORP (DE)
Reincorporated under the laws of Wisconsin 04/01/1999

COMMERCE GROUP GRAND IS INC (NE)
Merged out of existence 12/31/1986
Details not available

COMMERCE GROUP INC (MA)
Common 50¢ par split (2) for (1) by issuance of (1) additional share 06/28/1991
Common 50¢ par split (2) for (1) by issuance of (1) additional share 12/18/1992
Common 50¢ par split (2) for (1) by issuance of (1) additional share payable 06/09/2006 to holders of record 05/30/2006 Ex date - 06/12/2006
Merged into Corporacion MAPFRE S.A. 06/04/2008
Each share Common 50¢ par exchanged for $36.70 cash

COMMERCE GROUP INC (NE)
Stock Dividend - 10% 12/05/1979
Merged into First Commerce Bancshares, Inc. 09/30/1987
Each share Common $5 par exchanged for (1) share Common $1 par
First Commerce Bancshares, Inc. merged into Wells Fargo & Co. 06/16/2000

COMMERCE GROUP LINCOLN EAST INC (NE)
Name changed back to LBE Co. 05/23/1980
(See LBE Co.)

COMMERCE GROUP NATL FREMONT INC (NE)
Merged into Fremont Bancshares, Inc. 03/16/1981
Each share Common $2.50 par exchanged for $13 cash

COMMERCE GROUP ST FREMONT INC (NE)
Merged into Fremont Bancshares, Inc. 03/16/1981
Each share Common $2.50 par exchanged for $13 cash

COMMERCE INCOME SHS INC (TX)
Reorganized under the laws of Massachusetts as Commerce Income Shares and Common $1 par reclassified as Shares of Bene. Int. 1¢ par 08/26/1985

COMMERCE INSURANCE CO. (IL)
Completely liquidated 03/27/1969
Each share Common 10¢ par exchanged for first and final distribution of $0.00443322 cash

COMMERCE INVESTMENT CORP. (CO)
Charter revoked for failure to file reports and pay fees 10/13/1966

COMMERCE INVESTMENTS, INC.
Liquidated 00/00/1935
Details not available

COMMERCE LIFE INSURANCE CO. (TX)
Merged into Southern Republic Life Insurance Co. on a (0.6) for (1) basis 12/31/56
Southern Republic Life Insurance Co. merged into Southwest American Life Insurance Co. 2/21/58 which merged into Union Bankers Insurance Co. 2/14/61
(See Union Bankers Insurance Co.)

COMMERCE MOTOR CAR CO. (MI)
Charter declared inoperative and void for failure to file reports 00/00/1923

COMMERCE NATL BK (COLUMBUS, OH)
Under plan of reorganization each share Common $5 par automatically became (1) share CNBC Bancorp Common $5 par 08/23/1996
CNBC Bancorp merged into First Merchants Corp. 03/01/2003

COMMERCE NATL BK (NEWPORT BEACH, CA)
Location changed 05/23/2007
Location changed from Fullerton, CA to Newport Beach, CA 05/23/2007
Acquired by Sterling Financial Corp. 10/01/2013
Each share Common no par exchanged for $15.10 cash

COMMERCE NATL CORP (DE)
Merged into Wachovia Corp. (New) (Ctfs. dated between 05/20/1991 and 09/01/2001) 06/01/2000
Each share Common 10¢ par

exchanged for (0.8421) share Common $5 par
Wachovia Corp. (New) (Ctfs. dated between 05/20/1991 and 09/01/2001) merged into Wachovia Corp. (Ctfs. dated after 09/01/2001) 09/01/2001 which merged into Wells Fargo & Co. (New) 12/31/2008

COMMERCE OIL CO (UT)
Name changed 12/15/1982
Name changed from Commerce Oil of Kentucky, Inc. to Commerce Oil Co. 12/15/1982
Name changed to USIP.com, Inc. 02/04/2000
USIP.com, Inc. name changed to Eastern Environment Solutions, Corp. 12/28/2006 which recapitalized as Precicion Trim, Inc. 09/20/2016

COMMERCE ONE INC (DE)
Old Common $0.0001 par split (3) for (1) by issuance of (2) additional shares payable 12/23/1999 to holders of record 12/03/1999
Old Common $0.0001 par split (2) for (1) by issuance of (1) additional share payable 04/19/2000 to holders of record 03/24/2000
Each share old Common $0.0001 par exchanged for (0.1) share new Common $0.0001 par 09/17/2002
Plan of reorganization under Chapter 11 Federal Bankruptcy Code effective 08/09/2005
Each share new Common $0.0001 par received $0.11 cash
Note: Certificates were not required to be surrendered and are without value

COMMERCE ONLINE INC (DE)
Name changed to Cannabis Medical Solutions, Inc. 03/04/2010
Cannabis Medical Solutions, Inc. name changed to MediSwipe Inc. 07/08/2011 which name changed to Agritek Holdings, Inc. 05/20/2014

COMMERCE PPTYS INC (MO)
Name changed to Tower Properties Co. 05/01/1973
Tower Properties Co. merged into Commerce Bancshares, Inc. 01/29/1990

COMMERCE SEC BANCORP INC (DE)
Name changed to Eldorado Bancshares, Inc. 08/28/1998
Eldorado Bancshares, Inc. merged into Zions Bancorporation 03/30/2001 which merged into Zions Bancorporation, N.A. (Salt Lake City, UT) 10/01/2018

COMMERCE SOUTHWEST INC (DE)
Name changed to BancTEXAS Group Inc. 08/31/1982
BancTEXAS Group Inc. recapitalized as First Banks America, Inc. 08/31/1995
(See First Banks America, Inc.)

COMMERCE SPLIT CORP (ON)
Plan of reorganization effective 03/26/2010
Each Priority Equity Share no par had the option to receive either (1) share $5 Class I Preferred no par, (1) share $5 Class II Preferred no par, (0.5) 2011 Warrant expiring 02/28/2011 and (1) 2012 Warrant expiring 02/28/2012 or (1) new Priority Equity Share no par
Note: Option to receive new Priority Equity Share expired 02/26/2010
Each share old Class A no par had the option to receive either (0.7167721) Capital Share no par and (0.283228) share new Class A no par or (1) share new Class A no par
Note: Option to receive new Class A only expired 02/26/2010

New Class A no par called for redemption at $0.445 on 11/07/2012
New Priority Equity Shares no par called for redemption at $7.27725 plus $1.96875 accrued dividends on 11/07/2012
(Additional Information in Obsolete)

COMMERCE TITLE GTY CO (TN)
Each share Common $100 par exchanged for (10) shares Common $10 par 00/00/1955
Common $10 par changed to $12.50 par 02/11/1965
Acquired by Mid South Title Co. 00/00/1979
Details not available

COMMERCE TRUST CO. (FORT WORTH, TX)
Dissolved 09/24/1925
Details not available

COMMERCE TRUST CO. (KANSAS CITY, MO)
Each share Capital Stock $100 par exchanged for (5) shares Capital Stock $20 par 00/00/1944
Stock Dividends - 50% 08/01/1945; 100% 04/21/1960
Name changed to Commerce Bank (Kansas City, MO) 02/02/1970
Commerce Bank (Kansas City, MO) name changed to Commerce Bank of Kansas City, N.A. (Kansas City, MO) 06/30/1972
(See Commerce Bank of Kansas City, N.A. (Kansas City, MO))

COMMERCE UN BANCSHARES INC (TN)
Name changed to Reliant Bancorp, Inc. 01/02/2018

COMMERCE UN BK (NASHVILLE, TN)
Stock Dividends - 10% 04/01/1947; (9) for (11) 06/30/1951; 25% 02/12/1954; 20% 02/02/1956; 14.28571428 06/20/1959; 20% 12/23/1965; 15% 06/07/1968; 33.33333333% 03/26/1971
Reorganized as Tennessee Valley Bancorp, Inc. 05/15/1972
Each share Common $10 par exchanged for (1) share Common $10 par
Tennessee Valley Bancorp, Inc. name changed to Commerce Union Corp. 04/20/1982 which merged into Sovran Financial Corp. 11/01/1987 which merged into C&S/Sovran Corp. 09/01/1990 which merged into NationsBank Corp. (NC) 12/31/1991 which reincorporated in Delaware as BankAmerica Corp. (Old) 09/25/1998 which merged into BankAmerica (New) 09/30/1998 which name changed to Bank of America Corp. 04/28/1999

COMMERCE UN BK (SPRINGFIELD, TN)
Reorganized as Commerce Union Bancshares, Inc. 06/06/2012
Each share Common $1 par exchanged for (1) share Common $1 par
Commerce Union Bancshares, Inc. name changed to Reliant Bancorp, Inc. 01/02/2018

COMMERCE UN CORP (TN)
Stock Dividend - 100% 05/01/1986
Merged into Sovran Financial Corp. 11/01/1987
Each share Common $6.66666666 par exchanged for (0.91) share Common $5 par
Sovran Financial Corp. merged into C&S/Sovran Corp. 09/01/1990 which merged into NationsBank Corp. (NC) 12/31/1991 which reincorporated in Delaware as BankAmerica Corp. (Old) 09/25/1998 which merged into BankAmerica Corp. (New)

09/30/1998 which name changed to Bank of America Corp. 04/28/1999

COMMERCE UNION BANK (CHATTANOOGA, TN)
Acquired by Sovran Bank, N.A., (Richmond, VA) 00/00/1979
Details not available

COMMERCE VENTURES INC (CO)
Recapitalized as International Iron Carbide Corp. 11/29/1990
Each share Common $0.0001 par exchanged for (0.05) share Common 20¢ par
(See International Iron Carbide Corp.)

COMMERCEAMERICA CORP (IN)
Common no par split (2) for (1) issuance of (1) additional share 04/30/1986
Merged into Indiana National Corp. 08/29/1986
Each share Common no par exchanged for (0.75625) share Common no par
Indiana National Corp. name changed to INB Financial Corp. 04/26/1989 which merged into NBD Bancorp, Inc. 10/15/1992 which name changed to First Chicago NBD Corp. 12/01/1995 which merged into Bank One Corp. 10/02/1998 which merged into J.P. Morgan Chase & Co. 12/31/2000 which name changed to JPMorgan Chase & Co. 07/20/2004

COMMERCEBANCORP (CA)
$2 Conv. Preferred no par called for redemption 10/25/1989
Filed a petition under Chapter 7 Federal Bankruptcy Code 08/03/1994
Stockholders' equity unlikely

COMMERCEBANK (NEWPORT BEACH, CA)
Under plan of reorganization each share Common no par automatically became (1) share CommerceBancorp Common no par 07/31/1987
(See CommerceBancorp)

COMMERCEFIRST BANCORP INC (MD)
Merged into Sandy Spring Bancorp, Inc. 05/31/2012
Each share Common 1¢ par exchanged for $13.60 cash

COMMERCEHUB INC (DE)
Acquired by Great Dane Parent, LLC 05/21/2018
Each share Ser. A Common 1¢ par exchanged for $22.75 cash
Each share Ser. B Common 1¢ par exchanged for $22.75 cash
Each share Ser. C Common 1¢ par exchanged for $22.75 cash

COMMERCEPLANET INC (UT)
Each share old Common $0.001 par exchanged for (0.05) share new Common $0.001 par 01/30/2009
Company suspended operations 02/02/2009
Details not available

COMMERCESOUTH INC (DE)
Merged into BancTrust Financial Group, Inc. 12/30/2003
Each share Common 10¢ par exchanged for (0.8015) share Common 1¢ par and $12.75 cash
BancTrust Financial Group, Inc. merged into Trustmark Corp. 02/15/2013

COMMERCETEL CORP (NV)
Common $0.001 par split (2) for (1) by issuance of (1) additional share payable 10/05/2010 to holders of record 10/05/2010
Name changed to Mobivity Holdings Corp. 08/23/2012

COMMERCEWEST BK N A (IRVINE, CA)
Common $5 par split (3) for (2) by issuance of (0.5) additional share payable 09/23/2004 to holders of record 09/10/2004
Name changed to CommerceWest Bank (Irvine, CA) 05/12/2017

COMMERCIAL & FARMERS BANK (RURAL HALL, NC)
Each share Common $50 par exchanged for (5) shares Common $20 par to effect a (5) for (1) split plus a 100% stock dividend paid 02/15/1972
Merged into First-Citizens Bank & Trust Co. (Raleigh, NC) 12/15/1981
Each share Common $20 par exchanged for (1) share 9% Conv. Preferred Ser. E $40 par
First Citizens Bank & Trust Co. (Raleigh, NC) reorganized as First Citizens Corp. (NC) 12/09/1982 which reincorporated in Delaware as First Citizens BancShares, Inc. 10/20/1986

COMMERCIAL & FARMERS NATIONAL BANK (OXNARD, CA)
Merged into Standard Chartered Bank Ltd. 01/23/1978
Each share Common $10 par exchanged for $29 cash

COMMERCIAL & FMRS BK (ELLICOTT CITY, MD)
Under plan of reorganization each share Common $10 par automatically became (1) share Patapsco Valley Bancshares Inc. Common 1¢ par 10/07/1996
Patapsco Valley Bancshares Inc. merged into F&M Bancorp 12/31/1999 which merged into Mercantile Bankshares Corp. 08/12/2003 which merged into PNC Financial Services Group, Inc. 03/02/2007

COMMERCIAL & INDL SECS INCOME TR (ON)
Trust Units split (3) for (1) by issuance of (2) additional Units payable 11/01/2004 to holders of record 10/29/2004
Merged into Sentry Select Canadian Income Fund 08/20/2008
Each Trust Unit received (0.4438) Ser. A Unit no par

COMMERCIAL & SVGS BK (BEL AIR, MD)
Acquired by First Virginia Banks, Inc. 06/02/1986
Each share Capital Stock $10 par exchanged for (5.93) shares Common $1 par
First Virginia Banks, Inc. merged into BB&T Corp. 07/01/2003

COMMERCIAL & SAVINGS BANK (GALLIPOLIS, OH)
Acquired by First National Cincinnati Corp. 08/01/1979
Each share Common $10 par exchanged for $60.50 cash

COMMERCIAL & SVGS BK CO (DANVILLE, OH)
Merged into Killbuck Bancshares Inc. 11/21/1998
Each share Common no par exchanged for (2.1585) shares Common no par

COMMERCIAL ACCEP CORP (GA)
Name changed to Modular Sciences, Inc. 11/17/1969
Modular Sciences, Inc. name changed to Valley Forge Corp. (GA) 04/28/1971 which reincorporated in Delaware 06/12/1997
(See Valley Forge Corp.)

COMMERCIAL ACCEPTANCE CORP. (MI)
Name changed to CAC Inc. 10/21/1965

CAC Inc. name changed to Purification Systems, Inc. 04/30/1970

COMMERCIAL ACCEPTANCE CORP. LTD. (QC)
Went into bankruptcy 03/25/1970

COMMERCIAL ALCOHOLS LTD. (CANADA)
Each share Common $100 par exchanged for (4) shares old Common no par 00/00/1927
Each share old Common no par exchanged for (5) share new Common no par 00/00/1933
Each share 8% Preferred $100 par exchanged for (20) shares 8% Preferred $5 par 00/00/1937
Acquired by Canadian International Paper Co. 05/20/1954
Each share 8% Preferred $5 par exchanged for $6.50 cash
Each share Common no par exchanged for $4 cash

COMMERCIAL ALLIANCE CORP (DE)
Common $1 par split (2) for (1) by issuance of (1) additional share 07/09/1969
Common $1 par changed to 10¢ par 12/17/1971
Common 10¢ par split (2) for (1) by issuance of (1) additional share 03/22/1982
$7 Preferred $1 par reclassified as $7 Conv. Preferred $1 par 12/15/1982
Common 10¢ par split (2) for (1) by issuance of (1) additional share 01/24/1984
Merged into First Interstate Bancorp 12/03/1984
Each share $7 Conv. Preferred $1 par exchanged for $75 cash
Each share Common 10¢ par exchanged for $18 cash
Each share Common 10¢ par received an additional distribution of $2.3387 cash 05/01/1986
$1.62 Preferred $1 par called for redemption 02/27/1985
Public interest eliminated

COMMERCIAL ASSETS INC (DE)
Merged into American Land Lease, Inc. 08/11/2000
Each share Common 1¢ par exchanged for either (0.4075) share Common 1¢ par or $5.75 cash
Note: Cash electors received cash for 70% of their holdings with the balance issued in stock
(See American Land Lease, Inc.)

COMMERCIAL ASSETS INC (MD)
Reincorporated under the laws of Delaware 06/10/1999
Commercial Assets, Inc. (DE) merged into American Land Lease, Inc. 08/11/2000
(See American Land Lease, Inc.)

COMMERCIAL ASSOCIATES, INC. (FL)
Name changed to Charter Bankshares Corp. 07/22/1968
Charter Bankshares Corp. name changed to Century Banks, Inc. 04/08/1976 which merged into Sun Banks of Florida, Inc. 07/01/1982 which name changed to Sun Banks, Inc. 05/02/1983 which merged into SunTrust Banks, Inc. 07/01/1985

COMMERCIAL BANCORP (OR)
Common $2.50 par changed to no par 04/15/1992
Common no par split (2) for (1) by issuance of (1) additional share 01/25/1993
Stock Dividend - 10% 04/25/1994
Under plan of merger name changed to West Coast Bancorp (New) 03/01/1995
(See West Coast Bancorp (New))

COMMERCIAL BANCORP GA INC (GA)
Merged into Colonial BancGroup, Inc. 07/03/1996
Each share Common $10 par exchanged for (0.6117) share Common $2.50 par
(See Colonial BancGroup, Inc.)

COMMERCIAL BANCORP INC (FL)
Stock Dividend - 25% 03/31/1971
Name changed to Florida Commercial Banks, Inc. 05/10/1971
(See Florida Comercial Banks Inc.)

COMMERCIAL BANCORPORATION (CO)
Class A Common $1 par split (3) for (2) by issuance of (0.5) additional share 05/04/1992
Stock Dividends - 10% 02/01/1980; 10% 02/01/1981
Merged into KeyCorp (New) 03/24/1994
Each share Class A $1 par exchanged for (0.899) share Common $1 par

COMMERCIAL BANCSHARES INC (NJ)
Common $5 par split (3) for (2) by issuance of (0.5) additional share 07/15/1985
Merged into United Jersey Banks (Princeton, NJ) 12/01/1986
Each share Common $5 par exchanged for (2.1871) shares Common $2.50 par
United Jersey Banks (Princeton, NJ) name changed to UJB Financial Corp. 06/30/1989 which name changed to Summit Bancorp 03/01/1996 which merged into FleetBoston Financial Corp. 03/01/2001 which merged into Bank of America Corp. 04/01/2004

COMMERCIAL BANCSHARES INC (OH)
Common $12.50 par changed to no par 04/09/1997
Common no par split (3) for (1) by issuance of (2) additional shares payable 06/30/1997 to holders of record 06/13/1997 Ex date - 07/01/1997
Stock Dividend - 10% payable 12/15/2001 to holders of record 12/01/2001 Ex date - 12/11/2001
Merged into First Defiance Financial Corp. 02/27/2017
Each share Common no par exchanged for (0.6999) share Common 1¢ par and $20.77 cash

COMMERCIAL BANCSHARES INC (TX)
Merged into Prosperity Bancshares, Inc. 02/24/2001
Each share Common exchanged for (155) shares Common $1 par

COMMERCIAL BANCSHARES INC (WV)
Stock Dividend - 10% payable 03/14/1997 to holders of record 02/28/1997
Merged into WesBanco, Inc. 03/31/1998
Each share Common $5 par exchanged for (2.85) shares Common $2.0833 par

COMMERCIAL BK & SVGS CO (FOSTORIA, OH)
Merged into Commercial National Bank (Fostoria, OH) 12/31/1984
Each share Capital Stock $12.50 par exchanged for $142.86 cash

COMMERCIAL BK & TR CO
Location changed 10/00/1981
Location changed from (Wilmington, MA) to (Lowell, MA) 10/00/1981
Bank failed 05/07/1994
No stockholders' equity

COMMERCIAL BK & TR CO (MIAMI, FL)
Acquired by First Union National Bank of Florida (Jacksonville, FL) 07/01/1988
Details not available

COMMERCIAL BK & TR CO (MUSKOGEE, OK)
Merged into Boatmen's Bancshares, Inc. 09/18/1993
Details not available

COMMERCIAL BK & TR CO (PITTSBURGH, PA)
Merged into Keystone Bank (Lower Burrell, PA) 11/03/1975
Each share Common $25 par exchanged for (0.75) share Common $13.50 par, $10 principal amount of 8.5% Capital Notes due 01/15/1982 through 01/15/1985 and $10.9625 cash
Keystone Bank (Lower Burrell, PA) merged into First Seneca Bank & Trust Co. (Oil City, PA) 08/15/1980 which reorganized into First Seneca Corp. 06/01/1982 which merged into Pennbancorp 12/31/1983 which merged into Integra Financial Corp. 01/26/1989 which merged into National City Corp. 05/03/1996 which was acquired by PNC Financial Services Group, Inc. 12/31/2008

COMMERCIAL BK & TR CO S C (COLUMBIA, SC)
Merged into First-Citizens Bank & Trust Co. of South Carolina (Columbia, SC) 04/15/1970
Each share Common $5 par exchanged for (0.5) share Conv. Preferred Ser. C $20 par
First-Citizens Bank & Trust Co. of South Carolina (Columbia, SC) reorganized as First Citizens Bancorporation of South Carolina, Inc. 03/04/1983 which name changed to First Citizens Bancorporation, Inc. 03/20/2004 which merged into First Citizens BancShares, Inc. 10/01/2014

COMMERCIAL BANK (APOPKA, FL)
Name changed to Combank/Apopka (Apopka, FL) 03/15/1973
(See Combank/Apopka (Apopka, FL))

COMMERCIAL BK (DAYTONA BEACH, FL)
Through voluntary exchange offer First at Orlando Corp. held all shares except directors' qualifying shares as of 12/15/1970
Public interest eliminated

COMMERCIAL BK (DELPHOS, OH)
Reorganized under the laws of Delaware as ComBanc, Inc. 08/31/1998
Each share Common $6.25 par exchanged for (0.2) share Common no par
(See ComBanc, Inc.)

COMMERCIAL BK (MIAMI, FL)
Name changed to Commercial Bank & Trust Co. (Miami, FL) 02/14/1969
(See Commercial Bank & Trust Co. (Miami, FL))

COMMERCIAL BANK (PINE CASTLE, FL)
Name changed to Combank/Pine Castle (Pine Castle, FL) 03/01/1973
(See Combank/Pine Castle (Pine Castle, FL))

COMMERCIAL BK (SALEM, OR)
Each share Capital Stock $50 par exchanged for (5) shares Capital Stock $10 par 03/15/1965
Capital Stock $10 par changed to $2.50 par and (3) additional shares issued 11/20/1978
Stock Dividends - 10% 02/15/1962; 10% 02/17/1969; 15.96%

04/10/1970; 10% 04/10/1972; 10% 04/12/1977
Reorganized as Commercial Bancorp 07/14/1982
Each share Capital Stock $2.50 par exchanged for (1) share Capital Stock $2.50 par
Commercial Bancorp name changed to West Coast Bancorp (New) 03/01/1995
(See West Coast Bancorp (New))

COMMERCIAL BK (SAN FRANCISCO, CA)
Common $7.50 par split (2) for (1) by issuance of (1) additional share 11/24/1980
Merged into International Bancorp of the Pacific 09/07/1990
Each share Common $7.50 par exchanged for $3.3656 cash

COMMERCIAL BK (SAN FRANCISCO, CA)
Stock Dividend - 10% payable 12/31/1999 to holders of record 12/15/1999
Merged into First Banks America, Inc. 10/31/2000
Each share Common no par exchanged for $17.75 cash

COMMERCIAL BK (TAMPA, FL)
Name changed to Commercial Marine Bank (Tampa, FL) 10/15/1971
Commercial Marine Bank (Tampa, FL) name changed to Flagship Bank of Tampa-East (Tampa, FL) 11/08/1974 which name changed to Sun Bank of Tampa Bay (Tampa, FL) 01/01/1984

COMMERCIAL BK (WINTER PARK, FL)
Name changed to Combank/Winter Park (Winter Park, FL) 02/12/1973
(See Combank/Winter Park (Winter Park, FL))

COMMERCIAL BK AUSTRALIA LTD (AUSTRALIA)
Merged into Bank of New South Wales 10/16/1981
Each ADR for Ordinary exchanged for (2) ADR's for Ordinary and AUD$1.50 cash
Bank of New South Wales name changed to Westpac Banking Corp. Ltd. 10/01/1982

COMMERCIAL BK N Y (NEW YORK, NY)
Stock Dividend - 5% payable 01/05/1996 to holders of record 12/15/1995
Merged into North Fork Bancorporation, Inc. 11/09/2001
Each share Common $5 par exchanged for $32 cash

COMMERCIAL BK NEV (LAS VEGAS, NV)
Merged into Colonial BancGroup, Inc. 06/03/1998
Each share Common exchanged for (1) share Common $2.50 par
(See Colonial BancGroup, Inc.)

COMMERCIAL BANK OF CALIFORNIA (HAWAIIAN GARDENS, CA)
Common $5 par changed to no par and (2) additional shares issued 04/19/1980
Location changed to (Los Angeles, CA) 07/15/1980
(See Commercial Bank of California (Los Angeles, CA))

COMMERCIAL BANK OF CALIFORNIA (LOS ANGELES, CA)
Declared insolvent and taken over by the FDIC 05/27/1983
Stockholders' equity unlikely

COMMERCIAL BANK OF COBB COUNTY (MARIETTA, GA)
Merged into First Railroad & Banking Co. of Georgia 12/26/1979
Each share Common $1 par

exchanged for (0.6433) share Common 66-2/3¢ par
First Railroad & Banking Co. of Georgia acquired by First Union Corp. 11/01/1986 which name changed to Wachovia Corp. (Ctfs. dated after 09/01/2001) 09/01/2001 which merged into Wells Fargo & Co. (New) 12/31/2008

COMMERCIAL BANK OF NORTH AMERICA (NEW YORK, NY)
Name changed to Bank of North America (New York, NY) (New) 03/15/1965
Bank of North America (New York, NY) (New) merged into National Bank of North America (New York, NY) 05/08/1967
(See National Bank of North America (New York, NY))

COMMERCIAL BANKSHARES CORP (MI)
Stock Dividends - 10% 05/17/1978; 10% 03/06/1985; 10% 06/12/1986
Merged into Trustcorp, Inc. 03/31/1987
Each share Common $5 par exchanged for (1.77) shares Common $20 par
Trustcorp, Inc. acquired by Society Corp. 01/05/1990 which merged into KeyCorp (New) 03/02/1994

COMMERCIAL BANKSHARES INC. (GA)
Merged into First Railroad & Banking Co. of Georgia 06/30/1983
Each share Common $5 par exchanged for (1) share Common $0.66666666 par, $15 principal amount of 9.25% Conv. Promissory Notes due 06/30/1993 and $14 cash
First Railroad & Banking Co. of Georgia acquired by First Union Corp. 11/01/1986 which name changed to Wachovia Corp. (Ctfs. dated after 09/01/2001) 09/01/2001 which merged into Wells Fargo & Co. (New) 12/31/2008

COMMERCIAL BANKSHARES INC (FL)
Common 8¢ par split (5) for (4) by issuance of (0.25) additional share payable 01/03/2003 to holders of record 12/10/2002 Ex date - 01/06/2003
Common 8¢ par split (5) for (4) by issuance of (0.25) additional share payable 01/02/2004 to holders of record 12/11/2003 Ex date - 01/04/2004
Stock Dividends - 5% payable 01/03/1997 to holders of record 12/10/1996; 5% payable 01/02/1998 to holders of record 12/11/1997; 5% payable 01/04/1999 to holders of record 12/10/1998; 5% payable 01/04/2000 to holders of record 12/14/1999
Merged into Colonial BancGroup, Inc. 06/01/2007
Each share Common 8¢ par exchanged for (1.0107) shares Common $2.50 par and $24.50 cash
(See Colonial BancGroup, Inc.)

COMMERCIAL BANKSTOCK INC (AR)
Merged into First Commercial Corp. 07/30/1982
Each share Common $5 par exchanged for (1) share Common $5 par
First Commercial Corp. merged into Regions Financial Corp. (Old) 07/31/1998 which merged into Regions Financial Corp. (New) 07/01/2004

COMMERCIAL BENEFIT INSURANCE CO. (AZ)
Name changed to Trans-Pacific Insurance Co. 00/00/1953
(See Trans-Pacific Insurance Co.)

COMMERCIAL BKG CORP (DE)
7% Preferred $20 par called for redemption 01/00/1950
(Additional Information in Active)

COMMERCIAL BOOKBINDING CO. (OH)
Name changed to World Publishing Co. 03/19/1946
World Publishing Co. was acquired by Times Mirror Co. (Old) 12/12/1963 which merged into Times Mirror Co. (New) 02/01/1995 which merged into Tribune Co. 06/12/2000
(See Tribune Co.)

COMMERCIAL CAP BANCORP INC (NV)
Common 1¢ par split (3) for (2) by issuance of (0.5) additional share payable 09/29/2003 to holders of record 09/15/2003 Ex date - 09/30/2003
Common 1¢ par split (4) for (3) by issuance of (0.33333333) additional share payable 02/20/2004 to holders of record 02/06/2004 Ex date - 02/23/2004
Merged into Washington Mutual, Inc. 10/01/2006
Each share Common 1¢ par exchanged for $16 cash

COMMERCIAL CAPITAL SYSTEMS, INC. (LA)
Name changed to First National Corp. 03/31/1977
(See First National Corp.)

COMMERCIAL CASUALTY INSURANCE CO., NEWARK, N.J.
Acquired by Firemen's Insurance Co. of Newark, N.J. 00/00/1929
Details not available

COMMERCIAL CHEMICAL CO., INC. (MN)
Name changed to Pollution Controls, Inc. (MN) 07/03/1967
Pollution Controls, Inc. (MN) name changed to Ensco, Inc. 08/13/1982 which reorganized as Environmental Systems Co. 08/18/1983
(See Environmental Systems Co.)

COMMERCIAL CHEMICAL CO. OF TENNESSEE
Dissolution approved 00/00/1937
Details not available

COMMERCIAL CO., INC. (SC)
Completely liquidated 12/31/1970
Each share Common 1¢ par received first and final distribution of $0.01 cash

COMMERCIAL COMPUTER CORP. (MN)
Merged into Data Systems, Inc. 03/12/1970
Each share Common 5¢ par exchanged for (0.66666666) share Common 10¢ par
(See Data Systems, Inc.)

COMMERCIAL CONCEPTS INC (UT)
SEC revoked common stock registration 04/06/2010

COMMERCIAL CONSOLIDATORS CORP (AB)
Placed in receivership 09/18/2002
Stockholders' equity unlikely

COMMERCIAL CR GROUP INC (DE)
Under plan of merger name changed to Primerica Corp. (DE) 12/15/1988
Primerica Corp. (DE) name changed to Travelers Inc. 12/31/1993 which name changed to Travelers Group Inc. 04/16/1995 which name changed to Citigroup Inc. 10/08/1998

COMMERCIAL CREDIT CO., INC. OF NEW ORLEANS
Liquidated 00/00/1931
Details not available

COMMERCIAL CREDIT CO. NEW (DE)
Under plan of reorganization each share Common 1¢ par automatically became (1) share Commercial Credit Group, Inc. Common 1¢ par 05/11/1988
Commercial Credit Group, Inc. name changed to Primerica Corp. (DE) 12/15/1988 which name changed to Travelers Inc. 12/31/1993 which name changed to Travelers Group Inc. 04/16/1995 which name changed to Citigroup Inc. 10/08/1998

COMMERCIAL CREDIT CO. OLD (DE)
Common no par changed to $10 par 00/00/1933
Each share 6.5% 1st Preferred $100 par exchanged for (1) share 5.5% Preferred $100 par and (0.2) share Common $10 par 00/00/1935
Each share 8% Class B Preferred $25 par exchanged for (0.25) share 5.5% Preferred $100 par and (0.1125) share Common $10 par 00/00/1935
Each share 6% Class A $50 par exchanged for (0.35) share 5.5% Preferred $100 par and (0.475) share Common $10 par 00/00/1935
Each 8% Preferred Share of Bene. Int. $25 par exchanged for (0.25) share 5.5% Preferred $100 par and (0.5) share Common $10 par 00/00/1935
Common $10 par changed to $5 par and (1) additional share issued 05/01/1961
Stock Dividend - 100% 07/29/1952
Merged into Control Data Corp. (DE) 08/17/1968
Each share 4.5% Conv. Preferred $100 par exchanged for (1) share 4.5% Conv. Preferred $100 par
Each share Common $5 par exchanged for (0.45) share Common $5 par
Control Data Corp. (DE) name changed to Ceridian Corp. (Old) 06/03/1992
(See Ceridian Corp. (Old))

COMMERCIAL CREDIT TRUST
Dissolved 00/00/1936
Details not available

COMMERCIAL DECAL INC (NY)
Dissolved by proclamation 09/27/1995

COMMERCIAL DISC CORP (DE)
Common no par changed to $1 par 00/00/1953
Common $1 par split (4) for (1) by issuance of (3) additional shares 12/31/1959
Through purchase offer 100% acquired by Automatic Canteen Co. of America 00/00/1960
6% Preferred $10 par called for redemption 01/02/1962
Public interest eliminated

COMMERCIAL E WASTE MGMT INC (NV)
Name changed to FluoroPharma Medical, Inc. 06/03/2011

COMMERCIAL FED CORP (NE)
Common 1¢ par split (3) for (2) by issuance of (0.5) additional share 05/09/1986
Common 1¢ par split (3) for (2) by issuance of (0.5) additional share payable 01/14/1997 to holders of record 12/31/1996 Ex date - 01/15/1997
Common 1¢ par split (3) for (2) by issuance of (0.5) additional share payable 12/15/1997 to holders of record 11/28/1997 Ex date - 12/16/1997
Merged into BancWest Corp. 12/02/2005
Each share Common 1¢ par exchanged for $34 cash

COMMERCIAL FILTERS CORP. (NY)
Merged into Carborundum Co. 04/01/1968
Each share Common $1.50 par exchanged for $15 cash

COMMERCIAL FILTERS CORP. OF CALIFORNIA (CA)
Merged into Commercial Filters Corp. 01/23/1968
Each share Common no par exchanged for $1.85 cash

COMMERCIAL FINANCE CO. (OK)
Voluntarily dissolved 10/29/1976
Details not available

COMMERCIAL FINANCE CORP.
Merged into General Investors Trust 00/00/1932
Details not available

COMMERCIAL FINANCE CORP. LTD. (ON)
Capital Stock no par split (4) for (1) by issuance of (3) additional shares 05/04/1962
Name changed to Commercial Financial Corp. Ltd. 07/14/1982
(See Commercial Financial Corp. Ltd.)

COMMERCIAL FINL LTD (ON)
Acquired by Montreal Trustco Inc. 07/10/1990
Each share Common no par exchanged for $5.20 cash

COMMERCIAL GOLD & SILVER CORP. (UT)
Recapitalized as Morningstar Corp. 09/10/1982
Each share Common 1¢ par exchanged for (0.1) share Common $0.001 par

COMMERCIAL GTY BANCSHARES INC (KS)
Merged into Enterbank Holdings, Inc. 06/23/2000
Each share Common exchanged for (2.1429) shares Common 1¢ par
Enterbank Holdings, Inc. name changed to Enterprise Financial Services Corp. 04/29/2002

COMMERCIAL GTY BK (MOBILE, AL)
Acquired by Alabama Financial Group, Inc. 12/29/1972
Each share Common $1 par exchanged for (0.16666666) share Common $10 par
Alabama Financial Group, Inc. name changed to Southern Bancorporation 04/17/1974 which name changed to Southern Bancorporation of Alabama 04/21/1975 which name changed to SouthTrust Corp. 09/18/1981 which merged into Wachovia Corp. (Ctfs. dated after 09/01/2001) 11/01/2004 which merged into Wells Fargo & Co. (New) 12/31/2008

COMMERCIAL INDL MINERALS LTD (ON)
Recapitalized as ICV Integrated Commercial Ventures Inc. 10/31/1994
Each share Common no par exchanged for (0.11111111) share Common no par
ICV Integrated Commercial Ventures Inc. recapitalized as Blue Gold International, Inc. 12/23/1997
(See Blue Gold International, Inc.)

COMMERCIAL INTL CORP (DE)
Each share Common 20¢ par exchanged for (0.2) share Common $1 par 02/06/1969
Charter cancelled and declared inoperative and void for non-payment of taxes 03/01/1994

COMMERCIAL INTERNATIONAL EXPORT CORP. (DE)
Name changed to Oil Exploration International, Inc. 08/19/1969

(See Oil Exploration International, Inc.)

COMMERCIAL INTERTECH CORP (OH)
Common $1 par split (3) for (2) by issuance of (0.5) additional share 09/15/1994
Each share Common $1 par received distribution of (1) share Cuno Inc. Common $0.001 par payable 09/10/1996 to holders of record 08/09/1996
Merged into Parker-Hannifin Corp. 04/11/2000
Each share Common $1 par exchanged for (0.4611) share Common 50¢ par

COMMERCIAL INVESTMENT CORP. (DE)
Recapitalized as Spiegl Farms, Inc. 10/27/1960
Each share 6% Preferred $10 par exchanged for $5 principal amount of 6.5% Conv. Debentures
Each share Common no par exchanged for (1) share Common no par
Spiegl Farms, Inc. recapitalized as Spiegl Foods, Inc. 01/02/1966
(See Spiegl Foods, Inc.)

COMMERCIAL INVESTMENT TRUST CORP. (DE)
Name changed to C.I.T. Financial Corp. 04/26/1945
C.I.T. Financial Corp. merged into RCA Corp. 01/31/1980
(See RCA Corp.)

COMMERCIAL LABOR MGMT INC (NV)
Each share Common 5¢ par exchanged for (0.05) share old Common $0.001 par 05/12/1998
Each share old Common $0.001 par exchanged for (0.2) share new Common $0.001 par 07/31/1998
Name changed to Zeros & Ones, Inc. 07/01/1999
Zeros & Ones, Inc. name changed to Voyant International Corp. 04/30/2007
(See Voyant International Corp.)

COMMERCIAL LEASING CORP. (CA)
Acquired by Rochester Capital Leasing Corp. 11/00/1962
Details not available

COMMERCIAL LEASING CORP. (UT)
Recapitalized as Commercial Gold & Silver Corp. 02/29/1980
Each share Common 1¢ par exchanged for (10) shares Common 1¢ par
Commercial Gold & Silver Corp. recapitalized as Morningstar Corp. 09/10/1982

COMMERCIAL LIFE INSURANCE CO. (AZ)
Merged into Pacific Standard Life Insurance Co. 11/03/1967
Each share Common $1 par exchanged for (1.5) shares Common $1 par
Pacific Standard Life Insurance Co. reorganized as Pacific Standard Life Co. (DE) 07/01/1969 which merged into Southmark Corp. 08/30/1983
(See Southmark Corp.)

COMMERCIAL LIFE INSURANCE CO. OF MISSOURI (MO)
Voting Trust terminated 08/15/1963
Each VTC exchanged for (1) share Common $1.40 par
Common $1.40 par changed to $1 par and (0.4) additional share issued 06/01/1964
Merged into Commercial State Life Insurance Co. 04/28/1965
Each share Common $1 par exchanged for (1) share Common $1 par

(See Commercial State Life Insurance Co.)

COMMERCIAL LIQUIDATORS INC (UT)
Charter suspended for failure to pay taxes 09/30/1976

COMMERCIAL MARINE BANK (TAMPA, FL)
Name changed to Flagship Bank of Tampa-East (Tampa, FL) 11/08/1974
Flagship Bank of Tampa-East (Tampa, FL) name changed to Sun Bank of Tampa Bay (Tampa, FL) 01/01/1984

COMMERCIAL MINERALS CORP. (DE)
Name changed to Commercial International Corp. 06/14/1957
(See Commercial International Corp.)

COMMERCIAL MINERALS LTD. (AB)
Recapitalized as Commercial Oil & Gas Ltd. 12/30/1960
Each share Common exchanged for (0.1) share Common
(See Commercial Oil & Gas Ltd.)

COMMERCIAL NATIONAL BANK & TRUST CO. (MUSKOGEE, OK)
Name changed to Commercial Bank & Trust Co. (Muskogee, OK) 08/31/1970
(See Commercial Bank & Trust Co. (Muskogee, OK))

COMMERCIAL NATIONAL BANK (ANAHEIM, CA)
(See Commercial National Bank (Buena Park, CA))

COMMERCIAL NATL BK (BUENA PARK, CA)
Common Capital Stock $10 par changed to $5 par and (1) additional share issued 06/30/1971
Merged into Wells Fargo & Co. (CA) 08/23/1974
Each share Common Capital Stock $5 par exchanged for (1.07) shares Common $5 par
Wells Fargo & Co. (CA) reincorporated in Delaware 06/30/1987 which merged into Wells Fargo & Co. (New) 11/02/1998

COMMERCIAL NATL BK (CHICAGO, IL)
Stock Dividends - 25% 12/00/1952; 50% 08/15/1960; 33.33333333% 01/20/1964; 20% 01/25/1968; 28% 03/01/1977
Acquired by River Forest Bancorp 12/31/1986
Each share Capital Stock $20 par exchanged for $425 cash

COMMERCIAL NATL BK (KANSAS CITY, KS)
Stock Dividends - 20% 01/10/1941; 10% 01/03/1944; 64.14% 12/20/1944; 15.38% 08/01/1945; 17.647% 01/14/1953; 50% 12/31/1957; 25% 02/15/1966; 20% 02/16/1968; 15.1% 03/01/1971; 12.5% 03/28/1975; 11.11111111% 03/31/1978
Reorganized as CNB Financial Corp. 07/26/1982
Each share Capital Stock $10 par exchanged for (1) share Common $1 par
CNB Financial Corp. merged into UMB Financial Corp. 06/25/1993

COMMERCIAL NATL BK (LITTLE ROCK, AR)
Common $20 par changed to $10 par and (1) additional share issued 03/28/1973
Common $10 par changed to $5 par and (1) additional share issued 03/13/1979
Stock Dividends - 100% 01/14/1947; 100% 01/22/1954; 25% 02/07/1961; 33.33333333% 01/19/1965; 10% 03/28/1969; 10% 03/01/1971
Reorganized as Commercial Bankstock, Inc. 10/21/1980

Each share Common $5 par exchanged for (1) share Common $5 par
Commercial Bankstock, Inc. merged into First Commercial Corp. 07/30/1983 which merged into Regions Financial Corp. (Old) 07/31/1998 which merged into Regions Financial Corp. (New) 07/01/2004

COMMERCIAL NATL BK (MUSKOGEE, OK)
Each share Capital Stock $100 par exchanged for (5) shares Capital Stock $20 par and a 33-1/3% stock dividend paid 00/00/1948
Each share Capital Stock $20 par exchanged for (1.5) shares Capital Stock $10 par 06/30/1953
Stock Dividends - 25% 12/13/1955; 20% 12/10/1957; 10% 12/31/1958
Name changed to Commercial National Bank & Trust Co. (Muskogee, OK) 02/01/1969
Commercial National Bank & Trust Co. (Muskogee, OK) name changed to Commercial Bank & Trust Co. (Muskogee, OK) 08/31/1970
(See Commercial Bank & Trust Co. (Muskogee, OK))

COMMERCIAL NATL BK (PEORIA, IL)
Common Capital Stock $20 par changed to $10 par and (1) additional share issued 02/26/1974
Stock Dividend - 20% 04/21/1967
Reorganized under the laws of Delaware as Commercial National Corp. 05/08/1975
Each share Common Capital Stock $10 par exchanged for (1) share Common $10 par
Commercial National Corp. merged into Midwest Financial Group, Inc. 02/08/1983 which merged into First of America Bank Corp. 11/01/1989 which merged into National City Corp. 03/31/1998 which was acquired by PNC Financial Services Group, Inc. 12/31/2008

COMMERCIAL NATL BK (SAN LEANDRO, CA)
Merged into First National Bank (San Jose, CA) 05/01/1972
Each share Common $10 par exchanged for (1.6) shares Capital Stock $5 par
First National Bank (San Jose, CA) reorganized as First National Bancshares Inc. 06/16/1976 which name changed to Bancwest Corp. 03/15/1979 which name changed to BWC Liquidating Corp. 03/18/1980
(See BWC Liquidating Corp.)

COMMERCIAL NATL BK (SHREVEPORT, LA)
Each share Capital Stock $100 par exchanged for (5) shares Capital Stock $20 par 00/00/1951
Under plan of merger each share Capital Stock $20 par exchanged for (1.28846) shares Capital Stock $25 par 00/00/1954
Each share Capital Stock $25 par exchanged for (2.857042) shares Capital Stock $10 par to effect a (5) for (2) split and 14.28571428% stock dividend 03/07/1966
Stock Dividends - 11.11111111% 06/27/1958; 50% 03/06/1970; (1) for (9) 03/23/1975; 20% 03/23/1977; (1) for (6) 03/23/1979
Reorganized as Commercial National Corp. 01/19/1982
Each share Capital Stock $10 par exchanged for (2) shares Common $5 par
(See Commercial National Corp.)

COMMERCIAL NATIONAL BANK (SPARTANBURG, SC)
Merged into First Commercial

National Bank of South Carolina (Columbia, SC) 12/31/1964
Each share Capital Stock $20 par exchanged for (1.65) shares Capital Stock $5 par
First Commercial National Bank of South Carolina (Columbia, SC) name changed to First National Bank of South Carolina (Columbia, SC) 12/10/1965 which reorganized as First Bankshares Corp. of S.C. 07/19/1969 which liquidated for South Carolina National Corp. 12/01/1984 which merged into Wachovia Corp. (New) (Ctfs. dated between 05/20/1991 and 09/01/2001) 12/06/1991 which merged into Wachovia Corp. (Ctfs. dated after 09/01/2001) 09/01/2001 which merged into Wells Fargo & Co. (New) 12/31/2008

COMMERCIAL NATL BK WESTMORELAND CNTY (LATROBE, PA)
Reorganized as Commercial National Financial Corp. 07/01/1990
Each share Common $10 par exchanged for (5) shares Common $2 par

COMMERCIAL NATIONAL CORP.
Liquidated 00/00/1936
Details not available

COMMERCIAL NATL CORP (DE)
Merged into Midwest Financial Group, Inc. 02/08/1983
Each share Common $10 par exchanged for (2.185) shares Common $5 par
Midwest Financial Group, Inc. merged into First of America Bank Corp. 11/01/1989 which merged into National City Corp. 03/31/1998 which was acquired by PNC Financial Services Group, Inc. 12/31/2008

COMMERCIAL NATL CORP (LA)
Merged into Deposit Guaranty Corp. 02/14/1990
Each share Common $5 par exchanged for $5.50 cash

COMMERCIAL NET LEASE RLTY INC (MD)
Reincorporated 06/03/1994
State of incorporation changed from (DE) to (MD) 06/03/1994
Name changed to National Retail Properties, Inc. 05/01/2006

COMMERCIAL OIL & GAS LTD (AB)
Assets sold for the benefit of creditors 11/01/1991
No stockholders' equity

COMMERCIAL PAC BK F S B (SANTA CRUZ, CA)
Name changed to Bank USA, FSB (Phoenix, AZ) 04/01/1998
Bank USA, FSB (Phoenix, AZ) name changed to Bank USA, N.A. (Phoenix, AZ) 01/01/2007
(See Bank USA, N.A. (Phoenix, AZ))

COMMERCIAL PROGRAMMING UNLIMITED INC (DE)
Reincorporated 05/22/1987
Common $0.025 par split (4) for (1) by issuance of (3) additional shares 08/24/1986
State of incorporation changed from (NY) to (DE) 05/22/1987
Name changed to Universal Franchise Opportunities Corp. 08/01/1994
Universal Francshise Opportunies Corp. name changed to Innovative Materials, Inc. 11/19/1997
(See Innovative Materials, Inc.)

COMMERCIAL PPTY CORP (DE)
Each share old Common 1¢ par exchanged for (0.01) share new Common 1¢ par 04/01/1998
Note: No holder received fewer than (50) post-split shares

New Common 1¢ par changed to $0.001 par 12/23/2004
Each share old Common $0.001 par exchanged for (2) shares new Common $0.001 par 03/00/2005
Name changed to Shandong Ruitai Chemical Co., Ltd. 11/15/2006
Shandong Ruitai Chemical Co., Ltd. name changed to China Ruitai International Holdings Co., Ltd. 04/09/2007
(See China Ruitai International Holdings Co., Ltd.)

COMMERCIAL RESINS CORP. (MN)
Merged into Interplastic Corp. 05/01/1962
Each share Common $1 par exchanged for (2) shares Common 10¢ par
(See Interplastic Corp.)

COMMERCIAL RES CORP (DE)
Name changed to Scotti Commercial Corp. 04/08/1975
(See Scotti Commercial Corp.)

COMMERCIAL SVGS BK (UPPER SANDUSKY, OH)
Under plan of reorganization each share Common $12.50 par automatically became (1) share Commercial Bancshares Inc. Common $12.50 par 04/13/1995
Commercial Bancshares Inc. merged into First Defiance Financial Corp. 02/27/2017

COMMERCIAL SEC BANCORPORATION (UT)
Common no par split (2) for (1) by issuance of (1) additional share 08/01/1986
Acquired by KeyCorp (NY) 12/31/1987
Each share Common no par exchanged for (2.736) shares Common $5 par
KeyCorp (NY) merged into KeyCorp (New) (OH) 03/01/1994

COMMERCIAL SEC BK (OGDEN, UT)
Each share Capital Stock $100 par exchanged for (5.333) shares Capital Stock $25 par 00/00/1945
Capital Stock $25 par changed to $6.25 par and (3) additional shares issued 01/15/1969
Stock Dividends - 12.5% 00/00/1946; 11.11111111% 00/00/1947; 150% 06/27/1957; 20% 09/07/1961; 11.11111111% 11/15/1962; 25% 02/15/1967
Reorganized as Commercial Security Bancorporation 08/31/1977
Each share Capital Stock $6.25 par exchanged for (2) shares Common no par
Commercial Security Bancorporation acquired by KeyCorp (NY) 12/31/1987 which merged into KeyCorp (New) (OH) 03/01/1994

COMMERCIAL SECURITY BANK OF SALT LAKE (SALT LAKE CITY, UT)
Through purchase offer Commercial Security Bancorporation held 93% as of 12/31/1974
Public interest eliminated

COMMERCIAL SHEARING & STAMPING CO. (OH)
Common $1 par split (2) for (1) by issuance of (1) additional share 04/01/1971
Stock Dividends - 100% 06/24/1947; 10% 12/20/1950; 10% 12/21/1951; 50% 10/25/1956; 10% 01/02/1964
Name changed to Commercial Shearing, Inc. 03/01/1972
Commercial Shearing, Inc. name changed to Commercial Intertech Corp. 02/23/1988 which merged into Parker-Hannifin Corp. 04/11/2000
(See Parker-Hannifin Corp.)

COMMERCIAL SHEARING INC (OH)
Stock Dividends - 10% 01/04/1977; 50% 05/27/1977; 25% 01/03/1978; 100% 01/03/1979; 10% 01/04/1980; 10% 01/05/1981
Name changed to Commercial Intertech Corp. 02/23/1988
Commercial Intertech Corp. merged into Parker-Hannifin Corp. 04/11/2000

COMMERCIAL SOLUTIONS INC (AB)
Acquired by Genuine Parts Co. 02/05/2014
Each share Common no par exchanged for $1.07 cash
Note: Unexchanged certificates will be cancelled and become without value 02/05/2020

COMMERCIAL SOLVENTS CORP (MD)
Each share Class B no par exchanged for (2) shares old Common no par 00/00/1927
Each share old Common no par exchanged for (10) shares new Common no par 00/00/1929
New Common no par changed to $1 par 04/07/1955
4.5% Conv. Preferred Ser. A $20 par called for redemption 01/31/1975
Merged into International Minerals & Chemical Corp. 05/14/1975
Each share Common $1 par exchanged for $45 cash

COMMERCIAL ST CORP (MO)
$1.50 Conv. Preferred $1 par called for redemption 11/01/1979
Merged into Gibraltar Life Insurance Co. 12/21/1979
Each share Common $1 par exchanged for $9 cash

COMMERCIAL ST LIFE INS CO (MO)
Through voluntary exchange offer 100% acquired by Commercial State Corp. as of 03/01/1970
Public interest eliminated

COMMERCIAL STATE BANK & TRUST CO. (NEW YORK, NY)
Stock Dividend - 10% 11/24/1953
Merged into Commercial Bank of North America (New York, NY) 09/05/1958
Each share Capital Stock $25 par exchanged for (3.617) shares Capital Stock $5 par
Commercial Bank of North America (New York, NY) name changed to Bank of North America (New York, NY) (New) 03/11/1965
(See Bank of North America (New York, NY) (New))

COMMERCIAL STATE BANK (MADISON, WI)
Stock Dividends - 25% 01/08/1946; 10% 07/01/1963; 10% 07/01/1964
98.97% acquired by Marine Corp. through exchange offer which expired 02/29/1980
Public interest eliminated

COMMERCIAL TECHNOLOGY INC (NV)
Each share old Common 1¢ par exchanged for (0.33333333) share new Common 1¢ par 10/26/1977
Liquidation completed
Each share new Common 1¢ par received initial distribution of (0.5) share Electric & Gas Technology, Inc. Common 1¢ par 10/00/1988
Each share new Common 1¢ par exchanged for second and final distribution of (0.1) share Electric & Gas Technology, Inc. Common 1¢ par 10/00/1989
(See Electric & Gas Technology, Inc.)

COMMERCIAL TELEPHONICS INC (NY)
Charter cancelled and proclaimed dissolved for failure to pay taxes 09/25/1991

COMMERCIAL TRANSPORT CORP. (DE)
Merged into American Commercial Barge Line Co. 08/01/1957
Each share 6% Preferred $100 par exchanged for (9) shares Common $3 par
Each share Common $3 par exchanged for (1) share Common $3 par
American Commercial Barge Line Co. name changed to American Commercial Lines Inc. 04/30/1964 which merged into Texas Gas Transmission Corp. 05/15/1968
(See Texas Gas Transmission Corp.)

COMMERCIAL TRUST CO. (TX)
Name changed to Consolidated Commercial Corp. 05/28/1958
(See Consolidated Commercial Corp.)

COMMERCIAL TR CO N J (JERSEY CITY, NJ)
Capital Stock $25 par changed to $10 par and (1.5) additional shares issued 02/01/1961
Capital Stock $10 par changed to $5 par and (1) additional share issued 08/15/1969
Stock Dividend - (3) for (17) 02/01/1958
Reorganized as Commercial Bancshares, Inc. (NJ) 06/30/1982
Each share Capital Stock $5 par exchanged for (1) share Common $5 par
Commercial Bancshares, Inc. (NJ) merged into United Jersey Banks 12/01/1986 which name changed to UJB Financial Corp. 06/30/1989 which name changed to Summit Bancorp 03/01/1996 which merged into FleetBoston Financial Corp. 03/01/2001 which merged into Bank of America Corp. 04/01/2004

COMMERCIAL URANIUM MINES, INC. (DE)
Recapitalized as Commercial Minerals Corp. 08/16/1956
Each share Common 1¢ par exchanged for (0.05) share Common 20¢ par
Commercial Minerals Corp. name changed to Commercial International Corp. 06/14/1957
(See Commercial International Corp.)

COMMERCIAL VENTURES LTD. (DE)
Name changed to Fin U.S.A., Inc. 12/15/1987
Fin U.S.A, Inc. recapitalized as I/Net, Inc. 10/08/1993 which recapitalized as Ardmore Holding Corp. 06/11/2007 which name changed to Yayi International Inc. 09/25/2008
(See Yayi International Inc.)

COMMERCIAL WHARF CO. (MA)
Liquidation completed 10/15/1963
Details not available

COMMITTED CAP ACQUISITION CORP (DE)
Name changed to The ONE Group Hospitality, Inc. 06/25/2014

COMMITTEE BAY RES LTD (AB)
Recapitalized as CBR Gold Corp. 03/02/2009
Each share Common no par exchanged for (0.2) share Common no par
CBR Gold Corp. name changed to Niblack Mineral Development Inc. 04/15/2010 which merged into Heatherdale Resources Ltd. 01/23/2012

COMMNET CELLULAR INC (CO)
Under plan of merger each share old Common $0.001 par exchanged for either (1) share new Common $0.001 par or $36 cash 02/10/1998
Note: Non-electing holders received cash
New Common $0.001 par split (5) for (1) by issuance of (4) additional shares payable 05/07/1998 to holders of record 04/20/1998
Merged into Vodafone AirTouch PLC 01/06/2000
Each share new Common $0.001 par exchanged for $32.2077 cash

COMMODITY FUND FOR CAPITAL GROWTH, INC. (DE)
No longer in existence having become inoperative and void for non-payment of taxes 04/01/1966

COMMODITY HLDG CORP (DE)
Each share Common $1 par exchanged for (20) shares Common 5¢ par 10/27/1954
Name changed to Metalux Industries, Inc. 03/13/1970
(See Metalux Industries, Inc.)

COMMODITY RESEARCH CORP. (MN)
Name changed to Professional Adjusting System of America, Inc. 04/14/1972
(See Professional Adjusting System of America, Inc.)

COMMODITY RES INC (DE)
Name changed to Tri-Valley Oil & Gas Corp. 06/17/1982
Tri-Valley Oil & Gas Corp. name changed to Tri-Valley Corp. 12/08/1986
(See Tri-Valley Corp.)

COMMODORE, INC.
In process of liquidation 00/00/1949
Details not available

COMMODORE APPLIED TECHNOLOGIES INC (DE)
Each share old Common $0.001 par exchanged for (0.05) share new Common $0.001 par 08/29/2005
Ceased operations 12/31/2011
No stockholders' equity

COMMODORE BUSINESS MACHS LTD (ON)
Reorganized as Commodore International Ltd. 08/20/1976
Each share Common no par exchanged for (1) share Capital Stock $1 par
(See Commodore International Ltd.)

COMMODORE CORP (DE)
Common $1 par changed to 50¢ par and (1) additional share issued 03/03/1969
Common 50¢ par changed to 5¢ par 11/30/1977
Plan of reorganization under Chapter 11 Federal Bankruptcy proceedings confirmed 05/05/1986
No stockholders' equity

COMMODORE EDL SYS LTD (BAHAMAS)
Voluntarily dissolved 00/00/1983
No stockholders' equity

COMMODORE ENVIRONMENTAL SVCS INC (DE)
Reincorporated 08/00/1998
State of incorporation changed from (UT) to (DE) and Common 10¢ par changed to 1¢ par 08/00/1998
SEC revoked common stock registration 02/19/2010

COMMODORE GROWTH FD INC (WA)
Completely liquidated 03/06/1973
Each share Common 10¢ par exchanged for first and final distribution of $4.87 cash

COMMODORE HLDGS LTD (BERMUDA)
Plan of reorganization under Chapter 11 Federal Bankruptcy Code effective 03/26/2002
No stockholders' equity

COMMODORE HOTEL, INC. (NY)
Merged into Zeckendorf Hotels Corp. for cash 09/05/1958
Note: Unexchanged certificates were

cancelled and became without value 05/31/1965

COMMODORE INTL LTD (BAHAMAS)
Capital Stock $1 par split (3) for (2) by issuance of (0.5) additional share 09/07/1979
Capital Stock $1 par split (3) for (2) by issuance of (0.5) additional share 02/29/1980
Capital Stock $1 par split (3) for (1) by issuance of (2) additional shares 11/12/1980
Capital Stock $1 par split (3) for (2) by issuance of (0.5) additional share 05/03/1982
Capital Stock $1 par split (2) for (1) by issuance of (1) additional share 06/09/1983
Company liquidated 00/00/1994
Stockholders' equity unlikely

COMMODORE INVTS INC (UT)
Name changed to World Tournament International, Inc. 03/14/1988
(See World Tournament International, Inc.)

COMMODORE MINERALS INC (NV)
Name changed to INTAC International, Inc. 10/14/2001
INTAC International, Inc. merged into HSW International, Inc. 10/02/2007 which name changed to Remark Media, Inc. 01/03/2012 which name changed to Remark Holdings, Inc. 04/11/2017

COMMODORE RES CORP (UT)
Reorganized under Chapter 11 Bankruptcy Code 09/02/1983
Each share old Common 10¢ par exchanged for (1) share new Common 10¢ par
Name changed to Commodore Environmental Services, Inc. (UT) 06/26/1987
Commodore Environmental Services, Inc. (UT) reincorporated in Delaware 08/00/1998
(See Commodore Environmental Services, Inc.)

COMMODORE SEPARATION TECHNOLOGIES INC (DE)
SEC revoked common stock registration 07/23/2010

COMMOIL, LTD. (AB)
Acquired by Commonwealth Petroleum Services Ltd. 12/20/1962
Each share Capital Stock no par exchanged for (1) share Capital Stock no par
Commonwealth Petroleum Services Ltd. acquired by Westburne International Industries Ltd. (AB) 09/30/1969 which reincorporated in Canada 10/18/1977
(See Westburne International Industries Ltd. (Canada))

COMMON HORIZONS INC (NV)
Old Common $0.001 par split (4) for (1) by issuance of (3) additional shares payable 06/10/2005 to holders of record 05/25/2005 Ex date - 06/13/2005
Reorganized under the laws of Delaware as Novelos Therapeutics, Inc. 06/14/2005
Each share new Common $0.001 par exchanged for (1) share Common $0.00001 par
Novelos Therapeutics, Inc. name changed to Cellectar Biosciences, Inc. 02/12/2014

COMMON STK FD ST BD & MTG CO (MD)
Capital Stock 50¢ par changed to 25¢ par and (1) additional share issued 03/14/1966
Name changed to State Bond Common Stock Fund, Inc. 04/29/1983
(See State Bond Common Stock Fund, Inc.)

COMMON STOCK TRUST SHARES SERIES A
Trust terminated 00/00/1932
Details not available

COMMONCACHE INC (FL)
Reorganized as Global Roaming Distribution, Inc. 12/03/2007
Each share Common $0.001 par exchanged for (4) shares Common $0.001 par

COMMONWEAL HLDGS LTD (MN)
Recapitalized as Sandy Steele Unlimited Inc. 10/15/2001
Each share Common 1¢ par exchanged for (1/6) share Common 1¢ par

COMMONWEALTH, INC. (OR)
Preferred $50 par called for redemption 12/31/1963
Common $10 par changed to $5 par and (1) additional share issued 03/24/1964
100% acquired by Amfac, Inc. 10/00/1972
Public interest eliminated

COMMONWEALTH & SOUTHERN CORP. (DE)
Completely liquidated 10/01/1949
Each share $6 Preferred no par exchanged for (2.8) shares Consumers Power Co. (ME) Common no par, (0.55) share Central Illinois Light Co. Common no par and $1 cash
Each share Common no par exchanged for (0.35) share Southern Co. Common $5 par and (0.06) share Ohio Edison Co. Common $8 par
(See each company's listing)

COMMONWEALTH ACCEPTANCE CORP. LTD. (BC)
Adjudicated bankrupt 02/28/1969
No stockholders' equity

COMMONWEALTH AIRCRAFT, INC.
Adjudicated bankrupt 00/00/1949
No stockholders' equity

COMMONWEALTH ALUM CORP (DE)
Name changed to Commonwealth Industries, Inc. 04/21/1997
Commonwealth Industries, Inc. merged into Aleris International, Inc. 12/09/2004
(See Aleris International, Inc.)

COMMONWEALTH AMERN FINL GROUP INC (DE)
Each share old Common 20¢ par exchanged for (1.5) shares new Common 20¢ par 10/03/2005
Stock Dividend - 15% payable 09/15/2005 to holders of record 08/31/2005 Ex date - 08/29/2005
Name changed to James Monroe Capital Corp. 05/30/2006

COMMONWEALTH ASSISTED LIVING INC (AB)
Reincorporated under the laws of Canada as EnWave Corp. 08/09/1999

COMMONWEALTH ASSOC GROWTH FD INC (MD)
Name changed to MicroCap Fund Inc. 10/31/1994
MicroCap Fund Inc. name changed to MicroCap Liquidating Trust 02/24/1997
(See MicroCap Liquidating Trust)

COMMONWEALTH ASSOC INC (NV)
Name changed to KCD Holdings Inc. 10/25/1994
KCD Holdings Inc. name changed to Sequester Holdings Inc. 04/01/1997 which recapitalized as China Biolife Enterprises Inc. 06/19/2006 which recapitalized as Asia Pacific Energy Inc. 12/07/2007

COMMONWEALTH ASSURANCE CO. (CA)
Merged into USLIFE Holding Corp. 09/28/1967
Each share Common $10 par exchanged for (1.5) shares Capital Stock $2 par
USLIFE Holding Corp. name changed to USLIFE Corp. 05/22/1970 which merged into American General Corp. 06/17/1997 which merged into American International Group, Inc. 08/29/2001

COMMONWEALTH BANCORP INC (PA)
Merged into Citizens Financial Group, Inc. 01/17/2003
Each share Common 1¢ par exchanged for $46.50 cash

COMMONWEALTH BANCSHARES CORP (PA)
Common $3.50 par split (3) for (2) by issuance of (0.5) additional share 01/23/1987
Acquired by Meridian Bancorp, Inc. 08/31/1993
Each share Common $3.50 par exchanged for (1.415) shares Common $5 par
Meridian Bancorp, Inc. merged into CoreStates Financial Corp 04/09/1996 which merged into First Union Corp. 04/28/1998 which name changed to Wachovia Corp. (Ctfs. dated after 09/01/2001) 09/01/2001 which merged into Wells Fargo & Co. (New) 12/31/2008

COMMONWEALTH BANK & TRUST CO. (PITTSBURGH, PA)
Merged into Union National Bank (Pittsburgh, PA) 02/28/1964
Each share Capital Stock $12.50 par exchanged for (1.56775) shares Common $10 par
Union National Bank (Pittsburgh, PA) reorganized as Union National Corp. 02/08/1982 which merged into Integra Financial Corp. 01/26/1989 which merged into National City Corp. 05/03/1996 which was acquired by PNC Financial Services Group, Inc. 12/31/2008

COMMONWEALTH BK & TR CO (MUNCY, PA)
Merged into Commonwealth Bank & Trust Co., N.A. (Williamsport, PA) 05/29/1981
Each share Common $3.50 par exchanged for (1) share Common $3.50 par
Commonwealth Bank & Trust Co., N.A. (Williamsport, PA) reorganized as Commonwealth Bancshares Corp. 03/01/1982 which was acquired by Meridian Bancorp, Inc. 08/31/1993 which merged into CoreStates Financial Corp 04/09/1996 which merged into First Union Corp. 04/28/1998 which name changed to Wachovia Corp. (Ctfs. dated after 09/01/2001) 09/01/2001 which merged into Wells Fargo & Co. (New) 12/31/2008

COMMONWEALTH BK & TR CO N A (WILLIAMSPORT, PA)
Under plan of reorganization each share Common $3.50 par automatically became (1) share Commonwealth Bancshares Corp. Common $3.50 par 03/01/1982
Commonwealth Bancshares Corp. acquired by Meridian Bancorp, Inc. 08/31/1993 which merged into CoreStates Financial Corp 04/09/1996 which merged into First Union Corp. 04/28/1998 which name changed to Wachovia Corp. (Ctfs. dated after 09/01/2001) 09/01/2001 which merged into Wells Fargo & Co. (New) 12/31/2008

COMMONWEALTH BANK (LOS ANGELES, CA)
Merged into City National Bank (Beverly Hills, CA) 11/02/1965
Each share Common $10 par exchanged for (1) share Capital Stock $5 par
(See City National Bank (Beverly Hills, CA))

COMMONWEALTH BK (RICHMOND, VA)
Common no par split (5) for (4) by issuance of (0.25) additional share payable 07/10/2002 to holders of record 06/10/2002
Merged into First Community Bancshares, Inc. (NV) 06/09/2003
Each share Common no par exchanged for either (0.7491465) share Common $1 par and $5.1545 cash or $30.50 cash
Note: Option to receive stock and cash expired 06/30/2003
First Community Bancshares, Inc. (NV) reincorporated in Virginia 10/09/2018

COMMONWEALTH BK (TORRANCE, CA)
Common $5 par changed to no par 10/10/1979
Common no par split (2) for (1) by issuance of (1) additional share 07/30/1982
Stock Dividends - 10% 04/30/1981; 10% 09/14/1981
Location changed from (Hawthorne, CA) to (Torrance, CA) 00/00/1982
Each share old Common no par exchanged for (0.05) share new Common no par 08/27/1987
Declared insolvent and taken over by FDIC 09/25/1987
Stockholders' equity undetermined

COMMONWEALTH BANKS, INC. (VA)
Name changed to Central Fidelity Banks, Inc. 06/01/1979
Central Fidelity Banks, Inc. merged into Wachovia Corp. (New) (Ctfs. dated between 05/20/1991 and 09/01/2001) 12/15/1997 which merged into Wachovia Corp. (Ctfs. dated after 09/01/2001) 09/01/2001 which merged into Wells Fargo & Co. (New) 12/31/2008

COMMONWEALTH BANKSHARES CAP TR I (DE)
8% Conv. Preferred Securities $5 par called for redemption at $5 plus $0.06666666 accrued dividends 12/15/2006

COMMONWEALTH BANKSHARES INC (VA)
Common $2.50 par split (3) for (2) by issuance of (0.5) additional share payable 05/27/1999 to holders of record 05/17/1999
Common $2.50 par changed to $2.273 par and (0.1) additional share issued payable 06/30/2006 to holders of record 06/19/2006 Ex date - 06/15/2006
Common $2.273 par changed to $2.066 par and (0.1) additional share issued payable 12/29/2006 to holders of record 12/18/2006 Ex date - 12/14/2006
Stock Dividends - 6% payable 04/30/1996 to holders of record 03/31/1996; 8% payable 04/28/1998 to holders of record 03/31/1998
SEC revoked common stock registration 07/31/2013

COMMONWEALTH BIOTECHNOLOGIES INC (VA)
Under plan of reorganization each share Common no par automatically became (1) share HedgePath Pharmaceuticals, Inc. (DE) Common $0.0001 par 08/23/2013

COMMONWEALTH BRASS CORP (MI)
Acquired by Essex Wire Corp. 00/00/1967
Details not available

COMMONWEALTH BUSINESS BK (LOS ANGELES, CA)
Common no par split (2) for (1) by issuance of (1) additional share payable 03/20/2015 to holders of record 03/12/2015 Ex date - 03/23/2015
Stock Dividends - 10% payable 03/03/2014 to holders of record 02/14/2014 Ex date - 02/12/2014; 10% payable 05/27/2016 to to holders of record 05/16/2016 Ex date - 05/12/2016
Reorganized as CBB Bancorp, Inc. 09/13/2017
Each share Common no par exchanged for (1) share Common $0.001 par

COMMONWEALTH CAP FD INC (DE)
Stock Dividend - 100% 11/15/1968
Name changed to American Express Capital Fund, Inc. 04/27/1970
American Express Capital Fund, Inc. name changed to Capital Fund of America, Inc. 07/25/1975 which merged into New Perspective Fund, Inc. (MD) 11/03/1978 which reincorporated in Delaware as New Perspective Fund 12/01/2012

COMMONWEALTH CAP LTD (CO)
Recapitalized as Phoenix Network, Inc. 11/09/1987
Each share Common $0.001 par exchanged for (0.01) share Common $0.001 par
Phoenix Network, Inc. merged into Qwest Communications International Inc. 03/30/1998 which merged into CenturyLink, Inc. 04/01/2011

COMMONWEALTH CASUALTY CO. (PA)
Merged into Independence Indemnity Co. 07/19/1931
Details not available

COMMONWEALTH CORP. (FL)
Merged into Commonwealth Savings Association 12/22/1981
Each share Common no par exchanged for $3.86 cash

COMMONWEALTH CORP. OF OREGON
Reorganized as Commonwealth, Inc. 00/00/1952
Each share Preferred $100 par exchanged for (2) shares Preferred $50 par
Each share Common $10 par exchanged for (2) shares new Common $10 par
(See Commonwealth, Inc.)

COMMONWEALTH CREDIT CORP. OF UTAH (UT)
Merged into Western States Thrift on a (1) for (8.1292) basis 11/28/1960
Western States Thrift name changed to Western States Thrift & Loan Co. 07/06/1966
(See Western States Thrift & Loan Co.)

COMMONWEALTH DOCTORS HOSP INC (VA)
Liquidation completed
Each share Capital Stock $10 par exchanged for initial distribution of $10 cash 02/11/1976
Each share Capital Stock $10 par received second distribution of $2.50 cash 07/07/1976
Each share Capital Stock $10 par received third and final distribution of $2.052272 cash 01/19/1979

COMMONWEALTH DRILLING (BC) LTD. (BC)
Completely liquidated 00/00/1979
Each share Capital Stock no par received first and final distribution of $23 cash

COMMONWEALTH DRILLING (NORTHERN) LTD. (ON)
Under plan of merger each share Common no par automatically became (1) share Commonwealth Drilling (Western) Ltd. 7% Non-Cum. Preference $2.03 par 04/30/1971
(See Commonwealth Drilling (Western) Ltd.)

COMMONWEALTH DRILLING (WESTERN) LTD. (ON)
Called for redemption 02/15/1972
Public interest eliminated

COMMONWEALTH EDISON CO (IL)
Capital Stock $100 par changed to $25 par and (3) additional shares issued 00/00/1937
Capital Stock $25 par reclassified as Common $25 par 00/00/1951
$1.32 Preferred $25 par called for redemption 08/01/1954
$1.40 Preferred $25 par called for redemption 08/01/1954
Common $25 par changed to $12.50 par and (1) additional share issued 11/01/1961
4.64% Preferred $100 par called for redemption 01/19/1962
5.25% Preferred $100 par called for redemption 12/06/1962
9.44% Prior Preferred $100 par called for redemption 03/20/1972
$10.875 Preference no par called for redemption 11/01/1989
$12.75 Preference no par called for redemption 08/01/1990
$11.125 Preference no par called for redemption 11/01/1991
$13.25 Preference Ser. B no par called for redemption 11/01/1991
$2.375 Preference no par called for redemption 06/28/1993
$2.875 Preference no par called for redemption 06/28/1993
$9.30 Preference no par called for redemption 11/01/1993
$11.70 Preference no par called for redemption 11/01/1993
Under plan of reorganization each share Common $12.50 par automatically became (1) share UniCom Corp. Common no par 09/01/1994
8.2% Preference no par called for redemption at $101 on 01/19/1999
$8.40 Preference Ser. B no par called for redemption at $101 on 01/19/1999
$1.90 Preference no par called for redemption at $25.25 on 01/19/1999
$1.96 Preference no par called for redemption at $17.11 on 01/19/1999
$2 Preference no par called for redemption at $26.04 on 01/19/1999
$7.24 Preference no par called for redemption at $101 on 01/19/1999
$8.38 Preference no par called for redemption at $100.16 on 01/19/1999
$8.40 Preference no par called for redemption at $101 on 01/19/1999
$2.425 Preference no par called for redemption at $25 on 08/01/1999
$6.875 Preference no par called for redemption at $100 on 05/01/2000
$1.425 Conv. Preferred no par called for redemption at $42 on 08/01/2000

COMMONWEALTH ENERGY CORP (AB)
Merged into Empire Energy Corp. (UT) 06/29/2001
Each share Common no par exchanged for (0.16666666) share new Common $0.001 par
Empire Energy Corp. (UT) reorganized in Nevada as Empire Energy Corp. International 04/26/2004

COMMONWEALTH ENERGY CORP (CA)
Conv. Preferred converted to Common no par 07/03/2004
Under plan of reorganization each share Common no par automatically became (1) share Commerce Energy Group, Inc. (DE) Common $0.001 par 07/06/2004
(See Commerce Energy Group, Inc. (DE))

COMMONWEALTH ENERGY INC (AB)
Name changed to Scimitar Hydrocarbons Corp. 02/08/1996
Scimitar Hydrocarbons Corp. acquired by Rally Energy Corp. 07/10/2002
(See Rally Energy Corp.)

COMMONWEALTH ENERGY SYS (MA)
9.80% Preferred $100 par called for redemption 07/01/1987
Common Shares of Bene. Int. $4 par split (2) for (1) by issuance of (1) additional Share payable 06/05/1996 to holders of record 05/15/1996 Ex date - 06/06/1996
Merged into NSTAR 08/25/1999
Each Common Share of Bene. Int. $4 par exchanged for either (1.05) shares Common $1 par, $44.10 cash, or a combination thereof
Note: Cash electors received 35.489% of total holdings in cash and the remaining 64.511% in stock
Holdings of (99) shares or fewer received cash only
Option to receive stock and cash or only expired 09/21/1999
NSTAR merged into Northeast Utilities 04/10/2012
(See Northeast Utilities)

COMMONWEALTH EQUITIES INC (DE)
Reorganized under the laws of Nevada as Sun Vacation Properties, Corp. 04/07/2003
Each share Common 10¢ par exchanged for (0.1) share Common 10¢ par
(See Sun Vacation Properties, Corp.)

COMMONWEALTH EQUITY TR (CA)
Reorganized as Peregrine Real Estate Trust 10/07/1994
Holdings of (25) to (200) Shares who failed to make an election received $0.20 cash per share
Holdings of (201) Shares or more exchanged for (0.0975) Share of Bene. Int. $1 par per Share
Holdings of (24) or fewer Shares did not participate and are without value
Note: Unexchanged certificates were cancelled and holders forfeited all rights to receive shares or cash 10/07/1995
(See Peregrine Real Estate Trust)

COMMONWEALTH EQUITY TR USA (CA)
Name changed to USA Real Estate Investment Trust 12/24/1994
(See USA Real Estate Investment Trust)

COMMONWEALTH FD INDENTS TR PLANS A & B (MA)
Trust terminated 08/11/1989
Details not available

COMMONWEALTH FD INDENTS TR PLANS C & D (MA)
Trust terminated 08/11/1989
Details not available

COMMONWEALTH FDG INC (DE)
Recapitalized as A.I.S., Inc. 09/19/1987
Each share Common $0.0001 par exchanged for (0.33333333) share Common $0.0001 par
A.I.S., Inc. name changed to Troll's Seafood Ltd. 06/02/1989 which name changed to Valdor Ltd. 05/00/1998 which name changed to Pear Technologies, Inc. 06/12/1998 which recapitalized as Sanswire Technologies Inc. 05/20/2002 which name changed to Wireless Holdings Group, Inc. 03/30/2005 which recapitalized as Vega Promotional Systems, Inc. (DE) 12/26/2006 which reorganized in Wyoming as Vega Biofuels, Inc. 07/29/2010

COMMONWEALTH FED SVGS BK (LOWELL, MA)
Common 1¢ par split (2) for (1) by issuance of (1) additional share 10/05/1983
Name changed to ComFed Savings Bank (Lowell, MA) 08/07/1984
ComFed Savings Bank (Lowell, MA) reorganized in Delaware as Comfed Bancorp, Inc. 04/01/1988
(See Comfed Bancorp, Inc.)

COMMONWEALTH FED SVGS BK (VALLEY FORGE, PA)
Name changed to Commonwealth Savings Bank (Valley Forge, PA) 06/30/1974
Commonwealth Savings Bank (Valley Forge, PA) reorganized as Commonwealth Bancorp, Inc. 06/17/1976
(See Commonwealth Bancorp, Inc.)

COMMONWEALTH FINL CORP (PA)
Common $10 par changed to $5 par 09/01/1960
Common $5 par changed to $1 par 11/24/1965
Declared insolvent 02/27/1970
No stockholders' equity

COMMONWEALTH FINL GROUP REAL ESTATE INVT TR (TX)
Name changed to First Continental Real Estate Investment Trust 06/28/1985
First Continental Real Estate Investment Trust merged into Parkway Inc. (TX) 06/14/1994 which reincorporated in Maryland as Parkway Properties, Inc. 08/02/1996

COMMONWEALTH FUND FOR GROWTH, INC. (DE)
Name changed to Ivy Fund, Inc. (DE) 03/29/1967
Ivy Fund, Inc. (DE) reincorporated in Massachusetts as Ivy Growth Fund 04/01/1984
(See Ivy Growth Fund)

COMMONWEALTH GAS & ELECTRIC COMPANIES
Dissolved 00/00/1938
Details not available

COMMONWEALTH GAS CORP (DE)
Liquidation completed
Each share Common $1 par received initial distribution of $0.40 cash 07/03/1973
Each share Common $1 par exchanged for second distribution of $12.60 cash 08/10/1973
Each share Common $1 par received third distribution of $0.60 cash 12/31/1973
Each share Common $1 par received fourth and final distribution of $0.575 cash 12/31/1976

COMMONWEALTH GEN LTD (DE)
Charter cancelled and declared inoperative and void for non-payment of taxes 03/01/1977

COMMONWEALTH GENERAL LLC (TURKS & CAICOS ISLANDS)
8.875% Monthly Income Preferred called for redemption 05/31/1999

COMMONWEALTH GOLD CORP (BC)
Merged into Aber Resources Ltd. (New) 04/19/1994
Each share Common no par exchanged for (0.33333333) share Common no par
Aber Resources Ltd. (New) name changed to Aber Diamond Corp.

08/18/2000 which name changed to Harry Winston Diamond Corp. 11/19/2007 which name changed to Dominion Diamond Corp. 03/27/2013
(See Dominion Diamond Corp.)

COMMONWEALTH HOLIDAY INNS CDA LTD (ON)
6.5% Conv. Preference $200 par called for redemption 03/19/1971
Common no par changed to $1 par 03/29/1971
Common $1 par changed to no par 06/13/1974
8% Conv. Preferred Ser. A $25 par called for redemption 07/20/1979
Each share old Common no par exchanged for (0.00003333) share new Common no par 06/23/1980
Note: In effect holders received $12.25 cash per share and public interest was eliminated

COMMONWEALTH ICE & COLD STORAGE CO. (MA)
Merged into Boston Fish Market Corp. 08/30/1957
Each share Common $100 par exchanged for (0.2) share Common $100 par
Boston Fish Market Corp. name changed to Fulham, Maloney & Co., Inc. 06/22/1973 which name changed to Fulham (John) & Sons, Inc. 12/18/1979
(See Fulham (John) & Sons, Inc.)

COMMONWEALTH INCOME FD (DE)
Name changed to American Express Income Fund, Inc. 04/27/1970
American Express Income Fund, Inc. name changed to American Income Investments, Inc. 07/25/1975 which merged into Income Fund of America, Inc. (DE) 07/31/1976 which reincorporated in Maryland 09/22/1983 which reorganized in Delaware as Income Fund of America 10/01/2010

COMMONWEALTH INDS CORP (DE)
Reincorporated 04/20/1981
Each share old Class A Common no par exchanged for (0.1) share new Class A Common no par 12/29/1978
State of incorporation changed from (IL) to (DE) 04/20/1981
New Class A Common no par split (3) for (2) by issuance of (0.5) additional share 08/05/1988
Each share new Class A Common no par exchanged again for (0.1) share new Class A Common no par 08/08/1989
Voluntarily dissolved 03/14/1996
Details not available

COMMONWEALTH INDS INC (DE)
Merged into Aleris International, Inc. 12/09/2004
Each share Common $1 par exchanged for (0.815) share Common 10¢ par
(See Aleris International, Inc.)

COMMONWEALTH INDS INC (PA)
Common no par split (5) for (4) by issuance of (0.25) additional share 05/04/1980
Name changed to Leader Healthcare Organization, Inc. 05/30/1980
(See Leader Healthcare Organization, Inc.)

COMMONWEALTH INSURANCE SHARES SERIES A & B
Trusts liquidated 00/00/1935
Details not available

COMMONWEALTH INSURANCE SHARES SERIES C
Trust liquidated 00/00/1936
Details not available

COMMONWEALTH INTERNATIONAL & GENERAL FUND, INC. (DE)
Name changed to Commonwealth Capital Fund, Inc. 06/21/1965
Commonwealth Capital Fund, Inc. name changed to American Express Capital Fund, Inc. 04/27/1970 which name changed to Capital Fund of America, Inc. 07/25/1975 which merged into New Perspective Fund, Inc. (MD) 11/03/1978 which reincorporated in Delaware as New Perspective Fund 12/01/2012

COMMONWEALTH INTERNATIONAL CORP., LTD. (CANADA)
Name changed to Eaton Commonwealth Fund Ltd. 04/15/1974
Eaton Commonwealth Fund Ltd. name changed to Eaton Bay Commonwealth Fund Ltd. 04/12/1978 which name changed back to Eaton Commonwealth Fund Ltd. 04/16/1986 which name changed to Viking Commonwealth Fund Ltd. 04/16/1987 which name changed to Laurentian Commonwealth Fund Ltd. 05/31/1993 which name changed to Strategic Value Commonwealth Fund Ltd. 06/05/1997 which name changed to StrategicNova Commonwealth Fund Ltd. 09/26/2000
(See StrategicNova Commonwealth Fund Ltd.)

COMMONWEALTH INTL LEVERAGE FD LTD (CANADA)
Common $1 par changed to 25¢ par and (3) additional shares issued 03/31/1969
Name changed to Eaton Leverage Fund Ltd. 04/15/1974
Eaton Leverage Fund Ltd. name changed to Eaton/Bay Leverage Fund Ltd. 04/12/1978

COMMONWEALTH INTL VENTURE FD LTD (ON)
Name changed to Eaton International Fund Ltd. 04/15/1974
Eaton International Fund Ltd. name changed to Eaton Bay International Fund Ltd. (ONT) 04/12/1978 which reincorporated in Canada 04/16/1980 which name changed back to Eaton International Fund 04/16/1986 which name changed to Viking International Fund Ltd. 04/16/1987 which name changed to Laurentian International Fund Ltd. 05/31/1993 which name changed to Strategic Value International Fund Ltd. 06/05/1997 which name changed to StrategicNova World Large Cap Fund Ltd. 09/26/2000
(See StrategicNova World Large Cap Fund Ltd.)

COMMONWEALTH INVT CO (DE)
Each share Capital Stock no par exchanged for (6) shares Capital Stock $1 par 00/00/1933
Name changed to American Express Investment Fund, Inc. 04/27/1970
American Express Investment Fund, Inc. name changed to American Balanced Fund, Inc. (MD) 07/25/1975 which reincorporated in Delaware as American Balanced Fund 03/01/2010

COMMONWEALTH INVESTMENT CORP. (SD)
Charter cancelled for failure to file reports 07/01/1970

COMMONWEALTH INVESTORS CORP.
Liquidated 00/00/1935
Details not available

COMMONWEALTH INVESTORS SYNDICATE LTD. (BC)
Adjudicated bankrupt 02/25/1969
No stockholders' equity

COMMONWEALTH LD TITLE INS CO (PA)
Common $5 par changed to $1.66666666 par and (2) additional shares issued 02/17/1964
Acquired by Provident National Corp. 10/31/1969
Each share 4% Preferred $100 par exchanged for (3.3) shares $1.80 Conv. Preferred $1 par
Each share Common $1.66666666 par exchanged for (1) share $1.80 Conv. Preferred $1 par
Provident National Corp. merged into PNC Financial Corp 01/19/1983 which name changed to PNC Bank Corp. 02/08/1993 which name changed to PNC Financial Services Group, Inc. 03/15/2000

COMMONWEALTH LEAD MINING CO. (UT)
Name changed to Commonwealth Resources Corp. 05/01/1962
(See Commonwealth Resources Corp.)

COMMONWEALTH LIFE INSURANCE CO. (OK)
Merged into First United Life Insurance Co. 00/00/1959
Details not available

COMMONWEALTH LIFE INS CO (KY)
Capital Stock $10 par changed to $2 par and (4) additional shares issued plus a 50% stock dividend paid 12/07/1955
Capital Stock $2 par changed to $1 par and (1) additional share issued 11/01/1963
Stock Dividends - 33.33333333% 10/31/1951; 33.33333333% 12/31/1957; 25% 10/05/1959
Through voluntary exchange offer 100% acquired by Capital Holding Corp. as of 12/31/1977
Public interest eliminated

COMMONWEALTH LIGHT & POWER CO.
In process of dissolution 00/00/1945
Details not available

COMMONWEALTH LN CO (IN)
Merged into Beneficial Indiana Inc. 09/28/1990
Each share 4% Preferred $100 par exchanged for $44.50 cash

COMMONWEALTH MINERALS LTD (BC)
Merged into Meridor Resources Ltd. 04/01/1985
Each share Common no par exchanged for (0.14) share Common no par
Meridor Resources Ltd. merged into Hughes Lang Corp. 08/01/1989 which merged into CanGold Resources Inc. (BC) 01/31/1994 which reorganized in Ontario as Amalgamated CanGold Inc. 07/31/1995 which merged into Central Asia Goldfields Corp. 01/08/1996
(See Central Asia Goldfields Corp.)

COMMONWEALTH MTG AMER L P (DE)
Partnership dissolved 06/22/1990
Unitholders are unlikely to receive any distributions

COMMONWEALTH MTG INC (MA)
Acquired by Commonwealth Mortgage Acquisition Inc. 07/25/1989
Each share Common 10¢ par exchanged for $8 cash

COMMONWEALTH NAT RES INC (VA)
$2 Conv. Preferred Ser. A $10 par called for redemption 12/26/1980
Merged into Columbia Gas System, Inc. 08/21/1981
Each share Common $5 par exchanged for (1.05) shares Common $10 par
Columbia Gas System, Inc. name changed to Columbia Energy Group 01/16/1998 which merged into NiSource Inc. 11/01/2000

COMMONWEALTH NATL BK (BOSTON, MA)
Common $22.50 par changed to $11.25 par and (1) additional share issued 03/13/1968
Reorganized as Commonwealth National Corp. 05/31/1969
Each share Common $11.25 par exchanged for (1) share Common $1 par
(See Commonwealth National Corp.)

COMMONWEALTH NATL BK (HARRISBURG, PA)
Common $10 par changed to $5 par and (1) additional share issued 04/02/1973
Under plan of reorganization each share Common $5 par automatically became (1) share Commonwealth National Financial Corp. Common $5 par 03/05/1982
(See Commonwealth National Financial Corp.)

COMMONWEALTH NATL BK (SAN FRANCISCO, CA)
Completely liquidated in 07/00/1970
Each share Capital Stock $10 par exchanged for first and final distribution of $21.67191133 cash

COMMONWEALTH NATL BK (WORCESTER, MA)
Under plan of reorganization each share Common $5 par automatically became (1) share CNB Financial Corp. Common $1 par 12/16/2005
CNB Financial Corp. merged into United Financial Bancorp, Inc. (MD) 12/04/2009 which merged into United Financial Bancorp, Inc. (CT) 05/01/2014

COMMONWEALTH NATL CORP (MA)
Merged into Patriot Bancorporation 06/09/1982
Each share Common $1 par exchanged for $56 cash

COMMONWEALTH NATL FINL CORP (PA)
Common $5 par split (2) for (1) by issuance of (1) additional share 08/10/1985
Merged into Mellon Bank Corp. 04/02/1986
Each share Common $5 par exchanged for $40 cash

COMMONWEALTH NATIONAL LIFE INSURANCE CO. (MS)
Reorganized as Commonwealth Corp. 06/18/1987
Each share Capital Stock $1 par exchanged for (1) share Common $1.50 par

COMMONWEALTH NATL RLTY TR (MD)
Name changed to Maryland Realty Trust 06/02/1975
Maryland Realty Trust reorganized in Delaware as Maxxus, Inc. 11/30/1983
(See Maxxus, Inc.)

COMMONWEALTH NATURAL GAS CORP. (VA)
Common no par changed to $5 par 00/00/1950
Common $5 par split (2) for (1) by issuance of (1) additional share 04/20/1959
Stock Dividend - 10% 09/01/1961
Under plan of reorganization name changed to Commonwealth Natural Resources Inc. 02/28/1977
Commonwealth Natural Resources Inc. merged into Columbia Gas System, Inc. 08/21/1981 which name changed to Columbia Energy Group 01/16/1998 which merged into NiSource Inc. 11/01/2000

COMMONWEALTH OIL & GAS CO. (CO)
Declared defunct and inoperative for non-payment of taxes 09/30/1958

COMMONWEALTH OIL CO. (FL)
Merged into Jupiter Corp. 3/1/62
Each share Common 1¢ par exchanged for (0.1) share $1.50 Conv. Preferred no par
Jupiter Corp. merged into Jupiter Industries, Inc. 11/12/71
(See Jupiter Industries, Inc.)

COMMONWEALTH OIL REFNG INC (PR)
Each share Common 10¢ par exchanged for (5) shares Common 2¢ par 03/01/1956
Common 2¢ par changed to $5 par 05/02/1966
Common $5 par changed to $1 par 08/24/1977
Plan of reorganization under Chapter 11 Federal Bankruptcy proceedings confirmed 03/01/1990
No stockholders' equity
8% Preferred called for redemption at $20 on 08/01/2006

COMMONWEALTH PETE SVCS LTD (CANADA)
Subord. Preferred $1 par called for redemption 12/10/1938
Acquired by Westburne International Industries Ltd. (AB) 09/30/1969
Each share Common no par exchanged for (2.5) shares Common $1 par and $4 cash
Westburne International Industries Ltd. (AB) reincorporated in Canada 10/18/1977
(See Westburne International Industries Ltd. (Canada))

COMMONWEALTH PETROLEUM LTD. (CANADA)
Name changed to Commonwealth Petroleum Services Ltd. 11/25/1959
Commonwealth Petroleum Services Ltd. acquired by Westburne International Industries Ltd. (AB) 09/30/1969 which reincorporated in Canada 10/18/1977
(See Westburne International Industries Ltd. (Canada))

COMMONWEALTH PICTURES CORP. (ME)
Charter revoked for failure to pay taxes in 1921

COMMONWEALTH POWER CORP.
Acquired by Commonwealth & Southern Corp. in 1930
Details not available

COMMONWEALTH RLTY TR (PA)
Merged into Country & Princeton, Inc. 03/14/1988
Each Class A Share of Bene. Int. no par exchanged for $17.514564 cash

COMMONWEALTH REIT (MD)
8.75% Preferred Ser. B 1¢ par called for redemption at $25 plus $0.401041 accrued dividends on 10/21/2010
7.125% Preferred Ser. C 1¢ par called for redemption at $25 plus $0.4453 accrued dividends on 08/24/2012
Name changed to Equity Commonwealth 08/01/2014

COMMONWEALTH RES CORP (UT)
Each share Capital Stock 10¢ par exchanged for (0.1) share Capital Stock $1 par 12/07/1964
Charter suspended for failure to file annual reports 12/31/1985

COMMONWEALTH SAVINGS & LOAN ASSOCIATION (CA)
Guarantee Stock $5 par changed to $2.50 and (1) additional share issued 8/27/82
Name changed to Del Amo Savings & Loan Association 12/1/82

Del Amo Savings & Loan Association merged into City Holding Co. 4/1/98

COMMONWEALTH SVGS & LN ASSN FLA FT LAUDERDALE (FL)
Placed in conservatorship 07/17/1989
No stockholders' equity

COMMONWEALTH SVGS & LN CORP (ON)
Name changed to Central Ontario Savings & Loan Corp. 07/30/1970
Central Ontario Savings & Loan Corp. merged into Ontario Trust Co. 12/31/1971 which merged into Canada Trust Co.-La Societe Canada Trust (London, ON) 12/31/1976

COMMONWEALTH SVGS ASSN HOUSTON (TX)
Placed in receivership by FSLIC 05/25/1989
No stockholders' equity

COMMONWEALTH SVGS BK (VY FORGE, PA)
Reorganized as Commonwealth Bancorp, Inc. 6/17/96
Each share Common 10¢ par exchanged for (2.077474) shares Common 1¢ par
(See Commonwealth Bancorp, Inc.)

COMMONWEALTH SECURITIES, INC.
Merged into Pathe Industries Inc. (OH) 00/00/1946
Each share 6% Preferred exchanged for (0.3) share 4% Preferred and (0.275) share new Common
Each share Common exchanged for (0.222) share new Common
Pathe Industries, Inc. (OH) name changed to Chesapeake Industries Inc. 04/30/1952 which name changed to America Corp. (OH) 04/29/1959 which recapitalized as America Corp. (DE) 12/31/1963 which name changed to Pathe Industries Inc. (DE) 11/20/1964
(See Pathe Industries Inc. (DE))

COMMONWEALTH SECURITY INVESTORS, INC. (KY)
Merged into Boone (Daniel) Fried Chicken, Inc. 05/00/1969
Details not available

COMMONWEALTH SILVER INC (ID)
Charter forfeited for failure to file reports 12/01/1989

COMMONWEALTH SILVER INDS LTD (DE)
Stock Dividend - 100% 06/30/1971
Name changed to Commonwealth General Ltd. 07/01/1972
(See Commonwealth General Ltd.)

COMMONWEALTH STEEL CO.
Merged into General Steel Castings Corp. 00/00/1929
Details not available

COMMONWEALTH STK FD INC (DE)
Stock Dividends - 200% 4/7/55; 100% 1/25/65
Name changed to American Express Stock Fund, Inc. 4/27/70
American Express Stock Fund, Inc. name changed to Stock Fund of America, Inc. 7/25/75 which merged into Investment Co. of America 6/25/76

COMMONWEALTH TEL CO (PA)
Common $10 par changed to $6.66-2/3 par and (0.5) additional share issued 08/24/1962
Stock Dividend - 10% 04/29/1964
Reorganized as Commonwealth Telephone Enterprises, Inc. (Old) 10/01/1979
Each share Common $6.66-2/3 par exchanged for (2) shares Common $1 par
Commonwealth Telephone Enterprises, Inc. (Old) name changed to C-TEC Corp. 04/24/1986 which recapitalized as Commonwealth Telephone Enterprises Inc. (New) 10/10/1997 which merged into Citizens Communications Co. 03/08/2007 which name changed to Frontier Communications Corp. 07/31/2008

COMMONWEALTH TEL CO VA (VA)
Merged into Continental Telephone Corp. 7/15/71
Each share Common $10 par exchanged for (1.875) shares Common $1 par
Continental Telephone Corp. name changed to Continental Telecom Inc. 5/6/82 which merged into Contel Corp. 5/1/86 which merged into GTE Corp. 3/14/91 which merged into Verizon Communications Inc. 6/30/2000

COMMONWEALTH TEL ENTERPRISES INC (PA)
Name changed to C-TEC Corp. 04/24/1986
C-TEC Corp. recapitalized as Commonwealth Telephone Enterprises Inc. (New) 10/10/1997 which merged into Citizens Communications Co. 03/08/2007 which name changed to Frontier Communications Corp. 07/31/2008

COMMONWEALTH TEL ENTERPRISES INC NEW (PA)
Each share Class B Common $1 par reclassified as (1.09) shares Common $1 par 09/04/2003
Merged into Citizens Communications Co. 03/08/2007
Each share Common $1 par exchanged for (0.768) share Common 25¢ par and $31.31 cash
Citizens Communications Co. name changed to Frontier Communications Corp. 07/31/2008

COMMONWEALTH TELEPHONE CO. (WI)
Name changed to General Telephone Co. of Wisconsin 00/00/1952
General Telephone Co. of Wisconsin merged into GTE MTO Inc. 03/31/1987 which name changed to GTE MTO Inc. 01/01/1988

COMMONWEALTH TELEPHONE CO. OF OHIO (OH)
Acquired by General Telephone & Electronics Corp. on a (2.25) for (1) basis 7/2/60
General Telephone & Electronics Corp. name changed to GTE Corp. 7/1/82 which merged into Verizon Communications Inc. 6/30/2000

COMMONWEALTH TELEPHONE CORP. (IN)
Liquidated 00/00/1950
Details not available

COMMONWEALTH THEATRES INC (MO)
Common $2.50 par split (5) for (4) by issuance of (0.25) additional share 2/15/80
Merged into Commonwealth Theatres Holdings, Inc. 4/26/83
Each share Common $2.50 par exchanged for $24 cash

COMMONWEALTH THEATRES OF PUERTO RICO, INC. (PR)
Merged into Wometco Commonwealth Corp. 11/4/68
Each share Common no par exchanged for (1) share Preferred 10¢ par
(See Wometco Commonwealth Corp.)

COMMONWEALTH TITLE CO. OF PHILADELPHIA (PA)
Each share Capital Stock $100 par exchanged for (1) share 4% Preferred $100 par and (5) shares Common $5 par 00/00/1946
Name changed to Commonwealth Land Title Insurance Co. 01/03/1956
Commonwealth Land Title Insurance Co. acquired by Provident National Corp. 10/31/1969 which merged into PNC Financial Corp 01/19/1983 which name changed to PNC Bank Corp. 02/08/1993 which name changed to PNC Financial Services Group, Inc. 03/15/2000

COMMONWEALTH TRUST CO. (VANCOUVER, BC)
Each Share $100 par exchanged for (0.1) share Class B Common $10 par 07/23/1964
Completely liquidated 01/01/1970
No stockholders' equity

COMMONWEALTH UTD CORP (DE)
Class A $1 par reclassified as Common $1 par 1/17/68
Recapitalized as Iota Industries, Inc. 12/29/72
Each share Common $1 par exchanged for (0.1) share Common $1 par
Conv. Preferred $1 par was affected by a change in name only
(See Iota Industries, Inc.)

COMMONWEALTH UTILITIES CORP.
Dissolved in 1946
Details not available

COMMONWEALTH WATER CO., INC. (KY)
Liquidation completed 1/25/56

COMMONWEALTH WATER CO. (NJ)
5-1/2% 1st Preferred $100 par called for redemption 02/05/1966
5-1/4% 1st Preferred $100 par called for redemption 02/05/1966
5-1/4% 1st Preferred 1958 Series $100 par called for redemption 02/05/1966

COMMONWEALTH WESTN CORP (NV)
Charter revoked for failure to file reports and pay fees 03/03/1980

COMMONWEALTHS DISTRIBUTION, INC.
Completely liquidated in December 1943
Each share Capital Stock exchanged for first and final distribution of 91¢ cash

COMMPAT FINL CORP (FL)
Name changed to Diversified Foodservice Distributors Inc. 11/6/87
(See Diversified Foodservice Distributors Inc.)

COMMSCOPE INC (DE)
Acquired by Cedar I Holding Co., Inc. 01/14/2011
Each share Common 1¢ par exchanged for $31.50 cash

COMMSTAR LTD. (ON)
Merged into Allied Cellular Technology Inc. of Missouri 7/6/98
Details not available

COMMTOUCH SOFTWARE LTD. (ISRAEL)
Each share Ordinary ILS 0.05 par exchanged for (0.33333333) share Ordinary ILS 0.15 par 01/02/2008
Name changed to CYREN Ltd. 02/24/2014

COMMTRON CORP (NJ)
Merged into Ingram Industries Inc. 06/19/1992
Each share Class A Common 1¢ par exchanged for $7.75 cash

COMMUNICARE CORP (FL)
Name changed to Oxford Educational Services, Inc. (FL) 08/06/1999
Oxford Educational Services, Inc. (FL) reincorporated in Delaware as Aspen Global Corp. 01/02/2008 which name changed to Diversified Mortgage Workout Corp. 08/08/2008 which recapitalized as Arem Pacific Corp. 07/29/2013

COMMUNICATE COM INC (NV)
Name changed to Live Current Media Inc. 08/04/2008

COMMUNICATENOW COM INC (DE)
Name changed to American Energy Partners, Inc. (DE) 06/11/2002
American Energy Partners, Inc. (DE) name changed to American Energy Production Inc. 07/16/2002
(See American Energy Production Inc.)

COMMUNICATION & STUDIES, INC. (GA)
Proclaimed dissolved for failure to file annual reports 03/30/1976

COMMUNICATION CABLE INC (NC)
Stock Dividend - 10% 04/30/1991
Merged into Kuhlman Corp. 06/28/1996
Each share Common $1 par exchanged for $14 cash

COMMUNICATION CHANNELS INC (NY)
Stock Dividend - 10% 01/09/1970
Each share old Common 1¢ par exchanged for (0.01666666) share new Common 1¢ par 11/08/1976
Note: In effect holders received $3.25 cash per share and public interest was eliminated

COMMUNICATION CORP AMER (DE)
Each share old Common $0.0001 par exchanged for (0.33333333) share new Common $0.0001 par 12/13/1996
Reorganized under the laws of Nevada as Hidalgo Mining International 04/13/2007
Each share new Common $0.0001 par exchanged for (0.02) share Common $0.0001 par
Hidalgo Mining International (NV) reincorporated in Delaware 01/05/2010 which name changed to Verde Media Group Inc. 09/15/2010

COMMUNICATION INTELLIGENCE CORP NEW (DE)
Name changed to iSign Solutions Inc. 12/14/2015

COMMUNICATION INTELLIGENCE CORP OLD (DE)
Class B Common 1¢ par reclassified as Common 1¢ par 11/01/1991
Reorganized as Communication Intelligence Corp. (New) 11/14/1994
Each share Common 1¢ par exchanged for (0.5) Unit consisting of (2) shares Common 1¢ par and (1) Common Stock Purchase Warrant expiring 12/15/1994
Communication Intelligence Corp. (New) name changed to iSign Solutions Inc. 12/14/2015

COMMUNICATION MUSIC INTEGRATED NETWORK INC (CO)
Administratively dissolved 06/01/2000

COMMUNICATION SCIENCES INC (MN)
Statutorily dissolved 01/17/2006

COMMUNICATION TECHNOLOGY COS INC (DE)
Recapitalized as Turquoise Development Co. 2/17/2006
Each share Common $0.001 par exchanged for (0.001) share Common $0.001 par

COMMUNICATIONS & CABLE INC (DE)
Name changed to IMNET, Inc. 03/22/1989
IMNET, Inc. name changed to IMGE, Inc. 10/07/1992 which name changed to nStor Technologies, Inc. 11/15/1996
(See nStor Technologies, Inc.)

COMMUNICATIONS & ENTMT CORP (NV)
Each share Class A Common 1¢ par exchanged for (0.6375) share old Common 1¢ par 00/00/1992
Each share old Common 1¢ par exchanged for (0.16666666) share new Common 1¢ par 03/18/1996
Name changed to Odyssey Pictures Corp. 01/21/1997
(See Odyssey Pictures Corp.)

COMMUNICATIONS CENT INC (GA)
Merged into Davel Communications Group, Inc. 02/03/1998
Each share Common 1¢ par exchanged for $10.50 cash

COMMUNICATIONS CONSULTANTS INC (MN)
Name changed to Other Telephone Co. 06/09/1971
Other Telephone Co. name changed to Eastern Electric Inc. 03/05/1975 which name changed to Texergy Corp. 05/04/1981

COMMUNICATIONS CORP AMER (NV)
Stock Dividend - 50% 05/18/1981
Liquidated and dissolved 07/06/1988
No stockholders' equity

COMMUNICATIONS CYBERNETICS CORP (CO)
Note: Although reported Communications Cybernetics Corp. changed its name from International Airlines, Inc. 00/00/1972, and stock was trading under that name for years, the name change was never filed with the Colorado Secretary of State
(See International Airlines, Inc.)

COMMUNICATIONS DVR INC (CANADA)
Name changed to Exploration Aurtois Inc. 11/08/2010

COMMUNICATIONS GROUP INC (DE)
Reincorporated 04/01/1988
State of incorporation changed from (PA) to (DE) 04/01/1988
Name changed to CTI Group (Holdings) Inc. 11/16/1995
(See CTI Group (Holdings) Inc.)

COMMUNICATIONS INC (DE)
Name changed to Communications Properties, Inc. 06/23/1969
(See Communications Properties, Inc.)

COMMUNICATIONS INDS INC (TX)
Each share Common 10¢ par exchanged for (3) shares Common 50¢ par 12/10/1964
Common 50¢ par split (3) for (2) by issuance of (0.5) additional share 07/03/1978
Common 50¢ par split (3) for (2) by issuance of (0.5) additional share 04/01/1980
Common 50¢ par split (3) for (2) by issuance of (05) additional share 01/02/1981
Common 50¢ par split (3) for (2) by issuance of (0.5) additional share 01/04/1982
Stock Dividend - 50% 01/02/1968
Merged into Pacific Telesis Group 02/28/1986
Each share Common 50¢ par exchanged for $32.59 cash

COMMUNICATIONS PPTYS INC (DE)
Merged into Times Mirror Co. (Old) 04/30/1980
Each share Common $1 par exchanged for $17 cash

COMMUNICATIONS RESH INC (NV)
Recapitalized as Stratus Entertainment, Inc. 04/11/2007
Each share Common $0.001 par exchanged for (0.00033333) share Common $0.001 par
Stratus Entertainment, Inc. name changed to Latin Television, Inc. (New) 09/10/2007 which recapitalized as Pure Play Music, Ltd. 07/10/2008
(See Pure Play Music, Ltd.)

COMMUNICATIONS SALES & LEASING INC (MD)
Name changed to Uniti Group Inc. 02/27/2017

COMMUNICATIONS SATELLITE CORP (DC)
Common Ser. 1 no par split (2) for (1) by issuance of (1) additional share 06/27/1983
Common Ser. 2 no par split (2) for (1) by issuance of (1) additional share 06/27/1983
Name changed to COMSAT Corp. 05/24/1993
COMSAT Corp. merged into Lockheed Martin Corp. 08/03/2000

COMMUNICATIONS SYS AMER INC (DE)
Charter cancelled and declared inoperative and void for non-payment of taxes 03/01/1975

COMMUNICATIONS SYS INTL INC (AB)
Name changed to CSI Wireless Inc. 07/07/2000
CSI Wireless Inc. name changed to Hemisphere GPS Inc. 05/15/2007 which name changed to AgJunction Inc. 05/29/2013

COMMUNICATIONS SYS INTL INC (CO)
Each share old Common no par exchanged for (0.25) share new Common no par 07/28/1998
Each share new Common no par exchanged again for (0.5) share new Common no par 08/31/1998
Name changed to Redijet, Inc. and new Common no par changed to $0.001 par 06/21/2007
Redijet, Inc. name changed to Umairco, Inc. 09/27/2013 which name changed to Digital Arts Media Network, Inc. 03/10/2015

COMMUNICATIONS TRANSMISSION INC (DE)
Assets sold for the benefit of creditors 00/00/1992
Stockholders' equity unlikely

COMMUNICATIONS WORLD INTL INC (CO)
Each share Class A Common no par exchanged for (0.1) share old Common no par 10/14/1992
Each share old Common no par exchanged for (0.2) share new Common no par 11/23/1993
Name changed to Active Link Communications Inc. 11/09/2000
(See Active Link Communications, Inc.)

COMMUNICORP CORP (ON)
Delisted from Toronto Stock Exchange 10/05/2004

COMMUNIQUE CORP (NV)
Name changed 10/10/1997
Name changed from Communique Wireless Corp. to Communique Corp. 10/10/1997
Name changed to Formal Systems America Inc. 12/17/1998
(See Formal Systems America Inc.)

COMMUNITIES FIRST FINL CORP (CA)
Each share Perpetual Preferred Ser. A $100 par exchanged for (11.025) shares Common no par 09/02/2015
(Additional Information in Active)

COMMUNITRONICS AMER INC (UT)
Each share Common 1¢ par exchanged for (0.01) share Common $1 par 08/14/2002
Reorganized under the laws of Nevada as RPM Advantage, Inc. 04/12/2006
Each share new Common no par exchanged for (0.00166666) share Common no par

(See RPM Advantage, Inc.)

COMMUNITRONICS HLDGS LTD (DE)
Recapitalized as Dr. Squeeze International Inc. 09/28/1998
Each share Common $0.0001 par exchanged for (0.01428571) share Common $0.0001 par
Dr. Squeeze International Inc. name changed to American Resource Management, Inc. 06/20/2001 which name changed to EffTec International, Inc. 09/21/2007

COMMUNITY ALLIANCE INC
SEC revoked common stock registration 02/20/2014

COMMUNITY BANC-CORP SHEBOYGAN INC (WI)
Merged into Heartland Financial USA, Inc. 01/16/2015
Each share Common no par exchanged for (0.844) share Common no par

COMMUNITY BANCORP (NV)
Chapter 7 bankruptcy proceedings terminated 03/15/2016
Stockholders' equity unlikely

COMMUNITY BANCORP INC (CT)
Merged into Landmark/Community Bancorp, Inc. 07/29/1988
Each share Common $3.33 par exchanged for (1) share Common 1¢ par

COMMUNITY BANCORP INC (DE)
Stock Dividends - 5% payable 11/30/1999 to holders of record 11/15/1999; 5% payable 11/30/2000 to holders of record 11/15/2000; 5% payable 11/30/2001 to holders of record 11/15/2001 Ex date - 11/13/2001; 5% payable 11/29/2002 to holders of record 11/15/2002 Ex date - 11/13/2002
Merged into First Community Bancorp (CA) 10/26/2006
Each share Common $0.625 par exchanged for (0.735) share Common no par
First Community Bancorp (CA) reincorporated in Delaware as PacWest Bancorp 05/14/2008

COMMUNITY BANCORP INC (MA)
Acquired by Citizens Financial Group, Inc. 10/31/2003
Each share Common $2.50 par exchanged for $19.75 cash

COMMUNITY BANCORP INC (PA)
Merged into USBANCORP, Inc. 03/23/1992
Each share Common 1¢ par exchanged for (0.2179) share Common $2.50 par and $9.45 cash
USBANCORP, Inc. name changed to AmeriServ Financial, Inc. 05/07/2001

COMMUNITY BANCORP INC N Y (NY)
Name changed to Hudson Chartered Bancorp, Inc. 09/30/1994
Hudson Chartered Bancorp, Inc. name changed to Premier National Bancorp, Inc. 07/17/1998 which merged into M&T Bank Corp. 02/09/2001

COMMUNITY BANCORP NEW JERSEY (PA)
Common $5 par split (3) for (2) by issuance of (0.5) additional share payable 09/20/2002 to holders of record 09/10/2002 Ex date - 09/11/2002
Stock Dividends - 3% payable 08/02/1999 to holders of record 07/19/1999; 5% payable 05/01/2000 to holders of record 04/17/2000; 5% payable 05/15/2001 to holders of record 04/23/2001; 5% payable 05/15/2002 to holders of record 04/23/2002 Ex date - 04/19/2002; 5% payable 05/15/2003 to holders of

record 04/28/2003 Ex date - 04/24/2003
Merged into Sun Bancorp, Inc. 07/08/2004
Each share Common $5 par exchanged for (0.8715) share Common $1 par
Sun Bancorp, Inc. merged into OceanFirst Financial Corp. 01/31/2018

COMMUNITY BANCORPORATION (OH)
Name changed to Westford Group, Inc. 06/08/1979
(See Westford Group, Inc)

COMMUNITY BANCORPORATION INC (SC)
Merged into Branch Corp. 07/14/1987
Each share Common 10¢ par exchanged for (1.3) shares Common $2.50 par
Branch Corp. name changed to BB&T Financial Corp. 05/10/1988 which merged into Southern National Corp. 02/28/1995 which merged into BB&T Corp. 05/19/1997

COMMUNITY BANCSHARES CORP (NJ)
Merged into First Fidelity Bancorporation (Old) 09/28/1985
Each share Common $5 par exchanged for (1) share Common $6.25 par
First Fidelity Bancorporation (Old) merged into First Fidelity Bancorporation (New) 02/29/1988 which merged into First Union Corp. 01/01/1996 which name changed to Wachovia Corp. (Ctfs. dated after 09/01/2001) 09/01/2001 which merged into Wells Fargo & Co. (New) 12/31/2008

COMMUNITY BANCSHARES INC (NC)
Stock Dividend - 100% 07/23/1995
Merged into United Community Bancorp 12/31/2002
Each share Common $5 par exchanged for (1.2575) shares Common $1 par
United Community Bancorp name changed to Integrity Financial Corp. 05/30/2003 which merged into FNB United Corp. 04/28/2006 which name changed to CommunityOne Bancorp 07/01/2013

COMMUNITY BANCSHARES INC (TN)
Merged into First Tennessee National Corp. 02/24/1995
Each share Common $1 par exchanged for (0.41468) share Common $2.50 par
First Tennessee National Corp. name changed to First Horizon National Corp. 04/20/2004

COMMUNITY BANCSHARES WEST GA INC (GA)
Company's sole asset placed in receivership 06/26/2009
Stockholders' equity unlikely

COMMUNITY BANK & TRUST CO. (NEW HAVEN, CT)
Merged into Second National Bank (New Haven, CT) 06/30/1961
Each share Capital Stock $25 par exchanged for (2) shares Common $12.50 par
Second National Bank (New Haven, CT) name changed to Second New Haven Bank (New Haven, CT) 09/01/1972 which was acquired by Colonial Bancorp, Inc. (CT) 04/12/1975 which merged into Bank of Boston Corp. 06/20/1985 which name changed to BankBoston Corp. 04/25/1997 which merged into Fleet Boston Corp. 10/01/1999 which name changed to to FleetBoston Financial Corp. 04/18/2000 which merged into Bank of America Corp. 04/01/2004

COMMUNITY BK & TR CO (FAIRMONT, WV)
Reorganized as CB&T Financial Corp. 04/01/1984
Each share Common $10 par exchanged for (2) shares Common $1 par
CB&T Financial Corp. acquired by Huntington Bancshares Inc. 06/25/1993

COMMUNITY BK & TR CO (PAOLI, PA)
Acquired by CP Financial Corp. 03/13/1970
Each share Capital Stock $10 par exchanged for (5.25) shares Common $1 par
CP Financial Corp. name changed to Central Penn National Corp. 05/06/1976 which merged into Meridian Bancorp, Inc. 06/30/1983 which merged into CoreStates Financial Corp 04/09/1996 which merged into First Union Corp. 04/28/1998 which name changed to Wachovia Corp. (Ctfs. dated after 09/01/2001) 09/01/2001 which merged into Wells Fargo & Co. (New) 12/31/2008

COMMUNITY BK & TR CO (RUTHERFORDTON, NC)
Common $2.50 par split (2) for (1) by by issuance of (1) additional share 00/00/1988
Merged into Carolina First Bancshares, Inc. 06/04/1998
Each share Common $2.50 par exchanged for (0.72716) share Common $2.50 par
Carolina First Bancshares, Inc. merged into First Charter Corp. 04/04/2000 which merged into Fifth Third Bancorp 06/06/2008

COMMUNITY BK & TR CO (WOLFEBORO, NH)
Merged into Chittenden Corp. 10/31/2007
Each share Common $1 par exchanged for $33.37 cash

COMMUNITY BK (BAD AXE, MI)
Stock Dividend - 10% 03/16/1971
Acquired by Peoples Banking Corp. 06/30/1981
Each share Common $10 par exchanged for $50 cash

COMMUNITY BANK (DIVERNON, IL)
Under plan of reorganization each share Common $1 par automatically became (1) share South Sangamon Banc Shares, Inc. Common $1 par 04/01/1983
South Sangamon Banc Shares, Inc. merged into Illini Community Bancorp, Inc. 09/14/1984 which name changed to Illini Corp. 04/21/1994
(See Illini Corp.)

COMMUNITY BK (GRANTS PASS, OR)
Common split (2) for (1) by issuance of (1) additional share payable 06/22/2000 to holders of record 03/01/2000 Ex date - 06/23/2000
Merged into Cascade Bancorp 01/02/2004
Each share Common exchanged for (1) share Common no par
Cascade Bancorp merged into First Interstate BancSystem, Inc. 05/30/2017

COMMUNITY BANK (GREENVILLE, SC)
Under plan of reorganization each share Common $10 par automatically became (1) share Community Bancorporation, Inc. Common $10 par 05/31/1985
Community Bancorporation, Inc. merged into Branch Corp. 07/14/1987 which name changed to BB&T Financial Corp. 05/10/1988 which merged into Southern National Corp. 02/28/1995 which merged into BB & T Corp. 05/19/1997

COMMUNITY BANK (INDIANOLA, MS)
Acquired by Community Bank, N.A. (Memphis, TN) 01/24/2005
Details not available

COMMUNITY BANK (LAKE OSWEGO, OR)
Merged into Pacwest Bancorp 12/31/1979
Each share Common $20 par exchanged for (1.625) shares Common $5 par
Pacwest Bancorp merged into KeyCorp (NY) 11/07/1986 which merged into KeyCorp (New) (NY) 03/01/1994

COMMUNITY BK (LEMONT, IL)
Placed in receivership 10/30/2009
Stockholders' equity unlikely

COMMUNITY BK (LINDEN, NJ)
Name changed to Community State Bank & Trust Co. (Linden, NJ) 03/31/1969
(See Community State Bank & Trust Co. (Linden, NJ))

COMMUNITY BK (LYNBROOK, NY)
Stock Dividend - 10% 12/17/1969
Merged into Marine Midland Grace Trust Co. (New York, NY) 10/01/1970
Each share Capital Stock $10 par exchanged for (2) shares Capital Stock $10 par
Marine Midland Grace Trust Co. (New York, NY) name changed to Marine Midland Bank (New York, NY) 10/14/1970
(See Marine Midland Bank (New York, NY))

COMMUNITY BK (NAPLES, FL)
Merged into Alabama National BanCorporation (DE) 12/31/1998
Each share Common $2.50 par exchanged for (0.53271) share Common $1 par
Alabama National BanCorporation (DE) merged into Royal Bank of Canada (Montreal, QUE) 02/22/2008

COMMUNITY BK (PASADENA, CA)
13% Preferred Ser. B no par called for redemption at $26.25 on 07/26/1999
Merged into CVB Financial Corp. 08/10/2018
Each share Common no par exchanged for (9.4595) shares Common no par and $56 cash

COMMUNITY BK (PILOT MOUNTAIN, NC)
Stock Dividend - 35% payable 02/23/2001 to holders of record 01/31/2001 Ex date - 02/26/2001
Merged into Southern Community Financial Corp. 01/12/2004
Each share Common $2.50 par exchanged for (1.7034) shares Common no par and $34.50 cash
(See Southern Community Financial Corp.)

COMMUNITY BANK (RENTON, WA)
Acquired by Moore Financial Group Inc. 01/31/1989
Each share Common $10 par exchanged for (5.16477651) shares Common $1 par
Moore Financial Group Inc. name changed to West One Bancorp 04/21/1989 which merged into U.S. Bancorp (OR) 12/26/1995 which merged into U.S. Bancorp (Old) (DE) 08/01/1997 which merged into U.S. Bancorp (New) 02/27/2001 merged into Branch Corp. 07/14/1987 which name changed to BB&T Financial Corp. 05/10/1988 which merged into Southern National Corp. 02/28/1995 which merged into BB & T Corp. 05/19/1997

COMMUNITY BANK (WINSLOW TOWNSHIP, NJ)
Acquired by Citizens Bancorp (NJ) 05/15/1981
Each share Capital Stock $10 par exchanged for (2) shares Capital Stock no par
(See Citizens Bancorp (NJ))

COMMUNITY BK BERGEN CNTY (MAYWOOD, NJ)
Common $5 par split (2) for (1) by issuance of (1) additional share payable 02/01/2006 to holders of record 01/04/2006 Ex date - 02/02/2006
Stock Dividends - 33.33333333% 10/07/1983; 20% 07/10/1986; 20% 02/13/1995; 5% payable 06/28/2013 to holders of record 06/14/2013 Ex date - 06/12/2013; 10% payable 04/27/2016 to holders of record 04/15/2016 Ex date - 04/13/2016
Merged into Sussex Bancorp 01/04/2018
Each share Common $5 par exchanged for (0.97) share Common no par
Sussex Bancorp mame changed to SB One Bancorp 05/02/2018

COMMUNITY BK CAROLINA (GREENSBORO, NC)
Capital Stock $10 par changed to $5 par and (1) additional share issued 04/15/1973
Stock Dividend - 10% 03/31/1980
Merged into Southern National Corp. 03/30/1984
Each share Capital Stock $5 par exchanged for (0.83) share Common $5 par
Southern National Corp. merged into BB&T Corp. 05/19/1997

COMMUNITY BK NATL ASSN (CARMICHAELS, PA)
Common $0.4167 par split (3) for (1) by issuance of (2) additional shares payable 05/10/1999 to holders of record 04/21/1999
Under plan of reorganization each share Common $0.4167 par automatically became (1) share CB Financial Services, Inc. Common $0.4167 par 01/03/2006

COMMUNITY BK NEW JERSEY (FREEHOLD TWP, NJ)
Under plan of reorganization each share Common $5 par automatically became (1) share Community Bancorp of New Jersey (PA) Common $5 par 07/01/1999
Community Bancorp of New Jersey (PA) merged into Sun Bancorp, Inc. 07/08/2004 which merged into OceanFirst Financial Corp. 01/31/2018

COMMUNITY BK NORTHN VA (STERLING, VA)
Common $1 par split (3) for (1) by issuance of (2) additional shares payable 05/01/2000 to holders of record 04/01/2000 Ex date - 05/05/2000
Merged into Mercantile Bankshares Corp. 05/18/2005
Each share Common $1 par exchanged for (0.2604451) share Common $2 par and $7.1251375 cash
Mercantile Bankshares Corp. merged into PNC Financial Services Group, Inc. 03/02/2007

COMMUNITY BK OF LEXINGTON INC (KY)
Merged into Pikeville National Corp. 02/02/1995
Each share Common no par exchanged for (2.25) shares Common $5 par
Pikeville National Corp. name changed to Community Trust Bancorp, Inc. 01/01/1997

COMMUNITY BK OF ORANGE NATL ASSN (MIDDLETOWN, NY)
Name changed to Greater Hudson Bank, N.A. (Middletown, NY) 11/04/2008
Greater Hudson Bank, N.A. (Middletown, NY) name changed to Greater Hudson Bank (Middletown, NY) 07/07/2015

COMMUNITY BK PINELLAS (SEMINOLE, FL)
Merged into Southeast Banking Corp. 09/30/1981
Each share Common $2 par exchanged for (0.6) share Common $5 par
(See Southeast Banking Corp.)

COMMUNITY BK SANTA MARIA (SANTA MARIA, CA)
Common no par split (2) for (1) by issuance of (1) additional share payable 02/15/2005 to holders of record 01/21/2005 Ex date - 02/16/2005
Under plan of reorganization each share Common no par automatically became (1) share Community Bancorp of Santa Maria Common no par 06/30/2017

COMMUNITY BK SHS IND INC (IN)
Stock Dividend - 10% payable 12/27/2004 to holders of record 12/10/2004
Name changed to Your Community Bankshares, Inc. 07/01/2015
Your Community Bankshares, Inc. merged into WesBanco, Inc. 09/09/2016

COMMUNITY BK SOUTH FLA INC (FL)
Merged into CenterState Banks, Inc. 03/01/2016
Each share Common 50¢ par exchanged for (0.8467928) share Common 1¢ par and $0.98947949 cash
CenterState Banks, Inc. name changed to CenterState Bank Corp. 09/08/2017

COMMUNITY BK SYS INC (NY)
Perpetual Preferred Ser. A $1 par called for redemption 03/10/1997 (Additional Information in Active)

COMMUNITY BANKERS ACQUISITION CORP (DE)
Name changed to Community Bankers Trust Corp. (DE) 06/02/2008
Community Bankers Trust Corp. (DE) reincorporated in Virginia 01/01/2014

COMMUNITY BANKERS TR CORP (DE)
Units separated 05/27/2011
Reincorporated under the laws of Virginia 01/01/2014

COMMUNITY BKS FLA INC (FL)
Common $1 par changed to 10¢ par 04/20/1976
Liquidation completed
Each share Common 10¢ par received initial distribution of $3 cash 07/25/1980
Each share Common 10¢ par received second distribution of (1) share Community Bank of Pinellas (Seminole, FL) Common $2 par 01/01/1981
(See Community Bank of Pinellas (Seminole, FL))
Each share Common 10¢ par exchanged for third and final distribution of $0.07 cash 05/22/1981

COMMUNITY BKS GA INC (GA)
Under plan of merger each share Common $5 par exchanged for $20.85 cash 9/19/2005
Note: Holders of (500) shares or more retained their interests

COMMUNITY BKS INC (PA)
Common $5 par split (6) for (5) by issuance of (0.2) additional share 06/03/1992
Common $5 par split (6) for (5) by issuance of (0.2) additional share 11/29/1994
Common $5 par split (3) for (2) by issuance of (0.5) additional share payable 05/10/1998 to holders of record 04/15/1998 Ex date - 05/11/1998
Stock Dividends - 10% payable 05/30/1996 to holders of record 05/15/1996 Ex date - 05/13/1996; 5% payable 04/08/1997 to holders of record 03/24/1997 Ex date - 03/20/1997; 5% payable 04/15/1999 to holders of record 03/31/1999; 5% payable 04/17/2000 to holders of record 03/31/2000; 5% payable 04/30/2001 to holders of record 04/16/2001; 5% payable 04/30/2002 to holders of record 04/16/2002; 5% payable 04/30/2003 to holders of record 04/16/2003 Ex date - 04/14/2003; 20% payable 01/30/2004 to holders of record 01/16/2004; 5% payable 04/30/2004 to holders of record 04/16/2004 Ex date - 04/14/2004; 5% payable 04/28/2006 to holders of record 04/14/2006 Ex date - 04/11/2006
Merged into Susquehanna Bancshares, Inc. 11/16/2007
Each share Common $5 par exchanged for (1.48) shares Common $2 par
Susquehanna Bancshares, Inc. merged into BB&T Corp. 08/01/2015

COMMUNITY BANKSHARES INC (NH)
Merged into CFX Corp. 08/29/1997
Each share Common $1 par exchanged for (2.113) shares Common $0.66666666 par
CFX Corp. merged into Peoples Heritage Financial Group, Inc. 04/10/1998 which name changed to Banknorth Group, Inc. (ME) 05/10/2000 which merged into TD Banknorth Inc. 03/01/2005
(See TD Banknorth Inc.)

COMMUNITY BANKSHARES INC (SC)
Common no par split (2) for (1) by issuance of (1) additional share payable 07/21/1997 to holders of record 07/02/1997 Ex date - 07/22/1997
Stock Dividend - 5% payable 01/31/2000 to holders of record 01/15/2000
Merged into First Citizens Bank & Trust Co., Inc. 10/31/2008
Each share Common no par exchanged for $21 cash

COMMUNITY BANKSHARES INC (VA)
Merged into SouthTrust Corp. 11/30/2001
Each share Common $3 par exchanged for (1.5608) share Common $2.50 par
SouthTrust Corp. merged into Wachovia Corp. (Ctfs. dated after 09/01/2001) 11/01/2004 which merged into Wells Fargo & Co. (New) 12/31/2008

COMMUNITY BANKSHARES MARYLAND INC (MD)
Merged into F & M National Corp. 01/25/2001
Each share Common exchanged for (0.75) share Common $2 par
F & M National Corp. merged into BB&T Corp. 08/09/2001

COMMUNITY BKG CO (NORTH BRANFORD, CT)
Common $10 par changed to $5 par and (1) additional share issued 04/01/1969
Common $5 par changed to $2.50 par and (1) additional share issued 10/06/1971
Stock Dividends - 10% 11/20/1979; 10% 01/15/1981
Merged into State National Bancorp Inc. (DE) 09/28/1981
Each share Common $2.50 par exchanged for (1.25) shares Common $1 par
(See State National Bancorp Inc. (DE))

COMMUNITY BUSINESS BK (WEST SACRAMENTO, CA)
Under plan of reorganization each share Common no par automatically became (1) share CBBC Bancorp Common no par 08/12/2016
(See CBBC Bancorp)

COMMUNITY CAP CORP (SC)
Stock Dividends - 5% payable 10/31/1998 to holders of record 09/30/1998 Ex date - 09/28/1998; 5% payable 07/31/2000 to holders of record 06/30/2000; 5% payable 06/20/2001 to holders of record 05/30/2001; 15% payable 11/16/2007 to holders of record 11/02/2007 Ex date - 10/31/2007
Merged into Park Sterling Corp. 11/01/2011
Each share Common $1 par exchanged for (0.6667) share Common $1 par
Park Sterling Corp. merged into South State Corp. 11/30/2017

COMMUNITY CARE AMER INC (DE)
Merged into IHS Acquisition XXVI 09/25/1997
Each share Common $0.0025 par exchanged for $4 cash

COMMUNITY CARE SVCS INC (NY)
Merged into LHS Merger Sub, Inc. 12/22/1999
Each share Common 1¢ par exchanged for $1.20 cash

COMMUNITY CENT BK CORP (MI)
Stock Dividends - 10% payable 04/30/1997 to holders of record 04/15/1997; 10% payable 05/06/1998 to holders of record 04/21/1998; 10% payable 04/21/1999 to holders of record 04/06/1999; 10% payable 04/21/2000 to holders of record 04/06/2000; 5% payable 06/01/2004 to holders of record 05/03/2004; 5% payable 06/01/2005 to holders of record 05/02/2005 Ex date - 04/28/2005; 5% payable 06/01/2007 to holders of record 05/01/2007 Ex date - 04/27/2007
Principal asset placed in receivership 04/29/2011
Stockholders' equity unlikely

COMMUNITY CHARGE PLAN (NJ)
Under plan of merger each share Common 25¢ par exchanged for $8.17 cash 01/08/1974

COMMUNITY COMPUTER CORP (PA)
Merged into TBC Industries Inc. 10/01/1979
Each share Class A 1¢ par exchanged for (0.3611) share Class A 1¢ par

COMMUNITY CR CO (MN)
Merged into Norwest Corp. 03/16/1994
Each share Common no par exchanged for (1.1996) shares Common $1.66666666 par
Norwest Corp. name changed to Wells Fargo & Co. (New) 11/02/1998

COMMUNITY DISCOUNT CENTERS, INC. (IL)
Each share Common 10¢ par exchanged for (0.2) share Common 50¢ par 07/12/1965
Merged into TSC Industries, Inc. 02/19/1968
Each share Common 50¢ par exchanged for (1) share 70¢ Conv. Preferred Ser. 1 $1 par
TSC Industries, Inc. acquired by National Industries, Inc. (KY) 12/06/1969 which merged into Fuqua Industries, Inc. 01/03/1978 which name changed to Actava Group Inc. 07/21/1993 which name changed to Metromedia International Group, Inc. 11/01/1995
(See Metromedia International Group, Inc.)

COMMUNITY EQUITIES CORP (UT)
Name changed to Atlantica, Inc. 03/26/1996

COMMUNITY EQUITIES INC (DE)
Charter cancelled and declared void for non-payment of taxes 03/01/1997

COMMUNITY FED BANCORP INC (DE)
Merged into First M&F Corp. 11/22/1999
Each share Common 1¢ par exchanged for (0.2855) share Common $5 par and $8.8457 cash
First M&F Corp. merged into Renasant Corp. 09/01/2013

COMMUNITY FED SVGS BK (STAUNTON, VA)
Under plan of reorganization each share Common 1¢ par automatically became (1) share Community Financial Corp. (VA) Common 1¢ par 01/31/1990
Community Financial Corp. (VA) merged into City Holding Co. 01/10/2013

COMMUNITY FINANCE SERVICE, INC.
Bankrupt 00/00/1930
Stockholders' equity unlikely

COMMUNITY FINL BANCORP INC (PA)
Merged into National Penn Bancshares Inc. 12/01/1993
Each share Common $10 par exchanged for $31 cash

COMMUNITY FINL CORP (GA)
Merged into Alabama National BanCorporation (DE) 10/02/1998
Each share Common $2.50 par exchanged for (0.351807) share Common $1 par
Alabama National BanCorporation (DE) merged into Royal Bank of Canada (Montreal, QC) 02/22/2008

COMMUNITY FINL CORP (IL)
Merged into First Financial Corp. 02/01/2002
Each share Common 1¢ par exchanged for $15.16 cash

COMMUNITY FINL CORP (VA)
Reincorporated 09/30/1996
Common 1¢ par split (2) for (1) by issuance of (1) additional share 11/23/1994
State of incorporation changed from (DE) to (VA) 09/30/1996
Common 1¢ par split (2) for (1) by issuance of (1) additional share payable 03/25/1998 to holders of record 03/11/1998
Common 1¢ par split (2) for (1) by issuance of (1) additional share payable 09/06/2006 to holders of record 08/23/2006 Ex date - 09/07/2006
Merged into City Holding Co. 01/10/2013
Each share Common 1¢ par exchanged for (0.1753) share Common $2.50 par

COMMUNITY FINL GROUP INC (TN)
Merged into Synovus Financial Corp. 07/31/2002
Each share Common $6 par exchanged for (0.969) share Common $1 par

COMMUNITY FINL HLDG CORP (NJ)
Stock Dividends - 5% payable 12/16/1996 to holders of record 12/02/1996; 5% payable 12/15/1997 to holders of record 12/01/1997
Merged into HUBCO, Inc. 08/14/1998
Each share Common $5 par exchanged for (0.695) share Common no par
HUBCO, Inc. name changed to Hudson United Bancorp 04/21/1999 which merged into TD Banknorth Inc. 01/31/2006
(See TD Banknorth Inc.)

COMMUNITY FINL SHS INC (MD)
Reincorporated 06/25/2013
Common no par split (2) for (1) by issuance of (1) additional share payable 12/27/2006 to holders of record 12/11/2006 Ex date - 12/28/2006
State of incorporation changed from (DE) to (MD) and Common no par changed to 1¢ par 06/25/2013
Merged into Wintrust Financial Corp. 07/24/2015
Each share Common 1¢ par exchanged for (0.013) share Common no par and $0.71 cash

COMMUNITY 1ST BANCORP (CA)
Merged into First Foundation Inc. 11/10/2017
Each share Common no par exchanged for (0.453) share Common $0.001 par

COMMUNITY FIRST BANCORP INC (PA)
Common 50¢ par split (5) for (4) by issuance of (0.25) additional share payable 10/09/1998 to holders of record 09/30/1998
Merged into Emclaire Financial Corp. 10/01/2018
Each share Common 50¢ par exchanged for (1.2008) shares Common $1.25 par and $6.95 cash

COMMUNITY FIRST BANCSHARES INC (AR)
Merged into Equity Bancshares, Inc. 11/10/2016
Each share Common 1¢ par exchanged for (7.261) shares Class A Common 1¢ par and $26.31 cash

COMMUNITY 1ST BK (AUBURN, CA)
Location changed 09/30/2009
Location changed from (Roseville, CA) to (Auburn, CA) 09/30/2009
Under plan of reorganization each share Common no par automatically became (1) share Community 1st Bancorp Common no par 12/31/2015
Community 1st Bancorp merged into First Foundation Inc. 11/10/2017

COMMUNITY FIRST BK (JACKSONVILLE, FL)
Stock Dividends - 20% 07/06/1993; 10% 09/12/1994
Under plan of reorganization each share Common $2 par automatically became (1) share CFB Bancorp Inc. Common 1¢ par 12/31/1994
CFB Bancorp Inc. merged into Compass Bancshares Inc. 08/23/1996

COMMUNITY FIRST BK (LYNCHBURG, VA)
Reorganized as Community First Financial Corp. 07/01/2002
Each share Common $4 par exchanged for (1) share Common no par
Community First Financial Corp. merged into American National Bankshares Inc. 04/04/2006

COMMUNITY FIRST BK (SOMERSET, NJ)
Stock Dividends - 10% payable 05/02/2011 to holders of record 04/22/2011 Ex date - 04/29/2011; 10% payable 05/07/2012 to holders of record 04/27/2012 Ex date - 04/25/2012; 10% payable 05/08/2013 to holders of record 04/26/2013 Ex date - 04/24/2013
Merged into Regal Bank (Livingston, NJ) 03/31/2016
Each share Common no par exchanged for either (0.3753) share Common or $5.30 cash

COMMUNITY FIRST BANKSHARES INC (DE)
7.75% Depositary Preferred called for redemption 03/31/1997
7.75% Conv. Preferred 1¢ par called for redemption 03/31/1997
Common 1¢ par split (2) for (1) by issuance of (1) additional share payable 05/15/1998 to holders of record 05/01/1998
Merged into BancWest Corp. 11/01/2004
Each share Common 1¢ par exchanged for $32.25 cash

COMMUNITY FIRST BKG CO (GA)
Common 1¢ par split (2) for (1) by issuance of (1) additional share payable 02/16/1999 to holders of record 02/01/1999
Merged into BB&T Corp. 12/12/2001
Each share Common 1¢ par exchanged for (0.98) share Common $5 par

COMMUNITY FIRST BKG CO (NJ)
Stock Dividends - 5% payable 12/22/1997 to holders of record 12/05/1997; 2% payable 06/29/1998 to holders of record 06/15/1998
Merged into Commerce Bancorp, Inc. 01/15/1999
Each share Common $5 par exchanged for (0.644) share Common $1.5625 par
Commerce Bancorp, Inc. merged into Toronto-Dominion Bank (Toronto, ON) 03/31/2008

COMMUNITY FIRST FINL BANCORP INC (OH)
Merged into Milton Banking Co. 03/31/2008
Each share Common no par exchanged for $4.46 cash

COMMUNITY FIRST FINL CORP (VA)
Stock Dividend - 20% payable 10/25/2004 to holders of record 10/15/2004
Merged into American National Bankshares Inc. 04/04/2006
Each share Common no par exchanged for $21 cash

COMMUNITY FIRST FINANCIAL INC. (KY)
Acquired by National City Bancshares, Inc. 08/31/1998
Each share Common no par exchanged for (32.0692) shares Common $3.33333333 par
National City Bancshares, Inc. name changed to Integra Bank Corp. 05/22/2000
(See Integra Bank Corp.)

COMMUNITY GAS & POWER CO.
Reorganized as Minneapolis Gas Co. 07/30/1948
Each share Class A Common 50¢ par or Class B Common 50¢ par exchanged for (0.05) share Common $1 par
Minneapolis Gas Co. name changed to Minnesota Gas Co. 05/10/1974
(See Minnesota Gas Co.)

COMMUNITY HEALTH COMPUTING CORP (DE)
Plan of reorganization under Chapter 11 Federal Bankruptcy proceedings confirmed 11/13/1999
Stockholders' equity unlikely

COMMUNITY HEALTH CORP (MD)
Name changed to CHC Corp. 11/23/1973
(See CHC Corp.)

COMMUNITY HEALTH FACILITIES, INC. (MD)
Name changed to Community Health Corp. 12/08/1972
Community Health Corp. name changed to CHC Corp. 11/23/1973
(See CHC Corp.)

COMMUNITY HEALTH SYS INC (DE)
Common 1¢ par split (4) for (3) by issuance of (0.33333333) additional share 12/15/1992
Common 1¢ par split (3) for (2) by issuance of (0.5) additional share 11/22/1993
Merged into FLCH Acquisition Corp. 07/22/1996
Each share Common 1¢ par exchanged for $52 cash

COMMUNITY HOMES INC (OH)
Adjudicated bankrupt 02/02/1977
Stockholders' equity unlikely

COMMUNITY HOTEL CORP. OF NEWPORT, R. I. (RI)
Adjudicated bankrupt 06/03/1974
No stockholders' equity

COMMUNITY IMPT PROGRAMS INC (OH)
Name changed to CIP Corp. 04/25/1972
(See CIP Corp.)

COMMUNITY INDPT BK INC (PA)
Common $5 par split (2) for (1) by issuance of (1) additional share payable 07/31/1998 to holders of record 07/17/1998
Merged into National Penn Bancshares Inc. 01/03/2001
Each share Common $5 par exchanged for (0.945) share Common $5 par

COMMUNITY MGMT SVCS INC (DE)
Merged into Texas State Network, Inc. 05/14/1969
Each share Common 10¢ par exchanged for (0.714285) shares Common no par
Texas State Network, Inc. name changed to TSN Liquidating, Inc. 02/29/1972
(See TSN Liquidating, Inc.)

COMMUNITY MED TRANS INC (DE)
Each share old Common $0.001 par exchanged for (0.16666666) share new Common $0.001 par 12/09/1998
Charter cancelled and declared inoperative and void for non-payment of taxes 03/01/2001

COMMUNITY NATL BANCORP INC (DE)
Each share old Common 1¢ par exchanged for (0.1) share new Common 1¢ par 07/31/1991
Declared insolvent and placed in receivership 11/08/1991
Stockholders' equity unlikely

COMMUNITY NATL BANCORPORATION (GA)
Merged into South Georgia Bank Holding Co. 06/15/2006
Each share Common no par exchanged for approximately $14.65 cash

COMMUNITY NATL BANCORPORATION TR I (IA)
Floating Rate Trust Preferred Securities called for redemption at $1,000 on 03/15/2007

COMMUNITY NATIONAL BANK & TRUST CO. (MIAMI BEACH, FL)
Through voluntary exchange offer 100% acquired by First Orlando Corp. as of 06/01/1973
Public interest eliminated

COMMUNITY NATIONAL BANK & TRUST CO. OF RICHMOND (STATEN ISLAND, NY)
Name changed to Community National Bank & Trust Co. of New York (Staten Island, NY) 07/01/1969
Community National Bank & Trust Co. of New York (Staten Island, NY) reorganized in Delaware as Community National Bancorp, Inc. 05/27/1988
(See Community National Bancorp, Inc.)

COMMUNITY NATL BK & TR CO NEW YORK (STATEN ISLAND, NY)
Common $8.25 par changed to $5.50 par and (0.5) additional share issued 06/10/1971
Common $5.50 par changed to $3.66666666 par and (0.5) additional share issued 06/12/1972
Common $3.66666666 par changed to $3.84 par 05/15/1973
Common $3.84 par changed to $1.92 par and (1) additional share issued 06/12/1973
Common $1.92 par changed to $3 par and (1) additional share issued for each (11) share held 07/15/1974
Common $3 par changed to $1 par 12/21/1978
Common $1 par changed to 3¢ par 07/14/1981
Common 3¢ par changed to 50¢ par 10/26/1981
Reorganized under the laws of Delaware as Community National Bancorp, Inc. 05/27/1988
Each share Adjustable Rate Conv. Preferred $10 par exchanged for (1) share Adjustable Rate Conv. Preferred $10 par
Each share Common 50¢ par exchanged for (1) share Common 1¢ par
(See Community National Bancorp, Inc.)

COMMUNITY NATL BK (BARTOW, FL)
Reorganized as Community One Bancshares, Inc. 09/30/1999
Each share Common $5 par exchanged for (1) share Common $5 par
(See Community One Bancshares, Inc.)

COMMUNITY NATIONAL BANK (DERBY LINE, VT)
Reorganized as Community Bancorp 10/01/1983
Each share Common $2.50 par exchanged for (1) share Common $2.50 par

COMMUNITY NATL BK (FRAMINGHAM, MA)
Name changed to Shawmut Community Bank, N.A. (Framingham, MA) 04/01/1975
(See Shawmut Community Bank, N.A. (Framingham, MA))

COMMUNITY NATL BK (FRANKLIN, OH)
Common $10 par changed to $2.50 par and (3) additional shares issued payable 01/05/1999 to holders of record 12/27/1998 Ex date - 02/11/1999
Reorganized as Community National Corp. 07/02/2001
Each share Common $2.50 par exchanged for (2) shares Common no par
Community National Corp. merged into NB&T Financial Group, Inc. 12/31/2009 which merged into Peoples Bancorp Inc. 03/06/2015

COMMUNITY NATL BK (GLASTONBURY, CT)
Common $5 par changed to $3.33333333 par and (0.5) additional share issued 10/15/1986

Under plan of reorganization each share Common $3.33333333 par automatically became (1) share Community Bancorp Inc. (CT) Common $3.33333333 par 05/21/1987
Community Bancorp Inc. merged into Landmark/Community Bancorp, Inc. 07/29/1988

COMMUNITY NATL BK (GREAT NECK, NY)
Merged into Bridge Bancorp, Inc. 06/19/2015
Each share Common $5 par exchanged for (0.79) share Common 1¢ par

COMMUNITY NATL BK (PONTIAC, MI)
Stock Dividends - 50% 07/01/1936; 66.66666666% 01/24/1941; 60% 10/06/1944; 50% 07/31/1953; 33.33333333% 08/31/1956; 20% 10/01/1957; 25% 01/16/1962; 37.93% 01/26/1965; 20% 02/03/1970; 33.33333333% 07/31/1973; 25% 10/17/1978
Merged into First of America Bank Corp. 07/01/1985
Each share Capital Stock $10 par exchanged for (0.5) share 11.25% Conv. Preferred Ser. D no par
(See First of America Bank Corp.)

COMMUNITY NATIONAL BK (SOUTH BOSTON, VA)
Stock Dividends - 10% payable 01/29/1999 to holders of record 12/13/1998; 10% payable 06/30/2000 to holders of record 05/31/2000 Ex date - 08/21/2000; 10% payable 07/31/2001 to holders of record 06/30/2001; 10% payable 10/31/2003 to holders of record 09/30/2003 Ex date - 11/03/2003
Merged into Carter Bank & Trust (Martinsville, VA) 12/29/2006
Each share Common $5 par exchanged for (4.35) shares Common

COMMUNITY NATL BK LAKEWAY AREA (MORRISTOWN, TN)
Reclassification effective 08/10/2010
Holders of old Common $1 par held in street name and record holders of (1,000) shares or more reclassified as new Common $1 par
Each record holder of (199) or fewer shares old Common $1 par exchanged for (1) share Class B Preferred no par
Each record holder of between (200) and (999) shares old Common $1 par exchanged for (1) share Class A Preferred no par
Acquired by TriSummit Bancorp, Inc. 07/01/2014
Each share Class A Preferred no par exchanged for $5.35 cash
Each share Class B Preferred no par exchanged for $5.35 cash
Each share Common $1 par exchanged for $5.35 cash

COMMUNITY NATL BK N J (WESTMONT, NJ)
Under plan of reorganization each share Common $5 par automatically became (1) share Community Financial Holding Corp. Common $5 par 05/01/1991
Community Financial Holding Corp. merged into HUBCO, Inc. 08/14/1998 which name changed to Hudson United Bancorp 04/21/1999 which merged into TD Banknorth Inc. 01/31/2006
(See TD Banknorth Inc.)

COMMUNITY NATIONAL BANK OF BAL HARBOUR (MIAMI BEACH, FL)
Name changed to Community National Bank & Trust Co. (Miami Beach, FL) 10/31/1964

(See Community National Bank & Trust Co. (Miami Beach, FL))

COMMUNITY NATL BK OF NORTHWESTN PA (ALBION, PA)
Acquired by Andover Bancorp, Inc. 10/01/2015
Each share Common $1 par exchanged for $105.56 cash

COMMUNITY NATL BK PASCO CNTY (ZEPHYRHILLS, FL)
Merged into CenterState Banks of Florida, Inc. 06/30/2000
Each share Common $5 par exchanged for (2.02) shares Common 1¢ par
CenterState Banks of Florida, Inc. name changed to Centerstate Banks, Inc. 06/17/2009 which name changed to CenterState Bank Corp. 09/08/2017

COMMUNITY NATL BK SOUTHN PA (LITTLESTOWN, PA)
Common $10 par changed to $5 par and (1) additional share issued 03/00/1981
Merged into CCNB Corp. 03/16/1988
Each share Common $5 par exchanged for (2.81) share Common $1 par
CCNB Corp. merged into PNC Financial Corp. 10/23/1992 which name changed to PNC Bank Corp. 02/08/1993 which name changed to PNC Financial Services Group, Inc. 03/15/2000

COMMUNITY NATL CORP (OH)
Merged into NB&T Financial Group, Inc. 12/31/2009
Each share Common no par exchanged for either (0.761) share Common no par, $11.41 cash, or a combination thereof
Note: Holders of (1,500) shares or fewer will receive $11.41 cash per share
NB&T Financial Group, Inc. merged into Peoples Bancorp Inc. 03/06/2015

COMMUNITY NATL CORP (TN)
Merged into Community National Bancorp Inc. 03/31/2000
Eash share Common $1 par exchanged for $14.75 cash

COMMUNITY NATL LIFE INS CO (OK)
Completely liquidated 07/02/1970
No stockholders' equity

COMMUNITY ONE BANCSHARES INC (FL)
Principal asset placed in receivership 08/20/2010
Stockholders' equity unlikely

COMMUNITY OWNED BASEBALL OF JACKSONVILLE, INC. (FL)
Assets liquidated for the benefit of creditors 11/14/1967
No stockholders' equity

COMMUNITY PARTNERS BANCORP (NJ)
Stock Dividends - 3% payable 09/01/2006 to holders of record 08/18/2006 Ex date - 08/16/2006; 3% payable 08/31/2007 to holders of record 08/10/2007 Ex date - 08/08/2007; 3% payable 10/17/2008 to holders of record 09/30/2008 Ex date - 09/26/2008; 3% payable 10/23/2009 to holders of record 09/25/2009 Ex date - 09/23/2009; 5% payable 10/22/2010 to holders of record 09/24/2010 Ex date - 09/22/2010; 3% payable 12/30/2011 to holders of record 12/13/2011 Ex date - 12/09/2011
Name changed to Two River Bancorp 06/28/2013

COMMUNITY PETROLEUMS LTD.
Acquired by Peak Oils Ltd. on a (10) for (1) basis 00/00/1952
Peak Oils Ltd. recapitalized as Consolidated Peak Oils Ltd.

00/00/1953 which was acquired by Western Allenbee Oil & Gas Co. Ltd. 06/20/1960 which name changed to Convoy Capital Corp. 04/28/1989 which recapitalized as Hariston Corp. 09/25/1992 which recapitalized as Midland Holland Inc. (Canada) 02/10/1999 which reincorporated in Yukon 03/11/1999 which name changed to Mercury Partners & Co. Inc. 02/22/2000 which name changed to Black Mountain Capital Corp. 05/02/2005 which recapitalized as Grand Peak Capital Corp. (YT) 11/20/2007 which reincorporated in British Columbia 04/27/2010

COMMUNITY POWER & LIGHT CO.
Each share 1st Preferred no par exchanged for (5) shares Common $1 par Common $10 par 00/00/1940
Each share Common no par exchanged for (1.8) shares Common $1 par 00/00/1940
Merged into Southwestern Public Service Co. 00/00/1942
Each share Common $1 par exchanged for (1) share Common $1 par
Southwestern Public Service Co. merged into New Century Energies, Inc. 08/01/1997 which merged into Xcel Energy Inc. 08/18/2000

COMMUNITY PSYCHIATRIC CTRS (NV)
Reincorporated 06/30/1972
State of incorporation changed from (CA) to (NV) 06/30/1972
Common no par changed to $1 par and (0.5) additional share issued 07/20/1972
Common $1 par split (2) for (1) by issuance of (1) additional share 07/26/1978
Common $1 par split (2) for (1) by issuance of (1) additional share 07/14/1980
Common $1 par split (3) for (2) by issuance of (0.5) additional share 01/15/1982
Common $1 par split (3) for (2) by issuance of (0.5) additional share 02/25/1983
Common $1 par split (3) for (2) by issuance of (0.5) additional share 07/10/1984
Common $1 par split (3) for (2) by issuance of (0.5) additional share 11/05/1987
Preferred Stock Purchase Rights declared for Common stockholders of record 02/15/1989 were redeemed at $0.01 per right 04/14/1995 for holders of record 03/31/1995
Name changed to Transitional Hospitals Corp. 11/14/1996
(See Transitional Hospitals Corp.)

COMMUNITY PUB SVC CO (TX)
Reincorporated 05/01/1963
Common Voting Trust Agreement terminated 12/16/1937
Common $25 par changed to $10 par and (2) additional shares issued 05/12/1950
Common $10 par split (3) for (2) by issuance of (0.5) additional share 02/10/1959
State of incorporation changed from (DE) to (TX) 05/01/1963
5.72% Preferred Ser. A $100 par called for redemption 09/26/1963
Stock Dividends - 30% 04/27/1940; 20% 01/13/1953; 10% 05/18/1971; 10% 02/22/1974
Name changed to Texas-New Mexico Power Co. 05/14/1981
Texas-New Mexico Power reorganized as TNP Enterprises, Inc. 10/03/1984
(See TNP Enterprises, Inc.)

COMMUNITY REDEV CORP (FL)
Each share old Common $0.001 par exchanged for (0.1) share new Common 06/23/1997
Recapitalized as Areawide Cellular, Inc. (FL) 04/14/1998
Each share new Common $0.001 par exchanged for (0.5) share Common $0.001 par
Areawide Cellular, Inc. (FL) reincorporated in Delaware 04/12/2002
(See Areawide Cellular, Inc.)

COMMUNITY RESEARCH & DEVELOPMENT, INC. (MD)
45¢ Preferred $5 par called for redemption 06/20/1966
Name changed to Rouse Co. 06/20/1966
(See Rouse Co.)

COMMUNITY SVGS BK (BRISTOL, CT)
Merged into New England Community Bancorp, Inc. 12/31/1997
Each share Common $4 par exchanged for $5.30 cash

COMMUNITY SVGS BK (HOLYOKE, MA)
Merged into Heritage NIS Bank for Savings (Northampton, MA) 06/03/1988
Each share Common 10¢ par exchanged for $19.50 cash

COMMUNITY SVGS BK (JACKSONVILLE, FL)
Merged into Compass Bancshares, Inc. 08/23/1996
Each share Common $2 par exchanged for (0.61106) share Common $2 par
Compass Bancshares, Inc. merged into Banco Bilbao Vizcaya Argentaria, S.A. 09/07/2007

COMMUNITY SVGS BANKSHARES INC NEW (DE)
Merged into BankAtlantic Bancorp 03/25/2002
Each share Common $1 par exchanged for $19 cash

COMMUNITY SVGS BANKSHARES INC OLD (FL)
Reorganized under the laws of Delaware as Community Savings Bankshares Inc. (New) 12/15/1998
Each share Common $1 par exchanged for (0.20445) share Common $1 par
(See Community Savings Bankshares Inc. (New))

COMMUNITY SVGS F A (NORTH PALM BEACH, FL)
Under plan of reorganization each share Common $1 par automatically became (1) share Community Savings Bankshares, Inc. (FL) Common $1 par 09/30/1997
Community Savings Bankshares, Inc. (FL) reorganized in Delaware as Community Savings Bankshares Inc. (New) 12/15/1998
(See Community Savings Bankshares Inc. (New))

COMMUNITY SVC COMMUNICATIONS INC (ME)
Each share old Common $10 par exchanged for (10) shares new Common $10 par 04/01/1999
Liquidation completed
Each share new Common $10 par received initial distribution of $2 cash payable 12/13/2004 to holders of record 12/06/2004 Ex date - 12/14/2004
Each share new Common $10 par received second distribution of $1.50 cash payable 12/05/2005 to holders of record 11/28/2005 Ex date - 12/06/2005
Each share new Common $10 par received third distribution of $1.50

cash payable 12/15/2006 to holders of record 12/04/2006 Ex date - 12/18/2006
Each share new Common $10 par received fourth distribution of $1 cash payable 12/10/2007 to holders of record 11/29/2007 Ex date - 12/11/2007
Each share new Common $10 par received fifth distribution of $0.75 cash payable 12/11/2008 to holders of record 12/01/2008 Ex date - 12/12/2008
Each share new Common $10 par received sixth distribution of $0.75 cash payable 12/10/2009 to holders of record 11/30/2009 Ex date - 12/11/2009
Each share new Common $10 par received seventh distribution of $2.25 cash payable 12/16/2010 to holders of record 12/06/2010 Ex date - 12/17/2010
Each share new Common $10 par received eighth distribution of $0.50 cash payable 12/13/2012 to holders of record 12/03/2012 Ex date - 11/29/2012
Each share new Common $10 par received ninth distribution of $0.25 cash payable 12/12/2013 to holders of record 12/02/2013
Each share new Common $10 par received tenth and final distribution of $0.31 cash payable 08/05/2015 to holders of record 07/27/2015 Ex date - 08/06/2015

COMMUNITY SVC TEL CO (ME)
Under plan of reorganization each share Common $10 par automatically became (1) share Community Service Communications, Inc. Common $10 par 10/01/1988
(See Community Service Communications, Inc.)

COMMUNITY SHS LTD (WI)
Common 10¢ par split (3) for (2) by issuance of (0.5) additional share 04/18/1986
Declared defunct 00/00/1990
No stockholders' equity

COMMUNITY SOUTHN BK (LAKELAND, FL)
Stock Dividend - 15% payable 10/04/2013 to holders of record 09/30/2013 Ex date - 09/26/2013
Under plan of reorganization each share Common $5 par automatically became (1) share Community Southern Holdings, Inc. Common 1¢ par 10/18/2013
(See Community Southern Holdings, Inc.)

COMMUNITY SOUTHN HLDGS INC (FL)
Acquired by Sunshine Bancorp, Inc. 06/30/2015
Each share Common 1¢ par exchanged for $11.66 cash

COMMUNITY ST BK (ALGOMA, WI)
Merged into F&M Bancorporation, Inc. 06/28/1996
Each share Common $10 par exchanged for (9.2) shares Common $1 par
F&M Bancorporation, Inc. merged into Citizens Banking Corp. 07/01/1997 which name changed to Citizens Republic Bancorp, Inc. 04/26/2007 which merged into FirstMerit Corp. 04/12/2013 which merged into Huntington Bancshares Inc. 08/16/2016

COMMUNITY ST BK (ALBANY, NY)
Name changed to First American Bank of New York (Albany, NY) 07/28/1982
(See First American Bank of New York (Albany, N.Y.))

COMMUNITY ST BK (TULSA, OK)
Name changed to Community Bank & Trust Co. (Tulsa, OK) 07/01/1975

COMMUNITY STATE BANK & TRUST CO. (LINDEN, NJ)
Stock Dividends - 10% 11/15/1971; 10% 01/04/1973
Liquidation completed
Each share Common $12.50 par exchanged for initial distribution of $27 cash 05/25/1979
Each share Common $12.50 par received second and final distribution of $0.26271 cash 01/11/1980

COMMUNITY STATE BANK (DOWAGIAC, MI)
Stock Dividends - 10% 02/18/1965; 10% 03/04/1968; 10% 03/24/1969
Merged into First Michigan Bank Corp. 12/31/1976
Each share Capital Stock $10 par exchanged for (2.5) shares Common $1 par
First Michigan Bank Corp. merged into Huntington Bancshares Inc. 09/30/1997

COMMUNITY TEL LTD (ON)
5.5% Preference Ser. C $100 par called for redemption 08/23/1968
6.5% Preference Ser. A $100 par called for redemption 08/23/1968
6.5% Preference Ser. B $100 par called for redemption 08/23/1968
Liquidation completed
Each share Common no par exchanged for initial distribution of (0.7084) share Continental Telephone Corp. Common $1 par and $0.09 cash 11/18/1968
Each share Common no par received second and final distribution of $0.10 cash 11/20/1971

COMMUNITY TR BK (PORTSMOUTH, VA)
Merged into Crestar Financial Corp. 02/04/1991
Each share Common $0.1175 par exchanged for (0.824) share Common $5 par
Crestar Financial Corp. merged into SunTrust Banks, Inc. 12/31/1998

COMMUNITY TR FINL SVCS CORP (GA)
Common $2.50 par split (2) for (1) by issuance of (1) additional share payable 01/28/2000 to holders of record 01/18/2000
Merged into GB&T Bancshares, Inc. 06/30/2001
Each share Common $2.50 par exchanged for (0.786) share Common $5 par
GB&T Bancshares, Inc. merged into SunTrust Banks, Inc. 05/01/2008

COMMUNITY TV SYSTEMS, INC. (DE)
No longer in existence having become inoperative and void for non-payment of taxes 04/01/1956

COMMUNITY UNIT FUND (BC)
Name changed to International Income Fund 11/01/1971

COMMUNITY VY BANCORP (CA)
Common no par split (4) for (3) by issuance of (0.33333333) additional share payable 09/30/2002 to holders of record 09/16/2002 Ex date - 10/01/2002
Common no par split (4) for (3) by issuance of (0.33333333) additional share payable 03/26/2004 to holders of record 03/02/2004 Ex date - 03/29/2004
Common no par split (2) for (1) by issuance of (1) additional share payable 05/16/2005 to holders of record 05/02/2005 Ex date - 05/17/2005
Ceased operations 08/20/2010
Stockholders' equity unlikely

COMMUNITY VY BK (EL CENTRO, CA)
Under plan of reorganization each share Common no par automatically became (1) share CMUV Bancorp Common no par 01/07/2016

COMMUNITY WATER SERVICE CO. (DE)
Each share Common $1 par exchanged for (0.05) share American Water Works Co., Inc. Common $5 par 00/00/1947
(See American Water Works Co., Inc.)

COMMUNITYONE BANCORP (NC)
Merged into Capital Bank Financial Corp. 10/26/2016
Each share Common no par exchanged for (0.43) share Class A Common 1¢ par

COMMUNITYSOUTH FINANCIAL CORP (SC)
Name changed 07/06/2007
Common 1¢ par split (5) for (4) by issuance of (0.25) additional share payable 01/16/2007 to holders of record 12/15/2006 Ex date - 01/17/2007
Name changed from CommunitySouth Bancshares, Inc. to CommunitySouth Financial Corp. 07/09/2007
Administratively dissolved 07/10/2014

COMMUTER AIRLS INC (IA)
Adjudicated bankrupt 03/23/1970
No stockholders' equity

COMNET CORP (MD)
$1.60 Conv. Preferred Ser. C 25¢ par called for redemption 03/16/1992
Under plan of merger name changed to Group 1 Software, Inc. (New) 09/28/1998
(See Group 1 Software, Inc. (New))

COMNET INC (UT)
Chapter 11 bankruptcy proceedings converted to Chapter 7 on 05/25/1990
Stockholders' equity undetermined

COMNETIX CAP CORP (QC)
Reorganized under the laws of Canada as Comnetix Inc. 04/22/2004
Each share Common no par exchanged for (0.2) share Common no par
(See Comnetix Inc.)

COMNETIX INC (CANADA)
Merged into L-1 Identity Solutions, Inc. 02/23/2007
Each share Common no par exchanged for USD$1.17 cash

COMO MINES CO (NV)
Each share Capital Stock exchanged for (0.2) share Capital Stock $1 par 00/00/1938
Capital Stock $1 par changed to 1¢ par 12/01/1977
Recapitalized as Founders Equitable Co. of America, Inc. 06/22/1979
Each share Capital Stock 1¢ par exchanged for (0.05) share Common 20¢ par
Founders Equitable Co. of America, Inc. name changed to Renaissance Group, Inc. 11/18/1985

COMORO CAP LTD (CANADA)
Plan of arrangement effective 07/22/1994
Each share Common no par exchanged for (0.2) share Patent Enforcement & Royalties Ltd. Common no par
Patent Enforcement & Royalties Ltd. name changed to Blue Pearl Mining Ltd. 04/15/2005 which name changed to Thompson Creek Metals Co., Inc. (ON) 05/15/2007 which reincorporated in British Columbia 07/29/2008 which merged into Centerra Gold Inc. 10/21/2016

COMORO EXPL LTD (NV)
Common 25¢ par changed to 1¢ par 11/02/1970
Recapitalized as AWR-America West Resources, Inc. 12/10/1993
Each share Common 1¢ par exchanged for (0.25) share Common 1¢ par
AWR-America West Resources, Inc. name changed to Integrated Information International Group Co. Ltd. 10/08/1999 which name changed to Intervest Group, Ltd. 04/21/2001
(See Intervest Group, Ltd.)

COMOX RES LTD (BC)
Recapitalized as Pacific Comox Resources Ltd. 09/09/1988
Each share Common no par exchanged for (0.5) share Common no par

COMP DATA INTL INC (BC)
Name changed to Armenian Express Canada Inc. 11/26/1987
Armenian Express Canada Inc. recapitalized as Armenex Resources Canada Inc. 07/04/1990 which recapitalized as Ecuadorean Copperfields Inc. 08/31/1994 recapitalized as Bronx Minerals Inc. 06/24/1996 which name changed to Las Vegas From Home.Com Entertainment Inc. 09/07/1999 which name changed to Jackpot Digital Inc. 06/18/2015

COMP ONE CORP (OH)
Common $10 par split (3.25) for (1) by issuance of (2.25) additional shares 01/14/1986
Merged into C&H Bancorp 12/31/1986
Each share Common $10 par exchanged for (1) share Common no par
C&H Bancorp acquired by Fifth Third Bancorp 04/01/1988

COMP SERV CO (CA)
Charter suspended for failure to file reports and pay taxes 12/01/1977

COMP TRONICS INC (FL)
Each share old Common 10¢ par exchanged for (0.02) share new Common 10¢ par 10/04/1977
Name changed to Silvatex, Inc. 01/07/1980
Silvatex, Inc. name changed to Grandma's Inc. 07/30/1982
(See Grandma's Inc.)
00/00/1977 & 00/00/1980 Our cards)

COMP U CARD INTL INC (DE)
Common 1¢ par split (3) for (2) by issuance of (0.5) additional share 03/18/1985
Common 1¢ par split (3) for (2) by issuance of (0.5) additional share 07/18/1986
Name changed to CUC International Inc. 06/18/1987
CUC International Inc. name changed to Cendant Corp. 12/17/1997 which reorganized as Avis Budget Group, Inc. 09/01/2006

COMP U CHECK INC (MI)
Each share old Common $1 par exchanged for (0.25) share new Common $1 par 05/27/1975
New Common $1 par changed to 10¢ par and (0.5) additional share issued 05/14/1982
Common 10¢ par split (3) for (2) by issuance of (0.5) additional share 02/24/1983
Common 10¢ par split (3) for (2) by issuance of (0.5) additional share 02/15/1984
Automatically dissolved 07/15/1995

COMP U TEST SOFTWARE LTD (BC)
Name changed to Nucore Resources Ltd. 12/17/1990
Nucore Resources Ltd. acquired by Norcan Resources Ltd. 08/19/1994 which recapitalized as Odyssey

Exploration Inc. 06/07/2000 which recapitalized as Consolidated Odyssey Exploration Inc. 12/08/2000 which reorganized as Odyssey Petroleum Corp. 08/25/2005 which recapitalized as Petrichor Energy Inc. 03/03/2011

COMPAC COMPUTER SYS INC (MN)
Merged into Comserv Corp. 11/00/1971
Each share Common 10¢ par exchanged for (0.16666666) share Common 10¢ par
(See Comserv Corp.)

COMPAC CORP (DE)
Acquired by Masco Corp. (DE) 11/03/1978
Each share Common 50¢ par exchanged for $21 cash

COMPACE CORP (MN)
Common 5¢ par changed to 1¢ par and (4) additional shares issued 12/17/1969
Each share old Common 1¢ par exchanged for (0.5) share new Common 1¢ par and (0.09) share Comstar Corp. Common 1¢ par 08/21/1972
Note: Company is now private

COMPACT CASSETTE CORP (CA)
Out of business 03/00/1975
Company has no assets

COMPACT ORGANIZATIONAL SYS INC (NV)
Reorganized as U.S. Cast Products, Inc. 05/21/1997
Each share Common $0.001 par exchanged for (1.1343) shares Common $0.001 par
(See U.S. Cast Products, Inc.)

COMPACT PWR HLDGS LTD (AB)
Name changed to Exceed Capital Holdings Ltd. 09/05/2000
Exceed Capital Holdings Ltd. name changed to Gallic Energy Ltd. 07/16/2007 which merged into Petromanas Energy Inc. 01/04/2013 which recapitalized as PMI Resources Ltd. 06/14/2016 which name changed to PentaNova Energy Corp. 06/05/2017 which recapitalized as CruzSur Energy Corp. 09/04/2018

COMPACT VIDEO INC (CA)
Name changed to Andrews Group Inc. 03/07/1988
(See Andrews Group Inc.)

COMPACT VIDEO SYSTEMS, INC. (CA)
Name changed to Compact Video Inc. 08/31/1981
Compact Video, Inc. name changed to Andrews Group Inc 03/07/1988
(See Andrews Group Inc.)

COMPAGNIE DE ST GOBAIN (FRANCE)
Name changed 10/08/1970
Stock Dividends - 10% 11/30/1965; 25% 12/12/1969
Name changed from Compagnie de Saint-Gobain to Compagnie de Saint-Gobain Pont-A-Mousson 10/08/1970
Depositary Agreement terminated 05/21/1982
Each ADR for Bearer $7.50 par exchanged for Floating Rate Bonds of Caisse Nationale de L'Industrie due 01/01/1997
(Additional Information in Active)

COMPAGNIE DE SUEZ (FRANCE)
ADR agreement terminated 07/28/1997
Each Sponsored ADR for Ordinary exchanged for $24.55 cash

COMPAGNIE DES MACHS BULL (FRANCE)
Each ADR for Ordinary exchanged for (0.1) ADR for Ordinary 12/19/2005

ADR agreement terminated 02/02/2015
Each ADR for Ordinary exchanged for $1.13777 cash

COMPAGNIE FINANCIERE DE SUEZ (FRANCE)
Name changed to Compagnie Financiere de Suez et de l'Union Parisienne 06/20/1967 which name changed back to Compagnie Financiere de Suez 05/30/1972
Stock Dividend - 10% 09/30/1977
Nationalized 00/00/1982
Details not available

COMPAGNIE FINANCIERE RICHEMONT AG (SWITZERLAND)
Basis changed from (1:0.01) to (1:1) 11/12/2001
ADR agreement terminated 01/17/2006
Each Sponsored ADR for A Units exchanged for $57.14372 cash

COMPAGNIE GENERALE DE GEOPHYSIQUE VERITAS (FRANCE)
Name changed 01/12/2007
Under plan of merger name changed from Compagnie Generale de Geophysique to Compagnie Generale de Geophysique-Veritas 01/12/2007
ADR basis changed from (1:0.2) to (1:1) 06/03/2008
Name changed to CGG 05/29/2013

COMPAGNIE GENERALE DES EAUX (FRANCE)
Name changed to Vivendi S.A. 05/15/1998
Vivendi S.A. merged into Vivendi Universal 12/08/2000 which name changed to Vivendi 04/24/2006
(See Vivendi)

COMPAGNIE GENERALE DES ESTABLISSEMENTS MICHELIN (FRANCE)
ADR agreement terminated 07/10/2005
No ADR holders' equity

COMPAGNIE GENERALE MARITIME (FRANCE)
Depositary agreement terminated 02/21/1992
Proceeds of share sale will be distributed on a pro rata basis upon surrender of Certificates

COMPAGNIE GENERALE TRAN-ATLANTIQUE (FRANCE)
Name changed to Compagnie Generale Maritime
(See Compagnie Generale Maritime)

COMPAGNIE MINIERE DE L UNGAVA (QC)
Merged into Ungava Minerals Corp. 12/04/1996
Each share Common no par exchanged for (0.66666666) share Common no par
Ungava Minerals Corp. name changed to Nearctic Nickel Mines Inc. 09/07/2007

COMPAGNIE MINIERE LIGNERIS (QC)
Charter annulled for failure to file reports and pay fees 06/28/1977

COMPAGNIE NATIONALE A PORTEFEUILLE SA (BELGIUM)
ADR agreement terminated 12/02/2011
No ADR's remain outstanding

COMPAIR OIL CO.
Dissolved 00/00/1948
Details not available

COMPANHIA CERVEJARIA BRAHMA (BRAZIL)
Merged into Companhia de Bebidas das Americas-AMBEV 09/14/2000
Each Sponsored ADR for Preferred exchanged for (1) Sponsored ADR for Preferred

Each Sponsored ADR for Ordinary exchanged for (1) Sponsored ADR for Ordinary
Companhia de Bebidas das Americas-AMBEV merged into Ambev S.A. 11/11/2013

COMPANHIA DE BEBIDAS DAS AMERS - AMBEV (BRAZIL)
ADR basis changed from (1:100) to (1:1) 08/02/2007
Sponsored ADR's for Preferred split (5) for (1) by issuance of (4) additional ADR's payable 12/27/2010 to holders of record 12/22/2010 Ex date 12/28/2010
Sponsored ADR's for Common split (5) for (1) by issuance of (4) additional ADR's payable 12/27/2010 to holders of record 12/22/2010 Ex date 12/28/2010
Stock Dividend - 20% payable 06/08/2005 to holders of record 05/31/2005 Ex date - 06/09/2005
Merged into Ambev S.A. 11/11/2013
Each Sponsored ADR for Preferred exchanged for (5) Sponsored ADR's for Common
Each Sponsored ADR for Ordinary exchanged for (5) Sponsored ADR's for Common

COMPANHIA DE GERACAO DE ENERGIA ELETRICA TIETE (BRAZIL)
Name changed to AES Tiete S.A. 11/07/2006
(See AES Tiete S.A.)

COMPANHIA DE GERACAO DE ENERGIA PARANAPANEMA (BRAZIL)
Name changed to Duke Energy International Geracao Paranapanema S.A. 09/22/2003

COMPANHIA DE SANEAMENTO DE MINAS GERAIS - COPASA MG (BRAZIL)
GDR agreement terminated 10/10/2017
No GDR's remain outstanding

COMPANHIA DE TECIDOS NORTE DE MINAS- COTEMINAS (BRAZIL)
Each Sponsored 144A GDR for Ordinary received distribution of $0.4841 cash payable 02/26/2003 to holders of record 10/02/2002
Each Reg. S Sponsored GDR for Ordinary received distribution of $0.4841 cash payable 02/26/2003 to holders of record 10/02/2002
ADR agreement terminated 12/06/2007
Each Sponsored ADR for Preferred exchanged for $4.8762 cash
GDR agreement terminated 12/06/2007
Each Sponsored 144A GDR for Ordinary exchanged for $4.8762 cash
Each Sponsored Reg. S GDR for Ordinary exchanged for $4.8762 cash

COMPANHIA ENERGETICA DE MINAS GERAIS (BRAZIL)
Each Reg. S. Sponsored ADR for Preferred exchanged for (0.949) Sponsored ADR for Non-Vtg. Preferred 04/21/1995
Stock Dividends - ADR for Pfd. Reg. S 265% 04/21/1995; 22.377% payable 06/08/1998 to holders of record 05/07/1998
Each Sponsored Reg. S ADR for Preferred exchanged for (1) Sponsored ADR for Non-Vtg. Ordinary Preferred 09/18/2001
ADR agreement terminated 10/22/2001
Each Sponsored 144A ADR for Preferred exchanged for $10.218509 cash
(Additional Information in Active)

COMPANHIA FABRICADORA DE PECAS (BRAZIL)
ADR agreement terminated 02/06/2002
Each Sponsored ADR for Preferred exchanged for $0.7056 cash

COMPANHIA FORCA E LUZ CATAGUAZES LEOPOLDINA (BRAZIL)
ADR agreement terminated 03/07/2007
No ADR's remain outstanding

COMPANHIA SIDERURGICA BELGO-MINEIRA (BRAZIL)
Each Sponsored ADR for Ordinary exchanged for $118.89362 cash 02/08/2006

COMPANHIA SIDERURGICA DE TUBARAO (BRAZIL)
Each 144A Sponsored ADR for Class B exchanged for (1.2) ADR's for Class B 05/10/1999
Each Reg. S Sponsored ADR for Class B exchanged for (1.2) ADR's for Preferred 05/10/1999
ADR agreement terminated 11/21/2005
Each ADR for Preferred exchanged for $77.238476 cash

COMPANHIA SUZANO DE PAPEL E CELULOSE S A (BRAZIL)
Each Sponsored ADR for Ordinary no par received distribution of (0.3) Suzano Petroquimica S.A. Sponsored ADR for Preferred payable 3/25/2003 to holders of record 4/1/2002 Ex date 3/26/2003
Name changed to Suzano Bahia Sul Papel e Celulose S.A. 9/23/2004
Suzano Bahia Sul Papel e Celulose S.A. name changed to Suzano Papel e Celulose S.A. 8/4/2004

COMPANHIA VALE DO RIO DOCE (BRAZIL)
Sponsored ADR's for Preferred split (3) for (1) by issuance of (2) additional ADR's payable 09/07/2004 to holders of record 08/23/2004 Ex date - 09/07/2004
Sponsored ADR's for Common split (3) for (1) by issuance of (2) additional ADR's payable 09/07/2004 to holders of record 08/23/2004 Ex date - 09/07/2004
Each Sponsored ADR's for Preferred received distribution of $0.01096 cash payable 09/24/2004 to holders of record 04/18/1997
Sponsored ADR's for Preferred split (2) for (1) by issuance of (1) additional ADR payable 06/06/2006 to holders of record 05/24/2006 Ex date - 06/07/2006
Sponsored ADR's for Common split (2) for (1) by issuance of (1) additional ADR payable 06/06/2006 to holders of record 05/24/2006 Ex date - 06/07/2006
Sponsored ADR's for Preferred split (2) for (1) by issuance of (1) additional ADR payable 09/12/2007 to holders of record 09/05/2007 Ex date - 09/13/2007
Sponsored ADR's for Common split (2) for (1) by issuance of (1) additional ADR payable 09/12/2007 to holders of record 09/05/2007 Ex date - 09/13/2007
Name changed to Vale S.A. 05/28/2009

COMPANIA ANONIMA NACIONAL TELEFONOS DE VENEZUELA (VENEZUELA)
ADR agreement terminated 04/20/2009
Each Sponsored ADR for Class D exchanged for $11.27 cash

COMPANIA BOLIVIANA DE ENERGIA ELECTRICA S A (NS)
Class A Preferred $10 par called for redemption 02/28/1977

Class B Preferred $100 par called for redemption 08/23/1977
Public interest eliminated

COMPANIA DE ALUMBRADO ELECTRICO DE SAN SALVADOR SA (EL SALVADOR)
Common Colones 100 par changed to Colones 10 par 08/00/1972
Nationalized 11/00/1986
Each share Common Colones 10 par received initial distribution of $0.313 cash 00/00/1992
Each ADR for Common received initial distribution of $0.313 cash 00/00/1992
Note: Details on additional distributions are not available

COMPANIA DE S A (CHILE)
Name changed 03/17/1995
Name changed from Compania de Telefonos de Chile S.A. to Compania de Telecomunicaciones de Chile S.A. 03/17/1995
Each old Sponsored ADR for Ser. A Common no par exchanged for (4.25) new Sponsored ADR's for Ser. A Common no par 01/02/1997
ADR agreement terminated 05/07/2009
Each new Sponsored ADR for Ser. A Common no par exchanged for $5.091624 cash

COMPANIA NAVIERA PEREZ COMPANC S A C F I M F A (ARGENTINA)
Name changed to Perez Companc S.A. (Old) 10/03/1995
Perez Companc S.A. (Old) name changed to Pecom Energia S.A. 07/24/2000
(See Pecom Energia S.A.)

COMPANIA SALITRERA ANGLO CHILENA
Merged into Anglo-Lautaro Nitrate Corp. 00/00/1951
Each share Ordinary P50 par exchanged for (1) share Class A $2.40 par
Anglo-Lautaro Nitrate Corp. reorganized as Anglo-Lautaro Nitrate Co. Ltd. 07/08/1968 which name changed to Anglo Co. Ltd. 05/10/1972 which name changed to Anglo Energy Ltd. (Bahamas) 12/17/1980 which reorganized in Delaware as Anglo Energy, Inc. 07/14/1986 which name changed to Nabors Industries, Inc. (DE) 03/07/1989 which reincorporated in Bermuda as Nabors Industries Ltd. 06/24/2002

COMPANIA SEVILLANA DE ELECTRICIDAD S A (SPAIN)
ADR agreement terminated 12/01/1998
Each Sponsored ADR for Ordinary exchanged for (2) shares Ordinary 500P par
Note: Unexchanged shares were sold and proceeds, if any, held for claim after 06/01/1999

COMPANIA TELEFONICA NACIONAL DE ESPANA S A (SPAIN)
Name changed to Telefonica de Espana, S.A. 05/26/1988
Telefonica de Espana, S.A. name changed to Telefonica, S.A. 04/15/1998

COMPANY DOCTOR (DE)
Merged into HealthSouth Corp. 06/29/1998
Each share Common 1¢ par exchanged for (0.142) share Common 1¢ par
HealthSouth Corp. name changed to Encompass Health Corp. 01/02/2018

COMPANYS COMING SNACK BARS LTD (CANADA)
Name changed to Comac Food Group Inc. 07/31/1990
Comac Food Group Inc. name changed to Canada's Pizza Delivery Corp. 01/22/2004
(See Canada's Pizza Delivery COrp.)

COMPAQ COMPUTER CORP (DE)
Common 1¢ par split (2) for (1) by issuance of (1) additional share 07/06/1990
Common 1¢ par split (3) for (1) by issuance of (2) additional shares 06/07/1994
Common 1¢ par split (5) for (2) by issuance of (1.5) additional share payable 07/28/1997 to holders of record 07/14/1997 Ex date - 07/29/1997
Common 1¢ par split (2) for (1) by issuance of (1) additional share payable 01/20/1998 to holders of record 12/31/1997 Ex date - 01/21/1998
Merged into Hewlett-Packard Co. 05/03/2002
Each share Common 1¢ par exchanged for (0.6325) share Common 1¢ par
Hewlett-Packard Co. name changed to HP Inc. 11/02/2015

COMPARATOR SYS CORP (CO)
Each share old Common 1¢ par exchanged for (0.2) share new Common 1¢ par 08/06/1990
SEC revoked common stock registration 04/12/2005
No stockholders' equity

COMPARE GENERIKS INC (DE)
Company terminated registration of common stock and is no longer public as of 02/07/2001

COMPAS ELECTRS INC (CANADA)
Acquired by AIM Safety Co., Inc. 12/08/1997
Each share Common no par exchanged for (0.1) share Common no par
AIM Safety Co., Inc. name changed to AimGlobal Technologies Co., Inc. 01/29/1999
(See AimGlobal Technologies Co., Inc.)

COMPASS BANCSHARES INC (DE)
Common $2 par split (3) for (2) by issuance of (0.5) additional share payable 04/02/1997 to holders of record 03/17/1997
Perpetual Preferred Ser. F $25 par called for redemption at $25.75 on 02/15/1999
Common $2 par split (3) for (2) by issuance of (0.5) additional share payable 04/02/1999 to holders of record 03/15/1999
Preferred Ser. E $25 par called for redemption at $25 on 11/15/1999
Merged into Banco Bilbao Vizcaya Argentaria, S.A. 09/07/2007
Each share Common $2 par exchanged for either (2.8) Sponsored ADR's for Ordinary or (1.12) Sponsored ADR's for Ordinary and $43.092 cash

COMPASS CAP GROUP (MA)
Merged into PNC Fund 01/13/1996
Details not available

COMPASS DATA SYS INC (NV)
Merged into Ethika Corp. 08/20/1996
Details not available

COMPASS DISTRG INC (NY)
Name changed to Grudge Music Group, Inc. 7/28/89
Grudge Music Group, Inc. name changed to Echo Springs Water Co., Inc. 9/21/93
(See Echo Springs Water Co., Inc.)

COMPASS DIVERSIFIED TR (DE)
Issue Information - 13,500,000 SHS BEN INT offered at $15 per share on 05/10/2006
Name changed to Compass Diversified Holdings 09/14/2007

COMPASS EMP FDS TR (DE)
Name changed to Victory Portfolios II and EMP Developed 500 Enhanced Volatility Weighted Index ETF, EMP Emerging Market High Dividend 100 Volatility Weighted Index ETF, EMP Emerging Market 500 Volatility Weighted Index ETF, EMP International High Dividend 100 Volatility Weighted Index ETF, EMP International 500 Volatility Weighted Index ETF, EMP U.S. Discovery 500 Enhanced Volatility Weighted Index ETF, EMP U.S. EQ Income 100 Enhanced Volatility Weighted Index ETF, EMP U.S. 500 Enhanced Volatility Weighted Index ETF, EMP U.S. 500 Volatility Weighted Index ETF, EMP U.S. Large Cap High Dividend 100 Volatility Weighted ETF, EMP U.S. Small Cap 500 Volatility Weighted Index ETF and EMP U.S. Small Cap High Dividend 100 Volatility Weighted Index ETF reclassified as CEMP Developed Enhanced Volatility Wtd Index ETF, CEMP Emerging Market High Div Volatility Wtd Index ETF, CEMP Emerging Market Volatility Wtd Index ETF, CEMP International High Dividend Volatility Wtd Index ETF, CEMP International Volatility Wtd Index ETF, CEMP US Discovery Enhanced Volatility Wtd Index ETF, CEMP US EQ Income Enhanced Volatility Wtd Index ETF, CEMP US 500 Enhanced Volatility Wtd Index ETF, CEMP US 500 Volatility Wtd Index ETF, CEMP US Large Cap High Div Volatility Wtd Index ETF, CEMP US Large Cap Div Volatility Wtd Index ETF or CEMP US Small Cap Volatility Wtd Index ETF respectively 10/28/2015

COMPASS ENERGY CORP (NV)
Common $0.001 par split (4) for (1) by issuance of (3) additional shares payable 9/4/2001 to holders of record 8/27/2001 Ex date - 8/22/2001
Recapitalized as In-Systcom, Inc. 6/8/2004
Each share Common $0.001 par exchanged for (0.0005) share Common $0.001 par

COMPASS GOLD CORP (BC)
Each share old Common no par exchanged for (0.2) share new Common no par 06/22/2009
Each share new Common no par exchanged again for (0.025) share new Common no par 09/21/2015
Each share new Common no par exchanged again for (0.2) share new Common no par 11/30/2017
Reincorporated under the laws of Ontario 12/04/2017

COMPASS GROUP PLC (UNITED KINGDOM)
Merged into Granada Group PLC 07/27/2000
Each Sponsored ADR for Ordinary 5p par exchanged for $9.6619 cash
(Additional Information in Active)

COMPASS GROWTH FUND, INC. (DE)
Acquired by Massachusetts Investors Growth Stock Fund, Inc. 9/29/75
Each share Capital Stock $1 par exchanged for (0.5212045) share Capital Stock $1 par

COMPASS INCOME FD (ON)
Under plan of merger each Trust Unit automatically became (1.69281793) MINT Income Fund Trust Units 03/21/2017

COMPASS INCOME FUND, INC. (DE)
Acquired by Compass Growth Fund, Inc. 11/01/1974
Each share Capital Stock $1 par exchanged for (1.5946) shares Capital Stock $1 par
Compass Growth Fund, Inc. acquired by Massachusetts Investors Growth Stock Fund, Inc. 09/29/1975

COMPASS INDS INC (NV)
Reincorporated 05/13/1983
State of incorporation changed from (CA) to (NV) 05/13/1983
Name changed to National Comprehensive Services, Inc. 08/19/1983
National Comprehensive Services, Inc. name changed to HMO America, Inc. 12/21/1984 which merged into United HealthCare Corp. 08/31/1993 which name changed to UnitedHealth Group Inc. (MN) 03/01/2000 which reincorporated in Delaware 07/01/2015

COMPASS INTL SVCS CORP (DE)
Merged into NCO Group, Inc. 08/20/1999
Each share Common 1¢ par exchanged for (0.23739) share Common no par
(See NCO Group, Inc.)

COMPASS INVT GROUP (FL)
Reorganized under the laws of Delaware as American Pacific Corp. 03/30/1981
Each Share of Bene. Int. 10¢ par exchanged for (0.25) share Common 10¢ par
(See American Pacific Corp.)

COMPASS INVESTMENTS OF ALBERTA LTD. (AB)
Through exchange offer 100% acquired by Paloma Petroleum Ltd. as of 12/00/1978
Public interest eliminated

COMPASS KNOWLEDGE HLDGS INC (NV)
Each share old Common $0.001 par exchanged for (0.00004) share new Common $0.001 par 05/19/2009
Merged into Embanet Corp. 11/04/2010
Each share new Common $0.001 par exchanged for $209,304.83 cash
Note: Each share new Common $0.001 par received initial distribution of $732.6847 cash from escrow 02/02/2011
Each share new Common $0.001 par received second distribution of $26,899.6476 cash from escrow 11/03/2011
Each share new Common $0.001 par received third distribution of $879.07 cash from escrow 12/13/2012
Each share new Common $0.001 par received fourth and final distribution of $6,934.55 cash from escrow 03/12/2015

COMPASS PETE LTD (AB)
Merged into Whitecap Resources Inc. 02/10/2012
Each share Common no par exchanged for (0.205) share Common no par

COMPASS PLASTICS & TECHNOLOGIES INC (DE)
Assets sold for the benefit of creditors 09/28/1999
Stockholders' equity unlikely

COMPASS RES INC (NV)
Name changed to Workshop Ltd. 08/01/1989
Workshop Ltd. name changed to Children's Creative Workshop, Ltd. 08/30/1989 which name changed to Kent Holdings Ltd. 06/20/1991
(See Kent Holdings Ltd.)

COMPASS RES LTD (BC)
Recapitalized as United Compass Resources Ltd. 06/09/1993
Each share Common no par exchanged for (0.33333333) share Common no par
United Compass Resources Ltd. recapitalized as Tartan Energy Inc. (BC) 10/02/1998 which reincorporated in Alberta 08/01/2001
(See Tartan Energy Inc.)

COMPASS TR III (DE)
7.35% Capital Securities called for redemption at $25 on 11/08/2007

COMPCO GENERAL CORP. (CO)
Declared defunct and inoperative for failure to pay taxes and file reports 10/21/1972

COMPDENT CORP (DE)
Merged into TAGYCR Acquisition, Inc. 06/17/1999
Each share Common 1¢ par exchanged for $15 cash

COMPELLENT TECHNOLOGIES INC (DE)
Acquired by Dell International L.L.C. 02/22/2011
Each share Common $0.001 par exchanged for $27.75 cash

COMPERIPHERALS INC (NY)
Name changed to Facit-Addo, Inc. 02/28/1973
(See Facit-Addo, Inc.)

COMPETITIVE ASSOC INC (DE)
Name changed to Seaboard Leverage Fund 04/12/1973
Seaboard Leverage Fund merged into Oppenheimer A.I.M. Fund, Inc. 12/07/1976 which name changed to Oppenheimer Global Fund 02/01/1987

COMPETITIVE CAP FD (DE)
Merged into Oppenheimer A.I.M. Fund, Inc. 12/07/1976
Each share Common $1 par exchanged for (0.4500629) share Capital Stock $1 par
Oppenheimer A.I.M. Fund, Inc. name changed to Oppenheimer Global Fund 02/01/1987

COMPETITIVE GAMES INTL INC (NV)
Each share old Common $0.001 par exchanged for (0.002) share new Common $0.001 par 03/14/2007
Each share new Common $0.001 par exchanged again for (0.001) share new Common $0.001 par 06/18/2009
Recapitalized as PacWest Equities, Inc. 05/07/2010
Each share new Common $0.001 par exchanged for (0.001) share Common $0.001 par
(See PacWest Equities, Inc.)

COMPETITIVE TECHNOLOGIES INC (DE)
Name changed to Calmare Therapeutics Inc. 06/04/2015

COMPEX TECHNOLOGIES INC (MN)
Merged into Encore Medical Corp. 02/24/2006
Each share Common 10¢ par exchanged for (1.40056) shares Common $0.001 par
(See Encore Medical Corp.)

COMPLEAT HEALTH CORP (CANADA)
Out of business 06/11/1990
Details not available

COMPLETE AUTOMOTIVE INC (FL)
Name changed to Candywyne Corp. 10/21/1974
(See Candywyne Corp.)

COMPLETE BUSINESS SOLUTIONS INC (MI)
Common no par split (2) for (1) by issuance of (1) additional share payable 03/19/1998 to holders of record 03/05/1998
Name changed to Covansys Corp. 06/07/2001
(See Covansys Corp.)

COMPLETE GENOMICS INC (DE)
Acquired by BGI-Shenzhen 03/18/2013
Each share Common $0.001 par exchanged for $3.15 cash

COMPLETE MGMT INC (NY)
Plan of reorganization under Chapter 11 Federal Bankruptcy effective 10/03/2003
No stockholders' equity

COMPLETE PRODTN SVCS INC (DE)
Merged into Superior Energy Services, Inc. 02/07/2012
Each share Common 1¢ par exchanged for (0.945) share Common $0.001 par and $7 cash

COMPLETE WELLNESS CTRS INC (DE)
Chapter 7 Federal Bankruptcy proceedings closed 08/19/2003
No stockholders' equity

COMPLETEL EUROPE N V (NETHERLANDS)
Program terminated 08/23/2002
Each New York Share exchanged for (1) share Ordinary

COMPLEX, INC.
Name changed to Amer-Tex Energy, Inc. 12/03/1981
(See Amer-Tex Energy, Inc.)

COMPLIANCE & RISK MGMT SOLUTIONS INC (DE)
Name changed to Nukkleus Inc. 07/27/2015

COMPLIANCE INDS INC (NV)
Recapitalized as Vintage Properties Inc. 04/03/1995
Each share Common $0.001 par exchanged for (0.01) share Common $0.001 par
Vintage Properties Inc. name changed to Xecom Corp. 10/24/1995 which name changed to AirStar Technologies, Inc. 04/28/1998
(See AirStar Technologies, Inc.)

COMPLIANCE RECYCLING INDS INC (NV)
Each share old Common $0.001 par exchanged for (0.2) share new Common $0.001 par 05/22/1989
Name changed to Enviroserve, Inc. 10/09/1992

COMPLIANCE RESOURCE GROUP INC (NY)
Reincorporated under the laws of Nevada as EnerBrite Technologies Group, Inc. 06/15/2007
Technologies Group, Inc. recapitalized as Limitless Venture Group Inc. 02/04/2013

COMPLIANCE SYS CORP (NV)
Each share old Common $0.001 par exchanged for (0.00100554) share new Common $0.001 par 10/03/2012
Name changed to SeanieMac International Ltd. 08/16/2013

COMPLINK LTD (NY)
Name changed to Netplex Group, Inc. 06/10/1996
(See Netplex Group, Inc.)

COMPO INDS INC (DE)
Common $1 par split (5) for (4) by issuance of (0.25) additional share 03/01/1979
Stock Dividends - 10% 05/24/1968; 20% 08/15/1972; 100% 08/15/1977
Merged into Ausimont Compo N.V. 11/04/1985
Each share Common $1 par exchanged for (1) share Common 5 Gldrs. par
Ausimont Compo N.V. name changed to Ausimont N.V. 05/08/1987
(See Ausimont N.V.)

COMPO SHOE MACHINERY CORP. (DE)
Common no par changed to $1 par 00/00/1932
5% Preferred $25 par called for redemption 03/01/1960
Each VTC for Common $1 par exchanged for (1) share Common $1 par 03/16/1965
Stock Dividend - 100% 10/00/1946
Name changed to Compo Industries, Inc. 05/01/1967
Compo Industries, Inc. merged into Ausimont Compo N.V. 11/14/1985 which name changed to Ausimont N.V. 05/08/1987
(See Ausimont N.V.)

COMPONENT HOUSING SYSTEMS, USA, INC. (ID)
Common 5¢ par changed to $0.001 par and (1) additional share issued 01/04/1988
Name changed to Virogen, Inc. 01/04/1988
(See Virogen, Inc.)

COMPONENT SYS INC (MN)
Completely liquidated 12/06/1986
Each share Common 5¢ par received first and final distribution of approximately $1.50 cash

COMPONENT TECHNOLOGY CORP (DE)
Acquired by a management group 06/16/1989
Each share Common 1¢ par exchanged for $17 cash

COMPONENTGUARD INC (NY)
Filed a petition under Chapter 11 Federal Bankruptcy Code 05/01/1992
Stockholders' equity unlikely

COMPONENTS CORP AMER (NY)
Each share Common $1 par exchanged for (0.33333333) share Capital Stock $1 par 06/13/1962
Stock Dividends - 10% 04/28/1961; 100% 07/26/1971
Merged into CCA Nucorp Holding, Inc. 12/31/1981
Each share Capital Stock $1 par exchanged for $2.50 cash

COMPONENTS INC (DE)
Common 50¢ par changed to 25¢ par and (1) additional share issued 4/11/69
Stock Dividend - 50% 10/22/69
Liquidation completed
Each share Common 25¢ par stamped to indicate initial distribution of (0.03915) share Corning Glass Works Common $5 par 6/18/71
Each share Stamped Common 25¢ par exchanged for second and final distribution of (0.010875) share Corning Glass Works Common $5 par 6/17/74
Corning Glass Works name changed to Corning Inc. 4/28/89

COMPONENTS SPECIALTIES INC (NY)
Merged into a private company 8/31/2001
Each share Common 10¢ par exchanged for $5 cash

COMPONOFORM INC (MA)
Assets assigned and sold for benefit of creditors 06/13/1973
No stockholders' equity

COMPOSITE AUTOMOBILE RESH LTD (AB)
Name changed to World Transport Authority, Inc. and (3) additional shares issued 09/01/2000

COMPOSITE BD & STK FD INC (WA)
Name changed in March 1952
Name changed from Composite Bond & Preferred Stock Fund, Inc. to Composite Bond & Stock Fund, Inc. in March 1952
Capital Stock $1 par changed to 50¢ par and (1) additional share issued 2/28/62
Capital Stock $1 par reclassified as Class A $0.0005 par in 1994
Under plan of reorganization each share Class A $0.0005 par or Class B $0.0005 par automatically became (1) share WM Trust I Bond & Stock Fund Class A or Bond & Stock Fund Class B respectively 3/20/98

COMPOSITE BOND FUND, INC. (WA)
Name changed to Composite Bond & Preferred Stock Fund, Inc. in August 1948
Composite Bond & Preferred Stock Fund, Inc. name changed to Composite Bond & Stock Fund, Inc. in March 1952

COMPOSITE CASH MGMT CO (WA)
Under plan of reorganization each share Money Market Portfolio Class A, Money Market Portfolio Class B, Tax-Exempt Portfolio Class A, or Tax-Exempt Portfolio Class B automatically became (1) share WM Trust I Money Market Fund Class A, Money Market Fund Class B, Tax-Exempt Bond Fund Class A, or Tax-Exempt Bond Fund Class B respectively 3/20/98

COMPOSITE DESIGN INC (NV)
Each share old Common $0.001 par exchanged for (0.001) share new Common $0.001 par 7/5/96
Recapitalized as Centraxx Inc. 5/18/99
Each (2.5) shares new Common $0.001 par exchanged for (1) share Common $0.001 par

COMPOSITE ENTERPRISES INC (UT)
Name changed to Kent Toys, Inc. (UT) 01/20/1986
Kent Toys, Inc. (UT) reorganized in Delaware as L.A. Group Inc. 03/20/1996 which name changed to ONTV, Inc. 04/03/2000 which name changed to True Product ID, Inc. 05/22/2006

COMPOSITE EQUITY SER INC (WA)
Common $1 par changed to 50¢ par and (1) additional share issued 1/31/60
Common 50¢ par reclassified as Class A $0.0005 par in 1994
Under plan of reorganization each share Class A $0.0005 par or Class B $0.0005 par automatically became (1) share WM Trust I Growth & Income Fund Class A or Growth & Income Fund Class B respectively 3/20/98

COMPOSITE HLDGS INC (NV)
Name changed to Gold Rock Holdings, Inc. 1/7/2005

COMPOSITE INCOME FD INC (WA)
Under plan of reorganization each share Class A 1¢ par or Class B 1¢ par automatically became (1) share WM Trust I Income Fund Class A or Income Fund Class B respectively 3/20/98

COMPOSITE INDS AMER INC (NV)
Recapitalized as Composite Holdings, Inc. 5/8/2002
Each (1.1) shares Common $0.001 par exchanged for (1) share Class A Common $0.001 par and (0.1) share Class B Common Ser. 1 $0.001 par
Composite Holdings, Inc. name changed to Gold Rock Holdings, Inc. 1/7/2005

COMPOSITE NORTHWEST FUND 50 INC (WA)
Name changed 3/15/90
Value Portfolio liquidated 4/30/89
Details not available
Name changed from Composite Select Fund Inc. to Composite Northwest Fund 50, Inc. 3/15/90
High Yield Portfolio liquidated 4/30/90
Details not available
Under plan of reorganization each share Class A $0.00001 par or Class B $0.00001 par automatically became (1) share WM Trust I Northwest Fund Class A or Northwest Fund Class B respectively 3/20/98

COMPOSITE PWR CORP (NV)
Charter revoked for failure to file reports and pay taxes 08/31/2010

COMPOSITE SOLUTIONS INC (FL)
Each share old Common $0.0001 par exchanged for (9.229876) shares new Common $0.0001 par 07/12/1999
Plan of reorganization under Chapter 11 Federal Bankruptcy Code effective 01/02/2007
Each share new Common $0.0001 par received approximately (0.00105418) share Composite Solutions, Inc. (New) Common, (0.00105418) share Composite Solutions of Nevada Common, and (0.00105418) share Trans-Science Corp. Common 01/02/2007

COMPOSITE STOCK FUND, INC. (WA)
Name changed to Composite Equity Series Inc. in 1951
Composite Equities Series Inc. reorganized as WM Trust I 3/20/98

COMPOSITE TAX EXEMPT BD FD INC (WA)
Under plan of reorganization each share Class A $0.0001 par or Class B $0.0001 par automatically became (1) share WM Trust I Tax-Exempt Bond Fund Class A or Tax-Exempt Bond Fund Class B respectively 3/20/98

COMPOSITE TECHNOLOGY CORP (NV)
Plan of reorganization under Chapter 11 Federal Bankruptcy proceedings effective 10/01/2014
No stockholders' equity

COMPOSITE U S GOVT SECS INC (WA)
Under plan of reorganization each share Class A $0.0001 par or Class B $0.0001 par automatically became (1) share U.S. Government Securities Fund Class A or U.S. Government Securites Fund Class B respectively 3/20/98

COMPOSITECH LTD (DE)
Assets sold for the benefit of creditors 11/13/2002
No stockholders' equity

COMPOST AMER HLDG INC (NJ)
Reorganized under the laws of Delaware as Phoenix Waste Services Co., Inc. 09/29/2000
Each share Common no par exchanged for (1) share Common $0.001 par
(See Phoenix Waste Services Co., Inc.)

COMPOUND NAT FOODS INC (NV)
SEC revoked common stock registration 12/19/2012

COMPREHENSIVE CANCER CARE CORP (DE)
Name changed to Compremedx Cancer Centers Corp. 12/20/85
(See Compremedx Cancer Centers Corp.)

COMPREHENSIVE CMNTYS CORP (FL)
Each share old Common 1¢ par exchanged for (0.33333333) share new Common 1¢ par 01/10/1973
Recapitalized as University Properties Investment Corp. 08/02/1979
Each share new Common 1¢ par exchanged for (0.2) share Common 1¢ par
University Properties Investment Corp. name changed to John Phillip Tuba Corp. 04/22/1983
(See John Phillip Tuba Corp.)

COMPREHENSIVE COMPUTER SYS INC (NY)
Common 10¢ par changed to 5¢ par and (1) additional share issued 09/03/1968
Charter cancelled and proclaimed dissolved for failure to pay taxes 06/24/1981

COMPREHENSIVE DESIGNERS INC (PA)
Name changed to CDI Corp. and Common no par and Class B Common no par changed to 10¢ par 10/01/1973
(See CDI Corp.)

COMPREHENSIVE EDL SYS INC (NY)
Recapitalized as Atlantic City Property Investors, Inc. 04/03/2013
Each share Common 1¢ par exchanged for (0.5) share Common 1¢ par
(See Atlantic City Property Investors, Inc.)

COMPREHENSIVE ENVIRONMENTAL SYS INC (DE)
Name changed to Windswept Environmental Group, Inc. 03/25/1997
(See Windswept Environmental Group, Inc.)

COMPREHENSIVE HEALTH SYS INC (CA)
Adjudicated bankrupt 02/22/1974
Stockholders' equity unlikely

COMPREHENSIVE HEALTHCARE SOLUTIONS INC (DE)
Common 10¢ par changed to 1¢ par 09/07/2006
Name changed to Hybrid Energy Holdings, Inc. 11/12/2009

COMPREHENSIVE MED DIAGNOSTICS GROUP INC (FL)
Recapitalized as My Vintage Baby, Inc. 06/01/2007
Each share Common $0.001 par exchanged for (0.002) share Common $0.001 par
(See My Vintage Baby, Inc.)

COMPREHENSIVE MED INTELLIGENCE INC (AB)
Merged into Rise HealthWare Inc. 10/30/2001
Each share Common no par exchanged for (0.28571428) share Common no par and (0.14285714) Common Stock Purchase Warrant Ser. A which expired 12/31/2004
Rise HealthWare Inc. merged into Med Access Inc. 10/27/2005

COMPREHENSIVE RESOURCE INC (MN)
Each share old Common 1¢ par exchanged for (0.5) share new Common 1¢ par 08/17/1987
Name changed to Allercare, Inc. 10/00/1988
(See Allercare, Inc.)

COMPREHENSIVE REVIEW TECHNOLOGY INC (FL)
Name changed to Progressive Health Management, Inc. 09/10/1991
(See Progressive Health Management, Inc.)

COMPREHENSIVE SOFTWARE INC (DE)
Charter cancelled and declared inoperative and void for non-payment of taxes 03/01/1987

COMPREMEDX CANCER CTRS CORP (DE)
Charter forfeited for failure to maintain a registered agent 07/15/1999

COMPRESS TECHNOLOGIES INC (NV)
Each share old Common $0.001 par exchanged for (0.01) share new Common $0.001 par 10/14/2009
Name changed to Stadium Entertainment Holdings, Inc. 02/18/2011

COMPRESSARIO CORP (ON)
Delisted from Toronto Venture Stock Exchange 06/20/2003

COMPRESSCO INC (DE)
Merged into TETRA Technologies, Inc. 07/15/2004
Each share Common $0.001 par exchanged for $358.15 cash

COMPRESSCO PARTNERS L P (DE)
Name changed to CSI Compressco L.P. 12/01/2014

COMPRESSED CONCRETE CONSTRUCTION CORP. (NY)
Name changed to Compression Industries Corp. 12/00/1960
(See Compression Industries Corp.)

COMPRESSED INDUSTRIAL GASES, INC.
Merged into National Cylinder Gas Co. 08/31/1940
Each share Capital Stock exchanged for (1.45) shares Common $1 par
National Cylinder Gas Co. name changed to Chemetron Corp. 05/06/1958 which merged into Allegheny Ludlum Industries, Inc. 11/30/1977 which name changed to Allegheny International Inc. 04/29/1981
(See Allegheny International Inc.)

COMPRESSENT CORP (FL)
SEC revoked common stock registration 08/05/2004

COMPRESSION INDS CORP (NY)
Company went private 00/00/1976
Details not available

COMPRESSION LABS INC (DE)
Reincorporated 00/00/1987
State of incorporation changed from (CA) to (DE) and Common 1¢ par changed to $0.001 par 00/00/1987
Acquired by VTEL Corp. 05/23/1997
Each share Common $0.001 par exchanged for (0.46) share Common 1¢ par
VTEL Corp. name changed to Forgent Networks, Inc. 01/18/2002 which recapitalized as Asure Software, Inc. 12/29/2009

COMPRESSION TECHNOLOGIES INC (AB)
Recapitalized as Compression & Encryption Technologies Inc. 07/17/1996
Each share Common no par exchanged for (0.2) share Common no par

COMPRESSION TECHNOLOGIES INC (DE)
Recapitalized as Oriental Focus International Ltd. 10/10/1994
Each share Common $0.005 par exchanged for (0.1) share Common $0.005 par
(See Oriental Focus International Ltd.)

COMPRO LTD (CANADA)
Under plan of merger each share Common no par exchanged for $7 cash 11/05/1976

$1.10 Preferred Ser. A $20 par called for redemption 11/04/1980
Public interest eliminated

COMPS COM INC (DE)
Merged into CoStar Group, Inc. 02/11/2000
Each share Common 1¢ par exchanged for $7.50 cash

COMPSCRIPT INC (FL)
Merged into Omnicare, Inc. 06/26/1998
Each share Common $0.0008 par exchanged for (0.12947) share Common $1 par
(See Omnicare, Inc.)

COMPTEC INDS LTD (BC)
Recapitalized as Integrated Communications Industries Inc. 05/09/2000
Each share Common no par exchanged for (0.11111111) share Common no par
(See Integrated Communications Industries Inc.)

COMPTEK RESH INC (NY)
Common 2¢ par split (2) for (1) by issuance of (1) additional share 05/15/1992
Merged into Northrop Grumman Corp. 09/01/2000
Each share Common 2¢ par exchanged for (0.2799) share Common $1 par
Northrop Grumman Corp. reorganized as Northrop Grumman Corp. (Holding Company) 04/02/2001

COMPTOMETER CORP. (IL)
Common $5 par changed to $1 par 01/29/1959
Merged into Victor Comptometer Corp. 10/30/1961
Each share Common $1 par exchanged for (1) share Common $1 par
Victor Comptometer Corp. merged into Kidde (Walter) & Co., Inc. (DE) 07/15/1977 which name changed to Kidde, Inc. 04/18/1980 which merged into Hanson Trust PLC 12/31/1987 which name changed to Hanson PLC (Old) 01/29/1988 which reorganized as Hanson PLC (New) 10/15/2003

COMPTON EXPLORATIONS LTD. (ON)
Completely liquidated 07/07/1971
Each share Capital Stock $1 par exchanged for (0.105263) share Avilla International Explorations Ltd. Capital Stock no par
(See Avilla International Explorations Ltd.)

COMPTON PETE CORP (AB)
Each share old Common no par exchanged for (0.005) share new Common no par 08/10/2011
Acquired by MFC Industrial Ltd. 09/12/2012
Each share new Common no par exchanged for $1.25 cash

COMPTRAN COMPUTER CORP (OK)
Name changed to Mentor Corp. (OK) 12/01/1971
(See Mentor Corp. (OK))

COMPTRONIX CORP (DE)
Plan of reorganization under Chapter 11 Federal Bankruptcy Code effective 06/04/1997
No stockholders' equity

COMPU-DAWN INC (DE)
Name changed to MyTurn.com 10/27/1999
(See MyTurn.com)

COMPU HOME SYS INTL INC (ON)
Name changed to Arrowlink Corp. 06/26/1993
Arrowlink Corp. name changed to Triarx Gold Corp. 04/24/1996
(See Triarx Gold Corp.)

COMPU PLAN INC (NJ)
Charter revoked for failure to file reports and pay fees 03/31/1994

COMPU-POUR INDS INC (AB)
Name changed to Business Systems International Inc. 10/22/1993
(See Business Systems International Inc.)

COMPU READER INC (DE)
Name changed to Intertech Group, Inc. 04/14/1978
(See Intertech Group, Inc.)

COMPU-SERV NETWORK, INC. (OH)
Common no par split (2) for (1) by issuance of (1) additional share 10/22/1976
Name changed to Compuserve Inc. 05/03/1977
Compuserve Inc. merged into Block (H & R), Inc. 05/12/1980

COMPU SORT SYS INC (DE)
Charter cancelled and declared inoperative and void for non-payment of taxes 03/01/1987

COMPU TAG INC (MN)
Statutorily dissolved 09/25/1991

COMPU TECH INTL INC (FL)
Involuntarily dissolved 11/16/1987

COMPUBOOK SYS INC (NJ)
Merged into Jersey Book Co., Inc. 02/24/1971
Each share Common 1¢ par exchanged for $0.175 cash

COMPUCARE INC (VA)
Acquired by Baxter Travenol Laboratories, Inc. 05/29/1985
Each share Common $0.025 par exchanged for (0.863) share Common $1 par
Baxter Travenol Laboratories, Inc. name changed to Baxter International Inc. 05/18/1988

COMPUCHARGE INC (DE)
Charter cancelled and declared inoperative and void for non-payment of taxes 03/01/1974

COMPUCHEK CORP (NY)
Dissolved by proclamation 03/24/1993

COMPUCHEM CORP (MA)
Acquired by Roche Biomedical Laboratories, Inc. 02/11/1992
Each share Common 1¢ par exchanged for $9.75 cash

COMPUCOLOR INC (NY)
Merged into Moore Business Forms, Inc. 09/14/1978
Each share Common 10¢ par exchanged for $4.40 cash

COMPUCOLOR NETWORK LTD (DE)
Name changed to Moonlight International Corp. 11/09/1995
(See Moonlight International Corp.)

COMPUCOM DEV CORP (IN)
Merged into IWC Resources Corp. 12/12/1986
Each share Common $1 par exchanged for (0.4318) share Common no par
IWC Resources Corp. merged into NIPSCO Industries, Inc. 03/25/1997 which name changed to NiSource Inc. (IN) which reincorporated in Delaware 11/01/2000

COMPUCOM SYS INC (DE)
Reincorporated 06/15/1989
State of incorporation changed from (MI) to (DE) and Common no par changed to 1¢ par 06/15/1989
Merged into CHR Holding Corp. 10/01/2004
Each share Common 1¢ par exchanged for $4.60 cash

COMPUCREDIT CORP (GA)
Name changed to CompuCredit Holdings Corp. 06/30/2009
CompuCredit Holdings Corp. name changed to Atlanticus Holdings Corp. 12/03/2012

COMPUCREDIT HLDGS CORP (GA)
Name changed to Atlanticus Holdings Corp. 12/03/2012

COMPUDAT SCIENTIFIC SYS INC (NY)
Name changed to Biorex Corp. 12/08/1972
(See Biorex Corp.)

COMPUDYNE CORP (PA)
3% Conv. Preferred $1 par converted into Common 25¢ par 00/00/1968
Each share Common 25¢ par exchanged for (0.33333333) share Common 75¢ par 06/29/1979
$6 Preference Ser. B no par called for redemption 01/08/1987
Merged into Gores Patriot Holdings, Inc. 09/21/2007
Each share Common 75¢ par exchanged for $7 cash

COMPUFLEX SYS INC (DE)
Each share old Common $0.001 par exchanged for (0.1) share new Common $0.001 par 10/26/1994
Each share new Common $0.001 par exchanged for (0.1) share new Common $0.001 par 06/10/1996
Merged into Techteam Acquisition 08/22/1997
Each share new Common $0.001 par exchanged for $2.49 cash

COMPUFLIGHT INC (DE)
Each share Common $0.001 par exchanged for (0.025) share Common 1¢ par 04/24/1990
Each share Common 1¢ par exchanged for (0.25) share Common $0.001 par 04/13/1993
Name changed to Navtech, Inc. 01/14/2000
(See Navtech, Inc.)

COMPUFLIGHT OPERATIONS SERVICE, INC. (NY)
Reincorporated under the laws of Delaware as Compuflight, Inc. 12/07/1987
Compuflight, Inc. name changed to Navtech, Inc. 01/14/2000
(See Navtech, Inc.)

COMPUGRAPHIC CORP (MA)
Common 5¢ par split (2) for (1) by issuance of (1) additional share 06/09/1978
Merged into Bayer AG 06/15/1988
Each share Common 5¢ par exchanged for $27 cash

COMPUGROUP MED AG (GERMANY)
Name changed to CompuGroup Medical S.E. 02/26/2016

COMPUGUIDE CORP (NJ)
Recapitalized as Chemfirst Corp. 10/10/1984
Each share Common 10¢ par exchanged for (0.5) share Common 1¢ par
(See Chemfirst Corp.)

COMPUKNIT INDS INC (NY)
Charter cancelled and proclaimed dissolved for failure to pay taxes 03/25/1981

COMPULOAN ORIGINATIONS INC (UT)
Involuntarily dissolved 07/01/1997

COMPUMARKETING SVCS CORP (DE)
Name changed to National Business Lists, Inc. 04/27/1973
(See National Business Lists, Inc.)

COMPUMAT INC (DE)
Merged into JWP Sub Inc. 10/31/1990
Each share Common 1¢ par exchanged for $3.25 cash

COMPUMATICS INC (IN)
Administratively dissolved 06/14/2000

COMPUMATIX, INC. (MO)
Merged into Siboney Corp. 08/21/1967
Each share Common $1 par exchanged for (1.5) shares 55¢ Conv. Preferred $1 par
(See Siboney Corp.)

COMPUMEDIC CTLS CORP (NY)
Charter cancelled and proclaimed dissolved for failure to pay taxes and file reports 12/15/1975

COMPUMETRICS, INC. (DE)
Charter cancelled and declared inoperative and void for non-payment of taxes 04/15/1973

COMPUPRINT INC (NC)
Reincorporated under the laws of Delaware as Terra Energy & Resource Technologies, Inc. 11/16/2006

COMPURAD INC (DE)
Merged into Lumisys Inc. 11/25/1997
Each share Common $0.001 par exchanged for (0.928) share Common $0.001 par
(See Lumisys Inc.)

COMPUSA INC (DE)
Merged into Grupo Sanborns, S.A. de C.V. 03/10/2000
Each share Common no par exchanged for $10.10 cash

COMPUSAMP INC (NY)
Charter cancelled and proclaimed dissolved for failure to pay taxes 12/30/1981

COMPUSAVE CORP (DE)
Common 1¢ par split (2) for (1) by issuance of (1) additional share 03/01/1985
Chapter 11 Federal Bankruptcy Code converted to Chapter 7 on 03/02/1987
No stockholders' equity

COMPUSCAN INC (DE)
Recapitalized as Enercon Data Corp. 02/01/1989
Each share Common 10¢ par exchanged for (0.2) share Common 10¢ par
(See Enercon Data Corp.)

COMPUSERVE CORP (DE)
Merged into WorldCom, Inc. 01/31/1998
Each share Common 1¢ par exchanged for (0.40625) share Common 1¢ par
WorldCom, Inc. name changed to MCI WorldCom, Inc. 09/14/1998 which name changed to WorldCom Inc. (New) 05/01/2000
(See WorldCom Inc. (New))

COMPUSERVE INC (OH)
Merged into Block (H & R), Inc. 05/12/1980
Each share Common no par exchanged for (0.8) share Common no par or $20 cash

COMPUSHOP INC (TX)
Merged into Bell Atlantic Corp. 06/03/1985
Each share Common 1¢ par exchanged for (0.07143) share Common $1 par
Bell Atlantic Corp. name changed to Verizon Communications Inc. 06/30/2000

COMPUSOFT CDA INC (AB)
Name changed to TraceAbility Solutions, Inc. 02/28/2001
(See TraceAbility Solutions, Inc.)

COMPUSOLV INC (WY)
Charter revoked 05/28/1992

COMPUSONICS CORP (CO)
Name changed 07/12/1984
Name changed from CompuSound, Inc. to Compusonics Corp. 07/12/1984
Proclaimed dissolved 01/01/1996

COMPUSTREND FD INC (MD)
Name changed to Stock Average Fund, Inc. 06/07/1976
(See Stock Average Fund, Inc.)

COMPUTALOG LTD (AB)
Name changed 07/17/1989
Common no par split (2) for (1) by issuance of (1) additional share 08/14/1985
Name changed from Computalog Gearhart Ltd. to Computalog Ltd. 07/17/1989
Each share old Common no par exchanged for (0.25) share new Common no par 05/24/1994
Acquired by Precision Drilling Corp. 07/28/1999
Each share new Common no par exchanged for either (0.38) share Common no par or $9 cash
Note: Non-electing holders received stock
(See Precision Drilling Corp.)

COMPUTATIONAL SYS INC (TN)
Merged into Emerson Electric Co. 12/29/1997
Each share Common no par exchanged for (0.425) share Common $1 par and $5.83 cash

COMPUTAX SVCS INC (DE)
Merged into Commerce Clearing House, Inc. 01/01/1976
Each share Common 10¢ par exchanged for $6 cash

COMPUTEK COMPUTING CORP (OK)
Acquired by Flint Resources 08/01/1984
Each share Common 10¢ par exchanged for $1.33 cash

COMPUTEL SYS LTD (CANADA)
Merged into Canada Systems Group Ltd. 05/18/1982
Each share Common no par exchanged for $16 cash

COMPUTER & COMMUNICATIONS TECHNOLOGY CORP (DE)
Stock Dividend - 100% 06/30/1981
Name changed to Sunward Technologies, Inc. and Common 40¢ par changed to 1¢ par 08/31/1990
Sunward Technologies, Inc. merged into Read-Rite Corp. 08/22/1994
(See Read-Rite Corp.)

COMPUTER & DATA COMPONENTS CORP (DE)
Name changed to Arts & Science Technology, Inc. 02/01/1972
Arts & Science Technology, Inc. reorganized as Litex Energy Inc. 11/17/1995 which recapitalized as International Ostrich Corp. 12/11/1997
(See International Ostrich Corp.)

COMPUTER ACCESS INTL INC (FL)
Recapitalized as Dispatch Auto Parts, Inc. 06/16/2005
Each share Common $0.001 par exchanged for (0.005) share Common $0.001 par
Dispatch Auto Parts, Inc. name changed to Environment Ecology Holding Co. of China 11/29/2007

COMPUTER ACCESS TECHNOLOGY CORP (DE)
Merged into LeCroy Corp. 10/29/2004
Each share Common $0.001 par exchanged for $6 cash

COMPUTER AGE INDS INC (VA)
Recapitalized as Vortex Corp. 06/01/1971
Each share Common 10¢ par exchanged for (0.33333333) share Common 10¢ par
(See Vortex Corp.)

COMPUTER AIDED TIME SH INC (MN)
Each share old Common no par

exchanged for (0.44713266) share new Common no par 10/12/1989
Name changed to Mirror Technologies, Inc. 01/08/1990
Mirror Technologies, Inc. name changed to Global Maintech Corp. (Old) 05/15/1995 which name changed to Singlepoint Systems Corp. 08/14/2000 which name changed to Global Maintech Corp. (New) 03/07/2001
(See Global Maintech Corp. (New))

COMPUTER APPLICATIONS INC (DE)
Stock Dividend - 100% 07/01/1964
Adjudicated bankrupt 10/05/1970
No stockholders' equity

COMPUTER ASSISTANCE INTL INC (DE)
Merged into Computer Assistance, Inc. 12/19/1986
Each share Common 10¢ par exchanged for $46 cash

COMPUTER ASSOC INTL INC (DE)
Common 10¢ par split (2) for (1) by issuance of (1) additional share 05/17/1983
Common 10¢ par split (2) for (1) by issuance of (1) additional share 05/08/1986
Common 10¢ par split (2) for (1) by issuance of (1) additional share 05/07/1987
Common 10¢ par split (2) for (1) by issuance of (1) additional share 06/16/1989
Common 10¢ par split (3) for (2) by issuance of (0.5) additional share 09/05/1995
Common 10¢ par split (3) for (2) by issuance of (0.5) additional share payable 07/15/1996 to holders of record 06/19/1996 Ex date - 07/16/1996
Common 10¢ par split (3) for (2) by issuance of (0.5) additional share payable 11/26/1997 to holders of record 11/05/1997 Ex date - 11/28/1997
Name changed to CA, Inc. 02/01/2006

COMPUTER AUDIT SYS INC (NJ)
Merged into Cullinane Corp. 04/19/1977
Each share Common 5¢ par exchanged for $0.40 cash

COMPUTER AUTOMATION INC (DE)
Charter cancelled and declared inoperative and void for non-payment of taxes 03/01/1994

COMPUTER AUTOMATION SYS INC (NV)
Recapitalized as Kahuna Network Security, Inc. 01/20/2004
Each share Common $0.001 par exchanged for (0.25) share Common $0.001 par
Kahuna Network Security, Inc. name changed to American Security Resources Corp. 08/24/2004

COMPUTER BROKERS CDA INC (ON)
Name changed to Globelle Corp. 04/19/1995
(See Globelle Corp.)

COMPUTER BUSINESS SUPPLIES WASH INC (DE)
Name changed 06/11/1973
Name changed from Computer Business Supplies, Inc. to Computer Business Supplies of Washington, Inc. 06/11/1973
Filed a petition under Chapter 7 Federal Bankruptcy Code 08/18/1989
Stockholders' equity unlikely

COMPUTER CAP CORP (NY)
Name changed to Talbryn Financial Corp. 01/16/1985
Talbryn Financial Corp. name changed to Zuccarelli Holophonics Corp. 02/17/1988

COMPUTER CAREERS INC (NY)
Voluntarily dissolved 02/20/2009
Details not available

COMPUTER CENTER CORP. (NY)
Name changed to Electronic Computer Programming Institute, Inc. 05/01/1965
(See Electronic Computer Programming Institute, Inc.)

COMPUTER CENTURY 1, INC. (DE)
Reincorporated 02/14/1972
State of incorporation changed from (IL) to (DE) 02/14/1972
Charter cancelled and declared inoperative and void for non-payment of taxes 03/01/1974

COMPUTER CIRCUITS CORP (NY)
Charter cancelled and proclaimed dissolved for failure to pay taxes 06/27/1979

COMPUTER COLLEGE TECHNOLOGY INC (DE)
Charter cancelled and declared inoperative and void for non-payment of taxes 03/01/1979

COMPUTER COMMUNICATIONS INC (DE)
Reincorporated 02/02/1988
Each share Common $10 par exchanged for (10) shares Common $1 par 07/16/1968
State of incorporation changed from (CA) to (DE) 02/02/1988
Recapitalized as Trendsetter Solar Products, Inc. 06/12/2006
Each share Common $1 par exchanged for (0.001) share Common $1 par

COMPUTER COMPLEX INC (DE)
Name changed to Houston Complex, Inc. 11/24/1972
(See Houston Complex, Inc.)

COMPUTER COMPONENTS CORP (DE)
Filed petition under Chapter 7 Federal Bankruptcy Code 12/16/1988
Stockholders' equity unlikely

COMPUTER CONCEPTS, INC. (DE)
Acquired by Computer Applications Inc. 10/01/1964
Each share Common 5¢ par exchanged for (1.7) shares Common 10¢ par
(See Computer Applications Inc.)

COMPUTER CONCEPTS CORP (DE)
Each share Common $0.001 par exchanged for (0.25) share Common $0.0001 par 09/22/1992
Each share Common $0.0001 par exchanged for (0.1) share Common $0.001 par 03/30/1998
Name changed to Direct Insite Corp. 08/23/2000
Direct Insite Corp. name changed to Paybox Corp. 11/14/2016
(See Paybox Corp.)

COMPUTER CONSOLES INC (DE)
Common 10¢ par split (2) for (1) by issuance of (1) additional share 03/31/1980
Common 10¢ par split (2) for (1) by issuance of (1) additional share 06/30/1983
Acquired by STC PLC 02/10/1989
Each share Common 10¢ par exchanged for $12.80 cash
(See STC PLC)

COMPUTER CONSULTANTS CORP. (DE)
Name changed to CCC, Inc. 04/27/1971
(See CCC, Inc.)

COMPUTER CONTROL CO., INC. (DE)
Completely liquidated 05/27/1966
Each share Common no par exchanged for first and final distribution of (0.285714) share Honeywell Inc. Common $1.50 par
Honeywell Inc. merged into Honeywell International Inc. 12/01/1999

COMPUTER CORP CARIBBEAN (DE)
Charter cancelled and declared inoperative and void for non-payment of taxes 04/15/1971

COMPUTER COUNSELING INC (MD)
Common 12¢ par changed to 6¢ par and (1) additional share issued 03/28/1969
Charter annulled for failure to file reports 12/15/1971

COMPUTER CR SYS INC (GA)
Administratively dissolved 04/29/1988

COMPUTER CTLS CORP (DE)
Name changed to Control Industries Corp. 12/23/1969
Control Industries Corp. name changed to Consurgico Corp. 02/18/1971 which name changed to Chase Development Corp. 04/09/1979
(See Chase Development Corp.)

COMPUTER DATA SYS INC (MD)
Common 10¢ par split (2) for (1) by issuance of (1) additional share 06/03/1982
Common 10¢ par split (2) for (1) by issuance of (1) additional share 03/08/1983
Common 10¢ par split (2) for (1) by issuance of (1) additional share 08/23/1993
Stock Dividend - 25% 03/06/1981
Merged into Affiliated Computer Services, Inc. 12/16/1997
Each share Common 10¢ par exchanged for (1.759) shares Class A Common 1¢ par
Affiliated Computer Services, Inc. merged into Xerox Corp. 02/08/2010

COMPUTER DATABANKS (DE)
Name changed to Applied Data Processing, Inc. 05/01/1977
Applied Data Processing, Inc. name changed to Applied Data, Inc. 09/01/1982
(See Applied Data, Inc.)

COMPUTER DEDUCTIONS INC (DE)
Adjudicated bankrupt 07/01/1971
Stockholders' equity unlikely

COMPUTER DEPOT INC (MN)
Filed petition under Chapter 7 Federal Bankruptcy Code 07/00/1987
No stockholders' equity

COMPUTER DESIGN CORP (CA)
Name changed to Compucorp 06/12/1974

COMPUTER DESIGNED SYS INC (MN)
Common 5¢ par split (2) for (1) by issuance of (1) additional share 06/15/1984
Merged into CDS Acquisition Corp. 11/30/1988
Each share Common 5¢ par exchanged for $0.625 principal amount of Computer Designed Systems, Inc. 14% Subordinated Debentures due 12/01/1993

COMPUTER DEVICES CORP (NY)
Name changed to Retreading International, Inc. 05/21/1974
(See Retreading International, Inc.)

COMPUTER DEVICES INC (MA)
Reorganized under the laws of Maryland 06/30/1986
Each share Common 1¢ par exchanged for (0.5) share Conv. Class A Common 1¢ par
Note: Shares acquired before 06/30/1985 exchanged for (0.5) share Class B Common 1¢ par
Unexchanged certificates were cancelled and became without value 06/28/1987
(See Computer Devices, Inc. (MD))

COMPUTER DEVICES INC (MD)
Charter forfeited for failure to file reports and pay fees 10/06/2000

COMPUTER DIALYSIS SYS INC (CO)
Charter suspended for failure to file annual reports 01/01/1989

COMPUTER DIMENSIONS INC (DE)
Merged into Itel Corp. (Old) 12/14/1976
Each share Common 10¢ par exchanged for (0.55) share Common $1 par
Itel Corp. (Old) reorganized as Itel Corp. (New) 09/19/1983 which name changed to Anixter International Inc. 09/01/1995

COMPUTER DIODE CORP (DE)
Reincorporated 06/26/1969
State of incorporation changed from (NJ) to (DE) and Class A 10¢ par reclassified as Common 10¢ par 06/26/1969
Name changed to Codi Corp. 05/08/1973
(See Codi Corp.)

COMPUTER DYNAMICS INC (CA)
Merged into Central Bank (Oakland, CA) 06/30/1980
Each share Capital Stock no par exchanged for (0.0007758) share Common $2.50 par
Note: In effect holders received $0.55 cash per share and public interest was eliminated

COMPUTER EASY INTL INC (UT)
Reorganized under the laws of Delaware as American Architectural Products Corp. 04/02/1997
Each share Common 1¢ par exchanged for (0.1) share Common $0.001 par
(See American Architectural Products Corp.)

COMPUTER ED INC (DE)
Name changed to Barbizon International, Inc. 10/13/1969
(See Barbizon International, Inc.)

COMPUTER EDL SVCS INC (DE)
Charter cancelled and declared inoperative and void for non-payment of taxes 03/01/1976

COMPUTER ELECTION SYS INC (CA)
Stock Dividend - 25% 07/14/1975
Merged into Hale Bros. Associates, Inc. 08/08/1977
Each share Common 10¢ par exchanged for $9.75 cash

COMPUTER ENGR CORP (FL)
Name changed to CEC Corp. 11/09/1970
CEC Corp. name changed to Douglass Industries, Inc. 07/18/1972
(See Douglass Industries, Inc.)

COMPUTER ENTERPRISES INC (DE)
Name changed to Jefferson National Corp. 07/28/1971
(See Jefferson National Corp.)

COMPUTER ENTRY SYS CORP (DE)
Acquired by BancTec, Inc. 02/10/1989
Each share Common 5¢ par exchanged for $8.50 cash

COMPUTER EQUIP CORP (CA)
8% Conv. Preferred Ser. D called for redemption 06/03/1972
Name changed to Cetec Corp. (CA) 05/29/1974
Cetec Corp. (CA) reincorporated in Delaware 05/12/1986
(See Cetec Corp. (DE)

COMPUTER EXCHANGE INC (NY)
Name changed to Chyron Corp. 11/28/1975
Chyron Corp. name changed to ChyronHego Corp. 05/23/2013

(See ChyronHego Corp.)

COMPUTER EXPOSITIONS INC (NY)
Merged into New York Asset Management Inc. 05/25/1972
Details not available

COMPUTER FACS LTD (PA)
Common no par split (2) for (1) by issuance of (1) additional share 03/30/1972
Name changed to Rotex Corp. 03/05/1973
(See Rotex Corp.)

COMPUTER FACTORY INC (NY)
Common 1¢ par split (4) for (3) by issuance of (0.33333333) additional share 08/06/1986
Common 1¢ par split (3) for (2) by issuance of (0.5) additional share 03/03/1987
Stock Dividend - 10% 10/28/1988
Merged into CompuCom Systems, Inc. 04/30/1991
Each share Common 1¢ par exchanged for $4.40 cash

COMPUTER FIELD EXPRESS INC (NY)
Adjudicated bankrupt 11/27/1972
Stockholders' equity unlikely

COMPUTER GIFTWARE CO (NV)
Each share old Common $0.001 par exchanged for (0.1) share new Common $0.001 par 03/21/1995
Charter revoked 04/01/2005

COMPUTER GRAPHICS INC (MN)
Merged into Advertising Unlimited, Inc. 12/04/1972
Each share Common 10¢ par exchanged for (0.4) share Common 10¢ par
(See Advertising Unlimited, Inc.)

COMPUTER GRAPHICS INC (PA)
Ceased operations 09/13/1985
Details not available

COMPUTER HORIZONS CORP (NY)
Old Common 10¢ par split (3) for (2) by issuance of (0.5) additional share 07/11/1983
Old Common 10¢ par split (3) for (2) by issuance of (0.5) additional share 04/13/1993
Old Common 10¢ par split (3) for (2) by issuance of (0.5) additional share 03/22/1994
Old Common 10¢ par split (3) for (2) by issuance of (0.5) additional share 05/30/1995
Old Common 10¢ par split (3) for (2) by issuance of (0.5) additional share payable 01/09/1996 to holders of record 12/22/1995
Old Common 10¢ par split (3) for (2) by issuance of (0.5) additional share payable 06/09/1997 to holders of record 05/22/1997
Stock Dividends - 100% 11/07/1980; 10% 01/24/1983
Liquidation completed
Each share old Common 10¢ par received initial distribution of $4 cash payable 03/27/2007 to holders of record 03/16/2007
Each share old Common 10¢ par received second distribution of $0.30 cash payable 02/11/2008 to holders of record 01/15/2008 Ex date - 02/12/2008
Each share old Common 10¢ par exchanged for (1) share new Common 10¢ par to reflect a (1) for (500) reverse split followed by a (500) for (1) forward split 02/11/2009
Note: Holders of (499) or fewer pre-split shares received $0.30 cash per share
Each share new Common 10¢ par received third distribution of $0.23 cash payable 04/21/2009 to holders of record 03/31/2009 Ex date - 04/22/2009
Each share new Common 10¢ par received fourth distribution of $0.07 cash payable 09/10/2010 to holders of record 08/23/2010 Ex date - 09/13/2010
Each share new Common 10¢ par received fifth and final distribution of $0.0709 cash payable 12/21/2012 to holders of record 12/07/2012
Note: Certificates were not required to be surrendered and are without value

COMPUTER HORIZONS INC (DE)
Name changed to CHI Research, Inc. 09/12/1989
(See CHI Research, Inc.)

COMPUTER IDENTICS CORP (MA)
Merged into Robotic Vision Systems, Inc. 08/30/1996
Each share Common 10¢ par exchanged for (0.19558572) share Common 1¢ par
(See Robotic Vision Systems, Inc.)

COMPUTER IMAGE CORP (DE)
Charter cancelled and declared void for failure to pay franchise taxes 03/01/1988

COMPUTER INDS INC (DE)
Merged into University Computing Co. (TX) 12/17/1969
Each share Common $1 par exchanged for (0.25) share Common no par
University Computing Co. (TX) reincorporated in Delaware 06/30/1972 which name changed to Wyly Corp. 05/25/1973 which name changed to Uccel Corp. 05/22/1984 which merged into Computer Associates International, Inc. 08/19/1987 which name changed to CA, Inc. 02/01/2006

COMPUTER INNOVATIONS DISTR INC (CANADA)
Acquired by SHL Systemhouse Inc. 08/17/1988
Each share Common no par exchanged for $3.60 cash

COMPUTER INPUT SVCS INC (PA)
Common 10¢ par split (3) for (2) by issuance of (0.5) additional share 01/11/1983
Chapter 11 Bankruptcy petition converted to Chapter 7 on 08/08/1984
Stockholders' equity unlikely

COMPUTER INSTALLATIONS CORP (DE)
Merged into CIC Acquisition Corp. 02/21/1984
Each share Common $1 par exchanged for $1.50 cash

COMPUTER INSTRS CORP (NY)
Under plan of partial liquidation each share Common 25¢ par received distribution of $0.50 cash 12/12/1977
Common 25¢ par changed to 10¢ par 01/30/1978
Acquired by MK Acquisition Inc. 12/28/1987
Each share Common 10¢ par exchanged for $5 cash

COMPUTER INTEGRATED MFG & DESIGN SYS INC (NV)
Charter permanently revoked 07/01/1994

COMPUTER INTEGRATION CORP (DE)
Merged into CompuCom Systems, Inc. 05/13/1998
Each share Common $0.001 par exchanged for $0.724 cash

COMPUTER INTERACTIONS INC (NY)
Name changed to Chevaning Mining & Exploration Co. Ltd. 11/02/1983
(See Chevaning Mining & Exploration Co. Ltd.)

COMPUTER INVS GROUP INC (NY)
Common 10¢ par split (2) for (1) by issuance of (1) additional share 05/10/1984
Name changed to TTS, Inc. 09/10/1984

COMPUTER KNOWLEDGE CORP (TX)
Charter forfeited for failure to pay taxes 03/10/1975

COMPUTER LANGUAGE RESH INC (TX)
Merged into Thomson Corp. 02/18/1998
Each share Common 1¢ par exchanged for $22.50 cash

COMPUTER LEARNING & SYS CORP (MD)
Name changed to Clasco, Inc. 05/18/1971
Clasco, Inc. merged into MCD Holdings, Inc. 10/01/1973 which name changed to Chesapeake Investors, Inc. 08/14/1980
(See Chesapeake Investors, Inc.)

COMPUTER LEARNING CTRS INC (DE)
Common 1¢ par split (3) for (2) by issuance of (0.5) additional share payable 04/14/1997 to holders of record 04/08/1997
Common 1¢ par split (2) for (1) by issuance of (1) additional share payable 01/08/1998 to holders of record 12/29/1997
Assets sold for the benefit of creditors 04/10/2002
Stockholders' equity unlikely

COMPUTER LEASING CO (DE)
Reincorporated 10/31/1968
State of incorporation changed from (TX) to (DE) 10/31/1968
Merged into University Computing Co. (TX) 12/17/1969
Each share Common no par exchanged for (0.1852) share Common no par
University Computing Co. (TX) reincorporated in Delaware 06/30/1972 which name changed to Wyly Corp. 05/25/1973 which name changed to Uccel Corp. 05/22/1984 which merged into Computer Associates International, Inc. 08/19/1987 which name changed to CA, Inc. 02/01/2006

COMPUTER LITERACY INC (DE)
Name changed to Fatbrain.com Inc. 03/29/1999
Fatbrain.com Inc. was acquired by Barnesandnoble.com Inc. 11/16/2000
(See Barnesandnoble.com Inc.)

COMPUTER LOGIC CORP (UT)
Recapitalized as Beacon Energy, Inc. 11/21/1980
Each share Common 1¢ par exchanged for (0.05) share Common $0.001 par
(See Beacon Energy, Inc.)

COMPUTER MACHINING TECHNOLOGY CORP (NJ)
Name changed to CMT Industries, Inc. 03/25/1974
CMT Industries, Inc. name changed to Matrix Corp. (NJ) 01/12/1979 which reincorporated in Delaware 04/19/1988
(See Matrix Corp. (DE))

COMPUTER MACHY CORP (CA)
Acquired by Pertec Corp. (CA) 03/30/1976
Each share Common 10¢ par exchanged for (0.3475) share Common 10¢ par
Pertec Corp. (CA) reincorporated in Delaware as Pertec Computer Corp. 09/24/1976
(See Pertec Computer Corp.)

COMPUTER MAGNETICS CORP (DE)
Merged into HCC Industries 12/29/1982

Each share Common 10¢ par exchanged for $3 cash

COMPUTER MANAGEMENT & SERVICES, INC. (PA)
Out of business 06/20/1970
No stockholders' equity

COMPUTER MGMT CORP (UT)
Each share Common 10¢ par exchanged for (0.1) share Common $1 par 01/23/1969
Name changed to CMC Industries 08/28/1969
CMC Industries name changed to Andersen 2000, Inc. (UT) 07/09/1970 which reorganized in Delaware 09/30/1971 which merged into Crown Andersen Inc. 01/31/1986
(See Crown Andersen Inc.)

COMPUTER MGMT SCIENCES INC (FL)
Common 1¢ par split (3) for (2) by issuance of (0.5) additional share payable 07/05/1996 to holders of record 06/21/1996
Common 1¢ par split (3) for (2) by issuance of (0.5) additional share payable 11/20/1996 to holders of record 11/04/1996
Merged into Computer Associates International, Inc. 03/17/1999
Each share Common 1¢ par exchanged for $28 cash

COMPUTER MARKETING INDS INC (VA)
Merged into Delta Automated Systems, Inc. 10/01/1970
Each share Common 10¢ par exchanged for (1) share Common 10¢ par
(See Delta Automated Systems, Inc.)

COMPUTER MARKETPLACE INC (DE)
Common $0.0001 par split (2) for (1) by issuance of (1) additional share 06/06/1994
Each share old Common $0.0001 par exchanged for (0.16666666) share new Common $0.0001 par 04/21/1997
Name changed to Emarketplace Inc. 10/01/1999
Emarketplace Inc. recapitalized as Smart Card Marketing Systems, Inc. 03/24/2006

COMPUTER MEASUREMENTS INC II (WY)
Charter forfeited for failure to pay taxes 02/15/1975

COMPUTER MEMORIES INC (DE)
Reincorporated 08/08/1986
Common no par split (3) for (2) by issuance of (0.5) additional share 05/31/1983
State of incorporation changed from (CA) to (DE) 08/08/1986
Stock Dividend - 50% 11/30/1982
Name changed to American Holdings Inc. NJ 07/30/1992
American Holdings Inc. NJ name changed to Pure World Inc. 09/27/1995
(See Pure World Inc.)

COMPUTER MERCHANTS INC (NY)
Common 1¢ par split (2) for (1) by issuance of (1) additional share 01/07/1986
Completely liquidated
Each share Common 1¢ par received first and final distribution of $0.03 cash payable 12/09/2002 to holders of record 11/29/2002 Ex date - 12/10/2002
Note: Certificates were not required to be surrendered and are now valueless

COMPUTER METHODS CORP (DE)
Charter cancelled and declared inoperative and void for non-payment of taxes 03/01/1975

COMPUTER MICRODATA CORP (NJ)
Company reported out of business 01/00/1978
Stockholders' equity unlikely

COMPUTER MICROFILM CORP (DE)
Common 25¢ par split (4) for (1) by issuance of (3) additional shares 08/06/1979
Reincorporated under the laws of Georgia 07/11/1985
(See Computer Microfilm Corp. (GA))

COMPUTER MICROFILM CORP (GA)
Stock Dividends - 10% 08/14/1987; 10% 07/18/1988
Merged into Microfilm Reprographics PLC 10/06/1988
Each share Common 25¢ par exchanged for $7.10 cash

COMPUTER MICROGRAPHICS INC (CA)
Merged into Anacomp, Inc. 09/28/1979
Each share Common no par exchanged for (0.7) share Common $1 par

COMPUTER MICROTECHNOLOGY INC (DE)
Liquidation completed
Each share Common 10¢ par exchanged for initial distribution of (0.0203) share Advanced Memory Systems, Inc. Common 10¢ par 05/31/1973
Each share Common 10¢ par received second and final distribution of (0.005857) share Intersil, Inc. (New) Common 10¢ par 07/01/1977
(See each company's listing)

COMPUTER MOTION INC (DE)
Merged into Intuitive Surgical, Inc. 06/30/2003
Each share Common $0.001 par exchanged for (0.25713471) share Common $0.001 par

COMPUTER MTGS AMER HLDGS CO (NV)
Recapitalized as Kensington Energy Corp. 07/01/2005
Each share Common $0.001 par exchanged for (0.001) share Common $0.001 par
Kensington Energy Corp. name changed to Emerald Organic Products Inc. 08/28/2012

COMPUTER NETWORK CORP (MD)
Each share Common 25¢ par exchanged for (0.5) share Common 50¢ par 09/24/1971
Name changed to Comnet Corp. 08/28/1985
Comnet Corp. name changed to Group 1 Software, Inc. (New) 09/28/1998
(See Group 1 Software, Inc. (New))

COMPUTER NETWORK SYS CORP (DE)
Name changed to Hetra Computer & Communications Industries, Inc. 11/13/1969
(See Hetra Computer & Communications Industries, Inc.)

COMPUTER NETWORK TECHNOLOGY CORP (MN)
Merged into McDATA Corp. 06/01/2005
Each share Common 1¢ par exchanged for (1.3) shares Class A Common 1¢ par
McDATA Corp. acquired by Brocade Communications Systems, Inc. 01/29/2007
(See Brocade Communications Systems, Inc.)

COMPUTER OPERATIONS INC (MD)
Charter forfeited for failure to file annual reports 10/15/1986

COMPUTER OPTICS INC (DE)
Each share Common 10¢ par exchanged for (0.2) share Common 50¢ par 12/28/1972
Each share old Common 50¢ par exchanged for (0.2) share new Common 50¢ par 12/13/1978
Under plan of reorganization each share new Common 50¢ par received $0.03204 cash 08/29/1980
Note: Certificates were not required to be surrendered and are without value

COMPUTER ORIENTED RESEARCH & ENGINEERING, INC. (PA)
Name changed to Computer Research, Inc. (Old) 10/10/1966
Computer Research, Inc. (Old) name changed to General Nursing Homes Corp. 08/04/1969
(See General Nursing Corp.)

COMPUTER OUTSOURCING SVCS INC (NY)
Name changed to Infocrossing Inc. 06/05/2000
(See Infocrossing Inc.)

COMPUTER PERIPHERAL PRODS INC (CO)
Filed a petition under Chapter 11 Federal Bankruptcy Code 12/16/1985
Stockholders' equity unlikely

COMPUTER PETE CORP (MN)
Merged into UCG Acquisition Corp. 08/23/1996
Each share Common 1¢ par exchanged for $3.8939 cash

COMPUTER PLUS INC (NV)
Name changed to Education Access Inc. 05/23/1997

COMPUTER PWR INC (NJ)
Chapter 11 bankruptcy proceedings terminated 02/06/2006
Stockholders' equity unlikely

COMPUTER PWR INTL CORP (DE)
Charter cancelled and declared inoperative and void for non-payment of taxes 03/01/1980

COMPUTER PREPARATIONS INC (DE)
Charter cancelled and declared inoperative and void for non-payment of taxes 03/01/1983

COMPUTER PRODS INC (FL)
Common 1¢ par split (6) for (5) by issuance of (0.2) additional share 11/15/1979
Common 1¢ par split (4) for (3) by issuance of (0.33333333) additional share 11/20/1981
Common 1¢ par split (2) for (1) by issuance of (1) additional share 03/29/1985
Stock Dividends - 20% 11/15/1976; 20% 11/15/1977; 20% 11/15/1978; 20% 11/17/1980
Name changed to Artesyn Technologies Inc. 05/06/1998
(See Artesyn Technologies Inc.)

COMPUTER PPTY CORP (DE)
Merged into Fairfield Communities Land Co. 12/30/1971
Each share Common $1 par exchanged for (1.8) shares Common 30¢ par
Fairfield Communities Land Co. name changed to Fairfield Communities, Inc. 08/26/1977
(See Fairfield Communities, Inc.)

COMPUTER RADIX CORP (NY)
Name changed to Boothe Data Systems, Inc. and Common 20¢ par changed to 10¢ par 02/22/1971
Boothe Data Systems, Inc. name changed to Infonational Inc. 09/05/1972
(See Infonational Inc.)

COMPUTER REPORTING SYS INC (CA)
Charter suspended for failure to pay franchise taxes 10/01/1971

COMPUTER RESEARCH, INC. (OLD) (PA)
Name changed to General Nursing Homes Corp. 08/04/1969
(See General Nursing Corp.)

COMPUTER RESH INC (PA)
Merged into CRI Acquisition Corp. 09/18/2000
Each share Common no par exchanged for $2.42 cash

COMPUTER RES INC (OH)
Name changed to Opus Computer Products, Inc. 03/21/1988
(See Opus Computer Products, Inc.)

COMPUTER RESPONSE CORP (DE)
Charter subsequently cancelled and declared inoperative and void for non-payment of taxes 03/01/1976

COMPUTER RETRIEVAL SYS INC (MD)
Name changed to Copycomposer Corp. 10/15/1970
(See Copycomposer Corp.)

COMPUTER SCIENCES CORP (NV)
Common 50¢ par changed to 20¢ par and (1.5) additional shares issued 10/13/1965
Common 20¢ par changed to 10¢ par and (1) additional share issued 06/21/1967
Common 10¢ par changed to 4¢ par and (1.5) additional shares issued 06/28/1969
Common 4¢ par changed to $1 par 08/11/1969
Common $1 par split (3) for (1) by issuance of (2) additional shares 01/12/1994
Common $1 par split (2) for (1) by issuance of (1) additional share payable 03/23/1998 to holders of record 03/02/1998 Ex date - 03/24/1998
Each share Common $1 par received distribution of (1) share CSRA Inc. $0.001 par payable 11/27/2015 to holders of record 11/18/2015 Ex date - 11/30/2015
Merged into DXC Technology Co. 04/03/2017
Each share Common $1 par exchanged for (1) share Common 1¢ par

COMPUTER SERVICENTERS INC (DE)
Each share Common 50¢ par exchanged for (0.2) share old Common 5¢ par 02/11/1972
Each share old Common 5¢ par exchanged for (0.05) share new Common 5¢ par 01/28/1981
Name changed to Comtrol Systems, Inc. 01/24/1983
Comtrol Systems, Inc. merged into American Physicians Service Group, Inc. 02/01/1984
(See American Physicians Service Group, Inc.)

COMPUTER SERVICES, INC. (NJ)
Merged into C-E-I-R, Inc. 05/01/1961
Each share Common 50¢ par exchanged for (0.2) share Common $1 par
C-E-I-R, Inc. acquired by Control Data Corp. (MN) 11/22/1967 which merged into Control Data Corp. (DE) 08/17/1968 which name changed to Ceridian Corp. (Old) 06/03/1992
(See Ceridian Corp. (Old))

COMPUTER SERVICES CORP. (IA)
Filed petition under Chapter X bankruptcy proceedings 02/25/1970
No stockholders' equity

COMPUTER SVCS CORP (MI)
Merged into Anacomp Inc. 05/31/1996
Each share Common no par exchanged for $0.90 cash

COMPUTER SHARING INC (PA)
Merged into Data Network Corp. 01/28/1970

Each share Common 10¢ par exchanged for (1) share Common 10¢ par
Data Network Corp. name changed to MegaSystems, Inc. 05/15/1970
(See MegaSystems, Inc.)

COMPUTER SKILLS INC (IA)
Charter cancelled for failure to file annual reports 11/22/1974

COMPUTER SOFTWARE INNOVATIONS INC (DE)
Acquired by Constellation Software Inc. 11/09/2012
Each share Common $0.001 par exchanged for $1.10 cash

COMPUTER SOFTWARE SYS INC (DE)
Name changed to National CSS, Inc. 07/07/1970
(See National CSS, Inc.)

COMPUTER SPECIALTIES CORP (DE)
Name changed to Barricini Inc. 01/29/1998

COMPUTER STATISTICS INC (TX)
Completely liquidated 06/13/1983
Each share Common $1 par exchanged for first and final distribution of $3.84 cash

COMPUTER STORE INC (MA)
Filed petition under Chapter 7 Federal Bankruptcy Code 03/27/1986
Stockholders' equity unlikely

COMPUTER STUDIES INC (NY)
Charter cancelled and proclaimed dissolved for failure to pay taxes 12/15/1975

COMPUTER SUPERSTORES INC (TX)
Charter forfeited for failure to pay taxes 02/26/1988

COMPUTER SYNERGY INC (CA)
Merged into Shared Medical Systems Corp. 05/18/1985
Each share Common $0.001 par exchanged for (0.33333333) share Common 1¢ par
(See Shared Medical Systems Corp.)

COMPUTER SYS DEV CORP (DE)
Name changed to International Equity Funding Corp. 11/09/1970
International Equity Funding Corp. name changed to American Land Equity, Inc. 10/05/1972
(See American Land Equity, Inc.)

COMPUTER SYS MGMT INC (NV)
Charter revoked for failure to file reports and pay fees 03/06/1972

COMPUTER SYSTEMS, INC. (MN)
Common $2 par changed to 20¢ par 07/14/1969
Transfers ceased 11/01/1971
Company no longer in existence
No stockholders' equity

COMPUTER TECHNOLOGIES, INC. (LA)
Name changed to Interstate Computing, Inc. 03/18/1970
(See Interstate Computing, Inc.)

COMPUTER TECHNOLOGY ADVISORS CORP (FL)
Reorganized as Hostnyc Inc. 09/11/2000
Each share Common $0.001 par exchanged for (6) shares Common $0.001 par
Hostnyc Inc. recapitalized as Lumiere International Corp. 12/31/2001 which name changed to Air Temp North America, Inc. 01/30/2007
(See Air Temp North America, Inc.)

COMPUTER TECHNOLOGY INC (DE)
Merged into University Computing Co. (TX) 12/31/1971
Each share Common 50¢ par exchanged for (0.3125) share Common no par

University Computing Co. (TX) reincorporated in Delaware 06/30/1972 which name changed to Wyly Corp. 05/25/1973 which name changed to Uccel Corp. 05/22/1984 which merged into Computer Associates International, Inc. 08/19/1987 which name changed to CA, Inc. 02/01/2006

COMPUTER TECHNOLOGY INTL INC (DE)
Charter cancelled and declared inoperative and void for non-payment of taxes 03/01/1985

COMPUTER TEL CO CHICAGO INC (IL)
Proclaimed dissolved for failure to pay taxes and file reports 11/16/1972

COMPUTER TEL CORP (MA)
Class 1 Common 1¢ par split (5) for (4) by issuance of (0.25) additional share 03/10/1995
Class 1 Common 1¢ par split (3) for (2) by issuance of (0.5) additional share 08/04/1995
Class 1 Common 1¢ par split (2) for (1) by issuance of (1) additional share 11/06/1995
Name changed to CTC Communications Corp. 09/27/1996
CTC Communications Corp. reorganized as CTC Communications Group Inc. (DE) 10/01/1999
(See CTC Communications Group Inc. (DE))

COMPUTER TERM CORP (TX)
Name changed to Datapoint Corp. (TX) 12/08/1972
Datapoint Corp. (TX) reincorporated in Delaware 01/20/1977 which name changed to Dynacore Holdings Corp. 05/08/2000 which name changed to CattleSale Co. 02/25/2003
(See CattleSale Co.)

COMPUTER TERM SYS INC (NY)
Stock Dividends - 50% 03/16/1981; 50% 05/03/1983
Reorganized under Chapter 11 Bankruptcy Code 09/26/1986
Each share old Common 10¢ par recieved distribution of (0.38022813) share new Common 10¢ par
Note: Old Common 10¢ par became without value 09/26/1986
Chapter 11 Federal Bankruptcy Code converted to Chapter 7 on 06/07/1988
No stockholders' equity

COMPUTER TIME SHARING CORP (CA)
Reincorporated under the laws of Delaware as CTC Computer Corp. and Capital Stock $2 par reclassified as Common $2 par 09/01/1969
(See CTC Computer Corp.)

COMPUTER TOOLS INC (NY)
Charter cancelled and proclaimed dissolved for failure to pay taxes 12/20/1977

COMPUTER TRANSCEIVER SYS INC (NY)
Reorganized under Chapter 11 Federal Bankruptcy Code 06/29/1987
Each share old Common 1¢ par received distribution of (0.25) share new Common 1¢ par
Note: Certificates were not required to be surrendered and are without value
Recapitalized as MPEL Holdings Corp. 02/26/1998
Each share new Common 1¢ par exchanged for (0.04) share Common 1¢ par
(See MPEL Holdings Corp.)

COMPUTER USAGE CO (DE)
Common 25¢ par split (5) for (2) by issuance of (1.5) additional shares 02/05/1965
Common 25¢ par changed to $0.16666666 par and (0.5) additional share issued 09/09/1983
Chapter 11 bankruptcy proceedings converted to Chapter 7 on 12/23/1986
Stockholders' equity unlikely

COMPUTER UTILS CORP (DE)
Under plan of liquidation each share Common 10¢ par exchanged for (4.314017) shares Western Union Computer Utilities, Inc. Common 10¢ par and (1) Liquidation Certificate of Computer Utilities Corp. 10/12/1972
(See Western Union Computer Utilities, Inc.)

COMPUTER VENDING INC (FL)
Recapitalized as RAD Source Technologies Inc. 12/31/1998
Each share Common $0.001 par exchanged for (0.1) share Common $0.001 par
(See RAD Source Technologies Inc.)

COMPUTER VISION SYS LABORATORIES CORP (FL)
Each share old Common $0.0001 par exchanged for (0.1) share new Common $0.0001 par 09/01/2011
Name changed to CVSL Inc. 05/28/2013
CVSL Inc. name changed to JRjr33, Inc. 03/07/2016

COMPUTERBASE INTL INC (CA)
Charter forfeited for failure to file reports and pay fees 10/03/1988

COMPUTERCRAFT INC (DE)
Acquired by Businessland, Inc. 07/12/1988
Each share Common no par exchanged for (0.33333333) share Common no par
Businessland, Inc. merged into JWP Inc. 11/13/1991
(See JWP Inc.)

COMPUTERCRAFT INC (TX)
Reincorporated under the laws of Delaware 09/11/1984
ComputerCraft, Inc. (DE) acquired by Businessland, Inc. 07/12/1988 which merged into JWP Inc. 11/13/1991
(See JWP Inc.)

COMPUTERIZED AUTOMOTIVE REPORTING SVC INC (DE)
Name changed to Dyatron Corp. 12/01/1980
Dyatron Corp. acquired by SunGard Data Systems Inc. 11/10/1989
(See SunGuard Data Systems, Inc.)

COMPUTERIZED BUYING NETWORK INC (DE)
Name changed to CBNI Development Co., Inc. 09/01/1993
CBNI Development Co., Inc. name changed to Affinity Teleproductions Inc. 02/28/1994 which name changed to Affinity Entertainment Inc. 07/03/1996 which name changed to Tour CFG Inc. 11/04/1997
(See Tour CFG Inc.)

COMPUTERIZED KNITWEAR INC (NY)
Name changed to Compuknit Industries, Inc. 03/30/1971
(See Compuknit Industries, Inc.)

COMPUTERIZED NAT RES INC (DE)
Name changed to CNR Corp. 04/24/1970
CNR Corp. name changed to Rosen Petroleum Corp. 01/20/1971
(See Rosen Petroleum Corp.)

COMPUTERIZED THERMAL IMAGING INC (NV)
Charter revoked for failure to file reports 11/06/2015

COMPUTEROLOGY INC (NY)
Name changed to W.S.C. Group, Inc. 02/04/1971
(See W.S.C. Group, Inc.)

COMPUTERPHONE INTL CORP (CO)
Declared defunct and inoperative for failure to pay taxes and file annual reports 01/01/1988

COMPUTERS FOR LESS INC (NY)
Name changed to Electrograph Systems Inc. 01/23/1990
Electrograph Systems Inc. merged into Bitwise Designs, Inc. 08/18/1994 which name changed to AuthentiDate Holding Corp. 03/23/2001 which name changed to Aeon Global Health Corp. 02/01/2018

COMPUTERS UNLIMITED INC (NY)
Recapitalized as Cross Country Industries, Inc. 07/19/1973
Each share Common 2¢ par exchanged for (0.1) share Common 2¢ par
(See Cross Country Industries, Inc.)

COMPUTERVISION CORP NEW (DE)
Merged into Parametric Technology Corp. 01/12/1998
Each share Common 1¢ par exchanged for (0.0866) share Common 1¢ par
Parametric Technology Corp. name changed to PTC Inc. 01/28/2013

COMPUTERVISION CORP OLD (DE)
Reincorporated 06/30/1975
State of incorporation changed from (MA) to (DE) 06/30/1975
Common 5¢ par split (2) for (1) by issuance of (1) additional share 07/06/1979
Common 5¢ par split (2) for (1) by issuance of (1) additional share 08/15/1980
Common 5¢ par split (2) for (1) by issuance of (1) additional share 06/19/1981
Merged into Prime Computer, Inc. 02/11/1988
Each share Common 5¢ par exchanged for $15 cash

COMPUTERXPRESS COM INC (NV)
Each share old Common $0.001 par exchanged for (0.01) share new Common $0.001 par 08/20/2001
Name changed to Aurora Precious Metals Inc. 02/12/2003
Aurora Precious Metals Inc. name changed to V-Net Beverage, Inc. 09/03/2003 which name changed to RushNet, Inc. 07/08/2005
(See RushNet, Inc.)

COMPUTEST CORP (DE)
Name changed to EB&B Liquidating Corp. 05/29/1973
(See EB&B Liquidating Corp.)

COMPUTEX LTD (DE)
Charter cancelled and declared inoperative and void for non-payment of taxes 03/01/1990

COMPUTILITY INC (DE)
Merged into Grumman Data Systems Corp. 12/31/1973
Each share Common 10¢ par exchanged for $0.3168 cash

COMPUTIME COMPUTER SVCS INC (NV)
Charter revoked for failure to file reports and pay fees 02/01/1987

COMPUTING & SOFTWARE INC (CA)
Common no par split (2) for (1) by issuance of (1) additional share 03/28/1969
Name changed to Cordura Corp. (CA) 03/02/1973

Cordura Corp. (CA) reincorporated in Delaware 06/27/1975
(See Cordura Corp. (DE))

COMPUTING DEVICES CDA LTD (ON)
Acquired by Control Data Corp. (DE) 12/22/1969
Each share Common no par exchanged for (0.2) share Common $5 par
Control Data Corp. (DE) name changed to Ceridian Corp. (Old) 06/03/1992
(See Ceridian Corp. (Old))

COMPUTING EFFICIENCY INC (NY)
Merged into Mohawk Data Sciences Corp. 03/05/1973
Each share Common 10¢ par exchanged for (0.196721) share Common 10¢ par
Mohawk Data Sciences Corp. name changed to Qantel Corp. 09/17/1987
(See Qantel Corp.)

COMPUTONE CORP (DE)
Each share old Common 1¢ par exchanged for (0.16666666) share new Common 1¢ par 11/30/1993
Name changed to Symbiat, Inc. 07/01/2002
(See Symbiat, Inc.)

COMPUTONE SYS INC (DE)
Reincorporated 08/31/1987
State of incorporation changed from (GA) to (DE) and each share Common 10¢ par received distribution of (0.1) share Common 1¢ par 09/01/1987
Note: Common 10¢ par certificates were not required to be surrendered and are without value
Name changed to World-Wide Technology Inc. 05/24/1988
World-Wide Technology Inc. name changed to Computone Corp. 05/03/1991 which name changed to Symbiat, Inc. 07/01/2002
(See Symbiat, Inc.)

COMPUTRAC INC (TX)
Common 1¢ par split (3) for (2) by issuance of (0.5) additional share 04/07/1986
Common 1¢ par split (2) for (1) by issuance of (1) additional share 03/24/1987
Merged into ASA International Ltd. 08/01/2002
Each share Common 1¢ par exchanged for (0.20648) share Common 1¢ par and $0.2156 cash
(See ASA International Ltd.)

COMPUTRAC INSTRS INC (DE)
Name changed to Quintel Corp. 06/05/1984
Quintel Corp. name changed to Arizona Instrument Corp. 03/05/1987

COMPUTRAC SYS INC (UT)
Recapitalized as Foureyes Holdings, Inc. 08/21/1997
Each share Common $0.001 par exchanged for (0.04) share Common $0.001 par
Foureyes Holdings, Inc. name changed to New Anaconda Co. 06/07/1999
(See New Anaconda Co.)

COMPUTRAIL CORP (NY)
Name changed to Sun Gold Industries of New York, Inc. 11/14/1972
(See Sun Gold Industries of New York, Inc.)

COMPUTRAV INC (NJ)
Name changed to Elinvest Inc. 02/11/1970
(See Elinvest Inc.)

COMPUTREX CENTRES LTD (BC)
Recapitalized as Camex Energy Corp. (BC) 10/05/2005
Each share Common no par

exchanged for (0.5) share Common no par
Camex Energy Corp. (BC) reorganized in Ontario as Desert Lion Energy Inc. 02/26/2018

COMPUTROL SYSTEMS, INC. (GA)
Merged into Squires-Sanders, Inc. 12/31/1968
Details not available

COMPUTRON INC (NV)
Name changed to Ho Wah Genting Group Ltd. 11/08/2016

COMPUTRON INDS INC (UT)
Recapitalized 01/22/1972
Recapitalized from Computron Corp. to Computron Industries, Inc. 01/22/1972
Each share Common 1¢ par exchanged for (0.1) share Common 10¢ par
Name changed to Star-Glo Industries, Inc. 06/20/1972
(See Star-Glo Industries, Inc.)

COMPUTRON SOFTWARE INC (DE)
Name changed to AXS-One Inc. 11/01/2000
AXS-One Inc. merged into Unify Corp. 06/30/2009 which name changed to Daegis Inc. 07/07/2011
(See Daegis Inc.)

COMPUTRONIC INDS CORP (DE)
Reincorporated 10/30/1968
State of incorporation changed from (TX) to (DE) and Common no par changed to 1¢ par 10/30/1968
Charter cancelled and declared inoperative and void for non-payment of taxes 04/15/1972

COMPUTRONICS INC (WI)
Voluntarily dissolved 12/13/1977
No stockholders' equity

COMPUWARE CORP (MI)
Common 1¢ par split (2) for (1) by issuance of (1) additional share payable 04/14/1997 to holders of record 04/04/1997
Common 1¢ par split (2) for (1) by issuance of (1) additional share payable 11/04/1997 to holders of record 10/22/1997
Each share Common 1¢ par received distribution of (0.14025466) share Covisint Corp. Common no par payable 10/31/2014 to holders of record 10/20/2014
Stock Dividend - 100% payable 02/26/1999 to holders of record 01/26/1999
Acquired by Project Copper Holdings, LLC 12/15/2014
Each share Common 1¢ par exchanged for $10.389188 cash

COMRES CORP (DE)
Charter cancelled and declared inoperative and void for non-payment of taxes 03/01/1989

COMRESS INC (MD)
Merged into Comten, Inc. 09/26/1974
Each share Common 5¢ par exchanged for (0.1389) share Common 5¢ par
Comten, Inc. merged into NCR Corp. 06/13/1979 which merged into American Telephone & Telegraph Co. 09/19/1991 which name changed to AT&T Corp. 04/20/1994 which merged into AT&T Inc. 11/18/2005

COMSAT CAP I L P (DC)
8.125% Monthly Income Preferred Securities called for redemption at $25 on 07/31/2001

COMSAT CORP (DC)
Ser. 1 Common no par split (2) for (1) by issuance of (1) additional share 06/24/1993
Each share Common Ser. 1 no par received distribution of (0.4888) share Ascent Entertainment Group, Inc. Common 1¢ par payable 06/27/1997 to holders of record 06/19/1997 Ex date - 06/30/1997
Merged into Lockheed Martin Corp. 08/03/2000
Each share Ser. 1 Common no par exchanged for (1) share Common $1 par

COMSEC FD INC (OH)
Name changed to Columbus Fund, Inc. 07/23/1974
(See Columbus Fund, Inc.)

COMSERV CORP (MN)
Stock Dividend - 50% 06/01/1981
Acquired by Management Science America, Inc. 02/17/1987
Each share Common 10¢ par exchanged for $2.21 cash

COMSERV INC (NV)
Completely liquidated
Each share Common received initial distribution of $1.50 cash payable 10/31/2000 to holders of record 10/23/2000
Each share Common exchanged for second and final distribution of $0.10 cash 03/16/2001

COMSHARE INC (MI)
Common $1 par split (3) for (2) by issuance of (0.5) additional share 08/03/1979
Common $1 par split (2) for (1) by issuance of (1) additional share 05/31/1990
Common $1 par split (3) for (2) by issuance of (0.5) additional share payable 11/20/1995 to holders of record 11/13/1995
Merged into Geac Computer Corp. Ltd. 08/14/2003
Each share Common $1 par exchanged for $4.60 cash

COMSIP CUSTOMLINE CORP (NJ)
Merged into CCC, Inc. 10/27/1975
Each share Common 10¢ par exchanged for $0.385 cash

COMSOUTH BANKSHARES INC (SC)
Common $1 par split (3) for (2) by issuance of (0.5) additional share payable 10/30/1997 to holders of record 10/15/1997 Ex date - 10/31/1997
Stock Dividends - 15% 07/17/1989; 10% payable 12/02/1996 to holders of record 11/15/1996 Ex date - 11/18/1996
Merged into Anchor Financial Corp. 08/31/1998
Each share Common $1 par exchanged for (0.75) share Common no par
Anchor Financial Corp. merged into South Financial Group, Inc. 06/07/2000 which merged into Toronto-Dominion Bank (Toronto, ON) 09/30/2010

COMSPACE CORP (NY)
Dissolved by proclamation 04/25/2012

COMSTAR CORP (MN)
Completely liquidated 10/03/1975
Each share Common 1¢ par exchanged for first and final distribution of $0.4506 cash

COMSTATE RES INCOME TR (AB)
Under plan of merger name changed to Bonterra Energy Income Trust (New) 02/01/2002
Bonterra Energy Income Trust (New) name changed to Bonterra Oil & Gas Ltd. 11/17/2008 which name changed to Bonterra Energy Corp. (New) 01/15/2010

COMSTATE RES LTD (BC)
Common no par split (2) for (1) by issuance of (1) additional share 08/10/1990
Common no par split (2) for (1) by issuance of (1) additional share 07/28/1992
Plan of arrangement effective 06/28/2001
Each share Common no par exchanged for (0.25) Comstate Resources Income Trust (ALTA) Trust Unit no par, (0.6) share Comaplex Minerals Corp. Common no par and $0.20 cash
(See each company's listing)

COMSTOCK BANCORP (NV)
Merged into First Security Corp. 06/01/1999
Each share Common 1¢ par exchanged for (0.675) share Common $1.25 par
First Security Corp. merged into Wells Fargo & Co. (New) 10/26/2000
(See Wells Fargo & Co. (New))

COMSTOCK BK (CARSON CITY, NV)
Stock Dividend - 10% 04/12/1995
Under plan of reorganization each share Common 50¢ par automatically became (2) shares Comstock Bancorp Common 1¢ par 06/16/1997
Comstock Bancorp merged into First Security Corp. 06/01/1999 which merged into Wells Fargo & Co. (New) 10/26/2000

COMSTOCK COAL INC (UT)
Each share old Common 5¢ par exchanged for (0.1) share new Common 5¢ par 01/31/2000
Name changed to Telkonet Inc. 09/01/2000

COMSTOCK-DEXTER MINES, INC. (AZ)
Charter revoked for failure to file reports and pay fees 02/12/1944

COMSTOCK-EMPIRE INTL INC (WA)
Recapitalized as Winners Internet Network, Inc. 07/15/1997
Each share Common $0.001 par exchanged for (0.01) share Common $0.001 par
Winners Internet Network, Inc. recapitalized as American Television & Film Co. 02/17/2004 which name changed to Spotlight Homes, Inc. 04/06/2004

COMSTOCK FD INC (MD)
Reincorporated 12/31/1978
State of incorporation changed from (DE) to (MD) 12/31/1978
Name changed to American General Comstock Fund, Inc. 08/31/1979
American General Comstock Fund, Inc. name changed to American Capital Comstock Fund, Inc. 09/12/1983

COMSTOCK GOLD SILVER & COPPER MINES INC (NV)
Each share old Common 2¢ par exchanged for (0.5) share new Common 2¢ par 05/00/1975
Charter revoked for failure to file report and pay fees 02/01/1985

COMSTOCK GROUP INC (NY)
Merged into Spie Batignolles 08/14/1989
Each share Common 25¢ par exchanged for $2.25 cash

COMSTOCK HOMEBUILDING COS INC (DE)
Name changed to Comstock Holding Companies, Inc. 06/25/2012

COMSTOCK INDS INC (FL)
Reincorporated 07/21/2000
State of incorporation changed from (NV) to (FL) and Common 10¢ par changed to $0.0001 par 07/21/2000
Administratively dissolved for failure to file annual report 09/25/2009

COMSTOCK INTL CORP (DE)
Charter cancelled and declared inoperative and void for non-payment of taxes 06/26/1990

COMSTOCK INVESTMENT CO.
Liquidation completed 00/00/1948

Details not available

COMSTOCK KENO MINES LTD (ON)
Name changed to Thornbury Capital Corp. 12/30/1994
Thornbury Capital Corp. recapitalized as International Uranium Corp. 05/09/1997 which name changed to Denison Mines Corp. 12/06/2006

COMSTOCK KEYSTONE MNG CO (NV)
Recapitalized as Memory Magnetics International 02/07/1969
Each share Common 10¢ par exchanged for (0.6) share Common 5¢ par

COMSTOCK LODE SILVER & COPPER MINES INC (NV)
Recapitalized as Pacific Resources, Inc. (NV) 01/29/1973
Each share Common 1¢ par exchanged for (0.5) share Common 2¢ par
Pacific Resources, Inc. (NV) name changed to Comstock Gold, Silver & Copper Mines, Inc. 10/26/1973
(See Comstock Gold, Silver & Copper Mines, Inc.)

COMSTOCK LTD. (NV)
Merged into Sierra Cascade Enterprises, Inc. 07/24/1970
Each share Capital Stock 10¢ par exchanged for (0.1) share Capital Stock 10¢ par
Sierra Cascade Enterprises, Inc. merged into Associated Smelters International 04/27/1972 which name changed to ASI 09/01/1978 which recapitalized as ASI Technology Corp. 09/01/2000 which recapitalized as Robertson Global Health Solutions Corp. 08/06/2010

COMSTOCK MINES & MILLING CO. (AZ)
Charter revoked for failure to file reports and pay fees 10/13/1926

COMSTOCK MINES CO. (SD)
Charter expired by time limitation 01/03/1923

COMSTOCK TUNL & DRAIN CO (NV)
Reincorporated 01/01/1984
Common 10¢ par changed to $1 par 00/00/1929
State of incorporation changed from (DE) to (NV) 01/01/1984
Each share Common $1 par exchanged for (1) share Common 50¢ par
Name changed to Comstock Resources, Inc. 11/16/1987

COMSTOCK URANIUM & OIL CORP. (UT)
Each share Capital Stock 2¢ par exchanged for (0.2) share Capital Stock 10¢ par 04/27/1956
Recapitalized as Cochise Enterprises, Inc. 05/12/1960
Each share Capital Stock 10¢ par exchanged for (0.1) share Capital Stock $1 par
Cochise Enterprises, Inc. merged into Bella Vista Ranches, Inc. 10/08/1975
(See Bella Vista Ranches, Inc.)

COMSYS IT PARTNERS INC (DE)
Merged into Manpower Inc. 04/05/2010
Each share Common 1¢ par exchanged for either (0.304) share Common 1¢ par or approximately (0.136) share Common 1¢ par and $9.76 cash
Note: Option to receive stock and cash expired 05/28/2010

COMTECH CAP INC (AB)
Name changed to Revere Communications Inc. 12/12/1997
(See Revere Communications Inc.)

COMTECH CONSLDTN GROUP INC (DE)
Common $0.001 par split (2) for (1) by issuance of (1) additional share payable 09/17/1997 to holders of record 09/15/1997
Recapitalized as Summit National Consolidation Group Inc. 11/05/2001
Each share Common $0.001 par exchanged for (0.02) share Common $0.001 par
Summit National Consolidation Group Inc. name changed to Superwipes, Inc. 10/12/2004
(See Superwipes, Inc.)

COMTECH GROUP INC (MD)
Each share old Common 1¢ par exchanged for (0.5) share new Common 1¢ par 01/14/2005
Name changed to Cogo Group, Inc. (MD) 05/13/2008
Cogo Group, Inc. (MD) reincorporated in Cayman Islands 08/03/2011 which name changed to Viewtran Group, Inc. 11/26/2013

COMTECH GROUP INTL LTD (CANADA)
Reincorporated 12/01/1981
Place of incorporation changed from (ONT) to (Canada) 12/01/1981
Name changed to Postech Corp. 12/30/1988
(See Postech Corp.)

COMTECH INC. (NY)
Reincorporated under the laws of Delaware as Comtech Telecommunications Corp. 04/23/1987

COMTECH LABORATORIES INC. (NY)
Name changed to Comtech Telecommunications Corp. (NY) 12/20/1977
Comtech Telecommunications Corp. (NY) name changed to Comtech Inc. (NY) 12/15/1983 which reincorporated in Delaware as Comtech Telecommunications Corp. 04/23/1987

COMTECH TELECOMMUNICATIONS CORP (NY)
Stock Dividend - 100% 04/15/1980
Name changed to Comtech Inc. (NY) 12/15/1983
Comtech Inc. (NY) reincorporated in Delaware as Comtech Telecommunications Corp. 04/23/1987

COMTEL CORP (DE)
Each share old Common 1¢ par exchanged for (0.1) share new Common 1¢ par 05/02/1972
Each share new Common 1¢ par exchanged for (0.01) share Common $1 par 05/29/1981
Under plan of merger each share Common $1 par exchanged for $1,500 cash 10/07/1985

COMTEN INC (MD)
Merged into NCR Corp. 06/13/1979
Each share Common 5¢ par exchanged for (0.38) share Common $5 par
NCR Corp. merged into American Telephone & Telegraph Co. 09/19/1991 which name changed to AT&T Corp. 04/20/1994 which merged into AT&T Inc. 11/18/2005

COMTERM INC (CANADA)
Name changed to Bytec-Comterm Inc. 12/08/1983 which name changed back to Comterm Inc. 07/25/1984
Declared bankrupt 10/00/1990
Details not available

COMTEX NEWS NETWORK INC (NY)
Name changed 12/02/1999
Name changed from Comtex Scientific Corp. to Comtex News Network, Inc. 12/02/1999

Reincorporated under the laws of Delaware 12/31/2002

COMTREX SYS CORP (NJ)
Reincorporated 02/00/1989
State of incorporation changed from (NJ) to (DE) and Common no par changed to $0.001 par 02/00/1989
Each share Common $0.001 par exchanged for (0.33333333) share Common $0.003 par 02/12/2001
Acquired by Zonal Hospitality Systems, Inc. 08/01/2018
Each share share Common $0.003 par exchanged for $8.02036416 cash

COMTRIX INC (NV)
Reorganized as Lusora Healthcare Systems Inc. 06/23/2006
Each share Common $0.001 par exchanged for (25) shares Common $0.001 par
Lusora Healthcare Systems Inc. name changed to Western Standard Energy Corp. 09/07/2007 which name changed to Dominovas Energy Corp. 04/24/2014

COMTROL INC (MN)
Name changed to National Feeders, Inc. 12/21/1977

COMTROL SYS INC (DE)
Merged into American Physicians Service Group, Inc. 02/01/1984
Each share Common 5¢ par exchanged for (1) share Common 10¢ par
(See American Physicians Service Group, Inc.)

COMTRON, INC. (UT)
Reincorporated under the laws of Delaware as Faircom Inc. and Common $0.001 par changed to 1¢ par 07/27/1984
Faircom Inc. merged into Regent Communications, Inc. 06/15/1998
(See Regent Communications, Inc.)

COMTRON ENTERPRISES INC (BC)
Recapitalized as Olympic Resources Ltd. (BC) 10/21/1993
Each share Common no par exchanged for (0.33333333) share Common no par
Olympic Resources Ltd. (BC) reincorporated in Wyoming 01/08/2003 which reorganized in Nevada as Whittier Energy Corp. 01/02/2004
(See Whittier Energy Corp.)

COMTRUST CORP (NV)
Name changed to Exclusive Cruises & Resorts, Inc. 04/23/1998
Exclusive Cruises & Resorts, Inc. recapitalized as Shotpak, Inc. 06/11/2007 which name changed to Shot Spirits Corp. 01/15/2009

COM21 INC (DE)
Chapter 11 bankruptcy proceedings converted to Chapter 7 on 12/10/2003
No stockholders' equity

COMUTRIX CORP (DE)
Charter cancelled and declared inoperative and void for non-payment of taxes 04/15/1970

COMVEN INC (AZ)
Merged into Fleet Call Inc. 02/25/1988
Each share Common no par exchanged for $3.68 cash

COMVERGE INC (DE)
Acquired by Peak Holding Corp. 05/15/2012
Each share Common $0.001 par exchanged for $1.75 cash

COMVERSE INC (DE)
Name changed to Xura, Inc. 09/09/2015
(See Xura, Inc.)

COMVERSE TECHNOLOGY INC (NY)
Each share Common 1¢ par exchanged for (0.1) share Common 10¢ par 02/26/1993
Common 10¢ par split (3) for (2) by issuance of (0.5) additional share payable 04/15/1999 to holders of record 03/31/1999
Common 10¢ par split (2) for (1) by issuance of (1) additional share payable 04/03/2000 to holders of record 03/27/2000
Each share Common 10¢ par received distribution of (0.1) share Comverse, Inc. Common 1¢ par payable 10/31/2012 to holders of record 10/22/2012 Ex date - 11/01/2012
Merged into Verint Systems Inc. 02/05/2013
Each share 144A Common 10¢ par exchanged for (0.1298) share Common $0.001 par
Each share Common 10¢ par exchanged for (0.1298) share Common $0.001 par

COMWEST CAP CORP (CANADA)
Merged into ComWest Enterprise Corp. 12/12/2005
Each share Common no par exchanged for (0.33333333) share Non-Vtg Class A no par and (1) share Class B no par
ComWest Enterprise Corp. name changed to Unisync Corp. 08/01/2014

COMWEST ENTERPRISE CORP (CANADA)
Each share old Non-Vtg. Class A no par exchanged for (0.2) share new Non-Vtg. Class A no par to reflect a (1) for (2,500) reverse split followed by a (500) for (1) forward split 10/19/2009
Note: Holders of (2,499) or fewer pre-split shares received $0.04 cash per share
Each share old Class B no par exchanged for (0.2) share new Class B no par to reflect a (1) for (2,500) reverse split followed by a (500) for (1) forward split 10/19/2009
Note: Holders of (2,499) or fewer pre-split shares received $0.04 cash per share
Note: Unexchanged certificates were cancelled and became without value 10/19/2015
Name changed to Unisync Corp. 08/01/2014

CON AM RES LTD (BC)
Struck off register and declared dissolved for failure to file returns 02/23/1983

CON KEY MINES LTD (ON)
Merged into Can-Con Enterprises & Explorations Ltd. 11/30/1970
Each share Capital Stock no par exchanged for (0.1) share Capital Stock no par
Can-Con Enterprises & Explorations Ltd. name changed to Aubet Resources Inc. 09/08/1981 which recapitalized as Aubet Explorations Ltd. 09/30/1998 which name changed to Visa Gold Explorations Inc. 08/25/1999
(See Visa Gold Explorations Inc.)

CON SHAWKEY GOLD MINES LTD (ON)
Name changed to Kenn Holdings & Mining Ltd. and Capital Stock $1 par changed to no par 09/15/1969
(See Kenn Holdings & Mining Ltd.)

CON-SPACE COMMUNICATIONS LTD (BC)
Merged into Turret Oy AB 11/02/2009
Each share Common no par exchanged for $0.03 cash

CON TECH INDS INC (DE)
Charter cancelled and declared inoperative and void for non-payment of taxes 03/01/1991

CON-TECH SYS INC (DE)
Charter cancelled and declared inoperative and void for non-payment of taxes 03/01/1994

CON-WAY INC (DE)
Acquired by XPO Logistics, Inc. 10/30/2015
Each share Common $0.625 par exchanged for $47.60 cash

CONA RES LTD (AB)
Acquired by Waterous Energy Fund (International) L.P. 05/23/2018
Each share Common no par exchanged for $2.55 cash
Note: Unexchanged certificates will be cancelled and become without value 05/23/2021

CONAC SOFTWARE CORP (BC)
Recapitalized as Lomiko Enterprises Ltd. 12/03/2004
Each share Common no par exchanged for (0.06666666) share Common no par
Lomiko Enterprises Ltd. recapitalized as Lomiko Resources Inc. 07/28/2006 which name changed to Lomiko Metals Inc. 09/29/2008

CONAGRA CAP L C (IA)
9% Preferred Ser. A no par called for redemption at $25 plus $0.15625 accrued dividends on 11/26/2001
9.35% Preferred Ser. C no par called for redemption at $25 plus $0.16233 accrued dividends on 11/26/2001
Adjustable Rate Preferred Ser. B no par called for redemption at $25 plus $0.0104 accrued dividends on 02/03/2005

CONAGRA FOODS INC (DE)
Reincorporated 01/12/1976
Name changed 09/28/2000
5% Preferred $50 par called for redemption 03/01/1973
State of incorporation changed from (NE) to (DE) 01/12/1976
Common $5 par split (3) for (2) by issuance of (0.5) additional share 03/16/1977
Common $5 par split (2) for (1) by issuance of (1) additional share 12/05/1980
Common $5 par split (3) for (2) by issuance of (0.5) additional share 12/01/1984
Common $5 par split (2) for (1) by issuance of (1) additional share 12/01/1986
Common $5 par split (3) for (2) by issuance of (0.5) additional share 12/01/1989
Common $5 par split (3) for (2) by issuance of (0.5) additional share 11/29/1991
Conv. Preferred Class E no par called for redemption 11/30/1995
$2.50 Conv. Preferred Ser. D no par called for redemption 01/31/1996
Common $5 par split (2) for (1) by issuance of (1) additional share payable 10/01/1997 to holders of record 09/05/1997 Ex date - 10/02/1997
Name changed from ConAgra, Inc. to ConAgra Foods, Inc. 09/28/2000
Each share Common $5 par received distribution of (0.33333333) share Lamb Weston Holdings, Inc. Common $1 par payable 11/09/2016 to holders of record 11/01/2016 Ex date - 11/10/2016
Name changed to Conagra Brands, Inc. 11/10/2016

CONAIR CORP (DE)
Common 10¢ par split (3) for (1) by issuance of (2) additional shares 08/26/1983
Stock Dividends - 50% 01/14/1978; 80% 02/09/1983

Acquired by Conair Acquisition Corp. 06/20/1985
Each share Common 10¢ par exchanged for $24.70 cash

CONAMER LIQUIDATING CO. (SD)
Liquidation completed
Each share Common 10¢ par exchanged for initial distribution of $0.82241 cash 07/24/1972
Each share Common 10¢ par received second and final distribution of $0.12004 cash 03/21/1973

CONAR OIL LTD (BC)
Reincorporated under the laws of Canada as Southfork Energy Corp. 05/06/1981
Southfork Energy Corp. recapitalized as United Southfork Energy Inc. 04/21/1982
(See United Southfork Energy Inc.)

CONBEAU RES LTD (BC)
Recapitalized as Inlet Resources Ltd. 12/03/1984
Each share Common no par exchanged for (0.14285714) share Common no par
Inlet Resources Ltd. name changed to Guerrero Ventures Inc. 08/19/2014

CONBOW CORP (NY)
Each share Common 10¢ par exchanged for (0.2) share Common 50¢ par 01/26/1971
Each share Common 50¢ par exchanged for (0.01) share Common $50 par 05/17/1976
Remaining shares acquired through exchange offer which expired 03/15/1977
Public interest eliminated

CONBRACO INDS INC (MI)
Acquired by Aalberts Industries U.S. Holding Corp. 07/15/2010
Each share Common $10 par exchanged for $725.11841 cash
Each share Common $10 par received an initial additional distribution of $173.6495 cash from escrow payable 09/01/2010 to holders of record 07/15/2010
Each share Common $10 par received second additional distribution of $27.3039 cash from escrow payable 03/24/2011 to holders of record 07/15/2010
Each share Common $10 par received third additional distribution of $36.7583 cash from escrow payable 08/22/2011 to holders of record 07/15/2010
Each share Common $10 par received fourth additional distribution of $50.5021 cash from escrow payable 09/21/2012 to holders of record 07/15/2010
Each share Common $10 par received fifth additional distribution of $43.6728 cash from escrow payable 12/31/2012 to holders of record 07/15/2010
Each share Common $10 par received sixth and final distribution of $2.7533 cash from escrow payable 09/10/2013 to holders of record 07/15/2010

CONCAP INC (TX)
Each share old Common $0.0001 par exchanged for (0.01) share new Common $0.0001 par 06/08/1998
Name changed to Elite Technologies, Inc. 04/29/1999
(See Elite Technologies, Inc.)

CONCENTRA CORP (DE)
Merged into Oracle Corp. 01/01/1999
Each share Common $0.0001 par exchanged for $7 cash

CONCENTRA MANAGED CARE INC (DE)
Merged into Yankee Acquisition Corp. 08/17/1999

Each share Common 1¢ par exchanged for $16.50 cash

CONCENTRAX INC (NV)
SEC revoked common stock registration 08/04/2011

CONCENTREX INC (OR)
Merged into Harland (John H.) Co. 08/28/2000
Each share Common no par exchanged for $7 cash

CONCENTRIC NETWORK CORP (DE)
Common $0.001 par split (2) for (1) by issuance of (1) additional share payable 05/21/1999 to holders of record 04/30/1999
Stock Dividend - in Preferred to holders of Preferred 3.375% payable 12/01/1999 to holders of record 11/16/1999
Merged into Nextlink Communications, Inc. 06/19/2000
Each share 13.5% Sr. Exchangeable Preferred Ser. B $0.001 par exchanged for (1) share Sr. Exchangeable Preferred Ser. E
Each share Common 1¢ par exchanged for (1.2868) shares Class A Common 2¢ par
Nextlink Communications, Inc. name changed to XO Communications, Inc. 10/26/2000 which name changed to XO Holdings, Inc. 03/02/2006
(See XO Holdings, Inc.)

CONCEPT CAP CORP (UT)
Reorganized under the laws of Nevada as Concept Ventures Corp. 07/10/2006
Each share Common $0.001 par exchanged for (0.06779661) share Common $0.001 par
Concept Ventures Corp. name changed to China Ritar Power Corp. 04/09/2007

CONCEPT DEV GROUP (DE)
Name changed to Vocalscape, Inc. 05/11/2004
Vocalscape, Inc. name changed to Nevstar Precious Metals, Inc. 11/07/2005 which recapitalized as Deploy Technologies Inc. (DE) 11/06/2008 which reincorporated in Nevada 09/15/2010 which recapitalized as Body & Mind Inc. 12/07/2017

CONCEPT DEV INC (MO)
Stock Dividend - 25% 06/11/1984
Name changed to Pantera's Corp. 02/03/1987
Pantera's Corp. reorganized as Pizza Inn, Inc. (MO) 09/05/1990 which name changed to Pizza Inn Holdings, Inc. 09/26/2011 which name changed to Rave Restaurant Group, Inc. 01/09/2015

CONCEPT DIGITAL INC (DE)
SEC revoked common stock registration 05/27/2011

CONCEPT GOLD INC (NV)
Recapitalized as Environmental Plasma Arc Technology Inc. 09/25/1992
Each share Common $0.001 par exchanged for (0.2) share Common $0.001 par
Environmental Plasma Arc Technology Inc. name changed to Earth Products & Technologies Inc. 11/05/1997 which name changed to China Shen Zhou Mining & Resources, Inc. 10/20/2006

CONCEPT HLDG CORP (NV)
Name changed to M101 Corp. 11/01/2017

CONCEPT INC (FL)
Common 50¢ par split (3) for (2) by issuance of (0.5) additional share 05/31/1976
Common 50¢ par split (3) for (2) by issuance of (0.5) additional share 07/15/1977
Common 50¢ par split (3) for (2) by issuance of (0.5) additional share 02/24/1978
Common 50¢ par split (5) for (4) by issuance of (0.25) additional share 02/16/1987
Common 50¢ par split (5) for (4) by issuance of (0.25) additional share 02/22/1988
Common 50¢ par split (5) for (4) by issuance of (0.25) additional share 02/20/1989
Stock Dividend - 10% 02/23/1979
Merged into Bristol-Myers Squibb Co. 06/30/1990
Each share Common 50¢ par exchanged for (0.3566) share Common 10¢ par

CONCEPT INDS INC (BC)
Name changed to Concept Wireless Inc. 06/23/2000
Concept Wireless Inc. recapitalized as Candao Enterprises Inc. 02/27/2003
(See Candao Enterprises Inc.)

CONCEPT 90 MARKETING INC (DE)
Charter cancelled and declared inoperative and void for non-payment of taxes 03/01/1991

CONCEPT RES LTD (AB)
Reincorporated 08/21/1978
Place of incorporation changed from (BC) to (AB) 08/21/1978
Name changed to Skyline Natural Resources Ltd. and Capital Stock no par reclassified as Class A Common no par 10/23/1987
Skyline Nautural Resources Ltd. recapitalized as Stellarton Energy Corp. 09/06/1996
(See Stellarton Energy Corp.)

CONCEPT TECHNOLOGIES GROUP INC (DE)
Name changed to Trans Global Services, Inc. 04/25/1996
(See Trans Global Services, Inc.)

CONCEPT TECHNOLOGIES INC (UT)
Reincorporated under the laws of Nevada as Concept Holding Corp. 02/10/2015
Concept Holding Corp. name changed to M101 Corp. 11/01/2017

CONCEPT VENTURES CORP (NV)
Name changed to China Ritar Power Corp. 04/09/2007

CONCEPT WIRELESS INC (BC)
Recapitalized as Candao Enterprises Inc. 02/27/2003
Each share Common no par exchanged for (0.1) share Common no par
(See Candao Enterprises Inc.)

CONCEPTRONIC INC (DE)
Name changed to Arguss Holdings, Inc. 05/09/1997
Arguss Holdings, Inc. name changed to Arguss Communications, Inc. 05/19/2000 which merged into Dycom Industries, Inc. 02/21/2002

CONCEPTS DIRECT INC (DE)
Common 10¢ par split (2) for (1) by issuance of (1) additional share 12/15/1994
Common 10¢ par split (2) for (1) by issuance of (1) additional share payable 03/31/1997 to holders of record 03/14/1997
Completely liquidated 03/02/2015
Each share Common 10¢ par exchanged for first and final distribution of $0.03 cash

CONCEPTUAL TECHNOLOGIES INC (NV)
Each share old Common $0.001 par exchanged for (0.07142857) share new Common $0.001 par 09/11/1997

Name changed to Novamed, Inc. 05/07/1998
Novamed, Inc. name changed to WWA Group, Inc. 10/03/2003 which recapitalized as Genie Gateway 09/09/2015

CONCEPTUALISTICS INC (DE)
Name changed to Morning Star Industries, Inc. 12/13/1988
Morning Star Industries, Inc. recapitalized as Eat at Joe's Ltd. 10/07/1996 which name changed to SPYR, Inc. 03/12/2015

CONCEPTUS INC (DE)
Acquired by Bayer HealthCare LLC 06/05/2013
Each share Common $0.003 par exchanged for $31 cash

CONCERN GALNAFTOGAZ (UKRAINE)
GDR agreement terminated 08/17/2017
Each Reg. S GDR for Ordinary exchanged for (500) shares Ordinary
Note: Unexchanged GDR's will be sold and the proceeds, if any, held for claim after 08/20/2018

CONCERO INC (DE)
Liquidation completed
Each share Common 1¢ par received initial distribution of $0.36 cash payable 01/12/2004 to holders of record 12/29/2003 Ex date - 01/27/2004
Each share Common 1¢ par exchanged for second and final distribution of $0.086 cash 10/14/2005

CONCERT CORP AMER (DE)
Charter cancelled and declared inoperative and void for non-payment of taxes 03/31/1974

CONCERT INDS LTD (CANADA)
Reincorporated 03/17/1995
Place of incorporation changed from (BC) to (Canada) 03/17/1995
Each share old Common no par exchanged for (0.25) share new Common no par 07/26/1996
Plan of Arrangement under Companies' Creditors Arrangement Act effective 12/31/2004
No stockholders' equity

CONCERT NETWORK INC (RI)
Common $1 par changed to 10¢ par 09/10/1959
Liquidation completed
Each share Common 10¢ par exchanged for initial distribution of $1.50 cash 06/29/1979
Each share Common 10¢ par received second and final distribution of $0.22 cash 12/30/1983

CONCERT RES INC (BC)
Name changed to Concert Industries Ltd. (BC) 09/30/1987
Concert Industries Ltd. (BC) reincorporated in Canada 03/17/1995
(See Concert Industries Ltd. (Canada))

CONCERTO SOFTWARE INC (DE)
Merged into Melita International Ltd. 02/09/2004
Each share Common 10¢ par exchanged for $12 cash

CONCHEMCO INC (DE)
Reincorporated 03/31/1969
State of incorporation changed from (MO) to (DE) 03/31/1969
Name changed to Latshaw Enterprises, Inc. 04/19/1988
(See Latshaw Enterprises, Inc.)

CONCHO RES & ENERGY INC (ON)
Name changed to Tellerian Capital Corp. 03/04/1999

Tellerian Capital Corp. name changed to Cogient Corp. 03/23/2001
(See Cogient Corp.)

CONCIERGE TECHNOLOGIES INC (CA)
Reincorporated under the laws of Nevada 10/05/2006

CONCOPPER ENTERPRISES INC (ON)
Name changed 03/12/1998
Name changed from Concopper Phosphate Inc. to Concopper Enterprises Inc. 03/12/1998
Merged into Micon Gold Inc. 01/01/2011
Each share Class A no par exchanged for (1.02) shares Class A no par
Micon Gold Inc. merged into Jubilee Gold Exploration Ltd. 01/25/2013

CONCOR-CHIBOUGAMAU MINES LTD. (ON)
Merged into Ver-Million Gold Placer Mining Ltd. 09/27/1960
Each share Common exchanged for (1) share Common
(See Ver-Million Gold Placer Mining Ltd.)

CONCORD & PORTSMOUTH R.R.
Acquired by Boston & Maine Railroad Co. and dissolved 00/00/1944
Details not available

CONCORD BANCSHARES INC (MO)
Acquired by First Illinois Bancorp, Inc. 03/19/2016
Each share Common no par exchanged for $13.9520265 cash

CONCORD BK (ST LOUIS, MO)
Under plan of reorganization each share Common automatically became (1) share Concord Bancshares, Inc. Common no par 05/23/2003
(See Concord Bancshares, Inc.)

CONCORD CAMERA CORP (NJ)
Old Common no par split (2) for (1) by issuance of (1) additional share payable 04/14/2000 to holders of record 03/27/2000
Each share old Common no par exchanged for (0.2) share new Common no par 11/21/2006
Liquidation completed
Each share new Common no par received initial distribution of $4.26 cash payable 05/03/2010 to holders of record 05/11/2009
Each share new Common no par received second distribution of $0.40 cash payable 10/12/2010 to holders of record 05/11/2009
Each share new Common no par received third distribution of $0.20 cash payable 05/22/2012 to holders of record 05/11/2009
Each share new Common no par received fourth distribution of $0.07 cash payable 06/21/2013 to holders of record 05/11/2009
Each share new Common no par received fifth and final distribution of $0.02 cash payable 07/09/2014 to holders of record 05/11/2009

CONCORD CAP CORP (ON)
Delisted from Toronto Stock Exchange 09/21/1992

CONCORD CAP INC (UT)
Each share old Common $0.001 par exchanged for (0.9138381) share new Common $0.001 par 05/10/1993
Each share new Common $0.001 par exchanged again for (0.03520047) share new Common $0.001 par 03/27/1996
Name changed to Amazon Natural Treasures Inc. (UT) 04/08/1996
Amazon Natural Treasures Inc. (UT) reincorporated in Nevada 08/18/1997 which recapitalized as Amazon Natural Treasures.com, Inc. 02/06/2001
(See Amazon Natural Treasures.com, Inc.)

CONCORD CASUALTY & SURETY CO.
Liquidated by New York State Insurance Dept. 00/00/1934
No stockholders' equity

CONCORD COMMUNICATIONS INC (MA)
Merged into Computer Associates International, Inc. 06/07/2005
Each share Common 1¢ par exchanged for $17 cash

CONCORD COMPUTING CORP (DE)
Reincorporated 03/22/1990
Common $1 par split (2) for (1) by issuance of (1) additional share 04/18/1988
State of incorporation changed from (MA) to (DE) 03/22/1990
Common $1 par changed to $0.33333333 par and (2) additional shares issued 04/08/1991
Name changed to Concord EFS, Inc. 02/24/1992
Concord EFS, Inc. merged into First Data Corp. (Old) 02/26/2004
(See First Data Corp. (Old))

CONCORD DEV CORP (MN)
Merged into Louisiana General Services, Inc. 10/01/1971
Each share Common 10¢ par exchanged for (0.1539) share Common $1 par
Louisiana General Services, Inc. merged into Citizens Utilities Co. 12/04/1990 which name changed to Citizens Communications Co. 05/18/2000 which name changed to Frontier Communications Corp. 07/31/2008

CONCORD DEVELOPMENT CORP., LTD.
Name changed to New Concord Development Corp., Ltd. 00/00/1952
(See New Concord Development Corp., Ltd.)

CONCORD EFS INC (DE)
Common $0.33333333 par split (3) for (2) by issuance of (0.5) additional share 09/16/1994
Common $0.33333333 par split (3) for (2) by issuance of (0.5) additional share 05/22/1995
Common $0.33333333 par split (3) for (2) by issuance of (0.5) additional share payable 01/18/1996 to holders of record 01/08/1996
Common $0.33333333 par split (3) for (2) by issuance of (0.5) additional share payable 06/28/1996 to holders of record 06/18/1996
Common $0.33333333 par split (3) for (2) by issuance of (0.5) additional share payable 06/08/1998 to holders of record 06/01/1998
Common $0.33333333 par split (3) for (2) by issuance of (0.5) additional share payable 09/22/1999 to holders of record 09/15/1999
Common $0.33333333 par split (2) for (1) by issuance of (1) additional share payable 09/28/2001 to holders of record 09/14/2001 Ex date - 10/01/2001
Merged into First Data Corp. (Old) 02/26/2004
Each share Common $0.33333333 par exchanged for (0.365) share Common 1¢ par
(See First Data Corp. (Old))

CONCORD ELEC CO (NH)
Each share Common $100 par exchanged for (5) shares Common no par 00/00/1927
Stock Dividend - 100% 06/04/1974
Merged into UNITIL Corp. 01/23/1985
Each share Common no par exchanged for (2) shares Common no par

CONCORD ENERGY CORP (BC)
Name changed to United Safety Technology Inc. 02/18/1988
United Safety Technology Inc. recapitalized as Consolidated United Safety Technology Inc. 01/03/1990 which recapitalized as Genetronics Biomedical Ltd. (BC) 10/04/1994 which reincorporated in Delaware as Genetronics Biomedical Corp. 06/21/2001 which name changed to Inovio Biomedical Corp. 03/31/2005 which name changed to Inovio Pharmaceuticals, Inc. 05/14/2010

CONCORD ENERGY INC (DE)
Each share old Common $0.0001 par exchanged for (0.2) share new Common $0.0001 par 12/01/1995
Plan of reorganization under Chapter 11 Federal Bankruptcy Code effective 01/18/2001
No stockholders' equity

CONCORD FABRICS INC (DE)
Reincorporated 05/27/1988
Stock Dividend - 10% 03/27/1969
State of incorporation changed from (NY) to (DE) 05/27/1988
Each share Common $1 par exchanged for (1) share Class A Common 50¢ par and (1) share Class B Common 50¢ par
Merged into Concord Merger Corp. 09/24/1999
Each share Class A Common 50¢ par exchanged for $7.875 cash
Each share Class B Common 50¢ par exchanged for $7.875 cash

CONCORD FD INC (MA)
Completely liquidated 09/30/1998
Each share Common $1 par exchanged for first and final distribution of $15.43 cash

CONCORD FINL CORP (NV)
Reincorporated under the laws of Delaware as Millennium Group Holdings, Inc. 03/25/1999
Millennium Group Holdings, Inc. recapitalized as Ronn Motor Co. 04/22/2008 which recapitalized as Vydrotech, Inc. 04/02/2012

CONCORD GAS CO. (NH)
Reorganized as Concord Natural Gas Corp. 00/00/1952
Each share 7% Preferred $100 par exchanged for (1) share 5.5% Preferred $100 par and (2.5) shares Common $10 par
Each share Common $100 par exchanged for (1) share Common $10 par
Concord Natural Gas Corp. merged into EnergyNorth, Inc. 09/30/1985
(See EnergyNorth, Inc.)

CONCORD HALL APARTMENTS, INC.
In process of liquidation 00/00/1943
Details not available

CONCORD HEALTH GROUP INC (DE)
Merged into Multicare Companies, Inc. 02/26/1996
Each share Common $0.001 par exchanged for $7.35 cash

CONCORD HLDG CORP (DE)
Merged into BISYS Group, Inc. 03/29/1995
Each share Common 1¢ par exchanged for (0.789) share Common 2¢ par
(See BISYS Group, Inc.)

CONCORD INCOME TR (MA)
Acquired by Home Group Trust 09/01/1989
Each National Tax Exempt Portfolio Share of Bene. Int. no par exchanged for (1) National Tax-Free Fund Share of Bene. Int. $0.001 par
U.S. Government Sercurities Portfolio Shares of Bene. Int. no par exchanged for Government Securities Fund on a dollar-for-dollar basis
Convertible Portfolio no par reorganized as Lexington Convertible Securities Fund 11/11/1992
Details not available

CONCORD INTL GROUP INC (DE)
Recapitalized as Maxnet Inc. 06/19/1997
Each share Common $0.00001 par exchanged for (0.02) share Common $0.00001 par
Maxnet Inc. name changed to MaxPlanet, Corp. 08/06/1999 which recapitalized as Youth Enhancement Systems, Inc. 06/21/2006 which name changed to Dynamic Response Group, Inc. 03/30/2007
(See Dynamic Response Group, Inc.)

CONCORD MILESTONE INCOME FD II INC (DE)
Merged into Milestone Properties, Inc. 12/18/1990
Details not available

CONCORD MINES LTD.
Acquired by Concord Development Corp. Ltd. 00/00/1951
Details not available

CONCORD MINING SYNDICATE LTD.
Succeeded by Concord Mines, Ltd. 00/00/1946
Details not available

CONCORD NAT GAS CORP (NH)
Common $10 par changed to $5 par and (1) additional share issued 03/27/1957
Merged into EnergyNorth, Inc. 09/30/1985
Each share 5.5% Preferred $100 par exchanged for (6.3) shares Common $1 par
Each share Common $5 par exchanged for (8.2) shares Common $1 par
(See EnergyNorth, Inc.)

CONCORD NATL BK (CONCORD, NC)
Merged into First Charter Corp. 10/00/1984
Details not available

CONCORD PAC GROUP INC (CANADA)
Acquired by Adex Securities Inc. 01/24/2003
Each share Common no par exchanged for $3.40 cash

CONCORD RES INC (UT)
Name changed to TRU, Inc. 08/14/1979
(See TRU, Inc.)

CONCORD SUPPLIES & EQUIPMENT CORP. (NY)
Proclaimed dissolved 12/15/1962

CONCORD TEL CO (NC)
Name changed to CT Communications, Inc. 10/00/1993
(See CT Communications, Inc.)

CONCORD VENTURES INC (CO)
Reincorporated under the laws of Delaware as Golden Dragon Holding Co. 05/13/2011
Golden Dragon Holding Co. name changed to CannaPharmaRx, Inc. 03/23/2015

CONCORDE CAREER COLLEGES INC (DE)
Each share old Common 10¢ par exchanged for (0.5) share new Common 10¢ par 11/21/2001
Merged into Liberty Higher Education LLC 09/01/2006
Each share new Common 10¢ par exchanged for $19.80 cash

CONCORDE COMMODITY FD INC (CO)
Name changed to Concorde Holdings Corp. 12/21/1983
Concorde Holdings Corp. name changed to Concorde Gaming Corp. 06/03/1994
(See Concorde Gaming Corp.)

CONCORDE EXPL LTD (QC)
Struck off register 07/17/1997

CONCORDE EXPLS LTD (BC)
Struck off register 02/25/1983

CONCORDE GAMING CORP (CO)
Name changed 12/21/1983
Name changed from Concorde Holdings Corp. to Concorde Gaming Corp. 12/21/1983
Company terminated registration of common stock and is no longer public as of 01/27/2004

CONCORDE RES CORP (NV)
Each share old Common $0.001 par exchanged for (0.22222222) share new Common $0.001 par 06/08/2006
Recapitalized as Real Hip Hop Matrix Corp. 11/03/2006
Each share new Common $0.001 par exchanged for (0.00471698) share Common $0.001 par
Real Hip Hop Matrix Corp. name changed to RHNMedia 01/12/2007 which name changed to Massive G Media Corp. 03/16/2007 which name changed to International Minerals Mining Group, Inc. 06/21/2007 which name changed to Advanced Content Services, Inc. 02/05/2008 which recapitalized as New Wave Holdings, Inc. 12/08/2014 which name changed to PAO Group, Inc. 06/29/2017

CONCORDE STRATEGIES GROUP INC (CO)
Recapitalized as W3 Group, Inc. (CO) 10/01/1999
Each share Common $0.0001 par exchanged for (0.03333333) share Common $0.0001 par
W3 Group, Inc. (CO) reincorporated in Delaware 05/07/2003 which name changed to Aftersoft Group, Inc. 01/19/2006 which name changed to MAM Software Group, Inc. 05/27/2010

CONCORDE VENTURES INC (CO)
Name changed to Winley Home Builders, Inc. 05/07/1987

CONCORDIA BK & TR CO (VIDALIA, LA)
Under plan of reorganization each share Common $5 par automatically became (1) share Concordia Capital Corp. Common $5 par 07/31/1997

CONCORDIA HEALTHCARE CORP (ON)
Name changed to Concordia International Corp. (ON) 06/30/2016
Concordia International Corp. (ON) reincorporated in Canada 06/22/2018

CONCORDIA INTL CORP (ON)
Reincorporated under the laws of Canada 06/22/2018

CONCORDIA PAPER HLDGS LTD (BERMUDA)
Placed in receivership and delcared insolvent 11/30/1998
No ADR holders' equity

CONCORDIA PORCUPINE GOLD MINES LTD.
Succeeded by Delcore Porcupine Mines Ltd. 00/00/1944
Each share Common exchanged for (0.33333333) share Common
(See Delcore Porcupine Mines Ltd.)

CONCORDIA RESOURCE CORP (BC)
Each share Common no par received distribution of (1) share Meryllion Resources Corp. Common no par payable 12/06/2013 to holders of record 12/06/2013
Recapitalized as Kaizen Discovery Inc. 12/06/2013
Each share Common no par exchanged for (0.2) share Common no par

CONCOURSE CORP (MN)
Recapitalized as Peoples Educational Holdings Inc. 12/31/1998
Each share Common 1¢ par exchanged for (0.05) share Common 1¢ par

CONCOURSE MINES LTD. (ON)
Merged into Coniston Explorations & Holdings Ltd. 02/28/1972
Each share Common no par exchanged for (0.33333333) share Common no par
(See Coniston Explorations & Holdings Ltd.)

CONCRETE CASTING INC (NV)
Name changed to Living 3D Holdings, Inc. 10/03/2013

CONCRETE DESIGNS, INC. (FL)
Company proclaimed dissolved for non-payment of taxes 08/28/1964

CONCRETE MAINTENANCE PRODUCTS, INC. (DE)
Adjudicated bankrupt 03/20/1967
Stockholders' equity unlikely

CONCRETE PRODUCTS, INC. (GA)
Reorganized under Chapter 11 Federal Bankruptcy Code 08/00/1990
No stockholders' equity

CONCRETE UNIT MANUFACTURING CO. (MI)
Proclaimed dissolved for failure to file reports 08/31/1933

CONCUR TECHNOLOGIES INC (DE)
Acquired by SAP S.E. 12/04/2014
Each share Common $0.001 par exchanged for $129 cash

CONCURRENT COMPUTER CORP NEW (DE)
Each share old Common 1¢ par exchanged for (0.1) share new Common 1¢ par 02/07/1992
Each share new Common 1¢ par exchanged again for (0.1) share new Common 1¢ par 07/09/2008
Name changed to CCUR Holdings, Inc. 01/11/2018

CONCURRENT COMPUTER CORP OLD (DE)
Merged into Massachusetts Computer Corp. 09/27/1988
Each share Common 1¢ par exchanged for $20 cash

CONDAKA METALS CORP (BC)
Recapitalized as Dakon Metals Inc. 09/16/1987
Each share Common no par exchanged for (0.5) share Common no par
(See Dakon Metals Inc.)

CONDE NAST PUBLICATIONS, INC. (NY)
Common no par changed to $1 par 11/18/1959
Stock Dividend - 200% 09/04/1946
Merged into Patriot Nast Publishing Co., Inc. 06/06/1967
Each share Common $1 par exchanged for $18.50 cash

CONDEC CORP (DE)
Reincorporated 03/02/1984
State of incorporation changed from (NY) to (DE) 03/02/1984
10% Conv. Preferred $25 par called for redemption 07/09/1984
Acquired by Farley Acquisition Subsidiary Corp. 07/10/1984
Each share Common 10¢ exchanged for $29 cash
Voluntarily dissolved 12/20/2002

Details not available

CONDECOR INC (IL)
Each share Common 25¢ par exchanged for (0.000008) share Common 25¢ par 07/30/1990
Note: In effect holders received 10¢ cash per share and public interest was eliminated

CONDEV LAND FUND LTD. (FL)
Partnership terminated 06/09/2000
Details not available

CONDEV LD GROWTH FD LTD (FL)
Partnership terminated 05/26/2000
Details not available

CONDOMINIUMS NORTHWEST INC (OR)
Adjudicated bankrupt 06/18/1974
Stockholders' equity unlikely

CONDOR CAP INC (NV)
Reincorporated 05/15/2000
Each share old Common no par exchanged for (0.005) share new Common no par 08/19/1993
State of incorporation changed from (CO) to (NV) and new Common no par changed to $0.001 par 05/15/2000
Charter permanently revoked 03/31/2006

CONDOR GOLD CORP (ON)
SEC revoked common stock registration 12/14/2009

CONDOR GOLD FIELDS INC (CANADA)
Recapitalized as Cloudbreak Resources Ltd. (Canada) 11/08/2002
Each share Common no par exchanged for (0.0625) share Common no par
Cloudbreak Resources Ltd. (Canada) reorganized in British Columbia 04/26/2010 which name changed to Petro One Energy Corp. 12/14/2010 which merged into Goldstrike Resources Ltd. 02/29/2016

CONDOR GOLD MINES, INC. (NV)
Charter revoked for failure to file reports and pay fees 01/06/1936

CONDOR HOSPITALITY TR INC (MD)
8% Preferred Ser. A 1¢ par called for redemption at $10 plus $2.08494 accrued dividends on 04/15/2016
10% Preferred Ser. B 1¢ par called for redemption at $10 plus $6.354167 accrued dividends on 04/15/2016
(Additional Information in Active)

CONDOR INTERNATIONAL INC. (DE)
Name changed back to Abela Venture Group, Inc. 01/28/1989
(See Abela Venture Group, Inc.)

CONDOR INTL RES INC (BC)
Recapitalized as Northern Empire Minerals Ltd. 05/03/1999
Each (15) shares Common no par exchanged for (1) share Common no par
Northern Empire Minerals Ltd. name changed to Stornoway Diamond Corp. (BC) 07/16/2003 which reincorporated in Canada 10/28/2011

CONDOR PRECIOUS METALS INC (BC)
Name changed to Condor International Resources Inc. 10/07/1991
Condor International Resources Inc. recapitalized as Northern Empire Minerals Ltd. 05/03/1999 which name changed to Stornoway Diamond Corp. (BC) 07/16/2003 which reincorporated in Canada 10/28/2011

CONDOR SVCS INC (DE)
Stock Dividend - 10% 12/29/1992

Merged into Amwest Insurance Group, Inc. 03/18/1996
Each share Common 1¢ par exchanged for (0.5) share Common 1¢ par
(See Amwest Insurance Group, Inc.)

CONDOR TECHNOLOGY SOLUTIONS INC (DE)
Each share old Common 1¢ par exchanged for (0.5) share new Common 1¢ par 01/18/2002
Dissolved 03/26/2003
No stockholders' equity

CONDOR WEST CORP (NV)
Recapitalized as Online International Corp. 10/08/1999
Each share Common $0.001 par exchanged for (0.02083333) share Common $0.001 par
Online International Corp. name changed to Finotec Group Inc. 02/14/2002

CONDUCTRON CORP (DE)
Class A Common 1¢ par reclassified as Common 1¢ par 04/29/1964
Common 1¢ par split (5) for (4) by issuance of (0.25) additional share 03/12/1965
Acquired by McDonnell Douglas Corp. 05/28/1971
Each share Common 1¢ par exchanged for (0.27) share Common $1.25 par
McDonnell Douglas Corp. merged into Boeing Co. 08/01/1997

CONDUCTRON CORP (MA)
Merged into Amersub Corp. 03/02/1987
Each share Common 1¢ par exchanged for $6 cash

CONDUCTUS INC (DE)
Merged into Superconductor Technologies Inc. 12/23/2002
Each share Common $0.0001 par exchanged for (0.6) share Common $0.001 par

CONDUIT PUB LTD CO (IRELAND)
GDR agreement terminated 03/21/2003
Each Reg. S GDR for Ordinary exchanged for $3.2094 cash
Each 144A GDR for Ordinary exchanged for $3.2094 cash

CONDUITS AMHERST LTD (ON)
Acquired by Aqua Gem Investments Ltd. 10/14/1984
Each share Common no par exchanged for $1.30 cash

CONDUITS CO. LTD.
Merged into Conduits National Co., Ltd. 00/00/1935
Details not available

CONDUITS NATL LTD (ON)
Merged into Conduits-Amherst Ltd. 03/11/1974
Each share Common $1 par exchanged for (3) shares Common no par
(See Conduits-Amherst Ltd.)

C1 FINL INC (FL)
Merged into Bank of the Ozarks, Inc. 07/21/2016
Each share Common $1 par exchanged for (0.6283) share Common 1¢ par
Bank of the Ozarks, Inc. reorganized as Bank of the Ozarks (Little Rock, AR) 06/27/2017 which name changed to Bank OZK (Little Rock, AR) 07/16/2018

CONE MIDSTREAM PARTNERS LP (DE)
Name changed to CNX Midstream Partners L.P. 01/04/2018

CONE MLS CORP (NC)
Plan of reorganization under Chapter 11 Federal Bankruptcy Code effective 05/03/2005
No stockholders' equity

CONE MLS CORP OLD (NC)
4% Preferred $20 par called for redemption 06/30/1972
Common $10 par split (2) for (1) by issuance of (1) additional share 09/09/1976
Merged into a private company 03/27/1984
Each share Common $10 par exchanged for $70 cash

CONE MT MINES LTD (BC)
Recapitalized as Cancal Mines, Ltd. 03/31/1979
Each share Common 50¢ par exchanged for (0.2) share Common no par
Cancal Mines, Ltd. name changed to Cancal Resources Ltd. 10/01/1981
(See Cancal Resources Ltd.)

CONECHO MINES LTD. (ON)
Merged into Consolidated Frederick Mines Ltd. 09/09/1957
Each share Capital Stock $1 par exchanged for (0.0625) share Capital Stock $1 par
(See Consolidated Frederick Mines Ltd.)

CONECTIV INC (DE)
Merged into Pepco Holdings Inc. 08/01/2002
Each share Common 1¢ par exchanged for (0.84882) share Common 1¢ par and $8.844792 cash
Each share Class A Common 1¢ par exchanged for (0.73642) share Common 1¢ par and $7.32942 cash
(See Pepco Holdings, Inc.)

CONEJO SAVINGS & LOAN ASSOCIATION (CA)
Acquired by United Financial Corp. of California 07/10/1969
Each share Guarantee Stock $10 par exchanged for (1.03293) shares Capital Stock $1 par
(See United Financial Corp. of California)

CONEJO VALLEY NATIONAL BANK (THOUSAND OAKS, CA)
Merged into Ventura County National Bancorp 12/30/1986
Each share Common $5 par exchanged for (1.4) shares Common no par
(See Ventura County National Bancorp)

CONEL CORP (PA)
Name changed to Plantation Corp. 04/24/1972
(See Plantation Corp.)

CONESCO INDS LTD (NJ)
Common 10¢ par changed to 5¢ par and (1) additional share issued 06/19/1981
Each share old Common 5¢ par exchanged for (0.25) share new Common 5¢ par 01/06/1992
Each share new Common 5¢ par exchanged for (0.005) share Common $40 par 12/04/1995
Note: In effect holders received $3.80 cash per share and public interest was eliminated

CONESTOGA BANCORP INC (DE)
Merged into Dime Savings Bank of Williamsburgh (Brooklyn, NY) 06/26/1996
Each share Common 1¢ par exchanged for $21.31 cash

CONESTOGA ENTERPRISES INC (PA)
Common $5 par split (3) for (2) by issuance of (0.5) additional share payable 05/14/1999 to holders of record 04/15/1999
$3.42 Conv. Preferred Ser. A $65 par called for redemption at $66.30 plus $0.0637 accrued dividends on 02/06/2002
Merged into D&E Communications, Inc. 05/24/2002
Each share Common $5 par exchanged for either (A) (0.95436) shares Common 16¢ par and $18.15 cash, (B) (0.69901568) share Common 16¢ par and $22.1232 cash, or (C) (2.1208) shares Common 16¢ par
Note: Option to receive (B) or (C) expired 06/03/2002
D&E Communications, Inc. merged into Windstream Corp. 11/10/2009 which name changed to Windstream Holdings, Inc. 09/03/2013

CONESTOGA NATL BK (LANCASTER, PA)
Capital Stock $20 par changed to $10 par and (1) additional share issued 04/14/1967
Stock Dividends - 50% 04/12/1946; 50% 01/28/1957
Merged into Commonwealth National Bank (Harrisburg, PA) 01/01/1970
Each share Capital Stock $10 par exchanged for (1.05) shares Common $10 par and $0.3675 cash
Commonwealth National Bank (Harrisburg, PA) reorganized as Commonwealth National Financial Corp. 03/05/1982
(See Commonwealth National Financial Corp.)

CONESTOGA TEL & TELEG CO (PA)
Under plan of reorganization each share Common $5 par automatically became (1) share Conestoga Enterprises, Inc. Common $5 par 01/02/1990
4.50% Preferred $100 par called for redemption 09/01/1992
Conestoga Enterprises, Inc. merged into D&E Communications, Inc. 05/24/2002 which merged into Windstream Corp. 11/10/2009 which name changed to Windstream Holdings, Inc. 09/03/2013

CONESTOGA TRACTION CO.
Merged into Conestoga Transportation Co. 00/00/1931
Details not available

CONESTOGA TRANSN CO (PA)
Common no par changed to $5 par 12/19/1955
Acquired by a group of private investors 09/26/1989
Each share Common $5 par exchanged for $60 cash

CONETTA MFG INC (DE)
Reorganized as Dynetics Corp. 11/07/1968
Each share Class A Common 10¢ par exchanged for (4) shares Common $0.025 par
Dynetics Corp. name changed to Nylacarb, Inc. 05/24/1973 which name changed to N.I. Liquidating Corp. 11/14/1974
(See N.I. Liquidating Corp.)

CONEX AUSTRALIA N L (AUSTRALIA)
Name changed to Sapphire Mines N.L. 11/10/1989
Sapphire Mines N.L. name changed to Sapphire Mines Ltd. 02/08/2002
(See Sapphire Mines Ltd.)

CONEX CONTL INC (ON)
Name changed to Dominion International Investments Inc. 03/05/2001
(See Dominion International Investments Inc.)

CONEX MD INC (NV)
Name changed to ROI Land Investments Ltd. 10/28/2013

CONEXANT SYS INC (DE)
Common $1 par split (2) for (1) by issuance of (1) additional share payable 10/29/1999 to holders of record 09/24/1999
Each share Common $1 par received distribution of (0.351) share Skyworks Solutions, Inc. Common 25¢ par payable 06/25/2002 to holders of record 06/25/2002
Ex date - 06/26/2002
Common $1 par changed to 1¢ par 02/26/2003
Each share Common 1¢ par received distribution of (1/3) share Mindspeed Technologies, Inc. Common 1¢ par payable 06/27/2003 to holders of record 06/20/2003 Ex date - 06/30/2003
Each share old Common 1¢ par exchanged for (0.1) share new Common 1¢ par 06/30/2008
Acquired by Gold Holdings, Inc. 04/19/2011
Each share new Common 1¢ par exchanged for $2.40 cash

CONEXCO CORP (CO)
Administratively dissolved 08/01/2001

CONEXUS CATTLE CORP (NV)
Name changed to Connexus Corp. 12/02/2015

CONEY ISLAND & BROOKLYN R.R. CO.
Acquired by the City of New York 00/00/1940
Details not available

CONFED DOLPHIN FD (ON)
Fund terminated 12/29/1989
Details not available

CONFEDERATE MTRS INC (DE)
Name changed to Curtiss Motorcycles Co., Inc. 02/20/2018

CONFEDERATE STATES INVESTMENT CO. (MS)
Name changed to Affiliated Investments, Inc. 08/25/1962
(See Affiliated Investments, Inc.)

CONFEDERATION ENERGY LTD (AB)
Struck off register for failure to file annual returns 07/01/1986

CONFEDERATION LIFE ASSOCIATION (CANADA)
Each share Capital Stock $100 par exchanged for (10) shares Capital Stock $10 par 00/00/1953
Plan of Mutualization completed 00/00/1962
Each share Capital Stock $10 par received $180 cash
Note: Certificates were not required to be surrendered and are without value

CONFEDERATION RESOURCES (1980) LTD. (AB)
Merged into Confederation Energy Corp. Ltd. 02/22/1982
Each share Common no par exchanged for (1) share Common no par
(See Confederation Energy Corp. Ltd.)

CONFERENCE CAP CORP (NV)
Name changed to International Fire Prevention, Inc. 05/01/1987
International Fire Prevention, Inc. name changed to Trident Media Group Inc. 12/30/1997
(See Trident Media Group Inc.)

CONFERTECH INTL INC (CO)
Each share old Common 1¢ par exchanged for (0.33333333) share new Common 1¢ par 05/12/1988
Acquired by ALC Communications Corp. 03/15/1995
Each share new Common 1¢ par exchanged for $8 cash

CONFETTI INC (UT)
Recapitalized as Liteglow Industries Inc. 08/26/1996
Each share Common $0.001 par exchanged for (0.16666666) share Common $0.001 par
(See Liteglow Industries Inc.)

CONFIDENTIAL CR CORP (DE)
Charter cancelled and declared inoperative and void for non-payment of taxes 04/15/1972

CONFIDENTIAL FINANCE CORP. (DE)
No longer in existence having become inoperative and void for non-payment of taxes 04/01/1958

CONG INDS INC (ON)
Name changed to Outer Edge Inc. 04/19/1996
Outer Edge Inc. recapitalized as Outer Edge International Inc. 07/15/1997 which recapitalized as Vision Global Solutions Inc. (ON) 02/05/2001 which reincorporated in Nevada 01/07/2005 which recapitalized as Eco-Stim Energy Solutions, Inc. 12/11/2013

CONGAREE BANCSHARES INC (SC)
Merged into Carolina Financial Corp. (New) 06/13/2016
Each share Common 1¢ par exchanged for either (0.4806) share Common 1¢ par, $8.10 cash, or a combination thereof

CONGENERIC CORP (DE)
Liquidation completed
Each share Capital Stock $1 par exchanged for initial distribution of $4 cash 05/29/1979
Each share Capital Stock $1 par received second distribution of $1.50 cash 01/24/1980
Each share Capital Stock $1 par received third distribution of $0.50 cash 07/15/1981
Each share Capital Stock $1 par received fourth distribution of $0.40 cash 09/08/1982
Each share Capital Stock $1 par received fifth and final distribution of $0.32 cash 12/09/1984

CONGER LEHIGH FUELS LTD.
Completely liquidated
Each share Capital Stock no par received initial distribution of $28.25 cash 07/00/1954
Each share Capital Stock no par received second distribution of $3 cash 04/26/1955
Each share Capital Stock no par received third and final distribution of undetermined amount 00/00/1955

CONGER LIFE INSURANCE CO. (FL)
Name changed to Florida Life Insurance Co. 10/09/1997
(See Florida Life Insurance Co.)

CONGLOMERATE FD AMER INC (NY)
Merged into Churchill Fund, Inc. 01/31/1973
Each share Common 1¢ par exchanged for (0.29625) share Capital Stock $1 par
Churchill Fund, Inc. name changed to Beacon Income Fund, Inc. 05/24/1978
(See Beacon Income Fund, Inc.)

CONGLOMERATES INC (DE)
Reincorporated 03/18/1968
Under plan of merger state of incorporation changed from (NV) to (DE) 03/18/1968
Each share Common 1¢ par exchanged for (17) shares Common 1¢ par
Name changed to National Computer Corp. 08/06/1969
(See National Computer Corp.)

CONGO CREST MINERAL CORP (WA)
Reorganized as New Wave Mobile, Inc. 11/22/2006
Each share Common $0.001 par exchanged for (10) shares Common $0.001 par
New Wave Mobile, Inc. name changed to New Wave Media, Inc.

03/26/2007 which name changed to CA Goldfields, Inc. 04/08/2008

CONGO INTERNATIONAL MANAGEMENT CORP. (DE)
Charter cancelled for non-payment of taxes 04/01/1964

CONGO URANIUM CO (UT)
Name changed to Dakota Minerals, Inc. 03/01/1969
(See Dakota Minerals, Inc.)

CONGOLEUM CORP NEW (DE)
Plan of reorganization under Chapter 11 Federal Bankruptcy proceedings effective 07/01/2010
No stockholders' equity

CONGOLEUM CORP OLD (DE)
Common 50¢ par split (3) for (2) by issuance of (0.5) additional share 08/04/1978
Completely liquidated 01/31/1980
Each share Common 50¢ par exchanged for first and final distribution of $38 cash

CONGOLEUM-NAIRN, INC. (NY)
Common no par changed to $5 par 06/02/1966
Common $5 par split (2) for (1) by issuance of (1) additional share 08/18/1966
Merged into Bath Industries, Inc. 09/30/1968
Each share Common $5 par exchanged for (0.33333333) share $5 Conv. Preferred Ser. A no par
(See Bath Industries, Inc.)

CONGRESS & SENATE CO.
In process of liquidation 00/00/1946
No stockholders' equity

CONGRESS BLDG CORP (IL)
Liquidation completed
Each share Common no par exchanged for initial distribution of $10 cash and (1) Trust Certificate 03/10/1972
Each Trust Certificate received second distribution of $5.50 cash 12/01/1972
Each Trust Certificate received third distribution of $2 cash 12/01/1973
Each Trust Certificate received fourth distribution of $2 cash 12/01/1974
Each Trust Certificate received fifth distribution of $2 cash 12/01/1975
Each Trust Certificate received sixth and final distribution of $2 cash 12/03/1976

CONGRESS CIGAR CO., INC.
Dissolved 00/00/1940
Details not available

CONGRESS CO. (AZ)
Name changed to Congress Life Corp. 08/02/1972
(See Congress Life Corp.)

CONGRESS INDS INC (FL)
Merged out of existence 06/19/1992
Details not available

CONGRESS LIFE CORP (AZ)
Completely liquidated 01/30/1980
Each share Common 50¢ par exchanged for first and final distribution of $0.10 cash

CONGRESS MINING & EXPLORATION CO. (UT)
Recapitalized as Federal Oil Shale Corp. 10/01/1967
Each share Capital Stock 1¢ par exchanged for (0.1) share Common 10¢ par
Federal Oil Shale Corp. reorganized as Thompson International Corp. 02/24/1969 which name changed to Inland Western Corp. 10/24/1974
(See Inland Western Corp.)

CONGRESS MINING CORP. LTD. (ON)
Merged into Staple Mining Co. Ltd. 08/11/1972
Each share Capital Stock no par exchanged for (0.25) share Capital Stock no par
Staple Mining Co. Ltd. merged into Gerrard Realty Inc. 01/28/1976

CONGRESS ROTISSERIE INC (CT)
Company advised private 00/00/1998
Details not available

CONGRESS STR FD INC (MA)
Capital Stock $1 par split (5) for (1) by issuance of (4) additional shares 07/16/1973
Name changed to Fidelity Congress Street Fund, Inc. 10/07/1980

CONGRESS STR PPTYS INC (DE)
Merged into Parkway Co. (TX) 11/29/1994
Each share Common 10¢ par exchanged for (0.29) share Common $1 par
Parkway Co. (TX) reincorporated in Maryland as Parkway Properties, Inc. 08/02/1996 which merged into Cousins Properties Inc. 10/06/2016

CONGRESS URANIUM CORP. (UT)
Name changed to Congress Mining & Exploration Co. 08/16/1956
Congress Mining & Exploration Co. recapitalized as Federal Oil Shale Corp. 10/01/1967 which recapitalized as Thompson International Corp. 02/24/1969 which name changed to Inland Western Corp. 10/24/1974
(See Inland Western Corp.)

CONGRESS VIDEO GROUP INC (FL)
Assets assigned for benefit of creditors 04/00/1991
No stockholders' equity

CONGRESSIONAL LIFE CO (DE)
Liquidation completed
Each share Common $1 par exchanged for initial distribution of $1.80 cash 10/01/1990
Each share Common $1 par received second and final distribution of $0.18 cash 12/01/1991

CONGRESSIONAL LIFE INS CO (NY)
Capital Stock $2 par changed to $1 par 11/19/1969
Merged into Bankers Security Life Insurance Society 12/31/1970
Each share Capital Stock $1 par exchanged for (0.33333333) share Common $1 par
Bankers Security Life Insurance Society merged into United Services Life Insurance Co. (DC) 12/20/1979 which reorganized in Virginia as USLICO Corp. 08/15/1984 which merged into NWNL Companies, Inc. 01/17/1995 which name changed to ReliaStar Financial Corp. 02/13/1995
(See ReliaStar Financial Corp.)

CONGRESSIONAL OIL CORP. (NV)
Company voluntarily dissolved 03/01/1924
No stockholders' equity

CONIAGAS MINES LTD (ON)
Each share Capital Stock $5 par exchanged for (2) shares Capital Stock $2.50 par 08/18/1955
Capital Stock $2.50 par changed to no par 07/02/1965
Merged into QSR Ltd. 09/07/1993
Each share Common no par exchanged for (0.32) share Common no par
QSR Ltd. name changed to Coniagas Resources Ltd. 06/25/1999 which name changed to Lithium One Inc. 07/23/2009
(See Lithium One Inc.)

CONIAGAS RES LTD (ON)
Name changed to Lithium One Inc. 07/23/2009
(See Lithium One Inc.)

CONIAURUM HOLDINGS LTD. (ON)
Name changed 03/17/1961
Name changed from Coniaurum Mines Ltd. to Coniaurum Holdings Ltd. 03/17/1961
Recapitalized as Canadian Coniaurum Investments Ltd. 05/01/1967
Each share Capital Stock no par exchanged for (0.2) share Capital Stock no par
Canadian Coniaurum Investments Ltd. name changed to MTS International Services Ltd. 03/01/1971 which name changed to MTS International Services Inc. (ON) 10/06/1971 which reincorporated in Canada as Epitek International Inc. 12/07/1981 which recapitalized as International Epitek Inc. 08/01/1987 which name changed to CompAS Electronics Inc. 07/29/1993 which was acquired by AIM Safety Co., Inc. 12/08/1997 which name changed to AimGlobal Technologies Co., Inc. 01/29/1999
(See AimGlobal Technologies Co., Inc.)

CONIC INVT LTD (HONG KONG)
Name changed to China Aerospace International Holdings Ltd. 07/27/1993
(See China Aerospace International Holdings Ltd.)

CONIFER GROUP INC NEW (MA)
Merged into Bank of New England Corp. 04/22/1987
Each share Common $1 par exchanged for (1.71) shares Common $5 par
(See Bank of New England Corp.)

CONIFER GROUP INC OLD (MA)
Name changed 02/17/1973
Name changed 01/01/1985
Name changed from Conifer/Essex Group, Inc. to Conifer Group Inc. (Old) 02/17/1973
Common $1 par split (3) for (2) by issuance of (0.5) additional share 05/29/1981
Common $1 par split (2) for (1) by issuance of (1) additional share 12/14/1984
Stock Dividends - 10% 06/01/1979; 10% 11/30/1979; 10% 08/29/1980; 10% 02/26/1982
Name changed to Conifer Group Inc. (New) 01/01/1985
Conifer Group Inc. (New) merged into Bank of New England Corp. 04/22/1987
(See Bank of New England Corp.)

CONIGO MINES LTD (ON)
Acquired by Amos Mines Ltd. 11/19/1971
Each share Capital Stock $1 par exchanged for (1) share Common $1 par
Amos Mines Ltd. merged into Jonpol Explorations Ltd. 04/28/1982 which merged into Eastern Platinum Ltd. 04/26/2005

CONILL CORP (DE)
Name changed to Continental Illinois Corp. 03/27/1972
Continental Illinois Corp. reorganized as Continental Illinois Holding Corp. 09/27/1984
(See Continental Illinois Holding Corp.)

CONISIL RES INC (ON)
Name changed 04/28/1986
Name changed from Conisil Mines Ltd. to Conisil Resources Inc. 04/28/1986
Name changed to Human Resources for Growth Inc. 11/16/1992
Human Resouces for Growth Inc. name changed to IBI Corp. 12/12/1994

CONISTON CAP CORP (BC)
Reincorporated 08/10/1995
Place of incorporation changed from (Canada) to (BC) 08/10/1995
Name changed to CPL Ventures Ltd. 08/08/1996
CPL Ventures recapitalized as Manfrey Capital Corp. 11/11/1996
(See Manfrey Capital Corp.)

CONISTON COPPER MINES LTD. (ON)
Merged into Coniston Explorations & Holdings Ltd. 02/28/1972
Each share Common $1 par exchanged for (0.4) share Common no par
(See Coniston Explorations & Holdings Ltd.)

CONISTON EXPLS & HLDGS LTD (ON)
Charter cancelled for failure to pay taxes and file returns 03/14/1978

CONIX WESTERN, INC. (UT)
Proclaimed dissolved for failure to pay taxes 09/30/1975

CONJECTURE INC (ID)
Name changed 03/31/1989
Name changed from Conjecture Mines Inc. to Conjecture, Inc. and Common 10¢ par changed to 5¢ par 03/31/1989
Merged into Coeur d'Alenes Co. 02/02/1993
Each share Common 5¢ par exchanged for (0.04) share Common no par
(See Coeur d'Alenes Co.)

CONJO YELLOWKNIFE MINES, LTD. (ON)
Charter revoked for failure to file reports and pay taxes 04/00/1957

CONJUCHEM BIOTECHNOLOGIES INC NEW (CANADA)
Discharged from receivership 07/14/2015
No stockholders' equity

CONJUCHEM BIOTECHNOLOGIES INC OLD (CANADA)
Reorganized as ConjuChem Biotechnologies Inc. (New) 08/28/2009
Each share Common no par exchanged for (1) share Common no par
(See ConjuChem Biotechnologies Inc. (New))

CONJUCHEM INC (QC)
Plan of arrangement effective 05/23/2006
Each share Common no par exchanged for (1) share ConjuChem Biotechnologies Inc. Common no par and (1) share 6550568 Canada Inc. Common no par
(See each company's listing)

CONJUROR BAY MINES LTD (BC)
Recapitalized as Philco Resources Ltd. 01/29/1975
Each share Common 50¢ par exchanged for (0.5) share Common no par
(See Philco Resources Ltd.)

CONLEY MINES LTD.
Merged into Gencona Mines Ltd. 00/00/1944
Each share Capital Stock no par exchanged for (0.23809523) share Capital Stock no par 00/00/1944
Gencona Mines Ltd. recapitalized as Kelly Lake Nickel Mines Ltd. 09/16/1968 which name changed to Albany Oil & Gas Ltd. (MB) 03/22/1971 which reincorporated in Alberta 11/10/1980 which name changed to Albany Corp. 05/17/1988 which merged into LifeSpace Environmental Walls Inc. 08/17/1993 which merged into SMED International Inc. 07/01/1996
(See SMED International Inc.)

CONLEY RES CORP (BC)
Struck off register and declared dissolved for failure to file returns 01/07/1994

CONLON CORP.
Merged into Conlon-Moore Corp. 00/00/1947
Each share 5% Preferred exchanged for (2) shares 6% Preferred $50 par
Each share Common exchanged for (1) share Common $1 par
(See Conlon-Moore Corp.)

CONLON MOORE CORP (DE)
Voluntarily dissolved 12/31/1985
Details not available

CONMAR EXPLS LTD (ON)
Charter cancelled for failure to pay taxes and file returns 04/09/1975

CONMAT, INC. (TN)
Charter revoked for failure to pay taxes 08/09/1967

CONMAT TECHNOLOGIES INC (FL)
Administratively dissolved for failure to file annual reports 09/21/2001

CONMED HEALTHCARE MGMT INC (DE)
Acquired by Correct Care Solutions, L.L.C. 08/29/2012
Each share Common $0.0001 par exchanged for $3.95 cash

CONN C G LTD (IN)
Common $100 par changed to no par 00/00/1931
Each share Common no par exchanged for (3) shares Common $5 par 00/00/1939
Common $5 par split (3) for (2) by issuance of (0.5) additional share 08/31/1964
Common $5 par split (3) for (2) by issuance of (0.5) additional share 06/01/1965
Stock Dividend - 10% 07/01/1957
Merged into Crowell Collier & Macmillan, Inc. 05/19/1969
Each share 7% Preferred $100 par exchanged for (2.8) shares $2.50 Conv. Preferred $1 par
Each share 6% 2nd Preferred Class A $100 par exchanged for (2.4) shares $2.50 Conv. Preferred $1 par
Each share Common $5 par exchanged for (0.2) share $2.50 Conv. Preferred $1 par and (0.5) share Common $1 par
Crowell Collier & Macmillan, Inc. name changed to Macmillan, Inc. 01/01/1973
(See Macmillan, Inc.)

CONN CHEM LTD (ON)
Common no par reclassified as Conv. Part. Spec. Class A no par 02/04/1976
Under plan of merger each share Conv. Part. Spec. Class A no par exchanged for $10 cash 02/06/1978
Under plan of merger each share Conv. Part. Spec. Class B no par exchanged for $10 cash 02/06/1978
Public interest eliminated

CONNA CORP (KY)
Stock Dividends - 10% 11/15/1980; 10% 11/15/1981
Merged into Dairy Mart Convenience Stores, Inc. 10/17/1986
Each share Common no par exchanged for $20 cash

CONNACHER OIL & GAS LTD (AB)
Reincorporated under the laws of Canada 03/30/2015

CONNAUGHT BIOSCIENCES INC (CANADA)
Acquired by Merieux Canada Holdings Ltd. 02/02/1990
Each share Common no par exchanged for $37 cash

CONNAUGHT FILMS LTD (NY)
Name changed to Capital Corporate Resources, Inc. 12/14/1970
(See Capital Corporate Resources, Inc.)

CONNAUGHT HOTEL CO. LTD.
Acquired by Cardy Corp. Ltd. 00/00/1947
Each share exchanged for (0.6) share Class A, $3.50 principal amount of debentures and $0.60 cash
Name changed to Sheraton Ltd. 00/00/1950
(See Sheraton Ltd.)

CONNECT CORP (NV)
Common $0.001 par split (6) for (1) by issuance of (5) additional shares payable 04/16/2009 to holders of record 04/16/2009
Name changed to IFCI International Corp. 01/26/2012

CONNECT EXPRESS INC (FL)
Recapitalized as 2Connect Express Inc. 05/06/1997
Each share Common no par exchanged for (0.5) share Common no par
(See 2Connect Express Inc.)

CONNECT INC (DE)
Each share old Common $0.001 par exchanged for (0.2) share new Common $0.001 par 02/26/1998
Name changed to Connectinc.Com Co. 08/12/1999
Connectinc.Com Co. merged into Calico Commerce, Inc. 02/01/2000
(See Calico Commerce, Inc.)

CONNECT INTER-TEL MEDIA INC (BC)
Delisted from Vancouver Stock Exchange 03/05/1993

CONNECT ONE TELCOM CORP (FL)
Name changed to Green Machine Development Corp. 07/01/1999

CONNECTAJET COM INC (NV)
SEC revoked common stock registration 09/08/2011

CONNECTICUT & PASSUMPSIC RIVERS RAILROAD CO.
Liquidated 00/00/1946
Details not available

CONNECTICUT BANCFEDERATION INC (CT)
Liquidation completed
Each share Common $10 par stamped to indicate initial distribution of (1) share FirstBancorp, Inc. (CT) Conv. Preferred no par and $5 cash 10/19/1979
(See FirstBancorp, Inc. (CT))
Each share Stamped Common $10 par received second distribution of $1 cash 09/15/1980
Each share Stamped Common $10 par received third distribution of $1.50 cash 03/18/1983
Each share Stamped Common $10 par received fourth distribution of $7.50 cash 03/29/1985
Each share Stamped Common $10 par exchanged for fifth and final distribution of $1.46 cash 11/22/1985

CONNECTICUT BANCORP INC NORWALK (DE)
Declared insolvent and taken over by the FDIC 04/24/1992
Stockholders' equity unlikely

CONNECTICUT BANCSHARES CORP (CT)
Liquidation completed
Each share Common 10¢ par received initial distribution of (0.3286) share CBT Corp. Common $1 par 03/01/1985
Each share Common 10¢ par exchanged for second distribution of $1 cash 01/06/1986
Each share Common 10¢ par received third and final distribution of $0.17 cash 12/15/1986

CONNECTICUT BANCSHARES INC (DE)
Merged into NewAlliance Bancshares, Inc. 04/02/2004
Each share Common 1¢ par exchanged for $52 cash

CONNECTICUT BK & TR CO (HARTFORD, CT)
Capital Stock $25 par changed to $12.50 par and (1) additional share issued 11/08/1955
Capital Stock $12.50 par changed to $10 par and (0.25) additional share issued 08/25/1967
Under plan of reorganization each share Capital Stock $10 par automatically became (1) share CBT Corp. Common $10 par 02/27/1970
CBT Corp. merged into Bank of New England Corp. 06/14/1985
(See Bank of New England Corp.)

CONNECTICUT BK COMM (STAMFORD, CT)
Closed by the Connecticut Department of Banking and FDIC appointed receiver 06/26/2002
No stockholders' equity

CONNECTICUT CASH CREDIT CORP.
Merged into Franklin Plan Corp. 00/00/1932
Details not available

CONNECTICUT CMNTY BK (GREENWICH, CT)
Common $10 par changed to $5 par and (1) additional share issued 06/23/1986
Merged into Gateway Financial Corp. 12/29/1989
Each share Common $5 par exchanged for $14.75 cash

CONNECTICUT DAILY TAX FREE INCOME FD INC (MD)
Common $0.001 par reclassified as Class A $0.001 par 01/26/1995
Completely liquidated 11/23/2009
Each share Class A $0.001 par received first and final distribution of net asset value
Each share Class B $0.001 par received first and final distribution of net asset value
Note: Certificates were not required to be surrendered and are without value

CONNECTICUT DEV CORP (BC)
Recapitalized as Mira Properties Ltd. 04/16/1999
Each share Common no par exchanged for (0.16666666) share Common no par
Mira Properties Ltd. recapitalized as Resolve Ventures, Inc. 08/19/2003

CONNECTICUT ELECTRIC SERVICE CO.
Merged into Connecticut Light & Power Co. 00/00/1935
Details not available

CONNECTICUT ENERGY CORP (CT)
Common $13.33333333 par changed to $1 par and (1) additional share issued 05/23/1984
Common $1 par split (3) for (2) by issuance of (0.5) additional share 10/23/1989
Merged into Energy East Corp. 02/08/2000
Each share Common $1 par exchanged for either (1.82) shares Common 1¢ par, $42 cash, or a combination thereof
Note: Option to receive stock and cash or cash only expired 02/10/2000
(See Energy East Corp.)

CONNECTICUT FINL SVCS CORP (CT)
Name changed to Citytrust Bancorp, Inc. 04/12/1978
(See Citytrust Bancorp, Inc.)

CONNECTICUT GAS & COKE SECURITIES CO.
Liquidated 00/00/1948
Details not available

CONNECTICUT GEN CORP (CT)
Merged into Cigna Corp. 04/01/1982
Each share Common $2.50 par exchanged for (1) share Common $1 par

CONNECTICUT GEN MTG & RLTY INVTS (MA)
Shares of Bene. Int. no par reclassified as Common no par 06/07/1973
Name changed to 745 Property Investments 10/19/1981
(See 745 Property Investments)

CONNECTICUT GENERAL INSURANCE CORP. (CT)
Common $5 par changed to $2.50 par and (1) additional share issued 12/19/1967
Stock Dividends - 50% 04/21/1969; 50% 04/23/1973; 50% 05/11/1978
Under plan of reorganization each share Common $2.50 par automatically became (1) share Connecticut General Corp. Common $2.50 par 07/01/1981
Connecticut General Corp. merged into Cigna Corp. 04/01/1982

CONNECTICUT GENERAL LIFE INSURANCE CO. (CT)
Each share Common $100 par exchanged for (10) shares Common $10 par 00/00/1929
Common $10 par changed to $5 par and (1) additional share issued 02/28/1962
Stock Dividends - 100% 10/03/1949; 100% 04/02/1956; 100% 04/07/1961
Under plan of merger name changed to Connecticut General Insurance Corp. 12/19/1967
Connecticut General Insurance Corp. reorganized as Connecticut General Corp. 07/01/1981 which merged into Cigna Corp. 04/01/1982

CONNECTICUT INVESTMENT MANAGEMENT CORP. (CT)
Acquired by Broad Street Investing Corp. 00/00/1954
Approximately (4.42) shares Common no par exchanged for (1) share Capital Stock $5 par
Broad Street Investing Corp. name changed to Seligman Common Stock Fund, Inc. 05/01/1982

CONNECTICUT LIMOUSINE SVC INC (CT)
Merged into U.S. Industries, Inc. 09/24/1969
Each share Common Ser. 1 $1 par exchanged for $12 cash

CONNECTICUT LT & PWR CO (CT)
Common $100 par changed to no par 00/00/1935
Common no par changed to $10 par 06/22/1967
Stock Dividend - 300% 08/14/1950
Merged into Northeast Utilities 12/26/1967
Each share Common $10 par exchanged for (2) shares Common $5 par
(See Northeast Utilities)
Note: Unexchanged certificates were cancelled and became without value 12/27/1972
15.04% Preferred Ser. M $50 par called for redemption 06/02/1987
Depositary Preferred called for redemption 10/02/1988
Adjustable Rate Preferred Ser. N $50 par called for redemption 10/02/1988
$5.52 Preferred Ser. L $50 par called for redemption 09/01/1992
$4.56 Preferred Ser. K $50 par called for redemption 09/22/1992

9.36% Preferred 1970 Ser. $50 par called for redemption 09/22/1992
9.60% Preferred 1974 Ser. $50 par called for redemption 09/22/1992
11.52% Preferred 1975 Ser. $50 par called for redemption 10/01/1992
10.48% Preferred Ser. 1980 $50 par called for redemption 12/18/1992
$3.80 Preferred Ser. J $50 par called for redemption 11/05/1993
$4.48 Preferred Ser. H $50 par called for redemption 11/05/1993
$4.48 Preferred Ser. I $50 par called for redemption 11/05/1993
7.60% Preferred 1971 Ser. $50 par called for redemption 11/05/1993
9.10% Preferred Class A $25 par called for redemption 11/05/1993
Class A Dutch Auction Rate Preferred 1989 Ser. $25 par called for redemption 00/00/1995
9% Class A Preferred $25 par called for redemption 00/00/1995
(Additional Information in Active)

CONNECTICUT MILLS CO.
Dissolved 00/00/1934
Details not available

CONNECTICUT MUT INVT ACCOUNTS INC (MD)
Name changed 11/06/1985
Name changed from Connecticut Mutual Liquid Account, Inc. to Connecticut Mutual Investment Accounts, Inc. 11/06/1985
Merged into Oppenheimer Money Market Fund Inc. 06/28/1995
Each Liquid Account Share 10¢ par exchanged for Common $1 par on a net asset basis

CONNECTICUT NAT GAS CORP (CT)
Common $12.50 par changed to $6.25 par and (1) additional share issued 01/23/1978
6% Preferred Ser. A $100 par called for redemption 00/00/1981
Common $6.25 par changed to $3.125 par and (1) additional share issued 06/02/1986
Under plan of reorganization each share Common $3.125 par automatically became (1) share CTG Resources Inc. Common no par 03/31/1997
CTG Resources Inc. merged into Energy East Corp. 09/01/2000
(See Energy East Corp.)
6% Preferred Ser. B $100 par called for redemption at $110 plus $1.50 accrued dividends on 11/30/2012
(Additional Information in Active)

CONNECTICUT NATL BK (BRIDGEPORT, CT)
Merged into Hartford National Corp. 10/30/1982
Each share Common Capital Stock $5 par exchanged for (1.66) shares Common $6.25 par
Hartford National Corp. merged into Shawmut National Corp. 02/29/1988 which merged into Fleet Financial Group Inc. (New) 11/30/1995 which name changed to Fleet Boston Corp. 10/01/1999 which name changed to FleetBoston Financial Corp. 04/18/2000 which merged into Bank of America Corp. 04/01/2004

CONNECTICUT POWER CO. (CT)
Each share Common $100 par exchanged for (4) shares Common $25 par 00/00/1928
Merged into Hartford Electric Light Co. 01/01/1958
Each share 4.5% Preferred $50 par exchanged for (1) share 4.5% Preferred $50 par
Each share Common $25 par exchanged for (0.75) share Common $25 par
(See Hartford Electric Light Co.)

CONNECTICUT PRINTERS INC (CT)
Common $10 par changed to $5 par and (1) additional share issued 02/27/1962
Through purchase offer 99.4% acquired by Robertson Paper Box Co., Inc. as of 06/04/1973
Public interest eliminated

CONNECTICUT RIV BANCORP (NH)
Acquired by Mascoma Mutual Financial Services Corp. 08/15/2014
Each share Common 20¢ par exchanged for $18.15 cash

CONNECTICUT RIV CMNTY BK (WETHERSFIELD, CT)
Acquired by Liberty Bank (Middletown, CT) 12/03/2010
Each share Common 1¢ par exchanged for $10.75 cash

CONNECTICUT RIVER POWER CO. OF NEW HAMPSHIRE
Acquired by Connecticut River Power Co. in 1932
Details not available

CONNECTICUT TELEPHONE & ELECTRIC CORP.
Acquired by Great American Industries, Inc. 12/31/42
Each share Common 10¢ par exchanged for (1) share Common 10¢ par
(See Great American Industries, Inc.)

CONNECTICUT UTILITIES CORP. (CT)
Dissolved 12/23/37
No stockholders' equity

CONNECTICUT VALLEY BREWING CORP. (DE)
Charter cancelled and declared inoperative and void for non-payment of taxes in 1938

CONNECTICUT VALLEY CO.
Dissolved in 1935

CONNECTICUT VALLEY PUBLISHING CO. (CT)
Voluntarily dissolved 5/1/67
Details not available

CONNECTICUT VENTURE CAP CORP (CT)
Assets assigned to the U.S. Government 06/00/1972
No stockholders' equity

CONNECTICUT WESTN MUT FD INC (MD)
Common $100 par changed to $10 par and (9) additional shares issued 03/05/1965
Common $10 par split (10) for (1) by issuance of (9) additional shares 01/00/1970
Name changed to Channing Bond Fund, Inc. 04/08/1971
Channing Bond Fund, Inc. name changed to American General Capital Bond Fund, Inc. 11/21/1975 which name changed to American Capital Corporate Bond Fund, Inc. (MD) 09/09/1983 which reincorporated in Delaware as Van Kampen American Capital Corporate Bond Fund 08/05/1995 which name changed to Van Kampen Corporate Bond Fund 07/14/1998

CONNECTICUT WOMEN'S BANK (GREENWICH, CT)
Name changed to Connecticut Community Bank (Greenwich, Conn.) 7/1/84
(See Connecticut Community Bank (Greenwich, Conn.))

CONNECTICUT WTR CO (CT)
Merged into Connecticut Water Service, Inc. 04/10/1975
Each share Common no par exchanged for (1.25) shares Common no par

CONNECTINC COM CO (DE)
Merged into Calico Commerce, Inc. 2/1/2000
Each share Common $0.001 par exchanged for (0.081) share Common $0.001 par
(See Calico Commerce, Inc.)

CONNECTION CHINA TRADING CORP. (NV)
Name changed to Asian Pacific Co., Ltd. 09/09/1992
(See Asian Pacific Co., Ltd.)

CONNECTION SPORTS INTL INC (CO)
Recapitalized as DCH Technology Inc. (CO) 05/21/1997
Each share Common no par exchanged for (1/3) share Common no par
DCH Technology Inc. (CO) reincorporated in Delaware 06/02/2000 which recapitalized as Medra Corp. 08/21/2006

CONNECTIVCORP (DE)
Each share old Common $0.001 par exchanged for (0.1) share new Common $0.001 par 03/12/2002
Name changed to Majesco Holdings Inc. 04/14/2004
Majesco Holdings Inc. name changed to Majesco Entertainment Co. 04/11/2005 which name changed to PolarityTE, Inc. 01/11/2017

CONNECTIVE THERAPEUTICS INC (DE)
Name changed to Connetics Corp. 5/15/97
(See Connetics Corp.)

CONNECTIVITY & TECHNOLOGIES INC (CO)
Recapitalized as Peacock Financial Corp. (CO) 02/27/1996
Each share Common $0.001 par exchanged for (0.005) share Common $0.001 par
Peacock Financial Corp. (CO) reorganized in Nevada as Broadleaf Capital Partners, Inc. 03/22/2002 which recapitalized as EnergyTek Corp. 07/23/2014 which recapitalized as TimefireVR Inc. 11/22/2016

CONNECTIVITY TECHNOLOGIES INC (DE)
SEC revoked common stock registration 06/06/2011

CONNECTONE BANCORP INC (NJ)
Merged into ConnectOne Bancorp, Inc. (New) 07/01/2014
Each share Common no par exchanged for (2.6) shares Common no par

CONNECTURE INC (DE)
Acquired by FP Healthcare Holdings, Inc. 04/25/2018
Each share Common $0.001 par exchanged for $0.35 cash

CONNELL (W.W.), INC. (OK)
Charter revoked for failure to file reports and pay fees 4/16/51

CONNELLY CONTAINERS INC (PA)
40¢ Preferred $1 par called for redemption 5/4/62
Merged into Family Acquisition Corp. 12/1/89
Each share Common 50¢ par exchanged for $20 cash

CONNER CORP (NC)
Plan of reorganization under Chapter 11 Federal Bankruptcy proceedings confirmed 06/12/1990
No stockholders' equity

CONNER HOMES CORP. (NC)
Common 10¢ par split (3) for (2) by issuance of (0.5) additional share 8/31/83
Stock Dividend - 10% 9/20/79
Name changed to Conner Corp. 3/28/85
(See Conner Corp.)

CONNER PERIPHERALS INC (DE)
Reincorporated 8/18/92
State of incorporation changed from (CA) to (DE) 8/18/92
Merged into Seagate Technology, Inc. 2/2/96
Each share Common no par exchanged for (0.442) share Common 1¢ par
Seagate Technology, Inc. merged into Veritas Software Corp. 11/22/2000 which merged into Symantec Corp. 7/2/2005

CONNETICS CORP (DE)
Merged into Stiefel Laboratories, Inc. 12/28/2006
Each share Common $0.001 par exchanged for $17.50 cash

CONNETRICIA GOLD MINES LTD.
Name changed to Connetricia Mines & Exploration Ltd. in 1944
(See Connetricia Mines & Exploration Ltd.)

CONNETRICIA MINES & EXPLORATION LTD. (ON)
Charter revoked for failure to file reports and pay taxes 00/00/1953

CONNING CORP (MO)
Merged into Metropolitan Life Insurance Co. 04/19/2000
Each share Common 1¢ par exchanged for $12.50 cash

CONNOHIO INC (OH)
Liquidation completed
Each share Common $1 par received initial distribution of $3 cash payable 09/17/2007 to holders of record 09/17/2007
Each share Common $1 par received second and final distribution of approximately $2 cash payable 12/31/2007 to holders of record 12/31/2007
Note: Certificates were not required to be surrendered and are without value

CONNOLLY SHOE CO. (MN)
Liquidation completed
Each share Common $1 par received initial distribution of $0.95 cash in 1967
Each share Common $1 par received second distribution of $0.15 cash 3/15/68
Each share Common $1 par received third and final distribution of (1) Trust Certificate 5/1/68
Each Trust Certificate received initial distribution of $0.09 cash 1/17/69
Each Trust Certificate received second distribution of $0.05 cash 1/17/70
Each Trust Certificate received third distribution of $0.11043 cash 1/18/71
Each Trust Certificate received fourth and final distribution of $0.007 cash 12/27/73
Certificates were not surrendered and are now valueless

CONNOR CLARK & LUNN CONSERVATIVE INCOME & GROWTH FD (ON)
Under plan of reorganization each Trust Unit automatically became (1) CC&L Core Income & Growth Fund Ser. C Unit 05/31/2012

CONNOR CLARK & LUNN FINL OPPORTUNITIES FD (ON)
Merged into Australian Banc Income Fund 06/11/2013
Each Class A Unit automatically became (0.557596) Class A Unit
Each Class F Unit automatically became (0.550557) Class F Unit
Australian Banc Income Fund name changed to Purpose Global Financials Income Fund 06/18/2018

CONNOR CLARK & LUNN GLOBAL FINANCIALS FD (ON)
Merged into Connor, Clark & Lunn Global Financials Fund II 02/04/2008
Each Unit received (1.136) Units Connor, Clark & Lunn Global Financials Fund II merged into Focused Global Trends Fund 10/05/2011 which merged into Australian Banc Income Fund 06/11/2013 which name changed to Purpose Global Financials Income Fund 06/18/2018

CONNOR CLARK & LUNN GLOBAL FINANCIALS FD II (ON)
Under plan of merger each Common Unit or Class F Unit automatically became (0.872876) Focused Global Trends Fund Class A Unit or (0.871693) Class F Unit respectively 10/05/2011
Focused Global Trends Fund name changed to Connor, Clark & Lunn Financial Opportunities Fund 10/05/2011 which merged into Australian Banc Income Fund 06/11/2013 which name changed to Purpose Global Financials Income Fund 06/18/2018

CONNOR CLARK & LUNN PRINTS TR (ON)
Under plan of merger name changed to Connor, Clark & Lunn Conservative Income & Growth Fund 06/14/2010
Connor, Clark & Lunn Conservative Income & Growth Fund reorganized as CC&L Core Income & Growth Fund 05/31/2012

CONNOR CLARK & LUNN REAL RETURN INCOME FD (ON)
Merged into ING Floating Rate Senior Loan Fund 01/07/2013
Each Unit received (0.732842) Class A Unit
ING Floating Rate Senior Loan Fund name changed to Voya Floating Rate Senior Loan Fund 08/25/2015 which name changed to Redwood Floating Rate Income Fund 12/20/2017 which name changed to Purpose Floating Rate Income Fund 06/18/2018

CONNOR CLARK & LUNN ROC PREF CORP (CANADA)
Redeemable Retractable Preferred called for redemption at $12.9841 on 12/22/2009

CONNOR CLARK & LUNN TIGERS TR (ON)
Completely liquidated 12/15/2005
Each Unit received first and final distribution of $17.5159 cash

CONNOR CLARK & LUNN CONSERVATIVE INCOME FD (ON)
Merged into Connor, Clark & Lunn Conservative Income & Growth Fund 02/04/2011
Each Unit received (0.398816) Trust Unit
Connor, Clark & Lunn Conservative Income & Growth Fund reorganized as CC&L Core Income & Growth Fund 05/31/2012

CONNOR CLARK & LUNN CONSERVATIVE INCOME FD II (ON)
Merged into Connor, Clark & Lunn Conservative Income & Growth Fund 06/14/2010
Each Unit automatically became (0.36926932) Trust Unit
Connor, Clark & Lunn Conservative Income & Growth Fund reorganized as CC&L Core Income & Growth Fund 05/31/2012

CONNOR CLARK LTD (ON)
Acquired by Royal Bank of Canada (Montreal, QC) 04/27/1999
Each share Non-Vtg. Class A Common no par exchanged for $6.85 cash

CONNORS BROS INCOME FD (ON)
Merged into Centre Partners Management, LLC 11/19/2008
Each Trust Unit no par exchanged for $8.50 cash

CONNORS BROS LTD (NB)
Class A no par and Class B no par reclassified as $2.85 Preference no par 03/25/1983
$2.85 Preference no par called for redemption 04/29/1983

CONNORS HOE & TOOL CO., INC. (OH)
Charter cancelled for failure to pay taxes 11/15/29

CONNREX CORP (DE)
Reincorporated 10/31/68
Common no par split for (3) for (2) by issuance of (0.5) additional share 1/22/68
Under plan of merger state of incorporation changed from (CT) to (DE) and each share Common no par exchanged for (1) share Common $5 par 10/31/68
Stock Dividends - 10% 4/30/70; 10% 5/3/71; 10% 5/5/72
Name changed to Chloride Connrex Corp. 8/27/73
(See Chloride Connrex Corp.)

CONNSURANCE CORP (CT)
Completely liquidated 12/20/1977
Each share Capital Stock $1 par exchanged for first and final distribution of $1.95 cash

CONOCO CDA RES LTD (CANADA)
Sr. Preference Ser. 1 no par called for redemption at $5 on 4/22/2002

CONOCO INC (DE)
$2 Conv. Preferred no par called for redemption 06/30/1981
Acquired by Du Pont (E.I.) De Nemours & Co. 09/30/1981
Each share Common $5 par exchanged for (1.7) shares Common $1.66666666 par
(See Du Pont (E.I.) De Nemours & Co.)
Class A Common 1¢ par reclassified as Common 1¢ par 10/08/2001
Class B Common 1¢ par reclassified as Common 1¢ par 10/08/2001
Merged into ConocoPhillips 08/30/2002
Each share new Common 1¢ par exchanged for (0.4677) share Common 1¢ par

CONOCO SILVER MINES LTD. (BC)
Recapitalized as Canalta Resources Ltd. 02/03/1975
Each share Common 50¢ par exchanged for (0.2) share Common no par
Canalta Resources Ltd. merged into Consolidated Ascot Petroleum Corp. 02/08/1982 which name changed to Ascot Investment Corp. 03/03/1987 which recapitalized as Pacific Western Investments Inc. 08/03/1990 which merged into Revenue Properties Co. Ltd. 01/01/1992 which merged into Morguard Corp. 12/01/2008

CONOLITE, INC. (DE)
Liquidation completed 7/31/64
Each share Class A 10¢ par exchanged for $7 cash

CONOR MEDSYSTEMS INC (DE)
Merged into Johnson & Johnson 02/01/2007
Each share Common $0.001 par exchanged for $33.50 cash

CONOR PAC GROUP INC (AB)
Name changed 12/20/2001
Name changed from Conor Pacific Environmental Technologies Inc. to Conor Pacific Group Inc. 12/20/2001
Plan of reorganization under the Companies' Creditors Arrangement Act effective 4/25/2001
Each share old Common no par exchanged for (0.02) share new Common no par
Name changed to Precision Assessment Technology Corp. 08/20/2003
(See Precision Assessment Technology Corp.)

CONPAK SEAFOODS INC (CANADA)
Name changed 04/10/1987
Name changed from Conpac Resources Ltd. to Conpak Seafoods Inc. and place of incorporation changed from (BC) to (Canada) 04/10/1987
Cease trade order effective 04/22/1998
Stockholders' equity unlikely

CONPOREC INC (CANADA)
Each share old Common no par exchanged for (0.1) share new Common no par 11/30/2007
Plan of Arrangement under the Companies' Creditors Arrangement Act effective 05/28/2009
No stockholders' equity

CONQUEROR HLDGS LTD (BC)
Merged into Med Net International Ltd. 7/31/2000
Each share Common no par exchanged for (0.085) share Ordinary 30¢ par
(See Med Net International Ltd.)

CONQUEST AIRLS CORP (DE)
Each share old Common $0.001 par exchanged for (0.2) share new Common $0.001 par 3/15/89
Name changed to Conquest Industries Inc. 9/1/94
(See Conquest Industries Inc.)

CONQUEST CAPITAL CORP. (UT)
Reorganized under the laws of Delaware as Barrington International, Inc. 7/1/87
Each (32.12293) shares Common 2¢ par exchanged for (1) share Common $0.001 par

CONQUEST EXPL CO (DE)
Merged into American Exploration Co. 02/11/1991
Each share Common 20¢ par exchanged for (0.3867) share Common 5¢ par and $0.2302 cash
American Exploration Co. merged into Louis Dreyfus Natural Gas Corp. 10/14/1997 which merged into Dominion Resources, Inc. (New) 11/01/2001 which name changed to Dominion Energy, Inc. 05/11/2017

CONQUEST EXPL LTD (BC)
Recapitalized as International Conquest Exploration Ltd. 04/29/1996
Each share Common no par exchanged for (0.33333333) share Common no par
International Conquest Exploration Ltd. recapitalized as Conquest Ventures Inc. 02/07/2000 which recapitalized as Bellhaven Ventures Inc. 11/26/2003 which name changed to Bellhaven Copper & Gold Inc. 10/06/2006 which merged into GoldMining Inc. 05/30/2017

CONQUEST EXPLORATIONS LTD. (ON)
Charter cancelled and company dissolved for default in filing returns 09/22/1966

CONQUEST INDS INC (DE)
Each share old Common $0.001 par exchanged for (0.1) share new Common $0.001 par 11/18/94
Charter forfeited for failure to maintain a registered agent 4/6/97

CONQUEST PETE INC (TX)
SEC revoked common stock registration 09/15/2014

CONQUEST VENTURES INC (BC)
Recapitalized as Bellhaven Ventures Inc. 11/26/2003
Each share Common no par exchanged for (0.5) share Common no par
Bellhaven Ventures Inc. name changed to Bellhaven Copper & Gold Inc. 10/06/2006 which merged into GoldMining Inc. 05/30/2017

CONQUEST VENTURES INC (CO)
Recapitalized as Probex Corp. (CO) 9/30/93
Each share Common no par exchanged for (0.005) share Common no par
Probex Corp. (CO) reincorporated in Delaware 9/1/2000
(See Probex Corp. (DE))

CONQUEST YELLOWKNIFE RES LTD (ON)
Recapitalized as Conquest Resources Ltd. 2/24/2000
Each share Common no par exchanged for (0.25) share Common no par

CONQUISTADOR MINES LTD NEW (YT)
Recapitalized as Western Platinum Holdings Ltd. 12/14/2001
Each share Common no par exchanged for (0.2) share Common no par
Western Platinum Holdings Ltd. recapitalized as Orsa Ventures Corp. (YT) 07/23/2002 which reincorporated in British Columbia 12/31/2007
(See Orsa Ventures Corp.)

CONQUISTADOR MINES LTD OLD (YT)
Reincorporated 07/21/1997
Place of incorporation changed from (BC) to (YT) 07/21/1997
Merged into Conquistador Mines Ltd. (New) 02/02/1998
Each share Common no par exchanged for (1.3) shares Common no par
Conquistador Mines Ltd. (New) recapitalized as Western Platinum Holdings Ltd. 12/14/2001 which recapitalized as Orsa Ventures Corp. (YT) 07/23/2002 which reincorporated in British Columbia 12/31/2007
(See Orsa Ventures Corp.)

CONQUISTADOR RES LTD (AB)
Recapitalized as Bandera Gold Ltd. 03/28/2001
Each share Common no par exchanged for (0.5) share Common no par
Bandera Gold Ltd. name changed to Jaeger Resources Corp. 07/09/2018

CONRAC CORP (NY)
Common 50¢ par split (5) for (4) by issuance of (0.25) additional share 05/30/1977
Common 50¢ par split (2) for (1) by issuance of (1) additional share 05/20/1983
$1.50 Conv. Preferred Ser. C $5 par called for redemption 04/01/1984
Stock Dividends - 10% 07/30/1976; 10% 05/25/1978; 10% 06/16/1986
Merged into Mark IV Industries, Inc. 06/22/1987
Each share Common 50¢ par exchanged for $27.50 cash

CONRAD-CARSON ELECTRONICS, INC. (CA)
Assets liquidated for benefit of creditors 1/1/65
No stockholders' equity

CONRAD NATL BK (KALISPELL, MT)
Merged into Western Bancorporation 7/1/80
Each share Capital Stock $10 par exchanged for (1) share Capital Stock $2 par
Western Bancorporation name changed to First Interstate Bancorp 6/1/81 which merged into Wells Fargo & Co. (Old) 4/1/96 which merged into Wells Fargo & Co. (New) 11/2/98

CONRAIL INC (PA)
Merged into CSX Corp. 06/02/1997
Each share Common $1 par exchanged for $115 cash

CONREX CORP (ON)
Merged into Falvo Corp. 06/30/1989
Each share Common no par exchanged for (0.2) share Common no par
Falvo Corp. reorganized as Conrex Steel Corp. 05/28/1999
(See Conrex Steel Corp.)

CONREX STL CORP (ON)
Merged into Conrex Steel Ltd. 01/01/2003
Each share Class A Common no par exchanged for $0.65 cash

CONRO DEVELOPMENT CORP. LTD. (QC)
Charter annulled for failure to file reports or pay fees 08/25/1973

CONROCK CO (DE)
Capital Stock $5 par split (2) for (1) by issuance of (1) additional share 05/18/1972
Capital Stock $5 par split (2) for (1) by issuance of (1) additional share 07/22/1981
Capital Stock $5 par reclassified as Common $5 par 04/28/1983
Merged into CalMat Co. 06/27/1984
Each share Common $5 par exchanged for (1.85) shares Common $1 par
(See CalMat Co.)

CONROE BK (CONROE, TX)
Under plan of reorganization each share Common $5 par exchanged for (2) shares Allied Bancshares, Inc. (TX) Common $1 par 12/29/1972
Allied Bancshares, Inc. (TX) reincorporated in Delaware 04/22/1987 which merged into First Interstate Bancorp 01/29/1988 which merged into Wells Fargo & Co. (Old) 04/01/1996 which merged into Wells Fargo & Co. (New) 11/02/1998

CONROY INC (DE)
Liquidation completed
Each share Common $1 par received initial distribution of $25 cash 01/25/1984
Each share Common $1 par received second distribution of $5 cash 03/26/1984
Each share Common $1 par received third distribution of $3.50 cash 11/12/1984
Each share Common $1 par received fourth distribution of $1.02 cash 12/28/1984
Assets transferred to Conroy Liquidating Trust and each share Common $1 par automatically became (1) Share of Bene. Int. $1 par 12/28/1984
Each Share of Bene. Int. $1 par received fifth distribution of $0.23 cash 06/15/1987
Each Share of Bene. Int. $1 par received sixth distribution of $0.55 cash 12/15/1987
Each Share of Bene. Int. $1 par received seventh and final distribution of $0.06 cash 08/15/1991
Note: Certificates were not required to be surrendered and are without value

CONROYAL GOLD MINES LTD.
Merged into Kirkroyale Gold Mines Ltd. 00/00/1936
Each share Common exchanged for (0.33333333) shares Common
(See Kirkroyale Gold Mines Ltd.)

CONSCIOUS CO (MN)
Name changed to American Environmental Energy, Inc. 05/06/2008

CONSCIOUS INTENTION INC (NV)
Name changed to Bancroft Uranium Inc. 10/01/2007
(See Bancroft Uranium Inc.)

CONSCO ENTERPRISES INC (NY)
Dissolved by proclamation 12/29/1999

CONSCOT RES LTD (BC)
Recapitalized as Masters Holdings Inc. 05/08/1992
Each share Common no par exchanged for (0.1) share Common no par
Masters Holdings Inc. name changed to Envirotreat Systems Inc. 01/15/1993 which recapitalized as Treat Systems Inc. 09/02/1999 which name changed to Mega Silver Inc. (BC) 12/18/2007 which reincorporated in Ontario as Mega Precious Metals Inc. 09/14/2009 which merged into Yamana Gold Inc. 06/24/2015

CONSECO FING TR I (DE)
Plan of reorganization under Chapter 11 Federal Bankruptcy Code effective 09/10/2003
Each 9.16% Trust Originated Preferred Security exchanged for initial distribution of approximately (0.019) share Conseco Inc. Common 1¢ par and (0.0775) Common Stock Purchase Warrant expiring 09/10/2008
(See Conseco Inc.)
Each 9.16% Trust Originated Preferred Security received second distribution of approximately $0.0222 cash payable 09/19/2005 to holders of record 09/10/2003
Each 9.16% Trust Originated Preferred Security received third distribution of approximately $0.1553 cash payable 09/22/2006 to holders of record 09/10/2003
Each 9.16% Trust Originated Preferred Security received fourth distribution of approximately $0.073 cash payable 09/30/2008 to holders of record 09/10/2003
Each 9.16% Trust Originated Preferred Security received fifth distribution of approximately $0.0162 cash payable 09/23/2010 to holders of record 09/10/2003
Each 9.16% Trust Originated Preferred Security received sixth and final distribution of approximately $0.0252 cash payable 03/08/2011 to holders of record 09/10/2003
Note: Unexchanged certificates were cancelled and became without value 09/10/2004

CONSECO FING TR IV (DE)
Plan of reorganization under Chapter 11 Federal Bankruptcy Code effective 09/10/2003
Each Trust Preferred Security exchanged for initial distribution of approximately approximately (0.0371) share Conseco, Inc. Common 1¢ par and (0.1678) Common Stock Purchase Warrant Ser. A expiring 09/10/2008
(See Conseco, Inc.)
Each Trust Preferred Security received second distribution of approximately $0.0452 cash payable 09/19/2005 to holders of record 09/10/2003
Each Trust Preferred Security received third distribution of approximately $0.3159 cash payable 09/22/2006 to holders of record 09/10/2003
Each Trust Preferred Security received fourth distribution of approximately $0.1485 cash payable 09/29/2008 to holders of record 09/10/2003
Each Trust Preferred Security received fifth distribution of approximately $0.0331 cash payable 09/23/2010 to holders of record 09/10/2003
Each Trust Preferred Security received sixth and final distribution of approximately $0.0513 cash payable 03/08/2011 to holders of record 09/10/2003
Note: Unexchanged certificates were cancelled and became without value 09/10/2004

CONSECO FING TR V (DE)
Plan of reorganization under Chapter 11 Federal Bankruptcy Code effective 09/10/2003
Each 8.70% Trust Originated Preferred Security exchanged for initial distribution of approximately (0.0193) share Conseco Inc. (DE) Common 1¢ par and (0.0773) Common Stock Purchase Warrant Ser. A expiring 09/10/2008
(See Conseco Inc.)
Each 8.70% Trust Originated Preferred Security received second distribution of approximately $0.0222 cash payable 09/19/2005 to holders of record 09/10/2003
Each 8.70% Trust Originated Preferred Security received third distribution of approximately $0.155 cash payable 09/22/2006 to holders of record 09/10/2003
Each 8.70% Trust Originated Preferred Security received fourth distribution of approximately $0.0728 cash payable 09/30/2008 to holders of record 09/10/2003
Each 8.70% Trust Originated Preferred Security received fifth distribution of approximately $0.0162 cash payable 09/23/2010 to holders of record 09/10/2003
Each 8.70% Trust Originated Preferred Security received sixth and final distribution of approximately $0.0251 cash payable 03/08/2011 to holders of record 09/10/2003
Note: Unexchanged certificates were cancelled and became without value 09/10/2004

CONSECO FING TR VI (DE)
Plan of reorganization under Chapter 11 Federal Bankruptcy Code effective 09/10/2003
Each 9% Trust Originated Preferred Security exchanged for initial distribution of approximately (0.0193) share Conseco Inc. Common 1¢ par and (0.0774) Common Stock Purchase Warrant Ser. A expiring 09/10/2008
(See Conseco Inc.)
Each 9% Trust Originated Preferred Security received second distribution of approximately $0.0222 cash payable 09/19/2005 to holders of record 09/10/2003
Each 9% Trust Originated Preferred Security received third distribution of approximately $0.155 cash payable 09/22/2006 to holders of record 09/10/2003
Each 9% Trust Originated Preferred Security received fourth distribution of approximately $0.0729 cash payable 09/30/2008 to holders of record 09/10/2003
Each 9% Trust Originated Preferred Security received fifth distribution of approximately $0.0162 cash payable 09/23/2010 to holders of record 09/10/2003
Each 9% Trust Originated Preferred Security received sixth and final distribution of approximately $0.0252 cash payable 03/08/2011 to holders of record 09/10/2003
Note: Unexchanged certificates were cancelled and became without value 09/10/2004

CONSECO FING TR VII (DE)
Plan of reorganization under Chapter 11 Federal Bankruptcy Code effective 09/10/2003
Each 9.44% Trust Originated Preferred Security exchanged for initial distribution of approximately (0.0194) share Conseco, Inc. Common 1¢ par and (0.0776) Common Stock Purchase Warrant Ser. A expiring 09/10/2008
(See Conseco, Inc.)
Each 9.44% Trust Originated Preferred Security received second distribution of approximately $0.0222 cash payable 09/19/2005 to holders of record 09/10/2003
Each 9.44% Trust Originated Preferred Security received third distribution of approximately $0.1555 cash payable 09/22/2006 to holders of record 09/10/2003
Each 9.44% Trust Originated Preferred Security received fourth distribution of approximately $0.0731 cash payable 09/29/2008 to holders of record 09/10/2003
Each 9.44% Trust Originated Preferred Security received fifth distribution of approximately $0.0163 cash payable 09/24/2010 to holders of record 09/10/2003
Each 9.44% Trust Originated Preferred Security received sixth and final distribution of approximately $0.0252 cash payable 03/08/2011 to holders of record 09/10/2003
Note: Unexchanged certificates were cancelled and became without value 09/10/2004

CONSECO INC (IN & DE)
$1.875 Conv. Preferred no par called for redemption 12/07/1989
$3.25 Conv. Preferred Ser. D no par called for redemption 09/20/1996
7% Preferred Increased Dividend Equity no par called for redemption at (3.42) shares Common no par on 02/01/1999
Common no par split (2) for (1) by issuance of (1) additional share 07/01/1991
Common no par split (2) for (1) by issuance of (1) additional share 04/01/1992
Common no par split (2) for (1) by issuance of (1) additional share payable 04/01/1996 to holders of record 03/20/1996 Ex date - 04/02/1996
Common no par split (2) for (1) by issuance of (1) additional share payable 02/11/1997 to holders of record 01/27/1997 Ex date - 02/12/1997
Each Income Pride no par exchanged for (1.1268) shares Common no par 02/12/2001
Plan of reorganization under Chapter 11 Federal Bankruptcy Code effective 09/10/2003
No stockholders' equity
Note: Conseco, Inc. (DE) was issued to Noteholders through Chapter 11 reorganization
Class A Sr. Conv. Exchangeable Preferred 1¢ par called for redemption at $25 plus $0.72916 accrued dividend on 06/11/2004

Each share 5.50% Conv. Ser. B Preferred 1¢ par automatically became (1.3699) shares Conseco, Inc. (DE) Common 1¢ par 05/15/2007
Name changed to CNO Financial Group, Inc. 05/11/2010

CONSECO STRATEGIC INCOME FD (MA)
Name changed to 40/86 Strategic Income Fund 09/04/2003
40/86 Strategic Income Fund name changed to Helios High Yield Fund (MA) 09/08/2009 which reorganized in Maryland as Brookfield High Income Fund Inc. 03/05/2014 which merged into Brookfield Real Assets Income Fund Inc. 12/05/2016

CONSENSUS CORP (UT)
Name changed to Micro Display Systems Inc. and Common $0.001 par changed to 1¢ par 03/20/1985
Micro Display Systems Inc. name changed to Genius Technologies, Inc. 11/12/1990
(See Genius Technologies, Inc.)

CONSEP INC (OR)
Merged into Verdant Brands, Inc. 12/7/98
Each share Common 1¢ par exchanged for (0.95) share Common 1¢ par
(See Verdant Brands, Inc.)

CONSERVATION ANGLERS MANUFACTURING, INC. (DE)
Name changed to Newport International Group Inc. 01/31/2001
Newport International Group Inc. name changed to Spare Backup, Inc. 08/16/2006
(See Spare Backup, Inc.)

CONSERVATIVE CREDIT SYSTEM INC. (DE)
Dissolved 07/18/1963
Details not available

CONSERVATIVE LIFE INSURANCE CO.
Acquired by American National Insurance Co. (TX) in 1949
Details not available

CONSERVATIVE SVGS BK (OMAHA, NE)
Under plan of reorganization each share Common 1¢ par automatically became (1) share Conservative Savings Corp. Common 1¢ par 12/31/1989
Conservative Savings Corp. acquired by Commercial Federal Corp. 02/01/1996
(See Commercial Federal Corp.)

CONSERVATIVE SVGS CORP (NE)
Common 1¢ par split (2) for (1) by issuance of (1) additional share 12/03/1993
Acquired by Commercial Federal Corp. 02/01/1996
Each share $1.52 Conv. Preferred Ser. A 1¢ par exchanged for (0.5544) share Common 1¢ par and $14.33 cash
Each share Common 1¢ par exchanged for (0.2453) share Common 1¢ par and $6.34 cash
(See Commercial Federal Corp.)

CONSERVE ENERGY CORP (AB)
Recapitalized as Biotech Holdings Ltd. 3/18/96
Each share Common no par exchanged for (0.5) share Common no par

CONSERVE INC (DE)
Recapitalized as NMxS.com Inc. (DE) 08/04/1999
Each (1.5) shares Common $0.001 par exchanged for (1) share Common $0.001 par
NMxS.com Inc. (DE) reincorporated in Nevada as New Mexico Software, Inc. 01/09/2006 which name changed to Net Medical Xpress Solutions, Inc. 01/10/2013

CONSERVER CORP OF AMER (DE)
Name changed to CCA Companies Inc. 12/2/97
CCA Companies Inc. recapitalized as Lottery & Wagering Solutions Inc. 10/1/2001

CONSIDER H. WILLETT, INC. (KY)
See - Willet (Consider H.) Inc.

CONSIGNEE AMER INC (CO)
Company believed out of business 06/08/1990
Details not available

CONSIL CORP (ID)
Name changed 11/15/1995
Name changed from Consolidated Silver Corp. to Consil Corp. 11/15/1995
Reorganized under the laws of Nevada as LumaLite Holdings, Inc. 03/22/2002
Each share Common 10¢ par exchanged for (0.04) share Common 10¢ par
LumaLite Holdings, Inc. name changed to MEMS USA, Inc. 01/19/2004 which name changed to Convergence Ethanol, Inc. 12/13/2006
(See Convergence Ethanol, Inc.)

CONSILIUM INC (CA)
Merged into Applied Materials Inc. 12/11/98
Each share Common no par exchanged for (0.165) share Common no par

CONSO INTL CORP (SC)
Name changed 11/9/98
Common no par split (3) for (2) by issuance of (0.5) additional share payable 10/4/96 to holders of record 9/16/96
Name changed from Conso Products Co. to Conso International Corp. 11/9/98
Merged into Citicorp Capital 3/6/2000
Each share Common no par exchanged for $9 cash

CONSO PRODUCTS, INC. (NY)
Common $1 par changed to 50¢ par and (1) additional share issued 03/25/1966
Stock Dividend - 10% 10/26/1965
Completely liquidated 02/02/1967
Each share Common 50¢ par exchanged for first and final distribution of (0.65) share Consolidated Foods Corp. Common $1.33333333 par
Consolidated Foods Corp. name changed to Sara Lee Corp. 04/02/1985 which recapitalized as Hillshire Brands Co. 06/29/2012
(See Hillshire Brands Co.)

CONSOL ENERGY INC OLD (DE)
Common 1¢ par split (2) for (1) by issuance of (1) additional share payable 05/31/2006 to holders of record 05/15/2006 Ex date - 06/01/2006
Each share Common 1¢ par received distribution of (0.125) share CONSOL Energy Inc. (New) Common 1¢ par payable 11/28/2017 to holders of record 11/15/2017 Ex date - 11/29/2017
Name changed to CNX Resources Corp. 11/29/2017

CONSOLIDATED A M R CORP LTD (BC)
Recapitalized as Consolidated A.M.R. Development Corp. 10/17/2000
Each share Common no par exchanged for (0.2) share Common no par
Consolidated A.M.R. Development Corp. recapitalized as West Hawk Development Corp. 01/09/2002

CONSOLIDATED A M R DEVL CORP (BC)
Recapitalized as West Hawk Development Corp. 01/09/2002
Each share Common no par exchanged for (0.3030303) share Common no par

CONSOLIDATED ABADDON RES INC (BC)
Name changed to Aben Resources Ltd. 01/13/2011

CONSOLIDATED ABITIBI RES LTD (ON)
Merged into Aur Resources Inc. 11/22/1999
Each share Common no par exchanged for (0.04545454) share Common no par
Aur Resources Inc. acquired by Teck Cominco Ltd. 09/28/2007 which name changed to Teck Resources Ltd. 04/27/2009

CONSOLIDATED ACCESSORIES CORP (TX)
Name changed to Dranoel, Inc. 12/06/1982
(See Dranoel, Inc.)

CONSOLIDATED ACCORD CAP CORP (AB)
Merged into Peak Energy Services Ltd. (Old) 06/14/1996
Each share Common no par exchanged for (1) share Common no par
Peak Energy Services Ltd. (Old) reorganized as Peak Energy Services Trust 05/01/2004 which reorganized as Peak Energy Services Ltd. (New) 01/06/2011
(See Peak Energy Services Ltd. (New))

CONSOLIDATED ACORN RES LTD (BC)
Struck off register and declared dissolved for failure to file returns 9/9/94

CONSOLIDATED AD ASTRA MINERALS LTD (CANADA)
Dissolved 00/00/1989
Details not available

CONSOLIDATED ADVANCED ECOLOGY CORP (BC)
Struck off register and declared dissolved for failure to file returns 10/29/93

CONSOLIDATED AERONAUTICS INC (DE)
Completely liquidated 12/16/1986
Each share Preferred $2 par exchanged for first and final distribution of $2 cash
Each share Class A Common 50¢ par exchanged for first and final distribution of $0.50 cash
Each share Class B Common 50¢ par exchanged for first and final distribution of $0.50 cash

CONSOLIDATED AEROSOL CORP. (NY)
Charter revoked for failure to file reports and pay fees 12/16/68

CONSOLIDATED AFRICAN MNG CORP (YT)
Reincorporated 12/08/1997
Place of incorporation changed from (BC) to (Yukon) 12/08/1997
Recapitalized as Excam Developments Inc. 01/19/2000
Each share Common no par exchanged for (0.1) share Common no par
(See Excam Developments Inc.)

CONSOLIDATED AGARWAL RES LTD (BC)
Completely liquidated
Each share Common no par received first and final distribution of (1.133) shares Norwood Resources Ltd. Restricted Common no par and (0.353) Restricted Common Stock Purchase Warrant payable 01/13/2005 to holders of record 01/13/2005
Note: Certificates were not required to be surrendered and are without value

CONSOLIDATED AGX RES CORP (BC)
Reincorporated 07/09/2007
Common no par split (7) for (1) by issuance of (6) additional shares payable 03/20/2007 to holders of record 03/13/2007 Ex date - 03/09/2007
Place of incorporation changed from (YT) to (BC) 07/09/2007
Name changed to Petro Rubiales Energy Corp. 07/17/2007
Petro Rubiales Energy Corp. name changed to Pacific Rubiales Energy Corp. 01/23/2008 which name changed to Pacific Exploration & Production Corp. 08/18/2015

CONSOLIDATED AIRBORNE SYS INC (NY)
Class A 10¢ par reclassified as Common 10¢ par 10/15/1970
Charter cancelled and proclaimed dissolved for failure to pay taxes 09/30/1981

CONSOLIDATED AIRCRAFT CORP.
Merged into Consolidated Vultee Aircraft Corp. on a share for share basis in 1943
Consolidated Vultee Aircraft Corp. merged into General Dynamics Corp. in 1954

CONSOLIDATED ALCOR RES LTD (AB)
Struck off register and declared dissolved for failure to file returns 07/31/1981

CONSOLIDATED ALICE LAKE MINES LTD (BC)
Name changed to International Sales Information Systems Inc. 6/1/94
International Sales Information Systems name changed to Versatile Mobile Systems (Canada) Inc. (BC) 9/18/2000 which reincorporated in Yukon Territory 2/23/2004 which reincorporated in British Columbia as Versatile Systems Inc. 11/16/2005

CONSOLIDATED ALLENBEE OIL & GAS CO. LTD. (CANADA)
Common $1 par changed to no par 00/00/1954
Recapitalized as Western Allenbee Oil & Gas Co. Ltd. 04/06/1960
Each share Common no par exchanged for (0.25) share Capital Stock no par
Western Allenbee Oil & Gas Co. Ltd. name changed to Convoy Capital Corp. 04/28/1989 which recapitalized as Hariston Corp. 09/25/1992 which recapitalized as Midland Holland Inc. (Canada) 02/10/1999 which reincorporated in Yukon 03/11/1999 which name changed to Mercury Partners & Co. Inc. 02/22/2000 which name changed to Black Mountain Capital Corp. 05/02/2005 which recapitalized as Grand Peak Capital Corp. (YT) 11/20/2007 which reincorporated in British Columbia 04/27/2010

CONSOLIDATED ALLIANCE RES CORP (BC)
Name changed to Dyna Haul Corp. 07/09/1999
(See Dyna Haul Corp.)

CONSOLIDATED ALTAIR DEV LTD (BC)
Recapitalized as Super Scoop Ice-Cream Corp. 9/13/76
Each share Capital Stock no par

exchanged for (0.2) share Capital Stock no par

Super Scoop Ice-Cream Corp. name changed to Trojan Energy Corp. 1/7/83 which recapitalized as International Trojan Development Corp. 4/18/85 which recapitalized as Trojan Ventures Inc. 6/20/91 which reorganized in Cayman Islands as Alcanta International Education Ltd. 3/26/99 which name changed to Access International Education Ltd. 1/17/2001

CONSOLIDATED AMERICAN CORP. (UT)
Merged into Dynamic American Corp. 12/21/82
Each share Common $1 par exchanged for (1) share Common $1 par
(See Dynamic American Corp.)

CONSOLIDATED AMERICAN FIDELITY CO. (MI)
Charter voided for failure to file report and pay taxes 05/15/1968

CONSOLIDATED AMERICAN INDUSTRIES, INC. (DE)
Incorporated 05/26/1955
Bankrupt 05/10/1957
No stockholders' equity

CONSOLIDATED AMERN INDS INC (DE)
Incorporated 04/19/1988
Each share old Common $0.00001 par exchanged for (0.2) share new Common $0.00001 par 03/15/1991
Name changed to Quality Products, Inc. 12/11/1991
(See Quality Products, Inc.)

CONSOLIDATED AMERN INDS INC (VA)
Charter cancelled and proclaimed dissolved for failure to maintain a resident agent 01/10/1984

CONSOLIDATED AMERN INS CO (SC)
Common $10 par changed to $11 par 12/11/1969
Common $11 par changed to $12 par 06/09/1971
Stock Dividends - 33.33333333% 03/12/1954; 25% 02/22/1955; 16.66666666% 12/08/1955
Each share Common $12 par exchanged for (0.005161) share Common $2,500 par 12/18/1972
Note: In effect holders received $33 cash per share and public interest was eliminated

CONSOLIDATED AMERICAN LIFE INSURANCE CO. OF ILLINOIS (IL)
Merged into Empire Life Insurance Co. (AL) 12/31/1964
Each share Common 25¢ par exchanged for (0.6) share Class A Common $1 par
Empire Life Insurance Co. (AL) name changed to Empire Life Insurance Co. of America (AL) 06/18/1965
(See Empire Life Insurance Co. of America (AL))

CONSOLIDATED AMERN LIFE INS CO (MS)
Stock Dividends - 10% 05/01/1972; 10% 04/16/1973; 10% 03/15/1976; 10% 04/01/1977; 10% 04/01/1978; 10% 04/02/1979; 10% 04/01/1980; 10% 04/01/1981; 10% 04/01/1982
Merged into First Continental Life & Accident Insurance Co. (UT) 09/22/1983
Each share Common $1 par exchanged for $6.75 cash

CONSOLIDATED AMERN RES DEV CORP (NV)
Charter permanently revoked 07/31/2009

CONSOLIDATED AMERICAN ROYALTY CO.
Dissolved 00/00/1949
Details not available

CONSOLIDATED AMERN SVCS INC (CA)
Stock Dividend - 20% 11/30/1962
Acquired by Automation Industries, Inc. (CA) 09/30/1968
Each share Common $1 par exchanged for (0.18181818) share Common $1 par
(See Automation Industries, Inc. (CA))

CONSOLIDATED AMHAWK ENTERPRISES LTD (BC)
Struck off register and declared dissolved for failure to file returns 08/05/1994

CONSOLIDATED AMUSEMENT CO., LTD. (HI)
Common $10 par changed to no par 00/00/1937
Stock Dividend - 33.33333333% 12/01/1941
Liquidation completed 06/22/1959
Details not available

CONSOLIDATED ANALYSIS CTRS INC (CA)
Stock Dividend - 200% 03/21/1969
Name changed to CACI, Inc. (CA) 11/12/1973
CACI, Inc. (CA) reincorporated in Delaware 11/19/1976 which merged into CACI, Inc. (DE) (New) 02/27/1981 which name changed to CACI International Inc. 12/23/1986

CONSOLIDATED ANDEX RES LTD (BC)
Struck off register and declared dissolved for failure to file returns 09/24/1993

CONSOLIDATED ANSLEY MINES, LTD. (ON)
Recapitalized as Ankeno Mines Ltd. 00/00/1951
Each share Capital Stock $1 par exchanged for (0.33333333) share Capital Stock $1 par
Ankeno Mines Ltd. recapitalized as Bankeno Mines Ltd. (ON) 04/04/1955 which reincorporated in Alberta 01/30/1979 which name changed to Bankeno Resources Ltd. 01/28/1987
(See Bankeno Resources Ltd.)

CONSOLIDATED ARIZONA SMELTING CO. (ME)
Charter revoked for failure to file reports and pay fees 00/00/1922

CONSOLIDATED ASCOT PETE CORP (BC)
Name changed to Ascot Investment Corp. 03/03/1987
Ascot Investment Corp. recapitalized as Pacific Western Investments Inc. 08/03/1990 which merged into Revenue Properties Co. Ltd. 01/01/1992 which merged into Morguard Corp. 12/01/2008

CONSOLIDATED ASHLEY MINERALS LTD. (ON)
Name changed to Daering Explorers Corp. Ltd. 08/20/1956
Daering Explorers Corp. Ltd. recapitalized as Consolidated Daering Enterprises & Mining Inc. 08/20/1971 which recapitalized as Sim-Tek Enterprises & Exploration Inc. 12/11/1981 which name changed to Bonaventure Technologies Inc. 09/14/1983
(See Bonaventure Technologies Inc.)

CONSOLIDATED ASIATEL RES LTD (CANADA)
Reincorporated under the laws of Yukon Territory as Sino Foods Corp. 12/21/1994
Sino Foods Corp. recapitalized as G.R. Pacific Resource Corp. (Yukon)

01/23/1997 which reincorporated in British Columbia as Pacific GeoInfo Corp. 02/03/2003

CONSOLIDATED ASSETS CO.
Dissolved 00/00/1939
Details not available

CONSOLIDATED ASSETS CORP (NY)
Dissolved 10/31/1968
Details not available

CONSOLIDATED ASTON RES LTD (BC)
Delisted from Toronto Venture Stock Exchange 11/14/2002

CONSOLIDATED ASTORIA MINES LTD. (QC)
Recapitalized as Canadian Astoria Minerals Ltd. 06/30/1955
Each share Capital Stock $1 par exchanged for (0.33333333) share Capital Stock $1 par
Canadian Astoria Minerals Ltd. recapitalized as Cam Mines Ltd. 12/02/1963 which recapitalized as Energy & Resources (Cam) Ltd./Energy & Resources (Cam) Ltee. 01/21/1980 which name changed to ERG Resources Inc. 10/09/1986
(See ERG Resources Inc.)

CONSOLIDATED AUTOMATIC MERCHANDISING CORP.
Merged into Peerless Weighing & Vending Machine Corp. 00/00/1936
Details not available

CONSOLIDATED AZURE RES LTD (BC)
Name changed to Caltech Data Ltd. 02/05/1988
Caltech Data Ltd. recapitalized as Roraima Gold Corp. 09/14/1994 which recapitalized as International Roraima Gold Corp. 06/13/1996
(See International Roraima Gold Corp.)

CONSOLIDATED BAHN FOODS INC (BC)
Discharged from bankruptcy 06/00/2002
No stockholders' equity

CONSOLIDATED BAKERIES OF CANADA LTD. (CANADA)
Acquired by Inter City Baking Co. Ltd. 06/06/1967
Each share Ordinary no par received $8 cash
Note: Certificates were not required to be surrendered and are without value

CONSOLIDATED BALSAM RES INC (BC)
Recapitalized as Bluebird Explorations Ltd. 10/01/1991
Each share Common no par exchanged for (0.33333333) share Common no par
Bluebird Explorations Ltd. recapitalized as Spire Ventures Ltd. 10/24/1995 which recapitalized as Consolidated Spire Ventures Ltd. 01/04/2001 which recapitalized as Berkwood Resources Ltd. 12/01/2010

CONSOLIDATED BANC SHS INC (WV)
Acquired by CB&T Financial Corp. 09/01/1989
Each share Common $5 par exchanged for (1.5) shares Common $1 par
CB&T Financial Corp. acquired by Huntington Bancshares Inc. 06/25/1993

CONSOLIDATED BK N A (HIALEAH, FL)
Merged into NationsBank of Florida, N.A. (Tampa, FL) 03/03/1995
Details not available

CONSOLIDATED BANKSHARES FLA INC (FL)
Common $1 par split (2) for (1) by issuance of (1) additional share 06/15/1972
Name changed to Landmark Banking Corp. of Florida 05/17/1973
Landmark Banking Corp. of Florida merged into Citizens & Southern Georgia Corp. 08/30/1985 which name changed to Citizens & Southern Corp. 05/20/1986 which merged into C&S/Sovran Corp. 09/01/1990 which merged into NationsBank Corp. (NC) 12/31/1991 which reincorporated in Delaware as BankAmerica Corp. (Old) 09/25/1998 which merged into BankAmerica Corp. (New) 09/30/1998 which name changed to Bank of America Corp. 04/28/1999

CONSOLIDATED BARD SILVER & GOLD LTD (BC)
Recapitalized as Bard Ventures Ltd. 5/15/2000
Each share Common no par exchanged for (0.2) share Common no par

CONSOLIDATED BARRIER REEF RES LTD (BC)
Name changed to M F C Mining Finance Corp. 05/05/1986
M F C Mining Finance Corp. merged into MinVen Gold Corp. 08/12/1988 which reorganized as Dakota Mining Corp. 09/15/1993
(See Dakota Mining Corp.)

CONSOLIDATED BATHURST INC (CANADA)
Name changed 11/23/1978
Common no par reclassified as Conv. Class A Common no par 12/01/1975
Name changed from Consolidated-Bathurst Ltd. to Consolidated-Bathurst Inc. and (2) additional shares issued 11/23/1978
Conv. Class A Common no par reclassified as Conv. Ser. A Common no par 06/15/1979
Conv. Class B Common no par reclassified as Conv. Ser. B Common no par 06/15/1979
Conv. Ser. A Common no par split (2) for (1) by issuance of (1) additional share 09/13/1984
Conv. Ser. A Common no par split (2) for (1) by issuance of (1) additional share 03/16/1987
Conv. Ser. B Common no par split (2) for (1) by issuance of (1) additional share 03/16/1987
$5.75 Retractable 2nd Preferred Ser. A no par called for redemption 04/15/1988
U.S. $5.25 Retractable 2nd Preferred Ser. B no par called for redemption 04/15/1988
6% Preferred 1966 Ser. $25 par called for redemption 04/13/1989
Merged into Stone Container Acquisition Corp. 04/13/1989
Each share 2nd Preferred Ser. C no par exchanged for $25 cash
Each share Conv. Ser. A Common no par exchanged for $25 cash
Each share Conv. Ser. B Common no par exchanged for $25 cash

CONSOLIDATED BEACON RES LTD (AB)
Reorganized under the laws of British Columbia as Zone Resources Inc. 07/24/2009
Each share Common no par exchanged for (0.03333333) share Common no par

CONSOLIDATED BEAR INDS LTD (BC)
Merged into Resource Service Group Ltd. 07/01/1977
Each share Common no par exchanged for (4) shares Common no par

(See Resource Service Group Ltd.)

CONSOLIDATED BEAR LAKE RES LTD (BC)
Name changed to Advance Tire Systems Inc. 11/29/1990
Advance Tire Systems Inc. recapitalized as ATS Wheel Inc. 11/17/1993 which name changed to JSS Resources, Inc. 07/20/1998 which name changed to WSI Interactive Corp. 07/26/1999 which recapitalized as iaNett International Systems Ltd. 05/07/2001 which name changed to Data Fortress Systems Group Ltd. 09/03/2002
(See Data Fortress Systems Group Ltd.)

CONSOLIDATED BEATTIE MINES LTD.
Merged into Beattie-Duquesne Mines Ltd. 01/01/1952
Each share Common $2 par exchanged for (0.4) share Capital Stock $1 par
Beattie-Duquesne Mines Ltd. recapitalized as Donchester-Duquesne Mines Ltd. 07/11/1972 which merged into Fundy Chemical International Ltd. 10/01/1973
(See Fundy Chemical International Ltd.)

CONSOLIDATED BEAULIEU MINES LTD (ON)
Charter cancelled and declared dissolved for failure to file returns and pay fees 10/23/1974

CONSOLIDATED BEAUMONT RES LTD (BC)
Recapitalized as Conbeau Resources Ltd. 09/18/1979
Each share Common no par exchanged for (0.33333333) share Common no par
Conbeau Resources Ltd. recapitalized as Inlet Resources Ltd. 12/03/1984 which name changed to Guerrero Ventures Inc. 08/19/2014

CONSOLIDATED BEL AIR RES LTD (BC)
Recapitalized as Blue Sky Resources Ltd. 12/13/1991
Each share Common no par exchanged for (0.33333333) share Common no par
Blue Sky Resources Ltd. name changed to Axion Communications Inc. 02/28/1996 which merged into Technovision Systems Inc. 12/01/2002 which merged into Uniserve Communications Corp. 11/20/2003

CONSOLIDATED BELLEKENO MINES LTD (ON)
Charter cancelled and declared dissolved for default in filing returns and paying fees 03/16/1976

CONSOLIDATED BETA GAMMA MINES LTD (SK)
Recapitalized as Beta Gamma Exploration & Development Ltd. 01/20/1969
Each share Common no par exchanged for (0.005) share Common no par
(See Beta Gamma Exploration & Development Ltd.)

CONSOLIDATED BG BARON GROUP INC (BC)
Name changed to In.Sync Industries Inc. 04/03/2000
In.Sync Industries Inc. name changed to Jet Gold Corp. 05/27/2003 which recapitalized as Deep-South Resources Inc. 11/16/2016

CONSOLIDATED BI-ORE MINES LTD. (ON)
Charter cancelled and company declared dissolved for default in filing returns 05/27/1965

CONSOLIDATED BIDCOP MNG LTD (ON)
Recapitalized 06/25/1970
Recapitalized from Consolidated Bidcop Mines Ltd. to Consolidated Bidcop Mining Corp. Ltd. 06/25/1970
Each share Capital Stock $1 par exchanged for (0.25) share Capital Stock $1 par
Recapitalized as Yorkshire Resources Ltd. 10/01/1974
Each share Capital Stock $1 par exchanged for (0.25) share Common $1 par
Yorkshire Resources Ltd. merged into Dolly Varden Minerals Inc. 12/21/1979 which recapitalized as New Dolly Varden Minerals Inc. 11/16/1992 which name changed to Dolly Varden Resources Inc. 04/17/2000 which name changed to DV Resources Ltd. 01/31/2012 which name changed to DLV Resources Ltd. 11/27/2017

CONSOLIDATED BIG VY RES INC (BC)
Name changed to Gold Bullion Development Corp. 01/31/2007
Gold Bullion Development Corp. name changed to Granada Gold Mine Inc. 01/16/2017

CONSOLIDATED BIOMEDICAL LABORATORIES INC. (OH)
Liquidation completed
Each share Common $1 par exchanged for initial distribution of $11.50 cash 02/06/1970
Each share Common $1 par received second distribution of $1.29 cash 10/30/1970
Each share Common $1 par received third and final distribution of $0.65 cash 10/03/1972

CONSOLIDATED BISCUIT CO.
Merged into Carr-Consolidated Biscuit Co. 00/00/1946
Each share Common $1 par exchanged for (1) share Common $1 par
(See Carr-Consolidated Biscuit Co.)

CONSOLIDATED BLDG LTD (AB)
Merged into City Savings & Trust Co. (Calgary, AB) 12/01/1978
Each share Common no par exchanged for $4.25 cash

CONSOLIDATED BLDRS SUPPLY CORP (CO)
Recapitalized as Global Business Information Directory, Inc. 03/24/1999
Each share Common $0.001 par exchanged for (0.2) share Common $0.001 par
Global Business Information Directory, Inc. recapitalized as Jimmy Vu's Take Out, Inc. 03/04/2005
(See Jimmy Vu's Take Out, Inc.)

CONSOLIDATED BOEING HLDGS & EXPLS LTD (ON)
Name changed to Academy Explorations Ltd. 04/10/1980
(See Academy Explorations Ltd.)

CONSOLIDATED BONANZA METALS LTD (QC)
Name changed to Mincor Resources Inc. 02/19/1995
(See Mincor Resources Inc.)

CONSOLIDATED BONNYVILLE LTD. (QC)
Acquired by Cold Lake Pipe Line Co. Ltd. 02/26/1964
Each share Common $1 par exchanged for (0.5) share Capital Stock no par
Cold Lake Pipe Line Co. recapitalized as Worldwide Energy Co. Ltd. (AB) 07/01/1967 which reincorporated in Delaware as Weco Development Corp. 07/17/1972 which name changed to Worldwide Energy Corp. 06/14/1977 which merged into Triton Energy Corp. (TX) 11/18/1986 which reincorporated in Delaware 05/12/1995
(See Tritin Energy Corp. (DE))

CONSOLIDATED BOTTLING CO (DE)
Charter cancelled and declared inoperative and void for non-payment of taxes 04/15/1970

CONSOLIDATED BOULDER MTN RES LTD (BC)
Merged into Rich Coast Resources Ltd. (BC) 01/25/1993
Each share Common no par exchanged for (0.1) share Common no par
Rich Coast Resources Ltd. (BC) reincorporated in Delaware as Rich Coast Inc. 09/16/1996 which reincorporated in Nevada 07/14/1998 which recapitalized as Media Pal Holdings, Corp. 03/16/2010

CONSOLIDATED BOUNDARY EXPL LTD (BC)
Recapitalized as Boundary Gold Corp. 03/07/1989
Each share Capital Stock no par exchanged for (0.2) share Common no par
(See Boundary Gold Corp.)

CONSOLIDATED BOWLING CORP (NY)
Name changed to Conbow Corp. 12/23/1969
(See Conbow Corp.)

CONSOLIDATED BRADBURY INTL EQUITES LTD (BC)
Recapitalized as Talus Ventures Corp. 04/17/2001
Each share Common no par exchanged for (0.25) share Common no par
Talus Ventures Corp. name changed to SolutionInc Technologies Ltd. (BC) 06/26/2002 which reincorporated in Nova Scotia 02/24/2004

CONSOLIDATED BRANER VENTURES INC (BC)
Name changed to Sunmakers Travel Group Inc. 05/13/1994
Sunmakers Travel Group Inc. name changed to Setanta Ventures Inc. 01/24/1996
(See Setanta Ventures Inc.)

CONSOLIDATED BRANLY RES INC (ON)
Name changed to CBR Holdings Inc. 06/20/1985

CONSOLIDATED BRASS CO (MI)
Name changed to Consolidated Valve Industries, Inc. 11/03/1975
Consolidated Valve Industries, Inc. name changed to ConBraCo Industries, Inc. 07/20/1977
(See ConBraCo Industries, Inc.)

CONSOLIDATED BRENZAC DEV CORP (BC)
Name changed to Borneo Gold Corp. 04/16/1996
Borneo Gold Corp. name changed to Nexttrip.com Travel Inc. 01/04/2000 which recapitalized as WorldPlus Ventures Ltd. 05/26/2003 which recapitalized as New Global Ventures Ltd. 06/07/2007 which recapitalized as New Global Ventures International Ltd. 03/14/2008 which name changed to Auro Resources Corp. 10/15/2010 which recapitalized as Tesoro Minerals Corp. 08/26/2013

CONSOLIDATED BREWIS MINERALS LTD (ON)
Merged into Beauty Counselors of Canada Ltd. 12/01/1981
Each share Common $1 par exchanged for (0.33333333) share Common no par
Beauty Counselors of Canada Ltd. name changed to Beauty Counselors International, Inc. 09/22/1982 which recapitalized as Century Technologies Inc. 01/10/1989
(See Century Technologies Inc.)

CONSOLIDATED BRIGHTWORK RES INC (BC)
Name changed to Petra Resource Corp. 11/18/1997
Petra Resource Corp. recapitalized as Olly Industries Inc. 01/20/2004 which name changed to Aurea Mining Inc. 06/16/2004 which was acquired by Newstrike Capital Inc. 06/26/2008 which merged into Timmins Gold Corp. 05/28/2015 which recapitalized as Alio Gold Inc. 05/16/2017

CONSOLIDATED BRINCO LTD (CANADA)
Class A Common no par reclassified as Common no par 12/27/1990
Each share Common no par received distribution of (1.4) shares Dorset Exploration Ltd. Common no par 01/08/1991
Merged into Hillsborough Resources Ltd. (ON) 02/06/1992
Each share new Common no par exchanged for (0.61538461) share Common no par
Hillsborough Resources Ltd. (ON) reincorporated in Canada 11/05/1997
(See Hillsborough Resources Ltd. (Canada))

CONSOLIDATED BRX MNG & PETE LTD (BC)
Struck off register and declared dissolved for failure to file returns 02/25/1994

CONSOLIDATED BUFFALO RED LAKE MINES LTD (ON)
Charter cancelled and declared dissolved for failure to pay taxes and file returns 11/08/1977

CONSOLIDATED BUILDING CORP. LTD. (ON)
Common no par split (3) for (1) by issuance of (2) additional shares 10/29/1962
Each share 6% Preference Ser. A $10 par exchanged for (4) shares Common no par 08/16/1971
Reincorporated under the laws of Alberta 09/13/1978
(See Consolidated Building Corp. Ltd. (AB))

CONSOLIDATED BULLET GROUP INC (BC)
Recapitalized as New Bullet Group, Inc. (BC) 09/04/1996
Each share Common no par exchanged for (0.22222222) share Common no par
New Bullet Group, Inc. (BC) reincorporated in Ontario as Amerix Precious Metals Corp. 05/31/2004 which recapitalized as Eagle Graphite Inc. 01/22/2015

CONSOLIDATED BULLION REEF RES LTD (BC)
Name changed to Canada Payphone Corp. 03/08/1996
(See Canada Payphone Corp.)

CONSOLIDATED BUSINESS SYSTEMS, INC. (DE)
Merged into Diebold, Inc. 04/29/1963
Each share Common 10¢ par exchanged for (0.075) share Common $1.25 par
Diebold, Inc. name changed to Diebold Nixdorf Inc. 12/12/2016

CONSOLIDATED C B A LTD (BC)
Delisted from Alberta Stock Exchange 10/25/1988

CONSOLIDATED CACHE D OR RES INC (BC)
Name changed to Exploration Auriginor Inc. (BC) 03/19/1993
Exploration Auriginor Inc. (BC) reincorporated in Canada 03/03/1998
(See Exploration Auriginor Inc.)

CONSOLIDATED CALLINAN FLIN FLON MINES LTD (CANADA)
Name changed to Callinan Mines Ltd. 03/10/1998
Callinan Mines Ltd. name changed to Callinan Royalties Corp. 07/14/2011 which merged into Altius Minerals Corp. 05/07/2015

CONSOLIDATED CAMBRIDGE MINES LTD (BC)
Name changed to Cambridge Environmental Systems Inc. (BC) 07/20/1993
Cambridge Environmental Systems Inc. (BC) reincorporated in Alberta 12/09/1993
(See Cambridge Environmental Systems Inc.)

CONSOLIDATED CDN EXPRESS LTD (ON)
Name changed to Canadian Express Ltd. (New) 05/18/2001
Canadian Express Ltd. (New) recapitalized as BNN Investments Ltd. 11/02/2001 which name changed to BAM Investments Corp. 07/05/2006 which name changed to Partners Value Fund Inc. 06/10/2013 which name changed to Partners Value Investments Inc. 05/25/2015 which reorganized as Partners Value Investments L.P. 07/04/2016

CONSOLIDATED CDN FARADY LTD (ON)
Name changed to Faraday Resources Inc. 08/02/1983
Faraday Resources Inc. merged into Conwest Exploration Co. Ltd. (New) (AB) 09/01/1993 which merged into Alberta Energy Co. Ltd. 01/31/1996 which merged into EnCana Corp. 01/03/2003

CONSOLIDATED CDN FORTUNE RES INC (AB)
Name changed to Canadian Fortune Resources Inc. (New) 03/15/1993
Canadian Fortune Resources Inc. (New) merged into Fortune Energy Inc. 09/01/1993
(See Fortune Energy Inc.)

CONSOLIDATED CDN VENTURE CORP (BC)
Reorganized under the laws of Cayman Islands as Primeline Energy Holdings Inc. 06/30/1995
Each share Common no par exchanged for (0.33333333) share Common $0.001 par

CONSOLIDATED CANARCTIC INDS LTD (BC)
Placed in receivership 11/12/1985
No stockholders' equity

CONSOLIDATED CANDEGO MINES LTD. (ON)
Acquired by East MacDonald Mines Ltd. 00/00/1954
Each share Common $1 par exchanged for (0.2) share Common $1 par
(See East MacDonald Mines Ltd.)

CONSOLIDATED CANORAMA EXPLS LTD (ON)
Charter cancelled for failure to pay taxes and file returns 02/20/1980

CONSOLIDATED CAP CORP (FL)
Conv. Preferred 10¢ par converted into (4) shares Common 10¢ par 10/24/1981
Proclaimed dissolved for failure to file reports and pay fees 08/25/1995

CONSOLIDATED CAP INCOME OPPORTUNITY TR (CA)
Name changed to Johnstown Consolidated Realty Trust 08/31/1986
Johnstown Consolidated Realty Trust name changed to Transcontinental Realty Investors (CA) 07/05/1989 which reorganized in Delaware as Transcontinental Realty Investors, Inc. 08/17/1990 which reincorporated in Nevada 03/24/1992

CONSOLIDATED CAP INCOME TR (CA)
Name changed to National Income Realty Trust 07/05/1989
National Income Realty Trust merged into Tarragon Realty Investors Inc. 10/21/1998 which name changed to Tarragon Corp. 07/01/2004
(See Tarragon Corp.)

CONSOLIDATED CAP INSTL PPTYS L P (DE)
Reincorporated 04/25/2008
State of organization changed from (CA) to (DE) 04/25/2008
Units of Limited Partnership Int. reclassified as Ser. A Units 04/30/2008
Merged into AIMCO Properties, L.P. 02/11/2011
Each Ser. A Unit exchanged for either (0.17) Common Unit or $4.31 cash
Merged into AIMCO Properties, L.P. 01/23/2012
Each Unit of Ltd. Partnership Int. 3 $250 par exchanged for either (2.67) Common Units or $61.30 cash
Note: Option to receive to Units expired 03/01/2012
(Additional Information in Active)

CONSOLIDATED CAP LTD (DE)
Charter cancelled and declared inoperative and void for non-payment of taxes 03/01/1977

CONSOLIDATED CAP PPTYS L P (CA & DE)
Reincorporated 04/23/2008
Units of Ltd. Partnership Int. V completely liquidated 03/29/2001
Details not available
Units of Ltd. Partnership Int. VI completely liquidated 11/07/2006
Details not available
Units of Ltd. Partnership Int. IV state of incorporation changed from (CA) to (DE) 04/23/2008
Units of Ltd. Partnership Int. III assets sold for the benefit of creditors 10/20/2010
No stockholders' equity
Merged into AIMCO Properties, L.P. 01/23/2012
Each Unit of Ltd. Partnership Int. IV exchanged for either (2.44) Common Units or $56.14 cash
Note: Option to receive to Units expired 03/01/2012

CONSOLIDATED CAP RLTY INVS (CA)
Shares of Bene. Int. no par split (3) for (1) by issuance of (2) additional shares 01/28/1983
Name changed to Vinland Property Trust (CA) 07/05/1989
Vinland Property Trust (CA) reincorporated in Nevada as Tarragon Realty Investors Inc. 07/25/1997 which name changed to Tarragon Corp. 07/01/2004
(See Tarragon Corp.)

CONSOLIDATED CAP SPL TR (CA)
Name changed to Continental Mortgage & Equity Trust 07/05/1989
Continental Mortgage & Equity Trust merged into Transcontinental Realty Investors, Inc. 11/30/1999

CONSOLIDATED CAPRIVE INDS & RES LTD (QC)
Charter annulled for failure to file reports or pay fees 11/11/1978

CONSOLIDATED CAPROCK RES LTD (BC)
Recapitalized as Minco Mining & Metals Corp. 03/12/1993
Each share Common no par exchanged for (0.33333333) share Common no par
Minco Mining & Metals Corp. name changed to Minco Gold Corp. 02/01/2007

CONSOLIDATED CAR-HEATING CO., INC.
Name changed to Consolidated Metal Products Corp. 00/00/1953
Consolidated Metal Products Corp. name changed to CMP Indstries, Inc. 11/01/1958
(See CMP Industries, Inc.)

CONSOLIDATED CARBON CORP.
Merged into Carbons Consolidated, Inc. 00/00/1930
Details not available

CONSOLIDATED CARE PT MED CENTRES LTD (BC)
Filed notice of intention to make a proposal under the Bankruptcy and Insolvency Act 07/06/2004
Stockholders' equity unlikely

CONSOLIDATED CARIBOU SILVER MINES, INC. (DE)
Name changed to Nederland Mines, Inc. 00/00/1954
(See Nederland Mines, Inc.)

CONSOLIDATED CARINA RES CORP (CANADA)
Recapitalized as United Carina Resources Corp. 09/22/1995
Each share Common no par exchanged for (0.25) share Common no par
United Carina Resources Corp. name changed to United Uranium Corp. (Canada) 07/25/2007 which reincorporated in Saskatchewan 11/05/2008 which reorganized in British Columbia as Karoo Exploration Corp. 09/15/2013 which recapitalized as Bruin Point Helium Corp 12/11/2017 which name changed to American Helium Inc. 05/11/2018

CONSOLIDATED CARLIN RES CORP (CANADA)
Recapitalized as Carlin Gold Corp. (Canada) 05/16/2000
Each share Common no par exchanged for (0.33333333) share Common no par
Carlin Gold Corp. (Canada) reincorporated in British Columbia 08/29/2007

CONSOLIDATED CARMA CORP (AB)
Name changed to Carma Corp. 05/15/1996
Carma Corp. merged into Brookfield Properties Corp. 09/20/2000 which name changed to Brookfield Office Properties Inc. 05/09/2011
(See Brookfield Office Properties Inc.)

CONSOLIDATED CASSANDRA RES INC (BC)
Reincorporated under the laws of Yukon Territory as Bolivar Goldfields Ltd. 09/27/1993
Bolivar Goldfields Ltd. name changed to Storage @ccess Technologies Inc. 02/09/2001 which recapitalized as BluePoint Data Storage, Inc. 01/31/2003 which name changed to BluePoint Data, Inc. 07/27/2009
(See BluePoint Data, Inc.)

CONSOLIDATED CEMENT CORP. (DE)
Reorganized 00/00/1935
Holders of old stock received only warrants to purchase stock of new Company
Each share Class A no par exchanged for (2) shares Common no par 00/00/1954
Common no par changed to $1 par 04/14/1955
Common $1 par split (5) for (2) by issuance of (1.5) additional shares 04/16/1956
Merged into General Portland Cement Co. 04/30/1959
Each share Common $1 par exchanged for (0.83333333) share Common $1 par
General Portland Cement Co. name changed to General Portland Inc. 05/31/1972
(See General Portland Inc.)

CONSOLIDATED CHEMICAL INDUSTRIES, INC. (DE)
Merged into Stauffer Chemical Co. 11/14/1955
Each share Class A Part. Preference no par exchanged for (3.25) shares Common $10 par
(See Stauffer Chemical Co.)

CONSOLIDATED CHIBOUGAMAU GOLDFIELDS LTD. (QC)
Acquired by Campbell Chibougamau Mines Ltd. 00/00/1954
Each share Capital Stock $1 par exchanged for (0.25) share Capital Stock $1 par
Campbell Chibougamau Mines Ltd. name changed to Campbell Resources Inc. 09/22/1980 which merged into Campbell Resources Inc. (New) 06/08/1983
(See Campbell Resources Inc. (New))

CONSOLIDATED CHOLLAR GOULD & SAVAGE MINING CO. (CA)
Name changed to Consolidated Chollar Industries and Capital Stock $1 par changed to 25¢ par 05/20/1959
(See Consolidated Chollar Industries)

CONSOLIDATED CHOLLAR INDS (CA)
Charter suspended for failure to pay taxes 10/01/1969

CONSOLIDATED CHURCHILL COPPER LTD (BC)
Merged into Teck Corp. 11/29/1979
Each share Common no par exchanged for $2 cash

CONSOLIDATED CHURCHILL ENTERPRISES INC (BC)
Recapitalized as Samia Ventures Inc. 10/05/1992
Each share Common no par exchanged for (0.14285714) share Common no par
(See Samia Ventures Inc.)

CONSOLIDATED CIGAR CORP (DE)
Common no par changed to $1 par 04/11/1957
Common $1 par split (2) for (1) by issuance of (1) additional share 11/20/1959
Common $1 par split (3) for (2) by issuance of (0.5) additional share 02/15/1962
$5 Preferred Ser. 1953 no par called for redemption 05/31/1962
Common $1 par split (2) for (1) by issuance of (1) additional share 12/19/1963
Stock Dividends - 20% 03/16/1950; 33.33333333% 12/05/1957
Merged into Gulf & Western Industries, Inc. (DE) 01/11/1968
Each share Common $1 par exchanged for (0.11111111) share $3.50 Conv. Preferred Ser. B $2.50 par and (0.2) 10-year Common Stock Purchase Warrant
(See Gulf & Western Industries, Inc. (DE))

CONSOLIDATED CIGAR HLDGS INC (DE)
Merged into Seita SA 01/22/1999
Each share Class A Common 1¢ par exchanged for $17.85 cash
Each share Class B Common 1¢ par exchanged for $17.85 cash

CONSOLIDATED CIMA RES LTD (BC)
Reincorporated under the laws of Canada as Hankin Atlas Industries Ltd. 08/15/1989
Hankin Atlas Industries Ltd. name changed to Hankin Water Technologies Ltd. 03/26/1999
(See Hankin Water Technologies Ltd.)

CONSOLIDATED CINOLA MINES LTD (BC)
Name changed to City Resources (Canada) Ltd. 12/09/1986
City Resources (Canada) Ltd. name changed to Misty Mountain Gold Ltd. 04/22/1994 which recapitalized as Misty Mountain Gold Inc. 11/10/1995 which name changed to Continental Minerals Corp. (Incorporated 02/07/1962) 10/18/2001
(See Continental Minerals Corp. (Incorporated 02/07/1962))

CONSOLIDATED CIRCUIT CORP. (NY)
Name changed to Consolidated Home & Garden Services Corp. 05/28/1964
Consolidated Home & Garden Services Corp. name changed to Lawn-A-Mat Chemical & Equipment Corp. 11/13/1967
(See Lawn-A-Mat Chemical & Equipment Corp.)

CONSOLIDATED CISCO RES LTD (BC)
Name changed to Inca Gold Ltd. 09/05/1991
Inca Gold Ltd. name changed to Airpro Industries Inc. 12/10/1992 which recapitalized as Camelot Industries Inc. 05/08/1995 which merged into DC Diagnosticare, Inc. 07/15/1996
(See DC Diagnosticare, Inc.)

CONSOLIDATED CITEX RES INC (BC)
Recapitalized as Pacific Foam Form, Inc. 12/17/1979
Each share Common no par exchanged for (0.2) share Common no par
(See Pacific Foam Form, Inc.)

CONSOLIDATED CLEVELAND RES LTD (BC)
Struck off register and declared dissolved for failure to file returns 02/04/1983

CONSOLIDATED CLIFTON RES CORP (BC)
Name changed to Taina Developments Corp. 09/27/1990
Taina Developments Corp. name changed to Double Eagle Entertainment Corp. 01/06/1994
(See Double Eagle Entertainment Corp.)

CONSOLIDATED CLINE DEV CORP (BC)
Name changed to Cline Mining Corp. 11/29/1996
(See Cline Mining Corp.)

CONSOLIDATED COAL CO. (MI)
In process of dissolution 00/00/1941
Details not available

CONSOLIDATED COAL CO. OF ST. LOUIS
Recapitalized as Ketay Manufacturing Corp. on a (10) for (1) basis 4/15/53
Ketay Manufacturing Corp. name changed to Ketay Instrument Corp. 9/10/54 which name changed to Norden-Ketay Corp. 2/11/55 which merged into United Aircraft Corp. 7/1/58 which name changed to United Technologies Corp. 4/30/75

CONSOLIDATED COAST SILVER MINES LTD (BC)
Recapitalized as Newcoast Silver Mines Ltd. 05/17/1976
Each share Common no par exchanged for (0.2) share Common no par
Newcoast Silver Mines Ltd. recapitalized as Southern Silver Exploration Corp. 07/16/2004

CONSOLIDATED COLOSSAL ENERGY INC (BC)
Name changed to Draco Gold Mines Inc. 05/02/1988
Draco Gold Mines Inc. merged into Stanford Energy Corp. 06/29/1990 which recapitalized as Stanford Oil & Gas Ltd. 07/10/1998 which merged into Hilton Petroleum Ltd. (BC) 03/31/1999 which reincorporated in Yukon 04/01/1999 which name changed to Hilton Resources Ltd. (YT) 03/02/2004 which reincorporated in British Columbia 11/23/2004 which recapitalized as Rochester Resources Ltd. 08/26/2005

CONSOLIDATED COLUMBIA RIV MINES LTD (BC)
Recapitalized as Ruth Vermont Mine Ltd. 11/21/1977
Each share Class A Preferred $10 par automatically became (1) share Class A Preferred $10 par
Each share Common no par exchanged for (0.1) share Common no par
(See Ruth Vermont Mine Ltd.)

CONSOLIDATED COMMERCIAL CORP. (TX)
Charter revoked for failure to file reports and pay fees 02/17/1966

CONSOLIDATED COMPUTER INC (ON)
Reorganized 03/28/1972
Reorganized from Consolidated Computer Ltd. to Consolidated Computer Inc. 03/28/1972
Each share Common no par exchanged for (0.1) share Common no par and (0.16666666) Conv. Special Share no par
Placed in receivership 03/12/1984
No stockholders' equity

CONSOLIDATED COMPUTER INDS INC (FL)
Merged into Cyber Corp. (NC) 05/19/1972
Each share Common 1¢ par exchanged for (4) shares Common 10¢ par
Cyber Corp. (NC) reincorporated in Nevada as Cyber International Corp. 06/18/1973
(See Cyber International Corp.)

CONSOLIDATED COMPUTER SERVICES, INC. (OH)
Merged into Pyramid Group, Inc. 01/04/1971
Each share Common no par exchanged for (200) shares Common no par
(See Pyramid Group, Inc.)

CONSOLIDATED COMPUTER SVCS LTD (ON)
Name changed to Consolidated Computer Ltd. 06/23/1970
Consolidated Computer Ltd. reorganized as Consolidated Computer Inc. 03/28/1972
(See Consolidated Computer Inc.)

CONSOLIDATED COPPER LODE DEVS INC (ON)
Name changed to Norbeau Mines Inc. 02/28/1984
(See Norbeau Mines Inc.)

CONSOLIDATED COPPERMINES CORP. (DE)
Acquired by Cerro De Pasco Corp. 03/25/1959
Each share Capital Stock $5 par exchanged for (0.107126) share Common $5 par, $14 principal amount of 5.5% Debentures and $0.02678 cash
Cerro De Pasco Corp. name changed to Cerro Corp. 01/01/1961 which merged into Cerro-Marmon Corp. 02/24/1976 which name changed to Marmon Group, Inc. 06/03/1977
(See Marmon Group, Inc.)

CONSOLIDATED COPPERSTONE RES CORP (BC)
Name changed to Bonanza Silver Corp. 03/14/2000
Bonanza Silver Corp. recapitalized as Bonanza Explorations Inc. 09/07/2001 which recapitalized as Bonanza Resources Corp. 05/29/2002 which name changed to BRS Resources Ltd. 02/18/2011

CONSOLIDATED CORDASUN OILS, LTD. (ON)
Merged into Okalta Oils, Ltd. 01/31/1958
Each share Capital Stock $1 par exchanged for (0.1) share Common 90¢ par
Okalta Oils, Ltd. recapitalized as Oakwood Petroleum Ltd. 06/10/1970 which was acquired by Sceptre Resources Ltd. 03/14/1989 which merged into Canadian Natural Resources Ltd. 08/15/1996

CONSOLIDATED CORTEZ SILVER MINES CO. (NV)
Charter revoked for failure to file reports and pay taxes 03/31/1933

CONSOLIDATED COS (MA)
Plan of reorganization under Chapter 11 Federal Bankruptcy proceedings confirmed 10/02/1990
No stockholders' equity

CONSOLIDATED COSMETICS, INC. (DE)
Name changed to Lanolin Plus, Inc. 06/03/1955
Lanolin Plus, Inc. merged into Bishop (Hazel) Inc. 01/23/1962 which name changed to Bishop Industries Inc. (NY) 05/19/1967
(See Bishop Industries Inc. (NY))

CONSOLIDATED COTTONBALLS CORP (AB)
Recapitalized as CTB Industries Inc. 05/12/1994
Each share Common no par exchanged for (0.11111111) share Common no par
(See CTB Industries Inc.)

CONSOLIDATED COVE RES CORP (BC)
Recapitalized as Derek Resources Corp. 05/11/1995
Each share Common no par exchanged for (0.2173913) share Common no par
Derek Resources Corp. recapitalized as Derek Oil & Gas Corp. 03/03/2003 which name changed to Newcastle Energy Corp. 07/02/2013 which name changed to Martello Technologies Group Inc. 09/12/2018

CONSOLIDATED CREDIT CORP. (NC)
Acquired by Liberty Loan Corp. 10/17/1967
Each share $1.40 Preferred Ser. A $20 par exchanged for (1) share $1.25 Conv. Preference $25 par
Each share Class B Common $1 par exchanged for (0.092455) share $1.25 Conv. Preference $25 par
Liberty Loan Corp. name changed to LLC Corp. 03/14/1980 which name changed to Valhi, Inc. 03/10/1987

CONSOLIDATED CSA MINERALS INC (CANADA)
Name changed to Pamorex Minerals Inc. 04/16/1987
Pamorex Minerals Inc. merged into Royal Oak Mines Inc. 07/23/1991 which recapitalized as Royal Oak Ventures Inc. 02/14/2000
(See Royal Oak Ventures Inc.)

CONSOLIDATED CUBAN PETROLEUM CORP. (DE)
Name changed to Consolidated Development Corp. (DE) 07/06/1959
Consolidated Development Corp. (DE) name changed to Libya-Mercury Petroleum Corp. 05/21/1968 which name changed back to Consolidated Development Corp. (DE) 09/29/1969
(See Consolidated Development Corp. (DE))

CONSOLIDATED CYLL INDS LTD (BC)
Recapitalized as RW Packaging Ltd. (BC) 01/31/1995
Each share Common no par exchanged for (0.2) share Common no par
RW Packaging Ltd. (BC) reincorporated in Canada 02/17/1995
(See RW Packaging Ltd.)

CONSOLIDATED CYN-TECH VENTURES LTD (BC)
Common no par split (3) for (1) by issuance of (2) additional shares payable 06/27/1996 to holders of record 06/27/1996 Ex date - 06/25/1996
Name changed to Trans-Orient Petroleum Ltd. (BC) 06/27/1996
Trans-Orient Petroleum Ltd. (BC) reincorporated in Yukon 09/26/1997 which reincorporated back in British Columbia 01/16/2006 which merged into TAG Oil Ltd. 12/16/2009

CONSOLIDATED DAERING ENTERPRISES & MNG INC (ON)
Recapitalized as Sim-Tek Enterprises Exploration Inc. 12/11/1981
Each share Common no par exchanged for (0.33333333) share Common no par
Sim-Tek Enterprises Exploration Inc. name changed to Bonaventure Technologies Inc. 09/14/1983
(See Bonaventure Technologies Inc.)

CONSOLIDATED DAIRY PRODUCTS CORP.
Acquired by National Dairy Products Corp. 00/00/1931
Details not available

CONSOLIDATED DAKOTA RES LTD (BC)
Merged into Colossus Resource Equities Inc. 12/08/1987
Each share Common no par exchanged for (1) share Common no par
Colossus Resource Equities Inc. merged into Prime Resources Corp. (BC) 02/01/1989 which recapitalized as Prime Resources Group Inc. 01/26/1990 which merged into HomeStake Mining Co. 12/03/1998 which merged into Barrick Gold Corp. 12/14/2001

CONSOLIDATED DALLAS EXPLS LTD (BC)
Struck off register and declared dissolved for failure to file returns 08/21/1992

CONSOLIDATED DASHER RES LTD (ON)
Name changed to TM Technologies Corp. 04/16/1993
TM Technologies Corp. name changed to TM Bioscience Corp. 07/29/1997 which merged into Luminex Corp. 03/01/2007

FINANCIAL INFORMATION, INC.

CONSOLIDATED DATA INC (CO)
Name changed to Your Bank Online.com, Inc. 02/18/2000
Your Bank Online.com, Inc. name changed to Secure Sign, Inc. 10/31/2000 which name changed to SVC Financial Services, Inc. 02/03/2004
(See SVC Financial Services, Inc.)

CONSOLIDATED DEARBORN CORP. (DE)
Liquidation completed 05/11/1962
Details not available

CONSOLIDATED DEER CREEK RES LTD (ON)
Recapitalized as Montemor Resources Inc. 10/21/1996
Each share Common no par exchanged for (0.33333333) share Common no par
Montemor Resources Inc. name changed to European Gold Resources Inc. (ON) 08/11/1997 which reincorporated in Canada as Galantas Gold Corp. 05/10/2004

CONSOLIDATED DEL NORTE VENTURES INC (BC)
Name changed to Idaho-Maryland Mining Corp. 04/15/1991
Idaho-Maryland Mining Corp. recapitalized as HMC Healthgard Marketing Corp. 06/23/1993 which recapitalized as Reward Mining Corp. 08/07/1996 which name changed to Riverdance Resources Corp. 03/11/1998 which recapitalized as Luminex Ventures Inc. 05/26/1999 which recapitalized as Lateegra Resources Corp. 06/12/2002 which recapitalized as Lateegra Gold Corp. 01/12/2006 which merged into Excellon Resources Inc. 08/05/2011

CONSOLIDATED DELIVERY & LOGISTICS INC (DE)
Name changed to CD&L, Inc. 06/15/2000
(See CD&L, Inc.)

CONSOLIDATED DENCAM DEV CORP (BC)
Name changed to Equinox Exploration Corp. 03/13/2009
Equinox Exploration Corp. name changed to Equinox Copper Corp. 02/01/2013 which recapitalized as Anfield Resources Inc. 09/23/2013 which recapitalized as Anfield Energy Inc. 12/27/2017

CONSOLIDATED DENISON MINES LTD. (ON)
Under plan of merger name changed to Denison Mines Ltd. 04/07/1960
Denison Mines Ltd. recapitalized as Denison Energy Inc. (ON) 05/30/2002 which reorganized in Alberta 03/08/2004 which name changed to Calfrac Well Services Ltd. 03/29/2004

CONSOLIDATED DENTAL SVCS CO (LA)
Common no par split (5) for (4) by issuance of (0.25) additional share 03/16/1970
Reincorporated under the laws of Delaware as Codesco Inc. and Common no par changed to Common 10¢ par 04/03/1972
Codesco Inc. merged into IU International Corp. 12/26/1973
(See IU International Corp.)

CONSOLIDATED DEV CORP (DE)
Name changed to Libya-Mercury Petroleum Corp. 05/21/1968 which name changed back to Consolidated Development Corp. (DE) 09/29/1969
Charter cancelled and declared inoperative and void for non-payment of taxes 03/01/2007

CONSOLIDATED DEVELOPMENT CORP. (FL)
Proclaimed dissolved for failure to pay taxes 06/26/1971

CONSOLIDATED DEVS LTD (QC)
Ceased operations 06/03/1978
Details not available

CONSOLIDATED DIESEL ELECTRIC CORP. (NY)
Name changed to Condec Corp. (NY) 11/23/1964
Condec Corp. (NY) reincorporated in Delaware 03/02/1984
(See Condec Corp. (DE))

CONSOLIDATED DISCOVERY YELLOWKNIFE MINES LTD. (ON)
Merged into Discovery Mines Ltd. (ON) 04/14/1964
Each share Capital Stock $1 par exchanged for (0.6) share Capital Stock $1 par
Discovery Mines Ltd. (ON) reincorporated in Canada 01/15/1982 which merged into Discovery West Corp. 03/01/1987
(See Discovery West Corp.)

CONSOLIDATED DISTRIBUTORS, INC.
Out of business 00/00/1929
Details not available

CONSOLIDATED DIVERSIFIED ENTERPRISES INC (CA)
Common $1 par changed to 1¢ par 08/10/1973
Reincorporated under the laws of Delaware as Walter Enterprises, Inc. 08/30/1973
(See Walter Enterprises, Inc.)

CONSOLIDATED DIVERSIFIED STD SECS LTD (CANADA)
Name changed to C.S.D. Securities Ltd. 12/20/1981
(See C.S.D. Securities Ltd.)

CONSOLIDATED DIXIE RES INC (ON)
Recapitalized as United Dixie Resources Inc. 12/15/1992
Each share Common no par exchanged for (0.4) share Common no par
United Dixie Resources Inc. merged into United Pacific Capital Resources Corp. 03/12/1998
(See United Pacific Capital Resources Corp.)

CONSOLIDATED DOLSAN MINES LTD (QC)
Reported out of business 00/00/1977
Details not available

CONSOLIDATED DRAGON OILS LTD (ON)
Acquired by Plains Petroleum Ltd. 03/27/1965
Each share Capital Stock $1 par exchanged for (1.5) shares Common no par
(See Plains Petroleum Ltd.)

CONSOLIDATED DRY GOODS CO. (MA)
Merged into Forbes & Wallace, Inc. 01/29/1962
Each share Preferred $100 par exchanged for (2.5) shares Class A no par
Each share Common no par exchanged for (2.5) shares Class B Common no par
(See Forbes & Wallace, Inc.)

CONSOLIDATED DUQUESNE MINING CO., LTD.
Merged into Beattie-Duquesne Mines Ltd. 00/00/1952
Each share Capital Stock $1 par exchanged for (0.66666666) share Capital Stock $1 par
Beattie-Duquesne Mines Ltd. recapitalized as Donchester-Duquesne Mines Ltd. 07/11/1972 which merged into Fundy Chemical International Ltd. 10/01/1973
(See Fundy Chemical International Ltd.)

CONSOLIDATED DURHAM MINES & RES LTD (ON)
Common $1 par changed to no par 08/28/1972
Merged into Durham Resources Inc. 03/28/1984
Each share Common no par exchanged for (0.44444444) share Subordinate Stock no par
Durham Resources Inc. name changed to Landmark Corp. (Old) 04/21/1987 which merged into Landmark Corp. (New) 01/31/1992 which recapitalized as Landmark Global Financial Corp. 07/05/1996

CONSOLIDATED E T C INDS LTD (BC)
Name changed to Highbank Resources Ltd. 07/25/2003

CONSOLIDATED EARTH STEWARDS INC (BC)
Recapitalized as Royal County Minerals Corp. 08/29/2002
Each share Common no par exchanged for (0.25) share Common no par
Royal County Minerals Corp. acquired by International Curator Resources Ltd. 08/01/2003 which recapitalized as Canadian Gold Hunter Corp. (BC) 12/30/2003 which reincorporated in Canada 07/29/2004 which name changed to NGEx Resources Inc. 09/22/2009

CONSOLIDATED EAST CREST OIL LTD (CANADA)
Completely liquidated 01/01/1972
Each share Capital Stock no par exchanged for first and final distribution of (0.1506) share Pan Ocean Oil Corp. Common 1¢ par
(See Pan Ocean Oil Corp.)

CONSOLIDATED EDISON CO N Y INC (NY)
Name changed 03/23/1936
Name changed from Consolidated Gas Co. of York to Consolidated Edison Co. of New York, Inc. 03/23/1936
4.12% Conv. Preference Ser. A $100 par called for redemption 09/11/1964
Common no par changed to $10 par and (1) additional share issued 03/01/1965
Common $10 par changed to $5 par and (1) additional share issued 06/30/1982
Common $5 par changed to $2.50 par and (1) additional share issued 06/30/1989
8.125% Preferred Ser. H $100 par called for redemption 00/00/1992
8.30% Preferred Ser. G $100 par called for redemption 06/03/1992
5.75% Preferred Ser. E $100 par called for redemption 03/30/1996
6.20% Preferred Ser. F $100 par called for redemption 03/30/1996
6% Conv. Preference Ser. B $100 par called for redemption at $100 plus $0.75 accrued dividends on 12/16/1997
Under plan of reorganization each share Common $2.50 par automatically became (1) share Consolidated Edison, Inc. Common 10¢ par 01/02/1998
7.20% Preferred Ser. I $100 par called for redemption at $102.88 on 11/01/1998
5.75% Preferred Ser. A $100 par called for redemption at $102 on 11/01/1998
5.25% Preferred Ser. B $100 par called for redemption at $102 on 11/01/1998
6.125% Preferred Ser. J $100 par called for redemption at $100 on 08/01/2002
7.75% Quarterly Income Capital Securities called for redemption at $25 on 01/12/2003
4.65% Preferred Ser. C $100 par called for redemption at $101 plus $1.1625 accrued dividends on 05/01/2012
4.65% Preferred Ser. D $100 par called for redemption at $101 on 05/01/2012
$5 Preferred no par called for redemption at $105 on 05/01/2012
Public interest eliminated

CONSOLIDATED EDL PUBG INC (NY)
Liquidation completed
Each share Common 10¢ par received initial distribution of $3 cash 11/27/1972
Each share Common 10¢ par exchanged for second and final distribution of $1 principal amount of Newcep, Inc. Promissory Note due 10/01/1977, (0.206984) share Educational Reading Aids Corp. Common 10¢ par and $1 cash 03/22/1973

CONSOLIDATED ELEC PWR ASIA LTD (HONG KONG)
ADR agreement terminated 02/13/1997
Each 144A Sponsored ADR for Ordinary exchanged for $23.8065 cash

CONSOLIDATED ELECTRIC & GAS CO.
Stock of Atlanta Gas Light Co. distributed under plan of simplification 00/00/1947
Details not available

CONSOLIDATED ELECTRODYNAMICS CORP (CA)
Merged into Bell & Howell Co. (IL) 01/15/1960
Each share Common 50¢ par exchanged for (1) share Common 50¢ par
Bell & Howell Co. (IL) reincorporated in Delaware 05/06/1977
(See Bell & Howell Co. (DE))

CONSOLIDATED ELECTRS INDS CORP (DE)
Under plan of merger each share Common $1 par exchanged for (1.25) shares Common $5 par 10/16/1959
Name changed to North American Philips Corp. 02/14/1969
(See North American Philips Corp.)

CONSOLIDATED ELEVATOR CO. (MN)
Assets acquired by General Mills, Inc. 00/00/1943
Details not available

CONSOLIDATED ELEVATOR CO. (WV)
Acquired by Consolidated Elevator Co. (MN) 00/00/1939
Details not available

CONSOLIDATED EMJAY PETROLEUMS LTD. (AB)
Recapitalized as New Emjay Petroleums Ltd. 02/04/1966
Each share Capital Stock 1¢ par exchanged for (0.005) share Capital Stock no par
(See New Emjay Petroleums Ltd.)

CONSOLIDATED EMPIRE INC. (FL)
Charter revoked for failure to file reports and pay fees 06/07/1966

CONSOLIDATED ENERGY & RES INC (NV)
Recapitalized as Hemkat Sports International Inc. 04/12/1994
Each share Common $0.001 par exchanged for (0.33333333) share Common $0.001 par
Hemkat Sports International Inc.

name changed to Market Basket Enterprises, Inc. 12/28/1995 which reorganized as J.T.'s Restaurants, Inc. 11/12/1996 which name changed to National Integrated Food Service Corp. 12/10/1998
(See National Integrated Food Service Corp.)

CONSOLIDATED ENERGY & TECHNOLOGY GROUP INC (NV)
Each share old Common $0.001 par exchanged for (0.22222222) share new Common $0.001 par 06/30/2003
Charter permanently revoked 06/01/2010

CONSOLIDATED ENERGY INC (NV)
Name changed to Pureco Energy, Inc. 07/14/1988

CONSOLIDATED ENERGY INC (WY)
Chapter 11 bankruptcy proceedings dismissed 12/03/2008
No stockholders' equity

CONSOLIDATED ENERGY PARTNERS L P (DE)
Dissolved and liquidated 11/30/1989
No stockholders' equity

CONSOLIDATED ENERGY SYS INC (CA)
Name changed to Epworld International, Inc. 06/26/1997

CONSOLIDATED ENFIELD CORP (ON)
Name changed to West Street Capital Corp. 06/29/2004
(See West Street Capital Corp.)

CONSOLIDATED ENGINEERING CORP. (CA)
Common $1 par changed to 50¢ par and (1) additional share distributed 00/00/1951
Stock Dividend - 15% 12/28/1950
Name changed to Consolidated Electrodynamics Corp. 11/07/1955
Consolidated Electrodynamics Corp. merged into Bell & Howell Co. (IL) 01/05/1960 which reincorporated in Delaware 05/06/1977
(See Bell & Howell Co. (DE))

CONSOLIDATED ENGINEERING SERVICE, INC. (MN)
Assets liquidated for benefit of creditors 07/13/1965
No stockholders' equity

CONSOLIDATED ENVIROWASTE INDS INC (BC)
Merged into 0865273 B.C. Ltd. 02/26/2010
Each share Common no par exchanged for $0.14 cash

CONSOLIDATED EPIX TECHNOLOGIES LTD (YT)
Reorganized under the laws of Alberta as Saxon Energy Services Inc. 11/26/2004
Each share Common no par exchanged for (0.33333333) share Common no par
(See Saxon Energy Services Inc.)

CONSOLIDATED EQUITIES, INC. (MA)
Liquidation completed 08/04/1955
Details not available

CONSOLIDATED EQUITIES, INC. (NV)
Name changed to Classic Golf Cars, Inc. 01/15/1988
(See Classic Golf Cars, Inc.)

CONSOLIDATED EQUITIES & MGMT INC (UT)
Proclaimed dissolved for failure to pay taxes 12/31/1974

CONSOLIDATED EQUITIES CORP (GA)
Proclaimed dissolved for failure to file annual reports 07/06/1997

CONSOLIDATED ESKAY GOLD CORP (BC)
Name changed to DBA Telecom Corp. 04/08/1993
DBA Telecom Corp. recapitalized as Magnum Minerals Corp. 09/20/2004 which name changed to Magnum Uranium Corp. 10/03/2005 which was acquired by Energy Fuels Inc. 07/02/2009

CONSOLIDATED EUREKA MNG CO (UT)
Name changed to Exxcel Energy Corp. 09/06/1977
Exxcel Energy Corp. name changed to Excel Energy Corp. 01/05/1979 which merged into Barrett Resources Corp. (CO) 11/07/1985 which reincorporated in Delaware 07/22/1987 which merged into Williams Companies, Inc. 08/02/2001

CONSOLIDATED EUROCAN VENTURES LTD (CANADA)
Reincorporated 04/19/1994
Place of incorporation changed from (BC) to (Canada) 04/19/1994
Name changed to Tenke Mining Corp. 01/27/1997
Tenke Mining Corp. merged into Lundin Mining Corp. 07/03/2007

CONSOLIDATED EWING INDS INC (BC)
Recapitalized as Sirius Resources Ltd. 04/26/1999
Each share Common no par exchanged for (0.1) share Common no par
Sirius Resources Ltd. recapitalized as Lyra Resources Ltd. 10/14/1999 which name changed to Cicada Ventures Ltd. 07/02/2008

CONSOLIDATED EXCELLERATED RES INC (BC)
Name changed to Amarillo Gold Corp. 11/21/2003

CONSOLIDATED EXPLORER PETE CORP (BC)
Name changed to PEC Energy Corp. 07/14/1989
PEC Energy Corp. reorganized in Delaware as Perennial Energy, Inc. 10/18/1991

CONSOLIDATED EXTENSION MINES CO. (CO)
Charter dissolved for failure to file annual reports 01/01/1947

CONSOLIDATED FELDSPAR CORP. (DE)
Acquired by International Minerals & Chemical Corp. 00/00/1952
Each share Preferred $100 par exchanged for (2) shares Common $5 par and $31 cash
Each share Common $1 par exchanged for (0.4) share Common $5 par
International Minerals & Chemical Corp. name changed to IMCERA Group Inc. 06/14/1990 which name changed to Mallinckrodt Group Inc. 03/15/1994 which name changed to Mallinckrodt Inc. 10/16/1996 which merged into Tyco International Ltd. (Bermuda) 10/17/2000 which reincorporated in Switzerland 03/17/2009 which merged into Johnson Controls International PLC 09/06/2016

CONSOLIDATED FENIMORE IRON MINES LTD (QC)
Recapitalized as New Fenimore Iron Mines Ltd. 09/20/1972
Each share Capital Stock $7 par exchanged for (0.005) share Capital Stock no par
(See New Fenimore Iron Mines Ltd.)

CONSOLIDATED FIBRES INC (DE)
Name changed to CFI Industries Inc. 12/03/1992

(See CFI Industries Inc.)

CONSOLIDATED FILM INDUSTRIES, INC.
Merged into Republic Pictures Corp. 00/00/1945
Each share Preferred no par exchanged for (1) share $1 Conv. Preferred $10 par, (2) shares Common $1 par and (0.13) of $100 principal amount of 4% Debentures
Each share Common $1 par exchanged for (0.75) share Common $1 par
Republic Pictures Corp. name changed to Republic Corp. (NY) 04/06/1960 which reincorporated in Delaware 03/21/1968 which merged into Triton Group Ltd. 02/15/1985
(See Triton Group Ltd.)

CONSOLIDATED FINL CORP (FL)
Common $5 par changed to $2.50 par and (1) additional share issued 03/31/1965
Merged into Baker, Fentress & Co. 03/31/1971
Each share Common $2.50 par exchanged for (1.7142) shares Common $1 par
Baker, Fentress & Co. name changed to BKF Capital Group Inc. 04/19/2000

CONSOLIDATED FINL CORP NEW (DE)
Name changed to ABE Industrial Holdings, Inc. 06/13/1991

CONSOLIDATED FIRE ALARM CO.
Merged into Automatic Fire Alarm Co. 00/00/1948
Details not available

CONSOLIDATED FIRST NORTHN DEVS INC (BC)
Recapitalized as Golden Temple Mining Corp. 03/15/1996
Each share Common no par exchanged for (0.2) share Common no par
Golden Temple Mining Corp. recapitalized as Amerigo Resources Ltd. 03/08/2002

CONSOLIDATED FIVE STAR RES LTD (AB)
Name changed to CFS International Inc. 12/05/1995
(See CFS International Inc.)

CONSOLIDATED FOOD PRODUCTS, LTD.
Reorganized as Stop & Shop, Ltd. 00/00/1932
Details not available

CONSOLIDATED FOODS CORP (MD)
5.25% Preferred $50 par called for redemption 09/04/1959
Common $1.33333333 par split (5) for (4) by issuance of (0.25) additional share 11/08/1961
Common $1.33333333 par split (3) for (2) by issuance of (0.5) additional share 11/10/1964
Common $1.33333333 par split (5) for (3) by issuance of (0.66666666) additional share 11/25/1974
$4.50 Conv. Preferred Ser. A no par called for redemption 01/28/1983
Common $1.33333333 par split (2) for (1) by issuance of (1) additional share 12/20/1983
Stock Dividend - 10% 10/31/1955
Name changed to Sara Lee Corp. 04/02/1985
Sara Lee Corp. recapitalized as Hillshire Brands Co. 06/29/2012
(See Hillshire Brands Co.)

CONSOLIDATED FORTRESS RES INC (BC)
Reincorporated under the laws of Canada as Fortress IT Corp. 07/31/2002
Fortress IT Corp. name changed to Fortress Minerals Corp. 06/28/2004

which name changed to Lundin Gold Inc. 12/18/2014

CONSOLIDATED FORTUNE CHANNEL MINES LTD (BC)
Recapitalized as United Fortune Channel Mines Ltd. 09/22/1975
Each share Capital Stock no par exchanged for (0.2) share Capital Stock no par
United Fortune Channel Mines Ltd. recapitalized as Surewin Resources Corp. 02/07/1984
(See Surewin Resources Corp.)

CONSOLIDATED FOUND LAKE MINES LTD. (ON)
Charter cancelled 07/30/1959

CONSOLIDATED FREDERICK MINES LTD. (ON)
Liquidation completed 10/23/1961
Each share Capital Stock no par exchanged for first and final distribution of $0.385 cash

CONSOLIDATED FREDONIA RES LTD (BC)
Name changed to Sun River Gold Corp. 02/20/1986
Sun River Gold Corp. recapitalized as Yellow Point Mining Corp. 03/11/1991 which recapitalized as Desert Sun Mining Corp. (BC) 08/26/1994 which reincorporated in Canada 03/20/2003 which was acquired by Yamana Gold Inc. 04/05/2006

CONSOLIDATED FREIGHTWAYS CORP (DE)
Plan of reorganization under Chapter 11 Federal Bankruptcy Code effective 12/13/2004
No stockholders' equity

CONSOLIDATED FREIGHTWAYS INC (DE)
Reorganized 11/06/1959
Each share old Common no par exchanged for (10) shares new Common no par 00/00/1950
New Common no par changed to $5 par 00/00/1951
Common $5 par changed to $2.50 par and (1) additional share issued 03/15/1956
Reorganized from under the laws of (WA) to (DE) 11/06/1959
Each share Common $2.50 par exchanged for (1) share Capital Stock $2.50 par
Capital Stock $2.50 par changed to $1.25 par and (1) additional share issued 05/27/1966
Capital Stock $1.25 par reclassified as Common $1.25 par 05/07/1968
Common $1.25 par changed to $0.625 par and (1) additional share issued 05/29/1972
Common $0.625 par split (2) for (1) by issuance of (1) additional share 07/25/1984
Common $0.625 par split (3) for (2) by issuance of (0.5) additional share 06/02/1986
Each share $1.54 Conv. Depositary Preferred Ser. C exchanged for (1) share Common $0.625 par 03/15/1995
Preferred Stock Purchase Rights declared for Common stockholders of record 11/07/1986 were redeemed at $0.01 per right 11/10/1995 for holders of record 11/06/1995
Each share Common $0.625 par received distribution of (0.5) share Consolidated Freightways Corp. Common no par payable 12/02/1996 to holders of record 11/15/1996
Ex date - 12/03/1996
Name changed to CNF Transportation Inc. 04/29/1997
CNF Transportation Inc. name changed to CNF Inc. 12/08/2000

which name changed to Con-Way Inc. 04/18/2006
(See Con-Way Inc.)

CONSOLIDATED FULBRO GOLD MINES LTD. (ON)
Recapitalized as Sycon Energy Corp. 01/15/1980
Each share Capital Stock $1 par exchanged for (0.5) share Common no par
Sycon Energy Corp. name changed to Sycon Corp. in 11/00/1987
(See Sycon Corp.)

CONSOLIDATED FUNDS CORP. (DE)
Dissolved 00/00/1937
Details not available

CONSOLIDATED FUNDS CORP. (NY)
Succeeded by Consolidated Funds Corp. (DE) 00/00/1934
Details not available

CONSOLIDATED GAS & EQUIPMENT CO. OF AMERICA (DE)
Common $10 par changed to 10¢ par 10/21/1963
Charter cancelled and declared inoperative and void for non-payment of taxes 04/15/1973

CONSOLIDATED GAS CO. (GA)
Liquidated 00/00/1954
Details not available

CONSOLIDATED GAS CO. OF THE CITY OF PITTSBURGH
Each share Preferred $50 par exchanged for (1) share Duquesne Light Co. 4% Preferred $50 par plus accrued dividends 00/00/1952
(See Duquesne Light Co.)

CONSOLIDATED GAS ELEC LT & PWR CO BALTIMORE (MD)
Stock Dividend - 200% 04/10/1950
Name changed to Baltimore Gas & Electric Co. 04/04/1955
Baltimore Gas & Electric Co. reorganized as Constellation Energy Group, Inc. 05/03/1999 which merged into Exelon Corp. 03/12/2012

CONSOLIDATED GAS UTILITIES CO.
Reorganized as Consolidated Gas Utilities Corp. 00/00/1935
Details not available

CONSOLIDATED GAS UTILITIES CORP. (DE)
Stock Dividend - 10% 12/07/1959
Merged into Arkansas Louisiana Gas Co. 08/31/1960
Each share Common $1 par exchanged for (1) share Preference $20 par
Arkansas Louisiana Gas Co. name changed to Arkla, Inc. 11/23/1981
(See Arkla, Inc.)

CONSOLIDATED GASCOME OILS LTD (AB)
Name changed to Reef Hydrocarbons Ltd. 10/02/1987
Reef Hydrocarbons Ltd. recapitalized as International Reef Resources Ltd. 09/29/1988 which merged into UTS Energy Corp. 06/30/1998 which merged into SilverBirch Energy Corp. 10/01/2010 which merged into SilverWillow Energy Corp. 04/04/2012
(See SilverWillow Energy Corp.)

CONSOLIDATED GEM EXPLS LTD (BC)
Recapitalized as Brendon Resources Ltd. 02/13/1973
Each share Capital Stock no par exchanged for (0.2) share Capital Stock no par
Brendon Resources Ltd. recapitalized as Brendex Resources Ltd. 09/13/1976
(See Brendex Resources Ltd.)

CONSOLIDATED GENCO INDS INC (BC)
Dissolved and struck from the register 10/01/1993

CONSOLIDATED GEN CORP (DE)
Recapitalized as GoldCorp Holdings, Co. 08/17/2007
Each share Common $0.0001 par exchanged for (0.1) share Common $0.0001 par
GoldCorp Holdings, Co. name changed to Goldland Holdings, Co. 10/20/2010 which name changed to Bravo Multinational Inc. 04/07/2016

CONSOLIDATED GEN CORP (NV)
Stock Dividends - 100% 03/31/1982; 10% 05/31/1985
Name changed to Chisholm Resources Inc. 03/24/1998
(See Chisholm Resources Inc.)

CONSOLIDATED GEN DIAMOND CORP (BC)
Recapitalized as Exxel Energy Corp. 10/15/2001
Each share Common no par exchanged for (0.25) share Common no par
Exxel Energy Corp. recapitalized as XXL Energy Corp. 05/30/2008

CONSOLIDATED GENERAL PRODUCTS, INC. (TX)
Common $1 par reclassified as Class A Common $1 par 12/29/1959
Class A Common $1 par reclassified as Common $1 par 05/18/1964
7% Preferred $10 par called for redemption 10/14/1966
Completely liquidated 12/06/1971
Each share Common $1 par exchanged for first and final distribution of $4.09 cash

CONSOLIDATED GEN SEA HARVEST CORP (BC)
Struck off register and declared dissolved for failure to file returns 10/22/1993

CONSOLIDATED GEN WESTN INDS LTD (BC)
Recapitalized as Danco Industries Ltd. 12/02/1991
Each share 10% Non-Cum. Conv. 1st Preferred Ser. A no par exchanged for (0.05) share Common no par
Each share Common no par exchanged for (0.1) share Common no par
(See Danco Industries Ltd.)

CONSOLIDATED GIANT METALLICS LTD (BC)
Struck off register and declared dissolved for failure to file returns 09/25/1978

CONSOLIDATED GILLIES LAKE MINES LTD (ON)
Merged into Associated Porcupine Mines Ltd. 11/05/1968
Each share Capital Stock $1 par exchanged for (0.165855) share Capital Stock no par
Associated Porcupine Mines Ltd. merged into American Reserve Mining Corp. 02/27/1989 which recapitalized as AMI Resources Inc. 12/21/1994 which name changed to Ashanti Sankofa Inc. 01/19/2017

CONSOLIDATED GLASS INDUSTRIES LTD. (CANADA)
Each share Common no par exchanged for $1.50 cash 08/24/1965

CONSOLIDATED GLOBAL CABLE SYS INC (BC)
Name changed to Chelsea Minerals Corp. 01/20/2010
Chelsea Minerals Corp. merged into Sennen Resources Ltd. 05/13/2011 which name changed to Sennen Potash Corp. 04/15/2013

CONSOLIDATED GLOBAL DIAMOND CORP (BC)
Each share old Common no par exchanged for (0.1) share new Common no par 09/15/2009
Name changed to Gem International Resources Inc. 10/30/2009

CONSOLIDATED GLOBAL MINERALS LTD (BC)
Reincorporated 12/16/2005
Place of incorporation changed from (AB) to (BC) 12/16/2005
Name changed to Global Minerals Ltd. 11/27/2006
Global Minerals Ltd. recapitalized as MK2 Ventures Ltd. 06/27/2016

CONSOLIDATED GLOBAL TECHNOLOGIES INC (BC)
Name changed to Garnet Point Resources Corp. 12/17/2003
Garnet Point Resources Corp. name changed to Hastings Resources Corp. 02/21/2008 which recapitalized as Trigen Resources Inc. 09/22/2010 which recapitalized as BlissCo Cannabis Corp. 03/02/2018

CONSOLIDATED GOLD CITY MNG CORP (BC)
Recapitalized as Gold City Industries Ltd. (BC) 08/26/1998
Each share Common no par exchanged for (0.14285714) share Common no par
Gold City Industries Ltd. (BC) reincorporated in Manitoba 06/21/2005 which merged into San Gold Corp. 07/07/2005
(See San Gold Corp.)

CONSOLIDATED GOLD FIELDS OF SOUTH AFRICA LTD. (ENGLAND)
6% 1st and 2nd Preference £1 par reclassified as 7% 1st and 2nd Preference £1 par 01/01/1959
Name changed to Consolidated Gold Fields PLC 12/12/1963
(See Consolidated Gold Fields PLC)

CONSOLIDATED GOLD FIELDS PLC (ENGLAND)
Ordinary 5s par and ADR's for Ordinary 5s par changed to 25p par per currency change 02/15/1971
7% 1st Preference £1 par called for redemption 02/09/1976
7% 2nd Preference £1 par called for redemption 02/09/1976
Merged into Hanson PLC (Old) 11/20/1989
Each ADR for Ordinary 25p par exchanged for $92.11 cash

CONSOLIDATED GOLD HAWK RES INC (CANADA)
Name changed to Gold Hawk Resources Inc./ Les Ressources Gold Hawk Inc. 05/14/1998
Gold Hawk Resources Inc./Les Ressources Gold Hawk Inc. name changed to Oracle Mining Corp. 08/16/2011

CONSOLIDATED GOLD STD RES INC (WY)
Name changed to Strategic Industries Inc. (WY) 01/18/1988
Strategic Industries Inc. (WY) reincorporated in Delaware 01/22/1990
(See Strategic Industries Inc. (DE))

CONSOLIDATED GOLD URANIUM CORP. (CO)
Merged into Queen Corp. 04/27/1959
Details not available

CONSOLIDATED GOLD VESSEL RES INC (CANADA)
Name changed to Golden Bear Minerals Inc. (New) 07/04/1995
Golden Bear Minerals Inc. (New) name changed to Augusta Gold Corp. 07/04/1997 which recapitalized as Pulse Data Inc.
10/15/1999 which name changed to Pulse Seismic Inc. 05/28/2009

CONSOLIDATED GOLD WIN VENTURES INC (BC)
Each share old Common no par exchanged for (0.1) share new Common no par 04/14/2008
Name changed to Encore Renaissance Resources Corp. 04/09/2009
Encore Renaissance Resources Corp. recapitalized as WestKam Gold Corp. 05/01/2012

CONSOLIDATED GOLDBANK VENTURES LTD (AB)
Name changed to NEMI Northern Energy & Mining Inc. (AB) 08/13/2003
NEMI Northern Energy & Mining Inc. (AB) reincorporated in British Columbia 04/15/2010
(See NEMI Northern Energy & Mining Inc.)

CONSOLIDATED GOLDEN ARROW MINES LTD (ON)
Name changed to Canadian Arrow Mines Ltd. 04/13/1970
Canadian Arrow Mines Ltd. merged into Tartisan Resources Corp. 02/02/2018 which name changed to Tartisan Nickel Corp. 03/23/2018

CONSOLIDATED GOLDEN LION RES LTD (BC)
Recapitalized as Americ Resources Corp. (BC) 09/11/1995
Each share Common no par exchanged for (0.22222222) share Common no par
Americ Resources Corp. (BC) reincorporated in Canada as Rolland Virtual Business Systems Ltd. 04/27/2001 which name changed to Rolland Energy Inc. 02/16/2007 which recapitalized as Gale Force Petroleum Inc. 06/04/2008 which merged into Montana Exploration Corp. 09/22/2015

CONSOLIDATED GOLDEN PYRAMID RES INC (BC)
Name changed to Data Dial International Inc. 12/14/1993
Data Dial International Inc. recapitalized as First Telecom Corp. 05/15/1997 which recapitalized as Sunorca Development Corp. 03/13/2002 which name changed to Wildflower Marijuana Inc. 06/16/2014 which name changed to Wildflower Brands Inc. 05/03/2018

CONSOLIDATED GOLDEN QUAIL RES LTD (BC)
Delisted from Vancouver Stock Exchange 01/20/1998

CONSOLIDATED GOLDEN THUNDER RES LTD (BC)
Name changed to GHG Resources Ltd. 5/10/2004
GHG Resources Ltd. name changed to Los Andes Copper Ltd. 3/29/2007

CONSOLIDATED GOLDEN UNICORN MNG CORP (BC)
Recapitalized as Kirkstone Ventures Ltd. 12/09/1999
Each share Common no par exchanged for (0.1) share Common no par
Kirkstone Ventures Ltd. name changed to Balaton Power Inc. 07/24/2000
(See Balaton Power Inc.)

CONSOLIDATED GOLDFIELDS CORP (MT)
Recapitalized as Brilliant Sands Inc. 03/16/2015
Each share Common $0.001 par exchanged for (0.33333333) share Common $0.001 par
Brilliant Sands Inc. name changed to NexGen Mining, Inc. 01/18/2018

CONSOLIDATED GOLDFIELDS MAN LTD (MB)
Charter cancelled 03/17/1977

CONSOLIDATED GOLDRITE MNG CORP (CANADA)
Reincorporated under the laws of Cayman Islands as Bestar International Group Ltd. 04/30/1996
(See Bestar International Group Ltd.)

CONSOLIDATED GOLDSEC EXPLS LTD (ON)
Charter cancelled for failure to file reports and pay taxes 05/12/1986

CONSOLIDATED GOLDSTACK INTL RES INC (BC)
Name changed to Zim-Gold Resources Ltd. 06/30/1995
Zim-Gold Resources Ltd. name changed to Noise Media Inc. 02/05/2001 which recapitalized as GFK Resources Inc. (BC) 01/17/2008 which reincorporated in Canada 07/13/2012 which name changed to Opus One Resources Inc. 07/31/2017

CONSOLIDATED GOLDWEST RES LTD (BC)
Recapitalized as Tenby Developments Ltd. 08/06/1992
Each share Common no par exchanged for (0.13333333) share Common no par
Tenby Developments Ltd. name changed to Porcher Island Gold Corp. 10/18/1996 which recapitalized as Tetra Metals Ltd. 01/08/1999 which recapitalized as Palladon Ventures Ltd. 11/02/2000

CONSOLIDATED GRANBY RES LTD (CANADA)
Reincorporated 05/16/1997
Place of incorporation changed from (BC) to (Canada) 05/16/1997
Recapitalized as CRA Phase II Ltd. 11/02/2000
Each share Common no par exchanged for (0.25) share Common no par
(See CRA Phase II Ltd.)

CONSOLIDATED GRAND NATL RES INC (BC)
Name changed to First Star Innovations Inc. 11/28/2000
First Star Innovations Inc. name changed to First Star Resources Inc. 12/16/2003

CONSOLIDATED GRANDVIEW INC (ON)
Name changed to Grandview Gold Inc. and (2) additional shares issued 07/06/2004
Grandview Gold Inc. recapitalized as PUDO Inc. 07/13/2015

CONSOLIDATED GRAPHICS INC (TX)
Common 1¢ par split (2) for (1) by issuance of (1) additional share payable 01/10/1997 to holders of record 12/31/1996
Merged into Donnelley (R.R.) & Sons Co. 01/31/2014
Each share Common 1¢ par exchanged for (1.651) shares Common $1.25 par and $34.44 cash

CONSOLIDATED GREASE CREEK PETROLEUMS, LTD. (BC)
Acquired by Share Oils Ltd. 00/00/1957
Each share Capital Stock 50¢ par exchanged for (1) share Common no par
Share Oils Ltd. name changed to Share Mines & Oil Ltd. (AB) 03/01/1965 which reincorporated in Ontario 11/20/1979 which recapitalized as Share Resources Inc. 07/04/1996
(See Share Resources Inc.)

CONSOLIDATED GROCERS CORP. (MD)
Each share Common no par exchanged for (3) shares Common $1.33333333 par 05/01/1946
Name changed to Consolidated Foods Corp. 02/24/1954
Consolidated Foods Corp. name changed to Sara Lee Corp. 04/02/1985 which recapitalized as Hillshire Brands Co. 06/29/2012
(See Hillshire Brands Co.)

CONSOLIDATED GROWERS & PROCESSORS INC (DE)
Each share old Common $0.0001 par exchanged for (0.2) share new Common $0.0001 par 10/25/1999
Filed a petition under Chapter 7 Federal Bankruptcy Code 03/07/2000
Stockholders' equity unlikely

CONSOLIDATED GULFSIDE RES INC (BC)
Name changed to Gulfside Minerals Ltd. 04/11/2007
Gulfside Minerals Ltd. name changed to Arrowstar Resources Ltd. 03/07/2012

CONSOLIDATED GUYANA MINES LTD. (ON)
Recapitalized as Latin American Mines Ltd. 12/09/1957
Each share Capital Stock $1 par exchanged for (0.2) share Common 50¢ par
(See Latin American Mines Ltd.)

CONSOLIDATED H2O ENTMT CORP (BC)
Name changed to Tri-River Ventures Inc. 07/30/2007

CONSOLIDATED HAIR PRODUCTS, INC. (CA)
Charter revoked for failure to file reports and pay fees 11/1/66

CONSOLIDATED HALE RES LTD (BC)
Name changed to Richco Investors Inc. (BC) 03/22/1994
Richco Investors Inc. (BC) reincorporated in Ontario 08/16/1994

CONSOLIDATED HALLIWELL LTD (QC)
Recapitalized as International Halliwell Mines Ltd. 10/02/1969
Each share Capital Stock $1 par exchanged for (0.1) share Capital Stock no par
(See International Halliwell Mines Ltd.)

CONSOLIDATED HALO URANIUM MINES LTD. (ON)
Ceased to do business 10/20/59; no assets
Charter cancelled and declared dissolved by default 10/10/61

CONSOLIDATED HAMMER DRY PLATE & FILM CO. (DE)
Name changed to Consolidated International Corp. 1/1/70
(See Consolidated International Corp.)

CONSOLIDATED HARLIN RES LTD (BC)
Struck off register and declared dissolved for failure to file returns 8/22/79

CONSOLIDATED HARPERS MALARTIC GOLD MINES LTD (ON)
Charter cancelled and declared dissolved for failure to file returns and pay fees 3/16/76

CONSOLIDATED HCO ENERGY LTD (CANADA)
Name changed to HCO Energy Ltd. 06/18/1993
HCO Energy Ltd. merged into Pinnacle Resources Ltd. (New) 10/20/1997 which merged into Renaissance Energy Ltd. 07/16/1998 which merged into Husky Energy Inc. 08/25/2000

CONSOLIDATED HEALTH CARE ASSOC INC (NV)
Name changed 06/16/1992
Each share Common $0.002 par exchanged for (1/6) share Common $0.012 par 06/10/1988
Name changed from Consolidated Imaging Corp. to Consolidated Health Care Associates Inc. 06/16/1992
Voluntarily dissolved 04/01/2003
Details not available

CONSOLIDATED HERON RES LTD (BC)
Recapitalized as Fintra Ventures Ltd. 02/08/1993
Each share Common no par exchanged for (0.5) share Common no par
Fintra Ventures Ltd. name changed to U.S. Diamond Corp. 06/21/1996
(See U.S. Diamond Corp.)

CONSOLIDATED HLDGS CORP (UT)
Each share old Common $0.001 par exchanged for (0.0001) share new Common $0.001 par 10/18/1993
Each share 10% Ser. A Preferred $0.001 par exchanged for (1) share new Common $0.001 par 10/21/1993
Each share Non-Dividend Ser. B Preferred $0.001 par exchanged for (1) share new Common $0.001 par 10/21/1993
Recapitalized as Pacific Diversified Holdings Corp. 03/17/1997
Each share new Common $0.001 par exchanged for (0.09090909) share Common $0.001 par
Pacific Diversified Holdings Corp. name changed to Agora Holdings, Inc. 05/01/1998

CONSOLIDATED HOME & GARDEN SERVICES CORP. (NY)
Name changed to Lawn-A-Mat Chemical & Equipment Corp. 11/13/67
(See Lawn-A-Mat Chemical & Equipment Corp.)

CONSOLIDATED HOMESTEAD OIL CO., LTD. (AB)
Recapitalized as Western Homestead Oils Ltd. on a (0.25) for (1) basis in August 1950
Western Homestead Oils Ltd. recapitalized as Canadian Homestead Oils Ltd. 3/1/54 which merged into Inter-City Gas Corp. (Man.) 4/14/80 which reorganized as Inter-City Products Corp. (Man.) 4/18/90 which reincorporated in Canada 6/5/92 which name changed to International Comfort Products Corp. 7/9/97
(See International Comfort Products Corp.)

CONSOLIDATED HOTELS, INC.
Liquidated in 1949

CONSOLIDATED HOWEY GOLD MINES LTD. (ON)
Name changed to Howey Consolidated Mines Ltd. 04/08/1960
(See Howey Consolidated Mines Ltd.)

CONSOLIDATED HYDRO INC (DE)
Merged into Raindancer, Inc. 11/21/1988
Each share Common no par exchanged for $13.50 cash
Note: Unexchanged certificates were cancelled and became valueless 10/23/1997
Plan of reorganization under Chapter 11 Federal Bankruptcy Code effective 11/07/1997
Each share 13.5% Conv. Exchangeable Preferred exchanged for CHI Energy Inc. Class B Common Stock Purchase Warrants expiring 11/06/2003 and Class C Common Stock Purchase Warrants expiring 11/07/2005

CONSOLIDATED ICE CO. (PA)
Recapitalized in 1935
Each share 6% Preferred $50 par exchanged for (1) share Part. Preferred no par and (1) share Common no par
Each share Common $50 par exchanged for (1) share Common no par
Dissolved in 1956
Details not available

CONSOLIDATED IMPACT RES INC (BC)
Name changed to InContext Systems Inc. 7/22/92
InContext Systems Inc. merged into EveryWare Development Canada Inc. 6/30/97
(See EveryWare Development Canada Inc.)

CONSOLIDATED IMPERIAL RES ENERGY LTD (QC)
Recapitalized as Consolidated Imperial Resources Inc./Ressources Consolidees Imperial Inc. 04/21/1988
Each share Conv. Preferred Ser. A $5 par exchanged for (0.5) share Conv. Preferred Ser. A $5 par
Each share Common no par exchanged for (0.25) share Common no par
(See Consolidated Imperial Resources Inc./Ressources Consolidees Imperial Inc.)

CONSOLIDATED IMPERIAL RES INC (QC)
Delisted from Alberta Stock Exchange 04/27/1993

CONSOLIDATED IMPERIAL RES LTD (QC)
Recapitalized 11/15/1979
Recapitalized from Consolidated Imperial Minerals Ltd. to Consolidated Imperial Resources Ltd.-Ressources Consolidees Imperial Ltee. 11/15/1979
Each share Common no par exchanged for (0.5) share Common no par
Recapitalized as Consolidated Imperial Resources Energy Ltd./Ressources Consolidees Imperial Energie Ltee. 03/22/1983
Each share Common no par exchanged for (0.125) share Common no par
Consolidated Imperial Resources Energy Ltd./Ressources Consolidees Imperial Energie Ltee. recapitalized as Consolidated Imperial Resources Inc./Ressources Consolidees Imperial Inc. 04/21/1988
(See Consolidated Imperial Resources Inc./Ressources Consolidees Imperial Inc.)

CONSOLIDATED INDEMNITY & INSURANCE CO. (NY)
Assets liquidated for benefit of creditors 7/17/57
No stockholders' equity

CONSOLIDATED INDESCOR CORP (BC)
Delisted from Vancouver Stock Exchange 10/06/1989

CONSOLIDATED INDUSTRIES, INC. (DE)
No longer in existence having become inoperative and void for non-payment of taxes 4/1/32

CONSOLIDATED INDUSTRIES, INC. (IN)
Each share 6% Preferred $5 par exchanged for (1.4) shares Common $1 par in 1953

Each share Common 10¢ par exchanged for (0.05) share Common $1 par in 1953
Acquired by Welbilt Corp. on a (0.5) for (1) basis 10/28/58
(See Welbilt Corp.)

CONSOLIDATED INDS (NV)
Name changed to Sorority Industries 09/15/1969
(See Sorority Industries)

CONSOLIDATED INDUSTRIES CORP.
Dissolved in 1940
Details not available

CONSOLIDATED INLAND RECOVERY GROUP LTD (BC)
Struck off register and declared dissolved for failure to file returns 9/24/93

CONSOLIDATED INSTRUMENT CO. OF AMERICA, INC.
Assets acquired by Bendix Aviation Corp. in 1930
Details not available

CONSOLIDATED INTERNATIONAL CORP.
Completely liquidated 03/09/1998
Each share Common received first and final distribution of $0.06 cash

CONSOLIDATED INTL CORP (DE)
Charter cancelled and declared inoperative and void for non-payment of taxes 05/18/1998

CONSOLIDATED INTL PETE CORP (BC)
Name changed to International Petroleum Corp. 6/30/86
International Petroleum Corp. acquired by Sands Petroleum AB 1/15/98

CONSOLIDATED INTERSTAT VENTURES INC (BC)
Name changed to Diamcor Mining Inc. 11/23/99

CONSOLIDATED INVESTMENT CORP. OF CANADA
Reorganized as United Corporations, Ltd. in 1933
Details not available

CONSOLIDATED INVT TR (MA)
Stock Dividends - 200% 06/15/1946; 200% 05/31/1956; 100% 10/29/1964
Completely liquidated 12/20/1982
Each share Capital Stock $1 par exchanged for first and final distribution of (0.9436986) Share of Bene. Int. of Putnam (George) Fund of Boston

CONSOLIDATED JABA INC (AB)
Name changed to Jaba Exploration Inc. 12/11/2003
Jaba Exploration Inc. recapitalized as Dundarave Resources Inc. 12/20/2004 which recapitalized as Nano One Materials Corp. 03/13/2015

CONSOLIDATED JALNA RES LTD (BC)
Recapitalized as Jalna Mining Corp. 04/16/1993
Each share Common no par exchanged for (0.25) share Common no par
Jalna Mining Corp. recapitalized as Kolyma Goldfields Ltd. 07/27/1998 which name changed to BidCrawler.com Online Inc. 03/01/2000 which recapitalized as TradeRadius Online Inc. 08/21/2001 which recapitalized as Jalna Resources Ltd. (New) 04/10/2003 which reorganized as Jalna Minerals Ltd. 06/01/2006 which recapitalized as Papuan Precious Metals Corp. 10/01/2010 which name changed to Ironside Resources Inc. 04/21/2015

CONSOLIDATED KAITONE HLDGS LTD (BC)
Recapitalized as Largo Resources Ltd. (BC) 05/08/2003
Each share Common no par exchanged for (0.33333333) share Common no par
Largo Resources Ltd. (BC) reincorporated in Ontario 06/10/2004

CONSOLIDATED KALCO VY MINES LTD (BC)
Recapitalized as Brace Resources Ltd. 11/27/1979
Each share Capital Stock no par exchanged for (0.33333333) share Capital Stock no par
Brace Resources Ltd. recapitalized as International Brace Resources Inc. 05/11/1988 which recapitalized as Prescott Resources Inc. (BC) 04/04/1997 which reincorporated in Yukon as Asia Sapphires Ltd. 06/29/1998
(See Asia Sapphires Ltd.)

CONSOLIDATED KASSAN RES INC (BC)
Name changed to East Africa Gold Corp. 01/16/1995
(See East Africa Gold Corp.)

CONSOLIDATED KELD OR RES LTD (BC)
Recapitalized as CKD Ventures Ltd. 03/18/1994
Each share Common no par exchanged for (0.2) share Common no par
CKD Ventures Ltd. recapitalized as Alchemy Ventures Ltd. (BC) 05/14/1999 which reincorporated in Canada as i-minerals inc. 01/22/2004 which name changed to I-Minerals Inc. 12/15/2011

CONSOLIDATED KEY OILS, LTD. (BC)
Name changed to Commonwealth Drilling (BC) Ltd. 02/09/1970
(See Commonwealth Drilling (BC) Ltd.)

CONSOLIDATED KNOBBY LAKE MINES LTD (CANADA)
Recapitalized as Kancana Ventures Ltd. 09/23/1988
Each share Common no par exchanged for (0.333333333) share Common no par
Kancana Ventures Ltd. recapitalized as Walron Minerals Corp. 12/21/1994
(See Walron Minerals Corp.)

CONSOLIDATED KOOKABURRA RES LTD (BC)
Name changed to Salazar Resources Ltd. 3/9/2007

CONSOLIDATED KRONOFUSION TECHNOLOGIES INC (YT)
Recapitalized as JER Envirotech International Corp. (YT) 09/22/2004
Each share Common no par exchanged for (0.5) share Common no par
JER Envirotech International Corp. (YT) reincorporated in British Columbia 02/13/2006
(See JER Envirotech International Corp.)

CONSOLIDATED KYLE RES INC (BC)
Recapitalized as Zappa Resources Ltd. 07/27/1992
Each share Common no par exchanged for (0.33333333) share Common no par
Zappa Resources Ltd. recapitalized as AKA Ventures Inc. 07/02/2008 which name changed to Phoenix Copper Corp. 09/07/2012 which recapitalized as Phoenix Metals Corp. 12/04/2013 which name changed to Envirotek Remediation Inc. 04/27/2018

CONSOLIDATED LAND CO., INC. (MA)
Completely liquidated 01/15/1965
Each share Common no par exchanged for first and final distribution of $0.20 cash

CONSOLIDATED LAUNDRIES CORP. (MD)
Common no par changed to $5 par in 1936
Common $5 par split (3) for (2) by issuance of (0.5) additional share 4/30/56
Common $5 par changed to $1.66-2/3 par and (2) additional shares issued 2/24/67
Stock Dividend - 10% 12/1/58
Name changed to Sears Industries, Inc. 4/3/68
(See Sears Industries, Inc.)

CONSOLIDATED LEAD & ZINC CO.
Dissolved in 1933

CONSOLIDATED LEASING CORP AMER (DE)
7% Conv. Preferred $10 par called for redemption 11/15/1965
Stock Dividend - 200% 01/31/1969
Name changed to CLC of America, Inc. 12/15/1972
CLC of America, Inc. merged into Archer-Daniels-Midland Co. 08/25/1988

CONSOLIDATED LEBEL ORO MINES LTD. (ON)
Recapitalized as Copper-Man Mines Ltd. 00/00/1952
Each share Capital Stock $1 par exchanged for (0.25) share Capital Stock $1 par
Copper-Man Mines Ltd. merged into Hartland Mines Ltd. 07/25/1974
(See Hartland Mines Ltd.)

CONSOLIDATED LIBERTY INC (CA)
Merged into Beverly Enterprises (CA) 3/12/81
Each share Common $4 par exchanged for (0.5) share Common 10¢ par
Beverly Enterprises (CA) reorganized as as Beverly Enterprises, Inc. 7/31/87
(See Beverly Enterprises, Inc.)

CONSOLIDATED LIFE INSURANCE COMPANIES OF THE SOUTH (MS)
Merged into Consolidated American Life Insurance Co. (Miss.) 12/31/64
Each share Common $1 par exchanged for (1) share Common $1 par
(See Consolidated American Life Insurance Co. (Miss.))

CONSOLIDATED LIFT SYS INC (NV)
Charter revoked for failure to file reports and pay fees 05/01/1989

CONSOLIDATED LIQUIDATING CORP. (CA)
Liquidation completed 07/31/1957
Details not available

CONSOLIDATED LOBSTER & CHEMICAL CO., INC. (MA)
Completely liquidated in December 1964
Each share Common no par received (33) shares Consolidated Land Co., Inc. Common no par and $10 cash
Note: Certificates were not required to be surrendered and are without value
(See Consolidated Land Co., Inc.)

CONSOLIDATED LOBSTER CO., INC. (MA)
Name changed to Consolidated Lobster & Chemical Co., Inc. 7/24/59
(See Consolidated Lobster & Chemical Co., Inc.)

CONSOLIDATED LOGAN MINES LTD (BC)
Recapitalized as Logan Resources Ltd. 1/29/2002
Each share Common no par exchanged for (0.2) share Common no par

CONSOLIDATED LONE STAR RESOURCE CORP (BC)
Struck off register and declared dissolved for failure to file returns 3/4/94

CONSOLIDATED LOUANNA GOLD MINES LTD (ON)
Delisted from Canadian Dealer Network 01/03/1995

CONSOLIDATED MACHINE TOOL CORP. (DE)
Voluntarily dissolved 12/31/54
Details not available

CONSOLIDATED MACHINE TOOL CORP. OF AMERICA
Reorganized as Consolidated Machine Tool Corp. in 1935
Details not available

CONSOLIDATED MADISON HLDGS LTD (BC)
Merged into Ourominas Minerals Inc. 06/27/1996
Each share Common no par exchanged for (0.6) share Common no par
Ourominas Minerals Inc. recapitalized as Thistle Mining Inc. 04/27/1999
(See Thistle Mining Inc.)

CONSOLIDATED MAGNA VENTURES LTD (BC)
Name changed to Skinny Technologies Inc. 01/10/2002
Skinny Technologies Inc. recapitalized as Pediment Exploration Ltd. 09/22/2004 which name changed to Pediment Gold Corp. 02/26/2009 which merged into Argonaut Gold Inc. 02/01/2011

CONSOLIDATED MAN MINES LTD (MB)
Charter cancelled and declared dissolved for failure to file returns 03/17/1977

CONSOLIDATED MANGO RES LTD (BC)
Reincorporated under the laws of Delaware as U.S. Cobalt Inc. and Common no par changed to $0.001 par 03/10/2000
U.S. Cobalt Inc. recapitalized as U.S. Geothermal Inc. 12/22/2003
(See U.S. Geothermal Inc.)

CONSOLIDATED MANITOU RES INC (BC)
Name changed to A.C.T. Industrial Corp. 07/05/1991
A.C.T. Industrial Corp. name changed to Rhona Online.com Inc. 07/06/2000 which recapitalized as Winchester Minerals & Gold Exploration Ltd. 04/16/2004

CONSOLIDATED MANN OIL INC (CANADA)
Charter dissolved 02/28/1997

CONSOLIDATED MANUS INDS INC (BC)
Recapitalized as Westmount Resources Ltd. (New) 02/08/1996
Each share Common no par exchanged for (0.2) share Common no par
Westmount Resources Ltd. (New) recapitalized as Mt. Tom Minerals Corp. 05/20/1998 which name changed to Global Net Entertainment Corp. 10/14/1999 which recapitalized as Guildhall Minerals Ltd. 02/21/2006 which name changed to Edge Resources Inc. 07/28/2009
(See Edge Resources Inc.)

CONSOLIDATED MARBENOR MINES LTD (ON)
Merged into Canhorn Mining Corp. 01/09/1986
Each share Capital Stock $1 par exchanged for (0.03742514) share Common no par
Canhorn Mining Corp. merged into Canhorn Chemical Corp. 04/26/1995 which merged into Nayarit Gold Inc. 05/02/2005 which merged into Capital Gold Corp. 08/02/2010 which merged into Gammon Gold Inc. (QC) 04/08/2011 which reincorporated in Ontario as AuRico Gold Inc. 06/14/2011

CONSOLIDATED MARCUS GOLD MINES LTD (ON)
Recapitalized as Marcus Energy Inc. 08/26/1988
Each share Common no par exchanged for (0.1) share Common no par
Marcus Energy Inc. recapitalized as Marcus Energy Holdings Inc. 11/27/2000 which name changed to Au Martinique Silver Inc. 07/21/2005

CONSOLIDATED MARINA EXPLS LTD (BC)
Name changed to Watson Bell Communications Inc. 02/25/1994
Watson Bell Communications Inc. recapitalized as Cosworth Ventures Ltd. (BC) 11/22/1995 which reincorporated in Yukon as Cosworth Minerals Ltd. 03/30/1998 which name changed to Palcan Fuel Cells Ltd. 02/13/2002 which name changed to Palcan Power Systems Inc. 08/10/2004

CONSOLIDATED MATARROW MINES LTD. (ON)
Recapitalized as Jeanette Minerals Ltd. on a (2) for (7) basis 6/16/55
(See Jeanette Minerals Ltd.)

CONSOLIDATED MATERIALS INC. (LA)
99% held by OKC Corp. as of 04/09/1973
Public interest eliminated

CONSOLIDATED MAYBRUN MINES LTD (ON)
Charter cancelled for failure to file reports and pay taxes 07/22/1999

CONSOLIDATED MAYFLOWER INC (NV)
Name changed to Gold/Platinum International, Inc. 5/21/71
Gold/Platinum International, Inc. name changed to Billington Thermal Sonic Energy Control Corp. 12/22/78
(See Billington Thermal Sonic Energy Control Corp.)

CONSOLIDATED MAYMAC PETE CORP (BC)
Reincorporated under the laws of Yukon as Northern Star Mining Corp. 01/16/2003
Northern Star Mining Corp. (Yukon) reincorporated in British Columbia 07/17/2006

CONSOLIDATED MCKINNEY RES INC (BC)
Recapitalized as AZTEK Technologies Inc. 12/09/1996
Each share Common no par exchanged for (0.2) share Common no par
AZTEK Technologies Inc. recapitalized as Aztek Resource Development Inc. 11/19/2004
(See Aztek Resource Development Inc.)

CONSOLIDATED MED INDS INC (DE)
Charter cancelled and declared inoperative and void for non-payment of taxes 4/15/72

CONSOLIDATED MED MGMT INC (MT)
Name changed to Adino Energy Corp. 04/04/2008

CONSOLIDATED MEDIA CORP (DE)
Charter cancelled and declared inoperative and void for non-payment of taxes 3/1/89

CONSOLIDATED MERCANTILE CORP (ON)
Recapitalized as Consolidated Mercantile Inc. 11/23/1998
Each share Common no par exchanged for (0.5) share Common no par
Preference not affected except for change of name
Consolidated Mercantile Inc. merged into Genterra Capital Inc. (New) 05/10/2010 which merged into Gencan Capital Inc. 10/30/2015

CONSOLIDATED MERCANTILE INC (ON)
Common no par split (1.75) for (1) by issuance of (0.75) additional share payable 07/30/2003 to holders of record 07/23/2003 Ex date - 07/21/2003
Each share Preference Ser. 1 no par exchanged for (0.5) share Non-Cum. Class A Preference no par 11/12/2003
Class A Preference no par called for redemption at $0.44 on 02/19/2010
Merged into Genterra Capital Inc. (New) 05/10/2010
Each share Common no par exchanged for (1) share Common no par
Genterra Capital Inc. (New) merged into Gencan Capital Inc. 10/30/2015

CONSOLIDATED METAL PRODUCTS CORP. (NY)
Capital Stock $100 par changed to $25 par and (3) additional shares issued 4/2/56
Name changed to CMP Industries, Inc. 11/1/58
(See CMP Industries, Inc.)

CONSOLIDATED MIC MAC OILS LTD. (AB)
Common no par changed to $1 par 05/14/1957
Merged into Mic Mac Oils (1963) Ltd. 02/17/1964
Each share Common $1 par exchanged for (1) share 5.5% Preferred $4.50 par
(See Mic Mac Oils (1963) Ltd.)

CONSOLIDATED MIDVALE EXPLS LTD (ON)
Merged into Lumsden Building Corp., Inc. (New) 08/15/1978
Each share Common no par exchanged for (0.16666666) share Common no par
(See Lumsden Building Corp., Inc. (New))

CONSOLIDATED MINERVA GOLD MINES LTD (BC)
Name changed to El Misti Gold Ltd. (BC) 06/03/1996
El Misti Gold Ltd. (BC) reincorporated in New Brunswick 12/06/1996 which recapitalized as Andean American Mining Corp. (NB) 10/21/1999 which reincorporated in British Columbia 08/22/2005 which name changed to Andean American Gold Corp. 09/07/2010 which merged into Lupaka Gold Corp. 10/01/2012

CONSOLIDATED MINES INTL INC (DE)
Each share old Common 1¢ par exchanged for (0.05) share new Common 1¢ par 12/24/1986
Merged into Upland Minerals & Chemical Corp. 11/05/1987
Details not available

CONSOLIDATED MINES SYNDICATE (ID)
Charter forfeited for failure to file reports 12/01/1959

CONSOLIDATED MINING & REFINING CO. (NV)
Dissolved 06/23/1931
Details not available

CONSOLIDATED MINING & SMELTING CO. OF CANADA LTD. (CANADA)
Each share Capital Stock $25 par exchanged for (5) shares Capital Stock $5 par 00/00/1936
Each share Capital Stock $5 par exchanged for (5) shares Capital Stock no par 00/00/1952
Name changed to Cominco Ltd. 05/16/1966
Cominco Ltd. merged into Teck Corp. 07/20/2001 which name changed to Teck Cominco Ltd. 09/12/2001 which name changed to Teck Resources Ltd. 04/27/2009

CONSOLIDATED MODDERFONTEIN MINES LTD (SOUTH AFRICA)
Stock Dividends - 7.5% payable 01/09/1996 to holders of record 12/15/1995; 10% payable 10/15/1996 to holders of record 09/20/1996
Merged into Harmony Gold Mining Co. Ltd. 07/31/1997
Each ADR for Ordinary exchanged for (0.06) Sponsored ADR for Ordinary and $0.016 cash

CONSOLIDATED MOGADOR MINES LTD (QC)
Charter cancelled 10/26/85

CONSOLIDATED MOGUL MINES LTD. (ON)
Name changed to Mogul Mines Ltd. 07/27/1967
Mogul Mines Ltd. merged into International Mogul Mines Ltd. 11/20/1968 which merged into Conwest Exploration Co. Ltd. (Old) (ON) 08/27/1982 which merged into Conwest Exploration Co. Ltd. (New) (AB) 09/01/1993 which merged into Alberta Energy Co. Ltd. 01/31/1996 which merged into EnCana Corp. 01/03/2003

CONSOLIDATED MONARCH METAL MINES LTD (BC)
Recapitalized as San Rafael Resources Ltd. 11/15/1977
Each share Capital Stock no par exchanged for (0.33333333) share Capital Stock no par
San Rafael Resources Ltd. recapitalized as Rafael Resources Ltd. 07/27/1984 which name changed to Biologix (B.C.) Ltd. 09/28/1986 which name changed to Biologix International Ltd. 05/01/1998
(See Biologix International Ltd.)

CONSOLIDATED MONPAS MINES LTD (QC)
Merged into Albarmont Mines Corp. 10/12/1971
Each share Capital Stock $1 par exchanged for (0.375) share Common no par
Albarmont Mines Corp. recapitalized as Albarmont (1985) Inc. 07/19/1985
(See Albarmont (1985) Inc.)

CONSOLIDATED MONTCLERG MINES LTD (ON)
Recapitalized as Montclerg Resources Ltd. 11/25/1986
Each share Capital Stock no par exchanged for (0.2) share Capital Stock no par
Montclerg Resources Ltd. recapitalized as Prospectors Alliance Corp. 09/17/1996 which recapitalized as Explorers Alliance Corp. 10/13/2000
(See Explorers Alliance Corp.)

CONSOLIDATED MONUMENTAL ACCEPTANCE CORP. (SC)
Dissolved 04/11/1963
Details not available

CONSOLIDATED MORRISON EXPLS LTD (ON)
Capital Stock $1 par changed to no par 05/30/1978
Name changed to Morrison Petroleums Ltd. 10/22/1980
Morrison Petroleums Ltd. merged into Northstar Energy Corp. 03/14/1997 which merged into Devon Energy Corp. (OK) 12/11/1998 which merged into Devon Energy Corp. (New) (DE) 08/17/1999

CONSOLIDATED MORTGAGE & INVESTMENT CORP. (DE)
Name changed to Outdoor Development Co., Inc. (DE) 04/14/1966
(See Outdoor Development Co., Inc. (DE))

CONSOLIDATED MORTGAGE CORP. (MI)
Name changed to Emil Coolidges Mortgages, Inc. 05/21/1983
(See Emil Coolidges Mortgages, Inc.)

CONSOLIDATED MORTGAGE FUND, INC. (DE)
Charter cancelled and declared inoperative and void for non-payment of taxes 04/15/1972

CONSOLIDATED MOSHER MINES LTD. (ON)
Merged into MacLeod Mosher Gold Mines Ltd. 06/15/1967
Each share Capital Stock $2 par exchanged for (0.33333333) share Common no par
MacLeod Mosher Gold Mines Ltd. acquired by Lake Shore Mines Ltd. 12/31/1968 which merged into LAC Minerals Ltd. (New) 07/29/1985 which was acquired by American Barrick Resources Corp. 10/17/1994 which name changed to Barrick Gold Corp. 01/18/1995

CONSOLIDATED MT HYLAND MINES & RES LTD (BC)
Name changed to Avance International Inc. 01/26/1976
Avance International Inc. recapitalized as Avance Venture Corp. 10/21/1999 which recapitalized as Santa Cruz Ventures Inc. 02/09/2004 which name changed to Lignol Energy Corp. 01/23/2007

CONSOLIDATED MURCHISON LTD (SOUTH AFRICA)
Name changed 08/03/1973
Name changed from Consolidated Murchison (Transvaal) Goldfields Murchison to Consolidated Murchison Ltd. 08/03/1973
ADR agreement terminated 03/29/2000
Each ADR for Ordinary exchanged for approximately $0.475 cash

CONSOLIDATED NAT GAS CO (DE)
Capital Stock $15 par changed to $10 par and (1) additional share issued 12/08/1954
Capital Stock $10 par changed to $8 par and (1) additional share issued 12/16/1966
Capital Stock $8 par reclassified as Common $8 par 09/18/1974
Common $8 par changed to $4 par and (1) additional share issued 06/08/1982
10.96% Preferred Ser. A $100 par called for redemption 03/26/1984
Common $4 par changed to $2.75 par and (1) additional share issued 06/11/1986
Merged into Dominion Resources Inc. (New) 01/28/2000
Each share Common $2.75 par

exchanged for either (1.52) shares Common no par, $66.60 cash, or a combination thereof
Note: Non-electors received cash only
Dominion Resources Inc. (New) name changed to Dominion Energy, Inc. 05/11/2017

CONSOLIDATED NATL SHOE CORP (MA)
Name changed to American Girl Fashions, Inc. 05/17/1973
(See American Girl Fashions, Inc.)

CONSOLIDATED NAVAL STORES CO. (FL)
Name changed to Consolidated Financial Corp. and each share Capital Stock $100 par reclassified as (20) shares Capital Stock $5 par 03/23/1961
Consolidated Financial Corp. merged into Baker, Fentress & Co. 03/31/1971 which name changed to BKF Capital Group Inc. 04/19/2000

CONSOLIDATED NBS INC (CANADA)
Name changed to SBN Systems, Inc. 05/14/1992
SBN Systems, Inc. name changed to NBS Technologies Inc. (Old) 04/14/1994 which name changed to Mist Inc. 11/01/2000 which name changed to NBS Technologies Inc. (New) 03/16/2004
(See NBS Technologies Inc. (New))

CONSOLIDATED NEGUS MINES LTD (ON)
Capital Stock $1 par changed to no par 07/13/1971
Acquired by Groundstar Resources Ltd. (BC) 08/31/1973
Each share Capital Stock no par exchanged for (0.05) share Capital Stock no par
Groundstar Resources Ltd. (BC) reincorporated in Alberta 10/28/2005

CONSOLIDATED NEV GOLDFIELDS CORP (CANADA)
Recapitalized as Real Del Monte Mining Corp. 05/14/1998
Each share Common no par exchanged for (0.1) share Common no par
(See Real Del Monte Mining Corp.)

CONSOLIDATED NEVADA-UTAH CORP. (VA)
Charter cancelled and proclaimed dissolved for failure to file reports 06/01/1948

CONSOLIDATED NEW PAC LTD (ON)
Name changed to Conuco Ltd. 12/22/1969
Conuco Ltd. merged into Brinco Ltd. 12/17/1979 which merged into Consolidated Brinco Ltd. 05/30/1986 which merged into Hillsborough Resources Ltd. (ON) 02/06/1992 which reincorporated in Canada 11/05/1997
(See Hillsborough Resources Ltd. (Canada))

CONSOLIDATED NEW SAGE RES LTD (CANADA)
Reincorporated 10/24/2003
Place of incorporation changed from (BC) to (Canada) 10/24/2003
Name changed to New Sage Energy Corp. 05/24/2007

CONSOLIDATED NEWEN ENTERPRISES INC (BC)
Recapitalized as North American Gold Inc. 04/07/2003
Each share Common no par exchanged for (0.2) share Common no par
North American Gold Inc. name changed to Northland Resources Inc. (BC) 09/07/2005 which reincorporated in Luxembourg as Northland Resources S.A. 06/14/2010

CONSOLIDATED NEWGATE RES LTD (BC)
Recapitalized as Antler Resources Ltd. 01/17/1996
Each share Common no par exchanged for (0.08333333) share Common no par
Antler Resources Ltd. merged into Winspear Resources Ltd. (New) 01/13/1997

CONSOLIDATED NEWJAY RES LTD (BC)
Name changed to Indo-Pacific Energy Ltd. (BC) 05/09/1995
Indo-Pacific Energy Ltd. (BC) reincoporated in Yukon 10/15/1997 which name changed to Austral Pacific Energy Ltd. (YT) 01/02/2004 which reincorporated in British Columbia 10/16/2006
(See Austral Pacific Energy Ltd.)

CONSOLIDATED NICHE PERIPHERALS INC (BC)
Delisted from Canadian Dealer Network 04/18/2001

CONSOLIDATED NICHOLSON MINES LTD (ON)
Recapitalized as Auric Resources Ltd. 02/04/1975
Each share Capital Stock no par exchanged for (0.33333333) share Capital Stock no par
Auric Resources Ltd. recapitalized as Chancellor Energy Resources Inc. 05/01/1978 which merged into HCO Energy Ltd. 04/02/1996 which merged into Pinnacle Resources Ltd. (New) 10/20/1997 which merged into Renaissance Energy Ltd. 07/16/1998 which merged into Husky Energy Inc. 08/25/2000

CONSOLIDATED NIRVANA INDS LTD (BC)
Recapitalized as Navasota Resources Ltd. 06/02/1995
Each share Common no par exchanged for (0.33333333) share Common no par
Navasota Resources Ltd. name changed to Anglo Aluminum Corp. 01/26/2010 which recapitalized as Navasota Resources Inc. 07/12/2013

CONSOLIDATED NOREX RES CORP (BC)
Acquired by Morgan Hydrocarbons Inc. 05/15/1992
Each share Common no par exchanged for (1.225) shares Common no par
Morgan Hydrocarbons Inc. acquired by Stampeder Exploration Ltd. 10/15/1996 which was acquired by Gulf Canada Resoues Ltd. 09/10/1997
(See Gulf Canada Reources Ltd.)

CONSOLIDATED NORSEMONT VENTURES LTD (BC)
Name changed to Norsemont Mining Inc. 01/27/2005
Norsemont Mining Inc. acquired by HudBay Minerals Inc. 07/05/2011

CONSOLIDATED NORTH COAST INDS LTD (BC)
Recapitalized as Great Basin Gold Ltd. 12/18/1997
Each share Common no par exchanged for (0.625) share Common no par
(See Great Basin Gold Ltd.)

CONSOLIDATED NORTHLAND MINES LTD. (ON)
Merged into Crestland Mines Ltd. 05/04/1965
Each share Capital Stock $1 par exchanged for (0.6) share Capital Stock $1 par
Crestland Mines Ltd. merged into PYX Explorations Ltd. 07/30/1976 which merged into Discovery Mines Ltd. (Canada) 01/15/1982
(See Discovery Mines Ltd. (Canada))

CONSOLIDATED NORTHLAND OILS LTD (AB)
Recapitalized as International Northland Resources Inc. (AB) 01/11/1996
Each share Common no par exchanged for (0.5) share Common no par
International Northland Resources Inc. (AB) reincorporated in (Bahamas) 09/10/1997 which merged into Combined Logistics International Ltd. 11/03/1997
(See Combined Logistics International Ltd.)

CONSOLIDATED NORTHN EXPL LTD (QC)
Cease trade order effective 02/20/1986
Stockholders' equity unlikely

CONSOLIDATED NOVELL MINES LTD (ON)
Charter cancelled and declared dissolved for failure to file returns and pay fees 03/16/1976

CONSOLIDATED NRD RES LTD (BC)
Delisted from Vancouver Stock Exchange 01/09/1998

CONSOLIDATED NU-MEDIA INDS INC (BC)
Reincorporated under the laws of Yukon as Pan Asia Mining Corp. 10/08/1997
Pan Asia Mining Corp. name changed to China Diamond Corp. 01/02/2004
(See China Diamond Corp.)

CONSOLIDATED NU-SKY EXPL INC (BC)
Reorganized under the laws of Alberta as Nu-Sky Energy Inc. 03/01/1995
Each share Common no par exchanged for (1) share Common no par
(See Nu-Sky Energy Inc.)

CONSOLIDATED NUCLEAR INC (WA)
Merged into FP Investments, Inc. 01/20/1983
Each share Common $0.005 par exchanged for (1) share Common 1¢ par
FP Investments, Inc. name changed to FP Industries, Inc. 07/29/1985
(See FP Industries, Inc.)

CONSOLIDATED OASIS RES INC (CANADA)
Each share Common no par received distribution of (0.1) share Oxford Resources Ltd. Common no par payable 02/16/1996 to holders of record 01/31/1996 Ex date - 01/29/1996
Name changed to Oasis Diamond Exploration Inc. 06/18/2001
Oasis Diamond Exploration Inc. recapitalized as Temoris Resources Inc. 03/27/2006 which name changed to Glen Eagle Resources Inc. 09/10/2008

CONSOLIDATED OBERG INDS LTD (BC)
Name changed to Hytec Flow Systems Inc. 01/16/1997
(See Hytec Flow Systems Inc.)

CONSOLIDATED ODYSSEY EXPL INC (BC)
Under plan of reorganization name changed to Odyssey Petroleum Corp. 08/25/2005
Odyssey Petroleum Corp. recapitalized as Petrichor Energy Inc. 03/03/2011

CONSOLIDATED OFFICE BLDGS. CO. (CA)
Liquidated 00/00/1960
Details not available

CONSOLIDATED OIL & GAS INC (CO)
Common 20¢ par split (2) for (1) by issuance of (1) additional share 05/27/1980
Acquired by Hugoton Energy Corp. 09/07/1995
Each share Common 20¢ par exchanged for (0.7916) share Common no par and $3.0273 cash
Hugoton Energy Corp. merged into Chesapeake Energy Corp. 03/10/1998

CONSOLIDATED OIL & GAS INC (NV)
Each share old Common $0.001 par exchanged for (2) shares new Common $0.001 par 07/14/2004
SEC revoked common stock registration 08/01/2012

CONSOLIDATED OIL & GAS INC (NV)
Name changed to Hampden Group Inc. 03/17/2003
Hampden Group Inc. recapitalized as myPhotoPipe.com, Inc. 10/06/2006
(See myPhotoPipe.com, Inc.)

CONSOLIDATED OIL & RESOURCES, INC. (CO)
Merged into Randex Consolidated Oil Co. 00/00/1956
Each share Common exchanged for (0.66666666) share Common
Randex Consolidated Oil Co. recapitalized as American-Caribbean Oil Co. 03/21/1958 which merged into Elgin Gas & Oil Co. 06/30/1959
(See Elgin Gas & Oil Co.)

CONSOLIDATED OIL CORP. (NY)
Name changed to Sinclair Oil Corp. 05/19/1943
Sinclair Oil Corp. merged into Atlantic Richfield Co. (PA) 03/04/1969 which reincorporated in Delaware 05/07/1985 which merged into BP Amoco PLC 04/18/2000

CONSOLIDATED OMAB ENTERPRISES LTD (BC)
Delisted from Vancouver Stock Exchange 03/02/1989

CONSOLIDATED OPHIR VENTURES INC (AB)
Reorganized under the laws of British Virgin Islands as CIC Energy Corp. 03/14/2006
Each share Common no par exchanged for (1) share Common no par
(See CIC Energy Corp.)

CONSOLIDATED ORIOLE COMMUNICATIONS INC (BC)
Name changed to Oriole Systems Inc. 03/26/1996
(See Oriole Systems Inc.)

CONSOLIDATED ORLAC MINES LTD. (ON)
Recapitalized as Abbican Mines Ltd. 05/18/1956
Each share Capital Stock $1 par exchanged for (0.16666666) share Capital Stock
(See Abbican Mines Ltd.)

CONSOLIDATED OROFINO RES LTD (ON)
Name changed to Orofino Resources Ltd. 03/08/1983
Orofino Resources Ltd. merged into CanGold Resources Inc. (BC) 01/31/1994 which reorganized in Ontario as Amalgamated CanGold Inc. 07/31/1995 which merged into Central Asia Goldfields Corp. 01/08/1996
(See Central Asia Goldfields Corp.)

CONSOLIDATED OURO BRASIL LTD (YT)
Name changed to Superior Diamonds Inc. (YT) 09/03/2002
Superior Diamonds Inc. (YT) reincorporated in British Columbia 06/30/2004 which name changed to

CONSOLIDATED PAC BAY MINERALS LTD (BC)
Name changed to Pacific Bay Minerals Ltd. (New) 07/22/2008

CONSOLIDATED PACE II INDS LTD (BC)
Reorganized as Canadian Pacer Petroleum Corp. 07/11/1988
Each share Common no par exchanged for (5) shares Common no par
Canadian Pacer Petroleum Corp. name changed to Providence Innovations Inc. 10/30/1989 which recapitalized as Providence Industries Inc. 10/04/1991 which merged into Gold City Mining Corp. 12/07/1994 which recapitalized as Consolidated Gold City Mining Corp. 10/24/1997 which recapitalized as Gold City Industries Ltd. (BC) 08/26/1998 which reincorporated in Manitoba 06/21/2005 which merged into San Gold Corp. 07/07/2005
(See San Gold Corp.)

CONSOLIDATED PACKAGING CORP (MI)
Common $10 par changed to $5 par 03/25/1965
Name changed to Old Packaging Corp. 01/10/1994
(See Old Packaging Corp.)

CONSOLIDATED PANTHER MINES LTD (ON)
Recapitalized as Panthco Resources Inc. 07/03/1987
Each share Capital Stock 20¢ par exchanged for (0.33333333) share Common no par
Panthco Resources Inc. merged into Ztest Electronics, Inc. 07/01/1996

CONSOLIDATED PAPER BOX CO.
Adjudicated bankrupt 00/00/1932
Details not available

CONSOLIDATED PAPER CO. (MI)
Name changed to Consolidated Packaging Corp. 08/01/1964
Consolidated Packaging Corp. name changed to Old Packaging Corp. 01/10/1994
(See Old Packaging Corp.)

CONSOLIDATED PAPER CORP. LTD. (CANADA)
Name changed to Consolidated-Bathurst Ltd. 09/30/1967
Consolidated-Bathurst Ltd. name changed to Consolidated-Bathurst Inc. 11/23/1978
(See Consolidated-Bathurst Inc.)

CONSOLIDATED PAPERS INC (WI)
Capital Stock $12.50 par split (2) for (1) by issuance of (1) additional share 06/05/1976
Capital Stock $12.50 par reclassified as Common $12.50 par 05/09/1980
Common $12.50 par changed to $6.25 par and (1) additional share issued 05/31/1980
Common $6.25 par changed to $3.125 par and (1) additional share issued 12/01/1984
Common $3.125 par changed to $1 par and (1) additional share issued 05/28/1988
Common $1 par split (2) for (1) by issuance of (1) additional share payable 05/22/1998 to holders of record 05/08/1998 Ex date - 05/26/1998
Merged into Stora Enso Oyj 08/31/2000
Each share Common $1 par exchanged for (3.621) Sponsored ADR's for Ser. R shs.

CONSOLIDATED PARKLANE RES INC (BC)
Reincorporated 04/15/1991
Place of incorporation changed from (AB) to (BC) 04/15/1991
Recapitalized as Micrologix Biotech Inc. 01/07/1993
Each share Common no par exchanged for (0.5) share Common no par
Micrologix Biotech Inc. name changed to Migenix Inc. 09/20/2004 which reorganized as BioWest Therapeutics Inc. 03/19/2010 which name changed to Carrus Capital Corp. 08/22/2011 which name changed to Global Blockchain Technologies Corp. 10/05/2017

CONSOLIDATED PAYETTE INTL RES LTD (BC)
Name changed to Celico Resources Ltd. 06/14/1979
(See Celico Resources Ltd.)

CONSOLIDATED PAYMASTER RES LTD (BC)
Recapitalized as Albany Resources Ltd. 07/05/1988
Each share Common no par exchanged for (0.22222222) share Common no par
Albany Resources Ltd. recapitalized as International Albany Resources Inc. (BC) 04/07/1995 which reincorporated in Bahamas as Brazilian Goldfields Ltd. 03/21/1997 which recapitalized as Brazilian International Goldfields Ltd. 11/27/1998 which recapitalized as Aguila American Resources Ltd. (Bahamas) 03/08/2002 which reincorporated in British Columbia 01/14/2008 which name changed to Aguila American Gold Ltd. 05/26/2011

CONSOLIDATED PAYTEL LTD (BC)
Recapitalized as Paytel Industries Ltd. 06/01/1994
Each share Common no par exchanged for (1/3) share Common no par
Paytel Industries Ltd. name changed to Rodera Diamond Corp. 04/19/1996 which merged into Pacific Rodera Ventures Inc. 03/01/1999 which name changed to Pacific Rodera Energy Inc. (BC) 06/22/2004 which reincorporated in Alberta 06/14/2006 which name changed to PRD Energy Inc. 08/12/2010

CONSOLIDATED PCR INDS LTD (BC)
Name changed to Oregon Resources Corp. 12/02/1988
Oregon Resources Corp. recapitalized as International Oregon Resources Corp. 01/10/1992 which recapitalized as Dalphine Enterprises Ltd. 03/16/1993 which name changed to Inflazyme Pharmaceuticals Ltd. 12/10/1993 which recapitalized as Eacom Timber Corp. 08/26/2008
(See Eacom Timber Corp.)

CONSOLIDATED PEAK OILS LTD. (ON)
Acquired by Western Allenbee Oil & Gas Co. Ltd. 06/20/1960
Each share Capital Stock $1 par exchanged for (0.125) share Capital Stock no par
Western Allenbee Oil & Gas Co. Ltd. name changed to Convoy Capital Corp. 04/28/1989 which recapitalized as Hariston Corp. 09/25/1992 which recapitalized as Midland Holland Inc. (Canada) 02/10/1999 which reincorporated in Yukon 03/11/1999 which name changed to Mercury Partners & Co. Inc. 02/22/2000 which name changed to Black Mountain Capital Corp. 05/02/2005 which recapitalized as Grand Peak Capital Corp. (YT) 11/20/2007 which reincorporated in British Columbia 04/27/2010

CONSOLIDATED PEMBERTON TECHNOLOGIES LTD (BC)
Recapitalized as CPT Pemberton Technologies Ltd. 06/22/1995
Each share Common no par exchanged for (0.2) share Common no par
CPT Pemberton Technologies Ltd. name changed to Pemberton Energy Ltd. 01/13/1999 which recapitalized as Brixton Energy Corp. 11/04/2010

CONSOLIDATED PERITRONICS MED INC (BC)
Recapitalized as Peritronics Medical Inc. (New) 11/15/1996
Each share Common no par exchanged for (0.5) share Common no par
(See Peritronics Medical Inc. (New))

CONSOLIDATED PERSHCOURT MNG LTD (QC)
Merged into Abcourt Metals Inc. 02/23/1971
Each share Capital Stock $1 par exchanged for (0.2) share Common no par
Abcourt Metals Inc. name changed to Les Mines d'Argent Abcourt Inc. 03/18/1980 which name changed to Abcourt Mines Inc.-Mines Abcourt Inc. 04/23/1985

CONSOLIDATED PETE INDS INC (DE)
Plan of reorganization under Chapter 11 Federal Bankruptcy proceedings confirmed 08/13/1984
Shareholders of record 03/28/1984 received an interest in a revenue bond established on their behalf
Note: All outstanding shares have been cancelled and are now without value

CONSOLIDATED PETROQUIN RES LTD (BC)
Name changed to Xemplar Energy Corp. 07/11/2005

CONSOLIDATED PHANTOM INDUSTRIES LTD. (ON)
Name changed to In. Mark Corp. Ltd. 07/30/1971
In. Mark Corp. Ltd. name changed to Gemini Food Corp. 03/30/1984
(See Gemini Food Corp.)

CONSOLIDATED PICTURES CORP (DE)
Name changed to Y-Tel International, Inc. 12/22/2004
Y-Tel International, Inc. recapitalized as NexHorizon Communications, Inc. 02/01/2007 which name changed to NX Capital Co. 09/16/2013 which recapitalized as NX Uranium, Inc. 09/29/2014

CONSOLIDATED PICTURES GROUP INC (NV)
SEC revoked common stock registration 09/24/2010

CONSOLIDATED PINE CHANNEL GOLD CORP (BC)
Name changed to Star Uranium Corp. 05/11/2006
Star Uranium Corp. name changed to Star Minerals Group Ltd. 10/11/2013 which name changed to Navis Resources Corp. 04/11/2016

CONSOLIDATED PIPE LINES CO (CANADA)
Common $1 par split (2) for (1) by issuance of (1) additional share 03/31/1986
Merged into Union Enterprises Ltd. 08/31/1988
Each share Common $1 par exchanged for $12 cash

CONSOLIDATED PLACER MINES INC (NV)
Recapitalized as ReCompute International Corp. 04/21/1998
Each share Common 1¢ par exchanged for (0.22222222) share Common 1¢ par
ReCompute International Corp. recapitalized as Pangea Pictures Corp. 10/10/2006 which name changed to Tintic Standard Gold Mines, Inc. 02/21/2008

CONSOLIDATED PLATINUM VENTURES INC (BC)
Name changed to Allied Strategies Inc. 05/25/1993
Allied Strategies Inc. recapitalized as Sleeman Breweries Ltd. 05/30/1996
(See Sleeman Breweries Ltd.)

CONSOLIDATED PLAYER RES INC (BC)
Recapitalized as Epping Realty Corp. 12/23/1988
Each share Common no par exchanged for (0.33333333) share Common no par
(See Epping Realty Corp.)

CONSOLIDATED PLENTECH ELECTRONICS INC (BC)
Delisted from Vancouver Stock Exchange 06/05/2002

CONSOLIDATED POPE VY HLDGS LTD (BC)
Name changed to Da Capo Resources Ltd. 05/05/1994
Da Capo Resources Ltd. merged into Vista Gold Corp. (BC) 11/01/1996 which reincorporated in Yukon 12/27/1997 which reincorporated back in British Columbia 06/12/2013

CONSOLIDATED PWR BATTERY CORP (WA)
Involuntarily dissolved 01/25/1999

CONSOLIDATED POWERGEM RESOURCE CORP (BC)
Merged into Eurus Resource Corp. 05/01/1990
Each share Common no par exchanged for (0.13333333) share Common no par
Eurus Resource Corp. merged into Crystallex International Corp. (BC) 09/29/1995 which reincorporated in Canada 01/23/1998

CONSOLIDATED PPM DEV CORP (BC)
Name changed to Consolidated Global Diamond Corp. 04/23/2004
Consolidated Global Diamond Corp. name changed to Gem International Resources Inc. 10/30/2009

CONSOLIDATED PRODS CORP (UT)
Name changed to Crown Video International, Inc. 02/24/1986
(See Crown Video International, Inc.)

CONSOLIDATED PRODS INC (IN)
Common no par split (3) for (2) by issuance of (0.5) additional share 10/06/1995
Common no par split (5) for (4) by issuance of (0.25) additional share payable 12/26/1997 to holders of record 12/15/1997
Common no par split (5) for (4) by issuance of (0.25) additional share payable 12/28/1998 to holders of record 12/14/1998 Ex date - 12/29/1998
Stock Dividends - 10% 01/04/1989; 10% 01/02/1990; 10% 01/21/1992; 10% 01/18/1993; 10% 01/28/1994; 10% payable 01/20/1995; 10% payable 01/15/1996 to holders of record 12/22/1995; 10% payable 01/20/1997 to holders of record 01/06/1997; 10% payable 01/12/2000 to holders of record 12/29/1999
Name changed to Steak n Shake Co. 02/12/2001

Steak n Shake Co. name changed to Biglari Holdings Inc. 04/08/2010

CONSOLIDATED PRODTN CORP (DE)
In process of liquidation
Each share Common $1 par exchanged for initial distribution of $8.50 cash 11/20/1972
Note: Details on subsequent distributions, if any, are not available

CONSOLIDATED PROFESSOR MINES LTD (ON)
Merged into Royal Oak Mines Inc. 05/06/1996
Each share Common no par exchanged for $0.80 cash

CONSOLIDATED PPTYS LTD (CANADA)
Reincorporated 08/26/1998
Place of incorporation changed from (AB) to (Canada) 08/26/1998
Each share old Common no par exchanged for (0.11111111) share new Common no par 04/15/2004
Acquired by Canadian Aspen Properties Ltd. 01/25/2005
Each share new Common no par exchanged for $2.75 cash

CONSOLIDATED PROPRIETARY MINES HLDGS LTD (ON)
Charter cancelled for failure to pay taxes and file returns 03/13/1979

CONSOLIDATED PRUDENTIAL MINES LTD. (BC)
Merged into Davenport Oil & Mining Ltd. 02/29/1972
Each share Capital Stock $1 par exchanged for (0.5) share Capital Stock 50¢ par
Davenport Oil & Mining Ltd. name changed to Davenport Industries Ltd. 11/01/1973 which recapitalized as DVO Industries Ltd. 08/19/1991
(See DVO Industries Ltd.)

CONSOLIDATED PUBG GROUP (NV)
Recapitalized as Asian Dragon Group, Inc. (Old) 04/10/2006
Each share Common 1¢ par exchanged for (0.001) share Common 1¢ par
Asian Dragon Group, Inc. (Old) name changed to Angkor Minerals, Inc. 08/22/2006 which name changed to Hemisphere Gold Inc. 11/29/2006
(See Hemisphere Gold Inc.)

CONSOLIDATED PUBG INC (CA)
Charter suspended for failure to file reports and pay fees 06/01/1987

CONSOLIDATED PUMA MINERALS CORP (BC)
Merged into Sage Gold Inc. 08/07/2009
Each share Common no par exchanged for (1.202) shares Common no par

CONSOLIDATED QDATA SYS INC (BC)
Name changed to Carbite Golf Inc. (BC) 01/12/1996
Carbite Golf Inc. (BC) reorganized in Yukon 10/12/2001
(See Carbite Golf Inc.)

CONSOLIDATED QUE SMLT & REFNG LTD (QC)
Name changed to Magnetics International Ltd. 05/02/1968
Magnetics International Ltd. name changed to Magnetics International Ltd.- Magnetique International Ltee. 11/20/1970 which name changed to Mavtech Holdings Inc. 08/31/1987
(See Mavtech Holdings Inc.)

CONSOLIDATED QUE YELLOWKNIFE MINES LTD (QC)
Charter cancelled for failure to file reports 05/04/1974

CONSOLIDATED QUEBEC GOLD MINING & METALS CORP. (QC)
Recapitalized as Commercial Holding & Metals Corp. 03/25/1964
Each share Common $2.50 par exchanged for (0.5) share Common $1 par

CONSOLIDATED RAIL CORP (PA)
Common $1 par split (2) for (1) by issuance of (1) additional share 09/15/1992
Under plan of reorganization name changed to Conrail Inc. 07/01/1993
(See Conrail Inc.)

CONSOLIDATED RAINDOR MINES LTD. (ON)
Charter cancelled and declared dissolved for failure to file returns and pay fees 07/27/1976

CONSOLIDATED RAMBLER MINES LTD (ON)
Acquired by Grand River Holdings Ltd. 01/28/1999
Each share Common no par exchanged for $20.75 cash

CONSOLIDATED RAMROD GOLD CORP (BC)
Name changed to Quest International Resources Corp. 04/09/1996
Quest International Resources Corp. recapitalized as Standard Mining Corp. 06/16/1999 which merged into Doublestar Resources Ltd. (YT) 11/01/2001 which reincorporated in British Columbia 10/10/2002 which merged into Selkirk Metals Corp. 07/23/2007
(See Selkirk Metals Corp.)

CONSOLIDATED RANWICK URANIUM MINES LTD. (ON)
Name changed to International Ranwick Ltd. 06/29/1955
International Ranwick Ltd. name changed to International Molybdenum Mines Ltd. 08/00/1959 which merged into Pax International Mines Ltd. 01/31/1962 which recapitalized as Geo-Pax Mines Ltd. 09/00/1968
(See Geo-Pax Mines Ltd.)

CONSOLIDATED RAPID RIV RES LTD (AB)
Struck off register for failure to file annual returns 11/30/1981

CONSOLIDATED REACTOR URANIUM MINES LTD (ON)
Name changed to Canaustra Gold Explorations Ltd. 10/23/1987
Canaustra Gold Explorations Ltd. merged into Cliff Resources Corp. 01/09/1989 which name changed to Mineral Resources Corp. 09/13/1995 which name changed to Minroc Mines Inc. 06/10/1998 which name changed to Cassiar Mines & Metals, Inc. 06/10/1999 which name changed to Cassiar Magnesium Inc. 04/25/2000 which name changed to Cassiar Resources Inc. 07/25/2001 which name changed to Troutline Investments Inc. (ON) 06/30/2003 which reorganized in Alberta as Innova Exploration Ltd. 04/16/2004
(See Innova Exploration Ltd.)

CONSOLIDATED REC CORP (DE)
Charter cancelled and declared inoperative and void for non-payment of taxes 03/01/1978

CONSOLIDATED RED POPLAR MINERALS LTD (ON)
Recapitalized as New Dimension Resources Ltd. 11/09/1971
Each share Capital Stock $1 par exchanged for (0.2) share Capital Stock no par
New Dimension Resources Ltd. recapitalized as New Dimension Industries Ltd. 09/19/1989 which recapitalized as Toxic Disposal Corp. 02/15/1994 which recapitalized as Global Disposal Corp. 03/29/1996
(See Global Disposal Corp.)

CONSOLIDATED REDDING EXPLS CORP (BC)
Name changed to Redex Gold Inc. 06/20/1996
Redex Gold Inc. name changed to Bravo Gold Inc. 07/31/1997 which recapitalized as International Bravo Resource Corp. 09/22/1998 which recapitalized as Bravo Venture Group Inc. 03/15/2002 which name changed to Bravo Gold Corp. 02/22/2010 which recapitalized as Homestake Resource Corp. 04/16/2012 which merged into Auryn Resources Inc. 09/07/2016

CONSOLIDATED REFNG INC (NY)
Liquidation completed
Each share Common 10¢ par received initial distribution of $24.50 cash 12/17/1982
Each share Common 10¢ par received second distribution of $0.44 cash 04/20/1984
Each share Common 10¢ par received third and final distribution of $0.1578 cash 09/25/1986
Note: Certificates were not required to be surrendered and are without value

CONSOLIDATED REGAL RES LTD (BC)
Recapitalized as Fresco Developments Ltd. 09/18/1992
Each share Common no par exchanged for (0.4) share Common no par
Fresco Developments Ltd. merged into Oromin Explorations Ltd. (New) 02/25/2002 which merged into Teranga Gold Corp. 10/08/2013

CONSOLIDATED REGCOURT MINES LTD (QC)
Completely liquidated 12/09/1968
Each share Capital Stock $1 par exchanged for (0.1) share Kelly Lake Nickel Mines Ltd. Capital Stock no par
Kelly Lake Nickel Mines Ltd. name changed to Albany Oil & Gas Ltd. (MB) 03/22/1971 which reincorporated in Alberta 11/10/1980 which name changed to Albany Corp. 05/17/1988 which merged into LifeSpace Environmental Walls Inc. 08/17/1993 which merged into SMED International Inc. 07/01/1996
(See SMED International Inc.)

CONSOLIDATED RENDERING CO. (ME)
Common no par split (4) for (1) by issuance of (3) additional shares 00/00/1946
Common no par changed to $6.25 par and (1) additional share issued 10/17/1956
Name changed to Corenco Corp. 07/01/1966
(See Corenco Corp.)

CONSOLIDATED RESEARCH & MANUFACTURING CORP. (DE)
Charter revoked for non-payment of taxes 04/01/1964

CONSOLIDATED RESOURCES CORP. (DE)
No longer in existence having become inoperative and void for non-payment of taxes 04/15/1968

CONSOLIDATED RES GROUP INC (FL)
Each share old Common $0.001 par exchanged for (0.01) share new Common $0.001 par 04/01/2003
New Common $0.001 par split (3) for (1) by issuance of (2) additional shares payable 02/08/2004 to holders of record 01/17/2004
Ex date - 02/09/2004

SEC revoked common stock registration 09/16/2009

CONSOLIDATED RES HEALTH CARE FD (GA)
Units of Ltd. Partnership Int. II completely dissolved 01/02/2008
Details not available
SEC revoked registrations of Units of Ltd. Partnership IV, V and VI 06/24/2011

CONSOLIDATED RETAIL SOLUTIONS INC (BC)
Name changed to Ventir Challenge Enterprises Ltd. 07/18/1994
Ventir Challenge Enterprises Ltd. recapitalized as Whistler Gold Corp. 02/03/2006 which name changed to Svit Gold Corp. 08/11/2008 which name changed to Catalyst Copper Corp. 02/02/2010 which merged into NewCastle Gold Corp. 05/27/2016 which merged into Equinox Gold Corp. 12/22/2017

CONSOLIDATED RETAIL STORES, INC. (DE)
Common no par changed to $5 par 00/00/1931
Common $5 par changed to old Common $1 par 00/00/1937
Each share 4.25% Preferred Ser. A $50 par exchanged for (1) share 5% Preferred $20 par and (4) shares new Common $1 par 10/02/1957
Each share old Common $1 par exchanged for (0.5) share new Common $1 par 10/02/1957
Under plan of merger name changed to Consolidated Sun Ray, Inc. 02/02/1959
Consolidated Sun Ray, Inc. recapitalized as Penrose Industries Corp. 10/23/1964
(See Penrose Industries Corp.)

CONSOLIDATED REXSPAR MINERALS & CHEMS LTD (ON)
Capital Stock $1 par changed to no par 05/06/1971
Name changed to Conrex Corp. 10/01/1987
Conrex Corp. merged into Falvo Corp. 06/30/1989 which reorganized as Conrex Steel Corp. 05/28/1999
(See Conrex Steel Corp.)

CONSOLIDATED RHODES RES LTD (BC)
Recapitalized as Fairhaven Resources Ltd. 03/04/1992
Each share Common no par exchanged for (0.2) share Common no par
Fairhaven Resources Ltd. recapitalized as International Fairhaven Resources Ltd. 05/29/2002
(See International Fairhaven Resources Ltd.)

CONSOLIDATED RIBAGO MINES LTD (ON)
Charter cancelled for failure to pay taxes and file returns 03/16/1976

CONSOLIDATED RICH CAP CORP (BC)
Delisted from Toronto Venture Stock Exchange 11/12/2002

CONSOLIDATED RICH COAST SULPHUR LTD (BC)
Merged into Rich Coast Resources Ltd. (BC) 01/25/1993
Each share Common no par exchanged for (1) share Common no par
Rich Coast Resources Ltd. (BC) reincorporated in Delaware as Rich Coast Inc. 09/16/1996 which reincorporated in Nevada 07/14/1998 which recapitalized as Media Pal Holdings, Corp. 03/16/2010

CONSOLIDATED RICHLAND MINES INC (BC)
Name changed to Apogee Minerals Ltd. (BC) 01/19/1999
Apogee Minerals Ltd. (BC) reincorporated in Ontario 01/21/2005 which name changed to Apogee Silver Ltd. 03/28/2011 which name changed to Apogee Opportunities Inc. 09/16/2016

CONSOLIDATED RIDEAU RES CORP (BC)
Recapitalized as Brymore Oil & Gas Ltd. (BC) 02/01/1995
Each share Common no par exchanged for (0.5) share Class A no par
Brymore Oil & Gas Ltd. (BC) reincorporated in Alberta 02/09/1995 which name changed to BXL Energy Ltd. 05/30/1996 which merged into Viking Energy Royalty Trust 06/21/2001 which merged into Harvest Energy Trust 02/07/2006
(See Harvest Energy Trust)

CONSOLIDATED RIMROCK OIL CORP. (CO)
Merged into Consolidated Oil & Gas, Inc. (CO) 04/30/1958
Each share Common no par exchanged for (0.15384615) share Common 20¢ par
Consolidated Oil & Gas, Inc. (CO) acquired by Hugoton Energy Corp. 09/07/1995 which merged into Chesapeake Energy Corp. 03/10/1998

CONSOLIDATED RIO PLATA RES LTD (BC)
Recapitalized as New Rio Resources Ltd. 10/28/1993
Each share Common no par exchanged for (0.25) share Common no par
New Rio Resources Ltd. name changed to Southern Rio Resources Ltd. 08/23/1994 which recapitalized as Silver Quest Resources Ltd. 12/15/2005
(See Silver Quest Resources Ltd.)

CONSOLIDATED RIPPLE RES LTD (BC)
Struck off register and declared dissolved for failure to file returns 08/13/1993

CONSOLIDATED ROCHETTE MINES LTD. (QC)
Recapitalized as Conro Development Corp. Ltd. 02/17/1955
Each share Common $1 par exchanged for (0.2) share Common $1 par
(See Conro Development Corp. Ltd.)

CONSOLIDATED ROCK PRODS CO (DE)
Reorganized 00/00/1945
Each share Preferred no par exchanged for (2.236) shares Capital Stock $1 par
Common no par had no equity
Each share Capital Stock $1 par exchanged for (0.3) share Capital Stock $5 par 08/13/1956
Stock Dividends - 10% 06/08/1962; 10% 04/05/1965
Name changed to Conrock Co. 04/21/1972
Conrock Co. merged into CalMat Co. 06/27/1984
(See CalMat Co.)

CONSOLIDATED ROYAL MINES INC (UT)
Name changed to Royal Silver Mines, Inc. 08/08/1995
Royal Silver Mines, Inc. recapitalized as Cadence Resources Corp. 06/01/2001 which name changed to Aurora Oil & Gas Corp. 05/24/2006
(See Aurora Oil & Gas Corp.)

CONSOLIDATED ROYALGROUP INC (ON)
Name changed to Aronos Multinational Inc. 11/08/1991
Aronos Multinational Inc. name changed to RDG Minerals Inc. 10/24/1996 which recapitalized as Netforfun.com, Inc. 08/09/2000

CONSOLIDATED RTY OIL CO (WY)
Capital Stock $10 par changed to no par 10/21/1959
Liquidation completed
Each share Capital Stock no par received initial distribution of (1) Conwest Partnership Participating Unit of Undivided Fractional Interest in Conwest Royalty Trust plus $0.50 cash 12/23/1966
Each share Capital Stock no par received second distribution of (1) share Conroy, Inc. Common $1 par 01/27/1967
Each share Capital Stock no par received third distribution of $0.40 cash 01/10/1968
Each share Capital Stock no par exchanged fourth and final distribution of $0.24 cash 06/29/1970

CONSOLIDATED RTYS INC (CA)
6% Preferred $10 par called for redemption 07/07/1974
In process of liquidation
Each share Common $1 par received initial distribution of (0.25) share Clark Oil Co. Common $1 par 07/22/1974
Each share Common $1 par received second distribution of $15.50 cash 11/28/1975
Each share Common $1 par received third distribution of $1 cash 01/21/1977
Each share Common $1 par received fourth distribution of $1.81 cash 06/01/1977
Details on subsequent distributions, if any, are not available

CONSOLIDATED RUSKIN DEVS LTD NEW (BC)
Name changed to Leisureways Marketing Ltd. (BC) 11/23/1992
Leisureways Marketing Ltd. (BC) reincorporated in Yukon 11/10/1997 which name changed to LML Payment Systems Inc. (YT) 07/15/1998 which reincorporated in British Columbia 09/07/2012
(See LML Payment Systems Inc.)

CONSOLIDATED RUSKIN DEVS LTD OLD (BC)
Merged into Consolidated Ruskin Developments Ltd. (New) 03/31/1992
Each share Common no par exchanged for (1) share Common no par
Consolidated Ruskin Developments Ltd. (New) name changed to Leisureways Marketing Ltd. (BC) 11/23/1992 which reincorporated in Yukon 11/10/1997 which name changed to LML Payment Systems Inc. (YT) 07/15/1998 which reincorporated in British Columbia 09/07/2012
(See LML Payment Systems Inc.)

CONSOLIDATED SAMARKAND RES INC (BC)
Recapitalized as Soho Resources Corp. 10/15/1999
Each share Common no par exchanged for (0.16666666) share Common no par
Soho Resources Corp. recapitalized as Telson Resources Inc. 01/17/2013 which name changed to Telson Mining Corp. 02/21/2018

CONSOLIDATED SAND & GRAVEL LTD. (ON)
All preferred $100 par acquired through voluntary exchange offer by Standard Paving & Materials Ltd. 00/00/1947

CONSOLIDATED SANNORM MINES LTD (ON)
Dissolved 02/18/1970
No stockholders' equity

CONSOLIDATED SARABAT GOLD CORP (BC)
Recapitalized as CSG Resources Ltd. 11/20/1998
Each share Common no par exchanged for (0.33333333) share Common no par
CSG Resources Ltd. name changed to Artgallerylive.com Management Ltd. 09/24/1999 which recapitalized as Adaptive Marketing Solutions Inc. 01/18/2001 which recapitalized as Permission Marketing Solutions Inc. 01/18/2002 which name changed to Pacific Asia China Energy Inc. 01/04/2006
(See Pacific Asia China Energy Inc.)

CONSOLIDATED SASHA TECHNOLOGY LTD. (CANADA)
Dissolved 05/06/2004
Details not available

CONSOLIDATED SEA GOLD CORP (BC)
Recapitalized as Sea Gold Resources Inc. 05/09/1990
Each share Common no par exchanged for (0.5) share Common no par
Sea Gold Resources Inc. recapitalized as Fairchild Investments Inc. (BC) 06/03/1994 which reincorporated in Bermuda as Fairchild Investments Ltd. 06/26/1995
(See Fairchild Investments Ltd.)

CONSOLIDATED SERENA RES LTD (BC)
Name changed to Capstone Gold Corp. 03/07/2003
Capstone Gold Corp. name changed to Capstone Mining Corp. 02/13/2006

CONSOLIDATED SVCS INC (CO)
Name changed to Scientex Corp. (CO) 11/22/1978
Scientex Corp. (CO) reincorporated in Nevada 07/27/1979
(See Scientex Corp. (NV))

CONSOLIDATED SHASTA RES INC (BC)
Name changed to Lima Gold Corp. 11/24/1994
Lima Gold Corp. recapitalized as International Lima Resources Corp. 09/20/1999 which name changed to Crosshair Exploration & Mining Corp. 03/01/2004 which name changed to Crosshair Energy Corp. 11/02/2011 which recapitalized as Jet Metal Corp. (BC) 09/23/2013 which reorganized in Canada as Canada Jetlines Ltd. 03/07/2017

CONSOLIDATED SHOSHONI GOLD CORP (BC)
Recapitalized as New Shoshoni Ventures Ltd. 01/07/2000
Each share Common no par exchanged for (0.1) share Common no par
New Shoshoni Ventures Ltd. recapitalized as Shoshoni Gold Ltd. 05/09/2012

CONSOLIDATED SHUNSBY MINES LTD (ON)
Recapitalized as MW Resources Ltd. 07/21/1975
Each share Capital Stock $1 par exchanged for (0.33333333) share Capital Stock no par
MW Resources Ltd. recapitalized as MW Capital Resources Corp. (ON) 09/14/1990 which reorganized in Alberta as Oro Nevada Resources Inc. 08/31/1996 which name changed to Martlett Venture Management Ltd. 09/02/1999
(See Martlett Venture Management Ltd.)

CONSOLIDATED SILVER BANNER MINES LTD. (ON)
Merged into Trans-Canada Explorations Ltd. 09/00/1955
Each share Capital Stock $1 par exchanged for (0.02) share Capital Stock $1 par
Trans-Canada Explorations Ltd. merged into Roman Corp. Ltd. 11/27/1964
(See Roman Corp. Ltd.)

CONSOLIDATED SILVER BUTTE MINES LTD (BC)
Name changed to Silver Butte Resources Ltd. 07/31/1989
Silver Butte Resources Ltd. recapitalized as Uniterre Resources Ltd. 08/17/1995 which name changed to NaiKun Wind Energy Group Inc. 11/03/2006

CONSOLIDATED SILVER RIDGE MINES LTD (BC)
Name changed to Northcal Resources Ltd. 10/22/1981
Northcal Resources Ltd. recapitalized as Calnor Resources Ltd. 09/20/1985 which recapitalized as Norcal Resources Ltd. 08/23/1991 which recapitalized as Troon Ventures Ltd. (BC) 06/18/2002 which reorganized in Ontario as Grenville Strategic Royalty Corp. 02/21/2014 which merged into LOGiQ Asset Management Inc. (AB) 06/07/2018 which reorganized in British Columbia as Flow Capital Corp. 06/11/2018

CONSOLIDATED SILVER STD MINES LTD (BC)
Name changed to Silver Standard Resources Inc. 04/09/1990
Silver Standard Resources Inc. name changed to SSR Mining Inc. 08/03/2017

CONSOLIDATED SILVER TUSK MINES LTD (YT)
Reincorporated 00/00/2000
Place of incorporation changed from (BC) to (Yukon) 00/00/2000
Struck off register 05/20/2005

CONSOLIDATED SILVERS, INC. (NV)
Name changed to Consolidated Mining & Refining Co. 05/19/1922
(See Consolidated Mining & Refining Co.)

CONSOLIDATED SKEENA MINES LTD (BC)
Merged into International Mariner Resources Ltd. 02/09/1971
Each share Common no par exchanged for (0.22222222) share Common no par and (0.11111111) Ser. C Common Stock Purchase Warrant expiring 07/31/1972
(See International Mariner Resources Ltd.)

CONSOLIDATED SMLT & REFNG CORP (ID)
Merged into Michelle Enterprises, Ltd. 06/18/1969
Each share Capital Stock 10¢ par exchanged for (0.1) share Capital Stock $1 par
Michelle Enterprises, Ltd. recapitalized as America's Beautiful Cities 09/01/1971
(See America's Beautiful Cities)

CONSOLIDATED SOFTWARE INC (DE)
Each share Common 20¢ par exchanged for (0.5) share Common 25¢ par 03/06/1970
Charter cancelled and declared inoperative and void for non-payment of taxes 04/15/1972

CONSOLIDATED SOUTHERN COMPANIES, INC. (GA)
Assets sold for benefit of creditors 00/00/1965
No stockholders' equity

CONSOLIDATED SPECTRA VENTURES LTD (BC)
Name changed to Tiger International Resources Inc. 12/27/1996

CONSOLIDATED SPIRE VENTURES LTD (BC)
Recapitalized as Berkwood Resources Ltd. 12/01/2010
Each share Common no par exchanged for (0.1) share Common no par

CONSOLIDATED ST SIMEON MINES LTD (QC)
Charter annulled for failure to file reports or pay fees 05/11/1974

CONSOLIDATED STAINLESS INC (DE)
Common 1¢ par split (3) for (2) by issuance of (0.5) additional share 06/02/1995
Chapter 11 bankruptcy proceedings converted to Chapter 7 on 11/10/1998
Stockholders' equity unlikely

CONSOLIDATED STANDARD CORP. (DE)
Name changed to Patents Unlimited, Inc. 04/21/1967
Patents Unlimited, Inc. name changed to Diversified Development Inc. which name changed to Ionicron Inc. 02/23/1981
(See Ionicron Inc.)

CONSOLIDATED STD MINES LTD (BC)
Recapitalized as Golden Standard Mines Ltd. 05/20/1975
Each share Capital Stock $1 par exchanged for (0.2) share Capital Stock no par
Golden Standard Mines Ltd. recapitalized as International Standard Resources Ltd. 02/27/1979 which recapitalized as First Standard Mining Ltd. 03/15/1988 which name changed to First Standard Ventures Ltd. 07/16/1993 which recapitalized as LRG Restaurant Group, Inc. 09/05/1995
(See LRG Restaurant Group, Inc.)

CONSOLIDATED STANFORD CORP (ON)
Liquidation completed
Each share Common no par received first and final distribution of $0.39 cash payable 12/01/2003 to holders of record 11/24/2003
Note: Certificates were not required to be surrendered and are without value

CONSOLIDATED STEEL CORP.
Name changed to Consolidated Western Steel Corp. 07/01/1948
Consolidated Western Steel Corp. name changed to Consolidated Liquidating Corp. 08/31/1948
(See Consolidated Liquidating Corp.)

CONSOLIDATED STIKINE SILVER LTD (BC)
Name changed to Stikine Resources Ltd. 09/20/1989
Stikine Resources Ltd. was acquired by Prime Resources Group Inc. 12/14/1993 which merged into HomeStake Mining Co. 12/03/1998 which merged into Barrick Gold Corp. 12/14/2001

CONSOLIDATED STOCK & DEBENTURE CO. INC.
Dissolved 00/00/1930
Details not available

CONSOLIDATED STONE INDS INC (BC)
Delisted from Toronto Venture Stock Exchange 06/05/2002

CONSOLIDATED STORES CORP (DE)
Common 1¢ par split (2) for (1) by issuance of (1) additional share 11/25/1985
Common 1¢ par split (2) for (1) by issuance of (1) additional share 06/16/1986
Common 1¢ par split (5) for (4) by issuance of (0.25) additional share payable 12/24/1996 to holders of record 12/10/1996 Ex date - 12/26/1996
Common 1¢ par split (5) for (4) by issuance of (0.25) additional share payable 06/24/1997 to holders of record 06/10/1997 Ex date - 06/25/1997
Reincorporated under the laws of Ohio as Big Lots, Inc. 05/16/2001

CONSOLIDATED STRATEGIC METALS INC (BC)
Each share old Common no par exchanged for (0.25) share new Common no par 02/14/1983
Recapitalized as New Strategic Metals Inc. 05/25/1983
Each share new Common no par exchanged for (1) share Common no par
New Strategic Metals Inc. name changed to P.S.M. Technologies Inc. 12/29/1986
(See P.S.M. Technologies Inc.)

CONSOLIDATED SUDBURY BASIN MINES LTD. (ON)
Merged into Giant Yellowknife Mines Ltd. 06/30/1960
Each share Capital Stock no par exchanged for (0.04) share Capital Stock no par
Giant Yellowknife Mines Ltd. merged into Royal Oak Mines Inc. 07/23/1991 which recapitalized as Royal Oak Ventures Inc. 02/14/2000
(See Royal Oak Ventures Inc.)

CONSOLIDATED SUMMIT MINES LTD (ON)
Merged into Barrick Resources Corp. 05/02/1983
Each share Common no par exchanged for (0.25) share Common no par
Barrick Resources Corp. recapitalized as American Barrick Resources Corp. 12/06/1985 which name changed to Barrick Gold Corp. 01/18/1995

CONSOLIDATED SUN RAY, INC. (DE)
Common $1 par changed to 10¢ par 08/07/1962
Recapitalized as Penrose Industries Corp. 10/23/1964
Each share Common 10¢ par exchanged for (0.05) share Common $2 par
5% Convertible Preferred $20 par affected by name change only
(See Penrose Industries Corp.)

CONSOLIDATED SUNTEC VENTURES LTD (BC)
Name changed to Vortex Energy Systems Inc. 10/03/1990
Vortex Energy Systems Inc. recapitalized as Autumn Industries Inc. 09/16/1994 which name changed to Altek Power Corp. 03/07/2001

CONSOLIDATED SYH CORP (ON)
Merged into Central Capital Corp. 10/25/1991
Each share Common no par exchanged for $0.25 cash

CONSOLIDATED T C RES LTD (BC)
Name changed to Cyclone Capital Corp. 05/20/1992
Cyclone Capital Corp. recapitalized as Nikos Explorations Ltd. 06/04/1996 which name changed to Labrador Gold Corp. 12/19/2017

CONSOLIDATED TACHE MINES & INVTS LTD (QC)
Name changed to Tache Resources Inc. 9/13/82
Tache Resources Inc. recapitalized as United North American Resources, Inc. 2/15/85 which reorganized in the United Kingdom as Alliance Resources plc 2/11/91 which merged into AROC Inc. 12/8/99
(See AROC Inc.)

CONSOLIDATED TAKEPOINT VENTURES LTD (YT)
Name changed to Lake Shore Gold Corp. (YT) 12/18/2002
Lake Shore Gold Corp. (YT) reincorporated in (BC) 06/30/2004 which reincorporated in (Canada) 07/18/2008 which merged into Tahoe Resources Inc. 04/07/2016

CONSOLIDATED TAKO RES LTD (BC)
Recapitalized as International Tako Industries Inc. (BC) 01/18/2000
Each share Common no par exchanged for (0.26315789) share Common no par
International Tako Industries Inc. (BC) reincorporated in Alberta 11/26/2002 which name changed to Ironhorse Oil & Gas Inc. 05/14/2004 which recapitalized as Pond Technologies Holdings Inc. 02/06/2018

CONSOLIDATED TALCORP LTD (CANADA)
Name changed to Sound Insight Enterprises Ltd. 12/7/90
Sound Insight Enterprises Ltd. merged into CamVec Corp. 9/11/92 which name changed to AMJ Campbell Inc. 8/14/2001
(See AMJ Campbell Inc.)

CONSOLIDATED TAYWIN RES LTD (BC)
Name changed to Inspiration Mining Corp. (BC) 04/29/1996
Inspiration Mining Corp. (BC) reincorporated in Ontario 08/18/2008

CONSOLIDATED TEAM RES CORP (BC)
Name changed to QHR Technologies Inc. (BC) 06/27/2000
QHR Technologies Inc. (BC) reincorporated in Canada as QHR Corp. 07/08/2013
(See QHR Corp.)

CONSOLIDATED TECHNOLOGIES HLDGS INC (BC)
Name changed to TigerTel Telecommunications Corp. (BC) 11/26/2001
TigerTel Telecommunications Corp. (BC) reincorporated in Canada as TigerTel Communications Inc. 05/01/2002
(See TigerTel Communications Inc.)

CONSOLIDATED TECHNOLOGY GROUP LTD (NY)
Recapitalized as Sagemark Companies Ltd. 8/9/99
Each (30) shares Common 1¢ par exchanged for (1) share Common 1¢ par

CONSOLIDATED TECHNOLOGY INC (AZ)
Name changed to Discom, Inc. 11/14/1968
(See Discom, Inc.)

CONSOLIDATED TECHNOLOGY INC (DE)
Merged into Tri Tec Plastics Corp. 12/05/1990
Each share Common $0.0001 par exchanged for (0.5) share Common 1¢ par
Tri Tec Plastics Corp. merged into Secom General Corp. 12/17/1991
(See Secom General Corp.)

CONSOLIDATED TELEPHONE CO. (KY)
100% acquired through voluntary exchange offer as of 05/22/1967
5.5% Preferred called for redemption 01/31/1959
Public interest eliminated

CONSOLIDATED TELEVISION & RADIO BROADCASTERS, INC. (IN)
Liquidation completed 05/26/1958
Details not available

CONSOLIDATED TEX NORTHN MINERALS LTD (BC)
Recapitalized as Rio Verde Industries Inc. 6/28/2000
Each share Common no par exchanged for (0.125) share Common no par

CONSOLIDATED TEXTILE CO., INC. (DE)
Stock Dividends - 10% 07/19/1948; 10% 03/10/1950; 20% 10/16/1950
Name changed to Windsor Industries, Inc. 01/03/1957
Windsor Industries, Inc. merged into Bates Manufacturing Co., Inc. 05/15/1965
(See Bates Manufacturing Co., Inc.)

CONSOLIDATED TEXTILE CORP.
Reorganized as Consolidated Textile Co. Inc. in 1938
Stockholders received subscription warrants only

CONSOLIDATED TEXTILE MLS LTD (CANADA)
Each share old Common no par exchanged for (4) shares new Common no par 00/00/1949
5% Preferred $20 par called for redemption 04/25/1964
New Common no par split (3) for (1) by issuance of (2) additional shares 04/06/1971
Stock Dividend - 50% 12/31/1971
Name changed to Consoltex Canada Inc. 07/23/1980
(See Consoltex Canada Inc.)

CONSOLIDATED THEATRES CORP.
Succeeded by Consolidated Theatres Ltd. 00/00/1928
Details not available

CONSOLIDATED THEATRES LTD (CANADA)
Each share old Common no par exchanged for (0.25) share new Common no par 00/00/1937
Each share new Common no par exchanged for (1) share Class A no par and (3) shares Class B no par 00/00/1947
Merged into Famous Players Ltd. 06/30/1980
Each share Class A no par exchanged for $10 cash
Each share Class B no par exchanged for $10 cash

CONSOLIDATED THERMO TECH INTL INC (BC)
Recapitalized as Thermo Tech Technologies Inc. (BC) 06/09/1992
Each share Common no par exchanged for (1/3) share Common no par
Thermo Tech Technologies Inc. (BC) reincorporated in Yukon 04/11/2000

CONSOLIDATED THOMPSON IRON MINES LTD (CANADA)
Acquired by Cliffs Natural Resources Inc. 05/12/2011
Each share Common no par exchanged for $17.25 cash

CONSOLIDATED THOMPSON LUNDMARK GOLD MINES LTD (CANADA)
Name changed to Consolidated

Thompson Iron Mines Ltd. 08/24/2006
(See Consolidated Thompson Iron Mines Ltd.)

CONSOLIDATED THOR MINES LTD. (ON)
Name changed to Nealon Mines Ltd. 01/18/1957
(See Nealon Mines Ltd.)

CONSOLIDATED THUNDERBIRD PROJS LTD (BC)
Name changed to Jenosys Enterprises, Inc. 08/16/1999
Jenosys Enterprises, Inc. recapitalized as Fintry Enterprises Inc. 12/10/2004 which recapitalized as Mesa Uranium Corp. 12/23/2005 which name changed to Mesa Exploration Corp. 03/30/2011

CONSOLIDATED TITLE CORP. (MD)
Under plan of merger name changed to Realty Title Insurance Co. Inc. 12/31/62
(See Realty Title Insurance Co., Inc.)

CONSOLIDATED TITLE SECURITIES CO. (DE)
Merged into Security Title Insurance & Guarantee Co. 12/31/1946
Each share 2% Preferred $15 par exchanged for (1/7) share 3% Preferred $100 par, (1) share Common 50¢ par and $2 cash
Each share Common exchanged for (0.891416428) share Common 50¢ par
Security Title Insurance & Guarantee Co. name changed to Security Title Insurance Co. 07/01/1952 which name changed to Financial Corp. of America 04/30/1962 which merged into General America Corp. 07/31/1964 which name changed to Safeco Corp. 04/30/1968
(See Safeco Corp.)

CONSOLIDATED TOMOKA LD CO (DE)
Common $1 par split (2) for (1) by issuance of (1) additional share 3/24/86
Common $1 par split (2) for (1) by issuance of (1) additional share 8/17/92
Stock Dividend - 25% 1/12/79
Reincorporated under the laws of Florida 5/1/93

CONSOLIDATED TOP GUN EXPLS INC (BC)
Name changed to Sterling Pacific Resources Inc. 9/13/93
Sterling Pacific Resources Inc. recapitalized as Tres-Or Resources Ltd. 1/11/99

CONSOLIDATED TOPAZ EXPL LTD (BC)
Recapitalized as Topaz Resources International Inc. 08/06/1991
Each share Common no par exchanged for (0.5) share Common no par
Topaz Resources International Inc. recapitalized as Pacific Topaz Resources Ltd. 07/21/1997 which recapitalized as Western Atlas Resources Inc. 06/20/2018

CONSOLIDATED TOPPER GOLD CORP (BC)
Name changed to Topper Resources Inc. (BC) 02/06/2002
Topper Resources Inc. (BC) reincorporated in Alberta 05/03/2006 which name changed to Century Energy Ltd. (AB) 05/19/2006 which reincorporated in British Columbia 10/20/2016

CONSOLIDATED TOWER RES LTD (BC)
Struck off register and declared dissolved for failure to file returns 3/18/83

CONSOLIDATED TRACTION CO.
Merged into Pittsburgh Railways Co. 9/30/50
Each share 6% Preferred $50 par exchanged for (4.2) shares Common no par and $5 cash
Pittsburgh Railways Co. name changed to Pittway Corp. (PA) 11/28/67 which merged into Pittway Corp. (DE) 12/28/89
(See Pittway Corp. (DE))

CONSOLIDATED TRACTION CO. (NJ)
Acquired by Public Service Coordinated Transport and Stock exchange for equal amount of 4% bonds in 1940

CONSOLIDATED TRANDIRECT COM TECHNOLOGIES INC (BC)
Name changed to International Samuel Exploration Corp. 6/20/2001

CONSOLIDATED TRANS-CDA RES LTD (AB)
Merged into Ranchmen's Resources Ltd. 09/30/1989
Each share Class A Common no par exchanged for (0.69) share Common no par
Ranchmen's Resources Ltd. name changed to Ranchmen's Resources (1975) Ltd. 08/28/1975 which merged into Ranchmen's Resources (1976) Ltd. 01/31/1977 which name changed to Ranchmen's Resources Ltd. 05/31/1985 which merged into Crestar Energy Inc. 10/11/1995 which was acquired by Gulf Canada Resources Ltd. 11/13/2000
(See Gulf Canada Resources Ltd.)

CONSOLIDATED TRANS COLUMBIA INDS LTD (BC)
Struck off register and declared dissolved for failure to file returns 12/05/1986

CONSOLIDATED TRAVEL SYS INC (DE)
Each share old Class A 1¢ par exchanged for (3) shares new Class A 1¢ par 05/20/1988
Recapitalized as Knobias, Inc. 11/17/2004
Each share new Class A 1¢ par exchanged for (1/3) Common 1¢ par
(See Knobias, Inc.)

CONSOLIDATED TRILLION RES LTD (AB)
Merged into Viceroy Exploration Ltd. 12/04/2003
Each share Common no par exchanged for (0.7) share Common no par
Note: Unexchanged certificates were cancelled and became without value 12/04/2009
Viceroy Exploration Ltd. acquired by Yamana Gold Inc. 10/31/2006

CONSOLIDATED TRILOGY VENTURES LTD (BC)
Name changed to Thyssen Mining Exploration Inc. 12/22/1998
Thyssen Mining Exploration Inc. name changed to Trilogy Metals Inc. (BC) 12/08/2000 which reincorporated in Canada as NWest Energy Inc. 03/07/2008 which recapitalized as NWest Energy Corp. 11/04/2010 which name changed to Ceylon Graphite Corp. 01/03/2017

CONSOLIDATED TUNGSTEN MINING CORP. OF CANADA LTD. (ON)
Recapitalized as Mount Wright Iron Mines Co. Ltd. 04/18/1958
Each share Common no par exchanged for (0.25) share Common no par
Mount Wright Iron Mines Co. Ltd. name changed to Mantaur Goldfields Corp. 04/30/1996 which name changed to Mantaur Petroleum Corp. 06/25/1997 which merged into Videoflicks.com Inc. 03/24/1999
(See Videoflicks.com Inc.)

CONSOLIDATED TVX MNG CORP (ON)
Reincorporated under the laws of Canada as TVX Gold Inc. 1/7/91
TVX Gold Inc. merged into Kinross Gold Corp. 1/31/2003

CONSOLIDATED UTD SAFETY TECHNOLOGY INC (BC)
Recapitalized as Genetronics Biomedical Ltd. (BC) 10/04/1994
Each share Common no par exchanged for (0.17857142) share Common no par
Genetronics Biomedical Ltd. (BC) reincorporated in Delaware as Genetronics Biomedical Corp. 06/21/2001 which name changed to Inovio Biomedical Corp. 03/31/2005 which name changed to Inovio Pharmaceuticals, Inc. 05/14/2010

CONSOLIDATED URANIUM CORP. (QC)
Merged into Continental Consolidated Mines & Oils Co. Ltd. on a (0.1) for (1) basis 10/4/57
(See Continental Consolidated Mines & Oils Ltd.)

CONSOLIDATED URANIUM MINES, INC. (NV)
Common 25¢ par changed to $0.075 par 00/00/1951
Charter revoked for non-payment of fees 03/02/1959

CONSOLIDATED UTILITIES, LTD.
Merged into City Gas & Electric Corp. Ltd in 1933
Details not available

CONSOLIDATED VA MNG CORP (QC)
Charter cancelled for failure to file reports 08/03/1974

CONSOLIDATED VAL D OR RES LTD (QC)
Delisted from Montreal Stock Exchange 12/11/1992

CONSOLIDATED VY VENTURES LTD (BC)
Name changed to CVL Resources Ltd. 03/12/1997
CVL Resources Ltd. recapitalized as Newport Exploration Ltd. 02/04/2002

CONSOLIDATED VALVE INDS INC (MI)
Name changed to ConBraCo Industries, Inc. 07/20/1977
(See ConBraCo Industries, Inc.)

CONSOLIDATED VAN ANDA GOLD LTD (BC)
Delisted from Toronto Venture Stock Exchange 03/15/2002

CONSOLIDATED VAN-CITY MARBLE LTD (BC)
Delisted from Canadian Dealer Network 08/03/2001

CONSOLIDATED VAN TOR RES LTD (BC)
Merged into International Mariner Resources Ltd. 02/09/1971
Each share Common no par exchanged for (0.11111111) share Common no par and (0.055555) Ser. C Common Stock Purchase Warrant expiring 07/31/1972
(See International Mariner Resources Ltd.)

CONSOLIDATED VAUZE MINES LTD. (ON)
Acquired by Vauze Mines Ltd. 06/23/1961
Each share Capital Stock $1 par exchanged for (1) share Capital Stock $1 par
Vauze Mines Ltd. name changed to North American Gas Ltd. 05/27/1965
(See North American Gas Ltd.)

CONSOLIDATED VENTURES LTD. (BC)
Name changed to West-Coast Resources Ltd. in 1959
(See West-Coast Resources Ltd.)

CONSOLIDATED VENTUREX HLDGS LTD (BC)
Name changed to Venturex Explorations Inc. 05/24/2007
Venturex Explorations Inc. recapitalized as Black Panther Mining Corp. 06/17/2008 which name changed to Canadian International Pharma Corp. 06/22/2015

CONSOLIDATED VIGOR MINES LTD (BC)
Struck off register and declared dissolved for failure to file reports 3/22/73

CONSOLIDATED VIRGINIA & ANDES CORP.
Acquired by Consolidated Virginia Mining Co. in 1935
Details not available

CONSOLIDATED VIRGINIA MINING CO. (NV)
Capital Stock $1 par changed to 10¢ par 01/06/1955
Charter revoked 03/00/1964

CONSOLIDATED VISCOUNT RES LTD (BC)
Recapitalized as Choice Resources Corp. (BC) 02/20/2001
Each share Common no par exchanged for (0.33333333) share Common no par
Choice Resources Corp. (BC) reincorporated in Alberta 09/29/2004 which merged into Buffalo Resources Corp. 08/03/2007 which merged into Twin Butte Energy Ltd. 10/15/2009

CONSOLIDATED VULTEE AIRCRAFT CORP. (DE)
Merged into General Dynamics Corp. on a (4/7) for (1) basis in 1954

CONSOLIDATED WAGON & MACHINE CO.
Dissolved in 1943
Details not available

CONSOLIDATED WATER CO. OF UTICA
Sold to the City of Utica, N.Y. in 1938
Details not available

CONSOLIDATED WATER POWER & PAPER CO. (WI)
Each share Capital Stock $100 par exchanged for (4) shares new Capital Stock $25 par 00/00/1937
Each share Capital Stock $25 par exchanged for (2) shares Capital Stock $12.50 par 00/00/1951
Stock Dividend - 100% 10/01/1955
Name changed to Consolidated Papers, Inc. 04/25/1962
Consolidated Papers, Inc. merged into Stora Enso Oyj 08/31/2000

CONSOLIDATED WELLINGTON RES LTD (BC)
Name changed to First Hospitality (Canada) Corp. 09/24/1987
First Hospitality (Canada) Corp. recapitalized as Southern Pacific Development Corp. 11/05/1991 which recapitalized as Southern Pacific Resource Corp. (BC) 03/03/2006 which reincorporated in Alberta 11/17/2006

CONSOLIDATED WEST HILL ENERGY INC (ON)
Merged into African Selection Mining Corp. (ON) 11/21/1997
Each share Common no par exchanged for (0.25) share Common no par
African Selection Mining Corp. (ON) reincorporated in Yukon 04/23/1998
(See African Selection Mining Corp.)

CONSOLIDATED WEST PETE LTD (ON)
Merged into Western Decalta Petroleum (1977) Ltd. 08/22/1977
Each share Common no par exchanged for $6.90 cash

CONSOLIDATED WESTERN STEEL CORP.
Name changed to Consolidated Liquidating Corp. in 1948
(See Consolidated Liquidating Corp.)

CONSOLIDATED WESTN & PAC RES CORP (BC)
Name changed to Synergy Resource Technologies Inc. 07/02/1996
Synergy Resource Technologies Inc. recapitalized as Synergy Renewable Resources Inc. 01/09/1997
(See Synergy Renewable Resources Inc.)

CONSOLIDATED WESTREX DEV CORP (BC)
Name changed to Westrex Energy Corp. (BC) 07/25/1991
Westrex Energy Corp. (BC) reincorporated in Alberta 05/12/1994 which recapitalized as Search Energy Corp. 01/09/1997 which merged into Advantage Energy Income Fund 05/24/2001 which reorganized as Advantage Oil & Gas Ltd. 07/09/2009

CONSOLIDATED WESTVIEW RES CORP (BC)
Each share old Common no par exchanged for (0.16666666) share new Common no par 06/19/2014
Name changed to Lithoquest Diamonds Inc. 11/29/2017

CONSOLIDATED WOODGREEN MINES LTD. (ON)
Recapitalized as Cumberland Mining Co. Ltd. on a (0.2) for (1) basis 4/20/64
(See Cumberland Mining Co. Ltd.)

CONSOLIDATED YUKENO MINES LTD.
Recapitalized as Yukeno Mines Ltd. 00/00/1951
Each share Capital Stock $1 par exchanged for (0.5) share Capital Stock $1 par
Yukeno Mines Ltd. recapitalized as Gradore Mines Ltd. 03/04/1966
(See Gradore Mines Ltd.)

CONSOLIDATED YUKON MINERALS CORP (AB)
Struck off register for failure to file annual returns 10/01/1994

CONSOLIDATED ZINC CORP. LTD. (ENGLAND)
Merged into Rio Tinto-Zinc Corp. Ltd. on a (58) for (20) basis 07/09/1962
Rio Tinto-Zinc Corp. PLC name changed to RTZ Corp. PLC 08/26/1987 which name changed to Rio Tinto PLC 06/02/1997

CONSOLIDATION CAP CORP (DE)
Name changed to Building One Services Corp. 9/17/98
Building One Services Corp. merged into Encompass Services Corp. 2/22/2000
(See Encompass Services Corp.)

CONSOLIDATION COAL CO., INC. (DE)
Merged into Pittsburgh Consolidation Coal Co. in 1945
Each share Common exchanged for $7.50 principal amount of 3-1/2% Debentures and (1) share Common $1 par
Pittsburgh Consolidation Coal Co. name changed to Consolidation Coal Co. 5/1/58
(See Consolidation Coal Co.)

CONSOLIDATION COAL CO. (PA)
Liquidation completed
Each share Common $1 par received initial distribution consisting of (0.0106) share American Electric Power Co., Inc. Common $6.50 par; (0.3533) share Chrysler Corp. Common $6.25 par; (0.1009) share Continental Oil Co. (DE) Common $5 par; (0.0067) share Ingersoll-Rand Co. (NJ) Common $2 par; (0.0051) share National Steel Corp. Capital Stock $5 par; (0.0140) share Toledo Edison Co. Common $5 par; (0.0111) share United States Steel Corp. (DE) Common $30 par and $48.30 cash 10/21/66
(See each company's listing)
Each share Common $1 par exchanged for second and final distribution of $0.955 cash 3/27/67

CONSOLIDATION SVCS INC (DE)
Each share old Common $0.001 par exchanged for (0.25) share new Common $0.001 par 12/31/2012
Name changed to Mongolia Holdings, Inc. 09/02/2014

CONSOLIN U S INC (DE)
Merged into CHI (U.S.) Inc. 01/08/1975
Each share Common 10¢ par exchanged for $1.62 cash

CONSOLITECH INVEST CORP (AB)
Recapitalized as HTN Inc. (AB) 07/19/2001
Each share Common no par exchanged for (0.5) share Common no par
HTN Inc. (AB) reincorporated in Ontario as Internet of Things Inc. 05/14/2015

CONSOLTEX CDA INC (CANADA)
Merged into CCI Acquisition Corp. 06/27/1991
Each share Common no par exchanged for $33 cash

CONSOLTEX GROUP INC (CANADA)
Merged into AIP/CGI Acquisition Corp. 10/25/99
Each share Common no par exchanged for $5.60 cash

CONSORCIO G GRUPO DINA S A DE C V (MEXICO)
Each old Sponsored ADR for Common no par exchanged for (0.1) new Sponsored ADR for Common no par 5/22/2000
Each old Sponsored ADR for L Shares no par exchanged for (0.1) new Sponsored ADR for L Shares no par 5/22/2000
ADR agreement terminated 8/14/2002
Each new Sponsored ADR for L Shares no par exchanged for $0.85014 cash
Each new Sponsored ADR for Ordinary no par exchanged for $0.85014 cash

CONSORCIO HOGAR S A DE C V (MEXICO)
ADR agreement terminated 01/22/2015
No ADR's remain outstanding

CONSORT ENERGY CORP (BC)
Recapitalized as International Consort Industries Inc. 04/27/1990
Each share Common no par exchanged for (0.5) share Common no par
International Consort Industries Inc. name changed to Cryopak Industries Inc. 11/12/1993
(See Cryopak Industries Inc.)

CONSORTIUM SVC MGMT GROUP INC (TX)
Name changed to CSMG Technologies, Inc. 03/14/2008
(See CSMG Technologies, Inc.)

CONSPIRACY ENTMT HLDGS INC (UT)
Each share old Common $0.001 par exchanged for (0.33333333) share new Common $0.001 par 04/22/2010
SEC revoked common stock registration 10/18/2013

CONSTANT CONTACT INC (DE)
Acquired by Endurance International Group Holdings, Inc. 02/09/2016
Each share Common 1¢ par exchanged for $32 cash

CONSTANT ENVIRONMENT INC (NV)
Name changed to Zentric, Inc. 01/04/2010

CONSTAR INTL INC NEW (DE)
Plan of reorganization under Chapter 11 Federal Bankruptcy Code effective 05/29/2009
No old Common stockholders' equity
Plan of reorganization under Chapter 11 Federal Bankruptcy Code effective 05/31/2011
No new Common stockholders' equity

CONSTAR INTL INC OLD (DE)
Common 50¢ par split (2) for (1) by issuance of (1) additional share 06/02/1992
Merged into Galaxy Acquisition Inc. 10/26/1992
Each share Common 50¢ par exchanged for $32.50 cash

CONSTELLATION BANCORP (NJ)
Common no par split (2) for (1) by issuance of (1) additional share 09/30/1986
Merged into CoreStates Financial Corp 03/16/1994
Each share Common no par exchanged for (0.4137) share Common $1 par
CoreStates Financial Corp merged into First Union Corp. 04/28/1998 which name changed to Wachovia Corp. (Ctfs. dated after 09/01/2001) 09/01/2001 which merged into Wells Fargo & Co. (New) 12/31/2008

CONSTELLATION BRANDS INC (DE)
Each share 5.75% Mandatory Conv. Preferred Ser. A converted into (1.4638) shares Class A Common 1¢ par 09/01/2006
(Additional Information in Active)

CONSTELLATION COPPER CORP (CANADA)
Each share old Common no par exchanged for (0.1) share new Common no par 03/16/2004
Filed an assignment in bankruptcy 12/23/2008
No stockholders' equity

CONSTELLATION ENERGY GROUP INC (MD)
Merged into Exelon Corp. 03/12/2012
Each share Common no par exchanged for (0.93) share Common no par

CONSTELLATION ENERGY PARTNERS LLC (DE)
Name changed to Sanchez Production Partners LLC 10/06/2014
Sanchez Production Partners LLC reorganized as Sanchez Production Partners L.P. 03/09/2015 which name changed to Sanchez Midstream Partners L.P. 06/05/2017

CONSTELLATION LIFE INSURANCE CO. (VA)
Merged into Allied Security Insurance Co. 04/29/1961
Each share Common 70¢ par exchanged for (0.16666666) share Common $1 par
Allied Security Insurance Co. merged into United Family Life Insurance Co. 12/31/1963 which reorganized as Interfinancial Inc. 07/01/1969
(See Interfinancial Inc.)

CONSTELLATION OIL & GAS CO (AB)
Recapitalized as International Sovereign Energy Corp. (AB) 05/31/2000
Each share Class A Common no par exchanged for (0.2) share Class A Common no par
International Sovereign Energy Corp. (AB) reorganized in Canada as Wi2Wi Corp. 02/05/2013

CONSTELLATION 3D INC (DE)
Reincorporated 02/08/2001
State of incorporation changed from (FL) to (DE) and Common $0.001 par changed to $0.00001 par 02/08/2001
Plan of reorganization under Chapter 11 Federal Bankruptcy Code effective 01/12/2006
No stockholders' equity

CONSTELLATION URANIUM CORP. (OK)
Recapitalized as Gold Seal International Inc. 06/10/1964
Each share Common 1¢ par exchanged for (0.1) share Common 1¢ par
Gold Seal International Inc. merged into Bonneville Medical Products, Inc. 01/10/1973 which recapitalized as Ametex Corp. 02/11/1974
(See Ametex Corp.)

CONSTITUTION BANCORP NEW ENGLAND INC (DE)
Name changed to Lafayette American Bancorp, Inc. 05/21/1991
Lafayette American Bancorp, Inc. reorganized as Lafayette American Bank & Trust Co. (Hamden, CT) 02/23/1994 which merged into HUBCO, Inc. 07/01/1996 which name changed to Hudson United Bancorp 04/21/1999 which merged into TD Banknorth Inc. 01/31/2006
(See TD Banknorth Inc.)

CONSTITUTION BK & TR CO (HARTFORD, CT)
Merged into Colonial Bancorp, Inc. 01/01/1977
Each share Common $10 par exchanged for $37.50 cash

CONSTITUTION EXCHANGE FUND, INC. (MA)
Name changed to Constitution Fund, Inc. 02/15/1972
Constitution Fund, Inc. merged into Keystone Custodian Funds 10/31/1980
(See Keystone Custodian Funds)

CONSTITUTION FD INC (MA)
Merged into Keystone Custodian Funds 10/31/1980
Each share Common $1 par exchanged for (8.1875) shares Keystone Growth Fund Ser. K-2 $1 par
(See Keystone Custodian Funds)

CONSTITUTION FEDERAL SAVINGS & LOAN (CA)
Placed in receivership by the RTC 06/29/1990
Stockholders' equity unlikely

CONSTITUTION LIFE INSURANCE CO. (CA)
Merged into Sterling Insurance Co. 10/09/1956
Each share Common $3 par exchanged for $18.37 cash

CONSTITUTION MNG CORP (DE)
Reincorporated 10/21/2009
State of incorporation changed from (NV) to (DE) 10/21/2009
Name changed to Goldsands Development Co. 04/01/2011

CONSTITUTION NATL BK (HARTFORD, CT)
Common $6.50 par changed to $10 par 03/13/1972
Name changed to Constitution Bank & Trust Co. (Hartford, CT) 06/20/1973

(See Constitution Bank & Trust Co. (Hartford, CT))

CONSTITUTION SVGS & LN ASSN (CA)
Name changed to Constitution Federal Savings & Loan 10/14/1981
(See Constitution Federal Savings & Loan)

CONSTON CORP (DE)
Class A Common 12¢ par split (5) for (4) by issuance of (0.25) additional share 10/04/1991
Filed petition under Chapter 11 Federal Bankruptcy Code 02/26/1992
No stockholders' equity

CONSTRUCTION CREDIT CORP. (MD)
Went into liquidation 12/01/1968
Details not available

CONSTRUCTION DESIGN, INC. (CA)
Name changed to Allied Builders Corp. 01/20/1967
(See Allied Builders Corp.)

CONSTRUCTION MATERIALS CORP.
Bankrupt 00/00/1934
Stockholders' equity unlikely

CONSTRUCTION PRODS INTL INC (FL)
Common $0.001 par split (7) for (1) by issuance of (6) additional shares payable 08/25/1999 to holders of record 08/18/1999
Recapitalized as Sports Pouch Beverage Co., Inc. 10/06/2004
Each share Common $0.001 par exchanged for (0.001) share Common $0.001 par

CONSTRUCTION PRODUCTS CORP. (FL)
Name changed to GF Industries, Inc. (FL) 11/22/1965
GF Industries, Inc. (FL) reorganized in Delaware 07/30/1976
(See GF Industries, Inc. (DE))

CONSTRUCTION PRODUCTS SALES (CA)
Charter revoked for failure to file reports and pay fees 09/01/1959

CONSTRUCTION TECHNOLOGY INDS INC (DE)
Chapter 11 Federal Bankruptcy Code converted to Chapter 7 on 09/26/1988
Stockholders' equity unlikely

CONSUL RESTAURANT CORP (MN)
Name changed 09/27/1984
Common 2¢ par changed to 1¢ par 02/02/1979
Name changed from Consul Corp. to Consul Restaurant Corp. 09/27/1984
Plan of reorganization under Chapter 11 Federal Bankruptcy proceedings rejected by the Court and a competing plan confirmed 10/22/1992
No stockholders' equity

CONSULIER ENGR INC (FL)
Name changed 04/01/1990
Name changed from Consulier Industries, Inc. to Consulier Engineering, Inc. 04/01/1990
Each share Common $0.001 par exchanged for (0.1) share Common 1¢ par 02/01/1995
Common 1¢ par split (2) for (1) by issuance of (1) additional share payable 04/15/1998 to holders of record 03/31/1998
Acquired by Consulier Interim Corp. 12/31/2013
Each share Common 1¢ par exchanged for $1.29 principal amount of a 6% 5-Year Note

CONSULTA SEARCH CORP (DE)
Merged into Globe Security Systems, Inc. (DE) 07/12/1972
Each share Common 5¢ par exchanged for $1.25 cash

CONSULTAMERICA INC (DE)
Common $0.001 par split (7.5) for (1) by issuance of (6.5) additional shares payable 10/21/2005 to holders of record 10/12/2005
Ex date - 10/24/2005
Name changed to VirtualScopics, Inc. 11/04/2005
(See VirtualScopics, Inc.)

CONSULTANT CAPACITIES GROUP INC (DE)
Each share Common $0.0001 par exchanged for (0.025) share Common $0.004 par 01/07/1985
Charter cancelled and declared inoperative and void for non-payment of taxes 03/01/1990

CONSULTANTS & DESIGNERS INC (NY)
Merged into Greyhound Corp. (DE) 10/23/1973
Each share Common $1 par exchanged for $14 cash

CONSULTANTS BUREAU ENTERPRISES, INC. (NY)
Name changed to Plenum Publishing Corp. (NY) and Class A Common 10¢ par reclassified as Common 10¢ par 04/14/1946
Plenum Publishing Corp. (NY) reincorporated in Delaware 03/23/1987
(See Plenum Publishing Corp.)

CONSULTANTS CAP CORP (DE)
Name changed to Protective Energy Programs, Inc. 06/15/1984
(See Protective Energy Programs, Inc.)

CONSULTANTS MUT INVT INC (MD)
Merged into Drexel Burnham Fund 06/16/1975
Each share Common 10¢ par exchanged for (1.230769) shares Common 10¢ par

CONSUMAT ENVIRONMENTAL SYS INC (VA)
Assets sold for benefit of creditors in 05/00/1999
Stockholders' equity undetermined

CONSUMAT SYS INC (VA)
Each share Common $1 par exchanged for (0.33333333) share Common $3 par 09/30/1992
Reorganized under Chapter 11 Federal Bankruptcy Code as Reorganized Consumat Systems, Inc. 03/12/1996
Each share Common $3 par exchanged for approximately (0.3194888) share Common $1 par
Reorganized Consumat Systems, Inc. name changed to Consumat Environmental Systems, Inc. 12/12/1996
(See Consumat Environmental Systems, Inc.)

CONSUMER & TECHNICAL INDS INC (DE)
Completely liquidated 07/14/1972
Each share Common 10¢ par received first and final distribution of (1) share Digitronics Corp. Capital Stock 10¢ par and $0.085 cash
Note: Certificates were not required to be surrendered and are without value

CONSUMER ACCEP & LN CORP (SC)
Liquidation completed
Each share Capital Stock $1 par exchanged for initial distribution of $1.30 cash 05/12/1988
Each share Capital Stock $1 par previously exchanged received second and final distribution of $0.12850031 cash 10/18/1996

CONSUMER ACCEP CORP (DE)
Name changed to Symmar Inc. 10/06/1970

Symmar Inc. name changed to Aspir-Air Inc. 05/23/1990
(See Aspir-Air Inc.)

CONSUMER ACCEPTANCE CORP. (RI)
Each share 60¢ Preferred $1 par exchanged for (2) shares 30¢ Preferred $1 par 02/06/1959
30¢ Conv. Preferred $1 par called for redemption 01/01/1966
Recapitalized under the laws of Delaware 09/13/1968
Holders of 6% Conv. Preferred $20 par had option to exchange each share for $7.60 cash or for (0.2) share Preferred $38 par
Holders of Class A Common 10¢ par had option to exchange each share for $0.75 cash or to continue as holders of Class A Common 10¢ par
Consumer Acceptance Corp. (DE) name changed to Symmar Inc. 10/06/1970 which name changed to Aspir-Air, Inc. 05/23/1990
(See Aspir-Air, Inc.)

CONSUMER CONSV CORP (UT)
Involuntarily dissolved 12/31/1983

CONSUMER CR CORP (FL)
Stock Dividend - Payable in Class A - 10% 11/30/1963
Bankrupt 09/13/1966
No stockholders' equity

CONSUMER CREDIT CORP. LTD. (ON)
Reorganized as Glengair Group Ltd. 02/25/1966
Each share 6.50% Preference Ser. A $5 par exchanged for (2) shares Common no par
Each share Common no par exchanged for (1) share Common no par
Glengair Group Ltd. merged into Jannock Corp. Ltd. 07/04/1973 which reorganized as Jannock Ltd. 07/05/1977
(See Jannock Ltd.)

CONSUMER DIRECT OF AMER (NV)
Each share old Common $0.001 par exchanged for (0.05) share new Common $0.001 par 02/17/2004
Name changed to Shearson Financial Network, Inc. 07/06/2006
(See Shearson Financial Network, Inc.)

CONSUMER FINANCE CORP. (NC)
Dissolved 00/00/1954
Details not available

CONSUMER FINANCE CORP. OF AMERICA (CO)
Acquired by General Acceptance Corp. (New) 06/09/1960
Each share 60¢ Preferred $5 par exchanged for (1) share 60¢ Preference no par
Each share Class A Common $5 par exchanged for (0.5) share 60¢ Preference no par
Each share Class B Common $1 par exchanged for (0.56) share Common $1 par
General Acceptance Corp. (New) name changed to GAC Corp. (PA) 07/01/1968 which reincorporated in Delaware 12/20/1973
(See GAC Corp. (DE))

CONSUMER PLASTICS CORP (DE)
Name changed to CPC-Rexcel, Inc. 10/14/1987
(See CPC-Rexcel, Inc.)

CONSUMERS AUTOMATIC VENDING INC (NY)
Proclaimed dissolved for failure to file reports and pay fees 12/15/1969

CONSUMERS BLDG MARTS INC (CO)
Name changed to C.B.M.I. Corp. 01/01/1976
(See C.B.M.I. Corp.)

CONSUMERS CO. (DE)
Incorporated 02/01/1937
Recapitalized 00/00/1947
Class A Common $50 par changed to $2.50 Preferred $50 par
Class B Common no par changed to Common no par
Merged into Union Chemical & Materials Corp. 00/00/1954
Each share Common no par exchanged for (9.4) shares Common $10 par
Union Chemical & Materials Corp. merged into Vulcan Materials Co. 12/31/1957

CONSUMERS CO. (DE)
Incorporated 12/09/1938
Dissolved and charter surrendered 00/00/1938

CONSUMERS CO. (IL)
Reorganized as Consumers Co. of Illinois 00/00/1937
Details not available

CONSUMERS CO. OF ILLINOIS
Name changed to Consumers Co. (DE) 00/00/1940
Consumers Co. (DE) merged into Union Chemical & Materials Corp. 00/00/1954 which merged into Vulcan Materials Co. 12/31/1957

CONSUMERS COOPERATIVE ASSOCIATION (KS)
4% 2nd Preferred $25 par called for redemption 04/15/1965
Name changed to Farmland Industries, Inc. 09/01/1966
(See Farmland Industries, Inc.)

CONSUMERS CORDAGE CO. LTD.
Assets acquired by Plymouth Cordage Co. 00/00/1938
Details not available

CONSUMERS DISTRG LTD (ON)
Common no par split (3) for (1) by issuance of (2) additional shares 06/25/1969
Common no par split (2) for (1) by issuance of (1) additional share 08/21/1972
Each share Common no par exchanged for (1) share Conv. Class A no par and (2) shares Class B no par 06/28/1983
Acquired by Provigo Inc. (Old) 12/16/1987
Each share Conv. Class A no par exchanged for $5.50 cash
Each share Class B no par exchanged for $5.50 cash

CONSUMERS DUNES CORP. (IN)
Liquidation completed 05/06/1957
Details not available

CONSUMERS ELECTRIC LIGHT & POWER CO.
Merged into New Orleans Public Service, Inc. 00/00/1926
Details not available

CONSUMERS ENERGY CO (MI)
$7.45 Preferred $100 par called for redemption at $101 on 09/15/1997
$7.68 Preferred $100 par called for redemption at $101 on 09/15/1997
$7.72 Preferred $100 par called for redemption at $101 on 09/15/1997
$7.76 Preferred $100 par called for redemption at $102.21 on 09/15/1997
$2.08 Class A Preferred $100 par called for redemption at $25 on 04/01/1999
$4.16 Preferred $100 par called for redemption at $103.25 plus $1.04 accrued dividends on 07/01/2013
(Additional Information in Active)

CONSUMERS ENERGY CO FING TR I (DE)
$2.09 Trust Originated Preferred Securities called for redemption at $25 plus $0.3251 accrued dividends on 02/25/2005

CONSUMERS ENERGY CO FING II (DE)
8.2% Trust Originated Preferred Securities called for redemption at $25 plus $0.3189 accrued dividends 02/25/2005

CONSUMERS ENERGY CO FING III (DE)
9.25% Trust Originated Preferred Securities called for redemption at $25 01/24/2005

CONSUMERS ENERGY CO FING IV (DE)
9% Trust Preferred Securities called for redemption at $25 plus $0.5625 accrued dividends 06/30/2006

CONSUMERS FINL CORP (NV)
Reincorporated 02/26/2008
8% Conv. Preferred $10 par called for redemption 08/30/1987
Each share $5 Conv. Preferred Ser. 1 $1 par exchanged for (0.74074074) share Common no par 05/31/1988
Each share old Common no par exchanged for (0.1) share new Common $0.001 par 11/21/2005
State of incorporation changed from (PA) to (NV) 02/26/2008
Each share new Common $0.001 par exchanged again for (0.002) share new Common $0.001 par 03/13/2008
SEC revoked preferred and common stock registration 03/16/2010

CONSUMERS GAS CO. (PA)
Merged into United Gas Improvement Co. 00/00/1952
Each share Capital Stock $25 par exchanged for (0.8) share Common $13.50 par
United Gas Improvement Co. name changed to UGI Corp. (Old) 07/01/1968 which reorganized as UGI Corp. (New) 04/10/1992

CONSUMERS GAS CO. OF TORONTO (ON)
Each share Capital Stock $100 par exchanged for (10) shares Capital Stock $10 par 00/00/1952
Recapitalized as Consumers' Gas Co. (ON) and Common $10 par changed to no par 11/18/1957
Consumers' Gas Co. (ON) name changed to Walker (Hiram)-Consumers Home Ltd. 04/14/1980
(See - Walker (Hiram)-Consumers Home Ltd.)

CONSUMERS GAS CO (ON)
Common no par split (3) for (1) by issuance of (2) additional shares 08/29/1960
Common no par split (2) for (1) by issuance of (1) additional share 07/01/1963
5.5% Preference Ser. A & B $100 par and 5% Preference Ser. C $100 par reclassified as 5.5% Preference Group 1, Ser. A & B $100 par and 5% Preference Group 1, Ser. C $100 par respectively 10/14/1969
Under plan of merger name changed to Walker (Hiram) -Consumers Home Ltd. 04/14/1980
(See Walker (Hiram) -Consumers Home Ltd.)

CONSUMERS GAS LTD (ON)
9.25% Retractable Preference Group 3 Ser. A no par called for redemption 09/19/1988
13.5% Preference Group 2 Ser. A $25 par called for redemption 07/01/1989
Merged into British Gas Holdings (Canada) Ltd. 01/18/1991
Each share old Common no par exchanged for $34.265 cash
7.6% Preference Group 3 Ser. B no par called for redemption 09/16/1993
7.69% Preference Group 2 Ser. B no par called for redemption 04/06/1994
Merged into IPL Energy Inc. 12/09/1996
Each share new Common no par exchanged for (0.5663) share Common no par and $1.50 cash
5.72% Retractable Preference Group 3 Ser. C $100 par called for redemption at $25 plus $0.3575 accrued dividend on 10/01/1998
5.5% Preferred Ser. A $100 par called for redemption at $101 on 07/05/1999
5.5% Preferred Ser. B $100 par called for redemption at $101 on 07/05/1999
6.45% Retractable Preference Group 2 Ser. C $100 par called for redemption at $25 plus $0.017671 accrued dividend on 07/05/1999
(Additional Information in Active)

CONSUMERS GLASS LTD (CANADA)
Each share Part. Preferred $100 par exchanged for (1.5) shares Common no par 00/00/1935
Each share Common no par exchanged for (0.1) share Common no par 00/00/1940
Common no par split (4) for (1) by issuance of (3) additional shares 09/06/1963
Common no par split (2) for (1) by issuance of (1) additional share 06/22/1979
Common no par split (2) for (1) by issuance of (1) additional share 08/08/1983
Name changed to Consumers Packaging Inc./ Emballages Consumers Inc. 07/02/1986
(See Consumers Packaging Inc./Emballages Consumers Inc.)

CONSUMERS ILL WTR CO (IL)
5.50% Preferred $100 par called for redemption at $107.50 on 12/01/2012

CONSUMERS INVT FD INC (DE)
Acquired by Steadman American Industry Fund, Inc. 09/14/1970
Each share Capital Stock 50¢ par received (0.89969) share Common $1 par
Note: Shares were automatically credited to holders' account evidencing ownership
Certificates were not retired and are now without value
Steadman American Industry Fund, Inc. name changed to Ameritor Industry Fund 09/23/1998
(See Ameritor Industry Fund)

CONSUMERS NATL CORP (DE)
Merged into Lincoln American Corp. (NY) 04/30/1973
Each share Common $1 par exchanged for $8.50 cash

CONSUMERS NATL LIFE INS CO (IN)
Each share old Common Capital Stock $1 par exchanged for (0.33333333) share new Common $1 par 12/31/1966
Under plan of reorganization each share Common $1 par automatically became (1) share Consumers National Corp. (DE) 02/01/1972
(See Consumers National Corp. (DE))

CONSUMERS NATURAL GAS CO.
Acquired by New Mexico Eastern Gas Co. 00/00/1938
Details not available

CONSUMERS OXYGEN CO.
Merged into National Cylinder Gas Co. 00/00/1937
Details not available

CONSUMERS PACKAGING INC (CANADA)
Petition under Bankruptcy and Insolvency Act effective 04/28/2003
No stockholders' equity

CONSUMERS PWR CO (MI)
Reincorporated 06/06/1968
Common no par split (2) for (1) by issuance of (1) additional share 04/27/1962
Stock Dividend - 10% 04/03/1967
State of incorporation changed from (ME) to (MI) and $4.52 Preferred no par changed to $100 par, $4.50 Preferred no changed to $100 par, $4.16 Preferred no par changed to $100 par and Common no par changed to $10 par 06/06/1968
$6 Conv. Preference $1 par called for redemption 08/01/1980
$5.50 Conv. Preference $1 par called for redemption 07/01/1982
$4 Preference $1 par called for redemption 12/01/1986
Under plan of reorganization each share Common $10 par automatically became (1) share CMS Energy Corp. Common 1¢ par 05/26/1987
$4.40 Preference $1 par called for redemption 06/01/1987
$2.50 Preference $1 par called for redemption 08/14/1987
$4.02 Preference $1 par called for redemption 09/01/1987
$3.85 Preference $1 par called for redemption 09/15/1987
$3.78 Preference $1 par called for redemption 10/01/1987
$9.25 Preferred $100 par called for redemption 10/01/1987
$85 Preferred $1 par called for redemption 10/01/1987
$3.98 Preference $1 par called for redemption 11/01/1987
$2.43 Preference $1 par called for redemption 11/10/1987
$2.23 Preference $1 par called for redemption 11/20/1987
$3.60 Preference $1 par called for redemption 01/01/1988
$8.625 Preferred $100 par called for redemption 04/01/1988
$9 Preferred $100 par called for redemption 04/01/1988
$4.52 Preferred $100 par called for redemption 01/01/1990
$9.70 Preferred $100 par called for redemption 01/01/1990
Name changed to Consumers Energy Co. 03/11/1997

CONSUMERS PWR CO FING I (DE)
Name changed to Consumers Energy Company Financing Trust I 03/11/1997
(See Consumers Energy Company Financing Trust I)

CONSUMERS PUB SVC CO (MO)
Recapitalized 00/00/1939
Each share 7% Preferred $100 par exchanged for (1) share 5% Preferred $50 par and (5) shares Common $10 par
Each share Common no par exchanged for (16) shares Common $10 par
Assets sold to three utility companies which were its only stockholders 03/04/1962

CONSUMERS SANITARY COFFEE & BUTTER STORES
Acquired by Kroger Grocery & Baking Co. 00/00/1928
Details not available

CONSUMERS SOLAR ELEC PWR CORP (DE)
Charter cancelled and declared inoperative and void for non-payment of taxes 03/01/1983

CONSUMERS STEEL PRODUCTS CORP.
In process of liquidation 00/00/1941
Details not available

CONSUMERS UTILITIES CORP. (FL)
In process of liquidation
Each share Common 10¢ par exchanged for initial distribution of $1.44 principal amount of Manatee County, FL 1% Ser. B Bonds due 09/01/2005 and $0.80 cash 12/27/1965
Note: Details on subsequent distributions, if any, are not available

CONSUMERS WATERHEATER INCOME FD (ON)
Under plan of reorganization each Unit no par automatically became (1) share EnerCare Inc. (Canada) Common no par 01/05/2011
(See EnerCare Inc.)

CONSUMERS WTR CO (ME)
Common $1 par split (2) for (1) by issuance of (1) additional share 09/30/1983
Common $1 par split (2) for (1) by issuance of (1) additional share 09/30/1986
Stock Dividends - 10% 05/01/1959; 33.33333333% 06/28/1967
Merged into Philadelphia Surburban Corp. 03/10/1999
Each share 5.25% Preferred Ser. A $100 par exchanged for (5.649) shares Common 50¢ par
Each share Common $1 par exchanged for (1.432) shares Common 50¢ par
Philadelphia Suburban Corp. name changed to Aqua America, Inc. 01/16/2004

CONSURGICO CORP (DE)
Name changed to Chase Development Corp. 04/09/1979
(See Chase Development Corp.)

CONSYGEN INC (TX)
Company ceased operations 00/00/2002
Stockholders' equity unlikely

CONSYNE CORP (DE)
Reincorporated 06/11/1974
Common $1 par changed to 50¢ par and (1) additional share issued 06/12/1972
State of incorporation changed from (CA) to (DE) 06/11/1974
Merged into American Hospital Supply Corp. 02/28/1977
Each share Common 50¢ par exchanged for (0.34) share Common no par
American Hospital Supply Corp. merged into Baxter Travenol Laboratories, Inc. 11/25/1985 which name changed to Baxter International Inc. 05/18/1988

CONTACT CAPITAL GROUP INC. (FL)
Administratively dissolved 04/28/2003

CONTACT DIAMOND CORP (ON)
Acquired by Stornoway Diamond Corp. (BC) 01/17/2007
Each share Common no par exchanged for (0.36) share Common no par
Stornoway Diamond Corp. (BC) reincorporated in Canada 10/28/2011

CONTACT EXPL INC (AB)
Merged into Kicking Horse Energy Inc. 12/24/2014
Each share Common no par exchanged for (0.075) share Common no par
Note: Unexchanged certificates were cancelled and became without value 12/24/2017
(See Kicking Horse Energy Inc.)

CONTACT GOLD MINES LTD. (SK)
Recapitalized as Contact Ventures Ltd. (SK) 07/07/1969
Each share Common no par exchanged for (0.75) share Common no par
Contact Ventures Ltd. (SK) reincorporated in Canada 09/09/1982 which recapitalized as

West Pride Industries Corp. 04/15/1988 which recapitalized as Big Horn Resources Ltd. 09/07/1993 which merged into Westlinks Resources Ltd. 08/16/2001 which name changed to Enterra Energy Corp. 12/18/2001 which recapitalized as Enterra Energy Trust 11/25/2003 which reorganized as Equal Energy Ltd. 06/03/2010
(See Equal Energy Ltd.)

CONTACT IMAGE CORP (AB)
Assets sold for the benefit of creditors 00/00/2007
Stockholders' equity unlikely

CONTACT MINERALS CORP (NV)
Common $0.001 par split (2) for (1) by issuance of (1) additional share payable 02/09/2009 to holders of record 02/09/2009
Name changed to WECONNECT TECH INTERNATIONAL INC. 11/07/2017

CONTACT VENTURES LTD (CANADA)
Reincorporated 09/09/1982
Place of incorporation changed from (SK) to (Canada) 09/09/1982
Recapitalized as West Pride Industries Corp. 04/15/1988
Each share Common no par exchanged for (0.25) share Common no par
West Pride Industries Corp. recapitalized as Big Horn Resources Ltd. 09/07/1993 which merged into Westlinks Resources Ltd. 08/16/2001 which name changed to Enterra Energy Corp. 12/18/2001 which recapitalized as Enterra Energy Trust 11/25/2003 which reorganized as Equal Energy Ltd. 06/03/2010
(See Equal Energy Ltd.)

CONTAINER CORP AMER (DE)
Recapitalized 00/00/1935
Each share Preferred $100 par exchanged for (5) shares Capital Stock $20 par
Each share Class A $20 par exchanged for (1) share Capital Stock $20 par
Each share Class B no par exchanged for (0.4) share Capital Stock $20 par
Capital Stock $20 par reclassified as Common $20 par 00/00/1947
Each share Common $20 par exchanged for (2) shares Common $10 par 00/00/1950
Common $10 par changed to $5 par and (3) additional shares issued 10/11/1956
Stock Dividend - 25% 05/27/1954
4% Preferred $100 par called for redemption 11/01/1965
Merged into Marcor Inc. 11/01/1968
Each share Common $5 par exchanged for (1) share $2 Conv. Preferred Ser. A $1 par
Marcor Inc. merged into Mobil Corp. 07/01/1976 which merged into Exxon Mobil Corp. 11/30/1999

CONTAINER FGHT CORP (CA)
Merged out of existence 11/04/1981
Details not available

CONTAINER INDS INC (DE)
Plan of reorganization under Chapter 11 Federal Bankruptcy proceedings confirmed 01/26/1988
No stockholders' equity

CONTAINER TRANS SYS INC (MI)
Each share Common 5¢ par exchanged for (4) shares Common $0.0125 par 05/18/1971
Recapitalized as M.T.P.R. Corp. 03/09/1977
Each share Common $0.0125 par exchanged for (1) share Common no par
(See M.T.R.P. Corp.)

CONTAINERS SECURITIES CO.
Dissolved 00/00/1936
Details not available

CONTANGO OIL & GAS CO (NV)
Reorganized under the laws of Delaware 12/01/2000
Each share old Common 4¢ par exchanged for (0.5) share new Common 4¢ par

CONTAX PARTICIPACOES S A (BRAZIL)
ADR basis changed from (1:1) to (1:0.05) 11/22/2007
ADR basis changed from (1:0.05) to (1:0.2) 01/21/2010
ADR agreement terminated 01/13/2012
Each Sponsored ADR for Preferred exchanged for $2.525138 cash

CONTECH INC (MN)
Common 2¢ par split (2) for (1) by issuance of (1) additional share 11/28/1975
Stock Dividend - 100% 11/30/1971
Acquired by Rexnord Inc. 08/31/1982
Each share Common 2¢ par exchanged for $9 cash

CONTEL CELLULAR INC (DE)
Class A Common $1 par split (2) for (1) by issuance of (1) additional share 06/15/1989
Merged into GTE Corp. 05/12/1995
Each share Class A Common $1 par exchanged for $25.50 cash

CONTEL CORP (DE)
Common $1 par split (2) for (1) by issuance of (1) additional share 08/31/1989
5% Preferred 1961 Ser. $25 par called for redemption 01/01/1991
80¢ Conv. Preferred Ser. C no par called for redemption 01/31/1991
$1 Conv. Preferred Ser. D no par called for redemption 01/31/1991
80¢ Conv. Preferred Ser. E no par called for redemption 01/31/1991
Merged into GTE Corp. 03/14/1991
Each share Common $1 par exchanged for (1.27) shares Common 5¢ par
GTE Corp. merged into Verizon Communications Inc. 06/30/2000

CONTEL OF CALIFORNIA, INC. (CA)
4.75% Preferred Ser. A $20 par called for redemption 03/01/1994
5.25% Preferred $20 par called for redemption 03/01/1994
5.95% Preferred Ser. B $20 par called for redemption 03/01/1994

CONTEMPORARY AMERN INVS INC (MO)
Charter forfeited for failure to maintain a registered agent 12/22/1987

CONTEMPORARY ENVIRONMENTS INC (CA)
Capital Stock $4.40 par changed to $1 par 12/04/1970
Charter suspended 02/01/1973

CONTEMPORARY SOLUTIONS INC (NV)
Each share old Common 1¢ par exchanged for (0.002) share new Common 1¢ par 06/16/2006
SEC revoked common stock registration 08/21/2006
Stockholders' equity unlikely
Note: Company is also known as Sienna Broadcasting Corp.

CONTENDER RES LTD (BC)
Name changed to Strategic Communications Ltd. 08/29/1986
Strategic Communications Ltd. recapitalized as Stratcomm Media Ltd. (BC) 07/05/1991 which reincorporated in Yukon 11/12/1997
(See Stratcomm Media Ltd.)

CONTESSA CORP (DE)
Stock Dividend - 30.208% payable 03/27/2000 to holders of record 02/24/2000
Name changed to Fullcomm Technologies, Inc. 07/05/2000
Fullcomm Technologies, Inc. recapitalized as Amalgamated Technologies, Inc. 10/08/2002 which name changed to ProLink Holdings Corp. 01/26/2006
(See ProLink Holdings Corp.)

CONTEX ENTERPRISE GROUP INC (CO)
Name changed to Transportation Logistics International, Inc. 01/28/2001
Transportation Logistics International, Inc. name changed to Global Concepts, Ltd. 11/08/2004
(See Global Concepts, Ltd.)

CONTEXT ENERGY INC (AB)
Recapitalized as Ravenwood Resources Inc. 03/06/2001
Each share Common no par exchanged for (0.5) share Common no par
(See Ravenwood Resources Inc.)

CONTEXT INDS INC (FL)
Common $1 par changed to 10¢ par 06/23/1971
Merged into New Sub Inc. 12/23/1986
Each share Common 10¢ par exchanged for $0.15 cash

CONTI-MAC MINES LTD. (ON)
Charter revoked for failure to file reports and pay taxes 00/00/1957

CONTICCA INTERNATIONAL CORP. (DE)
No longer in existence having become inoperative and void for non-payment of taxes 4/1/65

CONTICO INTL INC (MO)
Merged into MICI, Inc. 01/08/1981
Each share Common 20¢ par exchanged for $8 cash

CONTIFINANCIAL CORP (DE)
Secondary Offering - 2,800,000 shares COM offered at $33 per share on 05/29/1997
Plan of reorganization under Chapter 11 Federal Bankruptcy Code effective 4/10/2001
No stockholders' equity

CONTIFINANCIAL CORP LIQUIDATING TR (DE)
Liquidation completed
Each Unit of Bene. Int. received initial distribution of $0.0135 cash payable 7/2/2001 to holders of record 6/18/2001
Each Unit of Bene. Int. received second distribution of $0.033 cash payable 11/8/2001 to holders of record 10/24/2001
Each Unit of Bene. Int. received third distribution of $0.01862 cash payable 1/15/2002 to holders of record 12/31/2001
Each Unit of Bene. Int. received fourth distribution of (0.05263157) Unit of Bene. Int. and $0.001 cash payable 2/28/2002 to holders of record 2/13/2002
Each Unit of Bene. Int. received fifth distribution of $0.0025 cash payable 4/1/2002 to holders of record 3/15/2002
Each Unit of Bene. Int. received sixth distribution of $0.01 cash payable 10/1/2002 to holders of record 9/16/2002 Ex date - 9/12/2002
Each Unit of Bene. Int. received seventh distribution of $0.015 cash payable 12/17/2002 to holders of record 12/2/2002 Ex date - 11/27/2002
Each Unit of Bene. Int. received eighth distribution of $0.008 cash payable 4/1/2003 to holders of record 3/13/2003 Ex date - 3/13/2003
Each Unit of Bene. Int. received ninth distribution of $0.005 cash payable 7/1/2003 to holders of record 6/16/2003
Each Unit of Bene. Int. received tenth distribution of $0.008 cash payable 1/20/2004 to holders of record 1/5/2004 Ex date - 3/13/2003
Each Unit of Bene. Int. received eleventh distribution of $0.005 cash payable 10/1/2004 to holders of record 9/16/2004 Ex date - 9/14/2004
Each Unit of Bene. Int. received twelfth distribution of $0.035 cash payable 4/11/2005 to holders of record 3/28/2005 Ex date - 3/23/2005
Each Unit of Bene. Int. received thirteenth distribution of $0.011 cash payable 10/5/2005 to holders of record 9/20/2005 Ex date - 9/16/2005
Each Unit of Bene. Int. received fourteenth distribution of $0.012 cash payable 1/5/2006 to holders of record 12/21/2005 Ex date - 12/19/2005
Each Unit of Bene. Int. received fifteenth distribution of (0.01907) Unit of Bene. Int. and $0.00512 cash payable 4/17/2007 to holders of record 4/2/2007 Ex date - 3/29/2007
Each Unit of Bene. Int. received sixteenth and final distribution of $0.004433 cash payable 02/29/2008 to holders of record 02/14/2008
Note: Certificates were not required to be surrendered and are without value

CONTIKI RES LTD (BC)
Name changed to Goldengoals.Com Ventures Inc. 08/31/1999
Goldengoals.Com Ventures Inc. recapitalized as General Strategies Ltd. 04/27/2001 which reorganized as Landdrill International Inc. 03/14/2006
(See Landdrill International Inc.)

CONTINAN COMMUNICATIONS INC (NV)
Recapitalized as XXX Acquisition Corp. 06/09/2009
Each share Common $0.001 par exchanged for (0.01) share Common $0.001 par
XXX Acquisition Corp. name changed to NightCulture, Inc. 09/20/2011
(See NightCulture, Inc.)

CONTINENT GROUP INC (AB)
Name changed to Popi Group Inc. 04/30/1999
Popi Group Inc. recapitalized as Damian Capital Corp. (AB) 09/17/2003 which reincorporated in Canada as CPVC Financial Inc. 05/15/2006 which merged into CPVC Financial Corp. 11/06/2006
(See CPVC Financial Corp.)

CONTINENT RES INC (BC)
Reincorporated 08/18/2008
Place of incorporation changed from (AB) to (BC) 08/18/2008
Reincorporated under the laws of Canada as Copper One Inc. 10/13/2009

CONTINENTAL ACCEP CORP (NC)
Each share Class B Common $1 par exchanged for (0.5) share 5% Class B Preference $3 par 02/09/1968
Merged into NCNB Corp. 04/03/1970
Each share 7% Class A Conv. Preference $1 par exchanged for (0.119918) share Common $5 par
Each share 5% Class B Conv. Preference $3 par exchanged for (0.191864) share Common $5 par
Each share Common $1 par exchanged for (0.095932) share Common $5 par
NCNB Corp. name changed to NationsBank Corp. 12/31/91 (NC) which reincorporated in Delaware as

BankAmerica Corp. (Old) 09/25/1998 which merged into BankAmerica Corp. (New) 09/30/1998 which name changed to Bank of America Corp. 04/28/1999

CONTINENTAL ACQUISITIONS INC (CO)
Name changed to Continental Art Galleries, Inc. 2/24/86
Continental Art Galleries, Inc. name changed to Quest Systems, Inc. 3/17/80
(See Quest Systems, Inc.)

CONTINENTAL AIR FILTERS INC (DE)
Recapitalized 07/24/1962
Class A $5 par reclassified as Preferred $8 par
Class B Common $1 par reclassified as Common $1 par
Preferred $8 par reclassified as Common $1 par 06/00/1968
Completely liquidated 08/15/1968
Each share Common $1 par exchanged for first and final distribution of $20.59 cash

CONTINENTAL AIRLS CORP (DE)
9% Conv. Preferred 10¢ par called for redemption 04/14/1986
Acquired by Texas Air Corp. 02/06/1987
Each share Common 1¢ par exchanged for $16.50 cash

CONTINENTAL AIRLS FIN TR (DE)
Each 8.50% Trust Originated Preferred Security exchanged for (2.068) shares Continental Airlines, Inc. Class B Common 1¢ par 01/00/1999
Continental Airlines, Inc. merged into United Continental Holdings, Inc. 10/01/2010

CONTINENTAL AIRLS HLDGS INC (DE)
Plan of reorganization under Chapter 11 Federal Bankruptcy proceedings effective 04/27/1993
No stockholders' equity

CONTINENTAL AIRLS INC (NV)
Capital Stock $1.25 par changed to 50¢ par and (2) additional shares issued 05/19/1967
Stock Dividend - 10% 03/28/1975
Merged into Texas Air Corp. 10/28/1982
Each share Capital Stock 50¢ par exchanged for (0.2) share 15% Preferred 10¢ par and (0.4) share Common 1¢ par
Texas Air Corp. name changed to Continental Airlines Holdings, Inc. 06/11/1990
(See Continental Airlines Holdings, Inc.)
CONTINENTAL AIRLINES, INC. (DE)
Class A Common 1¢ par split (2) for (1) by issuance of (1) additional share payable 07/16/1996 to holders of record 07/02/1996 Ex date - 07/17/1996
Class B Common 1¢ par split (2) for (1) by issuance of (1) additional share payable 07/16/1996 to holders of record 07/02/1996 Ex date - 07/17/1996
Each share Class A Common 1¢ par exchanged for (1.32) shares Class B Common 1¢ par 01/22/2001
Merged into United Continental Holdings, Inc. 10/01/2010
Each share Class B Common 1¢ par exchanged for (1.05) shares Common 1¢ par

CONTINENTAL ALLIANCE CORP (DE)
Liquidation completed
Each share Common 50¢ par exchanged for initial distribution of $1.25 cash 1/17/85
Each share Common 50¢ par received second and final distribution of $0.29 cash 4/11/85

CONTINENTAL AMERN ASSN INC (UT)
Recapitalized as Fountain of Youth, Inc. 1/23/73
Each share Common 1¢ par exchanged for (0.05) share Common 1¢ par
(See Fountain of Youth, Inc.)

CONTINENTAL AMERN INDS CORP (MA)
Proclaimed dissolved for failure to file reports and pay taxes 08/31/1998

CONTINENTAL AMERICAN LIFE INSURANCE CO. (TX)
Merged into Western States Life Insurance Co. (TX) 04/29/1966
Each share Common no par exchanged for (0.727273) share Common no par
Western States Life Insurance Co. (TX) name changed to Western States Life Insurance Co. of Texas 05/24/1966 which merged into Western Preferred Life Insurance Co. 01/01/1968 which merged into Western Preferred Corp. 08/23/1973
(See Western Preferred Corp.)

CONTINENTAL AMERN LIFE INS CO (DE)
Capital Stock $10 par changed to $5 par and (1) additional share issued 4/21/64
Stock Dividends - 100% 5/9/55; 50% 2/24/61; 25% 3/5/69; 50% 3/7/73
Merged into Crown Central Petroleum Corp. 1/4/80
Each share Capital Stock $5 par exchanged for (1) share Conv. Preferred Ser. A no par
(See Crown Central Petroleum Corp.)

CONTINENTAL AMERN RTY CO (SD)
Name changed to Conamer Liquidating Co. 7/17/72
(See Conamer Liquidating Co.)

CONTINENTAL AMERN TRANSN INC (CO)
Each share old Common $0.001 par exchanged for (0.04) share new Common $0.001 par 06/21/1995
Stock Dividend - 3% payable 02/15/1996 to holders of record 01/30/1996
SEC revoked common stock registration 06/24/2011

CONTINENTAL ART GALLERIES LTD (DE)
Stock Dividend - 100% 2/15/69
Name changed to Quest Systems, Inc. 3/17/80
Each share Capital Stock 1¢ par exchanged for (1) share Capital Stock 1¢ par
(See Quest Systems, Inc.)

CONTINENTAL ASSOC INC (MI)
Liquidation completed
Each share Common $1 par exchanged for initial distribution of $2.50 cash 10/8/76
Each share Common $1 par received second and final distribution of $3.50 cash 3/4/77

CONTINENTAL ASSOCIATED INDUSTRIES (UT)
Ceased operations 12/31/1974
No stockholders' equity

CONTINENTAL ASSURN CO (IL)
Common $10 par changed to $5 par and (1) additional share issued in 1954
Stock Dividends - 100% 12/22/44; 50% 6/30/48; 33-1/3% 7/12/50; 25% 10/15/51; 30% 12/29/52; (3) for (13) 4/20/56; 25% 5/1/59; 50% 6/20/61; 20% 6/20/63; 20% 6/15/65
Merged into CNA Financial Corp. 12/31/67
Each share Common $5 par exchanged for (2) shares Common $2.50 par

CONTINENTAL-ATLANTIC CORP. (DE)
Liquidation completed
Each share Common no par received initial distribution of $70 cash 12/26/1963
Each share Common no par received second and final distribution of $25.24 cash 12/02/1964
Note: Certificates were not required to be surrendered and are without value

CONTINENTAL AVIATION & ENGR CORP (VA)
Merged into Continental Motors Corp. 03/19/1969
Each share Common $1 par exchanged for $16 cash

CONTINENTAL BAKING CO (DE)
Recapitalized in 1941
Each share Class A Common no par exchanged for (3) shares Common no par
Each share Class B Common no par exchanged for (0.1) share Common no par
Each share 8% Preferred $100 par exchanged for (1.05) shares $5.50 Preferred no par and $7.50 cash in 1945
Common no par changed to $5 par 3/30/56
Common $5 par changed to $2.50 par and (1) additional share issued 6/10/67
Stock Dividend - 10% 10/19/55
Merged into International Telephone & Telegraph Corp. (DE) 9/13/68
Each share $5.50 Preferred no par exchanged for (1) share $5.50 Preferred Ser. L no par
Each share Common $2.50 par exchanged for (0.25) share $4 Conv. Preferred Ser. K no par and (0.72) share Common $1 par
International Telephone & Telegraph Corp. (DE) name changed to ITT Corp. 12/31/83 which reorganized in Indiana as ITT Industries, Inc. 12/19/95

CONTINENTAL BAKING CORP.
Merged into Continental Baking Co. 03/08/1939
Each share 8% Non-Vtg. Preferred exchanged for (1) share 8% Preferred $100 par
Each share Class A Common exchanged for (1) share Class A Common no par
Each share Class B Common exchanged for (1) share Class B Common no par
Continental Baking Co. merged into International Telephone & Telegraph Corp. (DE) 09/13/1968 which name changed to ITT Corp. 12/31/1983 which reorganized in Indiana as ITT Industries, Inc. 12/19/1995 which name changed to ITT Corp. 07/01/2006

CONTINENTAL BANCOR, INC. (AZ)
Merged into Chase Manhattan Corp. 10/02/1986
Each share Common $25 par exchanged for $78.79 cash

CONTINENTAL BANCORP (CA)
Merged into Western Commercial (CA) 12/30/1983
Each share Common no par exchanged for (1.65) shares Common no par
Western Commercial (CA) reincorporated in Delaware as Western Commercial, Inc. 07/27/1987 which merged into ValliCorp Holdings, Inc. 11/30/1989 which merged into Westamerica Bancorporation 04/12/1997

CONTINENTAL BANCORP INC (PA)
Merged into Midlantic Corp. 01/30/1987
Each share Common $5 par exchanged for (1.4302) shares Common $3 par
Midlantic Corp. merged into PNC Bank Corp. 12/31/1995 which name changed to PNC Financial Services Group, Inc. 03/15/2000

CONTINENTAL BANCORPORATION (NJ)
Merged into Collective Bancorp, Inc. 10/01/1996
Each share Common $2 par exchanged for $5 cash

CONTINENTAL BANCORPORATION (NV)
Merged into First Security Corp. 11/29/1993
Details not available

CONTINENTAL BANK & TRUST CO. (SPRINGFIELD, VA)
Merged into Dominion Bankshares 00/00/1986
Details not available

CONTINENTAL BK & TR CO (HOUSTON, TX)
Name changed to Continental Bank (Houston, TX) 02/09/1966
Continental Bank (Houston, TX) reorganized as Allied Bancshares, Inc. (TX) 12/29/1972 which reincorporated in Delaware 04/22/1987 which merged into First Interstate Bancorp 01/29/1988 which merged into Wells Fargo & Co. (Old) 04/01/1996 which merged into Wells Fargo & Co. (New) 11/02/1998

CONTINENTAL BK & TR CO (NORRISTOWN, PA)
Name changed to Continental Bank (Norristown, PA) 07/17/1969
Continental Bank (Norristown, PA) reorganized as Continental Bancorp, Inc. 05/01/1982 which merged into Midlantic Corp. 01/30/1987 which merged into PNC Bank Corp. 12/31/1995 which name changed to PNC Financial Services Group, Inc. 03/15/2000

CONTINENTAL BK & TR CO (SALT LAKE CITY, UT)
Each share Capital Stock $100 par exchanged for (10) shares Capital Stock $10 par plus a 100% stock dividend paid 02/01/1952
Stock Dividends - 50% 07/15/1960; 20% 11/20/1962
Merged into Moore Financial Group Inc. 11/01/1985
Each share Capital Stock $10 par exchanged for $138.1466 cash
Note: An additional final distribution of $16.09 cash per share was made 11/03/1986

CONTINENTAL BK & TR CO NEW (MILWAUKEE, WI)
99% owned by Continental Bank & Trust Holding Co. as of 00/00/1984
Public interest eliminated

CONTINENTAL BK & TR CO OLD (MILWAUKEE, WI)
Merged into Continental Bank & Trust Co. (New) (Milwaukee, WI) 12/31/1983
Each share Common $5 par exchanged for (0.0914) share Common $10 par
(See Continental Bank & Trust Co. (New) (Milwaukee, WI))

CONTINENTAL BK (ALHAMBRA, CA)
Common $5 par changed to $2.50 par and (1) additional share issued 04/22/1974
Common $2.50 par changed to $1.25 par and (1) additional share issued 08/15/1978
Stock Dividends - 10% 06/01/1979; 12% 05/30/1980

Acquired by Tokai Bank of California (Los Angeles, CA) 12/18/1981
Each share Common $1.25 par exchanged for $23.50 cash

CONTINENTAL BK (CLEVELAND, OH)
Common $10 par changed to $5 par and (1) additional share issued 02/28/1969
Stock Dividend - 15% 10/15/1974
Name changed to Continental Western Reserve Co. 03/31/1976
(See Continental Western Reserve Co.)

CONTINENTAL BK (GARDEN CITY, NY)
Merged into Reliance Bancorp, Inc. 10/20/1997
Each share Common $5 par exchanged for (1.1) shares Common 1¢ par
Reliance Bancorp, Inc. merged into North Fork Bancorporation, Inc. 02/18/2000 which merged into Capital One Financial Corp. 12/01/2006

CONTINENTAL BK (HOUSTON, TX)
Common $10 par changed to $2.50 par and (4) additional shares issued plus a 10% stock dividend paid 11/15/1966
Reorganized as Allied Bancshares, Inc. (TX) 12/29/1972
Each share Common $2.50 par exchanged for (1) share Common $1 par
Allied Bancshares, Inc. (TX) reincorporated in Delaware 04/22/1987 which merged into First Interstate Bancorp 01/29/1988 which merged into Wells Fargo & Co. (Old) 04/01/1996 which merged into Wells Fargo & Co. (New) 11/02/1998

CONTINENTAL BK (LOS ANGELES, CA)
Common $10 par and VTC's for Common $10 par changed to $6.66666666 par and (0.5) additional share issued respectively 05/20/1964
Voting Trust Agreement terminated 03/01/1968
Each VTC for Common $6.66666666 par exchanged for (1) share Common $6.66666666 par
Merged into United States National Bank (San Diego, CA) 08/30/1968
Each share Common $6.66666666 par exchanged for (0.5435432) share Capital Stock $10 par
(See United States National Bank (San Diego, CA))

CONTINENTAL BK (NORRISTOWN, PA)
Under plan of reorganization each share Capital Stock $5 par automatically became (1) share Continental Bancorp, Inc. Common $5 par 05/01/1982
Continental Bancorp, Inc. merged into Midlantic Corp. 01/30/1987 which merged into PNC Bank Corp. 12/31/1995 which name changed to PNC Financial Services Group, Inc. 03/15/2000

CONTINENTAL BK (PHOENIX, AZ)
Common $5 par changed to $2.50 par and (1) additional share issued 10/31/1972
Acquired by Chase Manhattan Corp. 10/02/1986
Each share Common $2.50 par exchanged for $79.97 cash

CONTINENTAL BK CDA (TORONTO, ONT)
Floating Rate Retractable Class A Ser. II no par called for redemption 11/27/1989
In process of liquidation
Each share Common no par received initial distribution of (1) share Floating Rate Retractable Preferred Class A Ser. II no par 05/25/1987
Each share Common no par received second distribution of $0.50 cash 12/00/1992
Each share Common no par received third distribution of $0.50 cash 05/00/1994
Name changed to CBOC Continental Inc. 10/22/1996
CBOC Continental Inc. reorganized as Coastal Group Inc. 04/17/2001 which merged into Continental (CBOC) Corp. 08/30/2002 which name changed to Stonington Capital Corp. 06/22/2004 which merged into Pyxis Capital Inc. 02/27/2006
(See Pyxis Capital Inc.)

CONTINENTAL BK CORP (DE)
Merged into BankAmerica Corp. (Old) 08/31/1994
Each share Adjustable Rate Preferred Ser. 1 no par exchanged for (1) share Adjustable Rate Preferred Ser. 1 no par
(See BankAmerica Corp. (Old))
Each share Common $4 par exchanged for $38.297 cash
Depositary Preferred Ser. 2 called for redemption 12/15/1994
Adjustable Rate Preferred Ser. 2 no par called for redemption 12/15/1994
Public interest eliminated

CONTINENTAL BK NJ (GLOUCESTER TWP, NJ)
Each share old Common $2 par exchanged for (0.25) share new Common $2 par 11/01/1985
Reorganized as Continental Bancorporation 07/01/1989
Each share Common $2 par exchanged for (1) share Common $2 par
(See Continental Bancorporation)

CONTINENTAL BANK OF NEW JERSEY (MAPLE SHADE, NJ)
Common $10 par changed to $5 par and (1) additional share issued 02/18/1970
Reorganized as Citizens Bancorp (NJ) 02/14/1972
Each share Common $5 par exchanged for (1.4375) shares Capital Stock no par
(See Citizens Bancorp (NJ))

CONTINENTAL BANKERS LIFE INS CO (MN)
100% acquired by GL Enterprises, Inc. through voluntary exchange offer as of 04/30/1971
Public interest eliminated

CONTINENTAL BENEFIT CORP (UT)
Charter suspended for failure to file annual reports 02/01/1992

CONTINENTAL BEVERAGE & NUTRITION INC (DE)
SEC revoked common stock registration 10/07/2008

CONTINENTAL BOAT CORP. (FL)
Name changed to Continental Diversified Industries, Inc. (FL) 05/12/1961
Continental Diversified Industries, Inc. (FL) reincorporated in Delaware 08/02/1968
(See Continental Diversified Industries, Inc. (Del.))

CONTINENTAL BODY, INC. (MI)
Charter revoked for failure to file reports and pay fees 05/15/1966

CONTINENTAL BUILDING CORP. (MO)
Liquidation completed 00/00/1953
Details not available

CONTINENTAL CABLEVISION INC (DE)
Merged into U.S. West, Inc. (Old) 11/15/1996
Each share Class A Common 1¢ par exchanged for (0.246394) share Conv. Preferred Ser. D 1¢ par and (0.246394) share Common-Media Group 1¢ par
Each share Class B Common 1¢ par exchanged for (0.075076) share Conv. Preferred Ser. D 1¢ par, (0.841920) share Common-Media Group 1¢ par and $8.56586 cash
(See U.S. West, Inc. (Old))

CONTINENTAL CAN INC (DE)
Merged into Suiza Foods Corp. 05/29/1998
Each share Common 25¢ par exchanged for (0.629) share Common 1¢ par
Suiza Foods Corp. name changed to Dean Foods Co. (New) 12/21/2001

CONTINENTAL CAN INC (NY)
$4.25 2nd Preferred no par called for redemption 07/20/1954
Common no par changed to $20 par 00/00/1932
Common $20 par changed to $10 par 10/26/1956
$4.50 2nd Preferred no par called for redemption 02/20/1959
Common $10 par changed to $5 par 04/27/1966
Common $5 par split (3) for (2) by issuance of (0.5) additional share 09/15/1966
Each share $3.75 Preferred no par exchanged for (1) share $4.25 Preferred no par 04/23/1969
Common $5 par changed to $1 par 04/23/1969
Common $1 par split (3) for (2) by issuance of (0.5) additional share 09/14/1970
Stock Dividend - 100% 02/15/1956
Name changed to Continental Group, Inc. 04/27/1976
Continental Group, Inc. merged into KMI Continental Inc. 11/02/1984
(See KMI Continental Inc.)

CONTINENTAL CAP CORP (CA)
Capital Stock $10 par changed to $5 par and (1) additional share issued 02/21/1969
In process of liquidation
Each share Capital Stock $5 par received initial distribution of $7.50 cash 01/31/1980
Each share Capital Stock $5 par received second distribution of (0.16666666) share Dataproducts Corp. Common 10¢ par 08/01/1980
(See Dataproducts Corp.)
Assets transferred to Continental Capital Liquidating Trust 08/29/1980
(See Continental Capital Liquidating Trust)

CONTINENTAL CAP CORP (CO)
Recapitalized as RFID Ltd. 06/21/2005
Each share Common $0.001 par exchanged for (0.01) share Common $0.001 par
RFID Ltd. name changed to OptimizeRx Corp. (CO) 04/30/2008 which reincorporated in Nevada 09/04/2008

CONTINENTAL CAP RES INC (TX)
Name changed to Concap Inc. 08/29/1996
Concap Inc. name changed to Elite Technologies, Inc. 04/29/1999
(See Elite Technologies, Inc.)

CONTINENTAL CAPITAL LIQUIDATING TRUST (CA)
Liquidation completed
Each Unit of Bene. Int. received initial distribution of (1) share KLA Instruments Corp. Common $0.001 par 02/13/1981
Each Unit of Bene. Int. received second distribution of (0.1) share General Signal Corp. Common $1 par 12/15/1981
Each Unit of Bene. Int. received third distribution of (0.33333333) share Computer Associates International, Inc. Common 10¢ par 02/03/1983
Each Unit of Bene. Int. received fourth distribution of (0.25) share Masstor Systems Corp. (CA) Common no par 09/13/1983
Each Unit of Bene. Int. received fifth distribution of (0.5) share Baron Data Systems Common 10¢ par 01/31/1984
Each Unit of Bene. Int. received sixth distribution of $0.50 cash 04/10/1984
Each Unit of Bene. Int. received seventh distribution of $10 cash 09/11/1985
Each Unit of Bene. Int. received eighth distribution of $2 cash 12/10/1986
Each Unit of Bene. Int. received ninth distribution of $0.15 cash 08/31/1987
Each Unit of Bene. Int. received tenth and final distribution of $0.50 cash 11/30/1987

CONTINENTAL CAR-NA-VAR CORP. (IN)
Stock Dividend - 20% 11/28/1953
Under plan of merger name changed to Continental Industries, Inc. (IN) and Common $1 par changed to 10¢ par 08/31/1956
Continental Industries, Inc. (IN) name changed to Continental Vending Machine Corp. 03/08/1961
(See Continental Vending Machine Corp.)

CONTINENTAL CARETECH CORP (ON)
Name changed to Corona Gold Corp. (Old) 05/17/1996
Corona Gold Corp. (Old) reorganized as Corona Gold Corp. (New) 06/13/2002 which merged into Oban Mining Corp. 08/27/2015 which name changed to Osisko Mining Inc. 06/21/2016

CONTINENTAL CASH TECHNOLOGIES CORP (ON)
Reincorporated 07/06/2004
Place of incorporation changed from (AB) to (ON) 07/06/2004
Name changed to Cenit Corp. 12/29/2004
Cenit Corp. name changed to Superior Copper Corp. 01/24/2012 which merged into Nighthawk Gold Corp. 05/30/2016

CONTINENTAL CASUALTY CO. (IL)
Each share Common $50 par exchanged for (5) shares Common $10 par 00/00/1926
Common $10 par changed to $5 par 00/00/1932
Common $5 par changed to $10 par 00/00/1944
Common $10 par changed to $5 par and (1) additional share issued 00/00/1954
Stock Dividends - 25% 07/12/1950; 33.33333333% 12/29/1952; 25% 04/20/1956; 100% 12/10/1959; 25% 06/20/1961
Merged into CNA Financial Corp. 12/31/1967
Each share Common $5 par exchanged for (1) share $1.10 Conv. Preferred Ser. A no par and (0.8) share Common $2.50 par

CONTINENTAL CBOC CORP (CANADA)
Name changed to Stonington Capital Corp. 06/22/2004
Stonington Capital Corp. merged into Pyxis Capital Inc. 02/27/2006
(See Pyxis Capital Inc.)

CONTINENTAL CHICAGO CORP.
Recapitalized as Chicago Corp. and Common no par changed to $1 par 00/00/1932
Chicago Corp. name changed to

Champlin Oil & Refining Co. 12/31/1956 which mereged into Celanese Corp. of America 10/29/1964 which name changed to Celanese Corp. 04/13/1966
(See Celanese Corp.)

CONTINENTAL CHOICE CARE INC (NJ)
Name changed to Techsys, Inc. 08/23/2000
(See Techsys, Inc.)

CONTINENTAL CINCH MINES LTD (BC)
Recapitalized as Gladiator Resources Ltd. (Incorporated June 25, 1959) 02/18/1974
Each share Capital Stock no par exchanged for (0.14285714) share Capital Stock no par
(See Gladiator Resources Ltd. (Incorporated June 25, 1959))

CONTINENTAL CIRCUITS CORP (DE)
Merged into Hadco Corp. 03/25/1998
Each share Common 1¢ par exchanged for $23.90 cash

CONTINENTAL COAL LIMITED (AUSTRALIA)
Each old Sponsored ADR for Ordinary exchanged for (0.4) new Sponsored ADR for Ordinary 09/14/2011
Basis changed from (1:40) to (1:10) 09/14/2011
ADR agreement terminated 08/31/2016
ADR holders' equity unlikely

CONTINENTAL COFFEE CO (DE)
Name changed to CFS Continental, Inc. 02/09/1973
(See CFS Continental, Inc.)

CONTINENTAL COMMERCIAL CORP. (PA)
Acquired by General Acceptance Corp. (New) 10/18/1967
Each share 6.5% Preferred $10 par exchanged for (0.1) share $6.50 Preference no par
Each share 6% Conv. Preferred $25 par exchanged for (2.5) shares 60¢ Preference no par
Each share 60¢ Preferred $10 par exchanged for (1) share 60¢ Preference no par
Each share Common $1 par exchanged for (0.4) share $1 Conv. Preference no par
General Acceptance Corp. (New) name changed to GAC Corp. (PA) 07/01/1968 which reincorporated in Delaware 12/20/1973
(See GAC Corp. (DE))

CONTINENTAL COMMUNITY BANK & TRUST CO. (AURORA, IL)
Acquired by First Banks, Inc. 07/31/2004
Details not available

CONTINENTAL COMPUTER ASSOC INC (PA)
Name changed to Banister Continental Corp. 07/22/1969
Banister Continental Corp. acquired by Banister Continental, Ltd. (AB) 04/02/1973 which reincorporated in Canada 01/10/1978 which name changed to Banister Inc. 06/04/1990 which name changed to Banister Foundation Inc. 06/13/1994 which name changed to BFC Construction Corp. 06/10/1997
(See BFC Construction Corp.)

CONTINENTAL CONNECTOR CORP (NY)
Class A $1 par changed to 50¢ par and (1) additional share issued 09/30/1959
Class A 50¢ par reclassified as Common 50¢ par 09/11/1968
Name changed to Dunes Hotels & Casinos Inc. 06/15/1979
(See Dunes Hotels & Casinos Inc.)

CONTINENTAL CONS INC (CA)
Charter suspended for failure to file reports or pay taxes 10/01/1971

CONTINENTAL CONSOLIDATED MINES & OILS CORP. LTD. (SK)
Charter cancelled 09/22/1961

CONTINENTAL CONSOLIDATED MINES LTD. (BC)
Recapitalized as Continental Cinch Mines Ltd. 09/22/1967
Each share Capital Stock 50¢ par exchanged for (0.1) share Capital Stock no par
Continental Cinch Mines Ltd. recapitalized as Gladiator Resources Ltd. (Incorporated June 25, 1959) 02/18/1974
(See Gladiator Resources Ltd. (Incorporated June 25, 1959))

CONTINENTAL CONVEYOR & EQUIP CO (AL)
Stock Dividends - 50% 03/01/1972; 100% 09/15/1975; 25% 12/14/1976; 10% 12/14/1977
Merged into Goodrich (B.F.) Co. 07/21/1978
Each share Common $1 par exchanged for either (4.0835) shares $0.975 Preferred Ser. B $1 par, (1.823) shares Common $5 par or $40.8352 cash
Note: Option to receive Preferred or Common stock expired 07/20/1978
Goodrich (B.F.) Co. name changed to Goodrich Corp. 06/01/2001
(See Goodrich Corp.)

CONTINENTAL COPPER & STL INDS INC (DE)
Stock Dividends - 10% 09/12/1955; 20% 09/30/1967; 10% 10/01/1979; 10% 10/01/1980; 10% 10/01/1981
Name changed to CCX, Inc. 12/01/1982
(See CCX, Inc.)

CONTINENTAL COPPER CORP (BC)
Name changed to Continental Energy Corp. 10/23/1997

CONTINENTAL COPPER MINES LTD (QC)
Name changed to Continental Resources Ltd. 12/04/1995
Continental Resources Ltd. recapitalized as C2C Inc. 07/26/2004 which name changed to C2C Gold Corp. Inc. 02/27/2008 which recapitalized as Key Gold Holding Inc. 03/11/2010 which recapitalized as Pangolin Diamonds Corp. 03/20/2013

CONTINENTAL CORP (DE)
Name changed to Continental Eastern Corp. 05/14/1968
(See Continental Eastern Corp.)

CONTINENTAL CORP (NY)
Common $2 par changed to $1 par and (1) additional share issued 05/15/1978
$2.50 Conv. Preferred Ser. A $4 par called for redemption 03/13/1995
$2.50 Conv. Preferred Ser. B $4 par called for redemption 03/13/1995
Stock Dividend - 10% 10/29/1971
Acquired by CNA Financial Corp. 05/10/1995
Each share Common $1 par exchanged for $20 cash

CONTINENTAL CREDIT CO.
Succeeded by Continental Credit Corp. 00/00/1931
Details not available

CONTINENTAL CREDIT CORP.
Acquired by Contract Purchase Corp. 00/00/1939
Details not available

CONTINENTAL CUSHION SPRING CO.
Acquired by Signode Steel Strapping Co. 00/00/1943
Details not available

CONTINENTAL DATA SYS INC (PA)
Name changed to Step-Saver Data Systems Inc. 07/22/1986
(See Step-Saver Data Systems Inc.)

CONTINENTAL DATANET INC (BC)
Struck off register and declared dissolved for failure to file returns 03/19/1993

CONTINENTAL DEVICE CORP. (DE)
Acquired by Teledyne, Inc. 08/07/1967
Each share Common no par exchanged for (0.25) share Conv. Preferred Ser. B $1 par
(See Teledyne, Inc.)

CONTINENTAL DIAMOND DRILLING & EXPLORATION CO. LTD. (ON)
Name changed to Continental Exploration Ltd. 00/00/1949
Continental Exploration Ltd. name changed to Conty Exploration Ltd. 12/14/1956 which liquidated for Canadian Faraday Corp. Ltd. 01/04/1962 which merged into Consolidated Canadian Faraday Ltd. 05/04/1967 which name changed to Faraday Resources Inc. 08/02/1983 which merged into Conwest Exploration Co. Ltd. (New) (AB) 09/01/1993 which merged into Alberta Energy Co. Ltd. 01/31/1996 which merged into EnCana Corp. 01/03/2003

CONTINENTAL DIAMOND FIBRE CO. (DE)
Capital Stock no par changed to $5 par 00/00/1932
Name changed to Haveg Industries, Inc. 06/30/1955
Haveg Industries, Inc. acquired by Hercules Powder Co. 07/31/1964 which name changed to Hercules Inc. 04/29/1966
(See Hercules Inc.)

CONTINENTAL DIVERSIFIED INDUSTRIES (AZ)
Charter cancelled for failure to file reports or pay fees 06/28/1976

CONTINENTAL DIVERSIFIED INDS INC (DE)
Reincorporated 08/02/1968
Each share Common 10¢ par exchanged for (0.1) share Common $1 par 07/09/1964
State of incorporation changed from (FL) to (DE) 08/02/1968
Merged into CDI Acquisition Corp. 07/26/1985
Each share Common $1 par exchanged for $10 cash

CONTINENTAL DIVIDE DEVELOPMENT CO. (CO)
Charter dissolved for failure to file annual reports 10/15/1936

CONTINENTAL DIVIDE URANIUM CO., INC. (DE)
Dissolved 01/14/1958
Details not available

CONTINENTAL DRUG CORP (NY)
Dissolved by proclamation 09/25/1991

CONTINENTAL DYNAMICS INC (UT)
Reorganized under the laws of Nevada as Continental Dynamics, Ltd. 03/15/1971
Each share Capital Stock 1¢ par exchanged for (1) share Capital Stock 1¢ par
Note: After 05/25/1971 certificates surrendered for exchange must be accompanied by proof of ownership and when and from whom shares were obtained
(See Continental Dynamics, Ltd.)

CONTINENTAL DYNAMICS LTD (NV)
Charter revoked for failure to file reports and pay fees 11/01/1981

CONTINENTAL EASTERN CORP. (DE)
Charter cancelled and declared inoperative and void for non-payment of taxes 03/01/1978

CONTINENTAL ELECTRIC EQUIPMENT CO. (OH)
Each share old Class A no par exchanged for (10) shares new Class A no par 07/31/1953
Each share old Class B no par exchanged for (10) shares new Class B no par 07/31/1953
New Class A no par changed to Common no par 09/28/1954
New Class B no par changed to Common no par 09/28/1954
Common no par split (2) for (1) by issuance of (1) additional share 06/28/1957
Name changed to Multnomah Co. 10/17/1962
Multnomah Co. name changed to General Color Graphics, Inc. 12/10/1969
(See General Color Graphics, Inc.)

CONTINENTAL ELECTRS INC (MN)
Common 5¢ par changed to 1¢ par 12/11/1970
Name changed to Kwantra National, Inc. 07/13/1972
(See Kwantra National, Inc.)

CONTINENTAL EMBASSY ACQUISITIONS INC (UT)
Each share old Common $0.001 par exchanged for (0.001) share new Common $0.001 par 01/16/1995
Reorganized under the laws of Delaware as You Bet International, Inc. 12/06/1995
Each share new Common $0.001 par exchanged for (1.5) shares Common $0.001 par
You Bet International, Inc. name changed to Youbet.com, Inc. 01/22/1999 which merged into Churchill Downs, Inc. 06/02/2010

CONTINENTAL ENERGY & NUCLEAR CORP (MT)
Name changed to Casino Gaming Systems, Inc. 10/22/1979
Casino Gaming Systems, Inc. recapitalized as Allison Industries, Ltd. 10/07/1982
(See Allison Industries, Ltd.)

CONTINENTAL ENERGY CORP. (IL)
Proclaimed dissolved for failure to pay taxes and file reports 12/01/1982

CONTINENTAL ENERGY CORP (CO)
Adjudicated bankrupt 09/24/1973
Stockholders' equity unlikely

CONTINENTAL ENERGY CORP (TX)
Name changed to Absol, Co. 04/22/1987
Absol, Co. name changed to Group Nine Financial Corp. 06/16/1988
(See Group Nine Financial Corp.)

CONTINENTAL ENGINEERING & MANAGEMENT CORP.
Name changed to Republic Industries, Inc. 00/00/1945
(See Republic Industries, Inc.)

CONTINENTAL ENGINEERING CO.
Name changed to New Mexico Copper Mining Co. 00/00/1951
New Mexico Copper Mining Co. recapitalized as New Mexico Copper Corp. 00/00/1952
(See New Mexico Copper Corp.)

CONTINENTAL ENTERPRISES INC (DE)
Recapitalized as Daylight Industries, Inc. 07/15/1968
Each share Capital Stock 10¢ par exchanged for (0.5) share Capital Stock 20¢ par
Daylight Industries, Inc. recapitalized as ThermaFreeze Products Corp. 08/18/2006

CONTINENTAL EXPL & DEV LTD (ON)
Recapitalized as Conex Continental Inc. 04/25/1996
Each share Common no par exchanged for (0.2) share Common no par
Conex Continental Inc. name changed to Dominion International Investments Inc. 03/05/2001
(See Dominion International Investments Inc.)

CONTINENTAL EXPLORATION LTD. (ON)
Name changed to Conty Exploration Ltd. 12/14/1956
Conty Exploration Ltd. liquidated for Canadian Faraday Corp. Ltd. 01/04/1962 which merged into Consolidated Canadian Faraday Ltd. 05/04/1967 which name changed to Faraday Resources Inc. 08/02/1983 which merged into Conwest Exploration Co. Ltd. (New) (AB) 09/01/1993 which merged into Alberta Energy Co. Ltd. 01/31/1996 which merged into EnCana Corp. 01/03/2003

CONTINENTAL FASHION GROUP INC (AB)
Reorganized under the laws of Canada as Genoil Inc. 08/07/1996
Each share Common no par exchanged for (0.1) share Common no par

CONTINENTAL FDG CORP (CA)
Name changed to C F C Financial Corp. 10/28/1970
C F C Financial Corp. name changed to Madison & Burke Capital 01/01/1973
(See Madison & Burke Capital)

CONTINENTAL FED SVGS & LN ASSN OKLA CITY OKLA (USA)
Placed in receivership 07/13/1989
No stockholders' equity

CONTINENTAL FID LIFE INS CO (AZ)
Stock Dividends - 12.5% 04/24/1964; 10% 04/26/1965; 10% 03/14/1966
Name changed to Unilife Insurance Co. (AZ) 05/23/1980
Unilife Insurance Co. (AZ) reincorporated in Delaware as Unilife Corp. 09/30/1982
(See Unilife Corp. (DE))

CONTINENTAL FID LIFE INS CO (TX)
Each share old Common no par exchanged for (0.14285714) share new Common no par 07/10/1969
Merged into Western Preferred Corp. 01/01/1977
Each share new Common no par exchanged for (1.399972) shares 8% Conv. Preferred Ser. A $5 par
(See Western Preferred Corp.)

CONTINENTAL FINANCE CO.
In process of liquidation 00/00/1945
Details not available

CONTINENTAL FIRE & CASUALTY INSURANCE CO.
Merged into Insurance Co. of Texas 00/00/1952
Each share Common $10 par exchanged for (1) share new Common $10 par and $3 cash
Insurance Co. of Texas name changed to ICT Insurance Co. 00/00/1954
(See ICT Insurance Co.)

CONTINENTAL FOOD MKTS CALIF INC (CA)
Charter suspended for failure to file reports and pay taxes 08/01/1974

CONTINENTAL FOOD STORES, INC.
Acquired by Mac Marr Stores, Inc. 00/00/1929
Details not available

CONTINENTAL FOUNDRY & MACHINE CO. (DE)
Stock Dividends - 10% 11/26/1951; 25% 02/29/1952
Completely liquidated 11/25/1958
Liquidating distributions were paid to holders of record without surrender of certificates for cancellation

CONTINENTAL FUELS INC (NV)
Old Common $0.001 par split (3) for (1) by issuance of (2) additional shares payable 04/20/2007 to holders of record 04/13/2007
Ex date - 04/23/2007
Each share old Common $0.001 par exchanged for (0.1) share new Common $0.001 par 05/12/2008
SEC revoked common stock registration 06/16/2011

CONTINENTAL FUND, INC. (FL)
Name changed to Manufacturers & Investors Corp. 08/19/1963
Manufacturers & Investors Corp. name changed to Landban of Florida Corp. 07/21/1970 which name changed to Transamerica Business Corp. 01/26/1977
(See Transamerica Business Corp.)

CONTINENTAL FUND DISTRIBUTORS, INC. (NY)
Charter cancelled and proclaimed dissolved for failure to pay taxes and file reports 12/15/1967

CONTINENTAL GAS & ELECTRIC CORP.
Dissolution approved 00/00/1950
Details not available

CONTINENTAL GEN CORP (NE)
Merged into Western & Southern Life Insurance Co. 04/11/1990
Each share Common 1¢ par exchanged for $10 cash

CONTINENTAL GENERAL INSURANCE CO. (NE)
Common $5 par changed to $3 par and (1) additional share issued 05/15/1964
Common $3 par changed to $1 par and (2) additional shares issued 05/15/1970
Common $1 par split (3) for (1) by issuance of (2) additional shares 05/07/1986
Stock Dividends - 20% 05/15/1967; 10% 05/15/1969; 10% 06/01/1974; 10% 06/01/1975; 10% 06/01/1976; 10% 03/01/1985; 10% 04/01/1987
Under plan of reorganization each share Common $1 par automatically became (1) share Continental General Corp. Common 1¢ par 05/01/1988
(See Continental General Corp.)

CONTINENTAL GIN CO., INC. (DE)
Name changed to Continental/Moss-Gordin Gin Co. 01/20/1965
Continental/Moss-Gordin Gin Co. name changed to Continental/Moss-Gordin Inc. 02/28/1966
(See Continental/Moss-Gordin Inc.)

CONTINENTAL GOLD & SILVER CORP (UT)
Charter suspended for failure to file reports 12/31/1975

CONTINENTAL GOLD CORP NEW (BC)
Acquired by Placer Dome Ltd. 11/19/1990
Each share Common no par exchanged for $20 cash

CONTINENTAL GOLD CORP OLD (BC)
Merged into Continental Gold Corp. (New) 03/15/1989
Each share Common no par exchanged for (1) share Common no par
(See Continental Gold Corp. (New))

CONTINENTAL GOLD LTD NEW (BERMUDA)
Reorganized under the laws of Ontario as Continental Gold Inc. 06/12/2015
Each share Common $0.0001 par exchanged for (1) share Common no par

CONTINENTAL GOLD LTD OLD (BERMUDA)
Each share Common $0.0001 par exchanged for (0.37074111) share Continental Gold Ltd. (New) (Bermuda) Common $0.0001 par 03/30/2010
Continental Gold Ltd. (New) (Bermuda) reorganized in Ontario as Continental Gold Inc. 06/12/2015

CONTINENTAL GOURMET CORP (DE)
Stock Dividend - 100% 09/10/1975
Charter cancelled and declared inoperative and void for non-payment of taxes 03/01/1986

CONTINENTAL GRAPHICS CORP (DE)
Acquired by a group of investors 11/02/1988
Each share Common $0.125 par exchanged for $17 cash

CONTINENTAL GROUP INC (NY)
Common $1 par split (3) for (2) by issuance of (0.5) additional share 03/15/1984
Merged into KMI Continental Inc. 11/02/1984
Each share $4.25 Preferred no par exchanged for (1) share $4.25 Preferred no par
Each share $4.50 Preference Ser. C $1 par exchanged for (1) share $4.50 Preference Ser. C $1 par
Each share $2.10 Conv. Preference Ser. B $1 par exchanged for $43.875 cash
Each share $2 Conv. Preference Ser. A $1 par exchanged for $29.25 cash
Each share Common $1 par exchanged for $58.50 cash
(See KMI Continental Inc.)

CONTINENTAL GROWTH FD INC (MD)
Acquired by National Investors Corp. (MD) 12/7/64
Each share Capital Stock 1¢ par exchanged for (0.395772) share Capital Stock $1 par
National Investors Corp. (MD) name changed to Seligman Growth Fund, Inc. 5/1/82

CONTINENTAL HAIR PRODS INC (DE)
Stock Dividends - 15% 5/1/74; 20% 6/30/75
Name changed to Conair Corp. (DE) 5/21/76
(See Conair Corp. (DE))

CONTINENTAL HEALTH AFFILIATES INC (DE)
Stock Dividend - 25% 2/8/85
Recapitalized as Kuala Healthcare, Inc. 1/28/98
Each share Common 2¢ par exchanged for (1/3) share Common 2¢ par
(See Kuala Healthcare, Inc.)

CONTINENTAL HEALTHCARE SYS INC (DE)
Merged into TBG Inc. 6/10/86
Each share Common 1¢ par exchanged for $9 cash

CONTINENTAL HERITAGE CORP (DE)
Name changed to Visionquest Worldwide Holdings Corp. 08/12/1999
(See Visionquest Worldwide Holdings Corp.)

CONTINENTAL HOMES HLDG CORP (DE)
Merged into D.R. Horton Inc. 4/20/98
Each share Common 1¢ par exchanged for (2.25) shares Common 1¢ par

CONTINENTAL HOSTS LTD (DE)
Merged into Continental Hosts Acquisition Corp. 2/28/85
Each share Common 5¢ par exchanged for $12 cash
Note: An additional payment of $4.945373 cash per share in settlement of litigation was made in 1996

CONTINENTAL ILL CORP (DE)
Common $10 par changed to $5 par and (1) additional share issued 06/06/1977
Reorganized as Continental Illinois Holding Corp. 09/27/1984
Each share old Common $5 par exchanged for (1) share Common $1 par
(See Continental Illinois Holding Corp.)
Recapitalized as Continental Bank Corp. 12/13/1988
Each share new Common $1 par exchanged for (0.25) share Common $4 par
Preferred not affected except for change of name
Continental Bank Corp. merged into BankAmerica Corp. (Old) 08/31/1994
(See BankAmerica Corp. (Old))

CONTINENTAL ILL HLDG CORP (DE)
Charter dissolved 12/20/1989
No stockholders' equity

CONTINENTAL ILL NATL BK & TR CO (CHICAGO, IL)
Capital Stock $33-1/3 par changed to $10 par and (2-1/3) additional shares issued plus a 20% stock dividend paid 08/16/1963
Stock Dividends - 20% 12/28/1943; 25% 02/25/1952; 20% 02/27/1956; 11-1/9% 02/24/1958; 10% 02/15/1965; 10% 02/15/1968
Reorganized under the laws of Delaware as Conill Corp. 03/31/1969
Each share Capital Stock $10 par exchanged for (1) share Common $10 par
Conill Corp. name changed to Continental Illinois Corp. 03/27/1972 which reorganized as Continental Illinois Holding Corp. 09/27/1984
(See Continental Illinois Holding Corp.)

CONTINENTAL ILL PPTYS (CA)
Shares of Bene. Int. $1 par reclassified as Common $1 par 03/14/1977
Name changed to Pan-American Properties 10/01/1979
Pan-American Properties merged into Pan-American Properties, Inc. 01/15/1981
(See Pan-American Properties, Inc.)

CONTINENTAL ILL RLTY (CA)
Merged into W.L. Realty Co. 12/12/79
Each Share of Bene. Int. $1 par exchanged for $11 cash

CONTINENTAL ILLINOIS CO.
Liquidated in 1934
Details not available

CONTINENTAL INC (DE)
Merged into Guardian Industries Corp. 12/31/93
Details not available

CONTINENTAL INDEPENDENT TELEPHONE CORP. (DE)
5% Conv. Preferred $25 par called for redemption 9/3/64
Name changed to Continental Telephone Corp. 5/11/65
Continental Telephone Corp. name

FINANCIAL INFORMATION, INC.   CON-CON

changed to Continental Telecom Inc. 5/6/82 which name changed to Contel Corp. 5/1/86 which merged into GTE Corp. 3/14/91 which merged into Verizon Communications Inc. 6/30/2000

CONTINENTAL INDUSTRIES, INC. (DC)
Reorganized under the laws of Delaware as Ecological Recycling Co. 4/25/71
Each share Common 1¢ par exchanged for (0.2) share Common 1¢ par
(See Ecological Recycling Co.)

CONTINENTAL INDUSTRIES, INC. (IN)
Name changed to Continental Vending Machine Corp. 3/8/61
(See Continental Vending Machine Corp.)

CONTINENTAL INFORMATION SYS CORP NEW (NY)
Company terminated common stock registration and is no longer public as of 10/15/2003

CONTINENTAL INFORMATION SYS CORP OLD (NY)
Common 3¢ par split (3) for (2) by issuance of (0.5) additional share 12/13/1982
Common 3¢ par split (2) for (1) by issuance of (1) additional share 07/25/1983
Common 3¢ par split (2) for (1) by issuance of (1) additional share 06/03/1986
Stock Dividends - 10% 09/11/1978; 10% 12/15/1981; 10% 12/05/1984; 10% 10/16/1985; 10% 06/02/1987
Recapitalized as Continental Information Systems Corp. (New) 12/21/1994
Each (60) shares Common 3¢ par exchanged for (1) share Common 3¢ par
(See Continental Information Systems Corp. (New))

CONTINENTAL INS CO (NY)
Each share Common $25 par exchanged for (2.5) shares Common $10 par in 1927
Common $10 par changed to $2.50 par in 1932
Common $2.50 par changed to $10 par in 1945
Common $10 par changed to $5 par and (1) additional share issued 3/15/56
Stock Dividends - 25% 3/20/50; 10% 7/17/59
Acquired by Continental Corp. (NY) 12/1/69
Each share Common $5 par exchanged for $101 cash

CONTINENTAL INVESTMENT CORP. (OH)
Acquired for cash by General Contract Finance Corp. 8/1/64

CONTINENTAL INVT CORP (AZ)
Charter revoked for failure to file reports or pay fees 12/20/71

CONTINENTAL INVT CORP (GA)
Each share old Common 50¢ par exchanged for (1) share new Common 50¢ par 9/29/2000
Liquidation completed
Each share new Common 50¢ par received initial distribution of $0.27 cash payable 8/23/2002 to holders of record 8/16/2002
Each share new Common 50¢ par received second distribution of $0.37 cash payable 7/8/2004 to holders of record 7/1/2004 Ex date - 7/9/2004
Each share new Common 50¢ par received third and final distribution of $0.03 cash payable 5/25/2007 to holders of record 5/17/2007
Ex date - 5/29/2007
Note: Certificates were not required to be surrendered and are without value

CONTINENTAL INVT CORP (MA)
Common $1 par split (3) for (1) by issuance of (2) additional shares 08/20/1969
Reorganized as ConVest Energy Corp. 10/26/1981
Each share Common $1 par exchanged for (1) share Common 1¢ par and $2.60 cash
(See ConVest Energy Corp.)

CONTINENTAL INVS LIFE INS INC (CO)
Reorganized 11/9/77
Under plan of reorganization each share of Continental Investors Life Insurance Co. Inc. Common 1¢ par automatically became (1) share Continental Investors Life, Inc. Common $1 par 11/9/77
Common $1 par split (3) for (2) by issuance of (0.5) additional share 3/1/84
Common $1 par split (3) for (2) by issuance of (0.5) additional share 7/2/85
Common $1 par split (3) for (2) by issuance of (0.5) additional share 10/15/86
Stock Dividend - 50% 8/1/81
Name changed to Citizens, Inc. and Common $1 par reclassified as Class A Common no par 12/1/88

CONTINENTAL IRON & TITANIUM MINING LTD. (QC)
Name changed to Continental Titanium Corp. in 1960
(See Continental Titanium Corp.)

CONTINENTAL KIRKLAND MINES LTD (ON)
Charter cancelled and company declared dissolved for default in filing returns 12/30/1970

CONTINENTAL LEAD MINES LTD. (ON)
Charter cancelled by Province of Ontario for default in 1956

CONTINENTAL LEASING INC (MA)
Name changed to Continental Resources, Inc. 5/10/77

CONTINENTAL LIFE & ACC CO (ID)
Common $2 par and VTC's for Common $2 par changed to 50¢ par and (3) additional shares issued respectively 07/01/1964
Voting Trust terminated and each VTC for Common 50¢ par automatically became (1) share Common 50¢ par 08/11/1973
Common 50¢ par changed to $1 par 05/10/1982
Stock Dividends - 33-1/3% 03/12/1954; 16-2/3% 06/15/1962; 10% 07/25/1963; 10% 07/02/1965; 10% 05/20/1966; 10% 12/15/1969; 10% 02/25/1971; 10% 02/25/1972; 10% 02/26/1973; 10% 02/25/1974; 10% 02/27/1975
98.5% acquired by John Alden Life Insurance Co. through purchase offer which expired 01/13/1982
Public interest eliminated

CONTINENTAL LIFE INSURANCE CO. (DE)
Name changed to Continental American Life Insurance Co. (DE) in 1927
Continental American Life Insurance Co. (DE) merged into Crown Central Petroleum Corp. 1/4/80
(See Crown Central Petroleum Corp.)

CONTINENTAL LIFE INS CO (TX)
Acquired by United International Corp. (NV) 10/1/69
Each share Common $1 par exchanged for (0.5714) share Common $1 par
United International Corp. (NV) liquidated for Transport Life Insurance Co. 6/30/71
(See Transport Life Insurance Co.)

CONTINENTAL MGMT INC (NY)
Charter cancelled and proclaimed dissolved for failure to pay taxes 12/30/86

CONTINENTAL MFG CO (MO)
Name changed to Contico International, Inc. 9/12/69
(See Contico International, Inc.)

CONTINENTAL MCKINNEY MINES LTD (BC)
Recapitalized as Chandalar Resources Ltd. 6/13/73
Each share Capital Stock no par exchanged for (0.1) share Capital Stock no par
Chandalar Resources Ltd. merged into International Park West Financial Corp. 6/20/78
(See International Park West Financial Corp.)

CONTINENTAL MED SYS INC (DE)
Common 1¢ par split (3) for (2) by issuance of (0.5) additional share 11/15/1991
Merged into Horizon/CMS Healthcare Corp. 07/10/1995
Each share Common 1¢ par exchanged for (0.5397) share Common $0.001 par
Horizon/CMS Healthcare Corp. merged into HealthSouth Corp. 10/29/1997 which name changed to Encompass Health Corp. 01/02/2018

CONTINENTAL MINERALS CORP (BC)
Incorporated 02/07/1962
Acquired by Jinchuan Group Ltd. 04/29/2011
Each share Non-Vtg. Preferred no par exchanged for (0.5028) share Taseko Mines Ltd. Common no par
(See Taseko Mines Ltd.)
Each share Common no par exchanged for $2.60 cash
Note: Unexchanged certificates were cancelled and became without value 04/29/2017

CONTINENTAL MINERALS CORP (BC)
Incorporated 06/15/1970
Struck from the register and dissolved 03/06/1987

CONTINENTAL MINES LTD.
Acquired by Continental Kirkland Mines 00/00/1928
Each share Common exchanged for (0.2) share Common
(See Continental Kirkland Mines Ltd.)

CONTINENTAL MINING & OIL CORP. (DE)
Name changed to Cominol Industries, Inc. 12/29/1958
Cominol Industries, Inc. name changed to Shieldtron, Inc. 01/24/1962 which recapitalized as Ocean Research Equipment, Inc. 03/08/1968
(See Ocean Research Equipment, Inc.)

CONTINENTAL MINING CORP. LTD. (BC)
Merged into Continental Consolidated Mines Ltd. 00/00/1959
Each share Capital Stock exchanged for (0.33333333) share Capital Stock 50¢ par
Continental Consolidated Mines Ltd. recapitalized as Continental Cinch Mines Ltd. 09/22/1967 which recapitalized as Gladiator Resources Ltd. (Incorporated 06/25/1959) 02/18/1974
(See Gladiator Resources Ltd.)
(Incorporated 06/25/1959))

CONTINENTAL MINING EXPLORATION LTD. (ON)
Merged into Augustus Exploration Ltd. 11/26/1958
Each share Capital Stock $1 par exchanged for (1) share Capital Stock $1 par
Augustus Exploration Ltd. merged into Consolidated Canadian Faraday Ltd. 05/04/1967 which name changed to Faraday Resources Inc. 08/02/1983 which merged into Conwest Exploration Co. Ltd. (New) (AB) 09/01/1993 which merged into Alberta Energy Co. Ltd. 01/31/1996 which merged into EnCana Corp. 01/03/2003

CONTINENTAL MNG INC (DE)
Charter cancelled and declared inoperative and void for non-payment of taxes 03/01/1976

CONTINENTAL MTG & EQUITY TR (CA)
Each old Share of Bene. Int. no par exchanged for (0.33333333) new Share of Bene. Int. no par 03/26/1990
Beneficial Stock Purchase Rights declared for Beneficial holders redeemed at $0.03 per right for holders of record 01/15/1992
New Shares of Bene. Int. no par split (3) for (2) by issuance of (0.5) additional share payable 03/01/1996 to holders of record 02/15/1996
Merged into Transcontinental Realty Investors, Inc. 11/30/1999
Each new Share of Bene. Int. no par exchanged for (1.181) shares new Common 1¢ par

CONTINENTAL MORTGAGE GUARANTEE CO.
Liquidated 00/00/1937
Details not available

CONTINENTAL MORTGAGE GUARANTEE HOLDING CO.
Name changed to Continental Realty Investing Co., Inc. 00/00/1937
(See Continental Realty Investing Co., Inc.)

CONTINENTAL MTG INS INC (WI)
Over 99% owned by Verex Corp. 00/00/1972
Public interest eliminated

CONTINENTAL/MOSS-GORDIN GIN CO. (DE)
Name changed to Continental/Moss-Gordin Inc. 02/28/1966
(See Continental/Moss-Gordin Inc.)

CONTINENTAL MOSS GORDIN INC (DE)
Merged into Continental Merging Corp. 12/06/1976
Each share 4.5% Preferred $100 par exchanged for $100.82 cash
Each share Common no par exchanged for $90.01 cash

CONTINENTAL MOTOR COACH LINES, INC. (DE)
Each share Common no par exchanged for (2) shares Common $1 par 00/00/1950
Name changed to Continental-Atlantic Corp. 11/15/1962
(See Continental-Atlantic Corp.)

CONTINENTAL MTRS CORP (VA)
Common no par changed to $1 par 00/00/1935
Merged into Teledyne, Inc. 12/16/1969
Each share Common $1 par exchanged for $30 principal amount of 7% Subord. Debentures due 06/01/1999

CONTINENTAL MUT INVT FD INC (MD)
Completely liquidated 12/18/1995
Each share Capital Stock $1 par

received first and final distribution of $7.08 cash

CONTINENTAL NAT GAS INC (OK)
Merged into CMS Energy Corp. 10/15/1998
Each share Common 1¢ par exchanged for (0.224) share Common 1¢ par

CONTINENTAL NATL BK (FORT WORTH, TX)
Each share Capital Stock $60 par exchanged for (3) shares Capital Stock $20 par 00/00/1943
Each share Capital Stock $20 par exchanged for (2) shares Capital Stock $10 par 02/15/1954
Merged into Southwest Bancshares, Inc. 06/26/1972
Each share Capital Stock $10 par exchanged for (0.72) share Common $10 par
Southwest Bancshares, Inc. merged into MCorp 10/11/1984
(See MCorp)

CONTINENTAL NATL BK (LAS VEGAS, NV)
Reorganized as Continental Bancorporation 07/01/1992
Each share Common $1.39 par exchanged for (1) share Common 25¢ par
(See Continental Bancorporation)

CONTINENTAL NATIONAL BANK (LINCOLN, NE)
Each share Capital Stock $100 par exchanged for (4) shares Capital Stock $25 par 00/00/1942
Stock Dividends - 12% 01/02/1940; 14.28% 01/21/1942; 20% 12/26/1944
Merged into First Continental National Bank & Trust Co. (Lincoln, NE) 03/12/1960
Each share Capital Stock $25 par exchanged for (1.202) shares Capital Stock $20 par
First Continental National Bank & Trust Co. (Lincoln, NE) name changed to First National Bank & Trust Co. (Lincoln, NE) 06/11/1962 which reorganized as First National Lincoln Corp. 09/04/1973 which merged into FirsTier, Inc. 06/01/1984 which name changed to FirsTier Financial Inc. 05/18/1987 which merged into First Bank System, Inc. 02/16/1996 which name changed to U.S. Bancorp 08/01/1997

CONTINENTAL NATL BK (PHOENIX, AZ)
Common $10 par changed to $5 par and (1) additional share issued 11/07/1969
Name changed to Continental Bank (Phoenix, AZ) 08/01/1970
(See Continental Bank (Phoenix, AZ))

CONTINENTAL NICKEL LTD (CANADA)
Acquired by IMX Resources Ltd. 09/14/2012
Each share Common no par exchanged for (3.7) shares Ordinary and (0.5) Ordinary Stock Purchase Warrant expiring 09/14/2015
(See IMX Resources Ltd.)

CONTINENTAL OIL & ASPHALT CO (DE)
In process of liquidation
Each share Common received initial distribution of $2.80 cash 06/29/1999
Note: Details on subsequent distribution(s), if any, are not available

CONTINENTAL OIL & REFINING CO. (DE)
No longer in existence having become inoperative and void for non-payment of taxes 03/22/1922

CONTINENTAL OIL CO. (ME)
Assets acquired by Continental Oil Co. (DE) 06/26/1929
Details not available

CONTINENTAL OIL CO. OF CANADA LTD. (AB)
Recapitalized as New Continental Oil Co. of Canada Ltd. 00/00/1951
Each share Capital Stock no par exchanged for (0.5) share Capital Stock no par
New Continental Oil Co. of Canada Ltd. liquidated for Pan Ocean Oil Corp. 01/01/1972
(See Pan Ocean Oil Corp.)

CONTINENTAL OIL CO. OF MEXICO S.A.
Dissolved 00/00/1944
No stockholders' equity

CONTINENTAL OIL CO (DE)
Capital Stock no par changed to $5 par 00/00/1933
Capital Stock $5 par split (2) for (1) by issuance of (1) additional share 02/18/1957
Capital Stock $5 par reclassified as Common $5 par 10/21/1963
Common $5 par split (2) for (1) by issuance of (1) additional share 03/24/1969
Common $5 par split (2) for (1) issuance of (1) additional share 06/02/1976
Stock Dividend - 100% 06/14/1951
Name changed to Conoco Inc. 07/02/1979
Conoco Inc. acquired by Du Pont (E.I.) De Nemours & Co. 09/30/1981

CONTINENTAL OIL SHALE MINING & REFINING CO. (AZ)
Company officials indicted for fraud 01/00/1921
No stockholders' equity

CONTINENTAL PAC BK (VACAVILLE, CA)
Under plan of reorganization each share Common no par automatically became (1) share California Community Bancshares Corp. Common 10¢ par 03/14/1996
California Community Bancshares Corp. merged into SierraWest Bancorp 04/15/1998 which merged into BancWest Corp. (New) 07/01/1999
(See BancWest Corp. (New))

CONTINENTAL PAC RES INC (BC)
Recapitalized as Northern Continental Resources Inc. 12/12/1997
Each share Common no par exchanged for (0.125) share Common no par
Northern Continental Resources Inc. merged into Hathor Exploration Ltd. 11/23/2009
(See Hathor Exploration Ltd.)

CONTINENTAL PACIFIC RESOURCES (DE)
Name changed to Pacific Resources, Inc. (DE) 09/16/1996
(See Pacific Resources, Inc. (DE))

CONTINENTAL PASSENGER RAILWAY CO. OF PHILADELPHIA
Acquired by Philadelphia Transportation Co. 00/00/1940
Each share Common exchanged for $37.46 principal amount of 3%-6% Consolidated Mortgage Bonds and (0.3135) share $1 Part. Preferred $20 par
(See Philadelphia Transportation Co.)

CONTINENTAL PET INNOVATIONS INC (NJ)
Recapitalized as Scuffy Pet, Inc. 01/28/1972
Each share Common 1¢ par exchanged for (0.33333333) share Common 1¢ par
(See Scuffy Pet, Inc.)

CONTINENTAL PETROLEUMS, LTD.
Acquired by Gaspe Oil Ventures Ltd. 00/00/1948
Each share Capital Stock $1 par exchanged for (1) share Capital Stock $1 par
Gaspe Oil Ventures Ltd. acquired by New Associated Developments Ltd. 04/17/1963 which recapitalized as Consolidated Developments Ltd. 05/10/1971
(See Consolidated Developments Ltd.)

CONTINENTAL PHARMA CRYOSAN INC (CANADA)
Name changed to IBEX Technologies Inc. 08/10/1995

CONTINENTAL PLASTICS & CHEMS INC (NJ)
Each share Class A Common 10¢ par exchanged for (4) shares Common 5¢ par 01/06/1969
Each share Class B Common 10¢ par exchanged for (4) shares Common 5¢ par 01/06/1969
Plan of reorganization under Chapter 11 Federal Bankruptcy proceedings confirmed 06/12/1991
No stockholders' equity

CONTINENTAL POTASH LTD (ON)
Charter cancelled and declared dissolved for failure to file returns and pay fees 03/16/1976

CONTINENTAL PWR SYS INC (CO)
Administratively dissolved 01/01/1993

CONTINENTAL PPTYS INC (UT)
Charter suspended for failure to pay taxes 09/15/1970

CONTINENTAL PRISON SYS INC (NV)
Recapitalized as General Payment Systems, Inc. 09/03/2013
Each share Common $0.001 par exchanged for (0.01) share Common $0.001 par

CONTINENTAL PROMOTIONS INC (MN)
Name changed to Reeder Development Corp. 04/06/1971
Reeder Development Corp. name changed to RDI Corp. 08/08/1977
(See RDI Corp.)

CONTINENTAL PUBLIC SERVICE CO.
Acquired in reorganization by Sun Utility Co. 00/00/1940
No stockholders' equity

CONTINENTAL RADIANT GLASS HEATING CORP (MI)
Charter declared inoperative and void for failure to file reports 05/15/1986

CONTINENTAL RAIL CORP (NV)
Recapitalized as MediXall Group, Inc. 11/22/2016
Each share Common $0.001 par exchanged for (0.06666666) share Common $0.001 par

CONTINENTAL REALTY INVESTING CO. INC. (DE)
Recapitalized 00/00/1941
Each share Preferred $100 par exchanged for (2) shares Capital Stock $25 par
No Common stockholders' equity
Recapitalized 00/00/1945
Capital Stock $25 par changed to $1 par
Liquidation completed 00/00/1950
Details not available

CONTINENTAL RESH & DEV LTD (ON)
Reincorporated 07/23/1984
Place of incorporation changed from (AB) to (ON) 07/23/1984
Recapitalized as Continental Exploration & Development Ltd. 05/05/1994
Each share Common 2¢ par exchanged for (0.4) share Common no par
Continental Exploration & Development Ltd. recapitalized as Conex Continental Inc. 04/25/1996 which name changed to Dominion International Investments Inc. 03/05/2001
(See Dominion International Investments Inc.)

CONTINENTAL RES GROUP INC (DE)
Merged into Pershing Gold Corp. 03/04/2013
Each share Common $0.0001 par exchanged for (0.8) share Common $0.0001 par

CONTINENTAL RES INTL (NV)
Each share old Common 1¢ par exchanged for (4) shares new Common 1¢ par 04/02/1974
Note: Certificates were not actually exchanged but were overstamped to indicate new quantity
Charter revoked for failure to file reports and pay fees 03/01/1976

CONTINENTAL RES LTD (QC)
Recapitalized as C2C Inc. 07/26/2004
Each share Common $1 par exchanged for (1/3) share Common $1 par
C2C Inc. name changed to C2C Gold Corp. Inc. 02/27/2008 which recapitalized as Key Gold Holding Inc. 03/11/2010 which recapitalized as Pangolin Diamonds Corp. 03/20/2013

CONTINENTAL RIDGE RES INC (BC)
Name changed to Nevada Geothermal Power Inc. 05/13/2003
Nevada Geothermal Power Inc. recapitalized as Alternative Earth Resources Inc. 04/02/2013 which recapitalized as Black Sea Copper & Gold Corp. 09/28/2016

CONTINENTAL ROLL & STEEL FOUNDRY CO. (DE)
Name changed to Continental Foundry & Machine Co. 03/22/1944
(See Continental Foundry & Machine Co.)

CONTINENTAL SAVINGS & LOAN ASSOCIATION (CA)
Name changed to Continental Savings of America, A Savings & Loan Association (San Francisco, CA) 10/11/1983
(See Continental Savings of America, A Federal Savings & Loan Association (San Francisco, CA))

CONTINENTAL SVGS AMER A SVGS & LN ASSN (SAN FRANCISCO, CA)
Common no par split (3) for (1) by issuance of (2) additional shares 12/28/1987
Common no par split (3) for (1) by issuance of (2) additional shares 12/06/1988
Stock Dividend - 10% 11/14/1988
Closed by the RTC 00/00/1995
No stockholders' equity

CONTINENTAL SCREW CO (MA)
Stock Dividend - 25% 08/30/1968
Completely liquidated 09/15/1969
Each share Common $1 par exchanged for first and final distribution of (1.625) shares Amtel, Inc. Common 50¢ par
(See Amtel, Inc.)

CONTINENTAL SEC LIFE INS CO (MO)
Common $1 par changed to $1.80 par 00/00/1979
Administratively dissolved 02/01/1996

CONTINENTAL SECURITIES CORP. (AR)
Name changed to Homestead Nursing Centers of America, Inc. 11/13/1968
Homestead Nursing Centers of America, Inc. name changed to

Homestead International Inc. (AR) 12/23/1969 which reincorporated in Delaware as Candler Co. 04/16/1973
(See Candler Co.)

CONTINENTAL SECURITIES CORP. (MD)
Charter revoked for failure to file reports and pay fees 10/28/1941

CONTINENTAL SECURITIES HOLDING CORP.
Merged into Continental Securities Corp. (MD) 00/00/1931
Details not available

CONTINENTAL SEMICONDUCTOR INC (NY)
Name changed to CSR Industries, Inc. 10/14/1971
(See CSR Industries, Inc.)

CONTINENTAL SERVICE CO. (DE)
Name changed to Lone Star Investment Co. 00/00/1945
(See Lone Star Investment Co.)

CONTINENTAL SHARES, INC.
Assets acquired for liquidation by Liquidating Shares, Inc. 00/00/1940
Details not available

CONTINENTAL SHELF FUND, INC. (NY)
Charter cancelled and proclaimed dissolved for failure to pay taxes and file reports 12/15/1973

CONTINENTAL SILVER CORP (BC)
Merged into Arizona Silver Corp. 08/01/1985
Each share Capital Stock no par exchanged for (0.5) share Common no par
Arizona Silver Corp. recapitalized as ASC Industries Ltd. 06/06/1995 which name changed to Acero-Martin Exploration Inc. 11/24/2004 which name changed to AM Gold Inc. 06/08/2010
(See AM Gold Inc.)

CONTINENTAL SILVER MINING CO. (NY)
Charter cancelled and proclaimed dissolved for failure to pay taxes and file reports 04/02/1924

CONTINENTAL SOUTHN RES INC (NV)
Name changed to Endeavour International Corp. 02/27/2004
(See Endeavour International Corp.)

CONTINENTAL STL CORP (DE)
Chapter 11 bankruptcy proceedings converted to Chapter 7 on 02/25/1986
Stockholders' equity unlikely

CONTINENTAL STL CORP (IN)
7% Preferred called for redemption 01/01/1944
Each share Common no par exchanged for (2.5) shares Common $14 par 00/00/1946
Common $14 par changed to $7 par and (1) additional share issued 03/30/1960
Common $7 par split (2) for (1) by issuance of (1) additional share 07/01/1971
Merged into Penn-Dixie Industries, Inc. 05/11/1973
Each share Common $7 par exchanged for (1.5) shares Common $1 par and (1) Warrant expiring 05/01/1983
Penn-Dixie Industries, Inc. name changed to Continental Steel Corp. (DE) 03/18/1982
(See Continental Steel Corp. (DE))

CONTINENTAL STOVE CORP.
Bankrupt 00/00/1939
Details not available

CONTINENTAL STRATEGICS, INC. (TN)
Merged into Continental Strategics Corp. 01/02/1969
Each share Capital Stock 50¢ par exchanged for (1) share Common 14¢ par
Continental Strategics Corp. merged into Chadbourn Inc. 04/27/1970 which reorganized as Stanwood Corp. 06/12/1975 which was acquired by Delta Woodside Industries, Inc. (DE) 09/07/1988 which merged into Delta Woodside Industries, Inc. (SC) 11/15/1989
(See Delta Woodside Industries, Inc. (SC))

CONTINENTAL STRATEGICS CORP (NY)
Merged into Chadbourn Inc. 04/27/1970
Each share Common 14¢ par exchanged for (0.36363636) share Common $1 par
Chadbourn Inc. reorganized as Stanwood Corp. 06/12/1975 which was acquired by Delta Woodside Industries, Inc. (DE) 09/07/1988 which merged into Delta Woodside Industries, Inc. (SC) 11/15/1989
(See Delta Woodside Industries, Inc. (SC))

CONTINENTAL STS CORP (DE)
Charter cancelled and declared inoperative and void for non-payment of taxes 03/01/1988

CONTINENTAL SULPHUR & PHOSPHATE CORP. (DE)
Charter revoked for non-payment of taxes 04/01/1960

CONTINENTAL TELECOM INC (DE)
Name changed to Contel Corp. 05/01/1986
Contel Corp. merged into GTE Corp. 03/14/1991 which merged into Verizon Communications Inc. 06/30/2000

CONTINENTAL TELEPHONE CO. (DE)
Ctfs. dated prior to 08/08/1956
5% Preferred $20 par called for redemption at $22 on 08/08/1956
Merged into General Telephone Corp. 08/08/1956
Each share Common $10 par exchanged for (0.875) share Common $10 par
General Telephone Corp. name changed to General Telephone & Electronics Corp. 03/05/1959 which name changed to GTE Corp. 07/01/1982 which merged into Verizon Communications Inc. 06/30/2000

CONTINENTAL TELEPHONE CO. NEW (DE)
Ctfs. dated after 10/03/1962
Under plan of merger name changed to Continental Independent Telephone Corp. 03/31/1964
Continental Independent Telephone Corp. name changed to Continental Telephone Corp. 05/11/1965 which name changed to Continental Telecom Inc. 05/06/1982 which name changed to Contel Corp. 05/01/1986 which merged into GTE Corp. 03/14/1991 which merged into Verizon Communications Inc. 06/30/2000

CONTINENTAL TELEPHONE CO. OF CALIFORNIA (CA)
Under plan of merger each share Common $5 par exchanged for $73.02 cash 12/20/1983
Name changed to Contel of California, Inc. 02/19/1988
(See Contel of California, Inc.)

CONTINENTAL TELEPHONE CORP. (DE)
4% Conv. Preferred $25 par called for redemption 03/10/1966
Name changed to Continental Telecom Inc. 05/06/1982
Continental Telecom Inc. name changed to Contel Corp. 05/01/1986 which merged into GTE Corp. 03/14/1991 which merged into Verizon Communications Inc. 06/30/2000

CONTINENTAL TELEVISION CORP. (DE)
Charter forfeited for failure to file annual reports 00/00/1935

CONTINENTAL TESTING LABS INC (FL)
Merged into Allegheny Ludlum Industries, Inc. 06/01/1978
Each share Common 10¢ par exchanged for (1) Non-Transferable Ctf. and $5.48 cash
Each Non-Transferable Ctf. exchanged for $1.0478 cash 10/28/1981

CONTINENTAL TITANIUM CORP. (QC)
Declared bankrupt 08/10/1967
No stockholders' equity

CONTINENTAL TOB CO S C (SC)
Dissolved by forfeiture for non-payment of taxes 10/01/1971

CONTINENTAL TOB INC (DE)
Name changed to Continental Mining Co., Inc. 12/01/1969
(See Continental Mining Co., Inc. (DE))

CONTINENTAL TOBACCO CO., INC. (SC)
Name changed to Continental Tobacco Co. of South Carolina, Inc. 07/26/1966
(See Continental Tobacco Co. of South Carolina, Inc.)

CONTINENTAL TRANSN SYS INC (CA)
Adjudicated bankrupt 04/24/1972
No stockholders' equity

CONTINENTAL TRANSPORTATION LINES, INC. (PA)
Merged into Werner Continental, Inc. 03/01/1968
Each share Common $1 par exchanged for (1) share 4.75% Conv. Preferred $17 par
(See Werner Continental, Inc.)

CONTINENTAL TRAVEL LTD (DE)
Charter cancelled and declared inoperative and void for non-payment of taxes 03/15/1972

CONTINENTAL TRUST CO. (AZ)
Name changed to Continental Investment Corp. (AZ) 11/27/1961
(See Continental Investment Corp. (AZ))

CONTINENTAL TR CORP (KY)
Merged into Continental States Corp. 7/18/84
Each share Common no par exchanged for (0.23) share Common $1 par
(See Continental States Corp.)

CONTINENTAL TURPENTINE & ROSIN CORP (MS)
Voluntarily liquidated 12/00/1984
Details not available

CONTINENTAL TYRE LTD (BC)
Completely liquidated 11/22/1991
Each share Common no par exchanged for first and final distribution of (0.25811698) share Export Tyre Holding Co. (Old) Common $0.001 par
Export Tyre Holding Co. (Old) merged into Export Tyre Holding Co. (New) 01/31/1995
(See Export Tyre Holding Co. (New))

CONTINENTAL UNITED INDUSTRIES, INC.
Merged into Continental Copper & Steel Industries, Inc. in 1948
Each share Common $1 par exchanged for (0.2) share 5% Preferred $25 par and (1) share Common $2 par
Continental Copper & Steel Industries, Inc. name changed to CCX, Inc. 12/1/82
(See CCX, Inc.)

CONTINENTAL URANIUM, INC. (DE)
Name changed to Continental Materials Corp. 5/17/57

CONTINENTAL URANIUM CORP. LTD. (SK)
Merged into Continental Consolidated Mines & Oils Co. Ltd. on a (0.1) for (1) basis 10/4/57
(See Continental Consolidated Mines & Oils Co. Ltd.)

CONTINENTAL VENDING MACHINE CORP. (IN)
Stock Dividend - 15% 04/17/1961
Assets sold for the benefit of creditors 00/00/1964
No stockholders' equity

CONTINENTAL VENTURES INC (DE)
Reorganized as Unipac Corp. 11/08/1990
Each share Common $0.005 par exchanged for (0.5) share Common $0.005 par, (0.5) Class A Warrant expiring 11/07/1991 and (0.5) Class B Warrant expiring 11/07/1992
Unipac Corp. name changed to Hansen Natural Corp. 10/27/1992 which name changed to Monster Beverage Corp. (Old) 01/09/2012 which reorganized as Monster Beverage Corp. (New) 06/15/2015

CONTINENTAL VINYL INDS INC (PA)
Declared out of existence 5/2/77
Details not available

CONTINENTAL WASTE CONVERSION INC (AB)
Name changed to EnviroPower Industries Inc. 10/09/1997
(See EnviroPower Industries Inc.)

CONTINENTAL WASTE INDS INC (DE)
Reincorporated 2/28/94
State of incorporation changed from (NY) to (DE) 2/28/94
Common $0.001 par split (5) for (3) by issuance of (2/3) additional share 12/28/95
Merged into Republic Industries Inc. 12/30/96
Each share Common $0.001 par exchanged for (0.8) share Common 1¢ par
Republic Industries Inc. name changed to AutoNation, Inc. 4/6/99

CONTINENTAL WELLNESS CASINOS TRUST R E I T (CO)
Name changed 12/22/97
Name changed from Continental Wellness Casinos, Inc. to Continental Wellness Casinos Trust R.E.I.T. 12/22/97
Name changed to Countryland Wellness Resorts, Inc. 9/22/99
Countryland Wellness Resorts, Inc. recapitalized as Minerals Mining Corp. 11/6/2000

CONTINENTAL WESTERN RESERVE CO. (OH)
Liquidation completed
Each share Common $5 par received initial distribution of $13 cash 05/10/1976
Each share Common $5 par received second distribution of $2.50 cash 07/27/1976
Each share Common $5 par received third distribution of $1.25 cash 10/29/1976
Each share Common $5 par received

fourth distribution of $1.25 cash 02/02/1977
Each share Common $5 par received fifth distribution of $2 cash 10/26/1977
Each share Common $5 par received sixth distribution of $5.27 cash 03/08/1979
Each share Common $5 par received seventh distribution of $1 cash 09/27/1979
Each share Common $5 par received eighth distribution of $1 cash 01/07/1980
Each share Common $5 par received ninth and final distribution of $0.20 cash 12/30/1981
Note: Certificates were not required to be surrendered and are without value

CONTINENTAL WESTN CORP (DE)
Charter cancelled and declared inoperative and void for non-payment of taxes 3/1/76

CONTINENTAL WESTN INDS INC (IA)
Each share Common $5 par exchanged for (0.1) share Common $1 par plus a 1000% stock dividend paid 7/11/77
Merged into NN Corp. 2/10/78
Each share Common $1 par exchanged for (0.5) share $3.60 Preferred Ser. A no par or (0.8) share Common $5 par
Note: The above option expired 1/27/78 after which holders received Preferred only
NN Corp. merged into Armco Inc. 12/1/80 which merged into AK Steel Holding Corp. 9/30/99

CONTINENTAL WESTN LIFE INS CO (IA)
Each share old Common $1 par exchanged for (0.5) share new Common $1 par 06/21/1971
Through voluntary exchange offer over 99% acquired by Continental Western Industries, Inc. as of 06/24/1969
Public interest eliminated

CONTINENTAL WINGATE INC (DE)
Merged into BGC Inc. 2/27/81
Each share Common 10¢ par exchanged for $3 cash

CONTINENTS GOLD & RES INC (MT)
Recapitalized as Energy Development, Inc. 7/24/78
Each share Common 1¢ par exchanged for (0.2) share Common 5¢ par
Energy Development, Inc. name changed to Environmental Recycling Technologies Inc. 10/23/83 which name changed to Mason Dental Ceramics, Inc. 4/16/84 which recapitalized as Mason Dental Inc. 12/1/90
(See Mason Dental Inc.)

CONTINUCARE CORP (FL)
Merged into Metropolitan Health Networks, Inc. 10/04/2011
Each share Common $0.0001 par exchanged for (0.0414) share Common $0.001 par and $6.25 cash
(See Metropolitan Health Networks, Inc.)

CONTINUED CARE FACS INC (DE)
Charter cancelled and declared inoperative and void for non-payment of taxes 03/01/1995

CONTINUING CARE ASSOC INC (DE)
Charter cancelled and declared inoperative and void for non-payment of taxes 03/01/1990

CONTINUOUS CURVE CONTACT LENSES INC (CA)
Merged into Revlon, Inc. 08/27/1980
Each share Common no par exchanged for (1.275) shares Common $1 par
(See Revlon, Inc.)

CONTINUUM ARTS INC (BC)
Recapitalized as Continuum Resources Ltd. 05/13/1999
Each share Common no par exchanged for (1/3) share Common no par
Continuum Resources Ltd. acquired by Fortuna Silver Mines Inc. 03/06/2009

CONTINUUM GROUP B INC (NV)
Each (5.96) shares old Common $0.001 par exchanged for (1) share new Common $0.001 par 05/05/2000
Reorganized under the laws of Delaware as Horizon Wimba, Inc. 10/12/2004
Each share new Common $0.001 par exchanged for (0.56) share Common $0.001 par
Horizon Wimba, Inc. name changed to Hayse Corp. 09/08/2006
(See Hayse Corp.)

CONTINUUM GROUP C INC (NV)
Recapitalized as Premier Alliance Group, Inc. (NV) 01/26/2005
Each share Common $0.001 par exchanged for (0.14285714) share Common $0.001 par
Premier Alliance Group, Inc. (NV) reincorporated in Delaware 09/01/2011 which name changed to root9B Technologies, Inc. 12/01/2014 which recapitalized as root9B Holdings, Inc. 12/05/2016

CONTINUUM GROUP INC (DE)
Each share Common $0.001 par exchanged for (0.666) share old Common $0.015 par 08/03/1993
Each share old Common $0.015 par exchanged for (0.25) share new Common $0.015 par 08/14/1995
Under plan of reorganization each share new Common $0.015 par automatically became (0.048) share new Common $0.015 par 10/10/1999
Recapitalized as NuWeb Solutions, Inc. 05/04/2000
Each share new Common $0.015 par exchanged for (0.55555555) share Common $0.015 par
NuWeb Solutions, Inc. recapitalized as Pensador Resources Inc. 05/30/2008

CONTINUUM HEALTH CARE INC (AB)
Plan of arragement effective 12/18/2009
Each share Common no par exchanged for $0.29 cash
Note: Unexchanged certificates were cancelled and became without value 12/18/2015

CONTINUUM INC (DE)
Reincorporated 8/20/87
Common 10¢ par split (2) for (1) by issuance of (1) additional share 9/21/84
Common 10¢ par split (3) for (2) by issuance of (0.5) additional share 3/29/85
Stock Dividend - 100% 1/5/81
State of incorporation changed from (TX) to (DE) 8/20/87
Common 10¢ par split (2) for (1) by issuance of (1) additional share 7/20/90
Merged into Computer Sciences Corp. 8/1/96
Each share Common 10¢ par exchanged for (0.79) share Common $1 par

CONTINUUM RES LTD (BC)
Acquired by Fortuna Silver Mines Inc. 03/06/2009
Each share Common no par exchanged for (0.0564) share Common no par

CONTINUUS SOFTWARE CORP (DE)
Merged into Telelogic AB 12/08/2000
Each share Common $0.001 par exchanged for $3.46 cash

CONTOOCOOK MILLS CORP.
Liquidated 00/00/1934
Details not available

CONTOUR BLIND & SHADE (CANADA) LTD. (BC)
Name changed to Contour Consumer Products Inc. 12/17/1991
Contour Consumer Products Inc. reorganized as Home Products, Inc. 08/26/1992
(See Home Products, Inc.)

CONTOUR CONSUMER PRODS INC (BC)
Reorganized as Home Products, Inc. 08/26/1992
Each share Preference Ser. 4 no par automatically became (1) share Preference Ser. 4 no par
Each share Common no par exchanged for (0.2) share Common no par
(See Home Products, Inc.)

CONTOUR ENERGY CO (DE)
Each share $2.625 Conv. Exchangeable Preferred 1¢ par exchanged for (3) shares Common 1¢ par and $7.25 cash 12/4/2001
Plan of reorganization under Chapter 11 Federal Bankruptcy Code effective 12/31/2002
Each share Common 1¢ par received first and final distribution of $0.043323 cash payable 12/31/2002 to holders of record 9/27/2002
Ex date - 8/27/2003
Note: Certificates were not required to be surrendered and are now valueless

CONTOUR MED INC (NV)
Stock Dividend - 5% payable 04/01/1996 to holders of record 03/15/1996
Merged into Sun Healthcare Group, Inc. (Old) 06/30/1998
Each share Common $0.001 par exchanged for (0.524) share Common 1¢ par
(See Sun Healthcare Group, Inc. (Old))

CONTOUR TELECOM MGMT SVCS INC (CANADA)
Recapitalized as Tigertel Inc. 07/14/1999
Each share Common no par exchanged for (0.25) share Common no par
(See Tigertel Inc.)

CONTRACAP INC (NV)
Each share old Common $0.001 par exchanged for (0.125) share new Common $0.001 par 06/22/1993
Each share new Common $0.001 par exchanged again for (0.5) share new Common $0.001 par 12/27/1994
Name changed to I Love Pizza Inc. 01/09/1995
I Love Pizza Inc. recapitalized as Revenge Marine, Inc. 02/19/1998 which name changed to eTravelServe.com, Inc. 01/28/2000
(See eTravelServe.com, Inc.)

CONTRACT & INVESTMENT CO.
Merged into Detroit Mortgage & Realty Co. (MI) 00/00/1946
Each share Common exchanged for (10) shares Common $1 par
Detroit Mortgage & Realty Co. (MI) reorganized in Nevada as Boundary Bay Resources, Inc. 09/24/2007 which recapitalized as Wave Technology Group Inc. 05/06/2010 which name changed to eMamba International Corp. 07/27/2011

CONTRACT ELECTRONICS CORP. (CO)
Merged into Shiprock Industries, Inc. on a (0.07) for (1) basis 12/31/64

CONTRACT PACKAGING, INC. (IA)
Completely liquidated in 1979
Each share Common 50¢ par exchanged for first and final distribution of $0.635 cash

CONTRACT PURCHASE CORP.
Acquired by Pacific Finance Corp. of California 00/00/1952
Each share Preferred $100 par exchanged for (4) shares 5% Preferred $25 par
Each share Common $2.50 par exchanged for (1.25) shares Common $10 par
Pacific Finance Corp. of California name changed to Pacific Finance Corp. 00/00/1952 which name changed to Transamerica Financial Corp. 03/29/1968
(See Transamerica Financial Corp.)

CONTRACTED SVCS INC (FL)
Name changed to ONE Holdings, Corp. 08/13/2009
ONE Holdings, Corp. recapitalized as ONE Bio, Corp. 11/17/2009

CONTRAN CORP (DE)
Each share old Common $1 par exchanged for (0.1) share new Common $1 par 06/30/1977
Class B Preferred $10 par called for redemption 01/16/1978
Each share new Common $1 par exchanged again for (0.03333333) share new Common $1 par 12/19/1979
Each share new Common $1 par exchanged for (0.1) share new Common $1 par 04/26/1984
Note: In effect holders received $5,000 cash per share and Common public interest eliminated
$0.75 Preferred Ser. A $1 par called for redemption 09/01/1995
Public interest eliminated

CONTRANS CORP (ON)
Each share 7.50% Conv. Preference Ser. A no par exchanged for (13) shares Class A Common no par and (2) Class A Common Stock Purchase Warrants expiring 08/15/1995 on 07/15/1994
Each share old Class A Subordinate no par exchanged for (0.2) share new Class A Subordinate no par 02/01/1995
Merged into Contrans Income Fund 07/25/2002
Each share new Class A Subordinate no par exchanged for (4) Trust Units
Contrans Income Fund reorganized as Contrans Group Inc. 12/03/2009
(See Contrans Group Inc.)

CONTRANS GROUP INC (ON)
Acquired by TransForce Inc. 12/10/2014
Each share Class A Subordinate no par exchanged for $14.60 cash

CONTRANS INCOME FD (ON)
Reorganized as Contrans Group Inc. 12/03/2009
Each Trust Unit exchanged for (1) share Class A Subordinate no par
(See Contrans Group Inc.)

CONTRARIAN CAP CORP (AB)
Name changed to Octane Energy Services Ltd. 08/16/1999
Octane Energy Services Ltd. name changed to NX Capital Corp. 06/27/2005 which recapitalized as Newton Energy Corp. 02/18/2009

CONTROL ADVANCEMENTS INC (ON)
Name changed to Betacom Corp. Inc. 07/28/2000
(See Betacom Corp. Inc.)

CONTROL BUILDING SYSTEMS, INC. (CA)
Plan of Arrangement under Chapter XI bankruptcy proceedings confirmed 06/17/1974
No stockholders' equity

CONTROL CHIEF HLDGS INC (NY)
Old Common 50¢ par split (5) for (4) by issuance of (0.25) additional share payable 02/20/1998 to holders of record 02/06/1998
Each share old Common 50¢ par exchanged for (0.01) share new Common 50¢ par 11/01/2002
Note: In effect holders received $3.73 cash per share and public interest was eliminated

CONTROL CIRCUITS INC (DE)
Recapitalized as Kleer-Pak Corp. 09/11/1972
Each share Common 10¢ par exchanged for (0.5) share Common 10¢ par
(See Kleer-Pak Corp.)

CONTROL DATA CORP (DE)
Common $5 par changed to $1 par 05/14/1975
Common $1 par changed to 50¢ par and (1) additional share issued 10/30/1981
Name changed to Ceridian Corp. (Old) 06/03/1992
(See Ceridian Corp. (Old))

CONTROL DATA CORP (MN)
Common 50¢ par split (3) for (1) by issuance of (2) additional share 09/21/1961
Common 50¢ par split (3) for (2) by issuance of (0.5) additional share 09/30/1964
4% Conv. Preferred $50 par called for redemption 10/20/1967
Merged into Control Data Corp. (DE) 08/17/1968
Each share Common 50¢ par exchanged for (1) share Common $5 par
Control Data Corp. (DE) name changed to Ceridian Corp. (Old) 06/03/1992
(See Ceridian Corp. (Old))

CONTROL DATA SYS INC (DE)
Merged into CDSI Acquisition Corp. 9/23/97
Each share Common 1¢ par exchanged for $20.25 cash

CONTROL DEVICES INC (IN)
Common no par split (4) for (3) by issuance of (0.33333333) additional share payable 12/15/1997 to holders of record 12/01/1997
Common no par split (5) for (4) by issuance of (0.25) additional share payable 06/15/1998 to holders of record 05/29/1998
Merged into First Technology PLC 03/30/1999
Each share Common no par exchanged for $16.25 cash

CONTROL ELECTRONICS CO., INC. (NY)
Merged into Paradynamics, Inc. on a (1/12) for (1) basis 2/9/62
(See Paradynamics, Inc.)

CONTROL ENERGY CORP (BC)
Struck off register and declared dissolved for failure to file returns 3/26/93

CONTROL INDS CORP (DE)
Name changed to Consurgico Corp. 02/18/1971
Consurgico Corp. name changed to Chase Development Corp. 04/09/1979
(See Chase Development Corp.)

CONTROL INDS INC (MO)
Name changed to Telecom Midwest Corp. 06/01/1971
(See Telecom Midwest Corp.)

CONTROL LASER CORP (FL)
Common 1¢ par split (3) for (2) by issuance of (0.5) additional share 03/01/1979
Common 1¢ par split (3) for (2) by issuance of (0.5) additional share 12/15/1980
Stock Dividends - 10% 08/19/1976; 10% 09/30/1977; 10% 08/15/1978
Reincorporated under the laws of Delaware as Control Laser International Corp. 01/01/1987
Control Laser International Corp. merged into Quantronix Corp. 11/22/1988 which was acquired by Excel Technology, Inc. 10/01/1992
(See Excel Technology, Inc.)

CONTROL LASER INTL CORP (DE)
Merged into Quantronix Corp. 11/22/1988
Each share Common 1¢ par exchanged for (1/6) share Common 1¢ par
Quantronix Corp. acquired by Excel Technology, Inc. 10/01/1992
(See Excel Technology, Inc.)

CONTROL METALS CORP (UT)
Each share old Capital Stock 1¢ par exchanged for (0.1) share new Capital Stock 1¢ par 5/1/71
Note: Company did not actually request exchange of certificates
Old Ctfs. are numbered 72462 and lower
New Ctfs. are numbered 72463 and higher
Proclaimed dissolved for failure to pay taxes 3/31/85

CONTROL NETWORKS CORP (BC)
Struck off register and declared dissolved for failure to file returns 7/26/91

CONTROL PACKAGING CORP (MA)
Adjudicated bankrupt 09/13/1974
Stockholders' equity unlikely

CONTROL REMOTE EMBEDDED TECHNOLOGIES INC (AB)
Name changed to CORE Technologies Inc. 01/15/1998
CORE Technologies Inc. name changed to Image Sculpting International Inc. 10/19/1999
(See Image Sculpting International Inc.)

CONTROL RESOURCE INDS INC (DE)
Common 1¢ par split (2) for (1) by issuance of (1) additional share 3/31/86
Recapitalized as Wellstead Industries Inc. 5/13/93
Each share Common 1¢ par exchanged for (0.2) share Common 1¢ par
(See Wellstead Industries Inc.)

CONTROL SCIENCE CORP (CANADA)
Reincorporated under the laws of Yukon as Steppe Gold International Inc. 8/29/96 which name changed to Steppe Gold Resources Ltd. 6/7/96
(See Steppe Gold Resources Ltd.)

CONTROLADORA COMERCIAL MEXICANA S A DE CV (MEXICO)
GDR agreement terminated 12/18/2006
Each GDR for Units exchanged for $49.65314 cash

CONTROLEX CORP AMER (NY)
Merged into Incom International Inc. 11/02/1979
Each share Common 10¢ par exchanged for $6.485 cash

CONTROLLED ENERGY SYS INC (DE)
Name changed to Circadian Systems, Inc. 06/09/1986
Circadian Systems, Inc. name changed to Harbour Intermodal, Ltd. 03/03/1993
(See Harbour Intermodal, Ltd.)

CONTROLLED ENVIRONMENT AQUACULTURE TECHNOLOGY INC (CO)
Name changed to Ceatech USA, Inc. 9/7/2001

CONTROLLED ENVIRONMENT FARMING INTL LTD (BC)
Recapitalized as International Controlled Investments Inc. (BC) 10/09/1987
Each share Common no par exchanged for (1) share Common no par
International Controlled Investments Inc. (BC) reincorporated in Yukon as New Age Ventures Inc. 08/23/1991 which recapitalized as Great Panther Inc. 01/01/1998 which recapitalized as Great Panther Resources Ltd. (YT) 10/02/2003 which reincorporated in British Columbia 07/14/2004 which name changed to Great Panther Silver Ltd. 01/12/2010

CONTROLLED FOODS INTL LTD (DE)
Acquired by Keg Restaurants Ltd. 07/18/1984
Each share Common no par exchanged for CAD $5.50 cash
Note: Residents of (BC), (AB), (MB), (SK) and (ON) had the option to receive (1-1/8) shares of Keg Restaurants Ltd. Non-Vtg. Class A no par or (2/3) share Keg Restaurants Ltd. Non-Vtg. Class A no par and $2.50 cash
Above option expired 09/17/1984

CONTROLLED PWR CORP (MI)
Adjudicated bankrupt 03/30/1973
No stockholders' equity

CONTROLLED PRODS & ELECTRS INC (CA)
Merged into CCI Marquardt Corp. 06/14/1968
Each share Common no par exchanged for (1/3) share Common 50¢ par
CCI Marquardt Corp. name changed to CCI Corp. 09/26/1969
(See CCI Corp.)

CONTROLLED REACTION CORP (DE)
Charter cancelled and declared inoperative and void for non-payment of taxes 4/15/72

CONTROLLED WTR EMISSION SYS (CA)
100% acquired by Reed Irrigation Systems through purchase offer which expired 09/19/1975
Public interest eliminated

CONTROLS CO. OF AMERICA (DE)
Stock Dividend - 50% 8/10/59
Merged into General Precision Equipment Corp. 5/20/66
Each share Common $5 par exchanged for (0.1875) share $1.60 Conv. Preference no par and (0.5625) share Common $1 par
General Precision Equipment Corp. merged into Singer Co. (NJ) 7/11/68 which reincorporated in Delaware in 1988 which name changed to Bicoastal Corp. 10/16/89
(See Bicoastal Corp.)

CONTROLS FOR ENVIRONMENTAL POLLUTION INC (NM)
Common 5¢ par split (3) for (1) by issuance of (2) additional shares 06/11/1986
Charter revoked 01/23/2001

CONTROLS RESH CORP (DE)
Each share Common 10¢ par exchanged for (0.25) share Common 40¢ par 07/27/1971
Adjudicated bankrupt 11/25/1975
Stockholders' equity unlikely

CONTWOYTO GOLDFIELDS LTD (AB)
Recapitalized as Corridor Resources Inc. 05/13/1996
Each share Common no par exchanged for (0.2) share Common no par

CONTY EXPLORATION LTD. (ON)
Completely liquidated 01/04/1962
Each share Capital Stock exchanged for (0.02) share Canadian Faraday Corp Ltd. Capital Stock no par
Canadian Faraday Corp Ltd. merged into Consolidated Canadian Faraday Ltd. 05/04/1967 which name changed to Faraday Resources Inc. 08/02/1983 which merged into Conwest Exploration Co. Ltd. (New) (AB) 09/01/1993 which merged into Alberta Energy Co. Ltd. 01/31/1996 which merged into EnCana Corp. 01/03/2003

CONUCO LTD (ON)
Common $1 par changed to no par 07/30/1970
5.5% Preferred $100 par called for redemption 03/31/1972
Merged into Brinco Ltd. 12/17/1979
Each share Common no par exchanged for (0.33333333) share 7% Conv. Preferred Ser. A $5.50 par, (0.33333333) share Conv. Preferred Ser. B $5.50 par and (0.33333333) share Common no par
Brinco Ltd. merged into Consolidated Brinco Ltd. 05/30/1986 which merged into Hillsborough Resources Ltd. (ON) 02/06/1992 which reincorporated in Canada 11/05/1997
(See Hillsborough Resources Ltd. (Canada))

CONVA INDTY CO (OH)
Reorganized under the laws of Delaware as Columbus Insurance Holding Co. 12/29/1980
Each share Conv. Preferred Ser. A $1 par exchanged for (2) shares $0.225 Preferred Ser. A $3.75 par
Each share Class A Common no par exchanged for (2) shares Common $1 par
(See Columbus Insurance Holding Co.)

CONVAIRE INTL INC (DE)
Chapter 11 bankruptcy proceedings converted to Chapter 7 on 04/22/1988
Stockholders' equity unlikely

CONVALARIUMS AMER INC (DE)
Name changed to C-V American Corp. 11/13/1972
(See C-V American Corp.)

CONVALESCENT CARE CTRS INC (MD)
Name changed to Medical Services Corp. and Common 25¢ par changed to 10¢ par 12/05/1969
(See Medical Services Corp.)

CONVALESCENT NURSING CTRS AMER INC (AR)
Merged into Leisure Lodges, Inc. 12/31/1970
Each share Common 10¢ par exchanged for (1) share Common $1 par
(See Leisure Lodges, Inc.)

CONVALO HEALTH INTL CORP (BC)
Name changed to BLVD Centers Corp. 06/13/2017

CONVAN CORP (DE)
Charter cancelled and declared inoperative and void for non-payment of taxes 04/15/1972

CONVENIENCE, INC.
Liquidated 00/00/1949
Details not available

CONVENIENCE CONCEPTS INC (TX)
Each share old Common $0.001 par

exchanged for (0.01333333) share
new Common $0.001 par
10/06/1998
Name changed to Market Formulation
& Research Corp. (New) 11/12/1998
Market Formulation & Research Corp.
(New) reorganized as 649.com Inc.
05/27/1999 which name changed to
Infinite Holdings Group, Inc.
01/24/2007
(See Infinite Holdings Group, Inc.)

CONVENIENCE FOODS INC (DE)
Name changed to Convenience
Foods of Pennsylvania, Inc.
05/11/1970
Convenience Foods of Pennsylvania,
Inc. merged into Beatrice Foods Co.
01/22/1974 which name changed to
Beatrice Companies, Inc.
06/05/1984
(See Beatrice Companies, Inc.)

CONVENIENCE FOODS PA INC (DE)
Merged into Beatrice Foods Co.
01/22/1974
Each share Common 10¢ par
exchanged for (0.33333333) share
Common no par
Beatrice Foods Co. name changed to
Beatrice Companies, Inc.
06/05/1984
(See Beatrice Companies, Inc.)

CONVENIENCE TV INC (NV)
Common $0.00001 par split (7) for (1)
by issuance of (6) additional shares
payable 06/15/2010 to holders of
record 06/15/2010
SEC revoked common stock
registration 06/24/2015

CONVENIENT FOOD MART INC (IL)
Common 10¢ par split (5) for (4) by
issuance of (0.25) additional share
04/28/1986
Stock Dividends - 25% 09/02/1985;
10% 12/10/1986; 10% 06/01/1987;
10% 09/14/1987
Plan of reorganization under Chapter
11 bankruptcy proceedings
confirmed 12/13/1990
Stockholders' equity unknown

CONVENIENT INDS AMER INC (KY)
Stock Dividend - 50% 11/05/1979
Reorganized as Conna Corp.
11/08/1979
Each share Common no par
exchanged for (1) share Common
no par
(See Conna Corp.)

CONVENIENTCAST INC (NV)
Name changed to Dewmar
International BMC, Inc. 05/17/2012

CONVENTION ALL HLDGS INC (DE)
Name changed to MIT Holding, Inc.
05/09/2007

CONVENTION CTRS INC (MN)
Statutorily dissolved 06/03/2002

CONVENTURES LTD (AB)
Merged into Oakwood Petroleums
Ltd. 07/30/1985
Each share Common no par
exchanged for (1) share $0.675
Retractable Preferred Ser. C no par
Oakwood Petroleums Ltd. acquired
by Sceptre Resources Ltd.
03/14/1989 which merged into
Canadian Natural Resources Ltd.
08/15/1996

CONVERA CORP (DE)
Liquidation completed
Each share Class A Common 1¢ par
received initial distribution of $0.10
cash payable 02/16/2010 to holders
of record 02/08/2010 Ex date -
02/17/2010
Each share Class A Common 1¢ par
received second and final
distribution of (0.00003783) share
Vertical Search Works, Inc. Common
and $0.047 cash payable
04/25/2011 to holders of record
02/08/2010

CONVERDE ENERGY USA INC (NV)
Reorganized under the laws of
Colorado as American Energy
Partners, Inc. 08/17/2017
Each share Common $0.001 par
exchanged for (0.05) share Common
$0.0001 par

CONVERGE GLOBAL INC NEW (UT)
Name changed to Marijuana Co. of
America, Inc. 12/01/2015

CONVERGE GLOBAL INC OLD (UT)
Recapitalized as Converge Global,
Inc. (New) 09/03/2010
Each share Common $0.001 par
exchanged for (0.01) share Common
$0.001 par
Converge Global, Inc. (New) name
changed to Marijuana Co. of
America, Inc. 12/01/2015

CONVERGENCE ETHANOL INC (NV)
Filed a petition under Chapter 7
Federal Bankruptcy Code
12/21/2007
No stockholders' equity

CONVERGENCE INC (CO)
Recapitalized as DER Entertainment,
Inc. 04/25/1994
Each share Common $0.0001 par
exchanged for (0.00181818) share
Common $0.001 par
DER Entertainment, Inc. recapitalized
as Medical Laser Technologies Inc.
05/02/1995 which recapitalized as
MLT International Inc. (CO)
08/22/2000 which reincorporated in
Delaware as SkyMark Holdings, Inc.
07/26/2004
(See SkyMark Holdings, Inc.)

**CONVERGENCE TECHNOLOGIES
GROUP INC (NV)**
Each share old Common $0.001 par
exchanged for (0.00133333) share
new Common $0.001 par
01/20/2009
Recapitalized as Bookkeeper
International Equities Corp.
06/26/2009
Each share new Common $0.001 par
exchanged for (0.00190476) share
Common $0.001 par

**CONVERGENET TECHNOLOGIES
INC (CA)**
Merged into Dell Computer Corp.
10/20/1999
Each share Common exchanged for
(0.22616) share Common 1¢ par
Dell Computer Corp. name changed
to Dell Inc. 07/18/2003
(See Dell Inc.)

**CONVERGENT COMMUNICATIONS
INC (DE)**
Each share old Common no par
exchanged for (0.5) share new
Common no par 03/16/1999
Plan of reorganization under Chapter
11 Federal Bankruptcy Code
effective 05/09/2002
No stockholders' equity

CONVERGENT COS INC (UT)
Each share Common $0.001 par
exchanged for (0.1) share Common
$0.001 par
Each share old Common $0.001 par
exchanged for (0.33333333) share
new Common $0.001 par
03/04/1999
Name changed to Zerotree
Technologies, Inc. 01/17/2001
Zerotree Technologies, Inc.
recapitalized as Global Equity Fund,
Inc. 03/20/2006
(See Global Equity Fund, Inc.)

**CONVERGENT ENERGY SYS INC
(DE)**
Recapitalized as National Transtech
Corp. 12/26/1994
Each share Common $0.0001 par
exchanged for (0.125) share
Common $0.0001 par
(See National Transtech Corp.)

CONVERGENT GROUP CORP (DE)
Merged into Schlumberger
Technology Corp. 12/01/2000
Each share Common $0.001 par
exchanged for $8 cash

CONVERGENT INC (DE)
Acquired by Unisys Corp. 12/22/1988
Each share Common no par
exchanged for $7 cash

CONVERGENT SOLUTIONS INC (NY)
Merged into KTI Inc. 02/08/1995
Each share Common 1¢ par
exchanged for (1) share Common
1¢ par
KTI Inc. merged into Casella Waste
Systems, Inc. 12/15/1999

**CONVERGENT TECHNOLOGIES,
INC. (CA)**
Common no par split (3) for (2) by
issuance of (0.5) additional share
01/21/1983
Reorganized under the laws of
Delaware as Convergent Inc. and
Common no par changed to 1¢ par
05/22/1987
(See Convergent, Inc.)

CONVERGYS CORP (OH)
Merged into SYNNEX Corp.
10/05/2018
Each share Common no par
exchanged for (0.1263) share
Common $0.001 par and $13.25
cash

**CONVERIUM HLDG AG
(SWITZERLAND)**
Name changed to SCOR Holding
(Switzerland) Ltd. 09/17/2007
*(See SCOR Holding (Switzerland)
Ltd.)*

CONVERSANT INC (DE)
Merged into Alliance Data Systems
Corp. 12/11/2014
Each share Common $0.001 par
exchanged for (0.07037) share
Common $1 par and $15.14 cash

CONVERSE INC (DE)
Plan of reorganization under Chapter
11 Federal Bankruptcy Code
effective 07/31/2002
No stockholders' equity

CONVERSE INC (MA)
Merged into Interco Inc. 09/08/1986
Each share Common $1 par
exchanged for $28 cash

CONVERSE RUBBER CO.
Merged into Converse Rubber Corp.
00/00/1946
Details not available

CONVERSE RUBR CORP (MA)
Each share old Common no par
exchanged for (10) shares new
Common no par 04/26/1951
Acquired by Eltra Corp. 10/02/1971
Details not available

CONVERSION INDS INC (BC)
Each share old Common no par
exchanged for (0.33333333) share
new Common no par 05/30/1989
Filed a petition under Chapter 11
Federal Bankruptcy Code
05/19/1995
Stockholders' equity unlikely

CONVERSION SVCS INTL INC (DE)
Each share old Common $0.001 par
exchanged for (0.06666666) share
new Common $0.001 par
09/21/2005
Chapter 7 bankruptcy proceedings
terminated 08/07/2014
No stockholders' equity

**CONVERSION SOLUTIONS HLDGS
CORP (DE)**
SEC revoked common stock
registration 08/27/2009

**CONVERSION TECHNOLOGIES INTL
INC (DE)**
Filed a petition under Chapter 7
Federal Bankruptcy Code 4/11/2001

Stockholders' equity unlikely

CONVERSIT COM INC (NV)
Name changed to One Voice
Technologies, Inc. 09/27/1999
(See One Voice Technologies, Inc.)

CONVERTAWINGS, INC. (NY)
Completely liquidated 10/23/1970
Each share Common $1 par
exchanged for first and final
distribution of (2) shares Cosmic
Resources Corp. Common 1¢ par
Cosmic Resources Corp.
recapitalized as C R G Corp.
08/22/1972
(See C R G Corp.)

CONVERTED ORGANICS INC (DE)
Units separated 03/21/2007
Each share old Common $0.0001 par
exchanged for (0.1) share new
Common $0.0001 par 11/08/2011
Each share new Common $0.0001
par exchanged again for (0.002)
share new Common $0.0001 par
03/05/2012
Each share new Common $0.0001
par exchanged again for (0.002)
share new Common $0.0001 par
06/04/2013
Stock Dividends - 5% payable
04/05/2007 to holders of record
03/30/2007 Ex date - 03/28/2007;
5% payable 07/13/2007 to holders of
record 06/30/2007 Ex date -
06/27/2007; 5% payable 10/12/2007
to holders of record 09/28/2007
Ex date - 09/26/2007; 5% payable
01/14/2008 to holders of record
12/31/2007 Ex date - 12/27/2007;
5% payable 04/14/2008 to holders of
record 03/31/2008 Ex date -
03/27/2008; 15% payable
12/01/2008 to holders of record
11/17/2008 Ex date - 11/13/2008
Recapitalized as Finjan Holdings, Inc.
06/04/2013
Each share Common $0.0001 par
exchanged for (0.002) share
Common $0.0001 par

**CONVERTIBLE & YIELD
ADVANTAGE TR (ON)**
Trust terminated 10/31/2013
Each Unit received $23.4459 cash

**CONVERTIBLE DEBS INCOME FD
(ON)**
Under plan of merger each Trust Unit
automatically became (0.74627697)
share Canoe 'GO CANADA!' Fund
Corp. Canadian Asset Allocation
Class Ser. Z 04/22/2016

CONVERTIBLE HLDGS INC (MD)
Income Shares 10¢ par called for
redemption at $9.30 on 07/31/1997
Reorganized as Merrill Lynch
Convertible Fund, Inc. 08/04/1997
Each Capital Share 10¢ par
exchanged for (1) share Class A 10¢
par
Merrill Lynch Convertible Fund, Inc.
merged into Merrill Lynch Balanced
Capital Fund, Inc. 12/15/2000

**CONVERTIBLE SECS & INCOME INC
(MD)**
Name changed to Liberty Equity
Income Fund, Inc. 01/08/1993
Liberty Equity Income Fund, Inc.
name changed to Federated Equity
Income Fund, Inc. 03/31/1996

CONVERTIBLE SECS FD INC (DE)
Name changed to Harbor Fund, Inc.
(DE) 04/30/1969
Harbor Fund, Inc. (DE) reincorporated
in Maryland 12/31/1978 which name
changed to American General
Harbor Fund, Inc. 12/10/1980 which
name changed to American Capital
Harbor Fund, Inc. (MD) 09/12/1983
which reincorporated in Delaware as
Van Kampen American Capital
Harbor Fund 08/19/1995 which
name changed to Van Kampen
Harbor Fund 07/14/1998

CONVERTIBLE SECURITIES & GROWTH STOCK FUND, INC. (DE)
Name changed to Enterprise Fund, Inc. (DE) 03/31/1967
Enterprise Fund, Inc. (DE) reincorporated in Maryland as American General Enterprise Fund, Inc. 01/15/1979 which name changed to American Capital Enterprise Fund, Inc. (MD) 09/09/1983 which reincorporated in Delaware as Van Kampen American Capital Enterprise Fund 08/03/1995 which name changed to Van Kampen Enterprise Fund 08/31/1998

CONVERTIBLE TRACTOR CORP. (SD)
Charter expired by time limitation 00/00/1941

CONVEST ENERGY CORP (MA)
Merged into Convest Energy Partners, Ltd. 12/06/1988
Each share Common 1¢ par exchanged for (0.0969) Depositary Receipt and $0.087 cash
Convest Energy Partners, Ltd. recapitalized as Convest Energy Corp. 12/07/1990 which merged into Forcenergy Inc. 10/22/1997 which merged into Forest Oil Corp. 12/07/2000 which name changed to Sabine Oil & Gas Corp. 01/13/2015
(See Sabine Oil & Gas Corp.)

CONVEST ENERGY CORP (TX)
Merged into Forcenergy Inc. 10/22/1997
Each share Common 1¢ par exchanged for (0.254) share Common 1¢ par
Forcenergy Inc. merged into Forest Oil Corp. 12/07/2000 which name changed to Sabine Oil & Gas Corp. 01/13/2015
(See Sabine Oil & Gas Corp.)

CONVEST ENERGY PARTNERS LTD (TX)
Recapitalized as Convest Energy Corp. 12/07/1990
Each Depositary Receipt exchanged for (0.5) share Common 1¢ par
Convest Energy Corp. merged into Forcenergy Inc. 10/22/1997 which merged into Forest Oil Corp. 12/07/2000 which name changed to Sabine Oil & Gas Corp. 01/13/2015
(See Sabine Oil & Gas Corp.)

CONVEX COMPUTER CORP (DE)
Merged into Hewlett-Packard Co. (CA) 12/20/1995
Each share Common 1¢ par exchanged for (0.0593) share Common $1 par
Hewlett-Packard Co. (CA) reincorporated in Delaware 05/20/1998 which name changed to HP Inc. 11/02/2015

CONVIO INC (DE)
Acquired by Blackbaud, Inc. 05/04/2012
Each share Common $0.001 par exchanged for $16 cash

CONVOY CAP CORP (CANADA)
Recapitalized as Hariston Corp. 09/25/1992
Each share Common no par exchanged for (0.2) share Common no par
Hariston Corp. recapitalized as Midland Holland Inc. (Canada) 02/10/1999 which reincorporated in Yukon 03/11/1999 which name changed to Mercury Partners & Co. Inc. 02/22/2000 which name changed to Black Mountain Capital Corp. 05/02/2005 which recapitalized as Grand Peak Capital Corp. (YT) 11/20/2007 which reincorporated in British Columbia 04/27/2010

CONVOY RED LAKE MINES, LTD. (ON)
Charter revoked for failure to file reports and pay taxes 08/29/1960

CONWAY RES INC (QC)
Assets surrendered to creditors 10/24/2013
No stockholders' equity

CONWED CORP (DE)
Stock Dividend - 50% 03/28/1980
Merged into Cardiff Equities Corp. 03/25/1985
Each share Common $5 par exchanged for $28.50 cash

CONWEST EXPL LTD (ON)
Reincorporated 08/27/1982
Capital Stock no par reclassified as Class B Common no par 06/06/1980
Stock Distribution - (1) share Class A Common for each share Class B Common 06/25/1980
Under plan of merger place of incorporation changed from (Canada) to (ON) and each share Class A Common no par exchanged for (1) share Class A no par and each share Class B Common no par exchanged for (1) share Class B no par 08/27/1982
6% Conv. 1st Preference Ser. A $20 par called for redemption 06/01/1987
$2.40 Retractable 1st Preference Ser. B $20 par called for redemption 04/01/1988
Merged into Conwest Exploration Co. Ltd. (New) (AB) 09/01/1993
Each share Class A no par exchanged for (1) share Common no par
Each share Class B no par exchanged for (1) share Common no par
Conwest Exploration Co. Ltd. (New) merged into Alberta Energy Co. Ltd. 01/31/1996 which merged into EnCana Corp. 01/03/2003

CONWEST EXPL LTD NEW (AB)
Merged into Alberta Energy Co. Ltd. 01/31/1996
Each share Common no par exchanged for either (1.25) shares Common no par or $28 cash
Alberta Energy Co. Ltd. merged into EnCana Corp. 01/03/2003

CONWOOD CORP (DE)
Reorganized 12/01/1966
Reorganized from (NJ) to under the laws of Delaware 12/01/1966
Each share Preferred $100 par exchanged for $130 principal amount of 6% Subord. Debentures due 12/01/1991
Each share Common $8.33333333 par exchanged for (1) share Common $8.33333333 par
Common $8.33333333 par changed to $4.16666666 par and (1) additional share issued 05/12/1977
Common $4.16666666 par changed to $2.08333333 and (1) additional share issued 05/15/1981
Common $2.08333333 par split (2) for (1) by issuance of (1) additional share 07/05/1983
Acquired by Dalfort Corp. 09/13/1985
Each share Common $2.08333333 par exchanged for $36 cash

CONYERS PK ACQUISITION CORP (DE)
Units separated 07/07/2017
Merged into Simply Good Foods Co. 07/07/2017
Each share Class A Common $0.0001 par exchanged for (1) share Common 1¢ par

CONZINC RIOTINTO OF AUSTRALIA LTD. (AUSTRALIA)
Name changed to CRA Ltd. 08/00/1980
CRA Ltd. name changed to Rio Tinto Ltd. 06/02/1997
(See Rio Tinto Ltd.)

COOK CHEM CO (MO)
Name changed to Realex Corp. 10/01/1973
(See Realex Corp.)

COOK COFFEE CO. (DE)
Merged into Cook Coffee Co. (OH) 00/00/1951
Each share Common no par exchanged for (1) share Common $1 par
Cook Coffee Co. (OH) name changed to Cook United, Inc. 04/30/1969
(See Cook United, Inc.)

COOK COFFEE CO (OH)
Common $1 par split (2) for (1) by issuance of (1) additional share 09/05/1956
Common Stock $1 par reclassified as Common Shares $1 par 03/25/1965
Common Shares $1 par split (2) for (1) by issuance of (1) additional share 05/15/1968
Name changed to Cook United, Inc. 04/30/1969
(See Cook United, Inc.)

COOK DATA SVCS INC (DE)
Name changed to Blockbuster Entertainment Corp. 05/28/1986
Blockbuster Entertainment Corp. merged into Viacom Inc. (Old) 09/30/1994
(See Viacom Inc. (Old))

COOK ELEC CO (DE)
Reincorporated 07/01/1957
Each share Common $50 par exchanged for (2) shares Common $25 par 09/06/1949
Each share Common $25 par exchanged for (2) shares Common $12.50 par 00/00/1953
Each share Common $12.50 par exchanged for (2) shares Common $5 par 00/00/1954
State of incorporation changed from (IL) to (DE) 07/01/1957
Common $5 par changed to $2.50 par and (1) additional share issued 10/21/1957
Common $2.50 par changed to $1 par and (1.5) additional shares issued 09/30/1959
6% Prior Preferred called for redemption 02/28/1966
Stock Dividends - 10% 03/31/1953; 10% 03/31/1954
Merged into Northern Telecom Ltd.-Northern Telecom Ltee. 12/17/1976
Each share Common $1 par exchanged for $15 cash

COOK INDUSTRIES, INC. (DE)
Common $1 par split (3) for (2) by issuance of (0.5) additional share 10/09/1974
Name changed to Cook International Inc. 05/11/1981
(See Cook International Inc.)

COOK INTL INC (DE)
Acquired by an investor group 02/05/1985
Each share Common $1 par exchanged for $14.35 cash

COOK L L CO (WI)
Through 00/00/1969 purchase offer of $80 cash for each share Common $1 par, GAF Corp. has acquired all but (250) shares as of 07/06/1970
Public interest eliminated

COOK LAKE GOLD MINES LTD. (ON)
Charter cancelled 10/31/1960

COOK PAINT & VARNISH CO. (DE)
Common no par changed to $20 par and (1) additional share issued 05/09/1957
$3 Prior Preference Ser. A $60 par called for redemption 10/01/1961
Common $20 par changed to $15 par and (1) additional share issued 01/11/1962
Merged into CPVC Acquisition Corp. 10/12/1979
Each share Common $15 par exchanged for $36.25 cash

COOK PAINT & VARNISH CO. (MO)
Assets acquired by Cook Paint & Varnish Co. (DE) 00/00/1927
Details not available

COOK TREADWELL & HARRY INC (TN)
Each share Common 10¢ par exchanged for (0.001) share Common $100 par 02/08/1979
Note: In effect holders received $12.50 cash per share and public interest was eliminated

COOK UTD INC NEW (OH)
Reorganized under Chapter 11 Federal Bankruptcy Code 10/13/1986
Each share Common $1 par exchanged for (0.10182) share Common 1¢ par
Chapter 11 bankruptcy proceedings converted to Chapter 7 on 11/24/1987
Stockholders' equity unlikely

COOKE ENGR CO (DE)
Merged into Dynatech Corp. (Old) 04/07/1969
Each share Common 20¢ par exchanged for (0.71428571) share Common 20¢ par
Dynatech Corp. (Old) (MA) merged into Dynatech Corp. (New) (MA) 05/21/1998 which reincorporated in Delaware 09/08/1999 which name changed to Acterna Corp. 08/30/2000
(See Acterna Corp.)

COOKE TRUST CO., LTD. (HONOLULU, HI)
Merged into First National Bank of Hawaii (Honolulu, HI) 07/26/1966
Each share Capital Stock $20 par exchanged for (1.6) shares Common $10 par
First National Bank of Hawaii (Honolulu, HI) name changed to First Hawaiian Bank (Honolulu, HI) 01/02/1969 which reorganized as First Hawaiian, Inc. 07/01/1974 which name changed to BancWest Corp. (New) 11/01/1998
(See BancWest Corp. (New))

COOKER CONCEPTS INC (KY)
Each share old Common no par exchanged for (0.000004) share new Common no par 04/15/1991
Note: In effect holders received $0.01 cash per share and public interest was eliminated

COOKER RESTAURANT CORP (OH)
Each share old Common no par exchanged for (0.33333333) share new Common no par 04/29/1991
New Common no par split (2) for (1) by issuance of (1) additional share 04/13/1992
Plan of reorganization under Chapter 11 Federal Bankruptcy Code effective 09/25/2002
No stockholders' equity

COOKSON GROUP PLC (UNITED KINGDOM)
ADR agreement terminated 10/19/2005
Each Sponsored ADR for Ordinary exchanged for $3.4361 cash
Name changed to Vesuvius PLC 12/18/2012

COOKSVILLE CO. LTD. (CANADA)
Each share Preference $100 par exchanged for (1) share 2nd Preferred $100 par and (4) shares Common no par 00/00/1937
Each share Common no par exchanged for (1) share Class A no

par and (1) share Class B no par 00/00/1947
Acquired by Dominion Tar & Chemical Co. Ltd. 00/00/1954
Each share Class A no par exchanged for $20 cash
Each share Class B no par exchanged for $15 cash

COOKSVILLE SHALE BRICK CO.
Name changed to Cooksville Co. Ltd. 00/00/1928
(See Cooksville Co. Ltd.)

COOKYS STEAK PUBS INC (NY)
Merged into SCP Acquisition Corp. 03/25/1983
Each share Common 10¢ par exchanged for $4 cash

COOL CAN TECHNOLOGIES INC (MN)
Reorganized under the laws of Nevada as NorPac Technologies, Inc. 07/12/2004
Each share Common no par exchanged for (0.05) share Common $0.001 par
NorPac Technologies, Inc. name changed to Cellynx Group, Inc. 08/05/2008
(See Cellynx Group, Inc.)

COOL ENTMT INC (CO)
Reorganized under the laws of Delaware as E-Trend Networks, Inc. 02/22/2001
Each share Common no par exchanged for (0.01) share Common no par
E-Trend Networks, Inc. name changed to Wilmington Rexford Inc. 02/19/2002 which recapitalized as China Pharmaceuticals Corp. (DE) 03/25/2004 which reincorporated in British Virgin Islands as China Pharmaceuticals International Corp. 08/26/2004 which recapitalized as China Heli Resource Renewable Inc. 11/07/2008
(See China Heli Resource Renewable Inc.)

COOLBRANDS INTL INC (CANADA)
Reincorporated 03/27/2006
Place of incorporation changed from (NS) to (Canada) 03/27/2006
Multiple Shares no par reclassified as Common no par 06/04/2007
Subordinate Shares no par reclassified as Common no par 06/04/2007
Reorganized under the laws of Delaware as Swisher Hygiene Inc. 11/04/2010
Each share Common no par exchanged for (1) share Common $0.001 par

COOLIDGE BK & TR CO (WATERTOWN, MA)
Common $1.67 par changed to 60¢ par and (2) additional shares issued 02/09/1970
Reorganized as First Coolidge Corp. 06/01/1972
Each share Common 60¢ par exchanged for (1) share Common 60¢ par
(See First Coolidge Corp.)

COOLIDGE INVESTMENT CO. (KS)
Charter expired by time limitation 07/14/1908

COOLSAVINGS INC (DE)
Name changed 09/20/2001
Name changed from CoolSavings.com Inc. (MI) to CoolSavings, Inc. (DE) 09/20/2001
Merged into Landmark Communications, Inc. 12/15/2005
Each share Common no par exchanged for $0.80 cash

COOPER, TINSLEY LABORATORIES, INC. (DE)
Name changed to Cooper Laboratories, Inc. 01/23/1967
(See Cooper Laboratories, Inc.)

COOPER & CHYAN TECHNOLOGY INC (DE)
Merged into Cadence Design Systems Inc. 05/07/1997
Each share Common 1¢ par exchanged for (0.85) share Common 1¢ par

COOPER AGY INC (MI)
Voluntarily dissolved 05/04/1988
Details not available

COOPER-BESSEMER CORP. (OH)
Common no par changed to $5 par 00/00/1948
Common $5 par split (2) for (1) by issuance of (1) additional share 06/07/1957
Stock Dividends - 50% 06/24/1949; 10% 12/28/1950; 10% 12/28/1951; 20% 12/06/1956; 10% 04/08/1960
Name changed to Cooper Industries, Inc. (OH) 12/10/1965
Cooper Industries, Inc. (OH) reincorporated in Bermuda as Cooper Industries, Ltd. 05/22/2002 which reincorporated in Ireland as Cooper Industries PLC 09/08/2009 which merged into Eaton Corp. PLC 11/30/2012

COOPER CAMERON CORP (DE)
Common 1¢ par split (2) for (1) by issuance of (1) additional share payable 06/12/1997 to holders of record 05/19/1997 Ex date - 06/13/1997
Common 1¢ par split (2) for (1) by issuance of (1) additional share payable 12/15/2005 to holders of record 11/21/2005 Ex date - 12/16/2005
Name changed to Cameron International Corp. 05/05/2006
Cameron International Corp. merged into Schlumberger Ltd. 04/01/2016

COOPER CDA LTD (ON)
Common no par split (2) for (1) by issuance of (1) additional share 08/16/1983
Class A no par reclassified as Common no par 05/01/1987
Stock Dividend - In Class A to holders of Common 100% 05/30/1985
Merged into Les Industries Charan Inc. 06/04/1987
Each share Common no par exchanged for $6 cash

COOPER DEV CO (DE)
Each share old Common 10¢ par exchanged for (0.1) share new Common 10¢ par 07/27/1987
Each share new Common 10¢ par exchanged again for (0.002) share new Common 10¢ par 03/14/1997
Note: In effect holders received $1.50 cash per share and public interest was eliminated

COOPER ENERGY INC (DE)
Name changed to Cooper Resources & Energy, Inc. 08/24/1981
(See Cooper Resources & Energy, Inc.)

COOPER HLDG CORP (DE)
Recapitalized as Crednology Holding Corp. 05/03/2013
Each share Common $0.001 par exchanged for (0.01) share Common $0.001 par

COOPER HOLDINGS INC. LIQUIDATING TRUST (DE)
Each Share of Bene. Int. 10¢ par received initial distribution of $0.35 cash 06/25/1985
Each Share of Bene. Int. 10¢ par received second distribution of (0.042) share Cooper Development Co. Common 10¢ par 10/09/1987
Date and amount of any subsequent distributions, if any, are unavailable

COOPER INDS INC (OH)
Common $5 par split (2) for (1) by issuance of (1) additional share 11/04/1966
$5 Conv. Preferred Ser. A no par called for redemption 07/18/1975
Common $5 par split (2) for (1) by issuance of (1) additional share 03/26/1976
Common $5 par split (2) for (1) by issuance of (1) additional share 04/21/1980
$2.90 Conv. Preferred $1 par called for redemption 01/06/1986
Common $5 par split (2) for (1) by issuance of (1) additional share 04/10/1989
$2.50 Conv. Preferred Ser. B no par called for redemption 04/05/1990
$8 Conv. Exchangeable Preferred $1 par dividend rate changed to $1.60 on 05/04/1990
$1.60 Conv. Exchangeable Preferred $1 par split (5) for (1) by issuance of (4) additional shares 05/25/1990
Each share $1.60 Conv. Exchangeable Preferred $1 par exchanged for $22.70 principal amount of 7.05% Conv. Subord. Debentures due 01/01/2015 on 12/30/1994
Reincorporated under the laws of Bermuda as Cooper Industries, Ltd. and Common $5 par changed to Class A Common 1¢ par 05/22/2002
Cooper Industries, Ltd. (Bermuda) reincorporated in Ireland as Cooper Industries PLC 09/08/2009 which merged into Eaton Corp. PLC 11/30/2012

COOPER INDS LTD (BERMUDA)
Class A Common 1¢ par split (2) for (1) by issuance of (1) additional share payable 03/15/2007 to holders of record 02/28/2007 Ex date - 03/16/2007
Reincorporated under the laws of Ireland as Cooper Industries PLC and Class A Common 1¢ par reclassified as Ordinary 1¢ par 09/08/2009
Cooper Industries PLC merged into Eaton Corp. PLC 11/30/2012

COOPER INDUSTRIES PLC (IRELAND)
Merged into Eaton Corp. PLC 11/30/2012
Each share Ordinary 1¢ par exchanged for (0.77479) share Ordinary 1¢ par and $39.15 cash

COOPER JARRETT INC (MO)
Stock Dividends - 10% 03/11/1959; 20% 09/25/1965
Chapter 11 bankruptcy proceedings converted to Chapter 7 on 01/30/1985
Stockholders' equity unlikely

COOPER LABS INC (DE)
Common 10¢ par split (5) for (2) by issuance of (1.5) additional shares 05/02/1983
Stock Dividends - 100% 02/21/1969; 15% 04/05/1972
In process of liquidation
Each share Common 10¢ par exchanged for initial distribution of (1.3184) shares CooperBiomedical, Inc. Common 10¢ par, (1) share Cooper LaserSonics, Inc. Common 10¢ par, (0.0633) share Rorer Group Inc. Common no par and $3.15 cash 06/17/1985
(See each company's listing)
Assets transferred to Cooper Holdings Inc. Liquidating Trust and Common 10¢ par reclassified as Shares of Bene. Int. 10¢ par 06/17/1985
(See Cooper Holdings Inc. Liquidating Trust)

COOPER LAKE GOLD MINES LTD. (ON)
Declared dissolved 04/01/1963
No stockholders' equity

COOPER LIFE SCIENCES INC (DE)
Recapitalized 05/27/1988
Recapitalized from Cooper Lasersonics, Inc. to Cooper Life Sciences, Inc. 05/27/1988
Each share Common 10¢ par exchanged for (0.1) share Common 10¢ par
Name changed to Berkshire Bancorp, Inc. 04/06/1999

COOPER MINERALS INC (YT)
Reincorporated under the laws of British Columbia as United Coal Holdings Ltd. 05/28/2012

COOPER OF CANADA LTD. (ON)
Name changed to Cooper Canada Ltd. 6/29/77
(See Cooper Canada Ltd.)

COOPER PETER CORP (DE)
Name changed to Wilhelm Enterprises Corp. 11/12/1976
(See Wilhelm Enterprises Corp.)

COOPER RES & ENERGY INC (DE)
Merged into Brunswick Subsidiary Inc. 12/31/1984
Each share Common 10¢ par exchanged for $15.39 cash

COOPER RIVER BRIDGE, INC.
Property sold to Charleston County, S.C. 00/00/1941
Details not available

COOPER STD HLDGS INC (DE)
Each share 7% Conv. Accredited Investors Participating Preferred $0.001 par automatically became (4.34164) shares Common $0.001 par 11/15/2013
Each share 7% Conv. Participating Preferred $0.001 par automatically became (4.34164) shares Common $0.001 par 11/15/2013
(Additional Information in Active)

COOPER TIRE & RUBR CO (DE)
4-3/4% Conv. Preferred $20 par called for redemption 7/14/67
5% Conv. Preferred $25 par called for redemption 4/17/81
(Additional Information in Active)

COOPERATIVE BK SVGS INC (NC)
Common $1 par split (5) for (4) by issuance of (0.25) additional share 06/30/1992
Common $1 par split (2) for (1) by issuance of (1) additional share 10/30/1992
Common $1 par split (3) for (2) by issuance of (0.5) additional share 02/24/1993
Common $1 par split (3) for (2) by issuance of (0.5) additional share 02/24/1994
Name changed to Cooperative Bankshares Inc. 08/09/1994
(See Cooperative Bankshares Inc.)

COOPERATIVE BANKSHARES INC (NC)
Common $1 par split (2) for (1) by issuance of (1) additional share payable 09/22/1997 to holders of record 09/08/1997
Common $1 par split (3) for (2) by issuance of (0.5) additional share payable 02/24/2005 to holders of record 02/08/2005 Ex date - 02/25/2005
Common $1 par split (3) for (2) by issuance of (0.5) additional share payable 06/30/2006 to holders of record 06/12/2006 Ex date - 07/03/2006
Chapter 7 bankruptcy proceedings terminated 09/14/2015
No stockholders' equity

COOPERATIVE ENERGY DEV CORP (CANADA)
Name changed to Co-Enerco Resources Ltd. 05/14/1991
(See Co-Enerco Resources Ltd.)

COOPERATIVE SERVICES INC. (IN)
Administratively dissolved 09/22/1999

COOPERBIOMEDICAL INC (DE)
Name changed to Cooper Development Co. 4/22/86
(See Cooper Development Co.)

COOPERS PK CORP (CANADA)
Each share old Common no par exchanged for (0.025) share new Common no par 04/13/2007
Each share new Common no par exchanged again for (0.00000393) share new Common no par 05/26/2015
Note: In effect holders received $1.62071 cash per share and public interest was eliminated
Distributions of less than $10 will not be made

COOPERS PK REAL ESTATE CORP (CANADA)
Name changed to Coopers Park Corp. 08/09/2006
(See Coopers Park Corp.)

COOPERS RES N L (AUSTRALIA)
Name changed 11/04/1982
Name changed from Coopers Diamond Holdings N.L. to Coopers Resources N.L. and ADR's for Ordinary AUD $0.05 par changed to AUD $2 par 11/04/1982
Each ADR for Ordinary AUD $2 par exchanged for (1) old ADR for Ordinary AUD $0.50 par 10/15/1986
Each old ADR for Ordinary AUD $0.50 par exchanged for (1) new ADR for Ordinary AUD $0.50 par 10/15/1986
ADR agreement terminated 11/20/2000
Each new ADR for Ordinary AUD $0.50 par exchanged for $0.0045 cash

COOPERVISION INC (DE)
Stock Dividend - 10% 10/12/1983
Name changed to Cooper Companies, Inc. 06/22/1987

COORDINATED COMPUTER CONCEPTS INC (NY)
Charter cancelled and proclaimed dissolved for failure to pay taxes 6/24/81

COORDINATED ENTITIES INC (DE)
Recapitalized as Bavarian Technologies Inc. 8/15/86
Each share Common $0.0001 par exchanged for (0.1) share Common $0.0001 par
Bavarian Technologies Inc. name changed to Bavarian Properties Inc. 5/24/89
(See Bavarian Properties Inc.)

COORDINATED HEALTHCARE INC (FL)
Recapitalized as Isleuth.Com, Inc. 08/10/1998
Each share Common $0.001 par exchanged for (0.05) share Common $0.001 par
Isleuth.Com, Inc. name changed to BigHub.com Inc. 04/29/1999
(See BigHub.com Inc.)

COORDINATED PHYSICIAN SVCS INC (FL)
Name changed to Techlabs, Inc. 02/26/1999

COORS ADOLPH CO (DE)
Reincorporated 10/3/2003
State of incorporation changed from (CO) to (DE) and Class B Common no par changed to 1¢ par 10/3/2003
Under plan of merger name changed to Molson Coors Brewing Co. 2/9/2005

COORSTEK INC (DE)
Merged into Keystone Holdings LLC 3/18/2003
Each share Common 1¢ par exchanged for $26 cash

COOS BAY LUMBER CO. (DE)
Each share Common no par exchanged for (3) shares Common $10 par in 1945
Voluntarily dissolved 7/10/56
Details not available

COOSA RIVER NEWSPRINT CO. (AL)
Acquired by Kimberly-Clark Corp. on a (1.36) for (1) basis 5/31/62

COP MAC MINES LTD (BC)
Recapitalized as Cametin Industries Ltd. 07/31/1973
Each share Capital Stock no par exchanged for (0.25) share Capital Stock no par
(See Cametin Industries Ltd.)

COPANO ENERGY LLC (DE)
Common Units split (2) for (1) by issuance of (1) additional Unit payable 03/30/2007 to holders of record 03/15/2007 Ex date - 04/02/2007
Merged into Kinder Morgan Energy Partners, L.P. 05/01/2013
Each Common Unit exchanged for (0.4563) Unit of Ltd. Partnership
Kinder Morgan Energy Partners, L.P. merged into Kinder Morgan, Inc. 11/26/2014

COPART INC (CA)
Issue Information - 2,000,000 shares COM offered at $12 per share on 03/16/1994
Common no par split (2) for (1) by issuance of (1) additional share payable 01/28/1999 to holders of record 01/14/1999
Common no par split (2) for (1) by issuance of (1) additional share payable 01/24/2000 to holders of record 01/06/2000
Common no par split (3) for (2) by issuance of (0.5) additional share payable 01/21/2002 to holders of record 01/04/2002 Ex date - 01/22/2002
Reincorporated under the laws of Delaware and Common no par changed to $0.0001 par 01/10/2012

COPCONDA MINES LTD. (ON)
Name changed to Copconda Resources Inc. 7/23/79

COPCONDA RES INC (CANADA)
Reincorporated 08/13/1980
Place of incorporation changed from (ON) to (Canada) 08/13/1980
Acquired by Copconda-York Resources Inc. 02/25/1981
Each share Common exchanged for (2) shares Common no par
Copconda-York Resources Inc. recapitalized as Pacvest Capital Inc. 07/21/1987 which merged into First Toronto Mining Corp. 01/01/1989
(See First Toronto Mining Corp.)

COPCONDA YORK RES INC (CANADA)
Each share Class B Special Stock no par exchanged for (0.205) share Common no par 01/30/1985
Recapitalized as Pacvest Capital Inc. 07/21/1987
Each share Common no par exchanged for (0.25) share Common no par
Pacvest Capital Inc. merged into First Toronto Mining Corp. 01/01/1989
(See First Toronto Mining Corp.)

COPE INC (DE)
Name changed to Mount10, Inc. 10/20/2000
(See Mount10, Inc.)

COPELAND AL ENTERPRISES INC (TX)
Plan of reorganization under Chapter 11 Federal Bankruptcy proceedings confirmed 10/22/1992
No stockholders' equity

COPELAND CORP (DE)
Common $1 par split (2) for (1) by issuance of (1) additional share 2/12/73
Merged into Hillman Co. 7/1/81
Each share Common $1 par exchanged for $38.50 cash

COPELAND PROCESS LTD (NB)
Name changed to Copeland Systems Ltd.-Copeland Systems Ltee. 08/09/1976
Copeland Systems Ltd.-Copeland Systems Ltee. name changed to MSZ Resources Ltd. (NB) 12/10/1979 which reorganized in Alberta as Corrida Oils Ltd. 02/08/1982
(See Corrida Oils Ltd.)

COPELAND PRODUCTS, INC.
Assets sold 00/00/1933
Details not available

COPELAND REFRIG CORP (MI)
Common $1 par split (3) for (2) by issuance of (0.5) additional share 1/20/67
Merged into Copeland Corp. 1/26/72
Each share Common $1 par exchanged for (2) shares Common $1 par
(See Copeland Corp.)

COPELAND RES LTD (BC)
Name changed to Copeland Technologies Inc. 10/23/1991
Copeland Technologies Inc. name changed to Golden Chief Resources Inc. (BC) 09/16/1994 which reorganized in Ontario as Roscan Minerals Corp. 11/17/2004 which name changed to Roscan Gold Corp. 10/01/2018

COPELAND SILICA GEL CORP.
Dissolved 00/00/1930
Details not available

COPELAND SYS LTD (NB)
Name changed to MSZ Resources Ltd. (NB) 12/10/1979
MSZ Resources Ltd. (NB) reorganized in Alberta as Corrida Oils Ltd. 02/08/1982
(See Corrida Oils Ltd.)

COPELAND TECHNOLOGIES INC (BC)
Name changed to Golden Chief Resources Inc. (BC) 09/16/1994
Golden Chief Resources Inc. (BC) reorganized in Ontario as Roscan Minerals Corp. 11/17/2004 which name changed to Roscan Gold Corp. 10/01/2018

COPELCO FINL SVCS GROUP INC (DE)
Merged into Mediq Inc. 01/06/1989
Each share Common 10¢ par exchanged for $8.75 cash

COPENE PETROQUIMICA DO NORDESTE S A (BRAZIL)
Name changed to Braskem S.A. 09/02/2002

COPERNIC INC (ON)
Each share old Common no par exchanged for (1/7) share new Common no par 09/14/2009
Merged into Comamtech Inc. (ON) 11/04/2010
Each share new Common no par exchanged for (1) share Common no par
Comamtech Inc. (ON) reincorporated in Delaware as DecisionPoint Systems, Inc. (New) 06/22/2011

COPERNICAN BRIT BKS FD (ON)
Under plan of merger each Trust Unit automatically became (0.214028) Portland Global Banks Fund Ser. A2 Unit 12/13/2013

COPERNICAN INTL FINL SPLIT CORP. (ON)
Preferred Shares called for redemption at $6.362 on 12/02/2013
Class A Shares called for redemption 12/02/2013
No stockholders' equity

COPERNICAN INTL PREM DIVIDEND FD (ON)
Under plan of merger each Trust Unit automatically became (0.638547) Portland Global Dividend Fund Ser. A2 Unit 05/23/2014

COPERNICAN WORLD BKS INCOME & GROWTH TR (ON)
Under plan of merger each Unit automatically became (0.879911) Global Banks Premium Income Trust, Trust Unit 12/13/2010
Global Banks Premium Income Trust merged into Portland Global Income Fund 12/13/2013

COPERNICAN WORLD BKS SPLIT INC (ON)
Preferred Shares called for redemption at $4.69 on 12/02/2013
Class A Shares called for redemption 12/02/2013
No stockholders' equity

COPERNICAN WORLD FINL INFRASTRUCTURE TR (ON)
Trust terminated 03/05/2014
Each Trust Unit received $8.4192 cash

COPICO (CA)
Each share old Common $1 par exchanged for (0.001) share new Common $1 par 00/00/1978
Note: In effect holders received $5 cash per share and public interest was eliminated

COPLAY CEM MFG CO (PA)
Name changed 09/10/1979
Common $100 par changed to $20 par 00/00/1934
Preferred Vtg. Trust $100 par expired 00/00/1962
Common Vtg. Trust $100 par expired 00/00/1962
Each share 6% Preferred $100 par exchanged for (10) shares 6% Preferred $20 par 07/01/1963
Each share Common $20 par exchanged for (10) shares Common $10 par 07/01/1963
6% Preferred $20 par changed to $6.66666666 par and (2) additional shares issued 05/06/1968
Common $10 par changed to $3.33333333 par and (2) additional shares issued 05/06/1968
Common $3.33333333 par changed to $1 par and (0.5) additional share issued 07/10/1972
Name changed from Coplay Cement Manufacturing Co. to Coplay Cement Co. 09/10/1979
Company acquired 03/17/1989
Details not available

COPLEY FD INC (FL)
Reincorporated 09/01/1987
Reincorporated 05/19/1994
Name changed to Copley Tax Managed Fund, Inc. 02/01/1984 which name changed back to Copley Fund, Inc. 03/11/1987
State of incorporation changed from (MA) to (NY) 09/01/1987
State of incorporation changed from (NY) to (FL) 05/19/1994
Reincorporated under the laws of Nevada 12/05/2007

COPLEY PHARMACEUTICAL INC (DE)
Common 1¢ par split (3) for (2) by issuance of (0.5) additional share 06/08/1993
Merged into Teva Pharmaceutical Industries Ltd. 09/17/1999
Each share Common 1¢ par exchanged for $11 cash

COPLEY PPTYS INC (DE)
Merged into Eastgroup Properties 06/19/1996
Each share Common $1 par

exchanged for (0.70668) share Common $1 par
Eastgroup Properties reorganized as Eastgroup Properties, Inc. 06/05/1997

COPLEY RLTY INCOME PARTNERS LTD PARTNERSHIP (MA)
Units of Ltd. Partnership I completely liquidated 03/30/1999
Details not available
Units of Ltd. Partnership 3 completely liquidated 12/28/2000
Details not available
Units of Ltd. Partnership 3 completely liquidated 12/28/2000
Details not available
Units of Ltd. Partnership 2 completely liquidated 04/23/2001
Details not available

COPLEY TAX MANAGED FD INC (MA)
Name changed back to Copley Fund, Inc. (MA) 03/11/1987
Copley Fund, Inc. (MA) reincorporated in New York 09/01/1987 which reincorporated in Florida 05/19/1994 which reincorporated in Nevada 12/05/2007

COPLEY TR (DC)
Reincorporated under the laws of Massachusetts as Copley Fund, Inc. 02/27/1980
Copley Fund, Inc. name changed to Copley Tax Managed Fund, Inc. 02/01/1984 which name changed back to Copley Fund, Inc. (MA) 03/11/1987 which reincorporated in New York 09/01/1987 which reincorporated in Florida 05/19/1994 which reincorporated in Nevada 12/05/2007

COPPER BELT RES LTD (BC)
Name changed to CB Resources Ltd. 08/11/2008
CB Resources Ltd. recapitalized as Next Gen Metals Inc. 08/18/2009 which recapitalized as Namaste Technologies Inc. 03/02/2016

COPPER BOUNTY MINES LTD (BC)
Reorganized under the laws of Canada as Walmont Precious Metals Corp. 01/23/1984
Each share Capital Stock no par exchanged for (0.25) share Common no par
Walmont Precious Metals Corp. recapitalized as IGF Metals Inc. 08/01/1986 which name changed to Independent Growth Finders Inc. 07/10/1998
(See Independent Growth Finders Inc.)

COPPER CAMP CONSOLIDATED MINES, INC. (ID)
Charter forfeited for failure to file reports 12/01/1993

COPPER-CAN DEVELOPMENTS LTD. (BC)
Name changed to S.M.I. Processes Ltd. 12/20/1968
S.M.I. Processes Ltd. name changed to S.M. Industries Ltd. 03/26/1969
(See S.M. Industries Ltd.)

COPPER CANYON MINING CO. (DE)
Capital Stock $1 par changed to 10¢ par 00/00/1936
Adjudicated bankrupt 04/30/1958
No stockholders' equity

COPPER CANYON RES LTD (AB)
Merged into NovaGold Resources Inc. 05/20/2011
Each share Common no par exchanged for (0.0735) share Common no par, (0.25) share Omineca Mining & Metals Ltd. Common no par and $0.001 cash
Note: Unexchanged certificates were cancelled and became without value 05/20/2017

COPPER CLIFF CONSOLIDATED MINING CORP. (QC)
Merged into Copper Rand Chibougamau Mines Ltd. on a (0.5) for (1) basis 09/25/1956
Copper Rand Chibougamau Mines Ltd. merged into Patino Mining Corp. 11/26/1962 which reorganized as Patino N.V. 12/20/1971
(See Patino N.V.)

COPPER COWBOY RES INC (BC)
Name changed to True Zone Resources Inc. 07/14/2014

COPPER CREEK GOLD CORP (BC)
Reincorporated 11/06/2017
Each share old Common no par exchanged for (0.1) share new Common no par 03/04/2013
Place of incorporation changed from (Canada) to (BC) 11/06/2017
Each share new Common no par exchanged again for (0.2) share new Common no par 12/11/2017
Reorganized as Surge Exploration Inc. 05/01/2018
Each share new Common no par exchanged for (2) shares Common no par

COPPER CREEK VENTURES LTD (CANADA)
Reincorporated 08/13/1997
Place of incorporation changed from (BC) to (Canada) 08/13/1997
Name changed to Copper Creek Gold Corp. (Canada) 07/26/2010
Copper Creek Gold Corp. (Canada) reincorporated in British Columbia 11/06/2017 which reorganized as Surge Exploration Inc. 05/01/2018

COPPER DISTRICT POWER CO.
Merged into Upper Peninsula Power Co. 00/00/1947
Details not available

COPPER DOME MINES LTD (AB)
Reorganized under the laws of British Columbia as Dome Ventures Inc. 11/06/1998
Each share Common no par exchanged for (0.5) share Common no par
Dome Ventures Inc. (BC) reincorporated in Delaware as EComm Systems Corp. 01/17/2000 which name changed to Dome Ventures Corp. 04/17/2001 which merged into Metalline Mining Inc. 04/16/2010 which name changed to Silver Bull Resources, Inc. 05/02/2011

COPPER FOX METALS INC (AB)
Reincorporated under the laws of British Columbia 07/14/2010

COPPER GIANT MNG LTD (BC)
Merged into Long Lac Minerals Ltd. 11/02/1981
Each share Common 50¢ par exchanged for (0.22222222) share Common $1 par
Long Lac Minerals Ltd. merged into Lac Minerals Ltd. (Old) 12/31/1982 which merged into LAC Minerals Ltd. (New) 07/29/1985 which was acquired by American Barrick Resources Corp. 10/17/1994 which name changed to Barrick Gold Corp. 01/18/1995

COPPER GLANCE MINING CO. (AZ)
Charter expired by time limitations 07/03/1926

COPPER HILL CORP (ON)
Recapitalized as Viking Gold Exploration Inc. 02/17/2004
Each share Common no par exchanged for (0.25) share Common no par

COPPER HILL MINING CO., LTD. (ON)
Charter revoked for failure to file reports and pay taxes 10/01/1956

COPPER HORN MNG LTD (BC)
Recapitalized as Hitec Development Corp. 03/28/1974
Each share Capital Stock 50¢ par exchanged for (1) share Capital Stock no par
(See Hitec Development Corp.)

COPPER ISLAND MINING CO. LTD. (ON)
Merged into Continental Consolidated Mines & Oils Co. Ltd. on a (0.2) for (1) basis 10/04/1957
(See Continental Consolidated Mines & Co. Ltd.)

COPPER JIM MINES LTD (ON)
Charter cancelled for failure to pay taxes and file returns 07/27/1976

COPPER KING CO. (NV)
Name changed to Nevada King Copper Co. 11/27/1956
Nevada King Copper Co. name changed to Nevada King Co. 12/03/1971
(See Nevada King Co.)

COPPER KING MINES LTD. (BC)
Merged into Proto Explorations & Holdings Inc. 05/31/1972
Each share Capital Stock $1 par exchanged for (0.142857) share Common no par
Proto Explorations & Holdings Inc. name changed to Baxter Resources Corp. 06/26/1981 which merged into Baxter Technologies Corp. 12/31/1981 which name changed to Standard-Modern Technologies Corp. 10/08/1985
(See Standard-Modern Technologies Corp.)

COPPER LAKE EXPLS LTD (BC)
Name changed to Whitecap Energy Resources Ltd. 11/17/1978 which name changed back to Copper Lake Explorations Ltd. 05/28/1980
Struck off register and declared dissolved for failure to file returns 01/19/1996

COPPER LODE MINES INC (NV)
Name changed to Trade Industries, Inc. 02/11/1971
Trade Industries, Inc. recapitalized as Traco Corp. 03/21/1972 which name changed to Energy International, Inc. 03/01/1974
(See Energy International, Inc.)

COPPER LODE MINES LTD (ON)
Recapitalized as Consolidated Copper-Lode Developments Inc. 06/23/1977
Each share Capital Stock $1 par exchanged for (0.1) share Capital Stock no par
Consolidated Copper-Lode Developments Inc. name changed to Norbeau Mines Inc. 02/28/1984
(See Norbeau Mines Inc.)

COPPER MAN MINES LTD (ON)
Capital Stock $1 par changed to no par 05/17/1971
Merged into Hartland Mines Ltd. 07/25/1974
Each share Capital Stock no par exchanged for (0.33333333) share Capital Stock no par
(See Hartland Mines Ltd.)

COPPER MESA MNG CORP (BC)
Delisted from Toronto Stock Exchange 02/19/2010

COPPER MOUNTAIN CONSOLIDATED LTD. (BC)
Merged into Rocky Mountain Trench Mines Ltd. (New) 07/11/1973
Each share Capital Stock 50¢ par exchanged for (1) share Capital Stock no par
Rocky Mountain Trench Mines Ltd. (New) merged into New Copper Mountain Mines Ltd. 08/09/1974
(See New Copper Mountain Mines Ltd.)

COPPER MOUNTAIN MINES LTD.
Name changed to Copper Mountain Consolidated Ltd. 06/29/1962
Copper Mountain Consolidated Ltd. merged into Rocky Mountain Trench Mines Ltd. (New) 07/11/1973 which merged into New Copper Mountain Mines Ltd. 08/09/1974
(See New Copper Mountain Mines Ltd.)

COPPER MTN ENERGY INC (UT)
Proclaimed dissolved for failure to pay taxes 03/31/1989

COPPER MTN MINES LTD (BC)
Name changed to China Ventures Inc. 07/27/2000
China Ventures Inc. recapitalized as China Education Resources, Inc. 12/16/2004

COPPER MTN NETWORKS INC (DE)
Common $0.001 par split (2) for (1) by issuance of (1) additional share payable 12/09/1999 to holders of record 11/24/1999
Each share old Common $0.001 par exchanged for (0.1) share new Common $0.001 par 07/18/2002
Merged into Tut Systems, Inc. 06/01/2005
Each share new Common $0.001 par exchanged for (0.3269) share Common $0.001 par
(See Tut Systems, Inc.)

COPPER PASS MINES LTD (AB)
Struck off register 07/01/1985

COPPER PRINCE MINES LTD. (ON)
Recapitalized as Copper Prince Resources Inc. (ON) 08/17/1981
Each share Capital Stock $1 par exchanged for (0.1) share Common no par
Copper Prince Resources Inc. (ON) reincorporated in British Columbia 09/13/1983 which reorganized in Ontario as Churchill Growth AA Communications, Inc. 01/18/1986 which recapitalized as Telecommerce Corp. 06/23/1987 which recapitalized as E Ventures Inc. 02/25/1999
(See E Ventures Inc.)

COPPER PRINCE RES INC (BC)
Reincorporated 09/13/1983
Place of incorporation changed from (ON) to (BC) 09/13/1983
Reorganized under the laws of Ontario as Churchill Growth AA Communications, Inc. 01/18/1986
Each share Common no par exchanged for (0.25) share Common no par
Churchill Growth AA Communications, Inc. recapitalized as Telecommerce Corp. 06/23/1987 which recapitalized as E Ventures Inc. 02/25/1999
(See E Ventures Inc.)

COPPER QUEEN EXPLS LTD (BC)
Struck off register and declared dissolved for failure to file returns 05/25/1976

COPPER RAND CHIBOUGAMAU MINES LTD. (QC)
Merged into Patino Mining Corp. 11/26/1962
Each share Capital Stock 75¢ par exchanged for (0.15384615) share Capital Stock $6.50 par
Patino Mining Corp. reorganized as Patino N.V. 12/20/1971
(See Patino N.V.)

COPPER RANGE CO (MI)
Capital Stock $25 par changed to no par 00/00/1931
Capital Stock no par changed to $5 par and (1) additional share issued 03/18/1955
Stock Dividend - 25% 12/29/1950
Merged into Louisiana Land & Exploration Co. 05/24/1977

Each share Capital Stock $5 par exchanged for (0.825) share Capital Stock 15¢ par
Louisiana Land & Exploration Co. merged into Burlington Resources Inc. 10/22/1997 which merged into ConocoPhillips 03/31/2006

COPPER RD INC (NV)
Charter revoked for failure to file reports and pay fees 02/27/2009

COPPER RIDGE EXPLORATIONS INC (BC)
Each share old Common no par exchanged for (0.06666666) share new Common no par 11/03/2009
Name changed to Redtail Metals Corp. 05/31/2011
Redtail Metals Corp. merged into Golden Predator Mining Corp. (AB) 04/22/2014 which reincorporated in British Columbia 10/21/2015

COPPER RIDGE MINES LTD (BC)
Name changed to Northern Copper Ridge Mines Ltd. 06/18/1980
Northern Copper Ridge Mines Ltd. name changed to Ventec Resources Inc. 07/19/1982
(See Ventec Resources Inc.)

COPPER RIDGE SILVER ZINC MINES, LTD. (BC)
Recapitalized as Copper Ridge Mines Ltd. 05/02/1962
Each share Capital Stock 50¢ par exchanged for (0.25) share Capital Stock no par
Copper Ridge Mines Ltd. name changed to Northern Copper Ridge Mines Ltd. 06/18/1980 which name changed to Ventec Resources Inc. 07/19/1982

COPPER SOO MNG LTD (BC)
Recapitalized as Beaumont Resources Ltd. 07/07/1969
Each share Capital Stock no par exchanged for (0.2) share Common no par
Beaumont Resources Ltd. recapitalized as Consolidated Beaumont Resources Ltd. 07/23/1973 which recapitalized as Conbeau Resources Ltd. 09/18/1979 which recapitalized as Inlet Resources Ltd. 12/03/1984 which name changed to Guerrero Ventures Inc. 08/19/2014

COPPER STACK RES LTD (BC)
Recapitalized as Katlor Explorations Ltd. 05/29/1990
Each share Common no par exchanged for (0.25) share Common no par
Katlor Explorations Ltd. name changed to Katlor Environmental Tech. Inc. 07/06/1993 which recapitalized as Barbican Financial Corp. 06/20/1995
(See Barbican Financial Corp.)

COPPER STS RES INC (AB)
Recapitalized as American Coppermine Resources Ltd. 08/26/1996
Each share Common no par exchanged for (0.25) share Common no par
American Coppermine Resources Ltd. recapitalized as Carleton Resources Corp. 02/04/1997
(See Carleton Resources Corp.)

COPPER TOWN MINES LTD. (BC)
Struck off register and declared dissolved for failure to file returns 06/00/1974

COPPER VY MINERALS LTD (NV)
Common $0.001 par split (3) for (1) by issuance of (2) additional shares payable 11/07/2001 to holders of record 10/22/2001 Ex date - 11/08/2001
Name changed to Dtomi, Inc. 10/29/2001

Dtomi, Inc. name changed to Vocalscape Networks, Inc. 11/09/2005 which recapitalized as Kaleidoscope Venture Capital Inc. 07/14/2008

COPPERCONDA MINES CO. (AZ)
Charter revoked for failure to file reports or pay fees 06/18/1952

COPPERCORP LTD (ON)
Charter cancelled for failure to pay taxes and file returns 06/23/1980

COPPERCREST MINES LTD. (ON)
Name changed to Peerless Canadian Explorations Ltd. 00/00/1957
(See Peerless Canadian Explorations Ltd.)

COPPERFIELDS MNG CORP (CANADA)
Name changed 04/04/1974
Reincorporated 08/31/1983
Name changed from Copperfields Mining Corp. Ltd. to Copperfields Mining Corp. and Common $1 par changed to no par 04/04/1974
Place of incorporation changed from (ON) to (Canada) 08/31/1983
Merged into Teck Corp. 09/02/1983
Each share Common no par exchanged for (1.25) shares Class B Common no par
Teck Corp. name changed to Teck Cominco Ltd. 09/12/2001 which name changed to Teck Resources Ltd. 04/27/2009

COPPERQUEST INC (ON)
Reorganized under the laws of Alberta as Gastar Exploration Ltd. (AB) 05/16/2000
Each share Common no par exchanged for (0.16666666) share Common no par
Gastar Exploration Ltd. (AB) reincorporated in Delaware as Gastar Exploration, Inc. 11/15/2013

COPPERSTONE RES CORP (BC)
Recapitalized as Consolidated Copperstone Resources Corp. 12/10/1998
Each share Common no par exchanged for (0.25) share Common no par
Consolidated Copperstone Resources Corp. name changed to Bonanza Silver Corp. 03/14/2000 which recapitalized as Bonanza Explorations Inc. 09/07/2001 which recapitalized as Bonanza Resources Corp. 05/29/2002 which name changed to BRS Resources Ltd. 02/18/2011

COPPERSTREAM FRONTENAC MINES LTD (ON)
Charter cancelled for failure to pay taxes and file returns 06/20/1973

COPPERSTREAM MINES LTD. (ON)
Name changed to Copperstream-Frontenac Mines Ltd. 02/01/1962
(See Copperstream-Frontenac Mines Ltd.)

COPPERUST MINES LTD. (BC)
Name changed to Ark Energy Ltd. 10/20/1978
Ark Energy Ltd. recapitalized as Arcanna Industries Corp. 06/27/1990 which merged into Mercana Industries Ltd. (BC) 12/17/1993 which reincorporated in Ontario 06/28/1995
(See Mercana Industries Ltd.)

COPPERVILLE MNG LTD (ON)
Charter cancelled and declared dissolved for failure to file returns and pay fees 03/16/1976

COPPERWELD CORP (DE)
Reincorporated 01/16/1987
Common $2.50 par changed to $1.25 par and (1) additional share issued 05/12/1977

Common $1.25 par changed to $0.83333333 par and (0.5) additional share issued 05/18/1982
State of incorporation changed from (PA) to (DE) 01/16/1987
Each share $2.48 Conv. Exchangeable Preferred $1 par exchanged for $25 principal amount of 9.92% Conv. Subord. Debentures due 09/01/2008 on 05/18/1982
Merged into Imetal 08/01/1990
Each share Common $0.83333333 par exchanged for $17 cash

COPPERWELD STEEL CO. (PA)
Common no par changed to $10 par 00/00/1934
Each share Common $10 par exchanged for (2) shares Common $5 par 00/00/1939
5% Preferred $50 par called for redemption 12/14/1959
6% Preferred $50 par called for redemption 12/14/1959
Common $5 par changed to $2.50 par and (1) additional share issued 05/12/1965
Name changed to Copperweld Corp. (PA) 04/27/1973
Copperweld Corp. (PA) reincorporated in Delaware 01/16/1987
(See Copperweld Corp. (DE))

COPPERWOOD EXPL LTD (AB)
Merged into Consolidated Beacon Resources Ltd. (AB) 11/14/1990
Each share Common no par exchanged for (0.6083) share Common no par
Consolidated Beacon Resources Ltd. (AB) reorganized in British Columbia as Zone Resources Inc. 07/24/2009

COPTER SKYWAYS, INC. (PA)
Completely liquidated 09/30/1965
Details not available

COPY CTRS CORP (DE)
Charter cancelled and declared inoperative and void for non-payment of taxes 04/15/1972

COPY DATA SYS INC (NJ)
Adjudicated bankrupt 07/20/1976
Stockholders' equity unlikely

COPY SYS INC (NV)
Name changed to Granatelli (J.T.) Lubricants, Inc. 09/06/1996
Granatelli (J.T.) Lubricants, Inc. name changed to Nanotech Fuel Corp. 05/31/2001

COPYCAT CORP. (NY)
Acquired by Nashua Corp. (DE) 05/23/1962
Each share Common 10¢ par exchanged for (0.265) share Class A Common $1.66666666 par
Nashua Corp. (DE) reincorporated in Massachusetts 06/12/2002 which was acquired by Cenveo, Inc. 09/15/2009
(See Cenveo, Inc.)

COPYCOMPOSER CORP (MD)
Charter annulled for failure to file annual reports 12/15/1971

COPYMAT INC (UT)
Recapitalized as Global Ecosystems, Inc. (UT) 10/03/1994
Each share Common $0.001 par exchanged for (0.01) share Common $0.001 par
Global Ecosystems, Inc. reorganized in Delaware as Rose International Inc. 08/07/1995 which name changed to Securities Resolution Advisors, Inc. 07/14/1998 which name changed to Sales Online Direct, Inc. 03/16/1999 which name changed to Paid, Inc. 12/08/2003

COPYMATION, INC. (IL)
Common 50¢ par split (5) for (4) by issuance of (0.25) additional share 11/18/1963

Reorganized as A.T.I. Inc. (DE) 07/08/1968
Each share Common 50¢ par exchanged for (1) share Common 5¢ par
(See A.T.I. Inc. (DE))

COPYTELE INC (DE)
Common 1¢ par split (3) for (1) by issuance of (2) additional shares 11/08/1985
Common 1¢ par split (5) for (4) by issuance of (0.25) additional share 09/15/1987
Common 1¢ par split (2) for (1) by issuance of (1) additional share 03/18/1991
Common 1¢ par split (2) for (1) by issuance of (1) additional share payable 06/17/1996 to holders of record 06/04/1996
Name changed to ITUS Corp. 09/02/2014
ITUS Corp. name changed to Anixa Biosciences, Inc. 10/01/2018

COQUINA OIL CORP (NV)
Capital Stock $1 par changed to $0.66666666 par and (0.5) additional share issued 01/08/1974
Capital Stock $0.66666666 par changed to $0.53333333 par and (0.25) additional share issued 04/07/1976
Stock Dividend - 10% 04/10/1975
Merged into St. Joe Minerals Corp. 03/16/1977
Each share Capital Stock $0.53333333 par exchanged for (0.555) share Common $10 par
St. Joe Minerals Corp. merged into Fluor Corp. (Old) 08/03/1981 which name changed to Massey Energy Co. 11/30/2000 which merged into Alpha Natural Resources, Inc. 06/01/2011
(See Alpha Natural Resources, Inc.)

COQUINA SEARCH CORP (DE)
Under plan of merger name changed to Strategic Abstract & Title Corp. 03/00/1989
Strategic Abstract & Title Corp. recapitalized as SA Holdings, Inc. 02/18/1992 which name changed to SA Telecommunications, Inc. 08/03/1995
(See SA Telecommunications, Inc.)

COR EQUITY HLDGS INC (FL)
Each share old Common $0.001 par received distribution of (0.33333333) share Medical Home Products Inc. old Common no par payable 09/17/2004 to holders of record 09/03/2004 Ex date - 09/20/2004
Each share old Common $0.001 par received distribution of (0.02) share LaSalle Capital Corp. (FL) Common payable 04/22/2005 to holders of record 04/11/2005 Ex date - 04/19/2005
Each share old Common $0.001 par exchanged for (0.01) share new Common $0.001 par 10/05/2005
Name changed to 727 Communications, Inc. 02/13/2006

COR THERAPEUTICS INC (DE)
Common $0.0001 par split (2) for (1) by issuance of (1) additional share payable 08/15/2000 to holders of record 07/31/2000 Ex date - 08/16/2000
Merged into Millennium Pharmaceuticals, Inc. 02/12/2002
Each share Common $0.0001 par exchanged for (0.9873) share Common $0.001 par
(See Millennium Pharmaceuticals, Inc.)

CORA RES LTD (BC)
Recapitalized as Boss Gold Corp. 11/19/2003
Each share Common no par exchanged for (0.33333333) share Common no par

Boss Gold Corp. recapitalized as Boss Gold International Corp. 07/11/2005 which name changed to Boss Power Corp. 06/15/2007 which name changed to Eros Resources Corp. 07/29/2015

CORADIAN CORP (NY)
Acquired by Mitel Inc. 08/31/1990
Each share Conv. Preferred Ser. A $1 par exchanged for $0.36 cash
Each share Common 1¢ par exchanged for $0.36 cash
Each share old Conv. Preferred Ser. A $1 par received additional escrow payment of $0.027099 cash 09/19/1991
Each share Common 1¢ par received additional escrow payment of $0.027099 cash 09/19/1991

CORAL AGGREGATES CORP (FL)
Acquired by a foreign company 11/07/1986
Each share Common 10¢ par exchanged for $6.50 cash

CORAL COS INC (DE)
Each share Common $0.00001 par exchanged for (0.02) share Common $0.0005 par 07/20/1989
Reorganized under the laws of Nevada as CNH Holdings Co. 05/31/1996
Each share Common $0.0005 par exchanged for (0.001) share Common $0.001 par
CNH Holdings Co. name changed to Cistera Networks, Inc. 09/27/2005

CORAL ENERGY CORP (BC)
Name changed to Coral Gold Corp. 10/16/1987
Coral Gold Corp. recapitalized as Coral Gold Resources Ltd. 09/15/2004

CORAL ENTERPRISES INC (DE)
Name changed to Eastmont Group, Inc. 12/23/1987

CORAL GABLES FEDCORP INC (DE)
Merged into First Union Corp. 06/01/1995
Each share Common 1¢ par exchanged for $26.59 cash

CORAL GABLES 1ST NATL BK (CORAL GABLES, FL)
Each share Common $100 par exchanged for (8) shares Common $25 par to effect a (4) for (1) split and a 100% stock dividend 01/22/1946
Each share Common $25 par exchanged for (2.5) shares Common $10 par 10/10/51
Stock Dividends - 50% 02/07/1945; 50% 04/20/1950
Name changed to Central First National Bank (Coral Gables, FL) 04/01/1964
Central First National Bank (Coral Gables, FL) name changed back to Coral Gables First National Bank 02/07/1969 which name changed to Flagship First National Bank (Coral Gables, FL) 11/08/1974 which merged into Flagship National Bank of Miami (Miami Beach, FL) 05/01/1978 which location was changed to (Miami, FL) 03/18/1980 which name changed to Sun Bank/Miami, N.A. (Miami, FL) 04/01/1985
(See SunTrust Bank, Miami, N.A. (Miami, FL))

CORAL GOLD CORP (BC)
Recapitalized as Coral Gold Resources Ltd. 09/15/2004
Each share Common no par exchanged for (0.1) share Common no par

CORAL INC (NV)
Merged into Independent Entertainment Group Inc. 06/10/1992
Each share Common $0.001 par exchanged for (0.178) share new Common $0.0001 par
Independent Entertainment Group Inc. name changed to Independent TeleMedia Group Inc. 07/07/1993
(See Independent TeleMedia Group Inc.)

CORAL LEISURE GROUP LTD (UNITED KINGDOM)
Merged into Bass Ltd. 08/14/1981
Each ADR for Ordinary exchanged for (0.46153846)) share Ordinary 25p par

CORAL RIDGE NATL BK (FORT LAUDERDALE, FL)
Stock Dividend - 33.33333333% 03/03/1969
Acquired by Broward Bancshares, Inc. 05/28/1970
Each share Common $10 par exchanged for (2.15) shares Common $1 par
Broward Bancshares, Inc. name changed to Century Banks, Inc. 04/08/1976 which merged into Sun Banks of Florida, Inc. 07/01/1982 which name changed to Sun Banks Inc. 05/02/1983 which merged into SunTrust Banks, Inc. 07/01/1985

CORAL RIDGE PPTYS INC (FL)
60¢ Conv. Preferred $8 par called for redemption 08/01/1965
6% Preferred $1 par called for redemption 05/13/1966
Acquired by Westinghouse Electric Corp. 06/04/1966
Each share Class A Common 10¢ par exchanged for (0.103) share Common $6.25 par
Westinghouse Electric Corp. name changed to CBS Corp. 12/01/1997 which merged into Viacom Inc. (Old) 05/04/2000
(See Viacom Inc. (Old))

CORAL SEA RES INC (AB)
Name changed to Sagres Energy Inc. 04/14/2010
(See Sagres Energy Inc.)

CORALOC INDUSTRIES, INC. (DE)
Dissolved 06/29/1964
No stockholders' equity

CORALTA RES LTD (BC)
Common $1 par changed to no par 02/21/1980
Struck off register and declared dissolved for failure to file returns 02/19/1988

CORAM HEALTHCARE CORP (DE)
Plan of reorganization under Chapter 11 Federal Bankruptcy Code effective 12/01/2004
Each share Common $0.001 par exchanged for $0.32 cash
Note: Each share Common $0.001 par received an initial additional distribution of $0.40 cash payable 06/30/2006 to holders of record 06/26/2003

CORATOMIC INC (PA)
Common 50¢ par changed to 10¢ par 09/30/1985
Name changed to Biocontrol Technology, Inc. 01/12/1987
Biocontrol Technology, Inc. name changed to BICO, Inc. 10/11/2000 which name changed to MobiClear Inc. 11/30/2006 which name changed to Intelligent Communication Enterprise Corp. 12/22/2009 which name changed to One Horizon Group, Inc. (PA) 01/31/2013 which reorganized in Delaware 08/29/2013

CORAUTUS GENETICS INC (DE)
Each share old Common $0.001 par exchanged for (0.14285714) share new Common $0.001 par 03/11/2003
Recapitalized as VIA Pharmaceuticals, Inc. 06/06/2007
Each share new Common $0.001 par exchanged for (0.06666666) share Common $0.001 par
(See VIA Pharmaceuticals, Inc.)

CORAZON GOLD CORP (BC)
Each share old Common no par exchanged for (0.06666666) share new Common no par 03/26/2014
Each share new Common no par exchanged again for (0.2) share new Common no par 05/05/2014
Name changed to NanoSphere Health Sciences Inc. 12/05/2017

CORBAL CAP CORP NEW (ON)
Name changed to iSign Media Solutions Inc. 12/03/2009

CORBEL HLDGS INC (NV)
Name changed to BioTech Medics, Inc. 11/30/2004

CORBETT LAKE MINERALS INC (NV)
Name changed to Geoalert Inc. 05/01/2001
(See Geoalert Inc.)

CORBETTS COOL CLEAR WTR INC (FL)
Name changed 09/01/1998
Name changed from Corbetts Clear Cool Water, Inc. to Corbetts Cool Clear Water, Inc. 09/01/1998
Name changed to Canadian Cool Clear Water, Inc. 10/27/1998
Canadian Cool Clear Water, Inc. name changed to Canadian Cool Clear Wtaa, Inc. 02/05/1999 which name changed to WTAA International, Inc. 10/27/1999 which name changed to Gravitas International, Inc. (FL) 12/06/2001 which reorganized in Nevada as Formcap Corp. 10/12/2007

CORBVEN CORP (NV)
Recapitalized as Airtrac Inc. 03/14/2000
Each share Common $0.001 par exchanged for (0.03125) share Common $0.001 par

CORBY DISTILLERIES LTD (CANADA)
Common no par split (2) for (1) by issuance of (1) additional share 01/30/1980
Class B Common Non-Vtg. no par split (2) for (1) by issuance of (1) additional share 01/30/1980
Common no par split (3) for (1) by issuance of (2) additional shares 01/20/1986
Class B Common Non-Vtg. no par split (3) for (1) by issuance of (2) additional shares 01/20/1986
Name changed to Corby Spirit & Wine Ltd. 11/12/2013

CORBY H DISTILLERY LTD (CANADA)
Name changed to Corby Distilleries Ltd.-Les Distilleries Corby Ltee. 01/24/1969
Corby Distilleries Ltd.-Les Distilleries Corby Ltee. name changed to Corby Spirit & Wine Ltd. 11/12/2013

CORCAP (NV)
Name changed to August Financial Holding Co., Inc. 05/08/2002
(See August Financial Holding Co., Inc.)

CORCO INC (OH)
Common no par split (5) for (4) by issuance of (0.25) additional share 09/29/1975
Stock Dividend - 10% 03/29/1974
Merged into Willamette Industries, Inc. 05/27/1977
Each share Common no par exchanged for (0.4326) share Common 50¢ par
Note: An undetermined amount of shares were distributed from escrow 05/27/1981
(See Willamette Industries, Inc.)

CORCOM INC (IL)
Common no par split (2) for (1) by issuance of (1) additional share 06/24/1983
Merged into CII Technologies, Inc. 06/19/1998
Each share Common no par exchanged for $13 cash

CORCORAN (THOMAS J.) LAMP CO.
Name changed to Corcoran-Brown Lamp Co. 00/00/1931
(See Corcoran-Brown Lamp Co.)

CORCORAN-BROWN LAMP CO.
Liquidated 00/00/1936
Details not available

CORCORAN FIRE INSURANCE CO. OF D.C.
Liquidated 00/00/1942
Details not available

CORD BLOOD AMER INC (FL)
Each share old Common $0.0001 par exchanged for (0.01) share new Common $0.0001 par 05/09/2011
Name changed to CBA Florida, Inc. 05/29/2018

CORD CORP.
Name changed to Aviation & Transportation Corp. 00/00/1938
Aviation & Transporation Corp. acquired by Aviation Corp. 00/00/1941 which name changed to Avco Manufacturing Corp. 03/25/1947 which name changed to Avco Corp. 04/10/1959
(See Avco Corp.)

CORD INTL MINERALS LTD (AB)
Struck off register and declared dissolved for failure to file reports 05/29/1981

CORDA DIVERSIFIED TECHNOLOGIES INC (FL)
Proclaimed dissolved for failure to file reports and pay fees 11/01/1985

CORDAL RES LTD (BC)
Recapitalized as Skyharbour Developments Ltd. 11/04/1999
Each share Common no par exchanged for (0.25) share Common no par
Skyharbour Developments Ltd. name changed to Skyharbour Resources Ltd. 10/25/2002

CORDANT TECHNOLOGIES INC (DE)
Merged into Alcoa Inc. 05/25/2000
Each share Common $1 par exchanged for $57 cash

CORDASUN PETROLEUMS LTD. (ON)
Name changed to Consolidated Cordasun Oils, Ltd. 10/03/1950
Consolidated Cordasun Oils, Ltd. merged into Okalta Oils, Ltd. 01/31/1958 which recapitalized as Oakwood Petroleum Ltd. 06/10/1970 which was acquired by Sceptre Resources Ltd. 03/14/1989 which merged into Canadian Natural Resources Ltd. 08/15/1996

CORDATUM INC (MD)
Each share Common 1¢ par exchanged for (0.1) share Common 10¢ par 05/09/1990
Charter forfeited for failure to file annual reports 10/03/1991

CORDELL GOLD MINES LTD (ON)
Charter cancelled for failure to file reports and pay taxes 07/19/1993

CORDERO ENERGY INC (AB)
Merged into Ember Resources Inc. 09/10/2008
Each share Common no par exchanged for (1.0732) shares new Common no par
(See Ember Resources Inc.)

CORDERO INDS INC (DE)
Charter cancelled and declared void

for failure to pay franchise taxes 03/01/1991

CORDEX PETROLEUMS LTD (BC)
Filed a petition under the Bankruptcy and Insolvency Act 03/05/1999
Stockholders' equity unlikely

CORDEX PHARMA INC (NV)
SEC revoked common stock registration 10/27/2014

CORDEX VENTURE CORP (BC)
Reincorporated under the laws of Ontario as Brauch Database Systems, Inc. 01/07/2000
(See Brauch Database Systems, Inc.)

CORDIA BANCORP INC (VA)
Acquired by FC Merger Subsidiary I, Inc. 08/31/2016
Each share Common 1¢ par exchanged for $5.15 cash

CORDIALE RES INC (BC)
Name changed to Vioclone Biologicals Inc. 06/22/1989
(See Vioclone Biologicals Inc.)

CORDIANT COMMUNICATIONS GROUP PLC (UNITED KINGDOM)
Name changed 12/12/1997
Each Sponsored ADR for Ordinary received distribution of (0.3) Saatchi & Saatchi PLC (New) Sponsored ADR for Ordinary payable 12/15/1997 to holders of record 12/12/1997
Name changed from Cordiant PLC to Cordiant Communications Group PLC 12/12/1997
Merged into WPP Group PLC (United Kingdom) 08/01/2003
Each Sponsored ADR for Ordinary exchanged for (0.00487804) Sponsored ADR for Ordinary
WPP Group PLC (United Kingdom) reorganized in Jersey as WPP PLC (Old) 11/20/2008 which reorganized as WPP PLC (New) 01/02/2013

CORDILLERA CORP. (WA)
Charter cancelled and proclaimed dissolved for failure to pay fees 07/01/1977

CORDILLERA CORP. OF UTAH (UT)
Through purchase offer reverted to a private company 00/00/1984
Public interest eliminated

CORDILLERA CORP (UT)
Merged into Cordillera Corp. of Utah 03/18/1981
Each share Common $1 par exchanged for (0.004) share Common $250 par
(See Cordillera Corp. of Utah)

CORDILLERA INC (NV)
Recapitalized as Uni-Vite, Inc. 08/08/1988
Each share Common 1¢ par exchanged for (0.5) share Common 1¢ par
Uni-Vite, Inc. name changed to Lifeworks Holdings Inc. 03/29/1994
(See Lifeworks Holdings Inc.)

CORDILLERA MINING CO. (CO)
Merged into Rock Hill Oil Corp. 02/23/1968
Each share Common 5¢ par exchanged for (0.25) share Common 20¢ par
(See Rock Hill Oil Corp.)

CORDILLERAN DEV INC (WA)
Charter cancelled and proclaimed dissolved for failure to pay fees 05/20/1991

CORDIS CORP (FL)
Common no par split (20) for (1) by issuance of (19) additional shares 08/01/1967
Common no par split (3) for (1) by issuance of (2) additional shares 07/09/1969
Common no par changed to $1 par 10/29/1969

Common $1 par split (4) for (1) by issuance of (3) additional shares 07/20/1983
Stock Dividend - 100% 09/15/1977
Merged into Johnson & Johnson 02/23/1996
Each share Common $1 par exchanged for (1.1292) shares Common $1 par

CORDOBA DEVS LTD (BC)
Recapitalized as Gold Cup Resources Ltd. 02/02/1977
Each share Common no par exchanged for (0.5) share Common no par
(See Gold Cup Resources Ltd.)

CORDOBA MINES LTD. (MB)
Charter cancelled 00/00/1970

CORDON CORP (DE)
Reincorporated 12/05/1989
Each share old Common $0.001 par exchanged for (0.25) share new Common $0.001 par 11/14/1989
State of incorporation changed from (NV) to (DE) 12/05/1989
Name changed to Ameriserv Financial Corp. 02/28/1990
Ameriserv Financial Corp. recapitalized as Namibian Copper Mines, Ltd. 07/14/1995 which name changed to American Southwest Holdings Inc. 06/09/2000
(See American Southwest Holdings Inc.)

CORDON INTL CORP (DE)
Charter cancelled and declared inoperative and void for non-payment of taxes 03/01/1983

CORDOVA BANCSHARES INC (TN)
Name changed to Victory Bancshares Inc. 04/01/1996
Victory Bancshares Inc. merged into Deposit Guaranty Corp. 03/23/1998 which merged into First American Corp. 05/01/1998 which merged into AmSouth Bancorporation 10/01/1999 which merged into Regions Financial Corp. (New) 11/04/2006

CORDOVA INDS LTD (AB)
Reincorporated under the laws of Canada as Ameriplas Holdings Ltd. 11/24/2003
Ameriplas Holdings Ltd. recapitalized as Downtown Industries Ltd. (Canada) 07/13/2010 which reincorporated in British Columbia as Inform Resources Corp. 11/04/2010

CORDREY MFG. CO. (CA)
Name changed to California General, Inc. 01/08/1951
(See California General Inc.)

CORDURA CORP (DE)
Reincorporated 06/27/1975
State of incorporation changed from (CA) to (DE) 06/27/1975
Merged into BSA Inc. 08/12/1986
Each share Common no par exchanged for $35 cash

CORDUROY RUBR CO (DE)
Each share Class A $75 par exchanged for (1) share Prior Preferred no par and (1) share Part. Preferred no par 00/00/1931
Each share Class B $25 par exchanged for (0.25) share Prior Preferred no par and (0.25) share Part. Preferred no par 00/00/1931
Each share Class C $100 par exchanged for (1.25) shares Prior Preferred no par and (1.25) shares Part. Preferred no par 00/00/1931
Each share Common no par exchanged for (1) share new Common no par 00/00/1931
Part. Preferred no par called for redemption 10/05/1956
Prior Preferred no par called for redemption 07/02/1962

Voluntarily dissolved 08/24/1987
Details not available

CORDUROY TIRE CO.
Name changed to Corduroy Rubber Co. 00/00/1931
(See Corduroy Rubber Co.)

CORDWELL INTL DEVS LTD (ON)
Charter cancelled and declared dissolved for failure to file returns and pay fees 11/28/1973

CORDYNE CORP (OR)
Plan of reorganization under Chapter 11 Federal Bankruptcy Code dismissed 05/05/1988
No stockholders' equity

CORE CRAFT INC. (ND)
Insolvent 00/00/1963
No stockholders' equity

CORE ENERGY CORP (BC)
Name changed to Core Ventures Ltd. 07/22/1988
Core Ventures Ltd. recapitalized as Encore Ventures Ltd. 12/09/1991 which merged into Prime Equities International Corp. 01/26/1993 which name changed to Medera Life Science Corp. 08/11/1998 which name changed to Medbroadcast Corp. (Canada) 01/04/2000 which reorganized in Alberta as Rock Energy Inc. 02/18/2004 which merged into Raging River Exploration Inc. 07/26/2016 which merged into Baytex Energy Corp. 08/27/2018

CORE EXPLS LTD (AB)
Recapitalized as Kelsey's International Inc. 05/20/1993
Each share Common no par exchanged for (0.2) share Common no par
(See Kelsey's International Inc.)

CORE HEALTHCARE PRODS LTD (INDIA)
GDR agreement terminated 03/17/2009
Each 144A GDR for Ordinary exchanged for (1) Ordinary share
Each Reg. S GDR for Ordinary exchanged for (1) Ordinary share
Note: Unexchanged GDR's will be sold and the proceeds distributed on a pro rata basis

CORE INC (MA)
Merged into Fortis NL 07/12/2001
Each share Common 10¢ par exchanged for $4.92 cash

CORE INCOMEPLUS FD (ON)
Merged into YIELDPLUS Income Fund 09/27/2007
Each Trust Unit received (0.75597249) Trust Unit
YIELDPLUS Income Fund merged into MINT Income Fund 03/21/2017

CORE INDS INC (NV)
Common $1 par split (3) for (2) by issuance of (0.5) additional share 03/16/1979
Common $1 par split (3) for (2) by issuance of (0.5) additional share 03/19/1980
Common $1 par split (3) for (2) by issuance of (0.5) additional share 03/20/1981
Merged into United Dominion Industries Ltd. 10/01/1997
Each share Common $1 par exchanged for $25 cash

CORE INTL LTD (CO)
Recapitalized as Therma-Med, Inc. 12/31/2008
Each share Common $0.001 par exchanged for (0.01) share Common $0.001 par

CORE LABS INC (DE)
Common $1 par split (2) for (1) by issuance of (1) additional share 09/19/1978
Common $1 par split (2) for (1) by

issuance of (1) additional share 07/31/1980
Merged into Litton Industries, Inc. 02/15/1984
Each share Common $1 par exchanged for $33 cash

CORE MARK INTL INC (CANADA)
Reincorporated 06/14/1984
Place of incorporation changed from (BC) to (Canada) 06/14/1984
Each Non-Vtg. Share no par exchanged for (1) share Common no par 07/12/1988
Acquired by CMI Acquisition Corp. 09/05/1989
Each share 7.5% Conv. Preferred Ser. A no par exchanged for $25.36125 cash
Each share Common no par exchanged for $7 cash

CORE MATLS CORP (DE)
Name changed to Core Molding Technologies, Inc. 09/03/2002

CORE OIL CO. (CO)
Name changed to Core Mineral Recoveries, Inc. 09/12/1983
Core Mineral Recoveries, Inc. recapitalized as Core Ventures Inc. 07/24/1997 which name changed to FutureLink Distribution Corp. (CO) 02/07/1998 which reincorporated in Delaware as FutureLink Corp. 10/15/1999
(See FutureLink Corp.)

CORE PARENTERALS LTD (INDIA)
Name changed to Core Healthcare Products Ltd. 12/18/1994
(See Core Healthcare Products Ltd.)

CORE RES LTD (WY)
Recapitalized as Club Resources Ltd. 06/30/2008
Each share Common no par exchanged for (0.001) share Common no par

CORE SOLUTIONS INC (NV)
Each share old Common $0.001 par exchanged for (0.00004) share new Common $0.001 par 10/23/2002
Recapitalized as Sunshine Ventures Inc. 05/12/2003
Each share new Common $0.001 par exchanged for (0.00004) share Common $0.001 par
Sunshine Ventures Inc. name changed to Christine's Precious Petals Inc. 07/14/2003 which name changed to Global Business Markets, Inc. 09/05/2003 which name changed to GREM USA 03/03/2005

CORE SYS INC (NV)
Name changed to Angelaudio.com Inc. 04/18/2000
Angelaudio.com Inc. name changed to Whatsupmusic.com Inc. 11/28/2000 which name changed to New Millennium Development Group 05/14/2001 which name changed to Millennium National Events, Inc. 10/05/2004 which recapitalized as Extensions, Inc. 08/24/2007
(See Extensions, Inc.)

CORE TECHNOLOGIES INC (AB)
Recapitalized as Image Sculpting International Inc. 10/19/1999
Each share Common no par exchanged for (0.1) share Common no par
(See Image Sculpting International Inc.)

CORE TECHNOLOGIES PA INC (DE)
Company ceased operations 01/28/2000
Stockholders' equity unlikely

CORE VENTURES INC (CO)
Recapitalized 07/24/1997
Recapitalized from Core Mineral Recoveries, Inc. to Core Ventures Inc. 07/24/1997
Each share Common 1¢ par

exchanged for (0.005) share Common 1¢ par
Each share Common 1¢ par exchanged for (0.03333333) share Common $0.0001 par 12/02/1997
Name changed to FutureLink Distribution Corp. (CO) 02/07/1998
FutureLink Distribution Corp. (CO) reincorporated in Delaware as FutureLink Corp. 10/15/1999
(See FutureLink Corp.)

CORE VENTURES LTD (BC)
Recapitalized as Encore Ventures Ltd. 12/09/1991
Each share Common no par exchanged for (0.2) share Common no par
Encore Ventures Ltd. merged into Prime Equities International Corp. 01/26/1993 which name changed to Medera Life Science Corp. 08/11/1998 which name changed to Medbroadcast Corp. (Canada) 01/04/2000 which reorganized in Alberta as Rock Energy Inc. 02/18/2004 which merged into Raging River Exploration Inc. 07/26/2016 which merged into Baytex Energy Corp. 08/27/2018

CORECARE SYS INC (DE)
Reincorporated 01/24/1997
State of incorporation changed from (NV) to (DE) 01/27/1997
SEC revoked common stock registration 05/30/2013

CORECO INC (CANADA)
Merged into DALSA Corp. 04/26/2005
Each share Common no par exchanged for (0.5207) share Common no par
(See DALSA Corp.)

CORECOMM HOLDCO INC (DE)
Name changed to ATX Communications, Inc. 07/15/2002
(See ATX Communications, Inc.)

CORECOMM INC (DE)
Each share Common 1¢ par received distribution of (1) share CoreComm Ltd. Common 1¢ par payable 09/02/1998 to holders of record 08/31/1998
Name changed to Cellular Communications of Puerto Rico, Inc. (New) 09/02/1998
(See Cellular Communications of Puerto Rico, Inc. (New))

CORECOMM LTD. NEW (DE)
Reincorporated 09/29/2000
Common 1¢ par split (3) for (2) by issuance of (0.5) additional share payable 09/02/1999 to holders of record 08/30/1999
Reincorporated from Bermuda to under the laws of Delaware 09/29/2000
Merged into CoreComm Holdco, Inc. 07/01/2002
Each share Common 1¢ par exchanged for (0.02570694) share Common 1¢ par
CoreComm Holdco, Inc. name changed to ATX Communications, Inc. 07/15/2002
(See ATX Communications, Inc.)

CORECOMM SOLUTIONS INC (BC)
Name changed to VGrab Communications Inc. 02/13/2015

COREL CORP NEW (CANADA)
Each share old Common no par exchanged for (0.00000115) share new Common no par 01/26/2010
Note: In effect holders received USD$4 cash per share and public interest was eliminated

COREL CORP OLD (CANADA)
Name changed 07/20/1992
Name changed from Corel Systems Corp. to Corel Corp. 07/20/1992
Common no par split (2) for (1) by issuance of (1) additional share 12/08/1993
Common no par split (3) for (2) by issuance of (0.5) additional share 10/28/1994
Merged into Vector Capital Corp. 08/28/2003
Each share Common no par exchanged for $1.05 cash

CORELAND CAP INC (BC)
Recapitalized as Rathdowney Resources Ltd. 03/17/2011
Each share Common no par exchanged for (0.2) share Common no par

CORENCO CORP (ME)
Stock Dividends - 10% 08/31/1973; 50% 03/17/1975; 10% 03/16/1979
Merged into Canadian Pacific Investments Ltd.-Investissements Canadien Pacifique Ltee. 08/08/1979
Each share Common $6.25 par exchanged for $22.50 cash

COREO AG (GERMANY)
ADS agreement terminated 11/20/2017
Each Sponsored ADS for Bearer Shares exchanged for $0.19295 cash

CORESITE RLTY CORP (MD)
7.25% Preferred Ser. A 1¢ par called for redemption at $25 plus $0.292014 accrued dividends on 12/12/2017
(Additional Information in Active)

CORESOURCE STRATEGIES INC (NV)
Reincorporated under the laws of Oklahoma as NUGL, Inc. 12/11/2017

CORESTAFF INC (DE)
Common 1¢ par split (3) for (2) by issuance of (0.5) additional share payable 03/26/1996 to holders of record 03/14/1996
Common 1¢ par split (3) for (2) by isssuance of (0.5) additional share payable 09/20/1996 to holders of record 09/10/1996
Name changed to Metamor Worldwide Inc. 03/19/1998
Metamor Worldwide Inc. merged into PSINet Inc. 06/15/2000
(See PSINet Inc.)

CORESTATES FINL CORP (PA)
Common $1 par split (2) for (1) by issuance of (1) additional share 10/17/1983
Common $1 par split (2) for (1) by issuance of (1) additional share 10/15/1985
Preferred Ser. A no par called for redemption 05/03/1988
Common $1 par split (2) for (1) by issuance of (1) additional share 10/15/1993
Merged into First Union Corp. 04/28/1998
Each share Common $1 par exchanged for (1.62) shares Common $3.33-1/3 par
First Union Corp. name changed to Wachovia Corp. (Ctfs. dated after 09/01/2001) 09/01/2001 which merged into Wells Fargo & Co. (New) 12/31/2008

CORESTREAM ENERGY INC (NV)
Charter revoked for failure to file reports and pay taxes 10/01/2012

CORETEC INC (ON)
Acquired by DDi Corp. 12/31/2009
Each share Common no par exchanged for $0.38 cash

CORETEC MULTIMEDIA INC (AB)
Name changed to Totally Hip Software Inc. (AB) 12/05/1995
Totally Hip Software Inc. (AB) reincorporated in British Columbia 03/18/1999 which recapitalized as Totally Hip Inc. 06/05/2002 which recapitalized as Totally Hip Technologies Inc. 12/23/2003

CORETECH INDS LTD (NV)
Common 1¢ par split (3) for (1) by issuance of (2) additional shares payable 12/24/1999 to holders of record 12/24/1999
Name changed to At Home Holdings, Inc. 03/15/2001
At Home Holdings, Inc. name changed to Dover Petroleum Corp. 08/27/2001
(See Dover Petroleum Corp.)

CORETEK VENCAP INC (CANADA)
Recapitalized as Ungava Minerals Corp. 12/04/1996
Each share Common no par exchanged for (0.1) share Common no par
Ungava Minerals Corp. name changed to Nearctic Nickel Mines Inc. 09/07/2007

COREWAFER INDS INC (NV)
Each share old Common $0.001 par exchanged for (0.00666666) share new Common $0.001 par 08/28/2014
Stock Dividends - 5% payable 04/26/2013 to holders of record 04/12/2013 Ex date - 04/10/2013; 5% payable 05/13/2013 to holders of record 05/06/2013 Ex date - 05/02/2013
Recapitalized as Aluf Holdings, Inc. 08/31/2015
Each share new Common $0.001 par exchanged for (0.0004) share Common $0.001 par

COREX GOLD CORP (BC)
Merged into Minera Alamos Inc. 04/18/2018
Each share Common no par exchanged for (0.95) share Common no par
Note: Unexchanged certificates will be cancelled and become without value 04/18/2018

CORGEMINES LTD (QC)
Charter annulled for failure to file reports 03/22/1975

CORGENIX MED CORP (NV)
Each share old Common $0.001 par exchanged for (0.2) share new Common $0.001 par 01/15/2002
Acquired by Centennial Medical Holdings, Inc. 03/10/2015
Each share new Common $0.001 par exchanged for $0.27 cash

CORGENTECH INC (DE)
Each share old Common $0.001 par exchanged for (0.25) share new Common $0.001 par 12/16/2005
Name changed to Anesiva, Inc. 06/21/2006
(See Anesiva, Inc.)

CORGI INTL LTD (HONG KONG)
Each Sponsored ADR for Ordinary HKD $0.50 par exchanged for (0.16666666) Sponsored ADR for Ordinary HKD $3 par 12/21/2006
ADR agreement terminated 04/15/2010
No ADR holders' equity

CORILLIAN CORP (OR)
Merged into CheckFree Corp. (New) 05/15/2007
Each share Common no par exchanged for $5.15 cash

CORIMON S A C A (VENEZUELA)
Name changed 08/18/1993
Each 144A Sponsored GDR for B shares exchanged for (1) old Sponsored ADR for Common 03/16/1993
Name changed from Corimon C.A.S.A.C.A. to Corimon S.A.C.A. 08/18/1993
Basis changed from (1:25) to (1:30) on 08/18/1993
Basis changed from (1:30) to (1:35) on 06/30/1994
Basis changed from (1:35) to (1:25) on 07/28/1997
Stock Dividend - 16.66666666% 06/30/1994
Name changed to Corimon, C.A. 07/28/1997

CORINDUS VASCULAR ROBOTICS INC (NV)
Reincorporated under the laws of Delaware 06/28/2016

CORINNE ASBESTOS & CHROME CORP. LTD. (QC)
Charter annulled for failure to file reports 10/28/1978

CORINTH RES LTD (BC)
Name changed to BMP Technologies Ltd. 10/24/1984
BMP Technologies Ltd. name changed to Palomar Capital Corp. 05/26/1988
(See Palomar Capital Corp.)

CORINTHIAN BROADCASTING CORP (DE)
Acquired by Dun & Bradstreet, Inc. 05/27/1971
Each share Common $1 par exchanged for (0.675) share Common $1 par
Dun & Bradstreet, Inc. name changed to Dun & Bradstreet Companies, Inc. 05/31/1973 which name changed to Dun & Bradstreet Corp. 04/17/1979 which name changed to R.H. Donnelley Corp. 07/01/1998
(See R.H. Donnelley Corp.)

CORINTHIAN COLLEGES INC (DE)
Common $0.0001 par split (2) for (1) by issuance of (1) additional share payable 12/15/2000 to holders of record 11/30/2000 Ex date - 12/18/2000
Common $0.0001 par split (2) for (1) by issuance of (1) additional share payable 05/28/2002 to holders of record 05/09/2002 Ex date - 05/28/2002
Common $0.0001 par split (2) for (1) by issuance of (1) additional share payable 03/23/2004 to holders of record 03/04/2004 Ex date - 03/24/2004
Plan of reorganization under Chapter 11 bankruptcy proceedings effective 09/22/2015
No stockholders' equity

CORINTHIAN RES LTD (BC)
Name changed to Pacific Basin Development Corp. 02/04/1986
Pacific Basin Development Corp. recapitalized as Jersey Goldfields Corp. 07/20/1994 which name changed to Jersey Petroleum Inc. 03/04/1998 which recapitalized as International Choice Ventures Inc. (BC) 08/17/2000 which reincorporated in Alberta as Rhodes Resources Corp. 11/20/2002 which merged into Terra Energy Corp. 01/30/2004

CORIO INC (DE)
Merged into International Business Machines Corp. 03/15/2005
Each share Common $0.001 par exchanged for $2.82 cash

CORIXA CORP (DE)
Merged into GlaxoSmithKline PLC 07/12/2005
Each share Common $0.001 par exchanged $4.40 cash

CORK EXPL INC (AB)
Recapitalized as Profound Energy Inc. 11/22/2007
Each share Common no par exchanged for (0.25) share Common no par
Profound Energy Inc. merged into Paramount Energy Trust 08/19/2009

which reorganized as Perpetual Energy Inc. 07/06/2010

CORKEN INTL CORP (DE)
Name changed to Entrecap International Inc. 05/29/1991
(See Entrecap International Inc.)

CORKER RES INC (AB)
Name changed to TriQuest Energy Corp. 07/15/1999
(See TriQuest Energy Corp.)

CORLAC OILFIELD LEASING LTD (AB)
Name changed to Enhanced Energy Services Ltd. 03/31/2000
Enhanced Energy Services Ltd. recapitalized as EnSource Energy Services Inc. 03/12/2001 which was acquired by Enerflex Systems Ltd. (Canada) 07/24/2002 which reorganized in Alberta as Enerflex Systems Income Fund 10/02/2006 which merged into Toromont Industries Ltd. 02/26/2010

CORLESS PATRICIA GOLD MINES, LTD. (ON)
Charter cancelled 06/19/1962
No stockholders' equity

CORMAC CHEM CORP (NY)
Charter cancelled and proclaimed dissolved for non-payment of taxes 12/15/1969

CORMAC PHOTOCOPY CORP. (NY)
Acquired by Cormac Chemical Corp. 11/08/1961
Each share Common 10¢ par exchanged for (0.407) share Common 10¢ par
(See Cormac Chemical Corp.)

CORMAX BUSINESS SOLUTIONS INC (UT)
Stock Dividend - 10% payable 08/07/2002 to holders of record 07/29/2002 Ex date - 07/25/2002
Recapitalized as Sure Trace Security Corp. 02/04/2003
Each share Common $0.001 par exchanged for (0.06666666) share Common $0.001 par

CORN EXCHANGE BANK TRUST CO. (NEW YORK, NY)
Merged into Chemical Corn Exchange Bank (New York, NY) 10/18/1954
Each share Capital Stock $20 par exchanged for (2) shares Capital Stock $10 par
Chemical Corn Exchange Bank (New York, NY) merged into Chemical Bank New York Trust Co. (New York, NY) 09/08/1959 which reorganized as Chemical New York Corp. 02/17/1969 which name changed to Chemical Banking Corp. 04/29/1988 which name changed to Chase Manhattan Corp. (New) 03/31/1996 which name changed to J.P. Morgan Chase & Co. 12/31/2000 which name changed to JPMorgan Chase & Co. 07/20/2004

CORN EXCHANGE CORP.
Dissolved 00/00/1934
Details not available

CORN EXCHANGE NATIONAL BANK & TRUST CO. (PHILADELPHIA, PA)
Merged into Girard Trust Corn Exchange Bank (Philadelphia, PA) 06/18/1951
Each share Capital Stock $20 par exchanged for (1) share Capital Stock $15 par
Girard Trust Corn Exchange Bank (Philadelphia, PA) name changed to Girard Trust Bank (Philadelphia, PA) 03/09/1964 which reorganized as Girard Co. 06/30/1969 which merged into Mellon National Corp. 04/06/1983 which name changed to Mellon Bank Corp. 09/30/1984 which name changed to Mellon Financial Corp. 10/17/1999 which merged into Bank of New York Mellon Corp. 07/01/2007

CORN PRODS CO (DE)
Reincorporated 04/30/1959
State of incorporation changed from (NJ) to (DE) 04/30/1959
Common $1 par changed to 50¢ par and (1) additional share issued 05/19/1961
Name changed to CPC International Inc. 04/23/1969
CPC International Inc. name changed to BestFoods 01/01/1998
(See BestFoods)

CORN PRODUCTS INTL INC (DE)
Common 1¢ par split (2) for (1) by issuance of (1) additional share payable 01/25/2005 to holders of record 01/04/2005 Ex date - 01/26/2005
Name changed to Ingredion Inc. 06/04/2012

CORN PRODUCTS REFINING CO. (NJ)
Common $25 par changed to $10 par and (2) additional shares issued 05/20/1955
Merged into Corn Products Co. (NJ) 09/30/1958
Each share 7% Preferred $100 par exchanged for $175 principal amount of 4.625% Debentures
Each share Common $10 par exchanged for (1) share Common $1 par
Corn Products Co. (NJ) reincorporated in Delaware 04/30/1959 which name changed to CPC International Inc. 04/23/1969 which name changed to BestFoods 01/01/1998
(See BestFoods)

CORNAT INDS LTD (BC)
$1.20 Preference no par called for redemption 05/15/1978
Merged into Versatile Cornat Corp. (BC) 07/01/1978
Each share Common no par exchanged for (1) share Common no par
Versatile Cornat Corp. (BC) reincorporated in Canada as Versatile Corp. 02/09/1981 which reorganized in British Columbia as B.C. Pacific Capital Corp. 05/16/1988
(See B.C. Pacific Capital Corp.)

CORNBELT INSURANCE CO. (IL)
Recapitalized as Great Equity Life Insurance Co. 12/08/1964
Each share Common $1 par exchanged for (0.4) share Common 58¢ par
Great Equity Life Insurance Co. reorganized as Great Equity Financial Corp. 02/25/1971 which name changed to Ryan Insurance Group, Inc. 01/21/1976
(See Ryan Insurance Group, Inc.)

CORNBELT LIFE CO. (IL)
Name changed to First American Life Insurance Co. (IL) 08/02/1965
First American Life Insurance Co. (IL) name changed to Empire Life Insurance Co. of Illinois 11/27/1968 which merged into Empire General Corp. 09/22/1969
(See Empire General Corp.)

CORNELIA CORP (DE)
Charter cancelled and declared inoperative and void for non-payment of taxes 04/15/1972

CORNELIUS CO (MN)
Common 20¢ par split (4) for (1) by issuance of (3) additional shares 08/30/1968
Acquired by IMI plc 02/24/1982
Each share Common 20¢ par exchanged for $16.50 cash

CORNELL BUILDING CO. (IL)
Liquidation completed 11/14/1960
Details not available

CORNELL COMPANIES INC (DE)
Name changed 05/25/2000
Name changed from Cornell Corrections, Inc. to Cornell Companies, Inc. 05/25/2000
Merged into GEO Group, Inc. (Old) 08/12/2010
Each share Common $0.001 par exchanged for (1.3) shares Common 1¢ par
GEO Group, Inc. (Old) reorganized as GEO Group, Inc. (New) 06/27/2014

CORNELL INN CORP.
Dissolved 00/00/1936
Details not available

CORNELL MILLS
Liquidated 00/00/1931
Details not available

CORNELL OIL & GAS CORP. (DE)
Acquired by Delafran Industries Inc. 04/17/1970
Each share Common 1¢ par exchanged for (0.22222222) share Common 1¢ par
Delafran Industries Inc. recapitalized as Solar Age Manufacturing, Inc. (DE) 11/12/1982 which reincorporated in Nevada as Solar Age Industries, Inc. 08/20/1984 which name changed to Solar Group, Inc. 07/17/1998 which name changed to Forex365, Inc. 08/28/2008 which name changed to Fuer International Inc. 08/30/2010
(See Fuer International Inc.)

CORNELL PAPERBOARD PRODUCTS CO. (WI)
Merged into St. Regis Paper Co. 12/01/1959
Each share Capital Stock exchanged for (0.68) share Common $5 par
St. Regis Paper Co. name changed to St. Regis Corp. 04/28/1983 which merged into Champion International Corp. 11/20/1984 which merged into International Paper Co. 06/20/2000

CORNELL WOOD PRODUCTS CO. (WI)
Name changed to Cornell Paperboard Products Co. 00/00/1951
Each share Common $1 par exchanged for (2) shares Capital Stock $10 par
Cornell Paperboard Products Co. merged into St. Regis Paper Co. 12/01/1959 which name changed to St. Regis Corp. 04/28/1983 which merged into Champion International Corp. 11/20/1984 which merged into International Paper Co. 06/20/2000

CORNER BAY SILVER INC (ON)
Name changed 03/01/2001
Name changed from Corner Bay Minerals, Inc. to Corner Bay Silver, Inc. 03/01/2001
Merged into Pan American Silver Corp. 02/20/2003
Each share Common no par exchanged for (0.3846) share Common no par and (0.1923) Common Stock Purchase Warrant expiring 00/00/2007

CORNER BROADWAY-MAIDEN LANE, INC. (NY)
Charter cancelled and proclaimed dissolved for failure to pay taxes 12/15/1936

CORNERSTONE BANCORP (SC)
Stock Dividends - 10% payable 06/14/2002 to holders of record 05/31/2002 Ex date - 05/29/2002; 10% payable 04/17/2003 to holders of record 03/17/2003 Ex date - 03/13/2003; 10% payable 05/25/2004 to holders of record 05/11/2004 Ex date - 05/07/2004; 10% payable 05/27/2005 to holders of record 05/10/2005 Ex date - 05/06/2005; 10% payable 05/26/2006 to holders of record 05/09/2006 Ex date - 05/30/2006; 10% payable 05/25/2007 to holders of record 05/08/2007 Ex date - 05/04/2007; 5% payable 05/29/2009 to holders of record 05/12/2009 Ex date - 05/08/2009; 5% payable 05/28/2010 to holders of record 05/11/2010 Ex date - 05/07/2010; 5% payable 05/20/2016 to holders of record 04/20/2016 Ex date - 04/18/2016
Merged into First Community Corp. 10/20/2017
Each share Common no par exchanged for either (0.54) share Common $1 par, $11 cash or a combination thereof

CORNERSTONE BANCORP INC (CT)
Stock Dividend - 10% payable 06/14/2002 to holders of record 05/31/2002 Ex date - 05/29/2002
Merged into NewAlliance Bancshares, Inc. 01/02/2006
Each share Common 1¢ par exchanged for (0.7143707) share Common 1¢ par and $25.070304 cash
NewAlliance Bancshares, Inc. merged into First Niagara Financial Group, Inc. (New) 04/15/2011 which merged into KeyCorp (New) 08/01/2016

CORNERSTONE BANCSHARES INC (TN)
Common $1 par split (2) for (1) by issuance of (1) additional share payable 09/15/2004 to holders of record 08/16/2004 Ex date - 09/16/2004
Common $1 par split (2) for (1) by issuance of (1) additional share payable 12/18/2006 to holders of record 12/01/2006 Ex date - 12/19/2006
Conv. Preferred Ser. A no par called for redemption at $25 plus $1.042 accrued dividends on 08/31/2015
Stock Dividends - 0.842% payable 07/03/2009 to holders of record 06/12/2009 Ex date - 06/10/2009; 2% payable 10/02/2009 to holders of record 09/18/2009 Ex date - 09/16/2009
Name changed to SmartFinancial, Inc. 09/11/2015

CORNERSTONE BK (MOORESTOWN, NJ)
Stock Dividends - 5% payable 05/15/2007 to holders of record 04/02/2007 Ex date - 04/26/2007; 7.5% payable 05/15/2008 to holders of record 04/02/2008 Ex date - 04/04/2008
Reorganized as Cornerstone Financial Corp. 02/02/2009
Each share Common $5 par exchanged for (1) share Common no par

CORNERSTONE BK (STAMFORD, CT)
Stock Dividend - 10% payable 08/31/1998 to holders of record 07/31/1998
Under plan of reorganization each share Common 1¢ par automatically became (1) share Cornerstone Bancorp, Inc. Common 1¢ par 03/01/1999
Cornerstone Bancorp, Inc. merged into NewAlliance Bancshares, Inc. 01/02/2006 which merged into First Niagara Financial Group, Inc. (New) 04/15/2011 which merged into KeyCorp (New) 08/01/2016

CORNERSTONE BK (WILSON, NC)
Stock Dividends - 10% payable 05/15/2002 to holders of record 04/15/2002; 5% payable 05/15/2003 to holders of record 04/15/2003; 5%

payable 05/31/2004 to holders of record 04/30/2004
Under plan of reorganization each share Common no par automatically became (1) share CB Financial Corp. Common no par 06/08/2005

CORNERSTONE CAPITAL INC. (NV)
Reorganized under the laws of Florida as Medhealth Service Corp. 08/16/1991
Each share Common 1¢ par exchanged for (0.1) share Common 1¢ par
(See Medhealth Service Corp.)

CORNERSTONE CMNTY BK (RED BLUFF, CA)
Under plan of reorganization each share Common no par automatically became (1) share Cornerstone Community Bancorp Common no par 02/04/2015

CORNERSTONE ENTMT INC (NV)
Name changed to Beverly Hills Film Studios, Inc. 10/28/2003
Each share Common $0.001 par exchanged for (1) share Common $0.001 par
Beverly Hills Film Studios, Inc. name changed to Big Screen Entertainment Group, Inc. 04/01/2005

CORNERSTONE FINL CORP (NH)
Common no par split (2) for (1) by issuance of (1) additional share 01/21/1987
Merged into BayBanks, Inc. 12/01/1995
Each share Common no par exchanged for $8.80 cash

CORNERSTONE IMAGING INC (DE)
Name changed to Input Software, Inc. 08/10/1998
Input Software, Inc. name changed to ActionPoint, Inc. 04/24/2000 which name changed to Captiva Software Corp. 08/01/2002
(See Captiva Software Corp.)

CORNERSTONE INDL MINERALS CORP (ON)
Acquired by Seven Peaks Mining, Inc. 02/09/1999
Each share Common no par exchanged for $0.12 cash

CORNERSTONE INDS INTL INC (BC)
Cease trade order effective 06/13/2007
Stockholders' equity unlikely

CORNERSTONE INNOVATIONS INC (AB)
Reincorporated under the laws of Canada as EXI Technologies Inc. 06/11/1999
EXI Technologies Inc. name changed to EXI Wireless Inc. 09/12/2000 which was acquired by Applied Digital Solutions, Inc. 03/31/2005 which name changed to Digital Angel Corp. (New) 06/20/2008

CORNERSTONE INTERNET SOLUTIONS CO (DE)
Reorganized under Chapter 11 Federal Bankruptcy Code as Smave Solutions, Inc. 07/14/2003
Each share Common 1¢ par exchanged for (0.0071) share Common 1¢ par

CORNERSTONE METALS INC (BC)
Each share old Common no par exchanged for (0.5) share new Common no par 09/22/2017
Name changed to First Vanadium Corp. 09/25/2018

CORNERSTONE MINISTRIES INVTS INC (GA)
Plan of reorganization under Chapter 11 Federal Bankruptcy proceedings effective 09/25/2009
No stockholders' equity

CORNERSTONE NAT GAS INC (DE)
Merged into El Paso Natural Gas Co. 06/04/1996
Each share Common 10¢ par exchanged for $6 cash

CORNERSTONE PPTYS INC (NV)
Merged into Equity Office Properties Trust 06/19/2000
Each share Common no par exchanged for either (0.7009) share Common 1¢ par or $18 cash
(See Equity Office Properties Trust)

CORNERSTONE PROGRESSIVE RETURN FD (DE)
Each share old Common no par exchanged for (0.25) share new Common no par 12/29/2014
Merged into Cornerstone Strategic Value Fund, Inc. 06/29/2015
Each share new Common no par exchanged for (0.765785) share Common 1¢ par

CORNERSTONE PROPANE PARTNERS L P (DE)
Plan of reorganization under Chapter 11 Federal Bankruptcy proceedings effective 12/20/2004
No Unitholders' equity

CORNERSTONE RLTY INCOME TR INC (VA)
Conv. Preferred Ser. A no par called for redemption at $25 plus $0.5228 accrued dividends on 12/21/2004
Merged into Colonial Properties Trust 04/01/2005
Each share Common no par exchanged for (0.2581) Common Share of Bene. Int. 1¢ par
Colonial Properties Trust merged into Mid-America Apartment Communities, Inc. 10/01/2013

CORNERSTONE STRATEGIC RETURN FUND INC (MD)
Merged into Cornerstone Total Return Fund, Inc. 10/30/2002
Each share Common $0.001 par exchanged for (0.549) share Common 1¢ par

CORNERSTONE THERAPEUTICS INC (DE)
Acquired by Chiesi Farmaceutici S.p.A. 02/03/2014
Each share Common $0.001 par exchanged for $9.50 cash

CORNERSTONE VENTURES INC (DE)
Charter cancelled and declared inoperative and void for non-payment of taxes 03/01/1990

CORNET STORES (CA)
Each share old Common $2 par exchanged for (0.005) share new Common $2 par 02/04/1998
Note: In effect holders received $13.50 cash per share and public interest was eliminated

CORNHUSKER BK (OMAHA, NE)
Name changed to Nebraska State Bank of Omaha (Omaha, NE) 04/15/1978
(See Nebraska State Bank of Omaha (Omaha, NE))

CORNICHE CAP INC (AB)
Recapitalized as Printlux.com Inc. (AB) 08/28/2001
Each share Common no par exchanged for (0.5) share Common no par
Printlux.com Inc. (AB) reincorporated in Ontario as Allana Resources Inc. 12/10/2007 which name changed to Allana Potash Corp. 01/22/2010
(See Allana Potash Corp.)

CORNICHE GROUP INC (DE)
Common 10¢ par changed to $0.001 par 05/18/1998
Name changed to Phase III Medical, Inc. 07/30/2003
Phase III Medical, Inc. recapitalized as NeoStem, Inc. 08/31/2006 which name changed to Caladrius Biosciences, Inc. 06/08/2015

CORNICHE INDS CORP (CANADA)
Name changed 12/04/1989
Name changed from Corniche Minerals & Processing Inc. to Corniche Industries Corp. 12/04/1989
Struck off register and declared dissolved for failure to file returns 11/02/1995

CORNICHE RES LTD (BC)
Recapitalized as International Avalon Aircraft Inc. 04/18/1988
Each share Common no par exchanged for (0.1) share Common no par
(See International Avalon Aircraft Inc.)

CORNING DEL L P (DE)
6% Monthly Income Preferred Convertible Securities $100 par called for redemption at $51.80 on 03/23/1999

CORNING GLASS WKS (NY)
Each share Common $10 par exchanged for (4) shares Common $5 par 00/00/1945
Common $5 par split (5) for (2) by issuance of (1.5) additional shares 00/00/1955
Common $5 par split (5) for (2) by issuance of (1.5) additional shares 02/23/1973
3.5% Preferred Ser. 45 called for redemption 12/31/1977
3.5% Preferred Ser. 47 called for redemption 12/31/1977
Common $5 par split (2) for (1) by issuance of (1) additional share 02/11/1985
Common $5 par split (2) for (1) by issuance of (1) additional share 02/14/1989
Name changed to Corning Inc. and Common $5 par changed to $1 par 04/28/1989

CORNING INC (NY)
Each share Mandatory Conv. Preferred Ser. C $100 par exchanged for (50.813) shares Common 50¢ par 08/16/2005
(Additional Information in Active)

CORNING NAT GAS CORP (NY)
Each share Common $10 par exchanged for (2) shares Common no par 07/18/1955
Common no par changed to $5 par and (1) additional share issued 01/05/1964
Common $5 par split (2) for (1) by issuance of (1) additional share 02/20/1988
Common $5 par split (3) for (2) by issuance of (0.5) additional share payable 04/20/2011 to holders of record 04/01/2011 Ex date - 04/21/2011
Stock Dividends - 5% payable 12/30/2002 to holders of record 12/01/2002 Ex date - 11/26/2002; 5% payable 12/31/2003 to holders of record 12/01/2003 Ex date - 12/08/2003
Under plan of reorganization each share Common $5 par automatically became (1) share Corning Natural Gas Holding Corp. Common 1¢ par 12/17/2013

CORNING RES LTD (BC)
Struck off register and declared dissolved for failure to file returns 03/01/1996

CORNO MILLS CO.
Name changed to National Oats Co. 05/24/1935
National Oats Co. acquired by Liggett & Myers Tobacco Co. 10/04/1967 which name changed to Liggett & Myers Inc. 05/31/1968 which name changed to Liggett Group Inc. 04/28/1976
(See Liggett Group Inc.)

CORNUCOPIA GOLD MINES (WA)
Capital Stock 1¢ par changed to 5¢ par 00/00/1934
Adjudicated bankrupt 10/24/1958
No stockholders' equity

CORNUCOPIA GOLD MINES LTD (UT)
Name changed to Valley View Gold Mines Ltd. 08/19/1987
Valley View Gold Mines Ltd. recapitalized as Jefferson Valley Gold Mines Inc. 06/01/1988
(See Jefferson Valley Gold Mines Inc.)

CORNUCOPIA RES LTD (BC)
Common no par split (2) for (1) by issuance of (1) additional share 07/13/1987
Recapitalized as Stockscape.Com Technologies Inc. 07/13/1999
Each share Common no par exchanged for (0.1) share Common no par
Stockscape.Com Technologies Inc. merged into Quest Investment Corp. 07/04/2002 which merged into Quest Capital Corp. (BC) 06/30/2003 which reincorporated in Canada 05/27/2008 which name changed to Sprott Resource Lending Corp. 09/10/2010 which merged into Sprott Inc. 07/24/2013

CORNWALL EQUITIES LTD (DE)
Merged into Kaydak Corp. 04/25/1978
Each share Common $1 par exchanged for $18 cash

CORNWALL INTL INDS INC (DE)
Charter cancelled and declared inoperative and void for non-payment of taxes 03/01/1976

CORNWALL PETE & RES LTD (BC)
Common no par split (2) for (1) by issuance of (1) additional share 05/14/1981
Recapitalized as Rexplore Resources International Ltd. 11/09/1984
Each share Common no par exchanged for (0.2) share Common no par
Rexplore Resources International Ltd. name changed to Kemgas Sydney Inc. 12/29/1987 which name changed to Kemgas International Ltd. (BC) 02/15/1995 which reincorporated in Bermuda 06/23/1995 which name changed to Kemgas Ltd. 05/28/1996 which name changed to CalciTech Ltd. 07/25/2000

CORNWALL TIN & MNG CORP (DE)
Charter cancelled and declared inoperative and void for non-payment of taxes 03/01/1984

CORO INC (DE)
Reincorporated 01/07/1970
Common no par changed to $5 par 05/08/1956
Stock Dividend - 200% 07/03/1946
State of incorporation changed from (NY) to (DE) and Common $5 par changed to 10¢ par 01/07/1970
Name changed to Richton International Corp. 02/27/1970
(See Richton International Corp.)

COROLLA RES LTD (BC)
Struck off register and declared dissolved for failure to file returns 04/15/1994

COROMANDEL RES LTD (BC)
Recapitalized as International Coromandel Resources Ltd. 05/05/2000
Each share Common no par exchanged for (0.2) share Common no par
International Coromandel Resources Ltd. name changed to Sonora Gold

Corp. 08/17/2004 which
recapitalized as MetalQuest
Minerals Inc. 10/17/2007 which
recapitalized as Canada Gold Corp.
09/01/2009 which name changed to
STEM 7 Capital Inc. 07/12/2013
which name changed to South Star
Mining Corp. 12/22/2017

COROMETRICS MED SYS INC (DE)
Stock Dividends - 100% 12/18/1972;
50% 12/18/1973
Merged into American Home Products
Corp. 01/03/1975
Each share Common 1¢ par
exchanged for (0.5) share Common
$0.33333333 par
American Home Products Corp. name
changed to Wyeth 03/11/2002 which
was acquired by Pfizer Inc.
10/15/2009

CORONA CAP INC (NV)
Reincorporated 03/00/1988
State of incorporation changed from
(UT) to (NV) 03/00/1988
Name changed to Applied
Biosensors, Inc. (NV) 03/28/1988
Applied Biosensors, Inc. (NV)
reorganized in Delaware as Ansama
Corp. 08/25/1994 which name
changed to Nutrisystems.com, Inc.
10/04/1999 which name changed to
Nutri/System, Inc. 09/25/2000 which
name changed to NutriSystem, Inc.
05/13/2003

CORONA CORP (ON)
Recapitalized as International Corona
Corp. 06/11/1991
Each share Conv. 1st Preference Ser.
A no par automatically became (1)
share Conv. 1st Preference Ser. A
no par
Each share Conv. 1st Preference Ser.
B no par automatically became (1)
share Conv. 1st Preference Ser. B
no par
Each share Conv. 1st Preference Ser.
C no par automatically became (1)
share Conv. 1st Preference Ser. C
no par
Each share Conv. Class B Common
no par exchanged for (0.5) share
Conv. Class B Common no par
Each share Class A Subordinate no
par exchanged for (0.5) share Class
A Subordinate no par
(See International Corona Corp.)

CORONA EQUITIES INC (MN)
Name changed to Opti-Mag Substrate
Inc. 09/30/1988

CORONA GOLD CORP NEW (ON)
Merged into Oban Mining Corp.
08/27/2015
Each share Common no par
exchanged for (0.38355) share new
Common no par
Note: Unexchanged certificates will
be cancelled and become without
value 08/27/2021
Oban Mining Corp. name changed to
Osisko Mining Inc. 06/21/2016

CORONA GOLD CORP OLD (ON)
Plan of arrangement effective
06/13/2002
Each share Common no par
exchanged for (1) share Corona
Gold Corp. (New) Common no par
and (1) share Unisphere Waste
Conversion Ltd. Common no par
(See each company's listing)

CORONA INVTS INC (AB)
Name changed to Payment Services
Interactive Gateway Corp. (AB)
11/02/2000
Payment Services Interactive
Gateway Corp. (AB) reincorporated
in Ontario 08/03/2005
*(See Payment Services Interactive
Gateway Corp.)*

CORONA RES LTD (BC)
Common no par split (4) for (1) by
issuance of (3) additional shares
10/05/1981
Recapitalized as International Corona
Resources Ltd. (BC) 06/25/1982
Each share Common no par
exchanged for (0.25) share Common
no par
International Corona Resources Ltd.
(BC) reincorporated in Canada
08/01/1985 which merged into
Corona Corp. 07/01/1988 which
recapitalized as International Corona
Corp. 06/11/1991
(See International Corona Corp.)

CORONA SAVINGS & LOAN ASSOCIATION (CA)
Completely liquidated 08/27/1971
Each share Guarantee Stock $1 par
exchanged for first and final
distribution of $0.96 cash

CORONADO APARTMENT HOTEL CORP. (DE)
Dissolved 02/13/1959
Details not available

CORONADO BIOSCIENCES INC (DE)
Name changed to Fortress Biotech,
Inc. 04/28/2015

CORONADO CAP CORP (NV)
Name changed to Sionix Corp.
01/11/1995
Sionix Corp. name changed to
Automatic Control Corp. (NV)
02/14/1996 which reincorporated in
Utah as Sionix Corp. 04/22/1996
which reincorporated back in
Nevada 07/03/2003

CORONADO CORP. (UT)
Charter suspended for non-payment
of corporate taxes 03/30/1962

CORONADO CORP (NV)
Name changed to Vampt America,
Inc. 06/19/2012

CORONADO EXPLORATION CO. (UT)
Merged into R.C.M.Corp. 05/18/1971
Each share Common 10¢ par
exchanged for (0.2) share Common
5¢ par
R.C.M. Corp. name changed to RCM
Technologies, Inc. 08/01/1981

CORONADO EXPLORATIONS LTD (DE)
Recapitalized as Naturol Holdings
Ltd. 07/23/2002
Each share Common $0.001 par
exchanged for (0.2) share Common
$0.001 par
Naturol Holdings Ltd. name changed
to Integrated Environmental
Technologies, Ltd. (DE) 04/23/2004
which reincorporated in Nevada
01/11/2008

CORONADO FIRST BK NEW (CORONADO, CA)
Name changed to San Diego Private
Bank (Coronado, CA) 04/04/2013
San Diego Private Bank (Coronado,
CA) reorganized as Private Bancorp
of America, Inc. 12/03/2015

CORONADO FIRST BK OLD (CORONADO, CA)
Merged into Coronado First Bank
(Coronado, CA) (New) 11/16/2011
Each share Common no par
exchanged for (0.5925) share
Common no par
Coronado First Bank (Coronado, CA)
(New) name changed to San Diego
Private Bank (Coronado, CA)
04/04/2013 which reorganized as
Private Bancorp of America, Inc.
12/03/2015

CORONADO GOLD MINES, INC.
Out of existence 00/00/1937
Details not available

CORONADO HOTEL CO. (MO)
Recapitalized 00/00/1948
Each share Class A no par
exchanged for (1) share Preferred
no par and $50 cash
Each share Class B $5 par
exchanged for (1) share Common
$5 par
Name changed to St. Louis Sheraton
Corp. 00/00/1953
(See St. Louis Sheraton Corp.)

CORONADO INDS INC (NV)
Reincorporated 10/29/1996
State of incorporation changed from
(NY) to (NV) 10/29/1996
Each share old Common $0.001 par
exchanged for (0.1) share new
Common $0.001 par 02/21/2006
Each share new Common $0.001 par
exchanged again for (0.01) share
new Common $0.001 par
02/05/2007
Name changed to Continental Fuels
Inc. 03/23/2007
(See Continental Fuels Inc.)

CORONADO MINERALS CO (DE)
Name changed 01/15/1977
Name changed from Coronado Oil &
Minerals Co. to Coronado Minerals
Co. 01/15/1977
Stock Dividend - 100% 10/09/1981
Charter cancelled and declared
inoperative and void for
non-payment of taxes 03/01/1987

CORONADO RES INC (BC)
Certificates dtd. after 05/13/1994
Recapitalized as Habanero
Resources Inc. 10/27/1997
Each share Common no par
exchanged for (0.5) share Common
no par
Habanero Resources Inc.
recapitalized as Sienna Resources
Inc. 01/24/2014

CORONADO RES INC (BC)
Certificates dated prior to 12/07/1990
Recapitalized as Iron King Mines Inc.
12/07/1990
Each share Common no par
exchanged for (0.33333333) share
Common no par
Iron King Mines Inc. recapitalized as
Corriente Resources Inc. 04/23/1992
(See Corriente Resources Inc.)

CORONADO URANIUM CORP. (UT)
Each share Common 3¢ par
exchanged for (0.3) share Common
10¢ par 07/07/1955
Name changed to Coronado
Exploration Co. 06/28/1957
Coronado Exploration Co. merged
into R.C.M. Corp. 05/18/1971 which
name changed to RCM
Technologies, Inc. 08/01/1981

CORONADO VENTURES INC (NV)
Recapitalized as Weststar Group, Inc.
01/05/1990
Each share Common $0.001 par
exchanged for (0.5) share Common
$0.001 par
Weststar Group, Inc. recapitalized as
Arena Group, Inc. 08/15/1997 which
name changed to Elligent Consulting
Group, Inc. 08/13/1998 which name
changed to E-Vantage Solutions,
Inc. 07/16/2000
(See E-Vantage Solutions, Inc.)

CORONATION ALLIED INDS LTD (BC)
Struck off register and declared
dissolved for failure to filed returns
04/04/1977

CORONATION CR LTD (BC)
Common no par split (3) for (1) by
issuance of (2) additional shares
10/20/1961
Each share $1.50 Preference Ser. A
$25 par exchanged for (10) shares
6% Conv. Preference Ser. A $2.50
par 01/20/1969
Each share $1.20 Preference Ser. B
$20 par exchanged for (8) shares
6% Conv. Preference Ser. A $2.50
par 01/20/1969
Each share 6% 2nd Preference $8
par exchanged for (3) shares
Common no par 01/20/1969
Acquired by Cornat Industries Ltd.
11/26/1974
Each share Common no par
exchanged for $3.50 cash
6% Conv. Preference Ser. A $2.50 par
called for redemption 02/15/1979
Public interest eliminated

CORONATION GULF MINES LTD. (BC)
Common $1 par changed to no par
12/07/1970
Name changed to Coronation Allied
Industries Ltd. 08/09/1971
(See Coronation Allied Industries Ltd.)

CORONATION MINERALS INC (ON)
Reincorporated 04/23/2004
Place of incorporation changed from
(AB) to (ON) 04/23/2004
Name changed to Guyana Precious
Metals Inc. 08/18/2009
Guyana Precious Metals Inc. name
changed to GPM Metals Inc.
08/29/2013

CORONATION MORTGAGE CO. LTD. (BC)
Name changed to Coronation Credit
Corp. Ltd. 01/00/1961
(See Coronation Credit Corp. Ltd.)

CORONATION RES CDA INC (ON)
Charter cancelled for failure to file
reports and pay taxes 02/21/1989

CORONATION ROYALTIES LTD. (AB)
Merged into Amalgamated Oils Ltd.
00/00/1941
Each share Common no par
exchanged for (0.19) share Common
no par
(See Amalgamated Oils Ltd.)

CORONDOLET RLTY TR (TN)
Charter revoked 11/19/1982

CORONET CARPETS INC (CANADA)
Each share old Common no par
exchanged for (0.00000867) share
new Common no par 12/19/1990
Note: In effect holders received $4
cash per share and public interest
was eliminated

CORONET HOUSEWARES INC. (QC)
Company went private 00/00/1986
Details not available

CORONET INDS INC (DE)
Common 10¢ par split (2) for (1) by
issuance of (1) additional share
04/12/1966
Common 10¢ par split (2) for (1) by
issuance of (1) additional share
11/30/1968
Merged into RCA Corp. 02/24/1971
Each share Common 10¢ par
exchanged for (1) share Common
no par
(See RCA Corp.)

CORONET METALS INC (BC)
Each share old Common no par
exchanged for (0.08333333) share
new Common no par 01/07/2015
Each share new Common no par
exchanged again for (0.33333333)
share new Common no par
11/27/2015
Name changed to MegumaGold Corp.
06/04/2018

CORONET MINES LTD (BC)
Merged into Coralta Resources Ltd.
10/18/1973
Each share Common 50¢ par
exchanged for (0.25) share Common
$1 par
(See Coralta Resources Ltd.)

CORONET PETROLEUM CORP. (DE)
Completely liquidated 04/15/1965
Each share Common 20¢ par
exchanged for (0.172414) share
Texstar Corp. Common $1 par
(See Texstar Corp.)

CORONET PROCESSORS, INC. (NV)
Name changed to Faxline Holding Corp. 04/22/1988
Faxline Holding Corp. name changed to Fax-9 Holding Corp. 04/28/1989
(See Fax-9 Holding Corp.)

CORONET PRODUCTS CO. (MO)
Acquired by King Louie International, Inc. 09/01/1964
Each share Common 25¢ par exchanged for (0.83333333) share Common $1 par
(See King Louie International, Inc.)

CORONET RES LTD (BC)
Name changed to Thunder Engines Corp. 02/12/1986
Thunder Engines Corp. recapitalized as Golden Thunder Resources Ltd. 05/02/1996 which recapitalized as Consolidated Golden Thunder Resources Ltd. 12/04/2000 which name changed to GHG Resources Ltd. 05/10/2004 which name changed to Los Andes Copper Ltd. 03/29/2007

CORPAC MINERALS LTD (BC)
Struck off register and declared dissolved for failure to file returns 09/26/1986

CORPAS HLDGS INC (OK)
SEC revoked common stock registration 10/04/2006

CORPAS INVTS INC (FL)
Old Common $0.001 par split (4) for (1) by issuance of (3) additional shares payable 11/08/1999 to holders of record 10/27/1999
Each share old Common $0.001 par exchanged for (0.00666666) share new Common $0.001 par 01/22/2002
Reorganized under the laws of Oklahoma as Corpas Holdings Inc. 04/25/2002
Each share new Common $0.001 par exchanged for (2) shares Common $0.001 par

CORPBANCA S A (CHILE)
ADR agreement terminated 02/18/2005
Each 144A Sponsored ADR for Common exchanged for $26.81665 cash
ADR basis changed from (1:5,000) to (1:1,500) 02/23/2011
Sponsored ADR's for Common split (10) for (3) by issuance of (2.33333333) additional ADR's payable 02/22/2011 to holders of record 02/18/2011 Ex date - 02/23/2011
Name changed to Itau CorpBanca 04/01/2016

CORPFIN COM INC (DE)
Name changed to JPC Capital Partners, Inc. 07/22/2004
JPC Capital Partners, Inc. recapitalized as DIAS Holding, Inc. 08/22/2008
(See DIAS Holding, Inc.)

CORPHQ INC (CA)
Common no par split (10) for (1) by issuance of (9) additional shares payable 05/18/2004 to holders of record 05/17/2004
Recapitalized as American Nano Silicon Technology, Inc. 08/06/2007
Each (1,302) shares Common no par exchanged for (1) share Common no par

CORPORACION BANCARIA DE ESPANA S A (SPAIN)
Name changed to Argentaria Caja Postal y Banco Hipotecario S.A. 05/03/99
Argentaria Caja Postal y Banco Hipotecario S.A. merged into Banco Bilbao Viscaya Argentaria S.A. 1/31/2000

CORPORACION DURANGO SAB DE CV (MEXICO)
Name changed 04/13/2007
Name changed from Corporacion Durango, S.A. de C.V. to Corporacion Durango, S.A.B. de C.V. 04/13/2007
Name changed to Bio Pappel S.A.B. de C.V. 05/19/2014
(See Bio Pappel S.A.B. de C.V.)

CORPORACION FINANCIERA DEL VALLE S A (COLOMBIA)
Stock Dividends - In 144A Shares to holders of 144A Shares 6.63% payable 4/26/96 to holders of record 3/15/96; 9.9% payable 4/30/97 to holders of record 3/14/97; 9.68% payable 4/3/98 to holders of record 3/13/98; 0.008% payable 4/11/2000 to holders of record 3/29/2000
Name changed to Corporacion Financiera Colombiana S.A. 3/23/2006

CORPORACION FINANCIERA REUNIDA S A (SPAIN)
Name changed to NH Hoteles, S.A. 02/12/1999
NH Hoteles, S.A. name changed to NH Hotel Group, S.A. 07/03/2015
(See NH Hotel Group, S.A.)

CORPORACION GEO S A DE C V (MEXICO)
144A Sponsored ADR's for Class B split (5) for (1) by issuance of (4) additional ADR's payable 05/11/2004 to holders of record 05/07/2004 Ex date - 05/12/2004
Sponsored ADR's for Common split (5) for (1) by issuance of (4) additional ADR's payable 05/11/2004 to holders of record 05/07/2004 Ex date - 05/12/2004
ADR agreement terminated 10/29/2015
No 144A ADR's remain outstanding
Each Sponsored ADR for Common exchanged for $0.013465 cash

CORPORACION INDL SANLUIS S A D E C V (MEXICO)
Each old Sponsored ADR for Ser. A-1 exchanged for (1) new Sponsored ADR for Ser. A-1 06/28/1993
Each old Sponsored ADR for Ser. A-2 exchanged for (1) new Sponsored ADR for Ser. A-2 06/28/1993
Each new Sponsored ADR for Ser. A-1 exchanged for (0.43391666) new Sponsored ADR for 1995 Ser. A-1 03/06/1995
Each new Sponsored ADR for Ser. A-2 exchanged for (0.43391666) new Sponsored ADR for 1995 Ser. A-2 03/06/1995
Each new Sponsored ADR for 1995 Ser. A-1 exchanged for (1) Sponsored ADR for Ordinary Participation 04/22/1995
Each new Sponsored ADR for 1995 Ser. A-2 exchanged for (1) Sponsored ADR for Ordinary Participation 04/22/1995
ADR agreement terminated 11/21/1995
Each Sponsored ADR for Ordinary Participation exchanged for $352.65 cash
Name changed to Rassini S.A.B. de C.V. 02/27/2015

CORPORACION MAPFRE S A (SPAIN)
Name changed 02/26/2002
Sponsored ADR's for Common P500 par split (3) for (1) by issuance of (2) additional ADR's payable 09/27/2001 to holders of record 09/14/2001 Ex date - 09/28/2001
Name changed from Corporacion Mapfre-Compania Internacional de Reaseguros S.A. to Corporacion Mapfre S.A. 02/26/2002
Sponsored ADR's for Common P500 par split (5) for (1) by issuance of (4) additional ADR's payable 11/09/2006 to holders of record 10/27/2006 Ex date - 11/10/2006
ADR agreement terminated 02/02/2007
Each Sponsored ADR for Common exchanged for $0.7464 cash

CORPORACION MEXICANA DE AVIACION S A DE C V (MEXICO)
Merged into Cintra S.A. 06/26/1996
Details not available

CORPORATE BK (SANTA ANA, CA)
Merged into CU Bancorp 1/12/96
Each share Common no par exchanged for (1.297742) shares Common no par and $3.4606 cash
(See CU Bancorp)

CORPORATE CAP PFD FD (MA)
Voluntarily dissolved 07/09/1990
Details not available

CORPORATE CAP RES INC (DE)
Charter cancelled and declared inoperative and void for non-payment of taxes 3/1/99

CORPORATE CASH MGMT PLUS FD INC (MD)
Under plan of reorganization each share Common 1¢ par automatically became (1) share Corporate Cash Management Fund Inc. Flagship Basic Value Fund 1¢ par 10/15/87
(See Corporate Cash Management Fund Inc.)

CORPORATE CATALYST ACQUISITION INC (ON)
Recapitalized as Globalive Technology Inc. 06/13/2018
Each share Common no par exchanged for (0.15015015) share Common no par

CORPORATE DATA SCIENCES INC (CA)
Charter suspended for failure to file reports and pay fees 10/01/1992

CORPORATE DEV CTRS INC (NV)
Name changed to e-Perception, Inc. 01/29/2002
e-Perception, Inc. name changed to PeopleView Inc. 05/15/2003 which recapitalized as Auxilio, Inc. (NV) 06/21/2004 which reincorporated in Delaware as CynergisTek, Inc. 09/08/2017

CORPORATE DEV STRATEGIES INC (DE)
Each share old Common $0.0003 par exchanged for (0.1) share new Common $0.0003 par 9/7/2004
Name changed to Irwin Energy Inc. 12/8/2004
Irwin Energy Inc. recapitalized as Irwin Resources Inc. 11/20/2006

CORPORATE ENTERPRISES INC (DE)
Charter cancelled and declared inoperative and void for non-payment of taxes 3/1/76

CORPORATE EXECUTIVE BRD CO (DE)
Common 1¢ par split (2) for (1) by issuance of (1) additional share payable 09/15/2000 to holders of record 09/01/2000 Ex date - 09/18/2000
Name changed to CEB Inc. 05/15/2015
CEB Inc. merged into Gartner, Inc. 04/05/2017

CORPORATE EXPRESS INC (CO)
Common $0.0002 par split (3) for (2) by issuance of (0.5) additional share 06/21/1995
Common $0.0002 par split (3) for (2) by issuance of (0.5) additional share payable 01/31/1997 to holders of record 01/24/1997
Merged into Buhrmann NV 10/28/1999
Each share Common $0.0002 par exchanged for $9.70 cash

CORPORATE EXPRESS N V (NETHERLANDS)
99% acquired by Staples, Inc. through voluntary purchase offer which expired 07/16/2008
ADR agreement terminated 04/16/2012
Each Sponsored ADR for Ordinary exchanged for $11.502325 cash

CORPORATE FINL VENTURES INC (DE)
Each share Common $0.00025 par exchanged for (0.01) share Common $0.025 par 12/31/1993
Each share Common $0.025 par exchanged for (0.16666666) share Common 15¢ par 10/17/1994
Name changed to NAL Financial Group, Inc. 11/30/1994
(See NAL Financial Group, Inc.)

CORPORATE FOODS LTD (ON)
$2.75 Preference $49 par changed to no par 05/03/1984
Common no par split (10) for (1) by issuance of (9) additional shares 05/10/1984
Common no par split (5) for (1) by issuance of (4) additional shares 12/10/1987
$2.75 Preference no par called for redemption 08/07/1992
Name changed to Canada Bread Ltd. (New) 05/06/1997
(See Canada Bread Ltd. (New))

CORPORATE HIGH YIELD FD INC (MD)
Name changed to BlackRock Corporate High Yield Fund, Inc. 10/02/2006
BlackRock Corporate High Yield Fund, Inc. merged into BlackRock Corporate High Yield Fund VI, Inc. 11/18/2013 which name changed to BlackRock Corporate High Yield Fund, Inc. 03/03/2014

CORPORATE HIGH YIELD FD II INC (MD)
Reorganized as Corporate High Yield Fund, Inc. 05/05/2003
Each share Common 10¢ par exchanged for (0.912603) share Common 10¢ par
Corporate High Yield Fund, Inc. name changed to BlackRock Corporate High Yield Fund, Inc. 10/02/2006 which merged into BlackRock Corporate High Yield Fund VI, Inc. 11/18/2013 which name changed to BlackRock Corporate High Yield Fund, Inc. 03/03/2014

CORPORATE HIGH YIELD FD III INC (MD)
Name changed to BlackRock Corporate High Yield Fund III Inc. 10/02/2006
BlackRock Corporate High Yield Fund III Inc. merged into BlackRock Corporate High Yield Fund VI, Inc. 11/18/2013 which name changed to BlackRock Corporate High Yield Fund, Inc. 03/03/2014

CORPORATE HIGH YIELD FD IV (MD)
Reorganized as Corporate High Yield Fund V, Inc. 05/05/2003
Each share Common 10¢ par exchanged for (1.000691) shares Common 10¢ par
Corporate High Yield Fund V, Inc. name changed to BlackRock Corporate High Yield Fund V, Inc. 10/02/2006 which merged into BlackRock Corporate High Yield Fund VI, Inc. 11/18/2013 which name changed to BlackRock Corporate High Yield Fund, Inc. 03/03/2014

CORPORATE HIGH YIELD FD V INC (MD)
Name changed to BlackRock Corporate High Yield Fund V, Inc. 10/02/2006
BlackRock Corporate High Yield Fund V, Inc. merged into BlackRock Corporate High Yield Fund VI, Inc. 11/18/2013 which name changed to BlackRock Corporate High Yield Fund, Inc. 03/03/2014

CORPORATE HIGH YIELD FD VI INC (MD)
Name changed to BlackRock Corporate High Yield Fund VI, Inc. 10/02/2006
BlackRock Corporate High Yield Fund VI, Inc. name changed to BlackRock Corporate High Yield Fund, Inc. 03/03/2014

CORPORATE INCOME FD (MA & NY)
Trust terminated 04/22/1997
Each Unit of Undivided Int. 7th Preferred Ser. exchanged for cash value
Trust terminated 04/29/1997
Each Unit of Undivided Int. 8th Preferred Ser. exchanged for cash value
Each Unit of Undivided Int. 10th Preferred Ser. exchanged for cash value
Trust terminated 03/29/2001
Each Unit of Undivided Int. 213th Monthly Payment Ser. exchanged for $124.52 cash
Each Unit of Undivided Int. 256th Monthly Payment Ser. exchanged for $194.05 cash
Note: Details on all other series are not available

CORPORATE INVESTMENT ASSOCIATES
Liquidated 00/00/1927
Details not available

CORPORATE LEADERS TR FD (NY)
Name changed to Lexington Corporate Leaders Trust Fund 00/00/1988
Lexington Corporate Leaders Trust Fund name changed to Pilgrim Corporate Leaders Trust Fund 08/07/2000 which name changed to ING Corporate Leaders Trust Fund 03/01/2002

CORPORATE MGMT GROUP INC (FL)
Name changed to Charles (J.W.) Financial Services, Inc. 1/1/95
Charles (J.W.) Financial Services, Inc. merged into JWGenesis Financial Corp. 6/12/98

CORPORATE MASTER LTD (ON)
Common no par converted into 6% Preferred Ser. A no par 6/30/78
6% Preferred Ser. A no par called for redemption 12/27/78

CORPORATE MTG SOLUTIONS INC (DE)
Name changed to Big Apple Worldwide, Inc. 11/25/2005
Big Apple Worldwide, Inc. name changed to Fusion Restaurant Group, Inc. 02/24/2011

CORPORATE OFFICE PPTYS TR (MD)
10% Preferred Shares of Bene. Int. Ser. B 1¢ par called for redemption at $25 on 07/15/2004
10.25% Preferred Shares of Bene. Int. Ser. E called for redemption at $25 on 07/15/2006
9.875% Preferred Shares of Bene. Int. Ser. F 1¢ par called for redemption at $25 on 10/15/2006
8% Preferred Shares of Bene. Int. Ser. G 1¢ par called for redemption at $25 plus $0.12 accrued dividends on 08/06/2012
7.625% Preferred Shares of Bene. Int. Ser. J 1¢ par called for redemption at $25 plus $0.0424 accrued dividends on 04/22/2013
7.5% Preferred Shares of Bene. Int. Ser. H 1¢ par called for redemption at $25 plus $0.323 accrued dividends on 06/16/2014
7.375% Preferred Shares of Bene. Int. Ser. L 1¢ par called for redemption at $25 plus $0.3687 accrued dividends on 06/27/2017
(Additional Information in Active)

CORPORATE OFFICE PPTYS TR INC (MN)
Reincorporated under the laws of Maryland as Corporate Office Properties Trust 3/12/98

CORPORATE OIL & GAS LTD (MB)
Recapitalized as Charlie O Beverages Ltd. 12/09/1987
Each share Common no par exchanged for (0.2) share Common no par
Charlie O Beverages Ltd. reincorporated in Oklahoma as Charlie O Co., Inc. 02/13/1990 which recapitalized as Sooner Holdings Inc. 10/24/1995 which recapitalized as FlyingEagle PU Technical Corp. 01/30/2012

CORPORATE OUTFITTERS INC (DE)
Name changed to Liberty Capital Asset Management, Inc. 11/20/2008
Liberty Capital Asset Management, Inc. name changed to Las Vegas Railway Express (DE) 03/30/2010 which reorganized in Nevada as United Rail, Inc. 10/12/2018

CORPORATE PFD FD INC (MD)
Charter forfeited 10/10/90

CORPORATE PLAN LEASING LTD. (ON)
Charter cancelled for failure to pay taxes and file returns 12/22/80

CORPORATE PPTYS LTD (ON)
Name changed to Seamiles Ltd. 11/29/2006
Seamiles Ltd. named changed to Intellectual Capital Group Ltd. 04/03/2012

CORPORATE PPTY ASSOC (CA & DE)
Merged into Carey Diversified L.L.C. 01/01/1998
Each Unit of Limited Partnership 1 exchanged for (26.3) Listed Shares no par
Each Unit of Limited Partnership 2 exchanged for (27.96) Listed Shares no par
Each Unit of Limited Partnership 3 exchanged for (37.93) Listed Shares no par
Each Unit of Limited Partnership 4 exchanged for (32.97) Listed Shares no par
Each Unit of Limited Partnership 5 exchanged for (18.37) Listed Shares no par
Each Unit of Limited Partnership 6 exchanged for (69.03) Listed Shares no par
Each Unit of Limited Partnership 7 exchanged for (55.39) Listed Shares no par
Each Unit of Limited Partnership 8 exchanged for (69.55) Listed Shares no par
Each Unit of Limited Partnership 9 exchanged for (52.63) Listed Shares no par
Note: Limited Partners who did not elect to receive shares became Subsidiary Partnership Unitholders which were called for redemption at $8,377 on 07/15/1998
Carey Diversified L.L.C. name changed to W.P. Carey & Co. L.L.C. (DE) 06/28/2000 which reorganized in Maryland as W.P. Carey Inc. 09/28/2012

CORPORATE PPTY ASSOC 10 INC (MD)
Merged into Carey Institutional Properties Inc. 04/29/2002
Each share Common $10 par exchanged for (0.8445) share Ser. 11 Common $0.001 par
Carey Institutional Properties Inc. merged into Corporate Property Associates 15 Inc. 09/01/2004 which merged into W.P. Carey Inc. 09/28/2012

CORPORATE PPTY ASSOC (MD)
Each share Ser. 12 Common $0.001 par exchanged for (0.8692) share Ser. 14 Common $0.001 par 12/01/2006
Merged into Corporate Property Associates 16 Global Inc. 05/02/2011
Each share Ser. 14 Common $0.001 par exchanged for either (1.1932) shares Common $0.001 par or $10.50 cash
Note: Holders also received an additional distribution of $1 cash per share
Corporate Property Associates 16 Global Inc. merged into W.P. Carey Inc. 01/31/2014

CORPORATE PPTY ASSOC 15 INC (MD)
Merged into W.P. Carey Inc. 09/28/2012
Each share Common $0.001 par exchanged for (0.2326) share Common $0.001 par and $1.25 cash

CORPORATE PPTY ASSOCS 16 GLOBAL INC (MD)
Name changed 11/26/2003
Name changed from Corporate Property Associates 16 Inc. to Corporate Property Associates 16 Global Inc. 11/26/2003
Merged into W.P. Carey Inc. 01/31/2014
Each share Common $0.001 par exchanged for (0.183) share Common $0.001 par

CORPORATE QUEST INC (CO)
Name changed to United Houston Oil & Gas, Inc. 08/01/1987

CORPORATE RLTY INCOME FD I L P (DE)
Company terminated registration of depository units and is no longer public as of 06/06/2008

CORPORATE RLTY INCOME TR I (MA)
Merged into Lexington Corporate Properties Trust 1/6/98
Each Share of Bene. Int. 10¢ par exchanged for (1) Common Share of Bene. Int. $0.001 par
Lexington Corporate Properties Trust name changed to Lexington Realty Trust 12/31/2006

CORPORATE RECRUITERS INC (MN)
Reincorporated under the laws of Nevada as Connection China Trading Corp. and Common 10¢ par changed to $0.001 par 09/00/1989
Connection China Trading Corp. name changed to Asian Pacific Co., Ltd. 09/09/1992
(See Asian Pacific Co., Ltd.)

CORPORATE RENAISSANCE GROUP INC (DE)
Assets transferred to Corporate Renaissance Group Inc. Liquidating Trust 2/15/2000
Each share Common 1¢ par exchanged for (1) Unit of Bene. Int.

CORPORATE RENAISSANCE GROUP INC LIQUIDATING TR (DE)
Each Unit of Bene. Int. 1¢ par received initial distribution of $4.78 cash 02/15/2000
Each Unit of Bene. Int. 1¢ par received second distribution of $7.25 cash payable 03/08/2001 to holders of record 03/01/2001 Ex date - 03/09/2001
Each Unit of Bene. Int. 1¢ par received third distribution of $1.24 cash payable 07/18/2003 to holders of record 07/11/2003 Ex date - 09/29/2003
Each Unit of Bene. Int. 1¢ par received fourth and final distribution of $0.077 cash payable 12/17/2003 to holders of record 12/10/2003 Ex date - 12/18/2003

CORPORATE ROAD SHOW COM INC (NY)
Reorganized under the laws of Delaware as Rexahn Pharmaceuticals, Inc. 05/16/2005
Each share Common $0.001 par exchanged for (0.01) share Common $0.0001 par

CORPORATE SVCS GROUP PLC (ENGLAND)
Each old ADR for Ordinary exchanged for (0.05) new ADR for Ordinary 11/27/1991
Acquired by Impellam Group PLC 05/07/2008
Each ADR for Ordinary exchanged for $0.116766 cash

CORPORATE SOFTWARE INC (DE)
Merged into CS Acquisition Corp. 3/1/94
Each share Common 1¢ par exchanged for $15 cash

CORPORATE STEEL PRODUCTS LTD.
Liquidated 00/00/1933
Details not available

CORPORATE TOURS & TRAVEL INC (NV)
Name changed to Absolutefuture.com, Inc. 05/26/1999
(See Absolutefuture.com, Inc.)

CORPORATE VISION INC (CO)
Each (300) shares old Common $0.001 par exchanged for (1) share new Common $0.001 par 05/26/1998
Each share new Common $0.001 par received distribution of (10) shares Preferred Ser. A $0.001 par payable 12/18/1998 to holders of record 06/01/1998
New Common $0.001 par split (2) for (1) by issuance of (1) additional share payable 06/05/1999 to holders of record 06/02/1999
New Common $0.001 par split (2) for (1) by issuance of (1) additional share payable 08/17/1999 to holders of record 08/16/1999
Preferred Ser. A $0.001 par split (3) for (1) by issuance of (2) additional shares payable 12/30/1999 to holders of record 12/28/1999
New Common $0.001 par split (3) for (1) by issuance of (2) additional shares payable 12/30/1999 to holders of record 12/28/1999
Reincorporated under the laws of Oklahoma as Wastech, Inc. 03/18/2004
(See Wastech, Inc.)

CORPORATEFAMILY SOLUTIONS INC (TN)
Merged into Bright Horizons Family Solutions, Inc. (Old) 07/24/1998
Each share Common no par exchanged for (1) share Common 1¢ par
(See Bright Horizons Family Solutions, Inc. (Old))

CORPORATION CANADIENNE DE CAP PRODIGE (CANADA)
Merged into Fronsac Capital Inc. 07/13/2010
Each share Common no par exchanged for (0.5) share Common no par

Fronsac Capital Inc. reorganized as Fronsac Real Estate Investment Trust 07/04/2011

CORPORATION D EXPANSION FINANCIERE (QC)
Each share 5% Non-Cum. Preferred $1 par exchanged for (0.1) share 7% Preferred $10 par 06/22/1965
Common $9 par changed to no par 10/13/1971
Through exchange offer 100% acquired by York Lambton as of 11/21/1975
Public interest eliminated

CORPORATION FALCONBRIDGE COPPER (QC)
Name changed to Minnova Inc. 05/26/1987
Minnova Inc. merged into Metall Mining Corp. 05/05/1993 which name changed to Inmet Mining Corp. 05/04/1995 which was acquired by First Quantum Minerals Ltd. 04/09/2013

CORPORATION FOR ENTMT & LEARNING INC (NY)
Name changed to CEL Communications, Inc. 12/13/1985
(See CEL Communications, Inc.)

CORPORATION LITHOS (QC)
Name changed to Limtech Lithium Metal Technologies Inc. 08/25/1999
Limtech Lithium Metal Technologies Inc. recapitalized as Limtech Lithium Industries Inc. 12/16/2002
(See Limtech Lithium Industries Inc.)

CORPORATION OF AMERICAS LTD. (FL)
Merged into Exquisite Form Industries, Inc. 08/04/1969
Each share Common 10¢ par exchanged for (0.33333333) share Class A Capital Stock 10¢ par
Exquisite Form Industries, Inc. name changed to Summit Organization, Inc. 01/05/1970
(See Summit Organization, Inc.)

CORPORATION S (DE)
Merged into Recognition Equipment Inc. 10/31/74
Each share Common 10¢ par exchanged for $0.45 cash

CORPTECH INDS INC (BC)
Recapitalized as Forefront Ventures Ltd. 07/15/1992
Each share Common no par exchanged for (0.25) share Common no par
Forefront Ventures Ltd. recapitalized as First Echelon Ventures, Inc. 02/16/1999 which name changed to Aumega Discoveries Ltd. 12/12/2003 which recapitalized as Fortress Base Metals Corp. 01/10/2007 which name changed to Lions Gate Metals Inc. 07/21/2008 which name changed to Block X Capital Corp. 01/25/2018

CORPUS CHRISTI BANCSHARES INC (TX)
Common $5 par split (4) for (1) by issuance of (3) additional shares 10/20/1993
Merged into R.E. Holding 03/07/1997
Each share Common $5 par exchanged for $18.84 cash

CORPUS CHRISTI BK & TR CO (CORPUS CHRISTI, TX)
Capital Stock $100 par changed to $20 par 05/07/1952
Capital Stock $20 par changed to $10 par and (1) additional share issued plus a 50% stock dividend paid 08/28/1963
Capital Stock $10 par changed to $5 par and (1) additional share issued plus a 10% stock dividend paid 03/12/1970
Acquired by First City Bancorporation of Texas, Inc. (TX) 07/12/1973
Each share Capital Stock $5 par exchanged for (1.0275) shares Common $6.50 par
(See First City Bancorporation of Texas, Inc. (TX))

CORPUS CHRISTI DEVELOPMENT CO. (TX)
Recapitalized as Impro, Inc. 09/09/1960
Each share Common 10¢ par exchanged for (0.2) share Common 50¢ par
(See Impro, Inc.)

CORPUS CHRISTI GAS CO.
Acquired by the City of Corpus Christi, TX 00/00/1933
Details not available

CORPUS CHRISTI REFINING CO. (TX)
Name changed to Corpus Christi Development Co. 3/6/56
Corpus Christi Development Co. recapitalized as Impro, Inc. 9/9/60
(See Impro, Inc.)

CORPUS CHRISTI SAVINGS & LOAN ASSOCIATION (TX)
Each share Permanent Reserve Fund Stock $10 par exchanged for (4) shares Permanent Reserve Fund Stock $2.50 par 02/01/1972
99.6% acquired through voluntary exchange offer by First Texas Financial Corp. as of 12/29/1973
Public interest eliminated

CORPUS CHRISTI ST NATL BK (CORPUS CHRISTI, TX)
Capital Stock $25 par changed to $2.50 par and (9) additional shares issued 04/08/1969
Merged into Federated Texas Bancorporation, Inc. 05/01/1973
Each share Capital Stock $2.50 par exchanged for (1.26) shares Common $5 par
Federated Texas Bancorporation, Inc. merged into Federated Capital Corp. 01/29/1974 which merged into Mercantile Texas Corp. 12/30/1976 which name changed to MCorp 10/11/1984
(See MCorp)

CORPUS RES CORP (BC)
Name changed to NeoMedyx Medical Corp. 08/04/2009
NeoMedyx Medical Corp. name changed to Blue Marble Media Corp. 03/30/2010 which name changed to KBridge Energy Corp. 01/31/2012

CORRA CAP CORP (BC)
Reincorporated under the laws of Delaware as GATCO Technologies Inc. 8/6/2002

CORRAL AMUSEMENTS INC. (IN)
Voluntarily dissolved 6/20/83
Details not available

CORRECTIONAL PPTYS TR (MD)
Name changed to CentraCore Properties Trust 12/20/2005
(See CentraCore Properties Trust)

CORRECTIONAL SVCS CORP (DE)
Merged into GEO Group, Inc. (Old) 11/04/2005
Each share Common 1¢ par exchanged for $6 cash

CORRECTIONAL SYS INC (CA)
Merged into Cornell Companies, Inc. 04/01/2005
Each share Common no par exchanged for $0.674 cash
Note: Each share Common no par received an additional distribution of $0.142597 cash from escrow 08/30/2007

CORRECTIONS CORP AMER (MD)
Each share Common 1¢ par received distribution of (0.01) share 12% Conv. Preferred Ser. B 1¢ par payable 11/13/2000 to holders of record 11/06/2000
Each share old Common 1¢ par exchanged for (0.1) share new Common 1¢ par 05/18/2001
8% Preferred Ser. A 1¢ par called for redemption at $25 plus $0.36 accrued dividends on 03/19/2004
12% Conv. Preferred Ser. B 1¢ par called for redemption at $24.46 on 06/28/2004
New Common 1¢ par split (3) for (2) by issuance of (0.5) additional share payable 09/13/2006 to holders of record 09/01/2006 Ex date - 09/14/2006
New Common 1¢ par split (2) for (1) by issuance of (1) additional share payable 07/06/2007 to holders of record 06/29/2007 Ex date - 07/09/2007
Each share new Common 1¢ par received distribution of (0.17) share new Common 1¢ par payable 05/20/2013 to holders of record 04/19/2013 Ex date - 04/17/2013
Stock Dividends - in 12% Preferred to holders of 12% Preferred 3.3% payable 01/02/2001 to holders of record 12/22/2000; 3% payable 04/02/2001 to holders of record 03/19/2001; 3% payable 10/01/2001 to holders of record 09/17/2001; 3% payable 01/02/2002 to holders of record 12/21/2001; 3% payable 10/01/2002 to holders of record 09/20/2002; 3% payable 01/2/2003 to holders of record 12/20/2002; 3% payable 03/31/2003 to holders of record 03/17/2003; 3% payable 06/30/2003 to holders of record 06/16/2003; 3% payable 09/30/2003 to holders of record 09/16/2003 Ex date - 09/12/2003
Name changed to CoreCivic, Inc. 11/09/2016

CORRECTIONS CORP AMER (TN)
Reincorporated 05/14/1997
Common $1 par split (2) for (1) by issuance of (1) additional share 10/31/1995
Common $1 par split (2) for (1) by issuance of (1) additional share payable 07/02/1996 to holders of record 06/19/1996 Ex date - 07/03/1996
State of incorporation changed from (DE) to (TN) 05/14/1997
Merged into Prison Realty Corp. 12/31/1998
Each share Conv. Preferred Ser. B $1 par exchanged for (1) share Common 1¢ par
Each share Common $1 par exchanged for (1) share Common 1¢ par
Prison Realty Corp. name changed to Prison Realty Trust Inc. 05/11/1999 which name changed to Corrections Corp. of America (MD) 10/01/2000 which name changed to CoreCivic, Inc. 11/09/2016

CORRECTIONS SVCS INC (FL)
Name changed to Ram Venture Holdings Corp. 07/14/2000
(See Ram Venture Holdings Corp.)

CORRIDA OILS LTD (AB)
Plan of arrangement effective 11/08/1985
Each share Common no par exchanged for (0.01666666) share Oakwood Petroleums Ltd. $0.96 Conv. Retractable Preferred Ser. D no par and (0.13333333) share Nucorr Petroleums Ltd. Common no par
(See each company's listing)

CORRIDOR COMMUNICATIONS CORP (DE)
SEC revoked common stock registration 03/23/2010

CORRIE COPPER LTD. (BC)
Name changed to Corrie Resources Ltd. 03/14/1984

Corrie Resources Ltd. name changed to Golden Seven Industries Inc. 04/08/1987
(See Golden Seven Industries Inc.)

CORRIE RES LTD (BC)
Name changed to Golden Seven Industries Inc. and Common 50¢ par changed to no par 04/08/1987
(See Golden Seven Industries Inc.)

CORRIENTE RES INC (BC)
Plan of arrangement effective 06/18/2007
Each share old Common no par exchanged for (1) share new Common no par and (0.33333333) share Q2 Gold Resources Inc. Restricted Common no par
(See Q2 Gold Resources Inc.)
Acquired by CRCC-Tongguan Investment Co., Ltd. 08/04/2010
Each share new Common no par exchanged for $8.60 cash

CORRIGAN COMMUNICATIONS, INC. (CA)
Charter suspended for non-payment of taxes 01/02/1963

CORRIGAN MCKINNEY STEEL CO.
Acquired by Republic Steel Corp. in 1935
Details not available

CORRIGAN OIL & GAS CORP. (NY)
Charter cancelled and proclaimed dissolved for failure to pay taxes 12/15/56

CORROON & BLACK CORP (DE)
Common $1 par changed to 50¢ par and (1) additional share issued 12/05/1969
Common 50¢ par changed to 25¢ par and (1) additional share issued 05/20/1977
Common 25¢ par split (2) for (1) by issuance of (1) additional share 05/20/1986
Merged into Willis Corroon PLC 10/08/1990
Each share Common 25¢ par exchanged for (1.56) ADR's for Ordinary 12-1/2p par
Willis Corroon PLC name changed to Willis Corroon Group PLC 01/22/1992
(See Willis Corroon Group PLC)

CORROON & REYNOLDS CORP. (DE)
Common no par changed to $1 par 00/00/1933
Each share $6 Preferred no par exchanged for (6) shares $1 Preferred Ser. A no par 00/00/1946
$1 Preferred Ser. A no par called for redemption 10/01/1964
Name changed to Corroon & Black Corp. 02/29/1968
Corroon & Black Corp. merged into Willis Corroon PLC 10/08/1990 which name changed to Willis Corroon Group PLC 01/22/1992
(See Willis Corroon Group PLC)

CORROSION CTL INC (NY)
Dissolved by proclamation 3/24/93

CORRPRO COS INC (OH)
Common no par split (5) for (4) by issuance of (0.25) additional share payable 06/19/1998 to holders of record 06/05/1998 Ex date - 06/22/1998
Acquired by Insituform Technologies, Inc. 03/31/2009
Each share Common no par exchanged for $1.4245 cash

CORRUGATED CONTAINER CO (OH)
Stock Dividends - 20% 01/15/1968; 100% 12/02/1968
Name changed to Corco, Inc. 02/19/1969
Corco, Inc. merged into Willamette Industries, Inc. 05/27/1977
(See Willamette Industries, Inc.)

CORRUGATED PAPER BOX CO., LTD. (CANADA)
Common no par exchanged (5) for (1) in 1951
Acquired by Hinde & Dauch Paper Co. of Canada Ltd. in 1954
Each share Common no par exchanged for $17 cash

CORSA CAP LTD (BC)
Name changed to Corsa Coal Corp. (BC) 04/27/2011
Corsa Coal Corp. (BC) reincorporated in Canada 06/27/2011

CORSA COAL CORP (BC)
Reincorporated under the laws of Canada 06/27/2011

CORSAIR COMMUNICATIONS INC (DE)
Merged into Lightbridge, Inc. 02/07/2001
Each share Common $0.001 par exchanged for (0.5978) share Common 1¢ par
Lightbridge, Inc. name changed to Authorize.Net Holdings, Inc. 04/30/2007 which was acquired by CyberSource Corp. 11/01/2007
(See CyberSource Corp.)

CORSAIR EXPL LTD (AB)
Recapitalized 2/6/96
Recapitalized from Corsiar Petroleum Inc. to Corsair Explorations Ltd. 2/6/96
Each share Common no par exchanged for (0.2) share Common no par
Acquired by Unocal Corp. 7/19/2002
Each share new Common no par exchanged for $3 cash

CORSAIR MINERALS INC (BC)
Reorganized as Madalena Ventures Inc. (BC) 09/14/2001
Each share Common no par exchanged for (5.69) shares Common no par
Madalena Ventures Inc. (BC) reincorporated in Alberta 08/22/2006 which name changed to Madalena Energy Inc. 08/02/2013

CORSAIRE INC (DE)
Name changed 07/21/1997
Name changed from Corsaire Snowboard Inc. to Corsaire Inc. 07/21/1997
Name changed to Net Command Tech, Inc. (DE) 05/12/1999
Net Command Tech, Inc. (DE) reincorporated under the laws of Florida 02/01/2000
(See Net Command Tech, Inc.)

CORSAYRE CAP CORP (AB)
Name changed to CV Technologies Inc. (Old) 12/01/1997
CV Technologies Inc. (Old) merged into CV Technologies Inc. (New) 07/01/1998 which name changed to Afexa Life Sciences Inc. 04/03/2009
(See Afexa Life Sciences Inc.)

CORSON G & W H INC (DE)
Acquired by International Utilities Corp. 03/23/1972
Each share Capital Stock $1 par exchanged for (0.37) share Common $2.50 par and (1) Ctf. of Contingent Interest
International Utilities Corp. name changed to IU International Corp. 04/27/1973
(See IU International Corp.)

CORSON GOLD MINES, LTD. (ON)
Charter revoked for failure to file reports and pay taxes 11/00/1957

CORSPAN INC (DE)
Recapitalized as Oncthera Inc. 03/19/2003
Each share Common $0.001 par exchanged for (0.1) share Common $0.001 par
Oncthera Inc. name changed to Evolve Oncology Inc. 11/26/2003

which recapitalized as Reparotech, Inc. 09/26/2007 which name changed to Nextrata Energy Inc. 01/07/2010

CORT BUSINESS SVCS CORP (DE)
Merged into Wesco Financial Corp. 3/3/2000
Each share Common 1¢ par exchanged for $28 cash

CORTDEV INC (NV)
Each share Common $0.001 par received distribution of (0.01) share Coastal Holdings, Inc. new Common 1¢ par payable 08/01/2004 to holders of record 05/19/2004
Recapitalized as Botaniex, Inc. 04/15/2005
Each share Common $0.001 par exchanged for (0.004) share Common $0.001 par
Botaniex, Inc. name changed to HE-5 Resources Corp. 03/16/2006 which recapitalized as Fansfrenzy Corp. 12/05/2017

CORTECH COMMUNICATIONS INC (NY)
Name changed 02/24/1988
Name changed from CorTech Inc. to CorTech Communications Inc. 02/24/1988
Name changed to CineMasters Group Inc. (NY) 03/17/1995
CineMasters Group Inc. (NY) reincorporated in Delaware as Avenue Entertainment Group, Inc. 04/14/1997 which name changed to alpha-En Corp. 07/22/2008

CORTECH INC (DE)
Each share old Common $0.002 par exchanged for (0.1) share new Common $0.002 par 09/22/1998
New Common $0.002 par split (2) for (1) by issuance of (1) additional share payable 06/01/2001 to holders of record 05/22/2001 Ex date - 06/04/2001
Reincorporated under the laws of Nevada as Kent International Holdings, Inc. 06/08/2006
(See Kent International Holdings, Inc.)

CORTECS PLC (UNITED KINGDOM)
Reincorporated 12/10/1997
Name and place of incorporation changed from Cortecs International Ltd. (Australia) to under the laws of United Kingdom as Cortecs PLC 12/10/1997
Name changed to Provalis PLC 11/22/1999
(See Provalis PLC)

CORTERRA CORP (DE)
Assets transferred 10/08/1980
Liquidation completed
Each share Common 25¢ par received initial distribution of $0.80 cash 10/08/1980
Assets transferred to CorTerra Corp. Liquidating Corp. 10/08/1980
Each share Common 25¢ par received first and final distribution of $0.118 cash 10/01/1984
Note: Certificates were not required to be surrendered and are without value

CORTEX PHARMACEUTICALS INC (DE)
Each share old Common $0.001 par exchanged for (0.2) share new Common $0.001 par 01/11/1995
Name changed to RespireRx Pharmaceuticals Inc. 01/11/2016

CORTEX SYS INC (NV)
Common $0.0001 par split (6) for (1) by issuance of (5) additional shares payable 11/12/2002 to holders of record 11/05/2002 Ex date - 11/13/2002
Name changed to BGR Corp. 08/05/2003
BGR Corp. recapitalized as Franchise Capital Corp. 01/12/2005 which

name changed to Aero Performance Products, Inc. 01/24/2008
(See Aero Performance Products, Inc.)

CORTEZ DEVELOPMENT LTD (DE)
Common $0.0001 par split (6.959314) for (1) by issuance of (5.959314) additional shares payable 01/25/2001 to holders of record 01/11/2001 Ex date - 01/26/2001
Name changed to MoliChem Medicines, Inc. 02/21/2001
MoliChem Medicines, Inc. name changed to Medical Licensing International Corp. 06/25/2003 which name changed to EmergenSys Corp. 11/18/2003 which recapitalized as Spencer Pharmaceutical, Inc. 10/05/2009

CORTEZ EXPLORATIONS LTD. (ON)
Recapitalized as Marpic Explorations Ltd. on a (0.2) for (1) basis 9/27/57
(See Marpic Explorations Ltd.)

CORTEZ GOLD CORP (BC)
Name changed 09/18/2009
Name changed from Cortez Resources Corp. to Cortez Gold Corp. 09/18/2009
Each share old Common no par exchanged for (0.1) share new Common no par 11/15/2013
Merged into Starcore International Mines Ltd. 08/10/2015
Each share new Common no par exchanged for (3) shares Common no par
Note: Unexchanged certificates will be cancelled and become without value 08/07/2021

CORTEZ INTL LTD (AB)
Recapitalized 06/02/1986
Recapitalized from Cortez Corp. to Cortez International Ltd. 06/02/1986
Each share Common no par exchanged for (0.5) share Common no par
Struck off register and declared dissolved for failure to file returns 05/01/1990

CORTEZ URANIUM & MINING CORP. (CO)
Name changed to Core Oil Co. 2/25/57
Core Oil Co. name changed to Core Mineral Recoveries, Inc. 9/12/83 which recapitalized as Core Ventures Inc. 7/24/97 which name changed to FutureLink Distribution Corp. 2/7/98 which reincorporated in Delaware as FutureLink Corp. 10/15/99
(See FutureLink Corp.)

CORTICELLI SILK CO., INC.
Merged into Belding-Heminway Co. (Old) 00/00/1932
Details not available

CORTINA CAP CORP (CANADA)
Name changed to Ecolomondo Corp. 10/31/2017

CORTLAND CORP. (NY)
Completely liquidated 03/17/1961
Details not available

CORTLAND FIRST FINL CORP (NY)
Common $5 par split (3) for (1) by issuance of (2) additional shares payable 04/15/1996 to holders of record 04/08/1996
Merged into Alliance Financial Corp. 11/25/1998
Each share Common $5 par exchanged for (1) share Common $1 par
Alliance Financial Corp. merged into NBT Bancorp Inc. 03/08/2013

CORTLAND INDS INC (NY)
Name changed to Lanacort Corp. 5/2/72
(See Lanacort Corp.)

CORTLAND LINE CO. (NY)
Name changed to Cortland Industries, Inc. 1/11/62
Cortland Industries, Inc. name changed to Lanacort Corp. 5/2/72
(See Lanacort Corp.)

CORTLAND TR (MA)
Trust terminated 05/31/1989
Details not available

CORTLANDT HOTEL CO.
Liquidated 00/00/1947
Details not available

CORTLEY FROSTED FOODS, INC.
Bankrupt 00/00/1952
Stockholders' equity unlikely

CORTRONIC CORP (DE)
Charter cancelled and declared inoperative and void for non-payment of taxes 6/24/91

CORUM RESOURCE CORP (BC)
Recapitalized as El Nino Ventures Inc. 8/19/99
Each (12) shares Common no par exchanged for (1) share Common no par

CORUMEL MINERALS CORP (NV)
Name changed to Prospero Minerals Corp. 06/20/2006
Prospero Minerals Corp. recapitalized as Prospero Group 01/05/2009
(See Prospero Group)

CORUS BANKSHARES INC (MN)
Common 5¢ par split (2) for (1) by issuance of (1) additional share payable 12/15/2003 to holders of record 12/01/2003 Ex date - 12/16/2003
Common 5¢ par split (2) for (1) by issuance of (1) additional share payable 05/18/2006 to holders of record 05/01/2006 Ex date - 05/19/2006
Plan of reorganization under Chapter 11 Federal Bankruptcy proceedings effective 10/27/2011
No stockholders' equity

CORUS GROUP PLC (ENGLAND)
ADR basis changed from (1:10) to (1:2) 05/15/2006
Merged into Tata Steel Ltd. 04/19/2007
Each Sponsored ADR for Ordinary 50p par exchanged for $24.00505 cash

CORVAIR FURNITURE MFG CO (DE)
Each (5,832) shares Common 50¢ par exchanged for (1) share Common 50¢ par 12/13/79
Note: In effect holders received $5 cash per share and public interest was eliminated

CORVAL RES LTD (BC)
Recapitalized as Arizona Silver Corp. 05/03/1977
Each share Common 50¢ par exchanged for (0.33333333) share Common no par
Arizona Silver Corp. recapitalized as ASC Industries Ltd. 06/06/1995 which name changed to Acero-Martin Exploration Inc. 11/24/2004 which name changed to AM Gold Inc. 06/08/2010
(See AM Gold Inc.)

CORVALLIS INC (NV)
Each share old Common $0.001 par exchanged for (0.04) share new Common $0.001 par 07/21/1994
Each share new Common $0.001 par exchanged for (0.2) share Common $0.001 par 08/22/1995
Name changed to USAOneStar.Net, Inc. 12/11/2000
USAOneStar.Net, Inc. name changed to Palladium Communications, Inc. 12/25/2001 which name changed to Peak Entertainment Holdings, Inc. 05/20/2003 which name changed to

Encore Energy Systems, Inc. 08/20/2007
(See Encore Energy Systems, Inc.)

CORVAS INTL INC (CA)
Merged into Dendreon Corp. 07/30/2003
Each share Common no par exchanged for (0.45) share Common $0.001 par
(See Dendreon Corp.)

CORVETTE GOLD MINES LTD (ON)
Merged into Berkwater Explorations Ltd. 07/28/1976
Each share Common no par exchanged for (1.66) share Capital Stock no par
Berkwater Explorations Ltd. merged into Branly Enterprises Inc. 12/09/1976 which recapitalized as Consolidated Branly Resources Inc. 02/27/1984 which name changed to CBR Holdings Inc. 06/20/1985

CORVETTE PETE CORP (BC)
Recapitalized as Armor Development Corp. 05/17/1985
Each share Common no par exchanged for (0.14285714) share Common no par
(See Armor Development Corp.)

CORVIS CORP (DE)
Recapitalized as Broadwing Corp. 10/08/2004
Each share Common 1¢ par exchanged for (0.1) share Common 1¢ par
Broadwing Corp. merged into Level 3 Communications, Inc. 01/03/2007 which merged into CenturyLink, Inc. 11/01/2017

CORVITA CORP (FL)
Issue Information - 2,500,000 shares COM offered at $5 per share on 10/24/1994
Merged into Pfizer Inc. 7/1/96
Each share Common $0.001 par exchanged for $10.25 cash

CORVU CORP (MN)
Merged into Rocket Software, Inc. 5/18/2007
Each share Common 1¢ par exchanged for $0.40 cash

CORVUS MINES LTD (BC)
Struck off register and declared dissolved for failure to file returns 1/18/79

CORVUS SYS INC (CA)
Filed a petition under Chapter 11 Federal Bankruptcy Code 06/27/1988
Stockholders' equity unlikely

CORY CORP (DE)
Through various purchase offers over 99% acquired by Hershey Foods Corp. 11/01/1967
Public interest eliminated

CORZON INC (TX)
Recapitalized as LecStar Corp. 03/29/2001
Each (60) shares Common 1¢ par exchanged for (1) share Common 1¢ par
Conv. Preferred Ser. A 1¢ par was affected by a change in name only
(See LecStar Corp.)

COSCAN DEV CORP (CANADA)
Recapitalized as Brookfield Homes Ltd. 06/03/1996
Each share Common no par exchanged for (0.2) share Common no par
Preferred not affected except for name change
Brookfield Homes Ltd. merged into Brookfield Properties Corp. 05/09/1997 which name changed to Brookfield Office Properties Inc. 05/09/2011
(See Brookfield Office Properties Inc.)

COSCIENT GROUP INC (CANADA)
Each share old Common no par exchanged for (0.2) share new Common no par 12/21/1989
Name changed to Motion International Inc. and new Common no par reclassified as Class A Multiple no par 01/25/2000
(See Motion International Inc.)

COSCO CORP SINGAPORE LTD (SINGAPORE)
Name changed 11/30/2004
Name changed from Cosco Investment (Singapore) Ltd to Cosco Corp. (Singapore) Ltd. 11/30/2004
Sponsored ADR's for Ordinary split (2) for (1) by issuance of (1) additional ADR payable 01/27/2006 to holders of record 01/24/2006 Ex date - 01/30/2006
Name changed to COSCO Shipping International (Singapore) Co., Ltd. 05/01/2017

COSCO ESP INC (NV)
Common $0.001 par split (3) for (2) by issuance of (0.5) additional share payable 09/26/2005 to holders of record 09/19/2005 Ex date - 09/27/2005
Recapitalized as Budget Center Inc. 04/28/2009
Each share Common $0.001 par exchanged for (0.01) share Common $0.001 par
Budget Center Inc. recapitalized as Enabling Asia Inc. 11/08/2017

COSCO INC (IN)
Acquired by Kidde (Walter) & Co., Inc. 3/30/79
Each share Common no par exchanged for $12 cash

COSCO PAC LTD (BERMUDA)
Name changed to COSCO SHIPPING Ports Ltd. 09/07/2016

COSCO SHIPPING ENERGY TRANSN CO LTD (CHINA)
ADR agreement terminated 07/25/2017
Each 144A Sponsored ADR for Class H Shares exchanged for $21.947820 cash
Each Sponsored ADR for Class H Shares exchanged for $21.947820 cash

COSDEN & CO., INC.
Name changed to Cosden Oil Co. in 1929
Cosden Oil Co. name changed to Cosden Oil Corp. in 1933 which reorganized as Cosden Petroleum Corp. in 1937
(See Cosden Petroleum Corp.)

COSDEN OIL CO.
Name changed to Cosden Oil Corp. in 1933
Cosden Oil Corp. reorganized as Cosden Petroleum Corp. in 1937
(See Cosden Petroleum Corp.)

COSDEN OIL CORP.
Reorganized as Cosden Petroleum Corp. in 1937
Each share 7% Preferred exchanged for (0.5) share 5% Preferred $50 par and (2.75) shares new Common $1 par
Each share Common exchanged for (0.375) share new Common $1 par
(See Cosden Petroleum Corp.)

COSDEN PETROLEUM CORP. (DE)
Common $1 par split (2) for (1) by issuance of (1) additional share 9/5/56
Stock Dividends - 20% 8/25/53; 25% 8/24/54
Liquidation completed
Each share Common $1 par exchanged for initial distribution of $22.50 cash 5/6/63
Each share Common $1 par received second distribution of $1 cash 11/25/63
Each share Common $1 par received third distribution of $0.70 cash 11/15/65
Each share Common $1 par received fourth distribution of $0.72 cash 12/7/67
Each share Common $1 par received fifth and final distribution of $0.16864 cash 12/29/76

COSEKA RES LTD (BC)
6% Exchangeable Shares no par called for redemption 05/31/1976
Each share 7% Conv. Preferred Ser. A $10 par exchanged for (3.5) shares Common no par 01/18/1988
Acquired by NCO Acquisition Ltd. 01/10/1991
Each share Common no par exchanged for $0.16 cash

COSGRAVE EXPORT BREWERY CO., LTD.
Merged into Brewing Corp. of Canada Ltd. 00/00/1934
Details not available

COSGROVE COAL CO. (PA)
Name changed to Kirk Industries, Inc. in February 1955
(See Kirk Industries, Inc.)

COSGROVE-MEEHAN COAL CORP.
Reorganized as Cosgrove Coal Co. in 1942
No stockholders' equity

COSGROVE-MOORE BINDERY SVCS LTD (ON)
Filed a petition under the Bankruptcy and Insolvency Act 06/12/2000
Stockholders' equity unlikely

COSHOCTON SECURITIES CO. (DE)
Liquidation completed 12/31/1960
Details not available

COSI INC (DE)
Each share old Common 1¢ par exchanged for (0.25) share new Common 1¢ par 05/09/2013
Plan of reorganization under Chapter 11 Federal Bankruptcy proceedings effective 05/10/2017
No stockholders' equity

COSINE COMMUNICATIONS INC (DE)
Each share old Common $0.0001 par exchanged for (0.1) share new Common $0.0001 par 09/18/2002
Each share new Common $0.0001 par exchanged again for (1) share new Common $0.0001 par to reflect a (1) for (500) reverse split followed by a (500) for (1) forward split 01/21/2011
Note: Holders of (499) or fewer pre-split shares received $2.24 cash per share
Each share new Common $0.0001 par exchanged again for (1) share new Common $0.0001 par to reflect a (1) for (80,000) reverse split followed by a (80,000) for (1) forward split 12/29/2015
Note: In effect holders received $4.40 cash per share and public interest was eliminated

COSMETEX INDS INC (DE)
Charter cancelled and declared inoperative and void for non-payment of taxes 06/27/1980

COSMETEX INDS INC (MN)
Merged into Cosmetex Industries, Inc. (DE) 12/30/75
Each share Common 5¢ par exchanged for (1) share Class A Non-Voting Conv. Preferred 1¢ par
(See Cosmetex Industries, Inc.)

COSMETIC & FRAGRANCE CONCEPTS INC (DE)
Name changed to Cosmetic Center, Inc. 2/28/91
(See Cosmetic Center, Inc.)

COSMETIC CHEMS CORP (DE)
Charter cancelled and declared inoperative and void for non-payment of taxes 3/1/77

COSMETIC CTR INC (DE)
Common 1¢ par reclassified as (0.5) share Non-Vtg. Class A Common 1¢ par and (0.5) share Class B Common 1¢ par 03/13/1992
Each share Non-Vtg. Class A Common 1¢ par exchanged for (1) share Class C Common 1¢ par 04/25/1997
Each share Class B Common 1¢ par exchanged for (1) share Class C Common 1¢ par 04/25/1997
Chapter 11 bankruptcy proceedings converted to Chapter 7 on 09/15/1999
Stockholders' equity unlikely

COSMETIC GROUP U S A INC (CA)
Name changed to Zegarelli Group International Inc. 10/01/1997
Zegarelli Group International Inc. recapitalized as 2050 Motors, Inc. 05/05/2014

COSMETIC SCIENCES INC (NY)
Merged into Star Multi Care Services, Inc. 9/9/97
Each share Common 1¢ par exchanged for (0.25907006) share Common $0.001 par and $0.063826051 cash

COSMETICA INC (DE)
Charter cancelled and declared inoperative and void for non-payment of taxes 4/15/72

COSMETICALLY YOURS INC (NY)
Charter cancelled and proclaimed dissolved for failure to pay taxes 6/24/81

COSMETICS INTL INC (NJ)
Charter declared void for non-payment of taxes 1/14/82

COSMETICS INTL LTD (OK)
Charter suspended for failure to file reports and pay fees 03/08/1974

COSMIC INDUSTRIES LTD. (BC)
Struck off register and declared dissolved for failure to file returns 7/22/88

COSMIC-LODE MINES LTD. (BC)
Merged into Cosmic Nickel Mines Ltd. 02/23/1970
Each share Capital Stock 50¢ par exchanged for (0.1) share Capital Stock no par
Cosmic Nickel Mines Ltd. recapitalized as New Cosmic Industries Ltd. 05/16/1972 which name changed to Cosmic Industries Ltd. 08/08/1977
(See Cosmic Industries Ltd.)

COSMIC NICKEL MINES LTD. (BC)
Recapitalized as New Cosmic Industries Ltd. 05/16/1972
Each share Capital Stock no par exchanged for (0.1) share Capital Stock no par
New Cosmic Industries Ltd. name changed to Cosmic Industries Ltd. 08/08/1977
(See Cosmic Industries Ltd.)

COSMIC RES CORP (DE)
Recapitalized as C R G Corp. 08/22/1972
Each share Common 1¢ par exchanged for (0.5) share Common 2¢ par
(See C R G Corp.)

COSMIC VENTURE CORP (DE)
Each share Common 1¢ par exchanged for (0.2) share Common 5¢ par 9/29/96
Charter cancelled and declared inoperative and void for non-payment of taxes 3/1/89

COSMO BOOK DISTRG CO (NJ)
Merged into Wellington Computer Graphics, Inc. 6/16/69
Each share Common 10¢ par exchanged for (1/3) share Common $1 par
Wellington Computer Graphics, Inc. merged into Wellington Industries, Inc. 4/30/82
(See Wellington Industries, Inc.)

COSMO CAP CORP (AB)
Name changed to Reco International Group Inc. (Old) 12/17/2004
Reco International Group Inc. (Old) reorganized as Reco International Group Inc. (New) 04/08/2015

COSMO CAP INC (DE)
Name changed to Consolidated Medical Industries, Inc. 04/18/1969
(See Consolidated Medical Industries, Inc.)

COSMO OIL CO LTD (JAPAN)
ADR agreement terminated 11/02/2015
Each ADR for Ordinary exchanged for $5.395825 cash

COSMO RECORDS, INC. (NJ)
Charter revoked for failure to file reports and pay fees 2/23/50

COSMOCOLOR CORP. (DE)
No longer in existence having become inoperative and void for non-payment of taxes 4/1/56

COSMODYNE CORP (CA)
Common no par split (3) for (2) by issuance of (0.5) additional share 11/10/67
Reorganized under the laws of Delaware as Cordon International Corp. and Common no par changed to $1 par 7/30/71
(See Cordon International Corp.)

COSMOPOLITAN CAPITAL, INC. (CA)
Reincorporated under the laws of Delaware as Cosmo Capital Inc. 07/14/1962
Cosmo Capital Inc. name changed to Consolidated Medical Industries, Inc. 04/18/1969
(See Consolidated Medical Industries, Inc.)

COSMOPOLITAN CARE CORP (NY)
Merged into Norrell Corp. 10/04/1988
Each share Common 1¢ par exchanged for $4.035 cash

COSMOPOLITAN FIRE INSURANCE CO.
Merged into Knickerbocker Insurance Co. of New York in 1933
Details not available

COSMOTE INSURANCE CO. (IL)
Ordered into liquidation under court order 4/15/65
No stockholders' equity

COSMOPOLITAN INVS FDG CO (PA)
Completely liquidated 09/22/1978
Each share Common no par exchanged for first and final distribution of (0.171600) 20th Century Corp. Conv. Preference Unit and (0.147200) share Common no par
20th Century Corp. name changed to Consumers Financial Corp. (PA) 05/30/1980 which reincorporated in Nevada 02/26/2008
(See Consumers Financial Corp.)

COSMOPOLITAN LIFE INSURANCE CO. (TN)
Capital Stock $5 par changed to $1 par and (4) additional shares issued 5/1/58
Stock Dividend - 25% 4/2/56
Acquired by Cherokee Insurance Co. on a (1) for (4.5) basis 10/1/59
Cherokee Insurance Co. merged into Cherokee Equity Corp. 12/2/68

COSMOPOLITAN NATL BK (CHICAGO, IL)
Stock Dividends - 14-2/7% 01/08/1946; 25% 01/26/1949; 20% 01/26/1951; 25% 01/18/1952; 10% 05/07/1957; 10% 01/21/1958; 10% 02/08/1960; (0.101928374) for (1) 12/19/1961
Bank failed 05/18/1991
Stockholders' equity unlikely

COSMOPOLITAN PLAN CORP. (NY)
Merged into Associated Scranton Industries, Inc. 1/13/67
Each share Common 1¢ par exchanged for (1) share Common 1¢ par
(See Associated Scranton Industries, Inc.)

COSMOPOLITAN SPA INTL INC (TN)
Stock Dividend - 20% 03/06/1974
100% reacquired through purchase offer which expired 03/26/1975
Public interest eliminated

COSMOS BROADCASTING CORP (SC)
Stock Dividend - 20% 6/1/67
Acquired by Liberty Corp. (SC) 12/31/68
Each share Common $1 par exchanged for (1) share 40¢ Conv. Preferred $2 par and (3) shares Common $2 par
(See Liberty Corp. (SC))

COSMOS FUTURA INC (DE)
Charter cancelled and declared inoperative and void for non-payment of taxes 06/30/1981

COSMOS IMPERIAL MLS LTD (CANADA)
Capital Stock no par exchanged (2) for (1) 00/00/1949
Capital Stock no par exchanged (2) for (1) 00/00/1952
Out of business and declared defunct 01/26/1974
No stockholders' equity

COSMOS INDS INC (NY)
Charter cancelled and proclaimed dissolved for failure to pay taxes 09/30/1981

COSMOS RES INC (BC)
Delisted from Vancouver Stock Exchange 11/16/1990

COSMOS RES INC (DE)
Name changed to Homecare Management, Inc. 03/11/1988
Homecare Management, Inc. name changed to Health Management Inc. 10/28/1994
(See Health Management Inc.)

COSMOTE MOBILE TELECOMMUNICATIONS S A (GREECE)
Acquired by Hellenic Telecommunications Organization S.A. 05/20/2008
Each 144A GDR for Ordinary exchanged for $82.375 cash
Each Reg. S GDR for Ordinary exchanged for $82.375 cash

COSMOZ INFRASTRUCTURE SOLUTIONS INC (DE)
Name changed 04/16/2001
Name changed from Cosmoz.Com, Inc. to Cosmoz Infrastructure Solutions, Inc. 04/16/2001
Recapitalized as FinancialContent, Inc. 11/13/2001
Each share Common $0.001 par exchanged for (0.01666666 share Common $0.001 par
(See FinancialContent, Inc.)

COSNAT CORP. (DE)
Class A Common 10¢ par reclassified as Common 10¢ par 02/04/1963
Common 10¢ par changed to 5¢ par and (1) additional share issued 09/16/1963
Stock Dividend - 10% 03/01/1963
Recapitalized as Jubilee Industries, Inc. 08/26/1966
Each share Common 5¢ par exchanged for (0.66666666) share Common $0.075 par
(See Jubilee Industries, Inc.)

COSNAT RECORD DISTRIBUTING CORP. (DE)
Name changed to Cosnat Corp. 12/20/1961
Cosnat Corp. recapitalized as Jubilee Industries, Inc. 08/26/1966
(See Jubilee Industries, Inc.)

COSO URANIUM, INC. (CA)
Merged into T-R Industries, Inc. 04/28/1973
Each share Common 10¢ par exchanged for (0.05) share Common 1¢ par
T-R Industries, Inc. merged into Tenakill Associates, Inc. 10/02/1975
(See Tenakill Associates, Inc.)

COSSETTE INC (QC)
Name changed 02/18/2009
Name changed from Cossette Communication Group Inc. to Cossette Inc. 02/18/2009
Merged into Mill Road Capital, L.P. 12/23/2009
Each share Subordinate no par exchanged for $8.10 cash

COST CONTAINMENT TECHNOLOGIES INC (NV)
Recapitalized as American Diversified Holdings Corp. 10/16/2007
Each share Common $0.001 par exchanged for (0.00025) share Common $0.001 par

COST MISER CPNS INTL INC (BC)
Recapitalized as Integrated Media Communications Inc. 02/24/1994
Each share Common no par exchanged for (0.2) share Common no par
Integrated Media Communications Inc. recapitalized as IMC Ventures, Inc. (BC) 09/29/1998 which reincorporated in Yukon Territory as Triumph Gold Corp. 03/29/2004 which reincorporated in British Columbia 08/26/2004 which recapitalized as Kenai Resources Ltd. 05/01/2007 which merged into Serabi Gold PLC 07/22/2013

COST PLUS INC (CA)
Common 1¢ par split (3) for (2) by issuance of (0.5) additional share payable 03/11/1999 to holders of record 03/01/1999
Common 1¢ par split (3) for (2) by issuance of (0.5) additional share payable 10/11/1999 to holders of record 10/01/1999
Acquired by Bed Bath & Beyond Inc. 06/29/2012
Each share Common 1¢ par exchanged for $22 cash

COST-U-LESS INC (WA)
Merged into NWC (US) Holdings, Inc. 12/14/2007
Each share Common $0.001 par exchanged for $11.75 cash

COSTA ENERGY INC (AB)
Each share old Common no par exchanged for (0.1) share new Common no par 03/17/2009
Recapitalized as Artek Exploration Ltd. 01/20/2010
Each share new Common no par exchanged for (0.028947) share Common no par
Artek Exploration Ltd. merged into Kelt Exploration Ltd. 04/21/2015

COSTA INC (RI)
Acquired by Essilor International S.A. 02/03/2014
Each share Class A Common $1 par exchanged for $21.50 cash

COSTA RICA INTL INC (NV)
Name changed to Rica Foods, Inc. 08/24/1998
(See Rica Foods, Inc.)

COSTA RICA PARADISE INC (NV)
Name changed to Convenience TV Inc. 06/15/2010
(See Convenience TV Inc.)

COSTAIN (RICHARD) (CANADA) LTD. (CANADA)
Common no par split (2) for (1) by issuance of (1) additional share 09/30/1977
Name changed to Costain Ltd.-Costain Ltee. 06/19/1978
Costain Ltd.-Costain Ltee. name changed to Coscan Development Corp. 05/20/1987 which recapitalized as Brookfield Homes Ltd. 06/03/1996 which merged into Brookfield Properties Corp. 05/09/1997 which name changed to Brookfield Office Properties Inc. 05/09/2011
(See Brookfield Office Properties Inc.)

COSTAIN LTD (CANADA)
Common no par split (3) for (2) by issuance of (0.5) additional share 08/24/1979
Name changed to Coscan Development Corp. 05/20/1987
Coscan Development Corp. recapitalized as Brookfield Homes Ltd. 06/03/1996 which merged into Brookfield Properties Corp. 05/09/1997 which name changed to Brookfield Office Properties Inc. 05/09/2011
(See Brookfield Office Properties Inc.)

COSTAR CORP (MA)
Common 10¢ par split (3) for (2) by issuance of (0.5) additional share 09/16/1988
Common 10¢ par split (2) for (1) by issuance of (1) additional share 09/30/1991
Acquired by Corning Inc. 09/08/1993
Each share Common 10¢ par exchanged for (0.79239) share Common $1 par

COSTAR ENTMT INC (DE)
Charter cancelled and declared void for failure to pay franchise taxes 03/01/1998

COSTCO COS INC (DE)
Reincorporated under the laws of Washington as Costco Wholesale Corp. (New) 08/30/1999

COSTCO WHSL CORP (WA)
Reincorporated 09/01/1987
State of incorporation changed from (DE) to (WA) 09/01/1987
Common 1¢ par split (2) for (1) by issuance of (1) additional share 04/30/1991
Common 1¢ par split (3) for (2) by issuance of (0.5) additional share 03/06/1992
Under plan of merger name changed to Price/Costco, Inc. 10/21/1993
Price/Costco, Inc. name changed to Costco Companies, Inc. (DE) 02/06/1997 which reincorporated in Washington as Costco Wholesale Corp. (New) 08/30/1999

COSTILLA ENERGY INC (DE)
Plan of reorganization under Chapter 11 Federal Bankruptcy Code effective 10/01/2000
No stockholders' equity

COSTO INC (NV)
Common $0.001 par split (5) for (2) by issuance of (4) additional shares payable 06/13/2016 to holders of record 06/06/2016 Ex date - 06/14/2016
Name changed to Union Bridge Holdings Ltd. 06/21/2016

COSTPLUSFIVE COM INC (NV)
Name changed to

Computerxpress.com Inc. 03/24/2000
Computerxpress.com Inc. name changed to Aurora Precious Metals Inc. 02/12/2003 which name changed to V-Net Beverage, Inc. 09/03/2003 which name changed to RushNet, Inc. 07/08/2005
(See RushNet, Inc.)

COSWORTH MINERALS LTD (YT)
Reincorporated 03/30/1998
Reincorporated from Cosworth Ventures Ltd. (BC) to Cosworth Minerals Ltd. (YT) 03/30/1998
Name changed to Palcan Fuel Cells Ltd. 02/13/2002
Palcan Fuel Cells Ltd. name changed to Palcan Power Systems Inc. 08/10/2004

COTA BIOTECH INC (CO)
Recapitalized as Magnaco Enterprises International, Inc. 05/22/1991
Each share Common no par exchanged for (0.002) share Common no par

COTELLIGENT INC (DE)
Name changed 09/09/1998
Name changed from Cotelligent Group, Inc. to Cotelligent, Inc. 09/09/1998
Name changed to Watchit Media, Inc. 12/08/2005

COTHERIX INC (DE)
Merged into Actelion Ltd. 01/09/2007
Each share Common $0.001 par exchanged for $13.50 cash

COTIVITI HLDGS INC (DE)
Acquired by Verscend Technologies, Inc. 08/27/2018
Each share Common $0.001 par exchanged for $44.75 cash

COTLEY MINES LTD. (ON)
Charter canceled for failure to pay taxes and file returns 07/27/1976

COTT-A-LAP CO.
Dissolved 00/00/1936
Details not available

COTT BEVERAGE CORP (DE)
Merged into Cott Corp. (NH) share for share 11/18/1963
Cott Corp. (NH) merged into National Industries, Inc. (KY) 07/01/1968 which merged into Fuqua Industries, Inc. 01/03/1978 which name changed to Actava Group Inc. 07/21/1993 which name changed to Metromedia International Group, Inc. 11/01/1995
(See Metromedia International Group, Inc.)

COTT BEVERAGES LTD (CANADA)
Name changed to Cott Corp. 06/11/1991

COTT BOTTLING CO. OF NEW ENGLAND, INC. (NH)
Under plan of merger name changed to Cott Corp. (NH) 11/18/1963
Cott Corp. (NH) merged into National Industries, Inc. (KY) 07/01/1968 which merged into Fuqua Industries, Inc. 01/03/1978 which name changed to Actava Group Inc. 07/21/1993 which name changed to Metromedia International Group, Inc. 11/01/1995
(See Metromedia International Group, Inc.)

COTT CORP. (NH)
Merged into National Industries, Inc. (KY) 07/01/1968
Each share Common $1 par exchanged for (0.4) share 60¢ Conv. Preferred Ser. A $1 par
National Industries, Inc. (KY) merged into Fuqua Industries, Inc. 01/03/1978 which name changed to Actava Group Inc. 07/21/1993 which name changed to Metromedia International Group, Inc. 11/01/1995
(See Metromedia International Group, Inc.)

COTT CORP (DE)
Name changed to Beverage Liquidating Corp. 12/28/1978
(See Beverage Liquidating Corp.)

COTTAGE 83 CO. (DE)
Liquidation completed 11/20/1964
Details not available

COTTAGE INVTS INC (NV)
Recapitalized as Paving Stone Corp. 12/19/2001
Each share Common $0.00001 par exchanged for (0.00751879) share Common $0.00001 par
(See Paving Stone Corp.)

COTTAGE SVGS ASSN F A (CINCINNATI, OH)
Under plan of reorganization each share Common $1 par automatically became (1) share Tristate Bancorp Common $1 par 12/22/1989
Tristate Bancorp merged into Fifth Third Bancorp 12/22/1993

COTTON CONCENTRATION INC (TX)
Liquidation completed
Each share Common $5 par received initial distribution of $10 cash 05/01/1974
Each share Common $5 par received second distribution of $10 cash 07/01/1974
Each share Common $5 par exchanged for third and final distribution of (1) Cotton Concentration Shareholders Trust Ctf. of Bene. Int., (1) share Galveston Corp. Common $5 par and $13.20 cash 08/16/1974
(See each company's listing)

COTTON CONCENTRATION SHAREHOLDERS TRUST (TX)
Completely liquidated 09/16/1974
Each Ctf. of Bene. Int. exchanged for first and final distribution of $9 cash

COTTON PETE CORP (DE)
Stock Dividend - 20% 12/15/1975
Merged into United Energy Resources, Inc. 12/02/1976
Each share Common 10¢ par exchanged for (0.75) share Common $1 par
United Energy Resources, Inc. merged into MidCon Corp. 12/11/1985 which merged into Occidental Petroleum Corp. (CA) 04/01/1986 which reincorporated in Delaware 05/21/1986

COTTON STS LIFE INS CO (AL)
Merged into Federated Guaranty Life Insurance Co. (AL) 12/31/1973
Each share Common $2.50 par exchanged for (1.33333333) shares Common $1 par
Federated Guaranty Life Insuarance Co. (AL) reorganized in Delaware as Federated Guaranty Corp. 03/01/1984 which recapitalized as Alfa Corp. 04/20/1987
(See Alfa Corp.)

COTTON STS LIFE INS CO (GA)
Merged into COUNTRY Life Insurance Co. 01/01/2005
Each share Common $1 par exchanged for $20.25 cash

COTTON VY RES CORP (YT)
Reincorporated 02/09/1998
Place of incorporation changed from (ON) to (YT) 02/09/1998
Name changed to Aspen Group Resources Corp. 02/28/2000
(See Aspen Group Resources Corp.)

COTTON VY RES INC (BC)
Reincorporated 11/17/1982
Place of incorporation changed from (ON) to (BC) 11/17/1982
name changed to Metromedia International Group, Inc. 11/01/1995
(See Metromedia International Group, Inc.)

COTT CORP (DE)
Name changed to Beverage Liquidating Corp. 12/28/1978
(See Beverage Liquidating Corp.)

[Note: duplicate entries above appear in source]

Recapitalized as Conscot Resources Ltd. 12/17/1984
Each share Capital Stock $1 par exchanged for (0.5) share Common no par
Conscot Resources Ltd. recapitalized as Masters Holdings Inc. 05/08/1992 which name changed to Envirotreat Systems Inc. 01/15/1993 which recapitalized as Treat Systems Inc. 09/02/1999 which name changed to Mega Silver Inc. (BC) 12/18/2007 which reincorporated in Ontario as Mega Precious Metals Inc. 09/14/2009 which merged into Yamana Gold Inc. 06/24/2015

COTTONBALLS CORP (AB)
Recapitalized as Consolidated Cottonballs Corp. 02/07/1992
Each share Common no par exchanged for (0.14285714) share Common no par
Consolidated Cottonballs Corp. recapitalized as CTB Industries Inc. 05/12/1994
(See CTB Industries Inc.)

COTTONWOOD ENERGY DEV CORP (UT)
Proclaimed dissolved for failure to pay taxes 04/01/1990

COTTONWOOD PLACER LTD. (BC)
Struck off register and declared dissolved for failure to file returns 07/15/1974

COTTONWOOD URANIUM CORP. (NV)
Charter revoked for failure to file reports and pay fees 03/02/1957

CO2 SOLUTION INC (QC)
Name changed to CO2 Solutions Inc. 12/07/2011

COTY, INC. NEW (DE)
Merged into Pfizer (Chas.) & Co., Inc. 12/31/1963
Each share Common $1 par exchanged for (0.22222222) share Common $0.33333333 par
Pfizer (Chas.) & Co., Inc. (DE) name changed to Pfizer Inc. 04/27/1970

COTY, INC. OLD (DE)
Capital Stock no par changed to $1 par 00/00/1938
Under plan of reorganization each share Capital Stock $1 par exchanged for (1) share Coty, Inc. (New) Common $1 par and (1) share Coty International Corp. (DE) Common $1 par 00/00/1938
(See each company's listing)

COTY INTERNATIONAL CORP. (DE)
Completely liquidated 12/14/1962
Each share Common $1 par exchanged for first and final distribution of (1.2) shares Coty International Corp. (Panama) Class A 1¢ par
Coty International Corp. (Panama) merged into Pfizer (Chas.) & Co., Inc. (DE) 12/31/1963 which name changed to Pfizer Inc. 04/27/1970

COTY INTERNATIONAL CORP. (PANAMA)
Merged into Pfizer (Chas.) & Co., Inc. (DE) 12/31/1963
Each share Class A 1¢ par exchanged for (0.1) share Common $0.33333333 par
Pfizer (Chas.) & Co., Inc. (DE) name changed to Pfizer Inc. 04/27/1970

COUBRAN RES LTD (ON)
Reincorporated under the laws of Canada as Sanu Resources Ltd. 03/31/2004
Sanu Resources Ltd. merged into Canadian Gold Hunter Corp. 08/20/2009 which name changed to NGEx Resources Inc. 09/22/2009

COUGAR BIOTECHNOLOGY INC (DE)
Acquired by Johnson & Johnson 07/09/2009
Each share Common $0.0001 par exchanged for $43 cash

COUGAR DEVELOPMENT CORP. LTD. (SK)
Reincorporated under the laws of Alberta as American Chromium Ltd. 05/29/1978
American Chromium Ltd. merged into Rhonda Mining Corp. 01/31/1992 which name changed Rhonda Corp. 06/26/2000
(See Rhonda Corp.)

COUGAR ENTERPRISES INC (UT)
Involuntarily dissolved for failure to file annual reports 04/01/1989

COUGAR HLDGS INC (NV)
Acquired by Linuo Group Holdings Co., Ltd. 05/06/2016
Each share Common $0.001 par exchanged for $3.32 cash

COUGAR MINERALS CORP (BC)
Reincorporated 01/11/2016
Each share old Common no par exchanged for (0.1) share new Common no par 08/24/2012
Each share new Common no par exchanged again for (0.25) share new Common no par 12/31/2013
Each share new Common no par exchanged again for (0.1) share new Common no par 07/02/2015
Place of incorporation changed from (Canada) to (BC) 01/11/2016
Recapitalized as TrackX Holdings Inc. 05/30/2016
Each share new Common no par exchanged for (0.5) share Common no par

COUGAR OIL & GAS CDA INC (AB)
Common no par split (3) for (1) by issuance of (2) additional shares payable 02/25/2010 to holders of record 02/22/2010 Ex date - 02/26/2010
Placed in receivership 05/11/2012
Stockholders' equity unlikely

COUGAR OIL CO., INC. (DE)
Liquidation completed
Each share 3% Preferred $2 par received initial distribution of (1.93055) shares Blue Water Drilling Corp. Common 10¢ par and $3.56 cash 12/20/1963
Each share 3% Preferred $2 par received second and final distribution of $0.4592 cash 06/23/1964
Note: Certificates were not required to be surrendered and are without value
No Common stockholders' equity

COUGAR PETROLEUMS LTD. (ON)
Name changed to Jo-Ami Gold Mines Ltd. 07/17/1959
(See Jo-Ami Gold Mines Ltd.)

COULEE LEAD & ZINC MINES LTD (ON)
Each share old Capital Stock $1 par exchanged for (0.1) share new Capital Stock $1 par 02/10/1977
Merged into Wayfair Explorations Ltd. 11/00/1980
Each share new Capital Stock $1 par exchanged for (1) share Common no par
(See Wayfair Explorations Ltd.)

COULEE RIDGE CAP CORP (AB)
Name changed to Del Roca Energy, Inc. 11/04/1997
Del Roca Energy, Inc. merged into Del Roca Energy Ltd. 10/31/1998 which merged into Tusk Energy Inc. 02/01/2003
(See Tusk Energy Inc.)

COULTER PHARMACEUTICAL INC (DE)
Merged into Corixa Corp. 12/22/2000
Each share Common $0.001 par exchanged for (1.003) shares Common $0.001 par
(See Corixa Corp.)

COUNCIL BLUFFS SVGS BK (COUNCIL BLUFFS, IA)
100% acquired by Banks of Iowa, Inc. through exchange offer which expired 11/30/1971
Public interest eliminated

COUNCIL COMM CORP (NY)
Liquidation completed
Each share Common 1¢ par exchanged for initial distribution of $1 cash 07/12/2002
Each share Common 1¢ par received second distribution of $0.75 cash payable 04/15/2003 to holders of record 04/15/2003
Each share Common 1¢ par received third and final distribution of $0.45 cash payable 10/20/2003 to holders of record 10/20/2003

COUNSEL CORP (ON)
Common no par split (3) for (2) by issuance of (0.5) additional share 05/22/1987
Class C Preferred Ser. III $9 par called for redemption 05/28/1996
Each share Common no par received distribution of (0.33333333) share Class C Preferred Ser. III $9 par 01/01/1991
Each share Common no par received distribution of (0.1578) share American HomePatient Inc. Common 1¢ par payable 04/30/2000 to holders of record 04/19/2000
Each share Common no par received distribution of (0.0719) share Terra Firma Capital Corp. Common no par payable 01/01/2013 to holders of record 12/03/2012 Ex date - 11/29/2012
Each share Common no par received distribution of (0.2084) share Heritage Global Inc. Common 1¢ par payable 04/30/2014 to holders of record 04/01/2014 Ex date - 03/28/2014
Name changed to Street Capital Group Inc. 06/23/2015

COUNSEL RB CAP INC (FL)
Name changed to Heritage Global Inc. 08/29/2013

COUNSEL REAL ESTATE INVT TR (ON)
Name changed to Riocan Real Estate Investment Trust 07/01/1995

COUNSELLORS CAP APPRECIATION FD (MA)
Name changed to Warburg, Pincus Capital Appreciation Fund 02/26/1992
Warburg, Pincus Capital Appreciation Fund name changed to Credit Suisse Warburg Pincus Capital Appreciation Fund 03/16/2001 which name changed to Credit Suisse Capital Appreciation Fund 12/12/2001 which name changed to Credit Suisse Large Cap Growth Fund 11/27/2006
(See Credit Suisse Large Cap Growth Fund)

COUNSELLORS CASH RESV FD INC (MD)
Name changed to Warburg, Pincus Cash Reserve Fund, Inc. 02/28/1992
Warburg, Pincus Cash Reserve Fund, Inc. name changed to Credit Suisse Warburg Pincus Cash Reserve Fund, Inc. 03/26/2001 which name changed to Credit Suisse Cash Reserve Fund, Inc. 12/12/2001
(See Credit Suisse Cash Reserve Fund, Inc.)

COUNSELLORS EMERGING GROWTH FD INC (MD)
Name changed to Warburg Pincus Emerging Growth Fund, Inc. 02/28/1992
Warburg Pincus Emerging Growth Fund, Inc. name changed to Credit Suisse Emerging Growth Fund, Inc. 12/12/2001 which name changed to Credit Suisse Mid-Cap Growth Fund, Inc. 05/01/2004 which name changed to Credit Suisse Mid-Cap Core Fund, Inc. 11/27/2006
(See Credit Suisse Mid-Cap Core Fund, Inc.)

COUNSELLORS FIXED INCOME FD (MA)
Name changed to Warburg, Pincus Fixed Income Fund 02/28/1992
Warburg, Pincus Fixed Income Fund name changed to Credit Suisse Warburg Pincus Fixed Income Fund 03/26/2001 which name changed to Credit Suisse Fixed Income Fund 12/12/2001
(See Credit Suisse Fixed Income Fund)

COUNSELLORS GLOBAL FIXED INCOME FD INC (MD)
Name changed to Warburg, Pincus Global Fixed Income Fund, Inc. 02/28/1992
Warburg, Pincus Global Fixed Income Fund, Inc. name changed to Credit Suisse Warburg Pincus Global Fixed Income Fund, Inc. 03/26/2001 which name changed to Credit Suisse Global Fixed Income Fund, Inc. 12/12/2001
(See Credit Suisse Global Fixed Income Fund, Inc.)

COUNSELLORS INTER MAT GOVT FD INC (MD)
Name changed to Warburg, Pincus Intermediate Maturity Government Fund, Inc. 02/28/1992
Warburg, Pincus Intermediate Maturity Government Fund, Inc. name changed to Credit Suisse Warburg Pincus Intermediate Maturity Government Fund, Inc. 03/06/2001 which name changed to Credit Suisse Investment Grade Bond Fund, Inc. 11/15/2001 which merged into Credit Suisse Fixed Income Fund 10/10/2003
(See Credit Suisse Fixed Income Fund)

COUNSELLORS INTL EQUITY FD INC (MD)
Name changed to Warburg, Pincus International Equity Fund, Inc. 02/28/1992
Warburg, Pincus International Equity Fund, Inc. name changed to Credit Suisse Warburg Pincus International Equity Fund, Inc. 03/06/2001 which name changed to Credit Suisse International Equity Fund, Inc. 12/12/2001 which merged into Credit Suisse International Focus Fund, Inc. 04/26/2002

COUNSELLORS N Y MUN BD FD (MA)
Name changed to Warburg, Pincus New York Municipal Bond Fund 02/28/1992
Warburg, Pincus New York Municipal Bond Fund name changed to Credit Suisse Warburg Pincus New York Intermediate Municipal Fund 02/28/1995 which name changed to Credit Suisse Warburg Pincus New York Intermediate Municipal Fund 03/26/2001 which name changed to Credit Suisse New York Municipal Fund 12/12/2001
(See Credit Suisse New York Municipal Fund)

COUNSELLORS TANDEM SECS FD INC (MD)
7.25% Preferred 1¢ par called for redemption 02/21/1994
Completely liquidated 11/22/1996
Each share Common 1¢ par exchanged for first and final distribution of $19.65 cash

COUNSELORS INVT FD INC (DE)
Stock Dividends - 100% 02/15/1950; 100% 09/07/1954
Acquired by Pegasus Fund, Inc. 07/02/1973
Each share Common $1 par exchanged for (0.3035) share Capital Stock $1 par
Pegasus Fund, Inc. name changed to Vanderbilt Growth Fund, Inc. 07/01/1975 which merged into St. Paul Capital Fund, Inc. 06/14/1977 which name changed to AMEV Capital Fund, Inc. 05/01/1985 which reorganized as Fortis Equity Portfolios Inc. 02/22/1992
(See Fortis Equity Portfolios Inc.)

COUNSELORS SECURITIES TRUST
Trust terminated 00/00/1933
Details not available

COUNTERPATH SOLUTIONS INC (NV)
Name changed to CounterPath Corp. 10/17/2007

COUNTIES GAS & ELECTRIC CO.
Merged into Philadelphia Suburban Counties Gas & Electric Co. 00/00/1927
Details not available

COUNTRY BANK (CARMEL, NY)
Each share old Common $10 par exchanged for (0.005) share new Common $10 par 07/10/2000
Under plan of reorganization each share new Common $10 par automatically became (1) share Country Bank Holding Company, Inc. Common $10 par 01/16/2004

COUNTRY CAP GROWTH FD INC (MD)
Name changed to IAA Trust Growth Fund, Inc. 09/28/1992
IAA Trust Growth Fund, Inc. name changed to COUNTRY Growth Fund, Inc. (MD) 09/28/1992 which reincorporated in Delaware as COUNTRY Mutual Funds Trust 11/01/2001

COUNTRY CAP INCOME FD INC (MD)
Name changed to IAA Trust Income Fund, Inc. 09/28/1992
IAA Trust Income Fund, Inc. name changed to IAA Trust Asset Allocation Fund, Inc. 02/10/1993 which name changed to COUNTRY Asset Allocation Fund Inc. (MD) 09/25/2000 which reincorporated in Delaware as COUNTRY Mutual Funds Trust 11/01/2001

COUNTRY CAP INVT FD INC (MD)
Name changed to COUNTRY Capital Growth Fund, Inc. 09/10/1979
COUNTRY Capital Growth Fund, Inc. name changed to IAA Trust Growth Fund, Inc. 09/28/1992 which name changed to COUNTRY Growth Fund, Inc. (MD) 09/28/1992 which reincorporated in Delaware as COUNTRY Mutual Funds Trust 11/01/2001

COUNTRY CUPBOARD INC (NV)
Reincorporated 12/22/1970
Under plan of partial liquidation 68.42% of holders' old Common $2 par exchanged for new Common $2 par plus balance of 31.58% old Common no par redeemed for $11.63 cash per share 10/01/1970
State of incorporation changed from (TX) to (NV) 12/22/1970
Liquidation completed

Each share Common $2 par exchanged for initial distribution of (2.666666) shares Burgess Industries Inc. Common 50¢ par 11/26/1971
Each share Common $2 par received second and final distribution of (0.15748) share Burgess Industries Inc. Common 50¢ par and $0.096 cash 02/06/1975
(See Burgess Industries Inc.)

COUNTRY KITCHEN INTL INC (MN)
Common 10¢ par split (3) for (2) by issuance of (0.5) additional share 02/16/1976
Merged into Carlson Companies 11/17/1977
Each share Common 10¢ par exchanged for $10 cash

COUNTRY LAKE FOODS INC (DE)
Merged into LOL Acquisition Co. 11/13/1991
Each share Common 1¢ par exchanged for $15.30 cash

COUNTRY MAID FINL INC (WA)
Recapitalized 10/09/1998
Recapitalized from Country Maid Foods Inc. to Country Maid Financial, Inc. 10/09/1998
Each share old Common no par exchanged for (0.01) share new Common no par
Stock Dividend - 10% payable 04/14/1999 to holders of record 04/07/1999
Corporate license expired 04/30/2002

COUNTRY MISS INC (NY)
Merged into Hart Schaffner & Marx 01/07/1981
Each share Common $1 par exchanged for $15 cash

COUNTRY SET, INC. (MO)
Name changed to C-S Liquidating Co., Inc. 05/02/1968
(See C-S Liquidating Co., Inc.)

COUNTRY STAR RESTAURANTS INC (DE)
Each share 6% Conv. Preferred Ser. A $0.001 par exchanged for (6) shares Common $0.001 par 05/10/1997
Each share old Common $0.001 par exchanged for (0.1) share new Common $0.001 par 02/12/1998
Each share new Common $0.001 par exchanged for (0.005) share Common 1¢ par 12/16/1998
Merged into Go Call, Inc. (DE) 04/19/1999
Each share Common 1¢ par exchanged for (7) shares Common $0.001 par
Go Call, Inc. (DE) reorganized in Nevada as Medical Institutional Services Corp. 10/23/2006 which recapitalized as National Pharmaceuticals Corp. 12/04/2009 which recapitalized as Ghana Gold Corp. 07/11/2012 which name changed to BrightRock Gold Corp. 11/11/2013

COUNTRY STYLE COOKING RESTAURANT CHAIN CO LTD (CAYMAN ISLANDS)
Acquired by Country Style Cooking Restaurant Chain Holding Ltd. 04/20/2016
Each Sponsored ADR for Ordinary exchanged for $5.18 cash

COUNTRY WIDE TRANS SVCS INC (DE)
Each share Common 1¢ par exchanged for (0.5) share Common 2¢ par 05/09/1994
Each share Common 2¢ par exchanged for (0.2) share Common 10¢ par 05/15/1997
In process of liquidation
Each share Common 10¢ par received initial distribution of $0.60

cash payable 09/30/1999 to holders of record 09/30/1999
Note: Details on subsequent distributions, if any, are not available

COUNTRY WORLD CASINOS INC (NV)
SEC revoked common stock registration 08/28/2006

COUNTRYLAND WELLNESS RESORTS INC (CO)
Recapitalized as Minerals Mining Corp. 11/6/2000
Each share Common $0.003 par exchanged for (0.2) share Common $0.003 par

COUNTRYMARK COOP HLDG CORP (IN)
1st Preferred called for redemption at $50 on 09/30/2011
Preferred Ser. B called for redemption at $50 on 09/30/2011
Preferred Ser. F called for redemption at $20 on 09/30/2011

COUNTRYMARK INC (OH)
Merged out of existence 01/01/2002
Details not available

COUNTRYSIDE GEN INC (MN)
Statutorily dissolved 11/12/1991

COUNTRYSIDE PWR INCOME FD (ON)
Merged into Fort Chicago Energy Partners L.P. 08/15/2007
Each Unit received $9.60 cash

COUNTRYSIDE REVIEW INC (NV)
Reorganized as Falcon Natural Gas Corp. 04/12/2004
Each share Common $0.00001 par exchanged for (5) shares Common $0.00001 par
(See Falcon Natural Gas Corp.)

COUNTRYWIDE CAP IV (DE)
6.75% Trust Preferred Securities called for redemption at $25 plus $0.20625 accrued dividends on 08/15/2016

COUNTRYWIDE CAP V (DE)
7% Capital Securities called for redemption at $25 plus $0.1701389 accrued dividends on 06/06/2018

COUNTRYWIDE FINL CORP (DE)
Reincorporated 02/06/1987
Name changed 11/07/2002
Common 10¢ par changed to 5¢ par and (1) additional share issued 07/30/1971
Common 5¢ par split (3) for (2) by issuance of (0.5) additional share 10/16/1986
State of incorporation changed from (NY) to (DE) 02/06/1987
Common 5¢ par split (3) for (2) by issuance of (0.5) additional share 07/17/1992
Conv. Depositary Preferred 5¢ par called for redemption 07/06/1993
Common 5¢ par split (3) for (2) by issuance of (0.5) additional share 05/03/1994
Stock Dividends - 50% 10/18/1978; 50% 07/03/1979; 15% 11/30/1979; 15% 05/05/1980; 30% 11/28/1980; 30% 05/15/1981
Name changed from Countrywide Credit Industries, Inc. to Countrywide Financial Corp. 11/07/2002
Common 5¢ par split (4) for (3) by issuance of (0.33333333) additional share payable 12/17/2003 to holders of record 12/02/2003 Ex date - 12/18/2003
Common 5¢ par split (3) for (2) by issuance of (0.5) additional share payable 04/12/2004 to holders of record 03/26/2004 Ex date - 04/13/2004
Common 5¢ par split (2) for (1) by issuance of (1) additional share payable 08/30/2004 to holders of record 08/25/2004 Ex date - 08/31/2004
Merged into Bank of America Corp. 07/01/2008
Each share Common 5¢ par exchanged for (0.1822) share Common 1¢ par

COUNTRYWIDE INVT TR (MA)
Completely liquidated 09/30/1997
Each share Adjustable Rate U.S. Government Securities Fund Class C no par received net asset value
Completely liquidated 09/30/1998
Each share Global Bond Fund Class A no par received net asset value
Each share Global Bond Fund Class C no par received net asset value
Completely liquidated 05/01/2000
Each share Adjustable Rate U.S. Government Securities Fund Class A no par received net asset value
Name changed to Touchstone Investment Trust 05/01/2000

COUNTRYWIDE MTG INVTS INC (DE)
Reincorporated 02/06/1987
State of incorporation changed from (MD) to (DE) 02/06/1987
Name changed to CWM Mortgage Holdings, Inc. 05/18/1994
CWM Mortgage Holdings, Inc. name changed to INMC Mortgage Holdings, Inc. 07/01/1997 which name changed to IndyMac Mortgage Holdings, Inc. 05/20/1998 which name changed to IndyMac Bancorp, Inc. 07/03/2000
(See IndyMac Bancorp, Inc.)

COUNTRYWIDE REALTY, INC. (DE)
Completely liquidated 11/01/1967
Each share Common $1 par exchanged for first and final distribution of (0.2) share Realty Equities Corp. of New York Common $1 par
(See Realty Equities Corp. of New York)

COUNTY BANCORP, INC. (PA)
Merged into Commonwealth Bancshares Corp. 06/26/1987
Each share Common $3.50 par exchanged for (15.798) shares Common $3.50 par
Commonwealth Bancshares Corp. acquired by Meridian Bancorp, Inc. 08/31/1993 which merged into CoreStates Financial Corp 04/09/1996 which merged into First Union Corp. 04/28/1998 which name changed to Wachovia Corp. (Ctfs. dated after 09/01/2001) 09/01/2001 which merged into Wells Fargo & Co. (New) 12/31/2008

COUNTY BANCORP INC (WA)
Principal asset placed in receivership 09/24/2010
Stockholders' equity unlikely

COUNTY BANK & TRUST CO. (CAMBRIDGE, MA)
Merged into County Bank (N.A.) (Cambridge, MA) 02/24/1967
Each share Common $10 par exchanged for (1) share Common $10 par
County Bank N.A. (Cambridge, MA) name changed to Shawmut County Bank, N.A. (Cambridge, MA) 04/01/1975
(See Shawmut County Bank, N.A. (Cambridge, MA))

COUNTY BK & TR CO (BLUE ISLAND, IL)
Stock Dividend - 100% 02/27/1973
Name changed to Heritage/County Bank & Trust Co. (Blue Island, IL) 11/01/1974
(See Heritage/County Bank & Trust Co. (Blue Island, IL))

COUNTY BK & TR CO SOMERSET CNTY (BOUND BROOK, NJ)
Merged into Somerset Hills & County National Bank (Basking Ridge, NJ) 01/13/1969
Each share Capital Stock $10 par exchanged for (2) shares Common $5 par
Somerset Hills & County National Bank (Basking Ridge, NJ) merged into First National State Bancorporation 04/19/1973 which name changed to First Fidelity Bancorporation (Old) 05/01/1985 which merged into First Fidelity Bancorporation (New) 02/29/1988 which merged into First Union Corp. 01/01/1996 which name changed to Wachovia Corp. (Ctfs. dated after 09/01/2001) 09/01/2001 which merged into Wells Fargo & Co. (New) 12/31/2008

COUNTY BK (CHESTERFIELD, VA)
Merged into Community Bankshares Inc. 07/01/1997
Each share Common no par exchanged for (1.1054) shares Common no par
Community Bankshares Inc. merged into SouthTrust Corp. 11/30/2001 which merged into Wachovia Corp. (Ctfs. dated after 09/01/2001) 11/01/2004 which merged into Wells Fargo & Co. (New) 12/31/2008

COUNTY BK (MERCED, CA)
Stock Dividend - 15% 06/30/1995
Under plan of reorganization each share Common no par automatically became (1) share Capital Corp of the West Common no par 01/18/1996
(See Capital Corp of the West)

COUNTY BK (MONTROSE, PA)
Name changed 08/05/1991
Each share Capital Stock $25 par exchanged for (4) shares Capital Stock $6.25 par 03/15/1967
Name changed from County National Bank (Montrose, PA) to County Bank (Montrose, PA) 08/05/1991
Merged into Commonwealth Bancshares Corp. 01/01/1992
Details not available

COUNTY BANK (SANTA BARBARA, CA)
Liquidation completed
Each share Capital Stock $5 par exchanged for initial distribution of $33 cash 11/20/1974
Each share Capital Stock $5 par received second and final distribution of $0.505 cash 06/01/1978

COUNTY BK (SANTA CRUZ, CA)
Capital Stock $5 par changed to $2.50 par and (1) additional share issued plus a 10% stock dividend paid 03/31/1979
Stock Dividends - 10% 03/31/1977; 10% 06/30/1982
Reorganized as Cobanco, Inc. 02/01/1984
Each share Capital Stock $2.50 par exchanged for (1) share Common no par
Cobanco, Inc. merged into Pacific Western Bancshares (CA) 05/18/1987 which reincorporated in Delaware as Pacific Western Bancshares, Inc. 06/30/1989 which merged into Comerica, Inc. 03/30/1994

COUNTY BK A FED SVGS BK (SANTA BARBARA, CA)
Declared insolvent by Office of Thrift Supervision 03/27/1991
No stockholders' equity

COUNTY BK N A (CAMBRIDGE, MA)
Name changed to Shawmut County Bank, N.A. (Cambridge, MA) 04/01/1975
(See Shawmut County Bank, N.A. (Cambridge, MA))

COUNTY BKG & TR CO (ELKTON, MD)
Merged into Mercantile Bankshares Corp. 07/01/1983
Each share Class A Common $20 par exchanged for (14) shares Common $2 par
Each share Class B Common $20 par exchanged for (7) shares Common $2 par
Mercantile Bankshares Corp. merged into PNC Financial Services Group, Inc. 03/02/2007

COUNTY COMM BK (VENTURA, CA)
Common no par split (5) for (4) by issuance of (0.25) additional share payable 05/13/2004 to holders of record 04/30/2004 Ex date - 05/14/2004
Common no par split (5) for (3) by issuance of (0.66666666) additional share payable 03/17/2015 to holders of record 02/17/2015 Ex date - 03/18/2015
Stock Dividends - 5% payable 08/15/2008 to holders of record 07/31/2008 Ex date - 07/29/2008; 10% payable 04/30/2011 to holders of record 04/15/2011 Ex date - 04/13/2011; 10% payable 04/30/2013 to holders of record 03/28/2013 Ex date - 03/26/2013
Merged into CVB Financial Corp. 02/29/2016
Each share Common no par exchanged for (0.572) share Common no par and $8.175 cash

COUNTY FEDERAL SAVINGS & LOAN ASSOCIATION OF WESTPORT (USA)
Common no par split (3) for (2) by issuance of (0.5) additional share 04/16/1979
Through exchange offer majority of Common no par acquired by CFS Corp. as of 07/19/1982
Public interest eliminated

COUNTY FIRST BK (LA PLATA, MD)
Stock Dividends - 20% payable 05/03/1999 to holders of record 03/24/1999; 20% payable 05/01/2000 to holders of record 04/12/2000; 20% payable 05/01/2001 to holders of record 04/02/2001 Ex date - 03/29/2001; 0.8% payable 10/29/2014 to holders of record 10/22/2014 Ex date - 10/20/2014; 10% payable 05/05/2015 to holders of record 04/28/2015 Ex date - 04/24/2015
Merged into Community Financial Corp. 01/01/2018
Each share Common $1 par exchanged for (0.9543) share Common 1¢ par and $2.20 cash

COUNTY GAS CO. (NJ)
Recapitalized as New Jersey Natural Gas Co. 00/00/1952
Each share Common no par exchanged for (1) share new Common $10 par
New Jersey Natural Gas Co. reorganized as New Jersey Resources Corp. 01/29/1982

COUNTY LINE RES INC (NV)
Reorganized as County Line Energy Corp. 05/15/2006
Each share Common $0.001 par exchanged for (8) shares Common $0.001 par

COUNTY NATL BANCORPORATION (MO)
Common $10 par changed to $5 par and (1) additional share issued 04/01/1971
Name changed to County Tower Corp. 12/23/1981
(See County Tower Corp.)

COUNTY NATL BK (CLEARFIELD, PA)
Capital Stock $15.625 par changed to

$7.8125 par and (1) additional share issued 02/05/1974
Capital Stock $7.8125 par changed to $3.90625 par and (1) additional share issued 02/00/1980
Under plan of reorganization each share Common $3.390625 par automatically became (1) share CNB Financial Corp. Common $4 par 04/00/1984

COUNTY NATL BK (MIDDLETOWN, NY)
Under plan of merger name changed to Empire National Bank (Middletown, NY) 03/02/1970
(See Empire National Bank (Middletown, NY))

COUNTY NATL BK (NORTH MIAMI BEACH, FL)
Name changed to County National Bank of South Florida (North Miami Beach, FL) 06/01/1981
(See County National Bank of South Florida (North Miami Beach, FL))

COUNTY NATL BK (ORANGE CNTY, CA)
Merged into United States National Bank (San Diego, CA) 08/31/1968
Each share Capital Stock $5 par exchanged for (0.5089031) share Capital Stock $10 par
(See United States National Bank (San Diego, CA))

COUNTY NATIONAL BANK OF SOUTH FLORIDA (NORTH MIAMI BEACH, FL)
Acquired by Republic Security Bank (West Palm Beach, FL) 12/02/1997
Details not available

COUNTY SVGS BK (SANTA BARBARA, CA)
Name changed 01/19/1984
Name changed from County Savings & Loan Association to County Savings Bank (Santa Barbara, CA) 01/19/1984
Common $10 par changed to $1 par and (28) additional shares issued 08/15/1986
Stock Dividend - 10% 03/31/1988
Reorganized as County Bank, A Federal Savings Bank (Santa Barbara, CA) 05/24/1989
Each share Common $1 par exchanged for (1) share Common $1 par
(See County Bank, A Federal Savings Bank (Santa Barbara, CA))

COUNTY TOWER CORP (MO)
Merged into Commerce Bancshares, Inc. 01/03/1984
Each share Common $5 par exchanged for $61.50 cash

COUNTY TRUST CO. (GARFIELD, NJ)
Acquired by Midlantic National Bank/North (West Paterson, NJ) 03/31/1990
Details not available

COUNTY TRUST CO. OF MARYLAND (GLEN BURNIE, MD)
Merged into Maryland National Bank (Baltimore, MD) 11/14/1961
Each share Capital Stock $10 par exchanged for (0.8) share Capital Stock $10 par
Maryland National Bank (Baltimore, MD) reorganized as Maryland National Corp. 05/01/1969 which name changed to MNC Financial, Inc. 04/29/1987 which merged into NationsBank Corp. 10/01/1993 which reincorporated in Delaware as BankAmerica Corp. (Old) 09/25/1998 which merged into BankAmerica Corp. (New) 09/30/1998 which name changed to Bank of America Corp. 04/28/1999

COUNTY TR CO (SOMERSET, PA)
Merged into Pittsburgh National Corp. 12/10/1982
Each share Capital Stock $25 par exchanged for $950 cash

COUNTY TR CO (TENAFLY, NJ)
Common $10 par changed to $5 par and (1) additional share issued 01/25/1968
Merged into First National State Bancorporation 11/16/1973
Each share Common $5 par exchanged for (0.825) share Common $6.25 par
First National State Bancorporation name changed to First Fidelity Bancorporation (Old) 05/01/1985 which merged into First Fidelity Bancorporation (New) 02/29/1988 which merged into First Union Corp. 01/01/1996 which name changed to Wachovia Corp. (Ctfs. dated after 09/01/2001) 09/01/2001 which merged into Wells Fargo & Co. (New) 12/31/2008

COUNTY TR CO (WHITE PLAINS, NY)
Capital Stock $20 par changed to $25 par 00/00/1940
Each share Capital Stock $25 par exchanged for (2.5) shares Capital Stock $10 par 00/00/1945
Capital Stock $10 par changed to $12 par 00/00/1946
Under plan of merger Capital Stock $12 par changed to $16 par 07/30/1947
Capital Stock $16 par changed to $5 par and (3) additional shares issued 00/00/1954
Merged into Bank of New York Co., Inc. 05/29/1969
Each share Capital Stock $5 par exchanged for $15 principal amount of 6.25% Conv. Debentures due 09/01/1994 and (0.315) share Common $15 par
Bank of New York Co., Inc. merged into Bank of New York Mellon Corp. 07/01/2007

COUPONS COM INC (DE)
Name changed to Quotient Technology Inc. 10/21/2015

COUR-BAR MINES LTD. (ON)
Charter revoked for failure to file reports and pay taxes 00/00/1959

COURAGE ENERGY INC (AB)
Acquired by Samson Investment Co. 07/25/2001
Each share Common no par exchanged for $5.20 cash

COURAGEOUS EXPL INC (AB)
Merged into Rhonda Mining Corp. 01/31/1992
Each share Common no par exchanged for (0.1) share Common no par
Rhonda Mining Corp. name changed to Rhonda Corp. 06/26/2000
(See Rhonda Corp.)

COURAGEOUS GOLD MINES LTD. (ON)
Charter cancelled 04/20/1963

COURIER CORP (MA)
Common $1 par split (3) for (2) by issuance of (0.5) additional share 01/14/1985
Common $1 par split (3) for (2) by issuance of (0.5) additional share 07/14/1986
Common $1 par split (3) for (2) by issuance of (0.5) additional share payable 06/01/1998 to holders of record 05/15/1998
Common $1 par split (3) for (2) by issuance of (0.5) additional share payable 08/31/2001 to holders of record 08/10/2001 Ex date - 09/04/2001
Common $1 par split (3) for (2) by issuance of (0.5) additional share payable 12/05/2003 to holders of record 11/17/2003 Ex date - 12/08/2003
Common $1 par split (3) for (2) by issuance of (0.5) additional share payable 05/27/2005 to holders of record 05/06/2005 Ex date - 05/31/2005
Stock Dividends - 10% 01/03/1978; 25% 11/27/1978
Acquired by Donnelley (R.R.) & Sons Co. 06/08/2015
Each share Common $1 par exchanged for $23 cash

COURIER DISPATCH GROUP INC (DE)
Merged into CDG Acquisition Corp. 10/01/1991
Each share Common $0.001 par exchanged for $4.10 cash

COURIER EXPLORATIONS LTD. (ON)
Merged into Proto Explorations & Holdings Inc. 02/24/1972
Each share Capital Stock no par exchanged for (0.21739130) share Common no par
Proto Explorations & Holdings Inc. name changed to Baxter Resources Corp. 06/26/1981 which merged into Baxter Technologies Corp. 12/31/1981 which name changed to Standard-Modern Technologies Corp. 10/08/1985
(See Standard-Modern Technologies Corp.)

COURNOR MINING CO., LTD. (QC)
Each share old Common no par exchanged (0.52405) share new Common no par 00/00/1939
Recapitalized as Courvan Mining Co. Ltd. 08/17/1960
Each share new Common no par exchanged for (0.5) share Common no par
Courvan Mining Co. Ltd. name changed to Courvan Mining Co. Ltd./Societe Miniere Courvan Ltee. 02/24/1982 which recapitalized as Rutter Technologies Inc. (QC) 07/25/2002 which reorganized in Canada as Rutter Inc. 03/31/2004
(See Rutter Inc.)

COURT DOCUMENT SVCS INC (FL)
Name changed to ChinAmerica Andy Movie Entertainment Media Co. 10/15/2012

COURTAULDS PLC (ENGLAND)
Ordinary Reg. £1 par changed to 5s par and (3) additional shares issued 09/14/1964
Each ADR for Ordinary Reg. £1 par exchanged for (4) ADR's for Ordinary Reg. 5s par 09/14/1964
ADR's for Ordinary Reg. 5s par changed to 25p par per currency change 02/15/1971
ADR agreement terminated 08/07/1998
Each ADR for Ordinary 25p par exchanged for approximately $7.50 cash

COURTESY DRUG STORES INC (NY)
Merged out of existence 07/08/1985
Details not available

COURTESY FINANCE CORP. (UT)
Merged into Dumont Corp. 10/7/63
Each share Common $1 par exchanged for (0.45) share Class A Common 25¢ par and (0.05) share Class B Common 25¢ par
(See Dumont Corp.)

COURTESY PRODS CORP (CA)
Completely liquidated 11/14/1973
Each share Common $1 par exchanged for $4 principal amount Intermark, Inc. 8% Subord. Debentures due 09/30/1983 and (0.2) Common Stock Purchase Warrant expiring 12/31/1978

COURTLAND CAP CORP (BC)
Name changed to ForceLogix Technologies Inc. 12/10/2009
ForceLogix Technologies Inc. name changed to Courtland Capital Inc. (BC) 03/21/2011 which reorganized in Canada as Tree of Knowledge International Corp. 07/09/2018

COURTLAND CAP INC (BC)
Reorganized under the laws of Canada as Tree of Knowledge International Corp. 07/09/2018
Each share Common no par exchanged for (0.02034174) share Common no par
Note: Unexchanged certificates will be cancelled and become without value 07/09/2023

COURTLEIGH CAP INC (KS)
Each share Common no par received distribution of (0.01) share Andros Island Hotels & Casino, Inc. Common $0.001 par, (0.01) share Fifth Avenue Publishing, Inc. Common $0.001 par, (0.01) share Net World Marketing, Inc. Common $0.001 par, and (0.01) share Scotties Fish & Chips, Inc. Common $0.001 par payable 10/30/1997 to holders of record 09/30/1997
Reorganized under the laws of Nevada as Stockup.Com Inc. 02/22/1999
Each shares Common no par exchanged for (0.07692307) share Common no par
Stockup.Com Inc. reorganized as Preference Technologies Inc. 02/23/2000
(See Preference Technologies Inc.)

COURTLO OPERATING CORP. (NY)
Liquidation completed 06/14/1957
Details not available

COURTMONT GOLD MINES, LTD. (ON)
Charter cancelled 11/26/1969

COURTS BUILDING CORP.
Liquidation completed 00/00/1949
Details not available

COURTSIDE ACQUISITION CORP (DE)
Name changed to American Community Newspapers, Inc. 07/02/2007
(See American Community Newspapers, Inc.)

COURTSIDE PRODS INC (WA)
Reincorporated under the laws of Nevada as Smokefree Innotec, Inc. 03/05/2009

COURVAN MNG LTD (QC)
Name changed 04/24/1982
Name changed from Courvan Mining Co. Ltd. to Courvan Mining Co. Ltd./Societe Miniere Courvan Ltee. 04/24/1982
Recapitalized as Rutter Technologies Inc. (QC) 07/25/2002
Each share Common no par exchanged for (0.33333333) share Common no par
Rutter Technologies Inc. (QC) reorganized in Canada as Rutter Inc. 03/31/2004
(See Rutter Inc.)

COURVILLE MINES LTD. (QC)
Declared dissolved for failure to file annual reports 03/02/1974

COUS CREEK COPPER MINES LTD (BC)
Cease trade order effective 03/05/1986
Stockholders' equity unlikely

COUSINS HOME FURNISHINGS INC (DE)
Name changed to Furnishings 2000, Inc. 11/29/1988
(See Furnishings 2000, Inc.)

COUSINS LTD. (NS)
Class A no par exchanged for Class B no par share for share 5/31/63
Acquired by American Linen Supply Co. in July 1965

COUSINS MTG & EQUITY INVTS (GA)
Merged into Newcorp, Inc. 04/10/1979
Each Share of Bene. Int. $1 par exchanged for (1) share Common $1 par
Newcorp, Inc. name changed to Pier 1 Imports, Inc. (GA) 04/07/1980 which name changed to Pier 1 Inc. 07/13/1984 which reincorporated in Delaware as Pier 1 Imports, Inc. 09/19/1986

COUSINS PPTYS INC (GA)
Common $1 par and Class B Common $1 par split (2) for (1) by issuance of (1) additional share respectively 07/15/1968
Common $1 par and Class B Common $1 par split (2) for (1) by issuance of (1) additional share respectively 05/21/1969
Common $1 par split (3) for (2) by issuance of (0.5) additional share 06/08/1971
Stock Dividend - 25% 06/08/1972
State of incorporation changed from (DE) to (GA) 06/14/1972
7.75% Preferred Ser. A $1 par called for redemption at $25 plus $0.484375 accrued dividends on 05/13/2013
7.50% Preferred Ser. B $1 par called for redemption at $25 plus $0.30729 accrued dividends on 04/14/2014

COUVERDEN POINT RES LTD (BC)
Recapitalized as Kilkenney Resources Ltd. 06/26/1991
Each share Common no par exchanged for (0.4) share Common no par
Kilkenney Resources Ltd. name changed to Ghana Goldfields Ltd. 09/18/1995 which recapitalized Icon Industries Ltd. 11/18/1999 which name changed to ICN Resources Ltd. 11/16/2009 which merged into Corazon Gold Corp. 10/17/2012 which name changed to NanoSphere Health Sciences Inc. 12/05/2017

COUVRETTE & PROVOST LTEE (QC)
Each share Class A $5 par exchanged for (5) shares Class A $1 par 05/14/1965
Each share Class B $1 par exchanged for (5) shares Class B 20¢ par 05/14/1965
Class A $1 par and Class B 20¢ par reclassified as Common no par 08/10/1967
Name changed to Provigo Inc. (Old) 09/14/1970
Provigo Inc. (Old) name changed to Univa Inc. 05/22/1992 which name changed to Univa Provigo Inc. (New) 05/25/1994 which was acquired by Loblaw Companies Ltd. 12/10/1998

COVAD COMMUNICATIONS GROUP INC (DE)
Common $0.001 par split (3) for (2) by issuance of (0.5) additional share payable 05/18/1999 to holders of record 05/03/1999
Common $0.001 par split (3) for (2) by issuance of (0.5) additional share payable 03/31/2000 to holders of record 03/17/2000
Merged into CCGI Holding Corp. 04/16/2008
Each share Common $0.001 par exchanged for $1.02 cash

COVALENT GROUP INC (DE)
Reincorporated 07/01/2002
State of incorporation changed from (NV) to (DE) 07/01/2002
Name changed to Encorium Group, Inc. 10/30/2006
(See Encorium Group, Inc.)

COVANCE INC (DE)
Merged into Laboratory Corp. of America Holdings 02/19/2015
Each share Common 1¢ par exchanged for (0.2686) share Common 10¢ par and $75.76 cash

COVANSYS CORP (MI)
Merged into Computer Sciences Corp. 07/02/2007
Each share Common no par exchanged for $34 cash

COVANTA ENERGY CORP (DE)
Plan of reorganization under Chapter 11 Federal Bankruptcy effective 03/10/2004
No stockholders' equity

COVASORB BIONIC SURFACES INC (DE)
Charter cancelled and declared inoperative and void for non-payment of taxes 6/24/91

COVATA LTD (AUSTRALIA)
ADR agreement terminated 08/07/2017
Each Sponsored ADR for Ordinary exchanged for $0.3744 cash

COVE APPAREL INC
Merged into Euroseas Ltd. 3/27/2006
Each share Common $0.001 par exchanged for (0.102969) share Common 1¢ par and $0.01339 cash

COVE INDUSTRIES, INC. (NY)
Name changed to Illustrated World Encyclopedia, Inc. 05/19/1967
Illustrated World Encyclopedia, Inc. name changed to Magnus International, Inc. 03/22/1974 which name changed back to Illustrated World Encyclopedia, Inc. 07/05/1978
(See Illustrated World Encyclopedia, Inc.)

COVE RES CORP (BC)
Name changed 05/12/1988
Name changed from Cove Energy Corp. to Cove Resources Corp. 05/12/1988
Recapitalized as Consolidated Cove Resources Corp. 08/11/1992
Each share Common no par exchanged for (0.2) share Common no par
Consolidated Cove Resources Corp. recapitalized as Derek Resources Corp. 05/11/1995 which recapitalized as Derek Oil & Gas Corp. 03/03/2003 which name changed to Newcastle Energy Corp. 07/02/2013 which name changed to Martello Technologies Group Inc. 09/12/2018

COVE VITAMIN & PHARMACEUTICAL, INC. (NY)
Name changed to Cove Industries, Inc. 08/17/1964
Cove Industries, Inc. name changed to Illustrated World Encyclopedia, Inc. 05/19/1967 which name changed to Magnus International, Inc. 03/22/1974 which name changed back to Illustrated World Encyclopedia, Inc. 07/05/1978
(See Illustrated World Encyclopedia, Inc.)

COVEINOR MINES INC (QC)
Cease trade order effective 01/22/1996
Stockholders' equity unlikely

COVENANT BANCORP INC (NJ)
Stock Dividend - 4% payable 07/14/1997 to holders of record 06/24/1997
Merged into First Union Corp. 01/15/1998
Each share 6% Conv. Preferred Ser. A $25 par exchanged for (1.516) shares Common $3.33-1/3 par
Each share 6% Conv. Preferred Ser. B $25 par exchanged for (1.2) shares Common $3.33-1/3 par
Each share Common $5 par exchanged for (0.3813) share Common $3.33-1/3 par
First Union Corp. name changed to Wachovia Corp. (Ctfs. dated after 09/01/2001) 09/01/2001 which merged into Wells Fargo & Co. (New) 12/31/2008

COVENANT BK SVGS (HADDONFIELD, NJ)
Stock Dividends - 4% payable 06/15/1996 to holders of record 05/31/1996; 6% payable 12/16/1996 to holders of record 12/02/1996
Under plan of reorganization each share 6% Conv. Preferred Ser. A $25, 6% Conv. Preferred Ser. B $25 and Common $5 par automatically became (1) share Covenant Bancorp, Inc. 6% Conv. Preferred Ser. A $25, 6% Conv. Preferred Ser. B $25 par or Common $5 par respectively 06/13/1997
Covenant Bancorp, Inc. merged into First Union Corp. 01/15/1998 which name changed to Wachovia Corp. (Ctfs. dated after 09/01/2001) 09/01/2001 which merged into Wells Fargo & Co. (New) 12/31/2008

COVENANT ENVIRONMENTAL TECHNOLOGIES, INC. (UT)
Involuntarily dissolved 05/01/1998

COVENANT ENVIRONMENTAL TECHNOLOGIES INC (NV)
Reorganized under the laws of Tennessee as Neurochemical Research Corp. 06/07/2001
Each share Common $0.001 par exchanged for (0.05) share Common $0.001 par
Neurochemical Research Corp. recapitalized as MiNetwork Group, Inc. (TN) 12/15/2003 which reincorporated in Nevada 04/21/2004 which name changed to Green Earth Technologies, Inc. 08/08/2007

COVENANT FINL CORP (DE)
Name changed to Air-Q Wi-Fi Corp. 06/30/2003
Air-Q Wi-Fi Corp. name changed to AirRover Wi-Fi Corp. 06/04/2004 which name changed to Diamond I, Inc. 01/28/2005 which recapitalized as ubroadcast, inc. 02/09/2009 which name changed to Santeon Group Inc. 06/11/2010

COVENANT GROUP OF CHINA INC (NV)
SEC revoked common stock registration 12/23/2014

COVENANT RES LTD (BC)
Certificates dated after 06/12/2008
Name changed to Passport Energy Ltd. 12/13/2010
Passport Energy Ltd. merged into Powder Mountain Energy Ltd. 06/20/2014 which merged into Canamax Energy Ltd. 08/04/2015
(See Canamax Energy Ltd.)

COVENANT RES LTD (BC)
Ctfs. dated prior to 07/15/1991
Merged into El Condor Resources Ltd. 07/15/1991
Each share Common no par exchanged for (1) share Common no par
El Condor Resources Ltd. merged into Royal Oak Mines Inc. 01/15/1996 which recapitalized as Royal Oak Ventures Inc. 02/14/2000
(See Royal Oak Ventures Inc.)

COVENANT TRANS INC (NV)
Name changed to Covenant Transportation Group, Inc. 05/22/2007

COVENTRY CARE INC (PA)
Out of business 00/00/1994
Details not available

COVENTRY CHARTER CORP (YUKON)
Recapitalized as Monster Copper Corp. 05/21/2003
Each share Common no par exchanged for (0.5) share Common no par
Monster Copper Corp. merged into Mega Uranium Ltd. 06/06/2007

COVENTRY CO.
Acquired by Berkshire Fine Spinning Associates, Inc. 00/00/1929
Details not available

COVENTRY CORP (DE)
Common 1¢ par split (2) for (1) by issuance of (1) additional share 08/03/1994
Merged into Coventry Health Care Inc. 04/01/1998
Each share Common 1¢ par exchanged for (1) share Common 1¢ par
Coventry Health Care Inc. merged into Aetna, Inc. 05/07/2013

COVENTRY GOLD MINES, LTD. (ON)
Charter cancelled by Province of Ontario for default 05/00/1955

COVENTRY HEALTH CARE INC (DE)
Common 1¢ par split (3) for (2) by issuance of (0.5) additional share payable 01/30/2004 to holders of record 01/09/2004 Ex date - 02/02/2004
Common 1¢ par split (3) for (2) by issuance of (0.5) additional share payable 10/17/2005 to holders of record 10/03/2005 Ex date - 10/18/2005
Merged into Aetna, Inc. 05/07/2013
Each share Common 1¢ par exchanged for (0.3885) share Common 1¢ par and $27.30 cash

COVENTRY INDS CORP (FL)
Each share old Common $0.001 par exchanged for (0.125) share new Common $0.001 par 03/22/1999
Name changed to American Risk Management Group, Inc. 09/07/1999
American Risk Management Group, Inc. name changed to Comprehensive Medical Diagnostics Group Inc. 07/21/2000 which recapitalized as My Vintage Baby, Inc. 06/01/2007
(See My Vintage Baby, Inc.)

COVENTRY RES INC (BC)
Each share Common no par received distribution of (0.5054346) share Chalice Gold Mines Ltd. Ordinary payable 02/07/2014 to holders of record 02/04/2014 Ex date - 01/31/2014
Shares transferred to Australian share register 12/23/2014

COVENTRY VENTURES INC (BC)
Struck off register and declared dissolved for failure to file returns 07/03/1992

COVENTURE INTL INC (DE)
Name changed to China Natural Gas, Inc. 12/19/2005

COVER ALL TECHNOLOGIES INC (DE)
Merged into Majesco 06/26/2015
Each share Common 1¢ par exchanged for (0.21641) share Common $0.002 par

COVER GIRL MIAMI INC (FL)
Liquidation completed
Each share Common 1¢ par exchanged for initial distribution of (1) Non-Transferable Receipt and $2 cash 09/30/1974
Each Non-Transferable Receipt received second distribution of $0.54 cash 11/01/1975

Each Non-Transferable Receipt received third and final distribution of $0.13 cash 09/29/1976

COVERED WAGON CO. (MI)
Liquidation completed 12/17/1951
Details not available

COVESCO CAP CORP (ON)
2nd Preferred Ser. Y no par called for redemption 08/09/1996
Merged into Magra Computer Technologies Corp. 08/14/1996
Each share 1st Preferred Ser. A no par exchanged for (1) share 1st Preferred Ser. A no par
Each share Class A Special no par exchanged for (1) share Common no par
Each share Common no par exchanged for (1) share Common no par
(See Magra Computer Technologies Corp.)

COVEST BANCSHARES INC (DE)
Common 1¢ par split (3) for (2) by issuance of (0.5) additional share payable 12/01/1997 to holders of record 11/14/1997
Merged into First Midwest Bancorp, Inc. 01/02/2004
Each share Common 1¢ par exchanged for $27.45 cash

COVEX, INC. (MN)
Merged into Northwest Cinema Corp. 04/24/1972
Each share Common 10¢ par exchanged for (1) share Common 10¢ par
(See Northwest Cinema Corp.)

COVIDIEN LTD (BERMUDA)
Reincorporated under the laws of Ireland as Covidien PLC and Common 20¢ par reclassified as Ordinary 20¢ par 06/04/2009
Covidien PLC merged into Medtronic PLC 01/27/2015

COVIDIEN PLC (IRELAND)
Each share old Ordinary 20¢ par automatically became (1) share new Ordinary 20¢ par to reflect a (1) for (100) reverse split followed by a (100) for (1) forward split 03/21/2011
Note: Holders of (99) or fewer pre-split shares received $51.67 cash per share
Merged into Medtronic PLC 01/27/2015
Each share new Ordinary 20¢ par exchanged for (0.956) share Ordinary EUR 1 par and $35.19 cash

COVIK DEV CORP (BC)
Name changed to Monarch Energy Ltd. (BC) 10/23/2006
Monarch Energy Ltd. (BC) reincorporated in Ontario as ChroMedX Corp. 09/18/2014 which name changed to Relay Medical Corp. 07/09/2018

COVINGTON & CINCINNATI BRIDGE CO. (KY)
Liquidated 00/00/1953
Details not available

COVINGTON BROS TECHNOLOGIES (CA)
Name changed 05/08/1979
Common $1 par changed to 50¢ par and (1) additional share issued 05/25/1978
Common 50¢ par changed to 25¢ par and (1) additional share issued 09/11/1978
Common 25¢ par changed to $0.125 par and (1) additional share issued 01/22/1979
Name changed from Covington Brothers to Covington Brothers Technologies 05/08/1979
Name changed to Covington Technologies (CA) 05/22/1981
Covington Technologies (CA)

reorganized in Delaware as Covington Development Group, Inc. 05/26/1988
(See Covington Development Group, Inc.)

COVINGTON CAP CORP (NV)
Recapitalized as American Cold Light Technologies Corp. 10/06/1989
Each share Common $0.001 par exchanged for (0.1) share Common 1¢ par
American Cold Light Technologies Corp. name changed to Southern Land & Exploration, Inc. 12/21/1989 which name changed to Investment & Consulting International, Inc. (Old) 06/22/1991 which name changed to Currentsea 07/02/1991 which name changed back to Investment & Consulting International, Inc. (New) 06/02/1993 which recapitalized as KleenAir Systems, Inc. 04/11/1995 which recapitalized as Migami, Inc. 03/02/2006

COVINGTON CORP (DE)
Charter cancelled and proclaimed inoperative and void for non-payment of taxes 04/15/1971

COVINGTON DEV GROUP INC (DE)
Charter cancelled and declared inoperative and void for non-payment of taxes 03/01/1994

COVINGTON TECHNOLOGIES (CA)
Reincorporated under the laws of Delaware as Covington Development Group, Inc. and Common $0.125 par changed to 1¢ par 05/26/1988
(See Covington Development Group, Inc.)

COVISINT CORP (MI)
Acquired by Open Text Corp. 07/26/2017
Each share Common no par exchanged for $2.45 cash

COVOL TECHNOLOGIES INC (DE)
Common $0.001 par split (2) for (1) by issuance of (1) additional share payable 01/22/1996 to holders of record 01/22/1996
Name changed to Headwaters Inc. 09/13/2000
(See Headwaters Inc.)

COW GULCH OIL CO (WY)
Common $1 par changed to 10¢ par 00/00/1951
Merged into K.R.M. Petroleum Corp. 08/31/1973
Each share Common 10¢ par exchanged for (1.686) shares Common 1¢ par
K.R.M. Petroleum Corp. name changed to PrimeEnergy Corp. 05/17/1990

COWANSVILLE CAP INC (CANADA)
Recapitalized as Malette Industries Inc. 11/14/2005
Each share Common no par exchanged for (0.2800336) share Common no par
(See Malette Industries Inc.)

COWEN (SG) STANDBY RESERVE FUND, INC. (MD)
Completely liquidated 12/14/2001
Each share Common 1¢ par received net asset value

COWEN (SG) STANDBY TAX-EXEMPT RESERVE FUND, INC. (MD)
Completely liquidated 06/01/2001
Each share Common $0.001 par received net asset value

COWEN FDS INC (MD)
Merged into TCW Galileo Funds, Inc. 12/14/2001
Details not available
Completely liquidated 12/27/2001
Details not available

COWEN GROUP INC NEW (DE)
Each share old Class A Common 1¢ par exchanged for (0.25) share new Class A Common 1¢ par 12/05/2016
Name changed to Cowen Inc. 05/23/2017

COWEN GROUP INC OLD (DE)
Under plan of reorganization each share Common 1¢ par automatically became (1) share Cowen Group, Inc. (New) Class A Common 1¢ par 11/02/2009
Cowen Group, Inc. (New) name changed to Cowen Inc. 05/23/2017

COWEN INCOME & GROWTH FD INC (MD)
Merged into TCW Galileo Funds, Inc. 12/14/2001
Details not available

COWEN STANDBY RESV FD INC (MD)
Name changed to Cowen (SG) Standby Reserve Fund, Inc. 07/01/1998
(See Cowen (SG) Standby Reserve Fund, Inc.)

COWEN STANDBY TAX EXEMPT RESV FD INC (MD)
Name changed to Cowen (SG) Standby Tax-Exempt Reserve Fund, Inc. 07/01/1998
(See Cowen (SG) Standby Tax-Exempt Reserve Fund, Inc.)

COWICHAN COPPER LTD (BC)
Recapitalized as Cerna Copper Mines Ltd. 11/27/1968
Each share Capital Stock no par exchanged for (0.2) share Capital Stock no par
(See Cerna Copper Mines Ltd.)

COWIKEE MLS (AL)
Preferred $1 par called for redemption 07/12/1973
Merged into Avondale Mills 02/10/1975
Each share Common $1 par exchanged for (2) shares Common $1 par
Note: An additional and final (0.038814) share Common $1 par was distributed 12/27/1977
(See Avondale Mills)

COWLES BROADCASTING INC (FL)
Merged into H&C Communications, Inc. 01/07/1985
Each share Common 10¢ par exchanged for $46 cash

COWLES CHEM CO (OH)
Common no par changed to $5 par 00/00/1954
Common $5 par changed to $1 par and (1) additional share issued 04/16/1956
Stock Dividends - 20% 12/21/1951; 10% 12/10/1953; 25% 09/30/1963; 25% 09/30/1966
Acquired by Stauffer Chemical Co. 12/31/1967
Each share Common $1 par exchanged for (0.9) share $1.80 Conv. Preference Ser. A no par
(See Stauffer Chemical Co.)

COWLES COMMUNICATIONS, INC. LIQUIDATING TRUST (IA)
Liquidation completed
Each Share of Bene. Int. $1 par received initial distribution of $0.0068 cash 12/27/1984
Each Share of Bene. Int. $1 par received second distribution of $0.006776 cash 06/12/1985
Each Share of Bene. Int. $1 par received third distribution of $0.013577 cash 03/20/1986
Each Share of Bene. Int. $1 par received fourth and final distribution of $0.183420 cash 08/22/1986

COWLES COMMUNICATIONS INC (IA)
Liquidation completed

Each share Capital Stock $1 par exchanged for initial distribution of (1) share Cowles Broadcasting, Inc. Common 10¢ par, (0.655) share New York Times Co. Class A Common 10¢ par and $2.25 cash 01/14/1983
(See each company's listing)
Each share Capital Stock $1 par received second distribution of $0.55 cash 06/22/1983
Assets transferred to Cowles Communications, Inc. Liquidating Trust and Capital Stock $1 par reclassified as Shares of Bene. Int. $1 par 08/10/1983
(See Cowles Communications, Inc. Liquidating Trust)

COWLES DETERGENT CO.
Name changed to Cowles Chemical Co. 00/00/1948
Cowles Chemical Co. acquired by Stauffer Chemical Co. 12/31/1967
(See Stauffer Chemical Co.)

COWLES MAGAZINES & BROADCASTING, INC. (IA)
Name changed to Cowles Communications, Inc. 10/18/1965
Cowles Communications, Inc. assets transferred to Cowles Communications, Inc. Liquidating Trust
(See Cowles Communications, Inc. Liquidating Trust)

COWLES MEDIA CO (DE)
Common no par split (6) for (1) by issuance of (5) additional shares 08/13/1993
Non-Vtg. Common no par split (6) for (1) by issuance of (5) additional shares 08/13/1993
Merged into McClatchy Co. 03/19/1998
Each share Non-Vtg. Common no par exchanged for either (3.01677) shares Class A Common no par, $90.50 cash, or a combination thereof
Each share Common no par exchanged for either (3.01677) shares Class A Common no par, $90.50 cash, or a combination thereof
Note: Non-electing holders received stock only

COWLITZ BANCORPORATION (WA)
Old Common no par split (5) for (1) by issuance of (4) additional shares payable 10/27/1997 to holders of record 10/17/1997
Each share old Common no par exchanged for (0.1) share new Common no par 03/02/2010
SEC revoked common stock registration 09/30/2014

COX BROADCASTING CORP (GA)
Common $1 par split (2) for (1) by issuance of (1) additional share 02/02/1970
Common $1 par split (2) for (1) by issuance of (1) additional share 07/31/1980
Common $1 par split (2) for (1) by issuance of (1) additional share 10/15/1981
Name changed to Cox Communications, Inc. 09/01/1982
(See Cox Communications, Inc.)

COX CABLE COMMUNICATIONS INC (DE)
Merged into Cox Broadcasting Corp. 07/22/1977
Each share Common $1 par exchanged for for (0.46) share Common $1 par and $10.83 cash
Cox Broadcasting Corp. name changed to Cox Communications, Inc. 09/01/1982
(See Cox Communications, Inc.)

COX COMMUNICATIONS INC (GA)
Merged into Cox Enterprises, Inc. 09/03/1985
Each share Common $1 par exchanged for $75 cash

COX COMMUNICATIONS INC NEW (DE)
Class A Common $1 par split (2) for (1) by issuance of (1) additional share payable 05/21/1999 to holders of record 05/14/1999 Ex date - 05/24/1999
Each Income Pride exchanged for (1.4414) shares Class A Common $1 par 08/16/2002
Each Growth Pride exchanged for (1.4414) shares Class A Common $1 par 08/16/2002
Merged into Cox Enterprises, Inc. 12/09/2004
Each share Class A Common $1 par exchanged for $34.75 cash

COX DISTRG INC (NV)
Name changed to China Armco Metals, Inc. 06/27/2008
China Armco Metals, Inc. name changed to Armco Metals Holdings, Inc. 07/18/2013

COX ELECTR SYS INC (UT)
Each share old Common 1¢ par exchanged for (2) shares new Common 1¢ par 01/18/1973
Name changed to Universal Energy, Inc. 11/20/1979
(See Universal Energy, Inc.)

COX INSTRUMENTS CORP. (MI)
Merged into Lynch Corp. on a (1.05) for (1) basis 06/28/1963
Lynch Corp. name changed to LGL Group, Inc. (IN) 06/21/2006 which reincorporated in Delaware 08/31/2007

COX RADIO INC (DE)
Class A Common $1 par changed to 33¢ par and (2) additional shares issued payable 05/19/2000 to holders of record 05/12/2000
Acquired by Cox Enterprises, Inc. 05/29/2009
Each share Class A Common 33¢ par exchanged for $4.80 cash

COX RES CORP (CO)
Merged into Falcon Oil & Gas Co., Inc. 04/30/1985
Each share Common no par exchanged for (0.17543859) share Common 1¢ par
(See Falcon Oil & Gas Co., Inc.)

COX STORES CO., INC.
Acquired by Kroger Grocery & Baking Co. 00/00/1929
Details not available

COX TECHNOLOGIES INC (AZ)
Reincorporated 12/31/2000
State of incorporation changed from (AZ) to (NC) 12/31/2000
Liquidation completed
Each share Common no par exchanged for initial distribution of $0.14 cash 01/17/2005
Each share Common no par received second and final distribution of $0.0271 cash payable 04/14/2005 to holders of record 01/17/2005

COXE COMMODITY STRATEGY FD (ON)
Class A Combined Units separated 06/04/2008
Class F Combined Units separated 06/04/2008
Merged into Global Water Solutions Fund 10/07/2016
Each Class A Unit received (1.183932) Units
Each Class F Unit received (1.302514) Units

COXE GLOBAL AGRIBUSINESS INCOME FD (ON)
Trust terminated 10/18/2016
Each Unit received $7.8533 cash

COXHEATH GOLD HLDGS LTD (NS)
Class A no par reclassified as Common no par 11/20/1987
Declared bankrupt 08/00/1995
No stockholders' equity

COYNEX DEV LTD (BC)
Struck off register and declared dissolved for failure to file returns 02/08/1991

COYOTE ACQUISITIONS INC (CO)
Name changed to Kangaroo Franchises, Inc. 01/30/1990

COYOTE HILLS GOLF INC (NV)
Name changed to Spindle, Inc. 12/02/2011

COYOTE NETWORK SYS INC (DE)
Stock Dividend - 5% payable 11/04/1998 to holders of record 10/21/1998
Name changed to Quentra Networks, Inc. 07/31/2000
(See Quentra Networks, Inc.)

COYOTE OIL & GAS CORP (IA)
Proclaimed dissolved 10/26/1998

COYOTE RES INC (NV)
Common $0.001 par split (60) for (1) by issuance of (59) additional shares payable 09/02/2010 to holders of record 09/02/2010
SEC revoked common stock registration 07/25/2016

COYOTE SPORTS INC (NV)
Recapitalized as Techsecure Partners, Inc. 06/15/2005
Each share Common $0.001 par exchanged for (0.001) share Common $0.001 par
Techsecure Partners, Inc. name changed to Poker TV Network Inc. 08/11/2005 which recapitalized as PC Universe, Inc. 07/05/2006
(See PC Universe, Inc.)

COYOTE VENTURES CORP (NV)
Name changed to August Biomedical Corp. 12/31/2002
August Biomedical Corp. name changed to Pan American Energy Corp. 03/22/2004 which name changed to Morgan Beaumont, Inc. 08/06/2004 which recapitalized as NFinanSe Inc. 12/26/2006

COYOTENET COMMUNICATIONS GROUP INC (AB)
Reorganized under the laws of British Columbia as Magnate Ventures Inc. 09/01/2006
Each share Common no par exchanged for (0.15384615) share Common no par
Magnate Ventures Inc. merged into Thor Explorations Ltd. (New) 09/01/2009

COZUMEL FDG INC (DE)
Name changed to Apex Data, Inc. 07/28/1995
Apex Data, Inc. merged into SMART Modular Technologies, Inc. 07/28/1995 which merged into Solectron Corp. 12/01/1999 which merged into Flextronics International Ltd. 10/01/2007 which name changed to Flex Ltd. 09/28/2016

COZY FINL CORP (NV)
Name changed to Braintech, Inc. (New) 02/17/1994
(See Braintech, Inc. (New))

CP FINL CORP (PA)
Name changed to Central Penn National Corp. 05/06/1976
Central Penn National Corp. merged into Meridian Bancorp, Inc. 06/30/1983 which merged into CoreStates Financial Corp 04/09/1996 which merged into First Union Corp. 04/28/1998 which name changed to Wachovia Corp. (Ctfs. dated after 09/01/2001) 09/01/2001 which merged into Wells Fargo & Co. (New) 12/31/2008

CP HOLDRS (ON)
Completely liquidated
Each Depositary Receipt received first and final distribution of $104.756303 cash payable 12/09/2011 to holders of record 09/15/2011

CP NATL CORP (CA)
Common $5 par split (2) for (1) by issuance of (1) additional share 10/31/1983
10.80% Preferred $20 par called for redemption 09/15/1986
5% Preferred $20 par called for redemption 09/30/1988
Acquired by Alltel Corp. (OH) 12/30/1988
Each share Common $5 par exchanged for (1.15) shares Common $1 par
Alltel Corp. (OH) reincorporated in Delaware 05/15/1990
(See Alltel Corp.)

CP OVERSEAS INC (GA)
Recapitalized as United Fashions Inc. (GA) 09/28/1990
Each share Common 50¢ par exchanged for (0.25) share Common 50¢ par
United Fashions Inc. (GA) reorganized in Delaware as UniHolding Corp. 08/30/1993 which name changed to ULH Corp. 11/21/2000
(See ULH Corp.)

CP SHIPS LTD (CANADA)
Merged into TUI AG 12/20/2005
Each share Common no par exchanged for $21.50 cash

CP&L ENERGY INC (NC)
Name changed to Progress Energy, Inc. 12/11/2000
Progress Energy, Inc. merged into Duke Energy Corp. 07/02/2012

CPAC CARE HLDGS LTD (CANADA)
Acquired by Chartwell Seniors Housing Real Estate Investment Trust 07/12/2005
Each share Common no par exchanged for $1.55 cash

CPAC INC (NY)
Common 1¢ par split (5) for (4) by issuance of (0.25) additional share 01/12/1995
Common 1¢ par split (5) for (4) by issuance of (0.25) additional share payable 05/15/1996 to holders of record 05/03/1996
Merged into Buckingham CPAC, Inc. 04/13/2007
Each share Common 1¢ par exchanged for $8.65 cash

CPB INC (HI)
Common $5 par changed to no par and (1) additional share issued 05/25/1988
Common no par split (2) for (1) by issuance of (1) additional share payable 11/14/1997 to holders of record 10/20/1997
Common no par split (2) for (1) by issuance of (1) additional share payable 11/08/2002 to holders of record 10/15/2002 Ex date - 11/12/2002
Stock Dividend - 10% 01/20/1989
Name changed to Central Pacific Financial Corp. 04/23/2003

CPC INTL INC (DE)
Common 50¢ par changed to 25¢ par and (1) additional share issued 05/26/1981
Common 25¢ par split (2) for (1) by issuance of (1) additional share 01/23/1987
Preferred Stock Purchase Rights declared for Ser. A Jr. Participating Preferred stockholders of record 12/01/1986 were redeemed at $0.025 per right 04/25/1991 for holders of record 04/01/1991
Common 25¢ par split (2) for (1) by issuance of (1) additional share 04/24/1992
Each share Common 25¢ par received distribution of (0.25) share Corn Products International, Inc. Common 1¢ par payable 01/02/1998 to holders of record 12/15/1997 Ex date - 01/02/1998
Name changed to BestFoods 01/01/1998
(See BestFoods)

CPC-REXCEL INC (DE)
Liquidating plan of reorganization under Chapter 11 Federal Bankruptcy proceedings confirmed 00/00/1993
No stockholders' equity

CPEX PHARMACEUTICALS INC (DE)
Acquired by FCB I Holdings Inc. 04/05/2011
Each share Common 1¢ par exchanged for $27.25 cash

CPI CORP (DE)
Common 40¢ par split (2) for (1) by issuance of (1) additional share 03/16/1987
Stock Dividend - 100% 02/15/1983
Company filed a petition under Chapter 7 Federal Bankruptcy Code 05/01/2013
Stockholders' equity unlikely

CPI CROWN PPTYS INTL CORP (AB)
Each share old Common no par exchanged for (0.25) share new Common no par 02/28/2000
Delisted from Toronto Venture Stock Exchange 07/13/2009

CPI GROUP INC. (DE)
Merged into Automatic Data Processing, Inc. 11/24/1976
Each share Common 10¢ par exchanged for (0.237125) share Common 10¢ par

CPI INTL INC (DE)
Acquired by Catalyst Holdings, Inc. 02/11/2011
Each share Common 1¢ par exchanged for $19.50 cash

CPI PFD EQUITY LTD (AB)
Name changed to Atlantic Power Preferred Equity Ltd. 02/07/2012

CPI PLASTICS GROUP LTD (ON)
Subordinate no par reclassified as Common no par 05/30/2000
Multiple Voting no par reclassified as Common no par 05/30/2000
Placed in receivership 01/08/2009
Stockholders' equity unlikely

CPII INC (CANADA)
Reorganized under the laws of Manitoba as Whiterock Real Estate Investment Trust 07/04/2005
Each share Common no par exchanged for (0.2) Trust Unit
Whiterock Real Estate Investment Trust merged into Dundee Real Estate Investment Trust 03/02/2012 which name changed to Dream Office Real Estate Investment Trust 05/08/2014

CPL CAP INC (AB)
Name changed to CPL Technologies Inc. (AB) 12/19/2002
CPL Technologies Inc. (AB) reincorporated in Canada 09/01/2003 which name changed to Intema Solutions Inc. 01/13/2009

CPL CAP I (DE)
8% Quarterly Income Preferred Securities Ser. A called for redemption at $25 on 07/30/2004

CPL LONG TERM CARE REAL ESTATE INVT TR (ON)
Each Instalment Receipt exchanged for (1) Trust Unit 05/06/1998
Merged into Retirement Residences Real Estate Investment Trust 05/03/2002

CPL-CRA

FINANCIAL INFORMATION, INC.

Each Trust Unit exchanged for (1.2) Trust Units
(See Retirement Residences Real Estate Investment Trust)

CPL REAL ESTATE INVT TR (MA)
Liquidation completed
Each Share of Bene. Int. no par received initial distribution of $7 cash 02/03/1988
Each Share of Bene. Int. no par received second and final distribution of $0.91 cash 03/24/1988

CPL TECHNOLOGIES INC (CANADA)
Reincorporated 09/01/2003
Place of incorporation changed from (AB) to (Canada) 09/01/2003
Name changed to Intema Solutions Inc. 01/13/2009

CPL VENTURES LTD (BC)
Recapitalized as Manfrey Capital Corp. 11/11/1996
Each share Common no par exchanged for (0.5) share Common no par
(See Manfrey Capital Corp.)

CPS CHEM INC (NJ)
Each share old Common no par exchanged for (0.5) share new Common no par 06/27/1985
Merged into Chemical Acquisition Corp. 12/20/1986
Each share Common no par exchanged for $150 cash

CPS-CORPORATE PLANNING SVCS INC (DE)
Charter cancelled and declared inoperative and void for non-payment of taxes 05/30/1996

CPS SYS INC (TX)
Plan of reorganization under Chapter 11 Federal Bankruptcy Code effective 03/24/2001
No stockholders' equity

CPSM INC (NV)
Name changed to Astro Aerospace Ltd. 04/24/2018

CPT PEMBERTON TECHNOLOGIES LTD (BC)
Name changed to Pemberton Energy Ltd. 01/13/1999
Pemberton Energy Ltd. recapitalized as Brixton Energy Corp. 11/04/2010

CPU COMPUTER CORP (MA)
Voluntarily dissolved 12/23/1986
Details not available

CPU MICROMART INC (NV)
Name changed to Ebiz Enterprises, Inc. 05/06/1999
(See Ebiz Enterprises, Inc.)

CPVC BLACKCOMB INC (AB)
Name changed to Prestige Telecom Inc. 08/10/2007

CPVC BROMONT INC (AB)
Name changed to Pro-Trans Ventures Inc. 06/24/2009

CPVC FINL CORP (CANADA)
Acquired by 4506791 Canada Inc. 04/08/2009
Each share Common no par exchanged for $0.02 cash

CPVC FINL INC (CANADA)
Merged into CPVC Financial Corp. 11/06/2006
Each share Common no par exchanged for (1) share Common no par
(See CPVC Financial Corp.)

CPVC TREMBLANT INC (AB)
Merged into CPVC Financial Corp. 11/06/2006
Each share Common no par exchanged for (2.889) shares Common no par
(See CPVC Financial Corp.)

CPX CORP (DE)
Each share old Common $0.001 par exchanged for (0.001) share new Common $0.001 par 07/26/2001
Name changed to Steel Partners, Ltd. 07/03/2002
(See Steel Partners, Ltd.)

CQI-BIOMED INTL INC (CANADA)
Recapitalized as Bio-Med Laboratories Inc. 12/31/1999
Each share Common no par exchanged for (0.1) share Class A Common no par
(See Bio-Med Laboratories Inc.)

CR PL INC (DE)
Merged into CR/PL Acquisition Co. 06/29/1990
Each share Common 1¢ par exchanged for $1.40 cash

CRA LTD (AUSTRALIA)
Each old Unsponsored ADR for Ordinary exchanged for (1) new Unsponsored ADR for Ordinary 05/31/1983
Each new Unsponsored ADR for Ordinary exchanged for (0.25) Sponsored ADR for Ordinary 08/28/1989
Name changed to Rio Tinto Ltd. 06/02/1997
(See Rio Tinto Ltd.)

CRA MANAGED CARE INC (MA)
Merged into Concentra Managed Care, Inc. 08/29/1997
Each share Common 1¢ par exchanged for (1.786) shares Common 1¢ par
(See Concentra Managed Care, Inc.)

CRA PHASE II LTD (CANADA)
Dissolved for non-compliance 11/02/2005

CRA-Z PRODS INC (DE)
Recapitalized as Advanced Products Group Inc. 05/15/1999
Each share Common $0.001 par exchanged for (0.33333333) share Common $0.001 par
Advanced Products Group Inc. name changed to Cloudtech Sensors, Inc. 06/25/2007
(See Cloudtech Sensors, Inc.)

CRAB HOUSE INC (FL)
Merged into Capt. Crabs, Inc. 06/08/1984
Each share Common $0.001 par exchanged for (0.28571428) share Common $0.001 par
Capt. Crabs, Inc. name changed to Bayport Restaurant Group, Inc. 06/04/1990 which merged into Landry's Seafood Restaurants, Inc. 08/09/1996 which name changed to Landry's Restaurants, Inc. 06/05/2001
(See Landry's Restaurants, Inc.)

CRACK RES LTD (BC)
Struck off register and declared dissolved for failure to file returns 10/14/1994

CRACKER BARREL OLD CTRY STORE INC (TN)
Common 50¢ par split (3) for (2) by issuance of (0.5) additional share 06/30/1983
Common 50¢ par split (3) for (2) by issuance of (0.5) additional share 03/26/1987
Common 50¢ par split (3) for (2) by issuance of (0.5) additional share 02/13/1989
Common 50¢ par split (3) for (2) by issuance of (0.5) additional share 04/02/1990
Common 50¢ par split (3) for (2) by issuance of (0.5) additional share 03/22/1991
Common 50¢ par split (3) for (2) by issuance of (0.5) additional share 03/20/1992
Common 50¢ par split (3) for (2) by issuance of (0.5) additional share 03/19/1993
Under plan of reorganization each share Common 50¢ par automatically became (1) share CBRL Group Inc. Common 1¢ par 12/31/1998
CBRL Group Inc. name changed to Cracker Barrel Old Country Store, Inc. 12/08/2008

CRACKINGSTONE MINES LTD (ON)
Capital Stock $1 par reclassified as Common no par 12/18/1980
Merged into Sparton Resources Inc. 12/30/1982
Each share Common no par exchanged for (0.71428571) share Common no par

CRADDOCK-TERRY CO.
Reorganized as Craddock-Terry Shoe Corp. 00/00/1939
Details not available

CRADDOCK TERRY SHOE CORP (VA)
Each share Common no par exchanged for (3) shares Common $1 par 00/00/1948
Stock Dividends - 10% 12/17/1951; 10% 12/15/1952; 10% 12/14/1953; 100% 07/15/1965; 100% 10/01/1968
Merged into HH Holdings, Inc. 04/30/1986
Each share Common $1 par exchanged for $20 cash
5% Preferred $100 par called for redemption 07/01/1986
Public interest eliminated

CRADGENE MINING CORP. LTD. (ON)
Dissolved 06/25/1956
Details not available

CRADLE MTN CDA LTD (AB)
Recapitalized as Upper Canada Gaming Corp. 03/14/1997
Each share Common no par exchanged for (0.2) share Common no par
Upper Canada Gaming Corp. name changed to Q-Tel Wireless Inc. 09/11/2000
(See Q-Tel Wireless Inc.)

CRAFT BREWERS ALLIANCE INC (WA)
Name changed to Craft Brew Alliance, Inc. 01/12/2012

CRAFT ELECTRS INC (DE)
Common 5¢ par split (2) for (1) by issuance of (1) additional share 4/6/73
Charter forfeited for failure to maintain a registered agent 10/25/74

CRAFT GLAS POOLS, INC. (FL)
Proclaimed dissolved for non-payment of taxes 8/28/64

CRAFT HOUSE CORP (MI)
Merged into RPM, Inc. (OH) 03/10/1988
Each share Common 10¢ par exchanged for (1.2) shares Common no par
RPM, Inc. (OH) reincorporated in Delaware as RPM International Inc. 10/15/2002

CRAFT MASTER CORP. (OH)
Name changed to C.M. Co. 10/30/67
(See C.M. Co.)

CRAFT WORLD INTL INC (FL)
Acquired by Craft World Acquisition, Inc. 05/11/1989
Each share Common 1¢ par exchanged for $3.96 cash

CRAFTCLICK COM INC (DE)
Reorganized 05/07/2001
Reorganized from (UT) to under the laws of Delaware 05/07/2001
Each share old Common $0.001 par exchanged for (0.01) share new Common $0.001 par
Name changed to Mobilepro Corp. 06/19/2001

CRAFTECH MFG INC (CANADA)
Merged into Buhler Industries Inc. 2/1/94
Each share Common no par exchanged for (0.027412) share Common par

CRAFTMADE INTL INC (TX)
Reincorporated 12/27/1991
State of incorporation changed from (TX) to (DE) and Common 20¢ par changed to 1¢ par 12/27/1991
Common 1¢ par split (3) for (2) by issuance of (0.5) additional share payable 11/15/1997 to holders of record 10/31/1997
Common 1¢ par split (3) for (2) by issuance of (0.5) additional share payable 11/16/1998 to holders of record 10/30/1998
Acquired by Litex Industries, Ltd. 12/13/2011
Each share Common 1¢ par exchanged for $4.25 cash

CRAFTMATIC INDS INC (DE)
Name changed 06/01/1993
Name changed from Craftmatic/Contour Industries, Inc. to Craftmatic Industries, Inc. 06/01/1993
Plan of reorganization under Chapter 11 Federal Bankruptcy Code effective 07/10/1997
Each share Common 1¢ par received $0.01 cash
Note: Certificates were not required to be surrendered and are without value

CRAFTSMAN INSURANCE CO. (MA)
Each share Common $25 par exchanged for (2.5) shares Common $10 par 3/8/55
Stock Dividends - 100% 1/15/54; 100% 6/30/55
Name changed to Craftsman Life Insurance Co. 10/14/59
Craftsman Life Insurance Co. merged into Hanover Life Insurance Co. 3/31/67 which was acquired by State Mutual Life Assurance Co. 12/15/72
(See State Mutual Life Assurance Co.)

CRAFTSMAN LIFE INSURANCE CO. (MA)
Capital Stock $10 par changed to $2.50 par and (3) additional shares issued 2/28/62
Stock Dividends - 25% 3/31/60; 25% 6/28/63
Merged into Hanover Life Insurance Co. 3/31/67
Each (2.9) shares Capital Stock $2.50 par exchanged for (1) share Common $5 par
Hanover Life Insurance Co. acquired by State Mutual Life Assurance Co. 12/15/72
(See State Mutual Life Assurance Co.)

CRAFTY ADMIRAL ENTERPRISES LTD (NV)
Each share old Common $0.001 par exchanged for (3) shares new Common $0.001 par 01/20/2004
Each share new Common $0.001 par exchanged again for (2) shares new Common $0.001 par 10/04/2005
Name changed to Nordic Nickel Ltd. 03/09/2007
Nordic Nickel Ltd. name changed to Constitution Mining Corp. (NV) 11/15/2007 which reincorporated in Delaware 10/21/2009 which name changed to Goldsands Development Co. 04/01/2011

CRAGAR INDS INC (DE)
Merged into Global Entertainment Corp. 3/19/2004
Each share Common 1¢ par exchanged for (0.2091) share Common $0.001 par

CRAGIN FINL CORP (DE)
Common 1¢ par split (3) for (2) by issuance of (0.5) additional share 12/28/92
Merged into ABN AMRO North America, Inc. 6/1/94
Each share Common 1¢ par exchanged for $38 cash

CRAIBBE FLETCHER GOLD MINES LTD (ON)
Acquired by Placer Dome Inc. 12/30/1994
Each share Common no par exchanged for $0.80 cash

CRAIG CONSUMER ELECTRONICS INC (DE)
Assets sold for benefit of creditors in January 1998
No stockholders' equity

CRAIG CORP (NV)
Reincorporated 12/29/99
Common 25¢ par split (2) for (1) by issuance of (1) additional share 9/29/89
Each share Common 25¢ par received distribution of (1) share Class A Preference 1¢ par payable 2/5/98 to holders of record 1/5/98 Ex date - 2/6/98
State of incorporation changed from (DE) to (NV) 12/29/99
Merged into Reading International, Inc. 12/31/2001
Each share Class A Preference 1¢ par exchanged for (1.17) shares Non-Vtg. Class A 1¢ par
Each share Common 25¢ par exchanged for (1.17) shares Non-Vtg. Class A 1¢ par

CRAIG FOOD INDS INC (DE)
Completely liquidated 03/19/1990
Each share Common 2¢ par received first and final distribution of $0.215 cash
Note: Certificates were not required to be surrendered and are without value

CRAIG JENNY INC (DE)
Merged into J Acquisition Corp. 5/14/2002
Each share Common $0.000000005 par exchanged for $5.30 cash

CRAIG MICHAEL PERSONNEL INC (NY)
Charter cancelled and proclaimed dissolved for failure to pay taxes 12/20/1977

CRAIG MUSIC & ENTMT INC (MB)
Completely liquidated 03/28/2002
Each Subordinate A Share exchanged for first and final distribution of $5 cash

CRAIG SYSTEMS, INC. (MA)
Reincorporated under the laws of Delaware as LeFebure, Inc. 3/15/65
LeFebure, Inc. acquired by Kidde (Walter) & Co., Inc. (NY) 5/26/66 which in Delaware 7/2/68
(See Kidde (Walter) & Co., Inc. (DE))

CRAIGMONT MINES LTD (BC)
Acquired by M. Seven Industries 05/31/1985
Each share Common 50¢ par exchanged for $1.27 cash

CRAIGS TACO INDS INC (DE)
Common 1¢ par changed to $0.0002 par 07/29/1971
Recapitalized as Craig Food Industries, Inc. 04/01/1976
Each share Common $0.0002 par exchanged for (0.01) share Common $0.02 par
(See Craig Food Industries, Inc.)

CRAIN R L INC (CANADA)
Name changed 04/11/1975
Name changed 01/12/1981
1% Preferred $1 par called for redemption 06/30/1956
Each share old Common no par exchanged for (4) shares new Common no par 01/19/1959
1% Non-Cum. Preferred $1 par called for redemption 09/01/1965
New Common no par split (3) for (1) by issuance of (2) additional shares 05/24/1968
Name changed from Crain (R.L.) Ltd. to Crain (R.L.) Ltd.-Crain (R.L.) Ltee. 04/11/1975
Name changed from Crain (R.L.) Ltd.-Crain (R.L.) Ltee. to Crain (R.L.) Inc. 01/12/1981
Common no par reclassified as Subordinate no par 09/12/1986
Subordinate no par split (3) for (1) by issuance of (2) additional shares 09/16/1986
Merged into 169065 Canada Ltd. 02/09/1990
Each share Subordinate no par exchanged for $12 cash

CRAM EXPL CORP (CO)
Name changed to Sierra Exploration Co. 04/08/1983
Sierra Exploration Co. merged into Wichita River Oil Corp. (VA) (New) 11/04/1987 which reincorporated in Delaware 03/30/1990
(See Wichita River Oil Corp. (DE))

CRAMER (R.W.) CO., INC. (CT)
Name changed to Cramer Controls Corp. in 1956
Cramer Controls Corp. was acquired by Giannini Controls Corp. 5/26/61 which name changed to Conrac Corp. 4/14/67
(See Conrac Corp.)

CRAMER CONTROLS CORP. (CT)
Acquired by Giannini Controls Corp. 5/26/61
Each share Common $1 par exchanged for (0.55) share Common $1 par
Giannini Controls Corp. name changed to Conrac Corp. 4/14/67
(See Conrac Corp.)

CRAMER ELECTRS INC (MA)
Common $1 par split (2) for (1) by issuance of (1) additional share 10/6/69
Acquired by Arrow Electronics, Inc. 1/7/80
Each share Common $1 par exchanged for $2 cash

CRAMER INC (KS)
Common no par split (2) for (1) by issuance of (1) additional share 06/24/1983
Acquired by Rotherwood Ventures, LLC 03/10/2003
Each share Common no par exchanged for $0.05 cash

CRAMERTON MILLS, INC. (NC)
Merged into Burlington Mills Corp. 08/00/1946
Details not available

CRAMP (WM.) & SONS SHIP & ENGINE BUILDING CO.
Reorganized as Cramp Shipbuilding Co. in 1940
No stockholders' equity

CRAMP SHIPBUILDING CO. (PA)
Acquired by Harriman Ripley & Co. 7/28/52
Each share Common $5 par exchanged for $31 principal amount of 4% unsecured Promissory Notes due 7/1/62

CRAMPTON HARDWARE CO.
Acquired by Crampton Manufacturing Co. 00/00/1947
Details not available

CRAMPTON MANUFACTURING CO. (MI)
Stock Dividend - 10% 1/15/53
$5 Preferred $10 par called for redemption 12/1/61
6% Conv. Preferred $10 par called for redemption 6/1/64
Acquired by Gulf & Western Industries, Inc. (MI) 7/31/64
Each (5.25) shares Common $1 par exchanged for (1) share Common $1 par
Gulf & Western Industries, Inc. (MI) reincorporated under the laws of Delaware 7/12/67 which name changed to Gulf + Western Inc. 5/1/86 which name changed to Paramount Communications Inc. 6/5/89 which merged into Viacom Inc. (Old) 7/7/94
(See Viacom Inc. (Old))

CRAN-KOR METALS MINES LTD. (ON)
Acquired by Valray Explorations Ltd. 00/00/1956
Each share Capital Stock $1 par exchanged for (0.33333333) share Capital Stock no par
(See Valray Explorations Ltd.)

CRANBERRY CANNERS, INC.
Name changed to National Cranberry Association in 1946
National Cranberry Association name changed to Ocean Spray Cranberries, Inc. 8/28/59

CRANBERRY CORP.
Name changed to E T & W N C Transporation Co. in 1942
(See E T & W N C Transportation Co.)

CRANBERRY IRON & COAL CO.
Reorganized as Cranberry Corp. in 1939
Cranberry Corp. name changed to E T & W N C Transporation Co. in 1942
(See E T & W N C Transportation Co.)

CRANE CARRIER INDUSTRIES, INC. (DE)
Name changed to CCI Corp. 10/14/1963
CCI Corp. name changed to CCI Marquardt Corp. 06/12/1968 which name changed to CCI Corp. 09/26/1969
(See CCI Corp.)

CRANE CARRIER INDUSTRIES, INC. (PA)
Reincorporated under the laws of Delaware 10/23/1959
Crane Carrier Industries, Inc. (DE) name changed to CCI Corp. 10/14/1963 which name changed to CCI Marquardt Corp. 06/12/1968 which name changed to CCI Corp. 09/26/1969
(See CCI Corp.)

CRANE CO (IL)
Common $25 par split (2) for (1) by issuance of (1) additional share 10/28/1965
Common $25 par changed to $12.50 par and (1) additional share issued 05/25/1972
Common $12.50 par changed to $6.25 par and (1) additional share issued 05/26/1976
Stock Dividend - 20% 12/30/1966
3.75% Preferred $100 par called for redemption 04/15/1985
Reincorporated under the laws of Delaware 05/14/1985

CRANE (SUSAN) PACKAGING, INC. (TX)
Common no par changed to $1 par 05/24/1963
Merged into Cole National Corp. 07/25/1966
Each share Common $1 par exchanged for (1) share 45¢ Conv. Preferred Ser. A no par
(See Cole National Corp.)

CRANE-SIMPLEX CO., INC.
Property sold 00/00/1927
No stockholders' equity

CRANEFIELD INTL INC (CANADA)
Recapitalized as Thorncliff Ventures Ltd. (Canada) 03/02/2000
Each share Common no par exchanged for (0.5) share Common no par
Thorncliff Ventures Ltd. (Canada) reincorporated in Yukon as eMobile Data Corp. 03/22/2001
(See eMobile Data Corp.)

CRANES SOFTWARE INTL LTD (INDIA)
Reg. S GDR's for Ordinary split (5) for (1) by issuance of (4) additional GDR's payable 11/18/2005 to holders of record 11/10/2005
Reg. S GDR's for Ordinary split (2) for (1) by issuance of (1) additional GDR payable 02/08/2006 to holders of record 11/10/2005
GDR agreement terminated 08/30/2013
No GDR's remain outstanding

CRANFILL REYNOLDS CO.
Name changed to General Crude Oil Co. and Common no par changed to $2.50 par 00/00/1933
(See General Crude Oil Co.)

CRANGOLD MINES LTD. (ON)
Acquired by Valray Explorations Ltd. 00/00/1956
Each share Capital Stock $1 par exchanged for (0.25) share Capital Stock no par
(See Valray Explorations Ltd.)

CRANWELL OIL LTD (ON)
Name changed to North American Resource Capital Ltd. 03/03/1988
(See North American Resource Capital Ltd.)

CRATEO INC (CA)
Each share 6.75% Preferred 90¢ par exchanged for (0.05) share 6.75% Preferred $18 par 12/12/1967
Adjudicated bankrupt 08/08/1973
Stockholders' equity unlikely

CRATER NATL BK (MEDFORD, OR)
Merged into Western Bank (Coos Bay, OR) 12/11/1978
Each share Common $1.66666666 par exchanged for (1) share Class A Conv. Preferred $20 par
Western Bank (Coos Bay, OR) merged into Washington Mutual Inc. 01/31/1996
(See Washington Mutual, Inc.)

CRAVEN RES INC (BC)
Name changed 04/19/1990
Name changed from Craven Ventures Inc. to Craven Rrsources Inc. 04/19/1990
Name changed to Cascadia International Resources Inc. (BC) 06/21/1998
Cascadia International Resources Inc. (BC) reincorporated in Alberta 02/27/2004 which recapitalized as Cascadia Resources Inc. 02/06/2009 which recapitalized as Kaymus Resources Inc. 07/31/2014

CRAVENS PETROLEUM BLDG., INC. (DE)
Dissolved 00/00/1953
Details not available

CRAVER INDUSTRIES, INC. (SC)
Name changed to Southern General Corp. and Common 50¢ par changed to 1¢ par 05/26/1972
(See Southern General Corp.)

CRAWFORD ALLIED INDS LTD (ON)
Merged into Superior Crawford Sand & Gravel Ltd. 00/00/1990
Each share Common no par exchanged for $10.50 cash

CRAWFORD BANCORP INC (IL)
Merged into First Financial Corp. 08/01/1996
Each share Common $10 par

exchanged for (3.9375) shares Common no par

CRAWFORD CORP (DE)
Voluntarily dissolved 11/22/1991
Details not available

CRAWFORD COUNTY STATE BANK (ROBINSON, IL)
Reorganized as Crawford Bancorp, Inc. 09/30/1982
Each share Common $10 par exchanged for (1) share Common $10 par
Crawford Bancorp, Inc. merged into First Financial Corp. 08/01/1996

CRAWFORD COUNTY TRUST CO. (MEADVILLE, PA)
Merged into Northwest Pennsylvania Bank & Trust Co. (Oil City, PA) 04/30/1962
Each share Common $20 par exchanged for (1) share Common $20 par
Northwest Pennsylvania Bank & Trust Co. (Oil City, PA) reorganized as Northwest Pennsylvania Corp. 07/01/1981 which merged into Mellon National Corp. 04/12/1984 which name changed to Mellon Bank Corp. 09/30/1994 which name changed to Mellon Financial Corp. 10/17/1999 which merged into Bank of New York Mellon Corp. 07/01/2007

CRAWFORD ENERGY INC (TX)
Each share old Common 10¢ par exchanged for (0.2) share new Common 10¢ par 04/02/1993
Reorganized under the laws of Delaware as BLC Financial Services, Inc. 07/01/1993
Each share new Common 10¢ par exchanged for (1) share Common 1¢ par
BLC Financial Services, Inc. merged into Allied Capital Corp. (New) 01/02/2001 which merged into Ares Capital Corp. 04/01/2010

CRAWFORD LAKE MNG INC (NV)
Common $0.001 par split (3.6) for (1) by issuance of (2.6) additional shares payable 09/06/2006 to holders of record 09/05/2006
Ex date - 09/07/2006
Name changed to China VoIP & Digital Telecom, Inc. 11/22/2006
China VoIP & Digital Telecom, Inc. name changed to China Intelligence Information Systems, Inc. 11/24/2010

CRAWFORD ONT SAND & GRAVEL LTD (ON)
Name changed to Crawford Allied Industries Ltd. 12/10/1968
(See Crawford Allied Industries Ltd.)

CRAY COMPUTER CORP (DE)
Plan of reorganization under Chapter 11 Federal Bankruptcy Code 05/28/1996
No stockholders' equity

CRAY RESH INC (DE)
Common $1 par split (3) for (1) by issuance of (2) additional shares 12/19/1980
Common $1 par split (2) for (1) by issuance of (1) additional share 08/16/1985
Stock Dividend - 150% 11/30/1978
Merged into Silicon Graphics, Inc. 06/30/1996
Each share Common $1 par exchanged for (1) share Common $0.001 par
(See Silicon Graphics, Inc.)

CRAYFISH CO LTD (JAPAN)
Each old Sponsored ADR for Common exchanged for (0.1) new Sponsored ADR for Common 12/01/2000
ADR agreement terminated 11/24/2003

Each new Sponsored ADR for Common exchanged for $37.4111 cash

CRAZY EDDIE INC (DE)
Common 1¢ par split (2) for (1) by issuance of (1) additional share 07/31/1985
Common 1¢ par split (2) for (1) by issuance of (1) additional share 09/30/1986
Chapter 11 bankruptcy proceedings converted to Chapter 7 on 12/31/1991
No stockholders' equity

CRAZY HORSE INDS INC (BC)
Recapitalized as CBX Ventures Inc. 07/20/1999
Each share Common no par exchanged for (0.125) share Common no par
CBX Ventures Inc. reorganized as Alma Resources Ltd. 12/05/2005 which name changed to Remstar Resources Ltd. 05/15/2008 which name changed to Avarone Metals Inc. 02/03/2014

CRAZY HORSE RES INC (BC)
Each share old Common no par exchanged for (0.33333333) share new Common no par 10/22/2013
Recapitalized as Rockwealth Resources Corp. 06/08/2017
Each share Common no par exchanged for (0.1) share Common no par

CRC COMPUTER RADIX CORP (NY)
Name changed to Computer Radix Corp. 10/13/1970
Computer Radix Corp. name changed to Boothe Data Systems, Inc. 02/22/1971 which name changed to Infonational Inc. 09/05/1972
(See Infonational Inc.)

CRC CROSE INTL INC (OK)
Merged into AIC Corp. 04/23/1968
Each share Common $12.50 par exchanged for (211.9093) shares 6% Preferred $1 par and (247.2275) shares Common $1 par
AIC Corp. name changed to Crutcher Resources Corp. 12/31/1968
(See Crutcher Resources Corp.)

CRC LIQUIDATING CORP. (OH)
Liquidation completed
Each share Common $2.50 par exchanged for initial distribution of (0.52821) share Norton Co. Common $10 par 02/25/1975
Each share Common $2.50 par received second and final distribution of (0.0587) share Norton Co. Common $10 par 10/00/1976
(See Norton Co.)

CRDENTIA CORP (DE)
Each share old Common $0.0001 par exchanged for (0.33333333) share new Common $0.0001 par 06/29/2004
Each share new Common $0.0001 par exchanged again for (0.1) share new Common $0.0001 par 04/05/2006
Each share new Common $0.0001 par exchanged again for (0.001) share new Common $0.0001 par 09/05/2008
Plan of reorganization under Chapter 11 Federal Bankruptcy proceedings effective 06/02/2010
No stockholders' equity

CREAM MINERALS LTD (BC)
Recapitalized 12/22/1994
Recapitalized from Cream Silver Mines Ltd. to Cream Minerals Ltd. 12/22/1994
Each share Common no par exchanged for (0.2) share Common no par
Recapitalized as Agave Silver Corp. 10/03/2013
Each share Common no par

exchanged for (0.1) share Common no par
Agave Silver Corp. name changed to First Energy Metals Ltd. 12/20/2016

CREAM OF WHEAT CORP. (DE)
Capital Stock no par changed to $2 par 00/00/1939
Acquired by National Biscuit Co. 08/09/1961
Each share Capital Stock $2 par exchanged for (0.6) share Common $10 par
National Biscuit Co. name changed to Nabisco Inc. 04/27/1971 which merged into Nabisco Brands, Inc. 07/06/1981
(See Nabisco Brands, Inc.)

CREAMERIES OF AMERICA, INC. (DE)
Common no par changed to $1 par 00/00/1937
Merged into Beatrice Foods Co. 00/00/1953
Each share Common $1 par exchanged for (0.125) share 4.5% Preferred $100 par and (1) share Common $12.50 par
Beatrice Foods Co. name changed to Beatrice Companies, Inc. 06/05/1984 which was acquired by BCI Holdings Corp. 04/17/1986
(See BCI Holdings Corp.)

CREATION CASINOS INC (BC)
Reincorporated 12/16/2004
Place of incorporation changed from (AB) to (BC) 12/16/2004
Recapitalized as Orca Power Corp. (BC) 07/22/2008
Each share Common no par exchanged for (0.4) share Common no par
Orca Power Corp. (BC) reorganized in Canada as AFG Flameguard Ltd. 04/11/2012

CREATION VENTURES INC (AB)
Name changed to Creation Casinos Inc. (AB) 11/28/2003
Creation Casinos Inc. (AB) reincorporated in British Columbia 12/16/2004 which recapitalized as Orca Power Corp. (BC) 07/22/2008 which reorganized in Canada as AFG Flameguard Ltd. 04/11/2012

CREATIV GROUP OPEN JT STK CO (UKRAINE)
Basis changed from (1:0.0001) to (1:0.01) 05/30/2008
Basis changed from (1:0.01) to (1:1) 08/06/2010
GDR agreement terminated 12/19/2016
Each Sponsored Reg. S GDR for Ordinary exchanged for (1) share Ordinary
Note: Unexchanged GDR's will be sold and the proceeds, if any, held for claim after 04/21/2017

CREATIVE APP SOLUTIONS INC (NV)
Name changed to Capstone Financial Group, Inc. 09/06/2013

CREATIVE BAKERIES INC (NY)
Name changed to Brooklyn Cheesecake & Desserts Co., Inc. 02/15/2005
Brooklyn Cheesecake & Desserts Co., Inc. name changed to Meridian Waste Solutions, Inc. 04/16/2015 which name changed to Attis Industries Inc. 05/01/2018

CREATIVE BEAUTY SUPPLY INC (NJ)
Name changed to Global Digital Solutions, Inc. 3/23/2004

CREATIVE BEAUTY SUPPLY OF NEW JERSEY CORP (NJ)
Recapitalized as Gotham Capital Holdings, Inc. (NJ) 06/30/2015
Each share Common $0.001 par

exchanged for (0.5) share Common $0.001 par
Gotham Capital Holdings, Inc. (NJ) reincorporated in Nevada as IIOT-OXYS, Inc. 08/16/2017

CREATIVE BIOMOLECULES INC (DE)
Merged into Curis, Inc. 07/31/2000
Each share Common 1¢ par exchanged for (0.3) share Common 1¢ par

CREATIVE CAP CORP (DE)
Incorporated 8/30/68
Name changed to Clarion Capital Corp. 10/1/73
(See Clarion Capital Corp.)

CREATIVE CAP CORP NEW (DE)
Incorporated 03/18/1985
Name changed to Telshare International Inc. 04/28/1986
Telshare International Inc. recapitalized as Sunvest Resorts, Inc. (DE) 07/16/1996 which reorganized in Florida 08/06/1996 which name changed to US Data Authority, Inc. 06/23/2000
(See US Data Authority, Inc.)

CREATIVE CAPITAL CORP. (MN)
Name changed to Valentine, Sherman & Associates, Inc. 5/25/72
(See Valentine, Sherman & Associates, Inc.)

CREATIVE CLASSICS INTL (NV)
Each share old Common $0.001 par exchanged for (0.2) share new Common $0.001 par in May 1991
Each share new Common $0.001 par exchanged again for (0.1) share new Common $0.001 par 1/31/92
Each share new Common $0.001 par exchanged again for (0.01) share new Common $0.001 par 4/20/92
Charter revoked for failure to file reports and pay fees 3/1/93

CREATIVE COMPUTER APPLICATIONS INC (CA)
Each share old Common no par exchanged for (0.2) share new Common no par 04/12/1991
Name changed to Aspyra, Inc. 11/21/2005

CREATIVE COMPUTERS INC (CA)
Issue Information - 2,000,000 shares COM offered at $17 per share on 04/04/1995
Each share Common $0.001 par received distribution of (1) share UBID, Inc. Common $0.001 par payable 06/07/1999 to holders of record 05/24/1999
Name changed to IdeaMall, Inc. 06/13/2000
IdeaMall, Inc. name changed to PC Mall, Inc. 06/19/2001 which name changed to PCM, Inc. 01/02/2013

CREATIVE CONSULTING CORP INTL (DE)
Recapitalized as 3CI Inc. 02/16/1987
Each share Common $0.0001 par exchanged for (0.05) share Common 1¢ par
3CI Inc. recapitalized as Cordero Industries Inc. 06/01/1990
(See Cordero Industries Inc.)

CREATIVE EATERIES CORP (NV)
Recapitalized as Diners Acquisition Corp. 10/20/2006
Each share Common $0.001 par exchanged for (0.2) share Common $0.001 par
Diners Acquisition Corp. recapitalized as LaSalle Brands Corp. 07/10/2007
(See LaSalle Brands Corp.)

CREATIVE ENTERPRISES INTL INC (NV)
Name changed to Skinny Nutritional Corp. 12/27/2006
(See Skinny Nutritional Corp.)

CREATIVE ENTMT TECH INC (BC)
Struck off register and declared

dissolved for failure to file returns 05/17/2005

CREATIVE ENVIRONMENTS INC (NY)
Charter cancelled and proclaimed dissolved for failure to pay taxes 06/24/1983

CREATIVE FABRICS CORP (CA)
Name changed to Laguna Financial Corp. 11/7/74
Laguna Financial Corp. merged into Swanton (Norman F.) Associates, Inc. 1/30/76 which name changed to Swanton Corp. 8/9/76
(See Swanton Corp.)

CREATIVE FINL INC (UT)
Charter suspended for failure to file reports 12/31/1973

CREATIVE FINL SVCS INC (IL)
Plan of reorganization under Chapter 11 Federal Bankruptcy proceedings confirmed 09/14/1990
No stockholders' equity

CREATIVE GAMING INC (NJ)
Name changed 05/22/1997
Each share old Common no par exchanged for (0.25) share new Common no par 01/26/1994
Name changed from Creative Learning Products, Inc. to Creative Gaming, Inc. 05/22/1997
Each share old Common no par exchanged for (0.03333333) share new Common no par 10/30/1997
Recapitalized as Management Services Inc. 10/16/2006
Each share new Common no par exchanged for (0.002) share Common $0.001 par
Management Services Inc. recapitalized as Centriforce Technology Corp. 08/15/2008 which recapitalized as ADB International Group, Inc. (NJ) 05/20/2010 which reorganized in Delaware 08/04/2014 which name changed to E- Qure Corp. 10/09/2014

CREATIVE HLDGS & MKTG CORP (NV)
Name changed to American Racing Capital, Inc. 10/7/2005

CREATIVE HOST SVCS INC (CA)
Merged into Compass Group USA Investments, LLP 4/16/2004
Each share Common no par exchanged for $3.40 cash

CREATIVE IS INC
Merged into Infospace Inc. 07/03/2000
Each share Common exchanged for (0.03314666) share Common $0.0001 par
Infospace Inc. name changed to Blucora, Inc. 06/07/2012

CREATIVE LOGIC CORP (DE)
Voluntarily dissolved 4/9/76
No stockholders' equity

CREATIVE MGMT ASSOC INC (NY)
Merged into Josephson (Marvin) Associates, Inc. (NY) 12/31/1974
Each share Common 10¢ par exchanged for $6.10 cash

CREATIVE MARKETING EXECUTIVES INC (MN)
Name changed to C.M.E., Inc. 08/23/1973
(See C.M.E., Inc.)

CREATIVE MASTER INTL INC (DE)
Each share old Common $0.001 par exchanged for (0.75) share new Common $0.0001 par 12/14/1998
Recapitalized as PacificNet.com, Inc. 07/27/2000
Each share new Common $0.0001 par exchanged for (1/3) share Common $0.0001 par
PacificNet.com, Inc. name changed to PacificNet Inc. 04/23/2002
(See PacificNet Inc.)

CREATIVE MED DEV INC (DE)
Recapitalized as Omni Rail Products Inc. 3/12/99
Each share Common 1¢ par exchanged for (1/3) share Common 1¢ par

CREATIVE MED SYS INC (NJ)
Each share old Common no par exchanged for (0.1) share new Common no par 09/30/1987
Filed petition under Chapter 7 Federal Bankruptcy Code 03/01/1990

CREATIVE MEDIA INTL INC (DE)
Name changed to Corporate Media International, Inc. 7/25/2005

CREATIVE MERCHANDISING INC (CO)
Adjudicated bankrupt 05/10/1972
Stockholders' equity unlikely

CREATIVE OPPORTUNITIES INC (CO)
Name changed to Vertec International, Inc. 05/06/1988

CREATIVE PATENTS & PRODS LTD (ON)
Charter cancelled for failure to pay taxes and file returns 9/5/79

CREATIVE PLAYTHINGS, INC. (NY)
Acquired by Columbia Broadcasting System, Inc. 7/18/66
Each share Common $1 par exchanged for (0.62) share Common $2.50 par
Columbia Broadcasting System, Inc. name changed to CBS Inc. 4/18/74
(See CBS Inc.)

CREATIVE POLYMER PRODS CORP (DE)
Charter cancelled and declared inoperative and void for non-payment of taxes 3/1/76

CREATIVE PRODS INC (BC)
Struck off register and declared dissolved for failure to file returns 3/5/93

CREATIVE PROGRAMMING & TECHNOLOGY VENTURES INC (CO)
Company terminated registration of common stock and is no longer public as of 08/15/1997
Details not available

CREATIVE RECYCLING TECHNOLOGIES INC (GA)
Name changed to Ingen Technologies, Inc. 11/1/2004

CREATIVE RES INC (NV)
Permanently revoked for failure to file reports and pay fees 04/30/1999

CREATIVE RESTAURANTS CONCEPTS INC (OK)
Each share old Common $0.005 par exchanged for (0.05) share new Common $0.005 par 04/20/1998
Name changed to Cala Corp. 12/02/1999
(See Cala Corp.)

CREATIVE SVC & DEV CORP (DE)
Charter dissolved 10/4/77

CREATIVE SVCS INC (DE)
Name changed to Creative Service & Development Corp. 5/19/70
(See Creative Service & Development Corp.)

CREATIVE SOLUTIONS WITH ART INC (NV)
Common $0.001 par split (14) for (1) by issuance of (13) additional shares payable 05/09/2005 to holders of record 05/02/2005
Ex date - 05/10/2005
Name changed to GlobalOptions Group, Inc. (NV) 06/27/2005
GlobalOptions Group, Inc. (NV) reincorporated in Delaware 12/08/2006 which name changed to Patent Properties, Inc. 11/27/2013

which name changed to Walker Innovation Inc. 08/12/2015

CREATIVE TECHNOLOGIES CORP (NY)
Each share Common 1¢ par exchanged for (1/3) share Common 3¢ par 08/05/1992
Common 3¢ par split (2) for (1) by issuance of (1) additional share 06/08/1994
Each share Common 3¢ par exchanged for (1/3) share Common 9¢ par 09/05/1996
Company terminated common stock registration and is no longer public as of 05/11/2007

CREATIVE TELEFILMS & ARTISTS LTD. (ON)
Name changed to Seven Arts Productions Ltd. 08/12/1960
Seven Arts Productions Ltd. name changed to Warner Bros.-Seven Arts Ltd. 07/15/1967 which was acquired by Kinney National Service, Inc. 07/08/1969 which name changed to Kinney Services, Inc. (NY) 02/17/1971 which reincorporated in Delaware as Warner Communications Inc. 02/11/1972
(See Warner Communications Inc.)

CREATIVE VENDING CORP (FL)
Reincorporated under the laws of Nevada as TetriDyn Solutions, Inc. 03/22/2016
TetriDyn Solutions, Inc. name changed to Ocean Thermal Energy Corp. 05/25/2017

CREATIVE VENTURES CORP (DE)
Charter cancelled and declared inoperative and void for non-payment of taxes 4/15/69

CREATOR CAP INC (BC)
Reincorporated under the laws of Bermuda as Sky Games International Ltd. and Common no par changed to 1¢ par 01/26/1995
Sky Games International Ltd. name changed to Interactive Entertainment Ltd. 05/13/1997 which name changed to Creator Capital Ltd. 10/16/2000

CREDENCE SYS CORP (DE)
Common $0.001 par split (3) for (2) by issuance of (0.5) additional share 06/05/1995
Common $0.001 par split (2) for (1) by issuance of (1) additional share payable 05/17/2000 to holders of record 05/01/2000
Merged into LTX-Credence Corp. 08/29/2008
Each share Common $0.001 par exchanged for (0.6129) share Common 5¢ par
LTX-Credence Corp. name changed to Xcerra Corp. 05/22/2014 which merged into Cohu, Inc. 10/01/2018

CREDICO INC. (QC)
Declared bankrupt 02/24/1969
No stockholders' equity

CREDIT & INVESTMENT CORP.
Liquidated 00/00/1943
Details not available

CREDIT ACCEP CORP (DE)
Recapitalized in 1937
Each share 1st Preferred $25 par exchanged for (1) share Preferred $20 par
Each share 2nd Preferred $100 par exchanged for (7) shares Class A Common 25¢ par
Each share Common no par exchanged for (3.5) shares Class A Common 25¢ par and (3.5) shares Common 25¢ par
Recapitalized in 1948
Class A Common 25¢ par reclassified as Common $1 par
Common 25¢ par changed to $1 par

Common $1 par changed to $2.50 par 10/29/56
$1.40 Non-Cum. Preferred $20 par called for redemption 5/1/74
Dissolved 6/28/79
Details not available

CREDIT ACCEPTANCE CORP. LTD. (BC)
Each share old Ordinary Stock no par exchanged for (10) shares new Ordinary Stock no par 10/22/1964
Name changed to Commonwealth Acceptance Corp. Ltd. 03/26/1965
(See Commonwealth Acceptance Corp. Ltd.)

CREDIT BUR REPORTS INC (DE)
Under plan of merger each share Common 25¢ par exchanged for an undetermined amount of cash 09/00/1982

CREDIT FINANCE SERVICE, INC. (DE)
Acquired by Liberty Loan Corp. 4/1/64
Each share 6% Preferred $100 par exchanged for (4) shares 5% Preferred $25 par
Each (5-1/3) shares Class A and/or B exchanged for (1) share Common $1 par
Liberty Loan Corp. name changed to LLC Corp. 3/14/80 which name changed to Valhi, Inc. 3/10/87

CREDIT FONCIER FRANCO CANADIEN (QC)
Acquired by Montreal City & District Savings Bank (Montreal, QC) 04/19/1979
Each share Common no par exchanged for $140 cash

CREDIT INSURERS AMER INC (FL)
Completely liquidated 8/25/73
Each share Common 5¢ par exchanged for first and final distribution of (0.350877) share Indiana National Corp. Common no par
Indiana National Corp. name changed to INB Financial Corp. 4/26/89 which merged into NBD Bancorp, Inc. 10/15/92 which name changed to First Chicago NBD Corp. 12/1/95 which merged into Bank One Corp. 10/2/98 which merged into J.P. Morgan Chase & Co. 12/31/2000 which name changed to JPMorgan Chase & Co. 7/20/2004

CREDIT LIFE INSURANCE CO. OF CONNECTICUT (CT)
Name changed to Insurance City Life Co. 09/16/1955
(See Insurance City Life Co.)

CREDIT LYONNAIS CAP S C A (LUXEMBOURG)
Sponsored ADR's for Guaranteed Preference $2 par called for redemption at $25.105556 on 7/21/2003
144A Sponsored ADR's for Guaranteed Preference $2 par called for redemption at $25.105556 on 7/21/2003

CREDIT M-G INC. (QC)
In process of liquidation 00/00/1971
Stockholders' equity unlikely

CREDIT MGMT SOLUTIONS INC (DE)
Issue Information - 2,600,000 shares COM offered at $11.50 per share on 12/18/1996
Merged into First American Corp. (CA) 05/30/2001
Each share Common 1¢ par exchanged for (0.2841) share Common $1 par
First American Corp. (CA) reincorporated in Delaware as CoreLogic, Inc. 06/01/2010

CREDIT ST LAURENT INC (QC)
Completely liquidated 08/01/1968
Each share Class A no par received $0.03 cash

CREDIT SERVICE, INC.
Bankrupt in 1940
Details not available

CREDIT STORE INC (UT)
Chapter 11 Federal bankruptcy proceedings converted to Chapter 7 on 02/04/2003
Stockholders' equity unlikely

CREDIT SUISSE ASSET MGMT STRATEGIC GLOBAL INCOME FD INC (MD)
Merged into Credit Suisse Asset Management Income Fund, Inc. 5/14/2001
Each share Common $0.001 par exchanged for (1.2681) shares Common $0.001 par

CREDIT SUISSE CASH RESERVE FD INC (MD)
Name changed 12/12/2001
Name changed from Credit Suisse Warburg Pincus Cash Reserve Fund, Inc. to Credit Suisse Cash Reserve Fund, Inc. 12/12/2001
Completely liquidated 09/22/2009
Each share Class A $0.001 par received net asset value
Each share Class B $0.001 par received net asset value
Each share Class C $0.001 par received net asset value
Each share Common $0.001 par received net asset value

CREDIT SUISSE EMERGING MKTS FD INC (MD)
Name changed 12/12/2001
Name changed from Credit Suisse Warburg Pincus Emerging Markets Fund to Credit Suisse Emerging Markets Fund, Inc. 12/12/2001
Completely liquidated
Each share Class A $0.001 par received first and final distribution of $24.57 cash payable 12/27/2007 to holders of record 12/27/2007
Each share Common Class $0.001 par received first and final distribution of $24.64 cash payable 12/27/2007 to holders of record 12/27/2007
Each share Advisor Class $0.001 par received first and final distribution of $23.87 cash payable 12/27/2007 to holders of record 12/27/2007
Note: Certificates were not required to be surrendered and are without value

CREDIT SUISSE FIRST BOSTON USA INC (DE)
Merged into Credit Suisse First Boston, Inc. 08/22/2001
Each share CSFDirect Common exchanged for $6 cash

CREDIT SUISSE FIXED INCOME FD (MA)
Name changed 12/12/2001
Name changed from Credit Suisse Warburg Pincus Fixed Income Fund to Credit Suisse Fixed Income Fund 12/12/2001
Completely liquidated 12/22/2006
Each share Advisor Class $0.001 par received net asset value
Each share Class A $0.001 par received net asset value
Each share Class B $0.001 par received net asset value
Each share Class C $0.001 par received net asset value
Each share Common Class $0.001 par received net asset value

CREDIT SUISSE GLOBAL FIXED INCOME FD INC (MD)
Name changed 12/12/2001
Name changed from Credit Suisse Warburg Pincus Global Fixed Income Fund, Inc. to Credit Suisse Global Fixed Income Fund, Inc. 12/12/2001
Merged into Aberdeen Funds 07/20/2009

Details not available

CREDIT SUISSE GLOBAL POST-VENTURE CAPITAL FUND, INC. (MD)
Name changed 12/12/2001
Name changed from Credit Suisse Warburg Pincus Global Post-Venture Capital Fund, Inc. to Credit Suisse Global Post-Venture Capital Fund, Inc. 12/12/2001
Name changed to Credit Suisse Global Small Cap Fund 2/21/2005

CREDIT SUISSE INSTL HIGH YIELD FD INC (MD)
Name changed to Credit Suisse Global High Yield Fund Inc. 2/21/2005

CREDIT SUISSE INTL EQUITY FD INC (MD)
Name changed 12/12/2001
Name changed from Credit Suisse Warburg Pincus International Equity Fund, Inc. to Credit Suisse International Equity Fund, Inc. 12/12/2001
Merged into Credit Suisse International Focus Fund, Inc. 04/26/2002
Each share Advisor Class $0.001 par exchanged for (1.7038145) Advisor Shares $0.001 par
Each share Common Class $0.001 par exchanged for (1.19174745) Common Shares $0.001 par

CREDIT SUISSE INVT GRADE BD FD INC (MD)
Name changed 11/15/2001
Name changed from Credit Suisse Warburg Pincus Intermediate Maturity Government Fund, Inc. to Credit Suisse Investment Grade Bond Fund, Inc. and Advisor Class $0.001 par reclassified as Class A $0.001 par 11/15/2001
Merged into Credit Suisse Fixed Income Fund 10/10/2003
Each share Class A $0.001 par exchanged for (1.0427) shares Class A $0.001 par
Each share Class B $0.001 par exchanged for (1.0439) shares Class B $0.001 par
Each share Class C $0.001 par exchanged for (1.0452) shares Class C $0.001 par
Each share Common $0.001 par exchanged for (1.0429) shares Class A $0.001 par
(See Credit Suisse Fixed Income Fund)

CREDIT SUISSE JAPAN EQUITY FD (MD)
Name changed 05/27/2003
Name changed from Credit Suisse Japan Growth Fund, Inc. to Credit Suisse Japan Equity Fund, Inc. 05/27/2003
Completely liquidated
Each share Advisor Class $0.001 par received first and final distribution of $5.21 cash payable 04/21/2008 to holders of record 04/21/2008
Each share Class A $0.001 par received first and final distribution of $5.29 cash payable 04/21/2008 to holders of record 04/21/2008
Each share Common Class $0.001 par received first and final distribution of $5.31 cash payable 04/21/2008 to holders of record 04/21/2008
Note: Certificates were not required to be surrendered and are without value

CREDIT SUISSE LARGE CAP BLEND FD (MD)
Name changed 12/12/2001
Name changed 08/08/2005
Name changed from Credit Suisse Warburg Pincus Focus Fund, Inc. to Credit Suisse Select Equity Fund, Inc. 12/12/2001
Name changed from Credit Suisse Select Equity Fund, Inc. to Credit Suisse Large Cap Blend Fund, Inc. 08/08/2005
Merged into Aberdeen Funds 10/07/2011
Details not available

CREDIT SUISSE LARGE CAP GROWTH FD (MA)
Name changed 12/12/2001
Name changed 11/27/2006
Name changed from Credit Suisse Warburg Pincus Capital Appreciation Fund to Credit Suisse Capital Appreciation Fund 12/12/2001
Name changed from Credit Suisse Capital Appreciation Fund to Credit Suisse Large Cap Growth Fund 11/27/2006
Merged into Credit Suisse Large Cap Blend Fund, Inc. 10/08/2010
Details not available

CREDIT SUISSE MID CAP CORE FD INC (MD)
Name changed 05/01/2004
Name changed 12/01/2006
Name changed from Credit Suisse Emerging Growth Fund to Credit Suisse Mid-Cap Growth Fund, Inc. 05/01/2004
Name changed from Credit Suisse Mid-Cap Growth Fund, Inc. to Credit Suisse Mid-Cap Core Fund, Inc. 12/01/2006
Merged into Credit Suisse Large Cap Blend Fund, Inc. 10/08/2010
Details not available

CREDIT SUISSE N Y MUN FD (MA)
Name changed 12/12/2001
Name changed from Credit Suisse Warburg Pincus New York to Credit Suisse New York Intermediate Municipal Fund to Credit Suisse New York Municipal Fund 12/12/2001
Completely liquidated 10/17/2006
Each share Class A $0.001 par received net asset value
Each share Common Class $0.001 par received net asset value

CREDIT SUISSE WARBURG PINCUS JAPAN GROWTH FUND, INC. (MD)
Name changed to Credit Suisse Japan Growth Fund, Inc. 12/12/2001
Credit Suisse Japan Growth Fund, Inc. name changed to Credit Suisse Japan Equity Fund, Inc. 05/27/2003
(See Credit Suisse Japan Equity Fund, Inc.)

CREDIT SUISSE WARBURG PINCUS MAJOR FGN MKTS FD INC (MD)
Name changed to Credit Suisse International Focus Fund, Inc. 12/12/2001

CREDIT SUISSE WARBURG PINCUS OPPORTUNITY FDS (MD)
Each share Developing Markets Fund Class A, B, C, and Common Class R $0.001 par were liquidated at net asset value 04/01/2001
Each share High Income Fund Class A, B, C, D or Common Class $0.001 par automatically became (1) share Credit Suisse Opportunity Funds High Income Fund Class A, B, C or Common Class $0.001 par respectively 12/12/2001
International Equity II Fund Class A, B, C, D and Common Class R $0.001 par reorganized as Credit Suisse International Focus Fund, Inc. Class A, B, C, Common or Advisor Class $0.001 par respectively 12/12/2001
U.S. Government Money Fund $0.001 par reclassified as Credit Suisse Cash Reserve Fund Class A $0.001 par 9/4/2004
Municipal Money Fund $0.001 par reclassified as Credit Suisse Cash Reserve Fund Class A $0.001 par 12/15/2004

CREDIT SUISSE WARBURG PINCUS SMALL CO GROWTH FD INC (MD)
Name changed to Credit Suisse Small Cap Growth Fund, Inc. 12/12/2001

CREDITBANK INC (CUTLER RIDGE, FL)
Placed in receivership 1/26/90
No stockholders' equity

CREDITGROUP COM INC (DE)
Recapitalized as Tradex Global Financial Services Inc. 07/18/2006
Each share Common $0.001 par exchanged for (0.01) share Common $0.001 par
Preferred not affected except for name change
(See Tradex Global Financial Services Inc.)

CREDITHRIFT FINL CORP (IN)
Common $1 par split (3) for (2) by issuance of (0.5) additional share 02/21/1969
Common $1 par split (3) for (2) by issuance of (0.5) additional share 03/01/1971
Common $1 par changed to 50¢ par and (1) additional share issued 03/02/1973
Under plan of reorganization each share Common 50¢ par automatically became (1) share Credithrift Financial Inc. Common 50¢ par 05/29/1974
(See Credithrift Financial Inc.)
4.5% Preferred $100 par called for redemption 08/22/1988
Name changed to American General Finance Corp. 03/20/1989
(See American General Finance Corp.)

CREDITHRIFT FINL INC (IN)
Merged into American General Corp. 02/08/1982
Each share $2.75 Conv. Preferred Class A Ser. 1 no par exchanged for $32.3479 principal amount of 11% Conv. Debentures due 02/08/2007
Each share Common 50¢ par exchanged for $12.50 principal of 11% Conv. Debentures due 02/08/2007

CREDITO ITALIANO (ITALY)
Name changed to Unicredito Italiano S.p.A. 11/04/1998
Unicredito Italiano S.p.A. recapitalized as UniCredit S.p.A. 01/20/2012
(See UniCredit S.p.A.)

CREDITORS LIQUIDATION CORP.
Participation Certificates Series A paid off 00/00/1933
Public interest eliminated

CREDITRUST CORP (MD)
Reorganized as NCO Portfolio Management Inc. 02/22/2001
Each share Common 1¢ par exchanged for (0.1388) share Common 1¢ par
Note: Each share Common 1¢ par received an additional distribution of (0.02341375) share payable 10/16/2002 to holders of record 02/22/2001
NCO Portfolio Management Inc. merged into NCO Group, Inc. 03/26/2004
(See NCO Group, Inc.)

CREDO MNG LTD (QC)
Charter annulled for failure to file reports or pay fees 03/22/1975

CREDO PETE CORP (DE)
Reincorporated 04/10/2009
Each share Common 1¢ par exchanged for (0.1) share Common 10¢ par 10/29/1982
Common 10¢ par split (3) for (2) by issuance of (0.5) additional share payable 04/20/2004 to holders of

record 04/05/2004 Ex date - 04/21/2004
Common 10¢ par split (3) for (2) by issuance of (0.5) additional share payable 10/11/2005 to holders of record 09/26/2005 Ex date - 10/12/2005
Stock Dividend - 20% payable 04/23/2003 to holders of record 04/02/2003 Ex date - 03/31/2003
State of incorporation changed from (CO) to (DE) 04/10/2009
Acquired by Forestar Group Inc. 09/28/2012
Each share Common 10¢ par exchanged for $14.50 cash

CREDO PORCUPINE GOLD MINES LTD. (ON)
Charter revoked for failure to file reports and pay fees 12/26/1960

CREE LAKE MNG LTD (BC)
Name changed to Scarboro Resources Ltd. (BC) 02/27/1980
Scarboro Resources Ltd. (BC) reincorporated in Alberta 06/11/1980 which recapitalized as Hillcrest Resources Ltd. 10/05/1987 which was acquired by Mark Resources Inc. 05/09/1995 which was acquired by EnerMark Income Fund 04/09/1996 which merged into Enerplus Resources Fund 06/22/2001 which reorganized as Enerplus Corp. 01/03/2011

CREE MINING CORP. LTD. (SK)
Charter revoked for failure to file reports and pay fees 09/25/1964

CREE OIL OF CANADA LTD. (CANADA)
Merged into North Star Oil Ltd. 12/15/1958
Each share Capital Stock no par exchanged for either (0.33333333) share Class A no par or Common no par
(See North Star Oil Co. Ltd.)

CREE RESH INC (NC)
Common 1¢ par changed to $0.005 par and (1) additional share issued 08/15/1995
Common $0.005 par changed to $0.0025 par and (1) additional share issued payable 07/30/1999 to holders of record 07/26/1999
Name changed to Cree, Inc. 01/01/2000

CRE8TIVE WKS INC (NV)
Name changed to Optium Cyber Systems, Inc. 10/03/2017

CREENERGY CORP (NV)
Name changed to Peptide Technologies, Inc. 10/25/2011

CREIGHTON CORP (ON)
Reincorporated under the laws of Nevada as Pearlstar Corp. and Common no par changed to $0.001 par 12/14/2005

CREMA TOILET CORP. OF AMERICA (UT)
Name changed to United Empire Industries, Inc. 01/10/1969
United Empire Industries, Inc. recapitalized as Fli-Co Corp. 07/17/1969 which recapitalized as AutoBale America Corp. 01/18/1972
(See AutoBale America Corp.)

CREMER S A (BRAZIL)
GDR agreement terminated 09/24/2014
Each Sponsored Reg. S GDR for Common exchanged for $11.917518 cash

CREO INC (CANADA)
Name changed 02/20/2002
Name changed from Creo Products Inc. to Creo Inc. 02/20/2002
Merged into Eastman Kodak Co. 06/15/2005

Each share Common no par exchanged for $16.50 cash

CREOLE PETE CORP (DE)
Capital Stock no par changed to $5 par 00/00/1933
Capital Stock $5 par split (3) for (1) by issuance of (2) additional shares 05/25/1955
Merged into Exxon Corp. 06/23/1975
Each share Capital Stock $5 par exchanged for $11.50 cash

CREOLE SNOW LAKE MINES, LTD. (ON)
Charter revoked for failure to file reports and pay taxes in 1951

CREOLE SYNDICATE
Name changed to Creole Petroleum Corp. 00/00/1928
(See Creole Petroleum Corp.)

CREOSUS GOLD MINING CO. (ID)
Name changed to National Uranium Corp. (ID) and Common $1 par changed to 5¢ par 05/27/1954
(See National Uranium Corp. (ID))

CRESCENDE INTL INC (WY)
Recapitalized as Core Resources Ltd. 11/03/2006
Each share Common no par exchanged for (0.01) share Common no par
Core Resources Ltd. recapitalized as Club Resources Ltd. 06/30/2008

CRESCENDO CAP CORP (ON)
Name changed to Tragoes Inc. 07/24/1996
Tragoes Inc. name changed to Rightsmarket.com Inc. 07/30/1999 which name changed to RightsMarket Inc. 06/07/2000 which reorganized as RightsMarket Ltd. 12/31/2003

CRESCENDO PHARMACEUTICALS CORP (DE)
Merged into Alza Corp. 11/14/2000
Each share Class A Common 1¢ par exchanged for $20.27 cash

CRESCENT AIRCRAFT CORP. (NJ)
Company went bankrupt 08/00/1930
No stockholders' equity

CRESCENT AIRWAYS CORP (GA)
Plan of reorganization under Chapter 11 Federal Bankruptcy proceedings confirmed 08/00/1999
Stockholders' equity unlikely

CRESCENT COMMUNICATIONS INC (NV)
Recapitalized as Bluegate Corp. 11/23/2004
Each share Common $0.001 par exchanged for (0.05) share Common $0.001 par
Bluegate Corp. recapitalized as Logicquest Technology, Inc. 03/19/2015

CRESCENT CORP (DE)
Common $1 par split (5) for (1) by issuance of (4) additional shares 12/12/1956
Name changed to Crescent Petroleum Corp. 04/16/1958 which name changed back to Crescent Corp. 12/16/1963
Merged into National Industries, Inc. (KY) 07/01/1968
Each share 5% Conv. Preferred $25 par exchanged for (1) share $1.25 Conv. Preferred Ser. B $1 par
Each share Common $1 par exchanged for (0.75) share Common $1 par
National Industries, Inc. (KY) merged into Fuqua Industries, Inc. 01/03/1978 which name changed to Actava Group Inc. 07/21/1993 which name changed to Metromedia International Group, Inc. 11/01/1995
(See Metromedia International Group, Inc.)

CRESCENT EAGLE OIL CO (UT)
Recapitalized as Crescent General Corp. 05/26/1969
Each share Capital Stock 10¢ par exchanged for (0.2) share Capital Stock 50¢ par
(See Crescent General Corp.)

CRESCENT ENGINEERING & RESEARCH CORP. (CA)
Name changed to Crescent Technology Corp. 10/11/1966
Crescent Technology Corp. name changed to Moxon, Inc. 05/11/1970
(See Moxon, Inc.)

CRESCENT FINANCE CO., INC. (OH)
Charter cancelled for failure to pay taxes 03/09/1984

CRESCENT FINL BANCSHARES INC (DE)
Name changed to VantageSouth Bancshares, Inc. 07/22/2013
VantageSouth Bancshares, Inc. merged into Yadkin Financial Corp. 07/04/2014 which merged into F.N.B. Corp. 03/11/2017

CRESCENT FINL CORP (NC)
Common $1 par split (6) for (5) by issuance of (0.2) additional share payable 04/16/2004 to holders of record 03/12/2004 Ex date - 03/10/2004
Stock Dividends - 12.5% payable 04/15/2002 to holders of record 03/15/2002 Ex date - 03/13/2002; 15% payable 04/25/2003 to holders of record 04/11/2003 Ex date - 04/09/2003; 15% payable 04/27/2005 to holders of record 04/14/2005 Ex date - 04/12/2005; 15% payable 05/31/2011 to holders of record 05/18/2006 Ex date - 05/16/2006; 10% payable 05/22/2011 to holders of record 05/11/2011 Ex date - 05/09/2007
Reincorporated under the laws of Delaware as Crescent Financial Bancshares, Inc. 11/15/2011
Crescent Financial Bancshares, Inc. name changed to VantageSouth Bancshares, Inc. 07/22/2013 which merged into Yadkin Financial Corp. 07/04/2014 which merged into F.N.B. Corp. 03/11/2017

CRESCENT GEN CORP (UT)
Charter suspended for failure to pay taxes 09/30/1975

CRESCENT GOLD CORP (NV)
Name changed to In Store Media Systems, Inc. 10/00/1998
In Store Media Systems, Inc. reorganized as AFG Enterprises, Inc. 01/31/2005 which name changed to AFG Enterprises USA, Inc. (NV) 08/24/2005 which reincorporated in Delaware as FP Technology, Inc. 07/06/2006 which name changed to Firepond, Inc. 07/12/2007
(See Firepond, Inc.)

CRESCENT HILL CAP CORP (GA)
Reincorporated under the laws of Oklahoma as Definitive Rest Mattress Co. and Common $1 par changed to $0.0001 par 12/04/2013
Definitive Rest Mattress Co. recapitalized as Zerez Holdings 04/12/2016 which name changed to Smart Cannabis Corp. 09/06/2017

CRESCENT KIRKLAND GOLD MINES LTD.
Acquired by Golden Gate Mining Co. Ltd. 00/00/1940
Details not available

CRESCENT MINES LTD (BC)
Recapitalized as Redwing Resources Inc. 08/16/1985
Each share Capital Stock no par exchanged for (0.23255813) share Common no par
(See Redwing Resources Inc.)

CRESCENT NIAGARA CORP (NY)
Common 10¢ par changed to $5 par 04/27/1966
Merged into Cooper Industries, Inc. 12/31/1970
Each share Common $5 par exchanged for $16 cash

CRESCENT OIL & GAS CORP (DE)
Merged into Com-Tek Resources, Inc. 09/13/1991
Each share Common 1¢ par exchanged for (0.19) share Common 1¢ par
Com-Tek Resources, Inc. name changed to Powerhouse Resources Inc. 08/10/1995
(See Powerhouse Resources Inc.)

CRESCENT OPER INC (DE)
Plan of reorganization under Chapter 11 Federal Bankruptcy Code effective 01/19/2005
Each share Common 1¢ par exchanged for (0.05) share Crescent Real Estate Equities Co. Common 1¢ par
Note: Unexchanged certificates were cancelled and became without value 01/19/2007
(See Crescent Real Estate Equities Co.)

CRESCENT PETE CORP (CO)
Merged into Crescent Oil & Gas Corp. 08/15/1983
Each share Common 1¢ par exchanged for (1) Common Stock Unit consisting of (1) share Common 1¢ par and (1) Common Stock Purchase Warrant expiring 09/30/1985
Crescent Oil & Gas Corp. merged into Com-Tek Resources, Inc. 09/13/1991 which name changed to Powerhouse Resources Inc. 08/10/1995
(See Powerhouse Resources Inc.)

CRESCENT PETROLEUM CORP. (DE)
Name changed back to Crescent Corp. 12/16/1963
Crescent Corp. merged into National Industries, Inc. (KY) 07/01/1968 which merged into Fuqua Industries, Inc. 01/03/1978 which name changed to Actava Group Inc. 07/21/1993 which name changed to Metromedia International Group, Inc. 11/01/1995
(See Metromedia International Group, Inc.)

CRESCENT PIPE LINE CO.
Liquidated 00/00/1927
Details not available

CRESCENT PT ENERGY LTD (AB)
Under plan of merger each share Class A Common no par exchanged for (0.5) share Starpoint Energy Ltd. Common no par and (0.5) Crescent Point Energy Trust, Trust Unit no par 09/10/2003
Each share Class B Common no par exchanged for (0.75) share Starpoint Energy Ltd. Common no par and (0.75) Crescent Point Energy Trust, Trust Unit no par 09/10/2003
(See each company's listing)

CRESCENT PT ENERGY TR (AB)
Reorganized as Crescent Point Energy Corp. 07/07/2009
Each Trust Unit no par exchanged for (1) share Common no par

CRESCENT PUBLIC SERVICE CO.
Liquidation completed 00/00/1948
Details not available

CRESCENT REAL ESTATE EQUITIES CO (TX)
Reincorporated 12/31/1996
Name and state of incorporation changed from Crescent Real Estate Equities, Inc. (MD) to Crescent Real Estate Equities Co. (TX) 12/31/1996

Common 1¢ par split (2) for (1) by issuance of (1) additional share payable 03/26/1997 to holders of record 03/20/1997 Ex date - 03/27/1997
Each share Common 1¢ par received distribution of (0.01) share Crescent Operating, Inc. Common 1¢ par payable 06/26/1997 to holders of record 05/30/1997 Ex date - 06/27/1997
6.75% Conv. Preferred Ser. A 1¢ par called for redemption at $25 plus $0.3656 accrued dividends on 08/03/2007
9.50% Conv. Preferred Ser. B 1¢ par called for redemption at $25 plus $0.5146 accrued dividends on 08/03/2007
Merged into Morgan Stanley Real Estate 08/03/2007
Each share Common 1¢ par exchanged for $22.80 cash

CRESCENT RES CORP (BC)
Each share old Common no par exchanged for (0.25) share new Common no par 12/20/2010
Recapitalized as Coventry Resources Inc. 01/09/2013
Each share new Common no par exchanged for (0.2) share Common no par
(See Coventry Resources Inc.)

CRESCENT ST BK (CARY, NC)
Stock Dividends - 10% payable 05/12/2000 to holders of record 04/20/2000; 12.5% payable 05/25/2001 to holders of record 05/11/2001 Ex date - 05/09/2001
Reorganized as Crescent Financial Corp. (NC) 06/29/2001
Each share Common $5 par exchanged for (1) share Common $1 par 06/29/2001
Crescent Financial Corp. (NC) reincorporated in Delaware as Crescent Financial Bancshares, Inc. 11/15/2011 which name changed to VantageSouth Bancshares, Inc. 07/22/2013 which merged into Yadkin Financial Corp. 07/04/2014 which merged into F.N.B. Corp. 03/11/2017

CRESCENT TECHNOLOGY CORP (CA)
Common no par changed to 10¢ par 01/16/1969
Name changed to Moxon, Inc. 05/11/1970
(See Moxon, Inc.)

CRESCENT URANIUM MINES, INC. (DE)
Merged into Fremont Uranium Corp. (CO) 09/21/1955
Each share Common 10¢ par exchanged for (1) share Common 10¢ par
Fremont Uranium Corp. (CO) merged into King Oil, Inc. 09/05/1956 which recapitalized as Lane Wood, Inc. 08/10/1964
(See Lane Wood, Inc.)

CRESCOTT INC (DE)
Recapitalized as China Career Builder Corp. 11/17/2006
Each share Common $0.001 par exchanged for (0.05) share Common $0.001 par
China Career Builder Corp. recapitalized as iMing Corp. 06/08/2012

CRESO EXPLORATION INC (CANADA)
Reincorporated 09/29/2010
Place of incorporation changed from (ON) to (Canada) 09/29/2010
Merged into Dundee Sustainable Technologies, Inc. 04/08/2014
Each share Common no par exchanged for (0.5) Subordinate Share no par

Note: Non-Canadian residents will receive a pro rata distribution from the sale of shares

CRESSET PRECIOUS METALS INC (NV)
Each share old Common $0.001 par exchanged for (0.01052631) share new Common $0.001 par 07/20/2007
Name changed to Alternative Fuel Technologies, Inc. 03/14/2008

CRESSEY DOCKHAM & CO INC (MA)
Merged into Wetterau Inc. 08/02/1985
Each share Common $1 par exchanged for $17.78 cash

CRESSON CONS INC (CO)
Name changed 04/28/1972
Capital Stock $1 par changed to 10¢ par 06/17/1970
Name changed from Cresson Consolidated Gold Mining & Milling Co. to Cresson Consolidated, Inc. 04/28/1972
Completely liquidated 09/25/1978
Each share Capital Stock 10¢ par exchanged for first and final distribution of (0.0913) share Envirosearch Corp. Common 10¢ par and $0.03 cash
Envirosearch Corp. name changed to Evro Financial Corp. (CO) 09/26/1986 which reincorporated in Florida as Evro Corp. 03/01/1994 which name changed to Channel America Broadcasting, Inc. 10/25/1996 which recapitalized as DTG Industries, Inc. 03/22/2004 which name changed to DTG Multimedia, Inc. (FL) 06/04/2004 which reorganized in Nevada as Amazing Technologies Corp. 12/23/2004 which name changed to Mvive, Inc. 08/24/2007
(See Mvive Inc.)

CRESSY GOLD MINES, LTD. (ON)
Charter cancelled 08/00/1958

CREST ENERGY RESOURCES CORP. (DE)
Charter cancelled and declared inoperative and void for non-payment of taxes 03/01/1988

CREST FOAM CORP (NJ)
Merged into L&P Foam 1986 Acquisition Co. 02/13/1987
Each share Common no par exchanged for $14.50 cash

CREST INDS INC (FL)
Plan of reorganization under Chapter 11 Federal Bankruptcy Code effective 06/21/1993
Each share Common 1¢ par received an undetermined amount of M.G. Products, Inc. Common no par
(See M.G. Products, Inc.)

CREST INDS INC (MN)
Stock Dividend - 200% 12/15/1969
Adjudicated bankrupt 01/23/1973
Stockholders' equity unlikely

CREST INVT TR INC (MD)
Class B Common no par reclassified as Class A Common no par 11/30/1967
Placed in receivership 12/00/1974
No stockholders' equity

CREST PETE CORP (BC)
Each share old Common no par exchanged for (0.2) share new Common no par 11/28/2014
Name changed to GFG Resources Inc. 10/27/2016

CREST RES INC (UT)
Merged into Henderson Petroleum Corp. 12/07/1981
Each share Class A 5¢ par exchanged for (0.09174311) share Common 1¢ par
Each share Class B 5¢ par exchanged for (0.09174311) share Common 1¢ par

Henderson Petroleum Corp. recapitalized as Burkhart Petroleum Corp. 12/31/1985 which merged into ZG Energy Corp. (DE) 06/29/1987 which reorganized in Oklahoma as Vantage Point Energy, Inc. 04/30/1990
(See Vantage Point Energy, Inc.)

CREST RES LTD (BC)
Recapitalized as Sentinel Resources Ltd. (BC) 03/24/1992
Each share Common no par exchanged for (0.33333333) share Common no par
Sentinel Resources Ltd. (BC) reincorporated in Bahamas as Ulysses International Resources Ltd. 08/30/1995 which recapitalized as Auric Resources Ltd. (Bahamas) 03/05/1999 which reorganized in Yukon as Lalo Ventures Ltd. 11/02/2001 which reincorporated in British Columbia 07/29/2005 which name changed to Sunrise Minerals Inc. 12/20/2005 which recapitalized as Cronus Resources Ltd. (BC) 03/10/2008 which reincorporated in Ontario 06/25/2009 which merged into Continental Gold Ltd. (New) (Bermuda) 03/30/2010 which reorganized in Ontario as Continental Gold Inc. 06/12/2015

CREST ULTRASONICS CORP (NJ)
Common no par split (5) for (4) by issuance of (0.25) additional share 02/28/1979
Name changed to Crestek, Inc. (NJ) 01/23/1980
Crestek, Inc. (NJ) reincorporated in Delaware as IMM Energy Services & Technology, Inc. 08/03/1981 which recapitalized as Crestek, Inc. (DE) 12/24/1984
(See Crestek, Inc. (DE))

CREST VENTURES LTD (BC)
Recapitalized as VanSea Resources Ltd. 06/12/1974
Each share Common $1 par exchanged for (0.33333333) share Common no par
(See VanSea Resources Ltd.)

CRESTA BLANCA WINE CO.
Liquidated 00/00/1941
Details not available

CRESTAR ENERGY INC (CANADA)
Acquired by Gulf Canada Resources Ltd. 11/13/2000
Each share Common no par exchanged for (3.33333333) shares Ordinary no par and $3.25 cash
(See Gulf Canada Resources Ltd.)

CRESTAR FINL CORP (VA)
$2.75 Conv. Preferred Ser. A $25 par called for redemption 07/10/1989
Adjustable Rate Preferred $25 par called for redemption 12/23/1993
Common $5 par split (2) for (1) by issuance of (1) additional share payable 01/24/1997 to holders of record 01/03/1997 Ex date - 01/27/1997
Merged into SunTrust Banks, Inc. 12/31/1998
Each share Common $5 par exchanged for (0.96) share Common $1 par

CRESTAURUM MINES, LTD. (ON)
Name changed to United Comstock Lode Mines Ltd. 03/18/1964
(See United Comstock Lode Mines Ltd.)

CRESTBROOK FOREST INDS LTD (BC)
Common no par split (3) for (1) by issuance of (2) additional shares 05/10/1984
Merged into Tembec Inc. (QC) 04/01/1999
Each share Common no par exchanged for (0.51298) share Class A Common no par and (1)

Contingent Value Right or $4.50 cash
Tembec Inc. (QC) reorganized in Canada 02/29/2008 which merged into Rayonier Advanced Materials Inc. 11/21/2017

CRESTBROOK TIMBER LTD. (BC)
Recapitalized 12/31/1963
Each share 5.5% Preferred $50 par exchanged for $65 principal amount of 6.5% Sinking Fund Debentures
Under plan of merger Common no par certificates stamped Amalgamated Company 1965 share for share 06/30/1965
Name changed to Crestbrook Forest Industries Ltd. 05/01/1967
Crestbrook Forest Industries Ltd. merged into Tembec Inc. (QC) 04/01/1999 which reorganized in Canada 02/29/2008 which merged into Rayonier Advanced Materials Inc. 11/21/2017

CRESTED CORP (CO)
Name changed 08/09/1984
Name changed from Crested Butte Silver Mining, Inc. to Crested Corp. 08/09/1984
Merged into U.S. Energy Corp. 11/27/2007
Each share Common $0.001 par exchanged for (0.5) share Common 1¢ par

CRESTEK INC (NJ)
Common no par split (6) for (5) by issuance of (0.2) additional share 02/19/1980
Common no par split (4) for (3) by issuance of (1/3) additional share 01/29/1981
Reincorporated under the laws of Delaware as IMM Energy Services & Technology, Inc. 08/03/1981
IMM Energy Services & Technology, Inc. recapitalized as Crestek, Inc. (DE) 12/24/1984
(See Crestek, Inc. (DE))

CRESTEK INC NEW (DE)
SEC revoked common stock registration 01/03/2013

CRESTLAND MINES LTD (ON)
Merged into PYX Explorations Ltd. 07/30/1976
Each share Capital Stock $1 par exchanged for (0.06666666) share Capital Stock no par
PYX Explorations Ltd. merged into Discovery Mines Ltd. (Canada) 01/15/1982
(See Discovery Mines Ltd. (Canada))

CRESTLINE CAP CORP (DE)
Each share old Common 1¢ par exchanged for (1) share new Common 1¢ par to reflect a (1) for (100) reverse split followed by a (100) for (1) forward split 06/23/2000
Note: Holders of (99) or fewer pre-split shares received $19.1375 cash per share
Merged into Barcelo Gestion Hotelera, S.L. 06/07/2002
Each share new Common 1¢ par exchanged for $34 cash

CRESTLINE INC (CO)
Recapitalized as JRS Foods, Inc. (CO) 03/05/1990
Each share Common $0.0001 par exchanged for (0.00714285) share Common $0.0001 par
JRS Foods, Inc. (CO) reincorporated in Delaware as Southwest Food Products Inc. 02/04/1991

CRESTLINE INDS INC (UT)
Name changed to Gaensel Mining Industries, Inc. 06/19/1978
Gaensel Mining Industries, Inc. name changed to Gaensel Mining & Energy, Inc. 12/15/1987

CRESTLINE INVESTMENT CO. (NC)
Liquidation completed

CRESTMONT
Each share Common $1 par received initial distribution of $4.50 cash 12/02/1982
Each share Common $1 par received second and final distribution of $29.07 cash 03/07/1983
Note: Certificates were not required to be surrendered and are without value

CRESTLINE URANIUM & MNG CO (UT)
Name changed to Crestline Industries, Inc. 11/01/1969
Crestline Industries, Inc. name changed to Gaensel Mining Industries, Inc. 06/19/1978 which name changed to Gaensel Mining & Energy, Inc. 12/15/1987

CRESTMONT CONSOLIDATED CORP. (CA)
Name changed to Crestmont Oil & Gas Co. 07/09/1964
(See Crestmont Oil & Gas Co.)

CRESTMONT FED SVGS & LN ASSN SPRINGFIELD N J (USA)
Stock Dividend - 10% 06/30/1989
Under plan of reorganization each share Common $1 par automatically became (1) share Crestmont Financial Corp. Common $1 par 03/08/1991
Crestmont Financial Corp. merged into merged into Summit Bancorp 03/01/1996 which Summit Bancorporation 09/13/1994 which merged into FleetBoston Financial Corp. 03/01/2001 which merged into Bank of America Corp. 04/01/2004

CRESTMONT FINL CORP (NJ)
Merged into Summit Bancorporation 9/13/94
Each share Common $1 par exchanged for (1.059) shares Common no par
Summit Bancorporation merged into Summit Bancorp 3/1/96 which merged into FleetBoston Financial Corp. 3/1/2001 which merged into Bank of America Corp. 4/1/2004

CRESTMONT OIL & GAS CO (CA)
Common $1 par split (5) for (4) by issuance of (0.25) additional share 06/10/1977
Common $1 par split (2) for (1) by issuance of (1) additional share 06/05/1979
Merged into Occidental Petroleum Corp. 02/27/1981
Each share Common $1 par exchanged for $24 cash

CRESTMONT OIL CO. (CA)
Stock Dividend - 25% 04/29/1960
Name changed to Crestmont Consolidated Corp. 09/09/1960
Crestmont Consolidated Corp. name changed to Crestmont Oil & Gas Co. 07/09/1964
(See Crestmont Oil & Gas Co.)

CRESTON GOLD MINES LTD.
Name changed to Rossland Mines Ltd. 00/00/1947
Rossland Mines Ltd. recapitalized as Rossland Mining Co. Ltd. 00/00/1952 which recapitalized as Ross Island Mining Co. Ltd. 06/29/1972
(See Ross Island Mining Co. Ltd.)

CRESTON MINING & INVESTMENT CO. (IA)
Charter expired by time limitation 07/15/1919

CRESTON MOLY CORP (BC)
Merged into Mercator Minerals Ltd. 06/21/2011
Each share Common no par exchanged for (0.15) share Common no par and $0.08 cash
Note: Unexchanged certificates were cancelled and became without value 06/21/2017

CRESTON MUTUAL TELEPHONE CO. (IA)
Dissolved 09/24/1968
Details not available

CRESTON TECHNOLOGY INC (FL)
Name changed to EnerGcorp, Inc. 07/19/1990
(See EnerGcorp, Inc.)

CRESTONE CO. (MI)
Charter revoked for failure to file reports and pay fees 05/15/1962

CRESTSTREET PWR & INCOME FD (ON)
Acquired by Aquilo LP, ULC 07/10/2008
Each Limited Partnership Unit received $6.915 cash

CRESTSTREET 2008 LTD PARTNERSHIP (ON)
Under plan of merger each Unit of Ltd. Partnership automatically became (2.52496603) shares Creststreet Mutual Funds Ltd. Resource Fund Class A 05/28/2010

CRESTSTREET 2007 LTD PARTNERSHIP (ON)
Under plan of merger each Unit of Ltd. Partnership automatically became (0.08974819) share Creststreet Energy Opportunities Fund Ser. 2010 FE 05/31/2010

CRESTVIEW PETE CORP (AB)
Merged into Cube Energy Corp. 04/01/1995
Each share Common no par exchanged for (0.03333333) share Common no par
(See Cube Energy Corp.)

CRESTWELL RES INC (BC)
Recapitalized as Organic Garage Ltd. 10/24/2016
Each share Common no par exchanged for (0.25) share Common no par

CRESTWOOD BANK SHARES CORP. (MO)
Merged into Metro Bancholding Corp. 09/02/1980
Each share Common $1 par exchanged for (1.6) shares Common $1 par
(See Metro Bancholding Corp.)

CRESTWOOD KITCHENS LTD (BC)
Acquired by K.G.R. Holdings Ltd. 11/30/1976
Each share Common no par exchanged for $2.65 cash

CRESTWOOD METRO BANK (CRESTWOOD, MO)
Reorganized as Metro Bancholding Corp. 09/02/1980
Each share Capital Stock $10 par exchanged for (1) share Common $1 par
(See Metro Bancholding Corp.)

CRESTWOOD MIDSTREAM PARTNERS LP NEW (DE)
Merged into Crestwood Equity Partners L.P. 09/30/2015
Each Unit of Ltd. Partnership Int. exchanged for (2.75) Units of Ltd. Partnership Int.

CRESTWOOD MIDSTREAM PARTNERS LP OLD (DE)
Merged into Crestwood Midstream Partners L.P. (New) 10/08/2013
Each Common Unit exchanged for (1.07) Common Units and $1.03 cash
Crestwood Midstream Partners L.P. (New) merged into Crestwood Equity Partners L.P. 09/30/2015

CRESWEL MINES LTD (ON)
Recapitalized as Newcrest Developments Ltd. 01/16/1973
Each share Capital Stock $1 par exchanged for (0.2) share Capital Stock no par
(See Newcrest Developments Ltd.)

CREW B O S PRODS LTD (INDIA)
GDR agreement terminated 08/15/2014
No GDR's remain outstanding

CREW DEV CORP (YT)
Reincorporated 01/26/2000
Place of incorporation changed from (BC) to (YT) 01/26/2000
Each share Common no par received distribution of (0.05) share North Pacific GeoPower Corp. Common no par payable 12/21/2001 to holders of record 11/28/2001
Name changed to Crew Gold Corp. 01/26/2004
(See Crew Gold Corp.)

CREW GOLD CORP (YT)
Each share old Common no par exchanged for (0.125) share new Common no par 02/23/2009
Each share new Common no par exchanged again for (0.05) share new Common no par 08/05/2010
Merged into OAO Severstal 01/18/2011
Each share new Common no par exchanged for USD $4.65 cash

CREW LEVICK CO.
Merged into Cities Service Oil Co. 00/00/1936
Details not available

CREW MINERALS INC (BC)
Name changed to Asia-Pacific Resources Ltd. 04/20/1988
Each share Common no par exchanged for (1) share Common no par
Asia-Pacific Resources Ltd. name changed to Asia Pacific Resources Ltd. 09/22/1995
(See Asia Pacific Resources Ltd.)

CREW NAT RES LTD (BC)
Recapitalized as South Crofty Holdings Ltd. 10/05/1994
Each share Common no par exchanged for (0.5) share Common no par
South Crofty Holdings Ltd. name changed to North Pacific GeoPower Corp. 12/05/2001 which recapitalized as Western GeoPower Corp. 10/09/2003 which merged into Ram Power, Corp. 10/20/2009 which recapitalized as Polaris Infrastructure Inc. 05/19/2015

CREX CARPET CO.
Out of existence 00/00/1937
Details not available

CREXENDO INC (DE)
Reincorporated under the laws of Nevada 12/13/2016

CREXUS INVT CORP (MD)
Acquired by Annaly Capital Management, Inc. 05/23/2013
Each share Common 1¢ par exchanged for $13 cash

CRF CORP. (IL)
Liquidation completed 11/26/1958
Details not available

CRI INSD MTG ASSN INC (DE)
Reincorporated under the laws of Maryland as CRIIMI MAE Inc. 07/01/1993
(See CRIIMI MAE Inc.)

CRI INSD MTG INVTS II INC (DE)
Under plan of merger each share Common 1¢ exchanged for (1.107) shares CRI Insured Mortgage Association, Inc. Common 1¢ par or (1.107) shares CRI Liquidating REIT, Inc. Common 1¢ par 11/27/1989
(See each company's listing)

CRI INSD MTG INVTS LTD PARTNERSHIP (MD)
Merged into CRI Liquidating REIT, Inc. 11/27/1989
Each Beneficial Assignee Certificate no par exchanged for (1.0094) shares CRI Insured Mortgage Association, Inc. Common no par or (1.0094) shares CRI Liquidating REIT, Inc. Common no par
(See each company's listing)

CRI LIQUIDATING REIT INC (MD)
Reincorporated 07/01/1993
State of incorporation changed from (DE) to (MD) 07/01/1993
Completely liquidated 12/29/1997
Each share Common 1¢ par exchanged for first and final distribution of $0.164 cash

CRIBBEN & SEXTON CO (IL)
4-1/2% Preferred $25 par called for redemption 03/23/1964
Acquired by Waste King Corp. 03/31/1964
Each share Common $5 par exchanged for (0.5) share Common $1 par and $6.25 cash
(See Waste King Corp.)

CRICKET CAP CORP (BC)
Name changed to Cricket Resources Inc. 07/13/2016
Cricket Resources Inc. recapitalized as Eastern Zinc Corp. 07/17/2017

CRICKET MEDIA GROUP LTD (ON)
Acquired by Cricket Acquisition Group, Ltd. 05/12/2016
Each share Preferred Ser. A no par exchanged for $0.14 cash
Each share Common no par exchanged for $0.14 cash
Note: Unexchanged certificates will be cancelled and become without value 05/12/2022

CRICKET RES INC (BC)
Recapitalized as Eastern Zinc Corp. 07/17/2017
Each share Common no par exchanged for (0.1) share Common no pa

CRIIMI MAE INC (MD)
Each share old Common 1¢ par received distribution of (0.03) share Preferred Ser. F 1¢ par payable 11/05/1999 to holders of record 10/20/1999 Ex date - 11/03/1999
Each share old Common 1¢ par received distribution of (0.06) share Preferred Ser. G 1¢ par payable 11/13/2000 to holders of record 10/27/2000 Ex date - 11/14/2000
Each share 10.875% Conv. Preferred Ser. B 1¢ par received distribution of (0.7452) share Common 1¢ par payable 06/01/2001 to holders of record 05/21/2001
Each share old Common 1¢ par exchanged for (0.1) share new Common 1¢ par 10/17/2001
Preferred Ser. F 1¢ par called for redemption at $10 plus $0.30 accrued dividends on 04/28/2004
Preferred Ser. G 1¢ par called for redemption at $10 plus $0.375 accrued dividends on 04/28/2004
Merged into CDP Capital Financing Inc. 01/18/2006
Each share new Common 1¢ par exchanged for $20 cash
10.875% Conv. Preferred Ser. B 1¢ par called for redemption at $25 plus $0.68 accrued dividends on 09/29/2006
Public interest eliminated

CRIME CTL INC (IN)
Common no par changed to $1 par 05/10/1983
Liquidation completed
Each share Common $1 par exchanged for initial distribution of $0.537 cash 08/07/1987

Assets transferred to CCI Liquidating Corp. 08/08/1987
(See CCI Liquidating Corp.)

CRIMSON EXPL INC (DE)
Each share old Common $0.001 par exchanged for (0.1) share new Common $0.001 par 09/18/2006
Merged into Contango Oil & Gas Co. 10/02/2013
Each share new Common $0.001 par exchanged for (0.08288) share Common 4¢ par

CRIMSON FALCON CAP CORP (BC)
Name changed to Crimson Bioenergy Ltd. 10/20/2011

CRIMSON TIDE RES LTD (BC)
Name changed to H.E.R.O. Industries Ltd. (BC) 12/22/1986
H.E.R.O. Industries Ltd. (BC) reincorporated in Ontario as Middlefield Bancorp Ltd. 04/25/1997 which merged into Middlefield Tactical Energy Corp. 02/23/2012 which name changed to MBN Corp. 02/27/2012

CRIMSONSTAR MNG CORP (CANADA)
Recapitalized as Mountain View Ventures Inc. 05/21/1993
Each share Common no par exchanged for (0.2) share Common no par
Mountain View Ventures Inc. recapitalized as Blackrun Ventures Inc. 04/08/1997 which recapitalized as Blackrun Minerals Inc. 06/10/1999 which name changed to Diversified Industries Ltd. 03/29/2000
(See Diversified Industries Ltd.)

CRIMSONSTAR RES LTD (CANADA)
Merged into Crimsonstar Mining Corp. 06/19/1991
Each share Common no par exchanged for (0.5) share Common no par
Crimsonstar Mining Corp. recapitalized as Mountain View Ventures Inc. 05/21/1993 which recapitalized as Blackrun Ventures Inc. 04/08/1997 which recapitalized as Blackrun Minerals Inc. 06/10/1999 which name changed to Diversified Industries Ltd. 03/29/2000
(See Diversified Industries Ltd.)

CRIO GROUP DEVS INC (BC)
Name changed to Tele Pacific International Communications Corp. 10/14/1992
Tele Pacific International Communications Corp. name changed to Pacific AD-Link Corp. 12/17/1997 which name changed to Pacific E-Link Corp. 07/15/1999
(See Pacific E-Link Corp.)

CRIPPLE CREEK CENTRAL RWY. CO.
Dissolved 00/00/1936
Details not available

CRIPPLE CREEK GOLD PRODTN CORP (CO)
Name changed to Hunter Petroleum Corp. 12/14/1982
(See Hunter Petroleum Corp.)

CRIPPLE CREEK HOMESTAKE MINING & REDUCTION CO. (CO)
Charter dissolved for failure to file annual reports 01/01/1919

CRISAN RES LTD (BC)
Recapitalized as Starteck Industries Ltd. 08/15/1994
Each share Common no par exchanged for (0.33333333) share Common no par
Starteck Industries Ltd. recapitalized as International StarTeck Industries Ltd. 09/24/1999
(See International StarTeck Industries Ltd.)

CRISE MANUFACTURING CO. (OH)
Name changed to Acro Manufacturing Co. 00/00/1951
Acro Manufacturing Co. acquired by Robertshaw-Fulton Controls Co. 01/10/1957 which name changed to Robertshaw Controls Co. 04/10/1963
(See Robertshaw Controls Co.)

CRISPIN ENERGY INC (AB)
Acquired by Pengrowth Energy Trust 04/29/2005
Each share Common no par held by Canadian residents exchanged for (0.0725) Class B Trust Unit no par
Each share Common no par held by non-Canadian residents exchanged for (0.0512) Class A Trust Unit no par
Pengrowth Energy Trust reorganized as Pengrowth Energy Corp. 01/03/2011

CRISS CREEK MINES LTD. (BC)
Name changed to Topley Criss Mines Ltd. 11/04/1970
(See Topley Criss Mines Ltd.)

CRISTALERIAS DE CHILE S A (CHILE)
ADR agreement terminated 06/21/2005
Each Sponsored ADR for Common exchanged for $29.32831 cash

CRISTINA COPPER MINES, INC. (DE)
No longer in existence having become inoperative and void for non-payment of taxes 04/01/1956

CRISTOBAL RES INC (QC)
Recapitalized as Netgraphe Inc. 07/13/1999
Each share Common no par exchanged for (0.33333333) share Common no par
(See Netgraphe Inc.)

CRISWELL JACK RES LTD (BC)
Dissolved 03/16/1990
Details not available

CRITERION BUSINESS TR TA FD (ON)
Completely liquidated
Each Unit received first and final distribution of $6.27 cash payable 3/15/2007 to holders of record 3/15/2007

CRITERION DIVERSIFIED COMMODITIES CURRENCY HEDGED FUND (ON)
Name changed to First Asset Diversified Commodities Currency Hedged Fund 06/04/2012
(See First Asset Diversified Commodities Currency Hedged Fund)

CRITERION DOW JONES-AIG COMMODITY INDEX FD (ON)
Name changed to Criterion Diversified Commodities Currency Hedged Fund and Units reclassified as Class E Units 06/05/2006
Criterion Diversified Commodities Currency Hedged Fund name changed to First Asset Diversified Commodities Currency Hedged Fund 06/04/2012
(See First Asset Diversified Commodities Currency Hedged Fund)

CRITERION GLOBAL CLEAN ENERGY FUND (ON)
Merged into Criterion Utility Plus Fund 02/03/2011
Each Class F Unit received (0.5872) Class F Unit
Each Class H Unit received (0.5551) Class A Unit
Each Class P Unit received (0.6547) Class F Unit
Each Class U Unit received (0.6224) Class A Unit
Criterion Utility Plus Fund name changed to First Asset Utility Plus Fund 06/04/2012

CRITERION GLOBAL DIVIDEND FUND (ON)
Name changed to First Asset Global Dividend Fund 06/04/2012

CRITERION GROUP INC (DE)
Merged into Transamerica Corp. 06/16/1989
Each share Class A Common 1¢ par exchanged for $13 cash

CRITERION INS CO (DC)
Stock Dividend - 100% 04/22/1972
Merged into GEICO Corp. 01/25/1980
Each share Common $2 par exchanged for $35 cash

CRITERION REIT INCOME FUND (ON)
Name changed to First Asset REIT Income Fund 06/04/2012

CRITERION SPL SER INC (MD)
Merged into Transamerica Special Series, Inc. 07/03/1989
Details not available

CRITERION UTILITY PLUS FUND (ON)
Name changed to First Asset Utility Plus Fund 06/04/2012

CRITERION VENTURES INC (NV)
Merged into Larson Davis Inc. 11/02/1987
Each share Common $0.001 par exchanged for (0.04) share Common $0.001 par
Larson Davis Inc. recapitalized as Sensar Corp. 05/03/1999 which name changed to VitalStream Holdings, Inc. 07/26/2002 which merged into Internap Network Services Corp. 02/20/2007 which name changed to Internap Corp. 12/04/2014

CRITERION WATER INFRASTRUCTURE FUND (ON)
Merged into Criterion Utility Plus Fund 02/03/2011
Each Class A Unit received (0.6320) Class A Unit
Each Class B Unit received (0.6315) Class A Unit
Each Class C Unit received (0.6489) Class A Unit
Each Class D Unit received (0.6553) Class A Unit
Each Class F Unit received (0.6839) Class F Unit
Each Class L Unit received (0.6333) Class A Unit
Each Class M Unit received (0.6332) Class A Unit
Each Class N Unit received (0.6483) Class A Unit
Each Class O Unit received (0.6536) Class A Unit
Each Class P Unit received (0.6833) Class F Unit
Criterion Utility Plus Fund name changed to First Asset Utility Plus Fund 06/04/2012

CRITIC CLOTHING INC (WY)
Recapitalized as Deep Green Waste & Recycling, Inc. 09/27/2017
Each share Common $0.001 par exchanged for (0.001) share Common $0.001 par

CRITICAL CAP CORP (BC)
Name changed to Castle Peak Mining Ltd. 03/09/2011

CRITICAL CARE AMER INC (DE)
Merged into Medical Care America, Inc. 09/09/1992
Each share Common 10¢ par exchanged for (0.72) share Common 1¢ par
Medical Care America, Inc. merged into Columbia/HCA Healthcare Corp. 09/16/1994 which name changed to HCA - The Healthcare Co. 05/25/2000 which name changed to HCA Inc. (Ctfs. dated after 06/29/2001) 06/29/2001
(See HCA Inc. (Ctfs. dated after 6/29/2001))

CRITICAL CARE INC (NV)
Each share old Common $0.001 par exchanged for (0.01666666) share new Common $0.001 par 11/30/2006
Name changed to Cost Containment Technologies, Inc. 03/21/2007
Cost Containment Technologies, Inc. recapitalized as American Diversified Holdings Corp. 10/16/2007

CRITICAL DIGITAL DATA INC (NV)
Name changed to Solar Park Initiatives, Inc. 08/25/2010

CRITICAL HOME CARE INC (NV)
Common 25¢ par changed to $0.001 par 05/04/2004
Name changed to Arcadia Resources, Inc. 12/01/2004

CRITICAL INDS INC (DE)
Charter cancelled and declared inoperative and void for non-payment of taxes 03/01/2001

CRITICAL OUTCOME TECHNOLOGIES INC (ON)
Each share old Common no par exchanged for (0.1) share new Common no par 06/30/2017
Name changed to Cotinga Pharmaceuticals Inc. 01/10/2018

CRITICAL PATH INC (CA)
Each share old Common $0.001 par exchanged for (0.25) share new Common $0.001 par 08/01/2003
Merged into CP Holdco, LLC 04/30/2008
Each share old 5.75% Conv. Ser. E Preferred $0.001 par exchanged for (0.00001428) share new 5.75% Conv. Ser. E Preferred $0.001 par
Note: Holders (69,999) or fewer pre-split shares received $0.123945 cash per share
Each share Common $0.001 par exchanged for $0.102 cash and (1) Contingent Litigation Recovery Right

CRITICAL PWR SOLUTIONS INTL INC (FL)
Reincorporated under the laws of Delaware as Critical Solutions, Inc. and Common no par changed to 1¢ par 03/03/2008

CRITICAL PT RES INC (NV)
Each share old Common $0.001 par exchanged for (0.2) share new Common $0.001 par 06/26/2008
Note: Holders of between (100) and (499) shares received (100) shares
Holders of (99) shares or fewer were not affected
Each share new Common $0.001 par exchanged again for (0.05) share new Common $0.001 par 12/19/2008
Note: Holders of between (100) and (1,999) shares received (100) shares
Holders of (99) shares or fewer were not affected
Each share new Common $0.001 par exchanged again for (0.125) share new Common $0.001 par 03/10/2011
Reorganized as Renewable Energy Solution Systems, Inc. 02/24/2012
Each share new Common $0.001 par exchanged for (2) shares Common $0.001 par

CRITICAL THERAPEUTICS INC (DE)
Recapitalized as Cornerstone Therapeutics Inc. 11/03/2008
Each share Common $0.001 par exchanged for (0.1) share Common $0.001 par
(See Cornerstone Therapeutics Inc.)

CRITICALCONTROL SOLUTIONS CORP (AB)
Each share old Common no par exchanged for (0.33333333) share new Common no par 02/11/2009
Name changed to Critical Control Energy Services Corp. 07/03/2015

CRITICARE SYS INC (DE)
Merged into Opto Circuits (India) Ltd. 04/11/2008
Each share Common 4¢ par exchanged for $5.50 cash

CRITON CORP (WA)
Common no par split (3) for (2) by issuance of (0.5) additional share 09/18/1980
Each share old Common no par exchanged for (0.00003333) share new Common no par 01/28/1983
Note: In effect holders received $46 cash per share and public interest was eliminated

CRITTENDON APARTMENTS LIQUIDATION TRUST
Liquidation completed 00/00/1950
Details not available

CRM CAP INC (ON)
Recapitalized as Active Control Technology Inc. 04/01/1997
Each share Common no par exchanged for (0.5) share Common no par
(See Active Control Technology Inc.)

CRM HLDGS LTD (BERMUDA)
Name changed to Majestic Capital, Ltd. 05/24/2010

CRMNET COM INC (ON)
Recapitalized as Advanced Explorations Inc. 02/25/2005
Each share Common no par exchanged for (0.33333333) share Common no par
(See Advanced Explorations Inc.)

CROCKER-ANGLO NATIONAL BANK (SAN FRANCISCO, CA)
Stock Dividends - 25% 09/19/1958; 16.66666666% 12/20/1961
Under plan of merger name changed to Crocker-Citizens National Bank (San Francisco, CA) 11/01/1963
Crocker-Citizens National Bank (San Francisco, CA) reorganized in Delaware as Crocker National Corp. 04/21/1969
(See Crocker National Corp.)

CROCKER BURBANK & CO. ASSN. (MA)
Acquired by Weyerhaeuser Co. 07/02/1962
Each Receipt Ctf. exchanged for (10.5) shares Common $7.50 par

CROCKER CTZNS NATL BK (SAN FRANCISCO, CA)
Stock Dividend - 10% 03/24/1967
Under plan of reorganization each share Common Capital Stock $10 par automatically became (1) share Crocker National Corp. Common $10 par 04/21/1969
(See Crocker National Corp.)

CROCKER ESTATE CO. (CA)
Acquired by Foremost-McKesson, Inc. 10/26/1970
Details not available

CROCKER FIRST NATIONAL BANK (SAN FRANCISCO, CA)
Each share Capital Stock $100 par exchanged for (4) shares Capital Stock $25 par 00/00/1949
Stock Dividend - 33.33333333% 07/03/1953
Merged into Crocker-Anglo National Bank (San Francisco, CA) 02/10/1956
Each share Capital Stock $25 par exchanged for (3.6) shares Common Capital Stock $10 par
Crocker-Anglo National Bank (San Francisco, CA) merged into Crocker-Citizens National Bank (San Francisco, CA) 11/01/1963 which reorganized in Delaware as Crocker National Corp. 04/21/1969
(See Crocker National Corp.)

CROCKER-MC ELWAIN CO. (MA)
Name changed to Chemical Paper Manufacturing Corp. 06/17/1957

CROCKER NATL CORP (DE)
Each share Common 10¢ par exchanged for (0.54) share Adjustable Rate Preferred no par 05/24/1985
$2.1875 Conv. Preferred no par called for redemption 04/24/1986
$3 Conv. Preferred no par called for redemption 04/24/1986
Adjustable Rate Preferred no par called for redemption 05/29/1986
Public interest eliminated

CROCKER RLTY INVS INC (FL)
Merged into Crocker Realty Trust, Inc. 06/30/1995
Each share Common $0.001 par exchanged for (1) share Common 1¢ par
(See Crocker Realty Trust, Inc.)

CROCKER RLTY TR INC (FL)
Merged into Highwoods Properties, Inc. 09/20/1996
Each share Common $0.001 par exchanged for $11.05243 cash

CROCKER-WHEELER ELECTRIC MANUFACTURING CO.
Name changed to C. W. Liquidating Co. 12/29/1942
(See C. W. Liquidating Co.)

CROCODILE GOLD CORP (ON)
Reincorporated 12/04/2009
Place of incorporation changed from (YT) to (ON) 12/04/2009
Merged into Newmarket Gold Inc. (ON) 07/14/2015
Each share Common no par exchanged for (0.2456) share Common no par
Note: Unexchanged certificates will be cancelled and become without value 07/14/2021
Newmarket Gold Inc. recapitalized as Kirkland Lake Gold Ltd. 12/06/2016

CROCOTTA ENERGY INC (AB)
Each share old Common no par exchanged for (0.33333333) share new Common no par 10/15/2007
Merged into Long Run Exploration Ltd. 08/11/2014
Each share new Common no par exchanged for (0.415) share Common no par, (1) share Leucrotta Exploration Inc. Common no par and (0.2) Common Stock Purchase Warrant expiring 09/00/2014
(See each company's listing)
Note: Unexchanged certificates were cancelled and became without value 08/11/2017

CROE INC (UT)
Reincorporated under the laws of Nevada as Crypto Co. 10/25/2017

CROESUS GOLD INC (BC)
Reincorporated 11/17/2006
Common no par split (2) for (1) by issuance of (1) additional share payable 06/26/2006 to holders of record 06/23/2006 Ex date - 06/22/2006
Place of incorporation changed from (ON) to (BC) 11/17/2006
Name changed to Kenieba Goldfields Ltd. 06/23/2008
Kenieba Goldfields Ltd. name changed to EA Education Group Inc. (BC) 02/20/2015 which reincorporated in Canada 08/17/2015

CROESUS GOLD MINING & MILLING CO. (WV)
Voluntarily dissolved 11/30/1948
Details not available

CROESUS INDS INC (MA)
Proclaimed dissolved for failure to file reports and pay fees 08/31/1998

CROESUS RES INC (BC)
Recapitalized as International Croesus Ventures Corp. 11/10/1995
Each share Common no par exchanged for (0.25) share Common no par
International Croesus Ventures Corp. name changed to Zinco Mining Corp. 01/29/2007

CROFF ENTERPRISES INC (UT)
Common 10¢ par split (3) for (1) by issuance of (2) additional shares payable 07/24/2009 to holders of record 07/23/2009 Ex date - 07/27/2009
Name changed to AMHN, Inc. (UT) 09/29/2009
AMHN, Inc. (UT) reincorporated in Nevada 07/20/2010 which recapitalized as TherapeuticsMD, Inc. 10/03/2011

CROFF OIL CO (UT)
Name changed 00/00/1952
Name changed from Croff Mining Co. to Croff Oil Co. 00/00/1952
Each share old Common 10¢ par exchanged for (0.1) share new Common 10¢ par 11/01/1991
Name changed to Croff Enterprises, Inc. 02/28/1996
Croff Enterprises, Inc. name changed to AMHN, Inc. (UT) 09/29/2009 which reincorporated in Nevada 07/20/2010 which recapitalized as TherapeuticsMD, Inc. 10/03/2011

CROFT & ALLEN CORP.
Bankrupt 00/00/1930
Assets purchased by Bondholders' Committee

CROFT BREWING CO.
Name changed to Croft Co. 00/00/1952
Croft Co. merged into C & C Super Corp. 04/29/1954 which name changed to C & C Television Corp. 08/05/1957 which recapitalized as Television Industries, Inc. 06/18/1958 which name changed to Trans-Beacon Corp. 05/05/1966
(See Trans-Beacon Corp.)

CROFT CARPET MILLS, INC. (TN)
Name changed to Bemporad Carpet Mills, Inc. 12/18/1962
(See Bemporad Carpet Mills, Inc.)

CROFT CO. (DE)
Merged into C & C Super Corp. 04/29/1954
Each share Capital Stock $1 par exchanged for (0.33333333) share Common 10¢ par
C & C Super Corp. name changed to C & C Television Corp. 08/05/1957 which recapitalized as Television Industries, Inc. 06/18/1958 which name changed to Trans-Beacon Corp. 05/05/1966
(See Trans-Beacon Corp.)

CROFT URANIUM MINES LTD. (ON)
Merged into Bicroft Uranium Mines Ltd. 05/02/1955
Each share Capital Stock $1 par exchanged for (0.33333333) share Capital Stock $1 par
Bicroft Uranium Mines Ltd. merged into Macassa Gold Mines Ltd. 11/01/1961 which merged into Willroy Mines Ltd. 01/08/1971 which merged into Lac Minerals Ltd. (Old) 12/31/1982 which merged into LAC Minerals Ltd. (New) 07/29/1985 which was acquired by American Barrick Resources Corp. 10/17/1994 which name changed to Barrick Gold Corp. 01/18/1995

CROGHAN COLONIAL BK (FREMONT, OH)
Capital Stock $50 par changed to $25 par and (1) additional share issued plus a 50% stock dividend paid 12/01/1965
Capital Stock $25 par changed to $12.50 par and (1) additional share issued 04/01/1972
Stock Dividends - 33.33333333% 04/01/1956; 10% 07/10/1971; 20% 03/22/1974; 10% 03/24/1976; 10% 04/03/1978; 10% 04/01/1980; 20% 04/01/1982
Reorganized as Croghan Bancshares, Inc. 06/30/1984
Each share Capital Stock $12.50 par exchanged for (1) share Common $12.50 par

CROINOR PERSHING MINES LTD (QC)
Declared dissolved for failure to file reports or pay fees 07/22/1972

CROMPTON & KNOWLES CORP (MA)
Common no par split (2) for (1) by issuance of (1) additional share 05/19/1960
Common no par changed to $5 par and (1) additional share issued 04/15/1966
Common $5 par split (3) for (2) by issuance of (0.5) additional share 06/04/1981
Common $5 par changed to $1 par and (1) additional share issued 05/29/1987
Common $1 par split (2) for (1) by issuance of (1) additional share 06/16/1989
Common $1 par changed to 10¢ par 04/10/1990
Common 10¢ par split (2) for (1) by issuance of (1) additional share 08/23/1990
Common 10¢ par split (2) for (1) by issuance of (1) additional share 05/22/1992
Under plan of merger name changed to CK Witco Corp. and Common 10¢ par changed to 1¢ par 09/01/1999
CK Witco Corp. name changed to Crompton Corp. 04/27/2000 which name changed to Chemtura Corp. 07/01/2005
(See Chemtura Corp.)

CROMPTON & KNOWLES LOOM WORKS (MA)
Each share Common $100 par exchanged for (4) shares Common no par 00/00/1926
Stock Dividend - 100% 11/21/1950
Name changed to Crompton & Knowles Corp. 00/00/1956
Crompton & Knowles Corp. name changed to CK Witco Corp. 09/01/1999 which name changed to Crompton Corp. 04/27/2000 which name changed to Chemtura Corp. 07/01/2005
(See Chemtura Corp.)

CROMPTON CORP (DE)
Under plan of merger name changed to Chemtura Corp. 07/01/2005
(See Chemtura Corp.)

CROMPTON GREAVES LTD (INDIA)
Basis changed from (1:1) to (1:5) 08/21/2006
Reg. S GDR's for Ordinary split (7) for (5) by issuance of (0.4) additional GDR payable 01/04/2007 to holders of record 12/14/2006
Reg. S GDR's for Ordinary split (7) for (4) by issuance of (0.75) additional GDR payable 03/23/2010 to holders of record 03/08/2010 Ex date - 03/24/2010
Each Reg. S GDR for Ordinary received distribution of $5.656207 cash payable 06/20/2016 to holders of record 06/13/2016
Each 144A GDR for Ordinary received distribution of $5.656207 cash payable 06/20/2016 to holders of record 06/13/2016

Name changed to CG Power & Industrial Solutions Ltd. 03/17/2017

CROMPTON INC (DE)
Common no par split (2) for (1) by issuance of (1) additional share 02/25/1966
Common no par split (2) for (1) by issuance of (1) additional share 06/24/1971
Plan of reorganization under Chapter 11 Federal Bankruptcy proceedings confirmed 09/15/1988
No stockholders' equity

CROMWELL RES LTD (ON)
Delisted from NEX 12/18/2011

CROMWELL URANIUM & DEVELOPMENT CO., INC. (DE)
Charter cancelled and declared inoperative and void for non-payment of taxes 05/24/1956

CROMWELL URANIUM CORP (NV)
Common $0.001 par split (6.35) for (1) by issuance of (5.35) additional shares payable 07/05/2007 to holders of record 06/29/2007
Ex date - 07/06/2007
Name changed to US Uranium Inc. 08/24/2007
US Uranium Inc. name changed to California Gold Corp. 03/30/2009 which recapitalized as MV Portfolios, Inc. 09/08/2014

CRONAN MOTOR LODGES LTD. (CANADA)
Name changed to Orangeroof Canada Ltd. 06/03/1969
(See Orangeroof Canada Ltd.)

CRONEX SCIENTIFIC INC (DE)
Charter cancelled and declared inoperative and void for non-payment of taxes 3/1/88

CRONIN BABINE MINES LTD. (ON)
Recapitalized as New Cronin Babine Mines Ltd. 00/00/1957
Each share Capital Stock $1 par exchanged for (0.2) share Capital Stock $1 par
New Cronin Babine Mines Ltd. recapitalized as Sproatt Silver Mines Ltd. 06/26/1973 which recapitalized as Hecate Gold Corp. 07/06/1977 which merged into Host Ventures Ltd. 06/29/1982 which recapitalized as Hot Resources Ltd. 04/30/1984 which name changed to Inter-Globe Resources Ltd. 04/16/1985
(See Inter-Globe Resources Ltd.)

CRONOS GROUP (LUXEMBOURG)
Completely liquidated 08/01/2007
Each share Common $2 par exchanged for first and final distribution of $16 cash

CRONUS CORP (NV)
SEC revoked common stock registration 06/07/2010

CRONUS INDS INC (DE)
Name changed to Business Records Corp. Holding Co. 05/16/1990
Business Records Corp. Holding Co. name changed to BRC Holdings Inc. 05/16/1996
(See BRC Holdings Inc.)

CRONUS RES LTD (ON)
Reincorporated 06/25/2009
Place of incorporation changed from (BC) to (ON) 06/25/2009
Merged into Continental Gold Ltd. (New) (Bermuda) 03/30/2010
Each share Common no par exchanged for (0.42424653) share Common $0.0001 par
Continental Gold Ltd. (New) (Bermuda) reorganized in Ontario as Continental Gold Inc. 06/12/2015

CROOK (J.W.) STORES CO.
Assets sold to American Stores Co. (Old) 00/00/1932
Details not available

CROP GENETICS INTL CORP (DE)
Merged into Biosys Inc. 3/31/95
Each share $0.95 Conv. Exchangeable Preferred 10¢ par exchanged for (0.6723) share Common $0.001 par
Each share Common 10¢ par exchanged for (0.1905) share Common $0.001 par
(See Biosys Inc.)

CROP GROWERS CORP (DE)
Merged into Firemans Fund 08/13/1997
Each share Common 1¢ par exchanged for $10.25 cash

CROSBY PHILIP ASSOC INC (FL)
Common 1¢ par split (2) for (1) by issuance of (1) additional share 8/15/86
Merged into Proudfoot Acquisition Subsidiary, Inc. 4/24/89
Each share Common 1¢ par exchanged for $9.50 cash

CROSBY-TELETRONICS CORP. (NY)
Bankrupt in 1963
No stockholders' equity

CROSCOURT GOLD MINES, LTD. (ON)
Charter cancelled and dissolved 4/11/55
No stockholders' equity

CROSE-UNITED CORP. (OK)
Each share Common 25¢ par exchanged for (0.2) share Common $1.25 par 4/22/64
Recapitalized as CRC-Crose International, Inc. 6/1/66
Each share Common $1.25 par exchanged for (0.1) share Common $12.50 par
CRC-Crose International, Inc. merged into AIC Corp. 4/23/68 which name changed to Crutcher Resources Corp. 12/31/68
(See Crutcher Resources Corp.)

CROSLEY CORP.
Acquired by Aviation Corp. 11/30/46
Each share Common no par exchanged for (4) shares Common $3 par
Aviation Corp. name changed to Avco Manufacturing Corp. 3/25/47 which name changed to Avco Corp. 4/10/59
(See Avco Corp.)

CROSLEY MOTORS, INC. (OH)
Common no par changed to $6 par 00/00/1949
Each share Common $6 par exchanged for (0.05) share Common $10 par 00/00/1952
Merged into Aerojet-General Corp. 00/00/1953
Each share Common $10 par exchanged for (1.4) shares Common $10 par
Aerojet-General Corp. merged into General Tire & Rubber Co. 11/10/1972 which name changed to GenCorp. (OH) 03/30/1984 which reincorporated in Delaware 04/14/2014 which name changed to Aerojet Rocketdyne Holdings, Inc. 04/27/2015

CROSLEY RADIO CORP.
Name changed to Crosley Corp. 10/31/38
Crosley Corp. acquired by Aviation Corp. 11/30/46 which name changed to Avco Manufacturing Corp. 3/25/47 which name changed to Avco Corp. 4/10/59
(See Avco Corp.)

CROSS & TRECKER CORP (MI)
Common $1 par split (3) for (2) by issuance of (0.5) additional share 9/6/80
Merged into Giddings & Lewis, Inc. (New) 10/31/91
Each Depositary Receipt exchanged for (1) Depositary Receipt
Each share Conv. Exchangeable Preferred Ser. A $1 par exchanged for (1) share Conv. Sr. Preferred Ser. A 10¢ par
Each share Common $1 par exchanged for (0.2123) share Common 10¢ par
(See Giddings & Lewis, Inc. (New))

CROSS A T CO (RI)
Class A Common $1 par split (2) for (1) by issuance of (1) additional share 06/07/1978
Class A Common $1 par split (2) for (1) by issuance of (1) additional share 06/08/1987
Stock Dividend - 100% 06/03/1982
Name changed to Costa Inc. 09/23/2013
(See Costa Inc.)

CROSS ATLANTIC CAP INC (DE)
Name changed to Elgin E2 Inc. 09/30/1997
Elgin E2 Inc. name changed to Elgin Technologies Inc. 06/16/1998 which name changed to Inicia Inc. 12/05/2008 which name changed to Corporate Universe Inc. 09/21/2010

CROSS ATLANTIC LIFE & SCIENCE TECHNOLOGY INC (TX)
Common $0.001 par split (25) for (1) by issuance of (24) additional shares payable 8/19/2005 to holders of record 8/17/2005 Ex date - 8/22/2005
Name changed to Deep Earth Resources, Inc. 5/5/2006

CROSS BORDER CAP INC (AB)
Merged into Titan Digital Corp. 02/05/2003
Each share Common no par exchanged for (1) share Common no par
(See Titan Digital Corp.)

CROSS CDA INTL INC (ON)
Each share old Common no par exchanged for (0.1) share new Common no par 11/02/1995
Recapitalized as Senator Minerals Inc. (ON) 11/16/1998
Each share new Common no par exchanged for (0.1) share Common no par
Senator Minerals Inc. (ON) reincorporated in British Columbia 09/22/2014

CROSS CANYON ENERGY CORP (NV)
Plan of reorganization under Chapter 11 Federal Bankruptcy Code effective 03/22/2010
Each share Common $0.001 par received distribution of approximately (0.002) share Cross Canyon Energy Corp. (DE) Common $0.001 par
Note: Certificates were not required to be surrendered and are without value
Company is now privately held

CROSS CO (MI)
Common $1 par changed to $5 par and (1) additional share issued 2/15/56
Common $5 par split (2) for (1) by issuance of (1) additional share 2/16/73
Common $5 par split (3) for (2) by issuance of (0.5) additional share 6/15/78
Merged into Cross & Trecker Corp. 2/9/79
Each share Common $5 par exchanged for (2) shares Common $1 par
Cross & Trecker Corp. merged into Giddings & Lewis, Inc. (New) 10/31/91
(See Giddings & Lewis, Inc. (New))

CROSS-CONTINENT AUTO RETAILERS INC (DE)
Merged into Republic Industries Inc. 3/19/99
Each share Common no par exchanged for $10.70 cash

CROSS CORP. (DE)
No longer in existence having become inoperative and void for non-payment of taxes 4/1/51

CROSS CTRY INC (DE)
Issue Information - 7,812,500 shares COM offered at $17 per share on 10/24/2001
Name changed to Cross Country Healthcare, Inc. 5/8/2003

CROSS CTRY INDS INC (NY)
Charter cancelled and proclaimed dissolved for failure to pay taxes 09/26/1979

CROSS GEAR & MACHINE CO.
Name changed to Cross Co. in 1944
Cross Co. merged into Cross & Trecker Corp. 2/9/79 which merged into Giddings & Lewis, Inc. (New) 10/31/91
(See Giddings & Lewis, Inc. (New))

CROSS GENETICS TECHNOLOGIES INC (FL)
Common split (100) for (1) by issuance of (99) additional shares payable 11/20/2002 to holders of record 8/9/2002 Ex date - 11/21/2002
Name changed to Clared Gene Technologies Ltd., Inc. 4/15/2004

CROSS (C.H. & GEO. H.) INC.
Name changed to Cross Baking Co., Inc. in 1941

CROSS IS CORP (DE)
Merged into Golden Brands, Inc. 8/7/69
Each share Common 1¢ par exchanged for (1) share Common 1¢ par
(See Golden Brands, Inc.)

CROSS ISLAND LAND & INDUSTRIES CORP. (NY)
Dissolved 05/03/1965
Details not available

CROSS LAKE MINERALS LTD (BC)
Each share Common no par received distribution of (0.1) share Selkirk Metals Corp. Common no par and (0.025) Common Stock Purchase Warrant expiring 02/28/2006 payable 09/06/2005 to holders of record 08/30/2005
Each share old Common no par exchanged for (0.2) share new Common no par 06/14/2009
Name changed to 0373849 B.C. Ltd. 06/01/2009
(See 0373849 B.C. Ltd.)

CROSS LAKE MINING CO. LTD. (ON)
Charter revoked for failure to file reports and pay taxes 00/00/1958

CROSS MED PRODS INC (DE)
Merged into Interpore International 5/7/98
Each share Common 1¢ par exchanged for (1.275) shares new Common no par
(See Interpore International)

CROSS MEDIA MARKETING CORP (DE)
Each share old Common $0.001 par exchanged for (0.2) share new Common $0.001 par 10/25/2001
Plan of reorganization under Chapter 11 Federal Bankruptcy Code effective 7/23/2004
No stockholders' equity

CROSS-MKT OPPORTUNITY FD INC (MD)
Proclaimed dissolved 03/30/1990

CROSS PAC PEARLS INC (BC)
Struck off register and declared

dissolved for failure to file returns 9/29/95

CROSS TIMBERS OIL CO (DE)
Common 1¢ par split (3) for (2) by issuance of (0.5) additional share payable 03/20/1997 to holders of record 03/12/1997 Ex date - 03/21/1997
Common 1¢ par split (3) for (2) by issuance of (0.5) additional share payable 02/24/1998 to holders of record 02/12/1998 Ex date - 02/25/1998
Common 1¢ par split (3) for (2) by issuance of (0.5) additional share payable 09/18/2000 to holders of record 09/05/2000 Ex date - 09/19/2000
Conv. Preferred Ser. A 1¢ par called for redemption at $25.94 on 02/16/2001
Name changed to XTO Energy Inc. 05/16/2001
XTO Energy Inc. merged into Exxon Mobil Corp. 06/25/2010

CROSS W B LTD (ON)
Reverted to private company in 1975 Details not available

CROSSBOX INC (NV)
Name changed to Flikmedia, Inc. 07/31/2014

CROSSCOMM CORP (DE)
Merged into Olicom A/S 06/12/1997
Each share Common 1¢ par exchanged for (0.2667) share Common DKK 0.25 par, (0.1075) Common Stock Purchase Warrant, and $5 cash
(See Olicom A/S)

CROSSCUT EXPLS INC (ON)
Recapitalized as Renaissance Industrial Corp. 12/19/1984
Each share Common no par exchanged for (0.125) share Common no par
Renaissance Industrial Corp. name changed to D.A.S. Electronics Industries, Inc. 01/29/1988 which recapitalized as Pace Corp. 09/30/1993
(See Pace Corp.)

CROSSETT CO (DE)
Name changed to Independent Business Alliance Inc. 07/27/1990
Independent Business Alliance Inc. name changed to I.C.W. Industries, Inc. 07/28/1991
(See I.C.W. Industries, Inc.)

CROSSFIELD CAP CORP (AB)
Name changed to Royal Laser Corp. 09/12/2005
(See Royal Laser Corp.)

CROSSFIRE ENERGY SVCS INC (AB)
Reported out of business 05/31/2010
Stockholders' equity unlikely

CROSSFIRE HLDGS INC (AB)
Name changed to Crossfire Energy Services Inc. 07/01/2007
(See Crossfire Energy Services Inc.)

CROSSHAIR ENERGY CORP (BC)
Recapitalized as Jet Metal Corp. (BC) 09/23/2013
Each share Common no par exchanged for (0.1) share Common no par
Jet Metal Corp. (BC) reorganized in Canada as Canada Jetlines Ltd. 03/07/2017

CROSSHAIR EXPL & MNG CORP (BC)
Each share old Common no par exchanged for (0.25) share new Common no par 12/20/2010
Name changed to Crosshair Energy Corp. 11/02/2011
Crosshair Energy Corp. recapitalized as Jet Metal Corp. (BC) 09/23/2013

which reorganized in Canada as Canada Jetlines Ltd. 03/07/2017

CROSSKEYS SYS CORP (CANADA)
Merged into Orchestream Holdings PLC 04/11/2001
Each share Common no par exchanged for (0.453) Sponsored ADR for Ordinary 10p par
(See Orchestream Holdings PLC)

CROSSLAND FDG CORP (DE)
Charter cancelled and declared inoperative and void for non-payment of taxes 12/20/1988

CROSSLAND FED SVGS BK (BROOKLYN, NY)
Under plan of reorganization each share Common $1 par automatically became (1) share Brooklyn Bancorp, Inc. Common 1¢ par 04/28/1994
(See Brooklyn Bancorp, Inc.)

CROSSLAND FDG CORP II (DE)
Dutch Auction Rate Transferable Securities Preferred no par called for redemption 11/14/1988

CROSSLAND INDS CORP (BC)
Cease trade order effective 07/23/1987

CROSSLAND N Y FDG CORP (DE)
Dutch Auction Rate Transferable Securities Preferred no par called for redemption 07/10/1989

CROSSLAND N Y FDG CORP II (DE)
Dutch Auction Rate Transferable Securities Preferred no par called for redemption 02/27/1989

CROSSLAND N Y FDG CORP III (DE)
Dutch Auction Rate Transferable Securities Preferred no par called for redemption 04/24/1989

CROSSLAND N Y FDG CORP IV (DE)
Dutch Auction Rate Tranferable Securities Preferred no par called for redemption 06/19/1989

CROSSLAND SVGS FSB OLD (BROOKLYN, NY)
Receivership terminated 01/01/2001
No stockholders' equity

CROSSMANN CMNTYS INC (IN)
Common no par split (3) for (2) by issuance of (0.5) additional share payable 08/25/1997 to holders of record 08/18/1997
Merged into Beazer Homes USA, Inc. 04/17/2002
Each share Common no par exchanged for (0.3544) share Common 1¢ par and $17.60 cash

CROSSNET COMMUNICATIONS INC (CO)
Recapitalized as Cirond Technologies Inc. 07/01/2002
Each share Common no par exchanged for (0.06051505) share Common no par
Cirond Technologies Inc. name changed to Seaside Holdings Inc. 03/17/2003

CROSSOFF INC (NS)
Name changed to Nexient Learning Inc. 06/22/2016
(See Nexient Learning Inc.)

CROSSPOINT ENERGY CO (NV)
Plan of reorganization under Chapter 11 Federal Bankruptcy proceedings effective 02/16/2009
Holders are to receive a pro-rata distribution of shares representing 8% of new company

CROSSPOINT GROUP INC (NV)
Recapitalized as The Employer Inc. 03/08/2007
Each share Common $0.001 par exchanged for (0.002) share Common $0.001 par
The Employer Inc. recapitalized as Vana Blue, Inc. 02/21/2008 which name changed to Osyka Corp. 05/19/2010

CROSSROAD VENTURES INC (BC)
Acquired by Consolidated Goldbank Ventures Ltd. 01/08/2003
Each share Common no par exchanged for (0.66666666) share Common no par
Consolidated Goldbank Ventures Ltd. name changed to NEMI Northern Energy & Mining Inc. (AB) 08/13/2003 which reincorporated in British Columbia 04/15/2010
(See NEMI Northern Energy & Mining Inc.)

CROSSROADS BANCSHARES INC (GA)
Merged into SNB Bancshares Inc. 08/07/1998
Each share Common $10 par exchanged for (2.9) shares Common $1 par
SNB Bancshares Inc. name changed to Security Bank Corp. 06/03/2003
(See Security Bank Corp.)

CROSSROADS CAP INC (MD)
Assets transferred to Crossroads Liquidating Trust and Common $$0.001 par reclassified as Units of Bene. Int. 06/23/2017

CROSSROADS EXPLORATIONS INC (CANADA)
Name changed to New Horizon Uranium Corp. 04/16/2007

CROSSROADS INVTS INC (CO)
Each share old Common no par exchanged for (0.01) share new Common no par 12/22/1988
Recapitalized as Victory Waste Inc. 11/30/1993
Each share new Common no par exchanged for (0.04492161) share Common no par
Victory Waste Inc. name changed to Econometrics, Inc. (CO) 11/21/1997 which reorganized in Delaware 06/20/2008 which name changed to JinZangHuang Tibet Pharmaceuticals, Inc. 02/27/2009
(See JinZangHuang Tibet Pharmaceuticals, Inc.)

CROSSROADS OIL GROUP PLC (UNITED KINGDOM)
Name changed to Melrose Energy PLC 03/03/1995
Melrose Energy PLC name changed to Pentex Energy PLC 05/07/1997
(See Pentex Energy PLC)

CROSSROADS SYS INC OLD (DE)
Each share old Common $0.001 par exchanged for (0.25) share new Common $0.001 par 08/15/2011
Each share new Common $0.001 par exchanged again for (0.05) share new Common $0.001 par 06/20/2016
Under Chapter 11 plan of reorganization each share new Common $0.001 par automatically became (1) share Crossroads Systems, Inc. (New) Common $0.001 par 10/03/2017

CROSSSTREET DISTR INC (WY)
Common $0.001 par split (10) for (1) by issuance of (9) additional shares payable 06/21/2004 to holders of record 06/10/2004 Ex date - 06/22/2004
Recapitalized as Nine Muses Entertainment, Inc. 02/21/2006
Each share Common $0.001 par exchanged for (0.001) share Common $0.001 par
Nine Muses Entertainment, Inc. name changed to Quotezy, Inc. 03/03/2006 which recapitalized as Lord Tech, Inc. 04/23/2008
(See Lord Tech, Inc.)

CROSSTEX ENERGY INC (DE)
Common 1¢ par split (2) for (1) by issuance of (1) additional share payable 03/29/2004 to holders of record 03/16/2004

Common 1¢ par split (3) for (1) by issuance of (2) additional shares payable 12/15/2006 to holders of record 12/01/2006 Ex date - 12/18/2006
Merged into EnLink Midstream, LLC 03/10/2014
Each share Common 1¢ par exchanged for (1) Common Unit and $2.05 cash

CROSSTEX ENERGY L P (DE)
Common Units of Ltd. Partnership Int. split (2) for (1) by issuance of (1) additional Unit payable 03/29/2004 to holders of record 03/16/2004
Name changed to EnLink Midstream Partners, L.P. 03/10/2014

CROSSTOWN ENTERPRISES INC (MN)
Merged into C-E Holdings, Inc. 04/22/1988
Each share Class A Common 1¢ par exchanged for $2.55 cash

CROSSWALK COM INC (DE)
Name changed to AMEN Properties, Inc. 10/09/2002

CROSSWAVE COMMUNICATIONS INC (JAPAN)
Each old ADR for Common exchanged for (0.1) new ADR for Common 02/18/2003
Basis changed from (1:0.005) to (1:0.05) 02/18/2003
ADR agreement terminated 02/27/2004
No ADR holder's equity

CROSSWAY MTR HOTELS INC (DE)
Charter cancelled and declared inoperative and void for non-payment of taxes 04/15/1972

CROSSWIND VENTURE CORP (CA)
Charter cancelled for failure to file reports and pay taxes 11/03/1989

CROSSWORLDS SOFTWARE INC (DE)
Merged into International Business Machines Corp. 01/14/2002
Each share Common $0.001 par exchanged for $4.65 cash

CROSSZ SOFTWARE CORP (DE)
Name changed to QueryObject Systems Corp. 05/27/1998
(See QueryObject Systems Corp.)

CROTON GOLD & SILVER MINING CO. NO. 2 (NY)
Charter cancelled and proclaimed dissolved for failure to pay taxes 05/02/1924

CROUSE HINDS CO (NY)
Common $1.66666666 par split (2) for (1) by issuance of (1) additional share 05/18/1972
Common $1.66666666 par split (4) for (3) by issuance of (0.33333333) additional share 11/01/1977
Common $1.66666666 par split (3) for (2) by issuance of (0.5) additional share 11/23/1979
$3.35 Conv. Preferred no par called for redemption 03/09/1981
Stock Dividends - 100% 04/08/1966; 10% 08/01/1968; 10% 03/19/1976
Merged into Cooper Industries, Inc. (OH) 04/29/1981
Each share Common $1.66666666 par exchanged for (0.75) share Common $5 par and $0.12 cash
Cooper Industries, Inc. (OH) reincorporated in Bermuda as Cooper Industries, Ltd. 05/22/2002 which reincorporated in Ireland as Cooper Industries PLC 09/08/2009 which merged into Eaton Corp. PLC 11/30/2012

CROUTHAMEL INC (DE)
Charter cancelled and declared inoperative and void for non-payment of taxes 03/01/1982

CROW'S NEST PASS COAL CO. LTD. (CANADA)
Each share Capital Stock $100 par exchanged for (10) shares Capital Stock $10 par 07/05/1957
Capital Stock $10 par changed to $8 par and (0.25) additional share issued 02/02/1962
Name changed to Crows Nest Industries, Ltd. 05/11/1965
(See Crows Nest Industries, Ltd.)

CROWBANK MINES LTD (ON)
Recapitalized as Patmore Developments Ltd. 02/14/1974
Each share Capital Stock $1 par exchanged for (0.1) share Capital Stock $1 par
Patmore Developments Ltd. name changed to Patmore Group Ltd. 11/01/1976 which merged into Uranco Inc. 10/23/1980

CROWD 4 SEEDS INC (NV)
Name changed to Sheng Ying Entertainment Corp. 04/25/2017
Sheng Ying Entertainment Corp. reorganized as Vitalibis, Inc. 02/08/2018

CROWD SHS AFTERMARKET INC (NV)
Name changed to AAA Century Group USA, Inc. 12/09/2016

CROWDER COMMUNICATIONS CORP (BC)
Recapitalized as Sigmacom Systems Inc. 08/10/1988
Each share Common no par exchanged for (0.2) share Common no par
(See Sigmacom Systems Inc.)

CROWELL COLLIER & MACMILLAN INC (DE)
Common $1 par split (2) for (1) by issuance of (1) additional share 04/12/1968
Name changed to Macmillan, Inc. 01/01/1973
(See Macmillan, Inc.)

CROWELL-COLLIER PUBLISHING CO. (DE)
Common no par split (2) for (1) by issuance of (1) additional share 00/00/1946
Common no par changed to $5 par 04/11/1955
Common $5 par changed to $1 par 07/26/1955
Name changed to Crowell Collier & Macmillan, Inc. 05/07/1965
Crowell Collier & Macmillan, Inc. name changed to Macmillan, Inc. 01/01/1973
(See Macmillan, Inc.)

CROWELL PUBLISHING CO.
Name changed to Crowell-Collier Publishing Co. 00/00/1939
Crowell-Collier Publishing Co. name changed to Crowell Collier & Macmillan, Inc. 05/07/1965 which name changed to Macmillan, Inc. 01/01/1973
(See Macmillan, Inc.)

CROWFLIGHT MINERALS INC (ON)
Reincorporated 07/31/2003
Place of incorporation changed from (BC) to (ON) 07/31/2003
Reincorporated under the laws of British Columbia as CaNickel Mining Ltd. 06/23/2011

CROWLEY FINL SVCS INC (FL)
Each share old Common 1¢ par exchanged for (0.1) share new Common 1¢ par 03/31/1984
Administratively dissolved 08/23/1996

CROWLEY FOODS INC (NY)
Stock Dividend - 10% 01/07/1980
Merged into Koninklijke Wessanen N.V. 01/06/1983
Each share Common $5 par exchanged for $14 cash

CROWLEY MARITIME CORP (CA)
Class B Preferred called for redemption at $100 on 7/1/2002
Merged into Crowley Newco Corp. 5/9/2007
Each share Common 1¢ par exchanged for $2,990 cash

CROWLEY MILNER & CO (MI)
Common no par changed to $1 par 00/00/1942
Common $1 par split (3) for (2) by issuance of (0.5) additional share 06/28/1968
Common $1 par split (2) for (1) by issuance of (1) additional share 05/25/1994
Plan of reorganization under Chapter 11 Federal Bankruptcy proceedings confirmed 10/15/1999
No stockholders' equity

CROWLEY OIL & MINERAL CO.
Out of business 00/00/1946
Details not available

CROWLEYS MILK INC (NY)
Recapitalized as Crowley Foods, Inc. 02/01/1972
Each share Common $10 par exchanged for (2) shares Common $5 par
(See Crowley Foods, Inc.)

CROWN ALLIANCE CAP LTD (NV)
Common $0.001 par split (5) for (1) by issuance of (4) additional shares payable 04/01/2013 to holders of record 04/01/2013 Ex date - 04/02/2013
Merged into Crown Life Canada Ltd. 06/02/2014
Each share Common $0.001 par exchanged for (1) share Common
Note: Crown Life Canada Ltd. privately held

CROWN ALUM INDS CORP (DE)
Liquidation completed Option A
Each share Common 25¢ par exchanged for first and final distribution of (0.123456) share Whittaker Corp. (CA) Common $1 par 11/30/1967
Option B
Each share Common 25¢ par exchanged for initial distribution of (0.082644) share Whittaker Corp. (CA) Common $1 par 11/30/1967
Each share Common 25¢ par received second and final distribution of (0.192086) share Whittaker Corp. (CA) Common $1 par 03/30/1970
Note: Holders not filing an election form prior to 11/11/1967 will receive Option A
Whittaker Corp. (CA) reincorporated in Delaware 06/16/1986
(See Whittaker Corp. (DE))

CROWN AMERN RLTY TR (MD)
Issue Information - 2,500,000 SR PFD SHS BEN INT 11% offered at $50 per share on 07/03/1997
Merged into Pennsylvania Real Estate Investment Trust 11/20/2003
Each Sr. Preferred Share of Bene. Int. 1¢ par exchanged for (1) share 11% Sr. Preferred $1 par
Each Common Share of Bene. Int. 1¢ par exchanged for (1) Share of Bene. Int. $1 par

CROWN ANDERSEN INC (DE)
Each share old Common 10¢ par exchanged for (0.002) share new Common 10¢ par 10/26/2004
Note: In effect holders received $1.95 cash per share and public interest was eliminated

CROWN AUTO HLDGS INC (NV)
Voluntarily dissolved 12/31/2012
No stockholders' equity

CROWN AUTO INC (MN)
Common 25¢ par split (3) for (2) by issuance of (0.5) additional share 9/28/84
Acquired by Northern Pacific Corp. 5/3/88
Each share Common 25¢ par exchanged for $7 cash

CROWN AUTO STORES INC (MN)
Common 1¢ par split (2) for (1) by issuance of (1) additional share 4/15/72
Merged into Empire Associates, Inc. 12/3/75
Each share Common 1¢ par exchanged for (1) share Common 25¢ par
Empire Associates, Inc. name changed to Empire-Crown Auto, Inc. 5/26/76 which name changed to Crown Auto Inc. 5/18/84
(See Crown Auto Inc.)

CROWN BANCORP (CA)
Under plan of reorganization each share Common no par automatically became (1) share Bank of Coronado (Coronado, CA) Common no par 7/6/94

CROWN BOOKS CORP (DE)
Plan of reorganization under Chapter 11 Federal Bankruptcy Code effective 11/11/99
No stockholders' equity

CROWN BRANDS INC (NJ)
Acquired by CB Holdings Corp. 03/16/1992
Each share Common $0.001 par exchanged for $0.50 cash

CROWN-BREMSON INDUSTRIES, INC. (MD)
Acquired by Berkey Photo, Inc. 1/28/65
Each share Common $1 par exchanged for (1/6) share Common $1 par
Berkey Photo, Inc. name changed to Berkey, Inc. 9/20/85
(See Berkey, Inc.)

CROWN BUTTE RES LTD (CANADA)
Liquidation completed
Each share Common no par received initial distribution of $4.50 cash payable 3/11/99 to holders of record 1/14/98
Each share Common no par received second and final distribution of $0.1769 cash payable 5/16/2003 to holders of record 5/15/2003
Note: Certificates were not required to be surrendered and are without value

CROWN CALIF CORP (ID)
Charter forfeited for failure to file reports 12/2/91

CROWN CAPITAL CORP. (DE)
Merged into Crown Finance Co., Inc. 09/28/1950
Each share Class A Common $1 par exchanged for (1.25) shares Class A Common $1 par
Each share Class B Common 25¢ par exchanged for (1) share Class B Common 25¢ par
(See Crown Finance Co., Inc.)

CROWN CASINO CORP (TX)
Name changed to Crown Group, Inc. 10/02/1997
Crown Group, Inc. name changed to America's Car-Mart, Inc. 03/28/2002

CROWN CASTLE INTL CORP NEW (DE)
Each share 4.5% Mandatory Conv. Preferred 1¢ par exchanged for (1.188) shares Common 1¢ par 11/01/2016
(Additional Information in Active)

CROWN CASTLE INTL CORP OLD (DE)
Each share 6.25% Conv. Preferred 1¢ par received distribution of (0.035027) share Common 1¢ par payable 11/15/2000 to holders of record 11/01/2000
Each share 6.25% Conv. Preferred 1¢ par received distribution of (0.029277) share Common 1¢ par payable 02/15/2001 to holders of record 02/01/2001
Each share 6.25% Conv. Preferred 1¢ par received distribution of (0.037888) share Common 1¢ par payable 05/15/2001 to holders of record 05/01/2001
Each share 6.25% Conv. Preferred 1¢ par received distribution of (0.0834218) share Common 1¢ par payable 8/15/2001 to holders of record 08/01/2001
Each share 6.25% Conv. Preferred 1¢ par received distribution of (0.707499) share Common 1¢ par payable 11/15/2001 to holders of record 11/01/2001
Each share 6.25% Conv. Preferred 1¢ par received distribution of (0.109886) share Common 1¢ par payable 02/15/2002 to holders of record 02/01/2002 Ex date - 01/30/2002
Each share 6.25% Conv. Preferred 1¢ par received distribution of (0.121546) share Common 1¢ par payable 05/15/2002 to holders of record 05/01/2002 Ex date - 05/02/2002
Each share 6.25% Conv. Preferred 1¢ par received distribution of (0.315992) share Common 1¢ par payable 08/15/2002 to holders of record 08/01/2002
Each share 6.25% Conv. Preferred 1¢ par received distribution of (0.294374) share Common 1¢ par payable 11/15/2002 to holders of record 11/01/2002 Ex date - 10/30/2002
Each share 6.25% Conv. Preferred 1¢ par received distribution of (0.232119) share Common 1¢ par payable 02/17/2003 to holders of record 02/01/2003 Ex date - 01/29/2003
Each share 6.25% Conv. Preferred 1¢ par received distribution of (0.128375) share Common 1¢ par payable 05/15/2003 to holders of record 05/01/2003 Ex date - 04/29/2003
Each share 6.25% Conv. Preferred 1¢ par distribution of (0.082214) share Common payable 08/15/2003 to holders of record 08/01/2003
Each share 6.25% Conv. Preferred 1¢ par received distribution of (0.068763) share Common 1¢ par payable 11/17/2003 to holders of record 11/01/2003
12.75% Sr. Exchangeable Preferred called for redemption at $106.375 on 12/15/2003
Each share 6.25% Conv. Preferred 1¢ par received distribution of (0.066387) share Common 1¢ par payable 02/17/2004 to holders of record 02/01/2004
Each share 6.25% Conv. Preferred 1¢ par received distribution of (0.054906) share Common 1¢ par payable 05/17/2004 to holders of record 05/01/2004
Each share 6.25% Conv. Preferred 1¢ par received distribution of (0.059863) share Common 1¢ par payable 08/16/2004 to holders of record 08/01/2004
Each share 6.25% Conv. Preferred 1¢ par received distribution of (0.054398) share Common 1¢ par payable 11/15/2004 to holders of record 11/01/2004
Each share 6.25% Conv. Preferred 1¢ par received distribution of (0.049787) share Common 1¢ par payable 02/15/2005 to holders of record 02/01/2005

Each share 6.25% Conv. Preferred 1¢ par received distribution of (0.049527) share Common 1¢ par payable 05/16/2005 to holders of record 05/01/2005
Each share 6.25% Conv. Preferred 1¢ par exchanged for (1.3559) shares Common 1¢ par 02/24/2012
Stock Dividends - in 12.75% Sr. Exchangeable Preferred to holders of 12.75% Sr. Exchangeable Preferred 3.1875% payable 03/15/1999 to holders of record 03/01/1999; 3.1875% payable 06/15/1999 to holders of record 06/01/1999; 3.1875% payable 09/15/1999 to holders of record 09/01/1999; 3.1875% payable 12/15/1999 to holders of record 12/01/1999; 3.1875% payable 03/15/2000 to holders of record 03/01/2000; 3.1875% payable 06/15/2000 to holders of record 06/01/2000; 3.1875% payable 09/15/2000 to holders of record 09/01/2000; 3.1875% payable 12/15/2000 to holders of record 12/01/2000; 3.1875% payable 03/15/2001 to holders of record 03/01/2001; 3.1875% payable 06/15/2001 to holders of record 06/01/2001; 3.1875% payable 09/17/2001 to holders of record 09/01/2001 Ex date - 09/20/2001; 3.1875% payable 12/15/2001 to holders of record 12/01/2001 Ex date - 12/05/2001; 3.1875% payable 03/15/2002 to holders of record 03/01/2002 Ex date - 03/07/2002; 3.1875% payable 06/17/2002 to holders of record 06/01/2002 Ex date - 06/13/2002; 3.1875% payable 09/16/2002 to holders of record 09/01/2002 Ex date - 09/13/2002; 3.1875% payable 12/15/2002 to holders of record 12/01/2002 Ex date - 12/03/2002; 3.1875% payable 03/17/2003 to holders of record 03/01/2003 Ex date - 02/26/2003; 3.1875% payable 06/16/2003 to holders of record 06/01/2003 Ex date - 05/28/2003; 3.1875% payable 09/15/2003 to holders of record 09/01/2003 Ex date - 08/27/2003; 3.1875% payable 12/15/2003 to holders of record 12/01/2003 Ex date - 11/26/2003
Reorganized as Crown Castle International Corp. (New) 12/16/2014
Each share 4.5% Mandatory Conv. Preferred Ser. A 1¢ par exchanged for (1) share 4.5% Mandatory Conv. Preferred Ser. A 1¢ par
Each share Common 1¢ par exchanged for (1) share Common 1¢ par

CROWN CENT PETE CORP (MD)
$2.25 Conv. Exchangeable Preferred Ser. B no par called for redemption 05/19/1989
Conv. Preferred Ser. A no par called for redemption 07/24/1989
Common $5 par split (2) for (1) by issuance of (1) additional share 07/27/1979
Common $5 par reclassified as Class A Common $5 par 01/03/1980
Stock Distribution - (0.25) share Class B Common for each share Class A Common 01/09/1980
Merged into Rosemore Inc. 03/07/2001
Each share Class A Common $5 par exchanged for $10.50 cash
Each share Class B Common $5 par exchanged for $10.50 cash

CROWN CENTRAL PETROLEUM CORP. (DE)
Reorganized under the laws of Maryland 00/00/1937
Each share Common $1 par exchanged for (0.2) share Common $5 par
(See Crown Central Petroleum Corp. (MD))

CROWN CITY PICTURES INC (DE)
Recapitalized as World Poker Fund Holdings, Inc. 01/06/2015
Each share Common $0.0001 par exchanged for (0.00666666) share Common $0.0001 par

CROWN CITY PLATING CO (CA)
Common $10 par changed to $2.50 par and (3) additional shares issued 10/10/1963
Common $2.50 par changed to $1.25 par and (1) additional share issued 09/17/1971
Reported out of business 00/00/2004
Details not available

CROWN COLONY NATL CORP (NV)
Charter revoked for failure to file reports and pay fees 05/05/1973

CROWN CORK & SEAL INC (PA)
Reincorporated 08/04/1989
Each share Common no par exchanged for (2) shares Common $2.50 par 00/00/1948
$2 Conv. Preference no par called for redemption 10/31/1962
Common $2.50 par split (4) for (1) by issuance of (3) additional shares 12/17/1962
Common $2.50 par changed to $5 par and (4) additional shares issued 08/22/1969
$2 Preferred no par called for redemption 04/15/1971
Common $5 par split (3) for (1) by issuance of (2) additional shares 09/30/1988
State of incorporation changed from (NY) to (PA) 08/04/1989
Common $5 par split (3) for (1) by issuance of (2) additional shares 05/29/1992
Each share 4.5% Conv. Preferred $41.8875 par exchanged for (0.91116) share Common $5 par 02/26/2000
Under plan of reorganization each share Common $5 par automatically became (1) share Crown Holdings, Inc. Common $5 par 02/25/2003

CROWN CORK & SEAL LTD (ON)
Merged into Crown Cork & Seal Co., Inc. 04/28/1978
Each share Capital Stock no par exchanged for $280 cash

CROWN CORK INTERNATIONAL CORP. (DE)
Merged into Crown Cork & Seal Co., Inc. (NY) 10/31/1961
Each share Class A no par exchanged for (1.5) shares $2 Cum. Conv. Preferred no par and (0.25) share Common $2.50 par
Crown Cork & Seal Co., Inc. (NY) reincorporated in Pennsylvania 08/04/1989 which reorganized as Crown Holdings, Inc. 02/25/2003

CROWN CORP (HI)
Each share Common $1 par exchanged for (0.00000666) share Common $150,000 par 04/15/1983
Note: In effect holders received $3.30 cash per share and public interest was eliminated

CROWN COS (DE)
Name changed to Crown Gold Companies Group, Ltd. 09/25/1987
Crown Gold Companies Group, Ltd. recapitalized as Tigershark Enterprises Inc. 10/28/1997 which name changed to Great White Marine & Recreation, Inc. 05/14/1998
(See Great White Marine & Recreation, Inc.)

CROWN COTTON MLS (GA)
Common $100 par changed to no par and (9) additional shares issued 11/11/1970
Stock Dividend - 20% 11/11/1971
Recapitalized as CrownAmerica, Inc. 04/04/1972
Each share Common no par exchanged for (5) shares Common no par
(See CrownAmerica, Inc.)

CROWN CRAFTS INC (GA)
Common $1 par split (4) for (1) by issuance of (3) additional shares 09/14/1987
Common $1 par split (2) for (1) by issuance of (1) additional share 01/11/1990
Stock Dividends - 100% 06/05/1972; 10% 02/06/1989
Reincorporated under the laws of Delaware 11/06/2003

CROWN DEV CORP (NV)
Name changed to Crown International 10/09/1969
(See Crown International)

CROWN-DOMINION OIL CO., LTD. (ON)
Recapitalized as Reliance Petroleum Ltd. 00/00/1949
Each share Capital Stock no par exchanged for (0.33333333) share Class A no par and (0.33333333) share Class B no par
(See Reliance Petroleum Ltd.)

CROWN DRUG CO (DE)
Charter cancelled and declared inoperative and void for non-payment of taxes 03/01/1975

CROWN DRUG STORES, INC.
Merged into Crown Drug Co. 00/00/1934
Details not available

CROWN DYNAMICS CORP (DE)
Each share old Common $0.001 par exchanged for (3) shares new Common $0.001 par 01/03/2012
New Common $0.001 par changed to $0.0001 par 03/30/2012
Name changed to Airware Labs Corp. 11/09/2012
Airware Labs Corp. name changed to Item 9 Labs Corp. 04/27/2018

CROWN ENERGY CORP (UT)
Recapitalized 01/06/1995
Each share Common $0.001 par exchanged for (0.2) share Common 2¢ par 08/27/1987
Recapitalized from Crown Energy Corp. to Crown Energy Corporation 01/06/1995
Each share Common 2¢ par exchanged (0.25) share Common 2¢ par
Each share old Common 2¢ par exchanged for (0.001) share new Common 2¢ par 05/27/2005
Note: Minority holders received $0.012 cash per share
Name changed to Onyx Corp. 12/01/2005

CROWN FINANCE CO., INC. (DE)
Merged into Beneficial Finance Co. of New York, Inc. 09/30/1965
Each share Class A Common $1 par exchanged for $3.29 cash

CROWN FINL HLDGS INC (NJ)
Name changed 01/11/2005
Name changed from Crown Financial Group, to Crown Financial Holdings, Inc. 01/11/2005
Executed an assignment for the benefit of creditors 10/04/2005
Stockholders' equity unlikely

CROWN FOREST INDS LTD (BC)
Acquired by Fletcher Challenge Canada Inc. 01/01/1988
Each share Class A $2 par exchanged for (4) Exchangeable Shares, $80 cash or a combination of Shares and cash
Note: Option to receive cash or a combination of Shares and cash expired 02/19/1988
Fletcher Challenge Canada Inc. name changed to Fletcher Challenge Investments Inc. 09/14/1988
(See Fletcher Challenge Investments, Inc.)

CROWN GOLD CORP (CANADA)
Recapitalized as Crown Mining Corp. 06/30/2014
Each share Common no par exchanged for (0.1) share Common no par

CROWN GOLD COS GROUP LTD (DE)
Reorganized under the laws of Nevada as Tigershark Enterprises Inc. 10/28/1997
Each share Common 1¢ par exchanged for (0.03571428) share Common 1¢ par
Tigershark Enterprises Inc. name changed to Great White Marine & Recreation, Inc. 05/14/1998
(See Great White Marine & Recreation, Inc.)

CROWN GROUP INC (TX)
Name changed to America's Car-Mart, Inc. 03/28/2002

CROWN HILL CEMETERY ASSN (CO)
Merged into Texas International Co. 02/25/1972
Each (5) shares Class A Common $5 par exchanged for $37.50 principal amount of 5% Subord. Debentures Ser. A due 02/01/1984 and $12.50 cash
Note: Holders of fewer than (5) shares received $10 cash per share

CROWN HILL DIVID FD (ON)
Under plan of merger each Unit no par automatically became (1.1742) Crown Hill Fund Trust Units no par 12/31/2008
Crown Hill Fund merged into Citadel Income Fund 12/02/2009

CROWN HILL FD (ON)
Under plan of merger name changed to Citadel Income Fund 12/02/2009

CROWN INDUSTRIES, INC. (OH)
Voluntarily dissolved 12/27/2006
Details not available

CROWN INDS INC (FL)
Common 40¢ par split (3) for (2) by issuance of (0.5) additional share 10/01/1969
Stock Dividends - 25% 11/27/1967; 25% 11/27/1968; 10% 03/14/1974; 25% 05/31/1978; 25% 05/31/1979; 10% 05/29/1980; 10% 05/28/1981
Acquired by Talquin Corp. 06/19/1985
Each share Common 40¢ par exchanged for $17.25 cash

CROWN INTL (NV)
Charter revoked for failure to file reports and pay fees 03/04/1974

CROWN JEWEL RES CORP (DE)
Each share old Common $0.00005 par exchanged for (0.03333333) share new Common $0.00005 par 08/22/2001
Charter cancelled and declared void for failure to pay franchise taxes 03/01/2003

CROWN LABS INC (DE)
Each share old Common $0.00001 par exchanged for (0.4) share new Common $0.00001 par 01/15/1993
Each share new Common $0.00001 par exchanged for (0.4) share Common $0.001 par 07/27/1993
SEC revoked common stock registration 12/28/2005

CROWN LEASING CO., INC. (MO)
Charter forfeited for failure to file reports 01/01/1985

CROWN LIFE INS CO (CANADA)
Each share Common $100 par

exchanged for (10) shares old
Common $10 par plus a stock
dividend of (0.80995475) share paid
05/12/1955
Each share old Common $10 par
exchanged for (2) shares new
Common $10 par 05/11/1961
Each share new Common $10 par
exchanged for (10) shares Common
$1 par 05/13/1965
Merged into 3660257 Canada Ltd.
11/27/2000
Each share Common $1 par
exchanged for $123 cash
$2.50 Class I Ser. A Preferred $25
par called for redemption at $25 on
12/20/2001
Public interest eliminated

CROWN LIFE PPTYS INC (ON)
7.375% Retractable Preferred Ser. I
no par called for redemption
02/10/1992
Public interest eliminated

CROWN LTD (AUSTRALIA)
Name changed to Crown Resorts Ltd.
12/27/2013

CROWN MARKETING (WY)
Common no par split (10) for (1) by
issuance of (9) additional shares
payable 10/09/2012 to holders of
record 10/02/2012 Ex date -
10/10/2012
Name changed to America Great
Health 06/29/2017

CROWN-MEAKINS INC. (ON)
Reorganized as Medicorp Technology
Ltd. 01/05/1976
Each share Capital Stock no par
exchanged for (1) share Capital
Stock no par
Medicorp Technology Ltd. merged into
North American Combustion
Technology Corp. 08/19/1980
(See North American Combustion
Technology Corp.)

CROWN MED SYS INC (NV)
Name changed to PaperFree Medical
Solutions, Inc. 12/06/2004

CROWN MEDIA HLDGS INC (DE)
Acquired by Hallmark Cards, Inc.
05/02/2016
Each share Class A Common 1¢ par
exchanged for $5.05 cash

CROWN MINERALS INC (CANADA)
Under plan of merger name changed
to Crown Gold Corp. and Class A
Common no par reclassified as
Common no par 08/31/2010
Crown Gold Corp. recapitalized as
Crown Mining Corp. 06/30/2014

CROWN NATL VENTURES INC (UT)
Proclaimed dissolved for failure to file
annual report 03/01/1993

CROWN NORTHCORP INC (DE)
SEC revoked common stock
registration 02/07/2012

CROWN OIL & GAS INC (NV)
Each share old Common $0.001 par
exchanged for (18) shares new
Common $0.001 par 01/31/2008
SEC revoked common stock
registration 08/29/2012

CROWN OIL CO. (DE)
Charter cancelled and declared
inoperative and void for
non-payment of taxes 03/18/1925

CROWN OIL CO. (UT)
Completely liquidated 08/06/1968
Each share Capital Stock no par
exchanged for first and final
distribution of (1) share Bagdad
Chase, Inc. Common $1 par
(See Bagdad Chase, Inc.)

CROWN OIL CO (CO)
Acquired by Cow Gulch Oil Co.
05/28/1971
Each share Common 10¢ par
exchanged for (0.83333333) share
Common 10¢ par
Cow Gulch Oil Co. merged into
K.R.M. Petroleum Corp. 08/31/1973
which name changed to
PrimeEnergy Corp. 05/17/1990

**CROWN OVERALL
MANUFACTURING CO. (OH)**
Recapitalized 00/00/1933
Each share Preferred $100 par
exchanged for (1) share 6% Prior
Preferred $20 par and (1) share 6%
Part. Preferred $100 par
Common $100 par changed to no par
Name changed to Stonewall Co.
07/15/1962

CROWN PAC PARTNERS L P (DE)
Plan of reorganization under Chapter
11 Federal Bankruptcy Code
effective 12/31/2004
No Ltd. Partnership holders' equity

CROWN PARTNERS INC (NV)
Recapitalized as TaxMasters, Inc.
08/12/2009
Each share Common $0.001 par
exchanged for (0.05) share Common
$0.001 par
(See TaxMasters, Inc.)

CROWN PHOTO, INC. (MD)
Name changed to Crown-Bremson
Industries, Inc. 9/20/61
Crown-Bremson Industries, Inc.
acquired by Berkey Photo, Inc.
1/28/65 which name changed to
Berkey, Inc. 9/20/85
(See Berkey, Inc.)

CROWN PT VENTURES LTD (BC)
Reincorporated under the laws of
Alberta as Crown Point Energy Inc.
07/31/2012

CROWN RESOURCE CORP (CO)
Each share Common 1¢ par
exchanged for (0.2) share Common
5¢ par 7/27/87
Merged into Crown Resources Corp.
2/16/89
Each share Common 5¢ par
exchanged for (0.68) share Common
1¢ par
Crown Resources Corp. acquired by
Kinross Gold Corp. 8/31/2006

CROWN RES CORP (WA)
Plan of reorganization under Chapter
11 Federal Bankruptcy Code
effective 06/11/2002
Each share old Common 1¢ par
exchanged for (0.2) share new
Common 1¢ par
Note: Holders of (499) or fewer
shares will receive no distribution
Unexchanged certificates were
cancelled and became without value
05/30/2007
Acquired by Kinross Gold Corp.
08/31/2006
Each share new Common 1¢ par
exchanged for (0.32) share Common
1¢ par

CROWN RES MINES INC (NV)
Name changed to Computer Systems
Management, Inc. 1/2/70
(See Computer Systems
Management, Inc.)

**CROWN ROTATIONAL MOLDED
PRODS INC (AR)**
Merged into Crown Andersen Inc.
1/31/86
Each share Common 1¢ par
exchanged for (1) share Common
10¢ par
(See Crown Andersen Inc.)

**CROWN SELF SVC STORES INC
(MO)**
Common 10¢ par changed to no par
9/1/64
Name changed to McGuire Water
Conditioning Corp. and Common no
par changed to 5¢ par 1/30/68
(See McGuire Water Conditioning
Corp.)

CROWN SILVER DEV LTD (BC)
Recapitalized as Cerro Mining Ltd.
03/05/1969
Each share Common $1 par
exchanged for (0.2) share Common
no par
Cerro Mining Ltd. name changed to
Crownex International Ltd.
08/13/1969 which recapitalized as
Dison International Ltd. 12/10/1971
(See Dison International Ltd.)

**CROWN SILVER LEAD MINES LTD.
(BC)**
Name changed to Crown Silver
Development Ltd. 1/14/54
Crown Silver Development Ltd.
recapitalized as Cerro Mining Ltd.
3/5/69 which name changed to
Crownex International Ltd. 8/13/69
which recapitalized as Dison
International Ltd. 12/10/71
(See Dison International Ltd.)

CROWN TR CO (TORONTO, ON)
Each share old Common $100 par
exchanged for (0.5) share new
Common $100 par 00/00/1940
Each share new Common $100 par
exchanged for (10) shares Common
$10 par 02/10/1955
Common $10 par changed to $2 par
and (4) additional shares issued
03/25/1970
Order to wind up company issued
02/18/88
No stockholders' equity

CROWN URANIUM CO. (CO)
Recapitalized as Crown Oil Co. (CO)
01/20/1967
Each share Common 5¢ par
exchanged for (0.01) share Common
10¢ par
Crown Oil Co. (CO) acquired by Cow
Gulch Oil Co. 05/28/1971 which
merged into K.R.M. Petroleum Corp.
08/31/1973 which name changed to
PrimeEnergy Corp. 05/17/1990

CROWN VANTAGE INC (VA)
Plan of reorganization under Chapter
11 Federal Bankruptcy Code
effective 03/01/2002
Each share Common no par
exchanged for an undetermined
amount of non-transferable
uncertificated beneficial interests in
Crown Paper Liquidating Trust
Note: Unexchanged certificates were
cancelled and became without value
12/01/2003

CROWN VIDEO INTL INC (UT)
Charter cancelled and proclaimed
dissolved for failure to file reports
08/01/1988

CROWN-WAIPAHU, INC. (HI)
Name changed to Crown Corp.
09/22/1966
(See Crown Corp.)

CROWN WESTN INVTS INC (DE)
Acquired by Selected American
Shares, Inc. 1/30/75
Each share Dallas Fund Series
S3-Common $1 par exchanged for
(0.8539) share Common $1.25 par
Each share Diversified Fund Series
D2-Common $1 par exchanged for
(0.7993) share Common $1.25 par

**CROWN WILLAMETTE PAPER CO.
(DE)**
Merged into Crown Zellerbach Corp.
in 1937
Each share $7 1st Preferred
exchanged for (1.2) shares $5 Conv.
Preferred no par and (0.2) share
Common $5 par
Each share $6 Second Preferred
exchanged for (0.8) share $5 Conv.
Preferred no par and (2.5) shares
Common $5 par
Crown Zellerbach Corp. merged into
James River Corp. of Virginia
10/30/86 which name changed to
Fort James Corp. 8/13/97 which
merged into Georgia-Pacific Corp.
11/27/2000
(See Georgia-Pacific Corp.)

**CROWN ZELLERBACH CDA LTD
(BC)**
Each share Ordinary $10 par
exchanged for (5) shares Ordinary
$2 par 00/00/1956
Ordinary $2 par reclassified as Class
A $2 par 05/27/1958
6% Preferred $100 par called for
redemption 11/30/1976
Name changed to Crown Forest
Industries Ltd. 11/09/1983
Crown Forest Industries Ltd. acquired
by Fletcher Challenge Canada Inc.
01/01/1988 which name changed to
Fletcher Challenge Investments Inc.
09/14/1988
(See Fletcher Challenge Investments
Inc.)

CROWN ZELLERBACH CORP (NV)
Each share $6 Preference no par
exchanged for (1.025) shares $5
Preferred no par and (1) share
Common $5 par in 1937
Each share Common no par
exchanged for (1) share Common
$5 par in 1937
$5 Preferred no par called for
redemption 12/1/45
$4 2nd Preferred no par called for
redemption 11/1/50
Common $5 par split (3) for (2) by
issuance of (0.5) additional share
7/14/69
$4.20 Preferred no par called for
redemption 4/2/79
$3.05 Preferred Ser. B no par called
for redemption 5/20/83
$4.625 Conv. Preferred Ser. A no par
called for redemption 1/2/86
Each share $4.50 Conv.
Exchangeable Preferred Ser. C no
par exchanged for $50 principal
amount of 9% Conv. Subord.
Debentures due 4/1/2013 on 1/1/86
Stock Dividends - 100% 4/24/53; 50%
9/6/55; 10% 1/2/62
Merged into James River Corp. of
Virginia 10/30/86
Each share Common $5 par
exchanged for (1.6023) shares
Common 10¢ par

CROWNAMERICA INC (GA)
Liquidation completed
Each share Common no par received
initial distribution of $9 cash
06/05/1995
Each share Common no par received
second distribution of $2 cash
11/28/1995
Each share Common no par
exchanged for third and final
distribution of $1.55 cash
11/05/1996

CROWNBRIDGE INDS INC (ON)
Recapitalized 02/02/1979
Recapitalized from Crownbridge
Copper Mines Ltd. to Crownbridge
Industries Inc. 02/02/1979
Each share Common $1 par
exchanged for (0.1) share Common
no par
Each share old Common no par
exchanged for (0.1) share new
Common no par 03/25/1980
New Common no par split (4) for (1)
by issuance of (3) additional shares
03/23/1987
Delisted from Alberta Stock Exchange
07/17/1992

CROWNBUTTE WIND PWR INC (NV)
Name changed to Canna Brands, Inc.
09/30/2014
Canna Brands, Inc. name changed to
Canna Consumer Goods, Inc.
06/24/2015

CROWNE VENTURES INC (NV)
Each share old Common $0.001 par

exchanged for (0.0005) share new Common $0.001 par 09/16/2009
Recapitalized as Grand Capital Ventures, Inc. 11/07/2012
Each share new Common $0.001 par exchanged for (0.0001) share Common $0.001 par

CROWNEX INTL LTD (BC)
Recapitalized as Dison International Ltd. 12/10/1971
Each share Common no par exchanged for (0.2) share Common no par
(See Dison International Ltd.)

CROWNJOULE EXPL LTD (AB)
Merged into BelAir Energy Corp. 06/13/2000
Each share Common no par exchanged for (0.42) share new Common no par and $0.10 cash
BelAir Energy Corp. merged into Purcell Energy Ltd. (New) 09/04/2003
(See Purcell Energy Ltd. (New))

CROWNX INC (CANADA)
Class A Non-Vtg. no par split (2) for (1) by issuance of (1) additional share 06/20/1986
Name changed to Extendicare Inc. 11/17/1994
(See Extendicare Inc.)

CROWPAT MINERALS LTD (ON)
Recapitalized as Crowbank Mines Ltd. 7/29/68
Each share Capital Stock $1 par exchanged for (0.5) share Capital Stock $1 par
Crowbank Mines Ltd. recapitalized as Patmore Developments Ltd. 2/14/74 which name changed to Patmore Group Ltd. 11/1/76 which merged into Uranco Inc. 10/23/80

CROWS NEST INDS LTD (CANADA)
Acquired by Shell Canada Resources Ltd. 05/09/1978
Each share Common $8 par exchanged for $85 cash

CROWS NEST OILS LTD. (BC)
Struck off register and declared dissolved for failure to file returns 06/10/1948

CROWSHORE GOLD MINES LTD. (ON)
Recapitalized as Crowshore Patricia Gold Mines Ltd. on a (0.5) for (1) basis in May 1944
Crowshore Patricia Gold Mines Ltd. recapitalized as Crowpat Minerals Ltd. in March 1955 which recapitalized as Crowbank Mines Ltd. 7/29/68 which recapitalized as Patmore Developments Ltd. 2/14/74 which name changed to Patmore Group Ltd. 11/1/76 which merged into Uranco Inc. 10/23/80

CROWSHORE PATRICIA GOLD MINES LTD (ON)
Recapitalized as Crowpat Minerals Ltd. on a (0.25) for (1) basis in March 1955
Crowpat Minerals Ltd. reorganized as Crowbank Mines Ltd. 7/29/68 which recapitalized as Patmore Developments Ltd. 2/14/74 which name changed to Patmore Group Ltd. 11/1/76 which merged into Uranco Inc. 10/23/80

CROWSNEST ACQUISITION CORP (AB)
Name changed to QE2 Acquisition Corp. 11/05/2014
QE2 Acquisition Corp. name changed to Distinct Infrastructure Group Inc. 08/24/2015

CROYDON MERCANTILE CORP (BC)
Name changed to World Mahjong Ltd. 12/01/2015

CROYDON MINES LTD (BC)
Recapitalized as Aalenian Resources Ltd. 08/08/1973
Each share Capital Stock $1 par exchanged for (0.1) share Capital Stock no par
Aalenian Resources Ltd. recapitalized as Silverado Mines Ltd. 08/03/1977 which recapitalized as Silverado Gold Mines Ltd. 05/23/1997
(See Silverado Gold Mines Ltd.)

CROYDON ROUYN MINES LTD (BC)
Merged into Nuinsco Resources Ltd. (BC) 12/08/1980
Each (150) shares Capital Stock $1 par exchanged for (1) share Common no par
Nuinsco Resources Ltd. (BC) reincorporated in Ontario 07/26/1989

CROZER COAL & LD CO (WV)
Liquidation completed
Each share Capital Stock $40 par received initial distribution of $150 cash 02/18/1964
Each share Capital Stock $40 par received second distribution of $6 cash 09/30/1964
Each share Capital Stock $40 par exchanged for third and final distribution of $4.6633 cash 12/19/1967

CRP HLDG CORP (FL)
Recapitalized as American Food Holdings, Inc. 05/02/2007
Each share Common $0.001 par exchanged for (0.1) share Common $0.001 par
American Food Holdings, Inc. name changed to Plateau Mineral Development, Inc. 09/15/2008

CRS DESIGN ASSOCIATES, INC. (DE)
Name changed to CRS Group, Inc. 12/26/1978
CRS Group, Inc. name changed to CRS/Sirrine, Inc. 11/07/1983 which name changed to CRS Sirrine, Inc. 10/25/1984 which name changed to CRSS Inc. 11/01/1989
(See CRSS Inc.)

CRS ELECTRONICS INC (CANADA)
Placed in receivership 10/13/2015
Stockholders' equity unlikely

CRS FINL CORP (NV)
Common $0.001 par split (2) for (1) by issuance of (1) additional share payable 03/07/2005 to holders of record 03/04/2005 Ex date - 03/08/2005
Name changed to Global Media Productions, Inc. 07/18/2006

CRS III DEFD PFD TR (ON)
Deferred Preferred Unit no par called for redemption at $33.34 on 05/23/2003

CRS ROBOTICS CORP (ON)
Merged into Thermo Electron Corp. 04/29/2002
Each share Common no par exchanged for $5.75 cash

CRSS INC (DE)
Name changed 11/07/1983
Common $1 par split (3) for (2) by issuance of (0.5) additional share 02/25/1981
Name changed from CRS Group, Inc. to CRS/Sirrine, Inc. 11/07/1983
CRS/Sirrine, Inc. name changed to CRS Sirrine, Inc. 10/25/1984 which name changed to CRSS Inc. 11/01/1989
Common $1 par split (2) for (1) by issuance of (0.5) additional share 11/08/1989
Merged into American Tractebel Corp. 06/29/1995
Each share Common $1 par exchanged for $14.50 cash

CRT CORP (NV)
Each share old Common $0.001 par exchanged for (0.5) share new Common $0.001 par 06/10/1998
Each share new Common $0.001 par exchanged again for (0.33333333) share new Common $0.001 par 07/10/2002
Name changed to DCM Enterprises Inc. 01/07/2003
DCM Enterprises Inc. name changed to Digital Security, Inc. 06/03/2005 which name changed to DLR Funding, Inc. 03/25/2006
(See DLR Funding, Inc.)

CRT PPTYS INC (FL)
Merged into DRA CRT Acquisition Corp. 09/27/2005
Each share 8.5% Preferred Ser. A 1¢ par automatically became (1) share 8.5% Preferred Ser. A 1¢ par
(See DRA CRT Acquisition Corp.)
Each share Common 1¢ par exchanged for $27.80 cash

CRTC INC (CO)
Voluntarily dissolved 08/27/1999
Details not available

CRUCELL N V (NETHERLANDS)
Acquired by Johnson & Johnson 02/21/2012
Each Sponsored ADR for Ordinary exchanged for $32.430411 cash

CRUCIBLE STEEL CORP. (DE)
Merged into Colt Industries Inc. (DE) 10/17/1968
Each share Common $10 par exchanged for (0.23) share $4.25 Conv. Preferred Ser. D $1 par and (0.41) share Common $1 par
Colt Industries Inc. (DE) reincorporated in Pennsylvania 05/06/1976
(See Colt Industries Inc. (PA))

CRUCIBLE STL CO AMER (NJ)
Each share 7% Preferred $100 par exchanged for (1.4) shares 5% Preferred $100 par 00/00/1940
Common $100 par changed to no par
Common no par changed to $25 par 00/00/1951
Common $25 par changed to $12.50 par and (1) additional share issued 01/23/1957
Stock Dividend - 10% 12/28/1951
5.25% Conv. Preferred called for redemption 02/15/1966
Reincorporated under the laws of Delaware as Crucible Steel Corp. and Common $12.50 par changed to $10 par 04/29/1968
Crucible Steel Corp. merged into Colt Industries Inc. (DE) 10/17/1968 which reincorporated in Pennsylvania 05/06/1976
(See Colt Industries Inc. (PA))

CRUDE CARRIERS CORP (MARSHALL ISLANDS)
Issue Information - 13,500,000 shares COM offered at $19 per share on 03/11/2010
Merged into Capital Product Partners L.P. 09/30/2011
Each share Common $0.0001 par exchanged for (1.56) Common Units 1¢ par

CRUISE AMER INC (FL)
Merged into Budget Group, Inc. 01/28/1998
Each share Common 1¢ par exchanged for (0.28073) share Class A Common 1¢ par
(See Budget Group, Inc.)

CRUISE OF A LIFETIME USA INC (DE)
Reported out of business 00/00/1989
Stockholders' equity unlikely

CRUISER MINERALS LTD (BC)
Name changed to E.C.A Technology Ltd. 01/04/1993
E.C.A. Technology Ltd. name changed to Marine Bioproducts International Corp. (BC) 09/30/1997 which reorganized in Alberta as Phoenix Oilfield Hauling Inc. 06/06/2006 which name changed to Aveda Transportation & Energy Servives Inc. 06/25/2012 which merged into Daseke, Inc. 06/08/2018

CRUISER OIL & GAS LTD (AB)
Merged into One Exploration Inc. 11/21/2008
Each share Common no par exchanged for (0.0609) share Class A Common no par
One Exploration Inc. recapitalized as TriOil Resources Ltd. 04/07/2010
(See TriOil Resources Ltd.)

CRUISESTOCK INC (TX)
Reincorporated under the laws of Florida as Brookside Technology Holdings Corp. 07/06/2007
Brookside Technology Holdings Corp. name changed to Blueprint Technologies, Inc. 03/24/2011

CRUM & FORSTER (NY)
8% Preferred called for redemption 06/30/1959
Common $10 par changed to $5 par and (1) additional share issued 08/25/1961
Common $5 par changed to $2.50 par and (1) additional share issued 07/15/1969
Common $2.50 par changed to $1.25 par and (1) additional share issued 10/14/1971
Common $1.25 par changed to $0.625 par and (1) additional share issued 06/19/1980
$2.40 Conv. Preferred Ser. A $5 par called for redemption 11/18/1982
Merged into Xerox Corp. 01/11/1983
Each share Common $0.625 par exchanged for $55 cash

CRUM & FORSTER INSURANCE SHARES CORP. (DE)
Name changed to Crum & Forster Securities Corp. 00/00/1947
Crum & Forster Securities Corp. merged into Crum & Forster 11/04/1955
(See Crum & Forster)

CRUM & FORSTER SECURITIES CORP. (DE)
Merged into Crum & Forster 11/04/1955
Each share Class B Common $10 par exchanged for (1.4) shares Common $10 par
(See Crum & Forster)

CRUMBS BAKE SHOP INC (DE)
Chapter 11 bankruptcy proceedings converted to Chapter 7 on 06/22/2015
Stockholders' equity unlikely

CRUMP COS INC (TN)
Name changed 05/04/1984
Common no par split (2) for (1) by issuance of (1) additional share 08/21/1972
Stock Dividend - 10% 01/10/1978
Name changed from Crump (E.H.) Companies, Inc. to Crump Companies, Inc. 05/04/1984
Common no par split (2) for (1) by issuance of (1) additional share 01/18/1985
Merged into Sedgwick Group PLC 11/03/1986
Each share Common no par exchanged for $33 cash

CRUMPTON BUILDERS, INC. (FL)
Adjudicated bankrupt 01/15/1965
No stockholders' equity

CRUSADE PETE LTD (AB)
Liquidation completed 01/01/1972
Each share Capital Stock no par exchanged for (0.066) share Pan Ocean Oil Corp. Common 1¢ par

(See Pan Ocean Oil Corp.)

CRUSADER CORP. (CO)
Merged into Crusader Oil & Uranium Co. 04/20/1955
Each share Capital Stock 1¢ par exchanged for (1) share Capital Stock
Crusader Oil & Uranium Co. merged into Crusader Oil & Gas Co. 02/06/1959 which merged into Gold Empire Mining Co. 06/15/1968
(See Gold Empire Mining Co.)

CRUSADER ENERGY GROUP INC (NV)
Plan of reorganization under Chapter 11 Federal Bankruptcy proceedings effective 12/31/2009
No stockholders' equity

CRUSADER GOLD CORP (BC)
Recapitalized as Shorewood Explorations Ltd. 11/13/1992
Each share Common no par exchanged for (0.4) share Common no par
Shorewood Explorations Ltd. merged into International Broadlands Resources Ltd. 04/06/1995 which recapitalized as Broadlands Resources Ltd. (New) 03/15/1999 which recapitalized as Pinnacle Mines Ltd. (Ctfs. dated after 07/16/2003) 07/16/2003 which name changed to Jayden Resources Inc. (BC) 06/29/2010 which reincorporated in Cayman Islands 10/03/2012

CRUSADER HLDG CORP (PA)
Stock Dividends - 5% payable 08/28/1998 to holders of record 08/17/1998; 5% payable 10/14/1999 to holders of record 10/06/1999
Each share Common 1¢ par received a liquidation distribution of $10.50 cash payable 08/27/2001 to holders of record 08/21/2001
Each share old Common 1¢ par exchanged for (0.001) share new Common 1¢ par 09/27/2001
Note: In effect holders received $0.05 cash per share and public interest was eliminated

CRUSADER LIFE INSURANCE CO. (PA)
Recapitalized as Pittsburgh Life Insurance Co. 03/07/1966
Each share Capital Stock $10 par exchanged for (4) shares Capital Stock $2.50 par
Pittsburgh Life Insurance Co. name changed to Allnation Life Insurance Co. of Pennsylvania 04/04/1979
(See Allnation Life Insurance Co. of Pennsylvania)

CRUSADER MINES LTD (ON)
Charter cancelled for failure to pay taxes and file returns 12/12/1973

CRUSADER OIL & GAS CO. (DE)
Merged into Gold Empire Mining Co. 06/15/1968
Each share Common 25¢ par exchanged for (0.33333333) share Common 50¢ par
(See Gold Empire Mining Co.)

CRUSADER OIL & URANIUM CO. (CO)
Merged into Crusader Oil & Gas Co. 02/06/1959
Each share Common 1¢ par exchanged for (0.005) share Common 25¢ par
Crusader Oil & Gas Co. merged into Gold Empire Mining Co. 06/15/1968
(See Gold Empire Mining Co.)

CRUSADER PETROLEUMS, LTD.
Merged into Astral Mining & Resources Ltd. 00/00/1952
Each share Capital Stock $1 par exchanged for (0.01052631) share Common and (0.2) Escrow Receipt Astral Mining & Resources Ltd.

recapitalized as New Astral Mining & Resources Ltd. 10/00/1962
(See New Astral Mining & Resources Ltd.)

CRUSADER SVGS & LN ASSN ROSEMONT (PA)
Merged into Crusader Holding Corp. 06/13/1989
Each share Common $1 par exchanged for $28.49 cash

CRUSH INTERNATIONAL INC. (IL)
Acquired by Crush International Ltd. (ON) 10/29/1962
Each share Common $1 par exchanged for (40) shares Common no par
Crush International Ltd. (ON) reincorporated in British Columbia 02/19/1981 which name changed to Great Pacific Industries, Inc. 03/10/1981
(See Great Pacific Industries, Inc.)

CRUSH INTL LTD (BC)
Reincorporated 02/19/1981
6.5% Conv. Preference Ser. A $100 par called for redemption 03/01/1963
Common no par split (2) for (1) by issuance of (1) additional share 02/06/1964
Common no par split (3) for (1) by issuance of (2) additional shares 03/13/1969
Place of incorporation changed from (ON) to (BC) 02/19/1981
Name changed to Great Pacific Industries, Inc. 03/10/1981
(See Great Pacific Industries, Inc.)

CRUTCHER RES CORP (DE)
Common $1 par changed to no par 5/29/86
Chapter 11 bankruptcy proceedings converted to Chapter 7 on 3/23/87
Stockholders' equity unlikely

CRUX INDS INC (BC)
Name changed to Mont Blanc Resources Inc. 11/18/2005
Mont Blanc Resources Inc. name changed to Sonora Gold & Silver Corp. 07/17/2008

CRUZ CAP CORP (BC)
Common no par split (3) for (1) by issuance of (2) additional shares payable 11/23/2016 to holders of record 11/18/2016 Ex date - 11/16/2016
Name changed to Cruz Cobalt Corp. 02/23/2017

CRUZ SILVER MINES INC (AB)
Recapitalized as Gold Shield Exploration & Development Inc. 07/30/1986
Each share Common no par exchanged for (0.125) share Common no par
(See Gold Shield Exploration & Development Inc.)

CRUZAN INTL INC (DE)
Merged into Absolut Spirits Co., Inc. 3/22/2006
Each share Common 1¢ par exchanged for $28.37 cash

CRW FINL INC (DE)
Common $0.001 par split (3) for (1) by issuance of (2) additional shares payable 10/24/1996 to holders of record 10/14/1996
Merged into Telespectrum Worldwide Inc. 06/30/1999
Each share Common $0.001 par exchanged for (0.709) share Common 1¢ par
(See Telespectrum Worldwide Inc.)

CRY LAKE MINERALS LTD (BC)
Struck off register and declared dissolved for failure to file returns 3/18/83

CRYDERMAN GOLD INC (BC)
Name changed to Softfund Capital Partners Inc. 12/16/1992
Softfund Capital Partners Inc. recapitalized as Sand River Resources Ltd. 06/30/1994 which recapitalized as Rio Fortuna Exploration Corp. 11/30/1999 which recapitalized as Fortune River Resource Corp. 12/21/2005 which merged into Bravada Gold Corp. (New) 01/07/2011

CRYDERMAN GOLD MINES, LTD. (MB)
Charter cancelled 12/5/63
No stockholders' equity

CRYENCO SCIENCES INC (DE)
Each share old Common 1¢ par exchanged for (0.5) share new Common 1¢ par 8/13/92
Merged into Chart Industries, Inc. 7/31/97
Each share new Class A Common 1¢ par exchanged for $2.75 cash

CRYO FREEZE PRODS CO (OR)
Adjudicated bankrupt 03/17/1970
No stockholders' equity

CRYO THERM INC (DE)
Liquidation completed
Each share Common 1¢ par exchanged for initial distribution of (0.0367) share Common $1 par and (1) Non-transferable Ctf. of Contingent Interest of Armstrong Cork Co. 6/20/72
Note: Non-transferable Ctfs. of Contingent Interest were deemed worthless prior to 12/31/1976 and in effect the above distribution was the first and final
Armstrong Cork Co. name changed to Armstrong World Industries, Inc. (Old) 05/15/1980 which reorganized as Armstrong Holdings, Inc. 05/01/2000
(See Armstrong Holdings, Inc.)

CRYOCATH TECHNOLOGIES INC (QC)
Acquired by Medtronic, Inc. 11/13/2008
Each share Common no par exchanged for $8.75 cash

CRYOCON PAC CONTAINERS INC (BC)
Recapitalized 06/17/1993
Recapitalized from Cryocon Containers Inc. to Cryocon-Pacific Containers Inc. 06/17/1993
Each share Common no par exchanged for (0.2) share Common no par
Recapitalized as Alda Industries Corp. 05/06/1996
Each share Common no par exchanged for (0.5) share Common no par
Alda Industries Corp. recapitalized as Crux Industries Inc. 07/14/1999 which name changed to Mont Blanc Resources Inc. 11/18/2005 which name changed to Sonora Gold & Silver Corp. 07/17/2008

CRYOCOR INC (DE)
Merged into Boston Scientific Corp. 05/28/2008
Each share Common $0.001 par exchanged for $1.35 cash

CRYODYNAMICS INC (DE)
Charter cancelled and declared void for non-payment of taxes 3/1/91

CRYOGENIC ENGR CO (CO)
Class A Common 10¢ par reclassified as Common 10¢ par 1/11/63
Merged into Cryogenic Technology, Inc. 10/27/72
Each share Common 10¢ par exchanged for (0.52) share Common no par
Each share Common 10¢ par received additional distribution of (0.067292) share Common no par from contingency reserve 10/31/73
Cryogenic Technology, Inc. name changed to Helix Technology Corp. 6/7/76 which merged into Brooks Automation, Inc. 10/26/2005

CRYOGENIC ENTERPRISES LTD. (BC)
Recapitalized as Cryogenic Industries Ltd. 11/7/74
Each share Capital Stock no par exchanged for (0.1) share Capital Stock no par

CRYOGENIC SOLUTIONS INC (NV)
Name changed to CytoGenix, Inc. 01/20/2000
(See CytoGenix, Inc.)

CRYOGENIC TECHNOLOGY INC (DE)
Name changed to Helix Technology Corp. and Common no par changed to $1 par 6/7/76
Helix Technology Corp. merged into Brooks Automation, Inc. 10/26/2005

CRYOGENICS, INC. (FL)
Name changed to International Controls Corp. 12/20/66
(See International Controls Corp.)

CRYOLIFE INC (FL)
Issue Information - 400,000 shares PFD CONV offered at $50 per share on 03/15/2005
Each share 6% Conv. Preferred 1¢ par automatically became (6.2189) shares Common 1¢ par 06/25/2007 (Additional Information in Active)

CRYOMEDICAL SCIENCES INC (DE)
Each share old Common $0.001 par exchanged for (0.2) share new Common $0.001 par 6/16/2000
Name changed to BioLife Solutions, Inc. 9/30/2002

CRYOPAK INDS INC (BC)
Each share old Common no par exchanged for (0.16666666) share new Common no par 03/21/2005
Note: Holders of (5,999) or fewer pre-split shares received $0.0578 cash per share
Placed in receivership 10/02/2006
No stockholders' equity

CRYOTECH INDS INC (FL)
Charter cancelled for failure to file annual reports in August 1994

CRYPLEX INDS INC (NY)
Common 10¢ par split (3) for (1) by issuance of (2) additional shares 4/15/68
Charter cancelled and proclaimed dissolved for failure to pay taxes and file reports 12/15/75

CRYPTIC VENTURES INC (BC)
Reorganized under the laws of Yukon as Zen International Resources Ltd. 11/21/96
Each share Common no par exchanged for (0.2) share Common no par
Zen International Resources Ltd. (Yukon) reorganized in Alberta as Orca Petroleum Inc. 4/1/2002 which reorganized in British Columbia as Nautilus Minerals Inc. 5/10/2006

CRYPTO-SERVICES INC (NV)
Name changed to Fortune Valley Treasures, Inc. 03/30/2017

CRYPTOLOGIC EXCHANGE CORP (ON)
Each Exchangeable Share no par exchanged for (1) share CryptoLogic Ltd. Ordinary no par 04/10/2012
(See CryptoLogic Ltd.)

CRYPTOLOGIC INC (ON)
Preferred no par called for redemption at $0.10 on 12/21/1998
Plan of arrangement effective 06/01/2007
Each share Common no par exchanged for either (1) CryptoLogic

Ltd. Ordinary share or (1) CryptoLogic Exchange Corp. Exchangeable Share
Note: Option to receive CryptoLogic Exchange Corp. shares expired 05/22/2007
(See each company's listing)

CRYPTOLOGIC LTD (GUERNSEY)
Acquired by Amaya Gaming Group Inc. 07/31/2012
Each share Ordinary no par exchanged for USD$2.535 cash

CRYPTOSIGN INC (DE)
Name changed to NABUfit Global, Inc. 12/10/2015
NABUfit Global, Inc. name changed to NewBridge Global Ventures, Inc. 12/12/2017

CRYS TEL TELECOMMUNICATIONS COM INC (FL)
Recapitalized as Juma Technology, Inc. 04/17/2006
Each share Common $0.001 par exchanged for (0.001) share Common $0.001 par
Juma Technology, Inc. name changed to Silverton Mining Corp. Ltd. 07/05/2006 which recapitalized as Fleet Management Solutions Inc. 02/13/2009

CRYSTAL ASSET MGMT INC (OR)
Name changed to Leading - Edge Earth Products, Inc. 12/29/1992
Leading - Edge Earth Products, Inc. name changed to LEEP, Inc. 01/03/2005

CRYSTAL BRANDS INC (DE)
Filed petition under Chapter 11 Federal Bankruptcy Code 1/21/94
No stockholders' equity

CRYSTAL BROADCASTING INC (DE)
Name changed to Alliance Broadcasting Group, Inc. 12/4/96
Alliance Broadcasting Group, Inc. recapitalized as Emission Controls Corp. 2/15/2002

CRYSTAL CAP CORP (NV)
Recapitalized as Monarch Minerals & Mining Inc. 5/13/91
Each share Common $0.001 par exchanged for (0.5) share Common $0.001 par
(See Monarch Minerals & Mining Inc.)

CRYSTAL CHEMICAL CO.
Succeeded by Crystal Corp. in 1933
Details not available

CRYSTAL CITY GAS CO. (NY)
Name changed to Corning Natural Gas Corp. 06/24/1953
Corning Natural Gas Corp. reorganized as Corning Natural Gas Holding Corp. 12/17/2013

CRYSTAL CORP.
Acquired by Affiliated Products, Inc. in 1935
Details not available

CRYSTAL DAVID INC (DE)
Merged into General Mills, Inc. 09/23/1969
Each share Common $1 par exchanged for (0.9) share Common $1.50 par

CRYSTAL DYNAMICS INC
Merged into Eidos Interactive Inc. 11/5/98
Each share Preferred Ser. D exchanged for $3.75 cash
Each share Common exchanged for $0.641 cash

CRYSTAL EXPL INC. (BC)
Recapitalized as Benchmark Metals Inc. 05/29/2018
Each share Common no par exchanged for (0.33333333) share Common no par

CRYSTAL GAS STORAGE INC (LA)
Merged into El Paso Energy Corp. 01/05/2000

Each share Common 1¢ par exchanged for $57 cash
$0.06 Sr. Conv. Preferred 1¢ par called for redemption at $1 on 02/04/2000
Public interest eliminated

CRYSTAL GOLD LTD (CO)
Name changed to Morgan Medical Holdings, Inc. 7/21/89
Morgan Medical Holdings, Inc. merged into NMR of America, Inc. 9/14/95 which merged into Medical Resources Inc. 8/30/96

CRYSTAL GRAPHITE CORP (BC)
Placed in receivership 01/26/2006
Stockholders' equity unlikely

CRYSTAL INTL TRAVEL GROUP INC. (DE)
SEC revoked common stock registration 10/05/2011

CRYSTAL KIRKLAND MINES LTD. (ON)
Charter cancelled 11/30/1964
No stockholders' equity

CRYSTAL LAKE MINES LTD. (QC)
Charter annulled for failure to file annual reports in 1955

CRYSTAL LEAD MINES CO.
Merged into Day Mines, Inc. in 1947
Day Mines, Inc. merged into Hecla Mining Co. (Wash.) 10/20/81 which was reincorporated in Delaware 6/6/83

CRYSTAL MNG N L (AUSTRALIA)
Name changed to Oriental Crystal International Ltd. 12/22/1995
(See Oriental Crystal International Ltd.)

CRYSTAL MTN INC (WA)
Merged into Boyne USA, Inc. 4/1/97
Each share Class A Common $50 par exchanged for $65.52 cash

CRYSTAL MTN RES LTD (BC)
Struck off register and declared dissolved for failure to file returns 9/1/93

CRYSTAL OIL & LD CO (MD)
Each share $1.12 Preferred $2.50 par exchanged for (3) shares Capital Stock $1 par 07/19/1961
Common 10¢ par reclassified as Capital Stock $1 par 07/19/1961
Capital Stock $1 par reclassified as Common $1 par 10/31/1963
Name changed to Crystal Oil Co. (MD) 05/15/1969
Crystal Oil Co. (MD) reincorporated in Louisiana 05/04/1984 which name changed to Crystal Gas Storage, Inc. 06/21/1999
(See Crystal Gas Storage, Inc.)

CRYSTAL OIL CO (LA)
Reincorporated 05/04/1984
$1.50 Conv. Preferred Ser. A $5 par called for redemption 09/23/1977
Common $1 par split (2) for (1) by issuance of (1) additional share 07/20/1979
Common $1 par split (3) for (2) by issuance of (0.5) additional share 01/21/1980
Common $1 par split (3) for (2) by issuance of (0.5) additional share 07/18/1980
Common $1 par split (3) for (2) by issuance of (0.5) additional share 03/20/1981
State of incorporation changed from (MD) to (LA) 05/04/1984
Common $1 par changed to 1¢ par 12/05/1985
Reorganized under Chapter 11 Federal Bankruptcy Code 01/30/1987
Each share old Common 1¢ par exchanged for (1) share new Common 1¢ par, (3.868044) $0.125 Common Stock Purchase Warrants expiring 01/30/1999, (3.868044)

$0.15 Common Stock Purchase Warrants expiring 01/30/1999 and (3.868044) $0.25 Common Stock Purchase Warrants expiring 01/30/1999
Each share new Common 1¢ par exchanged again for (0.005) share new Common 1¢ par 01/28/1988
Each share new Common 1¢ par exchanged again for (0.01) share new Common 1¢ par 05/29/1992
New Common 1¢ par split (10) for (1) by issuance of (9) additional shares 05/29/1992
$0.06 Conv. Preferred Ser. A 1¢ par called for redemption 04/19/1994
$0.06 Sr. Conv. Preferred 1¢ par reclassified as Adjustable Rate Conv. Participating Preferred 1¢ par 04/19/1994
Name changed to Crystal Gas Storage Inc. 06/21/1999
(See Crystal Gas Storage Inc.)

CRYSTAL OIL REFINING CORP. (MD)
6% Preferred $100 par changed to $10 par 00/00/1935
Recapitalized as Crystal Oil & Land Co. (MD) 12/01/1955
Each share $6 Preferred $10 par exchanged for (4) shares $1.12 Preferred $2.50 par and (10) shares Common 10¢ par
Each share Common no par exchanged for (1) share Common 10¢ par
Crystal Oil & Land Co. (MD) name changed to Crystal Oil Co. (MD) 05/15/1969 which reincorporated in Louisiana 05/04/1984 which name changed to Crystal Gas Storage, Inc. 06/21/1999
(See Crystal Gas Storage, Inc.)

CRYSTAL PPTYS HLDGS INC (NV)
SEC revoked common stock registration 11/19/2010

CRYSTAL RIV CAP INC (MD)
Merged into Brookfield Asset Management Inc. 07/30/2010
Each share Common $0.001 par exchanged for $0.60 cash

CRYSTAL ROCK HLDGS INC (DE)
Acquired by Cott Corp. 03/23/2018
Each share Common $0.001 par exchanged for $0.97 cash

CRYSTAL SPRINGS BLEACHERY, INC. (GA)
Name changed to Crystal Springs Textiles, Inc. 11/15/1967
(See Crystal Springs Textiles, Inc.)

CRYSTAL SPRINGS TEXTILES, INC. (GA)
Acquired by Dan River Mills, Inc. 03/31/1969
Each share Common no par exchanged for $22 cash

CRYSTAL SYS SOLUTIONS LTD (ISRAEL)
Name changed to BluePhoenix Solutions Ltd. 08/11/2003
BluePhoenix Solutions Ltd. name changed to ModSys International Ltd. 01/23/2015

CRYSTAL TISSUE CO (OH)
8% Preferred $100 par called for redemption 01/01/1964
Acquired by Crystal Acquisition Corp. 02/14/1985
Each share Common no par exchanged for $175 cash

CRYSTAL VENTURE CORP (CO)
Recapitalized as Enhanced Services Co., Inc. 11/10/1992
Each share Common $0.0001 par exchanged for (0.1) share Common $0.0001 par

CRYSTAL-VINTAGE GROWTH CORP (CANADA)
Completely liquidated
Each share Common no par received first and final distribution of (1.25)

shares Mercator Transport Group Corp. Common no par payable 01/14/2008 to holders of record 08/20/2007
Note: Certificates were not required to be surrendered and are without value

CRYSTAL WTR UTILS CORP (CT)
Merged into Connecticut Water Service, Inc. 09/30/1999
Each share Common exchanged for (2.46) shares Common no par

CRYSTALITE PRODUCTS CO. OF CALIFORNIA
Dissolution approved 00/00/1943
Details not available

CRYSTALITE PRODUCTS CORP.
Reorganized as Crystalite Products Co. of California 00/00/1938
Details not available

CRYSTALIX GROUP INTL INC (NV)
Recapitalized as Seaena, Inc. 03/31/2006
Each share Common $0.001 par exchanged for (0.02857142) share Common $0.001 par
(See Seaena, Inc.)

CRYSTALLEX INTL CORP (BC)
Reincorporated under the laws of Canada 01/23/1998

CRYSTALLUME (CA)
Name changed to Electronic Designs Inc. 03/06/1996
Electronic Designs Inc. merged into White Electronic Designs Corp. 10/23/1998
(See White Electronic Designs Corp.)

CRYSTALOGRAPHY CORP (NJ)
Charter declared void for non-payment of taxes 01/05/1976

CRYTON OPTICS INC (NY)
Out of business 10/21/1975
No stockholders' equity

CS CHINA ACQUISITION CORP (CAYMAN ISLANDS)
Each Unit exchanged for (1) share Ordinary $0.0001 par and (2) Ordinary Stock Purchase Warrants expiring 08/10/2013 on 02/22/2010
Name changed to Asia Entertainment & Resources Ltd. 02/22/2010
Asia Entertainment & Resources Ltd. name changed to Iao Kun Group Holding Co. Ltd. 10/02/2013 which name changed to LiNiu Technology Group 04/27/2017

CS FIRST BOSTON INCOME FD INC (MD)
Name changed to BEA Income Fund, Inc. 07/31/1995
BEA Income Fund, Inc. name changed to Credit Suisse Asset Management Income Fund, Inc. 05/11/1999

CS FIRST BOSTON STRATEGIC INCOME FD INC (MD)
Name changed to BEA Strategic Income Fund, Inc. 07/31/1995
BEA Strategic Income Fund, Inc. name changed to BEA Strategic Global Income Fund, Inc. 05/13/1997 which name changed to Credit Suisse Asset Management Strategic Global Income Fund, Inc. 05/14/2001

CS GROUP INC (TX)
Recapitalized as DeCorp Inc. 10/29/1987
Each share Common 10¢ par exchanged for (0.025) share Common $0.0001 par
(See DeCorp Inc.)

CS-LIVE COM INC (ON)
Name changed to Intelligent Web Technologies Inc. 09/18/2001
(See Intelligent Web Technologies Inc.)

CS PRIMO CORP (DE)
Name changed to Dynasty Travel Group, Inc. 07/11/1991
Dynasty Travel Group, Inc. name changed to Phoenix Information Systems Corp. 09/29/1993
(See Phoenix Information Systems Corp.)

CS RES LTD (ON)
Merged into PanCanadian Petroleum Ltd. 07/17/1997
Each share Common no par exchanged for $16 cash

CS TELEVISION INC (DE)
Dissolved by proclamation 09/27/1995

CSA MGMT INC (ON)
Class A Common no par split (2) for (1) by issuance of (1) additional share 06/19/1995
Merged into Goldcorp Inc. (New) 11/01/2000
Each share Non-Vtg. Class A no par exchanged for (2.1) shares Common no par
Each share Class B no par exchanged for (6) shares Common no par

CSA MGMT LTD (CANADA)
Merged into CSA Management Inc. 03/31/1994
Each share Class A no par exchanged for (1) share Non-Vtg. Class A no par
CSA Management Inc. merged into Goldcorp Inc. (New) 11/01/2000

CSA MINERALS CORP (ON)
Reorganized under the laws of Canada as Consolidated CSA Minerals Inc. 01/23/1986
Each share Common no par exchanged for (0.25) share Common no par
Consolidated CSA Minerals Inc. name changed to Pamorex Minerals Inc. 04/16/1987 which merged into Royal Oak Mines Inc. 07/23/1991 which recapitalized as Royal Oak Ventures Inc. 02/14/2000
(See Royal Oak Ventures Inc.)

CSAM FUNDING I (CAYMAN ISLANDS)
Reg. S Preference called for redemption 07/30/2012

CSB CORP. (IA)
Voluntarily dissolved 01/15/1981
Details not available

CSB FINL CORP (DE)
Merged into One Valley Bancorp, Inc. 04/30/1996
Each share Common 1¢ par exchanged for (0.6774) share Common $10 par
One Valley Bancorp, Inc. merged into BB&T Corp. 07/06/2000

CSB FINL CORP (NJ)
Merged into Lakeland Bancorp, Inc. 08/25/2003
Each share Common no par exchanged for (1.781) share Common no par

CSB FINL GROUP INC (DE)
Merged into Midland States Bancorp 7/14/2000
Each share Common 1¢ par exchanged for $16 cash

CSC HLDGS INC (DE)
Depositary Preferred Ser. I called for redemption at $25.70 plus $0.183 accrued dividend on 11/02/1999
11.75% Exchangeable Preferred Ser. H 1¢ par called for redemption at $103.917 on 05/06/2004
11.125% Depositary Preferred Ser. M 1¢ par called for redemption at $103.708 on 05/06/2004
Public interest eliminated

CSC INDS INC (DE)
Recapitalized as Ridgecrest Healthcare Group, Inc. 10/25/2005
Each share Common 10¢ par exchanged for (0.005) share Common $0.001 par
Ridgecrest Healthcare Group, Inc. recapitalized as Liberty Technologies, Inc. 10/20/2009 which recapitalized as DomiKnow, Inc. 02/15/2013 which name changed to Gooi Global, Inc. 04/02/2015

CSD, INC. (NV)
Name changed to Capital Energy & Operating Co. 05/06/1981
(See Capital Energy & Operating Co.)

CSE CORP (DE)
Class A Common $2.50 par changed to $1.875 par and (0.33333333) additional share issued 06/09/1972
Stock Dividend - 10% 02/28/1980
Acquired by La Guarantie Mutuelle des Fonctionnaires 04/08/1981
Each share Class A Common $1.875 par exchanged for $40 cash

CSE LIQUIDATING CORP. (DE)
Liquidation completed
Each share Common 10¢ par exchanged for initial distribution of $5 cash 09/30/1976
Each share Common 10¢ par received second and final distribution of $0.421 cash 10/01/1977

CSF HLDGS INC (FL)
Class B Common 1¢ par split (5) for (4) by issuance of (0.25) additional share 06/29/1992
Class B Common 1¢ par split (3) for (2) by issuance of (0.5) additional share 10/26/1992
Class B Common 1¢ par split (3) for (2) by issuance of (0.5) additional share 02/22/1993
Class B Common 1¢ par split (5) for (4) by issuance of (0.25) additional share 06/29/1995
Acquired by NationsBank Corp. 01/10/1996
Each share Class B Common 1¢ par exchanged for $39.50 cash

CSG RES LTD (BC)
Name changed to Artgallerylive.com Management Ltd. 09/24/1999
Artgallerylive.com Management Ltd. recapitalized as Adaptive Marketing Solutions Inc. 01/18/2001 which recapitalized as Permission Marketing Solutions Inc. 01/18/2002 which name changed to Pacific Asia China Energy Inc. 01/04/2006
(See Pacific Asia China Energy Inc.)

CSI BUSINESS FIN INC (FL)
Each share old Common $0.001 par exchanged for (0.04) share new Common $0.001 par 06/05/2006
Reincorporated under the laws of Nevada as Natural Nutrition, Inc. 11/03/2006
Natural Nutrition, Inc. recapitalized as AppTech Corp. 11/16/2009

CSI COMPUTER SPECIALISTS INC (DE)
Merged into Interactive Systems, Inc. 05/24/2000
Each share Common $0.001 par exchanged for $1 cash

CSI CR SYS INTL INC (BC)
Acquired by Royal Bank of Canada (Montreal, QC) 02/23/2000
Each share Common no par exchanged for $1.30 cash

CSI TECHNOLOGIES INC (NV)
Company terminated registration of common stock and is no longer public as of 8/20/2003

CSI TELE MARKETING INC (DE)
Common 1¢ par split (5) for (1) by issuance of (4) additional shares 01/16/1985
Name changed to Precision Target Marketing Inc. 11/14/1986
(See Precision Target Marketing Inc.)

CSI WIRELESS INC (AB)
Name changed to Hemisphere GPS Inc. 05/15/2007
Hemisphere GPS Inc. name changed to AgJunction Inc. 05/29/2013

CSK AUTO CORP (DE)
Merged into O'Reilly Automotive, Inc. (Old) 07/11/2008
Each share Common 1¢ par exchanged for (0.4285) share Common 1¢ par and $1 cash
O'Reilly Automotive, Inc. (Old) reorganized as O'Reilly Automotive, Inc. (New) 12/29/2010

CSK HOLDINGS CORP (JAPAN)
Name changed 10/03/2005
Each Unsponsored ADR for Common exchanged for (1) Sponsored ADR for Common 08/01/1994
Name changed from CSK Corp. to CSK Holdings Corp. 10/03/2005
ADR agreement terminated 01/31/2006
Each Sponsored ADR for Common exchanged for $45.0835 cash

CSL LTG MFG INC (DE)
Each share old Common 1¢ par exchanged for (0.07692307) share new Common 1¢ par 09/03/1998
Company terminated registration of common stock and is no longer public 03/28/2000

CSM ENVIRONMENTAL SYS INC (DE)
Each share Common 40¢ par exchanged for (0.01) share Common $1 par 11/27/1995
Name changed to CSM Worldwide, Inc. 12/23/1998
(See CSM Worldwide, Inc.)

CSM JAPAN FD LTD (CANADA)
Name changed to AGF Japan Fund Ltd. 05/25/1973

CSM MED DEVICES INC (DE)
Merged into KCSM, Inc. 06/12/1978
Each share Common 15¢ par exchanged for $0.02 cash

CSM N V (NETHERLANDS)
Name changed to Corbion N.V. 10/31/2013

CSM SYS CORP (AB)
Each share old Common no par exchanged for (0.25) share new Common no par 06/14/2002
Recapitalized as Visionstate Corp. 09/16/2014
Each share new Common no par exchanged for (0.25) share Common no par

CSM SYS INC (DE)
Each share Common 10¢ par exchanged for (0.25) share Common 40¢ par 09/08/1980
Stock Dividends - 20% 04/17/1984; 25% 09/20/1985
Name changed to CSM Environmental Systems, Inc. 05/31/1990
CSM Environmental Systems, Inc. name changed to CSM Worldwide, Inc. 12/23/1998

CSM WORLDWIDE INC (DE)
Company advised private 03/00/2008
Details not available

CSMG TECHNOLOGIES INC (TX)
Under Chapter 11 plan of reorganization each share Common $0.0001 par received distribution of (0.004511) share BioFuse Medical Technologies, Inc. Common payable 12/23/2014 to holders of record 08/25/2014
Note: BioFuse Medical Technologies, Inc. is a privately held company

CSOP ETF TR
Trust terminated 09/28/2018
Each share CSOP China CSI 300 A-H Dynamic ETF received $27.3637766 cash

(Additional Information in Active)

CSPC PHARMACEUTICAL GROUP LTD (HONG KONG)
ADR agreement terminated 11/30/2017
Each Sponsored ADR for Ordinary exchanged for (50) shares Ordinary
Note: Unexchanged ADR's will be sold and the proceeds, if any, held for claim after 12/03/2018
(Additional Information in Active)

CSR CORP LTD (CHINA)
ADR agreement terminated 07/16/2015
Each ADR for Ordinary exchanged for $38.757283 cash

CSR INDS INC (NY)
Dissolved by proclamation 06/23/1993

CSR LTD (AUSTRALIA)
Each Unsponsored ADR for Ordinary exchanged for (0.25) Sponsored ADR for Ordinary 12/29/1989
Each Sponsored ADR for Ordinary received distribution of $11.71901 cash payable 05/15/2003 to holders of record 05/08/2003
ADR agreement terminated 10/03/2003
Each ADR for Ordinary exchanged for $5.71818 cash
(Additional Information in Active)

CSR PLC (UNITED KINGDOM)
Each Unsponsored ADR for Ordinary exchanged for (1) Sponsored ADR for Ordinary 08/05/2011
ADR agreement terminated 09/14/2015
Each Sponsored ADR for Ordinary exchanged for $55.2028 cash

CSRA CAPITAL CORP. (GA)
Stock Dividends - 18% 01/10/1969; 10% 03/15/1971
Completely liquidated 02/25/1982
No stockholders' equity

CSRA INC (NV)
Acquired by General Dynamics Corp. 04/03/2018
Each share Common $0.001 par exchanged for $41.25 cash

CST BRANDS INC (DE)
Acquired by Alimentation Couche-Tard Inc. 06/28/2017
Each share Common 1¢ par exchanged for $48.53 cash

CST COLDSWITCH TECHNOLOGIES INC (BC)
Name changed to Coldswitch Technologies Inc. 06/21/2001
Coldswitch Technologies Inc. name changed to Photon Control Inc. 08/09/2002

CST ENTMT INC (DE)
Name changed 04/24/1995
Name changed from CST Entertainment Imaging Inc. to CST Entertainment, Inc. 04/24/1995
Recapitalized as Legacy Holding, Inc. 06/11/2007
Each share Common 15¢ par exchanged for (0.00166666) share Common 15¢ par
Note: Holders of between (100) and (60,000) shares received (100) shares
Holders of (99) shares or fewer were not affected by the reverse split
(See Legacy Holding, Inc.)

CST HLDG CORP (CO)
Reincorporated under the laws of Delaware as WebXU, Inc. 10/17/2011

CSW VENTURES CORP (AB)
Name changed to Direct IT Canada Inc. (AB) 11/12/2001
Direct IT Canada Inc. (AB) reincorporated in Ontario 11/25/2002 which recapitalized as Rage Energy Ltd. 08/29/2006
(See Rage Energy Ltd.)

CSX CORP (VA)
$7 Conv. Preferred Ser. A no par called for redemption 07/31/1992 (Additional Information in Active)

CT & T TELECOMMUNICATIONS INC (BC)
Recapitalized as Global CT & T Telecommunications Inc. 02/12/1998
Each share Common no par exchanged for (0.25) share Common no par
(See Global CT & T Telecommunications Inc.)

CT COMMUNICATIONS INC (NC)
Class B Common 50¢ par split (3) for (2) by issuance of (0.5) additional share payable 08/29/1997 to holders of record 08/01/1997 Ex date - 09/02/1997
Each share Class B Common 50¢ par exchanged for (0.2272727) share new Common no par 01/28/1999
Each share old Common no par exchanged for (0.2272727) share new Common no par 01/28/1999
New Common no par split (2) for (1) by issuance of (1) additional share payable 04/05/2000 to holders of record 03/15/2000
Merged into Windstream Corp. 08/31/2007
Each share new Common no par exchanged for $31.50 cash

CT FINL SVCS INC (CANADA)
1st Adjustable Dividend Perpetual Preference Ser. 2 no par called for redemption 12/29/1995
Acquired by Toronto-Dominion Bank (Toronto, ON) 02/01/2000
Each share 1st Adjustable Dividend Perpetual Preference Ser. 4 no par exchanged for (1) share Class A 1st Preferred Ser. K no par
Each share 1st Adjustable Dividend Perpetual Preference Ser. 5 no par exchanged for (1) share Class A 1st Preferred Ser. L no par
Each share Common no par exchanged for $67 cash
Note: Non-Canadian residents received cash

CT HLDGS ENTERPRISES INC (DE)
Recapitalized 02/28/2007
Each share Common 1¢ par received distribution of (0.25) share Citadel Security Software Inc. Common 1¢ par payable 05/17/2002 to holders of record 05/06/2002
Recapitalized from CT Holdings, Inc. to CT Holdings Enterprises, Inc. 02/28/2007
Each share old Common 1¢ par exchanged for (0.01428571) share new Common 1¢ par
Recapitalized as Xcorporeal, Inc. 10/15/2007
Each share new Common 1¢ par exchanged for (0.12091898) share Common 1¢ par

CT HLDGS INC (DE)
Each share Common $0.001 par exchanged for (0.0005) share new Common $0.001 par 03/21/2011
SEC revoked common stock registration 07/13/2011

CTB INDS INC (AB)
Struck off register for failure to file annual returns 04/01/1996

CTB INTL CORP (DE)
Merged into Berkshire Hathaway Inc. 10/31/2002
Each share Common 1¢ par exchanged for $12.75 cash

CTBC FINL HLDG CO LTD (TAIWAN)
Stock Dividends - 6.27376% payable 10/07/2013 to holders of record 08/19/2013 Ex date - 08/15/2013; 3.34055% payable 11/19/2014 to holders of record 09/18/2014 Ex date - 09/16/2014; 7.14687% payable 09/25/2015 to holders of record 08/06/2015 Ex date - 08/04/2015; 6.99981% payable 11/22/2016 to holders of record 10/12/2016 Ex date - 10/07/2016
ADR agreement terminated 12/30/2016
Each Sponsored 144A GDR for Common exchanged for $12.96912 cash

CTBI PFD CAP TR (DE)
9% Trust Preferred Securities called for redemption at $25 on 03/31/2007

CTBI PFD CAP TR II (DE)
8.25% Trust Preferred Securities called for redemption at $10 plus $0.20625 accrued dividends on 03/31/2007

CTC 3 INC (FL)
Name changed to Ventech International Corp. 07/16/1998
Ventech International Corp. name changed to VDO.com, Inc. 06/15/1999 which name changed to Hundred Mile Plus, Ltd. 09/19/2001 which recapitalized as Ultra Pure Water Technologies, Inc. 05/24/2004

CTC COMMUNICATIONS CORP (MA)
Reorganized under the laws of Delaware as CTC Communications Group Inc. and Common 1¢ par changed to no par 10/01/1999
(See CTC Communications Group Inc.)

CTC COMMUNICATIONS GROUP INC (DE)
Common no par split (3) for (2) by issuance of (0.5) additional share payable 03/17/2000 to holders of record 03/06/2000
Plan of reorganization under Chapter 11 Federal Bankruptcy Code effective 12/16/2003
No stockholders' equity

CTC COMPUTER CORP (DE)
Under Chapter XI bankruptcy plan of arrangement each share Common $2 par received first and final distribution of (0.1190476) share Data Instruments Co. Common 25¢ par 06/17/1972
(See Data Instruments Co.)

CTC COSMETICS HLDGS INC (DE)
Each share old Common $0.004 par exchanged for (0.01) share new Common $0.004 par 05/15/2000
Note: Holders of (99) or fewer pre-split shares received (1) share
Name changed to Combine Corp. 11/02/2000
(See Combine Corp.)

CTC CROWN TECHNOLOGIES CORP (AB)
Struck off register for failure to file annual returns 07/01/2000

CTC MEDIA INC (DE)
Acquired by CTCM Merger Sub, Inc. 05/20/2016
Each share Common 1¢ par exchanged for $2.0503 cash

CTF TECHNOLOGIES INC (BC)
Reincorporated 08/11/2008
Place of incorporation changed from (YT) to (BC) 08/11/2008
Merged into FleetCor Technologies, Inc. 07/03/2012
Each share Common no par exchanged for (1) share FTC Cards Inc. Common no par and $2.11143544 cash

CTG COMPRESSION TECHNOLOGY GROUP INC (BC)
Struck off register and declared dissolved for failure to file returns 09/02/1994

CTG INC (ON)
Merged into British Telecommunications PLC 12/31/1985
Each share Common no par exchanged for $5.25 cash

CTG RES INC (CT)
Merged into Energy East Corp. 09/01/2000
Each share Common no par exchanged for either (a) (1.18) shares Common 1¢ par and $12.8994 cash or (b) (0.01848) share Common 1¢ par and $40.5625 cash
Note: Option to receive (b) expired 09/06/2000
(See Energy East Corp.)

C3 INC (MD)
Common 1¢ par split (2) for (1) by issuance of (1) additional share 07/13/1981
Each share Common 1¢ par exchanged for (1.4) shares 12% Exchangeable Preferred 1¢ par 11/21/1989
Stock Dividends - 12.3% 12/01/1990; 12% 12/01/1991
Name changed to Telos Corp. 05/11/1995

C3 INC (NC)
Name changed to Charles & Colvard, Ltd. 05/26/2000

C-3D DIGITAL INC (UT)
SEC revoked common stock registration 01/21/2011

C3D INC (FL)
Name changed to Constellation 3D, Inc. (FL) 12/28/1999
Constellation 3D, Inc. (FL) reincorporated in Delaware 02/08/2001
(See Constellation 3D, Inc. (DE))

CTI BIOPHARMA CORP (WA)
Each share Conv. Preferred Ser. N-1 no par automatically became (800) shares old Common no par 10/30/2015
Each share Conv. Preferred Ser. N-2 no par automatically became (909.09) shares old Common no par 12/31/2015
Each share old Common no par exchanged for (0.1) share new Common no par 01/03/2017
Reincorporated under the laws of Delaware, Conv. Preferred Ser. N-3 no par reclassified as Conv. Preferred Ser. N $0.001 par and Common no par changed to $0.001 par 01/29/2018

CTI DIVERSIFIED HLDGS INC (DE)
Name changed to Wescorp Energy Inc. 12/17/2003
(See Wescorp Energy Inc.)

CTI GROUP HLDG INC (DE)
Acquired by Enghouse Systems Ltd. 12/07/2016
Each share Class A Common 1¢ par exchanged for $0.61 cash

CTI INDS CORP (DE)
Issue Information - 1,500,000 shares COM offered at $4 per share on 11/05/1997
Each share Common $0.065 par exchanged for (1/3) share Common $0.195 par 11/05/1999
Reincorporated under the laws of Illinois and Common $0.195 par changed to no par 11/19/2001

CTI MOLECULAR IMAGING INC (DE)
Merged into Siemens A.G. 05/13/2005
Each share Common 1¢ par exchanged for $20.50 cash

CTI TECHNICAL INC (NV)
Charter delinquent for failure to file annual reports 1/1/2004

CTI TECHNOLOGY INC (NV)
Reorganized under Chapter 11 Federal Bankruptcy Code as Dover Holding Corp. 02/10/2003
Each share Common $0.001 par will receive an undetermined amount of Common $0.001 par
Note: Certificates were not required to be surrendered and are without value

CTL CR INC (DE)
Merged into Bay View Capital Corp. 06/14/1996
Each share Common 1¢ par exchanged for $18 cash

CTM CITRUS S A (BRAZIL)
ADR agreement terminated 1/17/2003
Each Sponsored ADR for Ordinary exchanged for $0.1419 cash

CTM MEDIA HOLDINGS INC (DE)
Each share old Class A Common 1¢ par exchanged for (0.05) share new Class A Common 1¢ par 12/13/2011
Each share old Class B Common 1¢ par exchanged for (0.05) share new Class B Common 1¢ par 12/13/2011
New Class A Common 1¢ par reclassified as new Class B Common 1¢ par 07/28/2015
New Class B Common 1¢ par split (10) for (1) by issuance of (9) additional shares payable 08/03/2015 to holders of record 08/03/2015 Ex date - 08/04/2015
Name changed to IDW Media Holdings, Inc. 08/10/2015

CTP INDS INC (NY)
Common 1¢ par changed to 10¢ par and (1) additional share issued 05/24/1968
Charter cancelled and proclaimed dissolved for failure to pay taxes 12/23/1992

CTS INTL LTD (NY)
Dissolved by proclamation 3/24/93

CTT INTL DISTRIBUTORS INC (DE)
Common $0.0001 par split (3) for (1) by issuance of (2) additional shares payable 5/17/2007 to holders of record 5/14/2007
Ex date - 5/18/2007
Name changed to SK3 Group, Inc. 5/23/2007

CTV INC (ON)
Acquired by BCE Inc. 05/26/2000
Each share Common no par exchanged for $38.50 cash

C2 GLOBAL TECHNOLOGIES INC (FL)
Name changed to Counsel RB Capital Inc. 02/04/2011
Counsel RB Capital Inc. name changed to Heritage Global Inc. 08/29/2013

C2 INC (WI)
Name changed to Total Logistics, Inc. 04/21/2004
(See Total Logistics, Inc.)

C2 TECHNOLOGIES INC (NV)
Name changed to Tidelands Oil & Gas Corp. 10/21/98

C2C GOLD CORP INC (QC)
Recapitalized as Key Gold Holding Inc. 03/11/2010
Each share Common no par exchanged for (0.1) share Common no par
Key Gold Holding Inc. recapitalized as Pangolin Diamonds Corp. 03/20/2013

C2C INC (QC)
Name changed to C2C Gold Corp. Inc. 02/27/2008
C2C Gold Corp. Inc. recapitalized as Key Gold Holding Inc. 03/11/2010 which recapitalized as Pangolin Diamonds Corp. 03/20/2013

C2C INDL PPTYS LTD (ON)
Each share old Common no par exchanged for (0.04) share new Common no par 04/11/2012
Merged into Dundee Industrial Real Estate Investment Trust 07/23/2013

Each share new Common no par exchanged for (0.4485) Unit Dundee Industrial Real Estate Investment Trust name changed to Dream Industrial Real Estate Investment Trust 05/08/2014

C2C MNG CORP (AB)
Name changed to C2C Zeolite Corp. 12/22/2000
C2C Zeolite Corp. name changed to Zeox Corp. 04/21/2006
(See Zeox Corp.)

C2C ZEOLITE CORP (AB)
Name changed to Zeox Corp. 04/21/2006
(See Zeox Corp.)

C2I SOLUTIONS INC (DE)
Issue Information - 1,000,000 shares COM offered at $6 per share on 02/24/1998
Name changed to Globaldigitalcommerce.com Inc. 12/22/99
Globaldigitalcommerce.com Inc. recapitalized as Dreamfield Holdings Inc. 11/18/2002 which name changed to Riverside Entertainment Inc. 5/24/2004 which recapitalized as Axis Technologies Group, Inc. 10/20/2006

CU BANCORP (CA)
Merged into Pacific Century Financial Corp. 07/03/1997
Each share Common no par exchanged for $15.34 cash

CU BANCORP (CA)
Merged into PacWest Bancorp 10/20/2017
Each share Common no par exchanged for (0.5308) share Common 1¢ par and $12 cash

CU INC (CANADA)
Preferred Ser. 2 no par called for redemption at $25 on 06/01/2014
(Additional Information in Active)

CU-KAM PORCUPINE MINES LTD. (ON)
Charter cancelled for failure to pay taxes and file returns 6/14/79

CUATRO INDUSTRIES CORP. (NV)
Name changed to International Cosmetics & Chemicals, Inc. 3/1/63
International Cosmetics & Chemicals, Inc. name changed to International Minerals Corp. 7/1/65 which name changed to Dynatron, Inc. 10/7/68
(See Dynatron, Inc.)

CUB AIRCRAFT CORP. LTD. (ON)
Name changed to Transvision-Television (Canada) Ltd. 03/00/1949
Transvision-Television (Canada) Ltd. recapitalized as Arcan Corp. Ltd. 00/00/1953
(See Arcan Corp. Ltd.)

CUB ENERGY INC (ON)
Reincorporated under the laws of Canada 02/28/2012

CUBA CANE SUGAR CORP.
Succeeded by Cuban Cane Products Co., Inc. in 1930
Details not available

CUBA CO (NJ)
Recapitalized in 1938
7% Preferred $100 par changed to $7 Preferred no par
Common no par changed to $1 par
Acquired by Compania Cubana on a (1) for (0.265625) basis 9/3/59

CUBA RR CO (NJ)
Charter revoked for failure to file reports and pay fees 02/05/1962

CUBA VENTURES CORP (BC)
Name changed to CUV Ventures Corp. 03/01/2018

CUBACAN EXPL INC (AB)
Cease trade order 06/20/2003

CUBAMINA LTD.
Merged into International Metal & Petroleum Corp. on a (1) for (2) basis 11/4/57
(See International Metal & Petroleum. Corp.)

CUBAN-AMERICAN MANGANESE CORP.
Liquidated in 1946
Details not available

CUBAN AMERICAN OIL CO. (DE)
Recapitalized as McCulloch Oil Corp. of California and Common 50¢ par changed to 10¢ par 11/28/1960
McCulloch Oil Corp. of California name changed to McCulloch Oil Corp. 05/09/1969 which name changed to MCO Holdings, Inc. 06/19/1980 which name changed to MAXXAM Inc. 10/06/1988
(See MAXXAM Inc.)

CUBAN-AMERICAN SUGAR CO. (NJ)
Name changed to North American Sugar Industries, Inc. 1/17/63
North American Sugar Industries, Inc. merged into Borden, Inc. 4/28/71
(See Borden, Inc.)

CUBAN ATLANTIC SUGAR CO. (DE)
Capital Stock $10 par changed to $7.50 par and $2.50 in cash paid in 1938
Capital Stock $7.50 par changed to $5 par in 1939
Capital Stock $5 par reclassified as Common $5 par in 1946
Stock Dividend - 100% 8/16/51
Liquidation completed
Each share Common $5 par received initial distribution of (0.0715) share Central Violeta Sugar Co., S.A. Capital Stock $9.50 par and $6 cash 5/7/58
Each share Common $5 par received second distribution of $9 cash 10/22/58
Each share Common $5 par exchanged for third and final distribution of (2) shares Compania Azucarera Atlantica Del Golfo Capital Stock P5 par and $1.47 cash 1/14/59

CUBAN CANE PRODUCTS CO., INC.
Merged into Cuban Atlantic Sugar Co. in 1935
Details not available

CUBAN DOMINICAN SUGAR CORP.
Reorganized as West Indies Sugar Corp. in 1932
No stockholders' equity

CUBAN NATIONAL SYNDICATE
Property sold in 1932
No stockholders' equity

CUBAN TEL CO (DE)
Charter cancelled and declared inoperative and void for non-payment of taxes 07/01/1969

CUBAN TOBACCO CO., INC. (DE)
Acquired by American Tobacco Co. 04/15/1963
Each share Common no par exchanged for (2) shares Common $6.25 par
American Tobacco Co. name changed to American Brands, Inc. (NJ) 07/01/1969 which reincorporated in Delaware 01/01/1986 which name changed to Fortune Brands, Inc. 05/30/1997 which name changed to Beam Inc. 10/04/2011

CUBAN VENEZUELAN OIL VTG TR (CUBA)
Trust terminated 06/01/1965
Each VTC for Common 12¢ par stamped to indicate payment of $0.0075 cash
Note: Additional distributions contingent on revival of democratic government in Cuba

CUBB PAC CORP (DE)
Name changed to Norseman Industries, Inc. 8/10/78
(See Norseman Industries, Inc.)

CUBE ENERGY CORP (AB)
Merged into Barrington Petroleum Ltd. 04/10/1997
Each share Common no par exchanged for $13 cash

CUBE RES LTD (BC)
Struck off register and declared dissolved for failure to file returns 10/09/1987

CUBESCAPE INC (NV)
Name changed to American Rebel Holdings, Inc. 11/16/2017

CUBESMART (MD)
7.75% Preferred Shares of Bene. Int. Ser. A 1¢ par called for redemption at $25 plus $0.17374 accrued dividends on 11/02/2016
(Additional Information in Active)

CUBEX INC (NJ)
Name changed 10/8/75
Name changed from Cube Ice, Inc. to Cubex, Inc. 10/8/75
Acquired by Losquadro Ice Co. 2/8/2002
Each share Common 1¢ par exchanged for $0.15 cash

CUBIC CORP (CA)
Capital Stock no par split (3) for (1) by issuance of (2) additional shares 6/23/61
Capital Stock no par reclassified as Common no par 6/3/68
Common no par split (4) for (3) by issuance of (1/3) additional share 3/25/77
Common no par split (4) for (3) by issuance of (1/3) additional share 11/16/81
Common no par split (2) for (1) by issuance of (1) additional share 10/1/82
Reincorporated under the laws of Delaware 2/12/85

CUBIC ENERGY INC (TX)
Plan of reorganization under Chapter 11 Federal Bankruptcy proceedings effective 03/01/2016
No stockholders' equity

CUBIST PHARMACEUTICALS INC (DE)
Acquired by Merck & Co., Inc. (New) 01/21/2015
Each share Common $0.001 par exchanged for $102 cash

CUBIX INVTS INC (BC)
Reincorporated under the laws of Bermuda as Cubix Investments Ltd. 01/19/2001
Cubix Investments Ltd. recapitalized as Q Investments Ltd. 11/10/2003

CUBIX INVTS LTD (BERMUDA)
Recapitalized as Q Investments Ltd. 11/10/2003
Each share Common $0.001 par exchanged for (0.1) share Common $0.001 par

CUC INTL INC (DE)
Common 1¢ par split (3) for (2) by issuance of (0.5) additional share 02/28/1991
Common 1¢ par split (3) for (2) by issuance of (0.5) additional share 07/02/1992
Common 1¢ par split (3) for (2) by issuance of (0.5) additional share 04/30/1993
Common 1¢ par split (3) for (2) by issuance of (0.5) additional share 06/30/1995
Common 1¢ par split (3) for (2) by issuance of (0.5) additional share payable 10/21/1996 to holders of record 10/07/1996
Under plan of merger name changed to Cendant Corp. 12/17/1997

Cendant Corp. reorganized as Avis Budget Group, Inc. 09/01/2006

CUCOS INC (LA)
Reincorporated under the laws of Nevada as Enzyme Environmental Solutions, Inc. and Common no par changed to $0.001 par 03/24/2008

CUDA CAP CORP (BC)
Recapitalized as August Metal Corp. 11/24/2009
Each share Common no par exchanged for (0.2) share Common no par
August Metal Corp. recapitalized as Ardonblue Ventures Inc. 11/20/2013 which name changed to Juggernaut Exploration Ltd. 10/23/2017

CUDA CONS INC (ON)
Name changed to FoodQuest Corp. 09/27/1994
FoodQuest Corp. recapitalized as FoodQuest International Corp. 11/30/1994 which recapitalized as Dealcheck.com Inc. 01/21/1999 which recapitalized as Bontan Corp. Inc. (ON) 04/17/2003 which reincorporated in British Virgin Islands as Portage Biotech Inc. 08/23/2013

CUDAHY CO (ME)
Under plan of merger each share 4.5% Preferred $100 par exchanged for (4.028) shares Common $5 par 11/29/1968
Merged into General Host Corp. 02/24/1972
Each share $1.25 Cv. Preferred Ser. A $2.50 par exchanged for $25 cash
Each share Common $5 par exchanged for $22 cash

CUDAHY PACKING CO. (ME)
Each share Common $100 par exchanged for (2) shares Common $50 par 00/00/1926
Common $50 par changed to $30 par 00/00/1940
Each share Common $30 par exchanged for (3) shares Common $10 par 00/00/1947
Common $10 par changed to $5 par 00/00/1954
Stock Dividend - 10% 11/01/1946
Name changed to Cudahy Co. 02/18/1966
(See Cudahy Co.)

CUE CAP CORP (BC)
Name changed to Cue Resources Ltd. 10/19/2007
Cue Resources Ltd. merged into Uranium Energy Corp. 03/30/2012

CUE INDUSTRIES, INC. (DE)
Merged into Guardian Industries Corp. 05/17/1988
Each share Common 10¢ par exchanged for $3 cash

CUE RES LTD (BC)
Merged into Uranium Energy Corp. 03/30/2012
Each share Common no par exchanged for (0.0195) share Common $0.001 par

CUELLAR FOODS, INC. (TX)
Name changed to El Chico Foods, Inc. 02/04/1957
El Chico Foods, Inc. name changed to El Chico Corp. 05/01/1962 which merged into Campbell Taggart, Inc. 09/29/1977
(See Campbell Taggart, Inc.)

CUGOLD VENTURES INC (BC)
Recapitalized as Firestone Ventures Inc. (BC) 12/05/1999
Each share Common no par exchanged for (0.33333333) share Common no par
Firestone Ventures Inc. (BC) reincorporated in Alberta 09/27/2005

CULANE ENERGY CORP (AB)
Acquired by Killam Acquisition Co. Ltd. 07/29/2011
Each share Common no par exchanged for $2.32 cash
Note: Unexchanged certificates were cancelled and became without value 07/29/2016

CULBRO CORP (NY)
Common $1 par split (2) for (1) by issuance of (1) additional share 12/02/1983
Each share Common $1 par received distribution of (1) share Griffin Land & Nurseries, Inc. Common 1¢ par payable 07/03/1997 to holders of record 06/25/1997 Ex date - 07/07/1998
Merged into General Cigar Holdings, Inc. 08/29/1997
Each share Common $1 par exchanged for (4.44557) shares Class B Common 1¢ par
(See General Cigar Holdings, Inc.)

CULINARY CAP CORP (CO)
Recapitalized as Centra Capital Corp. (CO) 04/12/1996
Each share Common no par exchanged for (0.01) share Common no par
Centra Capital Corp. (CO) reincorporated in Delaware 04/26/1996 which reincorporated in Nevada 07/02/1998
(See Centra Capital Corp.)

CULLATON LAKE GOLD MINES LTD (ON)
Merged into Royex Gold Mining Corp. 06/08/1984
Each share 10% Preferred Ser. A $5 par exchanged for (0.5) share Conv. 1st Preference Ser. A no par
Each share Common no par exchanged for (0.09090909) share Conv. 1st Preference Ser. A no par and (3) shares Common no par
Royex Gold Mining Corp. merged into Corona Corp. 07/01/1988 which recapitalized as International Corona Corp. 06/11/1991
(See International Corona Corp.)

CULLEN AGRIC HLDG CORP (DE)
Merged into Long Island Iced Tea Corp. 06/01/2015
Each share Common $0.0001 par exchanged for (0.06666666) share Common $0.0001 par
Long Island Iced Tea Corp. name changed to Long Blockchain Corp. 01/05/2018

CULLEN BANKERS INC (TX)
Merged into Cullen/Frost Bankers, Inc. 07/07/1977
Each share Common $10 par exchanged for (0.8) share Common $5 par

CULLIGAN INC (DE)
Common $1 par split (2) for (1) by issuance of (1) additional share 09/20/1968
Stock Dividend - 100% 09/21/1964
Name changed to Culligan International Co. 08/21/1970
Culligan International Co. merged into Beatrice Foods Co. 06/02/1978 which name changed to Beatrice Companies, Inc. 06/05/1984
(See Beatrice Companies, Inc.)

CULLIGAN INTL CO (DE)
Acquired by Beatrice Foods Co. 06/02/1978
Each share Common $1 par exchanged for (0.6634) share Common no par
Beatrice Foods Co. name changed to Beatrice Companies, Inc. 06/05/1984
(See Beatrice Companies, Inc.)

CULLIGAN WTR TECHNOLOGIES INC (DE)
Merged into United States Filter Corp. (New) 06/15/1998
Each share Common 1¢ par exchanged for (1.875) shares Common 1¢ par
(See United States Filter Corp. (New))

CULLINANE CORP. (MA)
Common 10¢ par split (2) for (1) by issuance of (1) additional share 11/10/1980
Name changed to Cullinane Database Systems Inc. 01/02/1981
Cullinane Database Systems Inc. name changed to Cullinet Software, Inc. 09/15/1983 which merged into Computer Associates International, Inc. 09/12/1989 which name changed to CA, Inc. 02/01/2006

CULLINANE DATABASE SYSTEMS INC. (MA)
Common 10¢ par split (2) for (1) by issuance of (1) additional share 10/26/1981
Common 10¢ par split (2) for (1) by issuance of (1) additional share 01/10/1983
Name changed to Cullinet Software, Inc. 09/15/1983
Cullinet Software, Inc. merged into Computer Associates International, Inc. 09/12/1989 which name changed to CA, Inc. 02/01/2006

CULLINET SOFTWARE INC (MA)
Common 10¢ par split (2) for (1) by issuance of (1) additional share 01/21/1985
Merged into Computer Associates International, Inc. 09/12/1989
Each share Common 10¢ par exchanged for (0.5) share Common 10¢ par
Computer Associates International, Inc. name changed to CA, Inc. 02/01/2006

CULLUM COS INC (TX)
Common $1 par split (2) for (1) by issuance of (1) additional share 09/14/1983
Common $1 par split (4) for (3) by issuance of (0.33333333) additional share 09/10/1985
Common $1 par split (3) for (2) by issuance of (0.5) additional share 09/10/1987
Stock Dividends - Paid in Common to holders of Preferred and Common - 15% 10/16/1978; 20% 09/14/1979; 20% 09/15/1980; 20% 09/14/1981
$1 Preferred Ser. A $16 par called for redemption 09/21/1988
Merged into Cullum Acquisition Corp. 11/30/1988
Each share Common $1 par exchanged for $22.50 cash

CULPEPPERS PLANTATION ENTERPRISES INC (DE)
Charter cancelled and declared inoperative and void for non-payment of taxes 03/01/1974

CULTOR LTD (FINLAND)
Name changed 05/06/1998
Name changed from Cultor Ltd. to Cultor Corp. 05/06/1998
ADR agreement terminated 09/27/1999
Each Sponsored ADR for Ordinary exchanged for $18.311 cash

CULTURAL ATTRACTIONS & PROMOTIONS INC (MN)
Name changed to Creative Marketing Executives, Inc. 07/10/1969
Creative Marketing Executives, Inc. name changed to C.M.E., Inc. 08/23/1973
(See C.M.E., Inc.)

CULTURALACCESSWORLDWIDE INC (DE)
Name changed to Access Worldwide Communications, Inc. 11/02/1998
(See Access Worldwide Communications, Inc.)

CULTURE MEDIUM HLDGS CORP (WY)
Reincorporated 07/01/2014
State of incorporation changed from (NV) to (WY) and Common $0.001 par changed to no par 07/01/2014
Recapitalized as Code Navy 02/13/2015
Each share Common no par exchanged for (0.0005) share Common no par
Code Navy name changed to Universal Power Industry Corp. 06/02/2016

CULTUS EXPLS LTD (AB)
Recapitalized as Newcan Minerals Ltd. 05/07/1976
Each share Common no par exchanged for (0.2) share Common no par
Newcan Minerals Ltd. name changed to World Aquathemes Ltd. 06/20/1985 which name changed to Telesis Corp. Inc. 09/02/1986 which recapitalized as P.C. Ventures Ltd. 02/23/1989
(See P.C. Ventures Ltd.)

CULVER CITY PROPERTIES CO.
Liquidation completed 00/00/1942
Details not available

CULVER CORP. (OH)
Each share Common $5 par exchanged for (2) shares Common $2 par 00/00/1953
Name changed to U.S. Railroad Securities Fund 04/15/1955
(See U.S. Railroad Securities Fund)

CULVER GOLD MINES LTD. (ON)
Charter cancelled for failure to pay taxes and file returns 10/11/1977

CUMBERLAND & WESTERNPORT TRANSIT CO. (MD)
Liquidated 00/00/1953
Details not available

CUMBERLAND ASSOCIATES, INC. (KY)
Merged into International Life Insurance Co. (Ky.) 10/18/67
Each share Common $2 par or VTC for Common $2 par exchanged for (0.5) share Common $1 par
International Life Insurance Co. (Ky.) merged into Union Bankers Insurance Co. 6/30/78
(See Union Bankers Insurance Co.)

CUMBERLAND BANCORP INC (TN)
Common 50¢ par split (2) for (1) by issuance of (1) additional share payable 04/22/2001 to holders of record 03/22/2001 Ex date - 04/25/2001
Name changed to Civitas BankGroup, Inc. 05/20/2003
Civitas BankGroup, Inc. merged into Green Bankshares, Inc. 05/18/2007 which merged into Capital Bank Financial Corp. 09/20/2012 which merged into First Horizon National Corp. 11/30/2017

CUMBERLAND CORP. (KY)
Reorganized as Burnside Corp. (DE) 00/00/1958
Details not available

CUMBERLAND COS INC (NV)
Name changed to Lone Star International Energy Inc. 1/30/97

CUMBERLAND COUNTY BANK (CROSSVILLE, TN)
Capital Stock $5 par changed to $1.25 par and (3) additional shares issued 03/15/1982
Acquired by BPC Corp. 00/00/1986
Details not available

CUMBERLAND CNTY NATL BK & TR CO (NEW CUMBERLAND, PA)
Stock Dividend - 10% 03/03/1960
Under plan of reorganization each share Common $10 par automatically became (3) shares CCNB Corp. Common $1 par 03/25/1970
CCNB Corp. merged into PNC Financial Corp. 10/23/1992 which name changed to PNC Bank Corp. 02/08/1993 which name changed to PNC Financial Services Group, Inc. 03/15/2000

CUMBERLAND COUNTY POWER & LIGHT CO.
Acquired by Central Maine Power Co. 00/00/1942
Details not available

CUMBERLAND FED BANCORPORATION INC (KY)
Merged into Fifth Third Bancorp 8/26/94
Each share Common $1 par exchanged for (1.10025) shares Common no par

CUMBERLAND FED SVGS BK (LOUISVILLE, KY)
Reorganized as Cumberland Federal Bancorporation Inc. 10/24/88
Each share Common $1 par exchanged for (1) share Common $1 par
Cumberland Federal Bancorporation Inc. merged into Fifth Third Bancorp 8/26/94

CUMBERLAND GAS CO. (DE)
Name changed to Tree Preservation Co., Inc. 10/19/1979
Tree Preservation Co., Inc. name changed to Tree Holdings 4, Inc. 11/16/1993
(See Tree Holdings 4, Inc.)

CUMBERLAND GAS CORP. (WV)
Merged into Cumberland Gas Co. 01/03/1964
Each share Common $1 par exchanged for (1) share 60¢ Preferred $1 par
Cumberland Gas Co. name changed to Tree Preservation Co., Inc. 10/19/1979 which name changed to Tree Holdings 4, Inc. 11/16/1993
(See Tree Holdings 4, Inc.)

CUMBERLAND GOLD GROUP INC (GA)
Merged into North Lily Mining Co. 1/3/89
Each share Common no par exchanged for (0.5) share Capital Stock 10¢ par
(See North Lily Mining Co.)

CUMBERLAND GROWTH FD INC (NY)
Merged into 44 Wall Street Equity Fund, Inc. 09/18/1992
Details not available

CUMBERLAND HEALTHCARE FD (DE)
Completely liquidated 12/31/1999
Details not available

CUMBERLAND HILLS LTD (NV)
Common $0.001 par split (2) for (1) by issuance of (1) additional share payable 04/10/2013 to holders of record 04/03/2013 Ex date - 04/11/2013
Name changed to American Heritage International Inc. 09/05/2013

CUMBERLAND HLDGS INC (FL)
Name changed to Cumberland Technologies, Inc. 01/30/1997
(See Cumberland Technologies, Inc.)

CUMBERLAND KENTUCKY OIL SYNDICATE (DE)
Charter cancelled and declared inoperative and void for non-payment of taxes 3/16/27

CUMBERLAND MNG LTD (ON)
Charter cancelled and declared dissolved for failure to file returns and pay fees 05/18/1976

CUMBERLAND MOTOR EXPRESS CORP. (MD)
Dissolved 00/00/1959
Details not available

CUMBERLAND MTN BANCSHARES INC (KY)
Merged into Commercial Bancgroup, Inc. 11/01/2001
Each share Common 1¢ par exchanged for $14.32 cash

CUMBERLAND NATL BK (BRIDGETON, NJ)
Under plan of reorganization each share Common Capital Stock $100 par exchanged for (34) shares United Jersey Banks Common $5 par 10/1/70
United Jersey Banks name changed to UJB Financial Corp. 6/30/89 which name changed to Summit Bancorp 3/1/96 which merged into FleetBoston Financial Corp. 3/1/2001 which merged into Bank of America Corp. 4/1/2004

CUMBERLAND OIL & GAS CO. (UT)
Recapitalized as Nature-All Corp. 12/30/83
Each share Common $0.001 par exchanged for (0.1) share Common 1¢ par

CUMBERLAND OIL & GAS LTD (AB)
Merged into Kallisto Energy Corp. 10/15/2012
Each share Common no par exchanged for (0.918) share Common no par
Note: Unexchanged certificates were cancelled and became without value 10/15/2015
Kallisto Energy Corp. name changed to Toro Oil & Gas Ltd. 11/25/2014
(See Toro Oil & Gas Ltd.)

CUMBERLAND PIPE LINE CO., INC.
Liquidation completed 00/00/1935
Details not available

CUMBERLAND RES INC (GA)
Recapitalized as Cumberland Gold Group, Inc. 12/09/1987
Each share Common no par exchanged for (0.2) share Common no par
Cumberland Gold Group, Inc. merged into North Lily Mining Co. 01/03/1989
(See North Lily Mining Co.)

CUMBERLAND RES LTD (BC)
Acquired by Agnico-Eagle Mines Ltd. 07/10/2007
Each share Common no par exchanged for (0.185) share Common no par
Agnico-Eagle Mines Ltd. name changed to Agnico Eagle Mines Ltd. 04/30/2013

CUMBERLAND SHOE CORP. (TN)
Acquired by Georgia Shoe Manufacturing Co., Inc. in March 1964
Details not available

CUMBERLAND TECHNOLOGIES INC (FL)
SEC revoked common stock registration 02/15/2006

CUMBRE VENTURES INC (ON)
Reincorporated under the laws of Alberta as Atlas Minerals Inc. 11/23/2007
Atlas Minerals Inc. (AB) reorganized as Cliffmont Resources Ltd. (BC) 02/22/2010

CUMETRIX DATA SYS CORP (CA)
Issue Information - 2,350,000 shares COM offered at $5 per share on 04/08/1998
Each share old Common no par exchanged for (0.01) share new Common no par 10/05/2007
Name changed to Banneker Inc. 01/09/2008

CUMEX MINES LTD (QC)
Name changed to Pacific Nickel Mines Ltd. 08/27/1968
(See Pacific Nickel Mines Ltd.)

CUMIS INS SOC INC (WI)
Common $8 par changed to $4 par 08/09/1976
Merged into CUNA Mutual Investment Corp. 11/05/1982
Each share Common $4 par exchanged for $30 cash

CUMMINGS & CO., THE INTERNATIONAL SIGN SERVICE, INC. (TN)
Common no par changed to $1 par and (0.5) additional share issued 12/11/68
Name changed to Cummings Inc., The International Sign Service 11/15/74
(See Cummings Inc., The International Sign Service)

CUMMINGS INC INTL SIGN SVC (TN)
Merged into Cummings Merger Corp. 4/22/83
Each share Common $1 par exchanged for $5.25 cash

CUMMINGS PPTYS LTD (CANADA)
Acquired by Trizec Corp. Ltd. 6/25/71
Each share Common no par or Class B Deferred no par exchanged for $4 principal amount of 7% Conv. Notes due 12/31/90, (4) shares Common no par and $8 cash
Trizec Corp. Ltd. name changed to Trizec Corp. Ltd./La Corporation Trizec Ltee. 4/1/77 which recapitalized as Trizec Ltd. (New) 7/25/94 which merged into Trizec Hahn Corp. 11/1/96 which was acquired by Trizec Canada Inc. 5/8/2002
(See Trizec Canada Inc.)

CUMMINS (R.) & CO., INC. (MI)
Charter dissolved for failure to file reports 5/15/41

CUMMINS CAP TR I (DE)
144A Conv. Quarterly Income Preferred Securities called for redemption at $51.75 on 6/15/2006
7% Quarterly Income Preferred Securities called for redemption at $51.75 on 6/15/2006

CUMMINS DISTILLERIES CORP.
Liquidation completed 00/00/1950
Details not available

CUMMINS ENGINE INC (IN)
4-1/2% Preferred 1st Ser. $100 par called for redemption 12/31/1955
Common $5 par split (5) for (4) by issuance of (0.25) additional share 12/21/1956
Common $5 par changed to $2.50 par and (1) additional share issued 04/22/1960
Common $2.50 par split (4) for (3) by issuance of (1/3) additional share 06/19/1964
Common $2.50 par split (2) for (1) by issuance of (1) additional share 11/11/1993
$7.50 Conv. Preference no par called for redemption 07/06/1977
$3.50 Conv. Depositary Preferred Ser. A no par called for redemption 02/23/1994
Conv. Exchangeable Preferred Ser. A no par called for redemption 02/23/1994
Stock Dividends - 20% 12/20/1950; 20% 12/20/1951; 10% 12/22/1952; 25% 12/21/1955; 10% 12/20/1957; 10% 12/28/1962; 25% 12/24/1962; 10% 01/27/1969; 10% 01/29/1970
Name changed to Cummins Inc. 04/05/2001

CUMO RES LTD (BC)
Common no par split (2) for (1) by issuance of (1) additional share 6/15/81
Struck off register and declared dissolved for failure to file returns 3/19/93

CUMONT MINES LTD (BC)
Merged into Nufort Resources Inc. 8/20/74
Each share Common 50¢ par exchanged for (0.833333) share Capital Stock no par
Nufort Resources Inc. name changed to Mikotel Networks Inc. 5/9/2000 which recapitalized as Wabi Exploration Inc. 3/4/2005

CUMULO ALTERNATE FD INC (CA)
Completely liquidated 04/28/1977
Each share Common 10¢ par received first and final distribution of $4.86 cash
Note: Certificates were not required to be surrendered and are without value

CUMULO FD INC (DE)
Completely liquidated 04/28/1977
Each share Common $1 par received first and final distribution of $3.41 cash
Note: Certificates were not required to be surrendered and are without value

CUMULUS MEDIA INC (DE)
Reincorporated 08/01/2002
State of incorporation changed from (IL) to (DE) 08/01/2002
13.75% Exchangeable Preferred Ser. A called for redemption at $106.875 on 07/07/2003
Ser. B Preferred 1¢ par called for redemption at $1,000 plus $10 accrued dividends on 10/30/2013
Each share old Class A Common 1¢ par exchanged for (0.125) share new Class A Common 1¢ par 10/13/2016
Each share old Class B Common 1¢ par exchanged for (0.125) share new Class B Common 1¢ par 10/13/2016
Each share old Class C Common 1¢ par exchanged for (0.125) share new Class C Common 1¢ par 10/13/2016
Stock Dividends - in Preferred to holders of Preferred 3.4375% payable 10/01/1999 to holders of record 09/15/1999; 3.4375% payable 01/01/2000 to holders of record 12/15/1999; 3.4375% payable 04/01/2000 to holders of record 03/15/2000; 3.4375% payable 07/02/2001 to holders of record 06/15/2001 Ex date - 07/16/2001; 3.4375% payable 10/01/2001 to holders of record 09/15/2001; 3.4375% payable 01/01/2002 to holders of record 12/15/2001 Ex date - 12/12/2001
Plan of reorganization under Chapter 11 Federal Bankruptcy proceedings effective 06/04/2018
No stockholders' equity
(Additional Information in Active)

CUMULUS VENTURES LTD (BC)
Recapitalized 05/04/1999
Recapitalized from Cumulus Technology Ltd. to Cumulus Ventures Ltd. 05/04/1999
Each share Common no par exchanged for (0.14285714) share Common no par
Cease trade order effective 09/20/2001

CUNARD STEAM SHIP LTD (ENGLAND)
Through voluntary exchange offer by Trafalgar House Investments Ltd. 100% acquired as of 08/24/1971
Public interest eliminated

CUNDILL VALUE FD LTD (CANADA)
Voluntarily dissolved 02/09/2006
Details not available

CUNEO PRESS INC (IL)
Common $10 par changed to no par 00/00/1927
Each share Common no par exchanged for (2) shares Common $5 par 00/00/1939
4.5% Preferred $100 par called for redemption 02/21/1946
Stock Dividends - 25% 12/05/1945; 100% 07/01/1946
Each share Common $5 par exchanged for (0.002) share Common $2,500 par 11/22/1983
Note: In effect holders received an undermined amount of cash and public interest was eliminated

CUNIPTAU MINES LTD. (ON)
Acquired by Ontario Nickel Mines Ltd. 00/00/1943
Each share Common no par exchanged for (0.33333333) share Common no par
(See Ontario Nickel Mines Ltd.)

CUNNINGHAM ART PRODS INC (GA)
Administratively dissolved 04/29/1988

CUNNINGHAM DRUG CO.
Merged into Economical-Cunningham Drug Stores, Inc. 00/00/1931
Details not available

CUNNINGHAM DRUG STORES INC (MI)
Common $2.50 par split (2) for (1) by issuance of (1) additional share 02/04/1966
Common $2.50 par split (3) for (2) by issuance of (0.5) additional share 02/09/1970
Stock Dividend - 100% 10/24/1947
Acquired by CD Acquisition Corp. 02/20/1981
Each share Common $2.50 par exchanged for $18 cash

CUNNINGHAM DRUG STORES LTD (BC)
Each share Common $10 par exchanged for (10) shares Common no par 00/00/1950
Each share Common no par exchanged for (0.9) share Class A no par and (0.1) share Class B no par 08/00/1959
5.5% 1st Preference $50 par called for redemption 04/30/1964
Each share Class A Common no par exchanged for (3) shares Common $2 par 06/26/1967
Each share Class B Common no par exchanged for (3) shares Common $2 par 06/26/1967
Acquired by Koffler Stores (B.C.) Ltd. 07/26/1971
Each share Common $2 par exchanged for $12 cash

CUNNINGHAM GRAPHICS INTL INC (NJ)
Merged into Automatic Data Processing, Inc. 06/14/2000
Each share Common no par exchanged for $22 cash

CUNNINGHAM LINDSEY GROUP INC (ON)
Merged into Fairfax Financial Holdings Ltd. 12/19/2007
Each share Subordinate no par exchanged for $3.20 cash

CUNNINGHAM NAT GAS CORP (NY)
Charter cancelled and proclaimed dissolved for failure to pay taxes 06/30/1982

CUNO ENGINEERING CORP. (CT)
Acquired by American Machine & Foundry Co. 08/18/1960
Each share $1 Preferred no par exchanged for (0.2958) share Common $7 par or $17 cash
Each share Common $1 par

exchanged for (0.4428) share
Common $7 par
American Machine & Foundry Co.
name changed to AMF Inc.
04/30/1970
(See AMF Inc.)

CUNO INC (DE)
Merged into 3M Co. 08/02/2005
Each share Common $0.001 par
exchanged for $72 cash

CUORO RES CORP (BC)
Name changed to Rockshield Capital
Corp. 05/30/2014

CUP CAP CORP (ON)
Name changed to GBLT Corp.
03/27/2018

CUP RES INC (AB)
Recapitalized 09/07/1988
Recapitalized from Cup Oil Ltd. to
Cup Resources Inc. 09/07/1988
Each share Common no par
exchanged for (0.25) share Common
no par
Delisted from Alberta Stock Exchange
05/14/1990

CUPERTINO NATL BANCORP (CA)
Merged into Greater Bay Bancorp
11/29/1996
Each share Common no par
exchanged for (0.81522) share
Common no par
Greater Bay Bancorp merged into
Wells Fargo & Co. 10/01/2007

CUPRIC MINES CO. (NJ)
Merged into Tintic Lead Co. share for
share 12/22/1964
Tintic Lead Co. name changed to
Tintic Minerals Resources, Inc.
06/27/1969 which merged into Horn
Silver Mines, Inc. 07/20/1983
(See Horn Silver Mines, Inc.)

CUPRUS MINES LTD. (CANADA)
Out of business 00/00/1954
Details not available

CURAFLEX HEALTH SVCS INC (DE)
Merged into Coram Healthcare Corp.
07/08/1994
Each share Common $0.001 par
exchanged for (0.33333333) share
Common $0.001 par
(See Coram Healthcare Corp.)

CURAGEN CORP (DE)
Common 1¢ par split (2) for (1) by
issuance of (1) additional share
payable 03/30/2000 to holders of
record 03/15/2000
Merged into Celldex Therapeutics,
Inc. 10/01/2009
Each share Common 1¢ par
exchanged for (0.2739) share
Common $0.001 par

CURATECH INDS INC (NV)
SEC revoked common stock
registration 11/15/2011

CURATIVE HEALTH SVCS INC NEW (MN)
Plan of reorganization under Chapter
11 Federal Bankruptcy Code
effective 06/07/2006
No stockholders' equity

CURATIVE HEALTH SVCS INC OLD (MN)
Name changed 05/30/1996
Name changed from Curative
Technologies, Inc. to Curative Health
Services, Inc. (Old) 05/30/1996
Under plan of reorganization each
share Common 1¢ par automatically
became (1) share Curative Health
Services, Inc. (New) Common 1¢
par 08/19/2003
(See Curative Health Services, Inc. (New))

CURATOR RES LTD (BC)
Recapitalized as International Curator
Resources Ltd. 10/08/1985
Each share Common no par
exchanged for (0.33333333) share
Common no par
International Curator Resources Ltd.
recapitalized as Canadian Gold
Hunter Corp. (BC) 12/30/2003 which
reincorporated in Canada
07/29/2004 which name changed to
NGEx Resources Inc. 09/22/2009

CURAXIS PHARMACEUTICAL CORP (NV)
Chapter 7 bankruptcy proceedings
terminated 01/19/2016
No stockholders' equity

CURBSTONE ACQUISITION CORP (DE)
Each share old Common $0.0001 par
exchanged for (0.01) share new
Common $0.0001 par 11/05/1996
Name changed to Electro-Optical
Systems Corp. 12/18/1997

CURION VENTURES CORP (BC)
Recapitalized as UC Resources Ltd.
10/31/2001
Each share Common no par
exchanged for (0.2) share Common
no par

CURIS RES LTD (BC)
Reincorporated 04/06/2011
Place of incorporation changed from
(ON) to (BC) 04/06/2011
Merged into Taseko Mines Ltd.
11/25/2014
Each share Common no par
exchanged for (0.438) share
Common no par
Note: Unexchanged certificates will
be cancelled and become without
value 11/25/2020

CURL UP & DRY INC (DE)
Charter cancelled and declared
inoperative and void for
non-payment of taxes 04/15/1972

CURLEE CLOTHING CO (DE)
4-1/2% Preferred $100 par called for
redemption 07/01/1963
Stock Dividend - 10% 11/30/1959
98% acquired through purchase offer
which expired 03/20/1978
Public interest eliminated

CURLEW LAKE RES INC (BC)
Each share old Common no par
exchanged for (0.1) share new
Common no par 07/09/2012
Each share new Common no par
exchanged again for (0.1) share new
Common no par 07/09/2012
Name changed to C21 Investments
Inc. 11/24/2017

CURLEY CO., INC. (PA)
Name changed to C.C. Liquidating
Co. 02/15/1963
(See C.C. Liquidating Co.)

CURON MED INC (DE)
Each share old Common $0.001 par
exchanged for (0.25) share new
Common $0.001 par 06/09/2006
Filed a petition under Chapter 7
Federal Bankruptcy Code
11/17/2006
No stockholders' equity

CURRAGH INC (ON)
Name changed 05/05/1992
Name changed from Curragh
Resources Inc. to Curragh Inc.
05/05/1992
Discharged from receivership
00/00/1995
No stockholders' equity

CURRAN BAY RESOURCE LTD (ON)
Recapitalized as Snackie Jack's Ltd.
(ON) 05/15/2003
Each share Common no par
exchanged for (0.05263157) share
Common no par
Snackie Jack's Ltd. (ON) reorganized
in Nevada as Rocky Mountain
Brands Inc. 12/23/2004 which name
changed to The Estate Vault, Inc.
01/24/2008
(See The Estate Vault, Inc.)

CURRENCY TECHNOLOGY CORP (DE)
Charter cancelled and declared
inoperative and void for
non-payment of taxes 03/01/1985

CURRENCYSHARES AUSTRALIAN DLR TR
Name changed to Invesco
CurrencyShares Australian Dollar
Trust 06/04/2018

CURRENCYSHARES BRIT POUND STERLING TR (NY)
Name changed to Invesco
CurrencyShares British Pound
Sterling Trust 06/04/2018

CURRENCYSHARES CDN DLR TR (NY)
Name changed to Invesco
CurrencyShares Canadian Dollar
Trust 06/04/2018

CURRENCYSHARES CHINESE RENMINBI TR (NY)
Name changed to Invesco
CurrencyShares Chinese Renminbi
Trust 06/04/2018

CURRENCYSHARES EURO TR (NY)
Name changed to Invesco
CurrencyShares Euro Trust
06/04/2018

CURRENCYSHARES JAPANESE YEN TR (NY)
Name changed to Invesco
CurrencyShares Japanese Yen Trust
06/04/2018

CURRENCYSHARES MEXICAN PESO TR (NY)
Trust terminated 03/23/2012
Each Share no par received $78.37
cash

CURRENCYSHARES RUSSIAN RUBLE TR (NY)
Trust terminated 03/23/2012
Each Share no par received $34.12
cash

CURRENCYSHARES SINGAPORE DLR TR (NY)
Name changed to Invesco
CurrencyShares Singapore Dollar
Trust 06/04/2018

CURRENCYSHARES SWEDISH KRONA TR (NY)
Name changed to Invesco
CurrencyShares Swedish Krona
Trust 06/04/2018

CURRENCYSHARES SWISS FRANC TR (NY)
Name changed to Invesco
CurrencyShares Swiss Franc Trust
06/04/2018

CURRENT INT INC (TX)
Reorganized as Transamerica Current
Interest Inc. 08/02/1989
Details not available

CURRENT TECHNOLOGY CORP (BC)
Reincorporated under the laws of
Canada 05/13/2004

CURRENTSEA (NV)
Name changed back to Investment &
Consulting International, Inc. (New)
06/02/1993
Investment & Consulting International,
Inc. (New) recapitalized as KleenAir
Systems, Inc. 04/11/1995 which
recapitalized as Migami, Inc.
03/02/2006

CURRIE MINES LTD. (ON)
Declared dissolved 12/24/1962
No stockholders' equity

CURRIE ROSE RES INC (CANADA)
Reincorporated 05/20/1980
Place of incorporation changed from
(ON) to (Canada) 05/20/1980
Reincorporated under the laws of
British Columbia 02/03/2006

CURRIES MFG INC (IA)
Common no par split (2) for (1) by
issuance of (1) additional share
05/20/1983
Stock Dividend - 25% 06/16/1978
Merged into Kidde, Inc. 04/11/1984
Each share Common no par
exchanged for $12.50 cash

CURRY GOLD CORP (NV)
Name changed to Virtus Oil & Gas
Corp. 08/30/2013

CURT BULLOCK BLDRS INC (NV)
Charter permanently revoked for
failure file reports and pay fees
10/31/2004

CURTICE-BURNS FOODS INC (NY)
Name changed 12/15/1986
Class A Common $5 par changed to
$3.33333333 par and (0.5)
additional share issued 12/06/1982
Class B Common $5 par changed to
$3.33333333 par and (0.5)
additional share issued 12/06/1982
Class A Common $3.33333333 par
changed to $2.22 par and (0.5)
additional share issued 12/05/1983
Class B Common $3.33333333 par
changed to $2.22 par and (0.5)
additional share issued 12/05/1983
Stock Dividend - 20% 08/02/1979
Name changed from Curtice-Burns,
Inc. to Curtice-Burns Foods, Inc.
12/15/1986
Class A Common $2.22 par changed
to $1.48 par and (0.5) additional
share issued 12/22/1987
Class B Common $2.22 par changed
to $1.48 par and (0.5) additional
share issued 12/22/1987
Class A Common $1.48 par changed
to 99¢ par and (0.5) additional share
issued 12/20/1989
Class B Common $1.48 par changed
to 99¢ par and (0.5) additional share
issued 12/20/1989
Merged into Pro-Fac Cooperative,
Inc. 11/03/1994
Each share Class A Common 99¢ par
exchanged for $19 cash
Each share Class B Common 99¢ par
exchanged for $19 cash

CURTIN FILM PARTNERS (FL)
Completely liquidated 1/20/89
Each unit of Ltd. Partnership
exchanged for first and final
distribution of $0.001 cash

CURTIN-HOWE CORP.
Liquidated 00/00/1944
Details not available

CURTIN INTL PRODTNS INC (FL)
Common $0.0001 changed to
$0.00001 par and (9) additional
shares issued 03/09/1987
Common $0.00001 par changed to
$0.000001 par and (9) additional
shares issued 10/16/1987
Name changed to CIP Holdings Inc.
01/20/1988
CIP Holdings Inc. recapitalized as
Pan-International Holdings, Inc.
04/11/1989 which recapitalized as
Curtin International Productions, Inc.
(New) 09/15/1989 which name
changed to First Response Medical,
Inc. 11/23/1989 which recapitalized
as RMS Titanic, Inc. 05/19/1993
which name changed to Premier
Exhibitions, Inc. 10/18/2004

CURTIN INTL PRODTNS INC NEW (FL)
Name changed to First Response
Medical, Inc. 11/23/1989
First Response Medical, Inc.
recapitalized as RMS Titanic, Inc.
05/19/1993 which name changed to
Premier Exhibitions, Inc. 10/18/2004

CURTIS COS INC (IA)
Each share Common no par
exchanged for (12.5) shares
Common $2 par in 1946
In process of liquidation

Each share Common $2 par received initial distribution of $9 cash 12/22/67
Each share Common $2 par received second distribution of $1 cash 8/10/68
Each share Common $2 par exchanged for third distribution of (1) receipt (evidencing right to additional distributions) and $5.50 cash 10/29/68
Holders of Receipts received fourth distribution of $1 cash 7/25/70
Amount or number of subsequent distributions, if any, are unavailable

CURTIS ELECTRO CORP (DE)
Merged into Dual-Lite, Inc. 06/30/1978
Each share Class A 50¢ par exchanged for $0.19323 cash

CURTIS HOOKER CORP (DE)
Name changed to Hooker American Inc. 5/5/75
(See Hooker American Inc.)

CURTIS INDUSTRIES, INC. (OH)
Merged into Curtis Noll Corp. 12/31/64
Each share Common no par exchanged for $11 cash

CURTIS INTL LTD (ON)
Merged into Herzog Group 09/14/2001
Each share Common no par exchanged for $0.60 cash

CURTIS LIGHTING, INC. (IL)
Common no par changed to $2.50 par in 1940
Assets sold and name changed to C-L Liq. Co., Inc. in 1959
(See C-L Liq. Co., Inc.)

CURTIS MANUFACTURING CO. (DE)
No longer in existence having become inoperative and void for non-payment of taxes 04/01/1934

CURTIS MANUFACTURING CO. (MO)
Each share Capital Stock $5 par exchanged (2) shares Capital Stock $4 par 09/30/1955
Capital Stock $4 par changed to Class A Common $4 par or Class B Common $4 par 09/04/1956
Merged into Wyle Laboratories 02/01/1971
Each share Class A Common $4 par or Class B Common $4 par exchanged for $46 cash

CURTIS MATHES CORP (TX)
Each share Common no par exchanged for (0.001) share Common no par 8/19/77
Note: In effect holders received $6.25 cash per share and public interest was eliminated

CURTIS MATHES HLDG CORP (TX)
Name changed to uniView Technologies Corp. 01/30/1998
uniView Technologies Corp. name changed to VPGI Corp. 08/14/2003
(See VPGI Corp.)

CURTIS MATHES MFG CO (TX)
Stock Dividend - 100% 10/1/63
Under plan of merger each share Common $1 par automatically became (1) share Curtis Mathes Corp. Common 10¢ par 1/19/70
(See Curtis Mathes Corp.)

CURTIS MATHES P R INC (NV)
Merged into Curtis Mathes Corp. 10/30/70
Each share Common 10¢ par exchanged for (1) share Common 10¢ par
(See Curtis Mathes Corp.)

CURTIS MILLER & CO. (VA)
Charter cancelled and proclaimed dissolved for failure to file reports in 1923

CURTIS MINERALS INC (UT)
Name changed to Trans World Media 06/07/1972
(See Trans World Media)

CURTIS NOLL CORP (OH)
Common no par split (5) for (2) by issuance of (1.5) additional shares 1/1/65
Common no par split (6) for (5) by issuance of (0.2) additional share 3/15/66
Common no par split (2) for (1) by issuance of (1) additional share 9/20/68
Stock Dividend - 50% 1/19/68
Merged into Congoleum Corp. 12/31/77
Each share Common no par exchanged for $25 cash

CURTIS PUBG CO (PA)
Each share old Common no par exchanged for (2) shares new Common no par 00/00/1929
New Common no par changed to $1 par 00/00/1952
Each share $1.60 Prior Preferred no par exchanged for (0.93) share Common no par 10/16/1972
Each share $4 Prior Preferred no par exchanged for (1.54) shares Common no par 10/16/1972
Each share Common $1 par exchanged for (0.1) share Common no par 10/16/1972
Each share old Common no par exchanged for (0.1) share new Common no par 07/15/1983
Merged into Servaas Interests, Inc. 02/28/1992
Each share new Common no par exchanged for $30 cash

CURTIS S & SON INC (CT)
Common $10 par changed to $5 par and (1) additional share issued 04/25/1962
Stock Dividends - 50% 04/16/1973; 10% 04/15/1974
Name changed to Curtiscorp, Inc. 07/01/1977
Curtiscorp, Inc. name changed to SCS Inc. 01/20/1981
(See SCS Inc.)

CURTIS TUNGSTEN INC (NV)
Charter revoked for failure to file reports and pay fees 9/1/94

CURTISCORP INC (CT)
Name changed to SCS Inc. 01/20/1981
(See SCS Inc.)

CURTISS AEROPLANE & MOTOR CO., INC.
Merged into Curtiss-Wright Corp. in 1929
Details not available

CURTISS AEROPLANE EXPORT CORP.
Name changed to Curtiss-Wright Export Corp. in 1930
(See Curtiss-Wright Export Corp.)

CURTISS AIRPORTS CORP.
Name changed to Curtiss-Wright Airports Corp. in 1930
(See Curtiss-Wright Airports Corp.)

CURTISS BREEDING SERVICE INC. (DE)
Acquired by Searle (G.D.) & Co. (Del.) 9/10/68
Each share Common $4 par exchanged for (0.77736) share Common $1 par
(See Searle (G.D.) & Co. (Del.))

CURTISS CANDY CO. (IL)
Called for redemption 5/22/74
Public interest eliminated

CURTISS-CAPRONI CORP.
Merged into Curtiss-Wright Corp. in 1929
Details not available

CURTISS FLYING SERVICE, INC.
Name changed to Curtiss-Wright Flying Service, Inc. in 1930
Curtiss-Wright Flying Service, Inc. name changed to Devon Corp. (DE) in 1932
(See Devon Corp. (DE))

CURTISS NATIONAL BANK (MIAMI SPRINGS, FL)
Capital Stock $10 par changed to $5 par 00/00/1967
Name changed to First National Bank (Miami Springs, FL) 11/27/1967
First National Bank (Miami Springs, FL) name changed to Southeast First National Bank (Miami Springs, FL) 02/01/1971
(See Southeast First National Bank (Miami Springs, FL))

CURTISS-REID AIRCRAFT CO., LTD.
Reorganized as Montreal Aircraft Industries, Ltd. in 1932
Details not available

CURTISS-ROBERTSON AIRPLANE MANUFACTURING CO.
Merged into Curtiss-Wright Corp. in 1929
Details not available

CURTISS-WRIGHT AIRPLANE CO.
Dissolved in 1936
Details not available

CURTISS-WRIGHT AIRPORTS CORP.
Liquidated in 1936
Details not available

CURTISS WRIGHT CDA INC (ON)
Merged into Curtiss-Wright Corp. 7/7/86
Each share Common no par exchanged for $9.25 cash

CURTISS WRIGHT CORP (DE)
Conv. Class A $1 par called for redemption 06/10/1981
(Additional Information in Active)

CURTISS-WRIGHT EXPORT CORP.
Dissolved in 1936
Details not available

CURTISS-WRIGHT FLYING SERVICE, INC.
Name changed to Devon Corp. (DE) in 1932
(See Devon Corp. (DE))

CURTLINE AMER INC (NY)
Out of business and assets assigned for benefit of creditors 05/23/1969
No stockholders' equity

CURV ENTMT GROUP INC (NV)
Name changed to SuperBox, Inc. 09/01/2011

CURVE WIRELESS CORP (CO)
Name changed to OTC Wireless, Inc. 8/7/2006

CUSA TECHNOLOGIES INC (NV)
Merged into Fiserv, Inc. 4/30/98
Each share Common $0.001 par exchanged for (0.02130476) share Common 1¢ par

CUSAC GOLD MINES LTD (BC)
Name changed 08/14/1995
Each share Adjustable Dividend Conv. Preferred no par exchanged for (14) shares Common no par 04/17/1995
Name changed from Cusac Industries Ltd. to Cusac Gold Mines Ltd. 08/14/1995
Merged into Hawthorne Gold Corp. (New) 04/15/2008
Each share Common no par exchanged for (0.05263157) share Common no par
Hawthorne Gold Corp. (New) name changed to China Minerals Mining Corp. 04/05/2011 which name changed to Wildsky Resources Inc. 08/22/2018

CUSCO MINES LTD. (ON)
Recapitalized as Probe Mines Ltd. 03/04/1965
Each share Capital Stock $1 par exchanged for (0.25) share Capital Stock $1 par
Probe Mines Ltd. merged into Goldcorp Inc. 03/17/2015

CUSEEME NETWORKS INC (DE)
Merged into First Virtual Communications, Inc. 6/19/2001
Each share Common 1¢ par exchanged for (1.254) shares Common $0.001 par
(See First Virtual Communications, Inc.)

CUSHING MLP TOTAL RETURN FD (DE)
Each share old Common $0.001 par exchanged for (0.2) share new Common $0.001 par 09/14/2015
Name changed to Cushing MLP & Infrastructure Total Return Fund 02/20/2018

CUSHING RTY & INCOME FD (DE)
Recapitalized as Cushing Energy Income Fund 09/14/2015
Each Common Share of Bene. Int. $0.001 par exchanged for (0.2) Common Share of Bene. Int. $0.001 par

CUSHMAN CHUCK CO. (CT)
Name changed to Cushman Industries, Inc. 03/18/1963
(See Cushman Industries, Inc.)

CUSHMAN ELECTRS INC (CA)
Completely liquidated and dissolved 12/31/1991
No stockholders' equity

CUSHMAN FOOD CO., INC. (SC)
Assets sold for benefit of creditors in March 1960
No stockholders' equity

CUSHMAN INDS INC (CT)
Acquired by Republic Drill Corp. 01/25/2005
Details not available

CUSHNOC BK & TR CO (AUGUSTA, ME)
Merged into Northeast Bancorp 10/24/97
Each share Common exchanged for (2.089) shares Common $1 par

CUSI MEXICANA MINING CO.
Out of business 00/00/1942
Details not available

CUSIL VENTURE CORP (BC)
Name changed to InNexus Biotechnology Inc. 07/03/2003

CUSTER CHANNEL WING CORP (MD)
Each share Class A $2 par exchanged for (40) shares Class A 5¢ par 04/07/1958
Each share Class B $2 par exchanged for (40) shares Class B 5¢ par 04/07/1958
Each share Class C no par exchanged for (40) shares Class C 5¢ par 04/07/1958
Charter forfeited for failure to file annual reports 10/03/1994

CUSTER-FRAZER CORP. (DE)
Charter cancelled and declared inoperative and void for non-payment of taxes 01/17/1963

CUSTER RES INC (DE)
Merged into Palliser International Energy Inc. 06/01/1982
Each share Common no par exchanged for (0.4) share Common no par
Palliser International Energy Inc. recapitalized as Elan Industries Inc. 12/19/1986 which recapitalized as Trylox Environmental Corp. (BC) 08/17/1990 which reincorporated in Wyoming 09/14/1990
(See Trylox Environmental Corp. (WY))

CUSTODIAL GUIDANCE SYS INC (NY)
Charter cancelled and proclaimed dissolved for failure to pay taxes 06/23/1993

CUSTOM ALLOY CORP (DE)
Name changed to Custom Energy Services, Inc. 01/04/1982
Custom Energy Services, Inc. name changed to Customedix Corp. 07/13/1987
(See Customedix Corp.)

CUSTOM ARRAYS CORP (NV)
Charter permanently revoked 08/31/1999

CUSTOM BRANDED NETWORKS INC (NV)
Name changed to Novastar Resources, Ltd. 05/10/2005
Novastar Resources, Ltd. name changed to Thorium Power, Ltd. 10/10/2006 which recapitalized as Lightbridge Corp. 09/29/2009

CUSTOM BUILT HOMES INC (LA)
Name changed to Pa-Tex, Inc. 08/05/1976
(See Pa-Tex, Inc.)

CUSTOM CHROME INC (DE)
Name changed to Global Motorsport Group Inc. 07/31/1997
(See Global Motorsport Group Inc.)

CUSTOM CLASSIC GOLF INC (FL)
Name changed to Berkshire International, Inc. 01/12/1999
Berkshire International, Inc. recapitalized as Rockstar Industries, Inc. (FL) 07/31/2006 which reincorporated in Nevada as Monster Motors, Inc. 09/22/2006 which name changed to Eco2 Forests, Inc. 09/08/2009 which recapitalized as International Display Advertising, Inc. 03/20/2013

CUSTOM COALS CORP (NV)
Charter permanently revoked 06/01/2004

CUSTOM COMMUNICATIONS SVCS INC (DE)
Name changed 03/08/1979
Name changed from Custom Communications System, Inc. to Custom Communications Services Inc. 03/08/1979
Charter cancelled and declared inoperative and void for non-payment of taxes 03/01/1983

CUSTOM COMPONENTS INC (NJ)
Merged into Lauriat Corp. 10/01/1970
Each share Common 10¢ par exchanged for (1) share Common $1 par
(See Lauriat Corp.)

CUSTOM COMPUTER SYS INC (NY)
Merged into Electrospace Corp. 06/21/1973
Each share Common 10¢ par exchanged for (0.175) share Common 25¢ par
(See Electrospace Corp.)

CUSTOM CR LTD (AUSTRALIA)
Merged into National Bank of Australasia Ltd. (Melbourne, Australia) 04/24/1974
Each share Preference AUD $1 par exchanged for AUD $2 cash
Each share Ordinary AUD 50¢ par or ADR exchanged for (0.75) share Ordinary AUD $1 par
National Bank of Australasia Ltd. (Melbourne, Australia) name changed to National Commercial Banking Corp. of Australia Ltd. 01/04/1983 which name changed to National Australia Bank Ltd. 10/04/1984

CUSTOM CRAFT MARINE CO (NY)
Adjudicated bankrupt 12/08/1964
No stockholders' equity

CUSTOM CREAMERY SYS INC (DE)
Each share old Common $0.001 par exchanged for (0.125) new Common $0.001 par 07/19/1985
Name changed to Orange Julius International, Inc. 12/24/1985
Orange Julius International, Inc. name changed to Crescott, Inc. 08/14/1987 which recapitalized as China Career Builder Corp. 11/17/2006 which recapitalized as iMing Corp. 06/08/2012

CUSTOM DIRECT INCOME FD (ON)
Completely liquidated
Each Unit received first and final distribution of $10.20 cash payable 06/19/2007 to holders of record 06/19/2007

CUSTOM ENERGY SVCS INC (DE)
Name changed to Customedix Corp. 07/13/1987
(See Customedix Corp.)

CUSTOM FID INC (CA)
Name changed to Consolidated Publishing Inc. and Common 10¢ par changed to no par 12/16/1977
(See Consolidated Publishing, Inc.)

CUSTOM LABS INC (MN)
Statutorily dissolved 11/13/1991

CUSTOM LEATHERS LAS VEGAS INC (NV)
Name changed to JC Gear.com 05/17/1999
(See JC Gear.com)

CUSTOM LINE HOMES, INC. (MD)
Charter annulled for failure to file reports and pay taxes 12/02/1964

CUSTOM PETE CORP (CANADA)
Dissolved 12/05/1995
Details not available

CUSTOM PRIVATE CABLE INC (CO)
Recapitalized as Universal Cable Television, Inc. 02/28/1990
Each share Common no par exchanged for (0.02) share Common no par

CUSTOM Q INC (NV)
Name changed to GreenHouse Holdings, Inc. 02/23/2010
GreenHouse Holdings, Inc. merged into Premier Alliance Group, Inc. 03/05/2012 which name changed to root9B Technologies, Inc. 12/01/2014 which recapitalized as root9B Holdings, Inc. 12/05/2016

CUSTOM SHELL HOMES, INC. (MD)
Name changed to Custom Line Homes, Inc. 02/02/1962
(See Custom Line Homes, Inc.)

CUSTOM TOUCH ELECTRONICS INC (NV)
Recapitalized as Intraco Systems, Inc. 04/05/1999
Each share Common no par exchanged for (0.002) share Common no par
Intraco Systems, Inc. recapitalized as Investco, Inc. 01/28/2002
(See Investco, Inc.)

CUSTOMEDIX CORP (DE)
Each share old Common 1¢ par exchanged for (0.1) share new Common 1¢ par 11/04/1991
Merged into CUS Acquisition Inc. 09/30/1996
Each share new Common 1¢ par exchanged for $2.375 cash

CUSTOMER ACQUISITION NETWORK HLDGS INC (DE)
Name changed to interCLICK, Inc. 07/07/2008
(See interCLICK, Inc.)

CUSTOMER SPORTS INC (UT)
SEC revoked common stock registration 12/28/2009

CUSTOMLINE CONTROL PANELS, INC. (NJ)
Name changed to Customline Control Products, Inc. 07/30/1965
Customline Control Products, Inc. name changed to Comsip Customline Corp. 07/29/1974
(See Comsip Customline Corp.)

CUSTOMLINE CTL PRODS INC (NJ)
Name changed to Comsip Customline Corp. 07/29/1974
(See Comsip Customline Corp.)

CUSTOMLINE PRODS INC (MN)
Stock Dividend - 100% 05/03/1971
Name changed to Raw Development Corp. of America, Inc. and Common 5¢ par changed to 1¢ par 11/02/1971
Raw Development Corp. of America, Inc. name changed to Holiday-Gulf Homes, Inc. 10/28/1977
(See Holiday-Gulf Homes, Inc.)

CUSTOMTRACKS CORP (TX)
Name changed to Zixit Corp. 09/16/1999
Zixit Corp. name changed to Zix Corp. 08/13/2002

CUT & CURL INC (NY)
Stock Dividends - 10% 02/14/1979; 50% 02/15/1980
Name changed to Cutco Industries Inc. 11/27/1981
Cutco Industries Inc. name changed to Yellowave Corp. (NY) 11/19/1999 which reincorporated in Nevada 06/07/2000 which name changed to Xologic, Inc. (NV) 01/23/2001 which reorganized in Washington as Doll Technology Group, Inc. 06/30/2005

CUT BANK GAS CO (MT)
Acquired by Energy, Inc. 11/05/2009
Details not available

CUT BANK LEASING & ROYALTY CORP. (WA)
Charter cancelled and proclaimed dissolved for failure to pay fees 07/01/1976

CUT UP CAPERS INC (NY)
Charter cancelled and proclaimed dissolved for failure to pay taxes and file reports 12/16/1974

CUTCO INDS INC (NY)
Common 10¢ par split (2) for (1) by issuance of (1) additional share 05/16/1983
Stock Dividends - 10% 02/15/1982; 10% 08/17/1987
Name changed to Yellowave Corp. (NY) 11/19/1999
Yellowave Corp. (NY) reincorporated in Nevada 06/07/2000 which name changed to Xologic, Inc. (NV) 01/23/2001 which reorganized in Washington as Doll Technology Group, Inc. 06/30/2005

CUTLASS EXPL LTD (BC)
Recapitalized as Great Hercules Resources Inc. 05/31/1977
Each share Common 50¢ par exchanged for (0.2) share Common no par
Great Hercules Resources Inc. name changed to Pacific Coast Funding & Resources Inc. 09/26/1979 which name changed to Alliance Resources Ltd. 04/23/1987 which recapitalized as Acrex Ventures Ltd. 10/19/1993 which recapitalized as Alba Minerals Ltd. 07/10/2014

CUTLASS INDS CORP (BC)
Name changed 02/12/1985
Name changed from Cutlass Resources Ltd. to Cutlass Industries Corp. 02/12/1985
Recapitalized as Triangle Industries Ltd. 01/09/1996
Each share Common no par exchanged for (0.25) share Common no par

CUTLER FED INC (DE)
Reincorporated 06/24/1975
State of incorporation changed from (PA) to (DE) and Common no par changed to $1 par 06/24/1975
Common $1 par split (3) for (2) by issuance of (0.5) additional share 04/15/1983
Stock Dividend - 100% 10/15/1980
Under plan of reorganization each share Common $1 par automatically became (1) share Holder International Industries Inc. Common $1 par 11/14/1985
(See Holder International Industries Inc.)

CUTLER HAMMER INC (DE)
Reincorporated 12/07/1928
Name and state of incorporation changed from Cutler-Hammer Manufacturing Co. (WI) to Cutler-Hammer, Inc. (DE) 12/07/1928
Common no par split (2) for (1) by issuance of (1) additional share 10/26/1937
Common no par changed to $10 par and (1) additional share issued 07/30/1956
Common $10 par changed to $5 par and (1) additional share issued 02/18/1965
Common $5 par split (3) for (2) by issuance of (0.5) additional share 09/14/1977
Merged into Eaton Corp. 01/02/1979
Each share Common $5 par exchanged for either $58 principal amount of 7.75% Promissory Notes due 5 to 15 years from issuance date or $58 cash

CUTLER RIDGE CORP (DE)
Each share Common 5¢ par exchanged for (0.1) share Common 50¢ par 09/21/1961
Completely liquidated 07/15/1981
Each share Common 50¢ par exchanged for first and final distribution of $1.65 cash

CUTTER & BUCK INC (WA)
Common no par split (3) for (2) by issuance of (0.5) additional share payable 06/15/1999 to holders of record 06/04/1999
Merged into New Wave Group AB 06/08/2007
Each share Common no par exchanged for $14.38 cash

CUTTER LABORATORIES (CA)
Each share Common no par exchanged for (3) shares Common $1 par 00/00/1951
Each share Common $1 par exchanged for (1) share LV Common $1 par and (1) share V Common $1 par 04/11/1955
LV Common and V Common $1 par reclassified as Class A Common $1 par and Class B Common $1 par respectively 10/24/1958
Reincorporated under the laws of Delaware as Cutter Laboratories, Inc. 05/10/1960
(See Cutter Laboratories, Inc.)

CUTTER LABS INC (DE)
4% Preferred $100 par called for redemption 05/10/1965
Merged into Rhinechem Corp. 02/22/1974
Each share Class A Common $1 par or Class B Common $1 par exchanged for $18.50 cash

CUTTER WOOD & SANDERSON INTL INC (MA)
Proclaimed dissolved for failure to file reports and pay fees 10/19/1983

CUTTY RES INC (BC)
Name changed to Hatco Capital Inc. 04/15/1991
Hatco Capital Inc. name changed to SoftQuad International Inc. (BC)

12/07/1992 which reincorporated in Ontario 08/31/1994 which reincorporated in New Brunswick 09/18/1998 which name changed to NewKidco International Inc. 01/28/1999
(See NewKidco International Inc.)

CUTTYS INC (IA)
Proclaimed dissolved for failure to file reports and pay fees 12/17/1993

CUTWATER CAP CORP (ON)
Recapitalized as OutdoorPartner Media Corp. 03/31/2006
Each share Common no par exchanged for (0.25) share Common no par

CUTWATER SELECT INCOME FD (DE)
Name changed to Insight Select Income Fund 12/29/2016

CUVIER MINES INC (QC)
Merged into Kam Creed Mines Ltd. 07/13/1988
Each share Common $1 par exchanged for (0.5) share Common no par
(See Kam Creed Mines Ltd.)

CUYAHOGA SVGS ASSN (OH)
Merged into CS Financial Corp. 01/12/1973
Each share Capital Stock $50 par exchanged for (10) shares Common $5 par
CS Financial Corp. merged into Charter One Financial, Inc. 10/16/1998
(See Charter One Financial, Inc.)

CUYAMACA BK N A (SANTEE, CA)
Name changed 06/05/1998
Name changed from Cuyamaca Bank (Santee, CA) to Cuyamaca Bank N.A. (Santee, CA) 06/05/1998
Stock Dividends - 5% payable 03/30/2001 to holders of record 03/16/2001; 5% payable 10/22/2002 to holders of record 10/01/2002; 5% payable 05/18/2004 to holders of record 05/04/2004 Ex date - 04/30/2004
Merged into Community Bancorp Inc. 10/04/2004
Each share Common no par exchanged for either (1.0439) shares Common $0.625 par or $26.68 cash
Community Bancorp Inc. merged into First Community Bancorp (CA) 10/26/2006 which reincorporated in Delaware as PacWest Bancorp 05/14/2008

CUYUNI GOLDFIELDS LTD. (CANADA)
Each share Common no par exchanged for (0.2) share Class A no par 00/00/1948
Deemed not to be a subsisting company by the Dominion Secretary of State 01/10/1954

CV 100 PRODS INC (UT)
Merged into American Scientific Industries International 06/19/1972
Each share Common 5¢ par exchanged for (0.5) share Common 10¢ par
(See American Scientific Industries International)

CV REIT INC (DE)
Merged into Kramont Realty Trust 06/16/2000
Each share Common 1¢ par exchanged for (1) share Common 1¢ par
(See Kramont Realty Trust)

CV SPORTSMARK INTL INC (BC)
Cease trade order effective 08/13/1987
Stockholders' equity unlikely

CV TECHNOLOGIES INC NEW (AB)
Name changed to Afexa Life Sciences Inc. 04/03/2009
(See Afexa Life Sciences Inc.)

CV TECHNOLOGIES INC OLD (AB)
Merged into CV Technologies Inc. (New) 07/01/1998
Each share Common no par exchanged for (1.506) shares Common no par
CV Technologies Inc. (New) name changed to Afexa Life Sciences Inc. 04/03/2009
(See Afexa Life Sciences Inc.)

CV THERAPEUTICS INC (DE)
Acquired by Gilead Sciences, Inc. 04/17/2009
Each share Common $0.001 par exchanged for $20 cash

CVAC INDS INC (BC)
Recapitalized as Saddlerock Resources Inc. 11/27/1995
Each share Common no par exchanged for (0.25) share Common no par
Saddlerock Resources Inc. name changed to MDX Medical Inc. 07/07/2000 which name changed to Urodynamix Technologies Ltd. 06/21/2006 which recapitalized as Venturi Ventures Inc. 08/29/2011
(See Venturi Ventures Inc.)

CVC CAYMAN VENTURES CORP (BC)
Recapitalized as Discovery Harbour Resources Corp. 04/03/2013
Each share Common no par exchanged for (0.33333333) share Common no par

CVC INC (DE)
Merged into Veeco Instruments Inc. 05/08/2000
Each share Common 1¢ par exchanged for (0.43) share Common 1¢ par

CVD FINL CORP (DE)
Name changed to Drummond Financial Corp. (DE) 10/15/1996
Drummond Financial Corp. (DE) reincorporated in Washington 02/22/2002
(See Drummond Financial Corp. (WA))

CVENT INC (DE)
Acquired by Papay Holdco, LLC 11/29/2016
Each share Common $0.001 par exchanged for $36 cash

CVF CORP (NV)
Name changed to CVF Technologies Corp. 09/22/1998

CVI ENERGY CORPORATION LTD (AUSTRALIA)
Declaration by Liquidator About Shares issued 05/30/2012
No stockholders' equity

CVI TECHNOLOGY INC (NV)
Name changed to VendingData Corp. 07/24/2000
VendingData Corp. name changed to Elixir Gaming Technologies, Inc. 09/12/2007 which name changed to Entertainment Gaming Asia Inc. 07/26/2010
(See Entertainment Gaming Asia Inc.)

CVL RES LTD (BC)
Recapitalized as Newport Exploration Ltd. 02/04/2002
Each share Common no par exchanged for (0.1) share Common no par

CVN COS INC (MN)
Acquired by QVC Network, Inc. 10/31/1989
Each share Common no par exchanged for (0.125) share Common 1¢ par and $19 cash
QVC Network, Inc. name changed to QVC, Inc. 06/29/1994

(See QVC, Inc.)

CVR INDS INC (NY)
98% acquired by Outdoor Supply Co., Inc. through exchange offer which expired 12/15/1971
Public interest eliminated

CVS CAREMARK CORP (DE)
Name changed 03/22/2007
Name changed 05/10/2007
Common $1 par changed to 1¢ par and (1) additional share issued payable 06/15/1998 to holders of record 05/25/1998 Ex date - 06/16/1998
Common 1¢ par split (2) for (1) by issuance of (1) additional share payable 06/06/2005 to holders of record 05/23/2005 Ex date - 06/07/2005
Under plan of merger name changed from CVS Corp. to CVS/Caremark Corp. 03/22/2007
Name changed from CVS/Caremark Corp. to CVS Caremark Corp. 05/10/2007
Name changed to CVS Health Corp. 09/04/2014

CVSL INC (FL)
Each share old Common $0.0001 par exchanged for (0.05) share new Common $0.0001 par 10/17/2014
Name changed to JRjr33, Inc. 03/07/2016

CVT CORP AMER (NY)
Merged into Studio City Holding Corp. 06/27/1996
Each share Common $0.002 par exchanged for either (0.1) share Class B Conv. Preferred $0.001 par or (1) share Common $0.002 par
Note: Option to receive Preferred expired 03/31/1998
(See Studio City Holding Corp.)

CVTECH GROUP INC (CANADA)
Name changed to NAPEC Inc. 09/11/2014
(See NAPEC Inc.)

CWC INDS INC (NY)
Stock Dividends - 10% 08/15/1974; 10% 10/15/1975; 10% 04/29/1977
Dissolved by proclamation 03/28/2001

CWC WELL SVCS CORP (AB)
Name changed to CWC Energy Services Corp. 05/22/2014

CWE BANCORP INC (MO)
Merged into Pulaski Financial Corp. 03/31/2006
Each share Common $1 par exchanged for $8.13 cash

CWE INC (CO)
Each share Common $0.0001 par exchanged for (0.18751171) share Common $0.026665 par 03/31/1993
Voluntarily dissolved 10/00/1997
Details not available

CWM MTG HLDGS INC (DE)
Name changed to INMC Mortgage Holdings, Inc. 07/01/1997
INMC Mortgage Holdings, Inc. name changed to IndyMac Mortgage Holdings, Inc. 05/20/1998 which name changed to IndyMac Bancorp, Inc. 07/03/2000
(See IndyMac Bancorp, Inc.)

CWN MNG ACQUISITION CORP (CANADA)
Name changed to GCC Global Capital Corp. 01/03/2018

CWT SPECIALTY STORES INC
Chapter 11 bankruptcy proceedings converted to Chapter 7 on 08/09/2000
Stockholders' equity unlikely

CXR CORP (DE)
Name changed to Microtel International Inc. 03/07/1995
Microtel International name changed to EMRISE Corp. 09/15/2004

CXR TELCOM CORP (DE)
Each share old Common $0.0033 par exchanged for (0.04) share new Common $0.0033 par 02/04/1988
Under plan of reorganization each share new Common $0.0033 par automatically became (1) share CXR Corp. Common $0.0033 par 11/01/1989
CXR Corp. name changed to Microtel International Inc. 03/07/1995 which name changed to EMRISE Corp. 09/15/2004

CX2 TECHNOLOGIES INC (NV)
Name changed to Green Equity Holdings, Inc. and Common $0.001 par changed to $0.0001 par 08/16/2010
Green Equity Holdings, Inc. recapitalized as Holdings Energy, Inc. 04/25/2012 which name changed to Grillit, Inc. 04/22/2013

CXW CAP CORP (ON)
Name changed to RoaDor Industries Ltd. 02/25/2003

CYALUME TECHNOLOGIES HLDGS INC (DE)
Units separated 04/25/2012
Acquired by CPS Performance Materials Corp. 09/08/2017
Each share Common $0.001 par exchanged for $0.213837 cash

CYAN CORP (AB)
Merged into Titan Digital Corp. 02/05/2003
Each share Common no par exchanged for (0.697951) share Common no par
(See Titan Digital Corp.)

CYAN INC (DE)
Merged into Ciena Corp. 08/03/2015
Each share Common $0.0001 par exchanged for (0.19936) share new Common 1¢ par and $0.63 cash

CYBEAR GROUP (DE)
Each share old Common $0.001 par exchanged for (0.25) share new Common $0.001 par 07/31/2001
Merged into Andrx Corp. (DE) 05/17/2002
Each share new Common $0.001 par exchanged for (0.00964) share Andrx Group Common $0.001 par
(See Andrx Corp. (DE))

CYBEAR INC (DE)
Merged into Andrx Corp. (DE) 09/07/2000
Each share Common $0.001 par exchanged (1) share Cybear Group Common $0.001 par
(See Andrx Corp. (DE))

CYBER-CENTURIAN INC (FL)
Administratively dissolved for failure to file annual report 10/16/1998

CYBER CORP. (NC)
Reincorporated under the laws of Nevada as Cyber International Corp. 06/18/1973
Each share 6% Conv. Preferred $50 par automatically became (1) share 6% Conv. Preferred $50 par
Each share Common 10¢ par exchanged for (0.1) share Common 2¢ par
(See Cyber International Corp.)

CYBER DEFENSE SYS INC (OK)
Reincorporated 12/19/2008
State of incorporation changed from (FL) to (OK) 12/19/2008
Each share old Common $0.001 par exchanged for (0.005) share new Common $0.001 par 02/04/2009
Name changed to Spoofem.com, Inc. 08/28/2009
Spoofem.com, Inc. name changed to Spoofem.com USA, Inc. 04/06/2010 which recapitalized as Hi-Tech Crime Solutions, Corp. 10/07/2011 which name changed to Montague

International Holding Ltd. 07/20/2012

CYBER DIAGNOSTICS INC (CO)
Name changed to CDX Corp. 12/01/1982
CDX Corp. name changed to CDX.Com, Inc. (CO) 01/08/2001 which reorganized in Oklahoma as Airguide, Inc. 08/29/2005 which name changed to Amerex Group, Inc. 03/01/2007
(See Amerex Group, Inc.)

CYBER GROUP NETWORK CORP (NV)
Each share old Common $0.001 par exchanged for (0.06666666) share new Common $0.001 par 11/23/2001
Recapitalized as Skystar Bio-Pharmaceutical Co. 02/16/2006
Each share new Common $0.001 par exchanged for (0.00251889) share Common $0.001 par

CYBER INFORMATION INC (NV)
Each share old Common $0.001 par exchanged for (0.25) share new Common $0.001 par 10/07/1997
Name changed to Biltmore Vacation Resorts Inc. 02/25/1998
Biltmore Vacation Resorts Inc. recapitalized as AbsoluteSKY Inc. 04/05/2006
(See AbsoluteSKY Inc.)

CYBER INFORMATIX INC (NV)
Recapitalized as Goldenway, Inc. 12/20/2011
Each share Common $0.001 par exchanged for (0.48175219) share Common $0.001 par

CYBER INTL CORP (NV)
Charter revoked for failure to file reports and pay fees 03/01/1975

CYBER KIOSK SOLUTIONS INC (FL)
Name changed to World Oil Group, Inc. 12/10/2014

CYBER LAW REPORTER INC (TX)
Name changed to Exousia Advanced Materials, Inc. 02/28/2007
(See Exousia Advanced Materials, Inc.)

CYBER MARK INTL CORP (NV)
Reincorporated 04/19/2002
Common $0.0001 par split (2) for (1) by issuance of (1) additional share payable 08/25/2000 to holders of record 08/11/2000
Common $0.0001 par split (10) for (1) by issuance of (9) additional shares payable 08/01/2001 to holders of record 07/19/2001 Ex date - 08/02/2001
State of incorporation changed from (DE) to (NV) 04/19/2002
Name changed to Casavant Mining Kimberlite International Inc. 01/29/2003
Casavant Mining Kimberlite International Inc. name changed to CMKM Diamonds Inc. 02/05/2004
(See CMKM Diamonds, Inc.)

CYBER MERCHANTS EXCHANGE INC (CA)
Each share old Common no par exchanged for (0.11764705) share new Common no par 07/22/2005
Note: Holders of between (100) and (850) pre-split shares will receive (100) shares
Holders of (99) or fewer shares were not affected by the reverse split
Each share new Common no par received distribution of (8.5) shares ASAP Show, Inc. Common $0.001 par payable 03/27/2006 to holders of record 08/18/2005 Ex date - 04/13/2006
(See ASAP Show, Inc.)
Name changed to Infosmart Group, Inc. 10/18/2006

CYBER PUB RELATIONS INC (FL)
Name changed to Entech Environmental Technologies, Inc. 03/22/2004
Entech Environmental Technologies, Inc. recapitalized as SkyPeople Fruit Juice, Inc. 06/09/2008 which name changed to Future FinTech Group Inc. 06/12/2017

CYBER SUPPLY INC (NV)
Common $0.00001 par split (5) for (1) by issuance of (4) additional shares payable 10/04/2011 to holders of record 10/03/2011 Ex date - 10/05/2011
Name changed to CiG Wireless Corp. 12/02/2011
(See CiG Wireless Corp.)

CYBER TRONICS INC (NY)
Merged into Dasa Corp. (MA) 12/18/69
Each share Common 10¢ par exchanged for (0.357142) share Common $1 par
(See Dasa Corp.)

CYBER-VITAMIN COM (CA)
Name changed to Nutra Pharma Corp. 11/7/2001

CYBER VLG INC (NV)
Merged into neXstage Corp. 09/30/2000
Each share Common $0.001 par exchanged for (2.35) shares Common $0.001 par
(See neXstage Corp.)

CYBER WRESTLING INC (NV)
Charter revoked for failure to file reports and pay fees 6/1/2004

CYBERADS INC (NV)
Reincorporated 08/19/2005
State of incorporation changed from (FL) to (NV) 08/19/2005
Recapitalized as Rhino Outdoor International, Inc. 08/30/2006
Each share Common $0.001 par exchanged for (0.01) share Common $0.001 par
Rhino Outdoor International, Inc. recapitalized as Xtreme Motorsports International, Inc. 08/12/2018
(See Xtreme Motorsports International, Inc.)

CYBERAMERICA CORP (NV)
Each share old Common $0.001 par exchanged for (0.1) share new Common $0.001 par 10/31/1997
Name changed to Axia Group, Inc. 12/07/2000
Axia Group, Inc. recapitalized as Artistmss International Group, Inc. 12/11/2012

CYBERBIZ INC (DE)
Name changed to Urbanfind, Inc. 11/06/2000
Urbanfind, Inc. name changed to Klondike Star Mineral Corp. 01/21/2004
(See Klondike Star Mineral Corp.)

CYBERBOTANICAL INC (NV)
Name changed to Wichita Development Corp. 10/12/2000
(See Wichita Development Corp.)

CYBERCARE INC (FL)
Name changed 06/26/2001
Name changed from Cyber-Care, Inc. to CyberCare, Inc. 06/26/2001
Plan of reorganization under Chapter 11 Federal Bankruptcy proceedings terminated 12/17/2009
No stockholders' equity

CYBERCASH INC (DE)
Under plan of reorganization name changed to CYCH, Inc. 05/04/2001
(See CYCH, Inc.)

CYBERCOM SYS INC (BC)
Delisted from NEX 06/25/2004

CYBERDEFENDER CORP (DE)
Reincorporated 05/27/2010
State of incorporation changed from (CA) to (DE) and Common no par changed to $0.001 par 05/27/2010
Plan of reorganization under Chapter 11 Federal Bankruptcy proceedings effective 12/03/2012
No stockholders' equity

CYBERECORD INC (FL)
Administratively dissolved 9/19/2003

CYBEREDGE ENTERPRISES INC (DE)
Old Common $0.0001 par split (2) for (1) by issuance of (1) additional share payable 11/10/2000 to holders of record 11/1/2000
Each share old Common $0.0001 par exchanged for (0.005) share new Common $0.0001 par 2/19/2002
Name changed to Wayne's Famous Phillies Inc. 3/10/2003

CYBERFAST SYS INC (FL)
Recapitalized as GulfStream Industries, Inc 04/05/2005
Each share Common 1¢ par exchanged for (0.002) share Common 1¢ par
GulfStream Industries, Inc. recapitalized as Single Source Investment Group, Inc. 01/03/2006
(See Single Source Investment Group, Inc.)

CYBERFUND INC (OK)
Reincorporated under the laws of Delaware as ROK Entertainment Group Inc. 12/31/2007
(See ROK Entertainment Group Inc.)

CYBERGAMES INC (FL)
Recapitalized as River Creek Holdings, Inc. 07/23/2004
Each share Common $0.0001 par exchanged for (0.0025) share Common $0.0001 par
River Creek Holdings, Inc. name changed to EQ Labs, Inc. 02/05/2009

CYBERGATE INC (NV)
SEC revoked common stock registration 08/25/2004

CYBERGOLD INC (DE)
Merged into MyPoints.com, Inc. 08/08/2000
Each share Common $0.00015 par exchanged for (0.48) share Common $0.001 par
(See MyPoints.com, Inc.)

CYBERGUARD CORP (FL)
Merged into Secure Computing Corp. 01/12/2006
Each share Common 1¢ par exchanged for (0.5) share Common 1¢ par and $2.73 cash
(See Secure Computing Corp.)

CYBERGUIDES INTL INC (MN)
Name changed to AJA Merchant Banking Corp. 02/26/1998
AJA Merchant Banking Corp. name changed to Image-Photo Systems Inc. 12/09/1998 which name changed to e-bidd.com, Inc. 09/08/1999 which name changed to xraymedia.com, Inc. 06/28/2000 which name changed Xraymedia, Inc. 12/04/2003 which recapitalized as T.W. Christian, Inc. 08/14/2007
(See T.W. Christian, Inc.)

CYBERHAND TECHNOLOGIES INTL INC (NV)
Each (300) shares old Common $0.001 par exchanged for (1) share new Common $0.001 par 04/05/2007
Name changed to ChromoCure, Inc. 07/09/2009

CYBERIA HLDGS INC (DE)
Each (50,000) shares old Common $0.0001 par exchanged for (1) share new Common $0.0001 par 2/10/2003
Note: In effect holders received $0.11 cash per share and public interest was eliminated

CYBERIAN OUTPOST INC (DE)
Merged into Fry's Electronics, Inc. 11/09/2001
Each share Common 1¢ par exchanged for $0.25 cash

CYBERION NETWORKING CORP (BC)
Name changed to NexMedia Technologies Inc. 12/30/1998
(See NexMedia Technologies Inc.)

CYBERKEY CORP (NV)
Each share old Common $0.002 par exchanged for (0.01) share new Common $0.002 par 09/24/2004
Name changed to CyberKey Solutions, Inc. 04/24/2006
(See CyberKey Solutions, Inc.)

CYBERKEY SOLUTIONS INC (NV)
Charter revoked for failure to file reports and pay taxes 09/30/2009

CYBERKINETICS NEUROTECHNOLOGY SYS INC (DE)
Company wound down operations and assets sold for the benefit of creditors 03/31/2009
Stockholders' equity unlikely

CYBERMARK SYS INC (DE)
Charter cancelled and declared inoperative and void for non-payment of taxes 03/01/1974

CYBERMATE INFOTEK LTD (INDIA)
GDR agreement terminated 04/22/2014
No GDR's remain outstanding

CYBERMATICS INC (DE)
Reincorporated 06/19/1974
State of incorporation changed from (NY) to (DE) 06/19/1974
Charter cancelled and declared inoperative and void for non-payment of taxes 03/01/1994

CYBERMEDIA INC (DE)
Merged into Network Associates, Inc. 09/08/1998
Each share Common 1¢ par exchanged for $9.50 cash

CYBERMEDIC INC (CO)
Each share old Common no par exchanged for (0.1) share new Common no par 3/26/90
Name changed to Colorado MEDtech, Inc. 5/28/93
(See Colorado MEDtech, Inc.)

CYBERMEDIX INC (ON)
Acquired by Cogeco Inc. 10/31/89
Each share Class B Subordinate no par exchanged for (0.6) share Class B Preferred Ser. 1 no par, (0.12) share Subordinate no par and $14.30 cash

CYBERMIND GROUP INC (ON)
Reincorporated under the laws of New Brunswick as InterOil Corp. 06/11/1997
InterOil Corp. (NB) reincorporated in Yukon 08/24/2007 which merged into Exxon Mobil Corp. 02/22/2017

CYBERN ED INC (IL)
Reorganized under Chapter X bankruptcy proceedings 09/09/1974
No stockholders' equity

CYBERNET INTERNET SVCS INTL INC (DE)
Reincorporated 09/18/1998
State of incorporation changed from (UT) to (DE) 09/18/1998
Company ceased operations 12/22/2003
Stockholders' equity unlikely

CYBERNETIC DEVS INC (DE)
Charter cancelled and declared

inoperative and void for non-payment of taxes 4/15/70

CYBERNETIC SVCS INC (DE)
Involuntary petition under Chapter 7 bankruptcy proceedings filed 4/23/97
No stockholders' equity

CYBERNETICS INTL CORP (DE)
Adjudicated bankrupt 03/29/1972
Stockholders' equity unlikely

CYBERNETICS PRODS INC (NY)
Each share Class A Conv. Preferred 1¢ par received distribution of (0.16) share Common 1¢ par 04/29/1994
Reorganized under the laws of Nevada as Dynamotion/ATI Corp. 12/29/1995
Each share Conv. Class A Preferred 1¢ par exchanged for (0.25) share Conv. Class A Preferred 1¢ par
Each share Common 1¢ par exchanged for (0.25) share Common 1¢ par
Dynamotion/ATI Corp. merged into Electro Scientific Industries, Inc. 06/09/1997

CYBEROAD COM CORP (FL)
Reincorporated under the laws of Delaware as Strata Capital Corp. 01/11/2008
Strata Capital Corp. name changed to Metrospaces, Inc. 02/13/2013

CYBERONICS INC (DE)
Merged into LivaNova PLC 10/19/2015
Each share Common 1¢ par exchanged for (1) share Ordinary £1 par

CYBEROPTICLABS INC (NV)
Name changed to Cordia Corp. 5/25/2001

CYBERPLEX INC (ON)
Recapitalized as EQ Inc. 06/19/2013
Each share Common no par exchanged for (0.125) share Common no par

CYBERSENSOR INTL INC (DE)
Recapitalized as Angel Telecom Corp. 6/6/2007
Each share Common $0.0001 par exchanged for (0.1) share Common $0.0001 par
Note: Holders of (9) or fewer pre-split shares will receive $0.24 cash per share

CYBERSENTRY INC (DE)
Each share Common $0.001 par received distribution of (0.0528846) First Australian Resources NL Sponsored ADR for Ordinary payable 06/23/2000 to holders of record 06/09/2000
Recapitalized as Ludvik Capital, Inc. 07/09/2007
Each share Common $0.001 par exchanged for (0.0001) share Common $0.0001 par
Ludvik Capital, Inc. name changed to SavWatt USA, Inc. 10/27/2010

CYBERSHOP COM INC (DE)
Name changed 6/8/99
Issue Information - 2,800,000 shares COM offered at $6.50 per share on 03/23/1998
Name changed from Cybershop International, Inc. to Cybershop.com, Inc. 6/8/99
Name changed to GSV Inc. 4/6/2000

CYBERSOURCE CORP (DE)
Merged into Visa Inc. 07/21/2010
Each share Common $0.001 par exchanged for $26 cash

CYBERSPACE VITA INC (NV)
Each share old Common $0.001 par exchanged for (10) shares new Common $0.001 par 10/15/2007
Each share new Common $0.001 par exchanged again for (0.05) share new Common $0.001 par 07/01/2009
Name changed to Green Spirit Industries Inc. 06/06/2017
Green Spirit Industries Inc. name changed to GSRX Industries Inc. 07/16/2018

CYBERSTAR COMPUTER CORP (MN)
Name changed to eNetpc, Inc. 8/16/2000
eNetpc, Inc. name changed to BDC Capital, Inc. 12/1/2004 which name changed to DigitalTown, Inc. 3/1/2007

CYBERSURF CORP (AB)
Company completed the sale of substantially all of its assets and is no longer operational 06/10/2009
Note: Proceeds will be used to defend and continue ongoing legal disputes

CYBERTEK CORP (DE)
Reincorporated 8/31/87
Reincorporated and name changed from Cybertek Computer Products, Inc. (CA) to Cybertek Corp. (DE) and Common no par changed to 1¢ par 8/31/87
Merged into C-Tek Acquisition Corp. 8/25/93
Each share Common 1¢ par exchanged for $15.10 cash

CYBERTEK INC (DE)
Filed voluntary bankruptcy petition and was declared insolvent 1/24/73

CYBERTEL CAP CORP (NV)
Each share old Common $0.001 par exchanged for (0.001) share new Common $0.001 par 08/20/2004
Each share new Common $0.001 par exchanged again for (0.002) share new Common $0.001 par 10/26/2005
Each share new Common $0.001 par exchanged for (0.001) share Common $0.00001 par 03/15/2007
Recapitalized as NW Tech Capital, Inc. 01/22/2008
Each share Common $0.00001 par exchanged for (0.001) share Common $0.00001 par

CYBERTEL COMMUNICATIONS CORP (NV)
Each share Common $0.001 par received distribution of (0.05) share Universal Broadband Communications Inc. Common payable 07/15/2003 to holders of record 09/24/2002
Name changed to Cybertel Capital Corp. 05/25/2004
Cybertel Capital Corp. recapitalized as NW Tech Capital, Inc. 01/22/2008

CYBERVEGAS COM (NV)
Name changed to Aerius 03/01/2007
Aerius name changed to Aerius International, Inc. 10/31/2007

CYBERWEB CAFE INC (DE)
Charter cancelled and declared inoperative and void for non-payment of taxes 03/01/1999

CYBEX COMPUTER PRODS CORP (AL)
Common $0.001 par split (3) for (2) by issuance of (0.5) additional share payable 04/28/1998 to holders of record 04/10/1998
Common $0.001 par split (3) for (2) by issuance of (0.5) additional share payable 12/15/1998 to holders of record 11/23/1998
Common $0.001 par split (3) for (2) by issuance of (0.5) additional share payable 02/18/2000 to holders of record 01/31/2000
Merged into Avocent Corp. 07/01/2000
Each share Common $0.001 par exchanged for (1) share Common $0.001 par
(See Avocent Corp.)

CYBEX INTL INC (NY)
Acquired by UM Holdings, Ltd. 02/08/2013
Each share Common 10¢ par exchanged for $2.55 cash

CYC CORP. (DE)
Liquidation completed
Each share Class A 20¢ par exchanged for first and final distribution of (0.170319) share Whittaker Corp. (CA) Common $1 par 4/14/67
Each share Common 20¢ par exchanged for initial distribution of (0.043096) share Whittaker Corp. (CA) Common $1 par 4/14/67
Each share Common 20¢ par received second and final distribution of (0.021507) share Whittaker Corp. (CA) Common $1 par 3/1/68
Whittaker Corp. (CA) reincorporated in Delaware 6/16/86
(See Whittaker Corp. (DE))

CYCARE SYS INC (DE)
Common 1¢ par split (2) for (1) by issuance of (1) additional share 04/26/1986
Merged into HBO & Co. 08/21/1996
Each share Common 1¢ par exchanged for (0.86) share Common 5¢ par
HBO & Co. merged into McKesson HBOC Inc. 01/12/1999 which name changed to

CYCH, INC. (DE)
Liquidation completed
Each share Common $0.001 par received initial distribution of $0.25 cash 12/24/2001
Each share Common $0.001 par received second distribution of $0.30 cash payable 05/17/2002 to holders of record 05/15/2002
Each share Common $0.001 par received third distribution of $0.05 cash payable 07/21/2003 to holders of record 07/18/2003 Ex date - 07/22/2003
Each share Common $0.001 par received fourth and final distribution of $0.0125 cash payable 12/30/2004 to holders of record 12/28/2004
Note: Certificates were not required to be surrendered and are without value

CYCLE & CARRIAGE LTD (SINGAPORE)
Each Unsponsored ADR for Ordinary exchanged for (1) Sponsored ADR for Ordinary 9/28/92
Name changed to Jardine Cycle & Carriage Ltd. 1/5/2004
(See Jardine Cycle & Carriage Ltd.)

CYCLE CTRY ACCESSORIES CORP (NV)
Name changed to ATC Venture Group Inc. 01/30/2012

CYCLE OIL & GAS CORP (UT)
Recapitalized as Frontier Energy Corp. 12/21/82
Each share Common 1¢ par exchanged for (0.2) share Common 5¢ par
(See Frontier Energy Corp.)

CYCLELOGIC INC (DE)
Plan of reorganization under Chapter 11 Federal Bankruptcy Code effective 7/23/2004
No stockholders' equity

CYCLICAL SPLIT NT CORP (ON)
Preferred Shares no par called for redemption at $25 on 12/15/2008
Capital Shares no par called for redemption at $118.36821 on 12/15/2008

CYCLO SHINE CORP (DE)
Charter cancelled and declared inoperative and void for non-payment of taxes 4/15/72

CYCLODEXTRIN TECHNOLOGIES DEV INC (FL)
Name changed to CTD Holdings, Inc. 04/12/2000

CYCLODRAMA, INC. (CA)
Charter revoked for failure to file reports and pay fees 6/1/67

CYCLONE CAP CORP (BC)
Recapitalized as Nikos Explorations Ltd. 06/04/1996
Each share Common no par exchanged for (0.2) share Common no par
Nikos Explorations Ltd. name changed to Labrador Gold Corp. 12/19/2017

CYCLONE DEVS LTD (BC)
Merged into Acheron Resources Ltd. 10/01/1982
Each share Common no par exchanged for (0.33333333) share Common no par
Acheron Resources Ltd. recapitalized as Abaddon Resources Inc. 09/12/1994 which recapitalized as Consolidated Abaddon Resources Inc. 01/31/2001 which name changed to Aben Resources Ltd. 01/13/2011

CYCLONE ENTMT LTD INC (TX)
Charter forfeited for failure to pay taxes 11/20/89

CYCLONE HLDGS INC (DE)
Recapitalized as digitiliti, Inc. 3/7/2007
Each share Common $0.001 exchanged for (0.005) share Common $0.001 par

CYCLONE RES EXPLS LTD (ON)
Recapitalized as Pirrana Corp. 04/23/1982
Each share Common no par exchanged for (0.25) share Common no par
(See Pirrana Corp.)

CYCLONIC INVTS CORP (CANADA)
Name changed to Imaflex Inc. 02/11/1999

CYCLOPS CORP (PA)
Common $1 par split (3) for (2) by issuance of (0.5) additional share 1/31/79
$6 Conv. Preferred Ser. A $1 par called for redemption 9/11/86
$1.15 Conv. Preferred Ser. B $1 par called for redemption 9/11/86
Merged into Dixons Group plc 6/30/87
Each share Common $1 par exchanged for $95 cash

CYCLOPS INDS INC (DE)
Acquired by Armco Inc. 4/24/92
Each share Common $1 par exchanged for (1.99) shares Common $1 par and $11 cash
Armco Inc. merged into AK Steel Holding Corp. 9/30/99

CYCLOPS STEEL CO.
Merged into Universal-Cyclops Steel Corp. in 1936
Details not available

CYCLOPSS CORP (DE)
Name changed 2/2/95
Each share old Common $0.001 par exchanged for (0.2) share new Common $0.001 par 9/8/93
Name changed from Cyclopss Medical Systems Inc. to Cyclopss Corp. 2/2/95
Suspended operations 7/2/2002
Stockholders' equity unlikely

CYCLOTRON CORP (CA)
Capital Stock no par split (2) for (1) by issuance of (1) additional share 05/31/1976
Capital Stock no par split (2) for (1)

CYC-CYP

by issuance of (1) additional share 12/15/1978
Plan of reorganization under Chapter 11 Federal Bankruptcy proceedings confirmed 11/25/1986
No stockholders' equity

CYCO NET INC (NV)
Name changed to Nexicon, Inc. 01/25/2005
(See Nexicon, Inc.)

CYCOMM INTL INC (WY)
Reincorporated 11/03/1995
Each share old Common no par exchanged for (0.2) share new Common no par 10/18/1995
Place of incorporation changed from (ON) to (WY) 11/03/1995
SEC revoked common stock registration 10/31/2006

CYFIT WELLNESS SOLUTIONS INC (NV)
Charter revoked for failure to file reports and pay fees 04/01/2003

CYGAM ENERGY INC (AB)
Filed an assignment in bankruptcy 04/02/2015
Stockholders' equity unlikely

CYGENE LABORATORIES INC (DE)
SEC revoked common stock registration 07/06/2011

CYGNAL TECHNOLOGIES CORP (ON)
Plan of Arrangement under Companies' Creditors Arrangement Act sanctioned 03/17/2008
No stockholders' equity

CYGNE DESIGNS INC (DE)
SEC revoked common stock registration 08/24/2012

CYGNI SYSTEMS CORP (NV)
Name changed to XL Generation International, Inc. 08/30/2005
XL Generation International, Inc. name changed to Ecolocap Solutions Inc. 11/13/2007

CYGNUS INC (DE)
Liquidation completed
Each share Common $0.001 par exchanged for initial distribution of $0.16 cash 12/15/2005
Each share Common $0.001 par received second and final distribution of $0.004694181 cash payable 03/28/2006 to holders of record 11/21/2005

CYGNUS LTD (CANADA)
5.5% Conv. Preferred $20 par called for redemption 09/10/1969
Merged into Consumers' Gas Co. (ON) 12/21/1979
Each share Class A no par exchanged for $29.95 cash
Each share Class B no par exchanged for $29.95 cash

CYGNUS OIL & GAS CORP (DE)
Plan of reorganization under Chapter 11 Federal Bankruptcy Code effective 10/10/2007
No stockholders' equity

CYGNUS THERAPEUTIC SYS (CA)
Reincorporated under the laws of Delaware as Cygnus, Inc. and Common no par changed to $0.001 par 09/11/1995
(See Cygnus, Inc.)

CYLINDER ENTERPRISES LTD (AB)
Name changed to Mondev Senior Living Inc. 02/16/2000
(See Mondev Senior Living Inc.)

CYLINK CORP (CA)
Merged into SafeNet, Inc. 02/05/2003
Each share Common 1¢ par exchanged for (0.05) share Common 1¢ par
(See SafeNet, Inc.)

CYLL INDS LTD (BC)
Recapitalized as Consolidated Cyll Industries Ltd. 12/22/1988
Each share Common no par exchanged for (0.33333333) share Common no par
Consolidated Cyll Industries Ltd. recapitalized as RW Packaging Ltd. (BC) 01/31/1995 which reincorporated in Canada 02/17/1995
(See RW Packaging Ltd.)

CYMAT CORP (ON)
Reorganized as Duntroon Energy Ltd. 08/08/2006
Each share Common no par exchanged for (0.02777777) share Common no par and (1) share Cymat Technologies Ltd. Common no par
(See each company's listing)

CYMER INC (NV)
Common $0.001 par split (2) for (1) by issuance of (1) additional share payable 09/11/1997 to holders of record 08/21/1997
Merged into ASML Holding N.V. 05/31/2013
Each share Common $0.001 par exchanged for (1.1502) new New York Registry Shares and $20 cash

CYMRIC PETROLEUMS LTD. (BC)
Merged into Cymric Resources Ltd. (BC) 09/23/1983
Each share Common no par exchanged for (0.5) share Common no par
Cymric Resources Ltd. (BC) reincorporated in Canada 04/29/1985 which name changed to Rimoil Corp. 12/06/1988 which merged Barrington Petroleum Ltd. 09/22/1995 which merged into Petrobank Energy & Resources Ltd. (Old) 07/18/2001 which reorganized as Petrobank Energy & Resources Ltd. (New) 01/07/2013 which recapitalized as Touchstone Exploration Inc. 05/20/2014

CYMRIC RES LTD (CANADA)
Reincorporated 04/29/1985
Place of incorporation changed from (BC) to (Canada) and Common no par reclassified as Class A Common no par 04/29/1985
Name changed to Rimoil Corp. 12/06/1988
Rimoil Corp. merged into Barrington Petroleum Ltd. 09/22/1995 which merged into Petrobank Energy & Resources Ltd. (Old) 07/18/2001 which reorganized as Petrobank Energy & Resources Ltd. (New) 01/07/2013 which recapitalized as Touchstone Exploration Inc. 05/20/2014

CYN TECH VENTURES LTD (BC)
Recapitalized as Consolidated Cyn-Tech Ventures Ltd. 06/29/1995
Each share Common no par exchanged for (0.2) share Common no par
Consolidated Cyn-Tech Ventures Ltd. name changed to Trans-Orient Petroleum Inc. (BC) 06/27/1996 which reincorporated in Yukon 09/26/1997 which reincorporated back in British Columbia 01/16/2006 which merged into TAG Oil Ltd. 12/16/2009

CYNAPSUS THERAPEUTICS INC (CANADA)
Each share old Common no par exchanged for (0.1) share new Common no par 03/01/2013
Each share new Common no par exchanged again for (0.0625) share new Common no par 05/21/2015
Note: Holders of (15) or fewer pre-split shares were cancelled and are without value
Acquired by Sunovion CNS Development Canada ULC 10/21/2016

Each share new Common no par exchanged for USD$40.50 cash
Note: Unexchanged certificates will be cancelled and become without value 10/21/2022

CYNERGI HLDGS INC (NV)
Each share old Common $0.00001 par exchanged for (11.5) shares new Common $0.00001 par 09/02/2008
Recapitalized as Sports Supplement Group, Inc. 02/02/2009
Each share new Common $0.00001 par exchanged for (0.125) share Common $0.00001 par
Sports Supplement Group, Inc. name changed to CarSmartt, Inc. 02/14/2018

CYNERGY INC (NV)
Recapitalized as Mercantile Factoring Credit Online Corp. 09/29/1999
Each share Common 1¢ par exchanged for (0.05623031) share Common 1¢ par
Mercantile Factoring Credit Online Corp. name changed to Incitations Inc. 10/03/2000 which recapitalized as Osprey Gold Corp. 05/16/2003 which recapitalized as Gilla Inc. 03/30/2007

CYNET INC (TX)
Chapter 11 bankruptcy proceedings terminated 08/15/2005
Stockholders' equity unlikely

CYNEX MFG CORP (NJ)
Common 10¢ par split (3) for (1) by issuance of (2) additional shares 12/30/1982
Merged into Planum Technology Corp. 07/11/1986
Each share Common 10¢ par exchanged for (0.03846153) share Common 1¢ par
(See Planum Technology Corp.)

CYNOSURE INC (DE)
Acquired by Hologic, Inc. 03/22/2017
Each share Class A Common $0.001 par exchanged for $66 cash

CYNTECH TECHNOLOGIES INC (UT)
SEC revoked common stock registration 11/24/2009

CYNTROX CORP. (UT)
Proclaimed dissolved for failure to pay taxes 09/30/1978

CYOKONOS CORP (NV)
Name changed 07/22/2003
Common $0.001 par split (2) for (1) by issuance of (1) additional share payable 03/22/2002 to holders of record 03/18/2002 Ex date - 04/08/2002
Name changed from Cyokaras Corp. to Cyokonos Corp. 07/22/2003
Name changed to EPOD International Inc. (NV) 07/07/2004
EPOD International Inc. (NV) reorganized in British Columbia as EPOD Solar Inc. 05/23/2008

CYOP SYS INTL INC (NV)
Each share old Common $0.0001 par exchanged for (5) shares new Common $0.0001 par 10/07/2003
SEC revoked common stock registration 03/21/2012

CYPANGO VENTURES LTD (BC)
Recapitalized as Techsite Strategies Corp. 02/24/2000
Each share Common no par exchanged for (0.1) share Common no par
Techsite Strategies Corp. name changed to Sola Resource Corp. (BC) 07/17/2003 which reincorporated in Alberta 07/28/2004 which recapitalized as Cancana Resources Corp. (AB) 01/24/2011 which reincorporated in British Columbia 08/12/2015 which reorganized as Meridian Mining S.E 11/28/2016

CYPER MEDIA INC (NY)
SEC revoked common stock registration 02/03/2010

CYPLASIN BIOMEDICAL LTD (NV)
Each share old Common $0.001 par exchanged for (0.025) share new Common $0.001 par 02/02/2009
Name changed to Compass Biotechnologies Inc. 03/29/2011

CYPOST CORP (DE)
Common $0.001 par split (3) for (2) by issuance of (0.5) additional share payable 10/08/1999 to holders of record 09/24/1999
Chapter 11 bankruptcy proceedings converted to Chapter 7 on 06/29/2005
Stockholders' equity unlikely

CYPRESS ABBEY CO (CA)
Merged into Cypress Holdings, Inc. 12/17/1981
Each share Common $2 par exchanged for $10 cash

CYPRESS BKS INC (FL)
Merged into SouthTrust Corp. 12/10/1993
Each share Common 10¢ par exchanged for (1.174) shares Common $2.50 par
SouthTrust Corp. merged into Wachovia Corp. (Ctfs. dated after 09/01/2001) 11/01/2004 which merged into Wells Fargo & Co. (New) 12/31/2008

CYPRESS BIOSCIENCE INC (DE)
Each share old Common 2¢ par exchanged for (0.125) share new Common 2¢ par 03/09/2001
New Common 2¢ par changed to $0.001 par 09/22/2003
Acquired by Ramius Value & Opportunity Advisors L.L.C. 01/14/2011
Each share Common $0.001 par exchanged for $6.50 cash

CYPRESS BROADCASTING CORP (DE)
Name changed to Colony Corp. 07/02/1971
(See Colony Corp.)

CYPRESS COAST BK (SEASIDE, CA)
Merged into Central Coast Bancorp 05/31/1996
Each share Common no par exchanged for (0.5249) share Common no par
(See Central Coast Bancorp)

CYPRESS COMMUNICATIONS CORP (DE)
Common no par changed to $1 par 10/25/1968
Merged into Warner Communications Inc. 09/30/1972
Each share Common $1 par exchanged for (0.5) share Common $1 par
Warner Communications Inc. merged into Time Warner Inc. (Old) 01/10/1990 which merged into AOL Time Warner Inc. 01/11/2001 which name changed to Time Warner Inc. (New) 10/16/2003 which merged into AT&T Inc. 06/15/2018

CYPRESS COMMUNICATIONS HLDG CO INC (DE)
Merged into TechInvest Holding Co., Inc. 06/30/2005
Each share Common $0.001 par exchanged for $1.71 cash

CYPRESS COMMUNICATIONS INC (DE)
Each share old Common $0.001 par exchanged for (0.1) share new Common $0.001 par 08/27/2001
Merged into U.S. RealTel, Inc. 02/22/2002
Each share new Common $0.001 par exchanged for $3.50 cash

CYPRESS DRILLING LTD (AB)
Recapitalized as Precision Drilling (1987) Ltd. 06/17/1987
Each share Class A Common no par exchanged for (0.2) share Class A Common no par
Precision Drilling (1987) Ltd. name changed to Precision Drilling Corp. 09/10/1992
(See Precision Drilling Corp.)

CYPRESS ENERGY INC (AB)
Merged into PrimeWest Energy Trust 05/29/2001
Each share Class A no par exchanged for (1.45) Trust Units no par
Each share Class B no par exchanged for (1.45) Trust Units no par
Note: Canadian holders option to receive Exchangeable Shares expired 05/22/2001
(See PrimeWest Energy Trust)

CYPRESS FD INC (MD)
Liquidation completed
Each share Common $0.001 par received first and final distribution of $5.83 cash 08/26/1991
Note: Certificates were not required to be exchanged and are without value

CYPRESS FINL SVCS INC (NV)
Name changed to RevCare, Inc. 8/9/2000
(See RevCare, Inc.)

CYPRESS HILLS GAS & OIL CO. LTD. (BC)
Recapitalized as Cypress Resources Ltd. 4/27/64
Each share Capital Stock no par exchanged for (0.2) share Capital Stock no par
Cypress Resources Ltd. recapitalized as Pacific Cypress Minerals Ltd. 3/14/77 which recapitalized as International Pacific Cypress Minerals Ltd. 3/4/85
(See International Pacific Cypress Minerals Ltd.)

CYPRESS HILLS RESOURCE CORP (YUKON)
Reincorporated under the laws of Alberta 7/26/2005

CYPRESS INTL INC (DE)
Reincorporated under the laws of Florida as Latitude Industries, Inc. 08/10/2005
Latitude Industries, Inc. recapitalized as Water Technologies International, Inc. 06/20/2011

CYPRESS LAWN IMPROVEMENT CO.
Merged into Cypress Abbey Co. 00/00/1934
Details not available

CYPRESS MINERALS CORP (BC)
Name changed 09/16/1999
Name and place of incorporation changed from Cypress Petroleum Corp. (SK) to Cypress Minerals Corp. (BC) 10/26/1995
Recapitalized as Cypress Development Corp. 09/16/1999
Each share Common no par exchanged for (0.11111111) share Common no par

CYPRESS PETROLEUM CO. OF CALIF.
Dissolved 00/00/1940
Details not available

CYPRESS RES LTD (BC)
Recapitalized as Pacific Cypress Minerals Ltd. 3/14/77
Each share Common no par exchanged for (0.2) share Common no par
Pacific Cypress Minerals Ltd. recapitalized as International Pacific Cypress Minerals Ltd. 3/4/85
(See International Pacific Cypress Minerals Ltd.)

CYPRESS SVGS ASSN (FL)
Stock Dividend - 20% 12/30/1983
Placed in receivership by FSLIC 11/10/1988
No stockholders' equity

CYPRESS SEMICONDUCTOR CORP (CA)
Reincorporated under the laws of Delaware and Common no par changed to 1¢ par 2/20/87

CYPRESS SHARPRIDGE INVTS INC (MD)
Name changed to CYS Investments, Inc. 09/01/2011
CYS Investments, Inc. merged into Two Harbors Investment Corp. 07/31/2018

CYPRIUM RES INC (NV)
Name changed to Digital Development Partners, Inc. 06/29/2009

CYPROS PHARMACEUTICAL CORP (CA)
Common no par split (5) for (2) by issuance of (1.5) additional shares 05/08/1995
Under plan of merger name changed to Questcor Pharmaceuticals, Inc. 11/18/1999
Questcor Pharmaceuticals, Inc. merged into Mallinckrodt PLC 08/14/2014

CYPRUS AMAX MINERALS CO (DE)
$4 Conv. Preferred Ser. A $1 par called for redemption at $51.60 plus $0.8778 accrued dividends on 11/19/1999
Merged into Phelps Dodge Corp. 12/02/1999
Each share Common no par exchanged for (0.35) share Common $6.25 par
Phelps Dodge Corp. merged into Freeport-McMoRan Copper & Gold Inc. 03/19/2007 which name changed to Freeport-McMoRan Inc. 07/14/2014

CYPRUS ANVIL MNG CORP (BC)
Through purchase offer 100% acquired by Hudson's Bay Oil & Gas Co. Ltd. 00/00/1981
Public interest eliminated

CYPRUS CAP CORP (CANADA)
Name changed to Everest Energy Corp. (Canada) 02/07/2001
Everest Energy Corp. (Canada) reincorporated in Alberta 12/21/2005 which recapitalized as Westbow Energy Inc. 02/06/2006 which name changed to Western Canada Energy Ltd. 04/07/2008
(See Western Canada Energy Ltd.)

CYPRUS CORP (DE)
Each share $1.70 Preference 10¢ par exchanged for (1) share $1.80 Preference 10¢ par 12/29/80
Each share Common 10¢ par exchanged for (1/3) share Common 30¢ par 12/29/80
Name changed to Astrotech International Corp. (Old) 4/6/84
Astrotech International Corp. (Old) recapitalized as Astrotech International Corp. (New) 8/19/88 which merged into Iteq Inc. 10/28/97
(See Iteq Inc.)

CYPRUS MINERALS CO (DE)
Common no par split (3) for (2) by issuance of (0.5) additional share 06/23/1989
$3.75 Conv. Exchangeable Preferred Ser. B $1 par called for redemption 10/31/1992
Under plan of merger name changed to Cyprus Amax Minerals Co. 11/15/1993
Cyprus Amax Minerals Co. merged into Phelps Dodge Corp. 12/02/1999 which merged into Freeport-McMoRan Copper & Gold Inc. 03/19/2007 which name changed to Freeport-McMoRan Inc. 07/14/2014

CYPRUS MINES CORP (NY)
Capital Stock $4 par split (3) for (1) by issuance of (2) additional shares 6/10/59
Capital Stock $4 par reclassified as Common $4 par 5/13/69
Common $4 par split (2) for (1) by issuance of (1) additional share 3/10/71
Merged into Standard Oil Co. (IN) 9/21/79
Each share Common $4 par exchanged for (0.619) share Capital Stock $12.50 par
Standard Oil Co. (IN) name changed to Amoco Corp. 4/23/85 which merged into BP Amoco p.l.c. 12/31/98 which name changed to BP PLC 5/1/2001

CYPRUS MINES LTD. (ON)
Name changed to Nemo Mines Ltd. 6/26/68
(See Nemo Mines Ltd.)

CYPRUS POPULAR BK PUB CO LTD (CYPRUS)
ADR agreement terminated 11/20/2015
No ADR holders' equity

CYRANO RES INC (BC)
Recapitalized as Cornucopia Resources Ltd. 11/14/1985
Each share Common no par exchanged for (0.5) share Common no par
Cornucopia Resources Ltd. recapitalized as Stockscape.Com Technologies Inc. 07/13/1999 which merged into Quest Investment Corp. 07/04/2002 which merged into Quest Capital Corp. (BC) 06/30/2003 which reincorporated in Canada 05/27/2008 which name changed to Sprott Resource Lending Corp. 09/10/2010 which merged into Sprott Inc. 07/24/2013

CYRIES ENERGY INC (AB)
Merged into Iteration Energy Ltd. 03/07/2008
Each share Common no par exchanged for (1.62) shares Common no par
Iteration Energy Ltd. merged into Chinook Energy Inc. (Old) 07/05/2010
(See Chinook Energy Inc. (Old))

CYRIX CORP (DE)
Merged into National Semiconductor Corp. 11/17/1997
Each share Common $0.004 par exchanged for (0.825) share Common 50¢ par
(See National Semiconductor Corp.)

CYRK INC (DE)
Name changed to Simon Worldwide, Inc. 5/23/2001

CYRUS INDS INC (NV)
Each share old Common $0.001 par exchanged for (0.02) share new Common $0.001 par 06/02/2000
Name changed to Sentinel Solutions, Inc. 09/02/2005
Sentinel Solutions, Inc. merged into Global Monitoring Systems, Inc. 04/17/2006 which name changed to Planet Signal, Inc. 11/21/2007
(See Planet Signal, Inc.)

CYS INVTS INC (MD)
Merged into Two Harbors Investment Corp. 07/31/2018
Each share 7.5% Preferred Ser. B 1¢ par exchanged for (1) share 7.5% Preferred Ser. E 1¢ par
Each share 7.75% Preferred Ser. A 1¢ par exchanged for (1) share 7.75% Preferred Ser. D 1¢ par
Each share Common 1¢ par exchanged for (0.468) share new Common 1¢ par and $0.0965 cash

CYSIVE INC (DE)
Common 1¢ par split (2) for (1) by issuance of (1) additional share payable 05/08/2000 to holders of record 04/27/2000
Merged into Snowbird Holdings, Inc. 12/01/2003
Each share Common 1¢ par exchanged for $3.23 cash

CYTATION COM INC (NY)
Reincorporated under the laws of Delaware as Collegelink.com, Inc. 11/16/99
Collegelink.com, Inc. name changed to Cytation Corp. (DE) 6/21/2001 which reincorporated in Florida as Deer Valley Corp. 7/28/2006

CYTATION CORP. (RI)
Charter revoked 09/22/1999

CYTATION CORP (DE)
Each share old Common $0.001 par exchanged for (0.00666666) share new Common $0.001 par 11/26/2002
Each share new Common $0.001 par received distribution of (1) share Solomon Technologies, Inc. Common $0.001 par payable 01/15/2004 to holders of record 12/23/2003 Ex date - 01/16/2004
New Common $0.001 par split (2) for (1) by issuance of (1) additional share payable 11/23/2005 to holders of record 11/14/2005 Ex date - 11/24/2005
Reincorporated under the laws of Florida as Deer Valley Corp. 07/28/2006

CYTEC INDS INC (DE)
Common 1¢ par split (3) for (1) by issuance of (2) additional shares payable 07/23/1996 to holders of record 07/02/1996 Ex date - 07/24/1996
Common 1¢ par split (2) for (1) by issuance of (1) additional share payable 09/17/2014 to holders of record 09/02/2014 Ex date - 09/18/2014
Acquired by Solvay S.A. 12/09/2015
Each share Common 1¢ par exchanged for $75.25 cash

CYTEK INFORMATION SYS CORP (NY)
Dissolved by proclamation 12/20/77

CYTEL CORP (DE)
Each share old Common 1¢ par exchanged for (1/7) share new Common 1¢ par 11/13/1998
Name changed to Epimmune Inc. 07/01/1999
Epimmune Inc. recapitalized as IDM Pharma, Inc. 08/16/2005
(See IDM Pharma, Inc.)

CYTERRA CAP CORP (BC)
Issue Information - 6,000,000 shares COM offered at $0.10 per share on 04/08/2010
Name changed to Caiterra International Energy Corp. 03/15/2012

CYTIVA SOFTWARE INC (BC)
Acquired by Taleo Corp. 04/01/2011
Each share Common no par exchanged for $0.42 cash

CYTO SKIN CARE CORP (DE)
Name changed to Chantal Skin Care Corp. 08/01/1994
Chantal Skin Care Corp. recapitalized as Utix Group, Inc. 11/21/2003
(See Utix Group, Inc.)

CYTO WAVE TECHNOLOGIES INC (DE)
Name changed to Accurexa Inc. (DE) 08/21/2014
Accurexa Inc. (DE) reincorporated in

Marshall Islands as Medisun Precision Medicine Ltd. 06/30/2017

CYTOCARE INC (DE)
Name changed to Medstone International, Inc. (New) 09/25/1995
Medstone International, Inc. (New) merged into Prime Medical Services, Inc. (New) 02/20/2004 which merged into HealthTronics, Inc. 11/10/2004
(See HealthTronics, Inc.)

CYTOCLONAL PHARMACEUTICS INC (DE)
Name changed to eXegenics Inc. 10/24/2001
eXegenics Inc. name changed to Opko Health, Inc. 6/11/2007

CYTOCORE INC (DE)
Each share old Common $0.001 par exchanged for (0.1) share new Common $0.001 par 11/28/2007
Name changed to Medite Cancer Diagnostics, Inc. 12/11/20014

CYTODYN INC (CO)
Reincorporated under the laws of Delaware and Common no par changed to $0.001 par 08/27/2015

CYTOGEN CORP (DE)
$2.50 Conv. Exchangeable Preferred 1¢ par called for redemption 10/15/1992
Each share old Common 1¢ par exchanged for (0.1) share new Common 1¢ par 10/28/2002
Merged inot EUSA Pharma, Inc. 05/09/2008
Each share Common 1¢ par exchanged for $0.62 cash

CYTOGENIX INC (NV)
SEC revoked common stock registration 08/01/2012

CYTOMEDIX INC (DE)
Plan of reorganization under Chapter 11 Federal Bankruptcy Code effective 07/11/2002
Each share old Common $0.0001 par exchanged for (0.2) share new Common $0.0001 par
Name changed to Nuo Therapeutics, Inc. 11/14/2014

CYTOPROBE CORP (UT)
Each share old Common 15¢ par exchanged for (0.16666666) share new Common 15¢ par 01/17/1994
Name changed to Medical Device Technologies, Inc. 04/20/1995
Medical Device Technologies, Inc. name changed to Miracor Diagnostics Inc. 10/12/1999
(See Miracor Diagnostics Inc.)

CYTOSORBENTS CORP (NV)
Reorganized under the laws of Delaware 12/05/2014
Each share Common $0.001 par exchanged for (0.04) share Common $0.001 par

CYTOTHERAPEUTICS INC (DE)
Name changed to StemCells, Inc. 05/25/2000
StemCells, Inc. recapitalized as Microbot Medical, Inc. 11/29/2016

CYTOVAX BIOTECHNOLOGIES INC (CANADA)
Name changed to Millenium Biologix Corp. 12/03/2004
(See Millenium Biologix Corp.)

CYTOX CORP (DE)
Plan of reorganization under Chapter 11 Federal Bankruptcy proceedings confirmed 12/29/1986
No stockholders' equity

CYTRON MORTGAGE CO.
Liquidated 00/00/1932
Details not available

CYTRX BIOPOOL LTD (DE)
Name changed to Biopool International, Inc. 06/30/1989
Biopool International, Inc. name changed to Xtrana, Inc. 06/22/2001 which recapitalized as Alpha Innotech Corp. 10/06/2005
(See Alpha Innotech Corp.)

CYTYC CORP (DE)
Common 1¢ par split (2) for (1) by issuance of (1) additional share payable 01/28/2000 to holders of record 01/14/2000
Common 1¢ par split (3) for (1) by issuance of (2) additional shares payable 03/02/2001 to holders of record 02/16/2001 Ex date - 03/05/2001
Merged into Hologic, Inc. 10/22/2007
Each share Common 1¢ par exchanged for (0.52) share Common 1¢ par and $16.50 cash

CZAR ENERGY, INC. (UT)
Name changed to Micro Enhancement International, Inc. (UT) 04/16/1985
Micro Enhancement International, Inc. (UT) reorganized in Washington 09/27/1995
(See Micro Enhancement International, Inc. (WA))

CZAR RES LTD (AB)
Common no par split (3) for (1) by issuance of (2) additional shares 09/22/1978
7.5% Conv. 1st Preference Ser. A $25 par called for redemption 01/31/1980
Acquired by Ranger Oil Ltd. 12/06/1995
Each share Common no par exchanged for $1.55 cash

CZECH FD (DE)
Recapitalized as Czech Industries Inc. 12/01/1994
Each share Common 1¢ par exchanged for (0.82685629) share Common 1¢ par
Czech Industries Inc. name changed to Eastbrokers International Inc. 12/10/1996 which name changed to Global Capital Partners, Inc. 02/02/2000
(See Global Capital Partners, Inc.)

CZECH INDS INC (DE)
Each share old Common 1¢ par exchanged for (0.2) share new Common 1¢ par 09/10/1996
Name changed to Eastbrokers International Inc. 12/10/1996
Eastbrokers International Inc. name changed to Global Capital Partners, Inc. 02/02/2000
(See Global Capital Partners, Inc.)

CZECH REP FD INC (MD)
Name changed to Central European Value Fund, Inc. 02/24/1998
Central European Value Fund, Inc. name changed to Cornerstone Strategic Return Fund, Inc. 07/06/2000 which merged into Cornerstone Total Return Fund, Inc. 10/30/2002

CZECH REP RESOURCE CORP (NV)
Each share old Common $0.001 par exchanged for (0.002) share new Common $0.001 par 02/16/2011
Name changed to Global Senior Enterprises Inc. 04/26/2013
Global Senior Enterprises Inc. recapitalized as World Financial Holding Group 05/01/2018

CZM CAP CORP (BC)
Recapitalized as Taku Gold Corp. 01/26/2010
Each share Common no par exchanged for (0.33333333) share Common no par

D

D / W BANKSHARES INC (GA)
Merged into Colonial BancGroup, Inc. 01/31/1997
Each share Common $1 par exchanged for (0.7256) share Common $2.50 par
(See Colonial BancGroup, Inc.)

D. P. CO., INC. (DE)
Reorganized as State Street Investment Corp. 02/21/1978
Each share Common $2 par exchanged for (0.370318) share Common $2.50 par
State Street Investment Corp. name changed to State Street Investment Trust 05/01/1989 which name changed to State Street Master Investment Trust 12/14/1989 which name changed to State Street Research Master Investment Trust 05/25/1995
(See State Street Research Master Investment Trust)

D & E COMMUNICATIONS INC (PA)
Merged into Windstream Corp. 11/10/2009
Each share Common 16¢ par exchanged for (0.65) share Common $0.0001 par and $5 cash
Windstream Corp. name changed to Windstream Holdings, Inc. 09/03/2013

D & K HEALTHCARE RES INC (DE)
Name changed 08/14/1997
Name changed from D & K Wholesale Drug, Inc. to D & K Healthcare Resources Inc. 08/14/1997
Common $1 par split (2) for (1) by issuance of (1) additional share payable 04/11/2002 to holders of record 03/29/2002 Ex date - 04/12/2002
Merged into McKesson Corp. 08/30/2005
Each share Common $1 par exchanged for $14.50 cash

D & N FINL CORP (DE)
Reorganized 07/31/1988
Under plan of reorganization each share D&N Savings Bank, FSB (Hancock, MI) Common 1¢ par automatically became (1) share D&N Financial Corp. Common 1¢ par 07/31/1988
Stock Dividend - 10% payable 01/13/1998 to holders of record 12/23/1997
Merged into Republic Bancorp Inc. 05/17/1999
Each share Common 1¢ par exchanged for (1.82) shares Common $5 par
Republic Bancorp Inc. merged into Citizens Banking Corp. 12/29/2006 which name changed to Citizens Republic Bancorp, Inc. 04/26/2007 which merged into FirstMerit Corp. 04/12/2013 which merged into Huntington Bancshares Inc. 08/16/2016

D & R INTERNATIONAL CORP. (FL)
Name changed to Compu-Tech International Inc. 12/19/1977
(See Compu-Tech International Inc.)

D A B INDS INC (MI)
Common $7.50 par changed to $1 par 05/17/1973
Common $1 par split (3) for (2) by issuance of (0.5) additional share 09/29/1978
Stock Dividends - 10% 12/20/1973; 100% 12/08/1975; 10% 12/28/1984
Acquired by J.P. Industries Inc. 10/04/1985
Each share Common $1 par exchanged for $9.93 cash

D A CONSULTING GROUP INC (TX)
Recapitalized as Suggestion Box Inc. 05/11/2006
Each share Common 1¢ par exchanged for (0.05) share Common 1¢ par

D.A.I. LIQUIDATING CORP (DE)
Completely liquidated 01/13/1975
Each share Common 10¢ par received first and final distribution of (1) share Digital Applications, Inc. (New) Common 1¢ par
Note: Certificates were not required to be surrendered and are without value
(See Digital Applications, Inc. (New))

D A S ELECTRS INDS INC (ON)
Recapitalized as Pace Corp. 09/30/1993
Each share Common no par exchanged for (0.04) share Common no par
(See Pace Corp.)

D-B LIQUIDATING CO. (CA)
Liquidation completed
Each share Common $1 par exchanged for initial distribution of $1.50 cash 07/07/1977
Each share Common $1 par received second distribution of $0.35 cash 05/00/1978
Each share Common $1 par received third and final distribution of $0.175 cash 12/04/1979

D.B.S. CARRIAGE & LIVERY CO., INC. (UT)
Recapitalized as National Quick Start, Inc. 03/13/1986
Each share Common $0.001 par exchanged for (0.5) share Common $0.001 par
(See National Quick Start, Inc.)

D C CORROSION CORP (AB)
Name changed to Total Telcom Inc. 06/10/1999

D C DIAGNOSTICARE INC (BC)
Acquired by Canadian Medical Laboratories Ltd. 01/18/2002
Each share Common no par exchanged for $0.60 cash

D C INTL INC (NE)
Common $1 par split (3) for (2) by issuance of (0.5) additional share 04/11/1966
Merged into T.I.M.E.-DC, Inc. 01/17/1969
Each share Common $1 par exchanged for (0.6) share Conv. Preferred Ser. A $10 par and (0.4) share Common $2 par
(See T.I.M.E.-DC, Inc.)

D C NATL BANCORP INC (DC)
Common $10 par split (3) for (1) by issuance of (2) additional shares 05/15/1984
Merged into Sovran Financial Corp. 03/10/1986
Each share Common $10 par exchanged for (2.0273) shares Common $5 par
Sovran Financial Corp. merged into C&S/Sovran Corp. 09/01/1990 which merged into NationsBank Corp. (NC) 12/31/1991 which reincorporated in Delaware as BankAmerica Corp. (Old) 09/25/1998 which merged into BankAmerica Corp. (New) 09/30/1998 which name changed to Bank of America Corp. 04/28/1999

D C TRADING & DEV CORP (DE)
Class B Common 20¢ par reclassified as Class A Common 20¢ par 08/16/1971
Name changed to D.C. Transit System, Inc. 11/16/1977
(See D.C. Transit System, Inc.)

D C TRAN SYS INC (DE)
Charter cancelled and declared inoperative and void for non-payment of taxes 03/01/1993

D E FREY GROUP INC (DE)
Assets sold for the benefit of creditors 12/31/2009
No stockholders' equity

D ELDONA RES LTD (ON)
Recapitalized as Western D'Eldona Resources Ltd. 06/01/1988
Each share Common no par exchanged for (0.33333333) share Common no par
(See Western D'Eldona Resources Ltd.)

D F I VENTURES LTD (BC)
Recapitalized as National Quick Lube Ltd. 01/17/1989
Each share Common no par exchanged for (0.5) share Common no par
National Quick Lube Ltd. recapitalized as NQL Drilling Tools Inc. 06/14/1994 which name changed to NQL Energy Services Inc. 07/11/2005
(See NQL Energy Services Inc.)

D-FENSE CAP LTEE (CANADA)
Name changed to Freyja Resources Inc. 04/19/2013
Freyja Resources Inc. name changed to Cyprium Mining Corp. 06/09/2014

D.G. CORP. (MI)
Liquidation completed
Each share Common $1 par exchanged for initial distribution of $18 cash 03/05/1965
Each share Common $1 par received second distribution of $4.50 cash 05/05/1965
Each share Common $1 par received third distribution of $1.70 cash 01/14/1966
Each share Common $1 par received fourth distribution of $0.30 cash 03/13/1967
Each share Common $1 par received fifth and final distribution of $0.5417 cash 11/01/1968

D G JEWELRY INC (ON)
Name changed 07/29/1999
Name changed from D.G. Jewellery of Canada Ltd. to D.G. Jewelry Inc. 07/29/1999
Placed in receivership 10/10/2002
Stockholders' equity unlikely

D H MARKETING & CONSULTING INC (NV)
Each share Common $0.001 par exchanged for (3) shares Common $0.0003 par 02/05/1997
Name changed to VersaTech Inc. 03/24/2000
VersaTech Inc. name changed to VersaTech USA 05/13/2013

D H Z CAP CORP (DE)
Recapitalized as Full House Resorts, Inc. 09/02/1992
Each share Common $0.0001 par exchanged for (0.005) share Common $0.0001 par

D I Y HOME WHSE INC (OH)
Name changed to FNF Industries Inc. 9/30/2003
(See FNF Industries Inc.)

D-LANZ DEV GROUP INC (DE)
Each share old Common $0.001 par exchanged for (0.01) share new Common $0.001 par 04/17/2000
Name changed to eWeb21 Corp. 11/24/2000
eWeb21 Corp. recapitalized as Texas Wyoming Drilling, Inc. 07/21/2008 which recapitalized as Drone USA, Inc. 05/19/2016

D-LINK CORP (TAIWAN)
Each old 144A Sponsored GDR for Common exchanged for (0.8) new 144A Sponsored GDR for Common and $0.311892 cash 02/19/2008
Each old Reg. S Sponsored GDR for Common exchanged for (0.8) new Reg. S Sponsored GDR for Common and $0.3111892 cash 02/19/2008
Stock Dividends - in 144A to holders of 144A 10% payable 09/17/1999 to holders of record 07/16/1999; 15% payable 08/29/2000 to holders of record 06/23/2000; 15% payable 09/07/2001 to holders of record 07/11/2001 Ex date - 07/09/2001; 10% payable 09/04/2002 to holders of record 07/09/2002 Ex date - 07/05/2002; 5.08495% payable 09/16/2004 to holders of record 07/12/2004 Ex date - 07/08/2004; 10% payable 08/18/2006 to holders of record 07/20/2006; 2% payable 09/11/2007 to holders of record 07/26/2007; in Reg. S 10% payable 09/17/1999 to holders of record 07/16/1999; 15% payable 08/29/2000 to holders of record 06/23/2000; 15% payable 09/07/2001 to holders of record 07/11/2001; 10% payable 09/04/2002 to holders of record 07/09/2002 Ex date - 07/05/2002; 5.08495% payable 09/16/2004 to holders of record 07/12/2004; 10% payable 09/30/2005 to holders of record 07/22/2005 Ex date - 07/20/2005; 10% payable 08/18/2006 to holders of record 07/20/2006; 2% payable holders of record 07/20/2006; 2% payable 09/11/2007 to holders of record 07/26/2007
ADR agreement terminated 12/31/2008
Each new 144A Sponsored GDR for Common exchanged for $4.108684 cash
GDR agreement terminated 12/31/2008
Each new Reg. S Sponsored GDR for Common exchanged for $4.108684 cash

D LITES OF AMER INC (GA)
Plan of reorganization under Chapter 11 confirmed 07/25/1988
No stockholders' equity

D.N.W., INC. (IN)
Completely liquidated and dissolved 09/30/1971
Each share Common $1 par received total distribution of $19.625 cash
Note: Certificates were not required to be surrendered and are without value

D O C OPTICS CORP (DE)
Common 10¢ par split (2) for (1) by issuance of (1) additional share 8/10/81
Common 10¢ par split (2) for (1) by issuance of (1) additional share 7/29/83
Merged into D.O.C. Acquisition Corp. 7/13/92
Each share Common 10¢ par exchanged for $9.375 cash

D OR VAL MINES LTD (BC)
Merged into Aurizon Mines Ltd. 08/24/1988
Each share Common no par exchanged for (0.4167) share Common no par
Aurizon Mines Ltd. merged into Hecla Mining Co. 06/01/2013

D R W ENVIRONMENTAL TECHNOLOGIES INC (AB)
Delisted from Alberta Stock Exchange 05/14/1996

D T M CORP. (IL)
Liquidation completed 11/10/60
Each share Common $2 par received initial distribution of $15 cash 12/22/59
Each share Common $2 par received second distribution of (0.73) share Oliver Corp. Common $1 par 2/15/60
Each share Common $2 par received third distribution of $5 cash 5/31/60
Each share Common $2 par exchanged for fourth and final distribution of (0.05) share Murray Corp. of America Common $10 par, $2.429 cash and a (1/385,882) Ctf. of Bene. Int. in the liquidating trust 11/10/60
(See Murray Corp. of America)

D TEKTAMATIC CORP (GA)
Administratively dissolved 5/13/88

D V HLDGS INC (NV)
Name changed to Iceberg Corporation of America 06/24/1999
Iceberg Corporation of America recapitalized as Royal Alliance Entertainment, Inc. 08/07/2006 which name changed to Infinity Medical Group, Inc. 06/06/2007
(See Infinity Medical Group, Inc.)

D-VINE LTD (DE)
Name changed to Monsterdaata.Com Inc. 03/29/1999
Monsterdaata.Com Inc. name changed to Monsterdaata Inc. 12/07/2000 which recapitalized as Enviro Global Corp. 08/08/2007

D W FILTERS INC (DE)
Charter cancelled and declared inoperative and void for non-payment of taxes 03/01/1997

D W G CIGAR CORP. (OH)
Common $5 par split (5) for (4) by issuance of (0.25) additional share 12/29/1959
Name changed to D W G Corp. 11/30/1966
D W G Corp. name changed to Triarc Companies, Inc. (OH) 10/27/1993 which reincorporated in Delaware 06/30/1994 which name changed to Wendy's/Arby's Group, Inc. 09/29/2008 which name changed to Wendy's Co. 07/11/2011

D W G CORP (OH)
Common $5 par split (7) for (4) by issuance of (0.75) additional share 08/08/1968
Common $5 par changed to $1 par 01/20/1973
Common $1 par changed to 10¢ par 11/24/1975
$0.35 Conv. Preferred 1974 Ser. $1 par called for redemption 03/18/1993
$0.60 Conv. Preferred $1 par called for redemption 03/18/1993
Common 10¢ par reclassified as Class A Common 10¢ par 04/26/1993
Stock Dividends - 10% 10/01/1975; 10% 04/01/1976; 10% 10/01/1976; 10% 04/01/1977; 10% 10/01/1977; 10% 04/01/1978; 10% 10/01/1978
Name changed to Triarc Companies, Inc. (OH) 10/27/1993
Triarc Companies, Inc. (OH) reincorporated in Delaware 06/30/1994 which name changed to Wendy's/Arby's Group, Inc. 09/29/2008 which name changed to Wendy's Co. 07/11/2011

D W I CORP (CA)
Charter suspended for failure to file reports and pay fees 02/01/2001

D&N CAP CORP (MI)
Exchangeable Preferred Ser. A $25 par called for redemption at $25 plus $0.01375 accrued dividend on 7/22/2002

D'AMICO & CO., INC. (NY)
Charter revoked for failure to file reports and pay fees 12/15/68

D'ARBONNE LUMBER & OIL CO. (DE)
Charter cancelled for failure to pay taxes in 1925

D'ARCY OIL & GAS LTD. (ON)
Name changed to Lariat Exploration & Development Ltd. 00/00/1953
Lariat Exploration & Development Ltd. acquired by Dominion Asbestos Mines Ltd. 00/00/1954 which name changed to Daine Mining Corp. Ltd. 09/11/1956 which recapitalized as Cable Mines & Oils Ltd. 08/15/1957 which merged into St. Fabien Copper Mines Ltd. 07/27/1967 which name changed to St. Fabien Explorations Inc. 02/11/1981 which recapitalized as Fabien Explorations Inc. 07/18/1983
(See Fabien Explorations Inc.)

D'ORE MILLS, INC. (NV)
Charter revoked for failure to file reports 3/1/76

DA CAPO RES LTD (BC)
Merged into Vista Gold Corp. (BC) 11/01/1996
Each share Common no par exchanged for (2) shares Common no par
Vista Gold Corp. (BC) reincorporated in Yukon 12/27/1997 which reincorporated back in British Columbia 06/12/2013

DA-JON INC. (UT)
Recapitalized as Omega Energy, Inc. 03/12/1979
Each share Common $0.001 par exchanged for (10) shares Common $0.0001 par
Omega Energy, Inc. recapitalized as Olivier International Energy, Inc. 01/07/1980

DAB INVTS LTD (SOUTH AFRICA)
Name changed to Ettington Investments Ltd. 8/23/93
(See Ettington Investments Ltd.)

DABLON MINING CORP. LTD. (CANADA)
Charter cancelled for failure to file annual returns 09/00/1961

DAC TECHNOLOGIES AMER INC (FL)
Name changed to DAC Technologies Group International, Inc. 5/26/2000

DACHA CAP INC (CANADA)
Common no par split (2) for (1) by issuance of (1) additional share payable 10/03/2002 to holders of record 09/30/2002
Each share Common no par received distribution of (1) share Distinction Group Inc. Common no par and (0.25) Common Stock Purchase Warrant expiring 09/30/2009 payable 11/29/2007 to holders of record 11/27/2007 Ex date - 11/23/2007
Name changed to Dacha Strategic Metals Inc. 09/28/2010
(See Dacha Strategic Metals Inc.)

DACHA STRATEGIC METALS INC (CANADA)
Plan of reorganization effective 08/19/2014
Each share Common no par exchanged for approximately (0.0842) share Merus Labs International Inc. (New) Common no par
Note: Non-Qualified Shareholders will receive cash from the sale of shares
Unexchanged certificates will be cancelled and become without value 08/19/2020
(See Merus Labs International Inc. (New))

DACHAMINE INC (CANADA)
Name changed to Dacha Capital Inc. 12/18/1997
Dacha Capital Inc. name change to Dacha Strategic Metals Inc. 09/28/2010
(See Dacha Strategic Metals Inc.)

DACHATECH INC (CANADA)
Recapitalized as Syscan International Inc. 10/31/1996
Each share Common no par exchanged for (0.5) share Common no par
(See Syscan International Inc.)

DAC-DAI

FINANCIAL INFORMATION, INC.

DACO INDS INC (NY)
Dissolved by proclamation 12/23/92

DACONICS CORP. (CA)
Merged into Xerox Corp. 11/20/75
Each share Common 40¢ par exchanged for (0.08712) share Common $1 par

DACOR CO. (DE)
Liquidation completed 08/12/1955
Details not available

DACOTAH BK HLDG CO (SD)
Name changed to Dacotah Banks Inc. 2/1/95

DACOTAH PACKING CO. (SD)
Voluntarily dissolved 10/1/28
Details not available

DADAN, INC. (NY)
Proclaimed dissolved for failure to file reports and pay taxes 12/16/68

DADE BEHRING HLDGS INC (DE)
Common 1¢ par split (2) for (1) by issuance of (1) additional share payable 08/29/2005 to holders of record 08/15/2005 Ex date - 08/30/2005
Merged into Siemens AG 11/07/2007
Each share Common 1¢ par exchanged for $77 cash

DADE COUNTY SECURITY CO.
Assets sold 00/00/1935
Details not available

DADE METAL FABRICATIONS, INC. (FL)
Recapitalized as Merada Industries, Inc. (FL) on a (0.25) for (1) basis 9/5/63
Merada Industries, Inc. (FL) reincorporated in Delaware 4/11/69 which name changed to First Quality Corp. 9/30/70
(See First Quality Corp.)

DADE NATL BK (MIAMI, FL)
Name changed to Central National Bank (Miami, FL) 2/17/69
Central National Bank (Miami, FL) name changed to Eagle National Bank (Miami,FL) 11/2/81

DADE PLASTICS CO. (FL)
Liquidation completed
Each share Common 10¢ par exchanged for initial distribution of (0.0555555) share United States Pipe & Foundry Co. Common $5 par 4/22/65
Each share Common 10¢ par received second and final distribution of (0.0029348) share United States Pipe & Foundry Co. Common $5 par and $0.03181 cash 5/12/66
United States Pipe & Foundry Co. merged into Walter (Jim) Corp. 8/30/69
(See Walter (Jim) Corp.)

DADSON LAKE CHIBOUGAMAU MINES LTD. (QC)
Name changed to Saucon Development Corp. 00/00/1960
Saucon Development Corp. name changed to Quebec Industrial Minerals Corp. 01/10/1964
(See Quebec Industrial Minerals Corp.)

DAEDALIAN ESOLUTIONS INC (AB)
Acquired by Telus Corp. 7/26/2001
Each share Common no par exchanged for (0.005341) Non-Vtg. Share no par

DAEDALUS ENTERPRISES INC (DE)
Merged into Sensys Technologies Inc. 6/9/98
Each share Common 1¢ par exchanged for (1) share Common 1¢ par
Sensys Technologies Inc. name changed to Sensytech Inc. 10/7/99 which name changed to Argon ST, Inc. 10/4/2004

DAEGIS INC (DE)
Acquired by Open Text Corp. 11/23/2015
Each share Common $0.001 par exchanged for $0.82 cash

DAER GOLD MINES LTD (BC)
Name changed to I.M.P.A.C.T. Minerals Inc. 11/28/91
I.M.P.A.C.T. Minerals Inc. recapitalized as IMPACT Minerals International Inc. 8/20/99 which name changed to IMPACT Silver Corp. 8/18/2005

DAERING EXPLORERS LTD (ON)
Recapitalized as Consolidated Daering Enterprises & Mining Inc. 08/20/1971
Each share Capital Stock $1 par exchanged for (0.25) share Capital Stock no par
Consolidated Daering Enterprises & Mining Inc. recapitalized as Sim-Tek Enterprises Exploration Inc. 12/11/1981 which name changed to Bonaventure Technologies Inc. 09/14/1983
(See Bonaventure Technologies Inc.)

DAEWOO SHIPBUILDING & MARINE ENGR CO LTD (KOREA)
GDR agreement terminated 08/23/2016
Each 144A Sponsored GDR for Common exchanged for $3.282357 cash

DAFFIN CORP. (DE)
6% Preferred 1952 Ser. $20 par called for redemption 1/26/62
Name changed to Farmhand, Inc. 9/21/66
Farmhand, Inc. merged into Arizona-Colorado Land & Cattle Co. 6/9/72 which name changed to AZL Resources, Inc. 5/17/77
(See AZL Resources, Inc.)

DAFOE CORP (NV)
Name changed to Davi Luxury Brand Group, Inc. 01/18/2011

DAG MEDIA INC (NY)
Issue Information - 1,325,000 shares COM offered at $6.50 per share on 05/13/1999
Name changed to Manhattan Bridge Capital, Inc. 07/24/2008

DAGE-BELL CORP. (NJ)
Liquidation completed
Each share Common 1¢ par exchanged for initial distribution of (0.3) share Raytheon Co. Common $5 par 8/6/65
Each share Common 1¢ par received second distribution of (0.0037453) share Raytheon Co. Common $5 par and $0.005 cash 3/1/66
Each share Common 1¢ par received third and final distribution of (0.00862068) share Raytheon Co. Common $5 par and $0.006 cash 11/10/67

DAGGER INDUSTRIES CORP. (DE)
Charter cancelled and declared inoperative and void for non-payment of taxes 3/1/76

DAGGETT CHOCOLATE CO. (MA)
Each share Common no par exchanged for (1) share Class A Common no par and (9) shares Class B Common no par 12/28/56
Reverted to private company by reacquiring its own stock in 1966
Details not available

DAGILEV CAP CORP (BC)
Name changed to Astur Gold Corp. 06/04/2010
Astur Gold Corp. name changed to Black Dragon Gold Corp. 10/14/2016

DAHAVA RES LTD (AB)
Ceast trade order 02/06/2005

DAHL URANIUM MINE, INC. (WA)
Merged into Spokane National Mines, Inc. on a (1) for (6) basis 6/2/58

DAHLBERG ELECTRONICS, INC. (MN)
Name changed to Dahlberg, Inc. 06/22/1984
(See Dahlberg, Inc.)

DAHLBERG INC (MN)
Common 10¢ par split (5) for (3) by issuance of (0.66666666) additional share 03/18/1991
Common 10¢ par split (6) for (5) by issuance of (0.2) additional share 03/19/1992
Merged into Bausch & Lomb Inc. 07/30/1993
Each share Common 10¢ par exchanged for $21 cash

DAHLMAN INC (MN)
Each share old Capital Stock 10¢ par exchanged for (0.1) share new Capital Stock 10¢ par 10/30/1975
Merged into NFD Inc. 10/31/1978
Each share new Capital Stock 10¢ par exchanged for (0.25) share Class A Common 1¢ par
(See NFD Inc.)

DAHLONEGA BANCORP INC (GA)
Recapitalized as Century South Banks, Inc. 11/30/89
Each share Common $1 par exchanged for (1) share Common $1 par
Century South Banks, Inc. merged into BB&T Corp. 6/7/2001

DAHLSTROM CORP (NY)
Name changed to Prior Coated Metals, Inc. 06/01/1976
(See Prior Coated Metals, Inc.)

DAHLSTROM MANUFACTURING CORP. (NY)
Name changed to Dahlstrom Corp. 07/14/1971
Dahlstrom Corp. name changed to Prior Coated Metals, Inc. 06/01/1976
(See Prior Coated Metals, Inc.)

DAHLSTROM METALLIC DOOR CO. (NY)
Name changed to Dahlstrom Manufacturing Corp. 05/13/1960
Dahlstrom Manufacturing Corp. name changed to Dahlstrom Corp. 07/14/1971 which name changed to Prior Coated Metals, Inc. 06/01/1976
(See Prior Coated Metals, Inc.)

DAI ICHI BK LTD (JAPAN)
Merged into Dai-Ichi Kangyo Bank, Ltd. 12/01/1971
Each ADR for Common exchanged for (1) ADR for Common
(See Dai-Ichi Kangyo Bank, Ltd.)

DAI ICHI KANGYO BK LTD (JAPAN)
Merged 9/22/2000
Details not available

DAI-ICHI LIFE INS CO LTD (JAPAN)
Name changed to Dai-ichi Life Holdings, Inc. 10/03/2016

DAIEI INC (JAPAN)
Each Unsponsored ADR for Common JPY 50 par exchanged for (0.5) Sponsored ADR for Common JPY 50 par 10/11/2002
Each old Sponsored ADR for Common JPY 50 par exchanged for (0.1) new Sponsored ADR for Common JPY 50 par 05/10/2005
Stock Dividends - 52-1/2% 06/15/1975; 10% 07/28/1978; 10% 06/29/1979; 10% 07/01/1980; 10% 06/10/1981; 17% 12/11/1987
ADR agreement terminated 03/31/2009
Each new Sponsored ADR for Common JPY 50 par exchanged for $10.210665 cash

DAIG CORP (MN)
Common 1¢ par split (2) for (1) by issuance of (1) additional share 03/08/1995
Merged into St. Jude Medical, Inc. 05/31/1996
Each share Common 1¢ par exchanged for (0.651773) share Common 10¢ par
St. Jude Medical, Inc. merged into Abbott Laboratories 01/04/2017

DAIHATSU MTR CO LTD (JAPAN)
ADR agreement terminated 08/23/2016
Each ADR for Common issued by Bank of New York exchanged for $29.223647 cash

DAIICHI SANKYO CO LTD OLD (JAPAN)
Each Unsponsored ADR for Common exchanged for (1) Daiichi Sankyo Co., Ltd. (New) Sponsored ADR for Common 11/14/2011

DAILEY CORP.
Bankrupt 00/00/1938
Details not available

DAILEY INTL INC (DE)
Name changed 10/07/1997
Name changed from Dailey Petroleum Services Corp. to Dailey International Inc. 10/07/1997
Acquired by Weatherford International Inc. (New) (DE) 08/31/1999
Each share Common 1¢ par exchanged for (0.02795) share Common $1 par
Note: Unexchanged certificates were cancelled and became without value 08/31/2001
Weatherford International Inc. (New) (DE) reincorporated in Bermuda as Weatherford International Ltd. 06/26/2002 which reincorporated in Switzerland 02/25/2009 which reincorporated in Ireland as Weatherford International PLC 06/18/2014

DAILY CASH TAX EXEMPT FD INC (MD)
Reorganized under the laws of Massachusetts as Centennial Tax Exempt Trust and Common 1¢ par reclassified as Shares of Bene. Int. no par 09/27/1985
(See Centennial Tax Exempt Trust)

DAILY INCOME FD INC (MD)
Merged into Short Term Income Fund, Inc. 06/21/1993
Details not available

DAILY MAIL & GEN TR PLC (UNITED KINGDOM)
ADR agreement terminated 04/07/2016
Each Sponsored ADR for Non-Vtg. Ordinary A Shares exchanged for $8.910662 cash

DAILY MIRROR INC. (NY)
Merged into Hearst Corp. 12/31/43
Details not available

DAILY MIRROR NEWSPAPERS LTD. (ENGLAND)
Merged into International Publishing Corp. Ltd. 04/26/1963
Each ADR for Ordinary exchanged for (1) ADR for Ordinary
International Publishing Corp. Ltd. acquired by Reed International PLC 08/21/1970 which name changed to Reed Elsevier PLC 04/22/2002 which reorganized as RELX PLC 07/01/2015

DAILY NEWS CORP. (NV)
Charter revoked for failure to file reports and pay fees 3/5/56

DAILY RECORD CO (MD)
Merged into Warfield Acquisition Co. 12/05/1989
Each share Common $10 par exchanged for $142 cash

DAIMLER AG (GERMANY)
ADR agreement terminated 01/05/2017
Each Sponsored ADR for Ordinary exchanged for either (1) Unsponsored ADR for Ordinary or (1) share Ordinary
Note: Unexchanged ADR's will be sold and the proceeds, if any, held for claim after 07/05/2017
(Additional Information in Active)

DAIMLER BENZ A G (GERMANY)
ADR's for Ordinary DM50 par split (7) for (1) by issuance of (6) additional ADR's 08/11/1986
Each Unsponsored ADR for Ordinary DM50 par exchanged for (0.1) Sponsored ADR for Ordinary DM50 par 10/05/1993
Merged into DaimlerChrysler AG 11/12/1998
Each share Ordinary DM50 par exchanged for (1.005) shares Ordinary no par
Each Sponsored ADR for Ordinary DM50 par exchanged for (1.005) shares Ordinary no par
DaimlerChrysler AG name changed to Daimler AG 10/19/2007

DAIMLER RES INC (BC)
Struck off register and declared dissolved for failure to file returns 05/27/1994

DAIMLERCHRYSLER AG (GERMANY)
Name changed to Daimler AG 10/19/2007

DAIN KALMAN & QUAIL INC (DE)
Reorganized as Inter-Regional Financial Group, Inc. 5/6/74
Each share Common $0.125 par exchanged for (1) share Common $0.125 par
Inter-Regional Financial Group, Inc. name changed to Interra Financial Inc. 2/4/97 which name changed to Dain Rauscher Corp. 1/2/98
(See Dain Rauscher Corp.)

DAIN RAUSCHER CORP (DE)
Merged into Royal Bank of Canada (Montreal, QC) 01/10/2001
Each share Common $0.125 par exchanged for $95 cash

DAINE INDS INC (DE)
Each share old Common $0.00001 par received distribution of (0.01) share Lite King Corp. Common $0.001 par payable 05/00/1999 to holders of record 11/30/1998
Each share old Common $0.00001 par exchanged for (0.005) share new Common $0.00001 par 07/24/2000
Reported out of business 00/00/2003
Stockholders' equity unlikely

DAINE MINING CORP. LTD. (QC)
Recapitalized as Cable Mines & Oils Ltd. 08/15/1957
Each share Capital Stock $1 par exchanged for (0.16666666) share Capital Stock $1 par
Cable Mines & Oils Ltd. merged into St. Fabien Copper Mines Ltd. 07/27/1967 which name changed to St. Fabien Explorations Inc. 02/11/1975 which recapitalized as Fabien Explorations Inc. 07/18/1983
(See Fabien Explorations Inc.)

DAINIPPON SCREEN MFG CO LTD (JAPAN)
Name changed to SCREEN Holdings Co., Ltd. 02/09/2015
(See SCREEN Holdings Co., Ltd.)

DAINTY MAID SLIPPERS, INC. (NY)
Name changed to Eastern Footwear Corp. 00/00/1937
(See Eastern Footwear Corp.)

DAIRENE INDS LTD (DE)
Charter cancelled and declared inoperative and void for non-payment of taxes 03/01/1986

DAIRENE INTL (NV)
Each share Common $0.001 par exchanged for (0.2) share Common $0.005 par 02/21/1996
Each share old Common $0.005 par exchanged for (0.01) share new Common $0.005 par 04/18/2006
Reorganized as Edgetech International Inc. 05/11/2006
Each share new Common $0.005 par exchanged for (2) shares Common $0.005 par
(See Edgetech International Inc.)

DAIRY CORP. OF CANADA LTD.
Name changed to Silverwood Western Dairies Ltd. 02/26/1945
Silverwood Western Dairies Ltd. acquired by Silverwood Dairies, Ltd. 00/00/1952
(See Silverwood Dairies, Ltd.)

DAIRY DALE CO.
Acquired by Borden Co. 00/00/1929
Details not available

DAIRY DAN, INC. (NJ)
Declared bankrupt 06/15/1964
No stockholders' equity

DAIRY DUKE CORP. (NJ)
Charter revoked for failure to file reports and pay fees 01/03/1967

DAIRY FARM INTL HLDGS (BERMUDA)
Each old Sponsored ADR for Ordinary exchanged for (0.9) new Sponsored ADR for Ordinary 10/12/1999
ADR agreement terminated 05/28/2004
Each new Sponsored ADR for Ordinary exchanged for $13.81903 cash
(Additional Information in Active)

DAIRY FRESH FARMS INC (NV)
Name changed to Energy 1 Corp. 04/28/2009

DAIRY MART CONVENIENCE STORES INC (DE)
Common 1¢ par reclassified as Class B Common 1¢ par 08/15/1985
Class A Common 1¢ par split (2) for (1) by issuance of (1) additional share 07/15/1986
Class B Common 1¢ par split (2) for (1) by issuance of (1) additional share 07/15/1986
Class A Common 1¢ par split (5) for (4) by issuance of (0.25) additional share 06/17/1991
Class B Common 1¢ par split (5) for (4) by issuance of (0.25) additional share 06/17/1991
Each share Class A Common 1¢ par exchanged for (1) share Common 1¢ par 02/09/2000
Each share Class B Common 1¢ par exchanged for (1.1) shares Common 1¢ par 02/09/2000
Stock Dividends - 10% 07/16/1984; 10% 07/15/1985
Plan of reorganization under Chapter 11 Federal Bankruptcy Code effective 03/13/2003
No stockholders' equity

DAIRY OPERATORS CO.
Aquired by United States Dairy Products Corp. 00/00/1932
Details not available

DAIRY QUEEN STORES INC (TX)
In process of liquidation
Each share Common 10¢ par received initial distribution of $0.90 cash 02/10/1979
Note: Details on subsequent distributions, if any, are not available

DAIRY SERVICE CORP. (FL)
Name changed to Citrus Service, Inc. 12/16/1983

DAIRY WHEY FOODS CORP (DE)
Name changed to Novar International Corp. 06/08/1984
(See Novar International Corp.)

DAIRYLAND BANCSHARES INC (WI)
Acquired by Associated Banc-Corp. 12/28/1984
Each share Common $10 par exchanged for $108 cash

DAIRYMEN'S FEED & SUPPLY CO.
Dissolved 00/00/1936
Details not available

DAIRYMEN'S OHIO FARMERS MILK CO. (OH)
Liquidation completed 12/23/1959
Details not available

DAISY CORP (GA)
Name changed 12/06/1972
Name changed from Daisy Foods, Inc. to Daisy Corp. 12/06/1972
Involuntarily dissolved 11/25/1980

DAISY MANUFACTURING CO. (NV)
Merged into Victor Comptometer Corp. 05/18/1967
Each share Common $2 par exchanged for (0.13) share $4 Conv. Preferred Ser. A $1 par and (0.25) share Common $1 par
Victor Comptometer Corp. merged into Kidde (Walter) & Co., Inc. (DE) 07/15/1977 which name changed to Kidde, Inc. 04/18/1980 which merged into Hanson Trust PLC 12/31/1987 which name changed to Hanson PLC (Old) 01/29/1988 which reorganized as Hanson PLC (New) 10/15/2003

DAISY SYS CORP (DE)
Reincorporated 11/03/1986
State of incorporation changed from (CA) to (DE) 11/03/1986
Plan of reorganization under Chapter 11 Federal Bankruptcy proceedings confirmed 00/00/1992
Stockholders' equity unlikely

DAISYFRESH CREATIONS INC (QC)
Company became private 00/00/1981
Details not available

DAISYTEK INTL CORP (DE)
Common 1¢ par split (2) for (1) by issuance of (1) additional share payable 03/02/1998 to holders of record 02/16/1998
Each share Common 1¢ par received distribution of (0.81) share PFSweb, Inc. Common $0.001 par payable 07/06/2000 to holders of record 06/19/2000
Plan of reorganization under Chapter 11 Federal Bankruptcy Code effective 03/30/2004
No stockholders' equity

DAITCH CRYSTAL DAIRIES INC (DE)
Each share Common $1 par exchanged for (2) shares Common 50¢ par 05/04/1959
Name changed to Shopwell, Inc. 05/03/1973
(See Shopwell, Inc.)

DAIWA ASSOC HLDGS LTD (HONG KONG)
ADR agreement terminated 04/13/2015
No ADR's remain outstanding

DAIWA DANCHI LTD (JAPAN)
ADR agreement terminated 06/13/2001
Each ADR for Ordinary exchanged for $23.647 cash

DAIWA SECS LTD (JAPAN)
Stock Dividends - 10% 12/21/1973; 10% 12/27/1974; 10% 12/24/1975; 10% 12/28/1976; 10% 01/02/1979; 20% 12/24/1979; 20% 01/06/1982; 20% 12/01/1983
Name changed to Daiwa Securities Group, Inc. 04/26/1999

DAIWA SEIKO INC (JAPAN)
Stock Dividends - 16% 08/19/1987; 15% 07/18/1989
Name changed to Globeride, Inc. 10/01/2009

DAKA INTL INC (DE)
Each share old Common 1¢ par exchanged for (0.1) share new Common 1¢ par 01/17/1992
Each share new Common 1¢ par received distribution of (1) share Unique Casual Restaurants, Inc. Common 1¢ par payable 07/17/1997 to holders of record 07/11/1997
(See Unique Casual Restaurants, Inc.)
Merged into Compass Group PLC 07/17/1997
Each share new Common 1¢ par exchanged for $7.50 cash

DAKAMONT EXPLORATION CORP. (DE)
Merged into Permian Corp. (TX) 05/31/1961
Each share Common $1 par exchanged for (0.09478672) share Common no par
Permian Corp. (TX) reincorporated in Delaware 11/17/1961 which merged into Occidental Petroleum Corp. (CA) 10/31/1966 which reincorporated in Delaware 05/21/1986

DAKAR ENTERPRISES INC (NY)
Dissolved by proclamation 06/24/1981

DAKAR RESOURCE CORP (BC)
Name changed to Jericho Oil Corp. 02/27/2014

DAKON METALS INC (BC)
Struck off register and declared dissolved for failure to file returns 10/19/1990

DAKOTA BANCORPORATION (ND)
Stock Dividend - 100% 04/07/1976
Charter cancelled for failure to file annual reports 08/01/1993

DAKOTA ENERGY CORP (BC)
Recapitalized as Consolidated Dakota Resources Ltd. 06/19/1987
Each share Common no par exchanged for (0.2) share Common no par
Consolidated Dakota Resources Ltd. merged into Colossus Resource Equities Inc. 12/08/1987 which merged into Prime Resources Corp. (BC) 02/01/1989 which recapitalized as Prime Resources Group Inc. 01/26/1990 which merged into HomeStake Mining Co. 12/03/1998 which merged into Barrick Gold Corp. 12/14/2001

DAKOTA EQUITIES LTD (CO)
Name changed to Sel-Drum International Inc. 02/01/1995
(See Sel-Drum International Inc.)

DAKOTA GOLD CORP (NV)
Old Common $0.001 par split (100) for (1) by issuance of (99) additional shares payable 12/17/2010 to holders of record 12/16/2010
Ex date - 12/20/2010
Each share old Common $0.001 par exchanged for (0.01) share new Common $0.001 par 06/16/2011
Name changed to American Magna Corp. 07/02/2013

DAKOTA GRAPHICS INC (CO)
Recapitalized as Homeskills, Inc. (Old) 06/08/2004
Each share Common $1 par exchanged for (0.05) share Common $1 par
Homeskills, Inc. (Old) name changed to Pegasus Wireless Corp. 12/14/2004 which name changed to Homeskills, Inc. (New) 05/31/2005 which name changed to Curve Wireless Corp. 01/12/2006 which

name changed to OTC Wireless, Inc. 08/07/2006

DAKOTA GRAPHICS INC (DE)
Name changed 04/13/1973
State of incorporation and name changed from Dakota Microfilm Service (SD) to Dakota Graphics, Inc. (DE) 04/13/1973
Reincorporated under the laws of Colorado 09/01/1992
Dakota Graphics Inc. (CO) recapitalized as Homeskills, Inc. (Old) 06/08/2004 which name changed to Pegasus Wireless Corp. 12/14/2004 which name changed to Homeskills, Inc. (New) 05/31/2005 which name changed to Curve Wireless Corp. 01/12/2006 which name changed to OTC Wireless, Inc. 08/07/2006

DAKOTA GROWERS PASTA CO INC (ND)
Merged into Viterra Inc. 05/05/2010
Each share Ser. D Preferred 1¢ par exchanged for $0.10 cash
Each share Common 1¢ par exchanged for $18.28 cash

DAKOTA IMAGING INC (ND)
Common $0.001 par split (5) for (1) by issuance of (4) additional shares payable 02/08/2002 to holders of record 02/07/2002 Ex date - 02/11/2002
Name changed to Voyager Entertainment International, Inc. (ND) 04/02/2002
Voyager Entertainment International, Inc. (ND) reincorporated in Nevada 06/23/2003

DAKOTA MINERALS INC (UT)
Each share Common 1¢ par exchanged for (0.2) share Common 5¢ par 02/08/1974
Proclaimed dissolved for failure to pay taxes 06/01/1999

DAKOTA MNG CORP (BC)
SEC revoked common stock registration 04/22/2009

DAKOTA-MONTANA OIL LEASEHOLDS, INC. (DE)
No longer in existence having become inoperative and void for non-payment of taxes 04/01/1955

DAKOTA PLAINS HLDGS INC (NV)
Chapter 11 bankruptcy proceedings terminated 01/03/2018
No stockholders' equity

DAKOTA RES INC (CO)
Merged into Valex Petroleum Inc. 09/29/1983
Each share Common 1¢ par exchanged for (0.60606060) share Common 1¢ par
(See Valex Petroleum Inc.)

DAKOTA RES LTD (AB)
Name changed to Dynamix Corp. 04/14/1998
(See Dynamix Corp.)

DAKOTA TELECOMMUNICATIONS GROUP INC (DE)
Merged into McLeodUSA Inc. 03/05/1999
Each share Common no par exchanged for (0.4328) share Common 1¢ par
(See McLeodUSA Inc.)

DAKOTA WILLISTON OIL CORP. (DE)
No longer in existence having become inoperative and void for non-payment of taxes 04/01/1955

DAKOTAH INC (SD)
SEC revoked common stock registration 08/01/2012

DAL INTL LTD (NV)
Charter revoked 03/31/2016

DAL PETE CO (NV)
Name changed to Sacramento Oil & Gas Co. 00/00/1990

DAL-TILE INTL INC (DE)
Merged into Mohawk Industries, Inc. 03/20/2002
Each share Common 1¢ par exchanged for (0.2213) share Common 1¢ par and $11 cash

DALA PETE CORP (DE)
Name changed to KonaTel, Inc. 02/16/2018

DALAB HLDGS INC (NV)
Charter permanently revoked 09/30/1999

DALCO LIQUIDS, INC. (DE)
Name changed to International Drilling & Energy Corp. 11/10/1980
(See International Drilling & Energy Corp.)

DALCO PETE CORP (NV)
Plan of reorganization under Chapter 11 Federal Bankruptcy proceedings confirmed 12/05/1985
No stockholders' equity

DALCO PETE LTD (AB)
Common no par split (2) for (1) by issuance of (1) additional share 06/15/1981
Name changed to Dynex Petroleum Ltd. 05/12/1982
(See Dynex Petroleum Ltd.)

DALE ELECTRS INC (DE)
Acquired by Dale Holdings, Inc. 10/31/1985
Each share Common 10¢ par exchanged for $26.06 cash

DALE ENERGY CORP (DE)
Each share old Common no par exchanged for (0.05) share new Common no par 05/31/1995
Voluntarily dissolved 05/03/2007
Details not available

DALE ESTATE LTD. (ON)
Name changed to Calvert-Dale Estates Ltd. 03/03/1965
Calvert-Dale Estates Ltd. name changed to Argyll Energy Corp. 06/21/1983
(See Argyll Energy Corp.)

DALE GOLD MINES LTD. (ON)
Charter cancelled 09/00/1961

DALE JARRETT RACING ADVENTURE INC (FL)
Name changed to 24/7 Kid Doc, Inc. 02/18/2016

DALE MARKEY & CO INC (DE)
Name changed to Rand Systems, Inc. 10/17/1989
(See Rand Systems, Inc.)

DALE MOUNTAIN MINES LTD. (ON)
Charter cancelled and company declared dissolved for default in filing returns 12/28/1964

DALE PARIZEAU INC (CANADA)
6% Preferred Ser. A $10 par called for redemption 04/15/1995

DALE ROSS HLDGS LTD (CANADA)
Common no par split (3) for (1) by issuance of (2) additional shares 06/03/1970
Merged into Sodarcan Ltd. 10/27/1980
Each share Common no par exchanged for $21 cash
Name changed to Dale-Parizeau Inc. 11/12/1985
(See Dale-Parizeau Inc.)

DALECO RES CORP (DE)
Reincorporated 10/01/1996
Place of incorporation changed from (BC) to (DE) and Common no par changed to 1¢ par 10/01/1996
Each share old Common 1¢ par exchanged for (0.1) share new Common 1¢ par 02/16/1998
Reincorporated under the laws of Nevada 04/01/2002

DALEEN TECHNOLOGIES INC (DE)
Merged into Daleen Holdings, Inc. 10/19/2004
Each share Common 1¢ par exchanged for $0.0384 cash

DALEIGH HLDGS CORP (UT)
SEC revoked common stock registration 04/08/2009

DALER MNG CORP (BC)
Merged into Brandon Gold Corp. 02/19/1998
Each share Common no par exchanged for (0.310559) share Common no par
Brandon Gold Corp. recapitalized as Redmond Ventures Corp. 09/16/1999 which recapitalized as Crown Point Ventures Ltd. (BC) 03/12/2002 which reincorporated in Alberta as Crown Point Energy Inc. 07/31/2012

DALEX LTD (ON)
7% Preferred $100 par called for redemption 07/15/1975
(Additional Information in Active)

DALEX MINES LTD (BC)
Struck off register and declared dissolved for failure to file returns 01/17/1977

DALFENS LTD (QC)
Each share Common $1 par exchanged for (0.1) share Common no par 01/14/1965
Common no par split (10) for (1) by issuance of (9) additional shares 02/28/1973
Shares reacquired 04/30/1993
Each share Common no par exchanged for $2.20 cash

DALFORT CORP (NV)
Each share Conv. Preferred Ser. BB 1¢ par exchanged for (1) share Common 1¢ par 07/21/1984
Each share Conv. Preferred Ser. EE 1¢ par exchanged for (1) share Common 1¢ par 12/15/1984
Acquired by Hyatt Air, Inc. 10/10/1986
Each share Common 1¢ par exchanged for $14 cash

DALHART BERYLLIUM MINES & METALS CORP. LTD. (ON)
Acquired by Canhart Mines Ltd. 03/25/1960
Each share Capital Stock $1 par exchanged for (0.1) share Capital Stock $1 par
(See Canhart Mines Ltd.)

DALHART MINERALS CORP. LTD. (ON)
Name changed to Dalhart Beryllium Mines & Metals Corp. Ltd. 00/00/1957
Dalhart Beryllium Mines & Metals Corp. Ltd. acquired by Canhart Mines Ltd. 03/25/1960
(See Canhart Mines Ltd.)

DALIER RES LTD (CANADA)
Name changed to Vescan Equities Inc. 12/15/1999
Vescan Equities Inc. recapitalized as Inouye Technologies (Canada) Inc. 01/26/2000
(See Inouye Technologies (Canada) Inc.)

DALIN PHARMACEUTICALS INC (NY)
Dissolved by proclamation 09/25/1991

DALJACK INDS INC (NY)
Dissolved by proclamation 12/23/1992

DALJO GOLD MINES LTD. (ON)
Charter cancelled 12/03/1962

DALKEITH INVTS INC (DE)
Name changed to Sino Shipping Holdings Inc. 03/31/2008
(See Sino Shipping Holdings Inc.)

DALLAS AIRMOTIVE INC (DE)
Merged into Cooper Industries, Inc. (OH) 08/31/1970

Each share Common $1 par exchanged for (0.85) share Common $5 par
Cooper Industries, Inc. (OH) reincorporated in Bermuda as Cooper Industries, Ltd. 05/22/2002 which reincorporated in Ireland as Cooper Industries PLC 09/08/2009 which merged into Eaton Corp. PLC 11/30/2012

DALLAS BUSINESS CAP CORP (NV)
Stock Dividends - 10% 05/19/1978; 10% 05/18/1979; 10% 05/16/1980; 10% 05/15/1981; 10% 05/14/1982
Reincorporated under the laws of Delaware as Bizcap Inc. 04/01/1983
Bizcap, Inc. name changed to Caribbean Marine Inc. 12/03/1986
(See Caribbean Marine Inc.)

DALLAS CARPARK, INC. (DE)
Charter cancelled and declared inoperative and void for non-payment of taxes 03/01/1977

DALLAS CORP (IN)
Merged into DCO Holdings Corp. 02/09/1990
Each share Common $1 par exchanged for $24 cash

DALLAS COUNTY STATE BANK (CARROLLTON, TX)
Merged into First International Bancshares, Inc. 12/21/1973
Each share Capital Stock $5 par exchanged for (1.3) shares Common $5 par
First International Bancshares, Inc. name changed to InterFirst Corp. 12/31/1981 which merged into First RepublicBank Corp. 06/06/1987
(See First RepublicBank Corp.)

DALLAS ENVIRO HEALTH SYS LTD (BC)
Recapitalized as Accu-Chem International Ltd. 12/01/1995
Each share Common no par exchanged for (0.1) share Common no par

DALLAS EXPLS LTD (BC)
Name changed to Consolidated Dallas Explorations Ltd. 11/28/1983
(See Consolidated Dallas Explorations (Ltd.)

DALLAS FD INC (TX)
Completely liquidated 01/30/1975
Each share Common $1 par exchanged for $2.3764797 value of Selected Special Shares, Inc. Common 25¢ par
Selected Special Shares, Inc. name changed to Selected International Fund, Inc. 05/01/2011

DALLAS FED FINL CORP (DE)
Merged into Bright Banc Savings Association 12/31/1985
Each share Common $1 par exchanged for $33 cash

DALLAS FED SVGS & LN ASSN TEX (USA)
Reorganized as Dallas Federal Financial Corp. 02/20/1985
Each share Common $1 par exchanged for (1) share Common $1 par
(See Dallas Federal Financial Corp.)

DALLAS GOLD & SILVER EXCHANGE INC (NV)
Name changed to DGSE Companies, Inc. 06/27/2001

DALLAS INTL BK (DALLAS, TX)
Name changed to Northwest Bank (Dallas, TX) 01/15/1987
(See Northwest Bank (Dallas, TX))

DALLAS INVTS INC (UT)
Reorganized under the laws of Delaware as Hawaiian Legend Inc. 11/17/1995
Each share Common $0.001 par exchanged for (0.33333333) share Common $0.001 par

Hawaiian Legend Inc. name changed to Liberty International Entertainment Inc. 01/09/2002

DALLAS MANUFACTURING CO.
Liquidation completed 00/00/1949
Details not available

DALLAS OFFICE & CLUB BLDG., INC.
Liquidated 00/00/1943
Details not available

DALLAS OIL & MINERALS INC (NV)
Each share Common $0.002 par exchanged for (0.1) share Common 2¢ par 07/01/1984
Merged into Lomak Petroleum, Inc. 12/19/1990
For holdings of (199) shares or fewer each share Common 2¢ par exchanged for $0.25 cash
For holdings of (200) shares or more each share Common 2¢ par exchanged for (1) share Common 1¢ par
Lomak Petroleum, Inc. name changed to Range Resources Corp. 08/25/1998

DALLAS OIL CO. OF TEXAS, INC. (DE)
Recapitalized as Dallas Oil Co., Inc. 01/18/1982
Each share Common 10¢ par exchanged for (0.01) share Common $0.001 par
(See Dallas Oil Co., Inc.)

DALLAS OIL INC (DE)
Charter cancelled and declared inoperative and void for non-payment of taxes 03/01/1984

DALLAS PWR & LT CO (TX)
$6 Preferred no par called for redemption 05/31/1945
7% Preferred $100 par called for redemption 08/01/1945
4.5% Preferred $100 par changed to $4.50 Preferred no par 00/00/1959
Under plan of merger each share $4 Preferred no par, $4.24 Preferred no par, $4.50 Preferred no par, $4.80 Preferred no par, $6.84 Preferred no par, $7.20 Preferred no par, $7.48 Preferred no par and $11.32 Preferred no par automatically became (1) share Texas Utilities Electric Co. $4 Preferred no par, $4.24 Preferred no par, $4.50 Preferred no par, $4.80 Preferred no par, $6.84 Preferred no par, $7.20 Preferred no par, $7.48 Preferred no par and $11.32 Preferred no par respectively 01/01/1984
Texas Utilities Electric Co. name changed to TXU Electric Co. 06/14/1999 which name changed to TXU US Holdings Co. 01/01/2002
(See TXU US Holdings Co.)

DALLAS RAILWAY & TERMINAL CO. (TX)
Each share Common $100 par exchanged for (5) shares Common $20 par in 1946
Name changed to Dallas Transit Co. and each share Common $20 par exchanged for (2) shares Common $10 par 9/30/55
(See listing for Dallas Transit Co.)

DALLAS SEMICONDUCTOR CORP (DE)
Common 2¢ par split (2) for (1) by issuance of (1) additional share payable 2/28/2000 to holders of record 2/7/2000
Merged into Maxim Integrated Products, Inc. 4/11/2001
Each share Common 2¢ par exchanged for (0.6515) share Common $0.001 par

DALLAS SUNBELT ENERGY INC (DE)
Name changed to Chapman Energy, Inc. 10/19/82

Chapman Energy, Inc. name changed to Coda Energy, Inc. 10/10/89
(See Coda Energy, Inc.)

DALLAS SUNBELT OIL & GAS INC (DE)
Merged into Chapman Energy, Inc. 6/29/84
Each share Common $0.001 par exchanged for $0.75 cash

DALLAS TANK CO., INC. (TX)
Each share Common $10 par exchanged for (4) shares Common $2.50 par in 1952
Name changed to Trinity Steel Co., Inc. and Common $2.50 par changed to $1 par 11/6/58
Trinity Steel Co., Inc. name changed to Trinity Industries, Inc. (Tex.) 6/15/66 which reincorporated in Delaware 3/31/87

DALLAS TITLE & GTY CO (TX)
Stock Dividend - 66-2/3% 10/31/1952
Completely liquidated 12/21/1970
Each share Capital Stock $10 par exchanged for first and final distribution of (2.2808) shares USLIFE Corp. Common $2 par
(See USLIFE Corp.)

DALLAS TRANSIT CO. (TX)
Liquidation completed
Each share Common $10 par exchanged for $21.10 in cash plus a Ctf. of Bene. Int. for (1) Unit in Dallas Transit Co. Trust No. One 12/1/64
Each share Common $10 par received second and final distribution of pro rata interest in American Factors, Ltd., Arundel Corp., Dillingham Corp., Honolulu Rapid Transit Co., Fort Worth Transit Co., Inc., Jacobs (F.L.) Co., Lewers & Cook Ltd., Lihue Plantation Co., Ltd. and Todd Shipyards Corp. 12/29/64
(See each company's listing)

DALLAS TRANSIT CO. TRUST NO. ONE (TX)
Completely liquidated 6/18/70
Each Ctf. of Bene. Int. no par exchanged for first and final distribution of $1.5121874 cash

DALLAS URANIUM & OIL CORP. (CO)
Name changed to International Airlines, Inc. 5/20/69
(See International Airlines, Inc.)

DALLAS YELLOWKNIFE GOLD MINES, LTD. (ON)
Charter revoked for failure to file reports and pay taxes 00/00/1954

DALLEA PETE INC (ND)
Charter cancelled for failure to file annual reports 08/06/2007

DALLY DEVELOPMENT CORP. (ON)
Name changed to TNK Resources Inc. 07/07/1993
TNK Resources Inc. recapitalized as Opus Minerals Inc. 05/18/1999 which name changed to Investolinks.com, Inc. 07/28/2000 which recapitalized as API Electronics Group Inc. (ON) 09/10/2001 which reorganized in Delaware as API Electronics Group Corp. 09/15/2004 which merged into API Nanotronics Corp. 11/07/2006 which name changed to API Technologies Corp. 10/27/2009
(See API Technologies Corp.)

DALMATIAN RES LTD (BC)
Recapitalized as Enwest Ventures Corp. 02/18/2002
Each share Common no par exchanged for (1/3) share Common no par
Enwest Ventures Corp. recapitalized as Bayswater Ventures Corp. 02/25/2003 which merged into Bayswater Uranium Corp. (Old)

08/15/2006 which merged into Bayswater Uranium Corp. (New) 07/24/2007

DALMID OIL & URANIUM, INC. (DE)
Reorganized as Paxco, Inc. 7/19/71
Each share Common 1¢ par exchanged for (1) share Common 1¢ par
(See Paxco, Inc.)

DALMYS CDA LTD (CANADA)
Conv. Class A Common no par reclassified as Common no par 1/16/80
Conv. Class B Common no par reclassified as Common no par 1/16/80
Conv. Class D Common no par reclassified as Conv. Class C Common no par 1/16/80
Stock Dividends - In Common 10% 1/9/81; 10% 7/5/84; 10% 10/24/86; In Conv. Class C Common - 10% 10/24/86
Acquired by Reitman's (Canada) Ltd. 3/2/96
Each share Conv. Class C Common no par exchanged for $0.25 cash
Each share Common no par exchanged for $0.25 cash

DALO OIL CO. LTD. (AB)
Stuck off register and dissolved for failure to file returns and pay fees 12/31/68

DALPHINE ENTERPRISES LTD (BC)
Name changed to Inflazyme Pharmaceuticals Ltd. 12/10/1993
Inflazyme Pharmaceuticals Ltd. recapitalized as Eacom Timber Corp. 08/26/2008
(See Eacom Timber Corp.)

DALRADIAN RES INC (ON)
Acquired by Orion Mine Finance 09/10/2018
Each share Common no par exchanged for $1.47 cash
Note: Unexchanged certificates will be cancelled and become without value 09/10/2021

DALRAY YELLOWKNIFE GOLD MINES, LTD. (ON)
Charter surrendered for failure to file reports and pay taxes 03/19/1959

DALSA CORP (ON)
Common no par split (2) for (1) by issuance of (1) additional share payable 05/19/2000 to holders of record 05/12/2000 Ex date - 05/10/2000
Merged into Teledyne Technologies Inc. 02/18/2011
Each share Common no par exchanged for $18.25 cash

DALT BRANDS INC (NY)
Dissolved by proclamation 12/23/1992

DALT CORP (NV)
Charter revoked for failure to file reports and pay fees 11/1/90

DALTEX MED SCIENCES INC (DE)
Recapitalized as iiGroup, Inc. 11/29/1999
Each share Common 1¢ par exchanged for (0.02) share Common 1¢ par
iiGroup, Inc. name changed to Travlang, Inc. 04/26/2001
(See Travlang, Inc.)

DALTO CORP. (DE)
Name changed to Dalto Electronics Corp. 1/18/61
(See Dalto Electronics Corp.)

DALTO ELECTRS CORP (DE)
Common $1 par changed to old Common 50¢ par 5/28/61
Old Common 50¢ par changed to 10¢ par 10/1/63
Each share Common 10¢ par exchanged for (0.2) share new Common 50¢ par 9/30/65
Charter cancelled and declared

inoperative and void for non-payment of taxes 4/15/72

DALTON / WHITFIELD BK & TR (DALTON, GA)
Reorganized as D/W Bankshares, Inc. 04/08/1994
Each share Common $1 par exchanged for (1.1) shares Common $1 par
D/W Bankshares, Inc. merged into Colonial BancGroup, Inc. 01/31/1997
(See Colonial BancGroup, Inc.)

DALTON (EDWARD) & CO.
Merged into Yates-American Machine Co. in 1940
Each share 7% Preferred exchanged for (14) shares Common $5 par
Each share Common exchanged for (3.25) shares Common $5 par
(See Yates-American Machine Co.)

DALTON ADDING MACHINE CO.
Merged into Remington Rand, Inc. 00/00/1927
Details not available

DALTON COMMUNICATIONS INC (DE)
Charter cancelled and declared inoperative and void for non-payment of taxes 3/1/91

DALTON DEVELOPMENT LTD. (BC)
Charter cancelled 03/31/1983

DALTON ENTERPRISES LTD (WY)
Reincorporated 01/17/1995
Place of incorporation changed from (BC) to (WY) 01/17/1995
Reincorporated under the laws of Delaware as Dalton Specialties, Ltd. 03/01/1996
(See Dalton Specialties, Ltd.)

DALTON FINANCE, INC. (MD)
Bankrupt in 1961
No stockholders' equity

DALTON INDS INC (MN)
Each share old Common $0.00001 par exchanged for (0.001) share new Common $0.00001 par 08/10/2015
Reincorporated under the laws of Nevada as Universal Media Group, Inc. 01/11/2016

DALTON INTL RES INC (NV)
Name changed to E-Commerce Group Inc. 08/20/1999
E-Commerce Group Inc. recapitalized as Yizhong Bioengineering (USA), Inc. 06/12/2006 which name changed to Tianxin Mining (USA), Inc. 07/12/2007
(See Tianxin Mining (USA), Inc.)

DALTON RES LTD (BC)
Name changed to Dalton Development Ltd. 05/24/1973
(See Dalton Development Ltd.)

DALTON RES LTD NEW (AB)
Merged into Tiverton Petroleums Ltd. 10/01/2000
Each share Common no par exchanged for (1.27) shares Class A Common no par
Tiverton Petroleums Ltd. merged into Arsenal Energy Inc. (New) 03/13/2006 which merged into Prairie Provident Resources Inc. 09/16/2016

DALTON RES LTD OLD (AB)
Merged into Dalton Resources Ltd. (New) 12/31/1995
Each share Common no par exchanged for (1) share Common no par
Dalton Resources Ltd. (New) merged into Tiverton Petroleums Ltd. 10/01/2000 which merged into Arsenal Energy Inc. (New) 03/13/2006 which merged into Prairie Provident Resources Inc. 09/16/2016

DAL-DAN
FINANCIAL INFORMATION, INC.

DALTON SPECIALTIES LTD (DE)
Charter cancelled and declared inoperative and void for non-payment of taxes 03/01/1998

DALY MINING CO. (UT)
Merged into United Park City Mines Co. share for share 6/28/57
(See United Park City Mines Co.)

DAM HLDGS INC (NV)
Name changed to Premier Beverage Group Corp. 11/25/2011

DAMARK INTL INC (MN)
Name changed to Provell Inc. 4/24/2001
(See Provell Inc.)

DAMASCUS CMNTY BK (DAMASCUS, MD)
Common $30 par changed to $3 par and (9) additional shares issued payable 07/01/2015 to holders of record 06/25/2015 Ex date - 07/02/2015
Under plan of reorganization each share Common $3 par automatically became (1) share DCB Bancshares, Inc. Common 1¢ par 09/21/2016
DCB Bancshares, Inc. merged into Old Line Bancshares, Inc. 07/28/2017

DAMASCUS MINES LTD. (ON)
Charter surrendered 08/00/1959
No stockholders' equity

DAMASCUS MINING & MILLING CO. (CO)
Proclaimed defunct and inoperative for failure to pay taxes 09/03/1913

DAMASCUS RES LTD (BC)
Recapitalized as International Damascus Resources Ltd. 07/16/1982
Each share Common no par exchanged for (0.25) share Common no par
International Damascus Resources Ltd. recapitalized as Ravenhead Recovery Corp. 07/13/1998
(See Ravenhead Recovery Corp.)

DAMEN FINL CORP (DE)
Merged into MidCity Financial Corp. 07/01/1999
Each share Common 1¢ par exchanged for $18.35 cash

DAMERON INC (MN)
Statutorily dissolved 10/04/1991

DAMES & MOORE GROUP (DE)
Name changed 08/12/1997
Name changed from Dames & Moore, Inc. to Dames & Moore Group 08/12/1997
Merged into URS Corp. 06/23/1999
Each share Common 1¢ par exchanged for $16 cash

DAMIAN CAP CORP (AB)
Reincorporated under the laws of Canada as CPVC Financial Inc. 05/15/2006
CPVC Financial Inc. merged into CPVC Financial Corp. 11/06/2006
(See CPVC Financial Corp.)

DAMON BIOTECH INC (DE)
Acquired by Abbott Laboratories 03/15/1990
Each share Common 1¢ par exchanged for $1.023686 cash

DAMON CAP CORP (BC)
Name changed to Arizona Silver Exploration Inc. 11/16/2016

DAMON CORP NEW (DE)
Each share old Common 1¢ par exchanged for (0.3) share new Common 1¢ par and (0.7) share Class A Common 1¢ par 08/06/1991
Adjustable Dividend Exchangeable Sr. Preferred Ser. A no par called for redemption 12/06/1991
Merged into Opera Acquisition Corp. 08/04/1993
Each share new Common 1¢ par exchanged for $23 cash
Each share Class A Common 1¢ par exchanged for $23 cash

DAMON CORP OLD (DE)
Common 25¢ par split (3) for (2) by issuance of (0.5) additional share 12/02/1969
Common 25¢ par split (3) for (2) by issuance of (0.5) additional share 09/16/1987
Merged into Nomad Partners, L.P. 05/30/1989
Each share Common 25¢ par exchanged for $26 cash

DAMON CREATIONS INC (NY)
Class A $1 par split (4) for (3) by issuance of (0.33333333) additional share 02/03/1969
Class A $1 par reclassified as Common $1 par 10/21/1976
Merged into Apparel Group, Ltd. 11/27/1990
Each share Common $1 par exchanged for $1 cash

DAMON ENGR INC (DE)
Common 25¢ par split (3) for (2) by issuance of (0.5) additional share 12/26/1968
Name changed to Damon Corp. 11/17/1969
(See Damon Corp.)

DAMON GROUP INC (CA)
Completely liquidated 08/29/1991
Each share Common 1¢ par exchanged for first and final distribution of (0.5929) share Damon Corp. (New) Common 1¢ par
Note: Additional distribution of $0.02 cash per share was made to former holders who exchanged certificates prior to 09/03/1992

DAMSON ENERGY CO L P (TX)
Liquidation completed
Each Class A Unit of Limited Partnership received initial distribution of (0.1403) share Parker & Parsley Petroleum Co. Common 1¢ par and $0.76 cash 02/19/1991
Merged into Parker & Parsley Petroleum Co. 02/19/1991
Each Class B Unit of Ltd. Partnership exchanged for (0.1656) share Common 1¢ par and $0.97 cash
Each Class A Unit of Limited Partnership received second and final distribution of $0.525 cash 12/20/1991
Parker & Parsley Petroleum Co. merged into Pioneer Natural Resources Co. 08/07/1997

DAMSON INCOME ENERGY LTD PARTNERSHIP (TX)
Merged into Parker & Parsley Petroleum Co. 02/19/1991
Each Unit of Ltd. Partnership exchanged for (0.4405) share Common 1¢ par and $2.57 cash
Parker & Parsley Petroleum Co. merged into Pioneer Natural Resources Co. 08/07/1997

DAMSON INSTL ENERGY LTD PARTNERSHIP (TX)
Merged into Parker & Parsley Petroleum Co. 02/19/1991
Each Unit of Ltd. Partnership exchanged for (0.3841) share Common 1¢ par and $2.24 cash
Parker & Parsley Petroleum Co. merged into Pioneer Natural Resources Co. 08/07/1997

DAMSON OIL CORP (DE)
$3.75 Delayed Conv. Preferred $1 par dividend rate changed to $2.50 on 03/29/1984
$3.75 Delayed Conv. Preferred Ser. 2 $1 par dividend rate changed to $3 on 02/01/1986
Common 40¢ par changed to 1¢ par 08/26/1986
Plan of reorganization under Chapter 11 Federal Bankruptcy proceedings confirmed 03/26/1992
No stockholders' equity

DAN RIV INC NEW (GA)
Merged into GHCL Inc. 01/27/2006
Each share Common 1¢ par exchanged for $0.85 cash

DAN RIVER INC (VA)
Merged into Dan River Holding Co. 05/24/1983
Each share $1.10 Conv. Preferred $5 par exchanged for $22.50 cash
Each share Common $5 par exchanged for $22.50 cash

DAN RIVER INC OLD (GA)
Plan of reorganization under Chapter 11 Federal Bankruptcy Code effective 02/14/2005
No stockholders' equity

DAN RIVER MLS INC (VA)
6% Preferred called for redemption 09/19/1946
Common $5 par split (2) for (1) by issuance of (1) additional share 08/05/1955
5% Conv. Preferred $20 par called for redemption 07/15/1966
Name changed to Dan River Inc. 07/01/1970
(See Dan River Inc.)

DANA ASSOC (ME)
Completely liquidated 06/11/1975
Each share Capital Stock $10 par exchanged for first and final distribution of (5.1691475) shares Chemical Fund, Inc. (DE) Common $0.125 par
Chemical Fund, Inc. (DE) reincorporated in Maryland 02/08/1979 which name changed to Alliance Fund, Inc. 04/01/1987 which name changed to Alliance Mid-Cap Growth Fund Inc. 02/01/2002 which name changed to AllianceBernstein Mid-Cap Growth Fund, Inc. 03/31/2003

DANA CORP (VA)
Common $1 par split (2) for (1) by issuance of (1) additional share 10/30/1959
Common $1 par split (2) for (1) by issuance of (1) additional share 05/15/1969
3.75% Preference Ser. A $100 par called for redemption 04/14/1973
Common $1 par split (2) for (1) by issuance of (1) additional share 02/13/1976
Common $1 par split (3) for (2) by issuance of (0.5) additional share 11/14/1983
Common $1 par split (2) for (1) by issuance of (1) additional share 06/15/1994
Stock Dividends - 66.66666666% 08/00/1947; 66.66666666% 03/18/1949
Plan of reorganization under Chapter 11 Federal Bankruptcy Code effective 01/31/2008
No stockholders' equity

DANA ELECTRS INC (CA)
Name changed to Jenoa Inc. 12/27/1977
Jenoa Inc. name changed to EIP Microwave, Inc. (CA) 09/30/1979 which reincorporated in Delaware 04/29/1987
(See EIP Microwave, Inc.)

DANA HLDG CORP (DE)
Name changed to Dana Inc. 08/01/2016

DANA LABS INC (CA)
Common no par split (5) for (4) by issuance of (0.25) additional share 02/05/1970
Name changed to Danalab, Inc. 12/29/1970
Danalab, Inc. name changed to Dana Electronics, Inc. 01/24/1975 which name changed to Jenoa Inc. 12/27/1977 which name changed to EIP Microwave, Inc. (CA) 09/30/1979 which reincorporated in Delaware 04/29/1987
(See EIP Microwave, Inc.)

DANA NIGUEL BK N A (DANA POINT, CA)
Common $5 par changed to $2.50 par and (0.5) additional share issued 12/20/1984
Name changed to Harbor National Bank (Dana Point, CA) 12/15/1999
(See Harbor National Bank (Dana Point, CA))

DANA WARP MILLS
Name changed to Dana Associates 05/00/1955
Dana Associates liquidated for Chemical Fund, Inc. (DE) 06/11/1975 which reincorporated in Maryland 02/08/1979 which name changed to Alliance Fund, Inc. 04/01/1987 which name changed to Alliance Mid-Capital Growth Fund Inc. 02/01/2002 which name changed to AllianceBernstein Mid-Capital Growth Fund, Inc. 03/31/2003

DANAC REAL ESTATE INVT CORP (MD)
Merged into Richmond Corp. 06/30/1972
Each share Capital Stock $1 par exchanged for (0.6) share Common $5 par
Richmond Corp. merged into Continental Group, Inc. 06/29/1977

DANAHER CORP (FL)
Reincorporated under the laws of Delaware 10/31/1986

DANALAB INC (CA)
Name changed to Dana Electronics, Inc. 01/24/1975
Dana Electronics, Inc. name changed to Jenoa Inc. 12/27/1977 which name changed to EIP Microwave, Inc. (CA) 09/30/1979 which reincorporated in Delaware 04/29/1987
(See EIP Microwave, Inc.)

DANARAY URANIUM MINES, LTD. (ON)
Declared dissolved 04/01/1963
No stockholders' equity

DANBEL INDS CORP (ON)
Recapitalized as Danbel Ventures Inc. 12/01/2011
Each share Common no par exchanged for (0.1) share Common no par
Danbel Ventures Inc. recapitalized as Maricann Group Inc. 04/24/2017

DANBEL VENTURES INC (ON)
Recapitalized as Maricann Group Inc. 04/24/2017
Each share Common no par exchanged for (0.10845986) share Common no par

DANBOURNE CORP (OR)
Each share Capital Stock 25¢ par exchanged for (0.005) share Capital Stock $50 par 08/18/1976
Voluntarily dissolved 12/04/1987
Details not available

DANBURY INDL CORP (CT)
In process of liquidation
Each share Common $10 par received initial distribution of $40 cash payable 06/23/2003 to holders of record 06/16/2003 Ex date - 06/24/2003
Each share Common $10 par received second distribution of $45 cash payable 10/20/2003 to holders of record 10/09/2003
Each share Common $10 par received third distribution of $7 cash payable 03/25/2004 to holders of record 03/22/2004

Each share Common $10 par received fourth distribution of $128 cash payable 04/22/2004 to holders of record 04/15/2004
Each share Common $10 par received fifth distribution of $200 cash payable 05/10/2004 to holders of record 05/03/2004
Each share Common $10 par received sixth distribution of $80 cash payable 11/16/2004 to holders of record 11/08/2004
Note: Details on subsequent distributions, if any, are not available

DANBURY PRODUCTS, INC (DE)
Completely liquidated 07/20/1961
Each share Preferred $100 par exchanged for first and final distribution of $76.25 cash
No Common stockholders' equity

DANBUS MAGNETIC SYS INC (CA)
Reorganized 03/04/1988
Reorganized 01/06/1989
Reorganized from Danbus Resources Inc. (BC) to Danbus Memory Systems Inc. (CA) 03/04/1988
Reorganized from Danbus Memory Systems to Danbus Magnetic Systems, Inc. 01/06/1989
Each share old Common no par exchanged for (2) shares new Common no par
Charter suspended for failure to file reports and pay fees 02/01/1991

DANCAP RES INC (AB)
Name changed to Storm Energy Inc. 10/01/1997
(See Storm Energy Inc.)

DANCIGER OIL & REFINING CO.
Acquired by Southern Production Co., Inc. 00/00/1950
Each share Capital Stock $1 par exchanged for (1) share new 4% Preferred $25 par
(See Southern Production Co., Inc.)

DANCING STAR RES LTD (BC)
Recapitalized as Alcor Resources Ltd. 07/09/2003
Each share Common no par exchanged for (0.5) share Common no par
Alcor Resources Ltd. name changed to Balto Resources Ltd. 06/16/2008

DANCO INDS INC (BC)
Delisted from Vancouver Stock Exchange 05/04/1994

DANDEES ENTERPRISES INC (CA)
Charter suspended for failure to file reports and pay fees 07/01/1993

DANDOR INTL INC (DE)
Charter cancelled and declared inoperative and void for non-payment of taxes 03/01/1975

DANDRIT BIOTECH USA INC (DE)
Name changed to Enochian Biosciences Inc. 03/19/2018

DANE EXPL INC (NV)
Name changed to Portus Corp. 03/24/2014

DANEK GROUP INC (IN)
Common no par split (2) for (1) by issuance of (1) additional share 02/13/1992
Name changed to Sofamor/Danek Group, Inc. 06/25/1993
Sofamor/Danek Group, Inc. merged into Medtronic, Inc. (MN) 01/27/1999 which reincorporated in Ireland as Medtronic PLC 01/27/2015

DANG VENTURES (NV)
Name changed to Executive Eagles Inc. 05/12/1988
Executive Eagles Inc. name changed to Santa Rita Corp. 04/13/1990
(See Santa Rita Corp.)

DANGERFIELD RES INC (AB)
Merged into Remington Energy Ltd. 07/01/1994
Each share Common no par exchanged for (0.4) share Common no par
(See Remington Energy Ltd.)

DANIA BK (DANIA, FL)
Through purchase offer over 99% acquired by certain individuals as of 05/12/1978
Public interest eliminated

DANIEL CONSTR INC (SC)
Stock Dividends - 25% 12/05/1969; 25% 12/29/1970
Name changed to Daniel International Corp. 03/01/1971
(See Daniel International Corp.)

DANIEL DIVERSIFIED LTD (ON)
Recapitalized as Kaolin of Canada Inc. 09/02/1983
Each share Capital Stock no par exchanged for (0.2) share Common no par
(See Kaolin of Canada Inc.)

DANIEL INDS INC (DE)
Reincorporated 03/21/1988
Common $5 par changed to $2.50 par and (1) additional share issued 10/30/1975
Common $2.50 par changed to $1.25 par and (1) additional share issued 03/17/1981
Stock Dividends - 15% 06/28/1974; 15% 06/27/1975; 15% 06/28/1976; 15% 06/27/1977; 15% 06/30/1978
State of incorporation changed from (TX) to (DE) 03/21/1988
Merged into Emerson Electric Co. 06/24/1999
Each share Common $1.25 par exchanged for $21.25 cash

DANIEL INTL CORP (SC)
Common $2 par split (5) for (4) by issuance of (0.25) additional share 10/29/1971
Common $2 par split (5) for (4) by issuance of (0.25) additional share 12/29/1972
Stock Dividend - 50% 03/29/1974
Merged into Fluor Southeast, Inc. 02/01/1978
Each share Common $2 par exchanged for $31 cash

DANIEL MINING CO. LTD. (ON)
Name changed to Daniel Diversified Ltd. 01/14/1969
Daniel Diversified Ltd. recapitalized as Kaolin of Canada Inc. 09/02/1983
(See Kaolin of Canada Inc.)

DANIELSON FED SVGS & LN ASSN (USA)
Merged into New London Trust Co. 01/01/1994
Each share Common $1 par exchanged for $2.50 cash

DANIELSON HLDG CORP (DE)
Reincorporated 05/01/1992
State of incorporation changed from (CA) to (DE) 05/01/1992
Name changed to Covanta Holding Corp. 09/20/2005

DANIELSON MANUFACTURING CO. (CT)
Liquidation completed 12/04/1957
Details not available

DANIS QUEBEC GOLD MINES, LTD. (ON)
Charter revoked for failure to file reports and pay taxes 01/00/1957

DANISCO A/S (DENMARK)
Acquired by Du Pont (E.I.) de Nemours & Co. 12/01/2011
Each ADR for Ordinary exchanged for $10.972139 cash

DANKA BUSINESS SYS PLC (ENGLAND & WALES)
Sponsored ADR's for Ordinary split (2) for (1) by issuance of (1) additional ADR 03/03/1993
Sponsored ADR's for Ordinary split (2) for (1) by issuance of (1) additional ADR 08/29/1994
Basis changed from (1:8) to (1:4) 08/29/1994
Completely liquidated
Each Sponsored ADR for Ordinary received first and final distribution of $0.12 cash payable 09/17/2010 to holders of record 09/10/2010

DANKER & WOHLK, INC. (NY)
Common 1¢ par split (2) for (1) by issuance of (1) additional share 08/18/1972
Name changed to Danker Laboratories, Inc. 03/28/1979
(See Danker Laboratories, Inc.)

DANKER LABS INC (NY)
Company advised it became private 00/00/1993
Details not available

DANKOE MINES LTD (BC)
Recapitalized as Emerald Dragon Mines Inc. 10/30/1996
Each share Common no par exchanged for (0.2) share Common no par
(See Emerald Dragon Mines Inc.)

DANLAX CORP (NV)
Common $0.001 par split (1.094891) for (1) by issuance of (0.094891) additional share payable 04/23/2015 to holders of record 04/20/2015
Ex date - 04/24/2015
Name changed to Akoustis Technologies, Inc. (NV) 05/01/2015
Akoustis Technologies, Inc. (NV) reincorporated in Delaware 12/16/2016

DANLOU MINES LTD. (ON)
Charter revoked for failure to file reports and pay fees 10/22/1965

DANLY MACH CORP (DE)
Reincorporated 10/20/1976
State of incorporation changed from (IL) to (DE) 10/20/1976
Merged into Ogden Corp. 08/27/1981
Each share Common $5 par exchanged for $70 cash

DANLY MACHINE SPECIALTIES, INC. (IL)
Name changed to Danly Machine Corp. (IL) 10/19/1966
Danly Machine Corp. (IL) reincorporated in Delaware 10/20/1976
(See Danly Machine Corp. (DE))

DANMONT CORP (DE)
Reincorporated 04/27/1972
State of incorporation changed from (NV) to (DE) and each share Common 10¢ par exchanged for (0.5) share Common 10¢ par 04/27/1972
Charter cancelled and declared inoperative and void for non-payment of taxes 03/01/1986

DANNEMANN FABRICS INC (DE)
Merged into Everfast, Inc. 07/05/1977
Each share Common 1¢ par exchanged for $1.25 cash

DANNER FOODS INC (TN)
Name changed to Shoney's Big Boy Enterprises, Inc. 05/28/1971
Shoney's Big Boy Enterprises, Inc. name changed to Shoney's Inc. 10/21/1976
(See Shoney's Inc.)

DANNERS INC (IN)
Merged into Danners Merging Corp. 12/29/1987
Each share Common no par exchanged for $3.50 cash

DANNIES MOBILE HOMES INC (OH)
Charter cancelled for non-payment of taxes 02/23/1977

DANNINGER MED TECHNOLOGY INC (DE)
Name changed to Cross Medical Products, Inc. 03/21/1997
Cross Medical Products, Inc. merged into Interpore International 05/07/1998
(See Interpore International)

DANOIL ENERGY LTD (AB)
Merged into Acclaim Energy Trust 04/20/2001
Each share Class A Subordinate no par exchanged for (1) Trust Unit no par
(See Acclaim Energy Trust)

DANRA RES LTD (ON)
Delisted from Vancouver Stock Exchange 03/01/1999

DANROD MALARTIC MINES LTD. (ON)
Charter revoked for failure to file reports and pay taxes 00/00/1956

DANSKER REALTY & SECURITIES CORP.
Name changed to Investors Funding Corp. of New York 00/00/1952
(See Investors Funding Corp. of New York)

DANSKIN INC (DE)
Stock Dividend - 8.34% payable 09/29/1997 to holders of record 09/22/1997
Name changed to Triumph Apparel Corp. 10/01/2007
(See Triumph Apparel Corp.)

DANSTAR RES LTD (BC)
Name changed 07/30/1982
Name changed from Danstar Mines Ltd. to Danstar Resources Ltd. 07/30/1982
Each share Common no par exchanged for (1) share Common no par
Recapitalized as Star Dance Resources Ltd. 05/21/1992
Each share Common no par exchanged for (0.22727272) share Common no par
Star Dance Resources Ltd. recapitalized as Dancing Star Resources Ltd. 01/13/1999 which recapitalized as Alcor Resources Ltd. 07/09/2003 which name changed to Balto Resources Ltd. 06/16/2008

DANT & RUSSELL INC (NV)
Plan of reorganization under Chapter 11 Federal Bankruptcy proceedings confirmed 07/22/1987
No stockholders' equity

DANTE EXPLORATIONS CO. (CO)
Charter revoked for failure to file reports and pay fees 10/30/1959

DANTE HOSPITAL, INC.
Property sold and company liquidated 00/00/1946
Details not avaialable

DANVERS BANCORP INC (DE)
Merged into People's United Financial, Inc. 07/01/2011
Each share Common 1¢ par exchanged for either (1.624) shares Common 1¢ par or $23 cash

DANVILLE (VA) TRACTION & POWER CO. (VA)
Completely liquidated 06/00/1977
Details not available

DANVILLE BANCORP, INC. (KY)
Merged into Bank One, N.A. (Lexington, KY) 08/22/1992
Details not available

DANVILLE BANCSHARES, INC. (DE)
97% acquired by First Midwest Bancorp, Inc. through exchange offer which expired 09/13/1982
Public interest eliminated

DANVILLE NATL BK (DANVILLE, PA)
Merged into Fidelity National Bank of

Pennsylvania (Williamsport, PA) 11/01/1968
Each share Capital Stock $100 par exchanged for (10) shares Common $10 par
Fidelity National Bank of Pennsylvania (Williamsport, PA) merged into Commonwealth Bank & Trust Co., N.A. (Williamsport, PA) 05/29/1981 which reorganized as Commonwealth Bancshares Corp. 03/01/1982 which was acquired by Meridian Bancorp, Inc. 08/31/1992 which merged into Corestates Financial Corp 04/09/1996 which merged into First Union Corp. 04/28/1998 which name changed to Wachovia Corp. (Ctfs. dated after 09/01/2001) 09/01/2001 which merged into Wells Fargo & Co. (New) 12/31/2008

DANZAR INVT GROUP INC (CO)
Recapitalized as Alexander Mark Investments (USA), Inc. 12/26/1996
Each share Common no par received (0.01) share Common no par
Note: Certificates were not required to be surrendered and are without value
Alexander Mark Investments (USA), Inc. reorganized as Wincroft, Inc. (CO) 05/18/1998 which reorganized in Nevada 02/12/2008 which name changed to Apollo Solar Energy, Inc. 11/03/2008

DANZER CORP (NY)
Reincorporated under the laws of Delaware as Obsidian Enterprises, Inc. 10/17/2001
(See Obsidian Enterprises, Inc.)

DAON CENTRE LTD PARTNERSHIP (BC)
Dissolved 00/00/1987
Details not available

DAON DEV CORP (BC)
Name changed 02/22/1982
Each share old Common no par exchanged for (1) share new Common no par and (1) share 75¢ Class A no par or (2) shares new Common no par 11/27/1975
Note: In absence of an election to receive (2) shares new Common holders were entitled to (1) share new Common and (1) share 75¢ Class A for each share old Common only
New Common no par split (2) for (1) by issuance of (1) additional share 07/22/1977
New Common no par split (2) for (1) by issuance of (1) additional share 02/20/1978
New Common no par split (2) for (1) by issuance of (1) additional share 03/05/1979
New Common no par split (2) for (1) by issuance of (1) additional share 02/28/1980
Name changed from Daon Development Corp. to Daon Development Corp. - Corporation D'Amenagement Daon 02/22/1982
Name changed to BCE Development Corp. - Corporation de Developpement BCE 02/21/1986
BCE Development Corp. - Corporation de Developpement BCE name changed to BF Realty Holdings Ltd. 08/19/1991
(See BF Realty Holdings Ltd.)

DAOU SYS INC (DE)
Merged into Proxicom, Inc. 10/28/2005
Each share Common $0.001 par exchanged for approximately $0.384 cash

DAPCO, INC. (PA)
Adjudicated bankrupt 05/05/1969
No stockholders' equity

DARA BIOSCIENCES INC (DE)
Each share old Common 1¢ par exchanged for (0.0625) share new Common 1¢ par 05/13/2010
Each share new Common 1¢ par exchanged again for (0.2) share new Common 1¢ par 02/10/2014
Merged into Midatech Pharma PLC 12/04/2015
Each share new Common 1¢ par exchanged for (0.136) Sponsored ADR for Ordinary and (1) Non-Transferable Contingent Value Right

DARAGON MINES LTD (ON)
Capital Stock $1 par changed to no par 08/03/1977
Recapitalized as Pennant Resources Ltd. 06/28/1978
Each share Capital Stock no par exchanged for (0.33333333) share Capital Stock no par
Pennant Resources Ltd. recapitalized as PNR Food Industries Ltd. 11/23/1987
(See PNR Food Industries Ltd.)

DARBY, MEDIA & CHESTER STREET RAILWAY CO.
Acquired by Philadelphia Transportation Co. in 1940
Each share Common exchanged for $2.92 principal amount of 3%-6% Consolidated Mortgage Bonds and (0.2085) share $1 Part. Preferred $20 par
(See Philadelphia Transportation Co.)

DARBY MINING CO. (NJ)
Dissolved 4/25/56

DARBY PETROLEUM CORP.
Merged into Sunray Oil Corp. 00/00/1944
Each share Common exchanged for (1) share 4.5% Preferred $40 par
(See Sunray Oil Corp.)

DARCO CORP.
Acquired by Atlas Powder Co. 00/00/1950
Each share 8% Preferred exchanged for (5) shares Common $20 par
Each share Common exchanged for $1 cash
Atlas Powder Co. recapitalized as Atlas Chemical Industries, Inc. 05/31/1961
(See Atlas Chemical Industries, Inc.)

DARCY COMMUNICATIONS INC. (NY)
Merged into Hutchins/Darcy Inc. 07/01/1971
Each share Common 10¢ par exchanged for (0.6) share Common 10¢ par
(See Hutchins/Darcy Inc.)

DARCY CORP (CO)
Reincorporated under the laws of Delaware as Cetek Technologies Inc. 05/25/1994
Cetek Technologies Inc. (DE) reincorporated in Nevada 04/11/2008 which name changed to High Velocity Enterprises, Inc. 06/24/2014 which reorganized as NanoTech Gaming, Inc. 04/23/2015

DARCY INDS INC (NY)
Assets liquidated for benefit of creditors 7/9/69
No stockholders' equity

DARDELET THREADLOCK CORP. (DE)
Name changed to Lock Thread Corp. in 1947
Lock Thread Corp. name changed to Shelby Universal Corp. (DE) 12/1/83 which recapitalized as NA American Technologies, Inc. 4/3/2006 which name changed to JSX Energy, Inc. 8/30/2006

DARDICK CORP. (DE)
No longer in existence having become inoperative and void for non-payment of taxes 4/1/63

DAREN INDS LTD (BC)
Discharged from receivership 05/13/2003
Stockholders' equity unlikely

DAREN RES LTD (BC)
Recapitalized as Daren Industries Ltd. 12/01/1999
Each share Common no par exchanged for (0.33333333) share Common no par
(See Daren Industries Ltd.)

DARFIELD INDS INC (DE)
Each share Common 1¢ par exchanged for (0.005) share Common $2 par 8/9/76
Each share Common $2 par exchanged for (1/110) share new Common $2 par 7/14/78
Note: In effect holders received $84 cash per share and public interest was eliminated

DARFORD INTL INC (AB)
Assets sold for the benefit of creditors 11/30/2012
Stockholders' equity unlikely

DARI DELITE INC (CA)
Charter cancelled for failure to file reports and pay taxes 4/1/76

DARI INTL INC (WA)
Charter cancelled and proclaimed dissolved for failure to pay fees 07/02/1981

DARIEN RESOURCE DEV CORP (BC)
Name changed to New Energy Metals Corp. 04/04/2018

DARIUS TECHNOLOGY LTD (CANADA)
Declared bankrupt 12/12/1995
Stockholders' equity unlikely

DARK BLUE SEA LTD (AUSTRALIA)
Acquired by Photon Group Ltd. 01/22/2010
Each Sponsored ADR for Ordinary exchanged for $6.374599 cash

DARK DYNAMITE INC (NV)
Each share Common $0.001 par exchanged for (0.0005) share old Common $0.0001 par 11/17/2004
Each share old Common $0.0001 par exchanged for (0.001) share new Common $0.0001 par 03/28/2005
Each share new Common $0.0001 par exchanged again for (0.25) share new Common $0.0001 par 11/03/2005
Name changed to China International Tourism Holdings, Ltd. 10/26/2007
China International Tourism Holdings, Ltd. name changed to China Logistics, Inc. (NV) 08/10/2009 which reorganized in British Virgin Islands as Hutech21 Co., Ltd. 03/21/2011

DARKHAWK DEV LTD (BC)
Acquired by Trans-Canada Resources Ltd. (BC) 04/12/1982
Each share Capital Stock no par exchanged for $1.15 cash

DARKHAWK MINES LTD. (BC)
Name changed to Darkhawk Development Corp. Ltd. and Capital Stock 50¢ par changed to no par 08/22/1972
(See Darkhawk Development Corp. Ltd.)

DARKWATER MINES LTD. (ON)
Dissolved 01/19/1959
No stockholders' equity

DARLING (ANN) BOWL, INC. (CA)
Charter suspended for non-payment of taxes 07/02/1962

DARLING (L.A.) CO. (DE)
Reorganized in 1937
Each share Class A exchanged for (10) shares Common $1 par
Each share Class B exchanged for (1.5) shares Common $1 par
Stock Dividends - 25% 12/22/54; 20% 12/22/55; 10% 12/21/56; 20% 6/17/60
Name changed to L.A.D. Corp. 11/29/63
(See L.A.D. Corp.)

DARLING INTL INC (DE)
Name changed to Darling Ingredients Inc. 05/08/2014

DARLINGTON CNTY BK (DARLINGTON, SC)
Under plan of reorganization each share Common no par automatically became (1) share Darlington County Bancshares, Inc. Common 1¢ par 7/1/99
(See Darlington County Bancshares, Inc.)

DARLINGTON MANUFACTURING CO. (SC)
Liquidation completed 10/11/57
Each share Common $5 par stamped to indicate initial distribution of $10 cash 12/15/56
Each share Stamped Common $5 par received second and final distribution of $13.20 cash 10/11/57

DARLINGTON MINES LTD (NV)
Name changed to Pulse Beverage Corp. 02/24/2011

DARNLEY BAY RES LTD (ON)
Each share old Common no par exchanged for (0.2) share new Common no par 12/31/2014
Name changed to Pine Point Mining Ltd. 08/08/2017
(See Pine Point Mining Ltd.)

DAROX CORP (DE)
Charter cancelled and declared inoperative and void for non-payment of taxes 3/1/93

DARSI MINES LTD (BC)
Recapitalized as Dasher Development Corp. 06/27/1974
Each share Common 50¢ par exchanged for (0.33333333) share Common no par
Dasher Development Corp. recapitalized as Nightwatch Resources Inc. 03/02/1977
(See Nightwatch Resources Inc.)

DART & KRAFT INC (DE)
Common $2.50 par changed to $1 par and (2) additional shares issued 06/14/1985
Name changed to Kraft, Inc. (New) 11/21/1986
(See Kraft, Inc. (New))

DART DRUG STORES INC (DE)
Charter cancelled and declared inoperative and void for non-payment of taxes 03/01/1992

DART ENERGY INC (AB)
Recapitalized as Eyelogic Systems Inc. 03/13/1998
Each share Class A Common no par exchanged for (0.25) share Class A Common no par
(See Eyelogic Systems Inc.)

DART GROUP CORP (DE)
Name changed 6/29/84
Class A Common $1 par split (5) for (4) by issuance of (0.25) additional share 1/30/70
Class A Common $1 par split (5) for (4) by issuance of (0.25) additional share 1/29/71
Class A Common $1 par split (3) for (2) by issuance of (0.5) additional share 11/12/71
Name changed from Dart Drug Corp. to Dart Group Corp. 6/29/84
Merged into Richfood Holdings, Inc. 5/18/98
Each share Class A Common $1 par exchanged for $160 cash

DART INDS INC (DE)
Under plan of reorganization each share $2 Conv. Preferred Ser. A $5 par and Common $1.25 par automatically became (1) share Dart & Kraft, Inc. Common $2.50 par 09/25/1980
Dart & Kraft, Inc. name changed to Kraft, Inc. (New) 11/21/1986
(See Kraft, Inc. (New))

DART INVESTMENT CORP. (MN)
Adjudicated bankrupt 1/6/72

DART NATL CORP (DE)
No longer in existence having become inoperative and void for non-payment of taxes 04/01/1966

DART PROFESSIONAL INC (NY)
Dissolved by proclamation 12/29/1982

DARTMOUTH BANCORP INC (NH)
Administratively dissolved 11/01/1993

DARTMOUTH MANUFACTURING CO.
Liquidated 00/00/1933
Details not available

DARTMOUTH PORCUPINE GOLD MINES LTD. (ON)
Bankrupt 00/00/1949
No stockholders' equity

DARTNELL CORP (DE)
Company became private 00/00/1982
Details not available

DARVA RES & DEV LTD (BC)
Name changed to Eldorado Minerals & Petroleum Corp. 02/22/1979
(See Eldorado Minerals & Petroleum Corp.)

DARWIN CAP CORP (BC)
Name changed to UniLink Tele.Com Inc. 10/18/2000
(See UniLink Tele.com Inc.)

DARWIN GOLD MINES, LTD.
Reorganized as New Darwin Gold Mines, Ltd. 00/00/1938
Details not available

DARWIN MINES LTD. (ON)
Merged into New Force Crag Mines Ltd. 11/22/1974
Each share Common $1 par exchanged for (0.86956521) share Common no par
(See New Force Crag Mines Ltd.)

DARWIN PROFESSIONAL UNDERWRITERS INC (DE)
Merged into Allied World Assurance Company Holdings, Ltd. 10/20/2008
Each share Common 1¢ par exchanged for $32 cash

DARWIN RES CORP (BC)
Merged into Tinka Resources Ltd. 07/28/2014
Each share Common no par exchanged for (0.1818) share Common no par
Note: Unexchanged certificates will be cancelled and become without value 07/28/2020

DARWIN RES CORP (DE)
Reincorporated 11/22/2005
State of incorporation changed from (NV) to (DE) 11/22/2005
Name changed to Health Benefits Direct Corp. and (0.317663818) additional share issued 12/02/2005
Health Benefits Direct Corp. name changed to InsPro Technologies Corp. 12/06/2010

DARWIN RES INC (DE)
Recapitalized as A Clean Slate, Inc. 12/10/2010
Each share Common $0.000001 par exchanged for (0.001) share Common $0.000001 par

DARYL INDS INC (FL)
Adjudicated bankrupt 06/15/1973
Trustee opined no stockholders' equity

DASA CORP (MA)
Reincorporated 04/01/1966
Each share Common $1 par exchanged for (0.2) share Common no par 07/26/1965
Under plan of merger reincorporated from (CA) to under the laws of Massachusetts and Common no par changed to $1 par 04/01/1966
Each share 5.5% Conv. Preferred $36 par exchanged for (4) shares Common $1 par 10/22/1968
Common $1 par changed to 1¢ par 12/20/1979
Proclaimed dissolved for failure to file reports and pay taxes 10/19/1983

DASH INDS INC (FL)
Common $0.00066 par split (6) for (5) by issuance of (0.2) additional share 03/23/1984
Name changed to Avenue Holdings, Inc. 11/19/2003
Avenue Holdings, Inc. recapitalized as Global Prospecting Ventures, Inc. (FL) 01/12/2004 which reincorporated in Nevada 06/04/2004 which name changed to Competitive Games International, Inc. 01/22/2007 which recapitalized as PacWest Equities, Inc. 05/07/2010
(See PacWest Equities, Inc.)

DASHCOVERS INC (NV)
Each share old Common $0.001 par exchanged for (0.2) share new Common $0.001 par 07/01/1992
Recapitalized as American Telecommunication Standards International Inc. 05/06/1994
Each share new Common $0.001 par exchanged for (0.025) share Common $0.001 par
American Telecommunication Standards International Inc. name changed to PSA Inc. 04/01/1998
PSA Inc. name changed to Shearson American REIT, Inc. 10/16/2009

DASHER DEV CORP (BC)
Recapitalized as Nightwatch Resources Inc. 03/02/1977
Each share Common no par exchanged for (0.33333333) share Common no par
(See Nightwatch Resources Inc.)

DASHER EXPL LTD (BC)
Name changed to New World Resource Corp. 06/27/2005

DASHER RES CORP (BC)
Name changed 10/03/2002
Name changed from Dasher Energy Corp. to Dasher Resources Corp. 10/03/2002
Recapitalized as Dasher Exploration Ltd. 04/16/2003
Each share Common no par exchanged for (0.1) share Common no par
Dasher Exploration Ltd. name changed to New World Resource Corp. 06/27/2005

DASHER RES LTD (ON)
Recapitalized as Consolidated Dasher Resources Inc. 07/26/1991
Each share Common no par exchanged for (0.25) share Common no par
Consolidated Dasher Resources Inc. name changed to TM Technologies Corp. 04/16/1993 which name changed to TM Bioscience Corp. 07/29/1997 which merged into Luminex Corp. 03/01/2007

DASHEW BUSINESS MACHS INC (DE)
Each share Common 10¢ par exchanged for (0.1) share Common $1 par 11/27/1967
Adjudicated bankrupt 04/20/1972
No stockholders' equity

DASI INC (DE)
Merged into ISAD, Inc. 12/23/1993

Each share Common 1¢ par exchanged for $3 cash

DASIBI CORP (DE)
Name changed to Habico Industries 02/16/1973
(See Habico Industries, Inc.)

DASIBI ENVIRONMENTAL CORP (CA)
Name changed to Pollution Research & Control Corp. 12/29/1989
Pollution Research & Control Corp. name changed to Universal Detection Technology 08/13/2003

DASSARO MINES LTD. (ON)
Charter cancelled 00/00/1956

DASSAULT SYS S A (FRANCE)
Each Sponsored ADR for Partial Dividend exchanged for (1) Sponsored ADR for Common 07/30/2000
(Additional Information in Active)

DASSEN GOLD RES LTD (BC)
Delisted from Vancouver Stock Exchange 03/15/1991

DASSERAT DEVS CORP (BC)
Recapitalized as Vantage Enterprises Corp. 04/11/1994
Each share Common no par exchanged for (0.25) share Common no par
Vantage Enterprises Corp. name changed to African Gemstones Ltd. 07/14/1998
(See African Gemstones Ltd.)

DASTUR GOLD MINES LTD. (ON)
Charter cancelled by Province of Ontario for default 04/00/1958

DATA ACCESS SYS INC NEW (NJ)
Each share new Common 5¢ par exchanged for (0.1) share new Common 5¢ par 10/25/1988
Reincorporated under the laws of Delaware as Authorized Distribution Network, Inc. 11/03/1988
(See Authorized Distribution Newtork, Inc.)

DATA ACCESS SYS INC OLD (NJ)
Stock Dividends - 10% 12/28/1979; 10% 01/19/1981
Reorganized under Chapter 11 Federal Bankruptcy Code as Data Access Systems, Inc. (NJ) (New) 11/05/1984
Each share old Common 5¢ par received (0.0625) share new Common 5¢ par and (0.125) Common Stock Purchase Warrant Ser. A expiring 11/05/1985
Note: Old Common 5¢ certificates were not required to be surrendered and are without value
Data Access Systems, Inc. (NJ) (New) reincorporated in Delaware as Authorized Network, Inc. 11/03/1988
(See Authorized Network, Inc.)

DATA ACQUISITION TECHNOLOGIES INC (MN)
Name changed to Autoco.com, Inc. 05/18/1999

DATA ARCHITECTS INC (MA)
Merged into Logica PLC 05/18/1988
Each share Common 1¢ par exchanged for $14 cash

DATA AUTOMATION INC (TX)
Common no par changed to 1¢ par 11/11/1974
Each share Common 1¢ par exchanged for (0.1) share Common 10¢ par 07/18/1980
Each share Common 10¢ par exchanged for (0.01) share Common $10 par 01/07/1988
Note: Company repurchased outstanding Common $10 par shares at $10 cash per share

DATA BASE INDS INC (UT)
Involuntarily dissolved 12/31/1986

DATA BROADCASTING CORP (DE)
Name changed to Interactive Data Corp. 06/20/2001
(See Interactive Data Corp.)

DATA CABLEVISION INC (NY)
Name changed to T.C.C., Inc. 07/22/1983
(See T.C.C., Inc.)

DATA CALL SYS INC (DE)
Name changed to Massachusetts Bay Co. 08/27/1971
(See Massachusetts Bay Co.)

DATA CAP CORP (CO)
Each share old Common $1 par exchanged for (0.2) share new Common $1 par 08/02/1975
Each share new Common $1 par exchanged for (0.2) share Common 1¢ par 04/01/1984
Charter suspended for failure to file annual reports 09/30/1989

DATA CARD CORP (DE)
Stock Dividends - 50% 04/04/1977; 50% 08/20/1980; 25% 03/20/1985
Acquired by Seedamm, Inc. 10/09/1987
Each share Common 10¢ par exchanged for $17.50 cash

DATA CAREERS INC (NY)
Voluntarily dissolved 04/09/1973
Details not available

DATA COMMUNICATIONS, INC. (OR)
U.S. District Court ordered all Common no par redeemed at approximately 70% of the price paid on 05/11/1970

DATA COMMUNICATIONS INC (MN)
Liquidation completed
Each share Common 10¢ par exchanged for initial distribution of (0.4) share CPT Corp. Common 5¢ par and $1.25 cash 06/18/1982
Each share Common 10¢ par received second and final distribution of $1.55 cash 07/05/1983
CPT Corp. reorganized as CPT Holdings, Inc. 07/23/1991
(See CPT Holdings, Inc.)

DATA COMMUNICATIONS SYS INC (MN)
Name changed to Carterfone Communications Corp. 05/14/1969
(See Carterfone Communications Corp.)

DATA COMPUTER SYS (CA)
Charter suspended for failure to file reports and pay fees 06/28/1974

DATA COMPUTER SYSTEMS, INC. (FL)
Charter cancelled and proclaimed dissolved for failure to file reports and pay taxes 10/21/1974

DATA CONVERSION INTERNATIONAL, INC. (UT)
Name changed to Aztec Energy Corp. (UT) 08/00/1991
Aztec Energy Corp. (UT) reorganized in Delaware as Blaze Energy Corp. 06/26/2007
(See Blaze Energy Corp.)

DATA CRITICAL CORP (DE)
Merged into General Electric Co. 09/20/2001
Each share Common $0.001 par exchanged for $3.75 cash

DATA CTL SYS INC (DE)
Common 10¢ par changed to 5¢ par and (1) additional share issued 01/29/1965
Name changed to Engineered Electronics, Inc. 07/23/1979
(See Engineered Electronics, Inc.)

DATA DESIGN LABS INC (DE)
Name changed 12/01/1986
Capital Stock $1 par changed to $0.33333333 par and (2) additional shares issued 03/04/1966

Capital Stock $0.33333333 par split (5) for (4) by issuance of (0.25) additional share 08/03/1979
Capital Stock $0.33333333 par split (5) for (4) by issuance of (0.25) additional share 08/04/1980
Capital Stock $0.33333333 par split (4) for (3) by issuance of (0.33333333) additional share 08/06/1981
Capital Stock $0.33333333 par split (5) for (4) by issuance of (0.25) additional share 08/06/1982
Capital Stock $0.33333333 par split (5) for (4) by issuance of (0.25) additional share 08/04/1983
Capital Stock $0.33333333 par split (4) for (3) by issuance of (0.33333333) additional share 09/06/1984
Name changed from Data-Design Laboratories (CA) to Data-Design Laboratories, Inc. (DE) and Capital Stock $0.33333333 par reclassified as Common $0.33333333 par 12/01/1986
Name changed to DDL Electronics, Inc. and Common $0.33333333 par changed to 1¢ par 12/17/1993
DDL Electronics, Inc. name changed to SMTEK International, Inc. 10/09/1998 which merged into CTS Corp. 02/01/2005

DATA DIAL INTL INC (BC)
Recapitalized as First Telecom Corp. 05/15/1997
Each share Common no par exchanged for (0.2) share Common no par
First Telecom Corp. recapitalized as Sunorca Development Corp. 03/13/2002 which name changed to Wildflower Marijuana Inc. 06/16/2014 which name changed to Wildflower Brands Inc. 05/03/2018

DATA DIMENSIONS INC (DE)
Common 10¢ par changed to 1¢ par 09/27/1991
Each share Common 1¢ par exchanged for (0.33333333) share Common $0.001 par 04/03/1996
Common $0.001 par split (3) for (1) by issuance of (2) additional shares payable 03/20/1997 to holders of record 03/05/1997
Merged into Lionbridge Technologies, Inc. 06/21/2001
Each share Common $0.001 par exchanged for (0.190884) share Common 1¢ par
(See Lionbridge Technologies, Inc.)

DATA DISC INC (DE)
Name changed to Amcomp, Inc. 06/04/1976
(See Amcomp, Inc.)

DATA DISPLAY CORP (CO)
Each share Common no par exchanged for (0.01) share Common 10¢ par 09/19/1994
Name changed to Zeon Corp. 07/05/1995
(See Zeon Corp.)

DATA DISPLAY INC. (MN)
Acquired by Control Data Corp. (MN) 01/05/1965
Each share Common 50¢ par exchanged for (0.1538462) share Common $1 par
Control Data Corp. (MN) merged into Control Data Corp. (DE) 08/17/1968 which name changed to Ceridian Corp. (Old) 06/03/1992
(See Ceridian Corp. (Old))

DATA DISPLAY SYS INC (DE)
Name changed to OCG Technology Inc. 03/28/1973
OCG Technology Inc. recapitalized as UraniumCore Co. 04/12/2006 which name changed to Horizon Health International Corp. 10/09/2009 which name changed to Horizons Holdings International, Corp. 04/16/2015

DATA DOCUMENTS INC (DE)
Merged into Corporate Express, Inc. 11/26/1997
Each share Common 1¢ par exchanged for (1.1) shares Common 1¢ par
(See Corporate Express, Inc.)

DATA DOCUMENTS INC (NE)
Through purchase offer 99% acquired by Dictaphone as of 10/22/1976
Public interest eliminated

DATA DOMAIN INC (DE)
Merged into EMC Corp. 07/23/2009
Each share Common $0.0001 par exchanged for $33.50 cash

DATA DYNAMICS INC (FL)
Proclaimed dissolved for failure to file reports and pay fees 11/09/1990

DATA-FIT INC (NV)
Recapitalized as Real Security Co., Inc. 12/12/2005
Each share Common $0.001 par exchanged for (0.05) share Common $0.001 par
(See Real Security Co., Inc.)

DATA FORTRESS SYS GROUP LTD (BC)
Company reported out of business 11/01/2009
Details not available

DATA GATHERING CAP CORP (ON)
Name changed to Carbiz.com Inc. 09/17/1999
Carbiz.com Inc. name changed to Carbiz Inc. 10/06/2003
(See Carbiz Inc.)

DATA GEN CORP (DE)
Common 1¢ par split (2) for (1) by issuance of (1) additional share 11/18/1983
Stock Dividend - 200% 03/22/1973
Merged into EMC Corp. 10/12/1999
Each share Common 1¢ par exchanged for (0.3262) share Common 1¢ par
EMC Corp. merged into Dell Technologies Inc. 09/07/2016

DATA GRAPH, INC. (MN)
Merged into Advance Circuits, Inc. 09/18/1980
Each share Common 1¢ par exchanged for (0.0173) share Common 10¢ par
Note: Holders entitled to fewer than (20) shares of Advance Circuits, Inc. received cash
(See Advance Circuits, Inc.)

DATA GROUP INC (ON)
Name changed to Data Group Ltd. 01/02/2014
Data Group Ltd. recapitalized as DATA Communications Management Corp. 07/07/2016

DATA GROUP INCOME FD (ON)
Under plan of reorganization each Trust Unit automatically became (1) share Data Group Inc. Common no par 01/03/2012
Data Group Inc. name changed to Data Group Ltd. 01/02/2014 which recapitalized as DATA Communications Management Corp. 07/07/2016

DATA GROUP INVTS LTD (AB)
Struck off register for failure to file annual returns 05/01/1991

DATA GROUP LTD (ON)
Recapitalized as DATA Communications Management Corp. 07/07/2016
Each share Common no par exchanged for (0.01) share Common no par

DATA GROWTH INC (NV)
Each share old Common $0.001 par exchanged for (0.01) share new Common $0.001 par 11/18/1996
Recapitalized as PhotoLoft.Com Inc. 02/26/1999
Each share new Common $0.001 par exchanged for (0.40650406) share Common $0.001 par
PhotoLoft.Com Inc. name changed to Brightcube Inc. 12/06/2000

DATA IMAGING SVCS INC (FL)
Administratively dissolved for failure to file reports 08/26/1994

DATA INDS CORP TEXAS (DE)
Adjudicated bankrupt 08/28/1974
No stockholders' equity

DATA INFORMATION SVCS INC (DE)
Charter cancelled and declared inoperative and void for non-payment of taxes 04/15/1972

DATA INSTRS CO (CA)
Each share old Common 25¢ par exchanged for (0.4) share new Common 25¢ par 03/14/1972
Each share new Common 25¢ par exchanged for (0.25) share Common 10¢ par 03/16/1973
Adjudicated bankrupt 03/13/1975
Stockholders' equity unlikely

DATA INVESTMENT CORP. (MN)
Name changed to Cavalier Corp. 05/25/1971
Cavalier Corp. name changed to Philmon & Hart Laboratories, Inc. 03/05/1975 which name changed to Spearhead Industries, Inc. 10/07/1980
(See Spearhead Industries, Inc.)

DATA LAW CO (IA)
Name changed to United Systems Technology, Inc. 11/21/1986
(See United Systems Technology, Inc.)

DATA LEASE FINL CORP (FL)
Administratively dissolved for failure to file annual reports 08/13/1993

DATA LEASING INC (MN)
Name changed to Data Communications, Inc. 05/12/1975
(See Data Communications, Inc.)

DATA LIQUIDATING CORP. (NY)
Name changed 12/28/1972
Name changed from Data Decisions Corp. to Data Liquidating Corp. 12/28/1972
Completely liquidated 12/28/1972
Each share Common 1¢ par exchanged for first and final distribution of (0.05) share Wall Street Computer Corp. Common 1¢ par, (0.05) Wall Street Computer Corp. Common Stock Purchase Warrant expiring 06/30/1976 and (0.1) share Incotel, Ltd. Common 1¢ par
Note: Actual issuance of the Incotel, Ltd. stock was delayed until 11/09/1973
(See each company's listing)

DATA MGMT INC (MN)
Statutorily dissolved 10/03/1991

DATA MEASUREMENT CORP (DE)
Common 1¢ par split (3) for (2) by issuance of (0.5) additional share 12/15/1986
Common 1¢ par split (4) for (3) by issuance of (0.33333333) additional share 04/28/1987
Acquired by Measurex Corp. 01/10/1996
Each share Common 1¢ par exchanged for $18.625 cash

DATA MED CLINICAL SUPPORT SVCS INC (MN)
Common 1¢ par split (3) for (1) by issuance of (2) additional shares 06/30/1987
Name changed to Health Outcomes Management, Inc. (MN) 10/16/1995
Health Outcomes Management, Inc. (MN) reorganized in Delaware as Hudson Holding Corp. 09/07/2005 which merged into Rodman & Renshaw Capital Group, Inc. 04/08/2011 which name changed to Direct Markets Holdings Corp. 06/01/2012
(See Direct Markets Holdings Corp.)

DATA MICRO CO (MN)
Each share Common 20¢ par exchanged for (0.1) share Common 25¢ par 02/08/1971
Registration cancelled for failure to file reports 08/15/1972

DATA NATL CORP (CO)
Each share old Common $0.001 par exchanged for (0.0025) share new Common $0.001 par 09/30/1996
Administratively dissolved 09/01/2001

DATA NETWORK CORP (NY)
Stock Dividend - 50% 01/28/1970
Name changed to MegaSystems, Inc. 05/15/1970
(See MegaSystems, Inc.)

DATA 100 CORP (MN)
Each share Preferred 1974 Ser. $1 par exchanged for (10) shares Common 50¢ par 05/27/1975
Merged into Northern Telecom Computers Inc. 11/22/1978
Each share Common 50¢ par exchanged for $20 principal amount of 7.75% Installment Notes or $20 cash
Note: Option to receive Notes expired 11/21/1978

DATA 1 INC (UT)
Each share old Common $0.001 par exchanged for (0.5) share new Common $0.001 par 01/18/1994
Name changed to Diversified Resources Group, Inc. 06/06/1999
Diversified Resources Group, Inc. name changed to AeroGroup Inc. 07/15/2003
(See AeroGroup Inc.)

DATA PAC CORP (OR)
Involuntarily dissolved for failure to pay fees 07/28/1983

DATA PACKAGING CORP (MA)
Common 10¢ par split (2) for (1) by issuance of (1) additional share 06/14/1969
Name changed to Costar Corp. 04/02/1986
Costar Corp. acquired by Corning Inc. 09/08/1993

DATA PLEX SYS INC (DE)
Name changed to TVC Image Technology Inc. 05/13/1981
(See TVC Image Technology Inc.)

DATA PWR INC (NY)
Name changed to Equity Planning Corp. and Common 1¢ par changed to 5¢ par 05/04/1973
(See Equity Planning Corp.)

DATA PROBE INC (NY)
Dissolved by proclamation 01/25/2012

DATA PROCESSING FINL & GEN CORP (DE)
Stock Dividend - 100% 11/14/1968
Name changed to DPF Inc. 10/27/1971
DPF Inc. name changed to Interstate Bakeries Corp. 11/30/1981 which name changed to Interstate Brands Corp. 06/02/1990
(See Interstate Brands Corp.)

DATA PROCESSING INC (MA)
Class A Common no par reclassified as Common 5¢ par 11/25/1968
Completely liquidated 04/20/1970
Each share Common 5¢ par exchanged for first and final distribution of (1) share American Aero-Liquids Corp. Common 1¢ par
(See American Aero-Liquids Corp.)

DATA PROCESSING RES CORP (CA)
Merged into Compuware Corp. 08/30/1999
Each share Common no par exchanged for $24 cash

DATA PRODS CORP (DE)
Name changed to Dataproducts Corp: 08/23/1974
(See Dataproducts Corp.)

DATA RACE INC (TX)
Filed a plan of liquidation under Chapter 7 Federal Bankruptcy Code 06/28/2002
No stockholders' equity

DATA REALTY INC (NJ)
Charter revoked for failure to file annual reports 08/31/1994

DATA RECOGNITION CORP (DE)
Charter cancelled and declared inoperative and void for non-payment of taxes 03/01/1975

DATA RECORDING TECHNOLOGY CORP (DE)
Filed a petition under Chapter 7 bankruptcy proceedings 08/07/1989
No stockholders' equity

DATA RESH ASSOC INC (MO)
Common 1¢ par split (3) for (2) by issuance of (0.5) additional share payable 08/19/1996 to holders of record 08/05/1996
Merged into SIRSI Holding Corp. 08/30/2001
Each share Common 1¢ par exchanged for $11 cash

DATA RESH CORP (FL)
Involuntarily dissolved 11/01/1985

DATA RES INC (DE)
Stock Dividend - 50% 03/23/1979
Merged into McGraw-Hill, Inc. 09/28/1979
Each share Common 10¢ par exchanged for $50 cash

DATA RETURN CORP (TX)
Merged into divine, inc. 01/09/2002
Each share Common $0.001 par exchanged for (1.9876) shares Class A Common $0.001 par
(See divine, inc.)

DATA RITE INDS INC (WA)
Chapter 11 bankruptcy proceedings converted to Chapter 7 on 11/11/1989
No stockholders' equity

DATA SCIENCES INC (NV)
Recapitalized as Digital Sciences Inc. 05/06/1994
Each share Common $0.001 par exchanged for (0.5) share Common $0.002 par
Digital Sciences Inc. merged into Intelligent Decision Systems, Inc. 04/01/1996
(See Intelligent Decision Systems, Inc.)

DATA SWITCH CORP (DE)
Common 1¢ par split (2) for (1) by issuance of (1) additional share 06/14/1983
Stock Dividend - 25% 12/10/1982
Merged into General Signal Corp. 11/09/1995
Each share Common 1¢ par exchanged for (0.14357) share Common $1 par
General Signal Corp. merged into SPX Corp. 10/06/1998

DATA SYS & SOFTWARE INC (DE)
Name changed to Acorn Factor, Inc. 09/25/2006
Acorn Factor, Inc. name changed to Acorn Energy, Inc. 01/01/2008

DATA SYS ANALYSTS INC (DE)
Merged into DSA Holding, Inc. 06/19/1980
Each share Common 10¢ par exchanged for $5.50 cash

DATA SYS DEPOT INC (DE)
Recapitalized as American Track Systems International Inc. 11/12/1996
Each share Common $0.001 par exchanged for (0.02) share Common $0.001 par
(See American Track Systems International Inc.)

DATA SYS INC (MN)
Each share old Common 10¢ par exchanged for (0.0005) share new Common 10¢ par 08/01/1984
Note: In effect holders received an undisclosed amount of cash per share and public interest was eliminated

DATA SYS NETWORK CORP (MI)
Merged into TekInsight Inc. 08/14/2000
Each share Common 1¢ par exchanged for (0.392) share Conv. Preferred Ser. A
TekInsight name changed to DynTek Inc. 12/31/2001

DATA SYSTEMS DEVICES OF BOSTON, INC. (MN)
Adjudicated bankrupt in September 1964
No stockholders' equity

DATA TECH AMER INC (AZ)
Charter revoked 12/16/1971

DATA TECHNOLOGY CORP (CA)
Merged into A & E Plastik Pak Co., Inc. 07/11/1977
Each share Common $1 par exchanged for $4.40 cash

DATA TECHNOLOGY CORP NEW (DE)
Name changed to QUME Corp. 08/29/1988
QUME Corp. name changed to DTC Data Technology Corp. 04/06/1994 which merged into Photonics Corp. (CA) 03/13/2000 which reincorporated in Nevada as Small Cap Strategies, Inc. 10/02/2006 which recapitalized as Bay Street Capital, Inc. 08/31/2010 which name changed to Los Angeles Syndicate of Technology, Inc. 10/14/2010 which name changed to Invent Ventures, Inc. 09/19/2012

DATA TECHNOLOGY INDUSTRIES, INC. (DC)
Merged into Science Management Corp. 8/8/79
Each share Common exchanged for (1.10197) shares Common 10¢ par
(See Science Management Corp.)

DATA TERM SYS INC (MA)
Common 20¢ par split (3) for (1) by issuance of (2) additional shares 1/31/78
Merged into National Semiconductor Corp. 5/31/83
Each share Common 20¢ par exchanged for $7.25 cash

DATA TRANSLATION INC NEW (DE)
Company terminated registration of common stock and is no longer public as of 4/21/2003

DATA TRANSLATION INC OLD (DE)
Reincorporated 4/12/96
Common 1¢ par split (4) for (3) by issuance of (1/3) additional share 1/8/87
Common 1¢ par split (2) for (1) by issuance of (1) additional share 7/31/95
State of incorporation changed from (MA) to (DE) 4/12/96
Each share Common 1¢ par received distribution of (0.25) share Data Translation, Inc. (New) Common 1¢ par payable 12/13/96 to holders of record 11/29/96
Name changed to Media 100 Inc. 12/3/96
(See Media 100 Inc.)

DATA TRANSMISSION NETWORK CORP (DE)
Merged into VS&A Communications Partners III, L.P. 4/25/2000
Each share Common $0.001 par exchanged for $29 cash

DATA TRAX SYS INC (AB)
Each share old Common no par exchanged for (0.1) share new Common no par 06/23/1998
Delisted from Alberta Stock Exchange 01/15/1999

DATA TREE CORP (CA)
Merged into First American Financial Corp. (CA) 06/03/1998
Each share Common no par exchanged for (0.632006) share Common $1 par
First American Financial Corp. (CA) name changed to First American Corp. (CA) 05/19/2000 which reincorporated in Delaware as CoreLogic, Inc. 06/01/2010

DATA TRENDS INC (DE)
Reincorporated 10/28/1968
State of incorporation changed from (NJ) to (DE) 10/28/1968
Assets sold for benefit of creditors 02/13/1974
No stockholders' equity

DATA WORLD CORP (AZ)
Charter revoked for failure to file reports and pay taxes 12/26/1972

DATABASE SOLUTIONS LTD (NV)
Each share old Common $0.00001 par exchanged for (0.05) share new Common $0.00001 par 07/26/2004
Recapitalized as Blue Data Group, Inc. 10/17/2007
Each share new Common $0.00001 par exchanged for (0.001) share Common $0.00001 par
Blue Data Group, Inc. name changed to Expert Group, Inc. 11/07/2007 which name changed to American Premium Water Corp. 12/19/2013

DATABASE TECHNOLOGIES INC (DE)
Recapitalized as Palm Desert Art, Inc. 7/31/98
Each share Common $0.001 par exchanged for (0.1) share Common $0.001 par
(See Palm Desert Art, Inc.)

DATACAPITAL S A DE C V (MEXICO)
Name changed to Grupo Dataflux S.A. de C.V. 06/07/1999
(See Grupo Dataflux S.A. de C.V.)

DATACOM INC (ID)
Charter revoked for failure to file reports and pay fees 12/01/1975

DATACOM WIRELESS CORP (CANADA)
Merged into BSM Technologies Inc. 09/28/2009
Each share Common no par exchanged for (4.2421) shares Common no par

DATACOPY CORP (CA)
Acquired by Xerox Corp. 06/30/1988
Each share Common 10¢ par exchanged for $6 cash

DATACRAFT CORP (FL)
Merged into Harris-Intertype Corp. 01/25/1974
Each share Common 25¢ par exchanged for $2.80 cash

DATADYNE CORP (DE)
Voluntarily dissolved 02/09/1990
Details not available

DATAFLEX CORP (NJ)
Stock Dividend - 10% 5/28/87
Merged into CompuCom Systems, Inc. 6/26/98
Each share Common no par exchanged for $4.10 cash

DATAFLO INC (FL)
Proclaimed dissolved for failure to file reports and pay fees 11/14/1986

DATAFORCE INTL INC (PANAMA)
Company dormant 00/00/1988
Details not available

DATAGUARD RECOVERY SVCS INC (KY)
Recapitalized as Strategia Corp. (KY) 07/29/1996
Each share Common no par exchanged for (0.5) share Common no par
Strategia Corp. (KY) reorganized in Nevada as Catthai Corp. 08/20/2008
(See Catthai Corp.)

DATAIMAGE INC (DE)
Merged into Judge Imaging Systems Inc. 02/29/1996
Each share Common 1¢ par exchanged for (0.03128826) share Common 1¢ par
Judge Imaging Systems Inc. merged into Judge Group Inc. 02/20/1997 which name changed to JUDGE.com Inc. 02/14/2000 which name changed to Judge Group, Inc. (New) 01/15/2001
(See Judge Group, Inc. (New))

DATAJACK INC (NV)
Each share old Common $0.001 par exchanged for (0.05) share new Common $0.001 par 02/21/2014
Name changed to Unified Signal, Inc. 11/28/2014

DATAJUNGLE SOFTWARE INC (NV)
Name changed to Blink Logic Inc. 11/08/2007
(See Blink Logic Inc.)

DATAKEY INC (MN)
Merged into SafeNet, Inc. 12/15/2004
Each share Common 5¢ par exchanged for $0.65 cash

DATALEX CORP (CANADA)
Dissolved for non-compliance 11/08/2007

DATALIGHT INC (CT)
Name changed to Waters Equipment, Inc. 03/29/1978
(See Waters Equipment, Inc.)

DATALINE COMPUTER PROCESSING ASSOCIATES, LTD. (NY)
Name changed to Dataline Computing Corp. 5/6/64
Dataline Computer Corp. name changed to Data Decisions Corp. 11/2/64 which name changed to Data Liquidating Corp. 12/28/72
(See Data Liquidating Corp.)

DATALINE COMPUTING CORP (NY)
Name changed to Data Decisions Corp. 11/2/64
Data Decisions Corp. name changed to Data Liquidating Corp. 12/28/72
(See Data Liquidating Corp.)

DATALINE INC (NE)
Reincorporated under the laws of Delaware as Data Transmission Network Corp. 11/13/87
(See Data Transmission Network Corp.)

DATALINE INC NEW (ON)
Name changed 5/31/83
Under plan of merger name changed from Dataline Inc. (Old) to Dataline Inc. (New) and each share Common no par exchanged for (1) share Class B Special Stock no par or $10.50 cash 5/31/83
Note: Option to receive stock expired 7/29/83
Class B Special Stock called for redemption 8/2/83
Public interest eliminated

DATALINE SYSTEMS LTD. (ON)
Name changed to Dataline Inc. (Old) 6/15/81

Dataline Inc. (Old) merged into Dataline Inc. (New) 5/31/83
(See Dataline Inc. (New))

DATALINK CAP CORP (FL)
Recapitalized 04/30/1987
Recapitalized from DataLink Systems, Inc. to DataLink Capital Corp. 04/30/1987
Each share Common $0.0001 par exchanged for (0.05) share Common $0.0001 par
Reincorporated under the laws of Nevada as DCC Acquisition Corp. 01/01/1999
DCC Acquisition Corp. recapitalized as ProHealth Medical Technologies, Inc. 11/01/1999 which name changed to Applied DNA Sciences, Inc. (NV) 11/18/2002 which reincorporated in Delaware 12/17/2008

DATALINK CORP (MN)
Acquired by Insight Enterprises, Inc. 01/06/2017
Each share Common $0.001 par exchanged for $11.25 cash

DATALINK NET INC (NV)
Name changed 08/05/1999
Each share Common $0.001 par exchanged for (0.1) share Common 1¢ par 02/09/1998
Name changed from Datalink Systems Corp. to Datalink.net, Inc. 08/05/1999
Common $0.001 par split (2) for (1) by issuance of (1) additional share payable 04/26/2000 to holders of record 04/10/2000
Name changed Semotus Solutions, Inc. 01/11/2001
Semotus Solutions, Inc. name changed to Flint Telecom Group, Inc. 10/21/2008

DATALOGGER INC (AB)
Recapitalized as ICE Drilling Enterprises Inc. 11/28/1997
Each share Common no par exchanged for (0.2) share Common no par
(See ICE Drilling Enterprises Inc.)

DATALOGIX INTL INC (NY)
Merged into Delphi Acquisition 1/1/97
Each share Common 1¢ par exchanged for $8 cash

DATAMAG INC (AZ)
Common no par split (3) for (2) by issuance of (0.5) additional share 7/1/87
Reorganized under Chapter 11 Federal Bankruptcy Code 1/1/92
Each share Common no par exchanged for (1) Common Stock Purchase Warrant which expired 1/21/92
Dissolved for failure to file annual report 11/10/97

DATAMAP INC (MN)
Name changed to VISTA Information Solutions, Inc. (MN) 05/23/1995
VISTA Information Solutions, Inc. (MN) reorganized in Delaware 03/27/1998 which recapitalized as Fidelity National Information Solutions Inc. 08/01/2001 which merged into Fidelity National Financial, Inc. 09/30/2003 which merged into Fidelity National Information Services, Inc. 11/09/2006

DATAMARINE INTL INC (WA)
Reincorporated 04/11/2000
State of incorporation changed from (MA) to (WA) 04/11/2000
Company terminated registration of common stock and is no longer public as of 08/19/2005

DATAMARK HLDG INC (DE)
Name changed to Digital Courier Technologies Inc. 09/16/1998
Digital Courier Technologies Inc.
recapitalized as TransAxis, Inc. 05/08/2003
(See TransAxis, Inc.)

DATAMARK INC (NY)
Name changed to D.M.I. Liquidating Corp. and assets assigned for the benefit of creditors 10/30/1970
No stockholders' equity

DATAMARK SYS GROUP INC (QC)
Name changed 08/22/1988
Name changed 07/02/1999
Name changed from Datamark Business Forms Ltd. to Datamark Inc. 08/22/1988
Name changed from Datamark Inc. to Datamark Systems Group Inc. 07/02/1999
Merged into Komunik Corp. 06/12/2007
Each share Common no par exchanged for either (1) share Common no par, $2.0275 cash, or a combination thereof
Note: Unexchanged certificates were cancelled and became without value 06/08/2013

DATAMATE COMPUTER SYS INC (DE)
Name changed to Saba Oil & Gas Corp. 1/12/81
(See Saba Oil & Gas Corp.)

DATAMATIC INDS INC (DE)
Charter cancelled and declared inoperative and void for non-payment of taxes 3/1/76

DATAMATION INC (NJ)
Adjudicated bankrupt 07/06/1963
No stockholders' equity

DATAMATION SERVICES, INC (NY)
Common 10¢ par split (2) for (1) by issuance of (1) additional share 12/06/1968
Charter cancelled and proclaimed dissolved for failure to pay taxes 10/28/2009

DATAMEDIA INTL INC (TX)
Name changed 9/1/71
Name changed from Datamedia Computer Service, Inc. to Datamedia International, Inc. 9/1/71
Adjudicated bankrupt 8/28/73
Stockholders' equity unlikely

DATAMEG CORP (DE)
Reincorporated 04/27/2005
Stock Dividend - 10% payable 06/09/2003 to holders of record 01/08/2003 Ex date - 01/06/2003
State of incorporation changed from (NY) to (DE) and Common 1¢ par changed to $0.0001 par 04/27/2005
Recapitalized as Natural Blue Resources, Inc. 07/24/2009
Each share Common $0.0001 par exchanged for (0.01) share Common $0.0001 par

DATAMETRICS CORP (DE)
Reincorporated 04/19/1987
Class A Common 50¢ par reclassified as Common no par 07/19/1979
Common no par split (2) for (1) by issuance of (1) additional share 05/06/1980
Stock Dividends - 10% 10/06/1977; 10% 03/15/1979
State of incorporation changed from (CA) to (DE) and Common no par changed to 1¢ par 04/19/1987
Each share old Common 1¢ par exchanged for (0.05) share new Common 1¢ par 04/26/2002
Each (30) shares new Common 1¢ par exchanged again for (1) share new Common 1¢ par 04/10/2006
SEC revoked common stock registration 08/09/2012

DATAMILL MEDIA CORP (NV)
Name changed to AvWorks Aviation Corp. (NV) 11/30/2011
AvWorks Aviation Corp. (NV)
reincorporated in Florida as Vapor Group, Inc. 04/29/2014

DATAMINERS CAP CORP (BC)
Reincorporated under the laws of Alberta 05/19/2017

DATAMIRROR CORP (ON)
Merged into International Business Machines Corp. 09/05/2007
Each share Common no par exchanged for $27 cash

DATAPAX COMPUTER SYS CORP (DE)
Charter cancelled and declared inoperative and void for non-payment of taxes 3/1/75

DATAPHAZ INC (DE)
Assets transferred to DPZ Liquidating Corp. and Common $0.001 par reclassified as Shares of Bene. Int. $0.001 par 4/15/91
(See DPZ Liquidating Corp.)

DATAPOINT CORP (DE)
Reincorporated 01/20/1977
Each share Common 10¢ par exchanged for (0.4) share Common 25¢ par 02/14/1973
State of incorporation changed from (TX) to (DE) 01/20/1977
Common 25¢ par split (2) for (1) by issuance of (1) additional share 04/11/1980
Common 25¢ par split (2) for (1) by issuance of (1) additional share 02/06/1981
Each share $4.94 Exchangeable Preferred $1 par exchanged for (0.75) share $1 Preferred $1 par and (2) shares Common 25¢ par 06/09/1992
Name changed to Dynacore Holdings Corp. 05/08/2000
Dynacore Holdings Corp. name changed to CattleSale Co. 02/25/2003
(See CattleSale Co.)

DATAPOWER INC (CA)
Charter cancelled for failure to file reports and pay taxes 12/3/71

DATAPOWER USA INC (CO)
Declared defunct and inoperative for failure to pay taxes and file annual reports 01/01/2003

DATAPRO LTD (ON)
Name changed to Real Time Datapro Ltd. 3/30/74
(See Real Time Datapro Ltd.)

DATAPRODUCTS CORP (DE)
Common 10¢ par split (2) for (1) by issuance of (1) additional share 03/15/1983
Merged into HND Corp. 05/21/1990
Each share Common 10¢ par exchanged for $10 cash

DATARAM CORP (NV)
Reincorporated 01/12/2016
Each share old Common 20¢ par exchanged for (0.2) share old Common $1 par 02/21/1975
Old Common $1 par split (4) for (1) by issuance of (3) additional shares 05/09/1980
Old Common $1 par split (3) for (1) by issuance of (2) additional shares 04/03/1992
Old Common $1 par split (2) for (1) by issuance of (1) additional share payable 12/03/1998 to holders of record 11/23/1998 Ex date - 11/04/1998
Old Common $1 par split (3) for (2) by issuance of (0.5) additional share payable 12/15/1999 to holders of record 11/24/1999
Each share old Common $1 par exchanged for (0.16666666) share new Common $1 par 03/18/2013
Stock Dividends - 10% 06/23/1978; 10% 11/16/1979
Note: Although change in name from Data-Ram Corp. (two words) has not
been filed with the State of New Jersey, certificates reading Dataram Corp. (one word) have been in circulation since 1972
State of incorporation changed from (NJ) to (NV) and new Common $1 par changed to $0.001 par 01/12/2016
Each share old Common $0.001 par exchanged for (0.33333333) share new Common $0.001 par 07/11/2016
Each share new Common $0.001 par exchanged again for (0.25) share new Common $0.001 par 05/08/2017
Name changed to U.S. Gold Corp. 06/26/2017

DATAREX SYS INC (DE)
Merged into Abitibi-Price Inc. 08/26/1988
Each share Common 1¢ par exchanged for $17.875 cash

DATASCAN INC (DE)
Merged into Dymo Industries, Inc. 08/03/1972
Each share Common 5¢ par exchanged for (0.7) share Common $1 par
(See Dymo Industries, Inc.)

DATASCENSION INC (NV)
Each share old Common $0.001 par exchanged for (0.1) share new Common $0.001 par 11/05/2004
SEC revoked common stock registration 11/06/2014

DATASCOPE CORP (DE)
Reincorporated 12/29/1989
Common 1¢ par split (3) for (2) by issuance of (0.5) additional share 11/05/1976
Common 1¢ par split (2) for (1) by issuance of (1) additional share 09/25/1980
Common 1¢ par split (3) for (2) by issuance of (0.5) additional share 09/22/1986
State of incorporation changed from (NY) to (DE) 12/29/1989
Common 1¢ par split (3) for (1) by issuance of (2) additional shares 01/03/1992
Merged into Getinge AB 01/30/2009
Each share Common 1¢ par exchanged for $53 cash

DATASERV INC (NY)
Ceased doing business 00/00/1973
Company has no assets
Stockholders' equity unlikely

DATASOUTH COMPUTER CORP (DE)
Reincorporated 04/26/1993
State of incorporation changed from (NC) to (DE) 04/26/1993
Merged into Bull Run Corp. 11/29/1994
Each share Common 1¢ par exchanged for (3) shares Common 1¢ par
Bull Run Corp. merged into Triple Crown Media, Inc. 12/30/2005
(See Triple Crown Media, Inc.)

DATASPAN TECHNOLOGY INC (AB)
Declared bankrupt 03/00/1993
No stockholders' equity

DATASPEED INC (CA)
Merged into Lotus Development Corp. 7/31/85
Each share Common no par exchanged for $1.5527 cash
Each share Common no par received an initial additional distribution of $0.10 cash in November, 1986
Each share Common no par received final distribution of $0.33 cash 11/15/89

DATASTAND TECHNOLOGIES INC (IN)
Each share old Common $0.001 par exchanged for (0.33333333) share

new Common $0.001 par 06/14/2004
Name changed to Metabolic Research, Inc. 02/16/2007

DATASTREAM SYS INC (DE)
Issue Information - 1,420,000 shares COM offered at $15 per share on 03/29/1995
Common 1¢ par split (2) for (1) by issuance of (1) additional share 9/12/95
Common 1¢ par split (2) for (1) by issuance of (1) additional share payable 1/30/98 to holders of record 1/20/98
Merged into Infor Global Solutions AG 3/31/2006
Each share Common 1¢ par exchanged for $10.26 cash

DATASYSTEMS SOFTWARE CORP (CA)
Charter suspended for failure to file reports and pay fees 10/01/1986

DATATAB INC (NY)
Stock Dividends - 100% 02/09/1968; 50% 02/15/1972
Company terminated registration of common stock and is no longer public as of 11/14/2003
Details not available

DATATEC SYS INC (DE)
Plan of reorganization under Chapter 11 Federal Bankruptcy proceedings effective 11/01/2005
No stockholders' equity

DATATECH SYS LTD (BC)
Merged into SHL Systemhouse Inc. 10/31/1994
Each share Common no par exchanged for $0.90 cash

DATATRACKER INTL INC (BC)
Name changed to California Gold Mines Inc. 02/04/1991
(See California Gold Mines Inc.)

DATATRAK INC (CA)
Each share old Common 5¢ par exchanged for (0.2) share new Common 5¢ par 01/19/1988
Assets transferred to Datatrak Liquidating Trust 09/27/1990
Details not available
Reorganized under the laws of Delaware as WGI Holdings, Inc. 03/16/2007
Each Share of Bene. Int. 5¢ par exchanged for (0.01) share Common $0.00001 par

DATATREND SVCS INC (DE)
Company terminated registration of common stock and is no longer public as of 03/27/1998
Details not available

DATATROL CORP. (MD)
Acquired by Control Data Corp. (MN) on a (1) for (5.15) basis 03/15/1965
Control Data Corp. (MN) merged into Control Data Corp. (DE) 08/17/1968 which name changed to Ceridian Corp. (Old) 06/03/1992
(See Ceridian Corp. (Old))

DATATROL INC (DE)
Merged into Applied Devices Corp. 8/5/76
Each share Common 4¢ par exchanged for (0.18519) share Common 1¢ par
(See Applied Devices Corp.)

DATATRON (CA)
Stock Dividend - 100% 2/28/70
Chapter 11 Federal Bankruptcy Code converted to Chapter 7 on 3/30/89
Stockholders' equity unlikely

DATATRON PROCESSING INC (DE)
Recapitalized as Emerald Green Corp. 6/25/73
Each share Common 10¢ par exchanged for (0.25) share Common 40¢ par
(See Emerald Green Corp.)

DATATRONICS INC (MA)
Adjudicated bankrupt 04/11/1973
Stockholders' equity unlikely

DATATRONIX FINL SVCS (CA)
Merged into Fiserv, Inc. 6/25/93
Each share Common no par exchanged for (1.69) shares Common 1¢ par

DATATYPE CORP (DE)
Adjudicated bankrupt 01/05/1977
Stockholders' equity unlikely

DATAVEND INC (DE)
Name changed to Choices Entertainment Corp. 03/14/1990
Choices Entertainment Corp. name changed to CECS Corp. 08/09/2000
(See CECS Corp.)

DATAVISION, INC. (DE)
Dissolved 10/31/91
Details not available

DATAVISION INC (MI)
Common 1¢ par split (2) for (1) by issuance of (1) additional share 10/17/80
Merged into Datavision, Inc. (DE) 9/30/87
Details not available

DATAWARE TECHNOLOGIES INC (DE)
Name changed to Leadingside, Inc. 10/03/2000
(See Leadingside, Inc.)

DATAWAVE INC (CO)
Recapitalized as Coastal Maine Holdings Corp. 11/07/1989
Each share Common no par exchanged for (0.004) share Common $0.001 par

DATAWAVE SYS INC (DE)
Name changed 01/15/1997
Reincorporated 09/19/2000
Reincorporated 02/23/2005
Name changed from DataWave Vending Inc. to DataWave Systems Inc. (BC) 01/15/1997
Place of incorporation changed from (BC) to (Yukon) 09/19/2000
Place of incorporation changed from (Yukon) to (DE) 02/23/2005
Merged into InComm Holdings, Inc. 01/05/2007
Each share new Common no par exchanged for $0.58593762 cash
Note: Each share new Common no par received an initial additional distribution of approximately $0.04 cash from escrow 09/06/2007
Each share new Common no par received a second and final additional distribution of $0.03187445 cash from escrow payable 01/25/2008 to holders of record 01/05/2007

DATAWEST SOLUTIONS INC (BC)
Acquired by Open Solutions Inc. 10/29/2004
Each share Common no par exchanged for $1.16 cash

DATAWORKS CORP (DE)
Reincorporated 10/30/1998
State of incorporation changed from (CA) to (DE) 10/30/1998
Merged into Platinum Software Corp. 12/31/1998
Each share Common no par exchanged for (0.794) share Common no par
Platinum Software Corp. name changed to Epicor Software Corp. 05/04/1999
(See Epicor Software Corp.)

DATAWORLD SOLUTIONS INC (DE)
Name changed to Defense Technology Systems, Inc. 07/08/2004
(See Defense Technology Systems, Inc.)

DATCHA HLDGS AMER INC (NV)
Charter revoked for failure to file reports and pay fees 10/01/1995

DATEC GROUP LTD OLD (AB)
Common no par split (2) for (1) by issuance of (1) additional share payable 10/09/2003 to holders of record 10/08/2003
Plan of arrangement effective 02/01/2006
Each share Common no par exchanged for (1) share Datec Group Ltd. (New) Common no par and (0.02153202) share eLandia, Inc. Common
(See each company's listing)

DATEL INDS INC (BC)
Struck off register and declared dissolved for failure to file returns 09/03/1993

DATEL SYS CORP (NY)
Reincorporated under the laws of Delaware as Gulfmark, Inc. 05/21/1987

DATELAND CAP GROUP INC (AB)
Recapitalized as Austrak International Canada Corp. 01/10/1992
Each share Common no par exchanged for (0.4) share Common no par
(See Austrak International Canada Corp.)

DATELINE CORP (SC)
Name changed to Epic Corp. 08/29/1972
(See Epic Corp.)

DATEQ INFORMATION NETWORK INC (GA)
Merged into DIN Acquisition Corp. 08/29/1995
Each share Common 1¢ par exchanged for $5.41 cash

DATEX RES INC (UT)
Name changed to Alert Products Inc. 03/30/1992
(See Alert Products Inc.)

DATEX TECHNOLOGIES CORP (CANADA)
Acquired by 2272107 Ontario Ltd. 03/22/2011
Each share Common no par exchanged for $0.04 cash

DATIGEN COM INC (UT)
Reincorporated under the laws of Nevada as Smart Energy Solutions, Inc. 09/02/2005
Smart Energy Solutions, Inc. name changed to CannaPowder, Inc. 07/11/2018

DATLASAKA MINES LTD. (AB)
Struck off register for failure to file annual returns 04/30/1977

DATOM INDS INC (NY)
Name changed to Barrie (Milton R.) & Co., Inc. 04/05/1971
(See Barrie (Milton R.) & Co., Inc.)

DATONE INC (DE)
Recapitalized as Qingdao Footwear, Inc. 06/10/2010
Each share Common $0.0001 par exchanged for (0.03703704) share Common $0.0001 par

DATREK MILLER INTL INC (FL)
Each share old Common $0.001 par exchanged for (0.5) share new Common $0.001 par 12/05/2005
Name changed to ForeFront Holdings, Inc. 07/28/2006
(See ForeFront Holdings, Inc.)

DATRICON CORP (OR)
Recapitalized as Scientific Technologies Inc. 01/27/1987
Each share Common 1¢ par exchanged for (0.1) share Common no par
(See Scientific Technologies Inc.)

DATRON CORP (MN)
Merged into GGHF, Inc. 11/27/1987
Each share Common 1¢ par exchanged for $6 cash

DATRON SYS INC (DE)
Reincorporated 10/08/1987
State of incorporation changed from (CA) to (DE) and Common no par changed to 1¢ par 10/08/1987
Merged into Titan Corp. 09/28/2001
Each share Common 1¢ par exchanged for (0.81919) share Common 1¢ par
(See Titan Corp.)

DATRON SYS INC (NJ)
Merged into International Controls Corp. 12/24/1979
Each share Common no par exchanged for $1.25 cash

DATRONIC EQUIP INCOME FD XVII L P (DE)
Completely liquidated 12/31/2001
Details not available

DATRONIC EQUIP INCOME FD XIX L P (DE)
Completely liquidated 12/31/2001
Details not available

DATRONIC RENT CORP (IL)
Each share Common no par exchanged for (0.5) share Common $1 par 11/21/1968
Common $1 par split (4) for (1) by issuance of (3) additional shares 07/31/1987
Involuntarily dissolved 09/07/1993

DATRONICS ENGINEERS INC (MD)
Capital Stock $1 par changed to 1¢ par 01/16/1970
Charter forfeited for failure to file annual reports 10/06/1983

DATUM INC (CA)
Merged into Symmetricom, Inc. 10/30/2002
Each share Common 25¢ par exchanged for (2.7609) shares Common $0.0001 par
(See Symmetricom, Inc.)

DATUMONE PETE LTD (BC)
Recapitalized as Mischief Enterprises Ltd. 10/10/1984
Each share Common no par exchanged for (0.2) share Common no par
Mischief Enterprises Ltd. name changed to CV Sportsmark International Inc. 07/15/1985
(See CV Sportsmark International Inc.)

DAUCUS, INC. (TX)
Charter forfeited for failure to pay taxes 03/22/1974

DAUGHERTY RES INC (BC)
Name changed to NGAS Resources Inc. 07/05/2004
NGAS Resources Inc. merged into Magnum Hunter Resources Corp. 04/13/2011
(See Magnum Hunter Resources Corp.)

DAUNTLESS CAP CORP (BC)
Name changed to Tigris Uranium Corp. 09/02/2010
Tigris Uranium Corp. recapitalized as Wolfpack Gold Corp. 05/21/2013 which reorganized as enCore Energy Corp. 08/20/2014

DAUPHIN CORP (DE)
Ceased operations 06/09/1971
No stockholders' equity

DAUPHIN DEP CORP (PA)
Common $10 par changed to $5 par and (1) additional share issued 04/29/1983
Common $5 par split (2) for (1) by issuance of (1) additional share 08/16/1985
Common $5 par split (2) for (1) by

issuance of (1) additional share 12/04/1992
Stock Dividend - 10% 09/15/1981
Merged into Allied Irish Banks, PLC 07/08/1997
Each share Common $5 par exchanged for (1) Sponsored ADR for Ordinary 4p par
(See Allied Irish Banks, PLC)

DAUPHIN DEP TR CO (HARRISBURG, PA)
Stock Dividends - 25% 04/01/1950; 20% 09/24/1953; 16-2/3% 02/21/1955; 30% 02/10/1958; 10% 02/14/1959; 100% 06/15/1967; 10% 02/07/1969; 10% 07/15/1970; 10% 09/18/1972
Under plan of reorganization each share Capital Stock $10 par automatically became (1) share Dauphin Deposit Corp. Common 10¢ par 01/01/1977
Dauphin Deposit Corp. merged into Allied Irish Banks, PLC 07/08/1997
(See Allied Irish Banks, PLC)

DAUPHIN INC (FL)
Recapitalized as RPS Enterprises Inc. 07/19/1994
Each share Common 1¢ par exchanged for (0.33333333) share Common 1¢ par
(See RPS Enterprises Inc.)

DAUPHIN IRON MINES LTD (QC)
Charter annulled for failure to file reports or pay fees 12/29/1973

DAUPHIN TECHNOLOGY INC (IL)
Name changed to GeoVax Labs, Inc. (IL) 10/12/2006
GeoVax Labs, Inc. (IL) reincorporated in Delaware 06/18/2008

DAUR & SHAVER, INC. (UT)
Name changed to Western Antenna Corp. 10/19/1987
Western Antenna Corp. name changed to Hortitech, Inc. 03/05/1990 which name changed to Microaccel, Inc. 02/02/2000 which name changed to Health Anti-Aging Lifestyle Options, Inc. 03/18/2002 which name changed to Previsto International Holdings, Inc. 12/07/2010

DAVAGE TECHNOLOGY INC (UT)
Name changed 05/26/1986
Name changed from Davage Oil & Gas Co. to Davage Technology Inc. 05/26/1986
Proclaimed dissolved for failure to pay taxes 11/01/1993

DAVCO RESTAURANTS INC (DE)
Merged into Davco Acquisition Holding Inc. 04/01/1998
Each share Common $0.001 par exchanged for $20 cash

DAVE & BUSTERS INC (MO)
Common 1¢ par split (3) for (2) by issuance of (0.5) additional share payable 09/15/1997 to holders of record 08/25/1997
Merged into Wellspring Capital Management LLC 03/08/2006
Each share Common 1¢ par exchanged for $18.05 cash

DAVEGA, INC.
Acquired by Atlas Stores Corp. 00/00/1929
Details not available

DAVEGA STORES CORP. (DE)
Merged into Davega Stores Corp. (NY) 01/14/1946
Each share Common $5 par exchanged for (1.2) shares Common $5 par
(See Davega Stores Corp. (NY))

DAVEGA STORES CORP. (NY)
Common $5 par changed to $2.50 par and (1) share 5% Preferred $20 par distributed for each (4) shares Common 00/00/1947

Stock Dividend - 10% 01/02/1951
Adjudicated bankrupt 04/16/1963
No stockholders' equity

DAVEL COMMUNICATIONS GROUP INC (IL)
Merged into Davel Communications, Inc. 12/23/1998
Each share Common no par exchanged for (1) share Common 1¢ par
(See Davel Communications, Inc.)

DAVEL COMMUNICATIONS INC (IL)
Each share old Common 1¢ par exchanged for (0.00000001) share new Common 1¢ par 03/31/2005
Note: In effect holders received $0.015 cash per share and public interest was eliminated

DAVENPORT BK & TR CO (DAVENPORT, IA)
Capital Stock $100 par changed to $10 par and (9) additional shares issued 09/02/1982
Capital Stock $10 par split (5) for (1) by issuance of (4) additional shares 07/30/1990
Acquired by Norwest Corp. 01/21/1992
Each share Capital Stock $10 par exchanged for (8.05555555) shares Common $1.66666666 par
Norwest Corp. name changed to Wells Fargo & Co. (New) 11/02/1998

DAVENPORT-BESLER CORP. (DE)
Each share Class A Common $25 par or Class B Common $25 par exchanged for (12) shares Class A Common $5 par or Class B Common $5 par 00/00/1947
Liquidation completed 11/27/1956
Details not available

DAVENPORT CO (DE)
Common $0.001 par split (2) for (1) by issuance of (1) additional share 05/08/1989
Name changed to Heartsoft Inc. 06/20/1989

DAVENPORT HOSIERY MILLS, INC. (DE)
7% Conv. Preferred $100 par called for redemption 04/01/1946
Common no par changed to $2.50 par and (1) additional share issued 08/08/1946
Merged into Chadbourn Gotham, Inc. on a (6) for (1) basis 07/11/1960
Chadbourn Gotham, Inc. name changed to Chadbourn Inc. 01/31/1969 which reorganized as Stanwood Corp. 06/12/1975 which was acquired by Delta Woodside Industries, Inc. (DE) 09/07/1988 which merged into Delta Woodside Industries, Inc. (SC) 11/15/1989
(See Delta Woodside Industries, Inc. (SC))

DAVENPORT INDS LTD (BC)
Recapitalized as DVO Industries Ltd. 08/19/1991
Each share Capital Stock 50¢ par exchanged for (0.2) share Common no par
(See DVO Industries Ltd.)

DAVENPORT LOCOMOTIVE & MANUFACTURING CORP.
Reorganized as Davenport-Beiser Corp. 00/00/1935
Details not available

DAVENPORT MACH TOOL INC (NY)
Each share Common $1 par exchanged for (40) shares Common $5 par 07/01/1967
Common $5 par changed to $2.50 par and (4) additional shares issued 12/12/1969
Acquired by Dover Corp. 08/01/1972
Each share Common $2.50 par exchanged for (0.2) share Common $1 par

DAVENPORT MINERALS CORP (NV)
Name changed to ReallyThere Technologies 11/05/1999
(See ReallyThere Technologies)

DAVENPORT OIL & MNG LTD (BC)
Name changed to Davenport Industries Ltd. 11/01/1973
Davenport Industries Ltd. recapitalized as DVO Industries Ltd. 08/19/1991
(See DVO Industries Ltd.)

DAVENPORT TURNHALLE HOLDING CO. (IA)
Charter cancelled for failure to file annual reports 04/02/1945

DAVENPORT VENTURES INC (NV)
Name changed to Royal Financial Corp. 08/18/1998
Royal Financial Corp. recapitalized as Patriot Motorcycle Corp. 07/16/2001
(See Patriot Motorcycle Corp.)

DAVENPORT WTR CO (DE)
Name changed to Iowa-American Water Co. 01/01/1987
(See Iowa-American Water Co.)

DAVENTO LTD (UKRAINE)
GDR agreement terminated 02/11/2016
Each 144A Sponsored GDR for Ordinary exchanged for (0.002) share Ordinary
Each Reg. S Sponsored GDR for Ordinary exchanged for (0.002) share Ordinary
Note: Unexchanged GDR's will be sold and the proceeds, if any, held for claim after 02/13/2017

DAVEY (W.H.) STEEL CO.
Liquidation completed 00/00/1944
Details not available

DAVI SKIN INC (NV)
Chapter 7 bankruptcy proceedings terminated 05/07/2012
No stockholders' equity

DAVIAN EXPLORATION LTD. (ON)
Charter cancelled and company declared dissolved for failure to file returns 07/29/1965

DAVIC ENTERPRISES INC (BC)
Recapitalized as RBD Enterprises Inc. 03/10/1997
Each share Common no par exchanged for (0.18181818) share Common no par
RBD Enterprises Inc. recapitalized as Texas Gas & Oil Inc. 05/11/2000 which name changed to Legend Power Systems Inc. 07/03/2008

DAVID & DASH INC (FL)
Common 10¢ par changed to 1¢ par 06/22/1970
Common 1¢ par changed to $0.0033 par and (2) additional shares issued 09/06/1974
Common $0.0033 par changed to $0.00066 par and (4) additional shares issued 07/31/1979
Stock Dividend - 10% 03/29/1972
Name changed to Dash Industries, Inc. 12/11/1979
Dash Industries, Inc. name changed to Avenue Holdings, Inc. 11/19/2003 which recapitalized as Global Prospecting Ventures, Inc. (FL) 01/12/2004 which reincorporated in Nevada 06/04/2004 which name changed to Competitive Games International, Inc. 01/22/2007 which recapitalized as PacWest Equities, Inc. 05/07/2010
(See PacWest Equities, Inc.)

DAVID & FRERE, LTD. (QC)
Class A no par called for redemption 08/21/1967
Public interest eliminated

DAVID COPPERFIELD EXPLORATIONS LTD. (ON)
Charter cancelled and dissolved 07/30/1962

No stockholders' equity

DAVID ENTERPRISES INC (DE)
Name changed to Great American Media Corp. 04/22/1991
(See Great American Media Corp.)

DAVID JAMISON CARLYLE CORP (CA)
Acquired by Lex Service, Inc. 11/23/1985
Each share Common 1¢ par exchanged for $1 cash

DAVID LOREN CORP (NV)
Each share old Common $0.001 par exchanged for (0.33333333) share new Common $0.001 par 10/29/2007
Recapitalized as Kibush Capital Corp. 08/23/2013
Each share new Common $0.001 par exchanged for (0.00444444) share Common $0.001 par

DAVID MINERALS LTD NEW (BC)
Name changed 10/01/1981
Capital Stock $1 par changed to no par 12/21/1979
Under plan of merger name changed from David Minerals Ltd. (Old) to David Minerals Ltd. (New) and each share Capital Stock no par exchanged for (1) share Common no par 10/01/1981
Placed in receivership 05/29/1986
No stockholders' equity

DAVID WADE INDS INC (DE)
Name changed to KBH Industries, Inc. 06/30/1971
(See KBH Industries, Inc.)

DAVID WHITE INC (WI)
Reincorporated 05/05/1992
State of incorporation changed from (DE) to (WI) 05/05/1992
Merged into Choucroute Partners LLC 07/30/1997
Each share Common $3 par exchanged for $12 cash

DAVIDGE CAP FD INC (DC)
Liquidation completed
Each share Common 10¢ par exchanged for initial distribution of $4.75 cash 12/20/1974
Each share Common 10¢ par received second and final distribution of $0.337 cash 12/05/1975

DAVIDGE EARLY BIRD FD (DC)
Merged into Stratton Growth Fund, Inc. (DE) 12/21/1977
Each Unit of Bene. Int. no par exchanged for (0.48) share Common 10¢ par
Stratton Growth Fund, Inc. (DE) reincorporated in Maryland 06/21/1985 which name changed to Stratton Multi-Cap Fund, Inc. 05/01/2006

DAVIDGE FUND (DC)
Name changed to Davidge Early Bird Fund 03/29/1973
Davidge Early Bird Fund merged into Stratton Growth Fund, Inc. (DE) 12/21/1977 which reincorporated in Maryland 06/21/1985 which name changed to Stratton Multi-Cap Fund, Inc. 05/01/2006

DAVIDS BRIDAL INC (FL)
Merged into May Department Stores Co. 08/11/2000
Each share Common no par exchanged for $20 cash

DAVIDS INC (KS)
Common $1 par changed to 25¢ par and (3) additional shares issued 11/29/1968
Name changed to MFY Industries, Inc. 07/25/1969
(See MFY Industries, Inc.)

DAVIDSON & ASSOC INC (CA)
Common $0.0005 par split (2) for (1)

by issuance of (1) additional share 09/06/1995
Merged into CUC International Inc. 07/25/1996
Each share Common $0.0005 par exchanged for (0.85) share Common 1¢ par
CUC International Inc. name changed to Cendant Corp. 12/17/1997 which reorganized as Avis Budget Group, Inc. 09/01/2006

DAVIDSON BISCUIT CO.
Name changed to Consolidated Biscuit Co. 00/00/1936
Consolidated Biscuit Co. merged into Carr-Consolidated Biscuit Co. 00/00/1946
(See Carr-Consolidated Biscuit Co.)

DAVIDSON-BOUTELL CO. (DE)
6% Conv. Preferred $100 par called for redemption 05/20/1966
Acquired by Biederman National Stores, Inc. 11/10/1966
Details not available

DAVIDSON BROS., INC. (MI)
Stock Dividend - 50% 07/30/1948
Name changed to Federal's Inc. 11/28/1966
(See Federal's Inc.)

DAVIDSON DIVERSIFIED REAL ESTATE L P (DE)
Company terminated registration of Units of Limited Partnership and is no longer public as of 08/14/2009
Details not available
Company terminated registration of Units of Limited Partnership III and is no longer public as of 03/30/2010
Company terminated registration of Units of Limited Partnership II and is no longer public as of 11/15/2010

DAVIDSON ENAMEL CO.
Name changed to Clyde Porcelain Steel Corp. 00/00/1943
Clyde Porcelain Steel Corp. merged into Whirlpool Corp. (NY) 00/00/1952 which merged into Whirlpool-Seeger Corp. 09/15/1955 which name changed to Whirlpool Corp. (DE) 04/01/1957

DAVIDSON MANUFACTURING CORP.
Liquidated 00/00/1950
Details not available

DAVIDSON OPTRONICS INC (CA)
Common $1 par changed to $0.33333333 par and (2) additional shares issued 07/28/1969
Common $0.33333333 par changed to no par 09/30/1969
Common no par changed to 25¢ par 12/17/1973
Stock Dividends - 25% 06/15/1984; 25% 11/22/1985
Name changed to DOI Holdings, Inc. 08/18/2010
(See DOI Holdings, Inc.)

DAVIDSON ORE MINING CO.
Acquired by Pittsburgh Coke & Iron Co. 00/00/1940
Details not available

DAVIDSON TISDALE LTD (ON)
Name changed 08/26/1992
Common no par split (2) for (1) by issuance of (1) additional share 05/25/1983
Name changed from Davidson Tisdale Mines, Ltd. to Davidson Tisdale, Ltd. 08/26/1992
Name changed to Northcott Gold Inc. 07/10/2002
Northcott Gold Inc. name changed to Laurion Gold Inc. 03/12/2004 which name changed to Laurion Mineral Exploration Inc. 11/03/2006

DAVIE YDS INC (CANADA)
Plan of arrangement under Companies' Creditors Arrangement Act effective 05/26/2015
Each share Common no par received pro-rata distribution in the amount specified by Plan

DAVIES (WILLIAM) CO., INC.
Acquired by Canada Packers Ltd. 00/00/1927
Details not available

DAVIES IRWIN LTD. (QC)
Name changed to Dilmont, Inc. 09/01/1972

DAVIES PETROLEUMS LTD. (AB)
Recapitalized as New Davies Petroleums Ltd. 06/30/1952
Each share Capital Stock no par exchanged for (1) share Capital Stock no par
New Davies Petroleums Ltd. recapitalized as Davoil Natural Resources Ltd. 03/20/1972 which merged into Ranchmen's Resources (1975) Ltd. 01/31/1977 which name changed to Ranchmen's Resources Ltd. 05/31/1985 which merged into Crestar Energy Inc. 10/11/1995 which was acquired by Gulf Canada Resources Ltd. 11/13/2000
(See Gulf Canada Resources Ltd.)

DAVIES THEO H & CO LTD (HI)
Each share Common $100 par exchanged for (5) shares Common $20 par 04/13/1956
Each share Common $20 par exchanged for (5) shares Common no par 06/30/1968
5.5% Preferred $20 par called for redemption 06/14/1963
Stock Dividends - 20% 09/05/1956; 10% 12/07/1959; 10% 06/23/1960; 10% 12/03/1962
Through purchase offer 99.9% acquired by Jardine Matheson & Co. as of 03/27/1974
Public interest eliminated

DAVIESS COUNTY DISTILLING CO., INC.
Assets sold 00/00/1940
Details not available

DAVIN COMPUTER CORP (DE)
Charter cancelled and declared inoperative and void for non-payment of taxes 03/01/1995

DAVIN ENTERPRISES INC (DE)
Each share old Common $0.0001 par exchanged for (0.01) share new Common $0.0001 par 05/29/1996
Recapitalized as Creative Master International Inc. 03/11/1998
Each share new Common $0.0001 par exchanged for (0.1) share Common $0.0001 par
Creative Master International Inc. recapitalized as PacificNet.com, Inc. 07/27/2000 which name changed to PacificNet Inc. 04/23/2002
(See PacificNet Inc.)

DAVIS ALVA C PETE INC (DE)
Voluntarily dissolved 05/03/1976
Details not available

DAVIS COAL & COKE CO.
Merged into Clinchfield Coal Corp. in 1952
Each share Capital Stock $50 par exchanged for (1) share Common $20 par
Clinchfied Coal Corp. merged into Pittston Co. (DE & VA) 12/28/86 which Delaware incorporation was rescinded 5/14/86 which name changed to Brink's Co. 5/5/2003

DAVIS COVENANT CORP (MN)
Each share old Common $0.001 par exchanged for (0.01) share new Common $0.001 par 01/05/1998
Reincorporated under the laws of Nevada as Boyd Energy Corp. 04/15/1998
Boyd Energy Corp. recapitalized as Barnett Energy Corp. 08/02/2001 which recapitalized as WorldWide Strategies Inc. 07/08/2005

DAVIS DISTRG LTD (ON)
Name changed 06/13/1973
Name changed from Davis Distributing & Vending Ltd. to Davis Distributing Ltd. 06/13/1973
Common no par reclassified as Class B Subordinate no par 07/08/1986
Class B Subordinate no par split (3) for (2) by issuance of (0.5) additional share 07/08/1986
Delisted from Canadian Dealer Network 01/14/2000

DAVIS FOOD SVC INC (GA)
Common 10¢ par split (3) for (2) by issuance of (0.5) additional share 10/03/1972
Merged into Heublein, Inc. 08/29/1973
Each share Common 10¢ par exchanged for (0.388381) share Common no par
Heublein, Inc. merged into Reynolds (R.J.) Industries, Inc. 10/13/1982 which name changed to RJR Nabisco, Inc. 04/25/1986 which merged into RJR Holdings Group, Inc. 04/28/1989
(See RJR Holdings Group, Inc.)

DAVIS H B CORP (DE)
Completely liquidated 05/00/1975
Details not available

DAVIS HENDERSON CORP (ON)
Name changed to DH Corp. 05/08/2014
(See DH Corp.)

DAVIS HENDERSON INCOME FD (ON)
Under plan of reorganization each Unit automatically became (1) share Davis + Henderson Corp. Common no par 01/04/2011
Davis + Henderson Corp. name changed to DH Corp. 05/08/2014
(See DH Corp.)

DAVIS INDUSTRIES (CA)
Charter suspended for non-payment of franchise taxes 03/02/1964

DAVIS INTERMEDIATE INVT GRADE BD FD INC (MD)
Name changed 08/02/1999
Name changed from Davis High Income Fund Inc. to Davis Intermediate Investment Grade Bond Fund, Inc. 08/02/1999
Reorganized as Evergreen Intermediate Term Bond Fund 03/17/2000
Each share Class A 1¢ par automatically became (0.428044) share Class A
Each share Class B 1¢ par automatically became (0.4246) share Class B
Each share Class C 1¢ par automatically became (0.427504) share Class C
Each share Class Y 1¢ par automatically became (0.0430047) share Class Y
(See Evergreen Intermediate Term Bond Fund)

DAVIS INTL SERS INC (MD)
Completely liqiudated 07/18/2003
Each share International Total Return Fund Class A received first and final distribution of $0.04 cash payable 07/18/2003 to holders of record 07/16/2003
Each share International Total Return Fund Class Y received first and final distribution of $0.058 cash payable 07/18/2003 to holders of record 07/16/2003
Note: Certificates were not required to be surrendered and are without value
No equity for holders of International Total Return Fund Classes B and C

DAVIS (JEFFERSON) INVESTMENT CO., INC. (LA)
Liquidation completed
Each share Common no par exchanged for initial distribution of $26.92 cash 10/04/1973
Each share Common no par received second and final distribution of $0.971789 cash 05/20/1974

DAVIS KEAYS MNG LTD (BC)
Name changed 11/06/1981
Name changed from Davis-Keays Mining Co. Ltd. to Davis-Keays Mining Ltd. 11/06/1981
Delisted from Vancouver Stock Exchange 05/21/1991

DAVIS LABORATORIES, INC. (NV)
Charter revoked for failure to file reports and pay fees 09/01/1997

DAVIS LEATHER CO. LTD. (CANADA)
Recapitalized 10/31/1958
Each share Class A no par exchanged for (0.5) share Common no par and $20 principal amount of 4% Debentures
Each share Class B no par exchanged for (1) share Common no par
Name changed to Tancord Industries Ltd. 06/03/1959
(See Tancord Industries Ltd.)

DAVIS MANUFACTURING, INC.
Dissolved 00/00/1950
Details not available

DAVIS MILLS
Merged into General Cotton Corp. 00/00/1930
Details not available

DAVIS NATIONAL BANK (MULLINS, SC)
Merged into M&M Financial Corp. 08/01/1994
Each share Common no par exchanged for (0.5) share Common $5 par
M&M Financial Corp. merged into Anchor Financial Corp. 08/31/1998 which merged into South Financial Group Inc. 06/07/2000 which merged into Toronto-Dominion Bank (Toronto, ON) 09/30/2010

DAVIS TAX-FREE HIGH INCOME FD INC (MD)
Reorganized as Evergreen Municipal Trust 03/17/2000
Each share Class A 1¢ par automatically became (1) share Tax-Free High Income Fund Class A
Each share Class B 1¢ par automatically became (1) share Tax-Free High Income Fund Class B
Each share Class C 1¢ par automatically became (1) share Tax-Free High Income Fund Class C

DAVIS THEATRES INC (IA)
Name changed to Multi-Media, Inc. 09/28/1976
(See Multi-Media, Inc.)

DAVIS TR CO (ELKINS, WV)
Common $100 par split (2) for (1) by issuance of (1) additional share payable 04/01/1999 to holders of record 03/06/1999
Stock Dividend - 100% 02/25/1980
Under plan of reorganization each share Common $100 par automatically became (1) share Davis Trust Financial Corp. Common $100 par 06/01/2000

DAVIS (JEFFERSON) WAREHOUSES, INC. (LA)
Liquidation completed
Each share Common no par exchanged for initial distribution of $59.62 cash 10/04/1973
Each share Common no par received second and final distribution of $1.952378 cash 05/20/1974

DAVIS WHOLESALE DRUG CO., INC. (LA)
Preferred no par called for redemption 10/01/1972
Common no par split (10) for (1) by issuance of (9) additional shares 10/01/1972
Charter revoked for failure to file annual reports 02/09/1987

DAVIS-WOOD OIL CORP. (WY)
Charter revoked for failure to file reports and pay fees 07/19/1927

DAVIS WTR & WASTE INDS INC (GA)
Common $1 par split (3) for (2) by issuance of (0.5) additional share 04/03/1985
Common $1 par split (3) for (2) by issuance of (0.5) additional share 08/29/1986
Common $1 par split (4) for (3) by issuance of (0.33333333) additional share 03/23/1987
Merged into United States Filter Corp. (New) 08/23/1996
Each share Common $1 par exchanged for (1.3995) shares new Common 1¢ par
(See United States Filter Corp. (New))

DAVISON CHEMICAL CO.
Reorganized as Davison Chemical Corp. 00/00/1936
Details not available

DAVISON CHEMICAL CORP. (MD)
Merged into Grace (W.R.) & Co. (CT) 00/00/1954
Each share 4.6% Preferred Ser. A $50 par exchanged for $50 principal amount of 4.25% Conv. Debentures and $5 cash
Each share Common $1 par exchanged for (1.4) shares Common no par
Grace (W.R.) & Co. (CT) reincorporated in New York 05/19/1988
(See Grace (W.R.) & Co.)

DAVISON COKE & IRON CO.
Name changed to Pittsburgh Coke & Iron Co. 00/00/1936
Pittsburgh Coke & Iron Co. name changed to Pittsburgh Coke & Chemical Co. (PA) 00/00/1944 which reincorporated under the laws of Delaware 08/19/1970
(See Pittsburgh Coke & Chemical Co. (DE))

DAVISON OILS LTD. (CANADA)
Acquired by Calvan Consolidated Oil & Gas Co. Ltd. 00/00/1954
Each share Capital Stock exchanged for (0.16666666) share Capital Stock $1 par
(See Calvan Consolidated Oil & Gas Co. Ltd.)

DAVITA HEALTHCARE PARTNERS INC (DE)
Name changed 11/02/2012
Common $0.001 par split (3) for (2) by issuance of (0.5) additional share payable 06/15/2004 to holders of record 06/01/2004 Ex date - 06/16/2004
Common $0.001 par split (2) for (1) by issuance of (1) additional share payable 09/06/2013 to holders of record 08/23/2013 Ex date - 09/09/2013
Name changed form DaVita Inc. to DaVita HealthCare Partners Inc. 11/02/2012
Name changed back to DaVita Inc. 09/01/2016

DAVNET LTD (AUSTRALIA)
Name changed to DVT Holdings Ltd. 10/01/2002
DVT Holdings Ltd. name changed to UXC Ltd. 12/31/2002
(See UXC Ltd.)

DAVNOR WTR TREATMENT TECHNOLOGIES LTD (AB)
Delisted from Toronto Venture Stock Exchange 06/20/2005

DAVOIL NAT RES LTD (AB)
Merged into Ranchmen's Resources (1975) Ltd. 01/31/1977
Each share Capital Stock no par exchanged for (0.16666666) share Class A Common no par
Ranchmen's Resources (1975) Ltd. name changed to Ranchmen's Resources Ltd. 05/31/1985 which merged into Crestar Energy Inc. 10/11/1995 which was acquired by Gulf Canada Resources Ltd. 11/13/2000
(See Gulf Canada Resources Ltd.)

DAVOL MILLS
Acquired by General Cotton Corp. 00/00/1935
Details not available

DAVORN INDS LTD (NY)
Adjudicated bankrupt 09/12/1978
Stockholders' equity unlikely

DAVOS INC (NY)
Common 10¢ par changed to 5¢ par and (1) additional share issued 01/31/1963
Name changed to Okuraya/Davos International, Inc. 05/08/1974
(See Okuraya/Davos International, Inc.)

DAVOX CORP (DE)
Common 10¢ par split (3) for (2) by issuance of (0.5) additional share payable 05/28/1997 to holders of record 05/13/1997
Name changed to Concerto Software, Inc. 05/02/2002
(See Concerto Software, Inc.)

DAVSTAR INDS LTD (ON)
Reincorporated under the laws of Delaware as Urohealth Systems, Inc. 07/27/1995
Urohealth Systems, Inc. name changed to Imagyn Medical Technologies, Inc. 09/29/1997
(See Imagyn Medical Technologies, Inc.)

DAVY CORP PLC (UNITED KINGDOM)
Merged into Trafalgar House PLC 00/00/1992
Each Sponsored ADR for Ordinary exchanged for approximately $3.10 cash

DAW TECHNOLOGIES INC (UT)
Each share old Common 1¢ par exchanged for (0.25) share new Common 1¢ par 07/02/2001
Chapter 11 bankruptcy proceedings converted to Chapter 7 on 09/13/2005
Stockholders' equity unlikely

DAWCIN INTL CORP (NY)
Each share Common $0.0001 par received distribution of (0.83) share First Equities Corp. Common 1¢ par payable 04/15/1997 to holders of record 12/10/1996
SEC revoked common stock registration 07/07/2006

DAWES BROTHERS, INC.
Liquidated 00/00/1938
Details not available

DAWMAC MINING & OILS LTD. (QC)
Merged into International Metal & Petroleum Corp. 11/04/1957
Each share Common exchanged for (1) share Common
(See International Metal & Petroleum Corp.)

DAWN PETES LTD (AB)
Dissolved 00/00/1972
No stockholders' equity

DAWN TECHNOLOGIES INC (DE)
Name changed 09/14/1993
Each share Common $0.00001 par exchanged for (0.01) share Common $0.001 par 06/16/1989
Name changed from Dawn Capital Corp. to Dawn Technologies Inc. 09/14/1993
Chapter 11 bankruptcy proceedings converted to Chapter 7 on 02/26/2002
Stockholders' equity unlikely

DAWSON CREEK CAP CORP (AB)
Reorganized under the laws of Jersey as Lydian International Ltd. 01/10/2008
Each share Common no par exchanged for (0.66666666) share Ordinary no par

DAWSON DEVS LTD (BC)
Name changed to Daon Development Corp. 01/10/1974
Daon Development Corp. name changed to Daon Development Corp.-Corporation D'Amenagement Daon 02/22/1982 which name changed to BCE Development Corp.- Corporation de Developpement BCE 02/21/1986 which name changed to BF Realty Holdings Ltd. 08/19/1991
(See BF Realty Holdings Ltd.)

DAWSON ELDORADO MINES LTD (CANADA)
Name changed 08/07/1985
Name and place of incorporation changed from Dawson Eldorado Gold Exploration Ltd. (BC) to Dawson Eldorado Mines Ltd. (Canada) 08/07/1985
Struck off register and declared dissolved for failure to file returns 03/06/2000

DAWSON GEOPHYSICAL CO OLD (TX)
Merged into Dawson Geophysical Co. (New) 02/12/2015
Each share Common $0.33333333 par exchanged for (1.76) shares Common 1¢ par

DAWSON GOLD MINES, LTD.
In process of liquidation 00/00/1943
Details not available

DAWSON PRODTN SVCS INC (TX)
Merged into Key Energy Group, Inc. 09/18/1998
Each share Common 1¢ par exchanged for $17.50 cash

DAWSON RANGE MINES LTD (BC)
Recapitalized as Carpenter Lake Resources Ltd. 02/13/1979
Each share Common 50¢ par exchanged for (0.2) share Common no par
Carpenter Lake Resources Ltd. recapitalized as Wayside Gold Mines Ltd. 02/21/1992 which recapitalized as International Wayside Gold Mines Ltd. 02/08/1994 which name changed to Barkerville Gold Mines Ltd. 01/21/2010

DAWSON SCIENCE CORP (NV)
Each share old Common $0.001 par exchanged for (0.1) share new Common $0.001 par 01/22/1996
Reorganized under the laws of Delaware as Integrated Transportation Network Group Inc. 06/30/1998
Each share new Common $0.001 par exchanged for (0.25) share Common 1¢ par
(See Integrated Transportation Network Group Inc.)

DAWSON-WHITE GOLD MINES LTD.
Succeeded by Dawson Gold Mines Ltd. 00/00/1939
Details not available

DAX CORP (UT)
Involuntarily dissolved 09/30/1975

DAY & MEYER, MURRAY & YOUNG, INC.
Reorganized as Day & Meyer, Murray & Young Corp. 00/00/1938
No stockholders' equity

DAY & NIGHT AUTO SAFETY SIGNAL CO. (DE)
Charter cancelled and declared inoperative and void for non-payment of taxes 07/01/1939

DAY & NIGHT MANUFACTURING CO.
Acquired by Dresser Industries, Inc. (PA) 00/00/1945
Each share 6% Preferred exchanged for (0.19607843) share Common 50¢ par
Each share 7% Preferred exchanged for (0.20408163) share Common 50¢ par
Each share Original Preferred exchanged for (0.33333333) share Common 50¢ par
Each share Common exchanged for (1.1) shares Common 50¢ par
(See Dresser Industries, Inc. (PA))

DAY BALDWIN INC (NJ)
Merged into Chesebrough-Pond's, Inc. 07/02/1969
Each share Common 10¢ par exchanged for (0.232558) share Common $1 par
(See Chesebrough-Pond's, Inc.)

DAY-BRITE LIGHTING, INC. (MO)
Acquired by Emerson Electric Manufacturing Co. 06/30/1960
Each share Common $1 par exchanged for (0.43) share Common $2 par
Emerson Electric Manufacturing Co. name changed to Emerson Electric Co. 02/06/1964

DAY INTL (MI)
Merged into Hanna (M.A.) Co. (New) 09/01/1987
Each share Common $1 par exchanged for $48 cash
$4.25 Conv. Preferred Ser. A no par called for redemption 10/12/1987
Public interest eliminated

DAY INTL GROUP INC (DE)
Stock Dividends - 3.0625% payable 12/15/1999 to holders of record 12/01/1999 Ex date - 12/21/1999; 3.0625% payable 03/15/2000 to holders of record 03/05/2000 Ex date - 03/16/2000; 3.0625% payable 06/15/2000 to holders of record 06/05/2000; 3.0625% payable 09/15/2000 to holders of record 09/05/2000; 3.0625% payable 12/15/2000 to holders of record 12/05/2000; 3.0625% payable 03/15/2001 to holders of record 03/00/2001; 3.0625% payable 06/15/2001 to holders of record 06/05/2001; 3.0625% payable 09/17/2001 to holders of record 09/05/2001; 3.0625% payable 12/15/2001 to holders of record 12/05/2001; 3.0625% payable 03/15/2002 to holders of record 03/05/2002; 3.0625% payable 06/15/2002 to holders of record 06/05/2002 Ex date - 06/17/2002; 3.0625% payable 09/16/2002 to holders of record 09/05/2002 Ex date - 09/13/2002; 3.0625% payable 12/15/2002 to holders of record 12/05/2002 Ex date - 12/12/2002; 3.0625% payable 03/17/2003 to holders of record 03/05/2003 Ex date - 03/18/2003; 3.4132% payable 05/12/2006 to holders of record 05/10/2006 Ex date - 05/19/2006; 3.0625% payable 08/11/2006 to holders of record 08/10/2006 Ex date - 08/08/2006; 3.0625% payable 09/26/2006 to holders of

record 09/25/2006 Ex date - 09/21/2006; 3.0625% payable 01/05/2007 to holders of record 01/02/2007; 3.0625% payable 03/26/2007 to holders of record 03/23/2007 Ex date - 03/22/2007 12.25% Sr. Exchangeable Preferred called for redemption at $1,035.86 on 05/31/2007

DAY MINES INC (ID)
Common 10¢ par split (3) for (2) by issuance of (0.5) additional share 12/18/1980
Merged into Hecla Mining Co. (WA) 10/20/1981
Each share Common 10¢ par exchanged for (1.8) shares Common 25¢ par
Hecla Mining Co. (WA) reincorporated in Delaware 06/06/1983

DAY RUNNER INC (DE)
Reincorporated 7/29/93
State of incorporation changed from (CA) to (DE) and Common no par changed to $0.001 par 07/29/1993
Old Common $0.001 par split (2) for (1) by issuance of (1) additional share payable 03/30/1998 to holders of record 03/18/1998
Each share old Common $0.001 par exchanged for (0.2) share new Common $0.001 par 05/01/2000
Merged into Keysun Inc. 09/27/2001
Each share new Common $0.001 par exchanged for $0.10 cash

DAY SOFTWARE HLDG AG (SWITZERLAND)
Acquired by Adobe Systems Inc. 10/28/2010
Each ADR for Ordinary exchanged for $31.907696 cash

DAY SPAS OF AMER INC (NV)
Each share old Common $0.001 par exchanged for (0.00416666) share new Common $0.001 par 04/25/2006
Charter permanently revoked 09/30/2010

DAY TELECOMMUNICATIONS INC (TX)
Chapter 11 bankruptcy proceedings converted to Chapter 7 on 04/17/1986
Stockholders' equity unlikely

DAY TRUST CO. (BOSTON, MA)
Capital Stock $100 par changed to $50 par 00/00/1937
Merged into Merchants National Bank (Boston, MA) 12/31/1956
Each share Capital Stock $50 par exchanged for (4.1) shares Capital Stock $10 par
Merchants National Bank (Boston, MA) merged into New England Merchants National Bank (Boston, MA) 12/31/1960 which automatically became New England Merchants Co., Inc. (DE) 06/18/1970 which reincorporated in Massachusetts 03/31/1971 which name changed to Bank of New England Corp. 05/01/1982
(See Bank of New England Corp.)

DAYAK GOLDFIELDS CORP (ON)
Merged into International Pursuit Corp. 05/22/1997
Each share Common no par exchanged for (0.36666666) Common no par
International Pursuit Corp. recapitalized as Apollo Gold Corp. (ON) 06/24/2002 which reincorporated in Yukon 05/28/2003 which recapitalized as Brigus Gold Corp. (YT) 06/25/2010 which reincorporated in Canada 06/09/2011
(See Brigus Gold Corp.)

DAYBREAK ENERGY CORP (AB)
Recapitalized as Result Energy Inc. 12/19/2001
Each share Common no par exchanged for (0.125) share Common no par
Result Energy Inc. merged into PetroBakken Energy Ltd. (Old) 04/01/2010 which reorganized as PetroBakken Energy Ltd. (New) 01/07/2013 which name changed to Lightstream Resources Ltd. 05/28/2013

DAYBREAK MINES INC (WA)
Name changed to Daybreak Oil & Gas, Inc. 10/26/2005

DAYBREAK RES CORP (AB)
Name changed to Daybreak Energy Corp. 06/30/2000
Daybreak Energy Corp. recapitalized as Result Energy Inc. 12/19/2001 which merged into PetroBakken Energy Ltd. (Old) 04/01/2010 which reorganized as PetroBakken Energy Ltd. (New) 01/07/2013 which name changed to Lightstream Resources Ltd. 05/28/2013

DAYBREAK URANIUM, INC. (WA)
Name changed to Daybreak Mines Inc. 04/18/1964
Daybreak Mines Inc. name changed to Daybreak Oil & Gas, Inc. 10/26/2005

DAYCO CORP (MI)
Reincorporated 05/01/1966
Reincorporated 08/31/1982
Class A $35 par called for redemption 01/25/1966
State of incorporation changed from (OH) to (DE) and Common 50¢ par changed to $1 par 05/01/1966
Common $1 par split (5) for (4) by issuance of (0.25) additional share 12/01/1966
Common $1 par split (3) for (2) by issuance of (0.5) additional share 07/31/1969
Stock Dividends - 10% 05/06/1978; 10% 05/04/1979
State of incorporation changed from (DE) to (MI) 08/31/1982
Name changed to Day International Corp. 02/23/1987
(See Day International Corp.)

DAYCOM CORP (OH)
Common no par split (2) for (1) by issuance of (1) additional share 01/15/1982
Chapter 11 bankruptcy proceedings converted to Chapter 7 on 10/04/1984
No stockholders' equity

DAYFIELD REALTY CORP.
Dissolved 00/00/1948
Details not available

DAY4 ENERGY INC (BC)
Reincorporated 06/28/2012
Place of incorporation changed from (Canada) to (BC) 06/28/2012
Name changed to 0944460 B.C. Ltd. 08/27/2012

DAYJON EXPLORERS LTD. (ON)
Name changed to Dayjon Explorations & Holdings Ltd. 04/11/1963
(See Dayjon Explorations & Holdings Ltd.)

DAYJON EXPLS & HLDGS LTD (ON)
Charter cancelled for failure to pay taxes and file returns 04/22/1980

DAYLIGHT ENERGY LTD (AB)
Plan of arrangement effective 09/26/2006
Each Exchangeable Share exchanged for (0.85843) Daylight Resources Trust, Trust Unit no par, (0.05389) share Trafalgar Energy Ltd. Common no par and (0.01561) Common Stock Purchase Warrant expiring 10/23/2006
(See Trafalgar Energy Ltd.)
Acquired by Sinopec International Petroleum Exploration & Production Corp. 12/23/2011
Each share Common no par exchanged for $10.08 cash

DAYLIGHT ENERGY TR (AB)
Plan of arrangement effective 09/26/2006
Each Trust Unit exchanged for (0.6642) Daylight Resources Trust, Trust Unit, (0.0417) share Trafalgar Energy Ltd. Common no par and (0.01208) Common Stock Purchase Warrant expiring 10/23/2006
(See each company's listing)

DAYLIGHT INDS INC (DE)
Recapitalized as ThermaFreeze Products Corp. 08/18/2006
Each share Common 20¢ par exchanged for (0.01) share Common 20¢ par

DAYLIGHT RES TR (AB)
Reorganized as Daylight Energy Ltd. 05/12/2010
Each Trust Unit exchanged for (1) share Common no par
Note: Unexchanged certificates were cancelled and became without value 05/12/2016
(See Daylight Energy Ltd.)

DAYLIN INC (DE)
Reincorporated 01/15/1971
Common no par split (2) for (1) by issuance of (1) additional share 01/15/1970
State of incorporation changed from (CA) to (DE) and Common no par changed to 35¢ par 01/15/1971
Merged into Grace (W.R.) & Co. 03/21/1979
Each share Common 35¢ par exchanged for $4.0625 cash

DAYPAC INDS INC (DE)
Adjudicated bankrupt 08/19/1970
No stockholders' equity

DAYROCK MINING CO.
Acquired by Day Mines, Inc. 00/00/1947
Details not available

DAYS INNS CORP (DE)
Each share Common 4¢ par exchanged for (2) shares Common 2¢ par 08/28/1986
Acquired by Reliance Capital Group L.P. 06/07/1988
Each share Common 2¢ par exchanged for $9 cash

DAYSTAR COMMUNICATIONS LTD (UT)
Recapitalized as Daystar International Holdings, Inc. 04/02/1987
Each share Common $0.001 par exchanged for (0.2) share Common $0.001 par
Daystar International Holdings, Inc. name changed to BDI Systems, Inc. 05/25/1995

DAYSTAR INDS INC (DE)
Name changed to Drage Industries, Inc. 10/31/1972
(See Drage Industries, Inc.)

DAYSTAR INTL HLDGS INC (UT)
Name changed to BDI Systems, Inc. 05/25/1995

DAYSTAR TECHNOLOGIES INC (DE)
Each share old Common 1¢ par exchanged for (0.11111111) share new Common 1¢ par 05/12/2010
Each share new Common 1¢ par exchanged again for (0.14285714) share new Common 1¢ par 04/09/2012
SEC revoked common stock registration 03/06/2017

DAYSTROM CORP.
Acquired by American Type Founders, Inc. 00/00/1945
Details not available

DAYSTROM INC (NJ)
Capital Stock $10 par redesignated as Common $10 par 00/00/1954
Acquired by Schlumberger, Ltd. 02/01/1962
Each share Common $10 par exchanged for (0.5) share Common $1 par

DAYTON & TROY ELECTRIC RWY. CO.
Ceased operations 00/00/1932
Details not available

DAYTON & WESTERN TRACTION CO.
Property sold 00/00/1936
No stockholders' equity

DAYTON AIRPLANE ENGINE CO. (DE)
Charter cancelled and declared inoperative and void for non-payment of taxes 04/01/1932

DAYTON AVIATION RADIO & EQUIP CORP (OH)
Common 50¢ par changed to no par 11/22/1965
Merged into Allied Technology, Inc. 02/28/1970
Each share Common no par exchanged for (0.4) share Common no par
Allied Technology, Inc. merged into TSC, Inc. 01/04/1982
(See TSC, Inc.)

DAYTON BILTMORE HOTEL LAND TRUST (OH)
5% Land Trust Ctfs. called for redemption 07/31/1965

DAYTON CO. (MN)
Name changed to Dayton Corp. 09/06/1967
Dayton Corp. name changed to Dayton-Hudson Corp. 06/20/1969 which name changed to Target Corp. 01/31/2000

DAYTON COMMUNICATIONS CORP (OH)
Name changed to Daycom Corp. 11/12/1981
(See Daycom Corp.)

DAYTON CONS MINES CO (NV)
Capital Stock $1 par changed to 25¢ par 12/24/1968
Name changed to Dayton Universal, Inc. 09/10/1969
(See Dayton Universal, Inc.)

DAYTON CORP (MN)
6% 1st Preferred Ser. A $100 par called for redemption 11/28/1967
6% 1st Preferred Ser. B $100 par called for redemption 11/28/1967
Common $1 par split (2) for (1) by issuance of (1) additional share 04/07/1969
Name changed to Dayton-Hudson Corp. 06/20/1969
Dayton-Hudson Corp. name changed to Target Corp. 01/31/2000

DAYTON COUNTRY CLUB CO. LAND TRUST (OH)
6% Land Trust Ctfs. called for redemption 10/31/1965

DAYTON CREEK SILVER MINES LTD (BC)
Reincorporated 11/18/1982
Place of incorporation changed from (AB) to (BC) 11/18/1982
Merged into Mintek Resources Ltd. 01/04/1983
Each share Common no par exchanged for (0.33333333) share Common no par
Mintek Resources Ltd. recapitalized as Coast Diamond Ventures Ltd. 10/19/1992 which recapitalized as Avcan Global Systems Inc. 07/04/1994 which recapitalized as ASC Avcan Systems Corp. 04/21/1999 which recapitalized as Avcan Systems Inc. (BC)

DAY-DBA

09/07/2001 which reincorporated in Canada as Optimal Geomatics Inc. 10/09/2003 which merged into Aeroquest International Ltd. 09/30/2009
(See Aeroquest International Ltd.)

DAYTON DEVS CORP (BC)
Common no par split (2) for (1) by issuance of (1) additional share 04/07/1988
Common no par split (3) for (2) by issuance of (0.5) additional share 11/15/1988
Name changed to Dayton Mining Corp. 08/29/1991
Dayton Mining Corp. merged into Pacific Rim Mining Corp. 04/11/2002 which merged into OceanaGold Corp. 12/02/2013

DAYTON FILMCORP (NV)
Each share old Common $0.001 par exchanged for (0.02) share new Common $0.001 par 09/02/1994
Recapitalized as Universal Marketing & Entertainment Inc. 11/09/1994
Each share new Common $0.001 par exchanged for (0.25) share Common $0.001 par
Universal Marketing & Entertainment Inc. recapitalized as Odyssey Capital Group Ltd. 05/11/2001 which name changed to Print Data Corp. (NV) 08/13/2001 which reorganized in Delaware 10/11/2002 which name changed to ACL Semiconductors Inc. 12/16/2003 which name changed to USmart Mobile Device Inc. 04/17/2013 which name changed to Eagle Mountain Corp. 05/06/2015

DAYTON HUDSON CORP (MN)
Common $1 par split (2) for (1) by issuance of (1) additional share 11/30/1981
Common $1 par split (2) for (1) by issuance of (1) additional share 07/22/1983
Common $1 par changed to $0.33333333 and (2) additional shares issued payable 07/17/1996 to holders of record 06/28/1996 Ex date - 07/18/1996
Common $0.33333333 par changed to $0.1667 par and (1) additional share issued payable 04/30/1998 to holders of record 04/10/1998 Ex date - 05/01/1998
Name changed to Target Corp. 01/31/2000

DAYTON INDS INC (AZ)
Merged into Galaxie National Corp. 12/24/1969
Each share Common $1 par exchanged for (1) share Common 10¢ par
Galaxie National Corp. reorganized as Marathon Office Supply, Inc. 05/12/1982
(See Marathon Office Supply, Inc.)

DAYTON MALLEABLE INC (OH)
Common no par split (3) for (2) by issuance of (0.5) additional share 08/10/1976
Common no par split (4) for (3) by issuance of (0.33333333) additional share 10/15/1981
Name changed to Amcast Industrial Corp. 12/14/1983
(See Amcast Industrial Corp.)

DAYTON MALLEABLE IRON CO. (OH)
Reorganized 00/00/1935
Each share Preferred $100 par exchanged for (1) share Common no par, $2.50 cash and (1) share Preferred $10 par
Each share Class A Common no par exchanged for (2) shares Common no par
Each share Class B Common no par exchanged for (0.5) share Common no par

Common no par split (5) for (4) by issuance of (0.25) additional share 10/02/1950
Common no par split (6) for (5) by issuance of (0.2) additional share 10/01/1951
Preferred $10 par called for redemption 04/01/1963
Common no par split (3) for (2) by issuance of (0.5) additional share 01/21/1964
Common no par split (2) for (1) by issuance of (1) additional share 10/15/1965
Name changed to Dayton Malleable Inc. 12/05/1973
Dayton Malleable Inc. name changed to Amcast Industrial Corp. 12/14/1983
(See Amcast Industrial Corp.)

DAYTON MNG CORP (BC)
Each share old Common no par exchanged for (0.05) share new Common no par 04/11/2000
Merged into Pacific Rim Mining Corp. 04/11/2002
Each share new Common no par exchanged for (1.76) shares new Common no par
Pacific Rim Mining Corp. merged into OceanaGold Corp. 12/02/2013

DAYTON PORCUPINE MINES LTD. (ON)
Name changed to Denom Resources Inc. (ON) 11/15/1982
Denom Resources Inc. (ON) reincorporated in British Columbia 04/26/1983 which reincorporated in Ontarioas ITM Corp. 02/04/1986 which recapitalized as IMC Integrated Marketing Communications Inc. 08/06/1987
(See IMC Integrated Marketing Communications Inc.)

DAYTON PWR & LT CO (OH)
Each share Common no par exchanged for (4) shares Common $7 par 00/00/1946
Common $7 par split (3) for (1) by issuance of (2) additional shares 06/07/1961
11.6% Preferred Ser. J $100 par called for redemption 10/01/1985
12.5% Preferred Ser. G $100 par called for redemption 10/01/1985
Under plan of reorganization each share Common $7 par automatically became (1) share DPL Inc. Common $7 par 04/21/1986
(See DPL Inc.)
7.375% Preferred Ser. F $100 par called for redemption 05/06/1994
7.48% Preferred Ser. D $100 par called for redemption 05/06/1994
7.7% Preferred Ser. E $100 par called for redemption 05/06/1994
8.625% Preferred Ser. H $100 par called for redemption 05/06/1994
9.375% Preferred Ser. I $100 par called for redemption 05/06/1994
3.75% Preferred Ser. A $100 par called for redemption at $102.50 plus $0.437499 accrued dividends on 10/13/2016
3.75% Preferred Ser. B $100 par called for redemption at $103 plus $0.437499 accrued dividends on 10/13/2016
3.9% Preferred Ser. C $100 par called for redemption at $101 plus $0.454999 accrued dividends on 10/13/2016

DAYTON RUBBER CO. (OH)
Stock Dividends - 10% 02/15/1956; 20% 11/30/1956
Name changed to Dayco Corp. (OH) 04/01/1960
Dayco Corp. (OH) reincorporated in Delaware 05/01/1966 which reincorporated in Michigan 08/31/1982 which name changed to Day International Corp. 02/23/1987

(See Day International Corp.)

DAYTON RUBBER MANUFACTURING CO.
Name changed to Dayton Rubber Co. 00/00/1947
Dayton Rubber Co. name changed to Dayco Corp. (OH) 04/01/1960 which reincorporated in Delaware 05/01/1966 which reincorporated in Michigan 08/31/1982 which name changed to Day International Corp. 02/23/1987
(See Day International Corp.)

DAYTON SCALE CO.
Merged into International Business Machines Corp. in 1933
Details not available

DAYTON STREET RAILWAY
Name changed to Dayton Street Transit Co. 00/00/1934
(See Dayton Street Transit Co.)

DAYTON STREET TRANSIT CO.
Assets acquired by City Railway Co. in 1941
Details not available

DAYTON SUPERIOR CAP TR (DE)
Completely liquidated 6/16/2000
Each 10% Guaranteed Trust Conv. Preferred Security exchanged for first and final distribution of $22.40 cash

DAYTON SUPERIOR CORP (OH)
Merged into Odyssey Investment Partners 06/16/2000
Each share Class A Common no par exchanged for $27 cash
DAYTON SUPERIOR CORP. (DE) Issue Information - 7,850,000 shares COM offered at $12 per share on 12/19/2006
Plan of reorganization under Chapter 11 Federal Bankruptcy proceedings effective 10/26/2009
No stockholders' equity

DAYTON UNVL INC (NV)
Each share old Capital Stock 25¢ par exchanged for (0.2) share new Capital Stock 25¢ par 04/26/1971
Charter revoked for failure to file reports and pay fees 06/01/1982

DAYTONA BEACH GEN HOSP INC (FL)
Merged into Health Delivery Systems, Inc. (IL) 06/28/1985
Each share Common 10¢ par exchanged for $6 cash

DAYTONA CAP CORP (AB)
Acquired by Hutchinson Acquisitions Corp. 1/22/2002
Each share Common no par exchanged for $0.15 cash

DAYTONA ENERGY CORP (AB)
Reincorporated 01/29/2005
Reincorporated 02/02/2007
Each share old Common no par exchanged for (0.16666666) share new Common no par 09/10/2002
Place of incorporation changed from (YT) to (BC) 01/29/2005
Place of incorporation changed from (BC) to (AB) 02/02/2007
Recapitalized as Riata Resources Corp. 09/01/2010
Each share new Common no par exchanged for (0.1) share Common no par
Riata Resources Corp. name changed to Petroforte International Ltd. 11/02/2011 which recapitalized as Canamax Energy Ltd. 02/21/2014
(See Canamax Energy Ltd.)

DAYTONA INTL SPEEDWAY CORP (FL)
Name changed to International Speedway Corp. 12/23/1968

DAYTONA LINEN SERVICE, INC. (FL)
Name changed to DLS, Inc. 7/12/84
(See DLS, Inc.)

DAYTONABRANDS INC (FL)
SEC revoked common stock registration 03/25/2010

DAYTRONICS, INC. (OK)
Charter revoked for failure to file reports and pay fees 5/27/66

DAZEY CORP. (DE)
Name changed to Dacor Co. in 1954
(See Dacor Co.)

DB-X EXCHANGE-TRADED FDS INC (MD)
db-X 2010 Target Date Fund $0.0001 par reclassified as db X-trackers 2010 Target Date Fund $0.0001 par 02/01/2013 db-X 2020 Target Date Fund $0.0001 par reclassified as db X-trackers 2020 Target Date Fund $0.0001 par 02/01/2013 db-X 2030 Target Date Fund $0.0001 par reclassified as db X-trackers 2030 Target Date Fund $0.0001 par 02/01/2013 db-X 2040 Target Date Fund $0.0001 par reclassified as db X-trackers 2040 Target Date Fund $0.0001 par 02/01/2013 db-X In-Target Date Fund $0.0001 par reclassified as db X-trackers In-Target Date Fund $0.0001 par 02/01/2013 db X-trackers 2010 Target Date Fund $0.0001 par reclassified as Deutsche X-trackers 2010 Target Date ETF $0.0001 par 08/11/2014 db X-trackers 2020 Target Date Fund $0.0001 par reclassified as Deutsche X-trackers 2020 Target Date ETF $0.0001 par 08/11/2014 db X-trackers 2030 Target Date Fund $0.0001 par reclassified as Deutsche X-trackers 2030 Target Date ETF $0.0001 par 08/11/2014 db X-trackers 2040 Target Date Fund $0.0001 par reclassified as Deutsche X-trackers 2040 Target Date ETF $0.0001 par 08/11/2014 db X-trackers In-Target Date Fund $0.0001 par reclassified as Deutsche X-trackers In-Target Date ETF $0.0001 par 08/11/2014
Trust terminated 05/27/2015
Each share Deutsche X-trackers 2010 Target Date ETF $0.0001 par received $25.751903 cash
Each share Deutsche X-trackers 2020 Target Date ETF $0.0001 par received $28.957584 cash
Each share Deutsche X-trackers 2030 Target Date ETF $0.0001 par received $29.976885 cash
Each share Deutsche X-trackers 2040 Target Date ETF $0.0001 par received $30.785604 cash
Each share Deutsche X-trackers In-Target Date ETF $0.0001 par received $29.054279 cash

DBA SYS INC (FL)
Common $0.33333333 par changed to 10¢ par 11/14/1980
Common 10¢ par split (3) for (2) by issuance of (0.5) additional share 06/30/1981
Common 10¢ par split (4) for (3) by issuance of (0.33333333) additional share 10/21/1982
Common 10¢ par split (3) for (2) by issuance of (0.5) additional share 06/24/1983
Merged into Titan Corp. 02/27/1998
Each share Common 10¢ par exchanged for (1.366667) shares Common 1¢ par
(See Titan Corp.)

DBA TELECOM CORP (BC)
Each share old Common no par exchanged for (0.25) share new Common no par 12/16/1998
Recapitalized as Magnum Minerals Corp. 09/20/2004
Each share new Common no par exchanged for (0.02) share Common no par
Magnum Minerals Corp. name changed to Magnum Uranium Corp.

10/03/2005 which was acquired by Energy Fuels Inc. 07/02/2009

DBL CASH FD INC (MD)
Name changed to Zweig Cash Fund Inc. 09/05/1989
Zweig Cash Fund Inc. reorganized as Zweig Series Trust (MA) 05/01/1994 which reincorporated in Delaware 04/19/1996 which name changed to Phoenix-Zweig Trust 01/19/1999 which name changed to Phoenix Trust 09/30/2002
(See Phoenix Trust)

DBL SR CARE INC (NV)
Old Common $0.001 par split (10) for (1) by issuance of (9) additional shares payable 08/17/2009 to holders of record 08/17/2009
Name changed to Elemental Protective Coatings Corp. 01/21/2010
Elemental Protective Coatings Corp. recapitalized as Bio-Carbon Solutions International Inc. 01/27/2011 which name changed to NSU Resources Inc. 12/22/2011 which recapitalized as Hemcare Health Services Inc. 05/05/2015 which recapitalized DLT Resolution Inc. 12/20/2017

DBL TAX FREE FD INC (MD)
Name changed 04/01/1985
Name changed from DBL Tax-Free Cash Fund Inc. to DBL Tax-Free Fund Inc. 04/01/1985
Name changed to Zweig Tax-Free Fund Inc. 09/05/1989
Zweig Tax-Free Fund Inc. merged into Industrial Series Trust 04/01/1991

DBRIT CORP (DE)
Charter cancelled and declared inoperative and void for non-payment of taxes 03/01/1998

DBS GROUP HLDGS LTD (SINGAPORE)
ADR agreement terminated 06/08/2009
No ADR's remain outstanding
ADR agreement terminated 12/29/2009
Each 144A Sponsored ADR for Ordinary exchanged for $11.148633 cash
(Additional Information in Active)

DBS HLDGS INC (NV)
Name changed to MIV Therapeutics Inc. 3/5/2002

DBS INDS INC (DE)
Each share Common $0.00001 par exchanged for (0.025) share Common $0.0004 par 02/15/1996
SEC revoked common stock registration 12/28/2005

DBS INVTS INC (UT)
Each share old Common $0.001 par exchanged for (0.1) share new Common $0.001 par 9/23/99
Each share new Common $0.001 par exchanged again for (0.1) share new Common $0.001 par 10/26/2001
Recapitalized as Valuesetters Inc. 5/18/2004
Each share new Common $0.001 par exchanged for (0.1) share Common $0.001 par

DBS LD LTD (SINGAPORE)
Merged into Capitaland Ltd. 3/23/2001
Each Sponsored ADR for Ordinary exchanged for (1) Sponsored ADR for Ordinary S$1 par

DBT ONLINE INC (PA)
Common 10¢ par split (2) for (1) by issuance of (1) additional share payable 10/14/1997 to holders of record 09/26/1997 Ex date - 10/15/1997
Merged into ChoicePoint Inc. 05/16/2000
Each share Common 10¢ par exchanged for (0.525) share Common 10¢ par
(See ChoicePoint Inc.)

DBX ETF TR (DE)
db-X MSCI Brazil Currency-Hedged Equity Fund no par reclassified as db X-trackers MSCI Brazil Hedged Equity Fund no par 02/01/2013 db X-trackers MSCI Brazil Hedged Equity Fund no par reclassified as Deutsche X-trackers MSCI Brazil Hedged Equity ETF no par 08/11/2014 db X-trackers MSCI Mexico Hedged Equity Fund no par reclassified as Deutsche X-trackers MSCI Mexico Hedged Equity ETF no par 08/11/2014 db X-trackers Regulated Utilities Index Fund no par reclassified as Deutsche X-trackers Regulated Utilities Index ETF no par 08/11/2014 db X-trackers Solactive Investment Grade Subordinated Debt Fund no par reclassified as Deutsche X-trackers Solactive Investment Grade Subordinated Debt ETF no par 08/11/2014
Trust terminated 09/21/2015
Each share Deutsche X-trackers Regulated Utilities Index ETF no par received $26.75901 cash
Each share Deutsche X-trackers Solactive Investment Grade Subordinated Debt ETF no par received $24.65457 cash
Trust terminated 05/26/2017
Each share Deutsche X-trackers Dow Jones Hedged International Real Estate ETF no par received $22.99027 cash
Each share Deutsche X-trackers Japan JPX-Nikkei 400 Hedged Equity ETF no par received $23.50368 cash
Each share Deutsche X-trackers MSCI Australia Hedged Equity ETF no par received $27.15981 cash
Each share Deutsche X-trackers MSCI Spain Hedged Equity ETF no par received $25.61475 cash
Each share Deutsche X-trackers S&P Hedged Global Infrastructure ETF no par received $25.82144 cash
Deutsche X-trackers MSCI Brazil Hedged Equity ETF no par reclassified as Xtrackers MSCI Brazil Hedged Equity ETF no par 10/02/2017
Deutsche X-trackers MSCI EAFE Small Cap Hedged Equity ETF no par reclassified as Xtrackers MSCI EAFE Small Cap Hedged Equity ETF no par 10/02/2017
Deutsche X-trackers MSCI Eurozone High Dividend Yield Hedged Equity ETF no par reclassified as Xtrackers MSCI Eurozone High Dividend Yield Hedged Equity ETF no par 10/02/2017
Deutsche X-trackers MSCI Mexico Hedged Equity ETF no par reclassified as Xtrackers MSCI Mexico Hedged Equity ETF no par 10/02/2017
Trust terminated 12/29/2017
Each share Xtrackers MSCI Emerging Markets High Dividend Yield Hedged Equity ETF no par received $23.83786 cash
Each share Xtrackers MSCI Eurozone High Dividend Yield Hedged Equity ETF no par received $26.5048 cash
Trust terminated 05/31/2018
Each share Xtrackers MSCI Brazil Hedged Equity ETF no par received $12.12978 cash
Each share Xtrackers MSCI EAFE Small Cap Hedged Equity ETF no par received $30.30194 cash
Each share Xtrackers MSCI Mexico Hedged Equity ETF no par received $17.77533 cash
(Additional Information in Active)

DC BRANDS INTL INC (CO)
Each share old Common $0.001 par exchanged for (0.1) share new Common $0.001 par 09/26/2007
Each share new Common $0.001 par exchanged again for (0.1) share new Common $0.001 par 07/28/2011
Each share new Common $0.001 par exchanged again for (0.005) share new Common $0.001 par 06/28/2012
Each share new Common $0.001 par exchanged again for (0.01) share new Common $0.001 par 04/30/2013
Each share new Common $0.001 par exchanged again for (0.01) share new Common $0.001 par 10/03/2013
Each share new Common $0.001 par exchanged again for (0.01) share new Common $0.001 par 09/09/2014
Ceased operations 11/19/2014
Stockholders' equity unlikely

DCA DEV CORP (DE)
Adjudicated bankrupt 06/27/1973
Stockholders' equity unlikely

DCA TOTAL RETURN FD (DE)
Name changed to Virtus Total Return Fund 12/22/2011
Virtus Total Return Fund merged into Virtus Total Return Fund Inc. 04/03/2017

DCAP GROUP INC (DE)
Each share old Common 1¢ par exchanged for (0.2) share new Common 1¢ par 08/26/2004
Name changed to Kingstone Companies, Inc. 07/02/2009

DCB BANCSHARES INC (MD)
Merged into Old Line Bancshares, Inc. 07/28/2017
Each share Common 1¢ par exchanged for (0.9269) share Common 1¢ par

DCB CAP INC (QC)
Name changed to Opsens Inc. 10/03/2006

DCB CORP (IN)
Acquired by Old National Bancorp 4/1/93
Each share Common no par exchanged for (6.405) shares Common no par

DCB FINL CORP (OH)
Merged into First Commonwealth Financial Corp. 04/03/2017
Each share Common no par exchanged for either (1.427) shares Common $1 par, $14.50 cash or a combination thereof

DCC ACQUISITION CORP (NV)
Recapitalized as ProHealth Medical Technologies, Inc. 11/01/1999
Each share Common $0.0001 par exchanged for (0.1) share Common $0.0001 par
Prohealth Medical Technologies, Inc. name changed to Applied DNA Sciences, Inc. (NV) 11/18/2002 which reincorporated in Delaware 12/17/2008

DCC COMPACT CLASSICS INC (CO)
Each share Common $0.0001 par exchanged for (0.02) share old Common $0.005 par 01/14/1991
Each share old Common $0.005 par exchanged for (0.0148571) share new Common $0.005 par 05/25/2000
Administratively dissolved 10/01/2003

DCCA INC (DE)
Charter cancelled and declared inoperative and void for non-payment of taxes 4/15/72

DCGR INTL HLDGS INC (DE)
Each (30) shares old Common 1¢ par exchanged for (1) share new Common 1¢ par 09/11/1998
Each share new Common 1¢ par exchanged again for (0.02) share new Common 1¢ par 05/15/2000
Each share new Common 1¢ par exchanged again for (0.005) share new Common 1¢ par 12/21/2001
Each share new Common 1¢ par exchanged exchanged again for (0.04) share new Common 1¢ par 11/18/2002
Recapitalized as American Way Home Based Business Systems, Inc. 04/12/2004
Each share new Common 1¢ par exchanged for (0.01) share Common 1¢ par
American Way Home Based Business Systems, Inc. name changed to American Way Business Development Corp. (DE) 09/30/2004 which reincorporated in Florida as Harvard Learning Centers, Inc. 10/30/2006 which name changed to Americas Learning Centers, Inc. 09/25/2007 which recapitalized as Hackett's Stores, Inc. 01/26/2009 which recapitalized as WiseBuys, Inc. 06/17/2010 which name changed to Empire Pizza Holdings, Inc. 04/20/2011 which recapitalized as Vestiage, Inc. 03/22/2013

DCH TECHNOLOGY INC (DE)
Reincorporated 06/02/2000
State of incorporation changed from (CO) to (DE) 06/02/2000
Recapitalized as Medra Corp. 08/21/2006
Each share Common 1¢ par exchanged for (0.001) share Common 1¢ par

DCI TELECOMMUNICATIONS INC (CO)
Each share old Common $0.0001 par exchanged for (0.0025) share new Common $0.0001 par 03/14/1996
Each share new Common $0.0001 par received distribution of (1) share Corzon Inc. Common 1¢ par payable 01/30/2001 to holders of record 12/06/2000 Ex date - 01/31/2001
Voluntarily dissolved 12/29/2006
Details not available

DCI USA INC (DE)
SEC revoked common stock registration 06/13/2012

DCL INC (DE)
Liquidation completed
Each share Common $0.03333333 par received initial distribution of $2.25 cash 06/25/1980
Each share Common $0.03333333 par exchanged for second distribution of $3.75 cash 01/19/1982
Each share Common $0.03333333 par received third distribution of $0.35 cash 04/10/1984
Each share Common $0.03333333 par received fourth and final distribution of $0.20 cash 02/12/1986

DCM ENTERPRISES INC (NV)
Name changed to Digital Security, Inc. 06/03/2005
Digital Security, Inc. name changed to DLR Funding, Inc. 03/25/2006
(See DLR Funding, Inc.)

DCNY CORP (DE)
Common $1 par changed to 50¢ par and (1) additional share issued 06/07/1985
Common 50¢ par changed to 25¢ par and (1) additional share issued 05/27/1987
Name changed to Discount Corp. of New York (DE) 01/01/1991
(See Discount Corp. of New York (DE))

DCP MIDSTREAM PARTNERS LP (DE)
Name changed to DCP Midstream, L.P. 01/23/2017

DCS COMPUTER SVCS INC (NY)
Adjudicated bankrupt 02/10/1975
Stockholders' equity unlikely

DCS FINL CORP (DE)
Merged into Aero Systems Avionics Corp. 07/22/1976
Each share Common 10¢ par exchanged for $1.25 cash

DCS INTL SYS CORP (BC)
Recapitalized as Step 2 Software Corp. 06/10/1993
Each share Common no par exchanged for (0.2) share Common no par
Step 2 Software Corp. recapitalized as Emergo Software Corp. 11/01/1999 which name changed to eTVtech.com Communications Inc. 03/21/2000 which name changed to eTV Technology Inc. 05/02/2001 which recapitalized as Ocean Park Ventures Corp. 04/02/2009 which recapitalized as Dunnedin Ventures Inc. 08/06/2013

DCT INDL TR INC (MD)
Each share old Common 1¢ par exchanged for (0.25) share new Common 1¢ par 11/18/2014
Merged into Prologis, Inc. 08/22/2018
Each share new Common 1¢ par exchanged for (1.02) shares Common 1¢ par

DCUSA CORP (DE)
Recapitalized as Redox Technology Corp. 06/25/1993
Each share Common $0.0001 par exchanged for (0.1) share Common $0.001 par
Redox Technology Corp. name changed to Midnight Holdings Group, Inc. 03/07/2006

DCW LTD (INDIA)
Reg. S GDR's for Ordinary split (5) for (1) by issuance of (4) additional GDR's payable 10/04/2005 to holders of record 09/26/2005
144A GDR's for Ordinary split (5) for (1) by issuance of (4) additional GDR's payable 10/04/2005 to holders of record 09/26/2005
GDR agreement terminated 11/16/2016
Each Reg. S GDR for Ordinary exchanged for $1.129749 cash
Each 144A GDR for Ordinary exchanged for $1.129749 cash

DCW TOTAL RETURN FD (DE)
Merged into DCA Total Return Fund 09/24/2010
Each share Common $0.001 par exchanged for (1.7527535) shares Common $0.001 par
DCA Total Return Fund name changed to Virtus Total Return Fund 12/22/2011 which merged into Virtus Total Return Fund Inc. 04/03/2017

DCX INC (CO)
Each share old Common no par exchanged for (0.004) share new Common no par 06/09/1989
Name changed to Integrated Spatial Information Solutions, Inc. 07/07/1998
Integrated Spatial Information Solutions, Inc. name changed to PlanGraphics, Inc. (CO) 04/30/2002 which reorganized in Florida as Integrated Freight Corp. 09/07/2010

DDC INDS INC (NV)
Name changed to PHI Mining Group, Inc. 12/19/2008
PHI Mining Group, Inc. name changed to PHI Gold Corp. 01/28/2011

DDD GROUP PLC (ENGLAND & WALES)
ADR agreement terminated 09/21/2016
Each Sponsored ADR for Ordinary exchanged for (10) shares Ordinary
Note: Unexchanged ADR's will be sold and the proceeds, if any, held for claim after 03/21/2017

DDI CORP (DE)
Plan of reorganization under Chapter 11 Federal Bankruptcy Code effective 12/12/2003
Each share Common 1¢ par exchanged for (0.00504783) share old Common $0.001 par
Each share old Common $0.001 par exchanged for (0.14285714) share new Common $0.001 par 02/03/2006
Acquired by Viasystems Group, Inc. 06/01/2012
Each share new Common $0.001 par exchanged for $13 cash

DDI INTL INC (NV)
Name changed to Key Gold Corp. 05/17/2004
Key Gold Corp. name changed to Strategic Resources, Ltd. 12/26/2006
(See Strategic Resources, Ltd.)

DDI PHARMACEUTICALS INC (DE)
Name changed to OXIS International, Inc. 09/08/1994
OXIS International, Inc. recapitalized as GT Biopharma, Inc. 08/21/2017

DDJ CDN HIGH YIELD FD (ON)
Name changed to DDJ High Yield Fund 11/29/2005
(See DDJ High Yield Fund)

DDJ HIGH YIELD FD (ON)
Trust terminated 08/15/2017
Each Trust Unit received $10.450215 cash

DDJ U S HIGH YIELD FD (ON)
Completely liquidated
Each Unit received first and final distribution of $8.70513 cash payable 05/25/2006 to holders of record 05/19/2006

DDL ELECTRS INC (DE)
Name changed to SMTEK International, Inc. 10/09/1998
SMTEK International, Inc. merged into CTS Corp. 02/01/2005

DDR CORP (OH)
7.50% Depositary Preferred Class I called for redemption at $25 plus $0.1875 accrued dividends on 08/20/2012
7.375% Depositary Preferred Class H called for redemption at $25 plus $0.2305 accrued dividends on 05/30/2014
(Additional Information in Active)

DDR SYS INC (WA)
Reorganized as Grand Prix Sports Inc. 03/30/2001
Each share Common $0.0001 par exchanged for (5) shares Common $0.0001 par
Grand Prix Sports Inc. recapitalized as Superclick, Inc. 10/10/2003
(See Superclick, Inc.)

DDS TECHNOLOGIES USA INC (NV)
Company terminated common stock registration and is no longer public as of 03/22/2010

DDS WIRELESS INTL INC (BC)
Acquired by Ghai Investments Ltd. 07/03/2014
Each share Common no par exchanged for $2.25 cash

DE BACA RES INC (BC)
Name changed to Care Point Medical Centres Ltd. 11/13/1985
Care Point Medical Centres Ltd. recapitalized as Consolidated Care Point Medical Centres Ltd. 09/18/1991
(See Consolidated Care Point Medical Centres Ltd.)

DE BARDELEBEN COAL CORP. (DE)
Liquidation completed
Each share Common $1 par exchanged for initial distribution of $100 cash 07/23/1962
Each share Common $1 par received second distribution of $100 cash 10/02/1962
Each share Common $1 par received third distribution of $12.89 cash 05/20/1963
Each share Common $1 par received fourth and final distribution of $0.06 cash 06/07/1963

DE BEERS CONS MINES LTD (SOUTH AFRICA)
Each American share exchanged for (0.4) share Deferred Reg. £2.10s par 05/17/1944
Each share Deferred Reg. £2.10s par exchanged for (10) shares Deferred Reg. 5s par 00/00/1946
Each share Deferred Reg. Rand-50 par exchanged for (10) shares Deferred Reg. Rand-5 par 06/09/1969
Each ADR for Deferred Reg. exchanged for (10) ADR's for Deferred Reg. 06/09/1969
Stock Dividend - ADR's for Deferred Reg. 100% 07/15/1964
Acquired by Anglo American PLC 05/31/2001
Each share Preference Rand-5 par exchanged for approximately $45.94 cash
Each share Deferred Rand-5 par exchanged for approximately $45.94 cash
Each ADR for Deferred Reg. exchanged for (1.784) ADR's for Ordinary and $15.36009 cash

DE BEIRA GOLDFIELDS INC (NV)
Common $0.001 par split (8) for (1) by issuance of (7) additional shares payable 03/23/2006 to holders of record 03/21/2006 Ex date 03/24/2006
Common $0.001 par split (3) for (2) by issuance of (0.5) additional share payable 06/15/2006 to holders of record 06/13/2006 Ex date - 06/16/2006
Name changed to Panex Resources Inc. 09/27/2010

DE BOLES NUTRITIONAL FOODS INC (NY)
Merged into DNF New Corp. 05/18/1992
Each share Common 5¢ par exchanged for $7.50 cash

DE ELECTRONICS INC (NY)
Charter cancelled and proclaimed dissolved for non-payment of taxes 12/15/1969

DE FOREST PHONOFILM CORP. (DE)
No longer in existence having become inoperative and void for non-payment of taxes 04/01/1955

DE FOREST RADIO CO. (DE)
No longer in existence having become inoperative and void for non-payment of taxes 04/01/1934

DE HAVILLAND HOLDINGS LTD. (ENGLAND)
Name changed 03/11/1955
Name changed from De Havilland Aircraft Co. Ltd. to De Havilland Holdings Ltd. 03/11/1955
Acquired by Hawker Siddeley Group Ltd. by exchange offer which expired 02/04/1960
Each share 5.25% Preference £1 par exchanged for (0.75) share 5.25% Preference £1 par and £1 cash
Ordinary £1 par exchanged share for share
(See Hawker Siddeley Group PLC)

DE JUR-AMSCO CORP. LIQUIDATING TRUST (NY)
Liquidation completed
Each share Class A $1 par received third and final distribution of $0.41712 cash 10/15/1980
Note: Previous distributions under De Jur-Amsco Corp.

DE JUR AMSCO CORP (NY)
Liquidation completed
Each share Class A $1 par received initial distribution of $5 cash 09/16/1977
Each share Class A $1 par exchanged for second distribution of $3 cash 10/09/1978
Assets transferred to De Jur-Amsco Corp. Liquidating Trust 06/30/1978
(See De Jur-Amsco Corp. Liquidating Trust)

DE LA RUE P L C (UNITED KINGDOM)
Each ADR for Ordinary Reg. exchanged for (2) ADR's for Ordinary Reg. 03/14/1978
ADR agreement terminated 03/08/2000
Each ADR for Ordinary exchanged for $4.681 cash
(Additional Information in Active)

DE LAURENTIIS ENTMT GROUP INC (DE)
Plan of reorganization under Chapter 11 Federal Bankruptcy proceedings confirmed 05/03/1990
No stockholders' equity

DE LAURENTIIS FILM PARTNERS L P (DE)
Charter cancelled and declared inoperative and void for non-payment of taxes 06/01/1997

DE LAVAL DEV CORP (NJ)
Dissolved and liquidated 05/07/1968
Details not available

DE LAVAL STEAM TURBINE CO. (NJ)
Each share Common $100 par exchanged for (5) shares Common no par 00/00/1952
Common no par split (3) for (2) by issuance of (0.5) additional share 06/30/1959
Name changed to De Laval Development Corp. 05/31/1962
(See De Laval Development Corp.)

DE LONG HOOK & EYE CO. (PA)
Each share Common $100 par exchanged for (5) shares Common $20 par 00/00/1946
Acquired by Scovill Manufacturing Co. 04/01/1955
Each share Common $20 par exchanged for (1.125) shares Common $25 par
Scovill Manufacturing Co. name changed to Scovill Inc. 07/06/1979
(See Scovill Inc.)

DE MUN ESTATE CORP (MO)
Charter dissolved 05/30/1985

DE NIGRIS JOHN ASSOC INC (NY)
Recapitalized as Wien Group, Inc. (NY) 10/17/1974
Each share Common 10¢ par exchanged for (0.166666) share Common 1¢ par
Wien Group, Inc. (NY) reincorporated in New Jersey as MM2 Group, Inc. 10/27/2005
(See MM2 Group, Inc.)

DE ORO MINES INC (NV)
Reorganized as Saf-T-Hammer Corp. 11/03/1998
Each share Common $0.001 par exchanged for (4) shares Common $0.001 par
Saf-T-Hammer Corp. name changed to Smith & Wesson Holding Corp. 03/13/2002 which name changed to

American Outdoor Brands Corp. 01/03/2017

DE PERE FED SVGS & LN ASSN (WI)
Under plan of reorganization each share Common $1 par automatically became (1) share Prime Federal Bank, FSB (De Pere, WI) Common $1 par 03/11/1991
Prime Federal Bank, FSB (De Pere, WI) merged into First Northern Savings Bank, S.A. (Green Bay, WI) 04/29/1994 which reorganized as First Northern Capital Corp. 12/20/1995 which merged into Bank Mutual Corp. (USA) 11/01/2000 which reorganized in Wisconsin 10/29/2003 which merged into Associated Banc-Corp 02/01/2018

DE PINNA (A.) CO.
Merged into Brooks Brothers, Inc. 03/04/1952
Each share 6% Conv. Cum. Preferred $10 par exchanged for (1) share 6% Conv. Cum. Preferred $10 par
Each share Common $1 par exchanged for (1) share Common $1 par
Brooks Brothers, Inc. merged into Garfinckel (Julius) & Co., Inc. 01/31/1957 which name changed to Garfinckel, Brooks Brothers, Miller & Rhoads, Inc. 12/05/1967
(See Garfinckel, Brooks Brothers, Miller & Rhoads, Inc.)

DE RIGO S P A (ITALY)
ADR agreement terminated 02/10/2006
Each Sponsored ADR for Ordinary exchanged for $5.95 cash

DE ROSE INDS INC (IN)
Stock Dividend - 10% 12/31/1970
Out of business 02/28/1995
Stockholders' equity unlikely

DE SANTIS GOLD MINING CO. LTD.
Recapitalized as De Santis Porcupine Mines Ltd. 00/00/1935
Each share Common exchanged for (0.5) share Common
De Santis Porcupine Mines Ltd. was acquired by New Hope Porcupine Gold Mines Ltd. 09/00/1960
(See New Hope Porcupine Gold Mines Ltd.)

DE SANTIS PORCUPINE MINES, LTD. (ON)
Acquired by New Hope Porcupine Gold Mines Ltd. 09/00/1960
Each share Capital stock $1 par exchanged for (0.2) share Capital stock $1 par
(See New Hope Porcupine Gold Mines Ltd.)

DE SOTO APARTMENT CO. (MD)
Common $100 par changed to $25 par 04/14/1943
7% Preferred $100 par called for redemption 04/01/1949
Assets sold and company subsequently liquidated 04/14/1982
Details not available

DE-STA-CO CORP. (MI)
Name changed to H.G.R. Corp. 12/13/1962
(See H.G.R. Corp.)

DE TOMASO INDS INC (MD)
Name changed to Trident Rowan Group, Inc. and Common $2.50 par changed to 1¢ par 08/22/1996
Trident Rowan Group, Inc. name changed to Comtech Group Inc. 08/02/2004 which name changed to Cogo Group, Inc. (MD) 05/13/2008 which reincorporated in Cayman Islands 08/03/2011 which name changed to Viewtran Group, Inc. 11/26/2013

DE VAUX-HALL MOTORS CORP.
Bankrupt 00/00/1933
Details not available

DE VEGH INCOME FUND, INC. (MD)
Name changed to De Vegh Investing Co., Inc. 03/27/1956
De Vegh Investing Co., Inc. merged into Pine Street Fund, Inc. 06/24/1963 which name changed to Winthrop Focus Funds Growth & Income Fund 07/10/1992 which name changed to DLJ Winthrop Opportunity Funds Growth & Income Fund 01/29/1999 which name changed to DLJ Opportunity Funds Growth & Income Funds 08/01/2000 which name changed to Credit Suisse Warburg Pincus Capital Funds 02/06/2001 which name changed to Credit Suisse Capital Funds 12/12/2001

DE VEGH INVESTING CO., INC. (MD)
Merged into Pine Street Fund, Inc. 06/24/1963
Each share Capital Stock $1 par exchanged for (1.5185) shares Common 50¢ par
Pine Street Fund, Inc. name changed to Winthrop Focus Funds Growth & Income Fund 07/10/1992 which name changed to DLJ Winthrop Opportunity Funds Growth & Income Fund 01/29/1999 which name changed to DLJ Opportunity Funds Growth & Income Funds 08/01/2000 which name changed to Credit Suisse Warburg Pincus Capital Funds 02/06/2001 which name changed to Credit Suisse Capital Funds 12/12/2001

DE VEGH MUT FD INC (MD)
Capital Stock $1 par split (3) for (1) by issuance of (2) additional shares 07/23/1985
Stock Dividend - 100% 06/23/1975
Merged into Winthrop Focus Funds 02/28/1996
Each share Capital Stock $1 par exchanged for Aggressive Growth Fund Class A 1¢ par on a net asset basis
Winthrop Focus Funds name changed to DLJ Winthrop Focus Funds 01/29/1999 which name changed to DLJ Focus Funds 08/01/2000 which reorganized as Credit Suisse Warburg Pincus Capital Funds 01/18/2001 which name changed to Credit Suisse Capital Funds 12/12/2001

DE VILBISS CO (OH)
Each share Common $10 par exchanged for (2) shares Common $5 par 00/00/1946
Common $5 par changed to $15 par 04/25/1955
Common $15 par split (2) for (1) by issuance of (1) additional share 05/13/1959
Common $15 par changed to $10 par and (1) additional share issued 10/04/1965
Stock Dividend - 25% 01/17/1955
Merged into Champion Spark Plug Co. 01/01/1970
Each share Common $10 par exchanged for (1) share Common $0.83333333 par
(See Champion Spark Plug Co.)

DE VORE AVIATION CORP (NY)
Name changed 05/01/1974
Name changed from De Vore Aviation Service Corp. to De Vore Aviation Corp. 05/01/1974
Reorganized under the laws of New Mexico as De Vore Aviation Corporation of America 00/00/1991
Each share Common 1¢ par exchanged for (1) share Common 1¢ par

DE WITT HOTEL INC (IL)
Liquidation completed 06/19/1954
Details not available

DEAD ON INC (NV)
Name changed to Conversit.com Inc. 07/13/1999
Conversit.com Inc. name changed to One Voice Technologies, Inc. 09/27/1999
(See One Voice Technologies, Inc.)

DEADMANS PT INC (NV)
Common $0.001 par split (30) for (1) by issuance of (29) additional shares payable 11/10/2000 to holders of record 11/09/2000
Name changed to CobraTech International, Inc. 11/15/2000
CobraTech International, Inc. recapitalized as MetaSource Group, Inc. 05/28/2002
(See MetaSource Group, Inc.)

DEAF-TALK INC (GA)
Merged into Hospico, Inc. 10/21/2014
Each share Common $0.001 par exchanged for (1) share Common 10¢ par
Note: Holders of (99) or fewer shares received $0.02 cash per share
No holder will receive less than $0.10 cash
Company is now private

DEAK NATL BK (FLEISCHMANNS, NY)
Each share Common $10 par exchanged for (2) shares Common $5 par 08/03/1970
Each share Common $5 par exchanged for (2) shares Common $2.50 par 12/31/73
Common $2.50 par changed back to $5 par 09/01/1978
Name changed to American National Bank of New York (Fleischmanns, NY) 06/17/1985
(See American National Bank of New York (Fleischmanns, NY))

DEAK RES CORP (ON)
Name changed 03/27/1989
Name changed from Deak International Resources Corp. to Deak Resources Corp. 03/27/1989
Name changed to AJ Perron Gold Corp. 10/07/1994
(See AJ Perron Gold Corp.)

DEAL CAP LTD (BC)
Name changed to Animas Resources Ltd. 07/16/2007
Animas Resources Ltd. merged into GoGold Resources Ltd. 04/23/2014

DEALCHECK COM INC (ON)
Recapitalized as Bontan Corp. Inc. (ON) 04/17/2003
Each share Common no par exchanged for (0.14285714) share Common no par
Note: Holders of (64) or fewer pre-split shares received $0.21 cash per share
Bontan Corp. Inc. (ON) reincorporated in British Virgin Islands as Portage Biotech Inc. 08/23/2013

DEALERADVANCE INC (NV)
Each share old Common $0.0001 par exchanged for (0.001) share new Common $0.0001 par 02/27/2009
Company terminated common stock registration and is no longer public as of 10/27/2008

DEALERS & CONSUMERS COAL CO. (DE)
Charter cancelled and declared inoperative and void for non-payment of taxes 00/00/1924

DEALERS DISC CORP (SC)
Name changed to Develco, Inc. 08/01/1968
Develco, Inc. name changed to Southern "500" Truck Stops, Inc. 10/31/1974
(See Southern "500" Truck Stops, Inc.)

DEALERTRACK TECHNOLOGIES INC (DE)
Name changed 12/10/2012
Name changed from DealerTrack Holdings, Inc. to Dealertrack Technologies, Inc. 12/10/2012
Acquired by Cox Automotive, Inc. 10/01/2015
Each share Common 1¢ par exchanged for $63.25 cash

DEALS ARE AMERN INC (NV)
Name changed to American Visual Appliances, Inc. 12/06/1990
(See American Visual Appliances, Inc.)

DEALS ARE GOOD INC (NV)
Name changed to Linkon Corp. 12/31/1990
Linkon Corp. recapitalized as Packetport.com, Inc. 12/08/1999 which name changed to Wyndstorm Corp. 05/05/2008
(See Wyndstorm Corp.)

DEAN & CO (DE)
6% Preferred $10 par called for redemption 01/01/1962
Liquidated and dissolved 04/25/1984
Details not available

DEAN (W.E.) & CO.
Name changed to Dean & Co. 00/00/1950
(See Dean & Co.)

DEAN BROTHERS PUMPS, INC. (IN)
Merged into Met-Pro Corp. (DE) 07/20/1984
Each share Common $5 par exchanged for (3) shares Common 10¢ par and $52.25 cash
Note: Option to receive either (8.65) shares Common 10¢ par, $80 cash or a combination thereof expired 07/30/1984
Met-Pro Corp. (DE) reincorporated in Pennsylvania 07/31/2003 which merged into CECO Environmental Corp. 08/27/2013

DEAN ELECTRIC CO. (OH)
Incorporated 00/00/1903
Proclaimed dissolved for failure to pay taxes 08/02/1907

DEAN ELECTRIC CO. (OH)
Incorporated 00/00/1906
Proclaimed dissolved for failure to pay taxes 09/22/1919

DEAN FOODS CO OLD (DE)
Reincorporated 05/23/1968
State of incorporation changed from (IL) to (DE) and Common no par changed to $1 par 05/23/1968
Common $1 par split (3) for (2) by issuance of (0.5) additional share 04/21/1976
Common $1 par split (3) for (2) by issuance of (0.5) additional share 05/03/1977
Common $1 par split (3) for (2) by issuance of (0.5) additional share 09/13/1978
Common $1 par split (2) for (1) by issuance of (1) additional share 05/08/1981
Common $1 par split (3) for (2) by issuance of (0.5) additional share 05/10/1983
Common $1 par split (3) for (2) by issuance of (0.5) additional share 04/24/1984
Common $1 par split (3) for (2) by issuance of (0.5) additional share 06/16/1986
Common $1 par split (3) for (2) by issuance of (0.5) additional share 09/03/1991
Merged into Dean Foods Co. (New) 12/21/2001
Each share Common $1 par exchanged for (0.429) share Common 1¢ par and $21 cash

DEAN INDS INC (DE)
Name changed to Autocafe Systems, Inc. 12/2/88
(See Autocafe Systems, Inc.)

DEAN MILK CO. (IL)
Each share old Common no par exchanged for (1.666666) shares new Common no par 5/15/61
Name changed to Dean Foods Co. (IL) 4/27/63
Dean Foods Co. (IL) reincorporated in Delaware 5/23/68 which merged into Dean Foods Co. (New) 12/21/2001

DEAN PHIPPS STORES INC (PA)
Acquired by General Acceptance Corp. 05/22/1968
Details not available

DEAN RESH CORP (MO)
Filed petition under Chapter 7 Federal Bankruptcy Code 07/00/1991
No stockholders' equity

DEAN VAN LINES, INC. (CA)
Name changed to Pan American Van Lines, Inc. 6/13/72
Pan American Van Lines, Inc. merged into MPS International Corp. 1/19/73
(See MPS International Corp.)

DEAN WITTER & CO. INC. (DE)
See - Witter (Dean) & Co. Inc.

DEAN WITTER AMER VALUE FD (MD)
Name changed 04/30/1987
Name changed from Dean Witter Industry-Valued Securities Inc. to Dean Witter American Value Fund 04/30/1987
Name changed to Morgan Stanley Dean Witter American Value Fund 05/00/997
Morgan Stanley Dean Witter American Value Fund name changed to Morgan Stanley Dean Witter American Opportunities Fund 03/12/1999 which name changed to Morgan Stanley American Opportunities Fund 06/18/2001

DEAN WITTER CAP GROWTH SECS (MA)
Shares of Bene. Int. 1¢ par reclassified as Shares of Bene. Int. Class B 1¢ par 03/04/1997
Merged into Morgan Stanley Dean Witter Capital Growth Securities 06/22/1998
Details not available

DEAN WITTER DISCOVER & CO (DE)
Common 1¢ par split (2) for (1) by issuance of (1) additional share payable 1/14/97 to holders of record 12/26/96 Ex date - 1/15/97
Under plan of merger name changed to Morgan Stanley, Dean Witter, Discover & Co. 5/31/97
Morgan Stanley, Dean Witter, Discover & Co. name changed to Morgan Stanley 6/20/2002

DEAN WITTER GOVT INCOME TR (MA)
Name changed to Morgan Stanley Dean Witter 12/21/1998
Morgan Stanley Dean Witter name changed to Morgan Stanley Trusts 12/20/2001
(See Morgan Stanley Trusts)

DEAN WITTER HIGH YIELD SECS INC (MD)
Common 10¢ par reclassified as Class D 1¢ par 07/28/1997
Name changed to Morgan Stanley Dean Witter High Yield Securities Inc. 06/22/1998
Morgan Stanley Dean Witter High Yield Securities Inc. name changed to Morgan Stanley High Yield Securities Inc. 06/18/2001 which name changed to Invesco High Yield Securities Fund 06/01/2010

DEAN WITTER ORGANIZATION INC. (DE)
See - Witter (Dean) Organization Inc.

DEAN WITTER RLTY YIELD PLUS L P (DE)
Partnership terminated registration of Units of Ltd Partnership Int. II on 01/01/2003
Details not available
Completely liquidated 03/26/2003
Each Unit of Ltd Partnership Int. received first and final distribution of approximately $0.41 cash

DEAN WITTER REYNOLDS ORGANIZATION INC. (DE)
See - Witter (Dean) Reynolds Organization Inc.

DEAN WITTER SEARS CALIF TAX FREE DAILY INCOME TR (CA)
Name changed to Dean Witter California Tax-Free Daily Income Trust 2/19/93

DEAN WITTER SEARS LIQUID ASSET FD INC (MD)
Name changed to Dean Witter Liquid Asset Fund Inc. 2/19/93

DEAN'S PRIDE, INC. (CO)
Name changed to Cloud Nine, Inc. 7/11/60
(See Cloud Nine, Inc.)

DEANS GEOGRAPHICS LTD. (BC)
Name changed to Deans Industries Ltd. 02/27/1975
Deans Industries Ltd. recapitalized as International Geographics Ltd. 10/12/1976 which was acquired by Geographics, Inc. (WY) 07/29/1991 which reincorporated in Delaware 10/18/2000
(See Geographics, Inc.)

DEANS INDS LTD (BC)
Recapitalized as International Geographics Ltd. 10/12/1976
Each share Common no par exchanged for (0.2) share Common no par
International Geographics Ltd. was acquired by Geographics, Inc. (WY) 07/29/1991 which reincorporated in Delaware 10/18/2000
(See Geographics, Inc.)

DEANS KNIGHT INCOME & GROWTH FD (ON)
Completely liquidated 09/29/2011
Each Unit received first and final distribution of $7.283 cash

DEARBORN BANCORP INC (MI)
Stock Dividends - 2% payable 01/15/1999 to holders of record 12/24/1998; 5% payable 06/15/2001 to holders of record 05/31/2001 Ex date - 05/29/2001; 5% payable 12/28/2001 to holders of record 12/07/2001 Ex date - 12/05/2001; 5% payable 06/21/2002 to holders of record 06/07/2002; 5% payable 01/17/2003 to holders of record 12/27/2002 Ex date - 12/24/2002; 5% payable 06/20/2003 to holders of record 06/06/2003 Ex date - 06/04/2003; 5% payable 12/19/2003 to holders of record 12/05/2003; Ex date - 12/03/2003; 5% payable 06/18/2004 to holders of record 06/04/2004; 5% payable 12/17/2004 to holders of record 12/03/2004; 5% payable 06/17/2005 to holders of record 06/03/2005 Ex date - 06/01/2005; 5% payable 12/16/2005 to holders of record 12/02/2005 Ex date - 11/30/2005; 5% payable 06/16/2006 to holders of record 06/02/2006 Ex date - 05/31/2006; 5% payable 12/22/2006 to holders of record 12/08/2006 Ex date - 12/06/2006
Filed a petition under Chapter 7 Federal Bankruptcy Code 03/11/2013
Stockholders' equity unlikely

DEARBORN BK & TR CO (DEARBORN, MI)
Reorganized as Alliance Financial Corp. 10/01/1983
Each share Common $10 par exchanged for (1) share Common $10 par
(See Alliance Financial Corp.)

DEARBORN CLARIDGE CO. (IL)
Liquidation completed
Each share Common no par exchanged for initial distribution of $75 cash 2/3/67
Each share Common no par received second distribution of $15 cash 3/21/68
Each share Common no par received third and final distribution of $5 cash 10/6/70

DEARBORN COMPUTER & MARINE CORP (DE)
Name changed to Dearborn-Storm Corp. 03/03/1971
Dearborn-Storm Corp. name changed to Storm Drilling & Marine, Inc. 04/09/1974
(See Storm Drilling & Marine, Inc.)

DEARBORN COMPUTER CORP (DE)
Name changed to Dearborn Computer & Marine Corp. 02/06/1969
Dearborn Computer & Marine Corp. name changed to Dearborn-Storm Corp. 03/03/1971 which name changed to Storm Drilling & Marine, Inc. 04/09/1974
(See Storm Drilling & Marine, Inc.)

DEARBORN FINL CORP (DE)
Common $10 par changed to $1 par and (1) additional share issued 03/18/1976
Preferred Ser. A no par called for redemption 05/01/1979
Liquidation completed
Each share Common $1 par exchanged for initial distribution of $17.32 cash 07/24/1981
Each share Common $1 par received second and final distribution of $10.5581 cash 04/05/1985

DEARBORN FINL CORP (IN)
Reorganized under the laws of Delaware as DSA Financial Corp. 7/28/2004
Each share Common 10¢ par exchanged for (3.3926) shares Common 1¢ par

DEARBORN SVGS ASSN F A (IN)
Name changed to Dearborn Financial Corp. (IN) 4/22/99
Dearborn Financial Corp. (IN) reorganized in Delaware as DSA Financial Corp. 7/28/2004

DEARBORN-STORM CORP (DE)
Common $4 par split (2) for (1) by issuance of (1) additional share 11/09/1971
Name changed to Storm Drilling & Marine, Inc. 04/09/1974
(See Storm Drilling & Marine, Inc.)

DEARBORN TRUCK CO. (DE)
Charter cancelled and declared inoperative and void for non-payment of taxes 3/17/26

DEARBORN URANIUM MINES LTD. (ON)
Charter cancelled 02/05/1980

DEARDORF DRILLING CORP. (DE)
Acquired by Deardorf Oil Corp. on a (0.25) for (1) basis in 1949
(See Deardorf Oil Corp.)

DEARDORF OIL CORP. (DE)
Became inoperative and void for non-payment of taxes 4/1/57

DEATH VALLEY RES LTD (BC)
Name changed to DVR Resources Ltd. 4/12/89
DVR Resources Ltd. recapitalized as Gresham Resources Inc. 6/14/93 which was acquired by True Energy Inc. 7/31/2002
(See True Energy Inc.)

DEB SHOPS INC (PA)
Common 1¢ par split (3) for (2) by issuance of (0.5) additional share 07/01/1985
Common 1¢ par split (2) for (1) by issuance of (1) additional share 04/17/1987
Merged into DSI Holdings, LLC 10/23/2007
Each share Common 1¢ par exchanged for $27.25 cash

DEB YELLOWKNIFE GOLD MINES, LTD. (ON)
Charter revoked for failure to file reports and pay taxes 11/7/55

DEBARDELEBEN MARINE CORP (DE)
Completely liquidated 02/19/1969
Each share Common 50¢ par exchanged for first and final distribution of (0.1) share Detsco, Inc. Common 10¢ par
(See Detsco, Inc.)

DEBARTOLO RLTY CORP (OH)
Merged into Simon DeBartolo Group, Inc. 08/09/1996
Each share Common 1¢ par exchanged for (0.68) share Common $0.0001 par
Simon DeBartolo Group, Inc. merged into Simon Property Group, Inc. (DE) 09/24/1998

DEBE SYS CORP (DE)
Common 10¢ par changed to 1¢ par and (3) additional shares issued 1/17/84
Charter cancelled and declared inoperative and void for non-payment of taxes 3/1/89

DEBENHAMS LTD. (ENGLAND)
Reorganized 02/26/1968
Each share 6.5% 1st Preference £1 par or 6.5% 2nd Preference £1 par exchanged for £100 principal amount of 7.25% Loan Stock due 07/25/2002/07
Each share 3rd Preference 10s par exchanged for £100 principal amount of 7.75% Loan Stock due 07/25/2002/07
Holders had following options:
Retain each share 6.5% 1st Preference £1 par which was reclassified as 6.5% A Preference £1 par and receive (0.015) additional share
Retain each share 6.5% 2nd Preference £1 par which was reclassified as 6.5% A Preference £1 par and receive (0.01) additional share Retain each share 7% 3rd Preference 10s par which was reclassified as 7% B Preference 10s par and receive (0.005) additional share Option to retain old stock expired 02/26/1968 after which date old stock could only be exchanged
(Additional Information in Active)

DEBENHAMS SECURITIES, LTD.
Acquired by Debenhams, Ltd. 00/00/1934
Details not available

DEBHOLD CDA LTD (ON)
Merged into Anglo American Corp. of Canada Ltd. 01/30/1980
Each share 6% Preference Ser. A $100 par exchanged for (1) share 6% Preference Ser. A $100 par
Each share 6.25% Preference Ser. B $100 par exchanged for (1) share 6.25% Preference Ser. B $100 par
Anglo American Corp. of Canada Ltd. name changed to Minorco Canada Ltd. 08/28/1981
(See Minorco Canada Ltd.)

DEBRON CORP (DE)
Merged into Bristol Steel & Ironworks Inc. 05/31/1978
Each share Common $5 par exchanged for $28 cash

DEBRON INVTS PLC (ENGLAND)
Merged into Interface Overseas Inc. 10/30/1987
Each ADR for Ordinary Reg. exchanged for $5.688 cash

DEBT STRATEGIES FD INC NEW (MD)
Name changed to BlackRock Debt Strategies Fund Inc. 10/02/2006

DEBT STRATEGIES FD INC OLD (MD)
Merged into Debt Strategies Fund Inc. (New) 11/06/2000
Each share Common 1¢ par exchanged for (0.847782) share Common 10¢ par
Debt Strategies Fund Inc. (New) name changed to BlackRock Debt Strategies Fund Inc. 10/02/2006

DEBT STRATEGIES FD II INC (MD)
Under plan of merger name changed to Debt Strategies Fund Inc. (New) 11/06/2000
Debt Strategies Fund Inc. (New) name changed to BlackRock Debt Strategies Fund Inc. 10/02/2006

DEBT STRATEGIES FD III INC (MD)
Merged into Debt Strategies Fund Inc. (New) 11/06/2000
Each share Common no par exchanged for (1.094308) shares Common 10¢ par
Debt Strategies Fund Inc. (New) name changed to BlackRock Debt Strategies Fund Inc. 10/02/2006

DEBTOR CORP. (NC)
Administratively dissolved 04/14/1993

DEBUT BROADCASTING CORP INC (NV)
SEC revoked common stock registration 07/08/2014

DECA ENERGY CORP (NV)
Acquired by K.R.M. Petroleum Corp. 11/20/1986
Each share Common 1¢ par exchanged for (0.2) share Common 10¢ par
K.R.M. Petroleum Corp. name changed to PrimeEnergy Corp. 05/17/1990

DECADE DEV LTD (BC)
Recapitalized as Decade International Development Ltd. 07/04/1986
Each share Common 50¢ par exchanged for (0.2) share Common no par
Decade International Development Ltd. recapitalized as Seymour Exploration Corp. 04/11/2002 which name changed to Independent Nickel Corp. (BC) 06/21/2006 which reincorporated in Ontario 09/11/2007 which merged into Victory Nickel Inc. 01/05/2009

DECADE FD 1967 INC (DE)
Charter cancelled and declared inoperative and void for non-payment of taxes 04/15/1973

DECADE INTL DEV LTD (BC)
Recapitalized as Seymour Exploration Corp. 04/11/2002
Each share Common no par exchanged for (1/7) share Common no par
Seymour Exploration Corp. name changed to Independent Nickel Corp. (BC) 06/21/2006 which reincorporated in Ontario 09/11/2007 which merged into Victory Nickel Inc. 01/05/2009

DECAIR CORP (DE)
Common 1¢ par split (5) for (2) by issuance of (1.5) additional shares 07/01/1986

Name changed to Lynton Group Inc. 06/27/1989
(See Lynton Group Inc.)

DECALTA OILS LTD. (CANADA)
Recapitalized as Canadian Decalta Gas & Oils Ltd. 04/28/1952
Each share Capital Stock no par exchanged for (0.33333333) share Capital Stock no par
Canadian Decalta Gas & Oils Ltd. recapitalized as Western Decalta Petroleum Ltd. 11/22/1956
(See Western Decalta Petroleum Ltd.)

DECATUR CAP CORP (GA)
Adjustable Rate Preferred $1 par called for redemption 03/01/1990
Public interest eliminated

DECATUR FINL INC (IN)
Merged into First Merchants Corp. 05/31/2000
Each share Common exchanged for (9.13) shares Common no par

DECCA LTD (ENGLAND)
Acquired by Racal Electronics Ltd. 09/07/1980
Details not available

DECCA RECORD CO. LTD. (ENGLAND)
Ordinary 4s par changed to 10s par 02/26/1959
Name changed to Decca Ltd. 04/02/1962
(See Decca Ltd.)

DECCA RECORDS, INC. (NY)
Each share Capital Stock $1 par exchanged for (2) shares Capital Stock 50¢ par 00/00/1946
Merged into MCA, Inc. 01/01/1966
Each share Capital Stock 50¢ par exchanged for $48.50 cash

DECCA RES LTD (BC)
Name changed to Sceptre Resources Ltd. (BC) 12/27/1977
Sceptre Resources Ltd. (BC) reincorporated in Canada 10/31/1979 which merged into Canadian Natural Resources Ltd. 08/15/1996

DECHERT DYNAMICS CORP (DE)
Acquired by Dechert Corp. 03/31/2000
Each share Common 10¢ par exchanged for $8 cash

DECICOM SYS INC (DE)
Name changed to Euclid Equipment Inc. 07/08/1981
Euclid Equipment Inc. merged into Wedtech Corp. 12/16/1985
(See Wedtech Corp.)

DECISION CAP CORP (DE)
Name changed to Acrodyne Holdings, Inc. 10/24/1994
Acrodyne Holdings, Inc. name changed to Acrodyne Communications, Inc. 06/09/1995
(See Acrodyne Communications, Inc.)

DECISION CAP FD INC (MD)
Name changed to Hopper Soliday Corp. 07/06/1987
(See Hopper Soliday Corp.)

DECISION DATA COMPUTER CORP (PA)
Reincorporated 01/31/1973
State of incorporation changed from (DE) to (PA) 01/31/1973
Name changed to Decision Industries Corp. 06/02/1986
(See Decision Industries Corp.)

DECISION DYNAMICS TECHNOLOGY LTD (CANADA)
Merged into Acorn Energy, Inc. 05/14/2010
Each share Common no par exchanged for (0.0162) share Common 1¢ par

DECISION INDS CORP (PA)
Acquired by Onset Corp. (NY) 04/29/1988

Each share Common 10¢ par exchanged for $11 cash

DECISION SYS INC (DE)
Stock Dividend - 50% 11/02/1978
Charter cancelled and declared inoperative and void for non-payment of taxes 03/01/1994

DECISIONLINK CORP (DE)
SEC revoked preferred and common stock registration 05/08/2008

DECISIONONE HLDGS CORP NEW (DE)
Plan of reorganization under Chapter 11 Federal Bankruptcy Code effective 04/18/2000
No stockholders' equity

DECISIONONE HLDS CORP OLD (DE)
Name changed 03/11/1996
Name changed from DecisionOne Corp. to DecisionOne Holdings Corp. (Old) 03/11/1996
Merged into Donaldson, Lufkin & Jenrette, Inc. (New) 08/07/1997
Each share Common 1¢ par exchanged for either (1) share DecisionOne Holdings Corp. (New) Common 1¢ par or $23 cash
Note: Option to receive stock expired 08/06/1997
(See DecisionOne Holdings Corp. (New))

DECISIONPOINT SYS INC NEW (DE)
Each share 8% Conv. Preferred Ser. D $0.001 par exchanged for (0.572185) share new Common $0.001 par 10/05/2016
(Additional Information in Active)

DECISIONPOINT SYS INC OLD (DE)
Merged into Comamtech Inc. (ON) 06/15/2011
Each share Common $0.001 par exchanged for (0.13826038) share Common no par
Comamtech Inc. (ON) reincorporated in Delaware as DecisionPoint Systems, Inc. (New) 06/22/2011

DECITRON ELECTRS CORP (NY)
Adjudicated bankrupt 06/10/1971
Stockholders' equity unlikely

DECKER (ALFRED) & COHN, INC.
Reorganized as Society Brand Clothes, Inc. 00/00/1946
Each share Common $10 par exchanged for (3) shares Common $1 par
Society Brand Clothes, Inc. name changed to Industrial Development Corp. 00/00/1954
(See Industrial Development Corp.)

DECKER (JACOB E.) & SONS
Assets sold 00/00/1935
Details not availbale

DECKER LAKE MINES LTD (BC)
Name changed to Decker Resources Ltd. 05/09/1983
(See Decker Resources Ltd.)

DECKER MFG CORP (MI)
Name changed to Decker Nut Manufacturing Corp. 12/24/1956
Decker Nut Manufacturing Corp. name changed to Decker Manufacturing Corp. 03/31/1971

DECKER MOHN INC (NY)
Name changed to Brighter Community, Inc. (NY) 09/18/1989
Brighter Community, Inc. (NY) reincorporated in Delaware 09/18/1989
(See Brighter Community, Inc.)

DECKER NUT MFG CORP (MI)
Stock Dividend - 200% 07/02/1965
Name changed to Decker Manufacturing Corp. 03/31/1971

DECKER RES LTD (BC)
Struck off register and declared dissolved for failure to file returns 09/18/1992

DECLAN RES INC (BC)
Each share old Common no par exchanged for (0.03333333) share new Common no par 07/19/2017
Name changed to Declan Cobalt Inc. 08/30/2018

DECO ALUM INC (PA)
Name changed to Deco Industries, Inc. 04/07/1969
Deco Industries, Inc. name changed to First Estate Group Ltd. (PA) 06/01/1985 which reincorporated in Colorado as Companies West Group Inc. 10/09/1986

DECO INDS INC (PA)
Name changed to First Estate Group Ltd. (PA) 06/01/1985
First Estate Group Ltd. (PA) reincorporated in Colorado as Companies West Group Inc. 10/09/1986

DECO PLANTMINDER INC (BC)
Recapitalized as Canterbury Resources Inc. 07/24/1986
Each share Common no par exchanged for (0.33333333) share Common no par
(See Canterbury Resources Inc.)

DECODE GENETICS INC (DE)
Plan of reorganization under Chapter 11 Federal Bankruptcy proceedings effective 06/10/2010
No stockholders' equity

DECOM SYS INC (CA)
Merged into Coded Communications Corp. 08/27/1993
Each share Common no par exchanged for (0.238) share Common no par
(See Coded Communications Corp.)

DECOMA INTL INC (ON)
Merged into Magna International Inc. 03/06/2005
Each share Class A Subordinate no par exchanged for (0.1453) share Class A Subordinate no par

DECOR CORP (OH)
Common 1¢ par split (3) for (2) by issuance of (0.5) additional share 07/03/1985
Acquired by Claire's Stores, Inc. (DE) 12/15/1989
Each share Common 1¢ par exchanged for (0.1224) share Common 5¢ par
Claire's Stores, Inc. (DE) reincorporated in Florida 06/30/2000
(See Claire's Stores, Inc.)

DECOR GROUP INC (DE)
Common $0.0001 par split (3) for (1) by issuance of (2) additional shares payable 12/20/1996 to holders of record 12/16/1996
Each share old Common $0.0001 par exchanged for (0.33333333) share new Common $0.0001 par 10/09/1997
Company terminated common stock registration 03/28/2000

DECOR PRODS INTL INC (NV)
Reorganized 05/25/2010
Reorganized from Florida to under the laws of Nevada 05/25/2010
Each share Common $0.001 par exchanged for (0.33333333) share Common $0.001 par
Recapitalized as ViaDerma, Inc. 05/06/2014
Each share Common $0.001 par exchanged for (0.02) share Common $0.001 par

DECORA INDS INC (DE)
Each share old Common no par exchanged for (0.2) share new Common 12/29/1997
Chapter 11 bankruptcy proceedings converted to Chapter 7 on 10/21/2002
Stockholders' equity unlikely

DECORATOR INDS INC (PA)
Common no par split (2) for (1) by issuance of (1) additional share 12/11/1967
Common no par split (2) for (1) by issuance of (1) additional share 03/20/1968
Common no par split (3) for (2) by issuance of (0.5) additional share 12/27/1968
Common no par changed to 10¢ par 06/30/1977
Each share Common 10¢ par exchanged for (0.5) share Common 20¢ par 07/30/1982
Common 20¢ par split (3) for (2) by issuance of (0.5) additional share 12/11/1984
Common 20¢ par split (2) for (1) by issuance of (1) additional share 04/22/1993
Common 20¢ par split (4) for (3) by issuance of (0.33333333) additional share payable 06/17/1996 to holders of record 06/10/1996 Ex date - 06/18/1996
Common 20¢ par split (5) for (4) by issuance of (0.25) additional share payable 06/13/1997 to holders of record 06/04/1997 Ex date - 06/16/1997
Common 20¢ par split (5) for (4) by issuance of (0.25) additional share payable 07/21/1998 to holders of record 07/07/1998 Ex date - 07/22/1998
Plan of reorganization under Chapter 11 Federal Bankruptcy proceedings effective 10/15/2012
No stockholders' equity

DECORIZE INC (DE)
Recapitalized as GuildMaster, Inc. 11/04/2009
Each share Common $0.001 par exchanged for (0.2) share Common $0.001 par
(See GuildMaster, Inc.)

DECORP INC (TX)
Merged into DCI Acquisition Co. 10/09/1990
Each share Common $0.0001 par exchanged for $2.9075502 cash

DECORSTONE INDS INC (BC)
Delisted from Vancouver Stock Exchange 03/02/1990

DECOURCY CAP CORP (BC)
Merged into Aztech Innovations Inc. 04/16/2010
Each share Common no par exchanged for (1) share Common no par

DECOURSEY-BREWIS MINERALS LTD. (ON)
Recapitalized as Consolidated Brewis Minerals Ltd. 01/20/1964
Each share Capital Stock $1 par exchanged for (0.8) shares Common $1 par
Consolidated Brewis Minerals Ltd. merged into Beauty Counselors of Canada Ltd. 12/01/1981 which name changed to Beauty Counselors International, Inc. 09/22/1982 which recapitalized as Century Technologies Inc. 01/10/1989
(See Century Technologies Inc.)

DECOY ENERGY, INC. (UT)
Recapitalized as New Health Technologies, Inc. 03/28/1984
Each share Common $0.0001 par exchanged for (1) share Common $0.001 par
(See New Health Technologies, Inc.)

DECRAFORM INC (FL)
Each share Common 2¢ par exchanged for (0.25) share Common 8¢ par 11/06/1972
Adjudicated bankrupt 03/07/1977
Stockholders' equity unlikely

DECRANE AIRCRAFT HLDGS INC (DE)
Merged into DeCrane Acquisition Co. 09/02/1998
Each share Common 1¢ par exchanged for $23 cash

DECS TR (DE)
Each Debt Equity Convertible Security exchanged for (1) share DIMON Inc. Common no par 08/15/2000
DIMON Inc. name changed to Alliance One International, Inc. 05/13/2005

DECS TR II (DE)
Each Debt Equity Convertible Security exchanged for (1) share Royal Group Technologies Ltd. Subordinate no par 11/15/2000
(See Royal Group Technologies Ltd.)

DECS TR IX (DE)
Each Debt Equity Convertible Security exchanged for (1) share LaBranche & Co., Inc. Common 1¢ par 02/15/2005

DECTRON INTERNATIONALE INC (CANADA)
Acquired by 6997007 Canada Inc. 08/18/2008
Each share Common no par exchanged for $4.20 cash

DEE CEE CORP. (LA)
Voluntarily dissolved 05/09/1963
Details not available

DEEAS RES INC (NV)
Reorganized as GTX Corp. 03/14/2008
Each share Common $0.001 par exchanged for (20.71) shares Common $0.001 par

DEEKS INC (UT)
Name changed to Major Petroleum Co. 03/26/1976
Major Petroleum Co. name changed to Tyche Petroleum Corp. 03/16/1977

DEELKRAAL GOLD MNG LTD (SOUTH AFRICA)
Each Unsponsored ADR for Ordinary exchanged for (1) Sponsored ADR for Ordinary 12/27/1994
Scheme of arrangement effective 12/21/1997
Each Sponsored ADR for Ordinary exchanged for (0.2) Elandsrand Gold Mining Co. Ltd. ADR for Ordinary or $0.7214 cash
Note: Unexchanged ADR's were sold and holders received $0.7214 cash per ADR after 06/21/1998
Elandsrand Gold Mining Ltd. merged into AngloGold Ltd. 06/29/1998 which name changed to AngloGold Ashanti Ltd. 04/26/2004

DEENA ENERGY INC (CANADA)
Recapitalized 06/29/1994
Recapitalized from Deena Explorations Ltd. to Deena Energy Inc. 06/29/1994
Each share Common no par exchanged for (0.25) share Common no par
Struck off register and declared dissolved for failure to file returns 09/12/2002

DEEP BASIN ENERGY INC (AB)
Recapitalized 09/28/1995
Recapitalized from Deep Basin Petroleum Corp. to Deep Basin Energy Inc. 09/28/1995
Each share Common no par exchanged for (0.25) share Common no par
Name changed to Calibre Energy Inc. 06/26/1997
(See Calibre Energy Inc.)

DEEP BLUE INC (NV)
Recapitalized as Bell Rose Capital, Inc. 03/05/2014
Each share Common $0.001 par exchanged for (0.00048496) share Common $0.001 par

DEEP DRAWING CORP. (MI)
Name changed to Metal Flo Corp. 05/28/1968
Metal Flo Corp. merged into AO Industries, Inc. 09/01/1971 which name changed to Aegis Corp. 06/01/1974
(See Aegis Corp.)

DEEP EARTH INC (NV)
Name changed to Castpro.com, Inc. 11/29/1999
Castpro.com, Inc. name changed to Thaon Communications, Inc. 11/27/2000 which recapitalized as PracticeXpert, Inc. 07/21/2003
(See PracticeXpert, Inc.)

DEEP GAS EXPL INC (UT)
Name changed to Ratex Resources Inc. 06/07/1985
(See Ratex Resources Inc.)

DEEP RES LTD (AB)
Merged into Choice Resources Corp. 08/01/2006
Each share Common no par exchanged for (0.285714) share Common no par and (0.1) Common Stock Purchase Warrant expiring 07/21/2007
Choice Resources Corp. merged into Buffalo Resources Corp. 08/03/2007 which merged into Twin Butte Energy Ltd. 10/15/2009

DEEP ROCK OIL & GAS INC (NV)
Voluntarily dissolved 09/15/2016
Details not available

DEEP ROCK OIL CORP. (DE)
Reorganized 00/00/1941
Each share Preferred no par exchanged for (2) shares Common $1 par
Common no par had no equity
Name changed to Crescent Corp. 07/13/1955
Crescent Corp. name changed to Crescent Petroleum Corp. 04/16/1958 which name changed back to Crescent Corp. 12/16/1963 which merged into National Industries, Inc. (KY) 07/01/1968 which merged into Fuqua Industries, Inc. 01/03/1978 which name changed to Actava Group Inc. 07/21/1993 which name changed to Metromedia International Group, Inc. 11/01/1995
(See Metromedia International Group, Inc.)

DEEP SEA TECHNIQUES INC (NY)
Dissolved by proclamation 06/27/1979

DEEP SHAFT TECHNOLOGY INTL INC (BC)
Name changed to Noram Environmental Solutions Inc. (BC) 11/10/1988
Noram Environmental Solutions Inc. (BC) reincorporated in Alberta 02/27/1997 which name changed to Alternative Fuel Systems Inc 07/07/1997
(See Alternative Fuel Systems Inc.)

DEEP SOUTH PETE INC (BC)
Recapitalized as Gold Texas Resources Ltd. 08/22/1985
Each share Common no par exchanged for (0.5) share Common no par
Gold Texas Resources Ltd. acquired by Crown Resources Corp. 12/01/1989 which was acquired by Kinross Gold Corp. 08/31/2006

DEEP WTR INVTS INC (NV)
Reorganized 09/17/2004
Reorganized from (Canada) to under the laws of Nevada 09/17/2004
Each share Common no par exchanged for (0.00333333) share Common $0.0001 par

Charter revoked for failure to file reports and pay fees 08/31/2006

DEEPGREEN MINERALS CORP N L (AUSTRALIA)
ADR agreement terminated 05/19/2000
Each ADR for Ordinary exchanged for $0.0043 cash

DEEPSKY WEBMARKET LTD (AUSTRALIA)
Name changed to Monteray Group Ltd. 12/18/2001
Monteray Group Ltd. name changed to Monteray Mining Group Ltd. 09/26/2011 which name changed to Norwood Systems Ltd. 03/31/2016

DEEPTECH INTL INC (DE)
Merged into El Paso Energy Corp. 08/14/1998
Each share Common 1¢ par exchanged for $14 cash

DEEPWELL ENERGY SVCS TR (AB)
Reorganized as Palko Environmental Ltd. 06/16/2010
Each Unit no par exchanged for (1) share Common no par
Note: Unexchanged certificates were cancelled and became without value 06/16/2016
(See Palko Environmental Ltd.)

DEER BAY RES INC (NV)
Name changed to Bioflamex Corp. (NV) 02/08/2011
Bioflamex Corp. (NV) reincorporated in Wyoming 02/20/2013 which name changed to Canamed4Pets, Inc. 03/25/2015

DEER CREEK ENERGY LTD (AB)
Merged into Total E&P Canada Ltd. 12/13/2005
Each share Common no par exchanged for $31 cash

DEER HORN METALS INC (CANADA)
Each share old Common no par exchanged for (0.1) share new Common no par 05/14/2014
Name changed to Deer Horn Capital Inc. 10/07/2014

DEER HORN MINES LTD (ON)
Capital Stock $1 par changed to no par 07/26/1972
Charter cancelled for failure to pay taxes and file returns 10/18/1978

DEER LAKE MINES LTD (BC)
Merged into Nithex Exploration Ltd. 06/08/1976
Each share Common 50¢ par exchanged for (1) share Common no par
Nithex Exploration Ltd. name changed to Lintex Minerals Ltd. 06/01/1983 which recapitalized as New Lintex Minerals Ltd. 12/07/1987 which merged into Globaltex Industries Inc. 03/05/1993 which name changed to Pine Valley Mining Corp. 05/14/2003

DEER PARK BAKING CO (NJ)
Stock Dividend - 10% 03/02/1970
Merged into HJ & Sons Ltd. 02/15/1984
Each share Common 25¢ par exchanged for $12.50 cash

DEER PK PRODUCTIONS INC (DE)
Name changed to Deer Park Technology, Inc. 08/02/2001
Deer Park Technology, Inc. name changed to Media Classics Group International, Inc. 09/08/2004 which recapitalized as Global Gaming Network, Inc. (DE) 08/29/2005 which reincorporated in Washington as Innovativ Media Group, Inc. 07/27/2015 which name changed to Demand Brands, Inc. 10/24/2018

DEER PK TECHNOLOGY INC (DE)
Name changed to Media Classics Group International, Inc. 09/08/2004
Media Classics Group International,

Inc. recapitalized as Global Gaming Network, Inc. (DE) 08/29/2005 which reincorporated in Washington as Innovativ Media Group, Inc. 07/27/2015 which name changed to Demand Brands, Inc. 10/24/2018

DEER TRAIL DEV CORP (UT)
Proclaimed dissolved for failure to pay taxes 01/01/1994

DEER TRAIL MINES INC. (UT)
Recapitalized as Deer Trail Development Corp. 01/01/1971
Each share Common 30¢ par received (0.1) share Common $3 par
Note: Old certificates were cancelled and new certificate issued in replacement
(See Deer Trail Development Corp.)

DEERBANK CORP (DE)
Common 1¢ par split (2) for (1) by issuance of (1) additional share 09/10/1993
Merged into NBD Bancorp, Inc. 07/01/1995
Each share Common 1¢ par exchanged for (1.409) shares Common $1 par
NBD Bancorp, Inc. name changed to First Chicago NBD Corp. 12/01/1995 which merged into Bank One Corp. 10/02/1998 which merged into J.P. Morgan Chase & Co. 12/31/2000 which name changed to JPMorgan Chase & Co. 07/20/2004

DEERBROOK INVTS LTD (AB)
Name changed to Liquidation World Inc. 03/24/1988
(See Liquidation World Inc.)

DEERBROOK PUBG GROUP INC (CO)
Name changed to Artup.com Network, Inc. (CO) 09/24/1999
Artup.com Network, Inc. (CO) reincorporated in Nevada as Deerbrook Publishing Group Inc. 12/10/1999 which name changed to VOLT, Inc. 04/06/2001 which name changed to Kore Holdings, Inc. 10/20/2004
(See Kore Holdings, Inc.)

DEERBROOK PUBG GROUP INC (NV)
Recapitalized as VOLT, Inc. 04/06/2001
Each share Common $0.001 par exchanged for (0.01) share Common $0.001 par
VOLT, Inc. name changed to Kore Holdings, Inc. 10/20/2004
(See Kore Holdings, Inc.)

DEERE & CO (IL)
Each share Preferred $100 par exchanged for (5) shares Preferred $20 par 03/15/1930
Each share Common $100 par exchanged for (5) shares Common no par 03/15/1930
Common no par split (2) for (1) by issuance of (1) additional share 10/31/1937
Each share Common no par exchanged for (2) shares Common $10 par 07/08/1952
Reorganized under the laws of Delaware 08/01/1958
Each (14) shares 7% Preferred $20 par exchanged for $500 principal amount of 4.5% Debentures
Common $10 par changed to $1 par

DEERFIELD APARTMENTS
Trust terminated 00/00/1951
Details not available

DEERFIELD BEACH BANK & TRUST CO. (DEERFIELD BEACH, FL)
Stock Dividend - 20% 08/01/1969
98.6% acquired by Southeast Bancorporation, Inc. as of 03/26/1971
Public interest eliminated

DEERFIELD CAP CORP (MD)
Each share old Common $0.001 par exchanged for (0.1) share new Common $0.001 par 10/17/2008
Reincorporated under the laws of Delaware as CIFC Deerfield Corp. 04/13/2011
CIFC Deerfield Corp. name changed to CIFC Corp. 07/19/2011 which reorganized as CIFC LLC 01/04/2016
(See CIFC LLC)

DEERFIELD FED SVGS & LN ASSN ILL (USA)
Reorganized under the laws of Delaware as Deerbank Corp. and Common $1 par changed to 1¢ par 02/28/1991
Deerbank Corp. merged into NBD Bancorp, Inc. 07/01/1995 which name changed to First Chicago NBD Corp. 12/01/1995 which merged into Bank One Corp. 10/02/1998 which merged into J.P. Morgan Chase & Co. 12/31/2000 which name changed to JPMorgan Chase & Co. 07/20/2004

DEERFIELD FINL SVCS INC (FL)
Name changed to Optical Concepts of America, Inc. 06/26/1998
Optical Concepts of America, Inc. recapitalized as IBSG International, Inc. 11/14/2003

DEERFIELD GLASSINE CO (DE)
Each share old Common no par exchanged for (25) shares new Common no par 00/00/1947
Each share new Common no par exchanged for (3) shares Common $10 par 00/00/1949
Common $10 par changed to $2 par and (4) additional shares issued 07/21/1969
Name changed to Deerfield Specialty Papers, Inc. 05/01/1972
Deerfield Specialty Papers, Inc. name changed to D. P. Co., Inc. 09/28/1973 which reorganized as State Street Investment Corp. 02/21/1978 which name changed to State Street Investment Trust 05/01/1989 which name changed to State Street Master Investment Trust 12/14/1989 which name changed to State Street Research Master Investment Trust 05/25/1995
(See State Street Research Master Investment Trust)

DEERFIELD PACKING CORP.
Name changed to Seabrook Farms Co. 00/00/1948
Seabrook Farms Co. merged into Seeman Brothers, Inc. 11/01/1960 which name changed to Seabrook Foods, Inc. 07/24/1970
(See Seabrook Foods, Inc.)

DEERFIELD RES LTD (NV)
Each share old Common $0.001 par exchanged for (0.2) share new Common $0.001 par 01/08/2009
New Common $0.001 par split (8.435582) for (1) by issuance of (7.435582) additional shares payable 02/05/2010 to holders of record 02/05/2010 Ex date - 02/08/2010
Name changed to China TMK Battery Systems Inc. 06/25/2010

DEERFIELD SPECIALTY PAPERS INC (DE)
Name changed to D. P. Co., Inc. 09/28/1973
D. P. Co., Inc. reorganized as State Street Investment Corp. 02/21/1978 which name changed to State Street Investment Trust 05/01/1989 which name changed to State Street Master Investment Trust 12/14/1989 which name changed to State Street Research Master Investment Trust 05/25/1995

(See State Street Research Master Investment Trust)

DEERFIELD TRIARC CAP CORP (MD)
Name changed to Deerfield Capital Corp. (MD) 12/20/2007
Deerfield Capital Corp. (MD) reincorporated in Delaware as CIFC Deerfield Corp. 04/13/2011 which name changed to CIFC Corp. 07/19/2011 which reorganized as CIFC LLC 01/04/2016
(See CIFC LLC)

DEERMONT OIL & GAS CO. LTD. (ON)
Charter revoked for failure to file reports and pay fees 03/11/1965

DEERPARK BREWERIES, INC. (DE)
No longer in existence having become inoperative and void for non-payment of taxes 04/01/1938

DEERWOOD BANCORPORATION, INC. (MN)
Acquired by Deerwood Bancshares, Inc. 01/02/1997
Details not available

DEETHREE EXPL INC (AB)
Name changed to DeeThree Exploration Ltd. 01/04/2010
(See DeeThree Exploration Ltd.)

DEETHREE EXPLORATION LTD (AB)
Plan of arrangement effective 05/21/2015
Each share Common no par exchanged for (0.5) share Boulder Energy Ltd. Common no par and (0.33333333) share Granite Oil Corp. Common no par
(See each company's listing)

DEEX INVESTMENT CORP. (BC)
Merged into Deex Resources Corp. 05/05/1983
Each share Common no par exchanged for (0.59273309) share Common no par
Deex Resources Corp. recapitalized as Seam Resources Corp. 05/22/1987

DEEX RES CORP (BC)
Recapitalized as Seam Resources Corp. 05/22/1987
Each share Common no par exchanged for (0.25) share Common no par

DEFAULT PROOF CR CARD SYS INC (FL)
Each share Common $0.001 par exchanged for (0.1) share Common 1¢ par 02/05/1999
Completely liquidated
Each share Common 1¢ par received first and final distribution of $0.04 cash payable 11/06/2012 to holders of record 10/26/2012 Ex date - 11/07/2012

DEFENDER PHOTO SUPPLY CO., INC.
Acquired by du Pont (E.I.) de Nemours & Co. 00/00/1945
Details not available

DEFENSE ELECTRS INC (DE)
Name changed to DEI Industries, Inc. 12/30/1968
(See DEI Industries, Inc.)

DEFENSE INDS INTL INC (NV)
SEC revoked common stock registration 05/14/2015

DEFENSE SOFTWARE & SYS INC (DE)
Common 1¢ par split (2) for (1) by issuance of (1) additional share 06/18/1993
Name changed to Data Systems & Software Inc. 07/01/1993
Data Systems & Software Inc. name changed to Acorn Factor, Inc. 09/25/2006 which name changed to Acorn Energy, Inc. 01/01/2008

DEFENSE SOLUTIONS HLDG INC (NV)
Recapitalized as Shanrong Biotechnology Corp. 09/25/2017
Each share Common $0.001 par exchanged for (0.01) share Common $0.001 par

DEFENSE TECHNOLOGY SYS INC (DE)
Charter cancelled and declared inoperative and void for non-payment of taxes 03/01/2007

DEFENSIVE INSTRS INC (PA)
Adjudicated bankrupt 08/31/1978
Stockholders' equity unlikely

DEFI GLOBAL INC (DE)
SEC revoked common stock registration 02/20/2014

DEFIANCE CAP CORP (BC)
Name changed to Defiance Silver Corp. 06/27/2011

DEFIANCE INC (DE)
Merged into General Chemical Group Inc. 02/24/1999
Each share Common 5¢ par exchanged for $9.50 cash

DEFIANCE INDS INC (OH)
Class B Common $1 par split (3) for (2) by issuance of (0.5) additional share 09/16/1968
Stock Dividend - Class B Common 12% 08/08/1962
Merged into El-Tronics, Inc. 10/03/1969
Each share Class A Common $5 par exchanged for (2.0633) shares Common no par
Each share Class B Common $1 par exchanged for (1) share Common no par
El-Tronics, Inc. name changed to ELT, Inc. 01/04/1974 which name changed to Dutch Boy, Inc. 02/23/1977 which name changed to Artra Group Inc. 12/31/1980 which merged into Entrade Inc. 09/23/1999
(See Entrade Inc.)

DEFIANCE MNG CORP (QC)
Merged into Rio Narcea Gold Mines, Ltd. 09/03/2004
Each share Common no par exchanged for (0.19047619) share Common no par
(See Rio Narcea Gold Mines, Ltd.)

DEFIANCE PRECISION PRODS INC (DE)
Name changed to Defiance Inc. 07/27/1989
(See Defiance Inc.)

DEFIANCE SPARK PLUG CORP. (OH)
Liquidated 00/00/1953
Details not available

DEFIANT ENERGY CORP (AB)
Plan of arrangement effective 12/21/2004
Each share Common no par exchanged for (0.201373) Advantage Energy Income Fund Trust Unit no par and (0.16666666) share Defiant Resources Corp. Common no par
(See each company's listing)

DEFIANT MINERALS INC (BC)
Name changed to Hillestad Pharmaceuticals Inc. 02/14/1991

DEFIANT RES CORP (AB)
Merged into Profound Energy Inc. 03/31/2008
Each share Common no par exchanged for (0.55) share Common no par
Profound Energy Inc. merged into Paramount Energy Trust 08/19/2009 which reorganized as Perpetual Energy Inc. 07/06/2010

DEFINED STRATEGY FD INC (MD)
Completely liquidated 09/15/2009
Each share Common $0.001 par

DEFINITION LTD (NV)
received first and final distribution of $11.114982 cash
Each share old Common $0.001 par exchanged for (0.04) share new Common $0.001 par 03/31/1999
Each share new Common $0.001 par exchanged again for (0.05) share new Common $0.001 par 01/11/1999
Name changed to Epersonnelmanagement.com 05/01/2000
Epersonnelmanagement.com name changed to Monogram Pictures, Inc. 10/03/2000 which name changed to Vitallabs, Inc. 05/20/2002 which name changed to America Asia Corp. (NV) 10/19/2004 which reincorporated in Washington as America Asia Energy Corp. 11/08/2005 which name changed to Renegade Energy Corp. 09/14/2006 which recapitalized as Carson Development Corp. 10/20/2008
(See Carson Development Corp.)

DEFINITIVE REST MATTRESS CO (OK)
Recapitalized as Zerez Holdings 04/12/2016
Each share Common $0.0001 par exchanged for (0.01) share Common $0.00001 par
Zerez Holdings name changed to Smart Cannabis Corp. 09/06/2017

DEFLECTA-SHIELD CORP (DE)
Merged into Lund International Holdings, Inc. 02/27/1998
Each share Common 1¢ par exchanged for $16 cash

DEFOE CORP. (NY)
Stock Dividend - 10% 01/24/1977
Merged into DeFoe Construction Co., Inc. 09/03/1980
Each share Common 1¢ par exchanged for $7 cash

DEFOREST RADIO CO. (DE)
Charter cancelled and declared inoperative and void for non-payment of taxes 04/01/1934

DEGA TECHNOLOGY INC (CO)
Declared defunct for failure to pay taxes and file annual reports 03/01/2003

DEGARO INNOVATIONS CORP (NV)
Name changed to Blue Water Petroleum Corp. 07/30/2013

DEGEN OIL & CHEMICAL CO. (NJ)
Acquired by Vertellus Performance Materials Inc. 07/01/2009
Details not available

DEGEORGE FINL CORP (DE)
Acquired by American Home Partners Inc. 03/15/2001
Each share Common 10¢ par exchanged for (0.1000162) share Common 10¢ par

DEGREKO INC (DE)
Stock Dividend - 20% payable 03/31/2006 to holders of record 03/24/2006 Ex date - 03/22/2006
Name changed to VOIP 5000, Inc. 06/06/2006
VOIP 5000, Inc. name changed to Target Development Group, Inc. (DE) 04/30/2007 which reincorporated in Wyoming 04/13/2009 which name changed to Hannover House, Inc. 04/03/2012

DEHAIER MEDICAL SYS LTD (BRITISH VIRGIN ISLANDS)
Name changed to Lianluo Smart Ltd. 11/21/2016

DEHY (M&I), INC. (IA)
Merged into ILO Ltd. 00/00/1979
Each share Common $1 par exchanged for $4.50 cash

DEI HLDGS INC (FL)
Each share old Common 1¢ par exchanged for (1) share new Common 1¢ par to reflect a (1) for (240) reverse split followed by a (240) for (1) forward split 12/06/2010
Note: Holders of (239) or fewer pre-split shares received $0.82 cash per share
Acquired by Charlesbank Capital Partners 06/21/2011
Each share new Common 1¢ par exchanged for $4.456968 cash

DEI INDS INC (DE)
Assets sold for benefit of noteholder 05/00/1973
No stockholders' equity

DEISEL-WEMMER-GILBERT CORP.
Recapitalized as D W G Cigar Corp. 00/00/1946
Each share Common $10 par exchanged for (2) shares Common $5 par
D W G Cigar Corp. name changed to D W G Corp. 11/30/1966 which name changed to Triarc Companies, Inc. (OH) 10/27/1993 which reincorporated in Delaware 06/30/1994 which name changed to Wendy's/Arby's Group, Inc. 09/29/2008 which name changed to Wendy's Co. 07/11/2011

DEJAY STORES, INC. (DE)
Each share Common $1 par exchanged for (2) shares Common 50¢ par 00/00/1945
Stock Dividends - 10% 07/01/1946; 50% 12/09/1955
Bankrupt 00/00/1963
No stockholders' equity

DEJOUR ENERGY INC (BC)
Recapitalized as DXI Energy Inc. 10/30/2015
Each share Common no par exchanged for (0.2) share Common no par

DEJOUR ENTERPRISES LTD (BC)
Reincorporated 08/16/2005
Each share old Common no par exchanged for (0.33333333) share new Common no par 10/02/2003
Place of incorporation changed from (ON) to (BC) 08/16/2005
Name changed to Dejour Energy Inc. 03/28/2011
Dejour Energy Inc. recapitalized as DXI Energy Inc. 10/30/2015

DEJOUR MINES LTD (ON)
Recapitalized as Dejour Enterprises Ltd. (ON) 10/30/2001
Each share Common no par exchanged for (1) share Common no par
Dejour Enterprises Ltd. (ON) reincorporated in British Columbia 08/16/2005 which name changed to Dejour Energy Inc. 03/28/2011 which recapitalized as DXI Energy Inc. 10/30/2015

DEK ELECTRS INC (MD)
Merged into Kaufman (H.W.) Financial Group, Inc. 01/20/1970
Each share Common 1¢ par exchanged for (1) share Common no par
(See Kaufman (H.W.) Financial Group, Inc.)

DEKALB AGRESEARCH INC. (DE)
Preferred Ser. A $1 par called for redemption 08/27/1971
Class A Common no par split (2) for (1) by issuance of (1) additional share 01/12/1973
Class B Common no par split (2) for (1) by issuance of (1) additional share 01/12/1973
Stock Dividend - 20% 10/15/1971
Name changed to Dekalb Corp. 12/17/1985
Dekalb Corp. name changed to Dekalb Energy Co. 09/06/1988 which merged into Apache Corp. 05/17/1995

DEKALB AGRICULTURAL ASSOCIATION, INC. (DE)
Name changed to Dekalb AgResearch Inc. 11/08/1968
Dekalb AgResearch Inc. name changed to Dekalb Corp. 12/17/1985 which name changed to Dekalb Energy Co. 09/06/1988 which merged into Apache Corp. 05/17/1995

DEKALB BANKSHARES INC (SC)
Merged into First Community Corp. 06/15/2006
Each share Common no par exchanged for (0.60705) share Common $1 par and $3.875 cash

DEKALB CORP. (DE)
Name changed to Dekalb Energy Co. 09/06/1988
Dekalb Energy Co. merged into Apache Corp. 05/17/1995

DEKALB ENERGY CO (DE)
Merged into Apache Corp. 05/17/1995
Each share Class A Common no par exchanged for (0.8764) share Common $1.25 par
Each share Class B Common no par exchanged for (0.8764) share Common $1.25 par

DEKALB GENETICS CORP (DE)
Class A Common no par split (3) for (1) by issuance of (2) additional shares payable 05/24/1996 to holders of record 05/10/1996
Class B Common no par split (3) for (1) by issuance of (2) additional shares payable 05/24/1996 to holders of record 05/10/1996
Class B Common no par split (2) for (1) by issuance of (1) additional share payable 08/08/1997 to holders of record 07/25/1997 Ex date - 08/11/1997
Merged into Monsanto Co. 12/04/1998
Each share Class A Common no par exchanged for $100 cash
Each share Class B Common no par exchanged for $100 cash

DEKALB-OGLE TELEPHONE CO. (IL)
Acquired by Continental Telephone Corp. 12/31/1966
Each share Common $10 par exchanged for (2.25) shares Common $1 par
Continental Telephone Corp. name changed to Continental Telecom Inc. 05/06/1982 which name changed to Contel Corp. 05/01/1986 which merged into GTE Corp. 03/14/1991 which merged into Verizon Communications Inc. 06/30/2000

DEKALB ST BK (TUCKER, GA)
Under plan of reorganization each share Common $4 par automatically became (1) share Georgia Bancshares, Inc. Common $4 par 08/05/1995
Georgia Bancshares, Inc. merged into First Sterling Banks Inc. (Old) 04/23/1999 which name changed to First Sterling Banks, Inc. (New) 05/24/2000 which name changed to Main Street Banks, Inc. (New) 01/02/2001

DEKANIA CORP (DE)
Completely liquidated 02/19/2009
Each Unit exchanged for first and final distribution of $10 cash
Each share Common $0.0001 par exchanged for first and final distribution of $10 cash

DEKCRAFT CORP (NY)
Common 75¢ par changed to 10¢ par 12/08/1967
Common 10¢ par split (2) for (1) by issuance of (1) additional share 11/08/1968
Common 10¢ par split (3) for (1) by issuance of (2) additional shares 03/07/1969
Charter cancelled and proclaimed dissolved for failure to pay taxes 12/20/1977

DEKON CORP (DE)
Merged into Mothercare Stores, Inc. 07/15/1976
Each share Common $1 par exchanged for $3 cash

DEL AMO SVGS & LN ASSN (CA)
Merged into City Holding Co. 04/01/1998
Each share Common $2.50 par exchanged for (0.47479) share Common $2.50 par

DEL AMO SVGS BK (TORRANCE, CA)
Merged into City Holding Co. 04/01/1998
Each share Guaranty Stock $2.50 par exchanged for (0.47479) share Common $2.50 par

DEL BONITA ASSOCIATED OILS LTD. (AB)
Struck off register for failure to file annual reports 10/30/1943

DEL CANO PPTYS TR (MD)
Acquired by Aspen Square Management Inc. 04/30/2002
Each share Preferred no par exchanged for approximately $7,202 cash

DEL CERRO ENTERPRISES INC (NV)
SEC revoked common stock registration 09/14/2011

DEL CORONADO GOLD INC (UT)
Proclaimed dissolved for failure to pay taxes 04/01/1987

DEL GLOBAL TECHNOLOGIES CORP (NY)
Name changed 02/14/1996
Common 10¢ par split (2) for (1) by issuance of (1) additional share 07/18/1961
Name changed from Del Electronics Corp. to Del Global Technologies Corp. 02/14/1996
Stock Dividends - 25% 02/24/1984; 3% payable 07/23/1996 to holders of record 07/12/1996; 3% payable 12/23/1996 to holders of record 12/04/1996
Recapitalized as DGT Holdings Corp. 01/10/2011
Each share Common 10¢ par exchanged for (0.02) share Common 10¢ par
Note: Holders of (49) or fewer pre-split shares received $0.78 cash per share
(See DGT Holdings Corp.)

DEL LABS INC (DE)
Common $1 par split (4) for (3) by issuance of (1/3) additional share 06/24/1983
Common $1 par split (4) for (3) by issuance of (1/3) additional share 03/26/1986
Common $1 par split (4) for (3) by issuance of (1/3) additional share 09/20/1991
Common $1 par split (4) for (3) by issuance of (1/3) additional share 06/29/1994
Common $1 par split (2) for (1) by issuance of (1) additional share 06/30/1995
Common $1 par split (4) for (3) by issuance of (1/3) additional share payable 11/29/1996 to holders of record 11/08/1996 Ex date - 12/02/1996
Common $1 par split (4) for (3) by issuance of (1/3) additional share payable 03/10/1998 to holders of record 02/20/1998 Ex date - 03/11/1998
Stock Dividends - 2% payable

12/28/1999 to holders of record 11/30/1999; 5% payable 12/27/2000 to holders of record 11/30/2000; 5% payable 12/28/2001 to holders of record 12/01/2001 Ex date - 11/28/2001; 5% payable 12/27/2002 to holders of record 11/29/2002; 5% payable 12/29/2003 to holders of record 12/01/2003
Merged into DLI Holding Co. 01/27/2005
Each share Common $1 par exchanged for $35 cash

DEL MAR ENERGY INC (AB)
Recapitalized as Aventura Energy Inc. 09/20/1999
Each share Common no par exchanged for (0.33333333) share Common no par
(See Aventura Energy Inc.)

DEL MAR PETE INC (DE)
Each share Common 10¢ par exchanged for (0.5) share Common 20¢ par 06/20/1972
Merged into Shenandoah Oil Corp. 05/31/1973
Each share Common 20¢ par exchanged for (0.27951) share $1.25 Conv. Preferred Ser. A no par
(See Shenandoah Oil Corp.)

DEL MONTE CORP (NY)
Merged into Reynolds (R.J.) Industries, Inc. 02/02/1979
Each share Capital Stock $2.50 par exchanged for $48.5331 cash

DEL MONTE FOODS CO (DE)
Acquired by Blue Acquisition Group, Inc. 03/08/2011
Each share Common 1¢ par exchanged for $19 cash

DEL MONTE PAC LTD (SINGAPORE)
ADR agreement terminated 11/30/2016
Each Sponsored ADR for Ordinary exchanged for $2.0568 cash

DEL MONTE PPTYS CO (CA)
Each share Capital Stock $100 par exchanged for (4) shares Capital Stock $25 par 00/00/1945
Capital Stock $25 par changed to Common $2.50 par and (9) additional shares issued 12/22/1965
Reincorporated under the laws of Delaware as Pebble Beach Corp. 03/30/1977
(See Pebble Beach Corp.)

DEL NORTE CHROME CORP (BC)
Recapitalized as Consolidated Del Norte Ventures Inc. 10/16/1989
Each share Common no par exchanged for (0.2) share Common no par
Consolidated Del Norte Ventures Inc. name changed to Idaho-Maryland Mining Corp. 04/15/1991 which recapitalized as HMC Healthgard Marketing Corp. 06/23/1993 which recapitalized as Reward Mining Corp. 08/07/1996 which name changed to Riverdance Resources Corp. 03/11/1998 which recapitalized as Luminex Ventures Inc. 05/26/1999 which recapitalized as Lateegra Resources Corp. 06/12/2002 which recapitalized as Lateegra Gold Corp. 01/12/2006 which merged into Excellon Resources Inc. 08/05/2011

DEL NORTE CO. LTD.
Liquidated 00/00/1949
Details not available

DEL PENN CO (DE)
Liquidation completed
Each share Common 5¢ par stamped to indicate initial distribution of $18 cash 05/07/1965
6% Conv. Preferred $7.50 par called for redemption 07/02/1965
Each share Stamped Common 5¢ par received second distribution of $0.36 cash 04/22/1966
Each share Stamped Common 5¢ par received third distribution of $1.15 cash 09/01/1966
Each share Stamped Common 5¢ par exchanged for fourth and final distribution of $0.40 cash 12/12/1969

DEL-PENN CORP. (TX)
Voluntarily dissolved 04/22/1977
Details not available

DEL REY OIL CO. (CA)
Capital Stock $1 par changed to 20¢ par 00/00/1942
Completely liquidated 10/23/1964
Details not available

DEL RIO INTL A RESOURCE & TECHNOLOGY CORP (AB)
Name changed to Money Works Inc. 01/01/1994
Money Works Inc. recapitalized as CanArgo Energy Inc. 07/14/1997 which merged into CanArgo Energy Corp. 07/15/1998
(See CanArgo Energy Corp.)

DEL RIO MINING CO. LTD.
Merged into Consolidated Duquesne Mining Co., Ltd. 00/00/1948
Each share Capital Stock no par exchanged for (2.66666666) shares Capital Stock $1 par
Consolidated Duquesne Mining Co., Ltd. merged into Beattie-Duquesne Mines Ltd. 00/00/1952 which recapitalized as Donchester-Duquesne Mines Ltd. 07/11/1972 which merged into Fundy Chemical International Ltd. 10/01/1973
(See Fundy Chemical International Ltd.)

DEL RIO NATL BK (DEL RIO, TX)
Acquired by Laredo National Bancshares, Inc. 12/01/2001
Details not available

DEL RIO PRODUCERS LTD. (AB)
Merged into Central-Del Rio Oils Ltd. 04/15/1957
Each share Capital Stock no par exchanged for (0.71428571) share Common no par
Central-Del Rio Oils Ltd. name changed to PanCanadian Petroleum Ltd. 11/24/1971 which name changed to PanCanadian Energy Corp. 10/01/2001 which name changed to EnCana Corp. 04/05/2002

DEL RIO RES LTD (AB)
Recapitalized as Del Rio International, A Resource & Technology Corp. 01/26/1988
Each share Common no par exchanged for (2) shares Common no par
Del Rio International, A Resource & Technology Corp. name changed to Money Works Inc. 01/01/1994 which recapitalized as CanArgo Energy Inc. 07/14/1997 which merged into CanArgo Energy Corp. 07/15/1998
(See CanArgo Energy Corp.)

DEL ROCA ENERGY INC (AB)
Merged into Del Roca Energy Ltd. 10/31/1998
Each share Common no par exchanged for (0.29875) share Common no par
Del Roca Energy Ltd. merged into Tusk Energy Inc. 02/01/2003
(See Tusk Energy Inc.)

DEL ROCA ENERGY LTD (AB)
Merged into Tusk Energy Inc. 02/01/2003
Each share Common no par exchanged for either (0.25) share Common no par or $0.64 cash
Note: Option to receive stock expires 03/31/2003
(See Tusk Energy Inc.)

DEL ROY COPPER MINING & SMELTING CO. (NM)
Voluntarily dissolved 06/14/1921
Details not available

DEL TACO RESTAURANTS INC (DE)
Incorporated 08/04/1983
Merged into DT Merger Corp. 09/11/1991
Each share Common 1¢ par exchanged for $3.25 cash

DEL VAL FINL CORP (DE)
Name changed to DVL, Inc. 01/04/1994

DELADAM GOLD MINES LTD. (ON)
Merged into Porcupine Southgate Mines Ltd. 00/00/1944
Each share Capital Stock $1 par exchanged for (0.2173913) share Capital Stock $1 par
Porcupine Southgate Mines Ltd. merged into Associated Porcupine Mines Ltd. 11/05/1968 which merged into American Reserve Mining Corp. 02/27/1989 which recapitalized as AMI Resources Inc. 12/21/1994 which name changed to Ashanti Sankofa Inc. 01/19/2017

DELAFRAN INDUSTRIES INC. (DE)
Recapitalized as Solar Age Manufacturing, Inc. (DE) 11/12/1982
Each share Common 1¢ par exchanged for (0.2) share Common 1¢ par
Solar Age Manufacturing, Inc. (DE) reincorporated in Nevada as Solar Age Industries, Inc. 08/20/1984 which name changed to Solar Group, Inc. 07/17/1998 which name changed to Forex365, Inc. 08/28/2008 which name changed to Fuer International Inc. 08/30/2010
(See Fuer International Inc.)

DELAHEY CONS NICKEL MINES LTD (ON)
Merged into Hoffman Exploration & Minerals Ltd. 06/29/1981
Each share Common no par exchanged for (1) share Common no par
Hoffman Exploration & Minerals Ltd. merged into Consolidated Thompson-Lundmark Gold Mines Ltd. 01/16/1986 which name changed to Consolidated Thompson Iron Mines Ltd. 08/24/2006
(See Consolidated Thompson Iron Mines Ltd.)

DELAINE CORP (NV)
Old Common $0.001 par split (6) for (1) by issuance of (5) additional shares payable 07/23/2012 to holders of record 07/16/2012 Ex date - 07/24/2012
Each share old Common $0.001 par exchanged for (0.05) share new Common $0.001 par 01/16/2015
Name changed to Car Monkeys Group 02/03/2015

DELANAIR INC (NJ)
Merged into Harvey's Stores, Inc. (DE) 03/20/1972
Each share Common 1¢ par exchanged for (0.09090909) share Common $1 par
Harvey's Stores, Inc. (DE) name changed to Nexus Industries, Inc. 03/04/1975 which reorganized as Shirt Shed, Inc. 12/19/1986 which merged into Signal Apparel Co., Inc. 07/22/1992
(See Signal Apparel Co., Inc.)

DELANCEY-CLINTON THEATRES OPERATING CORP.
Liquidation completed 00/00/1946
Details not available

DELANCO BANCORP INC (NJ)
Merged into First Bank (Hamilton, NJ) 05/01/2018
Each share Common 1¢ par exchanged for (1.11) shares Common $5 par

DELANCO BANCORP INC (USA)
Reorganized under the laws of New Jersey 10/17/2013
Each share Common 1¢ par exchanged for (0.5711) share Common 1¢ par
Delanco Bancorp, Inc. (NJ) merged into First Bank (Hamilton, NJ) 05/01/2018

DELANCO ELECTRIC MACHINE CO. INC. (NY)
Adjudicated bankrupt 08/17/1962
No stockholders' equity

DELAND ST BK & TR (DELAND, FL)
Name changed 08/00/1978
Each share Capital Stock $10 par exchanged for (2.1) shares Capital Stock $5 par 12/31/1975
Name changed from DeLand State Bank (DeLand, FL) to DeLand State Bank & Trust (DeLand, FL) 08/00/1978
Acquired by Sun Banks, Inc. 03/01/1984
Each share Capital Stock $5 par exchanged for $79.03 cash

DELANDORE MINES LTD.
Succeeded by Delandore Sulphur & Iron Mines Ltd. share for share 00/00/1941
Delandore Sulphur & Iron Mines Ltd. liquidated for Atlas Sulphur & Iron Co. Ltd. 00/00/1954 which recapitalized as International Atlas Development & Exploration Ltd. 06/26/1963
(See Atlas Development & Exploration Ltd.)

DELANDORE SULPHUR & IRON MINES LTD.
Wound up 00/00/1954
Each share Capital Stock $1 par received distribution of (0.16666666) share Atlas Sulphur & Iron Co. Ltd. Capital Stock $1 par
Atlas Sulphur & Iron Co. Ltd. recapitalized as International Atlas Development & Exploration Ltd. 06/26/1963
(See International Atlas & Exploration Ltd.)

DELANEY ENERGY SVCS CORP (AB)
Acquired by Integrated Production Services Ltd. 06/04/2001
Each share Common no par exchanged for $1.05 cash

DELANO TECHNOLOGY CORP (ON)
Merged into divine, inc. 08/01/2002
Each share Common no par exchanged for (0.04748) share new Class A Common $0.001 par
(See divine, inc.)

DELAVACO RESIDENTIAL PPTYS CORP (ON)
Name changed to Firm Capital American Realty Partners Corp. 08/02/2016

DELAWARE & BOUND BROOK RR CO (NJ)
Each share Capital Stock $100 par exchanged for (4) shares Capital Stock $25 par 00/00/1944
Liquidation completed
Each share Capital Stock $25 par received initial distribution of $25 cash 01/07/1982
Each share Capital Stock $25 par received second distribution of $9 cash 02/23/1982
Each share Capital Stock $25 par received third and final distribution of $8 cash 07/21/1982

DELAWARE & HUDSON CO (NY)
Capital Stock $100 par changed to no par and (2) additional shares issued 05/25/1956

Name changed to Champlain National Corp. 07/01/1968
Champlain National Corp. merged into International Industries, Inc. (DE) 03/27/1969 which merged into IHOP Corp. 09/17/1976
(See IHOP Corp.)

DELAWARE AIRCRAFT INDUSTRIES, INC. (DE)
No longer in existence having become inoperative and void for non-payment of taxes 04/01/1953

DELAWARE BANCSHARES INC (NY)
Common $10 par changed to $1.25 par and (1) additional share issued payable 10/02/1996 to holders of record 09/01/1996 Ex date - 10/03/1996
Stock Dividend - 10% 05/15/1990
Merged into Norwood Financial Corp. 07/31/2016
Each share Common $1.25 par exchanged for approximately (0.4012545) share Common 10¢ par and $5.9214 cash

DELAWARE BARREL & DRUM CO., INC. (DE)
Acquired by Container Corp. of America 09/28/1964
Each share Common 50¢ par exchanged for (0.2793296) share Common $5 par
Container Corp. of America merged into Marcor Inc. 11/01/1968 which merged into Mobil Corp. 07/01/1976 which merged into Exxon Mobil Corp. 11/30/1999

DELAWARE CHEMICAL ENGINEERING CORP. (DE)
Name changed to Delfi Management, Inc. and Common no par changed to $1 par 09/28/1967
Delfi Management, Inc. name changed to Delfi American Corp. 08/28/1969
(See Delfi American Corp.)

DELAWARE CNTY BK & TR CO (DELAWARE, OH)
Each share Common $2.50 par exchanged for (3) shares Common $1 par 06/14/1995
Reorganized as DCB Financial Corp. 03/17/1997
Each share Common $1 par exchanged for (3) shares Common no par
DCB Financial Corp. merged into First Commonwealth Financial Corp. 04/03/2017

DELAWARE CNTY NATL BK (CHESTER, PA)
Capital Stock $10 par changed to $3.33333333 par and (2) additional shares issued 02/15/1967
Stock Dividend - 15% 02/15/1965
Merged into Southeast National Bank of Pennsylvania (Chester, PA) 01/01/1970
Each share Capital Stock $3.33333333 par exchanged for (1) share Common $3.33333333 par
Southeast National Bank of Pennsylvania (Chester, PA) reorganized as Southeast National Bancshares of Pennsylvania 01/04/1982 which merged into Fidelcor, Inc. 06/30/1983 which merged into First Fidelity Bancorporation (New) 02/29/1988
(See First Fidelity Bancorporation (New))

DELAWARE FD INC (DE)
Stock Dividend - 100% 08/08/1955
State of incorporation changed from (DE) to (MD) 05/01/1983
Reorganized as Delaware Group Equity Funds I, Inc. 12/27/1999
Details not available

DELAWARE FIRST FINL CORP (DE)
Merged into Crown Bank FSB (Casselberry, FL) 07/30/1999

Each share Common 1¢ par exchanged for $15.50 cash

DELAWARE GENERAL CORP. (DE)
Recapitalized as 2 B System, Inc. 03/15/1968
Each share Common 10¢ par exchanged for (0.33333333) share Common 10¢ par
(See 2 B System, Inc.)

DELAWARE GROUP DIVID & INCOME FD INC (MD)
Name changed to Delaware Investments Dividend & Income Fund, Inc. 12/01/2001

DELAWARE INSURANCE CO.
Merged into Westchester Fire Insurance Co. 00/00/1928
Details not available

DELAWARE INVTS MINN MUN INCOME FD INC (MN)
Merged into Delaware Investments Minnesota Municipal Income Fund II Inc. 02/24/2006
Each Municipal Income Preferred Share received (1) Municipal Income Preferred Share Ser. C
Each share Common 1¢ par received (0.9806) share Common 1¢ par

DELAWARE INVTS MINN MUN INCOME FD II INC (MN)
Municipal Income Preferred Ser. A 1¢ par called for redemption at $50,000 on 11/05/2008
Municipal Income Preferred Ser. B 1¢ par called for redemption at $50,000 on 11/05/2008
Municipal Income Preferred Ser. C 1¢ par called for redemption at $50,000 on 11/05/2008
Municipal Income Preferred Ser. C 1¢ par called for redemption at $50,000 on 11/05/2008
Variable Rate MuniFund Term Preferred Ser. 2016 called for redemption at $100,000 plus $102.7671 accrued dividends on 02/01/2016
(Additional Information in Active)

DELAWARE INVTS MINN MUN INCOME FD III INC (MN)
Merged into Delaware Investments Minnesota Municipal Income Fund II Inc. 02/24/2006
Each Municipal Income Preferred Share received (1) Municipal Income Preferred Share Ser. D
Each share Common 1¢ par received (0.9299) share Common 1¢ par

DELAWARE INVTS ARIZ MUN INCOME FD INC (MN)
Merged into Delaware Investments National Municipal Income Fund 06/17/2011
Each share Common 1¢ par exchanged for (1.0396) shares Common 1¢ par

DELAWARE INVTS COLO INSD MUN INCOME FD (MN)
Name changed 01/02/2008
Name changed from Delaware Investments Colorado Insured Municipal Income Fund Inc. to Delaware Investments Colorado Municipal Income Fund, Inc. 01/02/2008
Municipal Income Preferred Ser. A called for redemption at $50,000 on 11/05/2008
Municipal Income Preferred Ser. B called for redemption at $50,000 on 11/05/2008
Variable Rate MuniFund Term Preferred Ser. 2016 called for redemption at $100,000 plus $102.7671 accrued dividends on 02/01/2016
(Additional Information in Active)

DELAWARE INVTS GLOBAL DIVID & INCOME FD INC (MD)
Name changed 12/01/2001
Name changed from Delaware Group Global Dividend & Income Fund, Inc. to Delaware Investments Global Dividend & Income Fund, Inc. 12/01/2001
Merged into Delaware Enhanced Global Dividend & Income Fund 10/21/2011
Each share Common 1¢ par exchanged for (0.5691) share Common no par

DELAWARE INVTS NATL MUN INCOME FD (MA)
Name changed 10/16/2007
Name changed from Delaware Investments Florida Insured Municipal Income Fund to Delaware Investments National Municipal Income Fund 10/16/2007
Municipal Income Preferred Ser. A called for redemption at $50,000 on 10/24/2008
Municipal Income Preferred Ser. B called for redemption at $50,000 on 10/24/2008
Variable Rate MuniFund Term Preferred Ser. 2017 called for redemption at $100,000 plus 102.7671 accrued dividends on 02/01/2016
(Additional Information in Active)

DELAWARE LACKAWANA & WESTN RR CO (PA)
Merged into Erie-Lackawanna Railroad Co. 10/17/1960
Each share Capital Stock $50 par exchanged for (1) share Common no par
Erie-Lackawanna Railroad Co. merged into Dereco, Inc. 04/01/1968
(See Dereco, Inc.)

DELAWARE MINES CORP. (ID)
Charter forfeited for failure to file reports 11/30/1970

DELAWARE-MONTGOMERY COUNTIES CO. FOR GUARANTEEING MORTGAGES
Name changed to Delaware-Montgomery Mortgage Co. 00/00/1940
(See Delaware-Montgomery Mortgage Co.)

DELAWARE MONTGOMERY MTG CO (PA)
Liquidation completed 00/00/1980
Details not available

DELAWARE MORTGAGE CO. (DE)
Liquidation completed
Each share Common no par received initial distribution of $4 cash 04/29/1960
Each share Common no par received second distribution of $1 cash 01/23/1961
Each share Common no par received third distribution of $1.20 cash 07/23/1962
Each share Common no par received fourth and final distribution of $0.22 cash 01/14/1964

DELAWARE MORTGAGE INVESTMENT CO. (DE)
Name changed to Delaware Mortgage Co. 00/00/1949
(See Delaware Mortgage Co.)

DELAWARE NATIONAL BANK (GEORGETOWN, DE)
Under plan of reorganization each share Common $5 par automatically became (1) share Delaware National Bankshares Corp. 06/03/1985
Delaware National Bankshares Corp. merged into Fulton Financial Corp. 08/31/1995

DELAWARE NATL BANKSHARES CORP (DE)
Merged into Fulton Financial Corp. 08/31/1995
Each share Common $5 par exchanged for (1.244) shares Common $2.50 par

DELAWARE NATL CORP (DE)
Merged into Biscayne National Corp. 11/27/1991
Each share Common 1¢ par exchanged for (1) share Common 1¢ par
(See Biscayne National Corp.)

DELAWARE-NEW JERSEY FERRY CO.
Liquidation completed 00/00/1953
Details not available

DELAWARE OTSEGO CORP (NY)
Common $1.25 par changed to $0.125 par and (9) additional shares issued 08/06/1986
Stock Dividends - 5% payable 03/20/1996 to holders of record 02/17/1996; 5% payable 03/31/1997 to holders of record 02/28/1997
Merged into a corporate group 10/03/1997
Each share Common $0.125 par exchanged for $22 cash

DELAWARE PACIFIC CORP. (DE)
Merged into Floseal Corp. 03/08/1955
Each share Capital Stock 50¢ par exchanged for (1) share Common 50¢ par
(See Floseal Corp.)

DELAWARE PWR & LT CO (DE)
Common $13.50 par changed to $6.75 par and (1) additional share issued 05/16/1960
Name changed to Delmarva Power & Light Co. 04/19/1966
Delmarva Power & Light Co. (DE) reincorporated under the laws of Delaware and Virginia 12/31/1979 which merged into Conectiv, Inc. 03/01/1998
(See Conectiv, Inc.)

DELAWARE PUNCH CO. OF AMERICA (DE)
Name changed to Delaware Punch Co. 04/03/1967
(See Delaware Punch Co.)

DELAWARE PUNCH CO (DE)
Company went private 00/00/1976
Details not available

DELAWARE RES CORP (BC)
Common no par split (3) for (1) by issuance of (2) additional shares 07/14/1988
Merged into Prime Resources Corp. (BC) 02/01/1989
Each share Common no par exchanged for (1) share Common no par
Prime Resources Corp. (BC) recapitalized as Prime Resources Group Inc. 01/26/1990 which merged into HomeStake Mining Co. 12/03/1998 which merged into Barrick Gold Corp. 12/14/2001

DELAWARE RIVER FERRY CO. (DE)
Each share Common no par exchanged for (5) shares Common $1 par 00/00/1949
Liquidaton completed
Each share Common $1 par exchanged for initial distribution of $6 cash 05/07/1965
Each share Common $1 par received second distribution of $1 cash 06/13/1967
Each share Common $1 par received third and final distribution of $0.65 cash 10/12/1967

DELAWARE RR CO (DE & MD)
Merged into Penn Central Corp. 10/24/1978
Each share Capital Stock $25 par exchanged for (0.53) share Conv.

Preference Ser. B $20 par, (0.24) share Common $1 par, $9.01 principal amount of 7% General Mortgage Bonds Ser. A due 12/31/1987, $1.49 principal amount of 7% General Mortgage Bonds Ser. B due 12/31/1987 and $3.70 cash
Note: a) Distribution is certain only for certificates surrendered prior to 05/01/1985 b) Distribution may also be made for certificates surrendered between 05/01/1985 and 12/31/1986 c) No distribution will be made for certificates surrendered after 12/31/1986
Penn Central Corp. name changed to American Premier Underwriters, Inc. 03/25/1994 which merged into American Premier Group, Inc. 04/03/1995 which name changed to American Financial Group, Inc. 06/09/1995 which merged into American Financial Group, Inc. (Holding Co.) 12/02/1997

DELAWARE SVGS BK F S B (WILMINGTON, DE)
Merged into Lehman Brothers Holdings Inc. 06/30/1999
Each share Common $1 par exchanged for $1.50 cash

DELAWARE TR CO (WILMINGTON, DE)
Each share Capital Stock $100 par exchanged for (4) shares Capital Stock $25 par 00/00/1942
Capital Stock $25 par changed to $10 par and (4) additional shares issued 04/30/1962
Merged into Meridian Bancorp, Inc. 01/01/1988
Each share Capital Stock $10 par exchanged for (40.7611) shares Common $5 par
Meridian Bancorp, Inc. merged into CoreStates Financial Corp 04/09/1996 which merged into First Union Corp. 04/28/1998 which name changed to Wachovia Corp. (Ctfs. dated after 09/01/2001) 09/01/2001 which merged into Wells Fargo & Co. (New) 12/31/2008

DELAWARE VALLEY BANK & TRUST CO. (BRISTOL, PA)
Each share Capital Stock $50 par exchanged for (5) shares Capital Stock $10 par 03/24/1955
Stock Dividend - 60% 05/29/1951
Merged into Philadelphia National Bank (Philadelphia, PA) 11/09/1956
Each share Capital Stock $10 par exchanged for (0.55) share Capital Stock $20 par
Philadelphia National Bank (Philadelphia, PA) reorganized as PNB Corp. 11/01/1969 which name changed to Philadelphia National Corp. 04/23/1973 which merged into CoreStates Financial Corp 05/02/1983 which merged into First Union Corp. 04/28/1998 which name changed to Wachovia Corp. (Ctfs. dated after 09/01/2001) 09/01/2001 which merged into Wells Fargo & Co. (New) 12/31/2008

DELAWARE VALLEY FINL CORP (PA)
Name changed to North Lake Corp. (PA) 5/22/69
North Lake Corp. (PA) merged into North Lake Corp. (DE) 2/15/80
(See North Lake Corp.)

DELAWARE VALLEY NATL BK (CHERRY HILL, NJ)
Merged into New Jersey National Corp. 05/31/1974
Each share Common $5 par exchanged for (1) share Common $5 par
New Jersey National Corp. acquired by CoreStates Financial Corp 10/30/1986 which merged into First Union Corp. 04/28/1998 which name changed to Wachovia Corp. (Ctfs. dated after 09/01/2001) 09/01/2001 which merged into Wells Fargo & Co. (New) 12/31/2008

DELAWARE VALLEY RLTY & MTG INVS (PA)
Under plan of reorganization each Share of Bene. Int. $1 par automatically became (1) share Del-Val Financial Corp. Common $1 par 7/5/78
Del-Val Financial Corp. name changed to DVL, Inc. 1/4/94

DELAWARE VALLEY UTILITIES CO.
Merged into Northeastern Water Co. in 1944
Each share 6% Preferred $100 par exchanged for (3) shares $2 Preferred no par
Each share $3 Preferred no par exchanged for (1) share $2 Preferred no par
Each share Common no par exchanged for (1) share Common $1 par
Northeastern Water Co. merged into American Water Works Co., Inc. 8/17/62
(See American Water Works Co., Inc.)

DELAWARE WATER CO.
Sold to City of Delaware, Ohio in 1936

DELBANCOR INDS INC (BC)
Delisted from Vancouver Stock Exchange 03/31/1998

DELBROOK CORP (NV)
Name changed to Argentex Mining Corp. (NV) 03/15/2004
Argentex Mining Corp. (NV) reincorporated in Delaware 11/05/2007 which reincorporated in Navada 06/03/2011 which reincorporated in British Columbia 06/08/2011 which merged into Austral Gold Ltd. 08/22/2016

DELCHAMPS INC (AL)
Merged into Jitney-Jungle Stores of America, Inc. 11/4/97
Each share Common 1¢ par exchanged for $30 cash

DELCO CORP (NY)
Common 1¢ par split (2) for (1) by issuance of (1) additional share 1/7/71
Name changed to Commercial Telephonics, Inc. 2/23/83
(See Commercial Telephonics, Inc.)

DELCO REMY INTL INC (DE)
Merged into Court Square Capital Ltd. 03/15/2001
Each share Class A Common no par exchanged for $9.50 cash

DELCOR INC. (UT)
Charter suspended for failure to pay taxes 09/15/1971

DELCORE PORCUPINE MINES LTD. (ON)
Charter cancelled for failure to pay taxes and file returns 11/24/1973

DELCORP RES INC (BC)
Recapitalized as Bahn Foods Inc. 11/20/1990
Each share Common no par exchanged for (0.25) share Common no par
Bahn Foods Inc. recapitalized as Consolidated Bahn Foods Inc. 10/21/1996
(See Consolidated Bahn Foods Inc.)

DELDONA GOLD MINES LTD (ON)
Capital Stock $1 par changed to no par 08/09/1971
Merged into D'Eldona Resources Ltd. 10/15/1984
Each share Capital Stock no par exchanged for (0.5) share Common no par
D'Eldona Resources Ltd. recapitalized as Western D'Eldona Resources Ltd. 06/01/1988
(See Western D'Eldona Resources Ltd.)

DELEHANTY EDL SYS INC (DE)
Adjudicated bankrupt 12/03/1981
No stockholders' equity

DELEK GROUP LTD OLD (ISRAEL)
Each Unsponsored ADR for Common exchanged for (1) Delek Group Ltd. (New) Sponsored ADR for Common 10/19/2009

DELEK RES INC (FL)
SEC revoked common stock registration 07/06/2011

DELEK US HLDGS INC (DE)
Under plan of merger each share Common 1¢ par automatically became (1) share Delek US Holdings, Inc. (New) Common 1¢ par 07/01/2017

DELENDO CORP.
Liquidation for cash completed in 1943

DELEON URANIUM CO. (CO)
Dissolved 7/12/57
No stockholders' equity

DELFI AMERN CORP (DE)
Merged into Provident Mutual Life Insurance Co. 10/29/1987
Each share Common $1 par exchanged for $40 cash

DELFI MANAGEMENT, INC. (DE)
Name changed to Delfi American Corp. 08/28/1969
(See Delfi American Corp.)

DELFOLD CORP (NY)
Name changed to Rembrandt Cosmetic Corp. 1/8/87
(See Rembrandt Cosmetic Corp.)

DELFT CAP FD LLC
Market Auction Preferred Ser. B 144A called for redemption at $500,000 on 2/22/2002
Market Auction Preferred Ser. C 144A called for redemption at $500,000 on 3/1/2002
Market Auction Preferred Ser. D 144A called for redemption at $500,000 on 3/8/2002
Market Auction Preferred Ser. E 144A called for redemption at $500,000 on 3/15/2002
Market Auction Preferred Ser. F 144A called for redemption at $500,000 on 3/22/2002
Market Auction Preferred Ser. G 144A called for redemption at $500,000 on 3/29/2002
Market Auction Preferred Ser. A 144A called for redemption at $500,000 on 4/5/2002

DELGER FINL CORP (UT)
Name changed 04/18/1975
Name changed to Delger Insurance Corp. to Delger Financial Corp. 04/18/1975
Involuntarily dissolved 09/30/1980

DELGRATIA MNG CORP (BC)
Name changed 04/18/1995
Name changed from Delgratia Developments Ltd. to Delgratia Mining Corp. 04/18/1995
Reincorporated under the laws of Yukon as Central Minera Corp. 02/01/1999

DELHAIZE AMER INC (NC)
Merged into Etablissements Delhaize Freres et Cile Le Lion S.A. 04/25/2001
Each share Class A Common 50¢ par exchanged for (0.4) Sponsored ADR for Ordinary
Each share Class B Common 50¢ par exchanged for (0.4) Sponsored ADR for Ordinary
Etablissements Delhaize Freres et Cile Le Lion S.A. merged into Koninklijke Ahold Delhaize N.V. 07/25/2016

DELHI AUSTRALIAN PETE LTD (DE)
Name changed to Delhi International Oil Corp. 04/24/1970
(See Delhi International Oil Corp.)

DELHI CHEMICALS, INC. (NY)
Name changed to Delhi Consolidated Industries, Inc. 04/02/1981
Delhi Consolidated Industries, Inc. name changed to Maritime Transport & Technology Inc. 03/08/1989 which name changed to Bank Store 07/24/1998 which name changed to Banker's Store Inc. 09/18/2001
(See Banker's Store Inc.)

DELHI CONS INDS INC (NY)
Each share Common 1¢ par exchanged for (0.5) share Class A Common 1¢ par 07/27/1983
Name changed to Maritime Transport & Technology Inc. 03/08/1989
Maritime Transport & Technology Inc. name changed to Bank Store 07/24/1998 which name changed to Banker's Store Inc. 09/18/2001
(See Banker's Store Inc.)

DELHI CONTRACT INDUSTRIES (DE)
Plan of exchange effective 12/19/80
For holdings of (9) shares or fewer each Ctf. of Bene. Int. exchanged for $0.50 cash
For holdings of (10) shares or more each Ctf. of Bene. Int. exchanged for (1) share Brady Energy Corp. Conv. Preferred Ser. B 1¢ par

DELHI (TEMAGAMI) GOLD MINES LTD. (ON)
Merged into New Delhi Mines Ltd. 00/00/1951
Each share Capital Stock $1 par exchanged for (0.25) share new Common $1 par
New Delhi Mines Ltd. recapitalized as Delhi Pacific Mines Ltd. 05/23/1961 which name changed to Delhi Pacific Resources Ltd. 01/12/1981
(See Delhi Pacific Resources Ltd.)

DELHI INTL OIL CORP (DE)
Common 10¢ par split (3) for (2) by issuance of (0.5) additional share 2/28/80
Acquired by Patson Investments Ltd. 11/20/81
Each share Common 10¢ par exchanged for $78 cash

DELHI MFG CORP (LA)
Merged into Woodstream Corp. 10/29/1971
Each share Common $1 par exchanged for (0.363636) share Common no par
(See Woodstream Corp.)

DELHI OIL CO. (KS)
Charter forfeited for failure to file annual report 12/29/23

DELHI OIL CORP. (DE)
Stock Dividend - 100% 6/10/52
Merged into Delhi-Taylor Oil Corp. share for share in 1955
(See Delhi-Taylor Oil Corp.)

DELHI PAC RES LTD (ON)
Name changed 01/12/1981
Capital Stock $1 par changed to no par 08/09/1971
Name changed from Delhi Pacific Mines Ltd. to Delhi Pacific Resources Ltd. and Capital Stock no par reclassified as Common no par 01/12/1981
Delisted from Toronto Stock Exchange 07/04/1986

DELHI-TAYLOR OIL CORP. (DE)
Liquidation completed
Each share Common $1 par exchanged for initial distribution of (1) Ctf. of Bene. Int. of Delhi

Contract Units and $20 cash 10/21/1964
Each share Common $1 par received second distribution of $0.93 cash 08/16/1965
Each share Common $1 par received third distribution of $0.70 cash 10/31/1967
Each share Common $1 par received fourth and final distribution of $0.069 cash 10/28/1968
(See Delhi Contract Units)

DELI SOLAR USA INC (NV)
Name changed to China Solar & Clean Energy Solutions, Inc. 11/05/2007

DELI TREE INC (NY)
Dissolved by proclamation 6/23/93

DELIA*S INC (DE)
Merged into dELiA*s Corp. 11/20/2000
Each share Common 1¢ par exchanged for (1.715) shares Class A Common 1¢ par
(See dELiA*s Corp.)

DELIAS CORP OLD (DE)
Merged into Alloy, Inc. 09/16/2003
Each share Class A Common 1¢ par exchanged for $0.928 cash

DELICIAS INTL INC (DE)
Adjudicated bankrupt 05/27/1975
Stockholders' equity unlikely

DELICIOUS ALTERNATIVE DESSERTS LTD (AB)
Delisted from Toronto Venture Stock Exchange 06/05/2002

DELICIOUS BRANDS INC (DE)
Name changed to Next Generation Technology Holdings Inc. 06/09/2000
(See Next Generation Technology Holdings Inc.)

DELICORP FOODSERVICE INC (ON)
Recapitalized as Noble House Communications Inc. 08/30/1996
Each share Common no par exchanged for (1/9) share Common no par
Noble House Communications Inc. name changed to Webengine Corp. (ON) 06/06/2000 which reorganized in Canada as Foccini International Inc. 11/13/2003 which name changed to Arch Biopartners Inc. 05/07/2010

DELIGHTFULLY FROZEN CORP (TX)
Common $0.001 par changed to no par and (4,999) additional shares issued payable 02/14/2005 to holders of record 02/11/2005 Ex date - 02/15/2005
Name changed to International Debt Exchange Associates, Inc. 02/15/2005
International Debt Exchange Associates, Inc. name changed to China Media Group Corp. 10/06/2005 which name changed to Median Group Inc. 05/25/2016

DELISLE LTD. (QC)
Name changed to Acklands (Quebec) Ltd. 1/1/68

DELIVERY NOW CORP (DE)
Common $0.0001 par split (10) for (1) by issuance of (9) additional shares payable 10/23/2003 to holders of record 10/20/2003 Ex date - 10/24/2003
Name changed to NS8 Corp. 12/18/2003

DELL COMPUTER CORP (DE)
Common 1¢ par split (3) for (2) by issuance of (0.5) additional share 04/09/2992
Common 1¢ par split (2) for (1) by issuance of (1) additional share 10/27/1995
144A Conv. Preferred Ser. A 1¢ par called for redemption 08/15/1996

Common 1¢ par split (2) for (1) by issuance of (1) additional share payable 12/06/1996 to holders of record 11/25/1996
Common 1¢ par split (2) for (1) by issuance of (1) additional share payable 07/25/1997 to holders of record 07/18/1997
Common 1¢ par split (2) for (1) by issuance of (1) additional share payable 03/06/1998 to holders of record 02/27/1998
Common 1¢ par split (2) for (1) by issuance of (1) additional share payable 09/04/1998 to holders of record 08/28/1998
Common 1¢ par split (2) for (1) by issuance of (1) additional share payable 03/05/1999 to holders of record 02/26/1999
Name changed to Dell Inc. 07/18/2003
(See Dell Inc.)

DELL HYDRO POWER CORP. (NY)
Charter cancelled and proclaimed dissolved for failure to pay taxes 12/15/49

DELL INC (DE)
Acquired by Denali Holding Inc. 10/29/2013
Each share Common 1¢ par exchanged for $13.75 cash

DELLATERRA RES LTD (BC)
Recapitalized as United America Enterprises Ltd. 06/25/1992
Each share Common no par exchanged for (0.2) share Common no par
United America Enterprises Ltd. name changed to United America eHealth Technologies Inc. 06/01/2000
(See United America eHealth Technologies Inc.)

DELLWOOD FOODS INC (NY)
Merged into DFI Holdings, Inc. 09/22/1982
Each share Common $1 par exchanged for $26.50 cash

DELMAGYARORSZAGI ARAMSZOLGALTATO RT - DEMASZ (HUNGARY)
Acquired by EDF International S.A. 12/21/2004
Each Reg. S GDR for Ordinary exchanged for $20.21342 cash

DELMAR MGMT INC (NV)
Name changed to 2energia Inc. 01/31/2003
2energia Inc. name changed to Coastal Holdings, Inc. 07/02/2003 which name changed to Canadian Blue Gold, Inc. 10/18/2007 which recapitalized as Boreal Water Collection, Inc. 03/19/2008
(See Boreal Water Collection, Inc.)

DELMARVA COMPUTER INDUSTRIES, INC. (MD)
Deed of Trust executed 01/28/1970
Assets sold for benefit of creditors 00/00/1972
No stockholders' equity

DELMARVA OIL & MINES CORP. (UT)
Name changed to Richtech Inc. 12/12/1972
(See Richtech Inc.)

DELMARVA PWR & LT CO (DE & VA)
Reincorporated 12/31/1979
Common $6.75 par changed to $3.375 par and (1) additional share issued 05/16/1966
State of incorporation changed from (DE) to (DE) and (VA) 12/31/1979
12.56% Preferred $100 par called for redemption 12/31/1985
8% Preferred $100 par called for redemption 06/30/1986
8.96% Preferred $100 par called for redemption 06/30/1986
Common $3.375 par changed to

$2.25 par and (0.5) additional share issued 05/28/1987
9% Preferred $100 par called for redemption 12/31/1990
7.84% Preferred $100 par called for redemption 12/01/1993
7.88% Preferred $100 par called for redemption 12/01/1993
7.52% Preferred $100 par called for redemption 12/13/1996
Merged into Conectiv, Inc. 03/01/1998
Each share Common $2.25 par exchanged for (1) share Common 1¢ par
Conectiv, Inc. merged into Pepco Holdings Inc. 08/01/2002
7.75% Preferred $100 par called for redemption at $25 on 12/30/2002
6.75% Preferred $100 par called for redemption at $100 on 12/01/2005
3.7% Preferred $100 par called for redemption at $104 on 01/18/2007
4% Preferred $100 par called for redemption at $105 on 01/18/2007
4.2% Preferred $100 par called for redemption at $103 on 01/18/2007
4.28% Preferred $100 par called for redemption at $104 on 01/18/2007
4.56% Preferred $100 par called for redemption at $105 on 01/18/2007
5% Preferred $100 par called for redemption at $104 on 01/18/2007

DELMARVA PWR FING I (DE)
8.125% Trust Preferred Capital Securities called for redemption at $25 plus $0.2594548 accrued dividend on 5/17/2004

DELMAY MNG CORP (AB)
Name changed to Delmay Energy Corp. 7/16/93

DELMED INC (MA)
Recapitalized as Fresenius USA, Inc. 12/30/91
Each share Common 1¢ par exchanged for (0.1) share Common 1¢ par
Fresenius USA, Inc. merged into Fresenius Medical Care AG 9/30/96 which name changed to Fresenius Medical Care AG & Co. KGaA 2/10/2006

DELMICAH MINES INC (DE)
Name changed to Delmicah, Inc. 2/8/89

DELMICO MINES LTD (ON)
Capital Stock $1 par changed to no par 06/10/1971
Charter cancelled and declared dissolved for failure to pay taxes and file returns 12/07/1977

DELNAUR GOLD MINES LTD. (ON)
Merged into Associated Porcupine Mines Ltd. 11/05/1968
Each share Capital Stock $1 par exchanged for (0.00696) share Capital Stock no par
Associated Porcupine Mines Ltd. merged into American Reserve Mining Corp. 02/27/1989 which recapitalized as AMI Resources Inc. 12/21/1994 which name changed to Ashanti Sankofa Inc. 01/19/2017

DELNITE MINES LTD. (ON)
Common $1 par changed to 80¢ par 07/08/1960
Liquidation completed
Each share Common 80¢ par exchanged for initial distribution of $0.50 cash 02/01/1965
Each share Common 80¢ par received second distribution of $0.30 cash 06/10/1965
Each share Common 80¢ par received third distribution of $0.05 cash 12/01/1965
Each share Common 80¢ par received fourth and final distribution of $0.1575 cash 11/19/1969

DELON RES CORP (BC)
Recapitalized as Gener8 Media Corp. 04/30/2013

Each share Common no par exchanged for (0.5) share Common no par
Gener8 Media Corp. name changed to Eight Solutions Inc. 02/03/2015

DELORO MINERALS LTD (AB)
Recapitalized as Deloro Resources Ltd. (ALTA) 08/23/2005
Each share Common no par exchanged for (0.5) share Common no par
Deloro Resources Ltd. (ALTA) reincorporated in British Columbia 03/10/2009

DELORO RES LTD (AB)
Reincorporated under the laws of British Columbia 03/10/2009

DELOS INTL GROUP INC (DE)
Merged into Automatic Data Processing, Inc. 04/14/1976
Each share Common 10¢ par exchanged for $5 cash

DELOSHA PORCUPINE MINES LTD. (ON)
Charter revoked for failure to file reports and pay taxes 00/00/1957

DELPET RES LTD (CANADA)
Each share old Common no par exchanged for (0.2) share new Common no par 08/31/1999
Name changed to HTI Ventures Corp. (Canada) 06/06/2000
HTI Ventures Corp. (Canada) reincorporated in British Columbia as Leagold Mining Corp. 08/31/2016

DELPHI AUTOMOTIVE PLC (JERSEY)
Each share Ordinary 1¢ par received distribution of (0.33333333) share Delphi Technologies PLC Ordinary 1¢ par payable 12/04/2017 to holders of record 11/22/2017 Ex date - 12/05/2017
Name changed to Aptiv PLC 12/05/2017

DELPHI AUTOMOTIVE SYS CORP (DE)
Name changed to Delphi Corp. 03/13/2002
(See Delphi Corp.)

DELPHI CORP (DE)
Plan of reorganization under Chapter 11 Federal Bankruptcy proceedings effective 10/06/2009
No stockholders' equity

DELPHI FINL GROUP INC (DE)
Class A Common 1¢ par split (3) for (2) by issuance of (0.5) additional share payable 12/22/2003 to holders of record 12/08/2003 Ex date - 12/23/2003
Class A Common 1¢ par split (3) for (2) by issuance of (0.5) additional share payable 06/01/2006 to holders of record 05/18/2006 Ex date - 06/02/2006
Stock Dividends - 20% payable 09/30/1996 to holders of record 09/16/1996; 2% payable 06/10/1997 to holders of record 05/27/1997; 2% payable 05/04/1998 to holders of record 04/20/1998; 2% payable 12/15/1998 to holders of record 12/01/1998; 2% payable 06/08/1999 to holders of record 05/25/1999; 2% payable 12/15/1999 to holders of record 12/01/1999
Acquired by Tokio Marine Holdings, Ltd. 05/15/2012
Each share Class A Common 1¢ par exchanged for $43.875 cash

DELPHI GROUP INC (DE)
Name changed to Sutton Corp. 7/15/74
(See Sutton Corp.)

DELPHI GROUP PLC (UNITED KINGDOM)
ADR agreement terminated 4/21/99

Each Sponsored ADR for Ordinary exchanged for $8.6798 cash

DELPHI INFORMATION SYS INC (DE)
Each share old Common 10¢ par exchanged for (0.2) share new Common 10¢ par 05/08/1998
Name changed to Ebix.com, Inc. 10/27/1999
Ebix.com, Inc. name changed to Ebix, Inc. 12/30/2003

DELPHI INTL LTD (BERMUDA)
Completely liquidated 03/22/2002
Each share Common 1¢ par exchanged for first and final distribution of $3 cash

DELPHI TR I (DE)
Plan of reorganization under Chapter 11 Federal Bankruptcy proceedings confirmed 01/25/2008
Each 8.25% Trust Preferred Security received $25 principal amount of Delphi Corp. 8.25% Jr. Subordinated Note due 10/15/2033

DELPHOS CTZNS BANCORP INC (DE)
Merged into United Bancshares Inc. 02/28/2001
Each share Common 1¢ par exchanged for (0.8749) share Common no par and $5.41 cash

DELRAND RES LTD (CANADA)
Each share old Common no par exchanged for (0.33333333) share new Common no par 05/16/2014
Each share new Common no par exchanged again for (0.5) share new Common no par 02/29/2016
Name changed to KuuHubb Inc. 06/16/2017

DELRAY BEACH NATL BK (DELRAY BEACH, FL)
94.8% acquired by Barnett Banks of Florida, Inc. through exchange offer which expired 11/15/1973
Public interest eliminated

DELRAY VENTURES INC (AB)
Reincorporated under the laws of British Columbia as Clydesdale Resources Inc. 08/08/2008

DELRINA CORP (ON)
Acquired by Symantec Corp. 11/21/95
Each share Common no par exchanged for (0.61) Delrina Corp. Exchangeable Share no par
Each Exchangeable Share no par exchanged for (1) share Symantec Corp. Common 1¢ par 11/22/2002

DELSECUR CORP (NV)
Voluntarily dissolved 06/18/2014
Details not available

DELSITE INC (TX)
Chapter 7 bankruptcy proceedings terminated 03/12/2012
No stockholders' equity

DELSOFT CONSULTING INC (GA)
Chapter 11 bankruptcy proceedings converted to Chapter 7 on 2/5/2002
Stockholders' equity unlikely

DELSTAR CORP (DE)
Charter cancelled and declared inoperative and void for non-payment of taxes 06/26/1985

DELTA & PINE LD CO (DE)
Common 10¢ par split (4) for (3) by issuance of (0.33333333) additional share 12/15/1995
Common 10¢ par split (3) for (2) by issuance of (0.5) additional share payable 04/15/1996 to holders of record 03/29/1996 Ex date - 04/16/1996
Common 10¢ par split (4) for (3) by issuance of (0.33333333) additional share payable 04/11/1997 to holders of record 03/31/1997 Ex date - 04/14/1997
Common 10¢ par split (4) for (3) by issuance of (0.33333333) additional share payable 11/20/1997 to holders of record 11/10/1997 Ex date - 11/21/1997
Merged into Monsanto Co. (New) 06/01/2007
Each share Common 10¢ par exchanged for $42 cash

DELTA ACCEPTANCE CORP. LTD. (ON)
Name changed to Avco Delta Corp. Canada Ltd. 11/01/1966
Avco Delta Corp. Canada Ltd. merged into Avco Financial Services Canada Ltd. 05/05/1971

DELTA AIR CORP. (LA)
Name changed to Delta Air Lines, Inc. (LA) 00/00/1945
Delta Air Lines, Inc. (LA) reincorporated in Delaware 06/30/1967
(See Delta Air Lines, Inc.)

DELTA AIR LINES INC (DE)
Reincorporated 06/30/1967
Common $3 par split (4) for (3) by issuance of (0.33333333) additional share 03/15/1962
Common $3 par split (3) for (2) by issuance of (0.5) additional share 03/04/1963
Common $3 par split (5) for (4) by issuance of (0.25) additional share 09/08/1964
Common $3 par split (2) for (1) by issuance of (1) additional share 12/13/1965
Stock Dividend - 25% 06/29/1956
State of incorporation changed from (LA) to (DE) 06/30/1967
Common $3 par split (3) for (1) by issuance of (2) additional shares 12/01/1967
Common $3 par split (2) for (1) by issuance of (1) additional share 11/30/1981
Common $3 par changed to $1.50 par and (1) additional share issued payable 11/16/1998 to holders of record 11/02/1998 Ex date - 11/17/1998
Depositary Preferred Ser. C called for redemption 07/11/1996
Conv. Preferred Ser. C $1 par called for redemption 07/11/1996
Common $1.50 par changed to 1¢ par 05/19/2005
Plan of reorganization under Chapter 11 Federal Bankruptcy Code effective 04/30/2007
No stockholders' equity
(Additional Information in Active)

DELTA AUTOMATED SYS INC (DE)
Adjudicated bankrupt 04/12/1972
Stockholders' equity unlikely

DELTA BK & TR CO (BELLE CHASE, LA)
Merged into Regions Financial Corp. (Old) 08/08/1996
Each share Common $5 par exchanged for (2.2568) shares Common $0.625 par
Regions Financial Corp. (Old) merged into Regions Financial Corp. (New) 07/01/2004

DELTA BK & TR CO (PORT SULPHUR, LA)
Merged into Regions Financial Corp. (Old) 08/08/1996
Each share Common $5 par exchanged for (2.2568) shares Common $0.625 par
Regions Financial Corp. (Old) merged into Regions Financial Corp. (New) 07/01/2004

DELTA BENCO LTD (ON)
Each share old Common no par exchanged for (0.00000625) share new Common no par 03/22/1985
Note: In effect holders received $0.04 cash per share and public interest was eliminated

DELTA CALIF INDS (CA)
Merged into Meridian Express Co. 07/01/1981
Each share Common 50¢ par exchanged for $13 cash

DELTA CAP CORP (LA)
Liquidation completed
Each share Common $1 par exchanged for initial distribution of (0.147131) share Dasa Corp. Common $1 par and $7 cash 07/11/1969
Each share Common $1 par received second and final distribution of $1.30 cash 01/05/1972

DELTA CAP TECHNOLOGIES INC (DE)
Old Common $0.001 par split (4) for (1) by issuance of (3) additional shares payable 03/15/1999 to holders of record 03/15/1999
Old Common $0.001 par split (3) for (1) by issuance of (2) additional shares payable 01/12/2001 to holders of record 01/05/2001 Ex date - 01/16/2001
Each share old Common $0.001 par exchanged for (0.01) share new Common $0.001 par 01/04/2002
Name changed to Newmark Ventures Inc. 02/20/2004
Newmark Ventures Inc. reorganized as Mangapets, Inc. 10/26/2005 which name changed to Intrepid Global Imaging 3D, Inc. 03/01/2007 which name changed to Spine Pain Management, Inc. 11/27/2009 which name changed to Spine Injury Solutions, Inc. 10/08/2015

DELTA COMPUTEC INC (NY)
Acquired by Alpha Microsystems 09/01/1998
Each share Common 1¢ par exchanged for approximately $0.32 cash

DELTA CORP (CO)
Each share Common 20¢ par exchanged for (0.05) share Common $1 par 09/20/1966
Name changed to A.I.D. Inc. (CO) 12/29/1972
(See A.I.D. Inc. (CO))

DELTA CORP AMER (FL)
Common 10¢ par split (5) for (4) by issuance of (0.25) additional share 04/19/1971
Common 10¢ par split (5) for (4) by issuance of (0.25) additional share 11/11/1971
Proclaimed dissolved for failure to file reports and pay fees 11/01/1985

DELTA DATA SYS CORP (PA)
Plan of reorganization under Chapter 11 Federal Bankruptcy proceedings confirmed 11/26/1992
No stockholders' equity

DELTA DATA SYSTEMS, INC. (MD)
Merged into Delta Automated Systems, Inc. 10/01/1970
Each share Common 1¢ par exchanged for (0.37564) share Common 10¢ par
(See Delta Automated Systems, Inc.)

DELTA DESIGN, INC. (CA)
Name changed to ABC Dissolution Corp. 06/15/1967
(See ABC Dissolution Corp.)

DELTA DEV & EXPL LTD (ON)
Liquidated and voluntarily dissolved 09/04/1971
Details not available

DELTA DRILLING CO (TX)
Name changed to DeltaUS Corp. 06/29/1984
(See DeltaUS Corp.)

DELTA DRUG CORP. OF CENTRAL GEORGIA (FL)
Proclaimed dissolved for failure to file reports and pay fees 05/22/1970

DELTA ELECTRIC CO. (IN)
Common $2.50 par changed to $7.50 par 00/00/1949
Name changed to Deltec Corp. Inc. 12/31/1964
(See Deltec Corp. Inc.)

DELTA ELECTRONICS THAILAND PLC (THAILAND)
ADR agreement terminated 05/26/2011
Details not available

DELTA ELECTRS LTD (ON)
Name changed to Delta-Benco Ltd. 12/10/1971
(See Delta-Benco Ltd.)

DELTA EXPL INC (BC)
Merged into Rockgate Capital Corp. 01/30/2009
Each share Common no par exchanged for (0.5) share Common no par
Rockgate Capital Corp. merged into Denison Mines Corp. 01/20/2014

DELTA FED SVGS F S B (DELTA, CO)
Merged into First Colorado Bancorp Inc. 09/30/1997
Each share Common 1¢ par exchanged for (1.56965337) shares Common 10¢ par
First Colorado Bancorp Inc. merged into Commercial Federal Corp. 08/14/1998
(See Commercial Federal Corp.)

DELTA FINL CORP (DE)
Preferred Ser. A called for redemption at $100 on 06/14/2004
Plan of reorganization under Chapter 11 Federal Bankruptcy Code effective 01/05/2009
No stockholders' equity

DELTA GOLD CORP (BC)
Each share Common no par received distribution of (0.5) Common Stock Purchase Warrant expiring 09/14/2017 payable 02/19/2013 to holders of record 02/13/2013
Recapitalized as Mission Gold Ltd. 07/09/2015
Each share Common no par exchanged for (0.0625) share Common no par

DELTA GOLD LTD (AUSTRALIA)
Name changed 01/11/2000
Name changed from Delta Gold N.L. to Delta Gold Ltd. 01/11/2000
ADR agreement terminated 02/15/2002
Each ADR for Ordinary exchanged for $1.2918 cash

DELTA GOLD MNG CORP (BC)
Class A no par reclassified as Common no par 07/25/1994
Merged into Chase Resource Corp. (New) 05/30/1997
Each share Common no par exchanged for (0.5) share Common no par
(See Chase Resource Corp. (New))

DELTA HOTELS LTD (BC)
Each share 6% Preference Class A no par exchanged for (0.5) share 12¢ Conv. Preference no par 11/12/1972
Through purchase offer 100% acquired by Oxford Properties (BC) Ltd. as of 11/00/1974
Public interest eliminated

DELTA INDUSTRIES, INC. (MS)
Merged into Weyerhaeuser Co. 06/08/1979
Each share Common $1 par exchanged for (1.55564) shares Common $1.875 par

DELTA INDS INC (OH)
Common no par split (2) for (1) by issuance of (1) additional share 12/02/1968
Adjudicated bankrupt 03/05/1971
Stockholders' equity unlikely

DELTA INSTRUMENT CORP. (NJ)
Adjudicated insolvent 03/08/1963
No stockholders' equity

DELTA INTL INDS CORP (BC)
Recapitalized as Delta Exploration Inc. 12/12/2003
Each share Common no par exchanged for (0.33333333) share Common no par
Delta Exploration Inc. merged into Rockgate Capital Corp. 01/30/2009 which merged into Denison Mines Corp. 01/20/2014

DELTA INTL MINERALS LTD (BC)
Struck off register and declared dissolved for failure to file returns 02/10/1975

DELTA INTL OIL & GAS INC (DE)
Name changed to CannAwake Corp. 08/09/2018

DELTA LLOYD NV (NETHERLANDS)
Stock Dividends - 2.91545% payable 09/09/2013 to holders of record 08/19/2013 Ex date - 08/15/2013; 2.39463% payable 09/10/2014 to holders of record 08/18/2014 Ex date - 08/14/2014; 4.53514% payable 09/24/2015 to holders of record 08/24/2015 Ex date - 08/20/2015
ADR agreement terminated 06/30/2017
Each ADR for Ordinary exchanged for $5.839841 cash

DELTA MGMT SYS INC (NJ)
Each share old Common no par exchanged for (0.5) share new Common no par 03/01/1993
Filed a petition under Chapter 11 Federal Bankruptcy Code 01/28/1994
Details not available

DELTA MINERALS CORP (QC)
Charter annulled for failure to file reports or pay fees 10/12/1974

DELTA MNG & EXPL CORP (NV)
Each share old Common $0.001 par exchanged for (0.01) share new Common $0.001 par 05/04/2007
SEC revoked common stock registration 08/13/2010

DELTA MUT INC (DE)
Recapitalized as Helvetia Pharmaceuticals, Inc. 08/21/2002
Each share Common $0.0001 par exchanged for (0.1) share Common $0.0001 par
Helvetia Pharmaceuticals, Inc. reorganized back as Delta Mutual, Inc. 02/06/2003
Old Common $0.0001 par split (5) for (1) by issuance of (4) additional shares payable 02/20/2003 to holders of record 02/19/2003 Ex date - 02/21/2003
Each share old Common $0.0001 par exchanged for (0.1) share new Common $0.0001 par 07/06/2009
Name changed to Delta International Oil & Gas Inc. 11/27/2013
Delta International Oil & Gas Inc. name changed to CannAwake Corp. 08/09/2018

DELTA NAT GAS INC (KY)
10% Preferred $10 par called for redemption 06/30/1987
Common $1 par split (2) for (1) by issuance of (1) additional share payable 05/01/2012 to holders of record 04/17/2012 Ex date - 05/02/2012
Acquired by PNG Companies LLC 09/20/2017
Each share Common $1 par exchanged for $30.50 cash

DELTA NATL BANCORP (CA)
Merged into Farmers & Merchants Bancorp 11/18/2016
Each share Common no par exchanged for (0.031748) share Common 1¢ par

DELTA NORTH TRANSN LTD (AB)
Struck off register and declared dissolved for failure to file returns 10/31/1995

DELTA OIL CO. OF UTAH (UT)
Completely liquidated 04/19/1963
Each share Common $1 par exchanged for first and final distribution of (1) share Bloomfield Royalty Corp. Common 20¢ par
Bloomfield Royalty Corp. name changed to Financial Technology, Inc. 12/29/1969 which name changed to Texon Energy Corp. 05/14/1974
(See Texon Energy Corp.)

DELTA P INC (DE)
Merged into Burgess Industries Inc. 11/24/1971
Each share Common 10¢ par exchanged for (0.4) share Common 50¢ par
(See Burgess Industries Inc.)

DELTA PAC CORP (NV)
Charter revoked for failure to file reports and pay fees 03/01/1971

DELTA PACIFIC BANK (PITTSBURG, CA)
Placed in receivership with FDIC 10/30/1987
No stockholders' equity

DELTA PETE & ENERGY CORP (DE)
Name changed 09/24/1980
Name changed from Delta Petroleum Corp. to Delta Petroleum & Energy Corp. and state of incorporation changed from (UT) to (DE) 09/24/1980
Name changed to PNX Industries, Inc. 12/15/1986
(See PNX Industries, Inc.)

DELTA PETE CORP (DE)
Reincorporated 07/31/2006
Each share old Common 1¢ par exchanged for (0.01) share new Common 1¢ par 12/18/1992
State of incorporation changed from (CO) to (DE) 01/31/2006
Plan of reorganization under Chapter 11 Federal Bankruptcy proceedings effective 08/31/2012
No stockholders' equity

DELTA QUEEN STEAMBOAT CO (DE)
Name changed to American Classic Voyages Co. 5/17/94
(See American Classic Voyages Co.)

DELTA QUEEN STEAMBOAT CO (OH)
Acquired by Equity Holdings 5/9/86
Each share Common 25¢ par exchanged for $17 cash

DELTA REFNG CORP (BC)
Assignment in bankruptcy filed 5/6/83
Stockholders' equity undetermined

DELTA RENT SYS INC (UT)
Each share old Common $0.001 par exchanged for (0.1) share new Common $0.001 par 8/21/89
Proclaimed dissolved for failure to file annual report 2/1/92

DELTA SAVINGS & LOAN ASSOCIATION (CA)
Placed in receivership by the RTC 3/25/94
Stockholders' equity unlikely

DELTA SEABOARD INTL INC (NV)
Recapitalized as American International Holdings Corp. 08/13/2012
Each share Common $0.0001 par exchanged for (0.01) share Common $0.0001 par

DELTA SONICS, INC. (CA)
Completely liquidated 2/16/67
Each share Common $1 par exchanged for first and final distribution of $2.42 cash

DELTA SS LINES INC (LA)
Completely liquidated 10/26/76
Each share Capital Stock $5 par exchanged for first and final distribution of $35.27 cash

DELTA STAR RES INC (BC)
Reorganized under the laws of Ontario as Accord Financial Corp. 4/10/92
Each share Common no par exchanged for (0.2) share Common no par

DELTA STS OIL INC (DE)
Name changed to WindsorTech Inc. 01/30/2002
WindsorTech Inc. name changed to QSGI, Inc. 10/18/2005
(See QSGI, Inc.)

DELTA SYS INC (AR)
Acquired by Delta Systems, Inc. (Canada) 03/21/2006
Each share Common $0.001 par exchanged for CAD $0.72 cash

DELTA SYS INC (CANADA)
Dissolved for non-compliance 06/29/2011
Stockholders' equity unlikely

DELTA TREND FD INC (DE)
Reincorporated under the laws of Maryland 5/1/83

DELTA VENTURE FD INC (CO)
Name changed to Able Telcom Holding Corp. (CO) 02/07/1989
Able Telcom Holding Corp. (CO) reincorporated in Florida 07/00/1991
Able Telcom Holding Corp. (FL) merged into Bracknell Corp. 12/22/2000
(See Bracknell Corp.)

DELTA VENTURES INC (DE)
Common $0.001 par split (100) for (1) by issuance of (99) additional shares 07/03/1991
Name changed to Krantor Corp. 10/21/1991
Krantor Corp. name changed to Synergy Brands Inc. 06/29/1998
(See Synergy Brands Inc.)

DELTA WESTERN 1985-A DRILLING FUND, A LIMITED PARTNERSHIP (OK)
Partnership terminated 11/07/2002
Details not available

DELTA WESTERN 1985-B DRILLING FUND, A LIMITED PARTNERSHIP (OK)
Partnership terminated 11/07/2002
Details not available

DELTA WESTN SYS INC (DE)
Charter cancelled and declared inoperative and void for non-payment of taxes 03/01/1988

DELTA WOODSIDE INDS INC (DE)
Merged into Delta Woodside Industries, Inc. (SC) 11/15/1989
Each share Common 1¢ par exchanged for (1.0095816) shares Common 1¢ par
(See Delta Woodside Industries, Inc. (SC))

DELTA WOODSIDE INDS INC NEW (SC)
Each share Common 1¢ par received distribution of (0.1) share Delta Apparel, Inc. Common 1¢ par and (0.1) share Duck Head Apparel Co., Inc. Common 1¢ par payable 06/30/2000 to holders of record 06/19/2000
Each share old Common 1¢ par exchanged for (0.25) share new Common 1¢ par 02/05/2002
Plan of reorganization under Chapter 11 Federal Bankruptcy Code effective 10/23/2007
No stockholders' equity

DELTAK CORP (MN)
Stock Dividend - 50% 01/20/1978
Acquired by a management group 05/02/1990
Each share Common 1¢ par exchanged for $15 cash

DELTAN LTD (CANADA)
Acquired by Prudel Ltd. 12/31/1977
Each share Common $2 par exchanged for $10 cash

DELTAPOINT INC (CA)
Name changed to Site Technologies Inc. 01/20/1998
(See Site Technologies Inc.)

DELTATHREE INC (DE)
Name changed 12/26/2000
Name changed from Deltathree.com, Inc. to Deltathree, Inc. 12/26/2000
Class B Common $0.001 par reclassified as Class A Common $0.001 par 06/28/2001
Class A Common $0.001 par reclassified as Common $0.001 par 08/06/2009
Acquired by D4 Holdings, LLC 07/13/2015
Each share Common $0.001 par exchanged for $0.01 cash

DELTAUS CORP (TX)
Plan of reorganization under Chapter 11 Federal Bankruptcy proceedings confirmed 12/06/1989
No stockholders' equity

DELTAVISION INC (NV)
Name changed to First Deltavision, Inc. 03/25/1997
First Deltavision, Inc. name changed to KyoMedix Inc. 04/04/2002 which name changed back to First Deltavision, Inc. 11/18/2002 which name changed to Integrated Healthcare Holdings, Inc. 03/04/2004
(See Integrated Healthcare Holdings, Inc.)

DELTEC CORP. INC. (IN)
Liquidation completed
Each share Common $7.50 par exchanged for initial distribution of (1) Ctf. of Bene. Int. no par and $15 cash 04/14/1965
Each share Common $7.50 par received second distribution of $2.70 cash 11/12/1965
Each share Common $7.50 par received third and final distribution of $0.32 cash 07/18/1968

DELTEC INTL LTD (ENGLAND)
Reorganized 09/28/1973
Common $7.50 par changed to no par 04/06/1972
Reorganized from Ontario to under the laws of England 09/28/1973
Each share Common no par exchanged for (1) ADR for Ordinary Reg.
In process of liquidation
Each ADR for Ordinary Reg. received initial and second distributions of (1) share Deltec Holdings, Inc. Capital Stock $1 par, (0.5) share Treasure Cay, Ltd. Ordinary 1¢ par and $3 cash 04/25/1978
(See each company's listing)
Each ADR for Ordinary Reg. received third distribution of $2.50 cash 02/28/1979
Each ADR for Ordinary Reg. received fourth distribution of $8 cash 07/31/1980
Each ADR for Ordinary Reg. exchanged for fifth distribution of $2 cash 02/24/1981
Each ADR for Ordinary Reg. received sixth distribution of $1.25 cash 05/14/1982
Each ADR for Ordinary Reg. received seventh distribution of $0.50 cash 01/16/1984
Each ADR for Ordinary Reg. received

eighth distribution of $0.50 cash 01/31/1985
Each ADR for Ordinary Reg. received ninth distribution of $0.50 cash 08/17/1987
Each ADR for Ordinary Reg. received tenth distribution of $0.20 cash 10/31/1988
Amount or number of subsequent distributions, if any, are unknown

DELTEC PANAMERICA S A (PANAMA)
5% Conv. Preferred $2.85 par called for redemption 3/23/82
6% Sr. Preferred $5 par called for redemption 3/23/82
  (Additional Information in Active)

DELTEC RES LTD (BC)
Recapitalized as Pacific Titan Resource Corp. 2/4/91
Each share Common no par exchanged for (0.5) share Common no par
(See Pacific Titan Resource Corp.)

DELTEK INC (DE)
Acquired by Project Diamond Holdings Corp. 10/10/2012
Each share Common $0.001 par exchanged for $13 cash

DELTEK INTERTRADE CORP (UT)
Involuntarily dissolved 05/01/1988

DELTEK SYS INC (VA)
Merged into DF Merger Co. 05/31/2002
Each share Common $0.001 par exchanged for $7.15 cash

DELTIC TIMBER CORP (DE)
Merged into Potlatch Corp. (New) 02/20/2018
Each share Common 1¢ par exchanged for (1.8) shares Common $1 par
Potlatch Corp. (New) name changed to PotlatchDeltic Corp. 02/23/2018

DELTON INDS INC (DE)
Merged into DFC Financial Corp. 08/02/1982
Each share Common 20¢ par exchanged for $13 cash

DELTONA CORP (DE)
$3 Conv. Preferred Ser. A $1 par called redemption 10/15/1969
Common $1 par split (2) for (1) by issuance of (1) additional share 06/06/1989
Each share old Common $1 par exchanged for (0.000002) share new Common $1 par 01/29/2004
Note: In effect holders received $0.40 cash per share and public interest was eliminated

DELTONA INDS INC (ON)
Delisted from Canadian Dealer Network 05/31/1996

DELTOWN FOODS INC (NY)
Common $1 par split (4) for (3) by issuance of (1/3) additional share 12/31/63
Name changed to Dellwood Foods, Inc. 5/3/76
(See Dellwood Foods, Inc.)

DELUXE CHECK PRINTERS INC (MN)
Each share Common $10 par exchanged for (10) shares Common $1 par 02/23/1956
Common $1 par split (10) for (1) by issuance of (9) additional shares 02/19/1963
Common $1 par split (2) for (1) by issuance of (1) additional share 12/04/1972
Common $1 par split (2) for (1) by issuance of (1) additional share 09/18/1981
Common $1 par split (2) for (1) by issuance of (1) additional share 03/14/1985
Common $1 par split (2) for (1) by issuance of (1) additional share 09/12/1986
Stock Dividend - 100% 06/07/1971
Name changed to Deluxe Corp. 05/18/1988

DELWOOD CAPITAL CORP. LTD. (CANADA)
Name changed to Indostar Gold Corp. and (1.5) additional shares issued 07/10/1996
Indostar Gold Corp. name changed to Petroflow Energy Ltd. 10/28/1997

DELWOOD FURNITURE INC (DE)
Merged into U.S. Industries, Inc. 12/31/1977
Each share Common $1 par exchanged for $7 cash

DELWOOD PORCUPINE GOLD MINES LTD. (ON)
Charter cancelled 08/00/1960

DEM INC (MD)
Liquidation completed
Each share Common received initial distribution of $14.50 cash 9/22/98
Each share Common received second and final distribution of $14.50 cash in December 1998

DEMAC INVTS INC (CO)
Recapitalized as Reliance Lodging, Inc. 02/05/1993
Each share Common no par exchanged for (0.2) share Common no par
(See Reliance Lodging, Inc.)

DEMAND FINL INTL LTD (NV)
Common $0.001 par split (2) for (1) by issuance of (1) additional share payable 10/16/2002 to holders of record 10/14/2002 Ex date - 10/17/2002
Name changed to Blue Fish Entertainment, Inc. 11/26/2002
Blue Fish Entertainment, Inc. name changed to Pacific Gold Corp. 9/8/2003

DEMAND GOLD LTD (BC)
Name changed 01/25/1995
Name changed from Demand Technologies Ltd. to Demand Gold Ltd. 01/25/1995
Recapitalized as Demand Ventures Ltd. 03/03/1999
Each share Common no par exchanged for (0.33333333) share Common no par
Demand Ventures Ltd. name changed to Knexa.com Enterprises Inc. 08/01/2000 which name changed to Knexa Solutions Inc. 02/18/2003 which name changed to ClearFrame Solutions Inc. 02/13/2004 which recapitalized as ClearFrame Solutions Corp. 05/02/2005 which name changed to Clear Gold Resources Inc. 02/25/2013

DEMAND MEDIA INC (DE)
Each share old Common $0.0001 par received distribution of (0.2) share Rightside Group, Ltd. Common $0.0001 par payable 08/01/2014 to holders of record 07/25/2014
Each share old Common $0.0001 par exchanged for (0.2) share new Common $0.0001 par 08/04/2014
Name changed to Leaf Group Ltd. 11/09/2016

DEMAND VENTURES LTD (BC)
Name changed to Knexa.com Enterprises Inc. 08/01/2000
Knexa.com Enterprises Inc. name changed to Knexa Solutions Inc. 02/18/2003 which name changed to ClearFrame Solutions Inc. 02/13/2004 which recapitalized as ClearFrame Solutions Corp. 05/02/2005 which name changed to Clear Gold Resources Inc. 02/25/2013

DEMANDSTAR COM INC (FL)
Merged into Onvia.com, Inc. 03/05/2001
Each share Common $0.0001 par exchanged for (0.6) share Common $0.0001 par
Onvia.com, Inc. name changed to Onvia, Inc. 06/25/2004
(See Onvia, Inc.)

DEMANDTEC INC (DE)
Acquired by International Business Machines Corp. 02/14/2012
Each share Common $0.001 par exchanged for $13.20 cash

DEMANDWARE INC (DE)
Acquired by salesforce.com, inc. 07/11/2016
Each share Common 1¢ par exchanged for $75 cash

DEMARCO BUSINESS FORMS INC (PA)
Completely liquidated 03/11/1968
Each share Class A Common no par exchanged for first and final distribution of (0.5152) share Safeguard Industries, Inc. Common 10¢ par
Safeguard Industries, Inc. name changed to Safeguard Scientifics, Inc. 05/15/1981

DEMARCO ENERGY SYS AMER INC (UT)
Name changed to Energy Vision International, Inc. 03/03/2006
(See Energy Vision International, Inc.)

DEMARK FINL CORP (DE)
Name changed to Home Lending Associates, Inc. 08/02/1993
Home Lending Associates, Inc. name changed to Microsure Inc. 11/27/1996 which recapitalized as 9A Investment Holding Corp. 08/31/2001 which name changed to Viking Power Services, Inc. 07/03/2006

DEMATCO INC (DE)
Each share Common $0.001 par received distribution of (0.00625) share Progressive Training, Inc. Common $0.0001 par payable 04/22/2008 to holders of record 03/25/2008 Ex date - 05/16/2008
Note: No holder will receive fewer than (100) shares
SEC revoked common stock registration 11/01/2013

DEMCAP INVTS INC (CANADA)
Name changed to iPerceptions Inc. 07/10/2007
(See iPerceptions Inc.)

DEMEGEN INC (CO)
Each share old Common $0.001 par exchanged for (0.02857142) share new Common $0.001 par 10/01/2004
Name changed to Par Advance Technologies Corp. 10/18/2004
Par Advance Technologies Corp. name changed to ACI Global Corp. 06/20/2005

DEMERT & DOUGHERTY INC (NV)
Charter permanently revoked 12/31/1998

DEMETER BIOTECHNOLOGIES LTD (CO)
Name changed to Demegen, Inc. 09/18/1998
Demegen, Inc. name changed to Par Advance Technologies Corp. 10/18/2004 which name changed to ACI Global Corp. 06/20/2005

DEMIL INTL INC (NV)
Acquired by CH2M Hill 00/00/2002
Details not available

DEMING CO. (OH)
Name changed to Deming Investment Corp. 08/01/1961
Deming Investment Corp. acquired by Massachusetts Investors Trust 09/12/1968

DEMING INVT CORP (OH)
Completely liquidated 09/17/1968
Each share Common $5 par exchanged for first and final distribution of (1.1987) shares Massachusetts Investors Trust Ctfs. of Bene. Int. $0.33333333 par and $0.10 cash

DEMIRBANK (TURKEY)
ADR agreement terminated 12/20/2000
ADR holders' equity unlikely

DEMLEIN CORP. (NY)
Name changed to Industrial Enterprises, Inc. (NY) 10/25/1955
Industrial Enterprises, Inc. (NY) name changed to Novo Industrial Corp. 04/28/1960 which name changed to Novo Corp. 05/05/1969
(See Novo Corp.)

DEMOBAG BRANDS INC (NV)
Recapitalized as China Gold Resource, Inc. 08/16/2007
Each share Common $0.001 par exchanged for (0.1) share Common $0.001 par
China Gold Resource, Inc. name changed to WiseMobi, Inc. 05/13/2008 which recapitalized as New Infinity Holdings, Ltd. 02/23/2015

DEMOCRASOFT INC (DE)
Name changed to Democrasoft Holdings, Inc. 04/22/2013

DEMPSEY CADILLAC GOLD MINES LTD.
Name changed to Dominion Malartic Gold Mines Ltd. 00/00/1944
(See Dominion Malartic Gold Mines Ltd.)

DEMPSEY OILS LTD. (AB)
Each share old Capital Stock no par exchanged for (0.02) share new Capital Stock no par 09/14/1964
Merged into General Petroleums Drilling Ltd. 09/01/1969
Each share new Capital Stock no par exchanged for (1) share 7% Class B Preferred $2.77 par
(See General Petroleums Drilling Ltd.)

DEMPSTER EXPLS LTD (ON)
Recapitalized as Tritex Petroleum Corp. 11/03/1981
Each share Capital Stock $1 par exchanged for (0.33333333) share Common no par
Tritex Petroleum Corp. recapitalized as Peregrine Instruments & Monitoring Inc. 02/05/1988 which name changed to Justice Electronic Monitoring Systems Inc. 04/05/1990 which recapitalized as Jemtec Inc. 04/28/1994

DEMPSTER INDS INC (NE)
Acquired by Dempster Industries LLC 08/00/2008
Details not available

DEMPSTER INVT CO (IL)
Voluntarily dissolved 10/09/1974
Details not available

DEMPSTER MILL MANUFACTURING CO. (NE)
Each share 7% Preferred $100 par exchanged for (1) share 5% Preferred $100 par 00/00/1936
5% Preferred $100 par called for redemption 00/00/1942
Each share Common $100 par exchanged for (5) shares Common $20 par 02/06/1956
Name changed to First Beatrice Corp. 10/03/1963
(See First Beatrice Corp.)

DEMPSTER MILL MFG. CO. (NE)
Name changed to Dempster Industries Inc. 02/01/1966
(See Dempster Industries Inc.)

DEMSEY MINES LTD (BC)
Struck off register and declared dissolved for failure to file returns 12/18/1978

DEN DANSKE BK AF 1871 AKTIESELSKAB (DENMARK)
Name changed to Danske Bank A/S 09/01/2000

DEN NORSKE BK AS (NORWAY)
Name changed to DNB Holding A.S.A. 12/21/1999
DNB Holding A.S.A. name changed to DnB NOR A.S.A. (Old) 12/04/2003
(See DnB NOR A.S.A. (Old))

DEN-RADO PRODUCTS, INC. (CO)
Reported out of business; declared defunct for non-payment of franchise taxes 09/27/1957

DEN TAL EZ INC (IA)
Common $1 par split (2) for (1) by issuance of (1) additional share 05/24/1971
Merged into Syntex Corp. 05/31/1979
Each share Common $1 par exchanged for (1) share Class B Conv. Preferred no par and (1) share Class C Preferred no par
(See Syntex Corp.)

DENAB LABORATORIES INC. (CO)
Common 50¢ par changed to no par 05/10/1966
Name changed to Stellar Industries, Inc. (CO) 12/00/1967
Stellar Industries, Inc. (CO) in Delaware 01/06/1970
(See Stellar Industries, Inc. (DE))

DENALI CONCRETE MGMT INC (NV)
Name changed to OphthaliX Inc. (NV) 02/01/2012
OphthaliX Inc. (NV) reincorporated in Delaware 04/02/2012 which name changed to Wize Pharma, Inc. 11/16/2017

DENALI FD INC (MD)
Auction Preferred Ser. A $0.0001 par called for redemption at $25,000 on 03/10/2015
Merged into Boulder Growth & Income Fund, Inc. 03/20/2015
Each share Common $0.0001 par exchanged for (2.439214) shares Common 1¢ par

DENALI INC (DE)
Plan of reorganization under Chapter 11 Federal Bankruptcy Code effective 12/10/2002
No stockholders' equity

DENALI PETES LTD (BC)
Merged into Windstar Energy Ltd. 04/30/1997
Each share Common no par exchanged for (1) share Common no par
Windstar Energy Ltd. merged into BelAir Energy Corp. 01/28/1998 which merged into Purcell Energy Ltd. (New) 09/04/2003
(See Purcell Energy Ltd. (New))

DENAMERICA CORP (GA)
Name changed to Phoenix Restaurant Group, Inc. 07/06/1999
Phoenix Restaurant Group, Inc. name changed to Hiru Corp. 11/18/2008

DENAR MINES LTD (BC)
Recapitalized as International Sinabarb Industries Ltd. 08/31/1987
Each share Common no par exchanged for (0.33333333) share Common no par
International Sinabarb Industries Ltd. recapitalized as Primero Industries Ltd. 10/15/1990 which recapitalized as PMI Ventures Ltd. 03/27/2001 which name changed to PMI Gold Corp. 05/23/2006 which merged into Asanko Gold Inc. 02/10/2014

DENARII RES INC (NV)
Common $0.001 par split (6) for (1) by issuance of (5) additional shares payable 03/16/2009 to holders of record 03/13/2009 Ex date - 03/17/2009
Name changed to Double Crown Resources 11/10/2011

DENAULT LIMITEE (QC)
Each share Class A $5 par exchanged for (5) shares Class A $1 par 06/05/1964
Acquired by Couvrette & Provost Ltee. 11/05/1969
Each share Class A $1 par exchanged for (2) shares Common no par
Each share Class B $1 par exchanged for (2) shares Common no par
Couvrette & Provost Ltee. name changed to Provigo Inc. (Old) 09/14/1970 which name changed to Univa Inc. 05/22/1992 which name changed to Provigo Inc. (New) 05/25/1994 which was acquired by Loblaw Companies Ltd. 12/10/1998

DENBRIDGE CAP CORP (CANADA)
Reincorporated 02/24/1994
Place of incorporation changed from (ON) to (Canada) 02/24/1994
Recapitalized as Atlantis Systems Corp. 06/11/2001
Each share Common no par exchanged for (0.025) share Common no par
(See Atlantis Systems Corp.)

DENBURY RES INC (CANADA)
Each share old Common no par exchanged (0.5) share new Common no par 10/17/1996
Reincorporated under the laws of Delaware and new Common no par changed to $0.001 par 04/21/1999

DENCAL DEV CORP (ON)
Recapitalized as Bestquipt Sports Inc. 02/04/1991
Each share Common no par exchanged for (0.2) share Common no par
Bestquipt Sports Inc. recapitalized as Big Hammer Group Inc. 08/29/2000
(See Big Hammer Group Inc.)

DENCAM DEV CORP (BC)
Recapitalized as Consolidated Dencam Development Corp. 01/19/1994
Each share Common no par exchanged for (0.4) share Common no par
Consolidated Dencam Development Corp. name changed to Equinox Exploration Corp. 03/13/2009 which name changed to Equinox Copper Corp. 02/01/2013 which recapitalized as Anfield Resources Inc. 09/23/2013 which recapitalized as Anfield Energy Inc. 12/27/2017

DENCOR ENERGY COST CTLS INC (CO)
Recapitalized as Reliable Power Systems, Inc. 04/11/2001
Each (18) shares Common no par exchanged for (1) share Common no par
(See Reliable Power Systems, Inc.)

DENCROFT MINES LTD. (ON)
Charter cancelled and company declared dissolved for failure to file returns 03/25/1965

DENDO GLOBAL CORP (NV)
Each share old Common $0.001 par exchanged for (5) shares new Common $0.001 par 03/21/2003
Name changed to TechAlt, Inc. 10/15/2004
TechAlt, Inc. name changed to All American Energy Holding, Inc. 10/23/2012 which recapitalized as All American Energy Corp. 11/14/2017 which name changed to Core Lithium Corp. 04/11/2018

DENDREON CORP (DE)
Plan of reorganization under Chapter 11 Federal Bankruptcy proceedings effective 06/10/2015
Stockholders' equity unlikely

DENDRITE INTL INC (NJ)
Common no par split (2) for (1) by issuance of (1) additional share payable 8/21/98 to holders of record 8/11/98
Common no par split (3) for (2) by issuance of (0.5) additional share payable 10/7/99 to holders of record 9/23/99
Merged into Cegedim S.A. 5/8/2007
Each share Common no par exchanged for $16 cash

DENEHURST LTD (AUSTRALIA)
ADR agreement terminated 10/02/2006
No ADR holders' equity

DENELCOR INC (CO)
Filed a petition under Chapter 7 of the Federal Bankruptcy Code 11/19/85
Stockholders' equity unlikley

DENHAM AIRCRAFT SVCS CORP II NEW (UT)
Proclaimed dissolved for failure to file reports 4/1/96

DENIES JOHN A SONS CO (TN)
Merged into Stewart Concrete & Material Co. 12/31/67
Each share Common $2 par exchanged for (1) share 5% Preferred $5 par
(See Stewart Concrete & Material Co.)

DENIM APPAREL GROUP INC (NV)
Recapitalized as Bolivar Mining Corp. 10/15/2007
Each share Common $0.001 par exchanged for (0.005) share Common $0.001 par

DENISON CO-OPERATIVE BUYERS' UNION (TX)
Charter forfeited for failure to pay taxes 4/13/50

DENISON COPPER MINES, LTD. (ON)
Acquired by Denison Nickel Mines Ltd. 09/23/1946
Each share Capital Stock $1 par exchanged for (0.5) share Capital Stock $1 par
Denison Nickel Mines Ltd. merged into North Denison Mines Ltd. 00/00/1949 which recapitalized as Consolidated Denison Mines Ltd. 00/00/1954 which name changed to Denison Mines Ltd. 04/07/1960 which recapitalized as Denison Energy Inc. (ON) 05/30/2002 which reorganized in Alberta 03/08/2004 which name changed to Calfrac Well Services Ltd. 03/29/2004

DENISON CORP. (FL)
Liquidated 11/01/1955
Details not available

DENISON ENERGY INC (AB)
Reorganized 03/08/2004
Reorganized and place of incorporation changed from Denison Mines Ltd. (ON) to Denison Energy Inc. (AB) 03/08/2004
Each share Common no par exchanged for (0.04761904) share new Common no par, (1) share Denison Mines Inc. Common no par and (0.2) share Forte Resources Inc. Common no par
Name changed to Calfrac Well Services Ltd. 03/29/2004

DENISON INTL PLC (UNITED KINGDOM)
ADR agreement terminated 03/29/2004
Each Sponsored ADR for Ordinary exchanged for $23.95 cash

DENISON MINES INC (ON)
Merged into Denison Mines Corp. 12/6/2006
Each share Common no par exchanged for (2.88) shares Common no par

DENISON MINES LTD (ON)
Capital Stock $1 par changed to no par and (3) additional shares issued 03/05/1979
Capital Stock no par reclassified as Common no par 07/26/1983
Common no par reclassified as Conv. Class A no par 02/27/1984
Each share Conv. Class A no par received distribution of (1) share Class B no par 03/07/1984
Each share 9.5% Preferred Ser. B no par exchanged for (25) shares new Common no par 01/02/1996
Each share 9.75% Preferred Ser. A no par exchanged for (25) shares new Common no par 01/02/1996
Each share Conv. Class A Common no par exchanged for (1) share new Common no par 01/02/1996
Each share Conv. Class B Common no par exchanged for (1) share new Common no par 01/02/1996
Recapitalized as Denison Energy Inc. (ON) 05/30/2002
Each share new Common no par exchanged for (0.05) share Common no par
Denison Energy Inc. (ON) reorganized in Alberta 03/08/2004 which name changed to Calfrac Well Services Ltd. 03/29/2004

DENISON NICKEL MINES LTD.
Merged into North Denison Mines Ltd. in 1949
Each share Capital Stock $1 par exchanged for (0.25) share Common $1 par
North Denison Mines Ltd. recapitalized as Consolidated Denison Mines Ltd. in 1954 which name changed to Denison Mines Ltd. 4/7/60 which recapitalized as Denison Energy Inc. (ONT) 5/30/2002 which reorganized in Alberta 3/8/2004 which name changed to Calfrac Well Services Ltd. 3/29/2004

DENIZBANK A S (TURKEY)
Stock Dividend - 9% payable 01/31/2005 to holders of record 01/14/2005
GDR agreement terminated 10/31/2016
No GDR's remain outstanding

DENLAKE MINING CO. LTD. (ON)
Charter cancelled and company declared dissolved for failure to file returns 3/24/58

DENMAN CREDIT FACTORS LTD. (BC)
Preference $100 par called for redemption 8/31/65
Completely liquidated in May 1966
Each share Class A no par or Class B no par exchanged for first and final distribution of (1.02) shares Diversified Charge Service Ltd. Class A no par and (0.004) share Class C no par

DENMAN OIL & DRILLING CORP. (NM)
Merged into Coastal Plains Oil Co. on a (1) for (8.33) basis 1/1/58
Coastal Plains Oil Co. recapitalized as Western Oil Corp. 7/25/60
(See Western Oil Corp.)

DENMAN TIRE & RUBBER CO. (DE)
Name changed to McCandless Corp. 02/00/1954
McCandless Corp. name changed to Food Resources, Inc. 10/06/1969
(See Food Resources, Inc.)

DENMAN TIRE & RUBBER CO. (IL)
Reorganized under the laws of Delaware in 1937
No stockholders' equity

DENMANS COM INC (CO)
Name changed to Impulse Media Technologies, Inc. 11/23/2001
Impulse Media Technologies, Inc. name changed to Napoli Enterprises, Inc. 11/25/2002 which name changed to Lion-Gri International, Inc. 10/20/2004 which recapitalized as Promotora Valle Hermoso, Inc. 07/24/2006 which name changed to UNR Holdings, Inc. 10/15/2009

DENNEY REYBURN CO (PA)
Common $5 par changed to $2.50 par and (1) additional share issued 04/20/1979
Merged into DRC Acquisition Co. 10/12/1988
Each share Common $2.50 par exchanged for $39.67 cash

DENNEY TAG CO. (PA)
Each share Common $20 par exchanged for (4) shares Common $5 par in 1951
Name changed to Denney-Reyburn Co. 1/12/61
(See Denney-Reyburn Co.)

DENNING MOBILE ROBOTICS INC (DE)
Each share Common $0.0001 par exchanged for (0.04) share Common 1¢ par 11/18/1986
Chapter 7 bankruptcy proceedings dismissed 09/14/1999
No stockholders' equity

DENNINGHOUSE INC (ON)
Filed for protection under Companies' Creditors Arrangement Act 08/16/2004
Stockholders' equity unlikely

DENNIS (RICHARD J.) & CO. PREFERRED FUTURES FUND II, L.P. (DE)
Fund was closed 11/16/88
Details not available

DENNISON INC (DE)
Charter cancelled and declared inoperative and void for non-payment of taxes 3/1/88

DENNISON MANUFACTURING CO. (MA)
Each share 7% Preferred $100 par exchanged for (1) share Prior Preferred $50 par, (4) shares Class A Common $5 par and $6 in cash in 1939
Each share 7% Part. Class A $10 par exchanged for (1.25) shares Class A Common $5 par in 1939
Each $10 face amount of Intrim Optional receipts exchanged for (1.25) shares Class A Common $5 par in 1939
Stock Distribution - Voting Common and Class A Common: 100% in Class A Common 5/6/60
Under plan of merger reincorporated under the laws of Nevada 6/29/62
Dennison Manufacturing Co. (NV) merged into Avery Dennison Corp. 10/16/90

DENNISON MFG CO (NV)
Common $5 par split (2) for (1) by issuance of (1) additional share 04/29/1966
Class A Common $5 par split (2) for (1) by issuance of (1) additional share 04/29/1966
Under plan of merger Common $5 par and Class A Common $5 par reclassified as Common $5 par 05/26/1967
Common $5 par split (4) for (3) by issuance of (0.33333333) additional share 03/10/1976

$1 Conv. Preferred $10 par called for redemption 12/09/1977
8% Debenture Stock $100 par called for redemption 12/09/1977
Common $5 par changed to $1 par and (1) additional share issued 03/09/1979
Common $1 par split (3) for (2) by issuance of (0.5) additional share 12/10/1984
Common Stock Purchase Rights declared for Common stockholders of record 05/05/1986 were redeemed at $0.05 per right 06/11/1990 for holders of record 05/24/1990
Merged into Avery Dennison Corp. 10/16/1990
Each share Common $1 par exchanged for (1.12) shares Common $1 par

DENNISON PERSONNEL INC (DE)
Recapitalized as Dennison, Inc. 7/30/83
Each (10) shares Common $0.001 par exchanged for (1) share Common 1¢ par
(See Dennison, Inc.)

DENNY'S RESTAURANTS, INC. (CA)
Common $1 par split (5) for (4) by issuance of (0.25) additional share 1/29/65
Common $1 par split (2) for (1) by issuance of (1) additional share 1/10/68
Common $1 par split (5) for (2) by issuance of (1.5) additional shares 8/14/68
Stock Dividend - 25% 1/27/67
Name changed to Denny's, Inc. 12/8/72
(See Denny's, Inc.)

DENNYS INC (CA)
$1 Conv. Preferred no par called for redemption 4/9/76
Common $1 par split (3) for (2) by issuance of (0.5) additional share 4/1/82
Acquired by DRD Corp. 1/25/85
Each share Common $1 par exchanged for $43 cash

DENOM RES INC (ON)
Reincorporated 4/26/83
Place of incorporation changed from (BC) to (ONT) 4/26/83
Reincorporated in Ontario as ITM Corp. 2/4/86 which recapitalized as IMC Integrated Marketing Communications Inc. 8/6/87
(See IMC Integrated Marketing Communications Inc.)

DENOVO CAP CORP (AB)
Reorganized under the laws of British Columbia as Horn Petroleum Corp. 09/23/2011
Each share Common no par exchanged for (0.65) share Common no par
Horn Petroleum Corp. name changed to Africa Energy Corp. 03/12/2015

DENOVO CORP (ON)
Each share old Common no par exchanged for (0.1) share new Common no par 08/10/1994
Recapitalized as Princeton Media Group Inc. 10/29/1996
Each share new Common no par exchanged for (0.05) share Common no par
(See Princeton Media Group Inc.)

DENOVO GOLD MINES LTD. (ON)
Name changed to Denovo Mining Corp. Ltd. 7/31/51
(See Denovo Mining Corp. Ltd.)

DENOVO MINING CORP. LTD. (ON)
Charter revoked for failure to file reports and pay fees 9/29/66

DENROW MINES LTD. (MB)
Dissolved 03/01/1973
Details not available

DENROY MFG LTD (ON)
Recapitalized as Denroy Resources Corp. (ON) 06/28/2005
Each (35) shares Common no par exchanged for (1) share Common no par
Denroy Resources Corp. (ON) reincorporated in Canada as Nevoro Inc. 05/17/2007 which was acquired by Starfield Resources, Inc. 10/08/2009

DENROY RES CORP (ON)
Reincorporated under the laws of Canada as Nevoro Inc. 05/17/2007
Nevoro Inc. acquired by Starfield Resources Inc. 10/08/2009

DENSE PAC MICROSYSTEMS INC (CA)
Each share old Common no par exchanged for (0.5) share new Common no par 07/13/1988
Name changed to DPAC Technologies Corp. 08/10/2001
(See DPAC Technologies Corp.)

DENSTONE MINERALS LTD (BC)
Recapitalized 03/04/1998
Recapitalized from Denstone Resources Ltd. to Denstone Minerals Ltd. 03/04/1998
Each share Common no par exchanged for (0.5) share Common no par
Recapitalized as Denstone Ventures Ltd. 02/04/2000
Each share Common no par exchanged for (0.014285714) share Common no par
Denstone Ventures Ltd. recapitalized as Mesa Resources Inc. 10/10/2002 which merged into LongBow Energy Corp. (New) 02/25/2004 which recapitalized as LongBow Resources Inc. 04/11/2007
(See LongBow Resources Inc.)

DENSTONE VENTURES LTD (BC)
Recapitalized as Mesa Resources Inc. 10/10/2002
Each share Common no par exchanged for (0.2) share Common no par
Mesa Resources Inc. merged into LongBow Energy Corp. (New) 02/25/2004 which recapitalized as LongBow Resources Inc. 04/11/2007
(See LongBow Resources Inc.)

DENTAL / MED DIAGNOSTIC SYS (DE)
Each (1.333) shares old Common 1¢ par exchanged for (1) share new Common 1¢ par 04/17/1997
Filed a petition under Chapter 7 Federal Bankruptcy Code 07/24/2001
Stockholders' equity unlikely

DENTAL & TOILET PRODUCTS CORP. (NY)
Charter cancelled and proclaimed dissolved for failure to pay taxes 12/16/29

DENTAL CARE ALLIANCE INC (DE)
Issue Information - 2,000,000 shares COM offered at $12 per share on 11/04/1997
Merged into Interdent, Inc. 3/11/99
Each share Common 1¢ par exchanged for (1.66) shares Common 1¢ par
(See Interdent, Inc.)

DENTAL DYNAMIC SYS (CA)
Name changed to Alto Communications, Inc. 6/11/73
(See Alto Communications, Inc.)

DENTAL HLTH AMER INC (DE)
Reorganized 9/18/89
Reorganized from (CO) to under the laws of (DE) 9/18/89
Each share Common $0.0001 par exchanged for (0.01) share Common $0.0001 par
Charter cancelled and declared inoperative and void for non-payment of taxes 6/24/91

DENTAL MGMT SVCS INC (SC)
Charter revoked for failure to pay taxes 10/05/1988

DENTAL RES INC (MN)
Each share old Common 1¢ par exchanged for (0.42553191) share new Common 1¢ par 07/23/2001
Name changed to DTLL, Inc. 03/20/2003
DTLL, Inc. name changed to Solstice Resorts Inc. 09/07/2007
(See Solstice Resorts Inc.)

DENTAL SVCS AMER INC (DE)
Each share Common $0.001 par exchanged for (0.2) share Common $0.005 par 01/01/1998
Charter cancelled and declared inoperative and void for non-payment of taxes 03/01/2001

DENTAL WORLD CTR INC (NY)
Chapter 11 Federal Bankruptcy proceedings converted to Liquidating Chapter 11 on 09/23/1988
No stockholders' equity

DENTALLOY INC (CA)
Common 10¢ par split (2) for (1) by issuance of (1) additional share 01/15/1979
Stock Dividend - 10% 01/15/1978
Charter suspended for failure to file reports and pay fees 09/03/1985

DENTALSERV COM (NV)
Recapitalized as MedPro Safety Products, Inc. 12/31/2007
Each share Common $0.001 par exchanged for (0.25) share Common $0.001 par

DENTEC INC (DE)
Name changed to ST Systems, Inc. 4/11/86
(See ST Systems, Inc.)

DENTISTS SUPPLY CO NEW YORK (NY)
Each share Common $10 par exchanged for (4) shares Common $2.50 par in 1946
Reincorporated under the laws of Delaware as Dentsply International Inc. and Common $2.50 par changed to $1 par 4/30/69
(See Dentsply International Inc.)

DENTLCARE MGMT INC (NV)
Each share old Common $0.001 par exchanged for (0.2) share new Common $0.001 par 05/15/1998
Charter revoked for failure to file reports and pay fees 03/01/2000

DENTMART GROUP INC (CO)
Reorganized under the laws of Delaware as Sitek, Inc. 7/14/98
Each (1.65) shares Common $0.001 par exchanged for (1) share Common $0.005 par
Sitek Inc. name changed to Prodeo Technologies, Inc. 6/5/2000 which reorganized as Findem, Inc. 10/31/2005

DENTO MED INDS INC (NY)
Common 1¢ par split (2) for (1) by issuance of (1) additional share 11/02/1970
Common 1¢ par split (2) for (1) by issuance of (1) additional share 07/30/1971
Common 1¢ par split (2) for (1) by issuance of (1) additional share 07/06/1983
Name changed to Hydron Technologies, Inc. 07/29/1993

DENTONIA MINES LTD. (CANADA)
Bankrupt 00/00/1948
Deemed not to be a subsisting company by the Dominion Secretary of State 12/14/1950

DENTORE GOLD MINES, LTD. (ON)
Charter cancelled in 1951

DENTSPLY INTL INC (DE)
Common 1¢ par split (2) for (1) by issuance of (1) additional share payable 10/29/1997 to holders of record 10/14/1997
Common 1¢ par split (3) for (2) by issuance of (0.5) additional share payable 01/31/2002 to holders of record 01/15/2002 Ex date - 02/01/2002
Common 1¢ par split (2) for (1) by issuance of (1) additional share payable 07/17/2006 to holders of record 06/26/2006 Ex date - 07/18/2006
Under plan of merger name changed to DENTSPLY SIRONA Inc. 03/01/2016

DENTSPLY INTL INC (DE)
Common $1 par split (3) for (2) by issuance of (0.5) additional share 3/17/70
Common $1 par split (3) for (2) by issuance of (0.5) additional share 3/7/73
Under plan of merger each share Common $1 par exchanged for $25.50 cash 12/23/82

DENVER & EPHRATA TEL & TELEG CO (PA)
Common $25 par changed to $5 par and (4) additional shares issued 09/12/1968
Common $5 par split (10) for (1) by issuance of (9) additional shares 06/30/1992
Common $5 par split (3) for (1) by issuance of (2) additional shares payable 06/07/1996 to holders of record 06/07/1996
Stock Dividends - 100% 05/31/1951; 100% 07/15/1959
Under plan of reorganization each share Common $5 par automatically became (1) share D&E Communications, Inc. Common 16¢ par 06/07/1996
D&E Communications, Inc. merged into Windstream Corp. 11/10/2009 which name changed to Windstream Holdings, Inc. 09/03/2013
4.5% Preferred Ser. A $100 par called for redemption at $100 plus $2 accrued dividends on 11/12/2009

DENVER & RIO GRANDE RAILROAD CO. (CO & UT)
Declared defunct and inoperative for failure to pay taxes and file annual reports 09/17/1929

DENVER & RIO GRANDE WESTN RR CO (DE)
Each share Common Escrow Certificate $100 exchanged for (3) shares Common no par 5/28/55
Common no par split (3) for (1) by issuance of (2) additional shares 5/29/59
Stock Dividend - 50% 12/30/53
Merged into Rio Grande Industries, Inc. 12/15/70
Each share Common no par exchanged for (1.5) shares Common $1 par
(See Rio Grande Industries, Inc.)

DENVER & SALT LAKE RAILWAY CO.
Merged into Denver & Rio Grande Western Railroad Co. in 1947
Each share Capital Stock exchanged for (1) share Preferred Escrow Certificate
(See Denver & Rio Grande Western Railroad Co.)

DENVER ACCEPTANCE CORP. (CO)
Declared defunct and inoperative for failure to pay franchise taxes 10/17/63

DENVER CHEM MFG CO (CO)
Recapitalized 05/06/1965
Capital Stock $1 par split (2) for (1) by issuance of (1) additional share
Voting Trust Agreement terminated and each VTC for Capital Stock $1 par exchanged for (2) shares Capital Stock $1 par
Completely liquidated 11/30/1967
Each share Capital Stock $1 par exchanged for first and final distribution of (0.28) share Factor (Max) & Co. Class A $1 par
Factor (Max) & Co. merged into Simon (Norton), Inc. 02/14/1973 which merged into Esmark, Inc. (Inc. 03/14/1969) 09/09/1983
(See Esmark, Inc. (Inc. 03/14/1969))

DENVER-CHICAGO TRUCKING CO., INC. (NE)
Common $1 par split (3) for (1) by issuance of (2) additional shares 12/06/1961
Name changed to DC International, Inc. 03/25/1966
DC International, Inc. merged into T.I.M.E.-DC, Inc. 01/17/1969
(See T.I.M.E.-DC, Inc.)

DENVER GOLDEN CORP (CO)
Each share Common 1¢ par exchanged for (0.1) share Common 10¢ par 8/1/61
Name changed to Brooks Industries, Inc. 8/3/70
(See Brooks Industries, Inc.)

DENVER-GOLDEN OIL & URANIUM CO. (CO)
Name changed to Denver-Golden Corp. 8/4/59
Denver-Golden Corp. name changed to Brooks Industries, Inc. 8/3/70
(See Brooks Industries, Inc.)

DENVER ICE & COLD STORAGE CO. (CO)
Name changed to Shattuck (S.W.) Chemical Co. 3/8/55
Shattuck (S.W.) Chemical Co. name changed to JPL Enterprises, Inc. 12/30/69
(See JPL Enterprises, Inc.)

DENVER INDUSTRIES, INC. (UT)
Recapitalized as M & M Hydroelectric Corp. 00/00/1987
Each share Common $0.001 par exchanged for (0.04) share Common $0.001 par
M & M Hydroelectric Corp. recapitalized as Fundamental Financial Corp. 03/14/1995 which name changed to Ikar Mineral Corp. (UT) 09/22/1997 which reincorporated in Delaware 03/31/1998 which recapitalized as Ethos Capital Inc. 11/02/2000 which name changed to Patriot Energy Corp. 02/04/2002 which name changed to BigBrews Holdings Inc. (DE) 02/18/2003 which reincorporated in Nevada as Patriot Energy Corp. 09/09/2003 which name changed to Healing Hand Network International, Inc. 12/22/2003 which name changed to Patriot Energy Corp. (NV) 10/10/2005
(See Patriot Energy Corp.)

DENVER NATIONAL FINANCIAL, INC. (CO)
Completely liquidated 08/14/1967
Each share Common 25¢ par or Class B Common 25¢ par exchanged for first and final distribution of (0.1132) share National Western Life Insurance Co. (CO) Class A Common $1 par
National Western Life Insurance Co. (CO) reincorporated in Delaware as National Western Life Group, Inc. 10/02/2015

DENVER NATIONAL LIFE INSURANCE CO. (CO)
Under plan of merger each share old Common 25¢ par exchanged for (0.25) share new Common 25¢ par 02/15/1963
Name changed to Denver National Financial, Inc. 05/20/1965
Denver National Financial, Inc. acquired by National Western Life Insurance Co. (CO) 08/14/1967 which reincorporated in Delaware as National Western Life Group, Inc. 10/02/2015

DENVER OIL & GAS INC (NV)
Reincorporated 09/22/1978
State of incorporation changed from (ID) to (NV) 09/22/1978
Charter revoked for failure to file reports and pay fees 05/01/1987

DENVER REAL ESTATE INVT ASSN (CO)
Each Share of Bene. Int. no par exchanged for (0.00005) Share of Bene. Int. no par 04/13/1981
Note: In effect holders received $37.15 cash per share and public interest was eliminated

DENVER ROCK DRILL MANUFACTURING CO.
Merged into Gardner-Denver Co. 00/00/1927
Details not available

DENVER SILVER INC (BC)
Recapitalized as Androne Resources Ltd. 10/5/84
Each share Capital Stock no par exchanged for (0.25) share Common no par
Androne Resources Ltd. merged into Pezgold Resource Corp. (New) 9/1/88 which recapitalized as Braiden Resources Ltd. 6/15/90 which recapitalized as Pure Pioneer Ventures Ltd. 6/14/2002

DENVER TRAMWAY CORP (DE)
In process of liquidation
Each share 1st Preferred no par exchanged for initial distribution of $25.50 cash 06/07/1971
Each share Preferred $100 par exchanged for initial distribution of $52.6125 cash 06/07/1971
Each share 1st Preferred no par received second distribution of $25.50 cash 12/16/1971
Each share Preferred $100 par received second distribution of 52.6125 cash 12/16/1971
Each share 1st Preferred no par received third distribution of $14.56 cash 11/20/1973
Each share Preferred $100 par received third distribution of $30 cash 11/20/1973
Each share 1st Preferred no par received fourth distribution of $10 cash 03/11/1974
Each share Preferred $100 par received fourth distribution of $20.65 cash 03/11/1974
Each share 1st Preferred no par received fifth distribution of $9.44 cash 10/01/1975
Each share Preferred $100 par received fifth distribution of $19.50 cash 10/01/1975
Each share 1st Preferred no par received sixth and final distribution of $3.127 cash 09/21/1978
Each share Preferred $100 par received sixth and final distribution of $6.4519 cash 09/21/1978
Each share Common no par exchanged for initial distribution of $20 cash 03/20/1979
Note: Details on additional distributions if any, are not available

DENVER U S BANCORPORATION INC (CO)
Name changed to United Banks of Colorado, Inc. 08/31/1970
United Banks of Colorado, Inc. merged into Norwest Corp. 04/19/1991 which name changed to Wells Fargo & Co. (New) 11/02/1998

DENVER UN CORP (CO)
Liquidation completed 9/6/2000
Each share Common no par received initial distribution of $25 cash 1/29/82
Each share Common no par received second distribution of $35 cash 6/1/83
Assets transferred to Denver Union Corp. Liquidating Trust 1/2/86
(See Denver Union Corp. Liquidating Trust)

DENVER UN STK YD CO (CO)
Common no par split (2) for (1) by issuance of (1) additional share 5/19/69
Stock Dividend - 20% 3/22/57
Name changed to Denver Union Corp. 4/7/70
(See Denver Union Corp.)

DENVER UNION CORP. LIQUIDATING TRUST (CO)
Liquidation completed 9/6/2000
Each share Common no par received third distribution of $6 cash 5/15/92
Each share Common no par received fourth distribution of $6 cash 12/15/97
Each share Common no par received fifth distribution of $18 cash in May 1999
Each share Common no par received sixth and final distribution of $2.9068 cash 9/6/2000

DENVER UNITED STATES NATIONAL BANK (DENVER, CO)
Stock Dividend - 12-1/2% 01/27/1961
Name changed to United Bank of Denver, N.A. (Denver, CO) 09/01/1970
(See United Bank of Denver, N.A. (Denver, CO))

DENWAY MTRS LTD (HONG KONG)
Merged into Guangzhou Automobile Group Co., Ltd. 08/25/2010
Each ADR for Common exchanged for $27.390394 cash

DENYVAN RES INC (CANADA)
Merged into Minorca Resources Inc. 12/30/1994
Each share Common no par exchanged for (1) share Common no par
Minorca Resources Inc. merged into McWatters Mining Inc. 10/26/1998
(See McWatters Mining Inc.)

DEOTEXIS INC (NV)
Company terminated registration of common stock and is no longer public as of 11/10/2000
Details not available

DEP CORP (DE)
Reincorporated 12/15/1987
Common no par split (3) for (2) by issuance of (0.5) additional share 04/15/1986
State of incorporation changed from (CA) to (DE) 12/15/1987
Common no par split (3) for (2) by issuance of (0.5) additional share 04/29/1988
Each share old Common no par reclassified as (0.5) share Non-Vtg Class A Common no par and (0.5) share Class B Common no par 12/15/1992
Plan of reorganization under Chapter 11 Federal Bankruptcy Code effective 11/04/1996
Each share Class A Common no par exchanged for (1) share Common no par
Each share Class B Common no par exchanged for (1) share Common no par
Merged into Henkel KGAA 09/18/1998
Each share Common no par exchanged for $5.25 cash

DEPA LTD
(UNITED ARAB EMIRATES)
GDR agreement terminated
02/23/2018
Each Reg. S GDR for Ordinary
exchanged for $1.992873 cash
Each 144A GDR for Ordinary
exchanged for $1.992873 cash

DEPARTMENT 56 INC (DE)
Name changed to Lenox Group Inc.
11/14/2005
(See Lenox Group Inc.)

DEPENDABLE BLDG MAINTENANCE CO (WA)
Name changed to D Industries, Inc.
06/01/1980

DEPENDABLE INS GROUP INC AMER (FL)
Merged into St. Regis Corp. 11/3/83
Each share Common 10¢ par
exchanged for (0.704) share
Common $5 par
St. Regis Corp. merged into
Champion International Corp.
11/20/84 which merged into
International Paper Co. 6/20/2000

DEPENDABLE TRUCK & TRACTOR CO. (DE)
Charter cancelled and declared
inoperative and void for
non-payment of taxes in 1925

DEPEW & LANCASTER LIGHT, POWER & CONDUIT CO.
Name changed to Western New York
Gas & Electric Corp. in 1928
(See Western New York Gas & Electric Corp.)

DEPHASIUM CORP (NV)
Recapitalized as Allied Ventures
Holdings Corp. 04/05/2016
Each share Common $0.0001 par
exchanged for (0.00133333) share
Common $0.0001 par
Allied Ventures Holdings Corp. name
changed to Longwen Group Corp.
01/26/2017

DEPILAN LTD (DE)
Charter cancelled and declared
inoperative and void for
non-payment of taxes 03/01/1975

DEPLOY TECHNOLOGIES INC (NV)
Reincorporated 09/15/2010
State of incorporation changed from
(DE) to (NV) 09/15/2010
Each share old Common $0.0001 par
exchanged for (0.1) share new
Common $0.0001 par 11/19/2014
Recapitalized as Body & Mind Inc.
12/07/2017
Each share new Common $0.0001
par exchanged for (0.33333333)
share Common $0.0001 par

DEPOMED INC (CA)
Reincorporated under the laws of
Delaware as Assertio Therapeutics,
Inc. and Common no par changed to
$0.0001 par 08/15/2018

DEPOSIT BK (DU BOIS, PA)
Merged into First Commonwealth
Financial Corp. 03/19/1984
Each share Capital Stock $5 par
exchanged for (1.75) shares
Common $5 par

DEPOSIT GTY CORP (MS)
Common $7.50 par changed to no par
and (0.65) additional share issued
03/26/1970
Common no par split (2) for (1) by
issuance of (1) additional share
10/01/1985
Common no par split (2) for (1) by
issuance of (1) additional share
12/14/1992
Common no par split (2) for (1) by
issuance of (1) additional share
payable 12/06/1996 to holders of
record 12/02/1996 Ex date -
12/09/1996

Merged into First American Corp.
(TN) 05/01/1998
Each share Common no par
exchanged for (1.17) shares
Common $5 par
First American Corp. (TN) merged
into AmSouth Bancorporation
10/01/1999 which merged into
Regions Financial Corp. (New)
11/04/2006

DEPOSIT GTY NATL BK (JACKSON, MS)
Common $10 par changed to $7.50
par and (0.33333333) additional
share issued 02/23/1966
Common $7.50 par changed to $5 par
and (0.5) additional share issued
plus a 10% stock dividend paid
03/16/1970
Merged into Deposit Guaranty Corp.
06/01/1997
Each share Common $5 par
exchanged for (9.667) shares
Common no par
Deposit Guaranty Corp. merged into
First American Corp. (TN)
05/01/1998 which merged into
AmSouth Bancorporation
10/01/1999 which merged into
Regions Financial Corp. (New)
11/04/2006

DEPOSIT GUARANTY BANK & TRUST CO. (JACKSON, MS)
Each share Common $100 par
exchanged for (10) shares Common
$10 par 00/00/1949
Stock Dividends - 21% 02/15/1940;
25% 04/16/1942; 16.66666666%
01/29/1948; 12.5% 12/15/1952;
11.11111111% 01/20/1956; 25%
01/15/1963
Name changed to Deposit Guaranty
National Bank (Jackson, MS)
10/11/1965
Deposit Guaranty National Bank
(Jackson, MS) merged into Deposit
Guaranty Corp. 06/01/1997 which
merged into First American Corp.
(TN) 05/01/1998 which merged into
AmSouth Bancorporation
10/01/1999 which merged into
Regions Financial Corp. (New)
11/04/2006

DEPOSIT NATL BK (DUBOIS, PA)
Stock Dividends - 25% 12/15/1973;
10% 06/15/1979
Name changed to Deposit Bank
(DuBois, PA) 01/02/1980
Deposit Bank (DuBois, PA) merged
into First Commonwealth Financial
Corp. 03/19/1984

DEPOSITED BANK SHARES (PA)
Series B-1 Trust Agreement
terminated and liquidated
00/00/1954
Series N-Y and N.Y.-A Trust
Agreements terminated and
liquidated 00/00/1956
Details not available

DEPOSITED BOND CERTIFICATES
Trust terminated 00/00/1933
Details not available

DEPOSITED INSURANCE SHARES (PA)
Series B Trust Agreement terminated
00/00/1941
Series A Trust Agreement terminated
and liquidated 00/00/1956
Details not available

DEPOSITORS CORP (ME)
Capital Stock $12.50 par changed to
$6.25 par and (1) additional share
issued 04/16/1968
Capital Stock $6.25 par split (5) for
(4) by issuance of (0.25) additional
share 01/26/1979
Capital Stock $6.25 par split (2) for
(1) by issuance of (1) additional
share 05/19/1982
Merged into Key Banks Inc.
02/29/1984

Each share Capital Stock $6.25 par
exchanged for (1.09) shares
Common $5 par
Key Banks Inc. name changed to
KeyCorp (NY) 08/28/1985 which
merged into KeyCorp (New) (OH)
03/01/1994

DEPOSITORS SAVINGS ASSOCIATION (MS)
Name changed to Depositors Savings
Bank (Jackson, MS) and Preferred
$1 par reclassified as Common $1
par 07/23/1985
Depositors Savings Bank (Jackson,
MS) name changed to Eastover
Bank for Savings (Jackson, MS)
08/01/1986 which reorganized as
EB, Inc. 02/28/1993 which merged
into Parkway Co. (TX) 04/27/1995
which reincorporated in Maryland as
Parkway Properties, Inc. 08/02/1996
which merged into Cousins
Properties Inc. 10/06/2016

DEPOSITORS SVGS BK (JACKSON, MS)
Name changed to Eastover Bank for
Savings (Jackson, MS) 08/01/1986
Eastover Bank for Savings (Jackson,
MS) reorganized as EB, Inc.
02/28/1993 which merged into
Parkway Co. (TX) 04/27/1995 which
reincorporated in Maryland as
Parkway Properties, Inc. 08/02/1996
which merged into Cousins
Properties Inc. 10/06/2016

DEPOSITORS TRUST CO. (AUGUSTA, ME)
Capital Stock $25 par changed to
$12.50 par and (1) additional share
issued 01/19/1961
Merged into Depositors Corp.
12/30/1966
Each share Capital Stock $12.50 par
exchanged for (1) share Common
$12.50 par
Depositors Corp. merged into Key
Banks Inc. 02/29/1984 which name
changed to KeyCorp (NY)
08/28/1985 which merged into
KeyCorp (New) (OH) 03/01/1994

DEPOSITORS TR CO (MEDFORD, MA)
Acquired by Co-Operative Bank
(Concord, MA) 06/03/1994
Each share Common $100 par
exchanged for $302.07 cash

DEPOTECH CORP (CA)
Acquired by Skyepharma PLC
03/12/1999
Each share Common no par
exchanged for (0.185676393)
Sponsored ADR for Ordinary
(See Skyepharma PLC)

DEPRENYL ANIMAL HEALTH INC (LA)
Reincorporated 11/27/1996
State of incorporation changed from
(MO) to (LA) 11/27/1996
Merged into Draxis Health Inc.
11/27/1996
Each share Common no par
exchanged for (1.35) shares
Common no par
(See Draxis Health Inc.)

DEPRENYL RESH LTD (CANADA)
Common no par split (2) for (1) by
issuance of (1) additional share
09/20/1991
Stock Dividend - 50% 08/27/1990
Under plan of merger name changed
to Draxis Health Inc. 05/27/1994
(See Draxis Health Inc.)

DEPRENYL USA INC (NJ)
Name changed to DUSA
Pharmaceuticals, Inc. 05/26/1993
(See DUSA Pharmaceuticals, Inc.)

DEPUY INC (DE)
Merged into Johnson & Johnson
11/04/1998

Each share Common 1¢ par
exchanged for $35 cash

DEQ SYS CORP (CANADA)
Acquired by Scientific Games Corp.
01/24/2017
Each share Common no par
exchanged for $0.38 cash
Note: Unexchanged certificates will
be cancelled and become without
value 01/24/2023

DER ENTMT INC (CO)
Recapitalized as Medical Laser
Technologies Inc. 05/02/1995
Each share Common $0.001 par
exchanged for (0.5) share Common
$0.001 par
Medical Laser Technologies Inc.
recapitalized as MLT International
Inc. (CO) 08/22/2000 which
reincorporated in Delaware as
SkyMark Holdings, Inc. 07/26/2004
(See SkyMark Holdings, Inc.)

DERANCO MINES LTD. (ON)
Charter cancelled for failure to pay
taxes and file returns 07/09/1969

DERAND EQUITY GROUP INC (FL)
Dissolved for failure to file annual
report 08/13/1993

DERAND REAL ESTATE INVT TR (MA)
Ceased operations 03/01/1999
Stockholders' equity unlikely

DERBY FARMS, INC. (UT)
Name changed to Commerce Oil of
Kentucky, Inc. 12/18/1981
Commerce Oil of Kentucky, Inc. name
changed to Commerce Oil Co.
12/15/1982 which name changed to
USIP.com, Inc. 02/04/2000 which
name changed to Eastern
Environment Solutions, Corp.
12/28/2006 which recapitalized as
Precicion Trim, Inc. 09/20/2016

DERBY GAS & ELECTRIC CORP. (DE)
Recapitalized 00/00/1941
Each share $6.50 Preferred no par
exchanged for (3) shares Common
no par
Each share $7 Preferred no par
exchanged for (3) shares Common
no par
Merged into Housatonic Public
Service Co. 00/00/1953
Each share Common no par
exchanged for (1) share Capital
Stock $15 par
Housatonic Public Service Co.
merged into Connecticut Light &
Power Co. 05/01/1961
(See Connecticut Light & Power Co.)

DERBY OIL & REFINING CORP.
Merged into Derby Oil Co. 01/17/1945
Each share Common exchanged for
(1) share Capital Stock
Derby Oil Co. merged into Colorado
Oil & Gas Corp. 11/04/1954
(See Colorado Oil & Gas Corp.)

DERBY OIL CO. (KS)
Common no par changed to $8 par
08/00/1946
Stock Dividends - 50% 09/30/1948;
10% 12/28/1951
Merged into Colorado Oil & Gas
Corp. 11/04/1954
Each share Common $8 par
exchanged for (1) share $1.25
Preferred $25 par
(See Colorado Oil & Gas Corp.)

DERBY SVGS BK (DERBY, CT)
Under plan of reorganization each
share Common $1 par automatically
became (1) share DS Bancor, Inc.
Common $1 par 09/01/1987
DS Bancor, Inc. merged into Webster
Financial Corp. 01/31/1997

DERECO INC (DE)
$5.20 Non-Cum. Part. Class A Conv.

Preferred Ser. 1 $20 par called for redemption 05/23/1984
$5.20 Non-Cum. Part. Class B Conv. Preferred Ser. 1 $20 par called for redemption 05/23/1984
Public interest eliminated

DEREK OIL & GAS CORP (BC)
Name changed to Newcastle Energy Corp. 07/02/2013
Newcastle Energy Corp. name changed to Martello Technologies Group Inc. 09/12/2018

DEREK RES CORP (BC)
Recapitalized as Derek Oil & Gas Corp. 03/03/2003
Each share Common no par exchanged for (0.33333333) share Common no par
Derek Oil & Gas Corp. name changed to Newcastle Energy Corp. 07/02/2013 which name changed to Martello Technologies Group Inc. 09/12/2018

DERLAK ENTERPRISES INC (ON)
Name changed 09/09/1998
Name changed from Derlak Gold Inc. to Derlak Enterprises Inc. 09/09/1998
Cease trade order effective 06/04/2003
Stockholders' equity unlikely

DERLAK RED LAKE GOLD MINES LTD (ON)
Capital Stock $1 par changed to no par 04/07/1981
Recapitalized as Derlak Gold Inc. 11/14/1991
Each share Capital Stock no par exchanged for (0.25) share Common no par
Derlak Gold Inc. name changed to Derlak Enterprises Inc. 09/09/1998
(See Derlak Enterprises Inc.)

DERLAN INDS LTD (ON)
Common no par split (2) for (1) by issuance of (1) additional share 06/11/1986
9.50% Ser. A Conv. Preferred called for redemption at $8.50 plus $0.1686 accrued dividends on 06/15/1998
Note: The redemption price will be paid by the issuance of (1.535404) shares Common no par in lieu of cash
Name changed to Northstar Aerospace Inc. 06/11/2002
(See Northstar Aerospace Inc.)

DERMA LOCK MED CORP (CO)
Each share Common $0.001 par exchanged for (0.1) share Common 1¢ par 10/01/1987
Name changed to Unilab Corp. (CO) 11/10/1988
Unilab Corp. (CO) merged into Unilab Corp. (New) (DE) 11/10/1993
(See Unilab Corp. (New) (DE))

DERMA SCIENCES INC (DE)
Reincorporated 06/03/1996
Reincorporated 09/14/2012
State of incorporation changed from (CO) to (PA) 06/03/1996
Each share old Common 1¢ par exchanged for (0.2) share new Common 1¢ par 08/02/1999
Each share new Common 1¢ par exchanged again for (0.125) share new Common 1¢ par 02/01/2010
State of incorporation changed from (PA) to (DE) 09/14/2012
Acquired by Integra LifeSciences Holdings Inc. 02/24/2017
Each share Conv. Preferred Ser. A 1¢ par exchanged for $32 cash
Each share Conv. Preferred Ser. B 1¢ par exchanged for $48 cash
Each share new Common 1¢ par exchanged for $7 cash

DERMALAY INDS INC (NV)
Recapitalized as International Luxury Products, Inc. 07/22/2005
Each share Common $0.001 par exchanged for (0.0025) share Common $0.001 par

DERMARX CORP (DE)
Each share old Common 5¢ par exchanged for (0.2) share new Common 5¢ par 12/07/1999
Recapitalized as GoPublicNow.com, Inc. 04/07/2000
Each share new Common 5¢ par exchanged for (0.2) share Common $0.001 par
GoPublicNow.com, Inc. name changed to GPN Network Inc. 11/08/2000 which name changed to IR BioSciences Holdings, Inc. 08/28/2003

DERMAXAR INC (NV)
SEC revoked common stock registration 03/22/2013

DERO INDS INC (NY)
Dissolved by proclamation 03/25/1981

DERO RESH & DEV CORP (NY)
Name changed to Dero Industries Inc. 02/10/1971
(See Dero Industries Inc.)

DEROSIER NICKEL & COPPER MINES LTD. (ON)
Acquired by Temagami Mining Co. Ltd. 00/00/1954
Each share Capital Stock $1 par exchanged for (0.33333333) share Capital Stock $1 par
Temagami Mining Co. Ltd. name changed to Copperfields Mining Corp. Ltd. 11/10/1964 which name changed to Copperfields Mining Corp. (ON) 04/04/1974 which reincorporated in Canada 08/31/1983 which merged into Teck Corp. 09/02/1983 which name changed to Teck Cominco Ltd. 09/12/2001 which name changed to Teck Resources Ltd. 04/27/2009

DERRICK ENERGY CORP (AB)
Recapitalized 11/14/1995
Recapitalized from Derrick Oil & Gas Ltd. to Derrick Energy Corp. 11/14/1995
Each share Common no par exchanged for (0.2) share Common no par
Reorganized as Derrick Resources Inc. 06/04/1999
Each share Common no par exchanged for (1) share Derrick Resources Inc. Common no par and $5 cash
(See Derrick Resources Inc.)

DERRICK INDS INC (NV)
Reincorporated 01/30/1989
State of incorporation changed from (UT) to (NV) 01/30/1989
Recapitalized as Processing Research Inc. 04/18/1995
Each share Common $0.001 par exchanged for (0.05) share Common 2¢ par
(See Processing Research Inc.)

DERRICK-PATAGONIA MINING CO. (NV)
Charter revoked for failure to file reports and pay fees 03/05/1928

DERRICK PETE CORP (BC)
Name changed to Earth Stewards, Inc. 09/29/1993
Earth Stewards, Inc. recapitalized as Consolidated Earth Stewards, Inc. 07/17/1997 which recapitalized as Royal County Minerals Corp. 08/29/2002 which was acquired by International Curator Resources Ltd. 08/01/2003 which recapitalized as Canadian Gold Hunter Corp. (BC) 12/30/2003 which reincorporated in Canada 07/29/2004 which name changed to NGEx Resources Inc. 09/22/2009

DERRICK PETROLEUM, INC. (UT)
Name changed to Derrick Industries, Inc. (UT) 07/10/1987
Derrick Industries, Inc. (UT) reincorporated in Nevada 01/30/1989 which recapitalized as Processing Research Inc. 04/18/1995
(See Processing Research Inc.)

DERRICK RES INC (AB)
Merged into EOG Resources Canada Inc. 06/27/2001
Each share Common no par exchanged for $4.82 cash

DERRY GOLD RES INC (ON)
Recapitalized as Selby Green International Ltd. 01/18/1993
Each share Common no par exchanged for (0.1) share Common no par
Selby Green International Ltd. recapitalized as Berkshire Griffin Inc. 11/02/1995 which name changed to China Wind Power International Corp. 08/05/2009
(See China Wind Power International Corp.)

DERWOOD INVESTMENT CORP. (MA)
Merged into Westminster Investing Corp. 07/10/1986
Each share Common no par exchanged for $11 cash

DERWOOD INVT TR (MA)
Name changed to Derwood Investment Corp. 07/10/1986
(See Derwood Investment Corp.)

DERYCZ SCIENTIFIC INC (NV)
Name changed to Research Solutions, Inc. 03/04/2013

DES BARATS MINING CO. LTD. (ON)
Charter revoked for failure to file reports and pay fees 11/11/1965

DES LACS WESTERN OIL CO. (ND)
Charter expired by time limitation 12/6/36

DES MOINES CABLE TELEVISION INC (IA)
Name changed to Hawkeye Communications, Inc. 3/13/72
Hawkeye Communications, Inc. name changed to Heritage Communications, Inc. 4/16/73 which was acquired by Tele-Communications, Inc. (Old) 8/11/87 which merged into Tele-Communications, Inc. (New) 8/5/94 which merged into AT&T Corp. 3/9/99 which merged into AT&T Inc. 11/18/2005

DES MOINES GAS CO.
Merged into Iowa Power & Light Co. 00/00/1938
Details not available

DES MOINES REGISTER & TRIBUNE CO (IA)
Name changed to R & T Liquidation, Inc. 7/12/85
(See R & T Liquidation, Inc.)

DES MOINES TRAN CO (IA)
Name changed to Iowa Regional Transit Corp. 7/1/70
(See Iowa Regional Transit Corp.)

DESARROLLADORA HOMEX S A DE C V (MEXICO)
Each old Sponsored ADR for Common exchanged for (0.1) new Sponsored ADR for Common 11/05/2015
ADR agreement terminated 12/09/2016
Each new Sponsored ADR for Common exchanged for $0.34416 cash

DESC S A DE C V (MEXICO)
Sponsored ADR's for Ser. C no par reclassified as Sponsored ADR's for Ser. B no par 3/8/2004
Stock Dividends - 2.08% payable 6/20/96 to holders of record 5/6/96; 1% payable 5/23/97 to holders of record 4/29/97
ADR agreement terminated 11/30/2004
Each Sponsored ADR for Ser. B no par exchanged for $5.040185 cash

DESCANSO AGY INC (NV)
Name changed to Pacific Blue Energy Corp. 11/06/2009

DESCAR CORP. LTD. (QC)
Voluntarily dissolved 1/10/41
Details not available

DESCARTES SYS GROUP INC (ON)
Reincorporated under the laws of Canada 07/05/2006

DESCO ENERGY LTD (AB)
Recapitalized as Arcan Resources Ltd. 01/09/2007
Each share Common no par exchanged for (0.36231884) share Common no par
(See Arcan Resources Ltd.)

DESCO EXPL LTD (AB)
Name changed to Celtic Exploration Ltd. 09/30/2002
Celtic Exploration Ltd. merged into Kelt Exploration Ltd. 02/26/2013

DESCO RESOURCES INC (AB)
Recapitalized as Manitok Energy Inc. 07/29/2010
Each share Common no par exchanged for (0.37495313) share Common no par

DESCO RES LTD (AB)
Name changed to Peyto Exploration & Development Corp. (Old) 12/04/1998
Peyto Exploration & Development Corp. (Old) name changed to Peyto Energy Trust 07/01/2003 which reorganized as Peyto Exploration & Development Corp. (New) 01/07/2011

DESCON VENTURES INC (AB)
Issue Information - 1,500,000 shares COM offered at $0.20 per share on 04/28/1997
Recapitalized as Emercor Building Systems Ltd. 2/2/99
Each share Common no par exchanged for (0.2) share Common no par

DESEN COMPUTER INDS INC (BC)
Struck off register and declared dissolved for failure to file returns 2/17/89

DESERET PEAK MINES LTD (BC)
Struck off register and declared dissolved for failure to file returns 02/00/1974

DESERET PHARMACEUTICAL INC (UT)
Common $1 par split (2) for (1) by issuance of (1) additional share 3/25/66
Common $1 par split (3) for (2) by issuance of (0.5) additional share 12/22/67
Common $1 par changed to 50¢ par and (1) additional share issued 8/11/72
Merged into W-L, Inc. 3/18/77
Each share Common 50¢ par exchanged for $38 cash

DESERT ARABIAN BLOODSTOCK INC (CO)
Declared defunct and inoperative for failure to pay taxes and file annual reports 01/01/1995

DESERT CANADIANS LTD (DE)
Name changed to eXp Realty International Corp. 09/09/2013 eXp Realty International Corp. name changed to eXp World Holdings, Inc. 05/09/2016

DESERT COML BK (PALM DESERT, CA)
Merged into First Foundation Inc. 08/15/2012
Each share Common no par exchanged for (0.20807) share Common
Note: Company is now privately held

DESERT CMNTY BK (VICTORVILLE, CA)
Common $8.75 par split (2) for (1) by issuance of (1) additional share payable 05/31/2003 to holders of record 04/30/2003 Ex date - 06/02/2003
Common $8.75 par split (2) for (1) by issuance of (1) additional share payable 04/17/2006 to holders of record 03/24/2006 Ex date - 04/18/2006
Stock Dividend - 10% payable 10/31/2002 to holders of record 09/30/2002 Ex date - 09/26/2002
Merged into East West Bancorp, Inc. 08/17/2007
Each share Common $8.75 par exchanged for (0.62160384) share Common no par

DESERT GATEWAY INC (DE)
Each share old Common $0.0001 par exchanged for (1/9) share new Common $0.0001 par 11/08/2011
Name changed to Retrophin, Inc. 02/21/2013

DESERT GOLD & ALUMINUM CORP. (WA)
Declared dissolved for non-payment of taxes 7/1/55

DESERT GOLD RES INC (BC)
Recapitalized as Desert Holdings Inc. 7/7/93
Each share Common no par exchanged for (1/3) share Common no par
Desert Holdings Inc. recapitalized as Tinka Resources Ltd. 2/11/2003

DESERT HEALTH PRODS INC (AZ)
Chapter 11 bankruptcy proceedings converted to Chapter 7 on 12/29/2006
Stockholders' equity unlikely

DESERT HLDGS INC (BC)
Recapitalized as Tinka Resources Ltd. 2/11/2003
Each share Common no par exchanged for (1/3) share Common no par

DESERT MNG INC (NV)
Each share old Common $0.001 par exchanged for (10) shares new Common $0.001 par 07/15/2003
SEC revoked common stock registration 01/17/2013

DESERT NATIVE DESIGNS INC (NV)
Reorganized as FiberNet Telecom Group, Inc. (NV) 11/25/1997
Each share Common $0.001 par exchanged for (3.5) shares Common $0.001 par
FiberNet Telecom Group, Inc. (NV) reincorporated in Delaware 02/03/2000
(See FiberNet Telecom Group, Inc.)

DESERT QUEEN URANIUM CO. (UT)
Charter revoked for failure to file reports and pay fees 9/30/57

DESERT ROCK URANIUM CORP. (UT)
Name changed to Capital Enterprises Inc. 9/10/58
Capital Enterprises Inc. name changed to International Petroleum Holding Corp. 8/11/59 which name changed to Federal Gold & Silver, Inc. 7/1/68
(See Federal Gold & Silver, Inc.)

DESERT ROSE RES INC (BC)
Reincorporated under the laws of Delaware as QSA Technology, Inc. and Common no par changed to 1¢ par 01/14/1989
(See QSA Technology, Inc.)

DESERT SPRINGS ACQUISITION CORP (CO)
Reincorporated under the laws of Nevada as iDial Networks, Inc. 01/14/2000
iDial Networks, Inc. name changed to GlobalNet Corp. 12/19/2003
(See GlobalNet Corp.)

DESERT STAR RES LTD NEW (BC)
Each share old Common no par exchanged for (0.5) share new Common no par 08/30/2016
Each share new Common no par exchanged again for (0.5) share new Common no par 05/01/2017
Name changed to Kutcho Copper Corp. 12/21/2017

DESERT STAR RES LTD OLD (BC)
Under plan of merger each share Common no par automatically became (1) share Desert Star Resources Ltd. (New) Common no par 04/15/2015
Desert Star Resources Ltd. (New) name changed to Kutcho Copper Corp. 12/21/2017

DESERT SUN MNG CORP (CANADA)
Reincorporated 3/20/2003
Common no par split (2) by (1) by issuance of (1) additional share payable 5/15/96 to holders of record 5/14/96
Place of incorporation changed from (BC) to (Canada) 3/20/2003
Acquired by Yamana Gold Inc. 4/5/2006
Each share Common no par exchanged for (0.6) share Common no par

DESERT WINDS ENTMT CORP (NV)
Name changed to SunnComm, Inc. 07/06/2000
SunnComm, Inc. reorganized as SunnComm Technologies Inc. 11/21/2002 which name changed to SunnComm International, Inc. 05/03/2004 which name changed to Amergence Group, Inc. 06/01/2007 which name changed to Altitude Organic Corp. 05/16/2011 which name changed to Tranzbyte Corp. 02/22/2012 which name changed to American Green, Inc. 07/01/2014

DESIGN A PHONE INC (DE)
Charter cancelled and declared inoperative and void for non-payment of taxes 4/15/72

DESIGN ARTS INTERNATIONAL (UT)
Name changed 8/20/75
Name changed from Design Arts, Inc. of Utah to Design Arts International 8/20/75
Involuntarily dissolved 12/31/84

DESIGN AUTOMATION SYS INC (TX)
Name changed to EpicEdge, Inc. 03/17/2000
(See EpicEdge, Inc.)

DESIGN BY ROBIN INC (NV)
Name changed to Neosphere Technologies Inc. 5/14/2001
Neosphere Technologies Inc. recapitalized as Microsmart Devices Inc. 7/6/2004

DESIGN CONCEPTS INC (NV)
Name changed to Royal Millennia Group Ltd. 10/21/1996
Royal Millennia Group Ltd. recapitalized as Viper International Holdings Ltd. 08/05/1998 which name changed to 50on.com, Inc. 06/13/2000 which reorganized as Design Marketing Concepts Inc. 10/31/2000 which name changed to WEB Pay-Per-View Inc. 05/30/2001 which name changed to U.S. Federal Financial Corp. 09/25/2001 which name changed to Vibe Records Inc. 04/23/2002 which name changed to Great Entertainment & Sports Inc. 03/07/2003 which name changed to Rockit!, Inc. 06/11/2007
(See Rockit!, Inc.)

DESIGN CTLS INC (DE)
Adjudicated bankrupt 03/01/1976
Stockholders' equity unlikely

DESIGN ENTERPRISES INC (UT)
Name changed to Jalan, Inc. 08/15/1988

DESIGN INST AMER INC (CO)
Each share old Common $0.001 par exchanged for (0.2) share new Common $0.001 par 04/14/1989
Plan of reorganization under Chapter 11 Federal Bankruptcy proceedings confirmed 07/31/1991
No stockholders' equity

DESIGN MARKETING CONCEPTS INC (NV)
Incorporated 09/28/2004
Charter revoked for failure to file reports and pay fees 09/30/2011

DESIGN MARKETING CONCEPTS INC (NV)
Incorporated 06/08/1994
Name changed to WEB Pay-Per-View Inc. 05/30/2001
WEB Pay-Per-View Inc. name changed to U.S. Federal Financial Corp. 09/25/2001 which name changed to Vibe Records Inc. 04/23/2002 which name changed to Great Entertainment & Sports Inc. 03/07/2003 which name changed to Rockit!, Inc. 06/11/2007
(See Rockit!, Inc.)

DESIGN MEDIA TECH INC (MI)
Merged into Burton Advertising, Inc. 04/02/1993
Details not available

DESIGN PRODN INC (NV)
Name changed to Tech Assets, Ltd. 03/05/1997
(See Tech Assets, Ltd.)

DESIGN PROFESSIONALS FINL CORP (CA)
Acquired by Orion Capital Corp. 7/10/84
Each share Common no par exchanged for $15.11 cash

DESIGN PROFESSIONALS INS CO (CA)
Merged into Design Professionals Financial Corp. 12/31/1975
Each share Capital Stock $2.50 par exchanged for (5) shares Common no par
(See Design Professionals Financial Corp.)

DESIGN SOURCE INC (NV)
Name changed to InVivo Therapeutics Holdings Corp. 10/28/2010

DESIGN WITHIN REACH INC (DE)
Each share old Common $0.001 par exchanged for (0.02) share new Common $0.001 par 08/27/2010
Acquired by HM Catalyst, Inc. 07/28/2014
Each share new Common $0.001 par exchanged for $23.9311 cash
Note: Each share new Common $0.001 par received an additional distribution of $0.028 cash from escrow 11/10/2014

DESIGNATRONICS INC (NY)
Common 10¢ par changed to 8¢ par and (0.25) additional share issued 5/22/67
Common 8¢ par changed to 4¢ par and (1) additional share issued 1/25/68
Common 4¢ par split (3) for (2) by issuance of (0.5) additional share 2/22/83
Stock Dividends - 10% 11/6/81; 10% 11/5/82; 10% 10/24/83
Merged into Dyson, Dyson & Dunn, Inc. 9/1/95
Each share Common 4¢ par exchanged for $6 cash

DESIGNCRAFT INDS INC (NY)
Name changed 8/31/83
Each share Common 1¢ par exchanged for (0.5) share Common 2¢ par 11/16/71
Stock Dividends - 10% 9/30/81; 10% 4/14/83; 10% 9/28/84; 10% 9/25/87
Name changed from Designcraft Jewel Industries, Inc. to Designcraft Industries, Inc. 8/31/83
Name changed to Sloan's Supermarkets, Inc. 9/23/93
Sloan's Supermarkets, Inc. name changed to Gristede's Sloan's, Inc. 10/30/97 which name changed to Gristede's Foods, Inc. 10/21/99
(See Gristede's Foods, Inc.)

DESIGNED DATA CDA INC (BC)
Recapitalized as Pier Mac Environment Management Inc. 05/03/1990
Each share Common no par exchanged for (0.33333333) share Common no par
Pier Mac Environment Management Inc. recapitalized as Ebony Gold & Gas Inc. 04/07/1995 which recapitalized as Running Foxes Petroleum Corp. 12/09/1998 which recapitalized as Running Fox Resource Corp. 10/17/2000

DESIGNER & DECORATOR HSE INC (DE)
Merged into Designer & Decorator House, LLC 03/18/2002
Details not available

DESIGNER EXPT INC (NV)
Common $0.001 par split (2.582781) for (1) by issuance of (1.582781) additional shares payable 07/21/2010 to holders of record 07/14/2010 Ex date - 07/22/2010
Name changed to China Bilingual Technology & Education Group Inc. 07/30/2010
China Bilingual Technology & Education Group Inc. name changed to Capstone Technologies Group, Inc. 05/19/2017

DESIGNER FIN TR (DE)
Issue Information - 2,400,000 TR ORIGINATED PFD SECS 6% offered at $50 per share on 11/01/1996
Plan of reorganization under Chapter 11 Federal Bankruptcy Code effective 2/4/2003
Each share 6% Trust Originated Preferred Security no par received (0.11175) share Warnaco Group Inc. Common 1¢ par

DESIGNER HLDGS LTD (DE)
Merged into Warnaco Group, Inc. 12/12/1997
Each share Common 1¢ par exchanged for (0.324) share Class A Common 1¢ par
(See Warnaco Group, Inc.)

DESIGNERS INTL CORP (UT)
Charter suspended for failure to file annual reports 11/01/1991

DESIGNHOUSE INTL INC (GA)
Plan of reorganization under Chapter 11 Federal Bankruptcy Code dismissed 06/08/1989
No stockholders' equity

DESIGNLINE CORP (DE)
Plan of reorganization under Chapter 11 Federal Bankruptcy proceedings effective 03/17/2014
No stockholders' equity

DESIGNS INC (DE)
Common 1¢ par split (3) for (2) by

issuance of (0.5) additional share 06/01/1992
Stock Dividend - 50% 06/22/1993
Reincorporated under the laws of Nevada as Casual Male Retail Group, Inc. 08/09/2002
Casual Male Retail Group, Inc. name changed to Destination XL Group, Inc. 02/25/2013

DESILU PRODUCTIONS INC. (CA)
Completely liquidated 7/25/67
Each share Common $1 par or Class B Common $1 par exchanged for first and final distribution of (0.1) share Gulf & Western Industries, Inc. (DE) $5.75 Preferred $2.50 par and (0.05) share $1.75 Conv. Preferred Ser. A $2.50 par
Gulf & Western Industries, Inc. (DE) name changed to Gulf + Western Inc. 5/1/86 which name changed to Paramount Communications Inc. 6/5/89 which merged into Viacom Inc. (Old) 7/7/94
(See Viacom Inc. (Old))

DESITV INC (NV)
Name changed to Xero Mobile, Inc. 04/10/2006
Xero Mobile, Inc. name changed to MYEZSMOKES, Inc. 05/06/2011 which name changed to Icon Vapor, Inc. 02/06/2014

DESJARDINS FINL CORP (QC)
Name changed 03/31/2003
Acquired by La Confederation des caisses populaires et d'economie Desjardins du Quebec 11/13/2000
Each share Class A Subordinate no par exchanged for $23.50 cash
Name changed from Desjardins-Laurentian Financial Corp. to Desjardins Financial Corp. 03/31/2003
Class A Preferred no par called for redemption at $25 plus $0.30978 accrued dividend on 12/16/2003

DESK CORP (NV)
Each share old Common $0.0001 par exchanged for (0.2) share new Common $0.0001 par 04/05/1999
Name changed to Miner Internet Technologies & Communications Inc. 04/30/1999
Miner Internet Technologies & Communications Inc. name changed to Imsure Network, Inc. 06/15/2000
(See Imsure Network, Inc.)

DESK TOP FINL SOLUTIONS INC (NJ)
Charter declared void for non-payment of taxes 12/31/93

DESKTOP BROKER INC (DE)
Charter forfeited for failure to maintain a registered agent 10/29/1991

DESKTOP DATA INC (DE)
Issue Information - 2,000,000 shares COM offered at $15 per share on 08/11/1995
Under plan of merger name changed to NewsEdge Corp. 2/24/98
(See Newsedge Corp.)

DESMARAIS ENERGY CORP (AB)
Received Notice of Intention to Enforce a Security under the Bankruptcy and Insolvency Act 12/23/2014
Stockholders' equity unlikely

DESMOND INVTS LTD (BC)
Name changed to DLC Holdings Corp. 02/07/2017

DESMONT MINING CORP. LTD. (ON)
Charter cancelled and company dissolved by default 03/30/1959

DESOTO INC (DE)
Name changed 05/09/1967
Name changed from DeSoto Chemical Coatings, Inc. to DeSoto, Inc. 05/09/1967

Merged into Keystone Consolidated Industries, Inc. 09/27/1996
Each share Common $1 par exchanged for (0.7465) share Common $1 par
(See Keystone Consolidated Industries, Inc.)

DESPERADO RES INC (BC)
Recapitalized as Skyway Resources Ltd. 10/08/1986
Each share Common no par exchanged for (0.66666666) share Common no par
Skyway Resources Ltd. recapitalized as Burrard Ventures Inc. 07/24/1989
(See Burrard Ventures Inc.)

DESSAUER GLOBAL EQUITY FD (DE)
Issue Information - 5,250,000 shares COM offered at $12.50 per share on 05/30/1997
Merged into Advisors Series Trust 10/25/2002
Details not available

DESSIR RES LTD (BC)
Recapitalized as Taurus Exploration Ltd. 06/07/1993
Each share Common no par exchanged for (0.2) share Common no par
Taurus Exploration Ltd. name changed to Trans Asia Resources Inc. 11/28/1997 which name changed to Municipal Solutions Group, Inc. 01/14/2002 which reorganized as CloudBench Applications, Inc. 07/21/2008 which name changed to BasicGov Systems, Inc. 12/24/2009 which name changed to Pedro Resources Ltd. 09/30/2010

DEST CORP (CA)
Plan of reorganization under Chapter 11 Federal Bankruptcy proceedings confirmed 05/07/1990
No stockholders' equity

DESTAFFANY TANTALUM BERYLLIUM MINES LTD. (CANADA)
Merged into Boreal Rare Metals Ltd. on a (1) for (5) basis in 1953
(See Boreal Rare Metals Ltd.)

DESTEC ENERGY INC (DE)
Merged into NGC Corp. 06/27/1997
Each share Common 1¢ par exchanged for $21.65 cash

DESTIA COMMUNICATIONS INC (DE)
Issue Information - 6,500,000 shares COM offered at $10 per share on 05/05/1999
Merged into Viatel, Inc. 12/8/99
Each share Common 1¢ par exchanged for (0.445) share Common 1¢ par
(See Viatel, Inc.)

DESTINATION RESORTS INC (AB)
Acquired by T.G.S. Properties Ltd. 11/22/2000
Each share Common no par exchanged for (0.575) share Common no par
(See T.G.S. Properties Ltd.)

DESTINATION TELEVISION INC (DE)
Name changed to Movie Studio, Inc. 06/09/2014

DESTINY EXPRESS, INC. (UT)
Name changed to Psychological Health Care, Inc. (UT) 10/11/1985
Psychological Health Care, Inc. (UT) reincorporated in Illinois as Pain Prevention 02/03/1989 which reincorporated in Utah as PPI Capital Corp. 11/15/1997 which recapitalized as PPI Capital Group, Inc. (UT) 06/01/1998 which reincorporated in Delaware as DirectPlacement Inc. 11/28/2001 which name changed to PCS Research Technology, Inc. 10/07/2002 which name changed to

Sagient Research Systems, Inc. 05/20/2004
(See Sagient Research Systems, Inc.)

DESTINY HOSPITALITY LTD (AB)
Recapitalized as Real Time Measurements Inc. 05/16/2003
Each share Common no par exchanged for (0.1149425) share Common no par

DESTINY MEDIA TECHNOLOGIES INC (CO)
Each share old Common $0.001 par exchanged for (3) shares new Common $0.001 par 12/30/1999
Reincorporated under the laws of Nevada 10/08/2014

DESTINY MINERALS INC (NV)
Reorganized as Amico Games Corp. 10/06/2009
Each share Common $0.00001 par exchanged for (6) shares Common $0.00001 par

DESTINY RESOURCE SVCS CORP (AB)
Each share old Common no par exchanged for (0.05) share new Common no par 04/07/2005
Name changed to Logan International Inc. 05/18/2010
(See Logan International Inc.)

DESTINY RES LTD (BC)
Common no par split (3) for (1) by issuance of (2) additional shares 01/06/1988
Recapitalized as Double Down Resources Ltd. 06/12/1990
Each share Common no par exchanged for (0.14825714) share Common no par
Double Down Resources Ltd. recapitalized as Meteor Creek Resources Inc. 01/11/2001
(See Meteor Creek Resources Inc.)

DESTOR-O'HARA MINES LTD. (ON)
Charter cancelled and proclaimed dissolved for failure to pay taxes and file returns 2/18/63

DESTOR VALLEY GOLD MINES, LTD. (QC)
Charter surrendered 12/18/57
No stockholders' equity

DESTORADA MINES, LTD. (ON)
Charter cancelled and company declared dissolved for default in filing returns 3/25/65

DESTORBELLE MINES LTD (ON)
Acquired by Excellon Resources Inc. (BC) 06/30/2004
Each share Common no par exchanged for (3.25) shares Common no par and $0.60 cash
Excellon Resources Inc. (BC) reincorporated in Ontario 06/05/2012

DESTRON FEARING CORP (DE)
Reincorporated 10/01/1993
Name changed 08/03/1994
Place of incorporation changed from Canada to Delaware 10/01/1993
Name changed from Destron/IDI Inc. to Destron Fearing Corp. 08/03/1994
Merged into Applied Digital Solutions, Inc. 09/08/2000
Each share Common no par exchanged for (1.5) shares Common $0.001 par
Applied Digital Solutions, Inc. name changed to Digital Angel Corp. (New) 06/20/2008

DESTRON INC (IL)
Chapter 11 Federal Bankruptcy Code converted to Chapter 7 on 09/09/1987
Stockholders' equity unlikely

DESTRON TECHNOLOGIES INC (CANADA)
Recapitalized as International Destron Technologies Inc. 05/20/1986

Each share Common no par exchanged for (0.33333333) share Common no par
International Destron Technologies Inc. recapitalized as Destron/IDI Inc. (Canada) 06/03/1988 which reincorporated in Delaware 10/01/1993 which name changed to Destron Fearing Corp. 08/03/1994 which merged into Applied Didital Solutions, Inc. 09/08/2000 which name changed to Digital Angel Corp. (New) 06/20/2008 which recapitalized as VeriTeQ Corp. 10/22/2013

DETACHABLE BIT CO.
Out of business 00/00/1943
Details not available

DETACHABLE BIT CORP. OF AMERICA, INC.
Dissolved 00/00/1937
Details not available

DETEC RES LTD (BC)
Name changed to Streamline Web Broadcasting Inc. 10/19/2000
Streamline Web Broadcasting Inc. recapitalized as Kavalmedia Services Ltd. 05/17/2005 which name changed to EmerGeo Solutions Worldwide Inc. 08/05/2008

DETECH CORP (AB)
Delisted from Toronto Venture Stock Exchange 06/20/2003

DETECTION SCIENCES INC (MN)
Name changed to Dahlberg Electronics, Inc. 12/01/1980
Dahlberg Electronics, Inc. name changed to Dahlberg, Inc. 06/22/1984
(See Dahlberg, Inc.)

DETECTION SEC SYS INC (WA)
Recapitalized as Nexis International Industries, Inc. 08/30/2007
Each share Common $0.001 par exchanged for (0.00006666) share Common $0.001 par
(See Nexis International Industries, Inc.)

DETECTION SYS INC (NY)
Common 5¢ par split (3) for (2) by issuance of (0.5) additional share 09/30/1980
Common 5¢ par split (5) for (4) by issuance of (0.25) additional share 08/07/1987
Common 5¢ par split (3) for (2) by issuance of (0.5) additional share payable 12/17/1996 to holders of record 11/27/1996
Stock Dividends - 25% 09/20/1979; 50% 06/12/1981
Merged into Robert Bosch GmbH 03/05/2001
Each share Common 5¢ par exchanged for $18 cash

DETECTO SCALES INC (NY)
Common $1 par changed to 1¢ par 06/07/1974
Completely liquidated 01/03/1979
Each share Common 1¢ par exchanged for first and final distribution of $0.40 cash

DETECTOGAS INSTRUMENTS, INC. (TX)
Merged into Pacific Union Gas Co. 01/10/1963
Each share Common exchanged for (0.1) share Common $1 par
Pacific Union Gas Co. acquired by Texas American Oil Corp. 09/27/1967 which reorganized as Texas American Energy Corp. 06/13/1980 which name changed to Kent Financial Services, Inc. (DE) 07/27/1990 which reincorporated in Nevada 12/15/2006
(See Kent Financial Services, Inc.)

DETECTOR ELECTRS CORP (MN)
Acquired by RHP Group PLC 01/05/1988

Each share Common 10¢ par exchanged for $9 cash

DETECTOR RES LTD (AB)
Recapitalized as Detector Exploration Ltd. 06/23/1999
Each share Common no par exchanged for (0.25) share Common no par

DETERMINISTICS INC (DE)
Name changed to Bright Star World Entertainment Inc. 06/19/1989
Bright Star World Entertainment Inc. name changed to Cyto Skin Care Corp. 03/15/1994 which name changed to Chantal Skin Care Corp. 08/01/1994 which recapitalized as Utix Group, Inc. 11/21/2003
(See Utix Group, Inc.)

DETEX SEC SYS INC (WA)
Name changed to Detection Security Systems, Inc. 05/15/2006
Detection Security Systems, Inc. recapitalized as Nexis International Industries, Inc. 08/30/2007
(See Nexis International Industries, Inc.)

DETHRONE RTY HLDGS INC (NV)
Name changed to High Performance Beverages Co. 01/09/2014

DETINU LIQUIDATING LIFE INSURANCE CO. (TX)
Acquired by United International Corp. (NV) 11/24/1970
Each share Common no par exchanged for (2) shares Common $1 par
United International Corp. (NV) liquidated for Transport Life Insurance Co. 06/30/1971
(See Transport Life Insurance Co.)

DETOMAC MINES LTD. (ON)
Charter cancelled 03/00/1965

DETOUR INC (CA)
Reorganized under the laws of Colorado as Detour Magazine, Inc. 09/20/1997
Each share Common $0.001 par exchanged for (0.207356038) share Common $0.001 par
Detour Magazine, Inc. name changed to Detour Media Group, Inc. 03/31/2001
(See Detour Media Group, Inc.)

DETOUR MEDIA GROUP INC (CO)
Name changed 03/31/2001
Name changed from Detour Magazine, Inc. to Detour Media Group, Inc. 03/31/2001
SEC revoked common stock registration 01/25/2007

DETREX CORP (MI)
Name changed 06/29/1956
Name changed 05/13/1986
7% Preferred $100 par called for redemption 06/30/1976
Preferred $2 par called for redemption 12/31/1979
Common $2 par split (2) for (1) by issuance of (1) additional share 02/24/1984
Stock Dividend - 100% 05/11/1959
Name changed from Detrex Corp. to Detrex Chemical Industries, Inc. 06/29/1956 which name changed back to Detrex Corp. 05/13/1986
Acquired by Italmatch USA Corp. 12/08/2017
Each share Common $2 par exchanged for $27 cash

DETROIT AIRCRAFT CORP.
Became inactive 00/00/1948
Stockholders' equity unlikely

DETROIT ALUM & BRASS CORP (MI)
Common $1.25 par changed to $7.50 par 03/06/1962
Stock Dividend - 15% 12/31/1963
Name changed to D.A.B. Industries, Inc. 06/30/1969
(See D.A.B. Industries, Inc.)

DETROIT & CANADA TUNNEL CO.
Reorganized as Detroit & Canada Tunnel Corp. 00/00/1936
No stockholders' equity

DETROIT & CDA TUNL CORP (MI)
Each share Common no par exchanged for (3) shares Common $10 par 00/00/1946
Each share Common $10 par exchanged for (2) shares Common $5 par 10/26/1955
Merged into Hyde Park Tunnel Holdings L.L.C. 03/31/1997
Each share Common $5 par exchanged for $54 cash

DETROIT & CLEVELAND NAVIGATION CO. (MI)
Common $10 par changed to $5 par 00/00/1942
Merged into Denver-Chicago Trucking Co., Inc. 10/05/1960
Each share Common $5 par exchanged for (0.71428571) share Common $1 par
Denver-Chicago Trucking Co., Inc. name changed to DC International, Inc. 03/25/1966 which merged into T.I.M.E.-DC, Inc. 01/17/1969
(See T.I.M.E.-DC, Inc.)

DETROIT & MACKINAC RY CO (MI)
Acquired by Huron Acquisition Co. 02/17/1992
Details not available

DETROIT & NORTHN SVGS F A HANCOCK MICH (USA)
Name changed to D&N Savings Bank, FSB (Hancock, MI) 04/28/1986
D&N Savings Bank, FSB (Hancock, MI) reorganized in Delaware as D&N Financial Corp. 07/31/1988 which merged into Republic Bancorp Inc. 05/17/1999 which merged into Citizens Banking Corp. 12/29/2006 which name changed to Citizens Republic Bancorp, Inc. 04/26/2007 which merged into FirstMerit Corp. 04/12/2013 which merged into Huntington Bancshares Bancshares Inc. 08/16/2016

DETROIT BK & TR CO (DETROIT, MI)
Stock Dividends - 10% 02/09/1965; 12.5% 04/08/1969; 25% 04/06/1971
Reorganized as Detroitbank Corp. 06/01/1973
Each share Common $10 par exchanged for (1) share Common $10 par
Detroitbank Corp. name changed to Comerica, Inc. 07/01/1982

DETROIT BANK (DETROIT, MI)
Each share Common $20 par exchanged for (2) shares Common $10 par 00/00/1953
Stock Dividends - 10% 02/15/1944; 16.66666666% 02/15/1947; 11.11111111% 02/15/1949; 10% 02/05/1954; 50% 02/08/1956
Merged into Detroit Bank & Trust Co. (Detroit, MI) 08/31/1956
Each share Common $10 par exchanged for (1) share Common $10 par
Detroit Bank & Trust Co. (Detroit, MI) reorganized as Detroitbank Corp. 06/01/1973 which name changed to Comerica, Inc. 07/01/1982

DETROIT BISCUIT CO., INC.
Dissolved 00/00/1946
Details not available

DETROIT COMPENSATING AXLE CORP.
Name changed to Differential Wheel Corp. 00/00/1939
(See Differential Wheel Corp.)

DETROIT CREAMERY CO.
Acquired by National Dairy Products Corp. 00/00/1929
Details not available

DETROIT CREAMERY REALTY CO. (MI)
Liquidation completed 00/00/1953
Details not available

DETROIT-CRIPPLE CREEK GOLD MINING CO.
In process of dissolution 00/00/1939
Details not available

DETROIT DIESEL CORP (DE)
Merged into DaimlerChrysler North American Holding Corp. 10/13/2000
Each share Common 1¢ par exchanged for $23 cash

DETROIT EDISON CO (MI & NY)
Reincorporated 06/01/1967
Each share Capital Stock $100 par exchanged for (5) shares Capital Stock $20 par 00/00/1941
Capital Stock $20 par reclassified as Common $20 par 05/08/1959
Common $20 par changed to $10 par and (1) additional share issued 01/14/1963
Stock Dividend - 10% 05/01/1947
State of incorporation changed from (NY) to (NY) and (MI) 06/01/1967
12.8% Preferred $100 par called for redemption 08/15/1986
15.68% Preferred $100 par called for redemption 08/15/1986
$4.12 Preference $1 par called for redemption 01/15/1987
$4 Preference $1 par called for redemption 04/15/1987
$3.12 Preference $1 par called for redemption 01/15/1988
$3.40 Preference $1 par called for redemption 01/15/1988
$3.42 Preference $1 par called for redemption 01/15/1988
$3.13 Preference $1 par called for redemption 10/15/1988
$3.24 Preference $1 par called for redemption 10/15/1988
$2.75 Preference $1 par called for redemption 07/15/1992
$2.75 Preference Ser. B $1 par called for redemption 01/15/1993
$2.28 Preference $1 par called for redemption 03/26/1993
9.6% Preference $1 par called for redemption 03/26/1993
9.72% Preferred $100 par called for redemption 03/26/1993
9.32% Preferred $100 par called for redemption 05/28/1993
5.5% Conv. Preferred $100 par called for redemption 10/15/1995
Under plan of reorganization each share Common $10 par automatically became (1) share DTE Energy Co. Common no par 01/02/1996
7.36% Preferred $100 par called for redemption 03/21/1996
7.45% Preferred $100 par called for redemption 03/21/1996
7.68% Preferred $100 par called for redemption 03/21/1996
7.75% Depositary Preferred called for redemption at $25 plus $0.13993 accrued dividends on 05/11/1998
7.75% Preferred $100 par called for redemption at $100 on 05/11/1998
7.74% Depositary Preferred called for redemption at $25 plus $0.263375 accrued dividends on 12/03/1998
7.74% Preferred $100 par called for redemption at $100 plus $0.263375 accrued dividends on 12/03/1998

DETROIT ELECTRIC CO.
Name changed to Detroit Majestic Products Corp. 00/00/1930
(See Detroit Majestic Products Corp.)

DETROIT ENGINE CORP (NV)
Name changed to Pacific Waste Management, Inc. 11/27/1990
(See Pacific Waste Management, Inc.)

DETROIT FIRE & MARINE INSURANCE CO.
Merged into Great American Insurance Co. 12/31/1958
Each share Common exchanged for (4.1) shares Capital Stock $5 par
(See Great American Insurance Co.)

DETROIT GARAGES, INC.
Dissolution approved 00/00/1947
No stockholders' equity

DETROIT GASKET & MANUFACTURING CO. (MI)
Stock Dividend - 50% 12/13/1955
Name changed to D.G. Corp. 01/30/1965
(See D.G. Corp.)

DETROIT GEAR & MACHINE CO.
Acquired by Borg-Warner Corp. (IL) 00/00/1934
Details not available

DETROIT GRAY IRON & STEEL FOUNDRIES, INC. (OLD) (MI)
Ctfs. dated prior to 05/26/1960
Name changed to Detroit Industrial Products Corp. 05/26/1960
Detroit Industrial Products Corp. name changed to Technical Tape, Inc. 07/31/1964
(See Technical Tape, Inc.)

DETROIT GRAY IRON & STL FDRYS INC NEW (MI)
Ctfs. dated after 09/18/1969
Adjudicated bankrupt 05/10/1974
Stockholders' equity unlikely

DETROIT GRAY IRON FOUNDRY CO. (MI)
Capital Stock no par changed to $5 par 00/00/1933
Each share Capital Stock $5 par exchanged for (5) shares Common $1 par 00/00/1937
Name changed to Detroit Gray Iron & Steel Foundries, Inc. (Old) 05/14/1958
Detroit Gray Iron & Steel Foundries, Inc. (Old) name changed to Detroit Industrial Products Corp. 05/26/1960 which name changed to Technical Tape, Inc. 07/31/1964
(See Technical Tape, Inc.)

DETROIT HARDWARE MANUFACTURING CO. (NEW) (MI)
Incorporated 08/08/1956
Name changed to J-K Industries, Inc. (MI) 01/15/1962
J-K Industries, Inc. (MI) recapitalized under the laws of Delaware 12/11/1963 which name changed to Agrow Industries, Inc. 09/16/1977
(See Agrow Industries, Inc.)

DETROIT HARDWARE MANUFACTURING CO. OLD (MI)
Incorporated 02/20/1924
Name changed to Trans Continental Industries, Inc. 07/06/1956
Trans Continental Industries, Inc. name changed to Republic-Transcon Industries, Inc. 01/22/1960 which was acquired by Briggs Manufacturing Co. 10/19/1965 which name changed to Panacon Corp. 04/09/1970
(See Panacon Corp.)

DETROIT HARVESTER CO. (MI)
Each share old Common $1 par exchanged for (2) shares new Common $1 par 00/00/1946
Stock Dividend - 10% 12/20/1951
Name changed to Dura Corp. 08/01/1959
(See Dura Corp.)

DETROIT, HILLSDALE & SOUTH WESTERN RAILROAD CO. (MI)
Liquidation completed
Each share Common $100 par received initial distribution of $2 cash 02/06/1961
Each (10) shares Common $100 par exchanged for second and final

DETROIT INDUSTRIAL PRODUCTS CORP. (MI)
Name changed to Technical Tape, Inc. 07/31/1964
(See Technical Tape, Inc.)

DETROIT INDS LTD (DE)
Name changed to Wain Resources Inc. 11/06/1970
(See Wain Resources Inc.)

DETROIT INTL BRDG CO (MI)
Reorganized 00/00/1940
Preferred $100 par and Common no par holders received only Warrants to purchase Common $1 par stock of reorganized company
Stock Dividends - 100% 05/07/1946; 100% 04/21/1954; 100% 08/01/1977
Merged into Central Cartage Co. 07/31/1979
Each share Common $1 par exchanged for $25 cash

DETROIT LELAND HOTEL CO. (MI)
Common no par changed to $2.50 par 00/00/1945
Liquidation completed
Each share Common $2.50 par received initial distribution of $2.50 cash 06/12/1964
Each share Common $2.50 par exchanged for second and final distribution of $0.3304 cash 12/21/1966

DETROIT MAJESTIC PRODUCTS CORP.
Acquired by Grigsby-Grunow Co. 00/00/1933
Details not available

DETROIT MFRS RR (MI)
Voluntarily dissolved 01/01/2007
Details not available

DETROIT-MICHIGAN STOVE CO. (MI)
Each share Preferred $100 par exchanged for (1.21) shares Preferred $40 par 00/00/1934
Each share Common no par exchanged for (0.4) share Common $1 par 00/00/1934
Stock Dividend - 25% 06/25/1946
Merged into Welbilt Corp. 05/17/1955
Each share Preferred $40 par exchanged for (3) shares 5% Cum. Conv. Preferred $10 par
Each share Common $1 par exchanged for (1) share Common $1 par
(See Welbilt Corp.)

DETROIT MTG & RLTY CO (MI)
Reorganized under the laws of Nevada as Boundary Bay Resources, Inc. 09/24/2007
Each share Common $1 par exchanged for (40) shares Common $0.001 par
Boundary Bay Resources, Inc. recapitalized as Wave Technology Group Inc. 05/06/2010 which name changed to eMamba International Corp. 07/27/2011

DETROIT MORTGAGE CORP. (DE)
Charter cancelled and declared inoperative and void for non-payment of taxes 03/17/1926

DETROIT MOTOR CO. (NJ)
Charter revoked for failure to file reports and pay fees 01/13/1926

DETROIT MOTORBUS CO.
Liquidation completed 00/00/1943
Details not available

DETROIT PALMETTO CO.
Liquidation completed 00/00/1946
Details not available

DETROIT PAPER PRODUCTS CORP.
Liquidated 00/00/1945
Details not available

distribution of $1,000 principal amount New York Central Railroad Co. 4% Ser. A Mortgage Bonds due 02/01/1998 02/06/1961

DETROIT PROPERTIES CORP. (MI)
Ceased operations 12/31/1929
Stockholders' equity unlikely

DETROIT RACE COURSE INC (MI)
Liquidation completed
Each share Common $2 par exchanged for initial distribution of $17 cash 01/29/1969
Each share Common $2 par received second distribution of $1.10 cash 09/30/1969
Each share Common $2 par received third and final distribution of $0.682085 cash 05/13/1971

DETROIT RAILWAY & HARBOR TERMINALS CO.
Reorganized 00/00/1930
No stockholders' equity

DETROIT RAILWAY & HARBOR TERMINALS LAND CO.
Reorganized as Detroit River Warehouse, Inc. 00/00/1935
Details not available

DETROIT RIVER WHSE INC (MI)
Common $7.50 par changed to $5 par 12/04/1944
Common $5 par changed to $1 par 05/01/1946
Name changed to Rosemont-Penrod Corp. 09/03/1971
(See Rosemont-Penrod Corp.)

DETROIT STAMPING CO. (MI)
Stock Dividend - 20% 01/27/1958
Name changed to De-Sta-Co Corp. 04/09/1962
De-Sta-Co Corp. name channed to H.G.R. Corp. 12/13/1962
(See H.G.R. Corp.)

DETROIT STEEL PRODUCTS CO. (MI)
Common no par changed to $10 par 00/00/1940
Stock Dividends - 100% 08/01/1947; 25% 12/31/1952
Name changed to Fenestra Inc. 03/28/1956
Fenestra Inc. name changed to Marmon Group, Inc. (MI) 12/07/1967 which reincorporated in Delaware 12/31/1970
(See Marmon Group, Inc. (Ctfs. dated after 12/31/1970))

DETROIT STL CORP (MI)
Each share Common $5 par exchanged for $10 principal amount of 6% S.F. Debentures due 00/00/1964 and (1) share Common $2 par 00/00/1944
Each share Common $2 par exchanged for (2) shares Common $1 par 00/00/1946
Stock Dividend - 100% 02/19/1952
Name changed to Cliffs-St. Clair Corp. 11/16/1970
Cliffs-St. Clair Corp. liquidated for Cleveland-Cliffs Iron Co. 03/15/1972 which reorganized as Cleveland-Cliffs Inc. (Old) 07/01/1975 which name changed to Cliffs Natural Resources Inc. 10/15/2008 which name changed to Cleveland-Cliffs Inc. (New) 08/25/2017

DETROIT SULPHITE PULP & PAPER CO. (MI)
Merged into Scott Paper Co. 00/00/1954
Each share Common $10 par exchanged for (0.6) shares Common no par
Scott Paper Co. merged into Kimberly-Clark Corp. 12/12/1995

DETROIT TESTING LAB INC (MI)
Merged into Comtel Corp. 10/14/1968
Each share Common $1 par exchanged for (0.75) share Common 1¢ par
(See Comtel Corp.)

DETROIT TEX GAS GATHERING CO (MI)
Plan of reorganization under Chapter 11 Federal Bankruptcy proceedings confirmed 02/23/1989
No stockholders' equity

DETROIT TRACTOR LTD (DE)
Class A Common $2 par changed to 5¢ par 02/28/1969
Name changed to Detroit Industries Ltd. 05/26/1969
Detroit Industries Ltd. name changed to Wain Resources Inc. 11/06/1970
(See Wain Resources Inc.)

DETROIT TRUST CO. (DETROIT, MI)
Merged into Detroit Wabeek Bank & Trust Co. (Detroit, MI) 08/01/1956
Each share Capital Stock $10 par exchanged for (2.625) shares Common $10 par
Detroit Wabeek Bank & Trust Co. (Detroit, MI) merged into Detroit Bank & Trust Co. (Detroit, MI) 08/31/1956 which reorganized as Detroitbank Corp. 06/01/1973 which name changed to Comerica, Inc. 07/01/1982

DETROIT UNION RAILROAD DEPOT & STATION CO.
Acquired by Pennsylvania Railroad Co. 12/31/54
Details not available

DETROIT UNITED RAILWAY
Sold at foreclosure to Eastern Michigan Railways in 1928 which reorganized in 1939 with no stockholders' equity

DETROIT WABEEK BANK & TRUST CO. (DETROIT, MI)
Merged into Detroit Bank & Trust Co. (Detroit, MI) 08/31/1956
Each share Common $10 par exchanged for (1) share Common $10 par
Detroit Bank & Trust Co. (Detroit, MI) reorganized as Detroitbank Corp. 06/01/1973 which name changed to Comerica, Inc. 07/01/1982

DETROIT WAX PAPER CO.
Name changed to Fabricon Products, Inc. 00/00/1945
(See Fabricon Products, Inc.)

DETROITBANK CORP (DE)
Common $10 par changed to $5 par and (1) additional share issued 03/31/1978
Stock Dividends - 10% 09/29/1973; 33.33333333% 09/30/1976
Name changed to Comerica, Inc. 07/01/1982

DETROITER MOBILE HOMES, INC. (MI)
Name changed to DMH Corp. 05/24/1967
DMH Corp. merged into National Gypsum Co. 07/31/1970
(See National Gypsum Co.)

DETROLA CORP.
Merged into International Detrola Corp. 12/31/1943
Each share Common exchanged for (0.55555555) share Common $1 par
International Detrola Corp. name changed to Newport Steel Corp. 03/04/1949 which name changed to Newcorp, Inc. (IN) 09/18/1956
(See Newcorp, Inc. (IN))

DETSCO INC (DE)
Merged into Comcar Industries, Inc. 05/31/1985
Each share Common 10¢ par exchanged for $3 cash

DETTA MINERALS LTD. (ON)
Name changed 00/00/1950
Name changed from Detta Red Lake Mines Ltd. to Detta Minerals Ltd. 00/00/1950
Recapitalized as Candore Explorations Ltd. 01/04/1957

Each share Capital Stock no par exchanged for (0.16666666) share Capital Stock no par
Candore Explorations Ltd. recapitalized as Golden Crescent Resources Corp. 12/31/1987 which recapitalized as Golden Crescent Corp. 05/20/1998
(See Golden Crescent Corp.)

DETWILER MITCHELL & CO (CA)
Each (600) shares old Common 1¢ par exchanged for (1) share new Common 1¢ par 05/26/2004
Note: Holders of (599) or fewer pre-split shares received $1.25 cash per share
Name changed to Detwiler Fenton Group, Inc. 10/20/2008

DEUCALION RESH INC (ND)
Reorganized under the laws of Delaware as Digital Fuel, Inc. 06/22/2000
Each (6,800) shares Common $0.0001 par exchanged for (1) share Common $0.0001 par
(See Digital Fuel, Inc.)

DEUTERIUM CORP (NV)
Charter revoked for failure to file reports and pay fees 10/1/98

DEUTSCHE BK CAP FDG TR VIII (DE)
6.375% Non-Cumulative Trust Preferred Securities called for redemption at $25 on 04/18/2015

DEUTSCHE BK CAP FDG TR IX (DE)
6.625% Non-Cumulative Trust Preferred Securities called for redemption at $25 on 02/20/2015

DEUTSCHE BK CAP FDG TR X (DE)
7.35% Non-Cumulative Trust Preferred Securities called for redemption at $25 on 03/17/2014

DEUTSCHE BK CONTINGENT CAP TR III (DE)
7.6% Trust Preferred Securities called for redemption at $25 on 02/20/2018

DEUTSCHE BETEILIGUNGS HLDG AG (GERMANY)
Reg. S Sponsored ADR's for Bearer Shares DM 5 changed to Reg. S Sponsored ADR's for Bearer Shares EUR 3 on 08/14/2003
ADR agreement terminated 12/01/2007
Each Reg. S Sponsored ADR for Bearer Shares EUR 3 par exchanged for $0.320069 cash

DEUTSCHE ERDOEL AKTIENGESELLSCHAFT (GERMANY)
Name changed to Deutsche Texaco Aktiengesellschaft 08/12/1970
(See Deutsche Texaco Aktiengesellschaft)

DEUTSCHE GLOBAL HIGH INCOME FD INC (MD)
Completely liquidated
Each share Common 1¢ par received first and final distribution of $8.823 cash payable 09/18/2017 to holders of record 09/08/2017

DEUTSCHE HIGH INCOME OPPORTUNITIES FD INC (MD)
Completely liquidated 03/19/2018
Each share Common 1¢ par received $15.036 cash

DEUTSCHE HIGH INCOME TR (MA)
Trust terminated 11/14/2016
Each share Common 1¢ par received $9.346 cash

DEUTSCHE MUN INCOME TR (MA)
Floating Rate Municipal Term Preferred Ser. 2015 1¢ par called for redemption at $5,000 on 06/01/2015
Preferred Shares of Bene. Int. Ser. B 1¢ par called for redemption at $5,000 on 06/12/2015
Preferred Shares of Bene. Int. Ser. C

1¢ par called for redemption at $5,000 on 06/12/2015
Preferred Shares of Bene. Int. Ser. E 1¢ par called for redemption at $5,000 on 06/15/2015
Name changed to DWS Municipal Income Trust (New) 07/02/2018

DEUTSCHE STRATEGIC MUN INCOME TR (MA)
Floating Rate Municipal Term Preferred 1¢ par called for redemption at $25,000 on 06/01/2015
Municipal Auction Rate Preferred 1¢ par called for redemption at $25,000 plus $0.408 accrued dividends on 06/08/2015
Name changed to DWS Strategic Municipal Income Trust (New) 07/02/2018

DEUTSCHE TEXACO A G (GERMANY)
Acquired by Rhine Westphalia Electric Power Corp. in 1988
Details not available

DEUTSCHE WOHNEN AG (GERMANY)
Name changed to Deutsche Wohnen SE 08/21/2017

DEV INVTS INC (AB)
Name changed to Indicator Minerals Inc. (AB) 03/02/2004
Indicator Minerals Inc. (AB) reincorporated in British Columbia 06/13/2005 which recapitalized as Bluestone Resources Inc. 01/11/2012

DEV-SEC INC (FL)
Name changed 06/01/2005
Each share Common 10¢ par exchanged for (1/3) share Common 30¢ par 09/28/1992
Each share old Common 30¢ par exchanged for (0.25) share new Common 30¢ par 11/30/1994
Name changed from Dev-Tech Corp. to Dev-Sec, Inc. 06/01/2005
SEC revoked common stock registration 07/06/2011

DEVAGO INC (NV)
Name changed to 12 Retech Corp. 06/22/2017

DEVAL AERODYNAMICS INC (DE)
Voluntarily dissolved 11/14/1979
Details not available

DEVANT HOLDINGS LTD. (ON)
Liquidation completed
Each share Common no par received initial distribution of (0.603) share Nashua Corp. (DE) Common $1 par 04/29/1974
Each share Common no par received second distribution of $0.127 cash 08/21/1975
Each share Common no par received third and final distribution of $0.015 cash 02/15/1977
Note: Certificates were not required to be surrendered and are without value
Nashua Corp. (DE) reincorporated in Massachusetts 06/12/2002 which was acquired by Cenveo, Inc. 09/15/2009
(See Cenveo, Inc.)

DEVCO COPPER CORP (NM)
Charter voluntarily suspended 07/16/1970

DEVCO ENTERPRISES INC (BC)
Recapitalized as SBI Skin Biology Inc. (BC) 11/03/1995
Each share Common no par exchanged for (0.25) share Common no par
SBI Skin Biology Inc. (BC) reincorporated in Yukon 08/22/1996 which reorganized in British Columbia as Realm Energy International Corp. 10/26/2009

which merged into San Leon Energy PLC 11/10/2011

DEVCON INTL CORP (FL)
Stock Dividend - 200% 08/08/1989
Merged into Golden Gate Capital 09/30/2009
Each share Common 10¢ par exchanged for $0.15 cash

DEVCORP CAP INC (AB)
Name changed to Great Prairie Energy Services Inc. 12/24/2013

DEVELCO, INC. (SC)
Name changed to Southern "500" Truck Stops, Inc. and Common $5 par changed to $1 par 10/31/1974
(See Southern "500" Truck Stops, Inc.)

DEVELCO INC (NV)
Charter revoked for failure to file reports and pay fees 03/07/1977

DEVELCON ELECTRS LTD (SK)
Merged into Vianet Technologies, Inc. 5/28/99
Each share Common no par exchanged for (0.03250325) share Class A Common $0.001 par
(See Vianet Technologies, Inc.)

DEVELOCAP INC (NV)
Name changed to Trai Thien USA Inc. 01/27/2010
Trai Thien USA Inc. name changed to Onassis Mining Group, Inc. 06/08/2015

DEVELOPED TECHNOLOGY RESOURCE INC (MN)
Each share old Common 1¢ par exchanged for (1/3) share new Common 1¢ par 12/12/95
Each share new Common 1¢ par received distribution of (1) share DTR-Med Pharma Corp. Common payable 5/15/2001 to holders of record 5/7/2001
Name changed to GelStat Corp. 7/16/2003

DEVELOPER VENTURES INC (AB)
Issue Information - 3,000,000 shares COM offered at $0.15 per share on 07/05/2001
Name changed to DevStudios International Inc. 2/4/2002

DEVELOPERS DIVERSIFIED RLTY CORP (OH)
Common no par split (2) for (1) by issuance of (1) additional share payable 08/03/1998 to holders of record 07/27/1998 Ex date - 08/04/1998
9.44% Depositary Preferred Class B called for redemption at $25 plus $0.196667 accrued dividends on 04/15/2002
Depositary Preferred Class A called for redemption at $25 plus $0.197917 accrued dividends on 04/15/2002
8-3/8% Depositary Preferred Class C called for redemption at $25 plus $0.255903 accrued dividends on 07/28/2003
8.68% Depositary Preferred Ser. D called for redemption at $25 plus $0.391806 accrued dividends on 08/20/2003
9.375% Preferred no par called for redemption at $25 plus $0.481771 accrued dividends on 09/15/2003
8.60% Depositary Preferred Class F called for redemption at $25 on 04/02/2007
Common no par changed to 10¢ par 08/06/2008
8% Depositary Preferred Class G called for redemption at $25 plus $0.105556 accrued dividends on 04/04/2011
Name changed to DDR Corp. 09/15/2011

DEVELOPERS OF ENERGY SYS CORP (NJ)
Charter revoked for failure to file annual reports 04/05/1991

DEVELOPERS SMALL BUSINESS INVESTMENT CORP. (NJ)
Completely liquidated 8/12/68
Each share Common 1¢ par exchanged for first and final distribution of (0.2) share Struthers Wells Corp. Common $1 par
(See Struthers Wells Corp.)

DEVELOPMENT BANCORP LTD (WA)
Each (165) shares old Common no par exchanged for (1) share new Common no par 08/31/1993
Name changed to Imatel Holdings Inc. 11/24/1997
Imatel Holdings Inc. recapitalized as Ovvio Better Life, Inc. 03/26/1999 which name changed to Animal Cloning Sciences, Inc. 11/21/2000
(See Animal Cloning Sciences, Inc.)

DEVELOPMENT BK SINGAPORE LTD (SINGAPORE)
Each Unsponsored ADR for Ordinary S$1.45 par exchanged for (0.25) Sponsored ADR for Ordinary S$1.45 par 12/19/91
Each Sponsored ADR for Ordinary S$1.45 par received distribution of (0.163) additional ADR payable 9/14/99 to holders of record 9/1/99
Stock Dividends - 20% 6/17/88; 10% 6/27/90; 25% 11/5/93; 10% payable 4/27/98 to holders of record 4/2/98
Reorganized as DBS Group Holdings Ltd. 9/18/99
Each Sponsored ADR for Ordinary S$1.45 par exchanged for (1) Sponsored ADR for Ordinary S$1 par

DEVELOPMENT CONSULTANTS, INC. (OH)
Recapitalized under the laws of Delaware as Harrington Research Corp. 4/6/70
Each share Common $8 par exchanged for (30) shares Common 25¢ par
(See Harrington Research Corp.)

DEVELOPMENT CORP. OF AMERICA (DE)
Certificates dated prior to 07/14/1960
$1.25 Preferred $1 par called for redemption 07/13/1960
Merged into Equity Corp. 07/14/1960
Each share Common $1 par exchanged for $7.91 cash

DEVELOPMENT CORP. OF AMERICA (DE)
Certificates dated after 06/25/1970
Common 10¢ par split (2) for (1) by issuance of (1) additional share 08/06/1971
Stock Dividend - 10% 02/18/1971
Reincorporated under the laws of Florida 07/30/1976
(See Development Corp. of America (FL))

DEVELOPMENT CORP AMER (FL)
Reincorporated under the laws of Delaware 6/25/70 which reincorporated back in Florida 7/30/76
Common 10¢ par split (2) for (1) by issuance of (1) additional share 6/16/80
Common 10¢ par split (2) for (1) by issuance of (1) additional share 6/21/83
Merged into Lennar Corp. 12/31/86
Each share Common 10¢ par exchanged for $15 cash

DEVELOPMENT CR CORP MD (MD)
Proclaimed dissolved for failure to file annual reports 12/23/1986

DEVELOPMENT FUNDING CORP. (OH)
Merged into Meridian Reserve, Inc. 12/20/1985
Each share Common no par exchanged for (4) shares Common 1¢ par
(See Meridian Reserve, Inc.)

DEVELOPMENT INTL CORP (DE)
Charter cancelled and declared inoperative and void for non-payment of taxes 3/1/76

DEVELOPMENT PARTNERS (MA)
Partnership terminated 12/31/2000
Details not available

DEVELOPMENT PARTNERS II (MA)
Partnership terminated 12/31/2000
Details not available

DEVELOPMENT TECHNOLOGY CORP (DE)
Name changed to Enncite Control, Inc. 1/15/85
Enncite Control, Inc. recapitalized as Oxford Knight International Inc. (DE) 2/10/98 reincorporated in Texas 11/20/2001 which name changed to Montrose National Partners Inc. 2/23/2004 which name changed to Cross Atlantic Life & Science Technology Inc. 8/19/2005 which name changed to Deep Earth Resources, Inc. 5/5/2006

DEVELOPMENTAL DESIGN INC (UT)
Voluntarily dissolved 3/3/93
Details not available

DEVELOPMENTAL VENTURE CAP CORP (FL)
Proclaimed dissolved for failure to file reports and pay fees 11/09/1990

DEVELOPMENTS BY JAYMAN INC (AB)
Name changed to Apex Land Corp. 07/02/1991
Apex Land Corp. name changed to Apex Corp. 09/10/1999
(See Apex Corp.)

DEVENISH PETROLEUM LTD. (CANADA)
Deemed not to be a subsisting corporation for failure to file returns 12/01/1933

DEVER EXPL INC (WY)
Reincorporated under the laws of Delaware as BayStar Petroleum Corp. 07/20/1984
(See BayStar Petroleum Corp.)

DEVERON RES LTD (ON)
Name changed to Deveron UAS Corp. 07/19/2016

DEVICE SEALS INC (CA)
Name changed to Intercell Industries, Inc. 12/28/1971
(See Intercell Industries, Inc.)

DEVIL CANYON URANIUM CORP. (UT)
Merged into Lisbon Valley Uranium Co. 08/05/1955
Each share Common exchanged for (0.2) share Capital Stock 1¢ par Lisbon Valley Uranium Co. recapitalized as Ocean Data Industries, Inc. 12/20/1968 which name changed to Universal Investment Properties, Inc. 10/18/1972
(See Universal Investment Properties, Inc.)

DEVILLIERS NUCLEAR CORP (NM)
Adjudicated bankrupt 06/20/1975
Stockholders' equity unlikely

DEVILS ELBOW MINES LTD (ON)
Recapitalized as New Devil's Elbow Mines Ltd. 08/12/1974
Each share Capital Stock $1 par exchanged for (0.25) share Capital Stock no par
New Devil's Elbow Mines Ltd. recapitalized as Lancer Resources

Inc. 06/09/1978 which recapitalized as V-Tech Diagnostics (Canada) Inc. 01/29/1991
(See V-Tech Diagnostics (Canada) Inc.)

DEVJO INDS INC (ON)
Merged into 2015929 Ontario Inc. 12/01/2002
Each share Common no par exchanged for $0.50 cash

DEVLAN EXPL INC (AB)
Plan of arrangement effective 07/01/2005
Each share Common no par exchanged for (0.25) share Cyries Energy Inc. Common no par and (0.5) share Dual Exploration Inc. Common no par
(See each company's listing)

DEVLAN EXPL LTD (AB)
Recapitalized as Devlan Exploration Inc. 11/02/1998
Each share Common no par exchanged for (0.25) share Common no par
(See Devlan Exploration Inc.)

DEVLIEG-BULLARD INC (DE)
Plan of reorganization under Chapter 11 Federal Bankruptcy Code effective 06/29/2000
No stockholders' equity

DEVNIC ENERGY INC (AB)
Merged into Fortune Energy Inc. 09/01/1993
Each share Common no par exchanged for (1.77) shares Common no par
(See Fortune Energy Inc.)

DEVOE & RAYNOLDS CO., INC. (NY)
Recapitalized 00/00/1944
Class A Common no par reclassified as Class A no par
Each share old Class B Common no par exchanged for (5) shares new Class B Common
Recapitalized 00/00/1945
Each share Class A no par exchanged for (2.5) shares Class A $12.50 par
Recapitalized 00/00/1950
Class A $12.50 par changed to $2 par
New Class B Common no par changed to $1 par
Recapitalized 10/19/1959
Each share Class A $2 par exchanged for (1) share Common $2 par
Each share Class B Common $1 par exchanged for (0.5) share Common $2 par
Common $2 par changed to $1 par and (1) additional share issued 03/26/1962
Stock Dividend - Class A and B - 10% 02/05/1951
Name changed to Revday Industries, Inc. 08/28/1964
(See Revday Industries, Inc.)

DEVON APPAREL INC (PA)
Common 20¢ par split (2) for (1) by issuance of (1) additional share 06/11/1971
Merged into Interco Inc. (Old) 01/11/1974
Each share Common 20¢ par exchanged for (0.359067) share Common no par
(See Interco Inc. (Old))

DEVON CORP. (DE)
Dissolved 00/00/1941
No stockholders' equity

DEVON CORP. (MI)
Liquidated 07/08/1952
Details not available

DEVON ENERGY CORP NEW (DE)
6.49% Preferred Ser. A $1 par called for redemption at $100 on 06/20/2008
(Additional Information in Active)

DEVON ENERGY CORP OLD (OK)
Reincorporated 06/07/1995
$1.94 Conv. Preferred $1 par called for redemption 11/03/1992
State of incorporation changed from (DE) to (OK) 06/07/1995
Merged into Devon Energy Corp. (New) (DE) 08/17/1999
Each share Common 10¢ par exchanged for (1) share Common 10¢ par

DEVON FING TR (DE)
6.5% Conv. Trust Preferred Securities called for redemption at $52.275 plus $0.68 accrueds dividend on 11/30/1999

DEVON GOLD MINES LTD.
Bankrupt 00/00/1943
Stockholders' equity unlikely

DEVON GROUP INC (DE)
Ctfs. dated prior to 05/04/1978
Common 70¢ par split (2) for (1) by issuance of (1) additional share 09/15/1978
Common 70¢ par split (2) for (1) by issuance of (1) additional share 05/04/1979
Merged into Devon Holding Corp. 12/30/1982
Each share Common 70¢ par exchanged for $28 cash
$3.60 Preferred $1 par called for redemption 01/29/1983
Public interest eliminated

DEVON GROUP INC NEW (DE)
Ctfs. dated after 08/13/1986
Merged into Applied Graphics Technologies, Inc. 05/27/1998
Each share Common 1¢ par exchanged for (0.6) share Common 1¢ par and $30 cash
(See Applied Graphics Technologies, Inc.)

DEVON INTL LTD (NY)
Went out of business due to insolvency 06/30/1971
Stockholders' equity unlikely

DEVON LEDUC OILS LTD. (MB)
Capital Stock no par changed to 25¢ par 00/00/1951
Name changed to Devon-Palmer Oils Ltd. 10/26/1956
(See Devon-Palmer Oils Ltd.)

DEVON OIL & GAS CO (WA)
Each share old Common $0.001 par exchanged for (0.1) share new Common $0.001 par 05/15/1985
Recapitalized as Secured Retirement International Inc. 05/22/1995
Each share new Common $0.001 par exchanged for (0.1) share Common $0.001 par

DEVON-PALMER OILS LTD. (MB)
Merged into Triad Oil Manitoba Ltd. 03/08/1967
Each share Capital Stock 25¢ par exchanged for (1) share 5.75% Preferred $2.25 par which was called 04/30/1967
5.75% Preferred certificates were not issued and Devon-Palmer holders actually received $2.25 (Canadian funds) in cash plus daily interest to date exchanged between 03/08/1967 and 04/30/1967

DEVON RESOURCE INVS L P (OK)
Reorganized under the laws of Delaware as Devon Energy Corp. 09/29/1988
Each Depositary Receipt exchanged for (0.5) share Common 10¢ par Devon Energy Corp. (DE) reincorporated in Oklahoma 06/07/1995 which merged into Devon Energy Corp. (New) 08/17/1999

DEVON STORES CORP (DE)
Common 1¢ par split (3) for (2) by issuance of (0.5) additional share 08/15/1983
Merged into Pantry Pride, Inc. (New) 05/25/1984
Each share Common 1¢ par exchanged for (1.6267) shares Common 1¢ par and $8.50 cash
Pantry Pride, Inc. (New) name changed to Revlon Group Inc. 04/07/1986
(See Revlon Group Inc.)

DEVON VENTURES CORP (BC)
Name changed to Pender Financial Group Corp. 06/23/2004
(See Pender Financial Group Corp.)

DEVONBROOK INC (DE)
Charter cancelled and declared inoperative and void for non-payment of taxes 03/01/1974

DEVONIAN GAS & OIL CO. (PA)
Merged into Devonian Gas & Oil Co. (DE) 12/20/1957
Each share Capital Stock 10¢ par exchanged for (0.1) share Capital Stock $1 par
(See Devonian Gas & Oil Co. (DE))

DEVONIAN GAS & OIL CO (DE)
Charter cancelled and declared inoperative and void for non-payment of taxes 04/15/1972

DEVONIAN OIL CO.
Dissolved 00/00/1949
Details not available

DEVONION RES LTD (BC)
Recapitalized as Koba Capital Corp. 09/01/1987
Each share Common no par exchanged for (0.4) share Common no par

DEVONSHIRE BUILDING TRUST
Sold at foreclosure 00/00/1945
No stockholders' equity

DEVONSHIRE HOTEL, INC.
Trust terminated 00/00/1950
Details not available

DEVONSHIRE INVESTING CORP.
Property and assets sold to Railway & Light Securities Co. 00/00/1931
Details not available

DEVONSHIRE RES LTD (BC)
Recapitalized as Gold Standard Ventures Corp. 11/18/2009
Each share Common no par exchanged for (0.25) share Common no par

DEVONSHIRE STR FD INC (MA)
Completely liquidated 09/17/1979
Each share Common $1 par exchanged for first and final distribution of (1.0539703) shares Investment Trust of Boston Share of Bene. Int. $1 par
Investment Trust of Boston name changed to TNE Funds Trust 04/01/1992 which name changed to New England Funds Trust II 04/18/1994 which name changed to Nvest Funds Trust II 02/01/2000 which name changed to CDC Nvest Funds Trust II 05/01/2001
(See CDC Nvest Funds Trust II)

DEVORE INDUSTRIES, INC. (DE)
Stock Dividend - 50% 06/15/1973
Through purchase offer 95% reacquired by the company as of 10/00/1978
Public interest eliminated

DEVRAN PETE LTD (CANADA)
Reincorporated 09/24/1986
Place of incorporation changed from (BC) to (Canada) 09/24/1986
Name changed to Reserve Royalty Corp. 11/16/1995
Reserve Royalty Corp. merged into PrimeWest Energy Trust 07/27/2000
(See PrimeWest Energy Trust)

DEVRY ED GROUP INC (DE)
Name changed 11/07/2013
Common 1¢ par split (2) for (1) by issuance of (1) additional share 06/21/1995
Common 1¢ par split (2) for (1) by issuance of (1) additional share payable 12/18/1996 to holders of record 12/02/1996 Ex date - 12/19/1996
Common 1¢ par split (2) for (1) by issuance of (1) additional share payable 06/19/1998 to holders of record 06/01/1998 Ex date - 06/22/1998
Name changed from DeVry Inc. to DeVry Education Group Inc. 11/07/2013
Name changed to Adtalem Global Education Inc. 05/24/2017

DEVRY INC (IL)
Merged into Keller Graduate School of Management Inc. 08/07/1987
Each share Common 10¢ par exchanged for $16.75 cash

DEVTEK CORP (ON)
Acquired by 1410740 Ontario 07/14/2000
Each share Multiple no par exchanged for $3.50 cash
Each share Subordinate no par exchanged for $3.50 cash

DEVX ENERGY INC (DE)
Each share old Common $0.0015 par exchanged for (0.0064102) share new Common $0.0015 par 10/26/2000
Merged into Comstock Resources, Inc. 12/18/2001
Each share new Common $0.0015 par exchanged for $7.32 cash

DEWALT, INC.
Assets sold to American Machine & Foundry Co. and liquidated 11/01/1949
Details not available

DEWANI LAURO MARINE PROD DEV CORP (CO)
Company's IPO determined to be fraudulent by SEC 07/27/1990
Stockholders' equity unlikely

DEWEY & ALMY CHEMICAL CO. (MA)
Each share Class A Preferred $100 par or Preferred $100 par exchanged for (1) share Class B Preferred no par and (1) share Class A Common no par 00/00/1935
Recapitalized 00/00/1938
Each share Class B Preferred no par exchanged for (1) share $5 Preferred no par and (0.5) share Common no par
Each share Prior Preference no par exchanged for (1) share $5 Preferred no par and (0.5) share Common no par
Class B Common no par changed to Common no par 00/00/1946
Each share Common no par exchanged for (2) shares Common $1 par 00/00/1951
Merged into Grace (W.R.) & Co. (CT) share for share 00/00/1954
Grace (W.R.) & Co. (CT) reincorporated in New York 05/19/1988
(See Grace (W.R.) & Co.)

DEWEY G C CORP (NY)
Name changed to Dewey Electronics Corp. 04/02/1969

DEWEY OIL & GAS INC (ON)
Merged into Southern Eagle Enterprises Inc. 10/01/1987
Each share Common no par exchanged for (0.75) share Non-Vtg. Class A no par and (0.43) share Common no par
Southern Eagle Enterprises Inc. merged into Equican Ventures Corp. 12/04/1987 which recapitalized as Equican Capital Corp. 01/27/1998 which name changed to Genterra Capital Corp. (Old) 08/23/1995

which merged into Genterra Capital Corp. (New) 02/28/1997 which recapitalized as Genterra Capital, Inc. 06/30/1998 which name changed to Genterra Investment Corp. 04/30/1999 which merged into Genterra Inc. 12/31/2003

DEWEY PORTLAND CEMENT CO. (DE)
Acquired by American-Marietta Co. 02/26/1960
Each share Class A Common $7.50 par exchanged for (0.825) share Common $2 par
Each share Class B Common $7.50 par exchanged for (0.825) share Common $2 par
American-Marietta Co. merged into Martin Marietta Corp. (Old) 10/10/1961 which merged into Martin Marietta Corp. (New) 04/02/1993 which merged into Lockheed Martin Corp. 03/15/1995

DEWEY PORTLAND CEMENT CO. (WV)
Each share Common $100 par exchanged for (9) shares Common $15 par 00/00/1937
Recapitalized under the laws of Delaware 04/30/1957
Each share Common $15 par exchanged for (2) shares Class A Common $7.50 par and (1) share Class B Common $7.50 par
Dewey Portland Cement Co. (DE) acquired by American-Marietta Co. 02/26/1960 which merged into Martin Marietta Corp. 10/10/1961 which merged into Martin Marietta Corp. (New) which merged into Lockheed Martin Corp. 03/15/1995

DEWEYS CANDY CO (OH)
Charter cancelled for failure to pay taxes 05/13/1999

DEWITT (E.C.) & CO., INC. (NY)
Capital Stock $10 par changed to $2.50 par 01/07/1964
Merged into DeWitt International Corp. 04/01/1969
Each share Capital Stock $2.50 par exchanged for (0.2) share Common $1 par
DeWitt International Corp. name changed to DeWitt Drug & Beauty Products, Inc. 11/03/1969 which name changed back to DeWitt International Corp. 09/13/1974 which merged into Church & Dwight Co., Inc. 06/05/1986

DEWITT DRUG & BEAUTY PRODUCTS, INC. (DE)
Name changed back to DeWitt International Corp. 09/13/1974
DeWitt International Corp. acquired by Church & Dwight Co., Inc. 06/05/1986

DEWITT INTERNATIONAL CORP. (DE)
Name changed to DeWitt Drug & Beauty Products, Inc. 11/03/1969 which name changed back to DeWitt International Corp. 09/13/1974
Each share Common $1 par exchanged for (0.1) share Common $10 par 11/14/1978
Acquired by Church & Dwight Co., Inc. 06/05/1986
Each share Common $10 par exchanged for (11.55) shares Common $1 par

DEWMELLA INC (AB)
Name changed to Contact Image Corp. 12/08/2004
(See Contact Image Corp.)

DEWOLFE COS INC (MA)
Common 1¢ par split (3) for (2) by issuance of (0.5) additional share payable 03/28/2002 to holders of record 03/12/2002 Ex date - 04/01/2002

Merged into Cendant Corp. 09/12/2002
Each share Common 1¢ par exchanged for $19 cash

DEWS LABS INC (TX)
Reincorporated under the laws of Delaware as Summa RX Laboratories, Inc. 01/12/1988
(See Summa RX Laboratories, Inc.)

DEWSON MINES, LTD. (ON)
Dissolved 02/24/1958
Details not available

DEX MEDIA INC NEW (DE)
Plan of reorganization under Chapter 11 Federal Bankruptcy proceedings effective 07/29/2016
No stockholders' equity

DEX MEDIA INC OLD (DE)
Merged into R.H. Donnelley Corp. 01/31/2006
Each share Common 1¢ par exchanged for (0.24154) share new Common $1 par and $12.30 cash
(See R.H. Donnelley Corp.)

DEX ONE CORP (DE)
Merged into Dex Media, Inc. (New) 04/30/2013
Each share Common $0.001 par exchanged for (0.2) share Common $0.001 par
(See Dex Media, Inc. (New))

DEX RAY RES INC (NV)
SEC revoked common stock registration 09/18/2009

DEXIT INC (ON)
Name changed to Hosted Data Transaction Solutions Inc. 08/17/2007
Hosted Data Transaction Solutions Inc. name changed to Posera-HDX Inc. (ON) 10/07/2010 which reincorporated in Alberta as Posera-HDX Ltd. 10/12/2011 which name changed to Posera Ltd. 04/14/2016

DEXLEIGH CORP (CA)
Merged into Trillon Financial 01/29/1999
Each share Common no par exchanged for $2 cash

DEXON INC (MN)
Statutorily dissolved 12/31/1993

DEXTER & NEWPORT RAILROAD
Acquired by Maine Central Railroad Co. 00/00/1939
Details not available

DEXTER & PISCATAQUIS RAILROAD
Acquired by Maine Central Railroad Co. 00/00/1939
Details not available

DEXTER CO. (IA)
Stock Dividend - 100% 04/04/1949
Merged into Philco Corp. 02/08/1954
Each share Common $5 par exchanged for (0.35) share Common $3 par
Philco Corp. was acquired by Ford Motor Co. 12/11/1961

DEXTER CORP. (SC)
Completely liquidated 10/18/1966
Details not available

DEXTER CORP (CT)
Common $1 par split (3) for (2) by issuance of (0.5) additional share 06/09/1969
Common $1 par split (3) for (2) by isuance of (0.5) additional share 10/05/1978
Common $1 par split (5) for (3) by issuance of (0.66666666) additional share 10/07/1983
Common $1 par split (3) for (2) by issuance of (0.5) additional share 10/10/1986
Merged into Invitrogen Corp. 09/14/2000
Each share Common $1 par exchanged for either (0.75) share Common 1¢ par and $17.50 cash, (1.0417) shares Common 1¢ par, or $62.50 cash
Note: Option to receive stock or cash only expired 10/05/2000
Invitrogen Corp. name changed to Life Technologies Corp. 11/21/2008
(See Life Technologies Corp.)

DEXTER RED LAKE GOLD MINES LTD.
Merged into Campbell Red Lake Mines Ltd. 00/00/1950
Each share Capital Stock exchanged for (0.1) share Capital Stock $1 par and $0.175 cash
Campbell Red Lake Mines Ltd. merged into Placer Dome Inc. 08/13/1987 which merged into Barrick Gold Corp. 03/08/2006

DEXTERITY SURGICAL INC (DE)
Each share old Common $0.001 par exchanged for (0.002) share new Common $0.001 par 04/25/2007
Name changed to China INSOline Corp. 03/17/2008
China INSOnline Corp. recapitalized as China Bio-Energy Corp. 02/03/2011 which name changed to Wave Sync Corp. 10/05/2015

DEXTON TECHNOLOGIES CORP (BC)
Name changed to Strategem Capital Corp. 11/14/2001

DEXTONE CO., INC. (DE)
Name changed to Achievement, Inc. and Common 10¢ par changed to 1¢ par 09/13/1970
(See Achievement, Inc.)

DEXTRA CORP (DE)
Each share old Common 10¢ par exchanged for (0.07502836) share new Common 10¢ par 08/19/1977
Charter cancelled and declared inoperative and void for non-payment of taxes 03/01/1980

DEXUS INC (ON)
Acquired by Trimin Enterprises Inc. (BC) 06/30/1993
Each share Non-Vtg. Class A no par exchanged for (1.42) shares Common no par
Each share Class B no par exchanged for (1.42) shares Common no par
Trimin Enterprises Inc. (BC) reorganized as Trimin Enterprises Inc. (Canada) 07/27/1998
(See Trimin Enterprises Inc.)

DEXX CORP (ON)
SEC revoked common stock registration 03/01/2011

DEXX ENERGY CORP (BC)
Cease trade order effective 07/23/1992
Stockholders' equity unlikely

DEYU AGRICULTURE CORP (NV)
Name changed to Luca, Inc. 01/08/2016

DF CHINA TECHNOLOGY INC (BRITISH VIRGIN ISLANDS)
Name changed to China Technology Global Corp. 02/04/2005
(See China Technology Global Corp.)

DF&R RESTAURANTS INC (TX)
Merged into Apple South, Inc. 11/17/1995
Each share Common 1¢ par exchanged for (1.5) shares Common 1¢ par
Apple South, Inc. name changed to Avado Brands Inc. 10/13/1998
(See Avado Brands Inc.)

DFA SMALL COMPANY FUND INC. (MD)
Name changed to DFA Investment Dimensions Group Inc. and Common 1¢ par reclassified as (1) U.S. 9-10 Small Company Portfolio Common 1¢ par 06/00/1983

DFC GLOBAL CORP (DE)
Acquired by LSF8 Sterling Parent, LLC 06/13/2014
Each share Common $0.001 par exchanged for $9.50 cash

DFI COMMUNICATIONS INC (NY)
Charter cancelled and proclaimed dissolved for failure to pay taxes 12/07/1976

DFSOUTHEASTERN INC (GA)
Acquired by First Union Corp. 01/15/1993
Each share Common $1 par exchanged for (0.82) share Common $3.33333333 par
First Union Corp. name changed to Wachovia Corp. (Ctfs. dated after 09/01/2001) 09/01/2001 which merged into Wells Fargo & Co. (New) 12/31/2008

DFW-CONSULTANTS.COM INC (NV)
Name changed to OG Nation, Inc. 07/27/2007
OG Nation, Inc. name changed to Hall of Fame Beverages, Inc. 03/31/2008

DG FASTCHANNEL INC (DE)
Name changed to Digital Generation, Inc. 11/07/2011
Digital Generation, Inc. merged into Sizmek Inc. 02/07/2014
(See Sizmek Inc.)

DG FDG TR
144A Floating Rate Trust Preferred Securities called for redemption at $10,000 on 03/31/2014

DGE TECHNOLOGIES CORP (AB)
Name changed to DKW Systems Corp. 12/03/1990
(See DKW Systems Corp.)

DGL INC (UT)
Recapitalized as Whitestar Resources, Inc. 04/23/2008
Each share Common $0.001 par exchanged for (0.02) share Common $0.001 par
Whitestar Resources, Inc. recapitalized as Charista Global Corp. 02/24/2009 which name changed to UBK Resources Co. 09/12/2011

DGM MINERALS CORP (BC)
Recapitalized as Less Mess Storage Inc. 05/05/2014
Each share Common no par exchanged for (0.08333333) share Common no par
(See Less Mess Storage Inc.)

DGR INVESTMENTS, INC. (UT)
Recapitalized as Worldwide Rescue Systems, Ltd. 09/04/1984
Each share Common $0.001 par exchanged for (0.1) share Common 1¢ par
(See Worldwide Rescue Systems, Ltd.)

DGS MINERALS INC (BC)
Each share old Common no par exchanged for (0.33333333) share new Common no par 08/05/2015
Name changed to Dragon Legend Entertainment (Canada) Inc. 02/13/2017

DGT CORP (NV)
Name changed to Blackrock Petroleum Corp. 09/20/2007
Blackrock Petroleum Corp. name changed to Nexgen Petroleum Corp. 06/09/2008 which recapitalized as Hubei Minkang Pharmaceutical Ltd. 10/21/2010

DGT HLDGS CORP (NY)
Old Common 10¢ par split (4) for (1) by issuance of (3) additional shares payable 01/10/2011 to holders of record 01/10/2011
Each share old Common 10¢ par exchanged for (1) share new Common 10¢ par to reflect a (1) for

(5,000) reverse split followed by a (5,000) for (1) forward split 03/06/2013
Note: Holders of (4,999) or fewer pre-split shares received $13.50 cash per share
Each share new Common 10¢ par exchanged again for (0.00001) share new Common 10¢ par 10/29/2015
Note: In effect holders received $18.30 cash per share and public interest was eliminated

DGW FINL LTD (DE)
Reorganized under the laws of Nevada as YNOT Education, Inc. (Old) 03/10/2006
Each share Common $0.001 par exchanged for (0.001) share Common $0.001 par
YNOT Education, Inc. (Old) name changed to Physiognomy Interface Technologies, Inc. 05/01/2006 which name changed to Ynot Education, Inc. (New) 01/10/2007 which name changed to King Media Holdings Inc. 10/04/2007 which recapitalized as Extreme Fitness, Inc. 10/09/2007
(See Extreme Fitness, Inc.)

DH CORP (ON)
Acquired by Vista Equity Partners 06/15/2017
Each share Common no par exchanged for $25.50 cash
Note: Unexchanged certificates will be cancelled and become without value 06/15/2023

DH TECHNOLOGY INC (CA)
Common no par split (3) for (2) by issuance of (0.5) additional share 10/02/1995
Merged into Axiohm S.A. 10/02/1997
Each share Common no par exchanged for $25 cash

DHANOA MINERALS LTD (NV)
Each share old Common $0.001 par exchanged for (5) shares new Common $0.001 par 10/10/2006
Name changed to Discovery Minerals Ltd. 08/30/2012

DHB INDS INC (DE)
Reincorporated 04/12/1995
Name changed 07/24/2001
State of incorporation changed from (NY) to (DE) 04/12/1995
Common $0.001 par split (3) for (2) by issuance of (0.5) additional share payable 07/16/1996 to holders of record 07/15/1996
Name changed from DHB Capital Group, Inc. to DHB Industries, Inc. 07/24/2001
Name changed to Point Blank Solutions, Inc. 11/01/2007
(See Point Blank Solutions, Inc.)

DHJ INDS INC (NY)
Merged into Dominion Textile Ltd.- Dominion Textile Ltee. 10/20/1975
Each share Common $1 par exchanged for $5.50 cash

DHS INDS INC (UT)
Each share old Common $0.001 par exchanged for (0.01) share new Common $0.001 par 06/18/1996
Name changed to Glenhills Corp. 04/02/1998
Glenhills Corp. name changed to Millennium Multi-Media.com Corp. 07/06/2000 which name changed to Voxcorp Inc. 02/13/2002

DHT HOLDINGS INC (MARSHALL ISLANDS)
Name changed 03/01/2010
Name changed from DHT Maritime, Inc. to DHT Holdings, Inc. 03/01/2010
Each share Participating Preferred Ser. A 1¢ par exchanged for (17) shares new Common 1¢ par 07/01/2013
(Additional Information in Active)

DI AN CTLS INC (MA)
Reincorporated under the laws of Florida as ER Urgent Care Holdings, Inc. 10/20/2004
(See ER Urgent Care Holdings, Inc.)

DI-ARIO INC (UT)
Charter expired 10/01/1987

DI ENCO INC (UT)
Charter expired 01/20/1988

DI GIORGIO CORP (DE)
Common $2.50 par split (3) for (2) by issuance of (0.5) additional share 07/11/1969
$2.25 Conv. Preferred no par called for redemption 12/27/1985
88¢ Conv. Preferred Ser. A no par called for redemption 07/11/1986
Merged into Rose Partners, L.P. 02/20/1990
Each share Common $2.50 par exchanged for $30 cash

DI GIORGIO FRUIT CORP. (DE)
Each share 7% Preferred $100 par exchanged for (1) share $3 Part. Preferred $100 par 00/00/1934
Each share Common no par exchanged for (0.33333333) share Common $10 par 00/00/1934
Each share Common $10 par exchanged for (1) share Class A Common $5 par and (1) share Class B Common $5 par 00/00/1945
$3 Part. Preferred $100 par called for redemption 01/01/1947
Class A and B Common $5 par changed to $2.50 par and (1) additional share issued 12/10/1958
Class A and B Common $2.50 par reclassified as Common $2.50 par 06/01/1960
$3 Preferred no par called for redemption 11/01/1964
Stock Dividends - (1) share Class B for each (4) shares Class A or B 07/01/1950 and 12/15/1953; 10% Class B for each share Class A or B 03/10/1960
Name changed to Di Giorgio Corp. 04/30/1965
(See Di Giorgio Corp.)

DI INDS INC (TX)
Name changed to Grey Wolf, Inc. 09/18/1997
Grey Wolf, Inc. acquired by Precision Drilling Trust 12/23/2008 which reorganized as Precision Drilling Corp. 06/03/2010

DI-NOC CHEMICAL ARTS, INC. (OH)
Merged into Minnesota Mining & Manufacturing Co. 01/02/1962
Each share Common $1 par exchanged for (0.8) share Common no par
Minnesota Mining & Manufacturing Co. name changed to 3M Co. 04/08/2002

DI-NOC CO. (OH)
Name changed to Di-Noc Chemical Arts, Inc. 08/17/1955
Di-Noc Chemical Arts, Inc. merged into Minnesota Mining & Manufacturing Co. 01/02/1962 which name changed to 3M Co. 04/08/2002

DI-NOC MANUFACTURING CO. (OH)
Name changed to Di-Noc Co. 00/00/1945
Di-Noc Co. name changed to Di-Noc Chemical Arts, Inc. 08/17/1955 which merged into Minnesota Mining & Manufacturing Co. 01/02/1962 which name changed to 3M Co. 04/08/2002

DIA BRAS EXPL INC (CANADA)
Each share old Common no par exchanged exchanged for (1/7) share new Common no par 12/08/2010
Name changed to Sierra Metals Inc. 12/07/2012

DIA MET MINERALS LTD (BC)
Common no par split (2) for (1) by issuance of (1) additional share 03/11/1994
Each share Common no par exchanged for (0.25) share Class A Subordinate no par and (1) share Class B Multiple no par 07/28/1994
Merged into BHP Billiton Ltd. 10/31/2001
Each share Class A Subordinate no par exchanged for $21 cash
Each share Class B Multiple no par exchanged for $21 cash

DIABETEX INTL CORP (NV)
Recapitalized as Petrone Worldwide, Inc. 02/26/2014
Each share Common $0.002 par exchanged for (0.002) share Common $0.001 par

DIABETIC MEDSERV INC (FL)
Common $0.001 par split (2) for (1) by issuance of (1) additional share payable 11/27/1996 to holders of record 11/20/1996
Name changed to Diversified Business & Medical Services Inc. 01/16/1998
(See Diversified Business & Medical Services Inc.)

DIABETIC TREATMENT CTRS AMER INC (DE)
Recapitalized as Signature Exploration & Production Corp. 05/05/2008
Each share Common $0.0001 par exchanged for (0.02) share Common $0.0001 par
Signature Exploration & Production Corp. name changed to GrowBLOX Sciences, Inc. 04/28/2014 which name changed to GB Sciences, Inc. 04/10/2017

DIABEX RES INC (QC)
Merged into Metco Resources Inc. 11/01/1999
Each share Common no par exchanged for (0.5) share Common no par
Metco Resources Inc. merged into Breakwater Resources Ltd. 04/15/2008
(See Breakwater Resources Ltd.)

DIABLO BK (DANVILLE, CA)
Acquired by Security Pacific Corp. 02/28/1987
Each share Common no par exchanged for (0.37507) share Common $10 par
Security Pacific Corp. merged into BankAmerica Corp. (Old) 04/22/1992 which merged into BankAmerica Corp. (New) 09/30/1998 which name changed to Bank of America Corp. 04/28/1999

DIABLO LABORATORIES (CA)
Recapitalized as U.S. Laboratories 06/23/1967
Each share Capital Stock $1 par exchanged for (0.1) share Capital Stock $2 par
(See U.S. Laboratories)

DIABLO OIL CO (CO)
Merged into Wichita River Oil Corp. (VA) (New) 11/04/1987
Each share Common 1¢ par exchanged for (0.004167) share Common no par
Wichita River Oil Corp. (VA) (New) reincorporated in Delaware 03/30/1990
(See Wichita River Oil Corp. (DE))

DIABLO STATE BANK (DANVILLE, CA)
Name changed to Diablo Bank (Danville, CA) and Common $6 par changed to no par 06/15/1983
Diablo Bank (Danville, CA) acquired by Security Pacific Corp. 02/28/1987 which merged into BankAmerica Corp. (Old) 04/22/1992 which merged into BankAmerica Corp. (New) 09/30/1998 which name changed to Bank of America Corp. 04/28/1999

DIABLO VY BK (DANVILLE, CA)
Common no par split (3) for (2) by issuance of (0.5) additional share payable 04/22/2005 to holders of record 04/08/2005
Ser. A Preferred no par called for redemption at $32 on 06/20/2007
Merged into Heritage Commerce Corp. 06/20/2007
Each share Common no par exchanged for (0.7852) share Common no par and $4.2361 cash

DIACRIN INC (DE)
Merged into GenVec, Inc. 08/21/2003
Each share Common 1¢ par exchanged for (1.5292) shares Common $0.001 par
GenVec, Inc. merged into Intrexon Corp. 06/16/2017

DIADEM MINES LTD. (ON)
Charter cancelled and company declared dissolved for default in filing returns 03/25/1965

DIADEM MINING CO. (WA)
Charter cancelled and proclaimed dissolved for non-payment of fees 07/01/1973

DIADUS INC. (WA)
Charter cancelled and proclaimed dissolved for failure to file annual reports 12/19/1988

DIAEM RES LTD (BC)
Merged into LKA International, Inc. 08/09/1988
Each share Common no par exchanged for (0.6204) share Common $0.001 par
LKA International, Inc. recapitalized as LKA Gold Inc. 03/15/2013

DIAGEM INC (CANADA)
Name changed 11/18/2004
Name and place of incorporation changed from Diagem Creek Silver Mines Ltd. (BC) to Diagem Inc. (Canada) 11/18/2004
Each share old Common no par exchanged for (0.1) share new Common no par 09/20/2007
Dissolved for non-compliance 09/18/2011

DIAGNOCURE INC (QC)
Placed in liquidation 06/06/2016
No stockholders' equity

DIAGNON CORP (DE)
Each share old Common 1¢ par exchanged for 0.16666666) share new Common 1¢ par 10/22/1997
Name changed to BIOQUAL Inc. 12/31/1999

DIAGNOSTEK INC (DE)
Merged into Value Health, Inc. 07/28/1995
Each share Common 1¢ par exchanged for (0.4975) share Common no par
(See Value Health, Inc.)

DIAGNOSTIC CENTERS, INC. (OR)
Involuntarily dissolved for failure to file reports and pay fees 12/27/1972

DIAGNOSTIC CORP AMER (DE)
Each share old Common $0.001 par exchanged for (0.02857142) share new Common $0.001 par 10/16/2006
Name changed to NF Energy Saving Corp. of America 04/27/2007

DIAGNOSTIC DATA INC (DE)
Reincorporated 02/11/1974
Capital Stock $1 par split (2) for (1) by issuance of (1) additional share 06/22/1972
State of incorporation changed from (CA) to (DE) 02/11/1974

Common $1 par changed to 50¢ par 05/27/1976
Name changed to DDI Pharmaceuticals, Inc. 04/01/1985
DDI Pharmaceuticals, Inc. name changed to OXIS International, Inc. 09/08/1994 which recapitalized as GT Biopharma, Inc. 08/21/2017

DIAGNOSTIC HEALTH SVCS INC (DE)
Reincorporated 11/23/1992
State of incorporation changed from (NJ) to (DE) and Common no par changed to $0.001 par 11/23/1992
Each share old Common $0.001 par exchanged for (0.45175443) share new Common $0.001 par 06/07/1993
Plan of reorganization under Chapter 11 Federal Bankruptcy Code effective 10/30/2000
No stockholders' equity

DIAGNOSTIC IMAGING INTL CORP (NV)
Name changed to Medical Imaging Corp. 07/11/2014

DIAGNOSTIC IMAGING SVCS INC (DE)
Reverted to private company 02/17/2004
Each share Common 1¢ par exchanged for $0.05 cash

DIAGNOSTIC INC (MN)
Common 1¢ par split (3) for (1) by issuance of (2) additional shares 11/18/1983
Name changed to Lifecore Biomedical, Inc. 01/01/1987
(See Lifecore Biomedical, Inc.)

DIAGNOSTIC MED EQUIP CORP (NY)
Name changed to Universal Medical Equipment Corp. 06/13/1983
(See Universal Medical Equipment Corp.)

DIAGNOSTIC MED INSTRS INC (NY)
Merged into Burdick Corp. 05/24/1994
Each share Common 1¢ par exchanged for $0.35 cash

DIAGNOSTIC PRODS CORP (CA)
Common no par split (3) for (2) by issuance of (0.5) additional share 09/26/1983
Common no par split (2) for (1) by issuance of (1) additional share 06/21/1989
Common no par split (2) for (1) by issuance of (1) additional share payable 06/18/2001 to holders of record 06/01/2001 Ex date - 06/19/2001
Merged into Siemens AG 07/27/2006
Each share Common no par exchanged for $58.50 cash

DIAGNOSTIC RESH INC (NY)
Merged into Corning Glass Works 07/13/1974
Each share Common 1¢ par exchanged for $4.50 cash

DIAGNOSTIC RETRIEVAL SYS INC (DE)
Common 1¢ par reclassified as Class A Common 1¢ par 07/08/1983
Each share Class A Common 1¢ par received distribution of (0.5) share Class B Common 1¢ par 07/15/1983
Conv. Class A Common 1¢ par reclassified as Common 1¢ par 04/01/1996
Class B Common 1¢ par reclassified as Common 1¢ par 04/01/1996
Stock Dividend - 100% 10/29/1982
Name changed to DRS Technologies, Inc. 08/01/1997
(See DRS Technologies, Inc.)

DIAGNOSTIC SCIENCES INC NEW (DE)
Name changed to DSI Industries Inc. 05/14/1992
DSI Industries Inc. name changed to Norton Drilling Services, Inc. 10/07/1997 which merged into UTI Energy Corp. 06/26/1999 which merged into Patterson- UTI Energy, Inc. 05/09/2001

DIAGNOSTIC VENTURES INC (DE)
Name changed to DVI Financial Corp. 08/24/1988
DVI Financial Corp. name changed to DVI Health Services Corp. 11/06/1991 which name changed to DVI, Inc. 06/17/1993
(See DVI, Inc.)

DIAGNOSTICOS DA AMERICA S A (BRAZIL)
Sponsored 144A ADR for Ordinary split (4) for (1) by issuance of (3) additional ADR's payable 01/11/2010 to holders of record 12/31/2009 Ex date - 01/12/2010
Sponsored Reg. S ADR for Ordinary split (4) for (1) by issuance of (3) additional ADR's payable 01/11/2010 to holders of record 12/31/2009
Sponsored 144A ADR for Ordinary split (4) for (1) by issuance of (3) additional ADR's payable 02/12/2010 to holders of record 02/04/2010 Ex date - 02/16/2010
Sponsored Reg. S ADR for Ordinary split (4) for (1) by issuance of (3) additional ADR's payable 02/12/2010 to holders of record 02/04/2010 Ex date - 02/16/2010
ADR agreement terminated 08/31/2015
Each 144A Sponsored ADR for Ordinary exchanged for $8.34158 cash
Each Reg S Sponsored ADR for Ordinary exchanged for $8.34158 cash

DIAGONAL DATA CORP (FL)
Merged into Hartford Steam Boiler Inspection & Insurance Co. 06/29/1989
Each share Common 1¢ par exchanged for $5 cash

DIAL A BRAND (NV)
Each share old Common $0.001 par exchanged for (0.1) share new Common $0.001 par 12/01/1989
Recapitalized as China Container Holdings Ltd. (NV) 05/22/1995
Each share new Common $0.001 par exchanged for (0.14285714) share Common $0.001 par
China Container Holdings Ltd. (NV) reincorporated in Delaware as Asiana Dragons, Inc. 12/22/2009 which recapitalized as Annabidiol Corp. 01/08/2018

DIAL-A-DISK, INC. (FL)
Charter cancelled and company proclaimed dissolved for non-payment of taxes 08/28/1964

DIAL-A-GIFT INC (UT)
Each share old Common $0.002 par exchanged for (0.125) share new Common $0.002 par 12/02/1991
Reorganized as Interactive Gift Express Inc. 12/05/1994
Each share new Common $0.002 par exchanged for (1.04) shares Common $0.002 par
Interactive Gift Express Inc. name changed to E-Data Corp. (UT) 11/08/1995 which reincorporated in Delaware 05/23/2002

DIAL CORP (IA)
Merged into Northwest Bancorporation 08/31/1982
Each share Common no par exchanged for $56 cash

DIAL CORP NEW (DE)
Merged into Henkel KGaA 03/29/2004
Each share Common 1¢ par exchanged for $28.75 cash

DIAL CORP OLD (DE)
Common $1.50 par split (2) for (1) by issuance of (1) additional share 07/01/1994
Name changed to Viad Corp. 08/15/1996

DIAL FIN CO (IA)
Common no par split (2) for (1) by issuance of (1) additional share 05/11/1965
Common no par split (2) for (1) by issuance of (1) additional share 05/10/1966
Name changed to Dial Financial Corp. 04/15/1970
Dial Financial Corp. reorganized as Dial Corp. 08/03/1977
(See Dial Corp.)

DIAL FINL CORP (IA)
Under plan of reorganization each share Common no par automatically became (1) share Dial Corp. Common no par 08/03/1977
(See Dial Corp.)

DIAL FOOD INC (NV)
Company reported out of business 00/00/1989
Details not available

DIAL GLOBAL INC (DE)
Name changed to Westwood One, Inc. (New) 11/25/2013
(See Westwood One, Inc. (New))

DIAL ONE ACQUISITION INC (DE)
Charter cancelled and declared inoperative and void for non-payment of taxes 03/01/1991

DIAL PAGE INC (DE)
Merged into Nextel Communications, Inc. 01/30/1996
Each share Common 1¢ par exchanged for (1.0704) shares Class A Common $0.001 par
Each share Non-Vtg. Class A Common $0.001 par exchanged for (1.0704) shares Class A Common $0.001 par
Nextel Communications, Inc. merged into Sprint Nextel Corp. 08/12/2005 which merged into Sprint Corp. (DE) 07/10/2013

DIAL REIT INC (MD)
Name changed to Mid-America Realty Investments, Inc. 04/28/1994
Mid-America Realty Investments, Inc. merged into Bradley Real Estate, Inc. 08/06/1998
(See Bradley Real Estate, Inc.)

DIAL-THRU INTL CORP (DE)
Name changed to Rapid Link, Inc. 11/28/2005
Rapid Link, Inc. name changed to Spot Mobile International Ltd. 06/10/2010
(See Spot Mobile International Ltd.)

DIALAPHONE (CA)
Name changed to Perini Electronic Corp. 06/21/1962
Perini Electronic Corp. name changed to Dasa Corp. (CA) 09/29/1964 which merged into Dasa Corp. (MA) 04/01/1966
(See Dasa Corp. (MA))

DIALCO CORP (DE)
Merged into North American Philips Corp. 12/31/1973
Each share Capital Stock 10¢ par exchanged for (0.13333333) share Common $5 par
(See North American Philips Corp.)

DIALEX MINERALS INC (FL)
Recapitalized as Reliant Home Warranty Corp. 03/16/2005
Each share Common $0.001 par exchanged for (0.04545454) share Common $0.001 par
Reliant Home Warranty Corp. name changed to Reliant Financial Service Corp. 06/14/2007

DIALIGHT CORP. (DE)
Merged into Consolidated Electronics Industries Corp. 09/14/1964
Each share Common $1 par or Class B Common $1 par exchanged for (0.465116) share Common $5 par Consolidated Electronics Industries Corp. name changed to North American Philips Corp. 02/14/1969
(See North American Philips Corp.)

DIALOC CORP AMER (FL)
Common 20¢ par changed to $0.075 par 08/25/1966
Each share old Common $0.075 par exchanged for (0.2) share new Common $0.075 par 03/15/1968
New Common $0.075 par changed to $0.0375 par 12/01/1972
Adjudicated bankrupt 10/25/1978
Details not available

DIALOG COMPUTING INC (DE)
Declared inoperative and void for non-payment of taxes 04/15/1972

DIALOG CORP PLC (ENGLAND)
Name changed to Bright Station PLC 05/08/2000
Bright Station PLC name changed to Smartlogik Group PLC 07/09/2001
(See Smartlogik Group PLC)

DIALOG GROUP INC (DE)
Each share old Common $0.001 par exchanged for (0.01) share new Common $0.001 par 09/18/2006
SEC revoked common stock registration 04/20/2011

DIALOG SEMICONDUCTOR PLC (GERMANY)
ADR agreement terminated 01/13/2007
Each Sponsored ADR for Ordinary exchanged for $1.6824 cash

DIALOGIC CORP (NJ)
Merged into Intel Corp. 07/13/1999
Each share Common no par exchanged for $44 cash

DIALOGIC INC (DE)
Each share old Common $0.001 par exchanged for (0.2) share new Common $0.001 par 09/17/2012
Acquired by Dialogic Group Inc. 11/24/2014
Each share new Common $0.001 par exchanged for $0.15 cash

DIALPOINT COMMUNICATIONS CORP (NV)
Common $0.001 par split (4) for (1) by issuance of (3) additional shares payable 03/13/2008 to holders of record 03/13/2008 Ex date - 03/14/2008
SEC revoked common stock registration 10/14/2011

DIALSCAN SYS INC (NY)
Charter cancelled and proclaimed dissolved for failure to pay taxes and file reports 12/15/1973

DIALYS AIDS SYS INC (NY)
Dissolved by proclamation 06/29/1993

DIALYSIS CORP AMER (FL)
Class A Common 1¢ par reclassified as Common 1¢ par 04/00/1996
Each share Class B Common 1¢ par exchanged for (1) share Common 1¢ par 04/00/1996
Common 1¢ par split (2) for (1) by issuance of (1) additional share payable 02/09/2004 to holders of record 01/28/2004 Ex date - 02/10/2004
Merged into U.S Renal Care, Inc. 06/03/2010
Each share Common 1¢ par exchanged for $11.25 cash

DIAMANT ART CORP (ON)
Each share old Common no par exchanged for (0.0002) share new Common no par 04/28/2010
Company terminated common stock registration and is no longer public as of 02/28/2011

DIAMANTE MINERALS INC (NV)
Name changed to iMine Corp. 05/04/2018

DIAMEDICA INC (CANADA)
Reincorporated 04/11/2016
Place of incorporation changed from (MB) to (Canada) 04/11/2016
Name changed to DiaMedica Therapeutics Inc. 12/29/2016

DIAMETRICS MED INC (MN)
Each share old Common 1¢ par exchanged for (0.01) share new Common 1¢ par 06/30/2006
Reincorporated under the laws of Delaware as Allegro Biodiesel Corp. 12/01/2006
(See Allegro Biodiesel Corp.)

DIAMOND ALKALI CO (DE)
Each share Common $20 par exchanged for (2) shares Common $10 par 00/00/1951
4.4% Preferred $100 par called for redemption 05/14/1956
Common $10 par changed to no par 04/30/1962
Common no par split (2) for (1) by issuance of (1) additional share 12/07/1965
Under plan of merger name changed to Diamond Shamrock Corp. 12/19/1967
Diamond Shamrock Corp. name changed to Maxus Energy Corp. 04/30/1987
(See Maxus Energy Corp.)

DIAMOND BATHURST INC (DE)
Common 1¢ par split (3) for (2) by issuance of (0.5) additional share 10/22/1985
Merged into Anchor Glass Container Corp. (Old) 08/13/1987
Each share Common 1¢ par exchanged for $25.50 cash

DIAMOND BAY HLDGS INC (NV)
Recapitalized as Shaan Xi Ding Cheng Science Holding Co., Ltd. 01/31/2007
Each share Common $0.001 par exchanged for (0.005) share Common $0.001 par
Shaan Xi Ding Cheng Science Holding Co., Ltd. name changed to China Ding Cheng Science Holdings Co., Ltd. 03/22/2007 which name changed to China Transportation International Holdings Group Ltd. 04/23/2010
(See China Transportation International Holdings Group Ltd.)

DIAMOND BEVERAGE CORP (CT)
Name changed 05/03/1971
Capital Stock $20 par changed to no par 06/24/1970
Name changed from Diamond Ginger Ale, Inc. to Diamond Beverage Corp. 05/03/1971
Voluntarily dissolved 06/11/1976
No stockholders' equity

DIAMOND CO. (DE)
Liquidation completed 06/10/1958
Details not available

DIAMOND COAL INC (VA)
Merged into Transcontinental Oil Corp. (Old) 05/30/1978
Each share Common 50¢ par exchanged for $10.25 cash

DIAMOND CRYSTAL SALT CO. (MI)
Incorporated 01/09/1889
Acquired by General Foods Corp. 00/00/1929
Details not available

DIAMOND CRYSTAL SALT CO (MI)
Incorporated 03/17/1953
Common $2.50 par changed to $1.25 par and (1) additional share issued 08/06/1984
Merged into DC Holdings Inc. 07/01/1988
Each share Common $1.25 par exchanged for $35 cash

DIAMOND ELECTRICAL MANUFACTURING CO. LTD.
Acquired by Square D Co. 00/00/1930
Details not available

DIAMOND ENTMT CORP (NJ)
Each share old Common no par exchanged for (0.05) share new Common no par 07/13/1993
Each share new Common no par exchanged again for (0.03333333) share new Common no par 03/27/2007
Name changed to Rx for Africa, Inc. 10/29/2007

DIAMOND EQUITIES INC (NV)
SEC revoked common stock registration 07/21/2010

DIAMOND EXPL INC (ON)
Reincorporated under the laws of British Columbia as Diamond International Exploration Inc. 10/29/2009
Diamond International Exploration Inc. name changed to Northaven Resources Corp. 03/14/2011

DIAMOND FIELDS INTL LTD (BC)
Reorganized 06/08/1998
Reorganized 03/27/2007
Reorganized from British Virgin Islands to Yukon Territory 06/08/1998
Each share Common no par exchanged for (0.25) share new Common no par 06/08/1998
Reorganized from (YT) to under the laws of British Columbia 03/27/2007
Each share old Common no par exchanged for (0.2) share new Common no par 09/25/2008
Each share new Common no par exchanged again for (0.2) share new Common no par 09/22/2016
Name changed to Diamond Fields Resources Inc. 12/07/2017

DIAMOND FIELDS RES INC (BC)
Common no par split (4) for (1) by issuance of (3) additional shares 10/10/1995
Merged into Inco Ltd. 08/21/1996
Each share Common no par exchanged for (0.557) share Common no par
(See Inco Ltd.)

DIAMOND FOODS INC (DE)
Merged into Snyder's-Lance, Inc. 02/29/2016
Each share Common $0.001 par exchanged for (0.775) share Common $0.83333333 par and $12.50 cash
(See Snyder's-Lance, Inc.)

DIAMOND FRANK EXPL INC (CANADA)
Name changed to AXE Exploration Inc. 04/08/2013

DIAMOND GARDNER CORP (DE)
Under plan of merger name changed to Diamond National Corp. 09/28/1959
Diamond National Corp. name changed to Diamond International Corp. 10/29/1964
(See Diamond International Corp.)

DIAMOND GROWTH FUND, INC. (CA)
Charter suspended for failure to file reports and pay taxes 11/01/1974

DIAMOND HAWK MNG CORP (AB)
Reincorporated under the laws of British Columbia 07/04/2005

DIAMOND HEAD RES INC (NV)
Name changed to AAON, Inc. 06/05/1990

DIAMOND HILL FINL TRENDS FD INC (MD)
Completely liquidated 03/22/2013
Each share Common $0.001 par exchanged for first and final distribution of $12.901373 cash

DIAMOND HILL INVT GROUP INC (FL)
Each share old Common no par exchanged for (0.2) share new Common no par 09/26/2001
Reincorporated under the laws of Ohio 05/06/2002

DIAMOND HILL OIL & GAS CO (UT)
Name changed to Diamond Hill Industries, Inc. 02/21/1984

DIAMOND HITTS PRODTN INC (NV)
Reincorporated 09/04/2001
State of incorporation changed from (FL) to (NV) 09/04/2001
Charter revoked for failure to file reports and pay fees 07/01/2005

DIAMOND HOME SVCS INC (DE)
Charter cancelled and declared inoperative and void for non-payment of taxes 03/01/2002

DIAMOND ICE & COAL CO. (DE)
All Common no par was acquired by American Consumer Industries, Inc. 00/00/1962
Details not available

DIAMOND INFORMATION INST INC (NJ)
Each share old Common $0.001 par exchanged for (0.001) share new Common $0.001 par 05/28/2010
Reorganized under the laws of Wyoming as Therapy Cells, Inc. 09/19/2011
Each share new Common $0.001 par exchanged for (0.00066666) share Common $0.001 par

DIAMOND INSULATION INDS INC (CO)
Name changed to Orion Industries, Ltd. 06/11/1980
Orion Industries, Ltd. name changed to American Resources Group, Inc. 07/07/1982

DIAMOND INTL CORP (DE)
Common $1 par changed to 50¢ par and (1) additional share issued 11/02/1964
Stock Dividend - 10% 06/15/1979
Merged into Generale Occidentale S.A. 12/03/1982
Each share Common 50¢ par exchanged for $44.50 cash
$1.20 Conv. Preferred Ser. A $1 par called for redemption 11/15/1983
Public interest eliminated

DIAMOND INTL EXPL INC (BC)
Name changed to Northaven Resources Corp. 03/14/2011

DIAMOND INTL GROUP INC (DE)
Each share old Common $0.0001 par exchanged for (0.2) share new Common $0.0001 par 06/06/2003
Name changed to Organetix, Inc. 11/26/2003
Organetix, Inc. name changed to Seafarer Exploration Corp. (DE) 07/18/2008 which reincorporated in Florida 07/05/2011

DIAMOND INTL INDS INC (BC)
Recapitalized as Vault Systems Inc. 12/02/1999
Each share Common no par exchanged for (0.125) share Common no par
Vault Systems Inc. recapitalized as Vault Minerals Inc. (BC) 06/18/2003 which reincorporated in Ontario 07/25/2005 which merged into Queenston Mining Inc. 04/23/2010 which merged into Osisko Mining Corp. 01/02/2013
(See Osisko Mining Corp.)

DIAMOND IRON WORKS, INC. (DE)
Name changed to Diamond Co. 00/00/1954
(See Diamond Co.)

DIAMOND JIM ENTERPRISES INC (CO)
Recapitalized as Linkletter (Robert), Inc. 12/29/1986
Each share Common $0.001 par exchanged for (0.25) share Common $0.001 par
(See Linkletter (Robert), Inc.)

DIAMOND LABS INC (IA)
Stock Dividend - 50% 04/03/1970
Liquidation completed
Each share Common $1 par exchanged for initial distribution of (0.3968) share Syntex Corp. Common $1 par 12/21/1971
Each share Common $1 par received second and final distribution of (0.0187) share Syntex Corp. Common $1 par 11/13/1972
(See Syntex Corp.)

DIAMOND LANE CORP (NV)
Name changed to General Products Holdings Inc. 04/11/1997
General Products Holdings Inc. name changed to Diamond Linx Inc. 03/00/1999 which reorganized back as General Products Holdings Inc. 02/03/2000
(See General Products Holdings Inc.)

DIAMOND LASER INTL LTD (NY)
Reorganized under the laws of Nevada as Access TradeOne.Com, Inc. 06/11/1999
Each share Common 1¢ par exchanged for (0.01) share Common $0.001 par
(See Access TradeOne.Com, Inc.)

DIAMOND LEDGE GOLD MINING CO. (ME)
Voluntarily dissolved 06/29/1904
Details not available

DIAMOND LINX INC (NV)
Reorganized as General Products Holdings Inc. 02/03/2000
Each share Common $0.001 par exchanged for (20) shares new Common $0.001 par
(See General Products Holdings Inc.)

DIAMOND M CO (DE)
Acquired by Kaneb Services, Inc. 05/12/1978
Each share Common $1 par exchanged for (3) shares Common no par
Kaneb Services, Inc. name changed to Xanser Corp. 08/07/2001 which name changed to Furmanite Corp. 05/17/2007 which merged into Team, Inc. 02/29/2016

DIAMOND M DRILLING CO. (DE)
Reincorporated 05/22/1972
State of incorporation changed from (TX) to (DE) 05/22/1972
Stock Dividend - 10% 12/10/1975
Name changed to Diamond M Co. 04/29/1977
Diamond M Co. merged into Kaneb Services, Inc. 05/12/1978 which name changed to Xanser Corp. 08/07/2001 which name changed to Furmanite Corp. 05/17/2007 which merged into Team, Inc. 02/29/2016

DIAMOND MGMT & TECHNOLOGY CONSULTANTS INC (DE)
Acquired by PricewaterhouseCoopers L.L.P. 11/02/2010
Each share Common $0.001 par exchanged for $12.50 cash

DIAMOND MATCH CO. (DE)
Each share 6% Preferred $25 par exchanged for (1) share $1.50 Preferred $25 par and (0.3) share Common no par 12/18/1950
Common no par changed to $1 par and (0.66666666) additional share issued 05/09/1955
Name changed to Diamond Gardner Corp. 11/04/1957
Diamond Gardner Corp. name changed to Diamond National Corp.

09/28/1959 which name changed to Diamond International Corp. 10/29/1964
(See Diamond International Corp.)

DIAMOND MATCH CO. (IL)
Recapitalized under the laws of Delaware 00/00/1930
Details not available

DIAMOND MULTIMEDIA SYS INC (DE)
Common $0.001 par split (3) for (2) by issuance of (0.5) additional share 04/11/1995
Merged into S3 Inc. 09/27/1999
Each share Common $0.001 par exchanged for (0.52) share Common $0.0001 par
S3 Inc. name changed to SONICblue Inc. 11/15/2000
(See SONICblue Inc.)

DIAMOND NATIONAL CORP. (DE)
$1.50 Preferred called for redemption 05/31/1962
Name changed to Diamond International Corp. 10/29/1964
(See Diamond International Corp.)

DIAMOND OILS, INC. (SD)
Merged into Diamond-B Industries, Inc. 2/14/61
Each share Common 25¢ par exchanged for (5.5) shares Common 25¢ par

DIAMOND ONE INC (CO)
Common $0.001 par split (2) for (1) by issuance of (1) additional share payable 10/03/2005 to holders of record 10/03/2005 Ex date - 10/04/2005
Reincorporated under the laws of Delaware as PureDepth, Inc. 05/11/2006
(See PureDepth, Inc.)

DIAMOND I INC (DE)
Recapitalized as ubroadcast, inc. 02/09/2009
Each share Common $0.001 par exchanged for (0.03125) share Common $0.001 par
ubroadcast, inc. name changed to Santeon Group Inc. 06/11/2010

DIAMOND P VIDEO INC (UT)
Merged into Diamond P Sports, Inc. 07/21/1990
Each share Common $0.005 par exchanged for $0.20 cash

DIAMOND PORTLAND CEMENT CO. (OH)
Common $1 par split (2) for (1) by issuance of (1) additional share 9/15/51
Stock Dividend - 10% 12/10/51
Merged into Flintkote Co. 8/31/60
Each share Common $1 par exchanged for (1) share $2.25 2nd Preferred Ser. B no par
(See Flintkote Co.)

DIAMOND POWERSPORTS INC (FL)
Name changed to Golden Dragon Holdings, Inc. 06/27/2008
Golden Dragon Holdings, Inc. name changed to China Food Services, Corp. (FL) 07/07/2010 which reorganized in Nevada as California Grapes International, Inc. 11/09/2011

DIAMOND PPTYS INC (CA)
Company acquired at $65 cash per share through purchase offer which expired 11/30/2006
Public interest eliminated

DIAMOND RANCH FOODS LTD (NV)
Each share old Common $0.0001 par exchanged for (0.0005) share new Common $0.0001 par 09/19/2008
Name changed to Plandai Biotechnology, Inc. 01/05/2012

DIAMOND RESORTS INTL INC (DE)
Acquired by Dakota Parent, Inc. 09/02/2016

Each share Common 1¢ par exchanged for $30.25 cash

DIAMOND RES INC (BC)
Name changed to Diamond International Industries Inc. 08/10/1989
Diamond International Industries Inc. recapitalized as Vault Systems Inc. 12/02/1999 which recapitalized as Vault Minerals Inc. (BC) 06/18/2003 which reincorporated in Ontario 07/25/2005 which merged into Queenston Mining Inc. 04/23/2010 which merged into Osisko Mining Corp. 01/02/2013
(See Osisko Mining Corp.)

DIAMOND RIVER MINES, INC. (DE)
No longer in existence having become inoperative and void for non-payment of taxes 4/1/67

DIAMOND ROBINSON EQUITIES LTD (BC)
Reorganized under the laws of Yukon as Seahawk Minerals Ltd. 11/12/1986
Each share Common no par exchanged for (0.3256056) share Common no par
(See Seahawk Minerals Ltd.)

DIAMOND SELECTION CALIF LTD (CA)
Charter suspended for failure to file reports and pay fees 12/01/1988

DIAMOND SHAMROCK CORP (DE)
Each share Conv. Special Common no par exchanged for (1) share Common no par 12/29/1972
$1.15 Conv. Preferred Ser. E no par called for redemption 09/15/1976
$2 Conv. Preferred Ser. C no par called for redemption 09/15/1976
$4 Conv. Preferred Ser. B no par called for redemption 09/15/1976
Common no par split (2) for (1) by issuance of (1) additional share 12/20/1976
$1.20 Conv. Preferred Ser. D no par called for redemption 12/15/1977
$2.07 Conv. Preferred no par changed to $1 par 08/31/1983
Common no par changed to $1 par 08/31/1983
Name changed to Maxus Energy Corp. 04/30/1987
(See Maxus Energy Corp.)

DIAMOND SHAMROCK INC (DE)
Name changed 02/01/1990
Name changed from Diamond Shamrock R&M, Inc. to Diamond Shamrock Inc. 02/01/1990
Common Stock Purchase Rights declared for Common stockholders of record 04/30/1987 were redeemed at $0.01 per right 03/31/1990
Each share $2 Conv. Exchangeable Preferred 1¢ par exchanged for $25 principal amount of 8% Conv. Subordinated Debentures due 06/15/2013 on 06/15/1990
Merged into Ultramar Diamond Shamrock Corp. 12/03/1996
Each share 5% Conv. Preferred 1¢ par exchanged for (1) share 5% Conv. Preferred 1¢ par
Each share Common 1¢ par exchanged for (1.02) shares Common 1¢ par
(See Ultramar Diamond Shamrock Corp.)

DIAMOND SHAMROCK OFFSHORE PARTNERS LTD PARTNERSHIP (DE)
Merged into Burlington Resources Inc. 07/26/1994
Each Depositary Receipt exchanged for $4.485 cash

DIAMOND SHOE CORP.
Merged into Beck (A.S.) Shoe Corp. in 1945
Each share Common exchanged for (0.12) share 4-3/4% Preferred $100 par and (1) share Common $1 par Beck (A.S.) Shoe Corp. name changed to Beck Industries Inc. 10/29/68
(See Beck Industries Inc.)

DIAMOND ST SECS CORP (DE)
Charter cancelled and declared inoperative and void for non-payment of taxes 09/11/1986

DIAMOND T MOTOR CAR CO. (IL)
Each share Common $20 par exchanged for (10) shares Common $2 par in 1936
Name changed to D T M Corp. 4/1/58
(See D T M Corp.)

DIAMOND TECHNOLOGIES INC (NV)
Name changed to Kallo Inc. 03/10/2011

DIAMOND TECHNOLOGY PARTNERS INC (DE)
Class A Common $0.001 par split (3) for (2) by issuance of (0.5) additional share payable 11/01/1999 to holders of record 10/25/1999
Name changed to DiamondCluster International Inc. 11/28/2000
DiamondCluster International Inc. name changed to Diamond Management & Technology Consultants, Inc. 08/01/2006
(See Diamond Management & Technology Consultants, Inc.)

DIAMOND TRADE CTR INC (NY)
Each share old Common 1¢ par exchanged for (1/3) share new Common 1¢ par 10/01/1991
Dissolved by proclamation 12/24/1991

DIAMOND TREE ENERGY LTD (AB)
Merged into Crocotta Energy Inc. 10/15/2007
Each share Common no par exchanged for (0.3175) share new Common no par and (1) share Upper Lake Oil & Gas Ltd. Common no par
(See each company's listing)

DIAMOND WEST CORP (UT)
Recapitalized 1/29/79
Recapitalized from Diamond West Energy Corp. to Diamond West Corp. 1/29/79
Each share Common 1¢ par exchanged for (0.2) share Common 5¢ par
Proclaimed dissolved for failure to pay taxes 7/1/87

DIAMOND WORLDWIDE INC (NV)
Name changed to FutureVest, Inc. 12/07/2004
Each share Common $0.001 par exchanged for (1) share Common $0.001 par
FutureVest, Inc. name changed to Barotex Technology Corp. 01/09/2008
(See Barotex Technology Corp.)

DIAMONDBACK FINL CORP (UT)
Involuntarily dissolved 12/31/1986

DIAMONDCLUSTER INTL INC (DE)
Class A Common $0.001 par reclassified as Common $0.001 par 09/23/2003
Class B Common $0.001 par reclassified as Common $0.001 par 09/23/2003
Name changed to Diamond Management & Technology Consultants, Inc. 08/01/2006
(See Diamond Management & Technology Consultants, Inc.)

DIAMONDEX RES LTD (BC)
Recapitalized as Canterra Minerals Corp. 12/09/2009
Each share Common no par exchanged for (0.1) share Common no par

DIAMONDHEAD CORP (DE)
Name changed to Purcell Co., Inc. 09/29/1980
(See Purcell Co., Inc.)

DIAMONDS NORTH RES LTD NEW (BC)
Merged into Adamera Minerals Corp. 02/19/2013
Each share Common no par exchanged for (0.1333) share Common no par

DIAMONDS NORTH RES LTD OLD (BC)
Plan of arrangement effective 07/28/2006
Each share Common no par automatically became (1) share Diamonds North Resources Ltd. (New) Common no par and received distribution of (1/6) share Uranium North Resources Corp. Common no par
Uranium North Resources Corp. merged into Adamera Minerals Corp. 02/19/2013

DIAMONDS TR (NY)
Name changed to SPDR Dow Jones Industrial Average ETF Trust 02/26/2010

DIAMONDWORKS LTD (YUKON)
Each share old Common no par exchanged for (0.05) share new Common no par 3/22/2001
Name changed to Energem Resources Inc. 6/9/2004

DIAMONITE INDUSTRIES, INC. (NY)
Name changed to Liquid Optics Corp. 7/5/67
(See Liquid Optics Corp.)

DIAMYD MED AB (SWEDEN)
Sponsored ADR's for Class B split (2) for (1) by issuance of (1) additional ADR payable 01/29/2010 to holders of record 01/28/2010 Ex date - 02/01/2010
Name changed to Mertiva AB 06/28/2013
(See Mertiva AB)

DIAN WEST 26TH STREET CORP.
Liquidation completed in 1944

DIANA CORP (DE)
Stock Dividends - 5% payable 01/05/1996 to holders of record 12/18/1995; 5% payable 10/02/1996 to holders of record 09/16/1996
Name changed to Coyote Network Systems, Inc. 11/20/1997
Coyote Network Systems, Inc. name changed to Quentra Networks, Inc. 07/31/2000
(See Quentra Networks, Inc.)

DIANA EXPLS LTD (BC)
Capital Stock 50¢ par changed to no par 05/30/1980
Merged into Equus Petroleum Corp. 11/09/1982
Each share Capital Stock no par exchanged for (0.64998375) share Common no par
Equus Petroleum Corp. recapitalized as Nuequus Petroleum Corp. 09/30/1997 which name changed to Equus Energy Corp. 11/28/2002 which recapitalized as Habibi Resources Corp. 08/27/2008 which recapitalized as One World Investments Inc. 10/07/2009 which name changed to One World Minerals Inc. 02/28/2017 which name name changed to One World Lithium Inc. 01/19/2018

DIANA RES LTD (BC)
Struck off register and declared dissolved for failure to file returns 08/20/1993

DIANA STORES CORP (NY)
Each share old Common $1 par exchanged for (2) shares new Common $1 par 00/00/1945

DIANA, INC. (was DIA-DIC)

Each share new Common $1 par exchanged for (2) shares Common 50¢ par 00/00/1946
Merged into Daylin, Inc. (CA) 03/21/1969
Each share Common 50¢ par exchanged for $21 principal amount of 5% Subord. Debentures due 03/21/1989 and (7/15) 1969 Ser. Stock Purchase Warrant expiring 03/21/1989

DIANOL, INC. (FL)
Charter revoked for failure to file reports and pay fees 5/16/57

DIANON SYS INC (DE)
Merged into Laboratory Corp. of America Holdings 1/17/2003
Each share Common 1¢ par exchanged for $47.50 cash

DIAPULSE MANUFACTURING CORP. OF AMERICA (DE)
Common 10¢ par changed to 5¢ par 12/20/61
Name changed to Diapulse Corp. of America 1/1/62

DIAS HLDG INC (DE)
SEC revoked common stock registration 12/18/2012

DIASENSE INC (NV)
Reincorporated 03/22/2007
State of incorporation changed from Pennsylvania to Nevada and Common 1¢ par changed to $0.001 par 03/22/2007
Each share old Common $0.001 par exchanged for (0.00008) share new Common $0.001 par 12/07/2007
Note: No holder received fewer than (100) shares
Reorganized as Truewest Corp. 04/07/2008
Each share Common $0.001 par exchanged for (20) shares Common $0.001 par
Truewest Corp. name changed to JD International Ltd. 12/05/2013

DIASONICS INC (DE)
Reincorporated 05/20/1988
State of incorporation changed from (CA) to (DE) and Common no par changed to 1¢ par 05/20/1988
Each share old Common 1¢ par exchanged for (0.2) share new Common 1¢ par 08/01/1991
Name changed to OEC Medical Systems Inc. 10/01/1993
OEC Medical Systems Inc. merged into General Electric Co. 11/29/1999

DIASONICS ULTRASOUND INC (DE)
Merged into Elbit Ltd. 10/19/1994
Each share Common 1¢ par exchanged for $5.512 cash

DIASORIN SPA (ITALY)
ADR agreement terminated 12/26/2017
No ADR's remain outstanding

DIASYN TECHNOLOGIES LTD (CANADA)
Merged into Structured Biologicals Inc. 07/27/1993
Each share Common no par exchanged for (0.2) share Common no par
Structured Biologicals Inc. recapitalized as Ben-Abraham Technologies Inc. 12/06/1996 which name changed to BioSante Pharmaceuticals, Inc. (WY) 12/17/1999 which reincorporated in Delaware 06/26/2001 which recapitalized as ANI Pharmaceuticals, Inc. 07/18/2013

DIASYS CORP (DE)
Common $0.001 par split (2) for (1) by issuance of (1) additional share payable 03/27/2000 to holders of record 03/08/2000
Company terminated common stock registration and is no longer public as of 03/07/2008

DIATEC RES LTD (BC)
Delisted from Vancouver Stock Exchange 11/06/1989

DIATECT INTL CORP (CA)
SEC revoked common stock registration 08/10/2010

DIATERRE GOLD MINES, LTD. (ON)
Charter revoked for failure to file reports and pay taxes 00/00/1956

DIATEST RESH INC (DE)
Name changed to Tiger Coal & Gas Inc. 03/29/2005
Tiger Coal & Gas, Inc. name changed to Halal Financial Services, Inc. 06/00/2005

DIATIDE INC (DE)
Merged into Schering A.G. 11/02/1999
Each share Common $0.001 par exchanged for $9.50 cash

DIATOM CORP (NV)
Reorganized as Planktos Corp. (NV) 03/08/2007
Each share Common $0.001 par exchanged for (1.5) shares Common $0.001 par
Planktos Corp. (NV) reincorporated in Delaware as Planktos Merger Co. 05/06/2014 which name changed to Solar Gold Ltd. 06/24/2014

DIAZ RES LTD (AB)
Reincorporated 04/14/1998
Place of incorporation changed from (BC) to (AB) 04/14/1998
Each share old Common no par exchanged for (0.25) share Class A Subordinate no par and (0.25) share Class B Multiple no par 05/06/1998
Class A Subordinate no par reclassified as new Common no par 06/15/2005
Class B Multiple no par reclassified as new Common no par 06/15/2005
Each share new Common no par exchanged again for (0.04) share new Common no par 12/18/2012
Merged into Tuscany Energy Ltd. (Old) 07/18/2013
Each share new Common no par exchanged for (0.31) share Common no par 07/18/2013
Note: Unexchanged certificates were cancelled and became without value 07/18/2016
Tuscany Energy Ltd. (Old) reorganized as Tuscany Energy Ltd. (New) 07/19/2013
(See Tuscany Energy Ltd. (New))

DIBBS ALUMINUM PRODUCTS, INC. (FL)
Each share Common 10¢ par exchanged for (0.25) share Common 40¢ par 06/15/1962
Name changed to Crown Industries, Inc. (FL) 02/05/1965
(See Crown Industries, Inc. (FL))

DIBI RES INC (BC)
Merged into Eden Roc Mineral Corp. 07/30/1985
Each share Common no par exchanged for (0.2) share Capital Stock no par
(See Eden Roc Mineral Corp.)

DIBOLL ST BANCSHARES INC (TX)
Merged into Southside Bancshares, Inc. 11/30/2017
Each share Common $1 par exchanged for (6.5021) shares Common $1.25 par and $28.12 cash

DIBRELL BROS INC (VA)
Common $10 par split (3) for (2) by issuance of (0.5) additional share 09/20/1983
Common $10 par changed to $1 par 00/00/1988
Common $1 par split (2) for (1) by issuance of (1) additional share 09/13/1991
Stock Dividends - 100% 02/15/1974; 100% 11/19/1975; 50% 09/18/1978;

50% 06/21/1982; 50% 06/14/1985; 100% 12/15/1988
Merged into DIMON Inc. 04/01/1995
Each share Common $1 par exchanged for (1.5) shares Common no par
DIMON Inc. name changed to Alliance One International, Inc. 05/13/2005 which name changed to Pyxus International, Inc. 09/12/2018

DIBZ INTL INC (NV)
Each share old Common $0.001 par exchanged for (0.0000923) share new Common $0.001 par 10/31/2014
Each share new Common $0.001 par exchanged again for (0.01785714) share new Common $0.001 par 07/24/2015
Name changed to Turbo Global Partners, Inc. 05/02/2017

DICE HLDGS INC (DE)
Name changed to DHI Group, Inc. 04/21/2015

DICE INC (DE)
Plan of reorganization under Chapter 11 Federal Bankruptcy Code effective 06/30/2003
The largest (130) shareholders will receive an undetermined amount of new Common and new Common Stock Purchase Warrants
Remaining shareholders will receive an undetermined amount of cash
Holders who are entitled to less than $5 will not receive any distribution
Note: Unexchanged certificates were cancelled and became without value 06/24/2008

DICED CREAM AMER CO (DE)
Each VTC for Common $1 par (under agreement which terminated 01/31/1959) exchanged for (1) share Common $1 par to 04/09/1965 after which date exchanged for cash only
Common $1 par changed to 10¢ par 07/22/1968
Name changed to Raydon Technology Corp. 06/12/1970
(See Raydon Technology Corp.)

DICEON ELECTRS INC (CA)
Name changed to Elexsys International, Inc. 03/02/1995
Elexsys International, Inc. merged into Sanmina Corp. 11/06/1997 which name changed to Sanmina-SCI Corp. 12/10/2001 which name changed back to Sanmina Corp. 11/15/2012

DICK & BROTHERS' QUINCY BREWERY CO.
Name changed to Dick Brothers Brewing Co. 00/00/1937
(See Dick Brothers Brewing Co.)

DICK A B CO (DE)
Acquired by General Electric Co. Ltd. (New) 04/10/1979
Each share 5% Preferred Ser. A $100 par exchanged for $100 cash
Each share 5% Preferred Ser. B $100 par exchanged for $100 cash
Each share Common $1 par exchanged for $16.50 cash

DICK BROTHERS BREWING CO.
Bankrupt 00/00/1951
No stockholders' equity

DICKENS DEV CORP (DE)
Recapitalized as Dasi, Inc. 01/08/1973
Each share Common 10¢ par exchanged for (0.1) share Common 1¢ par
(See Dasi, Inc.)

DICKENS URANIUM & DEVELOPMENT CORP. (DE)
Recapitalized as Dickens Development Corp. 04/23/1959
Each share Common 1¢ par exchanged for (0.1) share Common 10¢ par

Dickens Development Corp. recapitalized as Dasi, Inc. 01/08/1973
(See Dasi, Inc.)

DICKENSON MINES LTD NEW (ON)
Reorganized 10/31/1980
Capital Stock $1 par changed to no par 06/30/1978
Reorganized from Dickenson Mines Ltd. (Old) to Dickenson Mines Ltd. (New) 10/31/1980
Each share Capital Stock no par exchanged for (1) share Class A no par and (1) share Class B no par
Merged into Goldcorp Inc. (New) 03/31/1994
Each share Class A no par exchanged for (1) share Class A Subordinate no par
Each share Conv. Class B no par exchanged for (1) share Class B Multiple no par

DICKENSON RED LAKE MINES LTD. (ON)
Recapitalized as New Dickenson Mines Ltd. 06/20/1949
Each share Capital Stock $1 par value exchanged for (0.3) share Capital Stock $1 par value
New Dickenson Mines Ltd. merged into Dickenson Mines Ltd. (Old) 10/14/1960 which merged into Dickenson Mines Ltd. (New) 10/31/1980 which merged into Goldcorp Inc. (New) 03/31/1994

DICKERSON AUTOMATIC GOVERNOR CO. (UT)
Proclaimed dissolved for failure to pay taxes 11/09/1974

DICKEY-JOHN CORP (DE)
Common no par split (6) for (1) by issuance of (5) additional shares 04/11/1974
Common no par split (3) for (2) by issuance of (0.5) additional share 12/15/1980
Merged into Churchill Companies 04/19/1988
Each share Common no par exchanged for $21.75 cash

DICKEY W S CLAY MFG CO (DE)
Each share $1 Preferred no par exchanged for (1) share Common no par 00/00/1946
Common no par split (2) for (1) by issuance of (1) additional share 02/21/1964
Stock Dividends - 10% 11/30/1959; 10% 11/30/1962; 50% 10/15/1965
Merged into Hepworth Pipes Inc. 04/26/1977
Each share Common no par exchanged for $17.50 cash

DICKIE WALKER MARINE INC (DE)
Recapitalized as China Stationery & Office Supply, Inc. 07/19/2006
Each share Common $0.001 par exchanged for (0.15625) share Common $0.001 par
China Stationery & Office Supply, Inc. recapitalized as Global Arena Holding, Inc. 05/27/2011

DICKINSON HLDG CORP (DE)
Name changed to Synergistic Holdings Corp. 10/18/1995
Synergistic Holdings Corp. name changed to Salex Holding Corp. 03/03/1998
(See Salex Holding Corp.)

DICKINSON INDUSTRIAL SITE, INC. (IL)
Liquidation completed 07/31/1958
Details not available

DICKS HAMBURGERS INC (WA)
Name changed to Labor Ready Inc. 10/20/1989
Labor Ready Inc. name changed to TrueBlue, Inc. 12/18/2007

DICKSON ELECTRS CORP (DE)
Merged into Siemens Capital Corp. 03/04/1974
Each share Common no par exchanged for $13 cash

DICKSON OIL CO.
Recapitalized as Seneca Oil Co. 00/00/1949
Each share Common $1 par exchanged for (1) share Class A 50¢ par
(See Seneca Oil Co.)

DICKSON R S & CO (NC)
Merged into Ruddick Corp. 10/28/1968
Each share 5% Preferred $100 par exchanged for (1) share 56¢ Conv. Preference $5 par
Each share Common $10 par or Class B $10 par exchanged for (1.028) shares 56¢ Conv. Preference $5 par and (6.444) shares Common $1 par
Ruddick Corp. name changed to Harris Teeter Supermarkets, Inc. (New) 04/02/2012
(See Harris Teeter Supermarkets, Inc. (New))

DICO CORP (IA)
Name changed to First Main Corp. 10/31/1978
(See First Main Corp.)

DICO INC (NV)
Name changed to Peekay Boutiques, Inc. 01/28/2015
(See Peekay Boutiques, Inc.)

DICOM IMAGING SYS INC (NV)
Common $0.001 par split (3) for (1) by issuance of (2) additional shares payable 12/23/1999 to holders of record 02/22/1999
Common $0.001 par split (3) for (1) by issuance of (2) additional shares payable 04/05/2000 to holders of record 03/31/2000
Recapitalized as Reality Wireless Networks, Inc. 12/18/2001
Each share Common $0.001 par exchanged for (0.03703703) share Common $0.001 par
Reality Wireless Networks, Inc. recapitalized as Recab International, Inc. 05/15/2006 which recapitalized as Saudi American Holdings Corp. 06/29/2007

DICOMED CORP (MN)
Each share Common 1¢ par exchanged for (0.33333333) share Common 3¢ par 04/25/1972
Common 3¢ par split (3) for (2) by issuance of (0.5) additional share 05/27/1983
Stock Dividend - 50% 05/15/1981
Acquired by De La Rue Co. 01/22/1988
Each share Common 3¢ par exchanged for $3.05 cash

DICON SYS LTD (ON)
Name changed to Disys Corp. 10/16/1991
Disys Corp. merged into Kasten Chase Applied Research Ltd. (ON) 07/24/1996 which reincorporated in Alberta 07/24/2007 which recapitalized as Kasten Energy Inc. 03/02/2010

DICT O TAPE INC (NY)
Name changed to Cassette Magnetics Corp. 06/11/1970
(See Cassette Magnetics Corp.)

DICTAPHONE CORP (DE)
Acquired by Nuance Communications, Inc. 03/31/2006
Each share Common 1¢ par exchanged for $32.43 cash

DICTAPHONE CORP (NY)
Common no par changed to $5 par and (3) additional shares issued 04/23/1957
Common $5 par changed to $2.50 par and (1) additional share issued 09/03/1965
4% Preferred $100 par called for redemption 12/04/1967
Common $2.50 par changed to $1 par and (1) additional share issued 03/12/1968
Merged into Pitney Bowes Inc. 05/11/1979
Each share Common $1 par exchanged for (1) share $2.12 Conv. Preference no par

DICTATOR MINES LTD (BC)
Struck off register 04/15/1983

DICTOGRAPH PRODS INC (DE)
Common no par changed to $2 par 00/00/1933
Common $2 par changed to 10¢ par 12/06/1962
Name changed to Acousticon Systems Corp. 06/09/1969
(See Acousticon Systems Corp.)

DICTOGRAPH PRODUCTS CORP. (VA)
Acquired by Dictograph Products Inc. 00/00/1928
Details not available

DICTORE PORCUPINE GOLD MINES, LTD. (ON)
Charter revoked for failure to file reports and pay taxes 00/00/1957

DICUT INC (DE)
Recapitalized as Silver Falcon Mining, Inc. 11/01/2007
Each share Class A Common $0.0001 par exchanged for (0.005) share Class A Common $0.001 par

DIDAX INC (DE)
Name changed to Crosswalk.Com, Inc. 05/13/1999
Crosswalk.Com, Inc. name changed to AMEN Properties, Inc. 10/09/2002

DIE MESH CORP (NY)
Dissolved by proclamation 12/30/1981

DIEBOLD COMPUTER LEASING INC (DE)
Under plan of reorganization each share Class A Common $0.03333333 par automatically became (1) share DCL Inc. Common $0.03333333 par 08/13/1971
(See DCL Inc.)

DIEBOLD INC (OH)
Common $5 par split (3) for (1) by issuance of (2) additional shares 05/31/1956
Common $5 par split (4) for (3) by issuance of (0.33333333) additional share 05/08/1962
Common $5 par changed to $2.50 par and (1) additional share issued 04/30/1965
Common $2.50 par changed to $1.25 par 04/10/1969
Common $1.25 par split (3) for (2) by issuance of (0.5) additional share 05/28/1971
Common $1.25 par split (3) for (2) by issuance of (0.5) additional share 05/15/1981
Common $1.25 par split (3) for (2) by issuance of (0.5) additional share 02/01/1985
Common $1.25 par split (3) for (2) by issuance of (0.5) additional share 02/26/1993
Common $1.25 par split (3) for (2) by issuance of (0.5) additional share 02/22/1994
Common $1.25 par split (3) for (2) by issuance of (0.5) additional share payable 02/23/1996 to holders of record 02/09/1996
Common $1.25 par split (3) for (2) by issuance of (0.5) additional share payable 02/19/1997 to holders of record 02/07/1997 Ex date - 02/20/1997
Stock Dividends - 10% 08/23/1954; 10% 01/16/1956; 10% 01/16/1957
Name changed to Diebold Nixdorf, Inc. 12/12/2016

DIEBOLD SAFE & LOCK CO. (OH)
Name changed to Diebold, Inc. 00/00/1944
Diebold, Inc. name changed to Diebold Nixdorf Inc. 12/12/2016

DIEBOLD TECHNOLOGY VENTURE FD INC (DE)
Name changed to Diebold Venture Capital Corp. 01/14/1970
Diebold Venture Capital Corp. name changed to Claremont Capital Corp. 02/04/1977 which name changed to Bergstrom Capital Corp. 11/08/1988
(See Bergstom Capital Corp.)

DIEBOLD VENTURE CAP CORP (DE)
Name changed to Claremont Capital Corp. 02/04/1977
Claremont Capital Corp. name changed to Bergstrom Capital Corp. 11/08/1988
(See Bergstom Capital Corp.)

DIEDRICH COFFEE INC (DE)
Each share old Common 1¢ par exchanged for (0.25) share new Common 1¢ par 05/11/2001
Merged into Green Mountain Coffee Roasters, Inc. 05/11/2010
Each share new Common 1¢ par exchanged for $35 cash

DIEHL GRAPHSOFT INC (NJ)
Each share old Common no par exchanged for (0.75) share new Common no par 08/16/1994
Merged into Nemetschek Aktiengesellschaft 05/19/2000
Each share new Common no par exchanged for $9.50 cash

DIELECTRIC PRODUCTS ENGINEERING CO., INC. (MI)
55¢ Conv. Preferred $8 par called for redemption 06/06/1968
Merged into Sola Basic Industries, Inc. 07/15/1968
Each share Common $1 par exchanged for (0.5) share Common $1 par
Sola Basic Industries, Inc. merged into General Signal Corp. 09/30/1977 which merged into SPX Corp. 10/06/1998

DIEPDAUME MINES LTD (CANADA)
Cease trade order effective 06/12/1992

DIERKS FORESTS INC (DE)
Common no par split (6) for (5) by issuance of (0.2) additional share 09/02/1962
Common no par split (2) for (1) by issuance of (1) additional share 02/10/1969
Stock Dividends - 10% 12/01/1950; 10% 09/04/1951; 10% 12/29/1954; 20% 11/09/1959; 50% 12/01/1960; 20% 12/19/1963; 25% 12/27/1965
Completely liquidated 09/18/1969
Each share Common no par received first and final distribution of (1.43546) shares Weyerhaeuser Co. $6.75 Conv. Preferred Ser. A no par and $219.8248553 cash

DIESEL EQUIPMENT CORP.
Name changed to Aircraft & Diesel Equipment Corp. 00/00/1940
(See Aircraft & Diesel Equipment Corp.)

DIESEL POWER, INC. (PA)
Common $1 par changed to 50¢ par 11/15/1954
Dissolved 08/15/1960
No stockholders' equity

DIESEL TRUCK DRIVER TRAINING SCH INC (WI)
Name changed to Gyco Corp. 07/16/1975

DIET COFFEE INC (DE)
Recapitalized as Zevotek, Inc. 06/27/2008
Each share Common $0.001 par exchanged for (0.02) share Common $0.00001 par

DIET CTL CTRS INC (DE)
Common 1¢ par split (3) for (1) by issuance of (2) additional shares 12/10/1971
Name changed to Edcoa, Inc. 08/00/1986
(See Edcoa, Inc.)

DIET INST INC (NJ)
Each share old Common $0.001 par exchanged for (0.1) share new Common $0.001 par 05/03/1985
Chapter 11 bankruptcy proceedings converted to Chapter 7 on 09/04/1985
Stockholders' equity unlikely

DIETETIC INTL INC (DE)
Name changed to Citiwide Capital Corp. 09/30/1983
(See Citiwide Capital Corp.)

DIETRICH EXPL INC (CO)
Reorganized under the laws of Delaware as Dietrich Resources Corp. 05/15/1981
Each share Common 1¢ par exchanged for (1) share Common 1¢ par
Dietrich Resources Corp. name changed to DRX, Inc. 04/29/1987
(See DRX, Inc.)

DIETRICH RES CORP (DE)
Each share Common 1¢ par exchanged for (0.1) share Common 10¢ par 10/20/1983
Name changed to DRX, Inc. 04/29/1987
(See DRX, Inc.)

DIETWORKS OF AMER INC (NJ)
Charter revoked for failure to file reports and pay fees 09/14/1995

DIETZGEN CORP. (DE)
Charter cancelled and declared inoperative and void for non-payment of taxes 03/01/1976

DIETZGEN EUGENE CO (DE)
Name changed to Dietzgen Corp. 09/01/1971
(See Dietzgen Corp.)

DIF CORP. (DE)
Completely liquidated 10/28/1964
Each share Preferred $50 par exchanged for $54.25 cash
No Common stockholders' equity

DIFFERENCE CAP FDG INC (CANADA)
Recapitalized as Difference Capital Financial Inc. 06/17/2013
Each share Common no par exchanged for (0.1) share Common no par

DIFFERENTIAL WHEEL CORP. (DE)
No longer in existence having become inoperative and void for non-payment of taxes 04/01/1954

DIFFRACTION LTD., INC. (MA)
Completely liquidated 02/20/1968
Each share Class A Common $1 par or Class B Common $1 par exchanged for first and final distribution of (1) share Ealing Corp. Common 10¢ par
(See Ealing Corp.)

DIG-IT UNDERGROUND INC (NV)
Recapitalized as Eco Innovation Group, Inc. 08/29/2018
Each share Common $0.001 par exchanged for (0.001) share Common $0.001 par

DIGAGOGO VENTURES CORP (DE)
Common $0.0001 par split (10) for (1) by issuance of (9) additional shares payable 12/01/2010 to holders of record 12/01/2010
Recapitalized as 420 Property Management, Inc. 10/19/2015
Each share Common $0.0001 par

exchanged for (0.01) share Common $0.0001 par

DIGBY DOME MINES CO. LTD. (ON)
Recapitalized as New Digby Dome Mines 07/08/1955
Each share Capital Stock $1 par exchanged for (0.33333333) share Capital Stock $1 par
(See New Digby Dome Mines Ltd.)

DIGENE CORP (DE)
Merged into Qiagen N.V. 07/30/2007
Each share Common 1¢ par exchanged for either (3.545) shares Common Euro 0.01 par or $61.25 cash
Note: Option to receive cash expired 09/13/2007

DIGEX INC (DE)
Each share Class A Common 1¢ par received distribution of (0.184654) share Worldcom Inc. Worldcom Group Common 1¢ par and (0.007386) share Worldcom Inc. MCI Group Common 1¢ par payable 07/05/2001 to holders of record 06/29/2001
Each share Class A Common 1¢ par received distribution of (0.18838) share Worldcom Inc. Worldcom Group Common 1¢ par and (0.007535) share Worldcom Inc. MCI Group Common 1¢ par payable 07/20/2001 to holders of record 09/01/2000
Merged into WorldCom, Inc. (New) 11/19/2003
Each share Class A Common 1¢ par exchanged for $1 cash

DIGEX INC (DE)
Merged into Intermedia Communications, Inc. 07/11/1997
Each share Common 1¢ par exchanged for $13 cash

DIGI LINK TECHNOLOGIES INC (DE)
SEC revoked common stock registration 02/14/2005

DIGI LOG SYS INC (DE)
Common 1¢ par split (5) for (4) by issuance of (0.25) additional share 03/21/1980
Stock Dividend - 20% 10/10/1980
Name changed to Digilog, Inc. 03/02/1981
Digilog, Inc. merged into CXR Corp. 11/15/1989 which name changed to Microtel International Inc. 03/07/1995 which name changed to EMRISE Corp. 09/15/2004

DIGICALL GROUP LTD (AUSTRALIA)
ADR agreement terminated 11/20/1997
No stockholders' equity

DIGICOM COMMUNICATIONS INC (DE)
Charter forfeited for failure to maintain a registered agent 02/25/1991

DIGICOM CORP (DE)
Name changed to Emery Ferron Energy Corp. 06/27/1994
(See Emery Ferron Energy Corp.)

DIGICON INC (DE)
Reorganized under Chapter 11 Federal Bankruptcy Code 06/18/1991
Each share Common 10¢ par exchanged for (0.0002575) Common Stock Purchase Warrant expiring 07/05/1996
Each share old Common 1¢ par exchanged for (0.33333333) share new Common 1¢ par 01/17/1995
Name changed to Veritas DGC Inc. 08/30/1996
Veritas DGC Inc. merged into Compagnie Generale de Geophysique-Veritas 01/12/2007 which name changed to CGG 05/29/2013

DIGICORP (DE)
Reincorporated 10/15/2006
State of incorporation changed from (UT) to (DE) 10/15/2006
Name changed to China Youth Media, Inc. 10/16/2008
China Youth Media, Inc. recapitalized as Midwest Energy Emissions Corp. 10/07/2011

DIGICURVE INC (NV)
Each share old Common $0.001 par exchanged for (9.4) shares new Common $0.001 par 03/19/2007
Name changed to Fightersoft Multimedia Corp. 02/04/2008
(See Fightersoft Multimedia Corp.)

DIGIDESIGN INC (DE)
Merged into Avid Technology, Inc. 01/05/1995
Each share Common $0.001 par exchanged for (0.79) share Common no par

DIGIFONICA INTL CORP (FL)
Merged into Digifonica International Inc. (AB) 10/26/2007
Each share Common $0.001 par exchanged for (1) share Common no par
Digifonica International Inc. (AB) reincorporated in British Columbia as Dominion Energy Inc. 12/09/2013 which name changed to Dynamic Oil & Gas Exploration Inc. 06/30/2014 which recapitalized as Darien Business Development Corp. 03/14/2017

DIGIFONICA INTL INC (AB)
Each share old Common no par exchanged for (0.1) share new Common no par 05/11/2011
Reincorporated under the laws of British Columbia as Dominion Energy Inc. 12/09/2013
Dominion Energy Inc. name changed to Dynamic Oil & Gas Exploration Inc. 06/30/2014 which recapitalized as Darien Business Development Corp. 03/14/2017

DIGIGRAPHIC SYS CORP (MN)
Name changed to DSC Nortech, Inc. 09/12/1988
DSC Nortech, Inc. name changed to Nortech Systems Inc. 12/03/1990

DIGILAVA INC (NV)
Recapitalized as WGE Holdings Corp. 05/27/2015
Each share Common $0.001 par exchanged for (0.01) share Common $0.001 par

DIGILOG INC (DE)
Merged into CXR Corp. 11/15/1989
Each share Common 1¢ par exchanged for (1) share Common $0.0033 par
CXR Corp. name changed to Microtel International Inc. 03/07/1995 which name changed to EMRISE Corp. 09/15/2004

DIGIMARC CORP NEW (DE)
Reincorporated under the laws of Oregon 04/30/2010

DIGIMARC CORP OLD (DE)
Each share Common $0.001 par received distribution of (0.28571428) share DMRC Corp. Common $0.001 par payable 10/16/2008 to holders of record 08/01/2008
Merged into L-1 Identity Solutions, Inc. 08/13/2008
Each share Common $0.001 par exchanged for $12.25 cash

DIGIMEDIA USA INC (NV)
Each share old Common $0.00066666 par exchanged for (0.14285714) share new Common $0.00066666 par 05/10/1997
Name changed to Algorhythm Technologies Corp. 07/24/1997
Algorhythm Technologies Corp. name changed to Quikbiz Internet Group, Inc. 07/07/1998
(See Quikbiz Internet Group, Inc.)

DIGIMETRICS INC (NY)
Recapitalized as Control Chief Holdings Inc. 11/23/1992
Each share Common 50¢ par exchanged for (0.25) share Common 50¢ par
(See Control Chief Holdings Inc.)

DIGINAMICS CORP (MN)
Statutorily dissolved 10/04/1991

DIGITAL ANGEL CORP NEW (DE)
Each share old Common 1¢ par exchanged for (0.125) share new Common 1¢ par 11/10/2008
Recapitalized as VeriTeQ Corp. 10/22/2013
Each share new Common 1¢ par exchanged for (0.03333333) share Common 1¢ par

DIGITAL ANGEL CORP OLD (DE)
Merged into Applied Digital Solutions, Inc. 12/31/2007
Each share Common $0.005 par exchanged for (1.4) shares Common 1¢ par
Applied Digital Solutions, Inc. name changed to Digital Angel Corp. (New) 06/20/2008 which recapitalized as VeriTeQ Corp. 10/22/2013

DIGITAL APPLICATIONS INC (DE)
Incorporated 01/29/1968
Name changed to D.A.I. Liquidating Corp. 04/30/1974
(See D.A.I. Liquidating Corp.)

DIGITAL APPLICATIONS INC NEW (DE)
Incorporated 01/25/1974
Voluntarily dissolved 12/26/1986
Details not available

DIGITAL ARTS MEDIA NETWORK INC (CO)
Name changed to Digital Asset Monetary Network, Inc. 09/05/2018

DIGITAL ATHENEUM TECHNOLOGY CORP (CANADA)
Name changed to Nickel Petroleum Resources Ltd. 05/18/2004
(See Nickel Petroleum Resources Ltd.)

DIGITAL BIOMETRICS INC (DE)
Name changed to Visionics Corp. 02/20/2001
Visionics Corp. merged into Identix Inc. 06/25/2002 which merged into L-1 Identify Solutions, Inc. 08/30/2006
(See L-1 Identify Solutions, Inc.)

DIGITAL BRDG INC (NV)
Recapitalized as Tantivy Group, Inc. 03/25/2002
Each share Common $0.001 par exchanged for (0.05) share Common $0.001 par
Tantivy Group, Inc. recapitalized as Oretech, Inc. 04/01/2003
(See Oretech, Inc.)

DIGITAL BROADBAND NETWORKS INC (CO)
Reorganized under the laws of Delaware 06/06/2002
Each share Common $0.00001 par exchanged for (1) share Common $0.00001 par
Digital Broadband Networks, Inc. (DE) name changed to Secured Digital Applications, Inc. 02/03/2004
(See Secured Digital Applications, Inc.)

DIGITAL BROADBAND NETWORKS INC (DE)
Name changed to Secured Digital Applications, Inc. 02/03/2004
(See Secured Digital Applications, Inc.)

DIGITAL CADDIES INC (OK)
Name changed to IZON Network, Inc. and Common $0.001 par changed to $0.0001 par 09/19/2017

DIGITAL CINEMA DESTINATIONS CORP (DE)
Merged into Carmike Cinemas, Inc. 08/15/2014
Each share Class A Common 1¢ par exchanged for (0.1765) share Common 1¢ par
(See Carmike Cinemas, Inc.)

DIGITAL COLOR PRINT INC (DE)
Reorganized under the laws of Florida as Bell Buckle Holdings, Inc. 06/29/2007
Each share Common $0.0001 par exchanged for (0.01) share Common $0.001 par

DIGITAL COMM INTL INC (DE)
Name changed to NetCare Health Group, Inc. 04/05/2002
(See NetCare Health Group, Inc.)

DIGITAL COMMUNICATIONS ASSSOC INC (GA)
Common 10¢ par split (3) for (2) by issuance of (0.5) additional share 02/04/1986
Merged into DCA Holdings, Inc. 12/28/1993
Each share Common 10¢ par exchanged for $18.75 cash

DIGITAL COMMUNICATIONS INC (FL)
Chapter 11 bankruptcy proceedings converted to Chapter 7 on 02/14/1983
Stockholders' equity unlikely

DIGITAL COMMUNICATIONS TECHNOLOGY CORP (DE)
Each share old Common $0.0002 par exchanged for (0.1) share new Common $0.0002 par 12/09/1997
Stock Dividend - 5% payable 05/27/1996 to holders of record 05/17/1996 Ex date - 05/15/1996
SEC revoked common stock registration 04/22/2009
Stockholders' equity unlikely

DIGITAL COMPOSITION SYS LTD (BC)
Recapitalized as DCS International Systems Corp. 03/01/1990
Each share Common no par exchanged for (0.2) share Common no par
DCS International Systems Corp. recapitalized as Step 2 Software Corp. 06/10/1993 which recapitalized as Emergo Software Corp. 11/01/1999 which name changed to eTVtech.com Communications Inc. 03/21/2000 which name changed to eTV Technology Inc. 05/02/2001 which recapitalized as Ocean Park Ventures Corp. 04/02/2009 which recapitalized as Dunnedin Ventures Inc. 08/06/2013

DIGITAL COMPUTER CTLS INC (DE)
Common 1¢ par split (3) for (2) by issuance of (0.5) additional share 07/02/1971
Merged into Data General Corp. 01/25/1977
Each share Common 1¢ par exchanged for (0.168776) share Common 1¢ par
Data General Corp. merged into EMC Corp. 10/12/1999 which merged into Dell Technologies Inc. 09/07/2016

DIGITAL CONCEPTS INTL INC (FL)
SEC revoked common stock registration 05/31/2007

DIGITAL COURIER INTL CORP (AB)
Placed in receivership and assets subsequently sold 09/24/1998
No stockholders' equity

DIGITAL COURIER TECHNOLOGIES INC (DE)
Recapitalized as TransAxis, Inc. 05/08/2003
Each share Common $0.001 par exchanged for (0.01) share Common $0.001 par
(See TransAxis, Inc.)

DIGITAL CYBERNET CORP (ON)
Name changed to Canadian Everock Explorations Inc. 11/21/2000
Canadian Everock Explorations Inc. recapitalized as Everock Inc. (ONT) 11/22/2002 which reorganized in Nevada 12/12/2005

DIGITAL DATA NETWORKS INC (WA)
Name changed to i2 Telecom International, Inc. 03/05/2004
i2 Telecom International, Inc. recapitalized as Geos Communications, Inc. 10/01/2009
(See Geos Communications, Inc.)

DIGITAL DATA SYS CORP (DE)
Adjudicated bankrupt 03/06/1974
Stockholders' equity unlikely

DIGITAL DATACOM INC (DE)
Merged into Honeywell Inc. 11/20/1984
Each share Common 1¢ par exchanged for $4.6321 cash

DIGITAL DESCRIPTOR SYS INC (DE)
Recapitalized as Allied Security Innovations, Inc. 02/07/2007
Each share Common $0.001 par exchanged for (0.002) share Common $0.001 par

DIGITAL DEV GROUP CORP (NV)
SEC revoked common stock registration 11/01/2016

DIGITAL DEVICES INC (DE)
Charter cancelled and declared inoperative and void for non-payment of taxes 03/01/1993

DIGITAL DIAGNOSTIC SYS INC (DE)
Charter cancelled and declared inoperative and void for non-payment of taxes 03/01/1990

DIGITAL DIAGNOSTICS CORP (DE)
Charter forfeited for failure to maintain a registered agent 07/27/2007

DIGITAL DICTATION INC (DE)
Merged into MedQuist Inc. 07/31/1998
Each share Common 1¢ par exchanged for (0.1440899) share Common no par
MedQuist Inc. merged into MedQuist Holdings Inc. 10/18/2011 which name changed to MModal Inc. 01/25/2012
(See MModal Inc.)

DIGITAL DISPATCH SYS INC (BC)
Name changed to DDS Wireless International Inc. 03/05/2008
(See DDS Wireless International Inc.)

DIGITAL DJ HLDGS INC (NV)
Recapitalized as Beverly Holdings Inc. 05/23/2001
Each share Common 40¢ par exchanged for (0.04) share Common 40¢ par
(See Beverly Holdings Inc.)

DIGITAL DOMAIN MEDIA GROUP INC (FL)
Chapter 11 bankrutpcy proceedings converted to Chapter 7 on 07/29/2016
Stockholders' equity unlikely

DIGITAL DUPLICATION INC (ON)
Delisted from Toronto Venture Stock Exchange 06/25/2004

DIGITAL ECOSYSTEMS CORP (NV)
Each share old Common $0.001 par exchanged for (10) shares new Common $0.001 par 09/16/2005
Reincorporated under the laws of Maryland as PetroHunter Energy Corp. 08/21/2006
(See PetroHunter Energy Corp.)

DIGITAL ENERGY CORP (NV)
Chapter 11 bankruptcy proceedings converted to Chapter 7 on 07/11/1983
Stockholders' equity unlikely

DIGITAL EQUIP CORP (MA)
Common $1 par split (3) for (1) by issuance of (2) additional shares 06/27/1969
Common $1 par split (3) for (1) by issuance of (2) additional shares 11/08/1976
Common $1 par split (2) for (1) by issuance of (1) additional share 05/09/1986
Merged into Compaq Computer Corp. 06/11/1998
Each share Common $1 par exchanged for (0.945) share Common 1¢ par and $30 cash
8.875% Depositary Preferred Ser. A called for redemption at $25 on 04/01/1999
Compaq Computer Corp. merged into Hewlett-Packard Co. 05/03/2002 which name changed to HP Inc. 11/02/2015

DIGITAL FUEL INC (DE)
Ceased operations 12/31/2009
Stockholders' equity unlikely

DIGITAL FUSION INC (DE)
Merged into Kratos Defense & Security Solutions, Inc. 12/24/2008
Each share Common 1¢ par exchanged for (1.7933) shares Common $0.001 par

DIGITAL FUSION MULTIMEDIA CORP (CANADA)
Charter cancelled and declared dissolved for failure to file returns 03/06/2000

DIGITAL GAS INC (MI)
Chapter 11 bankruptcy proceedings converted to Chapter 7 on 11/12/2008
No stockholders' equity

DIGITAL GEM CORP (ON)
Name changed to Northern Financial Corp. 10/03/2000
Northern Financial Corp. recapitalized as Added Capital Inc. 07/23/2014

DIGITAL GENERATION INC (DE)
Merged into Sizmek Inc. 02/07/2014
Each share Common $0.001 par exchanged for (1) share Common $0.001 par and $3 cash
(See Sizmek Inc.)

DIGITAL GENERATION SYS INC (DE)
Reincorporated 12/31/2000
State of incorporation changed from (CA) to (DE) 12/31/2000
Each share old Common $0.001 par exchanged for (0.1) share new Common $0.001 par 05/30/2006
Name changed to DG FastChannel, Inc. 09/08/2006
DG FastChannel, Inc. name changed to Digital Generation, Inc. 11/07/2011 which merged into Sizmek Inc. 02/07/2014
(See Sizmek Inc.)

DIGITAL GRAPHIX INC (DE)
Common 1¢ par split (10) for (1) by issuance of (9) additional shares payable 11/03/1995 to holders of record 10/23/1995
Completely liquidated 04/07/2000
No stockholders' equity

DIGITAL HOME THEATER SYS INC (NV)
Name changed to Xenonics Holdings, Inc. 07/22/2003

DIGITAL IMAGING RES INC (DE)
Recapitalized as Boomerang Systems, Inc. 02/08/2008
Each share Common $0.001 par exchanged for (0.06666666) share Common $0.001 par
(See Boomerang Systems, Inc.)

DIGITAL IMPACT INC (DE)
Merged into Acxiom Corp. 05/09/2005
Each share Common $0.001 par exchanged for $3.50 cash

DIGITAL INFORMATION & VIRTUAL ACCESS INC (DE)
Recapitalized 03/03/1999
Reincorporated 04/27/2006
Recapitalized from Digital Information & Voice Access Inc. to Digital Information & Virtual Access Inc. 03/03/1999
Each share Common $0.001 par exchanged for (0.08333333) share Common $0.001 par
State of incorporation changed from (NV) to (DE) 04/27/2006
Recapitalized as Kimber-X Resources Corp. 11/30/2006
Each share Common $0.001 par exchanged for (0.001) share Common $0.001 par
Kimber-X Resources Corp. name changed to Radium Resources Corp. 12/21/2007

DIGITAL INFORMATION DEVICES INC (DE)
Out of business and assets sold due to foreclosure 07/27/1973
No stockholders' equity

DIGITAL INSIGHT CORP (DE)
Merged into Intuit Inc. 02/07/2007
Each share Common $0.001 par exchanged for $39 cash

DIGITAL IS INC (DE)
Merged into Cable & Wireless PLC 08/31/2001
Each share Common $0.001 par exchanged for $3.40 cash

DIGITAL LAUNCH INC (DE)
Name changed to Global e Tutor, Inc. 02/03/2000
Global e Tutor, Inc. recapitalized as Winning Brands Corp. 11/09/2005

DIGITAL LAVA INC (DE)
Completely liquidated
Each share Common $0.0001 par received first and final distribution of $0.009558 cash payable 02/06/2006 to holders of record 01/31/2006
Ex date - 02/07/2006
Note: Certificates were not required to be surrendered and are without value

DIGITAL LEARNING MGMT CORP (DE)
Reincorporated 09/23/2004
State of incorporation changed from (NV) to (DE) 09/23/2004
Common $0.001 par split (3) for (1) by issuance of (2) additional shares payable 08/28/2006 to holders of record 08/18/2006 Ex date - 08/29/2006
Recapitalized as Nutradyne Group, Inc. 10/25/2007
Each share Common $0.001 par exchanged for (0.08350786) share Common $0.001 par
Nutradyne Group, Inc. name changed to China Yongxin Pharmaceuticals Inc. 05/15/2008

DIGITAL LIFESTYLES GROUP INC (DE)
Name changed to TN-K Energy Group Inc. 10/29/2009

DIGITAL LIGHTHOUSE CORP (DE)
Plan of reorganization under Chapter 11 Federal Bankruptcy Code effective 04/07/2003
No stockholders' equity

DIGITAL LIGHTWAVE INC (DE)
Merged into Optel Acquisition Corp. 01/18/2010
Each share Common $0.0001 par exchanged for $0.055 cash

DIGITAL LINK CORP (CA)
Merged into DLZ Corp. 11/17/1999
Each share Common no par exchanged for $10.85 cash

DIGITAL MICROWAVE CORP (DE)
Common 1¢ par split (2) for (1) by issuance of (1) additional share payable 11/24/1997 to holders of record 11/06/1997
Name changed to DMC Stratex Networks, Inc. 08/15/2000
DMC Stratex Networks, Inc. name changed to Stratex Networks, Inc. 09/10/2002 which merged into Harris Stratex Networks, Inc. 01/26/2007 which name changed to Aviat Networks, Inc. 01/27/2010

DIGITAL MUSIC GROUP INC (DE)
Each share old Common 1¢ par exchanged for (0.33333333) share new Common 1¢ par 11/14/2007
Name changed to Orchard Enterprises, Inc. 02/08/2008
(See Orchard Enterprises, Inc.)

DIGITAL NERVOUS SYS INC (AB)
Acquired by Battery & Wireless Solutions Inc. 08/07/2003
Each share Common no par exchanged for (1) Unit consisting of (0.91081) share Common no par and (0.5) Common Stock Purchase Warrant expiring 08/07/2005

DIGITAL NETWORK ALLIANCE INTL INC (DE)
Each share old Common $0.001 par exchanged for (0.5) share new Common $0.001 par 09/22/2005
Name changed to Sino Assurance, Inc. 01/02/2009

DIGITAL OPTRONICS CORP (DE)
Charter cancelled and declared inoperative and void for non-payment of taxes 03/01/1992

DIGITAL ORIGIN INC (CA)
Merged into Media 100 Inc. 05/09/2000
Each share Common no par exchanged for (0.5347) share Common 1¢ par
(See Media 100 Inc.)

DIGITAL PAGING SYS INC (DE)
Merged into Graphic Scanning Corp. 04/01/1980
Each share Common 1¢ par exchanged for (0.25) share Common 1¢ par
(See Graphic Scanning Corp.)

DIGITAL PAINT INTL HLDG CO LTD (NV)
Each share old Common $0.001 par exchanged for (0.002) share new Common $0.001 par 07/18/2008
Recapitalized as Direct Coating, Inc. 07/06/2009
Each share Common $0.001 par exchanged for (0.025) share Common $0.001 par
(See Direct Coating, Inc.)

DIGITAL PWR CORP (CA)
Reincorporated under the laws of Delaware as DPW Holdings, Inc. and Common no par reclassified as Class A Common $0.001 par 01/02/2018

DIGITAL PWR HLDG CO (NV)
Each share old Common $0.001 par exchanged for (0.01) share new Common $0.001 par 05/07/1996
Name changed to I-Storm, Inc. 07/20/1998
(See I-Storm, Inc.)

DIGITAL PRECISION IMAGERY CORP (AB)
Recapitalized as Alava Ventures Inc. 12/04/1996
Each share Common no par exchanged for (0.04) share Common no par
(See Alava Ventures Inc.)

DIGITAL PROCESSING SYS INC (ON)
Merged into Leitch Technology Corp. 10/25/2000
Each share Common no par exchanged for either (0.25823) share Common no par or (0.1) share Common no par and $3.97 cash
Note: Option to receive stock and cash expired 11/20/2000
(See Leitch Technology Corp.)

DIGITAL PRODS CORP (FL)
Common 1¢ par split (2) for (1) by issuance of (1) additional share 06/11/1981
Each share Common 1¢ par exchanged for (0.4) share Common $0.025 par 02/05/1992
Stock Dividend - 100% 01/06/1981
Chapter 7 bankruptcy proceedings terminated 06/29/2004
Stockholders' equity unlikely

DIGITAL RLTY TR INC (MD)
8.5% Preferred Ser. A 1¢ par called for redemption at $25 plus $0.312850 accrued dividends on 08/24/2010
7.875% Preferred Ser. B 1¢ par called for redemption at $25 plus $0.377344 accrued dividends on 12/10/2010
Each share 4.375% Conv. Preferred Ser. C 1¢ par exchanged for (0.548) share Common 1¢ par 04/17/2012
Each share 5.5% Conv. Preferred Ser. D 1¢ par exchanged for (0.636) share Common 1¢ par 02/26/2013
7% Preferred Ser. E 1¢ par called for redemption at $25 plus $0.35972 accrued dividends on 09/15/2016
6.625% Preferred Ser. F 1¢ par called for redemption at $25 plus $0.0184 accrued dividends on 04/05/2017
(Additional Information in Active)

DIGITAL RECORDERS INC (NC)
Name changed to DRI Corp. 06/13/2007
(See DRI Corp.)

DIGITAL RECORDING CORP (DE)
Charter cancelled and declared inoperative and void for non-payment of taxes 03/01/1994

DIGITAL REPORTING INC (MN)
Each share old Common 10¢ par exchanged for (0.2) share new Common 10¢ par 06/26/1996
Each share new Common 10¢ par exchanged for (0.25) share Common $0.001 par 06/02/1997
Name changed to Cyberguides International Inc. 10/03/1997
Cyberguides International Inc. name changed to AJA Merchant Banking Corp. 02/26/1998 which name changed to to Image-Photo Systems Inc. 12/09/1998 which name changed to e-bidd.com, Inc. 09/08/1999 which name changed to xraymedia.com, Inc. 06/28/2000 which name changed to Xraymedia, Inc. 12/04/2003 which recapitalized as T.W. Christian, Inc. 08/14/2007
(See T.W. Christian, Inc.)

DIGITAL RIV INC (DE)
Acquired by Danube Private Holdings II, LLC 02/12/2015
Each share Common 1¢ par exchanged for $26 cash

DIGITAL ROOSTER COM INC (ON)
Recapitalized as Digital Rooster.com Ltd. 12/02/2002
Each share Common no par exchanged for (0.02) share Common no par
Digital Rooster.com Ltd. name changed to Phinder Technologies Inc. (ON) 02/07/2007 which reincorporated in Florida 01/19/2007 which name changed to Zupintra Corp., Inc. 06/21/2007
(See Zupintra Corp., Inc.)

DIGITAL ROOSTER COM LTD (ON)
Each share Common no par received distribution of (0.5) share Avrada Inc. Common no par and (0.5) Common Stock Purchase Warrant payable 04/28/2004 to holders of record 04/07/2004 Ex date - 05/03/2004
Common no par split (1.75) for (1) by issuance of (0.75) additional share payable 04/28/2004 to holders of record 04/07/2004 Ex date - 05/03/2004
Name changed to Phinder Technologies Inc. (ON) 02/07/2005
Phinder Technologies Inc. (ON) reincorporated in Florida 01/19/2007 which name changed to Zupintra Corp., Inc. 06/21/2007

DIGITAL SCIENCES INC (NV)
Merged into Intelligent Decision Systems, Inc. 04/01/1996
Each share Common $0.002 par exchanged for (1) share Common $0.001 par
(See Intelligent Decision Systems, Inc.)

DIGITAL SEC INC (NV)
Name changed to DLR Funding, Inc. 03/25/2006
(See DLR Funding, Inc.)

DIGITAL SHELF SPACE CORP (BC)
Each share old Common no par exchanged for (0.2) share new Common no par 10/30/2013
Name changed to Movit Media Corp. (BC) 07/09/2015
Movit Media Corp. (BC) reorganized in British Columbia as Ether Capital Corp. 04/19/2018

DIGITAL SIGN CORP (DE)
Recapitalized as Pawnbroker.Com, Inc. 06/11/1999
Each share Common 1¢ par exchanged for (0.25) share Common $0.001 par
Pawnbroker.Com, Inc. recapitalized as Orinoco Resources, Inc. 08/05/2005 which recapitalized as El Alacran Gold Mine Corp. 05/23/2006

DIGITAL SOLUTIONS INC (NJ)
Name changed to TeamStaff Inc. 07/01/1999
TeamStaff Inc. name changed to DLH Holdings Inc. 06/27/2012

DIGITAL SOUND CORP (CA)
Recapitalized as Pulsepoint Communications 4/10/98
Each share Common no par exchanged for (0.25) share Common no par
Pulsepoint Communications merged into Unisys Corp. 8/27/99

DIGITAL SWITCH CORP (DE)
Common 1¢ par split (3) for (1) by issuance of (2) additional shares 05/23/1983
Name changed to DSC Communications Corp. 04/22/1985
DSC Communications Corp. merged into Alcatel 09/04/1998 which name changed to Alcatel-Lucent 11/30/2006
(See Alcatel-Lucent)

DIGITAL SYS INTL INC (WA)
Name changed to Mosaix, Inc. 01/02/1997
Mosaix, Inc. merged into Lucent Technologies Inc. 07/15/1999 which merged into Alcatel-Lucent S.A. 11/30/2006

DIGITAL TECHNOLOGIES MEDIA GROUP INC (DE)
Plan of reorganization under Chapter 11 Federal Bankruptcy Code effective 05/08/2000
Each share Common 5¢ par received (0.0090909) share Central Capital Venture Corp. Common $0.001 par and (0.0090909) Common Stock Purchase Warrant expiring 06/01/2001
Note: Cetificates were not required to be exchanged and are without value
(See Central Capital Venture Corp.)

DIGITAL TECHNOLOGY CORP (NY)
Charter cancelled and proclaimed dissolved for failure to pay taxes 3/25/81

DIGITAL THEATER SYS INC (DE)
Name changed to DTS, Inc. 05/24/2005
(See DTS, Inc.)

DIGITAL TRANSERVICE CORP (DE)
Charter cancelled and declared inoperative and void for non-payment of taxes 3/1/90

DIGITAL TRANSMISSION INC (TX)
Involuntarily dissolved 05/06/1998

DIGITAL TRANSMISSION SYS INC (DE)
SEC revoked common stock registration 09/14/2006

DIGITAL VENTURES INC (BC)
Recapitalized as Castleworth Ventures Inc. 01/04/2002
Each share Common no par exchanged for (0.5) share Common no par
Castleworth Ventures Inc. name changed to Pan-Nevada Gold Corp. 01/20/2006 which merged into Midway Gold Corp. 04/13/2007
(See Midway Gold Corp.)

DIGITAL VIDEO DISPLAY TECHNOLOGY CORP (NV)
Recapitalized as Iconet, Inc. 07/09/2001
Each share Common $0.001 par exchanged for (0.005) share Common $0.001 par
Iconet, Inc. name changed to Anglotajik Minerals, Inc. 09/10/2003 which name changed to Intercontinental Resources, Inc. 05/31/2006 which name changed to China Valves Technology, Inc. 01/09/2008

DIGITAL VILLAGE WORLD TECHNOLOGIES INC (NV)
Name changed to Super Energy Investments Corp. and Common $0.001 par changed to $0.0004 par 09/23/2002
Super Energy Investments Corp. recapitalized as USA Signal Technology, Inc. 04/17/2006 which name changed to Icon Media Holdings, Inc. 06/10/2011

DIGITAL VYS CORP (NV)
Name changed to Circle Star Energy Corp. 07/01/2011

DIGITAL WORLD CUP INC (NV)
Each share old Common $0.001 par exchanged for (0.02) share new Common $0.001 par 07/15/2002
Recapitalized as Magnum D'or Resources Inc. 10/21/2002
Each share new Common $0.001 par exchanged for (0.00333333) share Common $0.001 par
(See Magnum D'or Resources Inc.)

DIGITAL WORLD TR (ON)
Recapitalized as Top 10 Canadian Financial Trust 8/5/2005
Each share Common no par exchanged for (0.2) Trust Unit no par

DIGITAL YEARBOOK INC (NV)
Name changed to Titan Iron Ore Corp. 06/17/2011
Titan Iron Ore Corp. recapitalized as iHookup Social, Inc. 04/29/2014 which name changed to Friendable, Inc. 10/27/2015

DIGITAL YOUTH NETWORK CORP (AB)
SEC revoked common stock registration 06/08/2011

DIGITALE TELEKABEL AG (GERMANY)
Name changed to DTA Holding AG 1/7/2003
(See DTA Holding AG)

DIGITALFX INTL INC (FL)
Name changed to ComF5 International, Inc. 04/01/2010

DIGITALGLOBE INC (DE)
Stock Dividends - in 8.5% Preferred to holders of 8.5% Preferred 2.125% payable 03/31/2003 to holders of record 03/17/2003 Ex date - 03/13/2003; 1.794% payable 06/30/2003 to holders of record 06/15/2003 Ex date - 06/11/2003
Merged into a private company 00/00/2003
Each share 144A 8.5% Conv. Preferred Ser. C $0.001 par exchanged for approximately $2 cash
Each share 8.5% Sr. Conv. Preferred Ser. C $0.001 par exchanged for approximately $2 cash
Each share old Common $0.001 par exchanged for (0.2) share new Common $0.001 par 04/28/2009
Merged into MacDonald, Dettwiler & Associates Ltd. (New) 10/05/2017
Each share new Common $0.001 par exchanged for (0.3132) share Common no par and $17.50 cash
MacDonald, Dettwiler & Associates Ltd. (New) name changed to Maxar Technologies Ltd. 10/10/2017

DIGITALNET HLDGS INC (DE)
Merged into BAE Systems North America, Inc. 10/25/2004
Each share Common $0.001 par exchanged for $30.25 cash

DIGITALPREVIEWS COM INC (NV)
Name changed to IntraOp Medical Corp. 01/22/2004
(See IntraOp Medical Corp.)

DIGITALREACH HLDGS INC (FL)
Name changed to People Dynamics Holdings Inc. 06/10/2003
(See People Dynamics Holdings Inc.)

DIGITALTHINK INC (DE)
Acquired by Convergys Corp. 05/03/2004
Each share Common $0.001 par exchanged for $2.40 cash

DIGITAS INC (DE)
Merged into Publicis Groupe S.A. (New) 01/31/2007
Each share Common 1¢ par exchanged for $13.50 cash

DIGITEC 2000 INC (NV)
SEC revoked common stock registration 09/25/2008

DIGITECH INC (DE)
Charter cancelled and declared inoperative and void for non-payment of taxes 06/27/1989

DIGITECH LTD (AB)
Recapitalized as Colin Energy Corp. 11/17/1987
Each share Common no par exchanged for (0.2) share Common no par
Colin Energy Corp. recapitalized as International Colin Energy Corp. 06/06/1990 which merged into Morgan Hydrocarbons Inc. 07/01/1996 which was acquired by Stampeder Exploration Ltd. 10/15/1996 which was acquired by Gulf Canada Resources Ltd. 09/10/1997
(See Gulf Canada Resources Ltd.)

DIGITEK CORP (CA)
Charter suspended for failure to file reports and pay fees 06/01/1987

FINANCIAL INFORMATION, INC.

DIGITEL LAS VEGAS INC (NV)
Name changed to HYTK Industries Inc. 05/22/1987
HYTK Industries Inc. name changed to Quest Resource Corp. 06/25/2000 which merged into PostRock Energy Corp. 03/05/2010

DIGITEXT INC (DE)
Charter cancelled and declared inoperative and void for non-payment of taxes 3/1/93

DIGITRAN SYS INC (DE)
Recapitalized as TGFIN Holdings, Inc. 09/30/2002
Each share Common 1¢ par exchanged for (0.04761904) share Common 1¢ par
Preferred not affected except for change of name
TGFIN Holdings, Inc. recapitalized as Redify Group, Inc. 02/28/2014

DIGITRONICS CORP (DE)
Class A 10¢ par reclassified as Capital Stock 10¢ par 5/29/59
Name changed to Dialco Corp. 7/17/72
Dialco Corp. merged into North American Philips Corp. 12/31/73
(See North American Philips Corp.)

DIGIWAVE TECHNOLOGIES INC (KOREA)
Name changed to Naraewin Co., Ltd. 08/13/2007
Naraewin Co., Ltd. name changed to G Learning Corp. 09/14/2012
(See G Learning Corp.)

DIGNITY PARTNERS INC (DE)
Name changed to Point West Capital Corp. 08/01/1997
(See Point West Capital Corp.)

DIGS INC (DE)
Name changed to iVideoNow, Inc. (DE) 06/15/2000
iVideoNow, Inc. (DE) reorganized in Florida as 99 Cent Stuff, Inc. 09/15/2003
(See 99 Cent Stuff, Inc.)

DIGSOUND INC (NV)
Recapitalized as Global Wind Corp. 11/14/2008
Each share Common $0.001 par exchanged for (0.002) share Common $0.001 par

DII GROUP INC (DE)
Common 1¢ par split (2) for (1) by issuance of (1) additional share payable 09/02/1997 to holders of record 08/15/1997
Merged into Flextronics International Ltd. 04/03/2000
Each share Common 1¢ par exchanged for (1.61) shares Ordinary SGD $0.01 par
Flextronics International Ltd. name changed to Flex Ltd. 09/28/2016

DIJJI CORP (NV)
Chapter 7 bankruptcy proceedings terminated 01/12/2015
No stockholders' equity

DIKETAN INC (CA)
Each share Common $5 par exchanged for (1) share Common 10¢ par 05/05/1973
Stock Dividend - 10% 02/06/1974
Name changed to Royal American Products Corp. 08/03/1978

DIKETAN LABORATORIES, INC. (CA)
Recapitalized as Diketan Inc. 3/4/70
Each share Common $1 par exchanged for (0.2) share Common $5 par
Diketan Inc. name changed to Royal American Products Corp. 8/3/78

DIKEWOOD FUND, INC. (DE)
Reincorporated under the laws of New Mexico as Edde Fund, Inc. 12/14/1973
(See Edde Fund, Inc.)

DIKOR MINES LTD. (QC)
Dissolved in 1957
No stockholders' equity

DIKROTEK INTL CORP (UT)
Involuntarily dissolved for failure to file annual reports 07/01/1988

DILBERT'S LEASING & DEVELOPMENT CORP. (DE)
Federal Court approved a Plan of Reorganization under Chapter X of the Bankruptcy Act whereby the Court ruled holders of Common Stock have no equity and shall not participate 7/28/64

DILBERT'S QUALITY SUPERMARKETS INC. (NY)
Reorganized 07/02/1965
No stockholders' equity
Stock certificates dated prior to 7/2/65 are without value
Name changed to Pan American Supermarkets Inc. 06/17/1968
(See Pan American Supermarkets Inc.)

DILLARD DEPT STORES INC (DE)
Class A Common $10 par changed to $5 par and (1) additional share issued 03/23/1983
Class A Common $5 par changed to no par 11/17/1983
Class A Common no par split (2) for (1) by issuance of (1) additional share 09/14/1984
Class A Common no par split (2) for (1) by issuance of (1) additional share 12/16/1985
Class A Common no par changed to 1¢ par and (2) additional shares issued 06/05/1992
Name changed to Dillard's Inc. 05/19/1997

DILLINGHAM CORP (HI)
Common no par split (2) for (1) by issuance of (1) additional share 07/31/1967
Common no par split (2) for (1) by issuance of (1) additional share 08/12/1968
$1.35 Conv. Preferred no par called for redemption 03/12/1971
$2 Conv. Preferred March 1968 Ser. no par and $2 Conv. Preferred October 1968 Ser. no par reclassified as $2 Conv. Preferred no par 01/19/1973
$2 Conv. Preferred no par called for redemption 06/12/1981
Under plan of partial liquidation each share Common no par received distribution of (1) Ala Moana Hawaii Properties Depositary Receipt 07/29/1981
Merged into Kohlberg, Kravis, Roberts & Co. 03/18/1983
Each share Common no par exchanged for $25 cash

DILLON (J.S.) & SONS STORES CO., INC. (KS)
Common $5 par changed to $1.25 par and (3) additional shares issued 04/10/1965
Name changed to Dillon Companies, Inc. 10/16/1968
Dillon Companies, Inc. merged into Kroger Co. 01/25/1983

DILLON COS INC (KS)
Common $1.25 par split (3) for (2) by issuance of (0.5) additional share 08/27/1979
Merged into Kroger Co. 01/25/1983
Each share Common $1.25 par exchanged for (0.8539) share Common $1 par

DILLON (LOU) GOLDFIELD MINING CO. (AZ)
Charter expired by time limitation 10/08/1931

DILLY MFG INC (DE)
Stock Dividend - 10% 06/15/1971
Merged into LC 4, Inc. 10/11/1972

Each share Common 5¢ par exchanged for $8.02142 cash

DILMAX CORP (NV)
Name changed to Drug Free Solution Inc. 01/09/2014

DIM INC (NV)
Each share old Common $0.001 par exchanged for (0.1) share new Common $0.001 par 01/14/1991
Name changed to Belize American Corp. Internationale 06/26/1991
Belize American Corp. Internationale name changed to American Energy Group, Ltd. 12/05/1994
(See American Energy Group, Ltd.)

DIMAC CORP (DE)
Merged into Arch Acquisition Corp. 02/21/1996
Each share Common 1¢ par exchanged for $28 cash

DIMAC RES CORP (BC)
Adjudicated bankrupt 01/20/1983
No stockholders' equity

DIMARK INC (NJ)
Common no par split (2) for (1) by issuance of (1) additional share 12/28/1993
Common no par split (5) for (4) by issuance of (0.25) additional share 05/15/1995
Stock Dividends - 10% 01/21/1993; 10% 07/27/1993
Merged into Harte-Hanks Communications, Inc. (New) 04/30/1996
Each share Common no par exchanged for (0.656) share Common $1 par
Harte-Hanks Communications, Inc. (New) name changed to Harte-Hanks, Inc. 05/05/1998

DIME BANCORP INC NEW (DE)
Each share Common 1¢ par received distribution of (1) Litigation Tracking Warrant expiring 00/00/2005 payable 12/29/2000 to holders of record 12/22/2000 Ex date - 01/02/2001
Merged into Washington Mutual, Inc. 01/04/2002
Each share Common 1¢ par exchanged for either (0.9929) share Common no par and $4.07 cash or $35.0884 cash
Note: Option to receive cash expired 01/03/2002
(See Washington Mutual, Inc.)

DIME BANCORP INC OLD (DE)
Merged into Dime Bancorp, Inc. (New) 01/13/1995
Each share Common 1¢ par exchanged for (1) share Common 1¢ par
Dime Bancorp, Inc. (New) merged into Washington Mutual, Inc. 01/04/2002
(See Washington Mutual, Inc.)

DIME BANK (AKRON, OH)
Merged into Akron-Dime Bank (Akron, OH) 11/01/1960
Each share Capital stock exchanged for (1) share Capital Stock
Akron-Dime Bank (Akron, OH) name changed to Akron National Bank & Trust Co. (Akron, OH) 12/01/1966 which name changed to Akron National Bank (Akron, OH) 02/01/1977
(See Akron National Bank (Akron, OH))

DIME BK (CANTON, OH)
Reorganized as Great Lakes Bancshares, Inc. 10/01/1974
Each share Capital Stock $10 par exchanged for (1.6) shares Common 10¢ par
(See Great Lakes Bancshares, Inc.)

DIME BANK SECURITIES CO. (DE)
Liquidated 09/26/1956
Details not available

DIME CMNTY BANCORP INC (DE)
Name changed to Dime Community Bancshares, Inc. 06/12/1998

DIME FDG CORP I (DE)
Dutch Auction Rate Transferable Securities Preferred no par called for redemption 12/02/1988

DIME FINL CORP (CT)
Merged into HUBCO, Inc. 08/21/1998
Each share Common $1 par exchanged for (1.0815) shares Common no par
HUBCO, Inc. name changed to Hudson United Bancorp 04/21/1999 which merged into TD Banknorth Inc. 01/31/2006
(See TD Banknorth Inc.)

DIME FINL CORP (PA)
Name changed to Chester County Bancshares Inc. 03/31/1990
Chester County Bancshares Inc. merged into State Bancshares, Inc. 03/29/1994 which name changed to JeffBanks, Inc. 05/22/1995 which merged into Hudson United Bancorp 11/30/1999 which merged into TD Banknorth Inc. 01/31/2006
(See TD Banknorth Inc.)

DIME SVGS BK (WALLINGFORD, CT)
Under plan of reorganization each share Common $1 par automatically became (1) share Dime Financial Corp. (CT) Common $1 par 12/02/1988
Dime Financial Corp. (CT) merged into HUBCO, Inc. 08/21/1998 which name changed to Hudson United Bancorp 04/21/1999 which merged into TD Banknorth Inc. 01/31/2006
(See TD Banknorth Inc.)

DIME SAVINGS BANK (WASHINGTON, DC)
Name changed to Bank of Commerce & Savings (Washington, DC) 02/24/1911
Bank of Commerce & Savings (Washington, DC) name changed to Bank of Commerce (Washington, DC) 03/01/1955 which merged into National Savings & Trust Co. (Washington, DC) 09/09/1966 which reorganized in Delaware as NS&T Bankshares, Inc. 11/16/1982
(See NS&T Bankshares, Inc.)

DIME SAVINGS BANK CO. (AKRON, OH)
Each share Capital Stock $100 par exchanged for (5) shares Capital Stock $20 par 00/00/1944
Stock Dividends - 15% 01/11/1945; 50% 01/02/1946
Name changed to Dime Bank (Akron, OH) 11/08/1951
Dime Bank (Akron, OH) merged into Akron-Dime Bank (Akron, OH) 11/01/1960 which name changed to Akron National Bank & Trust Co. (Akron, OH) 12/01/1966 which name changed to Akron National Bank (Akron, OH) 02/01/1977
(See Akron National Bank (Akron, OH))

DIME SVGS BK N Y FSB (NEW YORK, NY)
Under plan of reorganization each share Common $1 par automatically became (1) share Dime Bancorp, Inc. (Old) Common 1¢ par 05/25/1994
Each share 10.50% Exchangeable Preferred $1 par exchanged for $1,000 principal amount of 10-1/2% Sr. Notes due 11/15/2005 on 12/16/1994
Dime Bancorp, Inc. (Old) merged into Dime Bancorp, Inc. (New) 01/13/1995 which merged into Washington Mutual, Inc. 01/04/2002
(See Washington Mutual, Inc.)

DIMEDIX INC (UT)
Plan of dissolution and liquidation effective 02/29/1996
Stockholders' equity unlikely

DIMENSION BUSINESS SERVICE, INC. (UT)
Name changed to Triple O Seven Corp. 12/00/1986
Triple O Seven Corp. name changed to Supervision Entertainment Inc. 04/01/2003 which name changed to BioNeutra International, Ltd. 11/04/2013

DIMENSION DATA HLDGS LTD (SOUTH AFRICA)
Stock Dividend - 1.09% payable 12/01/1999 to holders of record 11/19/1999
Merged into Dimension Data Holdings PLC 10/30/2000
Each 144A GDR for Ordinary exchanged for approximately $25 cash
Each Reg. S GDR for Ordinary exchanged for approximately $25 cash

DIMENSION HOUSE INTL INC (BC)
Name changed to PII Photovision International, Inc. 09/04/1990
(See PII Photovision International, Inc.)

DIMENSION HSE INC (NV)
Common $0.001 par split (8) for (1) by issuance of (7) additional shares payable 01/05/1999 to holders of record 01/01/1999
Name changed to Presidents Telecom Inc. 10/28/1999
Presidents Telecom Inc. name changed to VoIP Telecom Inc. 04/19/2000 which name changed to Diversified Thermal Solutions Inc. 07/01/2002
(See Diversified Thermal Solutions Inc.)

DIMENSION LABS INC (UT)
Name changed 06/29/1989
Name changed from Dimension Industries, Inc. to Dimension Laboratories, Inc. 06/29/1989
Involuntarily dissolved 11/01/1992

DIMENSION OIL & GAS INC (UT)
Each share Common 1¢ par exchanged for (0.1) share Common 10¢ par 10/16/1972
Recapitalized as Dimension Industries, Inc. 11/09/1981
Each share Common 10¢ par exchanged for (0.00666666) share Common no par
Dimension Industries, Inc. name changed to Dimension Laboratories, Inc. 06/29/1989
(See Dimension Laboratories, Inc.)

DIMENSION THERAPEUTICS INC (DE)
Acquired by Ultragenyx Pharmaceutical Inc. 11/07/2017
Each share Common $0.0001 par exchanged for $6 cash

DIMENSIONAL COMMUNICATIONS CORP (PA)
Name changed to Diversified Marketing Group, Inc. 07/29/1974
Diversified Marketing Group, Inc. merged into Magic Marker Corp. (NY) 11/15/1979 which reincorporated in Delaware 09/00/1975
(See Magic Marker Corp. (DE))

DIMENSIONAL ENTMT CORP (FL)
Proclaimed dissolved for failure to file reports and pay fees 12/01/1977

DIMENSIONAL MEDICINE INC (MN)
Merged into Dynamic Healthcare Technologies Inc. 05/01/1996
Each share Common 15¢ par exchanged for $0.04 cash

DIMENSIONAL TEC INC (MN)
Statutorily dissolved 12/30/1994

DIMENSIONAL VISIONS INC (DE)
Recapitalized 01/15/1998
Recapitalized from Dimensional Visions Group Ltd. to Dimensional Visions Inc. 01/15/1998
Each share Common $0.001 par exchanged for (0.04) share old Common $0.001 par
Each share old Common $0.001 par exchanged for (0.01666666) share new Common $0.001 par 05/18/2004
Name changed to Studio One Media, Inc. 04/19/2006
Studio One Media, Inc. name changed to AfterMaster, Inc. 10/14/2015

DIMENSIONS WEST MARKETING INC (BC)
Name changed to Dimensions West Energy Inc. 11/14/1997

DIMETHAID RESH INC (ON)
Name changed to Nuvo Research Inc. 10/31/2005
Nuvo Research Inc. name changed to Nuvo Pharmaceuticals Inc. 03/07/2016

DIMGROUP COM INC (IN)
Name changed to Datastand Technologies Inc. 04/06/2001
Datastand Technologies Inc. name changed to Metabolic Research, Inc. 02/16/2007

DIMI TELEMATICS INTL INC (NV)
Old Common $0.001 par split (2) for (1) by issuance of (1) additional share payable 04/17/2012 to holders of record 04/16/2012 Ex date - 04/18/2012
Old Common $0.001 par split (2) for (1) by issuance of (1) additional share payable 05/17/2012 to holders of record 05/16/2012 Ex date - 05/18/2012
Each share old Common $0.001 par exchanged for (0.01) share new Common $0.001 par 02/24/2014
Each share new Common $0.001 par exchanged again for (0.33333333) share new Common $0.001 par 12/01/2015
Name changed to Bespoke Extracts, Inc. 03/10/2017

DIMIS INC (DE)
Charter cancelled and declared inoperative and void for non-payment of taxes 03/01/1989

DIMITRA DEVS CORP (BC)
Name changed to Jeda Petroleum Ltd. 08/22/1996
Jeda Petroleum Ltd. merged into Roseland Resources Ltd. 02/29/2000 which merged into Rival Energy Ltd. 06/16/2003 which merged into Zargon Energy Trust 01/23/2008 which reorganized as Zargon Oil & Gas Ltd. (New) 01/07/2011

DIMODE INDS INC (DE)
Charter cancelled and declared inoperative and void for non-payment of taxes 04/15/1972

DIMON INC (VA)
Under plan of merger name changed to Alliance One International, Inc. 05/13/2005
Alliance One International, Inc. name changed to Pyxus International, Inc. 09/12/2018

DIMPLES GROUP INC (BC)
Delisted from Vancouver Stock Exchange 03/06/1995

DIMUS PARTNERS INC (NV)
Name changed to China Xibolun Technology Holdings Corp. Inc. 11/29/2012
China Xibolun Technology Holdings Corp. Inc. name changed to Borneo Industrial Fishery Corp. 07/30/2015 which name changed to Shenzhen Yidian Double Way of Innovation Culture Media Corp. 04/26/2017

DINAMO CORP (NV)
Name changed to Oriental Magic Soup, Inc. 03/23/2015

DINEEQUITY INC (DE)
Name changed to Dine Brands Global, Inc. 03/01/2018

DINELLO RESTAURANT VENTURES INC (FL)
Name changed to AF Ocean Investment Management Co. 11/23/2011

DINERS ACQUISITION CORP (NV)
Recapitalized as LaSalle Brands Corp. 07/10/2007
Each share Common $0.001 par exchanged for (0.05) share Common $0.001 par
(See LaSalle Brands Corp.)

DINERS CLUB INC (NY)
Common $1 par split (2) for (1) by issuance of (1) additional share 12/16/1957
Merged into Continental Corp. (NY) 11/14/1975
Each share Common $1 par exchanged for $1 cash

DING-HOW MINES LTD. (ON)
Name changed to Eramosa Technology Corp. 04/30/1982
(See Eramosa Technology Corp.)

DINGMAN INDS INC (CANADA)
Struck off register and declared dissolved for failure to file returns 12/13/2004

DINGYI GROUP INVESTMENT LTD (BERMUDA)
ADR agreement terminated 02/12/2015
No ADR's remain outstanding

DINI PRODS INC (NV)
Recapitalized as ANV Security Group, Inc. 07/16/2009
Each share Common $0.0001 par exchanged for (0.01497005) share Common $0.005 par

DINNER BELL FOODS INC (OH)
Common no par split (2) for (1) by issuance of (1) additional share 05/28/1971
Common no par split (2) for (1) by issuance of (1) additional share 11/27/1978
Merged into BJF Group 06/03/1988
Each share Common no par exchanged for $26.50 cash

DINO MINICHIELLO FASHIONS INC (NV)
Name changed to Resort World Enterprises, Inc. 06/15/1998
Resort World Enterprises, Inc. name changed to Remedent USA, Inc. 10/22/1998 which recapitalized as Remedent, Inc. 06/06/2005

DINOSAUR CAVERNS INC (AZ)
Administratively dissolved 07/06/2004

DINOSAUR ENERGY LTD (AB)
Name changed to Battery & Wireless Solutions Inc. 12/23/1996

DINOSAURUS INC (DE)
Each share old Common $0.001 par exchanged for (0.4) share new Common $0.001 par 10/27/1997
Each share new Common $0.001 par exchanged again for (0.005) share new Common $0.001 par 05/16/2006
Reorganized under the laws of Nevada as Ethanoil & Gas Corp. 09/27/2006
Each share new Common $0.001 par exchanged for (4) shares Common $0.001 par
Ethanoil & Gas Corp. reorganized as Sympowerco Corp. 01/18/2008

DINOZINE VENTURES INC (NV)
Name changed to Zamage Digital Art Imaging, Inc. 04/05/2004

DIODES INC (CA)
Stock Dividend - 200% 08/25/1967
Reincorporated under the laws of Delaware and Capital Stock $0.66666666 par reclassified as Common $0.66666666 par 02/01/1969

DIOGENES SYS INC (CA)
Charter suspended 02/03/1992

DIOMED HLDGS INC (NV)
Reincorporated 05/13/2002
State of incorporation changed from (NV) to (DE) 05/13/2002
Each share old Common $0.001 par exchanged for (0.04) share new Common $0.001 par 06/17/2004
Plan of reorganization under Chapter 11 Federal Bankruptcy proceedings effective 12/24/2008
No stockholders' equity

DION ENTMT CORP (CANADA)
Each share old Common no par exchanged for (0.1) share new Common no par 03/25/1993
Petitioned into bankruptcy 11/05/2003
Stockholders' equity unlikely

DION KENNETH SCOTTSDALE INC (UT)
Reorganized under the laws of Delaware as Select Housing Associates, Inc. 02/02/1990
Each share Common $0.001 par exchanged for (0.1) share Common $0.001 par

DIONEX CORP (DE)
Reincorporated 12/26/1986
State of incorporation changed from (CA) to (DE) and Common no par changed to $0.001 par 12/26/1986
Common $0.001 par split (2) for (1) by issuance of (1) additional share 12/30/1986
Common $0.001 par split (2) for (1) by issuance of (1) additional share 12/29/1995
Common $0.001 par split (2) for (1) by issuance of (1) additional share payable 06/05/1998 to holders of record 05/13/1998
Acquired by Thermo Fisher Scientific Inc. 05/17/2011
Each share Common $0.001 par exchanged for $118.50 cash

DIORO EXPL N L (AUSTRALIA)
ADR agreement terminated 12/05/2007
Each ADR for Ordinary exchanged for $0.101011 cash
Acquired by Avoca Resources Ltd. 03/03/2010
Each share Ordinary exchanged for (0.325) share Ordinary and AUD $0.65 cash

DIOTRON, INC. (PA)
Adjudicated bankrupt 12/31/1962
No stockholders' equity

DIPEXIUM PHARMACEUTICALS INC (DE)
Recapitalized as PLx Pharma Inc. 04/20/2017
Each share Common $0.001 par exchanged for (0.125) share Common $0.001 par

DIPLOMAT DIRECT MARKETING CORP (DE)
Name changed 05/29/1998
Name changed from Diplomat Corp. to Diplomat Direct Marketing Corp. 05/29/1998
Name changed to Stylesite Marketing, Inc. 08/24/1999
(See Stylesite Marketing, Inc.)

DIPLOMAT ELECTRS CORP (NY)
Ctfs. dated prior to 04/29/1980
Stock Dividends - 20% 12/18/1973; 10% 10/07/1976; 10% 07/05/1978; 10% 07/10/1979
Merged into R&C Holding Corp. 04/29/1980
Each share Common 10¢ par exchanged for $8.08 cash

DIPLOMAT ELECTRS CORP NEW (NY)
Ctfs. dated after 03/29/1984
Dissolved by proclamation 12/24/1991

DIPLOMAT INDS CORP (DE)
Charter cancelled and declared inoperative and void for non-payment of taxes 03/01/1979

DIPLOMAT NATIONAL BANK (WASHINGTON, DC)
Name changed to Washington Bank, N.A. (Washington, DC) 04/25/1981
Washington Bank, N.A. (Washington, DC) merged into Security National Bank (Washington, DC) 01/01/1982 which reorganized as Security National Corp. (DE) 06/01/1982
(See Security National Corp. (DE))

DIPLOMAT RES INC (BC)
Recapitalized as Sway Resources Inc. 06/26/1991
Each share Common no par exchanged for (0.25) share Common no par
Sway Resources Inc. name changed to Orion International Minerals Corp. 01/26/1996 which recapitalized as Laurier Resources, Inc. 05/04/1998 which name changed to Zarcan International Resources Inc. 11/08/1999 which name changed to Bighorn Petroleum Ltd. 01/30/2006 which recapitalized as Sunset Pacific Petroleum Ltd. 05/07/2009

DIPPY FOODS INC (NV)
Charter revoked for failure to file reports and pay fees 02/28/2005

DIRECT ACTION MARKETING INC (NY)
Merged into Meadow Group, Inc. 10/06/1989
Each share Common 1¢ par exchanged for (17) shares Common $0.001 par and $4.70 cash
(See Meadow Group, Inc.)

DIRECT CHOICE T V INC (BC)
Reincorporated under the laws of Canada as Star Choice Communications Inc. 12/11/1996
Star Choice Communications Inc. merged into Canadian Satellite Communications 08/31/1999 which was acquired by Shaw Communications Inc. 04/02/2001

DIRECT COATING INC (NV)
Charter revoked for failure to file reports and pay taxes 07/29/2011

DIRECT CONNECT INTL HLDGS INC (DE)
Charter cancelled and declared inoperative and void for non-payment of taxes 03/01/2002

DIRECT CONNECT INTL INC (DE)
Name changed to Direct Connect International Holdings, Inc. 08/31/2000
(See Direct Connect International Holdings, Inc.)

DIRECT CONTROL VALVE CO.
Bankrupt 00/00/1932
Stockholders' equity unlikely

DIRECT DELIVERY SERVICE, INC. (DE)
Charter cancelled and declared inoperative and void for non-payment of taxes 03/01/1993

DIRECT DRIVE MOTOR CO. (DE)
Charter cancelled for non-payment of taxes 00/00/1922

DIRECT ENERGY (ON)
Completely liquidated 08/28/2000
Each Trust Unit received first and final distribution of $28 cash

DIRECT EQUITY CORP (ON)
Merged into Envirothermic Technologies Ltd. 10/01/1993
Each share Common no par exchanged for (0.5) share Common no par
Envirothermic Technologies Ltd. recapitalized as Environmental Reclamation Inc. 06/22/1998 which was acquired by Therma Freeze Inc. 02/28/2001 which name changed to Enviro-Energy Corp. 07/03/2001
(See Enviro-Energy Corp.)

DIRECT FOCUS INC (WA)
Common no par split (3) for (2) by issuance of (0.5) additional share payable 08/14/2000 to holders of record 07/31/2000
Common no par split (3) for (2) by issuance of (0.5) additional share payable 01/15/2001 to holders of record 01/02/2001 Ex date - 01/16/2001
Common no par split (3) for (2) by issuance of (0.5) additional share payable 08/13/2001 to holders of record 08/02/2001 Ex date - 08/14/2001
Name changed to Nautilus Group, Inc. 05/21/2002
Nautilus Group, Inc. name changed to Nautilus, Inc. 03/14/2005

DIRECT GEN CORP (TN)
Merged into Elara Holdings, Inc. 03/30/2007
Each share Common no par exchanged for $21.25 cash

DIRECT HIT TECHNOLOGIES INC (DE)
Merged into Ask Jeeves, Inc. 02/03/2000
Each share Common exchanged for (0.2279001) share Common $0.001 par
Ask Jeeves, Inc. merged into IAC/InterActiveCorp 07/19/2005

DIRECT INSITE CORP (DE)
Each share old Common $0.0001 par exchanged for (0.06666666) share new Common $0.0001 par 05/08/2001
Name changed to Paybox Corp. 11/14/2016
(See Paybox Corp.)

DIRECT IT CDA INC (ON)
Reincorporated 11/25/2002
Place of incorporation changed from (AB) to (ON) 11/25/2002
Recapitalized as Rage Energy Ltd. 08/29/2006
Each share Common no par exchanged for (0.5) share Common no par
(See Rage Energy Ltd.)

DIRECT LABS INC (NY)
Acquired by Mogul Corp. 03/10/1969
Details not available

DIRECT MKTS HLDGS CORP (DE)
Filed a petition under Chapter 7 Federal Bankruptcy Code 01/11/2013
Stockholders' equity unlikely

DIRECT MUSIC GROUP INC (NV)
Name changed to Cell Bio-Systems, Inc. 04/14/2004
Cell Bio-Systems, Inc. name changed to Tulip BioMed, Inc. (NV) 06/02/2006 which reorganized in Florida as Bitcoin Services, Inc. 03/21/2016

DIRECT PET HEALTH HLDGS INC (NV)
Recapitalized as Core Resource Management, Inc. 11/13/2012
Each share Common $0.001 par exchanged for (0.005) share Common $0.001 par

DIRECT PHARMACEUTICAL CORP (DE)
Charter cancelled and declared inoperative and void for non-payment of taxes 03/01/1995

DIRECT RESPONSE FINL SVCS INC (CO)
Recapitalized as Sleeping with the Enemy Inc. 08/17/2007
Each share Common no par exchanged for (0.01) share Common no par
Sleeping with the Enemy Inc. name changed to Healthy Coffee International, Inc. 12/13/2007

DIRECT SALES CO. (NY)
Name changed to Direct Laboratories, Inc. 00/00/1950
(See Direct Laboratories, Inc.)

DIRECT III MARKETING INC (DE)
Name changed to Education Lending Group, Inc. 05/21/2002
(See Education Lending Group, Inc.)

DIRECT WEST INC (NV)
Name changed to Frontier Oil Exploration Co. 09/00/1993
Frontier Oil Exploration Co. name changed to FX Energy Inc. 07/23/1996
(See FX Energy, Inc.)

DIRECT-WINTERS TRANSPORT LTD. (DE)
Acquired by Brink's Express Co. of Canada, Ltd. 02/23/1965
Details not available

DIRECT WIRELESS COMMUNICATIONS INC (TX)
Name changed to Health Discovery Corp. (TX) 11/06/2003
Health Discovery Corp. (TX) reincorporated in Georgia 07/12/2007

DIRECTCASH INCOME FD (AB)
Reorganized as DirectCash Payments Inc. 01/07/2011
Each Trust Unit exchanged for (1) share Common no par
Note: Unexchanged certificates were cancelled and became without value 01/07/2017
(See DirectCash Payments Inc.)

DIRECTCASH PMTS INC (AB)
Acquired by Cardtronics Holdings Ltd. 01/09/2017
Each share Common no par exchanged for $19 cash
Note: Unexchanged certificates will be cancelled and become without value 01/09/2020

DIRECTCOM INC (DE)
SEC revoked common stock registration 08/19/2011

DIRECTED ELECTRONICS INC (FL)
Name changed to DEI Holdings, Inc. 06/20/2008
(See DEI Holdings, Inc.)

DIRECTION TECHNOLOGIES INC (NV)
Name changed to Empyrean Communications, Inc. 04/23/2001
Empyrean Communications, Inc. name changed to Empyrean Holdings, Inc. 01/25/2005 which name changed to American Asset Development, Inc. 11/02/2010
(See American Asset Development, Inc.)

DIRECTOMAT INC (DE)
Adjudicated bankrupt 01/19/1970
No stockholders' equity

DIRECTORS CAP INC (DE)
Name changed 04/28/1980
Name changed from Directors Capital Fund, Inc. to Directors Capital Inc. 04/28/1980
Charter cancelled and declared inoperative and void for non-payment of taxes 03/01/1986

DIRECTORS DIVERSIFIED INDS (CA)
Common $4 par changed to $2 par and (1) additional share issued 07/31/1981
Merged into Careamerica Health Plans, Inc. 02/05/1987
Details not available

DIRECTPLACEMENT INC (DE)
Name changed to PCS Research Technology, Inc. 10/07/2002
PCS Research Technology, Inc. name changed to Sagient Research Systems, Inc. 05/20/2004
(See Sagient Research Systems, Inc.)

DIRECTRIX INC (DE)
Plan of reorganization under Chapter 11 Federal Bankruptcy code effective 01/15/2004
No stockholders' equity

DIRECTV (DE)
Each share Class A Common 1¢ par exchanged for (1) share Common 1¢ par 08/28/2012
Merged into AT&T Inc. 07/24/2015
Each share Common 1¢ par exchanged for (1.892) shares Common $1 par and $28.50 cash

DIRECTV GROUP INC (DE)
Merged into DIRECTV 11/20/2009
Each share Common 1¢ par exchanged for (1) share Class A Common 1¢ par
DIRECTV merged into AT&T Inc. 07/24/2015

DIRECTVIEW HLDGS INC (DE)
Old Common $0.001 par split (9) for (1) by issuance of (8) additional shares payable 11/15/2010 to holders of record 11/09/2010 Ex date - 11/16/2010
Reincorporated under the laws of Nevada and Common $0.001 par changed to $0.0001 par 06/24/2014

DIRECTVIEW INC (NV)
Reorganized under the laws of Delaware as GS Carbon Corp. 12/08/2006
Each share Common $0.0001 par exchanged for (0.004) share Common $0.0001 par
GS Carbon Corp. name changed to Seaway Valley Capital Corp. 08/17/2007

DIRECTVIEW TECHNOLOGY GROUP INC (FL)
Name changed to Green Bridge Technologies International, Inc. 08/25/2009
Green Bridge Technologies International, Inc. recapitalized as Paradise Ridge Hydrocarbons, Inc. 08/20/2012 which name changed to Grupo Resilient International, Inc. 08/10/2017

DIREKT-FORM CORP. (NJ)
Common 10¢ par exchanged for (0.025) share Common 1¢ par 06/24/1960
Charter voided for non-payment of taxes 02/05/1962

DIREXION SHS ETF TR (DE)
Trust terminated 12/07/2010
Each Daily 2 Year Treasury Bear 3x Share no par received $38.02065 cash
Each Daily 2 Year Treasury Bull 3x Share no par received $41.3603 cash
Trust terminated 10/17/2011
Each Airline Share no par received $25.43 cash
Daily BRIC Bear 2X Shares no par reclassified as Daily BRIC Bear 3X Shares no par 12/01/2011
Daily BRIC Bull 2X Shares no par reclassified as Daily BRIC Bull 3X Shares no par 12/01/2011

Daily India Bear 2X Shares no par reclassified as Daily India Bear 3X Shares no par 12/01/2011
Daily Natural Gas Related Bear 2X Shares no par reclassified as Daily Natural Gas Related Bear 3X Shares no par 12/01/2011
Daily Retail Bear 2X Shares no par reclassified as Daily Retail Bear 3X Shares no par 12/01/2011
S&P 500 Volatility Response Shares no par reclassified as S&P 500 DRRC Index Volatility Response Shares no par 06/15/2012
S&P 1500 Volatility Response Shares no par reclassified as S&P 1500 DRRC Index Volatility Response Shares no par 06/15/2012
S&P Latin America 40 Volatility Response Shares no par reclassified as S&P Latin America 40 DRRC Index Volatility Response Shares no par 06/15/2012
Trust terminated 09/05/2012
Each Daily Agribusiness Bear 3X Share no par received $22.07013 cash
Each Daily Agribusiness Bull 3X Share no par received $24.29916 cash
Each Daily Basic Materials Bear 3X Share no par received $24.60712 cash
Each Daily BRIC Bear 3X Share no par received $28.09432 cash
Each Daily BRIC Bull 3X Share no par received $18.72968 cash
Each Daily Healthcare Bear 3X Share no par received $20.09281 cash
Each Daily India Bear 3X Share no par received $27.1724 cash
Each Daily Latin America Bear 3X Share no par received $14.2102 cash
Each Daily Retail Bear 3X Share no par received $9.19762 cash
Trust terminated 01/25/2013
Each Large Cap Insider Sentiment Share no par received $43.2475 cash
Each S&P 1500 DRRC Index Volatility Response Share no par received $44.62903 cash
Each S&P Latin America 40 DRRC Index Volatility Response Share no par received $40.65844 cash
Each old Daily Natural Gas Related Bear 3X Share no par automatically became (0.25) new Daily Natural Gas Related Bear 3X Share no par 08/20/2013
S&P 500 DRRC Index Volatility Response Shares no par reclassified as S&P 500 Volatility Response Shares no par 08/01/2014
Trust terminated 09/29/2014
Each Daily Brazil Bear 3X Share no par received $32.05259 cash
Each FTSE Europe Bear 3X Share no par received $38.35466 cash
Each Daily Japan Bear 3X Share no par received $24.75005 cash
Each new Daily Natural Gas Related Bear 3X Share no par received $23.35591 cash
Each Daily South Korea Bear 3X Share no par received $23.44218 cash
Each old Daily Mid Cap Bull 2X Share no par automatically became (0.33333333) new Daily Mid Cap Bull 2X Share no par 11/18/2014
Each old Daily 7-10 Year Treasury Bull 2X Share no par automatically became (0.5) new Daily 7-10 Year Treasury Bull 2X Share no par 11/18/2014
New Daily Mid Cap Bull 2X Shares no par split (4) for (1) by issuance of (3) additional shares payable 05/19/2015 to holders of record 05/18/2015 Ex date - 05/20/2015
New Daily 7-10 Year Treasury Bull 2X

Shares no par split (2) for (1) by issuance of (1) additional share payable 05/19/2015 to holders of record 05/18/2015 Ex date - 05/20/2015
Daily Cyber Security Bull 2X Shares no par reclassified as Daily Cyber Security & IT Bull 2X Shares no par 03/08/2016
Trust terminated 05/27/2016
Each Daily Currency Hedged MSCI Europe Bull 2X Share no par received $31.09741 cash
Each Daily Currency Hedged MSCI Japan Bull 2X Share no par received $23.02804 cash
Trust terminated 10/27/2015
Each Daily Basic Materials Bull 3X Share no par received $42.97439 cash
Each new Daily Mid Cap Bull 2X Share no par received $30.79737 cash
Each new Daily 7-10 Year Treasury Bull 2X Share no par received $45.32112 cash
Daily Cyber Security Bear 2X Shares no reclassified as Daily Cyber Security & IT Bear 2X Shares no par 03/08/2016
Trust terminated 03/30/2016
Each share Value Line Conservative Equity ETF received $25.76852 cash
Each share Value Line Mid- and Large-Cap High Dividend ETF received $23.54268 cash
Each share Value Line Small- and Mid-Cap High Dividend ETF received $22.08123 cash
Trust terminated 07/22/2016
Each Daily Total Market Bear 1X Share received $17.53752 cash
Trust terminated 10/14/2016
Each Daily FTSE Developed Markets Bull 1.25X Share received $26.10076 cash
Each Daily FTSE Emerging Markets Bull 1.25X Share received $24.78472 cash
Each S&P 500 Volatility Response Share received $54.93867 cash
Trust terminated 04/07/2017
Each Daily Cyber Security & IT Bear 2X Shares no par received $22.54301 cash
Each Daily Pharmaceutical & Medical Bear 2X Share no par received $44.08728 cash
Each Daily Pharmaceutical & Medical Bull 2X Share no par received $23.89446 cash
Trust terminated 10/02/2017
Each Daily Consumer Staples Bear 1X Daily Consumer Staples Bear 1X Share received $23.50964 cash
Each Daily Cyber Security & IT Bull 2X Share received $48.61068 cash
Each Daily Energy Bear 1X Share received $20.61053 cash
Each Daily European Financials Bear 1X Share received $16.72359 cash
Each Daily Financial Bear 1X Share received $16.8241 cash
Each Daily Gold Miners Index Bear 1X Share received $24.51316 cash
Each Daily Healthcare Bear 3X Share received $20.65263 cash
Each Daily Homebuilders & Supplies Bear 3X Share received $13.51142 cash
Each Daily S&P Biotech Bear 1X Share received $25.82597 cash
Each Daily Silver Miners Index Bear 2X Share received $27.85668 cash
Each Daily Technology Bear 1X Share received $18.36565 cash
Each Daily Utilities Bear 1X Share received $22.07203 cash
Trust terminated 04/13/2018
Each share iBillionaire Index ETF no par received $32.62033 cash
Portfolio+ Total Bond Market ETF no par reclassified as PortfolioPlus

Total Bond Market ETF no par 06/28/2018
Trust terminated 10/01/2018
Each share Direxion Daily Emerging Markets Bond Bull 3X Shares received $20.93307 cash
Each share Direxion Daily Silver Miners Index Bull 2X Shares received $4.97657 cash
Each share PortfolioPlus Total Bond Markets ETF received $24.84006 cash
(Additional Information in Active)

DIREXION SHS ETF TR II (DE)
Trust terminated 12/30/2014
Each Daily Gold Bear 3X Share no par received $47.55125 cash
Note: An additional $0.00247 cash per Share was distributed 04/30/2015
Trust terminated 06/26/2015
Each Daily Gold Bull 3X Share no par received $27.22956 cash

DIRIGO BANK & TRUST CO. (AUGUSTA, ME)
Each share Capital Stock $15 par exchanged for (2) shares Capital Stock $5 par 07/01/1980
Merged into Bank of New England Corp. 12/05/1986
Each share Capital Stock $5 par exchanged for (1.48) shares Common $5 par
(See Bank of New England Corp.)

DIRT MTR SPORTS INC (DE)
Name changed to World Racing Group, Inc. 01/31/2008

DISABILITY ACCESS CORP (DE)
Reorganized under the laws of Nevada 11/30/2006
Each share Common $0.001 par exchanged for (10) shares Common $0.001 par
(See Disability Access Corp. (NV))

DISABILITY ACCESS CORP (NV)
SEC revoked common stock registration 07/16/2014

DISABOOM INC (CO)
Recapitalized as Cantor Group Inc. (CO) 09/09/2015
Each share Common $0.0001 par exchanged for (0.004) share Common $0.0001 par
Cantor Group Inc. (CO) reincorporated in Wyoming as MedX Holdings, Inc. 02/18/2016

DISANI CAP CORP (CANADA)
Reorganized under the laws of British Columbia as NeutriSci International Inc. 12/04/2014
Each share Common no par exchanged for (0.33333333) share Common no par

DISASTER PREPAREDNESS SYS INC (NV)
Charter revoked for failure to file reports and pay fees 12/01/2008

DISBRO EQUITY-LEASING CORP (OH)
Name changed 01/28/1969
Name changed from Disbro & Co. to Disbro Equity-Leasing Corp. 01/28/1969
Charter cancelled for failure to pay taxes 12/15/1987

DISC GRAPHICS INC (DE)
Merged into DG Acquisition Corp. 12/31/2002
Each share Common 1¢ par exchanged for $1.82 cash

DISC INC (CA)
Company terminated common stock registration and is no longer public as of 08/12/2003

DISC INC (DC)
Merged into Disc Inc. of America 04/09/1983
Each share 80¢ Conv. Preferred $1 par exchanged for either (1) share

Common $1 and $3 cash or $7.50 cash
Note: Option to receive cash only expired 05/09/1973
Each share Class A Common $1 par automatically became (1) share Common $1 par
Disc Inc. of America recapitalized as Dominion Holdings, Inc. 09/03/1974 which name changed to Brenner International, Inc. 09/30/1985
(See Brenner International, Inc.)

DISC INC AMER (DE)
Recapitalized as Dominion Holdings, Inc. 09/03/1974
Each share Common $1 par exchanged for (0.33333333) share Common $1 par
Note: Holders of (100) shares or fewer had the option to exchange each share for $1.38 cash. Option expired 12/05/1974
Dominion Holdings, Inc. name changed to Brenner International, Inc. 09/30/1985
(See Brenner International, Inc.)

DISC-TAPE LIQUIDATING CORP. (TX)
Completely liquidated 01/31/1980
Each share Common 2¢ par exchanged for first and final distribution of $0.16 cash

DISC TECHNOLOGY CORP (DE)
Chapter 11 Federal Bankruptcy Code converted to Chapter 7 on 10/25/1988
Stockholders' equity unlikely

DISCAS INC (DE)
Recapitalized as China SNX Organic Fertilizers Co. 03/03/2008
Each share Common $0.0001 par exchanged for (0.02222222) share Common $0.0001 par

DISCFACTORIES CORP (CANADA)
Name changed to Excalibur Resources Ltd. 02/20/2007
Excalibur Resources Ltd. recapitalized as Metalla Royalty & Streaming Ltd. (Canada) 12/07/2016 which reincorporated in British Columbia 11/16/2017

DISCO INDUSTRIES, INC. (DE)
No longer in existence having become inoperative and void for non-payment of taxes 04/01/1956

DISCO S A (ARGENTINA)
ADR agreement terminated 01/08/2000
Each Sponsored ADR for Ordinary exchanged for $21 cash

DISCOM INC (AZ)
Completely liquidated 12/31/1972
No stockholders' equity

DISCON CORP (FL)
Adjudicated bankrupt 10/12/1972
No stockholders' equity

DISCOUNT AUTO PTS INC (FL)
Acquired by Advance Auto Parts, Inc. 11/28/2001
Each share Common 1¢ par exchanged for (0.2577) share Common $0.0001 par and $7.50 cash

DISCOUNT CORP. OF CALIFORNIA
Company liquidated and charter forfeited 00/00/1943

DISCOUNT CORP NEW YORK (DE)
Merged into Zions Bancorporation 08/11/1993
Each share Common 25¢ par exchanged for initial distribution of $7 cash
Each share Common 25¢ par received second and final distribution of $1.004919 cash 10/26/1993

DISCOUNT CORP NEW YORK (NY)
Each share Capital Stock $100 par exchanged for (1) share Capital

Stock $40 par and $120 cash 00/00/1940
Capital Stock $40 par changed to $8 par and (4) additional shares issued 05/22/1968
Capital Stock $8 par changed to $4 par and (1) additional share issued 05/27/1971
Capital Stock $4 par changed to $2 par and (1) additional share issued 06/04/1980
Reorganized under the laws of Delaware as DCNY Corp. 06/15/1983
Each share Capital Stock $2 par exchanged for (2) shares Common $1 par
DCNY Corp. name changed to Discount Corp. of New York (DE) 01/01/1991
(See Discount Corp. of New York (DE))

DISCOUNT COUPONS CORP (FL)
Recapitalized as Ecom Products Group Corp. 01/13/2017
Each share Common $0.00001 par exchanged for (0.025) share Common $0.00001 par

DISCOUNT DENTAL MATLS INC (NV)
Common $0.001 par split (6.25) for (1) by issuance of (5.25) additional shares payable 03/21/2012 to holders of record 03/21/2012
Recapitalized as Cerebain Biotech Corp. 06/19/2014
Each share Common $0.001 par exchanged for (0.1) share Common $0.001 par

DISCOUNT FABRICS INC (OR)
Common no par split (5) for (4) by issuance of (0.25) additional share 05/01/1972
Stock Dividend - 10% 04/12/1974
Acquired by Fabri-Centers of America, Inc. 09/15/1981
Each share Common no par exchanged for $3.14 cash

DISCOUNT MTG SOURCE INC (TX)
Name changed to Endo Networks Inc. (TX) 11/14/2001
Endo Networks Inc. (TX) reincorporated in Nevada 12/13/2001 which name changed to China West Coal Energy, Inc. 01/05/2007 which name changed to Sino Clean Energy, Inc. 08/20/2007

DISCOUNT STORES, INC. (CO)
Name changed to House of Adler, Inc. 09/08/1965
(See House of Adler, Inc.)

DISCOUNT SUNDRY SALES, INC. (CA)
Name changed to Ames Mercantile Co., Inc. 03/31/1964
Ames Mercantile Co., Inc. acquired by Castle & Cooke, Inc. (Old) 10/31/1966 which name changed to Dole Food Co., Inc. (HI) 07/30/1991 which reincorporated in Delaware 07/01/2001
(See Dole Food Co., Inc. (Old) (DE))

DISCOVER CAP HLDGS CORP (DE)
Name changed to FSBO Media Holdings, Inc. 11/04/2005
FSBO Media Holdings, Inc. recapitalized as Guard Dog, Inc. 10/28/2008

DISCOVER FINL SVCS (DE)
6.5% Depositary Preferred Ser. B called for redemption at $25 on 12/01/2017
(Additional Information in Active)

DISCOVERWARE INC (AB)
Placed in receivership 03/05/2001
No stockholders' equity

DISCOVERY ACQUISITIONS CORP (CO)
Name changed to C-Net, Inc. 09/29/1987

DISCOVERY ACQUISITIONS INC (AB)
Recapitalized as Vision HRM Software Inc. 10/01/2002
Each share Common no par exchanged for (0.33333333) share Common no par
Vision HRM Software Inc. name changed to Serenic Corp. 01/13/2005 which name changed to OneSoft Solutions Inc. 08/01/2014

DISCOVERY AIR INC (CANADA)
Each share old Class A Common no par exchanged for (0.1) share new Class A Common no par 09/29/2011
Acquired by Clairvest Group Inc. 05/29/2017
Each share new Class A Common no par exchanged for $0.20 cash
Note: Unexchanged certificates will be cancelled and become without value 05/28/2020

DISCOVERY ASSOC INC (NV)
Each share old Common $0.001 par exchanged for (0.33333333) share new Common $0.001 par 08/31/1988
Reincorporated under the laws of Delaware as Leo's Industries, Inc. 09/07/1988
(See Leo's Industries, Inc.)

DISCOVERY BANCORP (CA)
Acquired by CommerceWest Bank N.A. (Irvine, CA) 07/30/2009
Each share Common $5 par exchanged for (0.6513) share Common $5 par
CommerceWest Bank N.A. (Irvine, CA) name changed to CommerceWest Bank (Irvine, CA) 05/12/2017

DISCOVERY BK (SAN MARCOS, CA)
Name changed 12/26/2002
Name changed from Discovery Valley Bank (San Marcos, CA) to Discovery Bank (San Marcos, CA) 12/26/2002
Under plan of reorganization each share Common no par automatically became (1) share Discovery Bancorp Common $5 par 07/14/2005
Discovery Bancorp acquired by CommerceWest Bank N.A. (Irvine, CA) 07/30/2009 which name changed to CommerceWest Bank (Irvine, CA) 05/12/2017

DISCOVERY CAP CORP (BC)
Completely liquidated
Each share Common no par received first and final distribution of $0.1575 cash and a Receipt for Residual Discovery Capital Assets representing $0.0779 cash payable 09/14/2007 to holders of record 09/11/2007 Ex date - 09/07/2007
Note: Certificates were not required to be surrendered and are without value

DISCOVERY CAP CORP (CO)
Each share old Common no par exchanged for (0.01) share new Common no par 10/16/1989
Name changed to Lasorda Foods Holding Corp. 08/13/1990
(See Lasorda Foods Holding Corp.)

DISCOVERY COMMUNICATIONS INC (DE)
Each share Ser. A Common 1¢ par received distribution of (1) share Ser. C Common 1¢ par payable 08/06/2014 to holders of record 07/28/2014 Ex date - 08/07/2014
Each share Ser. B Common 1¢ par received distribution of (1) share Ser. C Common 1¢ par payable 08/06/2014 to holders of record 07/28/2014 Ex date - 08/07/2014
Stock Dividend - In Ser. C to holders of Ser. C 100% payable 08/06/2014 to holders of record 07/28/2014 Ex date - 08/07/2014
Name changed to Discovery, Inc. 04/02/2018

DISCOVERY DISTRG CORP (BC)
Name changed to Discovery Technologies Corp. 07/29/1993
(See Discovery Technologies Corp.)

DISCOVERY GOLD EXPLS LTD (BC)
Delisted from Vancouver Stock Exchange 01/09/1989

DISCOVERY HLDG CO (DE)
Each share Ser. A Common 1¢ par received distribution of (0.05) share Ascent Media Corp. Ser. A Common 1¢ par payable 09/17/2008 to holders of record 09/17/2008
Each share Ser. B Common 1¢ par received distribution of (0.05) share Ascent Media Corp. Ser. B Common 1¢ par payable 09/17/2008 to holders of record 09/17/2008
Merged into Discovery Communications, Inc. 09/17/2008
Each share Ser. A Common 1¢ par exchanged for (0.5) share Ser. A Common 1¢ par and (0.5) share Ser. C Common 1¢ par
Each share Ser. B Common 1¢ par exchanged for (0.5) share Ser. B Common 1¢ par and (0.5) share Ser. C Common 1¢ par
Discovery Communications, Inc. name changed to Discovery, Inc. 04/02/2018

DISCOVERY INVTS INC (NV)
Common $0.001 par split (7) for (2) by issuance of (2.5) additional shares payable 05/08/2002 to holders of record 05/06/2002 Ex date - 05/09/2002
Name changed to China Evergreen Environmental Corp. 12/21/2004
China Evergreen Environmental Corp. name changed to China Water Group, Inc. 11/14/2006

DISCOVERY LABORATORIES INC NEW (DE)
Each share old Common $0.001 par exchanged for (0.06666666) share new Common $0.001 par 12/28/2010
Each share new Common $0.001 par exchanged again for (0.07142857) share new Common $0.001 par 01/22/2016
Name changed to Windtree Therapeutics, Inc. 04/19/2016

DISCOVERY MINES LTD (CANADA)
Reincorporated 01/15/1982
Capital Stock $1 par changed to no par 06/06/1978
Place of incorporation changed from (ON) to (Canada) 01/15/1982
Merged into Discovery West Corp. 03/01/1987
Each share Capital Stock no par exchanged for (1) share Conv. Vtg. Common no par
(See Discovery West Corp.)

DISCOVERY OIL LTD (DE)
Reincorporated 01/23/1981
State of incorporation changed from (WY) to (DE) and Common no par changed to 1¢ par 01/23/1981
Each share old Common 1¢ par exchanged for (0.25) share new Common 1¢ par 06/14/1984
Charter cancelled and declared inoperative and void for non-payment of taxes 03/01/2011

DISCOVERY PARTNERS INTL INC (DE)
Recapitalized as Infinity Pharmaceuticals, Inc. 09/13/2006
Each share Common $0.001 par exchanged for (0.25) share Common $0.001 par

DISCOVERY PGM EXPL LTD (BC)
Acquired by Marathon PGM Corp. 06/13/2008
Each share Common no par exchanged for (0.0794) share Common no par
Note: U.S. holders received USD$1.8302 cash per share
(See Marathon PGM Corp.)

DISCOVERY RLTY FD (OH)
Acquired by Republic Franklin Inc. 10/12/1978
Each Share of Bene. Int. no par exchanged for $8.50 principal amount of 8% S.F. Debentures due 11/01/1993

DISCOVERY STUDIO INC (DE)
Charter forfeited for failure to maintain a registered agent 11/05/1997

DISCOVERY TECHNOLOGIES CORP (BC)
Delisted from Vancouver Stock Exchange 03/05/1996

DISCOVERY TECHNOLOGIES INC (NV)
Name changed 05/11/1990
Reincorporated 10/16/2007
Name changed from Discovery Systems, Inc. to Discovery Technologies, Inc. 05/11/1990
Each share old Common 1¢ par exchanged for (0.1) share new Common $1 par 11/10/1993
New Common $1 par changed to no par 02/15/2007
Place of incorporation changed from (KS) to (NV) 10/16/2007
Each share Common no par exchanged for (0.11111111) share Common $0.001 par
Each share old Common $0.001 par exchanged for (0.14768867) share new Common $0.001 par 12/18/2007
Name changed to China Green Agriculture, Inc. 02/05/2008

DISCOVERY VENTURES INC (BC)
Name changed to MX Gold Corp. 06/06/2016

DISCOVERY WEST CORP (CANADA)
Each share Common no par received distribution of (1) share BlackRock Ventures Inc. Common no par payable 10/31/1996 to holders of record 10/28/1996 Ex date - 10/24/1996
Each share Non-Vtg. Common no par received distribution of (1) share BlackRock Ventures Inc. Non-Vtg. Common no par payable 10/31/1996 to holders of record 10/28/1996 Ex date - 10/24/1996
Acquired by Magin Energy Inc. (New) 05/07/1997
Each share Common no par exchanged for $2.56 cash
Each share Non-Vtg. Common no par exchanged for $2.56 cash

DISCOVERY YELLOWKNIFE MINES LTD. (ON)
Recapitalized as Consolidated Discovery Yellowknife Mines Ltd. 08/05/1952
Each share Capital Stock $1 par exchanged for (0.5) share Capital Stock $1 par
Consolidated Discovery Yellowknife Mines Ltd. merged into Discovery Mines Ltd. (ON) 04/14/1964 which reincorporated in Canada 01/15/1982 which merged into Discovery West Corp. 03/01/1987
(See Discovery West Corp.)

DISCOVERY ZONE INC (DE)
Old Common 1¢ par split (2) for (1) by issuance of (1) additional share 09/01/1993
Plan of reorganization under Chapter 11 Federal Bankruptcy Code effective 07/29/1997
No stockholders' equity for holders of old Common
Chapter 11 bankruptcy proceedings converted to Chapter 7 on 05/23/2000

No stockholders' equity for holders of new Common

DISCREET LOGIC INC (QC)
Common no par split (2) for (1) by issuance of (1) additional share 11/15/1995
Merged into Autodesk, Inc. 03/16/1999
Each share Common no par exchanged for (0.33333333) share Common 1¢ par

DISCRETE TIMESYSTEMS INC (BC)
Recapitalized as ADI Technologies, Inc. 03/09/1992
Each share Common no par exchanged for (0.04) share Common no par
(See ADI Technologies, Inc.)

DISCUS ACQUISITION CORP (MN)
Name changed 06/07/1994
Name changed from Discus Corp. to Discus Acquisition Corp. 06/07/1994
Name changed to Peerless Industrial Group Inc. 05/01/1996
(See Peerless Industrial Group Inc.)

DISEASE DETECTION INTL INC (DE)
Each share Common $0.001 par exchanged for (0.025) share Common 4¢ par 08/15/1990
Each share Common 4¢ par exchanged for (0.1) share Common 40¢ par 10/06/1993
Merged into Trinity Biotech PLC 10/14/1994
Each share Common 40¢ par exchanged for (1) Sponsored ADR for Ordinary 1p par

DISEASE SCIENCES INC (DE)
Each share old Common $0.001 par exchanged for (0.1) share new Common $0.001 par 01/07/2002
Name changed to IceWEB, Inc. 05/30/2002
IceWEB, Inc. recapitalized as UnifiedOnline, Inc. 01/05/2015

DISKEY SIGN CORP (IN)
Plan of reorganization under Chapter 11 Federal Bankruptcy proceedings effective 04/30/1993
No stockholders equity

DISMAL SWAMP CORP (VA)
Charter revoked for failure to file reports 06/01/1972

DISNEY STREET CORP. (OH)
Dissolved 11/16/1963
Details not available

DISNEY WALT CO (CA)
Name changed 02/12/1986
6% Preferred $25 par called for redemption 01/01/1951
Common $5 par changed to $2.50 par and (1) additional share issued 08/31/1956
Common $2.50 par changed to $1.25 par and (1) additional share issued 11/15/1967
Common $1.25 par split (2) for (1) by issuance of (1) additional share 02/27/1971
Common $1.25 par split (2) for (1) by issuance of (1) additional share 01/15/1973
Common $1.25 par changed to no par 03/08/1977
Name changed from Disney (Walt) Productions to Disney (Walt) Co. 02/12/1986
Common no par split (4) for (1) by issuance of (3) additional shares 03/05/1986
Reincorporated under the laws of Delaware and Common no par changed to 10¢ par 02/11/1987

DISON INTL LTD (BC)
Struck off register and declared dissolved for failure to file returns 09/20/1983

DISPATCH AUTO PARTS INC (FL)
Name changed to Environment Ecology Holding Co. of China 11/29/2007

DISPATCH MGMT SVCS CORP (DE)
SEC revoked common stock registration 01/03/2006

DISPERSIONS PROCESS, INC.
Acquired by United States Rubber Co. 00/00/1946
Details not available

DISPLAY COMPONENTS INC (MA)
Acquired by TDK U.S.A. Corp. 08/18/1988
Each share Common 5¢ par exchanged for $3 cash

DISPLAY SCIENCES, INC. (NY)
Charter annulled 09/27/1995

DISPLAY TECHNOLOGIES INC (NV)
Stock Dividends - 5% payable 11/30/1998 to holders of record 11/16/1998; 5% payable 12/20/1999 to holders of record 12/03/1999
91.8% acquired by Jeko International, Inc. as of 11/02/2006

DISPLEX INC (DE)
Merged into North Hills Electronics, Inc. 07/06/1983
Each share Common 1¢ par exchanged for (0.06) share Common 1¢ par
(See North Hills Electronics, Inc.)

DISPOSABLE RESH INDS (CA)
Common 20¢ par changed to $0.13333333 par and (0.5) additional share issued 05/28/1971
Charter cancelled for failure to file reports and pay taxes 05/01/1981

DISPOSABLE SVCS CORP (DE)
Name changed to Bracken (Eddie) Ventures of Florida, Inc. 12/08/1970
(See Bracken (Eddie) Ventures of Florida, Inc.)

DISPOSIT PRODS INC (NY)
Reorganized under the laws of Delaware as ISO Industries Corp. 09/25/1972
Each share Common 1¢ par exchanged for (0.33333333) share Common 1¢ par
(See ISO Industries Corp.)

DISSON INC (NC)
Name changed back to Automatic Service Co. 05/19/1969
Automatic Service Co. name changed to Bowen Investment Co. 09/29/1976
(See Bowen Investment Co.)

DISSTON (HENRY) & SONS, INC. (PA)
Liquidation completed 03/15/1965
Details not available

DISSTON INC (DE)
Merged into Sandatlantic, Inc. 08/25/1976
Each share Common $1 par exchanged for $13 cash

DISTICRAFT, INC.
Out of business 07/21/1954
Details not available

DISTILLED LIQUORS CORP.
Name changed to Hildick Products Corp. 00/00/1941
(See Hildick Products Corp.)

DISTILLERS & BREWERS CORP. OF AMERICA
Liquidated 00/00/1940
Details not available

DISTILLERS & VINTNERS CORP AMER (DE)
Name changed to U.S. Dynamics, Inc. 07/10/1969
(See U.S. Dynamics, Inc.)

DISTILLERS CORP SEAGRAMS LTD (CANADA)
Each share Common no par exchanged for (5) shares Common $2 par 00/00/1946
Common $2 par changed to $1 par and (1) additional share issued 12/11/1964
Common $1 par changed to no par and (1) additional share issued 12/10/1971
Name changed to Seagram Co. Ltd.-La Compagnie Seagram Ltee. 01/20/1975
Seagram Co. Ltd. -La Compagnie Seagram Ltee. merged into Vivendi Universal 12/08/2000 which name changed to Vivendi 04/24/2006
(See Vivendi)

DISTILLERS LTD (SCOTLAND)
Each share Ordinary Reg. £1 par exchanged for (5) shares Ordinary Reg. 4s par 00/00/1949
Ordinary Reg. 4s par changed to 6s8d par 00/00/1955
Ordinary Reg. 6s8d par changed to 10s par 12/11/1958
Ordinary Reg. 10s par changed to 50p par per currency change 02/15/1971
Stock Dividends - Ordinary Reg. - 50% 10/17/1949; 25% 12/18/1958; 20% 12/30/1960; 40% 01/10/1964; 20% 01/07/1966
Stock Dividends - ADR's - 50% 12/02/1949; 25% 12/29/1958; 20% 01/13/1961; 40% 01/23/1964; 20% 01/24/1966
Acquired by Guinness PLC 00/00/1986
Details not available

DISTINC CORP. (NV)
Charter revoked for failure to file reports and pay fees 08/01/1982

DISTINCTION GROUP INC (QC)
Acquired by Birch Hill Fund IV 01/01/2012
Each share Common no par exchanged for $4.50 cash
Note: Unexchanged certificates were cancelled and became without value 01/01/2018

DISTINCTIVE DEVICES INC (DE)
Reorganized 11/08/2002
Each share Conv. Preferred Ser. A $1 par exchanged for (3) shares Common 5¢ par 12/19/1992
Reorganized from (NY) to under the laws of Delaware 11/08/2002
Each share Common 5¢ par exchanged for (0.16666666) share Common $0.001 par
SEC revoked common stock registration 07/14/2011

DISTRIBUCION Y SERVICIO D&S S A (CHILE)
ADR basis changed from (1:15) to (1:60) 12/06/2004
ADR agreement terminated 07/29/2009
Each Sponsored ADR for Common no par exchanged for $24.535461 cash

DISTRIBUCO INC (DE)
Common no par changed to $1 par 07/16/1974
Stock Dividends - 10% 06/14/1974; 10% 06/30/1975; 10% 09/30/1976; 10% 09/30/1977; 100% 08/22/1980; 20% 08/28/1981; 20% 08/27/1982
Assets transferred to DTIB Liquidating Co. 10/29/1986
(See DTIB Liquidating Co.)

DISTRIBUTED COMPUTER SYS INC (DE)
Charter cancelled and declared inoperative and void for non-payment of taxes 03/01/1986

DISTRIBUTED DIAGNOSTICS INC (NV)
Common no par split (10) for (1) by issuance of (9) additional shares payable 10/12/2004 to holders of record 10/12/2004 Ex date - 10/18/2004
Name changed to Textrabet, Inc. 09/23/2005
Textrabet, Inc. recapitalized as First Platinum Card Corp. 09/26/2006 which recapitalized as First Platinum Retail Innovations, Inc. 02/16/2007
(See First Platinum Retail Innovations, Inc.)

DISTRIBUTED ENERGY SYS CORP (DE)
Chapter 11 bankruptcy proceedings dismissed 09/24/2010
No stockholders' equity

DISTRIBUTED LOGIC CORP (DE)
Reincorporated 04/09/1987
State of incorporation changed from (CA) to (DE) 04/09/1987
Charter cancelled and declared inoperative and void for non-payment of taxes 03/01/1994

DISTRIBUTED PWR INC (DE)
Old Common 1¢ par split (10) for (1) by issuance of (9) additional shares payable 03/26/2004 to holders of record 03/18/2004 Ex date - 03/29/2004
Each share old Common 1¢ par exchanged for (0.01) share new Common 1¢ par 10/23/2006
Name changed to Global Pay Solutions, Inc. 04/23/2007
Global Pay Solutions, Inc. recapitalized as China National Appliance of North America Corp. 03/26/2009

DISTRIBUTION INTL CORP (DE)
Company went out of business 00/00/1994
Details not available

DISTRIBUTION MGMT SVCS INC (FL)
Each share old Common $0.001 par exchanged for (0.0001) share new Common $0.001 par 11/19/2008
Reincorporated under the laws of Delaware as Corporate Management Solutions, Inc. 04/21/2011

DISTRIBUTION TERMINAL WAREHOUSE CO.
Merged into Connohio, Inc. 00/00/1946
Each share Common $1 par exchanged for (5) shares Preferred $10 par and (5) shares Common $1 par
(See Connohio, Inc.)

DISTRIBUTORS GROUP, INC. (DE)
Preferred 25¢ par called for redemption 10/30/1959
Each share Common 10¢ par exchanged for (2.1) shares Class A Common 5¢ par 11/05/1959
Merged into USLIFE Holding Corp. 01/18/1968
Each share Class A Common 5¢ par exchanged for (0.33333333) share Common $2 par
Each share Class B Common 5¢ par exchanged for (0.33333333) share Common $2 par
USLIFE Holding Corp. name changed to USLIFE Corp. 05/22/1970 which merged into American General Corp. 06/17/1997 which merged into American International Group, Inc. 08/29/2001

DISTRICT COLUMBIA NATL BK (WASHINGTON, DC)
Reorganized as D.C. National Bancorp, Inc. 05/17/1982
Each share Common $10 par exchanged for (1) share Common $10 par
D.C. National Bancorp, Inc. merged into Sovran Financial Corp. 03/10/1986 which merged into C&S/Sovran Corp. 09/01/1990 which merged into NationsBank Corp. 12/31/1991 which reincorporated in Delaware as BankAmerica Corp. (Old) 09/25/1998 which merged into BankAmerica Corp. (New) 09/30/1998 which name changed to Bank of America Corp. 04/28/1999

DISTRICT NATIONAL SECURITIES CORP. (VA)
Liquidation completed 03/16/1962
Details not available

DISTRICT OF COLUMBIA PAPER MANUFACTURING CO.
Reorganized as District of Columbia Paper Mills, Inc. 00/00/1937
Details not available

DISTRICT PHOTO INC (DC)
Common 10¢ par split (3) for (2) by issuance of (0.5) additional share 10/29/1971
Common 10¢ par split (2) for (1) by issuance of (1) additional share 09/29/1972
Common 10¢ par split (5) for (4) by issuance of (0.25) additional share 09/28/1973
Merged into Cohen Family Corp. 08/22/1979
Each share Common 10¢ par exchanged for $32 cash

DISTRICT THEATRES CORP (DE)
Merged into Glenmar Cinestate, Inc. 03/10/1978
Each share Common $1 par exchanged for $21.83 cash

DISTRICT TR CO (LONDON, ON)
Each share Capital Stock $10 par exchanged for (2.5) shares Conv. Class A no par 12/01/1975
Each share Conv. Class A no par received distribution of (0.2) share International By-Products Ltd. Common no par 12/29/1978
Completely liquidated 02/00/1992
No stockholders' equity

DISTRICT WHSL DRUG CORP WASHINGTON (MD)
Merged into Spectro Industries, Inc. 11/08/1968
Each share Class A Common no par exchanged for (1) share Common $1 par
(See Spectro Industries, Inc.)

DISYS CORP (ON)
Merged into Kasten Chase Applied Research Ltd. (ON) 07/24/1996
Each share Common no par exchanged for (1) share Common no par
Kasten Chase Applied Research Ltd. (ON) reincorporated in Alberta 07/24/2007 which recapitalized as Kasten Energy Inc. 03/02/2010

DIT-MCO INC. (MO)
Name changed to Xebec Corp. 06/07/1965
Xebec Corp. merged into Susquehanna Corp. 03/06/1968
(See Susquehanna Corp.)

DITECH COMMUNICATIONS CORP (DE)
Common $0.001 par split (2) for (1) by issuance of (1) additional share payable 02/16/2000 to holders of record 02/01/2000
Name changed to Ditech Networks, Inc. 05/18/2006
(See Ditech Networks, Inc.)

DITECH NETWORKS INC (DE)
Acquired by Nuance Communications, Inc. (New) 12/05/2012
Each share Common $0.001 par exchanged for $1.45 cash

DITEK SOFTWARE CORP (CANADA)
Name changed to HomeProject.com Inc. 03/17/2000
(See HomeProject.com Inc.)

DITTO, INC. (DE)
Merged into Bell & Howell Co. (IL) 06/01/1962
Each share Common $4 par exchanged for (0.2) share 4.25% Conv. Preferred $50 par and (0.6) share Common no par
Bell & Howell Co. (IL) reincorporated in Delaware 05/06/1977
(See Bell & Howell Co. (DE))

DITTO BIKE INC (UT)
Name changed to Breakthru Industries Group, Inc. (UT) 11/21/1988
Breakthru Industries Group, Inc. (UT) reorganized in Delaware 05/24/1990

DIVCO CORP. (MI)
Stock Dividend - 100% 03/01/1946
Name changed to Divco-Wayne Corp. 11/01/1956
Divco-Wayne Corp. merged into Boise Cascade Corp. 01/23/1968
(See Boise Cascade Corp.)

DIVCO-TWIN TRUCK CO.
Name changed to Divco Corp. 00/00/1944
Divco Corp. name changed to Divco-Wayne Corp. 11/01/1956 which merged into Boise Cascade Corp. 01/23/1968
(See Boise Cascade Corp.)

DIVCO WAYNE CORP (MI)
Common $1 par split (1.333) for (1) by issuance of (0.33333333) additional share 03/31/1964
Stock Dividend - 10% 03/06/1959
Merged into Boise Cascade Corp. 01/23/1968
Each share Common $1 par exchanged for (1) share $1.40 Conv. Preferred no par
(See Boise Cascade Corp.)

DIVCOM TECHNOLOGIES INC (AB)
Reincorporated under the laws of Canada as Divcom Lighting Inc. 11/27/2003

DIVERCO INC (DE)
Charter cancelled and declared inoperative and void for non-payment of taxes 03/01/1976

DIVERSA CORP (DE)
Name changed to Verenium Corp. 06/21/2007
(See Verenium Corp.)

DIVERSA GRAPHICS INC (DE)
Each share old Common 1¢ par exchanged for (0.037212) share new Common 1¢ par 10/02/1972
Charter forfeited for failure to maintain a registered agent 02/25/1991

DIVERSA INC (DE)
Adjudicated bankrupt 12/21/1972
Stockholders' equity unlikely

DIVERSAFILE INTL INC (ON)
Delisted from Canadian Dealer Network 01/14/2000

DIVERSAFLOW CORP LTD (AB)
Name changed to Iplayco Corp. Ltd. 05/18/2006

DIVERSCO INC (SC)
Common 1¢ par split (3) for (2) by issuance of (0.5) additional share 12/09/1988
Acquired by a management group 03/11/1993
Each share Common 1¢ par exchanged for $5.55 cash

DIVERSE HLDGS CORP (DE)
SEC revoked common stock registration 06/10/2011

DIVERSE MEDIA GROUP INC (DE)
Common $0.0001 par split (15) for (1) by issuance of (14) additional shares payable 04/20/2009 to holders of record 04/17/2009
Ex date - 04/21/2009
Recapitalized as Peerless Developments Ltd. 04/25/2017
Each share Common $0.0001 par exchanged for (0.00025) share Common 1¢ par
Peerless Developments Ltd. name changed to Blockchain Loyalty Corp. 05/03/2018

DIVERSEY CORP (DE)
Reincorporated 05/01/1970
Common $1 par split (2) for (1) by issuance of (1) additional share 05/09/1960
Common $1 par split (2) for (1) by issuance of (1) additional share 03/31/1969
Reincorporated from (IL) to under the laws of Delaware 05/01/1970
Stock Dividend - 50% 10/10/1975
Merged into Oron Inc. 07/14/1978
Each share Common $1 par exchanged for $30 cash

DIVERSICARE CORP AMER (DE)
Each share old Common 1¢ par exchanged for (0.1) share new Common 1¢ par 08/01/1989
Merged into Diversicare Ltd. 10/29/1990
Each share new Common 1¢ par exchanged for $2.40 cash

DIVERSICARE INC (DE)
Name changed to American HomePatient, Inc. (DE) 05/16/1994
American HomePatient, Inc. (DE) reincorporated in Nevada 06/30/2010
(See American HomePatient, Inc.)

DIVERSICON HLDGS CORP (DE)
SEC revoked common stock registration 08/01/2011

DIVERSIFAX CORP (NJ)
Completely liquidated 01/15/1970
Each share Common 25¢ par exchanged for first and final distribution of (1) share Vantex Corp. Common 10¢ par
(See Vantex Corp.)

DIVERSIFAX INC (DE)
Each share old Common $0.001 par exchanged for (0.01) share new Common $0.001 par 10/23/2006
Name changed to Gulf Resources, Inc. (DE) 02/20/2007
Gulf Resources, Inc. (DE) reincorporated in Nevada 12/10/2015

DIVERSIFIED ACQUISITIONS INC (NV)
Recapitalized as Vitalcare Diabetes Treatment Centers, Inc. 03/24/2008
Each share Common $0.001 par exchanged for (0.0032258) share Common $0.001 par
Vitalcare Diabetes Treatment Centers, Inc. recapitalized as China Advanced Technology 06/23/2010 which name changed to Goliath Film & Media Holdings 01/20/2012

DIVERSIFIED ALPHA FD II (ON)
Trust terminated 07/11/2014
Each Unit received $7.38 cash

DIVERSIFIED AMERN HLDGS INC (DE)
Recapitalized as Strateginet, Inc. 11/20/98
Each share Common $0.001 par exchanged for (0.1) share Common $0.001 par
Strateginet, Inc. recapitalized as Cemtrex Inc. 12/28/2004

DIVERSIFIED AMERICAN INDUSTRIES INC. (NV)
Each share old Common 40¢ par exchanged for (0.1) share new Common 40¢ par 06/03/1991
Name changed to Thunderstone Group Inc. 11/13/1995
Thunderstone Group Inc. name changed to Cronus Corp. 03/04/1996
(See Cronus Corp.)

DIVERSIFIED BAYWEST CAP CORP (CANADA)
Name changed to Nextwave Software Corp. 11/01/1991
Nextwave Software Corp. recapitalized as Stox Infolink Systems Inc. 07/21/1994 which name changed to stox.com Inc. 02/24/1999
(See stox.com Inc.)

DIVERSIFIED BUSINESS & MED SVCS INC (FL)
Administratively dissolved for failure to file annual report 09/19/2003

DIVERSIFIED CANADIAN FINL CORP (ON)
Class A Preferred Ser. 1 1¢ par called for redemption at $25.50 plus $0.2925 accrued dividends 12/01/2005

DIVERSIFIED CDN FINL II CORP (CANADA)
Sr. Preferred called for redemption at $25 on 01/04/2007

DIVERSIFIED CAP APPLICATIONS INC (DE)
Name changed to Wellness International Inc. 01/10/1985
(See Wellness International Inc.)

DIVERSIFIED CAP CORP (DE)
Charter cancelled and declared inoperative and void for non-payment of taxes 03/01/1989

DIVERSIFIED CAP INVTS INC (CO)
Name changed to America's Favorite Clothing, Inc. 03/08/1988

DIVERSIFIED CAPITAL RESOURCES CORP. (NV)
Name changed to Prestige Industries, Inc. 01/28/1984
Prestige Industries, Inc. name changed to Prestige Pictures Industries, Inc. (NV) 05/02/1984
(See Prestige Pictures Industries, Inc.)

DIVERSIFIED COLLATERAL CORP. (FL)
Adjudicated bankrupt 06/11/1965
No stockholders' equity

DIVERSIFIED COMPUTER & MGMT SVCS INC (DE)
Name changed to Diversitron, Inc. 05/04/1971
(See Diversitron, Inc.)

DIVERSIFIED COMPUTER SVCS INC (DC)
Reincorporated under the laws of Delaware as Diversified Computer & Management Services, Inc. 05/27/1969
Diversified Computer & Management Services, Inc. name changed to Diversitron, Inc. 05/04/1971
(See Diversitron, Inc.)

DIVERSIFIED COMPUTER SVCS INC (NY)
Name changed to DCS Computer Services, Inc. 04/24/1970
(See DCS Computer Services, Inc.)

DIVERSIFIED CONCEPTS INC. (NV)
Recapitalized as Medsearch Inc. (NV) 07/09/1998
Each share Common $0.001 par exchanged for (0.01) share Common $0.001 par
Medsearch Inc. (NV) reincorporated in Delaware as Medsearch Technologies Inc. 08/11/1999
(See Medsearch Technologies Inc.)

DIVERSIFIED COSMETICS INTL INC (AB)
Company dissolved
Each share Common no par received distribution of (0.1698658) share I Crystal, Inc. Common 1¢ par payable 08/00/2001 to holders of record 09/29/1999
I Crystal, Inc. name changed to ICrystal, Inc. 06/15/2000 which name changed to ALL Fuels & Energy Co. 05/07/2007

DIVERSIFIED CR LTD (ON)
Common no par reclassified as Special Shares no par 12/12/1980

Special Shares no par called for redemption 02/02/1981
Public interest eliminated

DIVERSIFIED CREATIONS INC (CA)
Common $10 par changed to no par 07/31/1969
Name changed to International American Industries 11/12/1969
(See International American Industries)

DIVERSIFIED DATA SVCS & SCIENCES INC (NY)
Merged into Nytronics, Inc. (DE) 12/29/1970
Each share Common 10¢ par exchanged for (1.6102) shares Capital Stock 50¢ par and (2) Capital Stock Purchase Warrants expiring 12/28/1975
Nytronics, Inc. (DE) merged into Bastian Industries, Inc. 11/24/1980
(See Bastian Industries, Inc.)

DIVERSIFIED DESIGN DISCIPLINES INC (TX)
Merged into Design Professionals, Inc. 03/14/1975
Each share Common $1 par exchanged for $7 cash

DIVERSIFIED DEVELOPMENT INC. (DE)
Name changed to Ionicron Inc. and Common 10¢ par changed to 1¢ par 02/23/1981
(See Ionicron Inc.)

DIVERSIFIED DISC & ACCEP CORP (MN)
Common $1 par changed to 50¢ par and (1) additional share issued 11/14/1969
Name changed to Investment Corp. of America, Inc. 01/05/1970
Investment Corp. of America, Inc. name changed to River Forest Bancorp 05/18/1982 which name changed to River Forest Bancorp, Inc. 04/29/1988 which name changed to Corus Bankshares, Inc. 06/10/1996
(See Corus Bankshares, Inc.)

DIVERSIFIED EARTH SCIENCES INC (CA)
Class A Common $1 par reclassified as Common 80¢ par 01/22/1971
Common 80¢ par split (5) for (4) by issuance of (0.25) additional share 02/01/1971
Liquidation completed
Each share Common 80¢ par received initial distribution of $5 cash 02/16/1979
Each share Common 80¢ par received second distribution of (1) share Algeran, Inc. Common 1¢ par and $0.60 cash 06/25/1979
Note: Under plan of liquidation assets transferred to a Trust and each share Common 80¢ par automatically became (1) Diversified Earth Sciences Liquidating Trust Share of Bene. Int. 80¢ par 06/25/1979
(See Diversified Earth Sciences Liquidating Trust)

DIVERSIFIED EARTH SCIENCES LIQUIDATING TRUST (CA)
Liquidation completed
Each Share of Bene. Int. 80¢ par received initial distribution of $0.25 cash 05/09/1980
Each Share of Bene. Int. 80¢ par received second distribution of $0.25 cash 01/15/1981
Each Share of Bene. Int. 80¢ par received third distribution of $0.195 cash 08/02/1982
Each Share of Bene. Int. 80¢ par received fourth and final distribution of $0.1061 cash 08/18/1989

DIVERSIFIED EDUCATIONAL SYSTEMS, INC. (DE)
Adjudicated bankrupt 05/10/1971
No stockholders' equity

DIVERSIFIED ENERGIES INC (MN)
Common $1 par split (2) for (1) by issuance of (1) additional share 06/10/1985
Common Stock Purchase Rights declared for Common stockholders of record 11/24/1989 were redeemed at $0.01 per right 12/10/1990 for holders of record 11/29/1990
Merged into Arkla, Inc. 11/29/1990
Each share Common $1 par exchanged for (1.752) shares Common $0.625 par
Arkla, Inc. name changed to NorAm Energy Corp. 05/11/1994 which merged into Houston Industries Inc. 08/06/1997 which name changed to Reliant Energy Inc. 02/08/1999 which reorganized as CenterPoint Energy, Inc. 08/31/2002

DIVERSIFIED ENERGY & FUEL INTL INC (NV)
Name changed to Zyrox Mining International, Inc. 08/21/2012

DIVERSIFIED ENERGY CORP (UT)
Name changed to Diversified Enterprises, Inc. 11/25/2008

DIVERSIFIED ENTMT INC (BC)
Struck off register 05/14/1993

DIVERSIFIED ENVIRONMENTAL RES INC (MT)
Recapitalized as Trade The Planet Corp. (MT) 05/01/2001
Each share Common $0.001 par exchanged for (0.02) share Common $0.001 par
Trade The Planet Corp. (MT) reincorporated in Nevada as Human Science Systems Inc. 04/04/2005 which recapitalized as Nutralogix Laboratories, Inc. 11/14/2005 which recapitalized as Matrix Denture Systems International, Inc. 10/09/2007

DIVERSIFIED EQUITY CORP. (IN)
Charter revoked for failure to file annual reports 06/30/1978

DIVERSIFIED FD ST BD & MTG CO (MD)
Name changed to State Bond Diversified Fund, Inc. 04/29/1983
(See State Bond Diversified Fund, Inc.)

DIVERSIFIED FDS INC (NV)
Reincorporated 01/00/2002
State of incorporation changed from (LA) to (NV) 01/00/2002
Recapitalized as Masterslink Communications, Inc. 01/17/2002
Each share Common no par exchanged for (0.0625) share Common $0.001 par
Masterslink Communications, Inc. name changed to IQue Intellectual Properties, Inc. 12/02/2003 which name changed to Safeguard Security Holdings, Inc. 01/05/2005
(See Safeguard Security Holdings, Inc.)

DIVERSIFIED FINANCIAL CORP. OF AMERICA (DE)
Name changed to Consolidated American Industries, Inc. 05/28/1956
(See Consolidated American Industries, Inc.)

DIVERSIFIED FINL CORP (IN)
Under plan of merger each share Common Capital Stock 50¢ par automatically became (1) share United Presidential Corp. Common 50¢ par 10/24/1980
(See United Presidential Corp.)

DIVERSIFIED FINL RES CORP (NV)
Reincorporated 05/12/2006
Each share old Common $0.001 par exchanged for (0.005) share new Common $0.001 par 02/07/2003
New Common $0.001 par changed to no par 06/00/2004
Each share old Common no par exchanged for (0.001) share new Common no par 11/01/2004
Each share new Common no par exchanged again for (0.0005) share new Common no par 08/25/2005
State of incorporation changed from (DE) to (NV) 05/12/2006
Each share old Common $0.001 par exchanged for (0.08) share new Common $0.001 par 07/12/2006
Name changed to China Fruits Corp. 09/08/2006

DIVERSIFIED FOOD CORP (NV)
Merged into Coast Produce Co. 05/15/1985
Each share Common 10¢ par exchanged for $19.5022 cash
Each share Common 10¢ par received initial additional distribution of $4.62 cash 04/00/1986
Each share Common 10¢ par received second and final additional distribution of $5.24 cash 11/00/1986

DIVERSIFIED FOOD MFRS LTD (DE)
Name changed to Hygenics Pharmaceuticals, Inc. 02/21/1995

DIVERSIFIED FOODS INC (DE)
Each share Common $0.001 par exchanged for (0.33333333) share Common $0.003 par 12/12/1988
Charter cancelled and declared inoperative and void for non-payment of taxes 03/01/1990

DIVERSIFIED FOODSERVICE DISTRS INC (FL)
Proclaimed dissolved for failure to file annual reports 10/09/1992

DIVERSIFIED FUNDING, INC. (NJ)
Charter revoked for failure to file reports and pay fees 02/03/1965

DIVERSIFIED FUNDS, INC. (DE)
Stock Dividend - Diversified Investment Fund 100% 10/20/1952
Under plan of merger each share Diversified Growth Stock Fund $1 par exchanged for (1) share Diversified Growth Stock Fund, Inc. Capital Stock $1 par, Diversified Common Stock Fund $1 par exchanged for Diversified Investment Fund, Inc. Capital Stock $1 par on the basis of respective asset values and each share Diversified Investment Fund $1 par exchanged for (1) share Diversified Investment Fund, Inc. Capital Stock $1 par 00/00/1954
(See each company's listing)

DIVERSIFIED GLOBAL HLDGS INC (NV)
Reincorporated under the laws of Delaware as Winwheel Bullion Inc. 11/25/2008
Winwheel Bullion Inc. name changed to Verdant Automotive Corp. 06/09/2011 which name changed to VRDT Corp. 02/09/2012
(See VRDT Corp.)

DIVERSIFIED GROWTH CORP (VA)
Charter cancelled and proclaimed dissolved for failure to file reports 06/01/1978

DIVERSIFIED GROWTH STK FD INC (DE)
Stock Dividend - 100% 08/23/1957
Name changed to Anchor Growth Fund, Inc. 09/02/1969
Anchor Growth Fund, Inc. merged into Amcap Fund, Inc. 08/31/1981

DIVERSIFIED HEALTH COS INC (OK)
Charter suspended for failure to pay taxes 11/28/1990

DIVERSIFIED HEALTH INDS INC (NY)
Dissolved by proclamation 09/28/1994

DIVERSIFIED HISTORIC INVS (PA)
Units of Ltd. Partnership Int.-V completely liquidated 09/10/2003
Details not available
Units of Ltd. Partnership Int.-III reincorporated under the laws of Delaware as Independence Tax Credit Plus L.P. III Beneficial Assignment Certificates 10/20/2009
Units of Ltd. Partnership Int.-IV reincorporated under the laws of Delaware as Independence Tax Credit Plus L.P. IV Beneficial Assignment Certificates 10/20/2009
Units of Ltd. Partnership Int.-90 reincorporated under the laws of Delaware as Independence Tax Credit Plus L.P. Beneficial Assignment Certificates 10/20/2009
SEC revoked registration of Units of Ltd. Partnership II on 09/14/2011
(Additional Information in Active)

DIVERSIFIED HOLDING CORP. (GA)
Merged into New Century Farms, LLC 01/25/1990
Details not available

DIVERSIFIED HUMAN RES GROUP INC (TX)
Stock Dividend - 10% 06/15/1989
Name changed to Diversified Corporate Resources, Inc. 12/05/1994

DIVERSIFIED INCOME SHARES (BC)
Placed in Receivership and in process of liquidation
Each share Series A no par received first and final distribution of $1.20 cash 08/22/1969
Certificates were not required to be surrendered and are now valueless
Each share Series B no par received initial distribution of $3.455 cash 09/12/1969
Each share Series B no par received second distribution of $1 cash 04/17/1972
Each share Series B no par received third distribution of $0.821949 cash 04/14/1975
Amount or number of subsequent distributions, if any, are unavailable

DIVERSIFIED INCOME STRATEGIES PORTFOLIO INC. (MD)
Name changed to BlackRock Diversified Income Strategies Fund, Inc. 10/02/2006
BlackRock Diversified Income Strategies Fund, Inc. merged into BlackRock Floating Rate Income Strategies Fund, Inc. 10/08/2012

DIVERSIFIED INCOME TR II (ON)
Merged into Premier Value Income Trust 08/01/2008
Each Trust Unit no par received (1.1864599) Trust Units no par
Premier Value Income Trust merged into Sentry Canadian Income Fund 02/04/2011

DIVERSIFIED INDUSTRIAL CORP. (DE)
Acquired by Diversified Industrial Corp. of Kansas, Inc. 04/16/1965
Each share Common 10¢ par exchanged for (0.1) share Common 10¢ par
(See Diversified Industrial Corp. of Kansas, Inc.)

DIVERSIFIED INDL CORP KANS INC (KS)
Liquidation completed
Each share Common 10¢ par received initial distribution of $20 cash 10/30/1991
Each share Common 10¢ par

FINANCIAL INFORMATION, INC.   DIV-DIV

received second distribution of $20 cash 12/21/1992
Each share Common 10¢ par exchanged for third and final distribution of $13.50 cash 08/25/1993

DIVERSIFIED INDUSTRIES, INC. (CA)
Acquired by Tronchemics Research Inc. 11/15/1962
Each share 7% Preferred $5 par exchanged for (3.6146) shares Common 50¢ par
Each share Common $1 par exchanged for (0.7229) share Common 50¢ par
(See Tronchemics Research Inc.)

DIVERSIFIED INDS INC (DE)
Plan of reorganization under Chapter 11 Federal Bankruptcy Code effective 2/1/95
No stockholders' equity

DIVERSIFIED INDS INC (UT)
Each share old Common 1¢ par exchanged for (0.2) share new Common 1¢ par 04/21/1997
Reorganized under the laws of Nevada as EZConnect Inc. 10/19/1999
Each share new Common 1¢ par exchanged for (0.4) share Common 1¢ par
EZConnect Inc. name changed to Encore Wireless, Inc. 02/08/2001
(See Encore Wireless, Inc.)

DIVERSIFIED INDS LTD (BC)
Each share old Common no par exchanged for (0.00000004) share new Common no par 01/14/2013
Note: In effect holders received $0.00071 cash per share and public interest was eliminated
Unexchanged certificates will be cancelled and become without value 01/14/2019

DIVERSIFIED INSURERS CO (MN)
Preferred $1 par called for redemption 11/29/1968
Proclaimed dissolved for failure to file annual reports 12/31/1985

DIVERSIFIED INVT CAP (NV)
Charter revoked for failure to file reports and pay fees 07/31/2008

DIVERSIFIED INVT FD INC (DE)
Name changed to Anchor Income Fund, Inc. 09/02/1969
Anchor Income Fund, Inc. merged into Income Fund of America, Inc. (DE) 07/31/1978 which reincorporated in Maryland 09/22/1983 which reorganized in Delaware as Income Fund of America 10/01/2010

DIVERSIFIED INVT GRADE INCOME TR SER 1 (ON)
Trust Units no par called for redemption at $8.95 on 10/09/2007

DIVERSIFIED INVT GROUP INC (PA)
Acquired by Star States Corp. 02/02/1990
Each share Common 1¢ par exchanged for $13.75 cash

DIVERSIFIED INVESTMENTS, INC.
Name changed to Telephone Bond & Share Co. in 1930
Telephone Bond & Share Co. name changed to Continental Telephone Co. 2/11/55 which merged into General Telephone Corp. 8/8/56 which name changed to General Telephone & Electronics Corp. 3/5/59 which name changed to GTE Corp. 7/1/82 which merged into Verizon Communications Inc. 6/30/2000

DIVERSIFIED INVS CORP (DE)
Each share old Common 10¢ par exchanged for (0.05) share new Common 10¢ par 01/02/1997

Name changed to Diverse Holdings Corp. 12/07/2007
(See Diverse Holdings Corp.)

DIVERSIFIED MGMT ACQUISITIONS INC (CO)
Recapitalized as Tierra Environmental Corp. 12/23/1992
Each share Common no par exchanged for (0.06666666) share Common no par
Tierra Environmental Corp. name changed to Hallmark Properties Inc. 10/16/1998 which name changed to Norton Motorcycles, Inc. 04/23/1999
(See Norton Motorcycles, Inc.)

DIVERSIFIED MGMT ACQUISITIONS II INC (CO)
Each share old Common no par exchanged for (0.005) share new Common no par 12/23/1992
Each share new Common no par exchanged again for (0.28571428) share new Common no par 05/15/1996
Name changed to Carpet Holdings, Inc. 07/25/1996
Carpet Holdings, Inc. name changed to IQ Holdings Inc. (CO) 05/05/1997 which reorganized in Texas as Scenario Systems International, Inc. 08/01/2007 which reorganized in Wyoming as Insight ID, Inc. 09/18/2013

DIVERSIFIED MANAGEMENT CORP. (TN)
Name changed to Downtowner Corp. 3/29/61
Downtowner Corp. name changed to Perkins Foods, Inc. 11/28/83
(See Perkins Foods, Inc.)

DIVERSIFIED MARKETING GROUP INC (PA)
Merged into Magic Marker Corp. (NY) 11/15/1979
Each share Common 1¢ par exchanged for (1) share Common 50¢ par
Magic Marker Corp. (NY) reincorporated in Delaware 09/00/1975
(See Magic Marker Corp. (DE))

DIVERSIFIED MARKETING SVCS INC (NV)
Name changed to inFOREtech Wireless Technology Inc. 01/03/2000
inFOREtech Wireless Technology Inc. name changed to GPS Industries, Inc. 10/01/2003
(See GPS Industries, Inc.)

DIVERSIFIED MED CORP (DE)
Name changed to Diversified Investors Corp. 12/22/1981
Diversified Investors Corp. name changed to Diverse Holdings Corp. 12/07/2007
(See Diverse Holdings Corp.)

DIVERSIFIED MED INVTS CORP (CO)
Charter suspended for failure to maintain a resident agent 08/09/1985

DIVERSIFIED MED TECHNOLOGIES INC (CO)
Chapter 11 bankruptcy proceedings converted to Chapter 7 on 3/18/86
Stockholders' equity unlikely

DIVERSIFIED MEDIA HLDGS INC (DE)
Recapitalized as TPI International, Inc. 1/3/2006
Each share Common 1¢ par exchanged for (0.001) share Common 1¢ par

DIVERSIFIED MEDIA INC (DE)
Liquidation completed
Each share Common 1¢ par received initial distribution of $0.30 cash 1/28/82
Each share Common 1¢ par received second distribution of $0.45 cash 3/25/82

Each share Common 1¢ par received third distribution of $0.30 cash 12/12/84
Each share Common 1¢ par received fourth distribution of $0.18 cash 5/12/86
Each share Common 1¢ par received fifth distribution of $0.10 cash 12/30/87
Each share Common 1¢ par received sixth and final distribution of $0.04 cash 2/5/90
Note: Certificates were not required to be surrendered and are now valueless

DIVERSIFIED METALS CORP. (MO)
Reincorporated under the laws of Delaware and Class B Conv. Common 50¢ par reclassified as Common 50¢ par 9/25/67
Diversified Metals Corp. (DE) name changed to Diversified Industries, Inc. 8/4/69
(See Diversified Industries, Inc.)

DIVERSIFIED METALS CORP (DE)
Class B Conv. Common 50¢ par reclassified as Common 50¢ par 9/25/67
Stock Dividend - 100% 5/27/68
Name changed to Diversified Industries, Inc. 8/4/69
(See Diversified Industries, Inc.)

DIVERSIFIED MICROWAVE APPLICATIONS INC (DE)
Charter cancelled and declared inoperative and void for non-payment of taxes 3/1/78

DIVERSIFIED MINERALS INC (UT)
Proclaimed dissolved for failure to file annual reports 3/1/89

DIVERSIFIED MINING INTERESTS (CANADA) LTD.
Recapitalized as Progress Diversified Minerals Ltd. 03/00/1949
Progress Diversified Minerals Ltd. name changed to Indigo Consolidated Gold Mines Ltd. 00/00/1949 which was acquired by Nationwide Minerals Ltd. 00/00/1952
(See Nationwide Minerals Ltd.)

DIVERSIFIED MONTHLY INCOME CORP (ON)
Monthly Income Dividend Shares no par called for redemption 9/30/99

DIVERSIFIED MTG INVS (MA)
Merged into Diversified Mortgage Investors, Inc. 08/31/1978
Each Share of Bene. Int. no par exchanged for (1) share Common 1¢ par
Diversified Mortgage Investors, Inc. reorganized as DMG Inc. 09/30/1980 which name changed to Danaher Corp. (FL) 09/26/1984 which reincorporated in Delaware 10/31/1986

DIVERSIFIED MTG INVS INC (FL)
Under plan of reorganization each share Common 1¢ par automatically became (1) share DMG Inc. Common 1¢ par 09/30/1980
DMG Inc. name changed to Danaher Corp. (FL) 09/26/1984 which reincorporated in Delaware 10/31/1986

DIVERSIFIED MTG WORKOUT CORP (DE)
Stock Dividend - 20% payable 10/15/2008 to holders of record 09/30/2008 Ex date - 09/26/2008
Recapitalized as Arem Pacific Corp. 07/29/2013
Each share Common $0.001 par exchanged for (0.00257731) share Common $0.001 par

DIVERSIFIED MOUNTAINEER CORP (WV)
Completely liquidated 09/26/1975
No stockholders' equity

DIVERSIFIED OIL & MINING CORP. (DE)
Acquired by Diversified Industrial Corp. 4/11/62
Each share Common 10¢ par exchanged for (0.086956) share Common 10¢ par
Diversified Industrial Corp. acquired by Diversified Industrial Corp. of Kansas, Inc. 4/16/65
(See Diversified Industrial Corp. of Kansas, Inc.)

DIVERSIFIED OPERATIONS INC (FL)
Proclaimed dissolved for failure to file reports and pay fees 12/11/76

DIVERSIFIED OPPORTUNITIES INC (DE)
Name changed to Sugarmade, Inc. 07/15/2011

DIVERSIFIED PFD SH TR (ON)
Name changed to Sentry Global Balanced Income Fund and Trust Units reclassified as Series X 05/24/2013

DIVERSIFIED PHOTOGRAPHIC INDS INC (DE)
Name changed to Spectrum Equities Inc. 02/26/1996
Spectrum Equities Inc. recapitalized as Imtek Office Solutions Inc. 04/22/1997
(See Imtek Office Solutions Inc.)

DIVERSIFIED PREFERRED FOODS LTD (BC)
Name changed to Diversified Publishing Ltd. 01/18/1990
(See Diversified Publishing Ltd.)

DIVERSIFIED PRIVATE EQUITY CORP (AB)
Class A Shares called for redemption at $4.500541 on 03/15/2012

DIVERSIFIED PROD INSPECTIONS INC (DE)
Certificates dated after 03/07/2001
Reincorporated 11/14/2008
State of incorporation changed from (FL) to (DE) 11/14/2008
Name changed to ProGreen Properties, Inc. 09/11/2009
ProGreen Properties, Inc. name changed to ProGreen US, Inc. 07/22/2016

DIVERSIFIED PROD INSPECTIONS INC (FL)
Ctfs. dated prior to 03/05/2001
Name changed to General Consumer Products, Inc. 03/05/2001
(See General Consumer Products, Inc.)

DIVERSIFIED PRODS CORP (AL)
Merged into Liggett Group Inc. 2/17/77
Each share Common 50¢ par exchanged for (0.4787) share Common $1 par
(See Liggett Group Inc.)

DIVERSIFIED PUBG LTD (BC)
Struck off register and declared dissolved for failure to file returns 07/09/1993

DIVERSIFIED REAL ASSET INCOME FD (MA)
Merged into Nuveen Real Asset Income & Growth Fund 09/11/2017
Each Common Share of Bene. Int. 1¢ par exchanged for (1.00249699) Common Shares of Bene. Int. 1¢ par

DIVERSIFIED REAL ESTATE INVESTMENT TRUST (CA)
Charter suspended for failure to file reports and pay taxes 02/00/1975

DIVERSIFIED RESH INC (NV)
Name changed to Immediate Entertainment Group, Inc. 04/01/1997
Immediate Entertainment Group, Inc. recapitalized as Strategic Growth

Ventures, Inc. 01/31/2005 which recapitalized as Beere Financial Group, Inc. 05/31/2006 which recapitalized as Steadfast Holdings Group, Inc. 10/01/2007 which recapitalized as Scorpex, Inc. 05/20/2011

DIVERSIFIED RESOURCES, INC. (CO)
Advertised defunct and inoperative for non-payment of franchise taxes 10/30/1959

DIVERSIFIED RESOURCES, INC. (DE)
Each share Common 10¢ par exchanged for (0.05) share Common 5¢ par 06/25/1966
Merged into W. I. D. E., Inc. 01/18/1968
Each share Common 5¢ par exchanged for (1) share Capital Stock 1¢ par

DIVERSIFIED RES CORP (NV)
Company reported out of business 00/00/1992
Details not available

DIVERSIFIED RES GROUP INC (UT)
Each share old Common $0.001 par exchanged for (0.2) share new Common $0.001 par 09/28/2001
Name changed to AeroGroup Inc. 07/15/2003
(See AeroGroup Inc.)

DIVERSIFIED RES INC (WY)
Recapitalized as Techtower Group, Inc. 07/20/1984
Each share Common 1¢ par exchanged for (0.33333333) share Common 1¢ par
(See Techtower Group, Inc.)

DIVERSIFIED RETAIL GROUP INC (MD)
Plan of reorganization under Chapter 11 Federal Bankruptcy proceedings confirmed 12/00/1992
No stockholders' equity

DIVERSIFIED SEC SOLUTIONS INC (DE)
Name changed to Henry Bros. Electronics, Inc. 08/08/2005
(See Henry Bros. Electronics, Inc.)

DIVERSIFIED SECURE VENTURES CORP (NV)
Recapitalized as Go Green Global Technologies Corp. 03/15/2012
Each share Common $0.001 par exchanged for (0.1) share Common $0.001 par

DIVERSIFIED SECURITIES TRUST
Liquidated in 1944

DIVERSIFIED SPECIALTY STORES CORP. (NY)
Name changed to Diversified Stores Corp. 1/9/59
Diversified Stores Corp. merged into City Stores Co. 1/30/60 which name changed to CSS Industries, Inc. 9/24/85

DIVERSIFIED SR SVCS INC (NC)
SEC revoked common stock registration 11/17/2009

DIVERSIFIED STANDARD SECURITIES LTD.
Merged into Consolidated Diversified Standard Securities Ltd. 00/00/1932
Details not available

DIVERSIFIED STORES CORP. (NY)
Merged into City Stores Co. 1/30/60
Each share Common 1¢ par exchanged for (0.1) share Common $5 par
City Stores Co. name changed to CSS Industries, Inc. 9/24/85

DIVERSIFIED STRATEGIES INC (CA)
Recapitalized as PPOL, Inc. 08/15/2002
Each share Common $0.001 par exchanged for (1/7) share Common $0.001 par
(See PPOL, Inc.)

DIVERSIFIED TECH INC (UT)
Name changed to DTI Medical Corp. 05/22/1989
(See DTI Medical Corp.)

DIVERSIFIED TECHNOLOGIES GROUP INC (NV)
Reincorporated 10/04/2000
Name changed 11/14/2000
State of incorporation changed from (DE) to (NV) 10/04/2000
Common $0.001 par split (4) for (1) by issuance of (3) additional shares payable 11/13/2000 to holders of record 11/10/2000 Ex date - 11/14/2000
Name changed from Diversified Technology Group Inc. to Diversified Technologies Group Inc. 11/14/2000
Name changed to X-Change Corp. 07/30/2001
X-Change Corp. name changed to Endocan Corp. 11/06/2013

DIVERSIFIED TECHNOLOGIES INC (WY)
Name changed to Tek Digitel Corp. 7/6/98

DIVERSIFIED TECHNOLOGIES MGMT INC (CO)
Charter suspended for failure to maintain a resident agent 11/12/85

DIVERSIFIED TECHNOLOGY INC (BC)
Name changed to Discrete TimeSystems Inc. 03/22/1988
Discrete TimeSystems Inc. recapitalized as ADI Technologies, Inc. 03/09/1992
(See ADI Technologies, Inc.)

DIVERSIFIED THERMAL SOLUTIONS INC (NV)
Merged into Fuzion 11/28/2011
Each share Common $0.0001 par exchanged for $0.005 cash

DIVERSIFIED TRUSTEE SHS (NY)
Original Series Trust Agreement terminated 00/00/1933
Series B Trust Agreement terminated 00/00/1937
Series D Trust Agreement terminated 00/00/1950
Series E Trust Agreement terminated 00/00/1960
Series C Trust Agreement terminated 02/01/1981
Each share Series C no par exchanged for stock or cash
Note: Option to receive stock expired 04/30/1981

DIVERSIFIED UTIL TR (ON)
Trust terminated 4/15/2004
Each Trust Unit no par received $28.89 cash

DIVERSIFIED WIRE & STL CORP AMER (CA)
Name changed to Diversified Earth Sciences, Inc. 07/15/1970
(See Diversified Earth Sciences, Inc.)

DIVERSIFOODS INC (NE)
Merged into Pillsbury Co. 08/06/1985
Each share Common 1¢ par exchanged for $11.50 cash

DIVERSIGLOBAL DIVIDEND VALUE FD (ON)
Under plan of merger each Trust Unit no par automatically became (0.7436) Dynamic Global Dividend Value Fund Series A Unit no par 03/26/2010

DIVERSINET CORP (ON)
Each share old Common no par exchanged for (0.25) share new Common no par 05/12/1997
Each share new Common no par exchanged again for (0.1) share new Common no par 01/28/2003
Completely liquidated
Each share new Common no par received first and final distribution of $0.0806 cash payable 12/31/2014 to holders of record 12/09/2014

DIVERSITRON (AZ)
Charter revoked for failure to file reports or pay fees 05/10/1977

DIVERSITRON INC (DE)
Charter cancelled and declared inoperative and void for non payment of taxes 03/01/1979

DIVERSITRUST ENERGY INCOME FD (ON)
Issue Information - 14,000,000 TR UNITS offered at $10 per Unit on 11/29/2004
Under plan of merger each Trust Unit no par automatically became (0.8028) Dynamic Energy Income Fund Series A Unit no par 03/26/2010

DIVERSITRUST INCOME FD (ON)
Under plan of merger each Trust Unit no par automatically became (0.835) Dynamic Strategic Yield Fund Series A Unit no par 03/26/2010

DIVERSITRUST INCOME PLUS FD (ON)
Under plan of merger each Trust Unit no par automatically became (0.6938) Dynamic Strategic Yield Fund Series A Unit no par 03/26/2010

DIVERSITRUST STABLE INCOME FD (ON)
Under plan of merger each Trust Unit no par automatically became (0.8224) Dynamic Strategic Yield Fund Series A Unit no par 03/26/2010

DIVERSITY CORP (AB)
Recapitalized 04/18/1994
Recapitalized from Diversity Capital Corp. to Diversity Corp. 04/18/1994
Each share Common no par exchanged for (0.1) share Common no par
Recapitalized as Pancontinental Energy Inc. 08/23/2002
Each share Common no par exchanged for (0.2) share Common no par
Pancontinental Energy Inc. recapitalized as Immunall Science Inc. (Old) 07/10/2007 which reorganized as Immunall Science Inc. (New) (AB) 03/31/2011 which reincorporated in British Columbia 06/30/2016 which recapitalized as AREV Nutrition Sciences 01/23/2017 which name changed to AREV Brands International Inc. 09/12/2018

DIVERSITY GROUP INTL INC (FL)
Each share old Common $0.001 par exchanged for (0.000002) share new Common $0.001 par 12/10/2008
New Common $0.001 par split (200) for (1) by issuance of (199) additional shares payable 12/12/2008 to holders of record 12/12/2008 Ex date - 12/15/2008
Recapitalized as Automotive Resource Network Holdings, Inc. 01/06/2012
Each share new Common $0.001 par exchanged for (0.001) share Common $0.001 par

DIVERSIYIELD INCOME FD (ON)
Under plan of merger each Trust Unit no par automatically became (0.6866) Dynamic Strategic Yield Fund Series A Unit no par 03/26/2010

DIVI HOTELS INC (DE)
Merged into WHDAC Inc. 3/2/98
Each share Common exchanged for $0.15 cash

DIVI HOTELS N V (NETHERLANDS ANTILLES)
Common $1 par split (3) for (2) by issuance of (0.5) additional share 10/31/85
Company went out of business in 1991
Details not available

DIVIDE EXTENSION CONSOLIDATED MINES CO. (NV)
Charter revoked for failure to file reports and pay fees 3/1/37

DIVIDEND & INCOME FD INC (MD)
Under plan of reorganization each share Common 1¢ par automatically became (1) share Dividend & Income Fund (DE) Common Shares of Bene. Int. 1¢ par 05/14/2012

DIVIDEND CAP GLOBAL RLTY EXPOSURE FD (DE)
Name changed 07/14/2008
Name changed from Dividend Capital Strategic Global Realty Fund to Dividend Capital Global Realty Exposure Fund 07/14/2008
Name changed to DCW Total Return Fund 03/16/2009
DCW Total Return Fund merged into DCA Total Return Fund 09/24/2010 which name changed to Virtus Total Return Fund 12/22/2011 which merged into Virtus Total Return Fund Inc. 04/03/2017

DIVIDEND CAP RLTY INCOME ALLOCATION FD (DE)
Issue Information - 12,100,000 shares COM offered at $15 per share on 02/23/2005
Name changed to DCA Total Return Fund 03/16/2009
DCA Total Return Fund name changed to Virtus Total Return Fund 12/22/2011

DIVIDEND CAP TR INC (MD)
Name changed to DCT Industrial Trust, Inc. 10/10/2006
DCT Industrial Trust, Inc. merged into Prologis, Inc. 08/22/2018

DIVIDEND SHS INC (MD)
Name changed to Bullock Dividend Shares, Inc. 01/01/1985
Bullock Dividend Shares, Inc. name changed to Alliance Dividend Shares, Inc. 03/13/1987 which name changed to Alliance Growth & Income Fund, Inc. 10/17/89 which name changed to AllianceBernstein Growth & Income Fund, Inc. 03/31/2003

DIVINE INC (DE)
Each share old Class A Common $0.001 par exchanged for (0.04) share new Class A Common $0.001 par 05/29/2002
Plan of reorganization under Chapter 11 Federal Bankruptcy proceedings effective 12/20/2004
No stockholders' equity

DIVINE INTERVENTURES INC (DE)
Issue Information - 14,285,000 shares CL A offered at $9 per share on 07/11/2000
Name changed to divine, inc. 2/27/2001
(See divine, inc.)

DIVINE SKIN INC (FL)
Recapitalized as DS Healthcare Group, Inc. 11/30/2012
Each share Common $0.001 par exchanged for (0.1) share Common $0.001 par

DIVIO HLDGS CORP (NV)
Name changed to Greenwood Hall, Inc. 07/01/2014

DIVOT GOLF CORP (DE)
Name changed to orbitTRAVEL.com Corp. 04/20/2000
orbitTRAVEL.com Corp. name

changed to Orbit Brands Corp. 10/12/2005
(See Orbit Brands Corp.)

DIVX INC (DE)
Acquired by Sonic Solutions 10/08/2010
Each share Common $0.001 par exchanged for (0.514) share Common no par and $3.75 cash
Sonic Solutions merged into Rovi Corp. 02/17/2011 which name changed to TiVo Corp. 09/08/2016

DIX HILLS EQUITIES GROUP INC (DE)
Name changed to Millennium Quest Inc. 03/22/2002
Millennium Quest Inc. recapitalized as American Lorain Corp. (DE) 07/25/2007 which reincorporated in Nevada 11/09/2009 which recapitalized as Planet Green Holdings Corp. 10/01/2018

DIX URANIUM CORP. (NV)
Recapitalized as Dix Mining Corp. 7/1/67
Each share Common 5¢ par exchanged for (0.2) share Common $1 par

DIXCOM INC (FL)
Proclaimed dissolved for failure to file reports and pay fees 06/00/1996

DIXEL INDS INC (DE)
Name changed to Weatherford International Inc. (Old) 02/17/1975
Weatherford International Inc. (Old) recapitalized as Weatherford Enterra, Inc. 10/05/1995 which merged into EVI Weatherford, Inc. 05/27/1998 which name changed to Weatherford International Inc. (New) (DE) 09/21/1998 which reincorporated in Bermuda as Weatherford International Ltd. 06/26/2002 which reincorporated in Switzerland 02/25/2009 which reincorporated in Ireland as Weatherford International PLC 06/18/2014

DIXICO INC (TX)
Common $1 par changed to 50¢ par and (1) additional share issued 12/23/1976
Acquired by Bell Fibre Products Corp. 08/26/1985
Each share Common 50¢ par exchanged for $10.50 cash

DIXIE ALUMINUM CORP. (GA)
Reorganized 06/12/1961
No stockholders' equity

DIXIE AUTO INSURANCE CO. (AL)
Merged into Specialty Insurance Co. 09/29/1978
Details not available

DIXIE CAROLINA MNG LTD (ON)
Charter cancelled and declared dissolved for failure to file returns and pay fees 07/27/1976

DIXIE CHEMTECH INC (TX)
Name changed to Chemtech Industries, Inc. 03/10/1970
Chemtech Industries, Inc. name changed to Waste Resources Corp. 05/03/1972 which merged into Warner Co. 07/06/1977
(See Warner Co.)

DIXIE CUP CO. (DE)
Stock Dividend - 100% 11/26/1951
Merged into American Can Co. 06/26/1957
Each share Common no par exchanged for (1.65) shares Common $12.50 par
American Can Co. name changed to Primerica Corp. (NJ) 04/28/1987 which was acquired by Primerica Corp. (DE) 12/15/1988 which name changed to Travelers Inc. 12/31/1993 which name changed to Travelers Group Inc. 04/16/1995

which name changed to Citigroup Inc. 10/08/1998

DIXIE DINETTES, INC. (VA)
Stock Dividend - 50% 02/20/1963
Acquired by National Service Industries, Inc. 01/03/1969
Each share Common $1 par exchanged for (0.33333333) share Common $1 par
(See National Service Industries, Inc.)

DIXIE EQUIP INC (AR)
Charter revoked for failure to file reports and pay fees 03/21/1990

DIXIE FIRE & CASUALTY CO. (SC)
Merged into Southern Home Insurance Co. 01/01/1964
Each share Capital Stock $10 par exchanged for (1) share Common $5 par

DIXIE FIRE INSURANCE CO.
Acquired by American Insurance Co. (NJ) 00/00/1929
Details not available

DIXIE FOODS INTL INC (FL)
Name changed to Preferred Restaurant Brands, Inc. 04/21/2015

DIXIE GAS & UTILITIES CO.
Merged into United Gas Corp. 00/00/1931
Details not available

DIXIE GULF GAS CO.
Acquired by United Gas Corp. 00/00/1930
Details not available

DIXIE HOME STORES (SC)
Stock Dividends - 100% 03/04/1948; 100% 02/23/1955
Merged into Winn-Dixie Stores, Inc. 11/14/1955
Each share Common $1 par exchanged for (1) share Common $1 par
(See Winn-Dixie Stores, Inc.)

DIXIE INDS (CA)
Name changed to Dymaco Corp. (CA) and Common no par changed to 1¢ par 01/16/1980
Dymaco Corp. (CA) reincorporated in Delaware as Agric Development Corp. 05/15/1981 which name changed to Wil Wright's Ice Cream, Inc. 04/15/1983
(See Wil Wright's Ice Cream, Inc.)

DIXIE LAND & TIMBER CORP. (GA)
Out of business 11/05/1974
No stockholders' equity

DIXIE LIME & STONE CO. (FL)
Completely liquidated 05/15/1967
Each share Common $1 par exchanged for first and final distribution of (0.2427184) share New York & Honduras Rosario Mining Co. Capital Stock $1 par
New York & Honduras Rosario Mining Co. name changed to Rosario Resources Corp. 04/27/1973 which merged into Amax Inc. 04/10/1980 which merged into Cyprus Amax Minerals Co. 11/15/1993 which merged into Phelps Dodge Corp. 12/02/1999 which merged into Freeport-McMoRan Copper & Gold Inc. 03/19/2007 which name changed to Freeport-McMoRan Inc. 07/14/2014

DIXIE MERCERIZING CO. (TN)
Recapitalized as Dixie Yarns, Inc. 12/31/1964
Each share Common no par exchanged for (3) shares Common no par
Dixie Yarns, Inc. name changed to Dixie Group, Inc. 05/02/1997

DIXIE MNG & MLG CORP (MI)
Recapitalized as Digital Gas, Inc. 12/21/1998
Each share Common $0.001 par exchanged for (0.0001) share Common $0.001 par
(See Digital Gas, Inc.)

DIXIE NAT RES INC (NY)
Dissolved by proclamation 12/24/1991

DIXIE NATL CORP (MS)
Stock Dividends - 10% 04/09/1982; 10% 04/08/1983; 50% 05/15/1984; 20% 04/25/1986; 20% 04/30/1987; 20% 04/28/1989
Name changed to Ethika Corp. 08/13/1996
Ethika Corp. recapitalized as Tradequest International, Inc. (MS) 04/16/2001 which reorganized in Nevada 10/11/2005
(See Tradequest International, Inc.)

DIXIE NATURAL GAS CORP. (NY)
Each share Common 1¢ par exchanged for (0.5) share Common 2¢ par 11/04/1960
Name changed to Dixie Natural Resources, Inc. 09/19/1976
(See Dixie Natural Resources, Inc.)

DIXIE PORTLAND CEMENT CO.
Acquired by Pennsylvania-Dixie Cement Corp. 00/00/1926
Details not available

DIXIE REFINING CO.
Dissolved 00/00/1938
Details not available

DIXIE SECURITIES CORP.
Merged into Dixie-Vortex Co. 12/30/1938
Each share Class A Common no par exchanged for (1) share Class A Common no par
Each share Common no par exchanged for (1) share Common no par
Dixie-Vortex Co. name changed to Dixie Cup Co. 00/00/1943 which merged into American Can Co. 06/26/1957 which name changed to Primerica Corp. (NJ) 04/28/1987 which was acquired by Primerica Corp. (DE) 12/15/1988 which name changed to Travelers Inc. 12/31/1993 which name changed to Travelers Group Inc. 04/16/1995 which name changed to Citigroup Inc. 10/08/1998

DIXIE TERMINAL CO. (OH)
Acquired by American Financial Corp. 00/00/1968
Details not available

DIXIE-VORTEX CO.
Name changed to Dixie Cup Co. 00/00/1943
Dixie Cup Co. merged into American Can Co. 06/26/1957 which name changed to Primerica Corp. (NJ) 04/28/1987 which was acquired by Primerica Corp. (DE) 12/15/1988 which name changed to Travelers Inc. 12/31/1993 which name changed to Travelers Group Inc. 04/16/1995 which name changed to Citigroup Inc. 10/08/1998

DIXIE YARNS INC (TN)
Common no par split (6) for (5) by issuance of (0.2) additional share 05/16/1978
Common no par split (2) for (1) by issuance of (1) additional share 06/09/1986
Common no par split (2) for (1) by issuance of (1) additional share 11/14/1986
Common no par changed to $3 par and (2) additional shares issued 11/25/1986
Name changed to Dixie Group, Inc. 05/02/1997

DIXILYN CORP (DE)
Name changed 02/15/1961
Name changed from Dixilyn Drilling Corp. to Dixilyn Corp. 02/15/1961
Merged into Panhandle Eastern Pipe Line Co. 05/05/1977
Each share Common 10¢ par exchanged for (0.278453039) share Common no par
Panhandle Eastern Pipe Line Co. reorganized as Panhandle Eastern Corp. 05/22/1981 which name changed to Panenergy Corp. 04/26/1996 which merged into Duke Energy Corp. (NC) 06/18/1997 which merged into Duke Energy Corp. (DE) 04/03/2006

DIXON BANCORP, INC. (DE)
Acquired by AMCORE Financial, Inc. 11/30/1992
Each share Common $10 par exchanged for $254.33 cash

DIXON CAP CORP (CO)
Administratively dissolved 12/01/2002

DIXON CHEM & RESH INC (NJ)
Name changed to Essex Chemical Corp. 06/20/1962
(See Essex Chemical Corp.)

DIXON CHEM INDS INC (NJ)
Name changed to Paulsboro Chemical Industries, Inc. 03/28/1963
Paulsboro Chemical Industries, Inc. merged into Essex Chemical Corp. 04/17/1970
(See Essex Chemical Corp.)

DIXON CREEK OIL & REFINING CO.
Merged into King Oil Co. (DE) 00/00/1936
Details not available

DIXON INDUSTRIES CORP. (DE)
Completely liquidated 12/17/73
Each share Common $1 par exchanged for first and final distribution of $24.413958 cash

DIXON JOSEPH CRUCIBLE CO (NJ)
Each share Common $100 par exchanged for (5) shares Common $20 par 01/00/1955
Each share Common $20 par exchanged for (2) shares Common $10 par 04/21/1969
Merged into Dixon Ticonderoga Co. 09/21/1983
Each share Common $10 par exchanged for $15 principal amount of 12.5% Subordinated Sinking Fund Debentures due 03/01/1993 and $29 cash

DIXON NATL BK (DIXON, IL)
Capital Stock $100 par split (3) for (1) by issuance of (2) additional shares 12/20/1943
Capital Stock $100 par changed to $20 par and (4) additional shares issued 01/18/1972
Stock Dividends - 100% 05/16/1958; 100% 01/18/1977
Reorganized as Dixon Bancorp, Inc. 01/10/1985
Each share Capital Stock $20 par exchanged for (1) share Common $10 par
(See Dixon Bancorp, Inc.)

DIXON OIL & GAS INC (NV)
Old Common $0.001 par split (4) for (1) by issuance (3) additional shares payable 06/23/2003 to holders of record 06/18/2003 Ex date - 06/24/2003
Each share old Common $0.001 par exchanged for (5) shares new Common $0.001 par 09/15/2003
Recapitalized as Galloway Energy Inc. 12/01/2006
Each share new Common $0.001 par exchanged for (0.001) share Common $0.001 par
(See Galloway Energy Inc.)

DIXON POWDERMAKER FURNITURE CO (FL)
Stock Dividend - 10% 05/01/1959
Through 00/00/1967 purchase offer and subsequent purchases all but (700) shares acquired by company and principals 04/12/1971
Public interest eliminated

DIXON TICONDEROGA CO (DE)
Common $1 par split (5) for (4) by issuance of (0.25) additional share 05/25/1987
Common $1 par split (2) for (1) by issuance of (1) additional share 07/22/1988
Merged into Pencil Acquisition Corp. 02/07/2005
Each share Common $1 par exchanged for $7 cash

DIXONS GROUP PLC (UNITED KINGDOM)
ADR's for Ordinary 10p par split (3.9) for (1) by issuance of (2.9) additional ADR's payable 03/08/2000 to holders of record 03/07/2000
Name changed to DSG International PLC 01/27/2006
DSG International PLC name changed to Dixons Retail PLC 09/21/2010

DIXONS RETAIL PLC (UNITED KINGDOM)
ADR agreement terminated 09/26/2014
Each ADR for Ordinary exchanged for $2.49704 cash

DIXSON INC (CO)
Each share Common 50¢ par exchanged for (0.25) share Common $2 par 01/18/1968
Stock Dividends - 25% 09/15/1976; 25% 04/15/1977; 15% 09/15/1984
Merged into Dixson Acquisition Corp. 08/24/1987
Each share Common $2 par exchanged for $3.15 cash

DJN INC (DE)
Recapitalized as Allen Energy Co. 09/27/1990
Each share Common 2¢ par exchanged for (0.02) share Common $0.001 par
(See Allen Energy Co.)

DJO INC (DE)
Name changed 05/26/2006
Issue Information - 9,000,000 shares COM offered at $17 per share on 11/14/2001
Name changed from DJ Orthopedics, Inc. to DJO, Inc. 05/26/2006
Merged into ReAble Therapeutics Finance LLC 11/20/2007
Each share Common 1¢ par exchanged for $50.25 cash

DK INDS INC (CO)
Name changed to GDC Group, Inc. 11/14/96
(See GDC Group, Inc.)

DK INVS INC (NY)
Common $1 par changed to $0.0001 par 03/30/2005
Under plan of partial liquidation each share Common $0.0001 par received distribution of $13.19 cash payable 02/06/2004 to holders of record 01/30/2004 Ex date - 02/09/2004
Reorganized under the laws of Nevada as Resource Acquisition Group, Inc. 08/05/2010
Each share Common $0.0001 par exchanged for (0.005) share Common $0.001 par
Note: No holder will receive fewer than (100) shares
Resource Acquisition Group, Inc. name changed to American Retail Group, Inc. 04/01/2011

DK PLATINUM CORP (BC)
Name changed to TEGL Systems Corp. 10/04/1990
(See TEGL Systems Corp.)

DK SINOPHARMA INC (NV)
Name changed to VGambling, Inc. 08/14/2014
VGambling, Inc. name changed to Esports Entertainment Group, Inc. 05/25/2017

DKS CO. (OH)
Liquidated 11/30/1960
Details not available

DKSH HLDG LTD (SWITZERLAND)
ADR agreement terminated 10/23/2018
No ADR's remain outstanding

DKW SYS CORP (AB)
Merged into APG Solutions & Technologies 06/30/1998
Each share Common no par exchanged for $0.47 cash

DLB OIL & GAS INC (OK)
Issue Information - 3,000,000 shares COM offered at $10 per share on 07/25/1995
Merged into Chesapeake Energy Corp. 04/28/1998
Each share Common $0.001 par exchanged for approximately (0.3854) share Common 1¢ par, (0.2277) share Bayard Drilling Technologies Inc. Common 1¢ par, (0.02) Bayard Drilling Technologies Inc. Common Stock Purchase Warrant expiring 07/10/2002, (0.8318) share WRT Energy Corp. Common 1¢ par and $1.35 cash
Each share Common $0.001 par received an initial additional distribution of (0.01814605) share Gulfport Energy Corp. new Common 1¢ par 01/28/2003
(See each company's listing)
Each share Common $0.001 par received a second additional distribution of $0.02620930 cash 03/19/2010

DLJ CAP TR I (DE)
8.42% Trust Preferred Securities called for redemption at $25 on 8/31/2001

DLR FUNDING INC (NV)
SEC revoked common stock registration 03/08/2016

DLS, INC. (FL)
Proclaimed dissolved for failure to file reports and pay fees 11/1/85

DM HLDGS INC (DE)
Merged into International Metals & Machines, Inc. 12/23/1982
Each share Common $1 par exchanged for $0.30 cash

DM MGMT CO (DE)
Common 1¢ par split (3) for (2) by issuance of (0.5) additional share payable 6/30/98 to holders of record 6/12/98
Name changed to J. Jill Group Inc. 6/1/99
(See J. Jill Group Inc.)

DM PRODS INC (NV)
Each share old Common $0.001 par exchanged for (0.00531914) share new Common $0.001 par 07/17/2013
Name changed to New Asia Holdings, Inc. 02/13/2015

DMA MINERALS INC (NV)
Name changed to Liberty Energy Corp. 06/11/2008

DMC STRATEX NETWORKS INC (DE)
Name changed to Stratex Networks, Inc. 09/10/2002
Stratex Networks, Inc. merged into Harris Stratex Networks, Inc. 01/26/2007 which name changed to Aviat Networks, Inc. 01/27/2010

DMC TAX-FREE INCOME USA INC (MD)
Name changed to Delaware Group Tax-Free Fund Inc. 6/1/92

DMD DIGITAL HEALTH CONNECTIONS GROUP INC (CANADA)
Acquired by 10653365 Canada Inc. 10/04/2018
Each share Common no par exchanged for $0.25 cash
Note: Unexchanged certificates will be cancelled and become without value 10/04/2024

DME INTERACTIVE HLDGS INC NEW (DE)
Charter cancelled and declared inoperative and void for non-payment of taxes 03/01/2009

DME INTERACTIVE HLDGS INC OLD (DE)
Each share old Common $0.001 par exchanged for (0.01) share new Common $0.001 par 12/27/2005
Name changed to VidShadow.com, Inc. 06/28/2007
VidShadow.com, Inc. name changed to DME Interactive Holdings, Inc. (New) 05/13/2008
(See DME Interactive Holdings, Inc. (New))

DMG INC (FL)
Name changed to Danaher Corp. (FL) 09/26/1984
Danaher Corp. (FL) reincorporated in Delaware 10/31/1986

DMG MORI SEIKI CO LTD (JAPAN)
Name changed to DMG Mori Co., Ltd. 07/02/2015

DMH CORP (MI)
Common $1 par split (4) for (3) by issuance of (0.33333333) additional share 06/25/1969
Merged into National Gypsum Co. 07/31/1970
Each share Common $1 par exchanged for (0.818) share Common 50¢ par
(See National Gypsum Co.)

DMI FURNITURE INC (DE)
Merged into Flexsteel Industries, Inc. 10/02/2003
Each share Common 10¢ par exchanged for $3.30 cash

DMI INC. (MA)
Completely liquidated 02/00/1976
No stockholders' equity

DMI INC (CO)
Each share old Common no par exchanged for (0.01) share new Common no par 7/17/89
Recapitalized as Dega Technology Inc. 12/26/97
Each share new Common no par exchanged for (0.001) share Common no par
(See Dega Technology Inc.)

DMI TECHNOLOGY INC (AB)
Cease trade order effective 11/22/2002

DML SVCS INC (NV)
Each share old Common $0.001 par exchanged for (4) shares new Common $0.001 par 11/25/2002
Name changed to El Capitan Precious Metals, Inc. 3/19/2003

DMR GROUP INC (CANADA)
Merged into Amdahl Corp. 10/19/1995
Each share Class A Subordinate no par exchanged for $12.50 cash

DMR RES LTD (ON)
Delisted from Toronto Venture Stock Exchange 06/05/2002

DMRC CORP (DE)
Name changed to Digimarc Corp. (DE) (New) 10/16/2008
Digimarc Corp. (DE) (New) reincorporated in Oregon 04/30/2010

DMS INDS INC (NY)
Name changed to Swissray International, Inc. (NY) 6/1/95
Swissray International, Inc. (NY) reincorporated in Delaware 7/11/2002
(See Swissray International, Inc.)

DMT ENERGY INC (NV)
SEC revoked common stock registration 12/17/2004

DMX INC (DE)
Merged into TCI Music, Inc. 07/11/1997
Each share Common 1¢ par exchanged for (0.25) share Ser. A Common 1¢ par
TCI Music, Inc. name changed Liberty Digital Inc. 09/10/1999 which merged into Liberty Media Corp. (New) 03/14/2002 which reorganized as Liberty Media Corp. (Incorporated 02/28/2006) 05/10/2006 which name changed to Liberty Interactive Corp. 09/26/2011 which name changed to Qurate Retail, Inc. 04/10/2018

DMYTRYK BOYD PRODTNS INC (NY)
Name changed to E-Z 8 Motels, Inc. 06/20/1974
(See E-Z 8 Motels, Inc.)

DNA BEVERAGE CORP (NV)
Each share Common $0.001 par received distribution of (1) share Imagine Media, Ltd. Common $0.00001 par payable 07/31/2008 to holders of record 08/23/2007
Ex date - 08/21/2007
Reorganized under the laws of Oklahoma as Digital Caddies, Inc. 11/14/2011
Each share Common $0.001 par exchanged for (0.0117647) share Common $0.001 par
Digital Caddies, Inc. name changed to IZON Network, Inc. 09/19/2017

DNA MED INC (UT)
Recapitalized as United Heritage Corp. (UT) 09/15/1987
Each share Common $0.0001 par exchanged for (0.1) share Common $0.001 par
United Heritage Corp. (UT) reincorporated in Delaware as Glen Rose Petroleum Corp. 06/05/2008

DNA PLT TECHNOLOGY CORP (DE)
Merged into DNAP Holding Corp. 9/26/96
Each share $2.25 Conv. Exchangeable Preferred 1¢ par exchanged for (0.68375133) share Common 1¢ par
Each share Common 1¢ par exchanged for (0.1) share Common 1¢ par
DNAP Holding Corp. name changed to Bionova Holding Corp. 4/29/99

DNA PRECIOUS METALS INC (NV)
Each share Common $0.001 par received distribution of (0.5) share DNA Canada Inc. Restricted Common payable 02/12/2015 to holders of record 02/03/2015
Name changed to Breathe Ecig Corp. 03/11/2015
Breathe Ecig Corp. recapitalized as White Fox Ventures, Inc. 06/22/2016

DNAP HLDG CORP (DE)
Name changed to Bionova Holding Corp. 4/29/99

DNAPRINT GENOMICS INC (UT)
Each share old Common $0.001 par exchanged for (0.05) share new Common $0.001 par 07/12/2005
Charter expired 02/17/2009

DNB NOR A.S.A. OLD (NORWAY)
Name changed 12/04/2003
Name changed from DNB Holding A.S.A. to DnB NOR A.S.A. (Old) 12/04/2003
ADR agreement terminated 10/25/2010
Each 144A Sponsored ADR for Ordinary exchanged for $170.979888 cash

DNB NOR ASA NEW (NORWAY)
Name changed to DnB A.S.A. 11/16/2011

DNC MULTIMEDIA CORP (GA)
Chapter 11 bankruptcy proceedings dismissed 06/30/2009
No stockholders' equity

DNE CORP (UT)
Recapitalized as NFS Services Inc. 01/06/1994
Each share Common $0.002 par exchanged for (0.2) share Common $0.002 par
NFS Services Inc. name changed to Walnut Financial Services Inc. 02/27/1995 which name changed to THCG, Inc. (UT) 11/01/1999 which reincorporated in Delaware 05/16/2000 which name changed to THCG Liquidating Trust 07/16/2001
(See THCG Liquidating Trust)

DNI HLDGS INC (BC)
Struck off register and declared dissolved for failure to file returns 09/03/1993

DNIB UNWIND INC (DE)
Plan of reorganization under Liquidating Chapter 11 Federal Bankruptcy proceedings effective 10/11/2016
No stockholders' equity

DNIPROAZOT JSC (UKRAINE)
Each old Reg. S Sponsored GDR for Ordinary exchanged for (0.008) new Reg. S Sponsored GDR for Ordinary 11/09/2006
Basis changed from (1:20) to (1:2,500) 11/09/2006
GDR agreement terminated 05/17/2017
Each new Reg. S Sponsored GDR for Ordinary exchanged for (2,500) shares Ordinary
Note: Unexchanged GDR's will be sold and the proceeds, if any, held for claim after 05/21/2018

DNIPROENERGO (UKRAINE)
Name changed to DTEK Dniproenergo PJSC 02/27/2014
(See DTEK Dniproenergo PJSC)

DNIPROSHYNA OJSC (UKRAINE)
GDR agreement terminated 11/10/2015
No GDR holders' equity

DNO INTL ASA (NORWAY)
Name changed to DNO A.S.A. 06/27/2014

DNP SELECT INCOME FD INC (MD)
Remarketed Preferred Ser. B $0.001 par called for redemption at $100,000 on 03/04/2009
Auction Rate Preferred Ser. T $0.001 par called for redemption at $25,000 on 03/25/2009
Auction Rate Preferred Ser. M $0.001 par called for redemption at $25,000 on 04/07/2009
Remarketed Preferred Ser. A $0.001 par called for redemption at $100,000 on 04/15/2009
Remarketed Preferred Ser. C $0.001 par called for redemption at $100,000 on 04/29/2009
Auction Rate Preferred Ser. W $0.001 par called for redemption at $25,000 on 05/28/2009
Auction Rate Preferred Ser. TH $0.001 par called for redemption at $25,000 on 12/21/2012
Auction Rate Preferred Ser. F $0.001 par called for redemption at $25,000 on 12/24/2012
Remarketed Preferred Ser. D $0.001 par called for redemption at $100,000 on 03/12/2014
Remarketed Preferred Ser. E $0.001 par called for redemption at $100,000 on 03/19/2014
(Additional Information in Active)

DNX CORP (DE)
Name changed to Chrysalis International Corp. 12/18/1996
Chrysalis International Corp. merged into Phoenix International Life Sciences, Inc. 04/30/1999 which merged into MDS Inc. 05/15/2000 which name changed to Nordion Inc. 11/01/2010
(See Nordion Inc.)

DOAK AIRCRAFT CO., INC. (CA)
Liquidation completed 07/02/1962
Details not available

DOAK PHARMACAL INC (NY)
Merged into BP Acquisition Corp. 01/11/1995
Each share Common 10¢ par exchanged for $1.74 cash

DOANE PET CARE CO (DE)
14.25% Sr. Exchangeable Preferred called for redemption at $103.32 on 11/22/2005

DOB CORP. (CA)
Acquired by Fairmont Foods Co. 12/22/1965
Each share Common no par exchanged for (0.3724) share Common 50¢ par
Fairmont Foods Co. merged into American Financial Corp. 07/24/1980
(See American Financial Corp.)

DOBBS HOUSES, INC. (TN)
Common $1 par changed to 50¢ par and (1) additional share issued 11/14/1958
Common 50¢ par changed to $0.16666666 par and (2) additional shares issued 03/23/1960
Stock Dividend - 10% 08/31/1951
Merged into Beech-Nut Life Savers, Inc. 06/30/1966
Each share Common $0.16666666 par exchanged for (0.5) share $2 Conv. Preferred $4.75 par
Beech-Nut Life Savers, Inc. merged into Squibb Beech-Nut, Inc. 01/15/1968 which name changed to Squibb Corp. 04/30/1971 which merged into Bristol- Myers Squibb Co. 10/04/1989

DOBECKMUN CO. (OH)
Common $1 par split (3) for (1) by issuance of (2) additional shares 00/00/1946
Stock Dividend - 10% 01/25/1957
Merged into Dow Chemical Co. 08/31/1957
Each share Common $1 par exchanged for (0.75) share Common $5 par
Dow Chemical Co. merged into DowDuPont Inc. 09/01/2017

DOBELL PORCUPINE MINES LTD. (ON)
Charter cancelled 00/00/1963

DOBHAI VENTURES INC (BC)
Name changed to Formation Fluid Management Inc. 09/08/2010
Formation Fluid Management Inc. merged into Robix Environmental Technologies, Inc. 10/26/2016

DOBI MED INTL INC (DE)
Plan of reorganization under Chapter 11 Federal Bankruptcy Code effective 10/15/2008
No stockholders' equity

DOBIE MINES, LTD. (ON)
Charter surrendered 02/00/1961
No stockholders' equity

DOBLIQUE INC (NV)
Common $0.001 par split (5) for (1) by issuance of (4) additional shares payable 03/04/2003 to holders of record 03/03/2003 Ex date - 03/05/2003
Name changed to Inyx, Inc. (NV) 05/08/2003
Inyx, Inc. (NV) reincorporated in Delaware 08/30/2006

DOBRANA RES LTD (BC)
Recapitalized as Big Star Energy Inc. 11/09/1998
Each share Common no par exchanged for (0.2) share Common no par
Big Star Energy Corp. recapitalized as Arcland Resources Inc. 02/19/2004

DOBRY (D.A.) SECURITIES CO.
Bankrupt 00/00/1931
No stockholders' equity

DOBSON COMMUNICATIONS CORP (OK)
Stock Dividends - in 12.25% Exchangeable Sr. Preferred to holders of 12.25% Exchangeable Sr. Preferred 3.13055% payable 10/15/1999 to holders of record 10/01/1999; 3.13% payable 01/15/2000 to holders of record 01/01/2000; 3.105% payable 04/15/2000 to holders of record 04/01/2000; 3.063% payable 07/15/2000 to holders of record 07/01/2000; 3.13% payable 10/15/2000 to holders of record 10/01/2000; 3.13% payable 01/15/2001 to holders of record 01/01/2001 Ex date - 12/27/2000; 3.062% payable 04/15/2001 to holders of record 04/01/2001 Ex date - 03/28/2001; 3.096% payable 07/15/2001 to holders of record 07/01/2001 Ex date - 06/27/2001; 3.13% payable 10/15/2001 to holders of record 10/01/2001 Ex date - 09/27/2001; 3.13% payable 01/15/2002 to holders of record 01/01/2002 Ex date - 12/27/2001; 3.062% payable 04/15/2002 to holders of record 04/01/2002 Ex date - 04/01/2002; 3.097% payable 07/15/2002 to holders of record 07/01/2002 Ex date - 06/27/2002; 3.13% payable 10/15/2002 to holders of record 10/01/2002 Ex date - 09/27/2002; 3.165% payable 01/16/2003 to holders of record 01/01/2003 Ex date - 12/27/2002; in 13% Exchangeable Sr. Preferred to holders of 13% Exchangeable Sr. Preferred 3.222% payable 08/02/2001 to holders of record 07/15/2001 Ex date - 07/11/2001; 3.322% payable 11/01/2001 to holders of record 10/15/2001 Ex date - 10/11/2001; 3.322% payable 02/01/2002 to holders of record 01/15/2002 Ex date - 01/11/2002; 3.214% payable 05/01/2002 to holders of record 04/15/2002 Ex date - 04/11/2002; 3.322% payable 08/01/2002 to holders of record 07/15/2002 Ex date - 07/11/2002; 3.22% payable 11/01/2002 to holders of record 10/15/2002 Ex date - 10/10/2002; 3.322% payable 02/01/2003 to holders of record 01/15/2003 Ex date - 01/13/2003; 3.214% payable 05/01/2003 to holders of record 04/15/2003 Ex date - 04/11/2003; 3.322% payable 08/01/2003 to holders of record 07/15/2003 Ex date - 07/11/2003; 3.322% payable 11/01/2003 to holders of record 10/15/2003 Ex date - 10/10/2003; 3.25% payable 05/01/2004 to holders of record 04/15/2004 Ex date - 04/13/2004; in Conv. Preferred Ser. F to holders of Conv. Preferred Ser. F 7% payable 09/12/2005 to holders of record 09/01/2005 Ex date - 08/30/2005; 3.5% payable 10/15/2005 to holders of record 09/30/2005 Ex date - 09/28/2005
12.25% Sr. Exchangeable Preferred called for redemption at $1,000 plus $220.38 accrued dividends on 03/01/2006
13% Sr. Exchangeable Preferred called for redemption at $1,043.33 plus $227.65 accrued dividends on 03/01/2006
Accredited Investors Conv. Preferred Ser. F $1 par called for redemption at $178.571 plus $5.1488 accrued dividends on 10/04/2007
Accredited Investors Preferred Ser. F $1 par called for redemption at $178.571 plus $5.1488 accrued dividends on 10/04/2007
Conv. Preferred Ser. F $1 par called for redemption at $178.571 plus $5.1488 accrued dividends on 10/04/2007
Merged into AT&T Inc. 11/16/2007
Each share Class A Common $0.001 par exchanged for $13 cash

DOC HOLLYWOOD KIDZ (NV)
Recapitalized as Doc Hollywood Studios, Inc. 10/06/2005
Each share Common $0.0001 par exchanged for (0.01) share Common $0.0001 par
Doc Hollywood Studios, Inc. name changed to Hollywood Studios International 03/24/2006

DOC HOLLYWOOD STUDIOS INC (NV)
Name changed to Hollywood Studios International 03/24/2006

DOC LIQUIDATION CORP. (DE)
Completely liquidated 03/11/1985
Each share Common 10¢ par exchanged for first and final distribution of $2.75 cash

DOCA CAP CORP (BC)
Name changed to Great Northern Gold Exploration Corp. (BC) 10/10/2012
Great Northern Gold Exploration Corp. (BC) reorganized in Ontario as Poydras Gaming Finance Corp. 05/08/2014 which reincorporated in British Columbia 11/12/2015 which name changed to Integrity Gaming Corp. 01/02/2018

DOCANA OILS & MINES, LTD. (ON)
Charter cancelled and proclaimed dissolved for failure to pay taxes and file returns 04/09/1975

DOCDATA NV (NETHERLANDS)
ADR agreement terminated 12/31/2002
Each NY Registry Share NLG exchanged for $2.54 cash

DOCENT INC (DE)
Each share old Common $0.001 par exchanged for (0.33333333) share new Common $0.001 par 10/28/2002
Merged into SumTotal Systems, Inc. 03/19/2004
Each share new Common $0.001 par exchanged for (0.7327) share Common $0.001 par
(See SumTotal Systems, Inc.)

DOCKTOR PET CTRS INC (PA)
Common no par changed to 1¢ par 02/25/1970
Each share Common 1¢ par exchanged for (0.25) share Common 4¢ par 03/02/1981
Each share Common 4¢ par exchanged for (0.00016666) share Common 4¢ par 04/20/1982
Note: In effect holders received $2.80 cash per share and public interest was eliminated

DOCPLANET COM INC (CO)
Declared defunct and inoperative for failure to pay taxes and file annual reports 08/01/2002

DOCPLUS NET CORP (DE)
Reorganized under the laws of

Nevada as Sucre Agricultural Corp. 04/21/2006
Each share Common $0.001 par exchanged for (0.01) share Common $0.001 par
Sucre Agricultural Corp. recapitalized as Bluefire Ethanol Fuels, Inc. 06/22/2006 which name changed to BlueFire Renewables, Inc. 10/25/2010

DOCSALES COM INC (CO)
Name changed to Docplanet.com Inc. 10/19/1999
(See Docplanet.com Inc.)

DR ABRAVANELS FORMULAS INC (NV)
Name changed to Infotopia, Inc. 04/27/2000
(See Infotopia, Inc.)

DR CHRISTOPHERS ORIG FORMULAS INC (NJ)
Recapitalized as NFI Holdings Inc. 12/11/2001
Each share Common $0.001 par exchanged for (0.1) share Common $0.001 par
NFI Holdings Inc. name changed to ICR Systems, Inc. 11/18/2002 which name changed to Redux Holdings, Inc. 05/30/2006

DOCTOR JACK POT MNG CO (WY)
Recapitalized as First International Corp. 09/11/1972
Each share Capital Stock $0.025 par exchanged for (1) share Capital Stock 1¢ par
(See First International Corp.)

DR OWL ONLINE INC (TX)
Reincorporated under the laws of Delaware as Green Power Energy Holdings Corp. 05/02/2003
Green Power Energy Holdings Corp. (DE) reorganized in Nevada as Axiom Management Inc. 06/15/2007 which name changed to Potential Holdings, Inc. 07/24/2007 which name changed to RightSmile, Inc. 08/28/2009

DR PEPPER BOTTLING CO SOUTHN CALIF (CA)
Merged into Dr Pepper Co. 02/23/1977
Each share Common 50¢ par exchanged for (0.8) share Capital Stock no par
(See Dr Pepper Co.)

DR PEPPER BOTTLING HLDGS INC (DE)
Merged into Tosca Acquisition Corp. 10/07/1999
Each share Class A Common 1¢ par exchanged for $25 cash

DR PEPPER CO (CO)
Each share old Capital Stock no par exchanged for (4) shares new Capital Stock no par 10/15/1936
Capital Stock no par split (2) for (1) by issuance of (1) additional share 04/03/1964
Capital Stock no par split (2) for (1) by issuance of (1) additional share 04/10/1968
Capital Stock no par split (3) for (1) by issuance of (2) additional shares 04/13/1970
Capital Stock no par split (2) for (1) by issuance of (1) additional share 11/09/1972
Dr. Pepper Co. name changed to Dr Pepper Co. 04/20/1976
Merged into Forstmann Little & Co. 02/28/1984
Each share Capital Stock no par exchanged for $22 cash

DR PEPPER CO NEW (DE)
Name changed to Dr Pepper/Seven Up Corp. 10/28/1992
(See Dr Pepper/Seven Up Corp.)

DR PEPPER/SEVEN-UP COS INC (DE)
Merged into Cadbury Schweppes plc 06/06/1995
Each share Common 1¢ par exchanged for $33 cash

DR PEPPER/SEVEN UP CORP (DE)
1.375% Exchangeable Sr. Preferred 1¢ par called for redemption 08/31/1994
Public interest eliminated

DR PEPPER SNAPPLE GROUP INC (DE)
Name changed to Keurig Dr Pepper Inc. 07/10/2018

DR REDDYS LABS LTD (INDIA)
Each 144A GDR for Ordinary exchanged for (2) Sponsored ADR's for Ordinary 07/09/2001
(Additional Information in Active)

DR SKEEN CHILD DEV CTRS INC (CO)
Declared defunct and inoperative for failure to pay taxes and file annual reports 09/30/1982

DR SOLOMONS GROUP PLC (UNITED KINGDOM)
Merged into Network Associates, Inc. 08/13/1998
Each Sponsored ADR for Ordinary 1p par exchanged for (0.82875) share Common 1¢ par
Network Associates, Inc. name changed to McAfee, Inc. 06/30/2004
(See McAfee, Inc.)

DR SQUEEZE INTL INC (DE)
Name changed to American Resource Management, Inc. 06/20/2001
American Resource Management, Inc. name changed to EffTec International, Inc. 09/21/2007

DRGOODTEETH COM (NV)
Reorganized as American Oil & Gas Inc. (New) 01/17/2003
Each share Common $0.001 par exchanged for (8.25) shares Common $0.001 par
American Oil & Gas Inc. (New) merged into Hess Corp. 12/17/2010

DOCTORS HOUSE CALLS INC (OK)
Name changed to Diversified Health Companies, Inc. 09/22/1987
(See Diversified Health Companies, Inc.)

DOCTORS OFFICENTERS CORP (DE)
Name changed to DOC Liquidation Corp. 03/05/1985
(See DOC Liquidation Corp.)

DOCTORS REHABILITATION CORP AMER (NV)
Name changed to DRCA Medical Corp. 01/11/1991
DRCA Medical Corp. name changed to Integrated Orthopaedics, Inc. 03/12/1997 which recapitalized as PowerBrief, Inc. 02/27/2001
(See PowerBrief, Inc.)

DOCTORS' HOSPITAL, INC. (VA)
Name changed to Washington Medical Center, Inc. 01/01/1967
(See Washington Medical Center, Inc.)

DOCU-FAX INTL INC (CANADA)
Recapitalized as International Telepresence (Canada) Corp. 09/14/1994
Each share Common no par exchanged for (0.2) share Common no par
International Telepresence (Canada) Corp. name changed to Isee3d Inc. 04/30/1999

DOCUCON INC (DE)
Each share old Common 1¢ par exchanged for (0.25) share new Common 1¢ par 06/11/1998
Each share new Common 1¢ par exchanged again for (0.06666666) share new Common 1¢ par 03/23/2005
Name changed to Issuer Direct Corp. 01/23/2008

DOCUCORP INTL INC (DE)
Merged into Skywire Software, LLC 02/23/2007
Each share Common 1¢ par exchanged for $10 cash

DOCUCORP SYS INC (CANADA)
Merged into 3623297 Canada Inc. 07/15/1999
Each share Common no par exchanged for $0.29 cash

DOCUGRAPHIX INC (CA)
Each share old Common no par exchanged for (0.06666666) share new Common no par 05/04/1992
Charter suspended for failure to file reports and pay fees 12/01/1995

DOCUMATION INC (DE)
Merged into Storage Technology Corp. 11/26/1980
Each share Common 1¢ par exchanged for (0.72) share Common 10¢ par
(See Storage Technology Corp.)

DOCUMENT CAPTURE TECHNOLOGIES INC (DE)
Completely liquidated 12/16/2015
Each share Common $0.001 par exchanged for first and distribution of $0.18 cash

DOCUMENT IMAGING SYS CORP (CA)
Name changed to DISC, Inc. 08/10/1995
(See DISC, Inc.)

DOCUMENT SCIENCES CORP (DE)
Merged into EMC Corp. 03/06/2008
Each share Common $0.001 par exchanged for $14.75 cash

DOCUMENT SYS INC (NY)
Charter cancelled and proclaimed dissolved for failure to pay taxes and file reports 12/20/1977

DOCUMENT TECHNOLOGIES INC (CA)
Charter suspended for failure to file reports and pay fees 01/02/2002

DOCUMENTATION INC. (MD)
Acquired by Leasco Data Processing Equipment Co. 05/10/1967
Each share Common 10¢ par exchanged for (0.14285714) share Common 25¢ par
Leasco Data Processing Equipment Co. name changed to Leasco Corp. 02/24/1971 which name changed to Reliance Group, Inc. 12/14/1973
(See Reliance Group, Inc.)

DOCUMENTUM INC (DE)
Common no par split (2) for (1) by issuance of (1) additional share payable 11/13/2000 to holders of record 11/01/2000 Ex date - 11/14/2000
Merged into EMC Corp. 12/19/2003
Each share Common no par exchanged for (2.175) shares Common 1¢ par
EMC Corp. merged into Dell Technologies Inc. 09/07/2016

DOCUPORT INC (DE)
Charter cancelled and declared inoperative and void for non-payment of taxes 03/01/2002

DOCUTEL CORP. (DE)
Common 10¢ par split (5) for (4) by issuance of (0.25) additional share 03/27/1981
Name changed to Docutel/Olivetti Corp. 09/14/1982
(See Docutel/Olivetti Corp.)

DOCUTEL OLIVETTI CORP (DE)
Acquired by Olivetti (Ing. C.) & C., S.p.A. 08/20/1985
Each share Common 10¢ par exchanged for $5.50 cash

DODGE & COX FUND (CA)
Beneficial Shares no par changed to $1 par 03/04/1950
Beneficial Shares $1 par split (2) for (1) by issuance of (1) additional share 05/31/1961
Name changed to Dodge & Cox Balanced Fund 04/30/1964

DODGE BROTHERS, INC.
Acquired by Chrysler Corp. 00/00/1928
Details not available

DODGE COPPER MINES LTD. (ON)
Charter cancelled and declared dissolved for failure to file returns and pay fees 03/16/1976

DODGE CORP (GA)
Liquidation completed 00/00/1981
Details not available

DODGE (F.W.) CORP. (NY)
Acquired by McGraw-Hill Publishing Co., Inc. 03/07/1961
Each VTC for Common $3 par exchanged for (0.16666666) share $5.50 Conv. Preferred $10 par and (0.43333333) share Common $3 par
McGraw-Hill Publishing Co., Inc. name changed to McGraw-Hill, Inc. 01/02/1964 which name changed to McGraw-Hill Companies, Inc. 04/28/1995 which name changed to McGraw Hill Financial, Inc. 05/02/2013 which name changed to S&P Global Inc. 04/28/2016

DODGE MANUFACTURING CO., LTD.
Acquired by United Steel Corp. Ltd. 00/00/1933
Details not available

DODGE MANUFACTURING CORP. (IN)
Each share Common no par exchanged for (2) shares Common $10 par 00/00/1946
Common $10 par changed to $5 par and (1) additional share issued 10/31/1956
Common $5 par changed to $2.50 par and (1) additional share issued 11/15/1964
Stock Dividends - 20% 11/14/1952; 25% 02/15/1956
$1.56 Conv. Preferred no par called for redemption 03/01/1962
Merged into Reliance Electric & Engineering Co. (OH) 09/29/1967
Each share Common $2.50 par exchanged for (1) share $3 Conv. Preferred Ser. A no par
Reliance Electric & Engineering Co. (OH) reincorporated in Delaware as Reliance Electric Co. 02/28/1969
(See Reliance Electric Co.)

DODGE THIRTEENTH RLTY CO (OH)
Over 90% acquired by company through purchase offer which expired 08/15/1974
Public interest eliminated

DODGE WIRE CORP. (IL)
Reorganized under the laws of Georgia as Dodge Corp. 08/18/1966
(See Dodge Corp.)

DOE SPUN INC (DE)
Merged into DSI Merger, Inc. 06/15/1981
Each share Common 10¢ par exchanged for $9.75 cash

DOEHLER DIE CASTING CO.
Merged into Doehler-Jarvis Corp. 12/30/1944
Each share Common no par exchanged for (2.5) shares Common $5 par
Doehler-Jarvis Corp. acquired by National Lead Co. 00/00/1953 which name changed to N L Industries, Inc. 04/16/1971

DOEHLER-JARVIS CORP. (MI)
Acquired by National Lead Co. 00/00/1953
Each share Common $5 par exchanged for (1.15) shares Common $5 par
National Lead Co. name changed to N L Industries, Inc. 04/16/1971

DOERNBECHER MANUFACTURING CO. (NV)
Stock Dividend - 100% 11/00/1946
Liquidation completed 10/15/1957
Details not available

DOES-MORE PRODUCTS CORP. (AR)
Adjudicated bankrupt 06/07/1965
No stockholders' equity

DOESKIN PRODUCTS, INC. (NY)
Stock Dividend - 10% 06/01/1957
Preferred $8.50 par called for redemption 07/01/1967
Completely liquidated 09/29/1967
Each share Common $1 par exchanged for first and final distribution of $6.35 cash

DOFASCO INC (CANADA)
Conv. Class A Common no par split (3) for (1) by issuance of (2) additional shares 01/31/1984
Conv. Class B Common no par split (3) for (1) by issuance of (2) additional shares 01/31/1984
Conv. Class A Common no par reclassified as Common no par 05/01/1985
Conv. Class B Common no par reclassified as Common no par 05/01/1985
$2.35 Preferred 1980 Ser. no par called for redemption 01/15/1986
$2.60 Class C Conv. Preferred Ser. 1 no par called for redemption at $32.50 on 06/04/1997
4.75% Preferred Ser. A $100 par called for redemption at $101 plus $0.98 accrued dividends on 10/15/2004
Acquired by Arcelor S.A. 3/9/2006
Each share Common no par exchanged for $71 cash

DOG 'N SUDS FOOD SERVICES LTD. (BC)
Dissolved 12/22/1987
No stockholders' equity

DOG VALLEY URANIUM CO. (NV)
Charter revoked for failure to pay fees 03/05/1962

DOG WORLD INC (CO)
Name changed to Medical Management Systems Inc. (CO) 04/25/1995
Medical Management Systems Inc. (CO) reincorporated in Delaware as Dominix, Inc. 07/26/2000 which recapitalized as 110 Media Group, Inc. 06/04/2004 which name changed to Web2 Corp. 07/31/2006 which recapitalized as Full Motion Beverage, Inc. 12/08/2008

DOGAN YAYIN HLDGS A S (TURKEY)
ADR agreement terminated 09/26/2014
Each ADR for Ordinary exchanged for $0.614623 cash

DOGINN INC (NV)
Common $0.001 par split (9) for (1) by issuance of (8) additional shares payable 01/17/2014 to holders of record 01/17/2014 Ex date - 01/21/2014
Name changed to Vapor Hub International Inc. 03/07/2014

DOGPATCH RESTAURANTS, INC. (KY)
Name changed to Kentucky Family Restaurants, Inc. 09/23/1964
(See Kentucky Family Restaurants, Inc.)

DOGPAW GOLD MINES LTD. (ON)
Acquired by Falnora Gold Mines Ltd. 00/00/1951
Each share Capital Stock exchanged for (0.2) share Capital Stock
(See Falnora Gold Mines Ltd.)

DOGS INTL (NV)
Common $0.001 par split (2) for (1) by issuance of (1) additional share payable 06/13/2003 to holders of record 06/09/2003 Ex date - 06/16/2003
Name changed to AFV Solutions, Inc. 02/11/2005
AFV Solutions, Inc. recapitalized as Pure Transit Technologies, Inc. 06/18/2008

DOGWOOD TREE CAP CORP (FL)
Name changed to EntrePort Corp. 08/18/1999
(See EntrePort Corp.)

DOHRMANN COMMERICAL CO. (CA)
Common no par exchanged (7) for (1) in 1952
Out of business 12/31/61
No stockholders' equity

DOI HLDGS INC (CA)
Completely liquidated 07/28/2017
Each share Common 25¢ par exchanged for first and final distribution of $1.70 cash

DOJA CANNABIS CO LTD (BC)
Name changed to Hiku Brands Co. Ltd. 01/31/2018
Hiku Brands Co. Ltd. merged into Canopy Growth Corp. 09/06/2018

DOL RES INC (WY)
Recapitalized as Omega Commercial Finance Corp. 08/22/2007
Each share Common 1¢ par exchanged for (0.1) share Common 1¢ par

DOLAN CO (DE)
Name changed 05/26/2010
Name changed from Dolan Media Co. to Dolan Co. 05/26/2010
Under plan of reorganization each share 8.5% Preferred Ser. B $0.001 par received initial distribution of $0.86725026 cash payable 08/05/2014 to holders of record 06/12/2014
Under plan of reorganization each share Common $0.001 par received initial distribution of $0.04276313 cash payable 08/05/2014 to holders of record 06/12/2014
Each share 8.5% Preferred Ser. B $0.001 par received second and final distribution of $0.31440483 cash payable 12/30/2015 to holders of record 06/12/2014
Each share Common $0.001 par received second and final distribution of $0.01432326 cash payable 12/30/2015 to holders of record 06/12/2014

DOLAT VENTURES INC (WY)
Reincorporated 03/20/2013
State of incorporation changed from (NV) to (WY) 03/20/2013
Each share old Common $0.001 par exchanged for (0.004) share new Common $0.001 par 07/21/2014
New Common $0.001 par changed to Common $0.0001 par 08/06/2014
Common $0.0001 par changed to Common $0.00001 par 12/02/2016
Name changed to JB&ZJMY Holding Co., Inc. 10/25/2017

DOLCE ENTERPRISES INC (AB)
Reorganized under the laws of British Columbia as Sinchao Metals Corp. 12/21/2006
Each share Common no par exchanged for (0.16666666) share Common no par
Sinchao Metals Corp. recapitalized as Southern Legacy Minerals Inc. (BC) 07/03/2012 which reorganized in Alberta as Regulus Resources Inc. (New) 10/03/2014

DOLCE FINL CORP (AB)
Name changed to Seaway Energy Services Inc. (AB) 01/31/2007
Seaway Energy Services Inc. (AB) reincorporated in British Columbia 08/15/2014

DOLCE VENTURES INC (UT)
Recapitalized as Sino Gas International Holdings, Inc. 11/17/2006
Each share Common $0.001 par exchanged for (0.00328471) share Common $0.001 par
(See Sino Gas International Holdings, Inc.)

DOLCO PACKAGING CORP (DE)
Common 1¢ par split (3) for (2) by issuance of (0.5) additional share 9/30/94
Merged into Packaging Acquisition Corp. 2/22/96
Each share Preferred 1¢ par exchanged for $4 cash
Each share Common 1¢ par exchanged for $21 cash

DOLD (JACOB) PACKING CO.
Liquidation completed 00/00/1943
Details not available

DOLE & CLARK BUILDING CO. (IL)
Voluntarily dissolved 12/8/77
Details not available

DOLE CORP. (HI)
Merged into Castle & Cooke, Inc. 06/01/1961
Each share 5% Preferred A $50 par exchanged for (1.4) shares Capital Stock $10 par
Each share Common $7.50 par exchanged for (0.6) share Capital Stock $10 par
Castle & Cooke, Inc. (Old) name changed to Dole Food Co., Inc. (HI) 07/30/1991 which reincorporated in Delaware 07/01/2001
(See Dole Food Co., Inc. (Old) (DE))

DOLE FOOD CO INC NEW (DE)
Issue Information - 35,715,000 shares COM offered at $12.50 per share on 10/22/2009
Acquired by DFC Holdings, LLC 11/01/2013
Each share Common $0.001 par exchanged for $13.50 cash

DOLE FOOD INC OLD (DE)
Reincorporated 07/01/2001
Each share Common no par received distribution of (0.33333333) share Castle & Cooke, Inc. (New) Common no par payable 12/28/1995 to holders of record 12/20/1995 Ex date - 12/29/1995
State of incorporation changed from (HI) to (DE) 07/01/2001
Merged into DHM Holding Co., Inc. 03/28/2003
Each share Common no par exchanged for $33.50 cash

DOLE JAMES CORP (NV)
Each share old Common no par exchanged for (0.182) share new Common no par 01/03/1978
Name changed to Newport Corp. 02/02/1981
(See Newport Corp.)

DOLE JAMES ENGR CO (NV)
Common $1 par changed to no par 08/30/1966
5% Conv. Preferred $2 par called for redemption 04/30/1969
Name changed to Dole (James) Corp. 08/25/1970
Dole (James) Corp. name changed to Newport Corp. 02/02/1981
(See Newport Corp.)

DOLESE & SHEPARD CO (IL)
Acquired by Vulcan Materials Co. 11/3/67
Details not available

DOLET HILLS CORP. (LA)
Charter revoked for failure to file annual reports 10/21/85

DOLL FD INC (DE)
Liquidation completed
Each share Common $1 par received initial distribution of $2.21 cash 09/04/1979
Each share Common $1 par received second and final distribution of $0.02 cash 12/04/1979
Note: Certificates were not required to be surrendered and are without value

DOLLAR ASSOC INC (CA)
Merged into Dollar (Robert) Co. 01/13/1975
Each share Capital Stock no par exchanged for $19.69 cash

DOLLAR BANCORP INC (DE)
Company's sole asset placed in receivership 02/14/2004
Stockholders' equity unlikely

DOLLAR DRY DOCK FDG CORP (NY)
Charter cancelled and proclaimed dissolved for failure to pay taxes 11/13/1995

DOLLAR FIN INC (DE)
Market Auction Preferred Stock no par called for redemption 11/13/1995

DOLLAR FINANCIAL CORP (DE)
Common $0.001 par split (3) for (2) by issuance of (0.5) additional share payable 02/04/2011 to holders of record 01/20/2011 Ex date - 02/07/2011
Name changed to DFC Global Corp. 08/24/2011
(See DFC Global Corp.)

DOLLAR GEN CORP OLD (TN)
Reincorporated 06/02/1998
Common 50¢ par split (2) for (1) by issuance of (1) additional share 04/14/1972
Common 50¢ par split (2) for (1) by issuance of (1) additional share 08/04/1983
Common 50¢ par split (5) for (4) by issuance of (0.25) additional share 04/15/1992
Common 50¢ par split (5) for (4) by issuance of (0.25) additional share 02/26/1993
Common 50¢ par split (5) for (4) by issuance of (0.25) additional share 09/17/1993
Common 50¢ par split (5) for (4) by issuance of (0.25) additional share 04/15/1994
Common 50¢ par split (5) for (4) by issuance of (0.25) additional share 03/06/1995
Common 50¢ par split (5) for (4) by issuance of (0.25) additional share payable 04/26/1996 to holders of record 04/10/1996 Ex date - 04/29/1996
Common 50¢ par split (5) for (4) by issuance of (0.25) additional share payable 02/12/1997 to holders of record 02/03/1997 Ex date - 02/13/1997
Common 50¢ par split (5) for (4) by issuance of (0.25) additional share payable 09/22/1997 to holders of record 09/08/1997 Ex date - 09/23/1997
Common 50¢ par split (5) for (4) by issuance of (0.25) additional share payable 03/23/1998 to holders of record 03/09/1998 Ex date - 03/24/1998
Common 50¢ par split (5) for (4) by issuance of (0.25) additional share payable 09/21/1998 to holders of record 09/07/1998 Ex date - 09/22/1998
Common 50¢ par split (5) for (4) by issuance of (0.25) additional share payable 05/24/1999 to holders of

DOL-DOM — FINANCIAL INFORMATION, INC.

record 05/10/1999 Ex date - 05/25/1999
Common 50¢ par split (5) for (4) by issuance of (0.25) additional share payable 05/22/2000 to holders of record 05/08/2000 Ex date - 05/23/2000
Stock Dividends - 10% 04/26/1976; 10% 03/31/1977; 10% 04/05/1978; 10% 04/03/1979 10% 04/03/1980; 10% 04/03/1981; 10% 04/02/1982; 100% 12/22/1982; 20% 06/18/1985; 10% 07/01/1991
State of incorporation changed from (KY) to (TN) 06/02/1998
Merged into Kohlberg Kravis Roberts & Co. L.P. 07/06/2007
Each share Common 50¢ par exchanged for $22 cash

DOLLAR RESVS INC (MD)
Name changed to Midas Dollar Reserves, Inc. 5/1/2003

DOLLAR SVGS & TR CO (YOUNGSTOWN, OH)
Each share Capital Stock $40 par exchanged for (4) shares Capital Stock $10 par 2/25/60
Stock Dividends - 100% 2/25/58; 100% 8/15/67; 50% 2/28/75
Reorganized as Ohio Bancorp 4/1/82
Each share Capital Stock $10 par exchanged for (1.05) shares Common $10 par
(See Ohio Bancorp)

DOLLAR SVGS ASSN NEW CASTLE (PA)
Merged into F.N.B. Corp. (PA) 4/19/91
Each share Common $1 par exchanged for (1.8848) shares Common $2 par
F.N.B. Corp. (PA) reincorporated in Florida 6/13/2001

DOLLAR STEAMSHIP LINES, INC.
Name changed to American President Lines Ltd. in 1938
American President Lines Ltd. merged into Natomas Co. 6/28/79 which merged into Diamond Shamrock Corp. 8/31/83 which name changed to Maxus Energy Corp. 4/30/87
(See Maxus Energy Corp.)

DOLLAR THRIFTY AUTOMOTIVE GROUP INC (DE)
Acquired by Hertz Global Holdings, Inc. 11/28/2012
Each share Common 1¢ par exchanged for $87.50 cash

DOLLAR TIME GROUP INC (NV)
Each share old Common $0.0001 par exchanged for (0.5) share new Common $0.0001 par 11/21/94
Each share new Common $0.0001 par exchanged again for (0.1) shares new Common $0.0001 par 6/9/95
Charter revoked for failure to file reports and pay fees 8/1/96

DOLLAR TREE STORES INC (VA)
Issue Information - 1,750,000 shares COM offered at $28.25 per share on 08/23/1995
Common 1¢ par split (3) for (2) by issuance of (0.5) additional share payable 04/19/1996 to holders of record 04/05/1996
Common 1¢ par split (3) for (2) by issuance of (0.5) additional share payable 07/21/1997 to holders of record 07/14/1997
Common 1¢ par split (3) for (2) by issuance of (0.5) additional share payable 06/29/1998 to holders of record 06/22/1998
Common 1¢ par split (3) for (2) by issuance of (0.5) additional share payable 06/19/2000 to holders of record 06/12/2000
Name changed to Dollar Tree, Inc. 03/03/2008

DOLLAR VENTURES INC (CO)
Name changed to Applied Research Corp. 1/22/88
Applied Research Corp. recapitalized as U.S. Wind Farming, Inc. 3/19/2004

DOLLARS WEST INC (NV)
Recapitalized as Jaguar Gaming Corp. 03/27/1998
Each share Common $0.001 par exchanged for (0.2) share Common $0.001 par
Jaguar Gaming Corp. recapitalized as Ideal Financial Solutions, Inc. 09/07/2004
(See Ideal Financial Solutions, Inc.)

DOLLINGER CORP (NY)
Class A Common $1 par and Class B Common $1 par reclassified as Common 50¢ par and (1) additional share issued 12/29/69
Merged into American Filtrona Corp. 1/31/83
Each share Common 50¢ par exchanged for $36 cash

DOLLY MADISON FOODS, INC. (MN)
Name changed to Dolly Madison Industries, Inc. (MN) 02/15/1966
Dolly Madison Industries, Inc. (MN) reincorporated in Delaware 03/13/1969
(See Dolly Madison Industries, Inc. (DE))

DOLLY MADISON INDS INC (DE)
Reincorporated 03/13/1969
Common $1 par split (3) for (2) by issuance of (0.5) additional share 11/07/1968
Stock Dividend - 100% 02/23/1966
State of incorporation changed from (MN) to (DE) 03/13/1969
Declared insolvent 08/02/1974
No stockholders' equity

DOLLY RESOURCES LTD. (BC)
Name changed to Dolly Varden Resources Ltd. 04/15/1977
Dolly Varden Resources Ltd. merged into Dolly Varden Minerals Inc. 12/21/1979 which recapitalized as New Dolly Varden Minerals Inc. 11/16/1992 which name changed to Dolly Varden Resources Inc. 04/17/2000 which name changed to DV Resources Ltd. 01/31/2012 which name changed to DLV Resources Ltd. 11/27/2017

DOLLY VARDEN MINERALS INC (ON)
Recapitalized as New Dolly Varden Minerals Inc. 11/16/1992
Each share Common no par exchanged for (0.2) share Common no par
New Dolly Varden Minerals Inc. name changed to Dolly Varden Resources Inc. 04/17/2000 which name changed to DV Resources Ltd. 01/31/2012 which name changed to DLV Resources Ltd. 11/27/2017

DOLLY VARDEN MINES LTD (BC)
Recapitalized as Silver Dolly Resources Ltd. 02/23/1976
Each share Capital Stock 50¢ par exchanged for (0.25) share Capital Stock no par
Silver Dolly Resources Ltd. recapitalized as Dolly Resources Ltd. 11/10/1976 which name changed to Dolly Varden Resources Ltd. 04/15/1977 which merged into Dolly Varden Minerals Inc. 12/21/1979 which recapitalized as New Dolly Varden Minerals Inc. 11/16/1992 which name changed to Dolly Varden Resources Inc. 04/17/2000 which name changed to DV Resources Ltd. 01/31/2012 which name changed to DLV Resources Ltd. 11/27/2017

DOLLY VARDEN RES INC (ON)
Name changed to DV Resources Ltd. 01/31/2012
DV Resources Ltd. name changed to DLV Resources Ltd. 11/27/2017

DOLLY VARDEN RES LTD (BC)
Merged into Dolly Varden Minerals Inc. 12/21/1979
Each share Capital Stock no par exchanged for (0.5024) share Conv. Class A Special Stock no par
Dolly Varden Minerals Inc. recapitalized as New Dolly Varden Minerals Inc. 11/16/1992 which recapitalized as Dolly Varden Resources Inc. 04/17/2000 which name changed to DV Resources Ltd. 01/31/2012 which name changed to DLV Resources Ltd. 11/27/2017

DOLMAC MINES LTD (ON)
Merged into Junction Explorations Ltd. 12/12/78
Each share Capital Stock $1 par exchanged for (0.125) share Common no par
(See Junction Explorations Ltd.)

DOLOMITE GLASS FIBRES INC (NY)
Ceased operations 02/01/1973
No stockholders' equity

DOLOMITE MARINE CORP.
Bankrupt 00/00/1941
No stockholders' equity

DOLPHIN DIGITAL MEDIA INC (FL)
Reincorporated 12/03/2014
State of incorporation changed from (NV) to (FL) 12/03/2014
Each share old Common $0.015 par exchanged for (0.05) share new Common $0.015 par 05/16/2016
Recapitalized as Dolphin Entertainment, Inc. 09/18/2017
Each share new Common $0.015 par exchanged for (0.5) share Common $0.015 par

DOLPHIN EXPLS LTD (ON)
Reincorporated 10/07/1988
Place of incorporation changed from (BC) to (ON) 10/07/1988
Recapitalized as American Gem Corp. 02/18/1994
Each share Common no par exchanged for (0.05) share Common no par
American Gem Corp. name changed to Digital Gem Corp. 10/27/1999 which name changed to Northern Financial Corp. 10/03/2000 which recapitalized as Added Capital Inc. 07/23/2014

DOLPHIN INCOME FUND (ON)
Name changed to Dolphin Mortgage Fund 04/01/1979
(See Dolphin Mortgage Fund)

DOLPHIN MARINE CORP. (DE)
Name changed to Med-Test Systems, Inc. 01/12/1983
Med-Test Systems, Inc. recapitalized as Enxuta Corp. of America 06/10/1992

DOLPHIN-MILLER MINES LTD. (ON)
Acquired by Langis Silver & Cobalt Mining Co. Ltd. 12/00/1983
Each share Capital Stock $1 par exchanged for (1) share Common no par
Langis Silver & Cobalt Mining Co. name changed to Aranka Gold Inc. 07/27/2005 which merged into Guyana Goldfields Inc. 01/28/2009

DOLPHIN MTG FD (ON)
Fund believed terminated 00/00/1988
Details not available

DOLPHIN PAINT & CHEM CO (OH)
Each share Class B 10¢ par exchanged for (0.1) share Class B $1 par 09/19/1962
Merged out of existence 12/30/1986
Details not available

DOLPHIN PAINT & VARNISH CO. (OH)
Name changed to Dolphin Paint & Chemical Co. 05/16/1960
(See Dolphin Paint & Chemical Co.)

DOLPHIN PRODUCTIONS INC (NV)
Name changed to Innocom Technology Holdings, Inc. 07/10/2006

DOLPHIN QUEST INC (ON)
Name changed to Naftex Energy Corp. (ON) 04/10/1997
Naftex Energy Corp. (ON) reincorporated in Yukon 09/16/1998
(See Naftex Energy Corp. (YT))

DOLPHIN YELLOWKNIFE MINES LTD. (ON)
Name changed to Dolphin-Miller Mines Ltd. 00/00/1958
Dolphin-Miller Mines Ltd. acquired by Langis Silver & Cobalt Mining Co. Ltd. 12/00/1983 which name changed to Aranka Gold Inc. 07/27/2005 which merged into Guyana Goldfields Inc. 01/28/2009

DOLSAN MINES LTD (QC)
Recapitalized as Consolidated Dolsan Mines Ltd. 03/04/1968
Each share Common $1 par exchanged for (0.2) share Common $1 par
(See Consolidated Dolsan Mines Ltd.)

DOMAC ENTERPRISES INC (DE)
Reincorporated 10/01/1975
State of incorporation changed from (NY) to (DE) 10/01/1975
Merged out of existence 06/16/1998
Details not available

DOMAIN ENERGY CORP (DE)
Merged into Range Resources Corp. 08/25/1998
Each share Common 1¢ par exchanged for (1.2083) shares Common 1¢ par

DOMAIN EXTREMES INC (NV)
Name changed to Mi1 Global Telco., Inc. 07/19/2017

DOMAIN INDS INC (WI)
Stock Dividends - 10% 03/20/1972; 20% 07/02/1976
Merged into Nor-Dom Corp. 12/29/1978
Each share Common $1 par exchanged for $28 cash

DOMAIN REGISTRATION CORP (NV)
Common $0.001 par split (10) for (1) by issuance of (9) additional shares payable 10/11/2007 to holders of record 10/10/2007 Ex date - 10/12/2007
Name changed to BioPharm Asia, Inc. 08/28/2009
(See BioPharm Asia, Inc.)

DOMAIN TECHNOLOGY INC (DE)
Charter cancelled and declared inoperative and void for non-payment of taxes 03/01/1994

DOMAN-FRASIER HELICOPTERS, INC. (DE)
Name changed to Doman Helicopters, Inc. 00/00/1949
Doman Helicopters, Inc. name changed to Berlin Doman Helicopters, Inc. 10/06/1967 which name changed back to Doman Helicopters, Inc. 11/14/1969
(See Doman Helicopters, Inc.)

DOMAN HELICOPTERS INC (DE)
Each share Common $1 par exchanged for (0.1) share Common 10¢ par 01/07/1960
Name changed to Berlin Doman Helicopters, Inc. 10/06/1967 which name changed back to Doman Helicopters, Inc. 11/14/1969
Charter cancelled and declared inoperative and void for non-payment of taxes 03/01/1981

DOMAN INDS LTD (BC)
Common no par split (2) for (1) by issuance of (1) additional share 04/23/1973
Common no par split (2) for (1) by issuance of (1) additional share 04/30/1976
6.5% Conv. Preferred Ser. A $10 par called for redemption 04/15/1977
Common no par reclassified as Class A no par 06/30/1983
Class A Common no par reclassified as Conv. Class A Common no par 04/03/1984
Each share Conv. Class A Common no par received distribution of (1) share Class B Ser. 2 no par 04/17/1984
7% Class A Preferred Ser. 2 no par called for redemption 09/01/1994
Plan of Compromise and Arrangement under Companies' Creditors Arrangement Act effective 07/27/2004
Each share Class A no par received Class C Warrants Tranche 1, 2, and 3 expiring 00/00/2009 on a pro rata basis
Each share Non-Vtg. Class B Ser. 2 no par received Class C Warrants Tranche 1, 2, and 3 expiring 00/00/2009 on a pro rata basis
Notes: Holders of fewer than (67) shares will not receive any distribution
Certificates were not required to be surrendered and are without value

DOMAR EXOTIC FURNISHINGS INC (NV)
Reorganized as Domark International, Inc. 06/27/2008
Each share Common $0.001 par exchanged for (2) shares Common $0.001 par

DOMCO TARKETT INC (CANADA)
Name changed 07/10/1996
Name changed 08/24/1999
Common no par split (3) for (1) by issuance of (2) additional shares 03/31/1986
Common no par reclassified as Class B Multiple no par 09/13/1994
Class B Multiple no par reclassified as Common no par 01/05/1995
Common no par split (2) for (1) by issuance of (1) additional share payable 02/09/1996 to holders of record 02/06/1996 Ex date - 02/02/1996
Name changed from Domco Industries Ltd.- Les Industries Domco Ltee. to Domco Inc. 07/10/1996
Name changed from Domco Inc. to Domco Tarkett, Inc. 08/24/1999
Merged into Tarkett Sommer AG 10/30/2003
Each share Common no par exchanged for $7.75 cash (Additional Information in Active)

DOME BABINE MINES LTD (BC)
Name changed to Babine International Resources Ltd. 03/04/1970
Babine International Resources Ltd. merged into Seneca Developments Ltd. 12/08/1972 which recapitalized as Award Resources Ltd. 02/08/1982 which recapitalized as Tomco Developments Inc. 06/16/1990

DOME CDA LTD (AB)
Name changed to Encor Energy Corp. Ltd. 07/03/1986
Encor Energy Corp. Ltd. name changed to Encor Energy Corp. Inc. 02/18/1987
(See Encor Energy Corp. Inc.)

DOME EXPLORATION (WESTERN) LTD. (CANADA)
Each share Capital Stock $1 par exchanged for (6) shares Capital Stock no par 00/00/1951
Capital Stock no par changed to $2.50 par 00/00/1951
Name changed to Dome Petroleum Ltd. 06/20/1958
(See Dome Petroleum Ltd.)

DOME MINES LTD (CANADA)
Each share old Capital Stock no par exchanged for (2) shares new Capital Stock no par 00/00/1938
New Capital Stock no par split (3) for (1) by issuance of (2) additional shares 05/27/1974
Capital Stock no par split (3) for (1) by issuance of (2) additional shares 06/25/1979
Capital Stock no par split (4) for (1) by issuance of (3) additional shares 06/01/1981
Merged into Placer Dome Inc. 08/13/1987
Each share Capital Stock no par exchanged for (0.851) share Common no par
Placer Dome Inc. merged into Barrick Gold Corp. 03/08/2006

DOME MTN RES LTD (ON)
Recapitalized as DMR Resources Ltd. 11/06/1996
Each share Common no par exchanged for (0.33333333) share Common no par
(See DMR Resources Ltd.)

DOME PETE LTD (CANADA)
Common $2.50 par changed to no par and (2) additional shares issued 08/25/1971
Common no par split (4) for (1) by issuance of (3) additional shares 05/25/1979
Common no par split (5) for (1) by issuance of (4) additional shares 06/02/1981
Acquired by Amoco Canada Petroleum Co. Ltd. 09/01/1988
Each share 7.76% Preferred Ser. A $25 par exchanged for $5.604859 principal amount of 7.375% Exchangeable Subordinated Debentures Ser. A due 09/01/2013
Each share 7.76% Preferred Ser. B $25 par exchanged for $5.604859 principal amount of 7.375% Exchangeable Subordinated Debentures Ser. A due 09/01/2013
Each share Common no par exchanged for $1.132766 principal amount of 7.375% Exchangeable Subordinated Debentures Ser. A due 09/01/2013

DOME RES LTD (CANADA)
$5.75 Preferred Class A Retractable no par called for redemption 3/25/83
Public interest eliminated

DOME URANIUM MINES, INC. (CO)
Charter revoked for non-payment of taxes 10/26/60

DOME VENTURES CORP (DE)
Merged into Metalline Mining Inc. 04/16/2010
Each share Common $0.001 par exchanged for (0.968818) share Common 1¢ par
Metalline Mining Inc. name changed to Silver Bull Resources, Inc. 05/02/2011

DOME VENTURES INC (BC)
Reincorporated under the laws of Delaware as EComm Systems Corp. and Common no par changed to $0.001 par 01/17/2000
EComm Systems Corp. name changed to Dome Ventures Corp. 04/17/2001 which merged into Metalline Mining Inc. 04/16/2010 which name changed to Silver Bull Resources, Inc. 05/02/2011

DOMEGO RES LTD (BC)
Reincorporated under the laws of Canada as Polysteel Building Systems Ltd. 10/30/1987
Polysteel Building Systems Ltd. name changed to Medical Pathways International Inc. 04/16/1999
(See Medical Pathways International Inc.)

DOMEQUITY GROWTH & CALGARY LTD (AB)
Reincorporated 05/30/1980
Mutual Fund Stock 25¢ par changed to no par 04/30/1980
Place of incorporation changed from (Canada) to (ALTA) 05/30/1980
Merged into Dominion Equity Resource Fund 12/20/1991
Details not available

DOMESTIC & FOREIGN INVESTORS CORP.
Dissolved in 1939
No stockholders' equity

DOMESTIC & OVERSEAS INVESTING CO., LTD. (DE)
Charter cancelled and declared inoperative and void for non-payment of taxes in 1935

DOMESTIC AIR CONDITIONING CO.
Out of business 00/00/1943
Details not available

DOMESTIC AIR EXPRESS INC (DE)
Name changed to Air Forwarders, Inc. 7/26/74
(See Air Forwarders, Inc.)

DOMESTIC CREDIT CORP. (DE)
Name changed to Domestic Finance Corp. (Del.) (New) and Class A Common redesignated as Common in 1950
Domestic Finance Corp. (Del.) (New) merged into American Investment Co. of Illinois 9/20/55 which name was changed to American Investment Co. 11/30/63 which was acquired by Leucadia National Corp. 12/3/80
(See American Investment Co.)

DOMESTIC ELECTRIC CO.
Acquired by Black & Decker Manufacturing Co. 00/00/1929
Details not available

DOMESTIC ENERGY CORP (FL)
Administratively dissolved 09/23/2011

DOMESTIC ENERGY INC (CO)
Merged into Dietrich Exploration Co., Inc. (CO) 03/04/1976
Each share Common 10¢ par exchanged for (4.4) shares Common 1¢ par
Dietrich Exploration Co., Inc. (CO) reorganized in Delaware as Dietrich Resources Corp. 05/15/1981 which name changed to DRX, Inc. 04/29/1987
(See DRX, Inc.)

DOMESTIC FINANCE CORP. (KY)
Name changed to Time Finance Co. in 1939
Time Finance Co. acquired by C.I.T. Financial Corp. 5/13/63 which merged into RCA Corp. 1/31/80
(See RCA Corp.)

DOMESTIC FINANCE CORP. NEW (DE)
Merged into American Investment Co. of Illinois and each (3.5) shares Common $1 par exchanged for (1) share new Common $1 par 9/20/55
American Investment Co. of Illinois name changed to American Investment Co. 11/30/63
(See American Investment Co.)

DOMESTIC FINANCE CORP. OLD (DE)
Name changed to Domestic Industries, Inc. in 1943
Domestic Industries Inc. name changed to Domestic Credit Corp. in 1946 which name was changed to Domestic Finance Corp. (DE) (New) in 1950 which merged into American Investment Co. of Illinois 9/20/55 which name was changed to to American Investment Co. 11/30/63
(See American Investment Co.)

DOMESTIC FINANCE GROUP, INC. (NC)
Stock Dividend - 10% 11/5/57
Name changed to First Southern Co. 9/18/58
First Southern Co. was liquidated by exchange for Liberty Loan Corp. 6/8/65 which name changed to LLC Corp. 3/14/80 which name changed to Valhi, Inc. 3/10/87

DOMESTIC INDUSTRIES, INC. (DE)
Under plan of merger each share old Preference exchanged for (1) share Preferred $25 par and (1) Class A Common Stock Purchase Warrant in 1943
Each share Common exchanged for (2) shares Class A Common $1 par in 1943
Name changed to Domestic Credit Corp. in 1946
Domestic Credit Corp. name changed to Domestic Finance Corp. (DE) (New) in 1950 which merged into American Investment Co. of Illinois 9/20/55 which name changed to American Investment Co. 11/30/63
(See American Investment Co.)

DOMGLAS LTD.-DOMGLAS LTEE. (CANADA)
Each share 7% Preferred $10 par exchanged for $14 cash 12/31/1974
Merged into Consolidated-Bathurst Ltd. 05/15/1978
Each share Common no par exchanged for $20 cash

DOMIKNOW INC (DE)
Name changed to Gooi Global, Inc. 04/02/2015

DOMINCO INDS CORP (BC)
Delisted from Vancouver Stock Exchange 03/04/1991

DOMINGUEZ & CIA CARACAS S A (VENEZUELA)
Stock Dividends - 10% 4/15/94; In Sponsored ADR's for Preferred to holders of Sponsored ADR's for Preferred 27.5% payable 9/3/97 to holders of record 8/26/97; In Sponsored ADR's for Ordinary to holders of Sponsored ADR's for Ordinary 12.5% payable 9/3/97 to holders of record 8/26/97; In Sponsored ADR's for Preferred to holders of Sponsored ADR's for Ordinary 20% payable 2/17/98 to holders of record 2/12/98
ADR agreement terminated 12/1/2003
Each Sponsored ADR for Preferred no par exchanged for (400) shares Preferred no par
Each Sponsored ADR for Ordinary no par exchanged for (100) Ordinary shares no par
Note: Unexchanged ADR's will be sold and proceeds held for claim after 12/1/2004

DOMINGUEZ OIL FIELDS CO. (DE)
Liquidation completed 7/12/63

DOMINGUEZ SVCS CORP (CA)
5% Class A Preferred $25 par called for redemption 3/15/96
Common $1 par split (3) for (2) by issuance of (0.5) additional share payable 1/1/98 to holders of record 12/15/97
Merged into California Water Service Group 5/25/2000
Each share Common $1 par exchanged for (1.38) shares Common no par

DOMINGUEZ WTR CORP (CA)
5% Preferred $25 par reclassified as 5% Class A Preferred $25 par 5/19/75

DOM-DOM — FINANCIAL INFORMATION, INC.

Common $5 par changed to $1 par and (1) additional share issued 9/16/85
Common $1 par split (3) for (2) by issuance of (0.5) additional share 9/21/87
Under plan of reorganization each share 5% Class A Preferred $25 par and Common $1 par automatically became (1) share Dominguez Services Corp. 5% Class A Preferred $25 par or Common $1 par respectively 6/12/90
Dominguez Services Corp. merged into California Water Service Group 5/25/2000

DOMINI SPORTSWEAR LTD (CANADA)
Assets sold for the benefit of creditors in May 1993
No stockholders' equity

DOMINICAN CIGAR CORP (DE)
Name changed to DCGR International Holdings, Inc. 06/01/1998
DCGR International Holdings, Inc. recapitalized as American Way Home Based Business Systems, Inc. 04/12/2004 which name changed to American Way Business Development Corp. (DE) 09/30/2004 which reincorporated in Florida as Harvard Learning Centers, Inc. 10/30/2006 which name changed to Americas Learning Centers, Inc. 09/25/2007 which recapitalized as Hackett's Stores, Inc. 01/26/2009 which recapitalized as WiseBuys, Inc. 06/17/2010 which name changed to Empire Pizza Holdings, Inc. 04/20/2011 which recapitalized as Vestiage, Inc. 03/22/2013

DOMINICK FD INC (DE)
Capital Stock $1 par split (2) for (1) by issuance of (1) additional share 03/18/1968
Merged into Putnam Investors Fund, Inc. 10/15/1974
Each share Capital Stock $1 par exchanged for (1.290225) shares Common $1 par

DOMINICKS PIZZA PLUS INC (DE)
Charter cancelled and declared inoperative and void for failure to maintain a registered agent 2/25/91

DOMINICKS SUPERMARKETS INC (DE)
Merged into Safeway Inc. 11/19/98
Each share Common no par exchanged for $49 cash

DOMINION ALLOY STEEL CORP. LTD.
Completely liquidated 07/10/1950
Each share Preferred no par or Common no par were paid a first and final distribution of $0.46 cash

DOMINION ASBESTOS MINES LTD. (QC)
Name changed to Daine Mining Corp. Ltd. 09/11/1956
Daine Mining Corp. Ltd. recapitalized as Cable Mines & Oils Ltd. 08/15/1957 which merged into St. Fabien Copper Mines Ltd. 07/27/1967 which name changed to St. Fabien Explorations Inc. 02/11/1981 which recapitalized as Fabien Explorations Inc. 07/18/1983
(See Fabien Explorations Inc.)

DOMINION ATLANTIC RAILWAY CO. (CANADA)
Sold in 1993
Details not available

DOMINION BAKERIES, LTD.
In voluntary liquidation in 1941

DOMINION BANK (TORONTO, ONT)
Each share Capital Stock $100 par exchanged for (10) shares Capital Stock $10 par in 1944
Merged into Toronto-Dominion Bank (Toronto, Ont.) 2/1/55
Each share Capital Stock $10 par exchanged for (1) share Capital Stock $10 par

DOMINION BK N A (ROANOKE, VA)
Merged into Dominion Bankshares Corp. 10/19/1984
Each share Common $10 par exchanged for $84.96 cash

DOMINION BANK OF NORTHERN VIRGINIA, N.A. (VIENNA, VA)
Acquired by First Union National Bank of Virginia (Roanoke, VA) 12/31/1990
Details not available

DOMINION BANKSHARES CORP (VA)
Common $10 par changed to $5 par and (1) additional share issued 01/10/1973
Common $5 par split (2) for (1) by issuance of (1) additional share 09/30/1986
Stock Dividend - 10% 09/10/1979
Merged into First Union Corp. 03/01/1993
Each share $2.50 Conv. Preferred Ser. A $25 par exchanged for (1) share $2.50 Conv. Preferred Ser. A no par
Each share Common $5 par exchanged for (0.58) share Common $3.33-1/3 par
First Union Corp. name changed to Wachovia Corp. (Ctfs. dated after 09/01/2001) 09/01/2001 which merged into Wells Fargo & Co. (New) 12/31/2008

DOMINION BRDG CORP (DE)
Charter cancelled and declared inoperative and void for non-payment of taxes 03/01/2000

DOMINION BRDG LTD (CANADA)
Each share Common $100 par exchanged for (5) shares old Common no par 00/00/1927
Each share old Common no par exchanged for (5) shares new Common no par 00/00/1954
New Common no par split (2) for (1) by issuance of (1) additional share 11/25/1974
New Common no par split (2) for (1) by issuance of (1) additional share 10/26/1976
New Common no par split (2) for (1) by issuance of (1) additional share 12/17/1979
Name changed to AMCA International Ltd.- AMCA International Ltee. 06/04/1981
AMCA International Ltd.-AMCA International Ltee. recapitalized as United Dominion Industries Ltd. 06/04/1990 which was acquired by SPX Corp. 05/24/2001

DOMINION CABLE CORP (GA)
Completely liquidated 07/27/1990
Each share Common 1¢ par received first and final distribution of $0.015 cash

DOMINION CAP CORP (DE)
Charter cancelled and declared inoperative and void for non-payment of taxes 03/01/1987

DOMINION CITRUS & DRUGS LTD (ON)
Common no par reclassified as Conv. Class A Special Common no par 07/18/1975
Conv. Class A Special Common no par split (2) for (1) by issuance of (1) additional share 11/15/1978
Conv. Class B Special Common no par split (2) for (1) by issuance of (1) additional share 11/15/1978
Conv. Class A Special Common no par reclassified as Common no par 01/23/1981
Conv. Class B Special Common no par reclassified as Common no par 01/23/1981
Merged into Algonquin Mercantile Corp. 11/02/1982
Each share Common no par exchanged for (1) share $0.66 Non-Vtg. Preference no par
Algonquin Mercantile Corp. name changed to Automodular Corp. 06/05/2001 which merged into HLS Therapeutics Inc. 03/14/2018

DOMINION CITRUS CO. LTD. (ON)
Name changed to Dominion Citrus & Drugs Ltd. 08/31/1971
Dominion Citrus & Drugs Ltd. merged into Algonquin Mercantile Corp. 11/02/1982 which name changed to Automodular Corp. 06/05/2001 which merged into HLS Therapeutics Inc. 03/14/2018

DOMINION CITRUS LTD (ON)
Each share Common no par received distribution of (0.05) share Ser. A Preference payable 03/28/2003 to holders of record 03/14/2003
Reorganized as Dominion Citrus Income Fund 01/06/2006
Each share Common no par exchanged for (1) Trust Unit (Additional Information in Active)

DOMINION CNG CAP TR I (DE)
7.8% Trust Preferred Shares called for redemption at $25 on 07/17/2007

DOMINION COAL LTD (NS)
Each share 7% Preferred $100 par exchanged for (8) shares 6% Preference $25 par 00/00/1935
In process of liquidation
Each share 6% Preference $25 par stamped to indicate initial distribution of $21 cash 09/11/1973
Each share Stamped 6% Preference $25 par stamped to indicate second distribution of $14 cash 09/20/1974
Note: Details on subsequent distributions, if any, are not available

DOMINION CORSET LTD (QC)
Each share Common no par exchanged for (2) shares Common $4 par 02/21/1964
Name changed to Daisyfresh Creations Inc.-Creations Daisyfresh Inc. 10/01/1976
(See Daisyfresh Creations Inc.-Creations Daisyfresh Inc.)

DOMINION DAIRIES LTD-LAITERIES DOMINION LTEE (CANADA)
Name changed 11/27/1974
Each share old Common no par exchanged for (3) shares new Common no par 11/24/1958
5% Preferred $35 par called for redemption 12/28/1972
Name changed from Dominion Dairies Ltd. to Dominion Dairies Ltd.-Laiteries Dominion Ltee. 11/27/1974
Common no par split (4) for (1) by issuance of (3) additional shares 12/16/1974
Acquired by Labatt (John) Ltd. 08/24/1981
Each share Common no par exchanged for $26.01 cash

DOMINION DEV CORP (FL)
Name changed to First Continental Oil & Gas Co. Inc. 05/10/1971
First Continental Oil & Gas Co. Inc. merged into Continental Resources, International 07/31/1972
(See Continental Resources, International)

DOMINION DIAMOND CORP (CANADA)
Acquired by Northwest Acquisitions ULC 11/02/2017
Each share Common no par exchanged for USD$14.25 cash
Note: Unexchanged certificates will be cancelled and become without value 11/02/2023

DOMINION ELEC CORP (OH)
Acquired by Scovill Manufacturing Co. 04/08/1969
Each share Class A Common $1 par or Class C Common $1 par exchanged for $6.677 cash

DOMINION ELECTROHOME INDUSTRIES LTD. (ON)
Each share old Common no par exchanged for (3) shares new Common no par 05/12/1959
Name changed to Electrohome Ltd. 06/06/1967
Electrohome Ltd. name changed to Electrohome Ltd.-Electrohome Ltee. 06/08/1977
(See Electrohome Ltd.-Electrohome Ltee.)

DOMINION ENERGY CORP (BC)
Struck off register and declared dissolved for failure to file returns 12/31/1987

DOMINION ENERGY INC (BC)
Name changed to Dynamic Oil & Gas Exploration Inc. 06/30/2014
Dynamic Oil & Gas Exploration Inc. recapitalized as Darien Business Development Corp. 03/14/2017

DOMINION ENGINEERING WORKS, LTD. (CANADA)
Each share Capital Stock $100 par exchanged for (5) shares Capital Stock no par 00/00/1927
Each share Capital Stock no par exchanged for (5) shares Capital Stock no par 11/26/1951
Stock Dividend - 100% 01/22/1962
Acquired by Canadian General Electric Co., Ltd. 00/00/1962
Each share Capital Stock no par exchanged for (1) share of $1.25 Conv. Preferred $28 par and $3 cash
Canadian General Electric Co., Ltd. name changed to Canadian General Electric Co. Ltd.-Compagnie Generale Electrique du Canada Ltee. 07/02/1965 which name changed to General Electric Canada Inc. 08/19/1987
(See General Electric Canada Inc.)

DOMINION ENVELOPES & CARTONS (WESTERN) LTD. (MB)
Recapitalized 00/00/1943
Each share 1st Preference $100 par exchanged for (1) share 7% Preference $50 par, (5) shares Common no par and $22 cash
Each share 2nd Preference $100 par exchanged for (15) shares Common no par
Each share Common no par exchanged for (1) share Common no par
Ceased business and charter surrendered 11/18/1958

DOMINION EQUITY INVTS LTD (CANADA)
Deferred $1 par changed to 25¢ par and (3) additional shares issued 04/19/1966
Common $1 par reclassified as Mutual Fund Stock 25¢ par and (3) additional shares issued 04/19/1966
Name changed to Domequity Growth & Calgary Ltd. (Canada) 09/26/1979
Domequity Growth & Calgary Ltd. (Canada) reincorporated in Alberta 05/30/1980
(See Domequity Growth & Calgary Ltd.)

DOMINION EXPLORERS INC (ON)
Merged into Dominion Explorers Inc. (New) 12/31/1994
Each share Subordinate no par exchanged for (0.8) share Common no par and (0.8) Participating Right Dominion Explorers Inc. (New) merged into Neutrino Resources Inc. 02/28/1997
(See Neutrino Resources Inc.)

DOMINION EXPLORERS LTD (ON)
Capital Stock $1 par changed to no par 11/03/1972
Merged into Dominion Explorers Inc. (Old) 07/19/1985
Each share Capital Stock no par exchanged for (1) share Subordinate no par
Dominion Explorers Inc. (Old) merged into Dominion Explorers Inc (New) 12/31/1994 which merged into Neutrino Resources Inc. 02/28/1997
(See Neutrino Resources Inc.)

DOMINION EXPLS INC NEW (AB)
Merged into Neutrino Resources Inc. 02/28/1997
Each share Common no par exchanged for (0.6) share Common no par
(See Neutrino Resources Inc.)

DOMINION FDRYS & STL LTD (CANADA)
Each share 8% Preference $100 par exchanged for (1.66666666) shares 6% Preference $100 par 00/00/1935
Each share Common $100 par exchanged for (4) shares Common no par 00/00/1936
Each share Common no par exchanged for (2) shares Common no par 00/00/1939
Each share Common no par exchanged for (4) shares Common no par 00/00/1951
Common no par split (4) for (1) by issuance of (3) additional shares 05/13/1964
Common no par reclassified as Conv. Class A Common no par 05/06/1975
Name changed to Dofasco Inc. 10/17/1980
(See Dofasco Inc.)

DOMINION FED SVGS & LN ASSN MCLEAN VA (USA)
Capital Stock 1¢ par split (5) for (1) by issuance of (4) additional shares 08/15/1986
Name changed to Trustbank Savings, F.S.B. (McLean, VA) 07/01/1989
Trustbank Savings, F.S.B. (McLean, VA) reorganized as Trustbank Federal Savings Bank (Tysons Corner, VA) 01/29/1991
(See Trustbank Federal Savings Bank (Tysons Corner, VA))

DOMINION FLUORIDATORS LTD. (ON)
Charter cancelled 12/08/1966

DOMINION GEN INVT CORP (ON)
Name changed to Hampton Financial Corp. and Common no par reclassified as Subordinate Shares 08/12/2016

DOMINION GLASS LTD (CANADA)
Each share 7% Preferred $100 par exchanged for (5) shares 7% Preferred $20 par 00/00/1946
Each share Common $100 par exchanged for (5) shares old Common no par 00/00/1946
Each share 7% Preferred $20 par exchanged for (2) shares 7% Preferred $10 par 00/00/1953
Each share old Common no par exchanged for (2) shares new Common no par 00/00/1953
New Common no par split (5) for (1) by issuance of (4) additional shares 03/08/1963
Name changed to Domglas Ltd.-Domglas Ltee. 07/07/1976
(See Domglas Ltd.-Domglas Ltee.)

DOMINION GOLD FIELDS LTD.
Out of business 00/00/1943
Details not available

DOMINION HLDGS INC (DE)
Name changed to Brenner International, Inc. 09/30/1985
(See Brenner International, Inc.)

DOMINION HOMES INC (OH)
Merged into Dominion Holding Corp. 06/12/2008
Each share Common no par exchanged for $0.65 cash

DOMINION INDUSTRIAL MINERAL CORP. (QC)
Adjudicated bankrupt 07/08/1966
No stockholders' equity

DOMINION INTL INVTS INC (ON)
Delisted from Toronto Venture Stock Exchange 06/05/2002

DOMINION INTL RES CORP (CO)
Proclaimed dissolved for failure to file reports 02/01/1999

DOMINION JUBILEE LTD (CANADA)
Each share Capital Stock $1 par exchanged for (0.2) share Common no par 10/25/1990
Dissolved 08/28/1997
Details not available

DOMINION LEASEHOLDS LTD (AB)
Capital Stock $1 par changed to no par 04/30/1962
Struck off register for failure to file returns 07/15/1974

DOMINION LIME LTD (QC)
Name changed to Domlim Inc. and Common $1 par reclassified as Conv. Class A Common no par 12/15/1977
(See Domlim Inc.)

DOMINION MAGNESIUM LTD (ON)
Name changed to Chromasco Corp. Ltd. 08/16/1971
Chromasco Corp. Ltd. merged into Chromasco Ltd. (ON) 07/15/1974 which reincorporated in Canada 07/23/1980 which name changed to Timminco Ltd.-Timminco Ltee. 02/09/1984

DOMINION MALARTIC GOLD MINES LTD. (ON)
Charter cancelled and company declared dissolved for failure to file returns 12/2/63

DOMINION MIDSTREAM PARTNERS LP (DE)
Name changed to Dominion Energy Midstream Partners, L.P. 05/15/2017

DOMINION MINERALS, INC. (VA)
Merged into Riverton Lime & Stone Co., Inc. 04/00/1953
Each share Common $1 par exchanged for (1) share 6% 2nd Preferred $10 par
Riverton Lime & Stone Co., Inc. acquired by Chadbourn Gotham, Inc. 07/25/1956 which name changed to Chadbourn Inc. 01/31/1969 which reorganized as Stanwood Corp. 06/12/1975 which was acquired by Delta Woodside Industries, Inc. (DE) 09/07/1988 which merged into Delta Woodside Industries, Inc. (SC) 11/15/1989
(See Delta Woodside Industries, Inc. (SC))

DOMINION MINERALS DEVELOPMENT LTD. (AB)
Recapitalized as New Dominion Minerals Development Ltd. on a (1) for (25) basis 6/27/62
(See New Dominion Minerals Development Ltd.)

DOMINION MNG LTD (AUSTRALIA)
Name changed 02/05/1987
Name changed from Dominion Mining & Oil N.L. to Dominion Mining Ltd. 02/05/1987
Each Unsponsored ADR for Ordinary AUD $0.40 par exchanged for (0.2) Sponsored ADR for Ordinary AUD $0.40 par 11/14/1988
Stock Dividend - 15% 01/09/1990
Merged into Kingsgate Consolidated Ltd. 02/07/2011
Each Sponsored ADR for Ordinary AUD $0.40 par exchanged for $2.945666 cash

DOMINION MTG & RLTY TR (MA)
Merged into Southmark Corp. 01/31/1986
Each Share of Bene. Int. no par exchanged for (0.55623) share Common $1 par
(See Southmark Corp.)

DOMINION NATL BK (VIENNA, VA)
Location changed 08/05/1974
Location changed from (Falls Church, VA) to (Vienna, VA) 08/05/1974
Name changed to Dominion Bank of Northern Virginia, N.A. (Vienna, VA) 05/21/1984
(See Dominion Bank of Northern Virginia, N.A. (Vienna, VA))

DOMINION NICKEL MINING CORP. LTD. (ON)
Recapitalized as New Dominion Nickel Mines Ltd. in 1953
Each share Capital Stock $1 par exchanged for (1/3) share Capital Stock $1 par
New Dominion Nickel Mines Ltd. name changed to New Dominion Resources Ltd. 4/24/78 which name changed to Epping Resources Ltd. 10/13/82 which name changed to Tri-D Automotive Industries Ltd. 12/1/86
(See Tri-D Automotive Industries Ltd.)

DOMINION OF CANADA GENERAL INSURANCE CO. (CANADA)
Each share Capital Stock $100 par exchanged for (10) shares Capital Stock $10 par 08/25/1955
Each share Capital Stock $10 par exchanged for (2) shares Capital Stock $5 par 03/17/1966
99% acquired by E-L Financial Corp. Ltd. through exchange offer which expired 10/18/1971
Public interest eliminated

DOMINION OF CANADA GUARANTEE & ACCIDENT INSURANCE CO.
Name changed to Dominion of Canada General Insurance Co. in 1929
(See Dominion of Canada General Insurance Co.)

DOMINION OIL CO., LTD.
Name changed to Crown-Dominion Oil Co., Ltd. 00/00/1930
Crown-Dominion Oil Co., Ltd. recapitalized as Reliance Petroleum, Ltd. 00/00/1949
(See Reliance Petroleum, Ltd.)

DOMINION OILCLOTH & LINOLEUM CO. LTD. (CANADA)
Name changed to Domco Industries Ltd.- Les Industries Domco Ltee. 11/1/67
Domco Industries Ltd.-Les Industries Domco Ltee. name changed to Domco, Inc. 7/23/96 which name changed to Domco Tarkett, Inc. 8/24/99

DOMINION POWER & MILLING CORP.
In process of liquidation in 1932

DOMINION POWER & TRANSMISSION CO. LTD.
Sold to Ontario Hydro-Electric Power Commission in 1930

DOMINION RES BLACK WARRIOR TR (DE)
Trust terminated 12/31/2016
No Unitholders' equity

DOMINION RES CAP TR II (DE)
Issue Information - 12,000,000 TR PFD SECS 8.4% offered at $25 per share on 01/10/2001
8.4% Trust Preferred Securities called for redemption at $25 on 10/17/2006

DOMINION RESOURCES DEVELOPMENT CO. (VA)
Charter revoked 6/1/61

DOMINION RES INC (DE)
Each share Common $0.001 par exchanged for (0.25) share Common 1¢ par 06/12/1992
Reorganized as Digital Imaging Resources Inc. 11/12/2004
Each share Common 1¢ par exchanged for (0.05) share Common $0.001 par
Digital Imaging Resources Inc. recapitalized as Boomerang Systems, Inc. 02/08/2008
(See Boomerang Systems, Inc.)

DOMINION RES INC NEW (VA)
Name changed 05/11/2017
Each Premium Income Equity Security received (0.817) share Common no par 11/16/2004
Common no par split (2) for (1) by issuance of (1) additional share payable 11/19/2007 to holders of record 11/09/2007 Ex date - 11/20/2007
Each 2013 Corporate Unit Ser. A automatically became (0.7728) share Common no par 04/01/2016
Each 2013 Corporate Unit Ser. B automatically became (0.7743) share Common no par 07/01/2016
Name changed from Dominion Resources, Inc. (New) to Dominion Energy, Inc. 05/11/2017
Each 2014 Corporate Unit Ser. A automatically became (0.6272) share Common no par 07/03/2017

DOMINION RES INC OLD (VA)
Common no par split (3) for (2) by issuance of (0.5) additional share 01/23/1992
Merged into Dominion Resources Inc. (New) 01/28/2000
Each share Common no par exchanged for either (1) share Common no par, $66 cash, or a combination thereof
Note: Non-electors received stock only
Dominion Resources Inc. (New) name changed to Dominion Energy, Inc. 05/11/2017

DOMINION SVGS BK FSB (FRONT ROYAL, VA)
Merged into GTR Atlantic Financial 8/25/2000
Each share Common no par exchanged for $3.18 cash

DOMINION SCOTTISH INVTS LTD (CANADA)
Common $25 par changed to $1 par 00/00/1934
Common $1 par changed to no par and (2) additional shares issued 01/27/1961
Common no par split (2) for (1) by issuance of (1) additional share 05/25/1962
5% Preference no par called for redemption 01/15/1988
Completely liquidated 05/24/1988
Details not available

DOMINION SECS LTD (CANADA)
Acquired by Royal Bank of Canada (Montreal, QC) 03/31/1988
Each share Common no par exchanged for (0.5459) share Common no par and $7.67 cash

DOMINION SEWER PIPE & CLAY INDUSTRIES
Merged into National Sewer Pipe Co., Ltd. 00/00/1928
Details not available

DOMINION SQUARE CORP. (QC)
Liquidation completed 1/12/57

DOMINION STEEL & COAL CORP., LTD. (NS)
Each share Class B Common $25 par

exchanged for (2) shares Ordinary no par in 1951
Acquired by Sidbec 8/22/69
Each share Ordinary Stock no par exchanged for $11 cash

DOMINION STEEL CORP., LTD.
Merged into Dominion Steel & Coal Corp., Ltd. in 1930
Details not available

DOMINION STORES, LTD. (CANADA)
Common no par exchanged (4) for (1) 00/00/1950
Common no par split (5) for (1) by issuance of (4) additional shares 08/11/1961
Name changed to Dominion Stores Ltd.- Les Supermarches Dominion Ltee. 08/24/1976
Dominion Stores Ltd. - Les Supermarches Dominion Ltee. reorganized as Argcen Holdings Inc. 08/30/1984 which merged into Hollinger Inc. 09/17/1985
(See Hollinger Inc.)

DOMINION STORES LTD (CANADA)
Under plan of reorganization each share Common no par automatically became (1) share Argcen Holdings Inc. Common no par 08/30/1984
Argcen Holdings Inc. merged into Hollinger Inc. 09/17/1985
(See Hollinger Inc.)

DOMINION TANNERS SALES CORP. (MB)
Preference $50 par called for redemption 00/00/1975
Merged into United Canadian Shares, Ltd. (Canada) 12/31/1979
Each share Common no par exchanged for (28) shares Common no par
United Canadian Shares, Ltd. (Canada) merged into Tanbridge Corp. 04/30/1999
(See Tanbridge Corp.)

DOMINION TAR & CHEM LTD (CANADA)
Each share 6.50% Preference $100 par exchanged for (1) share 5.50% Preference $100 par and (2) shares Common no par 00/00/1937
Common no par exchanged (4) for (1) 00/00/1953
Name changed to Domtar Ltd. 07/01/1965
Domtar Ltd. name changed to Domtar Ltd.-Domtar Ltee. 01/13/1972 which name changed to Domtar Inc. 02/23/1978 which reorganized as Domtar Corp. (DE) 03/07/2007

DOMINION TEXTILE CO., LTD. (CANADA)
Each share old Common no par exchanged for (9) shares new Common no par 00/00/1947
Name changed to Dominion Textile Ltd.- Dominion Textile Ltee. 10/31/1969
Dominion Textile Ltd.-Dominion Textile Ltee. name changed to Dominion Textile Inc. 01/02/1979
(See Dominion Textile Inc.)

DOMINION TEXTILE INC (CANADA)
Name changed 01/02/1979
Common no par split (3) for (1) by issuance of (2) additional shares 11/07/1972
Common no par reclassified as Conv. Class A Common no par 02/26/1975
Name changed from Dominion Textile Ltd. to Dominion Textile Inc. and Conv. Class A Common no par and Conv. Class B Common no par reclassified as Common no par respectively 01/02/1979
Merged into DT Acquisition 12/30/1997
Each share Common no par exchanged for $14.50 cash
7% Preferred $100 par called for redemption 01/29/1998

Public interest eliminated

DOMINION TRACTION & LIGHTING CO. LTD.
Dissolved in 1936

DOMINION URANIUM CORP. (QC)
Charter cancelled for failure to file reports 10/13/73

DOMINION WADDING CO. (CANADA)
Acquired by Stearns & Foster Co. 00/00/1971
Details not available

DOMINION WOOLLENS & WORSTEDS, LTD. (CANADA)
Assets sold 3/9/50
No stockholders' equity

DOMINIX INC (DE)
Common $0.0001 par split (10) for (1) by issuance of (9) additional shares payable 04/30/2001 to holders of record 04/20/2001 Ex date - 05/01/2001
Recapitalized as 110 Media Group, Inc. 06/04/2004
Each share Common $0.0001 par exchanged for (0.005) share Common $0.0001 par
110 Media Group, Inc. name changed to Web2 Corp. 07/31/2006 which recapitalized as Full Motion Beverage, Inc. 12/08/2008

DOMINO INVESTMENTS (UT)
Recapitalized as Uphill Down U.S.A., Inc. 7/1/86
Each share Common $0.001 par exchanged for (0.2) share Common $0.001 par

DOMINO PRTG SCIENCES PLC (UNITED KINGDOM)
ADR agreement terminated 07/13/2015
Each ADR for Ordinary exchanged for $14.285304 cash

DOMINO WYOMING OIL CO. (WY)
Administratively dissolved for failure to pay taxes 03/14/2009

DOMLIM INC (QC)
Conv. Class A Common no par and Conv. Class B Common no par reclassified as Class A Common no par 06/01/1979
Through purchase offer 100% acquired by Graylim Inc. as of 10/01/1980
5-3/4% Preferred $20 par called for redemption 10/06/1980
Public interest eliminated

DOMTAR CDA PAPER INC (BC)
Each old Exchangeable Share no par exchanged for (0.08333333) new Exchangeable Share no par 06/11/2009
Each new Exchangeable Share no par exchanged for (1) share Domtar Corp. new Common 1¢ par 06/02/2014

DOMTAR INC (CANADA)
Name changed 01/13/1972
Name changed 02/23/1978
Under plan of merger name changed from Domtar Ltd. to Domtar Ltd. - Domtar Ltee. 01/13/1972
Name changed from Domtar Ltd. - Domtar Ltee. to Domtar Inc. 02/23/1978
Common no par split (2) for (1) by issuance of (1) additional share 06/21/1985
Common no par split (2) for (1) by issuance of (1) additional share 05/22/1987
$1 Preference no par called for redemption 04/01/1992
Under plan of reorganization each share Common no par automatically became (1) share Domtar Corp. (DE) Common 1¢ par 03/07/2007
Note: Canadian residents had the option to receive Domtar (Canada)

Paper Inc. Exchangeable Shares in lieu of Common until 02/23/2007
(See Domtar (Canada) Paper Inc.)
$2.25 Preferred Ser. A no par called for redemption at $25 plus $0.4932 accrued dividends on 12/21/2007
Variable Rate Preferred Ser. B no par called for redemption at $25 plus $0.2466 accrued dividends on 12/21/2007

DOMTAR LTD.-DOMTAR LTEE. (CANADA)
Name changed to Domtar Inc. and $1 Preference $23.50 par changed to no par 2/23/78

DON CAMERON EXPLORATION CO. LTD. (ON)
Merged into Milestone Exploration Ltd. 07/23/1968
Each share Capital Stock no par exchanged for (0.122294) share Capital Stock no par
Milestone Exploration Ltd. merged into Jubilee Gold Inc. 01/01/2010 which merged into Jubilee Gold Exploration Ltd. 01/25/2013

DON MARCOS TRADING CO (FL)
Name changed to Saga Energy, Inc. 09/22/2011

DON MARTIC GOLD MINES, LTD. (ON)
Charter revoked for failure to file reports and pay taxes in 1951

DON MOTT ASSOCS INC
Merged into CED Tropical Packing Acquisition 3/9/2000
Each share Common exchanged for $33.53 cash

DON PRIMO INC (NV)
Reorganized as Bedford Energy, Inc. 4/26/2006
Each share Common $0.001 par exchanged for (2) shares Common $0.001 par

DON QUIJOTE CO LTD (JAPAN)
Name changed to Don Quijote Holdings Co., Ltd. 02/18/2014

DON SOPHISTICATES INC (NY)
Chapter 11 bankruptcy code converted to Chapter 7 on 7/8/82
Stockholders' equity unlikely

DON THE BEACHCOMBER ENTERPRISES (CA)
Name changed to Getty Financial Corp. 08/10/1972
(See Getty Financial Corp.)

DON WILL APARTMENTS, INC.
Liquidated in 1940

DONA PATRICIA GOLD MINES LTD. (ON)
Charter revoked for failure to file reports and pay taxes 00/00/1956

DONAHOES INC (DE)
Recapitalized in 1940
Each share 6% Preferred $100 par exchanged for (1) share 6% Preferred $25 par and (1) share old Common no par
Each share Class A exchanged for (0.1) share 6% Preferred $25 par and (0.1) share old Common no par
Each share old Common no par exchanged for (7.5) shares new Common no par
Due to financial difficulties this company went out of business 6/22/70
Charter revoked and proclaimed inoperative and void for non-payment of taxes 4/15/71

DONALD CORP (DE)
Charter cancelled and declared inoperative and void for non-payment of taxes 3/1/77

DONALDA COPPER MINES LTD.
Name changed to Donalda Mines Ltd. in 1943
Donalda Mines Ltd. recapitalized as

Aldona Mines Ltd. 3/20/72 which name changed to Aldona Resources Ltd. 6/9/94 which merged into TCF Energy Inc. 7/10/95 which merged into TriGas Exploration Inc. 6/26/96
(See TriGas Exploration Inc.)

DONALDA MINES LTD (QC)
Recapitalized as Aldona Mines Ltd. 03/20/1972
Each share Capital Stock $1 par exchanged for (1/9) share Capital Stock no par
Aldona Mines Ltd. name changed to Aldona Resources Ltd. 06/09/1994 which merged into TCF Energy Inc. 07/10/1995 which merged into TriGas Exploration Inc. 07/01/1996
(See TriGas Exploration Inc.)

DONALDSON LUFKIN & JENRETTE INC NEW (DE)
Common 10¢ par split (2) for (1) by issuance of (1) additional share payable 05/11/1998 to holders of record 04/27/1998 Ex date - 05/12/1998
Acquired by Credit Suisse Group 11/03/2000
Each share Common 10¢ par exchanged for $90 cash
Name changed to Credit Suisse First Boston (USA), Inc. 01/15/2001
(See Credit Suisse First Boston (USA), Inc.)
Adjustable Fixed Rate Preferred Ser. A 1¢ par called for redemption at $50 on 12/31/2001
Adjustable Fixed Rate Preferred Ser. B called for redemption at $50 on 02/28/2003
Public interest eliminated

DONALDSON LUFKIN & JENRETTE INC OLD (DE)
Merged into Equitable Life Assurance Society of the United States 1/17/85
Each share Common 10¢ par exchanged for $30 cash

DONAR ENTERPRISES INC (DE)
Each share old Common $0.001 par exchanged for (0.1) share new Common $0.001 par 4/15/2005
Name changed to Playlogic Entertainment, Inc. 8/1/2005

DONARD GOLD MINES, LTD. (ON)
Charter cancelled 6/18/62
No stockholders' equity

DONBAR DEV CORP (DE)
Class A Common 10¢ par and Class B Common 10¢ par reclassified as Common 10¢ par 4/22/65
Charter cancelled and declared inoperative and void for non-payment of taxes 3/1/75

DONCASTERS PLC (ENGLAND & WALES)
ADR agreement terminated 01/12/2002
Each Sponsored ADR for Ordinary 25p par exchanged for $27.50 cash

DONCHESTER DUQUESNE MINES LTD (QC)
Merged into Fundy Chemical International Ltd. 10/01/1973
Each share Capital Stock $1 par exchanged for (0.5) share Common no par
(See Fundy Chemical International Ltd.)

DONEGAL PETROLEUMS LTD. (ON)
Acquired by D'Arcy Oil & Gas Ltd. on a (1) for (2) basis 00/00/1953
D'Arcy Oil & Gas Ltd. name changed to Lariat Exploration & Development Ltd. 00/00/1953 which was acquired by Dominion Asbestos Mines Ltd. 00/00/1954 which name changed to Daine Mining Corp. Ltd. 09/11/1956 which recapitalized as Cable Mines & Oils Ltd. 08/15/1957 which merged into St. Fabien Copper Mines Ltd. 07/27/1967 which name

changed to St. Fabien Explorations Inc. 02/11/1981 which recapitalized as Fabien Explorations Inc. 07/18/1983
(See Fabien Explorations Inc.)

DONEGAL RES LTD (BC)
Recapitalized as Markway Resources Ltd. 5/11/84
Each share Common no par exchanged for (0.2) share Common no par
Markway Resources Ltd. name changed to So-Luminaire Systems Corp. 8/9/84
(See So-Luminaire Systems Corp.)

DONETSK METALLURGICAL PLANT (UKRAINE)
GDR agreement terminated 05/14/2018
Each Reg. S Sponsored GDR for Ordinary exchanged for (100) shares Ordinary
Note: Unexchanged GDR's will be sold and the proceeds, if any, held for claim after 11/13/2018

DONG ENERGY A/S (DENMARK)
Name changed to Orsted A/S 11/15/2017

DONG FANG MINERALS INC (NV)
Reorganized as Heli Electronics Corp. 05/13/2010
Each share Common $0.00001 par exchanged for (120) shares Common $0.00001 par
(See Heli Electronics Corp.)

DONG XIN BIO-TECH PHARMACEUTICAL INC (NV)
Recapitalized as GP Solutions, Inc. 10/02/2018
Each share Common $0.001 par exchanged for (0.005) share Common $0.001 par

DONGFANG ELEC CORP LTD (CHINA)
ADR agreement terminated 08/06/2018
No ADR's remain outstanding

DONGYUE GROUP LTD (CAYMAN ISLANDS)
ADR agreement terminated 12/26/2017
No ADR's remain outstanding

DONINI INC (NJ)
Each share old Common $0.001 par exchanged for (0.33333333) share new Common $0.001 par 03/07/2002
Each share new Common $0.001 par exchanged again for (0.002) share new Common $0.001 par 12/19/2008
Stock Dividend - 5% payable 12/01/2004 to holders of record 11/15/2004
Recapitalized as GD Entertainment & Technology, Inc. 05/08/2015
Each share new Common $0.001 par exchanged for (0.0001) share Common $0.00001 par

DONLAR BIOSYNTREX CORP (NV)
Merged into Donlar Corp. 02/27/2003
Each share Common $0.0001 par exchanged for (0.25998836) share Common no par
(See Donlar Corp.)

DONLAR CORP (IL)
Chapter 11 bankruptcy proceedings converted to Chapter 7 on 07/13/2004
Stockholders' equity unlikely

DONLEE MFG INDS LTD (ON)
Acquired by Arthur S. Donovan, John C. Donovan, Stephen J. Donovan, Ronald H. Burns, Paul L. Murray and 80903 Canada Ltd. 11/25/1977
Each share Common no par exchanged for $16.50 cash

DONNA KARAN INTL INC (DE)
Merged into LVMH Moet Hennessy Louis Vuitton Inc. 11/27/2001
Each share Common 1¢ par exchanged for $10.75 cash

DONNA MINES LTD (BC)
Recapitalized as Oliver Resources Ltd. 08/14/1978
Each share Capital Stock 50¢ par exchanged for (0.2) share Capital Stock no par
Oliver Resources Ltd. recapitalized as Dyna Gold Resources Inc. 01/29/1986
(See Dyna Gold Resources Inc.)

DONNACONA PAPER CO. LTD. (QC)
Each share Common no par exchanged for (0.1) share Class B no par in 1932
Class A no par and Class B no par changed to Common no par in 1942
Completely liquidated for cash 12/7/62

DONNEBROOKE CORP (DE)
Each share old Common $0.00001 par exchanged for (0.001) share new Common $0.00001 par 02/19/1999
Name changed to Virtual Academics.com Inc. 01/04/2000
Virtual Academics.com Inc. name changed to Cenuco, Inc. 12/16/2002 which name changed to Ascendia Brands, Inc. 05/12/2006
(See Ascendia Brands, Inc.)

DONNELL & MUDGE LTD. (ON)
Class A no par reclassified as old Common no par 12/12/1955
Each share old Common no par exchanged for (20) shares new Common no par 06/11/1956
Name changed to United Telefilms Ltd. 07/25/1958
United Telefilms Ltd. recapitalized as Creative Telefilms & Artists Ltd. 01/26/1960 which name changed to Seven Arts Productions Ltd. 08/12/1960 which name changed to Warner Bros.-Seven Arts Ltd. 07/15/1967 which was acquired by Kinney National Service, Inc. 07/08/1969 which name changed to Kinney Services, Inc. (NY) 02/17/1971 which reincorporated in Delaware as Warner Communications Inc. 02/11/1972
(See Warner Communications Inc.)

DONNELLEY ENTERPRISE SOLUTIONS INC (DE)
Merged into Bowne & Co., Inc. 7/6/98
Each share Common 1¢ par exchanged for $21 cash

DONNELLY CORP (MI)
Class A Common 10¢ par split (5) for (4) by issuance of (0.25) additional share 4/1/92
Class A Common 10¢ par split (5) for (4) by issuance of (0.25) additional share payable 1/30/97 to holders of record 1/6/97 Ex date - 1/31/97
Merged into Magna International Inc. 10/1/2002
Each share Class A Common 10¢ par exchanged for (0.459) share Class A Common no par
Each share Class B Common 10¢ par exchanged for (0.459) share Class A Common no par

DONNER METALS LTD (CANADA)
Reincorporated 01/25/2013
Place of incorporation changed from (BC) to (Canada) 01/25/2013
Each share old Common no par exchanged for (0.01666666) share new Common no par 12/30/2013
Name changed to Sphinx Resources Ltd. 10/07/2014

DONNER MINERALS LTD (BC)
Plan of arrangement effective 08/16/2005
Each share Common no par exchanged for (0.1) share Donner Metals Ltd. Common no par and (0.025) share Donner Petroleum Ltd. Common no par
(See each company's listing)

DONNER PETE LTD (AB)
Recapitalized as Crocotta Energy Inc. 01/12/2007
Each share Common no par exchanged for (0.074) share Common no par
(See Crocotta Energy Inc.)

DONNER RES LTD (BC)
Plan of arrangement effective 11/07/1997
Each share Common no par exchanged for (1) share Donner Minerals Ltd. Common no par and (0.16666666) share Denstone Resources Ltd. Common no par
(See each company's listing)

DONNER STEEL CO., INC.
Acquired by Republic Steel Corp. 00/00/1930
Details not available

DONNKENNY INC (DE)
Common 1¢ par split (2) for (1) by issuance of (1) additional share 12/18/1995
Each share old Common 1¢ par exchanged for (0.25) share new Common 1¢ par 04/20/2000
Plan of reorganization under Chapter 11 Federal Bankruptcy Code effective 10/24/2005
No stockholders' equity

DONNKENNY INC (NY)
Stock Dividends - 25% 11/01/1968; 15% 04/09/1971; 100% 04/21/1976; 10% 04/12/1977
Name changed to DK Investors, Inc. (NY) 11/30/1978
DK Investors, Inc. (NY) reorganized in Nevada as Resource Acquisition Group, Inc. 08/05/2010 which name changed to American Retail Group, Inc. 04/01/2011

DONNY OSMOND ENTMT CORP (TX)
Name changed to Entertainment Equity Corp. 06/30/1989
Entertainment Equity Corp. name changed to Enhanced Electronics Corp. 08/31/1993 which name changed to Curtis Mathes Holding Corp. 05/23/1994 which name changed to uniView Technologies Corp. 01/30/1998 which name changed to VPGI Corp. 08/14/2003

DONNYBROOK ENERGY INC (AB)
Each share Common no par received distribution of (0.025) share Donnycreek Energy Inc. Common no par payable 11/07/2011 to holders of record 11/04/2011
Each share Common no par received distribution of (0.0527) share Cequence Energy Ltd. Common no par payable 04/15/2013 to holders of record 04/12/2013 Ex date - 04/16/2013
Recapitalized as Stonehaven Exploration Ltd. 10/29/2014
Each share Common no par exchanged for (0.025) share Common no par
Stonehaven Exploration Ltd. name changed to Front Range Resources Ltd. 08/11/2016 which recapitalized as Arrow Exploration Corp. 10/05/2018

DONNYBROOK RES INC (BC)
Recapitalized as Rodinia Minerals Inc. (BC) 08/13/2003
Each share Common no par exchanged for (0.2) share Common no par
Rodinia Minerals Inc. (BC) reincorporated in Ontario 11/03/2009 which name changed to Rodinia Lithium Inc. 06/30/2010 which recapitalized as Routemaster Capital Inc. 09/20/2016

DONNYBROOKE INC (MN)
Adjudicated bankrupt 02/19/1974
Stockholders' equity unlikely

DONNYCREEK ENERGY INC (AB)
Merged into Kicking Horse Energy Inc. 12/24/2014
Each share Common no par exchanged for (0.6) share Common no par
Note: Unexchanged certificates were cancelled and became without value 12/24/2017
(See Kicking Horse Energy Inc.)

DONOBI INC (NV)
Recapitalized as Gottaplay Interactive, Inc. 07/25/2006
Each share Common $0.001 par exchanged for (0.16666666) share Common $0.001 par

DONOHOE COMPANIES, INC. (MD)
Name changed to Federal Center Plaza Corp. 12/31/1986

DONOHOE CONSTRUCTION CO., INC. (MD)
Name changed to Donohoe Companies, Inc. 07/31/1984
Donohoe Companies, Inc. name changed to Federal Center Plaza Corp. 12/31/1986

DONOHUE BROS LTD (QC)
Each share Capital Stock no par exchanged for (2) shares Capital Stock no par 12/22/1951
Each share Capital Stock no par exchanged for (2) shares Capital Stock $3.33333333 par 04/01/1957
Recapitalized as Donohue Brothers Ltd.-La Compagnie Donohue Ltee. 05/26/1964
Each share Capital Stock $3.33333333 par exchanged for (3) shares Capital Stock no par
Donohue Brothers Ltd.-La Compagnie Donohue Ltee. name changed to Donohue Co. Ltd.-La Compagnie Donohue Ltee. 06/13/1970 which name changed to Donohue Inc. 07/08/1978 which merged into Abitibi-Consolidated Inc. 04/18/2000 which merged into AbitibiBowater Inc. 10/29/2007
(See AbitibiBowater Inc.)

DONOHUE BROTHERS LTD.-LA COMPAGNIE DONOHUE LTEE. (QC)
Capital Stock no par reclassified as Common no par 08/01/1967
Name changed to Donohue Co. Ltd.-La Compagnie Donohue Ltee. 06/13/1970
Donohue Co. Ltd.-La Compagnie Donohue Ltee. name changed to Donohue Inc. 07/08/1978 which merged into Abitibi-Consolidated Inc. 04/18/2000 which merged into AbitibiBowater Inc. 10/29/2007

DONOHUE CO. LTD.-LA COMPAGNIE DONOHUE LTEE. (QC)
Name changed to Donohue Inc. 07/08/1978
Donohue Inc. merged into Abitibi-Consolidated Inc. 04/18/2000 which merged into AbitibiBowater Inc. 10/29/2007
(See AbitibiBowater Inc.)

DONOHUE INC (QC)
Common no par split (2) for (1) by issuance of (1) additional share 10/24/1984
Common no par split (2) for (1) by issuance of (1) additional share 08/09/1988
Common no par reclassified as Class B no par 04/27/1989
Class A Subordinate no par split (2) for (1) by issuance of (1) additional share 05/20/1994
Class B no par split (2) for (1) by

issuance of (1) additional share 05/20/1994
Class A Subordinate no par split (3) for (2) by issuance of (0.5) additional share payable 05/18/1999 to holders of record 05/04/1999
Class B no par split (3) for (2) by issuance of (0.5) additional share payable 05/18/1999 to holders of record 05/04/1999
Merged into Abitibi-Consolidated Inc. 04/18/2000
Each share Class A Subordinate no par exchanged for (1.8642) shares Common no par and $12 cash
Each share Class B no par exchanged for (1.8642) shares Common no par and $12 cash
Abitibi-Consolidated Inc. merged into AbitibiBowater Inc. 10/29/2007
(See AbitibiBowater Inc.)

DONOVAN COS INC (IA)
Merged into Midwest Energy Co. 01/08/1986
Each share Class A Common $1 par exchanged for $33 cash

DONOVAN WEISS INC (NV)
Name changed to QuickEX, Inc. 12/01/2003
QuickEX, Inc. name changed to Meshtech Wireless, Inc. 05/27/2005 which name changed to Sleep Healers Holdings, Inc. 08/17/2006 which name changed to Sleep Holdings, Inc. 10/09/2006 which name changed to ALL-Q-TELL Corp. 11/03/2010
(See ALL-Q-TELL Corp.)

DONRAND MINES LTD (ON)
Recapitalized as CRMnet.com Inc. 03/08/2000
Each share Common no par exchanged for (0.5) share Common no par
CRMnet.com Inc. recapitalized as Advanced Explorations Inc. 02/25/2005
(See Advanced Explorations Inc.)

DONTRELL CAP LTD (ON)
Reincorporated 12/18/1995
Place of incorporation changed from (Canada) to (ON) 12/18/1995
Name changed to Mond Industries Inc. 01/01/1996
Mond Industries Inc. name changed to Trailmobile Canada Ltd. 06/08/1999
(See Trailmobile Canada Ltd.)

DONUT KASTLE INC (AL)
Name changed to Yankee Doodle Enterprises, Inc. 10/27/1986
Yankee Doodle Enterprises, Inc. reorganized as Mexus, Inc. 11/18/1993 which name changed to Wittcomm Inc. 04/29/1997
(See Wittcomm Inc.)

DONWOOD LARDER MINES, LTD. (ON)
Charter revoked for failure to file reports and pay taxes 00/00/1951

DOOLEY EXCHANGE, INC. (NY)
Name changed to Super Distributing Corp. 08/17/1921
(See Super Distributing Corp.)

DOONER LABS INC (MA)
Merged into Rorer Group Inc. 12/15/1977
Each share Common 1¢ par exchanged for (0.906276) share Common no par
Rorer Group Inc. name changed to Rhone Poulenc-Rorer Inc. 07/31/1990
(See Rhone Poulenc-Rorer Inc.)

DOONSON GOLD MINES, LTD. (ON)
Charter revoked for failure to file reports and pay taxes 3/11/57

DOOR OPENINGS CORP (NJ)
Name changed to Jersey Patents, Inc. 05/28/1975
Jersey Patents, Inc. name changed to Solar Energy Systems, Inc. 04/27/1978
(See Solar Energy Systems, Inc.)

DOORNFONTEIN GOLD MNG LTD (SOUTH AFRICA)
Each ADR for Ordinary Reg. exchanged for (4) ADR's for Ordinary Reg. 11/06/1987
Merged into Blyvooruitzicht Gold Mining Co. Ltd. 11/06/1995
Each ADR for Ordinary exchanged for (0.5) ADR for Ordinary
Blyvooruitzicht Gold Mining Co. Ltd. merged into Durban Roodepoort Deep Ltd. 09/15/1997 which name changed to DRDGOLD Ltd. 12/06/2004

DOR BIOPHARMA INC (DE)
Name changed to Soligenix, Inc. 09/30/2009

DOR ENERGY 1988 LTD (ISRAEL)
ADR agreement terminated 00/00/2001
Details not available

DORA EXPLS LTD (BC)
Merged into Meridor Resources Ltd. 04/01/1985
Each share Capital Stock no par exchanged for (0.2231) share Common no par
Meridor Resources Ltd. merged into Hughes Lang Corp. 08/01/1989 which merged into CanGold Resources Inc. (BC) 01/31/1994 which reorganized in Ontario as Amalgamated CanGold Inc. 07/31/1995 which merged into Central Asia Goldfields Corp. 01/08/1996
(See Central Asia Goldfields Corp.)

DORADO MICRO SYS (CA)
Name changed to Onyx + Imi, Inc. 03/01/1982
Onyx + Imi, Inc. merged into Corvus Systems, Inc. 07/30/1985
(See Corvus Systems, Inc.)

DORADO RES LTD (BC)
Recapitalized as International Dorado Resources Ltd. 05/05/1987
Each share Common no par exchanged for (0.25) share Common no par
International Dorado Resources Ltd. recapitalized as Calco Resources Inc. 12/14/1990 which recapitalized as Berkshire International Mining Ltd. 02/19/1997 which recapitalized as Tyner Resources Ltd. 01/24/2002

DORADO URANIUM LTD. (BC)
Struck off register and declared dissolved 05/22/1958
No stockholders' equity

DORAL ENERGY CORP (NV)
Each share old Common $0.001 par exchanged for (0.16) share new Common $0.001 par 01/23/2009
Each share new Common $0.001 par exchanged again for (5) shares new Common $0.001 par 09/14/2009
Each share new Common $0.001 par exchanged again for (0.01818181) share new Common $0.001 par 12/27/2010
Name changed to Cross Border Resources, Inc. 01/06/2011

DORAL FINL CORP (PR)
Old Common $1 par split (2) for (1) by issuance of (1) additional share payable 05/20/1998 to holders of record 05/08/1998
Old Common $1 par split (3) for (2) by issuance of (0.5) additional share payable 09/14/2002 to holders of record 08/30/2002 Ex date - 09/16/2002
Old Common $1 par split (3) for (2) by issuance of (0.5) additional share payable 12/11/2003 to holders of record 11/21/2003 Ex date - 12/12/2003
Each share old Common $1 par exchanged for (0.05) share new Common 1¢ par 08/20/2007
Each share new Common 1¢ par exchanged again for (0.05) share new Common 1¢ par 07/01/2013
Plan of reorganization under Chapter 11 Federal Bankruptcy proceedings effective 10/28/2016
Stockholders' equity unlikely

DORAL INDS INC (DE)
Name changed to Magic Marker Industries, Inc. 03/11/1982
(See Magic Marker Industries, Inc.)

DORAL MINERAL INDUSTRIES LTD. (AUSTRALIA)
Acquired by Iwatani International Corp. 12/16/1996
Each share Ordinary $1 par exchanged for $0.26 cash

DORAL MNG EXPLS LTD (QC)
Charter annulled for failure to file reports or pay fees 01/12/1974

DORAN ENERGY CORP (TX)
Name changed to Wright Brothers Energy Inc. 10/30/85
(See Wright Brothers Energy Inc.)

DORATO RES INC (BC)
Recapitalized as Xiana Mining Inc. 10/23/2013
Each share Common no par exchanged for (0.05) share Common no par

DORATO RES INC (WY)
Reincorporated under the laws of British Columbia 08/21/2006
Dorato Resources Inc. (BC) recapitalized as Xiana Mining Inc. 10/23/2013

DORBASKA GOLD MINES, LTD. (ON)
Charter revoked for failure to file reports and pay taxes 00/00/1957

DORCHESTER CORP. (DE)
Under plan of merger name changed to Dorchester Gas Producing Co. 01/02/1962
Dorchester Gas Producing Co. merged into Panoil Co. 11/26/1968 which name changed to Dorchester Gas Corp. 02/01/1972
(See Dorchester Gas Corp.)

DORCHESTER ENERGY INC (AB)
Acquired by Celtic Exploration Ltd. 12/16/2002
Each share Common no par exchanged for either (0.14) share Common no par and $0.28 cash, or $0.70 cash
Note: Option to receive stock and cash expired 02/14/2003
Celtic Exploration Ltd. merged into Kelt Exploration Ltd. 02/26/2013

DORCHESTER GAS CORP (DE)
Conv. Special Stock no par called for redemption 10/21/1977
Common 10¢ par split (2) for (1) by issuance of (1) additional share 01/07/1981
Merged into Damson Oil Corp. 08/24/1984
Each share 5.5% Preferred Ser. A $25 par exchanged for $13.75 cash
Each share Common 10¢ par exchanged for $22.50 cash

DORCHESTER GAS PRODUCING CO (DE)
Merged into Panoil Co. 11/26/1968
Each share 5.5% Preferred Ser. A $25 par exchanged for (1) share 5.5% Preferred Ser. A $25 par
Each share Common Capital Stock $1 par exchanged for (3.5) shares Conv. Special Stock no par
Panoil Co. name changed to Dorchester Gas Corp. 02/01/1972
(See Dorchester Gas Corp.)

DORCHESTER HOTELS INC (BC)
Placed in receivership 03/00/1989
No stockholders' equity

DORCHESTER HUGOTON LTD (TX)
Depositary Receipts split (3) for (1) by issuance of (2) additional Depositary Receipts 10/30/1987
Depositary Receipts split (2) for (1) by issuance of (1) additional Depositary Receipt 08/05/1989
Reorganized under the laws of Delaware as Dorchester Minerals L.P. 01/31/2003
Each Depositary Receipt exchanged for (1) Common Unit and $1.90 cash

DORCHESTER RES LTD (BC)
Recapitalized as Taurus Resources Ltd. 12/22/1976
Each share Capital Stock 50¢ par exchanged for (0.2) share Capital Stock no par
Taurus Resources Ltd. recapitalized as International Taurus Resources Inc. 11/24/1988 which merged into American Bonanza Gold Corp. 03/31/2005 which merged into Kerr Mines Inc. 07/07/2014

DORE EXPLS INC (ON)
Merged into Dore-Norbaska Resources Inc. 12/23/1987
Each share Common no par exchanged for (1) share Common no par
Dore-Norbaska Resources Inc. merged into Griffin Corp. 02/23/1998
(See Griffin Corp.)

DORE NORBASKA RES INC (ON)
Merged into Griffin Corp. 02/23/1998
Each share Common no par exchanged for (0.04) share Common no par
(See Griffin Corp.)

DOREAL ENERGY CORP (AB)
Delisted from Toronto Venture Stock Exchange 11/14/2002

DOREMUS & CO (DE)
Stock Dividend - 25% 02/28/1978
Merged into BBDO International, Inc. 11/28/1980
Each share Common $1 par exchanged for (0.30769230) share Common 10¢ par
BBDO International, Inc. merged into Omnicom Group Inc. 08/29/1986

DOREVA GOLD MINES, LTD. (ON)
Charter revoked for failure to file reports and pay taxes 03/00/1951

DOREX MINERALS INC (BC)
Each share old Common no par exchanged for (0.1) share new Common no par 06/05/2017
Name changed to Cipher Resources Inc. 09/18/2017

DORIC CORP. (OH)
Adjudicated bankrupt 08/07/1967
No stockholders' equity

DORIC CORP (DE)
Reincorporated 09/26/1967
State of incorporation changed from (OK) to (DE) 09/26/1967
Common $10 par changed to $1 par and (0.5) additional share issued 08/13/1968
Each share 6% Preferred $10 par exchanged for $10 principal amount of 7.5% Jr. Subord. Debentures due 04/30/1991 on 05/19/1971
Common $1 par split (2) for (1) by issuance of (1) additional share 10/25/1974
Merged into Esmark, Inc. (Inc. 03/14/1969) 04/24/1975
Each share Common $1 par exchanged for (0.46) share Common $1 par
(See Esmark, Inc. (Inc. 03/14/1969))

DORIC DISTRS INC (NY)
Adjudicated bankrupt 09/20/1971
Stockholders' equity unlikely

DORION RED LAKE MINES LTD (ON)
Merged into Goldquest Exploration Inc. 08/09/1982
Each share Capital Stock $1 par exchanged (0.06414368) share Common no par
Goldquest Exploration Inc. merged into Goldcorp Inc. (New) 03/31/1994

DORITA SILVER MINES LTD (BC)
Name changed to Liberty Petroleums Inc. 11/01/1978
Liberty Petroleums Inc. acquired by Corrida Oils Ltd. 05/06/1982
(See Corrida Oils Ltd.)

DORMAN LONG & CO LTD (ENGLAND)
Stock Dividend - 50% 02/26/1960
Nationalized by the United Kingdom 08/08/1967
Each ADR for Ordinary exchanged for principal amount of 6.5% Treasury Stock due 01/28/1971

DORMITZER ELECTRIC & MANUFACTURING CORP.
Bankrupt 00/00/1949
No stockholders' equity

DORNE & MARGOLIN CORP (NY)
Merged into Granger Associates 01/15/1969
Each share Capital Stock $1 par exchanged for (0.6) share Capital Stock $1 par
Granger Associates merged into Digital Switch Corp. 06/27/1984 which name changed to DCS Communications Corp. 04/22/1985 which merged into Alcatel 09/04/1998 which name changed to Alcatel-Lucent 11/30/2006
(See Alcatel-Lucent)

DORNOCH INTL INC (BC)
Name changed to DNI Holdings Inc. 04/28/1988
(See DNI Holdings Inc.)

DORNOST PUBLISHING CO., INC. (NY)
Name changed to Communication Channels, Inc. 09/01/1968
(See Communication Channels, Inc.)

DORNS STORES INC (CA)
Stock Dividend - 50% 06/20/1953
Adjudicated bankrupt 06/27/1967
Stockholders' equity unlikely

DOROMIN RES LTD (BC)
Delisted from Vancouver Stock Exchange 03/14/1997

DORON EXPLS INC (BC)
Recapitalized as WEW Ventures, Inc. 03/01/1993
Each share Common no par exchanged for (0.2) share Common no par
WEW Ventures, Inc. name changed to Independence Resources Inc. 05/11/1994 which name changed to iLoveTV Entertainment Inc. 01/15/2002
(See iLoveTV Entertainment Inc.)

DORR CO., INC. (DE)
Merged into Dorr-Oliver, Inc. 00/00/1954
Each share Preferred $50 par exchanged for (0.61349693) share Preferred $32.50 par
Each share Common $1 par exchanged for (10) shares Common $7.50 par
Each $11.0447 of book value Tenure Stock $2 par exchanged for (1) share Common $7.50 par
(See Dorr-Oliver, Inc.)

DORR OLIVER INC (DE)
Common $7.50 par changed to $1 par 03/05/1971
$2 Conv. Preferred $32.50 par called for redemption 09/01/1972
Merged into Curtiss-Wright Corp. 05/31/1979
Each share Common $1 par exchanged for $23 cash

DORREEN GOLD MINES LTD.
Acquired by Dorreen Mines Ltd. 00/00/1951
Details not available

DORREEN MINES LTD. (BC)
Charter revoked for failure to file reports and pay fees 00/00/1963

DORRIGO ENERGY INC (AB)
Merged into Sunalta Energy Inc. 02/10/1995
Each share Common no par exchanged for (0.4) share Common no par
(See Sunalta Energy Inc.)

DORSET BUILDING CORP. (IL)
Liquidation completed 11/01/1958
Details not available

DORSET EXPL LTD (AB)
Merged into Baytex Energy Ltd. 10/21/1997
Each share Common no par exchanged for (0.48) share Class A no par
(See Baytex Energy Ltd.)

DORSET FABRICS, INC.
Acquired by Fuller (D.B.) & Co., Inc. 00/00/1950
Each share Capital Stock exchanged for (0.06) share 6% 2nd Preferred $5 par and (0.06) share Common 10¢ par
Fuller (D.B.) & Co., Inc. acquired by Stevens (J.P.) & Co., Inc. 06/28/1958
(See Fuller (D.B.) & Co., Inc.)

DORSET RES LTD (CANADA)
Recapitalized 12/10/1985
Each share Common no par exchanged for (1) share Class A Common no par and (0.04) Cassiar Mining Corp. Unit consisting of (1) share Common no par and (1) Common Stock Purchase Warrant Series I expiring 04/30/1986
Merged into Consolidated Brinco Ltd. 05/30/1986
Each share Class A Common no par exchanged for (0.1) share Class A Common no par
Consolidated Brinco Ltd. merged into Hillsborough Resources Ltd. (ON) 02/06/1992 which reincorporated in Canada 11/05/1997
(See Hillsborough Resources Ltd. (Canada))

DORSETT EDL SYS INC (OK)
Name changed 08/08/1968
Name changed from Dorsett Industries, Inc. to Dorsett Educational Systems, Inc. 08/08/1968
Name changed to Laid Back Enterprises, Inc. and Common 10¢ par changed to 1¢ par 01/04/1990
Laid Back Enterprises, Inc. name changed to Gift Liquidators Inc. (OK) 12/20/2002 which reincorporated in Maryland as Excellency Investment Realty Trust, Inc. 09/20/2006
(See Excellency Investment Realty Trust, Inc.)

DORSETT ELECTRONICS, INC. (DE)
Reincorporated 02/19/1968
Stock Dividend - 200% 10/10/1961
State of incorporation changed from (OK) to (DE) 02/19/1968
Name changed to LaBarge, Inc. 12/02/1968
(See LaBarge, Inc.)

DORSETT ELECTRONICS LABORATORIES, INC. (OK)
Name changed to Dorsett Electronics, Inc. (OK) 08/22/1961
Dorsett Electronics, Inc. (OK) reincorporated in Delaware 02/19/1968 which name changed to LaBarge, Inc. 12/02/1968
(See LaBarge, Inc.)

DORSETT LABORATORIES, INC. (OK)
Name changed to Dorsett Electronics Laboratories, Inc. 04/25/1960
Dorsett Electronics Laboratories, Inc. name changed to Dorsett Electronics, Inc. (OK) 08/22/1961 which reincorporated in Delaware 02/19/1968 which name changed to LaBarge, Inc. 12/02/1968
(See LaBarge, Inc.)

DORSEY CORP (DE)
Common $1 par changed to 50¢ par and (1) additional share issued 07/03/1969
Common 50¢ par split (2) for (1) by issuance of (1) additional share 06/01/1986
Name changed to Constar International Inc. (Old) 05/01/1987
(See Constar International Inc. (Old))

DORSEY TRAILERS INC (DE)
Chapter 11 bankruptcy proceedings converted to Chapter 7 on 09/12/2001
Stockholders' equity unlikely

DORSON SPORTS INC (NY)
Merged into Dorson Acquisition, Inc. 02/23/1987
Each share Common 1¢ par exchanged for $3.75 cash

DORVAL-SISCOE GOLD SYNDICATE, LTD. (ON)
Voluntarily dissolved 11/21/1938
Details not available

DOSKOCIL COS INC (DE)
Each share old Common 40¢ par exchanged for (0.1) share new Common 40¢ par par 04/20/1987
Reorganized under Chapter 11 Federal Bankruptcy Code 10/31/1991
Each share new Common 40¢ par exchanged for (0.053) share Common 1¢ par
Note: Unexchanged certificates were cancelled and became without value 10/31/1996
Name changed to Foodbrands America Inc. 05/15/1995
Foodbrands America Inc. merged into IBP, Inc. 05/07/1997
(See Foodbrands America Inc.)

DOSTAL FOUNDRY & MACHINE CO. (MI)
Liquidation completed
Each share Common $1 par received initial distribution of Ctf. for (1) Unit of Int. in Dostal Liquidation Trust (for attachment to Common Ctf.) and 20¢ cash 3/12/63
Second distribution - 10¢ per Unit paid to holders of Dostal Liquidation Trust 5/25/65
Third distribution - 10¢ per Unit paid to holders of Dostal Liquidation Trust 8/18/67
Fourth distribution - 10¢ per Unit paid to holders of Dostal Liquidation Trust 12/30/69
Each unit of Common $1 par and Ctf. of Int. in Dostal Liquidation Trust exchanged for fifth and final distribution of $0.0451 cash 7/24/72

DOSTAL PER-MOLD FOUNDRY CO.
Name changed to Dostal Foundry & Machine Co. in 1949
(See Dostal Foundry & Machine Co.)

DOT COM ENTMT GROUP INC (FL)
Reincorporated under the laws of Ontario as Parlay Entertainment Inc. 12/16/2004
Parlay Entertainment Inc. recapitalized as Oramericas Corp. (ON) 12/10/2012 which reincorporated in British Columbia 02/21/2014 which name changed to Backstageplay Inc. 02/09/2016

DOT COM TECHNOLOGIES INC (BC)
Recapitalized as BCS Collaborative Solutions Inc. 07/12/2002
Each share Common no par exchanged for (0.5) share Common no par
BCS Collaborative Solutions Inc. recapitalized as BCS Global Networks Inc. 09/02/2003
(See BCS Global Networks Inc.)

DOT HILL SYS CORP (DE)
Reincorporated 09/19/2001
State of incorporation changed from (NY) to (DE) and Common 1¢ par changed to $0.001 par 09/19/2001
Acquired by Seagate Technology PLC 10/06/2015
Each share Common $0.001 par exchanged for $9.75 cash

DOTCOM 2000 INC (ON)
Name changed to Konexus Technologies Ltd. 01/10/2002
(See Konexus Technologies Ltd.)

DOTHAN FED SVGS BK (DOTHAN, AL)
Merged into Colonial BancGroup, Inc. 07/09/1996
Each share Common exchanged for either (0.1937) share Common $2.50 par and approximately $6.51 cash or an amount of stock and cash to be determined by the company
(See Colonial BancGroup, Inc.)

DOTRONIX INC (MN)
Name changed to Wind Energy America, Inc. 04/10/2007
(See Wind Energy America, Inc.)

DOTWAP COM HLDG CORP (DE)
Charter cancelled and declared inoperative and void for non-payment of taxes 03/01/2003

DOUBLE A URANIUM MINING & DEVELOPMENT CO. LTD. (SK)
Stricken from the Saskachewan register in September 1961

DOUBLE ARROW OIL & GAS LTD (BC)
Name changed to Arrowhead Minerals Corp. 12/02/1996
Arrowhead Minerals Corp. recapitalized as Gemini Energy Corp. 10/25/1999 which merged into Bucking Horse Energy Inc. 03/03/2008

DOUBLE CHANCE RES LTD (BC)
Name changed to Calaveras Explorations Ltd. 03/15/1983
Calaveras Explorations Ltd. recapitalized as Cardinal Mineral Corp. Ltd. 06/11/1986 which recapitalized as Connecticut Development Corp. 11/08/1990 which recapitalized as Mira Properties Ltd. 04/16/1999 which recapitalized as Resolve Ventures, Inc. 08/19/2003

DOUBLE COIN HLDGS LTD (CHINA)
Name changed to Shanghai Huayi Group Corp. Ltd. 06/10/2016
(See Shanghai Huayi Group Corp. Ltd.)

DOUBLE CREEK MNG CORP (BC)
Recapitalized as Minaterra Minerals Ltd. 8/17/98
Each share Common no par exchanged for (1/3) share Common no par
Minaterra Minerals Ltd. recapitalized as Golden Cariboo Resources Ltd. 8/31/2000

DOUBLE DAY INC (UT)
Recapitalized 2/9/95
Double Day Mining & Energy Corp. recapitalized as Double Day, Inc. 2/9/95
Each share Common $0.005 par exchanged for (0.05) share Common $0.005 par

Name changed to Resource Recovery International Corp. 7/25/2001

DOUBLE DOWN RES LTD (BC)
Recapitalized as Meteor Creek Resources Inc. 01/11/2001
Each share Common no par exchanged for (0.25) share Common no par
(See Meteor Creek Resources Inc.)

DOUBLE EAGLE ACQUISITION CORP (CAYMAN ISLANDS)
Units separated 11/30/2017
Under plan of merger each share Ordinary $0.0001 par automatically became (1) share WillScot Corp. Class A Common $0.0001 par 11/30/2017

DOUBLE EAGLE ENERGY & RES LTD (BC)
Reincorporated under the laws of Canada as Double Eagle Technology Ltd. 05/04/1984
Double Eagle Technology Ltd. name changed to Chessminster Group Ltd. 05/07/1985 which name changed to Pyrok Group PLC 11/08/1989
(See Pyrok Group PLC)

DOUBLE EAGLE ENTMT CORP (BC)
Delisted from Vancouver Stock Exchange 12/23/1996

DOUBLE EAGLE HLDGS LTD (NV)
Name changed to Fuse Science, Inc. 11/03/2011

DOUBLE EAGLE INC (UT)
Name changed to Tesco American, Inc. 6/1/81
(See Tesco American, Inc.)

DOUBLE EAGLE PETE CO (MD)
Reincorporated 02/28/2001
Name changed 03/16/2001
Each share Common 1¢ par exchanged for (0.1) share Common 10¢ par 02/27/1984
Stock Dividend - 100% 08/10/1984
State of incorporation changed from (WY) to (MD) 02/28/2001
Name changed from Double Eagle Petroleum & Mining Co. to Double Eagle Petroleum Co. 03/16/2001
Name changed to Escalera Resources Co. 04/01/2014

DOUBLE EAGLE RES INC (CO)
Each share old Common $0.001 par exchanged for (0.01) share new Common $0.001 par 10/20/92
Name changed to Biomed Science International Corp. 5/14/93

DOUBLE EAGLE TECHNOLOGY LTD (CANADA)
Name changed to Chessminster Group Ltd. 05/07/1985
Chessminster Group Ltd. name changed to Pyrok Group PLC 11/08/1989
(See Pyrok Group PLC)

DOUBLE EXEMPT CAP CONSV FD INC (MN)
Reorganized as Voyageur Intermediate Tax Free Funds, Inc. 01/31/1990
Details not available

DOUBLE EXEMPT FLEX FD INC (MN)
Reorganized as Voyageur Tax Free Funds, Inc. 01/31/1990
Details not available

DOUBLE FIVE FINL CORP (MN)
Name changed to EXA International, Inc. (MN) 07/24/1998
EXA International, Inc. (MN) reincorporated in Florida as Exa Inc. 12/31/2002 which name changed to ATI Nationwide Holding Corp. 06/07/2017

DOUBLE HALO RES INC (NV)
Name changed to Shengrui Resources Co. Ltd. 08/20/2009
Shengrui Resources Co. Ltd. name changed to Richland Resources Corp. 04/18/2011

DOUBLE HELIX FILMS INC (NY)
Each share Common $0.001 par exchanged for (0.05) share Common 1¢ par 02/22/1989
Merged into Communications & Entertainment Corp. 09/06/1990
Each share Common 1¢ par exchanged for (1) share Common 1¢ par
Communications & Entertainment Corp. name changed to Odyssey Pictures Corp. 01/21/1997
(See Odyssey Pictures Corp.)

DOUBLE HULL TANKERS INC (MARSHALL ISLANDS)
Issue Information - 16,000,000 shares COM offered at $12 per share on 10/13/2005
Name changed to DHT Maritime, Inc. 07/03/2008
DHT Maritime, Inc. name changed to DHT Holdings, Inc. 03/01/2010

DOUBLE IMPACT COMMUNICATIONS CORP (CANADA)
Recapitalized as Next Millennium Commercial Corp. 08/20/1998
Each share Common no par exchanged for (0.25) share Common no par
Next Millennium Commercial Corp. name changed to Roadrunner Oil & Gas Inc. 07/17/2008 which name changed to Bowood Energy Inc. 06/21/2010 which recapitalized as LGX Oil + Gas Inc. (Canada) 08/22/2012 which reincorporated in Alberta 06/27/2013

DOUBLE O RES CORP (NV)
Charter revoked for failure to maintain a registered agent 03/06/1978

DOUBLE O TIMBER & MNG CO (NV)
Name changed to Double O Resources Corp. 1/30/70
(See Double O Resources Corp.)

DOUBLE R FAST FOODS INC (DE)
Liquidation completed
Each share Common 1¢ par received initial distribution of $0.14 cash 12/31/83
Each share Common 1¢ par received second distribution of $0.055 cash 12/29/86
Further details not available

DOUBLE RIV OIL & GAS CO (TX)
Each (30) shares Common $0.001 par exchanged for (1) share Common no par 05/20/1994
SEC revoked common stock registration 07/08/2011

DOUBLE STRIKE MINES, LTD. (ON)
Charter cancelled and company dissolved for failure to file returns 4/1/65

DOUBLE-TAKE SOFTWARE INC (DE)
Acquired by Vision Solutions, Inc. 07/23/2010
Each share Common $0.001 par exchanged for $10.55 cash

DOUBLE THREE INC (CO)
Name changed to Coral Petroleum Corp. 04/17/1990

DOUBLE X RANCH INC (CO)
Merged into Pollution Research & Control Corp. 1/3/73
Each share Common 10¢ par exchanged for (0.5) share Common 1¢ par
Pollution Research & Control Corp. name changed to McMartin Inc. 6/23/88
(See McMartin Inc.)

DOUBLECLICK INC (DE)
Common $0.001 par split (2) for (1) by issuance of (1) additional share payable 04/02/1999 to holders of record 03/22/1999
Common $0.0001 par split (2) for (1) by issuance of (1) additional share payable 01/10/2000 to holders of record 12/31/1999
Merged into Click Holding Corp. 07/13/2005
Each share Common $0.001 par exchanged for $8.50 cash

DOUBLEDAY & CO INC (NY)
Merged into Bertelsmann AG 12/16/1986
Each share Class A Preferred $100 par exchanged for $3,427.20 cash
Each share Common $1 par exchanged for $3,427.20 cash
Each share Class A Preferred $100 par received initial additional distribution of $40.40 cash 07/02/1987
Each share Common $1 par received initial additional distribution of $40.40 cash 07/02/1987
Each share Class A Preferred $100 par received second additional distribution of $10 cash 08/01/1989
Each share Common $1 par received second additional distribution of $10 cash 08/01/1989
Each share Class A Preferred $100 par received third and final additional distribution of $43.70 cash 10/25/1991
Each share Common $1 par received third and final additional distribution of $43.70 cash 10/25/1991

DOUBLEDAY DORAN & CO. INC.
Name changed to Doubleday & Co. in 1946
(See Doubleday & Co., Inc.)

DOUBLEDAY PAGE CO.
Merged into Doubleday Doran & Co., Inc. 00/00/1928
Details not available

DOUBLEJACK EXPLORATION, INC. (UT)
Involuntarily dissolved for failure to file annual reports 10/1/88

DOUBLESTAR RES LTD (BC)
Reincorporated 10/10/2002
Place of incorporation changed from (YT) to (BC) 10/10/2002
Merged into Selkirk Metals Corp. 07/23/2007
Each share Class A Common no par exchanged for (0.5) share Common no par
(See Selkirk Metals Corp.)

DOUBLETREE CORP (DE)
Issue Information - 3,000,000 shares COM offered at $13 per share on 07/01/1994
Secondary Offering - 5,600,000 shares Common offered at $39.25 per share on 11/05/1996
Merged into Promus Hotel Corp. (New) 12/19/1997
Each share Common 1¢ par exchanged for (1) share Common 1¢ par
Promus Hotel Corp. (New) merged into Hilton Hotels Corp. 11/30/1999
(See Hilton Hotels Corp.)

DOUCETTE DEVS CORP (BC)
Name changed to Traders International Franchise Systems Inc. 08/30/1995
Traders International Franchise Systems Inc. recapitalized as NewQuest Ventures Corp. 05/22/1998 which recapitalized as Aster Ventures Corp. 05/26/1999 which recapitalized as Knight Petroleum Corp. 03/22/2001 which name changed to Knight Resources Ltd. 03/07/2003 which recapitalized as Knight Metals Ltd. 05/25/2011 which name changed to Africa Hydrocarbons Inc. (BC) 02/02/2012 which reincorporated in Alberta 04/25/2013 which name changed to Blockchaink2 Corp. 05/30/2018

DOUGALL GAMING CORP (DE)
Name changed to G-VII Energy Corp. 07/03/1997
G-VII Energy Corp. name changed to Nathaniel Energy Corp. (Old) 07/00/1998 which reorganized as Nathaniel Energy Corp. (New) 12/00/1998 which name changed to Vista International Technologies, Inc. 12/20/2007

DOUGHBOY INDS INC (WI)
Name changed to Domain Industries, Inc. 06/18/1970
(See Domain Industries, Inc.)

DOUGHERTY BROS CO (NJ)
Common 25¢ par split (5) for (4) by issuance of (0.25) additional share 08/19/1977
Stock Dividends - 10% 01/14/1965; 20% 11/01/1976; 10% 11/10/1978; 10% 11/16/1979; 10% 11/14/1980; 10% 11/16/1981; 10% 11/15/1982
Merged into Owens-Illinois, Inc. 07/02/1984
Each share Common 25¢ par exchanged for (0.51849) share Common $3.125 par
(See Owens-Illinois, Inc.)

DOUGHTIE S FOODS INC (VA)
Common $1 par split (3) for (2) by issuance of (0.5) additional share payable 01/12/1998 to holders of record 12/12/1997
Stock Dividends - 20% 06/22/1976; 10% 06/30/1978; 10% 06/20/1980; 10% 07/01/1982; 10% 07/05/1983; 10% 07/03/1984; 20% 04/04/1987
Acquired by Sysco Corp. 08/30/1999
Each share Common $1 par exchanged for (0.54839) share Common $1 par
Note: Each share Common $1 par received an additional distribution of (0.13254) share Common $1 par and approximately $1.975 cash from escrow 05/10/2005

DOUGLAS & LOMASON CO (MI)
Common $10 par split (2) for (1) by issuance of (1) additional share 12/17/1936
Each share Common $10 par exchanged for (5) shares Common $2 par 00/00/1937
Common $2 par split (2) for (1) by issuance of (1) additional share 02/16/1946
Common $2 par split (2) for (1) by issuance of (1) additional share 10/11/1968
Common $2 par split (2) for (1) by issuance of (1) additional share 08/31/1983
Common $2 par split (3) for (2) by issuance of (0.5) additional share 04/02/1992
Stock Dividends - 10% 07/10/1959; 10% 08/10/1962; 10% 01/28/1966
Merged into Magna Acquisition Corp. 10/14/1996
Each share Common $2 par exchanged for $31 cash

DOUGLAS AIRCRAFT INC (DE)
Capital Stock no par split (2) for (1) by issuance of (1) additional share 00/00/1954
Capital Stock no par split (3) for (2) by issuance of (0.5) additional share 00/00/1955
Stock Dividend - 100% 05/29/1951
Merged into McDonnell Douglas Corp. 04/28/1967
Each share Capital Stock no par exchanged for (1.75) shares Common $1.25 par
McDonnell Douglas Corp. merged into Boeing Co. 08/01/1997

DOUGLAS (JOHN) CO.
Assets acquired by Briggs Manufacturing Co. and liquidated 00/00/1944
Details not available

DOUGLAS COMPUTER INTL (UT)
Proclaimed dissolved for failure to pay taxes 04/01/1994

DOUGLAS CORP. (CO)
Declared defunct and inoperative for failure to pay franchise taxes 10/13/1962

DOUGLAS COUNTY BANK (OMAHA, NE)
Name changed to Douglas County Bank & Trust Co. (Omaha, NE) 01/10/1974

DOUGLAS EQUITY FD LTD (CANADA)
Involuntarily dissolved for failure to file annual reports 01/14/1980

DOUGLAS HLDG AG (GERMANY)
ADR agreement terminated 03/14/2016
No ADR's remain outstanding

DOUGLAS INDS INC (CO)
Each share Common 10¢ par exchanged for (0.33333333) share Common 30¢ par 09/14/1978
Completely liquidated 01/14/1981
Each share Common 30¢ par exchanged for first and final distribution of $5.11 cash

DOUGLAS LAKE MINERALS INC (NV)
Name changed to Handeni Gold Inc. 02/14/2012

DOUGLAS LEASEHOLDS LTD (ON)
Merged into Chalet Oil Ltd. 11/01/1978
Each share Common no par exchanged for $5.34 cash

DOUGLAS MICROWAVE INC (NY)
Completely liquidated 01/15/1968
Each share Common 10¢ par exchanged for first and final distribution of (0.25) share Struthers Wells Corp. Common $1 par
(See Struthers Wells Corp.)

DOUGLAS MNG CO (ID)
Name changed to Douglas Mining Co. and Capital Stock $1 par changed to 10¢ par 11/28/51

DOUGLAS OIL CO. OF CALIFORNIA (CA)
Merged into Continental Oil Co. (DE) 05/01/1961
Each share Common $1 par exchanged for (0.2) share Capital Stock $5 par
Continental Oil Co. (DE) name changed to Conoco Inc. 07/02/1979 which was acquired by Du Pont (E.I.) De Nemours & Co. 09/30/1981

DOUGLAS-PECTIN CORP.
Name changed to Certo Corp. 00/00/1927
Certo Corp. was acquired by Postum Co., Inc. 04/30/1929 which name changed to General Foods Corp. 07/24/1929
(See General Foods Corp.)

DOUGLAS PHARMACAL INDS INC (CO)
Name changed to Douglas Industries, Inc. 08/18/1976
(See Douglas Industries, Inc.)

DOUGLAS RESOURCES CORP. (DE)
Name changed to Cleary Petroleum Corp. 07/02/1968
Cleary Petroleum Corp. merged into Grace (W.R.) & Co. (CT) 11/01/1973 which reincorporated in New York 05/19/1988
(See Grace (W.R.) & Co.)

DOUGLASS INDS INC (FL)
Proclaimed dissolved for failure to file reports and pay fees 05/23/1973

DOUGOILCO INC. (SD)
Charter cancelled for failure to file reports 07/01/1970

DOV PHARMACEUTICAL INC (DE)
Each share Common $0.0001 par received distribution of (1.1) Common Stock Purchase Warrants expiring 12/31/2009 payable 05/24/2007 to holders of record 05/10/2007
Merged into Euthymics Bioscience, Inc. 07/20/2010
Each share Ser. D Preferred $1 par exchanged for $2.4670802 cash
Note: Each share Ser. D Preferred $1 par received an additional distribution of $0.4353671 cash from escrow 11/19/2010
Each share Common $0.0001 par exchanged for $0.0129 cash
Note: Each share Common $0.0001 par received an additional distribution of $0.0022791 cash from escrow 11/19/2010

DOVALS INC. (DE)
Name changed to Sanitary Paper Mills, Inc. 07/30/1928
Sanitary Paper Mills, Inc. merged into Swanee Paper Corp. 02/20/1964 which merged into Potlatch Forests, Inc. (DE) 12/23/1968 which name changed to Potlatch Corp. (Old) 04/27/1973 which reorganized as Potlatch Corp. (New) 02/03/2006 which name changed to PotlatchDeltic Corp. 02/23/2018

DOVARRI INC (NV)
Voluntarily dissolved 10/31/2012
No stockholders' equity

DOVATRON INTL INC (DE)
Name changed to DII Group Inc. 02/01/1996
DII Group Inc. merged into Flextronics International Ltd. 04/03/2000 which name changed to Flex Ltd. 09/28/2016

DOVE ENTMT INC (CA)
Name changed 12/24/1996
Name changed from Dove Audio, Inc. to Dove Entertainment Inc. 12/24/1996
Name changed to Newstar Media, Inc. 05/14/1998
(See Newstar Media, Inc.)

DOVE LAKE MINES INC. (ON)
Merged into Staple Mining Co. Ltd. 08/11/1972
Each share Capital Stock no par exchanged for (0.2) share Capital Stock no par
Staple Mining Co. Ltd. merged into Gerrard Realty Inc. 01/28/1976

DOVECORP ENTERPRISES INC (ON)
Assets sold for the benefit of creditors 09/10/2007
No stockholders' equity

DOVER CONSTRUCTION CO. (OH)
Adjudicated bankrupt 11/07/1967
No stockholders' equity

DOVER DOWNS ENTMT INC (DE)
Common 10¢ par split (2) for (1) by issuance of (1) additional share payable 09/15/1998 to holders of record 08/10/1998 Ex date - 09/16/1998
Each share Common 10¢ par received distribution of (0.7) share Dover Downs Gaming & Entertainment, Inc. Common 10¢ par payable 03/28/2002 to holders of record 03/18/2002 Ex date - 04/01/2002
Each share Class A Common 10¢ par received distribution of (0.7) share Dover Downs Gaming & Entertainment, Inc. Class A Common 10¢ par payable 03/28/2002 to holders of record 03/18/2002 Ex date - 04/01/2002
Name changed to Dover Motorsports, Inc. 03/31/2002

DOVER ENTERPRISES LTD (AB)
Delisted from Alberta Stock Exchange 11/02/1992

DOVER GEN CORP (DE)
Recapitalized as IR Associates, Inc. 09/10/1968
Each share Common 10¢ par exchanged for (0.33333333) share Common 10¢ par
IR Associates, Inc. recapitalized as Epcom, Inc. 06/25/1980
(See Epcom, Inc.)

DOVER GLEN INC (DE)
Name changed to PetroAlgae Inc. 01/16/2009
PetroAlgae Inc. name changed to Parabel Inc. 04/03/2012
(See Parabel Inc.)

DOVER INDS LTD (CANADA)
Common no par split (2) for (1) by issuance of (1) additional share 07/03/1973
Common no par split (3) for (1) by issuance of (2) additional shares 05/27/1977
Common no par split (2) for (1) by issuance of (1) additional share 06/08/1983
Common no par split (2) for (1) by issuance of (1) additional share 08/20/1986
6% Preferred $10 par called for redemption at $10 on 06/30/2000
Common no par split (2) for (1) by issuance of (1) additional share payable 06/15/2006 to holders of record 06/08/2006 Ex date - 06/06/2006
Merged into Parrish & Heimbecker, Ltd. 02/06/2009
Each share Common no par exchanged for $19.25 cash

DOVER INVT CORP (DE)
Merged into Dover Acquisition Corp. 02/07/2005
Each share Class A Common 1¢ par exchanged for $31.30 cash
Each share Class B Common 1¢ par exchanged for $31.30 cash

DOVER LEASING FUND, 1-B (FL)
Voluntarily dissolved 12/16/1992
Details not available

DOVER PETE CORP (NV)
SEC revoked common stock registration 05/19/2008

DOVER REGL FINL SHS (MA)
Completely liquidated 12/27/1994
Each Share of Bene. Int. no par exchanged for first and final distribution of $6.69 cash

DOVER RESOURCES, INC. (UT)
Name changed to First Houston Capital Resources Fund, Inc. (UT) 10/29/1985
First Houston Capital Resources Fund, Inc. (UT) reincorporated in Nevada 05/15/1986
(See First Houston Capital Resources Fund, Inc. (NV))

DOVER SADDLERY INC (DE)
Acquired by Dover Saddlery Holdings, Inc. 07/01/2015
Each share Common $0.0001 par exchanged for $8.50 cash

DOVER TR CO (DOVER, NJ)
Acquired by United Jersey Banks 09/29/1972
Each share Capital Stock $25 par exchanged for (1.05) shares Common $5 par
United Jersey Banks name changed to UJB Financial Corp. 06/30/1989 which name changed to Summit Bancorp 03/01/1996 which merged into FleetBoston Financial Corp. 03/01/2001 which merged into Bank of America Corp. 04/01/2004

DOVERTON OILS LTD (CANADA)
Charter dissolved 09/10/1997

DOW BREWERY LTD. (CANADA)
Merged into Carling O'Keefe Ltd. 06/28/1974
Details not available

DOW CHEM CO (DE)
Reincorporated 00/00/1947
5% Preferred called for redemption 02/15/1944
Under plan of merger state of incorporation changed from (MI) to (DE), each share $4 Preferred Ser. A no par exchanged for (1) share $4 Preferred Ser. A no par and each share Common no par exchanged for (4) shares Common $15 par 00/00/1947
Each share Common $15 par exchanged for (3) shares Common $5 par 00/00/1952
$3.25 2nd Preferred no par called for redemption 07/01/1952
$4 Preferred Ser. A no par called for redemption 10/15/1954
Common $5 par split (3) for (2) by issuance of (0.5) additional share 08/05/1971
Common $5 par split (2) for (1) by issuance of (1) additional share 05/09/1973
Common $5 par changed to $2.50 par and (1) additional share issued 06/07/1976
Common $2.50 par split (3) for (2) by issuance of (0.5) additional share 11/20/1989
Each Contingent Value Right received $11.187 cash 09/30/1991
Common $2.50 par split (3) for (1) by issuance of (2) additional shares payable 06/16/2000 to holders of record 05/23/2000 Ex date - 06/19/2000
Merged into DowDuPont Inc. 09/01/2017
Each share Common $2.50 par exchanged for (1) share Common 1¢ par

DOW DRUG CO. (OH)
Each share Common $100 par exchanged for (10) shares Common no par 00/00/1927
Merged into Chamberlin Co. of America 10/01/1959
Each share 7% Preferred $100 par exchanged for (4.64) shares 5% Preferred $25 par
Each share Common no par exchanged for (2) shares Common $2.50 par
(See Chamberlin Co. of America (DE))

DOW JONES & CO INC (DE)
Common $5 par changed to $1 par and (9) additional shares issued 05/27/1963
Common $1 par split (3) for (1) by issuance of (2) additional shares 03/04/1964
Common $1 par split (3) for (2) by issuance of (0.5) additional share 09/01/1966
Common $1 par split (2) for (1) by issuance of (1) additional share 12/12/1969
Common $1 par split (2) for (1) by issuance of (1) additional share 04/28/1981
Common $1 par split (2) for (1) by issuance of (1) additional share 02/07/1983
Stock Dividend in Conv. Class B Common to holders of Common - 50% 06/01/1984; 50% 06/30/1986
Merged into News Corp. 12/13/2007
Each share Common $1 par exchanged for $60 cash
Each share Conv. Class B $1 par exchanged for $60 cash

DOW THEORY FUND
Trust terminated 00/00/1949
Details not available

DOW THEORY INVT FD INC (MA)
Reincorporated 11/09/1964
State of incorporation changed from (DE) to (MA) 11/09/1964
Name changed to Salem Fund, Inc. 11/13/1969
Salem Fund, Inc. merged into Fidelity Magellan Fund, Inc. 06/22/1981

DOW 30 PREM & DIVID INCOME FD INC (MD)
Under plan of merger each share Common $0.001 par automaticaly became (1) Nuveen Dow 30SM Dynamic Overwrite Fund Common Share of Bene. Int. 1¢ par 12/22/2014

DOW 30SM ENHANCED PREM & INCOME FD INC (MD)
Under plan of merger each share Common $0.001 par automaticaly became (0.86404614) Nuveen Dow 30SM Dynamic Overwrite Fund Common Share of Bene. Int. 1¢ par 12/22/2014

DOWAGIAC-KAL CO. (MI)
Dissolved 05/14/1962
Details not available

DOWDLE OIL CORP (DE)
Name changed to Western Natural Gas Co. (Ctfs. dated after 12/13/1979) 12/14/1979
Western Natural Gas Co. (Ctfs. dated after 12/13/1979) recapitalized as North American Gaming & Entertainment Corp. (DE) 10/17/1994 which reorganized in Nevada as China Changjiang Mining & New Energy Co., Ltd. 08/02/2010

DOWNE COMMUNICATIONS INC (DE)
Common $1 par split (3) for (1) by issuance of (2) additional shares 05/13/1969
Merged into Charter Co. 03/31/1978
Each share Common $1 par exchanged for $4.50 cash

DOWEN ZIER KNITS INC (NY)
Merged into EHG International, Inc. 04/25/1986
Each share Common 1¢ par exchanged for (1) share Common 1¢ par
EHG International, Inc. name changed to Uniforms for America Inc. 12/18/1995 which recapitalized as HomeFoodClub.com Inc. (NV) 07/12/1999 which reincorporated in Delaware as iKarma Inc. 02/02/2006 which recapitalized as Medtino, Inc. 10/12/2010 which name changed to IntelaKare Marketing, Inc. 03/01/2011

DOWNER AIRCRAFT CO. (MN)
Name changed to Bellanca Aircraft Corp. (MN) 07/25/1966
(See Bellanca Aircraft Corp. (MN).)

DOWNEY BANCORP (CA)
Stock Dividend - 9% payable 05/15/1998 to holders of record 05/01/1998
Merged into California Financial Bancorp 11/25/1998
Each share Common no par exchanged for $22.84 cash

DOWNEY DESIGNS INTL INC (IN)
Merged into DDI Acquisition Inc. 12/28/1988
Each share Common 1¢ par exchanged for $6 cash

DOWNEY FINL CAP TR I (DE)
10% Guaranteed Capital Securities called for redemption at $25 on 07/23/2004

DOWNEY FINL CORP (DE)
Common no par split (3) for (2) by issuance of (0.5) additional share payable 12/12/1996 to holders of record 11/15/1996 Ex date - 12/13/1996
Stock Dividends - 5% payable 05/22/1997 to holders of record 05/08/1997; 5% payable 05/22/1998 to holders of record 05/07/1998
Filed a petition under Chapter 7 Federal Bankruptcy Code 11/25/2008
Stockholders' equity unlikely

DOWNEY INDS INC (NV)
Name changed to Zevex International, Inc. (NV) 08/11/1988
Zevex International, Inc. (NV) reincorporated in Delaware 11/21/1997
(See Zevex International, Inc.)

DOWNEY SVGS & LN ASSN (CA)
Guarantee Stock 25¢ par changed to $0.16666666 par and (0.5) additional share issued 06/03/1976
Guarantee Stock $0.16666666 par changed to no par and (0.5) additional share issued 02/16/1978
Guarantee Stock no par split (3) for (2) by issuance of (0.5) additional share 06/29/1979
Guarantee Stock no par reclassified as Common no par 06/25/1984
Common no par split (3) for (2) by issuance of (0.5) additional share 01/03/1986
Common no par split (3) for (2) by issuance of (0.5) additional share 05/30/1986
Common no par split (3) for (2) by issuance of (0.5) additional share 10/27/1989
Under plan of reorganization each share Common no par automatically became (1) share Downey Financial Corp. (DE) Common 1¢ par 01/23/1995
(See Downey Financial Corp. (DE))

DOWNING (C.M.) & CO., INC. (DE)
Dissolved 07/12/1946
Details not available

DOWNINGTOWN NATL BK (DOWNINGTOWN, PA)
Under plan of reorganization each share Common $10 par automatically became (1) share DNB Financial Corp. Common $10 par 07/01/1983

DOWNSTREAM INC (UT)
Name changed to Q-Seven Systems Inc. 06/10/1999
(See Q-Seven Systems Inc.)

DOWNTOWN AMER FDG CORP (NV)
Name changed to Savior Energy Corp. 12/22/2006

DOWNTOWN BK (HOUSTON, TX)
Name changed to Franklin Bank (Houston, TX) 04/08/1970
(See Franklin Bank (Houston, TX))

DOWNTOWN CREDIT SERVICE LTD. (BC)
Name changed to Denman Credit Factors Ltd. 02/21/1964
(See Denman Credit Factors Ltd.)

DOWNTOWN FD INC (DE)
Name changed to Neuwirth Century Fund Inc. 04/20/1970
Neuwirth Century Fund Inc. merged into Neuwirth Fund, Inc. 03/31/1975 which reorganized as Winthrop Focus Funds 07/10/1992 which name changed to DLJ Winthrop Focus Funds 01/29/1999 which name changed to DLJ Focus Funds 08/01/2000 which reorganized as Credit Suisse Warburg Pincus Capital Funds 01/18/2001 which name changed to Credit Suisse Capital Funds 12/12/2001

DOWNTOWN HOTEL-MOTEL, INC. (MS)
Completely liquidated 12/10/1980
Each share Common $50 par exchanged for first and final distribution of $65 cash

DOWNTOWN INDS LTD (CANADA)
Reincorporated under the laws of British Columbia as Inform Resources Corp. 11/04/2010

DOWNTOWN PPTYS INC (MI)
Charter declared inoperative and void for failure to file reports 06/25/1987

DOWNTOWN REDEV CORP (MO)
Voting Trust Agreement terminated 12/01/1964
Each VTC for Capital Stock $100 par exchanged for (1) share Capital Stock $100 par
Merged into Tower Properties Co. 09/24/1999
Each share Common $100 par exchanged for $1,360 cash

DOWNTOWNER CORP (TN)
Common $5 par changed to $1 par 02/16/1965
Name changed to Perkins Foods, Inc. 11/28/1973
(See Perkins Foods, Inc.)

DOWTY GROUP PLC (ENGLAND)
ADR's for Ordinary Reg. split (2) for (1) by issuance of (1) additional ADR 11/27/1979
Stock Dividend - 50% 11/02/1981
Acquired by TI Group PLC 09/03/1992
Each ADR for Ordinary Reg. exchanged for $2.945 cash

DOWZER ELEC INC (IL)
Name changed to DZR Liquidation Corp. 02/05/1971
(See DZR Liquidation Corp.)

DOXSEE FOOD CORP (DE)
Acquired by Borden, Inc. 08/28/1986
Each share Common 10¢ par exchanged for $10.75 cash

DOYLE DANE BERNBACH GROUP INC (NY)
Under plan of merger name changed to Omnicom Group Inc. 08/29/1986

DOYLE DANE BERNBACH INC (NY)
Class A $1 par and Class B (Ser. 2, 3 & 4) $1 par changed to 50¢ par respectively and (1) additional share issued 06/23/1966
Class B-2 50¢ par reclassified as Class A 50¢ par 11/01/1966
Class B-3 50¢ par reclassified as Class A 50¢ par 11/01/1967
Class B-4 50¢ par reclassified as Class A 50¢ par 11/01/1968
Class A 50¢ par reclassified as Common 50¢ par 02/27/1969
Name changed to Doyle Dane Bernbach International Inc. 05/16/1978
Doyle Dane Bernbach International Inc. name changed to Doyle Dane Bernbach Group Inc. 05/21/1985 which name changed to Omnicom Group Inc. 08/29/1986

DOYLE DANE BERNBACH INTERNATIONAL INC. (NY)
Stock Dividends - 50% 10/13/1978; 100% 01/15/1981
Name changed to Doyle Dane Bernbach Group Inc. 05/21/1985
Doyle Dane Bernback Group Inc. name changed to Omnicom Group Inc. 08/29/1986

DOYLE MACHINE & TOOL CORP.
Name changed to Doyle Manufacturing Corp. 00/00/1944
(See Doyle Manufacturing Corp.)

DOYLE MANUFACTURING CORP. (NY)
Bankrupt 00/00/1948
No stockholders' equity

DOYLESTOWN NATL BK & TR CO (DOYLESTOWN, PA)
Merged into Continental Bank (Norristown, PA) 04/20/1970
Each share Capital Stock $5 par exchanged for (3) shares Capital Stock $5 par
Continental Bank (Norristown, PA) reorganized as Continental Bancorp, Inc. 05/01/1982 which merged into Midlantic Corp. 01/30/1987 which merged into PNC Bank Corp. 12/31/1995 which name changed to PNC Financial Services Group, Inc. 03/15/2000

DOYLESTOWN TR CO (DOYLESTOWN, PA)
Merged into Industrial Valley Bank & Trust Co. (Jenkintown, PA) 7/1/69
Each share Capital Stock $20 par exchanged for (6) shares Common $5 par
Industrial Valley Bank & Trust Co. (Jenkintown, PA) reorganized as IVB Financial Corp. 1/1/84
(See IVB Financial Corp.)

DP CHARTERS INC (NV)
Each share old Common $0.001 par exchanged for (5) shares new Common $0.001 par 12/01/2000
Each share new Common $0.001 par exchanged again for (2) shares new Common $0.001 par 03/19/2001
Each share new Common $0.001 par exchanged again for (0.5) share new Common $0.001 par 08/13/2001
Note: Holders of (100) or fewer pre-split shares received share for share
Holders of between (101) and (200) shares received (100) shares only
Each share new Common $0.001 par exchanged again for (0.01) share new Common $0.001 par 10/26/2001
Name changed to Nomadic Collaboration International, Inc. 04/08/2002
Nomadic Collaboration International, Inc. name changed to LiquidGolf Holding Corp. (NV) 06/09/2003 which reincorporated in Delaware 09/29/2003 which name changed to Horizon Holding Corp. 09/02/2004 which name changed to Inverted Paradigms Corp. 05/12/2006 which recapitalized as Transfer Technology International Corp. 12/07/2007 which name changed to Enviro-Serv, Inc. 04/23/2013

DP DEV CO (NV)
Name changed to Berten USA, Inc. 12/01/1988
(See Berten USA, Inc.)

DPA INC (TX)
Reincorporated under the laws of Delaware as Pioneer Texas Corp. 03/30/1973
(See Pioneer Texas Corp.)

DPAC TECHNOLOGIES CORP (CA)
Completely liquidated 10/31/2011
Each share Common no par exchanged for first and final distribution of $0.05 cash

DPC BIOSCIENCES CORP (ON)
Name changed to iGaming Corp. 09/05/2006
iGaming Corp. name changed to Big Stick Media Corp. 06/29/2007
(See Big Stick Media Corp.)

DPF INC (DE)
Name changed to Interstate Bakeries Corp. 11/30/1981
Interstate Bakeries Corp. name changed to Interstate Brands Corp. 06/02/1990
(See Interstate Brands Corp.)

DPF INDIA OPPORTUNITIES FD (ON)
Name changed to Dynamic Emerging Markets Fund and Trust Units reclassified as Ser. C Units 06/20/2014

DPI TECHNOLOGIES INC (CANADA)
Name changed to Dynex Power Inc. 08/16/1999

DPL INC (OH)
Common $7 par changed to 1¢ par

and (0.5) additional share issued 05/04/1990
Common 1¢ par split (3) for (2) by issuance of (0.5) additional share payable 09/23/1992
Common 1¢ par split (3) for (2) by issuance of (0.5) additional share payable 01/12/1998 to holders of record 12/16/1997 Ex date - 01/13/1998
Acquired by AES Corp. 11/28/2011
Each share Common 1¢ par exchanged for $30 cash

DPOLLUTION INTL INC (NV)
Recapitalized as Ecrid, Inc. 10/16/2017
Each share Common $0.0001 par exchanged for (0.01428571) share Common $0.0001 par

DPVC INC (CANADA)
Name changed to TitanStar Properties Inc. 10/19/2010

DPZ LIQUIDATING CORP. (DE)
In process of liquidation
Each share Common $0.001 par exchanged for initial distribution of $1.18 cash 6/3/91
Each share Common $0.001 par received second distribution of $0.053 cash 10/7/91
Note: Details on subsequent distribution(s), if any, are not available

DQE (PA)
Name changed 06/04/1990
Name changed from DQE, Inc. to DQE 06/04/1990
Common no par split (3) for (2) by issuance of (0.5) additional share 05/24/1995
Name changed to Duquesne Light Holdings, Inc. 09/30/2003
(See Duquesne Light Holdings, Inc.)

DR EUROPEAN EQUITY FD INC (MD)
Dissolved 04/27/1992
Details not available

DRA CRT ACQUISITION CORP (DE)
8.5% Preferred Ser. A 1¢ par called for redemption at $25 plus $0.10625 accrued dividends on 01/02/2015

DRACKETT CO. (OH)
Each share old Common $1 par exchanged for (2) shares new Common $1 par 4/15/46
4% Preferred Ser. A $25 par called for redemption 2/15/60
New Common $1 par changed to no par and (2) additional shares issued 3/1/62
Common no par split (3) for (2) by issuance of (0.5) additional share 6/12/64
Acquired by Bristol-Myers Co. 8/2/65
Each share Common no par exchanged for (0.46) share Common $1 par
Bristol-Myers Co. name changed to Bristol-Myers Squibb Co. 10/4/89

DRACO GOLD MINES INC (BC)
Merged into Stanford Energy Corp. 06/29/1990
Each share Common no par exchanged for (1) share Common no par
Stanford Energy Corp. recapitalized as Stanford Oil & Gas Ltd. 07/10/1998 which merged into Hilton Petroleum Ltd. (BC) 03/31/1999 which reincorporated in Yukon 04/01/1999 which name changed to Hilton Resources Ltd. (YT) 03/02/2004 which reincorporated in British Columbia 11/23/2004 which recapitalized as Rochester Resources Ltd. 08/26/2005

DRACO HLDG CORP (NV)
Reorganized 09/13/1999
Reorganized from Draco Corp. (UT) to Draco Holding Corp. (NV) 09/13/1999

Each share Common $0.001 par exchanged for (0.1) share old Common $0.001 par
Each share old Common $0.001 par exchanged for (0.04) share new Common $0.001 par
Name changed to China North East Petroleum Holdings Ltd. 07/26/2004
(See China North East Petroleum Holdings Ltd.)

DRACO MINES LTD. (ON)
Liquidation completed in 1949

DRAFTDAY FANTASY SPORTS INC (DE)
Name changed to Function(x) Inc. 06/13/2016

DRAFTTEAM DAILY FANTASY SPORTS CORP (BC)
Name changed to Fantasy Aces Daily Fantasy Sports Corp. 10/06/2015

DRAFTTEAM FANTASY SPORTS INC (BC)
Merged into DraftTeam Daily Fantasy Sports Corp. 03/13/2015
Each share Common no par exchanged for (0.4667) share Common no par
Note: Unexchanged certificates will be cancelled and become without value 03/13/2021
DraftTeam Daily Fantasy Sports Corp. name changed to Fantasy Aces Daily Fantasy Fantasy Sports Corp. 10/06/2015

DRAGE INDS INC (DE)
Stock Dividend - 100% 12/15/1972
Adjudicated bankrupt 04/05/1979
No stockholders' equity

DRAGON ACQUISITION CORP (CAYMAN ISLANDS)
Name changed to China Oumei Real Estate Inc. 08/06/2010

DRAGON BEVERAGE INC (NV)
Each share old Common $0.001 par exchanged for (12.5) shares new Common $0.001 par 03/28/2011
Name changed to E-Waste Systems, Inc. 05/17/2011

DRAGON CAP CORP (ON)
Name changed to Arehada Mining Ltd. 07/12/2007

DRAGON CEMENT CO., INC. (ME)
Common $10 par split (3) for (1) by issuance of (2) additional shares 09/24/1954
Acquired by American-Marietta Co. 10/01/1956
Each share Common $10 par exchanged (1.05) shares Common $2 par
American-Marietta Co. merged into Martin Marietta Corp. (Old) 10/10/1961 which merged into Martin Marietta Corp. (New) 04/02/1993 which merged into Lockheed Martin Corp. 03/15/1995

DRAGON CONS MNG CO (UT)
Name changed to Dragon Mining Corp. 1/3/85
Dragon Mining Corp. recapitalized as Dragon Diamond Corp. 8/1/98

DRAGON ENERGY GROUP LTD (NV)
Each share old Common $0.001 par exchanged for (0.5) share new Common $0.001 par 5/1/2003
Recapitalized as Seven Angels Ventures, Inc. 3/5/2004
Each share new Common $0.001 par exchanged for (1/3) share Common $0.001 par
Seven Angels Ventures, Inc. name changed to Twister Networks, Inc. 3/25/2004 which recapitalized as Reynaldos Mexican Food Co., Inc. 3/4/2005

DRAGON ENVIRONMENTAL CORP (FL)
Each share old Common $0.001 par

exchanged for (0.001) share new Common $0.001 par 07/23/2002
Name changed to Symposium Productions Corp. 09/27/2006
Symposium Productions Corp. name changed to Grid Cloud Solutions, Inc. 12/14/2010 which recapitalized as Great Rock Development Corp. 02/29/2012 which recapitalized as Comepay, Inc. 03/01/2018

DRAGON GEM CORP (BC)
Recapitalized as Consolidated Alliance Resource Corp. 4/15/98
Each share Common no par exchanged for (1/3) share Common no par
Consolidated Alliance Resource Corp. name changed to Dyna Haul Corp. 7/9/99
(See Dyna Haul Corp.)

DRAGON GOLD RES INC (NV)
Common $0.001 par split (7) for (1) by issuance of (6) additional shares payable 06/14/2004 to holders of record 06/14/2004
Recapitalized as Edgeline Holdings, Inc. 07/23/2007
Each share Common $0.001 par exchanged for (0.0125) share Common 8¢ par
Edgeline Holdings, Inc. name changed to Oncolin Therapeutics, Inc. 03/24/2008 which recapitalized as Bering Exploration, Inc. 10/14/2010 which name changed to Breitling Energy Corp. 01/22/2014

DRAGON GROUP INTERNATIONAL LTD (SINGAPORE)
ADR agreement terminated 10/05/2018
No ADR's remain outstanding

DRAGON HLDGS AG (GERMANY)
ADR agreement terminated 01/07/2016
Each Sponsored ADR for Ordinary exchanged for (0.2) share Ordinary
Note: Unexchanged ADR's will be sold and the proceeds, if any, held for claim after 05/09/2016

DRAGON INTL GROUP CORP (NV)
SEC revoked common stock registration 03/05/2013

DRAGON MNG CORP (UT)
Recapitalized as Dragon Diamond Corp. 8/1/98
Each share Common $1 par exchanged for (0.1) share Common $1 par

DRAGON OIL PLC (IRELAND)
ADR agreement terminated 01/15/2016
Each ADR for Ordinary issued by Bank of New York exchanged for $23.337483 cash
Note: ADR's issued by Citibank exchanged for $23.907557 cash

DRAGON OILS & GAS LTD. (ON)
Merged into Consolidated Dragon Oils Ltd. 12/30/1954
Each share Capital Stock $1 par exchanged for (0.33333333) shares Capital Stock $1 par
Consolidated Dragon Oils Ltd. acquired by Plains Petroleums Ltd. 03/27/1965
(See Plains Petroleums Ltd.)

DRAGON PHARMACEUTICAL INC (FL)
Merged into Chief Respect Ltd. 07/22/2010
Each share Common $0.001 par exchanged for $0.82 cash

DRAGON POLYMERS INC (NV)
Name changed to Hitec Corp. 11/04/2015
Hitec Corp. recapitalized as Lead Innovation Corp. 03/27/2018

DRAGON-TEX GROUP LTD (AB)
Reorganized under the laws of British

Columbia as Med BioGene Inc. 4/28/2006
Each share Common no par exchanged for (0.5) share Common no par

DRAGON VENTURE (NV)
Common $0.001 par split (10) for (1) by issuance of (9) additional shares payable 4/25/2005 to holders of record 4/18/2005
Name changed to Dragon Capital Group Corp. 12/13/2005

DRAGONFLY DISTRS INC (BC)
Recapitalized as Nu Lite Industries Ltd. 2/24/92
Each share Common no par exchanged for (1/7) share Common no par
Nu Lite Industries Ltd. name changed to Netseers Internet International Corp. 5/31/2000 which recapitalized as 1st Anyox Resources Ltd. 12/2/2003 which name changed to Victory Resources Corp. 2/28/2005

DRAGONS LAIR HLDGS INC (FL)
Name changed to Four Star Holdings, Inc. 04/08/2010
(See Four Star Holdings, Inc.)

DRAGOON RES LTD (BC)
Recapitalized as Seabridge Resources Inc. 05/20/1998
Each share Common no par exchanged for (0.1) share Common no par
Seabridge Resources Inc. name changed to Seabridge Gold Inc. (BC) 06/20/2002 which reincorporated in Canada 10/21/2002

DRAGOR SHIPPING CORP. (DE)
Merged into American Export Industries, Inc. 10/17/1967
Each share $1.25 Preferred Ser. A $25 par exchanged for (1) share $6 Preferred Ser. B no par
Each share Common $1 par exchanged for (0.565) share Common 40¢ par
American Export Industries, Inc. name changed to Aeicor, Inc. 03/31/1978 which name changed to Doskocil Companies Inc. 09/30/1983 which name changed to Foodbrands America Inc. 05/15/1995 which merged into IBP, Inc. 05/07/1997 which merged into Tyson Foods, Inc. 09/28/2001

DRAIG ENERGY LTD (AB)
Recapitalized 08/15/1997
Recapitalized from Draig Resource Ltd. to Draig Energy Ltd. 08/15/1997
Each share Common no par exchanged for (0.5) share new Common no par
Merged into NAL Oil & Gas Trust 07/24/2000
Each share Preferred Ser. A exchanged for (0.125) Trust Unit no par
Each share new Common no par exchanged for (0.2375) Trust Unit no par
NAL Oil & Gas Trust reorganized as NAL Energy Corp. 01/06/2011 which merged into Pengrowth Energy Corp. 06/05/2012

DRAKE ENERGY LTD (AB)
Filed a petition under Bankruptcy & Insolvency Act 05/26/2010
Stockholders' equity unlikely

DRAKE ENVIRONMENTAL RECOVERY LTD (AB)
Name changed 05/27/1993
Name changed from Drake Petroleums Ltd. to Drake Environmental Recovery Ltd. 05/27/1993
Common no par reclassified as Conv. Class A no par 01/17/1994
Name changed to Hydromet

DRA-DRE

Environmental Recovery Ltd. 03/16/1994
(See Hydromet Environmental Recovery Ltd.)

DRAKE GOLD RES INC (NV)
Common $0.002 par changed to $0.0001 par 07/29/2010
Name changed to Universal Apparel & Textile Co. 04/27/2015

DRAKE HLDG CORP (NV)
Recapitalized as Canopus BioPharma, Inc. 07/16/2007
Each share Common $0.002 par exchanged for (0.06666666) share Common $0.002 par

DRAKE PAC ENTERPRISES LTD (AB)
Name changed to Drake Energy Ltd. 07/08/2009
(See Drake Energy Ltd.)

DRAKE TOWERS, INC.
Liquidated 00/00/1947
Details not available

DRAKE YELLOWKNIFE GOLD MINES LTD. (ON)
Charter cancelled and declared dissolved for failure to file returns and pay fees 07/27/1976

DRAKENFELD (B.F.) & CO., INC. (NY)
Acquired by Hercules Powder Co. 04/01/1966
Details not available

DRAKO CAP CORP (AB)
Recapitalized as Amarok Energy Inc. 08/31/2012
Each share Common no par exchanged for (0.6) share Common no par
Amarok Energy Inc. recapitalized as Powder Mountain Energy Ltd. 06/20/2014 merged into Canamax Energy Inc. 08/04/2015
(See Canamax Energy Ltd.)

DRAMEX CORP (CANADA)
Class A Subordinate no par called for redemption 10/28/1996
Public interest eliminated

DRAMISKA MINES LTD. (QC)
Charter annulled for failure to file reports 10/07/1978

DRANETZ ENGINEERING LABORATORIES, INC. (NJ)
Stock Dividends - 100% 10/05/1978; 50% 10/10/1980; 50% 03/04/1983
Name changed to Dranetz Technologies, Inc. 06/06/1983
(See Dranetz Technologies, Inc.)

DRANETZ TECHNOLOGIES INC (NJ)
Common 10¢ par split (3) for (2) by issuance of (0.5) additional share 10/28/1983
Merged into Hawker Siddeley Group PLC 09/30/1988
Each share Common 10¢ par exchanged for $10.50 cash

DRANOEL INC (TX)
Completely liquidated 02/05/1988
Each share Common $1 par exchanged for first and final distribution of $13.33 cash

DRANSFIELD CHINA PAPER CORP (BRITISH VIRGIN ISLANDS)
Name changed to DF China Technology Inc. 04/28/2000
DF China Technology Inc. name changed to China Technology Global Corp. 02/04/2005
(See China Technology Global Corp.)

DRAPER CORP. (ME)
Each share Capital Stock $100 par exchanged for (2) shares Capital Stock no par 00/00/1926
Capital Stock no par split (3) for (1) by issuance of (2) additional shares 00/00/1950
Capital Stock no par split (2) for (1) by issuance of (1) additional share 05/26/1965

Merged into Rockwell-Standard Corp. (DE) 06/30/1967
Each share Capital Stock no par exchanged for (0.33333333) share $4.75 Conv. Preferred Ser. A $100 par
Rockwell-Standard Corp. (DE) merged into North American Rockwell Corp. 09/22/1967 which merged into Rockwell International Corp. (Old) 02/16/1973 which merged into Boeing Co. 12/06/1996

DRAPER LAKE FRONTENAC LEAD-ZINC MINES LTD. (ON)
Recapitalized as Lake Kingston Mines Ltd. 00/00/1957
Each share Capital Stock $1 par exchanged for (0.33333333) share Capital Stock $1 par
(See Lake Kingston Mines Ltd.)

DRAPERIES PLUS INC (NY)
Name changed to Buck-Man Electronics, Inc. 09/23/1974
Buck-Man Electronics, Inc. name changed to Frequency Control Products, Inc. 01/05/1981 which name changed to FCP Inc. 07/08/1985
(See FCP Inc.)

DRAVCO MNG INC (NV)
Common $0.00001 par split (2) for (1) by issuance of (1) additional share payable 06/20/2006 to holders of record 06/16/2006 Ex date - 06/21/2006
Name changed to Spire Technologies Inc. 10/15/2013

DRAVO CORP (PA)
6% Preferred $50 par called for redemption 01/01/1946
4% Preferred $50 par called for redemption 04/01/1965
Common $1 par split (2) for (1) by issuance of (1) additional share 12/29/1967
$2 Conv. Preferred no par called for redemption 04/01/1973
Common $1 par split (2) for (1) by issuance of (1) additional share 03/01/1976
Common $1 par split (3) for (2) by issuance of (0.5) additional share 03/02/1981
Stock Dividend - 100% 01/22/1964
Merged into Cermeuse Lime, Inc. 10/26/1998
Each share Common $1 par exchanged for $13 cash

DRAVON MED INC (OR)
Merged into a private company 01/23/1989
Each share Common no par exchanged for $1.25 cash

DRAW INTL RES CORP (BC)
Recapitalized 11/21/1985
Recapitalized from Draw Resource Corp. to Draw International Resources Corp. 11/21/1985
Each share Common no par exchanged for (4) shares Common no par
Struck off register and declared dissolved for failure to file returns 03/27/1992

DRAWSON RED LAKE GOLD MINES LTD. (ON)
Charter revoked for failure to file reports and pay fees 11/10/1966

DRAX INTL INC (CO)
Name changed 02/24/1987
Name changed from Drax Ventures, Inc. to Drax International Inc. 02/24/1987
Recapitalized as Nutrition Express Corp. of Colorado Inc. 01/02/1991
Each share Common $0.0001 par exchanged for (0.05714285) share Common $0.0001 par
Nutrition Express Corp. of Colorado Inc. merged into Nutrition for Life International, Inc. 06/24/1994 which reorganized as Advanced Nutraceuticals Inc. 03/15/2000 which recapitalized as Bactolac Pharmaceutical, Inc. 09/11/2006
(See Bactolac Pharmaceutical, Inc.)

DRAXIS HEALTH INC (CANADA)
Acquired by Jubilant Organosys Ltd. 05/29/2008
Each share Common no par exchanged for U.S.$6 cash

DRAYER-HANSON, INC. (CA)
Recapitalized 00/00/1950
Each share Class A $1 par exchanged for (1) share Common 40¢ par
Each share Common $1 par exchanged for (0.01) share Common 40¢ par
Merged into United States Radiator Corp. 00/00/1953
Each share Common 40¢ par exchanged for (6.25) shares Common $1 par
United States Radiator Corp. merged into National-U.S. Radiator Corp. 04/01/1955 which name was changed to Natus Corp. 02/01/1960 which name changed to Kirkeby-Natus Corp. 06/30/1961 which name changed to United Ventures, Inc. 06/24/1966 which merged into Federated Development Co. 07/31/1970
(See Federated Development Co.)

DRAYTON HBR REOURCES INC (NV)
Common $0.001 par split (4) for (1) by issuance of (3) additional shares payable 01/04/2008 to holders of record 01/03/2008 Ex date - 01/07/2008
Common $0.001 par split (5) for (2) by issuance of (1.5) additional shares payable 01/16/2009 to holders of record 01/16/2009
Name changed to LED Power Group, Inc. 02/05/2009
LED Power Group, Inc. recapitalized as Nyxio Technologies Corp. 06/14/2011

DRAYTON MILLS (SC)
Merged into Pacolet Industries, Inc. 12/03/1962
Each share Common $20 par exchanged for (0.21739130) share Common $10 par
(See Pacolet Industries, Inc.)

DRAYTON VY PWR INCOME FD (AB)
Each old Trust Unit no par exchanged for (0.25) new Trust Unit no par 07/20/1998
Acquired by Algonquin Power Income Fund 07/27/2001
Each new Trust Unit no par exchanged for $4.30 cash

DRC RES CORP (BC)
Name changed to New Gold, Inc. 06/01/2005

DRC SOUNDSTREAM INC (DE)
Name changed to Digital Recording Corp. 05/21/1981
(See Digital Recording Corp.)

DRCA MED CORP (NV)
Name changed to Integrated Orthopaedics, Inc. 03/17/1997
Integrated Orthopaedics, Inc. recapitalized as PowerBrief, Inc. 02/27/2001
(See PowerBrief, Inc.)

DREAM TEAM INTL INC (NV)
Common $0.001 par split (3.75) for (1) by issuance of (2.75) additional shares payable 12/28/1999 to holders of record 12/28/1999
Name changed to BioSyntech, Inc. (NV) 01/10/2000
BioSyntech, Inc. (NV) reincorporated in Canada 03/28/2006
(See BioSyntech, Inc.)

DREAM WIZARD INVTS INC (CANADA)
Name changed to AeroMechanical Services Ltd. 03/17/2003
AeroMechanical Services Ltd. name changed to FLYHT Aerospace Solutions Ltd. 05/17/2012

DREAMARTS INTL CORP (DE)
Charter cancelled and declared inoperative and void for non-payment of taxes 03/01/1990

DREAMCAR HLDGS INC (DE)
Charter cancelled and declared inoperative and void for non-payment of taxes 03/01/1992

DREAMFIELD HLDGS INC (DE)
Name changed to Riverside Entertainment Inc. 05/24/2004
Riverside Entertainment Inc. recapitalized as Axis Technologies Group, Inc. 10/20/2006

DREAMLIFE INC (DE)
Name changed to EOS International, Inc. 12/31/2001
(See EOS International, Inc.)

DREAMS INC (UT)
Each share old Common no par exchanged for (0.16666666) share new Common no par 01/30/2007
Acquired by Fanatics, Inc. 06/06/2012
Each share new Common no par exchanged for $3.45 cash

DREAMTEC INC (DE)
Cease trade order effective 08/01/2003
Stockholders' equity unlikely

DREAMWEAVER CAP CORP (BC)
Name changed to NV Gold Corp. 11/26/2009

DREAMWORKS ANIMATION INC (DE)
Acquired by Comcast Corp. (New) 08/22/2016
Each share Class A Common 1¢ par exchanged for $41 cash

DRECO ENERGY SVCS LTD (AB)
Each share Common 1¢ par exchanged for (0.25) share Class A Common 1¢ par 11/14/1988
Each share Class A Common 1¢ par exchanged for (0.9159) Exchangeable Share 09/25/1997
Each Exchangeable Share no par received distribution of (1) additional Share payable 11/18/1997 to holders of record 11/10/1997
Merged into National-Oilwell Inc. 09/25/2002
Each Exchangeable Share no par exchanged for (1) share Common 1¢ par
National-Oilwell Inc. name changed to National Oilwell Varco 03/11/2005

DREMAN/CLAYMORE DIVID & INCOME FD (DE)
Each share old Common 1¢ par exchanged for (0.2) share new Common 1¢ par 06/05/2009
Name changed to Claymore Dividend & Income Fund 06/24/2009
Claymore Dividend & Income Fund name changed to Guggenheim Enhanced Equity Strategy Fund 05/16/2011 which merged into Guggenheim Enhanced Equity Income Fund 03/20/2017

DREMAN MUT GROUP INC (MD)
Bond Portfolio 1¢ par reclassified as Fixed Income Portfolio 1¢ par 05/01/1992
Reorganized as Kemper-Dreman Fund, Inc. 08/28/1995
Details not available

DRESDEN MINES LTD. (ON)
Merged into Berkwater Explorations Ltd. 07/28/1976
Each share Capital Stock no par exchanged for (0.5) share Capital Stock no par
Berkwater Explorations Ltd. merged

into Branly Enterprises Inc.
12/09/1976 which recapitalized as
Consolidated Branly Resources Inc.
02/27/1984 which name changed to
CBR Holdings Inc. 06/20/1985

DRESDNER BK A G (GERMANY)
Each Unsponsored ADR for Bearer
exchanged for (10) Sponsored
ADR's for Bearer 05/11/1992
Merged into Allianz AG 07/11/2002
Each Sponsored ADR for Bearer
exchanged for $51.2167 cash
Each 144A Sponsored ADR for
Bearer exchanged for $51.2167
cash

DRESDNER RCM EUROPE FD INC (MD)
Reorganized as Dresdner RCM
Global Funds, Inc. 03/06/2001
Details not available

DRESDNER RCM GLOBAL STRATEGIC INCOME FD INC (MD)
Merged into RCM Strategic Global
Government Fund, Inc. 01/18/2002
Each share Common $0.001 par
exchanged for (0.6139455) share
Common $0.00001 par
RCM Strategic Global Government
Fund, Inc. name changed to PIMCO
Strategic Global Government Fund,
Inc. 03/19/2002 which name
changed to PIMCO Strategic Income
Fund, Inc. 03/03/2014

DRESHER INC (DE)
Common 1¢ par split (2) for (1) by
issuance of (1) additional share
11/14/1983
Common 1¢ par split (3) for (2) by
issuance of (0.5) additional share
05/25/1985
Common 1¢ par split (3) for (2) by
issuance of (0.5) additional share
02/25/1986
Common 1¢ par split (3) for (2) by
issuance of (0.5) additional share
08/25/1986
Merged into Leggett & Platt, Inc.
06/19/1990
Each share Common 1¢ par
exchanged for $2.50 cash

DRESS BARN INC (CT)
Common 5¢ par split (2) for (1) by
issuance of (1) additional share
05/03/1985
Common 5¢ par split (5) for (2) by
issuance of (1.5) additional shares
05/02/1986
Common 5¢ par split (2) for (1) by
issuance of (1) additional share
05/25/1987
Common 5¢ par split (2) for (1) by
issuance of (1) additional share
payable 05/31/2002 to holders of
record 05/17/2002 Ex date -
06/03/2002
Common 5¢ par split (2) for (1) by
issuance of (1) additional share
payable 03/31/2006 to holders of
record 03/17/2006 Ex date -
04/03/2006
Reincorporated under the laws of
Delaware as Ascena Retail Group,
Inc. and Common 5¢ par changed to
1¢ par 01/03/2011

DRESSEN BARNES ELECTRS CORP (CA)
Name changed to D-B Liquidating Co.
06/21/1977
(See D-B Liquidating Co.)

DRESSER INDUSTRIES, INC. (DE)
(In combination with Transnational
Ventures Ltd. (Liberia) Common
N.P.)
Dissolution of Transnational Ventures
Ltd. (Liberia) effective 05/10/1965
with no stockholders' equity
Each share of combined stock
exchanged for (1) share Dresser
Industries Inc. (DE) (Plain) (New)
Common 50¢ par

DRESSER INDUSTRIES, INC. (PA)
Each share Common $1 par
exchanged for (2) shares Common
50¢ par 00/00/1945
Reincorporated under the laws of
Delaware 08/01/1956
Dresser Industries, Inc. (DE) (Plain)
(Old) exchanged for combination
certificate of Dresser Industries, Inc.
(DE) and Transnational Ventures
Ltd. 01/14/1964
(See Dresser Industries Inc. in
combination with Transnational
Ventures Ltd.)

DRESSER INDUSTRIES, INC. OLD (DE)
Common 50¢ par split (2) for (1) by
issuance of (1) additional share
12/17/1956
Distribution of (1) share Transnational
Ventures Ltd. Common no par, for
each share Dresser Common 50¢
par held, effected by exchange of
each "plain" share Dresser for a
combination certificate of (1) share
Dresser Industries, Inc. Common
50¢ par and (1) share Transnational
Ventures Ltd. Common no par
01/14/1964
(See Dresser Industries, Inc. in
combination with Transnational
Ventures Ltd.)

DRESSER INDS INC NEW (DE)
Common 50¢ par changed to 25¢ par
and (1) additional share issued
11/26/1965
$2.20 Conv. Preference Ser. A no par
called for redemption 07/21/1975
$2 Conv. Preferred Ser. B no par
called for redemption 07/21/1975
Common 25¢ par split (2) for (1) by
issuance of (1) additional share
06/18/1976
Common 25¢ par split (2) for (1) by
issuance of (1) additional share
11/14/1980
Preferred Stock Purchase Rights
declared for Common stockholders
of record 04/28/1986 were
redeemed at $0.025 per right
10/22/1990 for holders of record
10/03/1990
Common 25¢ par split (2) for (1) by
issuance of (1) additional share
09/20/1990
Merged into Halliburton Co.
09/29/1998
Each share Common 25¢ par
exchanged for (1) share Common
$2.50 par

DRESSER MANUFACTURING CO. (PA)
Name changed to Dresser Industries,
Inc. (PA) and Common no par
changed to $1 par 00/00/1944
(See Dresser Industries, Inc. (PA))

DRESSER (S.R.) MANUFACTURING CO.
Recapitalized as Dresser
Manufacturing Co. (PA) 00/00/1939
Each share Class A exchanged for (2)
shares Common no par
Each share Class B exchanged for
(1) share Common no par
Dresser Manufacturing Co. (PA) name
changed to Dresser Industries, Inc.
(PA) 00/00/1944
(See Dresser Industries, Inc. (PA))

DRESSER-RAND GROUP INC (DE)
Acquired by Siemens A.G.
06/30/2015
Each share Common 1¢ par
exchanged for $85.20 cash

DREVER CO (PA)
Each share Class B Common Ser. 1
40¢ par automatically became (1)
share Common 40¢ par 03/31/1964
Each share Class B Common Ser. 2
40¢ par automatically became (1)
share Common 40¢ par 03/31/1965
Each share Class B Common Ser. 3
40¢ par automatically became (1)
share Common 40¢ par 03/31/1966
98.5% acquired by Superior-Drever
Co. through purchase offer which
expired 03/16/1973
Public interest eliminated

DREW CTI CORP (FL)
Filed a petition under Chapter 7
Federal Bankruptcy Code
04/03/1984
No stockholders' equity

DREW INDS INC (DE)
Each share old Common 1¢ par
exchanged for (0.1) share new
Common 1¢ par 05/02/1989
New Common 1¢ par split (2) for (1)
by issuance of (1) additional share
payable 03/21/1997 to holders of
record 03/04/1997 Ex date -
03/24/1997
New Common 1¢ par split (2) for (1)
by issuance of (1) additional share
payable 09/07/2005 to holders of
record 08/19/2005 Ex date -
09/08/2005
Name changed to LCI Industries
01/03/2017

DREW NATL CORP (DE)
Common $1 par changed to 1¢ par
08/08/1979
14% Conv. Class A Preferred $5 par
called for redemption 07/09/1983
Merged into Pratt Hotel Corp.
05/31/1985
Each share 6.5% Conv. Preferred $25
par exchanged for $10 cash
Each share Common 1¢ par
exchanged for (0.25) share Common
1¢ par
Pratt Hotel Corp. name changed to
Greate Bay Casino Corp.
12/31/1996
(See Greate Bay Casino Corp.)

DREW NATL LEASING CORP (DE)
Charter cancelled and declared
inoperative and void for
non-payment of taxes 03/01/1978

DREW PPTYS CORP (DE)
Class A $1 par reclassified as
Common $1 par 01/28/1965
Name changed to Drew National
Corp. 01/30/1968
Drew National Corp. merged into
Pratt Hotel Corp. 05/31/1985 which
name changed to Greate Bay
Casino Corp. 12/31/1996
(See Greate Bay Casino Corp.)

DREW RES INC (NV)
Each share old Common $0.001 par
exchanged for (2) shares new
Common $0.001 par 10/27/2000
Name changed to RagingMediaGroup
Inc. 07/27/2001
RagingMediaGroup Inc. name
changed to Dixon Oil & Gas Inc.
06/04/2003 which recapitalized as
Galloway Energy Inc. 12/01/2006
(See Galloway Energy Inc.)

DREWRY PHOTOCOLOR CORP (CA)
In process of liquidation
Each share Common 10¢ par
received initial distribution of $14
cash 10/10/1988
Each share Common 10¢ par
received second distribution of $1.75
cash 12/15/1989
Each share Common 10¢ par
received third distribution of $1 cash
12/14/1990
Note: Details on subsequent
distribution(s), if any, are not
available

DREWRY'S LIMITED, U.S.A., INC. (IN)
Merged into Associated Brewing Co.
12/31/1965
Each share Common $1 par
exchanged for (1) share Common
$1 par
Associated Brewing Co. name
changed to Armada Corp.
03/02/1973

DREXEL BD DEB TRADING FD (DE)
Name changed to 1838
Bond-Debenture Trading Fund
10/05/1988
1838 Bond-Debenture Trading Fund
name changed to Rivus Bond Fund
07/07/2006 which name changed to
Insight Select Income Fund
12/29/2016

DREXEL CAP CORP (BC)
Name changed to Drexel Resources
Ltd. 04/25/2011
Drexel Resources Ltd. name changed
to Blue Gold Mining Inc. 08/23/2011
which merged into Riverstone
Resources Inc. 12/17/2012 which
name changed to True Gold Mining
Inc. 02/25/2013 which merged into
Endeavour Mining Corp. 04/27/2016

DREXEL DYNAMICS CORP (PA)
Recapitalized as Drexel Industries,
Inc. (PA) 02/01/1972
Each share Common no par
exchanged for (0.33333333) share
Common 10¢ par
(See Drexel Industries, Inc. (PA))

DREXEL ENTERPRISE CORP (BC)
Recapitalized as Graffoto Industries
Corp. 06/28/1993
Each share Common no par
exchanged for (0.5) share Common
no par

DREXEL ENTERPRISES, INC. (DE)
Stock Dividend - 100% 11/30/1962
Completely liquidated 07/09/1968
Each share Common $2.50 par
exchanged for first and final
distribution of (0.8) share U.S.
Plywood-Champion Papers Inc.
$1.20 Conv. Preference $1 par and
(0.9) share Common $1 par
U.S. Plywood-Champion Papers Inc.
name changed to Champion
International Corp. 05/12/1972
which merged into International
Paper Co. 06/20/2000

DREXEL EQUITY FD INC (DE)
Under plan of merger name changed
to Drexel Burnham Fund 06/16/1975

DREXEL FURNITURE CO. (DE)
Name changed to Drexel Enterprises,
Inc. 11/01/1960
Drexel Enterprises, Inc. acquired by
U.S. Plywood-Champion Papers Inc.
07/09/1968 which name changed to
Champion International Corp.
05/12/1972 which merged into
International Paper Co. 06/20/2000

DREXEL HEDGE FD INC (DE)
Acquired by Standard &
Poor's/Intercapital Dynamics Fund,
Inc. 05/07/1973
Each share Common 10¢ par
exchanged for (0.54661) share
Capital Stock 10¢ par
Standard & Poor's/Intercapital
Dynamics Fund, Inc. acquired by
Tudor Hedge Fund 09/30/1975
which name changed to Tudor Fund
06/18/1980 which name changed to
WPG Tudor Fund 12/29/1989
(See WPG Tudor Fund)

DREXEL INDS INC (PA)
Merged into Clark Equipment Co.
04/30/1990
Each share Common 10¢ par
exchanged for $29.71 cash
Note: An initial escrow payment of
$2.33 cash per share was made
09/12/1991
Additional and final escrow payment
of $0.66377 cash per share was
made 07/15/1992

DREXEL INDS INC (UT)
Common 5¢ par changed to no par
01/30/1964
Common no par changed to 1¢ par
07/10/1967
Charter suspended for failure to pay
taxes 09/15/1970

DREXEL INVT FD INC (DE)
Merged into Drexel Burnham Fund 06/16/1975
Each share Common 10¢ par exchanged for (0.627828) share Common 10¢ par

DREXEL NATL BK (CHICAGO, IL)
Stock Dividends - 50% 12/26/1944; 66-2/3% 10/28/1946
Acquired by South Shore Bank (Chicago, IL) 12/16/1995
Details not available

DREXEL RES LTD (BC)
Name changed to Blue Gold Mining Inc. 08/23/2011
Blue Gold Mining Inc. merged into Riverstone Resources Inc. 12/17/2012 which name changed to True Gold Mining Inc. 02/25/2013 which merged into Endeavour Mining Corp. 04/27/2016

DREXEL UTIL SHS INC (DE)
Name changed to Energy & Utility Shares, Inc. (DE) 06/12/1980
Energy & Utility Shares, Inc. (DE) reincorporated in Maryland as Stratton Monthly Dividend Shares, Inc. 03/05/1985 which name changed to Stratton Monthly Dividend REIT Shares, Inc. 12/09/1997 which name changed to Stratton Real Estate Fund, Inc. 09/30/2009

DREXEL VILLA APARTMENTS LIQUIDATION TRUST
Liquidation completed in 1950

DREXLER TECHNOLOGY CORP (DE)
Reincorporated 09/17/1987
Common 20¢ par changed to 10¢ par and (1) additional share issued 07/10/1981
Common 10¢ par changed to 6-2/3¢ par and (0.5) additional share issued 07/14/1986
State of incorporation changed from (CA) to (DE) and Common 6-2/3¢ par changed to 1¢ par 09/17/1987
Name changed to LaserCard Corp. 10/01/2004
(See LaserCard Corp.)

DREXORE DEVS INC (BC)
Recapitalized as Cabo Ventures Inc. (BC) 11/2/89
Each share Common no par exchanged for (0.25) share Common no par
Cabo Ventures Inc. (BC) reincorporated in Yukon as Cabo Exploration Ventures Inc. 2/1/96 which recapitalized as Cabo Mining Corp. 7/15/98 which recapitalized as Cabo Mining Enterprises Corp. 1/5/2004 which name changed to Cabo Drilling Corp. 1/12/2006

DREYERS GRAND ICE CREAM HLDGS INC (DE)
Merged into Nestle Holdings Inc. 1/17/2006
Each share Common 1¢ par exchanged for $83.10 cash

DREYERS GRAND ICE CREAM INC (DE)
Common no par split (2) for (1) by issuance of (1) additional share 9/3/82
Common no par split (3) for (2) by issuance of (0.5) additional share 6/24/83
Common no par split (2) for (1) by issuance of (1) additional share 10/1/90
Common no par split (2) for (1) by issuance of (1) additional share payable 11/17/97 to holders of record 10/30/97
Reorganized as Dreyer's Grand Ice Cream Holdings Inc. 6/30/2003
Each share Common no par exchanged for (1) share Common 1¢ par

(See Dreyer's Grand Ice Cream Holdings Inc.)

DREYFUS CALIF MUN INCOME INC (MD)
Merged into Dreyfus Premier California Tax Exempt Bond Fund, Inc. 2/24/2005
Each share Common $0.001 par exchanged for Class Z shares at net asset value

DREYFUS CAPITAL GROWTH FD INC (MD)
Reincorporated 04/30/1974
Name change 06/29/1992
State of incorporation changed from (DE) to (MD) 04/30/1974
Name changed from Dreyfus Leverage Fund, Inc. to Dreyfus Capital Growth Fund, Inc. 06/29/1992
Reorganized as Premier Equity Funds, Inc. 01/02/1996
Details not available

DREYFUS CASH MGMT INC (MD)
Reorganized under the laws of Massachusetts as Dreyfus Cash Management 05/22/1987
Each share Common $0.001 par exchanged for (1) Share of Bene. Int. $0.001 par

DREYFUS CONV SECS FD INC (MD)
Merged into Dreyfus Growth & Income Fund, Inc. 09/17/1993
Details not available

DREYFUS CORP (NY)
Common $1 par changed to 33-1/3¢ par and (2) additional shares issued 02/18/1981
Common 33-1/3¢ par changed to 16-2/3¢ par and (1) additional share issued 10/06/1983
Common 16-2/3¢ par changed to 10¢ par and (2) additional shares issued 06/30/1986
Merged into Mellon Bank Corp. 08/24/1994
Each share Common 10¢ par exchanged for (0.88017) share Common 50¢ par
Mellon Bank Corp. name changed to Mellon Financial Corp. 10/17/1999 which merged into Bank of New York Mellon Corp. 07/01/2007

DREYFUS FOUNDERS FDS INC (MD)
Name changed to Dreyfus Discovery Fund 12/01/2008

DREYFUS GNMA FD INC (MD)
Under plan of reorganization each share Common 1¢ par automatically became (1) Dreyfus Premier GNMA Fund, Inc. Class Z Share 1¢ par 5/3/2007

DREYFUS GROUP EQUITY FUND, INC. (DE)
Name changed to Dreyfus Number Nine, Inc. 07/18/1977
Dreyfus Number Nine, Inc. name changed to Dreyfus Growth Opportunity Fund, Inc. (DE) 06/20/1983 which reincorporated in Maryland 07/30/1982 which name changed to Dreyfus Research Growth Fund, Inc. 12/01/2008

DREYFUS GROWTH OPPORTUNITY FD INC (MD)
Reincorporated 07/30/1982
Reincorporated from under the laws of Delaware to under the laws of Maryland and Capital Stock $1 par reclassified as Common 1¢ par 07/30/1982
Common 1¢ par reclassified as Class Z $0.001 par 09/30/2008
Name changed to Dreyfus Research Growth Fund, Inc. 12/01/2008

DREYFUS INTER BD FD INC (MD)
Name changed to Dreyfus A Bonds Plus Inc. 09/15/1978

DREYFUS INTER TAX EXEMPT BD FD INC (MD)
Name changed to Dreyfus Intermediate Municipal Bond Fund, Inc. 09/11/1990

DREYFUS INTERCONTINENTAL INVESTMENT FUND N.V. (NETHERLANDS)
Merged into Dreyfus Fund International Ltd. 07/00/1991
Details not available

DREYFUS INVT FDS (MA)
Boston Company International Core Equity Fund reclassified as Boston Company International Core Equity Fund Class I 09/01/2009
Completely liquidated 01/25/2011
Each share Boston Company International Core Equity Fund Class I received first and final distribution of $17.67 cash
(Additional Information in Active)

DREYFUS MICH MUN MONEY MKT FD INC (MD)
Under plan of reorganization each share Common $0.001 par automatically became Dreyfus Municipal Money Market Fund, Inc. Common $0.001 par on a net asset basis 07/22/1996

DREYFUS N J TAX EXEMPT BD FD INC (MD)
Name changed to Dreyfus New Jersey Municipal Bond Fund, Inc. 9/14/90

DREYFUS N J TAX EXEMPT BD FD L P (DE)
Reorganized under the laws of Maryland as Dreyfus New Jersey Tax Exempt Bond Fund, Inc. 08/17/1988
Each Ltd. Partnership Int. exchanged for (1) share Common $0.001 par Dreyfus New Jersey Tax Exempt Bond Fund, Inc. name changed to Dreyfus New Jersey Municipal Bond Fund, Inc. 09/14/1990

DREYFUS N J TAX EXEMPT MONEY MKT FD INC (MD)
Name changed to Dreyfus New Jersey Municipal Money Market Fund, Inc. 10/2/90

DREYFUS N Y INSD TAX EXEMPT BD FD (MA)
Merged into General New York Municipal Bond Fund, Inc. 09/23/1999
Details not available

DREYFUS N Y MUN INCOME INC (MD)
Merged into Dreyfus New York Tax Exempt Bond Fund Inc. 3/4/2005
Each share Common $0.001 par exchanged for Common $0.001 par shares at net asset value

DREYFUS N Y TAX EXEMPT INTER BD FD (MA)
Merged into Dreyfus New York Tax Exempt Bond Fund, Inc. 11/27/2007
Each Share of Bene. Int. $0.001 par exchanged for Common $0.001 par on a net asset basis

DREYFUS NUMBER NINE, INC. (DE)
Name changed to Dreyfus Growth Opportunity Fund, Inc. (DE) 06/20/1983
Dreyfus Growth Opportunity Fund, Inc. (DE) reincorporated in Maryland 07/30/1982 which name changed to Dreyfus Research Growth Fund, Inc. 12/01/2008

DREYFUS PREMIER GNMA FD (MD)
Merged into Dreyfus Premier GNMA Fund, Inc. 05/03/2007
Details not available

DREYFUS SPL INCOME FD INC (DE)
Name changed to Dreyfus Convertible Securities Fund, Inc. 06/02/1986

(See Dreyfus Convertible Securities Fund, Inc.)

DREYFUS STRATEGIC GOVTS INCOME INC (MD)
Name changed 12/31/89
Name changed from Dreyfus Strategic Government Income, Inc. to Dreyfus Strategic Governments Income, Inc. 12/31/89
Merged into Dreyfus A Bonds Plus, Inc. 10/20/2000
Each share Common $0.001 par exchanged for (0.7166) share Common 1¢ par

DREYFUS STRATEGIC INCOME (MA)
Reorganized as Dreyfus Income Funds 01/02/1996
Details not available

DREYFUS STRATEGIC WORLD REVS L P (DE)
Ceased operations 11/16/1992
Details not available

DREYFUS TAX EXEMPT BD FD INC (MD)
Name changed to Dreyfus Municipal Bond Fund Inc. 2/9/93

DREYFUS THIRD CENTY FD INC (DE)
Capital Stock $1 par changed to 33-1/3¢ par and (2) additional shares issued 11/28/80
Reincorporated under the laws of Maryland and Capital Stock 33-1/3¢ par reclassified as Common 33-1/3¢ par 7/30/82

DRG INC (BC)
Name changed 06/23/1981
Reincorporated 00/00/1982
Class A Common no par split (2) for (1) by issuance of (1) additional share 05/03/1972
Name changed from DRG Ltd. to DRG Inc. 06/23/1981
Place of incorporation changed from (Canada) to (BC) 00/00/1982
Merged into DRG Acquisitions Inc. 11/21/1987
Each share Class A Subordinate no par exchanged for $27 cash

DRI CORP (NC)
Plan of reorganization under Chapter 11 Federal Bankruptcy proceedings effective 01/01/2013
No stockholders' equity

DRI-STEAM PRODUCTS, INC. (DE)
Name changed to Drico Industrial Corp. 00/00/1946
(See Drico Industrial Corp.)

DRI-STEAM VALVE SALES CORP.
Merged into Dri-Steam Products, Inc. 00/00/1940
Details not available

DRICO INDL CORP (DE)
Liquidation completed
Each share Common $1 par exchanged for initial distribution of (1) share Viskon-Aire Corp. Common 10¢ par and $1 cash 10/26/1983
Each share Common $1 par received second distribution of $0.782 cash 11/01/1984
Each share Common $1 par received third distribution of $0.738 cash 11/08/1985
Each share Common $1 par received fourth distribution of $0.694 cash 11/04/1986
Each share Common $1 par received fifth and final distribution of $2.665 cash 07/30/1987
(See Viskon-Aire Corp.)

DRIEFONTEIN CONS LTD (SOUTH AFRICA)
Each ADR for Ordinary exchanged for (2) Unsponsored ADR's for Ordinary 11/27/1987
Each Unsponsored ADR for Ordinary

FINANCIAL INFORMATION, INC.   DRI-DRO

exchanged for (1) Sponsored ADR for Ordinary 12/27/1994
Name changed to Gold Fields Ltd. (New) 05/10/1999

DRIFT LAKE RES INC (ON)
Name changed to Sintana Energy Inc. 10/12/2011

DRIFTWOOD MINES LTD (BC)
Struck off register 08/26/1983

DRIFTWOOD VENTURES INC (DE)
Reincorporated 12/20/2007
State of incorporation changed from (NV) to (DE) 12/20/2007
Name changed to Zoo Entertainment, Inc. 01/27/2009
Zoo Entertainment, Inc. name changed to indiePub Entertainment, Inc. 05/25/2012

DRILCO OIL TOOLS INC (TX)
Merged into Smith Industries International, Inc. 12/01/1967
Each share Common $1 par exchanged for (1) share Capital Stock no par
Smith Industries International, Inc. name changed to Smith International, Inc. (CA) 05/13/1969 which reincorporated in Delaware 05/19/1983
(See Smith International, Inc.)

DRILCORP ENERGY LTD (AB)
Merged into Twin Butte Energy Ltd. 06/02/2006
Each share Common no par exchanged for (0.4224352) share Common no par and $0.09456176 cash

DRILCORP SLIMHOLE TECHNOLOGIES LTD (AB)
Name changed to Drilcorp Energy Ltd. 11/15/1999
Drilcorp Energy Ltd. merged into Twin Butte Energy Ltd. 06/02/2006

DRILEX INTL INC (DE)
Merged into Baker Hughes Inc. 07/14/1997
Each share Common 1¢ par exchanged for (0.4013) share Common $1 par
Baker Hughes Inc. merged into Baker Hughes, a GE company 07/05/2017

DRILEX OIL & GAS INC (CO)
Each share Capital Stock 1¢ par exchanged for (0.05) share Capital Stock 20¢ par 12/05/1989
Declared defunct and inoperative for failure to pay taxes and file annual reports 01/01/1997

DRILLERS INC (TX)
Name changed to DI Industries, Inc. 04/28/1987
DI Industries, Inc. name changed to Grey Wolf, Inc. 09/18/1997 which was acquired by Precision Drilling Trust 12/23/2008 which reorganized as Precision Drilling Corp. 06/03/2010

DRILLERS TECHNOLOGY CORP (AB)
Merged into Saxon Energy Services Inc. 11/21/2005
Each share Common no par exchanged for $1.85 cash

DRILLING & EXPLORATION CO., INC. (DE)
Stock Dividend - 800% 04/04/1952
Liquidation completed
Each share Common $1 par stamped to indicate initial distribution of $17 cash 10/25/1963
Each share Stamped Common $1 par exchanged for second and final distribution of $1.35 cash 09/14/1964

DRILLING INC (NV)
Each share old Common $0.001 par exchanged for (7.5) shares new Common $0.001 par 03/17/2004

Name changed to PivX Solutions, Inc. 05/11/2004
PivX Solutions, Inc. name changed to Adia Nutrition, Inc. 12/20/2011

DRILLSTAR INTL CORP (DE)
Name changed 11/14/1990
Name changed from Drillstar Corp. to Drillstar International Corp. 11/14/1990
Recapitalized as Mobile Services International Corp. 04/16/1993
Each share Common $0.0001 par exchanged for (0.2) share Common $0.0001 par
Mobile Services International Corp. recapitalized as International Communications & Technologies Corp. 03/15/1996 which recapitalized as GBS Com-Tech Corp. 05/15/1997
(See GBS Com-Tech Corp.)

DRIMEX INC (NV)
Name changed to MakingORG, Inc. 08/25/2014

DRINK WORLD INC (NV)
Reorganized as Aimrite Holdings Inc. 07/24/1995
Each share Common $0.001 par exchanged for (2) shares Common $0.001 par

DRINKS, INC. (DE)
Dissolved 11/14/1962
No stockholders' equity

DRINKS BY THE CASE INC. (PA)
Name changed to Acustar Corp. 12/01/1986
(See Acustar Corp.)

DRIVE PRODS INCOME FD (ON)
Acquired by 2256479 Ontario Inc. 11/17/2010
Each Trust Unit no par received $2.50 cash

DRIVEFONE INC (DE)
Each share Common $0.0001 par exchanged for (0.2) share Common $0.0005 par 01/23/1992
Name changed to Luxcel Group, Inc. 01/15/1993
(See Luxcel Group, Inc.)

DRIVEN CAP CORP (BC)
Recapitalized as Greenflag Ventures Inc. 04/24/2014
Each share Common no par exchanged for (0.1) share Common no par
Greenflag Ventures Inc. recapitalized as Prosalutis Holdings Inc. 05/02/2016

DRIVER (WILBUR B.) CO. (NJ)
Acquired by General Telephone & Electronics Corp. 09/08/1967
Each share Capital Stock no par exchanged for (9.572657) shares Common $3.33333333 par
General Telephone & Electronics Corp. name changed to GTE Corp. 07/01/1982 which merged into Verizon Communications Inc. 06/30/2000

DRIVER DEV LTD (AB)
Completely liquidated 01/29/1971
Each share Capital Stock no par exchanged for first and final distribution of (0.2) share Delta Hotels Ltd. Capital Stock no par
(See Delta Hotels Ltd.)

DRIVER ENERGY SVCS INC NEW (AB)
Recapitalized as Kodiak Energy Services Ltd. 11/24/2003
Each share Common no par exchanged for (0.5) share Common no par
(See Kodiak Energy Services Ltd.)

DRIVER ENERGY SVCS INC OLD (AB)
Merged into Driver Energy Services Inc. (New) 04/03/2002
Each share Common no par

exchanged for (1) share Common no par
Driver Energy Services Inc. recapitalized as Kodiak Energy Services Ltd. 11/24/2003
(See Kodiak Energy Services Ltd.)

DRIVER HARRIS CO (NJ)
Each share Common $100 par exchanged for (10) shares Common $10 par 00/00/1929
Common $10 par changed to $5 par and (1) additional share issued 07/01/1959
Common $5 par changed to $1.66666666 par and (2) additional shares issued 07/06/1965
Common 1.66666666 par changed to $0.83333333 par and (1) additional share issued 02/11/1985
Stock Dividend - 10% 07/22/1970
Plan of reorganization under Chapter 11 Federal Bankruptcy Code effective 12/04/2006
No stockholders' equity

DRIVER PASSPORT INC (ND)
Reincorporated under the laws of Nevada as Eco Global Corp. 05/08/2009
(See Eco Global Corp.)

DRIVER PETROLEUMS LTD. (AB)
Name changed to Driver Development Corp. Ltd. 03/00/1969
(See Driver Development Corp. Ltd.)

DRIVERSHIELD CORP (NY)
Name changed 02/04/2002
Name changed from Driversshield.com Corp. to DriverShield Corp. 02/04/2002
Name changed to Accessity Corp. (NY) 01/24/2003
Accessity Corp. (NY) reorganized in Delaware as Pacific Ethanol, Inc. 03/24/2005

DRKOOP COM INC (DE)
Filed a petition under Chapter 7 Federal Bankruptcy Code 12/17/2001
No stockholders' equity

DRM VENTURES INC (ON)
Completely liquidated
Each share Common no par received first and final distribution of (0.6511) share Patient Home Monitoring Corp. (AB) Common no par payable 11/22/2011 to holders of record 08/22/2011
Note: Certificates were not required to be surrendered and are without value
Patient Home Monitoring Corp. (AB) reincorporated in British Columbia 12/30/2013
(See Patient Home Monitoring Corp.)

DROMEDARY EXPL LTD (BC)
Name changed to HEC Hitech Entertainment Corp. 08/18/1993
HEC Hitech Entertainment Corp. name changed to Gleneagles Petroleum Corp. 02/03/1997 which name changed to Clickhouse.Com Online Inc. 07/29/1999 which recapitalized as Windridge Technology Corp. 09/19/2002 which name changed to Dajin Resources Corp. 01/19/2005

DROMOLAND DEV CORP (BC)
Name changed to Burndale Resources Ltd. 01/18/1985
Each share Common no par exchanged for (1) share Common no par
Burndale Resources Ltd. name changed to Tai Energy Resources Corp. 09/14/1989 which merged into Tai Energy Corp. 06/30/1993 which was acquired by Maxx Petroleum Ltd. 03/17/1995 which was acquired by Provident Energy Trust 05/25/2001 which reorganized as Provident Energy Ltd. (New)

01/03/2011 which merged into Pembina Pipeline Corp. 04/02/2012

DROPE LAKE EXPLORATIONS LTD. (ON)
Name changed to Drope Lake Metals & Holdings Ltd. 12/22/1970
(See Drope Lake Metals & Holdings Ltd.)

DROPE LAKE METALS & HLDGS LTD (ON)
Charter cancelled for failure to pay taxes and file returns 02/20/1980

DROVERS & MECHANICS BK (YORK, PA)
Name changed 02/14/1979
Capital Stock $10 par changed to $5 par and (1) additional share issued 10/01/1970
Stock Dividends - 20% 09/29/1961; 25% 02/09/1966; 50% 10/01/1970
Name changed from Drovers & Mechanics National Bank (York, PA) to Drovers & Mechanics Bank (York, PA) 02/14/1979
Stock Dividends - 20% 07/20/1979; 20% 06/30/1980
Under plan of reorganization each share Capital Stock $5 par automatically became (1) share Drovers Bancshares Corp. Common $5 par 10/27/1982
Drovers Bancshares Corp. merged into Fulton Financial Corp. 07/01/2001

DROVERS BANCSHARES CORP (PA)
Common $5 par split (3) for (2) by issuance of (0.5) additional share 09/07/1990
Common $5 par split (5) for (4) by issuance of (0.25) additional share 09/02/1994
Common $5 par split (5) for (4) by issuance of (0.25) additional share payable 08/16/1996 to holders of record 07/19/1996
Common $5 par split (3) for (2) by issuance of (0.5) additional share payable 05/29/1998 to holders of record 05/08/1998
Stock Dividends - 10% 02/05/1988; 5% payable 11/28/1997 to holders of record 11/14/1997; 5% payable 05/28/1999 to holders of record 05/07/1999; 5% payable 05/26/2000 to holders of record 05/05/2000
Ex date - 05/03/2000
Merged into Fulton Financial Corp. 07/01/2001
Each share Common $5 par exchanged for (1.302) shares Common $2.50 par

DROVERS NATL BK (CHICAGO, IL)
Each share Capital Stock $100 par exchanged for (10) shares Capital Stock $10 par 10/00/1950
Capital Stock $10 par changed to $8 par and (0.25) additional share issued 10/15/1970
Stock Dividends - 25% 02/18/1952; 20% 02/12/1953; 20% 09/26/1955; 11.11111111% 02/12/1958; (1) for (5.4) 01/20/1964; 12.5 % 02/10/1966; 11.11111111% 02/08/1967; 10% 02/12/1969
Declared insolvent and closed by the Comptroller of the Currency 01/19/1978
No stockholders' equity

DROVERS TRUST & SAVINGS BANK (CHICAGO, IL)
Each share Capital Stock $100 par exchanged for (10) shares Capital Stock $10 par 00/00/1950
Stock Dividends - 42.8571% 12/22/1943; 25% 02/18/1952; 20% 02/12/1953; 20% 09/23/1955; 11.11111111% 02/25/1958
Merged into Drovers National Bank (Chicago, IL) 07/02/1962
Each share Capital Stock $10 par

exchanged for (1) share Capital Stock $10 par
(See Drovers National Bank (Chicago, IL))

DRS INC (NV)
Ceased operations 02/10/2012
Stockholders' equity unlikely

DRS INDS INC (DE)
Name changed to Family Bargain Corp. 01/13/1994
Family Bargain Corp. merged into Factory 2-U Stores, Inc. 11/23/1998
(See Factory 2-U Stores, Inc.)

DRS TECHNOLOGIES INC (DE)
Merged into Finmeccanica SpA 10/22/2008
Each share Common 1¢ par exchanged for $81 cash

DRT RES LTD (BC)
Delisted from Vancouver Stock Exchange 03/05/1996

DRUCKER INDS INC (DE)
Reorganized 09/06/1991
Name changed 12/01/2000
Reorganized from Drucker Sound Design Corp. to Drucker Industries, Inc. 09/06/1991
Each share Common $0.001 par exchanged for (5) shares Common $0.001 par
Name changed from Drucker Industries Inc. to Drucker Inc. 12/01/2000
SEC revoked common stock registration 10/15/2012

DRUCOX PETE CORP (BC)
Name changed to Marketfax Infoservices Ltd. 10/17/1984
(See Marketfax Infoservices Ltd.)

DRUDE URANIUM MINES LTD. (ON)
Charter cancelled for failure to pay taxes and file returns 05/18/1976

DRUG, INC.
Stock of five new companies issued in exchange for stock of Drug, Inc. in accordance with the plan of segregation 00/00/1933
Details not available

DRUG & FOOD CAPITAL CORP. (IL)
Name changed to Advance Growth Capital Corp. 08/14/1962
(See Advance Growth Capital Corp.)

DRUG DETECTION SYS INC (NV)
Each share old Common $0.001 par exchanged for (0.14285714) share new Common $0.001 par 09/17/1991
Name changed to Eye Dynamics Inc. 07/14/1993
Eye Dynamics Inc. name changed to AcuNetx, Inc. 01/03/2006
(See AcuNetx, Inc.)

DRUG EMPORIUM INC (DE)
Common 10¢ par split (2) for (1) by issuance of (1) additional share 07/10/1989
Plan of reorganization under Chapter 11 Federal Bankruptcy Code effective 09/24/2001
No stockholders' equity

DRUG FAIR CMNTY DRUG INC (MD)
Stock Dividend - 50% 07/31/1960
Name changed to Drug Fair Inc. and Class A Common $1 par reclassified as Common $1 par 10/26/1970
(See Drug Fair Inc.)

DRUG FAIR INC (MD)
Stock Dividend - 10% 11/24/1976
Acquired by Gray Drug Stores, Inc. 05/28/1981
Each share Common $1 par exchanged for $20 cash

DRUG PRODS INC (NY)
Dissolved by proclamation 03/27/1979

DRUG RTY INC (NL)
Acquired by Inwest Investments Ltd. 04/29/2002
Each share Common no par exchanged for $3.05 cash

DRUG SCREENING SYS INC (PA)
Each share Common $0.001 par exchanged for (0.1) share Common 1¢ par 05/06/1993
Name changed to DSSI Corp. 06/30/1997
DSSI Corp. name changed to Collegiate Pacific Inc. (PA) 02/20/1998 which reincorporated in Delaware 07/21/1999 which name changed to Sport Supply Group, Inc. (New) 07/02/2007
(See Sport Supply Group, Inc. (New))

DRUG SYS INC (DE)
Common $1 par changed to 80¢ par and (0.25) additional share issued 01/24/1984
Name changed to Retailing Corp. of America 11/04/1987
(See Retailing Corp. of America)

DRUGMAX INC (NV)
Name changed 09/07/2001
Name changed from DrugMax.com, Inc. to DrugMax, Inc. 09/07/2001
Name changed to Familymeds Group, Inc. 07/10/2006

DRUGSTORE COM INC (DE)
Acquired by Walgreen Co. 06/06/2011
Each share Common $0.0001 par exchanged for $3.80 cash

DRUID LIFE INS CO (AL)
Voluntarily dissolved 05/04/1988
Details not available

DRUK CAP PARTNERS INC (BC)
Name changed to Falco Pacific Resource Group Inc. 09/25/2012
Falco Pacific Resource Group Inc. name changed to Falco Resources Ltd. 07/25/2014

DRUM FINL CORP (VA)
Merged into St. Regis Paper Co. 09/11/1981
Each share Common $1 par exchanged for (0.3455) share Common $5 par
St. Regis Paper Co. name changed to St. Regis Corp. 04/28/1983 which merged into Champion International Corp. 11/20/1984 which merged into International Paper Co. 06/20/2000

DRUMETCO INC (QC)
Declared bankrupt 01/10/1975
Stockholders' equity unknown

DRUMM CORP (UT)
Name changed to Horti-Tech Inc. 01/07/1986
(See Horti-Tech Inc.)

DRUMMER BOY INC (IA)
Ceased operations 00/00/1975
No stockholders' equity

DRUMMOND, MC CALL & CO., LTD. (CANADA)
Name changed to Drummond McCall Inc. 01/19/1979
Drummond McCall Inc. name changed to Marshall Drummond McCall Inc. 05/16/1984 which name changed to Marshall Steel Ltd. 03/09/1987 which name changed to Marshall-Barwick, Inc. 05/29/1996
(See Marshall-Barwick, Inc.)

DRUMMOND DIE & STAMPING LTD (QC)
Recapitalized as Drumetco Inc. 08/23/1972
Each share Common no par exchanged for (0.1) share Common no par
(See Drumetco Inc.)

DRUMMOND FINL CORP (WA)
Reincorporated 02/22/2002
State of incorporation changed from (DE) to (WA) 02/22/2002
Majority of shares acquired for $1.25 cash per share through purchase offer which expired 02/14/2003
Company terminated common stock registration and is now private

DRUMMOND MCCALL INC (CANADA)
Class A Conv. Common no par split (2) for (1) by issuance of (1) additional share 05/08/1979
Class B Conv. Common no par split (2) for (1) by issuance of (1) additional share 05/08/1979
Name changed to Marshall Drummond McCall Inc. 05/16/1984
Marshall Drummond McCall Inc. name changed to Marshall Steel Ltd. 03/09/1987 which name changed to Marshall-Barwick, Inc. 05/29/1996
(See Marshall-Barwick, Inc.)

DRUMMOND PEEL EQUITIES INC (UT)
Involuntarily dissolved 05/01/1988

DRUMMOND PETE LTD (AB)
Recapitalized as Excel Energy Inc. 06/02/1987
Each share Common no par exchanged for (0.1) share Common no par
Excel Energy Inc. merged into Ranchmen's Resources Ltd. 07/25/1995 which merged into Crestar Energy Inc. 10/11/1995 which was acquired by Gulf Canada Resources Ltd. 11/13/2000
(See Gulf Canada Resources Ltd.)

DRUMMOND STREET REALTY CORP.
Name changed to Hotel de La Salle, Inc. 00/00/1945
(See Hotel de La Salle, Inc.)

DRUMMOND WELDING & STL WKS LTD (QC)
Acquired by Industries Drummond Ltee. 07/22/1975
Each share Class A no par exchanged for $7 cash

DRURY'S VAN LINES, INC. (MI)
Name changed to Container Transport Systems, Inc. 02/27/1969
Container Transport Systems, Inc. name changed to M.T.P.R. Corp. 03/09/1977
(See M.T.P.R. Corp.)

DRUSILLA SEAFOOD RESTAURANTS INC (UT)
Name changed to Life Signs Group, Inc. 08/29/1991
(See Life Signs Group, Inc.)

DRX INC (DE)
Charter cancelled and declared void for failure to pay franchise taxes 03/01/1993

DRX INC (NV)
Name changed to Nussentials Holdings, Inc. 06/24/2005
Nussentials Holdings, Inc. recapitalized as Alternate Energy Holdings, Inc. 09/20/2006

DRY CLEANING DEPOT INC (UT)
Proclaimed dissolved for failure to file annual reports 08/01/1996

DRY CREEK EXPLORATION INC. (UT)
Recapitalized as Appalachian Oil & Gas Co., Inc. 06/18/1982
Each share Common $0.001 par exchanged for (2) shares Common $0.001 par
(See Appalachian Oil & Gas Co., Inc.)

DRY DAIRY INTL INC (UT)
Name changed to Dryden Industries, Inc. 10/01/1999
Dryden Industries, Inc. recapitalized as E Resources Inc. 03/31/2000 which name changed to Central Wireless Inc. 08/27/2002

DRY DOCK, EAST BROADWAY & BATTERY RAILROAD CO.
Reorganized as Dry Dock & Corlears Park Properties, Inc. 00/00/1932
Details not available

DRY DOCK & CORLEARS PARK PROPERTIES, INC. (NY)
Liquidation completed 00/00/1954
Details not available

DRY ICE HOLDING CORP.
Dissolved 00/00/1932
Details not available

DRY-MIX MATERIALS CO. (CA)
Bankruptcy proceedings closed 02/13/1973
No stockholders' equity

DRY-PACK CORP.
Dissolved 00/00/1946
Details not available

DRYCLEAN U S A INC (DE)
Merged into JGI Acquisition Corp. 07/01/1988
Each share Common 1¢ par exchanged for $12.40 cash

DRYCLEAN USA INC (DE)
Name changed to EnviroStar, Inc. 12/01/2009

DRYDEN INDS INC (UT)
Recapitalized as E Resources Inc. 03/31/2000
Each share Common $0.001 par exchanged for (0.05) share Common $0.001 par
E Resources Inc. name changed to Central Wireless Inc. 08/27/2002

DRYDEN RESOURCE CORP (BC)
Merged into Leicester Diamond Mines Ltd. 06/01/1993
Each share Common no par exchanged for (0.6451612) share Common no par
Leicester Diamond Mines Ltd. recapitalized as Target Exploration & Mining Corp. 04/30/2004 which merged into Crosshair Exploration & Mining Corp. 03/31/2009 which name changed to Crosshair Energy Corp. 11/02/2011 which recapitalized as Jet Metal Corp. (BC) 09/23/2013 which reorganized in Canada as Canada Jetlines Ltd. 03/07/2017

DRYER CO. OF AMERICA, INC. (PA)
Name changed to American Dryer Corp. 00/00/1957
American Dryer Corp. name changed to Utronics Corp. 03/28/1962 which was acquired by Defiance Industries, Inc. 07/10/1963 which merged into El-Tronics, Inc. 10/03/1969 which name changed to ELT, Inc. 01/04/1974 which name changed to Dutch Boy, Inc. 02/23/1977 which name changed to Artra Group Inc. 12/31/1980 which merged into Entrade Inc. 09/23/1999
(See Entrade Inc.)

DRYOMATIC CORP. OF AMERICA (MD)
Dissolved 00/00/1950
Details not available

DRYPERS CORP (DE)
Each share old Common $0.001 par exchanged for (0.25) share new Common $0.001 par 03/30/1994
Plan of reorganization under Chapter 11 Federal Bankruptcy Code effective 08/14/2001
No stockholders' equity

DRYWAVE TECHNOLOGIES INC (DE)
Recapitalized as Bionik Laboratories Corp. 02/13/2015
Each share Common $0.001 par exchanged for (0.83110527) share Common $0.001 par

DS BANCOR INC (DE)
Acquired by Webster Financial Corp. 01/31/1997
Each share Common $1 par exchanged for (1.14158) shares Common 1¢ par

DSC COMMUNICATIONS CORP (DE)
Common 1¢ par split (2) for (1) by issuance of (1) additional share 05/25/1994

Merged into Alcatel 09/04/1998
Each share Common 1¢ par exchanged for (0.815) Sponsored ADR for Ordinary
Alcatel name changed to Alcatel-Lucent 11/30/2006
(See Alcatel-Lucent)

DSC NORTECH INC (MN)
Each share old Common 5¢ par exchanged for (0.1) share new Common 5¢ par 09/14/1989
Name changed to Nortech Systems Inc. and new Common 5¢ par changed to 1¢ par 12/03/1990

DSET CORP (NJ)
Each share old Common no par exchanged for (0.25) share new Common no par 08/21/2001
Merged into NE Technologies, Inc. 12/30/2002
Each share new Common no par exchanged for $0.30 cash

DSG INTL PLC (UNITED KINGDOM)
Name changed to Dixons Retail PLC 09/21/2010

DSI CORP (TN)
Merged into Anacomp, Inc. 07/21/1982
Each share Common $0.16666666 par exchanged for $6.25 cash

DSI DATOTECH SYS INC (BC)
Company ceased operations 11/07/2002
Stockholders' equity unlikely

DSI DESIGNCARD SVCS INC (NY)
Dissolved by proclamation 09/30/1981

DSI DIRECT SALES INC (NV)
Each share old Common $0.001 par exchanged for (0.002) share new Common $0.001 par 07/02/2007
Each share new Common $0.001 par exchanged again for (0.000005) share new Common $0.001 par 12/23/2008
Charter revoked 06/30/2010

DSI INDS INC (DE)
Name changed to Norton Drilling Services, Inc. 10/07/1997
Norton Drilling Services, Inc. merged into UTI Energy Corp. 06/26/1999 which merged into Patterson-UTI Energy, Inc. 05/09/2001

DSI SYS INC (DE)
Name changed to Conolog Corp. 06/10/1975

DSI TOYS INC (TX)
Merged into DSI Acquisition Inc. 08/12/2003
Each share Common 1¢ par exchanged for $0.47 cash

DSL NET INC (DE)
Common $0.0005 par changed to $0.0001 par 01/30/2007
Merged into MegaPath Inc. 03/30/2007
Each share Common $0.0001 par exchanged for $0.001 cash

DSM N V (NETHERLANDS)
Sponsored ADR's for Ordinary split (3) for (1) by issuance of (2) additional ADR's payable 09/27/1999 to holders of record 09/20/1999
Sponsored ADR's for Ordinary split (2) for (1) by issuance of (1) additional ADR payable 09/08/2005 to holders of record 09/02/2005 Ex date - 09/09/2005
Name changed to Royal DSM N.V. 03/03/2006

DSP COMMUNICATIONS INC (DE)
Common $0.001 par split (2) for (1) by issuance of (1) additional share payable 03/25/1996 to holders of record 03/05/1996
Common $0.001 par split (2) for (1) by issuance of (1) additional share payable 12/02/1996 to holders of record 11/13/1996
Merged into Intel Corp. 11/19/1999
Each share Common $0.001 par exchanged for $36 cash

DSP TECHNOLOGY INC (CA)
Merged into MTS Systems Corp. 05/28/1999
Each share Common no par exchanged for (0.8005) share Common $25 par

DSSI CORP (PA)
Name changed to Collegiate Pacific Inc. (PA) 02/20/1998
Collegiate Pacific Inc. (PA) reincorporated in Delaware 07/21/1999 which name changed to Sport Supply Group, Inc. (New) 07/02/2007
(See Sport Supply Group, Inc. (New))

DST SYS INC (DE)
Common 1¢ par split (2) for (1) by issuance of (1) additional share payable 10/19/2000 to holders of record 10/06/2000 Ex date - 10/20/2000
Common 1¢ par split (2) for (1) by issuance of (1) additional share payable 06/08/2017 to holders of record 05/26/2017 Ex date - 06/09/2017
Acquired by SS&C Technologies Holdings, Inc. 04/16/2018
Each share Common 1¢ par exchanged for $84 cash

DST SYS INC (MO)
Common 1¢ par split (2) for (1) by issuance of (1) additional share 09/15/1987
Merged into DST Acquisition Corp. 08/27/1990
Each share Common 1¢ par exchanged for $15.85 cash

DSTAGE COM INC (DE)
Name changed to Camelot Entertainment Group, Inc. 05/12/2004

DT ASIA INVESTMENTS LTD (BRITISH VIRGIN ISLANDS)
Units separated 07/13/2016
Rights portion of Units received (0.1) share Ordinary no par
Name changed to China Lending Corp. 07/13/2016

DT ENERGY LTD (AB)
Merged into Delphi Energy Corp. 06/19/2003
Each share Common no par exchanged for (0.51) share Common no par

DT INDS INC (DE)
Plan of reorganization under Chapter 11 Federal Bankruptcy Code effective 12/09/2005
No stockholders' equity

DTA HLDG AKTIENGESELLSCHAFT (GERMANY)
ADR agreement terminated 02/20/2004
Each Sponsored ADR for Ordinary exchanged for $0.31149 cash

DTC DATA TECHNOLOGY CORP (DE)
Merged into Photonics Corp. (CA) 03/13/2000
Each share Common $0.001 par exchanged for (0.147853) share Common $0.001 par
Photonics Corp. (CA) reincorporated in Nevada as Small Cap Strategies, Inc. 10/02/2006 which recapitalized as Bay Street Capital, Inc. 08/31/2010 which name changed to Los Angeles Syndicate of Technology, Inc. 10/14/2010 which name changed to Invent Ventures, Inc. 09/19/2012

DTE ENERGY CO (MI)
Each 8.75% Equity Security Unit received (0.5343) share Common no par 08/16/2005
(Additional Information in Active)

PJSC DTEK DNIPROENERGO (UKRAINE)
ADR agreement terminated 11/24/2017
Each Sponsored ADR for Ordinary exchanged for (0.25) share Ordinary
Note: Unexchanged ADR's will be sold and the proceeds, if any, held for claim after 11/29/2018

DTF TAX-FREE INCOME INC (MD)
Remarketed Preferred called for redemption at $50,000 on 09/20/2013
(Additional Information in Active)

DTG MULTIMEDIA INC (FL)
Name changed 06/04/2004
Name changed from DTG Industries, Inc. to DTG Multimedia, Inc. 06/04/2004
Reorganized under the laws of Nevada as Amazing Technologies Corp. 12/23/2004
Each share Common no par exchanged for (0.001) share Common $0.001 par
Amazing Technologies Corp. name changed to Mvive, Inc. 08/24/2007
(See Mvive Inc.)

DTI DENTAL TECHNOLOGIES INC (BC)
Acquired by Healthpoint Capital, LLC 09/26/2006
Each share Common no par exchanged for $1.60 cash

DTI DOREX LTD. (NV)
Name changed to Computerized Thermal Imaging Inc. 11/00/1989
(See Computerized Thermal Imaging Inc.)

DTI INC (DE)
Recapitalized as Rockbands, Inc. 05/23/2008
Each share Common 1¢ par exchanged for (0.001) share Common $0.0001 par
Note: No holder received fewer than (100) shares
Rockbands, Inc. recapitalized as American Community Development Group, Inc. 02/05/2010 which name changed to Wialan Technologies, Inc. 01/22/2014

DTI MED CORP (UT)
Proclaimed dissolved for failure to pay taxes 01/01/1998

DTIB LIQUIDATING CO. (DE)
Liquidation completed
Each share Common $1 par exchanged for initial distribution of $7 cash 10/29/1986
Each share Common $1 par received second distribution of $0.50 cash 12/18/1986
Each share Common $1 par received third distribution of $0.20 cash 12/31/1986
Each share Common $1 par received fourth distribution of $0.35 cash 06/19/1987
Each share Common $1 par received fifth distribution of $0.75 cash 11/17/1988
Each share Common $1 par received sixth and final distribution of $1.75 cash 11/01/1989

DTLL INC (MN)
Name changed to Solstice Resorts Inc. 09/07/2007
(See Solstice Resorts Inc.)

DTM CORP (TX)
Merged into 3D Systems Corp. 08/24/2001
Each share Common $0.0002 par exchanged for $5.80 cash

DTM INFORMATION TECHNOLOGY GROUP INC (CANADA)
Name changed to Nexxlink Technologies Inc. 01/10/2001
(See Nexxlink Technologies Inc.)

DTOMI INC (NV)
Each share old Common no par exchanged for (0.05) share new Common no par 04/07/2003
Each share new Common no par exchanged again for (0.0025) share new Common no par 10/12/2005
Name changed to Vocalscape Networks, Inc. 11/09/2005
Vocalscape Networks, Inc. recapitalized as Kaleidoscope Venture Capital Inc. 07/14/2008

DTS CAP CORP (AB)
Recapitalized as Petroleum Capital Energy Inc. 05/28/1990
Each share Common no par exchanged for (0.2) share Common no par
(See Petroleum Capital Energy Inc.)

DTS INC (DE)
Acquired by Tessera Technologies, Inc. 12/01/2016
Each share Common $0.0001 par exchanged for $42.50 cash

DTVN HLDGS INC (DE)
Plan of reorganization under Chapter 11 Federal Bankruptcy Code effective 06/13/2003
Stockholders may receive a future distribution
Note: Certificates were not required to be surrendered and are without value

DU MONT BROADCASTING CORP. (DE)
Name changed to Metropolitan Broadcasting Corp. 05/13/1958
Metropolitan Broadcasting Corp. name changed to Metromedia, Inc. 03/29/1961
(See Metromedia, Inc.)

DU MONT (ALLEN B.) LABORATORIES, INC. (DE)
Each share Class A Common $1 par or Class B Common $1 par exchanged for (10) shares Class A Common 10¢ par or Class B Common 10¢ par 00/00/1943
Class A Common 10¢ par or Class B Common 10¢ par reclassified as Common $1 par 10/17/1955
Merged into Fairchild Camera & Instrument Corp. 07/05/1960
Each share 5% Preferred $20 par exchanged for (0.17543859) share Common $1 par
Each share Common $1 par exchanged for (0.06666666) share Common $1 par (91.5% in Stock Certificates and 8.5% in Interim Certificates)
(See Fairchild Camera & Instrument Corp.)

DU PONT CDA INC (CANADA)
Class A Common Ser. 1 no par split (2) for (1) by issuance of (1) additional share 05/23/1984
Class A Common Ser. 1 no par split (2) for (1) by issuance of (1) additional share 05/20/1987
Name changed to Dupont Canada Inc. 05/27/1993
(See Dupont Canada Inc.)

DU PONT CO. OF CANADA (1956) LTD. (CANADA)
Name changed to Du Pont of Canada Ltd. 12/31/1958
Du Pont of Canada Ltd. name changed to Du Pont of Canada Ltd. - Du Pont du Canada Ltee. 04/28/1966 which name changed to Du Pont Canada Inc. 07/03/1979 which name changed to Dupont Canada Inc. 05/27/1993
(See Dupont Canada Inc.)

DU PONT E I DE NEMOURS & CO (DE)
Each share Common $100 par exchanged for (2) shares Common no par 10/28/1926
Each share Common no par exchanged for (3.5) shares Common $20 par 01/21/1929
Each share Common $20 par exchanged for (4) shares Common $5 par 06/15/1949
Common $5 par changed to $1.66666666 par and (2) additional shares issued 06/28/1979
Common $1.66666666 par changed to 60¢ par and (2) additional shares issued 01/19/1990
Common 60¢ par changed to 30¢ par and (1) additional share issued payable 06/12/1997 to holders of record 05/15/1997 Ex date - 06/13/1997
Each share Common 30¢ par received distribution of (0.2) share Chemours Co. Common 1¢ par payable 07/01/2015 to holders of record 06/23/2015 Ex date - 07/01/2015
Merged into DowDuPont Inc. 09/01/2017
Each share Common 30¢ par exchanged for (1.282) shares Common 1¢ par
(Additional Information in Active)

DU PONT ENERGY CTL CORP (NV)
Charter revoked for failure to file reports and pay fees 01/01/1986

DU PONT OF CANADA LTD. (CANADA)
Name changed to Du Pont of Canada Ltd.- Du Pont du Canada Ltee. 04/28/1966
Du Pont of Canada Ltd. - Du Pont du Canada Ltee. name changed to Du Pont Canada Inc. 07/03/1979 which name changed to Dupont Canada Inc. 05/27/1993
(See Dupont Canada Inc.)

DU PONT OF CANADA LTD.-DU PONT DU CANADA LTEE. (CANADA)
Name changed to Du Pont Canada Inc. and 7-1/2% Preferred $50 par reclassified as Class A Preferred no par and Common no par reclassified as Class A Common Ser. 1 no par 07/03/1979
Du Pont Canada Inc. name changed to Dupont Canada Inc. 05/27/1993
(See Dupont Canada Inc.)

DU PONT OF CANADA SECURITIES LTD. (CANADA)
Name changed to Du Pont Co. of Canada (1956) Ltd. 12/31/1956
Du Pont Co. of Canada (1956) Ltd. name changed to Du Pont of Canada Ltd. 12/31/1958 which name changed to Du Pont of Canada Ltd. - Du Pont du Canada Ltee. 04/28/1966 which name changed to Du Pont Canada Inc. 07/03/1979 which name changed to Dupont Canada Inc. 05/27/1993
(See Dupont Canada Inc.)

DU-RITE SALES CO., INC. (MD)
Charter revoked for failure to file reports and pay fees 11/9/65

DU VAL'S CONSENSUS, INC. (NY)
Charter revoked for failure to file reports and pay fees 12/15/65

DU WELL RES LTD (BC)
Struck off register and declared dissolved for failure to file returns 11/23/90

DUAL DRILLING CO (DE)
Merged into ENSCO International Inc. (DE) 06/12/1996
Each share Common 1¢ par exchanged for (0.625) share Common 10¢ par

ENSCO International Inc. (DE) reorganized in England & Wales as Ensco International PLC 12/23/2009 which name changed to Ensco PLC 03/31/2010

DUAL EXPL INC (AB)
Each share Common no par received distribution of (0.5) share DualEx Energy International Inc. Common no par payable 05/31/2006 to holders of record 05/31/2006 Ex date - 05/26/2006
Acquired by Cyries Energy Inc. 12/13/2006
Each share Common no par exchanged for (0.167) share Common no par
Note: Non-qualified holders will receive the cash proceeds from the sale of shares
Cyries Energy Inc. merged into Iteration Energy Ltd. 03/07/2008 which merged into Chinook Energy Inc. (Old) 07/05/2010
(See Chinook Energy Inc. (Old))

DUAL LITE INC (CT)
Merged into Insilco Corp. 7/2/87
Each share Common no par exchanged for $26 cash

DUAL RES LTD (BC)
Name changed to Serengeti Diamonds Ltd. 1/7/94
Serengeti Diamonds Ltd. name changed to Serengeti Minerals Ltd. 4/26/99 which recapitalized as Serengeti Resources Inc. 3/22/2001

DUALEX ENERGY INTL INC (AB)
Recapitalized as Return Energy Inc. 12/20/2016
Each share Common no par exchanged for (0.1) share Common no par

DUALSTAR TECHNOLOGIES CORP (DE)
Ceased operations 02/11/2005
Stockholders' equity unlikely

DUANE READE INC (DE)
Merged into Duane Reade Acquisition Corp. 07/30/2004
Each share Common 1¢ par exchanged for $16.50 cash

DUANE STR CORP (DE)
Name changed to CUR Media, Inc. 02/11/2014

DUBAR EXPLORATION LTD. (MB)
Charter cancelled in November 1960
No stockholders' equity

DUBARRY INC (UT)
Involuntarily dissolved 11/01/1991

DUBCO INC (CO)
Name changed to B.C.S., Inc. 7/21/89
B.C.S. Inc. name changed to Triple Co. 9/30/90

DUBENSKI GOLD MINES LTD (CANADA)
Struck off register and declared dissolved for failure to file returns 12/14/2005

DUBILIER CONDENSER CORP.
Assets acquired by Cornell-Dubilier Electric Corp. and dissolved in 1941

DUBL-CHEK CORP. (DE)
No longer in existence having become inoperative and void for non-payment of taxes 4/1/61

DUBLI INC (NV)
Name changed to Ominto, Inc. 07/01/2015

DUBLIN ENGR CO (DE)
Common 10¢ par changed to 2¢ par and (1) additional share issued 03/08/1982
Charter forfeited for failure to maintain a registered agent 02/07/1984

DUBLIN OSAKA GROUP INC (NV)
Charter revoked for failure to file reports and pay fees 8/1/90

DUBOIS CHEMICALS, INC. (DE)
Completely liquidated 05/06/1964
Each share Common $1 par exchanged for (0.51) share Grace (W.R.) & Co. (CT) Common $1 par
Grace (W.R.) & Co. (CT) reincorporated in New York 05/19/1988
(See Grace (W.R.) & Co.)

DUBOIS COUNTY BANK (JASPER, IN)
Under plan of reorganization each share Capital Stock $10 par automatically became (1) share DCB Corp. Common no par 6/1/82
DCB Corp. acquired by Old National Bancorp 4/1/93

DUBOIS DEPOSIT NATIONAL BANK (DUBOIS, PA)
Each share Capital Stock $50 par exchanged for (2) shares Capital Stock $25 par 01/28/1958
Capital Stock $25 par changed to $5 par and (4) additional shares issued 10/20/1972
Stock Dividends - 50% 11/10/1950; 33.33333333% 11/10/1960; 25% 12/15/1962
Name changed to Deposit National Bank (DuBois, PA) 01/01/1973
Deposit National Bank (DuBois, PA) name changed to Deposit Bank (DuBois, PA) 01/02/1980 which merged into First Commonwealth Financial Corp. 03/19/1984

DUBOW CHEM CORP (NY)
Class A Capital Stock 1¢ par reclassified as Common 1¢ par 02/05/1969
Charter cancelled and proclaimed dissolved for failure to pay taxes and file reports 12/20/1977

DUBROW ELECTRONIC INDUSTRIES, INC. (NJ)
Merged into Teledyne, Inc. 04/09/1964
Each share Common 10¢ par exchanged for (0.06666666) share Common $1 par
Teledyne, Inc. merged into Allegheny Teledyne Inc. 08/15/1996 which name changed to Allegheny Technologies Inc. 11/29/1999

DUBUISSON GOLDFIELDS LTD (QC)
Recapitalized as Dubuisson Explorations Ltd. 1/6/74
Each share Capital Stock $1 par exchanged for (0.05) share Capital Stock no par

DUBUQUE BK & TR CO (DUBUQUE, IA)
90% owned by Heartland Bancorp as of 1985
(See Heartland Bancorp)

DUCATI MTR HLDGS SPA (ITALY)
Acquired by Performance Motorcycles S.p.A. 12/19/2008
Each Sponsored ADR for Ordinary exchanged for $23.91285 cash

DUCHESNE RED LAKE MINES LTD. (ON)
Merged into Goldquest Exploration Inc. 08/09/1982
Each share Capital Stock $1 par exchanged for (0.09460737) share Common no par
Goldquest Exploration Inc. merged into Goldcorp Inc. (New) 03/31/1994

DUCK BOOK COMMUNICATIONS LTD (BC)
Struck off register and declared dissolved for failure to file returns 03/22/1991

DUCK HEAD APPAREL CO INC (GA)
Merged into Tropical Sportswear International Corp. 08/09/2001
Each share Common 1¢ par exchanged for $4.75 cash

DUCK HILL BK (DUCK HILL, MS)
Merged into Union Planters Corp. 7/31/98
Each share Common exchanged for (10.6008) shares Common $5 par
Union Planters Corp. merged into Regions Financial Corp. (New) 7/1/2004

DUCK LACE MINING CO. LTD. (ON)
Charter cancelled for failure to file reports and pay taxes in 1956

DUCKBACK INDS INC (CO)
Name changed to Sinecure Financial Corp. 08/27/1991
(See Sinecure Financial Corp.)

DUCKTOWN CHEMICAL & IRON CO.
Liquidated in 1936

DUCKWALL ALCO STORES INC (KS)
Common $2.50 par split (5) for (4) by issuance of (0.25) additional share 10/15/1979
Common $2.50 par split (3) for (2) by issuance of (0.5) additional share 04/27/1984
Stock Dividends - 25% 07/06/1978; 25% 10/17/1980; 10% 10/16/1981
Acquired by a group of investors 09/30/1985
Each share Common $2.50 par exchanged for $17.75 cash

DUCKWALL-ALTO STORES INC (KS)
Name changed to ALCO Stores, Inc. 07/06/2012

DUCKWALL STORES, INC. (KS)
Name changed to Duckwall-Alco Stores Inc. 6/7/78
(See Duckwall-Alco Stores Inc.)

DUCO BANCSHARES INC (DE)
Merged into Amerimark Financial 3/6/97
Each share Common $10 par exchanged for $89.6356 cash

DUCOMMUN INC (DE)
Reincorporated under the laws of Delaware 12/31/70

DUCOMMUN METALS & SUPPLY CO. (CA)
Stock Dividend - 50% 2/19/59
Name changed to Ducommun, Inc. (Calif.) 7/1/62
Ducommun, Inc. (Calif.) reincorporated under the laws of Delaware 12/31/70

DUCORE MINES, LTD. (ON)
Charter revoked for failure to file reports and pay taxes in 1955

DUCROS MINES LTD (QC)
Merged into Brominco Inc. 06/01/1976
Each share Capital Stock $1 par exchanged for (0.02) share Capital Stock no par
Brominco Inc. merged into Aur Resources Inc. 05/16/1985 which was acquired by Teck Cominco Ltd. 09/28/2007 which name changed to Teck Resources Ltd. 04/27/2009

DUCT UTIL CONSTR & TECHNOLOGIES INC (CO)
Involuntarily dissolved 12/06/2007

DUDDY S INC (DE)
Charter forfeited for failure to maintain a registered agent 1/28/80

DUDEK MOTORS INC. (WA)
Charter revoked for failure to pay fees 7/1/57

DUDLEY LOCK CORP (IL)
$1.75 Preferred $20 par called for redemption on 08/15/1966
Completely liquidated
Each share Common $1 par exchanged for first and final distribution of $3.564 cash 08/29/1968

DUDLEY SPORTS INC (DE)
Merged into Athlone Industries, Inc. 10/24/1969

Each share Common 10¢ par exchanged for (0.33333333) share Common 10¢ par
Athlone Industries, Inc. merged into Allegheny Ludlum Corp. 11/10/1993 which merged into Allegheny Teledyne Inc. 08/15/1996 which name changed to Allegheny Technologies Inc. 11/29/1999

DUDLO MANUFACTURING CO.
Merged into General Cable Corp. 00/00/1927
Details not available

DUECRITT SILVER-COBALT MINES LTD.
Name changed to Niki Silver-Cobalt Ltd. in 1942
Niki Silver-Cobalt Ltd. was acquired by Ni-Ag-Co. Mines Ltd. in 1946
(See Ni-Ag-Co. Mines Ltd.)

DUELING GROUNDS ENTMT CORP (DE)
Reincorporated 12/20/1995
Reincorporated from Dueling Grounds Thoroughbred Racing Corp. (YT) to under the laws of Delaware as Dueling Grounds Entertainment Corp. 12/20/1995
Charter cancelled and declared inoperative and void for non-payment of taxes 03/01/1998

DUESENBERG CORP (NV)
Each share old Capital Stock 10¢ par exchanged for (0.25) share new Capital Stock 10¢ par 3/29/72
Charter revoked for failure to file reports and pay fees 3/3/75

DUFF & PHELPS CORP (DE)
Issue Information - 8,300,000 shares CL A COM offered at $16 per share on 09/28/2007
Acquired by Dakota Holding Corp. 04/23/2013
Each share Class A Common 1¢ par exchanged for $15.55 cash

DUFF & PHELPS CORP (DE)
Common 1¢ par split (3) for (2) by issuance of (0.5) additional share 03/10/1993
Name changed to Phoenix Duff & Phelps Corp. 11/01/1995
Phoenix Duff & Phelps Corp. name changed to Phoenix Investment Partners, Ltd. 05/11/1998
(See Phoenix Investment Partners, Ltd.)

DUFF & PHELPS CR RATING CO (IL)
Merged into Fimalac S.A. 06/01/2000
Each share Common no par exchanged for $100 cash

DUFF & PHELPS UTIL & CORPORATE BD TR INC (MD)
Auction Market Preferred Ser. T7 1¢ par called for redemption at $25,000 on 03/25/2009
Auction Market Preferred Ser. TH7 1¢ par called for redemption at $25,000 on 09/20/2013
(Additional Information in Active)

DUFF & PHELPS UTILS INCOME INC (MD)
Name changed 11/01/1990
Name changed from Duff & Phelps Selected Utilities Inc. to Duff & Phelps Utilities Income Inc. 11/01/1990
Name changed to DNP Select Income Fund Inc. 04/23/2002

DUFF & PHELPS UTILS TAX FREE INCOME INC (MD)
Name changed to DTF Tax-Free Income Inc. 06/03/2002

DUFF-NORTON CO. (NC)
Reincorporated 01/01/1963
State of incorporation changed from (PA) to (NC) 01/01/1963
Capital Stock no par split (3) for (1) by issuance of (2) additional shares 12/02/1963
Capital Stock no par split (2) for (1) by issuance of (1) additional share 08/06/1965
Acquired by American Sugar Co. (DE) 04/30/1968
Each share Capital Stock no par exchanged for (1) share $2.65 Conv. Preferred Ser. A no par
American Sugar Co. (DE) name changed to Amstar Corp. 10/29/1970
(See Amstar Corp.)

DUFF-NORTON MANUFACTURING CO. (PA)
Name changed to Duff-Norton Co. (PA) 03/01/1955
Duff-Norton Co. (PA) reincorporated in North Carolina 01/01/1963 which was acquired by American Sugar Co. (DE) 04/30/1968 which name changed to Amstar Corp. 10/29/1970
(See Amstar Corp.)

DUFFY MOTT INC (NY)
Each share Common $100 par exchanged for (100) shares Common $1 par 09/30/1958
Merged into American Tobacco Co. 04/08/1969
Each share Common $1 par exchanged for $40 cash

DUFO INC (LA)
Charter revoked for failure to file annual reports 10/31/1991

DUFORT CAP INC (CANADA)
Name changed to Odesia Group Inc. 12/30/2005

DUFRESNOY INDL MINERALS INC (QC)
Name changed 11/12/1993
Each share old Common no par exchanged for (0.2) share new Common no par 07/00/1993
Name changed from Dufresnoy Societe d'Exploration Miniere Inc. to Dufresnoy Industrial Minerals Inc. 11/12/1993
Name changed to Boreal Exploration Inc. 01/15/1997
Boreal Exploration Inc. recapitalized as TGW Corp. (QC) 01/08/2001 which reincorporated in Canada as GlobeStar Mining Corp. 12/18/2002
(See GlobeStar Mining Corp.)

DUFRESNOY MINES LTD (ON)
Charter cancelled for failure to pay taxes and file returns in 00/00/1969

DUFT BIOTECH CAP LTD (BC)
Name changed to ALDA Pharmaceuticals Corp. 11/27/2003
ALDA Pharmaceuticals Corp. name changed to Nuva Pharmaceuticals Inc. 07/26/2013 which name changed to Vanc Pharmaceuticals Inc. 08/07/2014

DUGAS ENGINEERING CORP.
Dissolved 00/00/1948
Details not available

DUGGAN HUGHES OIL SYNDICATE
Liquidated 00/00/1941
Details not available

DUIKER EXPL LTD (SOUTH AFRICA)
ADR agreement terminated 02/19/1996
Each ADR for Ordinary exchanged for $24.651 cash

DUJOUR PRODS INC (NV)
Each share old Common $0.001 par exchanged for (6) shares new Common $0.001 par 02/01/2007
Name changed to Endeavor Energy Corp. 07/20/2007
Endeavor Energy Corp. name changed to Holloman Energy Corp. 10/10/2007

DUKANE PRESS INC (FL)
Name changed to Hollywood Securities Corp. 05/11/1970
(See Hollywood Securities Corp.)

DUKE & CO INC (PA)
Common $5 par split (2) for (1) by issuance of (1) additional share 07/07/1986
Liquidation completed
Each share Common $5 par received initial distribution of $0.57 cash 05/13/1991
Each share Common $5 par received second distribution of $0.16 cash 12/26/1991
Each share Common $5 par received third distribution of $0.19 cash 12/28/1992
Each share Common $5 par exchanged for fourth and final distribution of $0.40 cash 12/28/1993

DUKE CAP CORP (BC)
Name changed to CCC Internet Solutions Inc. 10/31/2000

DUKE CAP FING TR I (DE)
Guaranteed Trust Originated Preferred Securities called for redemption at $25 on 06/30/2003

DUKE CAP FING TR II (DE)
7.375% Quarterly Income Preferred Securities called for redemption at $25 on 12/29/2003

DUKE CAP FING TR III (DE)
8.375% Trust Preferred Securities called for redemption at $25 on 08/31/2004

DUKE DIVERSIFIED INDS INC (DE)
Charter cancelled and declared inoperative and void for non-payment of taxes 03/01/1976

DUKE ENERGY CDA EXCHANGECO (CANADA)
Each Exchangeable Share no par received distribution of (0.5) Exchangeable Share for Spectra Energy Corp. no par payable 01/02/2007 to holders of record 12/18/2006 Ex date - 12/14/2006
Name changed to Spectra Energy Canada Exchangeco Inc. 01/25/2007
(See Spectra Energy Canada Exchangeco Inc.)

DUKE ENERGY CAP TR I (DE)
7.2% Trust Preferred Securities called for redemption at $25 on 03/26/2004

DUKE ENERGY CORP (NC)
Name changed 06/18/1997
5.36% Preferred Ser. B $100 par called for redemption 09/16/1964
Common no par split (2) for (1) by issuance of (1) additional share 10/09/1964
10.76% Preferred A 1975 Ser. $25 par called for redemption 06/16/1986
11% Preferred Ser. O $100 par called for redemption 06/16/1986
15.4% Preferred A 1982 Ser. $25 par called for redemption 03/16/1987
Common no par split (2) for (1) by issuance of (1) additional share 09/28/1990
6.75% Conv. Preference Ser. AA $100 par called for redemption 04/06/1992
8.84% Preferred Ser. N $100 par called for redemption 06/16/1992
8.2% Preferred Ser. J $100 par called for redemption 09/16/1992
8.375% Preferred Ser. L $100 par called for redemption 09/16/1992
8.7% Preferred Ser. F $100 par called for redemption 09/16/1992
8.84% Preferred Ser. M $100 par called for redemption 09/16/1992
7.35% Preferred Ser. I $100 par called for redemption 12/16/1992
8.28% Preferred Ser. K $100 par called for redemption 03/16/1993
7.8% Preferred Ser. H $100 par called for redemption 12/16/1993
7.875% Preferred Ser. P $100 par called for redemption 06/16/1993
8.2% Preferred Ser. G $100 par called for redemption 06/16/1993
Adjustable Rate Preferred Ser. A $100 par called for redemption 09/18/1995
7.12% Preferred Ser. Q $100 par called for redemption 09/18/1995
Under plan of merger name changed to from Duke Power Co. to Duke Energy Corp. 06/18/1997
5.72% Preferred Ser. D $100 par called for redemption at $101 on 12/16/1997
6.72% Preferred Ser. E $100 par called for redemption at $102 on 12/16/1997
7.5% Preferred Ser. R $100 par called for redemption at $105 on 12/16/1997
7.72% Preferred 1992 Ser. A $25 par called for redemption on 12/16/1997
5.95% Preferred 1992 Ser. B $25 par called for redemption at $25 on 09/16/1999
6.1% Preferred 1992 Ser. C $25 par called for redemption at $25 on 09/18/2000
6.2% Preferred Ser. T $100 par called for redemption at $100 on 12/18/2000
Common no par split (2) for (1) by issuance of (1) additional share payable 01/26/2001 to holders of record 01/03/2001 Ex date - 01/29/2001
6.2% Preferred Stock A 1992 Ser. D $25 par called for redemption 09/17/2001
6.3% Preferred Ser. U $100 par called redemption at $100 on 12/17/2001
Auction Market Preferred Ser. Unit 1000 called for redemption at $100 on 09/16/2002
Variable Rate Auction Market Preferred Ser A no par called for redemption at $100,000 on 09/16/2002
6.4% Preferred Ser. V $100 par called for redemption at $100 on 12/16/2002
Each 8.25% Corporate Unit received (0.6414) share Common no par 05/18/2004
Each 8% Corporate Unit received (0.6231) share Common no par 11/16/2004
6.75% Preferred Ser. X $100 par called for redemption at $103.66 on 12/16/2004
4.5% Preferred Ser. C $100 par called for redemption at $101 on 12/16/2005
6.375% 1993 Ser. Preferred Ser. A $25 par called for redemption at $25.64 on 12/16/2005
7% Preferred Ser. W $100 par called for redemption at $102.80 on 12/16/2005
7.04% Preferred Ser. Y $100 par called for redemption at $102.82 on 12/16/2005
7.85% Preferred Ser. S $100 par called for redemption at $102.75 on 12/16/2005
Merged into Duke Energy Corp. (DE) 04/03/2006
Each share Common no par exchanged for (1) share Common $0.001 par

DUKE ENERGY INCOME FD (AB)
Name changed to Spectra Energy Income Fund 01/02/2007

DUKE ENTERPRISES LTD. (BC)
Name changed to Bay Street Systems Ltd. 08/21/1992
Bay Street Systems Ltd. recapitalized as Pacific Bay Street Systems, Inc. 08/17/1993 which name changed to Pacific Bay Minerals Ltd. (Old) 07/17/1995 which recapitalized as Consolidated Pacific Bay Minerals Ltd. 08/29/2000 which name

changed to Pacific Bay Minerals Ltd. (New) 07/22/2008

DUKE FDG I LTD (CAYMAN ISLANDS)
144A Preference Shares called for redemption 11/10/2006

DUKE FDG III LTD (CAYMAN ISLANDS)
144A Preference Shares called for redemption 06/05/2006

DUKE MINERALS LTD (BC)
Name changed to Duke Enterprises Ltd. 07/06/1989
Duke Enterprises Ltd. name changed to Bay Street Systems Ltd. 08/21/1992 which recapitalized as Pacific Bay Street Systems, Inc. 08/17/1993 which name changed to Pacific Bay Minerals Ltd. (Old) 07/17/1995 which recapitalized as Consolidated Pacific Bay Minerals Ltd. 08/29/2000 which name changed to Pacific Bay Minerals Ltd. (New) 07/22/2008

DUKE MNG CO INC (DE)
Reorganized as KaChing KaChing, Inc. 06/07/2010
Each share Common $0.0001 par exchanged for (8.4627) shares Common $0.0001 par
KaChing KaChing, Inc. name changed to KS International Holdings Corp. 12/02/2013

DUKE MNG LTD (BC)
Merged into Rievaulx Holdings Ltd. 11/30/1981
Each share Capital Stock 50¢ par exchanged for $0.50 cash

DUKE OF ENERGY (UT)
Name changed to TU International, Inc. 02/03/1983
(See TU International, Inc.)

DUKE POWER CO. (NJ)
Common $100 par changed to no par 00/00/1942
Common no par split (2) for (1) by issuance of (1) additional share 02/08/1956
Stock Dividends - 200% 12/02/1952; 15% 01/29/1959
7% Preferred Ser. A $100 par called for redemption 04/01/1964
Reincorporated under the laws of North Carolina 06/15/1964
Duke Power Co. (NC) name changed to Duke Energy Corp. (NC) 06/18/1997 which merged into Duke Energy Corp. (DE) 04/03/2006

DUKE-PRICE POWER CO. (QC)
Name changed to Saguenay Power Co., Ltd. 00/00/1935
(See Saguenay Power Co., Ltd.)

DUKE RLTY CORP (IN)
Reincorporated 04/30/1992
Name changed 07/02/1999
Name changed 07/01/2001
Each Capital Share 1¢ par exchanged for (0.14285714) share Common 1¢ par 08/16/1988
Each Income Share 1¢ par exchanged for (1) share Common 1¢ par 08/16/1988
State of incorporation changed from (DE) to (IN) 04/30/1992
Each share old Common 1¢ par exchanged for (0.23809523) share new Common 1¢ par 10/04/1993
New Common 1¢ par split (2) for (1) by issuance of (1) additional share payable 08/25/1997 to holders of record 08/18/1997 Ex date - 08/26/1997
Under plan of merger name changed from Duke Realty Investments, Inc. to Duke-Weeks Realty Corp. 07/02/1999
Name changed from Duke-Weeks Realty Corp. to Duke Realty Corp. 07/01/2001
9.1% Depositary Preferred Ser. A called for redemption at $25 on 08/31/2001
8% Preference Ser. F called for redemption at $25 plus $0.038889 accrued dividends on 10/10/2002
8.25% Depositary Preferred Ser. E called for redemption at $25 plus $0.11458 accrued dividends on 01/20/2004
7.375% Depositary Preferred Ser. D called for redemption at $25 plus $0.38924 accrued dividends on 03/16/2004
8.45% Depositary Preferred Ser. I called for redemption at $25 plus $0.18191 accrued dividends on 02/01/2006
7.99% Depositary Preferred Ser. B called for redemption at $50 plus $0.0111 accrued dividends on 10/01/2007
7.25% Depositary Preferred Ser. N called for redemption at $25 plus $0.090625 accrued dividends on 07/18/2011
6.95% Depositary Preferred Ser. M called for redemption at $25 plus $0.313715 accrued dividends on 03/05/2012
8.375% Depositary Preferred Ser. O called for redemption at $25 plus $0.308247 accrued dividends on 02/22/2013
6.625% Depositary Preferred Ser. J called for redemption at $25 plus $0.299045 accrued dividends on 08/04/2014
6.6% Depositary Preferred Ser. L called for redemption at $25 plus $0.06875 accrued dividends on 12/15/2014
6.5% Depositary Preferred Ser. K called for redemption at $25 plus $0.108333 accrued dividends on 12/24/2014
(Additional Information in Active)

DUKEL GOLD MINES, LTD. (ON)
Charter cancelled and company declared dissolved for default in filing returns 07/08/1965

DUKELAND FOODS, INC. (MD)
Charter annulled for failure to file annual reports 01/28/1975

DUKELAND PACKING CO., INC. (MD)
Name changed to Dukeland Foods, Inc. 02/11/1971
(See Dukeland Foods, Inc.)

DUKESHIRE VENTURES INC (NV)
Name changed to InterActive Leisure Systems, Inc. 06/06/2013

DUKOR MODULAR SYS INC (DE)
Charter cancelled and declared inoperative and void for non-payment of taxes 04/15/1973

DULAMA GOLD MINES LTD. (ON)
Recapitalized as Ladulama Gold Mines Ltd. on a (1) for (2) basis 00/00/1950
Ladulama Gold Mines Ltd. recapitalized as Nudulama Mines Ltd. 00/00/1953 which recapitalized as Anglo Dominion Gold Exploration Ltd. 03/06/1979 which merged into QSR Ltd. 09/07/1993 which name changed to Coniagas Resources Ltd. 06/25/1999 which name changed to Lithium One Inc. 07/23/2009
(See Lithium One Inc.)

DULANY INDUSTRIES, INC. (DE)
Name changed to Proteus Foods & Industries, Inc. 02/25/1966
(See Proteus Foods & Industries, Inc.)

DULUTH BREWING & MALTING CO. (MN)
Liquidation completed
Each share Common $1 par exchanged for initial distribution of $4 cash 10/01/1966
Each share Common $1 par received second distribution of $1.30 cash 03/31/1967
Each share Common $1 par received third distribution of $1.50 cash 08/11/1967
Each share Common $1 par received fourth and final distribution of $0.3192928 cash 02/20/1968

DULUTH GROWTH CO (MN)
Statutorily dissolved 12/10/1990

DULUTH METALS LTD (ON)
Acquired by Antofagasta Investment Co. Ltd. 01/22/2015
Each share Common no par exchanged for $0.45 cash
Note: Unexchanged certificates will be cancelled and become without value 01/22/2021

DULUTH SOUTH SHORE & ATLANTIC RAILWAY CO.
Reorganized as Duluth South Shore & Atlantic Railroad Co. 00/00/1949
No stockholders' equity

DULUTH STEAM CORP. (DE)
Merged into General Waterworks Corp. 05/15/1962
Each share Common no par exchanged for (0.16666666) share $2 Conv. 2nd Preferred $1 par
General Waterworks Corp. merged into International Utilities Corp. 03/01/1968 which name changed to IU International Corp. 04/27/1973
(See IU International Corp.)

DULUTH STREET RAILWAY CO. (MN)
Reorganized as Duluth-Superior Transit Co. 09/01/1933
Each share 7% Preferred $100 par exchanged for (1) share Common no par
Duluth-Superior Transit Co. name changed to Northern Enterprises, Inc. 01/02/1963 which merged into Kodiak, Inc. 09/30/1968 which recapitalized as Kodicor, Inc. 05/10/1972
(See Kodicor, Inc.)

DULUTH-SUPERIOR TRANSIT CO. (MN)
Name changed to Northern Enterprises, Inc. 01/02/1963
Northern Enterprises, Inc. merged into Kodiak, Inc. 09/30/1968 which recapitalized as Kodicor, Inc. 05/10/1972
(See Kodicor, Inc.)

DUMA ENERGY CORP (NV)
Name changed to Hydrocarb Energy Corp. 02/18/2014

DUMAC MINES LTD. (BC)
Struck off register and declared dissolved for failure to file returns 04/11/1957

DUMAGAMI MINES LTD (QC)
Merged into Agnico-Eagle Mines Ltd. 12/19/1989
Each share Common $1 par exchanged for (1.7) shares Common no par
Agnico-Eagle Mines Ltd. name changed to Agnico Eagle Mines Ltd. 04/30/2013

DUMAR GOLD MINES, LTD. (ON)
Charter revoked for failure to file reports and pay taxes 00/00/1957

DUMAS MILNER CORP. (MS)
Acquired by American Cyanamid Co. 02/20/1963
Each share Class A Common $1 par exchanged for (0.25) share Common $10 par
(See American Cyanamid Co.)

DUMAURIER MINES & HOLDINGS LTD. (ON)
Charter cancelled 02/20/1980

DUMBARTON BRIDGE CO. (CA)
Completely liquidated 12/15/1951
Each share Capital Stock $10 par stamped to indicate first and final distribution $8.50 cash

DUMONT-AIRPLANE & MARINE INSTRUMENTS, INC. (NY)
Reorganized 10/29/1960
No stockholders' equity

DUMONT CORP (UT)
Involuntarily dissolved for failure to pay taxes 12/31/1979

DUMONT ELECTRIC CORP. (NY)
Merged into Dumont-Airplane & Marine Instruments, Inc. 04/06/1953
Each share 30¢ Preferred $1 par exchanged for (1) share new Ser. A Preferred $1 par
Each share Common 10¢ par exchanged for (0.38095238) share Common $1 par
(See Dumont-Airplane & Marine Instruments, Inc.)

DUMONT NICKEL INC (QC)
Name changed 07/31/1998
Recapitalized 09/01/1998
Name changed from Dumont Resources Inc. to Dumont Nickel Corp. 07/31/1998
Recapitalized from Dumont Nickel Corp. to Dumont Nickel Inc. 09/01/1998
Each share Common $1 par exchanged for (0.036) share Common no par
Recapitalized as DNI Metals Inc. 05/11/2010
Each share Common no par exchanged for (0.125) share Common no par

DUN & BRADSTREET CORP (DE)
Name changed 04/17/1979
Common $1 par split (2) for (1) by issuance of (1) additional share 07/03/1973
Name changed from Dun & Bradstreet Companies, Inc. to Dun & Bradstreet Corp. 04/17/1979
Common $1 par split (2) for (1) by issuance of (1) additional share 06/10/1983
Common $1 par split (2) for (1) by issuance of (1) additional share 06/09/1987
Each share Common $1 par received distribution of (0.33333333) share ACNielsen Corp. Common 1¢ par and (1) share Cognizant Corp. Common $1 par payable 11/01/1996 to holders of record 10/21/1996 Ex date - 11/04/1996
Each share Common $1 par received distribution of (1) share Dun & Bradstreet Corp. (New) Common 1¢ par payable 06/30/1998 to holders of record 06/17/1998 Ex date - 07/01/1998
Name changed to R.H. Donnelley Corp. 07/01/1998
(See R.H. Donnelley Corp.)

DUN & BRADSTREET CORP NEW (DE)
Each share Common 1¢ par received distribution of (0.05) share Dun & Bradstreet Corp. Common 1¢ par payable 10/02/2000 to holders of record 09/20/2000 Ex date - 10/03/2000
Name changed to Moody's Corp. 10/02/2000

DUN & BRADSTREET INC (DE)
Common no par changed to $1 par and (1) additional share issued 01/10/1956
Common $1 par split (2) for (1) by issuance of (1) additional share 12/15/1960
Common $1 par split (2) for (1) by issuance of (1) additional share 04/05/1965
Voting Trust Agreement terminated 08/31/1966
Each VTC for Common $1 par

exchanged for (1) share Common $1 par
Stock Dividend - 100% 05/00/1947
Under plan of reorganization each share Common $1 par automatically became (1) share Dun & Bradstreet Companies, Inc. Common $1 par 05/31/1973
Dun & Bradstreet Companies, Inc. name changed to Dun & Bradstreet Corp. 04/17/1979 which name changed to R.H. Donnelley Corp. 07/01/1998
(See R.H. Donnelley Corp.)

DUN VENTURES INC (NV)
Recapitalized as VideoRated Inc. 01/26/1987
Each share Common $0.001 par exchanged for (0.1) share Common $0.001 par
(See VideoRated Inc.)

DUNAMIS INC (CA)
Reorganized under the laws of Nevada as WordCruncher Internet Technologies, Inc. 07/14/1998
Each share Common no par exchanged for (3) shares Common $0.001 par
WordCruncher Internet Technologies, Inc. name changed to Logio Inc. 06/21/2000 which merged into Pacific WebWorks, Inc. 01/31/2001 which name changed to Heyu Biological Technology Corp. 06/28/2018

DUNAV RES LTD (BC)
Merged into Avala Resources Ltd. 10/02/2014
Each share Common no par exchanged for (1.0457) shares Common no par
Note: Unexchanged certificates will be cancelled and become without value 10/02/2020
Avala Resources Ltd. merged into Dundee Precious Metals Inc. 04/12/2016

DUNBAR LIFE INSURANCE CO. (OH)
Merged into Supreme Liberty Life Insurance Co. 01/01/1959
Each share Common $10 par exchanged for (0.66666666) share Common $10 par
Supreme Liberty Life Insurance Co. name changed to Supreme Life Insurance Co. of America 11/04/1960
(See Supreme Life Insurance Co. of America)

DUNCAN COFFEE CO. (TX)
Name changed to Duncan Foods Co. 7/16/63
Duncan Foods Co. acquired by Coca-Cola Co. 5/8/64

DUNCAN ELEC INC (IN)
Class A Common $2.50 par and Class B Common $2.50 par changed to no par 06/22/1973
Class A Common no par and Class B Common no par split (2) for (1) by issuance of (1) additional share respectively 09/28/1973
Stock Dividends - 10% 12/20/1959; 10% 11/10/1961
Through purchase offer 99% acquired by Amerogyr Inc. as of 07/03/1978
Public interest eliminated

DUNCAN ELECTRIC MANUFACTURING CO. (IL)
Each share Common $2.50 par exchanged for (2) shares Common $5 par in 1951
Merged into Duncan Electric Co., Inc. 10/8/56
Each share Common $5 par exchanged for (1) share Class A Common $2.50 par and (1) share Class B Common $2.50 par
(See Duncan Electric Co., Inc.)

DUNCAN ENERGY PARTNERS L P (DE)
Issue Information - 13,000,000 COM UNITS REPSTG LTD PARTNER INT offered at $21 per Unit on 01/30/2007
Merged into Enterprise Products Partners L.P. 09/07/2011
Each Common Unit exchanged for (1.01) Common Units

DUNCAN FOODS CO. (TX)
Acquired by Coca-Cola Co. on a (1) for (5.5) basis 5/8/64

DUNCAN GOLD RES INC (ON)
Delisted from Vancouver Stock Exchange 03/04/1992

DUNCAN HILL LTD (OH)
Merged out of existence 11/07/1997
Details not available

DUNCAN INDS INC (DE)
Reincorporated 04/30/1969
State of incorporation changed from (NY) to (DE) 04/30/1969
Name changed to Qonaar Corp. 05/01/1970
(See Qonaar Corp.)

DUNCAN PARKING METER CORP. (NY)
Name changed to Duncan Industries, Inc. (NY) 5/29/68
Duncan Industries, Inc. (NY) reincorporated in Delaware 4/30/69 which name changed to Qonaar Corp. 5/1/70
(See Qonaar Corp.)

DUNCAN RANGE IRON MINES LTD (ON)
Charter cancelled and declared dissolved for failure to pay taxes and file returns 11/08/1977

DUNCASTLE GOLD CORP (BC)
Each share old Common no par exchanged for (0.1) share new Common no par 08/30/2012
Name changed to Group Ten Metals Inc. 02/26/2015

DUNCO REALTY & EQUIPMENT CORP. (NY)
Merged into Victory Markets, Inc. 4/7/64
Each share Capital Stock $10 par exchanged for (1) share Common $2 par
Victory Markets, Inc. merged into LNC Industries Pty. Ltd. 9/22/86

DUNDARAVE RES INC (AB)
Recapitalized as Nano One Materials Corp. 03/13/2015
Each share Common no par exchanged for (0.5) share Common no par

DUNDARAVE RES INC (BC)
Recapitalized as SRR Mercantile Inc. 2/4/93
Each share Common no par exchanged for (0.3125) share Common no par
(See SRR Mercantile Inc.)

DUNDAS MACH INC (DE)
Common $0.001 par split (3) for (1) by issuance of (2) additional shares 6/30/86
Charter cancelled and declared inoperative and void for non-payment of taxes 3/1/99

DUNDEE ACQUISITION LTD (ON)
Units separated 06/01/2015
Completely liquidated 04/21/2017
Each Class A Restricted Vtg. Share received $10.04 cash

DUNDEE BANCORP INC (ON)
1st Preference Ser. no par called for redemption 1/12/92
Name changed to Dundee Corp. 12/14/2004

DUNDEE CAP CORP (ON)
Reacquired 4/21/93
Each share Common no par exchanged for $7.45 cash

DUNDEE CAP MKTS INC (ON)
Acquired by Dundee Corp. 02/01/2012
Each share Common no par exchanged for $1.125 cash

DUNDEE CORP (ON)
Plan of arrangement effective 05/30/2013
Each share 5% 1st Preference Ser. 1 no par automatically became (1) share 1st Preference Ser. 4 no par and (1) share DREAM Unlimited Corp. 1st Preference Ser. 1 no par (Additional Information in Active)

DUNDEE INDL REAL ESTATE INVT TR (ON)
Name changed to Dream Industrial Real Estate Investment Trust 05/08/2014

DUNDEE INTL REAL ESTATE INVT TR (ON)
Name changed to Dream Global Real Estate Investment Trust 05/12/2014

DUNDEE MINES LTD (BC)
Ctfs. dated prior to 05/03/1973
Acquired by Palliser Petroleums Ltd. 05/03/1973
Each share Capital Stock no par exchanged for (0.33333333) share Common 20¢ par
Palliser Petroleums Ltd. name changed to Dundee-Palliser Resources Inc. 05/17/1973 which recapitalized as Scorpion Minerals Inc. 04/01/1996 which name changed to Nextair Inc. 03/05/2001 which recapitalized as NXA Inc. 02/23/2005 which recapitalized as Ellipsiz Communications Ltd. 11/26/2015

DUNDEE MINES LTD (BC)
Certificates dated after 10/12/2007
Name changed to Duncastle Gold Corp. 05/28/2008
Duncastle Gold Corp. name changed to Group Ten Metals Inc. 02/26/2015

DUNDEE MLS INC (GA)
Each share Common $100 par exchanged for (4) shares Common $25 par in 1946
Merged into Springs Industries, Inc. 4/12/95
Each share Common $25 par exchanged for either (65.58442) shares Common 25¢ par or $2,525 cash
Note: Option to receive cash expired 5/24/95
(See Springs Industries, Inc.)

DUNDEE PALLISER RES INC (ON)
Common 20¢ par changed to no par 04/30/1974
Recapitalized as Scorpion Minerals Inc. 04/01/1996
Each share Common no par exchanged for (0.033333333) share Common no par
Scorpion Minerals Inc. name changed to Nextair Inc. 03/05/2001 which recapitalized as NXA Inc. 02/23/2005 which recapitalized as Ellipsiz Communications Ltd. 11/26/2015

DUNDEE PETE CORP (AB)
Acquired by City of Medicine Hat (AB, Canada) 09/22/2000
Each share Common no par exchanged for $0.40 cash

DUNDEE REAL ESTATE INVT TR (ON)
Note: CUSIP® changed due to voluntary offer 08/27/2007
Name changed to Dream Office Real Estate Investment Trust 05/08/2014

DUNDEE RLTY CORP (ON)
Each share old Common no par exchanged for (0.125) share new Common no par 06/18/2001
Plan of arrangement effective 06/30/2003
Each share new Common no par exchanged for (1) Dundee Real Estate Investment Trust Ser. A Unit no par and $3 cash
Dundee Real Estate Investment Trust name changed to Dream Office Real Estate Investment Trust 05/08/2014

DUNDEE RES CORP (BC)
Recapitalized as Clear View Ventures Inc. 01/20/1993
Each share Common no par exchanged for (0.2) share Common no par
Clear View Ventures Inc. name changed to Turbodyne Technologies Inc. (BC) 04/21/1994 which reincorporated in Canada 12/03/1996 which reincorporated in Delaware 07/24/1998 which reincorporated in Nevada 09/12/2002

DUNDEE WEALTH INC (ON)
Name changed 06/28/2007
Name changed from Dundee Wealth Management Inc. to DundeeWealth Inc. 06/28/2007
Each share Common no par received distribution of (1) share Dundee Capital Markets Inc. Common no par payable 01/31/2011 to holders of record 01/28/2011 Ex date- 01/31/2011
Acquired by Bank of Nova Scotia (Halifax, NS) 03/09/2011
Each share Common no par exchanged for (0.2) share 3.70% Preferred Ser. 32 no par and (0.2497) share Common no par
4.75% 1st Preference no par called for redemption at $26.50 plus $0.22589 accrued dividends on 09/07/2011
Public interest eliminated

DUNE BUGGY INC (CO)
Name changed to Unique Mobility, Inc. 3/19/71
Unique Mobility, Inc. name changed to UQM Technologies, Inc. 1/25/2001

DUNE ENERGY INC (DE)
Each share old Common $0.001 par exchanged for (0.5) share new Common $0.001 par 05/24/2004
Each share 10% Senior Conv. Preferred $0.001 par received distribution of (0.02999803) share 144A 10% Senior Conv. Preferred $0.001 par payable 03/01/2009 to holders of record 02/13/2009 Ex date - 02/23/2009
Each share 10% Senior Conv. Preferred $0.001 par received distribution of (0.03000162) share 144A 10% Senior Conv. Preferred $0.001 par payable 06/01/2009 to holders of record 05/01/2009 Ex date - 04/29/2009
Each share 10% Senior Conv. Preferred $0.001 par received distribution of (0.03010646) share 144A 10% Senior Conv. Preferred $0.001 par payable 09/01/2009 to holders of record 07/10/2009
Each share 10% Senior Conv. Preferred $0.001 par received distribution of (0.02999956) share 144A 10% Senior Conv. Preferred $0.001 par payable 12/01/2009 to holders of record 10/05/2009
Each share new Common $0.001 par exchanged again for (0.2) share new Common $0.001 par 12/01/2009
Each share 10% Senior Conv. Preferred $0.001 par received distribution of (0.03000626) share 144A 10% Senior Conv. Preferred $0.001 par payable 06/01/2011 to

holders of record 05/13/2011 Ex date - 05/27/2011
Each share 10% Senior Conv. Preferred $0.001 par received distribution of (0.03000348) share 144A 10% Senior Conv. Preferred $0.001 par payable 09/01/2011 to holders of record 08/10/2011 Ex date - 08/12/2011
Each share 10% Senior Conv. Preferred $0.001 par received distribution of (0.03000594) share 144A 10% Senior Conv. Preferred $0.001 par payable 12/01/2011 to holders of record 11/10/2011 Ex date - 11/30/2011
Each share 10% 144A Senior Conv. Preferred $0.001 par exchanged for (355.16037) shares Common $0.001 par and $24.31 cash 12/21/2011
Each share 10% Senior Conv. Preferred $0.001 par exchanged for (355.16037) shares Common $0.001 par and $24.31 cash 12/21/2011
Each share new Common $0.001 par exchanged again for (0.01) share new Common $0.001 par 01/03/2012
Stock Dividends - In 144A 10% Senior Conv. Preferred to holders of 144A 10% Senior Conv. Preferred 2.94398% payable 09/01/2007 to holders of record 08/15/2007; 2.50001% payable 12/01/2007 to holders of record 11/15/2007 Ex date - 11/13/2007; 2.50002% payable 03/01/2008 to holders of record 02/15/2008 Ex date - 02/13/2008; 2.7266% payable 06/01/2008 to holders of record 05/15/2008 Ex date - 05/22/2008; 2.99989% payable 09/01/2008 to holders of record 07/18/2008; 3.00073% payable 12/01/2008 to holders of record 10/02/2008 Ex date - 09/30/2008; 2.9998% payable 03/01/2009 to holders of record 02/13/2009 Ex date - 02/23/2009; 3.00016% payable 06/01/2009 to holders of record 05/01/2009 Ex date - 04/29/2009; 3.01064% payable 09/01/2009 to holders of record 07/10/2009; 2.99995% payable 12/01/2009 to holders of record 10/05/2009; 3.00062% payable 06/01/2011 to holders of record 05/13/2011 Ex date - 06/02/2011; 3.00034% payable 09/01/2011 to holders of record 08/10/2011 Ex date - 08/12/2011; 3.00059% payable 12/01/2011 to holders of record 11/10/2011 Ex date - 11/30/2011
In 10% Senior Conv. Preferred to holders of 10% Senior Conv. Preferred 2.50002% payable 03/01/2008 to holders of record 02/15/2008 Ex date - 02/13/2008; 2.7266% payable 06/01/2008 to holders of record 05/15/2008; Ex date - 05/22/2008; 2.99989% payable 09/01/2008 to holders of record 07/18/2008; 3.00073% payable 12/01/2008 to holders of record 10/02/2008 Ex date - 09/30/2008
Plan of reorganization under Chapter 11 bankruptcy proceedings effective 09/30/2015
No stockholders' equity

DUNE MINERAL CORP (BC)
Name changed to Goldwinn Resources Ltd. 05/20/1980
(See Goldwinn Resources Ltd.)

DUNE RES LTD (AB)
Recapitalized as Robson Petroleum Ltd. 12/23/1988
Each share Class A Common no par exchanged for (0.33333333) share Common no par
(See Robson Petroleum Ltd.)

DUNEAN MILLS
Merged into Stevens (J.P.) & Co., Inc. 09/06/1946
Each share Common $20 par exchanged for (5.17062) shares Capital Stock $15 par
(See Stevens (J.P.) & Co., Inc.)

DUNES HOTELS & CASINOS INC (NY)
Stock Dividend - 100% 07/16/1979
91% acquired by company at $30 cash per each share $7.50 Ser. B Preferred 50¢ par and $1.05 cash per each share Common 50¢ par through purchase offer which expired 11/30/2001
Public interest eliminated

DUNFORD ROUYN MINES LTD.
Merged into Joliet-Quebec Mines Ltd. 00/00/1952
Each share Capital Stock exchanged for (0.1111111) share Capital Stock $1 par and $0.0218 cash
Joliet-Quebec Mines Ltd. recapitalized as J-Q Resources Inc. 09/08/1978 which name changed to International Pursuit Corp. 09/21/1987 which recapitalized as Apollo Gold Corp. (ON) 06/24/2002 which reincorporated in Yukon 05/28/2003 which recapitalized as Brigus Gold Corp. (YT) 06/25/2010 which reincorporated in Canada 06/09/2011
(See Brigus Gold Corp.)

DUNFRAZIER GOLD EXPLS INC (ON)
Name changed to Interlock Consolidated Enterprises, Inc. 07/06/1992
(See Interlock Consolidated Enterprises, Inc.)

DUNGANNON EXPLS LTD (BC)
Merged into Claddagh Gold Ltd. 08/09/1989
Each share Common no par exchanged for (1) share Common no par
Claddagh Gold Ltd. recapitalized as Resorts Unlimited Management Inc. 09/01/2000
(See Resorts Unlimited Management Inc.)

DUNGANNON INTL INC (DE)
Name changed to CallKey International, Inc. 06/20/2006

DUNHALL PHARMACEUTICALS INC (AR)
Merged into Omni Products of Palm Beach Inc. 10/15/1997
Details not available

DUNHAM BUSH INC (CT)
5% Preferred $100 par called for redemption 11/10/1967
Merged into Signal Oil & Gas Co. 12/29/1967
Each share Common $2 par exchanged for (0.382) share Class A Common $2 par
Signal Oil & Gas Co. name changed to Signal Companies, Inc. 05/01/1968 which merged into Allied-Signal Inc. 09/19/1985 which name changed to AlliedSignal Inc. 04/26/1993 which name changed to Honeywell International Inc. 12/01/1999

DUNHAM (C.A.) CO. (IA)
Each share Class A Common $5 par exchanged for (3) shares Common $2 par 00/00/1950
Each share Class B Common $5 par exchanged for (1) share Common $2 par 00/00/1950
Merged into Dunham-Bush, Inc. 06/29/1956
Each share 5% Preferred $100 par exchanged for (1) share 5% Preferred $100 par
Each share Common $2 par exchanged for (1) share Common $2 par

Dunham-Bush, Inc. merged into Signal Oil & Gas Co. 12/29/1967 which name changed to Signal Companies, Inc. 05/01/1968 which merged into Allied- Signal Inc. 09/19/1985 which name changed to AlliedSignal Inc. 04/26/1993 which name changed to Honeywell International Inc.12/01/1999

DUNHILL COMPACT CLASSICS INC (CO)
Name changed to DCC Compact Classics Inc. 08/08/1989
(See DCC Compact Classics Inc.)

DUNHILL DEV CORP LTD (BC)
Acquired by Woodbridge Development Corp. 03/01/1974
Details not available

DUNHILL HLDGS INC (CO)
Recapitalized as Williamson (E.B.) & Co., Inc. 04/28/1989
Each share Common $0.0001 par exchanged for (0.001) share Common $0.0001 par
(See Williamson (E.B.) & Co., Inc.)

DUNHILL INDS INC (CANADA)
Recapitalized 08/08/1989
Recapitalized from Dunhill Alberta Capital Corp. to Dunhill Industries Inc. 08/08/1989
Each share Class A Common no par exchanged for (0.25) share Class A Common no par
Name changed to Immedia Infomatic International Inc. 05/22/1991
Immedia Infomatic International Inc. recapitalized as Immedia Infomatic Corp. 12/16/1991 which name changed to MPACT Immedia Corp. 01/18/1994 which name changed to BCE Emergis Inc. 01/21/1999 which name changed to Emergis Inc. 12/01/2004
(See Emergis Inc.)

DUNHILL INTERNATIONAL, INC. (DE)
Common no par changed to $1 par 00/00/1933
Common $1 par split (3) for (1) by issuance of (2) additional shares 00/00/1954
Name changed to Questor Corp. 12/01/1968
(See Questor Corp.)

DUNK DONUT CORP.
Bankrupt 00/00/1950
Stockholders' equity unlikely

DUNKIN DONUTS INC (DE)
Common $1 par split (2) for (1) by issuance of (1) additional share 03/26/1969
Common $1 par split (3) for (2) by issuance of (0.5) additional share 08/14/1981
Common $1 par split (3) for (2) by issuance of (0.5) additional share 01/24/1983
Common $1 par split (3) for (2) by issuance of (0.5) additional share 04/19/1985
Merged into Allied-Lyons PLC 01/02/1990
Each share Common $1 par exchanged for $47.25 cash

DUNKIRK RADIATOR CORP (NY)
Acquired by ECR International, Inc. 06/14/1999
Details not available

DUNLAP & ASSOC INC (DE)
Common $1 par split (3) for (2) by issuance of (0.5) additional share 12/01/1978
Stock Dividends - 10% 08/13/1976; 10% 06/15/1977; 10% 05/26/1978; 10% 08/17/1979; 10% 06/27/1980
Name changed to Reflectone, Inc. (DE) 08/01/1982
Reflectone, Inc. (DE) reincorporated in Florida 12/23/1985
(See Reflectone, Inc.)

DUNLAP ELECTRS (CA)
Merged into Advance Ross Corp. (Old) 01/09/1970
Each share Common $1 par exchanged for (0.8077) share Common 10¢ par
Advance Ross Corp. (Old) reorganized as Advance Ross Corp. (New) 06/17/1993 which merged into CUC International Inc. 01/10/1996 which name changed to Cendant Corp. 12/17/1997 which reorganized as Avis Budget Group, Inc. 09/01/2006

DUNLAP RES LTD (BC)
Reincorporated under the laws of Yukon as International Dunlap Minerals Corp. 02/11/1997
International Dunlap Minerals Corp. reorganized into Iriana Resources Corp. 08/13/1999 which merged into Polaris Geothermal Inc. 06/21/2004
(See Polaris Geothermal Inc.)

DUNLOP AUSTRALIA LTD (AUSTRALIA)
Name changed to Dunlop Olympic Ltd. 04/01/1982
Dunlop Olympic Ltd. name changed to Pacific Dunlop Ltd. 01/22/1986 which recapitalized as Ansell Ltd. 04/30/2002
(See Ansell Ltd.)

DUNLOP HLDGS PLC (ENGLAND)
5.5% Preference £1 par reclassified as 5.75% Preference £1 par 01/01/1971
Merged into BTR PLC 10/28/1985
Each (21) shares Ordinary Reg. 50p par exchanged for (4) shares Ordinary Reg. 25p par
Each (21) ADR's for Ordinary Reg. 50p par exchanged for (4) ADR's for Ordinary Reg. 25p par
BTR PLC merged into BTR Siebe PLC 02/12/1999 which name changed to Invensys PLC 04/16/1999

DUNLOP INDS INC (AB)
Struck off register for failure to file annual returns 02/01/1994

DUNLOP LTD (ENGLAND)
Name changed to Dunlop Holdings plc 01/01/1971
Dunlop Holdings plc merged into BTR PLC 10/28/1985 which merged into BTR Siebe PLC 02/12/1999 which name changed to Invensys PLC 04/16/1999

DUNLOP OLYMPIC LTD (AUSTRALIA)
Name changed to Pacific Dunlop Ltd. 01/22/1986
Pacific Dunlop Ltd. recapitalized as Ansell Ltd. 04/30/2002
(See Ansell Ltd.)

DUNLOP RUBBER CO. LTD. (ENGLAND)
Each share 6.5% Preference Ser. A £1 par exchanged for (1.375) shares 5.5% Preference £1 par 00/00/1954
Each share 7% Preference Ser. B £1 par exchanged for (1.4) shares 5.5% Preference £1 par 00/00/1954
Each share 10% Preference Ser. C 16s par exchanged for (1.5) shares 5.5% Preference £1 par 00/00/1954
Each share Ordinary Reg. 6s8d par exchanged for (0.5) share Ordinary Reg. 10s par 00/00/1954
Each share Ordinary Reg. £1 par exchanged for (2) shares Ordinary Reg. 10s par plus stock dividend of (1) additional share 00/00/1954
Stock Dividends - Ordinary Reg. - 25% 07/01/1959; 33.33333333% 07/07/1964
ADR's for Ordinary Reg. - 25% 07/03/1959; 33.33333333% 07/20/1964
Name changed to Dunlop Co. Ltd. 01/01/1967

Dunlop Co. Ltd. name changed to Dunlop Holdings PLC 01/01/1971 which merged into BTR PLC 10/28/1985 which merged into BTR Siebe PLC 02/12/1999 which name changed to Invensys PLC 04/16/1999

DUNMAR MINES LTD. (ON)
Merged into Garrison Creek Consolidated Mines Ltd. 12/09/1954
Each share Capital Stock no par exchanged for (0.06666666) share Common no par
Garrison Creek Consolidated Mines Ltd. merged into QSR Ltd. 09/07/1993 which name changed to Coniagas Resources Ltd. 06/25/1999 which name changed to Lithium One Inc. 07/23/2009
(See Lithium One Inc.)

DUNN COMPUTER CORP (DE)
Reincorporated under the laws of Virginia 05/01/1998
Dunn Computer Corp. (VA) name changed to SteelCloud Co. 10/19/2000 which name changed to SteelCloud Inc. 08/14/2001
(See SteelCloud Inc.)

DUNN COMPUTER CORP (VA)
Name changed to SteelCloud Co. 10/19/2000
SteelCloud Corp. name changed to SteelCloud Inc. 08/14/2001
(See SteelCloud Inc.)

DUNN ENGINEERING ASSOCIATES, INC. (MA)
Name changed to Dunn Engineering Corp. 01/26/1961
(See Dunn Engineering Corp.)

DUNN ENGINEERING CORP. (MA)
Class A Common $1 par and Class B Common $1 par split (3) for (1) by issuance of (2) additional shares respectively 10/13/1961
Adjudicated bankrupt 05/25/1962
No stockholders' equity

DUNN MAR OIL & GAS CO (PA)
Merged into International Management & Research Corp. 12/20/1971
Each share Common $1 par exchanged for (0.7) share Common 5¢ par
(See International Management & Research Corp.)

DUNN-PENN CO., INC. (DE)
No longer in existence having become inoperative and void for non-payment of taxes 03/18/1925

DUNN (THOMAS) REALTY CO. (MO)
Liquidated 00/00/1953
Details not available

DUNN STEEL PRODUCTS CO.
Merged into Townsend Co. 00/00/1951
Each share Capital Stock $1 par exchanged for (0.27586206) share Common $12.50 par
(See Townsend Co.)

DUNN YELLOWKNIFE MINES, LTD. (ON)
Charter revoked for failure to file reports and pay taxes 00/00/1952

DUNNE (W.H.) CO. (NY)
Each share Class A Common no par exchanged for (5) shares Class A Common $2 par 00/00/1957
Each share Class B Common no par exchanged for (5) shares Class B Common $2 par 00/00/1957
Name changed to Victory Markets, Inc. 01/30/1959
(See Victory Markets, Inc.)

DUNNINGCOLOR CORP. (CA)
Bankrupt 06/30/1954
Details not available

DUNNS SUPPLY STORE INC (TN)
Chapter 11 bankruptcy proceedings dismissed 07/15/1998
Stockholders' equity unlikely

DUNNVILLE CONSOLIDATED TELEPHONE CO. LTD. (ON)
Merged into Community Telephone Co. of Ontario Ltd. 06/28/1971
Each share Preference Ser. A $50 par, Preference Ser. B $50 par or Preference Ser. D $50 par exchanged for (50) shares 6.5% 1st Preference Ser. A $1 par
Each share Preference Ser. C $50 par exchanged for (50) shares 6% 1st Preference Ser. B $1 par

DUNOIL RES LTD (AB)
Name changed to Dune Resources Ltd. 06/26/1986
Dune Resources Ltd. recapitalized as Robson Petroleum Ltd. 12/23/1988
(See Robson Petroleum Ltd.)

DUNRAINE MINES LTD (CANADA)
Recapitalized as International Dunraine Ltd. 02/06/1990
Each share Capital Stock no par exchanged for (0.5) share Class A no par and (0.5) share Class B no par
International Dunraine Ltd. name changed to World Point Terminals Inc. 07/18/1996
(See World Point Terminals Inc.)

DUNRITE CAP CORP (DE)
Recapitalized as Consolidated Technology, Inc. 06/16/1989
Each share Common $0.0001 par exchanged for (0.2) share Common $0.0001 par
Consolidated Technology, Inc. merged into Tri Tec Plastics Corp. 12/05/1990 which merged into Secom General Corp. 12/17/1991
(See Secom General Corp.)

DUNROBIN, LTD.
In process of liquidation 00/00/1938
Details not available

DUNSMUIR VENTURES LTD (BC)
Reorganized under the laws of Canada as Peregrine Diamonds Ltd. 01/18/2006
Each share Common no par exchanged for (0.05) share Common no par
(See Peregrine Diamonds Ltd.)

DUNTERRA COPPER MINES LTD. (ON)
Acquired by Dunraine Mines Ltd. 08/28/1961
Each share Capital Stock no par exchanged for (0.5) share Capital Stock no par
Dunraine Mines Ltd. recapitalized as International Dunraine Ltd. 02/06/1990 which name changed to World Point Terminals Inc. 07/18/1996
(See World Point Terminals Inc.)

DUNTROON ENERGY LTD (ON)
Name changed to Brompton Corp. 04/07/2008

DUNVEGAN EXPL LTD (BC)
Cease trade order effective 03/25/1992
Stockholders' equity unlikely

DUNVEGAN MINES LTD (ON)
Charter cancelled for failure to pay taxes and file reports 03/16/1976

DUNWYNN EXPL INC (NV)
SEC revoked common stock registration 10/24/2011

DUNWYNN RES INC (NV)
Recapitalized as Dunwynn Exploration, Inc. 06/29/2005
Each share Common $0.001 par exchanged for (0.002) share Common $0.001 par and (0.0717) share Dunwynn Resources Corp. Restricted Common $0.001 par

(See Dunwynn Exploration, Inc.)

DUO INC (DE)
Name changed to Wetjet International Ltd. 06/09/1988
Wetjet International Ltd. name changed to W-J International Ltd. (DE) 04/01/1993 which reincorporated in Nevada 10/24/2003 which recapitalized as InZon Corp. 09/22/2004
(See InZon Corp.)

DUO TOOTHBRUSH CO. (MO)
Charter forfeited for failure to file annual reports 01/01/1952

DUOFOLD HEALTH UNDERWEAR, INC. (NY)
Name changed to Duofold, Inc. 04/22/1932
(See Duofold, Inc.)

DUOFOLD INC (NY)
Each share Common $100 par exchanged for (4) shares Common $25 par 00/00/1936
Each share Common $25 par exchanged for (3) shares Common $10 par 00/00/1948
Acquired by Cluett, Peabody & Co., Inc. 03/30/1979
Each share Common $10 par exchanged for $63.147 cash
Each share Common $10 par received additional distribution of $7.226 cash 03/30/1982

DUOMALARTIC GOLD MINES LTD. (ON)
Charter cancelled for failure to pay taxes and file returns 04/14/1975

DUONAS CORP (NV)
Name changed to Huahui Education Group Corp. 11/29/2017

DUOYUAN GLOBAL WTR INC (BRITISH VIRGIN ISLANDS)
ADR agreement terminated 11/20/2015
Each Sponsored ADR for Ordinary exchanged for (2) shares Ordinary
Note: Unexchanged ADR's will be sold and the proceeds, if any, held for claim after 05/20/2016

DUOYUAN PRTG INC (WY)
SEC revoked common stock registration 10/27/2014

DUPARQUET MINING CORP. LTD. (QC)
Charter annulled for failure to file annual reports 03/13/1976

DUPAS METALS LTD. (QC)
Involuntarily dissolved 07/31/1972

DUPEL MINES LTD. (ON)
Merged into Goldale Ltd. 06/18/1964
Each share Capital Stock $1 par exchanged for (0.08) share Capital Stock no par
Goldale Ltd. recapitalized as Canadian Goldale Corp. Ltd. 06/16/1965 which name changed to Hambro Canada (1972) Ltd. 01/09/1973 which name changed to Hambro Canada Ltd. 05/28/1974 which name changed to Hatleigh Corp. (Old) 08/03/1978 which merged into Hatleigh Corp. (New) 08/31/1978 which merged into Dexleigh Corp. 06/30/1984
(See Dexleigh Corp.)

DUPLAN CORP (DE)
Common no par changed to $1 par 02/03/1958
Each share Common $1 par exchanged for (1) share Common 75¢ par and $7 cash 02/02/1965
Common 75¢ par split (2) for (1) by issuance of (1) additional share 10/10/1968
Stock Dividend - 100% 10/24/1947
Reorganized under Chapter X Federal Bankruptcy Act as Panex Industries, Inc. 06/04/1981
(See Panex Industries, Inc.)

DUPLAN SILK CORP.
Name changed to Duplan Corp. 00/00/1941
Duplan Corp. reorganized as Panex Industries, Inc. 06/04/1981
(See Panex Industries, Inc.)

DUPLEX CONDENSER & RADIO CORP. (DE)
Charter revoked for failure to file reports and pay fees 04/01/1928

DUPLEX ENVELOPE CO. (VA)
Merged into Hammermill Paper Co. 03/19/1965
Each share Common $1 par exchanged for (0.83333333) share Common $2.50 par
(See Hammermill Paper Co.)

DUPLEX PAPER BAG CO (OH)
In process of liquidation Company's President advised an initial distribution of $70 cash per share had been paid 00/00/1970 and second and final distribution would be paid by 12/31/1970

DUPLEX PRINTING PRESS CO.
Acquired by Goss Printing Press Co. 00/00/1947
Details not available

DUPLEX PRODS INC (DE)
Common $1 par split (3) for (2) by issuance of (0.5) additional share 10/13/1978
Common $1 par split (2) for (1) by issuance of (1) additional share 04/08/1980
$1.45 Conv. Preferred Ser. A $1 par called for redemption 06/30/1983
Common $1 par split (2) for (1) by issuance of (1) additional share 07/09/1985
Merged into Reynolds & Reynolds Co. 05/20/1996
Each share Common $1 par exchanged for $12 cash

DUPLEX TRUCK CO. (MI)
Capital Stock no par changed to $1 par 00/00/1936
Merged into Warner & Swasey Co. 11/10/1955
Each share Capital Stock $1 par exchanged for (0.33333333) share Common $1 par
Warner & Swasey Co. merged into Bendix Corp. 03/31/1980 which merged into Allied Corp. 01/31/1983 which merged into Allied-Signal Inc. 09/19/1985 which name changed to AlliedSignal Inc. 04/26/1993 which name changed to Honeywell International Inc. 12/01/1999

DUPLEX VENDING CORP. (NY)
Name changed to Vamco Corp. 01/19/1962
(See Vamco Corp.)

DUPONT CDA INC (CANADA)
Class A Ser. 1 no par split (3) for (1) by issuance of (2) additional shares 06/07/1994
Class A Ser. 1 no par split (3) for (1) by issuance of (2) additional shares payable 05/24/2001 to holders of record 05/18/2001 Ex date - 05/16/2001
Merged into Du Pont (E.I.) de Nemours & Co. 07/29/2003
Each share Class A Ser. 1 no par exchanged for $21.75 cash

DUPONT CAP INC (CANADA)
Name changed to Advitech Inc. 07/15/2004
Advitech Inc. recapitalized as Botaneco Corp. 10/14/2011 which name changed to Natunola AgriTech Inc. 07/09/2013
(See Natunola AgriTech Inc.)

DUPONT DIRECT FINL HLDGS INC (GA)
Chapter 11 bankruptcy petition dismissed 09/26/2006
Stockholders' equity unlikely

DUPONT FABROS TECHNOLOGY INC (MD)
7.875% Perpetual Preferred Ser. A $0.001 par called for redemption at $25 plus $0.29 accrued dividends on 06/09/2016
7.625% Perpetual Preferred Ser. B $0.001 par called for redemption at $25 on 07/15/2016
Merged into Digital Realty Trust, Inc. 09/14/2017
Each share 6.625% Perpetual Preferred Ser. C $0.001 par exchanged for (1) share 6.625% Perpetual Preferred Ser. C $0.001 par
Each share Common $0.001 par exchanged for (0.545) share Common 1¢ par

DUPONT HODGSON GOLD MINES, LTD. (ON)
Charter cancelled 08/29/1960

DUPONT INSTRS CORP (UT)
Proclaimed dissolved for failure to pay taxes 06/01/1991

DUPONT MINING CO. LTD. (QC)
Declared dissolved for failure to file annual reports 11/04/1978

DUPONT PHOTOMASKS INC (DE)
Merged into Toppan Printing Co., Ltd. 04/22/2005
Each share Common 1¢ par exchanged for $27 cash

DUPONT VENTURES INC (CO)
Charter suspended for failure to file annual reports 12/01/1991

DUPORT MNG LTD (ON)
Merged into Consolidated Professor Mines Ltd. 06/22/1981
Each share Capital Stock no par exchanged for (0.5) share Capital Stock no par
(See Consolidated Professor Mines Ltd.)

DUPRESNOY MINES LTD. (QC)
Merged into Lake Dufault Mines Ltd. 03/15/1955
Each share Common $1 par exchanged for (0.028571) share Capital Stock $1 par
Lake Dufault Mines Ltd. merged into Falconbridge Copper Ltd. 12/16/1971 which name changed to Corporation Falconbridge Copper 07/09/1980 which name changed to Minnova Inc. 05/26/1987 which merged into Metall Mining Corp. 05/05/1993 which name changed to Inmet Mining Corp. 05/04/1995 which was acquired by First Quantum Minerals Ltd. 04/09/2013

DUPUIS FRERES LTEE (QC)
4.8% Preferred $25 par called for redemption 08/16/1965
Declared bankrupt 02/07/1978
No stockholders' equity

DUQUESNE BREWING CO PITTSBURGH (PA)
Stock Dividend - 100% 11/04/1948
Name changed to Duke & Co., Inc. 04/19/1973
(See Duke & Co., Inc.)

DUQUESNE CAP L P (DE)
8.375% Monthly Income Preferred Securities Ser. A called for redemption at $25 plus $0.116319 accrued dividends 05/21/2004

DUQUESNE GAS CORP.
Reorganized as Duquesne Natural Gas Co. (PA) 00/00/1933
Details not available

DUQUESNE LT CO (PA)
Each share 8% Preferred $100 par exchanged for (4) shares Common no par 00/00/1928
Each share Common $100 par exchanged for (4) shares Common no par 00/00/1928
Common no par changed to $10 par 00/00/1951
Common $10 par changed to $5 par and (1) additional share issued 01/23/1959
Common $5 par changed to $1 par 04/22/1969
$2.75 Preference $1 par called for redemption 08/01/1987
Under plan of reorganization each share Common $1 par automatically became (1) share DQE, Inc. Common $1 par 07/07/1989
$8.64 Preferred $50 par called for redemption 04/01/1990
$2.315 Preference $1 par called for redemption 04/01/1991
$2.10 Preference Ser. K $1 par called for redemption 01/14/1994
$7.50 Preference $1 par called for redemption 01/14/1994
$7.20 Preferred $50 par called for redemption 09/01/1995
DQE, Inc. name changed to DQE 06/04/1990 which name changed to Duquesne Light Holdings, Inc. 09/30/2003
(See Duquesne Light Holdings, Inc.)
4% Preferred $50 par called for redemption at $51.50 plus $0.15 accrued dividends on 07/06/2007
6.5% Preferred $50 par called for redemption at $50 plus $0.045139 accrued dividends on 04/06/2015
$2.10 Preferred Ser. A $50 par called for redemption at $51.84 plus $0.2275 accrued dividends on 11/09/2017
3.75% Preferred $50 par called for redemption at $51 plus $0.203125 accrued dividends on 11/09/2017
4.1% Preferred $50 par called for redemption at $51.75 plus $0.222083 accrued dividends on 11/09/2017
4.15% Preferred $50 par called for redemption at $51.73 plus $0.224792 accrued dividends on 11/09/2017
4.2% Preferred $50 par called for redemption at $51.71 plus $0.2275 accrued dividends on 11/09/2017

DUQUESNE LT HLDGS INC (PA)
Merged into DQE Holdings LLC 5/31/2007
Each share Common no par exchanged for $20 cash

DUQUESNE MINING CO. LTD.
Reorganized as Consolidated Duquesne Mining Co., Ltd. 00/00/1948
Each share Capital Stock $1 par exchanged for (0.33333333) share Capital Stock $1 par
Consolidated Duquesne Mining Co., Ltd. merged into Beattie-Duquesne Mines Ltd. 00/00/1952 which recapitalized as Donchester-Duquesne Mines Ltd. 07/11/1972 which merged into Fundy Chemical International Ltd. 10/01/1973
(See Fundy Chemical International Ltd.)

DUQUESNE NAT GAS CO (PA)
Common no par changed to 1¢ par in 1938
Each share $5 Preferred no par exchanged for (1) share $1.50 Cum. Conv. Preferred $25 par and (5) shares Common 1¢ par in 1954
Each share $4 Preference no par exchanged for (1) share $1.50 Conv. Preferred $25 par and (20) shares Common 1¢ par in 1954
Merged into Duquesne Natural Gas Co. (TX) 12/29/72
Each share $1.50 Conv. Preferred $25 par exchanged for (20) shares Common 1¢ par
Each share Common 1¢ par exchanged for (1) share Common 1¢ par
(See Duquesne Natural Gas Co. (TX))

DUQUESNE NAT GAS CO (TX)
Merged into Aegis Corp. 08/13/1976
Each share Common $1 par exchanged for $1.175 cash

DUQUESNE OIL CORP (DE)
Capital Stock $5 par changed to 25¢ par in 1938
Charter cancelled and declared inoperative and void for non-payment of taxes 4/15/70

DUQUESNE STEEL FOUNDRY CO.
Merged into Continental Roll & Steel Foundry Co. 00/00/1930
Details not available

DUQUESNE SYS INC (DE)
Common no par split (2) for (1) by issuance of (1) additional share 03/17/1986
Common no par split (2) for (1) by issuance of (1) additional share 02/27/1987
Merged into Legent Corp. 03/20/1989
Each share Common no par exchanged for (1) share Common 1¢ par
(See Legent Corp.)

DUQUESNE TRACTION CO.
Merged into Pittsburgh Railways Co. 9/30/50
Each share Common $50 par exchanged for (4.2) shares Common no par and $5 cash
Pittsburgh Railways Co. named changed to Pittway Corp. (PA) 11/28/67 which merged into Pittway Corp. (DE) 12/28/89
(See Pittway Corp. (DE))

DUQUESTO GOLD MINES, LTD. (ON)
Charter revoked for failure to file reports and pay taxes in 1958

DURA AUTOMOTIVE SYS CAP TR (DE)
Plan of reorganization under Chapter 11 Federal Bankruptcy Code effective 06/27/2008
No stockholders' equity

DURA AUTOMOTIVE SYS INC (DE)
Plan of reorganization under Chapter 11 Federal Bankruptcy Code effective 06/27/2008
No stockholders' equity

DURA CO. (OH)
Charter cancelled for non-payment of taxes 11/15/34

DURA CORP. (MI)
Common $1 par split (4) for (3) by issuance of (0.33333333) additional share 06/15/1964
Stock Dividends - 10% 06/14/1963; 10% 06/10/1965; 10% 06/13/1966
Completely liquidated 11/22/1966
Each share Common $1 par exchanged for first and final distribution of (0.4) share Kidde (Walter) & Co., Inc. (NY) $2.20 Conv. Preference Ser. A $1 par
Kidde (Walter) & Co., Inc. (NY) reincorporated in Delaware 07/02/1968 which name changed to Kidde, Inc. 04/01/1980
(See Kidde, Inc.)

DURA PHARMACEUTICALS INC (DE)
Reincorporated 05/27/1997
Common no par split (2) for (1) by issuance of (1) additional share payable 07/01/1996 to holders of record 06/17/1996 Ex date - 07/02/1996
State of incorporation changed from (CA) to (DE) and Common no par changed to $0.001 par 05/27/1997
Merged into Elan Corp., PLC 11/10/2000
Each share Common $0.001 par exchanged for (0.6715) Sponsored ADR for Ordinary Elan Corp., PLC merged into Perrigo Co. PLC 12/18/2013

DURA PRINT TECHNOLOGIES (UT)
Each share Common $0.001 par exchanged for (0.1) share Common 1¢ par 05/01/1986
Involuntarily dissolved 03/01/1991

DURA PRODS INTL INC (ON)
Recapitalized as Dexx Corp. 01/15/2004
Each share Common no par exchanged for (0.02) share Common no par
(See Dexx Corp.)

DURACELL INTL INC (MD)
Merged into Gillette Co. 12/31/96
Each share Common 1¢ par exchanged for (0.904) share Common $1 par
Gillette Co. merged into Procter & Gamble Co. 10/1/2005

DURACO INDS INC (UT)
Proclaimed dissolved for failure to pay taxes 11/09/1974

DURACOTE, INC. (TX)
Charter forfeited for failure to pay taxes 2/3/67

DURACOTE MANUFACTURING & SALES CO., INC. (FL)
Proclaimed dissolved for failure to file reports and pay fees 9/3/76

DURACRAFT CORP (MA)
Merged into Honeywell Inc. 5/1/96
Each share Common no par exchanged for $43.50 cash

DURAKON INDS INC (MI)
Common no par split (3) for (2) by issuance of (0.5) additional share 2/1/86
Merged into Littlejohn Partners IV, L.P. 7/26/99
Each share Common no par exchanged for $16 cash

DURAL ELECTR CTLS CORP (CT)
Recapitalized as Stevron Industries, Inc. (CT) 3/4/85
Each share Common no par exchanged for (0.5) share Common 1¢ par
Stevron Industries, Inc. (CT) reincorporated in Delaware 5/20/85
(See Stevron Industries, Inc.)

DURALITH CORP (NJ)
Merged into Lucas Industries, Inc. 07/01/1985
Each share Common no par exchanged for $20 cash

DURALOY CO (DE)
Stock Dividend - 10% 12/31/1953
Name changed to Bridge Street, Inc. 11/30/1973
(See Bridge Street, Inc.)

DURAMAX INC
Preferred called for redemption at $105 on 12/31/97

DURAMED PHARMACEUTICALS INC (DE)
Merged into Barr Laboratories, Inc. (NY) 10/24/2001
Each share Common 1¢ par exchanged for (0.2562) share Common 1¢ par
Barr Laboratories, Inc. (NY) reincorporated in Delaware as Barr Pharmaceuticals, Inc. 12/31/2003 which was acquired by Teva Pharmaceutical Industries Ltd. 12/23/2008

DURAMETALLIC CORP. (MI)
Merged into Duriron Co., Inc. 12/14/95
Each share Common $5 par exchanged for (3.1132) shares Common $1.25 par
Duriron Co., Inc. name changed to Durco International Inc. 4/24/97 which name changed to Flowserve Corp. 7/22/97

DURAN GOLD CORP (BC)
Recapitalized as Duran Ventures Inc. (BC) 08/08/2000
Each share Common no par exchanged for (0.5) share Common no par
Duran Ventures Inc. (BC) reincorporated in Canada 10/31/2008 which name changed to Peruvian Metals Corp. 09/05/2018

DURAN VENTURES INC (CANADA)
Reincorporated 10/31/2008
Place of incorporation changed from (BC) to (Canada) 10/31/2008
Each share old Common no par exchanged for (0.14285714) share new Common no par 05/09/2016
Name changed to Peruvian Metals Corp. 09/05/2018

DURANDEL MINERALS CORP (CANADA)
Recapitalized as Calliope Metals Corp. (Canada) 07/15/1996
Each share Common no par exchanged for (0.5) share Common no par
Calliope Metals Corp. (Canada) reincorporated in Yukon 06/17/1997 which merged into Argosy Minerals Inc. (YT) 05/07/1999 which reincorporated in British Columbia 05/26/2005 which reincorporated in Australia as Argosy Minerals Ltd. 03/18/2011

DURANGO APPAREL INC (DE)
Chapter 11 bankruptcy proceedings dismissed 02/05/2003
Stockholders' equity unlikely

DURANGO CAP CORP (BC)
Recapitalized as Falkirk Resources Corp. 04/06/2009
Each share Common no par exchanged for (0.1) share Common no par
Falkirk Resources Corp. recapitalized as Jemi Fibre Corp. 06/27/2013 which merged into CanWel Building Materials Group Ltd. 05/16/2016

DURANGO CAP INC (NV)
Recapitalized as U.T., Inc. 08/08/1989
Each share Common $0.001 par exchanged for (0.1) share Common $0.001 par

DURANIUM MINES, LTD. (ON)
Merged into Continental Consolidated Mines & Oils Co. Ltd. on a (0.1) for (1) basis 10/4/57
(See Continental Consolidated Mines & Oils Co. Ltd.)

DURANT ACCEPTANCE CORP.
Dissolved in 1929

DURANT MOTOR CO. (NJ)
Charter forfeited for non-payment of taxes in 1934

DURANT MOTOR CO. OF CALIFORNIA
Name changed to De Vaux-Hall Motors Corp. 00/00/1931
(See De Vaux-Hall Motors Corp.)

DURANT MOTOR CO. OF MICHIGAN (MI)
Acquired by Durant Motor Co. (NJ) in 1927
Details not available

DURANT MOTOR CO. OF NEW JERSEY (NJ)
Charter declared void for non-payment of taxes 1/2/34

DURANT MOTORS, INC. (DE)
No longer in existence having become inoperative and void for non-payment of taxes 4/1/34

DURASOURCE INDS INC (UT)
Proclaimed dissolved for failure to pay taxes 10/1/96

DURASWITCH INDS INC (NV)
Each share old Common $0.001 par exchanged for (0.23529411) share new Common $0.001 par 08/27/1999
Name changed to InPlay Technologies, Inc. 06/15/2005
(See InPlay Technologies, Inc.)

DURATA THERAPEUTICS INC (DE)
Merged into Actavis PLC 11/18/2014
Each share Common 1¢ par exchanged for (1) Non-transferable Contingent Value Right and $23 cash
Each Non-transferable Contingent Value Right received distribution of $1 cash 03/20/2015

DURATEK CORP (NY)
Name changed to GTS Duratek, Inc. 5/29/92
GTS Duratek, Inc. name changed to Duratek Inc. 1/22/2001
(See Duratek Inc.)

DURATEK INC (NY)
Merged into Energy Solutions, LLC 6/7/2006
Each share Common 1¢ par exchanged for $22 cash

DURATION MINES LTD (CANADA)
Reincorporated 11/3/86
Place of incorporation changed from (BC) to (Canada) 11/3/86
Delisted from Toronto Stock Exchange 3/20/91

DURAY REALTY CORP. (NY)
Dissolved 8/14/64

DURBAN ROODEPOORT DEEP LTD (SOUTH AFRICA)
Each Unsponsored ADR for Ordinary exchanged for (1) Sponsored ADR for Ordinary 08/12/1996
Name changed to DRDGOLD Ltd. 12/06/2004

DURCO INTL INC (NY)
Under plan of merger name changed to Flowserve Corp. 7/22/97

DUREX GOLD MINES, LTD. (ON)
Charter revoked for failure to file reports and pay taxes in 1956

DUREZ PLASTICS & CHEMICALS, INC. (NY)
Common no par changed to $5 par in 1939
Each share Common $5 par exchanged for (3) shares Common $1.66-2/3 par in 1946
Stock Dividends - 200% 8/23/44; 10% 2/10/55
Merged into Hooker Electrochemical Co. 4/29/55
Each share Common $1.66-2/3 par exchanged for (1) share Common $5 par
Hooker Electrochemical Co. name changed to Hooker Chemical Corp. 5/29/58 which was acquired by Occidental Petroleum Corp. (CA) 7/24/68
(See Occidental Petroleum Corp. (CA))

DURGA RES LTD (AB)
Name changed to Leader Mining Corp. 9/24/93
Leader Mining Corp. recapitalized as Leader Mining International Inc. 7/29/94

DURHAM AIRCRAFT SERVICE, INC. (NY)
Merged out of existence 4/30/2001
Details not available

DURHAM CAP CORP (AB)
Name changed to Sikanni Services Ltd. 01/12/2007
Sikanni Services Ltd. merged into EnQuest Energy Services Corp. 04/29/2008
(See EnQuest Energy Services Corp.)

DURHAM CORP (NC)
Common $5 par split (2) for (1) by issuance of (1) additional share 09/13/1984
Common $5 par split (3) for (2) by issuance of (0.5) additional share 05/19/1987
Merged into Capital Holding Corp. 11/14/1991
Each share Common $5 par exchanged for (0.25) share Conv. Jr. Preferred Ser. J $5 par
Capital Holding Corp. name changed to Providian Corp. 05/12/1994 which merged into Aegon N.V. 06/10/1997

DURHAM DUPLEX RAZOR CO.
Name changed to Durham-Enders Razor Corp. in 1942
(See Durham-Enders Razor Corp.)

DURHAM-ENDERS RAZOR CORP. (NY)
Liquidation completed 9/16/58
Class A stockholders had no equity

DURHAM EXPLORATIONS LTD. (ON)
Recapitalized as Consolidated Durham Mines & Resources Ltd. on a (1) for (5) basis in October 1959
Consolidated Durham Mines & Resources Ltd. merged into Durham Resources Inc. 3/28/84 which name changed to Landmark Corp. (Old) 4/21/87 which merged into Landmark Corp. (New) 1/31/92 which recapitalized as Landmark Global Financial Corp. 7/5/96

DURHAM HOSIERY MLS (NC)
Each share 7% Preferred $100 par exchanged for (1.125) shares 6% Preferred $100 par in 1929
Class A Common $100 par changed to no par in 1929
Each share Class B Common $50 par exchanged for (0.5) share Class B Common no par in 1929 6% Class A Preferred $100 par called for redemption 2/1/73
Each share Class A Common no par exchanged for (0.000222) share Common no par 1/12/81
Each share Class B Common no par changed for (0.000222) share Common no par 1/12/81
Note: In effect holders received $7 cash per share and public interest was eliminated

DURHAM LIFE INS CO (NC)
Each share Capital Stock $10 par exchanged for (3) shares Capital Stock $5 par 03/08/1965
Stock Dividends - 25% 08/23/1974; 20% 09/07/1977
Reorganized as Durham Corp. 12/31/1979
Each share Capital Stock $5 par exchanged for (1) share Common $5 par
Durham Corp. merged into Capital Holding Corp. 11/14/1991 which name changed to Providian Corp. 05/12/1994 which merged into Aegon N.V. 06/10/1997

DURHAM MARKETING CORP (NV)
Each share old Common $0.001 par exchanged for (0.1) share new Common $0.001 par 10/18/2004
SEC revoked common stock registration 04/04/2013

DURHAM RED LAKE GOLD MINES LTD. (ON)
Name changed to Durham Explorations Ltd. in 1954
Durham Explorations Ltd. recapitalized as Consolidated Durham Mines & Resources Ltd. in October 1959 which merged into Durham Resources Inc. 3/28/84 which name changed to Landmark Corp. (Old) 4/21/87 which merged into Landmark Corp. (New) 1/31/92 which recapitalized as Global Financial Corp. 7/5/96

DURHAM RES INC (ON)
Name changed to Landmark Corp. (Old) 4/21/87
Landmark Corp. (Old) merged into Landmark Corp. (New) 1/31/92 which recapitalized as Landmark Global Financial Corp. 7/5/96

DURHAM RES LTD (BC)
Merged into Gothic Resources Inc. (BC) 07/09/1991
Each share Common no par exchanged for (0.75) share Common no par
Gothic Resources Inc. (BC) reincorporated in Canada 08/01/1991 which reincorporated in Oklahoma as American Natural Energy Corp. (Ctfs. dtd. after 02/12/2002) 02/12/2002
(See American Natural Energy Corp. (Ctfs. dtd. after 02/12/2002)

DURIRON INC (NY)
5% Preferred $25 par called for redemption 7/29/55
Each share Common $5 par exchanged for (2) shares Common $2.50 par in 1951
Common $2.50 par changed to $1.25 par and (1) additional share issued 5/2/66
Common $1.25 par split (3) for (2) by issuance of (0.5) additional share 5/20/68
Common $1.25 par split (2) for (1) by issuance of (1) additional share 9/8/76
Common $1.25 par split (3) for (2) by issuance of (0.5) additional share 9/11/78
Common $1.25 par split (3) for (2) by issuance of (0.5) additional share 3/27/81
Common $1.25 par split (3) for (2) by issuance of (0.5) additional share 3/20/89
Common $1.25 par split (3) for (2) by suance of (0.5) additional share 3/25/94
Name changed to Durco International Inc. 4/24/97
Durco International Inc. name changed to Flowserve Corp. 7/22/97

DURKIN HAYES PUBG LTD (ON)
Recapitalized as Imark Corp. 10/27/98
Each share Common no par exchanged for (1/7) share Common no par
Imark Corp. merged into Maxim Atlantic Corp. 8/19/2003

DURO ENZYME PRODS INC (NV)
Common $0.001 par split (20) for (1) by issuance of (19) additional shares payable 03/08/2002 to holders of record 03/04/2002
Ex date - 03/11/2002
Recapitalized as EAPI Entertainment, Inc. 05/27/2003
Each share Common $0.001 par exchanged for (0.02) share Common $0.001 par
EAPI Entertainment, Inc. name changed to Organic Recycling Technologies, Inc. 11/15/2005 which name changed to Global 8 Environmental Technologies, Inc. 05/15/2008

DURO PEN CO., INC. (NY)
Stock Dividend - 10% 11/10/1966
Completely liquidated 10/04/1967
Each share Common 50¢ par exchanged for first and final distribution of (0.33859) share Diversified Metals Corp. (DE) Common 50¢ par
Diversified Metals Corp. (DE) name changed to Diversified Industries, Inc. 08/04/1969
(See Diversified Industries, Inc.)

DURO TEST CORP (NY)
Common $1 par changed to 15¢ par and (6) additional shares issued 05/01/1962
5% Preferred 1956 Ser. $25 par called for redemption 06/16/1986

Acquired by TCA Acquisition Corp. 03/25/1988
Each share Common 15¢ par exchanged for $14.183 cash

DUROC RED LAKE MINES LTD.
Name changed to Duranium Mines Ltd. in 1949
Duranium Mines Ltd. merged into Consolidated Mines & Oils Co. Ltd. 10/4/57
(See Consolidated Mines & Oils Co. Ltd.)

DUROCHER URANIUM CO. LTD. (AB)
Name changed to Infrationics Industries Ltd. 5/7/74
(See Infrationics Industries Ltd.)

DUROX MANAGEMENT CO. (MN)
Adjudicated bankrupt 04/29/1968
No stockholders' equity

DUROX OF MINNESOTA, INC. (CO)
Merged into Durox Management Co. 11/00/1963
Each share Common $1 par exchanged for (1) share Common
(See Durox Management Co.)

DUROX SOUTHN CALIF INC (CA)
Name changed to Southern California Durox, Inc. 1/18/80
(See Southern California Durox, Inc.)

DURR FILLAUER MED INC (DE)
Common 50¢ par split (5) for (4) by issuance of (0.25) additional share 6/28/85
Common 50¢ par split (5) for (4) by issuance of (0.25) additional share 1/4/91
Stock Dividends - 25% 5/15/80; 50% 5/21/81; 100% 12/15/82
Merged into Bergen Brunswig Corp. 10/5/92
Each share Common 50¢ par exchanged for $33 cash

DURST S F & CO INC (UT)
Declared bankrupt in 1971
Stockholders' equity unlikely

DURUM CONS ENERGY CORP (YUKON)
Name changed to TAG Oil Ltd. (Yukon) 6/12/2002
TAG Oil Ltd. (Yukon) reincorporated in British Columbia 10/12/2006

DURUM ENERGY CORP (YUKON)
Reincorporated 10/24/97
Place of incorporation changed from (BC) to (Yukon) 10/24/97
Recapitalized as Durum Consolidated Energy Corp. 10/27/98
Each share Common no par exchanged for (0.2) share Common no par
Durum Consolidated Energy Corp. name changed to TAG Oil Ltd. (Yukon) 6/12/2002 which reincorporated in British Columbia 10/12/2006

DURVADA RES LTD (AB)
Merged into Durga Resources Ltd. 5/21/92
Each share Common no par exchanged for (1.5) shares Common no par
Durga Resources Ltd. name changed to Leader Mining Corp. 9/24/93 which recapitalized as Leader Mining International Inc. 7/29/94

DURWOOD INC (DE)
Reorganized as SportsNuts.com International, Inc. 04/07/1999
Each share Common $0.0001 par exchanged for (2.213) shares Common $0.0001 par
SportsNuts.com International, Inc. name changed to SportsNuts, Inc. 10/06/2003 which recapitalized as FuelStream, Inc. 05/13/2010

DUSA PHARMACEUTICALS INC (NJ)
Acquired by Sun Pharmaceutical Industries Ltd. 12/20/2012

Each share Common no par exchanged for $8 cash

DUSKA THERAPEUTICS INC (NV)
Each share old Common $0.001 par exchanged for (0.05) share new Common $0.001 par 03/26/2007
Note: Holders of between (100) and (1,999) shares received (100) shares
Holders of (99) shares or fewer were not affected by the reverse split
Name changed to Cordex Pharma, Inc. 01/28/2009
(See Cordex Pharma, Inc.)

DUSOLO FERTILIZERS INC (BC)
Reincorporated 07/19/2016
Place of incorporation changed from (Canada) to (BC) 07/19/2016
Each share old Common no par exchanged for (0.1) share new Common no par 07/11/2017
Name changed to Fengro Industries Corp. 12/18/2017

DUSSAULT APPAREL INC (NV)
Common $0.001 par split (14) for (1) by issuance of (13) additional shares payable 06/12/2006 to holders of record 06/12/2007
Recapitalized as Prospect Ventures, Inc. 03/21/2014
Each share Common $0.001 par exchanged for (0.00125) share Common $0.001 par

DUSTBANE ENTERPRISES LTD (CANADA)
Common no par split (2) for (1) by issuance of (1) additional share 01/05/1970
100% acquired by Monteville Holdings Ltd. through purchase offer which expired 07/03/1981
Public interest eliminated

DUSTY MAC MINES LTD (BC)
Recapitalized as International Dusty Mac Enterprises Ltd. 05/21/1992
Each share Common 50¢ par exchanged for (0.2) share Common no par
International Dusty Mac Enterprises Ltd. name changed to Dusty Mac Oil & Gas Ltd. 05/10/1994 which name changed to Transglobe Energy Corp. (BC) 04/02/1996 which reincorporated in Alberta 06/09/2004

DUSTY MAC OIL & GAS LTD (BC)
Name changed to Transglobe Energy Corp. (BC) 04/02/1996
Transglobe Energy Corp. (BC) reincorporated in Alberta 06/09/2004

DUTCH BOY INC (PA)
Name changed to Artra Group Inc. 12/31/1980
Artra Group Inc. merged into Entrade Inc. 09/23/1999
(See Entrade Inc.)

DUTCH CREEK RES LTD (BC)
Placed in receivership 04/00/1990
No stockholders' equity

DUTCH GUIANA MINERALS CORP. (DE)
Merged into Paraguay Mining Corp. 04/09/1957
Each share Capital Stock 1¢ par exchanged for (1) share Capital Stock 1¢ par
(See Paraquay Mining Corp.)

DUTCH WEST INDIA CO. LTD. (DE)
Merged into Madison Industries, Inc. 11/13/1967
Each share Common 10¢ par exchanged for (0.2857) share Common 10¢ par
(See Madison Industries, Inc.)

DUTCHFORK BANKSHARES INC (DE)
Merged into First Community Corp. 10/05/2004
Each share Common 1¢ par

exchanged for (1.78125) shares Common $1 par

DUTHIE MINES (1946) LTD. (BC)
Bankrupt 00/00/1949
Details not available

DUTRON CORP. (CA)
Merged into Thompson (H.I.) Fiber Glass Co. 02/27/1961
Each share Common no par exchanged for (1) share Capital Stock no par
Thompson (H.I.) Fiber Glass Co. name changed to Hitco 02/19/1965 which merged into Armco Steel Corp. 12/31/1969 which name changed to Armco Inc. 07/01/1978 which merged into AK Steel Holding Corp. 09/30/1999

DUTTON (C.H.) CO.
Name changed to Hapman-Dutton Co. 00/00/1950
Hapman-Dutton Co. name changed to Hapman-Conveyors, Inc. 05/01/1958 which name changed to Hapman Corp. 10/01/1959
(See Hapman Corp.)

DUTTON A C LMBR CORP (NY)
Each share Common $100 par exchanged for (10) shares Common $10 par 00/00/1948
Filed a petition under Chapter 11 Federal Bankruptcy Code 03/03/1982
Stockholders' equity unlikely

DUTY FREE INTL INC (MD)
Common 1¢ par split (2) for (1) by issuance of (1) additional share 10/20/1989
Common 1¢ par split (2) for (1) by issuance of (1) additional share 07/05/1991
Merged into W&G Acquisition Corp. 09/02/1997
Each share Common 1¢ par exchanged for $24 cash

DUVAL CORP (TX)
Merged into Pennzoil United, Inc. 12/31/1970
Each share Capital Stock no par exchanged for (6.75) shares Common $0.83333333 par
Pennzoil United, Inc. name changed to Pennzoil Co. (DE) 06/01/1972 which name changed to PennzEnergy Co. 12/30/1998 which merged into Devon Energy Corp. (New) 08/17/1999

DUVAL SULPHUR & POTASH CO. (TX)
Stock Dividend - 14.28571428% 12/31/1953
Name changed to Duval Corp. 03/19/1963
Duval Corp. merged into Pennzoil United, Inc. 12/31/1970 which name changed to Pennzoil Co. (DE) 06/01/1972 which name changed to PennzEnergy Co. 12/30/1998 which merged into Devon Energy Corp. (New) 08/17/1999

DUVAL TEXAS SULPHUR CO. (TX)
Name changed to Duval Sulphur & Potash Co. 00/00/1950
Duval Sulphur & Potash Co. name changed to Duval Corp. 03/19/1963 which merged into Pennzoil United, Inc. 12/31/1970 which name changed to Pennzoil Co. (DE) 06/01/1972 which name changed to PennzEnergy Co.12/30/1998 which merged into Devon Energy Corp. (New) 08/17/1999

DUVAN COPPER LTD (QC)
Charter cancelled 09/11/1982

DUVAY GOLD MINES LTD.
Recapitalized as Duvex Oils & Mines Ltd. 00/00/1952
Each share Common $1 par exchanged for (0.25) share Common $1 par

Duvex Oils & Mines Ltd. recapitalized as United Duvex Oils & Mines Ltd. 06/09/1972
(See United Duvex Oils & Mines Ltd.)

DUVERNAY OIL CORP (AB)
Acquired by Shell Canada Ltd. 08/28/2008
Each share Common no par exchanged for $83 cash

DUVERNOY & SONS INC (NY)
5% Preferred $100 par reclassified as 6% Preferred $100 par 07/13/1966
6% Preferred $100 par reclassified as 7% Preferred $100 par 05/10/1974
Dissolved by proclamation 01/25/2012

DUVERNY EXPL INC (QC)
Merged into Exploration SEG Inc./SEG Exploration Inc. 01/01/1992
Each share Common no par exchanged for (0.26954177) share Common no par
Exploration SEG Inc./SEG Exploration Inc. name changed to West Africa Mining Exploration Inc. 07/06/1995 which name changed to Semafo Inc. 05/13/1997

DUVEX OILS & MINES LTD. (ON)
Recapitalized as United Duvex Oils & Mines Ltd. 06/09/1972
Each share Common $1 par exchanged for (0.1) share Common no par
(See United Duvex Oils & Mines Ltd.)

DUZ CO., INC.
Acquired by Procter & Gamble Co. 00/00/1929
Details not available

DV RES LTD (ON)
Name changed to DLV Resources Ltd. 11/27/2017

DVD INVTS LTD (ON)
Name changed to Mooncor Oil & Gas Corp. 10/22/2007
Mooncor Oil & Gas Corp. recapitalized as Sensor Technologies Inc. 10/24/2018

DVI INC (DE)
Name changed 11/06/1991
Name changed 06/17/1993
Name changed from DVI Financial Corp. to DVI Health Services Corp. 11/06/1991
Name changed from DVI Health Services Corp. to DVI, Inc. 06/17/1993
Plan of reorganization under Chapter 11 Federal Bankruptcy Code effective 12/10/2004
No stockholders' equity

DVO INDS LTD (BC)
Delisted from Vancouver Stock Exchange 01/06/1994

DVR RES LTD (BC)
Recapitalized as Gresham Resources Inc. 06/14/1993
Each share Common no par exchanged for (0.22222222) share Common no par
Gresham Resources Inc. acquired by True Energy Inc. 07/31/2002
(See True Energy Inc.)

DVT HLDGS LTD (AUSTRALIA)
Name changed to UXC Ltd. 12/31/2002
(See UXC Ltd.)

DWANGO NORTH AMER CORP (NV)
Name changed to Dijji Corp. 12/13/2005

DWELLING HOUSE ASSOCIATES (MA)
Liquidation completed 12/12/1960
Details not available

DWIGHT HEALTH CARE INC (DE)
Charter cancelled and declared inoperative and void for non-payment of taxes 03/01/1985

DWIGHT MANOR APTS INC (DE)
Voluntarily dissolved 12/30/1986
Details not available

DWIGHT MANUFACTURING CO.
Merged into Cone Mills Corp.
00/00/1951
Each share Capital Stock $12.50 par exchanged for (1) share 4% Preferred $20 par and (2) shares Common $10 par
(See Cone Mills Corp.)

DWS GLOBAL COMMODITIES STK FD INC (MD)
Name changed to DWS Enhanced Commodity Strategy Fund, Inc. 03/31/2010

DWS GLOBAL HIGH INCOME FD INC (MD)
Name changed to Deutsche Global High Income Fund, Inc. 08/11/2014
(See Deutsche Global High Income Fund, Inc.)

DWS HIGH INCOME OPPORTUNITIES FD INC (MD)
Name changed 11/08/2010
Each share old Common 1¢ par exchanged for (0.5) share new Common 1¢ par 08/10/2009
Name changed from DWS Dreman Value Income Edge Fund, Inc. to DWS High Income Opportunities Fund, Inc. 11/08/2010
Name changed to Deutsche High Income Opportunities Fund, Inc. 08/11/2014
(See Deutsche High Income Opportunities Fund, Inc.)

DWS HIGH INCOME TR (MA)
Each share old Common 1¢ par exchanged for (0.5) share new Common 1¢ par 08/10/2009
Name changed to Deutsche High Income Trust 08/11/2014
(See Deutsche High Income Trust)

DWS MULTI MKT INCOME TR (MA)
Name changed to Deutsche Multi-Market Income Trust 08/11/2014

DWS MUN INCOME TR OLD (MA)
100% of Remarketed Preferred Ser. A 1¢ par acquired through purchase offer which expired 11/16/2012
100% of Remarketed Preferred Ser. D 1¢ par acquired through purchase offer which expired 11/16/2012
Name changed to Deutsche Municipal Income Trust 08/11/2014
Deutsche Municipal Income Trust name changed to DWS Municipal Income Trust (New) 07/02/2018

DWS RREEF WORLD REAL ESTATE FD INC (MD)
Name changed 06/30/2010
Each share old Common 1¢ par exchanged for (0.5) share new Common 1¢ par 08/10/2009
Name changed from DWS RREEF World Real Estate & Tactical Stategies Fund, Inc. to DWS RREEF World Real Estate Fund, Inc. 06/30/2010
Merged into DWS Securities Trust 02/18/2011
Each share new Common 1¢ par exchanged for (2.43571428) shares Class M $0.001 par

DWS STRATEGIC INCOME TR (MA)
Name changed to Deutsche Strategic Income Trust 08/11/2014

DWS STRATEGIC MUN INCOME TR OLD (MA)
Name changed to Deutsche Strategic Municipal Income Trust 08/11/2014
Deutsche Strategic Municipal Income Trust name changed to DWS Strategic Municipal Income Trust (New) 07/02/2018

DWS U S GOVT SECS FD (MA)
Name changed to DWS Strategic Government Securities Fund 03/25/2008

DWYER-BAKER ELECTRONICS CORP. (FL)
Name changed to Advance Metal Products, Inc. 11/07/1967
(See Advance Metal Products, Inc.)

DWYER GROUP INC (OK)
Merged into Riverside Co. 10/31/2003
Each share Common 10¢ par exchanged for $6.75 cash

DY 4 SYS INC (ON)
Common no par split (3) for (1) by issuance of (2) additional shares 05/16/1994
Merged into C-MAC Industries Inc. 11/24/2000
Each share Common no par exchanged for (0.22515) share Common no par
C-MAC Industries Inc. merged into Solectron Corp. 12/03/2001 which merged into Flextronics International Ltd. 10/01/2007 which name changed to Flex Ltd. 09/28/2016

DYANSEN CORP (NY)
Merged out of existence 11/20/1987
Details not available

DYATRON CORP (DE)
Merged into SunGard Data Systems Inc. 11/10/1989
Each share Common $0.66666666 par exchanged for (0.9615) share Common 1¢ par
(See SunGard Data Systems Inc.)

DYAX CORP (DE)
Acquired by Shire PLC 01/22/2016
Each share Common 1¢ par exchanged for $37.30 cash and (1) Contingent Value Right

DYCAM INC (DE)
Each share old Common 1¢ par exchanged for (0.1) share new Common 1¢ par 11/01/2000
Recapitalized as Mekju Processing, Inc. (DE) 03/14/2006
Each share new Common 1¢ par exchanged for (0.004) share Common 1¢ par
Mekju Processing, Inc. (DE) reincorporated in Nevada as Axium Technologies Inc. 11/24/2006 which name changed to Wincash Resources, Inc. 01/05/2016 which name changed to Fovea Jewelry Holdings, Ltd. 02/06/2018

DYCO PETE CORP (MN)
Common 1¢ par split (3) for (2) by issuance of (0.5) additional share 11/26/1980
Stock Dividends - 50% 02/03/1978; 50% 03/21/1979; 50% 10/22/1979
Merged into Diversified Energies, Inc. 10/18/1985
Each share Common 1¢ par exchanged for (0.65) share Common $1 par
Diversified Energies, Inc. merged into Arkla, Inc. 11/29/1990 which name changed to NorAm Energy Corp. 05/11/1994 which merged into Houston Industries Inc. 08/06/1997 which name changed to Reliant Energy Inc. 02/08/1999 which reorganized as CenterPoint Energy, Inc. 08/31/2002

DYER-MILLS MINING CO. LTD.
Bankrupt in 1936

DYER (JOHN T.) QUARRY CO. (PA)
Acquired by Warner Co. 04/30/1969
Each share Common no par exchanged for $121 cash

DYERSBURG CORP (TN)
Chapter 7 bankruptcy proceedings terminated 04/30/2008
No stockholders' equity

DYESOL LTD (AUSTRALIA)
Name changed to Greatcell Solar Ltd. 07/13/2017

DYKE LAKE MINES, LTD. (ON)
Charter revoked for failure to file reports and pay taxes 9/18/61

DYKE MINES LTD (BC)
Struck off register and declared dissolved for failure to file returns 06/08/1981

DYLEX DIVERSIFIED 1967 LTD (CANADA)
Each share old Common no par exchanged for (3) shares Class A Part. Preference no par and (1) share new Common no par 11/28/68
Name changed to Dylex Diversified Ltd. 5/6/69
Dylex Diversified Ltd. name changed to Dylex Ltd. 8/1/72
(See Dylex Ltd.)

DYLEX LTD (CANADA)
Name changed 08/01/1972
Name changed from Dylex Diversified Ltd. to Dylex Ltd. 08/01/1972
Class A Part. Preference no par split (2) for (1) by issuance of (1) additional share 01/22/1973
Common no par split (2) for (1) by issuance of (1) additional share 01/22/1973
Class A Participating Preference no par split (3) for (1) by issuance of (2) additional shares 07/19/1985
Common no par split (3) for (1) by issuance of (2) additional shares 07/19/1985
Stock Dividend - in Class A Participating Preference 100% 04/12/1983
Restructuring under Canada Business Corporations Act effective 05/31/1995
For each (52.72319) shares Class A Participating Preference no par exchanged holders received (1) share new Common no par and (1) Common Stock Purchase Right
For each (158.62149) shares Class A Participating Preference no par exchanged holders received (1) Common Stock Purchase Warrant expiring 5/31/98
For each (52.72319) shares old Common no par exchanged holders received (1) share new Common no par and (1) Common Stock Purchase Right
For each (158.62149) shares old Common no par exchanged holders received (1) Common Stock Purchase Warrant expiring 05/31/1998
Acquired by Hardof Wolf Group Inc. 05/16/2001
Each share new Common no par exchanged for $1.30 cash

DYM ENERGY CORP (NV)
Name changed to Four G Holdings Corp. 09/09/2015

DYMACO CORP (CA)
Reincorporated under the laws of Delaware as Agric Development Corp. 05/15/1981
Agric Development Corp. name changed to Wil Wright's Ice Cream, Inc. 04/15/1983
(See Wil Wright's Ice Cream, Inc.)

DYMAT INTL CORP (DE)
Charter forfeited for failure to maintain a registered agent 12/07/1978

DYMO INDS INC (CA)
Capital Stock $1 par reclassified as Common $1 par 11/29/1966
Stock Dividend - 200% 05/31/1962
Merged into Oxford Pendaflex Development Corp. 10/20/1978
Each share Common $1 par exchanged for $30 cash

DYNA-CAM ENGINE CORP (NV)
Reorganized as Chiste Corp. 05/14/2004
Each share Common $0.001 par received (0.02) share Common $0.001 par
Note: Holders of (100) to (4,999) shares will receive (100) shares Holders of (99) or fewer were not affected by the reverse split
Chiste Corp. recapitalized as HydroGen Corp. 08/19/2005
(See HydroGen Corp.)

DYNA FLEX CORP (UT)
Class A Common $1 par and Class B Common $1 par reclassified as Common $1 par 08/10/1972
Name changed to Dynamic American Corp. 12/31/1974
Each share Common $1 par exchanged for (1) share Common $1 par
(See Dynamic American Corp.)

DYNA GOLD RES INC (BC)
Struck off register and declared dissolved for failure to file returns 12/13/1991

DYNA GRAPHIC INTL INC (UT)
Proclaimed dissolved for failure to file annual report 12/31/1977

DYNA HAUL CORP (BC)
Placed in receivership 5/29/2000
Details not available

DYNA JET CORP (DE)
Charter cancelled for non-payment of taxes 3/1/80

DYNA-MATION, INC. (MN)
Assets sold for benefit of creditors 1/5/67
No stockholders' equity

DYNA MECH SCIENCES INC (NY)
Name changed to Thompson (William), Inc. 08/18/1972

DYNA MOD ELECTRS CORP (NY)
Out of business 00/00/1972
No stockholders' equity

DYNA RAY CORP (DE)
Name changed to Trans Delta Corp. 08/07/1972
(See Trans Delta Corp.)

DYNA-SEAL CORP (NV)
Name changed to Interactive Buyers Network International Ltd. 07/21/1995
Interactive Buyers Network International Ltd. name changed to Vsource, Inc. (NV) 12/03/1999 which reincorporated in Delaware 11/08/2000 which name changed to Tri-Isthmus Group, Inc. 12/30/2005 which name changed to First Physicians Capital Group, Inc. 01/08/2010

DYNA-THERM CHEMICAL CORP. (NV)
Name changed to Dyna-Therm Corp. 9/23/64
Dyna-Therm Corp. name changed to Flamemaster Corp. 9/4/73

DYNA THERM CORP (NV)
Each share Capital Stock $1 par exchanged for (0.25) share Capital Stock $4 par 4/7/65
Capital Stock $4 par changed to no par 8/20/68
Name changed to Flamemaster Corp. 9/4/73

DYNABAZAAR INC (DE)
Under plan of merger name changed to Sielox, Inc. 07/31/2007
Sielox, Inc. name changed to Costar Technologies, Inc. 03/02/2012

DYNACARE INC (ON)
Plan of arrangement effective 05/14/1997
Each share Class B Subordinate no par exchanged for $6.45 cash
Merged into Laboratory Corp. of America Holdings 07/26/2002
Each share Common no par exchanged for approximately

(0.2328) share new Common 1¢ par and $11.50 cash

DYNA RES LTD (BC)
Struck off register and declared dissolved for failure to file returns 05/20/1980

DYNACOLOR CORP. (NY)
Common 50¢ par changed to 20¢ par and (2) additional shares issued 10/5/60
Acquired by Minnesota Mining & Manufacturing Co. on a (0.2) for (1) basis 9/6/63
Minnesota Mining & Manufacturing Co. name changed to 3M Co. 4/8/2002

DYNACOM TELECOMMUNICATIONS CORP (NV)
Name changed to Goldstate Corp. 11/07/1997
(See Goldstate Corp.)

DYNACORE ENTERPRISES LTD. (BC)
Recapitalized as Dynaco Resources Ltd. 02/09/1971
Each share Common no par exchanged for (0.33333333) share Common no par
(See Dynaco Resources Ltd.)

DYNACORE EXPLORATIONS LTD. (BC)
Under plan of merger name changed to Dynacore Enterprises Ltd. and 50¢ par changed to no par 7/15/67
Dynacore Enterprises Ltd. recapitalized as Dynaco Resources Ltd. 2/9/71
(See Dynaco Resources Ltd.)

DYNACORE HLDGS CORP (DE)
Plan of reorganization under Chapter 11 Federal Bankruptcy Code effective 12/18/2000
Each share Preferred $1 par received (3.663683) shares new Common 25¢ par and (0.545655) Patent Litigation Trust Unit of Bene. Int.
(See Patent Litigation Trust)
Each share old Common 25¢ par received (0.225177) share new Common 25¢ par
Note: Certificates were not required to be surrendered and are without value
Name changed to CattleSale Co. 02/25/2003
(See CattleSale Co.)

DYNACQ HEALTHCARE INC (DE)
Reincorporated under the laws of Nevada 03/20/2007

DYNACQ INTL INC (NV)
Each share old Common $0.001 par exchanged for (0.125) share new Common $0.001 par 03/08/1993
Each share new Common $0.001 par exchanged again for (0.25) share new Common $0.001 par 02/10/1998
New Common $0.001 par split (2) for (1) by issuance of (1) additional share payable 01/13/2000 to holders of record 01/10/2000
New Common $0.001 par split (2) for (1) by issuance of (1) additional share payable 03/16/2001 to holders of record 03/12/2001 Ex date - 03/19/2001
Reincorporated under the laws of Delaware as Dynacq Healthcare, Inc. 11/14/2003
Dynacq Healthcare, Inc. (DE) reincorporated in Nevada 03/20/2007

DYNADAPT SYS INC (CO)
Name changed to Sun River Energy, Inc. 08/31/2006

DYNAFUEL CORP (UT)
Name changed to Virtual Technologies Inc. (UT) 12/08/1995
Virtual Technologies Inc. (UT) reincorporated in Nevada

07/00/1996 which name changed to Solpower Corp. 01/06/1998 which name changed to Bitcoin Collect, Inc. 06/10/2014 which name changed to Good Vibrations Shoes Inc. 09/09/2014

DYNAGEN INC (DE)
Each share old Common 1¢ par exchanged for (0.1) share new Common 1¢ par 3/11/98
Name changed to Able Laboratories, Inc. 5/21/2001

DYNALECTRON CORP (DE)
Name changed to DynCorp 05/11/1987
(See DynCorp)

DYNALOGICS, INC. (NY)
Charter cancelled and proclaimed dissolved for failure to pay taxes and file reports 12/20/77

DYNALTA ENERGY CORP (CANADA)
Merged into Fossil Oil & Gas Ltd. 6/1/93
Each (1.88) shares 10% Conv. Preference no par exchanged for (1) share Common no par
Each (18.8) shares Common no par exchanged for (1) share Common no par
Fossil Oil & Gas Ltd. merged into Elk Point Resources Inc. 12/17/96 which merged into Acclaim Energy Trust 1/28/2003
(See Acclaim Energy Trust)

DYNALTA OIL & GAS LTD (AB)
Completely liquidated 1/1/72
Each share Capital Stock no par exchanged for first and final distribution of (0.1447) share Pan Ocean Oil Corp. Common 1¢ par
(See Pan Ocean Oil Corp.)

DYNALYST MFG CORP (TX)
Name changed to Universal Media Corp. 10/16/2009
Universal Media Corp. name changed to UMED Holdings Inc. 04/14/2011 which name changed to Greenway Technologies, Inc. 01/18/2018

DYNAMAR ENERGY LTD (AB)
Placed in receivership 05/16/1988
Stockholders' equity unlikely

DYNAMAX PETROCHEMICAL CORP (AB)
Recapitalized as Wildrose Ventures Inc. 12/18/1992
Each share Common no par exchanged for (0.125) share Common no par
(See Wildrose Ventures Inc.)

DYNAMED, INC. (MN)
Adjudicated bankrupt 06/07/1977
No stockholders' equity

DYNAMED, INC. (UT)
Reorganized under the laws of Delaware as Health International, Inc. 04/30/1987
Each (8.508355) shares Common $0.001 par exchanged for (1) share Common 10¢ par
(See Health International, Inc.)

DYNAMEX INC (DE)
Acquired by TransForce Inc. 02/23/2011
Each share Common 1¢ par exchanged for $25 cash

DYNAMIC ALERT LTD (NV)
Common $0.001 par split (40) for (1) by issuance of (39) additional shares payable 03/17/2008 to holders of record 03/17/2008 Ex date - 03/18/2008
Name changed to Brazil Gold Corp. 03/15/2010
Brazil Gold Corp. recapitalized as Conexus Cattle Corp. 01/12/2015 which name changed to Connexus Corp. 12/02/2015

DYNAMIC AMERN CORP (UT)
Each share Common $1 par exchanged for (0.05) share Common $0.001 par 06/22/1995
Involuntarily dissolved 12/01/1996

DYNAMIC APPLICATIONS CORP (DE)
Old Common $0.0001 par split (3) for (1) by issuance of (2) additional shares payable 02/12/2009 to holders of record 02/11/2009 Ex date - 02/13/2009
Old Common $0.0001 par changed to $0.00001 par 09/08/2011
Each share old Common $0.00001 par exchanged for (0.01) share new Common $0.00001 par 10/26/2012
Name changed to OWC Pharmaceutical Research Corp. 01/07/2015

DYNAMIC ASSOC INC (NV)
Each share Class A Common $0.001 par received distribution of (1) share MW Medical Inc. Common $0.001 par payable 03/11/1998 to holders of record 02/25/1998
Recapitalized as Legal Access Technologies Inc. 06/19/2001
Each share Class A Common $0.001 par exchanged for (0.00653594) share Common $0.001 par
Legal Access Technologies Inc. name changed to UnderSea Recovery Corp. 07/21/2010
(See UnderSea Recovery Corp.)

DYNAMIC BIOMETRIC SYS INC (NV)
Name changed to MemReg, Inc. 01/02/2015
MemReg, Inc. name changed to ORHub, Inc. 02/10/2017

DYNAMIC CABLE SYSTEMS (CA)
Bankrupt 04/16/1964
No stockholders' equity

DYNAMIC CAP CDA CORP (SK)
Name changed 11/21/2001
Name changed from Dynamic Capital Corp. to Dynamic Capital Canada Corp. 11/21/2001
Recapitalized as Churchill Energy Inc. (SK) 10/22/2004
Each share Class A Common no par exchanged for (0.2) share Class A Common no par
Churchill Energy Inc. (SK) reincorporated in Alberta 06/29/2006 which merged into Zargon Energy Trust 09/23/2009 which reorganized as Zargon Oil & Gas Ltd. (New) 01/07/2011

DYNAMIC CAP CORP (DE)
Charter cancelled and declared inoperative and void for non-payment of taxes 03/01/1991

DYNAMIC CAP CORP (ON)
Reorganized as Dundee Capital Corp. 05/11/1990
Each share Class A Subordinate no par exchanged for (1) share Common no par and (0.25) Common Stock Purchase Warrant expiring 06/30/1992 or $6.66 cash
Note: Option to receive cash expired 05/25/1990
(See Dundee Capital Corp.)

DYNAMIC CAPITALISM, INC. (CA)
Charter suspended for failure to file reports and pay taxes 02/01/1973

DYNAMIC CENTER ENGINEERING CO., INC. (GA)
Out of business 00/00/1967
Details not available

DYNAMIC CLASSICS LTD (NY)
Common 1¢ par split (5) for (2) by issuance of (1.5) additional shares 04/25/1972
Common 1¢ par split (2) for (1) by issuance of (1) additional share 09/23/1975
Reorganized under the laws of

Nevada as Dynamic International Ltd. 08/08/1996
Each share Common 1¢ par exchanged for (5.555) shares Common $0.001 par
Dynamic International Ltd. name changed to Emergent Group Inc. 08/06/2000
(See Emergent Group Inc.)

DYNAMIC COMPUTER SYS INC (TX)
Charter forfeited for failure to maintain a registered agent 09/01/1978

DYNAMIC CONS RES LTD (QC)
Delisted from Montreal Stock Exchange 01/25/1991

DYNAMIC CONSULTING CORP. (NV)
Recapitalized as Chase Revel, Inc. 09/21/1981
Each share Common $0.001 par exchanged for (2) shares Common $0.0005 par
Chase Revel, Inc. name changed to Entrepreneur Group, Inc. 11/06/1984
(See Entrepreneur Group, Inc.)

DYNAMIC DIGITAL DEPTH INC (AB)
Merged into DDD Group PLC 01/02/2002
Each share Common no par exchanged for (1) Ordinary share
(See DDD Group PLC)

DYNAMIC ELECTRONICS-NEW YORK INC (NY)
Name changed to Capehart Corp. (NY) 11/20/1959
Capehart Corp. (NY) name changed to Clavier Corp. 08/31/1964 which merged into Dero Research & Development Corp. 09/24/1969 which name changed to Dero Industries Inc. 02/10/1971
(See Dero Industries Inc.)

DYNAMIC ENERGY ALLIANCE CORP (FL)
Recapitalized as Elite Data Services, Inc. 12/31/2013
Each share Common $0.0001 par exchanged for (0.00076923) share Common $0.0001 par
Elite Data Services, Inc. recapitalized as WOD Retail Solutions Inc. 09/05/2018

DYNAMIC FD CDA LTD (CANADA)
Under plan of reorganization each Mutual Fund Share automatically became (1) share Dynamic Value Fund of Canada Mutual Fund Share 06/05/2001

DYNAMIC FILMS INC (NY)
Name changed to DFI Communications, Inc. 02/24/1969
(See DFI Communications, Inc.)

DYNAMIC FUEL SYS INC (ON)
Name changed to DynaCERT Inc. 12/31/2012

DYNAMIC GEAR INC (FL)
Proclaimed dissolved for failure to file reports and pay fees 10/13/1988

DYNAMIC GLOBAL HLDGS LTD (HONG KONG)
ADR agreement terminated 02/19/2013
No ADR's remain outstanding

DYNAMIC GOLD CORP (NV)
Name changed to Hartford Retirement Network Corp. 06/26/2017
Hartford Retirement Network Corp. name changed to HQDA Elderly Life Network Corp. 06/07/2018

DYNAMIC HEALTH PRODS INC (FL)
Each share Common 1¢ par received distribution of (0.626882) share DrugMax, Inc. Common $0.001 par payable 11/22/2002 to holders of record 10/10/2002 Ex date - 12/09/2002
Common 1¢ par split (4) for (1) by issuance of (3) additional shares

payable 08/12/2003 to holders of record 08/01/2003 Ex date - 08/13/2003
Each share Common 1¢ par received distribution of (0.1) share Vertical Health Solutions, Inc. Common $0.001 par payable 07/26/2004 to holders of record 07/16/2004
Merged into GeoPharma, Inc. 10/17/2007
Each share Common 1¢ par exchanged for (0.14285714) share Common 1¢ par
(See GeoPharma, Inc.)

DYNAMIC HEALTHCARE TECHNOLOGIES INC (FL)
Reincorporated 07/01/1996
State of incorporation changed from (NE) to (FL) 07/01/1996
Each share old Common 1¢ par exchanged for (0.33333333) share new Common 1¢ par 06/29/2001
Merged into Cerner Corp. 12/17/2001
Each share new Common 1¢ par exchanged for (0.0548) share Common 1¢ par

DYNAMIC HOMES INC (MN)
Merged into Dynamic Acquisition, Inc. 12/28/2000
Each share Common 10¢ par exchanged for $2.55 cash

DYNAMIC I-T INC (CO)
Common no par split (2) for (1) by issuance of (1) additional share payable 10/26/2001 to holders of record 10/25/2001 Ex date - 10/29/2001
Each share Common no par received distribution of (1) share Consolidated Communications Corp. PLC Common payable 10/26/2001 to holders of record 10/25/2001
Recapitalized as Artwork & Beyond, Inc. 02/10/2004
Each share Common no par exchanged for (0.05) share Common no par
Artwork & Beyond, Inc. recapitalized as Advance Nanotech, Inc. (CO) 12/02/2004 which reincorporated in Delaware 06/19/2006
(See Advance Nanotech, Inc.)

DYNAMIC IMAGING GROUP INC (FL)
Recapitalized as Greentech USA, Inc. 10/13/2003
Each share Common $0.001 par exchanged for (0.04) share Common $0.001 par
(See Greentech USA, Inc.)

DYNAMIC IMAGING SYS CORP (FL)
Name changed to Dynamic Media, Inc. 05/15/2000
Dynamic Media, Inc. name changed to Holoco, Inc. 09/22/2004

DYNAMIC INDUSTRIES, INC. (GA)
Adjudicated bankrupt 03/04/1974
Stockholders' equity unlikely

DYNAMIC INFORMATION SYS & EXCHANGE INC (UT)
Each share old Common $0.001 par exchanged for (0.5) share new Common $0.001 par 09/01/1995
Reincorporated under the laws of Nevada as Career Worth, Inc. 11/17/2000
Career Worth, Inc. name changed to U.S. Homes & Properties, Inc. 11/22/2002
(See U.S. Homes & Properties, Inc.)

DYNAMIC INSTR CORP (NY)
Stock Dividend - 10% 05/06/1974
Chapter 11 bankruptcy proceedings converted to Chapter 7 on 03/16/1983
Stockholders' equity unlikely

DYNAMIC INTL INC (DE)
Each share old Common $0.001 par exchanged for (0.00196078) share new Common $0.001 par 03/18/2005
Note: In effect holders received $47.57 cash per share and public interest was eliminated

DYNAMIC INTL LTD (NV)
Each share old Common $0.001 par exchanged for (0.2) share new Common $0.001 par 12/30/1997
Name changed to Emergent Group Inc. 08/06/2000
(See Emergent Group Inc.)

DYNAMIC LEISURE CORP (MN)
Ceased operations 11/21/2013
No stockholders' equity

DYNAMIC MATLS CORP (DE)
Reincorporated 08/15/1997
State of incorporation changed from (CO) to (DE) 08/15/1997
Common 5¢ par split (2) for (1) by issuance of (1) additional share payable 10/12/2005 to holders of record 10/05/2005 Ex date - 10/13/2005
Name changed to DMC Global Inc. 11/14/2016

DYNAMIC MEASUREMENTS CO. (PA)
Liquidation completed
Each share Common no par exchanged for initial distribution of (0.185873) share Servonic Instruments, Inc. Common no par 01/16/1963
Each share Common no par received second and final distribution of $0.150639 cash 04/21/1965
Servonic Instruments, Inc. acquired by Gulton Industries, Inc. (NJ) 07/31/1963 which reincorporated in Delaware 06/28/1968
(See Gulton Industries, Inc. (DE))

DYNAMIC MEDIA HLDGS INC (NV)
Each share old Common $0.0001 par exchanged for (0.002) share new Common $0.0001 par 02/07/2008
Name changed to Evermedia Group, Inc. 03/25/2009

DYNAMIC MEDIA INC NEW (FL)
Voluntarily dissolved 04/23/2007
Details not available

DYNAMIC MEDIA INC OLD (FL)
Name changed to Holoco, Inc. 09/22/2004

DYNAMIC MERCHANDISING INC (MN)
Statutorily dissolved 10/01/1991

DYNAMIC MNG EXPL LTD (QC)
Recapitalized as Dynamic Consolidated Resources Ltd./Ressources Dynamic Consolidee Ltee. 02/16/1987
Each share Capital Stock $1 par exchanged for (0.1) share Common no par
(See Dynamic Consolidated Resources Ltd./ Ressources Dynamic Consolidee Ltee.)

DYNAMIC NAT RES INC (NV)
Each share old Common $0.0001 par exchanged for (0.1) share new Common $0.0001 par 04/16/2008
Name changed to Universal Tracking Solutions, Inc. 10/31/2008

DYNAMIC NUTRA ENTERPRISES HLDGS INC (NV)
Recapitalized as IL2M International Corp. 01/08/2014
Each share Common $0.0001 par exchanged for (0.1) share Common $0.0001 par

DYNAMIC OIL & GAS EXPL INC (BC)
Recapitalized as Darien Business Development Corp. 03/14/2017
Each share Common no par exchanged for (0.1) share Common no par

DYNAMIC OIL & GAS INC (BC)
Name changed 09/21/1998
Name changed from Dynamic Oil Ltd.
to Dynamic Oil & Gas, Inc. 09/21/1998
Merged into Shellbridge Oil & Gas, Inc. 09/30/2005
Each share Common no par exchanged for (1) share Common no par and $1.71 cash
Shellbridge Oil & Gas, Inc. acquired by True Energy Trust 06/23/2006 which reorganized as Bellatrix Exploration Ltd. 11/02/2009

DYNAMIC OIL & URANIUM CORP. (UT)
Name changed to Dynamic Oil Production Co., Inc. 04/30/1962
(See Dynamic Oil Production Co., Inc.)

DYNAMIC OIL PRODUCTIONS CO., INC. (UT)
Charter suspended for failure to pay taxes 03/31/1966

DYNAMIC OPTICS INC (NY)
Name changed to Fairport Industries, Inc. 2/2/72
(See Fairport Industries, Inc.)

DYNAMIC PETE PRODS LTD (AB)
Completely liquidated 01/01/1972
Each share Common no par exchanged for first and final distribution of (0.0953) share Pan Ocean Oil Corp. Common 1¢ par
(See Pan Ocean Oil Corp.)

DYNAMIC PETROLEUMS LTD. (AB)
Acquired by Dynamic Petroleum Products Ltd. on a (4) for (1) basis in 1958
(See Dynamic Petroleum Products Ltd.)

DYNAMIC RES CORP (AB)
Recapitalized as Dunes Exploration Ltd. 06/13/2011
Each share Common no par exchanged for (0.025) share Common no par

DYNAMIC RESPONSE GROUP INC (FL)
Each share old Common $0.0001 par exchanged for (0.01) share new Common $0.0001 par 06/19/2009
Company entered into an irrevocable Assignment for the Benefit of Creditors under Chapter 727 of the Florida Statutes 01/11/2010
Stockholders' equity unlikely

DYNAMIC RX HEALTHCARE, INC. (OH)
Reincorporated under the laws of Florida as Nu-Wave Health Products, Inc. 04/01/1998
Nu-Wave Health Products, Inc. name changed to Dynamic Health Products, Inc. 06/15/1998 which merged into GeoPharma, Inc. 10/17/2007
(See GeoPharma, Inc.)

DYNAMIC SCIENCES INTL INC (NV)
Plan of reorganization under Chapter 11 Federal Bankruptcy proceedings confirmed 04/28/2008
Stockholders' equity unlikely

DYNAMIC SEC CORP (OH)
Merged into Independence National Corp. (DE) 12/7/76
Each (9.9) shares Class A Common no par exchanged for (1) share Class A no par
Each (9.9) shares Class B Common no par exchanged for (1) share Class B no par
Independence National Corp. (DE) merged into I.C.H. Corp. 4/18/85 which name changed to Southwestern Life Corp. (New) 6/15/94 which name changed to I.C.H. Corp. (New) 10/10/95
(See I.C.H. Corp. (New))

DYNAMIC VENDING CORP (NY)
Stock Dividend - 100% 08/15/1962
Name changed to Pan-American Dynamic Corp. 05/22/1969
Pan-American Dynamic Corp. name changed to Sharp International Corp. 02/23/1986
(See Sharp International Corp.)

DYNAMIC VENTURES INC (FL)
Proclaimed dissolved for failure to file reports and pay fees 11/4/88

DYNAMIC VENTURES INC (WA)
Common no par split (1.7) for (1) by issuance of (0.7) additional share payable 04/10/2003 to holders of record 04/09/2003 Ex date - 04/11/2003
Name changed to O2Diesel Corp. (WA) 06/10/2003
O2Diesel Corp. (WA) reincorporated in Delaware 08/16/2004
(See O2Diesel Corp.)

DYNAMIC VENTURES LTD (AB)
Recapitalized as Dynamic Resources Corp. 03/05/2004
Each share Common no par exchanged for (0.1) share Common no par
Dynamic Resources Corp. recapitalized as Dunes Exploration Ltd. 06/13/2011

DYNAMIC WORLD DISTRS INC (FL)
Name changed to Lottoworld Inc. 5/8/95
(See Lottoworld Inc.)

DYNAMICORP INC (CO)
Each share Common $0.0001 par exchanged for (0.05) share Common $0.001 par 5/10/94
Name changed to D-Bar Capital Corp. 10/15/98

DYNAMICS CORP. OF AMERICA (DE)
No longer in existence having become inoperative and void for non-payment of taxes 04/01/1932

DYNAMICS CORP AMER (NY)
$1 Preference $2 par called for redemption 4/30/68
Common $1 par changed to 10¢ par 11/22/74
Merged into CTS Corp. 10/16/97
Each share Common 10¢ par exchanged for either (0.88) share Common no par or $58 cash
Note: Option to receive cash expired 10/17/97

DYNAMICS RESH CORP (MA)
Common $1 par split (3) for (2) by issuance of (0.5) additional share 04/25/1969
Common $1 par changed to 10¢ par 05/28/1971
Common 10¢ par split (5) for (4) by issuance of (0.25) additional share 01/16/1986
Common 10¢ par split (5) for (4) by issuance of (0.25) additional share 02/09/1987
Common 10¢ par split (5) for (4) by issuance of (0.25) additional share 11/03/1987
Stock Dividends - 10% 04/10/1978; 10% 04/09/1979; 50% 04/08/1980; 10% 04/14/1981; 50% 10/16/1981; 10% 04/13/1982; 10% 10/15/1982; 10% 04/29/1983; 10% 10/14/1983; 25% 10/26/1984; 10% 02/10/1992; 10% 02/05/1993; 10% 05/20/1994; 10% payable 04/28/1997 to holders of record 04/14/1997; 20% payable 05/26/1998 to holders of record 05/11/1998
Acquired by Engility Corp. 01/31/2014
Each share Common 10¢ par exchanged for $11.50 cash

DYNAMICWEB ENTERPRISES INC (NJ)
Each share old Common $0.0001 par exchanged for (0.2608491) share new Common $0.0001 par 01/09/1998

DYN-DYN

FINANCIAL INFORMATION, INC.

Name changed to eB2B Commerce, Inc. 04/18/2000
eB2B Commerce, Inc. reorganized as Mediavest, Inc. (NJ) 02/08/2005 which reincorporated in Delaware as Mandalay Media, Inc. 11/21/2007 which name changed to NeuMedia, Inc. 06/21/2010 which name changed to Mandalay Digital Group, Inc. 02/28/2012 which name changed to Digital Turbine, Inc. 01/20/2015

DYNAMITE RESOURCES LTD NEW (CANADA)
Merged into Avion Resources Corp. 05/08/2009
Each share Common no par exchanged for (0.75) share Common no par
Avion Resources Corp. name changed to Avion Gold Corp. (BC) 06/05/2009 which reincorporated in Ontario 06/14/2011

DYNAMITE RES LTD OLD (CANADA)
Reorganized as Dynamite Resources Ltd. (New) 09/17/2007
Each share Common no par exchanged for (1) share Common no par
Note: Unexchanged certificates were cancelled and became without value 09/17/2013
Dynamite Resources Ltd. (New) merged into Avion Resources Corp. 05/08/2009 which name changed to Avion Gold Corp. (BC) 06/05/2009 which reincorporated in Ontario 06/14/2011

DYNAMIX CORP (AB)
Delisted from Toronto Venture Stock Exchange 06/05/2002

DYNAMO RES LTD (BC)
Struck off register and declared dissolved for failure to file returns 09/03/1993

DYNAMOTION / ATI CORP (NV)
Merged into Electro Scientific Industries, Inc. 06/09/1997
Each share Class A Conv. Preferred 1¢ par exchanged for (0.0543) share Common no par
Each share Common 1¢ par exchanged for (0.0543) share Common no par

DYNAMOTIVE TECHNOLOGIES CORP (BC)
Name changed to DynaMotive Energy Systems Corp. 06/26/2001

DYNAPAC INC (UT)
Proclaimed dissolved for failure to file annual reports in May 1994

DYNAPLEX CORP. (NJ)
Acquired by Teledyne, Inc. 03/19/1966
Each share Common 10¢ par exchanged for (0.09090909) share Common $1 par
Teledyne, Inc. merged into Allegheny Teledyne Inc. 08/15/1996 which name changed to Allegheny Technologies Inc. 11/29/1999

DYNARAD INC (DE)
Ceased operations and went out of business 10/04/1974
No stockholders' equity

DYNASCAN CORP (DE)
Common $1 par changed to $0.33333333 par and (2) additional shares issued 01/23/1976
Common $0.33333333 par split (3) for (2) by issuance of (0.5) additional share 06/19/1987
Name changed to Cobra Electronics Corp. 03/31/1993
(See Cobra Electronics Corp.)

DYNASCIENCES CORP (PA)
Class A Common no par reclassified as Common 10¢ par 07/01/1969

Merged into Whittaker Corp. (CA) 04/19/1974
Each share Common 10¢ par exchanged for $5.25 cash

DYNASEAL LIGHTING CORP. (DE)
No longer in existence having become inoperative and void for non-payment of taxes 4/1/62

DYNASIL CORP AMER (NJ)
Common $5 par changed to 10¢ par and (9) additional shares issued 04/01/1969
Common 10¢ par changed to $0.001 par and (0.5) additional share issued payable 06/01/1996 to holders of record 04/30/1996
Common $0.001 par changed to $0.0005 par and (1) additional share issued payable 11/01/1996 to holders of record 10/01/1996
Reincorporated under the laws of Delaware 06/30/2008

DYNASONICS CORP. (NY)
Completely liquidated
First and final distribution of (0.05) share Dynasonics Corp. (MN) Common 25¢ par paid 5/24/65 to holders of record 5/20/65
Note: Certificates were not required to be surrendered and are without value

DYNASONICS CORP (MN)
Each share Common 25¢ par exchanged for (0.01) share Common $25 par 12/10/1982
Common $25 par changed to 50¢ par and (49) additional shares issued 12/10/1982
Recapitalized as Energro, Inc. 10/27/1983
Each share Common 50¢ par exchanged for (0.4) share Common 10¢ par
(See Energro, Inc.)

DYNASTAR CORP (DE)
Charter cancelled and declared inoperative and void for non-payment of taxes 3/1/84

DYNASTY CAP CORP (FL)
Recapitalized as Visitors Services International Corp. 09/26/1996
Each share Common $0.0001 par exchanged for (0.06944444) share Common $0.0001 par
Visitors Services International Corp. name changed to Teleservices International Group, Inc. 03/10/1997 which name changed to Teleservices Internet Group, Inc. 07/12/1999 which recapitalized as Opus Magnum Ameris, Inc. 02/16/2012
(See Opus Magnum Ameris, Inc.)

DYNASTY CLASSICS CORP (CA)
Plan of reorganization under Chapter 11 Federal Bankruptcy Code effective 9/23/94
No stockholders' equity

DYNASTY COMPONENTS INC (CANADA)
Discharged from receivership 02/00/2004
No stockholders' equity

DYNASTY ENERGY RES INC (DE)
Recapitalized as Fifth Season International, Inc. 10/28/2010
Each share Common $0.00001 par exchanged for (0.05) share Common $0.00001 par

DYNASTY ENTERPRISES, INC. (IN)
Stock Dividend - 10% 6/28/65
Involuntarily dissolved for failure to reports and pay fees 12/13/88

DYNASTY EXPLS LTD (BC)
Common 50¢ par changed to $2 par 01/26/1966
Merged into Cyprus Anvil Mining Corp. 04/28/1975
Each share Common $2 par exchanged for (1) share Common no par
(See Cyprus Anvil Mining Corp.)

DYNASTY GAMING INC (CANADA)
Recapitalized as Blue Zen Memorial Parks Inc. 01/21/2011
Each share Common no par exchanged for (0.1) share Common no par

DYNASTY INTL CORP (NV)
Common $0.001 par split (10) for (1) by issuance of (9) additional shares payable 12/22/2003 to holders of record 12/19/2003 Ex date - 12/23/2003
Name changed to Bullion River Gold Corp. 01/20/2004
(See Bullion River Gold Corp.)

DYNASTY INVT CORP (MN)
Name changed to Super Dupes, Inc. 08/31/1979
(See Super Dupes, Inc.)

DYNASTY LIMOUSINE INC (FL)
Common $0.0001 par split (3) for (1) by issuance of (2) additional shares payable 03/30/2012 to holders of record 03/19/2012 Ex date - 04/02/2012
Name changed to Cyber Kiosk Solutions, Inc. 02/12/2013
Cyber Kiosk Solutions, Inc. name changed to World Oil Group, Inc. 12/10/2014

DYNASTY METALS & MNG INC (YUKON)
Reincorporated under the laws of British Columbia as Core Gold Inc. 09/28/2017

DYNASTY MOTORCAR CORP (CANADA)
Reincorporated 11/29/2002
Place of incorporation changed from (BC) to (Canada) 11/29/2002
Recapitalized as Comwest Capital Corp. 06/29/2004
Each share Common no par exchanged for (0.1) share Common no par
Comwest Capital Corp. merged into ComWest Enterprise Corp. 12/12/2005 which name changed to Unisync Corp. 08/01/2014

DYNASTY OIL & MINERALS CORP (UT)
Recapitalized as Dynasty TMT Corp. 06/26/1996
Each share Common 2¢ par exchanged for (0.0125) share Common 2¢ par
Dynasty TMT Corp. recapitalized as Global Telephone Communication Inc. (UT) 10/14/1997 which reincorporated in Nevada as Spirit Exploration, Inc. 08/14/2006

DYNASTY OIL & MINERALS INC (NV)
Merged into Dallas Oil & Minerals, Inc. 07/01/1984
Each share Common $0.001 par exchanged for (0.00846468) share Common 2¢ par
Dallas Oil & Minerals, Inc. merged into Lomak Petroleum, Inc. 12/19/1990 which name changed to Range Resources Corp. 08/25/1998

DYNASTY OIL CORP (DE)
Filed a petition under Chapter 7 Federal Bankruptcy Code 05/30/1986
No stockholders' equity

DYNASTY RES INC (CA)
Charter suspended for failure to file reports and pay fees 01/02/1986

DYNASTY TMT CORP (UT)
Each share old Common 2¢ par exchanged for (1.5) shares new Common 2¢ par 12/17/1996
Reorganized as Global Telephone Communication, Inc. (UT) 10/15/1997

Each share new Common 2¢ par exchanged for (6) shares Common 2¢ par
Global Telephone Communication, Inc. (UT) reincorporated in Nevada 11/24/1998 which recapitalized as Spirit Exploration, Inc. 08/14/2006

DYNASTY TRAVEL GROUP INC (DE)
Name changed to Phoenix Information Systems Corp. 09/29/1993
(See Phoenix Information Systems Corp.)

DYNASYNETICS, INC. (CA)
Charter suspended for failure to file reports and pay taxes 08/01/1974

DYNATEC CORP (ON)
Merged into Sherritt International Corp. (NB) 06/14/2007
Each share Common no par exchanged for (0.19) share Common no par and (0.0634) share FNX Mining Co. Inc. Common no par
Note: U.S. holders received approximately $2.73 cash
(See each company's listing)

DYNATEC INC (DE)
Name changed to Technapower Industries Corp. 11/00/1987
(See Technapower Industries Corp.)

DYNATEC INTL INC (UT)
Recapitalized 04/21/1983
Recapitalized from Dynatec Inc. to Dynatec International Inc. 04/21/1983
Each share Common $0.001 par exchanged for (0.5) share Common $0.002 par
Each share Common $0.002 par exchanged for (0.2) share old Common 1¢ par 10/05/1984
Each share old Common 1¢ par exchanged for (0.1) share new Common 1¢ par 07/21/1990
Each share new Common 1¢ par exchanged again for (0.2) share new Common 1¢ par 11/09/1992
New Common 1¢ par split (3) for (2) by issuance of (0.5) additional share payable 12/16/1996 to holders of record 12/12/1996
Plan of reorganization under Chapter 11 Federal Bankruptcy Code effective 01/01/2004
No stockholders' equity

DYNATECH CORP (DE)
Merged 05/21/1998
Reincorporated 09/08/1999
Common 20¢ par split (2) for (1) by issuance of (1) additional share 07/01/1977
Common 20¢ par split (2) for (1) by issuance of (1) additional share 12/01/1978
Common 20¢ par split (3) for (2) by issuance of (0.5) additional share 04/01/1982
Common 20¢ par split (3) for (2) by issuance of (0.5) additional share 03/01/1984
Common 20¢ par split (2) for (1) by issuance (1) additional share 03/15/1995
Merged from Dynatech Corp. (Old) (MA) to Dynatech Corp. (New) (MA) 05/21/1998
Each share Common 20¢ par exchanged for (0.5) share Common 20¢ par and $47.75 cash
Dynatech Corp. (New) (MA) reincorporated in Delaware and Common no par changed to 1¢ par 09/08/1999
Name changed to Acterna Corp. 08/30/2000
(See Acterna Corp.)

DYNATECH INDS INC (OH)
Name changed to Xyovest Inc. 07/15/1969
(See Xyovest Inc.)

DYNATEK INDS INC (NY)
Dissolved by proclamation 12/20/1977

DYNATEM INC (CA)
Acquired by Eurotech S.p.A. 05/31/2011
Each share Common no par exchanged for $0.75603556 cash
Each share Common no par received an additional distribution of $0.19285294 cash from escrow payable 01/31/2013 to holders of record 05/31/2011

DYNATION CORP (DE)
Charter cancelled and declared inoperative and void for non-payment of taxes 03/01/1986

DYNATRON INC (NV)
Charter revoked for failure to file reports and pay fees 03/01/1971

DYNATRONICS, INC. (FL)
Merged into General Dynamics Corp. 03/04/1966
Each share Common 20¢ par exchanged for (0.120017) share Common $1 par

DYNATRONICS LASER CORP (UT)
Name changed to Dynatronics Corp. 11/19/1993

DYNAVEX INC (NV)
Charter revoked for failure to file reports and pay fees 03/01/1989

DYNAVOX ELECTRS CORP (NY)
Merged into Tilar Industries, Inc. 12/31/1972
Each share Common 10¢ par exchanged for (0.33333333) share Common 10¢ par
(See Tilar Industries, Inc.)

DYNAVOX INC (DE)
Under plan of reorganization each share Class A Common 1¢ par received first and final distribution of $0.05 cash payable 04/27/2016 to holders of record 01/16/2015

DYNCORP (DE)
Acquired by DME Holdings, Inc. 09/09/1988
Each share Common 10¢ par exchanged for $10.45 principal amount of 16% Subordinated Jr. Debentures due 06/30/2003, (0.1992) share 17% Class A Preferred 10¢ par and $8.82 cash
17% Class A Preferred 10¢ par called for redemption 02/27/1992
Public interest eliminated

DYNCORP INTL INC (DE)
Merged into Delta Tucker Holdings, Inc. 07/07/2010
Each share Class A Common 1¢ par exchanged for $17.55 cash

DYNECO CORP (MN)
Recapitalized as Dynamic Leisure Corp. 03/06/2006
Each share Common 1¢ par exchanged for (0.03333333) share Common 1¢ par
(See Dynamic Leisure Corp.)

DYNEER CORP (DE)
Common $1 par split (3) for (2) by issuance of (0.5) additional share 10/31/1979
Name changed to DYR Liquidating Corp. 07/31/1986
(See DYR Liquidating Corp.)

DYNEGY INC (CO)
Merged into Dynegy Inc. (IL) 02/01/2000
Each share Common no par exchanged for (0.69) share Class A Common no par
Dynegy Inc. (IL) merged into Dynegy Inc. (DE) (Old) 04/02/2007 which reorganized as Dynegy Inc. (DE) (New) 10/01/2012 which merged into Vistra Energy Corp. 04/09/2018

DYNEGY INC (IL)
Class A Common no par split (2) for (1) by issuance of (1) additional share payable 08/21/2000 to holders of record 08/07/2000 Ex date - 08/22/2000
Merged into Dynegy Inc. (DE) (Old) 04/02/2007
Each share Class A Common no par exchanged for (1) share Class A Common 1¢ par
Dynegy Inc. (DE) (Old) reorganized as Dynegy Inc. (DE) (New) 10/01/2012 which merged into Vistra Energy Corp. 04/09/2018

DYNEGY INC NEW (DE)
Each share 5.375% Mandatory Conv. Preferred Ser. A 1¢ par automatically became (3.2258) shares Common 1¢ par 11/01/2017
Merged into Vistra Energy Corp. 04/09/2018
Each 7% Tangible Equity Unit automatically became (1) 7% Tangible Equity Unit
Each share Common 1¢ par exchanged for (0.652) share Common 1¢ par

DYNEGY INC OLD (DE)
Each share Class A Common 1¢ par exchanged for (0.2) share Common 1¢ par 05/25/2010
Plan of reorganization under Chapter 11 Federal Bankruptcy proceedings effective 10/01/2012
Each share Common 1¢ par exchanged for (0.00813936) share Dynegy Inc. (New) Common 1¢ par and (0.12703043) Common Stock Purchase Warrant expiring 10/02/2017
Note: Unexchanged certificates were cancelled and became without value 10/01/2014
Dynegy Inc. (New) merged into Vistra Energy Corp. 04/09/2018

DYNELL ELECTRS CORP (NY)
Common 10¢ par split (2) for (1) by issuance of (1) additional share 03/21/1969
Common 10¢ par split (3) for (2) by issuance of (0.5) additional share 06/30/1972
Common 10¢ par split (3) for (2) by issuance of (0.5) additional share 07/16/1976
Acquired by United Technologies Corp. 12/27/1977
Each share Common 10¢ par exchanged for $7.75 cash

DYNERGY CORP (DE)
Company became private 06/23/1994
Details not available

DYNETEK INDS LTD (AB)
Acquired by Luxfer Holdings PLC 09/17/2012
Each share Common no par exchanged for $0.24 cash

DYNETICS CORP (DE)
Name changed to Nylacarb, Inc. 05/24/1973
Nylacarb, Inc. name changed to N.I. Liquidating Corp. 11/14/1974
(See N.I. Liquidating Corp.)

DYNEX, INC. (NY)
Name changed to Ceco Industries, Inc. 01/31/1962
Ceco Industries, Inc. recapitalized as F & B/Ceco Industries, Inc. 10/30/1964
(See F & B/Ceco Industries, Inc.)

DYNEX CAP INC (VA)
Each share 9.75% Preferred Ser. A 1¢ par reclassified as (2.784) shares Preferred Ser. D 1¢ par and (0.6373) share new Common 1¢ par 05/19/2004
Each share 9.55% Preferred Ser. B 1¢ par reclassified as (2.842) shares Preferred Ser. D 1¢ par and (0.6506) share new Common 1¢ par 05/19/2004
Each share 9.73% Preferred Ser. C 1¢ par reclassified as (3.48) shares Preferred Ser. D 1¢ par and (0.7967) share new Common 1¢ par 05/19/2004
Note: Certificates were not required to be surrendered and are without value
Under plan of partial redemption each share 9.5% Ser. D Preferred 1¢ par exchanged for $10 cash, $0.0238 accrued dividends and a certificate representing unredeemed shares on a pro-rata basis 01/09/2006
Each share 9.5% Ser. D Preferred 1¢ par exchanged for (1) share new Common 1¢ par 10/15/2010
(Additional Information in Active)

DYNEX PETE LTD (AB)
Common no par reclassified as Class A no par 12/21/1982
Struck off register for failure to file annual returns 11/01/1994

DYNO MINES LTD. (ON)
Recapitalized as Canadian Dyno Mines Ltd. 12/06/1956
Each share Capital Stock $1 par exchanged for (0.25) share Capital Stock $1 par
Canadian Dyno Mines Ltd. merged into International Mogul Mines Ltd. 11/20/1968 which merged into Conwest Exploration Co. Ltd. (Old) (ON) 08/27/1982 which merged into Conwest Exploration Co. Ltd. (New) (AB) 09/01/1993 which merged into Alberta Energy Co. 01/31/1996 which merged into EnCana Corp. 01/03/2003

DYNOPTICS INTL INC (DE)
Name changed to Efoora Health Management Inc. 11/16/1994

DYNTEK INC (DE)
Each share Conv. Preferred Ser. A exchanged for (2.5) shares Common $0.0001 par 09/14/2005
(Additional Information in Active)

DYONIX GREENTREE TECHNOLOGIES INC (BC)
Voluntarily dissolved 03/02/1990
Details not available

DYR LIQUIDATING CORP. (DE)
Liquidation completed
Each share Common $1 par received initial distribution of $23.50 cash 09/09/1986
Each share Common $1 par received second distribution of $2 cash 12/22/1986
Assets transferred to DYR Liquidating Trust and Common $1 par reclassified as Units of Bene. Int. 04/14/1987
(See DYR Liquidating Trust)

DYR LIQUIDATING TRUST (DE)
Liquidation completed
Each Unit of Bene. Int. received third distribution of $1 cash 04/28/1987
Each Unit of Bene. Int. received fourth distribution of $0.25 cash 12/20/1988
Each Unit of Bene. Int. received fifth distribution of $0.90 cash 09/21/1989
Each Unit of Bene. Int. exchanged for sixth and final distribution of $0.57 cash 04/13/1990
(See DYR Liquidating Corp. for previous distributions)

DYSAN CORP (CA)
Merged into Xidex Corp. (DE) 02/14/1985
Each share Common no par exchanged for (0.875) share Common $0.0875 par
(See Xidex Corp. (DE))

DYSON-KISSNER CORP. (DE)
$5.50 Preferred $100 par called for redemption 1/4/66
Public interest eliminated

DZR LIQUIDATION CORP. (IL)
Completely liquidated 02/16/1971
Each share Common no par exchanged for first and final distribution of (0.6) share Sola Basic Industries, Inc. Common $1 par
Sola Basic Industries, Inc. merged into General Signal Corp. 09/30/1977 which merged into SPX Corp. 10/06/1998

E

E & B BREWING CO., INC. (MI)
Merged into Associated Brewing Co. 11/15/62
Each share Common $1 par exchanged for (0.2) share Common $1 par

E & B CARPET MILLS, INC. (TX)
Completely liquidated 12/01/1967
Each share Common $1 par or Class A Common $1 par exchanged for first and final distribution of (0.4) share Armstrong Cork Co. Common $1 par
Armstrong Cork Co. name changed to Armstrong World Industries, Inc. (Old) 05/15/1980 which reorganized as Armstrong Holdings, Inc. 05/01/2000
(See Armstrong Holdings, Inc.)

E & B SUPERMARKETS, INC. (DE)
Name changed to 564 Southern Boulevard Corp. 6/30/79
(See 564 Southern Boulevard Corp.)

E & E CAP FDG INC (CANADA)
Merged into GC-Global Capital Corp. 01/09/2006
Each share Common no par exchanged for (1) share Subordinate no par
GC-Global Capital Corp. name changed to Fountain Asset Corp. 09/02/2015

E & E MUT FD INC (DE)
Merged into Drexel Burnham Fund 12/29/1975
Each share Common $1 par exchanged for (0.319575) share Common 10¢ par

E & J PPTYS LTD (CA)
Completely liquidated 12/29/1998
Each Unit of Ltd. Partnership Int. received first and final distribution of $3.79 cash
Note: Certificates were not required to be surrendered and are without value

E A S TECHNOLOGIES INC (DE)
Charter cancelled and declared inoperative and void for non-payment of taxes 6/24/91

E AMIGOS COM INC (AB)
Merged into Learning Library Inc. 07/05/2002
Each share Common no par exchanged for (0.066667) share Common no par
Learning Library Inc. recapitalized as Street Resources Inc. 01/05/2005 which name changed to EXMIN Resources Inc. 07/19/2005 which merged into Dia Bras Exploration Inc. 10/01/2009 which name changed to Sierra Metals Inc. 12/07/2012

E & S HLDGS INC (NV)
Common $0.001 par split (10) for (1) by issuance of (9) additional shares payable 05/26/2005 to holders of record 05/16/2006 Ex date - 09/20/2005
Reorganized as Trilliant Inc. 01/26/2007
Each share Common $0.001 par exchanged for (4) shares Common $0.001 par
Trilliant Inc. name changed to USA Uranium Corp. 05/17/2007

(See USA Uranium Corp.)

E-ART NETWORK INC (FL)
Name changed to e-Travel Store Network Inc. 09/24/2002
e-Travel Store Network Inc. name changed to Hillsboro Group, Inc. 05/16/2003 which name changed to CapTech Financial Group, Inc. 07/28/2004 which name changed to Boo Koo Holdings, Inc. (FL) 08/13/2007 which reincorporated in Delaware 12/17/2007 which name changed to Performing Brands, Inc. 08/19/2008
(See Performing Brands, Inc.)

E-AUCTION GLOBAL TRADING INC (NV)
Name changed to Aucxis Corp. 06/12/2001
(See Aucxis Corp.)

E-AUCTION NETWORK INC (FL)
Name changed to Preventive Technologies Ltd., Corp. 6/7/2002
Preventive Technologies Ltd., Corp. recapitalized as Synergy Software Development, Inc. 2/20/2004 which name changed to Universal Media Holdings, Inc. 11/15/2004 which name changed to Lyric Jeans, Inc. 3/8/2006

E-AUTO NETWORK INC (FL)
Name changed to MetaSwarm, Inc. 4/12/2007

E B ENTERPRISES INC (PA)
Dissolved 7/1/75
Details not available

E-B LIQUIDATION CO.
Liquidated in 1942
Details not available

E B S DATA PROCESSING INC (DE)
Charter cancelled and declared inoperative and void for non-payment of taxes 6/23/86

E B V SYS INC (MD)
Name changed to EBV Liquidating Corp. 12/13/74
(See EBV Liquidating Corp.)

E-BAIT INC (CA)
Reorganized under the laws of Nevada as Barrington Foods International, Inc. 12/10/2001
Each share Common $0.001 par exchanged for (0.1) share Common $0.001 par
Barrington Foods International, Inc. recapitalized as U.S. Canadian Minerals, Inc. 01/20/2004 which name changed to Noble Consolidated Industries Corp. 01/15/2010
(See Noble Consolidated Industries Corp.)

E-BAND MEDIA INC (DE)
Recapitalized as Annec Green Refractories Corp. 04/18/2011
Each share Common $0.0001 par exchanged for (0.06956521) share Common $0.0001 par

E-BIDD COM INC (MN)
Name changed to xraymedia.com, Inc. 06/28/2000
xraymedia.com, Inc. name changed to Xraymedia, Inc. 12/04/2003 which recapitalized as T.W. Christian, Inc. 08/14/2007
(See T.W. Christian, Inc.)

E-BIZ SOLUTIONS INC (NV)
Name changed to Jaws Technologies Inc. (NV) 02/27/1998
Jaws Technologies, Inc. (NV) reincorporated in Delaware 07/07/2000 which name changed to Jawz Inc. 10/02/2000 which recapitalized as Ponderosa Lumber, Inc. (DE) 07/27/2006 which reincorporated in Nevada as National Automation Services, Inc. 10/11/2007 which name changed to National Energy Services, Inc. 07/15/2015

E-BIZ VENTURE CORP (DE)
Each share old Common $0.0001 par exchanged for (0.00613496) share new Common $0.0001 par 05/01/2002
Name changed to Workplace Compliance, Inc. and (1.5) additional shares issued 10/01/2002

E-BOOK NETWORK INC (FL)
Name changed to SinoFresh Corp. 08/22/2003
SinoFresh Corp. name changed to SinoFresh Healthcare, Inc. 09/19/2003
(See SinoFresh Healthcare, Inc.)

E C A TECHNOLOGY LTD (BC)
Name changed to Marine Bioproducts International Corp. (BC) 09/29/1997
Marine Bioproducts International Corp. (BC) reorganized in Alberta as Phoenix Oilfield Hauling Inc. 06/06/2006 which name change to Aveda Transportation & Energy Servives Inc. 06/25/2012 which merged into Daseke, Inc. 06/08/2018

E C AUTO CENTRES INC (BC)
Recapitalized as Python Oil & Gas Corp. 2/27/95
Each (3.5) shares Common no par exchanged for (1) share Common no par
Pyton Oil & Gas Corp. recapitalized as Goldex Resources Corp. 7/4/2003

E.C.I. ELECTRONICS COMMUNICATIONS INC. (NY)
Completely liquidated 5/1/67
Each share Common 10¢ par exchanged for first and final distribution of (0.35915) share Whittaker Corp. (CA) Common $1 par
Whittaker Corp. (CA) reincorporated in in Delaware 6/16/86
(See Whittaker Corp. (DE))

E C L INDS INC (PANAMA)
Name changed to Norlin Corp. 04/04/1970
Norlin Corp. name changed to Service Resources Corp. (Panama) 03/06/1986 which reorganized in Delaware as Ameriscribe Corp. 07/24/1990 which merged into Pitney-Bowes, Inc. 10/29/1993

E C L INDS LTD (BAHAMAS)
Reincorporated under the laws of the Republic of Panama as ECL Industries, Inc. and Ordinary Stock $5 par reclassified as Common $5 par 6/26/69
ECL Industries, Inc. name changed to Norlin Corp. 4/4/70 which name changed to Service Resources Corp. (Panama) 3/6/86 which reorganized in Delaware as Ameriscribe Corp. 7/24/90 which merged into Pitney-Bowes, Inc. 10/29/93

E C M PAYTEL LTD (BC)
Recapitalized as Consolidated Paytel Ltd. 02/22/1990
Each share Common no par exchanged for (0.1) share Common no par
Consolidated Paytel Ltd. recapitalized as Paytel Industries Ltd. 06/01/1994 which name changed to Rodera Diamond Corp. 04/19/1996 which merged into Pacific Rodera Ventures Inc. 03/01/1999 which name changed to Pacific Rodera Energy Inc. (BC) 06/22/2004 which reincorporated in Alberta 06/14/2006 which name changed to PRD Energy Inc. 08/12/2010

E.C.P.I., INC. (NY)
Common 25¢ par changed to 12-1/2¢ par and (1) additional share issued 3/12/62
Name changed to Computer Center Corp. 4/8/64
Computer Center Corp. name changed to Electronic Computer Programming Institute, Inc. 5/1/65
(See Electronic Computer Programming Institute, Inc.)

E-CASINO GAMING CORP (NV)
Name changed to e-Vegas.com, Inc. 08/02/1999
e-Vegas.com, Inc. name changed to 1st Genx.com, Inc. 07/20/2000 which name changed to 1st Genx, Inc. 03/06/2001 which recapitalized as Oasis Information Systems, Inc. 10/31/2001 which recapitalized as 777 Sports Entertainment, Corp. 02/07/2005 which recapitalized as NT Mining Corp. 11/04/2008 which recapitalized as Sanwire Corp. (NV) 03/07/2013 which reincorporated in Wyoming 07/07/2015

E-CENTER COM INC (UT)
Each share old Common $0.001 par exchanged for (2) shares new Common $0.001 par 11/18/99
Name changed to Merlin Software Technologies Holdings Inc. 11/30/99
Merlin Software Technologies Holdings Inc. name changed to Optika Investment Co. Inc. (NV) 1/25/2001 which reincorporated in Delaware as USA Broadband, Inc. 7/10/2001

E-CENTIVES INC (DE)
Recapitalized as Invenda Corp. 05/18/2007
Each share Common 1¢ par exchanged for (0.1) share Common 1¢ par

E-CHANNELS CORP (NV)
Recapitalized as ETI Expertise Technology Innovation Corp. 12/18/2001
Each share Common $0.001 par exchanged for (0.33333333) share Common $0.001 par
ETI Expertise Technology Innovation Corp. name changed to UC Hub Group, Inc. 06/21/2004
(See UC Hub Group, Inc.)

E-CITY SOFTWARE INC (NV)
Common $0.0001 par split (2) for (1) by issuance of (1) additional share payable 12/24/2001 to holders of record 12/17/2001 Ex date - 12/26/2001
Reorganized under the laws of Florida as Cyber Defense Systems, Inc. 09/08/2004
Each share Common $0.0001 par exchanged for (0.03333333) share Common $0.001 par
Cyber Defense Systems, Inc. (FL) reincorporated in Oklahoma 12/19/2008 which name changed to Spoofem.com, Inc. 08/28/2009 which name changed to Spoofem.com USA, Inc. 04/06/2010 which recapitalized as Hi-Tech Crime Solutions, Corp. 10/07/2011 which name changed to Montague International Holding Ltd. 07/20/2012

E-CLAIM SOLUTION INC (CANADA)
Name changed to BUS Systems Inc. 04/04/2007
BUS Systems Inc. name changed to SUB Capital Inc. 12/29/2008 which name changed to Inca One Metals Corp. 05/11/2011 which name changed to Inca One Resources Inc. 10/26/2011 which name changed to Inca One Gold Corp. 09/17/2014

E COM FORCE CORP (NV)
Common $0.001 par split (3) for (1) by issuance of (2) additional shares payable 11/03/2003 to holders of record 11/03/2003 Ex date - 11/04/2003
Name changed to Personal Portals Online, Inc. 02/09/2004
Personal Portals Online, Inc. recapitalized as E Trade Systems, Inc. 09/15/2005 which name changed to Enterprise Traders, Inc. 11/23/2005 which name changed to Micromint, Inc. 01/16/2007
(See Micromint, Inc.)

E COM INTL INC (OR)
Administratively dissolved 06/06/2003

E-COM TECHNOLOGIES CORP (NV)
Each share old Common $0.001 par exchanged for (0.5) share new Common $0.001 par 06/15/2004
Name changed to Eden Energy Corp. 08/16/2004

E COM VENTURES INC (FL)
Each share old Common 1¢ par exchanged for (0.25) share new Common 1¢ par 03/21/2002
Name changed to Perfumania Holdings, Inc. 08/11/2008
(See Perfumania Holdings, Inc.)

E-COMBIZ COM INC (CO)
Common $0.001 par split (2) for (1) by issuance of (1) additional share payable 01/21/2005 to holders of record 01/19/2005 Ex date - 01/24/2005
Recapitalized as NET NET NET.TV, Inc. 12/01/2006
Each share Common $0.001 par exchanged for (0.005) share Common $0.001 par

E-COMMERCE CHINA DANGDANG INC (CAYMAN ISLANDS)
Each Sponsored ADS for Class A Common exchanged for $6.65 cash 09/23/2016

E-COMMERCE GROUP INC (NV)
Recapitalized as Yizhong Bioengineering (USA), Inc. 06/12/2006
Each share Common $0.001 par exchanged for (0.01) share Common $0.001 par
Yizhong Bioengineering (USA), Inc. name changed to Tianxin Mining (USA), Inc. 07/12/2007
(See Tianxin Mining (USA), Inc.)

E-COMMERCE WEST CORP (UT)
Recapitalized as Interactive Broadcasting Network Group Inc. 01/28/2002
Each share Common no par exchanged for (0.16666666) share Common no par
Interactive Broadcasting Network Group Inc. name changed to Baymark Technologies Inc. 08/30/2002 which name changed to Implantable Vision, Inc. 01/03/2006 which name changed to Arcland Energy Corp. 08/25/2008
(See Arcland Energy Corp.)

E COMNETRIX INC (CANADA)
Name changed to Moving Bytes Inc. 07/29/2002
Moving Bytes Inc. recapitalized as China International Enterprises Inc. (Canada) 03/23/2006 which reincorporated in Delaware as China Software Technology Group Co., Ltd. 11/16/2006 which recapitalized as American Wenshen Steel Group, Inc. 10/12/2007
(See American Wenshen Steel Group, Inc.)

E-COMPASS ACQUISITION CORP (CAYMAN ISLANDS)
Merged into iFresh Inc. 02/13/2017
Each Unit exchanged for (1.1) shares Common $0.0001 par
Each share Ordinary $0.0001 par exchanged for (1) share Common $0.0001 par

E-CONNECT NETWORK INC (FL)
Common no par split (4) for (1) by issuance of (3) additional shares payable 02/20/2003 to holders of record 02/20/2003 Ex date - 02/21/2003
Name changed to GLUV Corp. 03/31/2003
GLUV Corp. name changed to Media Magic, Inc. 07/08/2005

E-CRUITER COM INC (CANADA)
Name changed to Workstream Inc. 11/19/2001
(See Workstream Inc.)

E D G INC (CA)
Liquidation completed
Each share Common no par received initial distribution of $25 cash 10/29/1976
Each share Common no par received second distribution of $8 cash 07/08/1977
Each share Common no par received third distribution of $5 cash 08/18/1977
Each share Common no par exchanged for fourth distribution of $1 cash 02/28/1979
Each share Common no par received fifth distribution of $1.50 cash 03/05/1980
Each share Common no par received sixth distribution of $0.50 cash 08/28/1980
Each share Common no par received seventh distribution of $0.50 cash 01/05/1981
Each share Common no par received eighth distribution of $0.50 cash 02/27/1981
Each share Common no par received ninth distribution of $0.50 cash 12/17/1981
Each share Common no par received tenth distribution of $0.50 cash 03/11/1982
Each share Common no par received eleventh distribution of $0.25 cash 03/01/1983
Each share Common no par received twelfth distribution of $0.25 cash 03/08/1984
Each share Common no par received thirteenth and final distribution of $0.05 cash 06/18/1985

E D P CORP. (FL)
Charter cancelled and proclaimed dissolved for non-payment of taxes 05/23/1973

E D P LEARNING SYS INC (NY)
Recapitalized as Picture Island Computer Corp. 02/13/1970
Each share Common 2¢ par exchanged for (0.05) share Common 1¢ par
(See Picture Island Computer Corp.)

E D SMITH INCOME FD (ON)
Acquired by TreeHouse Foods, Inc. 10/15/2007
Each Unit no par received $9.055 cash
Note: Each Unit no par received an additional distribution of $0.1206 cash from escrow 11/30/2007

E-DATA CORP (UT)
Reincorporated under the laws of Delaware 05/23/2002

E DEAL NET INC (NV)
Name changed to International Energy, Inc. 06/20/2005
International Energy, Inc. recapitalized as NDB Energy, Inc. 06/29/2011 which name changed to Armada Oil, Inc. 05/15/2012

E DEBIT GLOBAL CORP (CO)
Old Common no par split (5) for (1) by issuance of (4) additional shares payable 11/15/2010 to holders of record 11/15/2010
Name changed to GreenLink International Inc. 07/30/2018

E-DISPATCH INC (NV)
Reorganized as First China Pharmaceutical Group, Inc. 05/14/2010
Each share Common $0.001 par exchanged for (25) shares Common $0.001 par
(See First China Pharmaceutical Group, Inc.)

E-DOCS MD INC (DE)
Chapter 7 bankruptcy proceedings terminated 08/12/2009
No stockholders' equity

E E C MARKETING CORP (BC)
Name changed to Amera Industries Corp. 01/13/1992
Amera Industries Corp. recapitalized as International Amera Industries Corp. 02/10/1995 which recapitalized as IMA Resource Corp. 02/21/1996 which recapitalized as IMA Exploration Inc. 07/07/1998 which recapitalized as Kobex Minerals Inc. 09/30/2009 which name changed to Kobex Capital Corp. 08/29/2014 which name changed to Itasca Capital Ltd. 06/23/2016

E-18 CORP (DE)
Common $0.0001 par split (5) for (1) by issuance of (4) additional shares payable 06/17/2009 to holders of record 06/02/2009 Ex date - 06/18/2009
Name changed to Protectus Medical Devices, Inc. 10/26/2019
(See Protectus Medical Devices, Inc.)

E FOR M CORP (DE)
Merged into Marquette Electronics, Inc. 01/10/1996
Each share Common $0.001 par exchanged for $12 cash

E FUTURE HLDG INC (CAYMAN ISLANDS)
Name changed 02/04/2016
Name changed from eFuture Information Technology Inc. to eFuture Holding Inc. 02/04/2016
Acquired by Shiji (Hong Kong) Ltd. 01/11/2017
Each share Ordinary $0.0756 par exchanged for $6.42 cash

E G CAP INC (ON)
Recapitalized as Quantum International Income Corp. 03/14/2014
Each share Common no par exchanged for (0.1) share Common no par

E-GAME NETWORK INC (FL)
Name changed to Global Medical Marketing Inc. 02/10/2003
Global Medical Marketing Inc. recapitalized as Virtual Innovations, Inc. 12/30/2005 which name changed to University Health Industries, Inc. 05/09/2008 which name changed to Cognitiv, Inc. 09/19/2012

E-GIFT NETWORK INC (FL)
Name changed to Shadow Ridge Holdings Inc. 08/02/2002
Shadow Ridge Holdings Inc. name changed to LMWW Holdings, Inc. 07/02/2007

E GLOBAL MARKETING INC (NY)
Name changed to Alpha Lujo, Inc. 02/23/2011
Alpha Lujo, Inc. recapitalized as IBITX Software Inc. 01/22/2018

E H INTL INC (CA)
Name changed 01/13/1978
Capital Stock $1 par split (2) for (1) by issuance of (1) additional share 10/10/1967
Name changed from E-H Research Laboratories, Inc. to E-H International, Inc. 01/13/1978
Capital Stock $1 par reclassified as Common no par 00/00/1983

Charter cancelled for failure to file reports and pay taxes 12/01/1993

E-HOBBY NETWORK INC (FL)
Name changed to Rent Shield Corp. 04/27/2003
Rent Shield Corp. name changed to RS Group of Companies, Inc. 04/23/2004
(See RS Group of Companies, Inc.)

E-HOUSE CHINA HLDGS LTD (CAYMAN ISLANDS)
Each ADR for Ordinary received distribution of (0.05) Leju Holdings Ltd. Sponsored ADS for Ordinary payable 01/15/2015 to holders of record 12/03/2014 Ex date - 12/01/2014
ADR agreement terminated 09/12/2016
Each ADR for Ordinary exchanged for $6.80 cash

E.I. LIQUIDATING CORP. (PA)
Liquidation completed
Each share Common $1 par exchanged for initial distribution of $3 cash 12/16/1978
Each share Common $1 par received second distribution of $1 cash 01/19/1979
Each share Common $1 par received third and final distribution of $1.75 cash 10/31/1979

E I L INSTRS INC (MD)
Merged into Loveton Equities L.P. 11/20/1989
Each share Common 10¢ par exchanged for $9.75 cash

E-I MUTUAL ASSOCIATION (DE)
Dissolved 04/13/1962
Details not available

E-II HLDGS INC (DE)
Acquired by AMBR Holdings Inc. 02/29/1988
Each share Common 1¢ par exchanged for $17.05 cash

E-INTERNATIONAL FD MGMT INC (NV)
Name changed to Mobile Self Storage, Inc. 04/10/2001
(See Mobile Self Storage, Inc.)

E JET HLDGS INC (NV)
Name changed to China Global Distribution Corp. 07/06/2004
China Global Distribution Corp. name changed to Rodedawg International Industries, Inc. 07/26/2005

E K DESIGN CORP (DE)
Charter cancelled and declared inoperative and void for non-payment of taxes 03/01/1989

E K G SVC CORP (DE)
Name changed to Camseal, Inc. 10/16/1981
(See Camseal, Inc.)

E-KIDS NETWORK INC (FL)
Name changed to GenoMed, Inc. 10/15/2001

E-KONG GROUP LTD (HONG KONG)
ADR agreement terminated 10/15/2015
Each Sponsored ADR for Ordinary exchanged for $11.81 cash

E.L. PRODUCTS LTD. (BC)
Liquidation completed
Each share Class B $20 par exchanged for initial distribution of $2.54 cash 3/17/67
Each share Class A $20 par received second and final distribution of $0.03 cash 4/5/68

E L E ENERGY INC (BC)
Recapitalized as Maple Leaf Springs Water Corp. 11/12/1992
Each share Common no par exchanged for (0.25) share Common no par
Maple Leaf Springs Water Corp.

recapitalized as International Maple Leaf Springs Ltd. 02/24/1998
(See International Maple Leaf Springs Ltd.)

E-L FINL CORP LTD (ON)
Each share 5.3% Preference Ser. B no par exchanged for (1) share 1st Preference Ser. 1 no par 11/30/2004
(Additional Information in Active)

E L I COMPUTER SYS INC (DE)
Merged into Hers Apparel Industries, Inc. 12/30/1970
Each share Common 10¢ par exchanged for (0.5) share Common 10¢ par
(See Hers Apparel Industries, Inc.)

E L I INDS INC (DE)
Name changed to Hers Apparel Industries, Inc. 10/22/1970
(See Hers Apparel Industries, Inc.)

E L M GROUP INC (AB)
Recapitalized as Vivant Natural Spring Water Inc. 06/30/1992
Each share Common no par exchanged for (0.5) share Common no par
Vivant Natural Spring Water Inc. name changed to Vivant Group Inc. 09/28/1993
(See Vivant Group Inc.)

E-LITE TECHNOLOGIES INC (DE)
Recapitalized as Americare Transtech Inc. 08/16/1999
Each share Common no par exchanged for (0.01492537) share Common no par

E-LOAN INC (DE)
Merged into Popular, Inc. 11/01/2005
Each share Common $0.001 par exchanged for $4.25 cash

E M C CORP (MN)
Each share Common 5¢ par exchanged for (0.2) share Common 25¢ par 06/01/1964
Common 25¢ par changed to $0.0125 par and (19) additional shares issued 03/16/1994
Merged into Wicks Educational Publishing, LLC 04/18/2005
Each share Common $0.0125 par exchanged for $21 cash

E M F CORP (WA)
Merged into BT Acquisition Corp. 10/22/1986
Each share Common no par exchanged for $4.25 cash

E-MEDIASCOPE COM INC (NV)
Recapitalized as Sports Alumni, Inc. 04/07/2005
Each share Common $0.001 par exchanged for (0.01) share Common $0.001 par
Sports Alumni, Inc. recapitalized as CoMedia Corp. 05/17/2007
(See CoMedia Corp.)

E MEDSOFT COM INC (NV)
Name changed to Med Diversified, Inc. 01/09/2002
(See Med Diversified, Inc.)

E MERGENT INC (DE)
Merged into ClearOne Communications, Inc. 05/31/2002
Each share Common 1¢ par exchanged for approximately (0.1389) share Common $0.001 par and $1.1667 cash
ClearOne Communications, Inc. name changed to ClearOne, Inc. 12/13/2012

E-MFG NETWORKS INC (AB)
Delisted from Toronto Venture Stock Exchange 06/20/2003

E-MINERALS EXPL CORP (ON)
Name changed to Eminator Capital Corp. 09/08/2000
Eminator Capital Corp. recapitalized as Internet Shopping Catalog Inc. 02/26/2001

(See Internet Shopping Catalog Inc.)

E MOBILE INFORMATION TECHNOLOGIES INC (NV)
Each share old Common $0.001 par exchanged for (0.03333333) share new Common $0.001 par 05/26/2006
Name changed to Best Rate Travel, Inc. 07/27/2006
Best Rate Travel, Inc. name changed to Yora International, Inc. 07/27/2007

E-MONEE COM INC (NV)
Charter revoked 12/31/2012

E N PHILLIPS CO (DE)
Name changed to Nuoasis Gaming, Inc. 09/30/1994
Nuoasis Gaming, Inc. name changed to Group V Corp. 06/12/1997 which name changed to TotalAxcess.com, Inc. 05/17/1999
(See TotalAxcess.com, Inc.)

E NET CDA FINL SVCS LTD (ON)
Under plan of merger name changed to Basis 100 Inc. 10/29/1999
(See Basis 100 Inc.)

E-NET FINL COM CORP (NV)
Name changed 05/12/1999
Name changed 01/18/2000
Name changed 02/02/2000
Name changed from E-Net Corp. to E-Net Financial Corp. 05/12/1999
Common $0.001 par split (2) for (1) by issuance of (1) additional share payable 12/01/1999 to holders of record 11/30/1999
Name changed from E-Net Financial Corp. to e-Net.com Corp. 01/18/2000
Name changed from E-Net.com Corp. to e-Net Financial.com Corp. 02/02/2000
Name changed to Anza Capital, Inc. 01/01/2002
Anza Capital, Inc. recapitalized as Renhuang Pharmaceutical, Inc. 08/11/2006 which name changed to China Botanic Pharmaceutical Inc. 11/22/2010

E NET INC (DE)
Name changed to ZEROplus.com Inc. 02/15/2000
(See ZEROplus.com Inc.)

E-NEW MEDIA CO LTD (HONG KONG)
Name changed to ENM Holdings Ltd. 07/11/2005
(See ENM Holdings Ltd.)

E NUTRITION INC (NV)
Recapitalized as Torpedo Sports USA, Inc. 05/20/2002
Each share Common $0.001 par exchanged for (0.52993288) share Common $0.001 par
Torpedo Sports USA, Inc. name changed to Interactive Games, Inc. 03/09/2005 which name changed to China Nuvo Solar Energy, Inc. 08/13/2007 which name changed to SurgLine International, Inc. 01/27/2012

E NVIZION COMMUNICATIONS GROUP LTD (CO)
Common $0.0001 par split (3) for (1) by issuance of (2) additional shares payable 09/29/2000 to holders of record 09/15/2000 Ex date - 10/02/2000
SEC revoked common stock registration 01/07/2011

E ON AG (GERMANY)
Sponsored ADR's for Ordinary no par split (3) for (1) by issuance of (2) additional ADR's payable 03/28/2005 to holders of record 03/21/2005 Ex date - 03/29/2005
ADR basis changed from (1:1) to (1:03) 03/29/2005
ADR basis changed from (1:0.3) to (1:1) 08/06/2008

Name changed to E. ON SE 01/04/2013

E ON FINLAND OYJ (FINLAND)
ADR agreement terminated 08/20/2004
Each Sponsored ADR for Ordinary exchanged for (1) Ordinary Share
Note: Unexchanged ADR's will be sold and proceeds, if any, held for claim after 08/01/2005

E.P. ENTERPRISES, INC. (UT)
Name changed to F/X Bio-Med, Inc. 03/05/1987
(See F/X Bio-Med, Inc.)

E P A ENTERPRISES INC (BC)
Merged into Ecology Pure Air International Inc. 07/24/1996
Each share Common no par exchanged for (0.5) share Common no par
(See Ecology Pure Air International Inc.)

E P G COMPUTER SVCS INC (NY)
Adjudicated bankrupt 12/27/1972
No stockholders' equity

E P L ENTERPRISES INC (NV)
Name changed to Macrosonic, Inc. 11/04/1999
Macrosonic, Inc. name changed to Sunx Energy, Inc. 11/09/2007 which recapitalized as Suntex Enterprises, Inc. 01/23/2017

E-PAWN COM INC (NV)
Each share Common $0.0001 par received distribution of (1) share Caribbean Holdings International Corp. Common payable 02/28/2000 to holders of record 02/28/2000
Each share Common $0.001 par received distribution of (2) shares UbuyNetwork.com Inc. Common payable 04/18/2000 to holders of record 04/18/2000
Each share Common $0.001 par received distribution of (2) shares Ubuyhomes.com Inc. Common payable 05/01/2000 to holders of record 05/01/2000
Name changed to UbuyHoldings, Inc. 06/01/2001
(See UbuyHoldings, Inc.)

E-PERCEPTION INC (NV)
Name changed to PeopleView Inc. 05/15/2003
PeopleView Inc. recapitalized as Auxilio, Inc. (NV) 06/21/2004 which reincorporated in Delaware as CynergisTek, Inc. 09/08/2017

E-PHORIA ONLINE SYS INC (YT)
Struck off register 09/03/2008

E PIPHANY INC (DE)
Common $0.0001 par split (3) for (2) by issuance of (0.5) additional share payable 11/13/2000 to holders of record 10/30/2000 Ex date - 11/14/2000
Merged into SSA Global Technologies, Inc. 09/29/2005
Each share Common $0.0001 par exchanged for $4.20 cash

E-POWER INTL INC (UT)
Recapitalized as Integrated Services Group Inc. 01/29/2003
Each share Common 1¢ par exchanged for (0.05) share Common 1¢ par
(See Integrated Services Group Inc.)

E-QUISITIONS INC (AB)
Recapitalized as Central Alberta Well Services Corp. 09/28/2005
Each share Common no par exchanged for (0.05) share Common no par
Central Alberta Well Services Corp. name changed to CWC Well Services Corp. 07/12/2011

E R G LTD (AUSTRALIA)
Name changed 11/18/1997
Name changed from E.R.G. Australia Ltd. to E.R.G. Ltd. 11/18/1997
Each old Sponsored ADR for Ordinary exchanged for (0.2) new Sponsored ADR for Ordinary 12/22/1999
New Sponsored ADR for Ordinary split (3) for (1) by issuance of (2) additional ADR's payable 11/16/2000 to holders of record 11/08/2000
Each new Sponsored ADR for Ordinary exchanged again for (0.1) new Sponsored ADR for Ordinary 08/22/2003
ADR agreement terminated 11/15/2012
Each new Sponsored ADR for Ordinary exchanged for (5) shares Ordinary
Note: Unexchanged ADR's were sold and the proceeds, if any, held for claim after 11/15/2013

E R I EXPLS INC (ON)
Charter cancelled for failure to pay taxes and file returns 03/16/1976

E R I GOLD & SILVER CORP (CO)
Proclaimed dissolved for failure to file reports 04/01/2000

E RES INC (UT)
Each share old Common $0.001 par exchanged for (0.05) share new Common $0.001 par 07/25/2002
Name changed to Central Wireless Inc. 08/27/2002

E-REWARDS NETWORK INC (NV)
Name changed to Rewards Nexus Inc. 10/02/2013
Rewards Nexus Inc. recapitalized as One Step Vending, Corp. 04/06/2015

E-REX INC (NV)
SEC revoked common stock registration 06/08/2005

E.S. LIQUIDATING CO.
Liquidation completed 00/00/1948
Details not available

E S C ELECTRS CORP (NY)
Acquired by Simmonds Precision Products, Inc. 02/15/1968
Each share Common 10¢ par exchanged for (0.28299) share Common 25¢ par
Simmonds Precision Products, Inc. merged into Hercules Inc. 09/20/1983 which was acquired by Ashland Inc. (New) (KY) 11/13/2008 which reincorporated in Delaware as Ashland Global Holdings Inc. 09/20/2016

E S I INDS CORP (BC)
Dissolved 08/04/1989
Details not available

E S R INC (NJ)
Reincorporated under the laws of Delaware as Edu-Cards Corp. 06/30/1972
Edu-Cards Corp. merged into Binney & Smith Inc. 03/14/1973
(See Binney & Smith Inc.)

E-SHOP NETWORK INC (FL)
Common no par split (6) for (1) by issuance of (5) additional shares payable 12/08/2003 to holders of record 12/01/2003 Ex date - 12/09/2003
Name changed to Inflot Holdings Corp. 12/11/2003
Inflot Holdings Corp. recapitalized as iTrackr Technologies, Inc. 05/21/2009 which name changed to Delivery Technology Solutions, Inc. 03/16/2010

E-SIM LTD (ISRAEL)
Acquired by SKY MobileMedia, Inc. 02/07/2007
Details not available

E-SMART TECHNOLOGIES INC (NV)
Each share old Common $0.001 par

exchanged for (0.05) share new Common $0.001 par 10/05/2009
SEC revoked common stock registration 01/23/2012

E-SOL INTL CORP (NV)
Each share old Common $0.001 par exchanged for (0.001) share new Common $0.001 par 02/02/2015
Name changed to Burn Entertainment Corp. 04/27/2015

E SPIRE COMMUNICATIONS INC (DE)
Stock Dividends - in 14.75% Preferred to holders of 14.75% Preferred 3.6875% payable 9/30/99 to holders of record 9/15/99; in Jr. Redeemable Preferred to holders of Jr. Redeemable Preferred 3.1875% payable 10/15/99 to holders of record 10/1/99; in 14.75% Preferred to holders of 14.75% Preferred 3.6875% payable 12/30/99 to holders of record 12/15/99; in 14.75% Preferred to holders of 14.75% Preferred 3.6875% payable 3/31/2000 to holders of record 3/15/2000; in 14.75% Preferred to holders of 14.75% Preferred 3.6875% payable 12/31/2000 to holders of record 12/15/2000 Ex date - 12/13/2000; in 12.75% Jr. Redeemable Preferred 3.6875% payable 9/30/2000 to holders of record 9/15/2000; in 12.75% Redeemable Preferred 3.1875% payable 1/15/2001 to holders of record 1/1/2001 Ex date - 12/27/2000
Assets sold for benefit of creditors 6/5/2002
No stockholders' equity

E-STAMP CORP (DE)
Name changed to Learn2 Corp. 09/26/2001
Learn2 Corp. name changed to LTWC Corp. 09/06/2002
(See LTWC Corp.)

E-SYNC NETWORKS INC (DE)
Chapter 11 bankruptcy proceedings terminated 09/23/2004
Stockholders' equity unlikely

E SYS INC (DE)
Each share Common 50¢ par exchanged for (0.4) share Common $1.25 par 04/07/1973
Common $1.25 par split (8) for (5) by issuance of (0.6) additional share 10/04/1977
Common $1.25 par split (4) for (3) by issuance of (1/3) additional share 10/01/1979
Common $1.25 par changed to $1 par and (1) additional share issued 02/12/1982
Common $1 par split (2) for (1) by issuance of (1) additional share 06/01/1983
Common Stock Purchase Rights declared for Common stockholders of record 10/07/1994 were redeemed at $0.01 per right for holders of record 04/28/1995
Merged into Raytheon Co. 05/08/1995
Each share Common $1 par exchanged for $64 cash

E T & T LEASING INC (MD)
Declared insolvent 05/26/1976
No stockholders' equity

E T & W N C TRANSN CO (DE)
Each share old Capital Stock no par exchanged for (5) shares new Capital Stock no par 00/00/1951
Through purchase offer 99% acquired by Red Ball Motor Freight, Inc. as of 12/30/1977
Public interest eliminated

E T C INDS LTD (BC)
Recapitalized as Consolidated E.T.C. Industries Ltd. 1/28/2002
Each share Common no par

exchanged for (0.1) share Common no par
Consolidated E.T.C. Industries Ltd. name changed to Highbank Resources Ltd. 7/25/2003

E T CDA INC (DE)
Cease trade order effective 08/11/1993
Stockholders' equity unlikely

E T CAP INC (CO)
Recapitalized as eCom.com, Inc. (CO) 10/15/1999
Each share Common 1¢ par exchanged for (0.33333333) share Common 1¢ par
eCom.com, Inc. (CO) reincorporated in Nevada 06/10/2000 which recapitalized as E.T. Corp. 04/12/2002 which recapitalized as ParaFin Corp. 10/15/2004

E T CORP (NV)
Each share old Common $0.001 par received distribution of (1) share eSearchb2b.com, Inc. Restricted Common payable 9/21/2002 to holders of record 8/30/2002 Ex date - 8/28/2002
Each share old Common $0.001 par received distribution of (1) share Timeshare Internet Corp. Restricted Common payable 9/21/2002 to holders of record 8/30/2002 Ex date - 8/28/2002
Each share old Common $0.001 par exchanged for (0.05) share new Common $0.001 par 3/3/2003
Recapitalized as ParaFin Corp. 10/15/2004
Each share new Common $0.001 par exchanged for (0.02) share Common $0.001 par

E T NETWORK INC (CO)
Recapitalized as E.T. Capital Inc. 2/8/95
Each share Common 1¢ par exchanged for (0.02) share Common 1¢ par
E.T. Capital Inc. recapitalized as eCom.com, Inc. (CO) 10/15/99 which reincorporated in Nevada 6/10/2000 which recapitalized as E.T. Corp. 4/12/2002 which recapitalized as ParaFin Corp. 10/15/2004

E T RAILCAR CORP (DE)
Acquired by Emons Holdings Inc. 12/29/88
Each share Common $0.001 par exchanged for $35.70 cash

E TECH CAP CORP (UT)
Reorganized under the laws of Nevada as Ultra Capital Corp. 7/7/92
Each (305) shares Common $0.001 par exchanged for (1) share Common $0.001 par
Ultra Capital Corp. (NV) reincorporated under the laws of Delaware as Tracker Corp. of America 7/12/94

E-TECH INVTS INC (AB)
Issue Information - 1,000,000 shares COM offered at $0.20 per share on 09/24/1997
Name changed to Zone Entertainment Group Inc. 4/16/99

E-TEK DYNAMICS INC (DE)
Issue Information - 5,000,000 shares COM offered at $12 per share on 12/01/1998
Merged into JDS Uniphase Corp. 6/30/2000
Each share Common $0.001 par exchanged for (2.2) shares Common $0.001 par

E-THE MOVIE NETWORK INC (FL)
Name changed to Cell Power Technologies, Inc. 04/23/2004
(See Cell Power Technologies, Inc.)

E TRADE GROUP INC (DE)
Secondary Offering - 7,305,000 shares COM offered at $27.50 per share on 08/00/1997
Common 1¢ par split (2) for (1) by issuance of (1) additional share payable 01/29/1999 to holders of record 01/15/1999
Common 1¢ par split (2) for (1) by issuance of (1) additional share payable 05/21/1999 to holders of record 05/07/1999
Name changed to E*Trade Financial Corp. 10/01/2003

E TRADE SYS INC (NV)
Name changed to Enterprise Traders, Inc, 11/23/2005
Enterprise Traders, Inc. name changed to Micromint, Inc. 01/16/2007
(See Micromint, Inc.)

E-TRAVEL STORE NETWORK INC (FL)
Name changed to Hillsboro Group, Inc. 05/16/2003
Hillsboro Group, Inc. name changed to CapTech Financial Group, Inc. 07/28/2004 which name changed to Boo Koo Holdings, Inc. (FL) 08/13/2007 which reincorporated in Delaware 12/17/2007 which name changed to Performing Brands, Inc. 08/19/2008
(See Performing Brands, Inc.)

E-TREND NETWORKS INC (DE)
Name changed to Wilmington Rexford Inc. 02/19/2002
Wilmington Rexford Inc. recapitalized as China Pharmaceuticals Corp. (DE) 03/25/2004 which reincorporated in British Virgin Islands as China Pharmaceuticals International Corp. 08/26/2004 which recapitalized as China Heli Resource Renewable Inc. 11/07/2008
(See China Heli Resource Renewable Inc.)

E TRON CORP (DE)
Chapter 11 bankruptcy proceedings converted to Chapter 7 on 5/1/88
Stockholders' equity unlikely

E-TRONICS INC (AB)
Name changed to Western Lakota Energy Services Inc. 10/28/2004
Western Lakota Energy Services Inc. acquired by Savanna Energy Services Corp. 08/25/2006 which merged into Total Energy Services Inc. 06/23/2017

E TWOMEDIA COM (NV)
Each share old Common $0.002 par exchanged for (0.005) share new Common $0.002 par 11/09/2000
Name changed to Exus Networks, Inc. 12/19/2000
Exus Networks, Inc. recapitalized as Exus Global, Inc. 09/12/2003 which recapitalized as StarInvest Group, Inc. 01/14/2005
(See StarInvest Group, Inc.)

E-VANTAGE SOLUTIONS INC (NV)
Charter permanently revoked 03/30/2005

E-VEGAS COM INC (NV)
Name changed to 1st Genx.com, Inc. 07/20/2000
1st Genx.com, Inc. name changed to 1st Genx, Inc. 03/06/2001 which recapitalized as Oasis Information Systems, Inc. 10/31/2001 which recapitalized as 777 Sports Entertainment, Corp. 02/07/2005 which recapitalized as NT Mining Corp. 11/04/2008 recapitalized as Sanwire Corp. (NV) 03/07/2013 which reincorporated in Wyoming 07/07/2015

E VENTURES INC (ON)
Delisted from Canadian Venture Stock Exchange 10/13/2000

E-VIDEO NETWORK INC (FL)
Name changed to Foster Community Inc. 04/04/2003
Foster Community Inc. name changed to GainClients, Inc. 10/31/2003

E-VIDEOTV INC (DE)
Name changed to Hi Score Corp. (DE) 07/02/2008
Hi Score Corp. (DE) reincorporated in Florida 07/01/2010

E-WORLD USA HLDG INC (NV)
Name changed to Merion, Inc. 08/09/2017

E-XACT TRANSACTIONS LTD (DE)
Merged into Datadirect Holdings Ltd. 12/03/2010
Each share Common no par exchanged for CAD $0.30 cash

E Z 8 MOTELS INC (NY)
Dissolved by proclamation 06/23/1993

E Z EM INC (NY)
Old Common 10¢ par split (3) for (2) by issuance of (0.5) additional share 05/15/1986
Each share old Common 10¢ par exchanged for (0.5) share Class A Common 10¢ par and (1) share Class B Common 10¢ par 10/28/1992
Each share Class A Common 10¢ par and Class B Common 10¢ par received distribution of (0.03) share Class B Common 10¢ par 03/12/1993
Each share Class A Common 10¢ par exchanged for (1) share new Common 10¢ par 10/22/2002
Each share Class B Common 10¢ par exchanged for (1) share new Common 10¢ par 10/22/2002
Each share new Common 10¢ par received distribution of (0.856377) share AngioDynamics, Inc. Common 1¢ par payable 10/30/2004 to holders of record 10/11/2004 Ex date - 11/01/2004
Stock Dividends - In Class B Common to holders of Class A and B 3% payable 03/11/1994 to holders of record 02/11/1994; 3% payable 03/16/1995 to holders of record 02/24/1995; 3% payable 03/15/1996 to holders of record 02/23/1996; 3% payable 04/21/1997 to holders of record 03/31/1997; 3% payable 03/16/1998 to holders of record 02/26/1998 Ex date - 02/24/1998
Merged into Bracco Diagnostics, Inc. 04/01/2008
Each share Common 10¢ par exchanged for $21 cash

E Z PAINTR CORP (DE)
Common $1 par split (5) for (4) by issuance of (0.25) additional share 01/08/1970
Stock Dividend - 100% 01/10/1969
Merged into Newell Companies, Inc. 10/31/1974
Each share Common $1 par exchanged for (0.78) share Common $1 par
Newell Companies, Inc. name changed to Newell Co. 05/22/1985 which name changed to Newell Rubbermaid Inc. 03/24/1999 which name changed to Newell Brands Inc. 04/18/2016

E Z SERVE CORP (DE)
$6 Conv. Preferred Ser. C 1¢ par called for redemption 1/27/97
Merged into EBC Texas Acquisition Corp. 8/26/98
Each share Common 1¢ par exchanged for $0.60 cash

E Z VENTURES LTD (BC)
Name changed to Haglund Industries International Inc. 10/05/1987

(See Haglund Industries International Inc.)

E&B MARINE INC (DE)
Each share Common 1¢ par exchanged for (0.25) share Common $0.001 par 12/09/1993
Merged into West Marine, Inc. 06/17/1996
Each share Common $0.001 par exchanged for (0.15157) share Common $0.001 par
(See West Marine, Inc.)

E'TOWN CORP. (NJ)
Merged into Thames Water Plc 11/29/2000
Each share Common no par exchanged for $68 cash

EA ED GROUP INC (BC)
Reincorporated under the laws of Canada 08/17/2015

EA ENGR SCIENCE & TECHNOLOGY INC (DE)
Common 1¢ par split (3) for (2) by issuance of (0.5) additional share 02/23/1994
Common 1¢ par split (3) for (2) by issuance of (0.5) additional share 07/05/1994
Merged into EA Engineering Holdings, LLC 09/25/2001
Each share Common 1¢ par exchanged for $1.60 cash

EA INDS INC (NJ)
Each share old Common no par exchanged for (0.25) share new Common no par 12/27/1996
Plan of reorganization under Chapter 11 Federal Bankruptcy proceedings effective 06/19/2002
Stockholders' equity unlikely

EAC INDS INC (NY)
Each share old Common 10¢ par exchanged for (1) share new Common 10¢ par to reflect a (0.01) reverse split followed by a (100) for (1) forward split 12/29/1997
Note: Holders of (99) or fewer shares received $0.28125 cash per share
Company terminated common stock registration and is no longer public as of 05/03/2000

EACCESS LTD (JAPAN)
ADR agreement terminated 03/21/2014
No ADR's remain outstanding

EACOM TIMBER CORP (BC)
Acquired by ET Acquisition Corp. 09/05/2013
Each share Common no par exchanged for $0.38 cash

EAGC VENTURES CORP (ON)
Merged into Bema Gold Corp. 02/14/2003
Each share Common no par exchanged for (1) share Common no par
Bema Gold Corp. merged into Kinross Gold Corp. 02/27/2007

EAGER TECHNOLOGY INC (UT)
Involuntarily dissolved 05/01/1990

EAGLE & PHENIX MILLS
Assets sold and liquidation approved 00/00/1947
Details not available

EAGLE AUTOMOTIVE ENTERPRISES INC (NV)
Name changed to Chariot Entertainment Inc. 04/13/1994
Chariot Entertainment Inc. name changed to AutoCorp Equities Inc. 09/23/1994 which name changed to Homeland Security Network, Inc. 03/16/2005 which name changed to Global Ecology Corp. 01/05/2010

EAGLE BANCGROUP INC (DE)
Merged into First Busey Corp. 10/29/1999

Each share Common 1¢ par exchanged for $25.74 cash

EAGLE BANCORP (USA)
Reorganized under the laws of Delaware as Eagle Bancorp Montana, Inc. 04/05/2010
Each share Common 1¢ par exchanged for (3.8) shares Common 1¢ par

EAGLE BANCORP INC (DE)
Common 10¢ par split (2) for (1) by issuance of (1) additional share 05/14/1993
Merged into United Bankshares, Inc. 04/12/1996
Each share Common 10¢ par exchanged for (1.15) shares Common $2.50 par

EAGLE BANCORP INC (GA)
Merged into PAB Bankshares, Inc. 12/10/1998
Each share Common no par exchanged for (1) share Common no par
(See PAB Bankshares, Inc.)

EAGLE BANCORPORATION INC (DE)
Merged into Landmark Bancshares Corp. 06/01/1988
Each share Common $1 par exchanged for (0.64928) share Common no par and $2.80 cash
Landmark Bancshares Corp. merged into Magna Group, Inc. 12/20/1991 which merged into Union Planters Corp. 07/01/1998 which merged into Regions Financial Corp. (New) 07/01/2004

EAGLE BANCSHARES INC (GA)
Common $1 par split (2) for (1) by issuance of (1) additional share 06/08/1987
Common $1 par split (2) for (1) by issuance of (1) additional share 12/21/1995
Merged into Royal Bank of Canada (Montreal, QC) 07/22/2002
Each share Common 1¢ par exchanged for $26 cash

EAGLE BAY MINES LTD (BC)
Name changed to Leisure Developments Ltd. 06/29/1973
Leisure Developments Ltd. name changed to Leisure Gold Ltd. 09/19/1974 which recapitalized as United Leisure Gold Ltd. 04/14/1975 which recapitalized as Forum Resources Ltd. 04/17/1978 which name changed to Forum Beverages Inc. 02/16/1989
(See Forum Beverages Inc.)

EAGLE BLDG TECHNOLOGIES INC (NV)
Plan of reorganization under Chapter 11 Federal Bankruptcy proceedings effective 10/09/2005
No stockholders' equity

EAGLE BROADBAND INC (TX)
Each share old Common $0.001 par exchanged for (0.02857142) share new Common $0.001 par 05/12/2006
Chapter 7 bankruptcy proceedings terminated 08/03/2012
No stockholders' equity

EAGLE CAP INTL LTD (NV)
Each share old Common $0.001 par exchanged for (0.16666666) share new Common $0.001 par 02/02/2001
Name changed to Eagle Building Technologies, Inc. 05/14/2001
(See Eagle Building Technologies, Inc.)

EAGLE CLOTHES INC (NY)
Common $1 par split (3) for (2) by issuance of (0.5) additional share 01/08/1969
Plan of reorganization under Chapter 11 Federal Bankruptcy proceedings confirmed 03/06/1990

No stockholders' equity

EAGLE COMPUTER INC (DE)
Chapter 11 bankruptcy proceedings converted to Chapter 7 on 07/31/1986
Stockholders' equity unlikely

EAGLE CORP. LTD. (AUSTRALIA)
ADR's for Ordinary A$0.10 par changed to A$0.01 par 06/23/1989
Each ADR for Ordinary A$0.01 par exchanged for (0.02) ADR for Ordinary A$0.50 par 06/23/1989
Name changed to Rowlands Corp. Ltd. 01/25/1990
(See Rowlands Corp. Ltd.)

EAGLE CNTY DEV CORP (CO)
Name changed to Princeville Corp. 05/17/1973
(See Princeville Corp.)

EAGLE ENERGY CORP (AB)
Merged into Centurion Energy International Inc. 05/20/1997
Each share Common no par exchanged for (0.6) share Common no par
(See Centurion Energy International Inc.)

EAGLE ENERGY TR (AB)
Under plan of reorganization each Trust Unit automatically became (1) share Eagle Energy Inc. Common no par 02/01/2016

EAGLE ENTERPRISES INC (AZ)
Name changed to Media Systems Corp. and Common $1 par changed to 25¢ par 08/24/1970
(See Media Systems Corp.)

EAGLE ENTMT INC (CO)
Name changed to Eagle Holdings Inc. (CO) 01/17/1992
Eagle Holdings Inc. (CO) reincorporated in Nevada 10/21/1993 which name changed to Eagle Automotive Enterprises, Inc. 12/01/1993 which name changed to Chariot Entertainment Inc. 04/13/1994 which name changed to AutoCorp Equities Inc. 09/23/1994 which name changed to Homeland Security Network, Inc. 03/16/2005 which name changed to Global Ecology Corp. 01/05/2010

EAGLE ENVIRONMENTAL TECHNOLOGIES LTD (NV)
Each share old Common $0.001 par exchanged for (0.1) share new Common $0.001 par 01/09/1998
SEC revoked common stock registration 02/27/2006

EAGLE EXPL CO (CO)
Ctfs. dated prior to 05/12/1978
Merged into Century Oil & Gas Corp. (DE) (New) 05/12/1978
Each share Common 10¢ par exchanged for (0.1) share Class A 2¢ par
(See Century Oil & Gas Corp. (DE) (New))

EAGLE EYE ENTERPRISES INC (CO)
Recapitalized as Atlas Environmental Inc. 11/22/1994
Each share Common no par exchanged for (0.00251256) share Common no par
(See Atlas Environmental Inc.)

EAGLE FIN CORP (DE)
Recapitalized as United Environmental Energy Corp. 02/14/2006
Each share Common 1¢ par exchanged for (0.001) share Common 1¢ par

EAGLE FINL CORP (DE)
Stock Dividends - 10% 9/1/93; 10% 3/1/95
Merged into Webster Financial Corp. 4/15/98
Each share Common 1¢ par exchanged for (1.68) shares Common 1¢ par

EAGLE FIRE INSURANCE CO. (NJ)
Each share Capital Stock $20 par exchanged for (4) shares Capital Stock $5 par 12/19/1929
Capital Stock $5 par changed to $2.50 par 06/28/1932
Capital Stock $2.50 par changed to $1.55 par 07/30/1942
Capital Stock $1.55 par changed to $1.25 par 04/30/1951
Stock Dividends - 10% 02/15/1956; 10% 03/15/1957
Name changed to Eagle Insurance Co. 05/13/1964
(See Eagle Insurance Co.)

EAGLE FOOD CENTERS, INC. (DE)
Ctfs. dated prior to 05/26/1961
Acquired by Consolidated Foods Corp. 05/26/1961
Each share Common $2.50 par and/or Class B Common $2.50 par exchanged for (0.561797) share Common $1.33333333 par
Consolidated Foods Corp. name changed to Sara Lee Corp. 04/02/1985 which recapitalized as Hillshire Brands Co. 06/29/2012
(See Hillshire Brands Co.)

EAGLE FOOD CTRS INC (DE)
Ctfs. dated after 08/03/1989
Each share old Common 1¢ par exchanged for (0.25) share new Common 1¢ par 06/29/2001
Plan of reorganization under Chapter 11 Federal Bankruptcy Code effective 04/08/2004
No stockholders' equity

EAGLE GEN CORP (DE)
Common 10¢ par reclassified as Class B 10¢ par 06/15/1967 and (1) share Class A $1 par distributed 06/28/1967
Recapitalization 04/22/1968
Each share Class A $1 par exchanged for (1) share Capital Stock $1 par
Each share Class B 10¢ par exchanged for (0.5) share Capital Stock $1 par
Capital Stock $1 par changed to 50¢ par and (1) additional share issued 08/06/1969
Merged into Union Capital Corp. 05/29/1980
Each share Capital Stock 50¢ par exchanged for $5 cash

EAGLE GEOPHYSICAL INC (DE)
Plan of reorganization under Chapter 11 Federal Bankruptcy proceedings confirmed 07/10/2000
No old Common stockholders' equity
Plan of reorganization under Chapter 11 Federal Bankruptcy proceedings effective 04/21/2010
No new Common stockholders' equity

EAGLE GOLD MINES LTD (ON)
Merged into Agnico-Eagle Mines Ltd. 06/01/1972
Each share Capital Stock $1 par exchanged for (1.5) shares Common no par
Agnico-Eagle Mines Ltd. name changed to Agnico Eagle Mines Ltd. 04/30/2013

EAGLE GROWTH SHS INC (MD)
Completely liquidated
Each share Common 10¢ par received first and final distribution of $7.09 cash payable 06/17/2009 to holders of record 06/17/2009
Note: Certificates were not required to be surrendered and are without value

EAGLE HARDWARE & GARDEN INC (WA)
Common no par split (3) for (2) by issuance of (0.5) additional share 11/16/1992
Merged into Lowe's Companies, Inc. 04/02/1999
Each share Common no par exchanged for (0.64) share Common 50¢ par

EAGLE HEAD MINES LTD. (ON)
Merged into Jubilant Eagle Holdings & Explorations Ltd. 04/01/1968
Each share Common $1 par exchanged for (0.190476) share Capital Stock no par
(See Jubilant Eagle Holdings & Explorations Ltd.)

EAGLE HILL EXPL CORP (ON)
Reincorporated 08/20/2015
Each share old Common no par exchanged for (0.05) share new Common no par 01/21/2015
Place of incorporation changed from (BC) to (ON) 08/20/2015
Merged into Oban Mining Corp. 08/27/2015
Each share new Common no par exchanged for (0.5) share new Common no par and (5) Common Stock Purchase Warrants expiring 08/25/2018
Note: Unexchanged certificates will be cancelled and become without value 08/27/2021
Oban Mining Corp. name changed to Osisko Mining Inc. 06/21/2016

EAGLE HLDGS INC (MN)
Name changed 01/08/1990
Name changed from Eagle Industries, Inc. to Eagle Holdings, Inc. 01/08/1990
Name changed to Network Capital, Inc. 01/23/1997

EAGLE HLDGS INC (NV)
Reincorporated 10/21/1993
Each share Common no par exchanged for (0.1) share Common 10¢ par 08/26/1992
State of incorporation changed from (CO) to (NV) 10/21/1993
Name changed to Eagle Automotive Enterprises, Inc. 12/01/1993
Eagle Automotive Enterprises, Inc. name changed to Chariot Entertainment Inc. 04/13/1994 which name changed to AutoCorp Equities Inc. 09/23/1994 which name changed to Homeland Security Network, Inc. 03/16/2005 which name changed to Global Ecology Corp. 01/05/2010

EAGLE HOSPITALITY PPTYS TR INC (MD)
Merged into AP AIMCAP Holdings LLC 08/15/2007
Each share Common 1¢ par exchanged for $13.35 cash

EAGLE INC (FL)
Proclaimed dissolved for failure to file reports and pay fees 12/05/1978

EAGLE INDS LTD (BC)
Incorporated 00/00/1968
Acquired by Bralorne Resources Ltd. 12/00/1972
Each share Common no par exchanged for $6 cash

EAGLE INDS LTD (BC)
Incorporated 04/16/1980
Each share Class A Common no par exchanged for (0.33333333) share Class B Common no par 03/16/1992
Name changed to Innovative Waste Technologies Inc. and Class B Common no par reclassified as Common no par 06/08/1992
Innovative Waste Technologies Inc. recapitalized as International Tire & Manufacturing Corp. 06/08/1995 which recapitalized as Intirmac Industrial Corp. 12/05/1997 which name changed to Sniper Enterprises Inc. 12/07/1998 which name changed to TransAmerican Energy Inc. 08/16/2005 which recapitalized

as American Biofuels Inc. 09/12/2018

EAGLE INS CO (NJ)
Capital Stock $1.25 par changed to $1 par 12/06/1965
Capital Stock $1 par reclassified as Common $1 par 12/16/1966
Common $1 par changed to 50¢ par 04/27/1967
Under plan of merger each share $1.20 Conv. Preferred $5 par exchanged for (1) share $1.20 Non-Cum. Preferred $1 par 06/30/1968
Each share old Common 50¢ par exchanged for (0.5) share new Common 50¢ par 12/31/1969
Each share new Common 50¢ par exchanged for (0.33333333) share Common 55¢ par 08/25/1976
Each share Common 55¢ par exchanged for (0.5) share new Common 50¢ par 04/03/1980
Order of Liquidation and Declaration of Insolvency entered 08/08/2007
No stockholders' equity

EAGLE LAKE EXPLS LTD (AB)
Recapitalized as Canalta Minerals Ltd. 12/16/1991
Each share Common no par exchanged for (0.2) share Common no par
Canalta Minerals Ltd. name changed to New Energy West Corp. 11/14/1994 which was acquired by Gastar Exploration Ltd. (AB) 11/20/2001 which reincorporated in Delaware as Gastar Exploration, Inc. (Old) 11/15/2013 which reorganized as Gastar Exploration, Inc. (New) 02/03/2014

EAGLE LOCK CO.
Acquired by Bowser (S.F.) & Co., Inc. which name changed to Bowser, Inc. (IN) in 1943
Each share Capital Stock exchanged for $25 principal amount of Debentures due 7/1/63 and (0.5) share Common $1 par
Bowser, Inc. (IN) reincorporated in Delaware as Bowser Delaware Corp. 11/17/69
(See Bowser Delaware Corp.)

EAGLE MACOMBER MOTOR CAR CO. (DE)
Charter cancelled and declared inoperative and void for non-payment of taxes 03/16/1921

EAGLE MANUFACTURING CO. (KY)
Charter revoked for failure to file annual reports 02/17/1974

EAGLE MTN GOLD CORP (BC)
Merged into Goldsource Mines Inc. 03/05/2014
Each share Common no par exchanged for (0.52763) share Common no par
Note: Unexchanged certificates will be cancelled and become without value 03/05/2020

EAGLE MTN MNG INC (WA)
Recapitalized as Global Productions, Inc. 12/31/1990
Each share Common no par exchanged for (0.02) share Common no par
Global Productions, Inc. recapitalized as Northstar Network Inc. 10/07/1999
(See Northstar Network Inc.)

EAGLE MTN TROUT FARMS LTD (BC)
Name changed to Preferred Foods Ltd. 12/17/1987
Preferred Foods Ltd. recapitalized as Diversified Preferred Foods Ltd. 08/24/1988 which name changed to Diversified Publishing Ltd. 01/18/1990
(See Diversified Publishing Ltd.)

EAGLE NATIONAL LIFE INSURANCE CO. (FL)
Merged into National Life Insurance Co. of Florida 07/01/1967
Each share Common $1 par exchanged for (0.571421) share Common $1 par
National Life Insurance Co. of Florida reorganized as National Life of Florida Corp. 10/31/1968 which name changed to Voyager Group, Inc. 07/01/1980
(See Voyager Group, Inc.)

EAGLE OIL & REFINING CO., INC. (CA)
Name changed to American Eagle Corp. 05/08/1959
American Eagle Corp. merged into Acme Eagle Corp. 05/08/1964 which merged into Allied Products Corp. (MI) 04/05/1965 which reincorporated in Delaware 01/31/1968
(See Allied Products Corp. (DE))

EAGLE PAC INDS INC (MN)
Name changed to PW Eagle, Inc. 06/19/2000
(See PW Eagle, Inc.)

EAGLE PASS RES LTD (BC)
Recapitalized as Starcore Resources Ltd. 09/18/1992
Each share Common no par exchanged for (0.33333333) share Common no par
Starcore Resources Ltd. recapitalized as Starcore International Ventures Ltd. 02/02/2004 which name changed to Starcore International Mines Ltd. 02/01/2008

EAGLE PHARMACEUTICALS INC (NY)
Charter cancelled and proclaimed dissolved for failure to pay taxes 09/29/1993

EAGLE PICHER INDS INC (OH)
Name changed 00/00/1945
Name changed 04/01/1966
Name changed from Eagle-Picher Lead Co. to Eagle-Picher Co. 00/00/1945
Common $10 par changed to $5 par and (1) additional share issued 01/22/1960
Name changed from Eagle-Picher Co. to Eagle-Picher Industries, Inc. 04/01/1966
$1.40 Conv. Preference Ser. A no par called for redemption 04/02/1983
$1.40 Conv. Preference Ser. C no par called for redemption 11/02/1984
Common $5 par changed to $2.50 par and (1) additional share issued 04/12/1968
Common $2.50 par changed to $1.25 par and (1) additional share issued 04/20/1977
Stock Dividends - 10% 12/10/1951; 10% 04/01/1975
Plan of reorganization under Chapter 11 Federal Bankruptcy proceedings effective 11/26/1996
No stockholders' equity

EAGLE PLAINS DEVELOPMENTS LTD. (YT)
Charter revoked for failure to file reports and pay fees 10/31/1961

EAGLE POINT SOFTWARE CORP (DE)
Merged into JB Acquisitions LLC 12/21/2001
Each share Common 1¢ par exchanged for $6.40 cash

EAGLE PRECISION TECHNOLOGIES INC (ON)
Each share old Common no par exchanged for (0.000000001) share new Common no par 11/19/2003
Note: In effect holders received $0.00118 cash per share and public interest was eliminated

EAGLE RESOURCES LTD. (BC)
Name changed to Bardine Oils Ltd. 09/28/1978
(See Bardine Oils Ltd.)

EAGLE RIDGE RES LTD (BC)
Name changed to AIMS Biotech Corp. 09/12/1986
(See AIMS Biotech Corp.)

EAGLE RIDGE VENTURES INC (NV)
Name changed to AlgoDyne Ethanol Energy Corp. 11/06/2006
AlgoDyne Ethanol Energy Corp. recapitalized as Easylink Solutions, Corp. 12/05/2008

EAGLE RIV INTERACTIVE INC (DE)
Name changed to Mastering Inc. 10/16/1997
Mastering Inc. merged into PLATINUM Technology, Inc. 04/21/1998 which name changed to Platinum Technology International Inc. 01/04/1999 which merged into Computer Associates International, Inc. 06/29/1999 which name changed to CA, Inc. 02/01/2006

EAGLE RIV MINES LTD (BC)
Common 50¢ par changed to no par 05/6/1977
Recapitalized as Twin Eagle Resources Inc. 04/01/1985
Each share Common no par exchanged for (0.2) share Common no par
Twin Eagle Resources Inc. recapitalized as Cordal Resources Ltd. 05/17/1993 which recapitalized as Skyharbour Developments Ltd. 11/04/1999 which name changed to Skyharbour Resources Ltd. 10/25/2002

EAGLE RIV MNG CORP (NV)
Each share old Common $0.001 par exchanged for (20) shares new Common $0.001 par 12/13/2004
Name changed to China Media1 Corp. 01/14/2005
(See China Media1 Corp.)

EAGLE ROCK ENERGY PARTNERS LP (DE)
Merged into Vanguard Natural Resources, LLC 10/08/2015
Each Unit of Ltd. Partnership Int. exchanged for (0.185) Common Unit
(See Vanguard Natural Resources, LLC)

EAGLE ROCK ENTERPRISES INC (UT)
Name changed to Worldwide Food Services, Inc. 08/19/2009
Worldwide Food Services, Inc. name changed to Global Holdings, Inc. 10/29/2013 which name changed to Element Global, Inc. 08/06/2015

EAGLE ROCK EXPL LTD (AB)
Recapitalized as Wild Stream Exploration Inc. 11/16/2009
Each share Common no par exchanged for (0.03333333) share Common no par
(See Wild Stream Exploration Inc.)

EAGLE STAR MINERALS CORP (CANADA)
Name changed to DuSolo Fertilizers Inc. (Canada) 02/28/2014
DuSolo Fertilizers Inc. (Canada) reincorporated in British Columbia 07/19/2016 which name changed to Fengro Industries Corp. 12/18/2017

EAGLE STAR PETE CORP (CANADA)
Name changed to Eagle Star Minerals Corp. 07/06/2010
Eagle Star Minerals Corp. name changed to DuSolo Fertilizers Inc. (Canada) 02/28/2014 which reincorporated in British Columbia 07/19/2016 which name changed to Fengro Industries Corp. 12/18/2017

EAGLE STEVEDORE, INC. (FL)
Name changed to Eagle, Inc. 08/29/1960
(See Eagle, Inc.)

EAGLE SUPPLY GROUP INC (DE)
Merged into Gulfside Supply, Inc. 09/22/2004
Each share Common $0.0001 par exchanged for $2.20 cash

EAGLE TELEPHONICS INC (NY)
SEC revoked common stock registration 02/06/2017

EAGLE TEST SYS INC (DE)
Merged into Teradyne, Inc. 11/14/2008
Each share Common 1¢ par exchanged for $15.65 cash

EAGLE USA AIRFREIGHT INC (TX)
Common $0.001 par split (2) for (1) by issuance of (1) additional share payable 08/01/1996 to holders of record 07/24/1996
Common $0.001 par split (3) for (2) by issuance of (0.5) additional share payable 08/30/1999 to holders of record 08/23/1999
Name changed to EGL, Inc. 02/22/2000
(See EGL, Inc.)

EAGLE VENTURE ACQUISITIONS INC (CO)
Name changed to Network Real Estate of California, Inc. 05/14/1990
Network Real Estate of California, Inc. name changed to Network Financial Services, Inc. 06/22/1992 which name changed to Westmark Group Holdings Inc. 07/13/1994 which recapitalized as Viking Consolidated, Inc. (DE) 05/15/2006 which reincorporated in Nevada as Tailor Aquaponics World Wide, Inc. 08/15/2006 which recapitalized as Diversified Acquisitions, Inc. 08/20/2007 which recapitalized as Vitalcare Diabetes Treatment Centers, Inc. 03/24/2008 which recapitalized as China Advanced Technology 06/23/2010 which name changed to Goliath Film & Media Holdings 01/20/2012

EAGLE VENTURES INC (NV)
Each share Common $0.001 par exchanged for (0.06666666) share Common 3¢ par 07/22/1993
Name changed to Applied Logic Inc. 09/18/1992
Applied Logic Inc. name changed to Thunderstone Group Inc. 03/01/1996

EAGLE VENTURES INTL INC (NV)
Chapter 7 bankruptcy proceedings terminated 07/18/2012
No stockholders' equity

EAGLE WASH CORP. (MN)
Name changed to Gold Eagle Corp. 01/15/1962
(See Gold Eagle Corp.)

EAGLE WIRELESS INTL INC (TX)
Name changed to Eagle Broadband, Inc. 03/04/2002
(See Eagle Broadband, Inc.)

EAGLE WORLDWIDE MARKETING INC (WA)
Reincorporated 04/27/2005
State of incorporation changed from (DE) to (WA) 04/27/2005
Each share old Common $0.001 par exchanged for (0.002) share new Common $0.001 par 05/11/2005
Recapitalized as IPhone2, Inc. 07/18/2005
Each share new Common $0.001 par exchanged for (0.1) share Common $0.001 par
(See IPhone2, Inc.)

EAGLECREST EXPLS LTD (BC)
Each share old Common no par

exchanged for (0.1) share new Common no par 12/14/2009
Name changed to Colombia Crest Gold Corp. 02/14/2011

EAGLECREST RES INC (NV)
Common $0.001 par split (6) for (1) by issuance of (5) additional shares payable 08/06/2010 to holders of record 08/06/2010
Name changed to Oryon Holdings, Inc. 11/25/2011
Oryon Holdings, Inc. name changed to Oryon Technologies, Inc. 05/03/2012

EAGLEFORD ENERGY CORP (ON)
Recapitalized as Intelligent Content Enterprises Inc. 02/05/2016
Each share Common no par exchanged for (0.1) share Common no par
Intelligent Content Enterprises Inc. recapitalized as Novicius Corp. 05/29/2017

EAGLEFORD ENERGY INC (ON)
Common no par split (2) for (1) by issuance of (1) additional share payable 03/21/2012 to holders of record 03/16/2012 Ex date - 03/22/2012
Recapitalized as Eagleford Energy Corp. 08/25/2014
Each share Common no par exchanged for (0.1) share Common no par
Eagleford Energy Corp. recapitalized as Intelligent Content Enterprises Inc. 02/05/2016 which recapitalized as Novicius Corp. 05/29/2017

EAGLELUND GOLD MINES LTD. (ON)
Charter revoked for failure to file reports and pay fees 10/21/1963

EAGLES NEST MNG CO (NV)
Reincorporated 07/31/2001
State of incorporation changed from (ID) to (NV) 07/31/2001
Each share old Common no par exchanged for (12.5) shares new Common $0.001 par 11/15/2001
Name changed to Nanoscience Technologies, Inc. 05/23/2002
Nanoscience Technologies, Inc. name changed to American Films, Inc. 03/07/2012

EAGLESTAR VENTURES INC (BC)
Name changed to Waratah Coal Inc. 12/07/2006
(See Waratah Coal Inc.)

EAGLET MINES LTD (BC)
Struck off register and declared dissolved for failure to file returns 05/27/1994

EAGLETECH COMMUNICATIONS INC (NV)
Each share old Common $0.001 par exchanged for (0.33333333) share new Common $0.001 par 06/09/1999
SEC revoked common stock registration 07/07/2006

EAGLEVIEW VENTURES INC (CO)
Recapitalized as AgriBioTech, Inc. 02/16/1988
Each share Common $0.0001 par exchanged for (0.05555555) share Common no par
AgriBioTech, Inc. merged into FiberChem, Inc. (DE) 11/21/1989 which name changed to DecisionLink, Inc. 12/05/2000
(See DecisionLink, Inc.)

EAGLEWOOD ENERGY INC (AB)
Acquired by Transform Exploration Pty Ltd. 07/11/2014
Each share Common no par exchanged for $0.38 cash

EALING CORP (DE)
Acquired by a private company 12/19/1986

Each share Common 10¢ par exchanged for $8 cash

EANCO INC (PA)
Name changed to E.I. Liquidating Corp. 11/30/1978
(See E.I. Liquidating Corp.)

EAPI ENTMT INC (NV)
Name changed to Organic Recycling Technologies, Inc. 07/11/2005
Organic Recycling Technologies, Inc. name changed to Global 8 Environmental Technologies, Inc. 05/15/2008

EARFUL OF BOOKS INC (DE)
Chapter 11 bankruptcy proceedings converted to Chapter 7 on 10/22/2002
No stockholders' equity

EARL CLAY LABS INC (CA)
Charter suspended for failure to pay taxes 06/01/1989

EARL GOLD MINES, LTD. (ON)
Charter revoked for failure to file reports and pay taxes 00/00/1954

EARL MOTORS, INC. (DE)
Charter cancelled and declared inoperative and void for non-payment of taxes 03/17/1926

EARL OWENSBY STUDIOS INC (UT)
Involuntarily dissolved 11/03/1991

EARL RADIO CORP.
Assets sold at public auction 00/00/1930
No stockholders' equity

EARL RES LTD (CAYMAN ISLANDS)
Reorganized under the laws of British Columbia 03/02/2018
Each share Common no par exchanged for (0.33333333) share Common no par

EARLCREST RES LTD (BC)
Name changed to Amalgamated General Resources Ltd. 12/14/1979
(See Amalgamated General Resources Ltd.)

EARLY & DANIEL CO (OH)
Merged into Early & Daniel Industries, Inc. 11/18/1975
Each share Common no par exchanged for (2) shares Class A Common no par
(See Early & Daniel Industries, Inc.)

EARLY & DANIEL INDS INC (IN)
Charter revoked for failure to file annual reports 09/12/1990

EARLY AMERICAN LIFE INSURANCE CO. (IN)
Merged into Great Fidelity Life Insurance Co. 12/29/1967
Each share Common $1 par exchanged for (1) share Capital Stock $1 par
(See Great Fidelity Life Insurance Co.)

EARLY BIRD MINES LTD (BC)
Capital Stock $1 par changed to no par 08/31/1970
Recapitalized as Euro-American Financial Services Ltd. 10/25/1983
Each share Capital Stock no par exchanged for (0.33333333) share Common no par
(See Euro-American Financial Services Ltd.)

EARLY CALIF INDS INC (CA)
Name changed to Erly Industries, Inc. (CA) 10/31/1985
Erly Industries, Inc. (CA) reorganized in Delaware as Torchmail Communications, Inc. 05/24/2001 which name changed to Ohana Enterprises, Inc. 12/11/2002 which reorganized as Vinoble, Inc. 11/19/2004 which name changed to Matrixx Resource Holdings, Inc. 07/14/2003
(See Matrixx Resource Holdings, Inc.)

EARLY EQUINE INC (UT)
Name changed to All For One Media Corp. 11/17/2015

EARLY RES LTD (AB)
Merged into Lionheart Energy Corp. 11/17/1994
Each share Common no par exchanged for (0.1) share Common no par
Lionheart Energy Corp. merged into Search Energy Corp. 05/02/1997 which merged into Advantage Energy Income Fund 05/24/2001 which reorganized as Advantage Oil & Gas Ltd. 07/09/2009

EARLYRAIN INC (AB)
Dissolved 00/00/2005

EARMARK AUDIO RESOURCES, INC. (CT)
Name changed to Earmark, Inc. 05/17/1975
(See Earmark, Inc.)

EARMARK INC (CT)
Stock Dividend - 10% 05/15/1977
Completely liquidated 10/17/1986
Each share Common no par exchanged for first and final distribution of $3.22 cash

EARNGOLD MINES, LTD. (ON)
Charter revoked for failure to file reports and pay taxes 06/13/1960

EARTH BIOFUELS INC (DE)
Common $0.001 par changed to $0.0001 par 04/22/2009
Common $0.00001 par split (2) for (1) by issuance of (1) additional share payable 06/15/2009 to holders of record 06/10/2009 Ex date - 06/16/2009
Name changed to Evolution Fuels, Inc. 06/16/2009
Evolution Fuels, Inc. name changed to SC Holdings Corp. 06/20/2014

EARTH ENERGY INC (NV)
Charter revoked for failure to file reports and pay fees 09/01/1991

EARTH HEAT RES LTD (BC)
Name changed to Rampart Energy Ltd. 05/22/2013

EARTH KING RES INC (BC)
Reincorporated under the laws of Yukon as West African Gold Corp. 03/17/1997
West African Gold Corp. recapitalized as First AU Stategies Corp. 04/28/1999 which name changed to Cangold Ltd. (YT) 06/04/2003 which reincorporated in British Columbia 12/22/2007 which merged into Great Panther Silver Ltd. 05/27/2015

EARTH PRODS & TECHNOLOGIES INC (NV)
Each share old Common $0.001 par exchanged for (0.03333333) share new Common $0.001 par 03/01/2006
Name changed to China Shen Zhou Mining & Resources, Inc. 10/20/2006

EARTH RES CO (DE)
Stock Dividend - 20% 07/17/1980
Merged into Mapco Inc. 02/10/1981
Each share Common no par exchanged for (1.25) shares Common $1 par
Mapco Inc. merged into Williams Companies, Inc. 03/28/1998

EARTH SCIENCES INC (CO)
Each share Common 10¢ par exchanged for (1) share Common 1¢ par 12/15/1972
Each share Class A Common no par exchanged for (1.1) shares Common 1¢ par 12/15/1972
Each share Common 1¢ par received distribution of (0.1) share ADA-ES, Inc. Common no par payable 09/12/2003 to holders of record 08/29/2003 Ex date - 09/03/2003

SEC revoked common stock registration 08/05/2010
Stockholders' equity unlikely

EARTH SEARCH SCIENCES INC (UT)
Reincorporated under the laws of Nevada 10/20/2004

EARTH STAR DIAMONDS LTD (BC)
Merged into Nordic Diamonds Ltd. 11/24/2003
Each share Common no par exchanged for (0.33333333) share Common no par
Nordic Diamonds Ltd. recapitalized as Western Standard Metals Ltd. 06/12/2009 which merged into Terraco Gold Corp. (AB) 01/25/2011 which reincorporated in British Columbia 06/08/2011

EARTH STEWARDS INC (BC)
Recapitalized as Consolidated Earth Stewards, Inc. 07/17/1997
Each share Common no par exchanged for (0.2) share Common no par
Consolidated Earth Stewards, Inc. recapitalized as Royal County Minerals Corp. 08/29/2002 which was acquired by International Curator Resources Ltd. 08/01/2003 which recapitalized as Canadian Gold Hunter Corp. (BC) 12/30/2003 which reincorporated in Canada 07/29/2004 which name changed to NGEx Resources Inc. 09/22/2009

EARTH TECHNOLOGY CORP USA (DE)
Merged into Tyco International Ltd. 01/19/1996
Each share Common 10¢ par exchanged for $8 cash

EARTHCARE CO (DE)
Plan of reorganization under Chapter 11 Federal Bankruptcy Code effective 10/29/2003
No stockholders' equity

EARTHDATA, INC. (CA)
Adjudicated bankrupt 08/18/1980
No stockholders' equity

EARTHFIRST CDA INC (CANADA)
Plan of arrangement under Companies' Creditors Arrangement Act effective 03/02/2010
No stockholders' equity

EARTHFIRST TECHNOLOGIES INC (FL)
Plan of reorganization under Chapter 11 Federal Bankruptcy proceedings terminated 01/05/2017
Stockholders' equity unlikely

EARTHGRAINS CO (DE)
Common 1¢ par split (2) for (1) by issuance of (1) additional share payable 07/28/1997 to holders of record 05/30/1997 Ex date - 07/29/1997
Common 1¢ par split (2) for (1) by issuance of (1) additional share payable 07/20/1998 to holders of record 07/10/1998 Ex date - 07/21/1998
Merged into Sara Lee Corp. 08/14/2001
Each share Common 1¢ par exchanged for $40.25 cash

EARTHLINK HLDGS CORP (DE)
Merged into Windstream Holdings, Inc. 02/27/2017
Each share Common 1¢ par exchanged for (0.818) share Common $0.0001 par

EARTHLINK INC (DE)
Name changed to EarthLink Holdings Corp. 01/02/2014
EarthLink Holdings Corp. merged into Windstream Holdings, Inc. 02/27/2017

EARTHLINK NETWORK INC (DE)
Common 1¢ par split (2) for (1) by issuance of (1) additional share

payable 07/20/1998 to holders of record 07/15/1998 Ex date - 07/21/1998
Merged into EarthLink, Inc. 02/04/2000
Each share Common 1¢ par exchanged for (1.615) shares Common 1¢ par
EarthLink, Inc. name changed to EarthLink Holdings Corp. 01/02/2014 which merged into Windstream Holdings, Inc. 02/27/2017

EARTHNET TV INC (DE)
Each share old Common $0.0001 par exchanged for (0.01) share new Common $0.0001 par 7/20/2001
Name changed to Nocera Inc. 2/8/2002

EARTHNETMEDIA INC (NV)
Each share old Common $0.001 par exchanged for (6) shares new Common $0.001 par 01/21/2003
Name changed to International Telecommunications, Inc. 08/10/2005
International Telecommunications, Inc. name changed to International Technology Systems, Inc. 11/20/2006 which name changed to Immunotech Laboratories, Inc. 02/04/2009

EARTHQUAKE VENTURE CAP CORP (CANADA)
Name changed to Rutel Corp. 8/11/2000
Rutel Corp. recapitalized as Rutel Networks Corp. 11/25/2003

EARTHRAMP COM COMMUNICATIONS INC (AB)
Reincorporated 00/00/2001
Place of incorporation changed from (BC) to (AB) 00/00/2001
Name changed to Champlain Resources Inc. 09/18/2007
Champlain Resources Inc. recapitalized as Beacon Resources Inc. 04/20/2012

EARTHSHELL CORP (DE)
Each share old Common 1¢ par exchanged for (0.08333333) share new Common 1¢ par 10/30/2003
Plan of reorganization under Chapter 11 Federal Bankruptcy Code effective 08/01/2007
No stockholders' equity

EARTHWATCH INC (DE)
Stock Dividends - In Preferred to holders of Preferred 2.125% payable 9/30/2001 to holders of record 9/15/2001 Ex date - 9/17/2001; 2.125% payable 6/30/2002 to holders of record 6/15/2002 Ex date - 6/21/2002; 2.125% payable 9/30/2002 to holders of record 9/15/2002 Ex date - 9/18/2002; 2.125% payable 12/31/2002 to holders of record 12/15/2002 Ex date - 12/18/2002
Each share 144A Common exchanged for (0.21) share new 144A Ser. C Preferred 4/14/99
Each share old 144A Ser. C Preferred exchanged for (0.441) share new 144A Ser. C Preferred 4/14/99
Each share Ser. C Conv. Preferred exchanged for (0.441) share new 144A Ser. C Preferred 4/14/99
Name changed to DigitalGlobe Inc. 8/22/2002
(See DigitalGlobe Inc.)

EARTHWEB INC (DE)
Issue Information - 2,100,000 shares COM offered at $14 per share on 11/10/1998
Name changed to Dice Inc. 6/14/2001
(See Dice Inc.)

EARTHWORM TRACTOR INC (NY)
Name changed to Earthworm, Inc. 7/17/87

EASCO CORP (MD)
$2.25 Conv. Preferred 1968 Ser. B $1 par called for redemption 03/30/1979
Common $2.50 par split (3) for (2) by issuance of (0.5) additional share 10/04/1983
Merged into ES Acquisition Corp. 06/27/1986
Each share Common $2.50 par exchanged for $17.50 cash

EASCO HAND TOOLS INC (DE)
Merged into Danaher Corp. 06/07/1990
Each share Common 1¢ par exchanged for (0.4175) share Common 1¢ par

EASCO INC (DE)
Merged into Caradon PLC 09/08/1999
Each share Common 1¢ par exchanged for $15.20 cash

EASEL CORP (MA)
Merged into VMARK Software, Inc. 6/14/95
Each share Common 1¢ par exchanged for (0.2127454) share Common 1¢ par
VMARK Software, Inc. name changed to ARDENT Software, Inc. 2/10/98 which merged into Informix Corp. 3/1/2000 which name changed to Ascential Software Corp. 7/3/2001

EASLEY COTTON MILLS
Merged into Woodside Mills in 1948
Details not available

EASON OIL CO (DE)
Each share Common $25 par exchanged for (8) shares Common $1 par in 1936
$1.50 Conv. Preferred called for redemption 3/31/49
Common $1 par split (4) for (1) by issuance of (3) additional shares 7/15/68
Merged into International Telephone & Telegraph Corp. 8/30/77
Each share Common $1 par exchanged for (2.3) shares Common $1 par
International Telephone & Telegraph Corp. name changed to ITT Corp. 12/31/83 which reorganized in Indiana as ITT Industries Inc. 12/19/95 which name changed to ITT Corp. 7/1/2006

EAST AFRICA GOLD CORP (BC)
Merged into Spinifex Gold N.L. 08/31/1999
Each share Common no par exchanged for (1.63) shares Ordinary no par

EAST AMPHI GOLD MINES LTD (QC)
Charter cancelled 06/06/1981

EAST ANTELOPE CORP (UT)
Each share Capital Stock 10¢ par exchanged for (0.1) share Capital Stock $1 par 12/30/1969
Proclaimed dissolved for failure to file annual reports 06/22/2000

EAST ASIA GOLD CORP (ON)
Recapitalized as EAGC Ventures Corp. 5/28/2001
Each (14) shares Common no par exchanged for (1) share Common no par
EAGC Ventures Corp. merged into Bema Gold Corp. 2/14/2003 which merged into Kinross Gold Corp. 2/27/2007

EAST AVENUE CORP. (NY)
Name changed to Rochester Sheraton Corp. in 1953
Rochester Sheraton Corp. merged into Sheraton Corp. of America 3/1/60 which was acquired by International Telephone & Telegraph Corp. (DE) 2/29/68 which name changed to ITT Corp. 12/31/83 which reorganized in Indiana as ITT Industries Inc. 12/19/95 which name changed to ITT Corp. 7/1/2006

EAST BANK OF COLORADO SPRINGS, N.A. (COLORADO SPRINGS, CO)
All except (67) shares held by First National Bancorporation, Inc. as of 12/26/72
Public interest eliminated

EAST BASIN OIL & URANIUM CO. (OK)
Charter revoked for non-payment of taxes 5/18/62

EAST BAY COPPER CO. LTD.
Acquired by East Bay Gold, Ltd. on a (1) for (3) basis 00/00/1936
(See East Bay Gold, Ltd.)

EAST BAY GOLD LTD (CANADA)
Voluntarily dissolved 06/05/1997
Details not available

EAST BAY MINES OF RED LAKE LTD. (ON)
Acquired by Inore Gold Mines Ltd. 00/00/1945
Each share Capital Stock no par exchanged for (0.5) share Capital Stock no par 00/00/1945
Inore Gold Mines Ltd. merged into Goldquest Exploration Inc. 08/09/1982 which merged into Goldcorp Inc. (New) 03/31/1994

EAST BEAUMONT OIL & GAS CO. (TX)
Charter forfeited for failure to pay taxes 4/18/50

EAST BERLIN RAILROAD CO.
Road abandoned and operations ceased 00/00/1939
Stockholders' equity unlikely

EAST BOSTON CO. (MA)
Liquidation completed 7/10/61

EAST BUTTE COPPER MINING CO.
Liquidation completed in 1936

EAST BUTTE MINING CO.
Liquidated in 1934

EAST CAROLINA BK (ENGELHARD, NC)
Common $3.33 par changed to $3.50 par and (2) additional shares issued payable 07/22/1998 to holders of record 07/22/1998
Under plan of reorganization each share Common $3.50 par automatically became (1) share ECB Bancorp Inc. Common $3.50 par 07/22/1998
ECB Bancorp Inc. merged into Crescent Financial Bancshares, Inc. 04/01/2013 which name changed to VantageSouth Bancshares, Inc. which merged into Yadkin Financial Corp. 07/04/2014 which merged into F.N.B. Corp. 03/11/2017

EAST COAST BEVERAGE CORP (CO)
Reorganized under Chapter 11 Federal Bankruptcy Code as North American Food & Beverage Corp. 07/28/2003
Each share Common 1¢ par exchanged for (0.06666666) share Common 1¢ par and (0.06666666) Common Stock Purchase Warrant expiring 01/01/2008
North American Food & Beverage Corp. name changed to Liquor Group Wholesale, Inc. 01/11/2008
(See Liquor Group Wholesale, Inc.)

EAST COAST ELECTRIC CO.
Acquired by Virginia Electric & Power Co. 00/00/1949
Each share Common exchanged for (1) share Common no par plus $1.50 cash dividend
Virginia Electric & Power Co. reorganized as Dominion Resources, Inc. (Old) 05/19/1983
(See Dominion Resources, Inc. (Old))

Industries Inc. 12/19/95 which name changed to ITT Corp. 7/1/2006

EAST COAST ENERGY LTD (NS)
10% Conv. Preferred no par reclassified as 2nd Preference no par 11/14/1983
Class A no par reclassified as Common no par 11/14/1983
Placed in receivership 06/05/1985
Details not available

EAST COAST INS CO (NY)
Capital Stock $2.50 par changed to $1.25 par 12/16/1966
Merged into Lion Insurance Co. 12/31/1975
Details not available

EAST COAST PUBLIC SERVICE CO.
Liquidation completed in 1949

EAST COAST UTILITIES CO.
Reorganized as East Coast Public Service Co. in 1934
Details not available

EAST COEUR D ALENE SILVER MINES INC (ID)
Each share old Common 10¢ par exchanged (0.015625) share new Common 10¢ par 08/21/2000
Reincorporated under the laws of Nevada as zKid Network Co. and Common 10¢ par changed to $0.0001 par 02/28/2001
zKid Network Co. recapitalized as EATware Corp. 04/12/2006 which name changed to Star Metro Corp. 11/27/2006 which name changed to BioPack Environmental Solutions Inc. 02/27/2007 which recapitalized as Tristar Wellness Solutions Inc. 01/18/2013

EAST COLO SPRINGS NATL BK (COLORADO SPRINGS, CO)
Name changed to East Bank of Colorado Springs, N.A. (Colorado Springs, CO) 10/04/1972
(See East Bank of Colorado Springs, N.A. (Colorado Springs, CO))

EAST CNTY BK N A (ANTIOCH, CA)
Merged into CivicBank of Commerce (Oakland, CA) 02/29/2000
Each share Common $5 par exchanged for $23.98 cash

EAST COUNTY LINE ROAD CORP. (PA)
Liquidation completed 01/11/1965
Details not available

EAST CREST OIL CO., LTD. (CANADA)
Recapitalized as Consolidated East Crest Oil Co. Ltd. 00/00/1953
Each share Capital Stock no par exchanged for (0.1) share Capital Stock no par
Consolidated East Crest Oil Co. Ltd. liquidated for Pan Ocean Oil Corp. 01/01/1972
(See Pan Ocean Oil Corp.)

EAST DAGGAFONTEIN MINES LTD (SOUTH AFRICA)
Stock Dividend - 6.05355% payable 02/01/1996 to holders of record 12/08/1995
ADR agreement terminated 07/29/1996
Each ADR for Ordinary exchanged for $2.904 cash

EAST DALQUIER GOLD MINES LTD. (QC)
Charter revoked for failure to file reports and pay fees 06/29/1964

EAST DELTA RES CORP (DE)
SEC revoked common stock registration 02/17/2010

EAST DRIEFONTEIN GOLD MNG LTD (SOUTH AFRICA)
Merged into Driefontein Consolidated Ltd. 07/01/1981
Each ADR for Ordinary exchanged for (1) ADR for Ordinary
Driefontein Consolidated Ltd. name changed to Gold Fields Ltd. (New) 05/10/1999

EAS-EAS   FINANCIAL INFORMATION, INC.

EAST END INVT INC (NV)
Name changed to Theme Factory Inc. 10/20/1989
Theme Factory Inc. name changed to Geyser Group, Ltd. 03/12/2001 which recapitalized as XStream Beverage Group Ltd. 10/16/2001 which name changed to XStream Beverage Network, Inc. 10/06/2004 which name changed to Hull Energy, Inc. 05/12/2008 which name changed to Gemini Group Global Corp. 11/04/2013

EAST END PARK HOTEL, INC. (DE)
Liquidated 00/00/1954
Details not available

EAST END ST BK (HOUSTON, TX)
Capital Stock $20 par changed to $10 par and (1) additional share issued 02/06/1973
Stock Dividends - 33.33333333% 01/13/1955; 30% 01/08/1959; 25% 01/23/1961; 125% 01/08/1976
Name changed to Houston United Bank (Houston, TX) 03/01/1979
(See Houston United Bank (Houston, TX))

EAST ENERGY CORP (BC)
Name changed to Rare Earth Metals Inc. 12/16/2009
Rare Earth Metals Inc. name changed to Canada Rare Earth Corp. 02/08/2013

EAST HAMPTON SECURITIES CO.
Merged into Connecticut Investment Management Corp. 00/00/1931
Details not available

EAST HARTFORD CO.
Merged into Connecticut Investment Management Corp. 00/00/1931
Details not available

EAST INDIA HOTELS LTD (INDIA)
Name changed to EIH Ltd. 11/14/1996
(See EIH Ltd.)

EAST INDIES MNG CORP (ON)
Merged into Falcon Well Services, Ltd. 02/13/1998
Each share Common no par exchanged for (1) share Common no par
(See Falcon Well Services, Ltd.)

EAST KOOTENAY POWER CO., LTD. (CANADA)
Acquired by British Columbia Hydro & Power Authority 09/12/1966
Each share 7% Preferred $100 par exchanged for $275 cash
Each share Common no par exchanged for $29 cash

EAST LEDUC OIL CO. LTD.
Merged into Trans Empire Oils Ltd. 00/00/1950
Each share Capital Stock no par exchanged for (0.06666666) share new Capital Stock no par
Trans Empire Oils Ltd. name changed to West Canadian Oil & Gas Ltd. 03/10/1958 which merged into Canadian Delhi Oil Ltd. 01/01/1962 which recapitalized as CanDel Oil Ltd. 01/10/1972
(See CanDel Oil Ltd.)

EAST LIBERTY PROPERTIES CORP. (PA)
Liquidation completed
Each share Common $50 par exchanged for initial distribution of $105 cash 08/24/1967
Each share Common $50 par received second and final distribution of $5.67 cash 07/31/1968

EAST LISBON URANIUM CO. (UT)
Merged into Sun Uranium Mining Co. 12/15/1954
Each share Capital Stock 1¢ par exchanged for (0.125) share Capital Stock 50¢ par
Sun Uranium Mining Co. name changed to Sun Tide Corp. 07/22/1955 which name changed to Maxa Corp. 04/13/1974
(See Maxa Corp.)

EAST LYNN POST 291 BUILDING ASSOCIATION, INC. (MA)
Dissolved for failure to file annual reports 08/08/1963

EAST MACDONALD MINES LTD (QC)
Charter annulled for failure to file annual reports 10/23/1982

EAST MALARTIC MINES LTD (QC)
Name changed to Les Mines Est-Malartic Ltee. 08/24/1979
Les Mines Est-Malartic Ltee. merged into Lac Minerals Ltd. (Old) 12/31/1982 which merged into LAC Minerals Ltd. (New) 07/29/1985 which was acquired by American Barrick Resources Corp. 10/17/1994 which name changed to Barrick Gold Corp. 01/18/1995

EAST-MANITOU MINES LTD (QC)
Charter surrendered 00/00/1960

EAST MIDDLESEX STREET RWY. CO.
Liquidated 00/00/1940
Details not available

EAST MOLINE DOWNS INC (IL)
Adjudicated bankrupt 02/15/1975
No stockholders' equity

EAST OAK STREET HOTEL CO. (DE)
Liquidated 00/00/1950
Details not available

EAST ORANGE COMMUNITY BANK (EAST ORANGE, NJ)
Name changed to Lincoln State Bank (East Orange, NJ) 11/01/1975
(See Lincoln State Bank (East Orange, NJ))

EAST PA RR CO (PA)
Voluntarily dissolved 09/21/1981
Details not available

EAST PENN BK (EMMAUS, PA)
Common $1.25 par split (2) for (1) by issuance of (1) additional share payable 04/17/2000 to holders of record 03/16/2000 Ex date - 04/18/2000
Stock Dividend - 3% payable 04/28/1999 to holders of record 04/23/1999
Under plan of reorganization each share Common $1.25 par automatically became (1) share East Penn Financial Corp. Common $0.625 par 07/01/2003
East Penn Financial Corp. merged into Harleysville National Corp. 11/16/2007 which merged into First Niagara Financial Group, Inc. (New) 04/09/2010 which merged into KeyCorp (New) 08/01/2016

EAST PENN FINL CORP (PA)
Merged into Harleysville National Corp. 11/16/2007
Each share Common $0.625 par exchanged for either (0.8416) share Common $1 par or $14.50 cash
Note: Option to receive stock expired 11/02/2007
Harleysville National Corp. merged into First Niagara Financial Group, Inc. (New) 04/09/2010 which merged into KeyCorp (New) 08/01/2016

EAST PORTO RICAN SUGAR CO. (MD)
Name changed to Eastern Sugar Associates 04/16/1935
Eastern Sugar Associates name changed to Fajardo Eastern Sugar Associates 05/02/1958
(See Fajardo Eastern Sugar Associates)

EAST RANCHERIA MINING CO. LTD. (ON)
Charter cancelled and declared dissolved for default in filing returns 01/13/1971

EAST RAND CONS PLC (ENGLAND)
Name changed to London Finance & Investment Group PLC 10/15/1986
(See London Finance & Investment Group PLC)

EAST RAND GOLD & URANIUM LTD (SOUTH AFRICA)
Merged into AngloGold Ltd. 06/29/1998
Each ADR for Ordinary exchanged for (1) Sponsored ADR for Ordinary AngloGold Ltd. name changed to AngloGold Ashanti Ltd. 04/26/2004

EAST RAND PROPRIETARY MINES LTD (SOUTH AFRICA)
ADR agreement terminated 05/09/2007
No ADR holders' equity

EAST RIM NICKEL MINES LTD. (ON)
Recapitalized as Nickel Rim Mines Ltd. 00/00/1954
Each share Common $1 par exchanged for (0.5) share Common $1 par
(See Nickel Rim Mines Ltd.)

EAST RIVER CAP CORP (NY)
Each share Exchangeable Auction Preferred no par exchanged for $100,000 principal amount of Auction Rate Notes due 08/27/1997 effective 07/29/1987

EAST ROCK EXPLORATIONS LTD. (ON)
Merged into Staple Mining Co. Ltd. 08/11/1972
Each share Capital Stock no par exchanged for (0.25) share Capital Stock no par
Staple Mining Co. Ltd. merged into Gerrard Realty Inc. 01/28/1976

EAST ROUYN GOLD MINES LTD.
Reorganized as East Rouyn (Quebec) Ltd. 00/00/1938
Each share Capital Stock exchanged for (1) share Capital Stock
East Rouyn (Quebec) Ltd. was acquired by Rouyn Merger Gold Mines Ltd. 00/00/1944 which recapitalized as New Rouyn Merger Mines Ltd. 00/00/1947 which recapitalized as Goldrim Mining Co. Ltd. 06/08/1965
(See Goldrim Mining Co. Ltd.)

EAST ROUYN (QUEBEC) LTD. (QC)
Acquired by Rouyn Merger Gold Mines Ltd. 00/00/1944
Each (100) shares Capital Stock exchanged for (78) shares Capital Stock and $0.50 cash
Rouyn Merger Gold Mines recapitalized as New Rouyn Merger Mines Ltd. 00/00/1947 which recapitalized as Goldrim Mining Co. Ltd. 06/08/1965
(See Goldrim Mining Co. Ltd.)

EAST SHORE CHEMICAL CO., INC. (MI)
Each share Capital Stock $3.33 par exchanged for (3) shares Capital Stock $1.11 par 05/06/1976
Capital Stock $1.11 par changed to 27¢ par and (3) additional shares issued 03/22/1979
Merged into Appleton Papers Inc. 12/26/1986
Details not available

EAST SHORE DISTRS INC (NV)
Name changed to Crimson Forest Entertainment Group Inc. 07/03/2014

EAST SIDE BANK & TRUST (WICHITA, KS)
Acquired by Bank IV Wichita, N.A. (Wichita, KS) 04/30/1990
Details not available

EAST SIDE BK & TR CO (CHICAGO, IL)
Name changed 10/11/1972
Name changed from East Side Bank (Chicago, IL) to East Side Bank & Trust Co. (Chicago, IL) 10/11/1972
Common Capital Stock $15 par changed to $50 par 01/29/1980
Name changed to BankChicago (Chicago, IL) 09/01/2000
(See BankChicago (Chicago, IL))

EAST SIDE CAP INC (AB)
Name changed to Redex Inc. (AB) 02/13/2003
Redex Inc. (AB) reincorporated in Canada 10/21/2004
(See Redex Inc.)

EAST SIDE FINL INC (DE)
Reincorporated under the laws of Florida 11/10/2008

EAST SIDE NATL BK (WICHITA, KS)
Common $10 par changed to $5 par and (1) additional share issued 09/00/1972
Name changed to East Side Bank & Trust (Wichita, KS) 09/02/1976
(See East Side Bank & Trust (Wichita, KS))

EAST SIDE PACKING CO. (IL)
Name changed to Hunter Packing Co. 00/00/1932
Hunter Packing Co. name changed to Paco, Inc. (IL) 11/28/1959
(See Paco, Inc.)

EAST SIDE SAVINGS & LOAN ASSOCIATION (IL)
Reincorporated under the laws of Delaware as East Side Financial, Inc. 00/00/1991
East Side Financial, Inc. (DE) reincorporated in Florida 11/10/2008

EAST SIDE TENNIS CLUB INC (NY)
Common 1¢ par split (5) for (1) by issuance of (4) additional shares 07/14/1969
Charter cancelled and proclaimed dissolved for failure to pay taxes and file reports 12/15/1975

EAST ST LOUIS & INTERURBAN WTR CO (IL)
7% 1st Preferred called for redemption 06/03/1957
Name changed to Illinois American Water Co. 06/01/1978
(See Illinois American Water Co.)

EAST STANDARD MINING CO. (UT)
Name changed to East Standard Corp. (UT) 07/01/1955
East Standard Corp. (UT) reincorporated in Nevada as Off-Track Betting Corp. of America, Inc. 09/10/1973 which recapitalized as Midwestern Fuel Systems, Inc. 05/08/1981 which name changed to Midwestern Companies, Inc. 05/25/1983
(See Midwestern Companies, Inc.)

EAST STD CORP (UT)
Each share Capital Stock 10¢ par exchanged for (0.5) share Capital Stock 20¢ par 11/01/1956
Reincorporated under the laws of Nevada as Off-Track Betting Corp. of America, Inc. and Capital Stock 20¢ par changed to 2¢ par 09/10/1973
Off-Track Betting Corp. of America, Inc. recapitalized as Midwestern Fuel Systems, Inc. 05/08/1981 which name changed to Midwestern Companies, Inc. 05/25/1983
(See Midwestern Companies, Inc.)

EAST SULLIVAN MINES LTD (QC)
Name changed 10/30/1974
Capital Stock $1 par changed to no par and (0.1) additional share issued 09/15/1969
Name changed from East Sullivan

Mines Ltd. to East Sullivan Mines Ltd. - Mines East Sullivan Ltee. and Capital Stock no par reclassified as Conv. Class A Capital Stock no par 10/30/1974
Conv. Class A Capital Stock no par reclassified as Common no par 02/05/1980
Conv. Class B Capital Stock no par reclassified as Common no par 02/05/1980
Merged into Sullivan Mines Inc. - Mines Sullivan Inc. 07/01/1983
Each share Common no par exchanged for (1) share Common no par
(See Sullivan Mines Inc.-Mines Sullivan Inc.)

EAST TEMPLE CORP.
Merged into Temple Coal Co. 00/00/1938
Each share Common exchanged for (1) share Common
(See Temple Coal Co.)

EAST TENN NAT GAS CO (TN)
5.2% Preferred $25 par called for redemption 12/17/1959
Merged into Tenneco Inc. 12/20/1979
Each share Common $1 par exchanged for (0.78) share Common $5 par
Tenneco Inc. merged into El Paso Natural Gas Co. 12/12/1996 which reorganized as El Paso Energy Corp. 08/01/1998 which name changed to El Paso Corp. 02/05/2001

EAST TENNESSEE LIGHT & POWER CO.
Dissolved 00/00/1945
Details not available

EAST TEX BANCSHARES INC (TX)
Preferred called for redemption at $154 on 12/30/1999

EAST TEX FINL SVCS INC (DE)
Common 1¢ par split (3) for (2) by issuance of (0.5) additional share payable 03/25/1998 to holders of record 03/11/1998
Merged into Prosperity Bancshares, Inc. 01/01/2013
Each share Common 1¢ par exchanged for (0.406) share Common $1 par

EAST TEX IRON CO (TX)
Each share Class B no par exchanged for (2) shares Class A no par 07/15/1974
Merged into Great Northern Nekoosa Corp. 02/28/1975
Each share Class A no par exchanged for (11.267) shares Common $10 par
(See Great Northern Nekoosa Corp.)

EAST TINTIC COALITION MNG CO (UT)
Merged into North Lily Mining Co. 12/01/1976
Each share Capital Stock 5¢ par exchanged for (0.0089) share Capital Stock 10¢ par
(See North Lily Mining Co.)

EAST TINTIC CONSOLIDATED MINING CO.
Merged into Eureka Lilly Consolidated Mining Co. 00/00/1937
Each share Common exchanged for (0.514801) share Common 10¢ par
Eureka Lilly Consolidated Mining Co. merged into Eureka Standard Consolidated Mining Co. 11/25/1974 which merged into South Standard Mining Co. 07/29/1983 which merged into Chief Consolidated Mining Co. 07/01/1996
(See Chief Consolidated Mining Co.)

EAST TRINITY METALS & HLDGS LTD (QC)
Name changed 00/00/1971
Name changed from East Trinity Mining Corp. to East Trinity Metals & Holdings Ltd. 00/00/1971
Charter cancelled 03/20/1982

EAST UTAH MNG CO (UT)
Reincorporated under the laws of Pennsylvania as Intramerican Oil & Minerals, Inc. 06/24/1982
Intramerican Oil & Minerals, Inc. name changed to Intramerican Corp. 07/31/1990 which name changed to Hunter Resources Inc. 11/10/1992 which was liquidated by Magnum Petroleum, Inc. 11/01/1996 which name changed to Magnum Hunter Resources, Inc. 03/18/1997 which merged into Cimarex Energy Co. 06/07/2005

EAST VENTURES LTD (QC)
Charter annulled for failure to file reports or pay fees 01/12/1974

EAST WEST ADVANCED TECHNOLOGY FD INC (CA)
Charter suspended for failure to file reports and pay fees 09/01/1977

EAST WEST BANCORP INC (DE)
Each share Non-Vtg. Mandatorily Conv. Preferred Ser. C $0.001 par exchanged for (110.74197) shares Common $0.001 par 03/30/2010
Each share 8% Non-Cum. Conv. Perpetual Preferred Ser. A $0.001 par exchanged for (65.26754) shares Common $0.001 par 05/01/2013
(Additional Information in Active)

EAST-WEST BK (CUPERTINO, CA)
Under plan of reorganization each share Common no par automatically became (1) share East West Bancorp, Inc. (DE) Common $0.001 par 12/30/1998

EAST/WEST COMMUNICATIONS INC (DE)
Merged into Voicestream Wireless Corp. 02/28/2000
Each share Common $0.001 par exchanged (0.36678) share Common no par
Voicestream Wireless Corp. merged into Deutsche Telekom AG 05/31/2001

EAST-WEST FEDERAL BANK, F.S.B. (LOS ANGELES, CA)
Merged into Talley Industries, Inc. 01/30/1989
Each share Common no par exchanged for $16 cash

EAST-WEST FEDERAL SAVINGS & LOAN ASSOCIATION (CA)
Name changed to East-West Federal Bank, F.S.B. (Los Angeles, CA) 04/23/1986
(See East-West Federal Bank, F.S.B. (Los Angeles, CA))

EAST/WEST FUND, INC. (CA)
Name changed to East/West Advanced Technology Fund, Inc. 01/01/1974
(See East/West Advanced Technology Fund, Inc.)

EAST WEST GROWTH STK FD INC (CA)
Charter suspended for failure to file reports and pay fees 09/01/1977

EAST WEST MED PRODS INC (DE)
Merged into Ultrasonic Systems, Inc. 08/12/1974
Each share Common 1¢ par exchanged for (1) share Common 1¢ par
(See Ultrasonic Systems, Inc.)

EAST WEST RES CORP (ON)
Reincorporated 12/11/2005
Common no par split (2) for (1) by issuance of (1) additional share 05/23/1988
Place of incorporation changed from (BC) to (ON) 12/11/2005
Reorganized under the laws of British Columbia as Rainy Mountain Royalty Corp. 02/05/2010
Each share Common no par exchanged for (0.2) share Common no par

EASTBAY INC (WI)
Acquired by Woolworth Corp. 01/30/1997
Each share Common 1¢ par exchanged for $24 cash

EASTBRIDGE INVT GROUP CORP (DE)
Reincorporated 01/31/2013
Each share Common no par received distribution of (0.00303782) share Wonder International Education & Investment Group Corp. Common no par payable 03/01/2011 to holders of record 07/31/2009
Each share Common no par received distribution of (0.00205592) share Tsingda eEDU Corp. Restricted Common $0.00128 par payable 08/29/2011 to holders of record 03/15/2010
State of incorporation changed from (AZ) to (DE) 01/31/2013
Each share Common no par exchanged for (0.01) share new Common $0.001 par
Name changed to Cellular Biomedicine Group, Inc. 03/05/2013

EASTBROKERS INTL INC (DE)
Name changed to Global Capital Partners, Inc. 02/02/2000
(See Global Capital Partners, Inc.)

EASTCHESTER FINL CORP (DE)
Acquired by North Fork Bancorporation, Inc. 06/28/1991
Each share Common 1¢ par exchanged for $15.50 cash

EASTCO INC (NJ)
Name changed to Eastco Medical Equipment, Inc. 01/31/1972
(See Eastco Medical Equipment, Inc.)

EASTCO INDL SAFETY CORP (NY)
Common 1¢ par split (3) for (1) by issuance of (2) additional shares 01/22/1988
Common 1¢ par split (3) for (2) by issuance of (0.5) additional share 07/12/1989
Each share Common 1¢ par exchanged for (0.08333333) share Common 12¢ par 12/31/1992
Each share old Common 12¢ par exchanged for (0.1) share new Common 12¢ par 08/13/1996
Name changed to Worksafe Industries Inc. 12/17/1998
(See Worksafe Industries Inc.)

EASTCO MED EQUIP INC (NJ)
Over 97% reacquired by company 00/00/1979
Public interest eliminated

EASTCO SAFETY EQUIP INC (NY)
Name changed to Eastco Industrial Safety Corp. 12/22/1969
Eastco Industrial Safety Corp. name changed to Worksafe Industries Inc. 12/17/1998
(See Worksafe Industries Inc.)

EASTCOAST ENERGY CORP (BRITISH VIRGIN ISLANDS)
Name changed to Orca Exploration Group Inc. 04/04/2007

EASTCOURT GOLD MINES LTD. (QC)
Declared dissolved for failure to file reports and pay fees 00/00/1957

EASTECH INC (DE)
Name changed to Brooks Tech, Inc. 09/30/1976
(See Brooks Tech, Inc.)

EASTEK CORP (NJ)
Chapter 11 bankruptcy proceedings converted to Chapter 7 on 11/09/1989
Stockholders' equity unlikely

EASTERN & CHARTERED TRUST CO. (TORONTO, ON)
Merged into Canada Permanent Mortgage Corp. 12/01/1967
Each share Capital Stock $10 par exchanged for (3) shares Capital Stock $2 par
Canada Permanent Mortgage Corp. merged into Canada Trustco Mortgage Co. 12/31/1985
(See Canada Trustco Mortgage Co.)

EASTERN & PAC INDS CORP (WA)
Involuntarily dissolved 07/01/1978
No stockholders' equity

EASTERN AIR DEVICES INC (DE)
Name changed to Electro Audio Dynamics, Inc. 12/19/1974
(See Electro Audio Dynamics, Inc.)

EASTERN AIR LINES INC (DE)
Common $1 par split (2) for (1) by issuance of (1) additional share 06/30/1967
Stock Dividend - 300% 05/15/1946
Merged into Texas Air Corp. 11/25/1986
Each share Common $1 par exchanged for (0.15) share Depositary Preferred $1 par and $6.25 cash
(See Texas Air Corp.)
Each share $2.69 Preferred $1 par exchanged for (1) share $2.72 Preferred $1 par and $5.22 cash 11/25/1986
Each share $3 Conv. Jr. Preferred $1 par exchanged for (1) share $3.12 Jr. Preferred $1 par and $9.75 cash 11/25/1986
Each share $3.20 Preferred $1 par exchanged for (1) share $3.24 Preferred $1 par and $6.20 cash 11/25/1986
Depositary Preferred $1 par called for redemption 03/30/1987
1986 Conv. Jr. Preferred $1 par called for redemption 03/30/1987
Depositary Preferred, $2.72 Preferred $1 par, $3.12 Preferred $1 par and $3.24 Preferred $1 par cancelled through plan of reorganization under Chapter 11 of the Federal Bankruptcy Code effective 02/06/1995
No stockholders' equity

EASTERN ALUM MFG INC (NJ)
Name changed to Eastco, Inc. 03/27/1969
Eastco, Inc. name changed to Eastco Medical Equipment, Inc. 01/31/1972
(See Eastco Medical Equipment, Inc.)

EASTERN ASBESTOS LTD (QC)
Charter cancelled 10/00/1974

EASTERN BAKERIES LTD (NB)
Each share old Common no par exchanged for (3) shares new Common no par 03/04/1971
4% Preferred $100 par called for redemption 10/28/1977
New Common no par split (3) for (1) by issuance of (2) additional shares 12/28/1978
New Common no par split (3) for (1) by issuance of (2) additional shares 06/03/1986
Merged into Corporate Foods Ltd. 09/11/1989
Each share new Common no par exchanged for (0.9) share Common no par
Corporate Foods Ltd. name changed to Canada Bread Ltd. (New) 05/06/1997
(See Canada Bread Ltd. (New))

EASTERN BANCORP INC (DE)
Common 1¢ par split (3) for (2) by issuance of (0.5) additional share payable 06/19/1996 to holders of record 06/05/1996
Merged into Vermont Financial Services Corp. 06/26/1997
Each share Common 1¢ par

exchanged for (0.6272) share Common $1 par and $0.7613 cash
Vermont Financial Services Corp. merged into Chittenden Corp. 05/28/1999
(See Chittenden Corp.)

EASTERN BOWLING CORP. (DE)
Name changed to Eastern Davis Corp. 04/03/1967
Eastern Davis Corp. name changed to Davis (H.B.) Corp. 12/10/1971
(See Davis (H.B.) Corp.)

EASTERN CAMERA & PHOTO CORP. (DE)
Merged into Fotochrome Inc. 06/22/1965
Each share Common 10¢ par exchanged for (0.5) share Common $1 par
(See Fotochrome Inc.)

EASTERN CAN CO., INC. (NY)
Merged into United States Crown Corp. 06/17/1968
Each share Class A $1 par exchanged for (1) share Common 10¢ par
(See United States Crown Corp.)

EASTERN CANADA COASTAL STEAMSHIPS LTD.
Dissolved 00/00/1947
Details not available

EASTERN CANADA DEVELOPMENT LTD. (QC)
Adjudicated bankrupt 08/02/1962
Details not available

EASTERN CANADA GAS & OIL LTD. (QC)
Recapitalized as Southern Exploration & Development Corp. 10/19/1960
Each share Capital Stock $1 par exchanged for (0.1) share Capital Stock $1 par
Southern Exploration & Development Corp. name changed to Calvin Exploration & Development Corp. 01/01/1973
(See Calvin Exploration & Development Corp.)

EASTERN CDA SVGS & LN CO (CANADA)
Each share Capital Stock $100 par exchanged for (10) shares Capital Stock $10 par 00/00/1951
Each share Capital Stock $10 par exchanged for (10) shares Capital Stock $1 par 04/30/1965
Merged into Central & Eastern Trust Co. (Moncton, NB) 07/02/1976
Each share Capital Stock $1 par exchanged for (1) share Conv. Class A $4 par
Central & Eastern Trust Co. (Moncton, NB) merged into Central Trust Co. (Moncton, NB) 03/01/1981

EASTERN CLAY PRODUCTS, INC.
Acquired by International Minerals & Chemical Corp. 00/00/1951
Each share Common exchanged for (1.75) share Common $5 par
International Minerals & Chemical Corp. name changed to Imcera Group Inc. 06/14/1990 which name changed to Mallinckrodt Group Inc. 03/15/1994 which name changed to Mallinckrodt Inc. 10/16/1996 which merged into Tyco International Ltd. (Bermuda) 10/17/2000 which reincorporated in Switzerland 03/17/2009 which merged into Johnson Controls International PLC 09/06/2016

EASTERN CO (CT)
Common Stock Purchase Rights declared for Common stockholders of record 08/29/1986 were redeemed at $0.0167 per right 10/15/1986 for holders of record 09/30/1991
(Additional Information in Active)

EASTERN CONNECTICUT POWER CO.
Merged into Connecticut Light & Power Co. 00/00/1929
Details not available

EASTERN CORP. (ME)
Merged into Standard Packaging Corp. 09/15/1958
Each share Common $10 par exchanged for (1) share $1.20 Conv. Preferred $20 par and (0.8) share Common $1 par
Standard Packaging Corp. acquired by Saxon Industries, Inc. (NY) 10/22/1970 which reincorporated in Delaware 10/03/1975 which reorganized as Paper Corp. of America 04/01/1985
(See Paper Corp. of America)

EASTERN COTTON OIL CO.
Reorganized as Davison Chemical Corp. 00/00/1936
Details not available

EASTERN CR CORP (VA)
Placed in receivership 06/00/1970
Each share Common $1 par exchanged for initial distribution of $0.80 cash 09/10/1974
Each share Common $1 par received second and final distribution of $1.40314 cash 12/02/1974

EASTERN CUBA SUGAR CORP.
Merged into Cuban Atlantic Sugar Co. 00/00/1935
Details not available

EASTERN DAIRIES, INC.
Acquired by General Ice Cream Corp. 00/00/1928
Details not available

EASTERN DAIRIES LTD.
Merged into Dominion Dairies Ltd. 00/00/1943
Each share Preferred $100 par exchanged for (1) share 6% Preferred $25 par and (3) shares Common no par
Each share Common no par exchanged for (0.15) share Common no par
Dominion Dairies Ltd. name changed to Dominion Dairies Ltd.-Laiteries Dominion Ltee. 11/27/1974
(See Dominion Dairies Ltd.-Laiteries Dominion Ltee.)

EASTERN DAVIS CORP (DE)
Name changed to Davis (H.B.) Corp. 12/10/1971
(See Davis (H.B.) Corp.)

EASTERN DIVERSIFIED CORP (NY)
Charter cancelled and proclaimed dissolved for failure to pay taxes and file reports 12/15/1975

EASTERN DYNAMIC INDS INC (FL)
Each share old Common 1¢ par exchanged for (0.332) share new Common 1¢ par and (0.001) share Preferred $10 par 12/16/1970
Proclaimed dissolved for failure to file reports and pay fees 06/28/1971

EASTERN EDISON CO (MA)
13.6% Preferred $100 par called for redemption 08/18/1986
15.48% Preferred $100 par called for redemption 08/18/1986
8.32% Preferred $100 par called for redemption 06/01/1993
9% Preferred $100 par called for redemption 06/01/1993

EASTERN ELEC INC (MN)
Name changed to Texergy Corp. 05/04/1981

EASTERN ELECTRICITY PLC (UNITED KINGDOM)
Name changed to Eastern Group PLC 10/01/1994
(See Eastern Group PLC)

EASTERN ENGINEERING CO.
Merged into Eastern Industries, Inc.

(DE) (Incorporated 10/02/1946) 00/00/1946
Each share Preferred $5 par exchanged for (1) share Preferred $5 par
Each share Common exchanged for (0.5) share Common 50¢ par
Eastern Industries, Inc. merged into Laboratory for Electronics, Inc. 03/15/1961 which name changed to LFE Corp. 11/03/1969
(See LFE Corp.)

EASTERN ENTERPRISES (MA)
Acquired by KeySpan Corp. 11/08/2000
Each share Common $1 par exchanged for $64.558 cash

EASTERN ENVIRONMENT SOLUTIONS CORP (NV)
Each share Common $0.0001 par received distribution of (0.1) share Datone, Inc. Restricted Common $0.0001 par payable 04/01/2008 to holders of record 08/24/2006
Recapitalized as Precicion Trim, Inc. 09/20/2016
Each share Common $0.0001 par exchanged for (0.02) share Common $0.0001 par

EASTERN ENVIRONMENTAL SVCS INC (DE)
Merged into Waste Management, Inc. 12/31/1998
Each share Common 1¢ par exchanged for (0.6406) share Common $1 par

EASTERN EQUITIES CORP.
Liquidated 00/00/1945
Details not available

EASTERN EXPL CO (DE)
Common $0.0001 par split (4) for (1) by issuance of (3) additional shares payable 05/17/2007 to holders of record 05/17/2007 Ex date - 05/18/2007
Name changed to Max Entertainment Holdings, Inc. 06/25/2007
Max Entertainment Holdings, Inc. name changed to Cyclon Capital Corp. 12/15/2007

EASTERN FGHT WAYS INC (NY)
Common 20¢ par split (2) for (1) by issuance of (1) additional share 06/23/1972
Adjudicated bankrupt 08/26/1976
Shareholders' equity unlikely

EASTERN FIN CORP (VA)
Placed in receivership 06/00/1970
No stockholders' equity

EASTERN FOOTWEAR CORP. (NY)
Capital Stock $1 par reclassified as Common $1 par 00/00/1949
Charter revoked for failure to file reports and pay fees 12/15/1961

EASTERN GAS & ELECTRIC SECURITIES CORP.
Dissolved 00/00/1936
Details not available

EASTERN GAS & FUEL ASSOC (MA)
4.5% Prior Preference $100 par reclassified as 4.5% Preferred $100 par 00/00/1950
Each share 6% Preferred $100 par exchanged for (6) shares Common $10 par 00/00/1950
Each share Common no par exchanged for (0.169) share Common $10 par 00/00/1950
4.5% Preferred $100 par called for redemption 01/01/1964
Common $10 par changed to $3.33333333 par and (2) additional shares issued 04/24/1967
Common $3.33333333 par changed to $1 par and (1) additional share issued 05/09/1968
Common $1 par split (3) for (2) by issuance of (0.5) additional share 07/28/1975
Common $1 par split (3) for (2) by issuance of (0.5) additional share 08/27/1976
Name changed to Eastern Enterprises 04/28/1989
(See Eastern Enterprises)

EASTERN GOLDFIELDS LTD (CANADA)
Recapitalized as Target Vanguard Capital Inc. 08/17/1993
Each share Common no par exchanged for (0.5) share Common no par
Target Vanguard Capital Inc. recapitalized as Coretek Vencap Inc. 02/22/1995 which recapitalized as Ungava Minerals Corp. 12/04/1996 which name changed to Nearctic Nickel Mines Inc. 09/07/2007

EASTERN GROUP INTL CO LTD (DE)
Name changed to Telespace Ltd. 01/07/1997
Telespace Ltd. name changed to Qinnet.com, Inc. 01/10/2000 which name changed to Q-Net Technologies, Inc. 08/13/2001
(See Q-Net Technologies, Inc.)

EASTERN GROUP PLC (UNITED KINGDOM)
Acquired by Hanson PLC (Old) 01/02/1995
Each Sponsored ADR for Ordinary exchanged for $30.30 cash

EASTERN HARNESS RACING CLUB, INC. (DE)
No longer in existence having become inoperative and void for non-payment of taxes 04/01/1953

EASTERN INDIANA TELEPHONE CO. (IN)
Each share Common $100 par exchanged for (30) shares Common $10 par 08/01/1959
Completely liquidated 07/29/1963
Each share Common $10 par exchanged for first and final distribution of (2.25) shares General Telephone & Electronics Corp. Common $3.33333333 par
5% Preferred $100 par called for redemption 08/31/1963
General Telephone & Electronics Corp. name changed to GTE Corp. 07/01/1982 which merged into Verizon Communications Inc. 06/30/2000

EASTERN INDUSTRIES, INC. (DE)
Incorporated 10/02/1946
Common 50¢ par split (3) for (2) by issuance of (0.5) additional share 11/01/1956
Stock Dividend - 10% 08/29/1952
Merged into Laboratory for Electronics, Inc. 03/15/1961
Each share Common 50¢ par exchanged for (1/3) share Common $1 par
Laboratory for Electronics, Inc. name changed to LFE Corp. 11/03/1969
(See LFE Corp.)

EASTERN INDUSTRIES, INC. (DE)
Ctfs. dated after 05/01/1965
Through purchase offer 100% acquired by Eureka Stone Quarry, Inc. 00/00/1976
Public interest eliminated

EASTERN INDUSTRIES CORP. (MN)
Merged into Graphic Service, Inc. 08/31/1973
Each share Common 1¢ par exchanged for (0.1) share Common 1¢ par
(See Graphic Service, Inc.)

EASTERN INS HLDGS INC (PA)
Acquired by ProAssurance Corp. 01/02/2014
Each share Common no par exchanged for $24.50 cash

EASTERN INVESTORS, INC. (NC)
Name changed to Continental Acceptance Corp. 11/01/1965

Continental Acceptance Corp. merged into NCNB Corp. 04/03/1970 which name changed to NationsBank Corp. (NC) 12/31/1991 which reincorporated in Delaware as BankAmerica Corp. (Old) 09/25/1998 which merged into BankAmerica Corp. (New) 09/30/1998 which name changed to Bank of America Corp. 04/28/1999

EASTERN KANSAS UTILITIES, INC.
Liquidated 00/00/1952
Details not available

EASTERN LEAD CORP., INC. (ID)
Merged into Northwest Uranium Mines, Inc. 00/00/1956
Each share Common exchanged for (0.2) share Capital Stock
(See Northwest Uranium Mines, Inc.)

EASTERN LEASEHOLDS INC (BC)
Name changed to GLF Technologies (1979) Ltd. 03/07/1984
GLF Technologies (1979) Ltd. recapitalized as Blackberry Gold Resources Inc. 02/24/1986
(See Blackberry Gold Resources Inc.)

EASTERN LIFE INS CO N Y (NY)
Capital Stock $5 par changed to $3.50 par 00/00/1935
Capital Stock $3.50 par changed to $5.50 par 00/00/1952
Capital Stock $5.50 par changed to $5 par 09/08/1958
Capital Stock $5 par changed to $1 par and (4) additional shares issued 11/30/1961
Stock Dividends - 100% 12/02/1958; 10% 07/24/1959; 10% 03/27/1961; 10% 10/14/1961; 10% 08/14/1964; 50% 11/30/1965
Merged into USLIFE Corp. 09/30/1971
Each share Capital Stock $1 par exchanged for (0.566) share Common $2 par
USLIFE Corp. merged into American General Corp. 06/17/1997 which merged into American International Group, Inc. 08/29/2001

EASTERN LIGHTS RES LTD (BC)
Delisted from Vancouver Stock Exchange 01/09/1989

EASTERN LIME CORP (DE)
Common $2 par changed to $1 par and (1) additional share issued 10/15/1959
Name changed to Eastern Industries, Inc. 05/01/1965
(See Eastern Industries, Inc.)

EASTERN LT CAP INC (DE)
Each share Ser. A Preferred 1¢ par exchanged for (1.25) shares Common 1¢ par 02/23/2011
(Additional Information in Active)

EASTERN MACH SCREW CORP (CT)
Each share Common $100 par exchanged for (5) shares Common $20 par 00/00/1951
Liquidation completed
Each share Common $20 par exchanged for initial distribution of $38 cash 05/12/1967
Each share Common $20 par received second distribution of $5 cash 11/08/1967
Each share Common $20 par received third distribution of $0.50 cash 08/27/1968
Each share Common $20 par received fourth and final distribution of $0.35 cash 08/11/1970

EASTERN MAINE RAILWAY
Acquired by Maine Central Railroad Co. 00/00/1936
Details not available

EASTERN MALLEABLE IRON CO. (CT)
Each share Common $100 par exchanged for (8) shares Common $10 par and $20 cash 00/00/1930
Common $10 par changed to $5 par 00/00/1933
Each share Common $5 par exchanged for (0.1) share Common $25 par 00/00/1935
Stock Dividend - 25% 07/12/1951
Name changed to Eastern Co. 02/22/1961

EASTERN MANUFACTURING CO. (MA)
Reorganized under the laws of Maine as Eastern Corp. 00/00/1939
Each share Preferred exchanged for (4) shares Common $1 par
Each share Common exchanged for (0.5) share Common $1 par
Eastern Corp. (ME) merged into Standard Packaging Corp. 09/15/1958 which was acquired by Saxon Industries, Inc. (NY) 10/22/1970 which reincorporated in Delaware 10/03/1975 which reorganized as Paper Corp. of America 04/01/1985
(See Paper Corp. of America)

EASTERN MANUFACTURING CO. (ME)
Reorganized under the laws of Massachusetts as Eastern Manufacturing Co. 00/00/1935
Details not available

EASTERN MASS STR RY CO (MA)
Liquidation completed
Each share 1st Preferred Ser. A $100 par exchanged for first and final distribution of $156.50 cash 07/29/1968
Each share Preferred Ser. B $100 par exchanged for first and final distribution of $208.50 cash 07/29/1968
Each share Adjustment Stock $100 par exchanged for first and final distribution of (5) shares Union Street, Inc. Common $1 par 01/02/1969
No Common stockholders' equity

EASTERN MERIDIAN MNG CORP (AB)
Recapitalized as New Meridian Mining Corp. 11/22/2000
Each share Common no par exchanged for (0.1) share Common no par
New Meridian Mining Corp. name changed to Phillppine Metals Inc. (AB) 04/07/2010 which reincorporated in British Columbia 04/17/2018

EASTERN METALS CORP. LTD. (QC)
Recapitalized as Territory Mining Co. Ltd. 07/02/1959
Each share Capital Stock $1 par exchanged for (0.2) share Capital Stock $1 par
Territory Mining Co. Ltd. merged into St. Fabien Copper Mines Ltd. 07/27/1967 which name changed to St. Fabien Explorations Inc. 02/11/1981 which recapitalized as Fabien Explorations Inc. 07/18/1983
(See Fabien Explorations Inc.)

EASTERN MICHIGAN PROPERTIES CORP.
Acquired by City Coach Lines, Inc. (MI) 00/00/1948
Details not available

EASTERN MICHIGAN RAILWAYS
Reorganized 00/00/1939
No stockholders' equity

EASTERN MICHIGAN TRANSPORTATION CORP.
Liquidation completed 00/00/1944
Details not available

EASTERN MINES LTD (BC)
Merged into HLX Resources Ltd. 09/01/1989
Each share Common no par exchanged for (0.1519) share Common no par
HLX Resources Ltd. recapitalized as Emperor Gold Corp. 03/30/1992 which name changed to Emgold Mining Corp. 08/01/1997

EASTERN MINING & SMELTING CORP. LTD. (QC)
Recapitalized as Nickel Mining & Smelting Corp. 08/19/1958
Each share Capital Stock $1 par exchanged for (0.36363636) share Capital Stock $1 par
Nickel Mining & Smelting Corp. recapitalized as Metal Mines Ltd. 12/31/1963 which merged into Consolidated Canadian Faraday Ltd. 05/04/1967 which name changed to Faraday Resources Inc. 08/02/1983 which merged into Conwest Exploration Co. Ltd. (New) (AB) 09/01/1993 which merged into Alberta Energy Co. Ltd. 01/31/1996 which merged into EnCana Corp. 01/03/2003

EASTERN MINNESOTA POWER CORP.
Dissolved 00/00/1949
Details not available

EASTERN MISSOURI POWER CO.
Merged into Missouri Edison Co. 00/00/1945
Details not available

EASTERN MONTANA LIGHT & POWER CO.
Acquired by Montana-Dakota Power Co. 00/00/1928
Details not available

EASTERN MTN SPORTS INC (MA)
Common 1¢ par split (2) for (1) by issuance of (1) additional share 04/21/1976
Acquired by Franklin Mint Corp. 11/20/1979
Each share Common 1¢ par exchanged for $8.69 cash

EASTERN NATL BK (CINNAMINSON, NJ)
Name changed to Cherry Hill National Bank (Medford, NJ) 04/27/1987
Cherry Hill National Bank (Medford, NJ) merged into Meridian Bancorp, Inc. 04/16/1993 which merged into CoreStates Financial Corp 04/09/1996 which merged into First Union Corp. 04/28/1998 which name changed to Wachovia Corp. (Ctfs. dated after 09/01/2001) 09/01/2001 which merged into Wells Fargo & Co. (New) 12/31/2008

EASTERN NATL BK LONG ISLAND (SMITHTOWN, NY)
Common $5 par changed to $2.50 par and (1) additional share issued 07/14/1967
Merged into Chemical New York Corp. 03/03/1972
Each share Common $2.50 par exchanged for (0.5247) share Common $12 par
Chemical New York Corp. name changed to Chemical Banking Corp. 04/29/1988 which name changed to Chase Manhattan Corp. (New) 03/31/1996 which name changed to J.P. Morgan Chase & Co. 07/20/2004

EASTERN NEW JERSEY POWER CO.
Dissolved 00/00/1935
Details not available

EASTERN NEW YORK POWER CORP. (NY)
Liquidation completed 03/25/1959
Details not available

EASTERN NEW YORK UTILITIES CORP.
Dissolved 00/00/1933
Details not available

EASTERN NEWSSTAND CORP (NY)
Stock Dividend - 10% 08/15/1975
Merged into Restaurant Associates, Inc. 06/08/1976
Each share Common 5¢ par exchanged for $5.50 cash

EASTERN OFFICES, INC. (NY)
Dissolved 10/09/1953
Details not available

EASTERN OIL CO.
Dissolved 00/00/1935
Details not available

EASTERN OREGON LIGHT & POWER CO.
Assets sold to California-Pacific Utilities Co. 00/00/1946
Details not available

EASTERN OREGON NATURAL GAS CO. (OR)
Merged into Cascade Natural Gas Corp. 03/01/1960
Each share Common $5 par exchanged for (1) share Common $1 par
(See Cascade Natural Gas Corp.)

EASTERN PAC CORP (NY)
Name changed to Dmytryk-Boyd Productions, Inc. 09/17/1973
Dmytryk-Boyd Productions, Inc. name changed to E-Z 8 Motels, Inc. 06/20/1974
(See E-Z 8 Motels, Inc.)

EASTERN PAC ENERGY CORP (FL)
Name changed to Utilisource Corp. 09/08/1999
Utilisource Corp. name changed to Utilisource International Corp. 08/29/2007 which name changed to Whole In One Organics Corp., Inc. 08/19/2009 which name changed to Liberty International Holding Corp. 05/02/2012

EASTERN PETE CO (OH)
Each share old Class A Common no par exchanged for (0.0002) share new Class A Common no par 09/07/1993
Merged out of existence 02/04/1997
Details not available

EASTERN PETE CO (UT)
Each share Capital Stock $0.005 par exchanged for (0.05) share Capital Stock 10¢ par 06/07/1972
Completely liquidated 08/30/1977
Each share Capital Stock 10¢ par exchanged for first and final distribution of $0.2122076 cash

EASTERN PPTYS INC (DE)
Charter cancelled and declared inoperative and void for non-payment of taxes 03/01/1984

EASTERN PROVINCIAL AWYS LTD (NL)
Recapitalized as Newfoundland Capital Corp. Ltd. (NFLD) 01/23/1981
Each share 6% Conv. Preferred Ser. A $15 par automatically became (1) share 6% Conv. Preferred Ser. A $1 par
Each share Common no par exchanged for (1) share Class A Common no par and (1) share Class B Common no par
Newfoundland Capital Corp. Ltd. (NFLD) reincorporated in Canada 03/04/1987

EASTERN PUBLIC SERVICE CORP. (DE)
Charter cancelled and declared inoperative and void for non-payment of taxes 4/1/34

EASTERN QUEBEC URANIUM & NICKEL CORP. LTD. (QC)
Charter annulled for failure to file reports 10/28/78

EASTERN RACING ASSOCIATION, INC. (MA)
Each share old Common no par exchanged for (35) shares new

Common no par with privilege of exchange for Common $2 par in 1946
Completely liquidated 1/6/69
Each share Common $2 par or Common no par exchanged for first and final distribution of (0.366666) share Realty Equities Corp. of New York Common $1 par
Preferred no par called for redemption 1/10/69
Public interest eliminated
(See Realty Equities Corp. of New York)

EASTERN RES AUSTRALIA LTD (AUSTRALIA)
Recapitalized as Firstpac Ltd. 01/31/1990
Each ADR for Ordinary AUD $0.10 par exchanged for (0.5) ADR for Ordinary AUD $0.20 par
(See Firstpac Ltd.)

EASTERN ROLLING MILL CO.
Name changed to Eastern Stainless Steel Corp. in 1944
Eastern Stainless Steel Corp. name changed to Easco Corp. 4/29/69
(See Easco Corp.)

EASTERN RR INDS INC (DE)
Name changed to Computers & Railroads Inc. 11/29/1968

EASTERN SVCS HLDGS INC (DE)
Common $0.001 par split (10) for (1) by issuance of (9) additional shares payable 01/15/2008 to holders of record 01/15/2008 Ex date - 01/16/2008
Name changed to Fund.com Inc. and Common $0.001 par reclassified as Class A Common $0.001 par 02/05/2008

EASTERN SHARES CORP.
Liquidated in 1934

EASTERN SHOPPING CTRS INC (DE)
Each share Common $1 par exchanged for (0.2) share Common $5 par 12/26/68
Completely liquidated 10/7/71
Each share Common $5 par exchanged for first and final distribution of (1) Mortgage Growth Investors Share of Bene. Int. $1 par
Mortgage Growth Investors name changed to MGI Properties 2/10/88
(See MGI Properties)

EASTERN SHORE GAS CORP.
Acquired by Suburban Propane Gas Corp. 00/00/1946
Details not available

EASTERN SMELTING & REFINING CO. LTD. (QC)
Merged into Eastern Mining & Smelting Corp. Ltd. share for share 1/3/56
Eastern Mining & Smelting Corp. Ltd. recapitalized as Nickel Mining & Smelting Corp. 8/19/58 which recapitalized as Metal Mines Ltd. 12/31/63 which merged into Consolidated Canadian Faraday Ltd. 5/4/67 which name changed to Faraday Resources Inc. 8/2/83 which merged into Conwest Exploration Co. Ltd. (New) (ALTA) 9/1/93 which merged into Alberta Energy Co. Ltd. 1/31/96 which merged into EnCana Corp. 1/3/2003

EASTERN SOUND INC (NY)
Common 1¢ par split (5) for (2) by issuuance of (1.5) additional shares 12/05/1975
Name changed to Audio Media Corp. 08/17/1973
(See Audio Media Corp.)

EASTERN STAINLESS CORP (MD)
Proclaimed dissolved 3/28/95

EASTERN STAINLESS STL CORP (MD)
Common $5 par changed to $2.50 par and (1) additional share issued 04/15/1959
Name changed to Easco Corp. 04/29/1969
(See Easco Corp.)

EASTERN STAR GAS LTD (AUSTRALIA)
Acquired by Santos Ltd. 11/17/2011
Each Sponsored ADR for Ordinary exchanged for $18.012503 cash

EASTERN STAR HLDGS INC (NV)
Reorganized 08/09/1989
Name changed 05/28/1997
Reorganized from Eastern Star Mining Co. (ID) to Eastern Star Mines, Inc. (NV) 08/09/1989
Each share Common 10¢ par exchanged for (0.2) share Common $0.001 par
Each share Common $0.001 par exchanged for (0.1) share new Common $0.001 par 05/19/1997
Name changed from Eastern Star Mines, Inc. to Eastern Star Holdings Inc. 05/28/1997
Name changed to Fan Energy, Inc. 12/09/1997
Fan Energy, Inc. name changed to Quiet Tiger, Inc. 02/21/2003 which name changed to MediaMax Technology Corp. 04/01/2005 which recapitalized as Exchange Media Corp. 10/01/2008 which name changed to Empire Oil Refineries Corp. 03/31/2011

EASTERN STATES POWER CORP.
Name changed to Eastern States Corp. in 1935
Eastern States Corp. liquidated for St. Regis Paper Co. 6/26/69 which name changed to St. Regis Corp. 4/28/83 which merged into Champion International Corp. 11/20/84 which merged into International Paper Co. 6/20/2000

EASTERN STATES SHARES CORP.
Liquidated in 1931

EASTERN STATES WAREHOUSE & COLD STORAGE CO.
Ceased operations 00/00/1926
Details not available

EASTERN STEAMSHIP LINES, INC. (ME)
Common no par exchanged (3) for (1) in 1929
Liquidation completed 3/19/57

EASTERN STEEL CASTINGS CO.
Property sold 00/00/1935
Details not available

EASTERN STEEL PRODUCTS, LTD. (CANADA)
Under plan of reorganization each share Common no par exchanged for (1) share 6% Preferred $1 par 3/24/58
6% Preferred $1 par called for redemption in 1959
Public interest eliminated

EASTERN STONE PRODS LTD (ON)
Reincorporated 07/07/1995
Place of incorporation changed from (AB) to (ON) 07/07/1995
Recapitalized as Greenshield Resources Inc. 08/18/1995
Each share Common no par exchanged for (0.1) share Common no par
Greenshield Resources Inc. acquired by Greenshield Resources Ltd. 11/11/2002 which recapitalized as Greenshield Explorations Ltd. (ON) 06/13/2006 which reincorporated in British Columbia 10/19/2007

EASTERN STS CORP (MD)
Common no par changed to $1 par in 1952
$7 Preferred Ser. A no par called for redemption 2/1/69
$6 Preferred Ser. B no par called for redemption 2/1/69
Completely liquidated 6/26/69
Each share Common $1 par exchanged for first and final distribution of (1.61845) shares St. Regis Paper Co. Common $5 par
St. Regis Paper Co. name changed to St. Regis Corp. 4/28/83 which merged into Champion International Corp. 11/20/84 which merged into International Paper Co. 6/20/2000

EASTERN SUGAR ASSOCIATES (MD)
Stock Dividend - 35% 4/14/58
Name changed to Fajardo Eastern Sugar Associates 5/2/58 which merged into Brewer (C.) Co., Puerto Rico, Inc. for cash 7/27/61

EASTERN TELEGRAPH CO.
Merged into Cables & Wireless Ltd. in 1929
Details not available

EASTERN TELEPHONE & TELEGRAPH CO.
Merged into New England Telephone & Telegraph Co. in 1947
Details not available

EASTERN TERRA COTTA CO.
Sold at foreclosure in 1945
No stockholders' equity

EASTERN TEXAS ELECTRIC CO.
Dissolved in 1938

EASTERN THEATRES, LTD. (CANADA)
Common $25 par changed to $1 par in 1938
Liquidated for cash 12/29/62

EASTERN TIME TABLE & FOLDER DISTRIBUTING CO., INC. (NY)
Name changed to Time Table & Folder Distributors, Inc. 3/10/64
(See Time Table & Folder Distributors, Inc.)

EASTERN TIME TABLE DISTRIBUTING CO., INC. (NY)
Name changed to Eastern Time Table & Folder Distributing Co., Inc. 4/8/55
Eastern Time Table & Folder Distributing Co., Inc. name changed to Time Table & Folder Distributors, Inc. 3/10/64
(See Time Table & Folder Distributors, Inc.)

EASTERN TRACTOR MANUFACTURING CORP. (NY)
Liquidated in 1954

EASTERN TRANSVAAL CONS MINES LTD (SOUTH AFRICA)
ADR's for Ordinary split (20) for (1) by issuance of (19) additional ADR's issued 10/29/1990
Each ADR for Ordinary exchanged for (0.0440476) Avgold Ltd. ADR for Ordinary 01/03/1997
(See Avgold Ltd.)

EASTERN TR & BKG CO (BANGOR, ME)
Each share Common $1 par exchanged for (5) shares Capital Stock $20 par 1/20/65
Reorganized as Eastern Trust Financial Associates 3/18/69
Each share Capital Stock $20 par exchanged for (4) shares Common $5 par
Eastern Trust Financial Associates name changed to Northeastern Bankshare Association 3/21/69 which name changed to Northeast Bankshare Association 3/23/71 which merged into Norstar Bancorp Inc. 6/1/83 which merged into Fleet/Norstar Financial Group, Inc. 1/1/88 which name changed to Fleet Financial Group, Inc. (New) 4/15/92 which name changed to Fleet Boston Corp. 10/1/99 which name changed to FleetBoston Financial Corp. 4/18/2000 which merged into Bank of America Corp. 4/1/2004

EASTERN TRUST CO. (HALIFAX, NS)
Each share Capital Stock $100 par exchanged for (10) shares Capital Stock $10 par 00/00/1948
Merged into Eastern & Chartered Trust Co. (Toronto, ONT) 11/30/1963
Each share Capital Stock $10 par exchanged for (1) share Capital Stock $10 par
Eastern & Chartered Trust Co. (Toronto, ONT) merged into Canada Permanent Mortgage Corp. 12/01/1967 which merged into Canada Trustco Mortgage Co. 12/31/1985
(See Canada Trustco Mortgage Co.)

EASTERN TRUST FINANCIAL ASSOCIATES (ME)
Name changed to Northeastern Bankshare Association 3/21/69
Northeastern Bankshare Association name changed to Northeast Bankshare Association 3/23/71 which merged into Norstar Bancorp Inc. 6/1/83 which merged into Fleet/Norstar Financial Group, Inc. 1/1/88 which name changed to Fleet Financial Group, Inc. (New) 4/15/92 which name changed to Fleet Boston Corp. 10/1/99 which name changed to FleetBoston Financial Corp. 4/18/2000 which merged into Bank of America Corp. 4/1/2004

EASTERN UTILITIES INVESTING CORP.
Acquired by Associated Gas & Electric Co. 00/00/1937
Each share Prior Preferred exchanged for (1) share $5 Preferred
Each share $7 Preferred exchanged for (1) share $6.50 Preference
Each share $6 Preferred exchanged for (1) share $5.50 Preference
Each share Part. Preference exchanged for (1) share $4 Preference
Each share Class A Common exchanged for (1/3) share Class A
Associated Gas & Electric Co. reorganized as General Public Utilities (NY) 00/00/1946
(See General Public Utilities Corp.)

EASTERN UTILITY PREFERRED HOLDING CORP.
Name changed to Eastern Utilities Investing Corp. in 1927
Eastern Utilities Investing Corp. acquired by Associated Gas & Electric Co. 1937 which reorganized as General Public Utilities Corp. (NY) in 1946
(See General Public Utilities Corp. (NY))

EASTERN UTILS ASSOC (MA)
Merged into National Grid USA 04/19/2000
Each share Common $5 par exchanged for $31.459 cash

EASTERN UTILS LTD (PE)
3% 2nd Preference $100 par called for redemption 12/11/1961
5.5% 1st Preference $10 par called for redemption at $9.215 on 12/22/2000
Common no par changed to $10.50 par 10/19/1965
Acquired by National Grid Transco PLC 04/16/2000
Each share Common $10.50 par exchanged for USD$31.459 cash

EASTERN VA BANKSHARES INC (VA)
Merged into Southern National Bancorp of Virginia, Inc. 06/23/2017
Each share Common $2 par exchanged for (0.6313) share Common 1¢ par

EASTERN WORLD SOLUTIONS INC (NV)
Name changed to Banjo & Matilda, Inc. 10/16/2013

EASTERN YORK INC (DE)
Ceased operations 08/31/1979
No stockholders' equity

EASTEX ENERGY INC (DE)
Merged into El Paso Natural Gas Co. 09/12/1995
Each share Common 1¢ par exchanged for either (0.1601) share new Common $3 par or $4.50 cash
Note: Option to receive cash expired 09/15/1995
El Paso Natural Gas Co. reorganized as El Paso Energy Corp. 08/01/1998 which name changed to El Paso Corp. 02/05/2001 which merged into Kinder Morgan, Inc. (New) 05/25/2012

EASTGATE ACQUISITIONS CORP (NV)
Name changed to Eastgate Biotech Corp. 12/12/2014

EASTGATE HOTEL, INC. (IL)
In process of liquidation 00/00/1951
Details not available

EASTGROUP PPTYS (MD)
Shares of Bene. Int. $1 par split (3) for (2) by issuance of (0.5) additional share payable 04/07/1997 to holders of record 03/31/1997 Ex date - 04/08/1997
Under plan of reorganization each Share of Bene. Int. $1 par automatically became (1) share Eastgroup Properties, Inc. Common $0.0001 par 06/05/1997

EASTGROUP PPTYS INC (MD)
Issue Information - 1,500,000 shares PFD SER A 9% offered at $25 per share on 06/12/1998
9% Preferred Ser. A $0.0001 par called for redemption at $25 plus $0.51875 accrued dividends on 07/07/2003
7.95% Preferred Ser. D $0.0001 par called for redemption at $25 plus $0.011 accrued dividends on 07/02/2008
(Additional information in Active)

EASTHAMPTON RUBBER THREAD CO.
Merged into United Elastic Corp. 00/00/1927
Details not available

EASTLAND FINL CORP (RI)
Charter revoked for failure to file reports 01/25/1994

EASTLAND SVGS & LN ASSN (CA)
Name changed to Columbia Savings & Loan Association (Ctfs. dtd after 11/29/1976) 11/30/1976
(See Columbia Savings & Loan Association (Ctfs. dtd after 11/29/1976))

EASTLYNN MINES, LTD. (ON)
Charter cancelled 00/00/1953

EASTMAN CHEM CO (DE)
Preferred Stock Purchase Rights declared for Common stockholders of record 12/13/1993 were redeemed at $0.01 per right 01/02/2007 for holders of record 12/18/2006
(Additional Information in Active)

EASTMAN KODAK CO (NJ)
Each share Common no par exchanged for (5) shares Common $10 par 00/00/1947
6% Preferred $100 par called for redemption 05/22/1959
$3.60 Preferred $50 par called for redemption 01/31/1964
Common $10 par changed to $5 par and (1) additional share issued 05/21/1965
Common $5 par changed to $2.50 par and (1) additional share issued 05/24/1968
Common $2.50 par split (3) for (2) by issuance of (0.5) additional share 05/17/1985
Common $2.50 par split (3) for (2) by issuance of (0.5) additional share 10/19/1987
Stock Dividends - 10% 01/20/1951; 10% 01/26/1952; 100% 04/13/1959
Plan of reorganization under Chapter 11 Federal Bankruptcy proceedings effective 09/03/2013
No stockholders' equity
(Additional Information in Active)

EASTMAQUE GOLD MINES LTD (BC)
Merged into Equinox Resources Ltd. (New) 12/08/1992
Each share 8% Conv. Preference no par exchanged for (0.5) share 8% Conv. Preferred no par, (0.5) share Common no par and (0.5) Common Stock Purchase Warrant expiring 12/08/1996
Each share Common no par exchanged for (0.125) share Common no par
Equinox Resources Ltd. (New) merged into Hecla Mining Co. 04/11/1994

EASTMET CORP (MD)
Common $1 par split (3) for (2) by issuance of (0.5) additional share 01/04/1974
Common $1 par split (3) for (2) by issuance of (0.5) additional share 07/05/1974
Common $1 par split (3) for (2) by issuance of (0.5) additional share 09/05/1979
Under plan of reorganization each share Common $1 par received (0.2957608) share Eastern Stainless Corp. Class B Common $1 par 07/29/1988
(See Eastern Stainless Corp.)

EASTMIN RES INC (BC)
Struck off register and declared dissolved for failure to file returns 12/16/1994

EASTMONT GOLD MINES LTD. (ON)
Reorganized as Angoss Software Corp. 02/26/1993
Each share Common no par exchanged for (0.5) share Common no par
(See Angoss Software Corp.)

EASTMONT LARDER LAKE GOLD MINES LTD. (ON)
Name changed to Eastmont Gold Mines Ltd. 09/17/1986
Eastmont Gold Mines Ltd. reorganized as Angoss Software Corp. 02/26/1993
(See Angoss Software Corp.)

EASTON BANCORP INC (MD)
Merged into Easton Facilitation, Inc. 06/16/2004
Each share Common 10¢ par exchanged for $16.29 cash

EASTON INC (DE)
Each share old Common $0.001 par exchanged for (0.2) share new Common $0.001 par 03/22/2002
SEC revoked common stock registration 07/07/2006

EASTON NATL BK & TR CO (EASTON, PA)
Stock Dividends - 32.45% 02/15/1971; 50% 05/01/1973; (1) for (6) 05/01/1978; (1) for (7) 05/01/1979
Merged into Merchants Bancorp, Inc. (PA) 12/30/1983
Each share Common $10 par exchanged for (2.35) shares Conv. Class A Preferred $3 par
(See Merchants Bancorp, Inc. (PA))

EASTON-TAYLOR TRUST CO. (ST. LOUIS, MO)
Name changed to Central West End Bank (St. Louis, MO) 06/15/1965
Central West End Bank (St. Louis, MO) merged into City Bank (St. Louis, MO) 06/30/1974

EASTOVER BK FOR SVGS (JACKSON, MS)
Each share Common $1 par exchanged for (0.1) share Common $2 par 07/22/1988
Note: Holders of (499) or fewer pre-split shares received $1.75 cash per share
Under plan of reorganization each share Common $2 par automatically became (1) share EB, Inc. Common $2 par 02/28/1993
EB, Inc. merged into Parkway Co. (TX) 04/27/1995 which reincorporated in Maryland as Parkway Properties, Inc. 08/02/1996 which merged into Cousins Properties Inc. 10/06/2016

EASTOVER CORP (LA)
Stock Dividends - 20% 03/19/1982; 20% 03/18/1983
Merged into Eastgroup Properties 12/20/1994
Each Share of Bene. Int. no par exchanged for (0.6) Share of Bene. Int. $1 par
Eastgroup Properties reorganized as Eastgroup Properties, Inc. 06/05/1997

EASTPARK RLTY TR (DC)
Completely liquidated 04/06/1990
Each Share of Bene. Int. no par exchanged for first and final distribution of (0.3347) share Parkway Co. (TX) Common $1 par and $4.78 cash
Parkway Co. (TX) reincorporated in Maryland as Parkway Properties, Inc. 08/02/1996 which merged into Cousins Properties Inc. 10/06/2016

EASTPORT ENTERPRISES INC (UT)
Name changed to Landfill Resources Inc. 10/25/1987

EASTRON DIVERSIFIED INDUSTRIES (FL)
Proclaimed dissolved for failure to file reports and pay fees 09/03/1976

EASTSHORE ENERGY LTD (AB)
Each share Class B no par exchanged for (10) shares Class A no par 05/01/2007
Acquired by Crocotta Energy Inc. 06/11/2007
Each share Class A no par exchanged for $0.65 cash

EASTSIDE BK & TR CO (SNELLVILLE, GA)
Merged into First Sterling Banks, Inc. (Old) 07/31/1996
Each share Common exchanged for (1) share Common no par
First Sterling Banks, Inc. (Old) name changed to First Sterling Banks, Inc. (New) 05/24/2000 which name changed to Main Street Banks, Inc. (New) 01/02/2001

EASTVIEW MINES LTD. (ON)
Charter cancelled 01/31/1979

EASTVILLE GOLD MINES LTD (QC)
Merged into Societe Miniere Pershing Manitou Ltee. 06/30/1993
Details not available

EASTWARD HO COUNTRY CLUB, INC. (MA)
All stock redeemed 00/00/1961
Details not available

EASTWARD MINES LTD.
Acquired by Upper Canada Mines Ltd. 00/00/1946
Each share Capital Stock $1 par exchanged for (0.125) share Capital Stock $1 par
Upper Canada Mines Ltd. name changed to Upper Canada Resources Ltd. 10/05/1972 which reorganized as Challenger International Services Ltd. 07/07/1978
(See Challenger International Services Ltd.)

EASTWEBB MINES, LTD. (ON)
Charter cancelled for failure to file reports and pay taxes 09/09/1958

EASTWIND GROUP INC (DE)
Recapitalized as Magellan Energy Ltd. 12/02/2005
Each share Common 10¢ par exchanged for (0.001) share Common 10¢ par

EASTWOOD OIL CO. LTD. (AB)
Merged into Medallion Petroleums Ltd. 01/22/1960
Each share Class A 50¢ par exchanged for (0.9) share Common $1.25 par
Each share Ordinary Stock 50¢ par exchanged for (0.9) share Common $1.25 par
Medallion Petroleums Ltd. merged into Canadian Industrial Gas & Oil Ltd. 03/08/1965 which merged into Norcen Energy Resources Ltd. (AB) 10/28/1975 which reincorporated in Canada 04/15/1977 which merged into Union Pacific Resources Group Inc. 04/17/1998 which merged into Anadarko Petroleum Corp. 07/14/2000

EASY ACCESS INTL INC (FL)
Recapitalized as National Business Promotions, Inc. 10/10/2007
Each share Common $0.001 par exchanged for (0.1) share Common $0.001 par
(See National Business Promotions, Inc.)

EASY CD YEARBOOK INC (NV)
Name changed to VizStar, Inc. 03/30/2010
VizStar, Inc. recapitalized as Kimberly Parry Organics Corp. 04/03/2014

EASY CELLULAR INC (NV)
Name changed to Easy Phone Inc. (Old) 09/10/1997
Easy Phone Inc. (Old) recapitalized as Indian Wells Acquisitions, Ltd. 08/04/2005 which name changed to Nitro Lube, Inc. 11/25/2005 which name changed to Uranium City Mining Corp. 11/14/2007 which name changed to U.S. Mine Makers, Inc. (NV) 01/28/2008 which reincorporated in Wyoming as Vid3G, Inc. 02/13/2014 which recapitalized as Argus Worldwide Corp. 11/14/2016

EASY COM INC (NV)
Name changed to Royal Spring Water, Inc. 02/22/2006
(See Royal Spring Water, Inc.)

EASY COME EASY GO INC (UT)
Name changed to Missouri Illinois Mining Inc. 08/00/1987
(See Missouri Illinois Mining Inc.)

EASY GARDENER PRODS TR I (DE)
Liquidation completed
Each 9.4% Trust Preferred Security received initial distribution of $3.80 cash payable 12/22/2006 to holders of record 09/21/2006 Ex date - 12/28/2006
Each 9.4% Trust Preferred Security received second and final distribution of approximately $2.15 cash payable 08/03/2007 to holders of record 09/21/2006 Ex date - 08/06/2007

EASY GOLF CORP (NV)
Name changed to China Bio-Immunity Corp. 02/25/2008

EAS-EAT

EASY GROUPS LTD (NV)
Name changed to China Bionanometer Industries Corp. 07/24/2007
(See China Bionanometer Industries Corp.)

EASY ORGANIC COOKERY INC (NV)
Name changed to New York Sub Co. 12/03/2014

EASY PHONE INC NEW (NV)
Charter revoked for failure to file reports and pay fees 03/31/2008

EASY PHONE INC OLD (NV)
Recapitalized as Indian Wells Acquisitions, Ltd. 08/04/2005
Each share Common $0.001 par exchanged for (0.1) share Common $0.001 par
Indian Wells Acquisitions, Ltd. name changed to Nitro Lube, Inc. 11/25/2005 which name changed to Uranium City Mining Corp. 11/14/2007 which name changed to U.S. Mine Makers, Inc. (NV) 01/28/2008 which reincorporated in Wyoming as Vid3G, Inc. 02/13/2014 which recapitalized as Argus Worldwide Corp. 11/14/2016

EASY STR ADVENTURES INC (CANADA)
Dissolved 01/02/2003

EASY WASHING MACHINE CO. LTD. (ON)
Each share Preferred $100 par exchanged for (2) shares Preferred $10 par and (5) shares Common no par 00/00/1934
Each share Common no par exchanged for (0.2) share new Common no par 00/00/1934
Each share Common no par exchanged for (5) shares new Common no par 00/00/1949
Acquired by General Steel Wares Ltd. 00/00/1958
Each share Common no par exchanged for (1) share Common no par and $1 cash
5% 1st Preference Ser. A $20 par called for redemption 10/10/1963
General Steel Wares Ltd. name changed to GSW Ltd.-GSW Ltee. 01/02/1970 which name changed to GSW Inc. 10/01/1980
(See GSW Inc.)

EASY WASHING MACHINE CORP. (DE)
Merged into Union Chemical & Materials Corp. 08/31/1955
Each share Class A Common no par or Class B Common no par exchanged for (2) shares 5% Preferred $5 par and (0.5) share Common $10 par
Union Chemical & Materials Corp. merged into Vulcan Materials Co. 12/31/1957

EASY WIND OIL CO (UT)
Name changed to Derrick Petroleum, Inc. 02/05/1986
Derrick Petroleum, Inc. name changed to Derrick Industries, Inc. (UT) 07/10/1987 which reincorporated in Nevada 01/30/1989 which recapitalized as Processing Research Inc. 04/18/1995
(See Processing Research Inc.)

EASYHOME LTD (ON)
Common no par split (3) for (2) by issuance of (0.5) additional share payable 05/31/2005 to holders of record 05/27/2005 Ex date - 05/25/2005
Name changed to goeasy Ltd. 09/17/2015

EASYLINK SVCS CORP (DE)
Each share old Class A Common 1¢ par exchanged for (0.1) share new Class A Common 1¢ par 01/23/2002
Each share new Class A Common 1¢ par exchanged again for (0.2) share new Class A Common 1¢ par 08/28/2006
Merged into Internet Commerce Corp. 08/17/2007
Each share new Class A Common 1¢ par exchanged for $5.80 cash

EASYLINK SVCS INTL CORP (DE)
Acquired by Open Text Corp. 07/02/2012
Each share Class A Common 1¢ par exchanged for $7.25 cash

EASYMED SVCS INC (BC)
Recapitalized as EasyMed Technologies Inc. 10/21/2013
Each share Common no par exchanged for (0.2) share Common no par
EasyMed Technologies Inc. recapitalized as Easy Technologies Inc. 02/05/2016

EASYMED TECHNOLOGIES INC (BC)
Recapitalized as Easy Technologies Inc. 02/05/2016
Each share Common no par exchanged for (0.1) share Common no par

EASYNET DATA CORP (ON)
Each share Common no par exchanged for (0.1) share Class A no par 12/18/1987
Name changed to Vertigo 3D, Inc. 04/30/1996
Vertigo 3D, Inc. recapitalized as Vertigo Software Corp. 10/27/1998 which name changed to Even Technologies Inc. 06/22/2004

EASYQUAL COM CO (CO)
Name changed to Entrust Financial Services, Inc. (CO) 04/09/2001
Entrust Financial Services, Inc. (CO) reincorporated in Delaware as Enthrust Financial Services, Inc. 01/11/2007 which name changed to Rodman & Renshaw Capital Group, Inc. 08/31/2007 which name changed to Direct Markets Holdings Corp. 06/01/2012
(See Direct Markets Holdings Corp.)

EASYRIDERS INC (DE)
Plan of reorganization under Chapter 11 Federal Bankruptcy Code effective 04/01/2003
No stockholders' equity

EASYWEB INC (DE)
Reincorporated 05/16/2005
State of incorporation changed from (CO) to (DE) 05/16/2005
Each share old Common $0.001 par exchanged for (0.025) share new Common $0.001 par 08/24/2005
Name changed to ZIOPHARM Oncology, Inc. 09/13/2005

EAT AT JOES LTD (DE)
Name changed to SPYR, Inc. 03/12/2015

EATERIES INC (OK)
Each share old Common $0.002 par exchanged for (0.00006666) share new Common $0.002 par 09/28/2004
Note: In effect holders received $3.75 cash per share and public interest was eliminated

EATON & HOWARD CASH MGMT FD (MA)
Name changed to Eaton Vance Cash Management Fund 09/27/1982
(See Eaton Vance Cash Management Fund)

EATON & HOWARD GROWTH FD INC (MA)
Name changed to Eaton Vance Special Equities Fund, Inc. 09/24/1982
Eaton Vance Special Equities Fund, Inc. name changed to Eaton Vance Special Investment Trust 07/21/1992

EATON & HOWARD INCOME FD (MA)
Name changed to Eaton Vance High Yield Fund 02/18/1983
(See Eaton Vance High Yield Fund)

EATON & HOWARD MANAGEMENT FUND B
Trust terminated 00/00/1940
Details not available

EATON & HOWARD MANAGEMENT FUND F
Name changed to Eaton & Howard Stock Fund 00/00/1940
Eaton & Howard Stock Fund name changed to Eaton Vance Stock Fund 05/01/1989 which name changed to Eaton Vance Securities Trust 07/31/1994
(See Eaton Vance Securities Trust)

EATON & HOWARD STK FD (MA)
Shares of Bene. Int. $1 par split (2) for (1) by issuance of (1) additional share 00/00/1954
Shares of Bene. Int. $1 par changed to 50¢ par and (1) additional share issued 05/23/1960
Name changed to Eaton Vance Stock Fund 05/01/1989
Eaton Vance Stock Fund name changed to Eaton Vance Securities Trust 07/31/1994
(See Eaton Vance Securities Trust)

EATON & HOWARD VANCE SANDERS INC (MD)
Name changed to Eaton Vance Corp. 02/20/1981

EATON AXLE & SPRING CO.
Name changed to Eaton Manufacturing Co. 03/16/1932
Eaton Manufacturing Co. name changed to Eaton Yale & Towne Inc. 12/31/1965 which name changed to Eaton Corp. (OH) 04/21/1971 which reincorporated in Ireland as Eaton Corp. PLC 11/30/2012

EATON BAY COMWLTH FD LTD (CANADA)
Name changed back to Eaton Commonwealth Fund Ltd. 04/16/1986
Eaton Commonwealth Fund Ltd. name changed to Viking Commonwealth Fund Ltd. 04/16/1987

EATON BAY DIVID FD LTD (CANADA)
Name changed 04/16/1986
Name changed from Eaton/Bay Dividend Fund to Eaton Dividend Fund Ltd. 04/16/1986
Name changed to Viking Dividend Fund Ltd. 04/16/1987
Viking Dividend Fund Ltd. name changed to Laurentian Dividend Fund Ltd. 05/31/1993 which name changed to Strategic Value Dividend Fund Ltd. 06/05/1997 which name changed to StrategicNova Canadian Dividend Fund Ltd. 09/26/2000
(See StrategicNova Canadian Dividend Fund Ltd.)

EATON BAY GROWTH FD LTD (CANADA)
Name changed back to Eaton Growth Fund Ltd. 04/16/1986
Eaton Growth Fund Ltd. name changed to Viking Growth Fund Ltd. 04/16/1987

EATON BAY INCOME FD (ON)
Name changed back to Eaton Income Fund 04/16/1986
Eaton Income Fund name changed to Viking Income Fund 04/16/1987 which name changed to StrategicNova Income Fund 09/26/2000 which name changed to StrategicNova Canadian Bond Fund 12/00/2001
(See StrategicNova Canadian Bond Fund)

EATON BAY INTL FD LTD (CANADA)
Name changed 04/12/1978
Reincorporated 04/16/1980
Name changed 04/16/1986
Name changed from Eaton International Fund to Eaton Bay International Fund 04/12/1978
Place of incorporation changed from (ON) to (Canada) and Class A $1 par reclassified as Mutual Fund Units no par 04/16/1980
Name changed back from Eaton Bay International Fund to Eaton International Fund Ltd. 04/16/1986
Name changed to Viking International Fund Ltd. 04/16/1987
Viking International Fund Ltd. name changed to Laurentian International Fund Ltd. 05/31/1993 which name changed to Strategic Value International Fund Ltd. 06/05/1997 which name changed to StrategicNova World Large Cap Fund Ltd. 09/26/2000
(See StrategicNova World Large Cap Fund Ltd.)

EATON BAY MTG CORP (CANADA)
Name changed to Seaway Mortgage Corp.-La Corporation d'Hypotheque Seaway 02/03/1982
(See Seaway Mortgage Corp.-La Corporation d'Hypotheque Seaway)

EATON BAY TRUST CO. (CALGARY, AB)
Name changed to Eaton Trust Co. (Calgary, AB) 11/13/1985
Eaton Trust Co. (Calgary, AB) merged into Laurentian Bank of Canada (Montreal, QC) 02/04/1988

EATON BAY VENTURE FD LTD (CANADA)
Merged into Eaton Bay International Fund Ltd. 04/16/1980
Details not available

EATON BAY VIKING FD LTD (CANADA)
Mutual Fund Shares 70¢ par changed to no par 04/12/1978
Name changed back to Eaton Viking Fund Ltd. 04/16/1986
Eaton Viking Fund Ltd. name changed to Viking Canadian Fund Ltd. 04/16/1987 which name changed to Laurentian Canadian Equity Fund Ltd. 05/31/1993 which name changed to Strategic Value Canadian Equity Fund Ltd. 06/05/1997 which name changed to StrategicNova Canadian Large Cap Value Fund Ltd. 09/26/2000
(See StrategicNova Canadian Large Cap Value Fund Ltd.)

EATON COMMONWEALTH FUND LTD. (CANADA)
Name changed to Eaton/Bay Commonwealth Fund Ltd. and Common $1 par reclassified as Mutual Fund Shares no par 04/12/1978
Eaton/Bay Commonwealth Fund Ltd. name changed back to Eaton Commonwealth Fund Ltd. 04/16/1986 which name changed to Viking Commonwealth Fund Ltd. 04/16/1987 which name changed to Laurentian Commonwealth Fund Ltd. 05/31/1993 which name changed to Strategic Value Commonwealth Fund Ltd. 06/05/1997 which name changed to StrategicNova Commonwealth Fund Ltd. 09/26/2000
(See StrategicNova Commonwealth Fund Ltd.)

EATON CORP (OH)
Common 50¢ par split (3) for (2) by issuance of (0.5) additional share 10/02/1979
$2.30 Conv. Preferred Ser. A no par called for redemption 11/25/1983

4.75% Conv. Preferred $25 par called for redemption 11/25/1983
Common 50¢ par split (3) for (2) by issuance of (0.5) additional share 09/19/1988
$10 Conv. Preferred Ser. B 50¢ par called for redemption 10/31/1988
Stock Purchase Rights declared for Common stockholders of record 10/08/1985 were redeemed at $0.0633 per right 05/25/1993 for holders of record 05/10/1993
Common 50¢ par split (2) for (1) by issuance of (1) additional share 06/28/1993
Each share Common 50¢ par received distribution of (1.179023) share Axcelis Technologies, Inc. Common $0.001 par payable 12/29/2000 to holders of record 12/06/2000 Ex date - 01/02/2001
Common 50¢ par split (2) for (1) by issuance of (1) additional share payable 02/23/2004 to holders of record 02/09/2004 Ex date - 02/24/2004
Common 50¢ par split (2) for (1) by issuance of (1) additional share payable 02/28/2011 to holders of record 02/07/2011 Ex date - 03/01/2011
Reincorporated under the laws of Ireland as Eaton Corp. PLC and Common 50¢ par changed to Ordinary 1¢ par 11/30/2012

EATON CRANE & PIKE CO.
Name changed to Eaton Paper Co. 00/00/1932
(See Eaton Paper Co.)

EATON FINL CORP (MA)
Common 10¢ par split (5) for (4) by issuance of (0.25) additional share 09/18/1985
Common 10¢ par split (5) for (4) by issuance of (0.25) additional share 09/18/1986
Merged into American Telephone & Telegraph Co. 03/16/1989
Each share Common 10¢ par exchanged for (0.5043) share Common $1 par
American Telephone & Telegraph Co. name changed to AT&T Corp. 04/20/1994 which merged into AT&T Inc. 11/18/2005

EATON GROWTH FD LTD (CANADA)
Name changed to Eaton/Bay Growth Fund Ltd. and Mutual Fund Shares $1 par changed to no par 04/12/1978
Eaton/Bay Growth Fund Ltd. name changed back to Eaton Growth Fund Ltd. 04/16/1986 which name changed to Viking Growth Fund Ltd. 04/16/1987 which name changed to Laurentian American Equity Fund Ltd. 05/31/1993 which name changed to Strategic Value American Equity Fund Ltd. 06/05/1997 which name changed to StrategicNova U.S. Large Cap Growth Fund Ltd. 09/26/2000
(See StrategicNova U.S. Large Cap Growth Fund Ltd.)

EATON INCOME FD (ON)
Name changed to Eaton/Bay Income Fund 11/30/1977
Eaton/Bay Income Fund name changed back to Eaton Income Fund 04/16/1986 which name changed to Viking Income Fund 04/16/1987 which name changed to StrategicNova Income Fund 09/26/2000 which name changed to StrategicNova Canadian Bond Fund 12/00/2001
(See StrategicNova Canadian Bond Fund)

EATON INTL FD LTD (ON)
Name changed to Eaton Bay International Fund Ltd. (ON) 04/12/1978

Eaton Bay International Fund Ltd. (ON) reincorporated in Canada 04/16/1980 which name changed back to Eaton International Fund Ltd. 04/16/1986 which name changed to Viking International Fund Ltd. 04/16/1987 which name changed to Laurentian International Fund Ltd. 05/31/1993 which name changed to Strategic Value International Fund Ltd. 06/05/1997 which name changed to StrategicNova World Large Cap Fund Ltd. 09/26/2000
(See StrategicNova World Large Cap Fund Ltd.)

EATON LABORATORIES INC (NV)
Each share old Common $0.001 par received distribution of (1) share IVPSA Corp. Restricted Common payable 11/01/2006 to holders of record 10/30/2006
Each share Common $0.001 par received distribution of (1) share Basic Services Inc. Restricted Common $0.001 par payable 04/30/2007 to holders of record 04/24/2007
Name changed to Hydrogen Hybrid Technologies, Inc. 06/26/2007

EATON LEVERAGE FD LTD (CANADA)
Name changed to Eaton/Bay Leverage Fund Ltd. and Common 25¢ par reclassified as Mutual Fund Shares no par 04/12/1978

EATON MANUFACTURING CO. (OH)
Common no par changed to $4 par 00/00/1936
Each share Common $4 par exchanged for (2) shares Common $2 par 00/00/1948
Common $2 par changed to $1 par and (1) additional share issued 10/12/1959
Name changed to Eaton Yale & Towne Inc. 12/31/1965
Eaton Yale & Towne Inc. name changed to Eaton Corp. (OH) 04/21/1971 which reincorporated in Ireland as Eaton Corp. PLC 11/30/2012

EATON MNG & EXPL LTD (BC)
Recapitalized as Synco Development Corp. 07/27/1982
Each share Common no par exchanged for (0.25) share Common no par
(See Synco Development Corp.)

EATON PAPER CO.
Succeeded by Eaton Paper Corp. (MA) 00/00/1933
Details not available

EATON PAPER CORP. (MA)
Acquired through purchase offer by Gorham Corp. 05/15/1959

EATON SCIENTIFIC SYS INC (NV)
Recapitalized as Eco Science Solutions, Inc. 02/25/2014
Each share Common $0.0001 par exchanged for (0.001) share Common $0.0001 par

EATON TR CO (CALGARY, AB)
Merged into Laurentian Bank of Canada (Montreal, QC) 02/04/1988
Each share 10.75% Preferred Ser. A $10 par exchanged for (1) share Class A Preferred Ser. 3 no par
Each share Common no par exchanged for (0.182) share Common no par

EATON VANCE CALIF MUN INCOME TR (MA)
Auction Preferred Ser. A 1¢ par called for redemption at $25,000 on 03/26/2018
(Additional Information in Active)

EATON VANCE CALIF MUN BD FD II (MA)
Auction Preferred Ser. A 1¢ par called for redemption at $25,000 on 03/26/2018
(Additional Information in Active)

EATON VANCE CASH MGMT FD (MA)
Fund terminated 10/02/1996
Details not available

EATON VANCE CR OPPORTUNITIES FD (MA)
Auction Preferred Ser. A 1¢ par called for redemption at $25,000 on 03/12/2010
Merged into Eaton Vance Limited Duration Income Fund 03/12/2010
Each share Common 1¢ par exchanged for (0.651424) share Common 1¢ par

EATON VANCE EQUITY-INCOME TR (MA)
Trust terminated 10/02/1996
Details not available

EATON VANCE FLA PLUS MUN INCOME TR (MA)
Name changed 01/01/2008
Name changed from Eaton Vance Florida Municipal Income Trust to Eaton Vance Florida Plus Municipal Income Trust 01/01/2008
Name changed to Eaton Vance National Municipal Income Trust 06/19/2008
Eaton Vance National Municipal Income Trust merged into Eaton Vance Municipal Income Trust 05/28/2009

EATON VANCE FLOATING RATE INCOME TR (MA)
Auction Preferred Shares Ser. E 1¢ par called for redemption at $25,000 on 12/31/2012
Auction Preferred Shares Ser. A 1¢ par called for redemption at $25,000 on 01/02/2013
Auction Preferred Shares Ser. D 1¢ par called for redemption at $25,000 on 01/02/2013
Auction Preferred Shares Ser. D 1¢ par called for redemption at $25,000 on 01/03/2013
Auction Preferred Shares Ser. C 1¢ par called for redemption at $25,000 on 01/04/2013
(Additional Information in Active)

EATON VANCE GROWTH FD INC (MA)
Name changed to Eaton Vance Growth Trust 08/18/1992

EATON VANCE HIGH YIELD FD (MA)
Merged into Eaton Vance Municipals Trust II 07/24/1989
Details not available

EATON VANCE HIGH YIELD MUNS TR (MA)
Name changed to Eaton Vance National Municipals Fund 02/01/1991

EATON VANCE INCOME FD BOSTON INC (MD)
Name changed to Eaton Vance Series Trust II 10/3/2003

EATON VANCE INSD FLA PLUS MUN BD FD (MA)
Name changed 04/18/2008
Name changed from Eaton Vance Insured Florida Municipal Bond Fund to Eaton Vance Insured Florida Plus Municipal Bond Fund 04/18/2008
Auction Preferred Shares called for redemption at $25,000 on 12/15/2008
Merged into Eaton Vance Insured Municipal Bond Fund 12/16/2008
Each share Common 1¢ par exchanged for (1.067011) shares Common 1¢ par

EATON VANCE INSD CALIF MUN BD FD (MA)
Auction Preferred Ser. B called for redemption at $25,000 on 08/22/2008
Auction Preferred Ser. A called for redemption at $25,000 on 08/27/2008
Name changed to Eaton Vance California Municipal Bond Fund 01/29/2010
(Additional Information in Active)

EATON VANCE INSD CALIF MUN BD FD II
Name changed to Eaton Vance California Municipal Bond Fund II 01/29/2010

EATON VANCE INSD MUN BD FD (MA)
Auction Preferred Ser. D called for redemption at $25,000 on 08/22/2008
Auction Preferred Ser. E called for redemption at $25,000 on 08/25/2008
Auction Preferred Ser. A called for redemption at $25,000 on 08/26/2008
Auction Preferred Ser. B called for redemption at $25,000 on 08/27/2008
Auction Preferred Ser. C called for redemption at $25,000 on 08/28/2008
Name changed to Eaton Vance Municipal Bond Fund 01/29/2010
(Additional Information in Active)

EATON VANCE INSD NEW YORK MUN BD FD (MA)
Auction Preferred Ser. A called for redemption at $25,000 on 08/26/2008
Auction Preferred Ser. B called for redemption at $25,000 on 08/28/2008
Name changed to Eaton Vance New York Municipal Bond Fund 01/29/2010
(Additional Information in Active)

EATON VANCE INVS TR (MA)
Name changed 09/29/1993
Name changed from Eaton Vance Investors Fund, Inc. to Eaton Vance Investors Trust 09/29/1993
Reorganized as Eaton Vance Special Investment Trust 07/31/1995
Details not available

EATON VANCE MASS MUN BD FD (MA)
Name changed 01/29/2010
Name changed from Eaton Vance Insured Massachusetts Municipal Bond Fund to Eaton Vance Massachusetts Municipal Bond Fund 01/29/2010
Auction Preferred Ser. A 1¢ par called for redemption at $25,000 on 03/26/2018
(Additional Information in Active)

EATON VANCE MASS MUN INCOME TR (MA)
Auction Preferred Ser. A 1¢ par called for redemption at $25,000 on 03/26/2018
(Additional Information in Active)

EATON VANCE MICH MUN BD FD (MA)
Name changed 01/29/2010
Name changed from Eaton Vance Insured Michigan Municipal Bond Fund to Eaton Vance Michigan Municipal Bond Fund 01/29/2010
Auction Preferred Ser. A 1¢ par called for redemption at $25,000 on 03/26/2018
(Additional Information in Active)

EATON VANCE MICH MUN INCOME TR (MA)
Auction Preferred Ser. A 1¢ par called for redemption at $25,000 on 03/26/2018
(Additional Information in Active)

EATON VANCE MUN INCOME TERM TR (MA)
Name changed to Eaton Vance Municipal Income 2028 Term Trust 01/12/2015

EATON VANCE MUN INCOME TRUST (MA)
Auction Rate Preferred Ser. A 1¢ par called for redemption at $25,000 on 03/26/2018
Auction Rate Preferred Ser. B 1¢ par called for redemption at $25,000 on 03/26/2018
Auction Rate Preferred Ser. C 1¢ par called for redemption at $25,000 on 03/26/2018
(Additional Information in Active)

EATON VANCE MUN BD FD II (MA)
Name changed 01/29/2010
Name changed from Eaton Vance Insured Municipal Bond Fund II to Eaton Vance Municipal Bond Fund II 01/29/2010
Auction Preferred Ser. A 1¢ par called for redemption at $25,000 on 03/26/2018
Auction Preferred Ser. B 1¢ par called for redemption at $25,000 on 03/26/2018
(Additional Information in Active)

EATON VANCE N J MUN BD FD (MA)
Name changed 01/29/2010
Name changed from Eaton Vance Insured New Jersey Municipal Bond Fund to Eaton Vance New Jersey Municipal Bond Fund 01/29/2010
Auction Preferred Ser. A 1¢ par called for redemption at $25,000 on 03/26/2018
(Additional Information in Active)

EATON VANCE NATL MUN INCOME TR (MA)
Merged into Eaton Vance Municipal Income Trust 05/28/2009
Each share Auction Rate Preferred 1¢ par exchanged for (1) share Auction Rate Preferred Ser. C 1¢ par
Each Share of Bene. Int. 1¢ par exchanged for (1.180047) Shares of Bene. Int. 1¢ par

EATON VANCE NEW JERSEY MUN INCOME TR (MA)
Auction Preferred Ser. A 1¢ par called for redemption at $25,000 on 03/26/2018
(Additional Information in Active)

EATON VANCE NEW YORK MUN INCOME TR (MA)
Auction Preferred Ser. A 1¢ par called for redemption at $25,000 on 03/26/2018
(Additional Information in Active)

EATON VANCE N Y MUN BD FD II (MA)
Name changed 01/29/2010
Name changed from Eaton Vance Insured New York Municipal Bond Fund II to Eaton Vance New York Municipal Bond Fund II 01/29/2010
Auction Preferred Ser. A 1¢ par called for redemption at $25,000 on 03/26/2018
(Additional Information in Active)

EATON VANCE OHIO MUN BD FD (MA)
Name changed 01/29/2010
Name changed from Eaton Vance Insured Ohio Municipal Bond Fund to Eaton Vance Ohio Municipal Bond Fund 01/29/2010
Auction Preferred Ser. A 1¢ par called for redemption at $25,000 on 03/26/2018
(Additional Information in Active)

EATON VANCE OHIO MUN INCOME TR (MA)
Auction Preferred Ser. A 1¢ par called for redemption at $25,000 on 03/26/2018
(Additional Information in Active)

EATON VANCE PA MUN BD FD (MA)
Name changed 01/29/2010
Name changed from Eaton Vance Insured Pennsylvania Municipal Bond Fund to Eaton Vance Pennsylvania Municipal Bond Fund 01/29/2010
Auction Preferred Ser. A 1¢ par called for redemption at $25,000 on 03/26/2018
(Additional Information in Active)

EATON VANCE PA MUN INCOME TR (MA)
Auction Preferred Ser. A 1¢ par called for redemption at $25,000 on 03/26/2018
(Additional Information in Active)

EATON VANCE SECS TR (MA)
Name changed 07/31/1994
Name changed from Eaton Vance Stock Fund to Eaton Vance Securities Trust 07/31/1994
Reorganized as Eaton Vance Special Investment Trust 07/31/1995
Details not available

EATON VANCE SPL INVT TR (MA)
Name changed 07/21/1992
Capital Stock $1 par split (3) for (1) by issuance of (2) additional shares 10/25/1991
Name changed from Eaton Vance Special Equities Fund, Inc. to Eaton Vance Special Investment Trust 07/21/1992
Trust terminated 07/24/2009
Each share Capital & Income Strategies Fund Class A no par exchanged for $7.3865 cash
Each share Capital & Income Strategies Fund Class C no par exchanged for $7.3751 cash
Each share Capital & Income Strategies Fund Class I no par exchanged for $7.3832 cash

EATON VANCE TAX-ADVANTAGED DIVID INCOME FD (MA)
Auction Rate Preferred Ser. D 1¢ par called for redemption at $25,000 on 03/31/2008
Auction Rate Preferred Ser. A 1¢ par called for redemption at $25,000 on 04/01/2008
Auction Rate Preferred Ser. B 1¢ par called for redemption at $25,000 on 04/02/2008
Auction Rate Preferred Ser. G 1¢ par called for redemption at $25,000 on 04/03/2008
Auction Rate Preferred Ser. C 1¢ par called for redemption at $25,000 on 04/04/2008
Auction Rate Preferred Ser. F 1¢ par called for redemption at $25,000 on 04/07/2008
Auction Rate Preferred Ser. E 1¢ par called for redemption at $25,000 on 04/23/2008
(Additional Information in Active)

EATON VANCE TAX-ADVANTAGED GLOBAL DIVID INCOME FD (MA)
Auction Rate Preferred Ser. F 1¢ par called for redemption at $25,000 on 04/01/2008
Auction Rate Preferred Ser. G 1¢ par called for redemption at $25,000 on 04/01/2008
Auction Rate Preferred Ser. A 1¢ par called for redemption at $25,000 on 04/03/2008
Auction Rate Preferred Ser. B 1¢ par called for redemption at $25,000 on 04/04/2008
Auction Rate Preferred Ser. C 1¢ par called for redemption at $25,000 on 04/07/2008
Auction Rate Preferred Ser. D 1¢ par called for redemption at $25,000 on 04/09/2008
Auction Rate Preferred Ser. E 1¢ par called for redemption at $25,000 on 04/14/2008
(Additional Information in Active)

EATON VANCE TAX-ADVANTAGED GLOBAL DIVID OPPORTUNITIES FD (MA)
Auction Rate Preferred Ser. A 1¢ par called for redemption at $25,000 on 04/01/2008
Auction Rate Preferred Ser. B 1¢ par called for redemption at $25,000 on 04/02/2008
Auction Rate Preferred Ser. C 1¢ par called for redemption at $25,000 on 04/23/2008
(Additional Information in Active)

EATON VANCE TOTAL-RETURN TR (MA)
Name changed 08/22/1986
Name changed from Eaton Vance Tax-Managed Trust to Eaton Vance Total-Return Trust 08/22/1986
Shares of Bene. Int. no par split (2) for (1) by issuance of (1) additional share 08/22/1986
Reorganized as Eaton Vance Special Investment Trust 07/31/1995
Details not available

EATON VENTURE FD LTD (CANADA)
Name changed to Eaton/Bay Venture Fund Ltd. 04/12/1978
(See Eaton/Bay Venture Fund Ltd.)

EATON VIKING FD LTD (CANADA)
Name changed to Eaton/Bay Viking Fund Ltd. 11/30/1977
Eaton/Bay Viking Fund Ltd. name changed back to Eaton Viking Fund Ltd. 04/16/1986 which name changed to Viking Canadian Fund Ltd. 04/16/1987 which name changed to Laurentian Canadian Equity Fund Ltd. 05/31/1993 which name changed to Strategic Value Canadian Equity Fund Ltd. 06/05/1997 which name changed to StrategicNova Canadian Large Cap Value Fund Ltd. 09/26/2000
(See StrategicNova Canadian Large Cap Value Fund Ltd.)

EATON YALE & TOWNE INC (OH)
Common $1 par changed to 50¢ par and (1) additional share issued 08/04/1966
Name changed to Eaton Corp. (OH) 04/21/1971
Eaton Corp. (OH) reincorporated in Ireland as Eaton Corp. PLC 11/30/2012

EATONTOWN NATL BK (EATONTOWN, NJ)
Liquidation completed
Each share Capital Stock $10 par received initial distribution of $6 cash 07/00/1979
Each share Capital Stock $10 par received second and final distribution of $6.378 cash 11/00/1981

EATWARE CORP (NV)
Name changed to Star Metro Corp. 11/27/2006
Star Metro Corp. name changed to BioPack Environmental Solutions Inc. 02/27/2007 which recapitalized as Tristar Wellness Solutions Inc. 01/18/2013

EAU CLAIRE HOTEL CO. (WI)
Each VTC for Common $10 par exchanged for (1) share Common $10 par 00/00/1956
Dissolved 07/15/1968
Details not available

EAUTOCLAIMS INC (NV)
Name changed 07/29/2004
Name changed from eAutoclaims.com, Inc. to eAutoclaims, Inc. 07/29/2004
Company terminated common stock registration and is no longer public as of 01/23/2009

EAV VENTURES CORP (BC)
Name changed to VendTek Systems Inc. 10/05/1999
(See VendTek Systems Inc.)

EAZOR EXPRESS INC (PA)
Stock Dividend - 100% 12/31/1964
Declared bankrupt 00/00/1992
No stockholders' equity

EB INC (MS)
Merged into Parkway Co. (TX) 04/27/1995
Each share Common $2 par exchanged for (0.623) share Common $1 par and $8 cash
Parkway Co. (TX) reincorporated in Maryland as Parkway Properties, Inc. 08/02/1996 which merged into Cousins Properties Inc. 10/06/2016

EB&B LIQUIDATING CORP. (DE)
Completely liquidated 05/29/1973
Each share Common 10¢ par exchanged for first and final distribution of $5.10 cash

EBAK STORES, INC.
Acquired by Dejay Stores, Inc. 00/00/1932
Details not available

EBALOY, INC.
Reorganized 00/00/1951
No stockholders' equity

EBALOY FOUNDRIES, INC.
Name changed to Ebaloy, Inc. 00/00/1945
(See Ebaloy, Inc.)

EBANK FINL SVCS INC (GA)
Name changed 01/01/2003
Name changed from ebank.com, Inc. to ebank Financial Services, Inc. 01/01/2003
Company's sole asset placed in receivership 08/21/2009
Stockholders' equity unlikely

EBASCO INDS INC (NY)
Merged into Boise Cascade Corp. 08/31/1969
Each share Common $5 par exchanged for (1.25) shares Common $2.50 par
Boise Cascade Corp. name changed to OfficeMax Inc. 11/01/2004

EBASEONE CORP (DE)
Charter cancelled and declared inoperative and void for non-payment of taxes 03/01/2002

EBAY GMARKET CO LTD (KOREA)
ADR agreement terminated 12/16/2009
Each Sponsored ADR for Common exchanged for $21.24 cash

EBENEFITSDIRECT INC (DE)
Common 1¢ par split (2) for (1) by issuance of (1) additional share payable 06/28/2007 to holders of record 06/18/2007 Ex date - 06/29/2007
Recapitalized as Seraph Security, Inc. 12/02/2008
Each share Common 1¢ par exchanged for (0.00066666) share Common 1¢ par
Seraph Security, Inc. name changed to Commerce Online, Inc. 06/18/2009 which name changed to Cannabis Medical Solutions, Inc. 03/04/2010 which name changed to MediSwipe Inc. 07/08/2011 which name changed to Agritek Holdings, Inc. 05/20/2014

EBENX INC (MN)
Merged into SHPS, Inc. 02/06/2003
Each share Common 1¢ par exchanged for $4.85 cash

EBERHARD FOODS, INC. (MI)
Charter declared inoperative and void for failure to file reports 02/02/1993

EBERLINE INSTR CORP (NM)
Common $2 par changed to $0.66666666 par and (2) additional shares issued 12/07/1967
Acquired by Thermo Electron Corp. 04/11/1979

Each share Common $0.66666666 par exchanged for (0.4) share Common $1 par
Thermo Electron Corp. name changed to Thermo Fisher Scientific, Inc. 11/09/2006

EBERSTADT ENERGY RES FD INC (MD)
Name changed to Putnam Energy Resources Trust 03/21/1985

EBERSTADT FD INC (MD)
Under plan of merger name changed to Surveyor Fund, Inc. (MD) 09/10/1973
Surveyor Fund, Inc. (MD) name changed to Alliance Global Small Capital Fund, Inc. 09/17/1990 which name changed to AllianceBernstein Global Small Capital Fund, Inc. 03/31/2003
(See AllianceBernstein Global Small Capital Fund, Inc.)

EBH CAP TR I (DE)
9.4% Preferred Securities called for redemption at $18 on 12/15/2004

EBI CAP TR I (DE)
8.5% Trust Preferred Securities called for redemption at $25 on 9/30/2003

EBI CASH MGMT INC (GA)
Voluntarily dissolved 12/27/1989
Details not avialable

EBI EQUITY INC (GA)
Voluntarily dissolved 12/27/1989
Details not available

EBI INCOME INC (GA)
Voluntarily dissolved 12/27/1989
Details not available

EBINGER (D.A.) SANITARY MANUFACTURING CO.
Liquidated 00/00/1935
Details not available

EBINGER BAKING CO (NY)
Adjudicated bankrupt 08/31/1972
Stockholders' equity unlikely

EBISDOT COM INC (AB)
Recapitalized as WorkGroup Designs Ltd. 01/03/2002
Each share Common no par exchanged for (0.33333333) share Common no par

EBIX COM INC (DE)
Each share old Common 10¢ par exchanged for (0.125) share new Common 10¢ par 10/01/2002
Name changed to Ebix, Inc. 12/30/2003

EBIZ ENTERPRISES INC (NV)
Plan of reoganization under Chapter 11 Federal Bankruptcy proceedings effective 05/21/2002
Each share Common $0.001 par received approximately (0.09090909) Common Stock Purchase Warrant expring 07/20/2002
Note: Certificates were not required to be surrendered and are without value

EBIZ HK COM LTD (BERMUDA)
Name changed to Hai Xia Holdings Ltd. 11/07/2001
Hai Xia Holdings Ltd. name changed to China Gas Holdings Ltd. 08/02/2002
(See China Gas Holdings Ltd.)

EBIZWARE INC (DE)
Name changed to Visber57 Corp. 04/11/2017

EBONLINEINC COM (NV)
Name changed to MoneyZone.com (NV) 12/16/1999
MoneyZone.com (NV) reincorporated in Delaware as MoneyZone.com, Inc. 06/12/2001 which name changed to QT 5, Inc. 01/08/2003 which recapitalized as Addison-Davis Diagnostics, Inc. 11/18/2004
(See Addison-Davis Diagnostics, Inc.)

EBONY & GOLD VENTURES INC (NV)
Name changed to booktech.com inc. and Common $0.001 par changed to $0.00042 par 04/05/2000
(See booktech.com inc.)

EBONY GOLD & GAS INC (BC)
Recapitalized as Running Foxes Petroleum Corp. 12/09/1998
Each share Common no par exchanged for (0.33333333) share Common no par
Running Foxes Petroleum Corp. recapitalized as Running Fox Resource Corp. 10/17/2000

EBONY GOLD CORP (BC)
Recapitalized as Otis J. Explorations Corp. 06/24/1993
Each share Common no par exchanged for (0.2) share Common no par
Otis J. Explorations Corp. name changed to Sedex Mining Corp. 02/29/1996

EBONY OIL CO (UT)
Recapitalized as Amini Oil Co. 10/25/1971
Each share Common 5¢ par exchanged for (0.1) share Common 5¢ par
(See Amini Oil Co.)

EBOOKERS PLC (ENGLAND & WALES)
Name changed 12/10/2001
Name changed from ebookers.com PLC to ebookers PLC 12/10/2001
ADR agreement terminated 03/30/2005
Each Sponsored ADR for Ordinary exchanged for $12.1772 cash

EBOR URANIUM MINES LTD. (ON)
Charter cancelled and company declared dissolved for default in filing returns 07/08/1965

EBRO PULEVA SA (SPAIN)
Stock Dividend - 2.4451% payable 05/12/2009 to holders of record 04/30/2009 Ex date - 05/05/2009
Name changed to Ebro Foods S.A. 11/18/2010

EBT INTL INC (DE)
Liquidation completed
Each share old Common 1¢ par received initial distribution of $3 cash 12/13/2001
Each share old Common 1¢ par received second distribution of $0.30 cash payable 10/30/2002 to holders of record 10/24/2002
Each share old Common 1¢ par exchanged for (0.02) share new Common 1¢ par 06/10/2003
Note: Holders of (49) or fewer pre-split shares received $0.11 cash per share
Each share new Common 1¢ par received third and final distribution of $8.25 cash payable 05/31/2006 to holders of record 05/20/2006 Ex date - 06/01/2006

EB2B COMM INC (NJ)
Each share old Common $0.0001 par exchanged for (0.06666666) share new Common $0.0001 par 01/10/2002
Under Chapter 11 plan of reorganization each share new Common $0.0001 par automatically became (0.017545) share Mediavest, Inc. (NJ) Common $0.0001 par payable 06/13/2005 to holders of record 01/26/2005
Mediavest, Inc. (NJ) reincorporated in Delaware as Mandalay Media, Inc. 11/21/2007 which name changed to NeuMedia, Inc. 06/21/2010 which name changed to Mandalay Digital Group, Inc. 02/28/2012 which name changed to Digital Turbine, Inc. 01/20/2015

EBULLY INC (AB)
Completely liquidated 05/14/2004
Each share Common no par received first and final distribution of $0.151 cash

EBUX INC (FL)
Name changed to Petapeer Holdings Inc. 05/05/2001
Petapeer Holdings Inc. name changed to Studio Bromont Inc. 02/14/2002 which name changed to United American Corp. 03/01/2004

EBV LIQUIDATING CORP. (MD)
Liquidation completed
Each share Common no par exchanged for initial distribution of $0.02 cash 12/13/1974
Each share Common no par received second and final distribution of $0.031 cash 05/01/1975

EC DEV INC (DE)
SEC revoked common stock registration 05/21/2015

EC PWR INC (DE)
SEC revoked common stock registration 01/07/2011

ECAD INC (DE)
Name changed to Cadence Design Systems Inc. 04/08/1987

ECAREER HLDGS INC (NV)
Each share old Common $0.001 par exchanged for (0.08333333) share new Common $0.001 par 06/25/2013
SEC revoked common stock registration 03/08/2016

ECARFLY INC (TX)
Common no par split (10) for (1) by issuance of (9) additional shares payable 09/21/2006 to holders of record 09/18/2006 Ex date - 09/22/2006
Reincorporated under the laws of Nevada as Market 99 Ltd. 12/06/2007

ECASH INC (DE)
Each share old Common $0.001 par exchanged for (0.0025) share new Common $0.001 par 06/02/2006
Recapitalized as Pacific Green Technologies Inc. 06/13/2012
Each share new Common $0.001 par exchanged for (0.0005) share Common $0.001 par

ECB BANCORP INC (NC)
Merged into Crescent Financial Bancshares, Inc. 04/01/2013
Each share Common $3.50 par exchanged for (3.55) shares Common $1 par
Crescent Financial Bancshares, Inc. name changed to VantageSouth Bancshares, Inc. 07/22/2013 which merged into Yadkin Financial Corp. 07/04/2014 which merged into F.N.B. Corp. 03/11/2017

ECC CORP (TX)
Name changed to Teccor Electronics, Inc. 03/25/1976
(See Teccor Electronics, Inc.)

ECC ENERGY CORP (OK)
Name changed to WestAmerica Corp. 04/18/1994

ECC GROUP PLC (ENGLAND)
Name changed to English China Clays PLC (New) 05/14/1992
(See English China Clays PLC)

ECC INTL CORP (DE)
Common 10¢ par split (5) for (4) by issuance of (0.25) additional share 12/09/1988
Merged into Cubic Corp. 10/14/2003
Each share Common 10¢ par exchanged for $5.25 cash

ECCO CAP CORP (NV)
Each share old Common 2¢ par exchanged for (0.25) share new Common 2¢ par 05/30/1997
Recapitalized as Viper Powersports Inc. 03/11/2005
Each shares new Common 2¢ par exchanged for (0.00666666) share Common $0.001 par
Note: Holders of (149) or fewer shares will receive $5 cash per share
(See Viper Powersports Inc.)

ECCO ENERGY CORP (NV)
Recapitalized as Eagle Ford Oil & Gas, Corp. 07/27/2010
Each share Common $0.001 par exchanged for (0.1) share Common $0.001 par

ECCS INC (NJ)
Recapitalized as Storage Engine, Inc. 07/23/2001
Each share Common 1¢ par exchanged for (0.16666666) share Common 1¢ par
(See Storage Engine, Inc.)

ECHAPMAN INC (MD)
Name changed 01/22/2002
Name changed from eChapman.com, Inc. to eChapman, Inc. 01/22/2002
Charter forfeited for failure to file property return 10/08/2004

ECHELON CORP (DE)
Each share old Common 1¢ par exchanged for (0.1) share new Common 1¢ par 12/08/2015
Acquired by Adesto Technologies Corp. 09/14/2018
Each share new Common 1¢ par exchanged for $8.50 cash

ECHELON INDS INC (AB)
Struck off register 02/01/1999

ECHELON INTL CORP (FL)
Merged into ETA Holding LLC 03/08/2000
Each share Common no par exchanged for $34 cash

ECHELON PETE CORP (BC)
Each share old Common no par exchanged for (0.13333333) share new Common no par 06/02/2014
Each share new Common no par exchanged again for (0.18181818) share new Common no par 03/05/2015
Name changed to Trenchant Capital Corp. 05/10/2016

ECHELON RES LTD (AUSTRALIA)
Name changed to Fusion Resources Ltd. 08/27/2007
Fusion Resources Ltd. acquired by Paladin Energy Ltd. 02/16/2009
(See Paladin Energy Ltd.)

ECHEX WORLDWIDE CORP (NV)
Name changed to BBMF Corp. 04/09/2004

ECHLIN INC (CT)
Name changed 01/11/1982
Common $1 par split (2) for (1) by issuance of (1) additional share 08/07/1961
Common $1 par split (3) for (2) by issuance of (0.5) additional share 05/15/1970
Common $1 par split (2) for (1) by issuance of (1) additional share 04/15/1972
Common $1 par split (2) for (1) by issuance of (1) additional share 11/10/1978
Stock Dividend - 100% 04/02/1962
Name changed from Echlin Manufacturing Co. to Echlin Inc. 01/11/1982
Common $1 par split (2) for (1) by issuance of (1) additional share 08/07/1985
Merged into Dana Corp. 07/09/1998
Each share Common $1 par exchanged for (0.9293) share Common $1 par
(See Dana Corp.)

ECH-ECL   FINANCIAL INFORMATION, INC.

ECHO AUTOMOTIVE INC (NV)
SEC revoked common stock registration 09/19/2016

ECHO BAY FIN CORP (DE)
$1.75 Conv. Preferred Ser. A 1¢ par called for redemption 12/27/1995
Public interest eliminated

ECHO BAY MINES LTD (CANADA)
$3 Preferred no par called for redemption 05/22/1984
Common no par split (6) for (5) by issuance of (0.2) additional share 08/29/1983
Common no par split (2) for (1) by issuance of (1) additional share 07/24/1987
Merged into Kinross Gold Corp. 01/31/2003
Each share Common no par exchanged for (0.1733) share new Common no par

ECHO BAY MINING LTD. (BC)
Name changed to Echo Industries Ltd. 09/05/1972
(See Echo Industries Ltd.)

ECHO DOWNHOLE TECHNOLOGIES INC (AB)
Merged into Alpine Subsurface Electronics Inc. 08/31/1993
Each share Common no par exchanged for (0.33333333) share Common no par
Alpine Subsurface Electronics Inc. name changed to Alpine Oil Services Corp. 03/01/1994 which merged into Weatherford Oil Services, Inc. 08/10/2000 which was exchanged for Weatherford International Inc. (New) (DE) 04/20/2001 which reincorporated in Bermuda 06/26/2002 which reincorporated in Switzerland 02/25/2009 which reincorporated in Ireland as Weatherford International PLC PLC 06/18/2014

ECHO ENERGY CDA INC (ON)
Placed in receivership 10/21/2010
Stockholders' equity unlikely

ECHO HEALTHCARE ACQUISITION CORP (DE)
Name changed to Pet DRx Corp. 01/07/2008
(See Pet DRx Corp.)

ECHO-INDIN MINES, LTD. (ON)
Charter cancelled 09/18/1961

ECHO INDS LTD (BC)
Struck off register and declared dissolved for failure to file returns 06/13/1977

ECHO METRIX INC (DE)
Name changed to ProText Mobility, Inc. 12/31/2010

ECHO MTN RES LTD (BC)
Recapitalized as Acquisicorp Capital Ltd. 06/15/1988
Each share Common no par exchanged for (0.1) share Common no par
(See Acquisicorp Capital Ltd.)

ECHO OIL CORP (WY)
Merged into Maynard Oil Co. 04/20/1979
Each share Common no par exchanged for (0.39885) share Common 10¢ par
(See Maynard Oil Co.)

ECHO RES INC (DE)
Name changed to Fortress Exploration, Inc. (DE) 09/30/2009
Fortress Exploration, Inc. (DE) reincorporated in Nevada 06/04/2010 which name changed to Greenworld Development, Inc. 08/20/2010

ECHO RES INC (NV)
Name changed to Big Daddy's BBQ Racing Co. 01/07/1999
Big Daddy's BBQ Racing Co. name changed to Ehydrogen Solutions, Inc. 12/14/2009

ECHO SATELLITE COMMUNICATIONS INC (NV)
Recapitalized as SatMAX Corp. 05/05/2009
Each share Common $0.0001 par exchanged for (0.05) share Common $0.0001 par
SatMAX Corp. name changed to Green Energy Solution Industries, Inc. 03/02/2012

ECHO SPRINGS WTR CORP (CANADA)
Plan of Arrangement under Companies' Creditors Arrangement Act effective 01/28/2004
No stockholders' equity

ECHO SPRINGS WTR INC (NY)
Each share old Common $0.0001 par exchanged for (0.04) share new Common $0.0001 par 11/22/1996
Chapter 11 bankruptcy proceedings converted to Chapter 7 on 01/29/2002
Stockholders' equity unlikely

ECHO THERAPEUTICS INC (MN)
Reincorporated under the laws of Delaware 06/09/2008

ECHOCATH INC (NJ)
SEC revoked common stock registration 08/23/2010

ECHODRIVE INTERNET CORP (FL)
Name changed to Firstline Environmental Solutions Inc. 10/31/2001
Firstline Environmental Solutions Inc. name changed to Gemco Minerals, Inc. 04/10/2006

ECHOSTAR COMMUNICATIONS CORP NEW (NV)
Stock Dividend - In Sr. Exchangeable Ser. B to holders of Sr. Exchangeable Ser. B 12.125% payable 12/31/1997 to holders of record 12/24/1997
Each share 12.25% Sr. Exchangeable Preferred Ser. B 1¢ par exchanged for $1,001.01041657 principal amount of 12.125% Sr. Exchange Notes due 07/01/2004 on 01/04/1999
Class A Common 1¢ par split (2) for (1) by issuance of (1) additional share payable 07/19/1999 to holders of record 07/01/1999
Class A Common 1¢ par split (2) for (1) by issuance of (1) additional share payable 10/25/1999 to holders of record 10/18/1999
Class A Common 1¢ par split (2) for (1) by issuance of (1) additional share payable 03/22/2000 to holders of record 03/10/2000
Conv. Preferred Ser. C 1¢ par called for redemption at $51.929 on 07/06/2001
Each share Class A Common 1¢ par received distribution of (0.2) share EchoStar Holding Corp. Class A Common $0.001 par payable 01/01/2008 to holders of record 12/27/2007 Ex date - 01/02/2008
Name changed to DISH Network Corp. 01/22/2008

ECHOSTAR COMMUNICATIONS CORP OLD (NV)
Merged into Echostar Communications Corp. (New) 12/22/1995
Each share Class A Common 1¢ par exchanged for (0.75) share Class A Common 1¢ par
Echostar Communications Corp. (New) name changed to DISH Network Corp. 01/22/2008

ECHOSTAR HLDG CORP (NV)
Name changed to EchoStar Corp. 01/25/2008

ECI INDS (CA)
Charter suspended for failure to file reports and pay taxes 05/03/1976

ECI INTL INC (NV)
Name changed 04/18/1994
Name changed from ECI Environmental Inc. to ECI International Inc. 04/18/1994
Name changed to American Phoenix Group Inc. (NV) 12/01/1995
American Phoenix Group Inc. (NV) merged into American Phoenix Group Inc. (DE) 09/26/1996 which name changed to TAL Wireless Networks, Inc. 05/22/1997
(See TAL Wireless Networks, Inc.)

ECI TELECOM LTD (ISRAEL)
Ordinary NIS 0.0024 par changed to NIS 0.12 par and (1) additional share issued 04/16/1991
Ordinary NIS 0.12 par split (2) for (1) by issuance of (1) additional share 04/10/1992
Ordinary NIS 0.12 par split (2) for (1) by issuance of (1) additional share 11/12/1993
Each share Ordinary NIS 0.12 par received distribution of (0.0703) share ECtel Ltd. Ordinary payable 05/10/2004 to holders of record 05/05/2004
Each share Ordinary NIS 0.12 par received distribution of (0.024688) share ECtel Ltd. Ordinary payable 07/11/2006 to holders of record 06/29/2006
Merged into Epsilon 3 Ltd. 09/29/2007
Each share Ordinary NIS 0.12 par exchanged for $10 cash

ECKERD CORP (DE)
Common no par split (2) for (1) by issuance of (1) additional share payable 05/13/1996 to holders of record 04/22/1996 Ex date - 05/14/1996
Merged into Penney (J.C.) Co., Inc. 02/27/1997
Each share Common no par exchanged for (0.6604) share Common 50¢ par

ECKERD DRUGS FLA INC (FL)
Common 10¢ par split (2) for (1) by issuance of (1) additional share 06/22/1965
Common 10¢ par split (2) for (1) by issuance of (1) additional share 07/01/1967
Common 10¢ par split (2) for (1) by issuance of (1) additional share 08/14/1968
Common 10¢ par split (2) for (1) by issuance of (1) additional share 07/10/1969
Name changed to Eckerd (Jack) Corp. 12/01/1969
(See Eckerd (Jack) Corp.)

ECKERD DRUGS INC (NC)
Reincorporated 08/27/1976
Common 10¢ par split (2) for (1) by issuance of (1) additional share 12/07/1971
State of incorporation changed from (DE) to (NC) 08/27/1976
Common 10¢ par split (3) for (2) by issuance of (0.5) additional share 10/15/1976
Stock Dividend - 100% 01/26/1968
Merged into Eckerd (Jack) Corp. 01/08/1977
Each share Common 10¢ par exchanged for (0.6) share Common 10¢ par
(See Eckerd (Jack) Corp.)

ECKERD JACK CORP (FL)
Common 10¢ par split (2) for (1) by issuance of (1) additional share 07/15/1971
Common 10¢ par split (3) for (2) by issuance of (0.5) additional share 08/07/1981

Merged into Eckerd Holdings Inc. 04/30/1986
Each share Common 10¢ par exchanged for $33 cash

ECKERT PACKING CO (OH)
Name changed to Dinner Bell Foods, Inc. 04/30/1971
(See Dinner Bell Foods, Inc.)

ECKLAN CORP (TX)
Each share old Common $0.001 par exchanged for (1.9) shares new Common $0.001 par 01/29/2001
Reincorporated under the laws of Nevada as Mindset Interactive Corp. 03/28/2001
Mindset Interactive Corp. name changed to DeGreko, Inc. 12/07/2005 which name changed to VOIP 5000, Inc. 06/06/2006 which name changed to Target Development Group, Inc. (DE) 04/30/2007 which reincorporated in Wyoming 04/13/2009 which name changed to Hannover House, Inc. 04/03/2012

ECKLER INDS INC (FL)
Name changed to Smart Choice Automotive Group Inc. and Class A Common 1¢ par reclassified as Common 1¢ par 03/24/1997
(See Smart Choice Automotive)

ECKMAR CORP (DE)
Reincorporated 06/19/1967
State of incorporation changed from (IL) to (DE) 06/19/1967
Under plan of merger name changed to Medallion Group, Inc. 11/06/1975
Medallion Group, Inc. merged into Health-Chem Corp. 12/31/1979
(See Health-Chem Corp.)

ECKRICH PETER & SONS INC (IN)
Merged into Beatrice Foods Co. 01/07/1972
Each share Common no par exchanged for (1) share Common no par
Beatrice Foods Co. name changed to Beatrice Companies, Inc. 06/05/1984
(See Beatrice Companies, Inc.)

ECLAIR HLDGS CO (NV)
Name changed to Eldorado Resorts, Inc. 09/19/2014

ECLECTIX INC (NV)
Name changed to Loch Harris, Inc. 09/27/1988
(See Loch Harris, Inc.)

ECLIC INC (NV)
Name changed to AngioGenex, Inc. 03/09/2006

ECLICKMD INC (NV)
Reorganized under Chapter 11 Federal Bankruptcy Code as SecureCARE Technologies, Inc. 12/15/2003
Holders received a distribution of (150) shares Common $0.001 par regardless of number of shares held 06/00/2004
Note: Certificates were not required to be surrendered and are without value
SecureCARE Technologies, Inc. name changed to Scrypt, Inc. 03/11/2014

ECLIPS ENERGY TECHNOLOGIES INC (FL)
Each share old Common $0.0001 par exchanged for (0.00666666) share new Common $0.0001 par 08/25/2009
Reincorporated under the laws of Delaware as EClips Media Technologies, Inc. 05/13/2010
EClips Media Technologies, Inc. name changed to Silver Horn Mining Ltd. (DE) 04/27/2011 which reorganized in Nevada as Great West Resources, Inc. 04/21/2014 which

name changed to Orbital Tracking Corp. 02/20/2015

ECLIPS INC (ON)
Recapitalized as Cadillac Mining Corp. (ON) 07/10/2006
Each share Common no par exchanged for (0.125) share Common no par
Cadillac Mining Corp. (ON) reincorporated in British Columbia 05/22/2007 which merged into Pilot Gold Inc. 08/29/2014 which name changed to Liberty Gold Corp. 05/12/2017

ECLIPS MEDIA TECHNOLOGIES INC (DE)
Name changed to Silver Horn Mining Ltd. (DE) 04/27/2011
Silver Horn Mining Ltd. (DE) reorganized in Nevada as Great West Resources, Inc. 04/21/2014 which name changed to Orbital Tracking Corp. 02/20/2015

ECLIPSE CAP CORP (ON)
Merged into TD Capital Group Ltd. 11/14/2003
Each share Common no par exchanged for $4.7333275 cash
Note: Holders received additional merger consideration in the form of a $0.063 cash dividend paid prior to the merger

ECLIPSE ENERGY INC (UT)
Name changed to Orfa Corp. of America 09/14/1983
Each share Common $0.001 par exchanged for (1) share Common $0.001 par
(See Orfa Corp. of America)

ECLIPSE ENTMT GROUP INC (NV)
Each share old Common $0.001 par exchanged for (0.25) share new Common $0.001 par 05/03/1999
Name changed to Nations RX Inc. 04/28/2003
Nations RX Inc. name changed to Lifespan Inc. 04/06/2006
(See Lifespan Inc.)

ECLIPSE IDENTITY RECOGNITION CORP (NV)
Common $0.001 par split (1,000) for (1) by issuance of (999) additional shares payable 01/17/2013 to holders of record 01/17/2013
Name changed to Nudg Media Inc. 03/14/2014

ECLIPSE IMPORTS INC (DE)
Recapitalized as Neurochemical Research International, Inc. 02/19/1999
Each share Common $0.001 par exchanged for (0.1) share Common $0.001 par
Neurochemical Research International, Inc. name changed to Ultimate Sports Entertainment Inc. 04/12/1999

ECLIPSE MNG CORP (BC)
Struck from the register and declared dissolved for failure to file returns 10/28/1990

ECLIPSE SURGICAL TECHNOLOGIES INC (CA)
Name changed to Cardiogenesis Corp. (CA) 06/21/2001
(See Cardiogenesis Corp. (CA))

ECLIPSE TECHNOLOGY INC (CO)
Name changed to Growth Ventures, Inc. 02/10/1986

ECLIPSYS CORP (DE)
Merged into Allscripts Healthcare Solutions, Inc. 08/24/2010
Each share Common 1¢ par exchanged for (1.2) shares Common 1¢ par

ECO BLDG INTL INC (NV)
Name changed to Deyu Agriculture Corp. 06/02/2010

Deyu Agriculture Corp. name changed to Luca, Inc. 01/08/2016

ECO CORP (ON)
Recapitalized as American Eco Corp. 11/15/1993
Each share Common no par exchanged for (0.1) share Common no par
(See American Eco Corp.)

ECO-DYNAMICS INDS INC (AB)
Struck off register for failure to file annual returns 05/01/1997

ECO ELECTRICAL MFG CORP (FL)
Common 1¢ par split (4) for (1) by issuance of (3) additional shares 10/12/1978
Reincorporated under the laws of Delaware as Windsor Industries, Inc. 09/13/1982
Windsor Industries, Inc. name changed to Windsor Holding Corp. 12/16/1985
(See Windsor Holding Corp.)

ECO-FORM INTL INC (DE)
Name changed to SkinzWraps, Inc. 03/16/2006
SkinzWraps, Inc. recapitalized as Evolution Technology Resources, Inc. 04/24/2014

ECO FRIENDLY PWR TECHNOLOGIES CORP (DE)
Name changed to Digagogo Ventures Corp. 12/01/2010
Digagogo Ventures Corp. recapitalized as 420 Property Management, Inc. 10/19/2015

ECO GLOBAL CORP (NV)
SEC revoked common stock registration 02/19/2013

ECO GREEN TEAM INC (NV)
Name changed to Champion Investments, Inc. 06/28/2012

ECO HYBRID ENERGY INC (DE)
Name changed to Global Energy Resources, Inc. 06/08/2014
(See Global Energy Resources, Inc.)

ECO PETE SOLUTIONS INC (DE)
Name changed to Enzolytics Inc. 03/22/2018

ECO PLANET CORP (DE)
Recapitalized as Zosano, Inc. 10/22/2013
Each share Common $0.0001 par exchanged for (0.005) share Common $0.0001 par
Zosano, Inc. name changed to J.E.M. Capital Inc. 03/15/2017

ECO-RESOURCES INTL INC (NV)
Recapitalized as Magnesium Technologies, Inc. 04/23/1999
Each share Common $0.001 par exchanged for (0.05) share Common $0.001 par
Magnesium Technologies, Inc. recapitalized as Relax Investments Ltd. 09/20/2000

ECO-RX INC (DE)
Each share old Common $0.001 par exchanged for (0.05) share new Common $0.001 par 10/17/2001
Recapitalized as NuEarth Corp. 09/14/2009
Each shares Common $0.001 par exchanged for (0.02272727) share Common $0.001 par

ECO SOIL SYS INC (NE)
Chapter 7 bankruptcy proceeding terminated 12/15/2004
Stockholders' equity unlikely

ECO TECHNOLOGIES INTL INC (ON)
Delisted from Toronto Stock Exchange 07/05/2001

ECO 2 INC (CO)
SEC revoked common stock registration 08/22/2007

ECO VENTURES GROUP INC (NV)
Each share old Common $0.001 par exchanged for (0.025) share new Common $0.001 par 07/12/2012
Recapitalized as Petlife Pharmaceuticals, Inc. (Old) 08/12/2014
Each share new Common $0.001 par exchanged for (0.05) share Common $0.001 par
Petlife Pharmaceuticals, Inc. (Old) reorganized as Petlife Pharmaceuticals, Inc. (New) 09/12/2016

ECOBLU PRODS INC (CO)
Name changed to Eco Building Products, Inc. 07/15/2011

ECOCHILD INC (NV)
Name changed to Aivtech International Group Co. 07/02/2010

ECODYNE CORP (DE)
Merged into Trans Union Corp. 06/28/1977
Each share Common $1 par exchanged for (0.45) share Common $1 par
(See Trans Union Corp.)

ECOEMISSIONS SOLUTIONS INC (DE)
Common $0.001 par split (30) for (1) by issuance of (29) additional shares payable 07/10/2009 to holders of record 07/10/2009
Name changed to NuTech Energy Resources, Inc. 06/26/2015

ECOGATE INC (CA)
Each share old Common no par exchanged for (0.004) share new Common no par 09/27/2007
Reincorporated under the laws of Nevada as CareView Communications, Inc. and Common no par changed to $0.001 par 11/14/2007

ECOGEN INC (DE)
Each share old Common 1¢ par exchanged for (0.2) share new Common 1¢ par 01/30/1996
Each share new Common 1¢ par exchanged again for (0.1) share new Common 1¢ par 07/29/2002
Merged into ECGN Acquisition Inc. 03/30/2004
Each share new Common 1¢ par exchanged for $0.25 cash

ECOLAND INTL INC (NV)
Name changed to Novus Robotics Inc. 04/10/2012

ECOLLEGE COM INC (CO)
Merged into Pearson Education, Inc. 07/31/2007
Each share Common 1¢ par exchanged for $22.45 cash

ECOLOGIC TRANSN INC (NV)
Recapitalized as Peartrack Security Systems, Inc. 10/17/2014
Each share Common $0.001 par exchanged for (0.1) share Common $0.001 par

ECOLOGICAL ASSISTANCE CORP (DE)
Charter forfeited for failure to maintain a registered agent 09/19/1977

ECOLOGICAL MFG CORP (NY)
Voluntarily dissolved 03/23/1978
Details not available

ECOLOGICAL RECYCLING CO (DE)
Charter cancelled and declared inoperative and void for non-payment of taxes 03/01/1974

ECOLOGICAL RECYCLING INC (DE)
Recapitalized as Michigan Gold Mining Investments Inc. (DE) 01/23/2006
Each share Common $0.001 par exchanged for (0.001) share Common $0.001 par
Michigan Gold Mining Investments Inc. (DE) reincorporated in Nevada as Sarissa Resources Inc. 03/23/2007

ECOLOGICAL SCIENCE CORP (FL)
Common 5¢ par changed to 2¢ par and (1.5) additional shares issued 01/24/1969
Reincorporated under the laws of Delaware as Amicor Inc. 05/20/1974
Amicor Inc. recapitalized as Keystone Camera Products Corp. 06/20/1984
(See Keystone Camera Products Corp.)

ECOLOGICAL SVCS INC (DE)
Name changed to Stanford Capital Corp. 01/02/2003
Stanford Capital Corp. recapitalized as Skreem Entertainment Corp. (DE) 03/16/2004 which name changed to SKRM Interactive, Inc. 02/05/2007 which name changed to Sector 10, Inc. 04/14/2008

ECOLOGY COATINGS INC (NV)
Old Common $0.001 par split (1.573255) for (1) by issuance of (0.573255) additional share payable 06/18/2007 to holders of record 06/04/2007 Ex date - 06/19/2007
Each share new Common $0.001 par exchanged for (0.2) share new Common $0.001 par 02/18/2011
Recapitalized as Metu Brands, Inc. 08/13/2015
Each share new Common $0.001 par exchanged for (0.0002) share Common $0.001 par
Metu Brands, Inc. name changed to American BriVision (Holding) Corp. 01/14/2016

ECOLOGY DEV CORP (DE)
Charter cancelled and proclaimed inoperative and void for non-payment of taxes 03/01/1975

ECOLOGY INC (DE)
Charter cancelled and declared inoperative and void for non-payment of taxes 04/15/1973

ECOLOGY INDS INC (NY)
Merged into Environmental Services, Inc. (NY) 03/26/1970
Each share Common 10¢ par exchanged for (1) share Common 10¢ par

ECOLOGY PURE AIR INTL INC (DE)
Charter cancelled and declared inoperative and void for non-payment of taxes 03/01/1999

ECOM COM INC (NV)
Reincorporated 06/10/2000
State of incorporation changed from (CO) to (NV) and Common 1¢ par changed to Common $0.001 par 06/10/2000
Each share old Common $0.001 par exchanged for (0.1) share new Common $0.001 par 05/14/2001
Recapitalized as E.T. Corp. 04/12/2002
Each share new Common $0.001 par exchanged for (0.02) share Common $0.001 par
E.T. Corp. recapitalized as ParaFin Corp. 10/15/2004

ECOM CORP (NV)
Name changed to Columbia Bakeries, Inc. 05/13/2003
Columbia Bakeries, Inc. reorganized as Municipal Payment Systems Inc. (NV) 11/28/2006 which reorganized in Wyoming as Victura Construction Group, Inc. 07/21/2014

ECOM ECOM COM INC (FL)
Each share Common $0.0001 par received distribution of (0.05) share MyZipSoft Inc. Common $0.0001 par payable 06/02/2005 to holders of record 02/23/2004
Each share Common $0.0001 par received distribution of (0.05) share American Capital Holdings, Inc. Common $0.0001 par payable 08/07/2006 to holders of record 01/05/2004 Ex date - 08/08/2006

SEC revoked common stock registration 08/31/2012

ECOM INDUSTRIES, INC. (UT)
Name changed to Suisse International Entertainment Corp. 07/12/1983
(See Suisse International Entertainment Corp.)

ECOM SYS INC (NV)
Each share Common 5¢ par exchanged for (0.5) share Common 10¢ par 10/20/1977
Charter revoked for failure to file reports and pay fees 03/01/1988

ECOMAT INC (DE)
Reincorporated under the laws of Nevada 02/09/2007

ECOMAX ENERGY SVCS LTD (AB)
Each share old Common no par exchanged for (0.5) share new Common no par 10/17/2011
Reincorporated under the laws of British Columbia as Tasca Resources Ltd. 10/19/2011

ECOMED CORP (NV)
Common $0.001 par split (2) for (1) by issuance of (1) additional share payable 11/21/2000 to holders of record 11/21/2000
Name changed to Ranger Wireless Corp. 03/30/2005
Ranger Wireless Corp. name changed to International Ranger Corp. 07/14/2005

ECOMETRY CORP (FL)
Merged into SG Merger Co. 05/31/2002
Each share Common 1¢ par exchanged for $2.70 cash

ECOMM SYS CORP (DE)
Name changed to Dome Ventures Corp. 04/17/2001
Dome Ventures Corp. merged into Metalline Mining Inc. 04/16/2010 which name changed to Silver Bull Resources, Inc. 05/02/2011

ECOMMERCIAL COM INC (NV)
Reincorporated under the laws of Delaware as MindArrow Systems, Inc. 04/03/2000
MindArrow Systems, Inc. merged into Avalon Digital Marketing Systems, Inc. 10/01/2002

ECOMPARK INC (ON)
Name changed to NAME Inc. 09/27/2000
NAME Inc. merged into itemus inc. 06/08/2001
(See itemus inc.)

ECON VENTURES LTD (BC)
Recapitalized as Richcor Resources Ltd. (BC) 09/12/2000
Each share Common no par exchanged for (0.1) share Common no par
Richcor Resources Ltd. (BC) reincorporated in Canada 07/24/2001 which name changed Bioxel Pharma Inc. 08/13/2001
(See Bioxel Pharma Inc.)

ECONETICS INC (DE)
Charter cancelled and declared inoperative and void for non-payment of taxes 03/01/1984

ECONNECT (NV)
Each share old Common $0.001 par received distribution of (0.01) share eGS Inc. Common payable 05/15/2002 to holders of record 04/03/2002
Each share old Common $0.001 par exchanged for (0.01) share new Common $0.001 par 07/24/2002
Stock Dividend - 5% payable 09/20/1999 to holders of record 09/14/1999
Name changed to EyeCashNetworks, Inc. 01/24/2003
(See EyeCashNetworks, Inc.)

ECONO-CAR INTERNATIONAL, INC. (NJ)
Merged into Americar, Inc. 09/30/1966
Each share Class A Common 10¢ par or Class B Common 10¢ par exchanged for (1) share Common 50¢ par
Americar, Inc. merged into Westinghouse Electric Corp. 10/30/1970
(See Westinghouse Electric Corp.)

ECONO THERM ENERGY SYS CORP (MN)
Each share old Common 15¢ par exchanged for (0.33333333) share new Common 15¢ par 10/27/1981
Statutorily dissolved 10/04/1991

ECONO TRAVEL MTR HOTEL CORP (VA)
Merged into Onoce, Inc. 06/13/1983
Each share Common 10¢ par exchanged for $6.57 cash

ECONODRAFT CORP (UT)
Recapitalized as Ultrexx Corp. (UT) 07/01/1996
Each share Common $0.001 par exchanged for (0.2) share Common $0.001 par
Ultrexx Corp. (UT) reorganized in Nevada as IP Matrix Corp. 06/30/2004 which name changed to Airprotek International, Inc. (NV) 03/24/2005 which reorganized in Wyoming as Rafarma Pharmaceuticals, Inc. 11/20/2012

ECONOGREEN ENVIRONMENTAL SYS LTD (BC)
Name changed to Voisey Bay Resources Inc. 6/28/95
Voisey Bay Resources Inc. merged into Twin Gold Corp. 4/4/97 which name changed to Twin Mining Corp. 3/15/2000 which recapitalized as Atlanta Gold Inc. 3/28/2007

ECONOMETRICS INC (DE)
Reorganized 06/20/2008
Common no par changed to $0.001 par 04/16/2007
Reorganized from (CO) to under the laws Delaware 06/20/2008
Each share Common no par exchanged for (0.02) share Common no par
Name changed to JinZangHuang Tibet Pharmaceuticals, Inc. 02/27/2009
(See JinZangHuang Tibet Pharmaceuticals, Inc.)

ECONOMIC ADVISORS INC (NV)
Recapitalized as TS Industries, Inc. 06/27/1985
Each share Common $0.0001 par exchanged for (0.05) share Common 2¢ par
(See TS Industries, Inc.)

ECONOMIC CONSULTING INC (NV)
Each share Common $0.001 par exchanged for (0.05) share Common 2¢ par 04/26/1982
Recapitalized as International Economic Consultants, Inc. 12/18/1989
Each share Common 2¢ par exchanged for (0.125) share Common 2¢ par
International Economic Consultants, Inc. name changed to ECCO Capital Corp. 08/00/1995 which recapitalized as Viper Powersports Inc. 03/11/2005
(See Viper Powersports Inc.)

ECONOMIC INVT TR LTD (CANADA)
5% Preferred Ser. A $50 par called for redemption at $52.50 plus $0.625 accrued dividends on 11/30/2009 (Additional information in Active)

ECONOMICAL-CUNNINGHAM DRUG STORES, INC.
Name changed to Cunningham Drug Stores, Inc. 1936

(See Cunningham Drug Stores, Inc.)

ECONOMICAL DRUG CO.
Merged into Economical-Cunningham Drug Stores, Inc. in 1931
Details not available

ECONOMICS LAB INC (DE)
Each share Common no par exchanged for (2) shares Common $1 par 11/07/1956
4-1/2% Preferred Ser. A $20 par called for redemption 09/06/1965
4% Conv. Preferred Ser. A no par called for redemption 09/20/1965
Common $1 par split (2) for (1) by issuance of (1) additional share 07/15/1986
Stock Dividends - 300% 12/19/1952; 100% 04/15/1964; 50% 07/15/1966; 100% 04/15/1964; 100% 07/15/1968; 100% 01/15/1970
Name changed to Ecolab Inc. 12/01/1986

ECONOMY AUTO STORES, INC. (GA)
Common 25¢ par changed to $1 par 4/30/55
Acquired by McCrory Corp. for cash 12/27/61

ECONOMY BALER CO. (MI)
Stock Dividend - 30% 10/1/56
Merged into American Hoist & Derrick Co. 9/27/67
Each share Common $1 par exchanged for (0.125) share $4.75 Conv. Preferred Ser. A $100 par
American Hoist & Derrick Co. name changed to Amdura Corp. 2/13/89
(See Amdura Corp.)

ECONOMY BOOKBINDING CORP (NJ)
Charter declared void for non-payment of taxes 9/1/88

ECONOMY GROCERY STORES CORP.
Reorganized as Stop & Shop, Inc. in 1946
Each share Common no par exchanged for (2) shares Common $1 par
Stop & Shop, Inc. name changed to Stop & Shop Companies, Inc. 5/26/70
(See Stop & Shop Companies, Inc.)

ECONOMY INNS INC (BC)
Name changed to Mintel International Development Corp. 11/01/1985
Mintel International Development Corp. recapitalized as Golden Trump Resources Ltd. 04/05/1989 which recapitalized as Golden Triumph Resources Ltd. 09/11/2002
(See Golden Triumph Resources Ltd.)

ECONOMY SVGS BK PASA (ALIQUIPPA, PA)
Under plan of reorganization each share Common $1 par automatically became (1) share ESB Bancorp, Inc. Common 1¢ par 07/31/1990
ESB Bancorp, Inc. merged into PennFirst Bancorp, Inc. 03/25/1994 which name changed to ESB Financial Corp. 05/01/1998 which merged into WesBanco, Inc. 02/10/2015

ECONOSHARE INC (NV)
Name changed to Cellceutix Corp. 02/19/2008
Cellceutix Corp. name changed to Innovation Pharmaceuticals Inc. 06/09/2017

ECONTENT INC (DE)
Name changed to Earthworks Entertainment, Inc. and Common 8¢ par changed to $0.0015 par 01/15/2004

ECOPIA BIOSCIENCES INC (CANADA)
Recapitalized as Thallion Pharmaceuticals Inc. (Old) 03/14/2007

Each share Common no par exchanged for (0.1) share Common no par
Thallion Pharmaceuticals Inc. (Old) reorganized as Thallion Pharmaceuticals Inc. (New) 07/27/2009
(See Thallion Pharmaceuticals Inc. (New))

ECOPLUS INC (NV)
Common $0.001 par changed to $0.0001 par 05/11/2010
Each share Common $0.0001 par received distribution of (0.0014) share Conv. Preferred Ser. B $0.001 par payable 06/16/2010 to holders of record 05/28/2010
Each share Common $0.0001 par exchanged for (0.005) share Common $0.0000001 par 06/18/2010
Reincorporated under the laws of Wyoming 08/09/2010

ECOPROGRESS CDA HLDGS INC (BC)
Recapitalized as Consolidated Ecoprogress Technology Inc. 05/06/1998
Each share Common no par exchanged for (0.1) share Common no par

ECORSE-LINCOLN PARK BANK (LINCOLN PARK, MI)
Name changed to Security Bank (Lincoln Park, MI) 7/25/50
Security Bank (Lincoln Park, MI) name changed to Security Bank & Trust Co. (Southgate, MI) 2/4/65
(See Security Bank & Trust Co. (Southgate, MI))

ECORSE SAVINGS BANK (ECORSE, MI)
Stock Dividend - 25% 3/14/41
Name changed to Wayne County Bank 6/5/44
Wayne County Bank (Ecorse, MI) name changed to Ecorse-Lincoln Park Bank (Lincoln Park, MI) 6/13/44 which name changed to Security Bank (Lincoln Park, MI) 7/25/50 which name changed to Security Bank & Trust Co. (Southgate, MI) 2/4/65
(See Security Bank & Trust Co. (Southgate, MI))

ECORSE STATE BANK (ECORSE, MI)
Name changed to Peoples Wayne County Bank (Ecorse, MI) 03/18/1929
Peoples Wayne County Bank (Ecorse, MI) name changed to Ecorse Savings Bank (Ecorse, MI) 08/02/1934 which name changed to Wayne County Bank (Ecorse, MI) 06/05/1944 which name changed to Ecorse-Lincoln Park Bank (Lincoln Park, MI) 06/13/1944 which name changed to Security Bank (Lincoln Park, MI) 07/25/1950 which name changed to Security Bank & Trust Co. (Southgate, MI) 02/04/1965
(See Security Bank & Trust Co. (Southgate, MI))

ECOS GROUP INC (FL)
Reincorporated 02/22/2000
State of incorporation changed from (CO) to (FL) 02/22/2000
Recapitalized as Third Millennium Telecommunications, Inc. (FL) 10/01/2001
Each share Common $0.001 par exchanged for (0.05) share Common $0.001 par
Third Millennium Telecommunications, Inc. (FL) reincorporated in Delaware as TMTM Merger Co. 09/04/2009 which recapitalized as Green Processing Technologies, Inc. 06/16/2010 which recapitalized as Umbra Applied Technologies Group, Inc. 01/13/2014

ECOS RES LTD (BC)
Struck off register for failure to file annual returns 07/30/1993

ECOSAFE INNOTECH INC (NV)
Charter revoked for failure to file reports and pay fees 08/31/2009

ECOSCIENCE CORP (DE)
Each share old Common 1¢ par exchanged for (0.2) share new Common 1¢ par 9/30/98
Plan of reorganization under Chapter 11 Federal Bankruptcy Code effective 9/30/2001
No stockholders' equity

ECOSOLUTIONS INTL (NV)
Each share old Common $0.001 par exchanged for (0.1) share new Common $0.001 par 08/04/2011
Name changed to Hedgebrook 12/10/2012

ECOSSE ENERGY CORP (CANADA)
Dissolved for non-compliance 06/17/2015

ECOST COM INC (DE)
Issue Information - 3,465,000 shares COM offered at $5.80 per share on 08/27/2004
Merged into PFSweb, Inc. 2/1/2006
Each share Common no par exchanged for (1) share Common $0.001 par

ECOSYSTEM CORP (DE)
Each share old Common $0.001 par exchanged for (0.001) share new Common $0.001 par 12/04/2009
Recapitalized as Adarna Energy Corp. 07/07/2011
Each share new Common $0.001 par exchanged for (0.01) share Common $0.0001 par
(See Adarna Energy Corp.)

ECOTALITY INC (NV)
Each share old Common $0.001 par exchanged for (0.01666666) share new Common $0.001 par 11/24/2009
Plan of reorganization under Chapter 11 Federal Bankruptcy proceedings effective 04/10/2015
No stockholders' equity

ECOTECH ENERGY GROUP INC (NV)
Name changed to Dong Fang Hui Le Inc. 11/09/2017

ECO2 FSTS INC (NV)
Each share old Common $0.001 par exchanged for (0.0000625) share new Common $0.001 par 12/10/2012
Recapitalized as International Display Advertising, Inc. 03/20/2013
Each share new Common $0.001 par exchanged for (0.25) share Common $0.001 par

ECO2 PLASTICS INC (DE)
Plan of reorganization under Chapter 11 Federal Bankruptcy proceedings effective 06/28/2010
No stockholders' equity

ECOTYRE TECHNOLOGIES INC (DE)
Each share old Common $0.001 par exchanged for (1/7) share new Common $0.001 par 06/02/1997
Recapitalized as Midland Baring Financial Group Ltd. 11/25/2005
Each share new Common $0.001 par exchanged for (0.001) share Common $0.001 par
Midland Baring Financial Group Ltd. recapitalized as Level Vision Electronics, Ltd. 01/07/2009

ECOURIERCORPS INC (WA)
Name changed to Azul Studios International Inc. 09/15/2004
Azul Studios International Inc. name changed to Modern City Entertainment, Inc. 04/27/2007
(See Modern City Entertainment, Inc.)

ECP VENTURES INC (NV)
Name changed to 2-Track Global, Inc. and (3) additional shares issued 12/01/2004
2-Track Global, Inc. name changed to Organic Farm Group, Corp. 11/14/2013

ECR ALL ST LTD (DE)
Charter cancelled and declared inoperative and void for non-payment of taxes 3/1/87

ECR MINERALS PLC (UNITED KINGDOM)
Each old Sponsored ADR for Ordinary exchanged for (0.005) new Sponsored ADR for Ordinary 12/19/2016
ADR agreement terminated 10/09/2018
Each new Sponsored ADR for Ordinary exchanged for (200) shares Ordinary
Note: Unexchanged ADR's will be sold and the proceeds, if any, held for claim after 04/09/2019

ECRM INC (MA)
Merged into Addressograph-Multigraph Corp. 11/30/78
Each share Common 1¢ par exchanged for $4.50 cash

ECRYPT TECHNOLOGIES INC (CO)
Common $0.001 par split (4) for (1) by issuance of (3) additional shares payable 11/24/2009 to holders of record 11/12/2009 Ex date - 11/25/2009
Recapitalized as Bravatek Solutions, Inc. 12/04/2015
Each share Common $0.001 par exchanged for (0.1) share Common $0.001 par

ECS INDS INC (DE)
Stock Dividend - 3% payable 4/15/2000 to holders of record 3/31/2000
Recapitalized as Infoserve Global Holdings Corp. 2/6/2002
Each share Common $0.001 par exchanged for (0.002) share Common $0.001 par

ECSOFT GROUP PLC (ENGLAND)
ADR agreement terminated 05/24/2003
Each Sponsored ADR for Ordinary exchanged for $4.7784 cash

ECSTALL MNG CORP (BC)
Acquired by Mantle Resources Inc. 03/28/2007
Each share Common no par exchanged for (0.41) share Common no par
Note: U.S. holders will receive cash from the sale of stock
Mantle Resources Inc. name changed to Canada Zinc Metals Corp. 09/26/2008 which name changed to ZincX Resources Corp. 05/07/2018

ECTEL LTD (ISRAEL)
Merged into cVidya Networks Inc. 01/11/2010
Each share Ordinary NIS 0.04 par exchanged for $1.26 cash

ECU SILVER MNG INC (QC)
Merged into Golden Minerals Co. 09/02/2011
Each share Common no par exchanged for (0.05) share Common 1¢ par and CAD $0.000394 cash
Note: Unexchanged certificates were cancelled and became without value 09/02/2017

ECUADOR GOLD & COPPER CORP (BC)
Each share old Common no par exchanged for (0.1) share new Common no par 3/14/2016
Merged into Lumina Gold Corp. 11/01/2016
Each share new Common no par exchanged for (1.0433) shares Common no par
Note: Unexchanged certificates will be cancelled and become without value 11/01/2022

ECUADOR GOLD CORP (DE)
Each share old Common $0.001 par exchanged for (0.05) share new Common $0.001 par 04/30/1997
Name changed to International Mining & Exploration Corp. 06/03/1998
International Mining & Exploration Corp. recapitalized as SPY Depot International Inc. 03/08/2002 which name changed to Fortune Graphite Inc. (DE) 01/07/2003 which reorganized in British Columbia 05/01/2010

ECUADOREAN COPPERFIELDS INC (BC)
Recapitalized as Bronx Minerals Inc. 06/24/1996
Each share Common no par exchanged for (0.33333333) share Common no par
Bronx Minerals Inc. name changed to Las Vegas From Home.Com Entertainment Inc. 09/07/1999 which name changed to Jackpot Digital Inc. 06/18/2015

ECUADORIAN CORP. LTD. (BAHAMAS)
Stock Dividend - 100% 9/20/51
Name changed to ECL Industries, Ltd. 05/27/1966
ECL Industries, Ltd. reincorporated in Republic of Panama as ECL Industries, Inc. 06/26/1969 which name changed to Norlin Corp. 04/04/1970 which name changed to Service Resources Corp. (Panama) 03/06/1986 which reorganized as Ameriscribe Corp. 07/24/1990 which merged into Pitney-Bowes, Inc. 10/29/1993

ECUADORIAN MINERALS CORP (YT)
Name changed to International Minerals Corp. 01/24/2002
(See International Minerals Corp.)

ECUAGOLD RES LTD (BC)
Name changed to AndeanGold Ltd. 10/14/2008

ECUDOR SOCIETE MINIERE INC (QC)
Name changed to ECU Silver Mining Inc. 08/12/1999
ECU Silver Mining Inc. merged into Golden Minerals Co. 09/02/2011

ECUITY INC (NV)
Charter revoked for failure to file reports and pay fees 03/31/2009

ECYCLING TECHNOLOGIES INC (AB)
Name changed to Trius Investments Inc. (New) 10/18/2007

ED-PHILLS INC (NV)
Recapitalized as Vegas Ventures, Inc. 09/04/1992
Each share Common $0.001 par exchanged for (0.1) share Common $0.001 par
Vegas Ventures, Inc. recapitalized as Telemall Communications, Inc. 06/03/1996 which recapitalized as Stein's Holdings, Inc. 04/22/1999 which name changed to Crown Partners Inc. 01/22/2002 which recapitalized as TaxMasters, Inc. 08/12/2009
(See TaxMasters, Inc.)

ED TECH CORP (DE)
Name changed to Educational Computer Corp. (DE) 06/30/1976
Educational Computer Corp. (DE) name changed to ECC International Corp. 10/30/1987
(See ECC International Corp.)

ED U CARDS MFG CORP (NY)
Completely liquidated 10/26/1967
Each share Common 1¢ par exchanged for for first and final distribution of (0.2) share E.S.R., Inc. (NJ) Common 10¢ par
E.S.R., Inc. (NJ) reincorporated in Delaware as Edu-Cards Corp. 06/30/1972 which merged into Binney & Smith Inc. 03/14/1973
(See Binney & Smith Inc.)

EDAC TECHNOLOGIES CORP (WI)
Stock Dividend - 10% payable 07/01/1998 to holders of record 06/01/1998
Acquired by GB Aero Engine LLC 05/07/2013
Each share Common $0.0025 par exchanged for $17.75 cash

EDAN CORP. (DE)
Name changed to Edan Enterprise, Inc. 03/25/1971
(See Edan Enterprise, Inc.)

EDAN ENTERPRISE INC (DE)
Completely liquidated 05/13/1974
Each share Common 10¢ par exchanged for first and final distribution of $11.90 cash

EDATENOW COM INC (CO)
Name changed to Encounter.Com, Inc. 05/31/1999
Encounter.Com, Inc. name changed to Encounter Technologies Inc. 02/18/2010

EDCOA INC (DE)
Merged out of existence 06/25/1992
Details not available

EDDA RES INC (ON)
Name changed to Razore Rock Resources Inc. (ON) 05/02/2008
Razore Rock Resources Inc. (ON) reincorporated in British Columbia 06/14/2018

EDDE FUND, INC. (NM)
Voluntarily dissolved 12/31/1985
Details not available

EDDE SECURITIES CORP. (NM)
Name changed to Dike (S.H.) & Co., Inc. 06/07/1974
Note: Dike (S.H.) & Co., Inc. is privately held

EDDY MATCH LTD (CANADA)
Acquired by Warrington Products Ltd. 01/08/1976
Each share Common no par exchanged for $30 cash

EDDY PAPER CO. LTD. (CANADA)
Each share Common no par exchanged for (3) new shares Comon no par 05/12/1961
Acquired by Weston (George) Ltd. 12/06/1962
Each share Common no par exchanged for (1.5) shares Class A Common no par and $1.50 cash

EDDY PAPER CORP. (IL)
Merged into Weyerhaeuser Timber Co. 04/30/1957
Each share Capital Stock no par exchanged for (10) shares Capital Stock $25 par
Weyerhaeuser Timber Co. name changed to Weyerhaeuser Co. 09/01/1959

EDEK CORP. (TX)
Each share Common $1 par exchanged for (4) shares Common 25¢ par 00/00/1944
Charter revoked for failure to file reports and pay fees 11/30/1960

EDEK OIL CO.
Liquidation completed 00/00/1944
Details not available

EDELBROCK CORP (DE)
Stock Dividend - 10% payable 06/07/2002 to holders of record 05/28/2002 Ex date - 05/23/2002
Merged into Edelbrock Holdings, Inc. 12/22/2004

Each share Common 1¢ par exchanged for $16.75 cash

EDELMAN FINL GROUP INC (TX)
Acquired by Lee Summer Holdings II, Inc. 09/20/2012
Each share Common 1¢ par exchanged for $8.85 cash

EDEN BIOSCIENCE CORP (WA)
Each share old Common $0.0025 par exchanged for (0.33333333) share new Common $0.0025 par 04/19/2006
Each share new Common $0.0025 par exchanged again for (0.33333333) share new Common $0.0025 par 02/25/2008
Liquidation completed
Each share Common $0.0025 par exchanged for initial distribution of $1 cash 08/07/2009
Each share Common $0.0025 par received second distribution of $0.35 cash payable 03/30/2010 to holders of record 06/29/2009
Each share Common $0.0025 par received third and final distribution of $0.17751887 cash payable 06/28/2012 to holders of record 06/29/2009

EDEN EXPL LTD (AB)
Merged into Cannon Oil & Gas Ltd. 07/23/1999
Each share Common no par exchanged for (0.122642) share Common no par
Cannon Oil & Gas Ltd. acquired by G2 Resources Inc. 01/29/2007 which merged into Regal Energy Ltd. 07/10/2008 which recapitalized as Novus Energy Inc. 08/05/2009
(See Novus Energy Inc.)

EDEN INDS INTL LTD (ON)
Charter cancelled for failure to pay taxes and file returns 03/16/1976

EDEN RES LTD (BC)
Delisted from Vancouver Stock Exchange 04/12/1989

EDEN ROC MINERAL CORP (ON)
Each share old Common no par exchanged for (0.1) share new Common no par 03/10/2000
Delisted from Toronto Stock Exchange 02/19/2003

EDENBRIDGE CORP (ON)
Recapitalized as Integrated Asset Management Corp. 07/13/1999
Each share Common no par exchanged for (0.2) share Common no par

EDENTIFY INC (NV)
SEC revoked common stock registration 12/07/2010

EDENVILLE CREATIONS INC (NV)
Name changed to American Maxifact System, Inc. 08/10/1989
American Maxifact System, Inc. name changed to First American Co. 06/25/1990

EDF LONDON CAP L P
Guaranteed Quarterly Income Preferred Securities Ser. A called for redemption at $25 on 12/20/2002

EDG CAP INC (NY)
Name changed to Isotope Solutions Group, Inc. 11/20/2001
(See Isotope Solutions Group, Inc.)

EDGAR BROTHERS CO. (NJ)
Merged into Minerals & Chemicals Corp. of America 06/23/1954
Each share 3.5% Preferred $100 par exchanged for (7.5) shares Common $1 par
Each share Common $1 par exchanged for (2) shares Common $1 par
Minerals & Chemicals Corp. of America name changed to Minerals & Chemicals-Philipp Corp. 07/21/1960 which merged into Engelhard Minerals & Chemicals Corp. 09/27/1967 which name changed to Phibro Corp. 05/20/1981 which name changed to Phibro-Salomon Inc. 05/20/1982 which name changed to Salomon Inc. 05/07/1986 which merged into Travelers Group Inc. 11/28/1997 which name changed to Citigroup Inc. 10/08/1998

EDGAR FILING NET INC (NV)
Common $0.001 par split (6) for (1) by issuance of (5) additional shares payable 11/15/2004 to holders of record 09/01/2004 Ex date - 11/16/2004
Name changed to EZ2 Companies, Inc. (NV) 11/18/2004
EZ2 Companies, Inc. (NV) reincorporated in Georgia as Coastal Capital Acquisition Corp. 01/31/2008

EDGAR ONLINE INC (DE)
Acquired by Donnelley (R.R.) & Sons Co. 08/14/2012
Each share Common 1¢ par exchanged for $1.092 cash

EDGAR SVCS INC (NV)
Common $0.001 par split (3) for (1) by issuance of (2) additional shares payable 01/11/2005 to holders of record 01/10/2005 Ex date - 01/12/2005
Name changed to Applied Nanoscience, Inc. 09/23/2005

EDGARS CONS STORES LTD (SOUTH AFRICA)
Acquired by Bain Capital LLC 05/03/2007
Each Sponsored ADR for Ordinary exchanged for $6.5312 cash

EDGARTOWN NATL BK (EDGARTOWN, MA)
Under plan of reorganization each share Common 1¢ par automatically became (1) share Island Bancorp, Inc. Common 1¢ par 06/30/2000
(See Island Bancorp, Inc.)

EDGCOMB CORP (DE)
Merged into Metal Acquisition Corp. 08/04/1989
Each share Common $1.50 par exchanged for $8 cash

EDGCOMB STL CO (PA)
Merged into Williams Brothers Co. 10/16/1969
Each share Common $5 par exchanged for (1) share 80¢ Conv. Preferred Ser. A no par
Williams Brothers Co. name changed to Williams Companies (NV) 05/11/1971 which reincorporated in Delaware as Williams Companies, Inc. 06/01/1987
(See Williams Companies, Inc. (DE))

EDGCOMB STL NEW ENGLAND INC (NH)
Each share Common $10 par exchanged for (1) share Class A Common $5 par and (1) share Class B Common $5 par 1/15/58
Each share Class A Common $5 par or Class B Common $5 par exchanged for (1) share Common $5 par 12/11/70
Common $5 par changed to $2.50 par 5/7/76
Common $2.50 par split (3) for (1) by issuance of (2) additional shares 7/19/85
Stock Dividends - Class A Common - 300% 1/15/58
Class A & B Common - Payable in Class Common - 10% 1/22/63; 10% 1/22/65; 10% 1/20/67; 10% 4/29/70
Common - 10% 5/28/71; 10% 5/31/74; 15% 1/31/75; 100% 5/21/76; 20% 3/1/78; 10% 8/24/79; 20% 12/31/84
Merged into Edgecomb Corp. 1/22/86

Each share Common $2.50 par exchanged for $25 cash

EDGE ENERGY INC (AB)
Merged into Ventus Energy Ltd. 08/11/2000
Each share Common no par exchanged for (0.375) share Common no par
Ventus Energy Ltd. name changed to Navigo Energy Inc. 05/24/2002
(See Navigo Energy Inc.)

EDGE LTD (MD)
Completely liquidated 12/27/68
Each share Common 25¢ par exchanged for first and final distribution of (0.043478) share Transcontinental Investing Corp. Common $1 par
Transcontinental Investing Corp. merged into Omega-Alpha, Inc. 3/7/72
(See Omega-Alpha, Inc.)

EDGE PETE CORP (DE)
Issue Information - 2,400,000 shares COM offered at $16.50 per share on 02/25/1997
Plan of reorganization under Chapter 11 Federal Bankruptcy proceedings effective 12/31/2009
No stockholders' equity

EDGE RES INC (AB)
Discharged from receivership 02/01/2017
No stockholders' equity

EDGE RES LTD (BC)
Merged into Gothic Resources Inc. (BC) 07/09/1991
Each share Common no par exchanged for (0.5) share Common no par
Gothic Resources Inc. (BC) reincorporated in Canada 08/01/1991 which reincorporated in Oklahoma as American Natural Energy Corp. (Ctfs. dtd. after 02/12/2002) 02/12/2002
(See American Natural Energy Corp. (Ctfs. dtd. after 02/12/2002))

EDGE TECHNOLOGY GROUP INC (DE)
Name changed to Axtive Corp. 11/4/2002

EDGEFRONT REAL ESTATE INVT TR (ON)
Under plan of merger name changed to Nexus Real Estate Investment Trust 04/05/2017

EDGEFRONT RLTY CORP (ON)
Reorganized as Edgefront Real Estate Investment Trust 01/17/2014
Each share Common no par exchanged for (0.5) Trust Unit
Note: Unexchanged certificates will be cancelled and become without value 01/17/2019
Edgefront Real Estate Investment Trust name changed to Nexus Real Estate Investment Trust 04/05/2017

EDGELINE HLDGS INC (NV)
Name changed to Oncolin Therapeutics, Inc. and Common 8¢ par changed to $0.001 par 03/24/2008
Oncolin Therapeutics, Inc. recapitalized as Bering Exploration, Inc. 10/14/2010 which name changed to Breitling Energy Corp. 01/22/2014

EDGEMARK FINL CORP. (IL)
Merged into Old Kent Financial Corp. 5/2/94
Each share Common $1 par exchanged for (0.3118) share Common $1 par
Old Kent Financial Corp. merged into Fifth Third Bancorp 4/2/2001

EDGEMONT BK & TR CO (EAST ST. LOUIS, IL)
Name changed to MidAmerica Bank & Trust Co. of Edgemont (East St. Louis, IL) 10/1/78
MidAmerica Bank & Trust Co. of Edgemont (East St. Louis, IL) reorganized as MidAmerica Bancsystem, Inc. 8/31/82 which merged into Landmark Bancshares Corp. 11/27/86 which merged into Magna Group, Inc. 12/20/91 which merged into Union Planters Corp. 7/1/98 which merged into Regions Financial Corp. (New) 7/1/2004

EDGEMONT MINING & URANIUM CORP. (DE)
Liquidation completed 3/23/58

EDGEMONT RES CORP (BC)
Struck off register and declared dissolved for failure to file returns 08/21/1992

EDGEN GROUP INC (DE)
Acquired by Sumitomo Corp. 11/20/2013
Each share Class A $0.0001 par exchanged for $12 cash

EDGERLY J W & CO (IA)
Liquidation completed
Each share Common $2 par received initial distribution of $2.50 cash 05/25/1978
Each share Common $2 par exchanged for second distribution of $0.60 cash 01/08/1979
Each share Common $2 par received third and final distribution of $1.1690 cash 06/27/1979

EDGERTON, GERMESHAUSEN & GRIER, INC. (MA)
Stock Dividend - 100% 3/6/62
Name changed to EG&G, Inc. 4/5/66
EG&G, Inc. name changed to PerkinElmer, Inc. 10/25/99

EDGERTON MUSICAL AMPLIFIERS INC (CO)
Ceased operations 05/00/1998
Stockholders' equity unlikely

EDGETECH INTL INC (NV)
Charter revoked for failure to file reports and pay fees 11/02/2009

EDGETECH SVCS INC (NV)
Name changed to Inova Technology, Inc. 05/23/2007
(See Inova Technology, Inc.)

EDGEWATER BEACH APARTMENTS LIQUIDATION TRUST
Liquidation completed 12/29/53

EDGEWATER CORP (PA)
Stock Dividend - 10% 11/14/1977
Merged into Hillman Co. 03/10/1982
Each share Capital Stock no par exchanged for $95 cash

EDGEWATER FOODS INTL INC (NV)
Name changed to Ocean Smart, Inc. 06/22/2009

EDGEWATER MANOR APARTMENTS
Trust terminated 00/00/1950
Details not available

EDGEWATER MINING CO. LTD. (BC)
Capital Stock 50¢ par changed to no par 01/00/1970
Name changed to Canarctic Resources Ltd. 02/06/1970
Canarctic Resources Ltd. recapitalized as Concept Resources Ltd. (BC) 03/20/1972 which reincorporated in Alberta 08/21/1978 which name changed to Skyline Natural Resources Ltd. 10/23/1987 which recapitalized as Stellarton Energy Corp. 09/06/1996
(See Stellarton Energy Corp.)

EDGEWATER NATL BK (ENGLEWOOD CLIFFS, NJ)
Name changed 1/17/72
Capital Stock $5 par changed to $2 par and (1.5) additional shares issued 8/8/69
Name changed from Edgewater National Bank (Edgewater, NJ) to

Edgewater National Bank (Englewood Cliffs, NJ) 1/17/72
Under plan of reorganization each share Capital Stock $2 par automatically became (1) share Edgewater National Corp. Common no par 1/31/85
Edgewater National Corp. acquired by Commercial Bancshares, Inc. (NJ) 11/27/85 which merged into United Jersey Banks 12/1/86 which name changed to UJB Financial Corp. 6/30/89 which name changed to Summit Bancorp 3/1/96 which merged into FleetBoston Financial Corp. 3/1/2001 which merged into Bank of America Corp. 4/1/2004

EDGEWATER NATL CORP (NJ)
Acquired by Commercial Bancshares, Inc. (NJ) 11/27/85
Each share Common no par exchanged for (1.1925) shares Common $5 par
Commercial Bancshares, Inc. (NJ) merged into United Jersey Banks 12/1/86 which name changed to UJB Financial Corp. 6/30/89 which name changed to Summit Bancorp 3/1/96 which merged into FleetBoston Financial Corp. 3/1/2001 which merged into Bank of America Corp. 4/1/2004

EDGEWATER PETE LTD (DE)
Recapitalized as English Furniture Industries, Inc. 6/30/95
Each share Common $0.001 par exchanged for (0.25) share Common $0.001 par
(See English Furniture Industries, Inc.)

EDGEWATER RES LTD (BC)
Name changed to MI Software Corp. 03/30/1987
(See MI Software Corp.)

EDGEWATER STEEL CO. (PA)
Each share Capital Stock $100 par exchanged for (4) shares Capital Stock no par in 1930
Capital Stock no par split (2) for (1) by issuance of (1) additional share 12/29/66
Name changed to Edgewater Corp. 5/1/68
(See Edgewater Corp.)

EDGEWAVE INC (DE)
Reorganized as EWDE Holding, Inc. 08/12/2013
Each share Common 1¢ par exchanged for (1) share Common 1¢ par
Note: EWDE Holding, Inc. is private

EDGINGTON OIL CO (CA)
Name changed to EDG Inc. 08/31/1976
(See EDG Inc.)

EDIE LIONEL D CAP FD INC (DE)
Name changed to Merrill Lynch Capital Fund, Inc. (DE) 06/16/1976
Merrill Lynch Capital Fund, Inc. (DE) reincorporated in Maryland 07/29/1987 which name changed to Merrill Lynch Balanced Capital Fund, Inc. 07/01/2000 which name changed to BlackRock Balanced Capital Fund, Inc. 09/29/2006

EDIE LIONEL D READY ASSETS TR (MA)
Name changed to Merrill Lynch Ready Assets Trust 06/16/1976
Merrill Lynch Ready Assets Trust name changed to Ready Assets Prime Money Fund 05/04/2009

EDIE SPL GROWTH FD INC (DE)
Acquired by Price (T. Rowe) New Horizons Fund, Inc. 06/28/1979
Each share Common $1 par exchanged for (2.305268109) shares Common $1 par

EDIE SPL INSTL FD INC (DE)
Merged into Edie Special Growth Fund, Inc. 10/24/1975
Each share Common $1 par exchanged for (2.527) shares Common $1 par
Edie Special Growth Fund, Inc. acquired by Price (T. Rowe) New Horizons Fund, Inc. 06/28/1979

EDIETS COM INC (DE)
Each share old Common $0.001 par exchanged for (0.2) share new Common $0.001 par 06/01/2011
Merged into As Seen On TV, Inc. 03/11/2013
Each share new Common $0.001 par exchanged for (1.2667) shares Common $0.0001 par

EDIFICE AMER CORP (DE)
Charter cancelled and declared inoperative and void for non-payment of taxes 3/1/90

EDIFICE EXPLS LTD (ON)
Recapitalized as Goldmint Explorations Ltd. 06/14/1996
Each share Common no par exchanged for (0.1) share Common no par
Goldmint Explorations Ltd. name changed to AXcension Capital Corp. (ONT) 11/06/1998 which reorganized in Bermuda as Caspian Oil Tools Ltd. 08/30/1999
(See Caspian Oil Tools Ltd.)

EDIFY CORP (DE)
Merged into Security First Technologies Corp. 11/11/1999
Each share Common $0.001 par exchanged for (0.330969) share Common 1¢ par
Security First Technologies Corp. name changed to S1 Corp. 11/12/1999 which was acquired by ACI Worldwide, Inc. 02/13/2012

EDINA INTL LTD (BC)
Recapitalized as Chisholm Resources Inc. 03/13/1981
Each share Capital Stock no par exchanged for (0.33333333) share Capital Stock no par
(See Chisholm Resources Inc.)

EDINBURGH CAP INC (CO)
Each (300) shares old Common no par exchanged for (1) share new Common no par 5/1/94
Reorganized as Zeitgeist Werks Inc. 2/23/96
Each share new Common no par exchanged for (3.13) shares Common no par
Zeitgeist Werks name changed to Mediax Corp. 8/15/96

EDINER INC (MN)
Statutorily dissolved 12/31/92

EDINOV CORP (BC)
Recapitalized 4/27/93
Recapitalized as from Edinov Technologies Inc./Les Technologies Edinov Inc. to Edinov Corp. 4/27/93
Each share Common no par exchanged for (0.2) share Common no par
Plan of arrangement effective 9/30/93
Each share Common no par exchanged for (1) share Cedar Group, Inc. Common $0.001 par
Cedar Group, Inc. name changed to Dominion Bridge Corp. 8/1/96
(See Dominion Bridge Corp.)

EDISON BROS STORES INC (DE)
Each share Common no par exchanged for (3) shares Common $2 par 00/00/1937
5% Preferred $50 par called for redemption 08/24/1945
Each share Common $2 par exchanged for (2) shares Common $1 par 00/00/1946
Common $1 par split (2) for (1) by issuance of (1) additional share 01/07/1965
Common $1 par split (2) for (1) by issuance of (1) additional share 05/07/1968
Common $1 par split (3) for (1) by issuance of (2) additional shares 02/10/1978
Common $1 par split (2) for (1) by issuance of (1) additional share 01/05/1990
4.25% Preferred $100 par called for redemption at $104 on 04/24/1995
Plan of reorganization under Chapter 11 Federal Bankruptcy Code effective 09/26/1997
Each share old Common $1 par exchanged for (0.04545454) Common Stock Purchase Warrant expiring 09/26/2003 and (0.4504) Common Stock Purchase Right expiring 10/27/1997
Chapter 11 bankruptcy proceedings converted to Chapter 7 on 07/05/2000
Stockholders' equity unlikely

EDISON CAP CORP (CO)
Name changed to Interfashion, Inc. 12/15/88
Interfashion, Inc. recapitalized as Ceramic Technology Inc. 8/31/92
(See Ceramic Technology Inc.)

EDISON CTL CORP (NJ)
Each (66,666) shares old Common 1¢ par exchanged for (1) share new Common 1¢ par 8/5/2003
Note: In effect holders received $7 cash per share and public interest was eliminated

EDISON ELECTRIC ILLUMINATING CO. OF BOSTON
Name changed to Boston Edison Co. 00/00/1937
(See Boston Edison Co.)

EDISON ELECTRIC ILLUMINATING CO. OF BROCKTON
Name changed to Brockton Edison Co. in 1937
(See listing for Brockton Edison Co.)

EDISON (THOMAS A.) INC. (NJ)
Merged into McGraw-Edison Co. 01/02/1957
Each share Class A $3.33-1/3 par exchanged for (1) share Common $1 par
Each share Class B $3.33-1/3 par exchanged for (1) share Common $1 par
(See McGraw-Edison Co.)

EDISON (THOMAS) LIFE INSURANCE CO. (IA)
Merged into North American Life & Casualty Co. 5/29/68
Each share Common $1 par exchanged for (0.4) share Common $1 par
(See North American Life & Casualty Co.)

EDISON PORTLAND CEMENT CO.
Dissolved in 1931

EDISON RENEWABLES INC (NV)
Name changed to NextPhase Wireless, Inc. 01/26/2005
NextPhase Wireless, Inc. name changed to MetroConnect Inc. 02/02/2009
(See MetroConnect Inc.)

EDISON SAULT ELEC CO (MI)
Stock Dividends - 10% 10/15/1949; 10% 01/25/1956; 50% 09/02/1966
Under plan of reorganization each share Common $5 par automatically became (1) share Eselco, Inc. Common 1¢ par 01/11/1989
Eselco, Inc. merged into Wisconsin Energy Corp. 05/31/1998 which name changed to WEC Energy Group, Inc. 06/30/2015

EDISON SCHS INC (DE)
Merged into Liberty Partners, LP 11/14/2003
Each share Class A Common 1¢ par exchanged for $1.76 cash
Each share Class B Common 1¢ par exchanged for $1.76 cash

EDISON-SPLITDORF CORP.
Dissolved in 1948

EDISPATCH COM WIRELESS DATA INC (BC)
Reincorporated under the laws of Canada as AirIQ Inc. 07/31/2002

EDISTO RES CORP (DE)
$2.60 Sr. Conv. Preferred $1 par called for redemption 6/29/93
Reorganized under Chapter 11 Federal Bankruptcy Code 6/29/93
Each share old Common 1¢ par exchanged for (0.05) share new Common 1¢ par and Common Stock Purchase Warrants expiring in 1996
Merged into Forcenergy Inc. 10/22/97
Each share new Common 1¢ par exchanged for (0.14485) share Common 1¢ par and $4.886 cash
Forcenergy Inc. merged into Forest Oil Corp. 12/7/2000

EDITEK INC (DE)
Reincorporated 09/26/1996
State of incorporation changed from (CA) to (DE) 09/26/1996
Name changed to Medtox Scientific, Inc. 05/16/1997
(See Medtox Scientific, Inc.)

EDITWORKS LTD (NV)
Each share old Common $0.001 par exchanged for (10) shares new Common $0.001 par 09/25/2000
Reorganized as TriLucent Technologies Corp. 04/06/2001
Each share new Common $0.001 par exchanged for (2) shares Common $0.001 par
TriLucent Technologies Corp. recapitalized as Anza Innovations, Inc. 12/03/2002 which name changed to Gaofeng Gold Corp. 02/17/2004 which recapitalized as Sun Oil & Gas Corp. 01/03/2005 which recapitalized as China 3C Group 12/20/2005 which recapitalized as Yosen Group, Inc. 12/31/2012

EDLEUN GROUP INC (CANADA)
Name changed to BrightPath Early Learning Inc. 08/07/2013
(See BrightPath Early Learning Inc.)

EDLUND ENGINEERED PRODUCTS, INC. (FL)
Bankrupt 2/13/62
No stockholders' equity

EDMARK CORP (WA)
Each share old Common no par exchanged for (1/3) share new Common no par 12/1/89
New Common no par split (3) for (2) by issuance of (0.5) additional share 8/3/95
Merged into International Business Machines Corp. 12/17/96
Each share new Common no par exchanged for $15.50 cash

EDMOND MEANY HOTEL, INC.
Liquidation completed
Each share Preferred $1 par exchanged for first and final distribution of $1 cash 7/30/66
Each share Common $1 par exchanged for first and final distribution of $1.63 cash 11/15/66

EDMONTON CITY DAIRY LTD. (AB)
Merged into Silverwood Western Dairies Ltd. 00/00/1946
Details not available

EDMONTON CITY DAIRY LTD. (CANADA)
Reorganized under the laws of Alberta 00/00/1940

Preferred exchanged for like principal amount of 5-1/4% General Mortgage Bonds
Each share Common exchanged for (2) shares Common
(See Edmonton City Dairy Ltd. (ALTA))

EDMONTON CONCRETE BLOCK LTD (AB)
Through purchase offer all shares acquired by BACM Industries, Ltd. as of 09/00/1971
Public interest eliminated

EDMONTON INTL INDS LTD (AB)
Delisted from Alberta Stock Exchange 05/23/1989

EDMONTON NORTH OIL CO. LTD. (AB)
Name changed to Regent Uranium Lithium Explorations Ltd. 00/00/1956
(See Regent Uranium Lithium Explorations Ltd.)

EDMONTON-WAINWRIGHT OILS (CANADA)
Charter surrendered in 1957
No stockholders' equity

EDMOR MINES, LTD. (ON)
Charter cancelled in 1957

EDMOS CORP (NY)
Common $1 par split (3) for (2) by issuance of (0.5) additional share 3/22/71
Name changed to Bangor America Inc. 5/19/86
(See Bangor America Inc.)

EDMOS PRODS CORP (NY)
Name changed to Edmos Corp. 04/17/1970
Edmos Corp. name changed to Bangor America Inc. 05/19/1986
(See Bangor America Inc.)

EDMUND LABORATORIES, INC. (CO)
Each share Common no par exchanged for (3) shares Common 10¢ par 05/13/1970
Name changed to Automated Learning Inc. 06/18/1970
Automated Learning Inc. merged into Automated Information Industries, Inc. 01/26/1973 which name changed to Standard Oil & Exploration Delaware, Inc. 11/30/1987
(See Standard Oil & Exploration Delaware, Inc.)

EDMUNDS & JONES CORP.
Merged into Hall (C.M.) Lamp Co. (MI) in 1926
Details not available

EDNET INC (CO)
Reincorporated under the laws of Delaware as Entertainment Digital Network, Inc. 2/22/99
Entertainment Digital Network, Inc. merged into Visual Data Corp. 8/3/2001 which name changed to Onstream Media Corp. 1/1/2005

EDO CORP (NY)
Class A $1 par and Class B $1 par reclassified as Common $1 par 12/02/1960
Common $1 par split (3) for (2) by issuance of (0.5) additional share 04/20/1983
Common $1 par split (3) for (2) by issuance of (0.5) additional share 02/23/1984
Stock Dividends - 50% 10/18/1979; 10% 06/30/1981; 50% 09/30/1982
Merged into ITT Corp. 12/20/2007
Each share Common $1 par exchanged for $56 cash

EDOLLARS INC (NV)
Recapitalized as Forex Inc. 06/18/2007
Each share Common 1¢ par exchanged for (0.05) share Common 1¢ par
Forex Inc. name changed to Petrogulf Inc. 03/26/2008 which name changed to Novagant Corp. 01/02/2014

EDOLLARS INC (NV)
Name changed to Luvoo Int, Inc. 09/06/2006
(See Luvoo Int, Inc.)

EDOMAR RES INC (ON)
Recapitalized as Kazakstan Goldfields Corp. 10/09/1996
Each share Common no par exchanged for (0.38461538) share Common no par
(See Kazakstan Goldfields Corp.)

EDOORWAYS CORP (DE)
Name changed to eDoorways International Corp. (DE) 09/02/2010
eDoorways International Corp. (DE) reincorporated in Nevada 05/06/2013 which recapitalized as Escue Energy, Inc. 06/23/2015

EDOORWAYS INTL CORP (NV)
Reincorporated 05/06/2013
Each share old Common $0.001 par exchanged for (0.001) share new Common $0.0001 par 10/27/2011
State of incorporation changed from (DE) to (NV) and new Common $0.0001 par changed to $0.00001 par 05/06/2013
Recapitalized as Escue Energy, Inc. 06/23/2015
Each share Common $0.00001 par exchanged for (0.0005) share Common $0.00001 par

EDORAN OIL CORP. LTD. (AB)
Recapitalized as Kamalta Exploration Ltd. 7/26/65
Each share Common no par exchanged for (0.2) share Common no par
(See Kamalta Exploration Ltd.)

EDOT-COM COM INC (CO)
Common $0.001 par split (3.2) for (1) by issuance of (2.2) additional shares payable 05/12/2005 to holders of record 05/12/2005 Ex date - 05/13/2005
Reincorporated under the laws of Nevada as NanoViricides, Inc. 07/05/2005

EDP ASSOC INC (NY)
Ceased doing business 11/00/1972
Company has no assets
Stockholders' equity unlikely

EDP CENT INC (OR)
Adjudicated bankrupt 03/26/1970
Stockholders' equity unlikely

EDP DATA CENTRES LTD (BC)
Name changed to EDP Industries Ltd. 12/08/1969
(See EDP Industries Ltd.)

EDP-ELECTRICIDADE DE PORTUGAL S A (PORTUGAL)
Basis changed from (1:2) to (1:10) 07/20/2000
Name changed to EDP-Energias de Portugal, S.A. 10/21/2004

EDP INDS LTD (BC)
Each share old Common no par exchanged for (0.000025) share new Common no par 03/19/1975
Note: In effect holders received approximately $0.056 cash per share and public interest was eliminated

EDP OF CALIFORNIA INC. (MN)
Statutorily dissolved 12/30/1994

EDP RESOURCES, INC. (NY)
Common $1 par split (2) for (1) by issuance of (1) additional share 08/06/1968
Merged into Greyhound Corp. 04/27/1979
Each share Common $1 par exchanged for $8.25 cash

EDP SYS INC (OK)
Charter cancelled for failure to pay taxes 09/12/1988

EDP TECHNOLOGY INC (DE)
Recapitalized as ED-TECH Corp. 10/23/1973
Each share Common 1¢ par exchanged for (0.1) share Common 10¢ par
ED-TECH Corp. name changed to Educational Computer Corp. (DE) 06/30/1976 which name changed to ECC International Corp. 10/30/1987
(See ECC International Corp.)

EDPER ENTERPRISES LTD (ON)
Reincorporated 11/25/1988
Place of incorporation changed from (Canada) to (ON) 11/25/1988
Class A Subordinate no par split (3) for (2) by issuance of (0.5) additional share 06/28/1991
Name changed to HIL Corp. Ltd. 06/08/1995
HIL Corp. Ltd. merged into Hees International Bancorp Inc. 11/30/1995 which name changed to Edper Group Ltd. (New) 01/01/1997 which merged into EdperBrascan Corp. 08/01/1997 which name changed to Brascan Corp. 04/28/2000 which name changed to Brookfield Asset Management, Inc. 11/10/2005

EDPER GROUP LTD NEW (ON)
Under plan of merger name changed to EdperBrascan Corp. 08/01/1997
EdperBrascan Corp. name changed to Brascan Corp. 04/28/2000 which name changed to Brookfield Asset Management, Inc. 11/10/2005

EDPER GROUP LTD OLD (ON)
Merged into Edper Group Ltd. (New) 01/01/1997
Each 7% Installment Receipt exchanged for (1) 7% Installment Receipt
Each share Class A Special no par exchanged for (0.38) share Class A Limited Vtg. no par
Each share Class B Special no par exchanged for (0.38) share Class B Limited Vtg. no par

EDPERBRASCAN CORP (ON)
Class A Preference Ser. 6 called for redemption at $25.375 on 09/12/1997
Name changed to Brascan Corp. 04/28/2000
Brascan Corp. name changed to Brookfield Asset Management, Inc. 11/10/2005

EDS NUCLEAR INC (DE)
Stock Dividend - 25% 09/15/1975
Under plan of reorganization each share Common 2¢ par automatically became (1) share Impell Corp. Common 2¢ par 04/19/1977
(See Impell Corp.)

EDSON GOULD FD INC (MD)
Name changed to Greenway Fund, Inc. 06/28/1982
Greenway Fund, Inc. name changed to Sigma Value Shares, Inc. 06/10/1988 which name changed to ProvidentMutual Value Shares, Inc. 03/01/1990
(See ProvidentMutual Value Shares, Inc.)

EDSON OIL CO. LTD. (ON)
Charter cancelled for non-compliance 11/18/1963

EDT LEARNING INC (DE)
Name changed 08/02/2001
Name changed from e-dentist.com, Inc. to EDT Learning, Inc. 08/02/2001
Name changed to iLinc Communications, Inc. 02/05/2004
(See iLinc Communications, Inc.)

EDU CARDS CORP (DE)
Merged into Binney & Smith Inc. 03/14/1973
Each share Common 10¢ par exchanged for (0.08333333) share Common $2.50 par
(See Binney & Smith Inc.)

EDU-TRONICS, INC. (DE)
Merged into General Electronic Laboratories, Inc. 01/01/1967
Each share Common 10¢ par exchanged for (1) share Common no par
General Electronic Laboratories, Inc. merged into Sippican Corp. 12/31/1968 which name changed to TSC Corp. 11/09/1981
(See TSC Corp.)

EDUCASTING SYS INC (DE)
Charter forfeited for failure to maintain a registered agent 10/22/1979

EDUCATE INC (DE)
Merged into Edge Acquisition, LLC 06/14/2007
Each share Common 1¢ par exchanged for $8 cash

EDUCATION ALTERNATIVES INC (MN)
Under plan of merger name changed to TesseracT Group, Inc. 01/02/1998
(See TesseracT Group, Inc.)

EDUCATION HLDGS 1 INC (DE)
Plan of reorganization under Chapter 11 Federal Bankruptcy proceedings effective 03/13/2013
No stockholders' equity

EDUCATION INDS INC (DE)
Liquidation completed
Each share Common 10¢ par exchanged for initial distribution of $3.82 cash 02/02/1974
Each share Common 10¢ par received second and final distribution of $0.065 cash 12/30/1976

EDUCATION LENDING GROUP INC (DE)
Merged into CIT Group Inc. (New) 02/17/2005
Each share Common no par exchanged for $19.05 cash

EDUCATION MGMT CORP (PA)
Common 1¢ par split (2) for (1) by issuance of (1) additional share payable 12/29/1998 to holders of record 12/08/1998
Common 1¢ par split (2) for (1) by issuance of (1) additional share payable 12/22/2003 to holders of record 12/01/2003 Ex date - 12/23/2003
Merged into EM Acquisition Corp. 06/01/2006
Each share Common 1¢ par exchanged for $43 cash

EDUCATION RLTY TR INC (MD)
Each share old Common 1¢ par exchanged for (0.33333333) share new Common 1¢ par 12/01/2014
Acquired by Greystar Real Estate Partners, LLC 09/20/2018
Each share new Common 1¢ par exchanged for $41.50 cash

EDUCATION SYS & PUBNS CORP (NV)
Each share Common $0.001 par exchanged for (0.02) share Common 1¢ par 04/15/1976
Proclaimed dissolved for failure to file reports and pay fees 03/30/1992

EDUCATIONAL & RECREATIONAL SVCS INC (CA)
Merged into ARA Services, Inc. 09/28/1972
Each share Common no par exchanged for (0.0388) share Common 50¢ par
(See ARA Services, Inc.)

EDUCATIONAL AIDS INC (FL)
Merged into Drago/Newton, Inc. 05/23/1978
Each share Common 10¢ par exchanged for $3.93 cash

EDUCATIONAL APPLICATIONS INC (NY)
Stock Dividend - 100% 03/15/1969
Charter cancelled and proclaimed dissolved for failure to pay taxes and file reports 12/16/1974

EDUCATIONAL CAREER SYS INC (AZ)
Charter revoked for failure to file reports and pay fees 09/05/1974

EDUCATIONAL COMPUTER CORP (DE)
Holdings of (20) shares or fewer exchanged for $1.75 cash per share 06/22/1979
Note: Option to prevent redemption and retain shares by notifying company expired 06/22/1979
Common 10¢ par split (2) for (1) by issuance of (1) additional share 07/21/1983
Name changed to ECC International Corp. 10/30/1987
(See ECC International Corp.)

EDUCATIONAL COMPUTER CORP (PA)
Stock Dividend - 100% 07/29/1968
Merged into EDP Technology, Inc. 05/02/1969
Each share Common 10¢ par exchanged for (1) share Common 1¢ par
EDP Technology, Inc. recapitalized as ED-TECH Corp. 09/07/1973 which name changed to Educational Computer Corp. (DE) 06/30/1976 which name changed to ECC International Corp. 10/30/1987
(See ECC International Corp.)

EDUCATIONAL COMPUTER SYS INC (AZ)
Adjudicated bankrupt 04/28/1972
No stockholders' equity

EDUCATIONAL DATA PROCESSING CORP (NY)
Charter revoked for failure to file reports and pay fees 12/16/1968

EDUCATIONAL DESIGN INC (NY)
Each share Common $1 par exchanged for (0.002) share Common $5 par 07/18/1978
Merged into Caldon Educational Corp. 10/15/1979
Each share Common $5 par exchanged for $75 cash

EDUCATIONAL DEVELOPMENT CORP. (CA)
Completely liquidated 07/22/1968
Each share Capital Stock $1 par exchanged for first and final distribution of (1) share Educational Development Corp. (DE) Common 20¢ par

EDUCATIONAL GAMES INC (NY)
Charter cancelled and proclaimed dissolved for failure to pay taxes and file reports 12/15/1975

EDUCATIONAL HORIZONS INC (DE)
Charter cancelled and declared inoperative and void for non-payment of taxes 03/01/1976

EDUCATIONAL INDL FACS INC (NJ)
Charter declared void for non-payment of taxes 01/05/1976

EDUCATIONAL INSIGHTS INC (CA)
Merged into EI Acquisition Inc. 10/16/2006
Each share Common no par exchanged for approximately $1.90687 cash

EDUCATIONAL MGMT SVCS INC (MN)
Liquidation completed

Each share Common 3¢ par exchanged for initial distribution of $2.50 cash 06/21/1984
Each share Common 3¢ par received second and final distribution of $0.08788 cash 10/15/1984

EDUCATIONAL MED INC (DE)
Name changed to Quest Education Corp. 09/23/1998
(See Quest Education Corp.)

EDUCATIONAL MEDIA PRODUCTIONS INC (NV)
Name changed to American Cattle Co., Inc. 10/16/2006

EDUCATIONAL OPPORTUNITIES INC (DE)
Name changed to EOI Services Inc. 02/20/1973
(See EOI Services Inc.)

EDUCATIONAL PICTURES, INC. (DE)
Incorporated 02/04/1927
Recapitalized 00/00/1937
Each share Preferred $100 par exchanged for (5) shares new Common $1 par
Each (2) shares Common no par received a warrant to subscribe for (1) share new Common $1 par
Declared inoperative and void for non-payment of taxes 04/01/1941

EDUCATIONAL PICTURES, INC. (DE)
Incorporated 01/04/1946
No longer in existence having become inoperative and void for non-payment of taxes 04/01/1949

EDUCATIONAL PICTURES SECURITIES CORP.
Acquired by Educational Pictures, Inc. (Incorporated February 4, 1927) 00/00/1927
Details not available

EDUCATIONAL SCIENCES PROGRAMS INC (DE)
Name changed to Delehanty Educational Systems, Inc. 01/05/1971
(See Delehanty Educational Systems, Inc.)

EDUCATIONAL SECURITIES CORP. (CA)
Charter revoked for failure to file reports and pay fees 02/01/1966

EDUCATIONAL SVC PROGRAMS INC (CT)
Name changed to By-Word Corp. 05/25/1973
By-Word Corp. name changed to B.W. Group, Inc. 09/10/1984
(See B.W. Group, Inc.)

EDUCATIONAL SVCS INTL INC (MI)
Reorganized under the laws of Wyoming as WindPower Innovations, Inc. 11/18/2009
Each share Common 10¢ par exchanged for (0.05) share Common 10¢ par
WindPower Innovations, Inc. name changed to NexGen Holdings Corp. 01/10/2014

EDUCATIONAL SOUND SYS INC (DE)
Merged into Opto Mechanik, Inc. 01/01/1981
Each share Common 20¢ par exchanged for (0.2222) share Common 10¢ par
(See Opto Mechanik, Inc.)

EDUCATIONAL STORYBOOKS INTL INC (NV)
Recapitalized as U.S. Plastic Lumber Corp. 3/19/96
Each share Common $0.0001 par exchanged for (0.0625) share Common $0.0001 par, (0.0625) Common Stock Purchase Warrant Ser. A expiring 6/30/98 and (0.0625) Common Stock Purchase Warrant Ser. B expiring 6/30/98
(See U.S. Plastic Lumber Corp.)

EDUCATIONAL SUPPLY CO. (OH)
4% Prior Preference $100 par called for redemption 03/20/1964

EDUCATIONAL TECHNOLOGY INC (NY)
Name changed to Technology Equipment Corp. 03/14/1984
Technology Equipment Corp. recapitalized as Systems Equipment Corp. 10/10/1986 which merged into Firetector Inc. 08/23/1991 which name changed to Synergx Systems Inc. 05/24/2002
(See Synergx Systems Inc.)

EDUCATIONAL VIDEO CONFERENCING INC (DE)
Issue Information - 1,200,000 shares COM offered at $12 per share on 02/23/1999
Name changed to EVCI Career Colleges Inc. 5/23/2002
EVCI Career Colleges Inc. name changed to EVCI Career Colleges Holding Corp. 8/12/2004

EDUCATIONAL YOUTH DEV INC (DE)
Name changed to American Pet Co. 12/20/72
(See American Pet Co.)

EDUCATOR & EXECUTIVE ASSOCIATED INSURANCE CO. (OH)
Merged into Educator & Executive Insurers, Inc. 12/31/63
Each share Common $5 par exchanged for (0.25) share Common $5 par
Educators & Executive Insurers, Inc. name changed to Penney (J.C.) Casualty Insurance Co. 1/1/76
(See Penney (J.C.) Casualty Insurance Co.)

EDUCATOR & EXECUTIVE CO (OH)
Class A Common $1 par and Class B Common $1 par reclassified as Common $1 par 11/29/68
Common $1 par split (3) for (2) by issuance of (0.5) additional share 12/19/68
Stock Dividends - Payable in Class A Common - 10% 3/31/65 - Payable in Common - 100% 8/20/71; 50% 8/22/72
Merged into Penney (J.C.) Co., Inc. 7/10/73
Each share Common $1 par exchanged for (0.385) share Common 50¢ par

EDUCATOR & EXECUTIVE INSURERS, INC. (OH)
Name changed to Penney (J.C.) Casualty Insurance Co. 1/1/76
(See Penney (J.C.) Casualty Insurance Co.)

EDUCATOR BISCUIT INC (MA)
Recapitalized 7/20/71
Each share Prior Preferred $2 par exchanged for (0.63195) share Common 10¢ par
Each share Preferred Ser. A $1 par exchanged for (5.23365) shares Common 10¢ par
Each share Class A $10 par exchanged for (0.6302) share Common 10¢ par
Each share Common $1 par exchanged for (0.0442) share Common 10¢ par
Placed in bankruptcy 5/28/74
No stockholders' equity

EDUCATORS CO. FOR INSURANCE ON LIVES & GRANTING ANNUITIES (CO)
Common $5 par changed to $1 par 10/1/66
Under plan of merger name changed to Equity Educators Assurance Co. 12/31/69
(See Equity Educators Assurance Co.)

EDUCATORS INSURANCE CO. OF AMERICA (CA)
Name changed to Educators Life Insurance Co. of America 1/4/66

EDUCATORS INVESTMENT CORP. (FL)
Completely liquidated 12/30/80
Each share Common $1 par received first and final distribution of $0.093 cash
Note: Certificates were not required to be surrendered and are now valueless

EDUCATORS INVT CORP (WA)
Company believed out of business 12/30/1988
Details not available

EDUCATORS INVT CORP ALA (AL)
Name changed to Twenty Services, Inc. 09/30/1978
(See Twenty Services, Inc.)

EDUCATORS INVT SVC CORP (WV)
Proclaimed dissolved for non-payment of taxes 06/23/1975

EDUCATORS LIFE INS CO AMER (CA)
Each share Capital Stock $1.50 par exchanged for (0.002) share Capital Stock $750 par 03/31/1978
Note: In effect holders received $19.04 cash per share and public interest was eliminated

EDUCATORS MFG CO (CA)
Merged into Hauserman (E.F.) Co. 2/14/69
Each share Capital Stock $10 par exchanged for (1.09) shares Common $1 par
Hauserman (E.F.) name changed to Hauserman, Inc. 6/3/70
(See Hauserman, Inc.)

EDUCATORS NATL LIFE INS CO (ND)
Class A Common 50¢ par and Class B Common 50¢ par changed to 25¢ par in October 1967
Merged into Prairie States Life Insurance Co. 10/26/70
Each share Class A Common 25¢ par or Class B Common 25¢ par exchanged for (0.322580) share Common $1 par
Prairie States Life Insurance Co. merged into Laurentian Capital Corp. (FL) 2/14/86 which reincorporated in Delaware 7/24/87
(See Laurentian Capital Corp.)

EDUCATORS PREFERRED HOLDING CO. (OK)
Name changed to Epic Enterprises, Inc. 12/30/1970
Epic Enterprises, Inc. name changed to United Premium Finance Corp. 02/24/1978
(See United Premium Finance Corp.)

EDUCATORS SEC INS CO (NE)
Merged into Superior Equity Corp. 2/28/72
Each share Common $1 par exchanged for (0.858) share Common no par
(See Superior Equity Corp.)

EDUCOM CORP (NJ)
Name changed to CareerCom Corp. (NJ) 2/21/85
CareerCom Corp. (NJ) reincorporated in Pennsylvania 7/15/87
(See CareerCom Corp. (PA))

EDUCOR INC (DE)
Name changed to Vocational Advancement Services, Inc. 05/08/1972
(See Vocational Advancement Services, Inc.)

EDUCOR INTL INC (CANADA)
Name changed to LogicalOptions International Inc. 07/20/2000
(See LogicalOptions International Inc.)

EDUDATA CORP (DE)
Recapitalized as Dental/Medical Diagnostics Systems Inc. 01/13/1997
Each share Common 1¢ par exchanged for (0.45510035) share Common 1¢ par
(See Dental/Medical Diagnostics Systems Inc.)

EDULINK INC (NV)
Recapitalized as Learning Priority, Inc. 01/25/2008
Each (1,500) shares Common $0.001 par exchanged for (1) share Common $0.001 par
(See Learning Priority, Inc.)

EDUNETICS LTD. (ISRAEL)
Merged into Steck-Vaughn Publishing Corp. 4/30/96
Each share Ordinary Stock NIS0.006 par exchanged for $2 cash

EDUPLAY INC (KY)
Name changed to E P I Corp. 07/31/1981
(See E P I Corp.)

EDUSOFT LTD (ISRAEL)
Acquired by CINAR Corp. 03/00/1999
Each share Ordinary ILS 0.1 par exchanged for USD $8.3326 cash

EDUTECH VENTURES INC (DE)
Name changed to Bailey Corp. 1/21/86
(See Bailey Corp.)

EDUTREK INTL INC (DE)
Issue Information - 2,600,000 shares CL A offered at $14 per share on 09/23/1997
Merged into Career Education Corp. 1/2/2001
Each share Class A Common no par exchanged for (0.0901) share Common 1¢ par and $0.1877 cash
Each share Class B Common no par exchanged for (0.0901) share Common 1¢ par and $0.01877 cash

EDUVERSE COM (NV)
Name changed 06/07/1999
Name changed from Eduverse Accelerated Learning Systems Inc. to Eduverse.com 06/07/1999
Each share old Common $0.001 par exchanged for (0.02) share new Common $0.001 par 06/08/2001
Name changed to GeneMax Corp. 07/15/2002
GeneMax Corp. recapitalized as TapImmune Inc. (NV) 06/28/2007 which reincorporated in Delaware as Marker Therapeutics, Inc. 10/18/2018

EDWARDS A G & SONS INC (DE)
Common $1 par split (5) for (4) by issuance of (0.25) additional share 06/30/1978
Common $1 par split (3) for (2) by issuance of (0.5) additional share 05/06/1980
Common $1 par split (4) for (3) by issuance of (1/3) additional share 01/30/1981
Common no par split (4) for (3) by issuance of (1/3) additional share 10/30/1981
Common $1 par split (5) for (4) by issuance of (0.25) additional share 01/31/1983
Stock Dividends - 10% 10/31/1975; 15% 10/01/1977; 20% 03/31/1979
Under plan of reorganization each share Common $1 par automatically became (1) share Edwards (A.G.), Inc. Common $1 par 08/01/1983
Edwards (A.G.), Inc. merged into Wachovia Corp. (Ctfs. dated after 09/01/2001) 10/01/2007 which merged into Wells Fargo & Co. (New) 12/31/2008

EDWARDS A G INC (DE)
Common $1 par split (3) for (2) by issuance of (0.5) additional share 05/09/1986
Common $1 par split (3) for (2) by issuance of (0.5) additional share 06/28/1991
Common $1 par split (5) for (4) by issuance of (0.25) additional share 03/31/1992
Common $1 par split (5) for (4) by issuance of (0.25) additional share 01/03/1994
Common $1 par split (3) for (2) by issuance of (0.5) additional share payable 09/30/1997 to holders of record 09/05/1997
Stock Dividend - 10% 10/02/1989
Merged into Wachovia Corp. (Ctfs. dated after 09/01/2001) 10/01/2007
Each share Common $1 par exchanged for (0.9844) share Common $3.33-1/3 par and $35.80 cash
Wachovia Corp. (Ctfs. dated after 09/01/2001) merged into Wells Fargo & Co. (New) 12/31/2008

EDWARDS CONTAINER CORP. (CA)
Name changed to Great Western Container, Inc. 11/28/62
Great Western Container, Inc. name changed to Great Western General, Inc. 6/1/66 which name changed to Ropak West Inc. 12/21/81 which name changed to Ropak Corp. 5/17/85
(See Ropak Corp.)

EDWARDS ENGR CORP (DE)
Reincorporated 11/30/1961
State of incorporation changed from (LA) to (DE) 11/30/1961
Stock Dividend - 50% 09/16/1963
Merged into Burch Engineering Corp. 05/13/1977
Each share Common $1 par exchanged for $9 cash

EDWARDS GROUP LTD (CAYMAN ISLANDS)
Issue Information - 12,500,000 SPONSORED ADRS offered at $8 per ADR on 05/10/2012
Acquired by Atlas Copco Group 01/10/2014
Each Sponsored ADR for Ordinary exchanged for $9.20 cash
Note: Each Sponsored ADR for Ordinary received an additional distribution of $1.25 cash from escrow 03/17/2014

EDWARDS HIGH VACUUM INTL PLC (ENGLAND)
Acquired by British Oxygen Co. PLC 08/06/1968
Each ADR for Ordinary Reg. 4s par exchanged for (0.75) share Ordinary Reg. 5s par
British Oxygen Co. PLC name changed to BOC International PLC 04/16/1975 which name changed to BOC Group PLC 02/17/1982
(See BOC Group PLC)

EDWARDS INDS INC (OR)
Reorganized under Chapter 11 Federal Bankruptcy Code 12/30/1985
Each share Common 50¢ par exchanged for $0.625 cash
Note: Unexchanged certificates were cancelled and became without value 04/29/1986

EDWARDS J D & CO (DE)
Issue Information - 15,800,000 shares COM offered at $23 per share on 09/23/1997
Merged into PeopleSoft, Inc. 8/28/2003
Each share Common $0.001 par exchanged for (0.43) share Common 1¢ par and $7.05 cash
(See PeopleSoft, Inc.)

EDWARDS MANUFACTURING CO.
Acquired by Bates Manufacturing Co. 00/00/1946

Details not available

EDWARDS STL FABRICATORS INC (ON)
Assets sold for the benefit of creditors 06/01/1992
No stockholders' equity

EDY CORP (NC)
Acquired by Yaggy Corp. 11/30/1980
Each share Common $4 par exchanged for $25 cash

EECO INC (DE)
Reincorporated 12/1/86
Common $1 par split (3) for (2) by issuance of (0.5) additional share 12/1/80
Common $1 par split (3) for (2) by issuance of (0.5) additional share 9/8/86
State of incorporation changed from (CA) to (DE) 12/1/86
Charter cancelled and declared void for failure to pay franchise taxes 3/1/93

EEE-ENERGY CONSULTANTS INC (NV)
Name changed to Voyager Group USA-Brazil Ltd. 7/17/96
Voyager Group USA-Brazil Ltd. name changed to Voyager Group Ltd. 7/21/99 which recapitalized as Voyager Internet Group.com 1/31/2000 which name changed Save On Meds.Net 7/31/2000 which recapitalized as Voyager Group Inc. (New) 5/31/2001 which recapitalized as Neoteric Group Inc. 6/17/2002
(See Neoteric Group Inc.)

EES INC (TX)
Charter forfeited for failure to pay taxes 5/20/85

EEX CORP (TX)
Each share Common $1 par exchanged for (1/3) share Common 1¢ par 12/8/98
Merged into Newfield Exploration Co. 11/26/2002
Each share Common 1¢ par exchanged for (0.05703) share Common 1¢ par

EF HUTTON AMER INC (CO)
Name changed to HUTN, Inc. 10/17/2017

EF JOHNSON TECHNOLOGIES INC (DE)
Name changed 05/28/2008
Name changed from EFJ, Inc. to EF Johnson Technologies, Inc. 05/28/2008
Acquired by FP-EF Holding Corp. 08/13/2010
Each share Common 1¢ par exchanged for $1.50 cash

EFAX COM (DE)
Name changed 12/23/1999
Name changed from EFax.Com, Inc. to eFax.com 12/23/1999
Merged into j2 Global Communications, Inc. 11/29/2000
Each share Common 1¢ par exchanged for (0.266) share Common 1¢ par
j2 Global Communications, Inc. name changed to j2 Global, Inc. 12/05/2011

EFC BANCORP INC (DE)
Merged into MAF Bancorp Inc. 2/1/2006
Each share Common 1¢ par exchanged for $34.69 cash

EFCO INC (PA)
Company went private in 1997
Each share Common $10 par exchanged for approximately $31 cash

EFES BREWERIES INTL N V (NETHERLANDS)
Acquired by Anadolu Efes Biracilik Ve Malt Sanayi A.S. 10/13/2010
Each Sponsored 144A GDR for Ordinary exchanged for $17 cash
Each Sponsored Reg. S GDR for Ordinary exchanged for $17 cash

EFES SINAI YATIRIM HLDG A S (TURKEY)
Old Sponsored 144A GDR's for Ordinary split (7) for (1) by issuance of (6) additional GDR's payable 09/01/1998 to holders of record 08/03/1998
Old Sponsored Reg. S GDR's for Ordinary split (7) for (1) by issuance of (6) additional GDR's payable 09/01/1998 to holders of record 08/03/1998
Each old Sponsored 144A GDR for Ordinary exchanged for (0.05) new Sponsored 144A GDR for Ordinary 02/24/2000
Each old Sponsored Reg. S GDR for Ordinary exchanged for (0.05) new Sponsored Reg. S for Ordinary 02/24/2000
Stock Dividend - 30% payable 07/16/1999 to holders of record 05/10/1999
Merged into Coca-Cola Icecek A.S. 09/26/2008
Each Sponsored 144A GDR for Ordinary exchanged for (1.4476) Sponsored 144A GDR's for Class C
Each Sponsored Reg. S GDR for Ordinary exchanged for (1.4476) Sponsored Reg. S GDR's for Class C

EFFECTIVE MGMT SYS INC (WI)
Merged into IFS Americas, Inc. 12/27/99
Each share Common 1¢ par exchanged for $4.50 cash

EFFECTIVE PROFITABLE SOFTWARE INC (DE)
Common $0.001 par changed to $0.0001 par 09/30/2006
Common $0.0001 par split (2.479150872) for (1) by issuance of (1.479150872) additional shares payable 06/06/2008 to holders of record 06/03/2008 Ex date - 06/09/2008
Name changed to Money4Gold Holdings, Inc. 08/13/2008
Money4Gold Holdings, Inc. name changed to Upstream Worldwide Inc. 07/13/2010 which name changed to usell.com, Inc. 07/27/2012

EFFECTIVE SEARCH CORP (NY)
Charter cancelled and proclaimed dissolved for failure to pay taxes and file reports 12/15/1975

EFFICIENCY SYSTEMS INC. (OH)
Charter cancelled for failure to maintain a registered agent 4/7/81

EFFICIENT INDS CORP (OH)
Common no par split (2) for (1) by issuance of (1) additional share 09/30/1966
Stock Dividend - 100% 10/02/1967
Acquired by Teledyne, Inc. 02/11/1969
Each share Common no par exchanged for (0.1573) share Common $1 par
Teledyne, Inc. merged into Allegheny Teledyne Inc. 08/15/1996 which name changed to Allegheny Technologies Inc. 11/29/1999

EFFICIENT LEASING CORP (DE)
Reincorporated 8/11/71
State of incorporation changed from (NY) to (DE) 8/11/71
Name changed to Alanthus Corp. 9/9/71
(See Alanthus Corp.)

EFFICIENT NETWORKS INC (DE)
Issue Information - 4,000,000 shares COM offered at $15 per share on 07/14/1999
Merged into Siemens A.G. 4/2/2001

Each share Common $0.001 par exchanged for $23.50 cash

EFFINGHAM BK & TR (RINCON, GA)
Merged into Bank Corporation of Georgia 6/6/96
Each share Common no par exchanged for (0.59) share Common $1 par
Bank Corporation of Georgia merged into Century South Banks, Inc. 12/16/97 which merged into BB&T Corp. 6/7/2001

EFH GROUP INC (CO)
Name changed to EF Hutton America, Inc. 05/21/2015
EF Hutton America, Inc. name changed to HUTN, Inc. 10/17/2017

EFI ELECTRS CORP (DE)
Each share old Common $0.0001 par exchanged for (1/3) share new Common $0.0001 par 7/28/89
Merged into Square D Co. 5/12/2000
Each share new Common $0.0001 par exchanged for $1.50 cash

EFINANCIAL DEPOT COM INC (DE)
Name changed to Collaborative Financial Network Group, Inc. 06/28/2001
(See Collaborative Financial Network Group, Inc.)

EFIRD MANUFACTURING CO.
Merged into American & Efird Mills, Inc. 00/00/1952
Each share Class A Common exchanged for (11) shares Class A Common $1 par and (2) shares 4% Conv. Preferred
Each share Class B Common exchanged for (11) shares Class B Common $1 par and (2) shares 4% Conv. Preferred
American & Efird Mills, Inc. merged into Ruddick Corp. 10/28/1968 which name changed to Harris Teeter Supermarkets, Inc. (New) 04/02/2012
(See Harris Teeter Supermarkets, Inc. (New))

E5 RESOURCE CORP (BC)
Name changed to Enershare Technology Corp. 7/31/86
(See Enershare Technology Corp.)

EFL OVERSEAS INC (NV)
Each share old Common $0.001 par exchanged for (20) shares new Common $0.001 par 06/30/2010
Name changed to EFLO Energy, Inc. 04/26/2013

EFM FINL CORP (DE)
Name changed to Impact International, Inc. 8/1/77
(See Impact International, Inc.)

EFO INC (NV)
Name changed to Think.com, Inc. 03/03/1999
Think.com, Inc. name changed to Go Think.com, Inc. 06/14/1999 which recapitalized as Knowledge Transfer Systems Inc. 04/24/2001 which name changed Global General Technologies, Inc. 07/08/2005 which recapitalized as Turbine Aviation, Inc. 12/19/2014

EFOODSAFETY COM INC (NV)
Name changed to Nuvilex, Inc. 03/18/2009
Nuvilex, Inc. name changed to PharmaCyte Biotech, Inc. 01/08/2015

EFOTOXPRESS INC (NC)
Charter suspended for failure to pay taxes 10/30/2006

E4 ENERGY INC (AB)
Merged into Twin Butte Energy Ltd. 02/08/2008
Each share Common no par exchanged for (0.3673) share Common no par
Note: Unexchanged certificates were cancelled and became without value 02/08/2014

E4L INC (DE)
Chapter 11 Federal bankruptcy proceedings converted to Chapter 7 on 11/22/2002
Preferred stockholders' equity unlikely
Recapitalized as Holographic Storage Ltd. 11/25/2005
Each share Common 1¢ par exchanged for (0.001) share Common 1¢ par
(See Holographic Storage Ltd.)

E4WORLD CORP (NV)
Each (60) shares old Common $0.001 par exchanged for (1) share new Common $0.001 par 06/26/2006
Name changed to Xcelplus Global Holdings, Inc. 08/18/2006
Xcelplus Global Holdings, Inc. name changed to Clean Energy Pathways, Inc. 02/04/2011

EFT BIOTECH HLDGS INC (NV)
Name changed to EFT Holdings, Inc. 05/27/2011

EFT CDA (ON)
Acquired by 1422748 Ontario Inc. 03/15/2016
Each share Common no par exchanged for $0.105 cash
Note: Unexchanged certificates will be cancelled and become without value 03/15/2022

EFTC CORP (CO)
Reorganized under the laws of Delaware as Suntron Corp. 03/01/2002
Each share Common 1¢ par exchanged for (0.25) share Common 1¢ par
(See Suntron Corp.)

EFTEK CORP (NV)
Each share old Common $0.001 par exchanged for (1/3) share new Common $0.001 par 5/22/97
Each share new Common $0.001 par exchanged again for (0.1) share new Common $0.001 par 2/28/2003
Charter revoked for failure to file reports and pay fees 1/1/2007

EFUNDS CORP (DE)
Issue Information - 5,500,000 shares COM offered at $13 per share on 06/26/2000
Merged into Fidelity National Information Services, Inc. 09/12/2007
Each share Common 1¢ par exchanged for $36.50 cash

EFUSION INC
Merged into ITXC Corp. 10/12/2000
Each share Preferred Ser. C exchanged for (0.4605265) share Common $0.0001 par
ITXC Corp. merged into Teleglobe International Holdings Ltd. 6/1/2004
(See Teleglobe International Holdings Ltd.)

EG & G INC (MA)
Common $1 par split (2) for (1) by issuance of (1) additional share 10/25/1967
$4 Conv. Preferred Ser. A $1 par called for redemption 08/01/1979
Common $1 par split (2) for (1) by issuance of (1) additional share 02/01/1980
Common $1 par split (2) for (1) by issuance of (1) additional share 02/01/1982
Preferred Stock Purchase Rights declared for Common stockholders of record 02/09/1987 were redeemed at $0.01 per right 02/14/1995 for holders of record 02/08/1995
Common $1 par split (2) for (1) by issuance of (1) additional share 05/08/1992
Name changed to PerkinElmer, Inc. 10/25/1999

EGA EMERGING GLOBAL SHS TR (DE)
Emerging Global Shares INDXX India Mid Cap Index Fund reclassified as Emerging Global Shares INDXX India Small Cap Index Fund 01/26/2010
Emerging Global Shares Dow Jones Emerging Markets Energy Titans Index Fund split (2) for (1) by issuance of (1) additional share payable 09/15/2010 to holders of record 09/13/2010 Ex date - 09/16/2010
Emerging Global Shares Dow Jones Emerging Markets Financial Titans Index Fund split (2) for (1) by issuance of (1) additional share payable 09/15/2010 to holders of record 09/13/2010 Ex date - 09/16/2010
Emerging Global Shares Dow Jones Emerging Markets Metals & Mining Titans Index Fund split (3) for (1) by issuance of (2) additional shares payable 09/15/2010 to holders of record 09/13/2010 Ex date - 09/16/2010
Emerging Global Shares Dow Jones Emerging Markets Titans Composite Index Fund split (2) for (1) by issuance of (1) additional share payable 09/15/2010 to holders of record 09/13/2010 Ex date - 09/16/2010
Emerging Global Shares Dow Jones Emerging Markets Energy Titans Index Fund reclassified as EGShares Energy GEMS ETF 06/23/2011
Emerging Global Shares Dow Jones Emerging Markets Financial Titans Index Fund reclassified as EGShares Financials GEMS ETF no par 06/23/2011
Emerging Global Shares Dow Jones Emerging Markets Metals & Mining Titans Index Fund reclassified as EGShares Emerging Markets Metals & Mining ETF 06/23/2011
Emerging Global Shares Dow Jones Emerging Markets Titans Composite Index Fund reclassified as EGShares GEMS Composite ETF 06/23/2011
Emerging Global Shares Industrial GEMS ETF reclassified as EGShares Emerging Markets Metals & Mining ETF 06/23/2011
Emerging Global Shares Dow Jones Emerging Markets Consumer Titans Index Fund reclassified as EGShares Emerging Markets Consumer ETF 07/29/2011
Emerging Global Shares INDXX Brazil Infrastructure Index Fund reclassified as EGShares Brazil Infrastructure ETF 07/29/2011
Emerging Global Shares INDXX China Infrastructure Index Fund reclassified as EGShares China Infrastructure ETF 07/29/2011
Emerging Global Shares INDXX India Infrastructure Index Fund reclassified as EGShares India Infrastructure ETF 07/29/2011
Emerging Global Shares INDXX India Small Cap Index Fund reclassified as EGShares India Small Cap ETF 07/29/2011
EGShares Emerging Markets High Income Low Beta ETF reclassified as EGShares Low Volatility Emerging Markets Dividend ETF 10/31/2011
Trust terminated 10/07/2013
Each share EGShares Basic Materials GEMS ETF received $10.13508 cash
Each share EGShares Consumer Goods GEMS ETF received $23.38191 cash
Each share EGShares Emerging Markets Metals Mining ETF received $10.01214 cash
Each share EGShares Financials GEMS ETF received $20.10513 cash
Each share EGShares Health Care GEMS ETF received $24.28351 cash
Each share EGShares Industrials GEMS ETF received $18.70525 cash
Each share EGShares Technology GEMS ETF received $21.87971 cash
Each share EGShares Utilities GEMS ETF received $15.35344 cash
Trust terminated 10/15/2013
Each share EGShares Consumer Services GEMS ETF receieved $22.36981 cash
Each share EGShares Energy GEMS ETF received $22.33178 cash
Each share EGShares GEMS Composite ETF received $22.61404 cash
Each share EGShares Telecom GEMS ETF received $19.89452 cash
Each share EGShares Consumer Services GEMS ETF received additional distribution of $0.01307 cash payable 03/20/2014 to holders of record 10/15/2013
Each share EGShares Energy GEMS ETF received additional distribution of $0.04236 cash payable 03/20/2014 to holders of record 10/15/2013
Each share EGShares GEMS Composite ETF received additonal distribution of $0.01415 cash payable 03/20/2014 to holders of record 10/15/2013
Each share EGShares Telecom GEMS ETF received additional distribution of $0.35975 cash payable 03/20/2014 to holders of record 10/15/2013
Trust terminated 10/06/2014
Each share EGShares China Infrastructure ETF no par received $17.81981 cash
Each share EGShares TCW EM Intermediate Term Investment Grade Bond ETF no par received $20.48314 cash
Each share EGShares TCW EM Long Term Investment Grade Bond ETF no par received $20.84447 cash
Each share EGShares TCW EM Short Term Investment Grade Bond ETF no par received $20.0271 cash
Trust terminated 12/31/2014
Each share EGShares EM Dividend High Income ETF no par received $17.24707 cash
Each share EGShares Emerging Markets Dividend Growth ETF no par received $17.33172 cash
EGShares Low Volatility Emerging Markets Dividend ETF reclassified as EGShares EM Quality Dividend ETF 01/26/2015
Trust terminated 10/30/2015
Each share EGShares Blue Chip ETF no par received $18.2527 cash
Each share EGShares Brazil Infrastructure ETF no par received $6.17745 cash
EGShares Emerging Markets Domestic Demand ETF reclassified as EGShares EM Strategic Opportunities ETF 03/01/2016
Name changed to Columbia ETF Trust II and EGShares Beyond BRICs ETF, EGShares EM Core ex-China ETF, EGShares EM Quality Dividend ETF, EGShares EM Strategic Opportunities ETF, EGShares Emerging Markets Consumer ETF, EGShares Emerging Markets Core ETF, EGShares India Consumer ETF,

EGShares India Infrastructure ETF and EGShares India Small Cap ETF reclassified as Columbia Beyond BRICs ETF, Columbia EM Core ex-China ETF, Columbia EM Quality Dividend ETF, Columbia EM Strategic Opportunities ETF, Columbia Emerging Markets Consumer ETF, Columbia Emerging Markets Core ETF, Columbia India Consumer ETF, Columbia India Infrastructure ETF or Columbia India Small Cap ETF respectively 10/19/2016

EGAIN COMMUNICATIONS CORP (DE)
Each share old Common $0.001 par exchanged for (0.1) share new Common $0.001 par 08/20/2003
Name changed to eGain Corp. 11/13/2012

EGALITE VENTURES LTD (BC)
Name changed to Glory Explorations Ltd. 10/10/1980
Glory Explorations Ltd. recapitalized as National Fuelcorp Ltd. 07/13/1987 which recapitalized as Fuelcorp International Ltd. 07/31/1991 which name changed to Specialty Retail Concepts Inc. 05/27/1994 which recapitalized as Altoro Gold Corp. 01/09/1997 which merged into Solitario Resources Corp. 10/18/2000 which name changed to Solitario Exploration & Royalty Corp. 06/17/2008 which name changed to Solitario Zinc Corp. 07/18/2017

EGAMES INC (PA)
Name changed to Entertainment Games, Inc. 10/11/2011
Entertainment Games, Inc. recapitalized as Tamino Minerals Inc. 03/25/2013

EGAN MACHY CO (NJ)
Merged into Lessona Corp. 08/17/1978
Each share Common no par exchanged for $14 cash

EGAN SYS INC (DE)
Reorganized under the laws of Nevada as Goldtech Mining Corp. 11/17/2003
Each share Common $0.001 par exchanged for (0.01) share Common $0.001 par
Goldtech Mining Corp. recapitalized as China Industrial Waste Management, Inc. 5/15/2006

EGANA INTL HLDGS LTD NEW (HONG KONG)
Recapitalized 09/09/1997
Recapitalized from Egana International (Holdings) Ltd. (Old) to Egana International (Holdings) Ltd. (New) 09/09/1997
Each Sponsored ADR for Ordinary exchanged for (0.5) new Sponsored ADR for Ordinary
Each old Sponsored ADR for Ordinary exchanged for (0.33333333) new Sponsored ADR for Ordinary
Stock Dividend - 20% payable 07/02/1999 holders of record 06/15/1999
Name changed to Eganagoldpfeil Holdings Ltd. 04/25/2000
(See Eganagoldpfeil Holdings Ltd.)

EGANAGOLDPFEIL HLDGS LTD (HONG KONG)
Each old Sponsored ADR for Ordinary exchanged for (0.1) new Sponsored ADR for Ordinary 10/01/2002
ADR agreement terminated 07/06/2009
Each new Sponsored ADR for Ordinary exchanged for (300) shares Ordinary HKD$0.10 par
Note: Unexchanged ADR's will be sold and the proceeds, if any, held for claim after 07/06/2010

EGBERT & BACKUS EXCAVATING INC (UT)
Proclaimed dissolved for failure to pay taxes 09/30/1978

EGENE INC (NV)
Merged into Qiagen N.V. 07/09/2007
Each share Common $0.001 par exchanged for (0.0416) share Common Euro 0.01 par and $0.65 cash

EGENIX INC (DE)
Plan of reorganization under Chapter 11 Federal Bankruptcy proceedings effective 02/29/2016
Stockholders' equity unlikely

EGG HARBOR BK & TR CO (EGG HARBOR, NJ)
Stock Dividend - 100% 04/01/1960
Merged into First National State Bancorporation 11/29/1974
Each share Common $50 par exchanged for (8.5) shares Common $6.25 par
First National State Bancorporation name changed to First Fidelity Bancorporation (Old) 05/01/1985 which merged into First Fidelity Bancorporation (New) 02/29/1988 which merged into First Union Corp. 01/01/1996 which name changed to Wachovia Corp. (Ctfs. dated after 09/01/2001) 09/01/2001 which merged into Wells Fargo & Co. (New) 12/31/2008

EGG SAFETY CARTON CORP.
Acquired by Gair (Robert) Co., Inc. 00/00/1947
Details not available

EGGHEAD COM INC (WA)
Name changed 02/12/1998
Name changed from Egghead, Inc. to Egghead.com Inc. 02/12/1998
Merged into Egghead.Com, Inc. (DE) 11/22/1999
Each share Common 1¢ par exchanged for (0.565) share Common $0.001 par
(See Egghead.Com, Inc. (DE))

EGGHEAD COM INC NEW (DE)
Plan of reorganization under Chapter 11 Federal Bankruptcy Code effective 01/28/2003
No stockholders' equity

EGGO FOOD PRODS INC (CA)
Common $1 par changed to 10¢ par and a stock dividend of 33-1/3% paid 00/00/1947
Voluntarily dissolved 12/26/1969
Details not available

EGGO MILLING CO., INC. (CA)
Name changed to Eggo Food Products, Inc. 00/00/1941
(See Eggo Food Products, Inc.)

EGI CDA CORP (CANADA)
Each Exchangeable share no par exchanged for (1) share E*Trade Financial Corp. Common 1¢ par 12/21/2005

EGI FINL HLDGS INC (ON)
Ser. F Special Shares called for redemption at $1.0511 on 01/31/2006
Name changed to Echelon Financial Holdings Inc. 05/26/2015

EGIS PLC (HUNGARY)
ADR agreement terminated 12/27/2013
Each ADR for Ordinary exchanged for $25.32312 cash

EGL INC (TX)
Merged into CEVA Group PLC 08/02/2007
Each share Common $0.001 par exchanged for $47.50 cash

EGLOBE INC (DE)
Each share old Common $0.001 par exchanged for (0.2127659) share new Common $0.001 par 11/13/2000
Chapter 11 bankruptcy proceedings converted to Chapter 7 on 10/24/2001
Stockholders' equity unlikely

EGO MINES LTD. (ON)
Capital Stock $1 par changed to no par 07/23/1974
Name changed to Ego Resources Ltd. 08/09/1978
Ego Resources Ltd. name changed to Cobatec Inc. 09/09/1997
(See Cobatec Inc.)

EGO RES INC (DE)
Charter cancelled and declared inoperative and void for non-payment of taxes 03/01/1981

EGO RES LTD (ON)
Name changed to Cobatec Inc. 09/09/1997
(See Cobatec Inc.)

EGOLI CONS MINES LTD (SOUTH AFRICA)
ADR agreement terminated 03/07/1997
Each ADR for Ordinary exchanged for $0.032 cash

EGR COMMUNICATIONS INC (DE)
Charter cancelled and declared inoperative and void for non-payment of taxes 03/01/1979

EGREETINGS NETWORK INC (DE)
Merged into AmericanGreetings.com, Inc. 03/20/2001
Each share Common $0.001 par exchanged for $0.85 cash

EGRET ENERGY CORP (CO)
Recapitalized as Territorial Resources Inc. 07/08/1988
Each share Common no par exchanged for (0.02) share Common no par
(See Territorial Resources Inc.)

EGRET FD INC (MA)
Merged into Pioneer Fund, Inc. 07/24/1978
Each share Common $1 par exchanged for (0.723938) share Common $1 par
Pioneer Fund, Inc. name changed to Pioneer Fund 07/03/1992

EGRET GROWTH FUND INC. (MA)
Name changed to Egret Fund Inc. 12/12/1974
Egret Fund Inc. merged into Pioneer Fund, Inc. 07/24/1978 which name changed to Pioneer Fund 07/03/1992

EGRET SVC INC (DE)
Merged into Egret Holding Corp. 02/28/1972
Each share Common 10¢ par exchanged for $3.25 cash

EGRY REGISTER CO. (OH)
Each share Class A no par exchanged for (0.33333333) share 5.5% Preferred $100 par 00/00/1936
Each share Class B no par exchanged for (1) share Common no par 00/00/1936
Name changed to Allied-Egry Business Systems, Inc. 05/29/1962
(See Allied-Egry Business Systems, Inc.)

EGS PPTY DEV & MGMT CO (TURKEY)
144A Sponsored GDR's for Class B split (3.4) for (1) by issuance of (2.4) additional GDR's payable 08/21/2000 to holders of record 08/08/2000
Reg. S Sponsored GDR's for Class B split (3.4) for (1) by issuance of (2.4) additional GDR's payable 08/21/2000 to holders of record 08/08/2000
Stock Dividend - 73.91304% payable 05/24/1999 to holders of record 05/21/1999
GDR agreement terminated 03/10/2009
Each 144A Sponsored GDR's for Class B exchanged for (0.3) share Class B
Each Reg. S Sponsored GDR's for Class B exchanged for (0.3) share Class B
Note: Unexchanged GDR's will be sold and the proceeds, if any, held for claim after 06/10/2009

EGX FDS TRANSFER INC (DE)
SEC revoked common stock registration 05/13/2011

EHEALTH COM INC (NV)
Common $0.001 par changed to $0.0001 par 12/17/1998
Common $0.0001 par split (3) for (1) by issuance of (2) additional shares payable 04/10/1999 to holders of record 03/15/1999
Name changed to InternetStudios.com, Inc. 09/20/1999
(See InternetStudios.com, Inc.)

EHG INTL INC (NV)
Name changed to Uniforms for America Inc. 12/18/1995
Uniforms for America Inc. recapitalized as HomeFoodClub.com Inc. (NV) 07/12/1999 which reincorporated in Delaware as iKarma Inc. 02/02/2006 which recapitalized as Medtino, Inc. 10/12/2010 which name changed to IntelaKare Marketing, Inc. 03/01/2011

EHOLDING TECHNOLOGIES INC (NV)
Each share old Common $0.001 par exchanged for (0.005) share new Common $0.001 par 03/29/2007
Recapitalized as Pine Ridge Holdings, Inc. 03/10/2008
Each share Common $0.001 par exchanged for (0.002) share Common $0.001 par
Pine Ridge Holdings, Inc. name changed to Mike the Pike Productions, Inc. (NV) 08/05/2009 which reorganized in Wyoming 03/03/2011

EHR LITE CORP (DE)
Reincorporated 06/30/1972
State of incorporation changed from (NY) to (DE) and Common 10¢ par changed to 1¢ par 06/30/1972
Charter forfeited for failure to maintain a registered agent 02/24/1975

EHRENKRANTZ TR (MA)
Undiscovered Equities Fund merged into Growth Fund 05/31/1989
Details not available
Completely liquidated 12/09/2008
Each share Growth Fund received net asset value

EHRENREICH PHOTO OPTICAL INDS INC (NY)
Common 10¢ par split (3) for (2) by issuance of (0.5) additional share 09/21/1966
Common 10¢ par split (3) for (2) by issuance of (0.5) additional share 09/20/1968
Merged into Nippon Kogaku K.K. 06/16/1981
Each share Common 10¢ par exchanged for $14 cash

EHRLICH BOBER FINL CORP (DE)
Name changed to Benson Eyecare Corp. and Common $1 par changed to 1¢ par 10/20/1992
Benson Eyecare Corp. merged into BEC Group, Inc. 05/03/1996 which recapitalized as Lumen Technologies, Inc. 03/12/1998
(See Lumen Technologies, Inc.)

EI ENVIRONMENTAL ENGR CONCEPTS LTD (BC)
Delisted from Toronto Venture Stock Exchange 06/20/2003

EICHLER CORP. (CA)
Name changed 06/09/1966
60¢ Preferred called for redemption 10/14/1959
Name changed from Eichler Homes, Inc. to Eichler Corp. 06/09/1966
Adjudicated bankrupt 01/07/1970
No stockholders' equity

EICO ELECTR INSTR INC (NY)
Completely liquidated
Each share Common $1 par received first and final distribution of $0.91 cash payable 01/10/2003 to holders of record 12/16/2002 Ex date - 01/23/2003

EICON GROUP INC (NY)
Charter cancelled and proclaimed dissolved for failure to pay taxes 06/26/2002

EICON TECHNOLOGY CORP (CANADA)
Merged into i-data international a-s 11/21/2000
Each share Common no par exchanged for $5 cash

EIDOS PLC (ENGLAND & WALES)
Sponsored ADR's for Ordinary split (5) for (1) by issuance of (4) additional ADR's payable 02/02/2000 to holders of record 01/25/2000
Merged into SCi Entertainment Group PLC 10/06/2005
Each Sponsored ADR for Ordinary exchanged for $1.20813 cash

EIEIHOME COM INC (DE)
Name changed to Wireless Ventures, Inc. 09/25/2000
Wireless Ventures, Inc. name changed to Pivotal Self-Service Technologies Inc. 10/02/2001 which name changed to Phantom Fiber Corp. 07/21/2004 which recapitalized as Accelerated Technologies Holding Corp. 09/18/2017

EIF HLDGS INC (HI)
Reorganized under the laws of Delaware as U.S. Industrial Services Inc. 05/04/1998
Each share Common no par exchanged for (0.1) share Common no par
U.S. Industrial Services Inc. name changed to Nextgen Communications Corp. 08/07/2001 which name changed to Home Solutions of America, Inc. 12/23/2002
(See Home Solutions of America, Inc.)

EIFFEL TECHNOLOGIES LTD (AUSTRALIA)
Each old Sponsored ADR for Ordinary exchanged for (0.1) new Sponsored ADR for Ordinary 02/13/2008
Name changed to Telesso Technologies Ltd. 03/07/2008
(See Telesso Technologies Ltd.)

EIGER TECHNOLOGY INC (ON)
Reincorporated 11/00/2000
Place of incorporation changed from (BC) to (ON) 11/00/2000
Recapitalized as GameCorp Ltd. 06/24/2008
Each share Common no par exchanged for (0.1) share Common no par
GameCorp Ltd. name changed to DealNet Capital Corp. 09/13/2012

EIGHT BALL CORP (NV)
Common $0.001 par split (20) for (1) by issuance of (19) additional shares payable 01/22/2002 to holders of record 01/18/2002 Ex date - 01/23/2002
Common $0.001 par split (3) for (1) by issuance of (2) additional shares payable 11/14/2002 to holders of record 11/13/2002 Ex date - 11/15/2002
Name changed to CardioBioscience Corp. 01/08/2003
CardioBioscience Corp. name changed to Secure Blue, Inc. 02/07/2003 which name changed to RedHand International, Inc. 10/06/2003 which name changed to African Diamond Co., Inc. 04/17/2006
(See African Diamond Co., Inc.)

8 BALL, INC. (UT)
Name changed to American Personal Blood Savings Bank 01/06/1989
American Personal Blood Savings Bank name changed to Convergent Companies, Inc. 05/13/1991 which name changed to Zerotree Technologies, Inc. 01/17/2001
(See Zerotree Technologies, Inc.)

8X8 INC OLD (DE)
Name changed to Netergy Networks, Inc. 08/14/2000
Netergy Networks, Inc. name changed to 8x8, Inc. (New) 07/19/2001

8 CROWN CAP CORP (BC)
Name changed to Starfire Technologies International Inc. 12/17/1999
(See Starfire Technologies International Inc.)

EIGHT DRAGONS CO (NV)
Common $0.0001 par split (100) for (1) by issuance of (99) additional shares payable 12/10/2007 to holders of record 10/24/2007 Ex date - 12/11/2007
Name changed to Rokk3r Inc. 06/18/2018

8888 ACQUISITION CORP (NV)
Reincorporated 07/18/2006
State of incorporation changed from (FL) to (NV) 07/18/2006
Each share old Common $0.0001 par exchanged for (0.00030303) share new Common $0.0001 par 04/24/2007
Each share new Common $0.0001 par exchanged again for (0.01) share new Common $0.0001 par 08/13/2007
New Common $0.0001 par split (100) for (1) by issuance of (99) additional shares payable 10/25/2007 to holders of record 10/15/2007 Ex date - 10/26/2007
Acquired by New Materials Mergerco Inc. 01/18/2013
Each share new Common $0.0001 par exchanged for $1.07 cash

800 AMER COM INC (NV)
Charter revoked for failure to file reports and pay fees 01/01/2004

800 COMM INC (FL)
Name changed to Petrogress, Inc. (FL) 04/01/2016
Petrogress, Inc. (FL) reincorporated in Delaware 11/30/2016

850 LAKE SHORE CORP. TRUST
Completely liquidated 00/00/1950
Details not available

800-JR CIGAR INC (DE)
Merged into L&LR, Inc. 10/04/2000
Each share Common 1¢ par exchanged for $13 cash

870-7TH AVENUE CORP. (NY)
Name changed to Park Sheraton Corp. 09/00/1952
Park Sheraton Corp. merged into Sheraton Corp. of America 03/01/1960 which was acquired by International Telephone & Telegraph Corp. (DE) 02/29/1968 which name changed to ITT Corp. 12/31/1983 which reorganized in Indiana as ITT Industries, Inc. 12/19/1995 which name changed to ITT Corp. 07/01/2006

810 SOUTH SPRING BLDG CO (CA)
Dissolved 05/31/1976
No stockholders' equity

800 TRAVEL SYS INC (DE)
Plan of reorganization under Chapter 11 Federal Bankruptcy Code effective 05/05/2003
No stockholders' equity

8829 REALTY CORP.
Dissolved 00/00/1949
Details not available

1838 BD-DEB TRADING FD (DE)
Name changed to Rivus Bond Fund 07/07/2006
Rivus Bond Fund name changed to Cutwater Select Income Fund 12/09/2011 which name changed to Insight Select Income Fund 12/29/2016

1867 WESTN FINL CORP (CA)
$4.9725 Preferred no par called for redemption at $51 on 02/20/2008 (Additional Information in Active)

18TH & MKT CORP (MO)
Voluntarily dissolved 12/30/1976
Details not available

18 EAST 52ND STREET
Dissolved 00/00/1949
Details not available

18 EAST 41ST STREET CORP. (NY)
Liquidation completed 09/18/1964
Details not available

80TH & LAFLIN APARTMENTS, INC.
Liquidated 00/00/1941
Details not available

8POINT3 ENERGY PARTNERS LP (DE)
Acquired by Capital Dynamics, Inc. 06/19/2018
Each Class A Share exchanged for $12.35 cash

EIGHTWINDS PETE INC (NV)
Name changed to Embryonics Inc. 05/31/1984
Embryonics Inc. name changed to Emerald Instrument Corp. 11/04/1986
(See Emerald Instrument Corp.)

80 BROAD STREET, INC. (NY)
Liquidation completed 09/26/1962
Details not available

88 CAP CORP (BC)
Each share old Common no par exchanged for (0.125) share new Common no par 04/07/2014
Each share new Common no par exchanged again for (0.1) share new Common no par 06/07/2016
Name changed to Golden Ridge Resources Ltd. 10/19/2017

81ST & DREXEL, INC.
Liquidated 00/00/1941
Details not available

81ST & LOOMIS BUILDING
Liquidated 00/00/1940
Details not available

80 JOHN STREET CORP.
Reorganized 00/00/1947
No stockholders' equity

89 EAST FULTON CORP. (NY)
Reorganized under the laws of Delaware as YGAC Corp. 04/18/1969
YGAC Corp. name changed to Hargrom Services Corp. 05/19/1969
(See Hargrom Services Corp.)

87 ACQUISITION CORP (LA)
Reincorporated 01/24/1994
Each share Common $0.001 par exchanged for (0.01) share Common 1¢ par 01/18/1994
State of incorporation changed from (DE) to (LA) 01/24/1994
Charter revoked for failure to file annual reports 05/15/2002

EIH LTD (INDIA)
144A GDR's for Equity Shares split (5) for (1) by issuance of (4) additional GDR's payable 10/11/2006 to holders of record 09/19/2006
Reg. S GDR's for Equity Shares split (5) for (1) by issuance of (4) additional GDR's payable 10/11/2006 to holders of record 09/19/2006
GDR agreement terminated 02/23/2017
Each 144A GDRs for Equity Shares exchanged for (1) Equity Share
Each Reg. S GDR for Equity Shares exchanged for (1) Equity Share
Note: Unexchanged GDR's will be sold and the proceeds, if any, held for claim

EIH LTD (INDIA)
144A GDR's for Equity Shares split (5) for (1) by issuance of (4) additional GDR's payable 10/11/2006 to holders of record 09/19/2006
Reg. S GDR's for Equity Shares split (5) for (1) by issuance of (4) additional GDR's payable 10/11/2006 to holders of record 09/19/2006
GDR agreement terminated 02/23/2017
Each 144A GDRs for Equity Shares exchanged for (1) Equity Share
Each Reg. S GDR for Equity Shares exchanged for (1) Equity Share
Note: Unexchanged GDR's will be sold and the proceeds, if any, held for claim

EIKONIX CORP (DE)
Merged into Eastman Kodak Co. 05/23/1985
Each share Common 5¢ par exchanged for $16.12 cash

EIMO CORP (FINLAND)
ADR agreement terminated 03/25/2003
Each Sponsored ADR for Ordinary exchanged for $1,207.56071 cash

EIMO OYJ (FINLAND)
Recapitalized as Eimo Corp. 09/11/2002
Each Sponsored ADR for Ordinary exchanged for (0.01) Sponsored ADR for Ordinary
(See Eimo Corp.)

EINSON FREEMAN & DE TROY CORP (NJ)
Acquired by Electronic Assistance Corp. 07/15/1970
Each share 4% Preferred $10 par or 6% Preferred $10 par exchanged for $10 principal amount of 6.5% Conv. Subord. Debentures due 06/15/1985
Each share Common $1 par exchanged for $6.50 principal amount of 6.5% Conv. Subord. Debentures due 06/15/1985

EINSTEIN / NOAH BAGEL CORP (DE)
Name changed to ENBC Corp. 07/11/2001
(See ENBC Corp.)

EINSTEIN NOAH RESTAURANT GROUP INC (DE)
Acquired by JAB Beech Inc. 11/05/2014
Each share Common $0.001 par exchanged for $20.25 cash

EIP MICROWAVE INC (DE)
Reincorporated 04/29/1987
Common no par split (2) for (1) by issuance of (1) additional share 03/01/1983
State of incorporation changed from (CA) to (DE) and Common no par changed to 1¢ par 04/29/1987
Each share old Common 1¢ par

exchanged for (0.2) share new Common 1¢ par 02/10/1993
Chapter 11 bankruptcy proceedings converted to Chapter 7 on 08/05/1999
Stockholders' equity unlikely

EIRCELL 2000 PLC (UNITED KINGDOM)
Merged into Vodafone Group PLC (New) 06/01/2001
Each share Ordinary exchanged for (0.4739) Sponsored ADR for Ordinary

EIRCOM PLC (IRELAND)
Acquired by Valentia Telecommunications Ltd. 12/12/2001
Each Euro Sponsored ADR for Ordinary exchanged for $$5.46 cash

EIS CAP CORP (AB)
Name changed to Entrec Transportation Services Ltd. 08/02/2011
Entrec Transportation Services Ltd. name changed to ENTREC Corp. 06/04/2012

EIS FD INC (NY)
Under plan of merger name changed to Cornerstone Total Return Fund, Inc. 10/30/2002

EIS INTL INC (DE)
Merged into SER System AG 01/31/2000
Each share Common 1¢ par exchanged for $6.25 cash

EISEMANN CORP.
Merged into Jack & Heintz Precision Industries, Inc. 00/00/1946
Each share Common $1 par exchanged for (0.115) share Common $5 par
Jack & Heintz Precision Industries, Inc. name changed to Jack & Heintz, Inc. 00/00/1951 which merged into Siegler Corp. 02/03/1961 which name was changed to Lear Siegler, Inc. 06/05/1962
(See Lear Siegler, Inc.)

EISEMANN MAGNETO CORP.
Merged into Eisemann Corp. 00/00/1943
Details not available

EISENLOHR (OTTO) & BROTHERS, INC.
Name changed to Webster-Eisenlohr, Inc. 00/00/1928
Webster-Eisenlohr, Inc. name changed to Webster Tobacco Co., Inc. 00/00/1945 which name changed to Webster Investment Co. Inc. (PA) 00/00/1953 which reincorporated in Delaware as Webster Investors, Inc. 04/30/1956 which merged into American Manufacturing Co., Inc. 12/20/1960 which assets were transferred to American Manufacturing Co., Inc. Liquidating Trust 05/20/1980
(See American Manufacturing Co., Inc. Liquidating Trust)

EISENSTADT MFG CO (MO)
Recapitalized 00/00/1939
Each share Preferred $100 par exchanged for (1) share 1st Preferred $75 par and (1) share 2nd Preferred $1 par
Each share Common no par exchanged for (1) share Common $1 par
1st Preferred $75 par called for redemption 09/30/1971
2nd Preferred $1 par called for redemption 09/30/1971
Acquired by Roberts (John), Inc. 07/01/1971
Each share Common $1 par exchanged for $167.38 cash

EISLER ELECTRIC CORP.
Name changed to Callite Tungsten Corp. 00/00/1940
(See Callite Tungsten Corp.)

EITEL MC CULLOUGH INC (CA)
Stock Dividends - 10% 12/27/1954; 100% 08/31/1959
Merged into Varian Associates (CA) 08/02/1965
Each share Capital Stock $1 par exchanged for (0.5) share Capital Stock $1 par
Varian Associates (CA) reincorporated in Delaware as Varian Associates, Inc. 10/07/1976 which name changed to Varian Medical Systems Inc. 04/03/1999

EITINGON SCHILD CO., INC. (NY)
Recapitalized 00/00/1934
Each share 6.5% 1st Preferred $100 par exchanged for (2.75) shares Common no par
Each share 7% Class A Jr. Preferred $100 par exchanged for (1.75) shares Common no par
Each share 6% Class B Jr. Preferred $100 par exchanged for (0.75) share Common no par
Each share old Common no par exchanged for (0.15) share new Common no par
New Common worthless 00/00/1956
Charter revoked for failure to file reports and pay fees 12/15/1960

EIX TR I (DE)
7.875% Quarterly Income Preferred Securities called for redemption at $25 on 12/20/2004

EIX TR II (CA)
8.6% Quarterly Income Preferred Securities Ser. B called for redemption at $25 on 11/30/2004

EJH ENTMT INC (NV)
Each share old Common $0.0001 par exchanged for (0.05) share new Common $0.0001 par 09/14/1998
Name changed to Findex.com, Inc. 05/10/1999

EK CHOR CHINA MOTORCYCLE CO LTD (BERMUDA)
Merged into C.P. Pokphand Co. Ltd. 06/23/2003
Each share Common 10¢ par exchanged for $3.75 cash

EKATON INDS INC (AB)
Name changed 05/14/1986
Name changed from Ekaton Energy Ltd. to Ekaton Industries Inc. 05/14/1986
Struck off register for failure to file annual returns 01/01/1992

EKCO GROUP INC (DE)
Merged into Borden, Inc. 09/16/1999
Each share Common 1¢ par exchanged for $7 cash

EKCO OIL CO. (DE)
Liquidated 12/14/1961
Details not available

EKCO PRODS INC (DE)
Reincorporated 04/29/1960
Each share Common $5 par exchanged for (2) shares Common $2.50 par 00/00/1948
Stock Dividend - 10% 02/01/1956
State of incorporation changed from (IL) to (DE) 04/29/1960
Common $2.50 par split (2) for (1) by issuance of (1) additional share 01/03/1962
4.5% Preferred 2nd Ser. called for redemption 01/14/1963
4.5% Preferred 3rd Ser. called for redemption 01/14/1963
4.5% Preferred $100 par called for redemption 10/15/1964
Merged into American Home Products Corp. 09/30/1965
Each share Common $2.50 par exchanged for (1) share $2 Conv. Preferred $2.50 par
American Home Products Corp. name changed to Wyeth 03/11/2002 which was acquired by Pfizer Inc. 10/15/2009

EKHARDT & BECKER BREWING CO., INC. (MI)
Name changed to E & B Brewing Co. Inc. 00/00/1944
E & B Brewing Co. Inc. merged into Associated Brewing Co. 11/15/1962 which name changed to Armada Corp. 03/02/1973

EKNOWLEDGE GROUP INC (NV)
Name changed 05/09/2000
Name changed from eKnowledge.com Inc. to eKnowledge Group Inc. 05/09/2000
Each share old Common $0.0001 par exchanged for (0.01) share new Common $0.0001 par 02/20/2003
Recapitalized as Amazon Oil & Energy Corp. 09/21/2006
Each share Common $0.0001 par exchanged for (0.1) share Common $0.0001 par 09/21/2006
Amazon Oil & Energy Corp. name changed to AEC Holdings, Corp. 02/20/2007
(See AEC Holdings, Corp.)

EKSPORTFINANS ASA (NORWAY)
8.7% Preferred Capital Securities called for redemption at $25 on 03/20/2003

EKZ INVTS LTD (AB)
Name changed to E-Tronics Inc. 12/20/2000
E-Tronics Inc. name changed to Western Lakota Energy Services Inc. 10/28/2002 which was acquired by Savanna Energy Services Corp. 08/25/2006 which merged into Total Energy Services Inc. 06/23/2017

EL APPAREL INC (FL)
Recapitalized as NutriOne Corp. 07/27/2006
Each share Common 1¢ par exchanged for (0.001) share Common 1¢ par
(See NutriOne Corp.)

EL BONANZA MNG LTD (ON)
Name changed to Virgin Metals Inc. 11/10/1998
Virgin Metals Inc. recapitalized as Minera Alamos Inc. 05/15/2014

EL BRAVO RES INTL LTD (BERMUDA)
Reincorporated 07/03/1995
Name changed 11/07/1997
Place of incorporation changed from (BC) to (Bermuda) 07/03/1995
Name changed from El Bravo Gold Mining Ltd. to El Bravo Resources International Ltd. 11/07/1997
Recapitalized as Tri-X International Ltd. 09/18/2000
Each (14) shares Common no par exchanged for (1) share Common no par
(See Tri-X International Ltd.)

EL CAJON VALLEY BANK (EL CAJON, CA)
Name changed to American Valley Bank (El Cajon, CA) 09/01/1981
American Valley Bank (El Cajon, CA) reorganized as BSD Bancorp, Inc. (CA) 03/26/1982 which reincorporated in Delaware 09/02/1987

EL CALLAO MNG CORP (BC)
Merged into Crystallex International Corp. 08/19/2004
Each share Common no par exchanged for (0.01818) share Common no par

EL CAMINO BANCORP (CA)
Acquired by Citizens Holdings 03/15/1988
Each share Common no par exchanged for $8.10 cash

EL CAMINO BANK (ANAHEIM, CA)
Common $5 par changed to $2.50 par and (1) additional share issued 05/18/1981
Reorganized as El Camino Bancorp 08/16/1982
Each share Common $2.50 par exchanged for (1) share Common no par
(See El Camino Bancorp)

EL CAMINO FINL CORP (CA)
Charter cancelled for failure to file reports and pay taxes 12/15/1993

EL CAMINO NATL BK (LOMPOC, CA)
Acquired by Bank of Santa Maria (Santa Maria, CA) 01/10/1997
Each share Common $5 par exchanged for (0.7332) share Common no par
Bank of Santa Maria (Santa Maria, CA) reorganized as BSM Bancorp 03/11/1997 which merged into Mid-State Bancshares 07/10/1998
(See Mid-State Bancshares)

EL CAMINO RES INC (BC)
Reorganized as C.I.S. Technologies, Inc. (BC) 07/24/1985
Each share Common no par exchanged for (1) share Common no par
C.I.S. Technologies, Inc. (BC) reincorporated in Delaware 05/03/1989 which merged into National Data Corp. 05/31/1996 which name changed to NDCHealth Corp. 10/25/2001 which merged into Per-Se Technologies, Inc. 01/06/2006
(See Per-Se Technologies, Inc.)

EL CANADA COLOMBIA MINES CO. (DE)
Insolvent 03/28/1957
No stockholders' equity

EL CANADA GOLD MINES CORP. (DE)
Acquired in reorganization by El Canada Colombia Mines Co. 00/00/1948
Each share Capital Stock no par exchanged for (0.1) share Common $1 par
(See El Canada Colombia Mines Co.)

EL CANADA MINES, INC. (DE)
Acquired in reorganization by El Canada Colombia Mines Co. 00/00/1948
Each share Captial Stock no par and each (100) shares $1 par exchanged for (5) shares Common $1 par
(See El Canada Colombia Mines Co.)

EL CANADA MINES CO., LTD.
Acquired in reorganization by El Canada Colombia Mines Co. 00/00/1948
Each share Capital Stock no par exchanged for (0.1) share Common $1 par
(See El Canada Colombia Mines Co.)

EL CAP GOLD MINES LTD (BC)
Recapitalized as Lakeland Royalty & Petroleum Corp. 02/27/1997
Each share Common no par exchanged for (0.27027027) share Common no par
(See Lakeland Royalty & Petroleum Corp.)

EL CAPITAN BANCSHARES INC (CA)
Merged into Vallicorp Holdings Inc. 02/02/1996
Each share Common 1¢ par exchanged for (2.32) shares Common 1¢ par
ValliCorp Holdings, Inc. merged into Westamerica Bancorporation 04/12/1997

EL CHARRO INC (UT)
Name changed to Treachers (Arthur), Inc. 02/03/1984
Treachers (Arthur), Inc. name changed to Creative Development Corp. 07/31/2000

EL CHEM MACHY INC (NY)
Reorganized under the laws of Delaware as DCS Financial Corp. 10/25/1972
Each share Common 5¢ par exchanged for (0.142857) share Common 10¢ par
(See DCS Financial Corp.)

EL CHICO CANNING CO., INC. (TX)
Name changed to Cuellar Foods, Inc. 05/14/1953
Cuellar Foods, Inc. name changed to El Chico Foods, Inc. 02/04/1957 which name changed to El Chico Corp. 05/01/1962 which merged into Campbell Taggart, Inc. 09/29/1977
(See Campbell Taggart, Inc.)

EL CHICO CORP (TX)
Ctfs. dated prior to 09/29/1977
Stock Dividend - 10% 06/27/1977
Merged into Campbell Taggart, Inc. 09/29/1977
Each share Common no par exchanged for (0.66666666) share Common $1 par
(See Campbell Taggart, Inc.)

EL CHICO CORP NEW (TX)
Certificates dated after 06/30/1983
Common 10¢ par split (3) for (2) by issuance of (0.5) additional share 01/03/1984
Name changed to Southwest Cafes, Inc. 12/06/1990
Southwest Cafes, Inc. name changed to El Chico Restaurants, Inc. 10/12/1992
(See El Chico Restaurants, Inc.)

EL CHICO FOODS, INC. (TX)
Name changed to El Chico Corp. 05/01/1962
El Chico Corp. merged into Campbell Taggart, Inc. 09/29/1977
(See Campbell Taggart, Inc.)

EL CHICO RESTAURANTS INC (TX)
Merged into Cracken, Harkey & Co. 01/21/1998
Each share Common 10¢ par exchanged for $12.75 cash

EL COCO EXPLS LTD (BC)
Name changed to Dassen Gold Resources Ltd.-Ressources Auriferes Ltee. 11/14/1984
(See Dassen Gold Resources Ltd.-Ressources Auriferes Ltee.)

EL COCO EXPLS QUE LTD (ON)
Merged into El Coco Explorations Ltd. 11/00/1978
Each share Capital Stock $1 par exchanged for (1) share Common no par
El Coco Explorations Ltd. name changed to Dassen Gold Resources Ltd.-Ressources Auriferers Dassen Ltee. 11/14/1984
(See Dassen Gold Resources Ltd.-Ressources Auriferes Ltee.)

EL CONDOR MINERALS INC (BC)
Recapitalized as Worldwide Resources Corp. 06/08/2015
Each share Common no par exchanged for (0.06666666) share Common no par

EL CONDOR RES LTD (BC)
Merged into Royal Oak Mines Inc. 01/15/1996
Each share Common no par exchanged for (0.95) share Common no par and $2 cash
Royal Oak Mines Inc. recapitalized as Royal Oak Ventures Inc. 02/14/2000
(See Royal Oak Ventures Inc.)

EL DON CORP. (WA)
Acquired by Power Research & Development Co., Inc. 08/18/1970
Each share Capital Stock $1 par exchanged for (0.66666666) share Common no par

EL DORADO GOLD MINES, LTD. (NV)
Capital Stock $50 par changed to $1 par 10/15/1947
Charter revoked for failure to file reports and pay fees 03/00/1951

EL DORADO INTL INC (MN)
Name changed to Westamerica Inc. 06/30/1987
(See Westamerica Inc.)

EL DORADO MNG CO (UT)
Recapitalized as Apollo Industries, Inc. (UT) 10/17/1969
Each share Common 1¢ par exchanged for (0.1) share Common 10¢ par
(See Apollo Industries, Inc. (UT))

EL DORADO ST BK (NAPA, CA)
Acquired by Western Bancorporation 02/13/1970
Each share Common Capital Stock $20 par exchanged for (1) share Capital Stock $2 par
Western Bancorporation name changed to First Interstate Bancorp 06/01/1981 which merged into Wells Fargo & Co. (Old) 04/01/1996 which merged into Wells Fargo & Co. (New) 11/02/1998

EL DORADO SYS CDA INC (BC)
Delisted from Vancouver Stock Exchange 11/03/1988

EL FAVOR MINING CO. (AZ)
Charter expired by time limitation 07/11/1931

EL MIRAGE AIRPORT DEVELOPMENT CORP. (CA)
Name changed to Antelope Valley Enterprises, Inc. 05/07/1970
Antelope Valley Enterprises, Inc. name changed to Alfalfa-640 Trust 12/31/1972
(See Alfalfa-640 Trust)

EL MISTI GOLD LTD (NB)
Reincorporated 12/06/1996
Place of incorporation changed from (BC) to (NB) 12/06/1996
Recapitalized as Andean American Mining Corp. (NB) 10/21/1999
Each share Common no par exchanged for (0.05) share Common no par
Andean American Mining Corp. (NB) reincorporated in British Columbia 08/22/2005 which name changed to Andean American Gold Corp. 09/07/2010 which merged into Lupaka Gold Corp. 10/01/2012

EL PALENQUE VIVERO INC (NV)
Reorganized as A5 Laboratories Inc. 04/08/2010
Each share Common $0.001 par exchanged for (10) shares Common $0.001 par
A5 Laboratories Inc. name changed to Hydrogen Future Corp. 12/24/2013

EL PARAISO RES LTD (BC)
Name changed to Commonwealth Gold Corp. 10/28/1988
Commonwealth Gold Corp. merged into Aber Resources Ltd. (New) 04/19/1994 which name changed to Aber Diamond Corp. 08/18/2000 which name changed to Harry Winston Diamond Corp. 11/19/2007 which name changed to Dominion Diamond Corp. 03/27/2013
(See Dominion Diamond Corp.)

EL PASO CO (DE)
Merged into Burlington Northern Inc. 12/13/1983
Each share Common $3 par exchanged for (0.25) share Adjustable Rate Preferred no par and $12 cash
(See Burlington Northern Inc.)

EL PASO CORP (DE)
Each 9% Equity Security Unit automatically became (2.5063) shares Common $3 par 08/15/2005
Each share 4.99% 144A Conv. Perpetual Preferred 1¢ par exchanged for (77.2295) shares Common $3 par 03/11/2011
Each share 4.99% Conv. Perpetual Preferred 1¢ par exchanged for (77.2295) shares Common $3 par 03/11/2011
Merged into Kinder Morgan, Inc. (New) 05/25/2012
Each share Common $3 par exchanged for (0.4187) share Common 1¢ par and (0.64) Common Stock Purchase Warrant expiring 05/25/2017 and $14.65 cash

EL PASO CPG CO (DE)
Each Growth Preferred Redeemable Increased Dividend Equity Security exchanged for (0.662) share El Paso Corp. Common $3 par 08/16/2002
Each Income Preferred Redeemable Increased Dividend Equity Security exchanged for (0.662) share El Paso Corp. Common $3 par 08/16/2002

EL PASO ELEC CO (TX)
Stock Dividend - 100% 10/30/1951
Common no par changed to $5 par and (1) additional share issued 04/01/1957
Common $5 par changed to no par 05/19/1960
Common no par split (2) for (1) by issuance of (1) additional share 05/25/1961
$5.36 Preferred $100 par called for redemption 07/01/1963
$5.40 Preferred $100 par called for redemption 07/01/1963
Common no par split (3) for (2) by issuance of (0.5) additional share 05/28/1965
$10.75 Preferred no par called for redemption 01/02/1981
$8.44 Preferred no par called for redemption 10/01/1984
Plan of reorganization under Chapter 11 Federal Bankruptcy Code effective 02/12/1996
Each share $4.12 Preferred no par exchanged for (9.466) shares new Common no par
Each share $4.50 Preferred no par exchanged for (9.923) shares new Common no par
Each share $4.56 Preferred no par exchanged for (9.104) shares new Common no par
Each share $4.72 Preferred no par exchanged for (9.468) shares new Common no par
Each share $8.24 Preferred no par exchanged for (9.226) shares new Common no par
Each share $8.44 Preferred no par exchanged for (9.296) shares new Common no par
Each share $8.95 Preferred no par exchanged for (9.308) shares new Common no par
Each share $10.125 Preferred no par exchanged for (9.104) shares new Common no par
Each share 10.75% Preferred no par exchanged for (9.331) shares new Common no par
Each share old Common no par exchanged for (0.05064) share new Common no par
11.40% Preferred Ser. A $100 par called for redemption at $105.70 on 03/01/1999
(Additional Information in Active)

EL PASO ELECTRIC CO. (DE)
Dissolved 00/00/1944
Details not available

EL PASO ENERGY CORP (BC)
Recapitalized as E.L.E. Energy Corp. 10/05/1984
Each share Common no par exchanged for (0.5) share Common no par
E.L.E. Energy Corp. recapitalized as Maple Leaf Springs Water Corp. 11/12/1992 which recapitalized as International Maple Leaf Springs Ltd. 02/24/1998
(See International Maple Leaf Springs Ltd.)

EL PASO ENERGY CORP (DE)
Name changed to El Paso Corp. 02/05/2001
El Paso Corp. merged into Kinder Morgan, Inc. (New) 05/25/2012

EL PASO ENERGY PARTNERS L P (DE)
Preference Units called for redemption at $10.25 on 10/20/2000
Name changed to Gulfterra Energy Partners, L.P. 05/15/2003
Gulfterra Energy Partners, L.P. merged into Enterprise Products Partners L.P. 09/30/2004

EL PASO NAT GAS CO (DE)
Each share Common no par exchanged for (3) shares Common $3 par 00/00/1936
7% Preferred $100 par called for redemption 09/01/1946
$4.25 2nd Preferred 1950 Ser. no par called for redemption 11/01/1954
$4.40 2nd Preferred 1951 Ser. no par called for redemption 11/01/1954
$4.40 2nd Preferred 1952 Ser. no par called for redemption 01/03/1955
Common $3 par split (2) for (1) by issuance of (1) additional share 01/10/1957
$4.40 2nd Preferred 1954 Ser. no par called for redemption 04/26/1957
Class B Common $3 par reclassified as Common $3 par 01/01/1958
Common $3 par split (5) for (4) by issuance of (0.25) additional share 10/28/1960
4.1% 1st Preferred $100 par called for redemption 12/31/1965
4.25% 1st Preferred $100 par called for redemption 12/31/1965
5.36% 1st Preferred $100 par called for redemption 12/31/1965
5.5% 1st Preferred $100 par called for redemption 12/31/1965
5.5% 1st Preferred 1956 Ser. $100 par called for redemption 12/31/1965
5.65% 1st Preferred $100 par called for redemption 12/31/1965
5.68% 1st Preferred 1957 Ser. $100 par called for redemption 12/31/1965
6.4% 2nd Preferred 1957 Ser. $100 par called for redemption 12/31/1965
Stock Dividend - 200% 04/14/1949
Under plan of reorganization each share old Common $3 par automatically became (1) share El Paso Co. Common $3 par 06/13/1974
$5 2nd Preferred 1957 Ser. no par called for redemption 04/17/1980
14% Preference Ser. 1982 no par called for redemption 09/26/1985
15% Preferred 1981 Ser. no par called for redemption 09/26/1985
9.4% Depositary Preferred 1978 Ser. no par called for redemption 02/28/1986
9.4% Preferred 1978 Ser. no par called for redemption 02/28/1986
10.75% Preferred 1970 Ser. no par called for redemption 02/28/1986
5.125% Preferred 1965 Ser. no par called for redemption 12/01/1989
New Common $3 par split (2) for (1) by issuance of (1) additional share payable 04/01/1998 to holders of record 03/13/1998
Under plan of reorganization each share new Common $3 par automatically became (1) share El

Paso Energy Corp. Common $3 par 08/01/1998
El Paso Energy Corp. name changed to El Paso Corp. 02/05/2001 which merged into Kinder Morgan, Inc. (New) 05/25/2012

EL PASO NATL BK (EL PASO, TX)
Each share Capital Stock $100 par exchanged for (5) shares Capital Stock $20 par 00/00/1945
Stock Dividends - 11-11111111% 06/27/1945 50% 06/29/1946; 10% 01/18/1949; 20% 12/26/1950; 14.2857% 12/17/1952; 25% 11/05/1954; 16.66666666% 01/23/1958; 11.11111111% 04/03/1961
99.97% acquired by Trans Texas Bancorporation, Inc. through purchase offer which expired 12/31/1979
Public interest eliminated

EL PASO NATL CORP (TX)
Merged into Texas Commerce Bancshares, Inc. 09/01/1982
Each share Common $5 par exchanged for $62.50 cash

EL PASO PIPELINE PARTNERS L P (DE)
Merged into Kinder Morgan, Inc. 11/26/2014
Each Common Unit exchanged for (0.9451) share Common 1¢ par and $4.65 cash

EL PASO REAL ESTATE INVESTMENT TRUST (TX)
Name changed to Property Trust of America (TX) 04/06/1970
Property Trust of America (TX) reincorporated in Maryland 06/29/1982 which merged into Security Capital Pacific Trust 03/23/1995 which name changed to Archstone Communities Trust 07/07/1998 which name changed to Archstone-Smith Trust 10/29/2001
(See Archstone-Smith Trust)

EL PASO REFINERY L P (DE)
Chapter 11 bankruptcy proceedings converted to Chapter 7 on 11/10/1993
Stockholders' equity unlikely

EL PASO TENN PIPELINE CO (DE)
8.25% Ser. A Preferred no par called for redemption at $50 plus $0.55 accrued dividends on 05/18/2005

EL PEN-REY MINES, LTD.
Name changed to El Pen-Rey Oil & Mines, Ltd. 00/00/1950
(See El Pen-Rey Oil & Mines, Ltd.)

EL PEN-REY OIL & MINES, LTD. (ON)
Charter cancelled and company declared dissolved for default in filing returns 00/00/1961

EL POLLO ASADO INC (AZ)
Chapter 11 Federal Bankruptcy Code converted to Chapter 7 on 05/14/1990
No stockholders' equity

EL SEGUNDO FIRST NATIONAL BANK (EL SEGUNDO, CA)
Under plan of reorganization each share Common $5 par automatically became (1) share First Coastal Bank, N.A. (El Segundo, CA) Common $1 par 01/01/1994
First Coastal Bank, N.A. (El Segundo, CA) reorganized as First Coastal Bancshares 06/23/1997

EL SITIO INC (BRITISH VIRGIN ISLANDS)
Each share Common 1¢ par exchanged for (0.1) share Common 10¢ par 08/22/2001
Merged into Claxson Interactive Group Inc. 09/21/2001
Each share Common 10¢ par exchanged for (1) share Class A Common 1¢ par

(See Claxson Interactive Group Inc.)

EL SOL GOLD MINES, LTD. (ON)
Name changed to El Sol Mining Ltd. 06/27/1957
El Sol Mining Ltd. recapitalized as Tex-Sol Explorations Ltd. 09/14/1964 which merged into Dominion Explorers Inc. (Old) 07/19/1985 which merged into Dominion Explorers Inc. (New) 12/31/1994 which merged into Neutrino Resources Inc. 02/28/1997
(See Neutrino Resources Inc.)

EL SOL MINING LTD. (ON)
Recapitalized as Tex-Sol Explorations Ltd. 09/14/1964
Each share Capital Stock $1 par exchanged for (0.2) share Capital Stock $1 par
Tex-Sol Explorations Ltd. merged into Dominion Explorers Inc. (Old) 07/19/1985 which merged into Dominion Explorers Inc. (New) 12/31/1994 which merged into Neutrino Resources Inc. 02/28/1997
(See Neutrino Resources Inc.)

EL TACO MINN INC (MN)
Name changed to Zapata International Inc. 07/07/1969
Zapata International Inc. name changed to Zapata Foods Inc. 07/01/1971 which merged into Heublein, Inc. 07/17/1974 which merged into Reynolds (R.J.) Industries, Inc. 10/13/1982 which name changed to RJR Nabisco, Inc. 04/25/1986
(See RJR Nabisco, Inc.)

EL TEJON OIL & REFINING CORP.
Merged into Douglas Oil Co. of California 00/00/1946
Details not available

EL TIGRE DEV CORP (NV)
Recapitalized as Associated Media Holdings, Inc. 11/02/2005
Each share Common $0.001 par exchanged for (0.01) share Common $0.001 par
Associated Media Holdings, Inc. recapitalized as N I S Holdings, Corp. 03/16/2010 which name changed to E-Rewards Network Inc. 08/16/2013 which name changed to Rewards Nexus Inc. 10/02/2013 which recapitalized as One Step Vending, Corp. 04/06/2015

EL TIGRE SILVER CORP (BC)
Reincorporated 07/09/2013
Place of incorporation changed from (Canada) to (BC) 07/09/2013
Merged into Oceanus Resources Corp. 11/24/2015
Each share Common no par exchanged for (0.2839) share Common no par
Note: Unexchanged certificates will be cancelled and become without value 11/24/2021

EL TORITO RESTAURANTS INC (CA)
Merged into Grace (W.R.) & Co. 02/17/1987
Each share Common 1¢ par exchanged for $20.50 cash

EL TORO MINES LTD.
Reorganized as El Toro Yellowknife Mines Ltd. 00/00/1946
Each share Common exchanged for (60) shares Common
(See El Toro Yellowknife Mines Ltd.)

EL TORO YELLOWKNIFE MINES, LTD. (ON)
Charter cancelled and company declared dissolved for default in filing returns 03/00/1957

EL TRONICS INC (PA)
Each share 3% Preferred exchanged for (10) shares old Common no par 11/10/1960
Each share Common 5¢ par

exchanged for (0.2) share old Common no par 11/10/1960
Each share old Common no par exchanged for (0.33333333) share new Common no par 08/07/1968
Name changed to ELT, Inc. 01/04/1974
ELT, Inc. name changed to Dutch Boy, Inc. 02/23/1977 which name changed to Artra Group Inc. 12/31/1980 which merged into Entrade Inc. 09/23/1999
(See Entrade Inc.)

ELAN AIR CORP (MA)
Reorganized under Chapter 11 Federal Bankruptcy Code 03/25/1983
No stockholders' equity

ELAN CORP PLC (IRELAND)
Sponsored ADR's for Ordinary split (3) for (2) by issuance of (0.5) additional ADR 06/12/1987
Sponsored ADR's for Ordinary split (3) for (2) by issuance of (0.5) additional ADR 08/19/1992
Sponsored ADR's for Ordinary split (2) for (1) by issuance of (1) additional ADR payable 08/22/1996 to holders of record 08/15/1996
Ex date - 08/23/1996
Sponsored ADR's for Ordinary split (2) for (1) by issuance of (1) additional ADR payable 06/04/1999 to holders of record 05/27/1999
Ex date - 06/07/1999
Each Sponsored ADR for Ordinary received distribution of (0.02439024) share Prothena Corp. PLC Ordinary 1¢ par payable 12/21/2012 to holders of record 12/14/2012
Ex date - 12/21/2012
Merged into Perrigo Co. PLC 12/18/2013
Each Sponsored ADR for Ordinary exchanged for (0.07636) share Ordinary EUR 0.001 par and $6.25 cash

ELAN DEV INC (NV)
Common $0.001 par split (3) for (1) by issuance of (2) additional shares payable 03/05/2008 to holders of record 03/05/2008 Ex date - 03/05/2008
Name changed to Star Gold Corp. 06/25/2008

ELAN ENERGY INC (AB)
Merged into Ranger Oil Ltd. (Canada) 10/09/1997
Each share Common no par exchanged for (0.501913) share Common no par and $3.849442 cash
Ranger Oil Ltd. (Canada) merged into Canadian Natural Resources Ltd. 07/28/2000

ELAN INDS INC (BC)
Recapitalized as Trylox Environmental Corp. (BC) 08/17/1990
Each share Common no par exchanged for (0.25) share Common no par
Trylox Environmental Corp. (BC) reincorporated in Wyoming 09/14/1990
(See Trylox Environmental Corp. (WY))

ELAN PHARMACEUTICAL RESH CORP (DE)
Common 1¢ par split (3) for (2) by issuance of (0.5) additional share 02/04/1983
Merged into Elan Corp., PLC 02/01/1984
Each share Common 1¢ par exchanged for (1) Sponsored ADR for Ordinary
Elan Corp., PLC merged into Perrigo Co. PLC 12/18/2013

ELANA AGRIC LD OPPORTUNITY FD REIT (BULGARIA)
GDR agreement terminated 08/12/2014
No GDR's remain outstanding

ELANCRA MINES LTD.
Liquidated 00/00/1951
No stockholders' equity

ELANDIA INTL INC (DE)
Name changed 04/21/2008
Name changed from eLandia, Inc. to eLandia International, Inc. 04/21/2008
Each share old Common $0.00001 par exchanged for (0.0001) share new Common $0.00001 par 05/16/2012
Note: In effect holders received $0.65 cash per share and public interest was eliminated

ELANDSRAND GOLD MNG LTD (SOUTH AFRICA)
Merged into AngloGold Ltd. 06/29/1998
Each ADR for Ordinary ZAR 20 par exchanged for (1) Sponsored ADR for Ordinary ZAR 50 par
AngloGold Ltd. name changed to AngloGold Ashanti Ltd. 04/26/2004

ELANOR MANOR APT CO (DE)
Liquidation completed
Each share Common $1 par exchanged for initial distribution of $113 cash 08/15/1968
Each share Common $1 par received second and final distrubution of $4.50 cash 12/31/1968

ELANTEC SEMICONDUCTOR INC (DE)
Common 1¢ par split (2) for (1) by issuance of (1) additional share payable 04/21/2000 to holders of record 04/07/2000 Ex date - 04/24/2000
Merged into Intersil Corp. 05/14/2002
Each share Common 1¢ par exchanged for (1.24) shares Class A Common 1¢ par and $8 cash
(See Intersil Corp.)

ELAST TECHNOLOGIES INC (NV)
Each share old Common $0.001 par exchanged for (0.1) share new Common $0.001 par 12/20/2000
Recapitalized as PTS Inc. 6/28/2001
Each share Common $0.001 par exchanged for (0.05) share Common $0.001 par

ELASTIC NETWORKS INC (DE)
Merged into Paradyne Networks, Inc. 03/05/2002
Each share Common 1¢ par exchanged for (0.2288) share Common $0.001 par
Paradyne Networks, Inc. merged into Zhone Technologies, Inc. 09/01/2005 which name changed to DASAN Zhone Solutions, Inc. 09/12/2016

ELASTIC STOP NUT CORP.
Name changed to Elastic Stop Nut Corp. of America in 1943
Elastic Stop Nut Corp. of America merged into Amerace Esna Corp. 8/30/68 which name changed to Amerace Corp. 4/27/73
(See Amerace Corp.)

ELASTIC STOP NUT CORP. OF AMERICA (NJ)
6% Conv. Preferred $50 par called for redemption 8/15/46
Common $1 par split (2) for (1) by issuance of (1) additional share 4/25/67
Merged into Amerace Esna Corp. 8/30/68
Each share Common $1 par exchanged for (1) share $2.60 Conv. Preferred Ser. A $10 par
Amerace Esna Corp. name changed to Amerace Corp. 4/27/73

(See Amerace Corp.)

ELATERITE BASIN URANIUM CO. (UT)
Merged into Sun Tide Corp. 11/15/1957
Each share Capital Stock $2.50 par exchanged for (1) share Capital Stock 10¢ par
Sun Tide Corp. name changed to Maxa Corp. 04/13/1974
(See Maxa Corp.)

ELBA INTL INC (UT)
Involuntarily dissolved for failure to file reports and pay fees 12/01/1986

ELBA SYS CORP (CO)
Common no par split (2) for (1) by issuance of (1) additional share 3/31/69
Liquidation completed
Each share Common no par received initial distribution of $1 cash 9/30/75
Each share Common no par received second distribution of $1 cash 4/20/76
Each share Common no par received third distribution of $1 cash 8/18/76
Name changed to ESC Liquidating Co. 12/20/76
(See ESC Liquidating Co.)

ELBIT LTD (ISRAEL)
Name changed 7/2/91
Ordinary Stock IS3 par changed to NIS 0.003 par per currency change 1/1/86
Name changed from Elbit Computers Ltd. to Elbit Ltd. 7/2/91
Each share Ordinary NIS0.003 par received distribution of (1) share Elbit Medical Imaging Ltd. Common and (1) share Elbit Systems Ltd. Ordinary NIS1 par payable 11/27/96 to holders of record 11/26/96
Merged into Elron Electronic Industries Ltd. 5/15/2002
Each share Ordinary NIS0.003 par exchanged for (0.45) share Ordinary NIS0.003 par

ELBIT MED IMAGING LTD (ISRAEL)
Name changed to Elbit Imaging Ltd. 12/04/2007

ELBIT VISION SYS LTD (ISRAEL)
Each share Ordinary ILS 1 par exchanged for (0.1) share Ordinary ILS 10 par 03/27/2017
Acquired by Uster Technologies AG 04/25/2018
Each share Ordinary ILS 10 par exchanged for $3.40 cash

ELCO CORP (PA)
Reincorporated 11/30/1965
Reincorporated 12/30/1971
State of incorporation changed from (PA) to (DE) 11/30/1965
Common 25¢ par split (2) for (1) by issuance of (1) additional share 02/28/1966
State of incorporation changed from (DE) to (PA) 12/30/1971
Merged into Gulf & Western Industries, Inc. 08/16/1974
Each share Common 25¢ par exchanged for $8.50 cash

ELCO INDS INC (DE)
Common $5 par split (2) for (1) by issuance of (1) additional share 6/20/69
Common $5 par split (3) for (2) by issuance of (0.5) additional share 6/29/84
Common $5 par split (2) for (1) by issuance of (1) additional share 10/3/88
Merged into Textron Inc. 10/20/95
Each share Common $5 par exchanged for $36 cash

ELCO INVESTMENT CO. (OH)
Completely liquidated 12/27/1966
Each share Common $2.50 par exchanged for first and final distribution of (3.11) shares Scudder, Stevens & Clark Common Stock Fund, Inc. Capital Stock $1 par
Scudder, Stevens & Clark Common Stock Fund, Inc. name changed to Scudder Common Stock Fund, Inc. 03/07/1979 which name changed to Scudder Growth & Income Fund 12/31/1984
(See Scudder Growth & Income Fund)

ELCO TOOL & SCREW CORP (IL)
Reincorporated under the laws of Delaware as Elco Industries, Inc. 6/9/69
(See Elco Industries, Inc.)

ELCOR CORP (DE)
Name changed 10/26/76
Name changed from Elcor Chemical Corp. to Elcor Corp. 10/26/76
Common $1 par split (2) for (1) by issuance of (1) additional share 5/28/87
Common $1 par split (3) for (2) by issuance of (0.5) additional share payable 11/12/97 to holders of record 10/16/97 Ex date - 11/13/97
Common $1 par split (3) for (2) by issuance of (0.5) additional share payable 8/11/99 to holders of record 7/15/99 Ex date - 8/12/99
Name changed to ElkCorp 9/1/2002
(See ElkCorp)

ELCOR GOLD MINES LTD. (ON)
Charter cancelled 4/1/63

ELCORA RES CORP (CANADA)
Name changed to Elcora Advanced Materials Corp. 02/10/2016

ELCOTEL INC (DE)
Common 1¢ par split (3) for (2) by issuance of (0.5) additional share 5/14/87
Plan of reorganization under Chapter 11 Federal Bankruptcy Code effective 12/31/2003
No stockholders' equity

ELDEC CORP (WA)
Merged into Crane Co. 3/18/94
Each share Common 5¢ par exchanged for $13 cash

ELDER & JOHNSTON CO. (OH)
Name changed to Elder-Beerman Stores Corp. 5/4/62
(See Elder-Beerman Stores Corp.)

ELDER BEERMAN STORES CORP (OH)
7% Preferred $100 par called for redemption 2/1/65
Each share Common $10 par exchanged for (10) shares Common no par 9/1/66
Stock Dividends - 10% 7/30/76; 10% 7/29/77; 10% 7/28/78; 10% 7/30/82; 10% 1/16/84; 10% 1/21/85; 15% 1/21/86
Acquired by E-B Acquisition Corp. 8/31/87
Each share Common no par exchanged for $33 cash

ELDER BEERMAN STORES CORP NEW (OH)
Merged into Bon-Ton Stores, Inc. 10/24/2003
Each share Common no par exchanged for $8 cash

ELDER GOLD MINES LTD. (ON)
Name changed to Elder Mines, Ltd. in 1946
Elder Mines, Ltd. name changed to Elder Mines & Developments Ltd. 8/14/59 which name changed to Elder-Peel Ltd. 8/7/62 which recapitalized as Peel-Elder Ltd. 12/30/63 which merged into Hambro Canada Ltd. 12/5/74 which name changed to Hatleigh Corp. (Old) 8/3/78 which merged into Hatleigh Corp. (New) 8/31/78 which merged into Dexleigh Corp. 6/30/84
(See Dexleigh Corp.)

ELDER MFG CO (MO)
Each share Common $10 par exchanged for (0.25) share Common no par in 1927
Each share Common no par exchanged for (4) shares Common $7.50 par in 1946
Out of business in 1988
Details not available

ELDER MINES & DEVELOPMENTS LTD. (ON)
Name changed to Elder-Peel Ltd. 8/7/62
Elder-Peel Ltd. recapitalized as Peel-Elder Ltd. 12/30/63 which merged into Hambro Canada Ltd. 12/5/74 which name changed to Hatleigh Corp. (Old) 8/3/78 which merged into Hatleigh Corp. (New) 8/31/78 which merged into Dexleigh Corp. 6/30/84
(See Dexleigh Corp.)

ELDER MINES LTD. (ON)
Name changed to Elder Mines & Developments Ltd. 8/14/59
Elder Mines & Developments Ltd. name changed to Elder-Peel Ltd. 8/7/62 which recapitalized as Peel-Elder Ltd. 12/30/63 which merged into Hambro Canada Ltd. 12/5/74 which name changed to Hatleigh Corp. (Old) 8/3/78 which merged into Hatleigh Corp. (New) 8/31/78 which merged into Dexleigh Corp. 6/30/84
(See Dexleigh Corp.)

ELDER-PEEL LTD. (ON)
Recapitalized as Peel-Elder Ltd. 12/30/63
Each share Capital Stock $1 par exchanged for (0.1) share Capital Stock no par
Peel-Elder Ltd. merged into Hambro Canada Ltd. 12/5/74 which name changed to Hatleigh Corp. (Old) 8/3/78 which merged into Hatleigh Corp. (New) 8/31/78 which merged into Dexleigh Corp. 6/30/84
(See Dexleigh Corp.)

ELDER PHARMACEUTICALS LTD (INDIA)
GDR agreement terminated 04/23/2015
No GDR's remain outstanding

ELDER-RED LAKE GOLD MINES LTD.
Acquired by Britt-Malartic Gold Mines Ltd. in 1940
Details not available

ELDER TECHNOLOGIES LTD (BC)
Struck off register and declared dissolved for failure to file returns 02/21/1992

ELDERCARE CTRS INC (CA)
Name changed to National Accommodations, Inc. 9/21/70
(See National Accommodations, Inc.)

ELDERIDGE GOLD MINES LTD.
Acquired by Elder Mines Ltd. on a (0.125) for (1) basis in 1946
Elder Mines Ltd. name changed to Elder Mines & Developments Ltd. 8/14/59 which name was changed to Elder-Peel Ltd. 8/7/62 which was recapitalized as Peel-Elder Ltd. 12/30/63 which merged into Hambro Canada Ltd. which name changed to Hatleigh Corp. (Old) 8/3/78 which merged into Hatleigh Corp. (New) 8/31/78 which merged into Dexleigh Corp. 6/30/84
(See Dexleigh Corp.)

ELDERS IXL CDA INC (ON)
Name changed to Foster's Brewing Group Canada Inc. 02/18/1991
(See Foster's Brewing Group Canada Inc.)

ELDERS IXL LTD (AUSTRALIA)
Each Unsponsored ADR for Ordinary exchanged for (1) Sponsored ADR for Ordinary 04/01/1987
Stock Dividends - 33.33333333% 12/19/1986; 0.14285714% 05/29/1987; 25% 04/18/1988; 20% 11/18/1988; 16.66666666% 01/02/1990
Name changed to Foster's Brewing Group Ltd. 11/30/1990
Foster's Brewing Group Ltd. name changed to Foster's Group Ltd. 07/03/2001
(See Foster's Group Ltd.)

ELDERTRUST (MD)
Merged into Ventas, Inc. 02/05/2004
Each Common Share of Bene. Int. 1¢ par exchanged for $12.50 cash

ELDERWATCH INC (FL)
Common $0.001 par split (3) for (2) by issuance of (0.5) additional share payable 05/08/2006 to holders of record 05/08/2006 Ex date - 05/09/2006
Reincorporated under the laws of Nevada as Energtek Inc. 09/28/2006

ELDON INDS INC (DE)
Reincorporated 06/15/1987
Class B Common $1 par reclassified as Common $1 par 03/24/1969
Common $1 par split (3) for (2) by issuance of (0.5) additional share 12/15/1969
Common $1 par split (5) for (4) by issuance of (0.25) additional share 07/01/1985
Stock Dividends - 10% 09/30/1980; 10% 10/02/1981; 50% 07/01/1982; 25% 06/30/1983; 10% 06/29/1984
State of incorporation changed from (CA) to (DE) and Common $1 par changed to 1¢ par 06/15/1987
Common 1¢ par split (5) for (4) by issuance of (0.25) additional share 06/30/1987
Common 1¢ par split (5) for (4) by issuance of (0.25) additional share 06/30/1988
Common 1¢ par split (4) for (3) by issuance of (0.33333333) additional share 06/29/1989
Acquired by Rubbermaid, Inc. 10/29/1990
Each share Common 1¢ par exchanged for (0.632) share Common $1 par
Rubbermaid, Inc. merged into Newell Rubbermaid Inc. 03/24/1999 which name changed to Newell Brands Inc. 04/18/2016

ELDON RES LTD (BC)
Recapitalized as KSAT Satellite Networks, Inc. (BC) 02/09/1998
Each share Common no par exchanged for (0.33333333) share Common no par
KSAT Satellite Networks, Inc. (BC) reincorporated in Yukon 04/14/1998
(See KSAT Satellite Networks, Inc.)

ELDONA GOLD MINES LTD. (ON)
Recapitalized as D'Eldona Gold Mines Ltd. 00/00/1952
Each share Capital Stock $1 par exchanged for (0.33333333) share Capital Stock $1 par
D'Eldona Gold Mines Ltd. merged into D'Eldona Resources Ltd. 10/15/1984 which recapitalized as Western D'Eldona Resources Ltd. 06/01/1988
(See Western D'Eldona Resources Ltd.)

ELDORADO BANCORP (CA)
Common no par split (5) for (4) by issuance of (0.25) additional share 12/16/1981
Stock Dividends - 10% 01/19/1983; 10% 05/21/1986; 10% 04/17/1987; 10% 12/04/1987; 10% 02/24/1989; 10% 02/23/1990; 10% 12/26/1995
Merged into Commerce Security Bancorp, Inc. 06/06/1997
Each share Common no par exchanged for $23 cash

ELDORADO BANCSHARES INC (DE)
Each share Common 1¢ par exchanged for (0.5) share Common 1¢ par 09/04/1998
Merged into Zions Bancorporation 03/30/2001
Each share Common 1¢ par exchanged for (0.23) share Common no par
Zions Bancorporation merged into Zions Bancorporation, N.A. (Salt Lake City, UT) 10/01/2018

ELDORADO BK (TUSTIN, CA)
Capital Stock $5 par changed to $2.50 par and (1) additional share issued 07/12/1976
Capital Stock $2.50 par changed to $1.25 par and (1) additional share issued 05/26/1978
Stock Dividends - 10% 01/21/1977; 10% 01/20/1978; 10% 01/10/1979; 10% 01/09/1980; 20% 01/27/1981
Under plan of reorganization each share Capital Stock $1.25 par automatically became (1) share Eldorado Bancorp Common $1.25 par 08/06/1981
(See Eldorado Bancorp)

ELDORADO CORP (BERMUDA)
Reincorporated under the laws of Canada as Eldorado Gold Corp. (Old) 06/28/1996
Eldorado Gold Corp. (Old) merged into Eldorado Gold Corp. (New) 11/19/1996

ELDORADO ELECTRODATA CORP (CA)
Adjudicated bankrupt 01/02/1975
Stockholders' equity unlikely

ELDORADO FINL GROUP INC (NV)
Reincorporated 06/27/2001
State of incorporation changed from (FL) to (NV) 06/27/2001
Name changed to Composite Technology Corp. 12/03/2001
(See Composite Technology Corp.)

ELDORADO FUND, INC. (DE)
Completely liquidated 01/18/1980
Each share Common $1 par received first and final distribution of $8.052 cash

ELDORADO GEN CORP (CA)
Charter suspended for failure to file reports and pay fees 07/01/1982

ELDORADO GOLD & EXPL INC (FL)
Recapitalized as Eldorado Financial Group Inc. (FL) 01/13/1987
Each share Common $0.001 par exchanged for (0.05) share Common $0.001 par
Eldorado Financial Group Inc. (FL) reincorporated in Nevada 06/27/2001 which name changed to Composite Technology Corp. 12/03/2001
(See Composite Technology Corp.)

ELDORADO GOLD CORP OLD (CANADA)
Merged into Eldorado Gold Corp. (New) 11/19/1996
Each share Common no par exchanged for (1) share Common no par

ELDORADO INS CO (CA)
Capital Stock $1 par changed to $1.10 par 03/12/1969
Each share Capital Stock $1.10 par exchanged for (0.002) share Capital Stock $550 par 10/19/1970
Note: Holders of fewer than (500) shares received $3 cash per share

ELDORADO MANAGEMENT CO. (CA)
Acquired by Eldorado General Corp. 01/01/1969
Each share Common no par exchanged for (1) share Capital Stock $1 par
(See Eldorado General Corp.)

ELDORADO MINERALS & PETE CORP (BC)
Struck off register and declared dissolved for failure to file returns 05/28/1993

ELDORADO MINING & REFINING LTD.
Appropriated by the Canadian Government 00/00/1944
No stockholders' equity

ELDORADO MTR CORP (KS)
Charter forfeited for failure to file annual reports 01/15/1991

ELDORADO ORE CORP (WA)
Recapitalized as Adaptive Technologies Inc. (WA) 10/18/1995
Each share Common no par exchanged for (0.05) share Common no par
Adaptive Technologies Inc. (WA) name changed to Atlantic Pacific International Inc. 07/16/1997 which reincorporated in Nevada as API Dental, Inc. 07/30/1999
(See API Dental, Inc.)

ELDORADO URANIUM CORP. (NV)
Recapitalized as Al-Kem, Inc. 10/27/1955
Each share Common 1¢ par exchanged for (0.02887142) share Common 35¢ par
(See Al-Kem, Inc.)

ELDREDGE & CO INC (NY)
Dissolved by proclamation 03/25/1992

ELDRICH MINES LTD. (ON)
Name changed to Canadian-Australian Exploration Ltd. 04/01/1963
Canadian-Australian Exploration Ltd. recapitalized as Win-Eldrich Mines Ltd. 06/21/1965

ELE CAP CORP (BC)
Name changed to Lero Gold Corp. 07/27/2006
Lero Gold Corp. merged into European Minerals Corp. (British Virgin Islands) 06/19/2008 which name changed to Orsu Metals Corp. 07/14/2008

ELEC COMMUNICATIONS CORP (NY)
Name changed to Pervasip Corp. 02/21/2008

ELECSYS CORP (KS)
Acquired by Lindsay Corp. 01/22/2015
Each share Common 1¢ par exchanged for $17.50 cash

ELECTONE INC (DE)
Merged into Seltig, Inc. 01/31/1980
Each share Common 10¢ par exchanged for $3.75 cash

ELECTRA GOLD LTD (BC)
Each share old Common no par exchanged for (0.1) share new Common no par 07/21/2014
Name changed to Electra Stone Ltd. 02/02/2015

ELECTRA MED INTL INC (UT)
Each share old Common $0.001 par exchanged for (0.001) share new Common $0.001 par 12/27/1995
Reorganized as Sports Vision Technology, Inc. 04/02/1996
Each share new Common $0.001 par exchanged for (0.03333333) share Common $0.001 par

ELECTRA MNG CONS LTD (BC)
Recapitalized 08/21/1992
Recapitalized from Electra North West Resources Ltd. to Electra Mining Consolidated Ltd. 08/21/1992
Each share Common no par exchanged for (0.2) share Common no par
Name changed to Electra Gold Ltd. 02/19/1997
Electra Gold Ltd. name changed to Electra Stone Ltd. 02/02/2015

ELECTRA PORCUPINE GOLD MINES LTD. (ON)
Recapitalized as New Electra Porcupine Gold Mines Ltd. 00/00/1944
Each share Capital Stock $1 par exchanged for (0.33333333) share Capital Stock $1 par
New Electra Porcupine Gold Mines Ltd. merged into Pardee Amalgamated Mines Ltd. 12/00/1954 which liquidated for Rio Algom Mines Ltd. 11/09/1961 which name changed to Rio Algom Ltd. 04/30/1975
(See Rio Algom Ltd.)

ELECTRA RES CORP (BC)
Merged into Electra North West Resources Ltd. 12/01/1981
Each share Common no par exchanged for (1) share Common no par
Electra North West Resources Ltd. recapitalized as Electra Mining Consolidated Ltd. 08/21/1992 which name changed to Electra Gold Ltd. 02/07/1997 which name changed to Electra Stone Ltd. 02/02/2015

ELECTRA SYSTEMS CORP. (CA)
Dissolution approved 08/18/1964
No stockholders' equity

ELECTRA TITLE CORP (BC)
Recapitalized as B.I. Ventures Ltd. 02/13/1987
Each share Common no par exchanged for (0.2) share Common no par
(See B.I. Ventures Ltd.)

ELECTRA TRONICS INC (FL)
Common 75¢ par changed to $0.375 par and (1) additional share issued 01/02/1981
Each share Common $0.375 par exchanged for (3) shares Common $0.125 par 01/15/1985
Administratively dissolved 10/09/1992

ELECTRACAPITAL INC (NV)
SEC revoked common stock registration 03/25/2011

ELECTRADA CORP. (DE)
Common $1 par changed to no par 06/03/1964
Name changed to Sargent Industries, Inc. (DE) 05/26/1966
(See Sargent Industries, Inc. (DE))

ELECTRIC & GAS TECHNOLOGY INC (TX)
Each share old Common 1¢ par received distribution of (0.15873015) share Tech Electro Industries, Inc. Common $0.001 par payable 08/04/1992 to holders of record 03/10/1992
Each share old Common 1¢ par exchanged for (0.75) share new Common 1¢ par 06/11/2001
Company terminated common stock registration and is no longer public as of 11/14/2007

ELECTRIC & MUSICAL INDS LTD (ENGLAND)
Ordinary Reg. £1 par changed to 10s par 00/00/1934
Recapitalized 01/01/1962
4.5% 1st Preference £1 par reclassified as 5% Preference £1 par
5.5% 2nd Preference £1 par reclassified as 5.75% Preference £1 par
Ordinary Reg. 10s par split (2) for (1) by issuance of (1) additional share 06/12/1964
American Shares for Ordinary Reg. 10s par split (2) for (1) by issuance of (1) additional share 07/07/1964
Stock Dividends - Ordinary Reg. - 33.33333333% 12/11/1958; 50% 12/10/1959; American Shares for Ordinary Reg. - 33.33333333% 01/16/1959; 50% 01/20/1960
Name changed to EMI Ltd. 01/01/1971
EMI Ltd. merged into Thorn EMI Ltd. 03/28/1980 which name changed to EMI Group PLC 08/19/1996
(See EMI Group PLC)

ELECTRIC & PEOPLES TRACTION CO.
Acquired by Philadelphia Transportation Co. in 1940
Each Stock Trust Certificate exchanged for $168.22 principal amount of 3%-6% Consolidated Mortgage Bonds and (4.147) shares $1 Part. Preferred $20 par
Philadelphia Transportation Co. completed liquidation 11/20/73

ELECTRIC AQUAGENICS UNLIMITED INC (DE)
Name changed to EAU Technologies, Inc. 2/13/2007

ELECTRIC AUTO-LITE CO. (OH)
Common no par changed to $5 par in 1933
Merged into Eltra Corp. 6/28/63
Each share Common $5 par exchanged for (1.88) shares $1.40 Conv. Preferred $34.50 par
(See Eltra Corp.)

ELECTRIC AVE INC (MN)
Statutorily dissolved 12/30/94

ELECTRIC BOAT CO. (NJ)
Name changed to General Dynamics Corp. in 1952

ELECTRIC BOND & SHARE CO. (NY)
Each share Common no par exchanged for (0.333333) share Common $5 par in 1932
Each share $6 Preferred no par and $5 Preferred no par stamped to indicate a distribution of $30 per share and a reduction to $4.20 and $3.50 Preferred no par respectively 11/23/46
Name changed to Ebasco Industries Inc. 5/9/68
Ebasco Industries Inc. merged into Boise Cascade Corp. 8/31/69 which name changed to OfficeMax Inc. 11/1/2004

ELECTRIC BOND & SHARE SECURITIES CORP.
Merged into Electric Bond & Share Co. in 1929
Details not available

ELECTRIC CAR CO AMER INC (DE)
Charter cancelled and declared inoperative and void for non-payment of taxes 3/1/82

ELECTRIC CITY CORP (DE)
Old Common $0.0001 par split (2) for (1) by issuance of (1) additional share payable 07/30/1999 to holders of record 07/29/1999
Each (15) shares old Common $0.0001 par exchanged for (1) share new Common $0.0001 par 06/15/2006
Name changed to Lime Energy Co. 09/22/2006

ELECTRIC CITY SUPPLY CO. (CO)
Proclaimed defunct and inoperative for failure to pay taxes 10/11/61

ELECTRIC CONTROLLER & MANUFACTURING CO. (OH)
Each share Common no par exchanged for (3) shares Common $5 par in 1951
Merged into Square D Co. on a (1.5) for (1) basis 12/30/55

ELECTRIC ENTMT INTL INC (NV)
Recapitalized as Private Media Group Ltd. 12/16/1997
Each share Common $0.001 par exchanged for (0.2) share Common $0.001 par

(See Private Media Group Ltd.)

ELECTRIC FUEL CORP (DE)
Name changed to Arotech Corp. 9/16/2003

ELECTRIC HOSE & RUBR CO (DE)
Each share Common $100 par exchanged for (10) shares Common $10 par 00/00/1947
Common $10 par changed to $5 par and (1) additional share issued 06/05/1969
Stock Dividends - 50% 10/20/1950; 50% 12/21/1953; 25% 11/25/1955; 50% 12/17/1959; 25% 10/18/1963
Merged into Dayco Corp. (DE) 05/15/1978
Each share Common $5 par exchanged for (0.5121) share Common $1 par
Dayco Corp. (DE) reincorporated in Michigan 08/31/1982 which name changed to Day International Corp. 02/23/1987
(See Day International Corp.)

ELECTRIC HOUSEHOLD UTILITIES CORP.
Name changed to Thor Corp. (Ill.) in 1947
Thor Corp. (Ill.) name changed to Allied Paper Corp, 10/5/56
(See Allied Paper Corp.)

ELECTRIC INVESTORS, INC.
Acquired by Electric Bond & Share Co. in 1929
Details not available

ELECTRIC LIGHT & POWER CO. OF ABINGTON AND ROCKLAND
Merged into Eastern Utilities Associates 00/00/1928
Details not available

ELECTRIC LIGHTWAVE INC (DE)
Issue Information - 8,000,000 shares COM offered at $16 per share on 11/24/1997
Merged into Citizens Communications Co. 6/20/2002
Each share Class A Common 1¢ par exchanged for $0.70 cash

ELECTRIC M & R INC (DE)
Each share old Common $1 par exchanged for (0.00002) share new Common $1 par 12/30/96
Note: In effect holders received $0.25 cash per share and public interest was eliminated

ELECTRIC MAIL INC (BC)
Recapitalized as ELE Capital Corp. 03/31/2004
Each share Common no par exchanged for (0.1) share Common no par and $0.47 cash
ELE Capital Corp. name changed to Lero Gold Corp. 07/27/2006 which merged into European Minerals Corp. (British Virgin Islands) 06/19/2008 which name changed to Orsu Metals Corp. 07/14/2008

ELECTRIC METALS INC (BC)
Merged into Moimstone Corp. 09/12/2013
Each share Class A Common no par exchanged for (1) share Common no par
Moimstone Corp. name changed to Apivio Systems Inc. 05/23/2014
(See Apivio Systems Inc.)

ELECTRIC MOTO CORP (DE)
Recapitalized as Empire Diversified Energy, Inc. 12/22/2014
Each share Common $0.00001 par exchanged par

ELECTRIC NETWORK COM INC (DE)
Reincorporated 3/31/2004
State of incorporation changed from (NV) to (DE) 3/31/2004
Name changed to Solar Energy Sources, Inc. 6/21/2006
Solar Energy Sources, Inc. name changed to SES Solar, Inc. 8/21/2006

ELECTRIC POWER & LIGHT CORP.
Liquidated in 1949

ELECTRIC POWER ASSOCIATES, INC.
Dissolved in 1939

ELECTRIC POWER DOOR CO., INC. (MN)
Class A Common $5 par reclassified as Common 10¢ par 10/11/1960
Name changed to Electric Products, Inc. 06/14/1962
(See Electric Products, Inc.)

ELECTRIC POWER EQUIPMENT CORP. (DE)
Bankrupt in 1949

ELECTRIC PRODUCTS, INC. (MN)
Assets sold for the benefit of creditors 00/00/1962
No stockholders' equity

ELECTRIC PRODUCTS CORP.
Dissolved in 1943

ELECTRIC PROPERTIES, INC. (TX)
Liquidated in 1953

ELECTRIC PUBLIC SERVICE CO.
Reorganized as Crescent Public Service Co. 00/00/1934
Details not available

ELECTRIC PUBLIC UTILITIES CO.
Reorganized as Utilities Stock & Bond Corp. in 1933
Details not available

ELECTRIC RAILWAY SECURITIES CO.
Dissolved in 1933

ELECTRIC REEL CORP AMER INC (MN)
Name changed to Assisted Living Corp. 11/03/1993
Assisted Living Corp. name changed to Stealth Industries Inc. (MN) 12/13/1999 which reincorporated in Nevada 11/22/2000 which recapitalized as Precious Metals Exchange Corp. 01/23/2009 which name changed to Legends Food Corp. 07/19/2011 which name changed to Republic of Texas Brands, Inc. 11/07/2011 which name changed to Totally Hemp Crazy Inc. 08/05/2014 which name changed to Rocky Mountain High Brands Inc. 10/16/2015

ELECTRIC REFRIGERATION CORP.
Name changed to Kelvinator Corp. 00/00/1928
Kelvinator Corp. merged into Nash-Kelvinator Corp. 00/00/1936 which merged into American Motors Corp. 00/00/1954 which merged into Chrysler Corp. 08/05/1987 which merged into DaimlerChrysler AG 11/12/1998 which name changed to Daimler AG 10/19/2007

ELECTRIC SHAREHOLDINGS CORP.
Name changed to General Shareholdings Corp. in 1939
General Shareholdings Corp. merged into Tri-Continental Corp. in 1948

ELECTRIC SHOVEL COAL CORP.
Merged into Ayrshire Patoka Collieries Corp. 00/00/1939
Each share Preferred exchanged for (2) shares Common
Each share Common exchanged for (0.03333333) share Common
Ayrshire Patoka Collieries Corp. name changed to Ayrshire Collieries Corp. (DE) 00/00/1944 which reincorporated in Indiana 06/30/1965 which merged into American Metal Climax, Inc. 10/31/1969 which name changed to Amax Inc. 07/01/1974
(See Amax Inc.)

ELECTRIC SMELTING & ALUMINUM CO.
Succeeded by Cowles Detergent Co. 00/00/1937
Details not available

ELECTRIC SORTING MACHINE CO. (MI)
Name changed to Mandrel Industries, Inc. in 1956
Mandrel Industries, Inc. acquired by Ampex Corp. 3/12/64 which merged into Signal Companies, Inc. 1/15/81 which merged into Allied-Signal Inc. 9/19/85 which name changed to AlliedSignal Inc. 4/26/93 which name changed to Honeywell International Inc. 12/1/99

ELECTRIC SPRAYIT CO. (DE)
Merged into Thomas Industries Inc. in 1953
Each share 5% Preferred $100 par exchanged for (12.5) shares Common $1 par
Common no par had no equity
(See Thomas Industries Inc.)

ELECTRIC STEAM STERILIZING INC (DE)
Capital Stock $1 par changed to no par in 1939
Capital Stock no par changed to 10¢ par in 1940
Charter cancelled and declared inoperative and void for non-payment of taxes 4/15/70

ELECTRIC STORAGE BATTERY CO. (NJ)
Common no par changed to $10 par 4/20/55
Common $10 par split (5) for (4) by issuance of (0.25) additional share 12/18/56
Common $10 par changed to $6.66-2/3 par and (0.5) additional share issued 10/14/63
Reincorporated under the laws of Delaware as ESB Inc. 6/30/67
(See ESB Inc.)

ELECTRIC TRANSN SYS INC (CO)
Name changed to Kober Corp. 10/13/83
(See Kober Corp.)

ELECTRIC VACUUM CLEANER CO., INC.
Acquired by General Electric Co. on a (10) for (13) basis in 1945

ELECTRIC VEH RESH CORP (FL)
Recapitalized as Advanced Environmental Petroleum Producers, Inc. 10/13/2015
Each share Common $0.0001 par exchanged for (0.001) share Common $0.0001 par
Advanced Environmental Petroleum Producers, Inc. name changed to Oncolix, Inc. 11/29/2017

ELECTRICAL GENERATION TECHNOLOGY CORP (UT)
SEC revoked common stock registration 10/14/2010

ELECTRICAL PRECISION METER CORP (NY)
Charter cancelled and proclaimed dissolved for failure to pay taxes 09/25/1991

ELECTRICAL PRODUCTS CONSOLIDATED (WA)
Name changed to Epcon, Inc. 03/21/1966
Epcon, Inc. liquidated for Rexall Drug & Chemical Co. 11/30/1967 which name changed to Dart Industries, Inc. 04/22/1969 which reorganized as Dart & Kraft, Inc. 09/25/1980 which name changed to Kraft, Inc. (New) 11/21/1986
(See Kraft, Inc. (New))

ELECTRICAL PRODUCTS CORP. (CA)
Merged into Federal Sign & Signal Corp. (NY) 06/00/1962
Each share Common $4 par exchanged for (1) share $1.20 Conv. Prior Preferred no par
Federal Sign & Signal Corp. (NY) reincorporated in Delaware 04/01/1969 which name changed to Federal Signal Corp. 08/29/1975

ELECTRICAL PRODUCTS CORP. OF ARIZONA
Name changed to Claude Neon Electrical Products Corp., Ltd. 00/00/1928
(See Claude Neon Electrical Products Corp., Ltd.)

ELECTRICAL PRODUCTS CORP. OF COLORADO
Liquidated 00/00/1936
Details not available

ELECTRICAL PRODUCTS CORP. OF WASHINGTON
Liquidated 00/00/1935
Details not available

ELECTRIGLAS CORP. (NJ)
Charter revoked for failure to file reports and pay fees 02/02/1959

ELECTRIGO CORP (OK)
Charter cancelled for failure to pay taxes 05/14/1982

ELECTRO AIR CORP (GA)
99% acquired by Avnet, Inc. through purchase offer which expired 08/01/1968
Public interest eliminated

ELECTRO AUDIO DYNAMICS INC (DE)
Common $1 par changed to 25¢ par 06/25/1985
Charter cancelled and declared inoperative and void for non-payment of taxes 03/01/1990

ELECTRO BIOLOGY INC (DE)
Common $1 par split (3) for (2) by issuance of (0.5) additional share 03/31/1983
Merged into Biomet Acquisition Corp. 01/04/1988
Each share Common $1 par exchanged for $6.25 cash

ELECTRO BLEACHING GAS CO.
Merged into Niagara Alkali Co. 00/00/1941
Details not available

ELECTRO CARE INDS (CA)
Merged 06/30/1969
Merged from Electro-Care, Inc. to Electro-Care Industries, Inc. 06/30/1969
Each share Common $1 par exchanged for (1) share Common $1 par
Name changed to ECI Industries 12/16/1971
(See ECI Industries)

ELECTRO CATHETER CORP (NJ)
Common 10¢ par split (3) for (2) by issuance of (0.5) additional share 12/19/1984
Stock Dividends - 100% 01/29/1981; 50% 03/25/1983
Chapter 7 bankruptcy proceedings terminated 02/05/2002
Stockholders' equity unlikely

ELECTRO-CHEMICAL TECHNOLOGIES LTD (NV)
Each share old Common $0.001 par exchanged for (0.5) share new Common $0.001 par 08/08/2001
Chapter 11 bankruptcy proceedings terminated 12/07/2009
No stockholders' equity

ELECTRO-COMPONENTS CORP. OF AMERICA (DE)
No longer in existence having

become inoperative and void for non-payment of taxes 04/01/1956

ELECTRO CONSOLIDATED CORP. (DE)
Class A 50¢ par split (3) for (1) by issuance of (2) additional shares 01/15/1963
Stock Dividend - 50% 01/15/1963
Name changed to Curtis Electro Corp. 04/26/1963
(See Curtis Electro Corp.)

ELECTRO-COTE CO. (MN)
Acquired by Fuller (H.B.) Co. 12/30/1970
Each share Common 40¢ par exchanged for (0.0588235) share Common $1 par

ELECTRO CRAFT CORP (MN)
Merged into Napco Industries, Inc. 10/11/1977
Each (2.75) shares Common Capital Stock 20¢ par exchanged for (1) share Common $1 par
Note: Holders of (99) shares or fewer received $3.25 cash per share
Napco Industries, Inc. name changed to Mass Merchandisers, Inc. (IN) 05/11/1984 which merged into McKesson Corp. (MD) 10/29/1985 which reincorporated in Delaware 07/31/1987
(See McKesson Corp. (Old) (DE))

ELECTRO DATA INC (TX)
Adjudicated bankrupt 05/04/1973
Stockholders' equity unlikely

ELECTRO DENT INC (DE)
Charter cancelled and declared inoperative and void for non-payment of taxes 03/01/1976

ELECTRO DEVELOPMENT CO. (CA)
Merged into Teledyne, Inc. 09/06/1963
Each share Capital Stock $1 par exchanged for (0.08612) share Capital Stock $1 par
Teledyne, Inc. merged into Allegheny Teledyne Inc. 08/15/1996 which name changed to Allegheny Technologies Inc.

ELECTRO ED RES CORP (DE)
Adjudicated bankrupt 02/20/1970
Stockholders' equity unlikely

ELECTRO ENERGY INC (FL)
Each share old Common $0.001 par exchanged for (0.2) share new Common $0.001 par 07/09/2008
Filed a petition under Chapter 7 Federal Bankruptcy Code 03/26/2009
No stockholders' equity

ELECTRO FDS CORP (CO)
Name changed to CMS Enhancements, Inc. (CO) 01/06/1987
CMS Enhancements, Inc. (CO) reorganized in Delaware 06/01/1987 which name changed to AmeriQuest Technologies, Inc. 03/31/1994
(See AmeriQuest Technologies, Inc.)

ELECTRO FIBEROPTICS CORP (MA)
Name changed to Valtec Corp. 01/01/1972
Valtec Corp. acquired by M/A-Com, Inc. 09/24/1980 which merged into AMP Inc. 06/30/1995 which merged into Tyco International Ltd. (Bermuda) 04/01/1999 which reincorporated in Switzerland 03/17/2009 which merged into Johnson Controls International PLC 09/06/2016

ELECTRO HEAT RES CORP (NY)
Charter cancelled and proclaimed dissolved for failure to pay taxes 09/29/1993

ELECTRO INDUSTRIES, INC. (MD)
Charter annulled for failure to file reports and pay taxes 11/27/1963

ELECTRO INSTRUMENTS, INC. (DE)
Completely liquidated 04/27/1966
Each share Common $1 par exchanged for first and final distribution of (0.125) share Honeywell Inc. Common $1.50 par
Honeywell Inc. merged into Honeywell International Inc. 12/01/1999

ELECTRO KINETIC SYS INC (PA)
Name changed to Sterling Media Capital Group, Inc. (PA) 07/07/2000
Sterling Media Capital Group, Inc. (PA) reincorporated in Nevada as Sterling Capital Investment Group, Inc. 01/18/2001 which recapitalized as Crystal Properties Holdings Inc. 09/17/2008
(See Crystal Properties Holdings Inc.)

ELECTRO KNIT FABRICS LTD (CANADA)
Name changed 11/29/1980
Name changed from Electro-Knit Fabrics (Canada) Ltd. to Electro-Knit Fabrics Ltd. 11/29/1980
Placed into receivership 03/26/1982
No stockholders' equity

ELECTRO MANGANESE CORP. (DE)
Acquired by Foote Mineral Co. 03/20/1956
Each share Common $1 par exchanged for (1) share Common $1 par
(See Foote Mineral Co.)

ELECTRO-MATION CO. (MN)
Acquired by Fullview Industries, Inc. 04/04/1963
Each share Common 25¢ par exchanged for $0.7196 principal amount of 6.5% Subord. Conv. Debentures

ELECTRO-MEC INSTRUMENT CORP. (DE)
Acquired by Nytronics, Inc. (NJ) 08/01/1966
Each share Common 10¢ par exchanged for (0.11111111) share Capital Stock $1 par
Nytronics, Inc. (NJ) reincorporated in Delaware 01/04/1968 which merged into Bastian Industries, Inc. 11/24/1980
(See Bastian Industries, Inc.)

ELECTRO MECHANICAL CORP (NY)
Common 1¢ par changed to 10¢ par 02/24/1966
Name changed to General Shelter Corp. 07/02/1970
(See General Shelter Corp.)

ELECTRO-MECHANICAL SPECIALTIES CO., INC. (CA)
Merged into Hurletron Inc. 07/31/1961
Each share Capital Stock 20¢ par exchanged for (0.2) share Common 25¢ par
Hurletron Inc. name changed to Altair Corp. 04/19/1972

ELECTRO-MECHANICAL SYSTEMS, INC. (FL)
Name changed to EMS Industries, Inc. 12/14/1967
EMS Industries, Inc. name changed to Regal International Holding Co., Inc. 06/16/1975 which name changed to Regal One Corp. (FL) 06/13/1988 which reorganized in Maryland as Princeton Capital Corp. 03/23/2015

ELECTRO MECHANICS CO (TX)
Class B Common 20¢ par reclassified as Common 10¢ par 12/29/1967
Stock Dividend - 100% 12/31/1968
Name changed to Lem Corp. 07/31/1972
(See Lem Corp.)

ELECTRO-MED, INC. (MN)
Recapitalized as Knapic Electro-Physics, Inc. 03/12/1962
Each share Class A Common $1 par exchanged for (1) share Common 10¢ par
(See Knapic Electro-Physics, Inc.)

ELECTRO MINIATURES CORP (DE)
Completely liquidated 08/04/1967
Each share Common 10¢ par exchanged for first and final distribution of $5.76 cash

ELECTRO-NETIC STEEL, INC. (IL)
Name changed to Electronetics Corp. 09/08/1977
(See Electronetics Corp.)

ELECTRO NETWORKS, INC. (NY)
Common 10¢ par split (4) for (3) by issuance of (0.33333333) additional share 04/28/1967
Stock Dividends - 10% 08/25/1961; 10% 08/15/1963
Merged into Connrex Corp. (DE) 10/31/1968
Each share Common 10¢ par exchanged for (0.6735) share Common $5 par
Connrex Corp. (DE) name changed to Chloride Connrex Corp. 08/27/1973
(See Chloride Connrex Corp.)

ELECTRO-NEUTRONICS, INC. (CA)
Completely liquidated 04/25/1968
Each share Capital Stock $1 par exchanged for first and final distribution of (0.0382) share International Chemical & Nuclear Corp. Common $1 par
International Chemical & Nuclear Corp. name changed to ICN Pharmaceuticals, Inc. (CA) 04/13/1973 which reincorporated in Delaware 10/03/1986 which merged into ICN Pharmaceuticals, Inc. (New) 11/10/1994 which name changed to Valeant Pharmaceuticals International 11/12/2003 which merged into Valeant Pharmaceuticals International, Inc. (Canada) 09/28/2010 which reincorporated in British Columbia 08/09/2013

ELECTRO-NITE, INC. (PA)
Merged into Electro-Nite Engineering Co. 01/01/1965
Each share Common exchanged for (0.5) share Common
Electro-Nite Engineering Co. name changed to Electro-Nite Co. 04/26/1967
(See Electro-Nite Co.)

ELECTRO NITE CO (PA)
Stock Dividend - 10% 11/15/1977
Merged into Midland-Ross Corp. 10/26/1979
Each share Common no par exchanged for $16.50 cash

ELECTRO-NITE ENGINEERING CO. (PA)
Stock Dividends - 10% 10/30/1964; 10% 04/08/1966
Name changed to Electro-Nite Co. 04/26/1967
(See Electro-Nite Co.)

ELECTRO NUCLEAR SYSTEMS CORP. (MN)
Out of business 00/00/1963
No stockholders' equity

ELECTRO NUCLEONICS INC (NJ)
Common $0.075 par changed to $0.025 par and (2) additional shares issued 09/30/1968
Merged into Pharmacia Inc. 01/26/1989
Each share Common $0.025 par exchanged for $14.75 cash

ELECTRO-OPTICAL SCIENCES INC (DE)
Name changed to MELA Sciences, Inc. 04/30/2010
MELA Sciences, Inc. name changed to STRATA Skin Sciences, Inc. 01/05/2016

exchanged for (1) share Common 10¢ par
(See Knapic Electro-Physics, Inc.)

ELECTRO PLASTICS INC (DE)
Name changed to EPI International, Inc. 01/01/1989
(See EPI International, Inc.)

ELECTRO POWERPACS CORP (MA)
Merged into Menvier USA Holdings Inc. 04/26/1988
Each share Common 10¢ par exchanged for $3 cash

ELECTRO PROT CORP AMER (NJ)
Through purchase offer 100% acquired by Hawley Group Ltd. as of 01/03/1982
Public interest eliminated

ELECTRO PULSE TECHNOLOGIES COML INC (DE)
Company terminated common stock registration and is no longer public as of 01/27/2002

ELECTRO REFRACTORIES & ABRASIVES CORP. (DE)
Common no par changed to $1 par and (1) additional share issued 02/27/1956
Completely liquidated 03/28/1967
Each share Common $1 par exchanged for first and final distribution of $25 cash

ELECTRO REFRACTORIES & ALLOYS CORP.
Name changed to Electro Refractories & Abrasives Corp. 00/00/1951
(See Electro Refractories & Abrasives Corp.)

ELECTRO RENT CORP (CA)
Common 50¢ par changed to no par 09/25/1984
Common no par split (3) for (2) by issuance of (0.5) additional share 02/28/1992
Common no par split (3) for (2) by issuance of (0.5) additional share 02/25/1994
Common no par split (3) for (2) by issuance of (0.5) additional share 08/18/1995
Common no par split (2) for (1) by issuance of (1) additional share payable 05/12/1998 to holders of record 04/30/1998
Stock Dividends - 25% 11/10/1982; 25% 11/15/1983
Acquired by Elecor Intermediate Holding II Corp. 08/10/2016
Each share Common no par exchanged for $15.50 cash

ELECTRO SCIENCE INVS INC (TX)
Common $1 par split (3) for (1) by issuance of (2) additional shares 02/06/1962
Recapitalized as Escon, Inc. 09/01/1967
Each share Common $1 par exchanged for (0.2) share Common $1.25 par
Escon, Inc. acquired by LTV Ling Altec, Inc. 03/19/1968 which name changed to Altec Corp. 04/27/1972
(See Altec Corp.)

ELECTRO-SONIC LABORATORIES, INC. (NY)
Adjudicated bankrupt 06/03/1965
No stockholders' equity

ELECTRO TEC CORP (NJ)
Acquired by KDI Corp. 12/04/1967
Each share 6% Conv. Preferred $100 par exchanged for (10) shares Common 35¢ par
Each share Common 10¢ par exchanged for (0.44) share Common 35¢ par
(See KDI Corp.)

ELECTRO TEMP SYS INC (NY)
Dissolved by proclamation 12/15/1975

ELECTRO-VEND CORP. (HI)
Proclaimed dissolved for failure to file annual reports 07/17/1980

ELECTRO-VOICE, INC. (IN)
Completely liquidated 08/31/1967
Each share Capital Stock $2 par exchanged for first and final distribution of (0.24084) share Gulton Industries, Inc. (NJ) $2 Conv. Preferred Ser. A $50 par and (0.26091) share Common $1 par Gulton Industries, Inc. (NJ) reincorporated in Delaware 06/28/1968
(See Gulton Industries, Inc. (DE))

ELECTROBUSINESS COM INC (AB)
Name changed to Cortex Business Solutions Inc. 05/25/2007

ELECTROCHEMICAL INDUSTRIES (1952) LTD (ISRAEL)
Name changed 11/13/1996
Each share Ordinary Stock NIS 1 par received distribution of (0.2) share Ordinary Stock NIS 1 par payable 05/09/1996 to holders of record 05/07/1996 Ex date - 05/10/1996
Stock Dividends - 30% 05/11/1990; 20% 07/08/1991
Name changed from Electrochemical Industries (Frutarom) Ltd. to Electrochemical Industries (1952) Ltd. 11/13/1996
Filed for Stay of Proceedings 07/07/2003
Stockholders' equity unlikely

ELECTROCOM AUTOMATION INC (DE)
Merged into ECA Acquisition Corp. 09/16/1994
Each share Common 5¢ par exchanged for $10 cash

ELECTROCON INTL INC (BRITISH VIRGIN ISLANDS)
Each share old Common $0.0001 par exchanged for (0.02) share new Common $0.0001 par 10/01/1991
Name changed to Getgo Mail.com, Inc. 10/14/1999
Getgo Mail.com, Inc. name changed to GETGO Inc. 06/29/2001
(See GETCO Inc.)

ELECTROCOPY CORP (DE)
Stock Dividend - 100% 04/20/1968
Charter cancelled and declared inoperative and void for non-payment of taxes 03/01/1974

ELECTRODATA CORP. (CA)
Merged into Burroughs Corp. (MI) 07/01/1956
Each share Capital Stock $1 par exchanged for (0.5) share Common $5 par
Burroughs Corp. (MI) reincorporated in Delaware 05/30/1984 which name changed to Unisys Corp. 11/13/1986

ELECTROFUEL INC (ON)
Name changed to Electrovaya Inc. 04/02/2002

ELECTROGASDYNAMICS INC (NJ)
Name changed to Futuresat Industries, Inc. 10/26/1983
Futuresat Industries, Inc. recapitalized as Future Communications Inc. 05/01/1990
(See Future Communications Inc.)

ELECTROGEN INDS INC (NY)
Merged into American Lima Corp. 11/08/1968
Each share Common 10¢ par exchanged for (1) share Common 1¢ par
American Lima Corp. reorganized as Brooklyn Poly Industries, Inc. 11/10/1969
(See Brooklyn Poly Industries, Inc.)

ELECTROGESIC CORP (DE)
Each share old Common 1¢ par exchanged for (0.1) share new Common 1¢ par 01/31/1995
Recapitalized as Midrange Marketing Solutions Inc. 10/26/1998
Each share new Common 1¢ par exchanged for (0.01) share Common 1¢ par
Midrange Marketing Solutions Inc. recapitalized as Millennium Broadcast Corp. 09/20/1999 which recapitalized as Diversified Media Holdings Inc. 03/13/2003 which recapitalized as TPI International, Inc. 01/03/2006

ELECTROGLAS INC (DE)
Common 1¢ par split (2) for (1) by issuance of (1) additional share 11/30/1995
Chapter 11 bankruptcy proceedings effective 09/16/2010
No stockholders' equity

ELECTROGRAPH SYS INC (NY)
Merged into Bitwise Designs, Inc. 08/18/1994
Each share Common 1¢ par exchanged for (0.035) share Common $0.001 par
Bitwise Designs, Inc. name changed to AuthentiDate Holding Corp. 03/23/2001 which name changed to Aeon Global Health Corp. 02/01/2018

ELECTROGRAPHIC CORP (DE)
Common no par changed to $1 par 00/00/1932
Stock Dividends - 10% 11/20/1946; 33.33333333% 05/11/1950
Merged into Encyclopedia Britannica Publishers Inc. 09/19/1980
Each share Common $1 par exchanged for $32.25 cash

ELECTROHOME BROADCASTING INC (ON)
Merged into 1406236 Ontario Inc. 05/03/2000
Each share Class X no par exchanged for $32.17 cash
Each share Class Y no par exchanged for $32.17 cash

ELECTROHOME LTD (ON)
Name changed 06/08/1977
Common no par split (5) for (1) by issuance of (4) additional shares 06/14/1972
Common no par reclassified as Conv. Class A Common no par 05/06/1974
Name changed from Electrohome Ltd. to Electrohome Ltd.-Electrohome Ltee. 06/08/1977
Conv. Class A Common no par reclassified as Common no par 06/18/1980
Conv. Class B Common no par reclassified as Common no par 06/18/1980
Each share Common no par exchanged for (0.5) share Class X Common no par and (1) share Class Y Common no par 06/24/1981
Plan of arrangement effective 04/01/1998
Each share old Class X Common no par exchanged for (1) share new Class X Common no par and (1) share Electrohome Broadcasting Inc. Class X Common no par
Each share old Class Y Common no par exchanged for (1) share new Class Y Common no par and (1) share Electrohome Broadcasting Inc. Class Y Common no par
(See Electrohome Broadcasting Inc.)
Completely liquidated
Each share new Class X no par received first and final distribution of $0.065 cash payable 04/07/2009 to holders of record 10/01/2008
Each share new Class Y no par received first and final distribution of $0.065 cash payable 04/07/2009 to holders of record 10/01/2008
Note: Certificates were not required to be surrendered and are without value

ELECTROL, INC. (DE)
Name changed to Kingston Hydraulics, Inc. 10/13/1960
Kingston Hydraulics, Inc. acquired by Avien, Inc. 01/10/1961
(See Avien, Inc.)

ELECTROLIER CORP (QC)
Sylvannia Electric (Canada) Ltd. acquired 100% of Class A Preference no par through purchase offer of $14 cash per share as of 01/07/1966
Public interest eliminated

ELECTROLUX, INC.
Acquired by Electrolux Corp. 00/00/1938
Details not available

ELECTROLUX AB (SWEDEN)
Each old Unsponsored ADR for Ordinary exchanged for (2) new Unsponsored ADR's for Ordinary 09/09/1985
Each new Unsponsored ADR for Ordinary exchanged for (1) AB Electrolux Sponsored ADR for Ordinary 07/01/1987

ELECTROLUX CORP. (DE)
Common $1 par split (2) for (1) by issuance of (1) additional share 05/05/1964
Common $1 par split (2) for (1) by issuance of (1) additional share 05/12/1966
Merged into Consolidated Foods Corp. 07/01/1968
Each share Common $1 par exchanged for (0.32) share $4.50 Conv. Preferred Ser. A no par
(See Consolidated Foods Corp.)

ELECTROLUX DO BRASIL S A (BRAZIL)
ADR agreement terminated 09/23/2003
Each Sponsored ADR for Ordinary exchanged for $1.775796 cash

ELECTROMAGNETIC INDS INC (NY)
Acquired by Square D Co. (MI) 03/14/1974
Each share Common 10¢ par exchanged for (0.25) share Common $1.66666666 par
Square D Co. (MI) reincorporated in Delaware 06/16/1989
(See Square D Co. (DE))

ELECTROMAGNETIC OIL RECOVERY INC (OK)
Reorganized under the laws of Delaware as Fountain Oil Inc. 12/16/1994
Each share Common no par exchanged for (0.04) share Common no par
Fountain Oil Inc. merged into CanArgo Energy Corp. 07/15/1998
(See CanArgo Energy Corp.)

ELECTROMAGNETIC SCIENCES INC (GA)
Reincorporated 07/03/1989
Common 10¢ par split (4) for (3) by issuance of (1/3) additional share 05/25/1982
Common 10¢ par split (3) for (2) by issuance of (0.5) additional share 05/10/1983
Common 10¢ par split (4) for (3) by issuance of (1/3) additional share 05/28/1985
Common 10¢ par split (3) for (2) by issuance of (0.5) additional share 05/23/1986
Stock Dividend - 10% 05/26/1981
State of incorporation changed from (NV) to (GA) 07/03/1989
Name changed to EMS Technologies Inc. 03/15/1999
(See EMS Technologies Inc.)

ELECTROMASTER, INC.
Acquired by Philco Corp. 00/00/1949
Each share Common $1 par exchanged for (0.1136875) share Common $3 par
Philco Corp. acquired by Ford Motor Co. 12/11/1961

ELECTROMATIC INVESTMENT CO., INC. (CA)
Liquidation completed 07/15/1963
Details not available

ELECTROMATION COMPONENTS CORP (DE)
Merged into RAI Research Corp. 01/01/1973
Each share Common 10¢ par exchanged for (0.125) share Common 1¢ par
RAI Research Corp. acquired by Pall Corp. 09/30/1988
(See Pall Corp.)

ELECTROMED INC (QC)
Recapitalized as Evolved Digital Systems Inc. 10/10/2003
Each share Common no par exchanged for (0.125) share Common no par

ELECTROMEDICS INC (CO)
Common 10¢ par changed to 1¢ par 07/31/1980
Each share Common 1¢ par exchanged for (0.2) share Common 5¢ par 10/19/1987
Merged into Medtronic, Inc. (MN) 04/25/1994
Each share Common 5¢ par exchanged for (0.095172) share Common 10¢ par
Medtronic, Inc. (MN) reincorporated in Ireland as Medtronic PLC 01/27/2015

ELECTROMITE CORP (FL)
Proclaimed dissolved for failure to file reports and pay fees 05/23/1973

ELECTRON SOLAR ENERGY (NV)
Charter revoked 09/29/2010

ELECTRONATOM CORP. (NY)
Name changed to Seversky Electronatom Corp. 10/19/1967
(See Seversky Electronatom Corp.)

ELECTRONETICS CORP (IL)
Under bankruptcy proceedings assets sold for benefit of creditors only 10/19/1971
No stockholders' equity

ELECTRONIC & MISSILE FACS INC (NY)
Name changed to Plaza Group, Inc. 03/10/1969
(See Plaza Group, Inc.)

ELECTRONIC ACCOUNTING CARD CORP (NC)
Completely liquidated 05/28/1968
Each share Common $1 par exchanged for first and final distribution of (0.074074) share Control Data Corp. (MN) Common 50¢ par
Control Data Corp. (MN) merged into Control Data Corp. (DE) 08/17/1968 which name changed to Ceridian Corp. (Old) 06/03/1992
(See Ceridian Corp. (Old))

ELECTRONIC AIDS INC (MD)
Merged into American Standard Inc. 09/10/1970
Each share Common 10¢ par exchanged for (0.01) share Common $5 par
(See American Standard Inc.)

ELECTRONIC ARRAYS INC (CA)
Merged into Nippon Electric Co., Ltd. 12/06/1978
Each share Common $1 par exchanged for $5 cash

ELECTRONIC ARTS (CA)
Reincorporated under the laws of Delaware as Electronic Arts Inc. and Common no par changed to 1¢ par 09/19/1991

ELECTRONIC ASSEMBLY SVCS INC (GA)
Administratively dissolved 11/29/1992

ELECTRONIC ASSISTANCE CORP (NY)
Common 10¢ par split (2) for (1) by issuance of (1) additional share 03/11/1960
Common 10¢ par split (2) for (1) by issuance of (1) additional share 07/14/1961
Name changed to EAC Industries, Inc. 05/26/1976
(See EAC Industries, Inc.)

ELECTRONIC ASSOC CDA LTD (ON)
Assets sold for the benefit of creditors 12/24/1974
No stockholders' equity

ELECTRONIC ASSOC INC (NJ)
Capital Stock $1 par split (2) for (1) by issuance of (1) additional share 06/04/1964
Capital Stock $1 par reclassified as Common $1 par 05/03/1972
Common $1 par changed to no par 05/17/1994
Stock Dividends - 100% 07/01/1955; 100% 07/30/1957
Name changed to EA Industries, Inc. 10/25/1995
(See EA Industries, Inc.)

ELECTRONIC BUSINESS SVCS INC (DE)
Plan of reorganization under Chapter 11 Federal Bankruptcy Code effective 05/14/2001
No old Common stockholders' equity
Name changed to Tangent Solutions, Inc. 09/07/2001
(See Tangent Solutions, Inc.)

ELECTRONIC CLEARING HOUSE INC (NV)
Each share Common $0.001 par exchanged for (0.09090909) share old Common 1¢ par 06/21/1990
Each share old Common 1¢ par exchanged for (0.25) share new Common 1¢ par 09/11/2001
Merged into Intuit, Inc. 03/06/2008
Each share Common 1¢ par exchanged for $17 cash

ELECTRONIC COMMUNICATIONS, INC. (NJ)
6% Conv. Preferred $10 par called for redemption 07/31/1968
Stock Dividends - 50% 08/17/1959; 10% 12/21/1966
Merged into ECI Merger Corp. 12/29/1971
Each share Common $1 par exchanged for $26 cash

ELECTRONIC COMPONENTS, INC. (CA)
Acquired by Milo Electronics Corp. 12/31/1964
Each share Common no par exchanged for (0.2843) share 6.5% Conv. Preferred $10 par
(See Milo Electronics Corp.)

ELECTRONIC COMPUTER PROGRAMMING INST INC (NY)
Common $0.125 par changed to $0.08333333 par and (0.5) additional share issued 05/06/1966
Stock Dividends - 25% 05/07/1965; 25% 11/10/1965
Adjudicated bankrupt 03/16/1976
Stockholders' equity unlikely

ELECTRONIC CONCEPTS INC (VA)
Completely liquidated 07/24/1967
Each share Common 5¢ par exchanged for first and final distribution of (0.0882) share Automatic Sprinkler Corp. of America (OH) Common 10¢ par
Automatic Sprinkler Corp. of America (OH) name changed to A-T-O Inc. 10/29/1969 which name changed to Figgie International Inc. (OH) 06/01/1981 which reorganized in Delaware as Figgie International Holdings Inc. 07/18/1983 which name changed to Figgie International Inc. 12/31/1986 which name changed to Scott Technologies, Inc. 05/20/1998 which merged into Tyco International Ltd. (Bermuda) 05/03/2001 which reincorporated in Switzerland 03/17/2009 which merged into Johnson Controls International PLC 09/06/2016

ELECTRONIC CONCEPTS LABS CORP (CT)
Merged into XCL Corp. 02/13/1979
Each share Common no par exchanged for (0.5) share Common $0.001 par
XCL Corp. name changed to Sunbelt Oil & Gas Inc. 11/10/1980 which name changed to Dallas Sunbelt Oil & Gas, Inc. 05/08/1981
(See Dallas Sunbelt Oil & Gas, Inc.)

ELECTRONIC CORP. OF AMERICA (NY)
Adjudicated bankrupt 12/30/1949
No stockholders' equity

ELECTRONIC CTL SYS INC (WV)
Merged into Central Technologies of the United Kingdom 02/14/1991
Each share Capital Stock 10¢ par exchanged for $2.43 cash

ELECTRONIC CTLS INC (MD)
Name changed to T-Bar Inc. 04/29/1971
(See T-Bar Inc.)

ELECTRONIC DATA CTLS CORP (NC)
Administratively dissolved 01/28/1994

ELECTRONIC DATA PROCESSING CENTER, INC. (OR)
Name changed to American Data Services, Inc. 05/03/1961
(See American Data Services, Inc.)

ELECTRONIC DATA SYS CORP (DE)
Each Income Preferred Redeemable Increased Dividend Equity Security received (0.843) share Common 1¢ par 08/17/2004
Merged into Hewlett-Packard Co. 08/26/2008
Each share Common 1¢ par exchanged for $25 cash

ELECTRONIC DATA SYS CORP (TX)
Common no par split (2) for (1) by issuance of (1) additional share 07/20/1981
Common no par split (2) for (1) by issuance of (1) additional share 06/07/1983
Merged into General Motors Corp. 10/18/1984
Each share Common no par exchanged for $44 cash

ELECTRONIC DATA TECHNOLOGIES (NV)
Acquired by International Game Technology 01/31/1992
Each share Common 1¢ par exchanged for (0.1007) share Common $0.005 par
International Game Technology merged into International Game Technology PLC 04/07/2015

ELECTRONIC DESIGNS INC (CA)
Merged into White Electronic Designs Corp. 10/23/1998
Each share Common no par exchanged for (1.275) shares Common no par
(See White Electronic Designs Corp.)

ELECTRONIC DEV CORP (UT)
Assets sold 05/00/1973
No stockholders' equity

ELECTRONIC DEVICES INC (DE)
Each share Common 1¢ par exchanged for (0.01) share Common 50¢ par 08/09/1960
Merged into Rectisel Corp. 08/29/1980
Each share Common 50¢ par exchanged for (4) shares Common 10¢ par
(See Rectisel Corp.)

ELECTRONIC DIAGNOSTICS INC (NY)
Charter cancelled and proclaimed dissolved for failure to pay taxes and file reports 12/15/1975

ELECTRONIC ENGR CO CALIF (CA)
Common $1 par split (3) for (2) by issuance of (0.5) additional share 02/09/1968
Common $1 par split (3) for (2) by issuance of (0.5) additional share 06/01/1976
Common $1 par split (3) for (2) by issuance of (0.5) additional share 07/21/1978
Stock Dividend - 10% 03/20/1961
Name changed to EECO Inc. (CA) 05/02/1979
EECO Inc. (CA) reincorporated in Delaware 12/01/1986
(See EECO Inc.)

ELECTRONIC ENTERPRISES INC (NJ)
Charter declared void for non-payment of taxes 06/24/1986

ELECTRONIC FAB TECHNOLOGY CORP (CO)
Name changed to EFTC Corp. (CO) 05/28/1997
EFTC Corp. (CO) reorganized in Delaware as Suntron Corp. 03/01/2002
(See Suntron Corp.)

ELECTRONIC FINL SYS INC (FL)
Merged into Electronic Clearing House, Inc. 01/17/1986
Each share Class A Common 1¢ par exchanged for (1) share Common $0.001 par
(See Electronic Clearing House, Inc.)

ELECTRONIC FUEL CTL INC (GA)
Name changed to Save On Energy, Inc. 03/01/2001
Save On Energy, Inc. name changed to Hybrid Fuel Systems, Inc. 02/18/2004 which name changed to US Energy Initiatives Corp. (GA) 06/05/2006 which reincorporated in Delaware 05/26/2008 which reincorporated in Nevada as U.S. Energy Initiatives Corporation Inc. 04/03/2013

ELECTRONIC FUTURES INC (DE)
Completely liquidated 04/23/1968
Each share Common no par exchanged for first and final distribution of (0.527) share KMS Industries, Inc. Common 1¢ par
(See KMS Industries, Inc.)

ELECTRONIC GAME CARD INC (NV)
Each share Common $0.001 par received distribution of (1) share Scientific Energy Inc. Common $0.001 par payable 11/12/2004 to holders of record 11/19/2003
Chapter 7 bankruptcy proceedings terminated 07/29/2014
No stockholders' equity

ELECTRONIC HAIR STYLING INC (DE)
Name changed to Lamaur Corp. 03/26/1997
(See Lamaur Corp.)

ELECTRONIC HARDWARE CORP (NY)
Name changed to Hi-Tech Industries, Inc. 01/16/1970
(See Hi-Tech Industries, Inc.)

ELECTRONIC IDENTIFICATION INC (NV)
Each share old Common $0.001 par exchanged for (0.125) share new Common $0.001 par 03/21/2002
Name changed to Manakoa Services Corp. 03/22/2004
Manakoa Services Corp. recapitalized as TeslaVision Corp. 12/15/2008
(See TeslaVision Corp.)

ELECTRONIC INDS HLDG INC (MN)
Merged into Electronic Industries, Inc. 03/31/1995
Each share Common 1¢ par exchanged for $0.15 cash

ELECTRONIC INDS INC (NV)
Name changed to North American Industries, Inc. 08/25/1972
North American Industries, Inc. name changed to Colossus Corp. 08/27/1980
(See Colossus Corp.)

ELECTRONIC INFORMATION SYS INC (DE)
Name changed to EIS International, Inc. 04/28/1994
(See EIS International, Inc.)

ELECTRONIC INSTRUMENT CO., INC. (NY)
Name changed to Eico Electronic Instrument Co., Inc. 01/31/1962
(See Eico Electronic Instrument Co., Inc.)

ELECTRONIC KOURSEWARE INTL INC (DE)
SEC revoked common stock registration 07/22/2013

ELECTRONIC LABORATORIES, INC.
Declared bankrupt 00/00/1948
No stockholders' equity

ELECTRONIC LABORATORIES, INC. (DE)
Reincorporated 05/06/1969
State of incorporation changed from (TX) to (DE) 05/06/1969
Name changed to Telxon Corp. and Capital Stock 50¢ par changed to 1¢ par 09/23/1974
Telxon Corp. merged into Symbol Technologies, Inc. 12/01/2000
(See Symbol Technologies, Inc.)

ELECTRONIC MAIL CORP AMER (DE)
Charter cancelled and declared inoperative and void for non-payment of taxes 06/26/1990

ELECTRONIC MFG SOLUTIONS & SVCS INC (NV)
Name changed to Searchlight Solutions Ltd. 06/13/2003

ELECTRONIC MEDIA CENTRAL CORP (CA)
Name changed to Morris Business Development Co. 08/10/2007

ELECTRONIC MEDICAL SYSTEMS, INC. (MN)
Bankrupt 10/03/1962
No stockholders' equity

ELECTRONIC MEMORIES & MAGNETICS CORP (DE)
Common $1 par split (2) for (1) by issuance of (1) additional share 12/19/1969
Name changed to Titan Corp. and Common $1 par changed to 1¢ par 05/30/1985
(See Titan Corp.)

ELECTRONIC MEMORIES INC (CA)
Merged into Electronic Memories & Magnetics Corp. 07/11/1969
Each share Common $1 par exchanged for (1) share Common $1 par
Electronics Memories & Magnetics Corp. name changed to Titan Corp. 05/30/1985
(See Titan Corp.)

ELECTRONIC MICRO-LEDGER ACCOUNTING CORP. CORP. (NY)
Charter revoked for failure to file reports and pay fees 12/15/1960

ELECTRONIC MICRO SYS INC (CA)
Name changed to Dynasty Resources, Inc. and Capital Stock 10¢ par reclassified as Common no par 09/30/1982
(See Dynasty Resources, Inc.)

ELECTRONIC MODULES CORP (MD)
Stock Dividends - 50% 05/20/1981; 100% 07/23/1982
Merged into Rexnord Inc. 04/02/1985
Each share Common 10¢ par exchanged for (1.34) shares Common $1 par
(See Rexnord Inc.)

ELECTRONIC PROCESSING INC (MO)
Name changed to Epiq Systems, Inc. 06/12/2000
(See Epiq Systems, Inc.)

ELECTRONIC PRODTN & DEV INC (CA)
Name changed to EPD Industries, Inc. 03/15/1968
(See EDP Industries, Inc.)

ELECTRONIC PRODUCTS CORP. (CA)
Acquired by Jefferson Electric Co. (IL) 11/01/1957
Details not available

ELECTRONIC PRODUCTS CORP. (MD)
Assets sold by Internal Revenue Service for unpaid taxes 06/10/1964
Common stock is worthless

ELECTRONIC PUBG TECHNOLOGY (CO)
Proclaimed dissolved 01/01/1997

ELECTRONIC RESH ASSOC INC (NJ)
Class A Capital Stock 10¢ par reclassified as old Common 10¢ par 10/01/1965
Class B Capital Stock 10¢ par reclassified as old Common 10¢ par 10/01/1965
Each share old Common 10¢ par exchanged for (0.3) share new Common 10¢ par 11/20/1987
Merged into Three-Five Systems, Inc. 05/01/1990
Each share new Common 10¢ par exchanged for (0.25) share Common 1¢ par
(See Three-Five Systems, Inc.)

ELECTRONIC RETAILING SYS INTL INC (DE)
Acquired by Systems Merger Inc. 01/02/2002
Each share Common 1¢ par exchanged for $0.26 cash

ELECTRONIC SENSOR TECHNOLOGY INC (NV)
Plan of reorganization under Chapter 11 Federal Bankruptcy proceedings effective 05/11/2015
No stockholders' equity

ELECTRONIC SPECIALTY CO (CA)
Conv. Preferred Ser. A no par called for redemption 09/30/1968
Merged into International Controls Corp. 08/01/1969
Each share Common 50¢ par exchanged for (0.7) share Common 10¢ par and (1.5) 1974 Ser. A Common Stock Purchase Warrants
(See International Controls Corp.)

ELECTRONIC SPECIALTY PRODS INC (DE)
Each share Common $0.001 par exchanged for (0.1) share Common 1¢ par 12/28/1983
Name changed to Sport of Kings, Inc. (DE) 08/29/1991
Sport of Kings, Inc. (DE) reorganized in Nevada as Triad North America, Inc. 04/27/2006 which name changed to Kingslake Energy, Inc. 06/07/2006
(See Kingslake Energy, Inc.)

ELECTRONIC TABULATING CORP (NY)
Common 1¢ par split (2) for (1) by issuance of (1) additional share 04/07/1969
Liquidation completed
Each share Common 1¢ par exchanged for initial distribution of $8.50 cash 08/15/1984
Each share Common 1¢ par received second and final distribution of $4.95 cash 06/13/1985
Note: A supplemental distribution of $0.26 cash per share was made 07/17/1986

ELECTRONIC TECHNOLOGY GROUP INC (DE)
Each share old Common $0.0045 par exchanged for (0.16666666) share new Common $0.0045 par 03/17/1993
Charter cancelled and declared inoperative and void for non-payment of taxes 03/01/1995

ELECTRONIC THEATRE RESTAURANTS CORP (DE)
Recapitalized as Momentum, Inc. 12/22/1986
Each share Common 10¢ par exchanged for (0.2) share Common 10¢ par
Momentum, Inc. name changed to Specialty Chemical Resources Inc. 12/12/1991
(See Specialty Chemical Resources Inc.)

ELECTRONIC TRANSFER ASSOCS INC (CO)
SEC suspended trading of securities 01/29/1999
Stock is virtually worthless

ELECTRONIC TRANSISTORS CORP (NJ)
Common 10¢ par split (3) for (2) by issuance of (0.5) additional share 07/30/1971
Name changed to Orion Diversified Technologies, Inc. and Common 10¢ par changed to 1¢ par 04/01/1985
Orion Diversified Technologies, Inc. name changed to Ovale Group, Inc. 01/23/2008
(See Ovale Group, Inc.)

ELECTRONIC TRANSMISSION SYS INC (DE)
Charter cancelled and declared inoperative and void for non-payment of taxes 03/01/1975

ELECTRONIC TUBE CORP. (PA)
Merged into General Atronics Corp. 09/01/1961
Each share Common exchanged for (0.5) share Common no par
General Atronics Corp. acquired by Magnavox Co. 04/25/1969
(See Magnavox Co.)

ELECTRONIC WHSLRS INC (DE)
Name changed to Agora Industries, Inc. 09/10/1969
(See Agora Industries, Inc.)

ELECTRONICS, INC. (SD)
Acquired by Dura Corp. 09/01/1964
Each share Common 20¢ par exchanged for (0.11) share Common $1 par
Dura Corp. acquired by Kidde (Walter) & Co., Inc. (NY) 11/22/1966 which reincorporated in Delaware 07/02/1968
(See Kidde (Walter) & Co., Inc. (DE))

ELECTRONICS & NUCLEONICS, INC. (DE)
Name changed to Square Root Industries, Inc. 09/00/1954
(See Square Root Industries, Inc.)

ELECTRONICS BOUTIQUE HLDGS CORP (DE)
Merged into GameStop Corp. (New) 10/08/2005
Each share Common 1¢ par exchanged for (0.78795) share Class A Common $0.001 par and $38.15 cash

ELECTRONICS CAP CORP (MA)
Reincorporated under the laws of Delaware as Shelter Resources Corp. 03/31/1970
(See Shelter Resources Corp.)

ELECTRONICS COMMUNICATIONS CORP (DE)
Each share Common 1¢ par exchanged for (0.2) share Common 5¢ par 02/15/1995
Each share Common 5¢ par exchanged for (0.08333333) share Common 60¢ par 07/31/1997
Name changed to Northeast Digital Networks Inc. 06/16/1998
(See Northeast Digital Networks Inc.)

ELECTRONICS CORP. OF AMERICA (NV)
Charter revoked for failure to file reports and pay fees 03/02/1964

ELECTRONICS CORP AMER (MA)
6% Preferred $100 par called for redemption 12/31/1962
Stock Dividends - 50% 03/14/1980; 33.33333333% 02/27/1981
Merged into Rockwell International Corp. (Old) 11/25/1986
Each share Common $1 par exchanged for $52 cash

ELECTRONICS CORP ISRAEL LTD (ISRAEL)
Ordinary IS3.60 par split (3) for (2) by issuance of (0.5) additional share 02/27/1984
Name changed to ECI Telecom Ltd. 06/01/1985
(See ECI Telecom Ltd.)

ELECTRONICS DISCOVERY CORP. (DE)
Name changed to First Standard Corp. 09/16/1965
First Standard Corp. name changed to Mastercraft Electronics Corp. 01/04/1968
(See Mastercraft Electronics Corp.)

ELECTRONICS FUNDING CORP. (NY)
Merged into First Philadelphia Corp. 02/01/1963
Each share Common 10¢ par exchanged for (0.2) share Class A Common 10¢ par
(See First Philadelphia Corp.)

ELECTRONICS INTERNATIONAL CAPITAL LTD. (BERMUDA)
Completely liquidated 06/22/1965
Each share Capital Stock £1 par exchanged for (0.25) share Marathon Securities Corp. Common $1 par
(See Marathon Securities Corp.)

ELECTRONICS INVESTMENT CORP. (DE)
Name changed to Republic Technology Fund, Inc. 02/25/1965
Republic Technology Fund, Inc. name changed to Equity Progress Fund, Inc. 08/26/1970 which merged into Equity Growth Fund of America Inc. 08/01/1975 which merged into American General Enterprise Fund, Inc. 12/31/1979 which name changed to American Capital Enterprise Fund, Inc. (MD) 09/09/1983 which reincorporated in Delaware as Van Kampen American Capital Enterprise Fund 08/03/1995 which name changed to Van Kampen Enterprise Fund 08/31/1998

ELECTRONICS MFG GROUP INC (AB)
Name changed to Adeptron Technologies Corp. (AB) 01/02/2003
Adeptron Technologies Corp. (AB) reincorporated in Ontario 11/22/2011 which recapitalized as Artaflex Inc. 03/27/2012

(See Artaflex Inc.)

ELECTRONICS MISSILES & COMMUNICATIONS INC (DE)
Common 10¢ par changed to 5¢ par and (1) additional share issued 10/01/1971
Common 5¢ par changed to 1-2/3¢ par and (2) additional shares issued 10/02/1972
Name changed to EMCEE Broadcast Products, Inc. 09/13/1995
(See EMCEE Broadcast Products, Inc.)

ELECTRONICS WHSE INC (DE)
Charter cancelled and declared inoperative and void for non-payment of taxes 03/01/1985

ELECTRONIZED CHEMS CORP (DE)
Each share Common 10¢ par exchanged for (0.5) share Common 20¢ par 04/23/1968
Merged into High Voltage Engineering Corp. 07/07/1977
Each share Common 20¢ par exchanged for (1.25) shares Common $1 par
(See High Voltage Engineering Corp.)

ELECTRONOMIC INDS CORP (NY)
Reorganized 02/23/1979
Reorganized from Electronomic Industries Inc. (FL) to Electronomic Industries Corp. (NY) 02/23/1979
Name changed to Quantech Electronics Corp. (NY) 02/23/1983
Quantech Electronics Corp. (NY) reincorporated in Colorado 12/15/2003 whicn name changed to Signal Bay, Inc. 10/24/2014 which recapitalized as EVIO, Inc. 09/06/2017

ELECTROPHARMACOLOGY INC (DE)
Issue Information - 1,250,000 shares COM offered at $5 per share on 05/12/1995
Company ceased operations 03/00/2001
Stockholders' equity unlikely

ELECTROPURE INC (CA)
Name changed to Micro Imaging Technology, Inc. 3/14/2006

ELECTROSCOPE INC (CO)
Name changed to Encision Inc. 8/1/2000

ELECTROSOLIDS CORP (CA)
Adjudicated bankrupt 10/04/1967
No stockholders' equity

ELECTROSOUND GROUP INC (NY)
Filed a petition under Chapter 11 Federal Bankruptcy Code 05/09/1994
No stockholders' equity

ELECTROSOURCE INC (DE)
Each share Common 10¢ par exchanged for (0.1) share Common $1 par 07/22/1996
Plan of reorganization under Chapter 11 Federal Bankruptcy Code effective 09/29/2003
No stockholders' equity

ELECTROSPACE CORP (NY)
Reincorporated 06/30/1971
State of incorporation changed from (DE) to (NY) 06/30/1971
Common 25¢ par split (3) for (2) by issuance of (0.5) additional share 03/15/1972
Adjudicated bankrupt 05/24/1974
Stockholders' equity unlikely

ELECTROSPACE SYS INC (TX)
Common 10¢ par split (2) for (1) by issuance of (1) additional share 05/05/1983
Common 10¢ par split (5) for (4) by issuance of (0.25) additional share 09/24/1984
Common 10¢ par split (5) for (4) by issuance of (0.25) additional share 09/24/1985

Stock Dividends - 50% 09/25/1978; 20% 09/27/1979; 20% 09/25/1980; 25% 09/25/1981; 25% 09/24/1982
Merged into Chrysler Corp. 08/20/1987
Each share Common 10¢ par exchanged for $27 cash

ELECTROSTAR INC (FL)
Merged into Tyco International Ltd. 01/08/1997
Each share Common 1¢ par exchanged for $14 cash

ELECTROSVYAZ IRKUTSK REGION O A O (RUSSIA)
GDR agreement terminated 03/11/2003
Each Sponsored Reg. S GDR for Ordinary exchanged for (40) shares Ordinary

ELECTROSVYAZ OF NOVOSIBIRSK REGION OPEN JT STK (RUSSIA)
Name changed to Sibirtelecom OJSC 09/04/2001
(See Sibirtelecom OJSC)

ELECTROSVYAZ OF PRIMORSKY REGION OPEN JT STK (RUSSIA)
Name changed to Far East Electrosvyaz Co. OJSC 03/20/2002
Far East Electrosvyaz Co. OJSC name changed to Far East Telecommunications Co. OJSC 11/08/2004
(See Far East Telecommunications Co. OJSC)

ELECTROVISION CORP. (IL)
Merged into Monogram Precision Industries, Inc. 05/11/1962
Each share Common no par exchanged for (0.61538461) share Common $1 par
Monogram Precision Industries, Inc. name changed to Monogram Industries, Inc. (CA) 12/03/1962 which reincorporated in Delaware 11/28/1969 which merged into Nortek, Inc. (RI) 08/26/1983 which reincorporated in Delaware 04/23/1987 which reorganized as Nortek Holdings, Inc. 11/20/2002
(See Nortek Holdings, Inc.)

ELECTRUM INTL INC (DE)
Name changed to Consolidated Gems, Inc. 10/01/2012

ELECTRUM LAKE GOLD MINES LTD. (ON)
Charter revoked for failure to file reports and pay fees 12/29/66

ELECTRUM MNG LTD (NV)
Recapitalized as CrossPoint Energy Co. 11/27/2006
Each share Common $0.00001 par exchanged for (0.4222972) share Common $0.00001 par
(See CrossPoint Energy Co.)

ELECTRUM RES PLC (UNITED KINGDOM)
Name changed to ECR Minerals PLC 01/10/2011
(See ECR Minerals PLC)

ELECTRUM SPECIAL ACQUISITION CORP (BRITISH VIRGIN ISLANDS)
Units separated 06/06/2018
Completely liquidated 06/06/2018
Each share Ordinary no par exchanged for first and final distribution of $10.48 cash

ELEGANCE BUSINESS CORP (BC)
Delisted from Vancouver Stock Exchange 01/09/1989

ELEGANT BEAUTY INC (NV)
Plan of reorganization under Chapter 11 Federal Bankruptcy proceedings confirmed 02/14/1989
Each share old Common $0.001 par exchanged for (0.8) share new Common $0.001 par
Recapitalized as Summa Properties Corp. 05/26/1989
Each share new Common $0.001 par exchanged for (0.1) share Common $0.001 par
Summa Properties Corp. recapitalized as Nevatech Industries Inc. 12/14/1989

ELEGANT CONCRETE INC (NV)
Name changed to Security First International Holdings, Inc. 8/1/2005

ELEK-TEK INC (DE)
Filed petition under Chapter 11 Federal Bankruptcy Code 9/17/97
No stockholders' equity

ELEKTRA PWR INC (BC)
Dissolved and struck from registry 12/16/1988

ELEMENT FINL CORP (ON)
Each share Common no par received distribution of (1) share ECN Capital Corp. Common no par payable 10/03/2016 to holders of record 09/30/2016 Ex date - 10/04/2016
Name changed to Element Fleet Management Corp. 10/04/2016

ELEMENT ONE LTD (SOUTH AFRICA)
ADR agreement terminated 07/30/2015
No ADR's remain outstanding

ELEMENT 21 GOLF CO (DE)
Each share old Common 1¢ par exchanged for (0.05) share new Common 1¢ par 04/25/2008
Reincorporated under the laws of Nevada as American Rare Earths & Materials, Corp. 07/20/2010

ELEMENTAL PROT COATINGS CORP (NV)
Recapitalized as Bio-Carbon Solutions International Inc. 01/27/2011
Each share Common $0.001 par exchanged for (0.11111111) share Common $0.001 par
Bio-Carbon Solutions International Inc. name changed to NSU Resources Inc. 12/22/2011 which recapitalized as Hemcare Health Services Inc. 05/05/2015 which recapitalized as DLT Resolution Inc. 12/20/2017

ELEMENT92 RES CORP (WY)
Name changed to Yinfu Gold Corp. 11/18/2010

ELENEX INC (NY)
Acquired by Quality Corp. 02/24/1972
Each share Common 5¢ par exchanged for (0.192) share Common no par
(See Quality Corp.)

ELEPHANT & CASTLE GROUP INC (BC)
Each share old Common no par exchanged for (0.5) share new Common no par 3/27/2000
Merged into Repechage Investments Ltd. 4/20/2007
Each share new Common no par exchanged for $0.7982 cash

ELEPHANT TALK COMMUNICATIONS INC (DE)
Reincorporated 09/26/2011
Each share old Common no par exchanged for (0.04) share new Common no par 06/11/2008
State of incorporation changed from (CA) to (DE) and Common no par changed to $0.00001 par 09/26/2011
Name changed to Pareteum Corp. 11/03/2016

ELETROPAULO METROPOLITANA - ELETRICIDADE DE SAU PAULO S A (BRAZIL)
144A GDS for Class B Preferred split (2) for (1) by issuance of (1) additional GDS payable 04/11/2008 to holders of record 04/03/2008
Basis changed from (1:500) to (1:1) 04/11/2008
Each 144A GDS for Class B Preferred exchanged for (1) Sponsored ADR for Ordinary 11/30/2017
(Additional Information in Active)

ELEVATED CONCEPTS INC (NV)
Name changed to Bloggerwave Inc. 01/20/2010

ELEVATION CAP CORP (BC)
Completely liquidated
Each share Common no par received first and final distribution of approximately (0.315) Sora Capital Corp. Unit consisting of (1) share Common no par and (0.5) Common Stock Purchase Warrant expiring 11/02/2017 payable 12/04/2015 to holders of record 11/23/2015

ELEVATION ETF TR (DE)
Under plan of reorganization each share Dhandho Junoon ETF no par automatically became (1) share Cambria ETF Trust Dhandho Junoon ETF no par 01/19/2017
Trust terminated 04/02/2018
Each share Summit Water Infrastructure Multifactor ETF no par received $29.62508495 cash

ELEVATOR ELECTRIC, INC. (CA)
Merged into White (K.M.) Co. 7/6/65
Each share Common no par exchanged for (0.5) share Common no par
White (K.M.) Co. merged into Armor Elevator Co., Inc. 4/14/69 which merged into Smith (A.O.) Corp. for cash 4/10/70

ELEVEN BIOTHERAPEUTICS INC (DE)
Name changed to Sesen Bio, Inc. 05/17/2018

ELEVEN BUSINESS ACQUISITIONS INC (CANADA)
Name changed to Ivana Capital Corp. 07/30/1990
Ivana Capital Corp. recapitalized as First Ivana Technologies Ltd. 09/29/1992 which recapitalized as Vitamed Biopharmaceuticals Ltd. 04/06/1993 which name changed to Receptagen Ltd. (Canada) 07/12/1993 which reorganized in Florida as Spantel Communications Inc. 10/16/2001 which recapitalized as Systems America, Inc. 05/27/2010
(See Systems America, Inc.)

ELEVEN ELEVEN CORP (NJ)
Charter declared void for non-payment of taxes 04/14/1975

ELEVEN ELEVEN LAWRENCE CORP (IL)
Completely liquidated 12/01/1978
Each share Common no par exchanged for first and final distribution of $26.25 cash

1140-5TH AVENUE, INC.
Dissolved 00/00/1948
Details not available

1140 NORTH LASALLE CORP. (DE)
Called for redemption 04/01/1948
Public interest eliminated

ELEVEN PARK PLACE CO., INC. (NY)
Liquidated in 1954

ELEVENTH & BALTIMORE CORP. (MO)
Liquidated 12/1/55

ELEVENTH & ST STR CORP (MO)
Liquidation completed
Each share Capital Stock no par exchanged for initial distribution of $20 cash 06/08/1973
Each share Capital Stock no par received second and final distribution of $0.2087 cash 06/30/1975

ELEVON INC (DE)
Merged into SSA Global Technologies, Inc. 7/22/2003
Each share Common $0.001 par exchanged for $1.30 cash

ELEXIS CORP (DE)
Ceased operations 12/00/1999
Details not available

ELEXSYS INTL INC (CA)
Merged into Sanmina Corp. 11/06/1997
Each share Common no par exchanged for (0.33) share Common 1¢ par
Sanmina Corp. name changed to Sanmina-SCI Corp. 12/10/2001 which name changed back to Sanmina Corp. 11/15/2012

ELF AQUITAINE (FRANCE)
Acquired by Total Fina Elf S.A. 9/18/2000
Each (3) Sponsored ADR's for Ordinary 50 Frcs. par exchanged for (4) Sponsored ADR's for B Shares 50 Frcs. par

ELF AQUITAINE U K HLDGS PLC (UNITED KINGDOM)
Auction Market Preferred ADR Ser. H Unit 5 called for redemption at $500,000 on 12/20/99
Auction Market Preferred ADR Ser. B Unit 5 called for redemption at $500,000 on 12/21/99
Auction Market Preferred ADR Ser. E Unit 5 called for redemption at $500,000 on 12/23/99
Auction Market Preferred ADR Ser. I Unit 5 called for redemption at $500,000 on 12/27/99
Auction Market Preferred ADR Ser. C Unit 5 called of redemption at $500,000 on 12/28/99
(Additional Information in Active)

ELGEET OPTICAL CO., INC. (NY)
Adjudicated bankrupt 3/31/67
No stockholders' equity

ELGEN CORP. (FL)
Acquired by Dresser Industries, Inc. 04/11/1958
Each share Common 25¢ par exchanged for (0.29411764) share Common 50¢ par
(See Dresser Industries Inc. in combination with Transnational Ventures Ltd.)

ELGIN & OGDEN MINING CO. (ID)
Merged into Palm Beach Diversified Enterprises, Inc. 09/11/1970
Each share Capital Stock 5¢ par exchanged for (0.2) share Common $1.40 par
(See Palm Beach Diversified Enterprises, Inc.)

ELGIN E2 INC (DE)
Name changed to Elgin Technologies Inc. 06/16/1998
Elgin Technologies Inc. name changed to Inicia Inc. 12/05/2008 which name changed to Corporate Universe Inc. 09/21/2010

ELGIN GAS & OIL CO. (CO)
Plan of liquidation effected 12/15/1964
No stockholders' equity

ELGIN MNG INC (ON)
Merged into Mandalay Resources Corp. 09/11/2014
Each share Common no par exchanged for (0.4111) share Common no par
Note: Unexchanged certificates will be cancelled and become without value 09/11/2020

ELGIN MOTOR CAR CORP. (DE)
Charter cancelled and declared inoperative and void for non-payment of taxes 03/18/1925

ELGIN NATL INDS INC (DE)
Each share Common $5 par

exchanged for (0.33333333) share Common $1 par 05/23/1973
Common $1 par split (3) for (1) by issuance of (2) additional shares 10/22/1976
Stock Dividend - 10% 04/15/1977
Merged into Jupiter Corp. 06/30/1988
Each share Common $1 par exchanged for $17.25 cash

ELGIN NATL WATCH CO (DE)
Reincorporated 08/30/1968
Common $25 par changed to $15 par 00/00/1933
Common $15 par changed to $5 par 00/00/1954
Stock Dividend - 100% 04/01/1946
State of incorporation changed from (IL) to (DE) 08/30/1968
Under plan of merger name changed to Elgin National Industries, Inc. 02/28/1969
(See Elgin National Industries, Inc.)

ELGIN RES INC (BC)
Reincorporated 01/24/2005
Place of incorporation changed from (AB) to (BC) 01/24/2005
Merged into Eastern Platinum Ltd. 04/26/2005
Each share Common no par exchanged for (1) share Common no par

ELGIN SOFTENER CORP. (IL)
Acquired by Culligan, Inc. 09/01/1964
Each share 4% Preferred $100 par exchanged for (0.16666666) share Common $1 par
Each share Common $5 par exchanged for (0.68966) share Common $1 par
Culligan, Inc. name changed to Culligan International Co. 08/21/1970 which was acquired by Beatrice Foods Co. 06/02/1978 which name changed to Beatrice Companies, Inc. 06/05/1984
(See Beatrice Companies, Inc.)

ELGIN SWEEPER CO (DE)
Reorganized 03/01/1957
Each share Prior Preference no par exchanged for (6) shares Common no par 00/00/1946
Reorganized from (IL) to under the laws of Delaware 03/01/1957
Each share Common no par exchanged for (1) share Common $5 par
Common $5 par changed to $1 par and (4) additional shares issued 12/04/1979
Merged into Federal Signal Corp. 11/23/1982
Each share Common $1 par exchanged for $30 principal amount of 10% Conv. Debentures due 11/15/2002

ELGIN TECHNOLOGIES INC (DE)
Name changed to Inicia Inc. 12/05/2008
Inicia Inc. name changed to Corporate Universe Inc. 09/21/2010

ELGRANDE COM INC (NV)
Each share old Common $0.001 par exchanged for (0.1) share new Common $0.001 par 08/11/2003
Name changed to Elgrande International, Inc. 05/31/2005
Elgrande International, Inc. name changed to Intelligent Living Corp. 08/15/2007 which recapitalized as Occidental Development Group Inc. 08/19/2013

ELGRANDE INTL INC (NV)
Name changed to Intelligent Living Corp. 08/15/2007
Intelligent Living Corp. recapitalized as Occidental Development Group Inc. 08/19/2013

ELI ECO LOGIC INC (ON)
Recapitalized as Global Development Resources Inc. 03/11/2005
Each share Common no par exchanged for (0.2) share Common no par
Global Development Resources Inc. recapitalized as GDV Resources Inc. 12/21/2010 which name changed to Cardinal Capital Partners Inc. 09/13/2013

ELI ENTERPRISES INC (FL)
Recapitalized as Solei Systems, Inc. 03/19/2008
Each share Common $0.00001 par exchanged for (0.05) share Common $0.00001 par

ELI SCIENTIFIC INC (OR)
Each share old Common $0.005 par exchanged for (0.05) share new Common $0.005 par 06/29/1989
Name changed to Lazarus Holdings, Inc. 08/31/1989
(See Lazarus Holdings, Inc.)

ELI SECS CO (FL)
Completely liquidated 03/19/1984
Each share Common 10¢ par exchanged for first and final distribution of $10.03 cash

ELIAS BROS RESTAURANTS INC (MI)
Each share old Common no par exchanged for (0.008) share new Common no par 03/15/1983
Stock Dividend - 20% 10/20/1976
Reacquired 00/00/1986
Details not available

ELINE ENTERTAINMENT GROUP INC (NV)
Each share old Common $0.001 par exchanged for (0.05) share new Common $0.001 par 05/29/2001
Each share new Common $0.001 par exchanged again for (0.004) share new Common $0.001 par 11/28/2002
New Common $0.001 par split (3) for (2) by issuance of (0.5) additional share payable 11/06/2003 to holders of record 10/24/2003 Ex date - 11/07/2003
Each share new Common $0.001 par exchanged again for (3) shares new Common $0.001 par 02/24/2004
Reincorporated under the laws of Wyoming 06/21/2017

ELINE MUSIC COM INC (NV)
Name changed to Eline Entertainment Group, Inc. (NV) 04/25/2001
Eline Entertainment Group, Inc. (NV) reincorporated in Wyoming 06/21/2017

ELINEAR INC (DE)
Each share Common $0.001 par exchanged for (0.05) share Common 2¢ par 05/15/2001
Chapter 7 bankruptcy proceedings terminated 10/19/2012
No stockholders' equity

ELINVEST INC (NJ)
Charter declared void for non-payment of taxes 04/12/1973

ELION INSTRUMENTS, INC. (PA)
Adjudicated bankrupt 06/17/1965
No stockholders' equity

ELIOT SVGS BK (BOSTON, MA)
Placed in receivership 06/29/1990
No stockholders' equity

ELIOT STREET GARAGE CO. (MA)
Dissolved by the Supreme Judicial Court 11/20/1963
Stockholders' equity unlikely

ELISION INTL INC (UT)
Involuntarily dissolved for failure to file annual reports 06/01/1995

ELISSA RES LTD (BC)
Each share old Common no par exchanged for (0.33333333) share new Common no par 04/16/2015
Name changed to Nexoptic Technology Corp. 02/17/2016

ELITE ACQUISITIONS INC (NV)
Reincorporated under the laws of North Carolina as Flanders Corp. 01/29/1996
(See Flanders Corp.)

ELITE ARTZ INC (NV)
Each share old Common $0.001 par exchanged for (2) shares new Common $0.001 par 05/24/2007
Name changed to Clifford China Estates Inc. 03/06/2008
Clifford China Estates Inc. name changed to Asian Trends Media Holdings, Inc. 08/17/2009 which recapitalized as YUS International Group Ltd. 05/20/2013

ELITE BOOKS INC (NV)
Name changed to Elite Group, Inc. 03/29/2017

ELITE BRANDS INTL INC (NV)
Name changed to Aviation Innovations & Research, Inc. 10/03/2002
Aviation Innovations & Research, Inc. recapitalized as Immune-Tree International, Inc. 10/26/2004

ELITE CAP CORP (AB)
Name changed to Elite Technical Inc. 12/17/2001
(See Elite Technical Inc.)

ELITE COMPUTER SVCS INC (GA)
Name changed to Key Capital Corp. 04/08/1998

ELITE DATA SVCS INC (FL)
Recapitalized as WOD Retail Solutions Inc. 09/05/2018
Each share Common $0.0001 par exchanged for (0.00033333) share Common $0.0001 par

ELITE ELECTRS INC (NY)
Dissolved by proclamation 06/26/1991

ELITE FLIGHT SOLUTIONS INC (DE)
Each share old Common $0.001 par exchanged for (0.01) share new Common $0.001 par 05/01/2006
Name changed to Home Energy Savings Corp. 07/21/2006

ELITE INDS LTD (ISRAEL)
Stock Dividend - 16.6667% payable 06/23/2003 to holders of record 06/13/2003 Ex date - 06/11/2003
ADR agreement terminated 10/02/2003
Each Sponsored ADR for Ordinary exchanged for $26.4791 cash
Each Sponsored ADR for Ordinary exchanged for $26.4791 cash

ELITE INFORMATION GROUP INC (DE)
Merged into Thomson Corp. 05/16/2003
Each share Common 1¢ par exchanged for $14 cash

ELITE INS MGMT LTD (BC)
Merged into Morgan Financial Corp. (ON) 06/30/1988
Each share Common no par exchanged for (0.9) share Common no par
(See Morgan Financial Corp. (ON))

ELITE LOGISTICS INC (ID)
SEC revoked common stock registration 10/14/2010

ELITE NUTRITIONAL BRANDS INC (FL)
Reorganized under the laws of Delaware as Aspen Group, Inc. 03/05/2012
Each share Common $0.0001 par exchanged for (0.4) share Common $0.001 par

ELITE PHARMACEUTICALS INC (DE)
Each share old Common 1¢ par exchanged for (0.5) share new Common 1¢ par 03/30/1998
New Common 1¢ par changed to $0.001 par 10/26/2009

Reincorporated under the laws of Nevada 01/05/2012

ELITE REAL ESTATE CDA INC (CANADA)
Recapitalized as Far Eastern Energy Corp. 03/21/1995
Each share Common no par exchanged for (0.25) share Common no par
(See Far Eastern Energy Corp.)

ELITE RESOURCE CORP (BC)
Recapitalized as Myriad Concepts, Ltd. 03/20/1987
Each share Common no par exchanged for (0.5) share Common no par
(See Myriad Concepts, Ltd.)

ELITE TECHNICAL INC (AB)
Placed in receivership 11/10/2005
Stockholders' equity unlikely

ELITE TECHNOLOGIES INC (TX)
SEC revoked common stock registration 10/14/2010

ELITEGROUP VENTURES NEV INC (NV)
Name changed to Recfuel Holdings, Inc. 07/20/2007
(See Recfuel Holdings, Inc.)

ELIXIR GAMING TECHNOLOGIES INC (NV)
Name changed to Entertainment Gaming Asia Inc. 07/26/2010
(See Entertainment Gaming Asia Inc.)

ELIXIR INDS (CA)
Common $1 par split (3) for (2) by issuance of (0.5) additional share 05/24/1972
Under plan of merger each share Common $1 par exchanged for $10 cash 02/24/1982

ELIZABETH & TRENTON RAILROAD
Dissolved 00/00/1941
Details not available

ELIZABETH ARDEN INC (FL)
Acquired by Revlon, Inc. 09/07/2016
Each share Common 1¢ par exchanged for $14 cash

ELIZABETHTOWN & FLORIN STREET RAILWAY CO.
Merged into Conestoga Transportation Co. in 1932
Details not available

ELIZABETHTOWN CONSOLIDATED GAS CO. (NJ)
Each share Capital Stock $100 par exchanged for (5) shares Capital Stock $20 par 00/00/1953
Capital Stock $20 par changed to $10 par and (1) additional share issued 03/20/1962
Name changed to Elizabethtown Gas Co. 03/08/1966
Elizabethtown Gas Co. acquired by National Utilities & Industries Corp. 07/17/1969 which name changed to NUI Corp. (Old) 04/04/1983 which reorganized as NUI Corp. (New) 03/01/2001
(See NUI Corp. (New))

ELIZABETHTOWN GAS CO (NJ)
Stock Dividend - 10% 01/05/1968
Acquired by National Utilities & Industries Corp. 07/17/1969
Each share Capital Stock $10 par exchanged for (2) shares Common $10 par
National Utilities & Industries Corp. name changed to NUI Corp. (Old) 04/04/1983 which reorganized as NUI Corp. (New) 03/01/2001
(See NUI Corp. (New))

ELIZABETHTOWN WATER CO. CONSOLIDATED (NJ)
Each share Capital Stock $100 par exchanged for (5) shares Capital Stock $20 par 03/29/1956
Each share Capital Stock $20 par

ELI-ELL

exchanged for (2) shares Capital Stock no par 05/05/1960
Merged into Elizabethtown Water Co. 06/30/1961
Each share Capital Stock no par exchanged for (1.4) shares Common no par
Elizabethtown Water Co. reorganized as E'town Corp. 09/01/1985
(See E'town Corp.)

ELIZABETHTOWN WTR CO (NJ)
Common no par split (2) for (1) by issuance of (1) additional share 10/14/1976
Under plan of reorganization each share Common no par automatically became (1) share E'Town Corp. Common no par 09/01/1985
(See E'Town Corp.)
$5.90 Preferred $100 par called for redemption at $100 on 03/01/2004
Public interest eliminated

ELJER CO. (PA)
Dissolved 00/00/1953
Details not available

ELJER INDS INC (DE)
Merged into Zurn Industries Inc. 01/27/1997
Each share Common $1 par exchanged for $24 cash

ELK ASSOC FDG CORP (NY)
Reincorporated under the laws of Delaware as Ameritrans Capital Corp. and Common 1¢ par changed to $0.0001 par 12/17/1999

ELK CITY MNG INC (NV)
Name changed to Chill Tech Industries Inc. 10/05/1998
(See Chill Tech Industries Inc.)

ELK CNTY BK & TR CO (ST MARYS, PA)
Merged into First Laurel Bank (St. Mary's, PA) 07/01/1972
Each share Common $12.50 par exchanged for (3) shares Capital Stock $5 par
First Laurel Bank (St. Mary's, PA) merged into Pennsylvania Bank & Trust Co. (Titusville, PA) 03/01/1975 which reorganized as Pennbancorp 12/31/1980 which merged into Integra Financial Corp. 01/26/1989 which merged into National City Corp. 05/03/1996 which was acquired by PNC Financial Services Group, Inc. 12/31/2008

ELK EQUITIES INC (AB)
Name changed to Qeva Group Inc. 08/13/2002
Qeva Group Inc. recapitalized as Excelsior Energy Ltd. 09/06/2006
(See Excelsior Energy Ltd.)

ELK HORN COAL CORP (WV)
Merged into PHI Acquisition Corp. 08/16/1994
Each share Common no par exchanged for $59.25 cash

ELK LAKE METALS & HLDGS LTD (ON)
Charter cancelled for failure to pay taxes and file returns 02/20/1980

ELK LAKE MINES LTD. (ON)
Name changed to Elk Lake Metals & Holdings Ltd. and Capital Stock $1 par changed to no par 12/22/1970
(See Elk Lake Metals & Holdings Ltd.)

ELK MOUNTAIN URANIUM CORP. (NV)
Recapitalized as Central Oil & Mining Corp. 00/00/1956
Each share Common 1¢ par exchanged for (0.06666666) share Common 15¢ par

ELK OILS CO. LTD. (SK)
Liquidated 00/00/1954
Details not available

ELK POINT RES INC (AB)
Name changed 11/09/1993
Name changed from Elk Point Game Ranching Corp. to Elk Point Resources Inc. 11/09/1993
Each share old Class A Common no par exchanged for (0.25) share new Class A Common no par 07/05/1996
New Class A Common no par reclassified as Common no par 06/04/1997
Merged into Acclaim Energy Trust 01/28/2003
Each share Common no par exchanged for (0.88537) Acclaim Energy Trust Trust Unit, (0.5) share Burmis Energy Inc. Common no par and $0.25172 cash
(See each company's listing)

ELK RIDGE URANIUM CO. (UT)
Merged into Federal Uranium Corp. (NV) 01/25/1956
Each share Common 15¢ par exchanged for (0.28571428) share Capital Stock 50¢ par
Federal Uranium Corp. (NV) merged into Federal Resources Corp. 05/02/1960
(See Federal Resources Corp.)

ELK RUN CO.
Liquidation completed 00/00/1947
Details not available

ELKCORP (DE)
Merged into Building Materials Corp. of America 03/26/2007
Each share Common $1 par exchanged for $43.50 cash

ELKHART BANC SHARES, INC. (IL)
Acquired by Illini Community Bancorp, Inc. 00/00/1988
Details not available

ELKHART COMMUNITY BANK (ELKHART, IL)
Reorganized as Elkhart Banc Shares, Inc. 11/16/1983
Each share Capital Stock $10 par exchanged for (1) share Capital Stock $10 par
(See Elkhart Banc Shares, Inc.)

ELKHART HOTEL CORP. (IN)
Liquidation completed
Each share Common no par exchanged for initial distribution of $70 cash 08/02/1971
Each share Common no par received second distribution of $15 cash 12/27/1971
Each share Common no par received third and final distribution of $6.1383 cash 04/22/1972

ELKHORN ETF TR (MA)
Trust terminated 03/14/2017
Each share FTSE RAFI U.S. Equity Income ETF 1¢ par received $28.65896 cash
Each share S&P 500 Capital Expenditures Portfolio 1¢ par received $27.22967 cash
Trust terminated 09/26/2017
Each share S&P MidCap Consumer Discretionary Portfolio 1¢ par received $15.01 cash
Each share S&P MidCap Consumer Staples Portfolio 1¢ par received $14.03 cash
Each share S&P MidCap Energy Portfolio 1¢ par received $9.73 cash
Each share S&P MidCap Financials Portfolio 1¢ par received $14.38 cash
Each share S&P MidCap Health Care Portfolio 1¢ par received $17.67 cash
Each share S&P MidCap Industrials Portfolio 1¢ par received $15.65 cash
Each share S&P MidCap Information Technology Portfolio 1¢ par received $17.53 cash
Each share S&P MidCap Materials Portfolio 1¢ par received $16.07 cash
Each share S&P MidCap Utilities Portfolio 1¢ par received $15.85 cash
Name changed to Innovator ETFs Trust II 04/10/2018
Trust terminated 04/13/2018
Each share Commodity Rotation Strategy ETF 1¢ par received $26.61 cash
Each share Fundamental Commodity Strategy ETF 1¢ par received $28.36 cash

ELKHORN GOLD MINING CO. (CO)
Charter expired by time limitation 12/08/1906

ELKHORN GOLD MNG CORP (BC)
Recapitalized as Tulloch Resources Ltd. 03/09/2012
Each share Common no par exchanged for (0.2) share Common no par
Tulloch Resources Ltd. recapitalized as Tidal Royalty Corp. 07/18/2017

ELKIN WEISS & COS INC (UT)
Involuntarily dissolved 03/31/1994

ELKINS INST INC (TX)
Stock Dividend - 100% 12/19/1969
Adjudicated bankrupt 11/09/1976
Stockholders' equity unlikely

ELKINS PRODUCTIONS OF CANADA LTD. (ON)
Merged into Life Investors International Ltd. 06/00/1973
Each share Common no par exchanged for (0.5) share Class A Common no par and (0.5) share Common no par
Life Investors International Ltd. merged into Life Investors Ltd. 07/14/1973
(See Life Investors Ltd.)

ELKINS SINN CORP (DE)
Name changed to CSE Liquidating Corp. 09/30/1976
(See CSE Liquidating Corp.)

ELKO OIL DEVELOPMENT AND IMPROVEMENT COMPANY (NV)
Charter forfeited for non-payment of taxes 07/01/1924

ELKO VENTURES INC (NV)
Common $0.001 par split (3) for (1) by issuance of (2) additional shares payable 01/31/2008 to holders of record 01/31/2008
Name changed to North American Gold & Minerals Fund 09/28/2009
North American Gold & Minerals Fund recapitalized as Nationsmark Nextgen 09/25/2015 which name changed to NationsMark Nexgen 05/12/2017

ELKS INC (ON)
Assets liquidated for the benefit of creditors 00/00/1991
No stockholders' equity

ELKS STORES LTD. (ON)
Name changed to Elks Inc. 08/17/1981
(See Elks Inc.)

ELKTON BKG & TR CO (ELKTON, MD)
Name changed to County Banking & Trust Co. (Elkton, MD) 10/01/1977
County Banking & Trust Co. (Elkton, MD) merged into Mercantile Bankshares Corp. 07/01/1983 which merged into PNC Financial Services Group, Inc. 03/02/2007

ELKTON CO (CO)
Declared defunct and inoperative for failure to file reports and pay taxes 10/16/1971

ELKWATER RES LTD (AB)
Recapitalized as Striker Exploration Corp. 03/02/2015
Each share Common no par exchanged for (0.05) share Common no par
Striker Exploration Corp. merged into Gear Energy Ltd. 07/29/2016

ELLA RES INC (BC)
Name changed to Kinetic Energy Inc. 01/25/2001
Kinetic Energy Inc. recapitalized as Torque Energy Inc. 02/19/2003
(See Torque Energy Inc.)

ELLEIPSIS GLOBAL TRAVEL SOLUTIONS INC (NV)
Common $0.001 par split (3) for (1) by issuance of (2) additional shares payable 06/10/2008 to holders of record 06/06/2008 Ex date - 06/11/2008
Recapitalized as Resource Ventures, Inc. 02/23/2010
Each share Common $0.001 par exchanged for (0.0005) share Common $0.001 par

ELLEN GOLD MINES, LTD. (ON)
Charter cancelled 12/00/1957

ELLENSBURG TEL INC (WA)
Stock Dividends - 10% 12/12/1986; 10% 12/09/1988
Merged into Ellensburg Acquisition Corp. 04/30/1998
Each share Common $10 par exchanged for $127 cash
Note: An additional $6.39988109 cash per share was distributed 06/01/1999

ELLENVILLE ENTERPRISES INC (NY)
Recapitalized as Organic Petroleum Additive Corp. 09/25/1981
Each share Common 1¢ par exchanged for (0.1) share Common 1¢ par
Organic Petroleum Additive Corp. name changed to Stanton Industries, Inc. 05/11/1982 which name changed to International Monetary Funding Corp. 06/28/1982 which recapitalized as Hawaiian Sugar Technologies, Inc. 01/20/1983 which recapitalized as Entertainment Inns of America, Inc. 10/21/1983 which name changed to Tiger Marketing, Inc. 11/08/1984 which recapitalized as U.S. Health Services, Inc. 04/08/1986 which name changed to Diamond Trade Center, Inc. 10/30/1990
(See Diamond Trade Center, Inc.)

ELLER INDS INC (CO)
Each share old Common $0.0001 par exchanged for (0.0125) share new Common $0.0001 par 05/08/1998
Each share new Common $0.0001 par received distribution of (0.008) share Infinite Networks Corp. (New) Common $0.001 par payable 03/23/2007 to holders of record 02/28/2007 Ex date - 02/26/2007
Name changed to Qenex Communications, Inc. 07/31/2007

ELLERY & JAMES LTD (NV)
Name changed to ELR Technologies Inc. 10/01/1998
ELR Technologies Inc. reorganized as CES International Inc. 05/16/2005
(See CES International, Inc.)

ELLESMERE MINERALS LTD (AB)
Recapitalized as Matador Exploration Inc. 11/09/2004
Each share Common no par exchanged for (0.25) share Common no par
(See Matador Exploration Inc.)

ELLESMERE OIL & DEVELOPMENT LTD.
Merged into New Concord Development Corp. Ltd. 00/00/1952
Each share Capital Stock no par exchanged for (0.33333333) share Capital Stock no par

(See New Concord Development Corp. Ltd.)

ELLETT BROS INC (SC)
Merged into Ellett Holding Inc. 03/28/2002
Each share Common no par exchanged for $3.20 cash

ELLIGENT CONSULTING GROUP INC (NV)
Name changed to E-Vantage Solutions, Inc. 07/16/2000
(See E-Vantage Solutions, Inc.)

ELLIMAN DOUGLAS L & CO INC (DE)
Merged into DLE Corp. 09/18/1981
Each share Common 10¢ par exchanged for $4 cash

ELLIOS RES LTD (BC)
Name changed to Fjordland Minerals Ltd. 10/08/1996
Fjordland Minerals Ltd. recapitalized as Fjordland Exploration Inc. 05/03/2002

ELLIOT URANIUM MINES LTD. (ON)
Charter cancelled 05/08/1971

ELLIOTT AUTOMATION LTD (ENGLAND)
Stock Dividends - Ordinary 100% 03/26/1964; ADR's 100% 04/13/1964
Acquired by English Electric Co. Ltd. 12/22/1967
Each ADR for Ordinary exchanged for (0.3) ADR for Ordinary
English Electric Co. Ltd. merged into General Electric & English Electric Companies Ltd. 12/20/1968 which name changed to General Electric Co. PLC (New) 09/18/1970 which name changed to Marconi PLC 11/26/1999 which name changed to M (2003) PLC 01/16/2004
(See M (2003) PLC)

ELLIOTT BANCORP, INC. (IL)
Merged into Firstbank of Illinois Co. 10/31/1986
Each share Capital Stock $100 par exchanged for (23) shares Common $1 par
Firstbank of Illinois Co. merged into Mercantile Bancorporation, Inc. 07/01/1998 which merged into Firstar Corp. (New) 09/20/1999 which merged into U.S. Bancorp (New) 02/27/2001

ELLIOTT CO. (PA)
Merged into Carrier Corp. 07/31/1957
Each share 5% Preferred $50 par exchanged for (1.2) shares 4.5% Preferred $50 par
Each share 5% 2nd Preferred $50 par exchanged for (1.1) shares 4.8% 2nd Preferred $50 par
Each share Common $10 par exchanged for (0.65) share Common $10 par
Carrier Corp. acquired by United Technologies Corp. 07/06/1979

ELLIOTT CORE DRILLING CO.
Acquired by Byron Jackson Co. 00/00/1939
Details not available

ELLIOTT FISHER CO.
Merged into Underwood Elliott Fisher Co. 00/00/1927
Details not available

ELLIOTT MURDOCH INC (DE)
Charter cancelled and declared inoperative and void for non-payment of taxes 03/01/1989

ELLIOTT ST BK (JACKSONVILLE, IL)
Reorganized as Elliott Bancorp, Inc. 01/01/1983
Each share Capital Stock $100 par exchanged for (1) share Capital Stock $100 par
Elliott Bancorp, Inc. merged into Firstbank of Illinois Co. 10/31/1983 which merged into Mercantile Bancorporation, Inc. 07/01/1998 which merged into Firstar Corp. (New) 09/20/1999 which merged into U.S. Bancorp (DE) 02/27/2001

ELLIOTT TECHNOLOGIES INC (DE)
Name changed to Elliott-Murdoch, Inc. 11/14/1986
(See Elliott-Murdoch, Inc.)

ELLIS BANK OF INDIAN ROCKS (TAMPA, FL)
Location changed from (Indian Rocks, FL) to (Tampa, FL) 09/30/1983
Name changed to NCNB National Bank of Florida (Tampa, FL) 06/22/1984
NCNB National Bank of Florida (Tampa, FL) name changed to NationsBank of Florida, N.A. (Tampa, FL) 09/04/1992
(See NationsBank of Florida, N.A. (Tampa, FL))

ELLIS BKG CORP (FL)
Stock Dividend - 25% 07/31/1978
Merged into NCNB Corp. 03/16/1984
Each share Common $1 par exchanged for $22 cash

ELLIS NATIONAL BANK OF CENTRAL FLORIDA (TAMPA, FL)
Name changed 10/08/1982
Name changed from Ellis National Bank of Tampa (Tampa, FL) to Ellis National Bank of Central Florida (Tampa, FL) 10/08/1982
Acquired by NCNB National Bank of Florida (Tampa, FL) 05/18/1984
Details not available

ELLIS NATIONAL BANK OF PINELLAS COUNTY (ST. PETERSBURG, FL)
99% held by Ellis Banking Corp. as of 03/20/1972
Public interest eliminated

ELLIS PARK APARTMENTS, LTD.
Dissolution approved 00/00/1951
Details not available

ELLIS PERRY INTL INC (FL)
Common 1¢ par split (3) for (2) by issuance of (0.5) additional share payable 12/29/2006 to holders of record 12/12/2006 Ex date - 01/3/2007
Acquired by Feldenkreis Holdings LLC 10/22/2018
Each share Common 1¢ par exchanged for $27.50 cash

ELLMANS INC (GA)
Merged into Service Merchandise Co., Inc. 05/24/1985
Each share Common $1 par exchanged for $28 cash

ELLSWORTH FUND LTD (DE)
Name changed 02/17/2006
Name and state of incorporation changed from Ellsworth Convertible Growth & Income Fund, Inc. (MD) to Ellsworth Fund Ltd. (DE) and Common 1¢ par reclassified as Shares of Bene. Int. 1¢ par 02/17/2006
Name changed to Ellsworth Growth & Income Ltd. 01/26/2015

ELLWOOD FED SVGS BK (ELLWOOD CITY, PA)
Under plan of reorganization each share Common $1 par automatically became (1) share PennFirst Bancorp, Inc. Common 1¢ par 07/01/1991
PennFirst Bancorp, Inc. name changed to ESB Financial Corp. 05/01/1998 which merged into WesBanco, Inc. 02/10/2015

ELM BANCSHARES INC (DE)
Name changed to Elm Marine Bancshares, Inc. 05/25/1984
Elm Marine Bancshares, Inc. name changed to Illinios Marine Bancorp, Inc. 07/17/1985 which name changed to Illinois Regional Bancorp, Inc. 01/30/1987
(See Illinois Regional Bancorp, Inc.)

ELM CITY NURSERY CO. WOODMONT INDUSTRIES, INC. (CT)
Charter forfeited for failure to file reports 12/26/1933

ELM FINL SVCS INC (DE)
Acquired by St. Paul Bancorp, Inc. 02/23/1993
Each share Common 1¢ par exchanged for (0.4076) share Common 1¢ par and $12.35 cash
St. Paul Bancorp, Inc. merged into Charter One Financial, Inc. 10/01/1999
(See Charter One Financial, Inc.)

ELM MARINE BANCHARES INC (DE)
Name changed to Illinois Marine Bancorp, Inc. 07/17/1985
Illinois Marine Bancorp, Inc. name changed to Illinois Regional Bancorp, Inc. 01/30/1987
(See Illinois Regional Bancorp, Inc.)

ELM POINT MINES LTD. (ON)
Merged into Great Eagle Explorations & Holdings Ltd. 07/07/1969
Each share Common no par exchanged for (0.125) share Common no par
Great Eagle Explorations & Holdings Ltd. merged into Belle Aire Resource Explorations Ltd. 08/29/1978 which name changed to Sprint Resources Ltd. 09/23/1982 which name changed to Meacon Bay Resources Inc. 03/09/1987 which recapitalized as Advantex Marketing International Inc. 09/16/1991

ELM TECHNOLOGIES INC (NV)
Name changed to Perla Group International, Inc. 12/10/2010

ELM TREE CAP CORP (FL)
Recapitalized as Ocean Fresh Seafood Marketplace Inc. 12/31/1999
Each share Common $0.001 par exchanged for (0.1) share Common $0.001 par
Ocean Fresh Seaford Marketplace Inc. name changed to International Builders Ltd., Inc. 03/23/2004
(See International Builders Ltd., Inc.)

ELM TREE MINERALS INC (BC)
Each share old Common no par exchanged for (0.2) share new Common no par 07/04/2013
Name changed to Ximen Mining Corp. 08/23/2013

ELMAC MALARTIC MINES LTD (ON)
Charter cancelled and declared dissolved for failure to file returns and pay fees 11/09/1976

ELMAR ELECTRONICS, INC. (CA)
Completely liquidated 09/05/1967
Each share Common no par exchanged for first and final distribution of (0.1) share Wyle Laboratories $3.40 Conv. Preference Ser. A no par
(See Wyle Laboratories)

ELMER BANK & TRUST CO. (ELMER, NJ)
Stock Dividend - 100% 06/01/1967
Reorganized as Midlantic Banks Inc. 06/12/1970
Each share Common $10 par exchanged for (1.25) shares Common $10 par
Midlantic Banks Inc. merged into Midlantic Corp. 01/30/1987 which merged into PNC Bank Corp. 12/31/1995 which name changed to PNC Financial Services Group, Inc. 03/15/2000

ELMER TRUST CO. (ELMER, NJ)
Recapitalized as Elmer Bank & Trust Co. (Elmer, NJ) 03/07/1967
Each share Common $100 par exchanged for (10) shares Common $10 par
Elmer Bank & Trust Co. (Elmer, NJ) reorganized as Midlantic Banks Inc. 06/12/1970 which merged into Midlantic Corp. 01/30/1987 which merged into PNC Bank Corp. 12/31/1995 which name changed to PNC Financial Services Group, Inc. 03/15/2000

ELMERS RESTAURANTS INC (OR)
Stock Dividends - 5% payable 12/10/1999 to holders of record 11/30/1999; 10% payable 09/15/2000 to holders of record 08/18/2000; 5% payable 03/21/2002 to holders of record 03/07/2002
Merged into ERI Acquisition Corp. 04/21/2005
Each share Common no par exchanged for $7.50 cash

ELMET INC (NV)
Company reported out of business 00/00/1981
Details not available

ELMHURST NATL BK (ELMHURST, IL)
Capital Stock $25 par changed to $10 par and (1.5) additional shares issued 04/01/1968
Stock Dividends - 33.33333333% 01/19/1960; 25% 07/12/1965; 20% 02/08/1968; 14.285714% 03/27/1973; 100% 04/22/1977
Under plan of reorganization each share Capital Stock $10 par automatically became (1) share Elm Bancshares, Inc. Common $10 par 05/30/1981
Elm Bancshares, Inc. name changed to Elm Marine Bancshares, Inc. 05/25/1984 which name changed to Illinois Marine Bancorp, Inc. 07/17/1985 which name changed to Illinois Regional Bancorp, Inc. 01/30/1987
(See Illinois Regional Bancorp, Inc.)

ELMIRA & WILLIAMSPORT RR CO (PA)
Merged into Penndel Co. 07/01/1969
Each share Preferred $50 par exchanged for $55 cash
Each share Common $50 par exchanged for $38.50 cash

ELMIRA CORNING & WAVERLY RWY.
Ceased operations 00/00/1930
Details not available

ELMIRA LIGHT, HEAT & POWER CORP.
Merged into New York State Electric & Gas Corp. 00/00/1936

ELMIRA SHARES CORP.
Liquidated 00/00/1944
Details not available

ELMIRA WATER, LIGHT & RAILROAD CO.
Name changed to Elmira Light, Heat & Power Corp. 00/00/1932
(See Elmira Light, Heat & Power Corp.)

ELMONT INDS LTD (BC)
Merged into Kapok Corp. 09/23/1983
Each share Common no par exchanged for (0.23809523) share Common 10¢ par
Kapok Corp. name changed to Hampton Healthcare Inc. 11/03/1987 which reorganized as Hampton Resources Corp. 12/31/1991 which merged into Bellwether Exploration Co. 03/01/1995 which name changed to Mission Resources Corp. 05/16/2001
(See Mission Resources Corp.)

ELMORE CORP (NC)
Class A Common $5 par split (2) for

(1) by issuance of (1) additional share 03/15/1969
Class B Common $5 par split (2) for (1) by issuance of (1) additional share 03/15/1969
Acquired by Belding Heminway Co. (Old) 12/00/1974
Each share Class A Common $5 par exchanged for $8 cash
Each share Class B Common $5 par exchanged for $5 cash

ELMOS GOLD MINES LTD.
Merged into Tombill Gold Mines Ltd. 00/00/1941
Each share Capital Stock $1 par exchanged for (0.2) share Capital Stock $1 par
Tombill Gold Mines Ltd. name changed to Tombill Mines Ltd. 05/07/1959
(See Tombill Mines Ltd.)

ELMRIDGE MINES LTD. (ON)
Merged into Canuba Manganese Mines Ltd. 06/28/1956
Each share Capital Stock $1 par exchanged for (0.01) share Capital Stock $1 par
(See Canuba Manganese Mines Ltd.)

ELMVIEW MANOR APARTMENTS, INC.
Liquidated 00/00/1939
Details not available

ELMWOOD APARTMENTS CORP. (IL)
Dissolved 00/00/1953
Details not available

ELMWOOD BANCORP INC (PA)
Acquired by Keystone Financial, Inc. 01/10/1994
Each share Common $1 par exchanged for (0.74) share Common $2 par
Keystone Financial, Inc. merged into M&T Bank Corp. 10/06/2000

ELMWOOD CAP CORP (NV)
Reincorporated under the laws of Delaware as U.S. Environmental Solutions Inc. 03/19/1991
U.S. Environmental Solutions Inc. recapitalized as EnviroResolutions, Inc. 07/23/2007
(See EnviroResolutions, Inc.)

ELMWOOD CEMETERY CORP. (DE)
Completely liquidated 01/10/1966
Each share Capital Stock no par exchanged for first and final distribution of $35 cash

ELMWOOD FED SVGS BK (MEDIA, PA)
Under plan of reorganization each share Common $1 par automatically became (1) share Elmwood Bancorp Inc. Common $1 par 07/01/1992
Elmwood Bancorp Inc. acquired by Keystone Financial, Inc. 01/10/1994 which merged into M&T Bank Corp. 10/06/2000

ELMWOOD MINES LTD. (ON)
Merged into Milestone Exploration Ltd. 07/23/1968
Each share Capital Stock $1 par exchanged for (0.071942) share Capital Stock no par
Milestone Exploration Ltd. merged into Jubilee Gold Inc. 01/01/2010 which merged into Jubilee Gold Exploration Ltd. 01/25/2013

ELMWOOD RES LTD (ON)
Name changed to Easynet Data Corp. 07/03/1985
Easynet Data Corp. name changed to Vertigo 3D, Inc. 04/30/1996 which recapitalized as Vertigo Software Corp. 10/27/1998 which name changed to Even Technologies Inc. 06/22/2004

ELNIDO MINES, LTD. (ON)
Charter cancelled 03/00/1951

ELOCITY NETWORKS CORP (DE)
Name changed to Diversified Financial Resources Corp. (DE) 08/23/2002
Diversified Financial Resources Corp. (DE) reincorporated in Nevada 05/12/2006 which name changed to China Fruits Corp. 09/08/2006

ELODA CORP (CANADA)
Assets sold for the benefit of creditors 10/07/2009
Stockholders' equity unlikely

ELODA 2006 CORP (CANADA)
Name changed to Eloda Corp. 01/12/2007
(See Eloda Corp.)

ELONG INC (CAYMAN ISLANDS)
Acquired by China E-dragon Holdings Ltd. 06/01/2016
Each Sponsored ADR for Ordinary exchanged for $17.95 cash

ELOQUA INC (DE)
Acquired by Oracle Corp. 02/11/2013
Each share Common $0.0001 par exchanged for $23.50 cash

ELOQUENT INC (DE)
Preferred Stock Purchase Rights declared for Common stockholders of record 11/08/2000 were redeemed at $0.001 per right 06/14/2002 for holders of record 05/22/2002
Merged into Open Text Corp. 03/20/2003
Each share Common $0.001 par exchanged for $0.29414092 cash
Note: Each share Common $0.001 par received an additional distribution of $0.05571021 cash from escrow 04/12/2013

ELORAC CORP (DE)
Name changed to Innovo Group Inc. 09/07/1990
Innovo Group Inc. name changed to Joe's Jeans Inc. 10/15/2007 which recapitalized as Differential Brands Group Inc. 01/29/2016

ELOT INC (DE)
Company terminated common stock registration and is no longer public as of 12/31/2002

ELOT INC (VA)
Reorganized under Chapter 11 Federal Bankruptcy Code as eLOT, Inc. (DE) 12/31/2002
Each share Common 1¢ par will receive (0.00893) Common Stock Purchase Warrant Class B and (0.01429) Common Stock Purchase Warrant Class C if the reorganized company reaches certain financial milestones by 12/31/2005
Note: Certificates were not required to be surrendered and are without value
(See eLOT, Inc. (DE))

ELOX CORP. (MI)
Stock Dividend - 10% 11/23/1965
Completely liquidated 07/28/1967
Each share Common $1 par exchanged for first and final distribution of (0.5) share Colt Industries Inc. (PA) Common $3 par
Colt Industries Inc. (PA) reincorporated in Delaware 10/17/1968 which reincorporated back in Pennsylvania 05/06/1976

ELOX CORP. OF MICHIGAN (MI)
Class A Common no par and Class B Common no par changed to $1 par 04/22/1955
Class A Common $1 par and Class B Common $1 par reclassified as Common $1 par 09/09/1957
Stock Dividends - 10% 07/10/1961; 10% 06/15/1965
Name changed to Elox Corp. 09/23/1965
Elox Corp. acquired by Colt Industries Inc. (PA) 07/28/1967 which reincorporated in Delaware 10/17/1968 which reincorporated back in Pennsylvania 05/06/1976
(See Colt Industries Inc. (PA))

ELOY WATER CO. (AZ)
Sold to Town of Eloy and liquidated 00/00/1954
Details not available

ELOYALTY CORP (DE)
Each share old Common 1¢ par exchanged for (0.1) share new Common 1¢ par 12/19/2001
Name changed to Mattersight Corp. 06/01/2011
(See Mattersight Corp.)

ELPAC INC (CA)
Common $1 par split (3) for (1) by issuance of (2) additional shares 05/06/1966
Each share Common $1 par exchanged for (0.4) share Common $2.50 par 08/01/1969
Each share Common $2.50 par exchanged for (0.25) share Common 1¢ par 09/15/1970
Reorganized under the laws of Delaware 08/01/1974
Each share Common 1¢ par exchanged for (1) share Common 1¢ par
Elpac, Inc. (DE) merged into Newpark Resources, Inc. 08/27/1976

ELPAC INC (DE)
Merged into Newpark Resources, Inc. 08/27/1976
Each share Common 1¢ par exchanged for (0.5) share Common $2 par

ELPLATA CORP (NV)
Name changed 09/30/1999
Name changed from ElPlata Mining Corp. to ElPlata Corp. and Common 5¢ par changed to $0.001 par 09/30/1999
Name changed to Shimoda Resources Holdings, Inc. 04/17/2001
(See Shimoda Resources Holdings, Inc.)

ELR TECHNOLOGIES INC (NV)
Each share old Common $0.001 par exchanged for (0.02) share new Common $0.001 par 02/15/2003
New Common $0.001 par split (3) for (1) by issuance of (2) additional shares payable 08/30/2004 to holders of record 08/30/2004
Reorganized as CES International, Inc. 05/16/2005
Each share new Common $0.001 par exchanged for (2) shares Common $0.001 par
(See CES International, Inc.)

ELRICO URANIUM CORP. (UT)
Name changed to Auranthetic Corp. 04/01/1971
(See Auranthetic Corp.)

ELRON ELECTR INDS LTD (ISRAEL)
Conv. Preferred IS3 par split (3) for (2) by issuance of (0.5) additional share 02/04/1983
Conv. Preferred IS3 par called for redemption 08/19/1983
(Additional Information in Active)

ELROY GOLD MINES LTD.
Name changed to Belteco Kirkland Mines Ltd. 00/00/1944
(See Belteco Kirkland Mines Ltd.)

ELSAG BAILEY PROCESS AUTOMATION N V (NETHERLANDS)
Merged into ABB Ltd. 01/00/1999
Each share Common 1 Gldr. par exchanged for $39.30 cash

ELSBURG GOLD MNG LTD (SOUTH AFRICA)
Merged into Western Areas Gold Mining Co. Ltd. 06/12/1992
Each ADR for Ordinary exchanged for (0.65) ADR for Ordinary Western Areas Gold Mining Co. Ltd. name changed to Western Areas Ltd. 10/19/1998
(See Western Areas Ltd.)

ELSCINT LTD (ISRAEL)
Ordinary Share I£1 par changed to IS 0.10 par per currency change 00/00/1980
Ordinary Share IS 0.10 par changed to IS 0.05 par and (1) additional share issued 02/20/1981
Ordinary Share IS 0.05 par changed to IS 0.025 par and (1) additional share issued 12/03/1982
Ordinary Share IS 0.025 par changed to ILS 0.04 par 09/09/1983
Ordinary Share ILS 0.04 par changed to ILS 0.01 par 11/25/1986
Each share old Ordinary Share ILS 0.01 par exchanged for (0.2) share new Ordinary Share ILS 0.01 par 03/11/1996
Merged into Elbit Medical Imaging Ltd. 11/23/2005
Each Ordinary Share NIS 0.01 par exchanged for (0.53) Ordinary Share NIS 1 par
Elbit Medical Imaging Ltd. name changed to Elbit Imaging Ltd. 12/04/2007

ELSEVIER N V (NETHERLANDS)
Each old Sponsored ADR for Ordinary exchanged for (2.5) new Sponsored ADR's for Ordinary 10/06/1994
Name changed to Reed Elsevier N.V. 04/22/2002
Reed Elsevier N.V. reorganized as RELX N.V. 07/01/2015 which merged into RELX PLC 09/10/2018

ELSIN ELECTRONICS CORP. (NY)
Merged into Specialty Electronics Development Corp. 05/25/1959
Each share Common 2¢ par exchanged for (0.5) share Common 4¢ par
Specialty Electronics Development Corp. name changed to Spedcor Electronics, Inc. 11/21/1967 which merged into Entron, Inc. 12/31/1969
(See Entron, Inc.)

ELSINOR APARTMENTS, INC.
Liquidated 00/00/1940
Details not available

ELSINORE CATTLE CO. (DE)
Common $100 par changed to $10 par 07/11/1968
Charter cancelled and declared inoperative and void for non-payment of taxes 09/30/1990

ELSINORE CORP (NV)
Each share old Common no par exchanged for (0.2) share new Common no par 07/12/1991
Plan of reorganization under Chapter 11 Federal Bankruptcy Code effective 02/28/1997
Each shares new Common no par exchanged for (0.00456621) share Common $0.001 par
Note: Holdings of (219) shares or fewer were cancelled and are without value
Unexchanged shares were cancelled and became void 02/28/1999
Completely liquidated
Each share Common $0.001 par received first and final distribution of $0.10 cash payable 03/05/2004 to holders of record 03/02/2004
Ex date - 03/08/2004
Note: Certificates were not required to be surrendered and are without value
Uncashed distribution checks became null and void 05/12/2004

ELSINORE ROYALTY CO. (DE)
Merged into Elsinore Cattle Co. 07/09/1968
Each share Common $100 par exchanged for (1) share Common $100 par

(See Elsinore Cattle Co.)

ELSON ENERGY ENTERPRISES LTD (AB)
Name changed to MATRRIX Energy Technologies Inc. 09/21/2011

ELSTER GROUP SE (GERMANY)
Acquired by Melrose PLC 08/22/2012
Each Sponsored ADR for Ordinary exchanged for $23.682 cash

ELT INC (PA)
Name changed to Dutch Boy, Inc. 02/23/1977
Dutch Boy, Inc. name changed to Artra Group Inc. 12/31/1980 which merged into Entrade Inc. 09/23/1999
(See Entrade Inc.)

ELTEC, INC. (OR)
Assets sold for benefit of creditors 08/02/1973
No stockholders' equity

ELTRA CORP (NY)
Common 25¢ par changed to $0.125 par and (1) additional share issued 10/27/1967
Common $0.125 par split (3) for (2) by issuance of (0.5) additional share 03/30/1976
$1.40 Preferred $34.50 par called for redemption 09/28/1979
Merged into Allied Chemical Corp. 11/05/1979
Each share Common 12.5¢ par exchanged for $51.50 cash

ELTRAX SYS INC (MN)
Name changed to Verso Technologies, Inc. 10/02/2000
(See Verso Technologies, Inc.)

ELTRON ENERGY CORP (BC)
Name changed 02/22/1982
Name changed from Eltron Security Systems Corp. to Eltron Energy Corp. 02/22/1982
Delisted from Vancouver Stock Exchange 11/26/1984

ELTRON INTL INC (CA)
Common no par split (2) for (1) by issuance of (1) additional share 05/05/1995
Merged into Zebra Technologies Corp. 10/28/1998
Each share Common no par exchanged for (0.9) share Common 1¢ par

ELUTION TECHNOLOGIES INC (NV)
Name changed to Tankless Systems Worldwide, Inc. 07/25/2003
Tankless Systems Worldwide, Inc. name changed to Skye International, Inc. 11/11/2005
(See Skye International, Inc.)

ELVA INC (FL)
Common $0.0001 par split (2) for (1) by issuance of (1) additional share payable 09/29/2000 to holders of record 09/22/2000 Ex date - 10/02/2000
Name changed to Elva International, Inc. 03/02/2001

ELVERSON NATL BK (ELVERSON, PA)
Stock Dividends - 10% 01/15/1995; 5% payable 04/10/1998 to holders of record 04/03/1998
Merged into National Penn Bancshares Inc. 01/04/1999
Each share Common $2.50 par exchanged for (1.46875) shares Common $5 par
National Penn Bancshares Inc. merged into BB&T Corp. 04/01/2016

ELWELL PARKER ELEC CO (OH)
Completely liquidated
Each share Common no par received first and final distribution of $1.16 cash payable 12/31/2002 to holders of record 12/27/2002 Ex date - 1/28/2003
Note: Certificates were not required to be surrendered and are without value

ELWOOD MINING EXPLORATION CO. LTD. (QC)
Acquired by Amalgamated Mining Development Corp. Ltd. 00/00/1960
Each share Capital Stock $1 par exchanged for (0.15384615) share Capital Stock $1 par
Amalgamated Mining Development Corp. Ltd. acquired by Amalgamated Mining Western Ltd. 12/20/1984 which name changed to Westall Resources Ltd. 07/12/1994
(See Westall Resources Ltd.)

ELXSI LTD (BERMUDA)
Reincorporated under the laws of Delaware as ELXSI Corp. and Common $0.0125 par changed to $0.001 par 8/13/87

ELY CONSOLIDATED MINING CO. (AZ)
Charter expired by time limitation 4/14/31

ELY GOLD & MINERALS INC (BC)
Name changed to Ely Gold Royalties Inc. 11/22/2017

ELYRIA CO (OH)
Each share Common $4 par exchanged for (0.018181) share Common no par 10/21/69
Voluntarily dissolved 6/29/82
Details not available

ELYRIA IRON & STEEL CO.
Name changed to Steel & Tubes, Inc. in 1927
Steel & Tubes, Inc. acquired by Republic Iron & Steel Co. in 1928
(See Republic Iron & Steel Co.)

ELYRIA SAVINGS & TRUST CO. (ELYRIA, OH)
Common $40 par changed to $10 par and (3) additional shares issued 1/27/60
Name changed to Elyria Savings & Trust National Bank (Elyria, Ohio) 3/1/66
(See Elyria Savings & Trust National Bank (Elyria, Ohio))

ELYRIA SVGS & TR NATL BK (ELYRIA, OH)
Merged into First Bancorporation of Ohio, Inc. 12/12/1983
Each share Common $10 par exchanged for $63.375 cash

ELYSIUM INTERNET INC (UT)
Name changed to TheDirectory.com, Inc. 08/17/2011

EM ENERGY INC (NV)
Name changed to MJ Harvest, Inc. 10/02/2018

EM INTL ENTERPRISES CORP (DE)
Charter cancelled and declared inoperative and void for non-payment of taxes 03/01/2009

EM NET (UT)
Recapitalized as American Ostrich Corp. (UT) 10/04/1995
Each share Common no par exchanged for (2/3) share Common no par
American Ostrich Corp. (UT) reincorporated in Delaware as CallNOW.com, Inc. 04/06/1999
(See CallNOW.com, Inc.)

EM NET CORP (BC)
Reincorporated under the laws of Canada as T & E Theatre.com Inc. 11/25/1999
T & E Theatre.com Inc. recapitalized as Manele Bay Ventures Inc. 02/28/2002 which name changed to MBA Gold Corp. 07/15/2003 which name changed to MBA Resources Corp. 10/14/2005 which name changed to Thunderbird Energy Corp. 07/27/2006 which recapitalized as Gordon Creek Energy Inc. 10/24/2013

EM RES INC (ON)
Reorganized under the laws of British Virgin Islands as Rio Verde Minerals Development Corp. 07/28/2011
Each share Common no par exchanged for (0.5) share Ordinary no par
(See Rio Verde Minerals Development Corp.)

EMAC DATA PROCESSING CORP. (NY)
Acquired by Computer Applications Inc. 3/16/65
Each share Common 1¢ par exchanged for (0.042201) share Common 10¢ par
(See Computer Applications Inc.)

EMACHINES INC (DE)
Merged into EM Holdings, Inc. 1/2/2002
Each share Common $0.0000125 par exchanged for $1.06 cash

EMAGEON INC (DE)
Issue Information - 5,000,000 shares COM offered at $13 per share on 02/09/2005
Acquired by AMICAS, Inc. 04/02/2009
Each share Common $0.001 par exchanged for $1.82 cash

EMAGIN CORP (NV)
Reincorporated under the laws of Delaware 7/16/2001

EMAIL LTD (AUSTRALIA)
ADR agreement terminated 06/01/2001
Each Sponsored ADR for Ordinary exchanged for $3.0393 cash

EMAIL MTG COM INC (CO)
Common $0.001 par split (5) for (1) by issuance of (4) additional shares payable 05/25/2002 to holders of record 05/16/2002
Reincorporated under the laws of Nevada as Mariner Health Care, Inc. 07/08/2002
Mariner Health Care, Inc. name changed to Advanced Healthcare Technologies Inc. 08/12/2002 which recapitalized as Global Resource Corp. 09/14/2004
(See Global Resource Corp.)

EMAILTHATPAYS COM INC (FL)
Each share Common $0.005 par received distribution of (1) share VidKid Distribution Inc. Common $0.005 par payable 03/26/2001 to holders of record 02/14/2001
Reorganized under the laws of Delaware as Forge, Inc. 05/13/2002
Each share Common $0.005 par exchanged for (0.05) share Common $0.001 par
Forge, Inc. name changed to Encore Clean Energy, Inc. (DE) 12/19/2003 which reincorporated in Nevada 10/21/2005
(See Encore Clean Energy, Inc.)

EMAJI INC (DE)
Each share Common $0.001 par exchanged for (0.0025) share Common $0.0001 par 10/07/2011
Name changed to Broadside Enterprises, Inc. 12/01/2016

EMAJIX COM INC (OK)
Name changed to Enxnet Inc. 8/1/2001

EMAK WORLDWIDE INC (DE)
Plan of reorganization under Chapter 11 Federal Bankruptcy proceedings effective 06/30/2011
Distribution to holders to be determined

EMARKETPLACE INC (DE)
Recapitalized as Smart Card Marketing Systems, Inc. 03/24/2006
Each share Common $0.0001 par exchanged for (0.001) share Common $0.0001 par

EMAX CORP (DE)
Recapitalized as eMax Holdings Corp. 5/27/2004
Each (14) shares Common $0.001 par exchanged for (1) share Common $0.001 par

EMAZING INTERACTIVE INC (TX)
Reincorporated under the laws of Nevada as ChinaNet Online Holdings, Inc. 08/14/2009

EMB CORP (HI)
Each share old Common no par exchanged for (0.25) share new Common no par 09/27/1996
Each share new Common no par exchanged again for (0.0666666) share new Common no par 07/10/2000
Reorganized under the laws of Nevada as AMT Group, Inc. 03/15/2007
Each share new Common no par exchanged for (0.01) share Common $0.001 par
(See AMT Group, Inc.)

EMB ELECTRS INC (NJ)
Merged into Strauss Stores Corp. 09/23/1969
Each share Common 1¢ par exchanged for (1) share Common 10¢ par
(See Strauss Stores Corp.)

EMBARCADERO TECHNOLOGIES INC (DE)
Merged into EMB Holding Corp. 06/25/2007
Each share Common $0.001 par exchanged for $7.20 cash

EMBARK HLDGS INC (NV)
Each share old Common $0.001 par exchanged for (0.0005) share new Common $0.001 par 02/14/2013
Name changed to Muscle Warfare International, Inc. 06/28/2013
Muscle Warfare International, Inc. name changed to Cannabusiness Group, Inc. 02/18/2014

EMBARQ CORP (DE)
Merged into CenturyTel, Inc. 06/30/2009
Each share Common 1¢ par received (1.37) shares Common $1 par

EMBASSY ACQUISITIONS CORP (FL)
Name changed to Orthodontix, Inc. (FL) 04/16/1998
Orthodontix, Inc. name changed to Protalix BioTherapeutics, Inc. (FL) 03/01/2007 which reincorporated in Delaware 04/01/2016

EMBASSY CO.
Property sold in 1946

EMBASSY CORP. (DE)
Liquidation completed
Each share Capital Stock $5 par or VTC for Capital Stock $5 par exchanged for initial distribution of $27.50 cash 6/23/65
Each share Capital Stock $5 par or VTC for Capital Stock $5 par received second and final distribution of $3.98 cash 10/9/68

EMBASSY MINES LTD. (ON)
Merged into Bison Petroleum & Minerals Ltd. 06/17/1960
Each share Capital Stock exchanged for (0.1428571) share Capital Stock $1 par
Bison Petroleum & Minerals Ltd. recapitalized as United Bison Resources Ltd. 12/22/1987 which merged into Nalcap Holdings Inc. 04/25/1991 which recapitalized as Arbatax International Inc. (Canada) 03/28/1996 which reincorporated in Yukon 08/06/1996 which name changed to MFC Bancorp Ltd. (YT)

03/03/1997 which reincorporated in British Columbia 11/03/2004 which name changed to KHD Humboldt Wedag International Ltd. 11/01/2005 which reorganized as Terra Nova Royalty Corp. 03/30/2010 which name changed to MFC Industrial Ltd. 09/30/2011 which name changed to MFC Bancorp Ltd. (BC) 02/16/2016
(See MFC Bancorp Ltd. (BC))

EMBASSY PETES LTD (CANADA)
Merged into Cavalier Energy Inc. (ONT) 3/1/74
Each share Capital Stock 25¢ par exchanged for (0.282485) share Common no par
Cavalier Energy Inc. (ONT) reincorporated in Alberta as Cavalier Energy Ltd. 2/7/78
(See Cavalier Energy Ltd.)

EMBASSY RES LTD (ON)
Merged into Unicorp Canada Corp. 3/2/84
Each share Common no par exchanged for (0.6) share 80¢ Conv. Class II Ser. A Preference no par
Unicorp Canada Corp. recapitalized as Unicorp Energy Corp. 6/25/91 which name changed to Unicorp Inc. 5/28/99 which name changed to Wilmington Capital Management Inc. 3/8/2002

EMBER RES INC (AB)
Each share old Common no par exchanged for (0.4) share new Common no par 09/10/2008
Acquired by Brookfield Special Situations Group 06/10/2011
Each share new Common no par exchanged for $0.50 cash

EMBERCLEAR CORP (AB)
Filed a proposal under the Bankruptcy & Insolvency Act 05/05/2016
No stockholders' equity

EMBERCLEAR INC (AB)
Name changed to EmberClear Corp. 12/29/2010

EMBLEM CAP INC (CANADA)
Recapitalized as SQI Diagnostics Inc. 5/4/2007
Each share Common no par exchanged for (1/6) share Common no par

EMBLEM FD (MA)
Name changed to Society Funds (MA) and Inter Government Obligations Portfolio no par, Ohio Regional Equity Portfolio no par, Relative Value Equity Portfolio no par and Short/Intermediate Fixed Income Portfolio no par reclassified as U.S. Government Income Fund no par, Ohio Regional Equity Fund no par, Diversified Stock Fund no par and Limited Term Income Fund no par respectively 11/01/1993
Society Funds (MA) reincorporated in Delaware as Victory Portfolios 09/01/1994

EMBLEM PETROLEUM SYNDICATE INC. (DE)
No longer in existence having become inoperative and void for non-payment of taxes 3/19/24

EMBOTELLADORA ANDINA S A (CHILE)
Each Sponsored ADR for Common no par exchanged for (1) Sponsored ADR for Ser. A no par and (1) Sponsored ADR for Ser. B no par 4/7/97
(Additional Information in Active)

EMBOTELLADORA ARICA S A (CHILE)
ADR agreement terminated 5/17/2007
Each Sponsored ADR for Ser. B exchanged for (10) Ser. B shares
Note: Unexchanged ADR's will be sold and the proceeds, if any, held for claim after 6/15/2007

EMBRACE SYS CORP (DE)
Chapter 7 bankruptcy proceedings closed 07/27/2000
No stockholders' equity

EMBRAER-EMPRESA BRASILEIRA DE AERONAUTICA S.A. (BRAZIL)
Each Sponsored Partial Dividend ADR for Preferred exchanged for (1) Sponsored ADR for Preferred 03/27/2002
Sponsored ADR's for Preferred reclassified as Sponsored ADR's for Common 06/08/2006
Stock Dividend - 14.2106% payable 03/12/2002 to holders of record 03/05/2002 Ex date - 03/01/2002
Name changed to Embraer S.A. 12/06/2010

EMBRATEL PARTICIPACOES S A (BRAZIL)
Each old Sponsored ADR for Preferred exchanged for (0.2) new Sponsored ADR for Preferred 06/16/2003
Basis changed from (1:1,000) to (1:5,000) 06/16/2003
ADR agreement terminated 04/23/2007
Each new Sponsored ADR for Preferred exchanged for $19.07757 cash

EMBREX INC (NC)
Merged into Pfizer Inc. 01/19/2007
Each share Common no par exchanged for $17 cash

EMBRYO DEV CORP (DE)
SEC revoked common stock registration 12/07/2010

EMBRYONICS INC (NV)
Name changed to Emerald Instrument Corp. 11/04/1986
(See Emerald Instrument Corp.)

EMBURY LAKE MINING CO. LTD. (ON)
Charter cancelled 11/00/1961

EMC CORP (MA)
Common 1¢ par split (3) for (2) by issuance of (0.5) additional share 08/31/1987
Common 1¢ par split (3) for (2) by issuance of (0.5) additional share 11/24/1992
Common 1¢ par split (2) for (1) by issuance of (1) additional share 06/07/1993
Common 1¢ par split (2) for (1) by issuance of (1) additional share 12/10/1993
Common 1¢ par split (2) for (1) by issuance of (1) additional share payable 11/17/1997 to holders of record 10/31/1997 Ex date - 11/18/1997
Common 1¢ par split (2) for (1) by issuance of (1) additional share payable 05/28/1999 to holders of record 05/14/1999 Ex date - 06/01/1999
Common 1¢ par split (2) for (1) by issuance of (1) additional share payable 06/02/2000 to holders of record 05/19/2000 Ex date - 06/05/2000
Each share Common 1¢ par received distribution of (0.0368069) share McDATA Corp. Class A Common 1¢ par payable 02/07/2001 to holders of record 01/24/2001 Ex date - 02/08/2001
Merged into Dell Technologies Inc. 09/07/2016
Each share Common 1¢ par exchanged for (0.11146) share Class V Common 1¢ par and $24.05 cash

EMC DEV CORP (DE)
Recapitalized as EM International Enterprises Corp. 01/24/2008
Each share Common $0.001 par exchanged for (0.03333333) share Common $0.001 par
(See EM International Enterprises Corp.)

EMC ENERGIES INC (WY)
Each share Common 5¢ par exchanged for (0.2) share Common 25¢ par 12/05/1978
Reorganized under the laws of Nevada as Metwood Inc. 01/28/2000
Each share Common 25¢ par exchanged for (0.05) share Common $0.001 par

EMC GROUP INC (FL)
Each share old Common $0.0001 par exchanged for (0.04) share new Common $0.0001 par 04/12/1999
Reinorporated under the laws of Washington as Coattec Industries, Inc. 05/10/2004
(See Coattec Industries, Inc.)

EMC METALS CORP (BC)
Name changed to Scandium International Mining Corp. 11/28/2014

EMCARE HLDGS INC (DE)
Merged into Laidlaw Inc. 09/10/1997
Each share Common 1¢ par exchanged for $38 cash

EMCEE BROADCAST PRODS INC (DE)
Filed a petition under Chapter 7 Federal Bankruptcy Code 02/24/2003
Stockholders' equity unlikely

EMCEE ELECTRS INC (DE)
Each share old Common no par exchanged for (0.1) share new Common no par 03/05/1965
Merged into Delta Industries, Inc. 10/26/1981
Each share Common no par exchanged for $72 cash

EMCO LTD (ON)
Common no par split (2) for (1) by issuance of (1) additional share 06/10/1965
Common no par split (3) for (1) by issuance of (2) additional shares 08/05/1971
Common no par split (2) for (1) by issuance of (1) additional share 09/25/1986
Acquired by Blackfriars Corp. 04/14/2003
Each share Common no par exchanged for $16.60 cash

EMCOM INC (MN)
Merged into Shelter Video Corp. 03/18/1982
Each share Common 10¢ par exchanged for $0.25 cash

EMCON (CA)
Name changed 06/04/1991
Common no par split (3) for (2) by issuance of (0.5) additional share 11/17/1989
Name changed from Emcon Associates to Emcon 06/04/1991
Common no par split (3) for (2) by issuance of (0.5) additional share 09/27/1991
Merged into IT Group, Inc. 06/15/1999
Each share Common no par exchanged for $6.75 cash

EMCOR PETE INC (DE)
Merged into Quinico Oil & Gas Corp. 09/20/1985
Details not available

EMDEKO INTL INC (UT)
Liquidation completed
Each share Common no par stamped to indicate initial distribution of $0.40 cash 06/20/1979
Each share Stamped Common no par exchanged for second and final distribution of $0.195 cash 08/15/1980

EMDEON CORP (DE)
Name changed to HLTH Corp. 05/21/2007
HLTH Corp. merged into WebMD Health Corp. 10/23/2009
(See WebMD Health Corp.)

EMDEON INC (DE)
Acquired by Beagle Parent Corp. 11/02/2011
Each share Class A Common $0.00001 par exchanged for $19 cash

EME INDS INC (NY)
Charter cancelled and proclaimed dissolved for failure to pay taxes 12/20/1977

EMED MINING PUBLIC LTD (CYPRUS)
Recapitalized as Atalaya Mining PLC 10/21/2015
Each share Ordinary 25p par exchanged for (0.03333333) share Ordinary 25p par

EMEDIA NETWORKS INTL CORP (BC)
Each share old Common no par exchanged for (0.00000082) share new Common no par 01/28/2014
Note: In effect holders received $0.045 cash per share and public interest was eliminated

EMEL MTR HOTEL INC (WA)
Completely liquidated 09/10/1969
Each share Common no par exchanged for first and final distribution of $270 cash

EMEMBERDIRECT INC (DE)
Charter cancelled and declared inoperative and void for non-payment of taxes 03/01/2003

EMENEE CORP (NY)
Common $1 par changed to 50¢ par and (0.5) additional share issued 11/25/1968
Merged into Ohio Art Co. 04/30/1973
Each share Common 50¢ par exchanged for (0.53) share Common $1 par

EMENS (W.H.) MINING CORP. (ON)
Charter cancelled 00/00/1952

EMERALD ACQUISITION CORP. (CAYMAN ISLANDS)
Name changed to Oriental Dragon Corp. 08/27/2010

EMERALD CAP HLDGS INC (DE)
Each share old Common $0.001 par exchanged for (0.00833333) share new Common $0.001 par 03/29/1996
Charter cancelled and declared inoperative and void for non-payment of taxes 03/01/1997

EMERALD CAP INC (DE)
Reorganized under the laws of Nevada as CCC Globalcom Corp. 06/12/2000
Each share Common $0.001 par exchanged for (0.05) share Common $0.001 par
CCC Globalcom Corp. name changed to Bakken Water Transfer Services, Inc. 08/13/2015

EMERALD COAL & COKE CO. (DE)
Name changed to Hillman Coal & Coke Co. 02/19/1962
(See Hillman Coal & Coke Co.)

EMERALD DAIRY INC (NV)
SEC revoked common stock registration 10/27/2014

EMERALD DRAGON MINES INC (BC)
Delisted from Toronto Venture Stock Exchange 06/05/2002

EMERALD DYEING & FINISHING CORP. (NY)
Charter cancelled and proclaimed dissolved for failure to pay taxes 12/15/1944

EMERALD EAGLE CORP (CO)
Recapitalized as Nortech Forest Technologies Inc. 06/11/1993
Each share Common no par exchanged for (0.08) share Common no par
(See Nortech Forest Technologies Inc.)

EMERALD FINL CORP (OH)
Common no par split (2) for (1) by issuance of (1) additional share payable 05/15/1997 to holders of record 05/01/1997
Common no par split (2) for (1) by issuance of (1) additional share payable 05/15/1998 to holders of record 05/01/1998
Merged into Fifth Third Bancorp 08/06/1999
Each share Common no par exchanged for (0.3) share Common no par

EMERALD GLACIER MINES LTD. (BC)
Certificates dated prior to 06/14/1957
Reorganized under the laws of Ontario as Glacier Mining Ltd. 06/14/1957
Each share Capital Stock no par exchanged for (0.25) share Capital Stock $1 par
Glacier Mining Ltd. name changed to Glacier Explorers Ltd. 09/25/1957 which recapitalized as New Glacier Explorers Ltd. 01/10/1967
(See New Glacier Explorers Ltd.)

EMERALD GLACIER MINES LTD. (BC)
Certificates dated after 01/01/1966
Struck off register and declared dissolved for failure to file returns 12/22/1975

EMERALD GREEN CORP (DE)
Adjudicated bankrupt 05/01/1975
Stockholders' equity unlikely

EMERALD HOMES L P (DE)
Charter cancelled and declared inoperative and void for non-payment of taxes 12/31/1995

EMERALD INSTR CORP (NV)
Chapter 11 bankruptcy proceedings converted to Chapter 7 on 01/31/1991
No stockholders' equity

EMERALD ISLE BANCORP (MA)
Common $1 par split (5) for (4) by issuance of (0.25) additional share payable 02/03/1997 to holders of record 01/22/1997
Merged into Eastern Bank Corp. 02/27/1998
Each share Common $1 par exchanged for $33 cash

EMERALD LAKE MINES LTD. (ON)
Merged into Summit Explorations & Holdings Ltd. 09/19/1969
Each share Capital Stock $1 par exchanged for (0.2) share Capital Stock no par
Summit Explorations & Holdings Ltd. name changed to Summit Diversified Ltd. 03/03/1972 which merged into Sumtra Diversified Inc. 08/30/1978

EMERALD LAKE RES INC (BC)
Merged into Noramco Mining Corp. 01/01/1988
Each share Common no par exchanged for (1) share Common no par
Noramco Mining Corp. name changed to Quest Capital Corp. 01/03/1995 which name changed to Quest Oil & Gas Inc. 11/15/1996 which merged into EnerMark Income Fund 04/18/1997 which merged into Enerplus Resources Fund 06/22/2001 which reorganized as Enerplus Corp. 01/03/2011

EMERALD MED APPLICATIONS CORP (DE)
Name changed to Virtual Crypto Technologies Inc. 03/07/2018

EMERALD MTG INVTS CORP (MD)
Name changed to Homeplex Mortgage Investments Corp. 04/12/1990
Homeplex Mortgage Investments Corp. recapitalized as Monterey Homes Corp. 12/31/1996 which name changed to Meritage Corp. 09/16/1998 which name changed to Meritage Homes Corp. 09/14/2004

EMERALD OIL INC (DE)
Reincorporated 06/11/2014
Each share old Common $0.001 par exchanged for (0.14285714) share new Common $0.001 par 10/23/2012
State of incorporation changed from (MT) to (DE) 06/11/2014
Each share old Common $0.001 par exchanged for (0.05) share new Common $0.001 par 05/21/2015
Plan of reorganization under Chapter 11 Federal Bankruptcy proceedings effective 04/07/2017
No stockholders' equity

EMERALD POWERBOATS INC (TX)
Name changed to MRLD Holdings, Inc. 9/26/2005
MRLD Holdings, Inc. name changed to Taj Systems, Inc. 10/24/2005

EMERALD-SHADE INC (MN)
Name changed to Microbest, Inc. 3/11/97
(See Microbest, Inc.)

EMERALD STAR MNG EXPLS LTD (BC)
Recapitalized as ESM Resources Ltd. 03/28/1996
Each share Common no par exchanged for (0.28571428) share Common no par
ESM Resources Ltd. recapitalized as EAV Ventures Corp. 12/10/1998 which name changed to VendTek Systems Inc. 10/05/1999
(See VendTek Systems Inc.)

EMERALD VENTURES INC (BC)
Reincorporated under the laws of Yukon as Spatializer Audio Laboratories, Inc. 12/27/1991
Spatializer Audio Laboratories, Inc. (YT) reincorporated in Delaware 07/27/1994 which recapitalized as AMERI Holdings, Inc. 05/26/2015

EMERALD YELLOWKNIFE MINES, LTD. (ON)
Charter cancelled in 1955

EMERCAP VENTURES INC (BC)
Merged into VendTek Systems Inc. 04/26/2002
Each share Common no par exchanged for (0.36801236) share Common no par
(See VendTek Systems Inc.)

EMERGE CAP CORP (DE)
Reincorporated under the laws of Nevada as Turnaround Partners, Inc. 01/03/2007
Turnaround Partners, Inc. recapitalized as Advanced Clean Technologies, Inc. 01/12/2009 which name changed to Act Clean Technologies, Inc. 12/09/2009

EMERGE INTERACTIVE INC (DE)
Issue Information - 8,000,000 shares COM offered at $15 per share on 02/03/2000
Each (15) shares Class A Common $0.008 par exchanged for (1) share Common 1¢ par 06/01/2006
Plan of reorganization under Chapter 11 Federal Bankruptcy Code effective 05/23/2007
No stockholders' equity

EMERGE OIL & GAS INC (AB)
Merged into Twin Butte Energy Ltd. 01/09/2012
Each share Common no par exchanged for (0.585) share Common no par

EMERGE RES CORP (ON)
Each share old Common no par exchanged for (0.14285714) share new Common no par 10/09/2014
Recapitalized as Vaxil Bio Ltd. 03/10/2016
Each share new Common no par exchanged for (0.5) share Common no par

EMERGENCE RESORT CDA INC (CANADA)
Reincorporated 06/06/2006
Place of incorporation changed from (AB) to (Canada) 06/06/2006
Name changed to ACFAW.com Inc. 06/03/2009
ACFAW.com Inc. recapitalized as St-Georges Platinum & Base Metals Ltd. 05/04/2010 which name changed to St-Georges Eco-Mining Corp. 12/22/2017

EMERGENCY FILTRATION PRODS INC (NV)
Name changed to Nano Mask, Inc. 06/04/2009
Nano Mask, Inc. recapitalized as NMI Health, Inc. 06/05/2013

EMERGENCY MED SVCS CORP (DE)
Issue Information - 8,100,000 shares CL A offered at $14 per share on 12/15/2005
Acquired by CDRT Acquisition Corp. 05/25/2011
Each share Class A Common 1¢ par exchanged for $64 cash

EMERGENSYS CORP (DE)
Recapitalized as Spencer Pharmaceutical, Inc. 10/05/2009
Each share Common $0.0001 par exchanged for (0.04) share Common $0.0001 par

EMERGENT FINL GROUP INC (DE)
Each share old Common $0.001 par exchanged for (0.03333333) share new Common $0.001 par 08/20/2001
New Common $0.001 par split (5) for (1) by issuance of (4) additional shares payable 10/29/2001 to holders of record 10/24/2001
Ex date - 10/30/2001
Recapitalized as EGX Funds Transfer, Inc. 06/14/2002
Each share Common $0.001 par exchanged for (0.01428571) share Common $0.001 par
(See EGX Funds Transfer, Inc.)

EMERGENT GROUP INC (NV)
Each share Common $0.001 par exchanged for (0.025) share Common 4¢ par 08/29/2003
Stock Dividend - 100% payable 08/31/2000 to holders of record 08/28/2000
Acquired by Universal Hospital Services, Inc. (DE) 04/01/2011
Each share Common 4¢ par exchanged for $8.46 cash

EMERGENT GROUP INC (SC)
Each share old Common 5¢ par received (0.2) share new Common 5¢ par 10/03/1991
Note: Certificates dated prior to 10/03/1991 were not required to be surrendered and are without value
Each share new Common 5¢ par received distribution of (49) shares Class A Common 5¢ par 10/25/1991
Each share old Class A Common 5¢ par exchanged for (1/3) share new Class A Common 5¢ par 06/09/1995
Each share new Common 5¢ par exchanged for (1/3) share new Common 5¢ par 06/09/1995
New Class A Common 5¢ par reclassified as new Common 5¢ par 04/19/1996
Name changed to Homegold Financial Inc. 07/01/1998
(See Homegold Financial Inc.)

EMERGENT INFORMATION TECHNOLOGIES INC (CA)
Name changed to SM&A (CA) 01/29/2002
SM&A (CA) reincorporated in Delaware 11/30/2006
(See SM&A (DE))

EMERGEO SOLUTIONS WORLDWIDE INC (BC)
Delisted from Toronto Venture Stock Exchange 04/13/2015

EMERGING AFRICA GOLD EAG INC (QC)
Merged into Diagem International Resource Corp. (BC) 05/31/2002
Each share Common no par exchanged for (1) share Common no par
Diagem International Resource Corp. (BC) reincorporated in Canada as Diagem Inc. 11/18/2004
(See Diagem Inc.)

EMERGING ALBA RESOURCE CORP (AB)
Name changed to Renfield Enterprises Inc. 08/01/1995
(See Renfield Enterprises Inc.)

EMERGING ALPHA CORP (DE)
Name changed to Compressco Inc. 1/7/2000
(See Compressco Inc.)

EMERGING BETA CORP (DE)
Name changed to Starship Cruise Line, Inc. 03/15/1998
(See Starship Cruise Line, Inc.)

EMERGING COMMUNICATIONS INC (DE)
Merged into Innovative Communication Corp. 10/19/98
Each share Common no par exchanged for $10.25 cash

EMERGING ENTERPRISE SOLUTIONS INC (AZ)
SEC revoked common stock registration 05/03/2005

EMERGING GAMMA CORP (DE)
Name changed to Gamma Pharmaceuticals Inc. 09/05/2006
(See Gamma Pharmaceuticals Inc.)

EMERGING GERMANY FD INC (MD)
Under plan of reorganization each share Common $0.001 par automatically became (1) share Dresdner RCM Europe Fund, Inc. Common $0.001 par 05/03/1999
(See Dresdner RCM Europe Fund, Inc.)

EMERGING GROWTH FD INC (MD)
Reorganized under the laws of Delaware as Forum Funds 09/20/2002
Each share Class A no par exchanged for (1) share BrownIA Small Cap Growth Fund Class A no par
Each share Class B no par exchanged for (1) share BrownIA Small Cap Growth Fund Class B no par
Each share Class C no par exchanged for (1) share BrownIA Small Cap Growth Fund Class C no par
Each share BIAT Class no par exchanged for (1.918821569) shares BrownIA Small Cap Growth Fund Institutional Class no par
Each share Institutional Class no par exchanged for (1.919429082) shares BrownIA Small Cap Growth Fund Institutional Class no par

EMERGING GROWTH TECHNOLOGIES INC (BC)
Name changed to Mandorin Goldfields, Inc. (BC) 04/23/1996
Mandorin Goldfields, Inc. (BC) reincorporated in Yukon 06/11/1999 which name changed to Sphere Resources Inc. 11/27/2007

EMERGING HEALTHCARE SOLUTIONS INC (WY)
Administratively dissolved 10/10/2012

EMERGING MKTS CORP (DE)
SEC revoked common stock registration 05/30/2008

EMERGING MKTS FLOATING RATE FD INC (MD)
Name changed to Salomon Brothers Emerging Markets Floating Rate Fund Inc. 04/21/2003
Salomon Brothers Emerging Markets Floating Rate Fund Inc. name changed to Western Asset Emerging Markets Floating Rate Fund Inc. 10/09/2006 which merged into Western Asset Emerging Markets Debt Fund Inc. 09/14/2009

EMERGING MKTS INCOME FD INC (MD)
Name changed to Salomon Brothers Emerging Markets Income Fund Inc. 04/21/2003
Salomon Brothers Emerging Markets Income Fund Inc. name changed to Western Asset Emerging Markets Income Fund Inc. (Old) 10/09/2006 which merged into Western Asset Emerging Markets Income Fund Inc. (New) 11/03/2008 which merged into Western Asset Emerging Markets Debt Fund Inc. 12/19/2016

EMERGING MKTS INCOME FD II INC (MD)
Name changed to Salomon Brothers Emerging Markets Income Fund II, Inc. 04/21/2003
Salomon Brothers Emerging Markets Income Fund II, Inc. name changed to Western Asset Emerging Markets Income Fund II, Inc. 10/09/2006 which name changed to Western Asset Emerging Markets Income Fund Inc. (New) 11/03/2008 which merged into Western Asset Emerging Markets Debt Fund Inc. 12/19/2016

EMERGING MKTS INFRASTRUCTURE FD INC (MD)
Under plan of merger name changed to Emerging Markets Telecommunications Fund, Inc. (New) 11/03/2000
Emerging Markets Telecommunications Fund, Inc. (New) name changed to Aberdeen Emerging Markets Telecommunications Fund, Inc. 03/26/2010 which name changed to Aberdeen Emerging Markets Telecommunications & Infrastructure Fund, Inc. 11/04/2010 which name changed to Aberdeen Emerging Markets Smaller Company Opportunities Fund, Inc. 03/21/2013

EMERGING MKTS TELECOMMUNICATIONS FD INC NEW (MD)
Name changed to Aberdeen Emerging Markets Telecommunications Fund, Inc. 03/26/2010
Aberdeen Emerging Markets Telecommunications Fund, Inc. name changed to Aberdeen Emerging Markets Telecommunications & Infrastructure Fund, Inc. 11/04/2010 which name changed to Aberdeen Emerging Markets Smaller Company Opportunities Fund, Inc. 03/21/2013

EMERGING MKTS TELECOMMUNICATIONS FD INC OLD (MD)
Merged into Emerging Markets Telecommunications Fund, Inc. (New) 11/03/2000
Each share Common $0.001 par exchanged for (0.9994) share Common $0.001 par
Emerging Markets Telecommunications Fund, Inc. name changed to Aberdeen Emerging Markets Telecommunications Fund, Inc. 03/26/2010 which name changed to Aberdeen Emerging Markets Telecommunications & Infrastructure Fund, Inc. 11/04/2010 which name changed to Aberdeen Emerging Markets Smaller Company Opportunities Fund, Inc. 03/21/2013 which reorganized as Aberdeen Emerging Markets Equity Income Fund, Inc. 04/30/2018

EMERGING MEDIA HLDGS INC (NV)
Each share old Common $0.001 par exchanged for (0.1) share new Common $0.001 par 10/12/2011
Stock Dividend - 20% payable 09/30/2010 to holders of record 09/15/2010 Ex date - 09/13/2010
Name changed to Lifestyle Medical Network Inc. 07/31/2012

EMERGING MEXICO FD INC (MD)
Completely liquidated 6/10/99
Each share Common 10¢ par exchanged for first and final distribution of $8.7773 cash

EMERGING SECS FD (DE)
Name changed to Engex, Inc. 04/14/1977
(See Engex, Inc.)

EMERGING TIGERS FD INC (MD)
Name changed to Merrill Lynch Emerging Tigers Fund, Inc. and Common 10¢ par reclassified as Class A Common 10¢ par 6/10/96
Merrill Lynch Emerging Tigers Fund Inc. merged into Merrill Lynch Dragon Fund, Inc. 5/19/2000

EMERGING VENTURES CORP (BC)
Reorganized under the laws of Ontario as QGX Ltd. 07/24/2002
Each share Common no par exchanged for (0.4) share Common no par
(See QGX Ltd.)

EMERGING VISION INC (NY)
Acquired by EMVI Holdings, L.L.C. 04/08/2011
Each share Common 1¢ par exchanged for $0.16 cash

EMERGIS INC (CANADA)
Acquired by TELUS Corp. 01/17/2008
Each share Common no par exchanged for $8.25 cash

EMERGISOFT HLDG INC (NV)
Each share old Common $0.001 par exchanged for (0.05) share new Common $0.001 par 03/31/2002
Merged into Emergisoft Acquisition, LLC 03/03/2009
Each share Common $0.001 par exchanged for $0.11542 cash

EMERGO SOFTWARE CORP (BC)
Name changed to eTVtech.com Communications Inc. 03/21/2000
Each share Common no par exchanged for (1) share Common no par eTVtech.com Communications Inc. name changed to eTV Technology Inc. 05/02/2001 which recapitalized as Ocean Park Ventures Corp. 04/02/2009 which recapitalized as Dunnedin Ventures Inc. 08/06/2013

EMERICK RES CORP (BC)
Name changed to Medgold Resources Corp. 12/17/2012

EMERITA GOLD CORP (BC)
Name changed to Emerita Resources Corp. 01/13/2014

EMERITE CORP (DE)
Merged into Plasmine Corp. 01/25/1982
Each share Common 10¢ par exchanged for (0.05) share Common 10¢ par
(See Plasmine Corp.)

EMERITUS CORP (WA)
Merged into Brookdale Senior Living Inc. 07/31/2014
Each share Common $0.0001 par exchanged for (0.95) share Common 1¢ par

EMERSON & CO., INC. (NY)
Dissolved 2/8/43

EMERSON-BRANTINGHAM CO.
Acquired by Emerson-Brantingham Corp. in 1927
Details not available

EMERSON-BRANTINGHAM CORP.
Liquidated in 1937

EMERSON DRUG CO.
Merged into Emerson Drug Co. of Baltimore City 00/00/1935
Details not available

EMERSON DRUG CO. OF BALTIMORE CITY (MD)
Merged into Warner-Lambert Pharmaceutical Co. 4/2/56
Each share Class A Common $2.50 par or Class B Common $2.50 par exchanged for (0.5) share Common $1 par
Warner-Lambert Pharmaceutical Co. name changed to Warner-Lambert Co. 11/13/70 which merged into Pfizer Co. 6/19/2000

EMERSON ELEC CO (MO)
$1 Conv. Preferred Ser. A $5 par called for redemption 7/1/68
$1.80 Conv. Preferred Ser. B $5 par changed to 90¢ Conv. Preferred Ser. B $2.50 par and (1) additional share issued 2/21/69
90¢ Conv. Preferred Ser. B $2.50 par called for redemption 1/2/74

EMERSON ELECTRIC MANUFACTURING CO. (MO)
Each share Common $100 par exchanged for (20) shares Common $4 par in 1937
Common $4 par split (5) for (4) by issuance of (0.25) additional share 9/28/56
7% Preferred called for redemption 4/1/59
Common $4 par changed to $2 par and (1) additional share issued 2/5/60
Common $2 par changed to $1 par and (1) additional share issued 2/2/62
Name changed to Emerson Electric Co. 2/6/64

EMERSON EXPL INC (BC)
Name changed to GBS Gold International, Inc. 9/19/2005

EMERSON FILMS INC (NV)
Charter revoked for failure to file list of officers 10/1/94

EMERSON OIL & GAS INC (NV)
Recapitalized as BioLife Remedies Inc. 01/19/2007
Each share Common $0.0001 par exchanged for (0.004) share Common $0.0001 par

EMERSON RADIO & PHONOGRAPH CORP. (NY)
Stock Dividends - 100% 3/2/48; 10% 12/23/49; 100% 6/23/50; 10% 12/15/50
Merged into National Union Electric Corp. 5/31/66
Each share Capital Stock $5 par exchanged for (1) share Common $1 par
(See National Union Electric Corp.)

EMERSON RADIO CORP (NJ)
Common 10¢ par split (3) for (2) by issuance of (0.5) additional share 11/13/1978
Common 10¢ par split (5) for (3) by issuance of (0.6) additional share 04/26/1982
Common 10¢ par split (5) for (3) by issuance of (2/3) additional share 04/01/1983
Common 10¢ par split (5) for (3) by issuance of (2/3) additional share 02/21/1984
Common 10¢ par split (2) for (1) by issuance of (1) additional share 10/16/1986
Common Stock Purchase Rights declared for Common stockholders of record 06/28/1999 were redeemed at $0.01 per right 04/03/1992 for holders of record 03/13/1992
Stock Dividends - 10% 07/29/1977; 10% 07/07/1978; 10% 06/15/1979; 10% 06/13/1980; 20% 05/15/1981; 10% 12/21/1984; 10% 12/04/1985
Plan of reorganization under Chapter 11 Federal Bankruptcy proceedings confirmed 03/31/1994
No stockholders' equity
Note: Stockholders received subscription rights to buy Emerson Radio Corp. (DE) Common 1¢ par expiring 09/19/1994

EMERSON'S BROMO-SELTZER, INC.
Merged into Emerson Drug Co. of Baltimore City 00/00/1935
Details not available

EMERSONS LTD (DE)
Common 1¢ par split (3) for (2) by issuance of (0.5) additional share 4/25/75
Chapter XI bankruptcy proceedings dismissed 3/10/87
No stockholders' equity

EMERTRON, INC. (DE)
Name changed to ERT Corp. 11/30/62
(See ERT Corp.)

EMERVAC CORP. (UT)
Name changed to American Component Industries, Inc. 9/29/83
(See American Component Industries, Inc.)

EMERY AIR FGHT CORP (DE)
Common 20¢ par split (2) for (1) by issuance of (1) additional share 07/26/1956
Common 20¢ par split (2) for (1) by issuance of (1) additional share 12/26/1963
Common 20¢ par split (2) for (1) by issuance of (1) additional share 12/28/1967
Common 20¢ par split (2) for (1) by issuance of (1) additional share 12/31/1971
Common 20¢ par split (2) for (1) by issuance of (1) additional share 05/26/1978
Stock Dividend - 25% 12/30/1959
Merged into Consolidated Freightways, Inc. 04/06/1989
Each share Common 20¢ par exchanged for $7.75 cash

EMERY COAL INC (UT)
Common 1¢ par changed to $0.002 par and (4) additional shares issued 2/27/76
Name changed to Emery Energy Inc. 7/15/79
Emery Energy Inc. name changed to Beryllium International Corp. (UT) 12/19/86 which reorganized in Florida as Wallstreet-Review Inc. 11/17/2000 which recapitalized as Champion American Energy Reserves, Inc. 10/15/2004

EMERY DATAGRAPHIC INC (CO)
Name changed to Northstar Acquisition Corp. 8/29/87
(See Northstar Acquisition Corp.)

EMERY ENERGY INC (UT)
Name changed to Beryllium International Corp. (UT) 12/19/86
Beryllium International Corp. (UT) reorganized in Florida as Wallstreet-Review Inc. 11/17/2000 which recapitalized as Champion American Energy Reserves, Inc. 10/15/2004

EMERY FERRON ENERGY CORP (DE)
Each share old Common 1¢ par exchanged for (0.001) share new Common 1¢ par 06/20/1996
Acquired by Premier Sports & Entertainment Acquisition Corp. 04/29/1997
Details not available

EMERY-HILL STORES (SC)
Name changed to Emery Stores, Inc.-Carolina 5/9/56
(See Emery Stores, Inc.-Carolina)

EMERY INDS INC (OH)
Common no par split (4) for (1) by issuance of (3) additional shares 01/15/1964
Common no par split (3) for (1) by issuance of (2) additional shares 07/31/1969
Merged into National Distillers & Chemical Corp. 05/19/1978
Each share Common no par exchanged for (1) share $1.85 Preference $1 par
Note: Prior to 05/16/1978 holders could elect to receive $22.25 cash per share in lieu of Preference Stock
National Distillers & Chemical Corp. name changed to Quantum Chemical Corp. 01/04/1988 which merged into Hanson PLC (Old) 10/01/1993 which reorganized as Hanson PLC (New) 10/15/2003
(See Hanson PLC (New))

EMERY STORES, INC.-CAROLINA (SC)
Voluntarily dissolved 5/13/77
Details not available

EMERYVILLE MARINA ENTERPRISES (CA)
Charter cancelled for failure to file reports and pay taxes 11/3/75

EMETT & CHANDLER COS INC (CA)
Common 50¢ par split (2) for (1) by issuance of (1) additional share 7/26/85
Merged into Jardine Matheson Holdings Ltd. 5/15/86
Each share Common 50¢ par exchanged for $19 cash

EMEX CORP (WY)
Stock Dividends - 5% payable 05/14/2001 to holders of record 04/16/2001; 2.5% payable 12/11/2001 to holders of record 11/13/2001 Ex date - 11/08/2001; 2.5% payable 03/28/2002 to holders of record 02/28/2002
Filed a petition under Chapter 7 Federal Bankruptcy Code 12/31/2002
No stockholders' equity

EMG CAP LTD (AB)
Name changed to Electronics Manufacturing Group Inc. 01/26/2000

EMHART CORP (CT)
Common $12.50 par changed to $6.25 par and (1) additional share issued 05/21/1965
Stock Dividends - 10% 12/22/1966; 10% 01/07/1969; 20% 01/10/1975
Under plan of merger each share Common $6.25 par automatically became (1) share Emhart Corp. (VA) Common $1 par 05/04/1976

(See Emhart Corp. (VA))

EMHART CORP (VA)
Common $1 par split (5) for (4) by issuance of (0.25) additional share 11/30/77
Common $1 par split (2) for (1) by issuance of (1) additional share 12/30/83
Common $1 par split (2) for (1) by issuance of (1) additional share 9/30/87
Stock Dividend - 10% 12/28/84
Money Market Preference Ser. A no par called for redemption 4/18/89
Merged into Black & Decker Corp. 7/18/89
Each share $2.10 Conv. Preference no par exchanged for $52.351 cash
Each share Common $1 par exchanged for $40 cash

EMHART MANUFACTURING CO. (DE)
Common no par changed to $7.50 par and (1) additional share issued plus a 20% stock dividend paid in 1953
Merged into Emhart Corp. (Conn.) 6/30/64
Each share Common $7.50 par exchanged for (1) share Common $12.50 par
Emhart Corp. (Conn.) reincorporated in Virginia 5/4/76
(See Emhart Corp. (Va.))

EMI ENERGY CORP (UT)
Name changed to EMI Inc. 9/11/85

EMI GROUP PLC (ENGLAND)
Each Sponsored ADR for Ordinary 25p par exchanged for (0.9) Sponsored ADR for Ordinary 14p par 07/18/1997
Acquired by Maltby Ltd. 08/01/2007
Each Sponsored ADR for Ordinary 14p par exchanged for $10.713246 cash

EMI LTD (ENGLAND)
Merged into Thorn EMI Ltd. 03/28/1980
Each (100) American Shares for Ordinary Reg. 50p par exchanged for (58) shares 7% Conv. 2nd Preference 1992/99 £1 par and (28) shares Ordinary 25p par or (58) shares 7% Conv. 2nd Preference 1992/93 £1 par plus £92.40 cash
Option to receive 7% Preference shares plus cash expired 04/18/1980
Thorn EMI PLC name changed to EMI Group PLC 08/19/1996
(See EMI Group PLC)

EMIL COOLIDGES MORTGAGES, INC. (MI)
Charter declared inoperative and void for failure to file reports 05/15/1984

EMILIE CORP. (DE)
Liquidation completed 1/15/59

EMILION ENTERPRISES, INC. (UT)
Involuntarily dissolved for failure to file annual reports 10/1/88

EMINATOR CAPITAL CORP. (ON)
Recapitalized as Internet Shopping Catalog Inc. 02/26/2001
Each share Common no par exchanged for (0.14970059) share Common no par and (0.14970059) Common Stock Purchase Warrant expiring 09/29/2004
(See Internet Shopping Catalog Inc.)

EMINENCE CAP I INC (ON)
Name changed to SonnenEnergy Corp. 09/13/2007

EMINENCE CAP II INC (ON)
Name changed to Xmet Inc. 06/07/2010

EMIR OILS LTD (AB)
Merged into Renaissance Energy Ltd. 5/29/92
Each share Common no par exchanged for either (0.0583) share Common no par or $0.70 cash
Note: Option to elect to receive stock expired 12/30/92
Renaissance Energy Ltd. merged into Husky Energy Inc. 8/25/2000

EMISSION CTL DEVICES INC (NV)
Recapitalized as Rocky Mountain Energy Corp. (NV) 6/5/2002
Each share Common $0.0001 par exchanged for (0.001) share Common $0.001 par
Note: Holders of (101) to (99,999) shares received (100) shares
Holders of (100) shares or fewer were not affected by the reverse split
(See Rocky Mountain Energy Corp. (NV))

EMISSION DIFFERENTIALS LTD (AB)
Recapitalized as Global Mainframe Corp. 06/13/2007
Each share Common no par exchanged for (0.01) share Common no par
(See Global Mainframe Corp.)

EMJ DATA SYS LTD (ON)
Acquired by Synnex Canada Ltd. 12/1/2004
Each share Common no par exchanged for $6.60 cash

EMJAY PETROLEUMS LTD. (AB)
Recapitalized as Canadian Emjay Petroleums Ltd. on a (1/3) for (1) basis in 1954
Canadian Emjay Petroleums Ltd. recapitalized as Consolidated Emjay Petroleums Ltd. 7/31/57 which recapitalized as New Emjay Petroleums Ltd. 2/4/66
(See New Emjay Petroleums Ltd.)

EMK INC (NY)
Dissolved by proclamation 3/24/92

EMLEN ARMS APARTMENT CORP. (PA)
Liquidation for cash completed 7/14/66

EMM ENERGY INC (AB)
Merged into SkyWest Energy Corp. 06/22/2010
Each share Common no par exchanged for (1.98) shares Common no par and $1.05 cash
SkyWest Energy Corp. recapitalized as Marquee Energy Ltd. (Old) 12/09/2011 which merged into Marquee Energy Ltd. (New) 12/08/2016

EMMA OIL & GAS INC (OR)
Involuntarily dissolved for failure to file reports and pay fees 04/18/1983

EMMA SILVER MINES CO.
Merged into Alta United Mines Co. 00/00/1932
Details not available

EMMART PACKING CO. (KY)
Merged into Klarer Co. share for share in 1957
Klarer Co. name changed to Klarer of Kentucky, Inc. 3/1/63
(See Klarer of Kentucky, Inc.)

EMMER GLASS CORP. (FL)
Reorganized as Richford Industries, Inc. and Class A Common 10¢ par reclassified as Common 10¢ par 5/6/66
Richford Industries, Inc. merged into Great American Industries, Inc. 3/12/81
(See Great American Industries, Inc.)

EMMERT MFG INC (IA)
Merged into Talbot-Carlson, Inc. 02/29/1980
Each share Common 66-2/3¢ par exchanged for $1.85 cash

EMMET INC (DE)
Charter cancelled and declared inoperative and void for non-payment of taxes 03/01/1995

EMMIS BROADCASTING CORP (IN)
Name changed to Emmis Communications Corp. 6/23/98

EMO MINES LTD. (ON)
Charter revoked for failure to file reports and pay fees 08/25/1966

EMOBILE DATA CORP (YUKON)
Acquired by Itron, Inc. 10/03/2002
Each share Common no par exchanged for USD$0.268 cash
Note: Each share Common no par received an additional distribution of approximately USD $0.02 cash 12/18/2002

EMONS HLDGS INC (DE)
Under plan of reorganization each share Preferred 1¢ par exchanged for (1) share Preferred Ser. A 1¢ par 9/27/89
Name changed to Emons Transportation Group Inc. 12/1/93
(See Emons Transportation Group Inc.)

EMONS INDS INC (NY)
Stock Dividends - 25% 8/12/77; 50% 12/29/77; 25% 5/9/79
Reorganized under the laws of Delaware as Emons Holdings Inc. 12/31/86
Each share $1.1875 Conv. Preferred 1¢ par exchanged for (0.027415) share Common 1¢ par
Each share Common 1¢ par exchanged for (0.02463) share Common 1¢ par
Note: Unexchanged certificates became valueless 6/30/87
Emons Holdings Inc. name changed to Emons Transportation Group Inc. 12/1/93

EMONS TRANSN GROUP INC (DE)
Each $0.14 Conv. Preferred Ser. A 1¢ par exchanged for (1.1) shares Common 1¢ par 6/29/99
Merged into Genesee & Wyoming, Inc. 2/25/2002
Each share Common 1¢ par exchanged for $2.50 cash

EMORY CAP CORP (DE)
Name changed to Sargent, Inc. (Old) 11/29/90
Sargent, Inc. (Old) reorganized as Sargent, Inc. (New) 7/25/94 which name changed to National Quality Care Inc. 5/28/96

EMORY GOLD MINING CO., LTD. (ON)
Charter cancelled 03/30/1959

EMPAQUES PONDEROSA S A (MEXICO)
ADR agreement terminated 06/01/1996
Each 144A Sponsored ADR for Ordinary no par exchanged for $12.117 cash
Each Sponsored ADR for Ordinary no par exchanged for $12.117 cash

EMPAQUES PONDEROSA S A DE C V (MEXICO)
ADR agreement terminated 6/1/2000
Each Sponsored ADR for Ordinary no par exchanged for $12.9584 cash

EMPCO INC (DE)
Completely liquidated 12/9/70
Each Unit exchanged for first and final distribution of $5.19 cash

EMPEIRIA ACQUISITION CORP (DE)
Issue Information - 8,500,000 UNITS consisting of (1) share COM and (1) WT offered at $10 per Unit on 06/15/2011
Name changed to Integrated Drilling Equipment Holdings Corp. 05/17/2013

EMPEROR ENTMT HOTEL (HONG KONG)
Name changed 08/24/2005
Name changed from Emperor (China Concept) Investments Ltd. to

Emperor Entertainment Hotel
08/24/2005
ADR agreement terminated
10/24/2005
No ADR's remain outstanding

EMPEROR GOLD CORP (BC)
Name changed to Emgold Mining Corp. 08/01/1997

EMPEROR INTL HLDGS LTD (BERMUDA)
Basis changed from (1:1) to (1:10) 01/04/2005
ADR agreement terminated 11/30/2017
Each Sponsored ADR for Common exchanged for (10) shares Common
Note: Unexchanged ADR's will be sold and the proceeds, if any, held for claim after 12/03/2018

EMPEROR MINERALS LTD (BC)
Name changed to Emperor Oil Ltd. 08/24/2012

EMPEROR MINES LTD (AUSTRALIA)
Stock Dividends - 25% 05/27/1980; 10% 12/12/1980; 33-1/3% 07/21/1987
Merged into Intrepid Mines Ltd. 03/11/2008
Each ADR for Ordinary A$0.10 par exchanged for $0.03874 cash

EMPEROR MINES LTD (BC)
Recapitalized as Taronga Resources Ltd. 06/00/1973
Each share Common no par exchanged for (0.2) share Common no par
(See Taronga Resources Ltd.)

EMPHATIC MERGERS INC (NV)
Name changed to First National Realty Associates, Inc. 04/11/1990
First National Realty Associates, Inc. name changed to 1st Realty Investments, Inc. 07/13/2000 which recapitalized as Great Western Land & Recreation, Inc. 02/05/2004
(See Great Western Land & Recreation, Inc.)

EMPHESYS FINL GROUP INC (DE)
Merged into HEW, Inc. 10/13/95
Each share Common 1¢ par exchanged for $37.50 cash

EMPI INC (MN)
Common 10¢ par split (3) for (2) by issuance of (0.5) additional share 10/21/83
Common 10¢ par changed to 1¢ par 6/7/90
Common 1¢ par split (3) for (2) by issuance of (0.5) additional share 8/16/91
Common 1¢ par split (2) for (1) by issuance of (1) additional share 6/11/93
Merged into El Merger Corp. 9/1/99
Each share Common 1¢ par exchanged for $26.50 cash

EMPIRE & BAY STS TELEG CO (NY)
Company went private 00/00/1982
Details not available

EMPIRE AIRLINES, INC. (NY)
Incorporated 7/17/43
Charter cancelled and proclaimed dissolved for failure to pay taxes 12/16/63

EMPIRE AIRLS INC (NY)
Incorporated 12/27/74
Merged into Piedmont Aviation, Inc. 2/1/86
Each share Common 40¢ par exchanged for $15 cash

EMPIRE ALLIANCE PPTYS INC (ON)
Cease trade order effective 03/11/2002

EMPIRE AMERICAN SECURITIES CORP.
Merged into Allied International Investing Corp. in 1947
Each share Preferred exchanged for (0.3404) share Capital Stock $1 par
Each share Common exchanged for (0.0008) share Capital Stock $1 par
Allied International Investing Corp. name changed to Dorsey Corp. 3/26/59 which name changed to Constar International Inc. 5/1/87
(See Constar International Inc.)

EMPIRE APPAREL STORES INC (DE)
Charter cancelled and declared inoperative and void for non-payment of taxes 3/1/85

EMPIRE ASBESTOS LTD. (QC)
Declared dissolved for failure to file reports or pay fees 5/25/74

EMPIRE ASSOC INC (MN)
Common 50¢ par changed to 25¢ par and (1) additional share issued 1/15/73
Name changed to Empire-Crown Auto, Inc. 5/26/76
Empire-Crown Auto, Inc. name changed to Crown Auto Inc. 5/18/84
(See Crown Auto Inc.)

EMPIRE BANC CORP (DE)
Stock Dividends - 10% 4/28/88; 33-1/3% 10/31/89; 10% 12/23/91; 10% 9/30/93
Merged into Huntington Bancshares Inc. 6/28/2000
Each share Common $5 par exchanged for (2.0355) shares Common no par

EMPIRE BANCORP (CA)
Common no par split (5) for (4) by issuance of (0.25) additional share 07/07/1986
Common no par split (6) for (5) by issuance of (1.2) additional shares 01/30/1990
Stock Dividend - 10% 06/22/1989
Acquired by California State Bank (Covina, CA) 12/03/1990
Each share Common no par exchanged for (0.93) share Common no par
California State Bank (Covina, CA) merged into First Security Corp. 05/30/198 which which merged into Wells Fargo & Co. (New) 10/26/2000

EMPIRE BK (SPRINGFIELD, MO)
Capital Stock $10 par changed to $5 par and (1) additional share issued 11/22/68
Over 99% acquired by Central Bancompany in August 1980
Public interest eliminated

EMPIRE BK CORP (HOMERVILLE, GA)
Merged into Flag Financial Corp. 12/11/1998
Each share Common $10 par exchanged for (42.5) shares Common $1 par
(See Flag Financial Corp.)

EMPIRE BOND & MORTGAGE CO.
Adjudicated bankrupt 00/00/1932
No stockholders' equity

EMPIRE BRASS MANUFACTURING CO. LTD. (ON)
Recapitalized 00/00/1951
Each share Class A no par exchanged for (1) share 5% Preference $22 par
Class B no par redesignated as Common no par
Name changed to Emco Ltd. 02/01/1957
(See Emco Ltd.)

EMPIRE BREEDERS INC (NY)
Name changed to Empire National Corp. (Incorporated February 7, 1980) 05/25/1983
(See Empire National Corp. (Incorporated February 7, 1980))

EMPIRE CAP CORP (BC)
Reincorporated under the laws of Canada as Zonte Metals Inc. 08/02/2011

EMPIRE CAP CORP (DE)
Recapitalized as Interfund Resources, Ltd. 07/20/1998
Each share Common $0.001 par exchanged for (0.16666666) share Common $0.001 par
Interfund Resources, Ltd. name changed to Interactive Technologies.Com, Ltd. (DE) 03/01/1999 which reorganized in Florida as International Coastal Biofuels, Inc. 04/09/2008 which recapitalized as IMD Companies Inc. 10/12/2010

EMPIRE CAPITAL CORP.
Dissolved 00/00/1943
Details not available

EMPIRE CHAIR CO.
In process of liquidation 00/00/1934
Details not available

EMPIRE COMMUNICATIONS CORP (NV)
Name changed to Front Porch Digital, Inc. 05/02/2000
Front Porch Digital, Inc. name changed to Incentra Solutions, Inc. 10/29/2004
(See Incentra Solutions, Inc.)

EMPIRE CORP.
Dissolved 00/00/1935
Details not available

EMPIRE CORP. (CO)
Merged into Crusader Oil & Uranium Co. 04/20/1955
Each share Common $1 par exchanged for (1) share Common $1 par
Crusader Oil & Uranium Co. merged into Crusader Oil & Gas Co. 02/06/1959 which merged into Gold Empire Mining Co. 06/15/1968
(See Gold Empire Mining Co.)

EMPIRE CROWN AUTO INC (MN)
Stock Dividend - 40% 02/27/1980
Name changed to Crown Auto Inc. 05/18/1984
(See Crown Auto Inc.)

EMPIRE DEVICES, INC. (NY)
Completely liquidated 09/20/1963
Each share Common $1 par exchanged for first and final distribution of (0.192724) share Singer Co. Capital Stock $10 par
(See Singer Co.)

EMPIRE DIST ELEC CO (KS)
Common $10 par split (3) for (2) by issuance of (0.5) additional share 12/14/1956
Common $10 par split (3) for (2) by issuance of (0.5) additional share 12/13/1963
4.75% Preferred $100 par and 5% Preferred $100 par changed to $10 par and (9) additional shares issued respectively 11/30/1971
Common $10 par split (3) for (2) by issuance of (0.5) additional share 06/29/1973
Common $10 par changed to $1 par 04/29/1981
9.16% Preferred $10 par called for redemption 06/01/1986
Common $1 par split (2) for (1) by issuance of (1) additional share 01/29/1992
9% Preferred $10 par called for redemption 06/01/1992
4.75% Preferred $10 par called for redemption at $10.20 on 08/02/1999
5% Preferred $10 par called for redemption at $10.50 on 08/02/1999
8.125% Preferred $10 par called for redemption at $10 on 08/02/1999
Acquired by Algonquin Power & Utilities Corp. 12/30/2016
Each share Common $1 par exchanged for $34 cash

EMPIRE DIST ELEC TR I (DE)
8.5% Trust Preferred Securities called for redemption at $25 on 06/28/2010

EMPIRE ENERGY CORP (UT)
Each share old Common $0.001 par exchanged for (2.5) shares new Common $0.001 par 09/30/1999
Reorganized under the laws of Nevada as Empire Energy Corp. International 04/26/2004
Each share new Common $0.001 par exchanged for (0.1) share Common $0.001 par

EMPIRE EQUITIES INC (CA)
Stock Dividend - 10% 01/04/1971
Name changed to Columbia Equities, Inc. 09/16/1986
Columbia Equities, Inc. merged into International Turbo Center, Inc. 05/15/1990

EMPIRE EXPL CO (UT)
Recapitalized as Tellco Information Services 03/30/1973
Each share Common 1¢ par exchanged for (4) shares Common 1¢ par
(See Tellco Information Services)

EMPIRE EXPLORATIONS, INC. (WA)
Name changed to Comstock-Empire International Inc. 07/22/1988
Comstock-Empire International Inc. recapitalized as Winners Internet Network, Inc. 07/15/1997 which recapitalized as American Television & Film Co. 02/17/2004 which name changed to Spotlight Homes, Inc. 04/06/2004

EMPIRE EXPLORATIONS LTD. (BC)
Each share Capital Stock $2 par exchanged for (2) shares Capital Stock $1 par 02/00/1956
Merged into Castle Oil & Gas Ltd. 05/00/1956
Each share Capital Stock $2 par exchanged for (0.1) share Capital Stock no par
(See Castle Oil & Gas Ltd.)

EMPIRE FARMS, INC.
Sold at public auction 00/00/1942
Details not available

EMPIRE FDG CORP (NV)
Market Auction Preferred no par called for redemption 10/10/1989
Public interest eliminated

EMPIRE FED BANCORP INC (DE)
Merged into Sterling Financial Corp. 03/03/2003
Each share Common 1¢ par exchanged for (0.9392) share Common $1 par
Sterling Financial Corp. merged into Umpqua Holdings Corp. 04/18/2014

EMPIRE FILM GROUP INC (FL)
Recapitalized as Tarsin Mobile, Inc. 07/09/2015
Each share Common $0.001 par exchanged for (0.0001) share Common $0.001 par

EMPIRE FINANCE CO.
Merged into Ohio Finance Co. 00/00/1929

EMPIRE FINANCIAL CORP. (DE)
Common $1 par split (5) for (4) by issuance of (0.25) additional share 02/20/1962
Common $1 par split (5) for (4) by issuance of (0.25) additional share 05/15/1970
Stock Dividends - 10% 02/20/1965; 10% 02/21/1966
Liquidation completed
Each share Common $1 par exchanged for initial distribution of $16.05 cash 07/31/1975
Each share Common $1 par received second distribution of $0.92 cash 08/25/1976
Each share Common $1 par received

third distribution of $0.62 cash 07/21/1977
Each share Common $1 par received fourth and final distribution of $0.0755 cash 02/01/1979

EMPIRE FINL CORP (CO)
Recapitalized as Duckback Industries, Inc. 08/31/1990
Each share Common $0.0001 par exchanged for (0.1) share Common $0.0001 par
Duckback Industries, Inc. name changed to Sinecure Financial Corp. 08/27/1991
(See Sinecure Financial Corp.)

EMPIRE FINL CORP (NJ)
Charter void by proclamation 07/30/1993

EMPIRE FINL HLDG CO (FL)
Name changed to Jesup & Lamont, Inc. 01/02/2008
(See Jesup & Lamont, Inc.)

EMPIRE FIRE & MARINE INS CO (NE)
Each share old Common $1 par exchanged for (2) shares new Common $1 par 03/20/1972
New Common $1 par changed to Common $2 par 12/27/1972
6% Preferred $5 par called for redemption 10/02/1970
7% Preferred $5 par called for redemption 10/02/1970
Merged into Zurich Insurance Co. 11/13/1979
Each share Common $2 par exchanged for $21 cash

EMPIRE FIRE INSURANCE CO. OF BROOKLYN
Acquired by Public Fire Insurance Co. (Newark) 00/00/1931
Details not available

EMPIRE GAS CORP (MO)
Certificates dated prior to 11/04/1980
Each share Common $1 par exchanged for (3) shares Common no par 08/09/1966
5.5% Conv. Preferred $100 par called for redemption 03/02/1970
Common no par split (2) for (1) by issuance of (1) additional share 03/01/1978
Common no par split (2) for (1) by issuance of (1) additional share 03/14/1980
Stock Dividend - 50% 09/12/1968
Name changed to Empire, Inc. and Common no par changed to $1 par 11/04/1980
(See Empire, Inc.)

EMPIRE GAS CORP (MO)
Certificates dated after 04/08/1986
Merged into EGAI Inc. 12/01/1989
Each share Common $0.001 par exchanged for $3.75 cash

EMPIRE GEN CORP (DE)
Merged into Protective Life Insurance Co. 05/12/1978
Each share Capital Stock $1 par exchanged for $4 cash

EMPIRE GLOBAL CORP (DE)
Name changed to Newgioco Group, Inc. 02/16/2017

EMPIRE GOLD INC (IN)
Administratively dissolved 05/19/2004

EMPIRE GOLD MINES LTD. (ON)
Merged into Associated Porcupine Mines Ltd. 11/05/1968
Each share Capital Stock $1 par exchanged for (0.193936) share Capital Stock no par
Associated Porcupine Mines Ltd. merged into American Reserve Mining Corp. 02/27/1989 which recapitalized as AMI Resources Inc. 12/21/1994 which name changed to Ashanti Sankofa Inc. 01/19/2017

EMPIRE GOLD RES CORP (BC)
Struck off register and declared dissolved for failure to file returns 03/28/1991

EMPIRE HEALTH CARE PRODS INC (DE)
Charter cancelled and declared inoperative and void for non-payment of taxes 03/01/1987

EMPIRE HOME LOANS, INC. (GA)
100% acquired by Associated Madison Companies, Inc. through exchange offer which expired 02/01/1971
Public interest eliminated

EMPIRE INC (MO)
Acquired by a group of investors 06/09/1983
Each share Common $1 par exchanged for $9 principal amount of Empire, Inc. 9% Subord. Debentures due 12/31/2007 and $22 cash

EMPIRE INDUSTRIES, INC. (UT)
Charter revoked for failure to file reports and pay fees 03/31/1966

EMPIRE INDUSTRIES LTD OLD (AB)
Plan of arrangement effective 06/30/2016
Each share Common no par exchanged for (0.25) share Empire Industries Ltd. (New) Common no par and (0.125) share Tornado Global Hydrovacs Ltd. Common no par

EMPIRE INS CO (CA)
Merged into American Liberty Insurance Co. 07/19/1974
Each share Common $1 par exchanged for $0.385 cash

EMPIRE INS CO NEW (NY)
Each share Common $1 par exchanged for (0.01) share Common $100 par 08/15/1988
Reacquired 12/18/1991
Each share Common $100 par exchanged for $1,365.01 cash

EMPIRE INTL INC (CO)
Adjudicated bankrupt 05/09/1973
Stockholders' equity unlikely

EMPIRE LEASING CORP. (OK)
Charter revoked for failure to file reports and pay fees 05/11/1968

EMPIRE LEE MNG CO (CO)
Charter revoked for failure to file reports and pay fees 10/13/1967

EMPIRE LIFE INSURANCE CO. (AL)
Under plan of merger name changed to Empire Life Insurance Co. of America (AL) 06/18/1965
(See Empire Life Insurance Co. of America (AL))

EMPIRE LIFE INSURANCE CO. OF AMERICA (AR)
Merged into Empire Life Insurance Co. of America (AL) 06/18/1965
Each share Capital Stock no par exchanged for (0.9) share Class A Common $1 par
(See Empire Life Insurance Co. of America (AL))

EMPIRE LIFE INSURANCE CO. OF ILLINOIS (IL)
Merged into Empire General Corp. 09/22/1969
Each share Common $1 par exchanged for (0.1) share Capital Stock $1 par
(See Empire General Corp.)

EMPIRE LIFE INS CO (CA)
Common 20¢ par changed to 25¢ par 06/28/1967
Common 25¢ par changed to 30¢ par 03/27/1969
Each share Common 30¢ par exchanged for (0.001) share Common $300 par 09/11/1972
Note: In effect holders received $4.75 cash per share and public interest was eliminated

EMPIRE LIFE INS CO AMER (AL)
Class B Common $20 par changed to $10 par 09/11/1969
Placed in receivership 06/29/1972
No stockholders' equity

EMPIRE LIFE INS CO OHIO (OH)
Merged into Empire General Corp. 04/30/1968
Each share Common 20¢ par exchanged for (0.41322314) share Capital Stock $1 par
(See Empire General Corp.)

EMPIRE LTD (NS)
Variable Rate Conv. Retractable Preferred Ser. 1 no par called for redemption at $25 on 08/15/1997
Variable Rate Preferred Ser. 3 $25 par called for redemption at $25 plus $0.50 accrued dividends on 01/23/2001
Variable Rate Preferred Ser. 2 $25 par called for redemption at $25.14 on 01/23/2012
(Additional Information in Active)

EMPIRE MERCURY CORP. LTD. (BC)
Name changed to Empire Metals Corp. Ltd. 12/17/1970
Empire Metals Corp. Ltd. recapitalized as Sovereign Metals Corp. 03/15/1976 which recapitalized as Barytex Resources Corp. 04/29/1986 which recapitalized as International Barytex Resources Ltd. 07/06/1993 which merged into Kobex Minerals Inc. 09/30/2009 which name changed to Kobex Capital Corp. 08/29/2014 which name changed to Itasca Capital Ltd. 06/23/2016

EMPIRE METALS LTD (BC)
Recapitalized as Sovereign Metals Corp. 03/15/1976
Each share Capital Stock no par exchanged for (0.2) share Capital Stock no par
Sovereign Metals Corp. recapitalized as Barytex Resources Corp. 04/29/1986 which recapitalized as International Barytex Resources Ltd. 07/06/1993 which merged into Kobex Minerals Inc. 09/30/2009 which name changed to Kobex Capital Corp. 08/29/2014 which name changed to Itasca Capital Ltd. 06/23/2016

EMPIRE MILLWORK CORP. (NY)
Name changed to Empire National Corp. 11/01/1960
Empire National Corp. name changed to Bruce (E.L.) Co., (Inc.) 09/22/1961 which merged into Cook Industries, Inc. 03/21/1969 which name changed to Cook International Inc. 05/11/1981
(See Cook International Inc.)

EMPIRE MINERALS CORP (DE)
Name changed to Dominion Minerals Corp. 02/14/2008

EMPIRE MINERALS INC (QC)
Charter annulled for failure to file reports or pay fees 05/00/1982

EMPIRE MINES CO (UT)
Merged into North Lily Mining Co. 12/01/1976
Each share Capital Stock 5¢ par exchanged for (0.0265) share Capital Stock 10¢ par
(See North Lily Mining Co.)

EMPIRE MNG CORP (BC)
Name changed to Columbus Copper Corp. 01/10/2013
Columbus Copper Corp. merged into EnerGulf Resources Inc. 10/05/2015

EMPIRE NATL BK (CLARKSBURG, WV)
Capital Stock $100 par changed to $20 par and (4) additional shares issued 01/30/1973
Capital Stock $20 par changed to $10 par and (1) additional share issued 03/10/1979
Stock Dividends - 100% 06/22/1955; 200% 01/31/1968; 20% 02/15/1974; 20% 03/10/1976
Merged into Mountaineer Bankshares of W. Va., Inc. 02/28/1985
Each share Capital Stock $10 par exchanged for (1) share Common $2.50 par
Mountaineer Bankshares of W. Va., Inc. merged into One Valley Bancorp of West Virginia, Inc. 01/28/1994 which name changed to One Valley Bancorp, Inc. 04/30/1996 which merged into BB&T Corp. 07/06/2000

EMPIRE NATL BK (ISLANDIA, NY)
Under plan of reorganization each share Common $1 par automatically became (1) share Empire Bancorp, Inc. Common 1¢ par 08/26/2013

EMPIRE NATIONAL BANK (LOS ANGELES, CA)
Closed by Comptroller of Currency and FDIC appointed receiver 07/30/1987
Stockholders' equity undetermined

EMPIRE NATL BK (MIDDLETOWN, NY)
Acquired by Bank of New York Co., Inc. 09/11/1980
Each share Common Capital Stock $5 par exchanged for $22 cash

EMPIRE NATL BK (TRAVERSE CITY, MI)
Merged into Empire Banc Corp. 05/31/1987
Each share Common $10 par exchanged for (2) shares Common $5 par
Empire Banc Corp. merged into Huntington Bancshares Inc. 06/28/2000

EMPIRE NATIONAL CORP. (NY)
Incorporated 04/20/1944
Name changed to Bruce (E.L.) Co., (Inc.) 09/22/1961
Bruce (E.L.) Co., (Inc.) merged into Cook Industries, Inc. 03/21/1969 which name changed to Cook International Inc. 05/11/1981
(See Cook International Inc.)

EMPIRE NATIONAL CORP. (NY)
Charter cancelled and proclaimed dissolved for failure to pay taxes 04/03/1985

EMPIRE OF AMER FED SVGS BK (BUFFALO, NY)
Placed in receivership 02/28/1990
No stockholders' equity

EMPIRE OF AMER FINL CORP (NV)
Market Auction Preferred no par called for redemption 09/25/1989
Public interest eliminated

EMPIRE OF CAROLINA INC (DE)
Common 10¢ par split (3) for (2) by issuance of (0.5) additional share 08/21/1989
Chapter 11 petition dismissed and assets sold for the benefit of creditors 02/25/2003
No stockholders' equity

EMPIRE OIL & GAS CO (CO)
Incorporated 04/14/1917
Declared defunct and inoperative for failure to pay taxes and file annual reports 10/14/1924

EMPIRE OIL & GAS CO (CO)
Incorporated 09/18/1979
Chapter 11 bankruptcy proceedings converted to Chapter 7 on 10/09/1985
Stockholders' equity unlikely

EMPIRE OIL & MINERALS INC. (QC)
Recapitalized as Empire Minerals Inc. 11/22/1965
Each share Capital Stock $1 par exchanged for (0.33333333) share Capital Stock $1 par

(See Empire Minerals Inc.)

EMPIRE OIL & REFINING CO. (DE)
Recapitalized as Cutler Ridge Corp. 05/16/1960
Each share Common 5¢ par exchanged for (0.2) share Common 50¢ par
(See Cutler Ridge Corp.)

EMPIRE OIL CO., INC. (NV)
Charter revoked for failure to file reports and pay fees 03/05/1962

EMPIRE OIL CORP. (DE)
Acquired by Capitol Holding Corp. 10/21/1968
Each share Common 5¢ par exchanged for (1) share Common $1 par
(See Capitol Holding Corp.)

EMPIRE OIL OF TEXAS, INC. (TX)
Dissolved 12/10/1954
Details not available

EMPIRE ORR INC (NY)
Filed a petition under Chapter 11 Federal Bankruptcy Code 01/10/1991
Details not available

EMPIRE PENCIL CORP (DE)
Merged into Empire Pencil Acquisition Corp. 02/28/1983
Each share Common 50¢ par exchanged for $19 cash

EMPIRE PETE CO (CO)
4% Preference Common $1 par reclassified as Common $1 par 12/14/1955
Name changed to Empire International, Inc. 07/15/1970
(See Empire International, Inc.)

EMPIRE PETROLEUMS, LTD. (AB)
Acquired by Texas Calgary Co. 00/00/1953
Each share Capital Stock no par exchanged for (0.2) share Capital Stock $1 par
Texas Calgary Co. was acquired by Texstar Corp. 10/02/1959
(See Texstar Corp.)

EMPIRE PIZZA HLDGS INC (FL)
Recapitalized as Vestiage, Inc. 03/22/2013
Each share Common $0.0001 par exchanged for (0.0000125) share Common $0.0001 par

EMPIRE POWER CORP.
Liquidation completed 00/00/1947
Details not available

EMPIRE PUBLIC SERVICE CORP.
Assets sold 00/00/1934
Details not available

EMPIRE RES INC (BC)
Recapitalized as Arabesque Resources Ltd. 08/15/1984
Each share Common no par exchanged for (0.33333333) share Common no par
(See Arabesque Resources Ltd.)

EMPIRE RES INC (DE)
Acquired by Ta Chen Stainless Pipe Co., Ltd. 05/09/2017
Each share Common 1¢ par exchanged for $7 cash

EMPIRE ROCK MINERALS INC (BC)
Name changed to Empire Metals Corp. 02/02/2017

EMPIRE ROOFING & SHEET METAL WORKS CO. (BC)
Liquidated 04/27/1962
No stockholders' equity

EMPIRE SVGS & LN ASSN (CA)
Acquired by Equitec Financial Group, Inc. 01/01/1985
Each share Guarantee Stock $8 par exchanged for $14.25 cash

EMPIRE SVGS BLDG & LN ASSN (CO)
Acquired by Baldwin (D.H.) Co. 11/00/1968

Details not available

EMPIRE SHEET & TIN PLATE CO.
Name changed to Empire Steel Corp. (New) 00/00/1944
Empire Steel Corp. (New) name changed to E.S. Liquidating Co. 00/00/1948
(See E.S. Liquidating Co.)

EMPIRE SOUTHERN GAS CO. (DE)
Common $1 par changed to $10 par 00/00/1945
Each share Common $10 par exchanged for (2) shares Common $5 par 00/00/1954
Acquired by Pioneer Natural Gas Co. 03/28/1958
Each share Common $5 par exchanged for (0.909091) share Common $7.50 par
Pioneer Natural Gas Co. name changed to Pioneer Corp. (TX) 04/18/1975 which liquidated for Mesa Limited Partnership 06/30/1986 which reorganized in Texas as Mesa Inc. 12/31/1991 which merged into Pioneer Natural Resources Co. 08/07/1997

EMPIRE SPORTS & ENTMT HLDGS CO (NV)
Common $0.0001 par split (2.51380043) for (1) by issuance of (1.51380043) additional shares payable 10/13/2010 to to holders of record 09/26/2010 Ex date - 10/14/2010
Name changed to Sagebrush Gold Ltd. 06/01/2011
Sagebrush Gold Ltd. name changed to Pershing Gold Corp. 03/26/2012

EMPIRE ST BK N A (NEWBURGH, NY)
Under plan of reorganization each share Common $5 par automatically became (1) share ES Bancshares, Inc. Common 1¢ par 08/15/2006

EMPIRE ST LIFE INS CO (NY)
Merged into Unity Mutual Life Insurance Co. 02/04/1993
Each share Common $1 par exchanged for $2.75 cash

EMPIRE ST OIL CO (WY)
Merged into Ashland Oil Canada Ltd. 06/29/1972
Each share Common $1 par exchanged for (2.25) shares Common 45¢ par
Ashland Oil Canada Ltd. name changed to Kaiser Petroleum Ltd. 03/23/1979
(See Kaiser Petroleum Ltd.)

EMPIRE STAR MINES CO. LTD. (DE)
Merged into Newmont Mining Corp. 05/06/1957
Each share Common $10 par exchanged for (0.25) share Capital Stock $10 par

EMPIRE STATE BANK (DALLAS, TX)
Each share Capital Stock $20 par exchanged for (2) shares Capital Stock $10 par 10/14/1959
Merged into National Bank of Commerce (Dallas, TX) 12/04/1967
Each share Capital Stock $10 par exchanged for (1) share 6% Conv. Preferred $22 par
National Bank of Commerce (Dallas, TX) reorganized as Commerce Southwest Inc. 03/16/1979 which name changed to BancTEXAS Group Inc. 08/31/1982 which recapitalized as First Banks America, Inc. 08/31/1995
(See First Banks America, Inc.)

EMPIRE STATE BANK (SALT LAKE CITY, UT)
Acquired by Guardian State Bank (Salt Lake City, UT) 04/09/1982
Details not available

EMPIRE STATE RAILROAD CORP.
Sold at foreclosure 00/00/1931

No stockholders' equity

EMPIRE STEEL CORP.
Reorganized as Empire Sheet & Tin Plate Co. 00/00/1933
Details not available

EMPIRE STEEL CORP. NEW
Name changed to E.S. Liquidating Co. 00/00/1948
(See E.S. Liquidating Co.)

EMPIRE STUDIOS, INC. (FL)
Each share Common $1 par exchanged for (2) shares Common 50¢ par 07/19/1955
Name changed to Consolidated Empire, Inc. 08/18/1961
(See Consolidated Empire, Inc.)

EMPIRE TECHNOLOGIES LTD (BC)
Reincorporated under the laws of Wyoming as Analytical Software Inc. 08/08/2000
(See Analytical Software Inc.)

EMPIRE TELEPHONE CO.
Merged into Southeastern Telephone Co. share for share in 1940
Southeastern Telephone Co. merged into Central Telephone Co. (New) 12/1/71
(See Central Telephone Co. (New))

EMPIRE TITLE & GUARANTEE CO.
Acquired by Home Title Guaranty Co. in 1949
Each share Capital Stock $25 par exchanged for (1) share Preferred which was redeemed at $41 per share

EMPIRE TRUST CO. (NEW YORK, NY)
Each share Capital Stock $10 par exchanged for (0.2) share Capital Stock $50 par 00/00/1940
Stock Dividends - 14-2/7% 02/09/1951; 12-1/2% 02/08/1952; 11-1/9% 02/13/1953
Merged into Bank of New York (New York, NY) 12/07/1966
Each share Capital Stock $50 par exchanged for (2.4285) shares $4 Conv. Preferred $75 par and (2.4285) shares Common $15 par
Bank of New York (New York, NY) reorganized as Bank of New York Co., Inc. 05/29/1969 which merged into Bank of New York Mellon Corp. 07/01/2007

EMPIRE VENTURES INC (CO)
Majority shares reacquired 00/00/1981
Public interest eliminated

EMPIRE VENTURES INC (DE)
Recapitalized as Soulfood Concepts, Inc. 12/26/1996
Each share Common $0.003 par exchanged for (1/3) share Common $0.003 par
(See Soulfood Concepts, Inc.)

EMPIRE VIDEO CORP (CO)
Name changed to Random Access, Inc. 2/12/88
Random Access, Inc. merged into Entex Information Services, Inc. 9/20/95

EMPIRE WESTERN CORP.
Liquidated in 1933

EMPIRE WHSES INC (DE)
Name changed to Empco, Inc. 10/27/69
(See Empco, Inc.)

EMPIRE WTR CORP (NV)
Voluntarily dissolved 02/20/2018
No stockholders' equity

EMPIRIC ENERGY INC (DE)
Issue Information - 361,500 UNITS consisting of (3) shares COM and (1) SER A WT offered at $10 per Unit on 06/13/1994
Each share old Common 1¢ par exchanged for (0.5) share new Common 1¢ par 01/14/2003

SEC revoked preferred and common stock registrations 08/05/2010
Stockholders' equity unlikely

EMPIRICAL INC (AB)
Received Notice of Intention to Enforce Security 01/08/2009
Stockholders' equity unlikely

EMPIRICAL RESH SYS INC (NV)
Each share old Common $0.005 par exchanged for (0.001) share new Common $0.005 par 04/15/1998
Note: Holdings of (999) or fewer pre-split shares were cancelled and are without value
Holdings of (99) or fewer post-split shares were rounded up to (100) shares
Charter revoked for failure to file reports and pay fees 06/30/2000

EMPIRICAL VENTURES INC (NV)
Recapitalized as Go-Page Corp. 06/06/2014
Each share Common $0.001 par exchanged for (0.02857142) share Common $0.001 par

EMPLOYEE BENEFIT PLANS INC (DE)
Merged into First Financial Management Corp. 10/19/1995
Each share Common 1¢ par exchanged for (0.1975) share Common 10¢ par
First Financial Management Corp. merged into First Data Corp. (Old) 10/27/1995
(See First Data Corp. (Old))

EMPLOYEE BENEFITS INC (DE)
Merged into Orion Capital Corp. 12/5/80
Each share Common $1 par exchanged for $32 cash

EMPLOYEE SOLUTIONS INC (AZ)
Common no par split (2) for (1) by issuance of (1) additional share payable 01/12/1996 to holders of record 01/02/1996
Common no par split (2) for (1) by issuance of (1) additional share payable 07/26/1996 to holders of record 07/12/1996
Chapter 7 bankruptcy proceedings terminated 05/25/2006
No stockholders' equity

EMPLOYEES CREDIT CORP. (DE)
Assets sold to Seaboard Finance Co. in 1951
(See listing for Seaboard Finance Co.)

EMPLOYERS CAS CO (TX)
Capital Stock $10 par changed to $5 par and (1) additional share issued 2/19/59
Capital Stock $5 par changed to $2.50 par and (1) additional share issued 5/12/72
Capital Stock $2.50 par changed to $1.25 par and (1) additional shares issued 7/15/86
Stock Dividends - 33-1/3% 2/1/38; 25% 2/1/39; 50% 3/2/48; 33-1/3% 3/4/50; 25% 3/20/54; 20% 3/19/55; 10% 2/19/70; 10% 2/15/73; 10% 2/14/74; 10.19% 2/19/75; 20% 2/16/77; 20% 2/16/78; 21.5% 2/15/79; 25% 2/14/80; 20% 2/18/81; 20% 2/17/82
Placed in receivership 2/11/94
No stockholders' equity

EMPLOYERS GEN INS GROUP INC (DE)
Merged into EGIG NuCorp 6/24/2005
Each share Common 1¢ par exchanged for $5 cash

EMPLOYERS GROUP ASSOC (MA)
Common no par split (2) for (1) by issuance of (1) additional share 4/30/60
Stock Dividends - 10% 5/15/54; 25% 4/30/62
Merged into ECU Corp. 1/1/72

Each share Common no par exchanged for $92.50 cash

EMPLOYERS GROUP FD INC (MA)
Common $1 par split (2) for (1) by issuance of (1) additional share 02/29/1968
Name changed to Egret Growth Fund Inc. 01/13/1969
Egret Growth Fund Inc. name changed to Egret Fund Inc. 12/12/1974 which merged into Pioneer Fund, Inc. 07/24/1978 which name changed to Pioneer Fund 07/03/1992

EMPLOYERS INDEMNITY CORP. (MO)
Name changed to Employers Reinsurance Corp. 00/00/1928
(See Employers Reinsurance Corp)

EMPLOYERS INS CO ALA (AL)
Each share Common $100 par exchanged for (10) shares Common $10 par in 1948
Merged into Employers Life Insurance Co. 12/31/82
Each share Common $10 par exchanged for (0.7483) share Common $7.50 par
(See Employers Life Insurance Co.)

EMPLOYERS LIFE INS CO (AL)
Proclaimed dissolved 10/2/2000

EMPLOYERS NATL LIFE INS CO (TX)
Common $5 par changed to $2.50 par and (1) additional share issued 06/22/1979
Stock Dividends - 12-1/2% 05/25/1972; 11.111111% 05/04/1973; 10% 05/03/1974; 16.67% 05/07/1976; 14.3% 05/06/1977; 25% 05/05/1978; 10% 05/02/1980; 10% 05/08/1981; 10% 05/07/1982; 20% 05/06/1983; 17.4% 03/05/1984; 10% 03/04/1985; 21.2% 03/03/1986; 10% 03/02/1987
Merged into Protective Life Insurance Group 03/01/1992
Each share Common $2.50 par exchanged for $44.46 cash

EMPLOYERS REINS CORP (MO)
Each share Capital Stock $10 par exchanged for (2) shares Capital Stock $5 par 2/7/56
Stock Dividends - 33-1/3% 2/15/41; 25% 2/25/55; 20% 2/25/56; 14-2/7% 3/1/62; 11-1/9% 5/6/68
Voluntary exchange offer in 1969 by ERC Corp.; held 95% as of 9/19/69
Each share Capital Stock $5 par exchanged for (0.001) share Capital Stock $5000 par 5/7/71
Public interest was eliminated

EMPORIUM (THE) (CA)
Name changed to Emporium Capwell Co. 12/4/36
Emporium Capwell Co. name changed to Broadway-Hale Stores, Inc. (CA) 8/27/70 which name changed to Carter Hawley Hale Stores Inc. (CA) 5/30/74 which reincorporated in Delaware 7/26/84 which name changed to Broadway Stores, Inc. 6/17/94 which merged into Federated Department Stores, Inc. 10/11/95 which name changed to Macy's, Inc. 6/1/2007

EMPORIUM CAPWELL CO (CA)
Each share Common no par exchanged for (2) shares Common $20 par 5/19/55
Common $20 par changed to $10 par and (1) additional share issued 11/27/59
Common $10 par changed to $5 par and (1) additional share issued 12/31/65
Under plan of merger name changed to Broadway-Hale Stores, Inc. (CA) 8/27/70
Broadway-Hale Stores, Inc. (CA) name changed to Carter Hawley Hale Stores Inc. (CA) 5/30/74 which reincorporated in Delaware 7/26/84 which name changed to Broadway Stores, Inc. 6/17/94 which merged into Federated Department Stores, Inc. 10/11/95 which name changed to Macy's, Inc. 6/1/2007

EMPORIUM CAPWELL CORP. (DE)
Merged into Emporium Capwell Co. share for share 1/31/40
Emporium Capwell Co. name changed to Broadway-Hale Stores, Inc. (CA) 8/27/70 which name changed to Carter Hawley Hale Stores Inc. (CA) 5/30/74 which reincoporated in Delaware 7/26/84 which name changed to Broadway Stores, Inc. 6/17/94 which merged into Federated Stores, Inc. 10/11/95

EMPORIUM CORP. (DE)
Name changed to Emporium Capwell Corp. 10/31/27
Emporium Capwell Corp. merged into Emporium Capwell Co. 1/31/40 which name changed to Broadway-Hale Stores, Inc. (CA) 8/27/70 which name changed to Carter Hawley Hale Stores Inc. (CA) 5/30/74 which reincorporated in Delaware 7/26/84 which name changed to Broadway Stores, Inc. 6/17/94 which merged into Federated Department Stores, Inc. 10/11/95 which name changed to Macy's, Inc. 6/1/2007

EMPOWER INDS INDIA LTD (INDIA)
Name changed to Empower India Ltd. 01/26/2011

EMPRESA NACIONAL DE ELECTRICIDAD (CHILE)
Each Sponsored ADR for Ordinary received distribution of (1) Endesa Americas S.A. Sponsored ADR for Common payable 04/26/2016 to holders of record 04/14/2016 Ex date - 04/27/2016
Name changed to Enel Generacion Chile S.A. 11/07/2016

EMPRESA NACIONAL DE ELECTRICIDAD S A (SPAIN)
Sponsored ADR's for Ordinary P800 par split (4) for (1) by issuance of (3) additional ADR's payable 07/31/1997 to holders of record 07/24/1997 Ex date - 08/01/1997
Name changed to Endesa, S.A. 09/04/1997
(See Endesa, S.A.)

EMPRESAS ICA SOCIEDAD CONTROLADORA S A DE C V (MEXICO)
Name changed to Empresas ICA, S.A. de C.V. 4/21/2005

EMPRESAS LA MODERNA S A DE C V (MEXICO)
Name changed to Savia S.A. de C.V. 4/13/99
(See Savia S.A. de C.V.)

EMPRESAS TELEX CHILE S A (CHILE)
Issue Information - 4,070,000 SPONSORED ADR's offered at $18.79 per ADR on 11/13/1994
Reorganized as Telex-Chile S.A. 5/8/2000
Each Sponsored ADR for Common no par exchanged for (0.2) Sponsored ADR for Ordinary no par
Telex-Chile S.A. name changed to Chilesat Corp. S.A. 2/14/2003
(See Chilesat Corp.)

EMPRESS CAP CORP (BC)
Reincorporated under the laws of Alberta as Daybreak Resources Corp. 05/19/2000
Daybreak Resources Corp. name changed to Daybreak Energy Corp. 06/30/2000 which recapitalized as Result Energy Inc. 12/19/2001 which merged into PetroBakken Energy Ltd. (Old) 04/01/2010 which reorganized as PetroBakken Energy Ltd. (New) 01/07/2013 which name changed to Lightstream Resources Ltd. 05/28/2013

EMPRESS CONSOLIDATED GOLD MINES, LTD. (ON)
Charter cancelled in 1956

EMPRESS INC. (UT)
Name changed to Zendora, Inc. 07/06/1988
Zendora, Inc. recapitalized as Inter*Act Communications Inc. 07/20/1994
*(See Inter*Act Communications Inc.)*

EMPRESS INTL LTD (DE)
Acquired by Thai Union International Inc. 07/29/2003
Each share Common 10¢ par exchanged for $36.26 cash
Note: Each share Common 10¢ par received an initial distribution of approximately $0.79 cash payable 09/14/2004 to holders of record 07/29/2003
Each share Common 10¢ par received a second distribution of approximately $0.07 cash payable 11/08/2004 to holders of record 07/29/2003
Each share Common 10¢ par received a third and final distribution of $6.66 cash payable 09/11/2012 to holders of record 07/29/2003

EMPRESS MANUFACTURING CO. LTD.
Acquired by Safeway Stores, Inc. 00/00/1939
Details not available

EMPS CORP (NV)
Common $0.001 par split (3) for (1) by issuance of (2) additional shares payable 01/18/2002 to holders of record 01/15/2002 Ex date - 01/22/2002
Each share Common $0.001 par received distribution of (0.1) share EMPS Research Corp. Common $0.001 par payable 07/31/2003 to holders of record 05/23/2003
Name changed to Caspian Services, Inc. 08/02/2005

EMPS RESH CORP (UT)
Name changed to Bekem Metals, Inc. 03/17/2005

EMPSON PACKING CO.
Merged into Kuner-Empson Co. 00/00/1937
Details not available

EMPYREAN BIOSCIENCE INC (DE)
Reincorporated 12/31/1996
Name changed 02/08/1999
Reincorporated 03/21/2001
Place of incorporation changed from (BC) to (WY) 12/31/1996
Name changed from Empyrean Diagnostics Ltd. to Empyrean Bioscience, Inc. 02/08/1999
State of incorporation changed from (WY) to (DE) 03/21/2001
SEC revoked common stock registration 06/10/2008

EMPYREAN COMMUNICATIONS INC (NV)
Each share old Common $0.001 par exchanged for (0.05) share new Common $0.001 par 10/31/2001
Each share new Common $0.001 par exchanged again for (0.05) share new Common $0.001 par 04/26/2002
Name changed to Empyrean Holdings, Inc. 01/25/2005
Empyrean Holdings, Inc. name changed to American Asset Development, Inc. 11/02/2010
(See American Asset Development, Inc.)

EMPYREAN HLDGS INC (NV)
Each share old Common $0.001 par exchanged for (0.02) share new Common $0.001 par 06/27/2006
Stock Dividend - 25% payable 08/30/2005 to holders of record 08/30/2005 Ex date - 08/31/2005
Name changed to American Asset Development, Inc. 11/02/2010
(See American Asset Development, Inc.)

EMR MICROWAVE TECHNOLOGY CORP (CANADA)
Dissolved for non-compliance 11/02/2005

EMS BREWING CO.
Acquired by Columbia Brewing Co. 00/00/1947
Each share Common exchanged for (0.5) share Capital Stock $5 par
Columbia Brewing Co. acquired by Falstaff Brewing Corp. (DE) 00/00/1948
(See Falstaff Brewing Corp. (DE))

EMS FIND INC (NV)
Name changed to Integrated Ventures, Inc. 07/27/2017

EMS INDS INC (FL)
Name changed to Regal International Holding Co., Inc. 06/16/1975
Regal International Holding Co., Inc. name changed to Regal One Corp. (FL) 06/13/1988 which reorganized in Maryland as Princeton Capital Corp. 03/23/2015

EMS PRODS INTERNATIONAL CORP (NV)
Recapitalized as Combined Companies International Corp. 11/21/1994
Each share Common 1¢ par exchanged for (0.04) share Common 1¢ par
(See Combined Companies International Corp.)

EMS SYS LTD (BC)
Struck off register and declared dissolved for failure to file returns 01/15/1993

EMS TECHNOLOGIES INC (GA)
Acquired by Honeywell International Inc. 08/22/2011
Each share Common 10¢ par exchanged for $33 cash

EMSCO DERRICK & EQUIPMENT CO. (CA)
Name changed to Emsco Manufacturing Co. 00/00/1953
Emsco Manufacturing Co. merged into Youngstown Sheet & Tube Co. 11/01/1956 which merged into Lykes-Youngstown Corp. 05/28/1969 which name changed to Lykes Corp. (DE) 05/11/1976 which merged into LTV Corp. (Old) 12/05/1978 which reorganized as LTV Corp. (New) 06/28/1993
(See LTV Corp. (New))

EMSCO MANUFACTURING CO. (CA)
Merged into Youngstown Sheet & Tube Co. 11/01/1956
Each share Common $5 par exchanged for (0.333333) share Common $5 par
Youngstown Sheet & Tube Co. merged into Lykes-Youngstown Corp. 05/28/1969 which name changed to Lykes Corp. (DE) 05/11/1976 which merged into LTV Corp. (Old) 12/05/1978 which reorganized as LTV Corp. (New) 06/28/1993
(See LTV Corp. (New))

EMTA HLDGS INC (NV)
Name changed to Green Planet Group, Inc. 07/08/2009

EMTEC INC. (OH)
Merged into Kuhlman Corp. (MI) 08/10/1973
Each share Common no par

exchanged for (2.712) shares
Common $1 par
Kuhlman Corp. (MI) reincorporated in
Delaware 06/09/1993
(See Kuhlman Corp.)

EMTECH LTD (BERMUDA)
Name changed to Ashurst Technology
Ltd. 07/09/1996
(See Ashurst Technology Ltd.)

EMTECH TECHNOLOGY CORP (BC)
Reorganized under the laws of
Bermuda as Emtech Ltd. 07/18/1994
Each share Common no par
exchanged for (1) Unit no par
Emtech Ltd. name changed to
Ashurst Technology Ltd. 07/09/1996
(See Ashurst Technology Ltd.)

EMULEX CORP (DE)
Reincorporated 02/18/1987
Common no par split (2) for (1) by
issuance of (1) additional share
02/23/1983
Common no par split (2) for (1) by
issuance of (1) additional share
02/28/1984
State of incorporation changed from
(CA) to (DE) and Common no par
changed to 10¢ par 02/18/1987
Each share Common 10¢ par
exchanged for (0.5) share Common
20¢ par 02/25/1994
Each share Common 20¢ par
received distribution of (1) share
QLogic Corp. Common 10¢ par
02/28/1994
Common 20¢ par split (2) for (1) by
issuance of (1) additional share
payable 08/30/1999 to holders of
record 08/16/1999
Common 20¢ par changed to 10¢ par
and (1) additional share issued
payable 12/15/1999 to holders of
record 11/30/1999
Common 10¢ par split (2) for (1) by
issuance of (1) additional share
payable 12/15/2000 to holders of
record 11/30/2000 Ex date -
12/18/2000
Acquired by Avago Technologies Ltd.
05/05/2015
Each share Common 10¢ par
exchanged for $8 cash

EMULTEK LTD (ISRAEL)
Name changed to e-SIM Ltd.
06/00/1999
(See e-SIM Ltd.)

EMUSIC COM INC (DE)
Merged into Universal Music Group,
Inc. 06/15/2001
Each share Common 1¢ par
exchanged for $0.57 cash

EMVELCO CORP (DE)
Name changed to Vortex Resources
Corp. 09/02/2008
Vortex Resources Corp. name
changed to Yasheng Eco-Trade
Corp. 07/15/2009 which
recapitalized as Eco-Trade Corp.
12/09/2010

EMYS SALSA AJI DISTR CO INC (NV)
Common $0.0001 par split (5) for (1)
by issuance of (4) additional shares
payable 11/12/2008 to holders of
record 11/10/2008 Ex date -
11/13/2008
Name changed to INVO BioScience,
Inc. 02/17/2009

EN / DRILL AMER INC (MN)
Merged into Jaguar Group Ltd.
12/31/1994
Each share Common no par
exchanged for (0.1) share Common
no par and (1) Common Stock
Purchase Warrant expiring
12/31/1997
Jaguar Group Ltd. name changed to
Tech Squared Inc. 05/09/1995 which
assets were transferred to Tech
Squared Liquidating Trust
12/17/1999

(See Tech Squared Liquidating Trust)

EN POINTE TECHNOLOGIES INC (DE)
Acquired by Din Global Corp.
08/07/2009
Each share Common $0.001 par
exchanged for $2.50 cash

EN-R-TECH INTL INC (BC)
Reorganized as International
En-R-Tech Inc. 11/16/1993
Each share Common no par
exchanged for (2) shares Common
no par
International En-R-Tech Inc.
recapitalized as National Telcom
Solutions Inc. 10/16/2000
(See National Telcom Solutions Inc.)

ENABLE HLDGS INC (DE)
Assets sold for the benefit of creditors
10/08/2010
Stockholders' equity unlikely

ENAMEL & HEATING PRODS LTD (CANADA)
Each share old Common no par
exchanged for (4) shares new
Common no par 00/00/1951
Each share new Common no par
exchanged for (1) share Class A
Common no par and (1) share Class
B Common no par 00/00/1956
Each share 4% Preferred $2.50 par
exchanged for (0.25) share Class A
Common no par 07/03/1962
Name changed to Enheat Ltd.
07/24/1974
Enheat Ltd. name changed to Enheat
Inc. 06/09/1980
(See Enheat Inc.)

ENAMEL PRODS CO (OH)
Charter cancelled 08/16/1985

ENAMELON INC (DE)
Plan of reorganization under Chapter
11 Federal Bankruptcy proceedings
effective 11/26/2001
No stockholders' equity

ENAMO-BORD PRODUCTS, INC. (WA)
Adjudicated bankrupt 04/21/1964
No stockholders' equity

ENBC CORP (DE)
Plan of reorganization under Chapter
11 Federal Bankruptcy proceedings
confirmed 03/27/2002
No stockholders' equity

ENBLAST PRODUCTIONS INC (CANADA)
Charter dissolved for non-compliance
06/10/2004

ENBRIDGE INC (CANADA)
7.6% Preferred Securities called for
redemption at $25 plus $0.3956
accrued dividends on 12/15/2004
8% Preferred Securities called for
redemption at $25 plus $0.4164
accrued dividends on 12/15/2004
7.8% Preferred Securities called for
redemption at $25 plus $0.2458
accrued dividends on 02/15/2007
(Additional Information in Active)

ENBRIDGE INCOME FD (AB)
Reorganized as Enbridge Income
Fund Holdings Inc. 12/17/2010
Each Trust Unit no par exchanged for
(1) share Common no par

ENCAD INC (DE)
Reincorporated 01/05/1998
Common no par split (2) for (1) by
issuance of (1) additional share
payable 05/31/1996 to holders of
record 05/17/1996
State of incorporation changed from
(CA) to (DE) 01/05/1998
Merged into Eastman Kodak Co.
01/24/2002
Each share Common no par
exchanged for (0.073046) share
Common $2.50 par

ENCAL ENERGY LTD (AB)
Merged into Calpine Canada Holdings
Ltd. 04/19/2001
Each share Common no par
exchanged for (0.1493)
Exchangeable Share no par
Calpine Canada Holdings Ltd.
exchanged for Calpine Corp.
05/27/2002
(See Calpine Corp.)

ENCANA CORP (CANADA)
8.5% Preferred Securities no par
called for redemption at $25 plus
$0.22705 accrued dividends on
08/09/2004
9.5% US$ Preferred Securities no par
called for redemption at $25 plus
$0.59375 accrued dividends on
09/30/2004
(Additional Information in Active)

ENCAP INVTS INC (BC)
Name changed to LCTI Low Carbon
Technologies International Inc.
02/15/2012

ENCEE GROUP LTD (AB)
Recapitalized as Liard Resources Ltd.
08/06/1996
Each share Class A Common no par
exchanged for (0.25) share Common
no par
Liard Resources Ltd. name changed
to CMX Gold & Silver Corp.
02/11/2011

ENCHANTED VLG INC (DE)
Each share Common $0.001 par
exchanged for (0.05) share Common
$0.002 par 05/07/1985
Each share $25 Conv. Preferred Ser.
A 1¢ par reclassified as (41.05)
shares old Common $0.002 par
12/08/2003
Class A Common $0.002 par
reclassified as old Common $0.002
par 12/08/2003
Each share old Common $0.002 par
exchanged for (0.025) share new
Common $0.002 par to reflect a (1)
for (4,000) reverse split followed by
a (100) for (1) forward split
12/08/2003
Note: No holder will receive fewer
than (100) shares
Recapitalized as SORL Auto Parts,
Inc. 07/16/2004
Each share Common $0.002 par
exchanged for (0.06666666) share
Common $0.002 par

ENCHANTING MERGERS INC (NV)
Name changed to Flea Fair USA, Inc.
12/12/1989
(See Flea Fair USA, Inc.)

ENCHIRA BIOTECHNOLOGY CORP (DE)
Plan of dissolution and liquidation
effective 01/20/2003
Stockholders' equity unlikely

ENCIBAR INC (UT)
Each share old Common $0.001 par
exchanged for (0.00134228) share
new Common $0.001 par
10/01/1999
Name changed to Versacom
International Inc. 04/10/2001
(See Versacom International Inc.)

ENCINO ENERGY & DEV CORP (TX)
Merged into Houston Oil Fields Co.
(DE) 08/20/1984
Each share Common 1¢ par
exchanged for (0.4) share Common
$10 par
Houston Oil Fields Co. (DE) merged
into Plains Resources Inc.
04/22/1987
(See Plains Resources Inc.)

ENCINO ST BK (ENCINO, CA)
Common no par split (5) for (2) by
issuance of (1.5) additional shares
payable 01/24/2000 to holders of
record 12/10/1999
Stock Dividends - 20% payable

05/15/2001 to holders of record
05/01/2001 Ex date - 04/27/2001;
20% payable 03/31/2003 to holders
of record 02/28/2003 Ex date -
02/26/2003
Merged into Boston Private Financial
Holdings, Inc. 10/01/2004
Each share Common no par
exchanged for $25.25 cash

ENCLAVE PRODS LTD (CO)
Recapitalized as IQ Medical Corp.
03/08/2005
Each share Common no par
exchanged for (0.005) share
Common no par
Note: No holder will receive fewer
than (100) post-split shares
IQ Medical Corp. name changed to IQ
Micro Inc. 10/23/2006
(See IQ Micro Inc.)

ENCLAVES GROUP INC (DE)
Each share old Common $0.001 par
exchanged for (0.002) share new
Common $0.001 par 08/18/2005
Charter cancelled and declared
inoperative and void for
non-payment of taxes 03/01/2007

ENCLEAN INC (DE)
Merged into Rust Acquisition Sub Inc.
08/06/1993
Each share Common 1¢ par
exchanged for $6.75 cash

ENCOM ENVIRONMENTAL & COMMUNICATIONS SYS LTD (BC)
Recapitalized as ST Systems Corp.
11/14/1994
Each share Common no par
exchanged for (0.18181818) share
Common no par
ST Systems Corp. recapitalized as
Sky Ridge Resources Ltd.
12/24/2007 which recapitalized as
Japan Gold Corp. 09/19/2016

ENCOMMERCE INC (CA)
Merged into Entrust Technologies,
Inc. 06/26/2000
Each share Preferred Ser. B
exchanged for (0.4316) share
Common 1¢ par
Each share Common exchanged for
(0.4316) share Common 1¢ par
Entrust Technologies, Inc. name
changed to Entrust, Inc. 06/05/2001
(See Entrust, Inc.)

ENCOMPASS GROUP AFFILIATES INC (FL)
Assets sold for the benefit of creditors
10/03/2011
Stockholders' equity unlikely

ENCOMPASS SVCS CORP (TX)
Plan of reorganization under Chapter
11 Federal Bankruptcy Code
effective 06/09/2003
No stockholders' equity

ENCON SYS INC (DE)
Company received notice that assets
will be sold for the benefit of
creditors 01/16/1997
Stockholders' equity unlikely

ENCOR ENERGY CORP. LTD. (AB)
Name changed to Encor Energy
Corp. Inc. and Common $1 par
changed to no par 02/18/1987
(See Encor Energy Corp. Inc.)

ENCOR ENERGY INC (AB)
Merged into TCLP Energy Ltd.
02/29/1988
Each share Common no par
exchanged for $9.375 cash

ENCOR INC (AB)
Acquired by Talisman Energy Inc.
05/21/1993
Each share Common no par
exchanged for (0.022) share
Common no par
(See Talisman Energy Inc.)

ENCORE ACQUISITION CO (DE)
Common 1¢ par split (3) for (2) by
issuance of (0.5) additional share

payable 07/12/2005 to holders of record 06/27/2005 Ex date - 07/13/2005
Merged into Denbury Resources Inc. 03/09/2010
Each share Common 1¢ par exchanged for approximately (2.4048) shares Common $0.001 par and $15 cash

ENCORE BANCSHARES INC (TX)
Acquired by Cadence Bancorp, LLC 07/02/2012
Each share Common $1 par exchanged for $20.62 cash

ENCORE CLEAN ENERGY INC (NV)
State of incorporation changed from (DE) to (NV) 10/21/2005
SEC revoked common stock registration 01/03/2013

ENCORE COMPUTER CORP (DE)
Completely liquidated
Each share Common 1¢ par received first and final distribution of $0.06233183 cash payable 12/2/2002 to holders of record 11/1/2002 Ex date - 12/3/2002
Note: Certificates were not required to be surrendered and are without value

ENCORE ENERGY PARTNERS LP (DE)
Merged into Vanguard Natural Resources, LLC 12/01/2011
Each share Common Unit of Ltd. Partnership Int. exchanged for (0.75) Common Unit
(See Vanguard Natural Resources, LLC)

ENCORE ENERGY SYS INC (NV)
Charter revoked for failure to file reports and pay fees 10/30/2010

ENCORE GROUP INC (OR)
Each share old Common no par exchanged for (0.002) share new Common no par 04/23/1996
Involuntarily dissolved 05/13/1999

ENCORE INDS INC (DE)
Charter cancelled and declared inoperative and void for non-payment of taxes 03/01/1988

ENCORE MARKETING INTL INC (DE)
Merged into Encore Marketing Holdings Inc. 03/17/2006
Each share 4% Conv. Preferred Ser. A $10 par exchanged for $2.97 cash
Each share Common 1¢ par exchanged for $3.24 cash

ENCORE MED CORP (DE)
Merged into Grand Slam Holdings, LLC 11/03/2006
Each share Common $0.001 par exchanged for $6.55 cash

ENCORE PRODS INC (BC)
Struck off register and declared dissolved for failure to file returns 11/12/1993

ENCORE RENAISSANCE RES CORP (BC)
Recapitalized as WestKam Gold Corp. 05/01/2012
Each share Common no par exchanged for (0.1) share Common no par

ENCORE TICKETS LTD (CANADA)
Struck off register and declared dissolved for failure to file returns 05/06/2004

ENCORE VENTURES INC (NV)
Each share old Common $0.001 par exchanged for (0.26217199) share new Common $0.001 par 07/26/2001
Name changed to Thinka Weight-Loss Corp. 08/01/2001
Thinka Weight-Loss Corp. name changed to TransWorld Benefits International, Inc. (NV) 10/28/2003 which reincorporated in California 01/15/2008
(See TransWorld Benefits International, Inc.)

ENCORE VENTURES LTD (BC)
Merged into Prime Equities International Corp. 01/26/1993
Each share Common no par exchanged for (0.4) share new Common no par
Prime Equities International Corp. name changed to Medera Life Science Corp. 08/11/1998 which name changed to Medbroadcast Corp. (Canada) 01/04/2000 which reorganized in Alberta as Rock Energy Inc. 02/18/2004 which merged into Raging River Exploration Inc. 07/26/2016 which merged into Baytex Energy Corp. 08/27/2018

ENCORE VENTURES LTD (CO)
Name changed to Cardiotronics Systems, Inc. 10/26/1989
(See Cardiotronics Systems, Inc.)

ENCORE WIRELESS INC (NV)
SEC revoked common stock registration 10/12/2010

ENCORIUM GROUP INC (DE)
Each share old Common $0.001 par exchanged for (0.125) share new Common $0.001 par 02/17/2010
SEC revoked common stock registration 11/10/2014

ENCOUNTER COM INC (CO)
Name changed to Encounter Technologies Inc. 02/18/2010

ENCOUNTER ENERGY INC (AB)
Merged into Impact Energy Inc. (Canada) 10/21/2002
Each share Common no par exchanged for (0.78) share Common no par
Impact Energy Inc. (Canada) merged into Thunder Energy Inc. 04/30/2004
(See Thunder Energy Inc.)

ENCOUNTER ENERGY RES LTD (AB)
Acquired by Conventures Ltd. 04/30/1985
Each share Common no par exchanged for $4.35 cash

ENCUE CAP CORP (AB)
Name changed to Visionwall Inc. and Common no par reclassified as Class A Subordinate no par 02/17/1997

ENCYSIVE PHARMACEUTICALS INC (DE)
Merged into Pfizer Inc. 06/13/2008
Each share Common $0.005 par exchanged for $2.35 cash

END RUST USA INC (NV)
Recapitalized as Wray-Tech Instruments Inc. 03/25/1991
Each share Common $0.002 par exchanged for (0.16666666) share Common $0.002 par

ENDAKO MINES LTD (BC)
Merged into Placer Development Ltd. 02/22/1971
Each share Capital Stock no par exchanged for (0.444444) share Common no par
Placer Development Ltd. merged into Placer Dome Inc. 08/13/1987 which merged into Barrick Gold Corp. 03/08/2006

ENDATA INC (TN)
Acquired by First Financial Management Corp. 10/30/1987
Each share Common 10¢ par exchanged for (0.464995) share Common 10¢ par and $2.48 cash
First Financial Management Corp. merged into First Data Corp. (Old) 10/27/1995
(See First Data Corp. (Old))

ENDATCOM VENTURES CORP (BC)
Common no par split (4) for (1) by issuance of (3) additional shares 11/07/1984
Name changed to Borkin Industries Corp. 06/07/1985
Each share Common no par exchanged for (1) share Common no par
(See Borkin Industries Corp.)

ENDAVO MEDIA & COMMUNICATIONS INC (DE)
Each share old Common $0.001 par exchanged for (0.025) share new Common $0.001 par 03/13/2006
Name changed to Integrated Media Holdings, Inc. (DE) 04/21/2006
Integrated Media Holdings, Inc. (DE) reorganized in Nevada as Arrayit Corp. 03/19/2009

ENDEAVOR ACQUISITION CORP (DE)
Name changed to American Apparel, Inc. 12/13/2007
(See American Apparel, Inc.)

ENDEAVOR ENERGY CORP (NV)
Name changed to Holloman Energy Corp. 10/10/2007

ENDEAVOR EXPLORATIONS INC (NV)
Common $0.001 par split (4) for (1) by issuance of (3) additional shares payable 11/23/2007 to holders of record 11/21/2007 Ex date - 11/26/2007
Name changed to Mobile Data Corp. 01/12/2010
Mobile Data Corp. name changed to GeoTraq Inc. 04/03/2014 which name changed to GoTraq Inc. 11/01/2016 which name changed to MJ Venture Partners, Inc. 04/10/2018

ENDEAVOR MINING CORP. LTD. (ON)
Merged into Mining Endeavor Co. Ltd. 03/28/1956
Each share Capital Stock $1 par exchanged for (1) share Capital Stock $1 par
(See Mining Endeavor Co. Ltd.)

ENDEAVOR OIL & GAS LTD (AB)
Name changed to Cubacan Exploration Inc. 08/18/1995
(See Cubacan Exploration Inc.)

ENDEAVOR PWR CORP (NV)
Each share old Common $0.001 par exchanged for (0.01) share new Common $0.001 par 08/16/2010
Name changed to Parallax Health Sciences, Inc. 01/29/2014

ENDEAVOR SER TR (MA)
Reorganized under the laws of Maryland as AEGON/Transamerica Series Fund, Inc. 05/01/2002

ENDEAVOR URANIUM INC (NV)
Common $0.0001 par split (65) for (1) by issuance of (64) additional shares payable 10/05/2007 to holders of record 10/05/2007
Name changed to Endeavor Power Corp. and Common $0.0001 par changed to $0.001 par 01/23/2009
Endeavor Power Corp. name changed to Parallax Health Sciences, Inc. 01/29/2014

ENDEAVOUR FINANCIAL CORP (CAYMAN ISLANDS)
Name changed 07/16/2008
Each Contingent Value Right received distribution of (0.0023) share Common 1¢ par payable 09/25/2003 to holders of record 09/10/2002
Name changed from Endeavour Mining Capital Corp. to Endeavour Financial Corp. 07/16/2008
Each Contingent Value Right exchanged for (0.01964) share Common 1¢ par 09/09/2008
Name changed to Endeavour Mining Corp. 09/20/2010

ENDEAVOUR GOLD CORP (BC)
Name changed to Endeavour Silver Corp. 09/13/2004

ENDEAVOUR INTL CORP (NV)
Each share old Common $0.001 par exchanged for (0.14285714) share new Common $0.001 par 11/18/2010
Chapter 11 bankruptcy proceedings dismissed 12/07/2015
Stockholders' equity unlikely

ENDEAVOUR RES INC (AB)
Merged into Aspen Group Resources Corp. 02/04/2002
Each share Common no par exchanged for (0.2375) share Common no par and (0.11875) Common Stock Purchase Warrant expiring 06/30/2003

ENDESA AMERS S A (CHILE)
Merged into Enel Americas S.A. 12/01/2016
Each Sponsored ADR for Ordinary exchanged for (1.68) shares Sponsored ADR for Ordinary

ENDESA S A (SPAIN)
ADR agreement terminated 12/24/2007
Each Sponsored ADR for Ordinary exchanged for $48.268372 cash

ENDEV ENERGY INC (AB)
Merged into Penn West Energy Trust 07/22/2008
Each share Common no par exchanged for (0.041) Trust Unit
Penn West Energy Trust reorganized as Penn West Petroleum Ltd. (New) 01/03/2011 which name changed to Obsidian Energy Ltd. 06/29/2017

ENDEV HLDGS INC (NV)
Common $0.001 par split (2) for (1) by issuance of (1) additional share payable 03/26/2012 to holders of record 03/26/2012
Name changed to MeeMee Media Inc. 05/16/2013

ENDEVCO CORP. (CA)
Acquired by Becton, Dickinson & Co. 12/31/1965
Each share Common no par exchanged for (0.555555) share Common $1 par

ENDEVCO INC (DE)
Reincorporated 06/14/1988
Stock Dividends - 10% 08/11/1986; 10% 10/27/1987
State of incorporation changed from (TX) to (DE) 06/14/1988
Reorganized as Cornerstone Natural Gas, Inc. 11/03/1993
Each share Common 10¢ par exchanged for (1) share Common 10¢ par
(See Cornerstone Natural Gas, Inc.)

ENDEVCO INC (TX)
Each share old Common no par exchanged for (0.01) share new Common no par 03/11/2008
SEC revoked common stock registration 03/05/2013

ENDEXELOPE, INC. (IL)
Involuntarily dissolved for failure to file reports and pay taxes 11/16/1972

ENDICOTT JOHNSON CORP (NY)
Each share 5% Preferred $100 par exchanged for (1) share 4% Preferred $100 par and $6 cash 00/00/1943
Each share Common $50 par exchanged for (2) shares Common $25 par 00/00/1947
Common $25 par changed to $10 par 03/20/1963
Merged into McDonough Co. 10/04/1971
Each share 4% Preferred $100 par exchanged for $100 principal

END-ENE

amount of 6% Subord. Debentures due 10/01/1986
Each share Common $10 par exchanged for (0.9) share Common $1 par
(See McDonough Co.)

ENDICOTT NATL BK (ENDICOTT, NY)
Merged into Bank of New York Co., Inc. 05/29/1969
Each share Capital Stock $25 par exchanged for $72.50 principal amount of 6.25% Conv. Debentures due 09/01/1994 and (0.25) share Common $15 par
Bank of New York Co., Inc. merged into Bank of New York Mellon Corp. 07/01/2007

ENDICOTT TRUST CO. (ENDICOTT, NY)
Capital Stock $100 par changed to $25 par and (9) additional shares issued 08/14/1961
Stock Dividends - 50% 01/22/1946; 25% 01/20/1947
Acquired by Charter New York Corp. 12/29/1967
Each share Capital Stock $25 par exchanged for (3.25) shares Common $10 par
Charter New York Corp. name changed to Irving Bank Corp. 10/17/1979 which merged into Bank of New York Co., Inc. 12/30/1988 which merged into Bank of New York Mellon Corp. 07/01/2007

ENDLESS ENERGY CORP (AB)
Name changed to Marauder Resources East Coast Inc. 08/11/2004

ENDLESS YOUTH PRODS INC (NV)
Each share old Common $0.001 par exchanged for (0.2) share new Common $0.001 par 05/22/1998
Reorganized under the laws of Bermuda as Glengarry Holdings Ltd. 02/16/2001
Each share new Common $0.001 par exchanged for (0.1) share Common 5¢ par
(See Glengarry Holdings Ltd.)

ENDO HEALTH SOLUTIONS INC (DE)
Name changed 05/23/2012
Name changed from Endo Pharmaceuticals Holdings Inc. to Endo Health Solutions Inc. 05/23/2012
Merged into Endo International PLC 03/03/2014
Each share Common 1¢ par exchanged for (1) share Ordinary USD$0.0001 par

ENDO LASE INC (DE)
Chapter 11 bankruptcy proceedings converted to Chapter 7 on 01/21/1987
No stockholders' equity

ENDO NETWORKS INC (NV)
Reincorporated 12/13/2001
State of incorporation changed from (TX) to (NV) 12/13/2001
Each share old Common $0.001 par exchanged for (0.2) share new Common $0.001 par 10/17/2006
Name changed to China West Coal Energy, Inc. 01/05/2007
China West Coal Energy, Inc. name changed to Sino Clean Energy, Inc. 08/20/2007

ENDO TECHNIC INTL CORP (DE)
Name changed to Laser Endo Technic Corp. 09/05/1991
Laser Endo Technic Corp. recapitalized as Laser Medical Technology Inc. 03/02/1992 which name changed to Biolase Technology, Inc. 05/24/1994 which name changed to Biolase, Inc. 05/29/2012

ENDOCARDIAL SOLUTIONS INC (DE)
Merged into St. Jude Medical, Inc. 01/13/2005
Each share Common 1¢ par exchanged for $11.75 cash

ENDOCARE INC (DE)
Each share old Common $0.001 par exchanged for (0.33333333) share new Common $0.001 par 08/21/2007
Merged into HealthTronics, Inc. 07/27/2009
Each share Common $0.001 par exchanged for either (0.530064) share Common no par and $0.43 cash, (0.7764) share Common no par, or $1.35 cash
Note: Option to receive stock or cash only expired 08/28/2009
(See HealthTronics, Inc.)

ENDOCHOICE HLDGS INC (DE)
Acquired by Boston Scientific Corp. 11/22/2016
Each share Common $0.001 par exchanged for $8 cash

ENDOGEN INC (MA)
Merged into PerBio Science AB 07/08/1999
Each share Common 1¢ par exchanged for $3.75 cash

ENDOREX CORP (DE)
Each share old Common $0.001 par exchanged for (0.06666666) share new Common $0.001 par 06/11/1997
Name changed to DOR BioPharma, Inc. 12/03/2001
DOR BioPharma, Inc. name changed to Soligenix, Inc. 09/30/2009

ENDOSONICS CORP (DE)
Reincorporated 08/14/1992
State of incorporation changed from (CA) to (DE) 08/14/1992
Merged into Jomed N.V. 09/21/2000
Each share Common no par exchanged for $11 cash

ENDOTRONICS INC (MN)
Common no par split (3) for (2) by issuance of (0.5) additional share 06/07/1985
Common no par split (3) for (2) by issuance of (0.5) additional share 10/21/1985
Common no par split (3) for (2) by issuance of (0.5) additional share 03/04/1986
Each share old Common no par exchanged for (0.44) share new Common no par 04/04/1988
Name changed to Cellex Biosciences Inc. (MN) 05/14/1993
Cellex Biosciences Inc. (New) reincorporated in Delaware as Biovest International, Inc. 05/07/2001
(See Biovest International, Inc.)

ENDOVASC INC (NV)
Each share Common $0.001 par received distribution of (0.25) share Series NDC Common $0.001 par payable 09/15/2003 to holders of record 08/29/2003
Chapter 7 bankrutpcy proceedings terminated 03/27/2017
No stockholders' equity

ENDOVASC LTD INC (DE)
Reorganized 07/01/2002
Reorganized from Nevada to under the laws of Delaware 07/01/2002
Each share old Common $0.001 par exchanged for (0.025) share new Common $0.001 par
Reorganized under the laws of Nevada as Endovasc, Inc. 03/31/2003
Each share new Common $0.001 par exchanged for (1.2) shares Common $0.001 par
(See Endovasc, Inc.)

ENDOVASCULAR TECHNOLOGIES INC (DE)
Merged into Guidant Corp. 12/19/1997
Each share Common $0.00001 par exchanged for (0.3154) share Common no par
Guidant Corp. merged into Boston Scientific Corp. 04/21/2006

ENDOWMENT LIFE INSURANCE CO. (NJ)
Name changed to Foundation Life Insurance Co. of America 03/03/1965
Foundation Life Insurance Co. of America reorganized as Foundation Financial Corp. 07/31/1972
(See Foundation Financial Corp.)

ENDOWMENTS (DE)
Under plan of merger each share Bond Portfolio automatically became Bond Fund of America, Inc. Class A $0.001 par on a net asset basis 02/19/2010
Under plan of merger each share Growth & Income Portfolio automatically became Capital Private Client Services Funds Capital U.S. Equity Fund on a net asset basis 04/01/2011
(See each company's listing)

ENDOWMENTS INC (DE)
Common $1 par split (100) for (1) by issuance of (99) additional shares 02/16/1988
Under plan of reorganization each share Common $1 par automatically became (1) share Endowments Growth & Income Portfolio 07/31/1998
(See Endowments)

ENDURANCE CANADIAN BALANCED FUND (ON)
Fund terminated 00/00/1992
Details not available

ENDURANCE CANADIAN EQUITY FUND (ON)
Fund terminated 00/00/1992
Details not available

ENDURANCE FD CORP (ON)
Name changed to Metals Creek Resources Corp. 03/13/2008

ENDURANCE GLOBAL EQUITY FUND (ON)
Fund terminated 00/00/1992
Details not available

ENDURANCE GOVERNMENT BOND FUND (ON)
Fund terminated 00/00/1992
Details not available

ENDURANCE MINERALS INC (BC)
Recapitalized as Takura Minerals Inc. 01/19/1994
Each share Common no par exchanged for (0.33333333) share Common no par
Takura Minerals Inc. recapitalized as Consolidated African Mining Corp. (BC) 08/28/1997 which reincorporated in Yukon 12/08/1997 which recapitalized as Excam Developments Inc. 01/19/2000
(See Excam Developments Inc.)

ENDURANCE SPECIALTY HLDGS LTD (BERMUDA)
7.75% Non-Cum. Preferred Ser. A $1 par called for redemption at $25 plus $0.048437 accrued dividends on 12/24/2015
7.5% Non-Cum. Preferred Ser. B $1 par called for redemption at $25 plus $0.39583 accrued dividends on 06/01/2016
Acquired by SOMPO Holdings, Inc. 03/28/2017
Each share Ordinary $1 par exchanged for $93 cash
6.35% Depositary Preferred Ser. C called for redemption at $25 plus $0.167569 accrued dividends on 10/23/2017
Public interest eliminated

ENDWAVE CORP (DE)
Each share old Common $0.001 par exchanged for (0.25) share new Common $0.001 par 06/28/2002
Merged into GigOptix, Inc. 06/17/2011
Each share new Common $0.001 par exchanged for (0.90852476) share Common $0.001 par
GigOptix, Inc. name changed to GigPeak, Inc. 04/06/2016
(See GigPeak, Inc.)

ENEL GREEN PWR S P A (ITALY)
ADR agreement terminated 05/02/2016
Each ADR for Common issued by Bank of New York exchanged for $10.1532 cash

ENEL SOCIETA PER AZIONI (ITALY)
ADR agreement terminated 04/11/2008
Each ADR for Ordinary exchanged for $32.716604 cash
(Additional Information in Active)

ENER CORE INC (NV)
Each share old Common $0.0001 par exchanged for (0.02) share new Common $0.0001 par 07/08/2015
Reincorporated under the laws of Delaware 09/03/2015

ENER CRAFT INC (NV)
Charter revoked for failure to file reports and pay fees 08/01/1993

ENER-GRID INC (CO)
Chapter 7 bankruptcy proceedings terminated 05/05/2003
Stockholders' equity unlikely

ENER MARK CORP (DE)
Charter cancelled and declared inoperative and void for non-payment of taxes 03/01/1990

ENERBRITE TECHNOLOGIES GROUP INC (NV)
Each share old Common $0.001 par exchanged for (0.001) share new Common $0.001 par 09/21/2007
Each share old Common $0.001 par exchanged again for (0.00001) share new Common $0.001 par 11/10/2008
Recapitalized as Limitless Venture Group Inc. 02/04/2013
Each share new Common $0.001 par exchanged for (0.001) share Common $0.001 par

ENERCAN GROUP INC (AB)
Delisted from Alberta Stock Exchange 05/26/1989

ENERCAP CORP (DE)
Each share old Common 10¢ par exchanged for (0.04) share new Common 10¢ par 03/05/1991
Charter cancelled and declared inoperative and void for non-payment of taxes 03/01/1993

ENERCARE INC (CANADA)
Merged into Brookfield Infrastructure Partners L.P. 10/17/2018
Each share Common no par exchanged for either (0.5509) Brookfield Infrastructure Partners Exchange L.P. Unit or $29 cash
Notes: Option to elect to receive Units expired 09/17/2018
Unexchanged certificates will be cancelled and become without value 10/17/2023

ENERCELL CORP (UT)
Involuntarily dissolved 11/01/1992

ENERCHEM INTL INC (AB)
Acquired by Trinity Capital Partners Ltd. 06/08/2010
Each share Common no par exchanged for $2.75 cash

ENERCO INC (CO)
Charter suspended for failure to file annual reports 09/30/1989

ENERCOMP INC (NJ)
Charter void by proclamation 09/13/1991

ENERCON DATA CORP (DE)
Charter cancelled and declared inoperative and void for non-payment of taxes 03/01/1992

ENERDINE INTL CORP (DE)
Charter cancelled and declared inoperative and void for non-payment of taxes 03/01/1984

ENERDINE VITAMIN CORP. (DE)
Name changed to Enerdine International Corp. 07/20/1981
(See Enerdine International Corp.)

ENERDYNE CORP (NM)
Name changed to Protalex Inc. (NM) 01/04/2000
Protalex Inc. (NM) reincorporated in Delaware 12/01/2004

ENERFLEX SYS INCOME FD (AB)
Merged into Toromont Industries Ltd. 02/26/2010
Each Trust Unit no par exchanged for either (0.2776) share Common no par and $6.926 cash or $14.25 cash

ENERFLEX SYS LTD (CANADA)
Common no par split (2) for (1) by issuance of (1) additional share payable 05/19/1997 to holders of record 05/14/1997
Reorganized under the laws of Alberta as Enerflex Systems Income Fund 10/02/2006
Each share Common no par exchanged for (2) Trust Units no par
Note: Canadian residents option to receive (2) Enerflex Holdings Ltd. Partnership Trust Units in lieu of above expired 09/25/2006
Enerflex Systems Income Fund merged into Toromont Industries Ltd. 02/26/2010

ENERFORCE ENERGY LTD (NV)
Each share old Common $0.00005 par exchanged for (0.05) share new Common $0.00005 par 09/09/1992
Recapitalized as Keystone Investment Management Group Inc. 02/16/1999
Each share Common $0.00005 par exchanged for (0.02857142) share Common $0.00005 par
Keystone Investment Management Group Inc. name changed to KIMG Management Group, Inc. 03/18/1999 which recapitalized as Fortune Real Estate Development Corp. 09/09/2004 which recapitalized as Andros Isle Development Corp. 04/18/2005
(See Andros Isle Development Corp.)

ENERGAS CO (TX)
Common no par split (2) for (1) by issuance of (1) additional share 06/12/1985
Name changed to Atmos Energy Corp. 10/01/1988

ENERGAS RES INC (DE)
Reincorporated 08/20/2001
Place of incorporation changed from (BC) to (DE) and Common no par changed to $0.001 par 08/20/2001
Recapitalized as Enerlabs, Inc. 01/25/2012
Each share Common $0.001 par exchanged for (0.1) share Common $0.001 par
Enerlabs, Inc. name changed to Energy & Environmental Services, Inc. 12/30/2016

ENERGCORP INC (FL)
Administratively dissolved 09/24/2010

ENERGEM RES INC (YT)
Reincorporated under the laws of British Columbia 07/21/2005

ENERGENTIA RES INC (BC)
Merged into Mega Uranium Ltd. 05/06/2008
Each share Common no par exchanged for (0.1) share Common no par

ENERGETICS HLDGS INC (DE)
Recapitalized as Pavilion Energy Resources, Inc. 07/25/2008
Each share Common 1¢ par exchanged for (0.1) share Common 1¢ par
Pavilion Energy Resources, Inc. recapitalized as Matchtrade, Inc. 05/02/2012
(See Matchtrade, Inc.)

ENERGETICS INC (DE)
Plan of reorganization under Chapter 11 Federal Bankruptcy proceedings confirmed 06/11/1985
Each share Ser. 1 Conv. Preferred $1 par exchanged for (3.3) shares Common 1¢ par
Each share Ser. 2 Conv. Preferred $1 par exchanged for (750) shares Common 1¢ par
Name changed to ENG Enterprises, Inc. 11/17/1999
ENG Enterprises, Inc. name changed to Global Online India, Inc. 08/17/2000
(See Global Online India, Inc.)

ENERGETICS MARKETING & MGMT ASSOC LTD (OR)
Name changed to Emma Oil & Gas Co., Inc. 11/25/1980
(See Emma Oil & Gas Co., Inc.)

ENERGEX MINERALS LTD (BC)
Delisted from Canadian Dealer Network 05/31/1996

ENERGIE HLDGS INC (DE)
Common 1¢ par changed to $0.0001 par 09/18/2014
Name changed to ExeLED Holdings Inc. 12/30/2015

ENERGIS PLC (UNITED KINGDOM)
Sponsored ADR's for Ordinary split (5) for (1) by issuance of (4) additional ADR's payable 07/21/2000 to holders of record 07/19/2000 Ex date - 07/20/2000
ADR agreement terminated 01/22/2007
No ADR holders' equity

ENERGIZ RENEWABLE INC (FL)
SEC revoked common stock registration 05/13/2015

ENERGIZER 500 INC (DE)
Name changed to Opportunity 21 on 06/16/1985
(See Opportunity 21)

ENERGIZER HLDGS INC OLD (MO)
Each share Common 1¢ par received distribution of (1) share Energizer Holdings, Inc. (New) Common 1¢ par payable 07/01/2015 to holders of record 06/16/2015 Ex date - 06/12/2015
Name changed to Edgewell Personal Care Co. 07/01/2015

ENERGIZER RES INC (MN)
Name changed to NextSource Materials Inc. (MN) 04/24/2017
NextSource Materials Inc. (MN) reincorporated in Canada 12/27/2017

ENERGIZER TENNIS INC (NV)
Common $0.001 par split (30) for (1) by issuance of (29) additional shares payable 03/10/2015 to holders of record 03/05/2015 Ex date - 03/11/2015
Recapitalized as West Coast Ventures Group Corp. 04/28/2016
Each share Common $0.001 par exchanged for (0.001) share Common $0.001 par

ENERGO ROSTOV ON DON PJSC (RUSSIA)
Name changed 08/18/2015
Name changed from Energosbyt Rostovenergo OAO to Energo Rostov-On-Don PJSC TNS 08/18/2015
GDR agreement terminated 05/23/2018
Each Reg. S GDR for Preference exchanged for (100) shares Preference
Each Reg. S GDR for Ordinary exchanged for (100) shares Ordinary
Note: Unexchanged GDR's will be sold and the proceeds, if any, held for claim after 11/23/2018

ENERGOLD MNG LTD (BC)
Name changed to Energold Drilling Corp. 10/03/2005

ENERGRO INC (MN)
Statutorily dissolved 10/05/1991

ENERGROUP TECHNOLOGIES CORP (UT)
Each share old Common $0.001 par exchanged for (0.05) share new Common $0.001 par 10/01/1999
Reorganized under the laws of Nevada as Energroup Holdings Corp. 08/21/2007
Each share new Common $0.001 par exchanged for (0.14285714) share Common $0.001 par
Note: Holders of between (100) and (699) shares or fewer received (100) shares
Holders of (99) shares or fewer were not affected by the reverse split

ENERGULF RES INC (YUKON)
Reincorporated 06/27/2003
Place of incorporation changed from (BC) to (Yukon) 06/27/2003
Reincorporated under the laws of British Columbia 10/05/2004

ENERGY & ENGINE TECHNOLOGY CORP (NV)
Chapter 7 bankruptcy proceedings terminated 06/03/2010
No stockholders' equity

ENERGY & ENVIROMENTAL COS INC (CO)
Common 1¢ par split (5) for (1) by issuance of (4) additional shares 06/19/1981
Recapitalized as Enerco, Inc. 04/30/1984
Each share Common 1¢ par exchanged for (0.2) share Common 1¢ par
(See Enerco, Inc.)

ENERGY & RES CAM LTD (QC)
Name changed to ERG Resources Inc. 10/09/1986
(See ERG Resources Inc.)

ENERGY & UTIL SHS INC (DE)
Reincorporated under the laws of Maryland as Stratton Monthly Dividend Shares, Inc. 05/31/1985
Stratton Monthly Dividend Shares, Inc. name changed to Stratton Monthly Dividend REIT Shares, Inc. 12/09/1997 which name changed to Stratton Real Estate Fund, Inc. 09/30/2009

ENERGY ABSORPTION SYS INC (DE)
Name changed to Quixote Corp. 07/31/1980
(See Quixote Corp.)

ENERGY AFRICA LTD (SOUTH AFRICA)
Acquired by Tullow Oil PLC 08/02/2004
Each 144A GDR for Ordinary exchanged for $24.5539 cash
Each Reg. S GDR for Ordinary exchanged for $24.5539 cash

ENERGY ASSETS INTL CORP (DE)
Merged into Torch Energy Advisors Inc. 02/08/1991
Each share Common 1¢ par exchanged for $0.50 cash

ENERGY ASSETS IV (TX)
Completely liquidated 07/02/1990
Each $10,000 Limited Partner Int. represented by Depositary Units exchanged for approximately (790) shares Nuevo Energy Co. Common 1¢ par
Nuevo Energy Co. merged into Plains Exploration & Production Co. 05/14/2004 which merged into Freeport-McMoRan Copper & Gold Inc. 05/31/2013 which name changed to Freeport-McMoRan Inc. 07/14/2014

ENERGY BIOSYSTEMS CORP (DE)
Each share old Common 1¢ par exchanged for (0.14285714) share new Common 1¢ par 12/21/1998
Name changed to Enchira Biotechnology Corp. 06/09/2000
(See Enchira Biotechnology Corp.)

ENERGY CAP DEV CORP (DE)
Reorganized 12/31/1980
Reorganized from Colorado to under the laws of Delaware 12/31/1980
Each share Common 1¢ par exchanged for (0.2) share Common 1¢ par
Each share Common 1¢ par exchanged for (0.1) share Common 10¢ par 10/30/1984
Name changed to ENERCAP Corp. 03/13/1989
(See ENERCAP Corp.)

ENERGY CLINIC CORP (DE)
Merged into Servamatic Solar Systems Inc. 7/7/82
Each share Common 1¢ par exchanged for (1) share Common no par
Servamatic Solar Systems Inc. name changed to Servamatic Systems, Inc. 5/1/84
(See Servamatic Systems, Inc.)

ENERGY CO NORTH AMER (DE)
Charter cancelled and declared inoperative and void for non-payment of taxes 03/01/1983

ENERGY COMPONENTS CORP. (NY)
Adjudicated bankrupt 8/6/64
No stockholders' equity

ENERGY COMPOSITES CORP (NV)
Name changed to Trailblazer Resources, Inc. 10/27/2011

ENERGY CONCEPTS INC (WY)
Name changed to CrossStreet Distribution, Inc. and (3) additional shares issued 04/20/2004
CrossStreet Distribution, Inc. recapitalized as Nine Muses Entertainment, Inc. 02/21/2006 which name changed to Quotezy, Inc. 03/03/2006 which recapitalized as Lord Tech, Inc. 04/23/2008
(See Lord Tech, Inc.)

ENERGY CONSV SYS INC (CO)
Name changed to Circle Energy, Inc. (CO) 09/15/1981
Circle Energy, Inc. (CO) reorganized in Delaware as Circle Corp. 04/22/1987

ENERGY CONSV TECHNOLOGIES INC (NV)
Recapitalized as ABCO Energy, Inc. 07/19/2013
Each share Common $0.001 par exchanged for (0.04347826) share Common $0.001 par

ENERGY CTL SYS AMER INC (DE)
Recapitalized as National Tax Accounting Inc. 02/28/1997
Each share Common 1¢ par exchanged for (0.02) share Common 1¢ par

ENERGY CTL TECH INC (DE)
Name changed to 5Fifty5.com, Inc. 09/26/2004
5Fifty5.com, Inc. recapitalized as Swap-A-Debt, Inc. 02/26/2008 which name changed to WikiLoan Inc. 06/26/2009 which name changed to Wiki Group, Inc. 03/26/2012 which recapitalized as Source Financial, Inc. 03/21/2013 which name changed to Alltemp, Inc. 04/27/2017

ENERGY CONVERSION DEVICES INC (DE)
Plan of reorganization under Chapter 11 Federal Bankruptcy proceedings effective 08/28/2012
No stockholders' equity

ENERGY CORP. INTERNATIONAL (UT)
Recapitalized as Garb-Oil Corp. of America 01/15/1981
Each share Common $1.50 par exchanged for (2/3) share Common no par
Garb-Oil Corp. of America name changed to Garb Oil & Power Corp. 10/31/1985

ENERGY CR OPPORTUNITIES INCOME FD (ON)
Name changed to Redwood Energy Credit Fund and Class A and U Units reclassified as ETF Currency Hedged or USD ETF Non-Currency Hedged Units respectively 02/15/2018
Redwood Energy Credit Fund name changed to Purpose Energy Credit Fund 06/18/2018

ENERGY DEV INC (MT)
Name changed to Environmental Recycling Technologies Inc. 10/23/1983
Environmental Recycling Technologies Inc. name changed Mason Dental Ceramics, Inc. 04/16/1984 which recapitalized as Mason Dental Inc. 12/01/1990
(See Mason Dental Inc.)

ENERGY DEV INC (UT)
Each share Common 1¢ par exchanged for (100) shares Common $0.0001 par 10/01/1979
Each share Common $0.0001 par exchanged for (0.2) share Common $0.0005 par 07/01/1981
Name changed to West Resources, Ltd. 11/08/1982
(See West Resources, Ltd.)

ENERGY DEV PARTNERS LTD (CO)
Merged into Hallwood Energy Partners, L.P. 5/10/90
Each Depositary Unit no par exchanged for (0.34) Depositary Receipt
Hallwood Energy Partners, L.P. reorganized as Hallwood Energy Corp. 6/8/99
(See Hallwood Energy Corp.)

ENERGY DRILLING INDS INC (NV)
Name changed to American International Industries Inc. 6/30/98

ENERGY EAST CAP TR I (DE)
8.25% Capital Securities called for redemption at $25 plus $0.48125 accrued dividends on 07/24/2006

ENERGY EAST CORP (NY)
Common 1¢ par split (2) for (1) by issuance of (1) additional share payable 04/01/1999 to holders of record 03/12/1999 Ex date - 04/05/1999
Merged into Iberdrola, S.A. 09/16/2008
Each share Common 1¢ par exchanged for $28.50 cash

ENERGY EXCHANGE CORP (DE)
Second Amended Plan of reorganization under Chapter 11 Federal Bankruptcy proceedings confirmed 12/09/1986
No stockholders' equity

ENERGY EXPL TECHNOLOGIES (AB)
Reincorporated 10/24/2003
Reincorporated from (NV) to under the laws of Alberta and Common $0.001 par changed to no par 10/24/2003
Name changed to NXT Energy Solutions Inc. 09/22/2008

ENERGY EXPLORER INC (AB)
Acquired by Great Plains Exploration Inc. (Old) 09/14/2004
Each share Common no par exchanged for either (0.571) share Common no par or $0.62 cash
Great Plains Exploration Inc. (Old) merged into Great Plains Exploration Inc. (New) (Canada) 07/29/2005 which reincorporated in Alberta 01/01/2009 which merged into Avenir Diversified Income Trust 11/10/2010 which reorganized as AvenEx Energy Corp. 01/07/2011 which merged into Spyglass Resources Corp. 04/04/2013

ENERGY FACTORS INC (CA)
Acquired by Sithe-Energies, L.P. 06/06/1988
Each share Common no par exchanged for $8.25 cash

ENERGY FINDERS INC (FL)
Common $0.001 par split (5) for (1) by issuance of (4) additional shares payable 09/08/2005 to holders of record 09/08/2005 Ex date - 09/12/2005
Reincorporated under the laws of Nevada 02/14/2006

ENERGY FUELS & MINERALS EXPL CORP (UT)
Name changed to Texas Western, Inc. and Common 1¢ par changed to 20¢ par 4/26/72
(See Texas Western, Inc.)

ENERGY GAS & OIL CORP (DE)
Name changed to Hiawatha Oil & Gas Corp. 11/18/82
Hiawatha Oil & Gas Corp. name changed to Hiawatha Industry Internet Corp. 6/21/96

ENERGY GAS SAVER INC (FL)
Name changed to Fun Time International, Inc. 06/10/1983

ENERGY GROUP PLC (UNITED KINGDOM)
Acquired by Texas Utilities Co. 8/7/98
Each Sponsored ADR for Ordinary exchanged for $54.54 cash

ENERGY INC (MT)
Reincorporated under the laws of Ohio as Gas Natural Inc. 07/09/2010
(See Gas Natural Inc.)

ENERGY INCOME & GROWTH FD (MA)
Issue Information - 1,600,000 shares COM offered at $27.25 per share on 11/19/2010
Name changed to First Trust Energy Income & Growth Fund 03/19/2012

ENERGY INDEXPLUS DIVID FD (AB)
Under plan of merger each Trust Unit automatically became (0.52583938) share Middlefield Mutual Funds Ltd. Global Infrastructure Fund Ser. A 06/16/2015

ENERGY INFRASTRUCTURE ACQUISITION CORP (DE)
Issue Information - 20,250,000 UNITS consisting of (1) share COM and (1) WT offered at $10 per Unit on 07/18/2006
Units separated 10/13/2006
Liquidation completed
Each share Common $0.0001 par received initial distribution of $10.0525 cash payable 11/13/2008 to holders of record 10/31/2008
Each share Common $0.0001 par received second and final distribution of $0.009446055 cash payable 03/03/2010 to holders of record 10/31/2008
Note: Certificates were not required to be surrendered and are without value

ENERGY INTL INC (NV)
Charter revoked for failure to file reports and pay fees 05/18/1987

ENERGY INTL OVERSEAS CORP (NY)
Common 1¢ par split (3) for (1) by issuance of (2) additional shares 12/15/1983
Recapitalized as Nova Continental Development Corp. 09/19/1994
Each share Common $0.001 par exchanged for (0.1) share Common $0.0005 par
(See Nova Continental Development Corp.)

ENERGY KING INC (NV)
Name changed to Godfather Media, Inc. 10/18/2011
Godfather Media, Inc. name changed to Embark Holdings, Inc. 08/20/2012 which name changed to Muscle Warfare International, Inc. 06/28/2013 which name changed to Cannabusiness Group, Inc. 02/18/2014

ENERGY LEADERS INCOME FD (ON)
Units separated 06/18/2012
Trust terminated 11/30/2017
Each Trust Unit received $6.2537 cash

ENERGY LEADERS PLUS INCOME ETF (ON)
Name changed to Harvest Energy Leaders Plus Income ETF 06/19/2018

ENERGY LEADERS PLUS INCOME FD (ON)
Under plan of reorganization each Class A Unit automatically became (1) Energy Leaders Plus Income ETF Class A Unit 10/24/2016
Energy Leaders Plus Income ETF name changed to Harvest Energy Leaders Plus Income ETF 06/19/2018

ENERGY MGMT CORP (CO)
Under plan of reorganization holders of $10 Conv. Preferred Ser. A and Common no par became entitled to receive rights to Class B Common 1¢ par on a percentage basis 12/15/1986
Merged into EMC Acquisition Corp. 09/01/1988
Each Right to receive Class B Common 1¢ par exchanged for $0.48 cash

ENERGY METALS CORP (BC)
Merged into Uranium One Inc. 08/10/2007
Each share Common no par exchanged for (1.15) shares Common no par
(See Uranium One Inc.)

ENERGY METHODS CORP (CO)
Reincorporated under the laws of Delaware as Emcor Petroleum, Inc. 05/01/1984
(See Emcor Petroleum, Inc.)

ENERGY MINERALS CORP (CO)
Stock Dividends - 10% 10/09/1980; 10% 10/13/1981
Acquired by Weeks Exploration Co. 01/03/1984
Each share Common 10¢ par exchanged for $7.50 cash

ENERGY MTR CTL INC (UT)
Involuntarily dissolved 10/31/1987

ENERGY NORTH INC NEW (AB)
Merged into Argo Energy Ltd. 7/30/2004
Each share Common no par exchanged for (0.3084) share Common no par
(See Argo Energy Ltd.)

ENERGY NORTH INC OLD (AB)
Reorganized as Energy North Inc. (New) 10/21/96
Each share Common no par exchanged for (1) share Common no par
Energy North Inc. (New) merged into Argo Energy Ltd. 7/30/2004
(See Argo Energy Ltd.)

ENERGY OIL INC (CO)
Reorganized under the laws of Delaware 08/16/1984
Each share Common 1¢ par exchanged for (0.2) share Common 1¢ par
Energy Oil, Inc. (DE) liquidated for Snyder Oil Partners L.P. 12/23/1986
(See Snyder Oil Partners L.P.)

ENERGY OIL INC (DE)
Completely liquidated 12/23/1986
Each share Common 1¢ par exchanged for first and final distribution of (0.54) Snyder Oil Partners L.P. Unit of Ltd. Partnership
(See Snyder Oil Partners L.P.)

ENERGY OPTICS INC (NM)
Each share old Common $0.001 par exchanged for (0.1) share new Common $0.001 par 08/22/1997
Name changed to American Millennium Corp. Inc. (NM) 06/11/1998
American Millennium Corp. Inc. (NM) reincorporated in Delaware 04/19/2004
(See American Millennium Corp. Inc.)

ENERGY PARTNERS LTD (DE)
Plan of reorganization under Chapter 11 Federal Bankruptcy proceedings effective 09/21/2009
Each share Common 1¢ par exchanged for (0.06166332) share new Common $0.001 par
Name changed to EPL Oil & Gas, Inc. 09/12/2012
EPL Oil & Gas, Inc. merged into Energy XXI (Bermuda) Ltd. 06/03/2014 which name changed to Energy XXI Ltd. 11/14/2014
(See Energy XXI Ltd.)

ENERGY PLUS INCOME TR (AB)
Merged into Energy Income Fund 10/04/2010
Each Trust Unit no par automatically became (1.2818) Trust Units no par

ENERGY PWR SYS LTD (ON)
Recapitalized as EnerNorth Industries, Inc. 02/12/2003
Each share Common no par exchanged for (1/3) share Common no par
(See EnerNorth Industries, Inc.)

ENERGY PRODTN CO (ON)
Recapitalized as FieldPoint Petroleum Corp. 12/31/1997
Each share Common 1¢ par exchanged for (0.01333333) share Common 1¢ par

ENERGY PRODUCERS INC (NV)
Name changed to EGPI Firecreek, Inc. 01/30/2004

ENERGY RECOVERY SYS INC (DE)
Recapitalized as Compuflex Systems Inc. 03/28/1994
Each share Common $0.001 par exchanged for (0.02) share Common $0.001 par
(See Compuflex Systems Inc.)

ENERGY RECYCLING CORP (DE)
Charter cancelled and declared inoperative and void for non-payment of taxes 03/01/1991

ENERGY RESH CORP (NY)
Each share Common $0.0001 par received distribution of (0.33333333) share Evercel, Inc. 12/14/1981

Common 1¢ par payable 02/22/1999 to holders of record 02/19/1999 Ex date - 02/17/1999
Reincorporated under laws of Delaware as FuelCell Energy, Inc. 09/21/1999

ENERGY RESH CORP (UT)
Name changed to Billings Energy Research Corp. 05/06/1974
Billings Energy Research Corp. name changed to Billings Energy Corp. 06/10/1976 which name changed to Billings Corp. 08/04/1981 which name changed to Hydrogen Energy Corp. 08/21/1985
(See Hydrogen Energy Corp.)

ENERGY RES CORP (NV)
Merged into ENERTEC Corp. 05/04/1984
Each share Common $1 par exchanged for (0.53) share Common 1¢ par
(See ENERTEC Corp.)

ENERGY RESOURCES DEVELOPMENT CORP. (UT)
Name changed to Energy Development, Inc. (UT) 04/07/1972
Energy Development, Inc. (UT) name changed to West Resources, Ltd. 11/08/1982
(See West Resources, Ltd.)

ENERGY RES N D INC (ND)
Each share Common 1¢ par exchanged for (0.2) share Common 5¢ par 09/01/1982
Name changed to Centrum Industries Inc. (ND) 09/16/1988
Centrum Industries Inc. (ND) reincorporated in Delaware 11/00/1990
(See Centrum Industries Inc.)

ENERGY RESV INC (AZ)
Name changed to Cox Technologies, Inc. (AZ) 03/31/1998
Cox Technologies, Inc. (AZ) reincorporated in North Carolina 12/31/2000
(See Cox Technologies, Inc.)

ENERGY RESVS GROUP INC (DE)
Merged into BHP Holdings (USA) Inc. 01/11/1985
Each share Common $0.03333333 par exchanged for $6.10 cash

ENERGY RIV CORP (NV)
Recapitalized as Global Freight Integrators Inc. 03/24/2003
Each share Common $0.001 par exchanged for (0.01) share Common $0.001 par

ENERGY SVGS INCOME FD (ON)
Units no par split (2) for (1) by issuance of (1) additional share payable 02/02/2004 to holders of record 01/30/2004 Ex date - 01/28/2004
Name changed to Just Energy Income Fund (ON) 06/01/2009
Just Energy Income Fund (ON) reorganized in Canada as Just Energy Group Inc. 01/04/2011

ENERGY SCIENCES CORP (WA)
Administratively dissolved for failure to file annual report and license renewal 08/08/1988

ENERGY SEARCH INC (TN)
Merged into EOG Resources, Inc. 07/20/2001
Each share 9% Conv. Redeemable Stock exchanged for $8.22 cash
Each share Common no par exchanged for $8.22 cash

ENERGY SEARCH INC (UT)
Reincorporated under the laws of Delaware as Med Search Inc. 05/23/1993
Med Search Inc. recapitalized as Prospect Medical Holdings, Inc. 02/10/1998
(See Prospect Medical Holdings, Inc.)

ENERGY SVC INC (DE)
Each share old Common 10¢ par exchanged for (0.25) share new Common 10¢ par 06/02/1994
$1.50 Conv. Exchangeable Preferred $1 par called for redemption 08/26/1994
Name changed to ENSCO International Inc. (DE) 05/26/1995
ENSCO International Inc. (DE) reorganized in England & Wales as Ensco International PLC 12/23/2009 which name changed to Ensco PLC 03/31/2010

ENERGY SVCS ACQUISITION CORP (DE)
Name changed to Energy Services of America Corp. 08/18/2008

ENERGY SHED INC (MN)
Statutorily dissolved 01/08/2007

ENERGY SOLUTIONS INC (DE)
Charter cancelled and declared inoperative and void for non-payment of taxes 03/01/1999

ENERGY SOURCE INC (NV)
SEC revoked common stock registration 11/03/2009

ENERGY SOURCES INC (DE)
Common no par split (3) for (2) by issuance of (0.5) additional share 02/27/1981
Stock Dividend - 10% 05/02/1980
Charter cancelled and declared inoperative and void for non-payment of taxes 03/01/1995

ENERGY SPLIT CORP INC (QC)
ROC Preferred Shares called for redemption at $25 on 09/15/2006
Ser. B Preferred Shares called for redemption at $21 on 09/16/2011
Capital Yield Shares called for redemption at $15.19 on 09/16/2011

ENERGY SPLIT CORP II INC (QC)
ROC Preferred Shares called for redemption at $13.74 on 12/16/2010
Capital Yield Shares called for redemption at $9.86 on 12/16/2010

ENERGY STOCK EXCHANGE (UT)
Name changed to Burke Oil Co. (UT) 04/20/1981
Burke Oil Co. (UT) reincorporated in Nevada as Centre Capital Corp. 09/06/1988 which name changed to Golden Health Holdings, Inc. 04/15/2004
(See Golden Health Holdings, Inc.)

ENERGY SYS INC (MN)
Statutorily dissolved 09/25/1998

ENERGY SYS UTD CORP (DE)
Charter cancelled and declared inoperative and void for non-payment of taxes 3/1/86

ENERGY TECHNOLOGIES INC (FL)
Voluntarily dissolved 06/10/1998
Details not available

ENERGY TELECOM INC (FL)
Each share old Common $0.0001 par exchanged for (0.16666666) share new Common $0.0001 par 01/11/2008
Each share new Common $0.0001 par exchanged again for (0.2) share new Common $0.0001 par 06/30/2010
Reorganized under the laws of Nevada as PFO Global, Inc. 07/06/2015
Each share new Common $0.0001 par exchanged for (0.01364708) share Common $0.0001 par

ENERGY TRANSFER EQUITY L P (DE)
Common Units of Ltd. Partnership split (2) for (1) by issuance of (1) additional Unit payable 01/24/2014 to holders of record 01/13/2014 Ex date - 01/27/2014
Common Units of Ltd. Partnership split (2) for (1) by issuance of (1) additional Unit payable 07/24/2015 to holders of record 07/15/2015 Ex date - 07/27/2015
Name changed to Energy Transfer L.P. 10/19/2018

ENERGY TRANSFER PARTNERS L P NEW (DE)
Name changed to Energy Transfer Operating, L.P. 10/19/2018
Merged into Energy Transfer L.P. 10/19/2018
Each Common Unit exchanged for (1.28) Common Units

ENERGY TRANSFER PARTNERS L P OLD (DE)
Common Units split (2) for (1) by issuance of (1) additional Unit payable 03/15/2005 to holders of record 02/28/2005 Ex date - 03/16/2005
Merged into Energy Transfer Partners, L.P. (New) 05/01/2017
Each Common Unit exchanged for (1.5) Common Units Energy Transfer Partners, L.P. (New) merged into Energy Transfer L.P. 10/19/2018

ENERGY VENTURES INC (DE)
Reincorporated 09/08/1980
State of incorporation changed from (MA) to (DE) 09/08/1980
Common $1 par split (4) for (1) by issuance of (3) additional shares 03/07/1990
Name changed to EVI, Inc. 05/06/1997
EVI, Inc. name changed to EVI Weatherford, Inc. 05/27/1998 which name changed to Weatherford International Inc. (New) (DE) 09/21/1998 which reincorporated in Bermuda as Weatherford International Ltd. 06/26/2002 which reincorporated in Switzerland 02/25/2009 which reincorporated in Ireland as Weatherford International PLC 06/18/2014

ENERGY VISION INTL INC (UT)
SEC revoked common stock registration 01/29/2007

ENERGY VISIONS INC (DE)
Name changed 07/23/2001
Name changed from Energy Ventures Inc. to Energy Visions Inc. 07/23/2001
Recapitalized as Lions Petroleum Inc. 11/09/2004
Each share Common $0.0001 par exchanged for (0.005) share Common $0.0001 par
(See Lions Petroleum Inc.)

ENERGY WEST INC (MT)
Old Common 15¢ par split (2) for (1) by issuance of (1) additional share 06/24/1994
Each share old Common 15¢ par exchanged for (1.5) shares new Common 15¢ par 02/01/2008
Name changed to Energy, Inc. (MT) 08/04/2009
Energy, Inc. (MT) reincorporated in Ohio as Gas Natural Inc. 07/09/2010
(See Gas Natural Inc.)

ENERGY WORLD CORP LTD (AUSTRALIA)
ADR agreement terminated 08/30/2017
Each Sponsored ADR for Ordinary exchanged for $3.59421 cash

ENERGY XXI GULF COAST INC (DE)
Acquired by MLCJR LLC 10/18/2018
Each share Common 1¢ par exchanged for $9.10 cash

ENERGY XXI LTD (BERMUDA)
Name changed 11/14/2014
Each share Common $0.001 par exchanged for (0.2) share Common $0.005 par 01/29/2010
Name changed from Energy XXI (Bermuda) Ltd. to Energy XXI Ltd. 11/14/2014
Plan of reorganization under Chapter 11 Federal Bankruptcy proceedings effective 12/30/2016
No stockholders' equity

ENERGYCONNECT GROUP INC (OR)
Acquired by Johnson Controls Holding Co., Inc. 07/01/2011
Each share Common no par exchanged for $0.2253 cash

ENERGYNORTH INC (NH)
Common $1 par split (3) for (2) by issuance of (0.5) additional share 08/22/1988
Merged into KeySpan Corp. 11/08/2000
Each share Common $1 par exchanged for $61.4587 cash

ENERGYSOLUTIONS INC (DE)
Acquired by Rockwell Holdco, Inc. 05/24/2013
Each share Common 1¢ par exchanged for $4.15 cash

ENERGYSOUTH INC (DE)
Reincorporated 02/01/2007
Common 1¢ par split (3) for (2) by issuance of (0.5) additional share payable 09/01/2004 to holders of record 08/16/2004 Ex date - 09/02/2004
State of incorporation changed from (AL) to (DE) 02/01/2007
Merged into Sempra Energy 10/01/2008
Each share Common 1¢ par exchanged for $61.50 cash

ENERGYTEC INC (NV)
Name changed 02/26/2002
Name changed from Energytec.com, Inc. to Energytec, Inc. 02/26/2002
Stock Dividends - 5% payable 07/01/2003 to holders of record 06/15/2003 Ex date - 06/11/2003; 6% payable 11/15/2004 to holders of record 11/01/2004 Ex date - 10/28/2004; 7% payable 10/31/2005 to holders of record 10/21/2005 Ex date - 10/19/2005
Plan of reorganization under Chapter 11 Federal Bankruptcy proceedings terminated 10/22/2014
No stockholders' equity

ENERGYTEK CORP (NV)
Recapitalized as TimefireVR Inc. 11/22/2016
Each share Common $0.001 par exchanged for (0.1) share Common $0.001 par

ENERJEX RES INC (NV)
Each share old Common $0.001 par exchanged for (0.2) share new Common $0.001 par 07/28/2008
Each share new Common $0.001 par exchanged again for (0.06666666) share new Common $0.001 par 06/02/2014
Each share 10% Perpetual Preferred Ser. A $0.001 par automatically became (10) shares new Common $0.001 par 03/26/2018
Recapitalized as AgEagle Aerial Systems, Inc. 03/27/2018
Each share new Common $0.001 par exchanged for (0.04) share Common $0.001 par

ENERJI LTD (AUSTRALIA)
ADR agreement terminated 08/03/2017
No ADR's remain outstanding

ENERLABS INC (DE)
Name changed to Energy & Environmental Services, Inc. 12/30/2016

ENERMARK INCOME FD (BC)
Merged into Enerplus Resources Fund 06/22/2001
Each Trust Unit no par exchanged for (0.173) Trust Unit Ser. G no par Enerplus Resources Fund

reorganized as Enerplus Corp. 01/03/2011

ENERMARK OIL LTD (OK)
Recapitalized as Quest Development, Inc. 08/08/1984
Each share Common $0.001 par exchanged for (0.06666666) share Common $0.015 par
(See Quest Development, Inc.)

ENERNOC INC (DE)
Acquired by Enel S.p.A. 08/07/2017
Each share Common $0.001 par exchanged for $7.67 cash

ENERNORTH INDS INC (ON)
Discharged from receivership 02/10/2011
No stockholders' equity

ENER1 INC (FL)
Each share Common 1¢ par received distribution of (0.01493) share Splinex Technology Inc. Common $0.001 par payable 01/24/2005 to holders of record 01/17/2005
Ex date - 01/12/2005
Each share old Common 1¢ par exchanged for (0.14285714) share new Common 1¢ par 04/24/2008
Plan of reorganization under Chapter 11 Federal Bankruptcy proceedings effective 03/30/2012
No stockholders' equity

ENERPHAZE CORP (OR)
Administratively dissolved 04/30/2004

ENERPLUS EXCHANGEABLE LTD PARTNERSHIP (AB)
Reorganized as Enerplus Corp. 01/03/2011
Each Class B Unit of Ltd. Partnership no par exchanged for (0.425) share Common no par

ENERPLUS RES CORP (AB)
Each Petroleum Royalty Unit Ser. A no par exchanged for (1) Petroleum Royalty Unit Ser. G no par 01/18/1990
Each Petroleum Royalty Unit Ser. B no par exchanged for (1.1) Petroleum Royalty Units Ser. G no par 01/18/1990
Each Petroleum Royalty Unit Ser. C no par exchanged for (1.35) Petroleum Royalty Units Ser. G no par 01/18/1990
Each Petroleum Royalty Unit Ser. D no par exchanged for (1.55) Petroleum Royalty Units Ser. G no par 01/18/1990
Each Petroleum Royalty Unit Ser. G no par exchanged for (1) Enerplus Resources Fund Trust Unit Ser. G no par 11/01/1994
Enerplus Resources Fund reorganized as Enerplus Corp. 01/03/2011

ENERPLUS RES FD (AB)
Each Trust Unit Ser. A no par exchanged for (1) old Trust Unit Ser. G no par 01/18/1990
Each Trust Unit Ser. B no par exchanged for (1.1) old Trust Units Ser. G no par 01/18/1990
Each Trust Unit Ser. C no par exchanged for (1.35) old Trust Units Ser. G no par 01/18/1990
Each Trust Unit Ser. D no par exchanged for (1.55) old Trust Units Ser. G no par 01/18/1990
Each old Trust Unit Ser. G no par exchanged for (0.16666666) new Trust Unit Ser. G no par 06/08/2000
Reorganized as Enerplus Corp. 01/03/2011
Each new Trust Unit Ser. G no par exchanged for (1) share Common no par

ENERSERV PRODS INC (TX)
Common $1 par changed to 1¢ par 12/30/1985
Merged into Franklin Land & Resources, Inc. 07/17/1987

Each share Common 1¢ par exchanged for $0.01 cash

ENERSHARE TECHNOLOGY CORP (BC)
Filed an assignment under the Bankruptcy & Insolvency Act 6/21/2004
No stockholders' equity

ENERSIS AMERS S A (CHILE)
Name changed 02/01/2016
Name changed from Enersis S.A. to Enersis Americas S.A. 02/01/2016
Each Sponsored ADR for Ordinary received distribution of (1) Enersis Chile S.A. Sponsored ADR for Common payable 04/26/2016 to holders of record 04/14/2016
Ex date - 04/27/2016
Under plan of merger name changed to Enel Americas S.A. 12/01/2016

ENERSIS CHILE S A (CHILE)
Name changed to Enel Chile S.A. 11/07/2016

ENERSTAR RES INC (AB)
Name changed to Net Shepherd Inc. 08/20/1996
Net Shepherd Inc. recapitalized as Flock Resources Ltd. 05/09/2002 which name changed to Endev Energy Inc. 07/11/2002 which merged into Penn West Energy Trust 07/22/2008 which reorganized as Penn West Petroleum Ltd. (New) 01/03/2011 which name changed to Obsidian Energy Ltd. 06/29/2017

ENERTEC CORP (DE)
Plan of reorganization under Chapter 11 Bankruptcy proceedings confirmed 08/08/1986
No stockholders' equity

ENERTEC RESOURCE SVCS INC (AB)
Merged into Veritas DGC Inc. 09/30/1999
Each share Common no par exchanged for (0.345) share Common 1¢ par
Veritas DGC Inc. merged into Compagnie Generale de Geophysique-Veritas 01/12/2007 which name changed to CGG 05/29/2013

ENERTECH INC (LA)
Charter revoked for failure to file annual reports 11/19/90

ENERTECK ENERGY TECHNOLOGIES CORP (BC)
Struck off register and declared dissolved for failure to file returns 05/13/1994

ENERTEX DEVS INC (ON)
Recapitalized as Marvas Developments Ltd. 03/02/1992
Each (12.6) shares Common no par exchanged for (1) share Common no par
Marvas Developments Ltd. reorganized as Pan American Resources Inc. 01/23/1996 which name changed to ONTZINC Corp. 08/08/2002 which recapitalized as HudBay Minerals Inc. (ONT) 12/24/2004 which reincorporated in Canada 10/25/2005

ENERTRAC INC (IL)
Proclaimed dissolved for failure to file reports and pay taxes 10/01/1987

ENERVEST DIVERSIFIED INCOME TR (AB)
Each old Trust Unit exchanged for (0.33333333) new Trust Unit 04/24/2009
Name changed to Canoe EIT Income Fund 11/06/2013

ENERVEST ENERGY & OIL SANDS TOTAL RETURN TR (AB)
Merged into Canoe 'GO CANADA!' Fund Corp. 11/19/2013

Each Unit received (0.758642) share Energy Income Class Ser. A

ENERVISION INC (NS)
Name changed to Helical Corp. Inc. 09/29/2004
Each share Common no par exchanged for (1) share Common no par

ENERWASTE MINERALS CORP (BC)
Name changed to Universal Gun-Loc Industries Ltd. 02/11/1994
Universal Gun-Loc Industries Ltd. recapitalized as UGL Enterprises Ltd. 04/25/2002 which name changed to Red Hill Energy Inc. 05/31/2006 (Red Hill Energy Inc.)

ENESCO GROUP INC (IL)
Reincorporated 07/31/2003
State of incorporation changed from (MA) to (IL) 07/31/2003
Chapter 11 bankruptcy proceedings converted to Chapter 7 on 07/28/2008
No stockholders' equity

ENETPC INC (MN)
Each share old Common 1¢ par exchanged for (0.2) share new Common 1¢ par 1/20/2004
Name changed to BDC Capital, Inc. 12/1/2004
BDC Capital, Inc. name changed to DigitalTown, Inc. 3/1/2007

ENEX RES CORP (DE)
Reincorporated 06/30/1992
Each share Common 1¢ par exchanged for (0.2) share Common 5¢ par 12/03/1987
State of incorporation changed from (CO) to (DE) 06/30/1992
Merged into 3TEC Energy Corp. 12/31/2001
Each share Common 5¢ par exchanged for $14 cash

ENEX RESOURCES LTD. (BC)
Name changed 12/01/1972
Name changed from Enex Mines Ltd. to Enex Resources Ltd. 12/01/1972
Capital Stock 50¢ par changed to no par 00/00/1978
Name changed to Enexco International Ltd. 10/26/1983
Enexco International Ltd. recapitalized International Enexco Ltd. 10/31/1991 which merged into Denison Mines Corp. 06/10/2014

ENEXCO INTL LTD (BC)
Recapitalized as International Enexco Ltd. 10/31/1991
Each share Capital Stock no par exchanged for (0.2) share Common no par
International Enexco Ltd. merged into Denison Mines Corp. 06/10/2014

ENEXI HLDGS INC (DE)
Recapitalized as Trinity3 Corp. 03/31/2003
Each share Common $0.0001 par exchanged for (0.2) share Common $0.0001 par
(See Trinity3 Corp.)

ENFIELD LTD (ON)
Common no par split (2) for (1) by issuance of (1) additional share 11/21/1986
Reorganized as Consolidated Enfield Corp. 07/09/1990
Each share 7% Conv. Class E Preferred Ser. 1 no par exchanged for (1) share 7% Conv. Class E Preferred Ser. 1 no par
Each share Common no par exchanged for (0.2) share Common no par
Consolidated Enfield Corp. name changed to West Street Capital Corp. 06/29/2004
(See West Street Capital Corp.)

ENFIELD RES INC (BC)
Recapitalized as Pacific Summa Capital Corp. 09/27/1989

Each share Common no par exchanged for (0.2) share Common no par
Pacific Summa Capital Corp. name changed to Pacific Summa Environmental Corp. 10/22/1991 which recapitalized as Truax Ventures Corp. 08/09/2000 which recapitalized as Aries Resource Corp. 09/02/2004 which recapitalized as Alderon Resource Corp. 09/24/2008 which name changed to Alderon Iron Ore Corp. 10/05/2011

ENFIN INC (OH)
Merged into Second Bancorp Inc. 08/20/1998
Each share Common no par exchanged for (0.95) share Common no par
Second Bancorp Inc. merged into Sky Financial Group, Inc. 07/02/2004 which merged into Huntington Bancshares Inc. 07/02/2007

ENFLEX INC (WA)
Recapitalized as Carrington Energy Development Corp. 11/09/1988
Each share Common $0.001 par exchanged (0.1) share Common 1¢ par

ENFLO CORP (DE)
Merged 10/13/1959
Under plan of merger each share Enflo Corp. (PR) Common $1 par exchanged for (2) shares Enflo Corp. (DE) Class B Common 10¢ par 10/13/1959
Class A Common 10¢ par and Class B Common 10¢ par reclassified as Common 10¢ par 06/30/1961
Each (330) shares Common 10¢ par exchanged for (1) share Common $33 par 08/26/1985
Stock Dividends - 10% 12/15/1967; 10% 09/10/1971
Merged into Wobeteam, Inc. 12/29/1987
Each share Common $33 par exchanged for $227 cash

ENG ENTERPRISES INC (DE)
Each share old Common $0.001 par exchanged for (0.005) share new Common $0.001 par 03/03/2000
New Common $0.001 par split (3) for (1) by issuance of (2) additional shares payable 08/17/2000 to holders of record 07/14/2000
Ex date - 08/18/2000
Name changed to Global Online India, Inc. 08/17/2000
(See Global Online India, Inc.)

ENGAGE INC (DE)
Name changed 04/28/2000
Common 1¢ par split (2) for (1) by issuance of (1) additional share payable 04/03/2000 to holders of record 03/20/2000
Name changed from Engage Technologies Inc. to Engage, Inc. 04/28/2000
Plan of reorganization under Chapter 11 Federal Bankruptcy Code effective 06/02/2004
No stockholders' equity

ENGEL GEN DEVELOPERS LTD (ISRAEL)
Issue Information - 3,600,000 CL A ORD shares offered at $9 per share on 09/30/1997
Under plan of merger each share Class A Ordinary ILS 0.1 par exchanged for $14 cash 06/12/2007

ENGEL INDS CORP (FL)
Charter cancelled for failure to file reports 09/03/1976

ENGELHARD CORP (DE)
Common $1 par split (3) for (2) by issuance of (0.5) additional share 3/31/87
Common $1 par split (3) for (2) by

issuance of (0.5) additional share 9/29/92
Common $1 par split (3) for (2) by issuance of (0.5) additional share 9/29/93
Common $1 par split (3) for (2) by issuance of (0.5) additional share 6/30/95
Merged into BASF A.G. 6/9/2006
Each share Common $1 par exchanged for $39 cash

ENGELHARD INDUSTRIES, INC. (DE)
Common $1 par split (5) for (4) by issuance of (0.25) additional share 1/24/66
Common $1 par split (5) for (4) by issuance of (0.25) additional share 1/25/67
Common $1 par split (2) for (1) by issuance of (1) additional share 8/30/67
Name changed to Engelhard Minerals & Chemicals Corp. 9/27/67
Engelhard Minerals & Chemicals Corp. name changed to Phibro Corp. 5/20/81 which name changed to Phibro-Salomon Inc. 5/20/82 which name changed to Salomon Inc. 5/7/86 which merged into Travelers Group Inc. 11/28/97 which name changed to Citigroup Inc. 10/8/98

ENGELHARD MINERALS & CHEMS CORP (DE)
Common $1 par split (2) for (1) by issuance of (1) additional share 1/20/69
$4.25 Conv. Preferred no par called for redemption 4/5/76
Common $1 par split (2.06) for (1) by issuance of (1.06) additional shares 12/31/79
Name changed to Phibro Corp. 5/20/81
Phibro Corp. name changed to Phibro-Salomon Inc. 5/20/82 which name changed to Salomon Inc. 5/7/86 which merged into Travelers Group Inc. 11/28/97 which name changed to Citigroup Inc. 10/8/98

ENGELS COPPER MINING CO.
Merged into California-Engels Mining Co. in 1936
Details not available

ENGEN LTD (SOUTH AFRICA)
ADR agreement terminated 1/22/99
Each Sponsored ADR for Ordinary Rand-50 par exchanged for $3.7767 cash

ENGENUITY TECHNOLOGIES INC (CANADA)
Acquired by CAE Inc. 06/01/2007
Each share Common no par exchanged for $1.20 cash

ENGESSER BREWING CO. (MN)
7% Part. Common $1 par and Class B Common no par reclassified as Common $1 par in 1935
Charter expired by time limitation in 1962

ENGEX INC (DE)
Completely liquidated
Each share Common 10¢ par received first and final distribution of (0.747537) share Enzo Biochem, Inc. Common 1¢ par and (0.16276) share Fortress Biotech, Inc. Common $0.001 par payable 04/02/2018 to holders of record 03/21/2018

ENGIL SOCIEDADE GESTORA DE PARTICIPACOES SOCIAIS SA (PORTUGAL)
ADR agreement terminated 5/21/2001
Each Sponsored ADR for Ordinary exchanged for (1) Ordinary share

ENGILITY HLDGS INC OLD (DE)
Merged into Engility Holdings, Inc. (New) 02/27/2015
Each share Common 1¢ par exchanged for (1) share Common 1¢ par

ENGINE DYNAMICS INC (NV)
Charter revoked for failure to file reports and pay fees 07/01/1990

ENGINE PWR CORP (NY)
Proclaimed dissolved 9/25/91

ENGINEER GOLD MINES, LTD. (DE)
Charter cancelled and declared inoperative and void for non-payment of taxes 4/1/33

ENGINEER ZINC CO. (MO)
Charter forfeited for failure to file reports 12/02/1913

ENGINEERED CONSTR INDS INC (UT)
Involuntarily dissolved for failure to file reports 12/31/1976

ENGINEERED ELECTRS INC (DE)
Liquidated 10/05/1982
No stockholders' equity

ENGINEERED PLASTICS CONTAINER CO., INC. (CA)
Name changed to R.G.G., Inc. 8/15/63
(See R.G.G., Inc.)

ENGINEERED STRUCTURES CORP (NV)
Recapitalized as React Systems, Inc. 10/30/73
Each share Capital Stock 5¢ par exchanged for (0.2) share Capital Stock 5¢ par
React Systems, Inc. name changed to Infrastructure International Inc. 9/12/97
(See Infrastructure International Inc.)

ENGINEERED SUPPORT SYS INC (MO)
Common 1¢ par split (5) for (4) by issuance of (0.25) additional share 09/09/1986
Common 1¢ par split (3) for (2) by issuance of (0.5) additional share payable 06/26/1998 to holders of record 06/12/1998
Common 1¢ par split (5) for (4) by issuance of (0.25) additional share payable 03/16/2001 to holders of record 02/16/2001 Ex date - 03/19/2001
Common 1¢ par split (3) for (2) by issuance of (0.5) additional share payable 10/31/2002 to holders of record 10/04/2002 Ex date - 11/01/2002
Common 1¢ par split (3) for (2) by issuance of (0.5) additional share payable 10/31/2003 to holders of record 10/03/2003 Ex date - 11/03/2003
Common 1¢ par split (3) for (2) by issuance of (0.5) additional share payable 04/15/2005 to holders of record 03/15/2005 Ex date - 04/18/2005
Acquired by DRS Technologies, Inc. 01/31/2006
Each share Common 1¢ par exchanged for (0.2628) share Common 1¢ par and $30.10 cash
(See DRS Technologies, Inc.)

ENGINEERED SYS & DEV CORP (DE)
Charter forfeited for failure to maintain a registered agent 02/25/1991

ENGINEERING & MANUFACTURING CORP. (DE)
No longer in existence having become inoperative and void for non-payment of taxes 4/1/55

ENGINEERING ANIMATION INC (DE)
Merged into Unigraphics Solutions Inc. 10/23/2000
Each share Common 1¢ par exchanged for $13.75 cash

ENGINEERING COM INC (ON)
Each share old Common no par exchanged for (0.00000285) share new Common no par 12/31/2013
Note: In effect holders received $0.03 cash per share and public interest was eliminated

ENGINEERING MEASUREMENTS CO (CO)
Merged into Advanced Energy Industries, Inc. 1/3/2001
Each share Common 1¢ par exchanged for $7.09 cash

ENGINEERING METAL PRODUCTS CORP. (IN)
Completely liquidated 04/01/1969
No stockholders' equity

ENGINEERING PWR SYS LTD (ON)
Recapitalized 01/29/1999
Recapitalized from Engineering Power Systems Group Inc. to Engineering Power Systems Ltd. 01/29/1999
Each share Common no par exchanged for (0.25) share Common no par
Recapitalized as Energy Power Systems Ltd. 02/06/2001
Each share Common no par exchanged for (0.25) share Common no par
Energy Power Systems Ltd. recapitalized as EnerNorth Industries, Inc. 02/12/2003
(See EnerNorth Industries, Inc.)

ENGINEERS EXPLORATION & MINING CORP.
Dissolution approved in 1940

ENGINEERS GOLD MINES, INC. (CO)
Charter revoked for failure to file reports and pay fees 10/17/63

ENGINEERS PUBLIC SERVICE CO. (DE)
Liquidation completed 2/18/57

ENGLANDER CO., INC. (DE)
Name changed to Pingro Corp. and dissolved 3/9/64

ENGLE HOMES INC (FL)
Merged into Technical Olympic USA, Inc. 11/22/2000
Each share Common 1¢ par exchanged for $19.10 cash

ENGLEFIELD RES LTD (BC)
Name changed to Valu Concepts International Corp. (BC) 04/22/1992
Valu Concepts International Corp. (BC) reorganized in Canada as Double Impact Communications Corp. 09/08/1994 which recapitalized as Next Millennium Commercial Corp. 08/20/1998 which name changed to Roadrunner Oil & Gas Inc. 07/17/2008 which name changed to Bowood Energy Inc. 06/21/2010 which recapitalized as LGX Oil + Gas Inc. (Canada) 08/22/2012 which reincorporated in Alberta 06/27/2013

ENGLEWOOD BK & TR (ENGLEWOOD, FL)
Stock Dividend - 10% 04/01/1975
Reorganized as First Southern Bank Corp. 07/01/1982
Each share Capital Stock $5 par exchanged for (1) share Common $5 par
First Southern Bank Corp. merged into Barnett Banks of Florida, Inc. 01/31/1984 which name changed to Barnett Banks, Inc. 04/24/1987 which merged into NationsBank Corp. (NC) 01/09/1998 which reincorporated in Delaware as BankAmerica Corp. (Old) 09/25/1998 which merged into BankAmerica Corp. (New) 09/30/1998 which name changed to Bank of America Corp. 04/28/1999

ENGLEWOOD BK (ENGLEWOOD, FL)
Common $1 par called for redemption at $5 on 11/18/97

ENGLEWOOD NATL BK & TR CO (ENGLEWOOD, NJ)
Merged into Midland Bank & Trust Co. (Paramus, NJ) 8/19/68
Each share Common Capital Stock $10 par exchanged for (1) share Common $5 par
Midland Bank & Trust Co. (Paramus, NJ) reorganized as Midland Bancorporation, Inc. 7/31/85 which merged into Valley National Bancorp 3/1/97

ENGLEWOOD SAVINGS & LOAN ASSOCIATION (CO)
Name changed to Key Savings & Loan Association 2/24/66

ENGLISH CHINA CLAYS P L C OLD (ENGLAND)
Name changed to ECC Group PLC 03/01/1990
ECC Group PLC name changed to English China Clays PLC (New) 05/14/1992
(See English China Clays PLC (New))

ENGLISH CHINA CLAYS PLC NEW (ENGLAND)
ADR agreement terminated 06/27/1997
Each Sponsored ADR for Ordinary 25p par exchanged for (3) Ordinary Shares 25p par
Note: Unexchanged ADR's will be sold and the proceeds, if any, held for claim after 06/27/1999

ENGLISH ELEC LTD (ENGLAND)
ADR agreement terminated 12/20/1968
Each ADR for Ordinary Reg. £1 par exchanged for (1.666666) General Electric & English Electric Companies Ltd. ADR's for Ordinary Reg. 5s par and 36s principal amount of 7-1/4% Conv. Unsecured Loan Stock due 1987/1992
General Electric & English Electric Companies Ltd. name changed to General Electric Co. PLC (New) 09/18/1970 which name changed to Marconi plc 11/26/1999 which name changed to M (2003) plc 01/16/2004
(See M (2003) plc)

ENGLISH ELECTRIC CO. OF CANADA LTD.
Acquired by Inglis (John) Co. Ltd. in 1948
Each share Class A exchanged for (2) shares Capital Stock no par and $3 in cash
Each (2) shares Class B exchanged for (1) share Capital Stock no par
Inglis (John) Co. Ltd. name changed to Inglis Ltd. 6/4/73
(See Inglis Ltd.)

ENGLISH FURNITURE INDS INC (DE)
Charter cancelled and declared inoperative and void for non-payment of taxes 3/1/96

ENGLISH GREENHOUSE PRODS CORP (DE)
Charter cancelled and declared inoperative and void for non-payment of taxes 6/26/90

ENGLISH LANGUAGE LEARNING & INSTRN SYS INC (DE)
Acquired by Pearson PLC 6/19/2006
Each share Common 1¢ par exchanged for $0.195 cash
Note: Holders may receive additional payments from escrow

ENGLISH OIL CO. (NV)
Completely liquidated 12/00/1962
Each share Common $1 par exchanged for first and final disribution of (0.4) share King Oil, Inc. Common $1 par

ENG-ENR

King Oil, Inc. recapitalized as Lane Wood, Inc. 08/10/1964
(See Lane Wood, Inc.)

ENGLISH SPEAKING WORLD, INC. (NY)
Proclaimed dissolved for failure to file reports and pay fees 12/16/29

ENGLOBE CORP (CANADA)
Acquired by ONCAP II L.P. 01/17/2011
Each share Common no par exchanged for $0.265 cash

ENGRAPH INC (NC)
Common $1 par split (5) for (4) by issuance of (0.25) additional share 1/16/78
Common $1 par split (5) for (4) by issuance of (0.25) additional share 2/25/83
Common $1 par split (5) for (4) by issuance of (0.25) additional share 2/24/84
Common $1 par split (5) for (4) by issuance of (0.25) additional share 3/22/85
Common $1 par split (5) for (4) by issuance of (0.25) additional share 3/21/86
Common $1 par split (5) for (4) by issuance of (0.25) additional share 9/16/88
Common $1 par split (4) for (3) by issuance of (1/3) additional share 6/16/89
Common $1 par split (5) for (4) by issuance of (0.25) additional share 6/15/90
Stock Dividends - 100% 1/6/76; 10% 5/22/81; 10% 5/21/82; 10% 3/27/87; 10% 3/18/88
Merged into Envoy Holdings, Inc. 10/21/93
Each share Common $1 par exchanged for $15.63 cash

ENGRAVING MASTERS INC (NV)
Name changed to Blue Line Protection Group, Inc. 05/20/2014

ENHANCE BIOTECH INC (DE)
Common $0.001 par split (3) for (2) by issuance of (0.5) additional share payable 03/05/2004 to holders of record 01/28/2004 Ex date - 03/08/2004
Company terminated registration of common stock and is no longer public as of 01/29/2007
Details not available

ENHANCE FINL SVCS GROUP INC (NY)
Common 10¢ par split (2) for (1) by issuance of (1) additional share payable 6/26/98 to holders of record 6/12/98
Merged into Radian Group Inc. 2/28/2001
Each share Common 10¢ par exchanged for (0.22) share Common $0.001 par

ENHANCE-YOUR-REPUTATION COM INC (FL)
Name changed to Force Protection Video Equipment Corp. 03/05/2015

ENHANCED ELECTRS CORP (TX)
Name changed to Curtis Mathes Holding Corp. 05/23/1994
Curtis Mathes Holding Corp. name changed to uniView Technologies Corp. 01/30/1998 which name changed to VPGI Corp. 08/14/2003
(See VPGI Corp.)

ENHANCED ENERGY SVCS LTD (AB)
Recapitalized as EnSource Energy Services Inc. 03/12/2001
Each share Common no par exchanged for (0.25) share Common no par
EnSource Energy Services Inc. acquired by Enerflex Systems Ltd. (Canada) 07/24/2002 which reorganized in Alberta as Enerflex Systems Income Fund 10/02/2006 which merged into Toromont Industries Ltd. 02/26/2010

ENHANCED EQUITY YIELD & PREM FD INC (MD)
Issue Information - 16,000,000 shares COM offered at $20 per share on 06/27/2005
Name changed to BlackRock Enhanced Equity Yield & Premium Fund, Inc. 10/02/2006
BlackRock Enhanced Equity Yield & Premium Fund, Inc. merged into BlackRock Enhanced Capital & Income Fund, Inc. 11/03/2008

ENHANCED EQUITY YIELD FD INC (MD)
Issue Information - 18,500,000 shares COM offered at $20 per share on 05/03/2005
Name changed to BlackRock Enhanced Equity Yield Fund, Inc. 10/02/2006
BlackRock Enhanced Equity Yield Fund, Inc. merged into BlackRock Enhanced Capital & Income Fund, Inc. 11/03/2008

ENHANCED GOVT FD INC (MD)
Issue Information - 12,000,000 shares COM offered at $20 per share at 10/26/2005
Name changed to BlackRock Enhanced Government Fund, Inc. 10/2/2006

ENHANCED IMAGING TECHNOLOGIES INC (DE)
Name changed to E for M Corp. 7/15/94
(See E for M Corp.)

ENHANCED OIL RES INC (BC)
Each share old Common no par exchanged for (0.1) share new Common no par 01/21/2015
Name changed to Hunter Oil Corp. 08/16/2016

ENHANCED RES 1986 INC (AB)
Recapitalized as Hockey Hose Athletic Inc. 5/14/91
Each share Common no par exchanged for (0.1) share Common no par
Hockey Hose Athletic Inc. recapitalized as Tri-Northern Pacific Resources Ltd. 10/4/93

ENHANCED S&P 500 COVERED CALL FD INC (MD)
Completely liquidated 05/24/2010
Each share Common $0.001 par exchanged for first and final distribution of $8.039734 cash

ENHANCED SYS TECHNOLOGIES LTD (AUSTRALIA)
ADR agreement terminated 07/01/2015
Each Sponsored ADR for Ordinary exchanged for $3.251547 cash

ENHEAT INC (CANADA)
Name changed 6/9/80
Name changed from Enheat Ltd. to Enheat Inc. 6/9/80
Each share Class A Common no par exchanged for (2) shares Class A Subordinate no par and (1) share Conv. Class B Multiple no par 8/1/86
Each share Class B Common no par exchanged for (2) shares Class A Subordinate no par and (1) share Conv. Class B Multiple no par 8/1/86
Acquired by Amherst Aerospace Inc. 8/31/88
Details not available

ENIGMA SOFTWARE GROUP INC (DE)
Name changed to City Loan, Inc. (DE) 06/05/2008
City Loan, Inc. (DE) reorganized in Nevada 09/17/2008

ENIRO AB (SWEDEN)
ADR agreement terminated 05/21/2018
No ADR's remain outstanding

ENJOY MEDIA HLDGS LTD (CA)
Name changed to Square Inn Budget Hotels Management, Inc. 06/29/2007

ENLIGHTEN SOFTWARE SOLUTIONS INC (CA)
Reorganized under the laws of Delaware as Diversified Opportunities, Inc. 02/12/2008
Each share Common no par exchanged for (0.04) share Common no par
Diversified Opportunities, Inc. name changed to Sugarmade, Inc. 07/15/2011

ENLIGHTENED GOURMET INC (NV)
SEC revoked common stock registration 05/01/2014

ENLIVEN MARKETING TECHNOLOGIES CORP (DE)
Merged into DG FastChannel, Inc. 10/02/2008
Each share Common $0.001 par exchanged for (0.03333333) share Common $0.001 par
DG FastChannel, Inc. name changed to Digital Generation, Inc. 11/07/2011 which merged into Sizmek Inc. 02/07/2014
(See Sizmek Inc.)

ENM HOLDINGS LTD (HONG KONG)
ADR agreement terminated 01/05/2015
No ADR's remain outstanding

ENNCITE CTL INC (DE)
Recapitalized as Oxford Knight International Inc. (DE) 2/10/98
Each share Common $0.001 par exchanged for (0.01) share Common $0.00001 par
Oxford Knight International Inc. (DE) reincorporated in Texas which name changed to Montrose National Partners Inc. 2/23/2004 which name changed to Cross Atlantic Life & Science Technology Inc. 8/19/2005 which name changed to Deep Earth Resources, Inc. 5/5/2006

ENNIS BRANDON COMPUTER SVCS INC (NV)
Name changed to Cardinal Corp. and Common $1 par changed to 10¢ par 05/02/1972
Cardinal Corp. recapitalized as Communications Corp. of America 11/19/1976
(See Communications Corp. of America)

ENNIS BUSINESS FORMS INC (TX)
Common $2.50 par split (2) for (1) by issuance of (1) additional share 12/10/69
Common $2.50 par split (3) for (2) by issuance of (0.5) additional share 6/25/79
Common $2.50 par split (2) for (1) by issuance of (1) additional share 7/11/83
Common $2.50 par split (2) for (1) by issuance of (1) additional share 7/17/85
Common $2.50 par split (3) for (2) by issuance of (0.5) additional share 3/20/87
Common $2.50 par split (3) for (2) by issuance of (0.5) additional share 7/24/89
Common $2.50 par split (3) for (2) by issuance of (0.5) additional share 7/31/91
Stock Dividends - 50% 12/1/63; 25% 12/1/64
Name changed to Ennis, Inc. 6/17/2004

ENNISTEEL CORP (ON)
Acquired by Acier Leroux Inc. 09/29/1994
Each share Class A Subordinate no par exchanged for $1.16 cash

ENODIS PLC (UNITED KINGDOM)
ADR agreement terminated 6/22/2005
Each Sponsored ADR for Ordinary exchanged for $8.97219 cash

ENOTE COM INC (DE)
Charter cancelled and declared void for failure to pay franchise taxes 3/1/2003

ENOTES SYS INC (DE)
Name changed to Veridigm, Inc. 12/07/2006
Veridigm, Inc. recapitalized as Mobile Media Unlimited Holdings Inc. 02/02/2009 which recapitalized as EnableTS, Inc. 04/18/2011

ENOVA CORP (CA)
Merged into Sempra Energy 6/26/98
Each share Common no par exchanged for (1) share Common no par

ENOVA HLDGS INC (NV)
SEC revoked common stock registration 02/19/2008

ENPAR TECHNOLOGIES INC (ON)
Name changed to Current Water Technologies Inc. 01/02/2018

ENPATH MED INC (MN)
Merged into Greatbatch, Inc. 06/18/2007
Each share Common 1¢ par exchanged for $14.38 cash

ENQUEST ENERGY SVCS CORP (AB)
Merged into TransForce Inc. 08/17/2010
Each share Common no par exchanged for $0.16 cash
Note: An additional $0.01 cash per share will be held in escrow for possible future distribution
Unexchanged certificates will be cancelled and become without value 08/17/2015

ENQUEST PLC (UNITED KINGDOM)
ADR agreement terminated 06/14/2018
No ADR's remain outstanding

ENQUIRER/STAR GROUP INC (DE)
Name changed to American Media, Inc. 11/18/94
(See American Media, Inc.)

ENRAY AUTOSYSTEMS INC (NV)
Name changed to KCM Holdings Corp. 04/16/2007

ENREC CORP (NM)
Charter revoked 8/12/99

ENRIC ENERGY EQUIPMENT HLDGS LTD (CAYMAN ISLANDS)
Name changed to CIMC Enric Holdings Ltd. 04/20/2010

ENRICH GOLD MINES LTD.
Acquired by Enrich Mines (1945) Ltd. on a (25) for (1) basis in 1945
(See Enrich Mines (1945) Ltd.)

ENRICH MINES (1945) LTD. (ON)
Charter cancelled for failure to pay taxes and file returns 3/5/75

ENROC INDS INC (CO)
Each share Common 1¢ par exchanged for (0.1) share Common 10¢ par 02/09/1972
Chapter XI bankruptcy proceedings dismissed 08/19/1980
No stockholders' equity

ENROL CORP (UT)
Name changed to E-Power International Inc. 01/22/2001
E-Power International Inc. recapitalized as Integrated Services Group Inc. 01/29/2003
(See Integrated Services Group Inc.)

ENRON CAP RES L P (DE)
Plan of reorganization under Chapter 11 Federal Bankruptcy Code effective 11/17/2004
Details not available

ENRON CAP TR I (DE)
Plan of reorganization under Chapter 11 Federal Bankruptcy Code effective 11/17/2004
Holders may receive a future distribution

ENRON CAP TR II (DE)
Plan of reorganization under Chapter 11 Federal Bankruptcy Code effective 11/17/2004
Holders may receive a future distribution

ENRON CORP (OR)
Reincorporated 07/01/1997
6.40% Preferred $100 par called for redemption 05/01/1987
6.84% Preferred $100 par called for redemption 05/01/1987
8.48% Preferred $100 par called for redemption 05/01/1987
5.60% Preferred $100 par called for redemption 10/01/1987
$10.50 2nd Preferred $100 par called for redemption 08/01/1989
Common $10 par split (2) for (1) by issuance of (1) additional share 12/30/1991
Common $10 par split (2) for (1) by issuance of (1) additional share 08/16/1993
State of incorporation changed from (DE) to (OR) and Common $10 par changed to no par 07/01/1997
Common no par split (2) for (1) by issuance of (1) additional share payable 08/13/1999 to holders of record 07/23/1999 Ex date - 08/16/1999
Plan of reorganization under Chapter 11 Federal Bankruptcy Code effective 11/17/2004
Stockholders' equity unlikely

ENRON GLOBAL PWR & PIPELINES L L C (DE)
Merged into Enron Corp. 11/18/97
Each share Common no par exchanged for (0.9189) share Common no par
(See Enron Corp.)

ENRON LIQUIDS PIPELINE L P (DE)
Name changed to Kinder Morgan Energy Partners, L.P. 02/15/1997
Kinder Morgan Energy Partners, L.P. merged into Kinder Morgan, Inc. 11/26/2014

ENRON OIL & GAS CO (DE)
Common 1¢ par split (2) for (1) by issuance of (1) additional share 6/15/94
Name changed to EOG Resources Inc. 9/15/99

ENROTEK CORP (NV)
Name changed 08/03/1992
Name changed 09/20/1993
Name changed from Enrotek Ltd. to Enrotek Properties, Inc. 08/03/1992
Name changed from Enrotek Properties, Inc. to Enrotek Corp. 09/20/1993
Charter revoked for failure to file reports and pay fees 12/01/2005

ENS BIO LOGICALS INC (CANADA)
Name changed to Enscor Inc. 6/3/87
Enscor Inc. name changed to Rose Corp. 6/1/98
(See Rose Corp.)

ENSCO INC (MN)
Under plan of reorganization each share Common 1¢ par automatically became (2) shares Environmental Systems Co. Common 1¢ par 8/18/83
(See Environmental Systems Co.)

ENSCO INTL INC (DE)
Common 10¢ par split (2) for (1) by issuance of (1) additional share payable 09/15/1997 to holders of record 09/02/1997 Ex date - 09/16/1997
Reorganized under the laws of England & Wales as Ensco International PLC 12/23/2009
Each share Common 10¢ par exchanged for (1) Sponsored ADR for Class A Ordinary
Ensco International PLC name changed to Ensco PLC 03/31/2010

ENSCO PLC (ENGLAND & WALES)
Name changed 03/31/2010
Name changed from Ensco International PLC to Ensco PLC 03/31/2010
ADR agreement terminated 05/22/2012
Each Sponsored ADR for Ordinary exchanged for (1) share Class A Ordinary USD $0.10 par
(Additional Information in Active)

ENSCOR INC (CANADA)
Name changed to Rose Corp. 06/01/1998
(See Rose Corp.)

ENSEC INTL INC (FL)
Recapitalized as Lotta Coal, Inc. 07/27/2006
Each share Common 1¢ par exchanged for (0.001) share Common 1¢ par
(See Lotta Coal, Inc.)

ENSECO ENERGY SVCS CORP (AB)
Each share old Common no par exchanged for (0.1) share new Common no par 10/20/2011
Discharged from receivership 08/25/2016
No stockholders' equity

ENSECO INC (DE)
Acquired by Corning Inc. 06/02/1989
Each share Common 1¢ par exchanged for (0.419) share Common $1 par

ENSEL CORP (AB)
Name changed to Surge Resources Inc. 05/04/2005
Surge Resources Inc. name changed to Eaglewood Energy Inc. 11/05/2007
(See Eaglewood Energy Inc.)

ENSERCH CORP (TX)
$10.32 Preferred Ser. A no par called for redemption 05/01/1987
Adjustable Rate Preferred Ser. D no par called for redemption 03/11/1994
Common $10 par changed to $6.66666666 par and (0.5) additional share issued 05/12/1978
Common $6.66666666 par changed to $4.45 par and (0.5) additional share issued 05/15/1981
Common $4.45 par changed to 1¢ par 08/04/1997
Each share Common 1¢ par received distribution of (1.4995056) shares Enserch Exploration, Inc. Common $1 par payable 08/18/1997 to holders of record 08/04/1997
Merged into Texas Utilities Co. 08/05/1997
Each share Common 1¢ par exchanged for (0.225) share Common no par
Texas Utilities Co. reorganized as Texas Utilities Co. (Holding Co.) 08/05/1997
Adjustable Depositary Preferred Ser. E called for redemption at $100 on 01/16/1998
Texas Utilities Co. (Holding Co.) name changed to TXU Corp. 05/16/2000
(See TXU Corp.)
Name changed to TXU Gas Co. 06/00/1999
(See TXU Gas Co.)

ENSERCH EXPL INC (TX)
Name changed to EEX Corp. 12/19/1997
EEX Corp. merged into Newfield Exploration Co. 11/26/2002

ENSERCH EXPL PARTNERS LTD (TX)
Reorganized as Enserch Exploration Inc. 12/30/1994
Each Depositary Unit exchanged for (1) share Common $1 par
Enserch Exploration Inc. name changed to EEX Corp. 12/19/1997 which merged into Newfield Exploration Co. 11/26/2002

ENSERCO ENERGY SVC CO INC (CANADA)
Acquired by Nabors Industries, Inc. 04/26/2002
Each share Common no par exchanged for $15.6529 cash

ENSERV CORP (AB)
Merged into Precision Drilling Corp. 05/27/1996
Each share Common no par exchanged for (0.56357) shares Common no par and $2.03 cash
(See Precision Drilling Corp.)

ENSIGN GOLD MINES, LTD. (ON)
Charter cancelled 08/04/1952

ENSIGN OILS LTD (AB)
Merged into Houston Oils Ltd. 02/02/1971
Each share Common no par exchanged for (1.333333) shares Capital Stock no par
Houston Oils Ltd. recapitalized as Bridger Petroleum Corp. Ltd. 10/09/1975
(See Bridger Petroleum Corp. Ltd.)

ENSIGN RESOURCE SVC GROUP INC (AB)
Common no par split (3) for (1) by issuance of (2) additional shares payable 06/04/2001 to holders of record 05/31/2001 Ex date - 05/29/2001
Name changed to Ensign Energy Services Inc. 06/07/2005

ENSIGN SVCS INC (NV)
SEC revoked common stock registation 03/05/2013

ENSOURCE ENERGY SVCS INC (AB)
Acquired by Enerflex Systems Ltd. (Canada) 07/24/2002
Each share Common no par exchanged for (0.26) share Common no par
Enerflex Systems Ltd. (Canada) reorganized in Alberta as Enerflex Systems Income Fund 10/02/2006 which merged into Toromont Industries Ltd. 02/26/2010

ENSOURCE INC (DE)
Each share Common 1¢ par exchanged for (1) share Common 10¢ par 05/15/1986
Acquired by United Meridian Corp. 09/12/1989
Each share Common $10 par exchanged for $10.50 cash

ENSR CORP (TX)
Merged into American NuKEM Corp. 06/01/1990
Each share Common 1¢ par exchanged for $8.25 cash

ENSTAR CORP (DE)
Stock Dividend - In Conv. Preferred Ser. A to holders of Common 10% 09/21/1983
Merged into Unimar Co. 09/25/1984
Each share Conv. Preferred Ser. A $1 par exchanged for (7) Indonesian Participating Units and $14 cash
Each share Common $1 par exchanged for (1) Indonesian Participating Unit and $2 cash
(See Unimar Co.)

ENSTAR CORP (MN)
Merged into North Star Universal Inc. 08/21/1985
Each share Common 10¢ par exchanged for (0.04) share $11 Preferred $100 par
(See North Star Universal Inc.)

ENSTAR GROUP INC (DE)
Plan of reorganization under Chapter 11 Federal Bankruptcy proceedings confirmed 02/24/1992
Existing shares were cancelled and are without value
Second amended plan of reorganization under Chapter 11 Federal Bankruptcy proceedings effective 03/27/1997
Holders of record 06/01/1992 will receive (0.1) share Enstar Group, Inc. (GA) Common 1¢ par for each share owned upon submitting a certification of ownership of cancelled stock prior to 12/31/1997

ENSTAR GROUP INC (GA)
Merged into Enstar Group Ltd. 01/31/2007
Each share Common 1¢ par exchanged for (1) share Ordinary $1 par

ENSTAR INC (MN)
Merged into Enstar Acquisition Inc. 12/01/1999
Each share Common no par exchanged for $12.50 cash

ENSTAR INCOME PROGRAM L P (GA)
Liquidation completed
Each Unit of Ltd. Partnership Int. II $250 par received initial distribution of $373 cash payable 11/04/2002 to holders of record 11/04/2002
Each Unit of Ltd. Partnership Int. II $250 par received second and final distribution of $124 cash payable 12/31/2002 to holders of record 12/31/2002

ENSTAR INDONESIA INC (DE)
Non-Vtg. Part. Preferred 1983 Ser. 1¢ par called for redemption 03/12/1991
Public interest eliminated

ENSTROM (R.J.) CORP. (MI)
Name changed to Enstrom Helicopter Corp. 03/01/1973
(See Enstrom Helicopter Corp.)

ENSTROM HELICOPTER CORP (MI)
Through purchase offer 100% acquired by Aircraft Management Associates, Inc. as of 03/01/1978
Public interest eliminated

ENSUN CORP (DE)
Charter cancelled and declared inoperative and void for non-payment of taxes 03/01/1994

ENSYS ENVIRONMENTAL PRODS INC (DE)
Name changed to Strategic Diagnostics Inc. (New) 01/02/1997
Strategic Diagnostics Inc. (New) name changed to Special Diversified Opportunities Inc. 09/19/2013 which recapitalized as Standard Diversified Opportunities Inc. 06/02/2017 which name changed to Standard Diversified Inc. 04/25/2018

ENTAREA INVT MGMT LTD (ON)
Name changed to Entarea Management Ltd. 05/29/1969

ENTEC PRODS CORP (CO)
Each share Common $0.001 par exchanged for (0.2) share Common no par 10/01/1982
Charter suspended for failure to maintain a registered agent 08/29/1983

ENTEC PRODS INTL INC (UT)
Proclaimed dissolved for failure to pay taxes 05/01/1990

ENTECH ENVIRONMENTAL TECHNOLOGIES INC (FL)
Recapitalized as SkyPeople Fruit Juice, Inc. 06/09/2008
Each share Common $0.001 par exchanged for (0.00304201) share Common $0.001 par
SkyPeople Fruit Juice, Inc. name changed to Future FinTech Group Inc. 06/12/2017

ENTECH INVTS INC (AB)
Merged into CAPVEST Income Corp. 01/01/2005
Each share Common no par exchanged for (1) share Common no par
(See CAPVEST Income Corp.)

ENTECH SOLAR INC (DE)
SEC revoked common stock registration 10/22/2014

ENTEGRIS INC (MN)
Reincorporated under the laws of Delaware 08/06/2005

ENTEK OIL & GAS LTD (BC)
Name changed to Amerivest Properties Inc. 04/16/1986
(See Amerivest Properties Inc.)

ENTELLUS MED INC (DE)
Acquired by Stryker Corp. 02/28/2018
Each share Common $0.001 par exchanged for $24 cash

ENTENMANNS INC (NY)
Common 1¢ par split (3) for (2) by issuance of (0.5) additional share 06/14/1978
Merged into W-L Products Co. 01/26/1979
Each share Common 1¢ par exchanged for $30 cash

ENTER, INC. (UT)
Recapitalized as Cornerstone Leisure Industries, Inc. 04/24/1986
Each share Common $0.001 par exchanged for (0.33333333) share Common 1¢ par

ENTER CORP (DE)
Name changed to Brainy Brands Co., Inc. 12/28/2010

ENTER TECH CORP (NV)
Charter revoked for failure to file reports and pay fees 04/01/2001

ENTERACTIVE INC (DE)
Name changed to Cornerstone Internet Solutions Co. 07/07/1998
Cornerstone Internet Solutions Co. reorganized as Smave Solutions, Inc. 07/14/2005

ENTERASYS NETWORKS INC (DE)
Each share old Common 1¢ par exchanged for (0.125) share new Common 1¢ par 10/28/2005
Merged into Gores ENT Holdings, Inc. 03/01/2006
Each share new Common 1¢ par exchanged for $13.92 cash

ENTERAYON INC (DE)
Recapitalized as North Bay Resources Inc. 02/07/2008
Each share Common exchanged for (0.1) share Common

ENTERBANK HLDGS INC (DE)
Common 1¢ par split (3) for (1) by issuance of (2) additional shares 09/29/1999
Name changed to Enterprise Financial Services Corp. 04/29/2002

ENTERCOM COMMUNICATIONS CAP TR (DE)
Term Income Deferrable Equity Securities called for redemption at $51.563 on 04/07/2003

ENTERCONNECT INC (NV)
Charter revoked for failure to file reports and pay taxes 11/30/2010

ENTERCOR ENTMT CORP (AB)
Recapitalized as Entercor Resource Corp. 02/25/2005
Each share Common no par exchanged for (0.2) share Common no par

ENTERGY ARK INC (AR)
$2.40 Preferred 1¢ par called for redemption 10/01/1996
8.84% Preferred $25 par called for redemption 10/01/1996
9.92% Preferred $25 par called for redemption at $25 on 06/01/1999
8.52% Preferred $100 par called for redemption at $100 on 11/01/1999
$1.96 Preferred 1¢ par called for redemption at $25 on 04/24/2006
7.32% Preferred $100 par called for redemption at $103.17 on 04/24/2006
$7.40 Preferred $100 par called for redemption at $102.80 on 04/24/2006
7.8% Preferred $100 par called for redemption at $103.25 on 04/24/2006
7.88% Preferred $100 par called for redemption at $103 on 04/24/2006
$6.08 Preferred $100 par called for redemption at $102.83 plus $1.249778 accrued dividends on 09/15/2016
6.45% Preferred $100 par called for redemption at $25 plus $0.331458 accrued dividends on 09/15/2016
(Additional Information in Active)

ENTERGY ARK CAP I (DE)
Issue Information - 2,400,000 GTD QUARTERLY INCOME PFD SECS A 8.50% offered at $25 per share on 08/08/1996
8.50% Guaranteed Quarterly Income Preferred Securities Ser. A called for redemption at $25 on 11/12/2004

ENTERGY CORP (DE)
Each 7.65% Equity Unit automatically became (0.6598) share Common 1¢ par 02/17/2009
(Additional Information in Active)

ENTERGY CORP (FL)
Reincorporated under the laws of Delaware and Common $5 par changed to 1¢ par 12/31/93

ENTERGY GULF STS CAP I (DE)
8.75% Guaranteed Quarterly Income Preferred Securities Ser. A called for redemption at $25 on 3/12/2005

ENTERGY GULF STS INC (TX)
$8.52 Preferred $100 par called for redemption 03/15/1997
$9.96 Dividend Preferred $100 par called for redemption 03/15/1997
$8.64 Dividend Preferred $100 par called for redemption at $101 on 03/15/1999
$8.80 Preferred $100 par called for redemption at $100 on 03/15/1999
$1.75 Preferred no par called for redemption on 05/16/2000
Adjustable Rate Preferred Ser. A $100 par called for redemption at $100 on 12/30/2007
Ser. B Depositary Preferred called for redemption at $50 on 12/30/2007
$4.20 Preferred $100 par called for redemption at $102.818 on 12/30/2007
$4.40 Preferred $100 par called for redemption at $103 on 12/30/2007
$4.40 Preferred 1944 Ser. $100 par called for redemption at $108 plus $4.40 accrued dividends on 12/30/2007
$4.44 Preferred $100 par called for redemption at $103.75 on 12/30/2007
$4.52 Preferred $100 par called for redemption at $103.57 on 12/30/2007
$5 Preferred $100 par called for redemption at $104.25 on 12/30/2007
$5.08 Preferred $100 par called for redemption at $104.63 plus $5.08 accrued dividends on 12/30/2007
$6.08 Preferred $100 par called for redemption at $103.34 on 12/30/2007
$7.56 Preferred $100 par called for redemption at $101.80 on 12/30/2007
Name changed to Entergy Gulf States Louisiana, LLC and 8.25% 144A Preference Ser. A no par reclassified as 8.25% 144A Membership Int. Preferred Ser. A 12/31/2007
(See Entergy Gulf States Louisiana, LLC)

ENTERGY GULF STS LA LLC (TX)
Reincorporated 09/21/2015
State of incorporation changed from (LA) to (TX) 09/21/2015
8.25% 144A Membership Int. Preferred Ser. A called for redemption at $100 plus $2.0625 accrued dividends on 09/28/2015

ENTERGY LA HLDGS INC (TX)
Reincorporated 12/31/2005
Name changed 2/13/2006
8.56% Preferred $100 par called for redemption 9/9/96
9.68% Preferred $25 par called for redemption 9/9/96
12.64% Preferred $25 par called for redemption 2/1/97
7% Preferred $25 par called for redemption at $100 on 2/1/99
8% Preferred Ser. 1991 $100 par called for redemption at $100 on 9/1/2001
State of incorporation changed from (LA) to (TX) 12/31/2005
Name changed from Entergy Louisiana, Inc. to Entergy Louisiana Holdings, Inc. 2/13/2006
4.44% Preferred $100 par called for redemption at $104.06 on 6/15/2006
4.96% Preferred $100 par called for redemption at $104.25 on 6/15/2006
5.16% Preferred $100 par called for redemption at $104.18 on 6/15/2006
5.40% Preferred $100 par called for redemption at $103 on 6/15/2006
6.44% Preferred $100 par called for redemption at $102.92 on 6/15/2006
7.36% Preferred $100 par called for redemption at $103.36 on 6/15/2006
7.84% Preferred $100 par called for redemption at $103.78 on 6/15/2006
8% Preferred Ser. 1992 $25 par called for redemption at $25 on 6/15/2006
4.16% Preferred $100 par called for redemption at $104.21 plus $0.508442 accrued dividends on 6/19/2006

ENTERGY LA LLC (TX)
6.95% Membership Int. Preferred Ser. A called for redemption at $100 plus $0.250972 accrued dividends on 09/28/2015
6.95% 144A Membership Int. Preferred Ser. A called for redemption at $100 plus $0.250972 accrued dividends on 09/28/2015

ENTERGY LONDON CAP L P
Name changed to EDF London Capital, L.P. 12/11/98
(See EDF London Capital, L.P.)

ENTERGY LA CAP I (DE)
Issue Information - 2,800,000 QUARTERLY INCOME PFD SECS SER A 9.00% offered at $25 per share on 07/10/1996
9% Quarterly Income Preferred Securities called for redemption at $25 on 11/4/2004

ENTERGY MISS INC (MS)
9.76% Preferred $100 par called for redemption 01/01/1997
9.16% Preferred $100 par called for redemption at $104.06 on 08/01/1997
7.44% Preferred $100 par called for redemption at $102.81 plus $1.673946 accrued dividends on 07/22/2005
8.36% Preferred $100 par called for redemption at $100 plus $1.880999 accrued dividends on 07/22/2005
6.25% Preferred $25 par called for redemption at $25 plus $0.329861 accrued dividends on 10/17/2016
(Additional Information in Active)

ENTERNET INC (NV)
Name changed to Secured Data, Inc. and (4) additional shares issued 05/31/2002
Secured Data, Inc. recaptialized as Huifeng Bio-Pharmaceutical Technology Inc. 10/12/2005

ENTEROMEDICS INC (DE)
Each share old Common 1¢ par exchanged for (0.16666666) share new Common 1¢ par 07/12/2010
Each share new Common 1¢ par exchanged again for (0.06666666) share new Common 1¢ par 01/07/2016
Each share new Common 1¢ par exchanged again for (0.01428571) share new Common 1¢ par 12/28/2016
Name changed to ReShape Lifesciences Inc. 10/23/2017

ENTERPRISE ACQUISITION CORP (DE)
Issue Information - 25,000,000 UNITS consisting of (1) share COM and (1) WT offered at $10 per Unit on 11/07/2007
Units separated 11/09/2009
Merged into ARMOUR Residential REIT, Inc. 11/09/2009
Each share Common $0.0001 par exchanged for (1) share Common $0.001 par

ENTERPRISE BANCORP (CA)
Stock Dividend - 15% 01/31/1983
Placed in receivership 04/26/1985
No stockholders' equity

ENTERPRISE BANCORP INC (NC)
Merged into Triangle Bank & Trust Co. (Raleigh, NC) 06/28/1991
Each share Common $1 par exchanged for (1) share Common $5 par
Triangle Bank & Trust Co. (Raleigh, NC) reorganized as Triangle Bancorp, Inc. 11/26/1991 which merged into Centura Banks, Inc. 02/18/2000 which merged into Royal Bank of Canada (Montreal, QC) 06/05/2001

ENTERPRISE BK & TR CO (LOWELL, MA)
Under plan of reorganization each share Class A Common $1 par automatically became (1) share Enterprise Bancorp, Inc. Class A Common 1¢ par 7/26/96

ENTERPRISE BK (ALLISON PARK, PA)
Under plan of reorganization each share Class A Common no par automatically became (1) share Enterprise Financial Services Group, Inc. Class A Common 1¢ par 11/13/2006

ENTERPRISE BK (KENILWORTH, NJ)
Name changed to Enterprise Bank N.J. (Kenilworth, NJ) 11/16/2006
Enterprise National Bank N.J. (Kenilworth, NJ) name changed to Enterprise Bank N.J. (Kenilworth, NJ) 03/10/2016

ENTERPRISE BANK CORP. (RESTON, VA)
Merged into Washington Bancorporation 12/31/86
Each share Common $2 par exchanged for (5) shares Common $2.50 par
(See Washington Bancorporation)

ENTERPRISE CAP CORP (AB)
Reorganized under the laws of British Columbia as Ecuador Gold & Copper Corp. 07/12/2012
Each share Common no par exchanged for (0.8) share Common no par
Ecuador Gold & Copper Corp. merged into Lumina Gold Corp. 11/01/2016

ENTERPRISE CAP CORP (FL)
Name changed to Pallet Management Systems Inc. 12/08/1994
(See Pallet Management Systems Inc.)

ENTERPRISE CAP TR I (DE)
Issue Information - 9,000,000 TR ORIG PFD SECS SER A 7.44% offered at $25 per share on 01/14/1998
7.44% Trust Originated Preferred Securities Ser. A called for redemption at $25 plus $0.036166 accrued dividends on 10/7/2005

ENTERPRISE CAP TR III (DE)
Issue Information - 6,000,000 TR ORIGINATED PFD SECS 7.25% SER C offered at $25 per share on 06/30/1998
7.25% Trust Originated Preferred Securities Ser. C called for redemption at $25 on 10/20/2005

ENTERPRISE CONSLDTN CORP (DE)
Name changed to Billiard Channel Inc. 03/14/2000
(See Billiard Channel Inc.)

ENTERPRISE DEV CORP (AB)
Delisted from Canadian Venture Exchange 05/31/2001

ENTERPRISE DEV CORP (BC)
Recapitalized as Magenta Development Corp. 03/28/1984
Each share Common no par exchanged for (0.2) share Common no par
(See Magenta Development Corp.)

ENTERPRISE DEV GROUP (MA)
Merged into Apex Oil Co. 08/10/1982
Each Share of Bene. Int. $1 par exchanged for $10.50 cash

ENTERPRISE ENERGY N L (AUSTRALIA)
Name changed 02/12/2004
Each Unsponsored ADR for Ordinary A$0.25 par exchanged for (1) Sponsored ADR for Ordinary A$0.25 par 12/17/1987
Name changed from Enterprise Gold Mines N.L. to Enterprise Energy N.L. 02/12/2004
ADR agreement terminated 02/20/2007
Each Sponsored ADR for Ordinary A$0.25 par exchanged for $0.0017 cash 10/02/2007

ENTERPRISE ENERGY RES LTD (BC)
Merged into LNG Energy Ltd. 08/20/2013
Each share Common no par exchanged for (5) shares Common no par
LNG Energy Ltd. recapitalized as Esrey Energy Ltd. 11/18/2013 which name changed to Esrey Resources Ltd. 10/16/2017

ENTERPRISE ENTMT GROUP INC (NV)
Recapitalized as Andromeda Capital Corp. 07/29/1994
Each share Common 1¢ par exchanged for (0.01) share Common 1¢ par
Andromeda Capital Corp. name changed to Home Capital Investment Corp. 12/16/1994
(See Home Capital Investment Corp.)

ENTERPRISE FD INC (DE)
Capital Stock $1 par split (3) for (1) by issuance of (2) additional shares 01/09/1968
Reincorporated under the laws of Maryland as American General Enterprise Fund, Inc. 01/15/1979
American General Enterprise Fund, Inc. name changed to American Capital Enterprise Fund, Inc. (MD) 09/09/1983 which reincorporated in Delaware as Van Kampen American Capital Enterprise Fund 08/03/1995 which name changed to Van Kampen Enterprise Fund 08/31/1998

ENTERPRISE FED BANCORP INC (OH)
Merged into Fifth Third Bancorp 06/04/1999
Each share Common 1¢ par exchanged for (0.68516) share Common 1¢ par

ENTERPRISE FINANCE LTD.
In process of liquidation in 1950

ENTERPRISE GP HLDGS L P (DE)
Issue Information - 12,600,000 UNITS LTD PARTNERSHIP INT offered at $28 per Unit on 08/23/2005
Merged into Enterprise Products Partners L.P. 11/22/2010
Each Unit of Ltd. Partnership Int. exchanged for (1.5) Common Units

ENTERPRISE GROUP FDS INC (MD)
Growth Portfolio $0.001 par reclassified as AXA Enterprise Growth Fund Class A $0.001 par 05/01/1995
Reorganized as Goldman Sachs Trust Capital Growth Fund 12/14/2007
Details not available

ENTERPRISE HOTEL DEV CORP (PR)
In process of liquidation
Each share Preferred no par received initial distribution of $141.35 cash 12/1/75
Each share Common no par received initial distribution of $1 cash 12/1/75
Note: Number or amount of subsequent distributions, if any, are not available

ENTERPRISE INC (NV)
Name changed to eHealth.com, Inc. 12/14/1998
eHealth.com, Inc. name changed to InternetStudios.com, Inc. 09/20/1999
(See InternetStudios.com, Inc.)

ENTERPRISE INNS (UNITED KINGDOM)
Name changed to Ei Group PLC 02/23/2017

ENTERPRISE MANUFACTURING CO. (GA)
Merged into Sibley-Enterprise Co. 00/00/1938
Details not available

ENTERPRISE MANUFACTURING CO. OF PENNSYLVANIA (PA)
Merged into Silex Co. 9/1/55
Each share Capital Stock $70 par exchanged for (7) shares 4-3/4% Conv. Preferred $10 par
Silex Co. name changed to Proctor-Silex Co. 3/1/60 which merged into SCM Corp. 6/30/66
(See SCM Corp.)

ENTERPRISE NATL BK (JACKSONVILLE, FL)
Merged into Compass Bancshares, Inc. 01/14/1997
Each share Common $5 par exchanged for (0.0823579) share Common $2 par
Compass Bancshares, Inc. merged into Banco Bilbao Vizcaya Argentaria, S.A. 09/07/2007

ENTERPRISE NATL BK (KENILWORTH, NJ)
Name changed to Enterprise Bank N.J. (Kenilworth, NJ) 03/10/2016

ENTERPRISE OIL & GAS CORP (NV)
Name changed to Enterprise Technologies Inc. 7/27/83
Enterprise Technologies Inc. reorganized as Enterprise Entertainment Group, Inc. 10/3/89 which recapitalized as Andromeda Capital Corp. 7/29/94

ENTERPRISE OIL LTD (AB)
Name changed to Enterprise Oilfield Group, Inc. 05/30/2007
Enterprise Oilfield Group, Inc. name changed to Enterprise Group, Inc. 07/30/2012

ENTERPRISE OIL PLC (UNITED KINGDOM)
Sponsored ADR's for Ser. A Preference l1 par called for redemption 8/6/97
ADR agreement terminated 10/10/2000
Each Sponsored ADR for Ser. B £0.25 par exchanged for $25.6476 cash
ADR agreement terminated 7/9/2002
Each Sponsored ADR for Ordinary exchanged for $33.300406 cash

ENTERPRISE OILFIELD GROUP INC (AB)
Name changed to Enterprise Group, Inc. 07/30/2012

ENTERPRISE RADIO INC (CT)
Involuntary petition under Chapter 7 of the Federal Bankruptcy Code filed 12/11/81
No stockholders' equity

ENTERPRISE RES INC (BC)
Recapitalized as ERI Ventures Inc. 5/6/93
Each share Common no par exchanged for (1/3) share Common no par
ERI Ventures Inc. name changed to Antam Resources International Ltd. 9/8/97 which recapitalized as International Antam Resources Ltd. 6/8/99 which name changed to Goldsource Mines Inc. (Yukon) 1/23/2004 which reincorporated in British Columbia 8/3/2005

ENTERPRISE SOFTWARE INC (DE)
Merged into Live Wire Acquisition Corp. 09/17/1999
Each share Common $0.0001 par exchanged for $9.25 cash

ENTERPRISE SOLUTIONS ASIA PAC LTD (AUSTRALIA)
Name changed to Deepsky Webmarket Ltd. 12/17/1999
Deepsky Webmarket Ltd. name changed to Monteray Group Ltd. 12/18/2001 which name changed to Monteray Mining Group Ltd. 09/26/2011 which name changed to Norwood Systems Ltd. 03/31/2016

ENTERPRISE SOLUTIONS INC (NV)
Common $0.001 par split (3) for (2) by issuance of (0.5) additional share payable 7/30/99 to holders of record 7/6/99
Name changed to Enterprises Solutions Inc. 9/1/99
(See Enterprises Solutions Inc.)

ENTERPRISE SYS INC (DE)
Secondary Offering - 600,000 shares COM offered at $23.50 per share on 10/11/1996
Merged into HBO & Co. 06/26/1997
Each share Common 1¢ par exchanged for (0.4579) share Common 5¢ par
HBO & Co. merged into McKesson HBOC Inc. 01/12/1999 which name changed to McKesson Corp. 07/30/2001

ENTERPRISE TECHNOLOGIES INC (NV)
Reorganized as Enterprise Entertainment Group, Inc. 10/03/1989
Each (100) shares Common 1¢ par exchanged for (1) Unit consisting of (1) share Common 1¢ par, (1) Class A Common Stock Purchase Warrant expiring 10/03/1991 and (1) NUOILCO., Inc. Unit consisting of (1) share Common 1¢ par and (1) Class A Common Stock Purchase Warrant expiring 10/03/1991
(See each company's listing)

ENTERPRISE TECHNOLOGIES INC (NV)
Name changed to PhytoMedical Technologies, Inc. 09/02/2004
PhytoMedical Technologies, Inc. recapitalized as Ceres Ventures, Inc. 12/12/2011

ENTERPRISE TRADERS INC (NV)
Name changed to Micromint, Inc. 01/16/2007
(See Micromint, Inc.)

ENTERPRISE VENTURE CORP (DE)
Name changed to Beaver Creek Silver Co., Inc. 03/09/1988
(See Beaver Creek Silver Co., Inc.)

ENTERPRISES SOLUTIONS INC (NV)
Agreement to sell company assets terminated 4/16/2002
Stockholders' equity unlikely

ENTERRA CORP (DE)
Reincorporated 02/04/1987
State of incorporation changed from (PA) to (DE) 02/04/1987
Merged into Weatherford Enterra, Inc. 10/05/1995
Each share Common $1 par exchanged for (0.845) share Common 10¢ par
Weatherford Enterra, Inc. merged into EVI Weatherford, Inc. 05/27/1998 which name changed to Weatherford International Inc. (New) (DE) 09/21/1998 which reincorporated in Bermuda as Weatherford International Ltd. 06/26/2002 which reincorporated in Switzerland 02/25/2009 which reincorporated in Ireland as Weatherford International PLC 06/18/2014

ENTERRA CORP OLD (DE)
Incorporated 12/08/2006
Name changed to VinCompass Corp. 04/27/2015
VinCompass Corp. name changed to Enterra Corp. (New) 11/13/2015

ENTERRA ENERGY CORP (AB)
Preferred Ser. I no par called for redemption 09/30/2003
Recapitalized as Enterra Energy Trust 11/25/2003
Each share Common no par exchanged for (2) Trust Units
Enterra Energy Trust reorganized as Equal Energy Ltd. 06/03/2010
(See Equal Energy Ltd.)

ENTERRA ENERGY TR (AB)
Reorganized as Equal Energy Ltd. 06/03/2010
Each Trust Unit exchanged for (0.33333333) share Common no par
Note: Unexchanged certificates were cancelled and became without value 06/03/2016
(See Equal Energy Ltd.)

ENTERTAINMENT / MEDIA ACQUISITION CORP (DE)
Name changed to Overseas Filmgroup, Inc. 10/31/1996
Overseas Filmgroup, Inc. name changed to First Look Media, Inc. 01/17/2001

ENTERTAINMENT & GAMING INTL INC (DE)
Name changed to Whitestone Industries Inc. (New) 06/16/1995

ENT-ENT

FINANCIAL INFORMATION, INC.

Whitestone Industries Inc. (New) recapitalized as Proformix Systems Inc. 07/15/1997 which name changed to Magnitude Information Systems, Inc. 12/03/1998 which name changed to Kiwibox.Com, Inc. 03/02/2010

ENTERTAINMENT AMER INC (FL)
Proclaimed dissolved for failure to file reports and pay fees 10/13/1989

ENTERTAINMENT ART INC (NV)
Name changed to Biozoom, Inc. 04/01/2013

ENTERTAINMENT BLVD INC (NV)
SEC revoked common stock registration 07/07/2006

ENTERTAINMENT CONCEPTS INTERNATIONAL (UT)
Name changed to Lord & Lazarus, Inc. 00/00/1988
Lord & Lazarus, Inc. name changed to Utility Communications International, Inc. 00/00/1996 which reorganized as Intermost Corp. (UT) 11/10/1998 which reincorporated in Wyoming 02/25/2003 which name changed to Uni Core Holdings Corp. 01/29/2010

ENTERTAINMENT CORP AMER (DE)
Each share Common $0.001 par received distribution of (0.0732824) share Media Entertainment, Inc. Common $0.0001 par payable 09/12/1997 to holders of record 03/15/1997
Recapitalized as CAC Homes Corp. (DE) 01/27/2006
Each share Common $0.001 par exchanged for (0.0005) share Common $0.001 par
CAC Homes Corp. (DE) reincorporated in Wyoming as Ostashkov Industrial Inc. 11/20/2013
(See Ostashkov Industrial Inc.)

ENTERTAINMENT DIGITAL NETWORK INC (DE)
Merged into Visual Data Corp. 8/3/2001
Each share Common $0.001 par exchanged for (0.1) share Common $0.0001 par
Visual Data Corp. name changed to Onstream Media Corp. 1/1/2005

ENTERTAINMENT DISTR CO INC (DE)
Recapitalized as EDCI Holdings, Inc. 08/26/2008
Each share Common 2¢ par exchanged for (0.1) share Common 2¢ par
(See EDCI Holdings, Inc.)

ENTERTAINMENT EQUITY CORP (TX)
Name changed to Enhanced Electronics Corp. 08/31/1993
Enhanced Electronics Corp. name changed to Curtis Mathes Holding Corp. 05/23/1994 which name changed to uniView Technologies Corp. 01/30/1998 which name changed to VPGI Corp. 08/14/2003
(See VPGI Corp.)

ENTERTAINMENT FACTORY INC (NV)
Reorganized under the laws of Delaware as Tri-Hub International, Ltd. 07/16/2008
Each share Common $0.001 par exchanged for (0.0025) share Common $0.001 par

ENTERTAINMENT FIN & SVCS INC (NV)
Name changed to Omni Entertainment Group, Inc. 02/13/2006
Omni Entertainment Group, Inc. name changed to Entertainment Financial Services, Inc. 03/29/2006
(See Entertainment Financial Services, Inc.)

ENTERTAINMENT FINL SVCS INC (NV)
Charter revoked for failure to file reports and pay taxes 06/30/2010

ENTERTAINMENT GAMES INC (PA)
Recapitalized as Tamino Minerals Inc. 03/25/2013
Each share Common no par exchanged for (0.1) share Common no par

ENTERTAINMENT GAMING ASIA INC (NV)
Each share old Common $0.001 par exchanged for (0.25) share new Common $0.001 par 06/12/2012
Each share new Common $0.001 par exchanged again for (0.25) share new Common $0.001 par 02/26/2015
Acquired by Melco International Development Ltd. 06/21/2017
Each share new Common $0.001 par exchanged for $2.35 cash

ENTERTAINMENT INNS AMER INC (NY)
Name changed to Tiger Marketing, Inc. 11/08/1984
Tiger Marketing, Inc. recapitalized as U.S. Health Services, Inc. 04/08/1986 which name changed to Diamond Trade Center, Inc. 10/30/1990
(See Diamond Trade Center, Inc.)

ENTERTAINMENT INTL LTD (NY)
Each share old Common 1¢ par exchanged for (0.05) share new Common 1¢ par 10/18/2001
Name changed to Clean Systems Technology Group, Ltd. 12/27/2001
(See Clean Systems Technology Group, Ltd.)

ENTERTAINMENT INTERNET INC (NV)
Each share old Common $0.001 par exchanged for (0.00333333) share new Common $0.001 par 01/23/2002
Name changed to SkyBridge Wireless Inc. 04/09/2003
SkyBridge Wireless Inc. recapitalized as SkyBridge Technology Group, Inc. 03/21/2006

ENTERTAINMENT MGMT INC (DE)
Charter cancelled and declared inoperative and void for non-payment of taxes 03/01/1998

ENTERTAINMENT MARKETING INC (TX)
Common 1¢ par split (2) for (1) by issuance of (1) additional share 12/29/1986
Name changed to KLH Computers, Inc. 01/27/1992
(See KLH Computers, Inc.)

ENTERTAINMENT ONE INCOME FD (ON)
Acquired by Entertainment One Ltd. 04/02/2007
Each Fund Unit received $3.57 cash
Note: An additional $0.03 cash per share was placed in escrow for possible future distribution

ENTERTAINMENT PPTYS TR (MD)
9.5% Preferred Ser. A 1¢ par called for redemption at $25 plus $0.389236 accrued dividends on 05/29/2007
7.75% Preferred Ser. B 1¢ par called for redemption at $25 plus $0.322917 accrued dividends on 08/31/2011
7.375% Preferred Ser. D 1¢ par called for redemption at $25 plus $0.18 accrued dividends on 11/05/2012
Name changed to EPR Properties 11/12/2012

ENTERTAINMENT PPTY INC
144A Preferred called for redemption at $865.16 on 03/30/1999

ENTERTAINMENT PUBG CORP (MI)
Common no par split (3) for (2) by issuance of (0.5) additional share 06/28/1991
Merged into CUC International Inc. 01/21/1992
Each share Common no par exchanged for (1.1) shares Common 1¢ par
CUC International Inc. name changed to Cendant Corp. 12/17/1997 which reorganized as Avis Budget Group, Inc. 09/01/2006

ENTERTAINMENT PUBNS INC (MI)
Reorganized as Entertainment Publishing Corp. 12/15/1988
Each share Common no par exchanged for (1) share Common no par and $16 cash
Entertainment Publishing Corp. merged into CUC International Inc. 01/21/1992 which name changed to Cendant Corp. 12/17/1997 which reorganized as Avis Budget Group, Inc. 09/01/2006

ENTERTAINMENT ROYALTIES INC (AB)
Delisted from Toronto Venture Stock Exchange 11/19/2003

ENTERTAINMENT SYS INC (FL)
Proclaimed dissolved for failure to file reports and pay fees 10/11/1991

ENTERTAINMENT TECHNOLOGIES & PROGRAMS INC (DE)
Filed a petition under Chapter 7 Federal Bankruptcy Code 11/06/2003
Stockholders' equity unlikely

ENTERTAINMENT TELECOMMUNICATIONS TELEVISION INC (UT)
Each share old Common $0.001 par exchanged for (0.02857142) share new Common $0.001 par 03/04/1996
Name changed to Tek Systems Inc. 01/14/1997
(See Tek Systems Inc.)

ENTERTAINMENT TONIGHT VIDEO EXPRESS LTD (DE)
Common $0.001 par split (10) for (1) by issuance of (9) additional shares 05/18/1987
Recapitalized as Sports International Ltd. 09/19/1994
Each share Common $0.001 par exchanged for (0.25) share Common $0.001 par
Sports International Ltd. name changed to Interactive Gaming & Communications Corp. (Old) 02/26/1996 which name changed to GlobSpan Technology Partners, Inc. 02/02/2000 which name changed to GlobeSpan Technology Partners, Inc. 02/10/2000 which name changed to Interactive Gaming & Communications Corp. (New) 09/27/2000 which recapitalized as Great American Financial Corp. 04/01/2003

ENTERTECH MEDIA GROUP INC (NV)
SEC revoked common stock registration 07/07/2006

ENTEST BIOMEDICAL INC (NV)
Each share old Common $0.001 par received distribution of (0.125) share old Ser. B Preferred $0.001 payable 03/17/2012 to holders of record 02/21/2012
Each share old Ser. B Preferred $0.001 par exchanged for (0.00666666) share new Ser. B Preferred $0.001 par 07/27/2015
Each share old Common $0.001 par exchanged for (0.00666666) share new Common $0.001 par 07/27/2015

Name changed to Entest Group, Inc. 02/14/2018

ENTEX ENERGY DEV LTD (TX)
Name changed to General Energy Development, Ltd. 08/10/1987
(See General Energy Development, Ltd.)

ENTEX INC (TX)
Common $5 par split (4) for (3) by issuance of (0.33333333) additional share 08/25/1976
Common $5 par changed to $1 par 10/28/1976
Common $1 par split (3) for (2) by issuance of (0.5) additional share 08/24/1977
Common $1 par split (2) for (1) by issuance of (1) additional share 08/25/1978
Common $1 par split (5) for (4) by issuance of (0.25) additional share 08/24/1979
Stock Dividend - 20% 08/29/1975
Acquired by Arkla, Inc. 02/02/1988
Each share Common $1 par exchanged for (1.15) shares Common $0.625 par
Arkla, Inc. name changed to NorAm Energy Corp. 05/11/1994 which merged into Houston Industries Inc. 08/06/1997 which name changed to Reliant Energy Inc. 02/08/1999 which reorganized as CenterPoint Energy, Inc. 08/31/2002

ENTEX INFORMATION SVCS INC (DE)
Merged into Siemens A.G. 04/21/2000
Each share Common $0.0001 par exchanged for $0.7538 cash
Note: Each share Common $0.0001 par received an initial additional distribution of approximately $0.1752 cash 04/15/2003
Each share Common $0.0001 par received a second additional distribution of approximately $0.1113 cash 10/18/2006

ENTHEOS TECHNOLOGIES INC (NV)
Each share old Common $0.00001 par exchanged for (0.04) share new Common $0.001 par 07/30/2001
Each share new Common $0.00001 par exchanged again for (6) shares new Common $0.00001 par 09/15/2004
Name changed to Janus Resources, Inc. 02/14/2011
Janus Resources, Inc. name changed to RenovaCare, Inc. 01/09/2014

ENTHRUST FINL SVCS INC (DE)
Name changed to Rodman & Renshaw Capital Group, Inc. 08/31/2007
Rodman & Renshaw Capital Group, Inc. name changed to Direct Markets Holdings Corp. 06/01/2012
(See Direct Markets Holdings Corp.)

ENTITY INC (CO)
Recapitalized as Boundless Motor Sports Racing, Inc. (CO) 08/12/2003
Each share Common $0.0001 par exchanged for (0.01) share Common $0.0001 par
Boundless Motor Sports Racing, Inc. (CO) reincorporated in Delaware as Dirt Motor Sports, Inc. 07/08/2005 which name changed to World Racing Group, Inc. 01/31/2008

ENTMT IS US INC (DE)
Charter cancelled and declared inoperative and void for non-payment of taxes 03/01/2006

ENTORIAN TECHNOLOGIES INC (DE)
Each share old Common $0.001 par exchanged for (0.08333333) share new Common $0.001 par 10/30/2009
Liquidation completed
Each share new Common $0.001 par

received initial distribution of $7 cash payable 12/17/2012 to holders of record 11/16/2012
Each share new Common $0.001 par received second distribution of $0.80 cash payable 03/08/2013 to holders of record 11/16/2012
Each share new Common $0.001 par received third and final distribution of $1.0225 cash payable 11/25/2014 to holders of record 11/16/2012

ENTOURAGE INTL INC (TX)
Recapitalized as Biozhem Cosmeceuticals Inc. 08/21/1998
Each share Common $0.001 par exchanged for (0.2) share Common $0.001 par
Biozhem Cosmeceuticals Inc. recapitalized as Islet Holdings, Inc. 05/28/2009

ENTOURAGE METALS LTD (BC)
Each share old Common no par exchanged for (0.16666666) share new Common no par 05/08/2014
Recapitalized as Genesis Metals Corp. 03/02/2016
Each share new Common no par exchanged for (0.66666666) share Common no par

ENTRAD LTD (AUSTRALIA)
Merged into Nardis Investments Ltd. 02/07/1985
Each ADR for Ordinary exchanged for $1.76 cash

ENTRADA CORP. (NV)
Common $1 par changed to 10¢ par 02/09/1961
Recapitalized as Pacific Energy Corp. 01/14/1976
Each share Common 10¢ par exchanged for (0.02) share Common $5 par
Pacific Energy Corp. name changed to Aimco, Inc. 09/01/1977 which recapitalized as Colt Technology, Inc. 03/31/1983

ENTRADA NETWORKS INC (DE)
Ceased operations 07/22/2005
Stockholders' equity unlikely

ENTRADA SOFTWARE INC (NV)
Recapitalized as Medlink Technologies, Inc. 04/04/2006
Each share Common $0.001 par exchanged for (0.001) share Common $0.001 par
Medlink Technologies, Inc. name changed to Cambridge Resources Corp. 06/21/2006
(See Cambridge Resources Corp.)

ENTRADE INC (PA)
SEC revoked common stock registration 08/19/2009

ENTRE COMPUTER CTRS INC (DE)
Merged into Intelligent Electronics, Inc. 01/04/1989
Each share Common 1¢ par exchanged for $6.10 cash

ENTREC TRANSN SVCS LTD (AB)
Name changed to ENTREC Corp. 06/04/2012

ENTRECAP INTL INC (DE)
Charter forfeited for failure to maintain a registered agent 10/15/1993

ENTREE CORP (DE)
Assets sold 02/03/1997
Details not available

ENTREE GOLD INC (BC)
Reincorporated 01/22/2003
Place of incorporation changed from (BC) to (Yukon) 01/22/2003 which reincorporated back in (BC) 05/27/2005
Plan of arrangement effective 05/12/2017
Each share Common no par exchanged for (1) share Entree Resources Ltd. Common no par and (0.45) share Mason Resources Corp. Common no par

Note: Unexchanged certificates will be cancelled and become without value 05/12/2023

ENTREE RES INC (BC)
Recapitalized as Entree Gold Inc. (BC) 10/10/2002
Each share Common no par exchanged for (0.5) share Common no par
Entree Gold Inc. (BC) reincorporated in Yukon 01/22/2003 which reincorporated back in British Columbia 05/27/2005 which reorganized as Entree Resources Ltd. 05/12/2017

ENTREMED INC (DE)
Each share old Common 1¢ par exchanged for (1) share new Common 1¢ par 07/01/2010
Name changed to CASI Pharmaceuticals, Inc. 06/16/2014

ENTREMETRIX CORP (NV)
Name changed to NeoTactix Corp. 01/07/2008
(See NeoTactix Corp.)

ENTREPLEX TECHNOLOGY CORP (AB)
Name changed to IVRnet Inc. (Old) 10/10/2000
IVRnet Inc. (Old) merged into IVRnet Inc. (New) 07/31/2003

ENTREPORT CORP (FL)
Each share old Common $0.001 par exchanged for (0.1) share new Common $0.001 par 05/31/2006
SEC revoked common stock registration 10/12/2010

ENTREPRENEUR GROUP INC (NV)
Each share Common $0.0005 par exchanged for (0.1) share Common $0.005 par 05/26/1987
Acquired by Entrepreneur Acquisition Corp. 03/28/1989
Each share Common $0.005 par exchanged for $1.56 cash

ENTREPRENEUR INC (DE)
Merged into Dial One Acquisition, Inc. 07/31/1989
Each share Common $0.001 par exchanged for (1) share Common $0.001 par
(See Dial One Acquisition, Inc.)

ENTRON INC (DE)
Under plan of merger each share Common 10¢ par exchanged for (0.33333333) share old Common 30¢ par 12/31/1969
Each share old Common 30¢ par exchanged for (0.01) share new Common $30 par 07/26/1978
Each share new Common $30 par exchanged for (1) share Common $300 par 04/04/1984
Note: In effect holders received $1,350 cash per share and public interest was eliminated

ENTRONICS CORP (DE)
Name changed to Inotek Technologies Corp. 11/01/1991
(See Inotek Technologies Corp.)

ENTROPIC COMMUNICATIONS INC (DE)
Merged into MaxLinear, Inc. 04/30/2015
Each share Common $0.001 par exchanged for (0.22) share Class A Common $0.0001 par and $1.20 cash

ENTROPIN INC (DE)
Reincorporated 06/14/2002
State of incorporation changed from (CO) to (DE) 06/14/2002
SEC revoked common stock registration 12/07/2010

ENTROPY LTD (CO)
Recapitalized as Solenergy Corp. 09/13/1984
Each share Common no par

exchanged for (0.05) share Common no par
Solenergy Corp. recapitalized as Carnegie International Corp. 05/03/1996
(See Carnegie International Corp.)

ENTRPRIZE CORP (DE)
Reincorporated under the laws of Indiana as Tprize, Inc. 08/18/2016

ENTRUST FINL SVCS INC (CO)
Each share old Common $0.0000001 par exchanged for (0.1) share new Common $0.0000001 par 02/01/2002
Each (28) shares new Common $0.0000001 par exchanged again for (1) share new Common $0.0000001 par 09/18/2006
Reincorporated under the laws of Delaware as Enthrust Financial Services, Inc. and Common $0.0000001 par changed to $0.001 par 01/11/2007
Enthrust Financial Services, Inc. name changed to Rodman & Renshaw Capital Group, Inc. 08/31/2007 which name changed to Direct Markets Holdings Corp. 06/01/2012
(See Direct Markets Holdings Corp.)

ENTRUST INC (MD)
Name changed 06/05/2001
Name changed from Entrust Technologies, Inc. to Entrust, Inc. 06/05/2001
Acquired by HAC Holdings, Inc. 07/28/2009
Each share Common 1¢ par exchanged for $2 cash

ENTRX CORP (DE)
Each share old Common 10¢ par received distribution of (0.5) share Surg II, Inc. Common 1¢ par payable 10/22/2002 to holders of record 10/11/2002 Ex date - 10/21/2002
Each share old Common 10¢ par exchanged for (1) share new Common 10¢ par to reflect a (1) for (500) reverse split followed by a (500) for (1) forward split 06/15/2009
Note: Holders of (499) or fewer pre-split shares received $0.35 cash per share
Name changed to Entrprize Corp. (DE) 06/04/2012
Entrprize Corp. (DE) reincorporated in Indiana as Tprize, Inc. 08/18/2016

ENTWISTLE CO (RI)
Merged into Corkin Corp. 09/20/1990
Each share Common 10¢ par exchanged for $46.40 cash

ENTWISTLE MANUFACTURING CO.
Acquired by Lowenstein (M.) & Sons, Inc. 00/00/1946
Details not available

EN2GO INTL INC (NV)
Each share old Common $0.00001 par exchanged for (0.1) share new Common $0.00001 par 09/15/2009
Name changed to Lyynks Inc. (NV) 05/14/2012
Lyynks Inc. (NV) reincorporated in Delaware as Vancord Capital Inc. 01/06/2015

ENUCLEUS INC (DE)
Plan of reorganization under Chapter 11 Federal Bankruptcy Code effective 04/10/2002
Each share old Common $0.001 par exchanged for (0.16666666) share new Common $0.001 par
Note: Unexchanged certificates were cancelled and became without value 10/15/2002
Each share new Common $0.001 par exchanged again for (0.1) share new Common $0.001 par 03/23/2004
Recapitalized as EC Development, Inc. 08/10/2010
Each share new Common $0.001 par

exchanged for (0.005) share Common $0.001 par
(See EC Development, Inc.)

ENUMERAL BIOMEDICAL HLDGS INC (DE)
Common $0.001 par split (4.62) for (1) by issuance of (3.62) additional shares payable 07/25/2014 to holders of record 07/24/2014
Ex date - 07/28/2014
Plan of reorganization under Chapter 11 Federal Bankruptcy proceedings effective 05/31/2018
No stockholders' equity

ENVENTIS CORP (MN)
Merged into Consolidated Communications Holdings, Inc. 10/16/2014
Each share Common no par exchanged for (0.7402) share Common no par

ENVIGRA INC (NV)
Recapitalized as Electron Solar Energy 01/19/2007
Each share Common $0.001 par exchanged for (0.01333333) share Common $0.001 par
(See Electron Solar Energy)

ENVIPCO AUTOMATED RECYCLING INC (BC)
Name changed to Automated Recycling Inc. 08/20/1999
Automated Recycling Inc. name changed to OceanLake Commerce Inc. 03/01/2001

ENVIRA MINERALS INC (AZ)
Reorganized under the laws of Nevada as KoreaStation Corp. 05/01/2000
Each (8.5) shares Common no par exchanged for (1) share Common $0.001 par
KoreaStation Corp. name changed to E4World Corp. 01/01/2001 which name changed to Xcelplus Global Holdings, Inc. 08/18/2006 which name changed to Clean Energy Pathways, Inc. 02/04/2011

ENVIREMATICS INC (DE)
Name changed to Familian Corp. 04/14/1971
(See Familian Corp.)

ENVIREMATICS INC (FL)
Merged into Enviremetics, Inc. (DE) 12/21/1970
Each share Common 10¢ par exchanged for (0.7) share Common 50¢ par
Enviremetics, Inc. (DE) name changed to Familian Corp. 04/14/1971
(See Familian Corp.)

ENVIRO/ANALYSIS CORP (NY)
Plan of reorganization under Chapter 11 Federal Bankruptcy proceedings confirmed 08/16/1990
No stockholders' equity

ENVIRO-CLEAN AMER INC (NV)
Name changed to Titanium Holdings Group, Inc. 9/7/2001

ENVIRO ENERGY CAP CORP (BC)
Name changed to Silver Sun Resource Corp. 04/14/2009
Silver Sun Resource Corp. name changed to Golden Sun Mining Corp. 02/01/2013

ENVIRO-ENERGY CORP (DE)
Each share Common $0.001 par received distribution of (0.00167785) share Reed Holdings Corp. Common 2¢ par payable 03/21/2003 to holders of record 02/21/2003
Ex date - 02/19/2003
SEC revoked preferred and common stock registration 05/07/2008

ENVIRO ENERGY INTL HLDGS LTD (CAYMAN ISLANDS)
ADR agreement terminated 12/22/2016

ENVIRO-FUELS TECHNOLOGY INC (NV)
Name changed to Environmental Technologies Group International (NV) 12/09/1993
Environmental Technologies Group International (NV) reincorporated in Delaware as Covol Technologies, Inc. 08/23/1995 which name changed to Headwaters Inc. 09/13/2000
(See Headwaters Inc.)

ENVIRO FX INC (AB)
Recapitalized as Niaski Environmental Inc. 12/31/1998
Each share Common no par exchanged for (0.33333333) share Common no par
Niaski Environmental Inc. recapitalized as Rimron Resources Inc. 11/22/2002 which recapitalized as Caribou Resources Corp. 01/22/2004 which merged into JED Oil Inc. 07/31/2007
(See JED Oil Inc.)

ENVIRO-GREEN TECH INC (NY)
Charter cancelled and proclaimed dissolved for failure to pay taxes 06/30/2004

ENVIRO GRO INC (DE)
Charter cancelled and declared inoperative and void for non-payment of taxes 3/1/80

ENVIRO-GUARD HLDG CORP (CO)
Recapitalized as Weston Hotels & Properties Inc. 8/7/97
Each share Common $0.00001 par exchanged for (0.0125) share Common $0.00001 par
Weston Hotels & Properties Inc. recapitalized as Irvine Pacific Corp. (CO) 8/30/2002 which reincorporated in Delaware as iMedia International, Inc. 11/26/2003

ENVIRO INDS INC (DE)
Recapitalized as Agiss Corp. 2/27/97
Each share Common $0.001 par exchanged for (0.25) share Common $0.001 par
(See Agiss Corp.)

ENVIRO-RECOVERY INC (TX)
SEC revoked common stock registration 02/15/2006

ENVIRO SOLUTIONS INTL INC (NV)
Each share old Common $0.001 par exchanged for (0.01) share new Common $0.001 par 1/20/95
Name changed to International Custom Pack Inc. 11/22/95
International Custom Pack Inc. name changed to Global Seafood Technologies Inc. 12/15/98

ENVIRO VORAXIAL TECHNOLOGY INC (ID)
Name changed to Enviro Technologies, Inc. 11/14/2017

ENVIRO WASTE TECHNOLOGIES INC (ON)
Merged into Compressario Corp. 03/07/2002
Each share Common no par exchanged for (0.18348623) share Common no par
(See Compressario Corp.)

ENVIROCARE INC (DE)
Charter cancelled and declared inoperative and void for non-payment of taxes 6/23/86

ENVIROCON MFG CO (CA)
Name changed to Traditional Industries, Inc. 07/09/1982
(See Traditional Industries, Inc.)

ENVIRODYNE INDS INC (AB)
Recapitalized 03/07/1991
Recapitalized from Envirodyne International Inc. to Envirodyne Industries Inc. 03/07/1991
Each share Common no par exchanged for (0.333333333) share Common no par
Recapitalized as Telesis Industrial Group Inc. 08/07/1992
Each share Common no par exchanged for (0.66666666) share Common no par
Telesis Industrial Group Inc. name changed to Merendon Canada Inc. 10/09/1998 which recapitalized as Richfield Explorations Inc. 03/03/2000
(See Richfield Explorations Inc.)

ENVIRODYNE INDS INC (DE)
Name changed 2/13/78
Each share Conv. Preferred Ser. A $1 par exchanged for (1) share Conv. Preferred Ser. B $1 par 07/04/1974
Stock Dividend - 150% 09/20/1972
Name changed from Envirodyne Inc. to Envirodyne Industries, Inc. 02/13/1978
Common 10¢ par split (2) for (1) by issuance of (1) additional share 07/10/1987
Merged into Emerald Acquisition Corp. 06/01/1989
Each share Common 10¢ par exchanged for $40 cash
Name changed to Viskase Companies, Inc. 09/08/1998
(See Viskase Companies, Inc.)

ENVIROFIL INC (DE)
Reincorporated 3/26/93
Each share old Common $0.002 par exchanged for (1/3) share new Common $0.002 par 9/20/91
State of incorporation changed from (NV) to (DE) 3/26/93
Merged into USA Waste Services Inc. 5/27/94
Each share Common $0.002 par exchanged for (0.2) share Common 1¢ par
USA Waste Services Inc. merged into Waste Management, Inc. 7/16/98

ENVIROFOOD INC (DE)
Adjudicated bankrupt 10/17/1975
Details not available

ENVIROGEN INC (DE)
Each share old Common 1¢ par exchanged for (1/6) share new Common 1¢ par 11/24/98
Merged into Shaw Environmental & Infrastructure, Inc. 3/19/2003
Each share new Common 1¢ par exchanged for $0.90 cash

ENVIROKARE TECH INC (NV)
Each share old Common $0.001 par exchanged for (0.5) share new Common $0.001 par 02/22/1999
New Common $0.001 par split (2) for (1) by issuance of (1) additional share payable 03/06/2000 to holders of record 03/01/2000
Recapitalized as Xemex Group, Inc. 07/02/2010
Each share new Common $0.001 par exchanged for (0.001) share Common $0.001 par

ENVIROMART COS INC (DE)
Name changed to eCard Inc. 10/30/2017

ENVIROMED CORP (DE)
Common 1¢ par split (2) for (1) by issuance of (1) additional share 5/18/71
Common 1¢ par split (3) for (1) by issuance of (2) additional shares 9/21/71
Charter cancelled and declared inoperative and void for non-payment of taxes 3/1/75

ENVIROMETRICS INC (DE)
Issue Information - 600,000 UNITS consisting of (1) share COM and (1) WT offered at $5 per Unit on 04/29/1994
Recapitalized as Rainwire Partners Inc. 07/27/2000
Each share Common no par exchanged for (0.1) share Common $0.001 par
(See Rainwire Partners Inc.)

ENVIROMINT HLDGS INC (FL)
Each (3.5) shares old Common $0.001 par exchanged for (1) share new Common $0.001 par 7/31/92
Each share new Common $0.001 par exchanged for (0.125) share Common $0.0001 par 4/6/94
Proclaimed dissolved for failure to file reports and pay fees 8/26/94

ENVIRON, INC. (CA)
Charter suspended for failure to file reports and pay fees 11/01/1993

ENVIRON CORP (UT)
Proclaimed dissolved for failure to pay taxes 12/31/77

ENVIRON ELECTR LABS INC (MN)
Each (13,000) shares old Common 50¢ par exchanged for (1) share new Common 50¢ par 09/23/1985
Note: In effect holders received $0.55 cash per share and public interest was eliminated

ENVIRONMENT CTL CORP (OH)
Common no par split (3) for (1) by issuance of (2) additional shares 7/30/71
Charter cancelled for failure to pay fees 5/8/91

ENVIRONMENT-ONE CORP (NY)
Stock Dividend - 100% 01/10/1972
Merged into EOC Acquisition Corp. 06/16/1998
Each share Common 10¢ par exchanged for $15.25 cash

ENVIRONMENT 2000 LTD (IA)
Charter cancelled for failure to file annual reports 05/10/1976

ENVIRONMENTAL & ECOLOGICAL SALES, INC. (UT)
Common 1¢ par changed to $0.001 par and (9) additional shares issued 10/11/1979
Name changed to Grease Monkey Holding Corp. 06/18/1980
(See Grease Monkey Holding Corp.)

ENVIRONMENTAL ALTERNATIVES CORP (DE)
Name changed to Healthspan Inc. 03/04/1997
Healthspan Inc. recapitalized as Riverside Information Technologies, Inc. (DE) 10/10/2006 which reincorporated in Nevada as Clean Coal Technologies, Inc. 10/12/2007

ENVIRONMENTAL APPLIED RESH TECHNOLOGY HSE-EARTH CDA CORP (CANADA)
Recapitalized as TORR Canada Inc. 11/08/2005
Each share Common no par exchanged for (0.2) share Common no par
TORR Canada Inc. name changed to ProSep Inc. 05/23/2008

ENVIRONMENTAL ASSET MGMT INC (NJ)
Company became private 00/00/2005
Details not available

ENVIRONMENTAL CAP LTD (BC)
Name changed to Mobiclear Technologies Ltd. 01/09/2006

ENVIRONMENTAL CHEMS GROUP INC (DE)
Charter cancelled and declared inoperative and void for non-payment of taxes 03/01/1997

ENVIRONMENTAL CMNTYS INC (CA)
Charter suspended for failure to file reports and pay taxes 09/01/1975

ENVIRONMENTAL CONSTR PRODS INTL INC (FL)
Each share old Common $0.001 par exchanged for (0.00666666) share new Common $0.001 par 10/16/2007
Name changed to Empire Film Group, Inc. 11/08/2007
Empire Film Group, Inc. recapitalized as Tarsin Mobile, Inc. 07/09/2015

ENVIRONMENTAL CONTAINMENT SYS LTD (AB)
Recapitalized as ATC Environmental Group Inc. 01/20/1994
Each share Common no par exchanged for (0.14285714) share Common no par
ATC Environmental Group Inc. name changed to ATC Petroleum Services International Inc. 09/25/2001 which recapitalized as Tiger Pacific Mining Corp. (AB) 02/03/2004 which reincorporated in British Columbia 07/29/2004 which recapitalized as Chantrell Ventures Corp. 08/31/2010

ENVIRONMENTAL CREDITS LTD (DE)
Reincorporated under the laws of Nevada as GlyEco, Inc. and Common 1¢ par changed to $0.0001 par 11/23/2011

ENVIRONMENTAL CTL GROUP INC (DE)
Charter cancelled and declared inoperative and void for non-payment of taxes 03/01/1995

ENVIRONMENTAL CTL PRODS INC (NC)
Chapter 11 bankruptcy proceedings converted to Chapter 7 on 04/22/1985
Stockholders' equity unlikely

ENVIRONMENTAL DEV CORP (NV)
Name changed to Millenium Istec Inc. 07/14/1998
(See Millenium Istec Inc.)

ENVIRONMENTAL DEVICES INC (DE)
Charter cancelled and declared inoperative and void for non-payment of taxes 03/01/1974

ENVIRONMENTAL DIAGNOSTICS INC (CA)
Each share Common no par exchanged for (0.06666666) share Common 15¢ par 11/02/1990
Name changed to Editek, Inc. (CA) 11/03/1992
Editek, Inc. (CA) reincorporated in Delaware 09/26/1996 which name changed to Medtox Scientific, Inc. 05/16/1997
(See Medtox Scientific, Inc.)

ENVIRONMENTAL DIGITAL SVCS INC (DE)
Reincorporated 07/01/2008
State of incorporation changed from (FL) to (DE) and Common no par changed to $0.001 par 07/01/2008
Recapitalized as Sabre Industrial, Inc. 04/12/2010
Each share Common $0.001 par exchanged (0.133333333) share Common $0.001 par
Sabre Industrial, Inc. name changed to Tsingyuan Brewery Ltd. 01/19/2011
(See Tsingyuan Brewery Ltd.)

ENVIRONMENTAL DYNAMICS INC (DE)
Charter cancelled and declared inoperative and void for non-payment of taxes 04/15/1973

ENVIRONMENTAL EARTH SOLUTIONS LTD (BC)
Name changed to Environmental Capital, Ltd. 09/09/2005
Environmental Capital, Ltd. name changed to Mobiclear Technologies, Ltd. 01/09/2006

ENVIRONMENTAL ELEMENTS CORP (DE)
Plan of reorganization under Chapter

11 Federal Bankruptcy proceedings effective 06/01/2006
No stockholders' equity

ENVIRONMENTAL ENERGY SVCS INC (DE)
SEC revoked common stock registration 05/07/2014

ENVIRONMENTAL FILTRATION CORP (NY)
Dissolved by proclamation 12/07/1976

ENVIRONMENTAL FUELS INC (UT)
Each share old Common $0.001 par exchanged for (0.5) share new Common $0.001 par 01/07/1991
Name changed to Geo-Environmental Resources, Inc. 05/09/1991
Geo-Environmental Resources, Inc. name changed to American Absorbents Natural Products, Inc. (UT) 06/05/1995 which reincorporated in Delaware as Earful of Books, Inc. 08/24/2001
(See Earful of Books, Inc.)

ENVIRONMENTAL HYDRONICS INC (DE)
Merged into Enhydron Acquisition Corp. 01/09/1985
Each share Common 10¢ par exchanged for $4.50 cash

ENVIRONMENTAL LANDFILLS INC (ID)
Charter forfeited for failure to file reports 12/01/1988

ENVIRONMENTAL LEASING CORP (DE)
Common 10¢ par split (3) for (2) by issuance of (0.5) additional share 05/28/1971
Charter cancelled and declared inoperative and void for non-payment of taxes 04/15/1973

ENVIRONMENTAL MGMT SOLUTIONS INC (CANADA)
Reincorporated 09/28/2004
Place of incorporation changed from (AB) to (Canada) 09/28/2004
Name changed to EnGlobe Corp. 04/20/2007
(See EnGlobe Corp.)

ENVIRONMENTAL MONITORING & TESTING CORP (DE)
Name changed to Netchoice, Inc. 05/13/2005
Netchoice, Inc. recapitalized as Xstream Mobile Solutions Corp. 01/31/2006

ENVIRONMENTAL OIL PROCESSING TECHNOLOGY CORP (UT)
Chapter 11 bankruptcy proceedings converted to Chapter 7 on 01/14/2003
Stockholders' equity unlikely

ENVIRONMENTAL OIL TECHNOLOGIES INC (FL)
Name changed to American Industrial Minerals Group, Inc. 01/14/1999
American Industrial Minerals Group, Inc. name changed to Networthusa.com, Inc. 04/06/1999 which name changed to EBUX Inc. 10/06/2000 which name changed to Petapeer Holdings Inc. 05/05/2001 which name changed to Studio Bromont Inc. 02/14/2002 which name changed to United American Corp. 03/01/2004

ENVIRONMENTAL PLASMA ARC TECHNOLOGY INC (NV)
Each share old Common $0.001 par exchanged for (0.1) share new Common $0.001 par 05/02/1997
Name changed to Earth Products & Technologies Inc. 11/05/1997
Earth Products & Technologies Inc. name changed to China Shen Zhou Mining & Resources, Inc. 10/20/2006

ENVIRONMENTAL PLUS INC (TX)
Recapitalized as TTI Industries Inc. 04/27/1998
Each share Common 25¢ par exchanged for (0.1) share Common 25¢ par
(See TTI Industries Inc.)

ENVIRONMENTAL POLLUTION RESH CORP (NY)
Common 1¢ par split (5) for (2) by issuance of (1.5) additional share 11/12/1971
Dissolved by proclamation 03/25/1981

ENVIRONMENTAL PWR CORP (DE)
Each share old Common 1¢ par exchanged for (0.14285714) share new Common 1¢ par 11/30/2004
Filed a petition under Chapter 7 Federal Bankrutpcy Code 07/29/2010
Stockholders' equity unlikely

ENVIRONMENTAL PROCESSING INC (TX)
Name changed to EPI Technologies, Inc. 05/05/1988
(See EPI Technologies, Inc.)

ENVIRONMENTAL PRODS & TECHNOLOGIES CORP (DE)
Common $0.025 par split (2) for (1) by issuance of (1) additional share payable 05/11/1998 to holders of record 05/04/1998
Charter cancelled and declared void for failure to pay franchise taxes 03/01/2003

ENVIRONMENTAL PRODS GROUP INC (DE)
SEC revoked common stock registration 05/05/2011

ENVIRONMENTAL PROT INDS INC (NV)
Charter revoked for failure to file reports and pay fees 05/01/1990

ENVIRONMENTAL PROTECTORS INC (OK)
Charter suspended for failure to pay taxes 01/21/1998

ENVIRONMENTAL PROTN SYS INC (NY)
Name changed to Enviro/Analysis Corp. 09/16/1987
(See Enviro/Analysis Corp.)

ENVIRONMENTAL PYROGENICS INC (NV)
Recapitalized as Northport Industries Inc. 01/28/1998
Each (157.8) shares Preferred no par exchanged for (1) share Preferred no par
Each (157.8) shares Common no par exchanged for (1) share Common no par
(See Northport Industries Inc.)

ENVIRONMENTAL RECLAMATION INC (ON)
Acquired by Therma Freeze Inc. 02/28/2001
Each share Common no par exchanged for (0.5039623) share Common no par
Therma Freeze Inc. name changed to Enviro-Energy Corp. 07/03/2001
(See Enviro-Energy Corp.)

ENVIRONMENTAL RECOVERY SYS INC (CO)
Recapitalized as Recycling Industries Inc. 06/27/1995
Each share Common $0.001 par exchanged for (0.2) share Common $0.001 par
(See Recycling Industries Inc.)

ENVIRONMENTAL RECYCLING TECHNOLOGIES INC (MT)
Name changed to Mason Dental Ceramics, Inc. 04/16/1984
Mason Dental Ceramics, Inc. recapitalized as Mason Dental Inc. 12/01/1990
(See Mason Dental Inc.)

ENVIRONMENTAL RECYCLING TECHNOLOGIES PLC (ENGLAND)
ADR agreement terminated 02/07/2014
Each Sponsored ADR for Ordinary exchanged for $0.054971 cash

ENVIRONMENTAL REMEDIATION HLDG CORP (CO)
Name changed to ERHC Energy Inc. 02/15/2005

ENVIRONMENTAL REMEDIATION SVCS INC (OK)
Charter suspended for failure to pay taxes 03/05/1992

ENVIRONMENTAL RESH & APPLICATIONS INC (DE)
Name changed to Hastings Industries, Inc. 03/08/1979
(See Hastings Industries, Inc.)

ENVIRONMENTAL RESH CORP (MN)
Stock Dividend - 100% 03/17/1972
Completely liquidated 06/13/1975
Each share Common 50¢ par exchanged for first and final distribution of $4.50 cash

ENVIRONMENTAL SAFEGUARDS INC (NV)
Each share old Common $0.001 par exchanged for (0.1) share new Common $0.001 par 08/02/1995
Each share new Common $0.001 par exchanged again for (10) shares new Common $0.001 par 01/24/1996
Recapitalized as One World Holdings, Inc. 08/30/2011
Each share new Common $0.001 par exchanged for (0.4) share Common $0.0025 par
One World Holdings, Inc. name changed to Tonner-One World Holdings, Inc. 07/28/2016

ENVIRONMENTAL SCIENCES CORP (WA)
Name changed to Hazleton Laboratories Corp. 02/01/1974
Hazleton Laboratories Corp. merged into Corning Glass Works 04/02/1987 which name changed to Corning Inc. 04/28/1989

ENVIRONMENTAL SVCS AMER INC (DE)
Each share Common $0.001 par exchanged for (0.1) share Common 1¢ par 09/29/1989
Each share Common 1¢ par exchanged for (0.5) share Common 2¢ par 11/19/1990
Merged into DRD Waste Corp. 05/07/1996
Each share Common 2¢ par exchanged for $1.66 cash

ENVIRONMENTAL SERVICES GROUP INC. (DE)
Charter cancelled and declared inoperative and void for non-payment of taxes 03/01/1998

ENVIRONMENTAL SVCS INC (PA)
Merged into Environmental Services, Inc. (NY) 03/26/1970
Each share Common 10¢ par exchanged for (1) share Common 10¢ par

ENVIRONMENTAL SVCS INC (UT)
Reincorporated under the laws of Delaware as Environmental Services of America, Inc. 07/25/1988
(See Environmental Services of America, Inc.)

ENVIRONMENTAL SHOWCASE LTD (NH)
Ceased operations 12/31/1999
No stockholders' equity

ENVIRONMENTAL SPECTRUM INC (NY)
Name changed to Recycling Resources, Inc. 11/10/1975
(See Recycling Resources, Inc.)

ENVIRONMENTAL STRATEGIES & TECHNOLOGIES INTL INC (FL)
Recapitalized as Tango Inc. 02/10/2003
Each share Common $0.001 par exchanged for (0.05) share Common $0.001 par
Tango Inc. recapitalized as AutoBidXL Inc. 10/24/2005 which name changed to Trophy Resources, Inc. 02/28/2006

ENVIRONMENTAL SYS CO (DE)
Common 1¢ par split (2) for (1) by issuance of (1) additional share 05/15/1985
Common 1¢ par split (2) for (1) by issuance of (1) additional share 04/18/1986
Merged into Brambles Acquisition, Inc. 04/08/1992
Each share Common 1¢ par exchanged for $17.50 cash
Conv. Exchangeable Preferred Ser. A called for redemption at $25 plus $0.4375 accrued dividends on 06/01/2002
Public interest eliminated

ENVIRONMENTAL SYS INTL INC (CA)
Each share Common 20¢ par exchanged for (0.2) share Common 1¢ par 11/22/1977
Name changed to Apexx Investing Group 10/12/1978
(See Apexx Investing Group)

ENVIRONMENTAL TECHNOLOGIES CORP (DE)
Name changed to EVTC, Inc. 00/00/1997
(See EVTC, Inc.)

ENVIRONMENTAL TECHNOLOGIES GROUP INTL (NV)
Each share old Common $0.001 par exchanged for (0.05) share new Common $0.001 par 06/14/1995
Reincorporated under the laws of Delaware as Covol Technologies, Inc. 08/23/1995
Covol Technologies, Inc. name changed to Headwaters Inc. 09/13/2000
(See Headwaters Inc.)

ENVIRONMENTAL TECHNOLOGIES INC (AB)
Delisted from Alberta Stock Exchange 02/20/1997

ENVIRONMENTAL TECHNOLOGIES INTL INC (ON)
Recapitalized as Eco Technologies International Inc. 04/24/1998
Each share Common no par exchanged for (0.00666666) share Common no par
(See Eco Technologies International Inc.)

ENVIRONMENTAL TECHNOLOGIES INTL INC (WV)
Each share old Common $0.001 par exchanged for (10) shares new Common $0.001 par 02/23/2002
New Common $0.001 par split (5) for (4) by issuance of (0.25) additional share payable 01/16/2006 to holders of record 01/16/2006 Ex date - 01/18/2006
Recapitalized as Atlantic Wind & Solar, Inc. 10/23/2008
Each share new Common $0.001 par exchanged for (0.01428571) share Common $0.001 par
Note: No holder will receive fewer than (10) post-split shares

ENVIRONMENTAL TECHNOLOGIES INVTS INC (ON)
Merged into Environmental Technologies International Inc. 11/29/1991
Each share Common no par exchanged for (1) share Common no par

Environmental Technologies International Inc. recapitalized as Eco Technologies International Inc. 04/24/1998
(See Eco Technologies International Inc.)

ENVIRONMENTAL TECHNOLOGIES USA INC (MN)
Each share old Common 1¢ par exchanged for (0.1) share new Common 1¢ par 08/02/1996
Company terminated registration of common stock and is no longer public as of 10/14/1997

ENVIRONMENTAL TECHNOLOGY SYS INC (NV)
Stock Dividend - 5% payable 02/28/1998 to holders of record 02/27/1998
Recapitalized as Tombao Antiques & Art Group 04/05/2012
Each share Common $0.001 par exchanged for (0.00333333) share Common $0.001 par

ENVIRONMENTAL TESTING & CERTIFICATION CORP (DE)
Common 10¢ par split (3) for (2) by issuance of (0.5) additional share 07/12/1985
Reorganized as Environmental Treatment & Technologies Corp. 07/01/1986
Each share Common 10¢ par exchanged for (1) share Common 10¢ par
Environmental Treatment & Technologies Corp. name changed to OHM Corp. (DE) 02/10/1989 which reincorporated in Ohio 05/20/1994 which merged into International Technology Corp. 06/11/1998 which name changed to IT Group, Inc. 12/24/1998
(See IT Group, Inc.)

ENVIRONMENTAL TREATMENT & TECHNOLOGIES CORP (DE)
Name changed to OHM Corp. (DE) 02/10/1989
OHM Corp. (DE) reincorporated in Ohio 05/20/1994 which merged into International Technology Corp. 06/11/1998 which name changed to IT Group, Inc. 12/24/1998
(See IT Group, Inc.)

ENVIRONMENTAL WASTE CTL INC (MI)
Name changed 05/30/1974
Common no par changed to 1¢ par 07/24/1973
Name changed from Environmental Waste Control Holding Corp. to Environmental Waste Control, Inc. 05/30/1974
Automatically dissolved for failure to file reports 07/15/2000

ENVIRONONICS INC (NV)
Charter revoked for failure to file reports and pay fees 03/07/1977

ENVIROPACT INC (FL)
Proclaimed dissolved for failure to file reports and pay fees 08/26/1994

ENVIROPAVE INTL LTD (AB)
Recapitalized as Rockex Mining Corp. (AB) 12/20/2010
Each share Common no par exchanged for (0.16666666) share Common no par
Rockex Mining Corp. (AB) reincorporated in Ontario 01/24/2011

ENVIROPOWER INDS INC (AB)
Delisted from Alberta Stock Exchange 06/15/1998

ENVIROQ CORP (DE)
Ctfs. dated prior to 04/18/1995
Common 44¢ par split (6) for (5) by issuance of (0.2) additional share 04/11/1991
Merged into Insituform Mid-America, Inc. 04/18/1995
Each share Common 44¢ par exchanged for (0.2) share Class A Common 1¢ par
Insituform Mid-America, Inc. merged into Insituform Technologies, Inc. 10/26/1995 which name changed to Aegion Corp. 10/26/2011

ENVIROQ CORP (DE)
Certificates dated after 04/18/1995
Merged into Intrepid Capital Corp. 01/12/1999
Each share Common 10¢ par exchanged for (1) share Common 1¢ par and $2.229098 cash

ENVIRORESOLUTIONS INC (DE)
SEC revoked common stock registration 03/19/2010

ENVIROSAFE CORP (NV)
Reincorporated 09/19/2008
Old Common $0.0001 par split (2) for (1) by issuance of (1) additional share payable 06/05/2006 to holders of record 05/05/2006 Ex date - 06/06/2006
Each share old Common $0.0001 par exchanged for (0.00333333) share new Common $0.0001 par 04/26/2007
State of incorporation changed from (DE) to (NV) 09/19/2008
Each share new Common $0.0001 par exchanged again for (0.125) share new Common $0.0001 par 10/31/2008
Name changed to China Education Technology, Inc. 04/09/2009
China Education Technology, Inc. recapitalized as Valentine Beauty, Inc. 12/11/2013

ENVIROSAFE SVCS INC (DE)
Merged into EnviroSource, Inc. 02/28/1992
Each share Common 1¢ par exchanged for (5) shares Common 5¢ par
EnviroSource, Inc. recapitalized as Envirosource, Inc. 06/22/1998
(See Envirosource, Inc.)

ENVIROSEARCH CORP (CO)
Common $1 par changed to 10¢ par 05/20/1974
Name changed to Evro Financial Corp. (CO) 09/26/1986
Evro Financial Corp. (CO) reincorporated in Florida as Evro Corp. 03/01/1994 which name changed to Channel America Broadcasting, Inc. 10/25/1996 which recapitalized as DTG Industries, Inc. 03/22/2004 which name changed to DTG Multimedia, Inc. (FL) 06/04/2004 which reorganized in Nevada as Amazing Technologies Corp. 12/23/2004 which name changed to Mvive, Inc. 08/24/2007
(See Mvive Inc.)

ENVIROSOLUTIONS HLDGS INC (DE)
Plan of reorganization under Chapter 11 Federal Bankruptcy Code effective 07/29/2010
No stockholders' equity

ENVIROSOURCE INC NEW (DE)
Recapitalized 06/22/1998
$7.25 Conv. Preferred Class G 25¢ par called for redemption 07/15/1996
Recapitalized from EnviroSource, Inc. (Old) to Envirosource, Inc. (New) 06/22/1998
Each share Common 5¢ par exchanged for (1/7) share Common 5¢ par
Merged into GSC Recovery II, L.P. 07/24/2001
Each share Common 5¢ par exchanged for $0.20 cash
Preferred Ser. A called for redemption at $92.5926 on 01/15/2004
Note: Each share Common 5¢ par received an initial additional distribution of $4.92790812 cash from escrow 11/22/2005
Each share Common 5¢ par received a second additional distribution of $7.027865 cash from escrow 12/20/2006
Each share Common 5¢ par received a third and final additional distribution of $7.07390447 cash from escrow 12/24/2007

ENVIROSURE MGMT CORP (DE)
Charter cancelled and declared inoperative and void for non-payment of taxes 03/01/1991

ENVIROTECH CORP (DE)
Merged into Baker International Corp. (CA) 03/02/1982
Each share Common $1 par exchanged for (0.4) share Common $1 par and $3 cash
Baker International Corp. (CA) reincorporated in Delaware 01/27/1983 which merged into Baker Hughes Inc. 04/03/1987 which merged into Baker Hughes, a GE company 07/05/2017

ENVIROTECH MFG CORP (DE)
Name changed to Alfa Utility Services Inc. 06/01/2001
(See Alfa Utility Services Inc.)

ENVIROTECH SYS INC (DE)
Charter forfeited for failure to maintain a registered agent 11/19/1999

ENVIROTEK (NV)
Name changed to Suffer 06/21/2010
Suffer recapitalized as Ophir Resources Co. 01/23/2013
(See Ophir Resources Co.)

ENVIROTEST SYS CORP (DE)
Merged into Environmental Systems Products, Inc. 10/16/1998
Each share Class A Common 1¢ par exchanged for $17.25 cash

ENVIROTHERMIC TECHNOLOGIES LTD (ON)
Recapitalized as Environmental Reclamation Inc. 06/22/1998
Each share Common no par exchanged for (0.0285714) share Common no par
Environmental Reclamation Inc. acquired by Therma Freeze Inc. 02/28/2001 which name changed to Enviro-Energy Corp. 07/03/2001
(See Enviro-Energy Corp.)

ENVIROTIRE INC (WA)
Charter cancelled and proclaimed dissolved for failure to pay fees 01/31/1998

ENVIROTRAIN CAP CORP (CANADA)
Name changed to Railpower Technologies Corp. 07/13/2001
(See Railpower Technologies Corp.)

ENVIROTREAT SYS INC (BC)
Recapitalized as Treat Systems Inc. 09/02/1999
Each share Common no par exchanged for (0.04) share Common no par
Treat Systems Inc. name changed to Mega Silver Inc. (BC) 12/18/2007 which reincorporated in Ontario as Mega Precious Metals Inc. 09/14/2009 which merged into Yamana Gold Inc. 06/24/2015

ENVIROTRONICS INC (CO)
Charter suspended for failure to file annual reports 09/30/1985

ENVIROWASTE INDS INC (BC)
Recapitalized as Consolidated Envirowaste Industries Inc. 03/24/1992
Each share Common no par exchanged for (0.33333333) share Common no par
(See Consolidated Envirowaste Industries, Inc.)

ENVIROWEST INC. (UT)
Petition under Chapter 7 United States Bankruptcy Code filed 06/26/1981
No stockholders' equity

ENVIROXTRACT INC (WY)
Reincorporated 08/19/2010
Each share old Common $0.0001 par exchanged for (0.002) share new Common $0.0001 par 03/11/2010
State of incorporation changed from (NV) to (WY) and Common $0.0001 par changed to $0.0000001 par 08/19/2010
Each share old Common $0.0000001 par exchanged for (0.001) share new Common $0.0000001 par 10/28/2010
Each share new Common $0.0000001 par exchanged again for (0.001) share new Common $0.0000001 par 04/15/2011
Recapitalized as Mission Mining Co. 01/04/2013
Each share new Common $0.0000001 par exchanged for (0.001) share Common $0.0000001 par

ENVIRX INDS INC (DE)
Name changed 06/23/1992
Name changed from Envirx Ltd. to Envirx Industries, Inc. 06/23/1992
Name changed to TransAmerican Waste Industries, Inc. 08/24/1992
TransAmerican Waste Industries, Inc. merged into USA Waste Services, Inc. 05/06/1998 which merged into Waste Management, Inc. 07/16/1998

ENVISION DEVL CORP (DE)
Company terminated registration of common stock and is no longer public as of 05/04/2001

ENVISION HEALTHCARE CORP (DE)
Each share 5.25% Mandatory Conv. Preferred Ser. A-1 1¢ par automatically became (1.8141) shares Common 1¢ par 07/03/2017
Acquired by Enterprise Parent Holdings Inc. 10/11/2018
Each share Common 1¢ par exchanged for $46 cash

ENVISION HEALTHCARE HLDGS INC (DE)
Merged into Envision Healthcare Corp. 12/02/2016
Each share Common 1¢ par exchanged for (0.334) share Common 1¢ par
(See Envision Healthcare Corp.)

ENVIT CAP GROUP INC (DE)
SEC revoked common stock registration 09/11/2009

ENVIVIO INC (DE)
Acquired by Ericsson 10/27/2015
Each share Common $0.001 par exchanged for $4.10 cash

ENVOY CAP GROUP INC (ON)
Merged into Merus Labs International Inc. (New) 12/22/2011
Each share Common no par exchanged for (1) share Common no par
Note: Unexchanged certificates were cancelled and became without value 12/22/2017
(See Merus Labs International Inc. (New))

ENVOY COMMUNICATIONS GROUP INC (ON)
Place of incorporation changed from (BC) to (ON) 12/05/1997
Each share old Common no par exchanged for (0.2) share new Common no par 02/10/2005
Name changed to Envoy Capital Group Inc. 04/05/2007
Envoy Capital Group Inc. merged into Merus Labs International Inc. (New) 12/22/2011

(See Merus Labs International Inc. (New))

ENVOY CORP NEW (DE)
Merged into Quintiles Transnational Corp. 03/30/1999
Each share Common no par exchanged for (1.166) shares Common $1 par
(See Quintiles Transnational Corp.)

ENVOY CORP OLD (DE)
Merged into First Data Corp. (Old) 06/06/1995
Each share Common $1 par exchanged for (0.25) share Common 1¢ par
(See First Data Corp.(Old))

ENVOY GROUP CORP (FL)
Common $0.0001 par split (10) for (1) by issuance of (9) additional shares payable 10/22/2014 to holders of record 10/22/2014 Ex date - 10/23/2014
Name changed to Black Cactus Global Inc. 12/27/2017

ENVOY RES LTD (BC)
Recapitalized as ERL Resources Ltd. 04/23/1979
Each share Capital Stock no par exchanged for (0.33333333) share Capital Stock no par
ERL Resources Ltd. name changed to Tenajon Silver Corp. 12/16/1980 which name changed to Tenajon Resources Corp. 09/15/1988 which merged into Creston Moly Corp. 08/26/2009 which merged into Mercator Minerals Ltd. 06/21/2011

ENWEST VENTURES CORP (BC)
Recapitalized as Bayswater Ventures Corp. 02/25/2003
Each share Common no par exchanged for (0.33333333) share Common no par
Bayswater Ventures Corp. merged into Bayswater Uranium Corp. (Old) 08/15/2006 which merged into Bayswater Uranium Corp. (New) 07/24/2007

ENWIN RES INC (NV)
Each share old Common $0.001 par exchanged for (10) shares new Common $0.001 par 05/16/2007
SEC revoked common stock registration 10/24/2012

ENWISEN COM INC (FL)
Reincorporated under the laws of Delaware as Enwisen, Inc. 05/28/2004
(See Enwisen, Inc.)

ENWISEN INC (DE)
Acquired by Lawson Software, Inc. (New) 12/31/2010
Each share Common $1 par exchanged for approximately $0.29 cash
Note: An additional initial distribution of approximately $0.0048 cash per share was paid from escrow 05/20/2011
An additional second distribution of approximately $0.0183 cash per share was paid from escrow 08/09/2011
An additional third distribution of approximately $0.0218 cash per share was paid from escrow 01/30/2012

ENZON INC (DE)
Name changed to Enzon Pharmaceuticals, Inc. 12/10/2002

ENZYMATICS INC (PA)
Merged into Universal Display Corp. 06/23/1995
Each share Common 1¢ par exchanged for (0.09118097) share Common 1¢ par

ENZYMES AMER HLDG CORP (DE)
Charter cancelled and declared inoperative and void for non-payment of taxes 03/01/1992

ENZYMOTEC LTD (ISRAEL)
Acquired by Frutarom Ltd. 01/11/2018
Each share Ordinary ILS 0.01 par exchanged for $11.90 cash

EOA AUTO FDG CORP (NV)
Asset Backed Short Term Auction Rate Preferred Ser. A no par called for redemption 12/11/1989

EOA SOUTH FDG CORP (NV)
Market Auction Preferred no par called for redemption 08/25/1989
Public interest eliminated

EOG RES INC (DE)
Money Market Preferred Ser. D called for redemption at $100,000 on 12/15/2004
100% of 7.195% Perpetual Preferred Ser. B 1¢ par acquired at $1,080 cash per share through purchase offer which expired 01/18/2008
(Additional Information in Active)

EOH HLDGS LTD (SOUTH AFRICA)
ADR agreement terminated 08/10/2017
No ADR's remain outstanding

EOI SVCS INC (DE)
Charter cancelled and declared inoperative and void for non-payment of taxes 03/01/2000

EON COMMUNICATIONS CORP (DE)
Each share Common $0.001 par received distribution of (0.1) share Cortelco Systems Puerto Rico, Inc. Common payable 07/31/2002 to holders of record 07/22/2002
Each share Common $0.001 par exchanged for (0.2) share Common $0.005 par 04/21/2008
Recapitalized as Inventergy Global, Inc. 06/09/2014
Each share Common $0.005 par exchanged for (0.5) share Common $0.001 par

EON CORP (NY)
Common $1 par changed to 1¢ par 02/17/1967
Filed a petition under Chapter 7 bankruptcy proceedings 12/28/1977
No stockholders' equity

EON LABS INC (DE)
Common 1¢ par split (2) for (1) by issuance of (1) additional share payable 06/01/2004 to holders of record 05/17/2004 Ex date - 06/02/2004
Merged into Novartis AG 07/26/2005
Each share Common 1¢ par exchanged for $31 cash

EOPTIMIZE ADVANCED SYSTEMS INC (BC)
Cease trade order effective 09/06/2005
Stockholders' equity unlikely

EOS INTL INC (DE)
Company terminated registration of common stock and is no longer public as of 04/19/2004

EOS PFD CORP (MA)
Completely liquidated
Each share 8.5% Non-Cum Exchangeable Preferred Ser. D 1¢ par received first and final distribution of $25 cash payable 04/09/2012 to holders of record 03/28/2012
Note: Certificates were not required to be surrendered and are without value

EOTT ENERGY LLC (DE)
Name changed to Link Energy LLC 10/01/2003
(See Link Energy LLC)

EOTT ENERGY PARTNERS L P (DE)
Issue Information - 10,000,000 UNITS LTD PARTNERSHIP INT offered at $20 per Unit on 03/18/1994
Plan of reorganization under Chapter 11 Federal Bankruptcy Code effective 3/1/2003
Each Unit of Limited Partnership Int. exchanged for (0.02) EOTT Energy LLC Common Unit and (0.05185) Common Unit Purchase Warrant expiring 3/1/2008
EOTT Energy LLC name changed to Link Energy LLC 10/1/2003
(See Link Energy LLC)

EP GLOBAL COMMUNICATIONS INC (DE)
Each share old Common $0.0001 par exchanged for (0.1) share new Common $0.0001 par 07/27/2012
Under plan of merger each share new Common $0.0001 par automatically became (0.0026) share InWith Corp. Common 05/11/2018
Note: InWith Corp. is privately held

EP MEDSYSTEMS INC (NJ)
Merged into St. Jude Medical, Inc. 07/07/2008
Each share Common no par exchanged for (0.0738) share Common 10¢ par
St. Jude Medical, Inc. merged into Abbott Laboratories 01/04/2017

EP TECHNOLOGIES INC (DE)
Merged into Boston Scientific Corp. 01/22/1996
Each share Common $0.001 par exchanged for (0.297) share Common 1¢ par

EP 2000 CONSV INC (QC)
Struck off register for failure to file reports or pay fees 05/06/2005

EPALS CORP (ON)
Recapitalized as Cricket Media Group Ltd. 07/10/2014
Each share Common no par exchanged for (0.04) share Common no par
(See Cricket Media Group Ltd.)

EPCO, INC. (IA)
Name changed to General Plastronics, Inc. 09/21/1961
(See General Plastronics, Inc.)

EPCOM INC (DE)
Chapter 11 bankruptcy proceedings converted to Chapter 7 on 05/22/1986
Stockholders' equity unlikely

EPCON, INC. (WA)
Completely liquidated 11/30/1967
Each share Common $5 par exchanged for first and final distribution of (0.774913) share Rexall Drug & Chemical Co. Common $1.25 par
Rexall Drug & Chemical Co. name changed to Dart Industries, Inc. 04/22/1969 which reorganized as Dart & Kraft, Inc. 09/25/1980 which name changed to Kraft, Inc. (New) 11/21/1986
(See Kraft, Inc. (New))

EPCOR PFD EQUITY INC (AB)
1st Preferred Ser. 1 called for redemption at $25 on 09/30/2007

EPCOR PWR EQUITY LTD (AB)
Name changed to CPI Preferred Equity Ltd. 11/09/2009
CPI Preferred Equity Ltd. name changed to Atlantic Power Preferred Equity Ltd. 02/07/2012

EPCOR PWR L P (ON)
Name changed to Capital Power Income L.P. 11/09/2009
Capital Power Income L.P. merged into Atlantic Power Corp. 11/09/2011

EPCOS AG (GERMANY)
ADR agreement terminated 12/17/2009
Each Sponsored ADR for Ordinary exchanged for $27.067486 cash

EPD INDS INC (CA)
Charter suspended for failure to file reports and pay fees 04/01/1981

EPERSONNELMANAGEMENT COM (NV)
Name changed to Monogram Pictures, Inc. 10/03/2000
Monogram Pictures, Inc. name changed to Vitallabs, Inc. 05/20/2002 which name changed to America Asia Corp. (NV) 10/19/2004 which reincorporated in Washington as America Asia Energy Corp. 11/08/2005 which name changed to Renegade Energy Corp. 09/14/2006 which recapitalized as Carson Development Corp. 10/20/2008
(See Carson Development Corp.)

EPHONE TELECOM INC (FL)
SEC revoked common stock registration 06/08/2005

EPHOTO IMAGE INC (NV)
Reorganized as GroveWare Technologies Ltd. 05/29/2012
Each share Common $0.001 par exchanged for (50) shares Common $0.001 par
(See GroveWare Technologies Ltd.)

EPHRATA & ADAMSTOWN RWY. CO.
Merged into Conestoga Transportation Co. 00/00/1932
Details not available

EPHRATA NATL BK (EPHRATA, PA)
Each share Common $10 par exchanged for (10) shares Common $1 par 03/16/1983
Common $1 par split (5) for (1) by issuance of (4) additional shares 04/19/1995
Reorganized as ENB Financial Corp. 07/03/2008
Each share Common $1 par exchanged for (1) share Common 20¢ par

EPI CORP (KY)
Merged into TAI Corp. 12/30/1985
Each share Common no par exchanged for $32.36 cash

EPI ENVIRONMENTAL TECHNOLOGIES INC (BC)
Each share old Common no par exchanged for (0.00000006) share new Common no par 09/23/2013
Note: In effect holders received $0.23 cash per share and public interest was eliminated

EPI HOLDINGS LTD (HONG KONG)
Basis changed from (1:100) to (1:1) 11/10/2006
Basis changed from (1:1) to (1:0.1) 07/25/2011
ADR agreement terminated 11/25/2015
Each Sponsored ADR for Ordinary exchanged for $0.000273 cash

EPI INTL INC (DE)
Charter cancelled and declared inoperative and void for non-payment of taxes 03/01/1992

EPI TECHNOLOGIES INC (TX)
Each share old Common 1¢ par exchanged for (0.05) share new Common 1¢ par 12/29/1989
Merged into Elk Sub Inc. 09/29/2000
Each share new Common 1¢ par exchanged for $0.03 cash

EPIC BANCORP (CA)
Stock Dividend - 7% payable 02/14/2007 to holders of record 01/31/2007 Ex date - 01/31/2007
Name changed to Tamalpais Bancorp 06/10/2008
(See Tamalpais Bancorp)

EPIC BEVERAGES LTD (AB)
Cease trade order in effect 09/25/1997

EPIC CAP GROUP INC (CO)
Name changed to Epic Energy Resources, Inc. 12/05/2006
(See Epic Energy Resources, Inc.)

EPIC CORP (SC)
Merged into Ecco, Inc. 12/02/1975
Each share Common 10¢ par exchanged for $1 cash

EPIC DATA INTL INC (BC)
Name changed 07/06/1992
Name changed from Epic Data Inc. to Epic Data International Inc. 07/06/1992
Plan of arangement effective 07/02/2013
Each share Common no par exchanged for (1) share Epic Fusion Corp. Common no par
Note: Unexchanged certificates were cancelled and became without value 07/02/2016

EPIC DESIGN TECHNOLOGY INC (CA)
Common no par split (2) for (1) by issuance of (1) additional share 11/15/1995
Merged into Synopsys, Inc. 02/28/1997
Each share Common no par exchanged for (0.7485) share Common 1¢ par

EPIC ENERGY INC (AB)
Reincorporated 04/15/1996
Place of incorporation changed from (BC) to (AB) 04/15/1996
Assets seized for the benefit of creditors and the company shut down 11/00/2007
No stockholders' equity

EPIC ENERGY RES INC (CO)
Plan of reorganization under Chapter 11 Federal Bankruptcy proceedings effective 03/05/2012
No stockholders' equity

EPIC ENTERPRISES, INC. (OK)
Name changed to United Premium Finance Corp. 02/24/1978
(See United Premium Finance Corp.)

EPIC FINL CORP (NV)
SEC revoked common stock registration 12/01/2010

EPIC HEALTH GROUP INC (NY)
Merged into Saga Acquisition Corp. 08/22/1990
Each share Common 1¢ par exchanged for $1.04 cash

EPIC HEALTHCARE GROUP INC (DE)
Merged into EPIC Holdings Inc. 03/25/1992
Each share Common 1¢ par exchanged for (1) share Common 1¢ par
(See EPIC Holdings Inc.)

EPIC HLDGS INC (DE)
Merged into HealthTrust Inc. - The Hospital Co. 00/00/1994
Each share Common 1¢ par exchanged for $7 cash

EPIC MANUFACTURING CORP. (MI)
Adjudicated bankrupt 12/07/1971
No stockholders' equity

EPIC MEDIA INC (CA)
Common no par split (10) for (1) by issuance of (9) additional shares payable 06/29/2005 to holders of record 06/25/2005 Ex date - 06/30/2005
Name changed to YouMee, Inc. 10/19/2006
YouMee, Inc. name changed to Liberty Presidental Investment Funds 02/23/2007 which name changed to American Pacific Rim Commerce Group (CA) 03/28/2008 which reincorporated in Florida as American Pacific Rim Commerce Corp. 11/21/2012

EPIC MINES LTD. (ON)
Charter cancelled and declared dissolved 03/04/1959
No stockholders' equity

EPIC OIL & GAS LTD (BC)
Recapitalized as Blue Parrot Energy Inc. 04/11/2003
Each share Common no par exchanged for (0.2) share Common no par
Blue Parrot Energy Inc. recapitalized as RIA Resources Corp. 05/19/2009 which reorganized as Qwest Diversified Capital Corp. 06/05/2013

EPIC RES B C LTD (BC)
Under plan of merger name changed to Epic Oil & Gas Ltd. 06/17/1998
Epic Oil & Gas Ltd. recapitalized as Blue Parrot Energy Inc. 04/11/2003 which recapitalized as Ria Resources Corp. 05/19/2009 which reorganized as Qwest Diversified Capital Corp. 06/05/2013

EPIC RES INC (NV)
Name changed to Semicon Tools, Inc. 04/21/1987
Semicon Tools, Inc. name changed to Seto Holdings, Inc. 08/18/1998

EPICEDGE INC (TX)
Chapter 7 bankruptcy proceedings terminated 04/24/2008
Stockholders' equity unlikely

EPICENTRIX TECHNOLOGIES INC (YT)
Name changed to Ventura Gold Corp. (YT) 07/05/2004
Ventura Gold Corp. (YT) reincorporated in British Columbia 10/07/2004 which merged into International Minerals Corp. 01/20/2010
(See International Minerals Corp.)

EPICEPT CORP (DE)
Each share old Common $0.0001 par exchanged for (0.33333333) share new Common $0.0001 par 01/15/2010
Recapitalized as Immune Pharmaceuticals Inc. 08/21/2013
Each share new Common $0.0001 par exchanged for (0.025) share Common $0.0001 par

EPICOR SOFTWARE CORP (DE)
Acquired by Eagle Parent, Inc. 05/16/2011
Each share Common $0.001 par exchanged for $12.50 cash

EPICORE BIONETWORKS INC (AB)
Acquired by Neovia S.A.S. 12/19/2017
Each share Common no par exchanged for $1.30 cash

EPICORE NETWORKS INC (AB)
Recapitalized as Epicore BioNetworks Inc. 08/28/2000
Each share Common no par exchanged for (0.25) share Common no par
(See Epicore BioNetworks Inc.)

EPICURE CHARCOAL INC (NV)
Each share old Common $0.001 par exchanged for (273) shares new Common $0.001 par 02/13/2015
Name changed to Immage Biotherapeutics Corp. 06/10/2015

EPICURE FOOD PRODS INC (BC)
Delisted from Vancouver Stock Exchange 03/04/1992

EPICURE FOODS, INC. (MN)
Name changed to Manning & Rudolph, Inc. 02/06/1969
Manning & Rudolph, Inc. name changed to Gordon-Miles Mining Co. 10/13/1970 which name changed to U.S. Coal Corp. 01/21/1975
(See U.S. Coal Corp.)

EPICURE INVTS INC (FL)
Name changed to V-GPO Inc. 01/01/2002
(See V-GPO Inc.)

EPICUS COMMUNICATIONS GROUP INC (FL)
Each share old Common 1¢ par exchanged for (0.001) share new Common 1¢ par 12/08/2005
SEC revoked common stock registration 12/07/2010

EPIDYNE INC (DE)
Reincorporated 09/27/1974
State of incorporation changed from (PA) to (DE) 09/27/1974
Name changed to Brady Energy Corp. 10/29/1979
(See Brady Energy Corp.)

EPIGEN INC (DE)
Each share Common $0.001 par exchanged for (0.04545454) share Common $0.0001 par 09/02/1997
Each share Common $0.0001 par exchanged for (0.1) share Common 1¢ par 11/14/2001
Name changed to Egenix, Inc. 12/16/2002
(See Egenix, Inc.)

EPIMMUNE INC (DE)
Recapitalized as IDM Pharma, Inc. 08/16/2005
Each share Common 1¢ par exchanged for (0.14285714) share Common 1¢ par
(See IDM Pharma, Inc.)

EPIPHARMA INC (NV)
Name changed to Strategic Healthcare Systems, Inc. 03/09/2006

EPIQ SYS INC (MO)
Common 1¢ par split (3) for (2) by issuance of (0.5) additional share payable 02/23/2001 to holders of record 02/08/2001 Ex date - 02/26/2001
Common 1¢ par split (3) for (2) by issuance of (0.5) additional share payable 11/30/2001 to holders of record 11/16/2001 Ex date - 12/03/2001
Common 1¢ par split (3) for (2) by issuance of (0.5) additional share payable 06/07/2007 to holders of record 05/24/2007 Ex date - 06/08/2007
Acquired by Document Technologies, LLC 09/30/2016
Each share Common 1¢ par exchanged for $16.50 cash

EPITAN LTD (AUSTRALIA)
Name changed to Clinuvel Pharmaceuticals Ltd. 03/03/2006

EPITEK INTL INC (CANADA)
Recapitalized as International Epitek Inc. 08/01/1987
Each share Capital Stock no par exchanged for (0.05) share Common no par
International Epitek Inc. name changed to CompAS Electronics Inc. 07/29/1993 which was acquired by AIM Safety Co., Inc. 12/08/1997 which name changed to AimGlobal Technologies Co., Inc. 01/29/1999
(See AimGlobal Technologies Co., Inc.)

EPITOPE INC (OR)
Common no par split (3) for (1) by issuance of (2) additional shares 04/08/1987
Each share Common no par received distribution of (0.2) share Agritope Inc. Common 1¢ par payable 01/07/1998 to holders of record 12/26/1997
Merged into OraSure Technologies, Inc. 09/29/2000
Each share Common no par exchanged for (1) share Common $0.000001 par

EPIX PHARMACEUTICALS INC (DE)
Name changed 09/07/2004
Name changed from EPIX Medical, Inc. to EPIX Pharmaceuticals, Inc. 09/07/2004
Each share old Common 1¢ par exchanged for (0.66666666) share new Common 1¢ par 08/17/2006
Filed an Assignment for the Benefit of Creditors 07/20/2009
No stockholders' equity

EPIX TECHNOLOGIES LTD (YT)
Recapitalized as Consolidated Epix Technologies Ltd. (Yukon) 03/20/2000
Each share Common no par exchanged for (0.1) share Common no par
Consolidated Epix Technologies Ltd. (Yukon) reorganized in Alberta as Saxon Energy Services Inc. 11/26/2004
(See Saxon Energy Services Inc.)

EPIXTAR CORP (FL)
Chapter 11 bankruptcy proceedings converted to Chapter 7 on 08/30/2010
No stockholders' equity

EPKO SHOES INC (OH)
Common $1 par split (1.333) for (1) by issuance of (0.333) additional share 06/11/1971
Stock Dividends - 10% 12/16/1963; 25% 06/18/1965; 10% 07/15/1968
Reincorporated under the laws of Nevada as Alnan, Inc. 10/08/1976
(See Alnan, Inc.)

EPL OIL & GAS INC (DE)
Merged into Energy XXI (Bermuda) Ltd. 06/03/2014
Each share Common $0.001 par exchanged for (0.584) share Common $0.005 par and $25.35 cash
Energy XXI (Bermuda) Ltd. name changed to Energy XXI Ltd. 11/14/2014
(See Energy XXI Ltd.)

EPL SYS INC (FL)
Name changed to Conmat Technologies, Inc. 12/18/98
(See Conmat Technologies, Inc.)

EPL TECHNOLOGIES INC (CO)
Each share old Common $0.001 par exchanged for (0.5) share new Common $0.001 par 03/17/1998
SEC revoked common stock registration 12/14/2009

EPL VENTURES CORP (FL)
Recapitalized as Industrial Rubber Innovations, Inc. 04/26/1999
Each share Common $0.001 par exchanged for (0.2) share Common $0.001 par
(See Industrial Rubber Innovations, Inc.)

EPLETT DAIRIES LTD (ON)
Merged into 816530 Ontario Inc. 04/20/1989
Each share 8.5% Conv. Preferred Ser. I no par exchanged for $10 cash
Each share Common no par exchanged for $1.30 cash

EPM MNG VENTURES INC (YT)
Reincorporated 05/20/2011
Place of incorporation changed from (ON) to (YT) 05/20/2011
Name changed to Crystal Peak Minerals Inc. 06/26/2015

EPOCH BIOSCIENCES INC (DE)
Name changed 08/17/2000
Name changed from Epoch Pharmaceuticals, Inc. to Epoch Biosciences Inc. 08/17/2000
Merged into Nanogen, Inc. 12/17/2004
Each share Common 1¢ par exchanged for (0.4673) share Common $0.001 par

FINANCIAL INFORMATION, INC. — EPO-EQU

(See Nanogen, Inc.)

EPOCH CAP CORP (BC)
Merged into Quest Capital Corp. 10/25/1996
Each share Common no par exchanged for (1) share Common no par and (0.1) Profco Resources Ltd. Common Stock Purchase Warrant expiring 12/31/1997
Quest Capital Corp. name changed to Quest Oil & Gas Inc. 11/15/1996 which merged into EnerMark Income Fund 04/18/1997 which merged into Enerplus Resources Fund 06/22/2001 which reorganized as Enerplus Corp. 01/03/2011

EPOCH CORP (UT)
Name changed to Osterloh & Durham Insurance Brokers of North America, Inc. 10/03/1973
(See Osterloh & Durham Insurance Brokers of North America, Inc.)

EPOCH HLDG CORP (DE)
Acquired by Toronto-Dominion Bank (Toronto, ON) 03/27/2013
Each share Common 1¢ par exchanged for $28 cash

EPOCRATES INC (DE)
Acquired by athenahealth, Inc. 03/12/2013
Each share Common $0.001 par exchanged for $11.75 cash

EPOD INTL INC (NV)
Common $0.001 par split (2) for (1) by issuance of (1) additional share payable 09/21/2004 to holders of record 09/20/2004 Ex date - 09/22/2004
Reorganized under the laws of British Columbia as EPOD Solar Inc. 05/23/2008
Each share Common $0.001 par exchanged for (1) share Common $0.001 par

EPOD SOLAR INC (NV)
Name changed to Hybrid Coating Technologies Inc. 09/07/2011

EPOLIN INC (NJ)
Acquired by Polymathes Holdings I L.L.C. 08/13/2012
Each share Common no par exchanged for $0.22 cash

EPPING RLTY CORP (BC)
Struck off register and declared dissolved for failure to file returns 07/16/1993

EPPING RES LTD (ON)
Name changed to Tri-D Automotive Industries Ltd. 12/01/1986
(See Tri-D Automotive Industries Ltd.)

EPPS INDUSTRIES, INC. (CA)
Acquired by MSL Industries, Inc. (MN) 11/20/1963
Each share Common $1 par exchanged for (0.142855) share Common no par
MSL Industries, Inc. (MN) reincorporated in Delaware 06/01/1973
(See MSL Industries, Inc. (DE))

EPR PPTYS (MD)
6.625% Preferred Ser. F 1¢ par called for redemption at $25 plus $0.299045 accrued dividends on 12/21/2017
(Additional Information in Active)

EPRESENCE INC (MA)
Liquidation completed
Each share Common 1¢ par received initial distribution of $4.05 cash payable 06/23/2004 to holders of record 06/14/2004
Each share Common 1¢ par received second distribution of approximately $0.10 cash payable 03/06/2006 to holders of record 06/14/2004
Each share Common 1¢ par received third distribution of $0.14 cash payable 12/28/2007 to holders of record 06/14/2004
Each share Common 1¢ par received fourth and final distribution of $0.0332 cash payable 04/06/2011 to holders of record 06/14/2004
Note: Certificates were not required to be surrendered and are without value

EPRISE CORP (DE)
Merged into divine, inc. 12/06/2001
Each share Common $0.001 par exchanged for (2.4233) shares Class A Common $0.001 par
(See divine, inc.)

EPROMO COM (NV)
Recapitalized as Asia Pacific Entertainment, Inc. 05/23/2007
Each share Common $0.001 par exchanged for (0.025) share Common $0.001 par
Asia Pacific Entertainment, Inc. name changed to Access Beverage Inc. 01/06/2009 which name changed to Unity Auto Parts Inc. 09/22/2009 which name changed to Unity Management Group, Inc. 01/08/2010 which name changed to Petrotech Oil & Gas, Inc. 03/26/2013

EPS CAP CORP (BC)
Reincorporated under the laws of Alberta as BioMS Medical Corp. and Common no par reclassified as Class A Common no par 07/31/2001
BioMS Medical Corp. name changed to Medwell Capital Corp. (AB) 07/08/2010 which reorganized in Canada as GDI Integrated Facility Services Inc. 05/14/2015

EPSCO INC (MA)
Common no par changed to $1 par 05/22/1981
Merged into Lucas Industries PLC 10/03/1988
Each share Common $1 par exchanged for $14 cash

EPSILON CORP (DE)
Name changed to Great East Energy, Inc. 09/16/2013
Great East Energy, Inc. name changed to GASE Energy, Inc. 06/13/2014

EPSILON DATA MGMT INC (DE)
Merged into American Express Co. 08/20/1990
Each share Common 1¢ par exchanged for (0.655) share Common 60¢ par

EPUBLISHEDBOOKS COM (NV)
Name changed to Mosaic Nutriceuticals Corp. and (2) additional shares issued 06/03/2004
Mosaic Nutriceuticals Corp. name changed to Mosaic Nutraceuticals Corp. 02/15/2005
(See Mosaic Nutraceuticals Corp.)

EQ RES LTD (ON)
Reorganized under the laws of Delaware as Teton Petroleum Co. 11/23/1998
Each share Common no par exchanged for (0.1) share Common $0.001 par
Teton Petroleum Co. name changed to Teton Energy Corp. 07/01/2005
(See Teton Energy Corp.)

EQCO2 INC (NV)
Common $0.001 par split (5) for (1) by issuance of (4) additional shares payable 07/30/2013 to holders of record 07/30/2013
SEC revoked common stock registration 08/08/2016

EQK GREEN ACRES L P (DE)
Reorganized as EQK Green Acres Trust 02/28/1994
Each Unit of Ltd. Partnership no par exchanged for (1) share Common no par
EQK Green Acres Trust name changed to Arbor Property Trust 05/16/1994 which merged into Vornado Realty Trust 12/16/1997

EQK GREEN ACRES TR (DE)
Name changed to Arbor Property Trust 5/16/94
Arbor Property Trust merged into Vornado Realty Trust 12/16/97

EQK RLTY INVS 1 (MA)
Plan of reorganization under Chapter 11 Federal Bankruptcy Code effective 10/02/2000
No stockholders' equity

EQSTRA HLDGS LTD (SOUTH AFRICA)
Each old Sponsored ADR for Ordinary exchanged for (0.1) new Sponsored ADR for Ordinary 01/02/2014
Basis changed from (1:1) to (1:10) 01/02/2014
Name changed to eXtract Group Ltd. 11/22/2016
(See eXtract Group Ltd.)

EQUAL ENERGY LTD (AB)
Acquired by Petroflow Energy Corp. 07/31/2014
Each share Common no par exchanged for USD$5.43 cash
Note: Unexchanged certificates will be cancelled and become without value 07/31/2020

EQUAL WEIGHT PLUS FD (AB)
Under plan of merger each Trust Unit no par automatically became (0.8028) Citadel Income Fund Trust Unit no par 12/02/2009

EQUALITY BANCORP INC (DE)
Merged into Allegiant Bancorp, Inc. 11/17/2000
Each share Common 1¢ par exchanged for (1.118) shares Common 1¢ par
Allegiant Bancorp, Inc. merged into National City Corp. 04/09/2004

EQUALITY PLASTICS, INC. (NY)
Acquired by United Whelan Corp. 06/30/1966
Each share Common 10¢ par exchanged for (0.2625) share Common $1.20 par
United Whelan Corp. name changed to Perfect Film & Chemical Corp. 05/31/1967 which name changed to Cadence Industries Corp. 10/22/1970
(See Cadence Industries Corp.)

EQUALITY SVGS & LN ASSN (MO)
Merged into Equality Bancorp Inc. 12/01/1997
Each share Common $1 par exchanged for (2.9724) shares Common 1¢ par
Equality Bancorp Inc. merged into Allegiant Bancorp, Inc. 11/17/2000 which merged into National City Corp. 04/09/2004

EQUALNET COMMUNICATIONS CORP (TX)
Name changed 06/30/1998
Name changed from Equalnet Holding Corp. to Equalnet Communications Corp. 06/30/1998
Chapter 11 bankruptcy proceedings converted to Chapter 7 on 06/06/2003
Stockholders' equity unlikely

EQUANT N V (NETHERLANDS)
Each New York Reg. for Ordinary Shares NLG0.02 par received distribution of (1) France Telecom Sponsored ADR for Contingent Value Rights payable 07/05/2001 to holders of record 06/28/2001 Ex date - 07/06/2001
Liquidation completed 05/25/2005
Each New York Reg. for Ordinary Shares NLG0.02 par exchanged for first and final distribution of approximately $5.3754 cash

EQUASHARE MGMT CORP (ON)
Recapitalized as Forest Hill Capital Corp. 02/23/1996
Each share Common no par exchanged for (0.025) share Common no par
(See Forest Hill Capital Corp.)

EQUATORIAL COMMUNICATIONS CO (CA)
Merged into Contel Corp. 12/10/1987
Each share Common no par exchanged for $3.75 cash

EQUATORIAL ENERGY INC (AB)
Each share old Common no par exchanged for (0.25) share new Common no par 07/20/1999
Name changed to Resolute Energy Inc. 11/14/2002
(See Resolute Energy Inc.)

EQUATORIAL RES LTD (BC)
Recapitalized as Intergold Resources Inc. 03/01/1976
Each share Capital Stock no par exchanged for (0.33333333) share Capital Stock no par
Intergold Resources Inc. name changed to Internetwork Realty Corp. 04/17/1979 which recapitalized as Skalbania Enterprises Ltd. 10/15/1980 which name changed to Selco International Properties Inc. 03/03/1988
(See Selco International Properties Inc.)

EQUESS COMMUNICATIONS INC (AB)
Delisted from Toronto Venture Stock Exchange 06/20/2003

EQUESTRIAN CTRS AMER INC (CA)
7.2% Conv. Preferred Ser. A $1 par called for redemption 03/27/1984
Charter suspended for failure to file reports 09/21/1988

EQUESTRIAN RESOURCES CORP. (UT)
Recapitalized as Optico Corp. 12/05/1983
Each share Common $0.001 par exchanged for (0.1) share Common 1¢ par
Optico Corp. name changed to Diamondback Financial Corp. 08/13/1984
(See Diamondback Financial Corp.)

EQUI VENTURES INC (BC)
Delisted from Vancouver Stock Exchange 05/01/1990

EQUICAN CAP CORP (BC)
Class A Subordinate no par split (5) for (1) by issuance of (4) additional shares 06/28/1991
Class B no par split (5) for (1) by issuance of (4) additional shares 06/28/1991
Name changed to Genterra Capital Corp. (Old) 08/23/1995
Genterra Capital Corp. (Old) merged into Genterra Capital Corp. (New) 02/28/1997 which recapitalized as Genterra Capital Inc. (Old) 06/30/1998 which name changed to Genterra Investment Corp. 04/30/1999 which merged into Genterra Inc. 12/31/2003 which merged into Genterra Capital Inc. (New) 05/10/2010 which merged into Gencan Capital Inc. 10/30/2015

EQUICAN VENTURES CORP. (ON)
Recapitalized as Equican Capital Corp. 01/27/1988
Each share Common no par exchanged for (0.33333333) share Common no par
Equican Capital Corp. name changed to Genterra Capital Corp. (Old) 08/23/1995 which merged into Genterra Capital Corp. (New) 02/28/1997 which recapitalized as Genterra Capital, Inc. 06/30/1998 which name changed to Genterra

Investment Corp. 04/30/1999 which merged into Genterra Inc. 12/31/2003

EQUICAN VENTURES INC (ON)
Merged into Equican Capital Corp. 12/04/1987
Each share Preference Class A no par exchanged for (0.32) Class A Subordinate no par
Each share Common no par exchanged for (0.32) share Common no par
Equican Capital Corp. name changed to Genterra Capital Corp. (Old) 08/23/1995 which merged into Genterra Capital Corp. (New) 02/28/1997 which recapitalized as Genterra Capital Inc. (Old) 06/30/1998 which name changed to Genterra Investment Corp. 04/30/1999 which merged into Genterra Inc. 12/31/2003 which merged into Genterra Capital Inc. (New) 05/10/2010 which merged into Gencan Capital Inc. 10/30/2015

EQUICAN VENTURES LTD. (ON)
Name changed to Equican Ventures Inc. 01/16/1979
Equican Ventures Inc. merged into Equican Capital Corp. 12/04/1987 which name changed to Genterra Capital Corp. (Old) 08/23/1995 which merged into Genterra Capital Corp. (New) 02/28/1997 which recapitalized as Genterra Capital Inc. (Old) 06/30/1998 which name changed to Genterra Investment Corp. 04/30/1999 which merged into Genterra Inc. 12/31/2003 which merged into Genterra Capital Inc. (New) 05/10/2010 which merged into Gencan Capital Inc. 10/30/2015

EQUICAP FINL CORP (BC)
Name changed to Zecotek Medical Systems, Inc. 02/10/2005
Zecotek Medical Systems, Inc. name changed to Zecotek Photonics Inc. 11/26/2007

EQUICAP INC (NV)
Reincorporated 01/25/2005
Each share old Common no par exchanged for (0.01) share new Common no par 07/31/1998
Each share new Common no par exchanged again for (2) shares new Common no par to reflect a (1) for (50) reverse and a subsequent (100) for (1) forward split 01/18/2000
State of incorporation changed from (CA) to (NV) and Common no par changed to $0.001 par 01/25/2005
Name changed to Zhongchai Machinery, Inc. 06/04/2010

EQUICO LESSORS INC (DE)
Name changed to Equitable Life Leasing Corp. 02/15/1983
(See Equitable Life Leasing Corp.)

EQUICORP INDS INC (ON)
Name changed 06/10/1974
Name changed from Equicorp Industries Ltd. to Equicorp Industries Inc. 06/10/1974
Recapitalized as Equican Ventures Ltd. 01/16/1978
Each share Class A Preference no par exchanged for (0.1) share Class A Preference no par
Each share Common no par exchanged for (0.1) share Common no par
Equican Ventures Ltd. name changed to Equican Ventures Inc. 01/16/1979 which merged into Equican Capital Corp. 12/04/1987 which name changed to Genterra Capital Corp. (Old) 08/23/1995 which merged into Genterra Capital Corp. (New) 02/28/1997 which recapitalized as Genterra Capital Inc. (Old) 06/30/1998 which name changed to Genterra Investment Corp. 04/30/1999 which merged into Genterra Inc. 12/31/2003 which merged into Genterra Capital Inc. (New) 05/10/2010 which merged into Gencan Capital Inc. 10/30/2015

EQUICREDIT CORP (DE)
Merged into Barnett Banks, Inc. 01/27/1995
Each share Common 1¢ par exchanged for $32 cash

EQUIDATA INC (OH)
Merged into Inland Systems, Inc. 02/28/1970
Each share Common no par exchanged for (1) share Common no par
(See Inland Systems, Inc.)

EQUIDYNAMICS INC (DE)
Name changed to Applied Equities, Inc. 08/01/1991
Applied Equities, Inc. name changed to Soma Technologies International Inc. 05/25/1993

EQUIDYNE CORP (DE)
Name changed to Cathay Merchant Group, Inc. 10/06/2004
Cathay Merchant Group, Inc. name changed to Mansfelder Metals Ltd. 02/21/2008

EQUIFUND-WRIGHT NATL FID EQUITY FDS (MA)
Name changed to Wright EquiFund Equity Trust 04/13/1995
(See Wright EquiFund Equity Trust)

EQUILINE CORP (NV)
Recapitalized as Chelsea Collection, Inc. 06/15/2005
Each share Common $0.001 par exchanged for (0.1) share Common $0.001 par
Chelsea Collection, Inc. recapitalized as G-H-3 International, Inc. 10/30/2006

EQUILINK CORP (DE)
Name changed to MacGregor Sporting Goods Inc. 01/03/1984
MacGregor Sporting Goods Inc. name changed to M Holdings Corp. 09/14/1989
(See M Holdings Corp.)

EQUIMARK CORP (DE)
Reorganized 03/24/1988
Common $5 par changed to $3.33333333 par and (0.5) additional share issued 06/19/1972
$2.10 Conv. Preferred $35 par called for redemption 06/30/1978
Common $3.33333333 par changed to $1 par 06/28/1985
$2 Conv. Preferred Ser. C $1 par called for redemption 02/25/1986
Reorganized from (PA) to under the laws of Delaware 03/24/1988
Each share $2.31 Conv. Preferred $1 par automatically became (1) share $2.31 Conv. Preferred $1 par
Each share Common $1 par exchanged for (0.25) share Common $1 par
Merged into Integra Financial Corp. 01/15/1993
Each share $2.31 Conv. Preferred $1 par exchanged for (1) share $2.31 Conv. Preferred $1 par
Each share new Common $1 par exchanged for (0.2) share Common $1 par
Integra Financial Corp. merged into National City Corp. 05/03/1996 which was acquired by PNC Financial Services Group, Inc. 12/31/2008

EQUIMED INC (DE)
Each share Common no par exchanged for (0.16666666) share Common $0.0001 par 08/11/1997
Reincorporated under the laws of Saint Kitts and Nevis 06/16/2008
(See EquiMed, Inc. (Saint Kitts and Nevis))

EQUIMED INC (SAINT KITTS AND NEVIS)
SEC revoked common stock registration 07/08/2010

EQUINE CORP (NY)
Name changed to Lexington Group, Inc. 04/24/1986
Lexington Group, Inc. name changed to Harris & Harris Group, Inc. 08/15/1988 which name changed to 180 Degree Capital Corp. 03/27/2017

EQUINE RES LTD (BC)
Recapitalized as Western Canadian Mining Corp. 01/21/1987
Each share Common no par exchanged for (0.3) share Common no par
Western Canadian Mining Corp. merged into Consolidated Brinco Ltd. 12/31/1990 which merged into Hillsborough Resources Ltd. (ON) 02/06/1992 which reincorporated in Canada 11/05/1997
(See Hillsborough Resources Ltd. (Canada))

EQUINETICS INC (NY)
Out of business 00/00/1987
Details not available

EQUINOX COPPER CORP (BC)
Recapitalized as Anfield Resources Inc. 09/23/2013
Each share Common no par exchanged for (0.1) share Common no par
Anfield Resources Inc. recapitalized as Anfield Energy Inc. 12/27/2017

EQUINOX ENTMT CORP (BC)
Name changed to Cancorp Enterprises Inc. 08/31/1988
Cancorp Enterprises Inc. name changed to G.E.M. Environmental Management Inc. (B.C.) 10/02/1989 which reincorporated in Delaware 07/13/1990
(See G.E.M. Environmental Management Inc.)

EQUINOX EXPL CORP (BC)
Name changed to Equinox Copper Corp. 02/01/2013
Equinox Copper Corp. recapitalized as Anfield Resources Inc. 09/23/2013 which recapitalized as Anfield Energy Inc. 12/27/2017

EQUINOX INTL INC (NV)
Name changed to Biostem U.S. Corp. 05/11/2010
(See Biostem U.S. Corp.)

EQUINOX MINERALS LTD (CANADA)
Acquired by Barrick Gold Corp. 07/19/2011
Each share Common no par exchanged for $8.15 cash

EQUINOX RES LTD NEW (BC)
Merged into Hecla Mining Co. 04/11/1994
Each share 8% Conv. Preferred no par exchanged for $1.50 principal amount of Unsecured Subord. Notes due 04/30/1997
Each share Common no par exchanged for (0.3) share Common 25¢ par

EQUINOX RES LTD OLD (BC)
Merged into Equinox Resources Ltd. (New) 12/08/1992
Each share Common no par exchanged for (1) share Common no par
Equinox Resources Ltd. (New) merged into Hecla Mining Co. 04/11/1994

EQUINOX SOLAR INC (FL)
Each share old Common 1¢ par exchanged for (0.25) share new Common 1¢ par 09/24/1985
Proclaimed dissolved for failure to file reports and pay fees 10/11/1991

EQUINOX SYS INC (FL)
Common 1¢ par split (3) for (2) by issuance of (0.5) additional share payable 06/10/1998 to holders of record 05/20/1998
Merged into Avocent Corp. 01/03/2001
Each share Common 1¢ par exchanged for $9.75 cash

EQUION CORP (DE)
Acquired by Equion Acquisition Corp. 03/31/1989
Each share Common 1¢ par exchanged for $9.75 cash

EQUIPMENT & SYS ENGR INC (FL)
Administratively dissolved 09/26/2014

EQUIPMENT CO AMER (FL)
Common 10¢ par split (5) for (4) by issuance of (0.25) additional share 10/25/1985
Common 10¢ par split (5) for (4) by issuance of (0.25) additional share 02/10/1987
Common 10¢ par split (5) for (4) by issuance of (0.25) additional share 02/19/1988
Stock Dividend - 30% 10/26/1984
Filed petition under Chapter 11 Federal Bankruptcy Code 02/26/1991
Case dismissed no stockholders' equity

EQUIPMENT LEASING & SALES CORP (WA)
Recapitalized as Intelispan Inc. 08/05/1998
Each share Common $0.0001 par exchanged for (0.2) share Common $0.0001 par
Intelispan Inc. merged into McLeodUSA Inc. 05/31/2001
(See McLeodUSA Inc.)

EQUIS ENERGY CORP (AB)
Merged into Magin Energy Inc. (New) 09/26/1996
Each share Common no par exchanged for (0.09090909) share Common no par
Magin Energy Inc. (New) acquired by NCE Petrofund 07/03/2001 which name changed to Petrofund Energy Trust 11/01/2003 which merged into Penn West Energy Trust 07/04/2006 which reorganized as Penn West Petroleum Ltd. (New) 01/03/2011 which name changed to Obsidian Energy Ltd. 06/29/2017

EQUISHARE DEV CORP (NV)
Recapitalized as Southland Financial Inc. 05/02/1995
Each share Common 1¢ par exchanged for (0.1) share Common 1¢ par
Southland Financial Inc. name changed to StarBridge Global Inc. 11/20/2000 which recapitalized as China Mulans Nano Technology Corp., Ltd. 01/29/2007

EQUISURE FINL NETWORK INC (ON)
Merged into ING Canada Inc. 01/22/2001
Each share Common no par exchanged for $7 cash

EQUISURE INC (MN)
Common 1¢ par split (2) for (1) by issuance of (1) additional share payable 11/29/1996 to holders of record 11/22/1996
Stock Dividend - 5% payable 05/30/1997 to holders of record 05/15/1997
Statutorily dissolved 09/25/2000

EQUITABLE BAG INC (NY)
Plan of reorganization under Chapter 11 Federal Bankruptcy Code effective 12/16/1994
Each share Common 1¢ par exchanged for (1) share Class B Common 1¢ par and (0.01) Class B

Common Stock Purchase Warrant expiring 12/16/1997
Plan of reorganization under Chapter 11 Federal Bankruptcy Code effective 07/09/1996
No Class B Common stockholders' equity
Assets sold for benefit of creditors 06/00/1999
New Common stockholders' equity undetermined

EQUITABLE BANCORPORATION (MD)
Common $5 par split (2) for (1) by issuance of (1) additional share 09/16/1983
Common $5 par split (3) for (2) by issuance of (0.5) additional share 04/15/1986
Adjustable Rate Preferred Ser. A $5 par called for redemption 12/15/1987
Adjustable Rate Preferred Ser. B $5 par called for redemption 04/01/1988
Stock Dividend - In Class B to holders of Common 10% 11/21/1984
Merged into MNC Financial, Inc. 01/18/1990
Each share Adjustable Rate Preferred Ser. C $5 par exchanged for (1) share Adjustable Rate Preferred Ser. CC $5 par
Each share Adjustable Rate Preferred Ser. D $5 par exchanged for (1) share Adjustable Rate Preferred Ser. DD $5 par
Each share Common $5 par exchanged for (1.41) shares Common $2.50 par
Each share Class B Common $2.50 par exchanged for (1.34655) shares Common $2.50 par
MNC Financial, Inc. merged into NationsBank Corp. (NC) 10/01/1993 which reincorporated in Delaware as BankAmerica Corp. (Old) 09/25/1998 which merged into BankAmerica Corp. (New) 09/30/1998 which name changed to Bank of America Corp. 04/28/1999

EQUITABLE BK (WHEATON, MD)
Stock Dividend - 5% payable 04/11/2000 to holders of record 03/28/2000
Merged into BB&T Corp. 03/14/2003
Each share Common 1¢ par exchanged for (1) share Common $5 par

EQUITABLE BANKSHARES COLO INC (CO)
Merged into WBH, Inc. 10/13/1994
Each share Common $10 par exchanged for $166.44 cash

EQUITABLE CASUALTY & SURETY CO.
Liquidated 00/00/1931
Details not available

EQUITABLE COS INC (DE)
Depositary Preferred Ser. C called for redemption 08/04/1997
$3 Conv. Preferred Ser. C $1 par called for redemption 08/04/1997
Conv. Preferred Ser. E $1 par called for redemption 08/04/1997
Name changed to AXA Financial Inc. 09/03/1999
AXA Financial Inc. merged into AXA S.A. 01/02/2001

EQUITABLE CR CORP (NY)
Recapitalized 00/00/1945
Each share Preference $3 par exchanged for (1) share Part. Preferred $2 par
Each share Prior Preferred $5 par exchanged for (3.1) shares Part. Preferred $2 par
Each share Common 1¢ par exchanged for (1) share Common $1 par
Each share Common $1 par exchanged for (8) shares Common 50¢ par 00/00/1948
Each share Common 50¢ par exchanged for (5) shares Common 25¢ par 07/17/1956
Merged into State Loan & Finance Corp. 09/30/1959
Each share 60¢ Preferred $5 par exchanged for (0.4) share 6% Preferred $25 par
Each share 50¢ Preferred $5 par exchanged for (0.33333333) share 6% Preferred $25 par
Each share Part. Preferred $2 par exchanged for (0.25) share Class A Common $1 par
Each share Common 25¢ par exchanged for (0.125) share Class A Common $1 par
State Loan & Finance Corp. name changed to American Finance System Inc. 05/01/1968 which merged into Security Pacific Corp. 12/15/1978 which merged into BankAmerica Corp. (Old) 04/22/1992 which into BankAmerica Corp. (New) 09/30/1998 which name changed to Bank of America Corp. 04/28/1999

EQUITABLE DEV CORP (FL)
Name changed to Solar Industries, Inc. 02/23/1977
Solar Industries, Inc. name changed to Pan American Gold, Inc. 04/10/1987
(See Pan American Gold, Inc.)

EQUITABLE DEVELOPMENT CORP. (DE)
Capital Stock 10¢ par changed to $0.001 par 05/15/1964
Recapitalized as TT & T Realty Equities, Inc. 12/12/1972
Each share Capital Stock $0.001 par exchanged for (0.666666) share Common $0.001 par
(See TT & T Realty Equities, Inc.)

EQUITABLE FED SVGS BK (WHEATON, MD)
Common 1¢ par split (2) for (1) by issuance of (1) additional share payable 02/12/1998 to holders of record 01/29/1998
Name changed to Equitable Bank (Wheaton, MD) 03/14/2000
Equitable Bank (Wheaton, MD) merged into BB&T Corp. 03/14/2003

EQUITABLE FINANCIAL CORP. (NJ)
Charter revoked for failure to file reports and pay fees 02/05/1963

EQUITABLE FINL CORP (USA)
Reorganized under the laws of Maryland 07/09/2015
Each share Common 1¢ par exchanged for (1.0911) shares Common 1¢ par

EQUITABLE FINL GROUP INC (FL)
Merged into 1st United Bancorp, Inc. 02/29/2008
Each share Common $7 par exchanged for (6.9855) shares Common 1¢ par
1st United Bancorp, Inc. merged into Valley National Bancorp 11/01/2014

EQUITABLE FINL SVCS AMER INC (FL)
Administratively dissolved for failure to file annual reports 11/09/1990

EQUITABLE FIRE INSURANCE CO. (SC)
Each share Capital Stock $50 par exchanged for (5) shares Capital Stock $10 par 00/00/1938
Acquired by Boston Insurance Co. 05/31/1957
Each share Capital Stock $10 par exchanged for (1) share Capital Stock $5 par
Boston Insurance Co. name changed to Bimar Corp. 06/06/1966
(See Bimar Corp.)

EQUITABLE GAS CO (PA)
4.5% Preferred $100 par called for redemption 02/09/1959
5.6% Preferred $100 par called for redemption 04/30/1965
4.36% Conv. Preferred $100 par changed to no par 06/01/1976
Common $8.50 par changed to $4.25 par and (1) additional share issued 06/29/1979
Common $4.25 par split (3) for (2) by issuance of (0.5) additional share 04/06/1981
4.36% Conv. Preferred no par called for redemption 03/05/1981
$4.60 Preferred no par called for redemption 03/05/1981
Common $4.25 par changed to no par and (0.5) additional share issued 01/31/1984
Name changed to Equitable Resources, Inc. 10/01/1984
Equitable Resources, Inc. name changed to EQT Corp. 02/09/2009

EQUITABLE GEN CORP (VA)
Merged into Gulf United Corp. 01/11/1979
Each share Common $3 par exchanged for (1) share $3.78 Conv. Preferred Ser. B $2.50 par
(See Gulf United Corp.)

EQUITABLE GROUP INC (ON)
Non-Cum. 5-Yr. Rate Reset Preferred Ser. 1 no par called for redemption at $25 on 09/30/2014
(Additional Information in Active)

EQUITABLE INVESTING CORP.
Liquidated 00/00/1934
Details not available

EQUITABLE INVESTMENT CORP. (OH)
Acquired by Transcontinental Investing Corp. 06/25/1963
Each share 7% Preferred $100 par exchanged for (10) shares Class A Common $1 par
Each share Class A or B Common $1 par exchanged for (1.17) shares Class A Common $1 par
Transcontinental Investing Corp. merged into Omega-Alpha, Inc. 03/07/1972
(See Omega-Alpha, Inc.)

EQUITABLE INVESTMENT CORP. MASSACHUSETTS
Merged into Eaton & Howard Stock Fund 00/00/1944
Details not available

EQUITABLE INVESTORS, INC.
Merged into Connecticut Investment Management Corp. 00/00/1931
Details not available

EQUITABLE INVESTORS SECURITIES, INC. (DE)
Charter cancelled and declared inoperative and void for non-payment of taxes 04/15/1968

EQUITABLE IOWA COS (IA)
Old Common no par reclassified as Non-Vtg. Class B Common no par and (0.24) share Class A Common no par distributed 04/25/1980
Class A Common no par reclassified as new Common no par 05/01/1992
Non-Vtg. Class B Common no par reclassified as new Common no par 05/01/1992
New Common no par split (2) for (1) by issuance of (1) additional share 06/02/1992
New Common no par split (2) for (1) by issuance of (1) additional share 06/01/1993
Stock Dividend - 50% 12/10/1986
Merged into ING Groep N.V. 10/24/1997
Each share new Common no par exchanged for either (1.5115) Sponsored ADR's for Ordinary or $68 cash

Note: Option to make a definitive election expired 10/30/1997

EQUITABLE IOWA COS CAP TR
8.70% Trust Originated Preferred Securities called for redemption at $25 on 08/28/2001

EQUITABLE LAND & OIL CO. THE (TX)
Charter forfeited for failure to pay taxes 04/19/1950

EQUITABLE LEASING CORP (NC)
Common 50¢ par changed to 25¢ par and (1) additional share issued 03/01/1961
Merged into First & Merchants Corp. 10/29/1973
Each share Common 25¢ par exchanged for $0.40 cash

EQUITABLE LIFE INSURANCE CO. OF CANADA (CANADA)
Mutualization completed 9/9/63

EQUITABLE LIFE INS CO IOWA (IA)
Name changed to Equitable of Iowa Companies and Common $1 par changed to no par 12/15/77
Equitable of Iowa Companies merged into ING Groep N.V. 10/24/97

EQUITABLE LIFE INS CO WASHINGTON D C (DC)
Each share Capital Stock $100 par exchanged for (10) shares Capital Stock $10 par 11/30/54
Capital Stock $10 par changed to $2 par and (4) additional shares issued 12/16/64
Capital Stock $2 par changed to $3 par 6/9/72
Capital Stock $3 par split (4) for (3) by issuance of (1/3) additional share 7/12/72
Reorganized as Equitable General Corp. 12/31/73
Each share Capital Stock $3 par exchanged for (1) share Common $3 par
Equitable General Corp. merged into Gulf United Corp. 1/11/79
(See Gulf United Corp.)

EQUITABLE LIFE LEASING CORP (DE)
Acquired by Lomas & Nettleton Financial Corp. 06/30/1987
Details not available

EQUITABLE LIFE MTG & RLTY INVS (MA)
Shares of Bene. Int. $1 par reclassified as Common $1 par 03/05/1975
Merged into Equitable Life Assurance Society of the United States 01/05/1983
Each share Common $1 par exchanged for $15.15 cash

EQUITABLE MONEY MKT ACCOUNT INC (MD)
Merged into Alliance Capital Reserves, Inc. (MD) 02/27/1987
Each share Common $0.001 par exchanged for (1) share Common $0.001 par
Alliance Capital Reserves, Inc. (MD) reincorporated in Massachusetts as AllianceBernstein Capital Reserves 04/07/2003
(See AllianceBernstein Capital Reserves)

EQUITABLE OFFICE BUILDING CORP. (NY)
Common no par exchanged (4) for (1) 00/00/1928
Each share Common no par exchanged for (0.2) share Common $1 par and the right to subscribe to (1.2) shares additional Common $1 par 00/00/1947
Merged into Webb & Knapp, Inc. 04/19/1955
Each share Common $1 par exchanged for $7 principal amount of 5% Debentures and $5 cash

EQU-EQU   FINANCIAL INFORMATION, INC.

EQUITABLE PETE CORP (DE)
Merged into Wichita River Oil Corp. (VA) (New) 03/30/1990
Each share Common 1¢ par exchanged for (1.6) shares new Common no par
Wichita River Oil Corp. (VA) (New) reincorporated in Delaware 03/30/1990
(See Wichita River Oil Corp. (DE))

EQUITABLE REAL ESTATE SHOPPING CTRS L P (DE)
Name changed to Midwest Real Estate Shopping Center L.P. 11/30/94
(See Midwest Real Estate Shopping Center L.P.)

EQUITABLE RES CAP TR I (DE)
Issue Information - 5,000,000 CAP SECS 7.35% offered at $25 per share on 04/16/1998
7.35% Capital Securities called for redemption at $25 on 4/23/2003

EQUITABLE RES INC (PA)
Common no par split (3) for (2) by issuance of (0.5) additional share 03/31/1987
Common no par split (3) for (2) by issuance of (0.5) additional share 01/25/1993
Common no par split (2) for (1) by issuance of (1) additional share payable 06/11/2001 to holders of record 05/11/2001 Ex date - 06/12/2001
Common no par split (2) for (1) by issuance of (1) additional share payable 09/01/2005 to holders of record 08/12/2005 Ex date - 09/02/2005
Name changed to EQT Corp. 02/09/2009

EQUITABLE SVGS & LN ASSN (CA)
Completely liquidated 12/20/1968
Each share Guarantee Stock $1 par exchanged for first and final distribution of (0.7) share LFC Financial Corp. Capital Stock $1 par
LFC Financial Corp. merged into Great Western Financial Corp. 12/22/1970 which merged into Washington Mutual Inc. 07/01/1997
(See Washington Mutual, Inc.)

EQUITABLE SVGS & LN ASSN (OR)
Reserve Fund Capital Stock $4 par changed to $2 par and (1) additional share issued 04/27/1973
Reserve Fund Capital Stock $2 par reclassified as Common $2 par 03/22/1977
Stock Dividends - 33-1/3% 12/10/1962; 25% 04/15/1965
Merged into Benjamin Franklin Savings & Loan Association 09/30/1982
To holdings of (250) shares of fewer:
Each share Common $2 par exchanged for $5 principal balance of 5.5% regular savings account passbook
To holdings of (251) shares or more:
In addition to above holders received an additional $5 principal amount divided between (3) certificate savings accounts

EQUITABLE SECS CORP (TN)
Merged into SunTrust Banks, Inc. 1/2/98
Each share Common $1 par exchanged for (24.24) shares Common $1 par

EQUITABLE SECURITY TRUST CO. (WILMINGTON, DE)
Stock Dividend - 10% 03/14/1958
Name changed to Bank of Delaware (Wilmington, DE) 04/11/1958
Bank of Delaware (Wilmington, DE) reorganized as Bank of Delaware Corp. 01/02/1983 which was acquired by PNC Financial Corp 03/31/1989 which name changed to PNC Bank Corp. 02/08/1993 which name changed to PNC Financial Services Group, Inc. 03/15/2000

EQUITABLE TR CO (BALTIMORE, MD)
Stock Dividends - 20% 2/1/51; 15% 2/1/54; 10% 2/1/55; 205.007236% 4/29/66
Reorganized as Equitable Bancorporation 2/1/72
Each share Capital Stock $10 par exchanged for (2) shares Common $5 par
Equitable Bancorporation merged into MNC Financial, Inc. 1/18/90 which merged into NationsBank Corp. 10/1/93 which reincorporated in Delaware as BankAmerica Corp. (Old) 9/25/98 which merged into BankAmerica Corp. (New) 9/30/98 which name changed to Bank of America Corp. 4/28/99

EQUITAS GROUP (NV)
Charter revoked for failure to file reports and pay fees 05/01/2004

EQUITAS RES CORP (BC)
Each share old Common no par exchanged for (0.33333333) share new Common no par 09/29/2014
Each share new Common no par exchanged again for (0.1) share new Common no par 01/03/2017
Name changed to Altamira Gold Corp. 04/18/2017

EQUITEC FD INC (CA)
Completely liquidated 00/00/1982
Details not available

EQUITEC FINL GROUP INC (CA)
Common 1¢ par split (2) for (1) by issuance of (1) additional share 05/07/1984
Plan of reorganization under Chapter 11 Federal Bankruptcy Code effective 09/30/1995
No stockholders' equity

EQUITEC REAL ESTATE INVS FD L P (CA)
Merged into Hallwood Realty Partners, L.P. 11/01/1990
Details not available

EQUITEC SIEBEL FD GROUP II (MA)
Merged into SunAmerica Fund Group II 06/30/1989
Details not available

EQUITEL INC (DE)
Charter cancelled and declared inoperative and void for non-payment of taxes 03/01/2003

EQUITEX INC (DE)
Common $0.001 par split (2) for (1) by issuance of (1) additional share 09/09/1985
Each share Common $0.001 par exchanged for (0.04) share Common 1¢ par 08/03/1992
Each share Common 1¢ par exchanged for (0.5) share Common 2¢ par 01/02/1996
Each share Common 2¢ par received distribution of (1) share Equitex 2000, Inc. Common 2¢ par payable 08/13/2001 to holders of record 07/20/2001
Each share Common 2¢ par exchanged for (1/6) share Common 1¢ par 01/25/2005
Each share Common 1¢ par received distribution of (0.5) Common Stock Purchase Warrant, Class A expiring 02/07/2010 and (0.5) Common Stock Purchase Warrant, Class B expiring 02/07/2010 payable 02/07/2005 to holders of record 02/07/2005
Name changed to Hydrogen Power International, Inc. 05/30/2006
Hydrogen Power International, Inc. name changed to Hydrogen Power, Inc. 12/26/2006
(See Hydrogen Power, Inc.)

EQUITEX 2000 INC (DE)
SEC revoked common stock registration 04/20/2016

EQUITIES INTL LIFE INS CO (TX)
Capital Stock $1 par changed to no par 07/09/1975
Merged into Citizens, Inc. 01/01/1989
Each share Common no par exchanged for (0.5) share Class A Common $1 par

EQUITORIAL CAP CORP (BC)
Name changed to Equitorial Exploration Corp. 07/04/2013

EQUITRAC CORP (FL)
Merged into Equity Investors LLC 8/13/99
Each share Common 1¢ par exchanged for $21 cash

EQUITRUST MONEY MKT FD INC (MD)
Merged into EquiTrust Series Fund, Inc. 08/31/2009
Each share Common $0.001 par exchanged for (1) share Money Market Portfolio Institutional Class $0.001 par

EQUITRUST MTG & SVGS CO (CANADA)
Merged into First City Mortgage Co. 01/01/1994
Details not available

EQUITY ANNUITY AGENCY, INC. OF NEVADA (NV)
Charter cancelled for failure to file reports and pay fees 3/1/65

EQUITY ANNUITY LIFE INSURANCE CO. (DC)
Acquired by Variable Annuity Life Insurance Co. of America (DC) 8/9/67
Each share Capital Stock $2 par exchanged for (1) share Capital Stock $1 par
Variable Annuity Life Insurance Co. of America (DC) reincorporated in Texas as Variable Annuity Life Insurance Co. 5/1/69 which merged into American General Insurance Co. 1/20/77 which reorganized as American General Corp. 7/1/80 which merged into American International Group, Inc. 8/29/2001

EQUITY AU INC (DE)
Each share old Common $0.001 par exchanged for (0.01) share new Common $0.001 par 09/24/1997
Name changed to Equity Technologies & Resources, Inc. 03/10/2000
Equity Technologies & Resources, Inc. recapitalized as VirtualHealth Technologies, Inc. 08/31/2006 which name changed to VHGI Holdings, Inc. 05/25/2010
(See VHGI Holdings, Inc.)

EQUITY BK (WETHERSFIELD, CT)
Stock Dividend - 10% 6/30/94
Merged into New England Community Bancorp, Inc. 11/30/95
Each share Common $10 par exchanged for (1.85) shares Class A Common 10¢ par
New England Community Bancorp, Inc. merged into Webster Financial Corp. 12/1/99

EQUITY CAP CO (MN)
Acquired by Kodiak, Inc. 11/1/68
Each share Common $1.25 par exchanged for (1.25) shares Common 50¢ par
Kodiak, Inc. recapitalized as Kodicor, Inc. 5/10/72
(See Kodicor, Inc.)

EQUITY CAP CORP
Completely liquidated 2/27/96
Each share Common exchanged for first and final liquidation of $1.09 cash

EQUITY CAP GROUP INC (NV)
Recapitalized as Voice Mobility International, Inc. 06/30/1999
Each share Common $0.001 par exchanged for (0.25) share Common $0.001 par

EQUITY CO-OPERATIVE EXCHANGE (ND)
Charter cancelled for failure to file annual reports 10/1/29

EQUITY COMWLTH (MD)
7.25% Preferred Ser. E 1¢ par called for redemption at $25 on 05/15/2016 (Additional Information in Active)

EQUITY COMPRESSION SVCS CORP (OK)
Name changed to OEC Compression Corp. 04/15/1998
OEC Compression Corp. merged into Hanover Compressor Co. 03/19/2001 which merged into Exterran Holdings, Inc. 08/20/2007 which name changed to Archrock, Inc. 11/04/2015

EQUITY CONCEPTS INC (CO)
Declared defunct and inoperative for failure to pay taxes and file annual reports 09/30/2004

EQUITY CORP.
Liquidation completed 01/09/1932
Details not available

EQUITY CORP (DE)
Each share $3 Preferred $1 par exchanged for (1) share $2 Preferred $1 par, (1) share Class A 10¢ par and (2) shares new Common 10¢ par 10/17/1950
Each share 20¢ Preferred 10¢ par exchanged for (0.1) share $2 Preferred $1 par 10/17/1950
Each share old Common 10¢ par exchanged for (1) share new Common 10¢ par 10/17/50
$2 Preferred $1 par called for redemption 08/09/1971
Under plan of merger name changed to Wheelabrator-Frye Inc. 11/04/1971
Wheelabrator-Frye Inc. merged into Signal Companies, Inc. 02/01/1983 which merged into Allied-Signal Inc. 09/19/1985 which name changed to AlliedSignal Inc. 04/26/1993 which name changed to Honeywell International Inc. 12/01/1999

EQUITY CORP INTL (DE)
Issue Information - 3,300,000 shares COM offered at $13 per share on 10/19/1994
Secondary Offering - 7,994,522 shares COM offered at $19.25 per share on 01/30/1997
Common 1¢ par split (3) for (2) by issuance of (0.5) additional share payable 10/2/96 to holders of record 9/23/96
Merged into Service Corp. International 1/19/99
Each share Common 1¢ par exchanged for (0.71053) share Common $1 par

EQUITY EDUCATORS ASSURN CO (CO)
Placed in receivership 03/20/1975
No stockholders' equity

EQUITY ENTERPRISES INC (DE)
Merged into New Equity, Inc. 11/01/1982
Each share Common 10¢ par exchanged for $3.50 cash

EQUITY EXPLORATIONS LTD. (ON)
Recapitalized as Eagle Gold Mines Ltd. 02/08/1967
Each share Capital Stock $1 par exchanged for (0.5) share Capital Stock $1 par
Eagle Gold Mines Ltd. merged into Agnico-Eagle Mines Ltd. 06/01/1972 which name changed to Agnico Eagle Mines Ltd. 04/30/2013

EQUITY FD INC (DE)
Common no par changed to 20¢ par 00/00/1933
Name changed to Safeco Equity Fund, Inc. (DE) 06/30/1973
Safeco Equity Fund, Inc. (DE) reincorporated in Washington 08/20/1987 which reincorporated back in Delaware 09/30/1993
(See Safeco Equity Fund, Inc.)

EQUITY FDG CORP AMER (DE)
Under plan of reorganization holders of Conv. Preferred Ser. B $100 par and Common 30¢ par who filed a timely proof of claim form prior to 03/31/1976 received shares of Orion Capital Corp. Common $1 par
(See Orion Capital Corp.)

EQUITY FIN HLDG CORP (BELIZE)
Name changed to Yantai Dahua Holdings Co. Ltd. 02/18/2003
Yantai Dahua Holdings Co. Ltd. name changed to China Agro-Technology Holdings, Ltd. 01/14/2008
(See China Agro-Technology Holdings, Ltd.)

EQUITY FINL HLDGS INC (CANADA)
Acquired by Smoothwater Capital Corp. 12/22/2017
Each share Common no par exchanged for $10.25 cash
Note: Unexchanged certificates will be cancelled and become without value 12/22/2020

EQUITY GENERAL INSURANCE CO. (CO)
Proclaimed defunct and inoperative for failure to pay taxes 10/10/62

EQUITY GENERAL INSURANCE CO. (FL)
Proclaimed dissolved for failure to file reports and pay fees 10/21/74

EQUITY GOLD INC (CO)
Involuntarily dissolved for failure to pay taxes and file annual reports 1/1/90

EQUITY GROUP INC (NY)
Recapitalized as Montebello Furniture Industries, Ltd. 07/01/1973
Each share Common 1¢ par exchanged for (0.2) share Common 5¢ par
(See Montebello Furniture Industries, Ltd.)

EQUITY GROWTH AMER INC (VA)
Name changed to Diversified Growth Corp. 5/1/76
(See Diversified Growth Corp.)

EQUITY GROWTH CORP (DE)
Charter cancelled and declared inoperative and void for non-payment of taxes 3/1/91

EQUITY GROWTH FD AMER INC (DE)
Common $1 par changed to 50¢ par and (1) additional share issued 05/15/1970
Merged into American General Enterprise Fund, Inc. 12/31/1979
Each share Common 50¢ par exchanged for (1.0257905434) shares Capital Stock $1 par
American General Enterprise Fund, Inc. name changed to American Capital Enterprise Fund, Inc. (MD) 09/09/1983 which reincorporated in Delaware as Van Kampen American Capital Enterprise Fund 08/03/1995 which name changed to Van Kampen Enterprise Fund 08/31/1998

EQUITY GROWTH SYS INC (DE)
Name changed to Amerinet Group.com Inc. 7/19/99
Amerinet Group.com Inc. name changed to Fields Technologies Inc. (DE) 7/3/2001 which reincorporated in Nevada as Park City Group, Inc. 8/8/2002

EQUITY INNS INC (TN)
9.5% Preferred Ser. A 1¢ par called for redemption at $25 on 08/11/2003
Under plan of merger each share 8% Preferred Ser. C 1¢ par or 8.75% Preferred Ser. B 1¢ par automatically became (1) share W2007 Grace Acquisition I, Inc. 8% Preferred Ser. C 1¢ par or 8.75% Preferred Ser. B 1¢ par respectively 10/25/2007
Merged into Grace Acquisition I, Inc. 10/25/2007
Each share Common 1¢ par exchanged for $23 cash

EQUITY INVT CORP (MD)
Name changed to Windjammer International Corp. and Class A Common 10¢ par reclassified as Common 10¢ par 9/25/68
(See Windjammer International Corp.)

EQUITY INV FD (MA & NY)
Name changed 04/22/1997
5th Utility Common Stock Series Units of Undivided Int. split (2) for (1) by issuance of (1) additional Unit 04/10/1986
6th Utility Common Stock Series Units of Undivided Int. split (2) for (1) by issuance of (1) additional Unit 04/10/1986
Units of Undivided Int. of First Exchange Series - AT&T Shares split (3) for (1) by issuance of (2) additional Units 10/14/1986
Trust terminated 01/17/1997
Each Unit of Undivided Int. Pacific Northwest Trust Concept Ser. received cash value
Trust terminated 02/26/1997
Each Unit of Undivided Int. Food Fund Concept Ser. received cash value
Trust terminated 09/12/1997
Each Unit of Undivided Int. 5th Utility Common Stock Series received cash value
Each Unit of Undivided Int. 6th Utility Common Stock Series received cash value
1st Utility Common Stock Series Units of Undivided Int. split (2) for (1) by issuance of (1) additional Unit 04/10/1986
2nd Utility Common Stock Series Units of Undivided Int. split (2) for (1) by issuance of (1) additional Unit 04/10/1986
3rd Utility Common Stock Series Units of Undivided Int. split (2) for (1) by issuance of (1) additional Unit 04/10/1986
4th Utility Common Stock Series Units of Undivided Int. split (2) for (1) by issuance of (1) additional Unit 04/10/1986
Name changed from Equity Income Fund to Equity Investor Fund 04/22/1997
Trust terminated 07/14/1998
Each Unit of Undivided Int. Concept Ser. Natural Gas Trust 2 received cash value
Trust terminated 08/20/1998
Each Unit of Undivided Int. Real Estate Income Fund received cash value
Trust terminated 06/02/2000
Each Unit of Undivided Int. Common Stock 1st Utility Ser. received $613.12 cash
Trust terminated 09/07/2001
Each Unit of Undivided Int. Common Stock 7th Utility Ser. received $0.4869 cash
Trust terminated 09/24/2001
Each Unit of Undivided Int. Common Stock 3rd Utility Ser. received $349.65 cash
Each Unit of Undivided Int. Common Stock 4th Utility Ser. received $277.01 cash
Trust terminated 11/02/2001
Each Unit of Undivided Int. Common Stock 2nd Utility Ser. received $377.84 cash
Trust terminated 08/01/2008
Each Unit of Undivided Int. AT&T 1st Exchange Ser. received $95.142 cash
Trust terminated 08/06/2008
Each Unit of Undivided Int. AT&T 2nd Exchange Ser. received $11.434 cash
(Additional Information in Active)

EQUITY INVESTORS, INC.
Name changed to Second Incorporated Equities in 1929
Second Incorporated Equities merged into Incorporated Investors Equities in 1930 which name changed to Consolidated Equities, Inc. in 1932

EQUITY INVESTORS CORP.
Merged into Equity Corp. (Old) 05/13/1931
Each share 6% Preferred $50 par exchanged for (1) share Preferred
Each share Common no par exchanged for (1) share Common
(See Equity Corp. (Old))

EQUITY LEASING CORP (DE)
Name changed to Equity Enterprises, Inc. 06/08/1970
(See Equity Enterprises, Inc.)

EQUITY LIFE & ANNUITY CO. (SC)
Capital Stock $25 par changed to 10¢ par 5/28/63
Merged into South Atlantic Corp. 11/1/81
Each share Capital Stock 10¢ par exchanged for $2.50 cash

EQUITY LIFE ASSURANCE OF CANADA
Acquired by Ontario Equitable Life & Accident Insurance Co. in 1929 which reorganized as Equitable Life Insurance Co. of Canada in 1936 which completed mutualization 9/9/63

EQUITY LIFE INSURANCE CO. (AL)
Merged into Founders Life Assurance Co. of Florida 3/31/66
Each share Common $1 par exchanged for (1.5) shares Capital Stock $1 par
Founders Life Assurance Co. of Florida merged into Founders Financial Corp. (Fla.) 6/16/69 which merged into Laurentian Capital Corp. (Fla.) 12/1/86 which reincorporated in Delaware 7/24/87

EQUITY LIFESTYLE PPTYS INC (MD)
8.034% Preferred Ser. A 1¢ par called for redemption at $25 plus $0.094846 accrued dividends on 10/18/2012
6.75% Depositary Preferred Ser. C called for redemption at $25 plus $0.412875 accrued dividends on 09/25/2017
(Additional Information in Active)

EQUITY MANAGEMENT CORP. (MD)
Charter cancelled for non-payment of taxes 7/3/74

EQUITY MARKETING INC (DE)
Reincorporated 04/07/1995
State of incorporation changed from (NY) to (DE) 04/07/1995
Name changed to EMAK Worldwide, Inc. 09/15/2004
(See EMAK Worldwide, Inc.)

EQUITY MEDIA HLDGS CORP (DE)
Chapter 11 bankruptcy proceedings converted to Chapter 7 on 06/21/2010
Stockholders' equity unlikely

EQUITY MIDWEST INC (DE)
Charter cancelled and declared inoperative and void for non-payment of taxes 3/1/90

EQUITY NATL FINL CORP (DE)
Name changed to Equity National Industries, Inc. 3/11/69
(See Equity National Industries, Inc.)

EQUITY NATL INDS INC (DE)
Charter cancelled and declared inoperative and void for non-payment of taxes 3/1/77

EQUITY NATIONAL LIFE INSURANCE CO. (GA)
Reincorporated under the laws of Delaware as Equity National Financial Corp. 7/1/68
Equity National Financial Corp. name changed to Equity National Industries, Inc. 3/11/69
(See Equity National Industries, Inc.)

EQUITY OFFICE PPTYS TR (MD)
Preferred Ser. D called for redemption at $25 plus $0.282187 accrued dividends on 11/14/2001
8.98% Preferred Ser. A 1¢ par called for redemption at $25 plus $0.261916 accrued dividends on 07/29/2002
8% Preferred Ser. F called for redemption at $25 plus $0.317187 accrued dividends on 06/27/2003
7.875% Preferred Ser. E called for redemption at $25 on 06/30/2003
8.625% Preferred Ser. C called for redemption at $25 plus $0.125781 accrued dividends on 01/05/2004
Merged into Blackstone Group 02/09/2007
Each share 5.25% Conv. Accredited Investors Preferred Ser. B 1¢ par exchanged for $50 cash
Each share 5.25% Conv. Preferred Ser. B exchanged for $50 cash
Each share 7.75% Preferred Ser. G 1¢ par exchanged for $25 cash
Each share Common 1¢ par exchanged for $55.50 cash

EQUITY OIL CO (CO)
Reincorporated 01/02/1958
State of incorporation changed from (UT) to (CO) 01/02/1958
Common $1 par split (2) for (1) by issuance of (1) additional share 04/04/1977
Stock Dividend - 300% 08/15/1980
Merged into Whiting Petroleum Corp. 07/20/2004
Each share Common $1 par exchanged for (0.185) share Common $0.001 par

EQUITY ONE INC (MD)
Merged into Regency Centers Corp. 03/01/2017
Each share Common 1¢ par exchanged for (0.45) share Common 1¢ par

EQUITY PLANNING CORP (NY)
Dissolved by proclamation 05/04/1994

EQUITY PRESERVATION CORP (BC)
Name changed to Brassie Golf Corp. (BC) 07/28/1993
Brassie Golf Corp. (BC) reorganized in Delaware as Divot Golf Corp. 06/16/1998 which name changed to orbitTRAVEL.com Corp. 04/20/2000 which name changed to Orbit Brands Corp. 10/12/2005
(See Orbit Brands Corp.)

EQUITY PROGRESS FD INC (DE)
Merged into Equity Growth Fund of America Inc. 08/01/1975
Each share Capital Stock $1 par exchanged for (0.41537) share Common 50¢ par
Equity Growth Fund of America Inc. merged into American General Enterprise Fund, Inc. 12/31/1979 which name changed to American Capital Enterprise Fund, Inc. (MD) 09/09/1983 which reincorporated in Delaware as Van Kampen American Capital Enterprise Fund 08/03/1995 which name changed to Van

Kampen Enterprise Fund 08/31/1998

EQUITY QUEST INC (DE)
Name changed to World Television, Inc. 06/03/1986
(See World Television, Inc.)

EQUITY RESIDENTIAL (MD)
Name changed 05/15/2002
$1.75 Conv. Preferred Ser. H called for redemption 06/30/1998
Each share $2.15 Conv. Preferred Ser. J 1¢ par exchanged for (0.6136) Share of Bene. Int. on 06/02/2000
9.375% Preferred Share of Bene. Int. Ser. A 1¢ par called for redemption at $25 plus $0.462239 accrued dividend on 06/25/2001
9.65% Preferred Share of Bene. Int. Ser. F 1¢ par called for redemption at $25 plus $0.475798 accrued dividend on 06/25/2001
Shares of Bene. Int. 1¢ par split (2) for (1) by issuance of (1) additional share payable 10/11/2001 to holders of record 09/21/2001 Ex date - 10/12/2011
Name changed from Equity Residential Properties Trust to Equity Residential 05/15/2002
7.625% Preferred Ser. L 1¢ par called for redemption at $25 plus $0.418315 accrued dividend on 06/19/2003
7.25% Conv. Depositary Preferred Ser. G 1¢ par called for redemption at $25.725 plus $0.357465 accrued dividend on 12/26/2003
9.125% Depositary Preferred Ser. B 1¢ par called for redemption at $25 plus $0.012673 accrued dividends on 10/17/2005
Depositary Preferred Ser. C called for redemption at $25 plus $0.354861 accrued dividends on 09/11/2006
8.6% Depositary Preferred Ser. D called for redemption at $25 plus $0.005972 accrued dividends on 07/16/2007
Each share $1.75 Conv. Preferred Ser. H 1¢ par exchanged for (1.448) Shares of Bene. Int. 1¢ par 10/29/2010
7% Conv. Preferred Shares of Bene. Int. 1¢ par called for redemption at $25 plus $0.1556 accrued dividends on 11/01/2010
6.48% Depositary Preferred Ser. N 1¢ par called for redemption at $25 plus $0.1575 accrued dividends on 08/20/2012
(Additional Information in Active)

EQUITY RESOURCES CORP. (OH)
Reorganized as Bancinsurance Corp. 03/01/1976
Each share Class A Common no par exchanged for (15) shares Common no par
(See Bancinsurance Corp.)

EQUITY RESV CORP (BC)
Merged into CanGold Resources Inc. (BC) 01/31/1994
Each share 7% Conv. Preferred Ser. A no par exchanged for (1) share 7% Conv. Preferred Ser. A no par
Each share Common no par exchanged for (1.666) shares Common no par
CanGold Resources Inc. (BC) reorganized in Ontario as Amalgamated CanGold Inc. 07/31/1995 which merged into Central Asia Goldfields Corp. 01/08/1996
(See Central Asia Goldfields Corp.)

EQUITY RETIREMENT DISTRS CDA LTD (ON)
Each share old Preferred no par exchanged for (0.05) share new Preferred no par 11/13/2003
Each share old Common no par exchanged for (0.05) share new Common no par 11/13/2003
Name changed to Infinity Mining Corp. 03/08/2006

EQUITY SAVINGS & LOAN ASSOCIATION, INC. (MD)
Name changed to Equity Investment Corp. 06/27/1961
Equity Investment Corp. name changed to Windjammer International Corp. 09/25/1968
(See Windjammer International Corp.)

EQUITY SAVINGS & LOAN CO. (OH)
Name changed to Equity Savings Association 00/00/1951
(See Equity Savings Association)

EQUITY SAVINGS ASSOCIATION (OH)
In process of liquidation 00/00/1953
Details not available

EQUITY SECS TR I (DE)
Trust terminated 11/15/2004
Each Equity Trust Security received (1) share Cablevision Systems Corp. Cablevision NY Group Class A Common 1¢ par

EQUITY SECS TR II (DE)
Trust terminated 02/15/2005
Each Equity Trust Security received distribution of (0.9762) Cablevision NY Group Class A Common 1¢ par

EQUITY SHARES, INC.
Dissolved 00/00/1938
Details not available

EQUITY SILVER MINES LTD (BC)
$1.60875 Conv. Preferred Ser. 1 no par called for redemption 02/15/1990
Common no par split (3) for (1) by issuance of (2) additional shares 06/08/1983
Common no par reclassified as Class A Common no par 05/01/1987
Merged into Placer Dome Ltd. 07/18/1995
Each share Class A Common no par exchanged for $0.85 cash

EQUITY STD CORP (ON)
Name changed to Bekeen Computer Corp. 09/15/1989
(See Bekeen Computer Corp.)

EQUITY STRATEGIES FD INC (MD)
Completely liquidated 04/26/1994
Each share Common $1 par received first and final distribution of (13,276,349) shares Nabors Industries, Inc. Common 10¢ par on a pro rata basis
Note: Certificates were not required to be surrendered and are without value

EQUITY SYS LTD (NV)
Each share old Common $0.001 par exchanged for (0.05) share new Common $0.001 par 08/14/1995
Recapitalized as North American Graphics Ltd. 11/25/1996
Each share new Common $0.001 par exchanged for (0.1) share Common $0.001 par
North American Graphics Ltd. name changed to Environmental Technology Systems Inc. 08/18/1997 which recapitalized as Tombao Antiques & Art Group 04/05/2012

EQUITY TECHNOLOGIES & RES INC (DE)
Each share old Common $0.001 par exchanged for (0.02) share new Common $0.001 par 08/04/2000
Each share new Common $0.001 par received distribution of (0.002) share Restricted Preferred payable 08/31/2001 to holders of record 07/16/2001
New Common $0.001 par changed to $0.0001 par 01/23/2003
Recapitalized as VirtualHealth Technologies, Inc. 08/31/2006
Each share new Common $0.0001 par exchanged for (0.01) share Common $0.001 par
VirtualHealth Technologies, Inc. name changed to VHGI Holdings, Inc. 05/25/2010
(See VHGI Holdings, Inc.)

EQUITY TRUST SHARES IN AMERICA
Trust terminated 00/00/1950
Details not available

EQUITY VENTURES INC (DE)
Recapitalized as EV Environmental Inc. 04/22/1992
Each share Common 1¢ par exchanged for (0.2) share Common 1¢ par
EV Environmental Inc. recapitalized as Burned Media Ltd. 11/25/2005

EQUITY WESTN FD INC (DE)
Name changed to SAFECO Western Fund, Inc. 06/26/1973
SAFECO Western Fund, Inc. name changed to SAFECO Special Bond Fund 01/28/1976
(See SAFECO Special Bond Fund)

EQUITYALERT COM INC (NV)
Recapitalized as InnoTech Corp. 07/31/2001
Each share Common no par exchanged for (0.04) share Common no par

EQUITYGUARD STK FD INC (MD)
Name changed to Capstone Equity Series, Inc. 05/21/1988
(See Capstone Equity Series, Inc.)

EQUIVEST FIN INC (FL)
12.50% Conv. Class A Preferred Ser. 1 $3 par called for redemption at $3 plus $0.75 accrued dividends on 2/13/98
Each share old Common 5¢ par exchanged for (0.25) share new Common 5¢ par 6/18/91
Merged into Cendant Corp. 2/11/2002
Each share new Common 5¢ par exchanged for $3 cash

EQUIVEST INC (GA)
Merged into Medical Resource Companies of America 03/24/1993
Each share Common 1¢ par exchanged for (1.5) Shares of Bene. Int. no par
Medical Resource Companies of America name changed to Greenbriar Corp. 03/27/1996 which name changed to CabelTel International Corp. 02/10/2005 which name changed to New Concept Energy, Inc. 06/03/2008

EQUIVEST INTL FINL CORP (BC)
Name changed to Allegro Property Inc. 03/25/1996
Allegro Property Inc. name changed to Valdor Fiber Optics Inc. 07/05/2000 which recapitalized as Valdor Technology International Inc. 07/21/2008

EQUIVISION INC (PA)
Merged into EquiMed, Inc. (DE) 02/02/1996
Each share Common no par exchanged for (0.5) share Common no par
EquiMed, Inc. (DE) reincorporated in Saint Kitts and Nevis 06/16/2008
(See EquiMed, Inc. (Saint Kitts and Nevis)

EQUUS ENERGY CORP (BC)
Recapitalized as Habibi Resources Corp. 08/27/2008
Each share Common no par exchanged for (0.1) share Common no par
Habibi Resources Corp. recapitalized as One World Investments Inc. 10/07/2009 which name changed to One World Minerals Inc. 02/28/2017 which name changed to One World Lithium Inc. 01/19/2018

EQUUS GAMING CO L P (VA)
Charter cancelled and proclaimed dissolved for failure to file reports 12/31/2008

EQUUS INDS INC (ON)
Recapitalized as Eros Financial Investments Inc. 03/04/1991
Each share Common no par exchanged for (0.1) share Common no par
Eros Financial Investments Inc. name changed to Eros Entertainment Inc. 06/02/1992 which name changed to Flying Disc Entertainment Inc. 06/28/1994 which name changed to Software Gaming Corp. 03/20/1998 which recapitalized as Xgen Ventures Inc. 11/26/2004
(See Xgen Ventures Inc.)

EQUUS INVTS INC (DE)
Merged into Equus II Inc. 06/30/1993
Each share Common $0.001 par exchanged for (0.54) share Common $0.001 par
Equus II Inc. name changed to Equus Total Return, Inc. 09/01/2006

EQUUS PETE CORP (BC)
Recapitalized as Nuequus Petroleum Corp. 09/30/1997
Each share Common no par exchanged for (0.2) share Common no par
Nuequus Petroleum Corp. name changed to Equus Energy Corp. 11/28/2002 which recapitalized as Habibi Resources Corp. 08/27/2008 which recapitalized as One World Investments Inc. 10/07/2009 which name changed to One World Minerals Inc. 02/28/2017 which name changed to One World Lithium Inc. 01/19/2018

EQUUS RES INC (CO)
Name changed to Quasar Aerospace Industries, Inc. 06/16/2009
Quasar Aerospace Industries, Inc. recapitalized as Green Energy Enterprises, Inc. 10/30/2015

EQUUS II INC (DE)
Stock Dividend - 10% payable 12/17/2001 to holders of record 12/03/2001
Name changed to Equus Total Return, Inc. 09/01/2006

ER URGENT CARE HLDGS INC (FL)
Each share old Common 10¢ par exchanged for (0.07692307) share new Common 10¢ par 04/23/2007
Proclaimed dissolved for failure to file reports and pay fees 09/25/2009

ERA CARBON OFFSETS LTD (BC)
Name changed to Offsetters Climate Solutions Inc. 03/04/2013
Offsetters Climate Solutions Inc. name changed to NatureBank Asset Management Inc. 10/20/2015

ERA CONSTR INDIA LTD (INDIA)
Name changed to Era Infra Engingeering Ltd. 06/25/2007
(See Era Infra Engineering Ltd.)

ERA INFRA ENGR LTD (INDIA)
GDR agreement terminated 04/23/2015
No GDR's remain outstanding

ERA RES INC (CANADA)
Each share old Common no par exchanged for (0.00000009) share new Common no par 06/15/2017
Notes: In effect holders received $0.25 cash per share and public interest was eliminated
Unexchanged certificates will be cancelled and become without value 06/13/2023

ERACON INDS INC (BC)
Name changed to Zcomm Industries, Inc. 06/02/1993
Zcomm Industries, Inc. recapitalized as Labrador International Mining Ltd.

08/25/1995 which recapitalized as Royal International Venture Corp. 03/18/1999 which recapitalized as RCOM Venture Corp. 07/28/2000 which name changed to Wellstar Energy Corp. 07/21/2005

ERAMONT PETROLEUMS LTD. (ON)
Charter cancelled and company declared dissolved for default in filing returns 12/23/1963

ERAMOSA TECHNOLOGY CORP (ON)
Merged into Hammond Manufacturing Co. Ltd. 05/29/1987
Each share Common no par exchanged for $0.33 cash

ERAWEST INC (NV)
Recapitalized as Securities Holding Corp. Inc. 02/09/2001
Each share Common $0.001 par exchanged for (0.1) share Common $0.001 par
Securities Holding Corp. name changed to Nationwide Safe T Propane, Inc. 03/26/2002 which recapitalized as EMP Solutions Inc. 03/10/2015

ERB LMBR CO (DE)
Reincorporated under the laws of Michigan and Common $1 par changed to 1¢ par 08/31/1975
(See Erb Lumber Co. (MI))

ERB LMBR CO (MI)
Common 1¢ par split (4) for (1) by issuance of (3) additional shares 07/11/1986
Merged into Fredco, Inc. 12/29/1986
Each share Common 1¢ par exchanged for $17 cash

ERBAMONT N V (NETHERLANDS ANTILLES)
Completely liquidated 05/14/1990
Each share Common $4 par received first and final distribution of $37 cash
Note: Certificates were not required to be surrendered and are without value

ERC CORP (DE)
Common $2.50 par split (2) for (1) by issuance of (1) additional share 10/10/1972
Merged into Getty Oil Co. 09/30/1980
Each share Common $2.50 par exchanged for $97 cash

ERC ENERGY RECOVERY CORP (DE)
Each share old Common $0.001 par exchanged for (0.0025) share new Common $0.001 par 09/30/1997
Each share new Common $0.001 par exchanged again for (0.00666666) share new Common $0.001 par 11/15/2007
New Common $0.001 par split (100) for (1) by issuance of (99) additional shares payable 11/15/2007 to holders of record 11/15/2007
Name changed to Go EZ Corp. and Common $0.001 par changed to $0.0001 par 06/09/2014

ERC ENVIRONMENTAL & ENERGY SVCS INC (DE)
Merged into Ogden Corp. 04/01/1991
Each share Common 5¢ par exchanged for $15.15 cash

ERC INDS INC NEW (DE)
Merged into John Wood Group 07/18/2000
Each share Common 1¢ par exchanged for $1.60 cash

ERC INDS INC OLD (DE)
Plan of reorganization under Chapter 11 Federal Bankruptcy Code effective 01/10/1989
No old Common stockholders' equity
Merged into ERC Industries, Inc. (New) 04/16/1993
Each share new Common 1¢ par exchanged for (1) share Common 1¢ par
(See ERC Industries, Inc (New))

ERC INTL INC (DE)
Acquired by Ogden Corp. 01/19/1990
Each share Common 5¢ par exchanged for (0.4067) share Common 50¢ par
Ogden Corp. name changed to Covanta Energy Corp. 03/14/2001
(See Covanta Energy Corp.)

ERCIYAS BIRACYLYK VE MALT SANAYI A S (TURKEY)
Sponsored 144A ADR's for Ordinary split (4) for (1) by issuance of (3) additional ADR's payable 03/11/1999 to holders of record 03/05/1999
Recapitalized as Anadolu Efes Biracilik Ve Malt Sanayi A.S. 07/24/2000
Each Sponsored 144A ADR for Ordinary exchanged for (0.08) Sponsored 144A ADR for Ordinary

ERCO RADIO LABS INC (NY)
Proclaimed dissolved 12/15/1971

ERD WASTE CORP (DE)
Charter cancelled and declared inoperative and void for non-payment of taxes 03/01/1999

ERDENE GOLD INC (CANADA)
Name changed to Erdene Resource Development Corp. 06/17/2008

ERDMAN, SMOCK, HOSLEY & REED, INC. (VA)
Name changed to Castle U.S. Corp. 08/08/1983
(See Castle U.S. Corp.)

ERE MGMT INC (NV)
Common $0.001 par changed to $0.0001 par and (29) additional shares issued payable 04/16/2012 to holders of record 04/16/2012 Ex date - 04/17/2012
Name changed to Guar Global Ltd. 10/08/2012

ERESEARCHTECHNOLOGY INC (DE)
Common 1¢ par split (3) for (2) by issuance of (0.5) additional share payable 07/16/2002 to holders of record 06/25/2002 Ex date - 07/17/2002
Common 1¢ par split (2) for (1) by issuance of (1) additional share payable 05/29/2003 to holders of record 05/06/2003 Ex date - 05/30/2003
Common 1¢ par split (3) for (2) by issuance of (0.5) additional share payable 11/26/2003 to holders of record 11/05/2003 Ex date - 11/28/2003
Common 1¢ par split (3) for (2) by issuance of (0.5) additional share payable 05/27/2004 to holders of record 05/06/2004
Acquired by Explorer Holdings, Inc. 07/03/2012
Each share Common 1¢ par exchanged for $8 cash

ERESERVATION SYS CORP (BC)
Each share old Common no par exchanged for (0.2) share new Common no par 07/06/2005
Name changed to Cobre Exploration Corp. 10/25/2007
Cobre Exploration Corp. name changed to Calico Resources Corp. 01/28/2011 which merged into Paramount Gold Nevada Corp. 07/07/2016

ERESOURCE CAP GROUP INC (DE)
Each share old Common 4¢ par exchanged for (0.14285714) share new Common 4¢ par 06/17/2002
Name changed to RCG Companies Inc. 11/14/2003
RCG Companies Inc. name changed to OneTravel Holdings, Inc. 06/08/2005
(See OneTravel Holdings, Inc.)

EREZ INC (AB)
Name changed to MCS Global Corp. (AB) 07/15/2003
MCS Global Corp. (AB) reorganized in British Columbia as Newstrike Capital Inc. 05/08/2006 which merged into Timmins Gold Corp. 05/28/2015 which recapitalized as Alio Gold Inc. 05/16/2017

ERG RES INC (QC)
Placed in receivership 11/27/1991
No stockholders' equity

ERG SPA (ITALY)
ADR agreement terminated 09/11/2017
No ADR's remain outstanding

ERGO SCIENCE CORP OLD (DE)
Reorganized as Ergo Science Corp. (New) 10/19/2001
Each share Common 1¢ par exchanged for (0.5) share Common 1¢ par

ERGONIC SYSTEMS, INC. (UT)
Name changed to North American & International Petroleum Corp., Inc. 07/02/1982
North American & International Petroleum Corp., Inc. name changed to North American Petroleum, Inc. 10/08/1982 which name changed to North American Consolidated, Inc. 12/06/1985

ERGONOMIC ENTERPRISES INC (MN)
Reincorporated under the laws of Texas as Ecarfly, Inc. 07/17/2006
Ecarfly, Inc. (TX) reincorporated in Nevada as Market 99 Ltd. 12/06/2007

ERGORESEARCH LTD (AB)
Name changed 03/05/2003
Name changed from Ergo Ventures Inc. to Ergoresearch Ltd. 03/05/2003
Acquired by 9332073 Canada Inc. 03/02/2018
Each share Common no par exchanged for $0.30 cash
Note: Unexchanged certificates will be cancelled and become without value 03/02/2024

ERGOVISION INC (DE)
Name changed to EyeCity.com, Inc. 05/11/1999

ERI VENTURES INC (BC)
Reincorporated under the laws of Yukon as Antam Resources International Ltd. 09/08/1997
Antam Resources International Ltd. recapitalized as International Antam Resources Ltd. 06/08/1999 name changed to Goldsource Mines Inc. (Yukon) 01/23/2004 which reincorporated in British Columbia 08/03/2005

ERIC'S STEAK HOUSE, INC. (WV)
Proclaimed dissolved for non-payment of taxes 08/22/1984

ERICA (NV)
Recapitalized as NPOWR Digital Media, Inc. 06/30/2005
Each share Common $0.001 par exchanged for (0.01) share Common $0.001 par
NPOWR Digital Media, Inc. name changed to NPW Development, Inc. 07/28/2005 which name changed to GreenZap, Inc. 11/7/2005 which name changed to Blue Star Opportunities Corp. 07/28/2008

ERICA RES LTD (BC)
Struck off register and declared dissolved for failure to file returns 12/09/1983

ERICKSEN ASHBY MINES LTD (BC)
Struck off register and declared dissolved for failure to file returns 08/26/1974

ERICKSON CORP (MN)
Each share Common 10¢ par exchanged for (0.0001) share Common $1,000 par 12/30/1981
Note: In effect holders received $1.10 cash per share and public interest was eliminated

ERICKSON GOLD MINES LTD (BC)
Reincorporated under the laws of Canada as Total Erickson Resources Ltd. and Capital Stock 1¢ par reclassified as Common no par 02/14/1986
Total Erickson Resources Ltd. merged into TOTAL Energold Corp. 09/19/1988
(See TOTAL Energold Corp.)

ERICKSON INC (DE)
Name changed 04/10/2014
Name changed from Erickson Air-Crane Inc. to Erickson Inc. 04/10/2014
Plan of reorganization under Chapter 11 Federal Bankruptcy proceedings effective 04/28/2017
No stockholders' equity

ERICKSON SUSPENSION WHEEL CORP. (DE)
No longer in existence having become inoperative and void for non-payment of taxes 03/17/1926

ERICKSON TIRE CORP. (DE)
No longer in existence having become inoperative and void for non-payment of taxes 03/18/1925

ERICSSON L M TEL CO (SWEDEN)
Each ADR exchanged for (5) ADR's for Ser. B 09/20/1990
ADR's for Ser. B split (4) for (1) by issuance of (3) additional ADR's 06/21/1995
Each old ADR for Ser. B exchanged for (0.1) new ADR for Ser. B 10/23/2002
Basis changed from (1:1) to (1:10) 10/23/2002
ADR's for Ser. B split (2) for (1) by issuance of (1) additional ADR payable 06/09/2008 to holders of record 06/04/2008 Ex date - 06/10/2008
Basis changed from (1:10) to (1:1) 06/09/2008
Stock Dividends - 25% 11/01/1965; 20% 10/10/1967; 20% 09/30/1969; 25% 10/00/1973; 25% 01/26/1977; 50% 11/30/1982; 100% payable 05/29/1998 to holders of record 05/27/1998; 300% payable 05/11/2000 to holders of record 05/10/2000
Name changed to Ericsson 04/05/2012

ERIE & PITTSBURGH RR CO (PA)
Merged into Penn Central Corp. 10/24/78
Each share Guaranteed Stock $50 par exchanged for (1.2) shares Conv. Preference Ser. B $20 par, (0.54) share Common $1 par, $24.05 principal amount of 7% General Mortgage Bonds Ser. A due 12/31/87 and $8.48 cash
Note: a) Distribution is certain only for certificates surrendered prior to 5/1/85 b) Distribution may also be made for certificates surrendered between 5/1/85 and 12/31/86 c) No distribution will be made for certificates surrendered after 12/31/86
Penn Central Corp. name changed to American Premier Underwriters, Inc. 3/25/94 which merged into American Premier Group, Inc. 4/3/95 which name changed to American Financial Group, Inc. 4/3/95 which name changed to American Financial Group, Inc. 6/9/95 which merged into American Financial Group, Inc. (Holding Co.) 12/2/97

ERIE BUS CO. (PA)
Liquidation completed 12/4/64

ERIE COACH CO. (PA)
Stock Dividend - 300% 10/11/48
Name changed to Erie Bus Co. which completed liquidation 12/4/64

ERIE CORP (IN)
Completely liquidated 06/01/1978
Each share Common Capital Stock received first and final distribution of $13 cash
Note: Option to receive Partnership Ctfs. expired 06/01/1978

ERIE DIVERSIFIED INDS LTD (ON)
Class A Preference no par and Common no par split (3) for (1) by issuance of (2) additional shares respectively 02/28/1969
Name changed to Lambda Mercantile Corp. Ltd. 10/23/1973
Lambda Mercantile Corp. Ltd. recapitalized as Lambda Mercantile Corp. 02/20/1979 which reorganized as Consolidated Mercantile Corp. 09/30/1987 which recapitalized as Consolidated Mercantile Inc. 11/23/1998 which merged into Genterra Capital Inc. (New) 05/10/2010 which merged into Gencan Capital Inc. 10/30/2015

ERIE FAMILY LIFE INS CO (PA)
Common 40¢ par split (3) for (1) by issuance of (2) additional shares 5/1/87
Common 40¢ par split (3) for (1) by issuance of (2) additional shares payable 5/10/96 to holders of record 5/2/96
Merged into Erie Idemnity Co. 5/31/2006
Each share Common 40¢ par exchanged for $32 cash

ERIE FDRY CO (PA)
Capital Stock $100 par changed to Common $10 par and (9) additional shares issued plus a 300% stock dividend paid 4/7/69
Name changed to Efco, Inc. 10/10/74
(See Efco, Inc.)

ERIE FLOORING & WOOD PRODUCTS LTD. (ON)
Name changed to Erie Diversified Industries Ltd. and Class B Common no par reclassified as Common no par 11/21/1968
Erie Diversified Industries Ltd. name changed Lambda Mercantile Corp. Ltd. 10/23/1973 which recapitalized as Lambda Mercantile Corp. 02/20/1979 which reorganized as Consolidated Mercantile Corp. 09/30/1987 which recapitalized as Consolidated Mercantile Inc. 11/23/1998 which merged into Genterra Capital Inc. (New) 05/10/2010 which merged into Gencan Capital Inc. 10/30/2015

ERIE FORGE & STL CORP (DE)
Common 10¢ par changed to $1 par 09/25/1957
Stock Dividend - 25% 04/13/1953
Adjudicated bankrupt 08/12/1969
No stockholders' equity

ERIE FORGE CO.
Name changed to Erie Forge & Steel Corp. in 1952
(See Erie Forge & Steel Corp.)

ERIE INVTS INC (IN)
Name changed to Erie Corp. 11/16/1973
(See Erie Corp.)

ERIE LACKAWANNA INC. LIQUIDATING TRUST (DE)
Liquidation completed
Each Share of Bene. Int. no par received fifth and final distribution of $1.47 cash 8/18/92
Note: Certificates were not required to be surrendered and are without value

(See Erie Lackawanna Inc. for previous distributions)

ERIE LACKAWANNA INC (DE)
Liquidation completed
Each share Capital Stock no par received initial distribution of $115 cash 11/30/1988
Each share Capital Stock no par received second distribution of $10 cash 04/06/1990
Each share Capital Stock no par received third distribution of $54 cash 05/31/1991
Each share Capital Stock no par received fourth distribution of $9.75 cash 01/02/1992
Assets transferred to Erie Lackawanna Liquidating Trust 01/02/1992
(See Erie Lackawanna Liquidating Trust)

ERIE LACKAWANNA RY CO (NY)
Merged into Dereco, Inc. 04/01/1968
Each share 5% Preferred Ser. A $100 par exchanged for (0.375) share Class A Conv. Preferred Ser. 1 $20 par
Each share 5% Preferred Ser. B $100 par exchanged for (0.385) share Class A Conv. Preferred Ser. 1 $20 par
Each share Common no par exchanged for (0.128) share Class B Conv. Preferred Ser. 1 $20 par
(See Dereco Inc.)

ERIE NAT GAS INC (DE)
Recapitalized as Oil Shale & Uranium Resources, Inc. 05/01/1968
Each share Common 50¢ par exchanged for (0.4) share Common 1¢ par
Oil Shale & Uranium Resources, Inc. name changed to Minerals & Industries, Inc. 06/18/1969 which name changed to Techno-Design, Ltd. 06/22/1987

ERIE RAILROAD CO. (NY)
Recapitalized in 1941
Each share 1st Preferred $100 par exchanged for (0.2) share Common no par
Each share 2nd Preferred $100 par exchanged for (0.2) share Common no par
Each share Common $100 par exchanged for (0.2) share Common no par
Under plan of merger name changed to Erie-Lackawanna Railroad Co. and each share Common no par received an additional (0.25) share Common no par 10/17/60
Erie-Lackawanna Railroad Co. merged into Dereco, Inc. 4/1/68
(See Dereco, Inc.)

ERIE RAILWAYS CO. (PA)
Reorganized as Erie Coach Co. 6/12/39
No stockholders' equity

ERIE REINFORCED PLASTIC PIPE CORP. (DE)
Name changed to Penn-Akron Corp. in 1957
Penn-Akron Corp. name changed to Heroes, Inc. 12/7/2000

ERIE RESISTOR CORP. (PA)
Common $5 par changed to $2.50 par and (1) additional share issued 4/30/57
Name changed to Erie Technological Products, Inc. 9/18/63
(See Erie Technological Products, Inc.)

ERIE SHARE CORP.
Acquired by Liberty Share Corp. in 1930
Details not available

ERIE STEAM SHOVEL CO.
Merged into Bucyrus-Erie Co. 00/00/1927

Details not available

ERIE TECHNOLOGICAL PRODS INC (PA)
$0.90 Conv. Preference 1957 Ser. $12.50 par called for redemption 06/15/1966
Merged into New Erie Corp. 12/24/1975
Each share Common $2.50 par exchanged for $10 cash

ERIENT RES INC (BC)
Recapitalized as First Idaho Resources Inc. 10/14/1987
Each share Common no par exchanged for (2) shares Common no par

ERIESHORE INDS INC (ON)
Merged into Portfield Industries Inc. 10/22/1980
Each share Common no par exchanged for (0.25) share Common no par
Portfield Industries Inc. recapitalized as Canmine Resources Corp. 05/01/1991
(See Canmine Resources Corp.)

ERIN EXPLS LTD (BC)
Common 50¢ par changed to no par 03/13/1974
Recapitalized as Intercon Petroleum Inc. 06/01/1981
Each share Common no par exchanged for (0.2) share Common no par
(See Intercon Petroleum Inc.)

ERIN KIRKLAND MINES LTD. (ON)
Charter revoked for failure to file reports and pay fees 03/30/1967

ERL RES LTD (BC)
Name changed to Tenajon Silver Corp. 12/16/1980
Tenajon Silver Corp. name changed to Tenajon Resources Corp. 09/15/1988 which merged into Creston Moly Corp. 08/26/2009 which merged into Mercator Minerals Ltd. 06/21/2011

ERLANGER MILLS CORP. (DE)
Plan of liquidation effective
Each share Prior Preferred $100 par received first and final distribution of $100.375 cash 06/30/1965
Each share Common $1 par received initial distribution of $18 cash plus an additional (0.58674) share Common 07/22/1965
Note: Details on additional distributions are not available

ERLY INDS INC (CA)
Stock Dividends - 10% 09/05/1986; 10% 09/24/1987; 10% 11/15/1988; 10% 12/20/1989; 10% 10/13/1990; 15% 10/06/1995; 10% payable 10/02/1996 to holders of record 09/23/1996; 10% payable 11/17/1997 to holders of record 10/31/1997
Reorganized under the laws of Delaware as Torchmail Communications, Inc. 05/24/2001
Each share Common 1¢ par exchanged for (0.01) share Common $0.001 par
Torchmail Communications, Inc. name changed to Ohana Enterprises, Inc. 12/11/2002 which reorganized as Vinoble, Inc. 11/19/2004 which name changed to Matrixx Resource Holdings, Inc. 07/14/2003
(See Matrixx Resource Holdings, Inc.)

ERMAN ENTERPRISES INC (UT)
Name changed to Genetic Technology, Inc. 04/27/1984

ERMITA SUGAR CO.
Property acquired by bond holders committee in 1933
No stockholders' equity

ERNDALE MINES LTD.
Recapitalized as Elancra Mines Ltd. 00/00/1949
Each share Capital Stock exchanged for (0.2) share Capital Stock
(See Elancra Mines Ltd.)

ERNST E C INC (DC)
Class A Common 50¢ par reclassified as Common 50¢ par 08/07/1975
Common 50¢ par changed to 40¢ par and (0.25) additional share issued 09/07/1977
Common 40¢ par changed to 1¢ par 12/09/1986
Merged into Philadelphia Bourse, Inc. 09/28/1987
Each share Common 1¢ par exchanged for $0.05 cash

ERNST HOME CTR INC (DE)
Plan of reorganization under Chapter 11 Federal Bankruptcy proceedings confirmed 07/09/1999
No stockholders' equity

ERNST INC (CA)
Name changed to Captech, Inc. 1/27/84
Captech, Inc. name changed to Matthews Studio Equipment Group 2/15/89
(See Matthews Studio Equipment Group)

ERO INC (DE)
Merged into Hedstrom Corp. 6/12/97
Each share Common 1¢ par exchanged for $11.25 cash

ERO INDUSTRIES, INC. (IL)
Stock Dividend - 100% 4/15/69
Reincorporated under the laws of Delaware 2/1/75
(See ERO Industries, Inc. (Del.))

ERO INDS INC (DE)
Common $1 par split (3) for (2) by issuance of (0.5) additional share 8/10/84
Common $1 par split (3) for (2) by issuance of (0.5) additional share 3/10/86
Common $1 par split (3) for (2) by issuance of (0.5) additional share 3/24/87
Stock Dividend - 25% 9/1/82
Acquired by GTC Leisure Holding Co. 7/15/88
Each share Common $1 par exchanged for $13 cash

ERO MANUFACTURING CORP. (IL)
Name changed to Ero Industries, Inc. (IL) 6/15/66
Ero Industries, Inc. (IL) reincorporated in Delaware 2/1/75
(See ERO Industries, Inc. (DE))

EROS ENTERPRISES INC. (DE)
Name changed to IQ Webquest, Inc. 03/03/2006
(See IQ Webquest, Inc.)

EROS ENTMT INC (ON)
Name changed 06/02/1992
Name changed from Eros Financial Investments Inc. to Eros Entertainment Inc. 06/02/1992
Name changed to Flying Disc Entertainment Inc. 06/28/1994
Flying Disc Entertainment Inc. name changed to Software Gaming Corp. 03/20/1998 which recapitalized as Xperia Corp. 11/09/2001 which recapitalized as Xgen Ventures Inc. 11/26/2004
(See Xgen Ventures Inc.)

EROS RED LAKE MINES LTD. (ON)
Charter cancelled and declared dissolved for failure to file returns and pay fees 07/27/1976

EROS RES LTD (BC)
Recapitalized as International Eros Holdings Ltd. 02/21/1992
Each share Common no par exchanged for (0.5) share Common no par

International Eros Holdings Ltd. name changed to Global Cable Systems, Inc. 04/12/1996 which recapitalized as Consolidated Global Cable Systems, Inc. 12/19/2000 which name changed to Chelsea Minerals Corp. 01/20/2010 which merged into Sennen Resources Ltd. 05/13/2011 which name changed to Sennen Potash Corp. 04/15/2013

EROX CORP (CA)
Name changed to Human Pheromone Sciences, Inc. 05/20/1998

ERROWANA GOLD MINES LTD. (ON)
Charter cancelled 09/30/1957

ERSKINE RES CORP (AB)
Acquired by Mark Resources Inc. 01/01/1989
Each share Common no par exchanged for (0.14084507) share Common no par and (0.07042253) Common Stock Purchase Warrant expiring 10/31/1991
Mark Resources Inc. acquired by EnerMark Income Fund 04/09/1996 which merged into Enerplus Resources Fund 06/22/2001 which reorganized as Enerplus Corp. 01/03/2011

ERSTE BK DER OESTERREICHISCHEN SPARKASSEN A G (AUSTRIA)
Sponsored 144A GDR's for Ordinary split (4) for (1) by issuance of (3) additional GDR's payable 07/09/2004 to holders of record 07/07/2004
Sponsored ADR's for Ordinary split (4) for (1) by issuance of (3) additional ADR's payable 07/09/2004 to holders of record 07/07/2004 Ex date - 07/12/2004
Name changed to Erste Group Bank 08/11/2008

ERT CORP. (DE)
Liquidation completed
Each share Common $1 par received initial distribution of $4 cash 05/11/1964
Each share Common $1 par exchanged for second and final distribution of $1 cash 12/14/1965

ERUPCION MINING CO.
Dissolved 00/00/1932
Details not available

ERXSYS INC (NV)
Name changed to Assured Pharmacy, Inc. 11/07/2005
(See Assured Pharmacy, Inc.)

ES&L BANCORP INC (DE)
Common 1¢ par split (3) for (2) by issuance of (0.5) additional share 09/01/1994
Common 1¢ par split (3) for (2) by issuance of (0.5) additional share payable 08/23/1996 to holders of record 08/16/1996
Merged into ESL Acquisition 08/11/2006
Each share Common 1¢ par exchanged for $50.75 cash

ESAFETYWORLD INC (NV)
Each share Common $0.001 par received distribution of (0.233) share Corpfin.com Inc. Common $0.001 par payable 04/01/2003 to holders of record 03/03/2003 Ex date - 02/27/2003
Recapitalized as EZ Auctions & Shipping, Inc. 02/28/2005
Each share Common $0.001 par exchanged for (0.02222222) share Common $0.001 par
(See EZ Auctions & Shipping, Inc.)

ESAOTE S P A (ITALY)
97.08% acquired by Bracco Bromed S.p.A. through a voluntary offer which expired 10/04/2002
Public interest eliminated

ESARTI ELEC TECHNOLOGIES CORP (NV)
Common $0.001 par split (6) for (1) by issuance of (5) additional shares payable 07/13/2000 to holders of record 07/13/2000
Name changed to Evader, Inc. (NV) 08/15/2003
Evader, Inc. (NV) reincorporated in Wyoming 05/25/2012 which name changed to Critic Clothing, Inc. 12/14/2015 which recapitalized as Deep Green Waste & Recycling, Inc. 09/27/2017

ESAT INC (NV)
Charter permanently revoked 06/30/2003

ESAT TELECOM GROUP PLC (IRELAND)
Merged into British Telecommunications PLC 07/10/2000
Each Sponsored ADR for Ordinary exchanged for $100 cash

ESAVINGSSTORE COM INC (NV)
Each share old Common $0.001 par exchanged for (0.5) share new Common $0.001 par 06/29/2007
Name changed to Immureboost, Inc. 07/19/2007
Immureboost, Inc. name changed to Fountain Healthy Aging, Inc. 10/09/2008
(See Fountain Healthy Aging, Inc.)

ESB BANCORP INC (DE)
Stock Dividends - 10% 04/15/1992; 10% 01/15/1993
Merged into PennFirst Bancorp, Inc. 03/25/1994
Each share Common 1¢ par exchanged for (0.972) share Common 1¢ par and $10.80 cash
PennFirst Bancorp, Inc. name changed to ESB Financial Corp. 05/01/1998 which merged into WesBanco, Inc. 02/10/2015

ESB BANCORP INC (NC)
Merged into Southern Bank & Trust Co. (Mount Olive, NC) 05/15/1998
Each share Common no par exchanged for $16 cash

ESB FINL CORP (PA)
Stock Dividends - 10% payable 05/29/1998 to holders of record 05/15/1998; 10% payable 05/31/2000 to holders of record 05/17/2000
Common 1¢ par split (6) for (5) by issuance of (0.2) additional share payable 05/30/2001 to holders of record 05/18/2001 Ex date - 05/16/2001
Common 1¢ par split (6) for (5) by issuance of (0.2) additional share payable 10/25/2002 to holders of record 09/30/2002 Ex date - 09/26/2002
Common 1¢ par split (6) for (5) by issuance of (0.2) additional share payable 05/15/2003 to holders of record 05/01/2003 Ex date - 04/29/2003
Common 1¢ par split (6) for (5) by issuance of (0.2) additional share payable 05/16/2011 to holders of record 05/05/2011
Common 1¢ par split (6) for (5) by issuance of (0.2) additional share payable 05/17/2013 to holders of record 05/03/2013 Ex date - 05/01/2013
Merged into WesBanco, Inc. 02/10/2015
Each share Common 1¢ par exchanged for (0.502) share Common $2.0833 par and $1.76 cash

ESB INC (DE)
Common $6.66666666 par split (2) for (1) by issuance of (1) additional share 08/18/1967
Merged into Inco Holdings Inc. 12/20/1974
Each share Common $6.66666666 par exchanged for $41 cash

ESC ENVIROTECH SYS CORP (BC)
Recapitalized as SWI Steelworks Inc. 03/29/1999
Each share Common no par exchanged for (0.1) share Common no par
(See SWI Steelworks Inc.)

ESC LIQUIDATING CO. (CO)
Liquidation completed
Each share Common no par received fourth distribution of $1.50 cash 10/07/1977
Each share Common no par received fifth distribution of $0.50 cash 07/11/1977
Each share Common no par received sixth distribution of $0.16 cash 12/31/1977
Each share Common no par received seventh distribution of $0.18 cash 12/30/1978
Each share Common no par received eighth and final distribution of $0.16 cash 04/01/1980
(See Elba Systems Corp. for previous distributions)

ESC MED SYS LTD (ISRAEL)
Ordinary ILS 0.10 par split (3) for (2) by issuance of (0.5) additional share payable 05/31/1996 to holders of record 05/30/1996
Name changed to Lumenis Ltd. 09/24/2001
(See Lumenis Ltd.)

ESCADA AG (GERMANY)
ADR agreement terminated 05/01/2008
Each Sponsored ADR for Bearer exchanged for $3.6789 cash

ESCAGENETICS CORP (DE)
Name changed 03/15/1988
Name changed from Escagen Corp. to Escagenetics Corp. 03/15/1988
Each share old Common $0.0001 par exchanged for (0.00714285) share new Common $0.0001 par 05/05/2003
Name changed to Krystal Digital Corp. 11/07/2003
Krystal Digital Corp. recapitalized as Sunningdale, Inc. 04/16/2004 which name changed to AdAI Group, Inc. 11/05/2004
(See AdAI Group, Inc.)

ESCALA GROUP INC (DE)
Name changed to Spectrum Group International, Inc. 05/21/2009

ESCALADE INC (DE)
Reincorporated under the laws of Indiana and Common $1 par changed to no par 07/23/1987

ESCALATOR INC (DE)
Each share old Common $0.001 par exchanged for (0.1) share new Common $0.001 par 04/12/1995
Name changed to Nu Electric Corp. 04/15/1998
Nu Electric Corp. name changed to Clean Water Technologies Inc. 04/02/2002 which name changed to SheerVision, Inc. 06/19/2006

ESCALON MED CORP (DE)
Reincorporated 11/17/1999
Each share old Common no par exchanged for (0.25) share new Common no par 11/24/1997
State of incorporation changed from (CA) to (DE) and Common no par changed to $0.001 par 11/17/1999
Reincorporated under the laws of Pennsylvania 11/07/2001

ESCAPE COM INC (CANADA)
Name changed to Escape Group Inc. 10/11/2001
Escape Group Inc. name changed to Escape Gold Inc. 07/26/2007 which

Merged into Inco Holdings Inc.
name changed to Rio Silver Inc. 11/15/2011

ESCAPE GOLD INC (CANADA)
Name changed to Rio Silver Inc. 11/15/2011

ESCAPE GROUP INC (CANADA)
Name changed to Escape Gold Inc. 07/26/2007
Escape Gold Inc. name changed to Rio Silver Inc. 11/15/2011

ESCHELON TELECOM INC (DE)
Merged into Integra Telecom Holdings, Inc. 08/31/2007
Each share Common 1¢ par exchanged for $30 cash

ESCO CORP (DE)
Voluntarily dissolved 08/20/1993
Details not available

ESCO ELECTRS CORP (MO)
Each Common Stock Trust Receipt exchanged for (1) share Common 1¢ par 01/17/2000
Name changed to ESCO Technologies Inc. 07/10/2000

ESCO TRANSPORTATION CO (DE)
Each share old Common $0.001 par exchanged for (10) shares new Common $0.001 par 12/17/1996
Chapter 11 bankruptcy proceedings converted to Chapter 7 on 10/15/2001
Stockholders' equity unlikely

ESCON INC (TX)
Completely liquidated 03/19/1968
Each share Common $1.25 par exchanged for first and final distribution of (1) share LTV Ling Altec, Inc. Conv. Preferred Ser. B $1 par and $17 cash
LTV Ling Altec, Inc. name changed to Altec Corp. 04/27/1972
(See Altec Corp.)

ESCONDIDO NATL BK (ESCONDIDO, CA)
Common $10 par changed to $5 par and (1) additional share issued 05/00/1970
Common $5 par changed to $1 par and (4) additional shares issued 01/15/1974
Name changed to First National Bank of San Diego County (Escondido, CA) 08/01/1976
(See First National Bank of San Diego County (Escondido, CA))

ESCUDO CAP CORP (BC)
Name changed to Aston Bay Holdings Ltd. 05/06/2013

ESD CO (CA)
Merged into Heath Tecna Corp. 02/04/1977
Each share Common $1 par exchanged for $13 cash

ESE CORP (NV)
Name changed to Renaissance Bioenergy, Inc. 03/04/2010
Renaissance Bioenergy, Inc. name changed to ASPA Gold Corp. 12/01/2010

ESELCO INC (MI)
Common 1¢ par split (3) for (2) by issuance of (0.5) additional share 05/14/1993
Stock Dividends - 3% payable 05/16/1996 to holders of record 05/01/1996; 3% payable 05/15/1997 to holders of record 05/01/1997
Merged into Wisconsin Energy Corp. 05/31/1998
Each share Common 1¢ par exchanged for (1.5114) shares Common 1¢ par
Wisconsin Energy Corp. name changed to WEC Energy Group, Inc. 06/30/2015

ESENJAY EXPL INC (OK)
12% Conv. Preferred 1¢ par called for redemption at $10 on 06/15/1998

ESG RE LTD (BERMUDA)
Ser. A Conv. Preferred 1¢ par called for redemption at $1.925 on 09/22/2000
Merged into ECM Acquisition Co. 04/26/2002
Each share Common 1¢ par exchanged for $2.84 cash

ESG RE LTD (BERMUDA)
Placed into liquidation 04/28/2011
Stockholders' equity unlikely

ESGRO INC (CA)
Common no par split (2) for (1) by issuance of (1) additional share 01/25/1967
Name changed to California Wholesale Electric Co. 06/21/1976
California Wholesale Electric Co. name changed to Chalet Gourmet Corp. 01/12/1982
(See Chalet Gourmet Corp.)

ESHARE COMMUNICATIONS INC (GA)
Name changed 06/08/2000
Name changed from eshare Technologies Inc. to eShare Communications Inc. 06/08/2000
Merged into divine, inc. 10/23/2001
Each share Common 1¢ par exchanged for (3.12) shares Class A Common $0.001 par
(See divine, inc.)

ESHED ROBOTEC (1982) LTD (ISRAEL)
Name changed to RoboGroup T.E.K. Ltd. 05/16/2001

ESHELMAN MOTORS CORP. (MD)
Charter annulled for failure to pay taxes 12/14/1961

ESHIPPERS COM MGMT LTD (BC)
Recapitalized as eShippers Management Ltd. 02/28/2003
Each share Common no par exchanged for (0.1) share Common no par

ESI ENTMT SYS INC (BC)
Acquired by 0979854 B.C. Ltd. 10/31/2013
Each share Common no par exchanged for $0.055 cash

ESI INDS INC (DE)
Reincorporated 09/18/1989
State of incorporation changed from (TX) to (DE) 09/18/1989
Name changed to Supreme Industries, Inc. 06/17/1993
(See Supreme Industries, Inc.)

ESIO WTR & BEVERAGE DEV CORP (NV)
Name changed to UPD Holding Corp. 03/01/2017

ESKAY GOLD CORP (BC)
Recapitalized as Consolidated Eskay Gold Corp. 10/05/1992
Each share Common no par exchanged for (0.55555555) share Common no par
Consolidated Eskay Gold Corp. name changed to DBA Telecom Corp. 04/08/1993 which recapitalized as Magnum Minerals Corp. 09/20/2004 which name changed to Magnum Uranium Corp. 10/03/2005 which was acquired by Energy Fuels Inc. 07/02/2009

ESKAY MNG CORP (BC)
Reincorporated under the laws of Ontario 11/02/2010

ESKER RES LTD (AB)
Acquired by Rider Resources Inc. 12/14/2001
Each share Common no par exchanged for (0.867) share Common no par
Rider Resources Inc. merged into Rider Resources Ltd. 02/21/2003 which merged into NuVista Energy Ltd. 03/04/2008

ESKEY INC (NV)
Merged into Yankee Companies, Inc. 01/02/1986
Each share $1 Conv. Preferred 1¢ par exchanged for (1) share $1.15 Preferred 10¢ par
Each share Common 10¢ par exchanged for (1) share $1.15 Preferred 10¢ par
Yankee Companies, Inc. reorganized as National Environmental Group Inc. 10/11/1989 which reorganized as Key Energy Group, Inc. 12/04/1992 which name changed to Key Energy Services Inc. (MD) 12/09/1998
(See Key Energy Services Inc. (MD))

ESKIMO COPPER MINES LTD (ON)
Charter cancelled for failure to pay taxes and file returns 03/16/1976

ESKIMO PIE CORP (VA)
Reincorporated 06/30/1996
Each share 7% Preferred $100 par exchanged for (1) share 5% Preferred $100 par and (21) shares Common no par 00/00/1948
Each share 5% Preferred $100 par exchanged for (20) shares Common $1 par 05/16/1962
Each share Class A Common no par or Class B Common no par exchanged for (0.33333333) share Common no par 00/00/1948
Common no par changed to $1 par 05/16/1962
Common $1 par split (5) for (2) by issuance of (1.5) additional share 03/17/1992
State of incorporation changed from (DE) to (VA) 06/30/1996
Merged into CoolBrands International Inc. 10/06/2000
Each share Common $1 par exchanged for $10.25 cash

ESKIMO RES LTD (BC)
Recapitalized as Ft. Lauderdale Resources Inc. 01/05/1987
Each share Common no par exchanged for (0.5) share Common no par
Ft. Lauderdale Resources Inc. recapitalized as Amcorp Industries Inc. 06/22/1990 which name changed to Molycor Gold Corp. 05/17/1996 which name changed to Nevada Clean Magnesium Inc. 04/17/2012

ESKOM (SOUTH AFRICA)
GDR agreement terminated 06/14/2007
Each GDR for Debt Security Ser. E168 exchanged for (10,000) shares Ordinary
Each GDR for Debt Security Ser. E170 exchanged for (10,000) shares Ordinary
Note: Unexchanged GDR's will be sold and the proceeds, if any, held for claim after 12/14/2007

ESL INC (CA)
Merged into TRW Inc. 06/09/1978
Each share Common 50¢ par exchanged for $47 cash

ESL TEACHERS INC (NV)
Name changed to Liberty Coal Energy Corp. 03/29/2010

ESM RES LTD (BC)
Recapitalized as EAV Ventures Corp. 12/10/1998
Each share Common no par exchanged for (0.2) share Common no par
EAV Ventures Corp. name changed to Vendtek Systems Inc. 10/05/1999
(See VendTek Systems Inc.)

ESMARK INC (DE)
Incorporated 02/24/1986
Merged into OAO Severstal 08/04/2008
Each share Common 1¢ par exchanged for $19.25 cash

ESMARK INC (DE)
Incorporated 03/14/1969
Common $1 par split (5) for (4) by issuance of (0.25) additional share 09/30/1975
4.75% Conv. Preferred Ser. A Class 1 $100 par called for redemption 10/30/1975
Common $1 par split (5) for (4) by issuance of (0.25) additional share 06/30/1981
Common $1 par split (5) for (4) by issuance of (0.25) additional share 11/30/1982
Common $1 par split (2) for (1) by issuance of (1) additional share 12/01/1983
Merged into Beatrice Companies, Inc. 08/07/1984
Each share $2.80 Conv. Class 2 Preferred Ser. B $1 par exchanged for $42.60 cash
Each share Common $1 par exchanged for $60 cash

ESMERALDA EXPL INC (BC)
Struck off register and declared dissolved for failure to file returns 07/09/1993

ESMOND MILLS, INC.
Name changed to Cantitoe Corp. 00/00/1948
(See Cantitoe Corp.)

ESMOR CORRECTIONAL SVCS INC (DE)
Common 1¢ par split (5) for (4) by issuance of (0.25) additional share 04/05/1995
Name changed to Correctional Services Corp. 08/01/1996
(See Correctional Services Corp.)

ESO URANIUM CORP (AB)
Recapitalized as Alpha Minerals Inc. 11/02/2012
Each share Common no par exchanged for (0.1) share Common no par
Alpha Minerals Inc. merged into Fission Uranium Corp. 12/06/2013

ESOFT INC (DE)
Name changed to Zvelo, Inc. 12/16/2010

ESOFTBANK COM INC (NV)
Name changed to Broadengate Systems Inc. 11/17/2001
Broadengate Systems Inc. name changed to Otter Lake Resources, Inc. 11/06/2006
(See Otter Lake Resources, Inc.)

ESOTERICS INC (DE)
Name changed to International Space Corp. 01/23/1989
(See International Space Corp.)

ESP INTL LTD (UT)
Proclaimed dissolved for failure to file reports 07/01/1989

ESPALAU MNG CORP (QC)
Name changed 05/00/1994
Name changed from Espalau Inc. to Espalau Mining Corp. 05/00/1994
Name changed to CED-Or Corp. 12/15/1998
(See CED-Or Corp.)

ESPEED INC (DE)
Name changed to BGC Partners, Inc. 04/01/2008

ESPERANZA (DOLORES) CORP. (ME)
Dissolved 02/27/1952
Details not available

ESPERANZA EXPLS LTD (BC)
Recapitalized as Columbia Gold Mines Ltd. 03/28/1990
Each share Common no par exchanged for (0.33333333) share Common no par
Columbia Gold Mines Ltd. recapitalized as Pacific Ridge Exploration Ltd. 05/12/1999

ESPERANZA MINES LTD. (BC)
Struck off register and declared dissolved for failure to file reports and pay fees 05/15/1969

ESPERANZA RESOURCE CORP (BC)
Merged into Alamos Gold Inc. (Old) 08/30/2013
Each share Common no par exchanged for (0.0265) Common Stock Purchase Warrant expiring 08/30/2018 and $0.85 cash

ESPERANZA SILVER CORP (BC)
Name changed to Esperanza Resources Corp. 07/19/2010
(See Esperanza Resources Corp.)

ESPERION THERAPEUTICS INC OLD (DE)
Merged into Pfizer Inc. 02/11/2004
Each share Common $0.001 par exchanged for $35 cash

ESPERO ENERGY CORP (DE)
Merged into Southwest Realty Trust 05/19/1995
Each share Common $0.005 par exchanged for $0.7392 cash
Note: An additional $0.02 cash per share was placed in escrow for future possible distribution

ESPEY MANUFACTURING CO., INC. (NY)
Name changed to Espey Mfg. & Electronics Corp. 04/06/1960

ESPINA COPPER DEVS LTD (BC)
Recapitalized as Northern Espina Resources Ltd. 09/13/1977
Each share Capital Stock 50¢ par exchanged for (0.25) share Capital Stock 50¢ par
Northern Espina Resources Ltd. name changed to Erica Resources Ltd. 01/09/1981
(See Erica Resources Ltd.)

ESPIRIT TELECOM GROUP PLC (ENGLAND & WALES)
Acquired by Global TeleSystems Group, Inc. 05/04/1999
Each Sponsored ADR for Ordinary exchanged for (0.89) share Common no par
Global TeleSystems Group, Inc. name changed to Global TeleSystems, Inc. 04/17/2000
(See Global TeleSystems, Inc.)

ESPIRITO SANTO FINL GROUP S A (LUXEMBOURG)
Name changed 09/30/1997
Sponsored ADR's for Ordinary split (2) for (1) by issuance of (1) additional ADR 08/02/1994
Name changed from Espirito Santo Financial Holding, S.A. to Espirito Santo Financial Group S.A. 09/30/1997
Stock Dividend - 1% payable 07/03/2002 to holders of record 06/14/2002 Ex date - 06/12/2002
ADR agreement terminated 06/26/2006
Each Sponsored ADR for Ordinary exchanged for $39.30666 cash

ESPO EAST CORP (NY)
Name changed to Paradigm System Solutions, Inc. 06/07/2011

ESPOIR EXPL CORP (AB)
Merged into Rockyview Energy Inc. 01/12/2006
Each share Class A no par exchanged for (0.5148) share Common no par
Each share Class B no par exchanged for (1.61379504) shares Common no par
(See Rockyview Energy Inc.)

ESPOON SAHKO OY (FINLAND)
Name changed to E.ON Finland OYJ 2/17/2004
(See E.ON Finland OYJ)

ESPORTBIKE COM INC (NV)
Recapitalized as Red Butte Energy, Inc. 04/10/2002
Each share Common $0.001 par exchanged for (0.125) share Common $0.001 par
Red Butte Energy, Inc. name changed to Canglobe International, Inc. 01/31/2003 which name changed to Globetech Environmental, Inc. 11/07/2005 which recapitalized as Global Gold Corp. 03/09/2009 which recapitalized as Fernhill Corp. 01/20/2012

ESPOS INC (NY)
Name changed to Integrated Performance Systems, Inc. (NY) 4/17/2001
Integrated Performance Systems, Inc. (NY) reorganized in Delaware as Global Innovation Corp. 11/17/2006

ESPOS LTD (NY)
Reorganized under the laws of Nevada as KMA Global Solutions International, Inc. 3/27/2006
Each share Common $0.001 par exchanged for (17) shares Common $0.001 par

ESPOS SURF & SPORT INC (NY)
Each share Common $0.001 par received distribution of (1) share Espo East Corp. Common $0.001 par payable 08/01/2008 to holders of record 07/21/2008 Ex date - 07/31/2008
Name changed to Bona Coffee Holdings Corp. 08/25/2008
Bona Coffee Holdings Corp. name changed to VuQo Holdings Corp. 05/09/2011 which name changed to WMAC Holdings Corp. (NY) 07/08/2013 which reincorporated in Nevada as Lighthouse Global Holdings Inc. 05/03/2018

ESPRE SOLUTIONS INC (DE)
Each share old Common $0.001 par exchanged for (3) shares new Common $0.001 par 05/02/2005
Plan of reorganization under Chapter 11 Federal Bankruptcy proceedings effective 05/12/2009
No stockholders' equity

ESPRIT ENERGY TR (AB)
Each Class A Trust Unit exchanged for (1) Trust Unit 07/05/2005
Each Class B Trust Unit exchanged for (1) Trust Unit 07/05/2005
Merged into Pengrowth Energy Trust 10/02/2006
Each Trust Unit no par exchanged for (0.53) Trust Unit no par
Pengrowth Energy Trust reorganized as Pengrowth Energy Corp. 01/03/2011

ESPRIT EXPL LTD (CANADA)
Plan of arrangement effective 10/01/2004
Each share Common no par exchanged for (0.25) share Esprit Energy Trust Class A Trust Unit, (0.2) share ProspEx Resources Ltd. Common no par and $0.22 cash
(See each company's listing)

ESPRIT FINL GROUP INC (NV)
Recapitalized as Monarc Corp. 02/13/2008
Each share Common $0.0001 par exchanged for (0.001) share Common $0.0001 par
Monarc Corp. recapitalized as Flexpower, Inc. 05/12/2014

ESPRIT RES LTD (AB)
Acquired by American Eagle Petroleums Ltd. 05/28/1990
Each share Common no par exchanged for $0.40 cash

ESPRIT SYS INC (DE)
Merged into Esprit Acquisition Corp. 07/12/1990

Each share Common 1¢ par exchanged for $0.17 cash

ESPS INC (DE)
Issue Information - 3,500,000 shares COM offered at $7.50 per share on 6/16/1999
Name changed to Liquent, Inc. 5/1/2001
(See Liquent, Inc.)

ESQUIRE COMMUNICATIONS LTD (DE)
Each share Common 1¢ par exchanged for (0.5) share Common 2¢ par 11/30/98
Filed a petition under Chapter 7 Federal Bankruptcy Code 3/19/2001
Stockholders' equity unlikely

ESQUIRE-CORONET, INC.
Name changed to Esquire, Inc. in 1939
(See Esquire, Inc.)

ESQUIRE INC (DE)
Common $1 par split (3) for (2) by issuance of (0.5) additional share 1/31/67
Common $1 par split (2) for (1) by issuance of (1) additional share 8/31/67
Common $1 par split (3) for (2) by issuance of (0.5) additional share 2/8/82
Common $1 par split (3) for (2) by issuance of (0.5) additional share 1/3/83
Common $1 par changed to 10¢ par 7/26/83
Common 10¢ par split (2) for (1) by issuance of (1) additional share 10/31/83
Merged into Gulf & Western Industries, Inc. 2/27/84
Each share Common 10¢ par exchanged for $23.50 cash

ESQUIRE RADIO & ELECTRS INC (DE)
100% acquired through purchase offer which expired 07/08/1994
Public interest eliminated

ESREY ENERGY LTD (BC)
Common no par split (50) for (1) by issuance of (49) additional shares payable 11/18/2013 to holders of record 11/18/2013
Name changed to Esrey Resources Ltd. 10/16/2017

ESS CAP INC (AB)
Name changed to Centillion Industries Inc. 12/09/2003
Centillion Industries Inc. name changed to Palo Duro Energy Inc. (AB) 05/29/2007 which reincorporated in British Columbia 12/19/2014 which recapitalized as CarbonOne Technologies Inc. 07/28/2015 which name changed to TekModo Industries Inc. 10/12/2016 which recapitalized as Lincoln Ventures Ltd. 07/16/2018

ESS TECHNOLOGY INC (CA)
Each share Common no par received distribution of (1.8) shares Vialta Inc. Class A Common no par payable 08/10/2001 to holders of record 07/23/2001
Merged into Imperium Master Fund, Ltd. 06/30/2008
Each share Common no par exchanged for $1.64 cash

ESSAR ENERGY PLC (UNITED KINGDOM)
ADR agreement terminated 06/17/2014
No ADR's remain outstanding

ESSAR PROJS LTD (INDIA)
GDR agreement terminated 03/06/2009
No GDR's remain outstanding

ESSAR SHIPPING PORTS & LOGISTICS LTD (INDIA)
Name changed 03/24/2008
Name changed from Essar Shipping Ltd. to Essar Shipping Ports & Logistics Ltd. 03/24/2008
GDR agreement terminated 10/01/2018
No GDR's remain outstanding

ESSEF CORP (OH)
Name changed 2/5/85
Name changed from ESSEF Industries, Inc. to ESSEF Corp. 2/5/85
Common no par split (2) for (1) by issuance of (1) additional share payable 9/9/97 to holders of record 8/22/97
Each share Common no par received distribution of (0.25) share Anthony & Sylvan Pools Corp. Common no par payable 8/10/99 to holders of record 8/10/99
Stock Dividends - 10% payable 2/28/97 to holders of record 2/7/97; 10% payable 3/3/98 to holders of record 2/12/98; 10% payable 3/10/99 to holders of record 2/19/99
Merged into Pentair Inc. 8/10/99
Each share Common no par exchanged for $18.97 cash

ESSELTE AB (SWEDEN)
Under plan of merger each ADR for Ordinary SKr12.5 par exchanged for $0.939331 cash 3/4/93

ESSELTE BUSINESS SYS INC (DE)
Acquired by Esselte AB 6/20/90
Each share Common $1 par exchanged for $48.06 cash

ESSENCE BIOTECHNOLOGIES INC (BC)
Name changed to American Sidewinder Oil Corp. 11/14/90
American Sidewinder Oil Corp. recapitalized as Texas Sidewinder Oil Corp. 11/23/92 which name changed to Archon Minerals Ltd. 7/2/93

ESSENCE PERFUME INC (UT)
Name changed to Essence International Inc. 4/10/91

ESSENCE RES INC (BC)
Name changed to Essence Biotechnologies Inc. 01/11/1988
Essence Biotechnologies Inc. name changed to American Sidewinder Oil Corp. 11/14/1990 which recapitalized as Texas Sidewinder Oil Corp. 11/23/1992 which name changed to Archon Minerals Ltd. 07/02/1993

ESSENDON SOLUTIONS INC (AB)
Name changed to ESO Uranium Corp. 06/27/2005
ESO Uranium Corp. recapitalized as Alpha Minerals Inc. 11/02/2012 which merged into Fission Uranium Corp. 12/06/2013

ESSENTIAL ENERGY SVCS TR (AB)
Reorganized as Essential Energy Services Ltd. 05/05/2010
Each Trust Unit exchanged for (1) share Common no par
Note: Unexchanged certificates were cancelled and became without value 05/05/2015

ESSENTIAL ENTERPRISES CORP. (DE)
Merged into Automatic Steel Products, Inc. 7/17/63
Each share Class A Common $1 par or Class B Common $1 par exchanged for (1.2) shares Common $1 par
Automatic Steel Products, Inc. name changed to Aspro, Inc. 11/26/69 which name changed to Dyneer Corp. 11/29/78 which name changed to DYR Liquidating Corp. 7/31/86
(See DYR Liquidating Corp.)

ESSENTIAL REALITY INC (NV)
Reorganized under the laws of Delaware as Alliance Distributors Holding Inc. 11/22/2004
Each share Common $0.001 par exchanged for (0.02272727) share Common $0.001 par
Alliance Distributors Holding Inc. name changed to Alliance Media Holdings Inc. 06/26/2015

ESSENTIAL RES INC (NV)
Common $0.001 par split (2) for (1) by issuance of (1) additional share payable 08/28/1996 to holders of record 08/26/1996
Charter permanently revoked for failure to file reports and pay fees 03/31/2000

ESSENTIAL TECHNOLOGIES INC (NV)
Each (15) shares old Common $0.001 par exchanged for (1) share new Common $0.001 par 11/14/1994
Name changed to Forbidden City Holdings, Inc. 02/03/1995
Forbidden City Holdings, Inc. name changed to Life Industries Inc. 05/26/1995 which recapitalized as Quill Industries Inc. 09/19/1997 which recapitalized as Ostrich Products of America, Inc. 06/01/2005 which name changed to PayPro, Inc. 07/11/2005 which name changed to Panamersa Corp. 02/16/2007 which recapitalized as Eagle Worldwide Inc. 01/12/2012

ESSENTIAL THERAPEUTICS INC (DE)
Plan of reorganization under Chapter 11 Federal Bankruptcy Code effective 10/21/2003
No stockholders' equity

ESSEX & HUDSON GAS CO.
Merged into Public Service Electric & Gas Co. 00/00/1939
Details not available

ESSEX ACQUISITION CORP (NV)
Name changed to B Squared Technologies Inc. 10/07/1999
B Squared Technologies Inc. recapitalized as Metropolis Technologies Corp. 02/20/2003 which recapitalized as Impact E-Solutions Corp. 02/08/2007
(See Impact E-Solutions Corp.)

ESSEX ANGEL CAP INC (CANADA)
Each share old Common no par exchanged for (0.05) share new Common no par 01/24/2014
Name changed to Block One Capital Inc. 11/09/2017

ESSEX BANCORP (DE)
Ser. A Preferred called for redemption 9/18/95
Merged into Essex Acquisition Corp. 8/31/2001
Each share Common 1¢ par exchanged for $1.45 cash

ESSEX BANCORP INC (MA)
Common $10 par split (2) for (1) by issuance of (1) additional share 12/29/78
Common $10 par changed to $5 par and (1) additional share issued 12/30/81
Merged into Conifer/Essex Group, Inc. 2/17/83
Each share Common $5 par exchanged for (0.6218) share Common $1 par
Conifer/Essex Group, Inc. name changed back to Conifer Group Inc. (New) 1/1/85

ESSEX BK (WEST ORANGE, NJ)
Liquidation completed
Each share Capital Stock $5 par exchanged for initial distribution of $18 cash 08/31/1983
Each share Capital Stock $5 par received second and final

distribution of $1.25 cash 03/30/1984

ESSEX BREWING CO., INC.
Bankrupt in 1938

ESSEX CHEM CORP (NJ)
6% Conv. 2nd Preferred Ser. A $100 par called for redemption 01/01/1966
6% Conv. Preferred Ser. A $100 par called for redemption 12/31/1976
Conv. Preferred Ser. A no par called for redemption 07/11/1977
Common $1 par split (5) for (4) by issuance of (0.25) additional share 09/27/1985
Common $1 par split (5) for (4) by issuance of (0.25) additional share 09/26/1985
Common $1 par changed 80¢ par and (0.25) additional share issued 12/11/1987
Common 80¢ par changed back to $1 par 05/03/1988
Stock Dividends - 10% 02/10/1981; 10% 12/18/1981; 10% 12/17/1982; 10% 12/19/1983; 10% 12/19/1984
Merged into Dow Chemical Co. 10/21/1988
Each share Common $1 par exchanged for $36 cash

ESSEX COMMUNICATIONS CORP (DE)
Merged into ECC Holding Corp. 03/31/1988
Each share Class A Common 1¢ par exchanged for $17.85 cash
Each share Class A Common 1¢ par received an additional distribution of $2.98 cash 04/12/1989
Each share Class A Common 1¢ par received second and final additional distribution of $0.355 cash 12/18/1989

ESSEX CORP (VA)
Merged into Northrop Grumman Corp. 01/25/2007
Each share Common 10¢ par exchanged for $24 cash

ESSEX CNTY BK & TR CO (LYNN, MA)
Stock Dividends - 10% 2/15/68; 10% 2/17/70
Reorganized as Essex Bancorp, Inc. 2/3/72
Each share Capital Stock $10 par exchanged for (1) share Common $10 par
Essex Bancorp, Inc. merged into Conifer/ Essex Group, Inc. 2/17/83 which name changed back to Conifer Group Inc. (New) 1/1/85

ESSEX COUNTY ELECTRIC CO. (MA)
Merged into Merrimack-Essex Electric Co. share for share 7/30/57
Merrimack-Essex Electric Co. Common acquired by New England Electric System 6/30/59
(See New England Electric Systems)

ESSEX CNTY GAS CO (MA)
Common $5 par changed to $2.50 par and (1) additional share issued 4/1/87
Merged into Eastern Enterprises 9/30/98
Each share Common $2.50 par exchanged for (1.183985) shares Common $1 par
(See Eastern Enterprises)

ESSEX CNTY ST BK (WEST ORANGE, NJ)
Name changed to Essex Bank (West Orange, NJ) and Capital Stock $10 par changed to $5 par 03/01/1976
(See Essex Bank (West Orange, NJ))

ESSEX COURT APARTMENTS
Trust terminated in 1949
Details not available

ESSEX ENTERPRISES INC (DE)
Reorganized as Veronique Inc. 12/13/1996

Each share Common $0.001 par exchanged for (2) shares Common $0.001 par
Veronique Inc. name changed to Digital Launch Inc. 04/13/1999 which name changed to Global e Tutor, Inc. 02/03/2000 which recapitalized as Winning Brands Corp. 11/09/2005

ESSEX FD INC (MA)
Merged into Magellan Fund, Inc. 06/25/1976
Each share Capital Stock $1 par exchanged for (0.434) share Capital Stock $1 par
Magellan Fund, Inc. merged into Fidelity Magellan Fund, Inc. 06/22/1981

ESSEX FIDELITY & PLATE GLASS INSURANCE CO.
Dissolved in 1936

ESSEX FINL PARTNERS L P (DE)
Merged into Essex Bancorp, Inc. 1/18/95
Each Unit of Ltd. Partnership exchanged for (0.5) share Common 1¢ par
(See Essex Bancorp, Inc.)

ESSEX FIRE INSURANCE CO. (NJ)
Acquired by Sussex Fire Insurance Co. in 1931
Details not available

ESSEX INTL INC (DE)
Issue Information - 5,750,000 shares COM offered at $17 per share on 04/17/1997
Merged into Superior Trust I 3/31/99
Each share Common 1¢ par exchanged for (0.64) share 8.50% Conv. Preferred 1¢ par
(See Superior Trust I)

ESSEX INTL INC (MI)
Common $1 par split (2) for (1) by issuance of (1) additional share 03/09/1973
Merged into United Aircraft Corp. 02/05/1974
Each share $2.84 Conv. Preferred Ser. A $1 par exchanged for (1) share $2.84 Conv. Prior Preferred $1 par
Each share Common $1 par exchanged for (0.2) share $8 Conv. Preferred $1 par
United Aircraft Corp. name changed to United Technologies Corp. 04/30/1975

ESSEX INVT CO (NJ)
Each share old Capital Stock $10 par exchanged for (0.01) share new Capital Stock $10 par 12/10/82
Note: In effect holders received $300 cash per share and public interest was eliminated

ESSEX OFFSHORE INC (DE)
Liquidation completed
Each share Common 10¢ par received initial distribution of $6 cash 10/31/91
Each share Common 10¢ par received second distribution of $7 cash 10/23/92
Each share Common 10¢ par received third distribution of $4 cash 10/25/93
Each share Common 10¢ par received fourth distribution of $7 cash 2/24/94
Each share Common 10¢ par received fifth and final distribution of $5 cash 11/14/94
Note: Certificates were not required to be surrendered and are without value

ESSEX PACKERS LTD (ON)
Declared bankrupt 00/00/1976
No stockholders' equity

ESSEX PETE CORP (BC)
Name changed to Fibertech Industries Corp. 11/18/1985

Fibertech Industries Corp. recapitalized as Solar Pharmaceutical Ltd. 08/11/1989

ESSEX PRODUCTS, INC. (NJ)
Each share Capital Stock 50¢ par exchanged for (5) shares Capital Stock 10¢ par in January 1954
Dissolved 1/31/65
No stockholders' equity

ESSEX PPTY TR INC (MD)
7.8125% Preferred Ser. F $0.0001 par called for redemption at $25 on 05/30/2011
Each share 4.875% Preferred Ser. G $0.0001 par exchanged for (0.19301) share Common $0.0001 par 05/14/2014
7.125% Preferred Ser. H $0.0001 par called for redemption at $25 on 04/15/2016
(Additional Information in Active)

ESSEX RESOURCE CORP (BC)
Recapitalized as Maximus Ventures Ltd. 04/08/2002
Each share Common no par exchanged for (0.1) share Common no par
Maximus Ventures Ltd. merged into Bear Lake Gold Ltd. 09/17/2008 which merged into Kerr Mines Inc. 05/26/2014

ESSEX SYS INC (NY)
Common 10¢ par split (2) for (1) by issuance of (1) additional share 5/23/68
Charter cancelled and proclaimed dissolved for failure to pay taxes 6/24/81

ESSEX TRUST CO. (LYNN, MA)
Stock Dividend - 10% 2/25/60
Name changed to Essex County Bank & Trust Co. (Lynn, MA) 1/20/64
Essex County Bank & Trust Co. (Lynn, MA) reorganized as Essex Bancorp, Inc. 2/3/72 which merged into Conifer/Essex Group, Inc. 2/17/83 which name changed back to Conifer Group Inc. (New) 1/1/85

ESSEX UNIVERSAL CORP. (DE)
Each share Common 10¢ par exchanged for (0.0666666) share Common $1 par 5/31/57
Acquired by Blauner's 12/29/61
Each share Common $1 par exchanged for (1/3) share Common 50¢ par
Blauner's name changed to Gale Industries, Inc. 11/11/63
(See Gale Industries, Inc.)

ESSEX WIRE CORP (MI)
Common $1 par split (2) for (1) by issuance of (1) additional share 05/19/1967
Name changed to Essex International, Inc. 12/19/1968
Essex International, Inc. merged into United Aircraft Corp. 02/05/1974 which name changed to United Technologies Corp. 04/30/1975

ESSICK INVT CO (CA)
98% acquired by private interests 00/00/1979
Public interest eliminated

ESSILOR INTL S A (FRANCE)
ADR's for Ordinary split (2) for (1) by issuance of (1) additional ADR payable 07/23/2007 to holders of record 07/20/2007 Ex date - 07/24/2007
Name changed to EssilorLuxottica 10/09/2018

ESSROC FIN CORP
Asset Backed Short Term Auction Rate Preferred Ser. A called for redemption at $1,000,000 on 12/3/97
Asset Backed Short Term Auction Rate Preferred Ser. B called for redemption at $1,000,000 on 12/10/97

Asset Backed Short Term Auction Rate Preferred Ser. C called for redemption at $1,000,000 on 12/17/97

ESSROC OFFSHORE LTD
Money Market Preference Ser. 1 called for redemption at $500,000 on 8/26/99
Money Market Preference Ser. 2 called for redemption at $500,000 on 8/26/99

ESSTRA INDS CORP (AB)
Reincorporated 05/07/1993
Place of incorporation changed from (BC) to (AB) 05/07/1993
Each share Common no par received distribution of (1) share Antarex Metals Ltd. Common no par payable 09/11/1997 to holders of record 09/03/1997
Name changed to Esstra Industries Inc. 09/11/1997

ESSXSPORT CORP (NV)
Name changed to Giant Jr. Investments, Corp. 05/28/2004
Giant Jr. Investments, Corp. name changed to Financial Media Group, Inc. 09/14/2005 which name changed to Clicker Inc. 07/08/2009
(See Clicker Inc.)

ESTABROOKS (T.H.) CO. LTD. (CANADA)
Name changed to Brooke Bond Canada (1959) Ltd. 5/13/59
Brooke Bond Canada (1959) Ltd. name changed to Brooke Bond Canada Ltd. 7/9/61 which name changed to Brooke Bond Foods Ltd. 11/7/69 which name changed to Brooke Bond Inc. 1/12/81
(See Brooke Bond Inc.)

ESTATE COFFEE HLDGS CORP (NV)
Name changed to Fresh Traffic Group Inc. 11/04/2010
Fresh Traffic Group Inc. recapitalized as Synergetics, Inc. 08/31/2012

ESTATE FUND MANAGEMENT CORP. (UT)
Completely liquidated 9/29/70
Each share Capital Stock $1.25 par exchanged for first and final distribution of $1.25 cash

ESTATE LIFE INS CO AMER (VA)
Merged into Founders Financial Corp. (FL) 6/30/81
Each share Common 25¢ par exchanged for (0.25) share Common $1 par
Founders Financial Corp. (FL) merged into Laurentian Capital Corp. (FL) 12/1/86 which reincorporated in Delaware 7/24/87
(See Laurentian Capital Corp.)

ESTATES, INC. (NV)
Charter revoked for failure to file reports and pay fees 03/03/1958

ESTATES LIFE OF WASHINGTON (WA)
Each share Voting Common $10 par or Non-Voting Common $10 par exchanged for (0.41) share new Common $10 par in 1960
Name changed to Preferred Life Insurance Co. 12/16/61
Preferred Life Insurance Co. recapitalized as Washington Preferred Life Insurance Co. 8/16/65 which merged into Northern National Life Insurance Co. 9/7/71 which name changed to Manhattan National Life Insurance Co. 1/1/82
(See Manhattan National Life Insurance Co.)

ESTATION COM INC (ON)
Each share old Common no par exchanged for (0.25) share new Common no par 06/30/2000
Name changed to eStation Network Services Inc. 10/30/2001
(See eStation Network Services Inc.)

ESTATION NETWORK SVCS INC (ON)
Assets foreclosed upon 06/30/2004
Stockholders' equity unlikely

ESTAURUM MINES LTD (CANADA)
Name changed to Westaurum Industries Inc. 07/22/1991
Westaurum Industries Inc. recapitalized as Opal Energy Inc. 10/14/1993 which was acquired by Founders Energy Ltd. 01/12/1999 which reorganized as Provident Energy Trust 03/06/2001 which reorganized as Provident Energy Ltd. (New) 01/03/2011 which merged into Pembina Pipeline Corp. 04/02/2012

ESTEBAN'S MEXICAN FOODS, INC. (MN)
Name changed to Esteban Foods Inc. 8/6/84
Esteban Foods Inc. name changed to Arden International Kitchens, Inc. 7/10/85
(See Arden International Kitchens, Inc.)

ESTEBANS FOODS INC (MN)
Name changed to Arden International Kitchens, Inc. 7/10/85
(See Arden International Kitchens, Inc.)

ESTEC SYS CORP (AB)
Reincorporated 12/19/2005
Place of incorporation changed from (BC) to (AB) 12/19/2005
Acquired by 2000067 Alberta Ltd. 12/20/2016
Each share Common no par exchanged for $0.12 cash
Note: Unexchanged certificates will be cancelled and become without value 12/19/2019

ESTEEM SOFTWARE SOLUTIONS INC (FL)
Common $0.0001 par split (4) for (1) by issuance of (3) additional shares payable 10/26/1999 to holders of record 10/24/1999
Recapitalized as Wavescribe International Corp. 01/29/2002
Each (90) shares Common $0.0001 par exchanged for (1) share Common $0.0001 par
Wavescribe International Corp. recapitalized as Security Financing Services, Inc. 09/29/2006 which recapitalized as Echo Satellite Communications, Inc. 02/11/2008 which recapitalized as SatMAX Corp. 05/05/2009 which name changed to Green Energy Solution Industries, Inc. 03/02/2012

ESTELLA MINES LTD. (BC)
Recapitalized as United Estella Mines Ltd. 00/00/1955
Each share Common $1 par exchanged for (0.2) share Common $1 par
(See United Estella Mines Ltd.)

ESTELLE REYNA INC (NV)
Name changed to Karma Media, Inc. 09/24/2003
Karma Media, Inc. recapitalized as Pit BOSS Entertainment, Inc. 07/18/2005 which name changed to US Energy Holdings, Inc. 03/08/2006 which name changed to Lonestar Group Holdings, Co. 01/10/2007 which recapitalized as Guardian Angel Group, Inc. 12/14/2007 which recapitalized as Ree International, Inc. 06/29/2011

ESTER PORCUPINE GOLD MINES LTD. (ON)
Dissolved 00/00/1958
Details not available

ESTERBROOK PEN CO (NJ)
Name changed 00/00/1946
Name changed from Esterbrook Steel Pen Manufacturing Co. to Esterbrook Pen Co. 00/00/1946
Merged into Venus Esterbrook Corp. 11/29/1967
Each share Common no par exchanged for (1) share $1.50 Conv. Preferred $40 par
Venus Esterbrook Corp. name changed to Domac Enterprises Inc. (NY) 10/05/1973 which reincorporated in Delaware 10/01/1975
(See Domac Enterprises Inc.)

ESTERLINE CORP (DE)
Common 20¢ par split (3) for (2) by issuance of (0.5) additional share 5/9/80
Common 20¢ par split (3) for (2) by issuance of (0.5) additional share 12/1/80
Name changed to Esterline Technologies Corp. 3/7/91

ESTEY CORP. (DE)
Name changed to Estey Electronics, Inc. 7/6/60
(See Estey Electronics, Inc.)

ESTEY ELECTRONICS, INC. (DE)
Each share Common 1¢ par exchanged for (0.05) new share Common 10¢ par 5/29/61
Adjudicated a bankrupt 2/5/65
Common Stock is valueless

ESTEY ORGAN CORP. (DE)
Recapitalized as Estey Corp. on a (1) for (10) basis 3/23/59
Estey Corp. name changed to Estey Electronics, Inc. 7/6/60
(See Estey Electronics, Inc.)

ESTEY ORGAN CORP. (VT)
Reincorporated under laws of Delaware and Common $1 par changed to 1¢ par 10/29/56
Estey Organ Corp. (DE) recapitalized as Estey Corp. 3/23/59 which name changed to Estey Electronics, Inc. 7/6/60
(See Estey Electronics, Inc.)

ESTEY-WELTE CORP.
Name changed to Welte Co., Inc. 00/00/1927
(See Welte Co., Inc.)

ESTRELLA GOLD CORP (ON)
Merged into Alianza Minerals Ltd. 04/30/2015
Each share Common no par exchanged for (1) share Common no par
Note: Unexchanged certificates will be cancelled and become without value 04/30/2021

ESTRELLA INTL ENERGY SVCS LTD (AB)
Reincorporated 07/21/2011
Place of incorporation changed from (AB) to (ON) 07/21/2011
Each share old Common no par exchanged for (0.01) share new Common no par 11/01/2013
Each share new Common no par exchanged again for (0.00000071) share new Common no par 12/30/2016
Note: In effect holders received $0.19 cash per share and public interest was eliminated
No distributions of less than $1 will be made
Unexchanged certificates will be cancelled and become without value 12/30/2019

ESTRELLAS U.S.A., INC. (NY)
In process of liquidation in 1954

ESURE GROUP PLC (ENGLAND & WALES)
ADR agreement terminated 08/06/2018
No ADR's remain outstanding

ESYNCH CORP (DE)
Recapitalized as Mergence Corp. 2/13/2004
Each share Common $0.001 par exchanged for (0.025) share Common $0.001 par

ESYS HLDGS INC (DE)
Name changed to PERF Go-Green Holdings, Inc. 05/09/2008

ET VOILA EUROPEAN CAFES INC (NV)
Name changed to Celtron International, Inc. 04/16/2002
Celtron International, Inc. name changed to Satellite Security Corp. 05/31/2006 which name changed to Mobicom Corp. 05/22/2008
(See Mobicom Corp.)

ETABLISSEMENTS DELHAIZE FRERES ET CIE LE LION S A (BELGIUM)
Sponsored ADR's for Ordinary split (4) for (1) by issuance of (3) additional ADR's payable 04/04/2014 to holders of record 04/01/2014 Ex date - 04/07/2014
Basis changed from (1:1) to (1:0.25) 04/07/2014
Merged into Koninklijke Ahold Delhaize N.V. 07/25/2016
Each Sponsored ADR for Ordinary exchanged for (1.1875) new Sponsored ADR's for Ordinary

ETAC SALES LTD (CANADA)
Wound up 12/04/2000
No stockholders' equity

ETANA TECHNOLOGIES CORP (BC)
Recapitalized as Techtana Capital Ltd. 07/29/1991
Each share Common no par exchanged for (0.5) share Common no par
Techtana Capital Ltd. recapitalized as Forum Ventures Ltd. 12/21/1995 which recapitalized as Forum Development Corp. 10/15/2001 which name changed to Forum Uranium Corp. 06/27/2006 which name changed to Forum Energy Metals Corp. 02/28/2018

ETC (ELECTRONIC TELE-COMMUNICATIONS CORP.) (DE)
Name changed to ETC. Technologies Corp. 7/24/87
(See ETC. Technologies Corp.)

ETC ENTERPRISES INC (CO)
Name changed to Chartwell Capital Corp. 12/20/1988
(See Chartwell Capital Corp.)

ETC TECHNOLOGIES CORP (DE)
Charter cancelled and declared inoperative and void for non-payment of taxes 3/1/93

ETC TRANSACTION CORP (AB)
Reincorporated under the laws of Delaware as Electronic Transmission Corp. and Common no par changed to $0.001 par 02/11/1997

ETEC SYS INC (NV)
Merged into Applied Materials Inc. 3/29/2000
Each share Common 1¢ par exchanged for (1.298) shares Common no par

ETELCHARGE COM (NV)
Common $0.003 par split (4) for (1) by issuance of (3) additional shares payable 04/04/2005 to holders of record 03/29/2005 Ex date - 04/05/2005
SEC revoked common stock registration 03/05/2013

ETELECARE GLOBAL SOLUTIONS INC (PHILIPPINES)
Basis changed from (1:2) to (1:1) 09/03/2007
ADR agreement terminated 04/27/2009
Each Sponsored ADR for Common exchanged for $8.85 cash

ETELOS INC (DE)
Name changed to Cloudward, Inc. 08/24/2012

ETERNAL ENERGY CORP (NV)
Recapitalized as American Eagle Energy Corp. 12/20/2011
Each share Common $0.001 par exchanged for (0.22222222) share Common $0.001 par
(See American Eagle Energy Corp.)

ETERNAL IMAGE INC (DE)
Each share old Common $0.001 par exchanged for (0.05) share new Common $0.001 par 01/16/2008
Each share new Common $0.001 par exchanged again for (0.05) share new Common $0.001 par 01/07/2011
Involuntary Chapter 7 bankruptcy proceedings terminated 01/06/2015
No stockholders' equity

ETERNAL TECHNOLOGIES GROUP INC (NV)
SEC revoked common stock registration 03/09/2011

ETERNALITE INC (LA)
Recapitalized 10/26/1956
Each share Class AA Preferred $100 par exchanged for (29.7) shares Class A Common 50¢ par
Each share Class A Common no par exchanged for (13.5) shares Class A Common 50¢ par
Charter revoked for failure to file annual reports 05/13/1982

ETERNIT S A (BRAZIL)
Sponsored ADR's for Ordinary split (2) for (1) by issuance of (1) additional ADR payable 10/02/2014 to holders of record 09/30/2014 Ex date - 10/03/2014
ADR agreement terminated 06/15/2015
Each Sponsored ADR for Ordinary exchanged for $0.460536 cash

ETF ADVISORS TR (DE)
Completely liquidated
Each Treasury FITR 1 received first and final distribution of $0.561542 cash payable 5/30/2003 to holders of record 5/27/2003
Each Treasury FITR 2 received first and final distribution of $2.02682 cash payable 5/30/2003 to holders of record 5/27/2003
Each Treasury FITR 5 received first and final distribution of $3.720206 cash payable 5/30/2003 to holders of record 5/27/2003
Each Treasury FITR 10 received first and final distribution of $5.756008 cash payable 5/30/2003 to holders of record 5/27/2003
Note: Certificates were not required to be surrendered and are without value

ETF MANAGERS TR (DE)
Trust terminated 12/23/2016
Each share The Restaurant ETF received $28.1725 cash
PureFunds ETFx HealthTech ETF reclassified as ETFMG ETFx HealthTech ETF 08/01/2017
Trust terminated 08/01/2017
Each share PureFunds ISE Big Data ETF received $27.701 cash
Each share Purefunds Solactive FinTech ETF received $29.0968 cash
Trust terminated 09/07/2017
Each share ETFMG ETFx HealthTech ETF received $28.4325 cash
Trust terminated 06/20/2018
Each share Spirited Funds/ETFMG Whiskey & Spirits ETF received approximately $32.31 cash
(Additional Information in Active)

ETF SER SOLUTIONS (DE)
Trust terminated 07/15/2016
Each share Falah
Russell-IdealRatings U.S.Large Cap
ETF received $26.03822 cash
Under plan of reorganization each
share Master Income ETF
automatically became (1) share
GraniteShares ETF Trust HIPS US
High Income ETF 12/18/2017
Trust terminated 06/29/2018
Each share AlphaClone International
ETF received $25.2532 cash
(Additional Information in Active)

ETF SER TR (DE)
Name changed to Recon Capital
Series Trust 06/08/2015
Recon Capital Series Trust name
changed to Horizons ETF Trust I
02/28/2017

ETFIS SER TR I (DE)
Trust terminated 08/31/2017
Each share Tuttle Tactical
Management Multi-Strategy Income
ETF no par received $22.81318
cash
Each share Tuttle Tactical
Management U.S. Core ETF no par
received $22.67507 cash
Trust terminated 10/01/2018
Each share iSectors Post-MPT
Growth ETF received $27.31 cash
(Additional Information in Active)

ETFS ASIAN GOLD TR (NY)
Trust terminated 08/12/2015
Each ETFS Physical Asian Gold
Share received $106.70912 cash

ETFS GOLD TR (NY)
Name changed to Aberdeen Standard
Gold ETF and Physical Swiss Gold
Shares no par reclassified as
Physical Swiss Gold Shares ETF
10/01/2018

ETFS PALLADIUM TR (NY)
Name changed to Aberdeen Standard
Palladium ETF Trust and Physical
Palladium Shares no par reclassified
as Physical Palladium Shares ETF
10/01/2018

ETFS PRECIOUS METALS BASKET TR (NY)
Name changed to Aberdeen Standard
Precious Metals Basket ETF Trust
and Physical PM Basket Shares no
par reclassified as Physical Precious
Metals Basket Shares ETF
10/01/2018

ETFS SILVER TR (NY)
Name changed to Aberdeen Standard
Silver ETF Trust and Physical Silver
Shares no par reclassified as
Physical Silver Shares ETF
10/01/2018

ETFS TR (DE)
Trust terminated 11/28/2016
Each share Diversified-Factor
Developed Europe Index Fund
received $21.9842 cash
Each share Diversified-Factor U.S.
Large Cap Index Fund received
$26.2911 cash
Trust terminated 01/30/2017
Each share Zacks Earnings
Large-Cap U.S. Index Fund received
$27.4985186 cash
Each share Zacks Earnings
Small-Cap U.S. Index Fund received
$26.8834234 cash
Name changed to Aberdeen Standard
Investments ETFs 10/01/2018

ETFS WHITE METALS BASKET TR (NY)
Trust terminated
Each ETFS Physical WM Basket
Share received $28.96033 cash
payable 06/07/2016 to holders of
record 03/03/2016

ETG CORP (NV)
Name changed to AIMS Worldwide,
Inc. 12/17/2002
(See AIMS Worldwide, Inc.)

ETG INTL INC (MN)
Reincorporated 01/11/1995
State of incorporation changed from
(IA) to (MN) 01/11/1995
Recapitalized as SolutionNet
International, Inc. 03/29/1999
Each share Common no par
exchanged for (0.025) share
Common no par
(See SolutionNet International, Inc.)

ETHAN ALLEN INC (NY)
Merged into Interco Inc. (Old) 1/28/80
Each share Class A $1 par
exchanged for (0.5) share $7.75
Conv. Preferred Ser. D no par
Each share Class B $1 par
exchanged for (0.5) share $7.75
Conv. Preferred Ser. D no par
(See Interco Inc. (Old))

ETHANEX ENERGY INC (NV)
Each share old Common $0.001 par
exchanged for (0.1) share new
Common $0.001 par 01/24/2008
Plan of reorganization under Chapter
11 Federal bankruptcy proceedings
effective
Each share new Common $0.001 par
received $0.6795153 cash payable
10/02/2014 to holders of record
04/08/2014

ETHANOIL & GAS CORP (NV)
Reorganized as Sympowerco Corp.
01/18/2008
Each share Common $0.001 par
exchanged for (1.1) shares Common
$0.001 par

ETHEL COPPER MINES LTD (ON)
Charter cancelled for failure to pay
taxes and file returns 04/09/1975

ETHEL GOLD MINING CO. (WY)
Charter revoked for failure to pay
taxes 11/27/23

ETHELDA RED LAKE GOLD MINES LTD. (ON)
Charter cancelled 00/00/1955

ETHICAL HLDGS PLC (ENGLAND)
Each old Sponsored ADR for Ordinary
10p par exchanged for (0.1) new
Sponsored ADR for Ordinary 10p
par 10/19/1998
Name changed to Amarin Corp. PLC
01/10/2000

ETHICORP RES LTD (AB)
Recapitalized as Central Explorers
Inc. 10/26/1987
Each share Common no par
exchanged for (0.33333333) share
Common no par
(See Central Explorers Inc.)

ETHIGEN CORP (CA)
Charter suspended for failure to file
reports and pay fees 04/01/1991

ETHIKA CORP (MS)
Recapitalized as Tradequest
International, Inc. (MS) 04/16/2001
Each share Common $1 par
exchanged for (0.02) share Common
no par
Tradequest International, Inc. (MS)
reorganized in Nevada 10/11/2005
(See Tradequest International, Inc.)

ETHIOPIAN POTASH CORP (ON)
Name changed to AgriMinco Corp.
07/15/2013

ETHOS CAP CORP (BC)
Name changed to Ethos Gold Corp.
04/04/2012

ETHOS CAP INC (DE)
Name changed to Patriot Energy
Corp. 02/04/2002
Patriot Energy Corp. name changed
to BigBrews Holdings Inc. (DE)
02/18/2003 which reincorporated in
Nevada as Patriot Energy Corp.
09/09/2003 which name changed to
Healing Hand Network International,
Inc. 12/22/2003 which name
changed to Patriot Energy Corp.
(NV) 10/10/2005
(See Patriot Energy Corp.)

ETHOS ENVIRONMENTAL INC (NV)
Name changed to Regeneca, Inc.
06/14/2011
(See Regeneca, Inc.)

E3 ENERGY INC (CANADA)
Under plan of merger each share
Common no par exchanged for
(0.0488) share Mission Oil & Gas
Inc. Common no par and (0.11)
StarPoint Energy Trust, Trust Unit
01/07/2005
(See each company's listing)

ETHYL CORP (VA)
Class A Common $5 par changed to
$3 par and (1) share Class B
Common $3 par issued 6/17/63
Class B Common $5 par changed to
$3 par and (1) additional share
issued 6/17/63
Class A Common $3 par changed to
$1 par and (2) shares Class B
Common $1 par issued 1/10/65
Class B Common $3 par changed to
$1 par and (2) additional shares
issued 1/10/65
Class A Common $1 par and Class B
Common $1 par reclassified as
Common $1 par 6/24/65
6% Preferred Ser. A, B, C and D $100
par called for redemption 6/24/65
5% Preferred Ser. B $100 par called
for redemption 7/1/71
Common $1 par split (2) for (1) by
issuance of (1) additional share
12/31/77
$4 Conv. 2nd Preferred Ser. B $10
par called for redemption 3/29/83
Common $1 par split (2) for (1) by
issuance of (1) additional share
4/11/83
Common $1 par split (2) for (1) by
issuance of (1) additional share
4/1/85
Common $1 par split (2) for (1) by
issuance of (1) additional share
5/30/86
$2.40 Conv. 2nd Preferred Ser. A $10
par called for redemption 9/21/90
6% 1st Preferred Ser. A $100 par
called for redemption 1/31/95
Each share old Common $1 par
exchanged for (0.2) share new
Common $1 par 7/1/2002
Under plan of reorganization each
share new Common $1 par
automatically became (1) share
NewMarket Corp. Common no par
6/18/2004

ETI EXPERTISE TECHNOLOGY INNOVATION CORP (NV)
Each share old Common $0.001 par
exchanged for (0.25) share new
Common $0.001 par 04/29/2003
Name changed to UC Hub Group,
Inc. 06/21/2004
(See UC Hub Group, Inc.)

ETINUUM INC (DE)
Name changed to Digital Lighthouse
Inc. 9/8/2000

ETNA RES INC (BC)
Name changed to Pan American
Lithium Corp. 01/21/2010
Pan American Lithium Corp. name
changed to First Potash Corp.
11/26/2012
(See First Potash Corp.)

ETNA STORES, INC.
Liquidated in 1947

ETON LODGE CORP.
Property sold in 1949
No stockholders' equity

ETOWAH BK (CANTON, GA)
Merged into Regions Financial Corp.
(Old) 9/10/98
Each share Common no par
exchanged for (3.2) shares Common
$0.625 par
Regions Financial Corp. (Old) merged
into Regions Financial Corp. (New)
7/1/2004

ETOYS INC (DE)
Plan of reorganization under Chapter
11 Federal Bankruptcy Code
effective 11/05/2002
No stockholders' equity

ETRAVELSERVE COM INC (NV)
SEC revoked common stock
registration 10/14/2010

ETRAVNET COM INC (NY)
Name changed to REZconnect
Technologies, Inc. (NY) 08/29/2001
REZconnect Technologies, Inc. (NY)
reincorporated in Delaware as YTB
International, Inc. 01/04/2005
(See YTB International, Inc.)

ETRIALS WORLDWIDE INC (DE)
Merged into Merge Healthcare Inc.
07/20/2009
Each share Common $0.0001 par
exchanged for (0.3448) share
Common 1¢ par and $0.80 cash
(See Merge Healthcare Inc.)

ETRUSCAN RES INC (BC)
Reincorporated 09/11/1997
Reincorporated from Etruscan
Enterprises Ltd. (BC) to under the
laws of Nova Scotia as Etruscan
Resources Inc. 09/11/1997
Merged into Endeavour Financial
Corp. 09/14/2010
Each share Common no par
exchanged for (0.0932) share
Ordinary USD $0.01 par and $0.26
cash
Note: U.S. residents will receive pro
rata proceeds from the sale of
shares
Endeavour Financial Corp. name
changed to Endeavour Mining Corp.
09/20/2010

ETS-HOKIN & GALVAN, INC. (CA)
Name changed to Ets-Hokin Corp.
6/27/63
Ets-Hokin Corp. name changed to
Techo Corp. 3/18/74
(See Techo Corp.)

ETS HOKIN CORP (CA)
Name changed to Techo Corp.
3/18/74
(See Techo Corp.)

ETS INTL INC (VA)
Name changed to InfraCorps Inc.
08/20/1998
InfraCorps Inc. name changed to
InfraCor Inc. 08/09/2000
(See InfraCor Inc.)

ETS PAYPHONES INC (DE)
Name changed to Payphone Wind
Down Corp. 02/12/2007
(See Payphone Wind Down Corp.)

ETTINGTON INVTS LTD (SOUTH AFRICA)
ADR agreement terminated 5/15/2007
No ADR holders' equity

ETV TECHNOLOGY INC (BC)
Name changed 05/02/2001
Name changed from eTVtech.com
Communications Inc. to eTV
Technology Inc. 05/02/2001
Recapitalized as Ocean Park
Ventures Corp. 04/02/2009
Each share Common no par
exchanged for (0.25) share Common
no par
Ocean Park Ventures Corp.
recapitalized as Dunnedin Ventures
Inc. 08/06/2013

E21 GROUP INC (ON)
Recapitalized as Green
Environmental Technologies, Inc.
08/14/2003
Each share Common no par
exchanged for (0.33333333) share
Common no par

ETWINE HLDGS INC (DE)
Name changed to Snap Interactive, Inc. 12/14/2007
Snap Interactive, Inc. name changed to PeerStream, Inc. 03/12/2018

E2OPEN INC (DE)
Acquired by Eagle Parent Holdings, LLC 03/26/2015
Each share Common $0.001 par exchanged for $8.60 cash

ETZ LAVUD LTD (ISRAEL)
Each share Ordinary Stock IS5.25 par exchanged for (1) share Class A Common NIS 0.17 par and (1) share Common NIS 0.17 par 11/01/1991
Company terminated registration of Common stock and is no longer public as of 06/27/2003
Details not available

EUBIX TECHNOLOGIES INC (NV)
Name changed to Nettel, Inc. 06/10/1999
Nettel, Inc. name changed to One Touch Total Communications Inc. 09/27/1999 which name changed to One Touch Total Development, Inc. 06/10/2004 which name changed to Carbon Jungle, Inc. 03/27/2006 which recapitalized as Global New Energy Industries Inc. 01/17/2013 which name changed to Coin Citadel 11/06/2014

EUCATEX SA INDUSTRIA E COMERCIO (BRAZIL)
ADR agreement terminated 01/14/2009
Each Sponsored ADR for Ordinary exchanged for $14.70349 cash

EUCLID-DOAN CO. (OH)
Dissolved 5/1/57

EUCLID EQUIP INC (DE)
Merged into Wedtech Corp. 12/16/85
Each share Preferred Ser. B $1 par exchanged for $1.1209 principal amount of Promissory Notes due 5/31/88 and (0.411) share Common 1¢ par
Each share Common 1¢ par exchanged for $0.21 principal amount of Promissory Notes due 5/31/88 and (0.077) share Common 1¢ par
(See Wedtech Corp.)

EUCLID NATL BK (EUCLID, OH)
Common Capital Stock $10 par changed to $5 par and (1) additional share issued 8/15/69
Merged into Winters National Corp. 10/1/75
Each share Common Capital Stock $5 par exchanged for (1) share Conv. Preferred Ser. A $10 par
(See Winters National Corp.)

EUCLID SVCS CORP (DE)
Merged into Homestead National Corp. 10/5/95
Each share 40¢ Preferred 10¢ par exchanged for $5 cash
Each share Common 10¢ par exchanged for $24.5149 cash

EUFAULA BANCCORP INC (DE)
Common 10¢ par split (2) for (1) by issuance of (1) additional share payable 12/20/1996 to holders of record 12/13/1996
Common 10¢ par split (3) for (2) by issuance of (0.5) additional share payable 11/15/1997 to holders of record 10/30/1997
Name changed to CommerceSouth, Inc. 06/01/2002
CommerceSouth, Inc. merged into BancTrust Financial Group, Inc. 12/30/2003 which merged into Trustmark Corp. 02/15/2013

EUGENE SCIENCE INC (DE)
SEC revoked common stock registration 04/24/2012

EUGENIC CORP (ON)
Name changed to Eagleford Energy Inc. 12/01/2009
Eagleford Energy Inc. recapitalized as Eagleford Energy Corp. 08/25/2014 which recapitalized as Intelligent Content Enterprises Inc. 02/05/2016 which recapitalized as Novicius Corp. 05/29/2017

EULER HERMES GROUP (FRANCE)
Name changed 07/08/2015
Name changed from Euler Hermes S.A. to Euler Hermes Group 07/08/2015
ADR agreement terminated 05/23/2018
Each ADR for Ordinary exchanged for $72.1425 cash

EUMAY INC (OH)
Liquidated 11/00/1972
Details not available

EUNITS 2 YR U S EQUITY MKT PARTN TR UPSIDE TO CAP / BUFFERED DOWNSIDE (MA)
Trust terminated 01/27/2014
Each Unit of Bene. Int. 1¢ par received $11.7914 cash

EUNITS 2 YR U S MKT PARTN TR II UPSIDE TO CAP / BUFFERED DOWNSIDE (MA)
Trust terminated 05/21/2014
Each Unit of Bene. Int. 1¢ par received $12.0586 cash

EUNIVERSE INC (DE)
Reincorporated 1/9/2003
State of incorporation changed from (NV) to (DE) 1/9/2003
Name changed to Intermix Media, Inc. 7/12/2004
(See Intermix Media, Inc.)

EUOKO GROUP INC (NV)
Recapitalized as Dermaxar Inc. 12/31/2010
Each share Common $0.001 par exchanged for (1/6) share Common $0.001 par
(See Dermaxar Inc.)

EUOKO INC (NV)
Name changed to Euoko Group Inc. 01/10/2008
Euoko Group Inc. recapitalized as Dermaxar Inc. 12/31/2010
(See Dermaxar Inc.)

EUPA INTL CORP (NV)
Each share old Common $0.001 par exchanged for (0.00012501) share new Common $0.001 par 01/26/2007
Note: In effect holders received $0.40 cash per share and public interest was eliminated

EUPHONIX INC (CA)
Issue Information - 1,875,000 shares COM offered at $8 per share on 08/22/1995
Completely liquidated 09/15/2010
Stockholders' equity unlikely

EURAM CAP CORP (CO)
Common $0.0001 par changed to $0.00005 par and (1) additional share issued 12/21/88
Name changed to Basic Natural Resources, Inc. in December 1990
Basic Natural Resources, Inc. name changed to Synaptix Systems Corp. 3/27/97 which name changed to Affiliated Resources Corp. 1/12/99

EURAMPEX INDS INC (UT)
Each share Common $0.001 par exchanged for (0.1) share Common 1¢ par 3/4/88
Involuntarily dissolved 7/1/92

EURAND N V (NETHERLANDS)
Issue Information - 7,000,000 shs. ORD offered at $16 per share on 05/16/2007
Merged into Axcan Holdings Inc. 02/28/2011
Each share Ordinary EUR 0.01 par exchanged for $10.90 cash

EURASIA DESIGN INC (NV)
Name changed to Prince Mexico S.A., Inc. 01/22/2013
Prince Mexico S.A., Inc. name changed to Luve Sports Inc. 09/20/2013
(See Luve Sports Inc.)

EURASIA DRILLING CO LTD (RUSSIA)
GDR agreement terminated 11/20/2015
Each Sponsored 144A GDR for Ordinary exchanged for $11.75 cash
Each Sponsored Reg. S GDR for Ordinary exchanged for $11.75 cash

EURASIA ENERGY LTD (NV)
Reincorporated under the laws of British West Indies 12/31/2007

EURASIA GOLD CORP (YT)
Reincorporated 06/17/1999
Place of incorporation changed from (AB) to (YT) 06/17/1999
Reorganized under the laws of Canada as Eurasia Gold Inc. 05/25/2006
Each share Common no par exchanged for (0.1) share Common no par
Eurasia Gold Inc. (Canada) reincorporated in British Columbia 04/05/2007
(See Eurasia Gold Inc. (BC))

EURASIA GOLD FIELDS INC (FL)
SEC revoked common stock registration 08/23/2010

EURASIA GOLD INC (BC)
Reincorporated 04/05/2007
Place of incorporation changed from (Canada) to (BC) 04/05/2007
Merged into Kazakhmys PLC 07/06/2007
Each share Common no par exchanged for $0.85 cash

EURASIACOM INC (CO)
Each share old Common no par exchanged for (0.005) share new Common no par 04/15/2002
Recapitalized as Supertel Communications, Ltd. 06/24/2002
Each share new Common no par exchanged for (0.0005) share Common no par
Supertel Communications, Ltd. name changed to Premier Platforms Holding Co., Inc. 09/24/2002 which name changed to Paolo Nevada Enterprises, Inc. (CO) 02/17/2005 which reorganized in Nevada as David Loren Corp. 11/13/2006 which recapitalized as Kibush Capital Corp. 08/23/2013

EURASIAN MINERALS INC (BC)
Reincorporated 09/24/2004
Place of incorporation changed from (AB) to (BC) 09/24/2004
Name changed to EMX Royalty Corp. 07/19/2017

EURASIAN NAT RES CORP (UNITED KINGDOM)
ADR agreement terminated 06/14/2016
Each ADR for Common exchanged for $1.766106 cash

EURBID COM INC (DE)
Each share old Common 10¢ par exchanged for (0.025) share new Common 10¢ par 12/12/2000
Name changed to Junum Inc. 12/14/2000
Junum Inc. recapitalized as WinWin Gaming Inc. 12/31/2002
(See WinWin Gaming Inc.)

EUREKA BK (PITTSBURGH, PA)
Under plan of reorganization each share Common 10¢ par automatically became (1) share Eureka Financial Corp. (USA) Common 10¢ par 04/01/2003
Eureka Financial Corp. (USA) reorganized in Maryland 03/01/2011
(See Eureka Financial Corp. (MD))

EUREKA BULLION MNG CO (UT)
Merged into North Lily Mining Co. 12/1/76
Each share Capital Stock 5¢ par exchanged for (0.0088) share Capital Stock 10¢ par
(See North Lily Mining Co.)

EUREKA CAP CORP I (NV)
Exchangeable Extendible Auction Preferred Ser. A $1 par called for redemption 01/09/1992
Exchangeable Extendible Auction Preferred Ser. B $1 par called for redemption 01/09/1992
Public interest eliminated

EUREKA CO. (NV)
Charter revoked for failure to file reports and pay fees 3/6/61

EUREKA CORP. LTD. (NS)
Liquidated 01/16/1964
Each share Common 25¢ par or Common $1 par exchanged for (0.1) share Silver Eureka Corp. Capital Stock 10¢ par
(See Silver Eureka Corp.)

EUREKA FELDSPAR MINING & MILLING CO. INC. (CT)
Liquidation completed 12/24/1969
No stockholders' equity

EUREKA FINL CORP (MD)
Acquired by NexTier, Inc. 01/08/2016
Each share Common 1¢ par exchanged for $28.50 cash

EUREKA FINL CORP (USA)
Reorganized under the laws of Maryland 03/01/2011
Each share Common 10¢ par exchanged for (1.0457) shares Common 1¢ par
(See Eureka Financial Corp. (MD))

EUREKA HAMBURG DEVELOPMENT CO. (NV)
Name changed to Eureka Western Mines and Capital Stock 10¢ par changed to 1¢ par 12/13/1968
(See Eureka Western Mines)

EUREKA HAMBURG MINING CO. (NV)
Name changed to Eureka Hamburg Development Co. 05/27/1959
Eureka Hamburg Development Co. name changed to Eureka Western Mines 12/13/1968
(See Eureka Western Mines)

EUREKA LEAD & ZINC MINING CO. (MO)
Charter forfeited for failure to file reports 12/02/1913

EUREKA LILLY CONS MNG CO (UT)
Merged into Eureka Standard Consolidated Mining Co. 11/25/1974
Each share Common 10¢ par exchanged for (1/3) share Capital Stock 10¢ par
Eureka Standard Consolidated Mining Co. merged into South Standard Mining Co. 07/29/1983 which merged into Chief Consolidated Mining Co. 07/01/1996
(See Chief Consolidated Mining Co.)

EUREKA LILLY MINING CO.
Merged into Eureka Lilly Consolidated Mining Co. 00/00/1937
Each share exchanged for (1.1737) shares Common 10¢ par
Eureka Lilly Consolidated Mining Co. merged into Eureka Standard Consolidated Mining Co. 11/25/1974 which merged into South Standard Mining Co. 07/29/1983 which merged into Chief Consolidated Mining Co. 07/01/1996
(See Chief Consolidated Mining Co.)

EUREKA MINES CO (UT)
Charter expired 07/16/2003

EUREKA NEVADA RAILWAY
Road abandoned 00/00/1938
Stockholders' equity unlikely

EUREKA PRODS CO (NJ)
Stock Dividend - 100% 09/20/1973
Ceased operations and declared insolvent 06/24/1976
No stockholders' equity

EUREKA SMELTING & MINING CO.
Capital Stock exchanged for stock of Eureka Smelting Co. in 1928 which company was foreclosed in 1930
No stockholders' equity

EUREKA STD CONS MNG CO (UT)
Merged into South Standard Mining Co. 07/29/1983
Each share Capital Stock 10¢ par exchanged for (0.2857) share Capital Stock 10¢ par
South Standard Mining Co. merged into Chief Consolidated Mining Co. 07/01/1996
(See Chief Consolidated Mining Co.)

EUREKA SWANSEA EXTENSION MINING CO. (UT)
Merged into North Lily Mining Co. 12/1/76
Each share Common 10¢ par exchanged for (0.0091) share Capital Stock 10¢ par
(See North Lily Mining Co.)

EUREKA VACUUM CLEANER CO. (MI)
Name changed to Eureka Williams Corp. in 1946
Eureka Williams Corp. name changed to Wardell Corp. in 1954 which merged into Amerace Corp. 5/29/57 which name changed to Amerace Esna Corp. 8/30/68 which name changed back to Amerace Corp. 4/27/73
(See Amerace Corp.)

EUREKA WESTERN MINES (NV)
Charter revoked for failure to file reports and pay fees 3/3/80

EUREKA WILLIAMS CORP. (MI)
Name changed to Wardell Corp. in 1954
Wardell Corp. merged into Amerace Corp. 5/29/57 which name changed to Amerace Esna Corp. 8/30/68 which name changed back to Amerace Corp. 4/27/73
(See Amerace Corp.)

EURIPIDES DEV CORP (PA)
Recapitalized as Transworld Telecommunications Inc. 3/2/92
Each share Common $0.001 par exchanged for (0.1) share Common $0.001 par

EURO-AD SYS INC (BC)
Recapitalized as Sun Devil Gold Corp. 07/03/1997
Each share Common no par exchanged for (0.5) share Common no par
Sun Devil Gold Corp. name changed to Cardero Resource Corp. 05/13/1999

EURO AMERN EXPL CORP (CO)
Name changed to 2 I Inc. 01/07/1993
(See 2 I Inc.)

EURO AMERN FINL SVCS LTD (BC)
Struck off register and declared dissolved for failure to file returns 02/19/1988

EURO ASIA CAP LTD (BC)
Recapitalized as Asiamerica Holdings Ltd. 01/18/1989
Each share Common no par exchanged for (0.33333333) share Common no par
Asiamerica Holdings Ltd. name changed to Stone Mark Capital Inc.

(BC) 11/17/1989 which reincorporated in Yukon 03/04/1994
(See Stone Mark Capital Inc. (Yukon))

EURO BANC CAP SECS TR (ON)
Merged into Global Capital Securities Trust 02/04/2016
Each Unit automatically became (0.382254) Class A Unit
Global Capital Securities Trust name changed to Redwood Global Financials Income Fund 12/20/2017
(See Redwood Global Financials Income Fund)

EURO CURRENCY TR (NY)
Name changed to CurrencyShares Euro Trust 09/26/2006
CurrencyShares Euro Trust name changed to Invesco CurrencyShares Euro Trust 06/04/2018

EURO GROUP COS (DE)
SEC revoked common stock registration 06/10/2015

EURO INDS LTD (CO)
Name changed to Destiny Media Technologies, Inc. (CO) 10/19/1999
Destiny Media Technologies, Inc. (CO) reincorporated in Nevada 10/08/2014

EURO INDS LTD (DE)
Name changed to Dairene Industries Ltd. 1/9/73
(See Dairene Industries Ltd.)

EURO NEVADA MNG LTD (ON)
Common no par split (2) for (1) by issuance of (1) additional share payable 07/12/1996 to holders of record 07/11/1996
Common no par split (2) for (1) by issuance of (1) additional share payable 08/14/1997 to holders of record 08/14/1997
Merged into Franco-Nevada Mining Corp. Ltd. (New) 09/20/1999
Each share Common no par exchanged for (0.77) share Common no par
Franco-Nevada Mining Corp. Ltd. (New) merged into Newmont Mining Corp. 02/16/2002

EURO PAC RESOURCE GROUP INC (BC)
Recapitalized as Holt International Investments Ltd. 05/21/1996
Each share Common no par exchanged for (0.2) share Common no par
Holt International Investments Ltd. name changed to Argent Resources Ltd. 11/04/1998 which recapitalized as Argent Mining Corp. 04/07/2006 which recapitalized as Avion Resources Corp. 06/21/2007 which name changed to Avion Gold Corp. (BC) 06/05/2009 which reincorporated in Ontario 06/14/2011 which merged into Endeavour Mining Corp. 10/18/2012

EURO PETE CORP (BC)
Recapitalized as Morgan Petroleum Inc. 02/19/1991
Each share Common no par exchanged for (0.2) share Common no par
Morgan Petroleum Inc. recapitalized as Mortlock Resources Corp. 05/28/1993 which name changed to NovaDx International Inc. 01/20/1995 which recapitalized as NovaDx Ventures Corp. 12/02/2004
(See NovaDx Ventures Corp.)

EURO TRADE & FORFAITING INC (UT)
Plan of dissolution effective 9/2/2004
No stockholders' equity

EURO TREND INC (NV)
Recapitalized as Data Storage Corp. 01/27/2009
Each share Common $0.001 par exchanged for (1/7) share Common $0.001 par

EUROAMERICAN GROUP INC (DE)
Recapitalized as Sycamore Ventures, Inc. 6/19/2006
Each share Common $0.001 par exchanged for (0.001) share Common $0.001 par

EUROBANCSHARES INC (PR)
Principal asset placed in receivership 04/30/2010

EUROCAN HLDGS LTD (NV)
Name changed to Eastside Distilling, Inc. 12/05/2014

EUROCAN VENTURES LTD (BC)
Recapitalized as Consolidated Eurocan Ventures Ltd. (BC) 2/7/91
Each share Common no par exchanged for (0.1) share Common no par
Consolidated Eurocan Ventures Ltd. (BC) reincorporated in Canada 4/19/94 which name changed to Tenke Mining Corp. 1/27/97

EUROCAPITAL CORP (DE)
Recapitalized as Alternative Distributors Corp. 12/26/91
Each share Common 1¢ par exchanged for (0.04) share Common $0.025 par
(See Alternative Distributors Corp.)

EUROCAR IMPORTS CORP (NY)
Dissolved by proclamation 6/23/93

EUROCONTROL TECHNICS INC (ON)
Reincorporated 10/11/2006
Place of incorporation changed from (BC) to (ON) 10/11/2006
Name changed to Eurocontrol Technics Group Inc. 08/22/2011

EURODYNAMICS CORP (UT)
Recapitalized as U-Ship Inc. 06/16/1992
Each share Common 1¢ par exchanged for (0.04) share Common 1¢ par
U-Ship Inc. name changed to United Shipping & Technology, Inc. (UT) 05/03/1999 which reincorporated in Delaware as Velocity Express Corp. 01/14/2002
(See Velocity Express Corp.)

EUROFINA LTD (DE)
Name changed to Euro Industries, Ltd. 7/20/71
Euro Industries, Ltd. name changed to Dairene Industries Ltd. 1/9/73
(See Dairene Industries Ltd.)

EUROFUND INC (MD)
Name changed to Eurofund International, Inc. 4/28/69
Eurofund International, Inc. merged into International Telephone & Telegraph Corp. 3/29/71 which name changed to ITT Corp. 12/31/83 which reorganized in Indiana as ITT Industries Inc. 12/19/95 which name changed to ITT Corp. 7/1/2006

EUROFUND INTL INC (MD)
Merged into International Telephone & Telegraph Corp. 3/29/71
Each share Common $1 par exchanged for (0.3549) share Common $1 par
International Telephone & Telegraph Corp. name changed to ITT Corp. 12/31/83 which reorganized in Indiana as ITT Industries, Inc. 12/19/95 which name changed to ITT Corp. 7/1/2006

EUROGAS CORP (CANADA)
Plan of arrangement effective 06/11/2004
Each share old Common no par exchanged for (1) share new Common no par and (0.2) share Great Plains Exploration Inc. (Old) Common no par
Each share Common no par received distribution of (0.2) share Eurogas International Inc. Common no par

payable 03/31/2009 to holders of record 08/05/2008 Ex date - 07/31/2008
Name changed to Dundee Energy Ltd. 06/22/2011

EUROGAS INC (UT)
SEC revoked common stock registration 04/20/2011

EUROGOLD RES INC (BC)
Name changed to Superior Pipeline Corp. (BC) 05/13/1992
Superior Pipeline Corp. (BC) reincorporated in Yukon as Superior Mining Corp. 02/10/1998 which recapitalized as Superior Mining International Corp. (Yukon) 05/10/2006 which reincorporated in British Columbia 02/18/2008

EUROMED INC (NV)
Name changed to Institutional Equity Holdings, Inc. 04/26/1999
Institutional Equity Holdings, Inc. recapitalized as Shing-Mei International, Inc. 04/03/2008 which name changed to Triad Pro Innovators, Inc. 01/25/2012

EUROMIN CDA LTD (CANADA)
Reincorporated 04/28/1989
Place of incorporation changed from (BC) to (Canada) 04/28/1989
Recapitalized as International Euromin Corp. 06/03/1994
Each share Common no par exchanged for (0.2) share Common no par
International Euromin Corp. merged into Eurogas Corp. 06/30/1995 which name changed to Dundee Energy Ltd. 06/22/2011

EURONAV NV (BELGIUM)
ADR agreement terminated 07/29/2015
No ADR's remain outstanding
(Additional Information in Active)

EURONET SVCS INC (DE)
Name changed to Euronet Worldwide, Inc. 5/24/2001

EURO909 COM A/S (DENMARK)
Name changed to EuroTrust A/S 12/10/2001
(See EuroTrust A/S)

EUROPA CRUISES CORP (DE)
Each share Preferred Ser. S no par received distribution of (0.06815) share Common $0.001 par payable 09/15/1999 to holders of record 09/15/1999
Name changed to Diamondhead Casino Corp. 12/09/2002

EUROPA GROUP INC (DE)
Charter cancelled and declared inoperative and void for non-payment of taxes 3/1/78

EUROPA HAIR INC. (DE)
Name changed to Europa Group, Inc. 1/29/73
(See Europa Group, Inc.)

EUROPA PETE LTD (BC)
Merged into Orbit Oil & Gas Ltd. 11/8/84
Each share Common no par exchanged for (0.2) share Common no par
(See Orbit Oil & Gas Ltd.)

EUROPA PETROLEUM, INC. (DE)
Merged into Europa Petroleum Ltd. 10/1/82
Each (10) shares Common exchanged for (1.8) shares Common no par

EUROPA RES INC (NV)
Name changed to EWRX Internet Systems, Inc. 05/19/1999
EWRX Internet Systems, Inc. name changed to DLD Group, Inc. 06/05/2013

EUROPA TRADE AGY LTD (NV)
Reorganized as Ironclad Performance Wear Corp. 05/09/2006
Each share Common $0.001 par exchanged for (3.454895) shares Common $0.001 par
Ironclad Performance Wear Corp. name changed to ICPW Liquidation Corp. 11/20/2017

EUROPA TRADING CORP (NY)
Dissolved by proclamation 3/20/96

EUROPE FD INC (MD)
Name changed to BlackRock Europe Fund, Inc. 10/02/2006
BlackRock Europe Fund, Inc. merged into BlackRock EuroFund 11/06/2006

EUROPE 2001 HOLDRS TR (DE)
Trust terminated
Each Depositary Receipt received first and final distribution of $58.341107 cash payable 01/08/2013 to holders of record 12/24/2012

EUROPEAN & NORTH AMERICAN RWY. (ME)
Assets sold and company liquidated 8/30/55

EUROPEAN AERONAUTIC DEFENCE & SPACE CO EADS NV (NETHERLANDS)
ADR's for Ordinary split (4) for (1) by issuance of (3) additional ADR's payable 10/16/2013 to holders of record 10/15/2013 Ex date - 10/17/2013
Basis changed from (1:1) to (1:0.25) 10/17/2013
Name changed to Airbus Group 01/02/2014
Airbus Group name changed to Airbus S.E. 04/19/2017

EUROPEAN AMERN LEASING CORP (NV)
Name changed to Sunny Land Tours Inc. 03/16/1978
Sunny Land Tours Inc. recapitalized as InterAllied Restaurant Group, Inc. 11/15/1993 which name changed to InterAllied Group, Inc. (NV) 02/08/1999 which reincorporated in Delaware as Pilot Therapeutics Holdings, Inc. 12/06/2001
(See Pilot Therapeutics Holdings, Inc.)

EUROPEAN AMERN RES INC (DE)
SEC revoked common stock registration 02/07/2011

EUROPEAN AUTO CLASSICS LTD (DE)
Charter cancelled and declared inoperative and void for non-payment of taxes 3/1/83

EUROPEAN COML REAL ESTATE LTD (ON)
Reorganized as European Commercial Real Estate Investment Trust 05/03/2017
Each share Common no par exchanged for (0.032) Unit
Note: Unexchanged certificates will be cancelled and become without value 05/02/2023

EUROPEAN DAY SPA & TANNING SALON HLDG INC (NV)
Name changed to European Diversified Holding Co. 07/18/2002
European Diversified Holding Co. recapitalized as NavStar Technologies, Inc. 07/30/2007 which recapitalized as Energy Revenue America, Inc. 08/01/2012

EUROPEAN DIVERSIFIED HLDG CO (NV)
Recapitalized as NavStar Technologies, Inc. 07/30/2007
Each (24) shares Common $0.001 par exchanged for (1) share Common $0.001 par
NavStar Technologies, Inc. recapitalized as Energy Revenue America, Inc. 08/01/2012

EUROPEAN ELECTRIC CORP. LTD.
Liquidated in 1940

EUROPEAN ELECTRIC MANAGEMENT CORP. LTD.
Liquidation completed in 1951

EUROPEAN GARNET LTD (BC)
Recapitalized as Indo Metals Ltd. 12/16/1996
Each share Common no par exchanged for (0.5) share Common no par
Indo Metals Ltd. recapitalized as Blue Lagoon Ventures Inc. 03/14/2001 which recapitalized as VMX Resources Inc. 12/08/2004 which name changed to Monster Uranium Corp. 09/07/2007

EUROPEAN GAS & ELEC CO (DE)
Charter surrendered 07/20/1984

EUROPEAN GATEWAY ACQUISITION CORP (DE)
Name changed to Bogen Communications International, Inc. 8/24/95

EUROPEAN GOLD RES INC (ON)
Reincorporated under the laws of Canada as Galantas Gold Corp. 5/10/2004

EUROPEAN GOLDFIELDS LTD (BC)
Merged into Eldorado Gold Corp. 02/24/2012
Each share Common no par exchanged for (0.85) share Common no par and $0.0001 cash
Note: Unexchanged certificates were cancelled and became without value 02/24/2018

EUROPEAN MICRO HLGS INC (NV)
In process of liquidation
Each share Common 1¢ par received initial distribution of approximately $0.039764 cash payable 09/01/2005 to holders of record 08/01/2005
Note: Details on additional distribution(s), if any, are not available

EUROPEAN MIDDLE IND VENTURE CAP INC (DE)
Name changed to Minpetro Ltd. 03/25/1991
(See Minpetro Ltd.)

EUROPEAN MINERALS CORP (BRITISH VIRGIN ISLANDS)
Name changed to Orsu Metals Corp. 07/14/2008

EUROPEAN MINERALS CORP (YUKON)
Reincorporated under the laws of British Virgin Islands 04/08/2005
European Minerals Corp. (British Virgin Islands) name changed to Orsu Metals Corp. 07/14/2008

EUROPEAN ORIG N Y SELTZER LTD (BC)
Struck off register and declared dissolved for failure to file returns 4/26/88

EUROPEAN PREM DIVID FD (ON)
Under plan of merger each Unit automatically became (1.23092) Copernican International Premium Dividend Fund Trust Units 12/13/2010
Copernican International Premium Dividend Fund merged into Portland Global Dividend Fund 05/23/2014

EUROPEAN SECURITIES & TRADING GROUP INC (CO)
Administratively dissolved 02/01/2001

EUROPEAN SHARES, INC.
Dissolved in 1928

EUROPEAN STRATEGIC BALANCED FD (ON)
Trust terminated 01/09/2017
Each Unit received $9.8814 cash

EUROPEAN TECHNOLOGIES INTL INC (AB)
Name changed to Steely Group Inc. 6/1/2001
(See Steely Group Inc.)

EUROPEAN URANIUM RES LTD (BC)
Recapitalized as Azarga Metals Corp. 05/31/2016
Each share Common no par exchanged for (0.1) share Common no par

EUROPEAN VENTURES INC (BC)
Recapitalized as Cugold Ventures Inc. 12/01/1994
Each share Common no par exchanged for (0.25) share Common no par
Cugold Ventures Inc. recapitalized as Firestone Ventures Inc. (BC) 12/05/1999 which reincorporated in Alberta 09/27/2005

EUROPEAN WT FD INC (MD)
Name changed to Julius Baer Global Equity Fund Inc. 07/01/2004
Julius Baer Global Equity Fund Inc. reorganized as Artio Global Investment Funds Global Equity Fund Inc. 10/13/2008 (Artio Global Investment Funds)

EUROPEJKI FUNDUSZ LEASINGOWY S A (POLAND)
99.79% acquired by Credit Agricole Deveurope B.V. through cash purchase offer which expired 10/30/2001
Public interest eliminated

EUROPIX INTL LTD (NY)
Assets assigned for benefit of creditors 03/07/1975
No stockholders' equity

EUROPRIME CAP CORP (BC)
Recapitalized as International Europrime Capital Corp. 7/4/95
Each share Common no par exchanged for (0.04) share Common no par
(See International Europrime Capital Corp.)

EUROSEEK INC (DE)
Charter cancelled and declared inoperative and void for non-payment of taxes 3/1/2001

EUROSOFT CORP (FL)
Reincorporated 9/15/97
State of incorporation changed from (NV) to (FL) 9/15/97
Reacapitalized as Herbalpharm Inc. 10/4/2006
Each share Commom $0.0001 par exchanged for (0.001) share Common $0.001 par
Herbalpharm Inc. reorganized as Herbalpharm Holdings, Inc. 2/22/2007 which name changed to MitoPharm Corp. 3/9/2007

EUROTECH RES INC (DE)
Charter cancelled and declared inoperative and void for non-payment of taxes 03/01/1991

EUROTECH TECHNOLOGIES INC (BC)
Recapitalized 09/16/1992
Recapitalized from Eurotech Building Products Inc. to Eurotech Technologies Inc. 09/16/1992
Each share Common no par exchanged for (0.5) share Common no par
Recapitalized as Artemis Venture Inc. 04/29/1996
Each share Common no par exchanged for (0.25) share Common no par
Artemis Venture Inc. recapitalized as Paradym Ventures Inc. 01/04/1999 which recapitalized as Pacific Paradym Energy Inc. 10/01/2007

EUROTELECOM COMMUNICATIONS INC (DE)
Recapitalized as BENE IO, Inc. 07/24/2006
Each share Common 1¢ par exchanged for (0.001) share Common $0.001 par
(See BENE IO, Inc.)

EUROTRONICS HLDGS INC (UT)
Each share old Common $0.0001 par exchanged for (0.00196078) share new Common $0.0001 par 10/31/97
Name changed to Legalopinion.com 8/16/99
Legalopinion.com recapitalized as Drayton Richdale Corp. 4/14/2004

EUROTRUST A/S (DENMARK)
Each old Sponsored ADR for Ordinary exchanged for (0.16666666) new Sponsored ADR for Ordinary 08/29/2002
ADR basis changed from (1:1) to (1:6) 08/29/2002
ADR basis changed from (1:6) to (1:1) 06/24/2005
ADR agreement terminated 08/01/2007
Each Sponsored ADR for Ordinary exchanged for $0.36932 cash

EUROTUNNEL PLC (UNITED KINGDOM)
ADR agreement terminated 12/31/2003
Each Sponsored ADR for Ordinary exchanged for $0.6196718 cash

EUROWEB INTL CORP (DE)
Each share old Common $0.001 par exchanged for (0.2) share new Common $0.001 par 08/31/2001
Name changed to EMVELCO Corp. 01/08/2007
EMVELCO Corp. name changed to Vortex Resources Corp. 09/02/2008 which name changed to Yasheng Eco-Trade Corp. 07/15/2009 which recapitalized as Eco-Trade Corp. 12/09/2010

EUROWIND ENERGY INC (NY)
Name changed to First Petroleum & Pipeline Inc. 03/31/2005
First Petroleum & Pipeline Inc. recapitalized as Luke Entertainment, Inc. 11/15/2007 which name changed to Greene Concepts, Inc. 01/14/2011

EUROWORK GLOBAL LTD (DE)
Common $0.001 par split (5) for (1) by issuance of (4) additional shares payable 10/09/2006 to holders of record 09/25/2006 Ex date - 10/10/2006
Name changed to Quintessence Holdings, Inc. 07/25/2007
Quintessence Holdings, Inc. name changed to Terminus Energy, Inc. 12/04/2009

EUROZINC MNG CORP (BC)
Merged into Lundin Mining Corp. 11/1/2006
Each share Common no par exchanged for (0.0952) share Common no par and $0.0001 cash

EURUS RESOURCE CORP (BC)
Merged into Crystallex International Corp. (BC) 9/29/95
Each share Common no par exchanged for (0.15513146) share Common no par and (0.15513146) Common Stock Purchase Warrant expiring 9/20/96
Crystallex International Corp. (BC) reincorporated in Canada 1/23/98

EUTHENICS SYS CORP (PA)
Name changed to Baker (Michael) Corp. 04/16/1975
(See Baker (Michael) Corp.)

EUTRO GROUP HLDG INC (FL)
Name changed to Strategic Alliance Group Inc. 10/18/99
Strategic Alliance Group Inc. name

changed to CruiseCam International, Inc. 7/30/2004

EV ENERGY PARTNERS L P (DE)
Plan of reorganization under Chapter 11 Federal Bankruptcy proceedings effective 06/04/2018
Each Common Unit received (0.00973704) share Harvest Oil & Gas Corp. Common 1¢ par and (0.01557926) Common Stock Purchase Warrant expiring 06/04/2023

EV ENVIRONMENTAL INC (DE)
Recapitalized as Burned Media Ltd. 11/25/2005
Each share Common 1¢ par exchanged for (0.001) share Common 1¢ par

EV INNOVATIONS INC (NV)
Recapitalized as Li-ion Motors Corp. 02/01/2010
Each share Common $0.001 par exchanged for (0.5) share Common $0.001 par
Li-ion Motors Corp. recapitalized as Terra Inventions Corp. 12/21/2012
(See Terra Inventions Corp.)

EV TRADITIONAL WORLDWIDE HEALTH SCIENCES FD INC (MD)
Reorganized as Eaton Vance Growth Trust 09/01/1997
Details not available

EVA LAKE GOLD MINES, LTD. (ON)
Dissolved 8/18/58

EVADER INC (WY)
Reincorporated 05/25/2012
State of incorporation changed from (NV) to (WY) 05/25/2012
Name changed to Critic Clothing, Inc. 12/14/2015
Critic Clothing, Inc. recapitalized as Deep Green Waste & Recycling, Inc. 09/27/2017

EVALUATION RESH CORP (VA)
Stock Dividend - 25% 7/10/83
Reincorporated under the laws of Delaware as ERC International Inc. and Class One Common 5¢ par reclassified as Common 5¢ par 2/1/85
ERC International Inc. acquired by Ogden Corp. 1/19/90 which name changed to Covanta Energy Corp. 3/14/2001
(See Covanta Energy Corp.)

EVANDER GOLD MINES LTD (SOUTH AFRICA)
Merged into Harmony Gold Mining Co. Ltd. 8/28/98
Each ADR for Ordinary Rand-1 par exchanged for either (0.583) Sponsored ADR for Ordinary Rand-50 par or (0.264) Sponsored ADR for Ordinary Rand-50 par and $7.4046 cash
Note: Option to receive cash and ADR's expired 9/2/98

EVANS & MITCHELL INDS INC (GA)
Adjudicated bankrupt 3/31/75
Stockholders' equity unlikely

EVANS (E.S.) & CO., INC.
Name changed to Evans Auto Loading Co., Inc. 00/00/1927
Evans Auto Loading Co., Inc. name changed to Evans Products Co. 00/00/1931
(See Evans Products Co.)

EVANS ARISTOCRAT INDS INC (NJ)
Common $1 par split (5) for (4) by issuance of (0.25) additional share 3/15/73
Common $1 par split (5) for (4) by issuance of (0.25) additional share 5/31/78
Stock Dividends - 10% 9/14/76; 15% 10/4/77; 20% 3/31/79; 20% 3/19/80; 10% 1/20/82
Merged into Masco Corp. 12/23/82

Each share Common $1 par exchanged for $18.25 cash

EVANS AUTO LOADING CO., INC.
Name changed to Evans Products Co. in 1931
(See Evans Products Co.)

EVANS BREWING CO INC (DE)
Name changed to I-ON Communications Corp. 08/02/2018

EVANS COLEMAN & GILLEY BROTHERS, LTD. (CANADA)
Each (2) shares Common no par exchanged for (1) share Class A no par and (3) shares Class B Common no par in 1947
Acquired by Ocean Cement & Supplies Ltd. share for share 12/30/57
(See Ocean Cement & Supplies Ltd.)

EVANS CREEK OIL & GAS CO. (OH)
Charter cancelled for failure to pay taxes 2/15/24

EVANS ENVIRONMENTAL CORP (CO)
Each share old Common $0.001 par exchanged for (0.25) share new Common $0.001 par 01/02/1996
Name changed to ECOS Group, Inc. (CO) 11/01/1996
ECOS Group, Inc. (CO) reincorporated in Florida 02/22/2000 which recapitalized as Third Millennium Telecommunications, Inc. (FL) 10/01/2001 which reincorporated in Delaware as TMTM Merger Co. 09/04/2009 which recapitalized as Green Processing Technologies, Inc. 06/16/2010 which recapitalized as Umbra Applied Technologies Group, Inc. 01/13/2014

EVANS HEALTH GROUP LTD (ON)
Merged into FoxMeyer Canada Inc. 06/29/1994
Each share Common no par exchanged for (1) share Common no par
FoxMeyer Canada Inc. name changed to Healthstreams Technology Inc. 10/04/1996 which name changed to MediSolution Ltd. 09/18/1997
(See MediSolution Ltd.)

EVANS INC (DE)
Common $1 par changed to 20¢ par and (8) additional shares issued 08/13/1985
Each share old Common 20¢ par exchanged for (0.25) share new Common 20¢ par 12/09/1998
Assets sold for the benefit of creditors 05/09/2000
No stockholders' equity

EVANS INDS INC (DE)
Merged into Evinco, Inc. 10/29/1976
Each share Common 10¢ par exchanged for $0.20 cash

EVANS LEAD CO.
Merged into Evans-Wallower Lead Co. in 1928
Details not available

EVANS PRODS CO (DE)
Common $5 par split (3) for (1) by issuance of (2) additional shares 10/19/1955
Common $5 par split (3) for (2) by issuance of (0.5) additional share 01/19/1966
Common $5 par changed to $1 par 05/22/1970
$4 Conv. Preferred no par called for redemption 08/30/1971
Common $1 par split (2) for (1) by issuance of (1) additional share 12/28/1971
Plan of reorganization under Chapter 11 Federal Bankruptcy proceedings confirmed 07/02/1986
No stockholders' equity

EVANS RULE CO. (NJ)
Under plan of merger name changed to Evans-Aristocrat Industries, Inc. 6/15/64
(See Evans-Aristocrat Industries, Inc.)

EVANS SYS INC (TX)
Each share Common 1¢ par exchanged for (0.1) share Common $0.001 par 08/14/2006
Stock Dividend - 5% payable 01/20/1997 to holders of record 12/31/1996
Name changed to WatchIt Technologies, Inc. (TX) and Common $0.001 par changed to $0.0001 par 08/24/2007
WatchIt Technologies, Inc. (TX) reincorporated in Nevada 09/05/2007
(See WatchIt Technologies, Inc.)

EVANS-WALLOWER LEAD CO.
Reorganized as Evans Wallower Zinc, Inc. in 1937
Each share Preferred exchanged for (4) shares new Common $5 par
Common received warrants which expired in 21 days
(See Evans Wallower Zinc, Inc.)

EVANS WALLOWER ZINC, INC. (DE)
Capital Stock $5 par changed to $1 par and $1.70 in cash distributed in 1940
Liquidation completed 6/28/56

EVANS WITHYCOMBE RESIDENTIAL INC (MD)
Issue Information - 8,685,000 shares COM offered at $20 per share on 08/10/1994
Merged into Equity Residential Properties Trust 12/23/97
Each share Common 1¢ par exchanged for (0.5) Share of Bene. Int. 1¢ par
Equity Residential Properties Trust name changed to Equity Residential 5/15/2002

EVANSTON BLOCK CORP. (IL)
Liquidation completed
Each share Common $5 par exchanged for $29 cash 7/24/46
Each share Common $5 par received second and final distribution of $0.92 cash 12/29/48

EVANSVILLE & OHIO VALLEY RAILWAY CO.
Property sold in 1939
No stockholders' equity

EVANSVILLE AUTO HOTEL, INC.
In process of liquidation in 1948

EVANSVILLE FED SVGS BK (EVANSVILLE, IN)
Under plan of reorganization each share Common no par automatically became (1) share Fidelity Federal Bancorp Common no par 11/8/93
(See Fidelity Federal Bancorp.)

EVC VENTURES INC (FL)
Name changed to Invnsys Holding Corp. 10/27/1998
Invnsys Holding Corp. name changed to iBIZ Technology Corp. 01/22/1999
(See iBIZ Technology Corp.)

EVCARCO INC (NV)
Each share old Common $0.001 par exchanged for (0.002) share new Common new Common $0.001 par 07/06/2012
SEC revoked common stock registration 05/14/2015

EVCI CAREER COLLEGES INC (DE)
Name changed to EVCI Career Colleges Holding Corp. 8/12/2004

EVELYNN NICKEL MINES LTD. (ON)
Name changed to Hardiman Bay Mines Ltd. 12/27/1962
(See Hardiman Bay Mines Ltd.)

EVEN-GLO CHARCOAL CO., INC. (KY)
Assets sold for benefit of creditors 01/21/1971
No stockholders' equity

EVEN RES LTD (BC)
Recapitalized as Plata Minerals Corp. 2/27/98
Each share Common no par exchanged for (1/7) share Common no par
Plata Minerals Corp. name changed to Briyante Software Corp. 10/5/2001 which merged into Imagis Technologies Inc. (BC) 11/25/2003 which reincorporated in Canada as Visiphor Corp. 7/7/2005

EVENING NEWS ASSOCIATION, INC. (MI)
Merged into Gannett Co., Inc. (Old) 02/18/1986
Each share Common no par exchanged for $1,583.04 cash

EVENING STAR HOTELS INC (DE)
Name changed to NuEnergy Group, Inc. 02/07/2003
NuEnergy Group, Inc. recapitalized as Rising India Inc. 05/14/2009 which name changed to Rising Biosciences, Inc. 05/31/2018

EVENING STAR MINES LTD.
Liquidated in 1949

EVENLODE MINES LTD (ON)
Name changed 08/11/1961
Name changed from Evenlode Gold Mines Ltd. to Evenlode Mines Ltd. 08/11/1961
Charter cancelled 08/31/1987

EVENTEMP CORP (NV)
Each share old Common 10¢ par exchanged for (0.01538461) share new Common 10¢ par 12/15/2000
Name changed to Westside Energy Corp. 03/31/2004
Westside Energy Corp. name changed to Crusader Energy Group Inc. 06/27/2008
(See Crusader Energy Group Inc.)

EVENTS INTL HLDG CORP (CANADA)
Name changed to Dynasty Gaming Inc. 12/09/2005
Dynasty Gaming Inc. recapitalized as Blue Zen Memorial Parks Inc. 01/21/2011

EVENTURE CAP CORP (BC)
Recapitalized as Invicta Oil & Gas Ltd. 11/28/2006
Each share Common no par exchanged for (0.5) share Common no par
Invicta Oil & Gas Ltd. name changed to LNG Energy Ltd. 03/28/2008 which recapitalized as Esrey Energy Ltd. 11/18/2013 which name changed to Esrey Resources Ltd. 10/16/2017

EVENTURES GROUP INC (DE)
Name changed to Novo Networks Inc. 12/12/2000
Novo Networks Inc. recapitalized as Berliner Communications, Inc. 09/19/2005 which name changed to UniTek Global Services, Inc. 07/06/2010
(See UniTek Global Services, Inc.)

EVEOLUTION VENTURES INC (BC)
Reincorporated under the laws of Yukon as Bear Creek Mining Corp. 11/14/2002
Bear Creek Mining Corp. (Yukon) reincorporated in British Columbia 7/16/2004

EVERBANK FINL CORP (DE)
Acquired by Teachers Insurance and Annuity Association of America 06/09/2017
Each 6.75% Depositary Preferred Share exchanged for $25 cash

Each share Common 1¢ par exchanged for $19.50 cash

EVERCLEAR CAP LTD (BC)
Name changed to Avrupa Minerals Ltd. 07/14/2010

EVERCLEAR INTL INC (DE)
Charter cancelled and declared inoperative and void for non-payment of taxes 03/01/2003

EVERCORE PARTNERS INC (DE)
Name changed to Evercore Inc. 08/30/2017

EVERDEEN RES LTD (ON)
Merged into Hendricks Minerals Canada Ltd. 03/22/1994
Each share Common no par exchanged for (1) share Class A Subordinate no par
Hendricks Minerals Canada Ltd. recapitalized as MCK Mining Corp. 05/09/1997 which name changed to PhosCan Chemical Corp. (ON) 08/01/2006 which reincorporated in Canada 10/19/2006
(See PhosCan Chemical Corp.)

EVEREADY INC (AB)
Acquired by Clean Harbors, Inc. 07/31/2009
Each share Common no par exchanged for (0.1304) share Common 1¢ par and $3.30 cash

EVEREADY INCOME FD (AB)
Reorganized as Eveready Inc. 01/07/2009
Each Unit no par exchanged for (0.2) share Common no par
Note: Unexchanged certificates were cancelled and became without value 01/07/2011
Eveready Inc. acquired by Clean Harbors, Inc. 07/31/2009

EVEREADY INDS INDIA LTD (INDIA)
GDR agreement terminated 04/23/2015
No GDR's remain outstanding

EVEREL PROPELLER CORP. (MD)
Liquidation completed in December 1955

EVEREN CAPITAL CORP (DE)
Each share Ser. A Preferred 1¢ par exchanged for $25 principal amount of 13.5% Jr. Subordinated Debentures due 09/15/2007 on 06/17/1996
Common 1¢ par split (2) for (1) by issuance of (1) additional share payable 06/16/1998 to holders of record 06/02/1998 Ex date - 06/17/1998
Merged into First Union Corp. 10/01/1999
Each share Common 1¢ par exchanged for (0.8286) share Common $3.33-1/3 par
First Union Corp. name changed to Wachovia Corp. (Ctfs. dated after 09/01/2001) 09/01/2001 which merged into Wells Fargo & Co. (New) 12/31/2008

EVEREST & JENNINGS INTL LTD (DE)
Reincorporated 5/27/87
Common $1 par reclassified as Conv. Class B Common $1 par 11/17/80
Stock Dividends - 75% 10/31/80; In Class A Common to Conv. Class B Common 100% 12/1/80
State of incorporation changed from (CA) to (DE), Class A Common $1 par and Conv. Class B Common $1 par changed to 1¢ par 5/27/87
Each share Class A Common 1¢ par exchanged for (1) share Common 1¢ par 11/18/93
Each share Class B Common 1¢ par exchanged for (1) share Common 1¢ par 11/18/93
Each share old Common 1¢ par exchanged for (0.1) share new Common 1¢ par 6/5/96
Merged into Graham-Field Health Products, Inc. 11/27/96
Each share new Common 1¢ par exchanged for (0.35) share Common 2-1/2¢ par
(See Graham-Field Health Products, Inc.)

EVEREST ENERGY CORP (AB)
Reincorporated 12/21/2005
Place of incorporation changed from (Canada) to (AB) 12/21/2005
Recapitalized as Westbow Energy Inc. 02/06/2006
Each share Common no par exchanged for (0.10269892) share Common no par
Westbow Energy Inc. name changed to Western Canada Energy Ltd. 04/07/2008
(See Western Canada Energy Ltd.)

EVEREST EQUITY INC (AB)
Name changed to V. Fund Investments Ltd. 12/21/92

EVEREST FD INC (MA)
Name changed to Fidelity Equity-Income Funds, Inc. 7/22/75

EVEREST FDG CORP (NV)
Each share old Common $0.001 par exchanged for (0.1) share new Common $0.001 par 7/24/95
Name changed to Everest Security Systems Corp. 11/18/95
Everest Security Systems Corp. name changed to Guardian International Inc. 8/28/96
(See Guardian International Inc.)

EVEREST INCOME FD INC (MA)
Name changed to Everest Fund, Inc. 2/14/69
Everest Fund, Inc. name changed to Fidelity Equity-Income Fund, Inc. 7/22/75

EVEREST INTL INC (DE)
Name changed to Comstock International, Inc. 10/21/88
(See Comstock International, Inc.)

EVEREST MED CORP (MN)
Merged into Gyrus Group PLC 5/15/2000
Each share Common 1¢ par exchanged for $4.85 cash

EVEREST MINES & MINERALS LTD (BC)
Recapitalized as First Narrows Resources Corp. 4/4/2000
Each share Common no par exchanged for (0.1) share Common no par

EVEREST MINING & EXPLORATION LTD. (SK)
Name changed to Everest Resources Ltd. in February 1970
(See Everest Resources Ltd.)

EVEREST RE CAP TR (DE)
7.85% Guaranteed Trust Preferred Securities called for redemption at $25 on 11/15/2007

EVEREST RE CAP TR II (DE)
Issue Information - 11,200,000 TR PFD SECS 6.20% offered at $25 per share on 03/24/2004
6.20% Trust Preferred Securities called for redemption at $25 on 05/24/2013

EVEREST REINS HLDGS INC (DE)
Under plan of merger each share Common 1¢ par automatically became (1) share Everest Re Group, Ltd. Common 1¢ par 2/23/2000

EVEREST RES CORP (NV)
Name changed to Covenant Group of China Inc. 02/10/2010
(See Covenant Group of China Inc.)

EVEREST RESOURCES LTD. (SK)
Struck off register for failure to file annual reports 9/28/73

EVEREST RES LTD (BC)
Recapitalized as Northfork Ventures Ltd. 09/27/1989
Each share Common no par exchanged for (1/3) share Common no par
Northfork Ventures Ltd. name changed to Medsana Medical Systems, Inc. 11/26/1993 which recapitalized as Connect Inter-Tel Media Inc. 01/22/1996
(See Connect Inter-Tel Media Inc.)

EVEREST SEC SYS CORP (NV)
Name changed to Guardian International Inc. 8/28/96
(See Guardian International Inc.)

EVEREST VENTURES CORP (AB)
Recapitalized as Estrella International Energy Services Ltd. (AB) 07/05/2010
Each share Common no par exchanged for (0.18952854) share Common no par
Estrella International Energy Services Ltd. (AB) reincorporated in Ontario 07/21/2011

EVEREST VENTURES INC (BC)
Each share old Common no par exchanged for (0.33333333) share new Common no par 05/04/2016
Name changed to Halio Energy Inc. 06/28/2016

EVERETT RES LTD (BC)
Recapitalized as Elm Tree Minerals Inc. 03/20/2012
Each share Common no par exchanged for (0.08333333) share Common no par
Elm Tree Minerals Inc. name changed to Ximen Mining Corp. 08/23/2013

EVERETT TRUST & SAVINGS BANK (EVERETT, WA)
Each share Capital Stock $100 par exchanged for (10) shares Capital Stock $20 par to effect a (5) for (1) split and 100% stock dividend 12/31/48
Capital Stock $20 par split (2) for (1) by issuance of (1) additional share 3/31/63
Each share Capital Stock $20 par exchanged for (4) shares Capital Stock $10 par to effect a (2) for (1) split and 100% stock dividend 3/31/70
Stock Dividend - 25% 3/31/52
Name changed to Olympic Bank (Everett, WA) 1/1/77
Olympic Bank (Everett, WA) merged into First Interstate Bancorp 1/28/85 which merged into Wells Fargo & Co. (Old) 4/1/96 which merged into Wells Fargo & Co. (New) 11/2/98

EVEREX SYS INC (DE)
Plan of reorganization under Chapter 11 Federal Bankruptcy proceedings confirmed 06/16/1994
No stockholders' equity

EVERFRONT VENTURES CORP (ON)
Name changed to DataMetrex AI Ltd. 09/27/2017

EVERGLADES BK & TR CO (FORT LAUDERDALE, FL)
Merged into Southeast Bancorporation, Inc. 06/02/1969
Each share Common $10 par exchanged for (1.1) shares Common $5 par
Southeast Bancorporation, Inc. name changed to Southeast Banking Corp. 04/22/1971
(See Southeast Banking Corp.)

EVERGO HLDGS LTD (BERMUDA)
Reorganized 3/13/89
Reorganized from Evergo Industrial Enterprise Ltd. (Hong Kong) to under the laws of Bermuda as Evergo Holdings Ltd. 3/13/89
Each ADR for Ordinary HK$1 par exchanged for (1) ADR for Ordinary HK$1 par
Company went private in 1993
Details not available

EVERGOLD RES INC (BC)
Recapitalized as Westrend Natural Gas Inc. 11/03/1992
Each share Common no par exchanged for (0.2) share Common no par
Westrend Natural Gas Inc. recapitalized as Westrend Oil & Gas Technologies Corp. 08/12/1999
(See Westrend Oil & Gas Technologies Corp.)

EVERGOOD PRODS CORP (DE)
Common 1¢ par split (2) for (1) by issuance of (1) additional share 10/22/1982
Common 1¢ par split (3) for (2) by issuance of (0.5) additional share 09/20/1983
Terminated common stock registration and is no longer public as of 09/17/2002

EVERGRANDE REAL ESTATE GROUP LTD (CAYMAN ISLANDS)
Name changed to China Evergrande Group 07/29/2016

EVERGREEN-AGRA INC (NV)
Reincorporated under the laws of Delaware as Evergreen-Agra Global Investments, Inc. 11/14/2017

EVERGREEN BANCORP INC (DE)
Common $5 par changed to $3.33-1/3 par and (0.5) additional share issued 06/20/1986
Common $3.33-1/3 par split (3) for (2) by issuance of (0.5) additional share 09/15/1987
Common $3.33-1/3 par split (3) for (2) by issuance of (0.5) additional share 09/15/1989
Common $3.33-1/3 par split (2) for (1) by issuance of (1) additional share payable 09/16/1996 to holders of record 08/30/1996
Merged into BankNorth Group, Inc. (DE) 12/31/1998
Each share Common $3.33-1/3 par exchanged for (0.9) share Common $1 par
BankNorth Group, Inc. (DE) merged into Banknorth Group, Inc. (ME) 05/10/2000 which merged into TD Banknorth Inc. 03/01/2005
(See TD Banknorth Inc.)

EVERGREEN BANCSHARES INC (FL)
Company's sole asset placed in receivership 03/12/2004
Stockholders' equity unlikely

EVERGREEN BK (SEATTLE, WA)
Under plan of reorganization each share Common $10 par automatically became (1) share EvergreenBancorp, Inc. Common no par 6/20/2001

EVERGREEN ENERGY INC (DE)
Each (12) shares old Common $0.001 par exchanged for (1) share new Common $0.001 par 08/20/2010
Filed a petition under Chapter 7 Federal Bankruptcy Code 01/23/2012
Stockholders' equity unlikely

EVERGREEN ENERGY RES LTD (ON)
Recapitalized as Evergreen International Corp. 08/08/1984
Each share Common no par exchanged for (0.25) share Common no par
(See Evergreen International Corp.)

EVERGREEN FD FOR TOTAL RETURN (DE)
Name changed to Evergreen Equity Income Fund 4/6/99

EVERGREEN FSTS LTD (NEW ZEALAND)
ADR agreement terminated 7/27/2006
Each Sponsored ADR for Ordinary exchanged for $4.0268 cash

EVERGREEN GAS & OIL CO. (ID)
Name changed to Evergreen Minerals, Inc. 09/30/1968

EVERGREEN GLOBAL DIVID OPPORTUNITY FD (DE)
Name changed to Wells Fargo Advantage Global Dividend Opportunity Fund 07/09/2010
Wells Fargo Advantage Global Dividend Opportunity Fund name changed to Wells Fargo Global Dividend Opportunity Fund 12/15/2015

EVERGREEN HEALTHCARE INC (GA)
Merged into GranCare, Inc. 7/20/95
Each share Common 1¢ par exchanged for (0.775) share Common no par
GranCare, Inc. merged into Vitalink Pharmacy Services, Inc. 2/12/97 which merged into Genesis Health Ventures, Inc. 8/28/98
(See Genesis Health Ventures, Inc.)

EVERGREEN INCOME ADVANTAGE FD (DE)
Name changed to Wells Fargo Advantage Income Opportunities Fund 07/09/2010
Wells Fargo Advantage Income Opportunities Fund name changed to Wells Fargo Income Opportunities Fund 12/15/2015

EVERGREEN INFORMATION TECHNOLOGIES INC (CO)
Administratively dissolved 02/16/1996

EVERGREEN INTER TERM BD FD (DE)
Merged into Wells Fargo Advantage Funds 07/12/2010
Details not available

EVERGREEN INTL BALANCED INCOME FD (DE)
Issue Information - 10,750,000 shares COM offered at $20 per share on 10/26/2005
Completely liquidated
Each share Common no par received first and final distribution of $15.88 cash payable 08/16/2010 to holders of record 08/16/2010
Note: Certificates were not required to be surrendered and are without value

EVERGREEN INTL CORP (ON)
Delisted from Toronto Stock Exchange 07/19/1989

EVERGREEN INTL TECHNOLOGY INC (BC)
Name changed to Jot-It! Software Corp. 2/1/97
Jot-It! Software Corp. name changed to Sideware Systems Inc. (BC) 2/18/98 which reincorporated in Yukon 1/2/2002 which reincorporated in Delaware as Knowledgemax, Inc. 5/21/2002
(See Knowledgemax, Inc.)

EVERGREEN MEDIA CORP (DE)
Class A Common 1¢ par split (3) for (2) by issuance of (0.5) additional share payable 08/26/1996 to holders of record 08/19/1996 Ex date - 08/27/1996
$3 Conv. Exchangeable Preferred 1¢ par called for redemption 12/27/1996
Under plan of merger name changed to Chancellor Media Corp. 09/15/1997
Chancellor Media Corp. name changed to AMFM, Inc. 07/13/1999 which merged into Clear Channel Communications, Inc. 08/30/2000
(See Clear Channel Communications, Inc.)

EVERGREEN MULTI SECTOR INCOME FD (DE)
Name changed 05/14/2007
Name changed from Evergreen Managed Income Fund to Evergreen Multi-Sector Income Fund 05/14/2007
Name changed to Wells Fargo Advantage Multi-Sector Income Fund 07/09/2010
Wells Fargo Advantage Multi-Sector Income Fund name changed to Wells Fargo Multi-Sector Income Fund 12/15/2015

EVERGREEN MUN TR (DE)
Reincorporated 09/17/1997
Tax Exempt Money Market Fund-California $0.001 par reclassified as Short Intermediate Municipal Fund Class Y 01/03/1994
State of incorporation changed from (MA) to (DE) 09/17/1997
Tax Exempt Money Market Fund $0.0001 par exchanged for Evergreen Money Market Trust Class Y on a net asset basis 01/12/1998

EVERGREEN NAT RES FD (DE)
Completely liquidated 12/4/98
Each share Class A $0.001 par exchanged for first and final distribution of $7.79 cash
Each share Class B $0.001 par exchanged for first and final distribution of $7.52 cash
Each share Class C $0.001 par exchanged for first and final distribution of $7.51 cash

EVERGREEN NETWORK COM INC (CO)
Administratively dissolved 03/01/2003

EVERGREEN RES INC (CO)
Each share old Common no par exchanged for (0.05) share new Common no par 3/3/86
Each share new Common no par exchanged again for (0.025) share new Common no par 8/28/90
New Common no par split (2) for (1) by issuance of (1) additional share payable 9/15/2003 to holders of record 8/29/2003 Ex date - 9/15/2003
Merged into Pioneer Natural Resources Co. 9/28/2004
Each share new Common no par exchanged for (0.58175) share Common no par and $19.98 cash

EVERGREEN SMALL CAP EQUITY FD (DE)
Name changed to Evergreen Small Cap Value Fund 4/6/99

EVERGREEN SOLAR INC (DE)
Issue Information - 3,000,000 shares COM offered at $14 per share on 11/01/2000
Each share old Common 1¢ par exchanged for (1/6) share new Common 1¢ par 01/03/2011
Plan of reorganization under Chapter 11 Federal Bankruptcy proceedings effective 07/16/2012
No stockholders' equity

EVERGREEN TITLE INC (WA)
Merged into ETC Acquisition Corp. 4/20/99
Each share Common no par exchanged for $11.25 cash

EVERGREEN TOTAL RETURN FD (MD)
Name changed 7/31/86
Name changed from Evergreen Total Return Fund, Inc. to Evergreen Total Return Fund 7/31/86
Reincorporated under the laws of Delaware as Evergreen Income & Growth Fund 2/6/97

EVERGREEN TR (DE)
Aggressive Growth Fund Class Y reclassified as Aggressive Growth Fund Class I 05/11/2001
Completely liquidated 08/25/2006
Details not available

EVERGREEN UTILS & HIGH INCOME FD (DE)
Auction Preferred Ser. M28 called for redemption at $25,000 on 05/20/2008
Name changed to Wells Fargo Advantage Utilities & High Income Fund 07/09/2010
Wells Fargo Advantage Utilities & High Income Fund name changed to Wells Fargo Utilities & High Income Fund 12/15/2015

EVERGREEN WESTERN (CA)
Merged into S.O. Systems, Inc. (CA) 11/27/64
Each share Capital Stock $1 par exchanged for (0.01232) share Common $1 par
S.O. Systems, Inc. (CA) acquired by Kalvar Corp. (LA) 4/3/68 which reincorporated in Delaware 11/12/81
(See Kalvar Corp. (DE))

EVERGREENBANCORP INC (WA)
Common no par split (3) for (2) by issuance of (0.5) additional share payable 07/23/2001 to holders of record 07/01/2001
Common no par split (5) for (4) by issuance of (0.25) additional share payable 11/30/2004 to holders of record 11/15/2004 Ex date - 12/01/2004
Common no par split (4) for (3) by issuance of (1/3) additional share payable 10/25/2005 to holders of record 10/11/2005 Ex date - 10/26/2005
Stock Dividends - 15% payable 07/15/2002 to holders of record 07/08/2002 Ex date - 07/03/2002; 10% payable 11/26/2003 to holders of record 11/14/2003 Ex date - 11/12/2003; 5% payable 12/03/2008 to holders of record 11/19/2008 Ex date - 11/17/2008
Chapter 7 Federal Bankruptcy proceedings terminated 02/05/2013
Stockholders' equity unlikely

EVERLAST FILTRATION SYS INC (AB)
Delisted from Alberta Stock Exchange 11/29/1991

EVERLAST WORLDWIDE INC (DE)
Merged into Brands Holdings Ltd. 09/20/2007
Each share Common $0.002 par exchanged for $33 cash

EVERLASTIK, INC.
Liquidation completed in 1950

EVERNU RUBBER HEEL CORP.
Adjudicated bankrupt in 1928

EVEROCK INC (ON)
Reorganized under the laws of Nevada 12/12/2005
Each share Common no par exchanged for (0.025) share Common $0.001 par

EVERON, INC. (UT)
Recapitalized as Nuclear Resources, Inc. 12/26/68
Each share Common Capital Stock 1¢ par exchanged for (0.1) share Common Capital Stock 1¢ par
Nuclear Resources, Inc. name changed to Unicept, Inc. 6/15/72 which name changed to Power Train, Inc. 11/29/76 which name changed to Scanner Energy Exploration Corp. 8/28/80 which name changed to Odin-Phoenix, Ltd. 10/18/82

EVERSHARP INC (DE)
Common $1 par split (2) for (1) by issuance of (1) additional share 10/2/63
5% Preferred $20 par called for redemption 10/31/63
Stock Dividends - 100% 5/19/45; 50% 4/15/46
Acquired by Warner-Lambert Pharmaceutical Co. 5/15/70
Each share Common $1 par exchanged for (0.4419) share Warner-Lambert Pharmaceutical Co. Common $1 par and (0.3362) share Frawley Enterprises, Inc. Common $1 par
(See each company's listing)

EVERSHARP PEN CO. (CA)
99.4% of Common $1 par was held by Parker Pen Co. as of 12/31/57 and balance was acquired by 1968

EVERSWEET CORP. (FL)
Name changed to Eversweet Foods, Inc. 2/16/62
Eversweet Foods, Inc. merged into Capitol Food Industries, Inc. 3/15/65
(See Capitol Food Industries, Inc.)

EVERSWEET FOODS, INC. (FL)
Merged into Capitol Food Industries, Inc. 3/15/65
Each share Common 10¢ par exchanged for (0.1) share 6% Convertible Preferred $10 par
(See Capitol Food Industries, Inc.)

EVERTON CAP CORP (NV)
Reorganized as CleanTech Innovations, Inc. (NV) 07/02/2010
Each share Common $0.00001 par exchanged for (8) shares Common $0.00001 par
CleanTech Innovations, Inc. (NV) reincorporated in Delaware as 6D Global Technologies, Inc. 06/29/2014

EVERTON RES INC (AB)
Reincorporated under the laws of Canada 04/16/2004

EVERTRUST FINL GROUP INC (WA)
Common no par split (3) for (2) by issuance of (0.5) additional share payable 01/16/2004 to holders of record 01/02/2004 Ex date - 01/20/2004
Merged into KeyCorp (New) 10/15/2004
Each share Common no par exchanged for $25.6016 cash

EVERYBODYS PHONE CO (TX)
Each share old Common $0.001 par exchanged for (0.001) share new Common $0.001 par 07/22/2013
Name changed to SW Innovative Holdings, Inc. 07/23/2014

EVERYDAY HEALTH INC (DE)
Acquired by j2 Global, Inc. 12/05/2016
Each share Common 1¢ par exchanged for $10.50 cash

EVERYMAN FD INC (OH)
Completely liquidated 05/03/1974
Each share Common no par received first and final distribution of $4.64 cash
Note: Certificates were not required to be surrendered and are now without value

EVERYWARE DEV CDA CORP (CANADA)
Merged into EveryWare Development Canada Inc. 06/30/1997
Each share Common no par exchanged for (0.1) share Common no par
(See EveryWare Development Canada Inc.)

EVERYWARE DEV CDA INC NEW (CANADA)
Merged into Pervasive Acquisition Corp. 11/13/1998
Each share Common no par exchanged for $1.20 cash

EVERYWARE GLOBAL INC (DE)
Under Chapter 11 plan of reorganization each share Common $0.0001 par received distribution of $0.06 cash payable 06/03/2015 to holders of record 06/02/2015

EVI INC (DE)
Common $1 par split (2) for (1) by issuance of (1) additional share payable 05/19/1997 to holders of record 05/12/1997 Ex date - 05/20/1997
Under plan of merger name changed to EVI Weatherford, Inc. 05/27/1998
EVI Weatherford, Inc. name changed to Weatherford International Inc. (New) (DE) 09/21/1998 which reincorporated in Bermuda as Weatherford International Ltd. 06/26/2002 which reincorporated in Switzerland 02/25/2009 which reincorporated in Ireland as Weatherford International PLC 06/18/2014

EVI WEATHERFORD INC (DE)
Name changed to Weatherford International Inc. (New) (DE) 09/21/1998
Weatherford International Inc. (New) (DE) reincorporated in Bermuda as Weatherford International Ltd. 06/26/2002 which reincorporated in Switzerland 02/25/2009 which reincorporated in Ireland as Weatherford International PLC 06/18/2014

EVICA RESOURCES, INC. (UT)
Name changed to American Arms, Inc. 04/05/1984
American Arms, Inc. name changed to American Industries Inc. 03/29/1988 which name changed to Dolce Ventures Inc. 05/21/2002 which recapitalized as Sino Gas International Holdings, Inc. 11/17/2006
(See Sino Gas International Holdings, Inc.)

EVIRUS SOFTWARE CORP (BC)
Name changed to Durango Capital Corp. 11/15/2002
Durango Capital Corp. recapitalized as Falkirk Resources Corp. 04/06/2009 which recapitalized as Jemi Fibre Corp. 06/27/2013 which merged into CanWel Building Materials Group Ltd. 05/16/2016

EVISION INTL INC (CO)
Name changed 02/26/2002
Name changed from eVision USA.Com, Inc. to eVision International, Inc. 02/26/2002
SEC revoked common stock registration 02/07/2011
Stockholders' equity unlikely

EVN ENERGIE-VERSORGUNG NIEDEROSTERREICH AG (AUSTRIA)
Name changed to EVN AG 9/1/98

EVOKE COMMUNICATIONS INC (DE)
Each share old Common $0.0015 par exchanged for (0.66666666) share new Common $0.0015 par 07/13/2000
Name changed to Raindance Communications Inc. 05/17/2001
(See Raindance Communications Inc.)

EVOLUCIA INC (NV)
SEC revoked common stock registration 10/06/2017

EVOLUTION FUELS INC (CO)
Reincorporated 10/18/2012
Each share old Common $0.001 par received distribution of (1) share Restricted Common $0.001 par payable 06/15/2009 to holders of record 06/10/2009
Old Common $0.0001 par changed to $0.00001 07/31/2009
Each share old Common $0.00001 par exchanged for (0.00166666) share new Common $0.00001 par 11/27/2009
Each share new Common $0.00001 par received distribution of (0.2) share Big Star Media Group, Inc. Common $0.00001 par payable 02/25/2010 to holders of record 12/28/2009
State of incorporation changed from (DE) to (CO) 10/18/2012
Each share new Common $0.00001 par exchanged again for (0.00005) share new Common $0.00001 par 02/11/2013
Name changed to SC Holdings Corp. 06/20/2014

EVOLUTION RES INC (NV)
Recapitalized as Tapinator, Inc. 11/14/2013
Each share Common $0.001 par exchanged for (0.002) share Common $0.001 par

EVOLUTION TECHNOLOGIES INC (CO)
Plan of reorganization confirmed 12/08/1983
No stockholders' equity

EVOLUTIONS INC (DE)
Filed a petition under Chapter 7 Federal Bankruptcy Code 01/05/1998
Stockholders' equity unlikely

EVOLVE ONCOLOGY INC (DE)
Common $0.001 par split (2) for (1) by issuance of (1) additional share payable 04/06/2004 to holders of record 03/01/2004 Ex date - 04/07/2004
Recapitalized as Reparotech, Inc. 09/26/2007
Each share Common $0.001 par exchanged for (0.01) share Common $0.001 par
Reparotech, Inc. name changed to Nextrata Energy Inc. 01/07/2010

EVOLVE ONE INC (DE)
Each share old Common $0.00001 par exchanged for (0.004) share new Common $0.00001 par 01/31/2003
New Common $0.00001 par split (8) for (1) by issuance of (7) additional shares payable 12/06/2004 to holders of record 12/03/2004 Ex date - 12/07/2004
New Common $0.00001 par changed to $0.0001 par 00/00/2005
Each share old Common $0.0001 par exchanged for (0.01) share new Common $0.0001 par 06/29/2006
Name changed to China Direct, Inc. (DE) 09/19/2006
China Direct, Inc. (DE) reincorporated in Florida 06/21/2007 which name changed to China Direct Industries, Inc. 05/29/2009 which name changed to CD International Enterprises, Inc. 02/29/2012

EVOLVE SOFTWARE INC (DE)
Issue Information - 5,000,000 shares COM offered at $9 per share on 08/09/2000
Each share old Common $0.001 par exchanged for (0.025) share new Common $0.001 par 12/19/2002
Plan of liquidation under Chapter 11 Federal Bankruptcy Code effective 10/28/2003
No stockholders' equity

EVON (H.H.) CO. (AR)
Plan of arrangement under Chapter XI Federal Bankruptcy Act dismissed 01/12/1977
No stockholders' equity

EVOQ PPTYS INC (DE)
Acquired by DTLA Parent JV LLC 10/09/2014
Each share Common 1¢ par exchanged for $11.63435233 cash
Note: Each share Common 1¢ par received additional distribution of $1.28669232 cash from escrow 08/07/2015

EVRAZ GROUP S A (RUSSIA)
GDR agreement terminated 02/08/2012
Each Sponsored 144A GDR for Ordinary exchanged for $15.101324 cash
Each Sponsored Reg. S GDR for Ordinary exchanged for $15.101324 cash

EVRAZ HIGHVELD STL & VANADIUM LTD (SOUTH AFRICA)
ADR agreement terminated 01/08/2016
Each Sponsored ADR for Ordinary exchanged for (1) share Ordinary
Note: Unexchanged ADR's will be sold and the proceeds, if any, held for claim after 05/12/2016

EVRO CORP (FL)
Reorganized 03/01/1994
Each share old Common 10¢ par exchanged for (0.2) share new Common 10¢ par 10/15/1992
Reorganized from Evro Financial Corp. (CO) to Evro Corp. (FL) and Common 10¢ par changed to no par 03/01/1994
Each share old Common no par exchanged for (0.05) share new Common no par 01/26/1995
Name changed to Channel America Broadcasting, Inc. 10/25/1996
Channel America Broadcasting, Inc. recapitalized as DTG Industries, Inc. 03/22/2004 which name changed DTG Multimedia, Inc. (FL) 06/04/2004 which reorganized in Nevada as Amazing Technologies Corp. 12/23/2004 which name changed to Mvive, Inc. 08/24/2007
(See Mvive Inc.)

EVTC, INC. (DE)
Charter cancelled and declared inoperative and void for non-payment of taxes 3/1/2003

EV3 INC (DE)
Issue Information - 11,765,000 shares COM offered at $14 per share on 06/16/2005
Merged into Covidien Group S.A.R.L. 07/12/2010
Each share Common 1¢ par exchanged for $22.50 cash

EWA PLANTATION CO (HI)
Merged into Castle & Cooke, Inc. (Old) 05/21/1968
Each share Capital Stock $20 par exchanged for (1.125) shares Common $10 par
Castle & Cooke, Inc. (Old) name changed to Dole Food Co., Inc. (HI) 07/30/1991 which reincorporated in Delaware 07/01/2001
(See Dole Food Co., Inc. (Old) (DE))

EWAN 1 INC (NV)
Name changed to Advanced Technetix, Inc. 09/26/2006
Advanced Technetix, Inc. name changed to AccessKey IP, Inc. 03/26/2007
(See AccessKey IP, Inc.)

EWEB21 CORP (DE)
Recapitalized as Texas Wyoming Drilling, Inc. 07/21/2008
Each share Common $0.001 par exchanged for (0.00285714) share Common $0.001 par
Note: Holders of (349) or fewer shares received $0.003 cash per share
Texas Wyoming Drilling, Inc. recapitalized as Drone USA, Inc. 05/19/2016

EWING BK & TR CO (WEST TRENTON, NJ)
Capital Stock $5 par changed to $2 par 12/13/72
Name changed to Independent Bank & Trust Co. (West Trenton, NJ) 1/1/78
Independent Bank & Trust Co. (West Trenton, NJ) merged into Franklin Bancorp 9/30/83 which was acquired by United Jersey Banks 1/24/86 which name changed to UJB Financial Corp. 6/30/89 which name changed to Summit Bancorp 3/1/96 which merged into FleetBoston Financial Corp. 3/1/2001 which merged into Bank of America Corp. 4/1/2004

EWING OIL CORP (BC)
Recapitalized as Consolidated Ewing Industries Inc. 12/06/1989
Each share Common no par exchanged for (0.2) share Common no par
Consolidated Ewing Industries Inc. recapitalized as Sirius Resources Ltd. 04/26/1999 which recapitalized as Lyra Resources Ltd. 10/14/1999 which name changed to Cicada Ventures Ltd. 07/02/2008

EWMC INTL INC (ON)
Name changed to Environmental Waste International Inc. 09/27/2001

EWORLD INTERACTIVE (FL)
Old Common no par split (4.6) for (1) by issuance of (3.6) additional shares payable 01/12/2007 to holders of record 01/01/2007 Ex date - 01/30/2007
Each share old Common no par exchanged for (0.025) share new Common no par 09/21/2009
New Common no par changed to $0.001 par 03/25/2011
Recapitalized as Green Energy Renewable Solutions, Inc. 01/26/2012
Each share Common $0.001 par exchanged for (0.2) share Common $0.001 par
Green Energy Renewable Solutions, Inc. name changed to Cirque Energy, Inc. 07/01/2015

EWORLD TRAVEL CORP (NV)
Each share old Common $0.001 par exchanged for (0.1) share new Common $0.001 par 04/17/2001
Each share new Common $0.001 par exchanged again for (0.01) share new Common $0.001 par 09/27/2001
Each share new Common $0.001 par exchanged again for (0.1) share new Common $0.001 par 09/18/2002
Name changed to GYK Ventures, Inc. 10/15/2002
GYK Ventures, Inc. name changed to Diatom Corp. 08/08/2005 which reorganized as Planktos Corp. (NV) 03/08/2007 which reincorporated in Delaware as Planktos Merger Co. 05/06/2014 which name changed to Solar Gold Ltd. 06/24/2014

EWORLDMEDIA HLDGS INC (NV)
Each (300) shares old Common $0.001 par exchanged for (1) share new Common $0.001 par 01/24/2005
Each (20,000) shares new Common $0.001 par exchanged again for (0.00005) share new Common $0.001 par 05/16/2005
Name changed to Liberty Diversified Holdings, Inc. 01/09/2006
Liberty Diversified Holdings, Inc. name changed to Nutripure Beverages, Inc. 01/17/2008

EWRX INTERNET SYS INC (NV)
Name changed to DLD Group, Inc. 06/05/2013

EX CEL RES INC (DE)
Each share old Common 1¢ par exchanged for (0.01) share new Common 1¢ par 3/16/94
Name changed to Physician's Laser Services, Inc. 5/6/96

EX-CELL-O AIRCRAFT & TOOL CORP. (MI)
Name changed to Ex-Cell-O Corp. in April 1937
(See Ex-Cell-O Corp.)

EX CELL O CORP (MI)
Common $3 par split (2) for (1) by issuance of (1) additional share 3/31/55
Common $3 par split (2) for (1) by issuance of (1) additional share 4/1/57
Common $3 par split (2) for (1) by issuance of (1) additional share 11/17/67
Common $3 par split (3) for (2) by issuance of (0.5) additional share 5/15/81
Stock Dividends - 50% 4/1/50; 10% 4/1/52; 10% 4/1/53, 10% 4/1/54; 50% 7/1/57
Merged into Textron Inc. 9/30/86
Each share Common $3 par exchanged for $77.50 cash

EX FD A CAP CORP (BC)
Name changed to Discovery Capital Corp. 07/28/2000
(See Discovery Capital Corp.)

EX LAX INC (NY)
Merged into General Cigar Co., Inc. 09/03/1971
Each share 6% Preferred $10 par exchanged for $25.80 cash
Each share Class A Common $10 par exchanged for $672 cash
Class B Common $10 par exchanged for $672 cash

EX-LAX MANUFACTURING CO. (NY)
Name changed to Ex-Lax, Inc. 10/31/31
(See Ex-Lax, Inc.)

EX-MOTHER LODE MINES LTD. (QC)
Merged into Opemisca Dufault Mines Ltd. on a (1) for (4) basis 5/10/62
(See Opemisca Dufault Mines Ltd.)

EXA CORP (DE)
Acquired by Dassault Systemes S.A. 11/17/2017
Each share Common $0.001 par exchanged for $24.25 cash

EXA INC (FL)
Name changed to ATI Nationwide Holding Corp. 06/07/2017

EXA INTL INC (MN)
Each share old Common 1¢ par exchanged for (0.33333333) share new Common 1¢ par 07/10/2000
Reincorporated under the laws of Florida as Exa Inc. and new Common 1¢ par changed to $0.001 par 12/31/2002
Exa Inc. (FL) name changed to ATI Nationwide Holding Corp. 06/07/2017

EXABYTE CORP (DE)
Each share old Common $0.001 par received distribution of (1) share CreekPath Systems Common payable 12/22/2000 to holders of record 12/22/2000
Each share old Common $0.001 par exchanged for (0.1) share new Common $0.001 par 10/31/2005
Name changed to MidgardXXI, Inc. 11/21/2006
(See MidgardXXI, Inc.)

EXACT ELECTRS INC (OR)
Merged into Vector Management Corp. 8/29/69
Each share Common no par exchanged for (1) share Common no par
Vector Management Corp. name changed to Hinkle Northwest, Inc. 6/25/73 which name changed to Hinkle & Lamear, Inc. 5/27/83 which name changed L & H Capital Services Corp. 6/18/84
(See L & H Capital Services Corp.)

EXACT ENERGY RES INC (NV)
Charter revoked for failure to file reports and pay taxes 12/31/2009

EXACT IDENTIFICATION CORP (NV)
Recapitalized as Powin Corp. 07/08/2008
Each share Common $0.001 par exchanged for (0.04) share Common $0.001 par
Powin Corp. name changed to Powin Energy Corp. 02/10/2017

EXACT WEIGHT SCALE CORP (OH)
Stock Dividend - 20% 11/14/1967
Acquired by Franklin Electric Co., Inc. 05/26/1971
Each share Common $5 par exchanged for (1.6425) shares Common no par

EXACTA INC (UT)
Name changed to Meadowbrook Golf, Inc. (UT) 10/25/1995
Meadowbrook Golf, Inc. (UT) reorganized in Delaware as Meadowbrook Golf Group Inc. 03/17/1997
(See Meadowbrook Golf Group Inc.)

EXACTECH INC (FL)
Common 1¢ par split (2) for (1) by issuance of (1) additional share payable 02/28/2003 to holders of record 02/14/2003 Ex date - 03/03/2003
Acquired by Osteon Holdings, L.P. 02/14/2017
Each share Common 1¢ par exchanged for $49.25 cash

EXACTIS COM INC (DE)
Merged into 24/7 Media, Inc. 06/29/2000
Each share Common 1¢ par exchanged for (0.6) share Common 1¢ par
24/7 Media, Inc. name changed to 24/7 Real Media Inc. 12/10/2001
(See 24/7 Real Media Inc.)

EXACTLY SPORTSWEAR INC (NV)
Recapitalized as Seirios International, Inc. 04/02/1997
Each share Common $0.001 par exchanged for (1/3) share Common $0.001 par
(See Seirios International, Inc.)

EXACTTARGET INC (DE)
Issue Information - 8,500,000 shares COM offered at $19 per share on 03/21/2012
Acquired by salesforce.com, Inc. 07/12/2013
Each share Common $0.0005 par exchanged for $33.75 cash

EXADOR RES INC (CANADA)
Merged into Tymar Resources Inc. 10/31/1989
Each share Common no par exchanged for (0.07142857) share Common no par
Tymar Resources Inc. recapitalized as Baja Gold, Inc. 01/25/1993 which merged into Viceroy Resource Corp. 05/30/1996 which merged into Quest Capital Corp. (BC) 06/30/2003 which reincorporated in Canada 05/27/2008 which name changed to Sprott Resource Lending Corp. 09/10/2010 which merged into Sprott Inc. 07/24/2013

EXALL ENERGY CORP (AB)
Reincorporated 11/06/2007
Place of incorporation changed from (ON) to (AB) 11/06/2007
Placed in receivership 03/25/2015
Stockholders' equity unlikely

EXALL RES LTD (ON)
Each share Common no par received distribution of (0.2) share Exall Energy Corp. Common no par payable 01/30/2007 to holders of record 12/14/2006 Ex date - 12/12/2006
Merged into Gold Eagle Mines Ltd. 12/27/2006
Each share Common no par exchanged for (0.5428) share Common no par
Note: Unexchanged certificates were cancelled and became without value 12/27/2008
Gold Eagle Mines Ltd. acquired by Goldcorp Inc. 09/25/2008

EXALT CAP CORP (BC)
Name changed to Astron Connect Inc. 08/30/2018

EXALTA ENERGY INC (AB)
Merged into Galleon Energy Inc. 01/22/2008
Each share Common no par exchanged for (0.118) share Class A Common no par
Galleon Energy Inc. name changed to Guide Exploration Ltd. 11/04/2011 which merged into Long Run Exploration Ltd. 10/29/2012
(See Long Run Exploration Ltd.)

EXALTISTICS INC (DE)
Name changed to International Standards Group, Inc. 03/15/1991
International Standards Group, Inc. name changed to Total World Telecommunications, Inc. 10/16/1996 which name changed to Whitehall Enterprises Inc. 02/10/1999
(See Whitehall Enterprises Inc.)

EXAM USA INC (NV)
Name changed to Pachinko World, Inc. 03/31/2006
(See Pachinko World, Inc.)

EXAMWORKS GROUP INC (DE)
Acquired by Gold Parent, L.P. 07/27/2016
Each share Common $0.0001 par exchanged for $35.05 cash

EXAR COMMUNICATION INC (NV)
Charter revoked for failure to file reports and pay fees 03/01/1990

EXAR CORP (DE)
Reincorporated 02/27/1992
State of incorporation changed from (CA) to (DE) 02/27/1992
Common $0.0001 par split (3) for (2) by issuance of (0.5) additional share 10/11/1994
Common $0.0001 par split (3) for (2) by issuance of (0.5) additional share payable 02/15/2000 to holders of record 01/25/2000
Common $0.0001 par split (2) for (1) by issuance of (1) additional share payable 10/19/2000 to holders of record 10/02/2000 Ex date - 10/20/2000
Acquired by MaxLinear, Inc. 05/12/2017
Each share Common $0.0001 par exchanged for $13 cash

EXARG CORP. (DE)
Liquidation completed
Each share Common $1 par received initial distribution of $2 cash 2/13/76
Each share Common $1 par exchanged for second and final distribution of $1.10 cash 2/16/77

EXBUD SKANSKA S A (POLAND)
ADR agreement terminated 11/22/2002
Each Sponsored ADR for Ordinary exchanged for $5.3014 cash

EXBUS ASSET MGMT NYRT (HUNGARY)
ADR agreement terminated 02/27/2007
Each Sponsored ADR for Ordinary exchanged for $0.4526 cash

EXCAL ENTERPRISES INC (DE)
Company terminated common stock registration and is no longer public as of 06/28/2002

EXCALIBER ENTERPRISES LTD (NV)
Name changed to VistaGen Therapeutics, Inc. 06/10/2011

EXCALIBUR CONTRACTING INC (FL)
Reincorporated under the laws of Delaware as Nation Energy Inc. 3/20/2000
Nation Energy Inc. (DE) reincorporated in Wyoming 6/13/2003

EXCALIBUR ENERGY CORP (CANADA)
Name changed 02/23/1981
Name and place of incorporation changed from Excalibur Development Ltd. (BC) to Excalibur Energy Corp. (Canada) and Common 50¢ par changed to no par 02/23/1981
Company went out of business 00/00/1982
Details not available

EXCALIBUR HLDG CORP (DE)
Ctfs. dated prior to 10/11/1993
Name changed to Winners Entertainment Inc. 10/11/1993
Winners Entertainment Inc. name changed to MTR Gaming Group, Inc. 10/18/1996 which merged into Eldorado Resorts, Inc. 09/19/2014

EXCALIBUR HLDG CORP (DE)
Ctfs. dated after 10/11/93
Auction Market Preferred Ser. C 144A called for redemption at $25,000 on 11/4/2004
Auction Market Preferred Ser. D 144A called for redemption at $25,000 on 11/12/2004
Auction Market Preferred Ser. E 144A called for redemption at $25,000 on 11/18/2004
Auction Market Preferred Ser. F 144A called for redemption at $25,000 on 11/26/2004
Auction Market Preferred Ser. G 144A called for redemption at $25,000 on 12/2/2004
Auction Market Preferred Ser. A 144A called for redemption at $25,000 on 12/9/2004
Auction Market Preferred Ser. B 144A called for redemption at $25,000 on 12/16/2004

EXCALIBUR INDS INC (DE)
Recapitalized as Shumate Industries, Inc. 10/20/2005
Each share Common $0.001 par exchanged for (1/7) share Common $0.001 par
Shumate Industries, Inc. name changed to Hemiwedge Industries, Inc. 02/19/2009 which name changed to HII Technologies, Inc. 01/17/2012
(See HII Technologies, Inc.)

EXCALIBUR RES LTD (CANADA)
Each share old Common no par exchanged for (0.125) share new Common no par 01/11/2010
Recapitalized as Metalla Royalty & Streaming Ltd. (Canada) 12/07/2016
Each share new Common no par exchanged for (0.33333333) share Common no par
Metalla Royalty & Streaming Ltd. (Canada) reincorporated in British Columbia 11/16/2017

EXCALIBUR SEC SVCS INC (DE)
Reorganized as Excalibur Holding Corp. 12/19/1991
Each share Common $0.00001 par exchanged for (1) share Common $0.00001 par
Excalibur Holding Corp. name

changed to Winners Entertainment Inc. 10/11/1993 which name changed to MTR Gaming Group, Inc. 10/18/1996 which merged into Eldorado Resorts, Inc. 09/19/2014

EXCALIBUR TECHNOLOGIES CORP (DE)
Each share old Common 1¢ par exchanged for (0.1) share new Common 1¢ par 04/03/1987
Under plan of reorganization each share new Common 1¢ par automatically became (1) share Convera Corp. Class A Common 1¢ par 12/21/2000
(See Convera Corp.)

EXCAM DEVS INC (YT)
Dissolved 12/31/2004

EXCAPSA SOFTWARE INC (BC)
Reincorporated under the laws of Canada 02/28/2005

EXCEED CAP HLDGS LTD (AB)
Name changed to Gallic Energy Ltd. 07/16/2007
Gallic Energy Ltd. merged into Petromanas Energy Inc. 01/04/2013 which recapitalized as PMI Resources Ltd. 06/14/2016 which name changed to PentaNova Energy Corp. 06/05/2017 which recapitalized as CruzSur Energy Corp. 09/04/2018

EXCEED ENERGY INC (AB)
Each share Class B Common no par automatically became (10) shares Class A Common no par 02/02/2009
Merged into WestFire Energy Ltd. 12/29/2009
Each share Class A Common no par exchanged for (0.01) share Common no par
WestFire Energy Ltd. name changed to Long Run Exploration Ltd. 10/29/2012
(See Long Run Exploration Ltd.)

EXCEL BANCORP INC QUINCY MASS (DE)
Under plan of reorganization each share Common 10¢ par automatically became (1) share Quincy Savings Bank (Quincy, MA) Common 10¢ par 9/28/92
(See Quincy Savings Bank (Quincy, MA))

EXCEL COMMUNICATIONS INC (DE)
Merged into Excel Communications, Inc. (VA) 10/14/97
Each share Common $0.001 par exchanged for (1) share Common $0.001 par
Excel Communications, Inc. (VA) merged into Teleglobe Inc. 11/10/98 which was acquired by BCE Inc. 11/1/2000

EXCEL COMMUNICATIONS INC NEW (VA)
Merged into Teleglobe Inc. 11/10/98
Each share Common $0.001 par exchanged for (0.885) share Common no par
Teleglobe Inc. acquired by BCE Inc. 11/1/2000

EXCEL ENERGY CORP (UT)
Merged into Barrett Resources Corp. (CO) 11/7/85
Each share Common 1¢ par exchanged for (0.901197) share Common $0.001 par
Barrett Resources Corp. (CO) reincorporated in Delaware 7/22/87 which merged into Williams Companies, Inc. 8/2/2001

EXCEL ENERGY INC (AB)
Merged into Ranchmen's Resources Ltd. 07/25/1995
Each share Common no par exchanged for (0.3) share Common no par
Ranchmen's Resources Ltd. merged into Crestar Energy Inc. 10/11/1995 which was acquired by Gulf Canada Resources Ltd. 11/13/2000
(See Gulf Canada Resources Ltd.)

EXCEL ENTERPRISES, LTEE. (QC)
Charter annulled for failure to file report 8/26/72

EXCEL GLOBAL BALANCED ASSET ALLOCATION ETF (ON)
Trust terminated 05/30/2018
Each Class E Unit received $24.2949 cash

EXCEL GLOBAL GROWTH ASSET ALLOCATION ETF (ON)
Trust terminated 05/30/2018
Each Class E Unit received $24.9858 cash

EXCEL GLOBAL INC (NV)
Common $0.001 par changed to $0.0001 par 09/27/2010
Name changed to Empire Sports & Entertainment Holdings Co. 10/06/2010
Empire Sports & Entertainment Holdings Co. name changed to Sagebrush Gold Ltd. 06/01/2011 which name changed to Pershing Gold Corp. 03/26/2012

EXCEL INDIA GROWTH & INCOME FD (ON)
Under plan of merger each Unit automatically became (2.5005) Excel Group of Funds India Balanced Fund Ser. X Units 07/11/2017

EXCEL INDIA TR (ON)
Under plan of merger each Trust Unit automatically became (0.365848) Excel Funds India Fund Ser. A Unit 08/27/2010

EXCEL INDS INC (IN)
Common no par split (5) for (4) by issuance of (0.25) additional share 01/26/1987
Stock Dividends - 10% 01/21/1985; 10% 01/27/1986; 10% 01/23/1989
Merged into Dura Automotive Systems, Inc. 03/23/1999
Each share Common no par exchanged for either (0.8) share Common 1¢ par, $25.50 cash, or a combination thereof
(See Dura Automotive Systems, Inc.)

EXCEL INTERFINANCIAL CORP (NV)
Under plan of recapitalization each share old Common 1¢ par exchanged for (0.0416666) share new Common 1¢ par 10/12/89
Merged into Excel Realty Trust 7/25/94
Each share new Common 1¢ par exchanged for $20 cash

EXCEL INVT CO (IA)
Each share Common 50¢ par exchanged for (0.2) share Common $2.50 par 07/15/1970
Stock Dividend - 10% 12/28/1970
Merged into FMIC Corp. (NC) 12/31/1973
Each share Common $2.50 par exchanged for (1) share Common no par
FMIC Corp. (NC) name changed to United Guaranty Corp. 12/30/1974 which merged into American International Group, Inc. 10/01/1981

EXCEL LATIN AMER BD FD (ON)
Merged into Excel High Income Fund 09/03/2015
Each Ser. A Unit automatically became (1.183819) Ser. A Units
Each Ser. F Unit automatically became (1.225281) Ser. F Units.

EXCEL LATIN AMER BD FD II (ON)
Merged into Excel High Income Fund 09/03/2015
Each Ser. A Unit automatically became (1.146293) Ser. A Units
Each Ser. F Unit automatically became (1.166523) Ser. F Units

EXCEL LEGACY CORP (DE)
Merged into Price Legacy Corp. 9/18/2001
Each share Common 1¢ par exchanged for (0.6667) share Common $0.0001 par

EXCEL MARITIME CARRIERS LTD (LIBERIA)
Each share Class A Common 1¢ par received distribution of (0.01) share Class B Common payable 12/27/1999 to holders of record 12/13/1999
Plan of reorganization under Chapter 11 Federal Bankruptcy proceedings effective 02/14/2014
No stockholders' equity

EXCEL MIDAS GOLD SHS INC (MN)
Reincorporated under the laws of Maryland as Midas Fund, Inc. 08/25/1995
Midas Fund, Inc. (MD) reorganized in Delaware as Midas Series Trust 10/12/2012

EXCEL PETES LTD (AB)
Class A Stock 50¢ par reclassified as Ordinary Stock 50¢ par 06/29/1967
Recapitalized 08/14/1967
Each share Ordinary Stock 50¢ par exchanged for (1) share Ordinary Stock no par and (1) share General Petroleums Drilling Ltd. Common no par
Name changed to Westburne Petroleum & Minerals Ltd. 12/31/1969
(See Westburne Petroleum & Minerals Ltd.)

EXCEL PUBG INC (NV)
Recapitalized as FullCircle Registry, Inc. 04/17/2002
Each share Common $0.001 par exchanged for (0.06666666) share Common $0.001 par
FullCircle Registry, Inc. recapitalized as Galaxy Next Generation, Inc. 09/18/2018

EXCEL RLTY TR INC (MD)
Issue Information - 4,000,000 shares PFD SER A offered at $25 per share on 01/30/1997
Each share Common 1¢ par received distribution of (1) share Excel Legacy Corp. Common 1¢ par payable 3/31/98 to holders of record 3/2/98 Ex date - 4/1/98
Stock Dividend - 20% payable 7/15/98 to holders of record 7/1/98
Under plan of merger name changed to New Plan Excel Realty Trust, Inc. 9/28/98

EXCEL RES INC (NV)
Charter revoked for failure to file reports and pay fees 9/1/98

EXCEL SWITCHING CORP (MA)
Issue Information - 4,500,000 shares COM offered at $21 per share on 11/04/1997
Merged into Lucent Technologies Inc. 11/3/99
Each share Common 1¢ par exchanged for (0.558) share Common no par
Lucent Technologies Inc. merged into Alcatel-Lucent S.A. 11/30/2006

EXCEL-TECH LTD (CANADA)
Acquired by Natus Medical Inc. 11/30/2007
Each share Common no par exchanged for $3.25 cash

EXCEL TECHNOLOGY INC (DE)
Conv. Preferred Ser. 1 $0.001 par called for redemption 07/01/1996
Merged into GSI Group Inc. 09/08/2008
Each share Common $0.001 par exchanged for $32 cash

EXCEL TRANSCONTINENTAL CORP (AB)
Struck off register 11/01/1996

EXCEL TR INC (MD)
7% Conv. Perpetual Preferred Ser. A 1¢ par called for redemption at $28.8993 on 07/31/2015
8.125% Preferred Ser. B 1¢ par called for redemption at $25 plus $0.0846 accrued dividends on 07/31/2015
Acquired by Blackstone Property Partners L.P. 07/31/2015
Each share Common 1¢ par exchanged for $15.85 cash

EXCELAN INC (DE)
Merged into Novell, Inc. 06/20/1989
Each share Common 1¢ par exchanged for (0.5649961) share Common 10¢ par
(See Novell, Inc.)

EXCELLENCY INVT RLTY TR (MD)
SEC revoked common stock registration 09/02/2011

EXCELLERATED RES INC (BC)
Recapitalized as Consolidated Excellerated Resources Inc. 02/28/2000
Each share Common no par exchanged for (0.17241379) share Common no par
Consolidated Excellerated Resources Inc. name changed to Amarillo Gold Corp. 11/21/2003

EXCELLEX CORP (FL)
Merged into Central & Southern Holding Co., Inc. 11/7/87
Each share Class A Common 10¢ par exchanged for (0.4) share Class A Common $1 par
(See Central & Southern Holding Co., Inc.)

EXCELLIGENCE LEARNING CORP (DE)
Merged into ELC Holdings Corp. 12/1/2006
Each share Common 1¢ par exchanged for $13 cash

EXCELLIUM INC (CANADA)
Name changed to XL-ID Solutions Inc. 01/24/2014
(See XL-ID Solutions Inc.)

EXCELLO TIRE & RUBBER CO. (DE)
Charter cancelled and declared inoperative and void for non-payment of taxes 1/23/24

EXCELLON RES INC (BC)
Reincorporated under the laws of Ontario 06/05/2012

EXCELON CORP (DE)
Each share old Common $0.001 par exchanged for (0.125) share new Common $0.001 par 10/07/2002
Merged into Progress Software Corp. 12/20/2002
Each share new Common $0.001 par exchanged for $3.19 cash

EXCELSIOR BIOTECHNOLOGY INC (NV)
Name changed to Targetviewz, Inc. 03/03/2006
Targetviewz, Inc. recapitalized as Greenway Energy 11/15/2007 which name changed to Greenway Technology 09/19/2008

EXCELSIOR CAP CORP (CO)
Name changed to Demeter Biotechnologies Ltd. 9/14/92
Demeter Biotechnologies Ltd. name changed to Demegen, Inc. 9/18/98 which name changed to Par Advance Technologies Corp. 10/18/2004 which name changed to ACI Global Corp. 6/20/2005

EXCELSIOR CORP (NV)
Name changed to Legal Software Solutions Inc. 4/12/88
(See Legal Software Solutions Inc.)

EXCELSIOR ENERGY LTD (AB)
Acquired by Athabasca Oil Sands Corp. 11/09/2010

Each share Common no par exchanged for $0.36 cash

EXCELSIOR-HENDERSON MOTORCYCLE MFG CO (MN)
Plan of reorganization under Chapter 11 Federal Bankruptcy Code effective 9/14/2000
No stockholders' equity

EXCELSIOR INCOME SHS INC (NY)
Name changed to EIS Fund, Inc. 4/17/2001
EIS Fund, Inc. name changed to Cornerstone Total Return Fund, Inc. 10/3/2002

EXCELSIOR INSURANCE CO. OF NEW YORK (NY)
Capital Stock $5 par changed to $6 par in 1951
Capital Stock $6 par changed to $4 par 5/10/66
Capital Stock $4 par changed to $2 par and (1) additional share issued 11/30/79
Name changed to Excelsior Insurance Co. 5/20/80
(See Excelsior Insurance Co.)

EXCELSIOR INS CO (NY)
Capital Stock $2 par changed to $3 par 5/15/81
Merged into Peerless Holdings, Inc. 12/28/83
Each share Capital Stock $3 par exchanged for $22.36 cash

EXCELSIOR LIFE INS CO (ON)
Name changed to Aetna Life Insurance Co. of Canada 01/16/1989
(See Aetna Life Insurance Co. of Canada)

EXCELSIOR PETROLEUM CORP. (CO)
Merged into Elgin Gas & Oil Co. 06/05/1959
Each share Common exchanged for (0.1) share Common 10¢ par
(See Elgin Gas & Oil Co.)

EXCELSIOR REFINERIES LTD. (AB)
Acquired by Richwell Petroleums Ltd. 04/30/1958
Each share Capital Stock no par exchanged for (1) share Capital Stock no par
Richwell Petroleums Ltd. merged into North West Pacific Developments Ltd. 06/25/1962 which recapitalized as N.W.P. Developments Ltd. 02/28/1966 which recapitalized as N.W.P. Resources Ltd. 06/17/1981 which merged into Golden North Resource Corp. 08/30/1984 which merged into Caledonia Mining Corp. (BC) 02/04/1992 which reincorporated in Canada 03/29/1995 which reincorporated in Jersey as Caledonia Mining Corp. PLC 03/24/2016

EXCELSIS INVTS INC (NV)
Each share old Common $0.001 par exchanged for (0.1) share new Common $0.001 par 04/09/2015
Name changed to Stealth Technologies, Inc. 07/06/2016

EXCEPTICON INC (KY)
Merged into Forum Group, Inc. 09/08/1981
Each share Capital Stock no par exchanged for (1) share Common no par
(See Forum Group, Inc.)

EXCEPTIONAL ENTERPRISES INC (DE)
Name changed to Cabaret Royale Corp. 11/2/93
Cabaret Royale Corp. name changed back to Exceptional Enterprises, Inc. 7/18/97
Charter cancelled and declared inoperative and void for non-payment of taxes 3/1/99

EXCEPTIONAL OIL CO. (CO)
Charter dissolved for failure to file annual reports 1/1/26

EXCEPTIONAL TECHNOLOGIES FD 5 VCC INC (BC)
Completely liquidated
Each share Common no par received first and final distribution of approximately (0.19751182) share TIR Systems Ltd. Common no par, (0.67407137) share Vigil Health Solutions Inc. Common no par and (1) Receipt payable 03/30/2007 to holders of record 03/15/2007
(See each company's listing)
Note: Each Receipt represents an interest in privately held companies whose proceeds will be distributed on a pro rata basis upon liquidation of assets

EXCERPTA ENTERPRISES, INC. (UT)
Reincorporated under the laws of Nevada as Atlantic Energy, Inc. 11/04/1985
Atlantic Energy, Inc. name changed to Cherokee Atlantic Corp. 03/03/1988

EXCESS INSURANCE CO. OF AMERICA (NJ)
Merged into Excess Insurance Co. of 00/00/1939
Each share Capital Stock $5 par exchanged for (1) share Capital Stock $5 par
Excess Insurance Co. of America (NY) merged into American Motorists Insurance Co. 00/00/1953 which was acquired by Kemperco, Inc. 05/31/1968 which name changed to Kemper Corp. (Old) 01/15/1974
(See Kemper Corp. (Old))

EXCESS INSURANCE CO. OF AMERICA (NY)
Merged into American Motorists Insurance Co. 00/00/1953
Each share Capital Stock $5 par exchanged for (1) share Capital Stock $3 par
American Motorists Insurance Co. acquired by Kemperco, Inc. 05/31/1968 which name changed to Kemper Corp. (Old) 01/15/1974
(See Kemper Corp. (Old))

EXCHANGE APPLICATIONS INC (DE)
Old Common $0.001 par split (2) for (1) by issuance of (1) additional share payable 03/17/2000 to holders of record 03/03/2000
Each share old Common $0.001 par exchanged for (0.03333333) share new Common $0.001 par 03/18/2002
Chapter 7 bankruptcy filing dismissed 01/19/2005
Stockholders' equity unlikely

EXCHANGE BANCORP INC (DE)
Common $1 par split (5) for (4) by issuance of (0.25) additional share 2/16/89
Acquired by Algemene Bank Nederland N.V. 1/30/90
Each share Common $1 par exchanged for $24 cash

EXCHANGE BANCORPORATION INC TAMPA (FL)
Common $5 par changed to $2.50 par and (1) additional share issued 12/31/1969
Stock Dividends - 10% 09/15/1980; 10% 09/01/1981
Merged into NCNB Corp. 12/31/1982
Each share Common $2.50 par exchanged for $31.92 cash

EXCHANGE BANCSHARES INC (OH)
Stock Dividends - 5% payable 06/15/1998 to holders of record 05/31/1998; 5% payable 06/18/1999 to holders of record 05/29/1999; 5% payable 06/15/2000 to holders of record 06/02/2000 Ex date - 05/31/2000
Merged into Rurban Financial Corp. 12/31/2005
Each share Common $5 par exchanged for either (1.555) shares Common no par, $22 cash, or a combination thereof
Note: Holders of (100) or fewer shares received cash
Rurban Financial Corp. name changed to SB Financial Group, Inc. 04/25/2013

EXCHANGE BK & TR CO (DALLAS, TX)
Stock Dividend - 100% 05/22/1958
99.97% held by Fort Worth National Corp. as of 11/30/1973
Public interest eliminated

EXCHANGE BK & TR CO (FRANKLIN, PA)
Each share Capital Stock $100 par exchanged for (10) shares Capital Stock $10 par 04/09/1963
Merged into Pennsylvania Bank & Trust Co. (Titusville, PA) 01/01/1971
Each share Capital Stock $10 par exchanged for (1.4) shares Capital Stock $10 par
Pennsylvania Bank & Trust Co. (Titusville, PA) reorganized as Pennbancorp 12/31/1980 which merged into Integra Financial Corp. 01/26/1989 which merged into National City Corp. 05/03/1996 which was acquired by PNC Financial Services Group, Inc. 12/31/2008

EXCHANGE BK (KINGSTREE, SC)
Merged into First Citizens Bancorporation of South Carolina, Inc. 08/11/1999
Each share Common exchanged for approximately (0.7) share Common $5 par
First Citizens Bancorporation of South Carolina, Inc. name changed to First Citizens Bancorporation, Inc. 03/20/2004 which merged into First Citizens BancShares, Inc. 10/01/2014

EXCHANGE BUFFET CORP (NY)
Dissolved by proclamation 9/29/82

EXCHANGE INDL GROUP INC (MB)
Recapitalized as Exchange Industrial Income Fund (MB) 05/10/2004
Each share Common no par exchanged for (0.05) Class A Trust Unit no par
Exchange Industrial Income Fund (MB) reorganized in Canada as Exchange Income Corp. 07/31/2009

EXCHANGE INDL INCOME FD (MB)
Reorganized under the laws of Canada as Exchange Income Corp. 07/31/2009
Each Class A Trust Unit no par exchanged for (1) share Common no par
Note: Unexchanged certificates were cancelled and became without value 07/31/2015

EXCHANGE INS CO (NY)
Class A Common $1 par called for redemption at $5 on 12/15/98
Public interest eliminated

EXCHANGE INTL CORP (DE)
Common $1 par split (3) for (2) by issuance of (0.5) additional share 12/6/85
Common $1 par split (2) for (1) by issuance of (1) additional share 11/24/86
8% Conv. Preferred Ser. B $18 par called for redemption 12/14/87
Stock Dividend - 10% 3/2/88
Name changed to Exchange Bancorp, Inc. 5/17/88
(See Exchange Bancorp, Inc.)

EXCHANGE INVT CORP (IL)
Merged into Fiduciary & General Corp. 10/22/81

Each (1.1) shares Class A Common 50¢ par exchanged for (1) share Common 25¢ par
Note: Surrender of certificates not requested until 11/11/81
(See Fiduciary & General Corp.)

EXCHANGE LEASING CORP. (NY)
Acquired by Coburn Corp. of America 2/27/68
Each share Class A Common 5¢ par or Class B Common 5¢ par exchanged for (0.5) share Common $1 par
Coburn Corp. of America name changed to Lincoln American Corp. (NY) 5/1/72 which merged into American General Corp. 9/1/80 which merged into American International Group, Inc. 8/29/2001

EXCHANGE LISTED FDS TR (DE)
Name changed 07/01/2015
Trust terminated 03/26/2015
Each share Horizons S&P Financial Select Covered Call ETF received $42.3425 cash
Name changed from Exchange Traded Concepts Trust II to Exchange Listed Funds Trust 07/01/2015
Trust terminated 02/13/2017
Each share GaveKal Knowledge Leaders Emerging Markets ETF received $23.4715891 cash
Under plan of reorganization each share Exchange Listed Funds Trust Horizons S&P 500 Covered Call ETF automatically became (1) share Horizons ETF Trust I Horizons S&P 500 Covered Call ETF 07/10/2017
(Additional Information in Active)

EXCHANGE MEDIA CORP (NV)
Name changed to Empire Oil Refineries Corp. 03/31/2011

EXCHANGE MOBILE TELECOMMUNICATIONS CORP (NV)
Recapitalized as Anything Technologies Media, Inc. 09/20/2010
Each share Common $0.001 par exchanged for (0.05) share Common $0.001 par

EXCHANGE NATL BANCSHARES INC (MO)
Common $1 par split (3) for (2) by issuance of (0.5) additional share payable 10/13/1999 to holders of record 10/07/1999
Common $1 par split (2) for (1) by issuance of (1) additional share payable 06/12/2000 to holders of record 06/05/2000 Ex date - 06/13/2000
Common $1 par split (3) for (2) by issuance of (0.5) additional share payable 07/15/2003 to holders of record 07/02/2003 Ex date - 07/16/2003
Name changed to Hawthorn Bancshares, Inc. 06/18/2007

EXCHANGE NATL BK (CHICAGO, IL)
Each share Capital Stock $100 par exchanged for (10) shares Capital Stock $20 par to effect a (5) for (1) split and 100% stock dividend 9/5/56
Capital Stock $20 par changed to $10 par and (1) additional share issued plus a 20% stock dividend paid 1/18/62
Capital Stock $10 par changed to $5 par and (1) additional share issued 1/21/64
Capital Stock $5 par changed to $3.33-1/3 par and (0.5) additional share issued 1/30/70
Stock Dividends - 100% 11/1/45; 25% 2/1/60; 25% 1/13/61
Reorganized under the laws of Delaware as Exchange International Corp. 12/31/72
Each share Capital Stock $3.33-1/3

par exchanged for (1) share Common $1 par
Exchange International Corp. name changed to Exchange Bancorp, Inc. 5/17/88
(See Exchange Bancorp, Inc.)

EXCHANGE NATL BK (COLORADO SPRINGS, CO)
Each share Capital Stock $20 par exchanged for (2) shares Capital Stock $10 par 08/01/1966
99% acquired by Mountain Banks, Ltd. through exchange offer which expired 04/17/1972
Public interest eliminated

EXCHANGE NATIONAL BANK (JEFFERSON CITY, MO)
Capital Stock $100 par changed to $10 par and (9) additional shares issued 1/15/64
Capital Stock $10 par changed to $1 par and (9) additional shares issued 6/14/89
Under plan of reorganization each share Capital Stock $1 par automatically became (1) share Exchange National Bancshares Inc. Capital Stock $1 par 4/7/93

EXCHANGE NATL BK (MOORE, OK)
Under plan of reorganization each share Common $1 par automatically became (1) share Exchange Bancshares of Moore Inc. Common $1 par 9/14/2000

EXCHANGE NATL BK (OLEAN, NY)
Each share Capital Stock $50 par exchanged for (6) shares Capital Stock $10 par 01/27/1960
Merged into Bank of New York Co., Inc. 05/29/1969
Each share Capital Stock $10 par exchanged for $42.50 principal amount of 6-1/4% Conv. Debentures due 09/01/1994 and (0.1667) share Common $15 par
Bank of New York Co., Inc. merged into Bank of New York Mellon Corp. 07/01/2007

EXCHANGE NATL BK (TAMPA, FL)
Each share Capital Stock $100 par exchanged for (25) shares Capital Stock $10 par to effect a (10) for (1) split and 150% stock dividend 12/27/1967
Stock Dividend - 60% 03/30/1957
99% acquired by Exchange Bancorporation, Inc. through purchase offer which expired 04/07/1969
Public interest eliminated

EXCHANGE OIL & GAS CORP (DE)
Merged into Georgia-Pacific Corp. 11/10/75
Each share Common $1 par exchanged for (0.30003) share Common 80¢ par
(See Georgia-Pacific Corp.)

EXCHANGE RES LTD (AB)
Acquired by Mannville Oil & Gas Ltd. 9/30/94
Each share Common no par exchanged for $2.75 cash

EXCHANGE SEC BK (BIRMINGHAM, AL)
Stock Dividends - 10% 12/15/58; 10% 12/21/59; 10% 12/15/60; 10% 12/22/61
Name changed to First Alabama Bank (Birmingham, AL) 2/1/75
(See First Alabama Bank (Birmingham, AL))

EXCHANGE TRADED CONCEPTS TR (DE)
VelocityShares Equal Risk Weighted Large Cap ETF reclassified as Janus Equal Risk Weighted Large Cap ETF 01/23/2015
Under plan of reorganization each share Yorkville High Income Infrastructure MLP ETF and Yorkville High Income MLP ETF automatically became (1) Market Vectors ETF Trust High Income Infrastructure MLP ETF no par or High Income MLP ETF no par respectively 02/22/2016
Trust terminated 02/25/2016
Each share Janus Equal Risk Weighted Cap ETF received $47.9796 cash
Trust terminated 09/30/2016
Each share CrowdInvest Wisdom ETF received $25.0001 cash
Trust terminated 06/06/2017
Each share REX Gold Hedged FTSE Emerging Markets ETF received $27.1229 cash
Each share old REX VolMAXX Long VIX Weekly Futures Strategy ETF automatically became (0.125) share new REX VolMAXX Long VIX Weekly Futures Strategy ETF 08/17/2017
REX VolMAXX Long VIX Weekly Futures Strategy ETF reclassified as REX VolMAXX Long VIX Futures Strategy ETF 04/25/2018
Trust terminated 06/22/2018
Each share REX Gold Hedged S&P 500 ETF received $33.5954 cash
Trust terminated 07/27/2018
Each share REX VolMAXXTM Long VIX Futures Strategy ETF received $18.5818 cash
(Additional Information in Active)

EXCHANGEBANC FINANCIAL CORP.
Liquidated in 1934

EXCHANGEBLVD COM INC (DE)
Recapitalized as WorldWide Auction Solutions, Inc. 09/26/2008
Each (15) shares Common $0.001 par exchanged for (1) share Common $0.001 par

EXCHEQUER INC (DE)
Recapitalized as Royal Seafood Enterprises, Inc. 01/03/1988
Each (34) shares Common $0.0001 par exchanged for (1) share Common $0.0001 par
Royal Seafood Enterprises, Inc. recapitalized as DataMark Holding, Inc. 01/11/1995 which name changed to Digital Courier Technologies Inc. 09/16/1998 which recapitalized as TransAxis, Inc. 05/08/2003
(See TransAxis, Inc.)

EXCHEQUER RESOURCE CORP (CANADA)
Reincorporated 10/25/2004
Place of incorporation changed from (AB) to (Canada) 10/25/2004
Recapitalized as CBD MED Research Corp. 07/18/2014
Each share Common no par exchanged for (0.1) share Common no par

EXCITE INC (CA)
Common no par split (2) for (1) by issuance of (1) additional share payable 7/20/98 to holders of record 7/6/98
Merged into At Home Corp. 5/28/99
Each share Common no par exchanged for (1.041902) shares Common Ser. A 1¢ par
(See At Home Corp.)

EXCLAMATION INTERNATIONAL INC (ON)
Name changed to Points International Ltd. (Ont) 7/16/2002
Points International Ltd. (Ont) reincorporated in Canada 11/10/2004

EXCLUSIVE APPAREL INC (NV)
Name changed to Helmer Directional Drilling Corp. 08/30/2011

EXCLUSIVE BLDG SVCS INC (NV)
Common $0.001 par split (31.25) for (1) by issuance of (30.25) additional shares payable 03/19/2012 to holders of record 03/17/2012
Ex date - 03/20/2012
Name changed to Dethrone Royalty Holdings, Inc. 08/27/2012
Dethrone Royalty Holdings, Inc. name changed to High Performance Beverages Co. 01/09/2014

EXCLUSIVE CRUISES & RESORTS INC (NV)
Recapitalized as Shotpak, Inc. 06/11/2007
Each (175) shares Common $0.001 par exchanged for (1) share Common $0.001 par
Shotpak, Inc. name changed to Shot Spirits Corp. 01/15/2009

EXCLUSIVE INCENTIVES INC (DE)
Each (250) shares Common $0.00001 par exchanged for (1) share Common $0.0025 par 07/02/1991
Charter cancelled and declared inoperative and void for non-payment of taxes 03/01/1994

EXCLUSIVELY FOR MEN INC (CO)
Name changed to Dynamicorp, Inc. 6/19/87
Dynamicorp, Inc. name changed to D-Bar Capital Corp. 10/15/98

EXCO ENERGY LTD (CANADA)
Struck off register for failure to file annual returns 03/13/1999

EXCO RES INC (TX)
Each share Common 1¢ par exchanged for (0.5) share Common 2¢ par 4/1/98
Merged into Exco Holdings Inc. 7/30/2003
Each share Common 2¢ par exchanged for $18 cash
(Additional Information in Active)

EXCOA OIL & GAS INC (CO)
Each share old Common $0.001 par exchanged for (0.02) share new Common $0.001 par 11/20/87
Name changed to Lexington Industries, Inc. 7/15/88
(See Lexington Industries, Inc.)

EXE TECHNOLOGIES INC (DE)
Issue Information - 8,000,000 shares COM offered at $8 per share on 08/04/2000
Each share old Common 1¢ par exchanged for (0.14285714) share new Common 1¢ par 01/02/2003
Merged into SSA Global Technologies, Inc. 12/19/2003
Each share new Common 1¢ par exchanged for $7.10 cash

EXECUFIRST BANCORP INC (PA)
Under plan of merger name changed to First Republic Bancorp, Inc. 6/7/96
First Republic Bancorp, Inc. name changed to Republic First Bancorp, Inc. 7/15/97

EXECUSTAFF INC (NV)
Name changed to Pinnacle Developments, Inc. 08/19/2004
Pinnacle Developments, Inc. recapitalized as Prime Petroleum Group, Inc. 08/14/2007
(See Prime Petroleum Group, Inc.)

EXECUSTAY CORP (MD)
Issue Information - 2,650,000 shares COM offered at $10 per share on 08/27/1997
Merged into Marriott International Inc. (New) 3/26/99
Each share Common 1¢ par exchanged for $14 cash

EXECUTEL CORP (DE)
Name changed to Protoqwik Inc. 11/09/1989

EXECUTIVE BOULEVARD CORP. (IN)
Voting Trust Agreement terminated 10/25/1963
Each VTC for Common no par exchanged for (1) share Common no par

Liquidation completed
Each share Common no par exchanged for initial distribution of (0.721755) share Super Valu Stores, Inc. 2nd Preferred Ser. A no par 10/27/1963
Each share Common no par received second and final distribution of (0.080195) share Super Valu Stores, Inc. 2nd Preferred Ser. A no par 05/22/1968
(See Super Valu Stores, Inc.)

EXECUTIVE COMMUNICATIONS INTERNATIONAL, INC. (IN)
Charter revoked for failure to file annual reports 6/6/78

EXECUTIVE DATA SYS INC (IA)
Name changed to Health Management Services, Inc. 7/31/74
(See Health Management Services, Inc.)

EXECUTIVE DETAIL CORP (NV)
Name changed to CEO America, Inc. 1/6/2005

EXECUTIVE EAGLES LTD (NV)
Name changed to Santa Rita Corp. 4/13/90
(See Santa Rita Corp.)

EXECUTIVE EMI CORP. (NV)
Each share Common 20¢ par exchanged for (0.05) share Common 1¢ par 5/21/77
Name changed to Nevada Silver Refinery 8/9/77
(See Nevada Silver Refinery)

EXECUTIVE EQUIP CORP (NY)
Name changed to Industralease Corp. 2/19/70
(See Industralease Corp.)

EXECUTIVE EXPLORATIONS LTD. (ON)
Merged into Boeing Holdings & Explorations Ltd. 12/13/1968
Each share Capital Stock $1 par exchanged for (0.2) share Common no par
Note: on 12/10/1968 company recapitalized as Executive Explorations (1968) Ltd. on a (0.2) for (1) basis changing the Capital Stock $1 par to no par
Certificates were not surrendered at time of recapitalization
Executive Explorations (1968) Ltd. merged into Boeing Holdings & Explorations Ltd. on a share for share basis
Subsequently as a result of the merger each share Executive Explorations Ltd. Capital Stock $1 par (which actually represents (0.2) share Executive Explorations (1968) Ltd. Capital Stock no par) is exchanged for (0.2) share Boeing Holdings & Explorations Ltd. Common no par
Boeing Holdings & Explorations Ltd. recapitalized as Consolidated Boeing Holdings & Explorations Ltd. 01/06/1972 which name changed to Academy Explorations Ltd. 04/10/1980
(See Academy Explorations Ltd.)

EXECUTIVE EXPLORATIONS (1968) LTD. (ON)
Merged into Boeing Holdings & Explorations Ltd. 12/13/1968 (For complete details see listing for Executive Explorations Ltd.)

EXECUTIVE GROWTH PLANS INC (NJ)
Name changed to Rotex International, Inc. 2/21/74
(See Rotex International, Inc.)

EXECUTIVE HELP SVCS INC (DE)
Name changed to AdZone Research Inc. 08/10/2001
(See AdZone Research Inc.)

EXECUTIVE HOSPITALITY CORP (DE)
Recapitalized as Forest Resources Management Corp. 08/09/2006
Each share Common 1¢ par exchanged for (0.01) share Common 1¢ par
(See Forest Resources Management Corp.)

EXECUTIVE HOUSE INC (DE)
Name changed to EXTECH Corp. 09/25/1991
EXTECH Corp. name changed to DCAP Group Inc. 02/25/1999 which name changed to Kingstone Companies, Inc. 07/02/2009

EXECUTIVE INDS INC (CA)
Common 25¢ par changed to 12-1/2¢ par and (1) additional share issued 5/19/72
Common 12-1/2¢ par split (3) for (2) by issuance of (0.5) additional share 10/18/76
Merged into Executive Merger Corp. 3/26/84
Each share Common 12-1/2¢ par exchanged for $3.90 cash

EXECUTIVE INN GROUP CORP (CANADA)
Each (2,744,950) shares old Common no par exchanged for (1) share new Common no par 07/26/2007
Note: In effect holders received $0.97 cash per share and public interest was eliminated

EXECUTIVE INVS INC (IN)
Proclaimed dissolved for failure to file annual reports 4/18/89

EXECUTIVE INVS TR (MA)
Merged into First Investors Tax Exempt Funds 04/28/2006
Details not available

EXECUTIVE LIFE & DISABILITY CO. OF CANADA (ON)
Acquired by Income Disability & Reinsurance Co. of Canada (New) 01/13/1968
Each VTC for Common $5 par exchanged for (1) VTC for Common $5 par (holders were not advised to surrender certificates until 05/08/1970)
Income Disability & Reinsurance Co. of Canada (New) name changed to Canadian General Life Insurance Co. 11/01/1973
(See Canadian General Life Insurance Co.)

EXECUTIVE LIFE INSURANCE CO. (CA)
Each share old Common $2 par exchanged for (0.001) share new Common $2 par 12/31/1968
Note: Minority interests were eliminated as there was only holders of fewer than (1,000) shares and cash was paid in lieu of fractional shares
Now a wholly owned subsidiary of First Executive Corp.

EXECUTIVE LIFE INS CO N Y (NY)
95% acquired by First Executive Corp. through exchange offer which expired 04/01/1971
Public interest eliminated

EXECUTIVE NATL DEV CORP (FL)
SEC revoked common stock registration 11/24/2010

EXECUTIVE NATL LIFE INS CO (IL)
Each share Common $2 par exchanged for (0.9672978) share Common $1 par 03/31/1967
Merged into Commonwealth Industries Corp. (DE) 08/10/1986
Each share Common $1 par exchanged for (0.75) share Class A Common no par
(See Commonwealth Industries Corp.)

EXECUTIVE OFFICE GROUP INC (NV)
Each share Common $0.001 par exchanged for (0.05) share Common 1¢ par 8/2/91
Name changed to Alliance National Inc. 4/24/96
Alliance National Inc. name changed to Vantas Inc. 7/23/99
(See Vantas Inc.)

EXECUTIVE RES INC (NV)
Name changed to JB Capital Corp. 11/25/88
JB Capital Corp. name changed to Computer Plus, Inc. 8/21/90 which name changed to Education Access Inc. 5/23/97

EXECUTIVE RISK INC (DE)
Merged into Chubb Corp. 07/19/1999
Each share Common 1¢ par exchanged for (1.235) shares Common $1 par
Chubb Corp. merged into Chubb Ltd. 01/15/2016

EXECUTIVE SECS CORP (FL)
Common 10¢ par split (3) for (1) by issuance of (2) additional shares 5/15/70
Proclaimed dissolved for failure to file reports and pay fees 12/11/76

EXECUTIVE SECURITY LIFE INSURANCE CO. (MO)
Merged into Roosevelt National Investment Co. (IL) 06/01/1973
Each share Capital Stock $1 par exchanged for (1.55) shares Class A $1 par
Roosevelt National Investment Co. (IL) reorganized in Delaware as Universal Guaranty Investment Co. 06/14/1990
(See Universal Guaranty Investment Co.)

EXECUTIVE SPORTSMENS CLUB LTD (NV)
Name changed to Executive E.M.I. Corp. 3/10/75
Executive E.M.I. Corp. name changed to Nevada Silver Refinery 8/9/77
(See Nevada Silver Refinery)

EXECUTIVE SUITES HLDGS INC (NY)
Dissolved by proclamation 9/23/92

EXECUTIVE SYS INC (DE)
Merged out of existence 12/29/2005
Details not available

EXECUTIVE TELECARD CORP FLA (FL)
Recapitalized as Xelex Corp. 01/13/1997
Each (14) shares Common $0.001 par exchanged for (1) share Common $0.001 par
Xelex Corp. recapitalized as Automax Group, Inc. 02/16/2001 which recapitalized as Heritage Capital Credit Corp. 04/01/2004 which recapitalized as Protective Capital Structures Corp. 12/11/2008

EXECUTIVE TELECARD INC (DE)
Stock Dividends - 100% 3/16/90; 10% 8/14/92; 10% 2/5/93; 10% 8/27/93; 10% 2/4/94; 10% 8/25/95; 10% payable 8/5/96 to holders of record 6/14/96
Name changed to Eglobe, Inc. 9/18/98
(See Eglobe, Inc.)

EXECUTIVE TELECOMMUNICATIONS INC (DE)
Charter cancelled and declared inoperative and void for non-payment of taxes 3/1/87

EXECUTIVE TRANSPORT CONSULTANTS, INC. (TX)
Charter forfeited for failure to maintain a registered agent 3/2/78

EXECUTONE INC (NY)
Common $1 par split (3) for (2) by issuance of (0.5) additional share 1/12/70
Stock Dividend - 25% 9/14/65
Merged into Continental Telephone Corp. 4/20/79
Each share Common $1 par exchanged for (1.2) shares Common $1 par
Continental Telephone Corp. name changed to Continental Telecom Inc. 5/6/82 which name changed to Contel Corp. 5/1/86 which merged into GTE Corp. 3/14/91 which merged into Verizon Communications Inc. 6/30/2000

EXECUTONE INFORMATION SYS INC (VA)
Reincorporated 06/00/1989
State of incorporation changed from (DE) to (VA) 06/00/1989
7.5% Conv. Preferred Ser. A 1¢ par called for redemption 12/31/1993
Name changed to eLOT, Inc. (VA) 01/04/2000 eLOT, Inc. (VA) reorganized in Delaware 12/31/2002
(See eLOT, Inc. (DE))

EXEGENICS INC (DE)
Name changed to Opko Health, Inc. 6/11/2007

EXEL EXPLS LTD (BC)
Recapitalized as Northern Lights Resources Ltd. 11/01/1977
Each share Common 50¢ par exchanged for (0.2) share Common no par
Northern Lights Resources Ltd. recapitalized as Larch Resources Ltd. 03/25/1986 which recapitalized as Manticore Petroleum Corp. 01/28/1987 which recapitalized as Dexx Energy Corp. 05/31/1988
(See Dexx Energy Corp.)

EXEL LTD (CAYMAN ISLANDS)
Ordinary Stock 1¢ par split (2) for (1) by issuance of (1) additional share payable 07/26/1996 to holders of record 07/12/1996
Name changed to XL Capital Ltd. (Cayman Islands) 02/01/1999
XL Capital Ltd. (Cayman Islands) reorganized in Ireland as XL Group PLC 07/01/2010 which reincorporated in Bermuda as XL Group Ltd. 07/25/2016
(See XL Group Ltd.)

EXEL PLC (UNITED KINGDOM)
ADR agreement terminated 06/15/2000
Each Sponsored ADR for Ordinary 6.66p par exchanged for $22.864 cash

EXELIS INC (IN)
Each share Common 1¢ par received distribution of (0.05555555) share Vectrus, Inc. Common 1¢ par payable 09/27/2014 to holders of record 09/18/2014 Ex date - 09/29/2014
Merged into Harris Corp. 05/29/2015
Each share Common 1¢ par exchanged for (0.1025) share Common $1 par and $16.625 cash

EXELON CORP (PA)
Each Corporate Unit automatically became (1.4309) shares Common no par 06/01/2017
(Additional Information in Active)

EXELTECH AEROSPACE INC (CANADA)
Filed an assignment in bankruptcy 05/29/2010
No stockholders' equity

EXEMPLAR INTL INC (NV)
Recapitalized as Now Corp. 12/4/2006
Each share Common $0.001 par exchanged for (0.001) share Common $0.001 par

EXERCYCLE CORP (DE)
Charter dissolved 03/01/1979

EXETER & HAMPTON ELEC CO (NH)
Each share Common $100 par exchanged for (5) shares Common $20 par in 1948
Each share Common $20 par exchanged for (2) shares Common $10 par 10/17/62
Each share Common $10 par exchanged for (2) shares Common $5 par 9/28/73
Merged into UNITIL Corp. 1/23/85
Each share Common $5 par exchanged for (2.15) shares Common no par

EXETER CAP CORP (AB)
Recapitalized as DGE Technologies Corp. 5/25/89
Each share Common no par exchanged for (0.25) share Common no par
DGE Technologies Corp. name changed to DKW Systems Corp. 12/3/90
(See DKW Systems Corp.)

EXETER MFG CO (NH)
Each share Common $50 par exchanged for (10) shares Common $5 par 12/00/1953
Acquired by Milliken & Co. 00/00/1966
Details not available

EXETER MINES LTD (BC)
Recapitalized as Tinta Hills Mines Ltd. 06/27/1975
Each share Capital Stock no par exchanged for (0.2) share Capital Stock no par
Tinta Hills Mines Ltd. name changed to Anchor Petroleum Corp. 04/30/1980 which reorganized as Logo Resources Ltd. 05/30/1983
(See Logo Resources Ltd.)

EXETER MNG INC (BC)
Struck off register and declared dissolved for failure to file returns 8/22/94

EXETER OIL & GAS LTD (BC)
Reorganized under the laws of Alberta as Terradyne Energy Corp. 4/11/2000
Each share Common no par exchanged for (1/3) share Common no par
(See Terradyne Energy Corp.)

EXETER OIL LTD (CA)
Reincorporated 12/31/1973
Class B Common $1 par changed to 1¢ par 00/00/1953
State of incorporation changed from (DE) to (CA) and Class A $1 par and Class B 1¢ par changed to 25¢ par 12/31/1973
Merged into Sun Co., Inc. 01/10/1984
Each share Class A 25¢ par exchanged for $36 cash

EXETER REFINING CO.
Dissolved in 1948

EXETER RESOURCE CORP (BC)
Each share Common no par received distribution of (1) share Extorre Gold Mines Ltd. Common no par payable 03/23/2010 to holders of record 03/22/2010 Ex date - 03/24/2010
Merged into Goldcorp Inc. (New) 08/08/2017
Each share Common no par exchanged for (0.12) share Common no par
Note: Unexchanged certificates will be cancelled and become without value 08/02/2023

EXFO ELECTRO-OPTICAL ENGR INC (CANADA)
Issue Information - 7,000,000 SUB VTG SHS offered at $26 per share on 06/29/2000
Name changed to EXFO Inc. 03/08/2010

EXHAUST CTLS INC (MN)
Charter cancelled for failure to file reports 03/02/1971

EXHAUST TECHNOLOGIES INC (WA)
Each share old Common $0.00001 par exchanged for (0.00005) share new Common $0.00001 par 04/28/2014
Note: In effect holders received $0.85 cash per share and public interest was eliminated

EXHIBITORS FILM FINANCIAL GROUP, INC. (DE)
Liquidated 11/5/56

EXHIBITRONIX INC (NV)
Each share old Common $0.001 par exchanged for (0.2) share new Common $0.001 par 5/7/97
Name changed to VPN Communications Corp. 3/31/2000
VPN Communications Corp. name changed to Resource Asset Management Corp. 4/16/2002

EXI TECHNOLOGIES INC (CANADA)
Name changed to EXI Wireless Inc. 09/12/2000
EXI Wireless Inc. acquired by Applied Digital Solutions, Inc. 03/31/2005 which name changed to Digital Angel Corp. (New) 06/20/2008 which recapitalized as VeriTeQ Corp. 10/22/2013

EXI WIRELESS INC (CANADA)
Acquired by Applied Digital Solutions, Inc. 03/31/2005
Each share Common no par exchanged for (3.0295) shares Common no par
Applied Digital Solutions, Inc. name changed to Digital Angel Corp. (New) 06/20/2008 which recapitalized as VeriTeQ Corp. 10/22/2013

EXIDE ELECTRS GROUP INC (DE)
Merged into BTR PLC 11/19/1997
Each share Common 1¢ par exchanged for $29 cash

EXIDE SECURITIES CORP.
Name changed to Allied Atlas Corp. in 1931
(See Allied Atlas Corp.)

EXIDE TECHNOLOGIES (DE)
Name changed 08/01/2001
Name changed from Exide Corp. to Exide Technologies 08/01/2001
Plan of reorganization under Chapter 11 Federal Bankruptcy Code effective 05/05/2004
No old Common stockholders' equity
Plan of reorganization under Chapter 11 Federal Bankruptcy Code proceedings effective 04/30/2015
No new Common stockholders' equity

EXIDYNE INC (NM)
Recapitalized as Good Software Corp. 3/22/88
Each share Common $0.001 par exchanged for (0.05) share Common no par
(See Good Software Corp.)

EXIGENT INTL INC (DE)
Merged into Harris Corp. 6/18/2001
Each share Common 1¢ par exchanged for $3.55 cash

EXILE RES INC (CANADA)
Recapitalized as Oando Energy Resources Inc. 07/30/2012
Each share Common no par exchanged for (0.06144116) share Common no par, (0.06144116) Common Stock Purchase Warrant expiring 07/24/2013 and (0.06144116) Common Stock Purchase Warrant expiring 07/24/2014
Note: Unexchanged certificates were cancelled and became without value 07/30/2018
(See Oando Energy Resources Inc.)

EXIM INTERNET GROUP INC (NV)
Each share old Common $0.001 par exchanged for (10) shares new Common $0.001 par 10/03/2005
SEC revoked common stock registration 05/20/2011

EXIT INC (UT)
Name changed to Parker Energy Technology, Inc. 05/25/1984
Parker Energy Technology, Inc. recapitalized as Source Energy Corp. 06/06/1997 which name changed to Innuity, Inc. (UT) 12/20/2005 which reincorporated in Washington 11/21/2008
(See Innuity, Inc.)

EXIT ONLY INC (NV)
Name changed to Bayport International Holdings, Inc. 11/05/2012

EXITO ENERGY INC (AB)
Recapitalized as Artisan Energy Corp. 12/06/2012
Each share Common no par exchanged for (0.5) share Common no par
(See Artisan Energy Corp.)

EXITO ENERGY II INC (AB)
Reorganized under the laws of British Columbia as Good Life Networks Inc. 01/31/2018
Each share Common no par exchanged for (0.5) share Common no par

EXITO MINERALS LTD (BC)
Name changed to eVirus Software Corp. 08/27/1999
eVirus Software Corp. name changed to Durango Capital Corp. 11/15/2002 which recapitalized as Falkirk Resources Corp. 04/06/2009 which recapitalized as Jemi Fibre Corp. 06/27/2013 which merged into CanWel Building Materials Group Ltd. 05/16/2016

EXMAILIT COM (NV)
Name changed to Cirond Corp. 10/16/2003
Cirond Corp. recapitalized as Amarium Technologies, Inc. 08/31/2006 which recapitalized as Calissio Resources Group, Inc. 10/06/2014

EXMAR RES LTD (BC)
Merged into Mishibishu Gold Corp. 10/27/1989
Each share Common no par exchanged for (0.5334) share Common no par
Mishibishu Gold Corp. recapitalized as Messina Minerals Inc. 04/07/2003 which merged into Canadian Zinc Corp. 12/20/2013 which name changed to NorZinc Ltd. 09/11/2018

EXMIN RES INC (ON)
Merged into Dia Bras Exploration Inc. 10/01/2009
Each share Common no par exchanged for (0.204) share Common no par
Dia Bras Exploration Inc. name changed to Sierra Metals Inc. 12/07/2012

EXMOCARE INC (NV)
Name changed to Second Solar, Inc. 07/01/2009
(See Second Solar, Inc.)

EXMOOR OIL & GAS CORP (CANADA)
Recapitalized as Koala Kreme Inc. 02/16/1990
Each share Common no par exchanged for (0.5) share Common no par
Koala Kreme Inc. recapitalized as Sur American Gold Corp. (Canada) 06/15/1995 which reincorporated in British Columbia as Cadan Resources Corp. 08/28/2007 which name changed to Rizal Resources Corp. 10/07/2016

EXMOUTH CAP CORP (BC)
Completely liquidated 03/22/2004
Each share Common no par exchanged for first and final distribution of (0.488564) share PhotoChannel Networks Inc. Common no par
PhotoChannel Networks Inc. name changed to PNI Digital Media Inc. 06/09/2009
(See PNI Digital Media Inc.)

EXO-WEB COM (NV)
Recapitalized as Pan American Gold Resources Corp. 5/24/2004
Each (30) shares Common no par exchanged for (1) share Common no par
Pan American Gold Resource Corp. name changed to Dragon Venture 4/18/2005 which name changed to Dragon Capital Group Corp. 12/13/2005

EXODUS COMMUNICATIONS INC (DE)
Issue Information - 4,500,000 shares COM offered at $15 per share on 03/18/1998
Common $0.001 par split (2) for (1) by issuance of (1) additional share payable 4/12/99 to holders of record 3/19/99
Common $0.001 par split (2) for (1) by issuance of (1) additional share payable 8/12/99 to holders of record 7/29/99
Common $0.001 par split (2) for (1) by issuance of (1) additional share payable 12/14/99 to holders of record 11/30/99
Common $0.001 par split (2) for (1) by issuance of (1) additional share payable 6/20/2000 to holders of record 6/7/2000 Ex date - 6/21/2000
Plan of reorganization under Chapter 11 Federal Bankruptcy Code effective 6/19/2002
No stockholders' equity

EXODYNE ENTERPRISES INC. (DE)
Declared inoperative and void for non-payment of taxes 4/1/64

EXOGEN INC (DE)
Issue Information - 2,500,000 shares COM offered at $11 per share on 07/20/1995
Merged into Smith & Nephew Acquisition, Inc. 9/9/99
Each share Common $0.0001 par exchanged for $5.15 cash

EXOL INDS INC (BC)
Recapitalized as BY & G Ventures Corp. 07/19/1991
Each share Common no par exchanged for (0.33333333) share Common no par
BY & G Ventures Corp. recapitalized as Load Resources Ltd. 11/19/1997 which name changed to GIS Global Imaging Solutions Inc. 05/31/2000 which name changed to Segami Images Inc. 02/05/2001
(See Segami Images Inc.)

EXOLIFESTYLE INC (NV)
Recapitalized as Sun Pacific Holding Corp. 10/13/2017
Each share Common $0.0001 par exchanged for (0.02) share Common $0.0001 par

EXOLON ESK CO (DE)
Reorganized 4/27/84
Each share old Common no par exchanged for (4) shares new Common no par in 1937
New Common no par split (2) for (1) by issuance of (1) additional share 11/16/60
New Common no par changed to $1 par and (1) additional share issued 6/12/64
Reorganized from Exolon Co. (MA) to under the laws of (DE) as Exolon-Esk Co. 4/27/84
Merged into Washington Mills Co., Inc. 8/16/2001
Each share Common $1 par exchanged for $13.24 cash

EXOR DATA INC (BC)
Recapitalized as Conac Software Corp. 04/22/1998
Each share Common no par exchanged for (1/3) share Common no par
Conac Software Corp. recapitalized as Lomiko Enterprises Ltd. 12/03/2004 which recapitalized as Lomiko Resources Inc. 07/28/2006 which name changed to Lomiko Metals Inc. 09/29/2008

EXOSPHERE AIRCRAFT CO INC (FL)
Name changed to Business Continuity Solutions Inc. 07/14/2011
Business Continuity Solutions Inc. name changed to Tall Trees LED Co. 08/05/2016 which recapitalized as Light Engine Design Corp. 12/21/2016

EXOTACAR INC (NV)
Name changed to Phoenix Energy Resource Corp. 07/18/2008
Phoenix Energy Resource Corp. name changed to China Forestry Industry Group, Inc. 02/02/2011 which name changed to Silvan Industries, Inc. 12/20/2011
(See Silvan Industries, Inc.)

EXOTECH INC (DE)
Charter cancelled and declared inoperative and void for non-payment of taxes 03/01/2005

EXOTIC BODIES INC (NV)
Recapitalized as Eftek Corp. 8/22/94
Each (17) shares Common $0.001 par exchanged for (1) share Common $0.001 par
(See Eftek Corp.)

EXOTICS COM INC (NV)
Each share old Common $0.0001 par exchanged for (0.2) share new Common $0.0001 par 11/08/2001
Each share new Common $0.0001 par exchanged for (0.06666666) share Common $0.001 par 03/24/2003
Company terminated common stock registration and is no longer public as of 05/19/2004

EXOUSIA ADVANCED MATLS INC (TX)
SEC revoked common stock registration 09/05/2013

EXOVIR INC (NY)
Merged out of existence 07/03/1987
Details not available

EXP RLTY INTL CORP (DE)
Common $0.00001 par split (35) for (1) by issuance of (34) additional shares payable 09/09/2013 to holders of record 09/09/2013
Name changed to eXp World Holdings, Inc. 05/09/2016

EXP RES LTD (AB)
Recapitalized as Maxim Resources Inc. (AB) 07/07/2003
Each share Common no par exchanged for (0.05) share Common no par
Maxim Resources Inc. (AB) reincorporated in Ontario 01/16/2015

EXPANDED SHALE PRODUCTS, INC. (CO)
Bankrupt 1/23/61

EXPANDER MINES & PETES LTD (AB)
Recapitalized as Northrim Mines Ltd. 11/28/73
Each share Capital Stock no par exchanged for (0.05) share Capital Stock no par

(See Northrim Mines Ltd.)

EXPATRIATE RES LTD (BC)
Each share Common no par received distribution of (0.1186268) share Stratagold Corp. Common no par payable 11/04/2003 to holders of record 10/29/2003
Each share Common no par received distribution of (0.092025) share Pacifica Resources Ltd. Common no par payable 12/16/2004 to holders of record 12/08/2004
Name changed to Yukon Zinc Corp. 12/20/2004
(See Yukon Zinc Corp.)

EXPEDIA INC (DE)
Each share Common $0.001 par exchanged for (0.5) share Common $0.0001 par and (0.5) share TripAdvisor, Inc. Common $0.001 par 12/21/2011
Name changed to Expedia Group, Inc. 03/27/2018

EXPEDIA INC (WA)
Issue Information - 5,200,000 shares COM offered at $14 per share on 11/09/1999
Acquired by USA Networks, Inc. 2/4/2002
Each share Class B Common 1¢ par exchanged for (0.380232) share Conv. Preferred Ser. A 1¢ par, (0.596582) share Common 1¢ par and (0.4229) Common Stock Purchase Warrant expiring 2/4/2009
USA Networks, Inc. name changed to USA Interactive 5/9/2002
(See USA Interactive)
Class A Common 1¢ par split (2) for (1) by issuance of (1) additional share payable 3/10/2003 to holders of record 2/24/2003 Ex date - 3/11/2003
Merged into InterActiveCorp 8/8/2003
Each share Class A Common 1¢ par exchanged for (1.93875) shares Common 1¢ par
InterActiveCorp name changed to IAC/InterActiveCorp 7/14/2004

EXPEDIACOM GLOBAL INC (NV)
Recapitalized as COi Solutions, Inc. 12/03/1998
Each share Common $0.001 par exchanged for (0.0025) share Common $0.001 par
COi Solutions, Inc. recapitalized as Alternate Energy Corp. 05/20/2003 which recapitalized as Treaty Energy Corp. 01/27/2009

EXPEDITER SYS INC (DE)
Each (7,500) shares Common $1 par exchanged for (1) share Common $75 par 12/31/1981
Note: In effect holders received $9 cash per share and public interest was eliminated

EXPEDITION ENERGY INC (AB)
Acquired by Salvo Energy Corp. 11/02/2007
Each share Common no par exchanged for $0.34 cash

EXPEDITION LEASING INC (FL)
Reincorporated under the laws of Nevada as Weikang Bio-Technology Group Co., Inc. 06/18/2008

EXPEDITION MNG INC (BC)
Each share old Common no par exchanged for (0.2) share new Common no par 06/23/2014
Each share new Common no par exchanged again for (0.33333333) share new Common no par 06/17/2015
Name changed to Imagin Medical Inc. 02/24/2016

EXPEDITOR RESOURCE GROUP LTD (BC)
Recapitalized as Mt. Expeditor Resources Ltd. 08/02/1989
Each share Common no par exchanged for (0.2) share Common no par
Mt. Expeditor Resources Ltd. name changed to Envirowaste Industries Inc. 03/29/1990 which recapitalized as Consolidated Envirowaste Industries Inc. 03/24/1992
(See Consolidated Envirowaste Industries Inc.)

EXPENSE MGMT & CTL INC (TX)
Recapitalized under Chapter 11 Federal Bankruptcy Code as Integrated Travel Systems Inc. 02/12/1990
Each share Common no par exchanged for (0.3783) share Common no par
(See Integrated Travel Systems Inc.)

EXPERIAN GROUP LTD (UNITED KINGDOM)
Name changed to Experian PLC 07/21/2008

EXPERIENTIAL AGY INC (NV)
Recapitalized as XA, Inc. 12/09/2004
Each share Common $0.001 par exchanged for (0.05) share Common $0.001 par
(See XA, Inc.)

EXPERT GROUP INC (NV)
Each share old Common $0.001 par exchanged for (0.002) share new Common $0.001 par 01/09/2009
Name changed to American Premium Water Corp. 12/19/2013

EXPERT SOFTWARE INC (DE)
Issue Information - 2,700,000 shares COM offered at $12 per share on 04/11/1995
Merged into Activision, Inc. 6/22/99
Each share Common 1¢ par exchanged for $2.65 cash

EXPERTELLIGENCE INC (NV)
Reincorporated 06/26/2006
Each share old Common no par exchanged for (0.01) share new Common no par 10/02/1995
State of incorporation changed from (CA) to (NV) and Common no par changed to $0.0001 par 06/26/2006
Each share old Common $0.0001 par exchanged for (0.005) share new Common $0.0001 par 11/19/2007
Reorganized as Pay Mobile, Inc. 07/07/2011
Each share new Common $0.0001 par exchanged for (2) shares Common $0.0001 par
Pay Mobile, Inc. name changed to Dephasium Corp. 04/18/2013 which recapitalized as Allied Ventures Holdings Corp. 04/05/2016 which name changed to Longwen Group Corp. 01/26/2017

EXPLOGAS INC (AB)
Recapitalized as EXP Resources Ltd. 09/25/1996
Each share Common no par exchanged for (0.16666666) share Common no par
EXP Resources Ltd. recapitalized as Maxim Resources Inc. (AB) 07/07/2003 which reincorporated in Ontario 01/16/2015

EXPLOGAS LTD (CANADA)
Recapitalized as MD Multimedia Inc. 09/08/2000
Each share Common no par exchanged for (0.1) share Common no par
(See MD Multimedia Inc.)

EXPLORATION AIGUEBELLE INC (QC)
Name changed to Aiguebelle Resources Inc. 12/21/1983
(See Aiguebelle Resources Inc.)

EXPLORATION AURIGINOR INC (CANADA)
Reincorporated 03/03/1998
Place of incorporation changed from (BC) to (Canada) 03/03/1998
Dissolved for non-compliance 04/15/2005

EXPLORATION CAMBIEX INC (QC)
Name changed to Hope Bay Gold Corp. Inc. 07/17/2000
Hope Bay Gold Corp. Inc. merged into Miramar Mining Corp. 05/23/2002
(See Miramar Mining Corp.)

EXPLORATION CO (DE)
Name changed 05/18/1999
Each share old Common 1¢ par exchanged for (0.02) share new Common 1¢ par 03/29/1993
Each share new Common 1¢ par received distribution of (0.2) share ExproFuels, Inc. Common 1¢ par payable 09/03/1997 to holders of record 09/13/1996
Name changed from Exploration Co. to Exploration Co. of Delaware, Inc. and state of incorporation changed from (CO) to (DE) 05/18/1999
Name changed to TXCO Resources Inc. 05/14/2007
(See TXCO Resources Inc.)

EXPLORATION CO LA INC (DE)
Reincorporated 00/00/1988
State of incorporation changed from (LA) to (DE) 00/00/1988
Name changed to XCL Ltd. (Old) 07/01/1994
XCL Ltd. (Old) recapitalized as XCL Ltd. (New) 12/17/1997
(See XCL Ltd. (New))

EXPLORATION DENN OR INC (QC)
Recapitalized as Sulliden Exploration Inc. - Exploration Sulliden Inc. 11/18/1992
Each share Common no par exchanged for (0.2) share Common no par
Sulliden Exploration Inc. - Exploration Sulliden Inc. name changed to Sulliden Gold Corp. Ltd. 11/06/2009
(See Sulliden Gold Corp. Ltd.)

EXPLORATION DRILLING INTL INC (NV)
SEC revoked common stock registration 03/08/2012

EXPLORATION ESSOR INC (CANADA)
Recapitalized as Orco Ressources Inc. 05/03/1991
Each share Common no par exchanged for (0.1) share Common no par
Orco Ressources Inc. merged into Minorca Resources Inc. 12/30/1994 which merged into McWatters Mining Inc. 10/26/1998
(See McWatters Mining Inc.)

EXPLORATION ORBITE VSPA INC (CANADA)
Name changed to Orbite Aluminae Inc. 10/17/2011
Orbite Aluminae Inc. name changed to Orbite Technologies Inc. 06/17/2015

EXPLORATION OREX INC (QC)
Merged into Anaconda Mining Inc. 05/24/2017
Each share Common no par exchanged for (0.85) share Common no par
Note: Unexchanged certificates will be cancelled and become without value 05/24/2023

EXPLORATION ROGI INC (QC)
Recapitalized as International Alliance Resources Inc. 9/20/91
Each share Common no par exchanged for (0.2) share Common no par
International Alliance Resources Inc. name changed to Groupe Covitec Inc. 8/27/93
(See Groupe Covitec Inc.)

EXPLORATION SEG INC (QC)
Name changed to West Africa Mining Exploration Inc. 7/6/95
West Africa Mining Exploration Inc. name changed to Semafo Inc. 5/13/97

EXPLORATION SULLIDEN INC (QC)
Name changed to Sulliden Gold Corp. Ltd. 11/06/2009
(See Sulliden Gold Corp. Ltd.)

EXPLORATION SURVEYS INC (TX)
Name changed to ESI Industries, Inc. (TX) 06/14/1985
ESI Industries, Inc. (TX) reincorporated in Delaware 09/18/1989 which name changed to Supreme Industries, Inc. 06/17/1993
(See Supreme Industries, Inc.)

EXPLORATION TERRENEX INC (AB)
Recapitalized as Terrenex Ventures Inc. 11/16/1993
Each share Common no par exchanged for (0.1) share Common no par
Terrenex Ventures Inc. merged into Terrenex Acquisition Corp. 08/22/1995 which reorganized as Terrenex Ltd. 11/27/2007 which was acquired by Questerre Energy Corp. 04/29/2008

EXPLORATION VENT D OR INC (QC)
Merged into Acabit Explorations Inc. 02/15/1990
Each share Common no par exchanged for (0.35269) share Common no par
Acabit Explorations Inc. name changed to Western Pacific Mining Exploration Inc. 10/17/1996 which recapitalized as Sierra Minerals Inc. 12/05/2002 which recapitalized as Goldgroup Mining Inc. 05/07/2010

EXPLORATIONS ABIOR INC (QC)
Recapitalized as Explorations Diabior Inc. 09/27/1993
Each share Common no par exchanged for (0.33333333) share Common no par
Explorations Diabior Inc. merged into Mines D'Or Virginia Inc.-Virginia Gold Mines Inc. (Canada) 06/01/1996
(See Mines D'Or Virginia Inc.-Virginia Gold Mines Inc. (Canada))

EXPLORATIONS BANQUE OR INC (QC)
Name changed to Golden Tiger Mining Exploration Co. Inc. 03/31/1984
Golden Tiger Mining Exploration Co. Inc. recapitalized as Tiger Resources Inc. 06/23/1988
(See Tiger Resources Inc.)

EXPLORATIONS DIABIOR INC (QC)
Merged into Mines D'Or Virginia Inc.-Virginia Gold Mines Inc. (Canada) 06/01/1996
Each share Common no par exchanged for (0.5) share Common no par and (0.1) share of Explorations Abior Inc. a wholly owned subsidiary
(See Mines D'Or Virginia Inc.-Virginia Gold Mines Inc. (Canada))

EXPLORATIONS ENTMT GROUP INC (FL)
Each share old Common $0.001 par exchanged for (0.5) share new Common $0.001 par 4/18/97
Recapitalized as Worldwide Equipment Corp. 4/21/97
Each share Common $0.001 par exchanged for (0.5) share Common $0.001 par
Worldwide Equipment Corp. name changed to OnCure Technologies Corp. (FL) 3/19/2001 which reincorporated in Delaware as Oncure Medical Corp. 4/21/2003
(See Oncure Medical Corp.)

EXPLORATOR RES INC (ON)
Reincorporated 06/22/2007
Place of incorporation changed from (AB) to (ON) 06/22/2007
Acquired by Sociedad Punta del Cobre S.A. 05/19/2011
Each share Common no par exchanged for $0.685 cash
Note: Unexchanged certificates were cancelled and became without value 05/19/2017

EXPLORE ANYWHERE HLDG CORP (NV)
Common $0.001 par split (15) for (1) by issuance of (14) additional shares payable 11/10/2010 to holders of record 11/10/2010
Recapitalized as Multimedia Platforms, Inc. 01/16/2015
Each share Common $0.001 par exchanged for (0.03333333) share Common $0.001 par

EXPLORE TECHNOLOGIES INC (NV)
Each share old Common $0.001 par exchanged for (0.1) share new Common $0.001 par 09/25/2001
Name changed to Pan Asia Communications Corp. 06/10/2002
Pan Asia Communications Corp. recapitalized as Hubei Pharmaceutical Group Ltd. 04/02/2003 which name changed to Amersin Life Sciences Corp. 01/14/2005 which recapitalized as Golden Tech Group, Ltd. 05/21/2007 which name changed to Mega Win Investments, Inc. 03/02/2018 which name changed to Invech Holdings, Inc. 08/07/2018

EXPLORER FD INC (MD)
Reincorporated 04/01/1973
State of incorporation changed from (DE) to (MD) 04/01/1973
Stock Dividend - 100% 12/15/1978
Name changed to Vanguard Explorer Fund, Inc. (MD) 02/28/1990
Vanguard Explorer Fund, Inc. (MD) reorganized in Delaware as Vanguard Explorer Fund 06/30/1998

EXPLORER PETE CORP (BC)
Recapitalized as Consolidated Explorer Petroleum Corp. 01/10/1986
Each share Common no par exchanged for (0.2) share Common no par
Consolidated Explorer Petroleum Corp. name changed to PEC Energy Corp. (BC) 07/14/1989 which reorganized in Delaware as Perennial Energy, Inc. 10/18/1991

EXPLORERS ALLIANCE CORP (ON)
Delisted from Toronto Venture Stock Exchange 06/05/2002

EXPLORERS ALLIANCE LTD. (MB)
Charter revoked for failure to file reports and pay fees 12/5/63

EXPLOREX CAP LTD (BC)
Name changed to Explorex Resources Inc. 06/12/2012

EXPLORO MINERALS CORP LTD (YUKON)
Delisted from Canadian Dealer Network 10/13/2000

EXPLORTEX ENERGY INC (NV)
SEC revoked common stock registration 10/08/2013

EXPLOSIVE FABRICATORS INC (CO)
Each share Common 1¢ par exchanged for (0.2) share Common 5¢ par 08/27/1990
Name changed to Dynamic Materials Corp. (CO) 12/01/1994
Dynamic Materials Corp. (CO) reincorporated in Delaware 08/15/1997 which name changed to DMC Global Inc. 11/14/2016

EXPO IRON LTD (QC)
Charter cancelled 01/25/1986

EXPO LTD (AUSTRALIA)
Recapitalized 06/03/1988
Name changed 12/05/1988
Each ADR for Ordinary A$0.20 par exchanged for (0.1) ADR for Ordinary A$2 par 03/20/1987
Recapitalized from Expo Oil N.L. to Expo Oil Ltd. 06/03/1988
Each (10) ADR's for Ordinary A$2 par exchanged for (8) ADR's for Ordinary A$1 par
Name changed from Expo Oil Ltd. to Expo Ltd. 12/05/1988
Struck off the register 03/10/1990

EXPO UNGAVA MINES LTD (ON)
Capital Stock $1 par changed to no par 12/08/1972
Merged into Exroy Resources Ltd. 07/29/1980
Each share Capital Stock no par exchanged for (0.125) share Capital Stock no par
Exroy Resources Ltd. recapitalized as Birim Goldfields Inc. 09/30/1994 which merged into Volta Resources Inc. 03/31/2008 which merged into B2Gold Corp. 12/27/2013

EXPORT EREZ USA INC (DE)
Acquired by Pawnbrokers Exchange, Inc. 03/25/2002
Details not available

EXPORT NICKEL CORP. OF CANADA LTD. (ON)
Declared dissolved by default 11/27/61
No stockholders' equity

EXPORT TYRE HLDG CO NEW (DE)
Merged into Arizona/Guam Investment Co. 1/31/95
Details not available

EXPORT TYRE HLDG CO OLD (DE)
Each share old Common $0.001 par exchanged for (0.2) share new Common $0.001 par 05/07/1990
Merged into Export Tyre Holding Co. (New) 01/31/1995
Each share Preferred Ser. A no par exchanged for (1) share Preferred Ser. A no par
Each share new Common $0.001 par exchanged for (1) share Common Ser. B $0.001 par
(See Export Tyre Holding Co. (New))

EXPOSAIC INDS INC (NC)
Common no par split (3) for (2) by issuance of (0.5) additional share 3/4/86
Stock Dividends - 10% 4/15/87; 10% 4/15/88
Name changed to Insteel Industries, Inc. 5/3/88

EXPRESS AMER HLDGS CORP (DE)
Name changed to Pilgrim America Capital Corp. 04/28/1997
Pilgrim America Capital Corp. name changed to Pilgrim Capital Corp. 06/21/1999 which merged into ReliaStar Financial Corp. 10/29/1999
(See ReliaStar Financial Corp.)

EXPRESS CAP CONCEPTS INC (DE)
Recapitalized as Greystone Digital Technology Inc. 12/22/99
Each (41.66667) shares Common $0.0001 par exchanged for (1) share Common $0.0001 par

EXPRESS CASH INTL CORP (DE)
Acquired by Cash America International, Inc. 06/30/1993
Each share Common $0.001 par exchanged for $4.5875 cash

EXPRESS-1 EXPEDITED SOLUTIONS INC (DE)
Recapitalized as XPO Logistics, Inc. 09/02/2011
Each share Common $0.001 par exchanged for (0.25) share Common $0.001 par

EXPRESS RES LTD (BC)
Recapitalized as First Star Energy Ltd. 06/23/1988
Each share Common no par exchanged for (0.5) share Common no par
First Star Energy Ltd. name changed to First Star Capital Corp. 04/03/1990
(See First Star Capital Corp.)

EXPRESS SCRIPTS INC (DE)
Class A Common 1¢ par split (2) for (1) by issuance of (1) additional share 06/24/1994
Class A Common 1¢ par split (2) for (1) by issuance of (1) additional share payable 10/30/1998 to holders of record 10/20/1998
Class A Common 1¢ par reclassified as Common 1¢ par 05/23/2001
Common 1¢ par split (2) for (1) by issuance of (1) additional share payable 06/22/2001 to holders of record 06/08/2001 Ex date - 06/25/2001
Common 1¢ par split (2) for (1) by issuance of (1) additional share payable 06/24/2005 to holders of record 06/10/2005 Ex date - 06/27/2005
Common 1¢ par split (2) for (1) by issuance of (1) additional share payable 06/22/2007 to holders of record 06/08/2007 Ex date - 06/25/2007
Common 1¢ par split (2) for (1) by issuance of (1) additional share payable 06/07/2010 to holders of record 05/21/2010 Ex date - 06/08/2010
Under plan of merger name changed to Express Scripts Holding Co. 04/02/2012

EXPRESS SYS CORP (NV)
Common $0.001 par split (2) for (1) by issuance of (1) additional share payable 12/11/2006 to holders of record 12/06/2006 Ex date - 12/12/2006
Name changed to Manas Petroleum Corp. 04/02/2007
Manas Petroleum Corp. name changed to MNP Petroleum Corp. 01/20/2014

EXPRESS TECHNOLOGIES INC (DE)
Each share Common $0.0001 par exchanged for (1/300) share Common $0.001 par 3/29/93
Note: No shareholder of record will receive fewer than (100) post-split shares
Name changed to Dougall Gaming Corp. 10/3/94
Dougall Gaming Corp. name changed to G-VII Energy Corp. 7/3/97

EXPRESSIONS GRAPHICS INC (NV)
Common $0.001 par split (4) for (1) by issuance of (3) additional shares payable 01/03/2002 to holders of record 01/03/2002 Ex date - 01/04/2002
Recapitalized as Continental Southern Resources, Inc. 05/31/2002
Each share Common $0.001 par exchanged for (0.2) share Common $0.001 par
Continental Southern Resources, Inc. name changed to Endeavour International Corp. 02/27/2004
(See Endeavour International Corp.)

EXPRESSJET HLDGS INC (DE)
Issue Information - 30,000,000 shares COM offered at $16 per share on 04/17/2002
Each share old Common 1¢ par exchanged for (0.1) share new Common 1¢ par 10/02/2008
Acquired by SkyWest, Inc. 11/12/2010
Each new Common 1¢ par exchanged for $6.75 cash

EXPRESSWAY CAMPSITES INC (MI)
Name changed to RSA Corp. 03/08/1972
(See RSA Corp.)

EXPROFUELS INC (DE)
SEC revoked common stock registration 01/03/2007

EXQUISITE FORM BRASSIERE CDA LTD (ON)
5% 2nd Non-Cum. Preference $50 par called for redemption 01/00/1970
6% 1st Preference Ser. A $10 par conversion privilege expired 12/01/1970
Placed in receivership 04/12/1983
No stockholders' equity

EXQUISITE FORM INDS INC (NY)
Name changed to Summit Organization, Inc. and Class A Capital Stock 10¢ par reclassified as Common 10¢ par 01/05/1970
(See Summit Organization, Inc.)

EXROY RES LTD (ON)
Recapitalized as Birim Goldfields Inc. 09/30/1994
Each share Common no par exchanged for (0.25) share Class A Common no par
Birim Goldfields Ltd. merged into Volta Resources Inc. 03/31/2008 which merged into B2Gold Corp. 12/27/2013

EXSORBENT INDS INC (ID)
Name changed to Consolidated Eco-Systems Inc. 1/23/97

EXSTAR FINL CORP (DE)
Merged into Exstar Newco Inc. 7/26/2001
Each share Common 1¢ par exchanged for $0.25 cash

EXTANT INVTS INC (BC)
Name changed to Sydney Resource Corp. 11/14/2001
Sydney Resource Corp. merged into West Timmins Gold Corp. 09/18/2006 which merged into Lake Shore Gold Corp. 11/05/2009 which merged into Tahoe Resources Inc. 04/07/2016

EXTARE CORP (IA)
Reorganized under the laws of Minnesota as Infi-Shield International, Inc. 01/04/1995
Each share Common no par exchanged for (0.01) share Common no par

EXTECH CORP (DE)
Name changed to DCAP Group Inc. 02/25/1999
DCAP Group Inc. name changed to Kingstone Companies, Inc. 07/02/2009

EXTEK LIQUIDATING TRUST (NV)
Liquidation completed
Each share Common 5¢ par received second distribution of $0.80 cash 8/5/92
Each share Common 5¢ par received third and final distribution of $0.17 cash 12/27/93
Note: Certificates were not required to be surrendered and are without value

EXTEK MICROSYSTEMS INC (NV)
Each share old Common 5¢ par exchanged for (0.1) share new Common 5¢ par 04/03/1975
In process of liquidation
Each share new Common 5¢ par received initial distribition of $6 cash 02/04/1991
Assets transferred to Extek Liquidating Trust 03/13/1991
(See Extek Liquidating Trust)

EXTEN INDS INC (DE)
Recapitalized 08/09/1991
Each share old Common 1¢ par

exchanged for (1/7) share new
Common 1¢ par 08/31/1990
Recapitalized from Exten
Ventures,Inc. to Exten Industries Inc.
08/09/1991
Each share new Common 1¢ par
exchanged for (0.5) share Common
1¢ par
Each share old Common 1¢ par
exchanged for (0.1) share new
Common 1¢ par 11/30/1992
Name changed to MultiCell
Technologies, Inc. 04/01/2004

EXTENDED PROD LIFE INC (CO)
Name changed to EPL Technologies
Inc. 09/30/1994
(See EPL Technologies Inc.)

EXTENDED STAY AMER INC (DE)
Common 1¢ par split (2) for (1) by
issuance of (1) additional share
payable 07/19/1996 to holders of
record 07/05/1996
Merged into BHAC Capital IV, LLC
05/11/2004
Each share Common 1¢ par
exchanged for $19.625 cash

EXTENDED SYS INC (DE)
Merged into Sybase, Inc. 10/26/2005
Each share Common $0.001 par
exchanged for $4.460847 cash

EXTENDICARE INC (CANADA)
Each share Common no par
exchanged for (2) Multiple Shares
no par 04/25/1996
Each share Class A Common no par
exchanged for (1) Subordinate
Share no par 04/25/1996
8% Conv. Preferred Ser. I no par
called for redemption 12/23/1996
Ser. 2 Preferred no par called for
redemption at $25 plus $0.1646
accrued dividends on 10/13/2006
Note: Right to receive redemption
funds expired 10/13/2012
Adjustable Dividend Class II Ser. 1 no
par called for redemption at $25 plus
$0.243 accrued dividends on
10/13/2006
Note: Right to receive redemption
funds expired 10/13/2012
Adjustable Dividend Preferred Ser. 3
no par called for redemption at $25
plus $0.1138 accrued dividends on
10/13/2006
Note: Right to receive redemption
funds expired 10/13/2012
Adjustable Dividend Preferred Ser. 4
no par called for redemption at $25
plus $0.1669 accrued dividends on
10/13/2006
Note: Right to receive redemption
funds expired 10/13/2012
Plan of arrangement effective
11/10/2006
Each Multiple Share no par
exchanged for (1.075) Extendicare
Real Estate Investment Trust (ON)
Trust Units no par and (1) share
Assisted Living Concepts, Inc. (Ctfs.
dated after 11/10/2006) Class B
Common 1¢ par
Each share Subordinate no par
exchanged for (1) Extendicare Real
Estate Investement Trust (ON) Trust
Unit no par and (1) share Assisted
Living Concepts, Inc. (Ctfs. dated
after 11/10/2006) Class A Common
1¢ par
Note: Canadian residents had the
option to receive Exchangeable
Class B Units of Ltd. Partnership in
lieu of Trust Units
(See each company's listing)
(Additional Information in Active)

EXTENDICARE INC (DE)
Common 33-1/3¢ par changed to
16-2/3¢ par and (1) additional share
issued 1/21/69
Name changed to Humana Inc.
1/18/74

EXTENDICARE LTD (CANADA)
Name changed 03/18/1974
Common no par split (2) for (1) by
issuance of (1) additional share
05/16/1973
Name changed from Extendicare
(Canada) Ltd. to Extendicare Ltd.
03/18/1974
Each share Common no par
exchanged for (1) share Class A
Non-Voting no par and (1) share
Conv. Common no par 01/22/1979
Name changed to Crownx Inc.
12/01/1983
Crownx Inc. name changed to
Extendicare Inc. 11/17/1994
(See Extendicare Inc.)

EXTENDICARE REAL ESTATE INVT TR (ON)
Each Class B Unit of Ltd. Partnership
exchanged for (1) Trust Unit
11/10/2011
Each Trust Unit exchanged for (1)
share Extendicare Inc. (Canada)
Common no par 07/05/2012
Note: Unexchanged certificates were
cancelled and became without value
07/05/2018

EXTENSION ENERGY CO., INC. (ID)
Name changed to Extension Gold Inc.
2/2/83
Extension Gold Inc. name changed to
Extension Enterprises Inc. 12/17/84
which name changed to
International Measurement & Control
Co. 12/5/85 which reorganized as
Laser Technology, Inc. (ID) 5/11/89
which reincorporated in Delaware
5/30/97

EXTENSION ENTERPRISES INC (ID)
Common 1¢ par split (2) for (1) by
issuance of (1) additional share
9/19/85
Name changed to International
Measurement & Control Co. 12/5/85
International Measurement & Control
Co. reorganized as Laser
Technology, Inc. (ID) 5/11/89 which
reincorporated in Delaware 5/30/97

EXTENSION GOLD INC. (ID)
Each share Common 1¢ par
exchanged for (0.05) share Common
20¢ par 11/16/84
Name changed to Extension
Enterprises Inc. and Common 20¢
par changed to 1¢ par 12/17/84
Extension Enterprises Inc. name
changed to International
Measurement & Control Co. 12/5/85
which reorganized as Laser
Technology, Inc. (ID) 5/11/89 which
reincorporated in Delaware 5/30/97

EXTENSIONS INC (NV)
Common $0.001 par split (20) for (1)
by issuance of (19) additional
shares payable 12/29/2008 to
holders of record 12/15/2008
Ex date - 12/30/2008
Charter revoked 02/28/2013

EXTENSITY INC (DE)
Issue Information - 4,000,000 shares
COM offered at $20 per share on
01/26/2000
Merged into Geac Computer Corp.
Ltd. 3/6/2003
Each share Common $0.001 par
exchanged for $1.75 cash

EXTENWAY SOLUTIONS INC (CANADA)
Deemed to have filed an assignment
in bankruptcy 04/13/2016
Stockholders' equity unlikely

EXTERRA ENERGY INC (NV)
Each share old Common $0.001 par
exchanged for (0.01666666) share
new Common $0.001 par
05/07/2009
Note: Holders also received (100)
shares Restricted Common $0.001
par
Plan of reorganization under Chapter
11 bankruptcy proceedings effective
11/27/2012
No stockholders' equity

EXTERRAN HLDGS INC (DE)
Each share Common 1¢ par received
distribution of (0.5) share Exterran
Corp. Common 1¢ par payable
11/03/2015 to holders of record
10/27/2015 Ex date - 11/04/2015
Name changed to Archrock, Inc.
11/04/2015

EXTERRAN PARTNERS L P (DE)
Name changed to Archrock Partners,
L.P. 11/04/2015
Archrock Partners, L.P. merged into
Archrock, Inc. 04/26/2018

EXTORRE GOLD MINES LTD (CANADA)
Merged into Yamana Gold Inc.
08/22/2012
Each share Common no par
exchanged for (0.0467) share
Common no par and $3.50 cash
Note: Unexchanged certificates were
cancelled and became without value
08/22/2018

EXTOTAL RES INC (BC)
Recapitalized as Luxor Resources
Ltd. 11/01/1989
Each share Common no par
exchanged for (0.5) share Common
no par
Luxor Resources Ltd. name changed
to Luxor Industrial Corp. 03/30/1992

EXTR@CT INC (DE)
Charter cancelled and declared
inoperative and void for
non-payment of taxes 03/01/2005

EXTRACARE CORP (CANADA)
Name changed to South Pacific
Resources Inc. 06/17/1994
South Pacific Resources Inc. name
changed to South Pacific Resources
Corp. 10/24/1994 which
recapitalized as Lexacal Investment
Corp. 07/24/1998 which name
changed to New West Energy
Services Inc. 10/26/2007

EXTRACORPOREAL MED SPECIALTIES INC (PA)
Common no par split (2) for (1) by
issuance of (1) additional share
4/26/71
Stock Dividend - 100% 11/26/73
Merged into Johnson & Johnson
5/26/78
Each share Common no par
exchanged for (0.3088) share
Common $2.50 par

EXTRACT GROUP LTD (SOUTH AFRICA)
Each Sponsored ADR for Ordinary
received distribution of $1.69936
cash payable 12/19/2016 to holders
of record 12/12/2016 Ex date -
12/20/2016
ADR agreement terminated
10/18/2017
Each Sponsored ADR for Ordinary
exchanged for $0.027031 cash

EXTRACT PHARMACEUTICALS INC (DE)
Name changed to Token Communities
Ltd. 03/21/2018

EXTRACT RES LTD (AUSTRALIA)
Acquired by Miraculum Mineral Ltd.
05/24/2012
Each share Ordinary exchanged for
$8.65 cash

EXTRACTIVE FUELS INC (WY)
Charter revoked for failure to pay
taxes 03/31/1987

EXTREME CCTV INC (CANADA)
Merged into Robert Bosch GmbH
02/29/2008
Each share Common no par
exchanged for $5 cash

EXTREME ENERGY CORP (AB)
Merged into C1 Energy Ltd.
12/16/2004
Each share Common no par
exchanged for (0.22) share Common
no par
C1 Energy Ltd. merged into Penn
West Energy Trust 09/25/2007

EXTREME FITNESS INC (NV)
Charter revoked 01/31/2010

EXTREME HOME STAGING INC (NV)
Name changed to Q Lotus Holdings,
Inc. 07/19/2010
(See Q Lotus Holdings, Inc.)

EXTREME INNOVATIONS INC (NV)
Recapitalized as Silverhawk
Entertainment Group, Inc.
07/27/2006
Each share Common $0.001 par
exchanged for (0.05) share Common
$0.001 par
Silverhawk Entertainment Group, Inc.
name changed to Acme Sports &
Entertainment, Inc. 06/27/2007
which recapitalized as Casa
Havana, Inc. 06/17/2008 which
name changed to Design Marketing
Concepts, Inc. 12/09/2009
(See Design Marketing Concepts, Inc.)

EXTREME MEDIA INC (NJ)
Recapitalized as Media Holdings
International, Inc. 12/17/2004
Each share Common no par
exchanged for (0.05) share Common
no par

EXTREME MOBILE COATINGS CORP LTD (UNITED KINGDOM)
Common $0.001 par split (2) for (1)
by issuance of (1) additional share
payable 11/26/2008 to holders of
record 11/26/2008
Reincorporated under the laws of
Delaware as Extreme Mobile
Coatings Worldwide Corp. and
Common $0.001 par changed to
$0.0001 par 04/08/2009
Extreme Mobile Coatings Worldwide
Corp. recapitalized as Structural
Enhancement Technologies Corp.
06/18/2010 which recapitalized as
Eco-Petroleum Solutions, Inc.
02/07/2013 which name changed to
Enzolytics Inc. 03/22/2018

EXTREME MOBILE COATINGS WORLDWIDE CORP (DE)
Common $0.0001 par split (5) for (1)
by issuance of (4) additional shares
payable 04/08/2009 to holders of
record 04/08/2009
Recapitalized as Structural
Enhancement Technologies Corp.
06/18/2010
Each share Common $0.0001 par
exchanged for (0.01) share Common
$0.0001 par
Structural Enhancement Technologies
Corp. recapitalized as
Eco-Petroleum Solutions, Inc.
02/07/2013 which name changed to
Enzolytics Inc. 03/22/2018

EXTREME POKER LTD (NV)
Recapitalized as China Capital
Holdings Corp. 02/28/2006
Each share Common $0.001 par
exchanged for (0.001) share
Common $0.001 par
(See China Capital Holdings Corp.)

EXTREME TECHNOLOGIES INC (BC)
Name changed to Portacom Wireless,
Inc. (BC) 12/5/95
Portacom Wireless, Inc. (BC)
reincorporated in Delaware 12/23/96
(See Portacom Wireless, Inc. (DE))

EXTRUDO-FILM CORP. (NY)
Acquired by Standard Oil Co. (NJ)
01/19/1962
Each share Common 10¢ par
exchanged for (0.081168) share
Capital Stock $7 par

Standard Oil Co. (NJ) name changed to Exxon Corp. 11/01/1972 which name changed to Exxon Mobil Corp. 11/30/1999

EXTRUDYNE INC (NY)
Dissolved by proclamation 12/29/82

EXULT INC (DE)
Merged into Hewitt Associates, Inc. 10/01/2004
Each share Common $0.0001 par exchanged for (0.2) share Common 1¢ par
Hewitt Associates, Inc. merged into Aon Corp. (DE) 10/01/2010 which reorganized in England & Wales as Aon PLC 04/02/2012

EXUS GLOBAL INC (NV)
Recapitalized 09/12/2003
Recapitalized from Exus Networks, Inc. to Exus Global, Inc. 09/12/2003
Each share Common $0.001 par exchanged for (0.14285714) share Common $0.001 par
Each (15) shares new Common $0.001 par exchanged again for (1) share new Common $0.001 par 03/04/2004
Recapitalized as StarInvest Group, Inc. 01/14/2005
Each share Common $0.001 par exchanged for (0.005) share Common $0.001 par
(See StarInvest Group, Inc.)

EXX INC (NV)
Class A Common 1¢ par split (5) for (1) by issuance of (4) additional shares payable 03/07/2000 to holders of record 12/16/1999
Class B Common 1¢ par split (5) for (1) by issuance of (4) additional shares payable 03/07/2000 to holders of record 12/16/1999
Shares reacquired 06/21/2010
Each share Class A Common 1¢ par exchanged for $1.55 cash
Each share Class B Common 1¢ par exchanged for $1.55 cash

EXXADON TECHNOLOGY CORP (ON)
Name changed to E.W.M.C. International Inc. 12/03/2014
E.W.M.C. International Inc. name changed to Environmental Waste International Inc. 09/27/2001

EXXAU MINERALS INC (CANADA)
Name changed to Getty Copper Corp. 9/3/92
Getty Copper Corp. recapitalized as Getty Copper Inc. 3/7/2003

EXXCEL ENERGY CORP (UT)
Name changed to Excel Energy Corp. 1/5/79
Excel Energy Corp. merged into Barrett Resources Corp. (CO) 11/7/85 which reincorporated in (DE) 7/22/87 which merged into Williams Companies, Inc. 8/2/2001

EXXEL ENERGY CORP (BC)
Common no par split (6) for (1) by issuance of (5) additional shares payable 02/15/2006 to holders of record 02/10/2006 Ex date - 02/08/2006
Recapitalized as XXL Energy Corp. 05/30/2008
Each share Common no par exchanged for (0.05) share Common no par

EXXETER RES CORP (CANADA)
Merged into Cable Satisfaction International Inc. 6/30/96
Each share Common no par exchanged for (0.04) Subordinate no par
(See Cable Satisfaction International Inc.)

EXXON ASSET MGMT CO
Preferred Class C Voting Trust Certificates called for redemption at $100,000 on 11/23/2005
Accredited Investors Class B Preferred called for redemption at $100,000 on 12/7/2005

EXXON CORP (NJ)
Capital Stock $7 par changed to no par and (1) additional share issued 07/23/1976
Capital Stock no par split (2) for (1) by issuance of (1) additional share 06/11/1981
Capital Stock no par split (2) for (1) by issuance of (1) additional share 09/14/1987
Capital Stock no par split (2) for (1) by issuance of (1) additional share payable 04/11/1997 to holders of record 03/14/1997 Ex date - 04/14/1997
Under plan of merger name changed to Exxon Mobil Corp. 11/30/1999

EXXON PROJ INVT CORP
Accredited Investors Money Market Preferred Ser. A called for redemption at $100,000 on 10/27/2005
Accredited Investor Money Market Preferred Ser. B called for redemption at $100,000 on 11/10/2005

EYE CARE CTRS AMER INC (TX)
Acquired by Sears, Roebuck & Co. 12/22/1987
Each share Common 10¢ par exchanged for $2.50 cash

EYE CARE INTL INC (FL)
Each share old Class A Common $0.001 par exchanged for (0.2) share new Class A Common $0.001 par 6/19/2003
Name changed to Amacore Group, Inc. 3/31/2005

EYE DYNAMICS INC (NV)
Name changed to AcuNetx, Inc. 01/03/2006
(See AcuNetx, Inc.)

EYE ON MEDIA NETWORK INC (FL)
Name changed to Ethos Media Network, Inc. 07/10/2017

EYE TECHNOLOGY INC (DE)
Each share old Common 1¢ par exchanged for (0.1) share new Common 1¢ par 04/01/1993
Name changed to Star Scientific, Inc. 12/15/1998
Star Scientific, Inc. name changed to Rock Creek Pharmaceuticals, Inc. 06/04/2014

EYECARE ACQUISITION CORP (DE)
Recapitalized as Homecare United Inc. 2/17/98
Each share Common 1¢ par exchanged for (0.5) share Common 1¢ par
Homecare United Inc. name changed to Oasis Holdings Inc. 2/8/2000

EYECASHNETWORKS INC (NV)
SEC revoked common stock registration 09/23/2004
Stockholders' equity unlikely

EYELOGIC SYS INC (AB)
Completely liquidated
Each share Class A Common no par received initial distribution of $0.33 cash payable 12/21/2015 to holders of record 12/11/2015
Each share Class A Common no par received second and final distribution of $0.04 cash payable 09/15/2016 to holders of record 12/11/2015
Note: Certificates were not required to be surrendered and are without value

EYEMAKERS INC (NV)
Name changed to Homeland Security Technology, Inc. 06/30/2004
Homeland Security Technology, Inc. merged into Amnis Energy Inc. 03/15/2005 which name changed to Homeland Security Group International, Inc. 10/10/2005 which recapitalized as Domestic Energy Corp. 04/07/2008
(See Domestic Energy Corp.)

EYEQ NETWORKING INC (DE)
Reincorporated 02/00/1998
State of incorporation changed from (CO) to (DE) 02/00/1998
Name changed to Aviation Holdings Group, Inc. 09/14/1998
(See Aviation Holdings Group, Inc.)

EYETECH PHARMACEUTICALS INC (DE)
Issue Information - 6,500,000 shares COM offered at $21 per share on 01/29/2004
Merged into OSI Pharmaceuticals, Inc. 11/14/2005
Each share Common 1¢ par exchanged for (0.12275) share Common 1¢ par and $15 cash
(See OSI Pharmaceuticals, Inc.)

EYETEL TECHNOLOGIES INC (WY)
Reincorporated 06/23/1994
Place of incorporation changed from (BC) to (WY) 06/23/1994
Charter revoked for failure to file reports and maintain a registered agent 08/14/2000

EYI INDS INC (NV)
Charter permanently revoked for failure to file reports and pay taxes 06/30/2009

EYRE TRADING GROUP LTD (CO)
Name changed to Natural Born Carvers, Inc. 05/08/1997
Natural Born Carvers, Inc. name changed to Carv Industries, Inc. 06/12/1998 which recapitalized as Carv.com, Inc. (CO) 12/14/1998 which reincorporated in Nevada as PacificTradingPost.Com, Inc. 02/26/1999 which recapitalized as IDC Technologies Inc. 11/23/2001 which name changed to Jill Kelly Productions Holding, Inc. 08/20/2003 which name changed to eWorldCompanies, Inc. 03/13/2007

EZ AUCTIONS & SHIPPING INC (NV)
SEC revoked common stock registration 03/06/2006

EZ COMMUNICATIONS INC (VA)
Merged into American Radio Systems Corp. 04/04/1997
Each share Class A Common 1¢ par exchanged for (0.9) share Class A Common 1¢ par and $11.75 cash
American Radio Systems Corp. merged into American Tower Systems Corp. 06/04/1998 which name changed to American Tower Corp. (Old) 06/17/1998 which reorganized as American Tower Corp. (New) 01/03/2012

EZ ENGLISH ONLINE INC (DE)
Name changed to Panglobal Brands, Inc. 2/6/2007

EZ TRAVEL INC (NV)
Name changed to World Information Technology Inc. 02/27/2003
(See World Information Technology Inc.)

EZCHIP SEMICONDUCTOR LTD. (ISRAEL)
Acquired by Mellanox Technologies, Ltd. 02/23/2016
Each share Common ILS 0.02 par exchanged for $25.50 cash

EZCOMM ENTERPRISES INC (DE)
Name changed 7/19/2004
Name changed from Ezcomm Inc. to Ezcomm Enterprises Inc. 7/19/2004
Recapitalized as Eugene Science, Inc. 1/13/2006
Each share Common $0.0001 par exchanged for (0.1) share Common $0.001 par

EZCONNECT INC (NV)
Name changed to Encore Wireless, Inc. 02/08/2001
(See Encore Wireless, Inc.)

EZCONY INTERAMERICA INC (BRITISH VIRGIN ISLANDS)
Filed a Petition for Assignment for the Benefit of Creditors 03/22/2002
Stockholders' equity unlikely

EZEKIEL EXPLS LTD (BC)
Recapitalized as Aurex Resources Corp. 12/11/1991
Each share Common no par exchanged for (0.2) share Common no par
Aurex Resources Corp. recapitalized as Cobre Mining Co., Inc. 03/10/1997
(See Cobre Mining Co., Inc.)

EZENET CORP (AB)
Merged into Cognicase Corp. 9/24/2001
Each share Common no par exchanged for (0.57) share Common no par
(See Cognicase Corp.)

EZFOODSTOP COM (NV)
Name changed to Far East Energy Corp. and (17) additional shares issued 01/01/2002
(See Far East Energy Corp.)

EZIX COM INC (UT)
Name changed to E-Center.com Inc. 07/19/1999
E-Center.com Inc. name changed to Merlin Software Technologies Holdings Inc. 11/30/1999 which name changed to Optika Investment Co. Inc. (NV) 01/25/2000 which reincorporated in Delaware as USA Broadband, Inc. 07/10/2001

EZJR INC (NV)
Recapitalized as Her Imports 01/31/2017
Each share Common $0.001 par exchanged for (0.5) share Common $0.001 par

EZRA HLDGS LTD (SINGAPORE)
Stock Dividend - 4% payable 01/06/2015 to holders of record 12/22/2014 Ex date - 12/18/2014
ADR agreement terminated 10/17/2018
Each ADR for Ordinary exchanged for (20) shares Ordinary
Note: Company filed Chapter 11 on 03/18/2017. Depositary will attempt to sell unexchanged ADR's after 04/17/2019.

EZTALK INC (FL)
Name changed to Billyweb Corp. 05/03/2000
Billyweb Corp. name changed to Poseidis, Inc. 08/28/2002
(See Poseidis, Inc.)

EZTRADER INC (NV)
Reincorporated under the laws of Delaware as EZTD Inc. 12/29/2015

EZ2 COS INC (NV)
Reincorporated under the laws of Georgia as Coastal Capital Acquisition Corp. 01/31/2008

EZUTILITIES CORP (TX)
Name changed to Texas Commercial Resources, Inc. (TX) 09/18/2001
Texas Commercial Resources, Inc. (TX) reincorporated in Delaware as Petrosearch Corp. 08/28/2003 which reorganized in Nevada as Petrosearch Energy Corp. 12/31/2004 which merged into Double Eagle Petroleum Co. 08/06/2009

F

F. & F. FINANCE CO., INC. (NC)
Each share Common $5 par

exchanged for (10) shares Common 50¢ par 06/30/1957
Name changed to Field Financial Corp. (NC) 12/21/1961
Field Financial Corp. (NC) name changed to Cyber Corp. (NC) 11/01/1971 which reincorporated in Nevada as Cyber International Corp. 06/18/1973
(See Cyber International Corp.)

F. & W. GRAND 5-10-25 CENT STORES
Merged into F. & W. Grand-Silver Stores, Inc. in 1929
Details not available

F. & W. GRAND PROPERTIES CORP.
Property sold under bankruptcy proceedings to Properties Realization Corp. in 1934
(See Porperties Realization Corp.)

F. & W. GRAND-SILVER STORES, INC.
Sold in bankruptcy in 1934
Details not available

F. P. E. NOTEHOLDERS CORP. (MI)
Liquidation completed 10/30/61

F & B CECO INDS INC (NY)
Plan of reorganization under Chapter 11 Federal Bankruptcy proceedings confirmed 07/15/1985
No stockholders' equity

F & C INTL INC (OH)
Common no par split (4) for (3) by issuance of (1/3) additional share 06/03/1992
Plan of reorganization under Chapter 11 Federal Bankruptcy Code effective 07/02/1994
No stockholders' equity

F & E RESOURCE SYS TECHNOLOGY INC (MD)
Each share old Common 1¢ par exchanged for (0.25) share new Common 1¢ par 10/27/1994
Stock Dividend - 50% 05/03/1993
Name changed to Wastemasters Inc. (MD) 06/05/1996
Wastemasters Inc. (MD) reincorporated in Delaware as Environmental Energy Services Inc. 06/29/2001
(See Environmental Energy Services Inc.)

F & G INVESTORS INC. (AZ)
Charter revoked for failure to file reports or pay fees 6/28/63

F & M BANCORP (IN)
Merged into First Financial Bancorp (OH) 4/1/96
Each share Common exchanged for (64.507739) shares Common 10¢ par

F & M BANCORPORATION (OK)
Reincorporated under the laws of Delaware 09/00/2003

F & M BANCORPORATION INC (DE)
Merged into Prosperity Bancshares, Inc. 04/01/2014
Each share Common 1¢ par exchanged for (0.88453) share Common $1 par and $9.18 cash
Each share Accredited Investors Common 1¢ par exchanged for (0.88453) share Common $1 par and $9.18 cash

F & M BANCORPORATION INC (WI)
Stock Dividends - 10% payable 06/10/1996 to holders of record 05/24/1996; 10% payable 06/09/1997 to holders of record 05/23/1997; 10% payable 09/01/1998 to holders of record 08/14/1998
Merged into Citizens Banking Corp. 11/01/1999
Each share Common $1 par exchanged for (1.303) shares Common $10 par
Citizens Banking Corp. name changed to Citizens Republic Bancorp, Inc. 04/26/2007 which merged into FirstMerit Corp. 04/12/2013 which merged into Huntington Bancshares Inc. 08/16/2016

F & M BK (JEFFERSON, WI)
Name changed 05/28/1998
Name changed from Farmers & Merchants Bank (Jefferson, WI) to F & M Bank (Jefferson, WI) 05/28/1998
Acquired by F&M Bancorporation Inc. 01/03/2000
Details not available

F & M FINL SVCS CORP (WI)
Common $1 par split (3) for (2) by issuance of (0.5) additional share 12/24/86
Common $1 par split (5) for (4) by issuance of (0.25) additional share 5/2/90
Merged into Associated Banc-Corp 5/8/92
Each share Common $1 par exchanged for (0.8) share Common 1¢ par

F & M NATL CORP (VA)
Common $2 par split (2) for (1) by issuance of (1) additional share 6/29/87
Stock Dividend - 3% payable 10/26/99 to holders of record 9/24/99
Merged into BB&T Corp. 8/9/2001
Each share Common $2 par exchanged for (1.09) shares Common $5 par

F & T FINL SVCS INC (NV)
Merged into Pan American Bank (Los Angeles, CA) 07/31/2015
Each share Common 1¢ par exchanged for (3.853) shares new Common $5 par
(See Pan American Bank (Los Angeles, CA))

F.A. CORP. (MD)
Liquidation completed
Each share Common no par exchanged for initial distribution of $5 cash 9/20/80
Each share Common no par received second and final distribution of $0.361 cash 4/14/81

F A O INC (DE)
Plan of reorganization under Chapter 11 Federal Bankruptcy Code effective 4/23/2003
Each (15) shares old Common no par exchanged for (1) share new Common no par
Plan of reorganization under Chapter 11 Federal Bankruptcy Code effective 11/18/2004
No stockholders' equity

F.A.R. LIQUIDATING CORP.
Liquidated 00/00/1950
Details not available

F A TUCKER GROUP INC (DE)
Charter cancelled and declared inoperative and void for non-payment of taxes 3/1/99

F B P PUBG INC (NY)
Name changed to Money Growth Institute, Inc. 06/16/1982
(See Money Growth Institute, Inc.)

F B TRUCK LINE CO (UT)
Stock Dividend - 25% 05/25/1977
Merged into Eagle Motor Lines Inc. 07/06/1979
Each share Common no par exchanged for $17.56 cash

F-D CAPITAL FUND (NV)
Merged into Pine Tree Fund, Inc. 11/27/1972
Each Share of Bene. Int. no par exchanged for (1) share Common 10¢ par
(See Pine Tree Fund, Inc.)

F D G MNG INC (BC)
Name changed to Tango Gold Mines Inc. 05/08/2013
Tango Gold Mines Inc. name changed to Tango Mining Ltd. 11/24/2014

F.E.D. CORP.
Liquidated in 1939

F F O FINL GROUP INC (FL)
Merged into Republic Bancshares, Inc. 9/19/97
Each share Common 10¢ par exchanged for (0.29) share Common $2 par
Republic Bancshares, Inc. merged into BB&T Corp. 4/14/2004

F.G. TRADING CORP.
Dissolved in 1939

F G MUT FD (CA)
Acquired by New World Fund, Inc. 12/31/1976
Each share Capital Stock $1 par exchanged for (0.65341) share Common $1 par
New World Fund, Inc. merged into Investment Co. of America 01/23/1981

F.H.G. LIQUIDATING CORP. (KY)
Liquidation completed
Each share Common no par exchanged for initial distribution of $14 cash 9/27/74
Each share Common no par received second and final distribution of $0.89675 cash 4/2/76

F H INDS CORP (DE)
Name changed to Diana Corp. 07/17/1985
Diana Corp. name changed to Coyote Network Systems, Inc. 11/20/1997 which name changed to Quentra Networks, Inc. 07/31/2000
(See Quentra Networks, Inc.)

F I C FD INC (QC)
Each share Class A $10 par exchanged for (1) share Part. Preferred $10 par 04/15/1969
Each share Class B $5 par exchanged for (1) share Common $5 par 04/15/1969
Part. Preferred $10 par called for redemption 03/31/1981
Acquired by a private company 09/01/1979
Details not available

F M RES LTD (BC)
Name changed to Designed Data (Canada) Inc. 10/20/1987
Designed Data (Canada) Inc. recapitalized as Pier Mac Environment Management Inc. 05/03/1990 which recapitalized as Ebony Gold & Gas Inc. 04/07/1995 which recapitalized as Running Foxes Petroleum Corp. 12/09/1998 which recapitalized as Running Fox Resource Corp. 10/17/2000

F M-STEREO GUIDE, INC. (PA)
Adjudicated bankrupt 7/31/62
No stockholders' equity

F N B CORP (PA)
Common $10 par changed to $2 par and (4) additional shares issued 09/09/1982
Stock Dividends - 5% payable 05/31/1996 to holders of record 05/01/1996; 5% payable 05/31/1997 to holders of record 05/01/1997; 5% payable 05/24/1998 to holders of record 04/20/1998; 5% payable 06/21/1999 to holders of record 06/04/1999; 5% payable 05/31/2000 to holders of record 04/28/2000; 5% payable 05/31/2001 to holders of record 05/03/2001 Ex date - 05/01/2001
Reincorporated under the laws of Florida and Common $2 par changed to 1¢ par 06/13/2001
Conv. Preferred Ser. B $2 par called for redemption at $25 plus $0.23 accrued dividend on 04/30/2003

F N B CORP (VA)
Stock Dividends - 10% payable 09/17/1999 to holders of record 08/27/1999; 6% payable 03/08/2002 to holders of record 02/26/2002 Ex date - 02/22/2002
Merged into StellarOne Corp. 02/28/2008
Each share Common $5 par exchanged for (1.585) shares Common $1 par
StellarOne Corp. merged into Union First Market Bankshares Corp. 01/02/2014 which name changed to Union Bankshares Corp. 04/28/2014

F P SPL ASSETS LTD (HONG KONG)
ADR's for Ordinary USD $0.01 par changed to USD $0.001 par and (9) additional ADR's issued 08/24/1990
Name changed to Asia Orient Co. Ltd. 08/08/1991
(See Asia Orient Co. Ltd.)

F R CORP (NY)
Completely liquidated 5/19/69
Each share Common 50¢ par exchanged for first and final distribution of (0.225) share Technology, Inc. Common no par
Technology, Inc. name changed to Krug International Corp. 7/22/86 which name changed to Sunlink Health Systems, Inc. 8/20/2001

F-R PUBLISHING CORP.
Reorganized as New Yorker Magazine, Inc. 3/20/47
Each share Common no par exchanged for (3) shares Common $1 par
(See New Yorker Magazine, Inc.)

F/X BIO-MED INC (UT)
Involuntarily dissolved 02/01/1990

F-X OF NEW YORK, INC. (NY)
Charter revoked for failure to file reports and pay fees 12/15/67

F Y I INC (DE)
Secondary Offering - 2,420,000 shares COM offered at $20 per share on 12/12/1996
Name changed to SOURCECORP Inc. 2/15/2002
(See SOURCECORP Inc.)

F&C BANCSHARES INC (FL)
Merged into First of America Bank Corp. 12/31/1994
Each share Common $1 par exchanged for (0.6436) share Common $10 par
First of America Bank Corp. merged into National City Corp. 03/31/1998 which was acquired by PNC Financial Services Group, Inc. 12/31/2008

F&C/CLAYMORE PFD SECS INCOME FD INC (MD)
Issue Information - 36,500,000 COM SHS offered at $25 per share on 01/28/2003
Name changed to Flaherty & Crumrine/Claymore Preferred Securities Income Fund Inc. 11/13/2003
Crumrine/Claymore Preferred Securities Income Fund Inc. name changed to Flaherty & Crumrine Preferred Securities Income Fund Inc. 02/22/2013

F&H LIQUIDATING CORP. (NJ)
Liquidation completed
Each share Capital Stock $1 par exchanged for initial distribution of $7 cash 6/26/63
Each share Capital Stock $1 par received second distribution of $1.49 cash 5/25/64
Each share Capital Stock $1 par received third distribution of $1.32 cash 12/7/65
Each share Capital Stock $1 par

F&M BANCORP (MD)
received fourth and final distribution of $0.14 cash 5/23/69
Common $5 par split (2) for (1) by issuance of (1) additional share 8/12/88
Stock Dividends - 5% payable 8/8/97 to holders of record 7/25/97; 5% payable 7/29/98 to holders of record 7/8/98; 5% payable 7/28/99 to holders of record 7/15/99
Merged into Mercantile Bankshares Corp. 8/12/2003
Each share Common $5 par exchanged for $50.3703 cash

F&M BANK & TRUST CO. (TULSA, OK)
Stock Dividends - 20% 00/00/1972; 13.6% 03/10/1974
Reorganized as F & M Bancorporation, Inc. (OK) 04/17/1975
Each share Common $10 par exchanged for (1) share Common $1 par
F & M Bancorporation, Inc. (OK) reincorporated in Delaware 09/00/2003

F&M DISTRS INC (MI)
Plan of reorganization under Chapter 11 Federal Bankruptcy proceedings confirmed 09/06/1996
No stockholders' equity

F&M IMPORTING INC (CA)
Recapitalized as MarCor Development Co., Inc. (CA) 11/03/1986
Each share Common no par exchanged for (0.25) share Common no par
MarCor Development Co., Inc. (CA) reincorporated in Nevada 08/31/1988 which name changed to MarCor Resorts, Inc. 07/13/1989 which name changed to Rio Hotel & Casino Inc. 03/02/1992 which merged into Harrah's Entertainment, Inc. 01/01/1999
(See Harrah's Entertainment, Inc.)

FA COMPUTER TECHNOLOGIES INC (DE)
Name changed to Gates/FA Distributing Inc. 1/1/91
Gates/FA Distributing Inc. acquired by Arrow Electronics, Inc. 8/29/94

FA PWR FD (ON)
Merged into First Asset PowerGen Fund 06/18/2008
Each Unit no par received (1.0527) Units no par
First Asset PowerGen Fund merged into Sprott Power Corp. 02/03/2011 which name changed to Renewable Energy Developers Inc. 07/02/2013 which merged into Capstone Infrastructure Corp. 10/07/2013

FAB GLOBAL INC (GA)
Name changed to Dupont Direct Financial Holdings, Inc. 03/10/2000
(See Dupont Direct Financial Holdings, Inc.)

FAB INDS INC (DE)
Common 20¢ par split (3) for (2) by issuance of (0.5) additional share 04/02/1971
Common 20¢ par split (3) for (2) by issuance of (0.5) additional share 03/23/1979
Common 20¢ par split (5) for (3) by issuance of (0.66666666) additional share 08/03/1983
Common 20¢ par split (2) for (1) by issuance of (1) additional share 06/14/1991
Liquidation completed
Each share Common 20¢ par received initial distribution of $10 cash payable 06/24/2002 to holders of record 06/10/2002
Each share Common 20¢ par received second distribution of $4 cash payable 08/22/2003 to holders of record 08/11/2003 Ex date - 08/25/2003
Each share Common 20¢ par received third distribution of $3 cash payable 03/10/2004 to holders of record 02/28/2004 Ex date - 03/11/2004
Each share Common 20¢ par received fourth and final distribution of $3.15 cash payable 05/27/2005 to holders of record 05/27/2005
Note: Certificates were not required to be surrendered and are without value

FAB METAL MINES LTD (ON)
Charter cancelled and declared dissolved for failure to file returns and pay fees 03/16/1976

FABER (A.W.)-CASTELL PENCIL CO., INC. (NJ)
Capital Stock $100 par changed to $25 par and (3) additional shares issued 12/3/64
Capital Stock $25 par changed to $10 par and (1.5) additional shares issued 4/30/75
Merged into Newell Co. 10/18/94
Each share Capital Stock $10 par exchanged for $143 cash

FABER COE & GREGG INC (NY)
Merged out of existence 05/03/1991
Details not available

FABERGE INC (MN)
Common 40¢ par split (2) for (1) by issuance of (1) additional share 6/30/69
Merged into McGregor Corp. 8/23/84
Each share Common 40¢ par exchanged for $32 principal amount of 15-1/2% Sinking Fund Subordinated Notes due 8/31/94

FABI LTD. (CANADA)
Name changed to Sintra Ltd. 06/30/1967
(See Sintra Ltd.)

FABIEN CORP (NJ)
Charter revoked for failure to file reports and pay fees 5/10/95

FABIEN EXPLS INC (QC)
Delisted from Canadian Dealer Network 08/31/1992

FABIEN TEXTILE PRINTING CORP. (NJ)
Common no par changed to $1 par in 1947
Name changed to Fabien Corp. 1/16/61
(See Fabien Corp.)

FABREX CORP. (DE)
Liquidation completed
Each share Capital Stock $1 par exchanged for initial distribution of $6.50 cash 1/4/63
Each share Capital Stock $1 par received second distribution of $1.21 cash 11/12/63
Each share Capital Stock $1 par received third and final distribution of $0.065 cash 4/9/70

FABRI CTRS AMER INC (OH)
Common no par split (3) for (2) by issuance of (0.5) additional share 12/05/1969
Common no par split (3) for (2) by issuance of (0.5) additional share 02/23/1976
Common no par split (3) for (2) by issuance of (0.5) additional share 11/12/1982
Common no par split (3) for (2) by issuance of (0.5) additional share 01/25/1991
Each share Common no par reclassified as (1) share Class A Common and (1) share Non-Vtg. Class B Common no par 08/02/1995
Name changed to Jo-Ann Stores, Inc. 09/01/1998
(See Jo-Ann Stores, Inc.)

FABRI-GLAS, INC. (UT)
Proclaimed dissolved for failure to pay taxes 9/30/76

FABRI TEK INC (WI)
Common 25¢ par changed to 10¢ par and (1.5) additional shares issued 06/28/1965
Merged into TSC Holdings, Inc. 04/28/1982
Each share Common 10¢ par exchanged for $6 cash

FABRIC MART DRAPERIES INC (IL)
Common $1 par changed to no par 6/25/74
Filed for Chapter XI bankruptcy proceedings 6/29/79 subsequently discharged 12/11/79
No stockholders' equity

FABRIC SUPERMART INC (NE)
Liquidation completed
Each share Common 10¢ par received initial distribution of $0.14285714 cash 12/14/1973
Each share Common 10¢ par exchanged for second and final distribution of $0.428571 cash 03/07/1974

FABRIC WHSLRS INC (OR)
Common no par split (2) for (1) by issuance of (1) additional share 6/20/83
Common no par split (2) for (1) by issuance of (1) additional share 6/20/85
Stock Dividend - 20% 3/5/71
Name changed to Fabricland, Inc. 10/26/87
Fabricland, Inc. merged into House of Fabrics, Inc. (Old) 7/16/91 which reorganized as House of Fabrics, Inc. (New) 7/31/96
(See House of Fabrics, Inc. (New))

FABRICLAND INC (OR)
Stock Dividend - 20% 1/4/90
Merged into House of Fabrics, Inc. (Old) 7/16/91
Each share Common no par exchanged for (0.8314) share Common 10¢ par
House of Fabrics, Inc. (Old) reorganized as House of Fabrics, Inc. (New) 7/31/96
(See House of Fabrics, Inc. (New))

FABRICON PRODUCTS, INC. (MI)
Dissolved 00/00/1954
Details not available

FABRICS FINISHING CORP.
Property sold in 1931
No stockholders' equity

FABRICS LIQUIDATION CORP.
Liquidated in 1936

FABRICS NATL INC (DE)
Name changed to Three D Departments, Inc. 07/15/1976
(See Three D Departments, Inc.)

FABRON CORP. (NY)
Name changed to Ross-Smith Corp. in 1947
Ross-Smith Corp. name changed to Photoex, Inc. in 1949 which was recapitalized as Universal Mineral Resources, Inc. 3/6/58
(See Universal Mineral Resources, Inc.)

FABULOUS INNS AMER (CA)
Common $1 par split (2) for (1) by issuance of (1) additional share 06/10/1988
Chapter 7 bankruptcy proceedings terminated 03/13/2000
Stockholders' equity unlikely

FABULOUS MERGERS INC (NV)
Reincorporated under the laws of Delaware as Sigma Alpha Entertainment Group Ltd. 01/02/1991
Sigma Alpha Entertainment Group Ltd. name changed to Sigma Alpha Group Ltd. 09/06/1995 which name changed to Clariti Telecommunications International Ltd. 03/03/1998 which reorganized as Integrated Data Corp. 11/12/2002

FAC RLTY TR INC (MD)
Reincorporated 12/18/97
Reincorporated from Fac Realty Inc. (DE) to Fac Realty Trust, Inc. (MD) 12/18/97
Name changed to Konover Property Trust, Inc. 8/10/98
(See Konover Property Trust, Inc.)

FACE BIOMETRICS INC (WA)
Name changed to WIDE Entertainment, Inc. 03/10/2005
WIDE Entertainment, Inc. name changed to Omega Mining & Exploration Corp. (WA) 09/12/2005 which reincorporated in Nevada as Cardio Infrared Technologies, Inc. 08/06/2007 which reorganized in Wyoming 07/15/2010 which recapitalized as Enchanted World, Inc. 12/08/2014

FACE PLACE INC. (UT)
Recapitalized as Tyco International, Inc. 12/7/82
Each share Common 1¢ par exchanged for (4.5) shares Common $0.001 par
Tyco International, Inc. name changed to Stinson & Farr Thoroughbred Management Co. 10/1/84

FACELIFTERS HOME SYS INC (NY)
Each share old Common 1¢ par exchanged for (0.125) share new Common 1¢ par 5/31/91
Merged into AMRE, Inc. 4/25/96
Each share new Common 1¢ par exchanged for (1) share Common 1¢ par

FACEPRINT GLOBAL SOLUTIONS INC (WY)
Each share old Common no par exchanged for (0.02) share new Common no par 08/08/2007
SEC revoked common stock registration 02/13/2013

FACET BIOTECH CORP (DE)
Merged into Abbott Laboratories 04/21/2010
Each share Common 1¢ par exchanged for $27 cash

FACET ENERGY INC (AB)
Merged into Raider Resources Inc. 11/29/1988
Each share Common no par exchanged for (1) share Common no par
Raider Resources Inc. recapitalized as Raider Resources Ltd. 06/24/1994 which merged into Shiningbank Energy Income Fund 06/01/2000 which merged into PrimeWest Energy Trust 07/13/2007
(See PrimeWest Energy Trust)

FACET ENTERPRISES INC (DE)
Merged into Pennzoil Co. 5/26/88
Each share Common $1 par exchanged for $32 cash

FACIT ADDO INC (NY)
Merged into USF Business Products, Inc. 12/31/1975
Each share Common 10¢ par exchanged for $0.25 cash

FACIT GROUP HLDGS INC (NV)
Charter revoked for failure to file reports and pay fees 9/1/99

FACS LTD. (ON)
Petitioned in bankruptcy 02/09/1970
Assets subsequently sold for benefit of creditors and trustee discharged 08/03/1973
No stockholders' equity

FACS RECORDS STORAGE INCOME FD (BC)
Each Installment Receipt plus final

payment of $4 cash received (1)
Trust Unit prior to April 1988
Completely liquidated 2/8/2001
Each Trust Unit exchanged for first and final distribution of $8.0367 cash

FACSIANO FD INC (MD)
Acquired by Neuberger Berman Inc. 03/23/2001
Each share Common 1¢ par exchanged for (1) share Common 1¢ par
Neuberger Berman Inc. merged into Lehman Brothers Holdings Inc. 10/31/2003
(See Lehman Brothers Holdings Inc.)

FACSIMILE & ELECTRONICS CORP.
Bankrupt in 1952
Details not available

FACT FINANCE CO. (OH)
Merged into Pyramid Group, Inc. 9/30/70
Each share Common 50¢ par exchanged for (1) share Common no par
(See Pyramid Group, Inc.)

FACTOR MAX & CO (DE)
Class A $1 par and Common $1 par split (3) for (2) by issuance of (0.5) additional share 12/30/1964
Class A $1 par split (3) for (2) by issuance of (0.5) additional share 06/30/1969
Stock Dividend - 50% 12/29/1961
Merged into Simon (Norton), Inc. 02/14/1973
Each share Class A $1 par exchanged for (1.115) shares Common $1 par
Simon (Norton), Inc. merged into Esmark, Inc. (Inc. 03/14/1969) 09/09/1983
(See Esmark, Inc. (Inc. 03/14/1969))

FACTORSHARES 2X GOLD BULL/S&P500 BEAR (DE)
Trust terminated 11/22/2013
Each Common Unit of Bene. Int. received $5.381602 cash
Each Common Unit of Bene. Int. received an additional distribution of $0.033166 cash 12/20/2013

FACTORSHARES 2X OIL BULL/S&P500 BEAR (DE)
Trust terminated 11/22/2013
Each Common Unit of Bene. Int. received $3.976077 cash
Each Common Unit of Bene. Int. received an additional distribution of $0.065893 cash 12/20/2013

FACTORSHARES 2X S&P500 BULL/TBOND BEAR (DE)
Trust terminated 11/22/2013
Each Common Unit of Bene. Int. received $12.967926 cash
Each Common Unit of Bene. Int. received an additional distribution of $0.132621 cash 12/20/2013

FACTORSHARES 2X S&P500 BULL/USD BEAR (DE)
Trust terminated 11/22/2013
Each Common Unit of Bene. Int. received $27.525718 cash
Each Common Unit of Bene. Int. received an additional distribution of $0.132623 cash 12/20/2013

FACTORSHARES 2X TBOND BULL/S&P500 BEAR (DE)
Trust terminated 11/22/2013
Each Common Unit of Bene. Int. received $5.602903 cash
Each Common Unit of Bene. Int. received an additional distribution of $0.132565 cash 12/20/2013

FACTORSHARES TR (DE)
Trust terminated 01/24/2014
Each share PureFunds ISE Diamond/Gemstone ETF received $21.1245657 cash
Each share PureFunds ISE Mining Service ETF received $15.04108191 cash
Name changed to ETF Managers Trust 06/27/2016

FACTORY CARD OUTLET & PARTY CORP (DE)
Common 1¢ par split (2) for (1) by issuance of (1) additional share payable 10/21/2003 to holders of record 10/07/2003 Ex date - 10/22/2003
Merged into Amscan Holdings, Inc. 11/16/2007
Each share Common 1¢ par exchanged for $16.50 cash

FACTORY CARD OUTLET CORP (DE)
Issue Information - 2,627,000 shares COM offered at $9 per share on 12/12/1996
Plan of reorganization under Chapter 11 Federal Bankruptcy Code effective 04/09/2002
Each share Common no par exchanged for (0.00999587104) share Factory Card Outlet & Party Corp. Common 1¢ par, and approximately (0.005) Common Stock Purchase Warrant Ser. A expiring 04/09/2006, (0.005) Common Stock Purchase Warrant Ser. B expiring 04/09/2008, (0.005) Common Stock Purchase Warrant Ser. C expiring 04/09/2010, and (0.005) Common Stock Purchase Warrant Ser. D expiring 04/09/2010
(See Factory Card Outlet & Party Corp.)

FACTORY POINT BANCORP INC (DE)
Common $1 par split (2) for (1) by issuance of (1) additional share payable 06/30/1995 to holders of record 06/05/1995
Common $1 par split (2) for (1) by issuance of (1) additional share payable 12/05/1997 to holders of record 11/28/1997
Common $1 par split (5) for (4) by issuance of (0.25) additional share payable 12/12/2003 to holders of record 11/28/2003 Ex date - 12/15/2003
Common $1 par split (5) for (4) by issuance of (0.25) additional share payable 12/10/2004 to holders of record 11/26/2004 Ex date - 12/13/2004
Common $1 par split (5) for (4) by issuance of (0.25) additional share payable 12/16/2005 to holders of record 12/09/2005 Ex date - 12/19/2005
Stock Dividends - 10% payable 12/20/1996 to holders of record 11/29/1996; 10% payable 12/11/1998 to holders of record 11/27/1998; 10% payable 12/13/1999 to holders of record 11/26/1999; 10% payable 12/15/2000 to holders of record 12/01/2000 Ex date - 11/29/2000; 10% payable 12/14/2001 to holders of record 11/30/2001 Ex date - 11/28/2001; 10% payable 12/13/2002 to holders of record 11/29/2002 Ex date - 11/26/2002
Merged into Berkshire Hills Bancorp, Inc. 09/21/2007
Each share Common $1 par exchanged for (0.5844) share Common 1¢ par

FACTORY POINT NATL BK (MANCHESTER CENTER, VT)
Under plan of reorganization each share Common $12.50 par automatically became (1) share Factory Point Bancorp, Inc. Common $1 par 01/01/1985
Factory Point Bancorp, Inc. merged into Berkshire Hills Bancorp, Inc. 09/21/2007

FACTORY STORES AMER INC (DE)
Name changed to Fac Realty Inc. (DE) 7/16/96
Fac Realty Inc. (DE) reincorporated in Maryland as Fac Realty Trust, Inc. 12/18/97 which name changed to Konover Property Trust. 8/10/98
(See Konover Property Trust, Inc.)

FACTORY 2-U STORES INC (DE)
Chapter 11 bankruptcy proceedings converted to Chapter 7 on 01/26/2005
No stockholders' equity

FACTSYSTEM INC (DE)
Assets sold for benefit of creditors 06/22/1970
No stockholders' equity

FACTUAL DATA CORP (CO)
Issue Information - 1,200,000 Units consisting of (1) share COM and (1) WT offered at $5.60 per Unit on 05/13/1998
Merged into Kroll Inc. 8/21/2003
Each share Common no par exchanged for (0.1497) share Common 1¢ par and $14 cash
(See Kroll Inc.)

FADA RADIO & ELECTRIC CORP.
Out of business 00/00/1935
Details not available

FAE INSTR CORP (NY)
Merged into Gyro Dynamics Corp. 8/19/68
Each share Common 10¢ par exchanged for (1) share Preferred 1¢ par
Gyro Dynamics Corp. reorganized as I.A.F.A., Inc. 2/16/84
(See I.A.F.A., Inc.)

FAFCO INC (CA)
Each share old Common $0.125 par exchanged for (0.001) share new Common $0.125 par 11/24/2003
Note: In effect holders received $0.70 cash per share and public interest was eliminated

FAFIC INVESTMENT CO., LTD.
Liquidation completed in 1943

FAFNIR BEARING CO. (CT)
Each share Common $25 par exchanged for (5) shares Common $10 par to effect a (2.5) for (1) split and 100% stock dividend in 1947
Under plan of merger Common $10 par exchanged share for share in 1954
Stock Dividends - 20% 7/27/55; 100% 5/6/59
Completely liquidated 1/4/68
Each share Common $10 par exchanged for first and final distribution of (1.3) shares Textron Inc. (Del.) $2.08 Conv. Preferred Ser. A no par

FAGEOL MOTORS CO.
Sold in bankruptcy in 1932

FAHNESTOCK VINER HLDGS INC (ON)
Name changed to Oppenheimer Holdings Inc. (ONT) 09/02/2003
Oppenheimer Holdings Inc. (ONT) reincorporated in Canada 05/11/2005 which reincorporated in Delaware 05/11/2009

FAHRENHEIT ENTMT INC (NV)
Reincorporated 01/24/2002
State of incorporation changed from (FL) to (NV) 01/24/2002
Name changed to Firesky Media Corp. 05/05/2006
Firesky Media Corp. name changed to Sky440, Inc. 02/12/2008

FAHRENHEIT MINING CO. LTD. (ON)
Charter cancelled for failure to pay taxes and file returns 04/00/1962

FAI INSURANCES LTD (AUSTRALIA)
Each Unsponsored ADR for Ordinary exchanged for (1) Sponsored ADR for Ordinary 07/31/1987
Each old Sponsored ADR for Ordinary exchanged for (1) new Sponsored ADR for Ordinary 03/07/1988
Each new Sponsored ADR for Ordinary exchanged again for (4) new Sponsored ADR's for Ordinary 03/06/1997
Stock Dividend - 100% 07/10/1987
ADR agreement terminated 06/10/1999
Each new Sponsored ADR for Ordinary exchanged for $9.2009 cash

FAILURE GROUP INC (DE)
Name changed to Exponent Inc. 3/9/98

FAIM INFORMATION SVCS INC (NY)
Ceased operations 11/30/1977
No stockholders' equity

FAIR GROUNDS CORP (LA)
Common $1 par changed to no par 07/25/1967
Old Common no par split (6) for (5) by issuance of (0.2) additional share 04/26/1991
Each share old Common no par exchanged for (0.005) share new Common no par 12/15/2000
Note: Holders of (199) or fewer pre-split shares received $40 cash
Liquidation completed
Each share new Common no par received initial distribution of $2,233 cash payable 09/26/2008 to holders of record 09/22/2008 Ex date - 09/29/2008
Each share new Common no par exchanged for second and final distribution of $202.967 cash 01/14/2013

FAIR HARBOUR MNG CORP (BC)
Recapitalized as Fair Resources Group Inc. 12/17/1991
Each share Common no par exchanged for (0.2) share Common no par
Fair Resources Group Inc. name changed to Southhampton Enterprises Corp. 12/02/1992 which recapitalized as Antigua Enterprises Inc. (BC) 06/13/1997 which reincorporated in Yukon 07/17/1998
(See Antigua Enterprises Inc.)

FAIR ISAAC & CO INC (DE)
Common 1¢ par split (2) for (1) by issuance of (1) additional share 06/26/1995
Common 1¢ par split (3) for (2) by issuance of (0.5) additional share payable 06/04/2001 to holders of record 05/14/2001 Ex date - 06/05/2001
Common 1¢ par split (3) for (2) by issuance of (0.5) additional share payable 06/05/2002 to holders of record 05/15/2002 Ex date - 06/06/2002
Name changed to Fair Isaac Corporation 04/01/2003

FAIR LANES INC (MD)
Class A Common $1 par split (3) for (2) by issuance of (0.5) additional share 05/01/1968
Class A Common $1 par reclassified as Common $1 par 11/29/1968
Common $1 par split (3) for (2) by issuance of (0.5) additional share 03/17/1969
Common $1 par split (3) for (2) by issuance of (0.5) additional share 09/15/1970
Common $1 par split (4) for (3) by issuance of (1/3) additional share 09/15/1971
Common $1 par split (3) for (2) by issuance of (0.5) additional share 01/31/1973
Common $1 par split (5) for (4) by issuance of (0.25) additional share 12/15/1976

Common $1 par split (4) for (3) by issuance of (1/3) additional share 02/15/1978
Common $1 par split (5) for (4) by issuance of (0.25) additional share 11/15/1978
Common $1 par split (5) for (4) by issuance of (0.25) additional share 11/15/1982
Common $1 par split (5) for (4) by issuance of (0.25) additional share 05/24/1983
Common $1 par split (2) for (1) by issuance of (1) additional share 02/15/1984
Merged into Northern Pacific Corp. 03/26/1987
Each share Common $1 par exchanged for (1.3043) shares BTR Realty, Inc. Common $1 par
BTR Realty, Inc. merged into Mid-Atlantic Realty Trust 09/13/1993
FAIR LANES INC (New) (MD)
Plan of Reorganization under Chapter 11 Federal Bankruptcy Code effective 02/07/1995
Each share new Common received $4 cash

FAIR OIL CO. (DE)
No longer in existence having become inoperative and void for non-payment of taxes 3/19/24

FAIR PLAY-MOUNT SHERIDAN & LEADVILLE RAILWAY CO. (CO)
Charter dissolved for failure to file annual reports 01/01/1919

FAIR RES GROUP INC (BC)
Name changed to Southhampton Enterprises Corp. 12/02/1992
Southhampton Enterprises Corp. recapitalized as Antigua Enterprises Inc. (BC) 06/13/1997 which reincorporated in Yukon 07/17/1998
(See Antigua Enterprises Inc.)

FAIR SKY RES INC (AB)
Receiver discharged 07/30/2009
No stockholders' equity

FAIR TEX MLS INC (PA)
Liquidation completed
Each share Common 10¢ par received initial distribution of $2.40 cash 03/23/1983
Each share Common 10¢ par received second distribution of $1.75 cash 01/05/1984
Each share Common 10¢ par exchanged for third and final distribution of $0.088667 cash 01/24/1985

FAIRBANCO HLDG INC (GA)
Merged into United Community Banks, Inc. 6/3/2004
Each share Common $5 par exchanged for (1.2261) shares Common $5 par and $3.56 cash

FAIRBANKS FINL INC (NV)
Name changed to Eastern Goldfields, Inc. 10/25/2005

FAIRBANKS GOLD LTD (BC)
Acquired by Amax Gold Inc. 01/06/1992
Each share Common no par exchanged for (0.5) share Common 1¢ par and (0.25) Common Stock Purchase Warrant expiring 01/08/1996
Amax Gold Inc. merged into Kinross Gold Inc. 06/01/1998

FAIRBANKS INC (FL)
Name changed to Jet Vacations, Inc. 4/18/97
Jet Vacations, Inc. name changed to Precom Technology, Inc. 4/21/98 which name changed to International Trust & Financial Systems, Inc. (FL) 10/15/2002 which reincorporated in Nevada as Marmion Industries Corp. 7/14/2004

FAIRBANKS MORSE & CO. (IL)
Stock Dividend - 100% 12/21/51
Acquired by Colt Industries Inc. (Pa.) on a (1.5) for (1) basis 5/15/64
Colt Industries Inc. (Pa.) reincorporated in Delaware 10/17/68 then reincorporated in Pennsylvania 5/6/76
(See Colt Industries Inc. (Pa.))

FAIRBANKS MORSE CDA LTD (CANADA)
Acquired by Colt Industries Inc. 01/26/1970
Each share Common exchanged for $9 cash

FAIRBANKS URANIUM MINES LTD. (ON)
Charter cancelled 04/02/1962

FAIRBANKS WHITNEY CORP. (PA)
Recapitalized as Colt Industries Inc. (PA) 05/15/1964
Each share $1.60 Conv. Preferred $40 par exchanged for (1) share $1.60 Conv. Preferred $40 par
Each share Common $1 exchanged for (0.33333333) share Common $3 par
Colt Industries Inc. (PA) reincorporated in Delaware 10/17/1968 which reincorporated back in Pennsylvania 05/06/1976
(See Colt Industries Inc. (PA))

FAIRBANKS WIRE CO., INC. (NY)
Name changed to Fairbanks Industries, Inc. 12/04/1968

FAIRBANKS YELLOWKNIFE GOLD MINES LTD. (ON)
Name changed to Fairbanks Uranium Mines Ltd. 00/00/1952
(See Fairbanks Uranium Mines Ltd.)

FAIRBORN MINES LTD (BC)
Struck off register and declared dissolved for failure to file returns 07/26/1976

FAIRBORNE ENERGY LTD NEW (AB)
Name changed to Santonia Energy Inc. 01/11/2013
Santonia Energy Inc. merged into Tourmaline Oil Corp. 04/29/2014

FAIRBORNE ENERGY LTD OLD (AB)
Plan of arrangement effective 06/06/2005
Each share Common no par exchanged for (1) Fairborne Energy Trust, Trust Unit no par and (0.333) share Fairquest Energy Ltd. Common no par
Note: Canadian residents option to receive Exchangeable Shares in lieu of Common expired 05/20/2005
(See each company's listing)
Each Exchangeable Share no par exchanged for (1.35931) shares Fairborne Energy Ltd. (New) Common no par 12/19/2007

FAIRBORNE ENERGY TR (AB)
Merged into Fairborne Energy Ltd. (New) 12/19/2007
Each Trust Unit no par exchanged for (1) share Common no par
Fairborne Energy Ltd. (New) name changed to Santonia Energy Inc. 01/11/2013 which merged into Tourmaline Oil Corp. 04/29/2014

FAIRCHILD AIRCRAFT LTD.
Liquidation completed 00/00/1950
Each share Capital Stock receieved $2.07 cash

FAIRCHILD AVIATION CORP.
Name changed to Fairchild Camera & Instrument Corp. in 1944
(See Fairchild Camera & Instrument Corp.)

FAIRCHILD CAMERA & INSTR CORP (DE)
Common $1 par split (2) for (1) by issuance of (1) additional share 12/02/1959
Common $1 par split (2) for (1) by issuance of (1) additional share 11/17/1961
Each share Interim Ctf. for Common $1 par exchanged for (2) shares Stamped Interim Ctf. for Common $1 par 11/17/1961
Escrow Agreement terminated 03/27/1967
Each share Stamped Interim Ctf. for Common $1 par exchanged for (0.4876) share Common $1 par
Common $1 par split (3) for (2) by issuance of (0.5) additional share 05/18/1967
Stock Dividend - 10% 12/24/1953
Merged into Schlumberger Ltd. 09/28/1979
Each share Common $1 par exchanged for $66 cash

FAIRCHILD CORP (DE)
Plan of liquidation under Chapter 11 Federal Bankruptcy proceedings effective 01/07/2010
No stockholders' equity

FAIRCHILD ENGINE & AIRPLACE CORP. (MD)
Name changed to Fairchild Stratos Corp. 5/15/61
Fairchild Stratos Corp. name changed to Fairchild Hiller Corp. 10/1/64 which name changed to Fairchild Industries, Inc. (MD) 5/10/71 which reincorporated in (DE) 3/19/87 which merged into Banner Industries, Inc. (DE) 8/18/89
(See Banner Industries, Inc. (DE))

FAIRCHILD GOLD CORP (BC)
Recapitalized as First International Metals Corp. 12/07/1990
Each share Capital Stock no par exchanged for (1/3) share Common no par
First International Metals Corp. recapitalized as Mill Bay Ventures Inc. 07/17/2000 which recapitalized as Great Thunder Gold Corp. 04/16/2013

FAIRCHILD HILLER CORP. (MD)
Name changed to Fairchild Industries, Inc. (MD) 5/10/71
Fairchild Industries, Inc. (MD) reincorporated in (DE) 3/19/87 which merged into Banner Industries, Inc. (DE) 8/18/89
(See Banner Industries, Inc. (DE))

FAIRCHILD INDS INC (DE)
Reincorporated 5/4/87
Common $1 par split (5) for (4) by issuance of (0.25) additional share 6/22/79
Common $1 par split (2) for (1) by issuance of (1) additional share 5/27/80
State of incorporation changed from (MD) to (DE) and Common $1 par changed to 1¢ par 5/4/87
Merged into Banner Industries, Inc. (DE) 8/18/89
Each share Common 1¢ par exchanged for $18 cash
Merged into Shared Technologies Fairchild Inc. 3/13/96
Each share $3.60 Conv. Preferred Ser. A no par exchanged for $45 cash
Each share $4.25 Preferred Ser. C no par exchanged for $45 cash
Public interest eliminated

FAIRCHILD INTL CORP (NV)
Each share old Common $0.001 par exchanged for (10) shares new Common $0.001 par 9/10/99
Each share new Common $0.001 par exchanged again for (0.04) share new Common $0.001 par 2/10/2005
Name changed to Syngas International Corp. 1/9/2006
Syngas International Corp. recapitalized as Energy Quest Inc. 5/31/2007

FAIRCHILD INVESTMENTS LTD. (BERMUDA)
Name changed to Stone Resources Ltd. 11/12/2009

FAIRCHILD INVTS INC (BC)
Reincorporated under the laws of Bermuda as Fairchild Investments Ltd. 06/26/1995
Fairchild Investments Ltd. name changed to Stone Resources Ltd. 11/12/2009

FAIRCHILD RES INC (BC)
Name changed to Fairchild Gold Corp. 11/18/1988
Fairchild Gold Corp. recapitalized as First International Metals Corp. 12/07/1990 which recapitalized as Mill Bay Ventures Inc. 07/17/2000 which recapitalized as Great Thunder Gold Corp. 04/16/2013

FAIRCHILD SEMICONDUCTOR INTL INC (DE)
Class A Common 1¢ par reclassified as Common 1¢ par 05/16/2003
Acquired by ON Semiconductor Corp. 09/19/2016
Each share Common 1¢ par exchanged for $20 cash

FAIRCHILD SONS INC (NY)
Acquired by International Funeral Services, Inc. 04/06/1970
Details not available

FAIRCHILD STRATOS CORP. (MD)
Name changed to Fairchild Hiller Corp. 10/1/64
Fairchild Hiller Corp. name changed to Fairchild Industries, Inc. (MD) 5/10/71 which reincorporated in (DE) 3/19/87 which merged into Banner Industries, Inc. (DE) 8/18/89
(See Banner Industries, Inc. (DE))

FAIRCOM INC (DE)
Merged into Regent Communications, Inc. 06/15/1998
Each share Common 1¢ par exchanged for (0.1409916) share $5 Conv. Preferred Ser. C 1¢ par
(See Regent Communications, Inc.)

FAIRCOURT INCOME & GROWTH SPLIT TR (ON)
Merged into Faircourt Split Trust 09/30/2010
Each share Preferred no par automatically became (1) share 6.25% Ser. B Preferred no par
Each Unit no par automatically became (0.954377) Unit no par

FAIRCOURT INCOME SPLIT TR (ON)
Trust Units no par split (3) for (1) by issuance of (2) additional Units payable 08/12/2005 to holders of record 08/12/2005 Ex date - 08/10/2005
Merged into Faircourt Income & Growth Split Trust 01/31/2007
Each Preferred Security no par automatically became (1) Preferred Security no par
Each Trust Unit no par automatically became (0.60851) Unit no par
Faircourt Income & Growth Split Trust merged into Faircourt Split Trust 09/30/2010

FAIRCOURT SPLIT FIVE TR (ON)
Merged into Faircourt Income & Growth Split Trust 01/31/2007
Each 6% Preferred Security no par automatically became (1) Preferred Security no par
Each Unit no par automatically became (1.6547) Units no par
Faircourt Income & Growth Split Trust merged into Faircourt Split Trust 09/30/2010

FAIRCOURT SPLIT SEVEN TR (ON)
Merged into Faircourt Income & Growth Split Trust 01/31/2007
Each 6.25% Preferred Security no par automatically became (1) Preferred Security no par

FAI-FAI — FINANCIAL INFORMATION, INC.

FAIRCOURT SPLIT TR (ON) (cont.)
Each Unit no par automatically became (1.42055) Units no par Faircourt Income & Growth Split Trust merged into Faircourt Split Trust 09/30/2010

FAIRCOURT SPLIT TR (ON)
Preferred no par called for redemption at $10 plus $0.0736 accrued dividends on 09/30/2010
6.25% Preferred Ser. B called for redemption at $10 on 12/31/2014
(Additional Information in Active)

FAIREY AVIATION CO. LTD. (ENGLAND)
Stock Dividend - 100% 06/08/1956
Name changed to Fairey Co. Ltd. 04/01/1959
(See Fairey Co. Ltd.)

FAIREY LTD (ENGLAND)
ADR's for Ordinary Reg. 10s par changed to 50p par per currency change 02/15/1971
ADR's for Ordinary Reg. 50p par changed to 25p par 04/01/1972
Placed in receivership 00/00/1977
ADR holders' equity unlikely

FAIRFAX AIRPORTS, INC.
Liquidated in 1941

FAIRFAX BK & TR CO (VA)
Under plan of reorganization each share Common $1.25 par automatically became (1) share FB&T Financial Corp. Common $1.25 par 7/1/94
FB&T Financial Corp. merged into F & M National Corp. 3/29/96 which merged into BB&T Corp. 8/9/2001

FAIRFAX CAP INC (BC)
Name changed to Free Energy International Inc. 02/14/2008
Free Energy International Inc. name changed to Darelle Online Solutions Inc. 04/18/2016

FAIRFAX CNTY NATL BK (SEVEN CORNERS, VA)
Stock Dividends - 20% 2/10/64; 10% 2/21/66
Merged into Virginia National Bankshares, Inc. 11/15/76
Each share Capital Stock $20 par exchanged for $24.555 cash

FAIRFAX GROUP INC (FL)
Name changed to Diversified Product Inspections, Inc. (Ctfs. dated after 03/07/2001) (FL) 03/07/2001
Diversified Product Inspections, Inc. (Ctfs. dated after 03/07/2001) (FL) reincorporated in Delaware 11/14/2008 which name changed to ProGreen Properties, Inc. 09/11/2009 which name changed to ProGreen US, Inc. 07/22/2016

FAIRFAX MINES LTD. (ON)
Charter cancelled for failure to pay taxes and file returns 07/27/1976

FAIRFIELD CAP CORP (CO)
Reorganized under the laws of Delaware as Space Wif Corp. 2/27/89
Space Wif Corp. recapitalized as Gateways To Space Inc. 5/1/92 which recapitalized as eMax Corp. 2/18/2000 which recapitalized as eMax Holdings Corp. 5/27/2004

FAIRFIELD CMNTYS INC (DE)
Name changed 08/26/1977
Reorganized 09/01/1992
Each share Common 30¢ par exchanged for (0.2) share Common $1.50 par 02/28/1974
Common $1.50 par changed to 10¢ par 07/09/1976
Name changed from Fairfield Communities Land Co. to Fairfield Communities, Inc. 08/26/1977
Common 10¢ par split (3) for (2) by issuance of (0.5) additional share 02/28/1983
Common 10¢ par split (2) for (1) by issuance of (1) additional share 08/10/1983
Plan of reorganization under Chapter 11 Federal Bankruptcy proceedings confirmed 08/14/1992
No stockholders' equity for holders of Common 10¢ par
Secondary Offering - 2,077,153 shares COM offered at $21.625 per share on 11/21/1996
Common 1¢ par split (3) for (2) by issuance of (0.5) additional share payable 07/15/1997 to holders of record 07/01/1997 Ex date - 07/16/1997
Common 1¢ par split (2) for (1) by issuance of (1) additional share payable 01/30/1998 to holders of record 01/15/1998 Ex date - 02/02/1998
Merged into Cendant Corp. 04/02/2001
Each share Common 1¢ par exchanged for $16 cash

FAIRFIELD CNTY BANCORP INC (CT)
Placed in receivership and FDIC appointed receiver 04/09/1992
No stockholders' equity

FAIRFIELD CNTY NATL BK (NORWALK, CT)
Merged into CBT Corp. 2/26/73
Each share Common $12.50 par exchanged for (2) shares Common $10 par
CBT Corp. merged into Bank of New England Corp. 6/14/85
(See Bank of New England Corp.)

FAIRFIELD CNTY TR CO (STAMFORD, CT)
Capital Stock $10 par changed to $5 par and (1) additional share issued 12/30/1964
Merged into Union Trust Co. (New Haven, CT) 10/01/1969
Each share Capital Stock $5 par exchanged for (1) share Capital Stock $5 par
Union Trust Co. (New Haven, CT) reorganized as Northeast Bancorp, Inc. 12/29/1972 which merged into First Fidelity Bancorporation (New) 05/03/1993 which merged into First Union Corp. 01/01/1996 which name changed to Wachovia Corp. (Ctfs. dated after 09/01/2001) 09/01/2001 which merged into Wells Fargo & Co. (New) 12/31/2008

FAIRFIELD FD INC (NY)
Stock Dividends - 100% 9/28/67; 100% 12/22/80; 25% 8/10/81
Reorganized under the laws of Massachusetts as National Aggressive Growth Fund Inc. 12/1/89
Each share Capital Stock $1 par exchanged for (1) share Common $1 par
National Aggressive Growth Fund Inc. name changed to National Worldwide Opportunities Fund 12/17/90 which merged into Phoenix Worldwide Opportunities Fund 12/31/93

FAIRFIELD FDG CORP (NV)
Name changed to Nite & Day Technologies, Inc. 9/27/88
Nite & Day Technologies, Inc. recapitalized as SDI Virtual Reality Corp. 11/2/93

FAIRFIELD FIRST BK & TR CO (SOUTHPORT, CT)
Each (52) shares old Common $5 par exchanged for (1) share new Common $5 par 12/29/1995
Stock Dividend - 10% 07/17/1989
Placed in receivership and FDIC appointed receiver 07/12/1996
Stockholders' equity unlikely

FAIRFIELD GEN CORP (NJ)
Placed in receivership 2/1/74
No stockholders' equity

FAIRFIELD MFG INC (DE)
Stock Dividends - 5.625% payable 9/15/2001 to holders of record 9/1/2001; 5.625% payable 3/15/2002 to holders of record 3/1/2002 Ex date - 3/15/2002
Company terminated registration of Preferred stock and is no longer public as of 10/14/2003

FAIRFIELD MINERALS LTD (BC)
Reincorporated under the laws of Ontario as Almaden Minerals Ltd. 02/11/2002

FAIRFIELD NATL BK (FAIRFIELD, NJ)
Merged into New Jersey Bank (N.A.) (Clifton, NJ) 10/31/74
Each share Capital Stock $2.50 par exchanged for $12 cash

FAIRFIELD NOBLE CORP (NY)
Common 10¢ par split (4) for (3) by issuance of (1/3) additional share 1/15/68
Dissolved by proclamation 9/29/93

FAIRFIELD SECURITIES, INC. (NY)
Capital Stock $1 par split (2) for (1) by issuance of (1) additional share 2/7/66
Stock Dividend - 400% 10/15/62
Name changed to Fairfield Fund, Inc. 3/2/67
Fairfield Fund, Inc. reorganized in Massachusetts as National Aggressive Growth Fund Inc. 12/1/89 which name changed to National Worldwide Opportunities Fund 12/17/90
(See National Worldwide Opportunities Fund)

FAIRFIELD SECURITIES CORP. (MA)
Dissolved 12/29/58
Details not available

FAIRFIELD TECHNOLOGY CORP (DE)
Charter cancelled and declared inoperative and void for non-payment of taxes 4/15/72

FAIRHAVEN INTL LTD (BERMUDA)
ADR agreement terminated 2/28/95
Each ADR for Ordinary 25¢ par exchanged for $0.399 cash

FAIRHAVEN RES LTD (BC)
Recapitalized as International Fairhaven Resources Ltd. 05/29/2002
Each share Common no par exchanged for (0.2) share Common no par
(See International Fairhaven Resources Ltd.)

FAIRHAVEN SVGS BK (FAIRHAVEN, MA)
Acquired by Citizens Financial Group, Inc. 06/30/1988
Each share Common 10¢ par exchanged for $17 cash

FAIRHILL ASSOCIATES, INC. (DE)
Charter cancelled and declared inoperative and void for non-payment of taxes 5/30/96

FAIRLADY ENERGY INC (CANADA)
Reincorporated 02/10/1988
Place of incorporation changed from (BC) to (Canada) 02/10/1988
Cease trade order issued 02/12/1990
Stockholders' equity unlikely

FAIRLANE INDS INC (TX)
Name changed to Reliability Inc. 05/01/1980

FAIRLANE TRANSN INC (BC)
Recapitalized as Excellerated Resources Inc. 11/24/1998
Each share Common no par exchanged for (0.25) share Common no par
Excellerated Resources Inc. recapitalized as Consolidated Excellerated Resources Inc. 02/28/2000 which name changed to Amarillo Gold Corp. 11/21/2003

FAIRLAWN HEIGHTS CO. (OH)
Dissolved in 1953

FAIRLEY RED LAKE GOLD MINES LTD. (ON)
Dissolved 10/22/1962
No stockholders' equity

FAIRLINE ENERGY SVCS INC (CANADA)
Name changed 04/08/1998
Name changed from Fairline Financial International Corp. to Fairline Energy Services Inc. 04/08/1998
Merged into Wellco Energy Services Inc. (BC) 12/31/1999
Each share Common no par exchanged for (1.5) shares Common no par
Wellco Energy Services Inc. (BC) reorganized in Alberta as Wellco Energy Services Trust 08/06/2002 which merged into Peak Energy Services Trust 03/12/2008 which reorganized as Peak Energy Services Ltd. (New) 01/06/2011
(See Peak Energy Services Ltd. (New))

FAIRMARKET INC (DE)
Issue Information - 5,000,000 shares COM offered at $17 per share on 03/13/2000
Name changed to Dynabazaar, Inc. 09/04/2003
Dynabazaar, Inc. name changed to Sielox, Inc. 07/31/2007 which name changed to Costar Technologies, Inc. 03/02/2012

FAIRMILE GOLD INC. (CANADA)
Name changed 03/07/1996
Name changed from Fairmile Acquisitions Inc. to Fairmile Gold Corp. 03/07/1996
Recapitalized as Fairmile Goldtech Inc. (Canada) 07/10/2000
Each share Common no par exchanged for (0.1) share Common no par
Fairmile Goldtech Inc. (Canada) reincorporated in British Columbia 02/23/2005

FAIRMILE GOLDTECH INC (CANADA)
Reincorporated under the laws of British Columbia 02/23/2005

FAIRMONT CREAMERY CO. (DE)
Name changed to Fairmont Foods Co. 5/3/47
Fairmont Foods Co. merged into American Financial Corp. 7/24/80

FAIRMONT FINL INC (CA)
Common no par split (5) for (3) by issuance of (2/3) additional share 07/07/1986
Merged into Transamerica Corp. 05/21/1987
Each share Common no par exchanged for (0.555) share Common $1 par
Transamerica Corp. merged into Aegon N.V. 07/21/1999

FAIRMONT FOODS CO (DE)
Common no par changed to $1 par 06/06/1955
Common $1 par changed to 50¢ par and (1) additional share issued 07/14/1961
4% Preferred $100 par called for redemption 11/01/1961
5% Jr. Preferred $50 par called for redemption 12/31/1963
Merged into American Financial Corp. 07/24/1980
Each share $1 Preferred no par exchanged for (1.33333333) shares $1 Preferred Ser. D $10.50 par plus (1.33333333) Non-Transferable Units of Contingent Debentures
Each share Common 50¢ par

exchanged for $14.50 principal amount of 12% Ser. A Debentures due 09/03/1999 and $4 cash
(See American Financial Corp.)

FAIRMONT GAS & OIL CORP (BC)
Recapitalized as Cater Energy, Inc. 05/23/1984
Each share Common no par exchanged for (0.2) share Common no par
Cater Energy, Inc. recapitalized as Houston Metals Corp. 10/27/1986 which recapitalized as Pacific Houston Resources, Inc. 03/30/1989
(See Pacific Houston Resources, Inc.)

FAIRMONT HOTEL CORP. (DE)
Liquidated in 1945

FAIRMONT HOTELS RESORTS INC (CANADA)
Merged into Kingdom Hotels International 05/11/2006
Each share Common no par exchanged for USD$45 cash

FAIRMONT RES INC (AB)
Name changed to Endeavour Resources Inc. 01/08/1996
Endeavour Resources Inc. merged into Aspen Group Resources Corp. 02/04/2002

FAIRMONT RY MTRS INC (MN)
Acquired by Harsco Corp. 06/22/1979
Each share Common $100 par exchanged for (137.5) shares Common $1.25 par

FAIRMOUNT BANCORP INC (MD)
Acquired by Hamilton Bancorp, Inc. 09/11/2015
Each share Common 1¢ par exchanged for $30 cash

FAIRMOUNT CHEM INC (NJ)
Common $1 par split (3) for (2) by issuance of (0.5) additional share 05/05/1975
Involuntary petition under Chapter 7 bankruptcy proceedings filed 01/10/2007
No stockholders' equity

FAIRMOUNT ENERGY INC (CANADA)
Merged into Delphi Energy Corp. 11/30/2009
Each share Common no par exchanged for (0.3571) share Common no par
Note: U.S. residents will receive pro rata proceeds from the sale of shares

FAIRMOUNT PARK & HADDINGTON PASSENGER RAILWAY CO.
Acquired by Philadelphia Transportation Co. in 1940
Each share Common exchanged for $21.67 principal amount of 3%-6% Consolidated Mortgage Bonds and (0.181) share $1 Participating Preferred $20 par
(See Philadelphia Transportation Co.)

FAIRMOUNT PARK TRANSIT CO.
Name changed to Philadelphia Park Amusement Co. in 1946
(See Philadelphia Park Amusement Co.)

FAIRMOUNT SANTROL HLDGS INC (DE)
Merged into Covia Holdings Corp. 06/01/2018
Each share Common 1¢ par exchanged for (0.2) share Common 1¢ par and approximately $0.73 cash

FAIRMOUNT TOOL & FORGING CO.
Acquired by Frontier Industries, Inc. (NY) in 1948
Details not available

FAIRPOINT COMMUNICATIONS INC (DE)
Plan of reorganization under Chapter 11 Federal Bankruptcy proceedings effective 01/24/2011
No old Common stockholders' equity
Merged into Consolidated Communications Holdings, Inc. 07/03/2017
Each share new Common 1¢ par exchanged for (0.73) share Common 1¢ par

FAIRPORT INDUSTRIES, INC. (NY)
Out of business 03/13/1973
No stockholders' equity

FAIRPORT PAINESVILLE & EASTN RR CO (OH)
Each share Capital Stock $100 par exchanged for (5) shares Capital Stock $20 par and 50% stock dividend 11/3/55
Acquired by New York Central Railroad Co. (DE) and Norfolk & Western Railway Co. in August 1967
Details not available

FAIRQUEST ENERGY LTD (AB)
Merged into Fairborne Energy Trust 06/06/2007
Each share Common no par exchanged for (0.39) Trust Unit no par
Fairborne Energy Trust merged into Fairborne Energy Ltd. (New) 12/19/2007 which name changed to Santonia Energy Inc. 01/11/2013 which merged into Tourmaline Oil Corp. 04/29/2014

FAIRSTAR EXPLS INC (CANADA)
Each share Common no par received distribution of (0.0667) share Branchez-Vous! Inc. Common no par payable 01/16/2001 to holders of record 01/15/2001
Each share Common no par received distribution of (0.15407494) share American Bonanza Gold Corp. Common no par payable 04/08/2005 to holders of record 04/07/2005
Ex date - 04/05/2005
Merged into FairWest Energy Corp. 08/18/2005
Each share Common no par exchanged for (0.14875197) share Common no par
(See FairWest Energy Corp.)

FAIRVIEW AMALGAMATED GOLD MINES LTD.
Bankrupt in 1943

FAIRVIEW CAP CORP (MB)
Name changed to Bald Eagle Golf Corp. and Class A Common no par reclassified as Common no par 06/15/2001
(See Bald Eagle Golf Corp.)

FAIRVIEW CORP CDA LTD (CANADA)
Common no par split (1.4) for (1) by issuance of (0.4) additional share 06/19/1974
Merged into Cadillac Fairview Corp. Ltd. 03/08/1976
Each share Common no par exchanged for (1) share Common no par
(See Cadillac Fairview Corp. Ltd.)

FAIRVIEW ENERGY CORP INC (NV)
Reorganized under the laws of Delaware as Akeena Solar, Inc. 08/21/2006
Each share Common $0.001 par exchanged for (1.084609) shares Common $0.001 par
Akeena Solar, Inc. recapitalized as Westinghouse Solar, Inc. 04/14/2011 which name changed to Andalay Solar, Inc. 09/27/2013

FAIRVIEW POTOMAC CORP.
Liquidated in 1943

FAIRWAY AUTOMOTIVE INDS LTD (ON)
Recapitalized as Fairway Industries Ltd. 02/26/1988
Each share Common no par exchanged for (0.33333333) share Common no par
Fairway Industries Ltd. recapitalized as Pharmaglobe Inc. (ON) 03/14/1994 which reincorporated in Delaware 03/01/2001 which name changed to Pharmaglobe America Group, Inc. 05/12/2004

FAIRWAY DIVERSIFIED INCOME & GROWTH TR (ON)
Under plan of merger each Unit no par automatically became (1.30587) Crown Hill Fund Trust Units no par 01/23/2009
Crown Hill Fund merged into Citadel Income Fund 12/02/2009

FAIRWAY ENTERPRISES INC (NV)
Recapitalized as Associated Golf Management Inc. 01/12/1999
Each share Common $0.001 par exchanged for (0.33333333) share Common $0.001 par
Associated Golf Management Inc. name changed to Vidmar Acquisitions Inc. 08/15/2001 which recapitalized as Online Transaction Systems, Inc. 08/05/2003 which name changed to Delta Mining & Exploration Corp. 01/28/2004
(See Delta Mining & Exploration Corp.)

FAIRWAY FLINFLON MINES LTD. (ON)
Charter cancelled 12/30/1970

FAIRWAY GROUP HLDGS CORP (DE)
Plan of reorganization under Chapter 11 Federal Bankruptcy proceedings effective 07/03/2016
No stockholders' equity

FAIRWAY INDS LTD (ON)
Recapitalized as Pharmaglobe Inc. (ON) 03/14/1994
Each share Common no par exchanged for (0.33333333) share Common no par
Pharmaglobe Inc. (ON) reincorporated in Delaware 03/01/2001 which name changed to Pharmaglobe America Group, Inc. 05/12/2004

FAIRWAY INVT GRADE INCOME FD (ON)
Under plan of merger each Redeemable Unit no par automatically became (0.678498) Fairway Diversified Income & Growth Trust Unit no par 06/29/2007
Fairway Diversified Income & Growth Trust merged into Crown Hill Fund 01/23/2009 which merged into Citadel Income Fund 12/02/2009

FAIRWAY MART, INC. (DE)
No longer in existence having become inoperative and void for non-payment of taxes 04/01/1965

FAIRWAY PPTYS INC (NV)
Name changed to Medient Studios, Inc. 10/17/2012
(See Medient Studios, Inc.)

FAIRWEST ENERGY CORP (CANADA)
Received Notice of Intention to Enforce Security 09/17/2013
Stockholders' equity unlikely

FAIRYOUNG HLDGS LTD (HONG KONG)
Name changed to Dynamic Global Holdings Ltd. 07/23/2002
(See Dynamic Global Holdings Ltd.)

FAIRYTALE VENTURES INC (NV)
Each share old Common $0.001 par exchanged for (1.84356289) shares new Common $0.001 par 07/21/2008
Reorganized as Aviation Surveillance Systems, Inc. 05/11/2009
Each share new Common $0.001 par exchanged for (1.6) shares Common $0.001 par
Aviation Surveillance Systems, Inc. name changed to Harmonic Energy, Inc. 07/29/2010 which name changed to THC Therapeutics, Inc. 02/07/2017 which name changed to Millennium BlockChain, Inc. 02/07/2018

FAITH INVESTMENT CO. (CO)
Charter suspended for failure to file annual reports 09/30/1984

FAITH MINES LTD (BC)
Recapitalized as Panterra Minerals Inc. 02/28/1996
Each share Common no par exchanged for (0.1) share Common no par
Panterra Minerals Inc. recapitalized as Neodym Technologies Inc. 05/03/2001 which recapitalized as Neoteck Solutions Inc. 09/06/2012 which recapitalized as Hello Pal International Inc. 05/13/2016

FAITH SPRING VENTURE INC (BC)
Recapitalized as Viscount Mining Corp. 07/25/2013
Each share Common no par exchanged for (0.5) share Common no par

FAITHSHARES TR (DE)
Trust terminated 07/27/2011
Each share FaithShares Baptist Values Fund received $29.44 cash
Each share FaithShares Catholic Values Fund received $30.57 cash
Each share FaithShares Lutheran Values Fund received $29.31 cash
Each share FaithShares Methodist Values Fund received $30.30 cash
Trust terminated 09/14/2011
Each share FaithShares Christian Values Fund received $25.576758 cash

FAJANA RES LTD (AB)
Name changed to KolVox Communications Inc. 7/13/93
KolVox Communications Inc. merged into Wildcard Technologies Inc. 7/2/96

FAJARDO EASTERN SUGAR ASSOCIATES (MD)
Merged into Brewer (C.) Co., Puerto Rico Inc. for cash 7/27/61

FAJARDO SUGAR CO. (PR)
Merged into Fajardo Eastern Sugar Associates on a (0.5) for (1) basis 5/1/58
(See Fajardo Eastern Sugar Associates)

FAJARDO SUGAR CO. OF PORTO RICO
Recapitalized as Fajardo Sugar Co. on a share for share basis 1/6/49 which merged into Fajardo Eastern Sugar Associates 5/1/58 which merged into Brewer (C.) Co., Puerto Rico, Inc. for cash 7/27/61

FAJITA JCT INC (CO)
Name changed to Tostel Corp. 03/23/1995
Tostel Corp. merged into Polus, Inc. 06/22/1998
(See Polus, Inc.)

FAL EXPL CORP (NV)
Recapitalized as Vapir Enterprises Inc. 10/03/2014
Each share Common $0.001 par exchanged for (0.2) share Common $0.001 par
Vapir Enterprises Inc. name changed to Gratitude Health, Inc. 03/23/2018

FALAISE LAKE MINES LTD (BC)
Recapitalized as Rosmac Mines Ltd. 11/15/1973
Each share Capital Stock no par exchanged for (0.2) share Capital Stock no par
Rosmac Mines Ltd. name changed to Rosmac Resources Ltd. 08/09/1979 which merged into Golden North

Resource Corp. 08/30/1984 which merged into Caledonia Mining Corp. (BC) 02/04/1992 which reincorporated in Canada 03/29/1995 which reincorporated in Jersey as Caledonia Mining Corp. PLC 03/24/2016

FALCO PAC RESOURCE GROUP INC (BC)
Name changed to Falco Resources Ltd. 07/25/2014

FALCON BLDG PRODS INC (DE)
Issue Information - 5,803,500 shares CL A offered at $12 per share on 11/02/1994
Merged into Investcorp 6/17/97
Each share Class A Common 1¢ par exchanged for $17.75 cash
Called for redemption at $28.16 on 12/30/99
Public intrest eliminated

FALCON BRONZE CO. (OH)
Dissolved in 1953
Details not available

FALCON CABLE SYS CO (CA)
Completely liquidated 7/23/96
Each Unit of Ltd. Partnership Int. exchanged for first and final distribution of $9.02 cash

FALCON CREST ENERGY INC (NV)
Recapitalized as Cherubim Interests, Inc. 06/16/2015
Each share Common $0.001 par exchanged for (0.06666666) share Common $0.0001 par

FALCON DRILLING INC (DE)
Common 1¢ par split (2) for (1) by issuance of (1) additional share payable 07/15/1997 to holders of record 07/09/1997 Ex date - 07/16/1997
Merged into R&B Falcon Corp. 12/31/1997
Each share Common 1¢ par exchanged for (1) share Common 1¢ par
R&B Falcon Corp. merged into Transocean Sedco Forex Inc. 01/31/2001 which name changed to Transocean Inc. (Old) 05/09/2002 which merged into Transocean Inc. (New) (Cayman Islands) 11/27/2007 which reorganized in Switzerland as Transocean Ltd. 12/18/2008

FALCON ELEC CORP
Filed plan of liquidation under Chapter 7 Federal Bankruptcy Code 8/24/2000
Stockholders' equity is unlikely

FALCON ENERGY INC (NV)
Recapitalized as Red Truck Entertainment Inc. 2/12/2007
Each share Common $0.0001 par exchanged for (0.01) share Common $0.001 par

FALCON ENTERPRISES INC (UT)
Name changed to Falcon Sciences, Inc. 7/16/82
(See Falcon Sciences, Inc.)

FALCON ENTMT CORP (DE)
SEC revoked common stock registration 07/02/2009

FALCON FD INC (CO)
Name changed to Armanino Foods of Distinction, Inc. 11/15/88

FALCON FINL INVT TR (MD)
Merged into iStar Financial Inc. 03/03/2005
Each share Common 1¢ par exchanged for $7.50 cash

FALCON GROUP LTD (ON)
Delisted from Canadian Dealer Network 01/03/1995

FALCON ISLAND MINING CO. LTD. (MB)
Charter cancelled for failure to file annual reports 00/00/1955

FALCON LEAD MINING CO.
Defunct and inoperative in 1937

FALCON MEDIA SVCS LTD (UNITED KINGDOM)
Name changed to Extreme Mobile Coatings Corp., Ltd. (United Kingdom) 11/26/2008
Extreme Mobile Coatings Corp., Ltd. (United Kingdom) reincorporated in Delaware as Extreme Mobile Coatings Worldwide Corp. 04/08/2009 which recapitalized as Structural Enhancement Technologies Corp. 06/18/2010 which recapitalized as Eco-Petroleum Solutions, Inc. 02/07/2013 which name changed to Enzolytics Inc. 03/22/2018

FALCON MINES CORP. (CO)
Dissolved 12/31/59

FALCON NAT GAS CORP (NV)
SEC revoked common stock registration 10/14/2009

FALCON NATIONAL LIFE INSURANCE CO. (CO)
Merged into Denver National Life Insurance Co. 02/15/1963
Each share Capital Stock 25¢ par exchanged for (0.5) share new Common 25¢ par
Denver National Life Insurance Co. name changed to Denver National Financial, Inc. 05/20/1965 which was acquired by National Western Life Insurance Co. (CO) 08/14/1967 which reincorporated in Delaware as National Western Life Group, Inc. 10/02/2015

FALCON OIL & GAS INC (CO)
Each share old Common 1¢ par exchanged for (0.1) share new Common 1¢ par 01/30/1986
Involuntarily dissolved 07/01/1998

FALCON POINT RES LTD (ON)
Recapitalized as Ontario Hose Specialties Inc. (ON) 05/12/1998
Each share Common no par exchanged for (0.125) share Common no par
Ontario Hose Specialties Inc. (ON) reincorporated in British Columbia as Bordeaux Energy, Inc. 03/13/2007 which recapitalized as Enterprise Energy Resources Ltd. 11/10/2008 which merged into LNG Energy Ltd. 08/20/2013 which recapitalized as Esrey Energy Ltd. 11/18/2013 which name changed to Esrey Resources Ltd. 10/16/2017

FALCON PRODS INC (DE)
Reincorporated 12/2/74
State of incorporation changed from (MO) to (DE) 12/2/74
Common 2¢ par split (5) for (3) by issuance of (2/3) additional share 3/26/90
Common 2¢ par split (3) for (2) by issuance of (0.5) additional share 1/19/93
Stock Dividends - 10% 2/29/80; 10% 10/18/90; 10% 1/2/96
Plan of reorganization under Chapter 11 Federal Bankruptcy Code effective 11/15/2005
No stockholders' equity

FALCON RES INC (BC)
Recapitalized as International Falcon Resources Inc. 4/23/86
Each share Common no par exchanged for (0.4) share Common no par

FALCON RIDGE DEV INC (NV)
Each share old Common $0.001 par exchanged for (0.005) share new Common $0.001 par 08/16/2006
SEC revoked common stock registration 01/17/2013

FALCON SCIENCES INC (UT)
Proclaimed dissolved for failure to pay taxes 3/31/85

FALCON SEABOARD DRILLING CO (DE)
Name changed to Falcon Seaboard Inc. 4/15/70
Falcon Seaboard Inc. acquired by Diamond Shamrock Corp. 2/23/79 which name changed to Maxus Energy Corp. 4/30/87
(See Maxus Energy Corp.)

FALCON SEABOARD INC (DE)
Common $1.50 par split (2) for (1) by issuance of (1) additional share 6/11/76
Common $1.50 par changed to 50¢ par and (1) additional share issued 6/23/77
Acquired by Diamond Shamrock Corp. 2/23/79
Each share Common 50¢ par exchanged for (1.65) shares Common no par
Diamond Shamrock Corp. name changed to Maxus Energy Corp. 4/30/87
(See Maxus Energy Corp.)

FALCON SPEEDWAYS CORP (NY)
Merged into Technibiotics, Inc. 2/6/74
Each share Common 1¢ par exchanged for (0.25) share Common 1¢ par
(See Technibiotics, Inc.)

FALCON STEEL CO.
Acquired by Empire Steel Corp. (Old) in 1927
Details not available

FALCON SUPER FAX GRAPHICS INC (ON)
Reorganized as Falcon Group Ltd. 04/29/1992
Each share Common no par exchanged for (2) shares Common no par
(See Falcon Group Ltd.)

FALCON VENTURES INC (BC)
Reincorporated under the laws of Alberta as Falcon Ventures International Inc. 06/26/2008
Falcon Ventures International Inc. (AB) reorganized in British Columbia as Firebird Resources Inc. 11/05/2009

FALCON VENTURES INTL CORP (BC)
Recapitalized as Falcon Ventures Inc. (BC) 12/24/2002
Each share Common no par exchanged for (0.1) share Common no par
Falcon Ventures Inc. (BC) reincorporated in Alberta as Falcon Ventures International Inc. 06/26/2008 which reorganized in British Columbia as Firebird Resources Inc. 11/05/2009

FALCON VENTURES INTL INC (AB)
Reorganized under the laws of British Columbia as Firebird Resources Inc. 11/05/2009
Each share Common no par exchanged for (0.2) share Common no par

FALCON WELL SVCS LTD (ON)
Placed in receivership 03/27/2003
No stockholders' equity

FALCONBRIDGE COPPER LTD (QC)
Name changed to Corporation Falconbridge Copper 07/09/1980
Corporation Falconbridge Copper name changed to Minnova Inc. 05/26/1987 which merged into Metall Mining Corp. 05/05/1993 which name changed to Inmet Mining Corp. 05/04/1995 which was acquired by First Quantum Minerals Ltd. 04/09/2013

FALCONBRIDGE LTD NEW (ON)
Reorganized as Falconbridge Ltd. (New) 2005 on 7/1/2005
Each share Common no par exchanged for (1.77) shares Common no par
Preferreds not affected except for change of name
(See Falconbridge Ltd. (New) 2005)

FALCONBRIDGE LTD NEW 2005 (ON)
Each share old Jr. Preference Ser. 1 no par exchanged for (1) share new Jr. Preference Ser. 1 no par and U.S. $0.1083 accrued dividends on 04/26/2006
Each share old Jr. Preference Ser. 2 no par exchanged for (1) share new Jr. Preference Ser. 2 no par and U.S. $0.1128 accrued dividends on 04/26/2006
Each share old Jr. Preference Ser. 3 no par exchanged for (1) share new Jr. Preference Ser. 3 no par and U.S. $0.1174 accrued dividends on 04/26/2006
New Jr. Preference Ser. 1 no par called for redemption at U.S. $25.25 plus U.S. $0.3658 accrued dividends on 06/28/2006
New Jr. Preference Ser. 2 no par called for redemption at U.S. $25.25 plus U.S. $0.381 accrued dividends on 06/28/2006
New Jr. Preference Ser. 3 no par called for redemption at U.S. $25.25 plus U.S. $0.3962 accrued dividends on 06/28/2006
Acquired by Xstrata PLC 09/05/2006
Each share Common no par exchanged for $62.50 cash
Preferred Ser. F no par called for redemption at $25.50 plus $0.115 accrued dividends on 11/01/2006
Preferred Ser. G no par called for redemption at $25 plus $0.38125 accrued dividends on 11/01/2006
Preferred Ser. 1 no par called for redemption at $10 plus $0.01340 accrued dividends on 11/01/2006
Name changed to Xstrata Canada Corp. (Old) 10/24/2007
Xstrata Canada Corp. (Old) reorganized as Xstrata Canada Corp. (New) 06/01/2008

FALCONBRIDGE LTD OLD (ON)
Common no par split (5) for (1) by issuance of (4) additional shares 5/10/85
Acquired by FL Acquisition Corp. 10/6/89
Each share Common no par exchanged for $37 cash

FALCONBRIDGE NICKEL MINES LTD. (ON)
Capital Stock no par reclassified as Common no par 07/20/1976
Common no par reclassified as Conv. Class A Common no par 05/16/1977
Name changed to Falconbridge Nickel Mines Ltd.-Les Mines Falconbridge Nickel Ltee. and Conv. Class A Common no par, Conv. Class B Common no par reclassified as Common no par respectively 04/29/1980
Falconbridge Nickel Mines Ltd.-Les Mines Falconbridge Nickel Ltee. name changed to Falconbridge Ltd. 02/10/1983
(See Falconbridge Ltd.)

FALCONBRIDGE NICKEL MINES LTD.-LES MINES FALCONBRIDGE NICKEL LTEE. (ON)
Name changed to Falconbridge Ltd. 2/10/83
(See Falconbridge Ltd.)

FALCONCREST RES INC (ON)
Recapitalized as SFP Communications Group Inc. 8/21/98
Each share Common no par exchanged for (0.25) share Common no par
SFP Communications Group Inc. name changed to Motivus Inc. 5/23/2001

FINANCIAL INFORMATION, INC.   **FAL-FAM**

(See Motivus Inc.)

FALCONER CO (MD)
Merged into McCorquodale Inc.
09/30/1975
Each share Common $1 par
exchanged for $9 cash

FALECK & MARGOLIES LTD (ON)
Cease trade order effective
06/01/1989
Details not available

FALK CORP. (WI)
Common $10 par changed to $2.50
par and (3) additional shares issued
4/23/62
Stock Dividend - 33-1/3% 12/9/66
Completely liquidated 12/31/68
Each share Common $2.50 par
exchanged for first and final
distribution of (0.4921) share
Sundstrand Corp. (DE) $3.50 Conv.
Preferred no par and (0.33599)
share Common $1 par
Sundstrand Corp. (DE) merged into
United Technologies Corp. 6/10/99

FALKEN INVT AG (NV)
Name changed to Holter Technologies
Holding, AG 03/00/1999
Holter Technologies Holding, AG
recapitalized as International
Consortium Corp. 06/17/2008
(See International Consortium Corp.)

FALKIRK RES CORP (BC)
Recapitalized as Jemi Fibre Corp.
06/27/2013
Each share Common no par
exchanged for (0.1) share Common
no par
Jemi Fibre Corp. merged into CanWel
Building Materials Group Ltd.
05/16/2016

FALL RIV RES LTD (BC)
Reincorporated 12/23/2004
Place of incorporation changed from
(AB) to (BC) 12/23/2004
Each share old Common no par
exchanged for (0.33333333) share
new Common no par 01/13/2010
Name changed to Earth Heat
Resources Ltd. 07/29/2010
Earth Heat Resources Ltd. name
changed to Rampart Energy Ltd.
05/22/2013

FALL RIVER BLEACHERY
Business discontinued and property
sold 00/00/1938
Stockholders' equity unlikely

FALL RIVER ELEC LT CO (MA)
5.80% Preferred $100 par called for
redemption 10/18/65
Acquired by Eastern Utilities
Associates 6/30/67
Each share Common $25 par
exchanged for (1.375) shares
Common $10 par
(See Eastern Utilities Associates)

FALL RIVER EXPL & MNG CO (CO)
Name changed to Fall River
Industries, Inc. and Capital Stock no
par changed to 1¢ par 6/23/70
(See Fall River Industries, Inc.)

FALL RIVER GAS CO (MA)
Common $10 par changed to $5 par
and (1) additional share issued
11/00/1965
Common $5 par changed to
$1.66666666 par and (2) additional
shares issued 01/00/1988
Common $1.66666666 par changed
to $0.83333333 par and (1)
additional share issued 01/14/1994
Merged into Southern Union Co.
(New) 09/28/2000
Each share Common $0.83333333
par exchanged for (1.19848) shares
Common $1 par
Southern Union Co. (New) merged
into Energy Transfer Equity, L.P.
03/26/2012 which name changed to
Energy Transfer L.P. 10/19/2018

FALL RIVER GAS WORKS CO. (MA)
Common $100 par changed to $25
par and (3) additional shares issued
09/00/1924
Reorganized as Fall River Gas Co.
07/25/1955
Each share Common $25 par
exchanged for (2.5) shares Common
$10 par
Fall River Gas Co. merged into
Southern Union Co. (New)
09/28/2000 which merged into
Energy Transfer Equity, L.P.
03/26/2012 which name changed to
Energy Transfer L.P. 10/19/2018

FALL RIVER INDS INC (CO)
Each share Capital Stock 1¢ par
exchanged for (0.1) share Capital
Stock 10¢ par 10/5/71
Proclaimed dissolved for failure to
pay taxes and file annual reports
1/31/77

**FALL RIVER NATL BK
(FALL RIVER, MA)**
Common $25 par changed to $10 par
and (2.5) additional shares issued
plus a 60% stock dividend paid
2/14/73
Merged into New England Merchants
Co., Inc. 5/9/75
Each share Common $10 par
exchanged for either (2) shares
Common $5 par or $30 cash
Note: Option to receive cash expired
2/24/75
New England Merchants Co., Inc.
name changed to Bank of New
England Corp. 5/1/82
(See Bank of New England Corp.)

**FALL RIVER TR CO
(FALL RIVER, MA)**
Capital Stock $100 par changed to
$20 par and (4) additional shares
issued 10/16/1972
Stock Dividends - 25% 08/15/1963;
10% 04/26/1965; 20% 04/14/1969;
25% 04/15/1971; 25% 10/16/1972;
20% 04/09/1973; 16-2/3%
04/12/1974; 14-2/7% 04/14/1975
Merged into Bank of Boston Corp.
11/21/1983
Each share Capital Stock $20 par
exchanged for (2.666) shares
Common $4.50 par
Bank of Boston Corp. name changed
to BankBoston Corp. 04/25/1997
which merged into Fleet Boston
Corp. 10/01/1999 which name
changed to FleetBoston Financial
Corp. 04/18/2000 which merged into
Bank of America Corp. 04/01/2004

**FALLBROOK NATL BK
(FALLBROOK, CA)**
Common $5 par split (2) for (1) by
issuance of (1) additional share
06/01/1995
Stock Dividend - 5% payable
12/11/1998 to holders of record
11/30/1998
Reorganized as Community Bancorp
Inc. 06/25/1999
Each share Common $0.625 par
exchanged for (1) share Common
$0.625 par
Community Bancorp Inc. merged into
First Community Bancorp (CA)
10/26/2006 which reincorporated in
Delaware as PacWest Bancorp
05/14/2008

FALLINGER CORP (QC)
Name changed to Sogevex Inc.
07/08/1976
(See Sogevex Inc.)

FALLINGER MINING CORP. (QC)
Name changed to Fallinger Corp.
02/12/1973
Fallinger Corp. name changed to
Sogevex Inc. 07/08/1976
(See Sogevex Inc.)

FALLMAC NICKEL MINES LTD. (ON)
Charter cancelled and declared
dissolved for failure to file returns
and pay fees 03/16/1976

FALLON GAS CORP. (CO)
Each share Common 5¢ par
exchanged for (0.1) share Common
5¢ par 8/27/57
Each share Common 5¢ par
exchanged for (0.001) share
Common 5¢ par 1/7/61
Name changed to Fallon Smith Corp.
1/28/66
Fallon Smith Corp. name changed to
Imperial Investment Corp. 8/7/69
(See Imperial Investment Corp.)

FALLON SMITH CORP (CO)
Name changed to Imperial Investment
Corp. 8/7/69
(See Imperial Investment Corp.)

FALLS BUDGET CORP. (NY)
Name changed to Falls Resources
Corp. 5/10/68
Falls Resources Corp. name changed
to Chemold Corp. 3/6/69
(See Chemold Corp.)

**FALLS CHURCH BANK
(FALLS CHURCH, VA)**
Merged into First Virginia Bankshares
Corp. 9/5/69
Each share Capital Stock $75 par
exchanged for (6) shares Common
$1 par
First Virginia Bankshares Corp. name
changed to First Virginia Banks, Inc.
9/1/78 which merged into BB&T
Corp. 7/1/2003

FALLS CITY INDS INC (KY)
Name changed 01/31/1979
Common $100 par changed to $25
par and (3) additional shares issued
plus a 200% stock dividend paid
05/16/1973
Name changed from Falls City
Brewing Co. to Falls City Industries
Inc. 01/31/1979
Acquired by MFI Leasing Co.
04/21/1992
Each share Preferred $50 par
exchanged for $50 cash
Each share Common $25 par
exchanged for $25 cash

FALLS FINL INC (OH)
Common 1¢ par split (2) for (1) by
issuance of (1) additional share
3/12/93
Merged into Fifth Third Bancorp
7/24/95
Each share Common 1¢ par
exchanged for (0.4791) share
Common no par

FALLS RES CORP (NY)
Name changed to Chemold Corp.
03/06/1969
(See Chemold Corp.)

FALLS SPRING & WIRE CO.
Merged into Standard Steel Spring
Co. in 1949
Each share Common exchanged for
(1) share Common $1 par
Standard Steel Spring Co. merged
into Rockwell Spring & Axle Co.
9/30/53 which name changed to
Rockwell-Standard Corp. (PA)
4/21/58 reincorporated in Delaware
7/31/64 which merged into North
American Rockwell Corp. 9/22/67
which merged into Rockwell
International Corp. (Old) 2/16/73
which merged into Boeing Co.
12/6/96

FALMOUTH BANCORP INC (DE)
Merged into Independent Bank Corp.
(MA) 7/16/2004
Each share Common 1¢ par
exchanged for (1.28) shares
Common 1¢ par

**FALMOUTH COOP BK
(FALMOUTH, MA)**
Under plan of reorganization each
share Common 10¢ par
automatically became (1) share
Falmouth Bancorp, Inc. (DE)
Common 1¢ par 10/7/97
Falmouth Bancorp, Inc. (DE) merged
into Independent Bank Corp. (MA)
7/16/2004

FALMOUTH PETE LTD (CANADA)
Name changed to RoyShel Properties
Ltd. (Canada) 10/16/1989
RoyShel Properties Ltd. (Canada)
reincorporated in British Columbia
12/23/1996 which recapitalized as
ATC Technologies Corp. 05/30/1997
(See ATC Technologies Corp.)

FALNORA GOLD MINES LTD. (ON)
Charter cancelled 05/25/1967
No stockholders' equity

FALSTAFF BREWING CORP. (MD)
Merged into Falstaff Brewing Corp.
(DE) 00/00/1936
Each share First and Second
Preferred exchanged for (1) share
6% Preferred $1 par 00/00/1936
(See Falstaff Brewing Corp. (DE)

FALSTAFF BREWING CORP (DE)
Capital Stock $1 par reclassified as
Common $1 par 00/00/1936
Common $1 par split (2) for (1) by
issuance of (1) additional share
01/08/1965
Stock Dividends - 100% 01/22/1948;
100% 10/31/1949
Merged into S&P Co. 05/16/1989
Each share Common $1 par
exchanged for $12 cash

FALVO CORP (ON)
Plan of arrangement effective
05/28/1999
Each share Common no par
exchanged for either (1) share
Conrex Steel Corp. Class A
Common no par or C$0.92 cash
Note: Option to receive stock expired
05/20/1999
(See Conrex Steel Corp.)

FAM REAL ESTATE INVT TR (ON)
Name changed to Slate Office REIT
03/16/2015

FAMIGLIA BRANDS INC (DE)
Charter cancelled and declared
inoperative and void for
non-payment of taxes 3/1/90

FAMIGLIA INDUSTRIES, INC. (DE)
Name changed to Famiglia Brands,
Inc. 2/16/88
(See Famiglia Brands, Inc.)

FAMILIAN CORP (DE)
Each share Common 50¢ par
exchanged for (1/3) share Common
$1.50 par 8/10/72
Common $1.50 par split (5) for (4) by
issuance of (0.25) additional share
8/26/74
Merged into Nufam Corp. 1/18/85
Each share Common $1.50 par
exchanged for $14 cash

**FAMILY ACHIEVEMENT INST INC
(UT)**
Name changed to Intermountain
Industries, Inc. 12/3/70
Intermountain Industries, Inc.
recapitalized as Dynapac, Inc.
9/22/71
(See Dynapac, Inc.)

FAMILY BANCORP (MA)
Common 10¢ par split (3) for (2) by
issuance of (0.5) additional share
11/27/1995
Merged into Peoples Heritage
Financial Group, Inc. 12/06/1996
Each share Common 10¢ par
exchanged for (1.26) shares
Common 1¢ par
Peoples Heritage Financial Group,
Inc. name changed to Banknorth
Group, Inc. (ME) 05/10/2000 which
merged into TD Banknorth Inc.
03/01/2005
(See TD Banknorth Inc.)

COPYRIGHTED MATERIAL   NO UNAUTHORIZED REPRODUCTION

FAMILY BK (HALLANDALE, FL)
Merged into Republic Security Financial Corp. 06/30/1997
Each share Common exchanged for (13) shares Common 1¢ par
Republic Security Financial Corp. merged into Wachovia Corp. (New) (Ctfs. dated between 05/20/1991 and 09/01/2001) 03/01/2001 which merged into Wachovia Corp. (Ctfs. dated after 09/01/2001) 09/01/2001 which merged into Wells Fargo & Co. (New) 12/31/2008

FAMILY BARGAIN CENTERS, INC. (NY)
Reincorporated under the laws of Delaware as Kenton Corp. and Common $1 par changed to 50¢ par 11/13/68
(See Kenton Corp.)

FAMILY BARGAIN CORP (DE)
Each share Common $0.0001 par exchanged for (0.16666666) share Common 1¢ par 05/02/1994
Merged into Factory 2-U Stores, Inc. 11/23/1998
Each share 9.5% Conv. Preferred Ser. A 1¢ par exchanged for (1) share Common 1¢ par
Each share Conv. Jr. Preferred Ser. B 1¢ par exchanged for (173.33) shares Common 1¢ par
Each share Common 1¢ par exchanged for (0.30133) share Common 1¢ par
(See Factory 2-U Stores, Inc.)

FAMILY BUILDING CREDITS LTD. (CANADA)
Merged into Interprovincial Building Credits Ltd. 01/12/1956
Each share Common no par exchanged for (0.33333333) share Common no par
Interprovincial Building Credits, Ltd. name changed to Traders Homeplan Ltd. 01/02/1969
(See Traders Homeplan Ltd.)

FAMILY CIRCLE ASSOCIATES, INC. (NJ)
Class A & B Common 10¢ par reclassified as Common 10¢ par 12/18/62
Completely liquidated for cash 6/10/65

FAMILY CR CORP (DE)
6% Pr. Preferred $100 par called for redemption 04/26/1968
4%-6% Preferred $10 par called for redemption 04/26/1968
Acquired by Credithrift Financial Corp. 04/27/1968
Each share Common no par exchanged for (1.4) shares Common $1 par
Credithrift Financial Corp. name changed to American General Finance Corp. 03/20/1989
(See American General Finance Corp.)

FAMILY DIGEST, INC. (NY)
Dissolved by proclamation 12/16/68

FAMILY DLR STORES INC (DE)
Common 10¢ par split (2) for (1) by issuance of (1) additional share 06/09/1971
Common 10¢ par split (2) for (1) by issuance of (1) additional share 05/31/1972
Common 10¢ par split (3) for (2) by issuance of (0.5) additional share 10/15/1981
Common 10¢ par split (3) for (2) by issuance of (0.5) additional share 01/14/1983
Common 10¢ par split (2) for (1) by issuance of (1) additional share 07/20/1983
Common 10¢ par split (3) for (2) by issuance of (0.5) additional share 02/22/1985
Common 10¢ par split (2) for (1) by issuance of (1) additional share 02/26/1992
Common 10¢ par split (3) for (2) by issuance of (0.5) additional share payable 07/31/1997 to holders of record 07/15/1997 Ex date - 08/01/1997
Common 10¢ par split (2) for (1) by issuance of (1) additional share payable 04/30/1998 to holders of record 04/16/1998 Ex date - 05/01/1998
Merged into Dollar Tree, Inc. 07/06/2015
Each share Common 10¢ par exchanged for (0.2484) share Common 1¢ par and $59.60 cash

FAMILY ENTMT CORP (FL)
Recapitalized as Airborne Security & Protective Services, Inc. (Ctfs. dated prior to 09/30/2009) 09/16/2008
Each share Common $0.001 par exchanged for (0.02) share Common $0.001 par
Airborne Security & Protective Services, Inc. (Ctfs. dated prior to 09/30/2009) name changed to Harbor Brewing Co., Inc. 09/30/2009 which name changed to CTGX Mining, Inc. 02/28/2013

FAMILY ENTMT CTRS INC (CA)
Chapter 11 bankruptcy proceedings converted to Chapter 7 on 3/5/86
Stockholders' equity unlikely

FAMILY FIN CORP (DE)
Common no par changed to $1 par in 1946
$1.50 Preferred Ser. A no par called for redemption 10/1/46
$1.50 Preferred Ser. B no par called for redemption 10/1/46
4-1/2% Preference Ser. A $50 par called for redemption 1/2/59
5% Preference Ser. B $50 par called for redemption 1/2/59
Common $1 par split (2) for (1) by issuance of (1) additional share 11/8/61
Stock Dividend - 100% 12/18/47
Name changed to Aristar Inc. 6/29/73
(See Aristar Inc.)

FAMILY FINANCE, INC. (IN)
Common $100 par changed to $10 par 11/30/60
Liquidation completed
Each share Common $10 par stamped to indicate initial distribution of $13 cash 8/20/60
Each share Stamped Common $10 par stamped to indicate second distribution of $5 cash 4/5/63
Each share Stamped Common $10 par exchanged for third distribution of $5.25 cash 7/1/63
Each share Stamped Common $10 par received fourth and final distribution of $0.45 cash 8/9/65

FAMILY FINANCE CO.
Acquired by Gotham Credit Corp. 00/00/1939
Details not available

FAMILY FIRST FED SVGS BK (CLIFTON, NJ)
Merged into Great Falls Bancorp 04/07/1995
Each share Common no par exchanged for (0.1643) share Common $1 par
Great Falls Bancorp name changed to Greater Community Bancorp 07/01/1996 which merged into Valley National Bancorp 07/02/2008

FAMILY FUND LIFE INSURANCE CO. (GA)
Merged into United Family Life Insurance Co. 4/9/62
Each share Common $1 par exchanged for (2) shares Common $1 par
United Family Life Insurance Co. reorganized as Interfinancial Inc. 7/1/69
(See Interfinancial Inc.)

FAMILY GOLF CTRS INC (DE)
Issue Information - 1,200,000 shares COM offered at $5 per share on 11/16/1994
Common 1¢ par split (3) for (2) by issuance of (0.5) additional share payable 05/04/1998 to holders of record 04/20/1998 Ex date - 05/05/1998
Plan of reorganization under Chapter 11 Federal Bankruptcy Code effective 07/10/2003
No stockholders' equity

FAMILY GROUP BROADCASTING L P (DE)
Voluntarily dissolved 12/22/1994
Details not available

FAMILY HEALTH SYS INC (DE)
Common 1¢ par changed to $0.00167 par and (5) additional shares issued 09/07/1994
Each share old Common $0.00167 par exchanged for (0.1) share new Common $0.00167 par 04/30/1993
Name changed to Armitec, Inc. 09/13/2000
(See Armitec, Inc.)

FAMILY HEALTHCARE SOLUTIONS INC (NV)
Name changed to Mega Media Group, Inc. 08/24/2007
(See Mega Media Group, Inc.)

FAMILY LIFE ASSURANCE CO.-LA FAMILIALE COMPAGNIE D'ASSURANCE-VIE (CANADA)
Acquired by Sovereign Life Insurance Co./ La Souveraine, Compagnie D'Assurance-Vie 12/13/1984
Details not available

FAMILY LIFE INS CO (WA)
Common $10 par and Class A Common $10 par changed to $1 par and (9) additional shares issued respectively 04/03/1964
Each share $8 Preferred $50 par exchanged for (2) shares Class A Common $1 par 09/15/1964
Stock Dividends - 100% 08/16/1965; 50% 12/31/1971
Merged into Merrill Lynch & Co., Inc. 11/13/1974
Each share Common $1 par or Class A Common $1 par exchanged for (1.61) shares Common $1.33-1/3 par
Merrill Lynch & Co., Inc. acquired by Bank of America Corp. 01/02/2009

FAMILY LOAN SOCIETY, INC.
Name changed to Family Finance Corp. in 1943
Family Finance Corp. name changed to Aristar Inc. 6/29/73
(See Aristar Inc.)

FAMILY LOOM, INC. (UT)
Merged into Alta Industries Corp. 4/30/71
Each share Common $1 par exchanged for (0.8) share Common $5 par
Alta Industries Corp. reorganized as Alta Industries Ltd. 9/13/79

FAMILY MED TREATMENT CTRS AMER INC (DE)
Name changed to National HMO Corp. 12/14/1984
National HMO Corp. name changed to National Home Health Care Corp. 12/24/1991
(See National Home Health Care Corp.)

FAMILY MEMS INC (ON)
Reincorporated 12/16/2014
Place of incorporation changed from (ON) to (BC) 12/16/2014
Merged into Thunder River Enterprises Inc. 02/09/2018
Each share Common no par exchanged for (1) share Common no par
Note: Unexchanged certificates will be cancelled and become without value 02/09/2020

FAMILY MORTGAGE CO. (CANADA)
Name changed to Traders Mortgage Co. 4/25/63

FAMILY MUT SVGS BK (HAVERHILL, MA)
Under plan of reorganization each share Common 10¢ par automatically became (1) share Family Bancorp Common 10¢ par 12/06/1996
Family Bancorp merged into Peoples Heritage Financial Group, Inc. 12/06/1996 which name changed to Banknorth Group, Inc. (ME) 05/10/2000 which merged into TD Banknorth Inc. 03/01/2005
(See TD Banknorth Inc.)

FAMILY PRODUCTS CORP.
Dissolved in 1939

FAMILY RECORD PLAN INC (CA)
Name changed to Hiller Aviation, Inc. 01/24/1980
(See Hiller Aviation, Inc.)

FAMILY RESORTS INC (FL)
Charter cancelled for non-payment of taxes 09/03/1976

FAMILY RESTAURANTS INC (DE)
Under plan of merger name changed to Koo Koo Roo Enterprises, Inc. 10/30/1998
Koo Koo Roo Enterprises, Inc. name changed to Prandium, Inc. 04/01/1999
(See Prandium, Inc.)

FAMILY SHOPPING NETWORK INC (DE)
Charter cancelled and declared inoperative and void for non-payment of taxes 3/1/90

FAMILY SHOWTIME THEATRES INC (NY)
Plan of reorganization under Chapter 11 Federal Bankruptcy proceedings confirmed 11/28/1990
No stockholders' equity

FAMILY STEAK HOUSES FLA INC (FL)
Common 1¢ par split (3) for (2) by issuance of (0.5) additional share 12/03/1986
Common 1¢ par split (2) for (1) by issuance of (1) additional share 03/16/1987
Common 1¢ par split (3) for (2) by issuance of (0.5) additional share 06/10/1987
Each share old Common 1¢ par exchanged for (0.2) share new Common 1¢ par 03/04/1998
Name changed to EACO Corp. 07/20/2004

FAMILY UNDERWRITERS CORP. (WA)
Dissolved 11/1/58

FAMILYMART CO LTD (JAPAN)
Name changed to FamilyMart UNY Holdings Co., Ltd. 09/01/2016

FAMILYWARE INTL INC (NV)
Each share old Common $0.0005 par exchanged for (0.01) share new Common $0.0005 par 07/31/1998
Reorganized as CentroCom Corp. (NV) 03/02/1999
Each share Common $0.0005 par exchanged for (6) shares Common $0.0005 par
CentroCom Corp. (NV) reorganized in Delaware as JMI Telecom Corp. 08/06/2007 which name changed to UA Multimedia Inc. 06/05/2012

FAMISE CORP. (DE)
Recapitalized in 1936
Class A no par changed to $2 par

Common no par changed to 50¢ par Dissolved 10/19/54

FAMOUS ARTISTS SCHS INC (NY)
Stock Dividends - 10% 7/26/66; 100% 3/15/68
Name changed to FAS International Inc. 5/13/69
Fas International Inc. name changed to Bowline Corp. 4/20/78
(See Bowline Corp.)

FAMOUS FIXINS INC (NY)
Name changed to Warning Model Management, Inc. 05/15/2003
Warning Model Management, Inc. name changed to Warning Management Services, Inc. 09/27/2004
(See Warning Management Services, Inc.)

FAMOUS FOOD GROUP INC (DE)
Recapitalized as Kootenai Corp. 07/05/2006
Each share Common $0.001 par exchanged for (0.001) share Common $0.001 par
Note: No holder will receive fewer than (100) shares
Kootenai Corp. reorganized as BizAuctions, Inc. 08/17/2006 which name changed to CannaGrow Holdings, Inc. 11/05/2014

FAMOUS INTERNET MALL INC (NV)
Common $0.001 par split (5) for (2) by issuance of (1.5) additional shares payable 11/22/1999 to holders of record 11/19/1999
Name changed to Yellowbubble.com Inc. (NV) 01/04/2000
Yellowbubble.com Inc. (NV) reorganized in Florida as Reality Racing, Inc. 08/02/2005
(See Reality Racing, Inc.)

FAMOUS PLAYERS CDN LTD (CANADA)
Each share old Common no par exchanged for (3) shares new Common no par in 1946
New Common no par split (4) for (1) by issuance of (3) additional shares 3/24/69
Name changed to Canadian Cablesystems Ltd. 4/5/71
Canadian Cablesystems Ltd. name changed to Rogers Cablesystems Inc. 2/13/81 which name changed to Rogers Communications Inc. 4/24/86

FAMOUS PRODS INC (CO)
Name changed to DNA Brands, Inc. 08/04/2010

FAMOUS RESTAURANTS INC (DE)
Plan of reorganization under Chapter 11 Federal Bankruptcy proceedings confirmed 06/02/1993
No stockholders' equity

FAMOUS SAMS GROUP INC (NV)
Each share old Common $0.001 par exchanged for (0.2) share new Common $0.001 par 11/06/1997
Name changed to BioProgress Technology International, Inc. (NV) 12/22/1997
BioProgress Technology International, Inc. (NV) reincorporated in England & Wales as BioProgress PLC 05/21/2003 which name changed to Meldex International PLC 09/28/2007

FAMOUS UNCLE ALS HOT DOGS & GRILLE INC (DE)
Each share old Common $0.001 par exchanged for (0.00217391) share new Common $0.001 par 07/29/2010
Name changed to American Standard Energy Corp. 11/10/2010
(See American Standard Energy Corp.)

FAN ENERGY INC (NV)
Each (15) shares old Common $0.001 par exchanged for (1) share new Common $0.001 par 12/27/2001
New Common $0.001 par split (9.3563) for (1) by issuance of (8.3563) additional shares payable 10/29/2002 to holders of record 06/28/2002 Ex date - 10/30/2002
Name changed to Quiet Tiger, Inc. 02/21/2003
Quiet Tiger, Inc. name changed to MediaMax Technology Corp. 04/01/2005 which recapitalized as Exchange Media Corp. 10/01/2008 which name changed to Empire Oil Refineries Corp. 03/31/2011

FAN-TAN MINES LTD. (BC)
Struck off register and declared dissolved for failure to file returns 10/15/1974

FANATICS ONLY INC (CO)
SEC revoked common stock registration 07/02/2009

FANCAMP RES LTD (BC)
Recapitalized as Fancamp Exploration Ltd. 11/4/99
Each share Common no par exchanged for (0.5) share Common no par

FANCY INDS INC (NY)
Dissolved by proclamation 01/25/2012

FANESS INDS INC (NY)
Completely liquidated 01/12/1978
Each share Common 1¢ par exchanged for first and final distribution of $0.30 cash

FANESS LEASING CORP. (NY)
Name changed to Faness Industries, Inc. 08/17/1970
(See Faness Industries, Inc.)

FANEX RES LTD (QC)
Declared disticoven for failure to file reports and pay fees 06/26/1989

FANFARE CORP (CA)
Stock Dividends - 10% 04/01/1971; 10% 01/20/1972
Charter suspended for failure to file reports and pay fees 05/03/1976

FANFARE FILM PRODTNS INC (CA)
Name changed to Fanfare Corp. 2/19/71
(See Fanfare Corp.)

FANNER MANUFACTURING CO. (OH)
Each share Common $100 par exchanged for (30) shares Common $5 par 00/00/1948
Each share Common $5 par exchanged for (4.20408) shares Common $1 par 00/00/1950
Stock Dividend - 100% 10/25/1951
Merged into Textron Inc. (RI) 01/24/1958
Each share Common $1 par exchanged for (0.5) share Common 25¢ par
Textron Inc. (RI) reincorporated in Delaware 01/02/1968

FANNIN BANCSHARES INC (TX)
Merged into InterFirst Corp. 12/2/82
Each share Common $1 par exchanged for (2.62) shares Common $5 par
InterFirst Corp. merged into First RepublicBank Corp. 6/6/87
(See First RepublicBank Corp.)

FANNIN BK (HOUSTON, TX)
Each share Capital Stock $20 par exchanged for (2) shares Capital Stock $10 par 6/25/65
Stock Dividends - 10% 6/10/65; 33-1/3% 1/25/68; 25% 1/30/70; 20% 1/29/71; 16-2/3% 2/22/72; 25% 3/29/74; 20% 3/12/76; 16-2/3% 3/11/77; 14.29% 3/23/78; 25% 3/22/79
Merged into Fannin Bancshares, Inc. 2/29/80
Each share Capital Stock $10 par held by non-residents of Texas exchanged for $43 cash
Each share Capital Stock $10 par held by residents of Texas exchanged for $16 principal amount of 10% Subordinated Conv. Debentures due 2/29/92 and (1) share Common $1 par
Fannin Bancshares, Inc. merged into InterFirst Corp. 12/2/82 which merged into First RepublicBank Corp. 6/6/87
(See First RepublicBank Corp.)

FANNIN STATE BANK (HOUSTON, TX)
Stock Dividends - 25% 3/3/58; 50% 12/28/59
Recapitalized as Fannin Bank (Houston, TX) 2/22/62
Each share Capital Stock $20 par exchanged for (1/3) share Capital Stock $20 par
Fannin Bank (Houston, TX) merged into Fannin Bancshares, Inc. 2/29/80 which merged into InterFirst Corp. 12/2/82 which merged into First RepublicBank Corp. 6/6/87
(See First RepublicBank Corp.)

FANNY FARMER CANDY SHOPS INC (NY)
Each share Common no par exchanged for (4) shares Common $1 par in 1934
Common $1 par split (5) for (4) by issuance of (0.25) additional share 6/30/64
Stock Dividend - 10% 3/7/75
Merged into Amoskeag Co. 1/28/80
Each share Common $1 par exchanged for $19.50 cash

FANNY HILL ENTERPRISES INC (NY)
Name changed to Cinetron Corp. 1/16/69
(See Cinetron Corp.)

FANO MNG & EXPL INC (QC)
Recapitalized as Fanex Resources Ltd. 08/26/1971
Each share Capital Stock $1 par exchanged for (0.14285714) share Capital Stock $1 par
(See Fanex Resources Ltd.)

FANO URANIUM MINES LTD. (ON)
Charter surrendered 09/08/1958

FANON ELECTRS INDS INC (NY)
Acquired by Whittaker Corp. (CA) 12/15/67
Each share Common 20¢ par exchanged for (0.090991) share Common $1 par
Whittaker Corp. (CA) reincorporated in Delaware 6/16/86
(See Whittaker Corp. (DE))

FANSPORT INC (FL)
Common $0.0001 par split (20) for (1) by issuance of (19) additional shares payable 02/27/2013 to holders of record 02/25/2013 Ex date - 02/28/2013
Name changed to Media Analytics Corp. 09/03/2013
Media Analytics Corp. recapitalized as Jade Global Holdings, Inc. 03/06/2017

FANSTEEL INC. (NY)
Common $5 par split (3) for (1) by issuance of (2) additional shares 9/20/83
Common $5 par changed to $2.50 par and (1) additional share issued 1/30/84
Reincorporated under the laws of Delaware 5/13/85

FANSTEEL INC (DE)
Reincorporated 05/13/1985
State of incorporation changed from (NY) to (DE) 05/13/1985
Plan of reorganization under Chapter 11 Federal Bankruptcy Code effective 01/23/2004
Each share Common $2.50 par exchanged for (0.098288) share Common 1¢ par
Each share old Common 1¢ par exchanged for (0.00013333) share new Common 1¢ par 02/17/2010
Note: Holders of (7,499) or fewer pre-split shares received $0.46 cash per share
Company is now private

FANSTEEL METALLURGICAL CORP (NY)
$5 Preferred no par called for redemption 1/30/46
Common no par changed to $5 par in 1954
Common $5 par split (3) for (2) by issuance of (0.5) additional share 12/14/61
Stock Dividend - 100% 2/27/46
Name changed to Fansteel Inc. (NY) 5/7/68
Fansteel Inc. (NY) reincorporated in Delaware 5/13/85

FANSTEEL PRODUCTS CO., INC.
Name changed to Fansteel Metallurgical Corp. in 1935
Fansteel Metallurgical Corp. name changed to Fansteel Inc. (N.Y.) 5/7/68 which reincorporated in Delaware 5/13/85

FANTASTIC FOODS INTL INC (CO)
Recapitalized as DCI Telecommunications, Inc. 01/11/1995
Each share Common $0.0001 par exchanged for (0.05) share Common $0.0001 par
(See DCI Telecommunications, Inc.)

FANTASTIC FUN INC (FL)
Name changed to Global Profit Technologies, Inc. 02/13/2008

FANTASTICON (NV)
Recapitalized as USCorp 03/06/2002
Each share Common $0.001 par exchanged for (0.1) share Common $0.001 par

FANTASY 6 SPORTS INC (BC)
Name changed to Victory Square Technologies Inc. 06/09/2017

FANTATECH INC (DE)
Each share old Common $0.001 par exchanged for (0.5) share new Common $0.001 par 06/30/2004
Completely liquidated
Each share new Common $0.001 par received first and final distribution of $0.128 cash payable 12/18/2008 to holders of record 11/13/2008
Note: Certificates were not required to be surrendered and are without value

FANTOM TECHNOLOGIES INC (ON)
Filed a Plan of Arrangement under Companies' Creditors Arrangement Act 10/25/2001
Stockholders' equity unlikely

FANTONIX ENTERPRISES INC (NY)
Adjudicated bankrupt 01/06/1971
No stockholders' equity

FANUC LTD (JAPAN)
ADR's for Common split (3) for (1) by issuance of (2) additional ADR's payable 12/03/2010 to holders of record 11/26/2010 Ex date - 12/06/2010
Name changed to Fanuc Corp. 07/12/2011

FAR-BEN S A DE C V (MEXICO)
ADR agreement terminated 08/26/2004
Each Sponsored ADR for Ser. B shares exchanged for (2) Ser. B shares

FAR EAST ENERGY CORP (NV)
Filed a petition under Chapter 7 Federal Bankruptcy proceedings 11/10/2015
Stockholders' equity unlikely

FAR EAST GOLD INC (ON)
Merged into KWG Resources Inc. 03/31/1997
Each share Common no par exchanged for (0.38022813) share Common no par and (0.33333333) Common Stock Purchase Warrant expiring 12/31/1997

FAR EAST HOSPITALITY TR (SINGAPORE)
ADR agreement terminated 04/19/2018
No ADR's remain outstanding

FAR EAST MINERALS LTD (BC)
Struck off register and declared dissolved for failure to file returns 00/00/1979

FAR EAST NATL BK (LOS ANGELES, CA)
Stock Dividends - 12% 2/10/93; 10% 1/20/94; 10% 1/20/95; 10% payable 1/26/96 to holders of record 1/12/96
Merged into Bank SinoPac 8/15/97
Each share Common $10 par exchanged for $15.48 cash
Note: An additional distribution of $0.053598 cash per share was made in 1998

FAR EAST OIL DEVELOPMENT CO. INC. (PHILIPPINES)
Name changed to Philippine Oil Development Co., Inc. 00/00/1948
(See Philippine Oil Development Co., Inc.)

FAR EAST RES CORP (BC)
Struck off register and declared dissolved for failure to file returns 09/28/1990

FAR EAST SHIPPING CO O A O (RUSSIA)
GDR agreement terminated 12/10/2012
No GDR's remain outstanding

FAR EAST TELECOMMUNICATIONS CO OPEN JT STK CO (RUSSIA)
Name changed 11/08/2004
Name changed from Far East Electrosvyaz Co. OJSC to Far East Telecommunications Co. OJSC 11/08/2004
Sponsored ADR's for Ordinary split (6) for (1) by issuance of (5) additional ADR's payable 07/31/2008 to holders of record 07/24/2008 Ex date - 08/01/2008
Merged into Rostelecom OJSC 04/13/2011
Each Sponsored ADR for Ordinary exchanged for $28.882173 cash

FAR EAST VENTURES INC (NV)
Name changed to Nico Telecom, Inc. 02/05/2001
Nico Telecom, Inc. name changed to Far East Ventures Trading Co. 10/09/2007
(See Far East Ventures Trading Co.)

FAR EAST VENTURES TRADING CO. (NV)
SEC revoked common stock registration 10/08/2008

FAR EASTN ENERGY CORP (CANADA)
Involuntarily dissolved for failure to file annual returns 07/12/2004

FAR EASTN TEXTILE LTD (TAIWAN)
Stock Dividends - In Sponsored 144A GDR's for Ordinary to holders of Sponsored 144A GDR's for Ordinary 11.68% payable 11/15/2000 to holders of 08/07/2000; 4.051% payable 10/12/2001 to holders of record 07/30/2001; 5% payable 10/31/2002 to holders of record 08/28/2002 Ex date - 08/26/2002; 7% payable 10/27/2003 to holders of record 08/20/2003 Ex date - 08/18/2003; 6.97% payable 11/09/2004 to holders of record 08/25/2004; 8% payable 11/21/2005 to holders of record 08/18/2005; 6% payable 10/23/2006 to holders of record 08/17/2006; 3% payable 11/28/2007 to holders of record 08/23/2007 Ex date - 08/21/2007; 2% payable 11/10/2008 to holders of record 08/21/2008 Ex date - 08/19/2008; 2% payable 10/20/2009 to holders of record 08/25/2009 Ex date - 08/21/2009
In Sponsored Reg. S GDR's for Ordinary to holders of Sponsored Reg. S GDR's for Ordinary 11.68% payable 11/15/2000 to holders of record 08/07/2000; 4.051% payable 10/12/2001 to holders of record 07/30/2001 Ex date - 08/01/2001; 5% payable 10/31/2002 to holders of record 08/28/2002 Ex date - 08/26/2002; 7% payable 10/27/2003 to holders of record 08/20/2003 Ex date - 08/18/2003; 6.97% payable 11/09/2004 to holders of record 08/25/2004; 8% payable 11/21/2005 to holders of record 08/18/2005; 6% payable 10/23/2006 to holders of record 08/17/2006; 3% payable 11/28/2007 to holders of record 08/23/2007; 2% payable 11/10/2008 to holders of record 08/21/2008; 2% payable 10/20/2009 to holders of record 08/25/2009 Ex date - 08/21/2009
Name changed to Far Eastern New Century Corp. 01/04/2010

FAR GROUP INC (WA)
Common $0.0001 par split (6) for (1) by issuance of (5) additional shares payable 09/10/2001 to holders of record 08/31/2001 Ex date - 09/11/2001
Name changed to North American Natural Gas, Inc. 03/05/2003
North American Natural Gas, Inc. name changed to PureRay Corp. 08/27/2008

FAR-MAR-CO., INC. (KS)
Merged out of existence 00/00/1985
Details not available

FAR NORTH EXPLORATION LTD. (AB)
Recapitalized as New Far North Exploration Ltd. 02/02/1959
Each share Common no par exchanged for (0.2) share Common no par
(See New Far North Exploraton Ltd.)

FAR VISTA INTERACTIVE CORP (NV)
Name changed to Far Vista Petroleum Corp. 05/30/2013

FAR WEST FINL CORP (DE)
Common $1 par split (3) for (1) by issuance of (2) additional shares 5/30/86
Name changed to Westminster Capital, Inc. 7/13/92
(See Westminster Capital, Inc.)

FAR WEST GROUP INC (NV)
Name changed to Capacitive Deionization Technology Systems, Inc. 8/1/2001

FAR WEST INDUSTRIES, INC. (UT)
Name changed to Hudco Telecommunications, Inc. 11/02/1981
Hudco Telecommunications, Inc. name changed to Centauri Communications, Inc. 10/18/1982

FAR WEST INDS INC (BC)
Merged into Digital Dispatch Systems Inc. 11/04/2003
Each share Common no par exchanged for (0.05) share Common no par
Digital Dispatch Systems Inc. name changed to DDS Wireless International Inc. 03/05/2008
(See DDS Wireless International Inc.)

FAR WEST MINERALS, INC. (UT)
Recapitalized as Pacific Minerals & Chemical Inc. 6/24/94
Each share Common $0.001 par exchanged for (0.25) share Common $0.001 par
Pacific Minerals & Chemical Inc. recapitalized as Nevada Magic Holdings Inc. 1/7/97 which name changed to To4c Corp. (UT) 6/29/99 which reorganized in Nevada as Aplox Corp. 4/27/2001 which name changed to Mirador Inc. 7/25/2001 which recapitalized as VWAY International 7/5/2004 which name changed to WorldWide Cannery & Distribution, Inc. 2/8/2006 which name changed to Global Diamond Exchange Inc. 9/22/2006

FAR WEST MNG LTD (BC)
Reincorporated 05/17/2006
Place of incorporation changed from (AB) to (BC) 05/17/2006
Merged into Capstone Mining Corp. 06/17/2011
Each share Class A Common no par exchanged for (1.825) shares Common no par and $1 cash
Note: Unexchanged certificates were cancelled and became without value 06/17/2017

FAR WEST RES INC (UT)
Reincorporated under the laws of Nevada as American Alliance Corp. and Common $0.001 par changed to $0.00001 par 08/01/1997
American Alliance Corp. name changed to WhatsOnline.com, Inc. 05/14/1999 which name changed to Entheos Technologies Inc. 07/31/2000 which name changed to Janus Resources, Inc. 02/14/2011 which name changed to RenovaCare, Inc. 01/09/2014

FAR WEST VENTURES INC (NV)
Each share old Common $0.001 par automatically became (0.00052405) share new Common $0.001 par 03/30/1993
Name changed to Advanced Materials Group, Inc. 06/11/1993
Note: Certificates reflecting the reverse split and name change will be issued; all outstanding shares are without value
(See Advanced Materials Group, Inc.)

FAR WESTN BK (TUSTIN, CA)
Closed by the State Banking Department and the FDIC was appointed receiver 12/14/90
Stockholders' equity undetermined

FARADAY INC (DE)
Each share old Common 10¢ par exchanged for (0.002) share new Common 10¢ par 6/6/74
Merged into Fostoria Corp. 10/15/76
Each share Common 10¢ par exchanged for $83 cash

FARADAY LABS INC (NJ)
Common 1¢ par split (2) for (1) by issuance of (1) additional share 09/30/1983
Stock Dividend - 100% 12/20/1975
Merged into ICN Pharmaceuticals, Inc. 06/12/1987
Each share Common 1¢ par exchanged for $4.005 cash
Note: An additional $0.445 cash is being held in escrow for possible distribution in one year

FARADAY NATIONAL CORP. (DE)
Acquired by De La Rue Co. PLC 01/01/1993
Details not available

FARADAY RES INC (ON)
$1.20 Conv. Retractable 1st Preference Ser. A no par called for redemption 07/20/1993
Merged into Conwest Exploration Co. Ltd. (New) (AB) 09/01/1993
Each share Common no par exchanged for (0.42) share Common no par
Conwest Exploration Co. Ltd. (New) merged into Alberta Energy Co. Ltd. 01/31/1996 which merged into EnCana Corp. 01/03/2003

FARADAY URANIUM MINES LTD. (ON)
Recapitalized as Canadian Faraday Corp. Ltd. 12/23/1963
Each share Capital Stock $1 par exchanged for (0.4) share Capital Stock no par
Canadian Faraday Corp. Ltd. merged into Consolidated Canadian Faraday Ltd. 05/04/1967 which name changed to Faraday Resources Inc. 08/02/1983 which merged into Conwest Exploration Co. Ltd. (New) (AB) 09/01/1993 which merged into Alberta Energy Co. Ltd. 01/31/1996 which merged into EnCana Corp. 01/03/2003

FARADYNE ELECTRS CORP (NJ)
Common 5¢ par split (3) for (1) by issuance of (2) additional shares 04/01/1986
Name changed to Total-Tel U.S.A. Communications, Inc. 11/06/1991
Total-Tel U.S.A Communications, Inc. name changed to Covista Communications, Inc. 10/16/2000

FARAH INC (TX)
Name changed 3/10/87
Common $4 par split (2) for (1) by issuance of (1) additional share 1/29/71
Name changed from Farah Manufacturing Co., Inc. to Farah Inc. 3/10/87
Merged into Tropical Sportswear International Corp. 6/10/98
Each share Common $4 par exchanged for $9 cash

FARALLON COMMUNICATIONS INC (DE)
Name changed to Netopia, Inc. 11/17/97
(See Netopia, Inc.)

FARALLON MINING LTD (BC)
Acquired by Nyrstar N.V. 03/09/2011
Each share Common no par exchanged for $0.80 cash

FARALLON RES LTD (BC)
Name changed to Farallon Mining Ltd. 06/16/2009
(See Farallon Mining Ltd.)

FARALLONE PACKING CO.
Sold to Broval, Inc. in 1941
Details not available

FARATRON CORP (DE)
Charter cancelled and declared inoperative and void for non-payment of taxes 3/1/80

FARAWAY GOLD MINES LTD (BC)
Struck off register and declared dissolved for failure to file returns 07/09/1993

FARBENFABRIKEN BAYER A G (GERMANY)
Stock Dividend - 50% 06/02/1965
Name changed to Bayer AG 06/30/1972

FARBWERKE HOECHST A G (GERMANY)
Name changed to Hoechst AG 07/09/1974
Hoechst AG merged into Aventis 12/15/1999 which merged into Sanofi-Aventis 12/31/2004

FARCROFT MINES LTD. (ON)
Charter cancelled and company declared dissolved for default in filing returns 11/09/1964

FARED SYS INC (DE)
Reorganized 3/28/88
Each share Common $0.001 par

exchanged for (0.2) share Common no par 10/1/83
State of incorporation changed from (CO) to (DE), name changed from Fared Robot Systems, Inc. to Fared Systems, Inc. and Common no par changed to 1¢ par 3/28/88
Charter forfeited for failure to maintain a registered agent 10/29/91

FARGO CAPITAL CORP (BC)
Name changed to Pacific Coast Nickel Corp. 07/16/2007
Pacific Coast Nickel Corp. recapitalized as Prophecy Platinum Corp. 06/20/2011 which name changed to Wellgreen Platinum Ltd. 12/19/2013 which name changed to Nickel Creek Platinum Corp. 01/11/2018

FARGO ELECTRONICS INC (DE)
Issue Information - 5,000,000 shares COM offered at $15 per share on 02/10/2000
Merged into Assa Abloy, Inc. 8/3/2006
Each share Common 1¢ par exchanged for $25.50 cash

FARGO ENERGY CORP (NV)
Name changed to Western Reserves, Inc. 04/29/1983
Western Reserves, Inc. recapitalized as Great Western Equities Group, Inc. 06/10/1986 which name changed to American International Marketing, Inc. 09/21/1989

FARGO MNG CORP (WA)
Charter cancelled and proclaimed dissolved for failure to pay fees 07/02/1981

FARGO NATL BK & TR CO (FARGO, ND)
Through voluntary exchange offer 97% acquired by Northern Plains Bancshares, Inc. as of 12/28/1978
Public interest eliminated

FARGO NATIONAL BANK (FARGO, ND)
Name changed to Fargo National Bank & Trust Co. (Fargo, N.D.) 4/30/68
(See Fargo National Bank & Trust Co. (Fargo, N.D.))

FARGO OILS LTD. (AB)
Common no par changed to 25¢ par 00/00/1952
Class B Common $1 par changed to Common $1 par 08/16/1956
Common 25¢ par changed to $1 par 08/16/1956
Acquired by Reserve Oil & Gas Co. 06/10/1968
Each share Common $1 par exchanged for (0.43) share Common $1 par
(See Reserve Oil & Gas Co.)

FARGO RES LTD (BC)
Recapitalized as Lang Bay Resources Ltd. 09/13/1991
Each share Common no par exchanged for (0.25) share Common no par
Lang Bay Resources Ltd. recapitalized as Hibright Minerals Inc. 11/06/1995 which name changed to Frontier Pacific Mining Corp. 10/25/1996 which was acquired by Eldorado Gold Corp. (New) 07/15/2008

FARINI GROUP INC (ON)
Recapitalized as Farini Companies Inc. 09/08/1997
Each share Common no par exchanged for (0.1) share Common no par

FARINON CORP (CA)
Merged into Harris Corp. 02/15/1980
Each share Common no par exchanged for (0.8) share Common $1 par

FARINON ELECTRIC (CA)
Stock Dividend - 200% 5/17/72
Name changed to Farinon Corp. 5/24/77
Farinon Corp. merged into Harris Corp. 2/15/80

FARLAND APARTMENTS
Trust terminated in 1950
Details not available

FARLEY NORTHWEST INDS INC (DE)
Name changed to Fruit of the Loom, Inc. (DE) 02/26/1987
Fruit of the Loom, Inc. (DE) reincorporated in Cayman Islands 03/04/1999
(See Fruit of the Loom, Inc. (Cayman Islands))

FARM & HOME AGENCY, INC. (IN)
Completely liquidated 9/11/68
Each share Capital Stock $1 par received first and final distribution of $0.2254 cash
Certificates were not retired and are now without value

FARM & HOME FINL CORP (DE)
Recapitalized 09/30/1991
Each share 13% Exchangeable Preferred Ser. A 1¢ par exchanged for $35 principal amount of 13% Subordinated Debentures due 09/30/2016
Common $1 par split (3) for (2) by issuance of (0.5) additional share 06/18/1993
Merged into Roosevelt Financial Group, Inc. 06/30/1994
Each share Common $1 par exchanged for (2.01) shares Common 1¢ par
Roosevelt Financial Group, Inc. merged into Mercantile Bancorporation, Inc. 07/01/1997 which merged into Firstar Corp. (New) 09/20/1999 which merged into U.S. Bancorp (DE) 02/27/2001

FARM & HOME INSURANCE CO. (IN)
Acquired by Alexander National Group, Inc. 11/22/68
Each share Common 65¢ par exchanged for (1.75) shares Common 25¢ par
Alexander National Group, Inc. name changed to ANG, Inc. 2/2/81
(See ANG, Inc.)

FARM & HOME LIFE INS CO (AZ)
Stock Dividends - 10% 06/21/1965; 10% 06/20/1966; 10% 06/20/1967; 10% 06/20/1968; 10% 06/20/1969
Completely liquidated 08/05/1991
No stockholders' equity

FARM & HOME SVGS ASSN NEVADA (MO)
Reorganized under the laws of Delaware as Farm & Home Financial Corp. 10/24/88
Farm & Home Financial Corp. merged into Roosevelt Financial Group, Inc. 6/30/94 which merged into Mercantile Bancorporation, Inc. 7/1/97 which merged into Firstar Corp. (New) 9/20/99 which merged into U.S. Bancorp (New) 2/27/2001

FARM & RANCH FINL INC (KS)
Completely liquidated 10/19/1979
Each share Common no par exchanged for first and final distribution of $10.50 cash

FARM BUR GROWTH FD INC (MD)
Name changed to FBL Series Fund, Inc. and Capital Stock $1 par reclassified as Growth Common Stock Portfolio Common $0.001 par 12/01/1987
FBL Series Fund, Inc. name changed to EquiTrust Series Fund, Inc. 05/01/1998

FARM BUR LIFE INS CO MICH (MI)
Class A Common called for redemption at $100 on 11/16/2009

FARM BUR MUT FD INC (MD)
Merged into Challenger Investment Fund, Inc. 04/28/1977
Each share Capital Stock $1 par exchanged for (80.61) shares Capital Stock $1 par
Challenger Investment Fund, Inc. name changed to Farm Bureau Growth Fund, Inc. 07/31/1978 which name changed to FBL Series Fund, Inc. 12/01/1987 which name changed to EquiTrust Series Fund, Inc. 05/01/1998

FARM CREST BAKERIES, INC. (DE)
Merged into Ward Foods, Inc. 12/25/65
Each share Common $1 par exchanged for (1) share Common $1 par
4% Preferred $100 par called for redemption 1/1/66
(See Ward Foods, Inc.)

FARM ENERGY CORP (AB)
Name changed to High Energy Ventures Inc. 02/09/2001
(See High Energy Ventures Inc.)

FARM EQUIPMENT ACCEPTANCE CORP. (IL)
Each share Common $50 par exchanged for (5) shares Common $10 par 00/00/1953
Acquired by Atkinson Finance Corp. 03/00/1959
Each share Common $10 par exchanged for $12.50 cash

FARM FAMILY HLDGS INC (DE)
Issue Information - 2,786,000 shares COM offered at $16 per share on 07/23/1996
Merged into America National Insurance Co. 4/10/2001
Each share Common 1¢ par exchanged for $44 cash

FARM FISH INC (MS)
Completely liquidated
Each share Common no par received first and final distribution of $0.52 cash payable 1/26/2004 to holders of record 1/15/2004 Ex date - 3/5/2004
Note: Certificates were not required to be surrendered and are without value

FARM FRESH INC (VA)
Common 1¢ par split (3) for (2) by issuance of (0.5) additional share 7/12/83
Merged into FF Holdings Corp. 9/27/88
Each share Common 1¢ par exchanged for $3 principal amount of 16.5% Subordinated Debentures due 9/15/2004 and $10.50 cash

FARM HAND, INC. (UT)
Recapitalized as Old Yeller, Inc. 02/09/1983
Each share Capital Stock $0.001 par exchanged for (0.2) share Common $0.001 par
(See Old Yeller, Inc.)

FARM HOUSE FOODS CORP (WI)
Common 5¢ par split (5) for (4) by issuance of (0.25) additional share 10/10/1972
Common 5¢ par split (2) for (1) by issuance of (1) additional share 08/15/1975
Common 5¢ par split (3) for (2) by issuance of (0.5) additional share 04/15/1976
Common 5¢ par split (5) for (4) by issuance of (0.25) additional share 11/14/1977
Common 5¢ par split (5) for (4) by issuance of (0.25) additional share 01/26/1981
Conv. Preferred Ser. A $1 par called for redemption 02/24/1981
Stock Dividends - 10% 09/29/1978; 10% 03/30/1979; 10% 11/27/1981; 10% 11/11/1982
Administratively dissolved 04/06/1993

FARM LDS GUINEA INC (NV)
Name changed to Farm Lands of Africa, Inc. 03/28/2012

FARM SALES & MORTGAGE CO.
Liquidated in 1942

FARMACIA CORP (NV)
Common $0.0001 par split (33) for (1) by issuance of (32) additional shares payable 01/07/2013 to holders of record 01/07/2013
Ex date - 01/08/2013
Name changed to American Copper Corp. 01/14/2013
American Copper Corp. name changed to Black River Petroleum Corp. 11/04/2013 which name changed to Viva Entertainment Group, Inc. 08/02/2016

FARMAX INDIA LTD (INDIA)
GDR basis changed from (1:5) to (1:25) 08/05/2010
GDR agreement terminated 06/15/2015
Each Sponsored GDR for Equity Shares exchanged for (25) Equity Shares
Note: Unexchanged GDR's will be sold and the proceeds, if any, held for claim after 06/18/2015

FARMER BROS CO (CA)
Common $1 par split (3) for (2) by issuance of (0.5) additional share 05/03/1976
Common $1 par split (10) for (1) by issuance of (9) additional shares payable 05/10/2004 to holders of record 04/42/2004
Stock Dividends - 15% 12/28/1953; 10% 12/28/1956
Reincorporated under the laws of Delaware 02/24/2004

FARMER IN THE DELL ENTERPRISES DEL INC (DE)
Charter cancelled and declared inoperative and void for non-payment of taxes 6/29/83

FARMERS & MECHANICS BK (MIDDLETOWN, CT)
Merged into Citizens Financial Group, Inc. 11/6/96
Each share Common 1¢ par exchanged for $32 cash

FARMERS & MECHANICS-CITIZENS NATIONAL BANK (FREDERICK, MD)
Each share Common $25 par exchanged for (6) shares Common $10 par to effect a (2-1/2) for (1) split and a 140% stock dividend 01/31/1953
Stock Dividend - 60% 01/05/1960
Name changed to Farmers & Mechanics National Bank (Frederick, MD) 04/25/1963
Farmers & Mechanics National Bank (Frederick, MD) reorganized as F&M Bancorp 07/01/1984 which merged into Mercantile Bankshares Corp. 08/12/2003 which merged into PNC Financial Services Group, Inc. 03/02/2007

FARMERS & MECHANICS NATL BK (FREDERICK, MD)
Common $10 par changed to $5 par and (1) additional share issued 02/10/1971
Common $5 par split (3) for (2) by issuance of (0.5) additional share 11/08/1974
Stock Dividend - 20% 02/28/1966
Reorganized as F&M Bancorp 07/01/1984
Each share Common $5 par exchanged for (1) share Common $5 par
F&M Bancorp merged into Mercantile Bankshares Corp. 08/12/2003 which merged into PNC Financial Services Group, Inc. 03/02/2007

FARMERS & MERCHANTS BANK, INC. (AMHERST, VA)
Merged into First Virginia Banks, Inc. 1/2/81
Each share Common $2.50 par exchanged for (1.8) shares Common $1 par
First Virginia Banks, Inc. merged into BB&T Corp. 7/1/2003

FARMERS & MERCHANTS BANK & TRUST CO. (TULSA, OK)
Stock Dividends - 14.2857% 06/30/1969; 10% 00/00/1970
Name changed to F&M Bank & Trust Co. (Tulsa, OK) 02/02/1971
F&M Bank & Trust Co. (Tulsa, OK) reorganized as F & M Bancorporation, Inc. (OK) 04/17/1975 which reincorporated in Delaware 09/00/2003

FARMERS & MERCHANTS BK (HANNIBAL, MO)
Under plan of reorganization each share Common 1¢ par automatically became (1) share Farmers & Merchants Bancorp, Inc. Common 1¢ par 01/29/1999

FARMERS & MERCHANTS BK (HONESDALE, PA)
Merged into Harleysville National Corp. 03/01/1996
Each share Common $10 par exchanged for (0.619) share Common $1 par
Harleysville National Corp. merged into First Niagara Financial Group, Inc. (New) 04/09/2010 which merged into KeyCorp (New) 08/01/2016

FARMERS & MERCHANTS BK (KEYSER, WV)
Merged into F & M National Corp. 6/1/92
Each share Common $25 par exchanged for (1.988) shares Common $2 par
F & M National Corp. merged into BB&T Corp. 8/9/2001

FARMERS & MERCHANTS BK (MORGANTOWN, WV)
Reorganized as Financial Management Bancshares of West Virginia, Inc. 11/15/1983
Each share Common $5 par exchanged for (1) share Common $5 par
Financial Management Bancshares of West Virginia, Inc. acquired by One Valley Bancorp of West Virginia, Inc. 07/31/1986 which name changed to One Valley Bancorp, Inc. 04/30/1996 which merged into BB&T Corp. 07/06/2000

FARMERS & MERCHANTS BK (STATESBORO, GA)
Under plan of reorganization each share Common $1 par automatically became (1) share FMB Equibanc, Inc. Common $10 par 11/01/2000

FARMERS & MERCHANTS BK (SUMMERVILLE, GA)
Merged into Premier Bancshares Inc. 11/9/99
Each share Common exchanged for (4.028) shares Common $1 par
Premier Bancshares Inc. merged into BB&T Corp. 1/13/2000

FARMERS & MERCHANTS BK (UPPERCO, MD)
Common $10 par split (5) for (4) by issuance of (0.25) additional share payable 10/29/1999 to holders of record 10/01/1999
Common $10 par split (2) for (1) by issuance of (1) additional share payable 10/11/2013 to holders of record 09/10/2013 Ex date - 10/14/2013
Stock Dividends - 1% payable 06/29/2001 to holders of record 05/25/2001 Ex date - 06/01/2001; 1.16% payable 06/30/2003 to holders of record 05/30/2003 Ex date - 06/09/2003; 20% payable 09/15/2004 to holders of record 08/27/2004 Ex date - 08/25/2004
Under plan of reorganization each share Common $10 par automatically became (1) share Farmers & Merchants Bancshares, Inc. Common $10 par 11/02/2016

FARMERS & MERCHANTS BK CENT CALIF (LODI, CA)
Common $20 par changed to $10 par and (1) additional share issued plus a 20% stock dividend paid in January 1961
Preferred $100 par called for redemption 3/31/65
Common $10 par changed to $5 par and (1) additional share issued 3/7/75
Stock Dividends - 16-2/3% January 1963; 14-2/7% March 1968; 12-1/2% 3/3/69; 11-1/9% 3/2/70; 5% payable 5/20/96 to holders of record 4/2/96; 5% payable 5/18/98 to holders of record 4/7/98
Under plan of reorganization each share Common 1¢ par automatically became (1) share Farmers & Merchants Bancorp (DE) Common 1¢ par 4/30/99

FARMERS & MERCHANTS BANK-EASTERN SHORE (ONLEY, VA)
Merged into Mercantile Bankshares Corp. 11/30/1990
Each share Capital Stock $5 par exchanged for (2.133) shares Common $2 par
Mercantile Bankshares Corp. merged into PNC Financial Services Group, Inc. 03/02/2007

FARMERS & MERCHANTS BANK OF SOUTHERN COUNTIES (LONG BEACH, CA)
Acquired by Farmers & Merchants Bank (Long Beach, Calif.) for cash 4/13/62

FARMERS & MERCHANTS COMPRESS & WAREHOUSE CO. (DE)
In process of liquidation
Each share Common $5 par exchanged for initial distribution of $2.41 cash 07/00/1980
Note: Details on additional distribution(s), if any, are not available

FARMERS & MERCHANTS NATIONAL BANK (ABILENE, TX)
Stock Dividend - 100% 1/22/54
Name changed to First National Bank (Abilene, TX) 6/28/57
First National Bank (Abilene, TX) merged into First Abilene Bankshares, Inc. 4/24/73 which name changed to First Financial Bankshares, Inc. 10/26/93

FARMERS & MERCHANTS NATL BK (BENTON HARBOR, MI)
Common $20 par changed to $10 par and split (2) for (1) plus a (1) for (8) stock dividend paid effected by exchange of each share Common $20 par for (2.125) shares Common $10 par 10/01/1964
Stock Dividends - 100% 03/17/1944; 33-1/3% 12/11/1944; 100% 01/13/1955; 50% 07/07/1970
Through voluntary Exchange Offer over 98% acquired by National Detroit Corp. as of 01/02/1980
Public interest eliminated

FARMERS & MERCHANTS NATL BK (BRIDGETON, NJ)
Common $20 par changed to $5 par and (3) additional shares issued 02/01/1972
Stock Dividends - 25% 01/22/1958; 20% 10/31/1960; 33-1/3% 12/09/1963; 50% 01/24/1969; 100% 09/10/1974
Reorganized as Southern Jersey Bancorp 05/22/1984
Each share Common $5 par exchanged for (1) share Common $5 par
Southern Jersey Bancorp merged into Hudson United Bancorp 12/01/1999 which which merged into TD Banknorth Inc. 01/31/2006
(See TD Banknorth Inc.)

FARMERS & MERCHANTS NATL BK (MATAWAN, NJ)
Common $1 par changed to $1.50 par 2/27/70
Merged into Franklin State Bank (Franklin Township, NJ) 8/23/71
Each share Common $1.50 par exchanged for (0.526315) share Capital Stock $3.50 par
(See Franklin State Bank (Franklin Township, NJ))

FARMERS & MERCHANTS NATL BK (WINCHESTER, VA)
Under plan of reorganization each share Capital Stock $10 par automatically became (1) share F & M National Corp. Common $2 par 1/1/70
F & M National Corp. merged into BB&T Corp. 8/9/2001

FARMERS & MERCHANTS ST BK (FREDERICKSBURG, VA)
Each share Common $50 par exchanged for (5) shares Common $10 par 8/27/49
Common $10 par changed to $5 par and (1) additional share issued in March 1969
Stock Dividends - 10% 11/15/66; 100% 3/31/72
Merged into First Virginia Bank (Falls Church, VA) 6/6/83
Each share Common $5 par exchanged for $79 cash

FARMERS & MERCHANTS STATE BANK (TULSA, OK)
Capital Stock $20 par changed to $10 par and (1) additional share issued 00/00/1961
Stock Dividends - 66-2/3% 10/23/1951; 20% 09/13/1954; 20% 00/00/1956; 16-2/3% 00/00/1958; 14-2/7% 06/30/1959; 25% 00/00/1961
Name changed to Farmers & Merchants Bank & Trust Co. (Tulsa, OK) 04/08/1965
Farmers & Merchants Bank & Trust Co. (Tulsa, OK) name changed to F&M Bank & Trust Co. (Tulsa, OK) 02/02/1971 which reorganized as F & M Bancorporation, Inc. (OK) 04/17/1975 which reincorporated in Delaware 09/00/2003

FARMERS & MERCHANTS TRUST CO. LTD. (CALGARY, AB)
Name changed to Farmers & Merchants Trust Co.-La Campagnie Trust Farmers & Merchants (Calgary, AB) 06/17/1975
Farmers & Merchants Trust Co.-La Compagnie Trust Farmers & Merchants (Calgary, AB) name changed to Commerce Capital Trust Co.-Compagnie Trust Commerce Capital (Calgary, AB) 11/01/1976 which name changed to Eaton Bay Trust Co. (Calgary, AB) 05/05/1981 which name changed to Eaton Trust Co. (Calgary, AB) 11/13/1985 which merged into Laurentian Bank of Canada (Montreal, QC) 02/04/1988

FARMERS & MERCHANTS TR CO (CALGARY, ALTA)
Name changed to Commerce Capital Trust Co.-Compagnie Trust Commerce Capital (Calgary, Alta.) 11/1/76
Commerce Capital Trust Co.-Compagnie Trust Commerce Capital (Calgary, Alta.) name changed to Eaton Bay Trust Co. (Calgary, Alta.) 5/5/81 which name changed to Eaton Trust Co. (Calgary, Alta.) 11/13/85 which merged into Laurentian Bank of Canada (Montreal, Que.) 2/4/88

FARMERS & MERCHANTS TR CO (CHAMBERSBURG, PA)
Stock Dividends - 33-1/3% 02/24/1961; 10% 01/29/1966; 20% 02/20/1969; 10% 00/00/1971; 10% 03/20/1973; 10% 03/15/1975
Under plan of reorganization each share Common $10 par automatically became (1) share Franklin Financial Services Corp. Common $10 par 01/16/1984

FARMERS & MERCHANTS UN BK (COLUMBUS, WI)
Under plan of reorganization each share Common automatically became (1) share Jewel Box Financial Services, Inc. Common 03/06/1998

FARMERS & TRADERS LIFE INSURANCE CO. (NY)
Pursuant to 20 year plan of mutualization 100% acquired by the company as of 10/17/74

FARMERS BANC CORP (NJ)
Merged into Susquehanna Bancshares, Inc. 02/28/1997
Each share Common $10 par exchanged for (2.281) shares Common $2 par
Susquehanna Bancshares, Inc. merged into BB&T Corp. 08/01/2015

FARMERS BANCSHARES INC (LA)
Company's sole asset placed in receivership 12/17/2002
Stockholders' equity unlikely

FARMERS BANK & TRUST CO. (HENDERSON, KY)
Merged into Old National Bancorp 11/1/90
Each share Common $50 par exchanged for (28) shares Common no par

FARMERS BANK & TRUST CO. (LANCASTER, PA)
Merged into Lancaster County Farmers National Bank (Lancaster, PA) 12/11/1963
Each share Capital Stock $10 par exchanged for (1) share Common $10 par
Lancaster County Farmers National Bank (Lancaster, PA) merged into National Central Bank (Lancaster, PA) 12/07/1970 which reorganized as National Central Financial Corp. 12/31/1972 which merged into CoreStates Financial Corp 05/02/1983 which merged into First Union Corp. 04/28/1998 which name changed to Wachovia Corp. (Ctfs. dated after 09/01/2001) 09/01/2001 which merged into Wells Fargo & Co. (New) 12/31/2008

FARMERS BK & TR CO (HANOVER, PA)
Stock Dividend - 20% 6/1/67
Acquired by FB&T Corp. 11/13/1981
Each share Capital Stock $50 par exchanged for (1) share Common $1 par
FB&T Corp. merged into Dauphin Deposit Corp. 07/01/1992 which merged into Allied Irish Banks, PLC 07/08/1997

FARMERS BK & TR CO (HUMMELSTOWN, PA)
Acquired by Dauphin Deposit Corp. 04/01/1988
Each share Capital Stock $10 par exchanged for (15.9) shares Common $5 par

Dauphin Deposit Corp. merged into Allied Irish Banks, PLC 07/08/1997
(See Allied Irish Banks, PLC)

FARMERS BK & TR CO (INDIANA, PA)
Liquidation completed
Each share Common $10 par exchanged for initial distribution of $110 cash 11/20/1973
Each share Common $10 par received second and final distribution of $61.36 cash 01/14/1974

FARMERS BK (WINDSOR, VA)
Under plan of reorganization each share Common $0.625 par automatically became (1) share Farmers Bankshares, Inc. Common $0.625 par 04/01/2014

FARMERS BK MARDELA SPRINGS (MARDELA SPRINGS, MD)
Merged into Mercantile Bankshares Corp. 07/01/1997
Each share Common no par exchanged for (1.875) shares Common $2 par
Mercantile Bankshares Corp. merged into PNC Financial Services Group, Inc. 03/02/2007

FARMERS BANK OF NANSEMOND (SUFFOLK, VA)
Merged into Seaboard Citizens National Bank (Norfolk, VA) 10/18/63
Each share Capital Stock $100 par exchanged for (1) share Capital Stock $5 par
Seaboard Citizens National Bank (Norfolk, VA) merged into United Virginia Bankshares, Inc. 1/1/67 which name changed to Crestar Financial Corp. 9/1/87 which merged into SunTrust Banks, Inc. 12/31/98

FARMERS BK ST DEL (DOVER, DE)
Each share Capital Stock $50 par exchanged for (10) shares Capital Stock $5 par 10/1/58
Stock Dividends - 200% 8/26/63; 11-1/9% 5/7/65; 20% 5/16/66; 100% 5/15/68
Acquired by Girard Co. 12/30/81
Each share Capital Stock $5 par exchanged for $23.25 cash

FARMERS BKG CO (LAKEVIEW, OH)
Reorganized as FBC Bancshares, Inc. 05/31/1985
Each share Common $5 par exchanged for (1) share Common $5 par
FBC Bancshares, Inc. acquired by Mid Am, Inc. 06/09/1989 which merged into Sky Financial Group, Inc. 10/02/1998 which merged into Huntington Bancshares Inc. 07/02/2007

FARMERS CAP BK CORP (KY)
Common $1.25 par changed to 25¢ par and (4) additional shares issued 07/01/1987
Common 25¢ par changed to $0.125 par and (1) additional share issued payable 07/01/1998 to holders of record 06/01/1998
Fixed Rate Preferred Ser. A no par called for redemption at $1,000 plus $5.75 accrued dividends on 06/08/2015
Merged into Wesbanco, Inc. 08/20/2018
Each share Common $0.125 par exchanged for (1.053) shares Common $2.0833 par and $5 cash

FARMERS FIRST BK (LITITZ, PA)
Under plan of reorganization each share Common $5 par automatically became (1) share Susquehanna Bancshares, Inc. 09/08/1982
Susquehanna Bancshares, Inc. merged into BB&T Corp. 08/01/2015

FARMERS FIRST NATIONAL BANK (LITITZ, PA)
Common $10 par changed to $5 par and (1) additional share issued 04/00/1974
Name changed to Farmers First Bank (Lititz, PA) 07/01/1974
Farmers First Bank (Lititz, PA) reorganized as Susquehanna Bancshares, Inc. 09/08/1982 which merged into BB&T Corp. 08/01/2015

FARMERS GROUP CAP (DE)
8.45% Guaranteed Quarterly Income Preferred Securities Ser. A no par called for redemption at $25 on 11/25/2003

FARMERS GROUP CAP II (DE)
Guaranteed Quarterly Income Preferred Securities called for redemption at $25 on 11/25/2003

FARMERS GROUP INC (NV)
Each share $3 Conv. Preferred $1 par exchanged for (3) shares Common $1 par 03/12/1976
Common $1 par split (2) for (1) by issuance of (1) additional share 06/10/1986
Stock Dividends - 200% 02/11/1972; 200% 07/16/1976
Acquired by B.A.T. Industries PLC 12/16/1988
Each share Common $1 par exchanged for $75 cash

FARMERS GROUP PURCHASING INC (KS)
Through purchase offer 100% acquired by FGP Holding Co., Inc. 00/00/1971
Public interest eliminated

FARMERS HYBRID COMPANIES, INC. (IA)
Acquired by Monsanto Co. 6/30/69
Each share Common no par exchanged for (0.2) share Common $2 par
Monsanto Co. name changed to Pharmacia Corp. 3/31/2000 which merged into Pfizer Inc. 4/16/2003

FARMERS LIQUIDATING CORP.
Liquidation completed in 1945

FARMERS LUMBER CO. (IA)
Charter cancelled for failure to file annual reports 4/4/85

FARMERS NATL BANCORP (MD)
Common $10 par split (2) for (1) by issuance of (1) additional share 11/1/83
Common $10 par split (2) for (1) by issuance of (1) additional share 5/28/86
Stock Dividend - 100% 12/15/87
Merged into First Virginia Banks, Inc. 12/28/94
Each share Common $10 par exchanged for (1.5) shares Common $1 par
First Virginia Banks, Inc. merged into BB&T Corp. 7/1/2003

FARMERS NATL BANCORP INC (DE)
Merged into Norwest Corp. 03/24/1997
Each share Common $5 par exchanged for (1.971657) shares Common $1-2/3 par
Norwest Corp. name changed to Wells Fargo & Co. (New) 11/02/1998

FARMERS NATL BANCORP INC (PA)
Merged into ACNB Corp. 3/1/99
Each share Common no par exchanged for (2.266) shares Common $2.50 par

FARMERS NATL BK & TR CO (ASHTABULA, OH)
Stock Dividends - 10% 5/3/66; 10% 5/31/67; 10% 5/31/68
Merged into Society Corp. 8/15/70
Each (2.25) shares Capital Stock $20 par exchanged for (1) share $4.50 Conv. Preferred Ser. C $100 par Society Corp. merged into KeyCorp (New) 3/1/94

FARMERS NATL BK (ANNAPOLIS, MD)
Stock Dividends - 100% 2/27/70; 50% 6/28/73; 28.2% 8/10/76; 25% 2/7/78; 20% 10/7/80
Reorganized as Farmers National Bancorp 8/1/82
Each share Capital Stock $10 par exchanged for (1) share Common $10 par
Farmers National Bancorp merged into First Virginia Banks, Inc. 12/28/94 which merged into BB&T Corp. 7/1/2003

FARMERS NATIONAL BANK (BEAVER FALLS, PA)
Merged into Union National Bank (Pittsburgh, PA) 12/04/1959
Each share Capital Stock $20 par exchanged for (1.43) shares Common $10 par
Union National Bank (Pittsburgh, PA) reorganized as Union National Corp. 02/08/1982 which merged into Integra Financial Corp. 01/26/1989 which merged into National City Corp. 05/03/1996 which was acquired by PNC Financial Services Group, Inc. 12/31/2008

FARMERS NATL BK (SALEM, OH)
Stock Dividends - 10% 05/15/1953; 25% 12/15/1969
Merged into First Steuben Bancorp, Inc. 01/02/1974
Each share Common $25 par exchanged for (4.825) shares Common $5 par
First Steuben Bancorp, Inc. name changed to Heritage Bancorp, Inc. 04/05/1979 which merged into Banc One Corp. (DE) 04/01/1983 which reincorporated in Ohio 05/01/1989 which merged into Bank One Corp. 10/02/1998 which merged into J.P. Morgan Chase & Co. 12/31/2004 which name changed to JPMorgan Chase & Co. 07/20/2004

FARMERS NATIONAL BANK (SALINA, KS)
Name changed to First National Bank & Trust Co. (Salina, KS) 01/01/1963

FARMERS NATIONAL BANK (WINCHESTER, TN)
Merged into Hamilton Bancshares, Inc. 1/28/74
Each share Common $5 par exchanged for (3) shares Common no par
(See Hamilton Bancshares, Inc.)

FARMERS NATL LIFE INS CO (FL)
Reincorporated 06/04/1965
Common $2.50 par changed to $1 par and (1.5) additional shares issued 03/22/1965
State of incorporation changed from (GA) to (FL) 06/04/1965
Proclaimed dissolved for failure to file reports and pay fees 12/01/1977

FARMERS NEW WORLD LIFE INS CO (WA)
Capital Stock $10 par changed to $1 par and (9) additional shares issued 4/29/65
Stock Dividends - 10% 8/6/65; 100% 9/16/68; 25% 6/25/71
Merged into Farmers Group, Inc. 12/21/77
Each share Capital Stock $1 par exchanged for (2.3) shares Common $1 par
(See Farmers Group, Inc.)

FARMERS SVGS & TR CO (MANSFIELD, OH)
First Banc Group of Ohio, Inc. acquired all except directors qualifying shares through voluntary exchange offer as of 09/15/1968
Public interest eliminated

FARMERS SVGS BK (NORTHWOOD, OH)
Acquired by Mid Am, Inc. 06/04/1994
Details not available

FARMERS SAVINGS BANK CO. (STONY RIDGE, OH)
Name changed to Farmers Savings Bank (Stony Ridge, Ohio) 1/9/74

FARMERS ST BANCORP (OH)
Merged into ANB Corp. 4/22/99
Each share Common no par exchanged for (5.4) shares Common no par
ANB Corp. merged into Old National Bancorp 3/13/2000

FARMERS ST BK (NEW WASHINGTON, OH)
Merged into First Citizens Banc Corp. 04/28/1998
Each share Common $20 par exchanged for (6.06) shares Common no par
First Citizens Banc Corp. Name changed to Civista Bancshares, Inc. 05/04/2015

FARMERS STANDARD CARBIDE CO., INC. (NY)
Proclaimed dissolved for failure to file reports and pay fees 12/16/29

FARMERS STATE BANK (FARMERSVILLE, CA)
Name changed to United Valley Bank (Farmersville, CA) 11/9/87
(See United Valley Bank (Farmersville, CA))

FARMERS TITLE GUARANTEE & MORTGAGE CO. (NY)
Liquidated in 1936

FARMERS TR CO (CARLISLE, PA)
Common $10 par changed to $3.33-1/3 par and (2) additional shares issued 11/15/73
Common $3.33-1/3 par changed to $5 par 4/10/79
Stock Dividends - 100% 4/15/66; 100% 10/1/70
Under plan of reorganization each share Common $5 par automatically became (1) share Financial Trans Corp. Common $5 par 11/3/82
Financial Trans Corp. name changed to Financial Trust Corp. 5/16/85 which merged into Keystone Financial, Inc. 5/30/97 which merged into M&T Bank Corp. 10/6/2000

FARMERS TR CO (LEBANON, PA)
Common $25 par changed to $5 par and (4) additional shares issued 01/31/1969
Stock Dividend - 10% 11/18/1975
Merged into Fulton Financial Corp. 01/31/1984
Each share Common $5 par exchanged for (5) shares Common $2.50 par

FARMERS UNDERWRITERS ASSN (NV)
Common $1 par split (5) for (4) by issuance of (0.25) additional share 6/11/65
Stock Dividend - 10% 9/1/54
Under plan of merger name changed to Farmers Group, Inc. 12/31/70
(See Farmers Group, Inc.)

FARMERS UNION CENTRAL WAREHOUSE CO., LTD. (LA)
Charter revoked for failure to file annual reports 10/1/85

FARMERS UNION COOPERATIVE MARKETING ASSOCIATION (KS)
Merged into Far-Mar-Co., Inc. 05/31/1968
Each share 6% Class A Preferred $10 par or Class B Preferred $10 par exchanged for (1) share Preferred $10 par
Each share Common $10 par exchanged for (0.1) share Common $100 par

(See Far-Mar-Co., Inc.)

FARMERS UNION TELEPHONE CO. (WI)
Name changed to Mid-Plains Telephone, Inc. 3/19/66
Mid-Plains Telephone, Inc. name changed to Mid-Plains Inc. 4/29/96 which name changed to Chorus Communications Group Ltd. 6/1/97
(See Chorus Communications Group Ltd.)

FARMHAND INC (DE)
Merged into Arizona-Colorado Land & Cattle Co. 06/09/1972
Each share Common no par exchanged for (1.25) shares $0.48 Conv. Preferred Ser. A no par
Arizona-Colorado Land & Cattle Co. name changed to AZL Resources, Inc. 05/17/1977
(See AZL Resources, Inc.)

FARMINGTON VALLEY SAVINGS & LOAN ASSOCIATION (CT)
Stock Dividend - 25% 11/22/85
Merged into Bank of New England Corp. 12/24/86
Each share Common $5 par exchanged for (0.95) share Common $5 par
(See Bank of New England Corp.)

FARMINGTON VALLEY TELEPHONE CO.
Property sold to Southern New England Telephone Co. in 1939
(See Southern New England Telephone Co.)

FARMLAND INDS INC (KS)
2% 3rd Preferred $25 par called for redemption 08/01/1975
Plan of reorganization under Chapter 11 Federal Bankruptcy Code effective 05/01/2004
Each share 5.5% Preferred $25 par exchanged for approximately $5 cash
Each share 6% Preferred $25 par exchanged for approximately $5 cash
No stockholders' equity for Common $25 par
Note: Unexchanged certificates were cancelled and became without value 04/30/2005

FARMSTEAD INTL CORP (DE)
Recapitalized as FIC Acquisition Corp. 10/9/92
Each share Common 1¢ par exchanged for (0.01) share Common 10¢ par
FIC Acquisition Corp. name changed to Florida West Airlines, Inc. 7/7/93
(See Florida West Airlines, Inc.)

FARMSTEAD TEL GROUP INC (DE)
Each share old Common $0.001 par exchanged for (0.1) share new Common $0.001 par 08/13/1996
Name changed to One IP Voice, Inc. 07/31/2006
(See One IP Voice, Inc.)

FARNELL ELECTRONICS PLC (UNITED KINGDOM)
Name changed to Premier Farnell PLC 4/11/96
(See Premier Farnell PLC)

FARNSWORTH BANCORP INC (NJ)
Stock Dividends - 20% payable 08/28/2003 to holders of record 08/18/2003 Ex date - 08/14/2003; 20% payable 04/08/2004 to holders of record 03/29/2004 Ex date - 03/25/2004
Merged into Sterling Banks, Inc. 03/19/2007
Each share Common 10¢ par exchanged for (0.59043026) share Common $2 par and $20.62726679 cash
(See Sterling Banks, Inc.)

FARNSWORTH TELEVISION, INC.
Reorganized as Farnsworth Television & Radio Corp. 00/00/1939
Details not available

FARNSWORTH TELEVISION & RADIO CORP.
Name changed to F.A.R. Liquidating Corp. 00/00/1949
(See F.A.R. Liquidating Corp.)

FAROUDJA INC (DE)
Issue Information - 3,000,000 shares COM offered at $6 per share on 10/30/1997
Merged into Sage Inc. 6/7/2000
Each share Common $0.001 par exchanged for (0.285) share Common 1¢ par
Sage Inc. merged into Genesis Microchip Inc. (DE) 2/20/2002

FARQUHAR (A.B.) CO.
Acquired by Oliver Corp. in 1951
Each share Common $5 par exchanged for (0.25) share Common $1 par
Oliver Corp. name changed to Cletrac Corp. 10/31/60 which merged into Hess Oil & Chemical Corp. 5/23/62 which merged into Amerada Hess Corp. 6/20/69 which name changed to Hess Corp. 5/3/2006

FARR ALPACA CO.
Liquidation completed in 1942

FARR CO (DE)
Reincorporated 6/5/87
Common $1 par changed to 10¢ par and (0.25) additional share issued 6/20/86
Stock Dividends - 20% 9/20/77; 20% 9/24/80; 20% 6/17/83
State of incorporation changed from (CA) to (DE) 6/5/87
Common 10¢ par split (5) for (4) by issuance of (0.25) additional share 9/7/90
Common 10¢ par split (3) for (2) by issuance of (0.5) additional share payable 3/28/97 to holders of record 3/7/97
Common 10¢ par split (3) for (2) by issuance of (0.5) additional share payable 5/29/98 to holders of record 5/8/98
Merged into Forvaltnings AB Ratos 5/8/2000
Each share Common 10¢ par exchanged for $17.45 cash

FARRAGUT BUILDING TRUST (MA)
Name changed to Farragut Real Estate Trust in 1948

FARRAGUT MTG INC (MA)
Name changed to Merchants Mortgage Co., Inc. 3/1/90 which name changed back to Farragut Mortgage Co., Inc. 3/4/91
Each (2.53837) shares old Common 10¢ par exchanged for (1) share new Common 10¢ par 2/25/92
Proclaimed dissolved for failure to file reports and pay taxes 8/31/98

FARRAH RES LTD (BC)
Struck off register and declared dissolved for failure to file returns 09/26/1988

FARREL-BIRMINGHAM CO., INC. (CT)
Each share Common $25 par exchanged for (2) shares Common $12.50 par in 1948
Stock Dividend - 10% 12/27/61
Name changed to Farrel Corp. 4/1/63
Farrel Corp. merged int USM Corp. 12/31/68
(See USM Corp.)

FARREL CORP (CT)
Stock Dividends - 100% 9/1/64; 10% 2/1/68
Merged into USM Corp. 12/31/68
Each share Common $12.50 par exchanged for (1) share $2.10 Conv. Preference no par
Each VTC for Common $12.50 par exchanged for (1) share $2.10 Conv. Preference no par
(See USM Corp.)

FARREL CORP (DE)
Merged into a private investor group 02/23/2007
Each share Common 1¢ par exchanged for $2.75 cash
Note: An additional distribution of $0.25 cash per share was made from escrow 03/01/2010

FARRELL OILS LTD. (AB)
Struck off register and proclaimed dissolved 11/29/1958

FARRIE (VAUGHAN E.), INC. (NY)
Charter cancelled and proclaimed dissolved for failure to pay taxes and file reports 12/15/66

FARRIER INDS INC (PA)
Filed petition in bankruptcy 00/00/1978
Trustee in Bankruptcy opined no stockholders' equity

FARRINGTON BK (NORTH BRUNSWICK, NJ)
Merged into United National Bancorp 2/28/97
Each share Common $5 par exchanged for (0.7647) share Common $2.50 par
(See United National Bancorp)

FARRINGTON MANUFACTURING CO. (MA)
5-1/2% Preferred $50 par changed to $25 par in 1953
Recapitalized in 1954
5-1/2% Preferred $25 par reclassified as $1.375 Preferred no par
Class A Common $10 par changed to $1 par
Common $10 par changed to $1 par
Class A Common $1 par reclassified as Common $1 par 12/22/58
Common $1 par changed to no par and (3) additional shares issued 3/1/60
$1.375 Preferred no par called for redemption 12/18/68
5-1/2% 2nd Preferred $5 par called for redemption 12/19/68
Reincorporated under the laws of Delaware 6/20/69
(See Farrington Manufacturing Co. (DE))

FARRINGTON MFG CO (DE)
Declared insolvent 11/26/71
No stockholders' equity

FARROW INC. (NV)
Recapitalized as Ener Craft, Inc. 5/4/88
Each share Common 1¢ par exchanged for (0.25) share Common $0.001 par
(See Ener Craft, Inc.)

FARWELL ST SVGS BK (FARWELL, MI)
Merged into IBT Bancorp, Inc. 10/4/2006
Each share Common $1.25 par exchanged for (3.0382) shares Common $6 par and $29 cash

FARWEST MNG LTD (BC)
Struck off register and declared dissolved for failure to file returns 03/17/1975

FARWEST TUNGSTEN COPPER MINES LTD. (BC)
Name changed to Farwest Mining Ltd. 00/00/1959
(See Farwest Mining Ltd.)

FAS INTL INC (NY)
Each share old Common 2¢ par exchanged for (0.05) share new Common 2¢ par 8/15/73
Name changed to Bowline Corp. 4/20/78
(See Bowline Corp.)

FAS INTL LTD (AB)
Company's sole asset sold for the benefit of creditors 10/00/2002
Stockholders' equity unlikely

FASHION & TIME PRODS INC (NY)
Merged into Omnisource, Inc. 4/15/87
Details not available

FASHION CHANNEL NETWORK INC (DE)
Charter cancelled and declared inoperative and void for non-payment of taxes 6/10/92

FASHION CO.
Acquired by Allied Stores Corp. in 1948
Each share Common no par exchanged for (1) share Common no par
(See Allied Stores Corp.)

FASHION DYNAMICS CORP (NV)
Each share old Common $0.001 par exchanged for (6) shares new Common $0.001 par 3/30/98
Name changed to eMagin Corp. (NV) 3/17/2000 eMagin Corp. (NV) reincorporated in Delaware 7/16/2001

FASHION FABRICS INC (DE)
Common 10¢ par split (5) for (4) by issuance of (0.25) additional share 3/26/71
Charter cancelled and declared inoperative and void for non-payment of taxes 3/1/79

FASHION FLAIR STORES, INC. (DE)
Filed bankruptcy petition in 1962
Declared no longer in existence having become inoperative and void for non-payment of taxes 4/1/62

FASHION HANDBAGS INC COM (FL)
Name changed to Southwestern Medical Solutions Inc. 3/10/2003

FASHION HOMES, INC. (NJ)
Liquidated for cash in 1964

FASHION HSE HLDG INC (CO)
Chapter 11 bankruptcy proceedings dismissed 09/08/2009
No stockholders' equity

FASHION IN PTS INC (DE)
Charter forfeited for failure to maintain a registered agent 11/28/83

FASHION NET INC (NV)
Name changed to Mimvi, Inc. 05/26/2010
Mimvi, Inc. name changed to Adaptive Medias, Inc. 11/19/2013

FASHION PARK ASSOCIATES, INC.
Assets sold at bankruptcy sale 00/00/1933
Stockholders' equity unlikely

FASHION TECH INTL INC (NV)
Reorganized 04/28/1999
Reorganized from (UT) to under the laws of Nevada 04/28/1999
Each share Common $0.005 par exchanged for (0.01) share old Common $0.001 par 04/28/1999
Each share old Common $0.001 par exchanged for (0.1) share new Common $0.001 par 06/20/2008
Name changed to China Nutrifruit Group Ltd. 08/25/2008

FASHION TRESS INC (OH)
Common no par changed to 5¢ par 03/18/1970
Name changed to FT Industries, Inc. 08/18/1975
FT Industries, Inc. name changed to Claire's Stores, Inc. (DE) 09/19/1983 which reincorporated in Florida 06/30/2000
(See Claire's Stores, Inc.)

FASHION TWO TWENTY INC (OH)
Plan of reorganization under Chapter 11 Federal Bankruptcy proceedings confirmed 09/13/1982
No stockholders' equity

FAS-FAY

FASHION WEEK INC (CA)
Company believed out of business 00/00/1977
Details not available

FASHIONMALL COM INC (DE)
Issue Information - 3,000,000 shares COM offered at $13 per share on 05/21/1999
Each (800,000) shares old Common no par exchanged for (1) share new Common no par 9/23/2003
Note: In effect holders received $0.54 cash per share and public interest was eliminated

FAST EDDIE RACING STABLES INC (FL)
Common 1¢ par changed to $0.001 par 08/19/2004
Each share old Common $0.001 par exchanged for (0.05) share new Common $0.001 par 02/24/2005
Name changed to National Investment Managers Inc. 03/15/2005
(See National Investment Managers Inc.)

FAST FOOD OPERATORS INC (NY)
Charter cancelled and proclaimed dissolved for failure to pay taxes 12/31/2003

FAST FOODS, INC. (KY)
Charter revoked for failure to file annual reports 1/30/86

FASTCLICK INC (DE)
Merged into ValueClick, Inc. 09/30/2005
Each share Common $0.001 par exchanged for (0.7928) share Common $0.001 par
ValueClick, Inc. name changed to Conversant, Inc. 02/05/2014 which merged into Alliance Data Systems Corp. 12/11/2014

FASTCOMM COMMUNICATIONS CORP (VA)
Chapter 11 bankruptcy proceedings converted to Chapter 7 on 8/27/2002
Stockholders' equity unlikely

FASTCRETE CORP (DE)
Charter cancelled and declared inoperative and void for non-payment of taxes 3/1/86

FASTFOOT INDS LTD (BC)
Recapitalized as Fab-Form Industries Ltd. 12/14/2001
Each share Common no par exchanged for (0.33333333) share Common no par

FASTLANE INTL ENTERPRISES INC (WY)
Reincorporated 05/10/1993
Place of incorporation changed from (BC) to (WY) 05/10/1993
Each share Common no par exchanged for (0.16666666) share Common 1¢ par 09/22/1994
Each share Common 1¢ par exchanged for (0.2) share Common no par 02/03/1997
Administratively dissolved for non-payment of taxes 08/14/2000

FASTLINE INC (NY)
Charter cancelled and proclaimed dissolved for failure to pay taxes 12/15/1970

FASTNET CORP (PA)
Issue Information - 4,000,000 shares COM offered at $12 per share on 02/08/2000
Plan of reorganization under Chapter 11 Federal Bankruptcy Code effective 4/11/2005
No stockholders' equity

FASTWAY FASTENERS, INC. (OH)
Through purchase offer 100% acquired by Thomas Industries Inc. as of 07/25/1977
Public interest eliminated

FATBRAIN COM INC (DE)
Acquired by Barnesandnoble.com Inc. 11/16/2000
Each share Common $0.001 par exchanged for (0.8557) share Class A Common $0.001 par and $1.0625 cash
(See Barnesandnoble.com Inc.)

FATHOM OCEANOLOGY LTD (CANADA)
Merged into Indal Technologies Ltd. 11/21/1989
Each share Capital Stock no par exchanged for $3 cash

FATIMA FERTILIZER CO LTD (PAKISTAN)
ADR agreement terminated 12/31/2012
Each Sponsored ADR for Ordinary exchanged for $11.904614 cash

FATIMA MINING CO. LTD. (ON)
Recapitalized as Texmont Mines Ltd. on a (0.5) for (1) basis 05/22/1964
Texmont Mines Ltd. recapitalized as New Texmont Explorations Ltd. (ONT) 03/20/1979 which reincorporated in Canada 03/19/1982
(See New Texmont Explorations Ltd.)

FAULDING F H & CO LTD (AUSTRALIA)
Stock Dividend - 10% 06/15/1995
ADR agreement terminated 02/05/2002
Each ADR for Ordinary exchanged for $30.1324 cash

FAULDING INC (DE)
Each (7,924,385) shares old Common 1¢ par exchanged for (1) share new Common 1¢ par 1/13/98
Note: In effect holders received $13.50 cash per share and public interest was eliminated

FAULKENHAM LAKE GOLD MINES LTD. (ON)
Recapitalized as New Faulkenham Mines Ltd. 00/00/1948
Each share Capital Stock $10 par exchanged for (0.25) share Capital Stock $10 par
New Faulkenham Mines Ltd. acquired by Starratt Nickel Mines Ltd. 07/09/1963 which recapitalized as Starratt Resources Ltd. 10/31/1994
(See Starratt Resources Ltd.)

FAULTFINDERS INC (NY)
Merged into Fairchild Camera & Instrument Corp. 09/29/1978
Each share Common 25¢ par exchanged for $10 cash

FAULTLESS CASTER CORP. (IN)
Acquired by Bliss & Laughlin Inc. 1/1/65
Each share Common $1 par exchanged for (1/3) share Common $2.50 par
Bliss & Laughlin Inc. name changed to Bliss & Laughlin Industries Inc. (Old) 5/7/65 which name changed to Axia Inc. 5/6/82
(See Axia Inc.)

FAULTLESS RUBBER CO. (OH)
Each share Common no par exchanged for (2) shares Common $1 par in 1946
Completely liquidated 11/1/66
Each share Common $1 par exchanged for first and final distribution of (0.75) share Abbott Laboratories Common no par

FAUQUIER NATL BK (WARRENTON, VA)
Common $25 par changed to $6.25 par and (3) additional shares issued 02/15/1996
Under plan of reorganization each share Common $6.25 par automatically became (1) share Fauquier National Bankshares, Inc. Common $6.25 par 05/24/1996

Fauquier National Bankshares, Inc. name changed to Fauquier Bankshares, Inc. 01/29/1998

FAUQUIER NATL BANKSHARES INC (VA)
Name changed to Fauquier Bankshares, Inc. 01/29/1998

FAVCO INC (MN)
Reacquired 00/00/1986
Each share Common 10¢ par exchanged for $0.75 cash

FAVOURABLE MINES LTD. (ON)
Merged into Alchib Developments Ltd. 07/10/1969
Each share Capital Stock no par exchanged for (0.12) share Capital Stock no par
Alchib Developments Ltd. merged into Kalrock Developments Ltd. 10/23/1978 which merged into Kalrock Resources Ltd. 08/08/1990 which merged into Cercal Minerals Corp. 07/09/1993
(See Cercal Minerals Corp.)

FAVRILLE INC (DE)
Issue Information - 6,000,000 shares COM offered at $7 per share on 02/02/2005
Name changed to MMR Information Systems, Inc. 04/22/2009
MMR Information Systems, Inc. name changed to MMRGlobal, Inc. 08/16/2010

FAWICK AIRFLEX CO., INC.
Merged into Federal Fawick Corp. on a share for share basis in 1952
Federal Fawick Corp. name changed to Fawick Corp. in 1954 which merged into Eaton Yale & Towne Inc. 3/31/68 which name changed to Eaton Corp. 4/21/71

FAWICK CORP. (MI)
Common $2 par split (6) for (5) by issuance of (0.2) additional share 12/10/65
Merged into Eaton Yale & Towne Inc. 3/31/68
Each share Common $2 par exchanged for (0.875) share Common 50¢ par
Eaton Yale & Towne Inc. name changed to Eaton Corp. 4/21/71

FAWN BAY DEV LTD (BC)
Recapitalized as Can-Trac Industries Ltd. 02/28/1973
Each share Common no par exchanged for (0.2) share Common no par
(See Can-Trac Industries Ltd.)

FAWN MINING CO. LTD. (BC)
Struck off register and declared dissolved for failure to file reports 1971

FAX-9 HLDG CORP (NV)
Charter revoked for failure to file reports and pay fees 11/01/2005

FAX BROADCASTING NETWORK CORP (NV)
Charter revoked for failure to file reports and pay fees 12/1/97

FAX UTILS SYS & SVCS CORP (FL)
Name changed to Netlist Corp. of Florida 3/19/99
(See Netlist Corp. of Florida)

FAXLINE HLDG CORP (NV)
Name changed to Fax-9 Holding Corp. 04/28/1989
(See Fax-9 Holding Corp.)

FAXMATE COM INC (AB)
Delisted from Toronto Venture Stock Exchange 06/20/2003

FAXSAV INC (DE)
Issue Information - 1,500,000 shares COM offered at $8 per share on 10/11/1996
Name changed to Netmoves Corp. 06/21/1999
Netmoves Corp. merged into Mail.Com, Inc. 02/09/2000 which name changed to EasyLink Services Corp. 04/03/2001
(See EasyLink Services Corp.)

FAYETTE BANCORP (IN)
Merged into Merchants National Corp. 05/20/1987
Each share Common no par exchanged for (2.5782) shares Common no par
Merchants National Corp. merged into National City Corp. 05/02/1992 which was acquired by PNC Financial Services Group, Inc. 12/31/2008

FAYETTE BK & TR CO (UNIONTOWN, PA)
Merged into BT Financial Corp. 9/5/86
Each share Capital Stock $5 par exchanged for (1.07) shares Common $5 par
BT Financial Corp. name changed to Promistar Financial Corp. 11/15/2000 which merged into F.N.B. Corp. (FL) 1/18/2002

FAYETTE CNTY BANCSHARES INC (GA)
Name changed to First Community Banking Services Inc. 1/29/97
First Community Banking Services Inc. merged into Regions Financial Corp. (Old) 9/10/98 which merged into Regions Financial Corp. (New) 7/1/2004

FAYETTE COURT CORP (NY)
Liquidation completed
Each share Common no par received initial distribution of $25 cash 12/10/1971
Each share Common no par received second distribution of $22.40 cash 01/25/1972
Each share Common no par received third distribution of $20 cash 01/25/1973
Each share Common no par exchanged for fourth and final distribution of $10.5389 cash 09/21/1973

FAYETTE FED SVGS BK (CONNERSVILLE, IN)
Merged into First Financial Bancorp 01/01/1991
Each share Common 1¢ par exchanged for (0.901071) share Common 10¢ par

FAYETTE NATIONAL BANK & TRUST CO. (UNIONTOWN, PA)
Each share Capital Stock $20 par exchanged for (4) shares Capital Stock $5 par 8/4/58
Stock Dividend - 33-1/3% 1/9/58
Name changed to Fayette Bank & Trust Co. (Uniontown, PA) 12/23/63
Fayette Bank & Trust Co. (Uniontown, PA) merged into BT Financial Corp. 9/5/86 which name changed to Promistar Financial Corp. 11/15/2000 which merged into F.N.B. Corp. (FL) 1/18/2002

FAYLESS INVS INC (NY)
Completely liquidated 11/18/87
Each share Common $1 par exchanged for first and final distribution of (1.701) shares Merrill Lynch Municipal Bond Fund, Inc. High Yield Portfolio Common 10¢ par

FAYMAR CAP CORP (AB)
Name changed to Valu-Net Corp. 10/30/1997
Valu-Net Corp. name changed to BSM Technologies Inc. 07/12/2001

FAYS INC (NY)
Name changed 07/01/1989
Common 10¢ par split (3) for (2) by issuance of (0.5) additional share 03/15/1977
Common 10¢ par split (2) for (1) by

issuance of (1) additional share 01/14/1983
Common 10¢ par split (2) for (1) by issuance of (1) additional share 09/02/1983
Stock Dividends - 10% 06/29/1978; 10% 06/15/1979; 10% 08/10/1980; 10% 08/10/1981; 10% 08/09/1982; 10% 06/28/1988
Name changed from Fay's Drug Co., Inc. to Fay's Inc. 07/01/1989
Common 10¢ par split (5) for (4) by issuance of (0.25) additional share 06/19/1992
Stock Dividend - 10% 07/03/1989
Merged into Penney (J.C.) Co., Inc. 10/11/1996
Each share Common 20¢ par exchanged for (0.2379286) share Common 50¢ par

FB CAP TR (DE)
9.75% Preferred Securities called for redemption at $10 on 11/4/2002

FB&T CORP (PA)
Stock Dividends - 10% 06/10/1987; 10% 09/10/1988; 10% 09/20/1989
Merged into Dauphin Deposit Corp. 07/01/1992
Each share Common $1 par exchanged for (0.9437) share Common $5 par
Dauphin Deposit Corp. merged into Allied Irish Banks, PLC 07/08/1997
(See Allied Irish Banks, PLC)

FB&T FINL CORP (VA)
Merged into F & M National Corp. 3/29/96
Each share Common $1.25 par exchanged for (1.983) shares Common $2 par
F & M National Corp. merged into BB&T Corp. 8/9/2001

FBA VENTURES LTD (NL)
Name changed to Nexstar Automation Inc. 04/15/1994
Nexstar Automation Inc. merged into Zygo Corp. 09/12/1996
(See Zygo Corp.)

FBC BANCSHARES INC (OH)
Acquired by Mid Am, Inc. 06/09/1989
Each share Common $5 par exchanged for (1.86459) shares Common no par
Mid Am, Inc. merged into Sky Financial Group, Inc. 10/02/1998 which merged into Huntington Bancshares Inc. 07/02/2007

FBD LIQUIDATING TR (DE)
Liquidation completed
Each Unit of Bene. Int. received initial distribution of $1.25 cash payable 12/06/2013 to holders of record 11/16/2012
Each Unit of Bene. Int. received second distribution of $0.375 cash payable 06/05/2014 to holders of record 11/16/2012
Each Unit of Bene. Int. received third distribution of $0.12 cash payable 12/19/2014 to holders of record 11/16/2012
Each Unit of Bene. Int. received fourth and final distribution of $0.03833 cash payable 12/29/2015 to holders of record 11/16/2012

FBI FRESH BURGERS INTL (CA)
Name changed to American Ammunition, Inc. (CA) 10/04/2001
American Ammunition, Inc. (CA) reorganized in Nevada 01/09/2006
(See American Ammunition, Inc.)

FBL MONEY MKT FD INC (MD)
Name changed to EquiTrust Money Market Fund, Inc. 05/01/1998
EquiTrust Money Market Fund, Inc. merged into EquiTrust Series Fund, Inc. 08/31/2009

FBL SER FD INC (MD)
Aggressive Growth Common Stock Portfolio merged into Value Growth Portfolio 11/22/1991
Details not available
Ginnie Mae Portfolio merged into High Quality Bond Portfolio 11/22/1991
Details not available
High Quality Bond Portfolio $0.001 par reclassified as High Grade Bond Portfolio $0.001 par 11/22/1991
Name changed to EquiTrust Series Fund, Inc. and Blue Chip Index Portfolio Traditional Class $0.001 par, Growth Common Stock Portfolio Traditional Class $0.001 par, High Grade Bond Portfolio Traditional Class $0.001 par, High Yield Bond Portfolio Traditional Class $0.001 par, Managed Portfolio Traditional Class $0.001 par, Money Market Portfolio Traditional Class $0.001 par, Value Growth Portfolio Institutional Class $0.001 par reclassified as Blue Chip Portfolio Class A $0.001 par, Value Growth Portfolio Class A $0.001 par, High Grade Bond Portfolio Class A $0.001 par, Strategic Yield Portfolio Class A $0.001 par, Managed Portfolio Class A $0.001 par, Money Market Portfolio Class A $0.001 par and Value Growth Portfolio Class A $0.001 par respectively 05/01/1998

FBO AIR INC (NV)
Name changed to FirstFlight, Inc. 01/30/2007
FirstFlight, Inc. name changed to Saker Aviation Services Inc. 10/02/2009

FBR & CO (VA)
Name changed 06/15/2011
Name changed from FBR Capital Markets Corp. to FBR & Co. 06/15/2011
Each share old Common $0.001 par exchanged for (0.25) share new Common Common $0.001 par 02/28/2013
Merged into B. Riley Financial, Inc. 06/01/2017
Each share new Common $0.001 par exchanged for (0.671) share Common $0.0001 par

FBR AMERN GAS INDEX FD INC (MD)
Merged into FBR Funds 02/27/2004
Details not available

FBR ASSET INVT CORP (VA)
Merged into Friedman, Billings, Ramsey Group, Inc. (New) 03/31/2003
Each share Common 1¢ par exchanged for (3.65) shares Class A Common 1¢ par
Friedman, Billings, Ramsey Group, Inc. (New) name changed to Arlington Asset Investment Corp. 06/10/2009

FBR CAP CORP (NV)
Name changed to Vitrix, Inc. 10/07/1999
Vitrix, Inc. name changed to Time America, Inc. Inc. 12/09/2003 which name changed to NETtime Solutions, Inc. 05/11/2007 which name changed to Tempco, Inc. 10/14/2008 which name changed to Esio Water & Beverage Development Corp. 01/18/2013 which name changed to UPD Holding Corp. 03/01/2017

FBR FD FOR GOVT INVS INC (MD)
Merged into FBR Funds 02/27/2004
Details not available

FBR RUSHMORE FD INC (MD)
Completely liquidated 11/28/2003
Each share Total Return Bond Fund $0.001 par received net asset value

FBT BANCORP INC (IN)
Stock Dividends - 10% 02/14/1975; 10% 02/16/1976; 10% 02/15/1978; 10% 02/15/1980
Name changed to 1st Source Corp. 04/29/1982

FBT BANCORP OF INDIANA, INC. (IN)
Name changed to FBT Bancorp, Inc. 4/17/72
FBT Bancorp, Inc. name changed to 1st Source Corp. 4/29/82

FBT BANCSHARES INC (OK)
Each share Common 33-1/3¢ par exchanged for (0.005) share Common $66.66 par 11/20/1978
Note: In effect holders received $3.40 cash per share and public interest was eliminated

FBX CORP (DE)
Merged into Pittway Corp. (DE) 6/19/90
Each share Common 1¢ par exchanged for $0.75 cash

FC BANC CORP (OH)
Old Common $2.50 par split (2) for (1) by issuance of (1) additional share payable 08/21/1998 to holders of record 08/14/1998
Each share old Common $2.50 par exchanged for (1) share new Common $2.50 par to reflect a (1) for (500) reverse split followed by a (500) for (1) forward split 01/06/2006
Note: Holders of (499) or fewer pre-split shares received $29.12 cash per share
Stock Dividends - 10% payable 04/26/2006 to holders of record 04/14/2006 Ex date - 04/11/2006; 10% payable 02/23/2007 to holders of record 02/02/2007 Ex date - 01/31/2007
Merged into CNB Financial Corp. 10/11/2013
Each share Common $2.50 par exchanged for (1.754) shares Common no par

FC FINL CORP (BC)
Recapitalized as West F.C. Financial Corp. 12/13/1991
Each share Common no par exchanged for (0.1) share Common no par
(See West F.C. Financial Corp.)

FC FINL SVCS INC (NV)
Common $0.00001 par split (5) for (1) by issuance of (4) additional shares payable 12/21/2005 to holders of record 12/19/2005 Ex date - 12/22/2005
Name changed to ICP Solar Technologies Inc. 12/05/2006
(See ICP Solar Technologies Inc.)

FCA HOLDING CORP. (DE)
Each share Class A Common $5 par exchanged for (0.01) share Class A Common $500 par 3/21/84
Each share Class B Common $5 par exchanged for (0.01) share Class B Common $500 par 3/21/84
Assets purchased by Finance Company of America L.P. in 1987
Stockholders' equity not determined

FCA INDS INC (DE)
Merged into Pacific Holding Corp. 4/28/76
Each share Capital Stock 50¢ par exchanged for $1.20 cash

FCA INTL LTD (CANADA)
Common no par reclassified as Class A Common no par 00/00/1983
Class A Common no par split (2) for (1) by issuance of (1) additional share 03/31/1986
Merged into FCA Acquisition Corp. 05/12/1998
Each share Class A Common no par exchanged for $9.60 cash

FCB BANCORP (CA)
Merged into First California Financial Group, Inc. 03/12/2007
Each share Common no par exchanged for (1.7904) shares Common 1¢ par
First California Financial Group, Inc. merged into PacWest Bancorp 05/31/2013

FCB BANCORP INC (KY)
Merged into MainSource Financial Group, Inc. 04/30/2017
Each share Common $1 par exchanged for (0.9) share Common no par and $7 cash

FCB FINL CORP (WI)
Merged into Anchor BanCorp Wisconsin Inc. 06/07/1999
Each share Common 1¢ par exchanged for (1.83) shares Common 10¢ par
(See Anchor BanCorp Wisconsin Inc.)

FCB FINL INC (FL)
Stock Dividend - 10% payable 12/17/2001 to holders of record 11/21/2001 Ex date - 12/03/2001
Administratively dissolved 09/27/2013

FCB/NC CAP TR II (DE)
8.40% Trust Preferred Securities called for redemption at $25 on 10/31/2006

FCE CDA INC (AB)
Name changed to FuelCell Energy, Ltd. 08/20/2004
Each Exchangeable Share no par exchanged for (1) Exchangeable Share no par
FuelCell Energy, Ltd. exchanged for FuelCell Energy, Inc. 10/29/2004

FCF, INC. (NV)
Charter revoked for failure to file reports and pay fees 12/1/2002

FCF CAP INC (AB)
Recapitalized as Founders Advantage Capital Corp. 05/19/2016
Each share Class A Common no par exchanged for (0.06666666) share Class A Common no par

FCFT INC (DE)
Under plan of reorganization each share Common $5 par automatically became (1) share First Community Bancshares Inc. (NV) Common $1 par 09/30/1997
First Community Bancshares Inc. (NV) reincorporated in Virginia 10/09/2018

FCI DEVELOPMENT CORP. (PHILIPPINES)
Merged into PHINMA Property Holdings Corp. 00/00/1987
Details not available

FCMI FINL CORP (ON)
Each share Common no par exchanged for (0.75) share Non-Vtg. Class A Common no par and (0.25) share Class B Common no par 09/22/1987
Merged into FFC Amalgamation Inc. 03/31/1997
Each share Non-Vtg. Class A Common no par exchanged for $4.60 cash
Each share Class B Common no par exchanged for $4.60 cash

FCMI PRECIOUS METALS FDS INC (BC)
Completely liquidated 11/08/2007
Each share Class A 1¢ par received net asset value

FCNB CAP TR (DE)
8.25% Trust Preferred Securities called for redemption at $25 on 4/1/2005

FCNB CORP (MD)
Stock Dividends - 10% 1/17/90; 10% payable 10/31/97 to holders of record 10/24/97
Merged into BB&T Corp. 1/8/2001
Each share Common $1 par

exchanged for (0.725) shares Common $5 par

FCP INC (NY)
Charter cancelled and proclaimed dissolved for failure to pay taxes 03/25/1992

FCR AUTOMOTIVE GROUP INC (CA)
Reorganized under the laws of Delaware as Simco America Inc. 10/18/2005
Each (85) shares Common exchanged for (1) share Common
Simco America Inc. name changed to Leo Motors, Inc. 11/05/2007

FCS FINANCIAL CORP. (GA)
Acquired by Georgia Bank Financial Corp. 01/01/1993
Details not available

FCS INDUSTRIES, INC. (AZ)
Name changed to FCS Laboratories, Inc. 10/24/1985
(See FCS Laboratories, Inc.)

FCS LABS INC (AZ)
Each share Common no par received distribution of (1) share I.R.I. Corp. Common no par payable 12/26/1997 to holders of record 12/15/1997
SEC revoked common stock registration 05/19/2009

FCSTONE GROUP INC (DE)
Issue Information - 5,100,000 shares COM offered at $24 per share on 03/16/2007
Common $0.0001 par split (3) for (2) by issuance of (0.5) additional share payable 09/27/2007 to holders of record 09/17/2007 Ex date - 09/28/2007
Merged into International Assets Holding Corp. 09/30/2009
Each share Common $0.0001 par exchanged for (0.295) share Common 1¢ par
International Assets Holding Corp. name changed to INTL FCStone Inc. 03/02/2011

FDI CORP (CO)
Name changed to Petrolift Corp. 02/25/1987
(See Petrolift Corp.)

FDI INC (DE)
Recapitalized as Interlee, Inc. 12/18/1981
Each share 5% Conv. Preferred $1 par exchanged for (1/6) share Common no par
Each share Conv. Special Preferred $100 par automatically became (1) share Interlee, Inc. Conv. Special Preferred $100 par
Each share Common $1 par exchanged for (1/6) share Common no par
(See Interlee, Inc.)

FDN INC (CO)
Each share old Common $0.001 par exchanged for (0.02025000) share new Common $0.001 par 10/08/2004
SEC revoked common stock registration 12/18/2006

FDP CORP (FL)
Common 1¢ par split (3) for (2) by issuance of (0.5) additional share payable 12/10/96 to holders of record 11/26/96
Merged into SunGard Data Systems Inc. 4/28/99
Each share Common 1¢ par exchanged for (0.4114) share Common 1¢ par
(See SunGard Data Systems Inc.)

FDS HLDG CO (IL)
Merged into American Brands, Inc. (NJ) 02/14/1979
Each share Common $2 par exchanged for (0.5) share $2.75 Preferred no par and (0.5) share $2.67 Conv. Preferred no par

American Brands, Inc. (NJ) reincorporated in Delaware 01/01/1986 which name changed to Fortune Brands, Inc. 05/30/1997 which name changed to Beam Inc. 10/04/2011
(See Beam Inc.)

FDX CORP (DE)
Common 10¢ par split (2) for (1) by issuance of (1) additional share payable 05/06/1999 to holders of record 04/15/1999 Ex date - 05/07/1999
Name changed to FedEx Corp. 01/19/2000

FEARLESS INTL INC (NV)
Chapter 7 bankruptcy proceedings terminated 12/15/2014
Stockholders' equity unlikely

FEARN FOODS INC (IL)
Common $5 par changed to $2.50 par and (1) additional share issued 05/17/1967
Name changed to Fearn International Inc. 05/05/1969
Fearn International Inc. merged into Kellogg Co. 10/30/1970

FEARN INTL INC (IL)
Merged into Kellogg Co. 10/30/1970
Each share Common $2.50 par exchanged for (2/3) share Common 50¢ par

FEARN LABORATORIES, INC.
Name changed to Fearn Foods, Inc. in 1951
Fearn Foods, Inc. name changed to Fearn International Inc. 5/5/69 which merged into Kellogg Co. 10/30/70

FEATHER GOLD RES LTD (BC)
Recapitalized as Sovereign Chief Ventures Ltd. 10/05/1995
Each share Common no par exchanged for (0.2127659) share Common no par
Sovereign Chief Ventures Ltd. name changed to Saxon Oil Co. Ltd. 04/21/2006
(See Saxon Oil Co. Ltd.)

FEATHER INDS INC (CO)
Each share Common $0.00001 par exchanged for $0.0001 cash 6/18/91
Note: Unexchanged certificates were cancelled and became without value 8/6/91

FEATHER RIV ST BK (YUBA CITY, CA)
Common $6.75 par changed to no par and (1.2) additional shares issued 5/21/80
Common no par split (3) for (2) by issuance of (0.5) additional share 2/14/90
Common no par split (5) for (4) by issuance of (0.25) additional share 5/26/94
Stock Dividend - 10% 12/88
Under plan of reorganization each share Common no par automatically became (1) share California Independent Bancorp Common no par 5/2/95
California Independent Bancorp merged into Humboldt Bancorp 1/6/2004 which merged into Umpqua Holdings Corp. 7/10/2004

FEATHER RIVER PINE MILLS, INC.
Acquired by Georgia-Pacific Corp. for cash in July 1955

FEATHER RIVER POWER CO.
Acquired by Pacific Gas & Electric Co. in 1931
Details not available

FEATHERLITE INC (MN)
Name changed 5/7/98
Issue Information - 1,700,000 shares COM offered at $6 per share on 09/28/1994
Name changed from Featherlite

Manufacturing, Inc. to Featherlite Inc. 5/7/98
Common no par split (3) for (2) by issuance of (0.5) additional share payable 5/4/2005 to holders of record 4/22/2005 Ex date - 5/5/2005
Merged into Universal Trailer Holdings Corp. 10/27/2006
Each share Common no par exchanged for $6.50 cash

FEATHEROCK INC (QC)
Each share Preferred $10 par exchanged for (4) shares Common $1 par 12/22/1961
Each share Common no par exchanged for (2) shares Common $1 par 12/22/1961
Charter annulled for failure to file annual reports 10/20/1973

FEATHERSTONE RESOURCE LTD (BC)
Recapitalized as Newcastle Minerals Ltd. 05/03/2002
Each share Common no par exchanged for (1/3) share Common no par
Newcastle Minerals Ltd. recapitalized as GoldON Resources Ltd. 03/07/2013

FEATHERTOUCH E COMM INC (CANADA)
Dissolved 06/10/2004
Details not available

FECC INC (MN)
Name changed to Argus Industries, Inc. 1/6/87
(See Argus Industries, Inc.)

FECHTOR DETWILER MITCHELL & CO INC (CA)
Recapitalized as Detwiler, Mitchell & Co. 03/27/2001
Each share Common 1¢ par exchanged for (0.25) share Common 1¢ par
Detwiler, Mitchell & Co. name changed to Detwiler Fenton Group, Inc. 10/20/2008

FECKER BREWING CO.
Bankrupt in 1940

FECOR INDS LTD (PA)
Reincorporated 08/20/1973
State of incorporation changed from (NY) to (PA) 08/20/1973
Name changed to Farrier Industries, Inc. 02/13/1976
(See Farrier Industries, Inc.)

FED-MART LIFE INSURANCE CO. (TX)
Name changed to First Financial Life Insurance Co. 3/26/65
First Financial Life Insurance Co. name changed to United General Life Insurance Co. 1/1/74
(See United General Life Insurance Co.)

FEDDER DATA CTRS INC (MD)
Common 10¢ par split (2) for (1) by issuance of (1) additional share 7/1/69
Assets assigned for the benefit of creditors 11/26/75
No stockholders' equity

FEDDERS CORP (DE)
Reincorporated 01/02/1985
5-1/2% Preferred $50 par called for redemption 05/29/1959
Common $1 par split (2) for (1) by issuance of (1) additional share 05/29/1968
Common $1 par split (2) for (1) by issuance of (1) additional share 06/03/1969
State of incorporation changed from (NY) to (DE) 01/02/1985
$1.75 Conv. Exchangeable Preferred $1 par called for redemption 05/01/1989
Each share Common $1 par received distribution of (0.5) share Non-Vtg. Class A Common $1 par 09/09/1994

Each share Common $1 par received distribution of (0.25) share Non-Vtg. Class A Common $1 par 06/14/1995
Non-Vtg. Class A Common $1 par split (5) for (4) by issuance of (0.25) additional share 06/14/1995
Conv. Preferred called for redemption 09/19/1997
Each share Common $1 par exchanged for (1.1) shares Common 1¢ par 03/26/2002
Each share Class A Common $1 par exchanged for (1) share Common 1¢ par 03/26/2002
Plan of reorganization under Chapter 11 Federal Bankruptcy Code effective 09/05/2008
No stockholders' equity

FEDDERS MANUFACTURING CO., INC. (NY)
Name changed to Fedders-Quigan Corp. 00/00/1946
Fedders-Quigan Corp. name changed to Fedders Corp. (NY) 12/16/1958 which reincorporated in Delaware 01/02/1985
(See Fedders Corp.)

FEDDERS-QUIGAN CORP. (NY)
Name changed to Fedders Corp. (NY) 12/16/1958
Fedders Corp. (NY) reincorporated in Delaware 01/02/1985
(See Fedders Corp.)

FEDERAL AFFORDABLE HSG CORP (MN)
Name changed to American Dream Entertainment, Inc. 09/03/1999
(See American Dream Entertainment, Inc.)

FEDERAL AMERICAN CO.
Succeeded by American Co. in 1938
Details not available

FEDERAL ASPHALT PRODS INC (MI)
Stock Dividend - 35% 06/20/1975
Name changed to Federal Enterprises, Inc. 07/30/1984
(See Federal Enterprises, Inc.)

FEDERAL AVIATION CORP.
Dissolved in 1931

FEDERAL BAKE SHOPS, INC. (DE)
Recapitalized in 1936
Each share 7% Preferred $100 par exchanged for (1) share 5% Preferred $30 par (10) shares new Common no par and $1.50 in cash
Each share Common no par exchanged for (0.05) share new Common no par
Recapitalized in 1946
Each share Common no par exchanged for (4) shares Capital Stock $1 par
Under plan of liquidation each share Capital Stock $1 par exchanged for $7 Jupiter Corp. 6-1/4% S.F. Sub. Debs. 5/6/63

FEDERAL BEARINGS INC (NY)
Name changed to Schatz Federal Bearings Co., Inc. 9/1/76
(See Schatz Federal Bearings Co., Inc.)

FEDERAL BOND & MORTGAGE CO.
Out of business in 1931
Details not available

FEDERAL BOWLING CENTERS, INC. (DE)
Charter revoked for non-payment of taxes 4/1/61

FEDERAL-BRANDES, INC.
Name changed to Kolster Radio Corp. in 1928
(See Kolster Radio Corp.)

FEDERAL CHEMICAL CO. (KY)
Common $100 par changed to no par 00/00/1936
Acquired by National Distillers & Chemical Corp. 01/06/1961
Each share Preferred $100 par

exchanged for (4.247) shares Common $5 par
Each share Common no par exchanged for (8) shares Common $5 par
National Distillers & Chemical Corp. name changed to Quantum Chemical Corp. 01/04/1988 which merged into Hanson PLC (Old) 10/01/1993 which reorganized as Hanson PLC (New) 10/15/2003
(See Hanson PLC (New))

FEDERAL CHIBOUGAMAU MINES LTD. (ON)
Recapitalized as New Federal Chibougamau Mines Ltd. 06/28/1968
Each share Capital Stock no par exchanged for (0.1) share Capital Stock no par
(See New Federal Chibougamau Mines Ltd.)

FEDERAL CO (DE)
Common $12 par split (2) for (1) by issuance of (1) additional share 12/1/73
Common $12 par split (2) for (1) by issuance of (1) additional share 11/26/80
Common $12 par split (2) for (1) by issuance of (1) additional share 2/27/86
Name changed to Holly Farms Corp. 9/10/87
(See Holly Farms Corp.)

FEDERAL COAL CO (WV)
Capital Stock $10 par changed to $1 par in 1941
Reorganized under Chapter X Bankruptcy proceedings in August 1973
No stockholders' equity

FEDERAL COMPRESS & WAREHOUSE CO. (DE)
Each share Common $100 par exchanged for (4) shares Common no par in 1929
Common no par changed to $25 par in 1933
Common $25 par changed to $12 par and a 200% stock dividend paid 9/1/56
Name changed to Federal Co. 3/1/69
Federal Co. name changed to Holly Farms Corp. 9/10/87
(See Holly Farms Corp.)

FEDERAL CONCRETE PIPE CO. (OH)
Completely liquidated for cash 8/19/63

FEDERAL CRUDE OIL CO. (TX)
Charter forfeited for failure to pay taxes 4/26/50

FEDERAL DATA PROCESSING CORP (DE)
Name changed to Color Systems Technology Inc. 01/03/1983
Color Systems Technology Inc. name changed to CST Entertainment Imaging Inc. 04/30/1992 which name changed to CST Entertainment, Inc. 04/24/1995 which recapitalized as Legacy Holding, Inc. 06/11/2007
(See Legacy Holding, Inc.)

FEDERAL DESIGN CORP. (NY)
Name changed to Peak Industries Inc. (NY) 02/13/1964
Peak Industries Inc. (NY) reorganized in Delaware 10/19/1972
(See Peak Industries Inc.)

FEDERAL DISCOUNT CORP. (DE)
Acquired by General Discount Corp. (MI) 12/01/1932
Details not available

FEDERAL DIVERSIPLEX LTD (CANADA)
Merged into Hardee Farms International Ltd. 12/16/1978
Each share Common no par exchanged for (3) shares Common no par
Hardee Farms International Ltd. name changed to Cobi Foods Inc. 05/15/1986
(See Cobi Foods Inc.)

FEDERAL ELECTRIC CO., INC.
Name changed to Federal-Enterprises, Inc. in 1948
Federal Enterprises, Inc. name changed to Federal Sign & Signal Corp. (N.Y.) in 1954 which reincorporated under the laws of Delaware 4/1/69 which name changed to Federal Signal Corp. 8/29/75

FEDERAL ELECTRIC PRODUCTS CO. (DE)
Name changed to Federal Pacific Electric Co. in 1954
Federal Pacific Electric Co. merged into United States Smelting Refining & Mining Co. (New) 4/14/72 which name changed to UV Industries, Inc. Liquidating Trust 3/25/80
(See UV Industries, Inc. Liquidating Trust)

FEDERAL ENERGY CORP (CO)
Charter suspended for failure to file corporate reports 12/14/1979

FEDERAL ENERGY CORP LTD (AB)
Reincorporated under the laws of British Columbia as Glenhaven Resources Inc. 07/31/1997
Glenhaven Resources Inc. recapitalized as Glenhaven Minerals Inc. 10/06/1999 which recapitalized as Glenhaven Ventures Inc. 01/30/2001 which name changed to Red Lake Resources Inc. 07/16/2002 which name changed to Silver Fields Resources Inc. 06/19/2006

FEDERAL ENTERPRISES, INC. (NY)
Name changed to Federal Sign & Signal Corp. (NY) in 1954
Federal Sign & Signal Corp. (NY) reincorporated in Delaware 4/1/69 which name changed to Federal Signal Corp. 8/29/75

FEDERAL ENTERPRISES INC (MI)
Merged into Newfed, Inc. 1/19/90
Each share Common $1 par exchanged for $5.80 cash

FEDERAL EQUIPMENT CO. (PA)
Name changed to Cutler-Federal, Inc. (PA) 07/10/1961
Cutler-Federal, Inc. (PA) reincorporated in Delaware 06/24/1975 which reorganized as Holder International Industries Inc. 11/14/1985
(See Holder International Industries Inc.)

FEDERAL EQUIPMENT CORP. (IL)
Assets liquidated for benefit of creditor 11/14/67
No stockholders' equity

FEDERAL EXPRESS CORP (DE)
Class A Common 20¢ par reclassified as Common 10¢ par and (1) additional share issued 10/12/1978
Common 10¢ par split (2) for (1) by issuance of (1) additional share 10/31/1980
Common 10¢ par split (2) for (1) by issuance of (1) additional share 10/31/1983
Common 10¢ par split (2) for (1) by issuance of (1) additional share payable 11/04/1996 to holders of record 10/15/1996 Ex date - 11/05/1996
Stock Dividend - 100% payable 11/04/1996 to holders of record 10/15/1996
Under plan of merger name changed to FDX Corp. 01/27/1998
FDX Corp. name changed to FedEx Corp. 01/19/2000

FEDERAL FACTORS, INC. (CA)
Incorporated 5/17/51
Charter revoked for failure to pay franchise or license taxes 1/2/53

FEDERAL FACTORS, INC. (CA)
Incorporated 12/12/57
Charter revoked for failure to pay franchise or license taxes 3/1/65

FEDERAL FARMS LTD (CANADA)
Name changed to Federal Diversiplex Ltd. 03/22/1971
Federal Diversiplex Ltd. merged into Hardee Farms International Ltd. 12/16/1978 which name changed to Cobi Foods Inc. 05/15/1986
(See Cobi Foods Inc.)

FEDERAL FAWICK CORP. (MI)
Name changed to Fawick Corp. in 1954
Fawick Corp. merged into Eaton Yale & Towne Inc. 3/31/68 which name changed to Eaton Corp. 4/21/71

FEDERAL FINANCE CORP. (CO)
Name changed to Leisure Services, Inc. and Common 25¢ par changed to 1¢ par 11/13/72
Leisure Services, Inc. name changed to Havelock Resources International, Inc. 5/7/82
(See Havelock Resources International, Inc.)

FEDERAL FOUNDRIES & STEEL CO. LTD.
Reorganized as Quality Steels (Canada) Ltd. share for share 00/00/1947
(See Quality Steels (Canada) Ltd.)

FEDERAL FOUNDRY SUPPLY CO. (OH)
Merged into Archer-Daniels-Midland Co. on a (7.25) for (1) basis 7/31/57

FEDERAL GLASS CO. (OH)
Acquired by Federal Paper Board Co., Inc. (NY) 6/30/58
Each share Common $20 par exchanged for (0.5) share 4.6% Preferred $25 par and (1.155) shares Common $5 par
Federal Paper Board Co., Inc. (NY) reincorporated in (NC) 4/20/94
(See Federal Paper Board Co., Inc.)

FEDERAL GOLD & SILVER (UT)
Involuntarily dissolved 12/31/79
Stockholders' equity unlikely

FEDERAL GOLD MINES, LTD. (BC)
Struck off register and dissolved by default 06/12/1952

FEDERAL GRAIN LTD (CANADA)
Recapitalized 00/00/1951
Each share 6.5% Preference $100 par exchanged for (5) shares $1.40 Preference $20 par
Class A Common no par and Class B Common no par exchanged for new Class A Common no par and Class B Common no par respectively
Class A Common no par and Class B Common no par split (10) for (1) by issuance of (9) additional shares 01/04/1965
$1.40 Preference $20 par called for redemption 08/03/1965
Each share Class A Common no par exchanged for (1) share Common no par 09/01/1966
Each share Class B Common no par exchanged for (1.5) shares Common no par 10/19/1966
Name changed to Federal Industries Ltd. 04/16/1973
Federal Industries Ltd. name changed to Russel Metals Inc. 06/01/1995

FEDERAL GRID CO UNI ENERGY SYS JT STK CO (RUSSIA)
Name changed to Federal Grid Co. of Unified Energy System PJSC 10/30/2015

FEDERAL HOME LN MTG CORP (USA)
Each share Participating Preferred $10 par exchanged for (4) shares Sr. Participating Preferred $2.50 par 12/08/1988
Sr. Participating Preferred $2.50 par reclassified as Common $1,000 par 08/09/1989
7.90% Preferred $1 par called for redemption on 07/01/1997
6.72% Preferred called for redemption on 02/12/1999
6.14% Preferred Ser. D called for redemption at $50 plus $0.35817 accrued dividends on 02/12/2007
(Additional Information in Active)

FEDERAL HYDRONICS INC (MN)
Assets assigned for benefit of creditors 12/15/1975
No stockholders' equity

FEDERAL INDUSTRIES, INC. (MI)
Liquidation completed
Each share Common $1 par exchanged for initial distribution of $4.65 cash 08/21/1958
Each share Common $1 par received second distribution of $0.32 cash 03/16/1959
Each share Common $1 par received third distribution of $0.09 cash 10/05/1959
Each share Common $1 par received fourth distribution of $0.09 cash 03/14/1960
Each share Common $1 par received fifth distribution of $0.09 cash 08/09/1960
Each share Common $1 par received sixth distribution of $0.10 cash 02/28/1961
Each share Common $1 par received seventh distribution of $0.10 cash 08/02/1961
Each share Common $1 par received eighth distribution of $0.12 cash 01/31/1962
Each share Common $1 par received ninth distribution of $0.16 cash 07/31/1962
Each share Common $1 par received tenth distribution of $0.15 cash 01/28/1963
Each share Common $1 par received eleventh distribution of $0.16 cash 07/30/1963
Each share Common $1 par received twelfth and final distribution of $0.047 cash 05/20/1965

FEDERAL INDUSTRIES INC. (NV)
Charter revoked for failure to file reports and pay fees 03/07/1977

FEDERAL INDS LTD (CANADA)
Common no par reclassified as Conv. Class A Common no par 11/14/1974
Conv. Class A Common no par split (2) for (1) by issuance of (1) additional share 09/06/1985
Conv. Class B Common no par split (2) for (1) by issuance of (1) additional share 09/06/1985
$2.0625 Conv. Class II Preferred Ser. B no par called for redemption 01/01/1987
7.5% Conv. Class II Preferred Ser. D no par called for redemption 03/31/1994
Name changed to Russel Metals Inc. 06/01/1995

FEDERAL INS CO (NJ)
Each share Capital Stock $100 par exchanged for (10) shares Capital Stock $10 par and a 33.33333333% stock dividend 00/00/1929
Under plan of merger each share Capital Stock $10 par exchanged for (4) shares Capital Stock $4 par 00/00/1953
Stock Dividend - 10% 11/23/1960
Acquired by Chubb Corp. 12/29/1967
Each share Capital Stock $4 par

exchanged for (1.075) shares Capital Stock $1 par
Chubb Corp. merged into Chubb Ltd. 01/15/2016

FEDERAL INVESTMENT TRUST
Name changed to Federated Capital Corp. in 1927
(See Federated Capital Corp.)

FEDERAL KIRKLAND MINES LTD (AB)
Recapitalized as Coexco Petroleum Inc. 12/23/1987
Each share Common no par exchanged for (0.1) share Common no par
Coexco Petroleum Inc. merged into Tesco Corp. 12/01/1993 which merged into Nabors Industries Ltd. 12/15/2017

FEDERAL KIRKLAND MINING CO., LTD. (ON)
Merged into Cadamet Mines Ltd. 11/17/1958
Each share Capital Stock $1 par exchanged for (0.2) share Capital Stock $1 par
Cadamet Mines Ltd. recapitalized as Terrex Mining Co. Ltd. 09/08/1966
(See Terrex Mining Co. Ltd.)

FEDERAL KNITTING MILLS CO.
Liquidation completed in 1939

FEDERAL LEATHER CO. (NJ)
Common no par changed to $1 par in 1951
Acquired by Textron Inc. (RI) 8/31/56
Each share Preferred $50 par exchanged for (2.4) shares Common 50¢ par
Each share Common $1 par exchanged for (2.5) shares Common 50¢ par
Textron Inc. (RI) reincorporated in Delaware 1/2/68

FEDERAL LIFE & CAS CO (MI)
Stock Dividend - 100% 12/12/1955
Acquired by Home Insurance Co. 09/00/1969
Details not available

FEDERAL LIFE INSURANCE CO. (IL)
Plan of mutualization completed 2/13/62

FEDERAL LIGHT & TRACTOR CO.
Liquidated in 1947

FEDERAL LIQUIDATING CORP.
Liquidation completed in 1952

FEDERAL LOAN CO. OF PITTSFIELD, INC. (MA)
Name changed to Signature Loan Co., Inc. in 1954
Signature Loan Co., Inc. merged into Budget Finance Plan 9/8/58 which name changed to Budget Capital Corp. 12/20/72
(See Budget Capital Corp.)

FEDERAL MACHINE & WELDER CO. (OH)
Stock Dividend - 100% 3/22/46
Merged into McKay Machine Co. 4/18/61
Each share Common $1 par exchanged for (0.0578) share Common no par
McKay Machine Co. merged into Wean Industries, Inc. 5/1/67 which name changed to Wean United, Inc. 5/1/68 which reincorporated in Delaware 9/16/87
(See Wean United, Inc.)

FEDERAL MANUFACTURING & ENGINEERING CORP. (NY)
Each share Common $1 par exchanged for (1) share Class A Capital Stock $1 par 9/25/56
Class A Capital Stock $1 par and Class B Capital Stock $1 par reclassified as Common $1 par 10/22/59
Common $1 par changed to 10¢ par 10/3/60

Merged into Victoreen Instrument Co. 5/31/63
Each share Common 10¢ par exchanged for (0.25) share Common $1 par
Victoreen Instrument Co. name changed to Victoreen Inc. 5/5/67 which name changed to Victoreen Leece Neville, Inc. 2/1/69 which name changed to VLN Corp. 4/29/70 which merged into Sheller-Globe Corp. 9/30/74
(See Sheller-Globe Corp.)

FED MART CORP (CA)
Merged into FM Holdings, Inc. 05/04/1981
Each share Common no par exchanged for $12.80 cash

FEDERAL MED INDS INC (UT)
Proclaimed dissolved for failure to pay taxes 5/1/90

FED MED SVCS CORP (AB)
Name changed to Elk Point Game Ranching Corp. 12/5/90
Elk Point Game Ranching Corp. name changed to Elk Point Resources Inc. 11/9/93 which merged into Acclaim Energy Trust 1/28/2003
(See Acclaim Energy Trust)

FEDERAL METALS CORP. (QC)
Recapitalized as Fedpen Ltee. 08/01/1978
Each share Capital Stock $1 par exchanged for (1) share Capital Stock no par
Fedpen Ltee. name changed to Mafricor Resources 02/17/1997
(See Mafricor Resources)

FEDERAL MILK CORP. (DE)
Charter cancelled and declared inoperative and void for non-payment of taxes 3/17/26

FEDERAL MINING & SMELTING CO. (DE)
Common $100 par changed to $10 par in 1936
Each share Common $10 par exchanged for (5) shares Common $2 par in 1939
Merged into American Smelting & Refining Co in 1953
Each share Common $2 par exchanged for (1.666666) shares Common no par
American Smelting & Refining Co. name changed to Asarco Inc. 4/23/75
(See Asarco Inc.)

FEDERAL-MOGUL-BOWER BEARINGS, INC. (MI)
Common $5 par split (2) for (1) by issuance of (1) additional share 11/13/1959
Name changed to Federal-Mogul Corp. (MI) 04/30/1965
(See Federal-Mogul Corp. (MI))

FEDERAL-MOGUL FING TR (DE)
Plan of reorganization under Chapter 11 Federal Bankruptcy Code effective 12/27/2007
Each 7% Guaranteed Trust Preferred Security exchanged for (0.07375591) Federal-Mogul Corp. Common Stock Purchase Warrant expiring 12/27/2014
Each 7% Accredited Investors Guaranteed Trust Preferred Security exchanged for (0.07375591) Federal-Mogul Corp. Common Stock Purchase Warrant expiring 12/27/2014
Each 7% 144A Guaranteed Trust Preferred Security exchanged for (0.07375591) Federal-Mogul Corp. Common Stock Purchase Warrant expiring 12/27/2014

FEDERAL MOGUL HLDGS CORP (DE)
Name changed 04/15/2014
Each share Common no par exchanged for (0.66666666) share Common $5 par 00/00/1939
Stock Dividends - 100% 07/01/1947; 50% 10/31/1952; 20% 05/20/1955
Under plan of merger name changed to Federal-Mogul-Bower Bearings, Inc. 07/29/1955 which name changed back to Federal-Mogul Corp. (MI) 04/30/1965
Common $5 par split (2) for (1) by issuance of (1) additional share 03/09/1979
Common $5 par split (2) for (1) by issuance of (1) additional share 06/09/1989
3.875% Conv. Exchangeable Preferred Ser. D no par called for redemption at $52.33 plus $0.839583 accrued dividends on 08/28/1997
Plan of reorganization under Chapter 11 Federal Bankruptcy Code effective
Each share 144A Common $5 par received (0.075528) Class A Common Stock Purchase Warrant expiring 12/27/2014 payable 12/27/2007 to holders of record 11/08/2007
Each share Common $5 par received distribution of (0.075528) Class A Common Stock Purchase Warrant expiring 12/27/2014 payable 12/27/2007 to holders of record 11/08/2007
Note: Certificates were not required to be surrendered and are without value
FEDERAL-MOGUL CORP. (DE) Name changed from Federal-Mogul Corp. (DE) & (MI) to Federal-Mogul Holdings Corp. (DE) 04/15/2014
Acquired by Icahn Enterprises L.P. 01/23/2017
Each share Common no par exchanged for $10 cash

FEDERAL MOTOR TRUCK CO. (MI)
Merged into Federal Fawick Corp. in 1952
Each share Capital Stock no par exchanged for (1) share Common $2 par
Federal Fawick Corp. name changed to Fawick Corp. in 1954 which merged into Eaton Yale & Towne Inc. 3/31/68 which name changed to Eaton Corp. 4/21/74

FEDERAL NATL MTG ASSN (USA)
6.41% Non-Cumulative Preferred Ser. A called for redemption at $50 plus $0.53417 accrued dividends on 03/01/2001
6.5% Non-Cumulative Preferred Ser. B called for redemption at $50 plus $0.51458 accrued dividends on 02/28/2002
6.45% Non-Cumulative Preferred Ser. C called for redemption at $50 on 07/31/2002
Variable Rate Preferred Ser. J called for redemption at $50 plus $0.5378 accrued dividends on 02/28/2007
Variable Rate Preferred Ser. K called for redemption at $50 on 04/02/2007
Each share 8.75% Non-Cumulative Mandatory Conv. Preferred Ser. 2008-1 exchanged for (1.8182) shares Common no par 05/13/2011
(Additional Information in Active)

FEDERAL OIL CO (NJ)
Charter revoked for failure to file reports and pay fees 5/31/94

FEDERAL OIL CO (NV)
Recapitalized as Federal Industries Inc. (NV) 7/5/72
Each share Common 5¢ par exchanged for (0.1) share Common 5¢ par

(See Federal Industries Inc.)

FEDERAL OIL SHALE CORP (UT)
Recapitalized as Thompson International Corp. 02/24/1969
Each share Common 10¢ par exchanged for (0.125) share Common 80¢ par
Thompson International Corp. name changed to Inland Western Corp. 10/24/1974
(See Inland Western Corp.)

FED ONE BANCORP INC (DE)
Merged into United Bankshares, Inc. 10/1/98
Each share Common 10¢ par exchanged for (1.5) shares Common $2.50 par

FED ONE BK (WHEELING, WV)
Reorganized under the laws of Delaware as Fed One Bancorp, Inc. 1/19/95
Each share Common 10¢ par exchanged for (2.239447) shares Common 10¢ par
Fed One Bancorp, Inc. merged into United Bankshares, Inc. 10/1/98

FED ONE SVGS BK FSB (WHEELING, WV)
Name changed to Fed One Bank (Wheeling, WV) 4/21/94
Fed One Bank (Wheeling, WV) reorganized as Fed One Bancorp, Inc. 1/19/95 which merged into United Bankshares, Inc. 10/1/98

FEDERAL PAC ELEC CO (DE)
Merged into United States Smelting Refining & Mining Co. (ME) (New) 04/14/1972
Each share 5-1/2% Conv. 2nd Preferred Ser. A $23 par exchanged for (1) share $1.265 Conv. Preferred $5 par
Each share Common $1 par exchanged for (0.9) share Common $1 par
United States Smelting Refining & Mining Co. (ME) (New) name changed to UV Industries, Inc. 06/09/1972 which name changed to UV Industries, Inc. Liquidating Trust 03/25/1980
(See UV Industries, Inc. Liquidating Trust)

FEDERAL PAPER BRD INC (NC)
Reincorporated 4/20/94
Common $5 par split (3) for (2) by issuance of (0.5) additional share 1/17/68
Common $5 par split (2) for (1) by issuance of (1) additional share 8/23/76
4.6% Preferred $25 par called for redemption 9/15/78
Common $5 par split (2) for (1) by issuance of (1) additional share 7/16/84
$2.3125 Conv. Exchangeable Class A Preferred $1 par called for redemption 3/13/87
Common $5 par split (2) for (1) by issuance of (1) additional share 7/14/88
State of incorporation changed from (NY) to (NC) 4/20/94
$2.875 Conv. Preferred $1 par called for redemption 8/9/95
$1.20 Conv. Preferred $1 par called for redemption 2/17/96
Merged into International Paper Co. 3/12/96
Each share Common $5 par exchanged for $55 cash

FEDERAL PEN LTE (QC)
Name changed to Mafricor Resources 02/17/1997
(See Mafricor Resources)

FEDERAL PETE INC (DE)
Class A Common $1 par split (2) for (1) by issuance of (1) additional share 03/22/1971

Class A Common $1 par reclassified as Common $1 par 05/19/1971
Merged into Doric Corp. 07/17/1972
Each share Common $1 par exchanged for $4.50 cash

FEDERAL PIONEER LTD (CANADA)
Reincorporated 01/27/1978
Place of incorporation changed from (MB) to (Canada) 01/27/1978
5.5% Conv. 1st Preference Ser. A $50 par called for redemption 07/15/1979
Class A no par reclassified as Common no par 00/00/1980
Common no par split (4) for (1) by issuance of (3) additional shares 06/04/1984
Common no par split (3) for (1) by issuance of (2) additional shares 01/06/1987
Merged into Schneider Canada Inc. 05/08/1990
Each share Common no par exchanged for $15 cash

FEDERAL PUBLIC SERVICE CORP.
Reorganized as American Utilities Service Corp. 00/00/1934
Details not available

FEDERAL PURCHASE CORP.
Liquidated in 1933

FEDERAL QUALITY HOMES, INC. (FL)
Adjudicated bankrupt 4/7/65
No stockholders' equity

FEDERAL RLTY INVT TR (MD)
Reincorporated 06/07/1999
Each old Common Share of Bene. Int. no par exchanged for (0.5) new Common Share of Bene. Int. no par 11/15/1971
New Common Shares of Bene. Int. no par split (2) for (1) by issuance of (1) additional share 08/31/1982
New Common Shares of Bene. Int. no par split (3) for (2) by issuance of (0.5) additional share 11/05/1985
Reincorporated under the laws of (DC) to (MD) and Preferred and Common Shares of Bene. Int. no par changed to 1¢ par 06/07/1999
7.95% Preferred Ser. A 1¢ par called for redemption at $25 plus $0.23959 accrued dividend on 06/13/2003
8.5% Preferred Ser. B 1¢ par called for redemption at $25 on 11/27/2006
(Additional Information in Active)

FEDERAL RES CORP (NV)
Common 50¢ par changed to 1¢ par 03/08/1984
Ceased operations 00/00/1998
Company's president advised no operating funds available

FEDERAL SVGS & LN CORP (ON)
98.5% held by Realty Capital Investments (Central) Ltd. as of 04/30/1971
Public interest eliminated

FEDERAL SVGS BK (NEW BRITAIN, CT)
Stock Dividend - 10% 4/3/89
Merged into MidConn Bank (Kensington, CT) 6/1/94
Each share Common 1¢ par exchanged for $15.50 cash

FEDERAL SVGS BK P R (BAYAMON, PR)
Acquired by Banco de Santander S.A. de Credito 03/13/1989
Each share Common $1 par exchanged for $21.50 cash

FEDERAL SEC PROTN SVCS INC (DE)
Name changed to Platina Energy Group, Inc. 06/17/2005
(See Platina Energy Group, Inc.)

FEDERAL SECURITY INSURANCE CO. (UT)
Each share Capital Stock $100 par exchanged for (10) shares Capital Stock $10 par in 1955
Name changed to Federated Security Insurance Co. in July 1957
(See Federated Security Insurance Co.)

FEDERAL SVCS ACQUISITION CORP (DE)
Issue Information - 21,100,000 UNITS consisting of (1) share COM and (2) WTS offered at $6 per Unit on 10/19/2005
Name changed to ATS Corp. 01/30/2007
(See ATS Corp.)

FEDERAL SERVICES FINANCE CORP. (DE)
Each share 7% Preferred $100 par exchanged for (1) share 6% Preferred $100 par and (0.4) share Common no par in 1936
Each share Common no par exchanged for (4) shares Class B Common no par in 1952
Class A & B Common no par changed to $1 par in 1956
Each share Class A & B Common $1 par exchanged for (2) shares Common 50¢ par in 1959
Common 50¢ par changed to 40¢ par and (0.25) additional share issued 11/20/64
Stock Dividend - 10% 1/15/49
Merged into Interstate Securities Co. (DE) 4/25/66
Each share 5% Preferred Ser. A $100 par exchanged for (5) shares 5% Preferred $20 par
Each share Common 40¢ par exchanged for (0.08) share 6% Conv. Preferred $100 par
(See Interstate Securities Co. (DE))

FEDERAL SHELL HOMES INC (FL)
Name changed to Federal Quality Homes, Inc. 7/30/62
(See Federal Quality Homes, Inc.)

FEDERAL SIGN & SIGNAL CORP (DE)
Reincorporated 4/1/69
Common $1 par split (2) for (1) by issuance of (1) additional share 11/17/59
$1.25 Preferred $10 par called for redemption 7/30/65
State of incorporation changed from (NY) to (DE) 4/1/69
$1.20 Conv. Prior Preferred no par called for redemption 5/1/69
Stock Dividends - 10% 9/1/55; 100% 2/6/68
Name changed to Federal Signal Corp. 8/29/75

FEDERAL SPORTS & ENTMT INC (NV)
Common $0.001 par split (20) for (1) by issuance of (19) additional shares payable 05/07/2010 to holders of record 04/19/2010 Ex date - 05/10/2010
Name changed to Universal Gold Mining Corp. 05/12/2010

FEDERAL STAMPINGS, INC. (MN)
Liquidated for cash 4/9/64

FEDERAL STL CORP (OH)
Completely liquidated 04/21/1967
Each share Common no par exchanged for first and final distribution of (0.116009) share Inland Steel Co. Capital Stock no par
Inland Steel Co. reorganized as Inland Steel Industries, Inc. 05/01/1986 which name changed to Ryerson Tull, Inc. (New) 02/26/1999 which name changed to Ryerson, Inc. 01/01/2006
(See Ryerson, Inc.)

FEDERAL STORAGE CO. (DE)
Under plan of merger name changed to Security Storage Co. of Washington (New) and each share Class A Common no par or Class B Common no par exchanged for (1) share Common no par 9/1/63

FEDERAL STR FD INC (MA)
Common $1 par split (20) for (1) by issuance of (19) additional shares 03/23/1962
Common $1 par split (3) for (1) by issuance of (2) additional shares 09/25/1972
Name changed to State Street Growth Fund, Inc. 03/11/1983
(See State Street Growth Fund, Inc.)

FEDERAL STREET & PLEASANT VALLEY PASSENGER RAILWAY CO.
Merged into Pittsburgh Railways Co. 9/30/50
Each share Common $25 par exchanged for (2.1) shares Common no par and $2.50 cash
Pittsburgh Railways Co. name changed to Pittway Corp. (PA) 11/28/67 which merged into Pittway Corp. (DE) 12/28/89
(See Pittway Corp. (DE))

FEDERAL SUGAR REFINING CO. OF NEW YORK
Acquired by Spreckels Sugar Corp. in 1929
Details not available

FEDERAL SURETY CO. (DAVENPORT, IA)
In receivership in 1931. Now out of business. Stock valueless

FEDERAL SYSTEM OF BAKERIES OF AMERICA, INC.
Acquired by Federal Bake Shops, Inc. 00/00/1929
Details not available

FEDERAL TELEGRAPH CO.
Merged into Federal-Brandes, Inc. in 1926
Details not available

FEDERAL TOOL & MANUFACTURING CO. (MN)
Name changed to Federal Stampings, Inc. 4/30/63
(See Federal Stampings, Inc.)

FEDERAL TR CO (WATERVILLE, ME)
Common $100 par changed to $25 par and (3) additional shares issued 11/29/1954
Common $25 par changed to $12.50 par and (1) additional share issued 09/27/1961
Stock Dividends - 25% 12/11/1944; 10% 12/16/1954
Merrill Bankshares Co. acquired 99.65% through exchange offer which expired 07/29/1971
Public interest eliminated

FEDERAL TR CORP (FL)
Stock Dividend - 2% payable 06/12/2006 to holders of record 06/01/2006 Ex date - 05/30/2006
Acquired by Hartford Financial Services Group, Inc. 06/24/2009
Each share Common 1¢ par exchanged for $1 cash

FEDERAL TRUSTCO INC (ON)
Name changed to RealCap Holdings Ltd. 10/02/1980

FEDERAL UTD CORP (DE)
$3 Preferred $1 par called for redemption at $55 plus $0.75 accrued dividend on 3/31/97
(Additional Information in Active)

FEDERAL URANIUM CORP. (NV)
Merged into Federal Resources Corp. share for share 05/02/1960

FEDERAL URANIUM CORP. (UT)
Each (25) shares Capital Stock 1¢ par exchanged for (1) share Capital Stock 25¢ par 01/00/1955
Merged into Federal Uranium Corp. (NV) on a (0.5) for (1) basis 04/28/1955
Federal Uranium merged into Federal Resources Corp. 05/02/1960

FEDERAL VENTURES LTD (BAHAMAS)
Company ceased operations 12/31/1991
No stockholders' equity

FEDERAL WATER & GAS CORP.
Liquidation completed in 1951
Details not available

FEDERAL WATER & GAS CORP. (DE)
Charter dissolved 8/21/48

FEDERAL WATER SERVICE CORP.
Recapitalized as Federal Water & Gas Corp. in 1941
Details not available

FEDERALE MYNBOU BEPERK (SOUTH AFRICA)
ADR agreement terminated 05/11/1995
Each ADR for Ordinary Rand-1 par exchanged for (1) share Ordinary Rand-1 par

FEDERALS INC (MI)
Common $1 par changed to 1¢ par 12/11/1973
Proclaimed dissolved for failure to file reports and pay fees 05/15/1980

FEDERATED ADJ RATE U S GOVT FD (MD)
Name changed to Federated Limited Duration Government Fund, Inc. 09/11/2000
Federated Limited Duration Government Fund, Inc. name changed to Federated Intermediate Government Fund, Inc. 04/30/2005

FEDERATED AMERN INS CO (WA)
Merged into Federated Merger Co., Inc. 12/5/84
Each share Common $10 par exchanged for $12 cash

FEDERATED BK S S B (WAUWATOSA, WI)
Merged into Firstar Corp. (Old) 09/11/1992
Each share Common 10¢ par exchanged for (0.353) share Common $1.25 par
Firstar Corp. (Old) merged into Firstar Corp. (New) 11/20/1998 which merged into U.S. Bancorp (DE) 02/27/2001

FEDERATED BUSINESS FORMS, INC. (NJ)
Out of business in August, 1962
No stockholders' equity

FEDERATED CAPITAL CORP.
Dissolved in 1935
Details not available

FEDERATED CAPITAL CORP. (DE)
Common $4 par split (11) for (8) by issuance of (0.375) additional share 2/12/74
Merged into Mercantile Texas Corp. 12/30/76
Each share Common $4 par exchanged for (0.1) share $3 Conv. Preferred Ser. A $50 par and (0.25) share Common $5 par
Mercantile Texas Corp. name changed to MCorp 10/11/84
(See MCorp)

FEDERATED COMMUNICATIONS CORP (DE)
Each share old Common 1¢ par exchanged for (0.1) share new Common 1¢ par 1/26/76
Charter cancelled and declared inoperative and void for non-payment of taxes 3/1/84

FEDERATED CORP. OF DELAWARE (DE)
Name changed to Norma Industries, Inc. and Class B Common $1 par changed to 10¢ par 12/1/66
Norma Industries, Inc. name changed to Gal Friday Services, Inc. 5/12/68

(See Gal Friday Services, Inc.)

FEDERATED DEPT STORES INC (DE)
Common 1¢ par split (2) for (1) by issuance of (1) additional share payable 6/9/2006 to holders of record 5/26/2006 Ex date - 6/12/2006
Name changed to Macy's, Inc. 6/1/2007

FEDERATED DEPT STORES INC NEW (DE)
Under plan of reorganization each share Common 1¢ par automatically became (1) share Federated Department Stores, Inc. Common 1¢ par 12/19/94
Federated Department Stores, Inc. name changed to Macy's, Inc. 6/1/2007

FEDERATED DEPT STORES INC OLD (DE)
Common no par changed to $5 par in 1948
4-1/4% Preferred $100 par called for redemption 9/8/54
Common $5 par changed to $2.50 par and (1) additional share issued 2/18/56
Common $2.50 par changed to $1.25 par and (1) additional share issued 9/29/60
Common $1.25 par split (2) for (1) by issuance of (1) additional share 7/26/68
Common $1.25 par split (2) for (1) by issuance of (1) additional share 5/11/87
Stock Dividends - 100% 8/12/46; 20% 6/29/51
Merged into Campeau Corp. 7/28/88
Each share Common $1.25 par exchanged for $73.50 cash

FEDERATED DEV CO (NY)
Each old Share of Bene. Int. no par exchanged for (0.025) new Share of Bene. Int. no par 12/07/1979
New Shares of Bene. Int. no par split (40) for (1) by issuance of (39) additional shares 12/28/1979
Merged into Federated Development Corp. (MD) 04/03/1987
Each new Share of Bene. Int. no par exchanged for $121.72 principal amount of Federated Development Co. 7-Year Secured Notes and $21 cash

FEDERATED DEV CORP (PA)
Merged into Federated Natural Resources Corp. 9/30/83
Each share Class B Common 25¢ par exchanged for (2.448) shares Class B Common 10¢ par
(See Federated Development Co.)

FEDERATED DUAL EXCHANGE FD INC (DE)
Capital Shares $25 par and Income Shares $25 par changed to $1.25 and (19) additional shares issued respectively 04/08/1968
Name changed to Pegasus Income & Capital Fund, Inc. 04/23/1974
Pegasus Income & Capital Fund, Inc. acquired by St. Paul Income Fund, Inc. 01/07/1981 which name changed to AMEV U.S. Government Securities Fund, Inc. 05/01/1985 which name changed to Fortis Income Portfolios, Inc. 02/22/1992
(See Fortis Income Portfolios, Inc.)

FEDERATED ELECTRS INC (NY)
Out of business 02/00/1965
No stockholders' equity

FEDERATED ENHANCED TREAS INCOME FD (DE)
Under plan of reorganization each Common Share of Bene. Int. 1¢ par automatically became (1) share Federated Income Securities Trust Enhanced Treasury Income Fund 10/23/2015

FEDERATED ENTERPRISES CORP (CA)
Capital Stock $100 par reclassified as Common $100 par 03/20/1963
Charter suspended for failure to file reports and pay taxes 02/03/1975

FEDERATED EQUITY FDS (MA)
Capital Appreciation Fund Class K reclassified as Class R 12/31/2010
Under plan of reorganization each share Capital Appreciation Fund Class A automatically became (0.90219302) share Federated Equity Income Fund, Inc. Class A 04/19/2013
Under plan of reorganization each share Capital Appreciation Fund Class B automatically became (0.85221531) share Federated Equity Income Fund, Inc. Class B 04/19/2013
Under plan of reorganization each share Capital Appreciation Fund Class C automatically became (0.85041109) share Federated Equity Income Fund, Inc. Class C 04/19/2013
Under plan of reorganization each Institutional Share Class automatically became (0.90041109) Federated Equity Income Fund, Inc. Institutional Share Class 04/19/2013
Under plan of reorganization each share Capital Appreciation Fund Class R automatically became (0.89375538) share Capital Appreciation Fund Class R 04/19/2013
(Additional Information in Active)

FEDERATED FD U S GOVT SECS INC (MD)
Under plan of reorganization each share Class A $0.001 par, Class B $0.001 par and Class C $0.001 par automatically became (1) share Federated Income Securities Trust Fund for U.S. Government Securities Class A, B, or C respectively 10/07/2002

FEDERATED FINANCIAL FUND LTD. (AB)
Name changed to NW Financial Fund Ltd. 03/06/1970
NW Financial Fund Ltd. name changed to NW Canadian Fund Ltd. 08/23/1972
(See NW Canadian Fund Ltd.)

FEDERATED FINL SVGS & LN ASSN (WI)
Name changed to Federated Bank, S.S.B. (Wauwatosa, WI) 02/23/1990
Federated Bank, S.S.B. (Wauwatosa, WI) merged into Firstar Corp. (Old) 09/11/1992 which merged into Firstar which merged into Firstar Corp. (New) 11/20/1998 which merged into U.S. Bancorp (DE) 02/27/2001

FEDERATED FLTG RATE TR (MA)
Name changed to Federated Income Securities Trust 03/09/1992

FEDERATED FRANCHISES INC (NJ)
Name changed to Sinequanon Corp. 08/04/1976
Sinequanon Corp. name changed to Synthetic Blood International Inc. (NJ) 11/05/1990 which reincorporated in Delaware as Oxygen Biotherapeutics, Inc. 07/01/2008 which name changed to Tenax Therapeutics, Inc. 09/19/2014

FEDERATED FUND (MA)
Merged into Income Foundation Fund, Inc. 12/31/1956
Each share Common $1 par exchanged for (4.263476) shares Capital Stock 10¢ par
Income Foundation Fund, Inc. name changed to Boston Foundation Fund Inc. 09/22/1969 which name changed to Federated Stock & Bond Fund, Inc. (Old) 01/01/1985 which name changed to Stock & Bond Fund, Inc. 04/17/1993 which name changed to Federated Stock & Bond Fund, Inc. (New) (MD) 03/31/1996 which reincorporated in Massachusetts as Federated Stock & Bond Fund 09/05/2008

FEDERATED FUND OF NEW ENGLAND (MA)
Name changed to Federated Fund 03/04/1956
Federated Fund merged into Income Foundation Fund, Inc. 12/31/1956 which name changed to Boston Foundation Fund Inc. 09/22/1969 which name changed to Federated Stock & Bond Fund, Inc. (Old) 01/01/1985 which name changed to Stock & Bond Fund, Inc. 04/17/1993 which name changed to Federated Stock & Bond Fund, Inc. (New) (MD) 03/31/1996 which reincorporated in Massachusetts as Federated Stock & Bond Fund 09/05/2008

FEDERATED GROUP INC (DE)
Common 10¢ par split (3) for (2) by issuance of (0.5) additional share 5/3/85
Merged into Atari Corp. 10/28/87
Each share Common 10¢ par exchanged for $6.25 cash

FEDERATED GROWTH FD INC (DE)
Name changed to Pligrowth Fund, Inc. 01/01/1971
Pligrowth Fund, Inc. merged into Plitrend Fund, Inc. 07/23/1982 which name changed to U.S. Trend Fund, Inc. (PA) 02/00/1986 which reincorporated in Maryland as Capstone U.S. Trend Fund, Inc. 05/11/1992 which name changed to Capstone Growth Fund, Inc. 08/26/1994 which name changed to Capstone Series Fund, Inc. 01/22/2002

FEDERATED GROWTH FUND LTD. (AB)
Name changed to NW Growth Fund Ltd. 3/6/70

FEDERATED GTY CORP (DE)
Common $1 par split (2) for (1) by issuance of (1) additional share 06/01/1984
Recapitalized as Alfa Corp. 04/20/1987
Each share Common $1 par exchanged for (1) share Common $1 par
(See Alfa Corp.)

FEDERATED GTY LIFE INS CO (AL)
Stock Dividend - 100% 03/01/1979
Under plan of reorganization each share Common $1 par automatically became (1) share Federated Guaranty Corp. (DE) Common $1 par 03/01/1984
Federated Guaranty Corp. (DE) recapitalized as Alfa Corp. 04/20/1987
(See Alfa Corp.)

FEDERATED HIGH INCOME SECS INC (MD)
Name changed to Liberty High Income Bond Fund Inc. 10/25/90
Liberty High Income Bond Fund Inc. name changed to Federated High Income Bond Fund, Inc. 3/31/96

FEDERATED INCOME & PRIVATE PLACEMENT FD (DE)
Merged into Federated High Income Securities, Inc. 11/21/83
Each share Capital Stock $1 par exchanged for (0.726) share Capital Stock 1¢ par
Federated High Income Securities, Inc. name changed to Liberty High Income Bond Fund Inc. 10/25/90 which name changed to Federated High Income Bond Fund, Inc. 3/31/96

FEDERATED INCOME SECS TR (MA)
California Municipal & Stock Fund Class A reclassified as Stock & California Municipal Fund Class A 12/04/2006
California Municipal & Stock Fund Class C reclassified as Stock & California Municipal Fund Class A 12/04/2006
Under plan of reorganization each share Stock & California Municipal Fund Class A and Class C automatically became shares of Muni & Stock Advantage Fund Class A or Class C on a net asset basis respectively 03/27/2009

FEDERATED INDS INC (MN)
Class A Common 5¢ par changed to 1-2/3¢ par and (2) additional shares issued 06/01/1970
Statutorily dissolved 12/09/1991

FEDERATED INTER GOVT TR (MA)
Name changed to Federated U.S Government Securities Fund: 2-5 Years 04/13/1995

FEDERATED INTER MUN TR (MA)
Name changed to Intermediate Municipal Trust 10/25/1993

FEDERATED INTL INC (FL)
Administratively dissolved 9/26/97

FEDERATED INVESTORS, INC. (CO)
Merged into Preferred-American Investors Co. on a (1.5) for (1) basis 3/31/60
(See Preferred-American Investors Co.)

FEDERATED INVS INC OLD (PA)
Class B Common 5¢ par split (2) for (1) by issuance of (1) additional share 3/13/70
Class B Common 5¢ par split (4) for (1) by issuance of (3) additional shares 1/21/81
Merged into Aetna Life & Casualty Co. 11/1/82
Each share Class B Common 5¢ par exchanged for (1.25) shares Common no par
Aetna Life & Casualty Co. name changed to Aetna, Inc. (CT) 7/19/96 which merged into ING Groep N.V. 12/13/2000

FEDERATED INVTS INC (AL)
Class A Common 10¢ par and Class B Common 10¢ par reclassified as Common 10¢ par 10/02/1970
Name changed to United Financing Corp. 02/22/1972

FEDERATED LTD DURATION GOVT FD INC (MD)
Name changed to Federated Intermediate Government Fund, Inc. 04/30/2005

FEDERATED MASTER TR (MA)
Merged into Money Market Obligations Trust 3/31/99
Each Share of Bene. Int. $1 par received Federated Master Trust shares on a net asset basis

FEDERATED MED INC (DE)
Name changed to Medical Depot, Inc. 11/20/89
(See Medical Depot, Inc.)

FEDERATED MEDIA INC (DE)
Liquidation completed
Each share Common 10¢ par exchanged for initial distribution of $7.55 cash 11/08/1974
Each share Common 10¢ par received second distribution of $0.27 cash 11/30/1977
Each share Common 10¢ par received third and final distribution of $0.26 cash 09/26/1980

FEDERATED METALS CORP.
Acquired by American Smelting & Refining Co. in 1932
Details not available

FEDERATED MNG LTD (BC)
Acquired by Northrim Mines Ltd. 00/00/1974
Each share Common 50¢ par exchanged for approximately (0.143918) share Capital Stock no par
(See Northrim Mines Ltd.)

FEDERATED MONEY MKT INC (MD)
Merged into Money Market Management, Inc. (MA) 05/16/1980
Each share Capital Stock 1¢ par exchanged for (1) share Capital Stock 1¢ par
Money Market Management, Inc. (MA) reorganized in Maryland as Money Market Management 06/29/1982 which merged into Money Market Obligations Trust 02/01/2000

FEDERATED MORTGAGE CORP. OF DELAWARE (DE)
Each share Class A Common $10 par or Class B Common $10 par exchanged for (10) shares Class A Common $1 par or Class B Common $1 par respectively 10/15/57
Name changed to Federated Corp. of Delaware in 1959
Federated Corp. of Delaware name changed to Norma Industries, Inc. 12/1/66 which name changed to Gal Friday Services, Inc. 5/12/68
(See Gal Friday Services, Inc.)

FEDERATED MTG INVS (NY)
Name changed to Federated Development Co. 07/22/1970
(See Federated Development Co.)

FEDERATED MUN HIGH YIELD ADVANTAGE FD INC (MD)
Name changed 08/01/2004
Name changed from Federated Municipal Opportunities Fund, Inc. to Federated Municipal High Yield Advantage Fund, Inc. 08/01/2004
Merged into Federated Municipal Securities Income Trust 11/10/2006
Each share Class A $0.001 par exchanged for (1) share High Yield Advantage Fund Class A no par
Each share Class B $0.001 par exchanged for (1) share High Yield Advantage Fund Class B no par
Each share Class C $0.001 par exchanged for (1) share High Yield Advantage Fund Class C no par
Each share Class F $0.001 par exchanged for (1) share High Yield Advantage Fund Class F no par

FEDERATED N J MUN SER TR (MA)
Trust terminated 09/20/1988
Details not available

FEDERATED NAT RES CORP (DE)
Liquidation completed
Each share Class B Common 10¢ par exchanged for initial distribution of $1.50 cash 5/12/89
Assets transferred to Federated Natural Resources Corp. Liquidating Trust and Class B Common 10¢ par reclassified as Shares of Ben. Int. 10¢ par 6/30/89
(See Federated Natural Resources Corp. Liquidating Trust)

FEDERATED NATL HLDG CO (FL)
Name changed to FedNat Holding Co. 06/07/2018

FEDERATED NATURAL RESOURCES CORP. LIQUIDATING TRUST (DE)
Liquidation completed
Each Share of Ben. Int. 10¢ par received initial distribution of $1 cash 1/26/90
Each Share of Ben. Int. 10¢ par received second and final distribution of $0.485 cash 6/30/92

FEDERATED OPT INCOME FD INC (MD)
Merged into Federated High Income Securities, Inc. 2/19/82
Each share Capital Stock 1¢ par exchanged for (1.2027) shares Capital Stock 1¢ par
Federated High Income Securities, Inc. name changed to Liberty High Income Bond Fund Inc. 10/25/90 which name changed to Federated High Income Bond Fund, Inc. 3/31/96

FEDERATED PETROLEUMS LTD. (AB)
Merged into Home Oil Co. Ltd. 00/00/1955
Each share Capital Stock no par exchanged for (0.5) share Class B no par
(See Home Oil Co. Ltd.)

FEDERATED PREMIER INTER MUN INCOME FD (PA)
Under plan of reorganization each share Auction Market Preferred Ser. A, 144A Preferred Ser 2014 and Common Share of Ben. Int. 1¢ par automaticallly became (1) share Federated Premier Municipal Income Fund Auction Market Preferred Ser. A, 144A Preferred Ser 2014 or (0.95005928) Common Share of Ben. Int. 1¢ par respectively 11/17/2017

FEDERATED PUBNS INC (DE)
Common no par split (3) for (1) by issuance of (2) additional shares 05/10/1960
Common no par split (3) for (1) by issuance of (2) additional shares 06/10/1964
Common no par split (2) for (1) by issuance of (1) additional share 01/02/1970
Merged into Gannett Co., Inc. (NY) 06/30/1971
Each share Common no par exchanged for (1.1) shares Common $1 par
Gannett Co., Inc. (NY) reincorporated in Delaware 05/29/1972 which name changed to TEGNA Inc. 06/26/2015

FEDERATED PURCHASER INC (NY)
Class A 10¢ par reclassified as Common 10¢ par 03/22/1962
Common 10¢ par split (5) for (4) by issuance of (0.25) additional share 02/02/1981
Common 10¢ par split (5) for (4) by issuance of (0.25) additional share 02/02/1982
Common 10¢ par split (5) for (4) by issuance of (0.25) additional share 10/11/1985
Merged out of existence 10/05/2001
Details not available

FEDERATED SEC INS CO (UT)
Each share Capital Stock $10 par exchanged for (10) shares Capital Stock $1 par 7/17/63
Charter revoked for failure to file reports 12/31/73

FEDERATED SHORT INTER GOVT TR (MA)
Name changed to Federated U.S. Government Securities Fund: 1-3 Years 04/20/1993

FEDERATED STK & BD FD INC NEW (MD)
Common no par reclassified as Class A no par 08/30/1996
Reincorporated under the laws of Massachusetts as Federated Stock & Bond Fund 09/05/2008

FEDERATED STK & BD FD INC OLD (MD)
Name changed to Stock & Bond Fund, Inc. 04/17/1993
Stock & Bond Fund, Inc. name changed to Federated Stock & Bond Fund, Inc. (New) (MD) 03/31/1996 which reincorporated in Massachusetts as Federated Stock & Bond Fund 09/05/2008

FEDERATED TAX FREE INCOME FD INC (MD)
Name changed to Liberty Municipal Securities Fund Inc. 12/23/92
Liberty Municipal Securities Fund Inc. name changed to Federated Municipal Securities Fund, Inc. 3/31/96

FEDERATED TAX FREE TR (MA)
Shares of Bene. Int. no par split (10) for (1) by issuance of (9) additional shares 05/03/1980
Trust terminated 03/21/2001
Details not available

FEDERATED TEX BANCORPORATION INC (TX)
Merged into Federated Capital Corp. 1/29/74
Each share Common $5 par exchanged for (1) share Common $4 par
Federated Capital Corp. merged into Mercantile Texas Corp. 12/30/76 which name changed to MCorp 10/11/84
(See MCorp.)

FEDERATED UTIL FD INC (MD)
Reorganized under the laws of Massachusetts as Federated Capital Income Fund, Inc. 12/20/2002

FEDERATED UTIL TR (MD)
Name changed to Fortress Utility Fund Inc. 05/30/1990
Fortress Utility Fund Inc. merged into Federated Utility Fund Inc. (MD) 06/01/1996 which reorganized in Massachusetts as Federated Capital Income Fund, Inc. 12/20/2002

FEDERATED VARIABLE RATE MTG SECS TR (MA)
Under plan of reorganization each Share of Bene. Int. no par automatically became Federated Income Trust Share of Bene. Int. Institutional Class no par on a net asset basis 04/26/1990

FEDERATION BANK & TRUST CO. (NEW YORK, NY)
Stock Dividends - (7) for (33) 12/28/44; 25% 11/5/45; 20% 11/1/54
Merged into Franklin National Bank (Mineola, NY) 6/30/67
Each share Capital Stock $10 par exchanged for (1) share $2.45 Conv. Preferred $25 par
Franklin National Bank (Mineola, NY) reorganized as Franklin New York Corp. 9/22/69
(See Franklin New York Corp.)

FEDERATION GROUP LTD (AUSTRALIA)
ADR agreement terminated 6/11/2007
No ADR holders' equity

FEDERATION RES N L (AUSTRALIA)
ADR agreement terminated 08/16/1999
Each ADR for Ordinary exchanged for $0.044 cash

FEDFIRST BANCSHARES INC (DE)
Acquired by Southern National Corp. 1/29/93
Each share Common 1¢ par exchanged for (2.3443) shares Common $5 par
Southern National Corp. name changed to BB&T Corp. 5/19/97

FEDFIRST FINL CORP (MD)
Merged into CB Financial Services Inc. 10/31/2014
Each share Common 1¢ par exchanged for (1.159) shares Common $0.4167 par

FEDFIRST FINL CORP (USA)
Reorganized under the laws of Maryland 09/21/2010
Each share Common 1¢ par exchanged for (0.4735) share Common 1¢ par

FEDONE SVGS BK F A (KANE, PA)
Name changed to First Federal Savings Bank (Kane, PA) 6/20/94
First Federal Savings Bank (Kane, PA) merged into Northwest Savings Bank (Warren, PA) 3/31/96 reorganized as Northwest Bancorp Inc. 2/18/98

FEDONICS INC (DE)
Charter cancelled and declared inoperative and void for non-payment of taxes 3/1/80

FEDORA INDS INC (BC)
Name changed to Airbomb.com Marketing Ltd. (BC) 02/21/2000
Airbomb.com Marketing Ltd. (BC) reincorporated in Delaware as airbomb.com inc. 05/09/2000

FEDSURE HLDGS LTD (SOUTH AFRICA)
ADR agreement terminated 7/30/2001
Each Sponsored ADR for Ordinary no par exchanged for (2) Ordinary shares

FEEL GOLF CO INC (CA)
Each share old Common $0.001 par exchanged for (0.01) share new Common $0.001 par 04/02/2012
Reincorporated under the laws of Nevada as Intelligent Living Inc. 08/26/2013
Intelligent Living Inc. recapitalized as Intelligent Living America Inc. 11/24/2014

FEEL GOOD CARS CORP (ON)
Name changed to Zenn Motor Co. Inc. 06/15/2007
Each share Common no par exchanged for (1) share Common no par
Zenn Motor Co. Inc. name changed to EEStor Corp. 04/06/2015

FEELGOODS INTL LTD (NV)
Each share old Common $0.001 par exchanged for (5) shares new Common $0.001 par 03/20/2006
Each share new Common $0.001 par exchanged again for (0.01) share new Common $0.001 par 03/14/2007
Each share new Common $0.001 par exchanged again for (0.01) share new Common $0.001 par 01/24/2008
Name changed to Premere Resources Corp. 01/22/2009
(See Premere Resources Corp.)

FEHR (FRANK) BREWING CO. (DE)
Recapitalized 00/00/1942
6% Part. Preference $1 par reclassified as 6% Part. Preferred $1 par
Common $1 par changed to 50¢ par
Reorganized 11/23/1959
6% Part. Preferred $1 par reclassified as 6% Preferred $1 par
No Common stockholders' equity
Assets liquidated for benefit of creditor 11/04/1965
No stockholders' equity

FEI CO (OR)
Acquired by Thermo Fisher Scientific Inc. 09/20/2016
Each share Common no par exchanged for $107.50 cash

FEI CORP (MN)
Name changed to Econo-Therm Energy Systems Corp. and Common 10¢ par changed to 5¢ par 12/12/1974
(See Econo-Therm Energy Systems Corp.)

FEIHE INTL INC (UT)
Acquired by Platinum Infant Formula Holding Ltd. 06/27/2013

Each share Common $0.001 par exchanged for $7.40 cash

FEINSTEIN REPORT INC (NV)
Recapitalized as United E&P, Inc. 04/17/2007
Each (43) shares Common $0.001 par exchanged for (1) share Common $0.001 par
(See United E&P, Inc.)

FELAFEL CORP (DE)
Common $0.0001 par split (7.5) for (1) by issuance of (6.5) additional shares payable 04/11/2012 to holders of record 04/09/2012 Ex date - 04/12/2012
Name changed to Valor Gold Corp. 04/19/2012
Valor Gold Corp. name changed to Vaporin, Inc. 02/07/2014 which merged into Vapor Corp. 03/05/2015

FELCO SPORTS PRODS INC (NY)
Dissolved by proclamation 3/25/92

FELCOR LODGING TR INC (MD)
9% Depositary Preferred Ser. B called for redemption at $25 on 09/12/2005
8% Depositary Preferred Ser. C called for redemption at $25 plus $0.072222 accrued dividends on 05/14/2015
Merged into RLJ Lodging Trust 08/31/2017
Each share $1.95 Conv. Preferred Ser. A 1¢ par exchanged for (1) share $1.95 Conv. Preferred Ser. A 1¢ par
Each share Common 1¢ par exchanged for (0.362) Common Sthare of Bene. Int. 1¢ par

FELCOR SUITE HOTELS INC (MD)
Reincorporated 06/23/1995
State of incorporation changed from (DE) to (MD) 06/23/1995
Under plan of merger name changed to FelCor Lodging Trust Inc. 07/28/1998
FelCor Lodging Trust Inc. merged into RLJ Lodging Trust 08/31/2017

FELD LEASING INC (KS)
Stock Dividends - 100% 08/20/1971; 100% 08/25/1972
Merged into Gelco-Feld Corp. 10/22/1974
Each share Common 50¢ par exchanged for (0.9) share Common 50¢ par
Gelco-Feld Corp. name changed back to Gelco Corp. 12/04/1975
(See Gelco Corp.)

FELDMAN MALL PPTYS INC (MD)
Name changed to Trade Street Residential, Inc. 06/18/2012
Trade Street Residential, Inc. merged into Independence Realty Trust, Inc. 09/17/2015

FELDMAN SALKIN WELCH & WINER INC (MD)
Name changed to Salkin, Welch & Co., Inc. 12/6/72
Salkin, Welch & Co., Inc. merged into Advest Group, Inc. 6/1/81 which merged into MONY Group Inc. 1/31/2001
(See MONY Group Inc.)

FELDSPAR-MICA-URANIUM CORP. (DE)
No longer in existence having become inoperative and void for non-payment of taxes 6/1/57

FELDT MANUFACTURING CO., INC. (TX)
Charter forfeited for failure to pay franchise taxes 3/17/64

FELLOWS CO. OF NEW YORK
Liquidated completed in 1951
Details not available

FELLOWS ENERGY LTD (NV)
Common $0.001 par split (7) for (1) by issuance of (6) additional shares payable 11/17/2003 to holders of record 11/14/2003 Ex date - 11/14/2003
SEC revoked common stock registration 01/17/2013

FELLOWS MED MFG INC (NY)
Capital Stock $100 par changed to $2 par 00/00/1944
Capital Stock $2 par changed to $1 par 04/03/1957
Merged into Chromalloy American Corp. (DE) 01/18/1971
Each share Capital Stock $1 par exchanged for (0.026088) share $5 Conv. Preferred $1 par
Chromally American Corp. (DE) merged into Sun Chemical Corp. 12/23/1986 which name changed to Sequa Corp. 05/08/1987
(See Sequa Corp.)

FELLOWSHIP BANK (MOUNT LAUREL TOWNSHIP, NJ)
Merged into Horizon Bancorp 5/29/81
Each share Capital Stock $10 par exchanged for $40 cash

FELMONT OIL CORP (DE)
Capital Stock $1 par split (3) for (1) by issuance of (2) additional shares 6/9/80
Merged into Homestake Mining Co. 6/19/84
Each share Capital Stock $1 par exchanged for (1.155) shares Common $1 par
Homestake Mining Co. merged into Barrick Gold Corp. 12/14/2001

FELMONT PETROLEUM CORP. (DE)
Under plan of merger name changed to Felmont Oil Corp. 6/30/65
Felmont Oil Corp. merged into Homestake Mining Co. 6/19/84 which merged into Barrick Gold Corp. 12/14/2001

FELSWAY CORP (DE)
Common 10¢ par split (3) for (2) by issuance of (0.5) additional share 7/14/69
Merged into Heck's, Inc. (WV) 10/5/78
Each share Common 10¢ par exchanged for (0.25) share Common 10¢ par and $20 cash
Heck's, Inc. (WV) reincorporated in Delaware as Hallwood Industries Inc. 7/2/90 which name changed to Steel City Products, Inc. 1/13/93
(See Steel City Products, Inc.)

FELSWAY SHOE CORP (DE)
Name changed to Felsway Corp. 6/23/69
Felsway Corp. merged into Heck's, Inc. (WV) 10/5/78 which reincorporated in Delaware as Hallwood Industries Inc. 7/2/90 which name changed to Steel City Products, Inc. 1/13/93
(See Steel City Products, Inc.)

FELT & TARRANT MANUFACTURING CO. (IL)
Name changed to Comptometer Corp. 5/10/57
Comptometer Corp. merged into Victor Comptometer Corp. 10/30/61 which merged into Kidde (Walter) & Co., Inc. 7/15/77 which name changed to Kidde, Inc. 4/18/80
(See Kidde, Inc.)

FELTERS CO (MA)
Common $100 par changed to $10 par and (9) additional shares issued in 1946
Common $10 par changed to $1 par 6/27/66
Name changed to Unisorb Inc. 12/22/93
(See Unisorb Inc.)

FELTON & SON, INC. (MA)
5% Preferred $100 par called 8/28/58

FEMALE HEALTH CO (WI)
Name changed to Veru Inc. 08/07/2017

FEMCO MINES LTD. (ON)
Charter cancelled and company declared dissolved for default in filing returns 07/08/1965

FEMINIQUE CORP (DE)
Recapitalized as Receivable Acquisition & Management Corp. 05/11/2004
Each share Common $0.001 par exchanged for (0.06666666) share Common $0.001 par
Receivable Acquisition & Management Corp. name changed to PwrCor, Inc. 03/29/2017

FEMONE INC (NV)
Name changed to ACTIS Global Ventures, Inc. 07/10/2006
(See ACTIS Global Ventures, Inc.)

FEMRX INC (DE)
Merged into Johnson & Johnson 11/13/98
Each share Common $0.001 par exchanged for $2.35 cash

FENARIO INC (NV)
Name changed to Ranger Gold Corp. 01/07/2010

FENCO INDS INC (DE)
Charter cancelled and declared inoperative and void for non-payment of taxes 3/1/83

FENESTRA INC. (MI)
Name changed to Marmon Group, Inc. (MI) 12/07/1967
Marmon Group, Inc. (MI) reincorporated in Delaware 12/31/1970
(See Marmon Group, Inc. (DE) (Ctfs. dated after 12/31/1970))

FENIMORE IRON MINES LTD. (QC)
Recapitalized as Consolidated Fenimore Iron Mines Ltd. 01/14/1955
Each share Common $1 par exchanged for (0.14285714) share Common $7 par
Consolidated Fenimore Iron Mines Ltd. recapitalized as New Fenimore Iron Mines Ltd. 09/20/1972
(See New Fenimore Iron Mines Ltd.)

FENIX PTS INC (DE)
Acquired by Stellex Capital Management L.P. 04/17/2018
Each share Common $0.001 par exchanged for $0.40 cash

FENLEY LTD (DE)
Each share Common 1¢ par exchanged for (0.5) share Common 2¢ par 04/14/1980
Merged into FLHC, Inc. 11/30/1983
Each share Common 2¢ par exchanged for $0.10 cash

FENNEL RES INC (NV)
Each share old Common $0.001 par exchanged for (1.5) shares new Common $0.001 par 02/17/2006
Recapitalized as 3P Networks, Inc. 09/20/2006
Each share new Common $0.001 par exchanged for (0.05) share Common $0.001 par
3P Networks, Inc. recapitalized as Kender Energy Inc. 10/07/2008 which recapitalized as Bettwork Industries Inc. 07/02/2014

FENNELL TEXAS OIL CO. (DE)
Charter cancelled for non-payment of taxes 06/26/1923

FENPRO INC (WA)
Charter cancelled and proclaimed dissolved for failure to pay fees 04/27/2001

FENTRESS COAL & COKE CO. (DE)
No longer in existence having become inoperative and void for non-payment of taxes 4/1/61

FENTRON HWY PRODS INC (WA)
Name changed to Fenpro, Inc. 05/01/1983

(See Fenpro, Inc.)

FENTURA BANCORP INC (MI)
Common $5 par changed to $2.50 par and (1) additional share issued payable 03/31/1998 to holders of record 03/18/1998
Stock Dividend - 20% payable 05/26/2000 to holders of record 04/26/2000 Ex date - 04/24/2000
Name changed to Fentura Financial, Inc. and Common $2.50 par changed to no par 05/01/2002

FENWAY RES LTD (BC)
Reincorporated 06/10/1998
Place of incorporation changed from (BC) to (DE) 06/10/1998
Assets acquired by Nevada/Utah Gold, Inc. 08/31/1998
Details not available

FENWICK FINANCIAL CORP. (CT)
Name changed to SBT Corp. 6/29/84
(See SBT Corp.)

FENWICK FINL INC (CO)
Name changed to Copilot Electronic Products, Inc. 6/21/89

FERALCO INDUSTRIES LTD. (CANADA)
Struck off register and declared dissolved for failure to file returns 12/16/1980

FERBER MNG CORP (BC)
Delisted from Vancouver Stock Exchange 03/02/1990

FERCO MINES LTD. (ON)
Charter cancelled and declared dissolved for failure to file returns and pay fees 7/27/76

FEREX CORP (TX)
Merged into Recycle Industries of Tyler, Inc. 5/28/98
Each share Class A Common 1¢ par exchanged for $1.7381017 cash

FERGUSON OIL & GAS INC (DE)
Merged into Kaneb Services, Inc. 08/18/1977
Each share Common 10¢ par exchanged for (1.1582776) shares Common no par
Kaneb Services, Inc. name changed to Xanser Corp. 08/07/2001 which name changed to Furmanite Corp. 05/17/2007 which merged into Team, Inc. 02/29/2016

FERIS INTL INC (NV)
Name changed to Stratus Media Group, Inc. 07/10/2008
Stratus Media Group, Inc. recapitalized as RestorGenex Corp. (NV) 03/10/2014 which reincorporated in Delaware 06/18/2015 which name changed to Diffusion Pharmaceuticals Inc. 01/25/2016

FERMAC GRAPHIC INDUSTRIES LTD. (ON)
Adjudicated bankrupt 10/30/1964
No stockholders' equity

FERMO GROUP INC (NV)
Name changed to Ubiquity Broadcasting Corp. 03/22/2013
Ubiquity Broadcasting Corp. recapitalized as Ubiquity, Inc. 04/24/2014

FERN GOLD MNG CO (WA)
Charter cancelled and proclaimed dissolved for failure to pay fees 1/31/2001

FERNLAND GOLD MINES LTD.
Acquired by Amalgamated Larder Mines Ltd. 00/00/1942
Each share Capital Stock $1 par exchanged for (0.1) share Capital Stock $1 par
Amalgamated Larder Mines Ltd. recapitalized as Larder Resources Inc. 09/08/1980 which merged into International Larder Minerals Inc.

05/01/1986 which merged into Explorers Alliance Corp. 10/13/2000
(See Explorers Alliance Corp.)

FERNMONT MINES LTD. (ON)
Charter revoked for failure to file reports and pay taxes in 1969

FERNWOOD FINL INC (NV)
Name changed to Exhibitronix, Inc. 9/30/88
Exhibitronix, Inc. name changed to VPN Communications Corp. 3/31/2000 which name changed to Resource Asset Management Corp. 4/16/2002

FERO INDS INC (CO)
Common $0.001 par split (5) for (1) by issuance of (4) additional shares payable 12/08/2008 to holders of record 12/08/2008
Common $0.001 par split (5) for (1) by issuance of (4) additional shares payable 05/28/2010 to holders of record 04/20/2010 Ex date - 06/01/2010
Name changed to PharmaRoth Labs, Inc. 05/02/2013

FEROMAC MINES LTD. (ON)
Charter revoked for failure to file reports and pay taxes 12/00/1970

FERRARA FOOD INC (DE)
Charter forfeited for failure to maintain a registered agent 9/25/97

FERRARI N V OLD (NETHERLANDS)
Under plan of reorganization each share Common EUR 0.01 par automatically became (1) share Ferrari N.V. (New) Common EUR 0.01 par 01/04/2016

FERREYROS S A (PERU)
Stock Dividends - 18.77% payable 09/24/1998 to holders of record 09/01/1998; 10.40951% payable 07/21/1999 to holders of record 06/18/1999; 26.6602% payable 07/16/2003 to holders of record 06/25/2003 Ex date - 07/17/2003; 6.3415% payable 07/07/2004 to holders of record 06/16/2004 Ex date - 06/14/2004; 11% payable 07/26/2005 to holders of record 06/17/2005 Ex date - 06/15/2005; 6.76915% payable 07/31/2006 to holders of record 06/23/2006 Ex date - 06/21/2006; 18.14% payable 10/09/2007 to holders of record 09/18/2007 Ex date - 09/14/2007; 23.77766% payable 07/02/2008 to holders of record 06/19/2008 Ex date - 06/19/2008; 12.454% payable 07/01/2009 to holders of record 06/18/2009 Ex date - 06/16/2009; 13.62372% payable 05/10/2011 to holders of record 07/15/2010 Ex date - 07/13/2010; 17.45401% payable 11/28/2011 to holders of record 11/18/2011 Ex date - 11/16/2011; 10% payable 12/05/2011 to holders of record 12/01/2011 Ex date - 11/29/2011
ADR agreement terminated 10/29/2012
Each Sponsored Reg. S ADR for Ordinary exchanged for (20) shares Ordinary
Each Sponsored 144A ADR for Ordinary exchanged for (20) shares Ordinary
Note: Unexchanged ADR's will be sold and the proceeds, if any, held for claim after 10/30/2013

FERRO DYNAMICS CORP. (NJ)
Name changed to Ferrodynamics Corp. (NJ) 06/05/1963
Ferrodynamics Corp. (NJ) merged into Ferrodynamics Corp. (DE) 07/01/1964 which name changed to Metex Corp. 03/08/1966 which merged into United Capital Corp. 03/03/1989
(See United Capital Corp.)

FERRO ENAMEL CORP.
Name changed to Ferro Corp. in 1951

FERRO ENAMELING CORP.
Name changed to Ferro Enamel Corp. in 1930 which was changed to Ferro Corp. in 1951

FERRO-FAB INC. (FL)
Proclaimed dissolved for failure to file reports and pay fees 06/28/1971

FERRO IRON ORE CORP (BC)
Reorganized under the laws of Ontario as Wolf Resource Development Corp. 07/19/2013
Each share Common no par exchanged for (0.25) share Common no par
Wolf Resource Development Corp. name changed to Fura Emeralds Inc. 03/09/2015 which name changed to Fura Gems Inc. 04/11/2017

FERRO MANUFACTURING CORP. (MI)
Acquired by Johnson Controls, Inc. 7/31/85
Each share Common $10 par exchanged for $87.59 cash

FERRO STAMPING CO. (MI)
Name changed to Ferro Manufacturing Corp. 6/15/65
(See Ferro Manufacturing Corp.)

FERRODYNAMICS CORP. (DE)
Name changed to Metex Corp. 03/08/1966
Metex Corp. merged into United Capital Corp. 03/03/1989
(See United Capital Corp.)

FERRODYNAMICS CORP. (NJ)
Merged into Ferrodynamics Corp. (DE) 07/01/1964
Each share Common or Class B Common 25¢ par exchanged for (1) share Common 25¢ par
Ferrodynamics Corp. (DE) name changed to Metex Corp. 03/08/1966 which merged into United Capital Corp. 03/03/1989
(See United Capital Corp.)

FERROFLUIDICS CORP (MA)
Each share Common $0.001 par exchanged for (0.25) share Common $0.004 par 11/15/89
Merged into Ferrotec Corp. 1/27/2000
Each share Common $0.004 par exchanged for $6.50 cash

FERRONICS INC (NY)
Common 10¢ par split (3) for (1) by issuance of (2) additional shares 6/16/71
Merged into Reeder (Samuel J.) Corp. 7/2/86
Each share Common 10¢ par exchanged for $0.12 cash

FERROVANADIUM CORP N L (AUSTRALIA)
Each ADR for Ordinary AUD $1 par exchanged for (0.1) ADR for Ordinary AUD $0.25 par 06/30/1983
Name changed to Great Australian Resources N.L. 09/12/1985
Great Australian Resources N.L. name changed to Trans-Global Resources N.L. 10/13/1988 which name changed to Trans-Global Interactive Ltd. 06/30/1999
(See Trans-Global Interactive Ltd.)

FERROX IRON LTD. (QC)
Charter annulled for failure to file annual reports 1/27/79

FERRUM AMERS MNG INC (CANADA)
Recapitalized as Toachi Mining Inc. 03/14/2016
Each share Common no par exchanged for (0.2) share Common no par

FERRY CAP & SET SCREW CO (OH)
Each share Common no par exchanged for (2) shares Common 50¢ par 00/00/1946
Common 50¢ par changed to $5 par 00/00/1950
Merged into Ferry Inc. 10/04/1991
Each share Common $5 par exchanged for $26.75 cash

FERRY MORSE SEED CO (MI)
Stock Dividend - 100% 04/15/1968
Acquired by Purex Corp., Ltd. 05/19/1969
Each share Capital Stock no par exchanged for (0.9) share Common $1 par
Purex Corp., Ltd. name changed to Purex Corp. (CA) 11/05/1973 which reincorporated in Delaware as Purex Industries, Inc. 10/31/1978
(See Purex Industries, Inc.)

FERRYBOAT LTD (DC)
Charter revoked for failure to file reports 09/09/1975

FERSOLIN CORP. (CA)
Assets assigned to noteholder 11/05/1963
No stockholders' equity

FERSON OPTICS, INC. (MA)
Merged into Ferson Optics of Delaware, Inc. on a share for share basis 03/31/1962
Ferson Optics of Delaware, Inc. liquidated for Bausch & Lomb Inc. 09/27/1968
(See Bausch & Lomb Inc.)

FERSON OPTICS DEL INC (DE)
Completely liquidated 09/27/1968
Each share Common $1 par exchanged for first and final distribution of (0.16626) share Bausch & Lomb Inc. Common $5 par
(See Bausch & Lomb Inc.)

FERTA-LAWN, INC. (UT)
Name changed to F.L. Energy, Corp. 11/3/80

FERTILITY & GENETICS RESH INC (IL)
Each share Non-Div. Non-Vtg. Conv. Preferred no par exchanged for (3) shares Common no par 3/23/89
(Additional Information in Active)

FERTILITY ADVANCEMENTS INC (NV)
Name changed to Eubix Technologies, Inc. 12/10/1990
Eubix Technologies, Inc. name changed to Nettel, Inc. 06/10/1999 which name changed to One Touch Total Communications Inc. 09/27/1999 which name changed to One Touch Total Development, Inc. 06/10/2004 which name changed to Carbon Jungle, Inc. 03/27/2006 which recapitalized as Global New Energy Industries Inc. 01/17/2013 which name changed to Coin Citadel 11/06/2014

FERTILO LTD. (CANADA)
Deemed not to be a subsisting company by the Dominion Secretary of State 12/28/60

FEST RES CORP (BC)
Recapitalized as Minvita Enterprises Ltd. 10/02/1992
Each share Common no par exchanged for (0.33333333) share Common no par
Minvita Enterprises Ltd. name changed to Silver Grail Resources Ltd. 02/27/2004

FESTINO VENTURE CORP (AB)
Name changed to Maskal Energy Inc. 08/01/2006
Maskal Energy Inc. recapitalized as Maskal Energy Ltd. 08/13/2007
(See Maskal Energy Ltd.)

FET RES LTD (AB)
Each Exchangeable Share exchanged for (1.473) Focus Energy Trust, Trust Units 01/16/2007
Focus Energy Trust merged into Enerplus Resources Fund 02/13/2008 which reorganized as Enerplus Corp. 01/03/2011

FETCHOMATIC GLOBAL INTERNET INC (NV)
Each share old Common $0.001 par exchanged for (0.16666666) share new Common $0.001 par 01/17/2001
SEC revoked common stock registration 06/22/2006

FEY INDS INC (MN)
Acquired by Normax Corp. 07/12/1984
Each share Common 5¢ par exchanged for $5.37 cash

FF BANCORP INC (FL)
Common 1¢ par split (3) for (1) by issuance of (2) additional shares 7/26/93
Stock Dividend - 10% 9/29/94
Merged into First National Bancorp (GA) 7/3/95
Each share Common 1¢ par exchanged for (0.825) share Common $1 par
First National Bancorp (GA) acquired by Regions Financial Corp. (Old) 3/1/96 which merged into Regions Financial Corp. (Old) which merged into Regions Financial Corp. (New) 7/1/2004

FFB CORP (DE)
Name changed to First Constitution Financial Corp. 05/02/1988
First Constitution Financial Corp. name changed to Aristotle Corp. 04/14/1993
(See Aristotle Corp.)

FFBS BANCORP INC (DE)
Merged into NBC Capital Corp. 08/31/1999
Each share Common 1¢ par exchanged for (0.875) share Common $1 par
NBC Capital Corp. name changed to Cadence Financial Corp. 06/28/2006
(See Cadence Financial Corp.)

FFC EQUITIES LTD (AB)
Name changed to Outrider Resources Ltd. 2/1/94
(See Outrider Resources Ltd.)

FFE FINL CORP (DE)
Issue Information - 402,500 shares COM offered at $10 per share on 07/15/1993
Merged into SouthTrust Corp. 03/29/1996
Each share Common 1¢ par exchanged for (0.645) share Common $2.50 par and $10.80 cash
SouthTrust Corp. merged into Wachovia Corp. (Ctfs. dated after 09/01/2001) 11/01/2004 which merged into Wells Fargo & Co. (New) 12/31/2008

FFLC BANCORP INC (DE)
Common $10 par split (5) for (3) by issuance of (2/3) additional share payable 11/14/1997 to holders of record 10/31/1997
Common $10 par split (3) for (2) by issuance of (0.5) additional share payable 03/14/2003 to holders of record 02/28/2003 Ex date - 03/17/2003
Merged into Colonial BancGroup, Inc. 05/18/2005
Each share Common $10 par exchanged for (2) shares Common $2.50 par
(See Colonial BancGroup, Inc.)

FFM FIN CORP (DE)
Voluntarily dissolved 08/27/1990
Details not available

FFM FIN CORP II (DE)
Voluntarily dissolved 08/27/1990

Details not available

FFM FIN CORP III (DE)
Short Term Auction Rate Preferred no par called for redemption 05/10/1990
Public interest eliminated

FFM FIN CORP IV (DE)
Short Term Auction Rate Preferred no par called for redemption 05/17/1990
Public interest eliminated

FFP MARKETING INC (TX)
Chapter 11 bankruptcy proceedings terminated 10/13/2009
Stockholders' equity unlikely

FFVA FINL CORP (VA)
Issue Information - 3,162,500 shares COM offered at $20 per share on 08/12/1994
Common 10¢ par split (2) for (1) by issuance of (1) additional share payable 6/5/96 to holders of record 5/15/96
Merged into One Valley Bancorp, Inc. 3/30/98
Each share Common 10¢ par exchanged for (1.05) shares Common $10 par
One Valley Bancorp, Inc. merged into BB&T Corp. 7/6/2000

FFY FINL CORP (DE)
Common 1¢ par split (2) for (1) by issuance of (1) additional share payable 03/05/1999 to holders of record 02/19/1999
Merged into First Place Financial Corp. 12/22/2000
Each share Common 1¢ par exchanged for (1.075) shares Common 1¢ par
(See First Place Financial Corp.)

FGI INVS INC (DE)
Reorganized 07/01/1981
Under plan of reorganization each FGI Investors (PA) Share of Bene. Int. $1 par automatically became (1) share FGI Investors, Inc. (DE) Common $1 par 07/01/1981
Merged into U.S. Lend Lease Inc. 12/09/1983
Each share Common $1 par exchanged for $5.50 cash

FGIC CORP (DE)
Merged into General Electric Capital Corp. 04/20/1989
Each share Common $1 par exchanged for $24 cash

FGX INTL HLDGS LTD (BRITISH VIRGIN ISLANDS)
Acquired by Essilor International S.A. 03/12/2010
Each share Ordinary no par exchanged for $19.75 cash

FHP INTL CORP (DE)
Name changed 01/16/1987
Name changed from FHP Corp. to FHP International Corp. 01/16/1987
Adjustable Rate Preferred Ser. B $1 par called for redemption 12/15/1995
Common 5¢ par split (2) for (1) by issuance of (1) additional share 12/13/1989
Stock Dividend - 10% 04/05/1991
Merged into PacifiCare Health Systems, Inc. (New) 02/14/1997
Each share Conv. Preferred Ser. A $1 par exchanged for (0.5) share Conv. Preferred Ser. A $1 par and $14.113 cash
Each share Common 5¢ par exchanged for (0.056) share Class A Common 1¢ par, (0.176) share Class B Common 1¢ par, and $17.50 cash
PacifiCare Health Systems, Inc. (New) merged into UnitedHealth Group Inc. 12/20/2005

FI LIQUIDATING INC (DE)
SEC revoked common stock registration 06/23/2009

FI-TEK II INC (DE)
Name changed to Online Network, Inc. 07/18/1989
(See Online Network, Inc.)

FI-TEK III INC (DE)
Name changed to VSI Enterprises, Inc. 12/26/1990
VSI Enterprises, Inc. name changed to Simtrol, Inc. 10/01/2001

FI TEK CORP (CO)
Name changed to Boston Technology, Inc. 06/10/1987
Boston Technology, Inc. merged into Comverse Technology, Inc. 01/14/1998 which merged into Verint Systems Inc. 02/05/2013

FI-TEK IV INC (DE)
Name changed to DBS Industries, Inc. 12/17/1992
(See DBS Industries, Inc.)

FI-TEK V (DE)
Each (32.4778) shares old Common $0.00001 par exchanged for (1) share new Common $0.00001 par 06/03/1999
Name changed to Laidlaw Global Corp. 06/09/1999
Laidlaw Global Corp. name changed to Allegro Group, Inc. 06/27/2006 which name changed to Brandt Inc. 03/13/2008

FI-TEK VI (DE)
Name changed to Global Water Technologies, Inc. 11/24/1997

FI-TEK VII INC (DE)
Recapitalized as Ronco Corp. 07/01/2005
Each (89) shares Common $0.00001 par exchanged for (1) share Common $0.00001 par
(See Ronco Corp.)

FIAC INC (DE)
Each share old Common 1¢ par exchanged for (0.05) share new Common 1¢ par 07/06/1992
Charter cancelled and declared inoperative and void for non-payment of taxes 03/01/1994

FIAT FRANCE S A (FRANCE)
Name changed 8/27/74
Name changed from FFSA to Fiat France S.A. 8/27/74
ADR agreement terminated 1/5/2000
Each ADR for Ordinary 100 Frcs. par exchanged for $89.13 cash

FIAT METAL MANUFACTURING CO., INC. (NY)
Name changed to FMM Co., Inc. 1/4/65
(See FMM Co., Inc.)

FIAT S P A (ITALY)
ADR agreement terminated 11/01/1949
Each old ADR for Capital Stock 500 Lire par exchanged for (3) shares Capital Stock 500 Lire par
Note: On 05/11/1962 all foreign shares were sold and each old ADR became exhangeable for $14.4445 cash plus accrued dividends
Each Unsponsored ADR for Preference exchanged for (0.2) Sponsored ADR for Preference 02/14/1989
Each Unsponsored ADR for Capital Stock exchanged for (0.2) old Sponsored ADR for Ordinary 02/14/1989
Each old Sponsored ADR for Preference exchanged for (0.5) new Sponsored ADR for Preference 08/23/1999
Each old Sponsored ADR for Savings Shares exchanged for (0.5) new Sponsored ADR for Savings Shares 08/23/1999
Each old Sponsored ADR for Ordinary exchanged for (0.5) new Sponsored ADR for Ordinary 08/23/1999
Stock Dividends - 100% 10/08/1984; 10% payable 08/11/1997 to holders of record 07/18/1997
ADR agreement terminated 02/25/2013
Each new Sponsored ADR for Preference exchanged for $5.7214 cash
Each new Sponsored ADR for Savings Shares exchanged for $5.7214 cash
Merged into Fiat Chrysler Automobiles N.V. 10/13/2014
Each new Sponsored ADR for Ordinary exchanged for (1) share Common EUR 0.01 par

FIATRON SYS INC (WI)
Acquired by LaBelle Industries Inc. 08/19/1983
Each share Common 10¢ par exchanged for $0.75 cash

FIB CAP TR (DE)
8.625% Trust Preferred Securities called for redemption at $25 plus $0.14975 accrued dividends on 04/25/2003

FIBER APPLICATION SYS TECHNOLOGY LTD (CO)
Reorganized under the laws of Florida as Innovative Food Holdings, Inc. 3/10/2004
Each share Common no par exchanged for (0.005) share Common $0.0001 par

FIBER CRAFT PRODUCTS CORP. (FL)
Stock Dividend - 10% 11/1/65
Recapitalized as Technological Industries Corp. 12/15/66
Each share Common 10¢ par exchanged for (0.2) share Common 5¢ par
Technological Industries Corp. reincorporated under the laws of Delaware 5/27/71 which name changed to T & I Companies, Inc. 6/16/72
(See T & I Companies, Inc.)

FIBER CRETE PRODS INC (OK)
Name changed to Great Spirit, Inc. 3/28/98

FIBER GLASS INDUSTRIES CORP. OF AMERICA (FL)
Name changed to Rocket/Atlas Corp. 07/14/1965
Rocket/Atlas Corp. recapitalized as Rocket Industries, Inc. 08/17/1966 which name changed to Polo Investment Corp. 04/30/1984 which name changed to Polo Investment Corp. of Missouri 05/30/1984 which name changed to Polo Equities Inc. (FL) 03/03/1997 which reincorporated in Nevada as Hybrid Fuels, Inc. 06/01/1998 which name changed to Nouveau Life Pharmaceuticals, Inc. 05/22/2012

FIBER GLASS PLASTICS CORP. (DE)
No longer in existence having become inoperative and void for non-payment of taxes 4/1/57

FIBER OPTIC SYS TECHNOLOGY INC (DE)
Name changed to Augusta Industries Inc. 10/31/2011
Augusta Industries Inc. recapitalized as IntellaEquity Inc. 10/04/2018

FIBER PRODUCTS, INC. (DE)
Merged into Wood Conversion Co. share for share 11/30/55
Wood Conversion Co. name changed to Conwed Corp. 8/1/67
(See Conwed Corp.)

FIBER TECH CORP (OR)
Name changed to Crystal Asset Management, Inc. 05/18/1989
Crystal Asset Management, Inc. name changed to Leading - Earth Products, Inc. 12/29/1992 which name changed to LEEP, Inc. 01/03/2005

FIBERCHEM INC (NM)
Merged into FiberChem, Inc. (DE) 12/28/1988
Each share Common no par exchanged for (1) share Common $0.0001 par
FiberChem, Inc. (DE) name changed to DecisionLink, Inc. 12/05/2000
(See DecisionLink, Inc.)

FIBERCHEM INC NEW (DE)
Each share old Common $0.0001 par exchanged for (0.02857142) share new Common $0.0001 par 04/17/1989
Name changed to DecisionLink, Inc. 12/05/2000
(See DecisionLink, Inc.)

FIBERCORE INC (NV)
Chapter 11 bankruptcy proceedings converted to Chapter 7 on 10/06/2004
Stockholders' equity unlikely

FIBERCORP INTL INC (DE)
Each share Common $0.001 par exchanged for (0.06) share Common 1¢ par 7/1/93
Charter cancelled and declared inoperative and void for non-payment of taxes 3/1/97

FIBERCRAFT, INC. (FL)
Name changed to Fiber Craft Products Corp. 1/16/60
Fiber Craft Products Corp. recapitalized as Technological Industries Corp. (FL) 12/15/66 which reincorporated in Delaware 5/27/71 which name changed to T & I Companies, Inc. 6/16/72
(See T & I Companies, Inc.)

FIBERGLASS HOMES AMER INC (MA)
Proclaimed dissolved for failure to file reports and pay fees 10/19/83

FIBERITE CORP (MN)
Merged into Beatrice Foods Co. 01/21/1980
Each share Common 30¢ par exchanged for $65.214 cash
Class B Common Ser. 1, 2, 3, 4 & 5, 30¢ par exchanged for $65.214 cash

FIBERLOID CORP.
Acquired by Monsanto Chemical Co. on a (7) for (12) basis in 1938 which name was changed to Monsanto Co. 4/1/64

FIBERMARK INC (DE)
Common $0.001 par split (3) for (2) by issuance of (0.5) additional share payable 5/13/97 to holders of record 5/6/97 Ex date - 5/14/97
Plan of reorganization under Chapter 11 Federal Bankruptcy Code effective 1/3/2006
No stockholders' equity

FIBERMATICS INC (DE)
Charter cancelled and declared inoperative and void for non-payment of taxes 04/15/1972

FIBERNET TELECOM GROUP INC (DE)
Reincorporated 02/03/2000
State of incorporation changed from (NV) to (DE) 02/03/2000
Each share old Common $0.001 par exchanged for (0.03333333) share new Common $0.001 par 05/12/2003
Each share new Common $0.001 par exchanged again for (0.1) share new Common $0.001 par 05/25/2005
Acquired by Zayo Group, LLC 09/09/2009
Each share Common $0.001 par exchanged for $11.45 cash

FIBEROPTIC MED SYS INC (CO)
Merged into FiberChem, Inc. (DE) 11/21/1989
Each (12.5) shares Common no par exchanged for (1) Unit consisting of (5) shares new Common $0.0001 par, (1) Class A Common Stock Purchase Warrant expiring 09/15/1991, (1) Class B Common Stock Purchase Warrant expiring 09/15/1992 and (1) Class C Common Stock Purchase Warrant expiring 09/15/1993
FiberChem, Inc. name changed to DecisionLink, Inc. 12/05/2000
(See DecisionLink, Inc.)

FIBEROPTIC ONE INC (CANADA)
Issue Information - 2,273,800 shares COM offered at $0.15 per share on 11/27/2001
Name changed to GlobeeCom International Inc. 9/20/2004

FIBERQUEST NETWORKS CORP (BC)
Name changed to StorageFlow Systems Corp. (BC) 08/17/2001
StorageFlow Systems Corp. (BC) reincorporated in Alberta 06/19/2002 which recapitalized as Northern Pine Ventures Inc. (AB) 11/21/2003 which reincorporated in British Columbia as Landmark Minerals Inc. 07/18/2005 which merged into Ucore Uranium Inc. 08/17/2007 which name changed to Ucore Rare Metals Inc. 06/29/2010

FIBERS INC (OR)
Involuntarily dissolved for failure to file reports and pay taxes 10/18/1972

FIBERSTARS INC (DE)
Reincorporated 11/27/2006
Issue Information - 1,000,000 shares COM offered at $4.50 per share on 08/18/1994
State of incorporation changed from CA to (DE) 11/27/2006
Name changed to Energy Focus, Inc. 5/9/2007

FIBERSTATICS CORP (NY)
Adjudicated bankrupt 03/06/1974
No stockholders' equity

FIBERTECH INDS CORP (BC)
Recapitalized as Solar Pharmaceutical Ltd. 08/11/1989
Each share Common no par exchanged for (0.25) share Common no par

FIBERTOWER CORP (DE)
Each share old Common $0.001 par exchanged for (0.1) share new Common $0.001 par 12/21/2009
Plan of reorganization under Chapter 11 Federal Bankruptcy proceedings effective 03/31/2014
No stockholders' equity

FIBERTREK INC (NV)
Name changed to Asset Capital Group, Inc. 08/01/2007
Asset Capital Group, Inc. name changed to Solutions Group, Inc. 12/15/2008

FIBRACAN INC. (QC)
Each share Preferred $10 par exchanged for (2) shares Preferred 5¢ par 11/16/73
Each share Common $1 par exchanged for (2) shares Common 50¢ par 11/16/73
Completely liquidated 3/29/85
Each share Preferred 5¢ par exchanged for first and final distribution of $0.05 cash
Each share Common 50¢ par exchanged for first and final distribution of $1.17 cash

FIBRE CONDUIT CO.
Name changed to Orangeburg Manufacturing Co., Inc. and each share Common $25 par exchanged for (3) shares Common $10 par in 1947
Orangeburg Manufacturing Co., Inc. was acquired by Flintkote Co. 12/1/58
(See Flintkote Co.)

FIBRE-KLAD INDS LTD (AB)
Merged into Tanqueray Resources Ltd. 05/16/1994
Each share Common no par exchanged for (0.94) share Common no par
Tanqueray Resources Ltd. recapitalized as Tanqueray Exploration Ltd. 09/13/2011 which name changed to ImmunoPrecise Antibodies Ltd. 12/29/2016

FIBRE PRODS CDA LTD (ON)
Name changed to Comtech Group International Ltd. (ON) 12/10/1969
Comtech Group International Ltd. (ON) reincorporated in Canada 12/01/1981 which name changed to Postech Corp. 12/30/1988
(See Postech Corp.)

FIBRE-TEK CORP. (CA)
Merged into Continental Consolidated Inc. 11/8/68
Each share Common $1 par exchanged for (0.5) share Common 10¢ par
(See Continental Consolidated Inc.)

FIBREBOARD CORP (DE)
Ctfs. dated prior to 6/27/78
Common no par split (2) for (1) by issuance of (1) additional share 11/1/68
Merged into Louisiana-Pacific Corp. 6/27/78
Each share Common no par exchanged for $17 cash

FIBREBOARD CORP NEW (DE)
Ctfs. dated after 6/26/88
Common 1¢ par split (2) for (1) by issuance of (1) additional share 5/19/95
Merged into Owens Corning (Old) 7/3/97
Each share Common 1¢ par exchanged for $55 cash

FIBREBOARD PAPER PRODUCTS CORP. (DE)
Name changed to Fibreboard Corp. 7/5/66
(See Fibreboard Corp.)

FIBRECOR INC (NY)
Charter cancelled and proclaimed dissolved for failure to pay taxes 03/25/1981

FIBREK INC (CANADA)
Merged into Resolute Forest Products Inc. 08/01/2012
Each share Common no par exchanged for (0.0284) share Common no par and $0.55 cash
Note: Unexchanged certificates were cancelled and became without value 08/01/2018

FIBREQUEST INTL LTD (BC)
Name changed to E.C.M. Paytel Ltd. 07/04/1988
E.C.M. Paytel Ltd. recapitalized as Consolidated Paytel Ltd. 02/22/1990 which recapitalized as Paytel Industries Ltd. 06/01/1994 which name changed to Rodera Diamond Corp. 04/19/1996 which merged into Pacific Rodera Ventures Inc. 03/01/1999 which name changed to Pacific Rodera Energy Inc. (BC) 06/22/2004 which reincorporated in Alberta 06/14/2006 which name changed to PRD Energy Inc. 08/12/2010

FIBRONICS INTL INC (DE)
Common 5¢ par split (3) for (2) by issuance of (0.5) additional share 6/12/85
Merged into Elbit Ltd. 12/30/94
Each share Common 5¢ par exchanged for (0.05) share Ordinary Stock NIS0.003 par
Elbit Ltd. merged into Elron Electronic Industries Ltd. 5/15/2002

FIBROTHANE INDS CORP (NY)
Name changed to A O K Enterprises Ltd. 9/20/84
A O K Enterprises Ltd. reorganized as Environmental Protective Industries Inc. 11/30/87
(See Environmental Protective Industries Inc.)

FIC ACQUISITION CORP (DE)
Name changed to Florida West Airlines, Inc. 7/7/93
(See Florida West Airlines, Inc.)

FICUL, INC. (NY)
Liquidation completed
Each share Class A Common $1 par or Class B Common $1 par exchanged for initial distribution of $11 cash 7/18/68
Each share Class A Common $1 par or Class B Common $1 par received second and final distribution of $0.95 cash 6/13/69

FIDATA CORP (DE)
Merged into Advanced Medical Technologies, Inc. 3/27/89
Each share Common 10¢ par exchanged for (0.3) share 10% Preferred 1¢ par, (1) share Common 1¢ par and $2 cash
Advanced Medical Technologies, Inc. name changed to Advanced Medical Inc. 9/7/90 which name changed to ALARIS Medical, Inc. 4/30/97 which name changed to ALARIS Medical Systems, Inc. 6/30/2003
(See ALARIS Medical Systems, Inc.)

FIDBANK CAP TR I (DE)
8.5% Guaranteed Capital Securities called for redemption at $10 plus $0.035416 accrued dividends on 10/15/2004

FIDELCO GROWTH INVS (PA)
Name changed to FGI Investors (PA) 05/29/1980
FGI Investors (PA) reorganized in Delaware as FGI Investors, Inc. 07/01/1981
(See FGI Investors, Inc.)

FIDELCOR INC (PA)
Common $1 par split (2) for (1) by issuance of (1) additional share 05/31/1985
Merged into First Fidelity Bancorporation (New) 02/29/1988
Each share $2.15 Conv. Preferred Ser. B $1 par exchanged for (1) share $2.15 Conv. Preferred Ser. B $1 par
Each share $3.25 Conv. Preferred Ser. A $1 par exchanged for (1) share $3.25 Conv. Preferred Ser. A $1 par
Each share Common $1 par exchanged for (1.16) shares Common $1 par
First Fidelity Bancorporation (New) merged into First Union Corp. 01/01/1996 which name changed to Wachovia Corp. (Ctfs. dated after 09/01/2001) 09/01/2001 which merged into Wells Fargo & Co. (New) 12/31/2008

FIDELIO BREWERY, INC. (NY)
Name changed to Greater New York Brewery, Inc. 11/15/40
Greater New York Brewery, Inc. name changed to Greater New York Industries, Inc. 12/19/44
(See Greater New York Industries, Inc.)

FIDELIO ENTERPRISE CORP (AB)
Merged into Exploration Terrenex Inc. 09/11/1991
Each share Common no par exchanged for (1) share Common no par
Exploration Terrenex Inc. recapitalized as Terrenex Ventures Inc. 11/16/1993 which merged into Terrenex Acquisition Corp. 08/22/1995 which reorganized as Terrenex Ltd. 11/27/2007 which was acquired by Questerre Energy Corp. 04/29/2008

FIDELITAS MGMT INC (NV)
Name changed to Archer Entertainment Media Communications Inc. 11/17/2005

FIDELITONE INC (IL)
Name changed to Fidelitone Microwave, Inc. 03/31/1961 and then changed back to Fidelitone, Inc. 10/17/1963
Through purchase offer 100% reacquired by company 04/06/1981
Public interest eliminated

FIDELITONE MICROWAVE, INC. (IL)
Name changed back to Fidelitone, Inc. 10/17/63
(See Fidelitone, Inc.)

FIDELITRON CORP. (DE)
No longer in existence having become inoperative and void for non-payment of taxes 4/1/67

FIDELITY & DEP CO MD (MD)
Capital Stock $50 par changed to $20 par in 1932
Each share Capital Stock $20 par exchanged for (2.5) shares Capital Stock $10 par to effect a (2) for (1) split and 25% stock dividend in 1949
Capital Stock $10 par changed to $5 par and (1) additional share issued plus a 12-1/2% stock dividend paid 6/30/59
Capital Stock $5 par changed to $2.50 par and (1) additional share issued 4/30/65
Stock Dividends - 33-1/3% 3/31/54; 11-1/9% 4/20/61
Merged into American General Insurance Co. 7/1/69
Each share Capital Stock $2.50 par exchanged for (0.4) share $1.80 Conv. Preferred $1.50 par and (2) shares Common $1.50 par
American General Insurance Co. reorganized as American General Corp. 7/1/80 which merged into American International Group, Inc. 8/29/2001

FIDELITY & GTY LIFE (DE)
Acquired by CF Corp. 11/30/2017
Each share Common 1¢ par exchanged for $31.10 cash

FIDELITY & GUARANTY FIRE CORP.
Name changed to Fidelity & Guaranty Insurance Corp. in 1947
Fidelity & Guaranty Insurance Corp. merged into United States Fidelity & Guaranty Co. in 1952 which reorganized as USF&G Corp. 10/1/81 which merged into St. Paul Companies, Inc. 4/24/98 which name changed to St. Paul Travelers Companies, Inc. 4/1/2004 which name changed to Travelers Companies, Inc. 2/27/2007

FIDELITY & GUARANTY INSURANCE CORP.
Merged into United States Fidelity & Guaranty Co. in 1952
Each share Capital Stock $10 par exchanged for (1.38) shares Common $10 par
United States Fidelity & Guaranty Co. reorganized as USF&G Corp. 10/1/81 which merged into St. Paul Companies, Inc. 4/24/98 which name changed to St. Paul Travelers Companies, Inc. 4/1/2004 which name changed to Travelers Companies, Inc. 2/27/2007

FIDELITY ACCEP CORP (MN)
6% Preferred Ser. E $25 par called for redemption 01/01/1971

6% Preferred Ser. F $22.75 par called for redemption 01/01/1971
6% Preferred Ser. G $25 par called for redemption 01/01/1971
7% Preferred Ser. H $25 par called for redemption 01/01/1971
Public interest eliminated

FIDELITY ADVISOR KOREA FD INC (MD)
Issue Information - 4,400,000 shares COM offered at $15 per share on 10/25/1994
Under plan of reorganization each share Common $0.001 par automatically became (1) share Fidelity Advisors Korea Fund, Series VIII Class A Korea Fund $0.001 par 6/30/2000

FIDELITY ADVISOR SER I (MA)
Merged into Fidelity Capital Trust 12/29/2001
Details not available
Merged into Fidelity Capital Trust 07/24/2015
Details not available
(Additional Information in Active)

FIDELITY ADVISOR SER III (MA)
Name changed to Fidelity Hanover Street Trust 04/23/2003

FIDELITY AGGRESSIVE INCOME FD (MA)
Name changed to Fidelity High Income Fund 01/09/1981

FIDELITY AMERN BANKSHARES INC (VA)
Merged into Commonwealth Banks, Inc. 12/31/1978
Each $6 Conv. Preferred Ser. A $100 par exchanged for (1) share $6 Conv. Preferred Ser. A $100 par
Each share Common $5 par exchanged for (1) share Common $5 par
Commonwealth Banks, Inc. name changed to Central Fidelity Banks, Inc. 06/01/1979 which merged into Wachovia Corp. (New) (Ctfs. dated between 05/20/1991 and 09/01/2001) 12/15/1997 which merged into Wachovia Corp. (Ctfs. dated after 09/01/2001) 09/01/2001 which merged into Wells Fargo & Co. (New) 12/31/2008

FIDELITY ASSET INVT TR (MA)
Name changed to Fidelity Discoverer Fund 12/30/1983
Fidelity Discoverer Fund name changed to Fidelity Value Fund 07/23/1986

FIDELITY ASSOCIATES UNDERWRITERS, INC. (IN)
Merged into Associates Life Insurance Co. 10/5/65
Each share Common no par exchanged for (2.5) shares Common $1 par
Associates Life Insurance Co. acquired by Alexander National Group, Inc. 12/13/71 which name changed to ANG, Inc. 2/2/81
(See ANG, Inc.)

FIDELITY ASSURANCE ASSOCIATION
Dissolution completed in 1952

FIDELITY AVIATION CORP (CO)
Recapitalized as China Infrastructure Construction Corp. 09/28/2009
Each share Common no par exchanged for (0.1) share Common no par

FIDELITY-BALTIMORE NATIONAL BANK & TRUST CO. (BALTIMORE, MD)
Stock Dividend - 10% 4/11/56
Name changed to Fidelity-Baltimore National Bank (Baltimore, MD) 1/15/57
Fidelity-Baltimore National Bank (Baltimore, MD) merged into Baltimore National Bank (Baltimore, MD) 6/24/60 which merged into Maryland National Bank (Baltimore, MD) 11/14/61 which reorganized as Maryland National Corp. 5/1/69 which name changed to MNC Financial, Inc. 4/29/87 which merged into NationsBank Corp. 10/1/93 which reincorporated in Delaware as BankAmerica Corp. (Old) 9/25/98 which merged into BankAmerica Corp. (New) 9/30/98 which name changed to Bank of America Corp. 4/28/99

FIDELITY-BALTIMORE NATIONAL BANK (BALTIMORE, MD)
Stock Dividend - 10% 1/21/59
Merged into Baltimore National Bank (Baltimore, MD) 6/24/60
Each share Capital Stock $10 par exchanged for (1) share Capital Stock $10 par
Baltimore National Bank (Baltimore, MD) merged into Maryland National Bank (Baltimore, MD) 11/14/61 which reorganized as Maryland National Corp. 5/1/69 which name changed to MNC Financial, Inc. 4/29/87 which merged into NationsBank Corp. (NC) 10/1/93 which reincorporated in Delaware as BankAmerica Corp. (Old) 9/25/98 which merged into BankAmerica Corp. (New) 9/30/98 which name changed to Bank of America Corp. 4/28/99

FIDELITY BANCORP INC (DE)
Common 1¢ par split (3) for (2) by issuance of (0.5) additional share payable 02/28/2002 to holders of record 02/06/2002
Merged into MAF Bancorp, Inc. 07/21/2003
Each share Common 1¢ par exchanged for (0.89) share Common 1¢ par
MAF Bancorp, Inc. merged into National City Corp. 09/01/2007 which was acquired by PNC Financial Services Group, Inc. 12/31/2008

FIDELITY BANCORP INC (PA)
Common 1¢ par split (5) for (4) by issuance of (0.25) additional share payable 03/31/1998 to holders of record 03/16/1998
Stock Dividends - 10% payable 05/31/1996 to holders of record 05/15/1996; 10% payable 05/28/1997 to holders of record 05/15/1997; 10% payable 05/29/2002 to holders of record 05/15/2002; 10% payable 05/28/2003 to holders of record 05/15/2003 Ex date - 05/13/2003; 10% payable 05/26/2004 to holders of record 05/14/2004; 10% payable 05/27/2005 to holders of record 05/13/2005 Ex date - 05/11/2005
Merged into WesBanco, Inc. 12/03/2012
Each share Common 1¢ par exchanged for (0.8275) share Common $2.0833 par and $4.50 cash

FIDELITY BANCORPORATION INC (OH)
Name changed to Resource General Corp. and Common 50¢ par changed to no par 6/19/85
Resource General Corp. name changed to PH Group Inc. 4/22/97
(See PH Group Inc.)

FIDELITY BANCSHARES INC TENN (TN)
Acquired by Union Planters Corp. 3/30/92
Each share Common $1 par exchanged for $23.50 cash

FIDELITY BANK, N.A. (OKLAHOMA CITY, OK)
Reorganized as Fidelity Corp. of Oklahoma 1/2/74
Each share Capital Stock $10 par exchanged for (1) share Common $10 par
Fidelity Corp. of Oklahoma name changed to Fidelity of Oklahoma, Inc. 12/2/77 which merged into BancOklahoma Corp. 10/15/84
(See BancOklahoma Corp.)

FIDELITY BANK & TRUST CO. (BATON ROUGE, LA)
Name changed to Fidelity National Bank (Baton Rouge, LA) 10/27/42
Fidelity National Bank (Baton Rouge, LA) reorganized as Fidelity National Financial Corp. 4/1/75 which merged into Hibernia Corp. 7/1/86 which merged into Capital One Financial Corp. 11/16/2005

FIDELITY BK & TR CO N J (PENNSAUKEN, NJ)
Common $5 par changed to $2.50 par and (1) additional share issued 07/01/1970
Acquired by Commercial Bancshares, Inc. (NJ) 08/31/1983
Each share Common $2.50 par exchanged for an Equity Contract, 13% Debentures due 02/28/1993 and cash
Note: If acceptance of the Equity Contract was not received by 09/31/1985 holders received cash only

FIDELITY BK (FUQUAY-VARINA, NC)
Under plan of reorganization each share Common $25 par automatically became (1) share Fidelity Bancshares (N.C.), Inc. Common $25 par 04/01/1988

FIDELITY BK (PHILADELPHIA, PA)
Reorganized as Fidelity Corp. of Pennsylvania 04/14/1969
Each share Capital Stock $10 par exchanged for (3) shares Common $1 par
Fidelity Corp. of Pennsylvania name changed to Fidelcor, Inc. 05/15/1974 which merged into First Fidelity Bancorporation (New) 02/29/1988 which merged into First Union Corp. 01/01/1996 which name changed to Wachovia Corp. (Ctfs. dated after 09/01/2001) 09/01/2001 which merged into Wells Fargo & Co. (New) 12/31/2008

FIDELITY BANK (WEST DELRAY BEACH, FL)
Over 97.9% acquired by Barnett Banks of Florida, Inc. through exchange offer which expired 11/15/1973
Public interest eliminated

FIDELITY BK COLONIE (LATHAM, NY)
Acquired by Manufacturers Hanover Corp. 2/1/73
Each share Capital Stock $15 par exchanged for (2) shares Common $7.50 par
Manufacturers Hanover Corp. merged into Chemical Banking Corp. 12/31/91

FIDELITY BANKERS LIFE INSURANCE CO. (VA)
Stock Dividends - 10% 12/18/64; 10% 2/11/66
Name changed to Fidelity Corp. 12/31/67
Fidelity Corp. name changed to Drum Financial Corp. 8/1/79 which was acquired by St. Regis Paper Co. 9/11/81 which name changed to St. Regis Corp. 4/28/83 which merged into Champion International Corp. 11/20/84 which merged into International Paper Co. 6/20/2000

FIDELITY BANKERS LIFE INSURANCE CORP. (VA)
Name changed to Fidelity Bankers Life Insurance Co. 6/15/62
Fidelity Bankers Life Insurance Co. name changed to Fidelity Corp. 12/31/67 which name changed to Drum Financial Corp. 8/1/79 which was acquired by St. Regis Paper Co. 9/11/81 which name changed to St. Regis Corp. 4/28/83 which merged into Champion International Corp. 11/20/84 which merged into International Paper Co. 6/20/2000

FIDELITY BANKERS TRUST CO. (KNOXVILLE, TN)
Merged into Valley Fidelity Bank & Trust Co. (Knoxville, TN) 5/1/64
Each share Capital Stock $25 par exchanged for (1) share Common $16 par and (0.1) share 5% Preferred $100 par

FIDELITY BANKSHARES INC NEW (DE)
Common 10¢ par split (3) for (2) by issuance of (0.5) additional share payable 01/14/2005 to holders of record 12/31/2004 Ex date - 01/18/2005
Merged into National City Corp. 01/05/2007
Each share Common 10¢ par exchanged for either (0.84094797) share Common $4 par and $9.23905 cash or $39.50 cash
Note: Option to receive stock and cash expired 01/05/2007
National City Corp. acquired by PNC Financial Services Group, Inc. 12/31/2008

FIDELITY BANKSHARES INC OLD (DE)
Reorganized as Fidelity Bankshares, Inc. (New) 05/15/2001
Each share Common 10¢ par exchanged for (2.4165) shares Common 10¢ par
Fidelity Bankshares, Inc. (New) merged into National City Corp. 01/05/2007 which was acquired by PNC Financial Services Group, Inc. 12/31/2008

FIDELITY BD DEB FD INC (MA)
Name changed to Fidelity Corporate Bond Fund, Inc. 04/26/1977
Fidelity Corporate Bond Fund, Inc. name changed to Fidelity Flexible Bond Fund 10/25/1985 which name changed to Fidelity Fixed Income Trust 04/15/1992

FIDELITY CAP CONCEPTS LTD (NV)
Common $0.0001 par split (8) for (1) by issuance of (7) additional shares payable 10/11/2004 to holders of record 10/08/2004 Ex date - 10/12/2004
Name changed to id-Confirm, Inc. 01/04/2005
(See id-Confirm, Inc.)

FIDELITY CAP FD INC (MA)
Stock Dividend - 100% 05/01/1962
Merged into Fidelity Trend Fund, Inc. 12/31/1979
Each share Capital Stock $1 par exchanged for (0.3547148) share Capital Stock $1 par
Fidelity Trend Fund, Inc. name changed to Fidelity Trend Fund 12/31/1984

FIDELITY CAP GROUP HLDGS INC (NV)
Name changed to Cyrus Industries Inc. 05/22/2000
Cyrus Industries Inc. name changed to Sentinel Solutions, Inc. 09/02/2005 which merged into Global Monitoring Systems, Inc. 04/17/2006 which name changed to Planet Signal, Inc. 11/21/2007
(See Planet Signal, Inc.)

FIDELITY CAP GROUP INC (DE)
Charter cancelled and declared inoperative and void for non-payment of taxes 3/1/89

FIDELITY CAPITAL CORP. (OR)
Name changed to Life Resources, Inc. 03/31/1971
(See Life Resources, Inc.)

FIDELITY CAP TR I (DE)
8.375% Trust Preferred Securities called for redemption at $10 on 11/24/2004

FIDELITY CO., LTD. (ID)
Charter forfeited for failure to file reports and pay taxes 12/1/33

FIDELITY CONV & SR SECS FD INC (MA)
Merged into Fidelity Equity-Income Fund, Inc. 09/12/1975
Each share Capital Stock $1 par exchanged for (0.636) share Capital Stock $1 par

FIDELITY CORP. (VA)
Common $1 par split (4) for (3) by issuance of (1/3) additional share 6/30/70
Name changed to Drum Financial Corp. 8/1/79
Drum Financial Corp. acquired by St. Regis Paper Co. 9/11/81 which name changed to St. Regis Corp. 4/28/83 which merged into Champion International Corp. 11/20/84 which merged into International Paper Co. 6/20/2000

FIDELITY CORP OKLA (DE)
Name changed to Fidelity of Oklahoma, Inc. 12/02/1977
Fidelity of Oklahoma, Inc. merged into BancOklahoma Corp. 10/15/1984
(See BancOklahoma Corp.)

FIDELITY CORP PA (PA)
Name changed to Fidelcor, Inc. 05/15/1974
Fidelcor, Inc. merged into First Fidelity Bancorporation (New) 02/29/1988 which merged into First Union Corp. 01/01/1996 which name changed to Wachovia Corp. (Ctfs. dated after 09/01/2001) 09/01/2001 which merged into Wells Fargo & Co. (New) 12/31/2008

FIDELITY CORPORATE BD FD INC (MA)
Name changed to Fidelity Flexible Bond Fund 10/25/1985
Fidelity Flexible Bond Fund name changed to Fidelity Fixed Income Trust 04/15/1992

FIDELITY DEP & DISC BK (DUNMORE, PA)
Common $1.5625 par split (2) for (1) by issuance of (1) additional share 05/12/1994
Common $1.5625 par split (2) for (1) by issuance of (1) additional share payable 06/10/1997 to holders of record 05/23/1997 Ex date - 06/11/1997
Reorganized as Fidelity D & D Bancorp, Inc. 06/30/2000
Each share Common $1.5625 par exchanged for (2) shares Common no par
Note: Unexchanged certificates were sold and the proceeds held for claim after 06/30/2002

FIDELITY DISCOUNT CORP.
Name changed to Fidelity Finance Co. in 1948 which was liquidated 6/30/53

FIDELITY DISCOVERER FD (MA)
Name changed to Fidelity Value Fund 07/23/1986

FIDELITY ELECTRONICS CORP. (NJ)
Bankrupt 8/6/63
No stockholders' equity

FIDELITY FED BANCORP (IN)
Common no par split (2.1) for (1) by issuance of (1.1) additional shares 4/14/95
Stock Dividends - 20% 7/15/94; 10% payable 5/27/96 to holders of record 5/10/96
Each (30,000) shares old Common no par exchanged for (1) share new Common no par 2/28/2005
Note: In effect holders received $1.85 cash per share and public interest was eliminated

FIDELITY FED BK FSB (GLENDALE, CA)
Each share old Class A Common 1¢ par exchanged for (0.25) share new Class A Common 1¢ par 2/14/96
Under plan of reorganization each share new Class A Common 1¢ par automatically became (1) share Bank Plus Corp. (DE) Common $1 par 3/14/96
12% Exchangeable Perpetual Preferred Ser. A called for redemption at $27.50 on 3/18/2002
(See Bank Plus Corp.)

FIDELITY FED SVGS & LN ASSN GLENDALE CALIF (USA)
Incorporated 00/00/1937
Reorganized as Citadel Holding Corp. (DE) 12/13/1983
Each share Common 1¢ par exchanged for (1) share Common 1¢ par
Citadel Holding Corp. (DE) reorganized in Nevada 01/05/2000 which merged into Reading International, Inc. 12/31/2001

FIDELITY FED SVGS & LN ASSN PHILADELPHIA PA (USA)
Incorporated 00/00/1940
Common 1¢ par split (6) for (5) by issuance of (0.2) additional share 04/10/1985
Common 1¢ par split (5) for (3) by issuance of (2/3) additional share 10/15/1985
Common 1¢ par split (6) for (5) by issuance of (0.2) additional share 10/01/1986
Reorganized under the laws of Pennsylvania as Diversified Investment Group, Inc. 12/28/1987
Each share Common 1¢ par exchanged for (1) share Common 1¢ par
(See Diversified Investment Group, Inc.)

FIDELITY FED SVGS & LN ASSN SEYMOUR (IN)
Acquired by Home Federal Savings Bank (Seymour, IN) 04/30/1990
Each share Common no par exchanged for $12.50 cash

FIDELITY FED SVGS & LN ASSN TENN NASHVILLE (USA)
Name changed to Fidelity Bancshares, Inc. 12/01/1989
(See Fidelity Bancshares, Inc.)

FIDELITY FED SVGS BK (CINCINNATI, OH)
Common 10¢ par split (3) for (2) by issuance of (0.5) additional share 10/04/1994
Merged into Fidelity Financial of Ohio, Inc. 03/04/1996
Each share Common 10¢ par exchanged for (2.25) shares Common 10¢ par
Fidelity Financial of Ohio, Inc. merged into Provident Financial Group, Inc. 02/04/2000 which merged into National City Corp. 07/01/2004 which was acquired by PNC Financial Services Group, Inc. 12/31/2008

FIDELITY FEDERAL SAVINGS BANK (DALTON, GA)
Acquired by Regions Financial Corp. (Old) 5/15/95
Each share Preferred no par exchanged for (0.456) share Common $0.625 par
Each share Common no par exchanged for (0.456) share Common $0.625 par
Regions Financial Corp. (Old) merged into Regions Financial Corp. (New) 7/1/2004

FIDELITY FED SVGS BK (MARION, IN)
Merged into First Financial Bancorp (OH) 09/21/1990
Each share Common 1¢ par exchanged for (0.527983) share Common 10¢ par

FIDELITY FED SVGS BK (RICHMOND, VA)
Common $1 par split (6) for (5) by issuance of (0.2) additional share 11/30/89
Common $1 par split (6) for (5) by issuance of (0.2) additional share 5/29/92
Common $1 par split (3) for (2) by issuance of (0.5) additional share 5/28/93
Under plan of reorganization each share Common $1 par automatically became (1) share Fidelity Financial Bankshares Corp. Common $1 par 5/26/95
Fidelity Financial Bankshares Corp. merged into Southern National Corp. 3/1/97 which name changed to BB&T Corp. 5/19/97

FIDELITY FED SVGS BK FLA (W PALM BEACH, FL)
Stock Dividend - 10% 11/30/1995
Under plan of reorganization each share Common $1 par automatically became (1) share Fidelity Bankshares, Inc. (Old) (DE) Common 10¢ par 01/29/1997
Fidelity Bankshares, Inc. (Old) (DE) reorganized as Fidelity Bankshares, Inc. (New) 05/15/2001 which merged into National City Corp. 01/05/2007 which was acquired by PNC Financial Services Group, Inc. 12/31/2008

FIDELITY FINANCE CO. (MI)
Liquidated 6/30/53

FIDELITY FINL BANKSHARES CORP (VA)
Merged into Southern National Corp. 3/1/97
Each share Common $1 par exchanged for (0.7137) share Common $5 par
Southern National Corp. name changed to BB&T Corp. 5/19/97

FIDELITY FINL CORP (CA)
Taken over by FSLIC 04/13/1982
Stockholders' equity unlikely

FIDELITY FINL OHIO INC (OH)
Merged into Provident Financial Group, Inc. 02/04/2000
Each share Common 10¢ par exchanged for (0.4939) share Common no par
Provident Financial Group, Inc. merged into National City Corp. 07/01/2004 which was acquired by PNC Financial Services Group, Inc. 12/31/2008

FIDELITY FLEXIBLE BD FD (MA)
Name changed to Fidelity Fixed Income Trust 04/15/1992

FIDELITY GEN INS CO (IL)
Declared insolvent and ordered liquidated 12/04/1970
No stockholders' equity

FIDELITY HLDGS INC (NV)
Common 1¢ par split (3) for (2) by issuance of (0.5) additional share payable 6/1/99 to holders of record 5/18/99
Common 1¢ par split (3) for (2) by issuance of (0.5) additional share payable 1/3/2000 to holders of record 12/17/99
Each share old Common 1¢ par exchanged for (1) share new Common 1¢ par 1/11/2000
Recapitalized as Major Automotive Companies, Inc. 5/2/2001
Each share Common 1¢ par exchanged for (0.2) share Common 1¢ par

FIDELITY INSURANCE CO. (SC)
Declared insolvent 10/13/1975
No stockholders' equity

FIDELITY INTERNATIONAL FUND (MA)
Name changed to Magellan Fund, Inc. 3/23/65
Magellan Fund, Inc. merged into Fidelity Magellan Fund, Inc. 6/22/81

FIDELITY INVESTMENT ASSOCIATES, INC. (DE)
Recapitalized as Pioneer Fund, Inc. (DE) 00/00/1951
Each share Capital Stock $5 par exchanged for (2) shares Capital Stock $2.50 par
Pioneer Fund, Inc. (DE) reincorporated in Massachusetts 04/01/1967 which name changed to Pioneer Fund 07/03/1992

FIDELITY INVESTMENT ASSOCIATION
Name changed to Fidelity Assurance Association in 1941 which completed liquidation in 1947

FIDELITY INVESTMENT CO. (AZ)
Acquired by Arizona Land Corp. 11/26/70
Each share Class A Common $1 par or Class B Common $1 par exchanged for (1) share Class A Common $1 par
Arizona Land Corp. adjudicated bankrupt 7/24/72

FIDELITY LIFE INSURANCE CO. (AL)
Acquired by All-States Life Insurance Co. in September 1931
Details not available

FIDELITY LIFE INSURANCE CORP.
Out of existence 00/00/1947
Details not available

FIDELITY LIQUIDATING TRUST
Liquidation completed in 1945

FIDELITY MED INC (DE)
Name changed 07/28/1983
Name changed from Fidelity Medical Services, Inc. to Fidelity Medical, Inc. 07/28/1983
Each share old Common 1¢ par exchanged for (0.25) share new Common 1¢ par 09/27/1991
Recapitalized as Corniche Group Inc. 10/01/1995
Each share new Common 1¢ par exchanged for (0.1) share Common 10¢ par
Corniche Group Inc. name changed to Phase III Medical, Inc. 07/30/2003 which recapitalized as NeoStem, Inc. 08/31/2006 which name changed to Caladrius Biosciences, Inc. 06/08/2015

FIDELITY MNG INVTS LTD (ON)
Recapitalized as New Fidelity Minerals Ltd. 06/00/1974
Each share Common no par exchanged for (0.005) share Common no par
(See New Fidelity Minerals Ltd.)

FIDELITY MTG & SVGS CORP (CANADA)
Common $10 par changed to $4 par and (1.5) additional shares issued 07/26/1972
Name changed to Equitrust Mortgage & Savings Co./Compagnie d'Hypotheque et d'Epargne Equitrust 03/06/1978
(See Equitrust Mortgage & Savings.

Co./ Compagnie d'Hypotheque et d'Epargne Equitrust)

FIDELITY MORTGAGE CO. (AR)
Completely liquidated 01/06/1975
Each share Capital Stock no par exchanged for first and final distribution of (0.5) share First Arkansas Bankstock Corp. Common $6.25 par and $200 cash
First Arkansas Bankstock Corp. name changed to Worthen Banking Corp. 10/23/1984 which merged into Boatmen's Bancshares, Inc. 02/28/1995 which merged into NationsBank Corp. (NC) 01/07/1997 which reincorporated in Delaware as BankAmerica Corp. (Old) 09/30/1998 which name changed to Bank of America Corp. 04/28/1999

FIDELITY MTG INVS (MA)
Under plan of merger each Share of Bene. Int. $1 par automatically became (1) share Lifetime Communities, Inc. Common 5¢ par 03/01/1978
Lifetime Communities, Inc. name changed to BEI Holdings Ltd. 05/30/1986 which name changed to Amresco Inc. 05/23/1994
(See Amresco Inc.)

FIDELITY MUN BD FD (MD)
Reorganized under the laws of Massachusetts as Fidelity Municipal Bond Fund and Capital Stock 1¢ par reclassified as Shares of Bene. Int. 1¢ par 08/01/1984

FIDELITY N Y F S B (GARDEN CITY, NY)
Acquired by Astoria Financial Corp. 01/31/1995
Each share Common 1¢ par exchanged for $29 cash

FIDELITY NATIONAL BANK & TRUST CO. (OKLAHOMA CITY, OK)
Each share Capital Stock $50 par exchanged for (5) shares Capital Stock $10 par 2/22/57
Stock Dividends - 20% 1/27/53; 33-1/3% 10/8/57; 25% 6/27/69
Name changed to Fidelity Bank, N.A. (Oklahoma City, OK) 7/1/70
Fidelity Bank, N.A. (Oklahoma City, OK) reorganized as Fidelity Corp. of Oklahoma 1/2/74 which name changed to Fidelity of Oklahoma, Inc. 12/2/77 which merged into BancOklahoma Corp. 10/15/84
(See BancOklahoma Corp.)

FIDELITY NATL BK (ARLINGTON, VA)
Acquired by Virginia Commonwealth Bankshares, Inc. 12/31/1968
Each share Common $10 par exchanged for (1.2) shares $1.20 Conv. Preferred Ser. A $20 par
Virginia Commonwealth Bankshares, Inc. name changed to Bank of Virginia Co. 07/17/1972
(See Bank of Virginia Co.)

FIDELITY NATL BK (BATON ROUGE, LA)
Common $25 par changed to $12.50 par and (1) additional share issued plus an 11-1/9% stock dividend paid 3/1/66
Common $12.50 par changed to $10 par and (0.25) additional share issued 3/3/69
Stock Dividends - 25% 3/1/55; 10% 4/5/57; 12-1/2% 12/31/62; 11-1/9% 2/26/68
Under plan of reorganization each share Common $10 par automatically became (1) share Fidelity National Financial Corp. Common $10 par 4/1/75
Fidelity National Financial Corp. merged into Hibernia Corp. 7/1/86 which merged into Capital One Financial Corp. 11/16/2005

FIDELITY NATL BK (LYNCHBURG, VA)
Though voluntary exchange offer Fidelity American Bankshares, Inc. acquired all but directors qualifying shares as of 05/03/1971

FIDELITY NATL BK (POMPANO BEACH, FL)
Merged into Pan American Bancshares, Inc. 5/1/80
Each share Capital Stock $10 par exchanged for $37.50 cash

FIDELITY NATL BK (SOUTH MIAMI, FL)
99.99987% acquired by First Bancshares of Florida, Inc. through exchange offer which expired 03/01/1974
Public interest eliminated

FIDELITY NATL BK (TWIN FALLS, ID)
Merged into Idaho First National Bank (Boise, ID) 7/1/70
Each share Capital Stock $100 par exchanged for (14.25) shares Capital Stock $5 par
Idaho First National Bank (Boise, ID) reorganized as Moore Financial Group Inc. 8/14/81 which name changed to West One Bancorp 4/21/89 which merged into U.S. Bancorp (OR) 12/26/95 which merged into U.S. Bancorp (Old) (DE) 8/1/97 which merged U.S. Bancorp (New) 2/27/2001

FIDELITY NATIONAL BANK (WEST FORT LAUDERDALE, FL)
Name changed to Plantation First National Bank (Plantation, Fla.) 7/1/63

FIDELITY NATIONAL BANK OF PENNSYLVANIA (WILLIAMSPORT, PA)
Common $10 par changed to $5 par and (1) additional share issued 03/05/1974
Stock Dividend - 50% 09/09/1969
Merged into Commonwealth Bank & Trust Co., N.A. (Williamsport, PA) 05/29/1981
Each share Common $5 par exchanged for (1.5) shares Common $3.50 par
Commonwealth Bank & Trust Co., N.A. (Williamsport, PA) reorganized as Commonwealth Bancshares Corp. 03/01/1982 which was acquired by Meridian Bancorp, Inc. 08/31/1993 which merged into CoreStates Financial Corp 04/09/1996 which merged into First Union Corp. 04/28/1998 which name changed to Wachovia Corp. (Ctfs. dated after 09/01/2001) 09/01/2001 which merged into Wells Fargo & Co. (New) 12/31/2008

FIDELITY NATIONAL CORP. (LA)
Merged into Republic Finance LLC 12/31/2002
Details not available

FIDELITY NATL CORP (GA)
Secondary Offering - 3,000,000 shares COM offered at $7.50 per share on 12/09/1997
Stock Dividend - 10% 10/9/95
Name changed to Fidelity Southern Corp. (New) 5/9/2003

FIDELITY NATL CORP (WA)
Merged into Western Preferred Corp. 9/22/76
Each share Common $1 par exchanged for (1) share 8% Conv. Preferred Ser. B $5 par
(See Western Preferred Corp.)

FIDELITY NATL FINL CORP (LA)
Stock Dividend - 10% 07/01/1982
Merged into Hibernia Corp. 07/01/1986
Each share Common $10 par exchanged for (1.02264) shares Class A Common no par
Hibernia Corp. merged into Capital One Financial Corp. 11/16/2005

FIDELITY NATL FINL INC NEW (DE)
Name changed 11/09/2006
Name changed from Fidelity National Title Group, Inc. to Fidelity National Financial, Inc. (New) 11/09/2006
Each share FNFV Group Common $0.0001 par received distribution of (0.17879) share Remy International, Inc. (Old) Common $0.0001 par payable 12/31/2014 to holders of record 12/23/2014 Ex date - 01/02/2015
Each share FNFV Group Common $0.0001 par received distribution of (0.17272) share J. Alexander's Holdings, Inc. Common $0.001 par payable 09/28/2015 to holders of record 09/22/2015 Ex date - 09/29/2015
Reorganized as Cannae Holdings, Inc. 11/20/2017
Each share FNFV Group Common $0.0001 par exchanged for (1) share Common $0.0001 par
(Additional Information in Active)

FIDELITY NATL FINL INC OLD (DE)
Common $0.0001 par split (4) for (3) by issuance of (0.33333333) additional share 03/30/1992
Common $0.0001 par split (3) for (2) by issuance of (0.5) additional share 02/03/1993
Common $0.0001 par split (3) for (2) by issuance of (0.5) additional share 12/23/1993
Common $0.0001 par split (5) for (4) by issuance of (0.25) additional share payable 05/23/2003 to holders of record 05/09/2003 Ex date - 05/27/2003
Each share Common $0.0001 par received distribution of (0.175) share Fidelity National Title Group, Inc. Class A Common $0.0001 par payable 10/17/2005 to holders of record 10/06/2005 Ex date - 10/18/2005
Each share Common $0.0001 par received distribution of (1.047732) shares Fidelity National Title Group, Inc. Class A Common $0.0001 par payable 10/24/2006 to holders of record 10/17/2006 Ex date - 10/25/2006
Stock Dividends - 10% 08/01/1991; 10% payable 02/02/1996 to holders of record 01/15/1996; 10% payable 01/07/1997 to holders of record 12/23/1996; 10% payable 01/14/1998 to holders of record 12/29/1997; 10% payable 01/12/1999 to holders of record 12/28/1998; 10% payable 08/23/2001 to holders of record 08/09/2001; 10% payable 05/23/2002 to holders of record 05/09/2002; 10% payable 02/26/2004 to holders of record 02/12/2004
Merged into Fidelity National Information Services, Inc. 11/09/2006
Each share Common $0.0001 par exchanged for (0.53741) share Common 1¢ par

FIDELITY NATL INFORMATION SOLUTIONS INC (DE)
Stock Dividend - 25% payable 05/23/2003 to holders of record 05/09/2003
Merged into Fidelity National Financial, Inc. 09/30/2003
Each share Common 1¢ par exchanged for (0.83) share Common $0.0001 par
Fidelity National Financial, Inc. merged into Fidelity National Information Services, Inc. 11/09/2006

FIDELITY NATL LIFE INS CO (OH)
Stock Dividend - 10% 06/17/1968
Each share Common $1 par exchanged for (0.000666) share Common $1,500 par 10/09/1972
Note: In effect holders received $2.50 cash per share and public interest was eliminated

FIDELITY NATL TITLE INS CO (TN)
Reacquired 12/31/98
Each share Common $2 par exchanged for $12.17 cash

FIDELITY OIL & REFINING CO. (KS)
Charter forfeited for failure to file annual reports 12/22/22

FIDELITY OIL COMPANY OF NEW JERSEY (NJ)
Out of business 2/20/25
No stockholders' equity

FIDELITY OKLA INC (DE)
Common $10 par changed to $5 par and (2) additional shares issued 03/31/1978
Stock Dividend - 100% 06/24/1982
Merged into BancOklahoma Corp. 10/15/1984
Each share Common $5 par exchanged for (0.632) share $2.50 Conv. Preferred Ser. A $1 par and (0.336056) share Common $2 par
(See BancOklahoma Corp.)

FIDELITY PARTNERSHIP 1993 (ON)
Partnership dissolved 03/31/2006
General Partner will distribute remaining assets to holders of record on a pro rata basis

FIDELITY PARTNERSHIP 1994 (ON)
Partnership dissolved 03/30/2007
General Partner will distribute remaining assets to holders of record on a pro rata basis

FIDELITY PARTNERSHIP 1995 (ON)
Partnership dissolved 03/31/2008
General Partner will distribute remaining assets to holders of record on a pro rata basis

FIDELITY PARTNERSHIP 1996 (ON)
Completely liquidated
Each Unit of Ltd. Partnership received first and final distribution of $0.28 cash payable 01/17/2012 to holders of record 12/31/2011

FIDELITY-PHENIX FIRE INSURANCE CO. (NY)
Each share Capital Stock $25 par exchanged for (2.5) shares Capital Stock $10 par in 1928
Capital Stock $10 par changed to $2.50 par in 1932
Capital Stock $2.50 par changed to $10 par in 1945
Capital Stock $10 par changed to $5 par and (1) additional share issued 3/15/56
Stock Dividend - 33-1/3% 3/20/50
Merged into Continental Insurance Co. 7/6/59
Each share Capital Stock $5 par exchanged for (1.17) shares Common $5 par
(See Continental Insurance Co.)

FIDELITY-PHILADELPHIA TRUST CO. (PHILADELPHIA, PA)
Each share Capital Stock $100 par exchanged for (5) shares Capital Stock $20 par 00/00/1948
Each share Capital Stock $20 par exchanged for (2) shares Capital Stock $10 par 01/28/1960
Name changed to Fidelity Bank (Philadelphia, PA) 04/03/1967
Fidelity Bank (Philadelphia, PA) reorganized as Fidelity Corp. of Pennsylvania 04/14/1969 which name changed to Fidelcor, Inc. 05/15/1974 which merged into First Fidelity Bancorporation (New) 02/29/1988 which merged into First Union Corp. 01/01/1996 which name changed to Wachovia Corp. (Ctfs.

dated after 09/01/2001) 09/01/2001 which merged into Wells Fargo & Co. (New) 12/31/2008

FIDELITY SVGS & LN ASSN (CA)
99.92% acquired by Fidelity Financial Corp. through exchange offer which expired 11/24/1969
Public interest eliminated

FIDELITY SVGS & LN ASSN (VA)
Merged into Washington-Lee Savings & Loan Association 08/31/1972
Each share Common 10¢ par exchanged for (1) share Ser. A Common $10 par
Washington-Lee Savings & Loan Association recapitalized as First Financial of Virginia Corp. 01/31/1974
(See First Financial of Virginia Corp.)

FIDELITY SAVINGS ASSOCIATION (PA)
Name changed to Fidelity Savings Bank (Pittsburgh, PA) 09/10/1990
Fidelity Savings Bank (Pittsburgh, PA) reorganized as Fidelity Bancorp, Inc. 08/19/1993 which merged into WesBanco, Inc. 12/03/2012

FIDELITY SVGS BK (ANTIGO, WI)
Stock Dividend - 100% 02/01/1976
Merged into Marine Corp. (WI) 12/30/1983
Each share Capital Stock $25 par exchanged for (3) shares $3 Conv. Preferred $1 par and (1.2) shares Common $10 par or $160 cash
Marine Corp. (WI) merged into Banc One Corp. (DE) 04/01/88 which reincorporated in Ohio 05/01/1989 which merged into Bank One Corp. 10/02/1998 which merged into J.P. Morgan Chase & Co. 12/31/2000 which name changed to JPMorgan Chase & Co. 07/20/2004

FIDELITY SVGS BK PASA (PITTSBURGH, PA)
Stock Dividends - 10% 05/08/1992; 10% 05/10/1993
Under plan of reorganization each share Common par automatically became (1) share Fidelity Bancorp, Inc. Common 1¢ par 08/19/1993
Fidelity Bancorp, Inc. merged into WesBanco, Inc. 12/03/2012

FIDELITY SMALL BUSINESS INVESTMENT CO. (MN)
Name changed to Minnesota Small Business Investment Co. 9/13/61
Minnesota Small Business Investment Co. name changed to Northeast Fidelity Investment Co. 10/7/75 which was acquired by Fidelity Securities & Investment Co. 3/29/76

FIDELITY SOUTHN CORP NEW (GA)
Fixed Rate Perpetual Preferred Ser. A no par called for redemption at $1,000 plus $2.083333 accrued dividends on 08/30/2013
(Additional Information in Active)

FIDELITY SOUTHN CORP OLD (GA)
Name changed to Fidelity National Corp. 8/1/95
Fidelity National Corp. name changed to Fidelity Southern Corp. (New) 5/9/2003

FIDELITY ST BK (TOPEKA, KS)
Name changed to Fidelity State Bank & Trust Co. (Topeka, Kans.) 3/18/68

FIDELITY TAX EXEMPT MONEY MKT TR (MA)
Name changed to Fidelity Beacon Street Trust 03/01/1990

FIDELITY THRIFT TR (MA)
Shares of Bene. Int. split (5) for (1) by issuance of (4) additional shares 8/27/76
Name changed to Fidelity Advisor Intermediate Bond Fund 8/30/76

FIDELITY TIRE & RUBBER CO. (IL)
Name changed to Denman Tire & Rubber Co. (IL) in 1930
(See Denman Tire & Rubber Co. (IL))

FIDELITY TITLE & MORTGAGE GUARANTEE CO. (RIDGEWOOD, NJ)
Taken over by State Commissioner of Banking in 1932

FIDELITY TREND FD INC (MA)
Name changed to Fidelity Trend Fund and Capital Stock $1 par reclassified as Shares of Bene. Int. no par 12/31/1984

FIDELITY TRUST CO. (BALTIMORE, MD)
Merged into Fidelity-Baltimore National Bank & Trust Co. (Baltimore, MD) 7/16/54
Each share Capital Stock $25 par exchanged for (1.6) shares Capital Stock $10 par
Fidelity-Baltimore National Bank & Trust Co. (Baltimore, MD) name changed to Fidelity-Baltimore National Bank (Baltimore, MD) 1/15/57 which merged into Baltimore National Bank (Baltimore, MD) 6/24/60 which merged into Maryland National Bank (Baltimore, MD) 11/14/61 which reorganized as Maryland National Co. 5/1/69 which name changed to MNC Financial, Inc. 4/29/87 which merged into NationsBank Corp. 10/1/93 which reincorporated in Delaware as BankAmerica Corp. (Old) 9/25/98 which merged into BankAmerica Corp. (New) 9/30/98 which name changed to Bank of America Corp. 4/28/99

FIDELITY TRUST CO. (PHILADELPHIA, PA)
Merged into Philadelphia Trust Co. under the name of Fidelity-Philadelphia Trust Co. (Philadelphia, PA) 07/08/1950
Each share Capital Stock $100 par exchanged for (1.5) shares Capital Stock $100 par
Fidelity-Philadelphia Trust Co. (Philadelphia, PA) name changed to Fidelity Bank (Philadelphia, PA) 04/03/1967 which reorganized as Fidelity Corp. of Pennsylvania 04/14/1969 which name changed to Fidelcor, Inc. 05/15/1974 which merged into First Fidelity Bancorporation (New) 02/29/1988 which merged into First Union Corp. 01/01/1996 which name changed to Wachovia Corp. (Ctfs. dated after 09/01/2001) 09/01/2001 which merged into Wells Fargo & Co. (New) 12/31/2008

FIDELITY TRUST CO. (PITTSBURGH, PA)
Under plan of merger each share Capital Stock $25 par exchanged for (2.5) shares Capital Stock $10 par 00/00/1954
Stock Dividend - 25% 04/15/1948
Merged into Pittsburgh National Bank (Pittsburgh, PA) 09/11/1959
Each share Capital Stock $10 par exchanged for (1-1/3) shares Capital Stock $20 par
Pittsburgh National Bank (Pittsburgh, PA) reorganized as Pittsburgh National Corp. 04/30/1969 which merged into PNC Financial Corp 01/19/1983 which name changed to PNC Bank Corp. 02/08/1993 which name changed to PNC Financial Services Group, Inc. 03/15/2000

FIDELITY TR CO (STAMFORD, CT)
Stock Dividend - 100% 5/1/79
Acquired by Shawmut Corp. 11/24/86
Each share Capital Stock $5 par exchanged for (2.54) shares Common $5 par
Shawmut Corp. merged into Shawmut National Corp. 2/29/88 which merged into Fleet Financial Group Inc. (New) 11/30/95 which name changed to Fleet Boston Corp. 10/1/99 which name changed to FleetBoston Financial Corp. 4/18/2000 which merged into Bank of America Corp. 4/1/2004

FIDELITY TRUST OF AMERICA (TX)
Charter forfeited for failure to pay taxes 7/24/59

FIDELITY TRUSTCO LTD (CANADA)
Voluntarily dissolved 03/14/1997
Details not available

FIDELITY UN BANCORPORATION (NJ)
Merged into First National State Bancorporation 04/05/1984
Each share Common $5 par exchanged for (1.3) shares Common $6.25 par
First National State Bancorporation name changed to First Fidelity Bancorporation (Old) 05/01/1985 which merged into First Fidelity Bancorporation (New) 02/29/1988 which merged into First Union Corp. 01/01/1996 which name changed to Wachovia Corp. (Ctfs. dated after 09/01/2001) 09/01/2001 which merged into Wells Fargo & Co. (New) 12/31/2008

FIDELITY UN LIFE INS CO (TX)
Common $10 par changed to $2.50 par and (3) additional shares issued 11/14/1966
Common $2.50 par changed to $1.25 par and (1) additional share issued 03/29/1968
Common $1.25 par changed to $1 par and (0.66666666) additional share issued 09/12/1969
Stock Dividend - 25% 09/10/1965
Merged into Allianz Versicherungs A.G. 10/09/1979
Each share Common $1 par exchanged for $72.50 cash

FIDELITY UN TR CO (NEWARK, NJ)
Capital Stock $10 par changed to $5 par and (1) additional share issued 03/01/1962
Stock Dividends - 12-1/2% 03/11/1952; 11-1/9% 01/30/1953; 50% 05/15/1969
Reorganized as Fidelity Union Bancorporation 01/04/1971
Each share Capital Stock $5 par exchanged for (1) share Common $5 par
Fidelity Union Bancorporation merged into First National State Bancorporation 04/05/1984 which name changed to First Fidelity Bancorporation (Old) 05/01/1985 which merged into First Fidelity Bancorporation (New) 02/29/1988 which merged into First Union Corp. 01/01/1996 which name changed to Wachovia Corp. (Ctfs. dated after 09/01/2001) 09/01/2001 which merged into Wells Fargo & Co. (New) 12/31/2008

FIDELITY UNION STOCK & BOND CO.
Name changed to Essex Investment Co. in 1945
(See Essex Investment Co.)

FIDELITY UNION TITLE & MORTGAGE GUARANTY CO.
Assets acquired by New Jersey Realty Co. in 1937
Details not available

FIDINAM PPTYS INC (ON)
Name changed to Bramalea Properties Inc. 06/05/1986
(See Bramalea Properties Inc.)

FIDUCIARIES INC (WI)
Merged into Triton, Inc. 03/05/1979
Each share Common 5¢ par exchanged for $8.91 cash

FIDUCIARY / CLAYMORE DYNAMIC EQUITY FD (DE)
Issue Information - 5,375,000 shares COM offered at $20 per share on 04/26/2005
Completely liquidated
Each share Common 1¢ par received first and final distribution of $4.207 cash payable 05/29/2009 to holders of record 04/24/2009

FIDUCIARY & GEN CORP (DE)
Charter cancelled and declared inoperative and void for non-payment of taxes 6/27/84

FIDUCIARY CAP CORP (DE)
Charter cancelled and declared inoperative and void for non-payment of taxes 3/1/77

FIDUCIARY CAP GROWTH FD INC (MI)
Name changed to FMI Common Stock Fund Inc. 12/15/2001

FIDUCIARY CORP.
Dissolved in 1943

FIDUCIARY FUND, INC.
Apparently dissolved in 1944

FIDUCIARY INCOME FDS INC (WI)
Fund dissolved in September 1988
Details not available

FIDUCIARY MANAGEMENT, INC. (DE)
Name changed to Resort Airlines, Inc. (DE) (Old) in 1953
Resort Airlines, Inc. name changed to Townsend Investment Co. 6/14/57 which name changed to Townsend Corp. of America 4/29/59 which name changed to Chatham Corp. 12/31/64

FIDUCIARY MUTUAL INVESTING CO., INC. (MD)
Capital Stock $1 par changed to 50¢ par and (1) additional share issued 6/5/63
Acquired by Steadman Fiduciary Investment Fund, Inc. 11/2/67
Each share Capital Stock 50¢ par exchanged for (1.06916) shares Common $1 par
Steadman Fiduciary Investment Fund, Inc. merged into Steadman Investment Fund, Inc. (New) 1/25/73 which name changed to Ameritor Investment Fund 9/23/98

FIDUCIARY TR CO INTL (NEW YORK, NY)
Each share Capital Stock $100 par exchanged for (10) shares Capital Stock $10 par in 1943
Stock Dividends - 100% 2/21/56; 10% 4/19/68; 100% 4/19/73
Name changed from Fiduciary Trust Co. (New York, NY) to Fiduciary Trust Co. International (New York, NY) and Capital Stock $10 par changed to $2.50 par 4/15/87
Common $2.50 par split (5) for (4) by issuance of (0.25) additional share 5/15/87
Common $2.50 par split (3) for (1) by issuance of (2) additional shares payable 9/27/96 to holders of record 9/16/96
Stock Dividend - 5% payable 3/9/99 to holders of record 2/22/99
Acquired by Franklin Resources, Inc. 4/10/2001
Each share Common $2.50 par exchanged for (2.7744) shares Common 10¢ par

FIDUCIARY VALQUEST FD INC (WI)
Name changed to Fiduciary Income Funds, Inc. 3/17/88
(See Fiduciary Income Funds, Inc.)

FIDUCIE DESJARDINS (QC)
Adjustable Rate Preferred Ser. 1 called for redemption at $25 plus

$0.07372 accrued dividends on 08/25/2004
(Additional Information in Active)

FIEDMONT RES LTD (ON)
Recapitalized as Advanced Recruitment Technologies Inc. 11/17/1992
Each share Common no par exchanged for (0.2) share Common no par
Advanced Recruitment Technologies Inc. name changed to Canadian States Gas Ltd. 12/19/1994 which name changed to Canadian States Resources Inc. 10/26/1995 which name changed to High North Resources Inc. 07/07/1997 which recapitalized as HNR Ventures Inc. 06/30/2000 which recapitalized as RMM Ventures Inc. (ON) 06/06/2006 which name changed to PetroCorp Group Inc. 12/23/2009

FIELD & STREAM PUBLISHING CO.
Merged into Holt (Henry) & Co., Inc. in 1951
Each share Common $2 par exchanged for (0.3) share 5-1/2% Preferred $10 par, (0.5) share Common $1 par and $7 cash
Holt (Henry) & Co., Inc. name changed to Holt, Rinehart & Winston, Inc. 3/1/60 which merged into Columbia Broadcasting System, Inc. 8/1/67 which name changed to CBS Inc. 4/18/74
(See CBS Inc.)

FIELD (MARSHALL) & CO. (DE)
See - Marshall Field & Co

FIELD EXPLORATIONS LTD. (ON)
Merged into Sakfield Mines & Investments Ltd. 01/17/1968
Each share Common $1 par exchanged for (0.33333333) share Capital Stock no par
(See Sakfield Mines & Investments Ltd.)

FIELD FINANCIAL CORP. (MN)
Merged into Heritage Nursing Centers, Inc. 11/19/68
Each share Common 25¢ par exchanged for (1) share Common 20¢ par
Heritage Nursing Centers, Inc. name changed to Heritage Rembrandt Corp. 1/23/70 which name changed to Rembrandt Enterprises, Inc. 1/31/72
(See Rembrandt Enterprises, Inc.)

FIELD FINL CORP (NC)
Name changed to Cyber Corp. (NC) and Common 50¢ par changed to 10¢ par 11/01/1971
Cyber Corp. (NC) reincorporated in Nevada as Cyber International Corp. 06/18/1973
(See Cyber International Corp.)

FIELD PETE CORP (BC)
Name changed to L & D Property Operations (Canada) Ltd. 04/12/1990
L & D Property Operations (Canada) Ltd. name changed to Uni-Way Pacific Holdings Inc. 04/06/1992 which recapitalized as New Uni-Way Holdings Ltd. 09/16/1993 which name changed to Full Riches Investments Ltd. 02/26/1998 which was acquired by Medoro Resources Ltd. 03/02/2004 which merged into Gran Colombia Gold Corp. 06/14/2011

FIELD-SCHLICK, INC. (DE)
Out of business 08/00/1979
Details not available

FIELDCREST CANNON INC (DE)
Name changed 6/30/86
Name changed from Fieldcrest Mills, Inc. to Fieldcrest Cannon, Inc. 6/30/86
Each share Capital Stock no par reclassified as (2) shares Common $1 par 9/30/86
Each share Class B Common $1 par converted into (1) share Common $1 par 12/1/93
Merged into Pillowtex Corp. 12/19/97
Each share $3 Conv. Preferred Ser. A $1 par exchanged for (0.269) share Common 1¢ par and $27 cash
Each share Common $1 par exchanged for (0.269) share Common 1¢ par and $27 cash
(See Pillowtex Corp.)

FIELDCREST CORP (DE)
Recapitalized as Softlock.Com, Inc. 8/10/98
Each share Common $0.00001 par exchanged for (0.02) share Common $0.00001 par
(See Softlock.Com, Inc.)

FIELDS AIRCRAFT SPARES INC (UT)
Plan of reorganization under Chapter 11 Federal Bankruptcy Code effective 11/19/2001
Company now known as Octagon Aerospace, Inc. which is privately held

FIELDS INDL GROUP INC (UT)
Recapitalized as Fields Aircraft Spares, Inc. 11/20/1995
Each share Common $0.001 par exchanged for (0.02) share Common 5¢ par
(See Fields Aircraft Spares, Inc.)

FIELDS NEBRASKA CORP (NV)
Proclaimed dissolved for failure to pay taxes 5/14/62

FIELDS PLASTICS & CHEMS INC (NY)
Name changed to Cleveland Calendering & Coating Corp. and Common $1 par changed to 50¢ par 04/25/1978
(See Cleveland Calendering & Coating Corp.)

FIELDS STORES LTD (BC)
Common no par split (3) for (1) by issuance of (2) additional shares 5/16/69
Each share old Common no par exchanged for (0.0005) share new Common no par 11/15/77
Note: In effect holders received $16.50 cash per share and public interest eliminated

FIELDS TECHNOLOGIES INC (DE)
Reincorporated under the laws of Nevada as Park City Group, Inc. 08/08/2002

FIELDSTONE INVT CORP (MD)
Merged into Credit-Based Asset Servicing & Securitization LLC 07/17/2007
Each share Common 1¢ par exchanged for $4 cash

FIELDWORKS INC (MN)
Issue Information - 2,125,000 shares COM offered at $6.50 per share on 3/20/1997
Name changed to Kontron Mobile Computing, Inc. 6/4/2001
(See Kontron Moblie Computing, Inc.)

FIERA HIGH INCOME TR (ON)
Trust terminated 11/12/2012
Each Trust Unit received $9.0501 cash

FIERA SCEPTRE INC (ON)
Name changed to Fiera Capital Corp. 04/16/2012

FIFE CORP (OK)
Common 10¢ par split (3) for (2) by issuance of (0.5) additional share 8/29/79
Stock Dividend - 20% 4/29/74
Merged into Clausing Corp. 8/15/80
Each share Common 10¢ par exchanged for (1) share Common $1 par
(See Clausing Corp.)

1518-20 LOCUST STREET CO. (PA)
Dissolution approved 00/00/1947
Details not available

1500 CORP. (PA)
Name changed to Seiler's, Inc. in 1956
Seiler's, Inc. name changed to Burk (Louis) Co. 9/18/67
(See Burk (Louis) Co.)

1500 WALNUT STREET CORP. (PA)
Merged into General Waterworks Corp. 6/28/57
Each share Preferred $1 par exchanged for (1) share 5% Preferred $100 par
Each share Common $1 par exchanged for (4) shares Common $1 par
General Waterworks Corp. merged into International Utilities Corp. 3/1/68 which name changed to IU International Corp. 4/27/73
(See IU International Corp.)

FIFTEEN OIL CO. (TX)
Acquired by Tennessee Gas Transmission Co. on a (0.365) for (1) basis 5/2/60
Tennessee Gas Transmission Co. name changed to Tenneco Inc. 4/11/66 which merged into El Paso Natural Gas Co. 12/12/96 which reorganized as El Paso Energy Corp. 8/1/98 which name changed to El Paso Corp. 2/5/2001

15 PARK AVE., INC. (NY)
Dissolved 08/13/1959
Details not available

15 PARK ROW CORP.
Property sold 00/00/1945
No stockholders' equity

1528 MORSE AVENUE BUILDING
Property sold 00/00/1948
Details not available

1528 WALNUT STREET BUILDING CORP. OLD
Merged into 1528 Walnut Street Building Corp. (New) 00/00/1948
Each share Preferred no par exchanged for (0.0909091) share new Common no par
Common no par did not participate and is without value
(See 1528 Walnut Street Building Corp. (New))

1528 WALNUT STREET BUILDING CORP. NEW
Dissolved 00/00/1950
Details not available

FIFTEENTH & FRISCO BUILDING CO. (DE)
Liquidation completed 1/2/63

FIFTH & PAC COS INC (DE)
Name changed to Kate Spade & Co. 02/26/2014
(See Kate Spade & Co.)

FIFTH AVE CARDS INC (NY)
Class A Capital Stock 10¢ par and Class B Capital Stock 10¢ par split (5) for (4) by issuance of (0.25) additional share respectively 12/22/69
Class A Capital Stock 10¢ par and Class B Capital Stock 10¢ par split (3) for (2) by issuance of (0.5) additional share respectively 5/3/71
Class A Capital Stock 10¢ par and Class B Capital Stock 10¢ par reclassified as Common 10¢ par 3/1/72
Stock Dividends - Class A & B - 20% 11/1/67; 25% 11/18/68
Reincorporated under the laws of Delaware as Fifth Retail Corp. 4/2/87
(See Fifth Retail Corp.)

FIFTH AVE COACH LINES INC (NY)
Name changed to South Bay Corp. 11/30/73
South Bay Corp. assets tranferred to South Bay Corp. Liquidating Trust 3/31/79
(See South Bay Corp. Liquidating Trust)

FIFTH AVE ELECTRS INC (NY)
Charter cancelled and proclaimed dissolved for failure to pay taxes and file reports 12/16/1974

FIFTH AVE INDS INC (NY)
Charter cancelled and proclaimed dissolved for failure to pay taxes and file returns 12/15/1971

FIFTH AVE VENTURES CORP (BC)
Recapitalized as Instar Energy Corp. 11/15/90
Each share Common no par exchanged for (0.2) share Common no par
(See Instar Energy Corp.)

FIFTH AVENUE & TWENTY EIGHTH STREET CORP.
Reorganized as 245 Fifth Avenue Corp. in 1952 which was liquidated in 1953

FIFTH AVENUE BANK (NEW YORK, NY)
Merged into Bank of New York & Fifth Avenue Bank (New York, NY) 04/30/1948
Each share Capital Stock exchanged for (4) shares Capital Stock $100 par
Bank of New York & Fifth Avenue Bank (New York, NY) name changed to Bank of New York (New York, NY) 05/01/1952 which reorganized as Bank of New York Co., Inc. 05/29/1969 which merged into Bank of New York Mellon Corp. 07/01/2007

FIFTH AVENUE BUS SECURITIES CORP.
Dissolved and assets distributed in 1936

5TH AVE CHANNEL CORP (FL)
Recapitalized as Simulated Environment Concepts, Inc. 01/16/2008
Each share Common $0.001 par exchanged for (0.01) share Common $0.001 par

FIFTH AVENUE PUBG INC (NV)
Issue Information - 10,000,000 shares COM offered at $0.10 per share on 03/02/1998
Name changed to New Horizons Airways Inc. 07/23/1999
(See New Horizons Airways Inc.)

FIFTH DIMENSION INC (NJ)
Common 50¢ par split (3) for (2) by issuance of (0.5) additional share 05/10/1991
Chapter 7 bankruptcy proceedings terminated 03/10/2009
Stockholders' equity unlikely

FIFTH ERA KNOWLEDGE INC (AB)
Recapitalized as Triton Capital Corp. 09/25/2003
Each share Common no par exchanged for (1/7) share Common no par
Triton Capital Corp. name changed to March Resources Corp. 09/30/2004 which recapitalized as Ranger Energy Ltd. (AB) 08/21/2009 which reorganized in Ontario as North Sea Energy Inc. 10/21/2011

FIFTH GENERATION SYS INC (BC)
Name changed to China Sea Resources Corp. 08/27/1986
(See China Sea Resources Corp.)

FIFTH RETAIL CORP (DE)
Charter cancelled and declared inoperative and void for non-payment of taxes 3/1/89

FIFTH ST FIN CORP (DE)
Name changed to Oaktree Specialty Lending Corp. 10/18/2017

FINANCIAL INFORMATION, INC.

FIFTH STR SR FLOATING RATE CORP (DE)
Name changed to Oaktree Strategic Income Corp. 10/18/2017

FIFTH STREET BUILDING (LOS ANGELES) (CA)
Racapitalized as Fifth Street Store in December 1944
Each share Common $100 par exchanged for (20) shares Common $5 par
Fifth Street Store name changed to Milliron's in May 1946
(See Milliron's)

FIFTH STREET STORE (LOS ANGELES) (CA)
Name changed to Milliron's in May 1946
(See Milliron's)

FIFTH THIRD BANCORP (OH)
Each share 8.50% Depositary Preferred Ser. G no par exchanged for (8.6393) shares Common no par 07/01/2013
(Additional Information in Active)

FIFTH 3RD BK (CINCINNATI, OH)
Common $10 par changed to $6-2/3 par and (0.5) additional share issued 3/21/69
Reorganized as Fifth Third Bancorp 4/15/75
Each share Common $6-2/3 par exchanged for (1) share Common $6.66 par

FIFTH THIRD CAP TR V (DE)
7.25% Trust Preferred Securities called for redemption at $25 on 08/15/2012

FIFTH THIRD CAP TR VI (DE)
7.25% Trust Preferred Securities called for redemption at $25 plus $0.422917 accrued dividends on 08/08/2012

FIFTH THIRD CAP TR VII (DE)
Guaranteed Trust Preferred Securities called for redemption at $25 on 06/15/2011

FIFTH 3RD UN TR CO (CINCINNATI, OH)
Each share Common $100 par exchanged for (4) shares Common $25 par plus a 14-2/7% stock dividend paid 10/26/51
Common $25 par changed to $10 par and (1.5) additional shares issued 3/6/64
Stock Dividends - 16-2/3% 11/4/47; 25% 1/25/55; 20% 1/31/61
Name changed to Fifth Third Bank (Cincinnati, OH) 3/12/69
Fifth Third Bank (Cincinnati, OH) reorganized as Fifth Third Bancorp 4/15/75

FIFTY ASSOC (MA)
Each share Common no par exchanged for (100) shares new Common no par 10/5/64
Common no par split (10) for (1) by issuance of (9) additional shares 6/9/89
Liquidation completed
Each share Common no par received initial distribution of $1.25 cash payable 6/16/2000 to holders of record 6/2/2000 Ex date - 5/31/2000
Each share Common no par received second distribution of $2.95 cash payable 9/29/2000 to holders of record 9/15/2000 Ex date - 9/20/2000
Each share Common no par received third distribution of $7.09 cash payable 12/28/2000 to holders of record 12/22/2000 Ex date - 12/20/2000
Each share Common no par received fourth distribution of $4 cash payable 3/29/2001 to holders of record 3/22/2001 Ex date - 3/20/2001
Each share Common no par received fifth distribution of $20 cash payable 6/28/2001 to holders of record 6/25/2001 Ex date - 6/29/2001
Each share Common no par received sixth distribution of $2 cash payable 9/28/2001 to holders of record 9/25/2001 Ex date - 10/1/2001
Each share Common no par received seventh distribution of $9.50 cash payable 12/19/2001 to holders of record 12/13/2001
Each share Common no par received eighth and final distribution of $1.12 cash payable 10/24/2002 to holders of record 12/19/2001 Ex date - 11/4/2002
Note: Certificates were not required to be surrendered and are now valueless

FIFTY ASSOCIATES CO. (OH)
Liquidation completed 6/1/57

FIFTY BROADWAY BUILDING, INC. (NY)
Common $10 par changed to $5 par by a capital distribution of $5 in cash in 1951
Liquidation completed 6/57

5847 DIVISION ST. BUILDING CORP. (IL)
Liquidation completed 07/02/1956
Details not available

5812-20 HIGGINS, INC.
Liquidated 00/00/1941
Details not available

5085 BROADWAY REALTY, LLC (NY)
Voluntarily dissolved 2/17/2005
Details not available

FIFTY FIFTH & DREXEL BLDG. CORP. (IL)
Liquidation completed 1/15/57

55 PARK AVENUE, INC.
Dissolved 00/00/1948
Details not available

5040 WASHINGTON CORP.
Liquidated 00/00/1943
Details not available

5401 TELEGRAPH ROAD CO. (CA)
Completely liquidated 01/23/1961
Details not available

59 EAST 54TH ST., INC.
Dissolved 00/00/1950
Details not available

5950 NORTH AVENUE BUILDING CORP. (IL)
Liquidation completed 02/03/1958
Details not available

50-OFF STORES INC (DE)
Reincorporated 12/22/1992
Common 1¢ par split (3) for (2) by issuance of (0.5) additional share 10/04/1991
State of incorporation changed from (TX) to (DE) 12/22/1992
Plan of reorganization under Chapter 11 Federal Bankruptcy Code effective 06/16/1997
No stockholders' equity for holders of old Common
Name changed to Lot$off Corp. 06/16/1997
(See Lot$off Corp.)

5151 CORP. (OH)
Liquidation completed
Each share Common $2 par exchanged for initial distribution of $18 cash 09/06/1967
Each share Common $2 par received second distribution of $1.10 cash 05/02/1968
Each share Common $2 par received third and final distribution of $0.70 cash 08/04/1969

FIFTY-PLUS NET INTL INC (CANADA)
Name changed to ZoomerMedia Ltd. 07/02/2008

5734 BLACKSTONE AVENUE BUILDING CORP. (IL)
Liquidation completed 01/21/1960
Details not available

5733 BROADWAY CORP.
Liquidated 00/00/1950
Details not available

57TH STR GEN ACQUISITION CORP (DE)
Name changed to Crumbs Bake Shop, Inc. 10/25/2011
(See Crumbs Bake Shop, Inc.)

56 PETROLEUM CORP. (MT)
Liquidation completed 00/00/1954
Details not available

53 ST STR CORP (MA)
Capital Stock $100 par reclassified as Common $100 par 12/18/1959
6% Preferred $100 par called for redemption 03/31/1968
Liquidation completed
Each share Common $100 par stamped to indicate initial distribution of $35 cash 06/10/1968
Each share Stamped Common $100 par exchanged for second distribution of $20 cash 09/30/1968
Each share Stamped Common $100 par received third and final distribution of $2.45 cash 10/31/1968

5332 BLACKSTONE, INC.
Liquidated 00/00/1943
Details not available

5222 HARPER AVENUE BUILDING CORP. (IL)
Liquidation completed 11/10/1958
Details not available

50 WEST BROAD, INC.
Property sold 00/00/1945
Details not available

50ON COM INC (NV)
Under plan of reorganization each share Common 1¢ par automatically became (0.5) share Common 1¢ par Design Marketing Concepts Inc. 10/31/2000
Design Marketing Concepts Inc. name changed to WEB Pay-Per-View Inc. 05/30/2001 which name changed to U.S. Federal Financial Corp. 09/25/2001 which name changed to Vibe Records Inc. 04/23/2002 which name changed to Great Entertainment & Sports Inc. 03/07/2003 which name changed to Rockit!, Inc. 06/11/2007
(See Rockit!, Inc.)

FIGGIE INTL INC (DE)
Name changed 12/31/1986
6% Preference 1st Ser. $100 par called for redemption 11/28/1983
Conv. Preference 2nd Ser. $1 par called for redemption 08/05/1985
Conv. Preference 3rd Ser. $1 par called for redemption 08/05/1985
Each share Common 10¢ par exchanged for (0.5) share Class B Common 10¢ par 01/23/1986
Each share Class B Common 10¢ par received distribution of (1) share Class A Common 10¢ par 01/23/1986
Name changed from Figgie International Holdings Inc. to Figgie International Inc. 12/31/1986
Class A Common 10¢ par split (3) for (1) by issuance of (2) additional shares 01/22/1990
Class B Common 10¢ par split (3) for (1) by issuance of (2) additional shares 01/22/1990
Name changed to Scott Technologies, Inc. 05/20/1998
Scott Technologies, Inc. merged into Tyco International Ltd. (Bermuda) 05/03/2001 which reincorporated in Switzerland 03/17/2009 which merged into Johnson Controls International PLC 09/06/2016

FIGGIE INTL INC (OH)
Conv. Preference 1st Ser. called for redemption at $100 on 12/03/1982
Under plan of reorganization each share Conv. Preference 2nd Ser. $1 par, Conv. Preference 3rd Ser. $1 par, 6% Preference 1st Ser. $100 par and Common 10¢ par automatically became (1) share Figgie International Holdings Inc. (DE) Conv. Preference 2nd Ser. $1 par, Conv. Preference 3rd Ser. $1 par, 6% Preference 1st Ser. $100 par and Common 10¢ par respectively 07/18/1983
Figgie International Holdings Inc. name changed to Figgie International Inc. 12/31/1986 which name changed to Scott Technologies, Inc. 05/20/1998 which merged into Tyco International Ltd. (Bermuda) 05/03/2001 which reincorporated in Switzerland 03/17/2009 which merged into Johnson Controls International PLC 09/06/2016

FIGHTERSOFT MULTIMEDIA CORP (NV)
SEC revoked common stock registration 12/07/2011

FIGO VENTURES INC (NV)
Recapitalized as Precious Investments, Inc. 08/10/2015
Each share Common $0.001 par exchanged for (0.05) share Common $0.001 par

FIGUERY GOLD MINES, LTD. (ON)
Charter surrendered 00/00/1956

FIGURETTE, LTD. (DE)
Name changed to Cal-Tech Systems, Inc. 2/3/61
Cal-Tech Systems, Inc. name changed to Fullview Industries, Inc. 8/31/62 which recapitalized as Darfield Industries, Inc. 3/9/72
(See Darfield Industries, Inc.)

FII INTL INC (NV)
Name changed to Amish Naturals, Inc. and (1.8) additional shares issued 10/27/2006
(See Amish Naturals, Inc.)

FII LIQUIDATING CO. (GA)
Liquidation completed
Each share $1 Class A Conv. Preferred $10 par exchanged for first and final distribution of $20 cash 05/01/1968
Each share Common $2 par exchanged for initial distribution of $7 principal amount of Allied Products Corp. (DE) 7% Subord. Debentures due 07/01/1984, (0.09) Common Stock Purchase Warrant and $3.10 cash 05/01/1968
Each share Common $2 par received second and final distribution of $0.0182 cash 03/31/1969

FIIC HLDGS INC (DE)
SEC revoked common stock registration 12/18/2012

FILA HLDG S P A (ITALY)
ADR basis changed from (1:5) to (1:1) 04/23/2001
Each Sponsored ADR for Ordinary EUR 0.50 par exchanged for (0.5) Sponsored ADR for Ordinary EUR 1 par 10/11/2002
Name changed to RCS Investimenti S.p.A. 01/01/2004
(See RCS Investimenti S.p.A.)

FILE LAKE EXPLS LTD (ON)
Struck off register and declared dissolved for failure to file returns 00/00/1976

FILENE'S (WM.) SONS CO.
Acquired by Federated Department Stores, Inc. in 1949
Each share Common no par exchanged for (1.25) shares Common $5 par

Federated Department Stores, Inc. name changed to Macy's, Inc. 6/1/2007

FILENES BASEMENT CORP (MA)
Plan of reorganization under Chapter 11 Federal Bankruptcy Code effective 03/17/2000
Stockholders' equity unlikely

FILENET CORP (DE)
Common 1¢ par split (2) for (1) by issuance of (1) additional share payable 6/12/98 to holders of record 5/29/98
Merged into International Business Machines Corp. 10/13/2006
Each share Common 1¢ par exchanged for $35 cash

FILICE WINERY INC (DE)
Name changed to Crown Companies, Inc. 03/04/1986
Crown Companies, Inc. name changed to Crown Gold Companies Group, Ltd. 09/25/1987 which recapitalized as Tigershark Enterprises Inc. 10/28/1997 which name changed to Great White Marine & Recreation, Inc. 05/14/1998
(See Great White Marine & Recreation, Inc.)

FILIGREE FOODS INC (DE)
Adjudicated bankrupt 09/08/1980
No stockholders' equity

FILING EQUIPMENT BUREAU, INC. (MA)
Dissolved 10/20/65

FILION GOLD MINES LTD. (ON)
Name changed to Teal Exploration Ltd. 03/20/1959
(See Teal Exploration Ltd.)

FILL R UP SYS INC (DE)
Name changed to Fort Atlantic Corp. 03/25/1982
(See Fort Atlantic Corp.)

FILLMORE OIL CO., LTD. (CA)
Company liquidated in 1987
Details not available

FILM & MUSIC ENTMT INC (NV)
SEC revoked common stock registration 05/19/2009

FILM AUTOMATIC MACHINE CO., INC.
Assets sold in 1940

FILM GROUP II, INC. (OH)
Charter cancelled for failure to pay taxes 12/29/95

FILM INSPECTION MACHINE CO., INC.
Dissolved in 1936

FILM MAKERS INTERNATIONAL INC. (UT)
Name changed to Multiphonic Corp. 5/9/85
(See Multiphonic Corp.)

FILM MICROELECTRONICS INC (MA)
Acquired by Sertech Corp. 06/30/1979
Each share Common 25¢ par exchanged for $5.25 cash

FILM ROMAN INC (DE)
Merged into IDT Entertainment, Inc. 3/30/2006
Each share Common 1¢ par exchanged for $0.08 cash

FILMACK CORP (IL)
Acquired by a private company in 1986
Holders received an undisclosed amount of cash

FILMAGIC ENTMT CORP (UT)
Each share old Common $0.0001 par exchanged for (0.1) share new Common $0.0001 par 08/25/1994
Name changed to InstaPay Systems Inc. and (2) additional shares issued 12/23/2002
(See InstaPay Systems Inc.)

FILMASTER INC (CA)
Charter suspended for failure to pay taxes 12/01/1970

FILMOHM CORP. (NY)
Completely liquidated 5/8/68
Each share Common 10¢ par exchanged for first and final distribution of (0.4) share Solitron Devices, Inc. (N.Y.) Common $1 par
Solitron Devices, Inc. (N.Y.) reincorporated in Delaware 8/20/87

FILMSTAR INC (DE)
Charter cancelled and declared inoperative and void for non-payment of taxes 03/01/1993

FILMTEC CORP (DE)
Common 10¢ par split (3) for (2) by Issuance of (0.5) additional share 09/15/1983
Merged into Dow Chemical Co. 08/07/1985
Each share Common 10¢ par exchanged for $21.75 cash

FILMVEST INTL INC (NV)
Each share old Common $0.001 par exchanged for (0.01) share new Common $0.001 par 10/7/92
Recapitalized as Golden Interstate Medical Management Inc. 3/17/93
Each share new Common $0.001 par exchanged for (1/3) share Common $0.001 par
(See Golden Interstate Medical Management Inc.)

FILMWAYS INC (DE)
Reincorporated 01/16/1969
State of incorporation changed from (NY) to (DE) 01/16/1969
Stock Dividend - 10% 04/22/1976
Name changed from Filmways, Inc. to Orion Pictures Corp. 07/30/1982
Orion Pictures Corp. merged into Metromedia International Group, Inc. 11/01/1995
(See Metromedia International Group, Inc.)

FILMWORLD INC (NV)
Name changed to SulphCo, Inc. 04/11/2001
(See SulphCo, Inc.)

FILMWORLD INTL INC (NV)
Name changed to Karting International Inc. 10/29/2003
(See Karting International Inc.)

FILOIL REFINERY CORP. (PHILIPPINES)
Taken over by Philippine Government 00/00/1973
Details not available

FILON CORP. (CA)
Name changed to Nolif Corp. 3/10/66
Nolif Corp. liquidated for Standard Oil Co. (Ohio) 10/31/68
(See Standard Oil Co. (Ohio))

FILTAKLEEN INC (UT)
Recapitalized as IPTV Corp. 10/31/2006
Each share Common $0.001 par exchanged for (0.0125) share Common $0.001 par

FILTER DYNAMICS INTL INC (DE)
Under plan of merger name changed to FDI, Inc. 10/15/1974
FDI, Inc. recapitalized as Interlee, Inc. 12/18/1981
(See Interlee, Inc.)

FILTER FLOW CORP (NY)
Stock Dividend - 10% 5/26/72
Completely liquidated 2/9/73
Each share Common 1¢ par exchanged for first and final distribution of (0.24158) share LCA Corp. Common 50¢ par
LCA Corp. merged into Kidde (Walter) Co., Inc. (DE) 3/4/76 which name changed to Kidde, Inc. 4/18/80
(See Kidde, Inc.)

FILTERED SOULS ENTMT INC (NV)
Name changed to Skyline Entertainment, Inc. 03/31/1999
Skyline Entertainment, Inc. name changed to Quotemedia.com, Inc. 08/19/1999 which name changed to QuoteMedia, Inc. 03/11/2003

FILTERTEK DE PUERTO RICO, INC. (DE)
See - Filtertek Inc

FILTERTEK INC NEW (DE)
Name changed to Schawk, Inc. 01/05/1995
Schawk, Inc. merged into Matthews International Corp. 07/29/2014

FILTERTEK INC OLD (DE)
Units split (3) for (2) by issuance of (0.5) additional Unit 05/15/1986
Note: Par value of both issues making up a Unit was changed from 25¢ par to $0.16666666 par and $0.012 par to $0.008 par respectively
Paired certificates separated 06/01/1994
Each Non-Separable Unit consisting of (1) share Filtertek, Inc. (Old) Common $0.16666666 par and (1) share Filtertek de Puerto Rico, Inc. Class A Common $0.008 par exchanged for (1) share Filtertek, Inc. (New) Common $0.008 par
Filtertek, Inc. (New) name changed to Schawk, Inc. 01/05/1995 which merged into Matthews International Corp. 07/29/2014

FILTORS, INC. (NY)
Merged into General Battery & Ceramic Corp. (N.Y.) on a (2/3) for (1) basis 12/29/61
General Battery & Ceramic Corp. (N.Y.) name changed to General Battery Corp. 10/3/69
(See General Battery Corp.)

FILTRA-SONIC CORP. (CA)
Stock Dividend - 10% 5/30/62
Adjudicated bankrupt 8/22/63
No stockholders' equity

FILTROL CO. OF CALIFORNIA (CA)
Merged into Filtrol Corp. in 1953
Each share Common $1 par exchanged for (3) shares Common $1 par
(See Filtrol Corp.)

FILTROL CORP (DE)
Common $1 par split (2) for (1) by issuance of (1) additional share 4/14/67
Merged into Newco Merging Corp. 6/19/79
Each share Common $1 par exchanged for $19 cash

FILTRONA PLC (ENGLAND)
Name changed to Essentra PLC 08/27/2013

FIMA INC (NV)
Common $0.001 par changed to $0.00001 par 03/22/2013
Name changed to International Spirit & Beverage Group, Inc. 04/01/2015
International Spirit & Beverage Group, Inc. recapitalized as International Spirits & Beverage Group, Inc. 09/12/2017

FIMACO INC (PA)
Adjudicated bankrupt 05/31/1979
Stockholders' equity unlikely

FIN RES INC (ON)
Recapitalized as Continental Precious Minerals Inc. 00/00/1987
Each share Common no par exchanged for (0.5) share Common no par

FIN SPORTS U S A INC (NV)
Each (6.5) shares old Common $0.001 par exchanged for (1) share new Common $0.001 par 2/10/99
Each share new Common $0.001 par exchanged again for (1.5384741) shares new Common $0.001 par 12/8/99
Name changed to Lifef/x, Inc. 12/14/99
(See Lifef/x, Inc.)

FIN U S A INC (DE)
Recapitalized as I/Net, Inc. 10/08/1993
Each share Common $0.001 par exchanged for (0.02222222) share Common $0.001 par
I/Net, Inc. recapitalized as Ardmore Holding Corp. 06/11/2007 which name changed to Yayi International Inc. 09/25/2008
(See Yayi International Inc.)

FINA INC (DE)
Class A $1 par split (2) for (1) by issuance of (1) additional share 05/16/1995
Merged into PetroFina S.A. 08/05/1998
Each share Class A $1 par exchanged for (1) ADR Purchase Warrant expiring 08/05/2003 and $60 cash

FINAL TEST INC (TX)
Charter forfeited for failure to maintain a resident agent 08/06/1990

FINAL WORD, INC. (UT)
Name changed to Utah Petrochemical Corp. (UT) 2/9/84
Utah Petrochemical Corp. (UT) reincorporated in Delaware as Premier Technology, Inc. 1/28/85 which name changed to Premier Technology Holdings, Inc. 5/5/86
(See Premier Technology Holdings, Inc.)

FINALCO GROUP INC (DE)
Majority of shares acquired by VAFS 00/00/1988
Details not available

FINANCE & THRIFT CO (CA)
Under plan of reorganization each share Common no par automatically became (1) share F&T Financial Services, Inc. (NV) Common 1¢ par 01/00/2002
F&T Financial Services, Inc. merged into Pan American Bank (Los Angeles, CA) 07/31/2015
(See Pan American Bank (Los Angeles, CA))

FINANCE AMERICA CORP. OF MINNESOTA INC. (MN)
Name changed to Investment Guaranty Corp. 10/28/92
(See Investment Guaranty Corp.)

FINANCE CO AMER (DE)
Name changed 12/01/1961
Each share 7% Preferred $5 par exchanged for (1) share 5-1/2% Preferred $5 par 00/00/1936
Class A & B Common no par changed to $5 par 00/00/1936
5-1/2% Preferred called for redemption 06/07/1943
Each (20) shares Class A or B Common $5 par exchanged for (1) share Class A or B Common $100 par respectively 00/00/1946
Each share Class A or B Common $100 par exchanged for (10) shares Class A or B Common $10 par respectively 00/00/1954
Class A & B Common $10 par changed to $5 par and (1) additional share issued respectively 02/24/1961
Stock Dividend - (3) shares A for each (7) shares A or B 09/15/1948
Name changed from Finance Co. of America at Baltimore to Finance Co. of America 12/01/1961
Name changed to FCA Holding Corp. 12/29/1983
(See FCA Holding Corp.)

FINANCE CO PA (PA)
Completely liquidated 08/31/2017

Each share Capital Stock $10 par received $133.26 cash

FINANCE ONE US INC (WY)
Name changed to PBC Inc. 11/16/2005
(See PBC Inc.)

FINANCIAL ACCEP CORP (MI)
Completely liquidated 12/03/1976
Each share Common $1 par exchanged for first and final distribution of $1.40 cash

FINANCIAL ACCESS SOLUTIONS TECHNOLOGY INC (NV)
Name changed to ABV Gold, Inc. 01/22/2007
ABV Gold, Inc. recapitalized as PharmaCom BioVet Inc. 09/10/2008

FINANCIAL BANCORP INC NEW (NY)
Merged into Dime Community Bancorp, Inc. 1/21/99
Each share Common 1¢ par exchanged for either (1.8282) shares Common 1¢ par, (0.3682) shares Common 1¢ par and $31.26 cash or $39.14 cash
Option to receive stock or cash only expired 1/13/99
Note: Holders of (49) shares or fewer received either stock and cash or cash only to be determined by the company

FINANCIAL BANCSHARES INC (MO)
Merged into Union Planters Corp. 12/2/96
Each share Common 1¢ par exchanged for (1.7415) shares Common $5 par
Union Planters Corp. merged into Regions Financial Corp. (New) 7/1/2004

FINANCIAL BD SHS INC (CO)
Bond Shares Portfolio Capital Stock 1¢ par reclassified as Select Income Portfolio Capital Stock 1¢ par 03/01/1985
Under plan of reorganization each High Yield Portfolio 1¢ par, Select Income Portfolio 1¢ par and U.S. Government Portfolio automatically became (1) INVESCO Income Funds, Inc. (MD) High Yield Fund 1¢ par, Select Income Fund 1¢ par or U.S. Government Securities Fund 1¢ par respectively 07/01/1993
(See INVESCO Income Funds, Inc.)

FINANCIAL BENEFIT GROUP INC (DE)
Stock Dividend - In Class A Common to holders of Class B Common 100% 6/12/86
Each share Class B Common 1¢ par converted into (1.35) shares Class A Common 1¢ par 4/8/96
Merged into AmVestors Financial Corp. 4/8/96
Each share Class A Common 1¢ par exchanged for (0.3822) share new Common no par, (0.0932) Common Stock Purchase Warrant expiring 4/2/2002 and $0.35 cash
AmVestors Financial Corp. merged into AmerUs Life Holdings, Inc. 12/19/97 which name changed to Amerus Group Co. 9/20/2000
(See Amerus Group Co.)

FINANCIAL BUSINESS COMPUTERS INC (NV)
Name changed to Prudential Resources Inc. 5/18/88
Prudential Resource Inc. name changed back to Acme International Corp. 8/13/91 which name changed to Beckett Industries Inc. 10/5/94 which name changed to International Supercell Ltd. 5/11/95 which name changed to Bargaincity.com, Inc. 3/25/99
(See Bargaincity.com, Inc.)

FINANCIAL CAP CORP (NJ)
Ceased operations 11/15/1976

No stockholders' equity

FINANCIAL COLLECTION AGYS LTD (CANADA)
Common no par split (3) for (1) by issuance of (2) additional shares 05/02/1969
Common no par split (2) for (1) by issuance of (1) additional share 07/11/1972
Stock Dividend - 10% 09/30/1971
Name changed to FCA International Ltd.- FCA Internationale Ltee. 10/17/1977
(See FCA International Ltd.- FCA Internationale Ltee.)

FINANCIAL COMM NETWORK INC (NV)
Each share old Common $0.001 par exchanged for (0.1) share new Common $0.001 par 09/13/2001
Name changed to Regions Oil & Gas Inc. 01/23/2007
Regions Oil & Gas Inc. recapitalized as American Green Group, Inc. 02/27/2008
(See American Green Group, Inc.)

FINANCIAL CONCEPTS BANCORP INC (WI)
Acquired by Norwest Corp. 04/01/1993
Details not available

FINANCIAL CONCEPTS INC (FL)
Proclaimed dissolved for failure to file reports and pay fees 11/10/1983

FINANCIAL CONGENERIC CORP (NV)
Charter revoked for failure to file reports and pay fees 03/07/1977

FINANCIAL CORP.
Liquidated 00/00/1933
Details not available

FINANCIAL CORP. (NC)
Name changed to Bancshares of North Carolina, Inc. 3/10/71
Bancshares of North Carolina, Inc. merged into NCNB Corp. 12/23/82 which name changed to NationsBank Corp. 12/3/91 which reincorporated in Delaware as BankAmerica Corp. (Old) 9/25/98 which merged into BankAmerica Corp. (New) 9/30/98 which name changed to Bank of America Corp. 4/28/99

FINANCIAL CORP. OF AMERICA (CA)
Stock Dividend - 20% 01/02/1964
Merged into General America Corp. 07/31/1964
Each share Common $1 par exchanged for (1) share 4-1/2% Conv. Preferred $20 par
General America Corp. name changed to Safeco Corp. 04/30/1968
(See Safeco Corp.)

FINANCIAL CORP. OF ARIZONA (AZ)
Capital Stock $5 par changed to no par 7/29/69
Recapitalized under the laws of Delaware and Capital Stock no par changed to 50¢ par 6/1/70
Financial Corp. of Arizona (Del.) name changed to FCA Industries, Inc. 4/24/75
(See FCA Industries, Inc.)

FINANCIAL CORP. OF ARIZONA (DE)
Name changed to FCA Industries, Inc. 4/24/75
(See FCA Industries, Inc.)

FINANCIAL CORP AMER (DE)
Common 50¢ par split (3) for (2) by issuance of (0.5) additional share 12/1/78
Common 50¢ par split (3) for (2) by issuance of (0.5) additional share 9/19/80
Common 50¢ par split (3) for (2) by issuance of (0.5) additional share 12/31/81

Common 50¢ par split (3) for (2) by issuance of (0.5) additional share 12/10/82
Common 50¢ par split (3) for (2) by issuance of (0.5) additional share 10/27/83
Chapter 11 Federal Bankruptcy Code converted to Chapter 7 on 3/3/89
No stockholders' equity

FINANCIAL CORP SANTA BARBARA (DE)
Capital Stock $1 par split (2) for (1) by issuance of (1) additional share 08/15/1978
Capital Stock $1 par reclassified as Common $1 par 04/30/1980
Common $1 par changed to 1¢ par 12/21/1989
Stock Dividend - 10% 04/23/1981
Plan of reorganization under Chapter 11 Federal Bankruptcy proceedings confirmed 03/31/1995
Stockholders' equity unlikely

FINANCIAL CREDIT CORP. (DE)
Charter cancelled and declared inoperative and void for non-payment of taxes 4/15/72

FINANCIAL CREDIT CORP. (VA)
Each share Common $1 par exchanged for (50) shares Common 1¢ par 10/30/51
Merged into Financial Credit Corp. (DE) in 1959
Each share 5% Preferred $20 par exchanged for (1) share 5% Preferred $20 par
Each share 6% Preferred $50 par exchanged for (1) share 6% Preferred $50 par
Each share Common 1¢ par exchanged for (2) shares Common 1¢ par
(See Financial Credit Corp. (DE))

FINANCIAL CTR BANCORP (CA)
Stock Dividends - 10% 1/18/89; 10% 8/16/89
Out of business in 1992
Details not available

FINANCIAL CTRS AMER INC (DE)
Charter cancelled and declared inoperative and void for non-payment of taxes 03/01/1988

FINANCIAL DAILY DIVID SHS INC (CO)
Merged into Financial Daily Income Shares, Inc. (CO) 11/20/1980
Each share Common 1¢ par exchanged for (1.018959) shares Capital Stock 1¢ par
Financial Daily Income Shares, Inc. (CO) reorganized in (MD) as Invesco Money Market Funds, Inc. 07/01/1993
(See Invesco Money Market Funds, Inc.)

FINANCIAL DAILY INCOME SHS INC (CO)
Reorganized under the laws of Maryland as Invesco Money Market Funds, Inc. and Common 1¢ par reclassified as Cash Reserves Fund 1¢ par 07/01/1993
(See Invesco Money Market Funds, Inc.)

FINANCIAL DATA CORP. (DE)
Merged into Indiana Industries Inc. 12/22/65
Each share Common 10¢ par exchanged for (0.1) share Common $1 par
Indiana Industries Inc. name changed to Bankshares of Indiana, Inc. 5/4/72 which name changed to Money Management Corp. 12/31/75 which merged into Banc One Corp. (DE) 7/1/86 which reincorporated in Ohio 5/1/89 which merged into Bank One Corp. 10/2/98 which merged into J.P. Morgan Chase & Co. 12/31/2000 which name changed to JPMorgan Chase & Co. 7/20/2004

FINANCIAL DATA SYS INC (DE)
Name changed to Individual Investors Group, Inc. 6/1/93
Individual Investors Group, Inc. name changed to Index Development Partners, Inc. 6/18/2002 which name changed to WisdomTree Investments, Inc. 9/22/2005

FINANCIAL DYNAMICS FD INC (CO)
Reincorporated under the laws of Maryland as INVESCO Dynamics Fund, Inc. 07/01/1993
INVESCO Dynamics Fund, Inc. name changed to INVESCO Capital Appreciation Funds, Inc. 07/03/1997
(See INVESCO Capital Appreciation Funds, Inc.)

FINANCIAL EMERGING GROWTH FD INC (MD)
Name changed to INVESCO Emerging Growth Fund, Inc. 07/01/1993
INVESCO Emerging Growth Fund, Inc. name changed to INVESCO Emerging Opportunity Funds, Inc. 12/02/1994
(See INVESCO Emerging Opportunity Funds, Inc.)

FINANCIAL ENGINES INC (DE)
Acquired by Edelman Financial, L.P. 07/19/2018
Each share Common $0.0001 par exchanged for $45 cash

FINANCIAL FD INC (WA)
Common 10¢ par changed to 5¢ par and (1) additional share issued 03/06/1970
In process of liquidation
Each share Common 5¢ par received an initial distribution of $2.50 cash 07/00/1976
Note: Details on additional distributions, if any, are not available

FINANCIAL FED CORP (NV)
Common 50¢ par split (3) for (2) by issuance of (0.5) additional share payable 01/30/1996 to holders of record 01/08/1996
Common 50¢ par split (3) for (2) by issuance of (0.5) additional share payable 07/30/1997 to holders of record 07/18/1997 Ex date - 07/31/1997
Common 50¢ par split (3) for (2) by issuance of (0.5) additional share payable 01/31/2006 to holders of record 01/05/2006 Ex date - 02/01/2006
Merged into People's United Financial, Inc. 02/19/2010
Each share Common 50¢ par exchanged for (1) share Common 1¢ par and $11.27 cash

FINANCIAL FED SVGS BK (HARTFORD, CT)
Placed in receivership 08/17/1990
No stockholders' equity

FINANCIAL FEDN INC (DE)
Capital Stock $1 par split (5) for (4) by issuance of (0.25) additional share 03/01/1962
Capital Stock $1 par split (5) for (4) by issuance of (0.25) additional share 04/01/1963
Merged into Great Western Financial Corp. 07/18/1983
Each share Capital Stock $1 par exchanged for (1.8) shares Capital Stock $1 par
Great Western Financial Corp. merged into Washington Mutual Inc. 07/01/1997
(See Washington Mutual, Inc.)

FINANCIAL 15 SPLIT CORP II (ON)
Name changed to North American Financial 15 Split Corp. 03/18/2015

FINANCIAL FIRE & CAS CO (FL)
Proclaimed dissolved for failure to file reports and pay fees 09/03/1976

FINANCIAL FREEDOM ENTERPRISES INC (CO)
Name changed to Cambridge Universal Corp. (CO) 07/15/1997
Cambridge Universal Corp. (CO) reorganized in Florida as Whitehall Limited, Inc. 06/23/1999
(See Whitehall Limited, Inc.)

FINANCIAL GEN BANKSHARES INC (VA)
Merged into FGB Holding Corp. 8/11/82
Each share Common 10¢ par exchanged for $33.80 cash
Each share Class A Common Ser. 1, 10¢ par exchanged for $28 cash
Name changed to First American Bankshares, Inc. 8/12/82
(See First American Bankshares, Inc.)

FINANCIAL GEN CORP (VA)
Name changed to Financial General Bankshares, Inc. 4/29/70
Financial General Bankshares, Inc. name changed to First American Bankshares, Inc. 8/12/82
(See First American Bankshares, Inc.)

FINANCIAL GROUP AMER (NV)
Capital Stock no par split (30) for (1) by issuance of (29) additional shares 05/01/1977
Merged into Financial Group of America, Inc. 08/05/1980
Each share Capital Stock no par exchanged for (1/60) share Common no par

FINANCIAL GROUP PORTFOLIOS INC (MD)
Name changed to Financial Strategic Portfolios, Inc. 02/11/1985
Financial Strategic Portfolios, Inc. name changed to INVESCO Strategic Portfolios Inc. 12/01/1994 which name changed to INVESCO Sector Funds, Inc. 10/29/1998
(See INVESCO Sector Funds, Inc.)

FINANCIAL INC (IN)
Common no par split (3) for (2) by issuance of (0.5) additional share 8/31/79
Stock Dividends - 50% 5/15/72; 10% 7/15/77
Under plan of merger name changed to Summit Bancorp 12/31/83
Summit Bancorp merged into SummCorp 4/24/84 which merged into NBD Bancorp, Inc. 7/1/92 which name changed to First Chicago NBD Corp. 12/1/95 which merged into Bank One Corp. 10/2/98 which merged into J.P. Morgan Chase & Co. 12/31/2000 which name changed to JPMorgan Chase & Co. 7/20/2004

FINANCIAL INDL FD INC (MD)
Name changed to Invesco Growth Fund Inc. 12/02/1994
(See Invesco Growth Fund Inc.)

FINANCIAL INDL INCOME FD INC (MD)
Stock Dividends - 100% 04/16/1962; 100% 05/16/1966
Name changed to INVESCO Industrial Income Fund, Inc. 12/02/1994
(See INVESCO Industrial Income Fund, Inc.)

FINANCIAL INDS CORP (TX)
Reincorporated 12/31/1980
State of incorporation changed from (OH) to (TX) 12/31/1980
Common $1 par changed to 20¢ par and (4) additional shares issued payable 11/19/1996 to holders of record 11/12/1996
Merged into Americo Life, Inc. 07/17/2008
Each share Common 20¢ par exchanged for $7.25 cash

FINANCIAL INSTN SVCS INC (TN)
Merged into Comp-U-Card International Inc. 12/9/85
Each share Common 10¢ par exchanged for (0.58) share Common 1¢ par
Comp-U-Card International Inc. name changed to CUC International Inc. 6/18/87 which name changed to Cendant Corp. 12/17/97 which reorganized as Avis Budget Group, Inc. 9/1/2006

FINANCIAL INSTNS INS GROUP LTD (DE)
Common $1 par split (2) for (1) by issuance of (1) additional share 2/24/94
Common $1 par split (6) for (5) by issuance of (0.2) additional share 8/24/95
Stock Dividend - 20% payable 2/22/96 to holders of record 1/25/96
Merged into Castle Harlan Partners II, L.P. 9/6/96
Each share Common $1 par exchanged for $16 cash

FINANCIAL INTL CORP (DE)
Each share Common 10¢ par exchanged for (0.1) share Common $1 par 09/01/1971
Liquidation completed
Each (10) shares Common $1 par exchanged for initial distribution of (8.17) shares Financial General Bankshares, Inc. Common 10¢ par and (1) share Financial Mortgage & Realty Corp. Common 10¢ par 01/23/1978
(See each company's listing)
Each share Common $1 par received second and final distribution of $0.54 cash 12/31/1979

FINANCIAL INTRANET INC (NV)
Each share old Common $0.001 par exchanged for (0.02857142) share new Common $0.001 par 04/02/2001
Name changed to Technest Holdings, Inc. (NV) 07/12/2001
Technest Holdings, Inc. (NV) reincorporated in Delaware as AccelPath, Inc. 05/09/2012

FINANCIAL INVS OF THE SOUTH INC (DE)
Common $1 par split (2) for (1) by issuance of (1) additional share payable 06/26/2000 to holders of record 06/26/2000 Ex date - 06/27/2000
Name changed to CapitalSouth Bancorp 09/28/2005
(See CapitalSouth Bancorp)

FINANCIAL LD CORP (OH)
Merged into Newco-FLC, Inc. 8/11/93
Each share Common no par exchanged for $0.55 cash

FINANCIAL LEISURE INC (NJ)
Name changed to Alliance Communications Group, Inc. 10/9/84
(See Alliance Communications Group, Inc.)

FINANCIAL LIFE INS CO (FL)
Completely liquidated 12/30/1975
Each share Common $1 par exchanged for first and final distribution of $3.14 cash

FINANCIAL MGMT BANCSHARES W VA INC (WV)
Acquired by One Valley Bancorp of West Virginia, Inc. 07/31/1986
Each share Common $5 par exchanged for (1.35) shares Common $10 par
One Valley Bancorp of West Virginia, Inc. name changed to One Valley Bancorp, Inc. 04/30/1996 which merged into BB&T Corp. 07/06/2000

FINANCIAL MEDIA GROUP INC (NV)
Name changed to Clicker Inc. 07/08/2009
(See Clicker Inc.)

FINANCIAL MODELS CO INC (ON)
Merged into SS&C Technologies, Inc. 04/19/2005
Each share Common no par exchanged for $17.70 cash

FINANCIAL MTG & RLTY CORP (DE)
Merged into United Financial Corp. of Virginia 5/31/79
Each share Common 10¢ par exchanged for (1) share Common 10¢ par
United Financial Corp. of Virginia merged into International Bank (Washington, DC) 6/30/81 which merged into USLICO Corp. 12/31/85 which merged into NWNL Companies, Inc. 1/17/95 which name changed to ReliaStar Financial Corp. 2/13/95
(See ReliaStar Financial Corp.)

FINANCIAL NATL BANCSHARES CO (DE)
Common $2.50 par changed to no par and (1) additional share issued 10/21/85
Name changed to FNW Bancorp, Inc. 12/9/86
FNW Bancorp, Inc. merged into NBD Bancorp, Inc. 10/1/91 which name changed to First Chicago NBD Corp. 12/1/95 which merged into Bank One Corp. 10/2/98 which merged into J.P. Morgan Chase & Co. 12/31/2000 which name changed to JPMorgan Chase & Co. 7/20/2004

FINANCIAL NEWS COMPOSITE FD INC (MD)
Name changed to Bull & Bear Financial News Composite Fund, Inc. 09/18/1989
(See Bull & Bear Financial News Composite Fund, Inc.)

FINANCIAL NEWS NETWORK INC (CA)
Reorganized as Data Broadcasting Corp. 06/26/1992
Each share Common no par exchanged for (0.66136188) share Common 1¢ par
Data Broadcasting Corp. name changed to Interactive Data Corp. 06/20/2001
(See Interactive Data Corp.)

FINANCIAL PERFORMANCE CORP (NY)
Each share Common 5¢ par exchanged for (0.2) share Common 1¢ par 09/23/1996
Reincorporated under the laws of Delaware as BrandPartners Group, Inc. 08/20/2001
(See BrandPartners Group, Inc.)

FINANCIAL PFD SECS CORP (AB)
Preferred Shares no par called for redemption at $13.72 on 06/13/2012

FINANCIAL PROGRAMS CORP. OF AMERICA (NY)
Charter cancelled and proclaimed dissolved for failure to pay taxes 12/15/69

FINANCIAL RES CORP (AZ)
In process of liquidation
Each share Common no par received initial distribution of $0.90 cash 6/25/82
Each share Common no par received second distribution of $0.15 cash 4/25/83
Note: Details on subsequent distributions, if any, are not available

FINANCIAL RES GROUP (NJ)
Merged into Financial Resources Group Inc. 11/18/96
Each share Common 10¢ par exchanged for $22.50 cash

FINANCIAL RESV INC (OK)
Each share Common 50¢ par exchanged for (10) shares Common 5¢ par 04/12/1968
Dissolved by Court Order 03/27/1975
Stockholders' equity unlikely

FINANCIAL SEC ASSURN HLDGS LTD (NY)
Issue Information - 7,500,000 shares COM offered at $20 per share on 05/06/1994
Acquired by Dexia S.A. 7/5/2000
Each share Common 1¢ par exchanged for $76 cash

FINANCIAL SEC CORP (DE)
Ctfs. dtd. after 12/29/92
Merged into Pinnacle Banc Group, Inc. 9/30/96
Each share Common 1¢ par exchanged for (0.9051) share Common $4.69 par
Pinnacle Banc Group, Inc. merged into Old Kent Financial Corp. 9/3/99 which merged into Fifth Third Bancorp 4/2/2001

FINANCIAL SEC CORP (DE)
Ctfs. dtd. prior to 6/20/69
Merged into International Bank (Washington, DC) 6/20/69
Each share Common 10¢ par exchanged for (1) share Class A Common $1 par
International Bank (Washington, DC) merged into USLICO Corp. 12/31/85 which merged into NWNL Companies, Inc. 1/17/95 which name changed to ReliaStar Financial Corp. 2/13/95
(See ReliaStar Financial Corp.)

FINANCIAL SEC CORP KANS INC (KS)
Name changed to Western Fidelity Corp. (KS) 04/26/1976
(See Western Fidelity Corp. (KS))

FINANCIAL SEC GROUP INC (DE)
Merged into International Bank (Washington, DC) 12/31/79
Each share Common 10¢ par exchanged for (1.8) shares Class A Common $1 par
International Bank (Washington, DC) merged into USLICO Corp. 12/31/85 which merged into NWNL Companies, Inc. 1/17/95 which name changed to ReliaStar Financial Corp. 2/13/95
(See ReliaStar Financial Corp.)

FINANCIAL SEC INS CO (HI)
Name changed 07/26/1979
Name changed from Financial Security Life Insurance Co. to Financial Security Insurance Co., Ltd. 07/26/1979
Placed in receivership 09/21/1984
No stockholders' equity

FINANCIAL SEC PLANNING CORP AMER (FL)
Name changed to Finsec Corp. 4/4/69
Finsec Corp. name changed to Zenith Funding Corp. 8/1/69 which name changed to Zenith American Corp. 5/30/73
(See Zenith American Corp.)

FINANCIAL SEC SVGS & LN ASSN (FL)
Class A Common $5 par changed to $2.50 par and (1) additional share issued 12/21/1984
Placed in receivership by FSLIC 10/06/1988
No stockholders' equity

FINANCIAL SECURITY CORP. (KY)
Common $1 par changed to 50¢ par and (1) additional share issued 05/07/1965
Merged into American Family Security Group, Inc. 02/15/1967
Details not available

FINANCIAL SECURITY FUND, INC. (MD)
Name changed to Financial Industrial Fund, Inc. 00/00/1941

FINANCIAL INFORMATION, INC.

Financial Industrial Fund, Inc. name changed to Invesco Growth Fund Inc. 12/02/1994
(See Invesco Growth Fund Inc.)

FINANCIAL SECURITY LIFE INSURANCE CO. (IL)
Acquired by Regency National, Ltd. 06/15/1972
Each share Capital Stock 12-1/2¢ par exchanged for (0.275) share Class A Common $1 par
Regency National, Ltd. recapitalized as Regency Financial Group, Inc. 08/23/1978
(See Regency Financial Group, Inc.)

FINANCIAL SER TR (MA)
International Growth Fund no par reorganized as INVESCO International Funds, Inc. 07/01/1993
Details not available
U.S. Government Money Fund no par reorganized as INVESCO Money Market Funds, Inc. 07/01/1993
Details not available
Name changed to INVESCO Value Trust and Equity Fund no par and Flex Fund no par reclassified as Value Equity Fund no par and Total Return Fund no par respectively 07/01/1993
(See INVESCO Value Trust)

FINANCIAL SVC CORP (GA)
Merged into Sunamerica Inc. 10/1/97
Each share Common exchanged for $48.875 cash
Note: An additional distribution of approximately $9.63 cash per share was made in 1999

FINANCIAL SVCS ACQUISITION CORP (DE)
Name changed to Maxcor Financial Group Inc. 6/18/97
(See Maxcor Financial Group Inc.)

FINANCIAL SVCS CORP MIDWEST (DE)
Merged into Mercantile Bancorporation, Inc. 08/03/1998
Each share Common $1 par exchanged for (6.8573) shares Common 1¢ par
Mercantile Bancorporation, Inc. merged into Firstar Corp. (New) 09/20/1999 which merged into U.S. Bancorp (DE) 02/27/2001

FINANCIAL SVCS INCOME STREAMS CORP (ON)
Capital Yield Shares called for redemption at $25 on 02/01/2011
Equity Dividend Shares called for redemption at $9.7723 on 02/01/2011

FINANCIAL SOUTH CORP (DE)
Assets sold for benefit of creditors 00/00/1971
No stockholders' equity

FINANCIAL STRATEGIC PORTFOLIOS INC (MD)
Under plan of reorganization each European Portfolio 1¢ par and Pacific Portfolio 1¢ par automatically became (1) INVESCO International Funds, Inc. European Fund 1¢ par or Pacific Basin Fund 1¢ par respectively 07/01/1993
(See INVESCO International Funds, Inc.)
Name changed to INVESCO Strategic Portfolios Inc. 12/01/1994
INVESCO Strategic Portfolios Inc. name changed to INVESCO Sector Funds, Inc. 10/29/1998
(See INVESCO Sector Funds, Inc.)

FINANCIAL SYS GROUP INC (DE)
SEC revoked common stock registration 10/12/2005

FINANCIAL SYS TECHNOLOGY PLC (ENGLAND)
ADR agreement terminated 00/00/1987
No ADR holders' equity

FINANCIAL TAX FREE INCOME SHS INC (CO)
Under plan of reorganization each share Common 1¢ par automatically became (1) INVESCO Tax-Free Income Funds, Inc. (MD) Long Term Bond Fund 1¢ par 07/01/1993
(See INVESCO Tax-Free Income Funds, Inc.)

FINANCIAL TAX FREE MONEY FD INC (CO)
Reorganized under the laws of Maryland as Invesco Money Market Funds, Inc. and Common 1¢ par reclassified as Tax-Free Money Fund 1¢ par 07/01/1993
(See Invesco Money Market Funds, Inc.)

FINANCIAL TECHNOLOGIES INDIA LTD (INDIA)
GDR agreement terminated 03/24/2014
Each 144A GDR for Equity Shares exchanged for (0.14285714) Equity Share
Each Reg. S GDR for Equity Shares exchanged for (0.14285714) Equity Share

FINANCIAL TECHNOLOGY INC (TX)
Name changed to Texon Energy Corp. 05/14/1974
(See Texon Energy Corp.)

FINANCIAL TELECOM LTD USA INC (NV)
Recapitalized as MKA Capital, Inc. 01/26/2006
Each share Common $0.001 par exchanged for (0.04) share Common $0.001 par
MKA Capital, Inc. name changed to Sancon Resources Recovery, Inc. 08/04/2006 which recapitalized as IGS Capital Group Ltd. 06/09/2017

FINANCIAL TRENDS FD INC (MD)
Name changed to Diamond Hill Financial Trends Fund, Inc. 01/15/2008
(See Diamond Hill Financial Trends Fund, Inc.)

FINANCIAL TRENDS MUTUAL FUND, INC. (CA)
Charter suspended for failure to file reports or pay taxes 08/02/1971

FINANCIAL TR CORP (PA)
Name changed 5/16/85
Name changed from Financial Trans Corp. to Financial Trust Corp. 5/16/85
Common $5 par split (2) for (1) by issuance of (1) additional share 6/28/85
Common $5 par split (3) for (2) by issuance of (0.5) additional share 10/17/88
Common $5 par split (3) for (2) by issuance of (0.5) additional share 6/1/92
Common $5 par split (4) for (3) by issuance of (1/3) additional share 8/29/94
Stock Dividends - 10% 8/30/93; 10% payable 6/17/96 to holders of record 6/3/96
Merged into Keystone Financial, Inc. 5/30/97
Each share Common $5 par exchanged for (1.65) shares Common $2 par
Keystone Financial, Inc. merged into M&T Bank Corp. 10/6/2000

FINANCIAL TRUSTCO CAP LTD (AB)
Each share old Common no par exchanged for (1/3) share new Common no par 07/26/1983
Name changed to FT Capital Ltd. 07/25/1989
(See FT Capital Ltd.)

FINANCIAL VENTURE FD INC (CO)
Merged into Financial Dynamics Fund, Inc. (CO) 07/18/1975

Each share Common $1 par exchanged for (1.04551) shares Capital Stock 1¢ par
Financial Dynamics Fund, Inc. (CO) reincorporated in Maryland as Invesco Dynamics Fund, Inc. 07/01/1993 which name changed to INVESCO Capital Appreciation Funds, Inc. 07/03/1997
(See INVESCO Capital Appreciation Funds, Inc.)

FINANCIALCONTENT INC (DE)
SEC revoked common stock registration 02/13/2013

FINANCIALWEB COM INC (NV)
SEC revoked common stock registration 04/23/2007

FINANCING FOR SCIENCE INTL INC (DE)
Merged into FINOVA Group Inc. 08/29/1996
Each share Common 1¢ par exchanged for $6.40 cash

FINANSBANK A S (TURKEY)
Old 144A Sponsored GDR's for Ordinary split (2.3) for (1) by issuance of (1.3) additional GDR's payable 04/21/1999 to holders of record 04/16/1999
Old Reg. S Sponsored GDR's for Ordinary split (2.3) for (1) by issuance of (1.3) additional GDR's payable 04/21/1999 to holders of record 04/16/1999
Each old 144A Sponsored GDR for Ordinary exchanged for (0.1) new 144A Sponsored GDR for Ordinary 08/09/2001
Each old Reg. S Sponsored GDR for Ordinary exchanged for (0.1) new Reg. S Sponsored GDR for Ordinary 08/09/2001
Basis changed from (1:5) to (1:50) 08/09/2001
Basis changed from (1:50) to (1:0.2) 01/03/2005
Stock Dividends - 90% payable 06/12/2000 to holders of record 05/26/2000; In 144A GDR's to holders of 144A GDR's 61.6% payable 06/08/2001 to holders of record 05/30/2001; In Reg. S GDR's to holders of Reg. S GDR's 61.6% payable 06/08/2001 to holders of record 05/30/2001; 29.0564% payable 11/21/2002 to holders of record 11/06/2002; In 144A GDR's to holders of 144A GDR's 19.8086% payable 01/05/2004 to holders of record 12/23/2003; In Reg. S GDR's to holders of Reg. S GDR's 19.8086% payable 01/05/2004 to holders of record 12/23/2003; 38.7517% payable 10/06/2004 to holders of record 09/24/2004; 61.02% payable 10/18/2005 to holders of record 10/11/2005; In Reg. S GDR's to holders of Reg. S GDR's 31.58% payable 08/03/2006 to holders of record 07/26/2006; 5% payable 07/17/2007 to holders of record 07/06/2007; 7% payable 09/06/2007 to holders of record 07/06/2007; 7.14285% payable 10/28/2008 to holders of record 10/21/2008
GDR agreement terminated 09/26/2016
No GDR's remain outstanding

FINANTRA CAP INC (DE)
Assets foreclosed upon 05/11/2001
Stockholders' equity unlikely

FINAVERA RENEWABLES INC (BC)
Recapitalized as Finavera Wind Energy Inc. 02/08/2011
Each share Common no par exchanged for (0.1) share Common no par
Finavera Wind Energy Inc. name changed to Finavera Solar Energy Inc. 07/03/2015 which name

changed to Solar Alliance Energy Inc. 02/01/2016

FINAVERA SOLAR ENERGY INC (BC)
Name changed to Solar Alliance Energy Inc. 02/01/2016

FINAVERA WIND ENERGY INC (BC)
Name changed to Finavera Solar Energy Inc. 07/03/2015
Finavera Solar Energy Inc. name changed to Solar Alliance Energy Inc. 02/01/2016

FINCA CONSULTING INC (CO)
Administratively dissolved 8/1/99

FINCH PRUYN & CO INC (NY)
6% Preferred $100 par called for redemption at $100 on 09/30/2007
In process of liquidation
Each share Class A Common $1 par received initial distribution of $800 cash payable 11/16/2007 to holders of record 08/02/2007
Each share Class B Common $1 par received initial distribution of $800 cash payable 11/16/2007 to holders of record 08/02/2007
Each share Class A Common $1 par received second distribution of $300 cash payable 03/31/2008 to holders of record 03/15/2008 Ex date - 05/15/2008
Each share Class B Common $1 par received second distribution of $300 cash payable 03/31/2008 to holders of record 03/15/2008 Ex date - 05/14/2008
Each share Class A Common $1 par received third distribution of $500 cash payable 11/20/2008 to holders of record 10/21/2008 Ex date - 12/03/2008
Each share Class B Common $1 par received third distribution of $500 cash payable 11/20/2008 to holders of record 10/21/2008 Ex date - 12/03/2008
Each share Class A Common $1 par received fourth distribution of $300 cash payable 03/27/2009 to holders of record 03/02/2009 Ex date - 03/27/2009
Each share Class B Common $1 par received fourth distribution of $300 cash payable 03/27/2009 to holders of record 03/02/2009 Ex date - 03/27/2009
Each share Class A Common $1 par received fifth distribution of $100 cash payable 12/21/2009 to holders of record 12/14/2009 Ex date - 12/31/2009
Each share Class B Common $1 par received fifth distribution of $100 cash payable 12/21/2009 to holders of record 12/14/2009 Ex date - 12/31/2009
Each share Class B Common $1 par received sixth distribution of $100 cash payable 12/15/2011 to holders of record 12/01/2011
Note: Details on additional distributions, if any, are not available
Voluntarily dissolved 01/10/2013

FINCH TELECOMMUNICATIONS, INC.
Name changed to Facsimile & Electronics Corp. in 1950
(See Facsimile & Electronics Corp.)

FINCORP CAP LTD (ON)
Wound up 05/01/1998
No stockholders' equity

FIND ENERGY LTD (AB)
Acquired by Shiningbank Energy Income Fund 09/22/2006
Each share Common no par exchanged for (0.465) Trust Unit
Note: U.S. holders received $8.29 cash from the sale of units 11/03/2006
Shiningbank Energy Income Fund merged into PrimeWest Energy Trust 07/13/2007

(See PrimeWest Energy Trust)

FIND SVP INC (NY)
Each share old Common $0.0001 par exchanged for (0.05) share new Common $0.0001 par 01/04/1989
Name changed to Guideline, Inc. 03/15/2006
(See Guideline, Inc.)

FIND THE WORLD INTERACTIVE INC (DE)
Name changed to China Interactive Education, Inc. 02/05/2010

FINDENT ENGR SEC LTD (CANADA)
Merged into Fox River Group, Inc. 07/13/2004
Each share Common no par exchanged for (5.541837) shares Common $0.0001 par
Fox River Group, Inc. recapitalized as Global Uranium Power, Corp. 03/25/2005
(See Global Uranium Power, Corp.)

FINDERS KEEPERS INC (NV)
Common $0.001 par split (2) for (1) by issuance of (1) additional share payable 04/19/2000 to holders of record 04/14/2000
Common $0.001 par split (7) for (1) by issuance of (6) additional shares payable 08/09/2000 to holders of record 08/07/2000 Ex date - 08/10/2000
Recapitalized as Bauer Partnership, Inc. 09/27/2001
Each (150) shares Common $0.001 par exchanged for (1) share Common $0.001 par
Bauer Partnership, Inc. name changed to Harbour Front Holdings, Inc. 01/27/2003 which recapitalized as American Eagle Manufacturing Co. 10/20/2003 which name changed to No Borders, Inc. 10/27/2004

FINDLAY WALLY GALLERIES INTL INC (DE)
Each share old Common 10¢ par exchanged for (0.00001169) share new Common 10¢ par 2/12/96
Note: In effect holders received $20 cash per share and public interest was eliminated

FINDORE GOLD RES LTD (ON)
Name changed to Ripped Canada Artists Inc. 11/03/2000
Ripped Canada Artists Inc. recapitalized as Condor Gold Corp. 10/03/2002
(See Condor Gold Corp.)

FINDORE MINERALS INC (ON)
Name changed to Cantex Energy Inc. 01/09/1998
Cantex Energy Inc. name changed to Outlook Resources Inc. 06/21/2001
(See Outlook Resources Inc.)

FINDWHAT COM (DE)
Reincorporated 09/03/2004
State of incorporation changed from (NV) to (DE) 09/03/2004
Name changed to MIVA, Inc. 06/13/2005
MIVA, Inc. name changed to Vertro, Inc. 06/09/2009 which merged into Inuvo, Inc. 03/01/2012

FINE AIR SVCS CORP (DE)
Plan of reorganization under Chapter 11 Federal Bankruptcy Code effective 5/8/2002
No stockholders' equity

FINE ART ACQUISITIONS LTD (NY)
Name changed to Dyansen Corp. 8/4/87
(See Dyansen Corp.)

FINE ART CORP AMER INC (DE)
Name changed to Petro-Art Ltd., Inc. 6/22/81
Petro-Art Ltd., Inc. name changed to Class, Inc. 6/7/93 which recapitalized as Avery Communications, Inc. 12/12/94
(See Avery Communications, Inc.)

FINE ARTS ACCEP CORP (PA)
Name changed to Commonwealth Financial Corp. 1/1/60
(See Commonwealth Financial Corp.)

FINE ARTS PICTURES, INC.
Liquidated in 1927
Details not available

FINE COM INTL CORP (WA)
Name changed 04/02/1998
Name changed from Fine.com Corp. to Fine.com International Corp. 04/02/1998
Merged into Aris Corp. 09/01/1999
Each share Common no par exchanged for (0.546) share Common no par and $1.115 cash
Aris Corp. merged into Ciber, Inc. 09/19/2001 which name changed to CMTSU Liquidation, Inc. 12/22/2017

FINE HOMES INTL L P (DE)
Merged into Merrill Lynch Mortgage Co. 10/31/89
Each Depositary Unit exchanged for $15.75 cash

FINE HOST CORP NEW (DE)
Ceased operations 00/00/2002
Details not available

FINE HOST CORP OLD (DE)
Plan of reoganization under Chapter 11 Federal Bankruptcy Code effective 05/27/1999
Each share Common 1¢ par exchanged for an undetermined amount of Common Stock Purchase Warrants expiring 05/27/2001

FINE ORGANICS INC (NY)
Merged into Hexcel Corp. (CA) 05/14/1973
Each share Common $1 par exchanged for $4.20 cash

FINE PRODS INC (GA)
Stock Dividends - 100% 04/15/1968; 100% 09/01/1969
Acquired by Coastal Management Corp. 03/31/1986
Each share Common $1 par exchanged for $2.25 cash

FINE PRODUCTS CORP. (GA)
Liquidation completed 1/5/66
Each share Common $2 par exchanged for first and final distribution of $25 cash

FINEART FOODS, INC.
Acquired by Pennsylvania Sugar Co. in 1931
Details not available

FINECOGROUP S P A (ITALY)
Name changed 12/04/2002
Name changed from Fineco S.p.A. to FinecoGroup S.p.A. 12/04/2002
ADR agreement terminated 11/24/2004
No ADR's remain outstanding

FINELINE HLDGS INC (DE)
SEC revoked common stock registration 08/23/2010

FINELINE PPTYS COM INC (NV)
Reorganized under the laws of Delaware as Fineline Holdings, Inc. 02/08/2005
Each share Common $0.001 par exchanged for (0.01) share Common $0.001 par
(See Fineline Holdings, Inc.)

FINELINE PPTYS INC (NV)
Name changed to Fineline Properties.com, Inc. (NV) 03/12/1999
Fineline Properties.com, Inc. (NV) reorganized in Delaware as Fineline Holdings, Inc. 02/08/2005
(See Fineline Holdings, Inc.)

FINEST FINL CORP (NH)
Merged into First Essex Bancorp, Inc. 12/30/1996
Each share Common $2.50 par exchanged for either (1.761) share Common 10¢ par, $20.25 cash, or a combination thereof
Note: Option to make a specific election expired 01/27/1997
(See First Essex Bancorp, Inc.)

FINEST HOUR INC (CA)
Chapter 11 bankruptcy proceedings confirmed 00/00/1992
Stockholders' equity unlikely

FINET COM INC (DE)
Name changed 05/28/1999
Each share old Common 1¢ par exchanged for (0.12667848) share new Common 1¢ par 11/08/1993
Each share new Common 1¢ par exchanged again for (0.5) share new Common 1¢ par 10/21/1996
Name changed from Finet Holdings Corp. to FiNet.com, Inc. 05/28/1999
Each share old Common 1¢ par exchanged for (0.08333333) share new Common 1¢ par 02/20/2001
Plan of reorganization under Chapter 11 Federal Bankruptcy Code effective 07/09/2004
No stockholders' equity

FINET INC (NY)
Name changed to Continental Waste Industries, Inc. (NY) 9/9/93
Continental Waste Industries, Inc. (NY) reincorporated under the laws of Delaware 2/28/94

FINEVEST FOODS INC (DE)
Common 1¢ par reclassified as Class A Common 1¢ par 07/09/1992
Name changed to GEV Corp. 05/21/1993
GEV Corp. recapitalized as Pioneer Companies Inc. 04/28/1995
(See Pioneer Companies Inc.)

FINGER LAKES BANCORP INC (USA)
Merged into First Niagara Financial Group, Inc. (Old) 01/17/2003
Each share Common 1¢ par exchanged for $20 cash

FINGER LAKES FINL CORP (DE)
Reincorporated 1/31/2000
Place of incorporation changed from (USA) to (DE) 1/31/2000
Reorganized as Finger Lakes Bancorp, Inc. 11/22/2000
Each share Common 1¢ par exchanged for (0.9643) share Common 1¢ par
(See Finger Lakes Bancorp, Inc.)

FINGER LAKES NATIONAL BANK (ODESSA, NY)
Merged into First National Bank (Rochester, NY) 1/1/82
Each (34.814) shares Common 50¢ par exchanged for (1) share Common $10 par
First National Bank (Rochester, NY) reorganized as FNB Rochester Corp. 9/10/84 which merged into M&T Bank Corp. 6/1/99

FINGERHUT CORP (MN)
Common $1 par split (2) for (1) by issuance of (1) additional share 2/9/73
Merged into American Can Co. 1/4/79
Each share Common $1 par exchanged for $20 cash

FINGERHUT COS INC (MN)
Common 1¢ par split (2) for (1) by issuance of (1) additional share 8/19/93
Each share Common 1¢ par received distribution of (0.3184) share Metris Companies Inc. Common 1¢ par payable 9/25/98 to holders of record 9/11/98 Ex date - 9/28/98
Merged into Federated Department Stores, Inc. 3/22/99
Each share Common 1¢ par exchanged for $25 cash

FINGERMATRIX INC NEW (NY)
Reorganized under the laws of Delaware as Finx Group, Inc. 7/17/2000
Each share Common 2¢ par exchanged for (0.1) share Common 1¢ par
Finx Group, Inc. recapitalized as Secure Technologies Group, Inc. 3/21/2005

FINGERMATRIX INC OLD (NY)
Reorganized under Chapter 11 Federal Bankruptcy Code as Fingermatrix Inc. (New) 04/17/1995
Each (11.2) shares Common 2¢ par exchanged for (1) share Common 2¢ par
Fingermatrix Inc. (New) reorganized in Delaware as Finx Group, Inc. 07/17/2000 which recapitalized as Secure Technologies Group, Inc. 03/21/2005
(See Secure Technologies Group, Inc.)

FINGERWARE CORP (NV)
Name changed to Seemless Technology, Inc. 10/25/2005

FINI GROUP INC (DE)
Name changed to Avalon Capital Holdings Corp. 08/24/2007
(See Avalon Capital Holdings Corp.)

FINISH LINE INC (IN)
Reincorporated 07/20/2004
Class A Common 1¢ par split (2) for (1) by issuance of (1) additional share payable 11/15/1996 to holders of record 10/18/1996
State of incorporation changed from (DE) to (IN) 07/20/2004
Class A Common 1¢ par split (2) for (1) by issuance of (1) additional share payable 11/17/2004 to holders of record 11/05/2004
Acquired by JD Sports Fashion PLC 06/18/2018
Each share Class A Common 1¢ par exchanged for $13.50 cash

FINISHING TOUCHES HOME GOODS INC (NV)
Name changed to Endeavor IP, Inc. 06/19/2013

FINISHMASTER INC (IN)
Reincorporated 12/20/1996
State of incorporation changed from (MI) to (IN) 12/20/1996
Acquired by Uni-Select Inc. 01/11/2011
Each share Common no par exchanged for $21 cash

FINITY HLDGS INC (DE)
Recapitalized as Patients & Physicians, Inc. 08/31/2006
Each share Common $0.001 par exchanged for (0.008) share Common $0.001 par
Patients & Physicians, Inc. name changed to Flagship Global Health, Inc. 01/24/2007
(See Flagship Global Health, Inc.)

FINK (A.) & SONS, INC.
Assets sold to Hygrade Food Products Corp. in 1934
(See Hygrade Food Products Corp.)

FINLAY ENTERPRISES INC (DE)
Each share old Class A Common 1¢ par exchanged for (2/3) share new Class A Common 1¢ par 03/07/1995
Plan of reorganization under Chapter 11 Federal Bankruptcy proceedings effective 08/02/2010
Stockholders' equity unlikely

FINLAYSON ENTERPRISES LTD (CANADA)
Class C $1 par called for redemption 12/01/1971
Class A no par reclassified as Common no par 12/15/1971
Class B no par reclassified as Common no par 12/15/1971
Stock Dividends - In Class C to

holders of Class B - (0.6) for (1) 03/29/1968; (8) for (1) 12/31/1968
Acquired by 147742 Canada Ltd. 03/27/1986
Each share Common no par exchanged for $0.10 cash

FINMECCANICA SPA (ITALY)
Name changed to Leonardo - Finmeccanica S.p.A. 05/27/2016
Leonardo - Finmeccanica S.p.A. name changed to Leonardo S.p.A. 01/06/2017

FINMETAL MNG LTD (NV)
Recapitalized as Amazon Goldsands Ltd. 06/09/2008
Each share Common $0.00001 par exchanged for (0.05) share Common $0.00001 par
Amazon Goldsands Ltd. name changed to First Colombia Gold Corp. 11/29/2010

FINNELL SYSTEM, INC. (IN)
Merged into Kent Finnell Industries Inc. 3/12/62
Each share Class A and/or B Preferred $10 par and/or Common $10 par exchanged for (0.392392953) share Common $10 par 3/12/62
Kent Finnell name changed to Keltec, Inc. 3/4/63
(See Keltec, Inc.)

FINNIGAN CORP (VA)
Reincorporated 03/28/1988
Common $1 par changed to no par and (1) additional share issued 09/22/1978
Common no par changed to 1¢ par and (1) additional share issued 02/23/1981
State of incorporation changed from (CA) to (VA) 03/28/1988
Merged into Thermo Instrument Systems Inc 09/14/1990
Each share Common 1¢ par exchanged for $20 cash

FINNIN MINING CO. LTD. (ON)
Charter cancelled and company declared dissolved for failure to file returns 05/13/1965

FINNING LTD (CANADA)
Common no par split (2) for (1) by issuance of (1) additional share 05/16/1989
Name changed to Finning International Inc. 04/25/1997

FINNING TRACTOR & EQUIPMENT CO. LTD. (CANADA)
Reorganized 11/12/1986
Old Common no par split (2) for (1) by issuance of (1) additional share 10/16/1972
Old Common no par split (2) for (1) by issuance of (1) additional share 04/21/1980
Old Common no par split (2) for (1) by issuance of (1) additional share 04/30/1981
Each share old Common no par exchanged for (0.5) share Conv. Class A no par and (0.5) share Conv. Class B no par 05/21/1981
Reorganized from (BC) to under the laws of Canada 11/12/1986
Each share Conv. Class A no par exchanged for (1) share Common no par
Each share Conv. Class B no par exchanged for (1) share Common no par
Name changed to Finning Ltd. 05/14/1987
Finning Ltd. name changed to Finning International Inc. 04/25/1997

FINNISH SUGAR LTD (FINLAND)
Name changed to Cultor Ltd. 03/23/1989
Cultor Ltd. name changed to Cultor Corp. 05/06/1998
(See Cultor Corp.)

FINOMIC INVT FD INC (TX)
Fund terminated 12/31/1985
Details not available

FINOR EXPL INC (CANADA)
Declared bankrupt 04/24/1989
No stockholders' equity

FINORE MNG INC (BC)
Each share old Common no par exchanged for (0.1) share new Common no par 06/16/2014
Recapitalized as Micron Waste Technologies Inc. 10/26/2017
Each share new Common no par exchanged for (0.5) share Common no par

FINOVA FIN TR (DE)
Plan of reorganization under Chapter 11 Federal Bankruptcy Code effective 08/21/2001
Each share 5.5% Trust Originated Preferred Conv. Securities exchanged for $11.25 principal amount of 7.5% Sr. Notes due 11/15/2016 and $26.25 cash

FINOVA GROUP INC (DE)
Common 1¢ par split (2) for (1) by issuance of (1) additional share payable 10/01/1997 to holders of record 09/01/1997 Ex date - 10/02/1997
Assets sold for the benefit of creditors 11/17/2009
No stockholders' equity

FINSEC CORP (FL)
Name changed to Zenith Funding Corp. 8/1/69
Zenith Funding Corp. name changed to Zenith American Corp. 5/30/73
(See Zenith American Corp.)

FINTECH ACQUISITION CORP (DE)
Units separated 08/01/2016
Name changed to CardConnect Corp. 08/01/2016
(See CardConnect Corp.)

FINTECH ACQUISITION CORP II (DE)
Units separated 07/27/2018
Name changed to International Money Express, Inc. 07/27/2018

FINTECH GROUP INC (FL)
Name changed to Capital Markets Technologies, Inc. 02/20/2007
(See Capital Markets Technologies, Inc.)

FINTECH INC (CO)
Recapitalized as Summa Metals Corp. 11/29/1991
Each share Common $0.0001 par exchanged for (0.0025) share Common 4¢ par
Summa Metals Corp. name changed to Casmyn Corp. (CO) 10/26/1994 which reorganized in Nevada as Aries Ventures Inc. 04/11/2000 which reincorporated in Delaware as Cardium Therapeutics, Inc. 01/23/2006 which name changed to Taxus Cardium Pharmaceuticals Group, Inc. 10/07/2014

FINTECH SOLUTIONS LTD (AB)
Name changed 11/17/2000
Name changed from Fintech Services Ltd. to Fintech Solutions Ltd. 11/17/2000
Name changed to Sylogist Inc. 08/15/2002
Sylogist Inc. recapitalized as Sylogist Ltd. 12/04/2002

FINTEX CORP. (MI)
Liquidation completed
Each share Common $1 par exchanged for initial distribution of $10 cash 6/20/63
Each share Common $1 par received second and final distribution of $4 cash 7/6/64

FINTRA VENTURES LTD (BC)
Name changed to U.S. Diamond Corp. 06/21/1996
(See U.S. Diamond Corp.)

FINTRY ENTERPRISES INC (BC)
Recapitalized as Mesa Uranium Corp. 12/23/2005
Each share Common no par exchanged for (0.5) share Common no par
Mesa Uranium Corp. name changed to Mesa Exploration Corp. 03/30/2011

FINX GROUP INC (DE)
Recapitalized as Secure Technologies Group, Inc. 03/21/2005
Each share Common 1¢ par exchanged for (0.004) share Common $0.0001 par
(See Secure Technologies Group, Inc.)

FIORE EXPL LTD (BC)
Reorganized as Fiore Gold Ltd. 09/26/2017
Each share Common no par exchanged for (0.265) share Common no par
Note: Unexchanged certificates will be cancelled and become without value 09/26/2023

FIR-TEX INSULATING BOARD, INC. (OR)
Liquidation completed 10/11/57
Details not available

FIR-TEX INSULATING BOARD CO. (OR)
Merged into Fir-Tex Insulating Board, Inc. 10/1/55
Each share Class A Common $100 par exchanged for (1) share Common $30 par
Each (30) shares Class B Common no par exchanged for (1) share Common $30 par
(See Fir-Tex Insulating Board, Inc.)

FIRAN CORP (ON)
Name changed 07/19/1982
Name changed from Firan-Glendale Corp. to Firan Corp. 07/19/1982
Name changed to Glendale International Corp. 08/31/1999
(See Glendale International Corp.)

FIRCREST RES LTD (BC)
Recapitalized as NTC Capital Corp. 10/30/1991
Each share Common no par exchanged for (0.2) share Common no par
NTC Capital Corp. name changed to Sungold Gaming Inc. 03/01/1994 which name changed to Sungold Gaming International Ltd. 05/26/1997 which name changed to Sungold Entertainment Corp. (BC) 03/20/2000 which reincorporated in Canada as Sungold International Holdings Corp. 12/12/2003

FIRE ASSOCIATION OF PHILADELPHIA (PA)
Capital Stock $10 par exchanged (5) for (14) in 1932
Stock Dividends - 20% 6/30/45; 20.777% 2/1/50; 12% 5/14/56
Name changed to Reliance Insurance Co. 1/1/58
(See Reliance Insurance Co.)

FIRE BOSS SVCS LTD (AB)
Name changed to Boss Energy Ltd. 03/03/1994
Boss Energy Ltd. merged into Canadian Leader Energy Inc. 11/02/1995 which merged into Centurion Energy International Inc. 05/20/1997
(See Centurion Energy International Inc.)

FIRE ENGINEERS INC (MN)
Name changed to F E I Corp. 11/06/1971
F E I Corp. name changed to Econo-Therm Energy Systems Corp. 12/12/1974
(See Econo-Therm Energy Systems Corp.)

FIRE ENVIRONMENTAL INC (TX)
Charter forfeited for failure to pay taxes 03/23/2001

FIRE FLY ENTERPRISES INC (DE)
Name changed to Geo-Energy Resources Inc. 2/29/76
Geo-Energy Resources Inc. name changed to Guild Mark Industries, Inc. 8/21/87 which merged into MG Gold Corp. 5/15/97 which name changed to MG Natural Resources Corp. 10/12/98 which name changed to Xenolix Technologies Inc. 6/14/2000 which name changed to Pershing Resources Co., Inc. 4/27/2004

FIRE MTN BEVERAGE CO (WA)
Each share old Common $0.0001 par exchanged for (0.01) share new Common $0.0001 par 11/21/2005
Each share new Common $0.0001 par exchanged again for (1) share new Common $0.0001 par 10/24/2008
Stock Dividend - 8% payable 10/12/2006 to holders of record 10/02/2006
Name changed to FG Fitness & Media Group, Inc. 12/05/2014

FIRE PROTN INC (DE)
Name changed back to Tel-O-Tronic Industries, Inc. 8/3/77
Tel-O-Tronic Industries, Inc. name changed to American Swiss International Inc. 6/20/86
(See American Swiss International Inc.)

FIRE RIV GOLD CORP (ON)
Recapitalized as Kingly Enterprises Inc. 02/05/1997
Each share Common no par exchanged for (0.25) share Common no par
(See Kingly Enterprises Inc.)

FIRE STAR ENTERPRISES INC (UT)
Recapitalized as Waste Processor Industries, Inc. 10/07/1991
Each share Common $0.001 par exchanged for (0.01118959) share Common $0.001 par
Waste Processor Industries, Inc. merged into American Ecology Corp. 03/09/1993 which name changed to US Ecology, Inc. 02/22/2010

FIRE TELECOMMUNICATIONS INC (CO)
Name changed to Terracom, Inc. 11/07/2000
Terracom, Inc. recapitalized as EurAsiaCom, Inc. 12/14/2001 which recapitalized as Supertel Communications, Ltd. 06/24/2002 which name changed to Premier Platforms Holding Co., Inc. 09/24/2002 which name changed to Paolo Nevada Enterprises, Inc. (CO) 02/17/2005 which reorganized in Nevada as David Loren Corp. 11/13/2006 which recapitalized as Kibush Capital Corp. 08/23/2013

FIRE UNDERWRITERS ASSN (CA)
Common 10¢ par split (5) for (4) by issuance of (0.25) additional share 6/11/65
Merged into Farmers Group, Inc. 12/31/70
Each share Common 10¢ par exchanged for (0.75) share Common $1 par
(See Farmers Group, Inc.)

FIREARMS TRAINING SYS INC (DE)
Issue Information - 6,000,000 shares CL A COM offered at $14 per share on 11/26/1996
Merged into Meggitt PLC 10/19/2006
Each share Common $0.000006 par exchanged for $1.08 cash

FIREBALL RES LTD (BC)
Struck off register and declared

dissolved for failure to file returns 06/26/1992

FIREBIRD CAP PARTNERS INC (BC)
Name changed to Firebird Energy Inc. 12/27/2012
Firebird Energy Inc. recapitalized as T-Bird Pharma Inc. 09/09/2014 which name changed to Emerald Health Therapeutics, Inc. 06/19/2015

FIREBIRD ENERGY INC (BC)
Common no par split (3) for (1) by issuance of (2) additional shares payable 01/30/2013 to holders of record 01/30/2013 Ex date - 01/28/2013
Recapitalized as T-Bird Pharma Inc. 09/09/2014
Each share Common no par exchanged for (0.06666666) share Common no par
T-Bird Pharma Inc. name changed to Emerald Health Therapeutics, Inc. 06/19/2015

FIREBRAND FINL GROUP INC (DE)
Company terminated common stock registration and is no longer public as of 03/06/2003

FIRECO SALES LTD (ON)
Common no par split (2) for (1) by issuance of (1) additional share 12/30/1971
Common no par reclassified as Class A Conv. no par 09/01/1973
Declared bankrupt 12/18/1982
Assets subsequently sold with no stockholders' equity

FIRECOM INC (NY)
Each share Common 1¢ par received distribution of (1) share Class A Common 1¢ par payable 12/17/1997 to holders of record 12/05/1997
Merged into ALRM Acquisition Inc. 07/19/2001
Each share Conv. Class A Common 1¢ par exchanged for $0.80 cash
Each share Common 1¢ par exchanged for $0.80 cash

FIREFISH INC (NV)
Each share old Common $0.001 par exchanged for (10) shares new Common $0.001 par 04/18/2012
Name changed to Gifa, Inc. 09/25/2018

FIREFLY MNG LTD (ON)
Charter cancelled and declared dissolved for failure to file returns and pay fees 03/16/1976

FIREFOX COMMUNICATIONS INC (DE)
Issue Information - 2,300,000 shares COM offered at $18 per share on 05/04/1995
Merged into FTP Software, Inc. 07/22/1996
Each share Common $0.001 par exchanged for (0.9498) share Common 1¢ par and $1.3458 cash
FTP Software, Inc. merged into NetManage, Inc. 08/27/1998
(See NetManage, Inc.)

FIRELIGHT CORP (AB)
Delisted from NEX 10/21/2008

FIREMAN'S FUND INSURANCE CO. (CA)
Each share Capital Stock $25 par exchanged for (1.5) shares Capital Stock $10 par 00/00/1942
Capital Stock $10 par changed to $7.50 par 00/00/1948
Each share Capital Stock $7.50 par exchanged for (2) shares Capital Stock $5 par 00/00/1950
Capital Stock $5 par changed to $2.50 par 00/00/1954
Capital Stock $2.50 par changed to $1.25 par and (1) additional share issued 02/25/1963
Stock Dividends - 20% 03/15/1954; 25% 01/15/1960

Under plan of merger name changed to Fund American Companies and Capital Stock $1.25 par reclassified as Common $1.25 par 01/04/1966
Fund American Companies acquired by American Express Co. 10/31/1968

FIREMANS FD CORP (DE)
Name changed to Fund American Companies, Inc. 12/08/1989
Fund American Companies, Inc. name changed to Fund American Enterprises Holdings, Inc. 06/19/1992 which name changed to White Mountains Insurance Group, Inc. (DE) 06/01/1999 which reincorporated in Bermuda as White Mountains Insurance Group, Ltd. 10/25/1999

FIREMANS INS CO NEWARK (NJ)
Each share Common $50 par exchanged for (5) shares Common $10 par 00/00/1927
Common $10 par changed to $5 par 00/00/1932
Common $5 par changed to $7.50 par 03/07/1955
Acquired by Continental Corp. (NY) 06/30/1971
Each share Common $7.50 par exchanged for $90 cash

FIREMEN'S INSURANCE CO. OF WASHINGTON & GEORGETOWN (DC)
Name changed to Firemen's Insurance Co. of Washington, D.C. 7/3/57
(See Firemen's Insurance Co. of Washington, D.C.)

FIREMENS INS CO WASHINGTON D C (DC)
Stock Dividends - 50% 07/15/1957; 10% 06/01/1960; 10% 06/01/1962; 10% 06/01/1964; 10% 06/01/1966; 22.91354% 02/01/1979
Merged into Berkley (W. R.) Corp. 04/02/1982
Each share Capital Stock $20 par exchanged for $120 cash

FIRENZE LTD (NV)
Each share old Common $0.001 par exchanged for (0.05) share new Common $0.001 par 10/18/1995
Each share new Common $0.001 par exchanged again for (0.05) share new Common $0.001 par 03/28/1997
Recapitalized as Internet Cable Corp. 09/12/1997
Each share new Common $0.001 par exchanged for (0.05) share Common $0.001 par
(See Internet Cable Corp.)

FIREPLACE MFRS INC (CA)
Merged into Desa International 8/19/98
Each share Common 1¢ par exchanged for $7.14 cash

FIREPOND INC (DE)
Incorporated 11/04/1999
Each share old Common 1¢ par exchanged for (0.1) share new Common 1¢ par 08/16/2002
Merged into Jaguar Technology Holdings, LLC 12/03/2003
Each share new Common 1¢ par exchanged for $3.16 cash

FIREPOND INC (DE)
Incorporated 08/31/2005
Filed a petition under Chapter 7 Federal Bankruptcy Code 03/31/2009
Stockholders' equity unlikely

FIREROCK CAP CORP (NV)
Name changed to Ameritech International Corp. 2/24/2005

FIRESAND RES LTD (ON)
Recapitalized as Talisman Enterprises Inc. 12/30/1997
Each share Common no par

exchanged for (0.22271714) share Common no par
(See Talisman Enterprises Inc.)

FIRESIDE SECS CORP (CA)
Merged into Teledyne, Inc. 09/10/1968
Each share 7% Preferred $10 par exchanged for (0.126334) share Common $1 par
Teledyne, Inc. merged into Allegheny Teledyne Inc. 08/15/1996 which name changed to Allegheny Technologies Inc. 11/29/1999

FIRESKY MEDIA CORP (NV)
Name changed to Sky440, Inc. 02/12/2008

FIRESPUR EXPLORATIONS LTD. (ON)
Recapitalized as Firesand Resources Ltd. 05/01/1989
Each share Common no par exchanged for (0.66666666) share Common no par
Firesand Resources Ltd. recapitalized as Talisman Enterprises Inc. 12/30/1997
(See Talisman Enterprises Inc.)

FIRESTEEL RES INC (AB)
Name changed to Nordic Gold Corp. 08/10/2018

FIRESTONE APSLEY RUBBER CO.
Name changed to Firestone Footwear Co. in 1926
(See Firestone Footwear Co.)

FIRESTONE BANCORP INC (DE)
Merged into Banc One Corp. (DE) 03/01/1982
Each share Common $10 par exchanged for (2.39) shares Common no par
Banc One Corp. (DE) reincorporated in Ohio 05/01/1989 which merged into Bank One Corp. 10/02/1998 which merged into J.P. Morgan Chase & Co. 12/31/2000 which name changed to JPMorgan Chase & Co. 07/20/2004

FIRESTONE BK (AKRON, OH)
Each share Capital Stock $100 par exchanged for (4) shares Capital Stock $25 par 00/00/1944
Capital Stock $25 par changed to $10 par and (1.5) additional shares issued plus a 20% stock dividend paid 02/02/1967
Stock Dividends - 200% 01/24/1940; 25% 01/19/1944; 100% 02/01/1955; 50% 02/20/1970
Under plan of reorganization each share Capital Stock $10 par automatically became (1) share Firestone Bancorp, Inc. Common $10 par 06/21/1973
Firestone Bancorp, Inc. merged into Banc One Corp. (DE) 03/01/1982 which reincorporated in Ohio 05/01/1989 which merged into Bank One Corp. 10/02/1998 which merged into J.P. Morgan Chase & Co. 12/31/2000 which name changed to JPMorgan Chase & Co. 07/20/2004

FIRESTONE BK (LISBON, OH)
Merged into Citizens Bancshares, Inc. (OH) 02/05/1994
Each share Common $40 par exchanged for (0.95) share Common no par
Citizens Bancshares, Inc. (OH) name changed Sky Financial Group, Inc. 10/02/1998 which merged into Huntington Bancshares Inc. 07/02/2007

FIRESTONE FOOTWEAR CO.
Dissolved in 1936

FIRESTONE PETROLEUMS LTD.
Merged into Amalgamated Oils Ltd. 00/00/1941
Each (500) shares Common exchanged for (33) shares Common

(See Amalgamated Oils Ltd.)

FIRESTONE RESOURCES INC. (NV)
Each share old Common no par exchanged for (40) shares new Common no par 09/25/1987
Name changed to U.S. Waste Management and Common no par changed to $0.00001 par 10/02/1987
U.S. Waste Management recapitalized as U.S. Waste Group 08/30/1988 which name changed to Genco Corp. 02/21/2008

FIRESTONE TIRE & RUBR CO (OH)
Common $10 par changed to $25 par in 1943
Common $25 par changed to $12.50 par and (1) additional share issued in 1951
Common $12.50 par changed to $6.25 par and (1) additional share issued in 1955
Common $6.25 par changed to no par and (2) additional shares issued 2/23/60
4-1/2% Preferred $100 par called for redemption 11/15/60
Common no par split (2) for (1) by issuance of (1) additional share 11/8/71
Merged into Bridgestone Corp. 5/5/88
Each share Common no par exchanged for $80 cash

FIRESTONE VENTURES INC (BC)
Reincorporated under the laws of Alberta 09/27/2005

FIRETECTOR INC (DE)
Each share old Common $0.001 par exchanged for (0.2) share new Common $0.001 par 08/23/1991
Each share new Common $0.001 par exchanged again for (0.25) share new Common $0.001 par 06/30/1992
Each share new Common $0.001 par exchanged again for (1/3) share new Common $0.001 par 09/24/1998
Name changed to Synergx Systems Inc. 05/24/2002
(See Synergx Systems Inc.)

FIREWORKS ENTMT INC (ON)
Merged into Canwest Global Communications Corp. 06/29/1998
Each share Class A Multiple no par exchanged for $3.50 cash
Each share Class B Subordinate no par exchanged for $3.50 cash

FIRM CAP MTG INVT TR (ON)
Name changed 04/17/2001
Name changed from Firm Capital Mortgage Investment Fund to Firm Capital Mortgage Investment Trust 04/17/2001
Under plan of reorganization each Unit no par automatically became (1) share Firm Capital Mortgage Investment Corp. (Canada) Common no par 01/05/2011

FIRM DEVELOPMENT, INC. (UT)
Name changed to Bingo USA Corp. 03/26/1986
Bingo USA Corp. recapitalized as Full Circle, Inc. (UT) 02/15/1989 which reorganized in Nevada as Hydro Grow Inc. 12/08/1998 which name changed to Asgard Alliance Corp. 09/22/1999 which name changed to Santa Fe Holding Co., Inc. 06/26/2007
(See Santa Fe Holding Co., Inc.)

FIRMA INC (CO)
Recapitalized as Hughes Resources Inc. (CO) 06/03/1991
Each share Common $0.0001 par exchanged for (0.03125) share Common $0.0001 par
Hughes Resources Inc. (CO) reincorporated in Nevada as Phoenix Resources Technologies, Inc. 02/29/1996

(See Phoenix Resources Technologies, Inc.)

FIRMATRON, INC. (NY)
Proclaimed dissolved for failure to file reports and pay taxes 12/15/67

FIRST & CTZNS NATL BK (ALEXANDRIA, VA)
Stock Dividends - 10% 9/11/59; 10% 2/3/61
Name changed to United Virginia Bank/ First & Citizens National (Alexandria, VA) 2/15/69
(See United Virginia Bank/First & Citizens National (Alexandria, VA))

FIRST & FMRS BK SOMERSET INC (SOMERSET, KY)
Merged into Union Planters Corp. 2/1/99
Each share Common no par exchanged for $45.58 cash

FIRST & MERCHANTS CORP (VA)
Common $10 par changed to $7.50 par and (1/3) additional share issued 5/10/72
Common $7.50 par changed to $3.75 par and (1) additional share issued 1/12/82
Merged into Sovran Financial Corp. 12/31/83
Each share $2.37 Conv. Preferred Ser. A $25 par exchanged for (1) share $2.37 Conv. Preferred Ser. A $25 par
Each share Common $3.75 par exchanged for (1) share Common $5 par
Sovran Financial Corp. merged into C&S/Sovran Corp. 9/1/90 which merged into NationsBank Corp. 12/31/91 which reincorporated in Delaware as BankAmerica Corp. (Old) 9/25/98 which merged into BankAmerica Corp. (New) 9/30/98 which name changed to Bank of America Corp. 4/28/99

FIRST & MERCHANTS NATL BK (RADFORD, VA)
Common $20 par changed to $10 par and (0.5) additional share issued 3/1/66
Common $10 par changed to $2.50 par and (3) additional shares issued 10/31/75
Merged into United Virginia Bankshares, Inc. 10/1/81
Each share Common $2.50 par exchanged for (0.71) share Common $10 par
United Virginia Bankshares, Inc. name changed to Crestar Financial Corp. 9/1/87 which merged into SunTrust Banks, Inc. 12/31/98

FIRST & MERCHANTS NATL BK (RICHMOND, VA)
Common $20 par changed to $10 par and (1) additional share issued plus a 25% stock dividend paid 7/31/62
Stock Dividends - 50% 2/1/56; 10% 2/15/65; 20% 10/22/68
Reorganized as First & Merchants Corp. 2/26/69
Each share Common $10 par exchanged for (1) share Common $10 par
First & Merchants Corp. merged into Sovran Financial Corp. 12/31/83 which merged into C&S/Sovran Corp. 9/1/90 which merged into NationsBank Corp. 12/31/91 which reincorporated in Delaware as BankAmerica Corp. (Old) 9/25/98 which merged into BankAmerica Corp. (New) 9/30/98 which name changed to Bank of America Corp. 4/28/99

FIRST & OCEAN BANCORP (MA)
Stock Dividends - 2.5% payable 10/1/98 to holders of record 9/15/98; 3% payable 10/1/99 to holders of record 9/15/99; 3% payable 4/1/2000 to holders of record 3/15/2000 Ex date - 4/20/2000; 3% payable 10/1/2000 to holders of record 9/15/2000; 3% payable 10/1/2001 to holders of record 9/14/2001 Ex date - 9/27/2001; 3% payable 4/1/2002 to holders of record 3/15/2002 Ex date - 3/26/2002; 3% payable 10/1/2002 to holders of record 9/16/2002 Ex date - 9/12/2002
Merged into Banknorth Group, Inc. 12/31/2003
Each share Common $12.50 par exchanged for $176 cash

FIRST & OCEAN NATL BK (NEWBURYPORT, MA)
Common $50 par changed to $12.50 par and (2) additional shares issued 2/26/80
Under plan of reorganization each share Common $12.50 par automatically became (1) share First & Ocean Bancorp Common $12.50 par in 1984
(See First & Ocean Bancorp)

FIRST ABILENE BANKSHARES INC (TX)
Common $10 par split (4) for (3) by issuance of (1/3) additional share 11/24/81
Common $10 par split (3) for (2) by issuance of (0.5) additional share 11/29/82
Common $10 par split (3) for (2) by issuance of (0.5) additional share 6/1/92
Stock Dividends - 50% 9/18/74; 25% 11/25/75; 20% 5/25/77; 20% 11/20/79; 20% 6/6/84; 10% 12/1/87
Name changed to First Financial Bankshares, Inc. 10/26/93

FIRST ACADIAN BANCSHARES INC (LA)
Merged into Union Planters Corp. 12/1/97
Each share Common exchanged for (2.422) shares Common $5 par
Union Planters Corp. merged into Regions Financial Corp. (New) 7/1/2004

FIRST ADVANCE CAP CORP (ON)
Recapitalized as Avonlee Capital Corp. 11/30/1994
Each share Common no par exchanged for (0.33333333) share Common no par
Avonlee Capital Corp. recapitalized as Internet Liquidators International Inc. 05/28/1996 which name changed to Bid.Com International, Inc. 07/17/1998 which recapitalized as ADB Systems International Inc. 10/18/2001 which name changed to ADB Systems International Ltd. 11/01/2002 which name changed to Northcore Technologies Inc. 07/18/2006

FIRST ADVANTAGE CORP (DE)
Acquired by First American Corp. (CA) 11/18/2009
Each share Class A Common $0.001 par exchanged for (0.58) share Common $1 par
First American Corp. (CA) reincorporated in Delaware as CoreLogic, Inc. 06/01/2010

FIRST AFFILIATED BANCORPORATION INC (WI)
Stock Dividend - 10% 10/01/1984
Merged into Marshall & Ilsley Corp. (Old) 11/28/1986
Each share Common $5 par exchanged for (2.67) shares Common $1 par
(See Marshall & Ilsley Corp. (Old))

FIRST AGRIC NATL BK BERKSHIRE CNTY (PITTSFIELD, MA)
Capital Stock $25 par changed to $12.50 par and (1) additional share issued 02/23/1965
Stock Dividends - 60.86% 03/15/1967; 10% 02/18/1969
Name changed to First Agricultural Bank (Pittsfield, MA) 01/24/1977
First Agricultural Bank (Pittsfield, MA) name changed to Multibank West (Pittsfield, MA) 07/01/1991
(See Multibank West (Pittsfield, MA))

FIRST AGRICULTURAL BANK (PITTSFIELD, MA)
Name changed to Multibank West (Pittsfield, MA) 07/01/1991
(See Multibank West (Pittsfield, MA))

FIRST AID DIRECT INC (FL)
Name changed to Total First Aid, Inc. 10/27/2003
Total First Aid, Inc. name changed to Spearhead Ltd., Inc. 06/29/2004 which recapitalized as Heritage Action Corp. 01/08/2016 which name changed to Heritage Printing Technology Corp. 06/28/2016 which recapitalized as Comerton Corp. 11/07/2017

FIRST AID DIRECT INC (NV)
Name changed to Platinum & Gold Inc. and (3) additional shares issued 12/21/1998
(See Platinum & Gold Inc.)

FIRST AID SELECT INC (FL)
Name changed to First Aid Direct, Inc. 11/22/1999
First Aid Direct, Inc. name changed to Total First Aid, Inc. 10/27/2003 which name changed to Spearhead Ltd., Inc. 06/29/2004 which recapitalized as Heritage Action Corp. 01/08/2016 which name changed to Heritage Printing Technology Corp. 06/28/2016 which recapitalized as Comerton Corp. 11/07/2017

FIRST ALA BANCSHARES INC (DE)
Common $2.50 par changed to $1.25 par and (1) additional share issued 6/1/84
Common $1.25 par changed to $0.625 par and (1) additional share issued 6/1/86
Stock Dividends - 10% 8/1/79; 10% 4/1/93
Name changed to Regions Financial Corp. (Old) 5/2/94
Regions Financial Corp. (Old) merged into Regions Financial Corp. (New) 7/1/2004

FIRST ALABAMA BANK (BIRMINGHAM, AL)
Merged into First Alabama Bancshares, Inc. 6/4/84
Each share Common $1 par exchanged for $29 cash

FIRST ALABAMA BANK OF HUNTSVILLE, N.A. (HUNTSVILLE, AL)
Through voluntary exchange offer First Alabama Bancshares, Inc. held 99.63% as of 08/16/1971
Public interest eliminated

FIRST ALABAMA BANK OF MONTGOMERY, N.A. (MONTGOMERY, AL)
100% acquired by First Alabama Bancshares, Inc. as of 12/28/1977
Public interest eliminated

FIRST ALBANY COS INC (NY)
Each share Common 1¢ par received distribution of (0.14285714) share Plug Power, Inc. Common 1¢ par payable 05/18/2004 to holders of record 05/04/2004
Stock Dividends - 5% payable 05/20/1996 to holders of record 05/06/1996; 5% payable 11/21/1996 to holders of record 11/07/1996; 5% payable 05/27/1997 to holders of record 05/12/1997; 5% payable 11/26/1997 to holders of record 11/12/1997; 5% payable 05/26/1998 to holders of record 05/12/1998; 5% payable 11/24/1998 to holders of record 11/10/1998; 5% payable 05/25/1999 to holders of record 05/11/1999; 5% payable 11/23/1999 to holders of record 11/09/1999; 5% payable 05/26/2000 to holders of record 05/12/2000; 5% payable 11/28/2000 to holders of record 11/14/2000; 5% payable 05/29/2001 to holders of record 05/15/2001 Ex date - 05/11/2001; 5% payable 11/29/2001 to holders of record 11/15/2001 Ex date - 11/13/2001; 5% payable 05/29/2002 to holders of record 05/15/2002 Ex date - 05/13/2002; 5% payable 11/29/2002 to holders of record 11/15/2002 Ex date - 11/13/2002
Name changed to Broadpoint Securities Group, Inc. 12/28/2007
Broadpoint Securities Group, Inc. name changed to Broadpoint Gleacher Securities Group, Inc. (NY) 06/05/2009 which reincorporated in Delaware as Gleacher & Co., Inc. 05/28/2010

FIRST ALERT INC (DE)
Issue Information - 3,600,000 shares COM offered at $17 per share on 03/28/1994
Common 1¢ par split (2) for (1) by issuance of (1) additional share 10/27/94
Merged into Sunbeam Corp. (New) 4/6/98
Each share Common 1¢ par exchanged for $5.25 cash

FIRST ALLEN PARISH BANCORP INC (DE)
Acquired by First Federal Bank of Louisiana (Lake Charles, LA) 11/1/2004
Each share Common 1¢ par exchanged for $33 cash

FIRST ALLIANCE / PREMIER BANCSHARES INC (GA)
Name changed to Premier Bancshares Inc. (New) 2/4/97
Premier Bancshares Inc. (New) merged into BB&T Corp. 1/13/2000

FIRST ALLIANCE BANCORP INC (GA)
Under plan of merger name changed to First Alliance/Premier Bancshares Inc. 8/31/96
First Alliance/Premier Bancshares Inc. name changed to Premier Bancshares Inc. (New) 2/4/97 which merged into BB&T Corp. 1/13/2000

FIRST ALLIANCE BK & TR CO (MANCHESTER, NH)
FDIC discharged from receivership 04/01/2003
No stockholders' equity

FIRST ALLIANCE CORP (DE)
Common 1¢ par split (3) for (2) by issuance of (0.5) additional share payable 10/31/97 to holders of record 10/15/97 Ex date - 11/3/97
Plan of reorganization under Chapter 11 Federal Bankruptcy Code effective 11/19/2002
Each share Common 1¢ par is expected to receive the lesser of $1.50 per share or the holder's purchase basis of such shares prior to cancellation

FIRST ALLIANCE CORP (KY)
Stock Dividend - 5% payable 6/30/2001 to holders of record 6/6/2001 Ex date - 7/16/2001
Merged into Citizens, Inc. 2/18/2003
Each share Common no par exchanged for (0.44984255) share Common no par

FIRST ALLIED CORP (FL)
Completely liquidated
Each share Common 1¢ par received initial distribution of $15 cash 3/31/86
Each share Common 1¢ par received

second distribution of $2 cash 4/9/86
Each share Common 1¢ par exchanged for third and final distribution of $3.03 cash 7/2/86

FIRST ALLIED RES CORP (BC)
Delisted from Vancouver Stock Exchange 07/07/1989

FIRST ALTA ENTERPRISES CORP (AB)
Recapitalized as Anitech Enterprises Inc. (AB) 02/06/1991
Each share Common no par exchanged for (0.5) share Common no par
Anitech Enterprises Inc. (AB) reorganized in Canada as IPICO Inc. 03/30/2006
(See IPICO Inc.)

FIRST AMARILLO BANCORPORATION INC (TX)
Acquired by Boatmen's Bancshares, Inc. 11/30/93
Each share Common $1 par exchanged for (0.912) share Common $1 par
Boatmen's Bancshares, Inc. merged into NationsBank Corp. 1/7/97 which reincorporated in Delaware as BankAmerica Corp. (Old) 9/25/98 which merged into BankAmerica Corp. (New) 9/30/98 which name changed to Bank of America Corp. 4/28/99

FIRST AMERI CABLE CORP (DE)
Completely liquidated 09/17/1990
Each share Common $0.001 par received first and final distribution of $0.15 cash

FIRST AMER BK CORP (MI)
Common $10 par split (3) for (2) by issuance of (0.5) additional share 07/30/1984
9% Conv. Preference $11 par called for redemption 01/07/1988
9% Conv. Preferred Ser. B $11 par called for redemption 01/07/1988
9-1/4% Conv. Preferred Ser. C no par called for redemption 01/07/1988
11-1/4% Conv. Preferred Ser. D no par called for redemption 07/02/1990
Common $10 par split (2) for (1) by issuance of (1) additional share 10/18/1990
9% Conv. Preferred Ser. H no par called for redemption 10/09/1992
9% Conv. Preferred Ser. G no par called for redemption 10/09/1992
10% Conv. Preferred Ser. E $19 par called for redemption 10/09/1992
Preferred $190 par called for redemption 12/31/1993
Common $10 par split (3) for (2) by issuance of (0.5) additional share payable 05/30/1997 to holders of record 05/09/1997 Ex date - 06/02/1997
Merged into National City Corp. 03/31/1998
Each share Common $10 par exchanged for (1.2) shares Common $4 par
National City Corp. acquired by PNC Financial Services Group, Inc. 12/31/2008

FIRST AMER CAP TR (DE)
8.5% Trust Preferred Securities called for redemption at $25 plus $0.53125 accrued dividend on 6/30/2003

FIRST AMERN BANCORP (AL)
Merged into Alabama National BanCorporation (DE) 11/30/1997
Each share Common 1¢ par exchanged for (0.7199) share Common $1 par
Alabama National BanCorporation (DE) merged into Royal Bank of Canada (Montreal, QUE) 02/22/2008

FIRST AMERN BANCORP (OH)
Acquired by Charter One Financial, Inc. 9/17/92
Each share Common $1 par exchanged for (0.88297) share Common 1¢ par
(See Charter One Financial, Inc.)

1ST AMERN BANCORP INC (DE)
Assets sold by FDIC 10/22/1990
No stockholders' equity

FIRST AMERICAN BANK & TRUST (BAYTOWN, TX)
Stock Dividend - 10% 05/01/1983
Declared insolvent by Federal Deposit Insurance Co. 03/10/1988
No stockholders' equity

FIRST AMERN BK & TR NORTH PALM BEACH (NORTH PALM BEACH, FL)
Taken over by the FDIC 12/15/89
Stockholders' equity unlikely

FIRST AMERN BK (AURORA, IL)
Acquired by Merchants Bancorp Inc. (DE) 2/29/84
Each share Common $10 par exchanged for $85 cash

FIRST AMERN BK (MEMPHIS, TN)
Capital Stock $1 par changed to 50¢ par and (1) additional share issued 4/10/73
Merged into Hamilton Bancshares, Inc. 6/17/74
Each share Capital Stock 50¢ par exchanged for (0.149993) share Common no par
(See Hamilton Bancshares, Inc.)

FIRST AMERICAN BANK (NORTH PALM BEACH, FL)
Common $10 par changed to $5 par and (1) additional share issued 2/28/73
Name changed to First American Bank of Palm Beach County (North Palm Beach, FL) 12/31/78
First American Bank of Palm Beach County (North Palm Beach, FL) name changed to First American Bank & Trust of Palm Beach (North Palm Beach, FL) 9/2/82
(See First American Bank & Trust of Palm Beach (North Palm Beach, FL))

FIRST AMERN BK (ROSEMEAD, CA)
Merged into First Community Bancorp 8/12/2005
Each share Common no par exchanged for $24.95 cash

FIRST AMERICAN BANK CORP. (IL)
Reincorporated under the laws of Delaware and Common Capital $10 par changed to no par 1/30/84

FIRST AMERN BK CORP (DE)
Merged into FABC, Inc. 12/19/2006
Each share Common no par exchanged for $340 cash

FIRST AMERN BK CORP (MI)
Name changed to First of America Bank Corp. 01/14/1983
First of America Bank Corp. merged into National City Corp. 03/31/1998 which was acquired by PNC Financial Services Group, Inc. 12/31/2008

1ST AMERN BK FOR SVGS (BOSTON, MA)
Under plan of reorganization each share Common 10¢ par automatically became (1) share 1st American Bancorp, Inc. (DE) 12/21/1987
(See 1st American Bancorp, Inc.)

FIRST AMERN BK INDIAN RIV CNTY (VERO BEACH, FL)
Merged into SouthTrust Corp. 12/11/1998
Each share Common $10 par exchanged for (1.887) shares Common $2.50 par
SouthTrust Corp. merged into Wachovia Corp. (Ctfs. dated after 09/01/2001) 11/01/2004 which merged into Wells Fargo & Co. (New) 12/31/2008

FIRST AMERN BK MD (SILVER SPRING, MD)
Merged into FABM Acquisition Bank 08/08/1988
Each share Common $10 par exchanged for $42 cash

FIRST AMERN BK N A (WASHINGTON, DC)
Acquired by First American Bankshares, Inc. 6/12/84
Each share Capital Stock $5 par exchanged for $30 cash

FIRST AMERN BK NY (ALBANY, NY)
Merged into Empire Shares Corp. 12/15/1982
Each share Common $10 par exchanged for $40 cash

FIRST AMERICAN BANK OF BROWARD COUNTY (HOLLYWOOD, FL)
Merged into First American Bank of Palm Beach County (North Palm Beach, FL) 9/1/82
Each share Common $10 par exchanged for (4) shares Class A Common $1 par
First American Bank of Palm Beach County (North Palm Beach, FL) name changed to First American Bank & Trust of Palm Beach County (North Palm Beach, FL) 9/2/82
(See First American Bank & Trust of Palm Beach County (North Palm Beach, FL))

FIRST AMERN BK PALM BEACH CNTY (NORTH PALM BEACH, FL)
Each share Common $5 par exchanged for (4) shares Class A Common $1 par and (1) share Class B Common $1 par 9/22/80
Stock Dividends - 10% 3/1/80; In Class A Common 10% 3/1/81; 20% 5/3/82
Name changed to First American Bank & Trust of Palm Beach County (North Palm Beach, Fla.) 9/2/82
(See First American Bank & Trust of Palm Beach County (North Palm Beach, FL))

FIRST AMERN BK VA (MCLEAN, VA)
Stock Dividend - 100% 12/30/1983
Merged into Virginia Bankshares, Inc. 05/27/1987
Each share Common $10 par exchanged for $42 cash

FIRST AMERICAN BANKSHARES, INC. (VA)
2.25% Preferred Ser. A $1 par called for redemption 7/1/85
Merged into First American Corp. 4/1/99
Details not available

1ST AMERN BUSINESS DEV GROUP INC (CO)
Common $0.001 par split (10) for (1) by issuance of (9) additional shares 9/7/88
Reorganized under the laws of Delaware as 21st Century Rehabilitation, Inc. 1/26/93
Each (220) shares Common $0.001 par exchanged for (1) share Common $0.022 par

FIRST AMERN CAP CORP (CO)
Struck off register and declared dissolved for failure to file reports 08/01/2002

FIRST AMERN CAP CORP (KS)
Each share Common 10¢ par exchanged for (1/3) share Common 1¢ par 04/16/2007
Name changed to Brooke Capital Corp. 06/12/2007
(See Brooke Capital Corp.)

FIRST AMERN CAP GROUP INC (BC)
Reincorporated under the laws of Wyoming as Rosetta Technologies Inc. and Common no par changed to 1¢ par 06/23/1993
Rosetta Technologies Inc. name changed to Tanisys Technology, Inc. 07/11/1994
(See Tanisys Technology, Inc.)

1ST AMERICAN CAPITAL CORP. (NV)
Charter revoked for failure to file reports and pay fees 03/04/1974

FIRST AMERN CLOCK CO (NV)
Reorganized as MangoSoft, Inc. 09/07/1999
Each share Common $0.001 par exchanged for (1.734) shares Common $0.001 par
MangoSoft, Inc. name changed to Mango Capital, Inc. 02/17/2011

FIRST AMERICAN CORP.
Acquired by Broad Street Investing Co., Inc. 00/00/1931
Details not available

FIRST AMERICAN CORP. (GA)
Completely liquidated 07/09/1998
No stockholders' equity

FIRST AMERICAN CORP. (IL)
Involuntarily dissolved 11/20/1973
No stockholders' equity

FIRST AMERN CORP (CA)
Name changed 05/19/2000
Common $1 par split (3) for (2) by issuance of (0.5) additional share 10/13/1978
Common $1 par split (2) for (1) by issuance of (1) additional share 06/05/1987
Common $1 par reclassified as Class A Common $1 par 08/23/1989
Each share Class A Common $1 par received distribution of (1) share Class B Common $1 par 11/20/1989
Each share Class A Common $1 par reclassified as (1.04) shares Common $1 par 09/24/1992
Class B Common $1 par reclassified as Common $1 par 09/24/1992
Common $1 par split (3) for (2) by issuance of (0.5) additional share payable 01/15/1998 to holders of record 01/01/1998 Ex date - 01/16/1998
Common $1 par split (3) for (1) by issuance of (2) additional shares payable 07/17/1998 to holders of record 07/07/1998 Ex date - 07/20/1998
Name changed from First American Financial Corp. to First American Corp. 05/19/2000
Each share Common $1 par received distribution of (1) share First American Financial Corp. Common $0.00001 par payable 06/01/2010 to holders of record 05/26/2010
Reincorporated under the laws of Delaware as CoreLogic, Inc. and Common $1 par changed to $0.00001 par 06/01/2010

FIRST AMERN CORP (FL)
Common $1 par changed to 1¢ par 12/30/1984
Name changed to Inamed Corp. (FL) 06/02/1986
Inamed Corp. (FL) reincorporated in Delaware 12/28/1998 which merged into Allergan, Inc. 03/23/2006 which merged into Actavis PLC 03/17/2015

FIRST AMERN CORP (TN)
Common $5 par split (3) for (2) by issuance of (0.5) additional share 08/22/1985
$2.375 Preferred no par called for redemption 09/02/1986
Common $5 par changed to $2.50 par and (1) additional share issued payable 05/09/1997 to holders of record 04/28/1997
Merged into AmSouth Bancorporation 10/01/1999

FINANCIAL INFORMATION, INC.

Each share Common $5 par exchanged for (1.871) shares Common $1 par
AmSouth Bancorporation merged into Regions Financial Corp. 11/04/2006

FIRST AMERN ENERGY INC (DE)
Charter cancelled and declared inoperative and void for non-payment of taxes 3/1/92

FIRST AMERN EQUITY CORP (PA)
Reincorporated 11/15/1974
State of incorporation changed from (DE) to (PA) 11/15/1974
Merged out of existence 03/31/1975
Details not available

FIRST AMERN FED SVGS & LN ASSN HUNTSVILLE ALA (USA)
Common 1¢ par split (2) for (1) by issuance of (1) additional share 03/14/1986
Under plan of reorganization each share Common 1¢ par automatically became (1) share First AmFed Corp. Common 1¢ par 06/24/1987
First AmFed Corp. acquired by Colonial BancGroup, Inc. 12/31/1993
(See Colonial BancGroup, Inc.)

FIRST AMERN FINL TEX INC (DE)
Merged into United Financial Group, Inc. (DE) 4/29/83
Each share Common no par exchanged for (0.7) share Common no par
(See United Financial Group, Inc. (DE))

FIRST AMERN GROUP INC (NV)
Common $0.001 par changed to $0.0001 par and (49) additional shares issued payable 03/12/2014 to holders of record 03/12/2014
Recapitalized as Loop Industries, Inc. 09/21/2015
Each share Common $0.0001 par exchanged for (0.25) share Common $0.0001 par

FIRST AMERN HEALTH CONCEPTS INC (AZ)
Common no par split (3) for (2) by issuance of (0.5) additional share 07/01/1986
Merged into Luxottica Group S.p.A. 06/01/2001
Each share Common no par exchanged for $9.06 cash

FIRST AMERN HOME CORP (MN)
Name changed to L-S-K Inns Corp. of America 5/10/77
(See L-S-K Inns Corp. of America)

FIRST AMERN INTL CORP (NY)
Merged into RBB Bancorp 10/15/2018
Each share Common $0.0001 par exchanged for (1.3472) shares Common no par and $15.30 cash

FIRST AMERICAN LIFE INSURANCE CO. (IL)
Name changed to Empire Life Insurance Co. of Illinois 11/27/68
Empire Life Insurance Co. of Illinois merged into Empire General Corp. 9/22/69

FIRST AMERN LIFE INS CO (TX)
Merged into American Capitol Insurance Co. (TX) 11/30/1977
Each share Capital Stock no par exchanged for (0.05) share Capital Stock no par
American Capital Insurance Co. (TX) reorganized in Delaware as Acap Corp. 10/31/1985 which merged into UTG, Inc. 11/14/2011

FIRST AMERN MINERALS CORP (ON)
Name changed to Multireal Properties Inc. 05/11/1987
Multireal Properties Inc. recapitalized XPF Development Inc. 06/09/1992 which recapitalized as GolfNorth Properties Inc. 01/12/1998

(See GolfNorth Properties Inc.)

FIRST AMERN MNG CORP (WY)
Reincorporated 05/05/1988
Place of incorporation changed from (BC) to (WY) 05/05/1988
Charter revoked for non-payment of taxes 01/31/1991

FIRST AMERN MINN MUN INCOME FD II INC (MN)
Auction Preferred Shares 1¢ par called for redemption at $25,000 plus $0.54 accrued dividends on 05/02/2014
Merged into Nuveen Minnesota Municipal Income Fund 10/06/2014
Each 144A Variable Rate MuniFund Term Preferred Share Ser. 2017 1¢ par exchanged for (1) 144A Variable Rate MuniFund Term Preferred Share Ser. 2017 1¢ par
Each share Common Share of Bene. Int. 1¢ par exchanged for (0.96710017) Common Share of Bene. Int. 1¢ par
Nuveen Minnesota Municipal Income Fund name changed to Nuveen Minnesota Quality Municipal Income Fund 12/28/2016

FIRST AMERN NATL BK (NASHVILLE, TN)
Stock Dividends - 25% 1946; 20% 1/17/56; 14-2/7% 8/26/58; 12-1/2% 1/12/61; 10% 10/3/62; 25% 10/10/67; 33-1/3% 9/10/70
Under plan of reorganization each share Common $10 par automatically became (1) share First American National Corp. Common $10 par 7/15/71
First American National Corp. name changed to First Amtenn Corp. 11/7/72 which name changed to First American Corp. (TN) 1/1/81 which merged into AmSouth Bancorporation 10/1/99 which merged into Regions Financial Corp. 11/4/2006

FIRST AMERICAN NATIONAL BANK (WAUSAU, WI)
Name changed to M&I First American National Bank (Wausau, Wisc.) 3/1/88

FIRST AMERN NATL CORP (TN)
Name changed to First Amtenn Corp. and Common $10 par changed to $5 par 11/7/72
First Amtenn Corp. name changed to First American Corp. (TN) 1/1/81 which merged into AmSouth Bancorporation 10/1/99 which merged into Regions Financial Corp. 11/4/2006

FIRST AMERN NATL CORP GA (DE)
Name changed to Williams (A.L.) Corp. 6/23/82
Williams (A.L.) Corp. merged into Primerica Corp. (DE) 1/1/89 which name changed to Travelers Inc. 12/31/93 which name changed to Travelers Group Inc. 4/16/95 which name changed to Citigroup Inc. 10/8/98

1ST AMERN RENT A CAR CORP (NV)
Name changed to 1st American Capital Corp. 6/18/71
Each share Capital Stock 10¢ par exchanged for (1) share Capital Stock 10¢ par
(See 1st American Capital Corp.)

FIRST AMERN RYS INC (NV)
Each share old Common $0.001 par exchanged for (0.001) share new Common $0.001 par 09/28/2005
Name changed to Spectrum Acquisition Holdings, Inc. 12/03/2007
Spectrum Acquisition Holdings, Inc. recapitalized as Nouveau Holdings, Ltd. 04/30/2013

FIRST AMERN SVGS BK F S B (CANTON, OH)
Under plan of reorganization each share Common $1 par automatically became (1) share First American Bancorp (OH) Common $1 par 6/30/90
First American Bancorp (OH) acquired by Charter One Financial, Inc. 9/17/92
(See Charter One Financial, Inc.)

FIRST AMERN SVGS F A (JENKINTOWN, PA)
Under plan of reorganization each share Common $1 par automatically became (1) share Flagship Financial Corp. Common 1¢ par 06/15/1989
(See Flagship Financial Corp.)

FIRST AMERN SILVER CORP (NV)
Common $0.001 par split (35) for (1) by issuance of (34) additional shares payable 06/16/2010 to holders of record 06/16/2010
Name changed to Century Cobalt Corp. 06/18/2018

FIRST AMERICAN STATE BANK (WAUSAU, WI)
Stock Dividends - 20% 6/26/40; 33-1/3% 6/15/44; 25% 1/14/53; 40% 12/29/61
Name changed to First American National Bank (Wausau, Wisc.) 11/10/64
First American National Bank (Wausau, Wisc.) name changed to M&I First American National Bank (Wausau, Wisc.) 3/1/88

FIRST AMERICAN TITLE CO. OF CENTRAL CALIFORNIA (CA)
Each share Preferred $10 par exchanged for (1.3) shares Common $10 par to effect the recapitalization of each share Preferred $10 par to (1) share Common $10 par plus payment of a 30% stock dividend 7/13/65
Merged into First American Title Insurance Co. 7/19/78
Each share Common $10 par exchanged for $3 cash
Note: Certificates not surrendered for exchange prior to 1/19/79 are now valueless

FIRST AMERN TITLE INS & TR CO (CA)
Each share Capital Stock $2.50 par exchanged for (3) shares Capital Stock $1 par 12/18/1964
Name changed to First American Financial Corp. (CA) 12/31/1968
First American Financial Corp. (CA) name changed to First American Corp. (CA) 05/19/2000 which reincorporated in Delaware as CoreLogic, Inc. 06/01/2010

FIRST AMERICANO FINL CORP (NJ)
Company's sole asset placed in receivership 07/31/2009
Stockholders' equity unlikely

FIRST AMERS GOLD CORP (BC)
Each share old Common no par exchanged for (0.33333333) share new Common no par 06/02/2015
Name changed to Intact Gold Corp. 02/03/2016

FIRST AMFED CORP (DE)
Acquired by Colonial BancGroup, Inc. 12/31/1993
Each share Common 1¢ par exchanged for (1) share Class A Common $2.50 par
(See Colonial BancGroup, Inc.)

FIRST AMTENN CORP (TN)
Common $5 par split (2) for (1) by issuance of (1) additional share 11/16/72
Name changed to First American Corp. (TN) 1/1/81
First American Corp. (TN) merged into AmSouth Bancorporation

10/1/99 which merged into Regions Financial Corp. 11/4/2006

1ST ANYOX RES LTD (BC)
Name changed to Victory Resources Corp. 02/28/2005

FIRST ARIZONA SECURITY CORP. (AZ)
Completely liquidated 11/30/74
Each share Common $1 par exchanged for first and final distribution of $2.26 cash

FIRST ARK BANKSTOCK CORP (AR)
Common $12.50 par changed to $6.25 par and (1) additional share issued 04/06/1972
Stock Dividends - 10% 04/02/1975; 20% 03/16/1977; 10% 01/29/1982
Name changed to Worthen Banking Corp. 10/23/1984
Worthen Banking Corp. merged into Boatmen's Bancshares, Inc. 02/28/1995 which merged into NationsBank Corp. (NC) 01/07/1997 which reincorporated in Delaware as BankAmerica Corp. (Old) 09/30/1998 which name changed to Bank of America Corp. 04/28/1999

FIRST ARK CAP CORP (DE)
Adjustable Rate Preferred $1 par called for redemption 11/20/1990
Public interest eliminated

FIRST ARK FDG CORP (DE)
Capital Market Preferred no par called for redemption 03/21/1988
Public interest eliminated

FIRST ARTISTS PRODTN LTD (DE)
Stock Dividend - 20% 8/31/77
Acquired by Mascot Industries Ltd. 3/23/82
Each share Capital Stock 10¢ par exchanged for $6.25 cash

FIRST ASHLAND CORP (KY)
Merged into First American Corp. (TN) 2/28/86
Each share Common $1 par exchanged for (0.636) share Common $5 par
First American Corp. (TN) merged into AmSouth Bancorporation 10/1/99 which merged into Regions Financial Corp. 11/4/2006

FIRST ASHLAND FINL CORP (DE)
Merged into Camco Financial Corp. 10/04/1996
Each share Common 1¢ par exchanged for (0.67492) share Common $1 par and $8.93736 cash
Note: An additional final distribution of (0.12) share for each share held was made 01/17/1997
(See Camco Financial Corp.)

FIRST ASIA INCOME FD (ON)
Name changed to Ravensource Fund 09/30/2003

FIRST ASSET / BLACK ROCK NORTH AMERN DIVIDEND ACHIEVERS TR (ON)
Merged into Criterion Global Dividend Fund 12/29/2009
Each Unit received (0.73904) Class D Unit
Criterion Global Dividend Fund name changed to First Asset Global Dividend Fund 06/04/2012

FIRST ASSET ACTIVE CDN REIT ETF (ON)
Trust terminated 08/31/2015
Each Common Unit received $9.741 cash
Each Advisor Class Unit received $9.7335 cash

FIRST ASSET ACTIVE CR FD (ON)
Name changed 12/22/2014
Each Class A Unit received distribution of (1) Warrant expiring 07/23/2009 payable 03/19/2009 to holders of record 03/02/2009
Ex date - 02/26/2009
Name changed from First Asset Yield

Opportunity Trust to First Asset Active Credit Fund 12/22/2014
Merged into First Asset Active Credit ETF 01/19/2015
Each Class A Unit automatically became (1.10586) Common Units
Each Class B Unit automatically became (0.41337) Common Unit USD

FIRST ASSET ALL CDA BD BARBELL INDEX ETF (ON)
Name changed 06/09/2014
Name changed from First Asset DEX All Canada Bond Barbell Index ETF to First Asset All Canada Bond Barbell Index ETF 06/09/2014
Trust terminated 08/31/2015
Each Common Unit received $9.8031 cash
Each Advisor Class Unit received $9.7892 cash

FIRST ASSET CAMBRIDGE CORE CDN EQUITY ETF (ON)
Trust terminated 08/21/2017
Each Unit received $20.4581 cash

FIRST ASSET CAN-ENERGY COVERED CALL ETF (ON)
Each old Common Unit automatically became (0.25) new Common Unit 11/09/2015
Each old Advisor Class Unit automatically became (0.25) new Advisor Class Unit 11/09/2015
Each new Advisor Class Unit automatically became (1.009) new Common Units 07/14/2017
Trust terminated 02/15/2018
Each new Common Unit received $7.9843 cash

FIRST ASSET CAN-FINANCIALS COVERED CALL ETF
Trust terminated 08/31/2015
Each Common Unit received $8.8105 cash
Each Advisor Class Unit received $8.7976 cash

FIRST ASSET CAN-60 COVERED CALL ETF (ON)
Trust terminated 08/31/2015
Each Common Unit received $6.4577 cash
Each Advisor Class Unit received $6.4598 cash

FIRST ASSET CDN DIVID LOW VOLATILITY INDEX ETF (ON)
Trust terminated 06/11/2018
Each Unit received $19.7218 cash

FIRST ASSET CDN REIT INCOME FD (ON)
Name changed to First Asset Canadian REIT ETF 07/14/2015

FIRST ASSET CANBANC INCOME ETF (ON)
Under plan of reorganization each ETF Share automatically became (1) share First Asset Fund Corp. CanBanc Income Class ETF 05/04/2016

FIRST ASSET CANBANC SPLIT CORP (ON)
Fund terminated 01/15/2016
Each Preferred Share received $10.0268 cash
Each Class A Share received $30.1588 cash

FIRST ASSET CORE BALANCED ETF (ON)
Trust terminated 01/16/2017
Each Common Unit received $18.9537 cash
Each Advisor Unit received $18.9443 cash

FIRST ASSET CORE FD CORP (ON)
Under plan of reorganization each share Canadian Equity Income ETF automatically became (1) share First Asset Fund Corp. Core Canadian Equity Income Class ETF 05/04/2016

FIRST ASSET CORPORATE BD BARBELL INDEX ETF (ON)
Name changed 06/09/2014
Name changed from First Asset DEX Corporate Bond Barbell Index ETF to First Asset Corporate Bond Barbell Index ETF 06/09/2014
Trust terminated 08/31/2015
Each Common Unit received $9.7546 cash
Each Advisor Class Unit received $9.7387 cash

FIRST ASSET DEX 1-5 YR LADDERED GOVT STRIP BD INDEX ETF (ON)
Name changed to First Asset 1-5 Year Laddered Government Strip Bond Index ETF 06/09/2014

FIRST ASSET DIVERSIFIED COMMODITIES CURRENCY HEDGED FUND (ON)
Fund terminated 10/31/2012
Each Class A, B, C, D, E and F Unit received respective net asset value

FIRST ASSET ENERGY & RESOURCE FD (ON)
Trust terminated 07/31/2017
Each Unit of Ltd. Partnership received $15.7407 cash

FIRST ASSET ENERGY & RESOURCE INCOME & GROWTH FD (ON)
Merged into First Asset Energy & Resource Fund 10/04/2007
Each Unit of Ltd. Partnership no par received (1.4819) Units of Ltd. Partnership no par
(See First Asset Energy & Resource Fund)

FIRST ASSET EQUAL WEIGHT PIPES & PWR INCOME FD (ON)
Name changed to First Asset Pipes & Power Income Fund 06/27/2006
First Asset Pipes & Power Income Fund name changed to First Asset Active Utility & Infrastructure ETF 01/16/2015

FIRST ASSET EQUAL WEIGHT REIT INCOME FD (ON)
Name changed to First Asset REIT Income Fund 08/31/2007
First Asset REIT Income Fund name changed to First Asset Canadian REIT Income Fund 06/22/2012 which name changed to First Asset Canadian REIT ETF 07/14/2015

FIRST ASSET EQUAL WEIGHT SMALL-CAP INCOME FD (ON)
Under plan of merger each Unit automatically became (0.6581) First Asset Equal Weight REIT Income Fund Unit 09/29/2006
First Asset Equal Weight REIT Income Fund name changed to First Asset REIT Income Fund 08/31/2007 which name changed to First Asset Canadian REIT Income Fund 06/22/2012 which name changed to First Asset Canadian REIT ETF 07/14/2015

FIRST ASSET FD CORP (ON)
Trust terminated 01/16/2017
Each share Global Momentum (CAD Hedged) Class ETF received $22.1589 cash
Each share Global Momentum Class ETF received $21.2517 cash
Each share Global Value (CAD Hedged) Class ETF received $25.2674 cash
Each share Global Value Class ETF received $24.2384 cash
(Additional Information in Active)

FIRST ASSET GLOBAL INFRASTUCTURE FD (ON)
Merged into Criterion Water Infrastructure Fund 12/29/2009
Each Unit received (0.95348) Class D Unit
Criterion Water Infrastructure Fund name changed to First Asset Utility Plus Fund 06/04/2012

FIRST ASSET GOVT BD BARBELL INDEX ETF (ON)
Name changed 06/09/2014
Name changed from First Asset DEX Government Bond Barbell Index ETF to First Asset Government Bond Barbell Index ETF 06/09/2014
Trust terminated 08/31/2015
Each Common Unit received $9.8812 cash
Each Advisor Class Unit received $9.8666 cash

FIRST ASSET HAMILTON CAP EUROPEAN BK ETF (ON)
Name changed to First Asset European Bank ETF 11/28/2016

FIRST ASSET HAMILTON CAP EUROPEAN BK FD (ON)
Name changed to First Asset Global Financial Sector ETF 04/25/2016

FIRST ASSET INCOME & GROWTH FD (ON)
Merged into Criterion Global Dividend Fund 12/29/2009
Each Unit received (1.01086) Class D Units
Criterion Global Dividend Fund name changed to First Asset Global Dividend Fund 06/04/2012

FIRST ASSET MGMT CORP (NY)
Reincorporated under the laws of Delaware as Largo Group, Ltd. 8/17/73
(See Largo Group, Ltd.)

FIRST ASSET MORNINGSTAR EMERGING MKTS COMPOSITE BD INDEX ETF (ON)
Trust terminated 08/31/2015
Each Common Unit received $8.7107 cash
Each Advisor Class Unit received $8.7016 cash

FIRST ASSET MORNINGSTAR U S CONSUMER DEFENSIVE INDEX FD (ON)
Name changed 04/03/2013
Name changed from First Asset Advantaged Morningstar U.S. Consumer Defensive Index Fund to First Asset Morningstar U.S. Consumer Defensive Index Fund 04/03/2013
Under plan of merger each Unit automatically became (0.562572) First Asset MSCI USA Low Risk Weighted ETF Common Unit 09/14/2018

FIRST ASSET OPPORTUNITY FD (ON)
Fund terminated 12/05/2007
Each Unit received $2.06 cash

FIRST ASSET PIPES & PWR INCOME FD (ON)
Each Unit no par received distribution of (1) Warrant expiring 07/23/2009 payable 03/19/2009 to holders of record 03/02/2009 Ex date - 02/26/2009
Name changed to First Asset Active Utility & Infrastructure ETF and Units reclassified as Common Units 01/16/2015

FIRST ASSET PWR FD (ON)
Merged into Sprott Power Corp. 02/03/2011
Each Unit no par received (5.35402342) shares Common no par
Sprott Power Corp. name changed to Renewable Energy Developers Inc. 07/02/2013 which merged into Capstone Infrastructure Corp. 10/07/2013

FIRST ASSET POWERGEN TR I (ON)
Name changed to FA Power Fund 03/14/2007
FA Power Fund merged into First Asset PowerGen Fund 06/18/2008 which merged into Sprott Power Corp. 02/03/2011 which name changed to Renewable Energy Developers Inc. 07/02/2013 which merged into Capstone Infrastructure Corp. 10/07/2013

FIRST ASSET POWERGEN TR III (ON)
Name changed to First Asset PowerGen Fund 03/14/2007
First Asset PowerGen Fund merged into Sprott Power Corp. 02/03/2011 which name changed to Renewable Energy Developers Inc. 07/02/2013 which merged into Capstone Infrastructure Corp. 10/07/2013

FIRST ASSET PROVINCIAL BD ETF (ON)
Name changed 06/09/2014
Name changed from First Asset DEX Provincial Bond Index ETF to First Asset Provincial Bond Index ETF 06/09/2014
Trust terminated 01/16/2017
Each Common Unit received $9.8869 cash
Each Advisor Unit received $9.8821 cash

FIRST ASSET REIT INCOME FD (ON)
Each Unit received distribution of (1) Warrant expiring 07/23/2009 payable 03/03/2009 to holders of record 03/02/2009 Ex date - 02/26/2009
Name changed to First Asset Canadian REIT Income Fund 06/22/2012
First Asset Canadian REIT Income Fund name changed to First Asset Canadian REIT ETF 07/14/2015

FIRST ASSET U S & CDA LIFECO INCOME FD (ON)
Name changed to First Asset U.S. & Canada LifeCo Income ETF and Units reclassified as Common Units 09/03/2014

FIRST ASSET U S EQUITY MULTI-FACTOR INDEX ETF (ON)
Trust terminated 06/11/2018
Each Unit received $22.7839 cash

FIRST AT ORLANDO CORP (FL)
Common $5 par changed to $2.50 par and (1) additional share issued 12/15/1969
Name changed to Sun Banks of Florida, Inc. 04/12/1974
Sun Banks of Florida, Inc. name changed to Sun Banks, Inc. 05/02/1983 which merged into SunTrust Banks, Inc. 07/01/1985

FIRST ATLANTA CORP (GA)
Common $5 par split (3) for (2) by issuance of (0.5) additional share 12/31/1981
Common $5 par split (3) for (2) by issuance of (0.5) additional share 09/30/1983
Common $5 par split (3) for (2) by issuance of (0.5) additional share 03/28/1985
Merged into First Wachovia Corp. 12/05/1985
Each share Common $5 par exchanged for (0.8) share Common $5 par
Adjustable Rate Preferred Ser. A $25 par called for redemption 11/01/1987
First Wachovia Corp. name changed to Wachovia Corp. (New) (Ctfs. dated between 05/20/1991 and 09/01/2001) 05/20/1991 which merged into Wachovia Corp. (Ctfs. dated after 09/01/2001) 09/01/2001 which merged into Wells Fargo & Co. (New) 12/31/2008

FIRST ATLANTIC ENTERPRISES INC (FL)
Proclaimed dissolved for failure to file reports and pay fees 11/9/90

FIRST ATLANTIC NATL BK (DAYTONA BEACH, FL)
Stock Dividends - 100% 01/25/1949; 100% 03/07/1955; 25% 01/29/1957; 16-2/3% 01/20/1959; 42% 01/12/1962
Through voluntary exchange offer 99.5% held by Atlantic Bancorporation as of 10/22/1973
Public interest eliminated

FIRST ATLAS CORP (FL)
Recapitalized as First Allied Corp. 07/06/1973
Each share Common 10¢ par exchanged for (0.2) share Common 1¢ par
(See First Allied Corp.)

FIRST AU STRATEGIES CORP (YT)
Name changed to Cangold Ltd. (YT) 06/04/2003
Cangold Ltd. (YT) reincorporated in British Columbia 12/22/2004 which merged into Great Panther Silver Ltd. 05/27/2015

FIRST AUGUST FINL CORP (OR)
Name changed to Mortgage Bankers Service Corp. N.A. 02/20/1996
Mortgage Bankers Service Corp. N.A. name changed to Harcourt-Symes Ltd. (OR) 05/03/1996 which reincorporated in Nevada as Nordic American Inc. 06/09/1997 which reorganized in Delaware as Stark Beneficial, Inc. 02/08/2008 which name changed to China Greenstar Corp. 01/22/2015

FIRST AUSTRALIA FD INC (MD)
Name changed to Aberdeen Australia Equity Fund, Inc. 5/1/2001

FIRST AUSTRALIA MUT FDS INC (MD)
Name changed to Keystone Australia Funds Inc. 01/01/1992
Keystone Australia Funds Inc. merged into Keystone America World Bond Fund 12/30/1994 which merged into Keystone America Strategic Income Fund (MA) 07/01/1997 which reincorporated in Delaware as Evergreen Strategic Income Fund 10/31/1997

FIRST AUSTRALIA PRIME INCOME FD INC (MD)
Name changed to Aberdeen Asia-Pacific Income Fund Inc. 05/01/2001

FIRST AUSTRALIA PRIME INCOME INVT LTD (COOK ISLANDS)
Name changed to Aberdeen Asia-Pacific Income Investment Co. Ltd. 5/15/2001

FIRST AUSTRALIAN RES N L (AUSTRALIA)
Name changed to FAR Ltd. 08/05/2011

FIRST AUTOMATED INC (UT)
Recapitalized as PBHG, Inc. 07/19/2004
Each share Common 6¢ par exchanged for (0.00333333) share Common 6¢ par
(See PBHG, Inc.)

FIRST AVE NETWORKS INC (DE)
Name changed to FiberTower Corp. 08/29/2006
(See FiberTower Corp.)

FIRST AVIATION SVCS INC (DE)
Each share Common 1¢ par exchanged for (1) share Class A Common 1¢ par 01/08/2010
Each share Class A Common 1¢ par exchanged for (0.05) share Class A Common 20¢ par 10/17/2011
Each share Class B Common 1¢ par exchanged for (0.05) share Class B Common 20¢ par 10/17/2011
Each share old Class A Common 20¢ par exchanged for (1) share new Class A Common 20¢ par to reflect a (1) for (10,000) reverse split followed by a (10,000) for (1) forward split 05/30/2014
Note: In effect holders received $8.40 cash per share and public interest was eliminated

FIRST B SHARES INC (ON)
Equity Dividend Shares no par called for redemption 04/23/1996

FIRST BANC GROUP OHIO INC (DE)
Common no par split (2) for (1) by issuance of (1) additional share 3/31/70
Stock Dividends - 10% 1/2/70; 10% 2/29/72; 10% 2/28/74; 10% 3/19/76; 10% 3/17/78
Name changed to Banc One Corp. (DE) 10/22/79
Banc One Corp. (DE) reincorporated in Ohio 5/1/89 which merged into Bank One Corp. 10/2/98 which merged into J.P. Morgan Chase & Co. 12/31/2000 which name changed to JPMorgan Chase & Co. 7/20/2004

FIRST BANC SECS INC (WV)
Common $5 par split (2) for (1) by issuance of (1) additional share 5/1/85
Common $5 par split (2) for (1) by issuance of (1) additional share 5/1/86
Merged into Huntington Bancshares Inc. 12/29/89
Each share Common $5 par exchanged for (1.62733) shares Common no par

FIRST BANCGROUP ALA INC (DE)
Name changed to Firstgulf Bancorp 3/30/84
(See Firstgulf Bancorp)

FIRST BANCORP BELLEVILLE INC (DE)
Common $12.50 par changed to $4 par and (2) additional shares issued 10/1/77
Name changed to Magna Group, Inc. 4/26/83
Magna Group, Inc. merged into Union Planters Corp. 7/1/98 which merged into Regions Financial Corp. (New) 7/1/2004

FIRST BANCORP INC. (DE)
Common $10 par changed to $2 par and (4) additional shares issued 2/21/72
Common $2 par changed to $1 par and (1) additional share issued 10/4/78
Merged into First International Bancshares, Inc. 9/11/81
Each share Common $1 par exchanged for (0.95238) share Common $5 par
First International Bancshares, Inc. name changed to InterFirst Corp. 12/31/81 which merged into First RepublicBank Corp. 6/6/87
(See First RepublicBank Corp.)

FIRST BANCORP INC (FL)
Name changed to Orion Bancorp, Inc. 12/16/2002
(See Orion Bancorp, Inc.)

FIRST BANCORP INC (PA)
Acquired by PNC Financial Corp. 02/29/1988
Each share Common $2 par exchanged for (1.9) shares Common $5 par
PNC Financial Corp. name changed to PNC Bank Corp. 02/08/1993 which name changed to PNC Financial Services Group, Inc. 03/15/2000

FIRST BANCORP IND INC OLD (IN)
Common no par split (3) for (2) by issuance of (0.5) additional share 5/29/92
Acquired by Huntington Bancshares Inc. 11/27/93
Each share Common no par exchanged for (1.9772) shares Common no par

1ST BANCORP (IN)
Common $1 par split (5) for (4) by issuance of (0.25) additional share 7/15/92
Stock Dividends - 5% payable 2/9/96 to holders of record 1/26/96; 5% payable 1/10/97 to holders of record 12/27/96; 5% payable 1/23/98 to holders of record 1/9/98
Merged into German American Bancorp 1/4/99
Each share Common $1 par exchanged for (1.8185) shares Common no par
German American Bancorp name changed to German American Bancorp Inc. 5/22/2006

FIRST BANCORP KANS (KS)
Common $100 par changed to $5 par and (19) additional shares issued 5/5/86
Name changed to Intrust Financial Corp. in May 1993
(See Intrust Financial Corp.)

FIRST BANCORP N H INC (NH)
Stock Dividends - 10% 05/15/1979; 10% 02/13/1981; 10% 11/16/1981; 100% 10/01/1982
Name changed to First NH Banks, Inc. 04/19/1983
(See First NH Banks, Inc.)

FIRST BANCORPORATION (NV)
Name changed to Nevada National Bancorporation 06/03/1976
(See Nevada National Bancorporation)

FIRST BANCORPORATION CLEVELAND INC (OH)
Merged into DSB Acquisition Corp. 1/22/99
Each share Common no par exchanged for $1.78 cash

FIRST BANCORPORATION INC (WI)
Common $1 par split (2) for (1) by issuance of (1) additional share payable 4/23/99 to holders of record 4/9/99 Ex date - 4/26/99
Each (3,700) shares old Common $1 par exchanged for (1) share new Common $1 par 11/21/2002
Note: In effect holders received $30.25 cash per share and public interest was eliminated

FIRST BANCORPORATION OHIO INC (OH)
Common $10 par changed to $5 par and (1) additional share issued 12/13/1985
Common $5 par changed to $3.33333333 par and (0.5) additional share issued 12/12/1986
Common $3.33333333 par changed to no par 04/14/1993
Common no par split (2) for (1) by issuance of (1) additional share 09/27/1993
Name changed to FirstMerit Corp. 12/26/1994
FirstMerit Corp. merged into Huntington Bancshares Inc. 08/16/2016

FIRST BANCSHARES CORP ILL (DE)
Acquired by Mercantile Bancorporation, Inc. 02/17/1987
Each share Common $5 par exchanged for (1.6254) shares Common $5 par
Mercantile Bancorporation, Inc. merged into Firstar Corp. (New) 09/20/1999 which merged into U.S. Bancorp (DE) 02/27/2001

FIRST BANCSHARES FLA INC (FL)
Common $1 par split (2) for (1) by issuance of (1) additional share 03/11/1971
Common $1 par split (3) for (2) by issuance of (0.5) additional share 04/20/1973
Under plan of reorganization each share Common $1 par exchanged for (1) share Gulfstream Banks, Inc. Common $1 par and (0.1009) share Southeast Banking Corp. $4.06 Conv. Preferred no par 12/31/1979
(See each company's listing)

FIRST BANCSHARES INC (CA)
Merged into Pacific Capital Bancorp (New) 07/25/2005
Each share Common no par exchanged for $48 cash

FIRST BANCSHARES INC OKLA (DE)
Merged into FB Merger, Inc. 10/20/1998
Details not available

FIRST BANCSHARES LA INC (LA)
Common $5 par split (3) for (2) by issuance of (0.5) additional share 5/24/84
Stock Dividends - 10% 6/30/82; 100% 3/22/83
Merged into Louisiana Bancshares, Inc. 1/10/85
Each share Common $5 par exchanged for (1) share Common no par
Louisiana Bancshares, Inc. name changed to Premier Bancorp, Inc. 4/15/87 which merged into Banc One Corp. 1/2/96 which merged into Bank One Corp. 10/2/98 which merged into J.P. Morgan Chase & Co. 12/31/2000 which name changed to JPMorgan Chase & Co. 7/20/2004

FIRST BANCSHARES TEX INC (TX)
Preferred Ser. B called for redemption at $10 on 12/31/96
Merged into Regions Financial Corp. (Old) 11/30/2001
Each share Common $1 par exchanged for (0.589) share Common $0.625 par
Regions Financial Corp. (Old) merged into Regions Financial Corp. (New) 7/1/2004

FIRST BANCTRUST CORP (DE)
Common 1¢ par split (2) for (1) by issuance of (1) additional share payable 05/21/2004 to holders of record 04/30/2004 Ex date - 05/24/2004
Under plan of merger holders of (249) or fewer shares exchanged for $11 cash per share 10/22/2008
Merged into First Mid-Illinois Bancshares, Inc. 05/01/2018
Each share Common 1¢ par exchanged for (0.8) share Common $4 par and $5 cash

FIRST BK & TRUST (BRYAN, TX)
Reorganized as First Financial Bancorporation, Inc. 10/14/1980
Each share Common $5 par exchanged for (1.04415) shares Common no par
First Financial Bancorporation, Inc. name changed to United Bankers Inc. 09/24/1981
(See United Bankers Inc.)

FIRST BK & TR (CLEVELAND, OH)
Name changed to First Bank N.A. (Cleveland, OH) 1/22/76
First Bank N.A. (Cleveland, OH) reorganized as First Intercity Banc Corp. 5/6/83
(See First Intercity Banc Corp.)

FIRST BANK & TRUST CO. (BELLEAIR BLUFFS, FL)
Merged into First Florida Banks, Inc. 02/01/1985
Each share Common Capital Stock $5 par exchanged for $75.176 cash

FIRST BANK & TRUST CO. (MADISON, NJ)
Merged into Trust Co. of Morris County (Morristown, NJ) 12/19/1958

Each share Capital Stock $20 par exchanged for (1.666666) shares Capital Stock $20 par
Trust Co. of Morris County (Morristown, NJ) name changed to Trust Co. National Bank (Morristown, NJ) 01/27/1967 which merged into American National Bank & Trust (Montclair, NJ) 07/10/1970 which reorganized as Princeton American Bancorp 01/01/1972 which name changed to Horizon Bancorp 12/31/1973
(See Horizon Bancorp)

FIRST BANK & TRUST CO. (PERTH AMBOY, NJ)
Stock Dividends - 100% 11/15/1948; 100% 11/03/1949; 100% 02/01/1955
Name changed to First Bank & Trust Co., N.A. (Fords, NJ) 01/31/1964
First Bank & Trust Co., N.A. (Fords, NJ) merged into National State Bank (Elizabeth, NJ) 08/18/1969 which reorganized as Constellation Bancorp 03/08/1958 which merged into CoreStates Financial Corp 03/16/1994 which merged into First Union Corp. 04/28/1998 which name changed to Wachovia Corp. (Ctfs. dated after 09/01/2001) 09/01/2001 which merged into Wells Fargo & Co. (New) 12/31/2008

FIRST BANK & TRUST CO. (SOUTH BEND, IN)
Each share Capital Stock $100 par exchanged for (5) shares Capital Stock $20 par 00/00/1941
Each share Capital Stock $20 par exchanged for (2) shares Capital Stock $10 par 00/00/1945
Stock Dividends - 33-1/3% 12/00/1945; 25% 01/25/1956; 10% 02/12/1960; 20% 10/10/1963
100% held by Associates Investment Co. through voluntary exchange offer as of 01/02/1964
Public interest eliminated

FIRST BK & TR CO (ASHLAND, KY)
Under plan of reorganization each share Capital Stock $10 par automatically became (1) share First Ashland Corp. Common $1 par 7/1/82
First Ashland Corp. merged into First American Corp. (TN) 2/28/86 which merged into AmSouth Bancorporation 10/1/99 which merged into Regions Financial Corp. 11/4/2006

FIRST BK & TR CO (CAIRO, IL)
Each share Capital Stock $100 par exchanged for (5) shares Capital Stock $20 par 08/10/1960
Stock Dividends - 50% 02/15/1968; 60% 02/07/1975
Acquired by Mid America Bank, N.A. (Davenport, IA) 06/01/1993
Details not available

FIRST BK & TR CO (HAVERHILL, MA)
Merged into Massachusetts Bay Bancorp, Inc. 12/29/72
Each share Capital Stock $5 par exchanged for (0.606060) share Common $1 par
Massachusetts Bay Bancorp, Inc. merged into New England Merchants Co., Inc. 5/31/80 which name changed to Bank of New England Corp. 5/1/82
(See Bank of New England Corp.)

FIRST BK & TR CO (JACKSONVILLE, FL)
Name changed to Southeast First Bank (Jacksonville, FL) 04/30/1971
(See Southeast First Bank (Jacksonville, FL))

FIRST BK & TR CO HAMPDEN CNTY (SPRINGFIELD, MA)
Through exchange offer 98.7%

acquired by Shawmut Association, Inc. 12/31/1969
Public interest eliminated

FIRST BK & TR CO N A (BOCA RATON, FL)
Stock Dividend - 10% 02/05/1968
100% acquired by First Bancshares of Florida, Inc. through voluntary exchange offers as 05/31/1972
Public interest eliminated

FIRST BK & TR CO N A (FORDS, NJ)
Common $10 par changed to $5 par and (1) additional share issued 07/14/1964
Merged into National State Bank (Elizabeth, NJ) 08/18/1969
Each share Common $5 par exchanged for (1) share Common $5 par
National State Bank (Elizabeth, NJ) reorganized as Constellation Bancorp 03/08/1985 which merged into CoreStates Financial Corp 03/16/1994 which merged into First Union Corp. 04/28/1998 which name changed to Wachovia Corp. (Ctfs. dated after 09/01/2001) 09/01/2001 which merged into Wells Fargo & Co. (New) 12/31/2008

FIRST BANK (HOUSTON, TX)
Merged into First State Bank of Texas (Houston, TX) 8/11/2000
Each share Common no par exchanged for $65 cash

FIRST BK (MARIETTA, OH)
Merged into First Bank of Ohio (Tiffin, OH) 9/30/99
Each share Common exchanged for (0.2) share Common

FIRST BK (WILLIAMSTOWN, NJ)
Location changed to (Hamilton, NJ) 02/01/2012

FIRST BK CENT JERSEY (NORTH BRUNSWICK, NJ)
Acquired by Synergy Financial Group 1/10/2003
Each share Common $5 par exchanged for $2.82 cash

FIRST BK COLONIA (COLONIA, NJ)
Acquired by Commercial Bancshares, Inc. (NJ) 1/31/86
Each share Common $5 par exchanged for (1.558) shares Common $5 par
Commercial Bancshares, Inc. (NJ) merged into United Jersey Banks 12/1/86 which name changed to UJB Financial Corp. 6/30/89 which name changed to Summit Bancorp 3/1/96 which merged into FleetBoston Financial Corp. 3/1/2001 which merged into Bank of America Corp. 4/1/2004

FIRST BK CORP (MI)
Merged into Detroitbank Corp. 07/01/1981
Each share Common $5 par exchanged for $42 cash

FIRST BK DEER PK (DEER PARK, TX)
Merged into Bayshore National Bank (La Porte, TX) 11/21/97
Each share Common $5 par exchanged for $69.0043 cash

FIRST BK DEL (WILMINGTON, DE)
Assets transferred to FBD Liquidating Trust and each share Common 5¢ par automatically became (1) Unit of Bene. Int. 11/16/2012
(See FBD Liquidating Trust)

FIRST BK FREDERICK MD (FREDERICK, MD)
Under plan of reorganization each share Common $10 par automatically became (1) share First Frederick Financial Corp. Common $1 par 8/5/96
First Frederick Financial Corp. merged into FCNB Corp. 8/19/99

which merged into BB&T Corp. 1/8/2001

FIRST BK GREATER PITTSTON (PITTSTON, PA)
Capital Stock $5 par split (5) for (1) by issuance of (4) additional shares 03/18/1974
Capital Stock $5 par changed to $2.50 par and (1) additional share issued 04/18/1986
Merged into Commonwealth Bancshares Corp. 11/01/1990
Each share Capital Stock $2.50 par exchanged for (3.6) shares Common $3.50 par
Commonwealth Bancshares Corp. acquired by Meridian Bancorp, Inc. 08/31/1993 which merged into CoreStates Financial Corp 04/09/1996 which merged into First Union Corp. 04/28/1998 which name changed to Wachovia Corp. (Ctfs. dated after 09/01/2001) 09/01/2001 which merged into Wells Fargo & Co. (New) 12/31/2008

FIRST BK IMMOKALEE (IMMOKALEE, FL)
Under plan of merger name changed to Florida Community Bank (Immokalee, FL) 07/26/1996
Florida Community Bank (Immokalee, FL) reorganized as Florida Community Banks, Inc. 04/16/2002
(See Florida Community Banks, Inc.)

FIRST BK N A (CLEVELAND, OH)
Reorganized as First Intercity Banc Corp. 5/6/83
Each share Common $4 par exchanged for (1) share Class A Common $4 par
(See First Intercity Banc Corp.)

FIRST BK NEW HAVEN (NEW HAVEN, CT)
Under plan of reorganization each share Common $5 par automatically became (1) share FirstBancorp, Inc. (CT) Common $5 par 2/1/79
FirstBancorp, Inc. (CT) merged into Hartford National Corp. 3/30/84 which merged into Shawmut National Corp. 2/29/88 which merged into Fleet Financial Group Inc. (New) 11/30/95 which name changed to Fleet Boston Corp. 10/1/99 which name changed to FleetBoston Financial Corp. 4/18/2000 which merged into Bank of America Corp. 4/1/2004

FIRST BANK OF CORDOVA (CORDOVA, AK)
Merged into National Bank of Alaska (Anchorage, Alaska) 6/2/75
Each share Common $10 par exchanged for (1.7) shares Common $10 par
National Bank of Alaska (Anchorage, Alaska) reorganized as National Bancorp of Alaska, Inc. 12/1/82

FIRST BANK OF HIALEAH GARDENS, N.A. (HIALEAH GARDENS, FL)
Name changed to Tower Bank, N.A. (Hialeah Gardens, FL) 06/03/1983
(See Tower Bank, N.A. (Hialeah Gardens, FL))

FIRST BANK OF HOLLYWOOD BEACH (HOLLYWOOD, FL)
Name changed to First American Bank of Broward County (Hollywood, FL) 8/1/81
First American Bank of Broward County (Hollywood, FL) merged into First American Bank of Palm Beach County (North Palm Beach, FL) 9/1/82 which name changed to First American Bank & Trust of Palm Beach County (North Palm Beach, FL) 9/2/82
(See First American Bank & Trust of Palm Beach County (North Palm Beach, FL))

FIRST BANK OF NORTH DAKOTA N.A. (FARGO, ND)
Acquired by First Bank, FSB (Fargo, ND) 02/21/1995
Details not available

FIRST BANK OF OAK PARK (OAK PARK, IL)
Acquired by Park National Bank (Chicago, IL) 01/01/2006
Details not available

FIRST BANK OF OAKLAND PARK (OAKLAND PARK, FL)
Name changed to Capital Bank of Broward County (Oakland Park, Fla.) 8/6/82
(See Capital Bank of Broward County (Oakland Park, Fla.))

FIRST BK PHILADELPHIA (PHILADELPHIA, PA)
Each share old Common 25¢ par exchanged for (0.1) share new Common 25¢ par 7/31/95
Merged into PSB Bancorp Inc. 10/12/99
Each share new Common 25¢ par exchanged for (0.857) share Common $1 par
(See PSB Bancorp Inc.)

FIRST BK PLANTATION (PLANTATION, FL)
Common $10 par changed to $5 par 03/30/1971
99.8434% acquired by Barnett Banks of Florida, Inc. through exchange offer which expired 09/19/1977
Public interest eliminated

FIRST BK SAN LUIS OBISPO (SAN LUIS OBISPO, CA)
Under plan of reorganization each share Common no par automatically became (1) share First Bancshares Inc. Common no par 7/1/99
(See First Bancshares Inc.)

FIRST BANK STOCK CORP. (DE)
Common $25 par changed to $10 par 00/00/1934
Common $10 par changed to $5 par and (1) additional share issued 05/18/1964
Name changed to First Bank System, Inc. 05/03/1968
First Bank System, Inc. name changed to U.S. Bancorp 08/01/1997

FIRST BK SYS INC (DE)
Common $5 par changed to $2.50 par and (1) additional share issued 05/19/1971
Common $2.50 par changed to $1.25 par and (1) additional share issued 05/17/1984
Common $1.25 par split (2) for (1) by issuance of (1) additional share 12/22/1986
Adjustable Rate Preferred Ser. 1983A $1 par called for redemption at $100.4875 plus accrued dividends on 10/27/1993
10.50% Preferred Ser. 1989A $1 par called for redemption 04/01/1994
Adjustable Rate Preferred Ser. 1989B $1 par called for redemption 04/01/1994
$3.5625 Conv. Preferred Ser 1991A $1 par called for redemption 12/31/1996
Under plan of merger name changed to U.S. Bancorp 08/01/1997

FIRST BK TR (BRIGHTON, CO)
Name changed 11/6/69
Name changed from First Bank of Brighton (Brighton, CO) to First Bank & Trust Co. (Brighton, CO) 11/6/69
Acquired by United Banks of Colorado, Inc. for cash 4/1/82
Details not available

FIRST BK WEST HARTFORD (HARTFORD, CT)
Merged into New England Community Bancorp, Inc. 8/8/97
Each share Common 1¢ par exchanged for (0.62) share Class A Common 10¢ par
New England Community Bancorp, Inc. merged into Webster Financial Corp. 12/1/99

FIRST BANKAMERICANO (ELIZABETH, NJ)
Under plan of reorganization each share Common no par automatically became (1) share First Americano Financial Corp. Common no par 04/02/2008
(See First Americano Financial Corp.)

FIRST BANKERS CORP FLA (FL)
Common $1 par split (5) for (4) by issuance of (0.25) additional share 06/28/1985
Stock Dividend - 10% 12/01/1980
Acquired by First Union Corp. 05/17/1986
Each share Common $1 par exchanged for $41 cash

FIRST BANKERS TR & SVGS ASSN (TX)
Placed in receivership 06/08/1990
No stockholders' equity

FIRST BKS AMER INC (DE)
Merged into First Banks, Inc. 12/31/2002
Each share Common 15¢ par exchanged for $40.54 cash

FIRST BKS INC (MO)
Increasing Rate Class C Preferred $1 par called for redemption at $25 on 12/01/1997
Public interest eliminated

FIRST BANKSHARES CORP S C (SC)
Stock Dividends - 20% 03/01/1971; 25% 12/28/1972; 25% 08/29/1977; 10% 09/29/1980
Completely liquidated 12/01/1984
Each share Common $5 par received first and final distribution of (0.4286) share South Carolina National Corp. Common $5 par and $48 cash
Note: Certificates were not required to be surrendered and are now valueless
South Carolina National Corp. merged into Wachovia Corp. (New) (Ctfs. dated between 05/20/1991 and 09/01/2001) 12/06/1991 which merged into Wachovia Corp. (Ctfs. dated after 09/01/2001) 09/01/2001 which merged into Wells Fargo & Co. (New) 12/31/2008

FIRST BANKSHARES INC (GA)
Merged into Regions Financial Corp. (Old) 6/1/97
Each share Common $1 par exchanged for (0.32) share Common $0.625 par
Regions Financial Corp. (Old) merged into Regions Financial Corp. (New) 7/1/2004

FIRST BANKSHARES INC (VA)
Merged into Xenith Bankshares, Inc. (Old) 12/22/2009
Each share Common $3.20 par exchanged for (1) share Common $1 par
Xenith Bankshares, Inc. (Old) merged into Xenith Bankshares, Inc. (New) 08/01/2016 which merged into Union Bankshares Corp. 01/01/2018

FIRST BANKSHARES WEST PT INC (GA)
Merged into Capital City Bank Group, Inc. 3/5/2001
Each share Common exchanged for (3.6419) shares Common 1¢ par and $17.7543 cash

FIRST BANKSHARES WYO (WY)
Merged into Wyoming National Corp. 12/15/1981
Each share Common no par exchanged for (0.44) share Common $1 par
Wyoming National Corp. name changed to Affiliated Bank Corp. of Wyoming 12/15/1981 which name changed to Wyoming National Bancorp 06/28/1988
(See Wyoming National Bancorp)

FIRST BATH CORP. (PA)
Merged into Meridian Bancorp, Inc. 12/10/1993
Each share Common $10 par exchanged for (1.45) shares Common $5 par
Meridian Bancorp, Inc. merged into CoreStates Financial Corp 04/09/1996 which merged into First Union Corp. 04/28/1998 which name changed to Wachovia Corp. (Ctfs. dated after 09/01/2001) 09/01/2001 which merged into Wells Fargo & Co. (New) 12/31/2008

FIRST BEATRICE CORP. (NE)
Voluntarily dissolved 12/29/72
Details not available

FIRST BEAUMONT CORP. (TX)
Stock issued as part of a Unit with First Security National Corp. Common $5 par represented by both names printed on the same certificate
First Beaumont Corp. merged into First Security National Corp. and each unit exchanged for (1) share First Security National Corp. Common $5 par 9/30/69
First Security National Corp. merged into First City Bancorporation of Texas, Inc. (TX) 12/3/79
(See First City Bancorporation of Texas, Inc. (TX))

FIRST BELL BANCORP INC (DE)
Merged into Northwest Merger Subsidary, Inc. 8/29/2003
Each share Common 1¢ par exchanged for $26.25 cash

FIRST BELLEFONTE BANK & TRUST CO. (BELLEFONTE, PA)
Merged into Mid-State Bank & Trust Co. (Altoona, PA) 12/31/65
Each share Capital Stock $10 par exchanged for (1.125) shares Capital Stock $10 par
Mid-State Bank & Trust Co. (Altoona, PA) reorganized as Mid-State Bancorp Inc. 1/12/82 which merged into Keystone Financial, Inc. 12/31/84 which merged into M&T Bank Corp. 10/6/2000

1ST BERGEN BANCORP (NJ)
Merged into Kearny Federal Savings Bank (Kearny, NJ) 3/31/99
Each share Common no par exchanged for $24 cash

FIRST BEVERLY BK (BEVERLY HILLS, CA)
Name changed to Capital Bank of California (Los Angeles, CA) in September 1985
(See Capital Bank of California (Los Angeles, CA))

FIRST BKG CO SOUTHEAST GA (GA)
Common $1 par split (8) for (5) by issuance of (0.6) additional share 5/15/95
Common $1 par split (5) for (4) by issuance of (0.25) additional share payable 6/30/97 to holders of record 6/15/97
Common $1 par split (5) for (4) by issuance of (0.25) additional share payable 5/29/98 to holders of record 5/15/98
Merged into BB&T Corp. 6/15/2000
Each share Common $1 par exchanged for (0.74) share Common $5 par

FIRST BKG CTR INC (WI)
Each share old Common $1 par exchanged for (0.0005) share new Common $1 par 01/31/2005
Note: Minority holders received $60 cash per share Administratively dissolved 09/10/2013

FIRST BLDRS BANCORP (CA)
Stock Dividend - 50% 10/28/1971
Name changed to American Magnetics Corp. 01/30/1980
American Magnetics Corp. name changed to Damon Group Inc. 04/05/1990 which liquidated for Damon Corp. (New) 08/29/1991
(See Damon Corp. (New))

FIRST BOND TRUST SHARES
Trust Agreement terminated in 1935
Details not available

FIRST BOSTON CORP (MA)
Each share Capital Stock $100 par exchanged for (10) shares Capital Stock $10 par 00/00/1934
Capital Stock $10 par changed to $6.66-2/3 par and (0.5) additional share issued 05/10/1968
Capital Stock $6.66-2/3 par changed to $3.33-1/3 par and (1) additional share issued 05/21/1969
Capital Stock $3.33-1/3 par changed to $1.66-2/3 par and (1) additional share issued 05/15/1972
Reincorporated under the laws of Delaware as First Boston Inc. 04/30/1976
(See First Boston Inc.)

FIRST BOSTON INC (DE)
Capital Stock $1.66-2/3 par reclassified as Common no par 5/3/83
Common no par split (2) for (1) by issuance of (1) additional share 5/4/83
Common no par split (2) for (1) by issuance of (1) additional share 7/17/85
Stock Dividend - 10% 1/15/82
Merged into CS First Boston, Inc. 12/22/88
Each share Common no par exchanged for $52.50 cash
Note: In addition holders will receive (1) Non-transferable Deferred Cash Consideration Right for possible additional payments

FIRST BOSTON INCOME FD INC (MD)
Name changed to CS First Boston Income Fund, Inc. 05/18/1994
CS First Boston Income Fund, Inc. name changed to BEA Income Fund, Inc. 07/31/1995 which name changed to Credit Suisse Asset Management Income Fund, Inc. 05/11/1999

FIRST BOSTON STRATEGIC INCOME FD INC (MD)
Name changed to CS First Boston Strategic Income Fund, Inc. 05/18/1994
CS First Boston Strategic Income Fund, Inc. name changed to BEA Strategic Income Fund, Inc. 07/31/1995 which name changed to BEA Strategic Global Income Fund, Inc. 05/13/1997 which name changed to Credit Suisse Asset Management Strategic Global Income Fund, Inc. 05/14/2001

FIRST BRANDON FINL CORP (VT)
Merged into New Hampshire Thrift Bancshares, Inc. 06/04/2007
Each share Common $20 par exchanged for (2.67) shares Common 1¢ par
New Hampshire Thrift Bancshares, Inc. name changed to Lake Sunapee Bank Group 06/01/2015 which merged into Bar Harbor Bankshares 01/13/2017

FIRST BRANDON NATL BK (BRANDON, VT)
Reorganized as First Brandon Financial Corp. 12/011/2005
Each share Common $20 par exchanged for (1) share Common $20 par
First Brandon Financial Corp. merged into New Hampshire Thrift Bancshares, Inc. 06/04/2007 which name changed to Lake Sunapee Bank Group 06/01/2015 which merged into Bar Harbor Bankshares 01/13/2017

FIRST BRANDS CORP (DE)
Common 1¢ par split (2) for (1) by issuance of (1) additional share payable 2/26/96 to holders of record 2/5/96 Ex date - 2/27/96
Merged into Clorox Co. 1/29/99
Each share Common 1¢ par exchanged for (0.349) share Common $1 par

FIRST BRISTOL CNTY NATL BK (TAUNTON, MA)
Common $10 par changed to $5 par and (1) additional share issued 4/1/83
Stock Dividends - 10% 2/1/84; 10% 2/1/85
Reorganized as First New England Bankshares Corp. 7/1/85
Each share Common $5 par exchanged for (3) shares Common $1 par
First New England Bankshares Corp. acquired by Hartford National Corp. 11/14/86 which merged into Shawmut National Corp. 2/29/88 which merged into Fleet Financial Group Inc. (New) 11/30/95 which name changed to Fleet Boston Corp. 10/1/99 which name changed to FleetBoston Financial Corp. 4/18/2000 which merged into Bank of America Corp. 4/1/2004

FIRST BUCKEYE BK N A (MANSFIELD, OH)
Merged into Toledo Trustcorp, Inc. 12/30/1982
Each share Capital Stock $5 par exchanged for (1) share $2.90 Conv. Preferred Ser. A no par
Toledo Trustcorp, Inc. name changed to Trustcorp, Inc. 04/10/1986 which was acquired by Society Corp. 01/05/1990 which merged into KeyCorp (New) 03/01/1994

FIRST BURLINGTON CORP (DE)
Acquired by First Illinois Corp. 06/30/1986
Each share Common $12.50 par exchanged for $115 cash

FIRST BUSEY CAP TR I (DE)
9% Guaranteed Trust Preferred Securities called for redemption at $10 on 6/19/2006

FIRST BUSEY CORP (DE)
Class A Common no par split (3) for (2) by issuance of (0.5) additional share 5/7/93
Reincorporated under the laws of Nevada 6/30/93

FIRST BUSINESS BK NATL ASSN (SAN DIEGO, CA)
Name changed to Bank of Southern California, N.A. (San Diego, CA) 08/12/2010

1ST BUSINESS CORP (CA)
Common no par split (3) for (2) by issuance of (0.5) additional share 3/22/83
Common no par split (5) for (4) by issuance of (0.25) additional share 6/3/85
Common no par split (5) for (4) by issuance of (0.25) additional share 6/23/86

Common no par split (5) for (4) by issuance of (0.25) additional share 3/14/88
Acquired by a private investor 7/28/89
Each share Common no par exchanged for $27 cash

FIRST BUSINESS FINL SVCS INC (WI)
Common Stock Purchase Rights declared for holders of record 06/02/2008 were redeemed at $0.0005 per right 03/08/2018 for holders of record 04/12/2018
(Additional Information in Active)

FIRST CALGARY PETES LTD (AB)
9% Conv. Preferred Ser. B $1 par reclassified as Class A Preferred $1 par 10/10/1985
Class A Preferred $1 par conversion privilege expired 12/31/1985
Common no par reclassified as Class A Common no par 10/10/1985
Each share Class A Preferred $1 par exchanged for (8.6) shares Class A Common no par and (7) Class A Common Stock Purchase Warrants expiring 08/31/1989 on 12/31/1987
Merged into Eni S.p.A. 11/21/2008
Each share Class A Common no par exchanged for $3.60 cash

FIRST CALIF BK (CAMARILLO, CA)
Under plan of reorganization each share Common no par automatically became (1) share FCB Bancorp Common no par 09/20/2005
FCB Bancorp merged into First California Financial Group, Inc. 03/12/2007 which merged into PacWest Bancorp 05/31/2013

FIRST CALIF BK (LA MESA, CA)
Declared insolvent and taken over by the FDIC 7/9/93

FIRST CALIF FINL GROUP INC (DE)
Merged into PacWest Bancorp 05/31/2013
Each share Common 1¢ par exchanged for (0.2966) share Common 1¢ par

FIRST CAMDEN NATL BK & TR CO (CAMDEN, NJ)
Common $12.50 par changed to $6.25 par and (1) additional share issued 2/23/55
Common $6.25 par changed to $5.625 par and (1/9) additional share issued 4/1/69
Stock Dividends - 33-1/3% 8/3/42; 25% 6/15/44
Name changed to South Jersey National Bank (Camden, NJ) 9/15/69
South Jersey National Bank (Camden, NJ) reorganized as Heritage Bancorporation 11/1/71
(See Heritage Bancorporation)

FIRST CDA FINL CORP (AB)
Common no par reclassified as Subordinate no par 11/30/1990
Recapitalized as Western Pacific Gold Inc. 06/04/1996
Each share Subordinate no par exchanged for (0.2) share Common no par
Western Pacific Gold Inc. recapitalized as WPI Gold Ltd. (AB) 03/17/2004 which reincorporated in British Columbia as Salmon River Resources Ltd. 07/13/2005
(See Salmon River Resources Ltd.)

FIRST CDN AMERN CR SVCS LTD (ON)
Reincorporated under the laws of Nevada as Galloway Oil & Gas Inc. and each share Preferred and Common no par received (19) additional shares respectively 05/17/2004
Galloway Oil & Gas Inc. name changed to Relay Capital Corp. 12/23/2004
(See Relay Capital Corp.)

FIRST CDN AMERN FINL SVCS INC (ON)
Reincorporated under the laws of Nevada as Koko Petroleum, Inc. and Common no par changed to $0.001 par 04/13/2004
(See Koko Petroleum, Inc.)

FIRST CDN AMERN HLDG CORP (WY)
Reincorporated 12/05/2004
Place of incorporation changed from (ON) to (WY) 12/05/2004
Each share old Common 1¢ par received distribution of (0.0001) share First Canadian American Trust Co. Ltd. Preferred $10 par and Common no par payable 06/30/2003 to holders of record 06/06/2003
Each share old Common 1¢ par received distribution of (0.0001) share New Wave Windmills Inc. Preferred no par and Common no par payable 06/30/2003 to holders of record 06/06/2003
Each share old Common 1¢ par received distribution of (0.0001) share Goodies Galore Packaging Inc. Preferred no par and Common no par payable 07/15/2003 to holders of record 06/30/2003
Each share old Common 1¢ par received distribution of (0.0001) share Warlock Holdings Inc. Preferred no par and Common no par payable 07/15/2003 to holders of record 07/08/2003
Each share old Common 1¢ par received distribution of (0.0001) share Fossil Graphics Inc. Preferred no par and Common no par payable 07/21/2003 to holders of record 07/07/2003
Each share old Common 1¢ par received distribution of (0.0001) share Berkshire Collection Inc. Preferred $0.001 par and Common $0.001 par payable 08/01/2003 to holders of record 07/15/2003
Each share old Common 1¢ par received distribution of (0.0001) share First Canadian American Credit Services Ltd. Preferred no par and Comon no par payable 08/01/2003 to holders of record 07/23/2003
Each share old Common 1¢ par received distribution of (0.0001) share Xcelarator Studios Inc. Preferred no par and Common no par payable 08/01/2003 to holders of record 07/21/2003
Each share old Common 1¢ par received distribution of (0.0001) share Goldberg Report Ltd. Preferred no par and Common no par payable 08/10/2003 to holders of record 07/28/2003
Each share old Common 1¢ par received distribution of (0.0001) share Microgenix Filtration Systems Inc. Preferred no par and Common no par payable 08/15/2003 to holders of record 07/30/2003
Each share old Common 1¢ par received distribution of (0.0001) share Seville Investment Funds Corp. Preferred no par and Common no par payable 08/15/2003 to holders of record 07/29/2003
Each share old Common 1¢ par received distribution of (0.0001) share First Public Securities Transfer Corp. Preferred no par and Common no par payable 09/01/2003 to holders of record 08/06/2003
Each share old Common 1¢ par received distribution of (0.0001) share First Xcelarator Marketing Inc. Preferred no par and Common no par payable 09/1/2003 to holders of record 08/05/2003
Each share old Common 1¢ par received distribution of (0.0001) share Broadspot World Wide Wireless Inc. Preferred no par and Common no par payable 09/15/2003 to holders of record 08/18/2003
Each share old Common 1¢ par received distribution of (0.0001) share Findent Engineering Security Ltd. Preferred no par and Common no par payable 09/15/2003 to holders of record 08/19/2003
Each share old Common 1¢ par received distribution of (0.0001) share Caribbean Mining Development Inc. Preferred no par and Common no par payable 09/15/2003 to holders of record 08/20/2003
Each share old Common 1¢ par received distribution of (0.0001) share First Eastern Energy Development Inc. Preferred no par and Common no par payable 09/15/2003 to holders of record 08/21/2003
Each share old Common 1¢ par received distribution of (0.0001) share First Mediterranean Gold Resources Inc. Preferred no par and Common no par payable 09/15/2003 to holders of record 08/22/2003
Each share old Common 1¢ par received distribution of (0.0001) share First Western Environmental Protection Inc. Preferred no par and Common no par payable 09/15/2003 to holders of record 08/25/2003
Each share old Common 1¢ par received distribution of (0.0001) share Josanden International Resources Inc. Preferred no par and Common no par payable 09/15/2003 to holders of record 08/26/2003
Each share old Common 1¢ par received distribution of (0.0001) share Second Bavarian Mining Consulting Services Inc. Preferred no par and Common no par payable 09/15/2003 to holders of record 08/27/2003
Each share old Common 1¢ par received distribution of (0.0001) share Second Colonial Mining & Engineering Services Inc. Preferred no par and Common no par payable 09/15/2003 to holders of record 08/28/2003
Each share old Common 1¢ par received distribution of (0.0001) share Second Mongolian Mining Security Services Inc. Preferred no par and Common no par payable 09/15/2003 to holders of record 08/29/2003
Each share old Common 1¢ par received distribution of (0.0001) share Central Asia Development & Construction Co. Ltd. Preferred no par and Common no par payable 11/01/2003 to holders of record 10/21/2003
Each share old Common 1¢ par received distribution of (0.0001) share Pearl Asian Mining Industries Inc. Preferred no par and Common no par payable 11/01/2003 to holders of record 10/21/2003
Each share old Common 1¢ par received distribution of (0.0001) share Energy Concepts, Inc. Common no par payable 01/06/2004 to holders of record 11/07/2003
Each share old Common 1¢ par received distribution of (0.00001) share Feinstein Report, Inc. Common no par payable 03/15/2004 to holders of record 01/26/2004
Each share old Common 1¢ par received distribution of (0.0001) share Sparrowtech Multimedia Inc. Common no par payable 04/01/2004 to holders of record 02/22/2004
Each share old Common 1¢ par exchanged for (0.0001) share new Common 1¢ par 03/21/2005
Name changed to Blackout Media Corp. 01/09/2006

FIRST CDN AMERN TR LTD (ON)
Reincorporated under the laws of Wyoming as Suncrest Energy, Inc. 09/10/2003
Suncrest Energy, Inc. name changed to Amerossi International Group, Inc. 01/30/2006 which recapitalized as Bio-Med Technologies, Inc. 11/19/2007
(See Bio-Med Technologies, Inc.)

FIRST CDN ENERGY CORP (BC)
Delisted from Vancouver Stock Exchange 03/02/1988

FIRST CDN ENERGY LTD (AB)
Reorganized under the laws of Canada as Northern Shield Resources Inc. 5/30/2003
Each share Common no par exchanged for (1) share Common no par

FIRST CDN FINL CORP (BC)
Recapitalized as Promax Communications Inc. (BC) 04/03/1997
Each share Class A Common no par exchanged for (0.2) share Class A Common no par
Promax Communications Inc. (BC) reincorporated in Yukon 00/00/1998 which reincorporated in Nevada 04/19/2007 which recapitalized as Sipp Industries, Inc. 08/24/2007

FIRST CDN FUTURES INC (ON)
Company went private 03/00/1987
Details not available

FIRST CDN GOLD INC (ON)
Common $1 par reclassified as Conv. Class B $1 par 06/24/1994
Conv. Class B $1 par called for redemption 12/31/1994
Merged into Compressario Corp. 03/07/2002
Each share Common no par exchanged for (1) share Common no par

FIRST CAPITAL CORP. (AZ)
Charter revoked for failure to file reports and pay fees 06/20/1967

FIRST CAP RES COM INC (NV)
Recapitalized as Hampton Berkshire Insurance & Financial Co. 03/25/2003
Each share Common $0.001 par exchanged for (0.1) share Common $0.001 par
Hampton Berkshire Insurance & Financial Co. recapitalized as Innovate Oncology, Inc. 10/05/2004 which name changed to Avantogen Oncology, Inc. 07/03/2006
(See Avantogen Oncology, Inc.)

FIRST CAPITAL BANCORP INC (VA)
Fixed Rate Perpetual Preferred Ser. A $4 par called for redemption at $1,000 plus $7.63884 accrued dividends on 01/10/2014
Common $4 par changed to 1¢ par 06/24/2014
Merged into Park Sterling Corp. 01/01/2016
Each share Common 1¢ par exchanged for (0.7748) share Common $1 par
Park Sterling Corp. merged into South State Corp. 11/30/2017

FIRST CAP BANCORP INC (GA)
Merged into Flag Financial Corp. 11/22/2005
Each share Common $1 par exchanged for (1.6) shares Common $1 par
(See Flag Financial Corp.)

FIRST CAP BANCORP INC (LA)
Merged into Deposit Guaranty Corp. 03/31/1997
Each share Common exchanged for (3.20624) shares Common no par

Deposit Guaranty Corp. merged into First American Corp. (TN) 05/01/1998 which merged into AmSouth Bancorporation 10/01/1999 which merged into Regions Financial Corp. (New) 11/04/2006

FIRST CAP BANCSHARES INC (OH)
Merged into LCNB Corp. 01/11/2013
Each share Common no par exchanged for (1.40114874) shares Common no par and $12.25448885 cash

FIRST CAP BK (RICHMOND, VA)
Common $4 par split (3) for (2) by issuance of (0.5) additional share payable 12/28/2005 to holders of record 12/15/2005 Ex date - 12/29/2005
Reorganized as First Capital Bancorp, Inc. 09/28/2006
Each share Common $4 par exchanged for (1) share Common $4 par
First Capital Bancorp, Inc. merged into Park Sterling Corp. 01/01/2016 which merged into South State Corp. 11/30/2017

FIRST CAP BK ARIZ (PHOENIX, AZ)
Stock Dividend - 5% payable 05/23/2000 to holders of record 04/28/2000 Ex date - 05/02/2000
Merged into CoBiz Inc. 03/12/2001
Each share Common $5 par exchanged for (2.266) shares Common 1¢ par
CoBiz Inc. name changed to CoBiz Financial Inc. 05/17/2007 which merged into BOK Financial Corp. 09/28/2018

FIRST CAP BK KY LOUISVILLE (LOUISVILLE, KY)
Under plan of reorganization each share Common $1 par automatically became (1) share FCB Bancorp, Inc. Common $1 par 05/31/2000
FCB Bancorp, Inc. merged into MainSource Financial Group, Inc. 04/30/2017

FIRST CAP CORP (MS)
Common $5 par changed to $2.50 par and (1) additional share issued 12/26/1984
Common $2.50 par changed to no par and (1) additional share issued 09/26/1986
Name changed to Trustmark Corp. 03/15/1990

FIRST CAPITAL CORP. OF SOUTH CAROLINA (SC)
Liquidation completed 04/01/1963 Details not available

FIRST CAP FINL CORP (FL)
Merged into Great American Management & Investment, Inc. 09/08/1983
Each share Common 1¢ par exchanged for $7 principal amount of 10% Subordinated Notes due 09/15/1993 and $9 cash

FIRST CAP HLDGS CORP (NV)
$2.0625 Conv. Preferred Ser. A 25¢ par called for redemption 11/10/1989
Plan of reorganization under Chapter 11 Federal Bankruptcy proceedings confirmed 12/00/1995
No stockholders' equity

FIRST CAPITAL INCOME PROPERTIES, LTD. (FL)
Charter voluntarily cancelled 12/27/2001

FIRST CAP INSTL REAL ESTATE LTD L P (FL & IL)
Fund terminated 07/16/1999
Each Unit of Ltd. Partnership Int. 3 received first and final distribution of approximately $117.97 cash Fund terminated 12/22/2000
Each Unit of Ltd. Partnership Int. 4 received first and final distribution of approximately $74 cash Fund terminated 03/15/2007
Each Unit of Ltd. Partnership Int. 1 received first and final distribution of $38.68 cash Fund terminated 03/15/2007
Each Unit of Ltd. Partnership Int. 2 received first and final distribution of $20.73 cash
Note: Certificates were not required to be surrendered and are without value
Partnerships 1, 2 and 3 were formed under the laws of Florida

FIRST CAP INTL INC (DE)
Each share old Common $0.001 par exchanged for (0.33333333) share new Common $0.001 par 08/07/2006
SEC revoked common stock registration 10/27/2014

FIRST CAPITAL SAVINGS & LOAN ASSOCIATION, LTD. (NC)
Merged into Scottish Savings & Loan Association, Inc. (New) 04/01/1981
Each share Common $6 par exchanged for (1.3223) shares Common $1 par
Scottish Savings & Loan Association, Inc. (New) merged into Southeastern Savings & Loan Co. 01/17/1984 which name changed to Southeastern Savings Bank, Inc. 07/13/1988
(See Southeastern Savings Bank, Inc.)

FIRST CAPITOL BK (YORK, PA)
Merged into Susquehanna Bancshares, Inc. 01/04/1999
Each share Common no par exchanged for (2.028) shares Common $2 par
Susquehanna Bancshares, Inc. merged into BB&T Corp. 08/01/2015

FIRST CAPITOL FINL CORP (DE)
Taken over by the RTC 05/04/1990
Stockholders' equity unlikely

FIRST CARIBBEAN MNG DEV INC (CANADA)
Reincorporated under the laws of Florida as Circular Logic Systems, Inc. 03/08/2005
Circular Logic Systems, Inc. name changed to Dynamic Media, Inc. (New) 09/15/2005
(See Dynamic Media, Inc. (New))

FIRST CAROLINA BANK & TRUST CO. (SANFORD, NC)
Merged into Centura Banks, Inc. 12/31/92
Each share Common $2.50 par exchanged for (0.395) share Common no par
Centura Banks, Inc. merged into Royal Bank of Canada (Montreal, QC) 6/5/2001

FIRST CAROLINA BANK FED SVGS BK (WALTERBORO, SC)
Name changed to First Federal of South Carolina Federal Savings Bank (Walterboro, SC) 3/15/97

FIRST CAROLINA FED SVGS BK (KINGS MOUNTAIN, NC)
Common 1¢ par split (5) for (4) by issuance of (0.25) additional share payable 11/24/97 to holders of record 10/24/97
Common 1¢ par split (2) for (1) by issuance of (1) additional share payable 8/3/98 to holders of record 7/3/98
Merged into First National Bank of Shelby (Shelby, NC) 4/2/99
Each share Common 1¢ par exchanged for $41.33 cash

FIRST CAROLINA INVS INC (DE)
Reorganized 07/01/1987
Reorganized from First Carolina Investors (SC) to under the laws of Delaware as First Carolina Investors, Inc. and Shares of Bene. Int. no par reclassified as Common no par 07/01/1987
Common no par split (2) for (1) by issuance of (1) additional share 03/14/1994
Liquidation completed
Each share Common no par received initial distribution of $3.57 cash payable 10/24/2011 to holders of record 10/21/2011
Each share Common no par exchanged for second and final distribution of $1.90 cash 11/23/2015

FIRST CAROLINA SAVINGS & LOAN ASSOCIATION, INC. (NC)
Merged into Scottish Savings & Loan Association, Inc. (New) 4/1/81
Each share Common $1 par exchanged for (1) share Common $1 par
Scottish Savings & Loan Association, Inc. (New) merged into Southeastern Savings & Loan Co. 1/17/84 which name changed to Southeastern Savings Bank, Inc. 7/13/88
(See Southeastern Savings Bank, Inc.)

FIRST CASH FINANCIAL SERVICES INC (DE)
Name changed 01/19/1999
Name changed from First Cash, Inc. to First Cash Financial Services Inc. 01/19/1999
Common 1¢ par split (3) for (2) by issuance of (0.5) additional share payable 04/05/2004 to holders of record 03/22/2004 Ex date - 04/06/2004
Common 1¢ par split (2) for (1) by issuance of (1) additional share payable 02/20/2006 to holders of record 02/06/2006 Ex date - 02/21/2006
Under plan of merger name changed to FirstCash, Inc. 09/02/2016

FIRST CENT BANCSHARES INC (TN)
Merged into United Community Banks, Inc. 3/31/2003
Each share Common $5 par exchanged for (1.506) shares Common $1 par and $16.46 cash

FIRST CENT BK (ST PETERSBURG, FL)
Merged into Colonial BancGroup, Inc. 02/11/1998
Each share Common $5 par exchanged for (2.103) shares Common $2.50 par
(See Colonial BancGroup, Inc.)

FIRST CENT BK, N.A. (LOS ANGELES, CA)
Merged into East West Bancorp, Inc. 05/28/1999
Each share Common $5 par exchanged for $23.12 cash

FIRST CENT COAST BK (SAN LUIS OBISPO, CA)
Merged into Wells Fargo Bank, N.A. (San Francisco, CA) 07/14/1979
Each share Common Capital Stock $10 par exchanged for $74.50 cash

FIRST CENT FINL CORP (NY)
Chapter 11 bankruptcy procedings converted to Chapter 7 on 04/30/1998
Stockholders' equity unlikely

FIRST CENTENNIAL BANCORP (CA)
Common no par split (5) for (4) by issuance of (0.25) additional share payable 04/30/2004 to holders of record 04/01/2004 Ex date - 05/03/2004
Common no par split (3) for (2) by issuance of (0.5) additional share payable 04/03/2006 to holders of record 03/03/2006 Ex date - 04/04/2006
Common no par split (3) for (2) by issuance of (0.5) additional share payable 05/15/2007 to holders of record 05/01/2007 Ex date - 05/16/2007
Stock Dividend - 7% payable 04/15/2005 to holders of record 03/15/2005 Ex date - 03/11/2005
Filed a petition under Chapter 7 Federal Bankruptcy Code 03/25/2009
Stockholders' equity unlikely

FIRST CENTENNIAL CORP (CO)
Class A Common $1 par split (5) for (4) by issuance of (0.25) additional share 06/17/1985
Acquired by Citizens, Inc. 07/31/1992
Each share 1988 Preferred Ser. 1 $1 par exchanged for (0.47143126) share Class A Common no par
Each share Class A Common $1 par exchanged for (0.20414829) share Class A Common $1 par

FIRST CENTRAL CORP. (PA)
Merged into Standard Toch Industries, Inc. 7/1/60
Each share Class A and/or B Common 1¢ par exchanged for (1) share Class A Common $1 par
(See Standard Toch Industries, Inc.)

FIRST CENTRAL TRUST CO. (AKRON, OH)
Charter cancelled for failure to pay taxes 10/15/51

1ST CENTY BANCSHARES INC (DE)
Acquired by Midland Financial Co. 07/01/2016
Each share Common 1¢ par exchanged for $11.22 cash

1ST CENTY BK N.A. (LOS ANGELES, CA)
Common no par split (2) for (1) by issuance of (1) additional share payable 02/28/2005 to holders of record 02/15/2005 Ex date - 03/01/2005
Reorganized under the laws of Delaware as 1st Century Bancshares, Inc. 12/19/2007
Each share Common no par exchanged for (1) share Common 1¢ par
(See 1st Century Bancshares, Inc.)

1ST CENTY HEALTHCARE INTL INC (AB)
Recapitalized as Pura Vida International Corp. 10/11/1995
Each share Common no par exchanged for (0.25) share Common no par

FIRST CENTY BANKSHARES INC (WV)
Acquired by Summit Financial Group, Inc. 04/01/2017
Each share Common $1.25 par exchanged for $22.50 cash

FIRST CHADRON BK CORP (NE)
Name changed to Chadron Energy Corp. 4/20/81

FIRST CHARLOTTE BK & TR CO (CHARLOTTE, NC)
Under plan of reorganization each share Common $1.25 par automatically became (1) share First Charlotte Financial Corp. Common $1.25 par 8/1/90
First Charlotte Financial Corp. acquired by Centura Banks, Inc. 12/31/93 which merged into Royal Bank of Canada (Montreal, QC) 6/5/2001

FIRST CHARLOTTE FINL CORP (NC)
Acquired by Centura Banks, Inc. 12/31/93
Each share Common $1.25 par exchanged for (0.627) share Common no par
Centura Banks, Inc. merged into Royal Bank of Canada (Montreal, QC) 6/5/2001

FIRST CHARTER BK N A (BEVERLY HILLS, CA)
Location changed 01/30/1990
Common $5 par changed to $4 par and (0.25) additional share issued 06/19/1986
Common $4 par changed to $3.20 par and (0.25) additional share issued 05/25/1989
Location changed from (Los Angeles, CA) to (Beverly Hills, CA) 01/30/1990
Common $3.20 par split (5) for (4) by issuance of (0.25) additional share 06/05/1990
Merged into First Community Bancorp (CA) 10/08/2001
Each share Common $3.20 par exchanged for (0.008635) share Common no par
First Community Bancorp (CA) reincorporated in Delaware as PacWest Bancorp 05/14/2008

FIRST CHARTER CORP (NC)
Common $5 par split (6) for (5) by issuance of (0.2) additional share 01/15/1993
Common $5 par split (4) for (3) by issuance of (1/3) additional share 12/16/1994
Common $5 par split (6) for (5) by issuance of (0.2) additional share payable 07/15/1997 to holders of record 06/20/1997
Common $5 par changed to no par 09/29/1998
Merged into Fifth Third Bancorp 06/06/2008
Each share Common no par exchanged for approximately (1.7412) shares Common no par

FIRST CHARTER FINL CORP (CA)
Common no par split (2) for (1) by issuance of (1) additional share 5/6/71
Merged into Financial Corp. of America 8/4/83
Each share Common no par exchanged for (0.14) share Floating Rate Preferred Ser. A $10 par and (0.606) share Common 50¢ par
(See Financial Corp. of America)

FIRST CHARTER NATL BK (EAST BRUNSWICK, NJ)
Capital Stock $6.25 par changed to $5 par and (0.25) additional share issued 8/20/69
Merged into Heritage Bancorporation 12/31/73
Each share Capital Stock $5 par exchanged for (2) shares Common no par
(See Heritage Bancorporation)

FIRST CHARTERED DEV CORP (BC)
Recapitalized as APAC Telecommunications Corp. 03/24/1995
Each share Common no par exchanged for (0.4347826) share Common no par
(See APAC Telecommunications Corp.)

FIRST CHATTANOOGA FINL CORP (TN)
Acquired by AmSouth Bancorporation 2/1/93
Each share Common $1 par exchanged for (1.26) shares Common $1 par and $1 cash
AmSouth Bancorporation merged into Regions Financial Corp. 11/4/2006

FIRST CHEROKEE BANCSHARES INC (GA)
Stock Dividend - 10% payable 4/1/96 to holders of record 3/7/96
Merged into First Cherokee Interim Corp. 12/22/2003
Each share Common $1 par exchanged for $23.60 cash

FIRST CHESAPEAKE FINL CORP (VA)
SEC revoked common stock registration 04/13/2006

FIRST CHESTER CNTY CORP (PA)
Merged into Tower Bancorp, Inc. 12/10/2010
Each share Common $1 par exchanged for (0.356) share Common no par
(See Tower Bancorp, Inc.)

FIRST CHICAGO BANK OF EVANSTON, N.A. (EVANSTON, IL)
Merged into First National Bank of Chicago (Chicago, IL) 04/25/1992
Details not available

FIRST CHICAGO CORP (DE)
Common $20 par changed to $10 par and (1) additional share issued 10/01/1971
Common $10 par changed to $5 par and (1) additional share issued 05/13/1974
$3.75 Conv. Preferred Ser. A no par called for redemption 09/02/1993
10% Preferred Ser. D no par called for redemption 07/01/1994
Preferred Adjustable Dividend no par called for redemption 08/31/1995
Merged into First Chicago NBD Corp. 12/01/1995
Each share Adjustable Dividend Preferred Ser. B no par exchanged for (1) share Adjustable Dividend Preferred Ser. B no par
Each share Adjustable Dividend Preferred Ser. C no par exchanged for (1) share Adjustable Dividend Preferred Ser. C no par
Each 5-3/4% Depositary Preferred Ser. B Share exchanged for (1) 5-3/4% Depositary Preferred Share Ser. E
Each share 5-3/4% Conv. Preferred Ser. B no par exchanged for (1) share 5-3/4% Conv. Preferred Ser. B no par
Each 8.45% Depositary Preferred Ser. E Share exchanged for (1) 8.45% Depositary Preferred Ser. E Share
Each share 8.45% Preferred Ser. E exchanged for (1) 8.45% Conv. Preferred Ser E
Each share Common $5 par exchanged for (1.81) shares Common $1 par
First Chicago NBD Corp. merged into Bank One Corp. 10/02/1998 which merged into J.P. Morgan Chase & Co. 07/01/2004 which name changed to JPMorgan Chase & Co. 07/20/2004

FIRST CHICAGO INVT CORP (AB)
Name changed to Graystone Corp. 02/25/2004
Graystone Corp. merged into Pyxis Capital Inc. 02/27/2006
(See Pyxis Capital Inc.)

FIRST CHICAGO NBD CORP (DE)
5.75% Depositary Preferred called for redemption 04/01/1997
5.75% Conv. Preferred Ser. B no par called for redemption 04/01/1997
8.45% Depositary Preferred Ser. E called for redemption at $25 plus $0.27 accrued dividends on 11/17/1997
Merged into Bank One Corp. 10/02/1998
Each share Adjustable Dividend Preferred Ser. B no par exchanged for (1) share Adjustable Dividend Preferred Ser. B 1¢ par
Each share Adjustable Dividend Preferred Ser. C no par exchanged for (1) share Adjustable Dividend Preferred Ser. C 1¢ par
Each 7.5% Preferred Purchase Unit exchanged for (1) 7.5% Preferred Purchase Unit
Each share Common $1 par exchanged for (1.62) shares Common 1¢ par
Bank One Corp. merged into J.P. Morgan Chase & Co. 07/01/2004 which name changed to JPMorgan Chase & Co. 07/20/2004

FIRST CHINA INVT CORP (BC)
Recapitalized as China First Capital Corp. 09/08/1987
Each share Common no par exchanged for (0.25) share Common no par
China First Capital Corp. merged into Black Hawk Mining Inc.-Compagnie Miniere Black Hawk Inc. 07/16/1990 which merged into Glencairn Gold Corp. 10/20/2003 which recapitalized as Central Sun Mining Inc. 12/05/2007 which was acquired by B2Gold Corp. 03/31/2009

FIRST CHINA PHARMACEUTICAL GROUP INC (NV)
Charter revoked 07/31/2015

FIRST CHOICE BK (CERRITOS, CA)
Stock Dividends - 4% payable 05/06/2015 to holders of record 04/15/2015 Ex date - 04/13/2015; 4% payable 07/22/2016 to to holders of record 07/01/2016 Ex date - 06/29/2016
Under plan of reorganization each share Common no par automatically became (1) share First Choice Bancorp Common no par 12/26/2017

1ST CHOICE FINL CORP (CO)
Merged into Wells Fargo & Co. (New) 06/13/2000
Each share Common exchanged for (0.406648) share Common $1-2/3 par

FIRST CHOICE INDS LTD (BC)
Recapitalized as Glen Hawk Minerals Ltd. 11/21/2003
Each share Common no par exchanged for (0.5) share Common no par
Glen Hawk Minerals Ltd. recapitalized as Oronova Resource Corp. 11/24/2009 which name changed to Oronova Energy Inc. 12/16/2016

FIRST CHROLD CORP.
Dissolved in 1934

FIRST CINCINNATI CORP.
Dissolved in 1943

FIRST CINCINNATI INC (OH)
Assets sold 02/02/2001
Details not available

FIRST CTZNS BANC CORP (OH)
Fixed Rate Perpetual Preferred Ser. A no par called for redemption at $1,000 on 02/15/2014
Stock Dividend - 300% payable 06/05/1996 to holders of record 04/16/1996 Ex date - 05/09/1996
Note: CUSIP® changed from (319459 10 3) at time of stock dividend
Name changed to Civista Bancshares, Inc. 05/04/2015

FIRST CTZNS BANCORP (TN)
Merged into BB&T Corp. 08/01/2006
Each share Common $1 par exchanged for (1.3) shares Common $5 par

FIRST CTZNS BANCORP INC (AL)
Merged into Banc Corp. 10/30/1998
Each share Common no par exchanged for (8.291) shares Common $0.001 par
Banc Corp. name changed to Superior Bancorp 05/19/2006
(See Superior Bancorp)

FIRST CITIZENS BANCORP OF INDIANA (IN)
Merged into KeyCorp (New) 12/13/94
Each share Common $1 par exchanged for (1.4286) shares Common $1 par

FIRST CTZNS BANCORPORATION INC (SC)
Name changed 03/20/2004
Name changed from First Citizens Bancorporation of South Carolina, Inc. to First Citizens Bancorporation, Inc. 03/20/2004
Recapitalized 01/12/2006
Holders of (170) or fewer shares exchanged for $735 cash per share
5% Conv. Preferred Ser. A $50 par called for redemption at $50 plus $0.21 accrued dividends on 08/01/2014
5% Conv. Preferred Ser. B $50 par called for redemption at $50 plus $0.21 accrued dividends on 08/01/2014
Conv. Preferred Ser. B $20 par called for redemption at $100 plus $0.63 accrued dividends on 08/01/2014
Conv. Preferred Ser. F $50 par called for redemption at $50 plus $0.21 accrued dividends on 08/01/2014
Non-Vtg. Preferred Ser. E called for redemption at $200 plus $0.84 accrued dividends on 08/01/2014
Preferred Ser. G called for redemption at $50 plus $0.21 accrued dividends on 08/01/2014
Merged into First Citizens BancShares, Inc. 10/01/2014
Each share Common $5 par exchanged for (4) shares Class A Common $1 par and $50 cash

FIRST CITIZENS BANCSTOCK INC (LA)
Stock Dividend - 10% 10/31/1994
Merged into Whitney Holding Corp. 03/08/1996
Each share Common $1 par exchanged for (1.6046) shares Common no par
Whitney Holding Corp. merged into Hancock Holding Co. 06/04/2011 which name changed to Hancock Whitney Corp. 05/25/2018

FIRST-CITIZENS BANK & TRUST CO. (RALEIGH, NC)
5% Conv. Preferred Ser. A $100 par called for redemption 03/14/1980
Reorganized as First Citizens Corp. (NC) 12/09/1982
Each share 5% Preferred Ser. C $20 par exchanged for (1) share 5% Ser. C Preferred $20 par
Each share 5% Conv. Preferred Ser. D $100 par exchanged for (1) share 5% Conv. Preferred Ser. D $100 par
Each share 9% Conv. Preferred Ser. E $40 par exchanged for (1) share 9% Ser. E Conv. Preferred $40 par
Each share 9% Conv. Preferred Ser. F $50 par exchanged for (1) share 9% Conv. Preferred Ser. R $50 par
Each share Common $100 par exchanged for (1) share Common $100 par
First Citizens Corp. (NC) reorganized in Delaware as First Citizens BancShares, Inc. 10/20/1986

FIRST-CITIZENS BANK & TRUST CO. (SMITHFIELD, NC)
Common $25 par changed to $50 par in January 1960
Common $50 par changed to $100 par 4/15/70
Stock Dividends - 50% 12/30/41; 33-1/3% in 1947; 15% 4/10/68; 25% 5/17/70
Location changed to (Raleigh, N.C.) 4/26/74
First-Citizens Bank & Trust Co. (Raleigh, N.C.) reorganized as First Citizens Corp. (N.C.) 12/9/82 which reorganized in Delaware as First Citizens BancShares, Inc. 10/20/86

FIRST CTZNS BK & TR CO S C (COLUMBIA, SC)
Reorganized as First Citizens Bancorporation of South Carolina, Inc. 03/04/1983

Each share Preferred Ser. A, B, D and F $50 par exchanged for (1) share Preferred Ser. A, B, D and F $50 par respectively
Each share Preferred Ser. C $20 par exchanged for (1) share Preferred Ser. C $20 par
Each share Common $5 par exchanged for (1) share Common $5 par
First Citizens Bancorporation of South Carolina, Inc. name changed to First Citizens Bancorporation, Inc. 03/20/2004 which merged into First Citizens BancShares, Inc. 10/01/2014

FIRST CTZNS BK (CLEVELAND, TN)
Under plan of reorganization each share Common $4 par automatically became (1) share First Citizens Bancorp Common $1 par 02/19/1990
First Citizens Bancorp merged into BB&T Corp. 08/01/2006

FIRST CTZNS BK (SHERMAN OAKS, CA)
Merged into Cal Fed Bancorp Inc. 10/18/96
Each share Common no par exchanged for $9.62 cash

FIRST CTZNS CORP (GA)
Common $1 par split (3) for (2) by issuance of (0.5) additional share payable 11/14/97 to holders of record 10/31/97
Merged into BB&T Corp. 7/9/99
Each share Common $1 par exchanged for (1.0789) shares Common $5 par

FIRST CTZNS CORP (NC)
Reorganized under the laws of Delaware as First Citizens BancShares, Inc. 10/20/1986
Each share 5% Ser. C Preferred $20 par, 5% Ser. D Conv. Preferred $100 par, 9% Ser. E Conv. Preferred $40 par and 9% Ser. F Conv. Preferred $50 par automatically became (1) share 5% Ser. C Preferred $20 par, 5% Ser. D Conv. Preferred $100 par, 9% Ser. E Conv. Preferred $40 par and 9% Ser. F Conv. Preferred $50 par respectively
Each share Common $10 par exchanged for (100) shares Class A Common $1 par and (25) shares Class B Common $1 par

FIRST CTZNS FINL CORP (DE)
Stock Dividends - 10% 06/05/1995; 10% payable 06/03/1996 to holders of record 05/03/1996
Merged into Provident Bankshares Corp. 08/22/1997
Each share Common 1¢ par exchanged for (0.7665) share Common $1 par
Provident Bankshares Corp. acquired by M&T Bank Corp. 05/26/2009

FIRST CITIZENS NATIONAL BANK (MANSFIELD, PA)
Under plan of reorganization each share Common $1 par automatically became (1) share Citizens Financial Services, Inc. Common $1 par 4/30/85

FIRST CITRUS BK (TAMPA, FL)
Under plan of reorganization each share Common $5 par automatically became (1) share First Citrus Bancorporation, Inc. Common $5 par 04/20/2007

FIRST CITY BANCORP INC. (GA)
Merged into Barnett Banks of Florida, Inc. 12/16/86
Each share Common $10 par exchanged for $422.793 cash

FIRST CITY BANCORP INC (TN)
Stock Dividend - 10% 5/30/92
$8.50 Preferred Ser. C no par called for redemption 3/8/96
Adjustable Dividend Preferred Ser. D no par called for redemption 3/8/96
Merged into First American Corp. (TN) 3/11/96
Each share Common no par exchanged for (0.6036) share Common $5 par
First American Corp. (TN) merged into AmSouth Bancorporation 10/1/99 which merged into Regions Financial Corp. 11/4/2006

FIRST CITY BANCORPORATION TEX INC (DE)
Each share Mandatory Conv. Jr. Preferred Ser. C $1 par exchanged for (1) share Common 1¢ par 10/20/88
Plan of reorganization under Chapter 11 bankruptcy proceedings effective 7/3/95
Each share Adjustable Rate Preferred Ser. E 1¢ par exchanged for (1.1085) shares FirstCity Financial Corp. Special Preferred 1¢ par, (0.77595) share Common 1¢ par, (0.1126) Common Stock Purchase Warrants expiring 7/3/99, and (1.1085) FirstCity Liquidating Trust Ctfs. of Bene. Int. Class B
Each share Increasing Rate Sr. Preferred Ser. A 1¢ par exchanged for 9% Sr. Subordinated Notes due 9/30/97 having a face amount equal to their full liquidation preference in increments of $100 face value
Each share $5.50 Conv. Preferred Ser. B 1¢ par exchanged for (1) share Special Preferred 1¢ par, (0.7) share Common 1¢ par, and (0.101588) Common Stock Purchase Warrant expiring 7/3/99
Each share Common 1¢ par exchanged for (0.03893779) share FirstCity Financial Corp. Common 1¢ par, (0.01318543) Common Stock Purchase Warrant expiring 7/3/99, and (0.03893779) FirstCity Liquidating Trust Ctf. of Bene. Int. Class C
Note: Holders of (129) or fewer Common will not receive a distribution; shares will be pooled for benefit of remaining holders
(See each company's listing)

FIRST CITY BANCORPORATION TEX INC (TX)
Common $10 par changed to $6.50 par and (0.5) additional share issued 04/15/1973
Common $6.50 par changed to $3.25 par and (1) additional share issued 04/14/1981
Reorganized 04/19/1988
Holders of Adjustable Rate Preferred Ser. A $10 par, Adjustable Rate Preferred Ser. B $10 par, $3.83 Conv. Preferred $10 par, $4.12 Conv. Preferred $10 par and Common $3.25 par received non-transferable rights to subscribe to shares of a new Delaware company of the same name. Such rights expired 07/25/1988
All outstanding shares were cancelled and without value

FIRST CITY BANK, N.A. (OKLAHOMA CITY, OK)
Declared insolvent 6/21/85
Stockholders' equity unlikely

FIRST CITY BK & TR CO (HOPKINSVILLE, KY)
Stock Dividend - 100% 2/12/74
Reorganized as Area Bancshares Corp. (Old) 4/1/82
Each share Common $5 par exchanged for (2) shares Common $2.50 par
(See Area Bancshares Corp. (Old))

FIRST CITY BK (NEW BRITAIN, CT)
Merged into Webster Financial Corp. 12/3/2004
Each share Common $5 par exchanged for either (0.46418862) share Common 1¢ par and $5.012118 cash or $27 cash
Note: Option to receive stock and cash expired 11/29/2004

FIRST CITY BK (ROSEMEAD, CA)
Stock Dividend - 25% 03/31/1978
Acquired by Golden State Sanwa Bank Ltd. (San Francisco, CA) 02/27/1981
Each share Common $7.50 par exchanged for $153.92 cash

FIRST CITY BANK (TAMPA, FL)
Name changed to Southeast Bank of Tampa (Tampa, FL) 02/02/1971
(See Southeast Bank of Tampa (Tampa, FL))

FIRST CITY CORP (AR)
Acquired by First United Bancshares, Inc. 08/15/1988
Each share Preferred $6 par exchanged for $7.50 cash
Each share Common $2 par exchanged for $50.91 cash

FIRST CITY FED SVGS & LN ASSN BRADENTON FLA (USA)
Merged into Metropolitan Savings Bank (New York, NY) 09/23/1983
Each share Common 1¢ par exchanged for $40 cash

FIRST CITY FINL CORP (NM)
Name changed to Moncor, Inc. 04/18/1984
(See Moncor, Inc.)

FIRST CITY FINL LTD (BC)
issuance of (1) additional share 05/16/1973
Common no par split (2) for (1) by issuance of (1) additional share 12/19/1980
Common no par reclassified as Class A Common no par 05/28/1984
Class A Common no par split (2) for (1) by issuance of (1) additional share 06/01/1984
$0.6125 1st Preferred Ser. A called for redemption 09/15/1985
Class A Common no par split (3) for (1) by issuance of (2) additional shares 11/17/1989
Merged into Harrowston Corp. 12/31/1991
Each share Class A Common no par exchanged for (0.1) share Common no par
Harrowston Corp. name changed to Harrowston Inc. 04/05/1993
(See Harrowston Inc.)

FIRST CITY GOLD CORP (CANADA)
Name changed to Ventech Healthcare Inc. 12/15/1986
Ventech Healthcare Inc. recapitalized as Ventech Healthcare International Inc. (Canada) 07/02/1987 which reincorporated in Ontario 08/11/1987 which name changed to Ventech Healthcare Corp. Inc. 09/10/1987 which name changed to NWE Capital Corp. 01/28/1992 which name changed to Petersburg Long Distance Inc. 12/31/1992 which name changed to PLD Telekom, Inc. (ON) 08/01/1996 which reincorporated in Delaware 02/28/1997 which merged into Metromedia International Group, Inc. 09/30/1999
(See Metromedia International Group, Inc.)

FIRST CITY INDS INC NEW (DE)
Merged into FCI Acquisition Corp. 7/26/94
Each share Common 10¢ par exchanged for $2.93 cash

FIRST CITY INDS INC OLD (DE)
Merged into First City Developments Corp. 01/30/1989
Each share Common 10¢ par exchanged for $13.10 cash

FIRST CITY NATL BK (BINGHAMTON, NY)
Stock Dividends - 25% 2/4/60; 10% 1/31/64
Merged into Lincoln First Group Inc. 5/16/67
Each share Capital Stock $20 par received (0.315) share Common $10 par
Each share Capital Stock $20 par then subsequently exchanged for (1) share Common $10 par
Lincoln First Group Inc. name changed to Lincoln First Banks Inc. 5/22/68 which merged into Chase Manhattan Corp. (Old) 7/1/84 which merged into Chase Manhattan Corp. (New) 3/31/96 which name changed to J.P. Morgan Chase & Co. 12/31/2000 which name changed to JPMorgan Chase & Co. 7/20/2004

FIRST CITY NATIONAL BANK (GADSDEN, AL)
Common $5 par changed to $2.50 par and (1) additional share issued plus a 30% stock dividend paid 3/17/70
Merged into First Alabama Bancshares, Inc. 8/7/74
Each share Common $2.50 par exchanged for (0.56) share Common $2.50 par
First Alabama Bancshares, Inc. name changed to Regions Financial Corp. (Old) 5/2/94 which merged into Regions Financial Corp. (New) 7/1/2004

FIRST CITY NATL BK (HOUSTON, TX)
Each share Common $20 par exchanged for (2) shares Common $10 par 2/9/60
Stock Dividend - (1) for (7.5) 4/6/70
Under plan of reorganization each share Common $10 par automatically became (1) share First City Bancorporation of Texas, Inc. (TX) Common $10 par 4/1/71
(See First City Bancorporation of Texas, Inc. (TX))

FIRST CITY NATIONAL BANK OF ARLINGTON (ARLINGTON, TX)
97% held by First City Bancorporation of Texas, Inc. as of 12/30/1988

FIRST CITY PPTYS INC (DE)
Name changed to First City Industries Inc. 05/31/1985
(See First City Industries Inc.)

FIRST CITY TR CO (CALGARY, AB)
11.25% Retractable 2nd Preferred Ser. 1
$8 par called for redemption 08/01/1986
Acquired by NAL Trustco Inc. 07/10/1992
Each share 8.32% Preferred Ser. B $10 par exchanged for $1.81 principal amount of Junior Notes due 01/01/2004
Each share 8.75% Preferred $8.50 par exchanged for $1.34 principal amount of Junior Notes due 01/01/2004
Each share 10.75% Preferred Ser. A $10 par exchanged for $1.82 principal amount of Junior Notes due 01/01/2004
Each share Common $2 par exchanged for $0.97 principal amount of Junior Notes due 01/01/2004

FIRST CITY TRUSTCO INC (CANADA)
Name changed to Talborne Capital Corp. 07/06/1992
(See Talborne Capital Corp.)

FIRST CLEVELAND CORP. (OH)
Class B $1 par changed to 1¢ par in 1938
Class B 1¢ par changed to $1 par in 1947

Class B $1 par changed to $5 par in 1952
6% Preferred $100 par called for redemption 10/1/63
Class A $10 par called for redemption 10/1/64
Merged into Cedar Point, Inc. 6/28/66
(See Cedar Point, Inc.)

FIRST CLOVER LEAF FINL CORP (MD)
Merged into First Mid-Illinois Bancshares, Inc. 09/08/2016
Each share Common 10¢ par exchanged for (0.495) share Common 10¢ par

FIRST COASTAL BANCSHARES (CA)
Reorganized 06/23/1997
Reorganized from First Coastal Bank, N.A. (El Segundo, CA) to First Coastal Bancshares and Common $1.15 par changed to no par 06/23/1997
Each share old Common no par exchanged for (0.2) share new Common no par 12/07/1998
Each share new Common no par exchanged again for (0.04) share new Common no par 06/30/2003
Conv. Preferred Ser. A called for redemption at $6.75 on 09/08/2003
Merged into CVB Financial Corp. 06/22/2007
Each share new Common no par exchanged for either (24.6201) shares Common no par or $276.73 cash
Note: Option to receive stock expired 05/31/2007

FIRST COASTAL BANKS, INC. (NH)
Acquired by Peoples Heritage Financial Group, Inc. 07/31/1989
Each share Common $1 par exchanged for $40.50 cash

FIRST COASTAL BANKSHARES INC (VA)
Merged into Centura Banks, Inc. 3/26/99
Each share Common 1¢ par exchanged for (0.34) share Common no par
Centura Banks, Inc. merged into Royal Bank of Canada (Montreal, QC) 6/5/2001

FIRST COASTAL CAP TR (DE)
11-7/8% Preferred Securities called for redemption at $20 on 11/30/2007

FIRST COASTAL CORP (DE)
Each share old Common $1 par exchanged for (0.1) share new Common $1 par 05/31/1995
Merged into Norway Bancorp, Inc. 08/31/2001
Each share Common $1 par exchanged for $21 cash

FIRST COBALT CORP (BC)
Reincorporated under the laws of Canada 09/04/2018

FIRST COINVESTORS INC (DE)
Common 10¢ par changed to 5¢ par and (1) additional share issued 6/2/75
Chapter 11 Federal Bankruptcy Code converted to Chapter 7 on 4/18/90
No stockholders' equity

FIRST COLEBROOK BANCORP INC (DE)
Common no par split (2) for (1) by issuance of (1) additional share payable 02/13/1996 to holders of record 01/29/1996
Common no par split (4) for (1) by issuance of (3) additional shares payable 09/21/2012 to holders of record 09/10/2012
Acquired by Bangor Bancorp, MHC 04/06/2018
Each share Common no par exchanged for $45 cash

FIRST COLO BANCORP INC (CO)
Merged into Commercial Federal Corp. 08/14/1998
Each share Common 10¢ par exchanged for (0.9847) share Common 1¢ par
(See Commercial Federal Corp.)

FIRST COLO BANKSHARES INC (CO)
Common $5 par split (5) for (2) by issuance of (0.25) additional share 5/25/71
Merged into Affiliated Bankshares of Colorado, Inc. 9/28/73
Each share Common $5 par exchanged for (0.85) share Common $5 par
Affiliated Bankshares of Colorado, Inc. merged into Banc One Corp. 11/2/92 which merged into Bank One Corp. 10/2/98 which merged into J.P. Morgan Chase & Co. 12/31/2000 which name change to JPMorgan Chase & Co. 7/20/2004

FIRST COLO FINL CORP (CO)
Assets liquidated 06/00/1990
No stockholders' equity

FIRST COLONIAL BANKSHARES CORP (DE)
Common $10 par changed to $5 par and (1) additional share issued 03/31/1983
Each share Common $5 par reclassified as (3) shares Class A Common $1.25 par and (1) share Class B Common $1.25 par 10/23/1984
Class A Common $1.25 par split (3) for (2) by issuance of (0.5) additional share 05/28/1986
Class B Common $1.25 par split (3) for (2) by issuance of (0.5) additional share 05/28/1986
Class A Common $1.25 par split (3) for (2) by issuance of (0.5) additional share 06/01/1987
Class B Common $1.25 par split (3) for (2) by issuance of (0.5) additional share 06/01/1987
Preferred Ser. A $57 par called for redemption 09/30/1993
Merged into Firstar Corp. (Old) 01/31/1995
Each share Depositary Preference Ser. C exchanged for (1) share Depositary Conv. Preferred Ser. D
Each share Class A Common $1.25 par exchanged for (0.7725) share Common $1.25 par
Each share Conv. Class B Common $1.25 par exchanged for (0.7725) share Common $1.25 par
Firstar Corp. (Old) merged into Firstar Corp. (New) 11/20/1998 which merged into U.S. Bancorp (DE) 02/27/2001

FIRST COLONIAL CORP AMER (DE)
Adjudicated bankrupt 9/8/70
Stockholders' equity unlikely

FIRST COLONIAL GROUP INC (PA)
Common $5 par split (2) for (1) by issuance of (1) additional share 04/18/1986
Common $5 par split (3) for (2) by issuance of (0.5) additional share 09/28/1987
Stock Dividends - 5% payable 06/19/1996 to holders of record 05/31/1996; 5% payable 06/19/1997 to holders of record 05/30/1997; 5% payable 06/25/1998 to holders of record 06/05/1998; 5% payable 06/24/1999 to holders of record 06/04/1999; 5% payable 06/22/2000 to holders of record 06/02/2000; 5% payable 06/22/2001 to holders of record 06/04/2001 Ex date - 05/31/2001; 5% payable 05/31/2002 to holders of record 05/17/2002 Ex date - 05/15/2002
Merged into KNBT Bancorp, Inc. 10/31/2003

Each share Common $5 par exchanged for (3.7) shares Common
KNBT Bancorp, Inc. merged into National Penn Bancshares, Inc. 02/01/2008

1ST COLONIAL NATL BK (COLLINGSWOOD, NJ)
Stock Dividend - 10% payable 01/15/2002 to holders of record 01/02/2002 Ex date - 12/28/2001
Under plan of reorganization each share Common $1 par automatically became (1) share 1st Colonial Bancorp, Inc. (PA) Common no par 06/30/2002

FIRST COLONIAL VENTURES LTD (UT)
Each share old Common $0.001 par exchanged for (0.1) share new Common $0.001 par 10/22/91
Each share new Common $0.001 par exchanged again for (0.05) share new Common $0.001 par 1/12/96
Reincorporated under the laws of Nevada as Nova Communications, Ltd. 8/11/99
Nova Communications, Ltd. name changed to Encompass Holdings, Inc. 1/31/2006

FIRST COLONY BANCSHARES (GA)
Merged into Main Street Banks, Inc. (GA) 5/22/2003
Each share Common exchanged for either (9.0321) shares Common no par or $192.2037 cash
Note: Option to receive stock expired 7/7/2003
Main Street Banks, Inc. (GA) merged into BB&T Corp. 6/1/2006

FIRST COLONY CORP (VA)
Merged into General Electric Capital Corp. 12/01/1996
Each share Common no par exchanged for $36.16 cash
Variable Term Preferred Ser. B no par called for redemption 12/23/1996
Variable Term Preferred Ser. C no par called for redemption 01/06/1997
Public interest eliminated

FIRST COLONY LIFE INS CO (VA)
Common $2.25 par changed to $1 par 12/7/61
Stock Dividend - 15% 12/15/80
Acquired by Ethyl Corp. 5/14/82
Each share Common $1 par exchanged for (0.3429) share $4 Conv. 2nd Preferred Ser. B $10 par and $55.50 cash

FIRST COLONY SAVINGS & LOAN ASSOCIATION, INC. (NC)
Assets sold 07/21/1986
No stockholders' equity

FIRST COLUMBIA FINL CORP (CO)
Liquidating plan of reorganization under Chapter 11 Federal Bankruptcy Code effective 3/29/94
Each share Common no par received $1.1905 cash
Note: Certificates were not required to be surrendered and are without value

FIRST COLUMBUS CMNTY BK & TR CO (GA)
Merged into SouthTrust Corp. 07/28/1994
Each share Common $5 par exchanged for (1) share Common $2.50 par
SouthTrust Corp. merged into Wachovia Corp. (Ctfs. dated after 09/01/2001) 11/01/2004 which merged into Wells Fargo & Co. (New) 12/31/2008

FIRST COMBINED ENTERPRISES INC (DE)
Reincorporated 6/30/70
State of incorporation changed from (NJ) to (DE) 6/30/70
Merged into G & G Real Estate, Inc. 4/12/77

Each share Common 1¢ par exchanged for $0.33 cash

FIRST COMM BANCORP (CA)
Acquired by Grandpoint Capital, Inc. 12/28/2010
Each share Common no par exchanged for $4.703 cash
Note: Holders may receive future additional consideration, if certain performance milestones are met

FIRST COMM BANCORP INC (GA)
Name changed to nBank Corp. 12/00/1999

FIRST COMM BANCSHARES INC (NE)
Each share Common $1 par received distribution of (4) shares Class B $1 par 10/26/1993
Common $1 par split (5) for (4) by issuance of (0.25) additional share payable 04/12/1999 to holders of record 03/31/1999
Merged into Wells Fargo & Co. 06/16/2000
Each share Common $1 par exchanged for (0.809172) share Common $1-2/3 par
Each share Class B Common $1 par exchanged for (0.809172) share Common $1-2/3 par

FIRST COMM BK (CHARLOTTE, NC)
Stock Dividend - 15% payable 10/01/1998 to holders of record 09/15/1998
Under plan of reorganization each share Common no par automatically became (1) share First Commerce Corp. Common no par 05/24/2001
First Commerce Corp. merged into Bank of Granite Corp. 07/18/2003 which merged into FNB United Corp. 10/24/2011 which name changed to CommunityOne Bancorp 07/01/2013 which merged into Capital Bank Financial Corp. 10/26/2016

FIRST COMM BK (LEWISBURG, TN)
Under plan of reorganization each share Common $1 par automatically became (1) share First Commerce Bancorp, Inc. Common $1 par 10/06/2006

FIRST COMM BK (LOS ANGELES, CA)
Under plan of reorganization each share Common no par automatically became (1) share First Commerce Bancorp Common no par 04/01/2004
(See First Commerce Bancorp)

FIRST COMM BKS FLA INC (FL)
Merged into Colonial BancGroup, Inc. 07/01/1997
Each share Common no par exchanged for (0.4326) share Common $2.50 par
(See Colonial BancGroup, Inc.)

FIRST COMM CMNTY BANKSHARES INC (GA)
Company's principal asset placed in receivership 09/17/2010
Stockholders' equity unlikely

FIRST COMM CORP (LA)
Reincorporated 5/21/74
Common $10 par changed to $5 par and (1) additional share issued 5/15/72
Stock Dividend - 10% 4/20/71
State of incorporation changed from (DE) to (LA) 5/21/74
Common $5 par split (4) for (3) by issuance of (1/3) additional share 10/3/83
Common $5 par split (3) for (2) by issuance of (0.5) additional share 1/11/93
7.25% Preferred no par called for redemption 1/2/97
Stock Dividends - 20% 4/15/80; 10% 9/30/81; 20% 9/14/82; 5% payable

11/15/96 to holders of record 10/31/96
Merged into Banc One Corp. 6/12/98
Each share Common $5 par exchanged for (1.408) shares Common no par
Banc One Corp. merged into Bank One Corp. 10/2/98 which merged into J.P. Morgan Chase & Co. 12/31/2004 which name changed to JPMorgan Chase & Co. 7/20/2004

FIRST COMM CORP (NC)
Common no par split (5) for (4) by issuance of (0.25) additional share payable 02/28/2002 to holders of record 01/31/2002
Stock Dividend - 10% payable 11/23/2001 to holders of record 11/13/2001 Ex date - 11/08/2001
Merged into Bank of Granite Corp. 07/18/2003
Each share Common no par exchanged for (0.5186) share Common $1 par and $9.37 cash
Bank of Granite Corp. merged into FNB United Corp. 10/24/2011 which name changed to CommunityOne Bancorp 07/01/2013 which merged into Capital Bank Financial Corp. 10/26/2016

FIRST COMM RLTY INVS (LA)
Name changed to Eastover Corp. 5/31/78
Eastover Corp. merged into Eastgroup Properties 12/20/94 which reorganized as Eastgroup Properties, Inc. 6/5/97

FIRST COML BANCORP INC (DE)
Reincorporated 03/30/1990
Stock Dividend - 10% 09/02/1981
Reincorporated from under the laws of (CA) to (DE) as First Commercial Bancorp Inc. and Common no par changed to 1¢ par 03/30/1990
Each share Common no par exchanged for (0.008) share Common $1.25 par 12/06/1996
Merged into First Banks America, Inc. 02/02/1998
Each share Common $1.25 par exchanged for (0.8888) share Common 15¢ par
(See First Banks America, Inc.)

FIRST COML BANCORPORATION (FL)
Administratively dissolved 10/11/91

FIRST COML BANCSHARES INC (DE)
Common $10 par changed to $1 par and (1) additional share issued 09/11/1987
Merged into Synovus Financial Corp. 12/31/1992
Each share Common $1 par exchanged for (1.5) shares Common $1 par

FIRST COML BK (ARLINGTON, VA)
Merged into United Bankshares, Inc. 10/31/95
Each share Common $5 par exchanged for either $26.25 cash and (1.0051) shares
Common $2.50 par or $52.57 cash
Note: Option to receive cash only expired 11/15/95

FIRST COML BK (CHICAGO, IL)
Each share old Common $20 par exchanged for (0.0001) share new Common $20 par 08/05/2003
Note: In effect holders received $229.11 cash per share and public interest was eliminated

FIRST COML BK (PHILADELPHIA, PA)
Merged into Marine Midland Bank (New York, NY) 2/27/99
Each share Common $5 par exchanged for $40.477 cash

FIRST COMMERCIAL BANK (SACRAMENTO, CA)
Reorganized as First Commercial Bancorp (CA) 9/2/80
Each share Common $7 par exchanged for (1) share Common no par
First Commercial Bancorp (CA) reincorporated in Delaware as First Commercial Bancorp Inc. 3/30/90
(See First Commercial Bancorp Inc. (DE))

FIRST COML BK (ST. PETERSBURG, FL)
Through voluntary exchange offer 100% acquired by Community Banks of Florida, Inc. 01/17/1978
Public interest eliminated

FIRST COML BK (TAMPA, FL)
Under plan of reorganization each share Common $5 par automatically became (1) share FCB Financial, Inc. Common 1¢ par 09/30/2000

FIRST COML BKS INC (NY)
Name changed to Key Banks Inc. 04/23/1979
Key Banks Inc. name changed to KeyCorp (NY) 08/28/1985 which merged into KeyCorp (New) (OH) 03/01/1994

FIRST COML CORP (AR)
Common $5 par split (2) for (1) by issuance of (1) additional share 7/16/85
Common $5 par changed to $3 par and (2/3) additional share issued 5/23/89
Common $3 par split (3) for (2) by issuance of (0.5) additional share 1/3/94
Stock Dividends - 10% 8/31/92; 7% payable 1/2/96 to holders of record 12/14/95; 5% payable 11/15/96 to holders of record 10/31/96; 5% payable 1/2/98 to holders of record 12/15/97
Merged into Regions Financial Corp. (Old) 7/31/98
Each share Common $3 par exchanged for (1.7) shares Common $0.625 par
Regions Financial Corp. (Old) merged into Regions Financial Corp. (New) 7/1/2004

FIRST COML FINL CORP (TX)
Company went private 11/15/2006
Each share Common $1 par exchanged for $37 cash

FIRST COML FINL GROUP INC (AB)
Name changed to Micron Metals Canada Corp. 10/03/1989
Micron Metals Canada Corp. name changed to USA Video Corp. (AB) 04/03/1992 which reincorporated in Wyoming as USA Video Interactive Corp. 02/23/1995 which recapitalized as Oculus VisionTech Inc. 01/26/2012

FIRST COML HLDG CORP (DE)
Stock Dividend - 10% 4/12/95
Merged into Centura Banks, Inc. 2/27/96
Each share Common $1 par exchanged for (0.63) share Common no par
Centura Banks, Inc. merged into Royal Bank of Canada (Montreal, QC) 6/5/2001

FIRST COMMERCIAL NATIONAL BANK OF SOUTH CAROLINA (COLUMBIA, SC)
Name changed to First National Bank of South Carolina (Columbia, SC) 12/10/1965
First National Bank of South Carolina (Columbia, SC) reorganized as First Bankshares Corp. of S.C. 07/19/1969 which liquidated for South Carolina National Corp. 12/01/1984 which merged into Wachovia Corp. (New) (Ctfs. dated between 05/20/1991 and 09/01/2001) 12/06/1991 which merged into Wachovia Corp. (Ctfs. dated after 09/01/2001) 09/01/2001 which merged into Wells Fargo & Co. (New) 12/31/2008

FIRST COMMONS BK N A (NEWTON, MA)
Merged into Brookline Bancorp, Inc. 03/01/2018
Each share Common 1¢ par exchanged for (1.089) shares Common 1¢ par

FIRST COMMONSTOCKS CORP.
Dissolved in 1936

1ST COMMONWEALTH BANK VIRGINIA (ARLINGTON, VA)
Merged into First Virginia Community Bank (Fairfax, VA) 10/19/2012
Each share Common exchanged for (0.17277) share Common $5 par
First Virginia Community Bank (Fairfax, VA) reorganized as FVCBankcorp, Inc. 11/02/2015

FIRST COMWLTH CORP (VA)
Each share old Common $1 par exchanged for (0.0025) share new Common $1 par 5/12/97
Merged into United Trust Group, Inc. (IL) 6/12/2002
Each share new Common $1 par exchanged for $250 cash

FIRST COMWLTH FD INC (MD)
Name changed to Aberdeen Commonwealth Income Fund, Inc. 5/1/2001
Aberdeen Commonwealth Income Fund, Inc. name changed to Aberdeen Global Income Fund, Inc. 7/1/2002

FIRST COMWLTH FINL CORP (DE)
Name changed to Global-Tron, Inc. 1/8/87
(See Global-Tron, Inc.)

FIRST COMWLTH INC (DE)
Merged into Guardian Life Insurance Co. of America 08/03/1999
Each share Common $0.001 par exchanged for $25 cash

FIRST CMNTY BANCORP (CA)
Reincorporated under the laws of Delaware as PacWest Bancorp and Common no par changed to 1¢ par 05/14/2008

FIRST CMNTY BANCORP INC (DE)
Common $10 par split (2) for (1) by issuance of (1) additional share 5/1/86
Common $10 par changed to 1¢ par 5/1/87
Acquired by Banc One Corp. 5/3/93
Each share Common 1¢ par exchanged for (0.6267) share Common no par
Banc One Corp. merged into Bank One Corp. 10/2/98 which merged into J.P. Morgan Chase & Co. 12/31/2000 which name changed to JPMorgan Chase & Co. 7/20/2004

FIRST CMNTY BANCORP INC (GA)
Merged into National Commerce Bancorporation 11/2/98
Each share Common $1 par exchanged for (3.2684) shares Common $2 par
National Commerce Bancorporation name changed to National Commerce Financial Corp. 4/25/2001 which merged into SunTrust Banks, Inc. 10/1/2004

FIRST CMNTY BANCORP INC (PA)
Common $5 par changed to $2.50 par and (1) additional share issued 11/15/85
Stock Dividends - 10% 12/10/86; 100% 11/10/87
Merged into Fulton Financial Corp. 3/26/90
Each share Common $2.50 par exchanged for (2.65) shares Common $2.50 par

1ST CMNTY BANCORP INC (MI)
Common $10 par split (5) for (4) by issuance of (0.25) additional share 5/16/94
Name changed to ChoiceOne Financial Services Inc. 5/30/97

FIRST CMNTY BANCORPORATION (MO)
Common $10 par changed to $5 par and (1) additional share issued plus a 50% stock dividend paid 02/04/1974
Merged into Mercantile Bancorporation Inc. 09/30/1983
Each share Common $5 par exchanged for (1.0638) share Common $5 par
Mercantile Bancorporation, Inc. merged into Firstar Corp. (New) 09/20/1999 which merged into U.S. Bancorp (DE) 02/27/2001

FIRST CMNTY BANCSHARES INC (DE)
Merged into FCFT, Inc. 05/09/1990
Each share Common $5 par exchanged for (1) share Common $5 par
FCFT, Inc. reorganized as First Community Bancshares Inc. (NV) 09/30/1997 which reincorporated in Virginia 10/09/2018

FIRST CMNTY BANCSHARES INC (IN)
Stock Dividend - 5% payable 02/02/1998 to holders of record 11/19/1997
Merged into MainSource Financial Group, Inc. 06/12/2003
Each share Common no par exchanged for $21 cash

FIRST CMNTY BANCSHARES INC (NV)
Common $1 par split (5) for (4) by issuance of (0.25) additional share payable 04/09/1999 to holders of record 03/31/1999
Stock Dividends - 10% payable 03/28/2002 to holders of record 03/01/2002 Ex date - 02/27/2002; 10% payable 08/15/2003 to holders of record 08/01/2003 Ex date - 07/30/2003
Reincorporated under the laws of Virginia 10/09/2018

FIRST COMMUNITY BANK (BOCA RATON, FL)
Name changed to First Marine Bank (Boca Raton, FL) 03/15/1976
First Marine Bank (Boca Raton, FL) merged into First Marine Bank & Trust Co. of the Palm Beaches (Riveria Beach, FL) 12/31/1977
(See First Marine Bank & Trust Co. of the Palm Beaches (Riviera Beach, FL))

FIRST CMNTY BK (GASTONIA, NC)
Merged into Centura Banks, Inc. 8/16/96
Each share Common $4.17 par exchanged for (0.96) share Common no par
Centura Banks, Inc. merged into Royal Bank of Canada (Montreal, QC) 6/5/2001

FIRST CMNTY BK (ROBERTA, GA)
Merged into Atlantic Southern Financial Group, Inc. 02/05/2007
Each share Common $4 par exchanged for (0.742555) share Common $5 par
(See Atlantic Southern Financial Group, Inc.)

FIRST CMNTY BK (WOODSTOCK, VT)
Merged into New Hampshire Thrift Bancshares, Inc. 10/01/2007
Each share Common $1 par

exchanged for (0.7477) share Common 1¢ par
New Hampshire Thrift Bancshares, Inc. name changed to Lake Sunapee Bank Group 06/01/2015 which merged into Bar Harbor Bankshares 01/13/2017

FIRST CMNTY BK CORP AMER (FL)
Additional Offering - 570,000 shares COM offered at $14 per share on 05/16/2005
Common 10¢ par changed to 8¢ par and (1) additional share issued payable 07/21/2003 to holders of record 07/01/2003
Common 8¢ par changed to 5¢ par and (0.5) additional share issued payable 01/20/2006 to holders of record 01/10/2006 Ex date - 01/23/2006
Each share 10% Conv. Perpetual Preferred Ser. B 1¢ par exchanged for (10) shares Common 5¢ par 03/31/2011
Stock Dividends - 5% payable 03/15/2005 to holders of record 03/01/2005 Ex date - 02/25/2005; 5% payable 02/28/2007 to holders of record 02/12/2007 Ex date - 02/08/2007
Completely liquidated
Each share Common 5¢ par received first and final distribution of $0.3114 cash payable 04/06/2012 to holders of record 03/24/2012
Note: Certificates were not required to be surrendered and are without value

FIRST CMNTY BK DESERT (YUCCA VY, CA)
Merged into First Community Bancorp (CA) 05/31/2000
Each share Common no par exchanged for (0.3) share Common no par
First Community Bancorp (CA) reincorporated in Delaware as PacWest Bancorp 05/14/2008

FIRST CMNTY BK JOLIET (JOILET, IL)
Under plan of reorganization each share Common $1 par automatically became (1) share First Community Financial Partners, Inc. Common $1 par 09/26/2006
First Community Financial Partners, Inc. merged into First Busey Corp. 07/03/2017

FIRST CMNTY BKG SVCS INC (GA)
Common $1 par split (2) for (1) by issuance of (1) additional share payable 2/20/98 to holders of record 1/30/98
Stock Dividend - 5% payable 11/3/97 to holders of record 10/14/97
Merged into Regions Financial Corp. (Old) 9/10/98
Each share Common $1 par exchanged for (0.625) share Common $0.625 par
Regions Financial Corp. (Old) merged into Regions Financial Corp. (New) 7/1/2004

FIRST CMNTY CORP (SC)
5% Perpetual Preferred Ser. T $1 par called for redemption at $1,000 plus $7.50 accrued dividends on 10/07/2012
(Additional Information in Active)

FIRST CMNTY FINL CORP (NC)
Merged into Capital Bank Corp. 01/22/2002
Each share Common no par exchanged for (0.84761) share Common no par and $21.86 cash
Capital Bank Corp. merged into Capital Bank Financial Corp. 09/24/2012 which merged into First Horizon National Corp. 11/30/2017

FIRST CMNTY FINL PARTNERS INC (IL)
Common $1 par split (2) for (1) by issuance of (1) additional share payable 12/18/2009 to holders of record 12/16/2009 Ex date - 12/21/2009
Merged into First Busey Corp. 07/03/2017
Each share Common $1 par exchanged for (0.396) share new Common $0.001 par and $1.35 cash

FIRST COMPUTER FD INC (DE)
Name changed to Idex, Inc. 11/21/1978
Idex, Inc. name changed to Globus Studios, Inc. 02/03/1988

FIRST CONCORD OF AMERICA (CA)
Charter suspended for failure to file reports and pay fees 11/3/75

FIRST CONN BANCORP INC (CT)
Common $10 par split (3) for (2) by issuance of (0.5) additional share 03/26/1982
Common $10 par split (3) for (2) by issuance of (0.5) additional share 03/30/1984
Stock Dividend - 50% 05/15/1979
Merged into Fleet Financial Group, Inc. (Old) 03/17/1986
Each share Common $10 par exchanged for (1.577) shares Common $1 par
Fleet Financial Group, Inc. (Old) merged into Fleet/Norstar Financial Group, Inc. 01/01/1988 which name changed to Fleet Financial Group, Inc. (New) 04/15/1992 which name changed to Fleet Boston Corp. 10/01/1999 which name changed to FleetBoston Financial Corp. 04/18/2000 which merged into Bank of America Corp. 04/01/2004

FIRST CONN BANCORP INC (MD)
Merged into People's United Financial, Inc. 10/01/2018
Each share Common 1¢ par exchanged for (1.725) shares Common 1¢ par

FIRST CONN CAP CORP (CT)
Name changed to FCCC, Inc. 6/4/2003

FIRST CONN SMALL BUSINESS INVT CO (CT)
Common $1 par changed to 50¢ par and (1) additional share issued 07/22/1968
Common 50¢ par changed to no par 06/25/1970
Name changed to First Connecticut Capital Corp. 01/28/1993
First Connecticut Capital Corp. name changed to FCCC, Inc. 06/04/2003

FIRST CONS SECS INC (NV)
Name changed to FCF, Inc. 12/15/2000
(See FCF, Inc.)

FIRST CONSORT HOTEL & INNS LTD (BC)
Struck off register and declared dissolved for failure to file returns 10/22/1993

1ST CONSTITUTION BK (CRANBURY, NJ)
Stock Dividends - 5% payable 01/31/1998 to holders of record 01/09/1998; 5% payable 01/28/1999 to holders of record 01/15/1999
Under plan of reorganization each share Common no par automatically became (1) share 1st Constitution Bancorp Common no par 07/01/1999

FIRST CONSTITUTION FINL CORP (DE)
Name changed to Aristotle Corp. 04/14/1993
(See Aristotle Corp.)

FIRST CONSULTING GROUP INC (DE)
Merged into Computer Sciences Corp. 01/11/2008
Each share Common $0.001 par exchanged for $13 cash

FIRST CONTL BANCSHARES INC (LA)
Acquired by Hibernia Corp. 8/1/94
Each share Common $1 par exchanged for (1.41) shares Class A Common no par
Hibernia Corp. merged into Capital One Financial Corp. 11/16/2005

FIRST CONTL CORP (TX)
Common no par changed to $1 par 01/27/1964
Name changed to First Continental Mortgage Co. 10/16/1967 which name changed to Western Financial Corp. 11/02/1970 which name changed back to First Continental Corp. 10/27/1971
Each share Common $1 par exchanged for (0.01) share Common $100 par 10/30/1975
Merged into FC Acquisition Corp. 03/16/1979
Each share Common $100 par exchanged for $1,000 cash

FIRST CONTL DEV CON INC (DE)
Charter cancelled and declared inoperative and void for non-payment of taxes 03/01/1976

FIRST CONTL LIFE & ACC INS CO (TX)
Common no par changed to $1 par 3/10/70
Merged into First Continental Life Group, Inc. 12/31/72
Each share Common $1 par exchanged for (1) share Common $1 par
(See First Continental Life Group, Inc.)

FIRST CONTL LIFE GROUP INC (DE)
Under plan of recapitalization each share Common $1 par automatically became (1) share $2 Preferred $1 par or (1) share Common 1980 Ser. $1 par 5/29/80
Note: Option to elect to receive Common 1980 Ser. expired 6/30/80
Part. Preferred Ser. A $1 par called for redemption 6/14/84
Merged into Lomas & Nettleton Financial Corp. 9/30/87
Each share Common 1980 Ser. $1 par exchanged for $154 cash
Part. Preferred Ser. B $1 par called for redemption 12/18/87
$2 Preferred $1 par called for redemption 12/18/87
Public interest eliminated

FIRST CONTL MTG CO (TX)
Name changed to First Continental Corp. 01/01/1964 which name changed back to First Continental Mortgage Co. 10/16/1967
Name changed to Western Financial Corp. 11/02/1970
Each share Common $1 par exchanged for (1) share Common $1 par
Western Financial Corp. name changed back to First Continental Corp. 10/27/1971
(See First Continental Corp.)

FIRST CONTL OIL & GAS INC (FL)
Merged into Continental Resources, International 7/31/72
Each share Common 1¢ par surrendered prior to 10/31/72, exchanged for (2.05) shares Common 1¢ par
Each share Common 1¢ par surrendered on or after 10/31/72 exchanged for (0.05) share Common 1¢ par
(See Continental Resources, International)

FIRST CONTL REAL ESTATE INVT TR (TX)
Under plan of merger name changed to Commonwealth Financial Group Real Estate Investment Trust 08/31/1983 which name changed back to First Continental Real Estate Investment Trust 06/28/1985
Merged into Parkway Co. (TX) 06/14/1994
Each Share of Bene. Int. $1 par exchanged for (14.25) shares Common $1 par
Parkway Co. (TX) reincorporated in Maryland as Parkway Properties, Inc. 08/02/1996 which merged into Cousins Properties Inc. 10/06/2016

FIRST COOLIDGE CORP (MA)
Each share 60¢ par exchanged for (0.2) share Common $3 par 06/01/1976
Each share Common $3 par exchanged for (0.05) share Common $60 par 12/01/1984
Merged into Colonial General Inc. 11/24/1986
Each share Common $60 par received $250 cash
Note: Certificates were not required to be surrendered and are without value

FIRST CORP (AL)
Stock Dividend - 5% payable 11/16/1998 to holders of record 10/30/1998
Merged into BancorpSouth Inc. 12/31/1998
Each share Common 5¢ par exchanged for (9.5758) shares Common $2.50 par
BancorpSouth Inc. reorganized as BancorpSouth Bank (Tupelo, MS) 11/01/2017

FIRST CORPORATE CAP INC (ON)
Merged into Genterra Capital Corp. (New) 02/28/1997
Each share Class A Subordinate no par exchanged for (0.69) share Class A Subordinate no par
Each share Class B Multiple no par exchanged for (0.759) share Class A Subordinate no par
Each share Conv. Class C Subordinate no par exchanged for (0.69) share Class A Subordinate no par
Each share Non-Vtg. Class D Special Share no par exchanged for (0.33333333) share Non-Vtg. Class D Preferred Ser. 1 no par and (1) share Non-Vtg. Class D Preferred Ser. 2 no par
Genterra Capital Corp. (New) recapitalized as Genterra Capital Inc. (Old) 06/30/1998 which name changed to Genterra Investment Corp. 04/30/1999 which merged into Genterra Inc. 12/31/2003 which merged into Genterra Capital Inc. (New) 05/10/2010 which merged into Gencan Capital Inc. 10/30/2015

FIRST CNTYS BK LAKESHORE DRIVE (CLEARLAKE, CA)
Stock Dividend - 5% payable 11/16/98 to holders of record 10/30/98
Merged into Westamerica Bancorporation 8/17/2000
Each share Common $2.50 par exchanged for (0.8035) share Common no par

FIRST CNTY BK (DOYLESTOWN, PA)
Merged into Univest National Bank & Trust Co. (Souderton, PA) 05/19/2003
Each share Common $2.50 par exchanged for $19.311797 cash

FIRST CNTY BK N J (NORTH BRUNSWICK, NJ)
Merged into First Jersey National Corp. 12/03/1984
Each share Common $2.50 par

exchanged for (0.519231) share Common $5 par
(See First Jersey National Corp.)

FIRST CNTY NATL BK & TR CO (WOODBURY, NJ)
Merged into National Bank & Trust Co. of Gloucester County (Woodbury, NJ) 07/17/1970
Each share Common $10 par exchanged for (1) share Capital Stock $10 par
National Bank & Trust Co. of Gloucester County (Woodbury, NJ) reorganized as Community Bancshares Corp. 10/01/1975 which merged into First Fidelity Bancorporation (Old) 09/28/1985 which merged into First Fidelity Bancorporation (New) 02/29/1988 which merged into First Union Corp. 01/01/1996 which name changed to Wachovia Corp. (Ctfs. dated after 09/01/2001) 09/01/2001 which merged into Wells Fargo & Co. (New) 12/31/2008

FIRST COUNTY NATIONAL BANK (BROCKTON, MA)
Name changed to Shawmut First County Bank, N.A. (Brockton, Mass.) 4/1/75

FIRST COWETA BK (NEWNAN, GA)
Placed in receivership 08/21/2009
Stockholders' equity unlikely

FIRST CREDIT CO.
Dissolved in 1945

FIRST CUSTODIAN SHARES CORP.
Liquidated in 1934

FIRST CYPRESS INC (NV)
Name changed 08/28/2003
Common $0.001 par split (5) for (1) by issuance of (4) additional shares payable 10/16/2002 to holders of record 10/14/2002 Ex date - 10/17/2002
Name changed from First Cypress Technologies, Inc. to First Cypress, Inc. 08/28/2003
Recapitalized as Otish Mountain Diamond Co. 10/23/2003
Each share Common $0.001 par exchanged for (0.005) share Common $0.001 par
Otish Mountain Diamond Co. name changed to Gulf Coast Oil & Gas, Inc. 01/27/2005

FIRST DATA CORP OLD (DE)
Common 1¢ par split (2) for (1) by issuance of (1) additional share payable 11/15/1996 to holders of record 11/01/1996 Ex date - 11/18/1996
Common 1¢ par split (2) for (1) by issuance of (1) additional share payable 06/04/2002 to holders of record 05/20/2002 Ex date - 06/05/2002
Each share Common 1¢ par received distribution of (1) share Western Union Co. Common 1¢ par payable 09/29/2006 to holders of record 09/22/2006 Ex date - 10/02/2006
Merged into New Omaha Holdings LP 09/24/2007
Each share Common 1¢ par exchanged for $34 cash

FIRST DATA MGMT INC (OK)
Merged into First Data Management Holding Co. 06/16/1987
Each (100) shares Common $1 par exchanged for $1,000 principal amount of 14.375% Sr. Subordinated Debentures due 06/15/2002
Note: Holdings of (99) or fewer shares exchanged for $10 cash per share

FIRST DATA RES INC (DE)
Merged into American Express Co. 10/30/1985

Each share Common 1¢ par exchanged for $38.25 cash

FIRST DEARBORN INCOME PPTYS L P (DE)
Filed Certification of Cancellation 01/14/2008
Details not available

FIRST DECATUR BANCSHARES INC (DE)
Merged into Main Street Trust, Inc. 03/23/2000
Each share Common $25 par exchanged for (1.638) shares Common 1¢ par
Main Street Trust, Inc. merged into First Busey Corp. 08/01/2007

FIRST DELTA INC (MN)
Recapitalized as Metropolitan Entertainment Corp. of America 1/31/90
Each share Common no par exchanged for (1/3) share Common no par
(See Metropolitan Entertainment Corp. of America)

FIRST DELTAVISION INC (NV)
Each share old Common $0.001 par exchanged for (4) shares new Common $0.001 par 04/04/2002
Name changed to KyoMedix Corp. 04/04/2002 which name changed back to First Deltavision, Inc. 11/18/2002
Name changed to Integrated Healthcare Holdings, Inc. 03/04/2004
(See Integrated Healthcare Holdings, Inc.)

FIRST DENVER MTG INVS (MA)
Name changed to Property Investors of Colorado 3/31/81
Property Investors of Colorado name changed to JFB Realty Trust 10/3/96

FIRST DEP BANCSHARES INC (GA)
Merged into Community First Banking Co. 5/23/2001
Each share Common no par exchanged for either (0.5155) share Common 1¢ par and $8.81 cash or $19.375 cash
Note: Option to receive stock and cash expired 6/22/2001
Community First Banking Co. merged into BB&T Corp. 12/12/2001

FIRST DES PLAINES CORP (DE)
Completely liquidated 09/20/1984
Holdings entitled to a distribution of $22,399 or less exchanged for $60.25 cash
Holdings entitled to a distribution of $22,400 or more exchanged for 8% Subord. Debs. due 10/31/1994 with warrants to purchase Boulevard Bancorp, Inc. Common expiring 11/01/1994, $60.25 cash or a combination thereof

FIRST DETROIT COMMERCIAL CORP. (MI)
Dissolved in 1931

FIRST DEVONIAN EXPLS LTD (AB)
Recapitalized as Cube Energy Corp. 12/22/1988
Each share Common no par exchanged for (0.1) share Common no par
(See Cube Energy Corp.)

FIRST DISCOUNT CORP. (IN)
5% Preferred $50 par called for redemption 13/31/65
Public interest eliminated

FIRST DOHERTY ORGANIZATION ANTICIPATION CO.
Dissolved in 1941

FIRST DOHERTY ORGANIZATION INVESTING CO.
Dissolved in 1941

FIRST DOMINION EQUITIES INC (DE)
Charter cancelled and declared inoperative and void for non-payment of taxes 3/1/89

FIRST DUBUQUE CORP (IA)
Merged into Hawkeye Bancorporation 05/03/1993
Each share Common no par exchanged for (3.01) shares Common $3 par
Hawkeye Bancorporation merged into Mercantile Bancorporation, Inc. 01/02/1996 which merged into Firstar Corp. (New) 09/20/1999 which merged into U.S. Bancorp (DE) 02/27/2001

FIRST DYNA CORP (PA)
Name changed to First Financial Group Inc. 04/28/1980
First Financial Group Inc. merged into Union National Corp. 01/22/1986 which merged into Integra Financial Corp. 01/26/1989 which merged into National City Corp. 05/03/1996 which was acquired by PNC Financial Services Group, Inc. 12/31/2008

FIRST DYNAMIC RESOURCES, INC. (DE)
Name changed to Cal-Star Financial Services, Inc. 4/19/84
(See Cal-Star Financial Services, Inc.)

FIRST DYNASTY MINES LTD (ON)
Name changed to Sterlite Gold Ltd. 05/21/2002
(See Sterlite Gold Ltd.)

FIRST DYNASTY VENTURES INC (CANADA)
Name changed to Firstfund Capital (1986) Corp. 11/07/1986
Firstfund Capital (1986) Corp. recapitalized as Consolidated Firstfund Capital Corp. 10/26/1988

FIRST EASTERN NATIONAL BANK (KINGSPORT, TN)
Merged into First American Corp. (TN) 9/30/82
Each share Common $10 par exchanged for $100 cash

FIRST EASTN BK N A (WILKES-BARRE, PA)
Stock Dividend - 10% 08/01/1975
Under plan of reorganization each share Common $10 par automatically became (1) share First Eastern Corp. Common $10 par 08/02/1982
(See First Eastern Corp.)

FIRST EASTN CAP CORP (DE)
Charter cancelled and declared inoperative and void for non-payment of taxes 03/01/1987

FIRST EASTN CORP (PA)
Common $10 par split (3) for (2) by issuance of (0.5) additional share 1/10/84
Common $10 par split (3) for (2) by issuance of (0.5) additional share 2/1/85
Common $10 par split (2) for (1) by issuance of (1) additional share 1/2/87
Acquired by PNC Bank Corp. 6/17/94
Each share Common $10 par exchanged for $27 cash

FIRST EASTN ENERGY DEV INC (CANADA)
Reincorporated under the laws of Nevada as Alliance Enterprise Corp. 6/17/2004

FIRST EASTN PPTY DEV INC (ON)
Recapitalized as First Eastern Equities, Inc. 07/22/1988
Each share Common no par exchanged for (0.2) share Common no par

FIRST ECHELON VENTURES INC (BC)
Recapitalized as Aumega Discoveries Ltd. 12/11/2003

Each share Common no par exchanged for (0.25) share Common no par
Aumega Discoveries Ltd. recapitalized as Fortress Base Metals Corp. 01/10/2007 which name changed to Lions Gate Metals Inc. 07/21/2008 which name changed to Block X Capital Corp. 01/25/2018

FIRST ECOM COM INC (NV)
Name changed to Brek Energy Corp. 01/31/2002
Brek Energy Corp. merged into Gasco Energy, Inc. 12/14/2007
(See Gasco Energy, Inc.)

FIRST ELBERT CORP. (GA)
Name changed to Pinnacle Financial Corp. (GA) 8/10/93

FIRST EMPIRE CORP (ON)
Recapitalized as Noble House Entertainment Inc. (ON) 11/01/2004
Each share Common no par exchanged for (0.1) share Common no par
Noble House Entertainment Inc. (ON) reincorporated in Canada as LiveReel Media Corp. 12/01/2006 which name changed to CordovaCann Corp. 08/08/2018

FIRST EMPIRE ENTMT COM INC (ON)
Recapitalized as First Empire Corp. 08/14/2003
Each share Common no par exchanged for (0.5) share Common no par
First Empire Corp. reorganized as Noble House Entertainment Inc. (ON) 11/01/2004 which reincorporated in Canada as LiveReel Media Corp. 12/01/2006

FIRST EMPIRE ST CORP (NY)
Common $5 par split (2) for (1) by issuance of (1) additional share 9/21/87
Name changed to M&T Bank Corp. 6/1/98

FIRST ENID INC (OK)
Company went out of business 11/06/1986
No stockholders' equity

1ST ENTERPRISE BK (LOS ANGELES, CA)
Merged into CU Bancorp 12/01/2014
Each share Common no par exchanged for (1.345) shares Common no par
CU Bancorp merged into PacWest Bancorp 10/20/2017

FIRST ENTERPRISE BANK (OAKLAND, CA)
Common $10 par changed to $5 par and (1) additional share issued 01/31/1974
Under plan of reorganization each share Common $5 par automatically became (1) share Enterprise Bancorp Common no par 05/28/1982
(See Enterprise Bancorp)

FIRST ENTERPRISE FINL GROUP INC (IL)
Involuntarily dissolved 3/4/99

FIRST ENTMT CORP (BC)
Recapitalized as MMX Ventures Inc. 07/12/1996
Each share Common no par exchanged for (0.2) share Common no par
MMX Ventures Inc. name changed to IP Applications Corp. 06/23/2000 which name changed to Monexa Technologies Corp. 10/28/2009 which name changed to Santa Rosa Resources Corp. 04/03/2012

FIRST ENTMT HLDG CORP (NV)
Name changed 12/15/1997
Each share old Common $0.008 par

exchanged for (0.5) share new Common $0.008 par 11/21/1994
Each share new Common $0.008 par exchanged again for (0.25) share new Common $0.008 par 05/14/1996
Name and state of incorporation changed from First Entertainment Inc. (CO) to First Entertainment Holding Corp. (NV) and Common $0.008 par changed to no par 12/15/1997
Name changed to F2 Broadcast Networks Inc. 01/04/2001
F2 Broadcast Networks Inc. name changed to Strat Petroleum, Ltd. 07/08/2004
(See Strat Petroleum, Ltd.)

FIRST ENUMCLAW BANCORPORATION (WA)
Merged into Puget Sound Bancorp 11/30/90
Each share Common $2 par exchanged for $40 cash

FIRST EQUITY CORP (OK)
Merged into Norin Corp. (DE) 11/03/1972
Each share Common 10¢ par exchanged for (0.085) share Common $1 par
Norin Corp. (DE) reorganized in Florida 05/31/1979
(See Norin Corp. (FL))

FIRST EQUITY FINL CORP (FL)
Merged into First Equity Merger Corp. 08/26/1986
Each share Common 10¢ par exchanged for $3 cash

FIRST EQUITY HLDG CORP (NV)
Recapitalized as Chilmark Entertainment Group, Inc. 06/23/2003
Each share Common $0.001 par exchanged for (0.001) share Common $0.001 par
Chilmark Entertainment Group, Inc. recapitalized as Integrated Bio Energy Resources, Inc. 03/13/2007 which name changed to Onslow Holdings, Inc. 01/30/2014

FIRST EQUITY INVTS PALM BEACH INC (FL)
Name changed to Chromalux Corp. 6/23/87
(See Chromalux Corp.)

FIRST EQUITY LIFE INSURANCE CO. OF MISSOURI (NEW) (MO)
Each share old Common $1 par exchanged for (0.75) share new Common $1 par 05/24/1974
Merged into Pan-Western Life Insurance Co. 06/11/1979
Details not available

FIRST EQUITY LIFE INSURANCE CO. OF MISSOURI (OLD) (MO)
Merged into First Equity Life Insurance Co. of Missouri (New) 02/04/1972
Each share Common $1 par exchanged for (0.53) share Common $1 par
(See First Equity Life Insurance Co. of Missouri (New))

FIRST EQUITY N J INC (NJ)
Recapitalized as Autobitter Group, Inc. 08/04/1992
Each (15) shares Common $0.0001 par exchanged for (1) share Common $0.0001 par
(See Autobitter Group, Inc.)

FIRST EQUITY SEC INVT CORP (IN)
Common $5 par changed to no par 9/21/67
Administratively dissolved 12/31/87

FIRST ESSEX BANCORP INC (DE)
Merged into Sovereign Bancorp, Inc. 02/06/2004
Each share Common 10¢ par exchanged for $48 cash

FIRST ESTATE CORP. (DE)
Name changed to Triex International Corp. 3/24/70
(See Triex International Corp.)

FIRST ESTATE GROUP LTD. (PA)
Reincorporated under the laws of Colorado as Companies West Group Inc. 10/09/1986

FIRST EVERGREEN CORP (DE)
Merged into Old Kent Financial Corp. 10/1/98
Each share Common $25 par exchanged for (32.0312) shares Common $1 par
Old Kent Financial Corp. merged into Fifth Third Bancorp 4/2/2001

FIRST EXECUTIVE BANCORP INC (PA)
Name changed to ExecuFirst Bancorp Inc. 11/02/1988
ExecuFirst Bancorp Inc. name changed to First Republic Bancorp, Inc. 06/07/1996 which name changed to Republic First Bancorp, Inc. 07/15/1997

FIRST EXECUTIVE CORP (DE)
Reincorporated 4/22/70
State of incorporation changed from (CA) to (DE) 4/22/70
1st Ser. Conv. Preference $1 par called for redemption 2/26/82
Common $2 par split (5) for (4) by issuance of (0.25) additional share 1/14/83
Common $2 par split (4) for (3) by issuance of (1/3) additional share 10/17/83
Common $2 par split (5) for (4) by issuance of (0.25) additional share 9/26/86
Stock Dividends - 10% 6/25/79; 50% 2/11/80; 50% 11/17/80; 100% 11/2/81
Plan of reorganization under Chapter 11 Federal Bankruptcy Code effective 9/1/92
Each holder of Adjustable Rate Preferred Ser. E $1 par, Depositary Preferred Ser. E $1 par, Preferred Ser. F $1 par, Depositary Preferred Ser. F $1 par, $1.5625 Conv. Preferred Ser. G $1 par, Depositary Preference Ser. H $1 par and Common $2 par received an undivided beneficial interest in FEC Shareholder Trust for possible distributions to be made on or before 9/11/97
Note: Certificates were not required to be surrendered and all outstanding shares have been cancelled and retired

FIRST EXPL CO (CO)
Administratively dissolved 02/06/1995

FIRST FACTOR DEVS INC (CANADA)
Name changed to Millrock Resources Inc. (Canada) 08/14/2007
Millrock Resources Inc. (Canada) reincorporated in British Columbia 07/24/2008

FIRST FAMILY BK FSB (EUSTIS, FL)
Under plan of reorganization each share Common $1 par automatically became (1) share First Family Financial Corp. Common 1¢ par 11/09/1994
First Family Financial Corp. merged into Colonial BancGroup, Inc. 01/09/1997
(See Colonial BancGroup, Inc.)

FIRST FAMILY FINL CORP (FL)
Merged into Colonial BancGroup, Inc. 01/09/1997
Each share Common 1¢ par exchanged for (0.2997) share Common $2.50 par and $11.75 cash
(See Colonial BancGroup, Inc.)

FIRST FAMILY GROUP INC (OH)
Reorganized as Home Centers, Inc. 7/2/90

Each share Common no par exchanged for (1) share Common no par
(See Home Centers, Inc.)

FIRST FARWEST CORP (OR)
Each share Common 50¢ par exchanged for (0.2) share Common $2.50 par 08/01/1976
Plan of reorganization under Chapter 11 Federal Bankruptcy proceedings confirmed 12/29/1989
No stockholders' equity

FIRST FD VA INC (VA)
Acquired by New York Venture Fund, Inc. 5/25/76
Each share Common 50¢ par exchanged for (1.15858) shares Capital Stock $1 par
New York Venture Fund, Inc. name changed to Davis New York Venture Fund, Inc. 10/1/95

FIRST FED ALA F S B (JASPER, AL)
Name changed to Pinnacle Bank (Jasper, AL) 1/8/96
Pinnacle Bank (Jasper, AL) reorganized as Pinnacle Bancshares, Inc. 1/31/97

FIRST FED BANC SOUTHWEST INC (DE)
Merged into Washington Federal, Inc. 2/13/2007
Each share Common 1¢ par exchanged for $24.14 cash

FIRST FED BANCORP INC (DE)
Taken over by the RTC 10/16/91
Stockholders' equity unlikely

FIRST FED BANCORP INC (OH)
Merged into Park National Corp. 12/31/2004
Each share Common no par exchanged for $13.25 cash

FIRST FED BANCORPORATION (MN)
Old Common 1¢ par split (3) for (2) by issuance of (0.5) additional share payable 12/18/97 to holders of record 12/5/97
Old Common 1¢ par split (3) for (2) by issuance of (0.5) additional share payable 5/20/99 to holders of record 5/5/99
Each (4,000) shares old Common 1¢ par exchanged for (1) share new Common 1¢ par 11/19/2003
Note: In effect holders received $14 cash per share and public interest was eliminated

FIRST FED BANCSHARES ARK INC (AR)
Old Common 1¢ par split (2) for (1) by issuance of (1) additional share payable 12/31/2003 to holders of record 12/17/2003 Ex date - 01/02/2004
Each share old Common 1¢ par exchanged for (0.2) share new Common 1¢ par 05/04/2011
State of incorporation changed from (TX) to (AR) 07/20/2011
Name changed to Bear State Financial, Inc. 06/03/2014
(See Bear State Financial, Inc.)

FIRST FED BANCSHARES DEFUNIAK SPRINGS INC (FL)
Proclaimed dissolved for failure to file reports and pay fees 08/26/1994

FIRST FED BANCSHARES INC (DE)
Merged into Heartland Bancorp, Inc. 2/28/2007
Each share Common 1¢ par exchanged for $23 cash

FIRST FED BANCSHARES OF EAU CLAIRE INC (WI)
Merged into Mutual Savings Bank of Milwaukee (Milwaukee, WI) 3/31/97
Each share Common 1¢ par exchanged for $18.85 cash

FIRST FEDERAL BANK, A FEDERAL SAVINGS BANK (VINCENNES, IN)
Under plan of reorganization each share Common $1 par automatically became (1) share 1st Bancorp Common $1 par 8/4/89
1st Bancorp merged into German American Bancorp 1/4/99 which name changed to German American Bancorp Inc. 5/22/2006

FIRST FED BK FOR SVGS (STARKVILLE, MS)
Merged into BancorpSouth, Inc. 07/31/1995
Each share Common $1 par exchanged for (0.698) share Common $2.50 par
BancorpSouth, Inc. reorganized as BancorpSouth Bank (Tupelo, MS) 11/01/2017

FIRST FED BK FSB (NASHUA, NH)
Acquired by New Hampshire Savings Bank Corp. 07/01/1988
Each share Common $1 par exchanged for (2.7692) shares Common $1 par
(See New Hampshire Savings Bank Corp.)

FIRST FED BK NORTHWEST GA FSB (CEDARTOWN, GA)
Merged into Regions Financial Corp. (Old) 4/1/96
Each share Common 1¢ par exchanged for (1.293) shares Common $0.625 par
Regions Financial Corp. (Old) merged into Regions Financial Corp. (New) 7/1/2004

FIRST FED BANKSHARES INC (DE)
In process of liquidation
Each share Common 1¢ par received initial distribution of $0.013 cash payable 03/26/2010 to holders of record 03/15/2010
Note: Details on additional distribution(s), if any, are not available

FIRST FED CAP CORP (WI)
Merged into Associated Banc-Corp. 01/26/2005
Each share Common 10¢ par exchanged for (0.9525) share Common 10¢ par

FIRST FED CAROLINAS F A HIGH PT N C (USA)
90¢ Conv. Preferred Ser. A $1 par called for redemption 05/15/1987
Reorganized under the laws of Delaware as Carolina Bancorp, Inc. 05/23/1988
Each share Common $1 par exchanged for (1) share Common 1¢ par
Carolina Bancorp, Inc. (DE) merged into BB&T Financial Corp. 08/20/1990 which merged into Southern National Corp. 02/28/1995 which merged into Southern National Corp. which name changed to BB&T Corp. 05/19/1997

FIRST FED ENERGY CORP (TN)
Charter revoked for non-payment of taxes 08/03/1984

FIRST FED ENTERPRISES INC (FL)
Merged into First Alabama Bancshares, Inc. 12/16/93
Each share Common $1 par exchanged for (0.363) share Common $0.625 par
First Alabama Bancshares, Inc. name changed to Regions Financial Corp. (Old) 5/2/94 which merged into Regions Financial Corp. (New) 7/1/2004

FIRST FED FINL BANCORP INC (DE)
Merged into Classic Bancshares, Inc. 6/20/2003
Each share Common 1¢ par exchanged for $24 cash

FIRST FED FINL CORP KY (KY)
Common $1 par split (2) for (1) by issuance of (1) additional share 07/20/1993

Common $1 par split (2) for (1) by issuance of (1) additional share payable 06/10/1996 to holders of record 06/03/1996
Stock Dividend - 10% payable 05/14/2003 to holders of record 04/28/2003 Ex date - 04/24/2003
Name changed to First Financial Service Corp. 06/01/2004
First Financial Service Corp. merged into Community Bank Shares of Indiana, Inc. 01/02/2015 which name changed to Your Community Bankshares, Inc. 07/01/2015 which merged into WesBanco, Inc. 09/09/2016

FIRST FED FINL SVCS INC (USA)
Merged into First Clover Leaf Financial Corp. 07/10/2006
Each share Common 10¢ par exchanged for (1.93621) shares Common 10¢ par
First Clover Leaf Financial Corp. merged into First Mid-Illinois Bancshares, Inc. 09/08/2016

FIRST FEDERAL FOREIGN BANKING CORP.
Liquidation completed in 1941

FIRST FEDERAL FOREIGN INVESTMENT TRUST
Name changed to First Federal Foreign Banking Corp. in 1929
(See First Federal Foreign Banking Corp.)

FIRST FEDERAL LIFE INSURANCE CO. (MD)
Name changed to First Federated Life Insurance Co. (Old) in 1958
First Federated Life Insurance Co. (Old) merged into Telephone Employees Life Insurance Co. 9/20/63 which name changed back to First Federated Life Insurance Co. (New) 9/30/63
(See First Federated Life Insurance Co. (New))

FIRST FED MICH DETROIT (USA)
Under plan of reorganization each share Common 1¢ par automatically became (1) share FirstFed Michigan Corp. Common 1¢ par 05/01/1989
FirstFed Michigan Corp. merged into Charter One Financial, Inc. 10/31/1995
(See Charter One Financial, Inc.)

FIRST FED NORTHN MICH BANCORP INC (MD)
Merged into Mackinac Financial Corp. 05/18/2018
Each share Common 1¢ par exchanged for (0.576) share Common no par

FIRST FED OLATHE BANCORP INC (KS)
Issue Information - 5,500,000 shares COM offered at $10 per share on 12/16/99
Under plan of merger each share Common 1¢ par exchanged for $33.60 cash 5/5/2004

FIRST FEDERAL SAVINGS & LOAN ASSOCIATION (NC)
Acquired by Old Stone Corp. 04/01/1985
Each share Common $1 par exchanged for (1) share Common $1 par
(See Old Stone Corp.)

FIRST FED SVGS & LN ASSN ALPENA (USA)
Under plan of reorganization each share Common $1 par automatically became (1) share Alpena Bancshares, Inc. (MI) Common $1 par 01/01/2001
Alpena Bancshares, Inc. (MI) reorganized in Maryland as First Federal Northern Michigan Bancorp, Inc. 04/01/2005 which merged into Mackinac Financial Corp. 05/18/2018

FIRST FED SVGS & LN ASSN ARIZ PHOENIX (USA)
Name changed to First Federal Savings Bank of Arizona (Phoenix, AZ) 07/19/1985
First Federal Savings Bank of Arizona (Phoenix, AZ) name changed to MeraBank, A Federal Savings Bank (Phoenix, AZ) 01/02/1986
(See MeraBank, A Federal Savings Bank (Phoenix, AZ))

FIRST FED SVGS & LN ASSN AUSTIN TEX (USA)
Placed in receivership 09/00/1988
No stockholders' equity

FIRST FED SVGS & LN ASSN BROOKSVILLE FLA (USA)
Merged into Mid-State Federal Savings & Loan Association 10/01/1987
Each share Common 1¢ par exchanged for (0.643) share Common $1 par and $12.03 cash
Mid-State Federal Savings & Loan Association reorganized as Mid-State Federal Savings Bank (Ocala, FL) 04/28/1989 which merged into AmSouth Bancorporation 12/09/1993 which merged into Regions Financial Corp. 11/04/2006

FIRST FED SVGS & LN ASSN CHARLESTON S C (USA)
Common $1 par split (2) for (1) by issuance of (1) additional share 03/24/1986
Stock Dividend - 10% 05/20/1985
Reorganized under the laws of Delaware as First Financial Holdings, Inc. 06/30/1988
Each share Common $1 par exchanged for (1) share Common 1¢ par
First Financial Holdings, Inc. (DE) merged into First Financial Holdings, Inc. (SC) 07/30/2013 which name changed to South State Corp. 06/30/2014

FIRST FED SVGS & LN ASSN CHICKASHA OKLA (USA)
Placed in conservatorship 03/22/1991
No stockholders' equity

FIRST FED SVGS & LN ASSN COEUR D ALENE (ID)
Common $1 par split (2) for (1) by issuance of (1) additional share 4/15/86
Stock Dividends - 10% 11/5/86; 10% 9/22/87; 10% 10/20/88
Under plan of reorganization name changed to Mountain West Savings Bank, F.S.B. (Coeur D'Alene, ID) 8/14/89
(See Mountain West Savings Bank, F.S.B. (Coeur D'Alene, ID))

FIRST FED SVGS & LN ASSN COLUMBIA (TN)
Under plan of reorganization each share Common $1 par automatically became (1) share First Chattanooga Financial Corp. Common $1 par 5/11/89
First Chattanooga Financial Corp. acquired by AmSouth Bancorporation 2/1/93 which merged into Regions Financial Corp. 11/4/2006

FIRST FED SVGS & LN ASSN EAST HARTFORD CONN (USA)
Merged into Connecticut Bancshares, Inc. 08/31/2001
Each share Common 1¢ par exchanged for $37.50 cash

FIRST FED SVGS & LN ASSN FT MYERS FLA (USA)
Common 1¢ par split (5) for (4) by issuance of (0.25) additional share 01/31/1986
Common 1¢ par split (4) for (3) by issuance of (1/3) additional share 01/12/1987
Stock Dividend - 20% 05/08/1985
Acquired by Society Corp. 01/22/1993
Each share Common 1¢ par exchanged for $45 cash

FIRST FED SVGS & LN ASSN GEORGETOWN S C (USA)
Merged into Carolina First Corp. 08/31/1990
Each share Common $1 par exchanged for (1.25) shares Common $1 par
Carolina First Corp. name changed to South Financial Group, Inc. 04/24/2000 which merged into Toronto-Dominion Bank (Toronto, ON) 09/30/2010

FIRST FED SVGS & LN ASSN HARRISBURG PA (USA)
Reorganized as First Harrisburg Bancor, Inc. 08/18/1989
Each share Common $1 par exchanged for (1) share Common 1¢ par
(See First Harrisburg Bancor, Inc.)

FIRST FED SVGS & LN ASSN LENAWEE CNTY MICH (USA)
Merged into Standard Federal Bank (Troy, MI) 08/07/1992
Each share Common $1 par exchanged for $27.94 cash

FIRST FED SVGS & LN ASSN MADISON (USA)
Name changed to First Federal Savings, F.A. 10/24/1984
First Federal Savings, F.A. name changed to Omnibank of Connecticut, Inc. 08/19/1987
(See Omnibank of Connecticut, Inc.)

FIRST FED SVGS & LN ASSN MICH KALAMAZOO (USA)
Acquired by Standard Federal Bank (Troy, MI) 01/03/1989
Each share Common 1¢ par exchanged for $29 cash

FIRST FED SVGS & LN ASSN MONT (USA)
Under plan of reorganization each share Common $1 par automatically became (1) share Big Sky Bancorp, Inc. Common 1¢ par 12/01/1994
Big Sky Bancorp, Inc. merged into Sterling Financial Corp. 11/13/1998
(See Sterling Financial Corp.)

FIRST FEDERAL SAVINGS & LOAN ASSOCIATION OF TORRINGTON (USA)
Reorganized under the laws of Delaware as Eagle Financial Corp. 02/10/1987
Eagle Financial Corp. merged into Webster Financial Corp. 04/15/1998

FIRST FED SVGS & LN ASSN PANAMA CITY (FL)
Name changed to Florida First Federal Savings Bank (Panama City, FL) 4/28/88
Florida First Federal Savings Bank (Panama City, FL) reorganized as Florida First Bancorp Inc. 5/1/95
(See Florida First Bancorp Inc.)

FIRST FED SVGS & LN ASSN RALEIGH (NC)
Stock Dividend - 10% 04/29/1983
Reorganized as Firstcorp, Inc. 05/01/1985
Each share Common $1 par exchanged for (1.5) shares Common $1 par
(See Firstcorp, Inc.)

FIRST FED SVGS & LN ASSN ROANOKE VA (USA)
Acquired by CorEast Savings Bank, FSB (Roanoke, VA) 04/01/1988
Each share Common 10¢ par exchanged for $25 cash

FIRST FED SVGS & LN ASSN S C GREENVILLE (USA)
Stock Dividends - 10% 04/15/1986; 10% 10/20/1987
Name changed to First Savings Bank, FSB (Greenville, SC) 12/14/1990
First Savings Bank, FSB (Greenville, SC) merged into Southern National Corp. 01/28/1994 which name changed to BB&T Corp. 05/19/1997

FIRST FED SVGS & LN ASSN SAN BERNARDINO (CA)
Merged into JNL Thrift Acquisition Corp. 11/9/98
Each share Common $1 par exchanged for $17.08 cash

FIRST FED SVGS & LN ASSN SANFORD N C (USA)
Merged into RS Financial Corp. 03/28/1989
Each share Common 1¢ par exchanged for $19 cash

FIRST FED SVGS & LN ASSN WINTER HAVEN FLA (USA)
Acquired by Philadelphia Saving Fund Society (Philadelphia, PA) 07/01/1985
Each share Common 1¢ par exchanged for $26.94227 cash

FIRST FED SVGS & LN ASSN WOOSTER OHIO (USA)
Under plan of reorganization each share Common $1 par automatically became (1) share FirstFederal Financial Services Corp. (OH) Common $1 par 07/21/1989
FirstFederal Financial Services Corp. name changed to Signal Corp. 06/16/1998 which merged into FirstMerit Corp. 02/12/1999 which merged into Huntington Bancshares Inc. 08/16/2016

FIRST FED SVGS & LN COLORADO SPRINGS (CO)
Common $1 par split (2) for (1) by issuance of (1) additional share 8/6/85
Common $1 par split (3) for (2) by issuance of (0.5) additional share 8/19/86
Name changed to First Colorado Financial Corp. 8/12/86
(See First Colorado Financial Corp.)

FIRST FED SVGS & LN DEFIANCE OH (USA)
Merged into First Defiance Financial Corp. 09/21/95
Each share Common 1¢ par exchanged for (2.1590231) shares Common 1¢ par

FIRST FED SVGS ARK F A (USA)
Placed in receivership 08/31/1989
Stockholders' equity unlikely

FIRST FED SVGS BK (BAINBRIDGE, GA)
Merged into PAB Bankshares, Inc. 01/01/1995
Each share Common 1¢ par exchanged for (1.05) shares Common no par
(See PAB Bankshares, Inc.)

FIRST FED SVGS BK (BRUNSWICK, GA)
Merged into NationsBank Corp. 4/15/97
Each share Common $1 par exchanged for (1.6) shares Common no par
NationsBank Corp. reincorporated in Delaware as BankAmerica Corp. (Old) 9/25/98 which merged into BankAmerica Corp. (New) 9/30/98 which name changed to Bank of America Corp. 4/28/99

FIRST FEDERAL SAVINGS BANK (CALHOUN, GA)
Acquired by AmSouth Bancorporation 4/8/94
Each share Common 1¢ par

exchanged for (0.9991) share Common $1 par
AmSouth Bancorporation merged into Regions Financial Corp. 11/4/2006

FIRST FED SVGS BK (DECATUR, AL)
Under plan of reorganization each share Common 1¢ par automatically became (1) share Alafirst Bancshares, Inc. (DE) Common 1¢ par 04/24/1991
Alafirst Bancshares, Inc. name changed to Bancfirst Corp. 03/01/1993 which name changed to BNF Bancorp, Inc. 03/02/1994 which was acquired by Union Planters Corp. 09/01/1994 which merged into Regions Financial Corp. (New) 07/01/2004

FIRST FED SVGS BK (DEFUNIAK SPRINGS, FL)
Under plan of reorganization each share Common $1 par automatically became (1) share First Federal Bancshares of Defuniak Springs Inc. Common $1 par 12/31/1992
(See First Federal Bancshares of Defuniak Springs Inc.)

FIRST FED SVGS BK (DICKSON, TN)
Each share old Common $1 par exchanged for (0.004) share new Common $1 par 5/13/94
Note: In effect holders received $13 cash per share and public interest was eliminated

FIRST FED SVGS BK (ELIZABETHTOWN, KY)
Under plan of reorganization each share Common $1 par automatically became (1) share First Federal Financial Corp. of Kentucky Common $1 par 06/01/1990
First Federal Financial Corp. of Kentucky name changed to First Financial Service Corp. 06/01/2004 which merged into Community Bank Shares of Indiana, Inc. 01/02/2015 which name changed to Your Community Bankshares, Inc. 07/01/2015 which merged into WesBanco, Inc. 09/09/2016

FIRST FED SVGS BK (HOPKINSVILLE, KY)
Acquired by Liberty National Bancorp, Inc. 11/30/93
Each share Common exchanged for (1.4705) shares Common no par Liberty National Bancorp, Inc. merged into Banc One Corp. 8/15/94 which merged into Bank One Corp. 10/2/98 which merged into J.P. Morgan Chase & Co. 12/31/2000 which name changed to JPMorgan Chase & Co. 7/20/2004

FIRST FED SVGS BK (KANE, PA)
Merged into Northwest Savings Bank (Warren, PA) 3/31/96
Each share Common 10¢ par exchanged for $32.40 cash

FIRST FED SVGS BK (MARIANNA, FL)
Under plan of reorganization each share Common $1 par automatically became (1) share First Federal Enterprises, Inc. Common $1 par 5/1/91
First Federal Enterprises, Inc. merged into First Alabama Bancshares, Inc. 12/16/93 which name changed to Regions Financial Corp. (Old) 5/2/94 which merged into Regions Financial Corp. (New) 7/1/2004

FIRST FED SVGS BK (NEW SMYRNA BEACH, FL)
Under plan of reorganization each share Common $1 par automatically became (1) share FF Bancorp Inc. Common 1¢ par 7/7/92
FF Bancorp Inc. merged into First National Bancorp (GA) 7/3/95 which was acquired by Regions Financial Corp. (Old) 3/1/96 which merged into Regions Financial Corp. (New) 7/1/2004

FIRST FED SVGS BK (PERRY, FL)
Under plan of reorganization each share Common $1 par automatically became (1) share First Financial Bancorp, Inc. Common $1 par 7/8/91
(See First Financial Bancorp, Inc.)

FIRST FED SVGS BK (SALT LAKE CITY, UT)
Name changed 10/25/89
Name changed from First Federal Savings & Loan Association of Salt Lake City (Salt (Salt Lake City, UT) to First Federal Savings Bank (Salt Lake City, UT) 10/25/89
Common $1 par split (3) for (2) by issuance of (0.5) additional share 4/6/92
Stock Dividend - 15% 6/14/91
Acquired by Washington Federal Savings Bank (Seattle, WA) 3/12/93
Each share Common $1 par exchanged for $17 cash

FIRST FED SVGS BK (SAN JUAN, PR)
Common $1 par changed to 1¢ par 08/06/1991
Common 1¢ par split (3) for (2) by issuance of (0.5) additional share 02/26/1993
Common 1¢ par split (3) for (2) by issuance of (0.5) additional share 11/15/1993
Stock Dividend - 10% 12/31/1992
Under plan of reorganization each share Common 1¢ par automatically became (1) share FirstBank Puerto Rico (San Juan, PR) 11/15/1994
FirstBank Puerto Rico (San Juan, PR) reorganized as First Bancorp. 10/01/1998

FIRST FED SVGS BK ARIZ (PHOENIX, AZ)
Name changed to MeraBank, A Federal Savings Bank (Phoenix, AZ) 01/02/1986
(See MeraBank, A Federal Savings Bank (Phoenix, AZ))

FIRST FED SVGS BK CALIF (SANTA MONICA, CA)
Common $1 par split (3) for (2) by issuance of (0.5) additional share 09/20/1985
Common $1 par split (3) for (2) by issuance of (0.5) additional share 07/28/1986
Reorganized under the laws of Delaware as FirstFed Financial Corp. and Common $1 par changed to 1¢ par 09/21/1987
(See FirstFed Financial Corp.)

FIRST FED SVGS BK CHARLOTTE CNTY (PUNTA GORDA, FL)
Stock Dividend - 10% 11/16/1989
Reorganized as F&C Bancshares Inc. 12/31/1991
Each share Common $1 par exchanged for (1) share Common $1 par
F&C Bancshares Inc. merged into First of America Bank Corp. 12/31/1994 which merged into National City Corp. 03/31/1998 which was acquired by PNC Financial Services Group, Inc. 12/31/2008

FIRST FED SVGS BK COLO (LAKEWOOD, CO)
Common $1 par split (3) for (2) by issuance of (0.5) additional share 10/20/93
Reorganized as First Colorado Bancorp Inc. 12/29/95
Each share Common $1 par exchanged for (3.03099353) shares Common 10¢ par
First Colorado Bancorp Inc. merged into Commercial Federal Corp. 8/14/98

(See Commercial Federal Corp.)

FIRST FED SVGS BK FT DODGE (FORT DODGE, IA)
Reorganized as North Central Bancshares, Inc. 03/21/1996
Each share Common 10¢ par exchanged for (1.0841375) shares Common 1¢ par
(See North Central Bancshares, Inc.)

FIRST FED SVGS BK GA (WINDER, GA)
Common $1 par split (3) for (2) by issuance of (0.5) additional share 3/30/87
Bank placed into conservatorship by the Office of Thrift Supervision 11/6/92
Stockholders' equity unlikely

FIRST FED SVGS BK LAGRANGE (LAGRANGE, GA)
Name changed 6/21/89
Name changed from First Federal Savings & Loan Association of LaGrange to First Federal Savings Bank of LaGrange (LaGrange, GA) 6/21/89
Common $1 par split (5) for (4) by issuance of (0.25) additional share 1/1/93
Common $1 par split (2) for (1) by issuance of (1) additional share 1/10/94
Under plan of reorganization each share Common $1 par automatically became (1) share Flag Financial Corp. Common $1 par 3/1/94
(See Flag Financial Corp.)

FIRST FED SVGS BK MONT (KALISPELL, MT)
Common 1¢ par changed to $0.0067 par and (0.5) additional share issued 1/22/86
Common $0.0067 par changed to $0.0044 par and (0.5) additional share issued 7/30/86
Common $0.0044 par split (3) for (2) by issuance of (0.5) additional share 11/30/89
Reincorporated under the laws of Delaware as Glacier Bancorp, Inc. (Old) 1/2/91
Glacier Bancorp, Inc. (Old) reorganized as Glacier Bancorp, Inc. (New) 7/8/98 which reincorporated in Montana 4/30/2004

FIRST FED SVGS BK NEW MEXICO (ROSWELL, NM)
Under plan of reorganization each share Common no par automatically became (1) share First Federal Banc of the Southwest, Inc. Common 1¢ par 8/13/98
(See First Federal Banc of the Southwest, Inc.)

FIRST FED SVGS BK NORTHWEST FLA (FT WALTON BEACH, FL)
Acquired by Central Bancshares of the South, Inc. 10/14/93
Each share Common $1 par exchanged for $10.89 cash

FIRST FEDERAL SAVINGS BANK OF PITT COUNTY (GREENVILLE, SC)
Acquired by BB&T Financial Corp. 9/1/90
Each share Common $1 par exchanged for (1.75) shares Common $2.50 par
BB&T Financial Corp. merged into Southern National Corp. 2/28/95 which name changed to BB&T Corp. 5/19/97

FIRST FED SVGS BK PROVISO TWP (HILLSIDE, IL)
Merged into First Banks Inc. 1/3/94
Each share Common $1 par exchanged for $39.16 cash

FIRST FED SVGS BK SIOUXLAND (SIOUX CITY, IA)
Common $1 par split (3) for (2) by issuance of (0.5) additional share

payable 5/16/97 to holders of record 5/1/97
Stock Dividends - 20% 6/22/95; 10% payable 11/18/96 to holders of record 11/1/96
Reorganized under the laws of Delaware as First Federal Bankshares, Inc. 4/13/99
Each share Common $1 par exchanged for (1.64696) shares Common $1 par

FIRST FED SVGS BK TENN TULLAHOMA (USA)
Merged into Trans Financial Bancorp, Inc. 03/26/1992
Each share Common $1 par exchanged for (1.3618729) shares Common no par
Trans Financial Bancorp, Inc. name changed to Trans Financial, Inc. 04/24/1995 which merged into Star Banc Corp. 08/21/1998 which merged into Firstar Corp. (New) 11/20/1998 which merged into U.S. Bancorp (DE) 02/27/2001

FIRST FED SVGS F A MADISON CONN (USA)
Common 1¢ par split (3) for (2) by issuance of (0.5) additional share 03/13/1985
Common 1¢ par split (2) for (1) by issuance of (1) additional share 05/16/1986
Name changed to OmniBank of Connecticut, Inc. 08/19/1987
(See OmniBank of Connecticut, Inc.)

FIRST FED WESTN PA SHARON (PA)
Merged into First Western Bancorp, Inc. 11/30/1990
Each share Common $5 par exchanged for either (0.76) share Common $5 par, $19 cash or a combination thereof
First Western Bancorp, Inc. merged into Sky Financial Group, Inc. 08/06/1999 which merged into Huntington Bancshares Inc. 07/02/2007

FIRST FEDERATED LIFE INSURANCE CO. OLD (MD)
Merged into Telephone Employees Life Insurance Co. on a (3.5) for (1) basis 9/20/63
Telephone Employees Life Insurance Co. name changed to First Federated Life Insurance Co. (New) 9/30/63
(See First Federated Life Insurance Co. (New))

FIRST FEDT LIFE INS CO NEW (MD)
Capital Stock $5 par changed to $3.75 par and (1/3) additional share issued 9/30/71
Stock Dividend - 10% 5/20/65
Merged into Monumental Corp. 7/15/83
Each share Capital Stock $3.75 par exchanged for $62.50 cash

FIRST FID ACCEP CORP (NV)
Charter revoked for failure to file reports and pay fees 11/1/2002

FIRST FID BANCORP INC FAIRMONT W VA (WV)
Stock Dividend - 10% 8/15/92
Merged into Wesbanco, Inc. 2/28/94
Each share Common $1.25 par exchanged for (0.9) share Common $4.1666 par

FIRST FID BANCORPORATION NEW (NJ)
$3.25 Conv. Preferred Ser. A $1 par called for redemption 10/07/1988
$4 Conv. Preferred Ser. C $1 par called for redemption 11/15/1988
Merged into First Union Corp. 01/01/1996
Each share Conv. Preferred Ser. B $1 par exchanged for (1) share Conv. Preferred Ser. B no par
Each share Adjustable Rate Preferred Ser. D $1 par exchanged for (1)

share Adjustable Rate Preferred Ser. D no par
Each Depositary Preferred Ser. F exchanged for (1) Depositary Preferred Ser. F
Each share 10.64% Preferred Ser. F $1 par exchanged for (1) share 10.64% Preferred Ser. F no par
Each share Common $1 par exchanged for (1.35) shares Common $3.33-1/3 par
First Union Corp. name changed to Wachovia Corp. (Ctfs. dated after 09/01/2001) 09/01/2001 which merged into Wells Fargo & Co. (New) 12/31/2008

FIRST FID BANCORPORATION OLD (NJ)
Common $6.25 par split (2) for (1) by issuance of (1) additional share 03/31/1986
$2.30 Conv. Preferred Ser. A no par called for redemption 07/01/1986
Merged into First Fidelity Bancorporation (New) 02/29/1988
Each share Adjustable Rate Preferred Ser. B no par exchanged for (1) share Adjustable Rate Preferred Ser. D $1 par
Each share $4 Conv. Preferred Ser. C no par exchanged for (1) share $4 Conv. Preferred Ser. C $1 par
Each share Common $6.25 par exchanged for (1) share Common $1 par
First Fidelity Bancorporation (New) merged into First Union Corp. 01/01/1996 which name changed to Wachovia Corp. (Ctfs. dated after 09/01/2001) 09/01/2001 which merged into Wells Fargo & Co. (New) 12/31/2008

FIRST FID CO (CA)
Name changed to First Zenith Mortgage Co. 10/2/72
(See First Zenith Mortgage Co.)

FIRST FID CORP (OK)
Name changed to Lincoln Plaza Corp. and Common $1 par changed to 50¢ par 08/29/1973
Lincoln Plaza Corp. name changed to Lincoln Plaza Resources, Inc. 06/03/1981
(See Lincoln Plaza Resources, Inc.)

FIRST FID INS CORP (OK)
Reorganized as First Fidelity Corp. (OK) 11/27/1963
Each share Common 50¢ par exchanged for (1) share Common $1 par
First Fidelity Corp. (OK) name changed to Lincoln Plaza Corp. 08/29/1973 which name changed to Lincoln Plaza Resources, Inc. 06/03/1981
(See Lincoln Plaza Resources, Inc.)

FIRST FID INVT CORP (CO)
Name changed to Newport Carpet Mills, Inc. 12/17/1990

FIRST FID INVT TR (MO)
Liquidation completed
Each Share of Bene. Int. no par exchanged for initial distribution of $6.50 cash 12/20/1978
Each Share of Bene. Int. no par received second distribution of $6.50 cash 02/15/1979
Each Share of Bene. Int. no par received third and final distribution of $0.598 cash 02/26/1982

FIRST FID SVGS & LN ASSOC WINTER PK (FL)
Name changed to American Pioneer Savings Bank (Orlando, FL) 07/01/1985
American Pioneer Savings Bank (Orlando, FL) reorganized as American Pioneer Inc. 10/03/1988
(See American Pioneer Inc.)

FIRST FIN CORP (MA)
Completely liquidated 10/30/1967

Each share Common $1 par exchanged for first and final distribution of (0.030303) share General Acceptance Corp. (New) Common $1 par
General Acceptance Corp. (New) name changed to GAC Corp. (PA) 07/01/1968 which reincorporated in Delaware 12/20/1973
(See GAC Corp. (DE))

FIRST FINL ASSOC INC (WI)
Each share Common $5 par exchanged for (2) shares Common $2.50 par 4/24/87
Stock Dividend - 10% 3/19/91
Acquired by Banc One Corp. 12/17/93
Each share Common $2.50 par exchanged for (1.418) shares Common no par
Banc One Corp. merged into Bank One Corp. 10/2/98 which merged into J.P. Morgan Chase & Co. 12/31/2000 which name changed to JPMorgan Chase & Co. 7/20/2004

FIRST FINL BANCORP (AR)
Reorganized 7/1/97
Under plan of reorganization each share First Financial Federal Savings & Loan Association Common $1 par automatically became (1) share First Financial Bancorp Common $1 par 7/1/97
Company went private 11/1/2000
Each share Common $1 par exchanged for $47.20 cash

FIRST FINL BANCORP (CA)
Merged into Placer Sierra Bancshares 12/10/2004
Each share Common no par exchanged for $25.4048 cash

FIRST FINANCIAL BANCORP INC. (WV)
Merged into Wesbanco, Inc. 10/16/87
Each share Common $10 par exchanged for (2.7) shares Common $4.1666 par

FIRST FINL BANCORP INC (DE)
Merged into Blackhawk Bancorp, Inc. 09/03/1998
Each share Common no par exchanged for $30 cash

FIRST FINL BANCORP INC (FL)
Stock Dividends - 10% 6/30/93; 10% 5/31/94
Merged into Capital City Bank Group, Inc. 7/1/96
Each share Common $1 par exchanged for $22 cash

FIRST FINL BANCORPORATION (IA)
Common $6.25 par changed to $1.25 par and (4) additional shares issued 04/00/1988
Merged into Mercantile Bancorporation Inc. 09/28/1998
Each share Common $1.25 par exchanged for (0.88) share Common 1¢ par
Mercantile Bancorporation, Inc. merged into Firstar Corp. (New) 09/20/1999 which merged into U.S. Bancorp (DE) 02/27/2001

FIRST FINL BANCORPORATION INC (DE)
Name changed to United Bankers Inc. 09/24/1981
(See United Bankers Inc.)

FIRST FINL BANCSHARES POLK CNTY INC (FL)
Common 1¢ par split (2) for (1) by issuance of (1) additional share 1/15/95
Merged into Barnett Banks, Inc. 1/18/96
Each share Common 1¢ par exchanged for 15.54 cash

FIRST FINL BROWARD INC (DE)
Company reported out of business 07/20/1990
Details not available

FIRST FINL CARIBBEAN CORP (PR)
Common $1 par split (2) for (1) by issuance of (1) additional share 12/10/1993
10.5% Conv. Preferred Ser. A $1 par called for redemption 05/10/1996
Common $1 par split (2) for (1) by issuance of (1) additional share payable 08/28/1997 to holders of record 08/18/1997
Name changed to Doral Financial Corp. 09/22/1997
(See Doral Financial Corp.)

FIRST FINANCIAL CORP. OF THE WEST OLD (CA)
Completely liquidated 9/11/68
Each share Capital Stock no par exchanged for first and final distribution of (0.2) share First Financial Corp. of the West (New) (CA) Capital Stock 50¢ par plus (1) share Huntington Savings & Loan Association Guarantee Stock 46¢ par
(See each company's listing)

FIRST FINL CORP (FL)
Name changed to First Florida Banks, Inc. 07/01/1977
First Florida Banks, Inc. merged into Barnett Banks, Inc. 12/07/1992 which merged into NationsBank Corp. reincorporated in Delaware as BankAmerica Corp. (Old) 09/25/1998 which merged into BankAmerica Corp. (New) 09/30/1998 which name changed to Bank of America Corp. 04/28/1999

FIRST FINL CORP (NV)
Charter revoked for failure to file reports and pay fees 2/17/72

FIRST FINL CORP (RI)
Merged into Washington Trust Bancorp, Inc. 4/16/2002
Each share Common $1 par exchanged for (0.842) share Common $0.0625 par and $16 cash

FIRST FINL CORP (TN)
Merged into National Commerce Bancorporation 8/4/99
Each share Common exchanged for (2.8502) shares Common $2 par
National Commerce Bancorporation name changed to National Commerce Financial Corp. 4/25/2001 which merged into SunTrust Banks, Inc. 10/1/2004

FIRST FINL CORP (TX)
Reported out of business 04/12/1976
Stockholders' equity unlikely

FIRST FINL CORP (WI)
Common $1 par split (2) for (1) by issuance of (1) additional share 10/14/85
Common $1 par split (2) for (1) by issuance of (1) additional share 4/16/92
Common $1 par split (2) for (1) by issuance of (1) additional share 3/5/93
Common $1 par split (5) for (4) by issuance of (0.25) additional share payable 12/30/96 to holders of record 12/16/96
Stock Dividend - 10% 3/31/89
Merged into Associated Banc-Corp 10/29/97
Each share Common $1 par exchanged for (0.765) share Common 1¢ par

FIRST FINL CORP WEST NEW (CA)
99% owned by Cooke Family as of 5/3/83
Public interest eliminated

FIRST FINL CORP WESTN MD (DE)
Common $1 par split (3) for (2) by issuance of (0.5) additional share 11/30/93
Merged into Keystone Financial, Inc. 5/29/97

Each share Common $1 par exchanged for $33.02 cash

FIRST FINL FD INC (MD)
Name changed to First Opportunity Fund, Inc. 10/13/2008
First Opportunity Fund, Inc. merged into Boulder Growth & Income Fund, Inc. 03/20/2015

FIRST FINL GROUP INC (PA)
Merged into Union National Corp. 01/22/1986
Each share Common $5 par exchanged for (4.7) shares Common $1 par
Union National Corp. merged into Integra Financial Corp. 01/26/1989 which merged into National City Corp. 05/03/1996 which was acquired by PNC Financial Services Group, Inc. 12/31/2008

FIRST FINL GROUP N H INC (NH)
Voting Trust Agreement terminated 10/1/74
Each VTC for Common $5 par automatically became (1) share Common $5 par
Name changed to Bankeast Corp. 4/22/81
(See BankEast Corp.)

FIRST FINL HLDGS INC (DE)
Common 1¢ par split (2) for (1) by issuance of (1) additional share 10/26/1993
Common 1¢ par split (2) for (1) by issuance of (1) additional share payable 03/27/1998 to holders of record 03/13/1998
Merged into First Financial Holdings, Inc. (SC) 07/30/2013
Each share Common 1¢ par exchanged for (0.4237) share Common $2.50 par
First Financial Holdings, Inc. (SC) name changed to South State Corp. 06/30/2014

FIRST FINL HLDGS INC (SC)
9% Perpetual Preferred Ser. A 1¢ par called for redemption at $1,000 plus $10.25 accrued dividends on 03/28/2014
Name changed to South State Corp. 06/30/2014

FIRST FINL LIFE INS CO (TX)
Common $1.50 par changed to $1 par 06/21/1966
Name changed to United General Life Insurance Co. 01/01/1974
(See United General Life Insurance Co.)

FIRST FINL MGMT CORP (GA)
Common 10¢ par split (3) for (2) by issuance of (0.5) additional share 06/20/1985
Common 10¢ par split (3) for (2) by issuance of (0.5) additional share 04/06/1987
Common 10¢ par split (3) for (2) by issuance of (0.5) additional share 03/30/1992
Merged into First Data Corp. (Old) 10/27/1995
Each share Common 10¢ par exchanged for (1.5859) shares Common 1¢ par
(See First Data Corp. (Old))

FIRST FINANCIAL NATIONAL BANK (TAMPA, FL)
Acquired by First National Bank of Florida (Tampa, Fla.) 7/1/77
Each share Common $10 par exchanged for (1.35) shares Capital Stock $5 par
(See First National Bank of Florida (Tampa, Fla.))

FIRST FINL SVGS ASSN (PA)
Under plan of reorganization each share Common $1 par automatically became (1) share Chester Valley Bancorp Inc. Common $1 par 05/16/1990

Chester Valley Bancorp Inc. merged into Willow Grove Bancorp, Inc. (New) 08/31/2005 which name changed to Willow Financial Bancorp, Inc. 09/22/2006 which merged into Harleysville National Corp. 12/08/2008 which merged into First Niagara Financial Group, Inc. (New) 04/09/2010 which merged into KeyCorp (New) 08/01/2016

FIRST FINL SVGS ASSN F A CINCINNATI (OH)
Under plan of reorganization each share Common $1 par automatically became (1) share First Savings Bancorp Common $1 par 03/01/1989
First Savings Bancorp merged into Tristate Bancorp 09/30/1992 which merged into Fifth Third Bancorp 12/22/1993

FIRST FINL SVC CORP (KY)
Stock Dividends - 10% payable 10/21/2005 to holders of record 10/07/2005 Ex date - 10/05/2005; 10% payable 09/14/2006 to holders of record 08/29/2006; 10% payable 09/14/2007 to holders of record 08/29/2007 Ex date - 08/27/2007
Merged into Community Bank Shares of Indiana, Inc. 01/02/2015
Each share Common $1 par exchanged for (0.513) share Common 10¢ par
Community Bank Shares of Indiana, Inc. name changed to Your Community Bankshares, Inc. 07/01/2015 which merged into WesBanco, Inc. 09/09/2016

1ST FINL SVCS CORP (NC)
Acquired by First Citizens BancShares, Inc. 01/02/2014
Each share Common $5 par exchanged for $0.39 cash

FIRST FINL SHS INC (DE)
Merged into Great Financial Corp. 07/14/1995
Each share Common $1 par exchanged for $50 cash

FIRST FINL VA CORP (VA)
Merged into Perpetual American Federal Savings & Loan Association 07/01/1982
Each share Common $5 par exchanged for $16 amount of an Unrestricted Savings Account
Note: Only certificates registered in Brokers and nominees' name were required to be surrendered along with a list of names and address of the beneficial owners

FIRST FINCORP INC (NC)
Merged into BB&T Financial Corp. 2/24/93
Each share Common $1 par exchanged for (0.276) share Common $2.50 par
BB&T Financial Corp. merged into Southern National Corp. 2/28/95 which name changed to BB&T Corp. 5/19/97

FIRST FITNESS INC (NV)
Each share old Common $0.001 par exchanged for (0.0002) share new Common $0.001 par 08/02/1994
Note: In effect holders receive $0.05 cash per share and public interest was eliminated

FIRST FIXTURES INC (NV)
Recapitalized as Stony Hill Corp. 10/24/2016
Each share Common $0.001 par exchanged for (0.1) share Common no par
Stony Hill Corp. name changed to Applied Biosciences Corp. 03/29/2018

FIRST FLA BANCORPORATION (FL)
Under plan of merger name changed to United First Florida Banks, Inc. 06/29/1973
United First Florida Banks, Inc. name changed to Flagship Banks, Inc. 06/30/1974 which merged into Sun Banks, Inc. 01/01/1984 which merged into SunTrust Banks, Inc. 07/01/1985

FIRST FLA BKS INC (FL)
Stock Dividend - 50% 5/15/78
Merged into Barnett Banks, Inc. 12/7/92
Each share Common $1 par exchanged for (1.42) shares Common $2 par

FIRST FLA COMMUNICATIONS INC (FL)
Each share old Common $0.0001 par exchanged for (0.05) share new Common $0.0001 par 05/27/1998
SEC revoked common stock registration 03/25/2002

FIRST FLIGHT CO. (TN)
Stock Dividends - 10% 4/2/62; 10% 5/3/63
Merged into Professional Golf Co. 12/31/66
Each share Capital Stock 50¢ par exchanged for (0.8) share Common 50¢ par
Professional Golf Co. name changed to ProGroup, Inc. 2/25/75 which name changed to Palmer (Arnold) Golf Co. (TN) 7/17/96
(See Palmer (Arnold) Golf Co. (TN))

FIRST FLIGHT INC (NV)
Name changed to Saker Aviation Services, Inc. 10/02/2009

FIRST FLORIDA SAVINGS & LOAN ASSOCIATION (FL)
Proclaimed dissolved for failure to file reports and pay fees 11/4/88

1ST FLOYD BANKSHARES INC
Merged into United Community Banks Inc. 8/27/99
Each share Common exchanged for (0.8477) share Common $1 par

FIRST FNDTN INC (CA)
Reincorporated under the laws of Delaware 10/28/2015

FIRST FORTUNE INVTS INC (BC)
Name changed to Hansa Resources Ltd. 09/18/2007

FIRST FOTO INC (DE)
Each share Common 1¢ par exchanged for (1/13,040) share Common $1 par 11/20/1979
Note: In effect holders received $3.35 cash per share and public interest was eliminated

FIRST FRANKLIN CORP (DE)
Common 1¢ par split (2) for (1) by issuance of (1) additional share 01/17/1995
Common 1¢ par split (3) for (2) by issuance of (0.5) additional share payable 05/10/1998 to holders of record 05/02/1998
Acquired by Cheviot Financial Corp. 03/16/2011
Each share Common 1¢ par exchanged for $14.50 cash

FIRST FREDERICK FINL CORP (MD)
Common $1 par split (2) for (1) by issuance of (1) additional share payable 10/19/98 to holders of record 10/2/98
Merged into FCNB Corp. 8/19/99
Each share Common $1 par exchanged for (1.0434) shares Common $1 par
FCNB Corp. merged into BB&T Corp. 1/8/2001

FIRST FREEPORT CORP. (TX)
Name changed to Texas Gulf Bancshares, Inc. 1/1/84
(See Texas Gulf Bancshares, Inc.)

FIRST FREEPORT CORP (DE)
Name changed to Premier Financial Services, Inc. 5/17/84
(See Premier Financial Services, Inc.)

FIRST FULTON BANCSHARES INC (GA)
Acquired by Barnett Banks, Inc. 2/11/88
Each share Class A Common $5 par exchanged for $72 cash

FIRST FULTON BANK & TRUST (PALMETTO, GA)
Reorganized as First Fulton Bancshares, Inc. 12/31/85
Each share Common $5 par exchanged for (1) share Class A Common $5 par
(See Fulton Bancshares, Inc.)

FIRST GALESBURG NATL BK & TR CO (GALESBURG, IL)
Capital Stock $100 par changed to $20 par and (4) additional shares issued 10/24/1969
Stock Dividends - 14-2/7% 12/15/1954; 25% 12/15/1959; 33-1/3% 11/25/1963; 50% 12/15/1970; 33-1/3% 11/13/1974; 25% 03/10/1977
Reorganized as First Illini Bancorp, Inc. 04/30/1984
Each share Capital Stock $20 par exchanged for (1) share Capital Stock $20 par
(See First Illini Bancorp, Inc.)

FIRST GASTON BK N C (GASTONIA, NC)
Stock Dividends - 20% payable 01/15/1999 to holders of record 12/15/1998; 10% payable 03/23/2001 to holders of record 03/02/2001 Ex date - 03/12/2001
Merged into United Community Bancorp 01/03/2002
Each share Common $4 par exchanged for (0.8934) share Common $1 par
United Community Bancorp name changed to Integrity Financial Corp. 05/30/2003 which merged into FNB United Corp. 04/28/2006 which name changed to CommunityOne Bancorp 07/01/2013

FIRST GEN CORP (DE)
Charter cancelled and declared inoperative and void for non-payment of taxes 04/15/1973

FIRST GEN MINE MGMT & GOLD CORP (CANADA)
Name changed to Laser Magic International Inc. 12/21/1989
(See Laser Magic International Inc.)

FIRST GEN REAL ESTATE & RES TR (MA)
Name changed to First General Resources Co. 02/24/1970

FIRST GEN REAL ESTATE TR (MA)
Name changed to First General Real Estate & Resources Trust 10/01/1968
First General Real Estate & Resources Trust name changed to First General Resources Co. 02/24/1970

FIRST GENERATION RES LTD (BC)
Name changed 10/09/1991
Name changed from First Generation Resources Ltd. to First Generation Financial Group Ltd. 10/09/1991
Plan of Arrangement effective 04/20/1993
Common no par became Class B Preferred no par and Class 1 Shares no par
Each share Class B Preferred no par received (0.0947) share Canadian Maple Leaf Financial Corp. Class A no par, (0.0973) share Katalor Explorations Ltd. Common no par, (0.005) share North American Environmental Group Inc. Common $0.001 par and $0.08 cash
(See each company's listing)
Each Class 1 Share no par exchanged for (0.33) share Canadian Maple Leaf Financial Corp. Class A no par
Canadian Maple Leaf Financial Corp. name changed to CML Global Capital Ltd. 10/26/1999
(See CML Global Capital Ltd.)

FIRST GENEVA INVTS INC (FL)
Name changed to Dragon Pharmaceutical, Inc. 10/02/1998
(See Dragon Pharmaceutical, Inc.)

1ST GENX INC (NV)
Name changed 03/06/2001
Name changed from 1st Genx.com, Inc. to 1st Genx, Inc. 03/06/2001
Each share old Common $0.001 par exchanged for (0.25) share new Common $0.001 par 06/10/2001
Recapitalized as Oasis Information Systems, Inc. 10/31/2001
Each share new Common $0.001 par exchanged for (0.5) share Common $0.001 par
Oasis Information Systems, Inc. recapitalized as 777 Sports Entertainment, Corp. 02/07/2005 which recapitalized as NT Mining Corp. 11/04/2008 which recapitalized as Sanwire Corp. (NV) 03/07/2013 which reincorporated in Wyoming 07/07/2015

FIRST GEORGIA BANCSHARES INC (GA)
Merged into First Railroad & Banking Co. of Georgia 06/26/1986
Each share Common $2.50 par exchanged for (1.22) shares Common 66-2/3¢ par
First Railroad & Banking Co. of Georgia acquired by First Union Corp. 11/01/1986 which name changed to Wachovia Corp. 09/01/2001 which merged into Wells Fargo & Co. (New) 12/31/2008

FIRST GEORGIA BK (ATLANTA, GA)
Acquired by First Georgia Bancshares, Inc. 08/01/1973
Each share Capital Stock $2.50 par exchanged for (1) share Common $2.50 par
First Georgia Bancshares, Inc. merged into First Railroad & Banking Co. of Georgia 06/26/1986 which was acquired by First Union Corp. 11/01/1986 which name changed to Wachovia Corp. (Ctfs. dated after 09/01/2001) 09/01/2001 which merged into Wells Fargo & Co. (New) 12/31/2008

FIRST GEORGIA CMNTY CORP (GA)
Company's sole asset placed in receivership 12/05/2008
Stockholders' equity unlikely

FIRST GEORGIA HLDG INC (GA)
Common $1 par split (3) for (2) by issuance of (0.5) additional share 5/9/94
Common $1 par split (3) for (2) by issuance of (0.5) additional share payable 2/29/96 to holders of record 2/12/96
Common $1 par split (3) for (2) by issuance of (0.5) additional share payable 2/28/97 to holders of record 1/31/97
Common $1 par split (3) for (2) by issuance of (0.5) additional share payable 6/15/98 to holders of record 5/26/98
Common $1 par split (3) for (2) by issuance of (0.5) additional share payable 5/19/99 to holders of record 4/30/99
Merged into United Community Banks, Inc. 5/1/2003
Each share Common $1 par

exchanged for (0.1519) share Common $1 par and $1.65 cash

FIRST GEORGIA SVGS BK F S B (BRUNSWICK, GA)
Reorganized as First Georgia Holding, Inc. 4/30/88
Each share Common $5 par exchanged for (1) share Common $1 par
First Georgia Holding, Inc. merged into United Community Banks, Inc. 5/1/2003

FIRST GLADES CORP (FL)
Merged into C & H Financial Inc. 7/31/96
Each share Common no par exchanged for $33.50 cash

FIRST GLEN BANCORP INC (DE)
Common $10 par changed to $5 par and (1) additional share issued 05/31/1985
Name changed to Evergreen Bancorp, Inc. 04/29/1986
Evergreen Bancorp, Inc. merged into BankNorth Group, Inc. (DE) 12/31/1998 which merged into Banknorth Group, Inc. (ME) 05/10/2000 which merged into TD Banknorth Inc. 03/01/2005
(See TD Banknorth Inc.)

FIRST GLOBAL FINL CORP (NV)
Common $0.001 par split (10) for (1) by issuance of (9) additional shares payable 04/03/2006 to holders of record 03/22/2006 Ex date - 04/04/2006
Recapitalized as Incorporated Productions 08/01/2013
Each share Common $0.001 par exchanged for (0.01) share Common $0.001 par

1ST GLOBAL PETE GROUP INC (DE)
Name changed to Commonwealth American Financial Group, Inc. 5/13/2005
Commonwealth American Financial Group, Inc. name changed to James Monroe Capital Corp. 5/30/2006

FIRST GNT CORP (DE)
Merged into Pittsburgh Coke & Chemical Co. 2/19/71
Each share Capital Stock no par exchanged for $37 cash

FIRST GOLD EXPL INC (CANADA)
Name changed to Critical Elements Corp. 02/18/2011

FIRST GOLD RES CORP (BC)
Name changed to Fastfoot Industries Ltd. 10/25/1999
Fastfoot Industries Ltd. recapitalized as Fab-Form Industries Ltd. 12/14/2001

FIRST GOLDEN BANCORPORATION (DE)
Name changed to Goldenbanks of Colorado, Inc. 10/21/1993
Goldenbanks of Colorado, Inc. merged into Norwest Corp. 05/01/1995 which name changed to Wells Fargo & Co. (New) 11/02/1998

FIRST GOLDWATER RES INC (BC)
Each share old Common no par exchanged for (0.0625) share new Common no par 11/14/2002
Name changed to Baja Mining Corp. 07/20/2004
Baja Mining Corp. recapitalized as Camrova Resources Inc. 10/17/2016

FIRST GRANITE BANCORPORATION INC (IL)
Common $10 par changed to $2.50 par and (3) additional shares issued 1/10/74
Merged into Magna Group, Inc. 8/31/87
Each share Common $2.50 par exchanged for (2.175) shares Common $2 par
Magna Group, Inc. merged into Union Planters Corp. 7/1/98 which merged into Regions Financial Corp. (New) 7/1/2004

FIRST GRANITE CITY NATL BK (GRANITE CITY, IL)
Stock Dividends - 33-1/3% 12/21/67; 50% 12/29/72; 10% 3/25/77
Reorganized as First Granite Bancorporation, Inc. 3/1/82
Each share Capital Stock $10 par exchanged for (1) share Common $10 par
First Granite Bancorporation, Inc. merged into Magna Group, Inc. 8/31/87 which merged into Union Planters Corp. 7/1/98 which merged into Regions Financial Corp. (New) 7/1/2004

FIRST GRAPHITE CORP (BC)
Recapitalized as Desert Star Resources Ltd. (Old) 01/21/2013
Each share Common no par exchanged for (0.5) share Common no par
Desert Star Resources Ltd. (Old) merged into Desert Star Resources Ltd. (New) 04/15/2015 which name changed to Kutcho Copper Corp. 12/21/2017

FIRST GREAT WESTN INVT CORP (AZ)
Name changed to Miller Medical Electronics, Inc. 8/19/76
(See Miller Medical Electronics, Inc.)

FIRST GREATWEST CORP (NE)
Merged into Pullman Inc. 4/25/78
Each share Common $4 par exchanged for $21 cash

FIRST GREENVILLE BANCSHARES INC (TX)
Out of business 07/23/1982
No stockholders' equity

FIRST GREENVILLE NATL BK (GREENVILLE, TX)
Reorganized as First Greenville Bancshares Inc. 07/25/1980
Each share Capital Stock $10 par exchanged for (1) share Preferred $20 par and (1) share Common no par
(See First Greenville Bancshares Inc.)

FIRST GROVES CORP (TX)
Merged into Southtrust of Alabama 8/13/99
Each share Common exchanged for $186.89782 cash

FIRST GROWTH HLDGS LTD (BC)
Filed an assignment in bankruptcy 07/17/2017
Stockholders' equity unlikely

FIRST GROWTH INVS INC (NV)
Recapitalized as Yuhe International, Inc. 04/07/2008
Each share Common $0.001 par exchanged for (0.06799961) share Common $0.001 par

FIRST GTY BK & TR CO (JACKSONVILLE, FL)
Stock Dividend - 50% 01/20/1972
Closed and FDIC appointed receiver 01/27/2012
Stockholders' equity unlikely

FIRST GTY BK (HAMMOND, LA)
Common $1 par split (3) for (2) by issuance of (0.5) additional share payable 09/29/1996 to holders of record 09/19/1996
Under plan of reorganization each share Common $1 par automatically became (1) share First Guaranty Bancshares, Inc. Common $1 par 07/27/2007

FIRST GUARDIAN FINL CORP (DE)
Common no par split (10) for (1) by issuance of (9) additional shares payable 03/31/2006 to holders of record 03/17/2006 Ex date - 04/03/2006
Name changed to New Capital Funding Corp. 05/07/2007
New Capital Funding Corp. recapitalized as Ulysses Holding Corp. 10/29/2007 which name changed to Ulysses Diversified Holdings Corp. 05/08/2008 which name changed to JNS Holdings Corp. 02/16/2012

FIRST GUARDIAN PETE CORP (BC)
Merged into Tai Energy Corp. 06/30/1993
Each share Common no par exchanged for (0.157968) share Common no par
Tai Energy Corp. acquired by Maxx Petroleum Ltd. 03/17/1995 which was acquired by Provident Energy Trust 05/21/2001 which reorganized as Provident Energy Ltd. (New) 01/03/2011 which merged into Pembina Pipeline Corp. 04/02/2012

FIRST GUARDIAN SECURITIES CORP.
Liquidated in 1950

FIRST GULF BEACH BK & TR CO (ST. PETERSBURG BEACH, FL)
Merged into First Florida Banks, Inc. 2/1/85
Each share Common $10 par exchanged for $136.7875 cash

FIRST GWINNETT BANCSHARES INC (GA)
Merged into Regions Financial Corp.(Old) 8/15/96
Each share Common $1 par exchanged for (1.1336) shares Common $0.625 par
Regions Financial Corp. (Old) merged into Regions Financial Corp. (New) 7/1/2004

FIRST HANOVER BANCORP INC (NC)
Declared insolvent and taken over by FDIC 10/25/91
Stockholders' equity unlikely

FIRST HANOVER BK (WILMINGTON, NC)
Reorganized as First Hanover Bancorp Inc. 10/1/90
Each share Common $4 par exchanged for (1) share Common $4 par
(See First Hanover Bancorp Inc.)

FIRST HARRISBURG BANCOR INC (PA)
Common 1¢ par split (2) for (1) by issuance of (1) additional share 1/17/95
Stock Dividends - 10% 11/15/89; 10% 11/15/91; 10% 11/13/92; 20% 11/15/93
Merged into Harris Savings Bank (Harrisburg, PA) 4/19/96
Each share Common 1¢ par exchanged for $14.77 cash

FIRST HARTFORD CORP (ME)
Under plan of reorganization each share Conv. Preferred Ser. A $1 par exchanged for (2.5) shares Common $1 par 6/27/84
(Additional Information in Active)

FIRST HARTFORD RLTY CORP (DE)
Common $1 par changed to 50¢ par and (1) additional share issued 08/15/1969
Completely liquidated 04/16/1971
Each share Common 50¢ par exchanged for first and final distribution of (0.5) share Wyandotte Industries Corp. Conv. Preferred Ser. A $1 par
Wyandotte Industries Corp. name changed to First Hartford Corp. 03/29/1972

FIRST HARVEST CORP (NV)
Each share old Common $0.001 par exchanged for (0.1) share new Common $0.001 par 09/26/2016
Name changed to Arias Intel Corp. 12/01/2017

FIRST HAWAII REAL ESTATE TR (HAWAII)
Completely liquidated 00/00/2004
Each Share of Bene. Int. received an undetermined amount of cash based upon total holdings in the Trust
Note: Certificates were not required to be surrendered and are without value

FIRST HAWAIIAN BK (HONOLULU, HI)
Common $10 par changed to $5 par and (1) additional share issued 1/15/69
Common $5 par split (2) for (1) by issuance of (1) additional share 8/29/72
Reorganized as First Hawaiian, Inc. 7/1/74
Each share Common $5 par exchanged for (1) share Common $5 par
First Hawaiian, Inc. name changed to BancWest Corp. (New) 11/1/98
(See BancWest Corp. (New))

FIRST HAWAIIAN INC OLD (DE)
Common $5 par split (2) for (1) by issuance of (1) additional share 10/22/1984
Common $5 par split (2) for (1) by issuance of (1) additional share 10/22/1986
Common $5 par split (2) for (1) by issuance of (1) additional share 01/26/1990
Stock Dividend - 10% 06/15/1981
Under plan of merger name changed to BancWest Corp. (New) 11/01/1998
(See BancWest Corp. (New))

FIRST HEALTH GROUP CORP (DE)
Merged into Coventry Health Care, Inc. 01/28/2005
Each share Common 1¢ par exchanged for (0.1791) share Common 1¢ par and $9.375 cash
Coventry Health Care, Inc. merged into Aetna, Inc. 05/07/2013

FIRST HERITAGE BK (SNOHOMISH, WA)
Common $1 par split (5) for (4) by issuance of (0.25) additional share payable 12/31/1997 to holders of record 12/11/1997
Common $1 par split (2) for (1) by issuance of (1) additional share payable 01/25/2001 to holders of record 12/13/2000
Stock Dividends - 5% payable 01/20/1999 to holders of record 12/09/1998; 5% payable 01/20/2000 to holders of record 12/08/1999
Bank closed and FDIC appointed receiver 05/27/2011
Stockholders' equity unlikely

FIRST HERITAGE INVESTMENT CORP. (AR)
Name changed to Monarc, Inc. 8/2/68
(See Monarc, Inc.)

FIRST HLDG INC (WI)
Name changed to Independence Bank Group, Inc. 11/12/1980
(See Independence Bank Group, Inc.)

FIRST HOME BANCORP INC (NJ)
Common no par split (4) for (3) by issuance of (0.33333333) additional share payable 02/14/1997 to holders of record 01/22/1997
Merged into Sovereign Bancorp, Inc. 07/31/1998
Each share Common no par exchanged for (1.779) shares Common no par
Sovereign Bancorp, Inc. merged into Banco Santander, S.A. 01/30/2009

1ST HOME BUY & SELL LTD (NV)
Common $0.001 par split (3) for (1) by issuance of (2) additional shares

payable 09/16/2008 to holders of record 09/15/2008 Ex date - 09/17/2008
Name changed to Infrastructure Developments Corp. 03/25/2010

1ST HOME CAP CORP (DE)
Adjustable Rate Preferred $1 par called for redemption 10/20/1989
Public interest eliminated

FIRST HOME FED SVGS & LN ASSN SEBRING FLA (USA)
Acquired by Huntington Bancshares Inc. 09/28/1990
Each share Common $1 par exchanged for (1.56086) shares Common no par

FIRST HOME INVT CORP KANS INC (KS)
Common $4.50 par changed to $4.25 par 9/30/67
Common $4.25 par changed to $4 par 10/15/68
Common $4 par changed to $3.75 par 9/30/69
Common $3.75 par changed to $3.50 par 9/30/70
Common $3.50 par changed to $3.25 par 9/30/71
Common $3.25 par changed to $3.13 par 3/31/72
Common $3.13 par changed to $3.01 par 9/30/72
Name changed to First Kansas Financial, Inc. 4/26/76
First Kansas Financial, Inc. merged into Central National Bancshares, Inc. 8/11/77 which name changed to United Central Bancshares Inc. 4/16/81 which name changed to First Interstate of Iowa, Inc. 6/24/85 which merged into Boatmen's Bancshares, Inc. 4/1/92 which merged into NationsBank Corp. 1/7/97 which reincorporated in Delaware as BankAmerica Corp. (Old) 9/25/98 which merged into BankAmerica Corp. (New) 9/30/98 which name changed to Bank of America Corp. 4/28/99

FIRST HOME SVGS BK SLA (PENNSVILLE, NJ)
Common $1 par split (4) for (3) by issuance of (1/3) additional share 01/31/1992
Common $1 par split (4) for (3) by issuance of (1/3) additional share 02/03/1993
Common $1 par split (4) for (3) by issuance of (1/3) additional share 02/15/1994
Under plan of reorganization each share Common $1 par automatically became (1) share First Home Bancorp Inc. Common no par 05/31/1996
First Home Bancorp Inc. merged into Sovereign Bancorp, Inc. 07/31/1998 which merged into Banco Santander, S.A. 01/30/2009

FIRST HOMESTEAD INC (FL)
Merged into HOH Acquisition 7/19/2006
Each share Common $1 par exchanged for $297.8186974 cash

FIRST HORIZON PHARMACEUTICAL CORP (DE)
Issue Information - 3,800,000 shares COM offered at $8 per share on 05/31/2000
Secondary Offering - 4,000,000 shares COM offered at $19.30 per share on 05/09/2001
Common $0.001 par split (3) for (2) by issuance of (0.5) additional share payable 09/24/2001 to holders of record 09/10/2001 Ex date - 09/25/2001
Name changed to Sciele Pharma, Inc. 06/19/2006
(See Sciele Pharma, Inc.)

FIRST HOSPITALITY CDA CORP (BC)
Recapitalized as Southern Pacific Development Corp. 11/05/1991
Each share Common no par exchanged for (0.2) share Common no par
Southern Pacific Development Corp. recapitalized as Southern Pacific Resource Corp. (BC) 03/03/2006 which reincorporated in Alberta 11/17/2006

FIRST HOST HOTEL CORP (AB)
Recapitalized as Vision SCMS Inc. 05/11/2001
Each share Common no par exchanged for (0.09548362) share Common no par
(See Vision SCMS Inc.)

FIRST HOUSTON BANCSHARES INC (TX)
Merged into Sterling Bancshares, Inc. 09/30/1997
Each share Common $1 par exchanged for (0.69) share Common $1 par
Sterling Bancshares, Inc. merged into Comerica, Inc. 07/28/2011

FIRST HOUSTON CAP RES FD INC (NV)
Charter revoked for failure to file reports and pay fees 07/01/1989

FIRST HOUSTON CAP RES FD INC (UT)
Reincorporated under the laws of Nevada 05/15/1986
(See First Houston Capital Resources Fund, Inc. (NV))

FIRST HOUSTON OIL & MINERALS LTD (AB)
Struck from the register 05/01/1985

FIRST HUNTINGTON NATL BK (HUNTINGTON, WV)
Capital Stock $12.50 par changed to $4.16-2/3 par and (2) additional shares issued 10/19/1970
Stock Dividend - 50% 02/15/1965
Reorganized as Key Bancshares of West Virginia, Inc. 12/12/1983
Each share Capital Stock $4.16-2/3 par exchanged for (2) shares Common $3 par
Key Bancshares of West Virginia, Inc. merged into Key Centurion Bancshares, Inc. 11/30/1985 which merged into Banc One Corp. 05/03/1993 which merged into Bank One Corp. 10/02/1998 which merged into J.P. Morgan Chase & Co. 12/31/2000 which name changed to JPMorgan Chase & Co. 07/20/2004

FIRST HUNTSVILLE CORP (DE)
Liquidated 5/14/93
Details not available

FIRST HUTCHINGS SEALY NATL BK (GALVESTON, TX)
Capital Stock $100 par changed to $10 par and (9) additional shares issued 5/3/65
Stock Dividend - 40% 7/31/68
Merged into First International Bancshares, Inc. 12/31/73
Each share Capital Stock $10 par exchanged for (1.7) shares Common $5 par
First International Bancshares, Inc. name changed to InterFirst Corp. 12/31/81 which merged into First RepublicBank Corp. 6/6/87
(See First RepublicBank Corp.)

FIRST IBERIAN FD INC (MD)
Name changed to Scudder Spain & Portugal Fund, Inc. 7/29/97
(See Scudder Spain & Portugal Fund, Inc.)

FIRST IDAHO CORP (ID)
Charter forfeited for failure to file annual reports 12/03/1990

FIRST ILL BANCSHARES CORP (DE)
Name changed to First Bancshares Corp. of Illinois 09/17/1979
First Bancshares Corp. of Illinois acquired by Mercantile Bancorporation, Inc. 02/17/1987 which merged into Firstar Corp. (New) 09/20/1999 which merged into U.S. Bancorp (DE) 02/27/2001

FIRST ILL CORP (DE)
Common $5 par split (5) for (4) by issuance of (0.25) additional share 4/1/84
Common $5 par split (3) for (2) by issuance of (0.5) additional share 5/25/85
Common $5 par split (3) for (2) by issuance of (0.5) additional share 10/15/85
Common $5 par split (3) for (2) by issuance of (0.5) additional share 3/15/86
Common $5 par changed to $1 par 4/23/86
Common $1 par split (5) for (4) by issuance of (0.25) additional share 9/15/86
Common $1 par split (5) for (4) by issuance of (0.25) additional share 12/30/87
Stock Dividends - 20.967742% 4/15/75; 10% 4/25/79; 10% 4/15/80; 10% 4/15/81; 25% 3/15/87
Acquired by Banc One Corp. 3/2/92
Each share $8.13 Conv. Preferred Ser. A no par exchanged for (18.41125) shares Common no par
Each share Common $1 par exchanged for (0.3575) share Common no par
Banc One Corp. merged into Bank One Corp. 10/2/98 which merged into J.P. Morgan Chase & Co. 12/31/2000 which name changed to JP Morgan Chase & Co. 7/20/2004

FIRST ILL TR (IL)
Out of business 08/31/1979
Details not available

FIRST ILLINI BANCORP INC (IL)
Acquired by First Interstate Corp. of Wisconsin 04/25/1990
Each share Capital Stock $20 par exchanged for $24.25 cash
Note: An additional $0.75 cash per share was placed in escrow for possible future distribution

FIRST IMPERIAL CORP. (IL)
Completely liquidated 3/27/75
Each share Class A $1 par exchanged for first and final distribution of (2) shares First United National Corp. Class A 40¢ par
First United National Corp. reorganized as United National Financial Corp. 9/1/77

FIRST IMPRESSION SINGLES NETWORK LTD (BC)
Name changed to Global Explorations Corp. 05/29/1997
Global Explorations Corp. merged into Trincomali, Ltd. 10/15/1999 which name changed to Global Explorations, Inc. 10/22/1999 which recapitalized as Malers, Inc. 05/17/2005 which name changed to Dot VN, Inc. 08/07/2006

FIRST IMPRESSIONS (NV)
Name changed to Fortis Enterprises 07/14/2003
Fortis Enterprises name changed to Renovo Holdings 06/14/2004 which name changed to Bebida Beverage Co. (NV) 10/14/2008 which reincorporated in Wyoming 12/03/2009

FIRST IND BANCORP (IN)
Acquired by Ameritrust Corp. 05/30/1970
Each share Common $10 par exchanged for (2.054) shares Common $3.33-1/3 par
Ameritrust Corp. merged into Society Corp. 03/16/1992 which merged into KeyCorp (New) 03/01/1994

FIRST IND BK A FED SVGS BK (INDIANAPOLIS, IN)
Common 1¢ par split (3) for (2) by issuance of (0.5) additional share 03/26/1986
Under plan of reorganization each share Common 1¢ par automatically became (1) share First Indiana Corp. Common 1¢ par 10/17/1986
(See First Indiana Corp.)

FIRST IND CORP (IN)
Common 1¢ par split (5) for (4) by issuance of (0.25) additional share 04/01/1987
Common 1¢ par split (5) for (4) by issuance of (0.25) additional share 03/19/1992
Common 1¢ par split (5) for (4) by issuance of (0.25) additional share 02/18/1993
Common 1¢ par split (4) for (3) by issuance of (1/3) additional share 03/17/1994
Common 1¢ par split (6) for (5) by issuance of (0.2) additional share payable 03/01/1996 to holders of record 02/21/1996
Common 1¢ par split (5) for (4) by issuance of (0.25) additional share payable 03/18/1997 to holders of record 03/03/1997
Common 1¢ par split (6) for (5) by issuance of (0.2) additional share payable 03/06/1998 to holders of record 02/19/1998
Common 1¢ par split (5) for (4) by issuance of (0.25) additional share payable 02/27/2002 to holders of record 02/13/2002 Ex date - 02/28/2002
Common 1¢ par split (5) for (4) by issuance of (0.25) additional share payable 02/27/2006 to holders of record 02/13/2006 Ex date - 02/28/2006
Merged into Marshall & Ilsley Corp. 01/02/2008
Each share Common 1¢ par exchanged for $32 cash

FIRST INDEPENDENCE BK FLA (FT MEYERS, FL)
Merged into Colonial BancGroup, Inc. 10/01/1997
Each share Common $5 par exchanged for (0.7257) share Common $2.50 par
(See Colonial BancGroup, Inc.)

FIRST INDEPENDENCE CORP (DE)
Common 1¢ par split (2) for (1) by issuance of (1) additional share payable 01/24/1997 to holders of record 01/10/1997
Acquired by Equity Bancshares, Inc. 10/09/2015
Each share Common 1¢ par exchanged for $17.65 cash

FIRST INDEPENDENCE CORP (FL)
Name changed to CodeSmart Holdings, Inc. 06/14/2013
(See CodeSmart Holdings, Inc.)

1ST INDEPENDENCE FINL GROUP INC (DE)
Merged into MainSource Financial Group, Inc. 08/29/2008
Each share Common 10¢ par exchanged for (0.7849) share Common no par and $4.418 cash
MainSource Financial Group, Inc. merged into First Financial Bancorp 04/02/2018

FIRST INDEPENDENCE NATL BK (DETROIT, MI)
Reorganized as First Independence Corp. 1/13/86
Each share Common $10 par exchanged for (1) share Common $10 par

FIRST INDEPENDENT BANK, N.A. (SARASOTA, FL)
Merged into First National Bank of Florida (Tampa, Fla.) 10/11/82
Each share Capital Stock $6 par exchanged for $59.21 cash

FIRST INDIA DIVERSIFIED HLDGS INC (NY)
Name changed to Cell Bio-Systems, Inc. 08/22/2003
Cell Bio-Systems, Inc. name changed to Franklin Scientific, Inc. 04/27/2004
(See Franklin Scientific, Inc.)

FIRST INDO-AMERICAN BK (SAN FRANCISCO, CA)
Name changed to Millenium Bank (San Francisco, CA) 8/7/95
(See Millenium Bank (San Francisco, CA))

FIRST INDL CAP CORP (AB)
Name changed to OnBus Technologies Inc. (AB) 01/08/2002
OnBus Technologies Inc. (AB) reorganized in British Columbia as Royal Monashee Gold Corp. 07/07/2006 which name changed to Plus8 Global Ventures, Ltd. 11/07/2012 which name changed to ParcelPal Technology Inc. 03/22/2016

FIRST INDL RLTY TR INC (MD)
9-1/2% Preferred Ser. A 1¢ par called for redemption at $25 plus $0.05872 accrued dividends on 04/09/2001
Depositary Preferred Ser. B called for redemption at $25 on 05/14/2002
7.95% Depositary Preferred Ser. D called for redemption at $25 on 06/07/2004
7.9% Depositary Preferred Ser. E called for redemption at $25 on 06/07/2004
8.625% Depositary Preferred Ser. C called for redemption at $25 plus $1.48541 accrued dividends on 06/07/2007
7.25% Depositary Preferred Ser. J called for redemption at $25 plus $0.45313 accrued dividends on 04/11/2013
7.25% Depositary Preferred Ser. K called for redemption at $25 plus $0.090625 accrued dividends on 07/18/2013
Depositary Preferred Ser. F called for redemption at $1,000 on 03/06/2014
Depositary Preferred Ser. G called for redemption at $1,000 plus $0.14472 accrued dividends on 03/31/2014
(Additional Information in Active)

FIRST INSURANCE CO. OF HAWAII LTD. (HI)
Capital Stock $8 par changed to $10 par 1/25/61
All except (3) shares acquired by Great American Insurance Co. per June 1963 exchange offer

FIRST INSURANSTOCKS CORP.
Liquidated in 1936

FIRST INTEGRATED ENTERPRISES LTD (AB)
Name changed to Kootenay Gold Inc. (AB) 03/07/2005
Each share Common no par exchanged for (1) share Common no par
Kootenay Gold Inc. (AB) reincorporated in British Columbia 11/09/2006 which name changed to Kootenay Silver Inc. 02/21/2012

FIRST INTER-BANCORP INC (DE)
Acquired by First Fidelity Bancorp 8/19/94
Each share Common $1 par exchanged for $24.20 cash

FIRST INTERACTIVE INC (ON)
Delisted from Canadian Dealer Network 04/14/2000

FIRST INTERCITY BANC CORP (OH)
Closed by the Comptroller of Currency 3/9/90
Stockholders' equity undetermined

FIRST INTERCONTINENTAL BK (DORAVILLE, GA)
Common $5 par split (111) for (100) by issuance of (0.11) additional share payable 01/22/2016 to holders of record 01/12/2016
Under plan of reorganization each share Common $5 par automatically became (1) share First IC Corp. Common $5 par 03/30/2017

FIRST INTERMOUNTAIN HLDG CORP (DE)
Recapitalized as United Bancorp, Inc. (DE) 01/31/1986
Each share Common 1¢ par exchanged for (0.02) share Common 1¢ par
United Bancorp, Inc. (DE) name changed to United London Group, Inc. 09/05/1991

FIRST INTL BANCORP INC (DE)
Secondary Offering - 1,700,000 shares COM offered at $13.50 per share on 09/22/1997
Merged into United Parcel Service, Inc. 8/7/2001
Each share Common 10¢ par exchanged for (0.1147) share Class B Common 1¢ par

FIRST INTL BANCSHARES INC (DE)
Common $5 par split (5) for (4) by issuance of (0.25) additional share 8/30/78
Common $5 par split (2) for (1) by issuance of (1) additional share 6/30/81
Name changed to InterFirst Corp. 12/31/81
InterFirst Corp. merged into First RepublicBank Corp. 6/6/87
(See First RepublicBank Corp.)

FIRST INTL CORP (WY)
Charter forfeited for failure to pay taxes 01/17/1980

FIRST INTL METALS CORP (BC)
Recapitalized as Mill Bay Ventures Inc. 07/17/2000
Each share Common no par exchanged for (0.2) share Common no par
Mill Bay Ventures Inc. recapitalized as Great Thunder Gold Corp. 04/16/2013

FIRST INTL OIL & GAS INC (TX)
Chapter 11 bankruptcy proceedings converted to Chapter 7 on 01/01/1987
Stockholders' equity unlikely

FIRST INTERNATIONAL SECURITIES CORP. (DE)
Charter forfeited for failure to maintain a registered agent in 1933

FIRST INTERNET BK (INDIANAPOLIS, IN)
Under plan of reorganization each share Common $1 par automatically became (1) share First Internet Bancorp Common no par 03/21/2006

FIRST INTEROCEANIC CORP. (IA)
Acquired by Archer-Daniels-Midland Co. in November 1969
Each share Common $5 par exchanged for (1.103) shares Common no par

FIRST INTERSTATE BANK OF ALBUQUERQUE (ALBUQUERQUE, NM)
Merged into Norwest Bank New Mexico, N.A. (Albuquerque, NM) in January 1994
Details not available

FIRST INTST BANCORP (DE)
Auction Preferred Ser. 1C no par called for redemption 01/02/1990
Auction Preferred Ser. 1A no par called for redemption 01/22/1990
Preferred Ser. A no par called for redemption 09/01/1992
Preferred Ser. B no par called for redemption 10/01/1993
Each share Class A Common 1¢ par exchanged for (0.0001) share Common $2 par 02/16/1993
Merged into Wells Fargo & Co. (Old) 04/01/1996
Each 9% Depositary Preferred Ser. G exchanged for (1) 9% Depositary Preferred Ser. G
Each share 9% Preferred Ser. G no par exchanged for (1) share 9% Preferred Ser. G no par
Each 9.875% Depositary Preferred Ser. F exchanged for (1) 9.875% Depositary Preferred Ser. F
Each share 9.875% Preferred Ser. F no par exchanged for (1) share 9.875% Preferred Ser. F no par
Each share Common $2 par exchanged for (0.66666666) share Common $5 par
Wells Fargo & Co. (Old) merged into Wells Fargo & Co. (New) 11/02/1998

FIRST INTST BK ALASKA (ANCHORAGE, AK)
Stock Dividends - 10% 1/31/84; 10% 1/5/85
Under plan of reorganization each share Capital Stock $2 par automatically became (1) share First Interstate Corp. of Alaska Common $2 par 8/1/85
(See First Interstate Corp. of Alaska)

FIRST INTST BK HAWAII (HONOLULU, HI)
Reorganized as First Interstate of Hawaii Inc. 12/31/85
Each share Capital Stock $10 par exchanged for (1) share Common $10 par
(See First Interstate of Hawaii Inc.)

FIRST INTST BK NORTHN IND N A (SOUTH BEND, IN)
Acquired by First Interstate Corp. of Wisconsin 1/17/89
Each share Capital Stock $10 par exchanged for $33 cash
Each share Capital Stock received a settlement distribution of $0.6988 cash 5/9/91

FIRST INTST BK SOUTHN LOUISIANA (THIBODAUX, LA)
Common $2.50 par changed to 10¢ par 4/20/93
Name changed to Argent Bank (Thibodaux, LA) 6/30/93
Argent Bank (Thibodaux, LA) merged into Hibernia Corp. 2/1/98 which merged into Capital One Financial Corp 11/16/2005

FIRST INTST BK WASHINGTON D C (WASHINGTON, DC)
Under plan of reorganization each share Common $5 par automatically became (1) share Franklin Bancorporation, Inc. Common 10¢ par 10/31/89
Franklin Bancorporation, Inc. merged into BB&T Corp. 7/1/98

FIRST INTST CORP ALASKA (AK)
Stock Dividend - 10% 1/31/86
Taken over by the FDIC 12/30/88
Stockholders' equity undetermined

FIRST INTST CORP WIS (WI)
Common $10 par changed to $2.50 par 04/18/1985
Common $2.50 par split (2) for (1) by issuance of (1) additional share 06/10/1986
Acquired by Norwest Corp. 04/30/1990
Each share Common $2.50 par exchanged for (1.166) shares Common $1-2/3 par
Norwest Corp. name changed to Wells Fargo & Co. (New) 11/02/1998

FIRST INTST HAWAII INC (HI)
Acquired by FIH, L.P. 02/14/1989
Each share Common $10 par exchanged for $111.42398 cash

FIRST INTST IOWA INC (IA)
Merged into Boatmen's Bancshares, Inc. 4/1/92
Each share Common $1 par exchanged for (0.17) share Common $1 par
Boatmen's Bancshares, Inc. merged into NationsBank Corp. 1/7/97 which reincorporated in Delaware as BankAmerica Corp. (Old) 9/25/98 which merged into BankAmerica Corp. (New) 9/30/98 which name changed to Bank of America Corp. 4/28/99

FIRST INTST N D INC (ND)
Acquired by Community First Bankshares, Inc. 05/31/1992
Details not available

FIRST INTST STAT TR I (DE)
144A Trust Preferred Securities called for redemption at $25 on 06/26/2012

FIRST INVESTMENT & SECURITY CORP.
Dissolved in 1943
Details not available

FIRST INVESTMENT CO. OF NEW HAMPSHIRE
Out of business in 1946
Details not available

FIRST INVT CO (OH)
Each share old Common exchanged for (0.01) share new Common 1/29/97
Note: In effect holders received $40 cash per share and public interest was eliminated

FIRST INVT CORP (VA)
Completely liquidated 12/1/77
Each share Common $1 par exchanged for first and final distribution of $0.13655 cash

FIRST INVESTMENT COUNSEL CORP. (MA)
Name changed to Scudder, Stevens & Clark Fund, Inc. 09/05/1939
Scudder, Stevens & Clark Fund, Inc. name changed to Scudder, Stevens & Clark Balanced Fund, Inc. 03/08/1963 which name changed to Scudder Income Fund, Inc. 03/02/1977 which name changed to Scudder Income Fund 12/31/1984
(See Scudder Income Fund)

FIRST INVT SECS CO (PA)
Name changed to Fisco, Inc. 04/23/1971
(See Fisco, Inc.)

FIRST INVS ADJUSTABLE PFD FD INC (NV)
Name changed to First Investors Qualified Dividend Fund, Inc. 04/22/1987
(See First Investors Qualified Dividend Fund, Inc.)

FIRST INVS BD APPRECIATION FD INC (MD)
Merged into First Investors High Yield Fund, Inc. 10/27/1989
Details not available

FIRST INVS CASH MGMT FD INC (MD)
Merged into First Investors Income Funds 01/27/2006
Details not available

FIRST INVESTORS CO. OF ILLINOIS
Liquidated in 1932
Details not available

FIRST INVESTORS CORP. (NY)
Name changed to Ficul, Inc. 6/19/68
(See Ficul, Inc.)

FINANCIAL INFORMATION, INC. FIR-FIR

FIRST INVS DISCOVERY FD INC (MD)
Merged into First Investors Global Fund, Inc. 12/27/1989
Details not available

FIRST INVS FD (MA)
Name changed to First Investors Series Fund Blue Chip Series 2/15/90

FIRST INVS FD GROWTH INC (MD)
Merged into First Investors Global Fund, Inc. 12/27/1989
Details not available

FIRST INVS FD INC (MD)
Name changed to First Investors Natural Resources Fund, Inc. 04/29/1981
First Investors Natural Resources Fund, Inc. merged into First Investors International Securities Fund, Inc. 11/30/1987
(See First Investors International Securities Fund, Inc.)

FIRST INVS FD INCOME INC (MD)
Reincorporated under the laws of Delaware as First Investors Income Funds and Common $1 par reclassified as Class A no par 08/18/2005

FIRST INVS FINL SVCS GROUP INC (TX)
Issue Information - 2,000,000 shares COM offered at $11 per share on 10/03/1995
Acquired by Aquiline Capital Partners L.L.C. 11/01/2012
Each share Common $0.001 par exchanged for $13.87 cash

FIRST INVS GOVT FD INC (MD)
Merged into First Investors Income Funds 08/18/2005
Details not available

FIRST INVS HIGH YIELD FD INC (MD)
Merged into First Investors Fund For Income, Inc. 03/14/2000
Details not available

FIRST INVS INSD TAX EXEMPT FD INC (MD)
Merged into First Investors Tax Exempt Funds 04/28/2006
Details not available

FIRST INVS INTL SECS FD INC (MD)
Merged into First Investors Global Fund, Inc. 12/27/1989
Details not available

FIRST INVS LIFE INS CO (NY)
98% acquired through purchase offer which expired 02/19/1982
Public interest eliminated

FIRST INVS LIFE SER FD (MA)
Reincorporated under the laws of Delaware as First Investors Life Series Funds 08/18/2005

FIRST INVS MULTI ST INSD TAX FREE FD (MA)
Merged into First Investors Tax Exempt Funds 10/28/2005
Details not available

FIRST INVS N Y INSD TAX FREE FD INC (MD)
Name changed 10/28/1988
Name changed from First Investors New York Tax Free Fund, Inc. to First Investors New York Insured Tax Free Fund, Inc. 10/28/1988
Common 1¢ par reclassified as Class A 1¢ par 01/12/1995
Class A 1¢ par reclassified as New York Insured Tax Free Fund Class A 1¢ par 08/15/2005
Class B 1¢ par reclassified as New York Insured Tax Free Fund Class B 1¢ par 08/15/2005
Merged into First Investors Tax Exempt Funds 04/28/2006
Details not available

FIRST INVS NAT RES FD INC (MD)
Merged into First Investors International Securities Fund, Inc. 11/30/1987
Each share Capital Stock $1 par exchanged for (1) share Common $1 par
(See First Investors International Securities Fund, Inc.)

FIRST INVS NINETY TEN FD INC (MD)
Name changed to First Investors Value Fund, Inc. 04/02/1987
(See First Investors Value Fund, Inc.)

FIRST INVS OPT FD INC (NY)
Merged into First Investors High Yield Fund, Inc. 11/01/1988
Each share Common $1 par exchanged for (1) share Common 1¢ par
(See First Investors High Yield Fund, Inc.)

FIRST INVS QUALIFIED DIVID FD INC (NV)
Fund terminated 02/04/1991
Details not available

FIRST INVS SER FD (MA)
Reincorporated under the laws of Delaware as First Investors Equity Funds 01/27/2006

FIRST INVS SPL BD FD INC (MD)
Reorganized as First Investors Life Series Funds 10/28/2005
Each share Common $1 par exchanged for (1) Special Bond Fund Class A no par

FIRST INVS STK FD INC (MD)
Name changed to First Investors Fund, Inc. 06/18/1968
First Investors Fund, Inc. name changed to First Investors Natural Resources Fund, Inc. 04/29/1981 which merged into First Investors International Securities Fund, Inc. 11/30/1987
(See First Investors International Securities Fund, Inc.)

FIRST INVS TAX EXEMPT FD INC (MD)
Name changed to First Investors Insured Tax Exempt Fund, Inc. 10/28/1988
(See First Investors Insured Tax Exempt Fund, Inc.)

FIRST INVS TAX EXEMPT MONEY MKT FD INC (MD)
Common 1¢ par reclassified as Tax Exempt Money Market Fund Class A 1¢ par 11/22/1993
Reincorporated under the laws of Delaware as First Investors Tax Exempt Funds 10/28/2005

FIRST INVS TREND FD INC (NY)
Name changed to First Investors Option Fund, Inc. 02/03/1979
First Investors Option Fund, Inc. merged into First Investors High Yield Fund, Inc. 11/01/1988
(See First Investors High Yield Fund, Inc.)

FIRST INVS U S GOVT PLUS FD (MA)
Completely liquidated 12/31/1998
Each Unit of Bene. Int. 1st Ser. no par exchanged for net asset value
Completely liquidated 12/31/1999
Each Unit of Bene. Int. 2nd Ser. no par exchanged for net asset value
Completely liquidated 12/31/2004
Each Unit of Bene. Int. 3rd Ser. no par exchanged for net asset value

FIRST INVS VALUE FD INC (MD)
Merged into First Investors Global Fund, Inc. 11/03/1989
Details not available

FIRST IPSWICH BANCORP (MA)
Each (15) shares old Common $1 par exchanged for (1) share new Common $1 par 03/18/1999
New Common $1 par split (10) for (1) by issuance of (9) additional shares payable 03/19/2004 to holders of record 02/28/2004 Ex date - 04/12/2004
Reclassification effective 12/21/2007
Common holders of (199) or fewer shares reclassified as Ser. A Preferred $1 par
Acquired by Brookline Bancorp, Inc. 03/01/2011
Each share Ser. A Preferred $1 par exchanged for $8.10 cash
Each share new Common $1 par exchanged for $8.10 cash

FIRST ISRAEL FD INC (MD)
Name changed to Aberdeen Israel Fund, Inc. 03/26/2010
Aberdeen Israel Fund, Inc. reorganized as Aberdeen Emerging Markets Equity Income Fund, Inc. 04/30/2018

FIRST IVANA TECHNOLOGIES LTD (CANADA)
Recapitalized as Vitamed Biopharmaceuticals Ltd. 04/06/1993
Each share Class A Common no par exchanged for (0.5) share Class A Common no par
Vitamed Biopharmaceuticals Ltd. name changed to Receptagen Ltd. (Canada) 07/12/1993 which reorganized in Florida as Spantel Communications Inc. 10/16/2001 which recapitalized as Systems America, Inc. 05/27/2010
(See Systems America, Inc.)

FIRST JERMYN CORP (PA)
Common $6.25 par changed to $1.25 par and (4) additional shares issued 12/29/89
Under plan of merger name changed to First Liberty Bank Corp. 6/26/98
First Liberty Bank Corp. merged into Community Bank System, Inc. 5/14/2001

FIRST JERSEY NATL BK (JERSEY CITY, NJ)
Capital Stock $7.50 par changed to $5 par and (0.5) additional share issued 1/15/69
Reorganized as First Jersey National Corp. 5/29/69
Each share Capital Stock $5 par exchanged for (1) share Common $5 par
(See First Jersey National Corp.)

FIRST JERSEY NATL CORP (NJ)
$3 Conv. Preferred Ser. A $1 par called for redemption 11/27/85
Merged into National Westminster Bank PLC 2/1/88
Each share $2.88 Conv. Preferred Ser. B $1 par exchanged for $82 cash
Each share Common $5 par exchanged for $82 cash

FIRST KANS FINL CORP (KS)
Merged into Landmark Bancorp, Inc. 04/01/2004
Each share Common 10¢ par exchanged for $19 cash

FIRST KANS FINL INC (KS)
Merged into Central National Bancshares, Inc. 8/11/77
Each share Common $3.01 par exchanged for (1) share Common $1 par
Central National Bancshares, Inc. name changed to United Central Bancshares Inc. 4/16/81 which name changed to First Interstate of Iowa, Inc. 6/24/85 which merged into Boatmen's Bancshares, Inc. 4/1/92 which merged into NationsBank Corp. 1/7/97 which reincorporated in Delaware as BankAmerica Corp. (Old) 9/25/98 which merged into BankAmerica Corp. (New) 9/30/98 which name changed to Bank of America Corp. 4/28/99

FIRST KEATING CORP (OK)
Recapitalized as 3DIcon Corp. 02/17/2004
Each share Common $0.002 exchanged for (0.1) share Common $0.0002 par
3DIcon Corp. recapitalized as Coretec Group Inc. 06/29/2017

FIRST KENT FINL CORP (DE)
Merged into Security First Corp. 04/10/2016
Each share Common 1¢ par exchanged for (1.7) shares Common 1¢ par
Security First Corp. merged into FirstMerit Corp. 10/23/1998 which merged into Huntington Bancshares Inc. 08/16/2016

FIRST KEYSTONE FINL INC (PA)
Common 1¢ par split (3) for (2) by issuance of (0.5) additional share payable 08/23/1996 to holders of record 08/06/1996
Common 1¢ par split (2) for (1) by issuance of (1) additional share payable 01/02/1998 to holders of record 12/16/1997
Merged into Bryn Mawr Bank Corp. 07/01/2010
Each share Common 1¢ par exchanged for (0.6973) share Common $1 par and $2.06 cash

FIRST KNOX BANC CORP (OH)
Common $3.125 par split (8) for (5) by issuance of (0.6) additional share 10/1/90
Common $3.125 par split (2) for (1) by issuance of (1) additional share 9/1/95
Stock Dividend - 5% payable 9/3/96 to holders of record 8/21/96
Merged into Park National Corp. 5/5/97
Each share Common $3.125 par exchanged for (0.5914) share Common no par

FIRST KNOX NATL BK (MT VERNON, OH)
Capital Stock $100 par changed to $50 par and (1) additional share issued plus a 20% stock dividend paid 11/7/51
Capital Stock $50 par changed to $25 par and (1) additional share issued 1/19/65
Capital Stock $25 par changed to $12.50 par and (1) additional share issued 2/5/70
Capital Stock $12.50 par changed to $6.25 par and (1) additional share issued 2/10/76
Capital Stock $6.25 par changed to $3.125 par 1/23/82
Capital Stock $3.125 par split (2) for (1) by issuance of (1) additional share 3/5/82
Stock Dividends - 11.1111% 2/6/57; 20% 2/28/62; 10% 1/24/64; 11.8881% 2/14/66; 10% 5/17/71
Reorganized as First-Knox Banc Corp. 1/19/85
Each share Capital Stock $3.125 par exchanged for (1) share Common $3.125 par
First-Knox Banc Corp. merged into Park National Corp. 5/5/97

FIRST KY NATL CORP (KY)
Common no par split (3) for (2) by issuance of (0.5) additional share 12/01/1976
Common no par split (3) for (2) by issuance of (0.5) additional share 01/20/1983
Common no par split (3) for (2) by issuance of (0.5) additional share 10/06/1983
Common no par split (3) for (2) by issuance of (0.5) additional share 02/07/1985
Common no par split (3) for (2) by issuance of (0.5) additional share 05/09/1986

Acquired by National City Corp. 07/29/1988
Each share Common no par exchanged for (0.8825) share Common $4 par
National City Corp. acquired by PNC Financial Services Group, Inc. 12/31/2008

FIRST LA MESA BANK (LA MESA, CA)
Name changed to First California Bank (La Mesa, CA) 07/12/1990
(See First California Bank (La Mesa, CA))

FIRST LABRADOR ACQUISITIONS INC (AB)
Recapitalized as Silver Spruce Resources Inc. 10/22/2003
Each share Common no par exchanged for (0.125) share Common no par

FIRST LAKE FOREST CORP (DE)
Merged into Northern Trust Corp. 12/31/1986
Each share Common $10 par exchanged for $60.52 cash

FIRST LAKESHORE DIVERSIFIED ASSET FD (MA)
Name changed to First Prairie Diversified Asset Fund 04/24/1989
(See First Prairie Diversified Asset Fund)

FIRST LAKESHORE MONEY MKT FD (MA)
Name changed to First Prairie Money Market Fund 04/24/1989
(See First Prairie Money Market Fund)

FIRST LAKESHORE TAX EXEMPT BD FD INC (MD)
Name changed to First Prairie Tax Exempt Bond Fund Inc. 06/14/1989
(See First Prairie Tax Exempt Bond Fund Inc.)

FIRST LAKESHORE TAX EXEMPT MONEY MKT FD (MA)
Name changed to First Prairie Tax Exempt Money Market Fund 04/24/1989

FIRST LANCASTER BANCSHARES INC (DE)
Merged into CKF Bancorp, Inc. 6/1/2001
Each share Common 1¢ par exchanged for $16.27 cash

FIRST LAPORTE FINL CORP (IN)
Merged into First of America Bank Corp. 12/12/1986
Each share Capital Stock $10 par exchanged for (1.611) shares Common $10 par
First of America Bank Corp. merged into National City Corp. 03/31/1998 which was acquired by PNC Financial Services Group, Inc. 12/31/2008

FIRST LAUREL BK (ST MARYS, PA)
Merged into Pennsylvania Bank & Trust Co. (Titusville, PA) 03/01/1975
Each share Capital Stock $5 par exchanged for (1) share Capital Stock $5 par
Pennsylvania Bank & Trust Co. (Titusville, PA) reorganized as Pennbancorp 12/31/1980 which merged into Integra Financial Corp. 01/26/1989 which merged into National City Corp. 05/03/1996 which was acquired by PNC Financial Services Group, Inc. 12/31/2008

FIRST LD & TIMBER CORP (AR)
Merged into FLT Acquisition 6/24/98
Each share Common $5 par exchanged for $601.3648 cash

FIRST LEESPORT BANCORP INC (PA)
Stock Dividend - 5% payable 01/17/2000 to holders of record 01/03/2000
Name changed to Leesport Financial Corp. 04/01/2002
Leesport Financial Corp. name changed to VIST Financial Corp. 03/03/2008 which merged into Tompkins Financial Corp. 08/01/2012

FIRST LEHIGH CORP (PA)
Acquired by Patriot Bank Corp. 1/22/99
Each share 5% Sr. Preferred 1¢ par exchanged for (0.482) share Common 1¢ par
Each share 5% Sr. Preferred Dividend Accrue from 01/01/96 exchanged for (0.482) share Common 1¢ par
Each share 5% Sr. Legend Dividend Accrue from 12/23/96 exchanged for (0.482) share Common 1¢ par
Each share Ser. A Preferred 1¢ par exchanged for (0.38562) share Common 1¢ par
Each share Common 1¢ par exchanged for (0.482) share Common 1¢ par
Patriot Bank Corp. merged into Susquehanna Bancshares, Inc. 6/10/2004

FIRST LEISURE CORP (DE)
Charter cancelled and declared inoperative and void for non-payment of taxes 3/1/74

FIRST LIBERTY BANCORP INC (DE)
Merged into WashingtonFirst Bank (Washington, DC) 09/05/2006
Each share Common 1¢ par exchanged for (1.049) shares Common $5 par and $2.65 cash
Note: Holders of (99) shares or fewer received $19.526 cash per share
WashingtonFirst Bank (Washington, DC) location changed to (Reston, VA) 05/01/2008 which reorganized as WashingtonFirst Bankshares, Inc. 09/10/2009 which merged into Sandy Spring Bancorp, Inc. 01/01/2018

FIRST LIBERTY BK CORP (PA)
Common $1.25 par split (4) for (1) by issuance of (3) additional shares payable 10/15/99 to holders of record 9/30/99
Merged into Community Bank System, Inc. 5/14/2001
Each share Common $1.25 par exchanged for (0.56) share Common no par

FIRST LIBERTY FINL CORP (DE)
7.75% Conv. Preferred Ser. A no par called for redemption 7/31/95
6% Conv. Preferred Ser. B no par called for redemption 3/7/97
Common $1 par split (3) for (2) by issuance of (0.5) additional share payable 10/1/96 to holders of record 9/15/96
Common $1 par split (3) for (2) by issuance of (0.5) additional share payable 4/27/98 to holders of record 4/13/98
Merged into BB&T Corp. 11/19/99
Each share Common $1 par exchanged for (0.87) share Common $5 par

FIRST LIFE ASSURN CO (OK)
Under plan of reorganization each share Common $1 par exchanged for (1) share American First Corp. Common $1 par 12/31/79
(See American First Corp.)

FIRST LINCOLN FINL CORP (CA)
Merged into American Continental Corp. 2/22/84
Each share Common no par exchanged for $20.83 cash

FIRST LINCOLNWOOD CORP. (IL)
Acquired by MB Financial, Inc. 04/06/2002
Each share Common exchanged for $351.11 cash

FIRST LITCHFIELD FINL CORP (DE)
Common 1¢ par split (5) for (2) by issuance of (1.5) additional shares 03/08/1995
Stock Dividends - 5% payable 12/31/1997 to holders of record 12/10/1997; 5% payable 12/31/1998 to holders of record 12/11/1998; 5% payable 12/30/1999 to holders of record 12/10/1999; 5% payable 12/29/2000 to holders of record 12/13/2000 Ex date - 12/11/2000; 5% payable 12/31/2001 to holders of record 12/14/2001 Ex date - 12/12/2001; 5% payable 12/31/2002 to holders of record 12/13/2002 Ex date - 12/12/2002; 5% payable 12/31/2003 to holders of record 12/15/2003 Ex date - 12/11/2003; 5% payable 12/31/2004 to holders of record 12/15/2004 Ex date - 12/13/2004; 5% payable 12/31/2005 to holders of record 12/15/2005 Ex date - 12/23/2005; 5% payable 12/29/2006 to holders of record 12/15/2006 Ex date - 12/19/2006; 5% payable 12/31/2007 to holders of record 12/14/2007 Ex date - 12/12/2007
Merged into Union Savings Bank (Danbury, CT) 04/07/2010
Each share Common 1¢ par exchanged for $15 cash

FIRST LITHIUM RES INC (BC)
Recapitalized as Golden Virtue Resources Inc. 10/11/2012
Each share Common no par exchanged for (0.1) share Common no par
Golden Virtue Resources Inc. name changed to Moseda Technologies, Inc. 04/23/2015 which name changed to Reliq Health Technologies Inc. 05/10/2016

FIRST LOS ANGELES BK (LOS ANGELES, CA)
Name changed 04/24/1974
Name changed from 1st Los Angeles Bank (Los Angeles, CA) to First Los Angeles Bank (Los Angeles, CA) 04/24/1974
Common $5 par changed to $2.50 par and (1) additional share issued 05/19/1977
Stock Dividends - 10% 09/29/1978; 25% 04/30/1981
Merged into Instituto Bancario San Paolo di Torino 12/31/1982
Each share Common $2.50 par exchanged for $37.8095 cash

FIRST LT RES INC (CO)
Name changed to Invercoal, Inc. 06/28/2006
Invercoal, Inc. recapitalized as Core International Ltd. 04/02/2007 which recapitalized as Therma-Med, Inc. 12/31/2008

FIRST LUMBER CORP. (NY)
Stock Dividend - 50% 10/20/59
Proclaimed dissolved for failure to file reports and pay fees 12/15/67

FIRST M&F CORP (MS)
Common $5 par split (2) for (1) by issuance of (1) additional share payable 05/15/2006 to holders of record 05/01/2006 Ex date - 05/16/2006
Merged into Renasant Corp. 09/01/2013
Each share Common $5 par exchanged for (0.6425) share Common $5 par

FIRST MACOMB BANCORP INC (MI)
Stock Dividend - 10% 11/15/1988
Merged into Huntington Bancshares Inc. 12/29/1989
Each share Common $2.50 par exchanged for (2.14286) shares Common no par

FIRST MACOMB CORP. (MI)
Stock Dividends - 10% 9/15/83; 10% 11/30/84; 10% 11/1/85
Name changed to First Macomb Bancorp, Inc. 5/30/86
First Macomb Bancorp, Inc. merged into Huntington Banchsares Inc. 12/29/89

FIRST MACON BK & TR CO (MACON, GA)
Merged into Colonial BancGroup, Inc. 10/01/1998
Each share Common no par exchanged for (4.3128) shares Common $2.50 par
(See Colonial BancGroup, Inc.)

FIRST MADISON BK FSB (DALLAS, TX)
Name changed to First Nationwide Bank, A Federal Savings Bank (Plano, TX) 09/30/1994
First Nationwide Bank, A Federal Savings Bank (Plano, TX) merged into California Federal Bank, A Federal Savings Bank (Los Angeles, CA) 01/03/1997 which name changed to Citibank (West) FSB (San Francisco, CA) 12/11/2002
(See Citibank (West) FSB (San Francisco, CA))

FIRST MAIN CORP (IA)
Liquidation completed
Each share Common $1 par exchanged for initial distribution of $1 cash 11/07/1978
Each share Common $1 par received second distribution of $3.10 cash 01/03/1979
Each share Common $1 par received third and final distribution of $1.16 cash 05/23/1979

FIRST MAINSTREET FINL LTD (CO)
Merged into Centennial Bank Holdings, Inc. 10/01/2005
Each share Common $25 par exchanged for (9.1694) shares Common $0.001 par
Centennial Bank Holdings, Inc. name changed to Guaranty Bancorp 05/12/2008

FIRST MAJESTIC RESOURCE CORP (BC)
Reincorporated 01/17/2005
Place of incorporation changed from (Yukon) to (BC) 01/17/2005
Name changed to First Majestic Silver Corp. 11/22/2006

FIRST MANHATTAN RES CORP (BC)
Recapitalized as Napier International Technologies Inc. 06/27/1990
Each share Common no par exchanged for (1.5) shares Common no par
Napier International Technologies Inc. name changed to Napier Environmental Technologies Inc. 01/03/2001
(See Napier Environmental Technologies Inc.)

FIRST MANISTIQUE CORP (MI)
Name changed to North Country Financial Corp. 4/14/98
North Country Financial Corp. recapitalized as Mackinac Financial Corp. 12/16/2004

FIRST MANITOWOC BANCORP INC NEW (WI)
Name changed to Bank First National Corp. 07/03/2014

FIRST MANITOWOC BANCORP INC OLD (WI)
Common $1 par split (5) for (4) by issuance of (0.25) additional share payable 04/16/1999 to holders of record 04/07/1999
Common $1 par split (2) for (1) by issuance of (1) additional share payable 06/30/2000 to holders of record 06/14/2000 Ex date - 07/03/2000

Common $1 par split (2) for (1) by issuance of (1) additional share payable 10/18/2002 to holders of record 10/01/2002 Ex date - 10/21/2002
Merged into First Manitowoc Bancorp, Inc. (New) 07/05/2005
Each share Common $1 par exchanged for $19.60 cash
Note: Holders of (1,000) shares or more will retain their interests
First Manitowoc Bancorp, Inc. (New) name changed to Bank First National Corp. 07/03/2014

FIRST MARATHON INC (ON)
Each share Common no par exchanged for (0.5) share Conv. Class A no par and (0.5) share Conv. Class B no par 10/04/1985
Conv. Class A no par reclassified as Non-Vtg. Class A no par 05/30/1986
Each share Conv. Class B no par exchanged for (0.6) share Non-Vtg. Class A no par and (0.4) share Conv. Class C no par 05/30/1986
Non-Vtg. Class A no par split (2) for (1) by issuance of (1) additional share 07/21/1987
Conv. Class C no par split (2) for (1) by issuance of (1) additional share 07/21/1987
Merged into National Bank of Canada (Montreal, QC) 08/13/1999
Each share Non-Vtg. Class A no par exchanged for either (1.3) shares Common no par, $26 cash or a combination thereof
Each share Conv. Class C no par exchanged for either (1.3) shares Common no par, $26 cash or a combination thereof
Note: Non-electing holders received cash

FIRST MARBLEHEAD CORP (DE)
Old Common 1¢ par split (3) for (2) by issuance of (0.5) additional share payable 12/04/2006 to holders of record 11/20/2006 Ex date - 12/05/2006
Each share old Common 1¢ par exchanged for (0.1) share new Common 1¢ par 12/03/2013
Acquired by FP Resources USA Inc. 08/22/2016
Each share new Common 1¢ par exchanged for $5.05 cash

FIRST MARINE BK & TR CO PALM BEACHES (RIVIERA BEACH, FL)
Merged into Barnett Bank of Palm Beach County (Riviera Beach, FL) 04/22/1983
Each share Common $10 par exchanged for $230.27 cash

FIRST MARINE BANK (BOCA RATON, FL)
Merged into First Marine Bank & Trust Co. of the Palm Beaches (Riveria Beach, FL) 12/31/77
Each share Capital Stock $10 par exchanged for (0.065) share Common $10 par
(See First Marine Bank & Trust Co. of the Palm Beaches (Riviera Beach, FL))

FIRST MARINE BKS INC (FL)
Merged into Barnett Banks of Florida, Inc. 06/15/1982
Each share Common $1 par exchanged for $15 cash

FIRST MARINER BANCORP (MD)
Stock Dividend - 10% payable 06/10/1998 to holders of record 05/26/1998
Plan of reorganization under Chapter 11 Federal Bankruptcy proceedings effective 12/09/2014
No stockholders' equity

FIRST MARITIME MNG LTD (NB)
Merged into Hunter Brook Holdings Ltd. 01/01/1999

Each share Common no par exchanged for $9.10 cash

FIRST MASTER FDG CORP N Y (NY)
Reincorporated under the laws of Delaware as Financial Centers of America Inc. 12/22/1971
(See Financial Centers of America Inc.)

FIRST MATAGORDA CORP (DE)
Reincorporated 06/01/1984
State of incorporation changed from (TX) to (DE) 06/01/1984
Merged into Sunshine Mining Co. 11/29/1984
Each share Common $1 par exchanged for (0.9656) share Capital Stock 50¢ par
Sunshine Mining Co. name changed to Sunshine Mining & Refining Co. 06/20/1994

FIRST MD BANCORP (MD)
Common $5 par split (5) for (4) by issuance of (0.25) additional share 3/3/80
Common $5 par split (2) for (1) by issuance of (1) additional share 12/30/85
Stock Dividends - 20% 6/17/77; 20% 3/15/88
Merged into Allied Irish Banks PLC 3/21/89
Each share Common $5 par exchanged for $39.25 cash
7.875% Preferred Ser. A $5 par called for redemption at $25 on 7/14/99
Public interest eliminated

FIRST-MECHANICS NATIONAL BANK (TRENTON, NJ)
Stock Dividends - 25% 09/23/1949; 50% 09/19/1950; 33-1/3% 12/24/1952; 25% 12/23/1954
Merged into First Trenton National Bank (Trenton, NJ) 08/29/1958
Each share Common $10 par exchanged for (1) share Common $10 par
First Trenton National Bank (Trenton, NJ) name changed to New Jersey National Bank (Trenton, NJ) 05/11/1970 which reorganized as NJN Bancorporation 07/01/1971 which name changed to New Jersey National Corp. 03/21/1972 which was acquired by CoreStates Financial Corp 10/30/1986 which merged into First Union Corp. 04/28/1998 which name changed to Wachovia Corp. (Ctfs. dated after 09/01/2001) 09/01/2001 which merged into Wells Fargo & Co. (New) 12/31/2008

FIRST MED CORP (GA)
Administratively dissolved 00/00/1993

FIRST MED DEVICES CORP (MN)
Merged into Westmark International Inc. 9/6/90
Each share Common no par exchanged for $0.97 cash

FIRST MED GROUP INC (DE)
Assets sold to AMCMC Acquisition Corp. 05/11/2000
Stockholders' equity unlikely

FIRST MED INTL INC (DE)
Charter cancelled and declared inoperative and void for non-payment of taxes 03/01/1992

FIRST MED MGMT LTD (BC)
Struck off register and declared dissolved for failure to file returns 05/22/1992

FIRST MEDITERRANEAN GOLD RES INC (ON)
Reorganized under the laws of Nevada as Advantage Opportunity Corp. 07/21/2004
Each share Common no par exchanged for (0.05) share Common $0.0001 par
Advantage Opportunity Corp. name changed to Kachina Gold Corp.

04/04/2005 which recapitalized as Osage Energy Corp. (NV) 05/15/2006 which reincorporated in Delaware as Osage Exploration & Development, Inc. 07/17/2007

FIRST MELVILLE BANCORP INC (MA)
Merged into Shawmut Corp. 10/1/81
Each share Common $1 par exchanged for (2) shares Common $5 par
Shawmut Corp. merged into Shawmut National Corp. 2/29/88 which merged into Fleet Financial Group Inc. (New) 11/30/95 which name changed to Fleet Boston Corp. 10/1/99 which name changed to FleetBoston Financial Corp. 4/18/2000 which merged into Bank of America Corp. 4/1/2004

FIRST MEMPHIS RLTY TR (MA)
Name changed to Towermarc 05/05/1980
(See Towermarc)

FIRST MENASHA BANCSHARES INC (WI)
Merged into Nicolet Bankshares, Inc. 04/28/2017
Each share Common $0.025 par exchanged for either (3.126) shares Common 1¢ par, $131.50 cash or a combination thereof

FIRST MERCANTILE CURRENCY FD INC (ON)
Under plan of recapitalization each share old Class A no par exchanged for (1) Unit consisting of (1) share new Class A no par and (1) Trust Unit 01/01/1990
Each share new Class A no par exchanged for (1) Combined Unit 06/30/1999
Each Trust Unit exchanged for (1) Combined Unit 06/30/1999
Completely liquidated 01/06/2010
Each Combined Unit exchanged for first and final distribution of $8.2918 cash

FIRST MERCANTILE NATL BK (LONGWOOD, FL)
Merged into Regions Financial Corp. (Old) 5/15/97
Each share Common no par exchanged for $30 cash

FIRST MERCHANTS ACCEP CORP (DE)
Plan of reorganization under Chapter 11 Federal Bankruptcy Code effective 03/31/1998
Each share Common 1¢ par received approximately (0.005) Ugly Duckling Corp. Common Stock Purchase Warrant expiring 04/01/2001
Note: Certificates were not required to be surrendered and are without value

FIRST MERCHANTS BANCORP INC (WV)
Merged into City Holding Co. 8/31/95
Each share Common no par exchanged for (1.6) shares Common $2.50 par

FIRST MERCHANTS CAP TR I (DE)
8.75% Guaranteed Trust Preferred Securities called for redemption at $25 on 06/30/2007

FIRST MERCHANTS NATIONAL BANK (ASBURY PARK, NJ)
Principal location changed from Asbury Park, NJ to Neptune Township, NJ 04/05/1971
First Merchants National Bank (Neptune Township, NJ) merged into Midlantic Banks Inc. 01/01/1979 which merged into Midlantic Corp. 01/30/1979
(See Midlantic Corp.)

FIRST MERCHANTS NATL BK (MICHIGAN CITY, IN)
Common $10 par changed to $5 par

and (1) additional share issued 02/18/1980
Stock Dividends - 10% 02/20/1970; 10% 02/19/1971; 10% 02/21/1973; 10% 02/22/1974; 10% 03/01/1977; 10% 02/23/1979
Merged into Horizon Bancorp 10/31/1983
Each share Common $5 par exchanged for (1) share Common no par
Horizon Bancorp name changed to Horizon Bancorp, Inc. 05/08/2018

FIRST MERCHANTS NATL BK (NEPTUNE TOWNSHIP, NJ)
Merged into Midlantic Banks Inc. 01/01/1979
Each share Common Capital $2.50 par exchanged for (0.53333) share $2 Conv. Preferred 2nd Ser. no par or (0.46578) share $2 Conv. Preferred 2nd Ser. no par and $2.62 in the form of cash or 8% Installment Notes due 12/31/1985
(See Midlantic Banks Inc.)

FIRST MERCURY FINL CORP (DE)
Acquired by Fairfax Financial Holdings Ltd. 02/09/2011
Each share Common 1¢ par exchanged for $16.50 cash

FIRST MET RLTY CORP (NY)
Dissolved by proclamation 3/24/93

FIRST METROPLEX CAP INC (TX)
Name changed to T Bancshares, Inc. 08/10/2007
(See T Bancshares, Inc.)

FIRST METROPOLITAN BANK (METAIRIE, LA)
Each share Capital Stock $10 par exchanged for (0.002) share Capital Stock $5,000 par 1/24/84
Note: In effect holders received $35 cash per share and public interest was eliminated

FIRST MFRS NATL BK LEWISTON & AUBURN (LEWISTON, ME)
Capital Stock $12.50 par changed to $10 par 2/15/63
Stock Dividend - 27% 2/15/63
Name changed to Northeast Bank N.A. of Lewiston & Auburn (Lewiston, ME) 12/31/71
(See Northeast Bank N.A. of Lewiston & Auburn (Lewiston, ME))

FIRST MICH BK & TR CO (ZEELAND, MI)
Each share Capital Stock $10 par exchanged for (2) shares Capital Stock $5 par 3/1/71
Reorganized as First Michigan Bank Corp. 3/1/74
Each share Capital Stock $5 par exchanged for (2) shares Common $1 par
First Michigan Bank Corp. merged into Huntington Bancshares Inc. 9/30/97

FIRST MICH BK CORP (MI)
Common $1 par split (4) for (3) by issuance of (1/3) additional share 02/28/1990
Common $1 par split (4) for (3) by issuance of (1/3) share 02/28/1994
Common $1 par split (4) for (3) by issuance of (1/3) additional share payable 07/26/1996 to holders of record 07/01/1996
Stock Dividends - 15% 05/27/1980; 5% payable 05/31/1996 to holders of record 04/30/1996; 5% payable 05/30/1997 to holders of record 04/30/1997
Merged into Huntington Bancshares Inc. 09/30/1997
Each share Common $1 par exchanged for (1.155) shares Common no par

FIRST MICH CAP CORP (DE)
Common 10¢ par split (3) for (2) by

issuance of (0.5) additional share 4/22/83
Common 10¢ par split (3) for (1) by issuance of (2) additional shares 8/29/83
Stock Dividends - 10% 10/30/80; 10% 1/18/94
Merged into Fahnestock Viner Holdings Inc. 7/31/97
Each share Common 10¢ par exchanged for $15 cash

FIRST MICH CORP (DE)
Reorganized as First of Michigan Capital Corp. 9/18/74
Each share Common 10¢ par exchanged for (1) share Common 10¢ par
(See First of Michigan Capital Corp.)

FIRST MIDWEST BANCORP INC (MO)
Common $10 par changed to $5 par and (1) additional share issued 04/15/1973
Common $5 par changed to $2.50 par and (1) additional share issued 04/15/1977
Common $2.50 par split (2) for (1) by issuance of (1) additional share 04/15/1979
Common $2.50 par changed to $1.25 par and (1) additional share issued 04/26/1983
Charter forfeited for failure to file reports 05/22/1990

FIRST MIDWEST CAPITAL CORP. (MN)
Stock Dividend - 25% 9/30/67
Name changed to First Midwest Corp. 10/16/70
(See First Midwest Corp.)

FIRST MIDWEST CORP. SHAREHOLDERS' TRUST (MN)
In process of liquidation
Details not available

FIRST MIDWEST CORP (MN)
Stock Dividend - 50% 8/7/81
Common $5 par changed to $1 par 8/17/82
Common $1 par split (3) for (2) by issuance of (0.5) additional share 9/15/83
In process of liquidation
Each share Common $1 par received initial distribution of (0.066) share Dicomed Corp. Common 3¢ par, (0.22) share HEI, Inc. Common 5¢ par and $0.60 cash 4/17/86
Assets transferred to First Midwest Corp. Shareholders' Trust and Common $1 par reclassified as Shares of Bene. Int. $1 par 4/30/86
(See First Midwest Corp. Shareholders Trust)

FIRST MIDWEST CORP (UT)
Merged into First Midwest Financial Corp. 12/10/1982
Each (174) shares Common $0.001 par exchanged for (1) share Common $0.001 par
(See First Midwest Financial Corp.)

FIRST MIDWEST CORP DEL (DE)
Common $5 par changed to $2.50 par and (1) additional share issued 04/19/1989
Common $2.50 par changed to $1.25 par and (1) additional share issued 04/03/1991
Common $1.25 par changed to 62-1/2¢ par and (1) additional share issued payable 04/30/1996 to holders of record 04/11/1996
Common 62-1/2¢ par changed to 1¢ par and (1) additional share issued payable 12/17/1997 to holders of record 11/17/1997
Name changed to Midwest Banc Holdings, Inc. 02/17/1998
(See Midwest Banc Holdings, Inc.)

FIRST MIDWEST FINL CORP (UT)
Involuntarily dissolved 06/01/1987

FIRST MIDWEST FINL INC (DE)
Common 1¢ par split (3) for (2) by issuance of (0.5) additional share payable 01/02/1997 to holders of record 12/16/1996
Name changed to Meta Financial Group, Inc. 01/28/2005

FIRST MIDWEST INVESTMENT CORP. (WI)
Completely liquidated 11/28/1972
No stockholders' equity

FIRST MIDWEST SMALL BUSINESS INVESTMENT CO. (MN)
Name changed to First Midwest Capital Corp. 9/27/61
First Midwest Capital Corp. name changed to First Midwest Corp. 10/16/70
(See First Midwest Corp.)

FIRST MILPITAS CORP. (CA)
Liquidation completed
Each share Capital Stock $2 par exchanged for initial distribution of $40 cash 3/18/68
Each share Capital Stock $2 par received second distribution of $4 cash 3/25/69
Each share Capital Stock $2 par received third and final distribution of $0.195 cash 11/19/70

FIRST MNG FIN CORP (BC)
Name changed to First Mining Gold Corp. 01/11/2018

1ST MIRACLE GROUP INC (ON)
Recapitalized as Miracle Entertainment, Inc. 11/16/2001
Each share Common no par exchanged for (0.00111111) share Common no par

FIRST MISS CORP (MS)
Common $1 par split (5) for (2) by issuance of (1.5) additional shares 12/17/1980
Stock Dividends - 50% 01/15/1974; 200% 12/17/1974
Each share Common $1 par received distribution of (1) share ChemFirst Inc. Common $1 par payable 01/06/1997 to holders of record 12/23/1996
Merged into Mississippi Chemical Corp. (New) 12/23/1996
Each share Common $1 par exchanged for (0.334026) share new Common 1¢ par
Mississippi Chemical Corp. (New) reorganized as Terra Industries Inc. 12/21/2004 which merged into CF Industries Holdings, Inc. 04/15/2010

FIRST MISS NATL BK (HATTIESBURG, MS)
Reorganized as First Mississippi National Corp. 04/08/1975
Each share Capital Stock $10 par exchanged for (1) share Common $1 par
First Mississippi National Corp. acquired by Bancorp of Mississippi 12/31/1986 which name changed to BancorpSouth, Inc. 10/06/1992 which reorganized as BancorpSouth Bank (Tupelo, MS) 11/01/2017

FIRST MISS NATL CORP (DE)
Stock Dividend - 10% 12/20/1976
Acquired by Bancorp of Mississippi 12/31/1986
Each share Common $1 par exchanged for (1.434786) shares Common $2.50 par
Bancorp of Mississippi name changed to BancorpSouth, Inc. 10/06/1992 which reorganized as BancorpSouth Bank (Tupelo, MS) 11/01/2017

FIRST MO BANCSHARES INC (DE)
Acquired by Linn County Bancshares, Inc. 01/01/2010
Details not available

FIRST MOLINE FINL CORP (DE)
Merged into Firstar Corp. (Old) 03/23/1995
Each share Common 1¢ par exchanged for (1.06) shares Common $1.25 par
Firstar Corp. (Old) merged into Firstar Corp. (New) 11/20/1998 which merged into U.S. Bancorp (DE) 02/27/2001

FIRST MONTAUK FINL CORP (NJ)
Each share old Common no par exchanged for (0.00990099) share new Common no par 07/16/2009
Note: Holders of (100) or fewer pre-split shares received $0.008 cash per share
Company terminated common stock registration and is no longer public as of 08//03/2009

FIRST MORRIS BK (MORRISTOWN, NJ)
Common $10 par split (2) for (1) by issuance of (1) additional share payable 10/17/2005 to holders of record 10/3/2005 Ex date - 10/18/2005
Stock Dividends - 10% payable 3/8/2001 to holders of record 3/2/2001 Ex date - 3/1/2001; 10% payable 3/14/2002 to holders of record 3/8/2002 Ex date - 3/6/2002; 10% payable 3/14/2003 to holders of record 3/7/2003 Ex date - 3/5/2003; 10% payable 3/12/2004 to holders of record 3/5/2004 Ex date - 3/4/2004; 10% payable 3/11/2005 to holders of record 3/4/2005 Ex date - 3/2/2005
Merged into Provident Financial Services, Inc. 4/2/2007
Each share Common $10 par exchanged for (2.1337) shares Common 1¢ par

FIRST MORTGAGE CORP. OF STUART (FL)
Adjudicated bankrupt 2/25/66
No stockholders' equity

FIRST MTG CORP (CA)
Common no par split (5) for (4) by issuance of (0.25) additional share 08/02/1993
Merged into Fin-West Group 03/31/2003
Each share Common no par exchanged for $4.77 cash

FIRST MORTGAGE GUARANTY & TITLE CO. (NEW ROCHELLE, NY)
Taken over by State Insurance Dept. in 1933

FIRST MTG INS CO (NC)
Under plan of reorganization each share Common $1 par automatically became (1) share FMIC Corp. (NC) Common no par 08/31/1973
FMIC Corp. (NC) name changed to United Guaranty Corp. 12/30/1974 which merged into American International Group, Inc. 10/01/1981

FIRST MTG INVS (MA)
Shares of Bene. Int. no par split (1.625) for (1) by issuance of (0.625) additional share 10/7/68
Reorganized under the laws of Florida as FMI Financial Corp. 12/30/80
Each Share of Bene. Int. no par exchanged for (1) share Common 1¢ par
FMI Financial Corp. name changed to Great American Communications Co.(Old) 10/12/87 which reorganized as Great American Communications Co. (New) 12/28/93 which name changed to Citicasters Inc. 6/8/94
(See Citicasters Inc.)

FIRST MTN BANCORP (CA)
Stock Dividends - 5% payable 06/20/2007 to holders of record 05/25/2007 Ex date - 05/23/2007; 3% payable 10/10/2008 to holders of record 09/15/2008 Ex date - 09/11/2008
Under plan of reorganization each share Common no par automatically became (1) share First Mountain Bank (Big Bear Lake, CA) (New)
Common no par 02/07/2013
First Mountain Bank (Big Bear Lake, CA) (New) merged into PBB Bancorp 01/29/2016

FIRST MTN BK NEW (BIG BEAR LAKE, CA)
Merged into PBB Bancorp 01/29/2016
Each share Common no par exchanged for (1) share Common no par and $1.05 cash

FIRST MTN BK OLD (BIG BEAR LAKE, CA)
Common no par split (5) for (4) by issuance of (0.25) additional share 12/01/1994
Common no par split (5) for (4) by issuance of (0.25) additional share payable 12/01/1998 to holders of record 10/30/1998 Ex date - 12/02/1998
Stock Dividends - 5% payable 06/25/2001 to holders of record 06/04/2001 Ex date - 05/31/2001; 5% payable 06/17/2002 to holders of record 05/23/2002; 5% payable 06/17/2003 to holders of record 05/23/2003 Ex date - 05/21/2003; 7% payable 06/17/2004 to holders of record 05/21/2004 Ex date - 05/19/2004; 7% payable 06/20/2005 to holders of record 05/25/2005 Ex date - 05/23/2005; 5% payable 06/20/2006 to holders of record 05/25/2006 Ex date - 05/23/2006
Under plan of reorganization each share Common no par automatically became (1) share First Mountain Bancorp Common no par 09/25/2006
First Mountain Bank (Big Bear Lake, CA) reorganized as First Mountain Bank (Big Bear Lake, CA) (New) 02/07/2013 which merged into PBB Bancorp 01/29/2016

FIRST MTN EXPL INC (AB)
Recapitalized as Point Loma Resources Ltd. 07/05/2016
Each share Common no par exchanged for (0.1) share Common no par

FIRST MTN EXPL LTD (AB)
Recapitalized as First Mountain Exploration Inc. 09/02/2014
Each share Common no par exchanged for (0.4) share Common no par
First Mountain Exploration Inc. recapitalized as Point Loma Resources Ltd. 07/05/2016

FIRST MULTIFUND AMER INC (NY)
Acquired by Oppenheimer Special Fund, Inc. (MD) 11/20/1979
Each share Common 1¢ par exchanged for (0.521699) share Capital Stock $1 par
Oppenheimer Special Fund, Inc. (MD) reincorporated in Massachusetts as Oppenheimer Special Fund 11/01/1985 which name changed to Oppenheimer Growth Fund 12/21/1994 which merged into Oppenheimer Capital Appreciation Fund 11/08/2007

FIRST MULTIFUND FOR DAILY INCOME INC (NY)
Acquired by Oppenheimer Monetary Bridge, Inc. 11/20/1979
Each share Common 1¢ par exchanged for (0.833290) share Capital Stock $1 par
Oppenheimer Monetary Bridge, Inc. name changed to Oppenheimer Money Market Fund Inc. 06/16/1980

FIRST MUNICH CAP LTD (ON)
Voluntarily dissolved 06/04/1990
Details not available

FIRST MUSKOGEE CORP (OK)
Merged into BOK Financial Corp. in June 1999
Details not available

FIRST MUT BANCORP INC (DE)
Merged into Union Planters Corp. 1/31/99
Each share Common 10¢ par exchanged for (0.398) share Common $5 par
Union Planters Corp. merged into Regions Financial Corp. (New) 7/1/2004

FIRST MUT BANCSHARES INC (WA)
Common $1 par split (5) for (4) by issuance of (0.25) additional share payable 10/04/2006 to holders of record 09/13/2006 Ex date - 10/05/2006
Stock Dividends - 10% payable 05/08/2002 to holders of record 04/17/2002; 10% payable 07/02/2003 to holders of record 06/11/2003 Ex date - 06/09/2003; 10% payable 04/07/2004 to holders of record 03/17/2004
Merged into Washington Federal, Inc. 02/02/2008
Each share Common $1 par exchanged for $26.8359 cash

FIRST MUT FDS (RI)
Name changed 11/14/1972
Name changed 07/03/1992
Name changed from First Mutual Fund of Rhode Island, Inc. to First Mutual Fund, Inc. 11/14/1972
Name changed from First Mutual Fund, Inc. to First Mutual Funds 07/03/1992
Reorganized as Trainer, Wortham First Mutual Funds 10/01/1996
Details not available

FIRST MUT INC (DE)
88.1% owned by officers as of 01/02/1998
Public interest eliminated

FIRST MUT SVGS ASSN FLA PENSACOLA (FL)
Common $1 par split (2) for (1) by issuance of (1) additional share 8/20/86
Stock Dividend - 10% 5/15/86
Acquired by AmSouth Bancorporation 11/1/87
Each share Common $1 par exchanged for (0.742) share Common $1 par or $23 cash
Note: Option to elect to receive either stock or cash expired 12/21/87
Non-electing holders will receive either option at the discretion of the company
AmSouth Bancorporation merged into Regions Financial Corp. 11/4/2006

FIRST MUT SVGS BK (BELLEVUE, WA)
Common $1 par split (3) for (2) by issuance of (0.5) additional share payable 11/05/1997 to holders of record 10/15/1997
Stock Dividends - 20% 04/05/1988; 15% 01/15/1990; 10% 12/01/1993; 15% 09/08/1994; 10% 08/16/1995; 20% payable 04/03/1996 to holders of record 03/13/1996; 10% payable 07/02/1997 to holders of record 06/11/1997; 10% payable 05/05/1999 to holders of record 04/14/1999
Under plan of reorganization each share Common $1 par automatically became (1) share First Mutual Bancshares Inc. Common $1 par 10/26/1999
(See First Mutual Bancshares Inc.)

FIRST MUTUAL TRUST FUND
Trust terminated in 1953
Details not available

FIRST N J BK (UNION, NJ)
Merged into Franklin State Bank (Franklin Township, NJ) 08/17/1973
Each share Capital Stock $5 par exchanged for (1.21) shares Capital Stock $3.50 par
(See Franklin State Bank (Franklin Township, NJ))

FIRST N Y BUSINESS BK CORP (DE)
Merged into First New York Bank for Business (New York, NY) 05/21/1992
Each share Common 10¢ par exchanged for (1) share Common $5 par
(See First New York Bank for Business (New York, NY))

FIRST NARROW GAUGE TRUST
Liquidated in 1949

FIRST NATL ALARMCAP INCOME FD (AB)
Each old Class A Trust Unit exchanged for (0.25) new Class A Trust Unit 12/16/2005
Completely liquidated 09/20/2013
Each new Class A Trust Unit exchanged for $0.74 cash

FIRST NATL BANCORP (GA)
Common $6.25 par split (2) for (1) by issuance of (1) additional share 5/1/85
Common $6.25 par split (2) for (1) by issuance of (1) additional share 9/1/86
Common $6.25 par changed to $1 par 4/20/88
Common $1 par split (3) for (2) by issuance of (0.5) additional share 11/16/92
Acquired by Regions Financial Corp. (Old) 3/1/96
Each share Common $1 par exchanged for (0.76) share Common $0.625 par
Regions Financial Corp. (Old) merged into Regions Financial Corp. (New) 7/1/2004

FIRST NATL BANCORP (OH)
Name changed to First United Financial Corp. and Class A Common $10 par reclassified as Common $5 par 12/3/71
(See First United Financial Corp.)

FIRST NATL BANCORP ALLENTOWN INC (PA)
Merged into Meridian Bancorp, Inc. 08/07/1984
Each share Common $1 par exchanged for (1.3) shares $2.50 Conv. Preferred Ser. A $25 par
(See Meridian Bancorp, Inc.)

FIRST NATL BANCORP GREENVILLE INC (AL)
Merged into Whitney Holding Corp. 08/21/1998
Each share Common exchanged for (42.3857) shares Common no par
Whitney Holding Corp. merged into Hancock Holding Co. 06/04/2011 which name changed to Hancock Whitney Corp. 05/25/2018

FIRST NATL BANCORP INC (IL)
Common $10 par split (7) for (5) by issuance of (0.4) additional share 03/28/1994
Common $10 par split (5) for (4) by issuance of (0.25) additional share payable 04/06/2000 to holders of record 03/23/2000
Merged into Bank of Montreal (Montreal, QC) 07/14/2001
Each share Common $10 par exchanged for $72.50 cash

FIRST NATL BANCORP INC (LA)
Each share Common $5 par received distribution of (1.5) additional shares 1/29/81
Common $5 par split (5) for (4) by issuance of (0.25) additional share 3/9/84
Merged into Louisiana Bancshares, Inc. 1/10/85
Each share Common $5 par exchanged for (1.60571) shares Common no par
Louisiana Bancshares, Inc. name changed to Premier Bancorp, Inc. 4/15/87 which merged into Banc One Corp. 1/2/96 which merged into Bank One Corp. 10/2/98 which merged into J.P. Morgan Chase & Co. 12/31/2000 which name changed to JPMorgan Chase & Co. 7/20/2004

FIRST NATL BANCORP INC (PA)
Merged into Northwest Savings Bank (Warren, PA) 4/12/96
Each share Common $1 par exchanged for $60 cash

FIRST NATL BANCORP INC (WI)
Merged into AMCORE Financial, Inc. 04/21/1997
Each share Common exchanged for (7.54) shares Common 33¢ par
(See AMCORE Financial, Inc.)

FIRST NATL BANCORPORATION INC (CO)
Common $10 par split (2) for (1) by issuance of (1) additional share 08/25/1978
Name changed to IntraWest Financial Corp. 10/01/1982
IntraWest Financial Corp. merged into United Banks of Colorado, Inc. 04/30/1987 which merged into Norwest Corp. 04/19/1991 which name changed to Wells Fargo & Co. (New) 11/02/1998

FIRST NATIONAL BANCSHARES INC. (DE)
Name changed to Bancwest Corp. 3/15/79
Bancwest Corp. name changed to BWC Liquidating Corp. 3/18/80
(See BWC Liquidating Corp.)

FIRST NATL BANCSHARES INC (AR)
Merged into First Commercial Corp. 07/30/1983
Each share Common $10 par exchanged for (1.52) shares Common $5 par
First Commercial Corp. merged into Regions Financial Corp. (Old) 07/31/1998 which merged into Regions Financial Corp. (New) 07/01/2004

FIRST NATL BANCSHARES INC (FL)
Common $5 par split (3) for (2) by issuance of (0.5) additional share payable 06/30/2004 to holders of record 06/01/2004 Ex date - 07/01/2004
Stock Dividends - 5% payable 10/01/1999 to holders of record 08/31/1999; 5% payable 09/29/2000 to holders of record 08/31/2000 Ex date - 08/29/2000; 5% payable 09/30/2001 to holders of record 08/31/2001 Ex date - 08/29/2001; 5% payable 09/30/2002 to holders of record 08/30/2002 Ex date - 08/28/2002; 5% payable 09/30/2003 to holders of record 09/08/2003 Ex date - 09/04/2003; 5% payable 09/30/2004 to holders of record 09/10/2004 Ex date - 09/08/2004
Merged into Whitney Holding Corp. 04/13/2006
Each share Common $5 par exchanged for (0.975) share Common no par
Whitney Holding Corp. merged into Hancock Holding Co. 06/04/2011

FIRST NATL BANCSHARES INC (SC)
Common 1¢ par split (3) for (2) by issuance of (0.5) additional share payable 03/01/2004 to holders of record 02/16/2004 Ex date - 03/02/2004
Common 1¢ par split (3) for (2) by issuance of (0.5) additional share payable 01/17/2006 to holders of record 01/03/2006 Ex date - 01/18/2006
Stock Dividends - 5% payable 09/29/2000 to holders of record 08/31/2000 Ex date - 08/29/2000; 10% payable 12/06/2002 to holders of record 11/22/2002; 5% payable 03/01/2004 to holders of record 02/16/2004 Ex date - 03/02/2004; 6% payable 05/15/2006 to holders of record 05/01/2006 Ex date - 04/27/2006; 7% payable 03/30/2007 to holders of record 03/16/2007 Ex date - 03/14/2007
Chapter 7 bankruptcy proceedings terminated 05/10/2017
Stockholders' equity unlikely

FIRST NATL BANCSHARES WETUMPKA INC (AL)
Merged into Union Planters Corp. 7/31/98
Each share Common exchanged for (4.179) shares Common $5 par
Union Planters Corp. merged into Regions Financial Corp. (New) 7/1/2004

FIRST NATIONAL BANK & TRUST CO. (BAY SHORE, NY)
Capital Stock $100 par changed to $50 par and (1) additional share issued 00/00/1947
Capital Stock $50 par changed to $25 par and (1) additional share issued 00/00/1948
Capital Stock $25 par changed to $10 par and (2) additional shares issued plus a 20% stock dividend paid 01/13/1960
Stock Dividend - 26% 02/19/1957
Name changed to First National Bank (Bay Shore, NY) 02/11/1960
First National Bank (Bay Shore, NY) merged into Manufacturers Hanover Corp. 09/01/1972 which merged into Chemical Banking Corp. 12/31/1991

FIRST NATIONAL BANK & TRUST CO. (CUMBERLAND, MD)
Under plan of merger name changed to First-Second National Bank & Trust Co. (Cumberland, MD) and Common $100 par changed to $20 par 03/08/1963
First-Second National Bank & Trust Co. (Cumberland, MD) name changed to First National Bank & Trust Co. of Western Maryland (Cumberland, MD) 05/01/1966 which merged into First Maryland Bancorp 09/04/1981
(See First Maryland Bancorp)

FIRST NATIONAL BANK & TRUST CO. (EUSTIS, FL)
Common $12.50 par changed to $10 par and (0.25) additional share issued 01/29/1970
Common $10 par changed to $5 par and (1) additional share issued 09/15/1972
Acquired by Barnett Banks of Florida, Inc. 01/10/1980
Each share Common $5 par exchanged for $30.47 cash

FIRST NATIONAL BANK & TRUST CO. (GREENFIELD, MA)
Name changed to First National Bank of Franklin County (Greenfield, MA) 03/01/1968

FIRST NATIONAL BANK & TRUST CO. (HANOVER, PA)
Merged into National Bank & Trust Co. of Central Pennsylvania (York, PA) 12/14/1964
Each share Capital Stock $10 par exchanged for (1.4) shares Capital Stock $10 par
National Bank & Trust Co. of Central Pennsylvania (York, PA) merged into National Central Bank (Lancaster, PA) 12/07/1970 which reorganized as National Central Financial Corp. 12/31/1972 which merged into CoreStates Financial Corp 05/02/1983 which merged into First Union Corp. 04/28/1998 which name changed to Wachovia Corp. (Ctfs. dated after 09/01/2001) 09/01/2001

which merged into Wells Fargo & Co. (New) 12/31/2008

FIRST NATIONAL BANK & TRUST CO. (LEXINGTON, KY)
Each share Capital Stock $50 par exchanged for (5) shares Capital Stock $12.50 par to effect a (4) for (1) split and a 25% stock dividend 06/21/1955
Merged into First Security National Bank & Trust Co. (Lexington, KY) 05/10/1961
Each share Capital Stock $12.50 par exchanged for (1.2) shares Capital Stock $12.50 par
First Security National Bank & Trust Co. (Lexington, KY) reorganized as First Security Corp. of Kentucky 10/14/1975 which was acquired by Banc One Corp. 08/21/1992 which merged into Bank One Corp. 10/02/1998 which merged into J.P. Morgan Chase & Co. 12/31/2000 which name changed to JPMorgan Chase & Co. 07/20/2004

FIRST NATIONAL BANK & TRUST CO. (NEW HAVEN, CT)
Each share Capital Stock $50 par exchanged for (5) shares Capital Stock $10 par 11/01/1955
Stock Dividends - 14.28571428% 10/24/1940; 25% 12/02/1941; (2) for (15) 01/28/1955
Merged into First New Haven National Bank (New Haven, CT) 09/27/1957
Each share Capital Stock $10 par exchanged for (1) share Common $10 par
First New Haven National Bank (New Haven, CT) name changed to First Bank of New Haven (New Haven, CT) 04/01/1977 which reorganized as FirstBancorp, Inc. (CT) 02/01/1979 which merged into Hartford National Corp. 03/30/1984 which merged into Shawmut National Corp. 02/29/1988 which merged into Fleet Financial Group Inc. (New) 11/30/1995 which name changed to Fleet Boston Corp. 10/01/1999 which name changed to FleetBoston Financial Corp. 04/18/2000 which merged into Bank of America Corp. 04/01/2004

FIRST NATIONAL BANK & TRUST CO. (SCRANTON, PA)
Under plan of merger name changed to Northeastern Pennsylvania National Bank & Trust Co. (Scranton, PA) 08/01/1958
Northeastern Pennsylvania National Bank & Trust Co. (Scranton, PA) name changed to Northeastern National Bank of Pennsylvania (Scranton, PA) 04/02/1971 which name changed to Northeastern Bank of Pennsylvania (Scranton, PA) 01/02/1974 which reorganized as Northeastern Bancorp, Inc. 08/12/1981 which merged into PNC Financial Corp. 01/30/1985 which name changed to PNC Bank Corp. 02/08/1993 which name changed to PNC Financial Services Group, Inc. 03/15/2000

FIRST NATL BK & TR CO (ALTON, IL)
Stock Dividends - 25% 01/17/1950; 33-1/3% 01/21/1958
Reorganized as First Illinois Bancshares Corp. 07/01/1974
Each share Capital Stock $25 par exchanged for (5) shares Common $5 par
First Illinois Bancshares Corp. name changed to First Bancshares Corp. of Illinois 09/17/1979 which was acquired by Mercantile Bancorporation, Inc. 02/17/1987 which merged into Firstar Corp. (New) 09/20/1999 which merged into U.S. Bancorp (DE) 02/27/2001

FIRST NATL BK & TR CO (AUGUSTA, GA)
Stock Dividend - 108.3% 3/28/77
Merged into Trust Co. of Georgia 8/17/78
Each share Common $10 par exchanged for (1.2764) shares Common $5 par
Trust Co. of Georgia merged into SunTrust Banks, Inc. 7/1/85

FIRST NATL BK & TR CO (BELLEAIR BLUFFS, FL)
Name changed to First Bank & Trust Co. (Belleair Bluffs, FL) 5/9/80
(See First Bank & Trust Co. (Belleair Bluffs, FL))

FIRST NATL BK & TR CO (BETHLEHEM, PA)
Stock Dividends - 10% 10/46; 10% 11/1/63
Reorganized as First Valley Corp. 7/1/69
Each share Common $10 par exchanged for (1) share Common $1 par
First Valley Corp. acquired by United Jersey Banks 1/29/88 which name changed to UJB Financial Corp. 6/30/89 which name changed to Summit Bancorp 3/1/96 which merged into FleetBoston Financial Corp. 3/1/2001 which merged into Bank of America Corp. 4/1/2004

FIRST NATL BK & TR CO (DUNEDIN, FL)
Name changed to Sun First National Bank (Dunedin, FL) 3/1/73
(See Sun First National Bank (Dunedin, FL))

FIRST NATL BK & TR CO (ENID, OK)
Capital Stock $100 par changed to $5 par and (19) additional shares issued 06/00/1968
Reorganized as First Enid, Inc. 12/31/1981
Each share Capital Stock $5 par exchanged for (1) share Common $1 par
(See First Enid, Inc.)

FIRST NATL BK & TR CO (EVANSTON, IL)
Each share Capital Stock $100 par exchanged for (5) shares Capital Stock $20 par in 1948
Capital Stock $20 par changed to $5 par and (3) additional shares issued 11/27/63
Stock Dividends - 25% 12/2/55; 11.11% 2/18/61
Reorganized as First Illinois Corp. 10/15/73
Each share Capital Stock $5 par exchanged for (1) share Common $5 par
First Illinois Corp. acquired by Banc One Corp. 3/2/92 which merged into Bank One Corp. 10/2/98 which merged into J.P. Morgan Chase & Co. 12/31/2000 which name changed to JPMorgan Chase & Co. 7/20/2004

FIRST NATL BK & TR CO (HAMILTON, OH)
Capital Stock $40 par changed to $8 par and (4) additional shares issued 9/2/69
Stock Dividends - 11-1/9% 4/5/48; 50% 11/12/53; 33-1/3% 4/1/65; 50% 4/1/71; 33-1/3% 4/1/76; 25% 4/18/79
Merged into First National Bank of Southwestern Ohio (Monroe, OH) 7/1/80
Each share Capital Stock $8 par exchanged for (1.21208) shares Common $10 par
First National Bank of Southwestern Ohio (Monroe, OH) reorganized as First Financial Bancorp 4/26/83

FIRST NATL BK & TR CO (ITHACA, NY)
Common $10 par changed to $5 par and (1) additional share issued 3/31/70
Acquired by Security New York State Corp. 3/31/71
Each share Common $5 par exchanged for (0.625) share $6 Conv. Preferred Ser. A $5 par
(See Security New York State Corp.)

FIRST NATL BK & TR CO (KALAMAZOO, MI)
Capital Stock $100 par changed to $10 par and (9) additional shares issued plus a 20% stock dividend paid 1/20/60
Stock Dividends - 25% 1940; 20% 1942; 33-1/3% 3/28/46; 10% 3/2/65; 10% 11/10/66; 100% 5/20/68
Name changed to First National Bank & Trust Co. of Michigan (Kalamazoo, MI) 3/2/70
(See First National Bank & Trust Co. of Michigan (Kalamozoo, MI))

FIRST NATL BK & TR CO (KEARNY, NJ)
Capital Stock $25 par changed to $10 par and (1.5) additional shares issued 2/18/69
Capital Stock $10 par changed to $5 par and (1) additional share issued 2/19/75
Stock Dividends - 20% 2/4/58; 16-2/3% 10/7/60; 12-1/2% 1/31/62
Merged into Valley National Bancorp 10/1/84
Each share Capital Stock $5 par exchanged for (1.85) shares Common no par

FIRST NATL BK & TR CO (LA PORTE, IN)
Capital Stock $25 par changed to $10 par and (1.5) additional shares issued 02/20/1972
Stock Dividends - 12-1/2% 04/12/1940; 33-1/3% 12/17/1943; 100% 11/22/1955; 12-1/2% 01/17/1962; 11% 01/20/1964; 33-1/3% 04/01/1966; 100% 03/31/1979
Reorganized as First LaPorte Financial Corp. 07/01/1983
Each share Capital Stock $10 par exchanged for (1) share Capital Stock $10 par
First LaPorte Financial Corp. merged into First of America Bank Corp. 12/12/1986 which merged into National City Corp. 03/31/1998 which was acquired by PNC Financial Services Group, Inc. 12/31/2008

FIRST NATL BK & TR CO (LAKE WORTH, FL)
Stock Dividend - 50% 01/25/1968
Acquired by General Financial Systems, Inc. 12/28/1973
Each share Capital Stock $10 par exchanged for (10) shares Common $1 par
General Financial Systems, Inc. name changed to First Marine Banks, Inc. 03/01/1976
(See First Marine Banks, Inc.)

FIRST NATL BK & TR CO (LIMA, OH)
Stock Dividend - 10% 3/1/64
Name changed to Huntington First National Bank (Lima, OH) 4/1/75
Huntington First National Bank (Lima, OH) merged into Huntington Bancshares Inc. 12/79

FIRST NATL BK & TR CO (LINCOLN, NE)
Name changed 06/11/1962
Name changed from First Continental National Bank & Trust Co. (Lincoln, NE) to First National Bank & Trust Co. (Lincoln, NE) 06/11/1962
Capital Stock $20 par changed to $10 par and (1) additional share issued 06/20/1963
Stock Dividend - 15% 02/11/1970
Reorganized as First National Lincoln Corp. 09/04/1973
Each share Capital Stock $10 par exchanged for (1) share Common $10 par
First National Lincoln Corp. merged into FirsTier, Inc. 06/01/1984 which name changed to FirsTier Financial Inc. 05/18/1987 which merged into First Bank System, Inc. 02/16/1996 which name changed to U.S. Bancorp 08/01/1997

FIRST NATL BK & TR CO (MACON, GA)
Stock Dividends - 14-2/7% 1/13/58; 25% 1/19/62; 60% 1/13/65; 50% 2/17/72; 66-2/3% 3/15/77
Merged into Trust Co. of Georgia 8/17/78
Each share Capital Stock $10 par exchanged for (1.3518) shares Common $5 par
Trust Co. of Georgia merged into SunTrust Banks, Inc. 7/1/85

FIRST NATL BK & TR CO (MUSKOGEE, OK)
Each share Capital Stock $100 par exchanged for (10) shares Capital Stock $10 par in 1946
Stock Dividends - 25% 7/7/48; 40% 1/24/57; 25% 1/22/65; 15% 1/23/70
Under plan of reorganization each share Capital Stock $10 par automatically became (1) share First of Muskogee Corp. Capital Stock $10 par 7/1/73
(See First of Muskogee Corp.)

FIRST NATL BK & TR CO (NAPLES, FL)
Each share Common Capital Stock $1 par exchanged for (1/29,000) share Common Capital Stock $100 par 6/15/82
Note: In effect holders received $20 cash per share and public interest was eliminated

FIRST NATL BK & TR CO (OKLAHOMA CITY, OK)
Stock Dividends - 20% 01/17/1950; 20% 01/25/1952; 33-1/3% 01/16/1956; 10% 01/28/1959; 36.36% 01/28/1964; 16.66% 05/29/1967; 11-1/9% 01/25/1971
99.99% acquired by First Oklahoma Bancorporation, Inc. through exchange offer which expired 00//1974
Public interest eliminated

FIRST NATL BK & TR CO (ONTARIO, CA)
Common $5 par changed to $2.50 par and (1) additional share issued 3/23/73
Common $2.50 par changed to $4 par 8/21/73
Common $4 par changed to $2 par and (1) additional share issued 11/24/78
Stock Dividend - 11% 4/21/72
Name changed to First Trust Bank (Ontario, CA) 4/2/79
(See First Trust Bank (Ontario, CA))

FIRST NATL BK & TR CO (PAULSBORO, NJ)
Merged into National Bank & Trust Co. of Gloucester County (Woodbury, NJ) 07/17/1970
Each share Capital Stock $25 par exchanged for (3) shares Capital Stock $10 par
National Bank & Trust Co. of Gloucester County (Woodbury, NJ) reorganized as Community Bancshares Corp. 10/01/1975 which merged into First Fidelity Bancorporation (Old) 09/28/1985 which merged into First Fidelity Bancorporation (New) 02/29/1988 which merged into First Union Corp. 01/01/1996 which name changed to Wachovia Corp. (Ctfs. dated after

09/01/2001) 09/01/2001 which merged into Wells Fargo & Co. (New) 12/31/2008

FIRST NATL BK & TR CO (PEKIN, IL)
Each share Common Capital Stock $100 par exchanged for (20) shares Common Capital Stock $10 par to effect a (10) for (1) split and a 100% stock dividend 9/28/74
Placed in receivership in 1995
No stockholders' equity

FIRST NATL BK & TR CO (RACINE, WI)
Common $100 par changed to $20 par and (4) additional shares issued plus a 20% stock dividend paid 02/04/1959
Common $20 par changed to $10 par and (1) additional share issued 01/14/1964
Stock Dividends - 25% 01/18/1950; 10% 01/17/1961; 100% 03/24/1971
Merged into Marine Corp. (WI) 11/21/1980
Each share Common $10 par exchanged for (1.75) shares $2 Conv. Preferred $1 par
Marine Corp. (WI) merged into Banc One Corp. (DE) 04/01/1988 which reincorporated in Ohio 05/01/1989 which merged into Bank One Corp. 10/02/1998 which merged into J.P. Morgan Chase & Co. 12/31/2000 which namge changed to JPMorgan Chase & Co. 07/20/2004

FIRST NATL BK & TR CO (ROCKFORD, IL)
Capital Stock $40 par changed to $10 par and (2) additional shares issued 1/28/75
Stock Dividends - 100% 9/2/58; 100% 6/11/62; 100% 2/8/71
Reorganized as First Community Bancorp, Inc. 8/2/82
Each share Capital Stock $10 par exchanged for (1) share Common $10 par
First Commmunity Bancorp, Inc. acquired by Banc One Corp. 5/3/93 which merged into Bank One Corp. 10/2/98 which merged into J.P. Morgan Chase & Co. 12/31/2000 which name changed to JPMorgan Chase & Co. 7/20/2004

FIRST NATL BK & TR CO (STEUBENVILLE, OH)
Stock Dividend - 100% 1945
Reorganized as First Steuben Bancorp, Inc. 8/29/69
Each share Capital Stock $10 par exchanged for (1) share Common $10 par
First Steuben Bancorp, Inc. name changed to Heritage Bancorp, Inc. 4/5/79 which merged into Banc One Corp. (DE) 4/1/83 which reincorporated in Ohio 5/1/89 which merged into Bank One Corp. 10/2/98 which merged into J.P. Morgan Chase & Co. 12/31/2000 which name changed to JPMorgan Chase & Co. 7/20/2004

FIRST NATL BK & TR CO (TROY, OH)
Stock Dividends - 20% 03/01/1968; 20% 03/01/1970; 10% 04/14/1972
Merged into First National Cincinnati Corp. 09/30/1976
Each share Capital Stock $10 par exchanged for $22.04 cash
Each share Capital Stock $10 par received an additional distribution of $22.04 cash 01/31/1977
Each share Capital Stock $10 par received an additional distribution of $0.3857 cash 07/25/1977

FIRST NATL BK & TR CO (TULSA, OK)
Each share Common $20 par exchanged for (2) shares Common $10 par in 1953
Stock Dividends - 12-1/2% 11/17/49; 100% 1/31/69
Reorganized as First Tulsa Bancorporation, Inc. 7/1/69
Each share Common $10 par exchanged for (1) share Common $10 par
First Tulsa Bancorporation, Inc. merged into Banks of Mid-America, Inc. 7/17/84 which reincorporated in Oklahoma as Liberty Bancorp Inc. 5/26/92 which merged into Banc One Corp. 6/1/97 which merged into Bank One Corp. 10/2/98 which merged into J.P. Morgan Chase & Co. 12/31/2000 which name changed to JPMorgan Chase & Co. 7/20/2004

FIRST NATL BK & TR CO (WASHINGTON, PA)
Reorganized as First Dyna-Corp. 06/11/1973
Each share Common $5 par exchanged for (1) share Common $5 par
First Dyna-Corp. name changed to First Financial Group Inc. 04/28/1980 which merged into Union National Corp. 01/22/1986 which merged into Integra Financial Corp. 01/26/1989 which merged into National City Corp. 05/03/1996 which was acquired by PNC Financial Services Group, Inc. 12/31/2008

FIRST NATL BK & TR CO (WAYNESBORO, PA)
Common $10 par changed to $5 par and (1) additional share issued 4/15/80
Under plan of reorganization each share Common $5 par automatically became (1) share Firstway Financial, Inc. Common $5 par 6/24/85
Firstway Financial, Inc. acquired by Financial Trust Corp. 11/2/87 which merged into Keystone Financial, Inc. 5/30/97 which merged into M&T Bank Corp. 10/6/2000

FIRST NATL BK & TR CO MICH (KALAMAZOO, MI)
Merged into First National Financial Corp. 06/20/1972
Each share Common $10 par exchanged for (2.5) shares Common $10 par
First National Financial Corp. merged into First American Bank Corp. 02/13/1978 which name changed to First of America Bank Corp. 01/14/1983 which merged into National City Corp. 03/31/1998 which was acquired by PNC Financial Services Group, Inc. 12/31/2008

FIRST NATL BK & TR CO WESTN MD (CUMBERLAND, MD)
Common $20 par changed to $10 par and (1) additional share issued 1/28/75
Common $10 par changed to $5 par and (1) additional share issued 4/10/79
Stock Dividends - 10% 2/10/69; 10% 2/9/73; 10% 5/2/77
Merged into First Maryland Bancorp 9/4/81
Each share Common $5 par exchanged for (1.75) shares Common $5 par
(See First Maryland Bancorp)

FIRST NATL BK (ABILENE, TX)
Capital Stock $20 par changed to $10 par and (1) additional share issued plus a 10% stock dividend paid 1/27/64
Stock Dividends - 25% 2/9/60; 11-1/9% 11/10/67
Under plan of reorganization each share Capital Stock $10 par automatically became (1) share First Abilene Bankshares, Inc. Common $10 par 4/24/73
First Abilene Bankshares, Inc. name changed to First Financial Bankshares, Inc. 10/26/93

FIRST NATL BK (ABSECON, NJ)
Stock Dividend - 5% payable 6/14/96 to holders of record 5/15/96
Under plan of reorganization each share Common $20 par automatically became (1) share Absecon Bancorp Common 10¢ par 4/1/97

FIRST NATL BK (AKRON, OH)
Capital Stock $5 par changed to $10 par plus a 25% stock dividend paid 00/00/1951
Stock Dividends - 25% 04/01/1959; 100% 10/15/1965
Reorganized as First Bancorporation of Ohio, Inc. 12/30/1981
Each share Capital Stock $10 par exchanged for (1) share Common $10 par
First Bancorporation of Ohio, Inc. name changed to FirstMerit Corp. 12/26/1994 which merged into Huntington Bancshares Inc. 08/16/2016

FIRST NATIONAL BANK (ALBANY, GA)
Merged into Trust Co. of Georgia 7/1/77
Each share Common $10 par exchanged for (2) shares Common $5 par
Trust Co. of Georgia merged into SunTrust Banks, Inc. 7/1/85

FIRST NATL BK (ALBEMARLE, NC)
Acquired by First Union Corp. 12/28/1981
Each share Common $5 par exchanged for $45 cash

FIRST NATL BK (ALBUQUERQUE, NM)
Each share Capital Stock $100 par exchanged for (8) shares Capital Stock $12.50 par plus a 12.5% stock dividend 00/00/1950
Each share Capital Stock $12.50 par exchanged for (2) shares Capital Stock $6.25 par 04/13/1978
Stock Dividends - 230% 02/00/1947; 33.33333333% 06/09/1958; 50% 07/26/1960; 25% 04/15/1979; 10% 04/15/1981
Reorganized as First National Financial Corp. (NM) 12/23/1985
Each share Capital Stock $6.25 par exchanged for (1) share Common $6.25 par
First National Financial Corp. (NM) merged into First Security Corp. 11/19/1993 which merged into Wells Fargo & Co. (New) 10/26/2000

FIRST NATIONAL BANK (ALLEGANY, NY)
Merged into First National Bank (Olean, NY) 1/1/63
Each share Capital Stock $100 par exchanged for (9) shares Capital Stock $12.50 par
First National Bank (Olean, NY) acquired by Manufacturers Hanover Corp. 7/25/73 which merged into Chemical Banking Corp. 12/31/91 which name changed to Chase Manhattan Corp. (New) 3/31/96 which name changed to J.P. Morgan Chase & Co. 12/31/2000 which name changed to JPMorgan Chase & Co. 7/20/2004

FIRST NATIONAL BANK (ALLENDALE, IL)
Under plan of reorganization each share Common $25 par automatically became (1) share Allendale Bancorp, Inc. Common 06/00/1994

FIRST NATL BK (ALLENTOWN, PA)
Common $10 par changed to $5 par and (1) additional share issued 09/25/1969
Common $5 par changed to $2.50 par and (1) additional share issued 01/30/1979
Stock Dividend - 20% 11/07/1960
Under plan of reorganization each share Common $2.50 par automatically became (1) share First National Bancorp of Allentown, Inc. Common $1 par 03/01/1982
First National Bancorp of Allentown, Inc. merged into Meridian Bancorp, Inc. 08/07/1984
(See Meridian Bancorp, Inc.)

FIRST NATL BK (ALTAVISTA, VA)
Reorganized as Pinnacle Bankshares Corp. 05/01/1997
Each share Common $2 par exchanged for (3) shares Common $3 par

FIRST NATL BK (ALTOONA, PA)
Each share Common $100 par exchanged for (10) shares Common $10 par 00/00/1948
Stock Dividend - 25% 02/02/1951
Merged into Central Counties Bank (State College, PA) 12/31/1974
Each share Common $10 par exchanged for (2.25) shares Common $5 par
Central Counties Bank (State College, PA) reorganized as CCB Bancorp, Inc. 07/01/1982 which merged into Mellon National Corp. 09/14/1983 which name changed to Mellon Bank Corp. 09/30/1984 which name changed to Mellon Financial Corp. 10/17/1999 which merged into Bank of New York Mellon Corp. 07/01/2007

FIRST NATL BK (AMARILLO, TX)
Each share Common $20 par exchanged for (2) shares Common $10 par in 1951
Stock Dividends - 50% 1/24/49; (10) for (27) 10/16/51; 20% 5/14/54; 66-2/3% 8/1/57; 25% 9/26/61; 14% 1/27/64; 16-2/3% 3/6/67; 20% 3/3/70; 25% 4/20/72; 40% 4/19/74; 12-1/2% 4/25/76; 15% 5/5/78; (1) for (6.67) 2/28/80; 100% 3/8/82
Under plan of reorganization each share Common $10 par automatically became (1) share First Amarillo Bancorporation, Inc. Common $1 par 11/1/82
First Amarillo Bancorporation, Inc. acquired by Boatmen's Bancshares, Inc. 11/30/93 which merged into NationsBank Corp. 1/7/97 which reincorporated in Delaware as BankAmerica Corp. (Old) 9/25/98 which merged into BankAmerica Corp. (New) 9/30/98 which name changed to Bank of America Corp. 4/28/99

FIRST NATL BK (AMHERST, MA)
Merged into Worcester Bancorp, Inc. 10/06/1972
Each share Capital Stock $10 par exchanged for (2.5) shares Common $1 par
Worcester Bancorp, Inc. acquired by Shawmut Corp. 05/03/1982 which merged into Shawmut National Corp. 02/29/1988 which merged into Fleet Financial Group Inc. (New) 11/30/1995 which name changed to Fleet Boston Corp. 10/01/1999 which name changed to FleetBoston Financial Corp. 04/18/2000 which merged into Bank of America Corp. 04/01/2004

FIRST NATL BK (ANCHORAGE, AK)
Capital Stock $100 par split (5) for (4) by issuance of (0.25) additional share 08/15/1981
Common $100 par split (2) for (1) by issuance of (1) additional share 05/01/1991
Stock Dividends - 100% 12/07/1951;

20% 01/31/1955; 66-2/3% 07/30/1958; 166-2/3% 00/00/1959; 100% 00/00/1969; 100% 02/25/1974; 100% 03/01/1977
Name changed to First National Bank Alaska (Anchorage, AK) 10/02/2001

FIRST NATL BK (ANNISTON, AL)
Stock Dividend - 25% 11/12/1964
Merged into Alabama Financial Group, Inc. 11/12/1973
Each share Capital Stock $25 par exchanged for (1.355932) shares Common $5 par
Alabama Financial Group, Inc. name changed to Southern Bancorporation 04/17/1974 which name changed to Southern Bancorporation of Alabama 04/21/1975 which name changed to SouthTrust Corp. 09/18/1981 which merged into Wachovia Corp. (Ctfs. dated after 09/01/2001) 11/01/2004 which merged into Wells Fargo & Co. (New) 12/31/2008

FIRST NATL BK (APPLETON, WI)
Stock Dividends - 50% 10/11/1950; 33.3333333% 12/08/1954; 50% 12/21/1960
98.98% held by First National Corp. (WI) and 1.02% by directors as of 02/02/1967
Public interest eliminated

FIRST NATL BK (ARLINGTON, TX)
Name changed to First City National Bank of Arlington (Arlington, TX) 01/01/1978
(See First City National Bank of Arlington (Arlington, TX))

FIRST NATL BK (ARLINGTON, VA)
Stock Dividends - 10% 02/02/1965; 10% 02/01/1966
Merged into Suburban National Bank of Virginia (McLean, VA) 08/31/1968
Each share Capital Stock $30 par exchanged for (3) shares Capital Stock $10 par
Suburban National Bank of Virginia (McLean, VA) merged into First & Merchants Corp. 08/01/1970 which merged into Sovran Financial Corp. 12/31/1983 which merged into C&S/Sovran Corp. 09/01/1990 which merged into NationsBank Corp. (NC) 12/31/1991 which reincorporated in Delaware as BankAmerica Corp. (Old) 09/25/1998 which merged into BankAmerica Corp. (New) 09/30/1998 which name changed to Bank of America Corp. 04/28/1999

FIRST NATL BK (ASHEBORO, NC)
Name changed to First National Bank of Randolph County (Asheboro, NC) 03/01/1976
(See First National Bank of Randolph County (Asheboro, NC))

FIRST NATL BK (ATLANTA, GA)
Stock Dividends - 11-1/9% 01/00/1947; 11-1/9% 03/15/1957; 10% 01/20/1961; 15% 02/01/1965
Reorganized as First National Holding Corp. (GA) 04/08/1969
Each share Capital Stock $10 par exchanged for (1) share Common $10 par
First National Holding Corp. (GA) name changed to First Atlanta Corp. 09/14/1979 which merged into First Wachovia Corp. 12/05/1985 which name changed to Wachovia Corp. (New) (Ctfs. dated between 05/20/1991 and 09/01/2001) 05/20/1991 which merged into Wachovia Corp. (Ctfs. dated after 09/01/2001) 09/01/2001 which merged into Wells Fargo & Co. (New) 12/31/2008

FIRST NATL BK (ATTLEBORO, MA)
Merged into First Bristol County National Bank (Taunton, MA) 6/30/70

Each share Capital Stock $50 par exchanged for (6) shares Common $10 par
First Bristol County National Bank (Taunton, MA) reorganized as First New England Bankshares Corp. 7/1/85 which was acquired by Hartford National Corp. 11/14/86 which merged into Shawmut National Corp. 2/29/88 which merged into Fleet Financial Group Inc. (New) 11/30/95 which name changed to Fleet Boston Corp. 10/1/99 which name changed to FleetBoston Financial Corp. 4/18/2000 which merged into Bank of America Corp. 4/1/2004

FIRST NATIONAL BANK (BALTIMORE, MD)
Stock Dividend - 50% 1/30/61
Name changed to First National Bank of Maryland (Baltimore, Md.) 7/20/62
First National Bank of Maryland (Baltimore, Md.) reorganized as First Maryland Bancorp 7/8/74
(See First Maryland Bancorp)

FIRST NATL BK (BAR HARBOR, ME)
Reorganized as FNB Bankshares 5/7/85
Each share Common $20 par exchanged for (5) shares Common $4 par
FNB Bankshares merged into First National Lincoln Corp. 1/14/2005

FIRST NATIONAL BANK (BARNESVILLE, OH)
Each share Common $100 par exchanged for (6) shares Common $20 par to effect a (5) for (1) split and 20% stock dividend 1/15/49
Stock Dividends - 25% 12/3/40; 33-1/3% 1/19/54; 20% 11/17/59; 16-2/3% 2/11/65; 50% 2/15/68
Acquired by Wesbanco, Inc. 7/17/92
Each share Common $20 par exchanged for (12) shares Common $4.1666 par

FIRST NATL BK (BARTLESVILLE, OK)
Each share Capital Stock $100 par exchanged for (5) shares Capital Stock $20 par 00/00/1948
Stock Dividends - 66-2/3% 01/29/1951; 66-2/3% 10/09/1957; 25% 04/01/1960; 33-1/3% 10/10/1963
Reorganized as First Bancshares, Inc. (DE) 01/01/1974
Each share Capital Stock $20 par exchanged for (10) shares Common $2 par
(See First Bancshares, Inc. (DE))

FIRST NATL BK (BAY CITY, TX)
Merged into Prosperity Bancshares, Inc. 11/1/2002
Each share Common $100 par exchanged for $16.47 cash

FIRST NATIONAL BANK (BAY HARBOR ISLANDS, FL)
Through voluntary exchange offer 96.3% held by Barnett Banks of Florida, Inc. as of 11/15/1973
Public interest eliminated

FIRST NATL BK (BAY SHORE, NY)
Capital Stock $10 par changed to $5 par and (1) additional share issued 12/10/69
Merged into Manufacturers Hanover Corp. 9/1/72
Each share Capital Stock $5 par exchanged for (1.6) shares Common $7.50 par
Manufacturers Hanover Corp. merged into Chemical Banking Corp. 12/31/91 which name changed to Chase Manhattan Corp. (New) 3/31/96 which name changed to J.P. Morgan Chase & Co. 12/31/2000 which name changed to JPMorgan Chase & Co. 7/20/2004

FIRST NATL BK (BAYTOWN, TX)
Name changed to First American Bank & Trust (Baytown, TX) 8/7/72
(See First American Bank & Trust (Baytown, TX))

FIRST NATIONAL BANK (BEAUMONT, TX)
Each share Capital Stock $100 par exchanged for (6) shares Capital Stock $25 par to effect a (4) for (1) split and 50% stock dividend 1/22/48
Stock Dividends - 33-1/3% 10/22/50; 50% 6/17/57
Under plan of merger name changed to First Security National Bank (Beaumont, TX) and Capital Stock $25 par changed to $20 par 10/28/61
(See First Security National Bank (Beaumont, TX))

FIRST NATL BK (BELLAIRE, TX)
Merged into Tradition Bancshares Inc. 10/1/2003
Each share Common exchanged for $26 cash

FIRST NATIONAL BANK (BELLE, WV)
Merged into National Banc of Commerce Co. 10/21/85
Each share Common $100 par exchanged for $203 cash

FIRST NATL BK (BELLEVILLE, IL)
Each share Common $100 par exchanged for (4) shares Common $25 par 1/13/42
Common $25 par changed to $12.50 par and (1) additional share issued plus a 25% stock dividend paid 7/1/70
Stock Dividends - 50% 2/15/60; 14.28% 3/1/66
Merged into First Bancorp of Belleville, Inc. 12/31/75
Each share Common $12.50 par exchanged for (1) share Common $12.50 par
First Bancorp of Belleville, Inc. name changed to Magna Group, Inc. 4/26/83 which merged into Union Planters Corp. 7/1/98 which merged into Regions Financial Corp. (New) 7/1/2004

FIRST NATL BK (BELLEVUE, OH)
Reorganized as First Bancshares, Inc. (OH) 5/1/83
Each share Common $20 par exchanged for (2) shares Common $10 par

FIRST NATIONAL BANK (BEVERLY HILLS, CA)
Name changed to Merchant Bank of California (Beverly Hills, CA) and Common $5 par changed to no par 04/04/1984
(See Merchant Bank of California (Beverly Hills, CA))

FIRST NATL BK (BIG RAPIDS, MI)
Name changed 01/17/1977
Name changed from First National Bank (Big Rapids, MI) to First National Bank & Trust (Big Rapids, MI) 01/17/1977
Acquired by Chemical Financial Corp. 05/01/1988
Each share Capital Stock $10 par exchanged for (1.26) shares Common $10 par

FIRST NATL BK (BIG SPRING, TX)
Each share Capital Stock $20 par exchanged for (4) shares Capital Stock $5 par 03/29/1966
Merged into Norwest Corp. 11/01/1995
Each share Common $5 par exchanged for $78.45 cash

FIRST NATL BK (BIRMINGHAM, AL)
Stock Dividend of (163/737) share paid followed by exchange of each share Common $25 par for (2.5) shares Common $10 par or total of

(3.0529173) shares of Common $10 par in 1955
Stock Dividends - 20% 1/13/50; 16-2/3% 7/1/52; 11-1/9% 2/1/57; 10% 1/20/59; (1) for (6.5) 2/15/63; 16-2/3% 2/9/65; 14-2/7% 1/17/67; 10% 2/27/70
Reorganized as Alabama Bancorporation 2/3/72
Each share Common $10 par exchanged for (1.5) shares Common $1 par
Alabama Bancorporation name changed to AmSouth Bancorporation 4/20/81 which merged into Regions Financial Corp. 11/4/2006

FIRST NATL BK (BLOOMINGTON, IN)
Stock Dividends - 200% 03/04/1974; 100% 05/24/1982
Under plan of reorganization each share Capital Stock $5 par automatically became (1) share First National Corp. (IN) Common $5 par 05/14/1985
First National Corp. (IN) acquired by Banc One Corp. (DE) 06/01/1987 which reincorporated in Ohio 05/01/1989 which merged into Bank One Corp. 10/02/1998 which merged into J.P. Morgan Chase & Co. 12/31/2000 which name changed to JPMorgan Chase & Co. 07/20/2004

FIRST NATL BK (BLUE ISLAND, IL)
Each share Capital Stock $100 par exchanged for (2) shares Capital Stock $50 par plus a 100% stock dividend paid 01/26/1956
Acquired by Great Lakes Financial Resources, Inc. 02/17/2001
Details not available

FIRST NATL BK (BLUEFIELD, WV)
Each share Capital Stock $50 par exchanged for (2) shares Capital Stock $25 par 00/00/1951
Each share Capital Stock $25 par exchanged for (2) shares Capital Stock $12.50 par 02/16/1960
Capital Stock $12.50 par changed to $6.25 par and (1) additional share issued plus a 25% stock dividend paid 02/10/1975
Stock Dividends - 25% 10/23/1945; 20% 11/10/1948; 11.11111111% 01/30/1950
Reorganized as Pocahontas Bankshares Corp. 03/01/1984
Each share Capital Stock $6.25 par exchanged for (1) share Capital Stock $6.25 par
Pocahontas Bankshares Corp. name changed to First Century Bankshares Inc. 07/08/1999
(See First Century Bankshares Inc.)

FIRST NATL BK (BOSTON, MA)
Stock Dividends - 25% 02/15/1960; 14-2/7% 11/15/1961; 50% 09/09/1965
Under plan of reorganization each share Capital Stock $12.50 par automatically became (1) share First National Boston Corp. Common $12.50 par 01/04/1971
First National Boston Corp. name changed to Bank of Boston Corp. 04/01/1983 which name changed to BankBoston Corp. 04/25/1997 which merged into Fleet Boston Corp. 10/01/1999 which name changed to FleetBoston Financial Corp. 04/18/2000 which merged into Bank of America Corp. 04/01/2004

FIRST NATL BK (BRADENTON, FL)
Through exchange offer 100% acquired by Ellis Banking Corp. 03/15/1972
Public interest eliminated

FIRST NATL BK (BRENHAM, TX)
Stock Dividend - 100% 2/16/73
Merged into Southwest Bancshares, Inc. 11/2/82
Each share Common $10 par

exchanged for (1.369) shares
Common $5 par
Southwest Bancshares, Inc. merged
into MCorp 10/11/84
(See MCorp)

**FIRST NATIONAL BANK
(BROOKSVILLE, FL)**
Merged into First National Bank of
Florida (Tampa, Fla.) 7/1/83
Each share Common $10 par
exchanged for $100 cash

FIRST NATL BK (BRUNSWICK, GA)
Merged into Trust Co. of Georgia
8/1/77
Each share Common Capital Stock
$25 par exchanged for (4.73) shares
Common $5 par
Trust Co. of Georgia merged into
SunTrust Banks, Inc. 7/1/85

FIRST NATL BK (CANTON, OH)
Capital Stock $10 par changed to
$10.80 par and (9) additional shares
issued 08/18/1942
Capital Stock $10.80 par changed to
$14 par 01/29/1943
Capital Stock $14 par changed to $20
par 01/24/1944
Capital Stock $20 par changed to $10
par and (1) additional share issued
01/19/1960
Stock Dividends - 100% 01/16/1952;
10% 02/04/1965
Merged into Central Bancorporation,
Inc. 10/31/1972
Each share Capital Stock $10 par
exchanged for (2.4) shares Common
$5 par
Central Bancorporation, Inc. merged
into PNC Financial Corp. 02/29/1988
which name changed to PNC Bank
Corp. 02/08/1993 which name
changed to PNC Financial Services
Group, Inc. 03/15/2000

FIRST NATL BK (CANTON, PA)
Reorganized as Canton Bancorp, Inc.
10/01/2003
Each share Common $10 par
exchanged for (1) share Common
$1 par
(See Canton Bancorp, Inc.)

**FIRST NATL BK
(CAPE CANAVERAL, FL)**
Thru purchase offer 99.027%
acquired by First Bankers Corp. of
Florida as of 1/1/79
Public interest eliminated

FIRST NATL BK (CARROLLTON, KY)
Under plan of reorganization each
share Common no par automatically
became (1) share Port Williams
Bancshares, Inc. Common no par
1/1/99

**FIRST NATIONAL BANK
(CASPER, WY)**
Merged into Western Bancorporation
7/1/80
Each share Common $20 par
exchanged for (21) shares Capital
Stock $2 par
Western Bancorporation name
changed to First Interstate Bancorp
6/1/81 which merged into Wells
Fargo & Co. (Old) 4/1/96 which
merged into Wells Fargo & Co.
(New) 11/2/98

FIRST NATL BK (CENTRE HALL, PA)
Merged into Northwest Savings Bank
(Warren, PA) 4/12/96
Each share Common $1 par
exchanged for $60 cash

FIRST NATL BK (CHAMPAIGN, IL)
Stock Dividend - 50% 04/08/1975
Reorganized under the laws of
Delaware as Champaign Bancorp,
Inc. 12/15/1981
Each share Common $25 par
exchanged for (1) share Common
$25 par
Champaign Bancorp, Inc. merged into
Midwest Financial Group, Inc.
02/08/1983 which merged into First
of America Bank Corp. 11/01/1989
which merged into National City
Corp. 03/31/1998 which was
acquired by PNC Financial Services
Group, Inc. 12/31/2008

FIRST NATL BK (CHICAGO, IL)
Capital Stock $100 par changed to
$20 par and (4) additional shares
issued 1/13/60
Stock Dividends - 66-2/3% 12/21/43;
20% 12/19/45; 25% 12/22/48; 20%
12/19/51; 11–1/9% 12/15/54; 25%
7/16/58; 20% 1/10/61; 16-2/3%
1/14/64; 14-2/7% 1/23/68
Reorganized under the laws of
Delaware as First Chicago Corp.
8/15/69
Each share Capital Stock $20 par
exchanged for (1) share Common
$20 par
First Chicago Corp. merged into First
Chicago NBD Corp. 12/1/95 which
merged into J.P. Morgan Chase &
Co. 7/1/2004 which name changed
to JPMorgan Chase & Co.
7/20/2004

**FIRST NATL BK
(CHRISTIANSBURG, VA)**
Under plan of reorganization each
share Common $5 par automatically
became (1) share FNB Corp.
Common $5 par 07/11/1996
FNB Corp. merged into StellarOne
Corp. 02/28/2008 which merged into
Union First Market Bankshares
Corp. 01/02/2014 which name
changed to Union Bankshares Corp.
04/28/2014

FIRST NATL BK (CICERO, IL)
Stock Dividend - 20% 01/19/1959
Acquired by First Cicero Banc Corp.
08/24/1979
Details not available

FIRST NATL BK (CINCINNATI, OH)
Each share Capital Stock $100 par
exchanged for (10) shares Capital
Stock $10 par 00/00/1949
Capital Stock $10 par changed to $5
par and (1) additional share issued
plus a 20% stock dividend paid
02/20/1970
Stock Dividends - 18% 12/01/1956;
25% 02/01/1961; 20% 11/01/1966
Reorganized as First National
Cincinnati Corp. 01/02/1974
Each share Capital Stock $5 par
exchanged for (1) share Common
$5 par
First National Cincinnati Corp. name
changed to Star Banc Corp.
04/13/1990 which merged into
Firstar Corp. (New) 11/20/1998
which merged into U.S. Bancorp
(DE) 02/27/2001

FIRST NATL BK (CLARKSVILLE, TN)
Capital Stock $100 par changed to
$50 par and (1) additional share
issued 08/20/1953
Capital Stock $50 par changed to $10
par and (4) additional shares issued
02/08/1972
Stock Dividends - 16-2/3%
01/25/1957; 14-2/7% 01/20/1959;
20% 12/11/1968; 33-1/3%
03/11/1975; 50% 04/15/1981
Reorganized as First National
Financial Corp. (TN) 03/01/1983
Each share Capital Stock $10 par
exchanged for (1) share Common
$10 par
First National Financial Corp. (TN)
merged into Dominion Bankshares
Corp. 05/01/1987 which merged into
First Union Corp. 03/01/1993 which
name changed to Wachovia Corp.
(Ctfs. dated after 09/01/2001)
09/01/2001 which merged into Wells
Fargo & Co. (New) 12/31/2008

FIRST NATL BK (CLAYTON, MO)
Stock Dividends - 42-6/7%
02/01/1943; 100% 04/30/1951;
33-1/3% 02/07/1967
Through purchase offer 99% acquired
by Central Bancompany as of
01/30/1979
Public interest eliminated

FIRST NATL BK (CLEARWATER, FL)
Common $50 par split (4) for (1) by
issuance of (3) additional shares
12/31/87
Stock Dividends - 50% 2/27/40;
33-1/3% 12/6/44; 25% 1/23/52;
100% 12/9/57; 25% 7/27/60; 10%
3/2/66; 50% 12/24/69; 33-1/3%
6/30/72; 150% 12/30/80; 300%
12/1/87
Acquired by AmSouth Bancorporation
10/14/93
Each share Common $50 par
exchanged for (6) shares Common
$1 par
AmSouth Bancorporation merged into
Regions Financial Corp. 11/4/2006

**FIRST NATL BK
(CLIFTON FORGE, VA)**
Merged into MainStreet BankGroup
Inc. 9/27/96
Each share Common $5 par
exchanged for (4.89) shares
Common $5 par
MainStreet BankGroup Inc. name
changed to MainStreet Financial
Corp. 6/1/98 which merged into
BB&T Corp. 3/8/99

FIRST NATL BK (CLINTON, IA)
Acquired by Mercantile
Bancorporation 08/17/1996
Details not available

**FIRST NATL BK
(COLORADO SPRINGS, CO)**
Each share Capital Stock $20 par
exchanged for (2) shares Capital
Stock $10 par 05/31/1960
Capital Stock $10 par changed to $5
par and (1) additional share issued
05/05/1964
Stock Dividend - 10% 12/18/1967
Through voluntary exchange offer
99.02% acquired by Affiliated
Bankshares of Colorado, Inc. as of
07/24/1970
Public interest eliminated

**FIRST NATIONAL BANK
(COLUMBIA, SC)**
Stock Dividend - 25% 05/15/1946
Merged into First National Bank of
South Carolina (Columbia, SC)
06/01/1984
Details not available

FIRST NATL BK (COLUMBUS, GA)
Capital Stock $10 par changed to $5
par and (1) additional share issued
01/01/1966
Stock Dividends - 20% 01/17/1962;
100% 03/15/1972
Reorganized as First South Bankcorp
11/03/1980
Each share Capital Stock $5 par
exchanged for (1) share Common
$5 par
First South Bankcorp merged into
First Railroad & Banking Co. of
Georgia 12/30/1982 which was
acquired by First Union Corp.
11/01/1986 which name changed to
Wachovia Corp. (Ctfs. dated after
09/01/2001) 09/01/2001 which
merged into Wells Fargo & Co.
(New) 12/31/2008

**FIRST NATIONAL BANK
(COMMERCE, GA)**
Reorganized as First Commerce
Bancorp, Inc. 9/15/80
Each share Common $10 par
exchanged for (1) share Common
$10 par
First Commerce Bancorp, Inc. name
changed to nBank Corp. in
December 1999

FIRST NATL BK (CORSICANA, TX)
Each share Capital Stock $100 par
exchanged for (10) shares Capital
Stock $10 par 2/14/56
Stock Dividends - 20% 1/25/64; 50%
2/26/70
Reorganized as First Bancorp Inc.
8/31/71
Each share Capital Stock $10 par
exchanged for (1) share Common
$10 par
First Bancorp Inc. acquired by First
International Bancshares, Inc.
9/11/81 which name changed to
InterFirst Corp. 12/31/81 which
merged into First RepublicBank
Corp. 6/6/87
(See First RepublicBank Corp.)

FIRST NATL BK (CORTLAND, NY)
Capital Stock $50 par changed to $10
par and (4) additional shares issued
10/07/1969
Capital Stock $10 par changed to $5
par and (1) additional share issued
03/01/1980
Stock Dividends - 25% 03/04/1952;
(5) for (51) 11/05/1954
Under plan of reorganization each
share Capital Stock $5 par
automatically became (1) share
Cortland First Financial Corp.
Common $5 par 09/30/1986
Cortland First Financial Corp. merged
into Alliance Financial Corp.
11/25/1998 which merged into NBT
Bancorp Inc. 03/08/2013

FIRST NATL BK (CROSSVILLE, TN)
Common $10 par changed to $2 par
06/04/1973
Acquired by Union Planters Corp.
01/01/1998
Details not available

FIRST NATL BK (DALLAS, TX)
Capital Stock $20 par changed to
$12.50 par in 1940
Capital Stock $12.50 par changed to
$16 par in 1950
Each share Capital Stock $16 par
exchanged for (1.6) shares Capital
Stock $10 par plus a stock dividend
of (1) share for each (7.5) shares
held paid in 1952
Stock Dividends - 20% 3/2/44;
14-2/7% 1/15/62; 25% 1/31/64; 10%
7/13/67; 10% 2/5/69
Reorganized as First International
Bancshares, Inc. 12/31/72
Each share Capital Stock $10 par
exchanged for (2) shares Common
$5 par
First International Bancshares, Inc.
name changed to InterFirst Corp.
12/31/81 which merged into First
RepublicBank Corp. 6/6/87
(See First RepublicBank Corp.)

FIRST NATL BK (DANVILLE, IL)
Stock Dividend - 16-2/3% 1/19/60
Acquired by private investors in 1977
Details not available

FIRST NATL BK (DANVILLE, VA)
Stock Dividends - 100% 1/17/55;
28.205128% 2/26/68
Merged into First & Merchants Corp.
9/30/71
Each share Capital Stock $10 par
exchanged for (2.25) shares
Common $10 par
First & Merchants Corp. merged into
Sovran Financial Corp. 12/31/83
which merged into C&S/Sovran
Corp. 9/1/90 which merged into
NationsBank Corp. 12/31/91 which
reincorporated in Delaware as
BankAmerica Corp. (Old) 9/25/98
which merged into BankAmerica
Corp. (New) 9/30/98 which name
changed to Bank of America Corp.
4/28/99

FIRST NATL BK (DAYTON, OH)
Stock Dividend - 10% 02/07/1967
Acquired by National City Corp.
12/29/1977
Each share Common $6.25 par

exchanged for (0.875) share
Common $4 par
National City Corp. acquired by PNC
Financial Services Group, Inc.
12/31/2008

FIRST NATL BK (DAYTON, TX)
Merged into Paradigm Bancorp
12/3/97
Each share Common no par
exchanged for $5.93 cash

FIRST NATL BK (DECATUR, IL)
Reorganized under the laws of
Delaware as First Decatur
Bancshares, Inc. 12/31/1980
Each share Common $25 par
exchanged for (1) share Common
$25 par
First Decatur Bancshares, Inc.
merged into Main Street Trust, Inc.
03/23/2000 which merged into First
Busey Corp. 08/01/2007

FIRST NATIONAL BANK (DEERWOOD, MN)
Under plan of reorganization each
share Capital Stock $100 par
automatically became (1) share
Deerwood Bancorporation, Inc.
Capital Stock $100 par 01/31/1984
(See Deerwood Bancorporation, Inc.)

FIRST NATL BK (DELRAY BEACH, FL)
100% acquired by First at Orlando
Corp. through exchange offer which
expired 07/19/1973
Public interest eliminated

FIRST NATL BK (DENVER, CO)
Under plan of merger each share
Capital Stock $100 par exchanged
for (2.505) shares Capital Stock $50
par 08/08/1958
Capital Stock $50 par changed to $20
par and (1.5) additional shares
issued plus 11-1/9% stock dividend
paid 10/11/1966
Stock Dividends - 13-1/3%
06/28/1963; 50% 02/27/1970
Merged into First National
Bancorporation, Inc. 01/19/1982
Each share Capital Stock $20 par
exchanged for (4.276) shares
Common $10 par
First National Bancorporation, Inc.
name changed to IntraWest
Financial Corp. 10/01/1982 which
merged into United Banks of
Colorado, Inc. 04/30/1987 which
merged into Norwest Corp.
04/19/1991 which name changed to
Wells Fargo & Co. (New) 11/02/1998

FIRST NATL BK (DES PLAINES, IL)
Capital Stock $100 par changed to
$50 par and (1) additional share
issued plus a 50% stock dividend
paid 2/16/51
Capital Stock $50 par changed to $20
par and (1.5) additional shares
issued plus a 20% stock dividend
paid 8/25/58
Capital Stock $20 par changed to $10
par and (1) additional share issued
1/17/66
Capital Stock $10 par changed to $5
par and (1) additional share issued
2/8/72
Stock Dividends - 50% 6/1/56;
12-1/2% 8/14/57; 25% 3/8/62; 10%
3/21/75
Reorganized as First Des Plaines
Corp. 12/19/80
Each share Capital Stock $5 par
exchanged for (1) share Capital
Stock $5 par
(See First Des Plaines Corp.)

FIRST NATL BK (DUBUQUE, IA)
Capital Stock $100 par changed to
$50 par and (1) additional share
issued 01/24/1961
Stock Dividends - 100% 06/22/1950;
33-1/3% 01/24/1961; 25%
01/24/1966; 20% 01/21/1970; 100%
01/15/1975; 100% 02/06/1981
Under plan of reorganization each
share Common $50 par
automatically became (1) share First
Dubuque Corp. no par 04/15/1985
First Dubuque Corp. merged into
Hawkeye Bancorporation
05/03/1993 which merged into
Mercantile Bancorporation, Inc.
01/02/1999 which merged into
Firstar Corp. (New) 09/20/1999
which merged into U.S. Bancorp
(DE) 02/27/2001

FIRST NATL BK (EAST HAMPTON, NY)
Name changed to Bank of the
Hamptons, N.A. (East Hampton, NY)
06/26/1980
Bank of the Hamptons, N.A. (East
Hampton, NY) reorganized as
Hamptons Bancshares, Inc.
09/04/1984 which merged into
Suffolk Bancorp 04/11/1994 which
merged into People's United
Financial, Inc. 04/01/2017

FIRST NATL BK (EAST ISLIP, NY)
Common $5 par changed to $2.50 par
8/8/72
Stock Dividends - 20% 6/2/69; 25%
9/28/72
Name changed to Bank of Long
Island, N.A. (East Islip, NY) 5/18/81
(See Bank of Long Island, N.A. (East Islip, NY))

FIRST NATL BK (EAST LANSING, MI)
Merged into Michigan National Corp.
12/29/75
Each share Common $10 par
exchanged for $74 cash

FIRST NATL BK (EAST LIVERPOOL, OH)
Each share Capital Stock $100 par
exchanged for (4) shares Capital
Stock $25 par 01/15/1952
Capital Stock $25 par changed to $5
par and (4) additional shares issued
01/21/1969
Stock Dividends - 100% 01/13/1948;
66-2/3% 01/15/1952; 100%
09/22/1977
Merged into Banc One Corp. (DE)
04/01/1984
Each share Capital Stock $5 par
exchanged for (1.36554) shares
Common no par
Banc One Corp. (DE) reincorporated
in Ohio 05/01/1989 which merged
into Bank One Corp. 10/02/1998
which merged into J.P. Morgan
Chase & Co. 12/31/2000 which
name changed to JPMorgan Chase
& Co. 07/20/2004

FIRST NATL BK (EAST ST. LOUIS, IL)
Each share Capital Stock the face of
which shows a $50 par value
exchanged for (5) shares Capital
Stock $12.50 par to effect a (4) for
(1) split and 25% stock dividend in
1951
Each share Capital Stock which on
the face did not state the $50 par
value received (3) additional shares
of Capital Stock $12.50 par value
plus a 25% stock dividend in 1951
Stock Dividends - 33-1/3% 1/13/59;
25% 2/8/66; 25% 2/12/74
Acquired by St. Clair Bancorporation,
Inc. 3/14/79
Each share Capital Stock $12.50 par
exchanged for $41 cash

FIRST NATL BK (EAU GALLIE, FL)
Through voluntary exchange offer all
but directors' qualifying shares
acquired by Consolidated
Bankshares of Florida, Inc. as of
10/19/1972
Public interest eliminated

FIRST NATL BK (EDMESTON, NY)
Merged into Central National Bank
(Canajoharie, NY) 6/30/72
Each share Common $25 par
exchanged for (3.3) shares Capital
Stock $10 par
Note: This ratio includes a 10% stock
dividend paid to holders of Central
National Bank 7/5/72
Central National Bank (Canajoharie,
NY) reorganized as CNB Financial
Corp. 1/5/93 which merged into NBT
Bancorp Inc. 11/9/2001

FIRST NATL BK (EFFINGHAM, IL)
Merged into First Banking Co. of
Southeast Georgia 8/27/96
Each share Common $10 par
exchanged for (0.892) share
Common $1 par
First Banking Co. of Southeast
Georgia merged into BB&T Corp.
6/15/2000

FIRST NATL BK (ELBERTON, GA)
Reorganized as First Elbert Corp.
9/1/83
Each share Capital Stock $10 par
exchanged for (1) share Common
$10 par
First Elbert Corp. name changed to
Pinnacle Financial Corp. (GA)
8/10/93

FIRST NATL BK (ELDRED, PA)
Common $100 par changed to $10
par 01/11/1972
Acquired by Hamlin Bank & Trust Co.
(Smethport, PA) 07/02/1984
Details not available

FIRST NATL BK (ELGIN, IL)
Common Capital Stock $100 par
changed to $20 par and (4)
additional shares issued 10/1/29
Common Capital Stock $20 par
changed to $5 par and (3) additional
shares issued 1/10/67
Common Capital Stock $5 par
changed to $2.50 par and (1)
additional share issued 4/27/79
Stock Dividend - 300% 1/25/65
Reorganized as Financial National
Bancshares, Co. 1/1/81
Each share Common Capital Stock
$2.50 par exchanged for (1) share
Common $2.50 par
First National Bancshares, Co. name
changed to FNW Bancorp, Inc.
12/9/86 which merged into NBD
Bancorp, Inc. 10/1/91 which name
changed to First Chicago NBD Corp.
12/1/95 which merged into Bank
One Corp. 10/2/98 which merged
into J.P. Morgan Chase & Co.
12/31/2000 which name changed to
JPMorgan Chase & Co. 7/20/2004

FIRST NATIONAL BANK (ELKHART, IN)
Each share Capital Stock $50 par
exchanged for (5) shares Capital
Stock $10 par 8/3/60
Name changed to First National Bank
of Elkhart County (Elkhart, IN)
8/15/64 which name changed back
to First National Bank (Elkhart, IN)
2/10/70
Stock Dividends - 50% 6/21/54; 50%
3/14/58; 20% 6/30/71
Merged into First Indiana Bancorp
11/5/82
Each share Capital Stock $10 par
exchanged for (1) share Common
$10 par
First Indiana Bancorp acquired by
Ameritrust Corp. 5/30/86 which
merged into Society Corp. 3/16/92
which merged into KeyCorp (New)
3/1/94

FIRST NATL BK (ELMER, NJ)
Under plan of reorganization each
share Common $25 par
automatically became (1) share
Elmer Bancorp, Inc. Common 10¢
par 1/2/2001

FIRST NATIONAL BANK (ENGLEWOOD, FL)
Merged into Exchange
Bancorporation, Inc. 6/30/82
Each share Common Capital Stock
$10 par exchanged for $37.90 cash

FIRST NATL BK (ENID, OK)
Stock Dividend - 100% 03/05/1952
Name changed to First National Bank
& Trust Co. (Enid, OK) 10/15/1968
First National Bank & Trust Co. (Enid,
OK) reorganized as First Enid, Inc.
12/31/1981
(See First Enid, Inc.)

FIRST NATL BK (ERIE, PA)
Each share Common $100 par
exchanged for (8) shares Common
$12.50 par 00/00/1945
Stock Dividends - 50% 11/30/1943;
100% 12/10/1968
Under plan of merger name changed
to First National Bank of
Pennsylvania (Meadville, PA)
03/01/1969
First National Bank of Pennsylvania
(Meadville, PA) reorganized as First
National Pennsylvania Corp.
11/19/1981 which merged into PNC
Financial Corp. 07/24/1992 which
name changed to PNC Bank Corp.
02/08/1993 which name changed to
PNC Financial Services Group, Inc.
03/15/2000

FIRST NATIONAL BANK (EXPORT, PA)
Merged into First National Bank of
Westmoreland (Greensburg, PA)
11/11/66
Each share Capital Stock $20 par
exchanged for (3) shares Capital
Stock $10 par
First National Bank of Westmoreland
(Greensburg, PA) merged into
Southwest National Bank of
Pennsylvania (Greensburg, PA)
6/30/70 which reorganized as
Southwest National Corp. (PA)
11/6/81 which merged into First
Commonwealth Financial Corp.
12/31/98

FIRST NATIONAL BANK (FARMINGDALE, NY)
Stock Dividend - 10% 1/29/60
Acquired by Bankers Trust Co. (New
York, NY) 9/9/63
Each share Capital Stock $100 par
exchanged for (12) shares Capital
Stock $10 par
Bankers Trust Co. (New York, NY)
acquired by BT New York Corp.
5/31/66 which name changed to
Bankers Trust New York Corp.
9/15/67 which name changed to
Bankers Trust Corp. 4/23/98
(See Bankers Trust Corp.)

FIRST NATL BK (FARMINGTON, NM)
Each share Capital Stock $25 par
exchanged for (2) shares Capital
Stock $12.50 par 3/15/70
Capital Stock $12.50 par split (5) for
(3) by issuance of (2/3) additional
share 4/21/80
Stock Dividends - (3) for (7) 3/12/73;
25% 3/17/75; 20% 4/14/76
Reorganized as First Place Financial
Corp. 8/31/84
Each share Capital Stock $12.50 par
exchanged for (1) share Common
no par
First Place Financial Corp. merged
into Wells Fargo & Co. (New)
1/18/2000

FIRST NATIONAL BANK (FENTON, MI)
Stock Dividends - 25% 9/12/73; 10%
6/16/74; 10% 11/23/79; 10% 6/13/83
Reorganized as FNB Bancorp, Inc.
12/31/84
Each share Common $10 par
exchanged for (1) share Common
$10 par
FNB Bancorp, Inc. liquidated for Banc
One Corp. 2/27/87 which merged
into Bank One Corp. 10/2/98 which
merged into J.P. Morgan Chase &

Co. 12/31/2000 which name changed to JPMorgan Chase & Co. 7/20/2004

FIRST NATL BK (FINDLAY, OH)
Stock Dividends - 42-6/7% 5/55; 33-1/3% 2/22/63; 25% 2/25/66
Merged into Fifth Third Bancorp 10/31/84
Each share Capital Stock $20 par exchanged for (2) shares Common no par or $100 cash

FIRST NATL BK (FLEISCHMANNS, NY)
Name changed to Deak National Bank (Fleischmanns, NY) 5/1/70
Each share Common $10 par exchanged for (1) share Common $10 par
Deak National Bank (Fleischmanns, NY) name changed to American National Bank of New York (Fleischmanns, NY) 6/17/85
(See American National Bank of New York (Fleischmanns, NY))

FIRST NATL BK (FLORENCE, AL)
Capital Stock $20 par changed to $10 par and (1) additional share issued plus a 25% stock dividend paid 1/21/66
Stock Dividends - 25% 3/9/60; 60% 2/27/70; 25% 2/28/74; 20% 2/28/77
Under plan of reorganization each share Capital Stock $10 par automatically became (1) share First United Bancorp Inc. Common $10 par 11/4/83
First United Bancorp Inc. merged into SunTrust Banks, Inc. 1/29/93

FIRST NATIONAL BANK (FOND DU LAC, WI)
Name changed to First Wisconsin National Bank (Fond Du Lac, WI) 03/01/1967
(See First Wisconsin National (Fond Du Lac, WI))

FIRST NATL BK (FORT COLLINS, CO)
Merged into Western Bancorporation 7/1/80
Each share Capital Stock $5 par exchanged for (1.75) shares Capital Stock $2 par
Western Bancorporation name changed to First Interstate Bancorp 6/1/81 which merged into Wells Fargo & Co. (Old) 4/1/96 which merged into Wells Fargo & Co. (New) 11/2/98

FIRST NATL BK (FORT LAUDERDALE, FL)
Stock Dividends - 40% 02/13/1959; 10% 03/01/1966; 10% 11/01/1968
Name changed to Landmark First National Bank (Fort Lauderdale, FL) 10/01/1974
(See Landmark First National Bank (Fort Lauderdale, FL))

FIRST NATL BK (FORT LEE, NJ)
Acquired by National Westminster Bank PLC 06/04/1988
Details not available

FIRST NATIONAL BANK (FORT MYERS, FL)
Stock Dividend - 30% 09/26/1958
99.9% acquired by Southwest Florida Banks, Inc. through exchange offer which expired 06/28/1973
Public interest eliminated

FIRST NATL BK (FORT SMITH, AR)
Stock Dividend - 100% 1/25/57
Reorganized as First Bank Corp. 3/30/90
Each share Capital Stock $100 par exchanged for (1) share Common $1 par

FIRST NATL BK (FORT WORTH, TX)
Each share Common $20 par exchanged for (2) shares Common $10 par 6/7/55
Stock Dividends - 25% 1/14/47; 16-2/3% 2/1/51; 12-1/2% 2/5/53; 10% 3/2/71
Reorganized as First United Bancorporation, Inc. 8/7/72
Each share Common $10 par exchanged for (1) share Common $10 par
First United Bancorporation, Inc. merged into InterFirst Corp. 6/28/83 which merged into First RepublicBank Corp. 6/6/87
(See First RepublicBank Corp.)

FIRST NATL BK (FREDERICKSBURG, PA)
Stock Dividends - 5% payable 03/09/2001 to holders of record 02/27/2001 Ex date - 04/03/2001; 10% payable 03/14/2002 to holders of record 02/26/2002 Ex date - 03/21/2002; 10% payable 03/11/2003 to holders of record 02/25/2003 Ex date - 03/25/2003; 2% payable 03/18/2005 to holders of record 02/22/2005 Ex date - 03/30/2005; 2% payable 03/17/2006 to holders of record 02/28/2006 Ex date - 04/03/2006; 2% payable 03/16/2007 to holders of record 02/27/2007 Ex date - 03/28/2007; 2% payable 03/13/2008 to holders of record 02/26/2008 Ex date - 04/03/2008
Merged into Citizens Financial Services, Inc. 12/11/2015
Each share Common $50 par exchanged for (12.6) shares Common $1 par

FIRST NATIONAL BANK (FREEHOLD, NJ)
Each share Common $25 par exchanged for (8) shares Common $5 par 12/31/1956
Merged into Monmouth County National Bank (Red Bank, NJ) 03/30/1962
Each share Common $5 par exchanged for (3.801137) shares Common $1 par
Monmouth County National Bank (Red Bank, NJ) name changed to Colonial First National Bank (Red Bank, NJ) 08/18/1972 which merged into Fidelity Union Bancorporation 06/28/1974 which merged into First National State Bancorporation 04/05/1984 which name changed to First Fidelity Bancorporation (Old) 05/01/1985 which merged into First Fidelity Bancorporation (New) 02/29/1988 which merged into First Union Corp. 01/01/1996 which name changed to Wachovia Corp. (Ctfs. dated after 09/01/2001) 09/01/2001 which merged into Wells Fargo & Co. (New) 12/31/2008

FIRST NATL BK (FREEPORT, IL)
Each share Common $20 par exchanged for (4) shares Common $5 par 2/18/75
Stock Dividend - 100% 10/1/71
Under plan of reorganization each share Common $5 par automatically became (1) share First Freeport Corp. Common $5 par 1/1/77
First Freeport Corp. name changed to Premier Financial Services, Inc. 5/17/84
(See Premier Financial Services, Inc.)

FIRST NATIONAL BANK (GADSEN, AL)
Merged into State National Bank of Alabama (Decatur, Ala.) 12/19/64
Each share Capital Stock $10 par exchanged for (1) share Common $10 par
State National Bank of Alabama (Decatur, Ala.) name changed to Central Bank of Alabama, N.A. (Decatur, Ala.) 6/4/73
(See Central Bank of Alabama, N.A. (Decatur, Ala.))

FIRST NATL BK (GAINESVILLE, FL)
100% acquired by Atlantic Bancorporation through exchange offer which expired 10/22/1973
Public interest eliminated

FIRST NATL BK (GALLATIN, MO)
Under plan of reorganization each share Common $20 par automatically became (1) share First National Bancshares Inc. of Gallatin Common $20 par 7/28/97

FIRST NATIONAL BANK (GEORGETOWN, DE)
Name changed to Delaware National Bank (Georgetown, Del.) 2/10/84
Delaware National Bank (Georgetown, Del.) reorganized as Delaware National Bankshares Corp. 6/3/85

FIRST NATL BK (GLEN FALLS, NY)
Common Capital Stock $20 par changed to $10 par and (1) additional share issued 04/03/1980
Stock Dividends - 10% 11/16/1970; 25% 11/16/1972; 25% 02/26/1976; 25% 03/31/1978
Reincorporated under the laws of Delaware as First Glen Bancorp Inc. and Common Capital Stock $10 par changed to Common $10 par 07/01/1981
First Glen Bancorp Inc. name changed to Evergreen Bancorp, Inc. 04/29/1986 which merged into BankNorth Group, Inc. (DE) 12/31/1998 which merged into Banknorth Group, Inc. (ME) 05/10/2000 which merged into TD Banknorth Inc. 03/01/2005
(See TD Banknorth Inc.)

FIRST NATL BK (GLEN HEAD, NY)
Stock Dividends - 100% 1/20/66; 50% 8/27/71
Name changed to First National Bank of Long Island (Glen Head, NY) 7/1/78
First National Bank of Long Island Glen Head, NY) reorganized as First of Long Island Corp. 5/1/84

FIRST NATL BK (GOSHEN, IN)
Merged into Midwest Commerce Corp. 11/1/82
Each share Common $10 par exchanged for (4) shares Common no par
Note: Option to receive $60 cash and/or Installment Obligations expired 11/29/82
(See Midwest Commerce Corp.)

FIRST NATL BK (GRAND FORKS, ND)
Capital Stock $10 par changed to $11 par in July 1964
Capital Stock $11 par changed to $12.50 par in January 1965
Capital Stock $12.50 par changed to $10 par and (0.25) additional share issued 11/20/79
Stock Dividends - 50% 3/12/37; 50% 12/4/44; 33-1/3% 10/31/47; 25% 1/26/51; 20% 1/28/54; 25% 2/5/59; 33-1/3% 1/29/62; 20% 2/4/66; 16-2/3% 2/1/69; 14-2/7% 2/5/71; 25% 11/20/74; 20% 11/8/77; 25% 11/20/79; 33-1/3% 8/11/81
Reorganized as First National Corp. (ND) 4/13/84
Each share Capital Stock $10 par exchanged for (2) shares Common $5 par
First National Corp. (ND) reorganized in Delaware as Alerus Financial Corp. 11/13/2001

FIRST NATIONAL BANK (GRAND JUNCTION, CO)
Stock Dividend - 20% 1/26/61
Merged into Baldwin (D.H.) Co. (Ohio) 4/29/74
Each share Common $100 par exchanged for (0.8) share 4% Class C Conv. Pfd. Ser. 2 $100 par *(See Baldwin (D.H.) Co. (Ohio))*

FIRST NATL BK (GREELEY, CO)
Each share Capital Stock $100 par exchanged for (10) shares Capital Stock $10 par 02/12/1959
Stock Dividends - 100% 12/19/1946; 100% 03/24/1955; 66-2/3% 12/28/1956; 20% 03/01/1966; 25% 04/01/1968
Merged into First National Bancorporation, Inc. 01/19/1982
Each share Capital Stock $10 par exchanged for (2.862) shares Common $10 par
First National Bancorporation, Inc. name changed to IntraWest Financial Corp. 10/01/1982 which merged into United Banks of Colorado, Inc. 04/30/1987 which merged into Norwest Corp. 04/19/1991 which name changed to Wells Fargo & Co. (New) 11/02/1998

FIRST NATL BK (GREENCASTLE, PA)
Reorganized as Tower Bancorp Inc. 11/02/1984
Each share Capital Stock $2.50 par exchanged for (1) share Common $2.50 par
(See Tower Bancorp, Inc.)

FIRST NATIONAL BANK (GREENSBURG, PA)
Capital Stock $25 par changed to $10 par and (1.5) additional shares issued plus a 11-1/9% stock dividend paid 8/26/63
Stock Dividends - 50% 1/22/54; 50% 2/17/61
Merged into First National Bank of Westmoreland (Greensburg, PA) 11/11/66
Each share Capital Stock $10 par exchanged for (1) share Capital Stock $10 par
First National Bank of Westmoreland (Greensburg, PA) merged into Southwest National Bank of Pennsylvania (Greensburg, PA) 6/30/70 which reorganized as Southwest National Corp. (PA) 11/6/81 which merged into First Commonwealth Financial Corp. 12/31/98

FIRST NATL BK (GREENVILLE, MS)
Merged into Grenada Bank (Grenada, MS) 7/1/84
Each (1.24) shares Common $5 par exchanged for (1) share Capital Stock $10 par
Grenada Bank (Grenada, MS) reorganized in Delaware as Grenada Sunburst System Corp. 5/20/86 which merged into Union Planters Corp. 12/30/94 which merged into Regions Financial Corp. (New) 7/1/2004

FIRST NATIONAL BANK (GREENVILLE, PA)
Stock Dividend - 42.85% 8/15/52
Name changed to First National Bank of Mercer County (Greenville, PA) 8/26/55
First National Bank of Mercer County (Greenville, PA) reorganized as F.N.B. Corp. (PA) 4/23/75 which reincorporated in Florida 6/13/2001

FIRST NATL BK (GREENWICH, NY)
Name changed to Chemical Bank-Eastern, N.A. (Greenwich, NY) 3/11/74
Chemical Bank-Eastern, N.A. (Greenwich, NY) acquired by Chemical New York Corp. 9/29/78 which name changed to Chemical Banking Corp. 4/29/88 which name changed to Chase Manhattan Corp. (New) 3/31/96 which name changed to J.P. Morgan Chase & Co. 12/31/2000 which name changed to JPMorgan Chase & Co. 7/20/2004

FIRST NATL BK (HARLINGEN, TX)
Merged into First International Bancshares, Inc. 10/31/73
Each share Capital Stock $20 par exchanged for (2.8125) shares Common $5 par
First International Bancshares, Inc. name changed to InterFirst Corp. 12/31/81 which merged into First RepublicBank Corp. 6/6/87
(See First RepublicBank Corp.)

FIRST NATIONAL BANK (HARRINGTON, DE)
100% acquired by Penney (J.C.) Co., Inc., in June 1983

FIRST NATL BK (HARTFORD CITY, IN)
Acquired by Town Financial Corp. 06/30/1976
Details not available

FIRST NATL BK (HARVEY, IL)
Each share Common $25 par exchanged for (5) shares Common $5 par 01/14/1964
Stock Dividends - 100% 02/04/1964; 10% 01/31/1968; 10% 09/02/1969; 10% 12/26/1970; 100% 03/01/1976
Acquired by Pinnacle Banc Group, Inc. 07/10/1993
Details not available

FIRST NATL BK (HATTIESBURG, MS)
Stock Dividend - 25% 01/19/1962
Name changed to First Mississippi National Bank (Hattiesburg, MS) 08/29/1969
First Mississippi National Bank (Hattiesburg, MS) reorganized as First Mississippi National Corp. 04/08/1975 which was acquired by Bancorp of Mississippi 12/31/1986 which name changed to BancorpSouth, Inc. 10/06/1992 which reorganized as BancorpSouth Bank (Tupelo, MS) 11/01/2017

FIRST NATIONAL BANK (HAZLETON, PA)
Merged into Peoples First National Bank & Trust Co. (Hazleton, PA) 5/31/66
Each share Capital Stock $100 par exchanged for (10) shares Capital Stock $10 par
People First National Bank & Trust Co. (Hazleton, PA) merged into First Eastern Corp. 8/8/88
(See First Eastern Corp.)

FIRST NATL BK (HIALEAH, FL)
Name changed to First National Bank of Greater Miami (Miami, FL) 09/01/1977
First National Bank of Greater Miami (Miami, FL) name changed to Consolidated Bank, N.A. (Hialeah, FL) 02/01/1982
(See Consolidated Bank, N.A. (Hialeah, FL))

FIRST NATIONAL BANK (HIGHLAND PARK, NJ)
Merged into First Bank & Trust Co., N.A. (Fords, NJ) 06/25/1965
Each share Capital Stock $25 par exchanged for (4.5) shares Common $5 par
First Bank & Trust Co., N.A. (Fords, NJ) merged into National State Bank (Elizabeth, NJ) 08/18/1969 which reorganized as Constellation Bancorp 03/08/1985 which merged into CoreStates Financial Corp 03/16/1994 which merged into First Union Corp. 04/28/1998 which name changed to Wachovia Corp. (Ctfs. dated after 09/01/2001) 09/01/2001 which merged into Wells Fargo & Co. (New) 12/31/2008

FIRST NATL BK (HIGHTSTOWN, NJ)
Merged into Colonial First National Bank (Red Bank, NJ) 08/18/1972
Each share Common $10 par exchanged for (13.5) shares Common $1 par

Colonial First National Bank (Red Bank, NJ) merged into Fidelity Union Bancorporation 06/28/1974 which merged into First National State Bancorporation 04/05/1984 which name changed to First Fidelity Bancorporation (Old) 05/01/1985 which merged into First Fidelity Bancorporation (New) 02/29/1988 which merged into First Union Corp. 01/01/1996 which name changed to Wachovia Corp. (Ctfs. dated after 09/01/2001) 09/01/2001 which merged into Wells Fargo & Co. (New) 12/31/2008

FIRST NATL BK (HOLLAND, MI)
Merged into First National Financial Corp. 03/26/1973
Each share Common $10 par exchanged for (65.5) shares Common $10 par
First National Financial Corp. merged into First American Bank Corp. 02/13/1978 which name changed to First of America Bank Corp. 01/14/1983 which merged into National City Corp. 03/31/1998 which was acquired by PNC Financial Services Group, Inc. 12/31/2008

FIRST NATL BK (HOLLYWOOD, FL)
Each share Common $100 par exchanged for (10) shares Common $10 par 08/16/1957
Stock Dividends - 20% 03/01/1962; 10% 07/03/1967; 100% 06/30/1972
99.83% acquired by Florida Bankshares, Inc. through exchange offer which expired 11/11/1973
Public interest eliminated

FIRST NATL BK (HOMESTEAD, FL)
Reorganized as First of Homestead Inc. 8/13/84
Each share Common $10 par exchanged for (1) share Common $1 par
(See First of Homestead Inc.)

FIRST NATL BK (HONEY BROOK, PA)
Completely liquidated 12/31/80
Each share Capital Stock $10 par exchanged for first and final distribution of $40 cash

FIRST NATL BK (HOUMA, LA)
Capital Stock $5 par changed to $2.50 par and (1) additional share issued 04/01/1974
Reorganized as First National Bankshares, Inc. 07/31/1982
Each share Capital Stock $2.50 par exchanged for (1) share Common $2.50 par
First National Bankshares, Inc. merged into Whitney Holding Corp. 02/28/1997 which merged into Hancock Holding Co. 06/04/2011 which name changed to Hancock Whitney Corp. 05/25/2018

FIRST NATL BK (HUNTSVILLE, AL)
Name changed to First Alabama Bank of Huntsville, N.A. (Huntsville, AL) 2/1/75
(See First Alabama Bank of Huntsville, N.A. (Huntsville, AL))

FIRST NATL BK (INDEPENDENCE, MO)
100% acquired by First Union, Inc. through voluntary exchange offer as of 06/15/1973
Public interest eliminated

FIRST NATIONAL BANK (IOWA CITY, IA)
Under plan of reorganization each share Common $6.25 par automatically became (1) share First Financial Bancorporation Common $6.25 par 12/31/85
First Financial Bancorporation merged into Mercantile Bancorporation, Inc. 9/28/98 which merged into Firstar

Corp. (New) 9/20/99 which merged into U.S. Bancorp (New) 2/27/2001

FIRST NATL BK (JACKSON, MS)
Common $10 par changed to $5 par and (1) additional share issued plus a 10% stock dividend paid 01/14/1963
Stock Dividends - 10% 06/30/1952; 10% 12/10/1961; 19.05% 01/29/1965; 10% 01/27/1967; 10% 05/31/1968
99.25% acquired by First Capital Corp. (MS) through exchange offer which expired 11/15/1968
Public interest eliminated

FIRST NATL BK (JACKSON, TN)
Acquired by First American Corp. (TN) 2/1/82
Each share Common $10 par exchanged for $60 principal amount of 11-3/4% Notes due 1/15/85 and $30 cash

FIRST NATL BK (JAMESTOWN, NY)
Each share Capital Stock $100 par exchanged for (5) shares Capital Stock $20 par 6/12/44
Stock Dividends - 400% 4/18/52; 25% 3/6/61
Merged into Lincoln First Group Inc. 5/16/67
Each share Capital Stock $20 par received (1.267) shares Common $10 par
Each share Capital Stock $20 par subsequently exchanged for (1) share Common $10 par
Lincoln First Group Inc. name changed to Lincoln First Banks Inc. 5/22/68 which merged into Chase Manhattan Corp. (Old) 7/1/84 which merged into Chase Manhattan Corp. (New) 3/31/96 which name changed to J.P. Morgan Chase & Co. 12/31/2000 which name changed to JPMorgan Chase & Co. 7/20/2004

FIRST NATL BK (JANESVILLE, WI)
Each share Common Capital Stock $100 par exchanged for (3) shares Common Capital Stock $50 par to effect a (2) for (1) split and 50% stock dividend 02/18/1953
Common Capital Stock $50 par changed to $10 par and (4) additional shares issued 02/00/1966
Stock Dividend - 33-1/3% 09/02/1959
Merged into Marine Corp. (WI) 01/14/1982
Each share Common Capital Stock $10 par exchanged for $44 cash

FIRST NATL BK (JASPER, AL)
Reorganized under the laws of Delaware as First Commercial Bancshares, Inc. 8/1/85
First Commercial Bancshares, Inc. merged into Synovus Financial Corp. 12/31/92

FIRST NATL BK (JERMYN, PA)
Under plan of reorganization each share Capital Stock $6.25 par automatically became (1) share First Jermyn Corp. Common $6.25 par 7/1/84
First Jermyn Corp. name changed to First Liberty Bank Corp. 6/26/98 which merged into Community Bank System, Inc. 5/14/2001

FIRST NATIONAL BANK (JERSEY CITY, NJ)
Each share Capital Stock $100 par exchanged for (4) shares Capital Stock $25 par in 1952
Each share Capital Stock $25 par exchanged for (2.5) shares Capital Stock $10 par 1/24/61
Capital Stock $10 par changed to $7.50 par and (1/3) additional share issued 3/2/65
Stock Dividend - 10% 1/30/58
Name changed to First Jersey National Bank (Jersey City, NJ) 7/1/68

First Jersey National Bank (Jersey City, NJ) reorganized as First Jersey National Corp. 5/29/69
(See First Jersey National Corp.)

FIRST NATL BK (JOLIET, IL)
Stock Dividends - 100% 2/7/45; 50% 8/20/46; 50% 1/20/54; 25% 1/17/56; 33-1/3% 9/4/58; 25% 2/15/64; 20% 4/15/67; 16-2/3% 4/15/70; 14.285% 4/16/73; 25% 4/16/76; 20% 5/15/79
Reorganized as First National Bancorp, Inc. 9/30/86
Each share Common $10 par exchanged for (1) share Common $10 par
(See First National Bancorp, Inc.)

FIRST NATL BK (JOPLIN, MO)
Merged into First Community Bancorporation 05/03/1971
Each share Common $20 par exchanged for (1) share Common $10 par
First Community Bancorporation merged into Mercantile Bancorporation, Inc. 09/30/1983 which merged into Firstar Corp. (New) 09/20/1999 which merged into U.S. Bancorp (DE) 02/27/2001

FIRST NATL BK (KANSAS CITY, MO)
Each share Capital Stock $100 par exchanged for (4) shares Capital Stock $25 par 00/00/1948
Stock Dividends - 50% 05/24/1945; (3) for (17) 07/15/1957; 50% 12/30/1958; 20% 12/30/1960; 11-1/9% 02/15/1962
100% acquired by First National Charter Corp. through exchange offer which expired 01/31/1970
Public interest eliminated

FIRST NATL BK (KENOSHA, WI)
Common $20 par changed to $10 par and (1) additional share issued 3/15/73
Common $10 par changed to $5 par and (1) additional share issued 3/15/78
Stock Dividends - 20% 1/10/55; 25% 1/15/60; 20% 1/27/65; 11-1/9% 2/27/70; 20% 2/19/75; 10% 4/15/80; 10% 4/20/83
Reorganized as First Financial Associates, Inc. 1/31/84
Each share Common $5 par exchanged for (1) share Common $5 par
First Financial Associates, Inc. acquired by Banc One Corp. 12/17/93 which merged into Bank One Corp. 10/2/98 which merged into J.P. Morgan Chase & Co. 12/31/2000 which name changed to JPMorgan Chase & Co. 7/20/2004

FIRST NATL BK (KEYSTONE, WV)
Placed in receivership and FDIC appointed receiver 09/01/1999
Stockholders' equity unlikely

FIRST NATIONAL BANK (KINGSPORT, TN)
Name changed to First National Bank of Sullivan County (Kingsport, Tenn.) 2/9/61
First National Bank of Sullivan County (Kingsport, Tenn.) name changed to First Eastern National Bank (Kingsport, Tenn.) 10/15/81
(See First Eastern National Bank (Kingsport, Tenn.))

FIRST NATL BK (KISSIMMEE, FL)
Merged into First Florida Banks, Inc. 9/1/85
Each share Common $100 par exchanged for $1,025 cash

FIRST NATL BK (KOKOMO, IN)
Common $10 par changed to $1 par and (9) additional shares issued 3/8/78
Common $1 par changed back to $10 par 1/92
Merged into FNBK National Merger Bank 12/20/96

Each share Common $10 par exchanged for $60 cash

FIRST NATL BK (LA GRANGE, IL)
Reorganized as F.N.B.C. of La Grange, Inc. 9/19/67
Each share Common $20 par exchanged for (1.2021) shares Common $7 par

FIRST NATL BK (LAFAYETTE, LA)
Each share Capital Stock $100 par exchanged for (10) shares Capital Stock $10 par 9/11/56
Stock Dividend - 33-1/3% 5/10/67
Acquired by First Commerce Corp. 9/30/92
Each share Capital Stock $10 par exchanged for $480 cash

FIRST NATL BK (LAKE ARIEL, PA)
Under plan of reorganization each share Common $5 par automatically became (1) share Lake Ariel Bancorp, Inc. Common $5 par 11/26/83
Lake Ariel Bancorp, Inc. merged into NBT Bancorp Inc. 2/17/2000

FIRST NATIONAL BANK (LAKE CHARLES, LA)
Common $25 par changed to $10 par and (1.5) additional shares issued plus a 25% stock dividend paid 2/15/68
Stock Dividends - 33-1/3% 3/1/76; 25% 4/16/79
Merged into First Commerce Corp. 9/27/85
Each share Common $10 par exchanged for $180 principal amount of 12-3/4% Conv. Debentures Ser. A due 12/1/2000

FIRST NATL BK (LAKE FOREST, IL)
Stock Dividend - 50% 2/26/80
Reorganized as First Lake Forest Corp. 5/4/84
Each share Common $10 par exchanged for (1) share Common $10 par
(See First Lake Forest Corp.)

FIRST NATIONAL BANK (LAKE WALES, FL)
Name changed to Sun First National Bank of Lake Wales (Lake Wales, FL) 03/01/1973
(See Sun First National Bank of Lake Wales (Lake Wales, FL))

FIRST NATIONAL BANK (LAKE WORTH, FL)
Stock Dividend - 20% 01/18/1961
Name changed to First National Bank & Trust Co. (Lake Worth, FL) 03/15/1967
First National Bank & Trust Co. (Lake Worth, FL) acquired by General Financial Systems, Inc. 12/28/1973 which name changed to First Marine Banks, Inc. 03/01/1976
(See First Marine Banks, Inc.)

FIRST NATL BK (LAPEER, MI)
Merged into Peoples Banking Corp. 6/7/77
Each share Common $1 par exchanged for $12.6025 cash

FIRST NATL BK (LARAMIE, WY)
Name changed to First Interstate Bank of Laramie, N.A. (Laramie, WY) 6/1/81

FIRST NATL BK (LAYTON, UT)
Each share old Common no par exchanged for (19) shares new Common no par 05/07/1996
Under plan of reorganization each share Common no par automatically became 1 share FNB Bancorp Common no par 11/20/2000

FIRST NATL BK (LEBANON, PA)
Capital Stock $25 par split (2) for (1) by issuance of (1) additional share 01/23/1956
Capital Stock $25 par changed to $12.50 par and (1) additional share issued 01/20/1966
Capital Stock $12.50 par changed to $6.25 par and (1) additional share issued 01/23/1970
Merged into Dauphin Deposit Trust Co. (Harrisburg, PA) 06/30/1972
Each share Capital Stock $6.25 par exchanged for (1.7) shares Capital Stock $10 par
Dauphin Deposit Trust Co. (Harrisburg, PA) reorganized as Dauphin Deposit Corp. 01/01/1977 which merged into Allied Irish Banks, PLC 07/08/1997
(See Allied Irish Banks, PLC)

FIRST NATL BK (LEESBURG, FL)
97.54% acquired by First At Orlando Corp. as of 04/12/1971
Public interest eliminated

FIRST NATL BK (LEWISTON, PA)
Merged into Central Counties Bank (State College, PA) 10/01/1976
Each share Common $5 par exchanged for (1) share Common $5 par
Central Counties Bank (State College, PA) reorganized as CCB Bancorp, Inc. 07/01/1982 which merged into Mellon National Corp. 09/14/1983 which name changed to Mellon Bank Corp. 09/30/1984 which name changed to Mellon Financial Corp. 10/17/1999 which merged into Bank of New York Mellon Corp. 07/01/2007

FIRST NATIONAL BANK (LINCOLN, NE)
Each share Capital Stock $100 par exchanged for (5) shares Capital Stock $20 par 07/02/1945
Stock Dividends - 50% 12/21/1943; 10% 12/14/1951; (7) for (33) 04/30/1954
Merged into First Continental National Bank & Trust Co. (Lincoln, NE) 03/12/1960
Each share Capital Stock $20 par exchanged for (1) share Capital Stock $20 par
First Continental National Bank & Trust Co. (Lincoln, NE) name changed to First National Bank & Trust Co. (Lincoln, NE) 06/11/1962 which reorganized as First National Lincoln Corp. 09/04/1973 which merged into FirsTier, Inc. 06/01/1984 which name changed to FirsTier Financial Inc. 05/18/1987 which merged into First Bank System, Inc. 02/16/1996 which name changed to U.S. Bancorp 08/01/1997

FIRST NATL BK (LINCOLNWOOD, IL)
Acquired by MB Financial, Inc. 04/06/2002
Each share Common $10 par exchanged for $185 cash

FIRST NATL BK (LISBON, NY)
Name changed to Upstate National Bank (Lisbon, NY) 4/22/98

FIRST NATL BK (LITCHFIELD, CT)
Reorganized under the laws of Delaware as First Litchfield Financial Corp. 12/02/1988
Each share Capital Stock $5 par exchanged for (1) share Common 1¢ par
(See First Litchfield Financial Corp.)

FIRST NATL BK (LITTLE ROCK, AR)
Capital Stock $25 par changed to $10 par and (1.5) additional shares issued 7/30/58
Capital Stock $10 par changed to $5 par and (1) additional share issued 2/15/67
Capital Stock $5 par reclassified as Common $10 par 3/27/75
Stock Dividends - 75% 6/30/50; 33-1/3% 2/25/59; 25% 2/27/69
Reorganized as First National Bancshares, Inc. 7/1/81
Each share Common $10 par exchanged for (1) share Common $10 par
First National Bancshares, Inc. merged into First Commercial Corp. 7/30/83 which merged into Regions Financial Corp. (Old) 7/31/98 which merged into Regions Financial Corp. (New) 7/1/2004

FIRST NATL BK (LOCKPORT, IL)
Acquired by Heritage Financial Services, Inc. 04/15/1996
Details not available

FIRST NATL BK (LOGANSPORT, IN)
Common $10 par changed to $5 par and (1) additional share issued 4/30/79
Stock Dividend - 10% 5/10/82
Under plan of reorganization each share Common $5 par automatically became (1) share First National Bankshares, Inc. (IN) Common $5 par 5/31/83
(See First National Bankshares, Inc. (IN))

FIRST NATL BK (LONGMONT, CO)
Under plan of reorganization each share Common $25 par automatically became (1) share First National Bank Holding Co. Common $25 par 01/01/1994
First National Bank Holding Co. name changed to First Mainstreet Financial Ltd. 01/01/2003 which merged into Centennial Bank Holdings, Inc. 10/01/2005 which name changed to Guaranty Bancorp 05/23/2008

FIRST NATIONAL BANK (LONGVIEW, TX)
Each share Capital Stock $100 par exchanged for (10) shares Capital Stock $10 par 1/30/62
Acquired by Southwest Bancshares, Inc. 7/1/71
(See Southwest Bancshares, Inc.)

FIRST NATL BK (LUBBOCK, TX)
Capital Stock $100 par changed to $10 par and (9) additional shares issued plus a 20% stock dividend paid 09/01/1965
Capital Stock $10 par split (3) for (2) by issuance of (0.5) additional share 02/26/1980
Stock Dividends - 100% 00/00/1946; 50% 00/00/1948; 75% 00/00/1951; 33-1/3% 00/00/1953; 15% 00/00/1957; 15% 08/05/1961; 50% 03/01/1970
Acquired by Western Bancshares, Inc. (TX) 02/12/2005
Details not available

FIRST NATL BK (MADISON, IN)
Acquired by Magna Group, Inc. 5/31/94
Each share Common $100 par exchanged for (412.135) shares Common $2 par
Magna Group, Inc. merged into Union Planters Corp. 7/1/98 which merged into Regions Financial Corp. (New) 7/1/2004

FIRST NATIONAL BANK (MADISON, WI)
Name changed to First Wisconsin National Bank (Madison, WI) 09/01/1970
(See First Wisconsin National Bank (Madison, WI))

FIRST NATIONAL BANK (MADISONVILLE, TX)
Acquired by First City Bancorporation of Texas, Inc. (TX) 09/30/1980
Each share Capital Stock $5 par exchanged for (0.875) share Common $6.50 par
(See First City Bancorporation of Texas, Inc. (TX))

FIRST NATL BK (MAITLAND, FL)
99.7% acquired by Southeast Banking Corp. through exchange offer which expired 09/30/1973
Public interest eliminated

FIRST NATL BK (MALDEN, MA)
Each share Capital Stock $100 par exchanged for (2) shares Capital Stock $50 par 01/00/1953
Merged into Malden Trust Co. (Malden, MA) 10/29/1982
Each share Capital Stock $25 par exchanged for $254.40 cash

FIRST NATL BK (MANSFIELD, OH)
Each share Capital Stock $25 par exchanged for (2.5) shares Capital Stock $10 par 4/13/55
Capital Stock $10 par changed to $5 par and (1) additional share issued 3/23/73
Stock Dividends - 10% 2/7/63; 10% 6/1/65; 10% 4/15/66; 10% 6/17/67
Name changed to First Buckeye Bank, N.A. (Mansfield, OH) 3/12/80
First Buckeye Bank, N.A. (Mansfield, OH) merged into Toledo Trustcorp. Inc. 12/30/82 that name changed to Trustcorp, Inc. 4/10/86 which was acquired by Society Corp. 1/5/90 which merged into KeyCorp (New) 3/1/94

FIRST NATL BK (MARGATE, FL)
99.994% acquired by First National Bankshares of Florida, Inc. through exchange offer which expired 08/31/1972
Public interest eliminated

FIRST NATL BK (MARION, IN)
Stock Dividends - 20% 01/17/1962; 16-2/3% 02/01/1965; 14.29% 02/01/1966; 10% 02/02/1970; 100% 11/01/1978
Under plan of reorganization each share Capital Stock $10 par automatically became (1) share Marion Bancorp Common no par 01/31/1985
Marion Bancorp merged into Banc One Corp. (DE) 10/01/1986 which reincorporated in Ohio 05/01/1989 which merged into Bank One Corp. 10/02/1998 which merged into Morgan Chase & Co. 12/31/2000 which name changed to JPMorgan Chase & Co. 07/20/2004

FIRST NATL BK (MARLTON, NJ)
Acquired by Citizens Bancorp (NJ) 11/2/72
Each share Common $5 par exchanged for (1) share Capital Stock no par
(See Citizens Bancorp (NJ))

FIRST NATL BK (MARSHALL, TX)
Capital Stock $8 par changed to $4 par and (1) additional share issued 9/28/78
Capital Stock $4 par changed to $2 par and (1.16) additional shares issued to reflect a (2) for (1) split and a 8% stock dividend 4/30/82
Reorganized as Firstshares of Texas, Inc. 1/1/89
Each share Capital Stock $2 par exchanged for (1) share Common $2 par
(See Firstshares of Texas, Inc.)

FIRST NATL BK (MARYSVILLE, PA)
Under plan of reorganization each share Common 50¢ par automatically became (2) shares First Perry Bancorp, Inc. Common 25¢ par 02/16/1999
First Perry Bancorp, Inc. merged into Riverview Financial Corp. (Old) 12/31/2008 which merged into Riverview Financial Corp. (New) 11/01/2013

FIRST NATL BK (MASSILLON, OH)
Common $5 par split (3) for (1) by issuance of (2) additional shares 05/23/1980

Merged into First Bancorporation of Ohio, Inc. 03/21/1989
Each share Common $5 par exchanged for (2.375) shares Common $3.33333333 par
First Bancorporation of Ohio, Inc. name changed to FirstMerit Corp. 12/26/1994 which merged into Huntington Bancshares Inc. 08/16/2016

FIRST NATL BK (MAYFIELD, KY)
Merged into Jackson Financial Corp. 11/28/83
Each share Capital Stock $25 par exchanged for $435 cash

FIRST NATL BK (McCONNELSVILLE, OH)
Reorganized as FNB Shares, Inc. 1/31/86
Each share Common $30 par exchanged for (2) shares Common no par

FIRST NATIONAL BANK (McKEESPORT, PA)
Under plan of merger each share Capital Stock $20 par exchanged for (5) shares Capital Stock $10 par 08/17/1954
Name changed to Western Pennsylvania National Bank (Pittsburgh, PA) 07/14/1956
Western Pennsylvania National Bank (Pittsburgh, PA) reorganized as WPNB Corp. 04/01/1969 which name changed to Equimark Corp. (PA) 05/10/71 which reorganized in Delaware 03/24/1988 which merged into Integra Financial Corp. 01/15/1993 which merged into National City Corp. 05/03/1996 which was acquired by PNC Financial Services Group, Inc. 12/31/2008

FIRST NATL BK (MEADVILLE, PA)
Merged into First National Bank of Pennsylvania (Meadville, PA) 03/01/1969
Each share Common $20 par exchanged for (1.1) shares 5% Conv. Preferred Ser. A $100 par
(See First National Bank of Pennsylvania (Meadville, PA))

FIRST NATL BK (MEMPHIS, TN)
Each share Common $100 par exchanged for (5) shares Common $20 par in 1944
Each share Common $20 par exchanged for (2) shares Common $10 par in 1954
Stock Dividends - 25% 10/13/50; 25% 1/20/59; 20% 1/19/66; 25% 1/15/68
Reorganized as First National Holding Corp. (TN) 1/17/69
Each share Common $10 par exchanged for (1) share Common $10 par
First National Holding Corp. (TN) name changed to First Tennessee National Corp. 10/27/71 which name changed to First Horizon National Corp. 4/20/2004

FIRST NATIONAL BANK (MERCER, PA)
Merged into Northwest Pennsylvania Bank & Trust Co. (Oil City, PA) 11/30/1963
Each share Capital Stock $25 par exchanged for (1) share Common $20 par
Northwest Pennsylvania Bank & Trust Co. (Oil City, PA) reorganized as Northwest Pennsylvania Corp. 07/01/1981 which merged into Mellon National Corp. 04/12/1984 which name changed to Mellon Bank Corp. 09/30/1984 which name changed to Mellon Financial Corp. 10/17/1999 which merged into Bank of New York Mellon Corp. 07/01/2007

FIRST NATIONAL BANK (MIAMI, FL)
Each share Common $100 par exchanged for (8) shares Capital Stock $25 par to effect a (4) for (1) split and a 100% stock dividend in 1946
Capital Stock $25 par changed to $10 par and (1.5) additional shares issued 1/28/55
Stock Dividends - 25% 1/24/44; 100% 1/21/46; 10% 2/11/52; 20% 1/31/63; 11-1/9% 2/18/66
Merged into Southeast Bancorporation, Inc. 10/2/67
Each share Capital Stock $10 par exchanged for (2) shares Common $5 par
Southeast Bancorporation, Inc. name changed to Southeast Banking Corp. 4/22/71
(See Southeast Banking Corp.)

FIRST NATIONAL BANK (MIAMI SPRINGS, FL)
Name changed to Southeast First National Bank (Miami Springs, FL) 02/01/1971
(See Southeast First National Bank (Miami Springs, FL))

FIRST NATL BK (MIDDLETOWN, OH)
Common $25 par changed to $10 par and (1.5) additional share issued 1/30/57
Stock Dividends - 48% 5/29/53; 13.6% 8/19/59; 11% 3/1/66; 50% 3/10/71; 20% 4/5/78
Under plan of merger name changed and location changed to First National Bank of Southwestern Ohio (Monroe, OH) 7/1/80
First National Bank of Southwestern Ohio (Monroe, OH) reorganized as First Financial Bancorp 4/26/83

FIRST NATL BK (MIDLAND, TX)
Each share Capital Stock $100 par exchanged for (10) shares Capital Stock $10 par 7/24/63
Capital Stock $10 par changed to $5 par and (1) additional share issued plus a 40% stock dividend paid 3/9/73
Stock Dividends - 20% 4/26/51; 42-6/7% 12/12/51; 25% 3/10/59; 10% 1/31/81; 10% 2/9/82
Declared insolvent by Federal Comptroller of currency 10/14/83
No stockholders' equity

FIRST NATL BK (MIFFLINTOWN, PA)
Under plan of reorganization each share Capital Stock $5 par automatically became (1) share First Community Financial Corp. Common $5 par 4/23/85

FIRST NATL BK (MILLVILLE, PA)
Acquired by Northern Central Bank (Williamsport, PA) 05/12/1979
Details not available

FIRST NATL BK (MINERSVILLE, PA)
Name changed to FNBM Financial Corp. 04/07/2000
FNBM Financial Corp. merged into GNB Financial Services, Inc. 03/27/2015

FIRST NATL BK (MINNEAPOLIS, MN)
Common $20 par changed to $30 par 01/25/1965
Common $30 par changed to $40 par 03/05/1971
Common $40 par changed to $50 par 08/28/1975
Stock Dividends - 87% 05/13/1955; 21.5% 05/12/1958
Acquired by U.S. Bancorp 08/01/1997
Details not available

FIRST NATIONAL BANK (MINOT, ND)
Merged into First National Bank of Bowbells (Bowbells, ND) 9/14/93
Details not available

FIRST NATL BK (MINOTOLA, NJ)
Reorganized as Minotola National Bank (Minotola, NJ) 04/03/1972
Each share Common $100 par exchanged for (50) shares Common $10 par
Minotola National Bank (Minotola, NJ) location changed to Vineland, NJ) 08/28/1974 which merged into Susquehanna Bancshares, Inc. 04/21/2006 which merged into BB&T Corp. 08/01/2015

FIRST NATL BK (MOBILE, AL)
Common $25 par changed to $12.50 par and (1) additional share issued plus a 50% stock dividend paid 5/8/65
Common $12.50 par changed to $6.25 par and (1) additional share issued 3/5/71
Stock Dividends - 25% 1/11/55; 25% 1/21/60; 20% 4/16/73
Reorganized as First Bancgroup-Alabama, Inc. 11/30/73
Each share Common $6.25 par exchanged for (2) shares Common $4 par
First Bancgroup-Alabama, Inc. name changed to Firstgulf Bancorp 3/30/84
(See Firstgulf Bancorp)

FIRST NATL BK (MOLINE, IL)
Capital Stock $100 par changed to $10 par and (9) additional shares issued plus a 100% stock dividend paid 9/12/63
Capital Stock $10 par changed to $5 par and (1) additional share issued 1/18/77
Reorganized under the laws of Delaware as Mid States Bancshares, Inc. 12/26/86
Each share Capital Stock $5 par exchanged for (1) share Common $5 par
Mid States Bancshares, Inc. merged into Banc One Corp. 6/9/94 which merged into Bank One Corp. 10/2/98 which merged into J.P. Morgan Chase & Co. 12/31/2000 which name changed to JPMorgan Chase & Co. 7/20/2004

FIRST NATL BK (MONACA, PA)
Name changed to National Bank of Beaver County (Monaca, PA) 09/01/1974
National Bank of Beaver County (Monaca, PA) merged into Century National Bank & Trust Co. (Rochester, PA) 12/09/1985 which reorganized as Century Financial Corp. 06/01/1988 which merged into Citizens Bancshares, Inc. 05/12/1998 which name changed to Sky Financial Group, Inc. 10/02/1998 which merged into Huntington Bancshares Inc. 07/02/2007

FIRST NATIONAL BANK (MONONGAHELA CITY, PA)
Merged into First National Bank (McKeesport, PA) 08/17/1954
Each share Capital Stock $100 par exchanged for (2) shares Capital Stock $10 par
First National Bank (McKeesport, PA) name changed to Western Pennsylvania National Bank (Pittsburgh, PA) 07/14/1956 which reorganized as WPNB Corp. 04/01/1969 which name changed to Equimark Corp. (PA) 05/10/1971 which reorganized in Delaware 03/24/1988 which merged into Integra Financial Corp. 01/15/1993 which merged into National City Corp. 05/03/1996 which was acquired by PNC Financial Services Group, Inc. 12/31/2008

FIRST NATL BK (MONROE, MI)
Capital Stock $100 par changed to $10 par and (9) additional shares issued 11/18/57
Stock Dividends - 20% in 1965; 25% in 1968; 20% in 1971; 25% in 1974; 100% in 1976
Merged into Security Bancorp, Inc. 3/28/83
Each share Capital Stock $10 par exchanged for $60 principal amount of Variable Rate 10-yr. Subordinated Installment Notes due 4/1/93

FIRST NATIONAL BANK (MONTCLAIR, NJ)
Each share Capital Stock $100 par exchanged for (5) shares Capital Stock $25 par to effect a (4) for (1) split and a 25% stock dividend 1/15/46
Merged into Montclair National Bank & Trust Co. (Montclair, NJ) 12/20/57
Each share Capital Stock $25 par exchanged for (2) shares Capital Stock $10 par
Montclair National Bank & Trust Co. (Montclair, NJ) merged into American National Bank & Trust (Montclair, NJ) 7/10/70 which reorganized as Princeton American Bancorp 1/1/72 which name changed to Horizon Bancorp 12/31/73
(See Horizon Bancorp)

FIRST NATL BK (MONTGOMERY, AL)
Each share Common $10 par exchanged for (2) shares Common $5 par 12/18/59
Stock Dividends - 50% 1/26/53; 16-2/3% 1/10/56; 12-1/2% 12/18/59; 10% 1/20/66; 10% 3/1/68; 10% 2/6/70
Name changed to First Alabama Bank of Montgomery, N.A. (Montgomery, AL) 2/1/75
(See First Alabama Bank of Montgomery, N.A. (Montgomery, AL))

FIRST NATL BK (MOORESTOWN, NJ)
Capital Stock $10 par changed to $5 par and (1) additional share issued 03/16/1971
Stock Dividend - 10% 02/16/1971
Merged into First National Bank of South Jersey (Pleasantville, NJ) 05/14/1973
Each share Capital Stock $5 par exchanged for $42.50 cash

FIRST NATL BK (MORGANTOWN, WV)
Capital Stock $10 par changed to $5 par and (1) additional share issued 3/31/81
Stock Dividends - 80% 7/12/57; 20% 2/25/65; 100% 2/26/71; 100% 9/15/77
Reorganized as First Banc Securities, Inc. 7/2/84
Each share Capital Stock $5 par exchanged for (1) share Common $5 par
First Banc Securities, Inc. merged into Huntington Bancshares Inc. 12/29/89

FIRST NATL BK (MORTON GROVE, IL)
Merged into Mid-Citco, Inc. 12/31/82
Each share Common $10 par exchanged for $41.50 cash

FIRST NATL BK (MOUNDSVILLE, WV)
Acquired by United Bankshares, Inc. 01/01/1993
Details not available

FIRST NATL BK (MOUNT CARMEL, PA)
Merged into First National Trust Bank (Sunbury, PA) 10/02/1972
Each share Common $10 par exchanged for (1.9) shares Common $6.25 par
First National Trust Bank (Sunbury, PA) reorganized as FNT Bancorp, Inc. 05/03/1984 which merged into Susquehanna Bancshares, Inc.

10/01/1985 which merged into BB&T Corp. 08/01/2015

FIRST NATIONAL BANK (MOUNT VERNON, NY)
Each share Common $100 par exchanged for (6) shares Common $25 par to effect a (4) for (1) split and 50% stock dividend in 1953
Stock Dividend - 33-1/3% 2/15/57
Merged into Chemical Bank New York Trust Co. (New York, NY) 2/25/64
Each share Common $25 par exchanged for (2.875) shares Capital Stock $12 par
Chemical Bank New York Trust Co. (New York, NY) reorganized as Chemical New York Corp. 2/17/69 which name changed to Chemical Banking Corp. 4/29/88 which name changed to Chase Manhattan Corp. (New) 3/31/96 which name changed to J.P. Morgan Chase & Co. 12/31/2000 which name changed to JPMorgan Chase & Co. 7/20/2004

FIRST NATL BK (MT CLEMENS, MI)
Capital Stock $25 par changed to $12.50 par and (1) additional share issued 3/15/69
Capital Stock $12.50 par changed to $3.125 par and (3) additional shares issued 5/30/86
Stock Dividends - 300% 8/3/45; 50% 1/12/54; 25% 1/2/59; 20% 3/15/68; 10% 4/30/76; 10% 4/29/78
Reorganized under the laws of Delaware as First National Bank Corp. 4/30/87
Each share Capital Stock $3.125 par exchanged for (1) share Common $3.125 par
First National Bank Corp. merged into Old Kent Financial Corp. 2/1/95 which merged into Fifth Third Bancorp 4/2/2001

FIRST NATL BK (NAPLES, FL)
Common Capital Stock $20 par changed to $10 par and (1) additional share issued 4/6/64
Common Capital Stock $10 par changed to $5 par and (1) additional share issued 10/18/67
Common Capital Stock $5 par changed to $2 par and (1.5) additional shares issued 6/12/69
Common Capital Stock $2 par changed to $1 par and (1) additional share issued 3/10/71
Name changed to First National Bank & Trust Co. (Naples, FL) 10/1/71
(See First National Bank & Trust Co. (Naples, FL))

FIRST NATL BK (NATICK, MA)
Common $50 par changed to $25 par and (1) additional share issued 4/1/66
Common $25 par changed to $6.25 par and (3) additional shares issued 9/14/67
Common $6.25 par changed to $3.125 par and (1) additional share issued 3/4/69
Merged into Guaranty-First Trust Co. (Waltham, MA) 1/1/73
Each share Capital Stock $3.125 par exchanged for (1) share Common $4 par
Guaranty-First Trust Co. (Waltham, MA) reorganized as New England Bancorp, Inc. 11/1/73
(See New England Bancorp, Inc.)

FIRST NATL BK (NEENAH, WI)
Stock Dividends - 20% 1/27/59; (1) for (7.5) 1/29/63
Acquired by Associated Bank Services, Inc. 6/1/70
Each share Capital Stock $20 par exchanged for (1.7) shares Common $1 par
Associated Bank Services, Inc. name changed to Associated Banc-Corp. 6/15/77

FIRST NATL BK (NEW BEDFORD, MA)
Reorganized as First Melville Bancorp, Inc. 5/10/74
Each share Common $5 par exchanged for (1) share Common $1 par
First Melville Bancorp, Inc. merged into Shawmut Corp. 10/1/81 which merged into Shawmut National Corp. 2/29/88 which merged into Fleet Financial Group Inc. (New) 11/30/95 which name changed to Fleet Boston Corp. 10/1/99 which name changed to FleetBoston Financial Corp. 4/18/2000 which merged into Bank of America Corp. 4/1/2004

FIRST NATL BK (NEW BRAUNFELS, TX)
Stock Dividend - 100% 3/8/74
Merged into Texas Commerce Bancshares, Inc. 4/16/76
Each share Capital Stock $5 par exchanged for (1) share Common $4 par
Texas Commerce Bancshares, Inc. acquired by Chemical New York Corp. 5/1/87 which name changed to Chemical Banking Corp. 4/29/88 which name changed to Chase Manhattan Corp. (New) 3/31/96 which name changed to J.P. Morgan Chase & Co. 12/31/2000 which name changed to JPMorgan Chase & Co. 7/20/2004

FIRST NATL BANK (NEW HOLLAND, OH)
Reorganized as Community First Financial Bancorp Inc. 07/31/2001
Each share Common no par exchanged for (4) shares Common no par
(See Community First Financial Bancorp Inc.)

FIRST NATL BK (NEWARK, OH)
Thru voluntary exchange offer 100% acquired by BancOhio Corp. as of 7/7/53
Public interest eliminated

FIRST NATL BK (NEWPORT, PA)
Common $2 par split (2) for (1) by issuance of (1) additional share payable 8/18/99 to holders of record 7/21/99
Merged into Orrstown Financial Services, Inc. 5/1/2006
Each share Common $2 par exchanged for (1.75) shares Common $1.25 par and $22.20 cash

FIRST NATIONAL BANK (NEWPORT NEWS, VA)
Common $100 par changed to $10 par plus a 100% stock dividend paid 8/29/58
Stock Dividend - 25% 7/25/61
Merged into First & Merchants National Bank (Richmond, VA) 10/31/62
Each share Common $10 par exchanged for (1.1) shares Common $10 par
First & Merchants National Bank (Richmond, VA) reorganized as First & Merchants National Corp. 2/26/69 which merged into Sovran Financial Corp. 12/31/83 which merged into C&S/Sovran Corp. 9/1/90 which merged into NationsBank Corp. 12/31/91 which reincorporated in Delaware as BankAmerica Corp. (Old) 9/25/98 which merged into BankAmerica Corp. (New) 9/30/98 which name changed to Bank of America Corp. 4/28/99

FIRST NATIONAL BANK (NILES, MI)
Name changed to First National Bank of Southwestern Michigan (Niles, Mich.) 4/1/66
First National Bank of Southwestern Michigan (Niles, Mich.) reorganized as Western Michigan Corp. 11/10/75 which merged into Pacesetter Financial Corp. (Del.) 2/1/78 which reincorporated in Michigan 3/10/80
(See Pacesetter Financial Corp. (Mich.))

FIRST NATL BK (NORFOLK, VA)
99% acquired by Dominion Bankshares Corp. through exchange offer which expired 04/30/1969
Public interest eliminated

FIRST NATL BK (NORTHAMPTON, MA)
Over 99% acquired by First Pioneer Bancorp, Inc. through purchase offer which expired 07/01/1973
Public interest eliminated

FIRST NATL BK (NORTHGLENN, CO)
Merged into First National Bancorporation, Inc. 01/19/1982
Each share Capital Stock $1 par exchanged for (0.467) share Common $10 par
First National Bancorporation, Inc. name changed to IntraWest Financial Corp. 10/01/1982 which merged into United Banks of Colorado, Inc. 04/30/1987 which merged into Norwest Corp. 04/19/1991 which name changed to Wells Fargo & Co. (New) 11/02/1998

FIRST NATIONAL BANK (OAKLAND, CA)
Merged into Security National Bank (Oakland, Calif.) 10/9/67
Each share Common $10 par exchanged for (1) share Common $4 par and $8 principal amount of 6% Conv. Debentures due 1982

FIRST NATL BK (OAKLAND, MD)
Stock Dividends - 25% 1/10/69; 25% 12/31/73; 100% 11/20/76
Reorganized as First United Corp. 7/1/85
Each share Common $10 par exchanged for (2) shares Common $5 par

FIRST NATL BK (ODESSA, TX)
Merged into First International Bancshares, Inc. 10/5/73
Each share Capital Stock $10 par exchanged for (1.7) shares Common $5 par
First International Bancshares, Inc. name changed to InterFirst Corp. 12/31/81 which merged into First RepublicBank Corp. 6/6/87
(See First RepublicBank Corp.)

FIRST NATL BK (OELWEIN, IA)
Each share old Common exchanged for (0.001) share new Common 9/30/2000
Note: In effect holders received $136.16 cash per share and public interest was eliminated

FIRST NATL BK (OLEAN, NY)
Each share Capital Stock $100 par exchanged for (5) shares Capital Stock $25 par to effect a (4) for (1) split and 25% stock dividend 1/23/56
Capital Stock $25 par changed to $12.50 par and (1) additional share issued 1/11/63
Acquired by Manufacturers Hanover Corp. 7/25/73
Each share Capital Stock $12.50 par exchanged for (2.5) shares Common $7.50 par
Manufacturers Hanover Corp. merged into Chemical Banking Corp. 12/31/91 which name changed to Chase Manhattan Corp. (New) 3/31/96 which name changed to J.P. Morgan Chase & Co. 12/31/2000 which name changed to JPMorgan Chase & Co. 7/20/2004

FIRST NATL BK (OMAHA, NE)
Capital Stock $20 par changed to $5 par and (3) additional shares issued 07/10/1962
Stock Dividends - 33-1/3% 01/20/1948; 25% 03/20/1951; 20% 06/29/1953
99.48% acquired by First National of Nebraska, Inc. through exchange offer which expired 07/29/1969
Public interest eliminated

FIRST NATL BK (ORLANDO, FL)
Capital Stock $20 par changed to $10 par and (1) additional share issued 01/31/1961
Stock Dividends - 25% 06/04/1941; 100% 01/29/1945; 25% 04/22/1949; 25% 01/22/1953; 20% 03/09/1954; 33-1/3% 10/20/1954
99.2% held by First At Orlando Corp. as of 04/02/1971
Public interest eliminated

FIRST NATL BK (OTTAWA, IL)
Stock Dividends - 100% 1/22/53; 25% 1/20/60
Under plan of reorganization each share Common $20 par automatically became (1) share First Ottawa Bancshares Inc. Common $20 par 10/1/99

FIRST NATIONAL BANK (OTTUMWA, IA)
91% acquired by Northwest Bancorporation through purchase offer which expired 01/28/1977
Public interest eliminated

FIRST NATL BK (PALM BEACH, FL)
Each share Capital Stock $100 par exchanged for (50) shares Capital Stock $10 par to effect a (10) for (1) split and a 400% stock dividend in 1945
Stock Dividends - 20% 2/4/57; 25% 2/10/60; 10% 2/6/63; 10% 2/11/65; 10% 3/1/67; 150% 2/12/69
Reorganized as First National Bank of Palm Beach, Inc. 9/10/81
Each share Capital Stock $10 par exchanged for (1) share Common $10 par
(See First National Bank of Palm Beach, Inc.)

FIRST NATL BK (PAMPA, TX)
Acquired by Boatmen's Bancshares, Inc. 5/31/95
Each share Common $1 par exchanged for (3.375) shares Common $1 par
Boatmen's Bancshares, Inc. merged into NationsBank Corp. 1/7/97 which reincorporated in Delaware as BankAmerica Corp. (Old) 9/25/98 which merged into BankAmerica Corp. (New) 9/30/98 which name changed to Bank of America Corp. 4/28/99

FIRST NATIONAL BANK (PARK RIDGE, IL)
Name changed to O'Hare International Bank (N.A.) (Chicago, Ill.) 4/11/66
O'Hare International Bank (N.A.) (Chicago, Ill.) reorganized as O'Hare Banc Corp. 10/21/80
(See O'Hare Banc Corp.)

FIRST NATIONAL BANK (PARMA, OH)
Common $20 par changed to $10 par and (1) additional share issued 2/7/66
Name changed to American National Bank (Parma, OH) 5/23/66
(See American National Bank (Parma, OH))

FIRST NATL BK (PEORIA, IL)
Each share old Capital Stock $100 par exchanged for (5) shares Capital Stock $20 par 12/16/1930
Capital Stock $20 par changed to $100 par 02/26/1975
Reorganized as First Peoria Corp. 04/01/1983
Each share Capital Stock $100 par exchanged for (10) shares Common $10 par

First Peoria Corp. merged into Commerce Bancshares, Inc. 06/01/1992

FIRST NATL BK (PETERBOROUGH, NH)
Reorganized under the laws of Delaware as First Peterborough Bank Corp. 06/18/1987
Each share Capital Stock $25 par exchanged for (10) shares Common $2.50 par
(See First Peterborough Bank Corp.)

FIRST NATIONAL BANK (PHILADELPHIA, PA)
Each share Common $100 par exchanged for (10) shares Common $10 par 00/00/1944
Stock Dividends - 25% 07/15/1949; (889) for (3,111) 05/20/1954
Merged into First Pennsylvania Banking & Trust Co. (Philadelphia, PA) 09/30/1955
Each share Common $10 par exchanged for (1) share Capital Stock $10 par
First Pennsylvania Banking & Trust Co. (Philadelphia, PA) reorganized as First Pennsylvania Corp. 01/31/1969 which merged into CoreStates Financial Corp 03/05/1990 which merged into First Union Corp. 04/28/1998 which name changed to Wachovia Corp. (Ctfs. dated after 09/01/2001) 09/01/2001 which merged into Wells Fargo & Co. (New) 12/31/2008

FIRST NATIONAL BANK (PISCATAWAY, NJ)
Acquired by Commercial Trust Co. of New Jersey (Jersey City, NJ) 12/26/75
Each share Capital Stock $10 par exchanged for $30 cash

FIRST NATL BK (PITTSFIELD, ME)
Merged into Maine National Bank (Portland, ME) 8/17/70
Each share Capital Stock $25 par exchanged for (4) shares Capital Stock $10 par
Maine National Bank (Portland, ME) reorganized as Maine National Corp. 2/18/83 which merged into Bank of New England Corp. 12/18/85
(See Bank of New England Corp.)

FIRST NATL BK (PITTSTON, PA)
Name changed to First Bank of Greater Pittston (Pittston, PA) and Capital Stock $25 par changed to $5 par 03/18/1974
First Bank of Greater Pittston (Pittston, PA) merged into Commonwealth Bancshares Corp. 11/01/1990 which was acquired by Meridian Bancorp, Inc. 08/31/1993 which merged into CoreStates Financial Corp 04/09/1996 which merged into First Union Corp. 04/28/1998 which name changed to Wachovia Corp. (Ctfs. dated after 09/01/2001) 09/01/2001 which merged into Wells Fargo & Co. (New) 12/31/2008

FIRST NATIONAL BANK (POMONA, CA)
Merged into California Bank (Los Angeles, CA) 03/05/1955
Each share Capital Stock $100 par exchanged for (12) shares Common $12.50 par
California Bank (Los Angeles, CA) merged into United California Bank (Los Angeles, CA) 02/24/1961 which merged into Western Bancorporation 01/16/1978 which name changed to First Interstate Bancorp 06/01/1981 which merged into Wells Fargo & Co. (Old) 04/01/1996 which merged into Wells Fargo & Co. (New) 11/02/1998

FIRST NATL BK (POMPANO BEACH, FL)
Stock Dividend - 50% 04/01/1971
99.597% held by First National Bankshares of Florida, Inc. through exchange offer which expired 08/31/1972
Public interest eliminated

FIRST NATL BK (PORT ARTHUR, TX)
Each share Capital Stock $100 par exchanged for (5) shares Capital Stock $20 par 10/9/51
Capital Stock $20 par changed to $10 par and (1) additional share issued plus a 15.38% stock dividend paid 2/15/71
Stock Dividends - 12-1/2% 2/24/59; 18.18% 3/4/67
Merged into Southwest Bancshares, Inc. 10/10/72
Each share Capital Stock $10 par exchanged for (1.5) shares Common $5 par
Southwest Bancshares, Inc. merged into MCorp 10/11/84
(See MCorp)

FIRST NATIONAL BANK (PORTLAND, ME)
Capital Stock $20 par changed to $10 par and (1) additional share issued plus a 10% stock dividend paid 2/28/66
Under plan of merger name changed to Maine National Bank (Portland, ME) 8/2/68
Maine National Bank (Portland, ME) reorganized as Maine National Corp. 2/18/83 which merged into Bank of New England Corp. 12/18/85
(See Bank of New England Corp.)

FIRST NATIONAL BANK (PORTLAND, OR)
Each share Common $100 par exchanged for (8) shares Common $12.50 par in 1943
Stock Dividends - 50% 1/26/42; 66-2/3% 5/29/50; 66-2/3% 4/1/52
Name changed to First National Bank of Oregon (Portland, OR) 8/1/58
First National Bank of Oregon (Portland, OR) merged into Western Bancorporation 7/1/80 which name changed to First Interstate Bancorp 6/1/81 which merged into Wells Fargo & Co. (Old) 4/1/96 which merged into Wells Fargo & Co. (New) 11/2/98

FIRST NATL BK (PORTSMOUTH, NH)
Common $6 par changed to $3 par and (1) additional share issued 02/10/1982
Reorganized as First Coastal Banks, Inc. 07/02/1984
Each share Common $3 par exchanged for (5) shares Common $1 par
(See First Coastal Banks, Inc.)

FIRST NATL BK (PRINCETON, NJ)
Capital Stock $100 par changed to $10 par 1/26/65
Capital Stock $10 par changed to $2.50 par and (3) additional shares issued 2/25/70
Stock Dividends - 33-1/3% 6/29/62; 10% 10/15/70
Merged into United Jersey Banks 11/1/71
Each share Capital Stock $2.50 par exchanged for (0.740740) share Common $5 par
United Jersey Banks name changed to UJB Financial Corp. 6/30/89 which name changed to Summit Bancorp 3/1/96 which merged into FleetBoston Financial Corp. 3/1/2001 which merged into Bank of America Corp. 4/1/2004

FIRST NATL BK (PUEBLO, CO)
Each share Capital Stock $100 par exchanged for (10) shares Capital Stock $10 par plus a 50% stock dividend paid 01/00/1955
Capital Stock $10 par changed to $17 par 02/01/1965
Stock Dividend - 100% 05/01/1947
Acquired by Mountain Banks Ltd. 04/17/1972
Each share Capital Stock $17 par exchanged for (2.606) shares Common $5 par
(See Mountain Banks Ltd.)

FIRST NATL BK (PUNTA GORDA, FL)
First Financial Corp. acquired all but (435) shares through exchange offer which expired 06/30/1974
Public interest eliminated

FIRST NATL BK (REIDSVILLE, NC)
Common $5 par changed to $1 par and (4) additional shares issued 10/08/1974
Stock Dividends - 50% 12/15/1970; 10% 10/29/1976
Reorganized as FNB Financial Services Corp. 12/31/1984
Each share Common $1 par exchanged for (1) share Common $1 par
FNB Financial Services Corp. merged into NewBridge Bancorp 07/31/2007 which merged into Yadkin Financial Corp. 03/01/2016 which merged into F.N.B. Corp. 03/11/2017

FIRST NATL BK (REYNOLDSVILLE, PA)
Common $100 par split (200) for (1) by issuance of (199) additional shares 12/31/1995
Under plan of reorganization each share Common $100 par automatically became (1) share Community First Bancorp Inc. Common 50¢ par 01/01/1996
Community First Bancorp Inc. merged into Emclaire Financial Corp. 10/01/2018

FIRST NATL BK (RICHMOND, IN)
Stock Dividends - 100% 1/27/53; 25% 2/1/66; 10% 3/15/77; 10% 3/15/78; 10% 4/20/79; 10% 4/21/80; 10% 4/20/81; 10% 4/19/82
Reorganized as Charter 17 Bancorp, Inc. 1/1/83
Each share Common $10 par exchanged for (1) share Common $10 par
Charter 17 Bancorp, Inc. merged into Banc One Corp. (DE) 8/31/87 which reincorporated in Ohio 5/1/89 which merged into Bank One Corp. 10/2/98 which merged into J.P. Morgan Chase & Co. 12/31/2000 which name changed to JPMorgan Chase & Co. 7/20/2004

FIRST NATIONAL BANK (RIO GRANDE CITY, TX)
Under plan of reorganization each share Common $1 par automatically became (1) share Rio Grande City Bancshares, Inc. Common $1 par 1/20/81
Rio Grande City Bancshares, Inc. merged into First Security Corp. 2/2/98 which merged into Wells Fargo & Co. (New) 10/26/2000

FIRST NATL BK (RIVERSIDE, NJ)
Name changed to First National Bank of Burlington County (Riverside, NJ) 05/20/1970
First National Bank of Burlington County (Riverside, NJ) changed location to First National Bank of Burlington County (Cinnaminson, NJ) 06/24/1971 which name changed to Friendly National Bank of New Jersey (Cinnaminson, NJ) 05/15/1974 which name changed to Eastern National Bank (Cinnaminson, NJ) 04/12/1983 which name changed to Cherry Hill National Bank (Medford, NJ) 04/27/1987 which merged into Meridian Bancorp, Inc. 04/16/1993 which merged into Corestates Financial Corp 04/09/1996 which merged into First Union Corp. 04/28/1998 which name changed to Wachovia Corp. (Ctfs. dated after 09/01/2001) 09/01/2001 which merged into Wells Fargo & Co. (New) 12/31/2008

FIRST NATL BK (ROCHESTER, NH)
Common Capital Stock $25 par split (2) for (1) by issuance of (1) additional share 01/23/1956
Common Capital Stock $25 par changed to $12.50 par and (1) additional share issued plus a 300% stock dividend paid 04/05/1968
96.73% acquired by Profile Bankshares Inc. through exchange offer which expired 05/27/1977
Public interest eliminated

FIRST NATL BK (ROCHESTER, NY)
Common $10 par changed to $7.50 par in July 1983
Reorganized as FNB Rochester Corp. 9/10/84
Each share Common $7.50 par exchanged for $7.50 principal amount of 10% Subordinated Debentures due 12/1/96 and (1) share Common $1 par
FNB Rochester Corp. merged into M&T Bank Corp. 6/1/99

FIRST NATL BK (ROCK ISLAND, IL)
Each share Capital Stock $100 par exchanged for (4) shares Capital Stock $25 par plus a 25% stock dividend paid 01/22/1958
Capital Stock $25 par changed to $10 par and (1.5) additional share issued 01/16/1973
Stock Dividends - 100% 01/10/1946; 100% 02/15/1965
Name changed to First National Bank of Quad Cities (Rock Island, IL) 10/02/1981
First National Bank of Quad Cities (Rock Island, IL) reorganized as Quad Cities First Co. 06/30/1982 which merged into First of America Bank Corp. 12/31/1988 which merged into National City Corp. 03/31/1998 which was acquired by PNC Financial Services Group, Inc. 12/31/2008

FIRST NATL BK (ROCKPORT, TX)
Acquired by Victoria Bankshares, Inc. 12/01/1992
Each share Common $5 par exchanged for (2) shares Common $10 par
Victoria Bankshares, Inc. merged into Norwest Corp. 04/11/1996 which name changed to Wells Fargo & Co. (New) 11/02/1998

FIRST NATL BANK (ROCKY MOUNT, VA)
Stock Dividends - 10% payable 07/31/2000 to holders of record 06/30/2000 Ex date - 08/16/2000; 10% payable 07/31/2001 to holders of record 06/29/2001; 10% payable 07/31/2002 to holders of record 07/30/2002 Ex date - 07/29/2002; 10% payable 10/31/2003 to holders of record 09/30/2003 Ex date - 11/03/2003
Merged into Carter Bank & Trust (Martinsville, VA) 12/29/2006
Each share Common $13.50 par exchanged for (1.613) shares Common

FIRST NATIONAL BANK (ROME, GA)
Merged into Trust Co. of Georgia 8/17/78
Each share Common $10 par exchanged for (1.1480) shares Common $5 par
Trust Co. of Georgia merged into SunTrust Banks, Inc. 7/1/85

FIRST NATIONAL BANK (ROYAL OAK, MI)
FDIC appointed as receiver and Bank out of business 7/3/31

FIRST NATL BK (SALEM, OH)
Each share Common $100 par exchanged for (5) shares Common $20 par 01/08/1946
Common $20 par changed to $4 par and (4) additional shares issued 07/31/1963
Stock Dividends - 100% 01/23/1969; 100% 03/01/1976
100% acquired by Society Corp. through purchase offer which expired 10/31/1983
Public interest eliminated

FIRST NATL BK (SAN ANTONIO, TX)
Each share Common $100 par exchanged for (10) shares Common $10 par 2/18/60
Stock Dividends - 13.3% 1/25/62; 10% 1/23/67
Merged into First International Bancshares, Inc. 6/19/81
Each share Common $10 par exchanged for (3.2) shares Common $5 par
First International Bancshares, Inc. name changed to InterFirst Corp. 12/31/81 which merged into First RepublicBank Corp. 6/6/87
(See First RepublicBank Corp.)

FIRST NATIONAL BANK (SAN DIEGO, CA)
Name changed to Southern California First National Bank (San Diego, CA) 8/18/67
Southern California First National Bank (San Diego, CA) reorganized as Southern California First National Corp. 2/28/69
(See Southern California First National Corp.)

FIRST NATL BK (SAN DIEGO, CA)
Common $100 par split (100) for (1) by issuance of (99) additional shares payable 02/15/2000 to holders of record 02/15/2000 Ex date - 04/20/2000
Merged into First Community Bancorp 09/10/2002
Each share Common $100 par exchanged for $10 cash

FIRST NATL BK (SAN JOSE, CA)
Capital Stock $100 par changed to $5 par and (19) additional shares issued 5/31/60
Stock Dividends - 10% 1/31/63; 10% 2/7/69
Under plan of reorganization each share Capital Stock $5 par automatically became (1) share First National Bancshares Inc. Common $5 par 6/16/76
First National Bancshares Inc. name changed to Bancwest Corp. 3/15/79 which name changed to BWC Liquidating Corp. 3/18/80
(See BWC Liquidating Corp.)

FIRST NATL BK (SANTA FE, NM)
Each share Capital Stock $100 par exchanged for (5) shares Capital Stock $20 par 01/00/1946
Capital Stock $20 par changed to $10 par and (1) additional share issued 01/14/1964
Stock Dividends - 30% 01/14/1946; 20% 04/21/1953; 25% 09/19/1962; 14-2/7% 03/15/1965; 10% 03/17/1969
Acquired by New Mexico Bancorporation, Inc. 05/14/1971
Each share Common $10 par exchanged for (2) shares Common $1 par
New Mexico Bancorporation, Inc. name changed to New Mexico Banquest Corp. 05/01/1980
(See New Mexico Banquest Corp.)

FIRST NATL BK (SAULT STE MARIE, MI)
Acquired by First National Financial Corp. 05/08/1974
Each share Common $10 par exchanged for (1.9022) shares Common $10 par
First National Financial Corp. merged into First American Bank Corp. 02/13/1978 which name changed to First of America Bank Corp. 01/14/1983 which merged into National City Corp. 03/31/1998 which was acquired by PNC Financial Services Group, Inc. 12/31/2008

FIRST NATIONAL BANK (SCRANTON, PA)
Each share Capital Stock $100 par exchanged for (4) shares Capital Stock $25 par 01/08/1929
Capital Stock $25 par changed to $18 par 06/00/1936
Stock Dividend - 33-1/3% 12/22/1929
Under plan of merger name changed to First National Bank & Trust Co. (Scranton, PA) 06/29/1956
First National Bank & Trust Co. (Scranton, PA) name changed to Northeastern Pennsylvania National Bank & Trust Co. (Scranton, PA) 08/01/1958 which name changed to Northeastern National Bank of Pennsylvania (Scranton, PA) 04/02/1971 which name changed to Northeastern Bank of Pennsylvania (Scranton, PA) 01/02/1974 which 01/02/1974 reorganized as Northeastern Bancorp, Inc. 08/12/1981 which merged into PNC Financial Corp. 01/30/1985 which name changed to PNC Bank Corp. 02/08/1993 which name changed to PNC Financial Services Group, Inc. 03/15/2000

FIRST NATIONAL BK (SHELBY, NC)
Common $10 par split (2) for (1) by issuance of (1) additional share payable 04/30/2001 to holders of record 03/20/2001 Ex date - 05/11/2001
Stock Dividend - 33.33333333% 12/00/1955
Merged into Bank of the Ozarks, Inc. 07/31/2013
Each share Common $10 par exchanged for (3.6199095) shares Common 1¢ par
Bank of the Ozarks, Inc. reorganized as Bank of the Ozarks (Little Rock, AR) 06/27/2017 which name changed to Bank OZK (Little Rock, AR) 07/16/2018

FIRST NATL BK (SHIPPENSBURG, PA)
Merged into Commonwealth National Bank (Harrisburg, PA) 4/1/80
Each share Common $2.50 par exchanged for (0.8) share Common $5 par and $5 cash
Commonwealth National Bank (Harrisburg, PA) reorganized as Commonwealth National Financial Corp. 3/5/82
(See Commonwealth National Financial Corp.)

FIRST NATL BK (SHREVEPORT, LA)
Each share Capital Stock $100 par exchanged for (4) shares Capital Stock $25 par in 1946
Each share Capital Stock $25 par exchanged for (2) shares Capital Stock $12.50 par 4/5/55
Stock Dividends - 33-1/3% 6/28/50; 25% 9/30/69; 10% 11/15/72; 10% 4/30/76; 100% 7/2/77; 10% 4/30/80
Under plan of reorganization each share Capital Stock $12.50 par automatically became (1) share First National Bancorp, Inc. Common $5 par 1/15/81
First National Bancorp, Inc. merged into Louisiana Bancshares, Inc. 1/10/85 which name changed to Premier Bancorp, Inc. 4/15/87 which merged into Banc One Corp. 1/2/96 which merged into Bank One Corp. 10/2/98 merged into J.P. Morgan Chase & Co. 12/31/2000 which name changed to JPMorgan Chase & Co. 7/20/2004

FIRST NATL BK (SIDNEY, OH)
Reorganized as First Sidney Banc Corp. 01/02/1987
Each share Capital Stock $10 par exchanged for (2) shares Common $5 par
First Sidney Banc Corp acquired by First National Cincinnati Corp. 01/29/1988 which name changed to Star Banc Corp. 04/13/1990 which merged into Firstar Corp. (New) 11/20/1998 which merged into U.S. Bancorp (DE) 02/27/2001

FIRST NATL BK (SIKESTON, MO)
Acquired by Continental Bancorporation, Inc. (MO) 04/01/1991
Details not available

FIRST NATL BK (SIOUX CITY, IA)
Stock Dividend - 100% 10/14/1963
Acquired by Banks of Iowa, Inc. 08/16/1976
Each share Common exchanged for $81.51 cash

FIRST NATL BK (SKOKIE, IL)
Stock Dividends - 10% in 1953; 20% in 1956; 100% 1/27/59; 42.857142% 2/7/63; 50% 1/22/68; 33-1/3% 10/2/69; 50% 1/2/73; 33-1/3% 12/1/75; 25% 9/15/77
Acquired by Citizens Financial Corp. (IL) 2/28/86
Each share Capital Stock $10 par exchanged for $42 cash

FIRST NATL BK (SLIDELL, LA)
Merged into Commercial Capital Systems, Inc. 10/7/72
Each share Common $10 par exchanged for (2) shares Common no par
Commercial Capital Systems, Inc. name changed to First National Corp. 3/31/77
(See First National Corp.)

FIRST NATL BK (SLIPPERY ROCK, PA)
Under plan of reorganization each share Common $3.33 par automatically became (1) share Slippery Rock Financial Corp. Common $1 par 06/30/1992
Slippery Rock Financial Corp. merged into F.N.B. Corp. (FL) 10/08/2004

FIRST NATIONAL BANK (SOUTH RIVER, NJ)
Each share Capital Stock $100 par exchanged for (4) shares Capital Stock $25 par 10/17/55
Stock Dividends - 100% 10/5/55; 30% 12/2/58
Name changed to First National Bank of Middlessex County (East Brunswick, NJ) 1/3/61
First National Bank of Middlesex County (East Brunswick, NJ) name changed to First Charter National Bank (East Brunswick, NJ) 4/1/69 which merged into Heritage Bancorporation 12/31/73
(See Heritage Bancorporation)

FIRST NATIONAL BANK (SOUTHGLENN, CO)
Each share Capital Stock 50¢ par exchanged for (0.1) share Capital Stock $5 par 12/22/1972
Merged into First National Bancorporation, Inc. 01/19/1982
Each share Capital Stock $5 par exchanged for (1.453) shares Common $10 par
First National Bancorporation, Inc. name changed to IntraWest Financial Corp. 10/01/1982 which merged into United Banks of Colorado, Inc. 04/30/1987 which merged into Norwest Corp. 04/19/1991 which name changed to Wells Fargo & Co. (New) 11/02/1998

FIRST NATL BK (SPRINGFIELD, IL)
Each share Common $100 par exchanged for (5) shares Common $20 par 00/00/1955
Common $20 par changed to $10 par and (1) additional share issued 02/27/1967
Common $10 par changed to $5 par and (1) additional share issued 02/14/1973
Stock Dividends - 100% 10/05/1955; 30% 12/02/1958; 20% 01/17/1961; 11% 02/15/1963
Reorganized as Firstbank of Illinois Co. 02/14/1975
Each share Common $5 par exchanged for (1) share Common $5 par
Firstbank of Illinois Co. merged into Mercantile Bancorporation, Inc. 07/01/1998 which merged into Firstar Corp. (New) 09/20/1999 which merged into U.S. Bancorp (DE) 02/27/2001

FIRST NATL BK (ST. LOUIS, MO)
Common $17 par changed to $20 par 00/00/1951
Common $20 par changed to $10 par and (1) additional share issued 01/30/1962
Stock Dividend - 10% 01/18/1960
99.64% acquired by Centerre Bancorporation through exchange offer which expired 06/30/1974
Public interest eliminated

FIRST NATL BK (ST. PETERSBURG, FL)
Each share Capital Stock $100 par exchanged for (10) shares Capital Stock $10 par 08/11/1954
Each share Capital Stock $10 par exchanged for (2) shares Capital Stock $5 par 12/14/1955
Stock Dividends - 100% 12/21/1951; 25% 08/11/1954; 20% 12/14/1955; 10% 03/01/1968
98.5% acquired by Charter Bankshares Corp. through exchange offer which expired 02/20/1976
Public interest eliminated

FIRST NATL BK (STEVENS POINT, WI)
Common $10 par changed to $5 par and (1) additional share issued plus a 20% stock dividend paid 02/27/1970
Stock Dividend - 25% 03/15/1973
Through voluntary exchange offer over 99% acquired by First Affiliated Bancorporation, Inc. as of 04/20/1979
First Affiliated Bancorporation, Inc. merged into Marshall & Ilsley Corp. (Old) 11/28/1986
(See Marshall & Ilsley Corp. (Old))

FIRST NATL BK (STRASBURG, PA)
Name changed to First National Bank of Lancaster County (Strasburg, PA) 09/01/1980
First National Bank of Lancaster County (Strasburg, PA) reorganized as Sterling Financial Corp. 07/01/1987
(See Sterling Financial Corp.)

FIRST NATL BK (SUFFIELD, CT)
Reorganized as First Suffield Financial, Inc. 9/1/2006
Each share Common $25 par exchanged for (1) share Common $25 par

FIRST NATL BK (SUNBURY, PA)
Each share Common $25 par exchanged for (5) shares Common $6.25 par to effect a (4) for (1) split

and a 25% stock dividend 06/07/1951
Under plan of merger name changed to First National Trust Bank (Sunbury, PA) 10/02/1972
First National Trust Bank (Sunbury, PA) reorganized as FNT Bancorp, Inc. 05/03/1984 which merged into Susquehanna Bancshares, Inc. 10/01/1985 which merged into BB&T Corp. 08/01/2015

FIRST NATL BK (TAMPA, FL)
Each share Capital Stock $100 par exchanged for (5) shares Capital Stock $20 par plus a 33-1/3% stock dividend paid 00/00/1952
Capital Stock $20 par changed to $5 par and (3) additional shares issued 02/09/1965
Stock Dividends - 20% 01/16/1946; 25% 05/04/1955; 20% 06/26/1958; 33-1/3% 01/08/1963; 10% 02/00/1966; 10% 02/17/1967
Name changed to First National Bank of Florida (Tampa, FL) 10/01/1976
(See First National Bank of Florida (Tampa, FL))

FIRST NATL BK (TITUSVILLE, FL)
Merged into First Florida Bancorporation 09/30/1971
Each share Common exchanged for (2.67) shares Common $1 par
First Florida Bancorporation name changed to United First Florida Banks, Inc. 06/29/1973 which name changed to Flagship Banks, Inc. 06/30/1974 which merged into Sun Banks, Inc. 01/01/1984 which merged into SunTrust Banks, Inc. 07/01/1985

FIRST NATL BK (TOLEDO, OH)
Capital Stock $25 par changed to $12.50 par and (1) additional share issued 2/18/70
Capital Stock $12.50 par changed to $6.25 par and (1) additional share issued 3/5/76
Stock Dividends - 10% 3/22/67; 10% 10/8/75; 10% 1/8/78
Reorganized as First Ohio Bancshares, Inc. 7/1/80
Each share Capital Stock $6.25 par exchanged for (1) share Capital Stock $6.25 par
First Ohio Bancshares, Inc. merged into Fifth Third Bancorp 11/30/89

FIRST NATL BK (TOMS RIVER, NJ)
Each share Capital Stock $25 par exchanged for (2.5) shares Capital Stock $10 par 9/22/49
Each share Capital Stock $10 par exchanged for (2) shares Capital Stock $5 par 1/8/57
Stock Dividends - 66-2/3% 4/24/61; 100% 6/12/72
Reorganized as Statewide Bancorp 8/16/82
Each share Capital Stock $5 par exchanged for (1) share Common $5 par
(See Statewide Bancorp)

FIRST NATL BK (TOPEKA, KS)
Stock Dividends - 100% 1/22/63; 20% 2/25/69
Reorganized as First Topeka Bankshares, Inc. 12/5/69
Each share Capital Stock $10 par exchanged for (1) share Common $10 par
First Topeka Bankshares, Inc. merged into Fourth Financial Corp. 12/17/85 which merged into Boatmen's Bancshares, Inc. 1/31/96 which merged into NationsBank Corp. 1/7/97 which reincorporated in Delaware as BankAmerica Corp. (Old) 9/25/98 which merged into BankAmerica Corp. (New) 9/30/98 which name changed to Bank of America Corp. 4/28/99

FIRST NATL BK (TUCKERTON, NJ)
Merged into Peoples National Bank of New Jersey (Westmont, NJ) 09/13/1971
Each share Common $18.75 par exchanged for (8) shares Common Capital Stock $3.75 par
Peoples National Bank of New Jersey (Westmont, NJ) name changed to First Peoples National Bank of New Jersey (Westmont, NJ) 06/30/1974 which name changed to First Peoples Bank of New Jersey (Westmont, NJ) 03/20/1978 which reorganized as First Peoples Financial Corp. 03/03/1987 which merged into CoreStates Financial Corp 09/03/1992 which merged into First Union Corp. 04/28/1998 which name changed to Wachovia Corp. (Ctfs. dated after 09/01/2001) 09/01/2001 which merged into Wells Fargo & Co. (New) 12/31/2008

FIRST NATL BK (TUSCALOOSA, AL)
Common $50 par changed to $12.50 par and (3) additional shares issued plus a 33-1/3% stock dividend paid 8/27/56
Common $12.50 par changed to $5 par and (1.5) additional shares issued 8/6/59
Stock Dividends - 25% 9/15/58; 50% 5/24/72
Under plan of reorganization each share Common $5 par automatically became (1) share First Tuskaloosa Corp. Common $5 par 7/18/83
First Tuskaloosa Corp. acquired by AmSouth Bancorporation 4/20/87 which merged into Regions Financial Corp. 11/4/2006

FIRST NATL BK (UVALDE, TX)
Merged into Praesidium Capital 1/18/2000
Each share Common exchanged for $28.57 cash

FIRST NATL BK (VENICE, FL)
Merged into Florida Westcoast Banks, Inc. 7/15/82
Each share Common $10 par exchanged for (1) share Common no par

FIRST NATL BK (VENTURA, CA)
Name changed to Bank of Ventura (Ventura, CA) 6/11/97

FIRST NATL BK (VICKSBURG, MS)
Stock Dividends - 10% 12/31/79; 10% 12/31/81
Reorganized as First National Financial Corp. 2/18/93
Each share Common $8 par exchanged for (2) shares Common $8 par
First National Financial Corp. merged into Trustmark Corp. 10/7/94

FIRST NATL BK (VIENNA, VA)
Merged into Suburban National Bank of Virginia (McLean, VA) 8/31/68
Each share Capital Stock $10 par exchanged for (0.75) share Capital Stock $10 par
Suburban National Bank of Virginia (McLean, VA) merged into First & Merchants Corp. 8/1/70 which merged into Sovran Financial Corp. 12/31/83 which merged into C&S/Sovran Corp. 9/1/90 which merged into NationsBank Corp. 12/31/91 which reincorporated in Delaware as BankAmerica Corp. (Old) 9/25/98 which merged into BankAmerica Corp. (New) 9/30/98 which name changed to Bank of America Corp. 4/28/99

FIRST NATIONAL BANK (VISTA, CA)
Stock Dividend - 10% 1/24/66
Merged into Liberty National Bank (San Francisco, CA) 12/15/67
Each share Capital Stock $3.33-1/3 par exchanged for (2) shares Common $2 par
(See Liberty National Bank (San Francisco, CA))

FIRST NATL BK (WACO, TX)
Each share Common $50 par exchanged for (5) shares Common $10 par 00/00/1951
Stock Dividend - 25% 06/30/1959
Merged into Pan National Group, Inc. 06/30/1975
Each share Common $10 par exchanged for $76 cash

FIRST NATIONAL BANK (WALLACE, ID)
Name changed to First National Bank of North Idaho (Wallace, ID) 03/08/1974
(See First National Bank of North Idaho (Wallace, ID))

FIRST NATL BK (WARREN, MI)
Reorganized as First National Bancorp 7/1/70
Each share Common $1 par exchanged for (1) share Class A Common $10 par
First National Bancorp name changed to First United Financial Corp. 12/3/71
(See First United Financial Corp.)

FIRST NATL BK (WASHINGTON, DC)
Capital Stock $50 par changed to $10 par and (4) additional shares issued plus a 33-1/3% stock dividend paid 1/21/64
Capital Stock $10 par changed to $5 par and (1) additional share issued 12/30/71
Stock Dividend - 10% 12/31/73
Under plan of merger name changed to Union First National Bank (Washington, DC) 1/1/76
Union First National Bank (Washington, DC) name changed to First American Bank, N.A. (Washington, DC) 3/17/80
(See First American Bank, N.A. (Washington, DC))

FIRST NATL BK (WATERLOO, NY)
Completely liquidated 12/23/82
Each share Capital Stock $10 par exchanged for first and final distribution of $50 cash

FIRST NATL BK (WAUKESHA, WI)
Capital Stock $25 par changed to $8.33-1/3 par and (2) additional shares issued 01/14/1964
Stock Dividends - 50% 12/30/1941; 11-1/9% 02/14/1952; 33-1/3% 01/17/1955; 37-1/2% 02/13/1959
Acquired by First Holding Co., Inc. 04/30/1968
Each share Capital Stock $8.33-1/3 par exchanged for (1) share Common $8.33-1/3 par
First Holding Co., Inc. name changed to Independence Bank Group, Inc. 11/12/1980
(See Independence Bank Group, Inc.)

FIRST NATL BK (WELLSTON, OH)
Common $2.50 par split (100) for (1) by issuance of (99) additional shares 08/00/1994
Reorganized as Midwest Bancshares, Inc. 04/02/2008
Each share Common $2.50 par exchanged for (1) share Common no par
Midwest Bancshares, Inc. merged into Peoples Bancorp Inc. 05/30/2014

FIRST NATL BK (WEST CHESTER, PA)
Reorganized as First West Chester Corp. 09/13/1984
Each share Common $20 par exchanged for (1) share Common $20 par
First West Chester Corp. name changed to First Chester County Corp. 06/01/2000 which merged into Tower Bancorp, Inc. 12/10/2010
(See Tower Bancorp, Inc.)

FIRST NATL BK (WESTWOOD, NJ)
Common $75 par changed to $5 par and (14) additional shares issued 1/23/51
Stock Dividend - 20% 6/12/56
Merged into New Jersey Bank (N.A.) (Clifton, NJ) 12/30/74
Each share Common $5 par exchanged for $75 cash

FIRST NATL BK (WICHITA, KS)
Stock Dividends - 100% 1/10/50; 100% 1/18/62; 100% 4/1/81; 100% 8/1/81
Reorganized as First Bancorp of Kansas 12/31/82
Each share Capital Stock $100 par exchanged for (1) share Common $100 par
First Bancorp of Kansas name changed to Intrust Financial Corp. in May 1993
(See Intrust Financial Corp.)

FIRST NATL BK (WILKES-BARRE, PA)
Stock Dividends - 25% 9/26/61; 10% 12/9/68
Name changed to First National Bank of Eastern Pennsylvania (Wilkes-Barre, PA) 4/1/71
First National Bank of Eastern Pennsylvania (Wilkes-Barre, PA) name changed to First Eastern Bank, N.A. (Wilkes-Barre, PA) 11/16/74 which reorganized as First Eastern Corp. 8/2/82
(See First Eastern Corp.)

FIRST NATL BK (WILLIAMSPORT, PA)
Merged into Fidelity National Bank of Pennsylvania (Williamsport, PA) 11/01/1968
Each share Common $10 par exchanged for (1) share Common $10 par
Fidelity National Bank of Pennsylvania (Williamsport, PA) merged into Commonwealth Bank & Trust Co., N.A. (Williamsport, PA) 05/29/1981 which reorganized as Commonwealth Bancshares Corp. 03/01/1982 which was acquired by Meridian Bancorp, Inc. 08/31/1993 which merged into CoreStates Financial Corp 04/09/1996 which merged into First Union Corp. 04/28/1998 which name changed to Wachovia Corp. (Ctfs. dated after 09/01/2001) 09/01/2001 which merged into Wells Fargo & Co. (New) 12/31/2008

FIRST NATIONAL BANK (WINTER PARK, FL)
Capital Stock $20 par changed to $10 par and (1) additional share issued 7/25/60
Stock Dividends - (1) for (5.5) 9/10/62; 25% 12/15/65
Thru voluntary exchange offer over 99% acquired by Barnett Banks of Florida, Inc. as of 5/20/71
Public interest eliminated

FIRST NATL BK (YONKERS, NY)
Each share Capital Stock $10 par exchanged for (4) shares Capital Stock $2.50 par and (6) additional shares distributed as a stock dividend 1/19/55
Stock Dividends - 20% 10/28/55; 10% 1/31/56; 10% 2/8/61; 10% 3/10/66
Merged into National Bank of North America (West Hempstead, NY) 10/13/70
Each share Capital Stock $2.50 par exchanged for (0.125) share C.I.T. Financial Corp. $5.50 Conv. Preferred 1970 Ser. no par and (0.3125) share Common no par
(See C.I.T. Financial Corp.)

FIRST NATL BK (YORK, PA)
Stock Dividends - 25% 9/8/61; 100% 2/1/64
Merged into Commonwealth National Bank (Harrisburg, PA) 1/1/70

Each share Capital Stock $10 par exchanged for (1) share Common $10 par and $1.24 cash
Commonwealth National Bank (Harrisburg, PA) reorganized as Commonwealth National Financial Corp. 3/5/82
(See Commonwealth National Financial Corp.)

FIRST NATL BK ANSON CNTY (WADESBORO, NC)
Merged into Southern National Corp. 3/31/84
Each share Common $10 par exchanged for (2.0355) shares Common $5 par
Southern National Corp. merged into BB&T Corp. 5/19/97

FIRST NATL BK ARIZ (PHOENIX, AZ)
Stock Dividends - 50% 11/18/53; 25% 8/2/55
Merged into Western Bancorporation 7/1/80
Each share Capital Stock $10 par exchanged for (3.1) shares Capital Stock $2 par
Western Bancorporation name changed to First Interstate Bancorp 6/1/81 merged into Wells Fargo & Co. (Old) 4/1/96 which merged into Wells Fargo & Co. (New) 11/2/98

FIRST NATL BK BEAR VALLEY (DENVER, CO)
Merged into First National Bancorporation, Inc. 01/19/1982
Each share Capital Stock $1 par exchanged for (0.298) share Common $10 par
First National Bancorporation, Inc. name changed to IntraWest Financial Corp. 10/01/1982 which merged into United Banks of Colorado, Inc. 04/30/1987 which merged into Norwest Corp. 04/19/1991 which name changed to Wells Fargo & Co. (New) 11/02/1998

FIRST NATL BK BREVARD (MERRITT ISLAND, FL)
Merged into First Florida Banks, Inc. 10/1/84
Each share Capital Stock $5 par exchanged for $46 cash

FIRST NATL BK CATAWBA CNTY (HICKORY, NC)
Each share Common $25 par exchanged for (6) shares Common $5 par to effect a (5) for (1) split and a 20% stock dividend 00/00/1954
Common $5 par changed to $2.50 par and (1) additional share issued 10/03/1973
Stock Dividends - 10% 03/15/1966; 10% 03/15/1968; 10% 10/17/1972; 10% 02/01/1979
Merged into First Union Corp. 11/01/1981
Each share Common $2.50 par exchanged for (1.5) shares Common $3.33-1/3 par
First Union Corp. name changed to Wachovia Corp. (Ctfs. dated after 09/01/2001) 09/01/2001 which merged into Wells Fargo & Co. (New) 12/31/2008

FIRST NATL BK CENT JERSEY (SOMERVILLE, NJ)
Common $12.50 par changed to $5 par and (2) additional shares issued 11/5/69
Stock Dividend - 10% 12/10/76
Location changed to First National Bank of Central Jersey (Bridgewater, NJ) 9/1/77
First National Bank of Central Jersey (Bridgewater, NJ) reorganized as Ultra Bancorporation 3/7/83
(See Ultra Bancorporation)

FIRST NATL BK CORP (DE)
Common $3.125 par split (4) for (3) by issuance of (1/3) additional share 11/24/93
Merged into Old Kent Financial Corp. 2/1/95
Each share Common $3.125 par exchanged for (1.0813) shares Common $1 par
Old Kent Financial Corp. merged into Fifth Third Bancorp 4/2/2001

FIRST NATL BK EASTN N C (JACKSONVILLE, NC)
Reorganized as Financial Corp. 3/14/69
Each share Common $10 par exchanged for (2) shares Common $5 par
Financial Corp. name changed to Bancshares of North Carolina, Inc. 3/10/71 which merged into NCNB Corp. 12/23/82 which name changed to NationsBank Corp. 12/31/91 which reincorporated in Delaware as BankAmerica Corp. (Old) 9/25/98 which merged into BankAmerica Corp. (New) 9/30/98 which name changed to Bank of America Corp. 4/28/99

FIRST NATL BK EASTN PA (WILKES-BARRE, PA)
Common $20 par changed to $10 par and (1) additional share issued 4/30/71
Name changed to First Eastern Bank, N.A. (Wilkes-Barre, PA) 11/16/74
First Eastern Bank, N.A. (Wilkes-Barre, PA) reorganized as First Eastern Corp. 8/2/82
(See First Eastern Corp.)

FIRST NATL BK ELKHART (ELKHART, IN)
Name changed to First National Bank (Elkhart, IN) 2/10/70
First National Bank (Elkhart, IN) merged into First Indiana Bancorp 11/5/82 which was acquired by Ameritrust Corp. 5/30/86 which merged into Society Corp. 3/16/92 which merged into KeyCorp (New) 3/1/94

FIRST NATL BK FRANKLIN CNTY (GREENFIELD, MA)
Through voluntary exchange offer 99.99% held by First Pioneer Corp. as of 07/01/1973
Public interest eliminated

FIRST NATL BK GREATER MIAMI (MIAMI, FL)
Name changed to Consolidated Bank, N.A. (Hialeah, FL) 02/01/1982
(See Consolidated Bank, N.A. (Hialeah, FL))

FIRST NATL BK HAWAII (HONOLULU, HI)
Each share Common $20 par exchanged for (2) shares Common $10 par 04/25/1960
Name changed to First Hawaiian Bank (Honolulu, HI) 01/02/1969
First Hawaiian Bank (Honolulu, HI) reorganized as First Hawaiian, Inc. 07/01/1974 which name changed to BancWest Corp. (New) 11/01/1998
(See BancWest Corp. (New))

FIRST NATL BK HLDG CO (CO)
Name changed to First Mainstreet Financial Ltd. 01/01/2003
First Maintstreet Financial Ltd. merged into Centennial Bank Holdings, Inc. 10/01/2005 which name changed to Guaranty Bancorp 05/12/2008

FIRST NATL BK JEFFERSON PARISH (GRETNA, LA)
Capital Stock $20 par changed to $10 par and (2) additional shares issued 9/12/67
Reorganized as First Continental Bancshares, Inc. 6/30/82
Each share Capital Stock $10 par exchanged for (1) share Conv. Preferred Series A $1 par and (1) share Common $1 par
First Continental Bancshares, Inc. acquired by Hibernia Corp. 8/1/94 which merged into Capital One Financial Corp. 11/16/2005

FIRST NATL BK JOHNS CREEK (SUWANEE, GA)
Merged into Main Street Banks, Inc. (GA) 12/11/2002
Each share Common exchanged for either (1.1823) shares Common no par or $24 cash
Note: Option to receive cash expired 2/14/2003
Main Street Banks, Inc. (GA) merged into BB&T Corp. 6/1/2006

FIRST NATL BK LANCASTER CNTY (STRASBURG, PA)
Common $2.50 par changed to $10 par 04/29/1983
Stock Dividend - 100% 05/31/1985
Under plan of reorganization each share Common $10 par automatically became (1) share Sterling Financial Corp. Common $5 par and (1) additional share issued 07/01/1987
(See Sterling Financial Corp.)

FIRST NATL BK LAWRENCE CNTY (NEW CASTLE, PA)
Capital Stock $10 par changed to $5 par and (1) additional share issued 11/30/1976
Name changed to First National Bank of Western Pennsylvania (New Castle, PA) 07/01/1980
First National Bank of Western Pennsylvania (New Castle, PA) reorganized as First Western PennBancorp, Inc. 04/04/1984 which name changed to First Western Bancorp, Inc. 04/08/1985 which merged into Sky Financial Group, Inc. 08/06/1999 which merged into Huntington Bancshares Inc. 07/02/2007

FIRST NATL BK LONG IS (GLEN HEAD, NY)
Reorganized as First of Long Island Corp. 05/01/1984
Each share Common $5 par exchanged for (1) share Common 10¢ par

FIRST NATL BK MANATEE (BRADENTON, FL)
Stock Dividend - 5% payable 08/31/1998 to holders of record 08/01/1998
Under plan of reorganization each share Common $5 par automatically became (2) shares First National Bancshares Inc. Common $5 par 01/01/1999
First National Bancshares Inc. merged into Whitney Holding Corp. 04/13/2006 which merged into Hancock Holding Co. 06/04/2011

FIRST NATL BK MARTINSVILLE & HENRY CNTY (MARTINSVILLE, VA)
Capital Stock $5 par split (10) for (1) by issuance of (9) additional shares in 1942
Capital Stock $10 par changed to $5 par and (1) additional share issued 2/2/70
Stock Dividends - 100% in 1945; 100% 8/25/55; 10% 1/8/61; 44.3% 1/14/65; 10% 4/17/72; 100% 3/20/76
Merged into United Virginia Bankshares, Inc. 12/1/82
Each share Capital Stock $5 par exchanged for (1) share $2.75 Conv. Preferred Ser. A $25 par and (0.582) share Common $10 par
United Virginia Bankshares, Inc. name changed to Crestar Financial Corp. 9/1/87 which merged into SunTrust Banks, Inc. 12/31/98

FIRST NATL BK MD (BALTIMORE, MD)
Common $10 par changed to $5 par and (1) additional share issued plus a 15% stock dividend paid 11/1/68
Stock Dividend - 20% 5/1/73
Under plan of reorganization each share Common $5 par automatically became (1) share First Maryland Bancorp Common $5 par 7/8/74
(See First Maryland Bancorp)

FIRST NATL BK MERCER CNTY (GREENVILLE, PA)
Capital Stock $25 par changed to $10 par and (1.5) additional shares issued 8/15/64
Reorganized as F.N.B. Corp. (PA) 4/23/75
Each share Capital Stock $10 par exchanged for (1) share Common $10 par
F.N.B. Corp. (PA) reincorporated in Florida 6/13/2001

FIRST NATL BK MIDDLESEX CNTY (EAST BRUNSWICK, NJ)
Capital Stock $25 par changed to $12.50 par and (1) additional share issued 2/3/66
Capital Stock $12.50 par changed to $6.25 par and (1) additional share issued 9/27/67
Stock Dividend - 11% 9/8/61
Name changed to First Charter National Bank (East Brunswick, NJ) 4/1/69
First Charter National Bank (East Brunswick, NJ) merged into Heritage Bancorporation 12/31/73
(See Heritage Bancorporation)

FIRST NATL BK N J (TOTOWA, NJ)
Capital Stock $10 par changed to $5 par and (1) additional share issued 10/28/77
Stock Dividends - 25% 12/1/76; 10% 7/21/78
Merged into First National State Bancorporation 9/6/83
Each share Capital Stock $5 par exchanged for $37.25 cash

FIRST NATL BK NEV (RENO, NV)
Stock Dividend - 10% 3/5/69
Merged into Western Bancorporation 10/1/79
Each share Common $10 par exchanged for (2.4) shares Capital Stock $2 par
Western Bancorporation name changed to First Interstate Bancorp 6/1/81 which merged into Wells Fargo & Co. (Old) 4/1/96 which merged into Wells Fargo & Co. (New) 11/2/98

FIRST NATL BK NORTH BROWARD CNTY (LIGHTHOUSE POINT, FL)
Stock Dividends - 10% 03/01/1966; 12-1/2% 03/01/1968; 16-2/3% 07/01/1968; 35.50136% 04/01/1970
Through voluntary exchange offer all but directors qualifying shares were acquired by First National Bankshares of Florida, Inc. as of 04/17/1972
Public interest eliminated

FIRST NATL BK NORTH CNTY (CARLSBAD, CA)
Merged into New First National Bank 7/1/97
Each share Common exchanged for $2.25 cash

FIRST NATL BK NORTHN CALIF (SOUTH SAN FRANCISCO, CA)
Name changed 10/00/1995
Name changed from First National Bank (Daly, CA) to First National Bank of Northern California (South San Francisco, CA) 10/00/1995
Stock Dividends - 5% payable 11/15/1997 to holders of record 10/15/1997; 5% payable 12/15/1999 to holders of record 10/20/1999; 5% payable 12/14/2001 to holders of record 11/30/2001 Ex date - 12/15/2001
Merged into FNB Bancorp 03/15/2002

Each share Common $1.25 par exchanged for (1) share Common no par
FNB Bancorp merged into TriCo Bancshares 07/06/2018

FIRST NATIONAL BANK OF BATH (BATH, PA)
Reorganized as First Bath Corp. 02/00/1983
Each share Capital Stock $10 par exchanged for (2) shares Common $10 par
First Bath Corp. merged into Meridian Bancorp, Inc. 12/10/1993 which merged into CoreStates Financial Corp 04/09/1996 which merged into First Union Corp. 04/28/1998 which name changed to Wachovia Corp. (Ctfs. dated after 09/01/2001) 09/01/2001 which merged into Wells Fargo & Co. (New) 12/31/2008

FIRST NATIONAL BANK OF BURLINGTON COUNTY (CINNAMINSON, NJ)
Name changed to Friendly National Bank of New Jersey (Cinnaminson, NJ) 05/15/1974
Friendly National Bank of New Jersey (Cinnaminson, NJ) name changed to Eastern National Bank (Cinnaminson, NJ) 04/12/1983 which name changed to Cherry Hill National Bank (Medford, NJ) 04/27/1987 which merged into Meridian Bancorp, Inc. 04/16/1993 which merged into CoreStates Financial Corp 04/09/1996 which merged into First Union Corp. 04/28/1998 which name changed to Wachovia Corp. (Ctfs. dated after 09/01/2001) 09/01/2001 which merged into Wells Fargo & Co. (New) 12/31/2008

FIRST NATIONAL BANK OF BURLINGTON COUNTY (RIVERSIDE, NJ)
Changed location to First National Bank of Burlington County (Cinnaminson, NJ) 06/24/1971
First National Bank of Burlington County (Cinnaminson, NJ) name changed to Friendly National Bank of New Jersey (Cinnaminson, NJ) 05/15/1974 which name changed to Eastern National Bank (Cinnaminson, NJ) 04/12/1983 which name changed to Cherry Hill National Bank (Medford, NJ) 04/27/1987 which merged into Meridian Bancorp, Inc. 04/16/1993 which merged into Corestates Financial Corp 04/09/1996 which merged into First Union Corp. 04/28/1998 which name changed to Wachovia Corp. (Ctfs. dated after 09/01/2001) 09/01/2001 which merged into Wells Fargo & Co. (New) 12/31/2008

FIRST NATIONAL BANK OF CENTRAL JERSEY (BRIDGEWATER, NJ)
Under plan of reorganization each share Common $5 par automatically became (1) share Ultra Bancorporation Common $5 par 3/7/83
(See Ultra Bancorporation)

FIRST NATIONAL BANK OF FLORIDA (TAMPA, FL)
Thru voluntary exchange offer 99.1% acquired by First Financial Corp. (Fla.) as of 6/30/77
Public interest eliminated

FIRST NATIONAL BANK OF LIBERTYVILLE (LIBERTYVILLE, IL)
Under plan of reorganization each share Common $10 par automatically became (1) share First Lake County Corp. Common $10 par 5/1/81

FIRST NATIONAL BANK OF NORTH COUNTY (CARLSBAD, CA)
Merged into First National Bank of Southern California (Riverside, CA) 11/11/2007
Details not available

FIRST NATIONAL BANK OF NORTH IDAHO (WALLACE, ID)
Stock Dividend - 10% 03/25/1977
Acquired by First Security Bank of Idaho, N.A. (Boise, ID) 01/25/1992
Details not available

FIRST NATIONAL BANK OF PUERTO RICO (SAN JUAN, PR)
Name changed to Banco Santander Puerto Rico (San Juan, PR) 05/02/1977
Banco Santander Puerto Rico (San Juan, PR) reorganized as Santander BanCorp 05/01/2000
(See Santander BanCorp)

FIRST NATIONAL BANK OF RANDOLPH COUNTY (ASHEBORO, NC)
Acquired by First National Bank & Trust Co. (Asheboro, NC) 10/01/1990
Details not available

FIRST NATIONAL BANK OF SOMERSET COUNTY (BOUND BROOK, NJ)
Location changed to First National Bank of Somerset County (Somerville, N.J.) in 1964
First National Bank of Somerset County (Somerville, N.J.) name changed to First National Bank of Central Jersey (Somerville, N.J.) 5/1/69 which changed location to First National Bank of Central Jersey (Bridgewater, N.J.) 9/1/77 which reorganized as Ultra Bancorporation 3/7/83
(See Ultra Bancorporation)

FIRST NATL BK OF THE GULF COAST (NAPLES, FL)
Reorganized as TGR Financial, Inc. 09/25/2012
Each share Common $5 par exchanged for (1) share Common $1 par

FIRST NATL BK OF VT (SPRINGFIELD, VT)
Reorganized as First National Vermont Corp. 2/28/81
Each share Common $10 par exchanged for (2) shares Common $1 par
First National Vermont Corp. name changed to Independent Bankgroup Inc. 4/24/86
(See Independent Bankgroup Inc.)

FIRST NATL BK ORANGE CNTY (ORANGE, CA)
Stock Dividend - 25% 10/20/73
Merged into Wells Fargo Bank, N.A. (San Francisco, CA) 5/6/78
Each share Common $6.25 par exchanged for $85.714 cash

FIRST NATL BK ORE (PORTLAND, OR)
Common $12.50 par changed to $7.50 par and (2/3) additional share issued 9/12/69
Common $7.50 par changed to $10 par 3/1/73
Stock Dividends - 12-1/2% 2/15/61; 20% 2/19/64; 25% 4/1/66; 12-1/2% 4/1/68
Merged into Western Bancorporation 7/1/80
Each share Common $10 par exchanged for (1.65) shares Capital Stock $2 par
Western Bancorporation name changed to First Interstate Bancorp 6/1/81 which merged into Wells Fargo & Co. (Old) 4/1/96 which merged into Wells Fargo & Co. (New) 11/2/98

FIRST NATL BK OSCEOLA CNTY (KISSIMMEE, FL)
Merged into CenterState Banks of Florida, Inc. 06/30/2000
Each share Common $5 par exchanged for (2) shares Common 1¢ par
CenterState Banks of Florida, Inc. name changed to Centerstate Banks, Inc. 06/17/2009 which name changed to CenterState Bank Corp. 09/08/2017

FIRST NATL BK PA (MEADVILLE, PA)
5% Conv. Preferred Ser. A $100 par called for redemption 03/01/1980
Stock Dividend - 100% 03/27/1972
Under plan of reorganization each share Common $12.50 par automatically became (1) share First National Pennsylvania Corp. Common $12.50 par 11/19/1981
First National Pennsylvania Corp. merged into PNC Financial Corp. 07/24/1992 which name changed to PNC Financial Services Group, Inc. 03/15/2000

FIRST NATL BK PALM BEACH INC (FL)
Merged into Southeast Banking Corp. 12/23/86
Each share Common $10 par exchanged for $175.0154395 cash

FIRST NATL BK PASCO (DADE CITY, FL)
Under plan of reorganization each share Common no par automatically became (1) share Florida Bancshares Inc. Common no par 5/31/97

FIRST NATL BK PASSAIC CNTY (TOTOWA, NJ)
Capital Stock $25 par changed to $10 par and (1.5) additional shares issued 4/10/67
Stock Dividends - 10% 2/10/61; 11-1/9% 1/28/64
Name changed to First National Bank of New Jersey (Totowa, NJ) 4/1/71
(See First National Bank of New Jersey (Totowa, NJ))

FIRST NATL BK PICKENS CNTY (EASLEY, SC)
Merged into Carolina First Corp. 09/29/1998
Each share Common no par exchanged for (35.2201) shares Common $1 par
Carolina First Corp. name changed to South Financial Group, Inc. 04/24/2000 which merged into Toronto-Dominion Bank (Toronto, ON) 09/30/2010

FIRST NATL BK POLK CNTY (WINTER HAVEN, FL)
Merged into CenterState Banks of Florida, Inc. 06/30/2000
Each share Common $5 par exchanged for (1.62) shares Common 1¢ par
CenterState Banks of Florida, Inc. name changed to Centerstate Banks, Inc. 06/17/2009 which name changed to CenterState Bank Corp. 09/08/2017

FIRST NATL BK PORT ALLEGANY (PORT ALLEGANY, PA)
Common $25 par split (4) for (1) by issuance of (3) additional shares payable 05/02/1995 to holders of record 04/18/1995
Common $25 par split (4) for (1) by issuance of (3) additional shares payable 05/16/2001 to holders of record 04/17/2001 Ex date - 06/04/2001
Reorganized as FNBPA Bancorp, Inc. 12/11/2009
Each share Common $25 par exchanged for (1) share Common $25 par
Note: Unexchanged certificates were cancelled and became without value 12/11/2011
FNBPA Bancorp, Inc. merged into Juniata Valley Financial Corp. 11/30/2015

FIRST NATL BK QUAD CITIES (ROCK ISLAND, IL)
Reorganized as Quad Cities First Co. 06/30/1982
Each share Capital Stock $10 par exchanged for (1) share Common $10 par
Quad Cities First Co. merged into First of America Bank Corp. 12/31/1988 which merged into National City Corp. 03/31/1998 which was acquired by PNC Financial Services Group, Inc. 12/31/2008

FIRST NATL BK SAN DIEGO CNTY (ESCONDIDO, CA)
Acquired by Mitsubishi Bank, Ltd. 3/7/81
Each share Common $1 par exchanged for $17 cash

FIRST NATL BK SC (COLUMBIA, SC)
Capital Stock $10 par changed to $5 par and (1) additional share issued 02/14/1962
Stock Dividends - 25% 06/07/1948; 10% 12/20/1956; 10% 06/15/1964; 10% 06/27/1966
Under plan of merger name changed to First Commercial National Bank of South Carolina (Columbia, SC) 12/31/1964 which name changed back to First National Bank of South Carolina (Columbia, SC) 12/10/1965
Reorganized as First Bankshares Corp. of S.C. 07/19/1969
Each share Capital Stock $5 par exchanged for (1) share Common $5 par
First Bankshares Corp. of S.C. liquidated for South Carolina National Corp. 12/01/1984 which merged into Wachovia Corp. (New) (Ctfs. dated between 05/20/1991 and 09/01/2001) 12/06/1991 which merged into Wachovia Corp. (Ctfs. dated after 09/01/2001) 09/01/2001 which merged into Wells Fargo & Co. (New) 12/31/2008

FIRST NATL BK SOMERSET CNTY (SOMERVILLE, NJ)
Common $25 par changed to $12.50 par and (1) additional share issued 2/3/65
Stock Dividend - 25% 12/27/68
Name changed to First National Bank of Central Jersey (Somerville, NJ) 5/1/69
First National Bank of Central Jersey (Somerville, NJ) location changed to First National Bank of Central Jersey (Bridgewater, NJ) 9/1/77 which reorganized as Ultra Bancorporation 3/7/83
(See Ultra Bancorporation)

FIRST NATL BK SOUTH JERSEY (PLEASANTVILLE, NJ)
Merged into First National State Bancorporation 12/31/1980
Each share Capital Stock $10 par exchanged for (0.2) share $2.30 Conv. Preferred Ser. A no par and (0.8) share Common $6.25 par
First National State Bancorporation name changed to First Fidelity Bancorporation (Old) 05/01/1985 which merged into First Fidelity Bancorporation (New) 02/29/1988 which merged into First Union Corp. 01/01/1996 which name changed to Wachovia Corp. (Ctfs. dated after 09/01/2001) 09/01/2001 which merged into Wells Fargo & Co. (New) 12/31/2008

FIRST NATL BK SOUTHWESTN MICH (NILES, MI)
Common $10 par changed to $5 par

and (1) additional share issued 3/1/67
Stock Dividends - 10% 3/2/70; 10% 11/1/74
Under plan of reorganization each share Common $5 par automatically became (1) share Western Michigan Corp. Capital Stock $5 par 11/10/75
Western Michigan Corp. merged into Pacesetter Financial Corp. (DE) 2/1/78 which reincorporated in Michigan 3/10/80
(See Pacesetter Financial Corp. (MI))

FIRST NATL BK SOUTHWESTN OHIO (MONROE, OH)
Reorganized as First Financial Bancorp 04/26/1983
Each share Common $10 par exchanged for (1.25) shares Common $8 par

FIRST NATL BK SPANGLER (SPANGLER, PA)
Merged into CNB Financial Corp. 8/18/99
Each share Common $20 par exchanged for (95) shares Common $2 par

FIRST NATL BK SULLIVAN CNTY (KINGSPORT, TN)
Common $25 par changed to $10 par and (2) additional shares issued 1/21/69
Stock Dividends - 27.27% 2/23/69; 25% 2/16/71; 20% 2/18/75; 20% 3/18/80
Name changed to First Eastern National Bank (Kingsport, TN) 10/15/81
(See First Eastern National Bank (Kingsport, TN))

FIRST NATL BK TRUSTEES LOUISVILLE KY (KY)
Trustee Ctfs. no par split (3) for (2) by issuance of (0.5) additional share 12/02/1968
Trustee Ctfs. no par split (3) for (2) by issuance of (0.5) additional share 12/01/1970
Trustee Ctfs. no par split (3) for (2) by issuance of (0.5) additional share 12/01/1972
Completely liquidated 09/09/1974
Each Trustee Ctf. no par exchanged for first and final distribution of (1) share First Kentucky National Corp. Common no par
First Kentucky National Corp. acquired by National City Corp. 07/29/1988 which was acquired by PNC Financial Services Group, Inc. 12/31/2008

FIRST NATL BK WESTERN PA (NEW CASTLE, PA)
Under plan of reorganization each share Capital Stock $5 par automatically became (1) share First Western PennBancorp, Inc. Common $5 par 04/04/1984
First Western PennBancorp, Inc. name changed to First Western Bancorp, Inc. 04/08/1985 which merged into Sky Financial Group, Inc. 08/06/1999 which merged into Huntington Bancshares Inc. 07/02/2007

FIRST NATL BK WESTMORELAND (GREENSBURG, PA)
Merged into Southwest National Bank of Pennsylvania (Greensburg, PA) 6/30/70
Each share Capital Stock $10 par exchanged for (1.5) shares Common $10 par
Southwest National Bank of Pennsylvania (Greensburg, PA) reorganized as Southwest National Corp. 11/6/81 which merged into First Commonwealth Financial Corp. 12/31/98

FIRST NATL BANKSHARES CORP NEW (WV)
Merged into Premier Financial Bancorp, Inc. 01/15/2016
Each share Common $1 par exchanged for (1.69) shares Common no par

FIRST NATL BANKSHARES CORP OLD (WV)
Common $1 par split (5) for (1) by issuance of (4) additional shares payable 09/24/1999 to holders of record 09/08/1999
Merged into First National Bankshares Corp. (New) 02/19/2004
Each share Common $1 par exchanged for $21.70 cash
Note: Holders of (1,500) or more shares retained their interests
First National Bankshares Corp. (New) merged into Premier Financial Bancorp, Inc. 01/15/2016

FIRST NATL BANKSHARES FLA INC (FL)
Name changed to First Bankers Corp. of Florida 05/06/1976
(See First Bankers Corp. of Florida)

FIRST NATL BANKSHARES FLA INC (FL)
Merged into Fifth Third Bancorp 1/1/2005
Each share Common 1¢ par exchanged for (0.5065) share Common no par

FIRST NATL BANKSHARES INC (IN)
Common $5 par split (2) for (1) by issuance of (1) additional share 12/21/87
Acquired by Merchants National Corp. 10/24/89
Each share Common $5 par exchanged for $40 cash

FIRST NATL BANKSHARES INC (LA)
Merged into Whitney Holding Corp. 02/28/1997
Each share Common $2.50 par exchanged for (0.56155) share Common no par
Whitney Holding Corp. merged into Hancock Holding Co. 06/04/2011 which name changed to Hancock Whitney Corp. 05/25/2018

FIRST NATL BOSTON CORP (MA)
Common $12.50 par changed to $6.25 par and (1) additional share issued 09/07/1972
Common $6.25 par changed to $4.50 par and (0.5) additional share issued 04/15/1982
Name changed to Bank of Boston Corp. 04/01/1983
Bank of Boston Corp. name changed to BankBoston Corp. 04/25/1997 which merged into Fleet Boston Financial Corp. 10/01/1999 which name changed to FleetBoston Financial Corp. 04/18/2000 which merged into Bank of America Corp. 04/01/2004

FIRST NATL CHARTER CORP (MO)
Common $12.50 par changed to $6.25 par and (1) additional share issued 5/12/78
Name changed to CharterCorp 6/25/82
CharterCorp merged into Boatmen's Bancshares, Inc. 1/28/85 which merged into NationsBank Corp. 1/7/97 which reincorporated in Delaware as BankAmerica Corp. (Old) 9/25/98 which merged into BankAmerica Corp. (New) 9/30/98 which name changed to Bank of America Corp. 4/28/99

FIRST NATL CINCINNATI CORP (DE)
Common $5 par split (2) for (1) by issuance of (1) additional share 04/01/1985
Common $5 par split (2) for (1) by issuance of (1) additional share 04/14/1989

Stock Dividends - 25% 03/30/1979; 10% 07/14/1984
Name changed to Star Banc Corp. 04/13/1990
Star Banc Corp. merged into Firstar Corp. (New) 11/20/1998 which merged into U.S. Bancorp (DE) 02/27/2001

FIRST NATL CITY BK (ALLIANCE, OH)
Each share Capital Stock $50 par exchanged for (2) shares Capital Stock $25 par 00/00/1950
Capital Stock $25 par changed to $12.50 par and (1) additional share issued 02/25/1969
Capital Stock $12.50 par changed to $4.16-2/3 par and (2) additional shares issued 03/14/1975
Capital Stock $4.16-2/3 par changed to $4 par 03/24/1981
Stock Dividends - 66-2/3% 00/00/1945; 25% 00/00/1950; 20% 00/00/1954; 25% 10/16/1957; 20% 10/17/1961; 20% 11/01/1965; 17.560749% 05/01/1981
Merged into Banc One Corp. (DE) 11/01/1983
Each share Capital Stock $4 par exchanged for (1.3314) shares Common no par
Banc One Corp. (DE) reincorporated in Ohio 05/01/1989 which merged into Bank One Corp. 10/2/98 which merged into J.P. Morgan Chase & Co. 12/31/2000 which which name changed to JPMorgan Chase & Co. 07/20/2004

FIRST NATL CITY BK (NEW YORK, NY)
Capital Stock $20 par changed to $13.50 par and (1) additional share issued 02/18/1965
Under plan of reorganization each share Capital Stock $13.50 par automatically became (1) share First National City Corp. Common $13.50 par 10/31/1968
First National City Corp. name changed to Citicorp 03/26/1974 which merged into Citigroup Inc. 10/08/1998

FIRST NATL CITY CORP (DE)
Common $13.50 par changed to $6.75 par and (1) additional share issued 04/27/1971
Common $6.75 par changed to $4 par and (1) additional share issued 04/27/1973
Name changed to Citicorp 03/26/1974
Citicorp merged into Citigroup Inc. 10/08/1998

FIRST NATL CMNTY BANCORP INC (PA)
Common $1.25 par split (2) for (1) by issuance of (1) additional share payable 01/31/2003 to holders of record 12/16/2002 Ex date - 02/03/2003
Stock Dividends - 10% payable 03/31/2006 to holders of record 03/20/2006 Ex date - 03/16/2006; 25% payable 12/27/2007 to holders of record 12/17/2007 Ex date - 12/28/2007
Name changed to FNCB Bancorp, Inc. 11/30/2016

1ST NATL CMNTY BK (EAST LIVERPOOL, OH)
Under plan of reorganization each share Common $6.25 par automatically became (1) share Tri-State 1st Bank Inc. Common no par 05/31/1996
Tri-State 1st Bank Inc. name changed to Tri-State 1st Banc, Inc. 04/17/2002 which merged into Farmers National Banc Corp. 10/01/2015

FIRST NATL CMNTY BK (DUNMORE, PA)
Stock Dividend - 10% payable 05/08/1996 to holders of record 04/03/1996
Under plan of reorganization each share Common $1.25 par automatically became (1) share First National Community Bancorp Inc. Common $1.25 par 07/01/1998
First National Community Bancorp Inc. name changed to FNCB Bancorp, Inc. 11/30/2016

FIRST NATIONAL CORP. OF PORTLAND, OREGON
Liquidated in 1938

FIRST NATL CORP (CA)
Stock Dividends - 10% 8/17/87; 10% 8/24/89; 10% 8/23/91
Reorganized as Boatracs, Inc. 1/12/95
Each share Common no par exchanged for (0.14285714) share Common no par
Boatracs, Inc. name changed to Advanced Remote Communication Solutions Inc.
(See Advanced Remote Communication Solutions Inc.)

FIRST NATL CORP (LA)
Charter revoked for failure to maintain a registered agent 5/18/99

FIRST NATL CORP (ND)
Common $5 par changed to $1 par in May 1993
Common $1 par split (2) for (1) by issuance of (1) additional share 10/20/87
Common $1 par changed to no par 4/12/88
Stock Dividends - 10% 8/23/85; 100% 10/20/87
Under plan of reorganization each share Common no par automatically became (1) share Alerus Financial Corp. (DE) Common $1 par 11/13/2000

FIRST NATL CORP (NV)
Recapitalized as Seal Fleet, Inc. 8/9/79
Each (10) shares Class A Common $1 par exchanged for (5) shares Class A Common 10¢ par
Seal Fleet, Inc. (NV) reorganized in Delaware as Seal Holdings Corp. 6/30/97 which name changed to Le@p Technology, Inc. 7/6/2000

FIRST NATL CORP (OH)
Stock Dividend - 25% 4/30/90
Name changed to C. A. Short International, Inc. 6/21/90
C. A. Short International, Inc. name changed to Pages, Inc. (OH) 11/16/92 which reincorporated in Delaware 10/13/94 which recapitalized as Media Source Inc. 3/9/99
(See Media Source Inc.)

FIRST NATL CORP (SC)
Common $5 par changed to $2.50 par and (1) additional share issued payable 05/30/1997 to holders of record 05/19/1997 Ex date - 06/02/1997
Stock Dividend - 10% payable 11/16/1998 to holders of record 11/02/1998
Name changed to SCBT Financial Corp. 02/20/2004
SCBT Financial Corp. name changed to First Financial Holdings, Inc. 07/30/2013 which name changed to South State Corp. 06/30/2014

FIRST NATIONAL CORP (VA)
5% Preferred Ser. A $1.25 par called for redemption at $1,000 plus $20.749999 accrued dividends on 11/06/2015
9% Preferred Ser. B $1.25 par called for redemption at $1,000 plus

$20.749999 accrued dividends on 11/06/2015
(Additional Information in Active)

FIRST NATL CORP (WI)
Common $10 par split (3) for (1) by issuance of (2) additional shares 04/20/1979
Common $10 par changed to $5 par 03/25/1980
Name changed to Firstar Corp. 06/01/1983
Firstar Corp. merged into Marine Corp. (WI) 09/23/1985 which merged into Banc One Corp. (DE) 04/01/1988 which reincorporated in Ohio 05/01/1989 which merged into Bank One Corp. 10/02/1998 which merged into J.P. Morgan Chase & Co. 12/31/2000 which name changed to JPMorgan Chase & Co. 07/20/2004

FIRST NATL CORP BLOOMINGTON (IN)
Acquired by Banc One Corp. (DE) 06/01/1987
Each share Capital Stock $5 par exchanged for (1.65) shares Common no par
Banc One Corp. (DE) reincorporated in Ohio 05/01/199 which merged into Bank One Corp. 10/02/1998 which merged into J.P. Morgan Chase & Co. 12/31/2000 which name changed to JPMorgan Chase & Co. 07/20/2004

FIRST NATL CORP WEST PT (MS)
Merged into NBC Capital Corp. 12/31/1998
Each share Common $5 par exchanged for (7.8072) shares Common $1 par
NBC Capital Corp. name changed to Cadence Financial Corp. 06/28/2006
(See Cadence Financial Corp.)

FIRST NATIONAL CRANDALL CORP. (NV)
Charter revoked for failure to file reports and pay fees 2/1/88

FIRST NATIONAL CREDIT BUREAU, INC. (MI)
Common $10 par changed to $1 par and (9) additional shares issued 02/01/1959
Merged into International Industries, Inc. (CA) 09/10/1968
Each share Common $1 par exchanged for (0.2) share Common no par
International Industries, Inc. (CA) reincorporated in Delaware 03/07/1969 which merged into IHOP Corp. 09/17/1976
(See IHOP Corp.)

FIRST NATL EMPLOYEES BENEFIT FD (DE)
Charter cancelled and declared inoperative and void for non-payment of taxes 4/2/75

FIRST NATL ENTMT CORP (CO)
Company terminated registration of common stock and is no longer public as of 02/23/2008

FIRST NATL EXCHANGE BK (ROANOKE, VA)
Stock Dividends - 10% payable 07/31/2001 to holders of record 06/30/2001 Ex date - 07/20/2001; 10% payable 07/31/2002 to holders of record 06/28/2002 Ex date - 07/29/2002; 10% payable 10/31/2003 to holders of record 09/30/2003 Ex date - 11/03/2003
Merged into Carter Bank & Trust (Martinsville, VA) 12/29/2006
Each share Common $5 par exchanged for (4.509) shares Common

FIRST NATL EXCHANGE BK VA (ROANOKE, VA)
Name changed to Dominion Bank, N.A. (Roanoke, VA) 07/20/1984
(See Dominion Bank, N.A. (Roanoke, VA))

FIRST NATL FD INC (DE)
Merged into Standard & Poor's/Intercapital Dynamics Fund, Inc. 10/27/1972
Each share Capital Stock $1 par exchanged for (0.62384) share Capital Stock 10¢ par
Standard & Poor's/Intercapital Dynamics Fund, Inc. acquired by Tudor Hedge Fund 09/30/1975 which name changed to Tudor Fund 06/18/1980 which name changed to WPG Tudor Fund 12/29/1989
(See WPG Tudor Fund)

1ST NATL FILM CORP (CO)
Each share Common $0.0001 par exchanged for (0.02) share Common $0.005 par 02/06/1992
Name changed to First National Entertainment Corp. 10/28/1994
(See First National Entertainment Corp.)

FIRST NATL FINL CORP (GA)
Merged into ABC Bancorp 08/30/1996
Each share Common $5 par exchanged for (1.2548) shares Common no par
ABC Bancorp name changed to Ameris Bancorp 12/01/2005

FIRST NATL FINL CORP (MI)
Merged into First American Bank Corp. 02/13/1978
Each share Common $10 par exchanged for (1) share Common $10 par
First American Bank Corp. name changed to First of America Bank Corp. 01/14/1983 which merged into National City Corp. 03/31/1998 which was acquired by PNC Financial Services Group, Inc. 12/31/2008

FIRST NATL FINL CORP (MS)
Merged into Trustmark Corp. 10/07/1994
Each share Common $8 par exchanged for (2.59736) shares Common $2.50 par and $0.79363 cash

FIRST NATL FINL CORP (NM)
Common $6.25 par reclassified as Class B Common $1 par 04/24/1990
Merged into First Security Corp. 11/19/1993
Each share Class B Common $1 par exchanged for (1.6696) shares Common $1.25 par
First Security Corp. merged into Wells Fargo & Co. (New) 10/26/2000

FIRST NATL FINL CORP (TN)
Stock Dividend - 50% 11/01/1985
Merged into Dominion Bankshares Corp. 05/01/1987
Each share Common 10¢ par exchanged for (4.065) shares Common $5 par
Dominion Bankshares Corp. merged into First Union Corp. 03/01/1993 which name changed to Wachovia Corp. (Ctfs. dated after 09/01/2001) 09/01/2001 which merged into Wells Fargo & Co. (New) 12/31/2008

FIRST NATL FINL INCOME FD (ON)
Under plan of reorganization each Unit no par automatically became (1) share First National Financial Corp. Common no par 01/04/2011

FIRST NATL GRANITE BK (AUGUSTA, ME)
Each share Common $100 par exchanged for (5) shares Common $20 par in 1945
Stock Dividends - 16-2/3% 5/24/56; 14-2/7% 1/25/62; 25% 2/1/65; 25% 6/1/66
Name changed to Bank of Maine, N.A. (Augusta, ME) 2/2/70
Bank of Maine, N.A. (Augusta, ME) reorganized as Banc of Maine Corp. 2/1/73
(See Banc of Maine Corp.)

FIRST NATL HLDG CORP (GA)
Common $10 par changed to $5 par and (1) additional share issued 11/17/1972
Common $5 par split (3) for (2) by issuance of (0.5) additional share 04/28/1978
Name changed to First Atlanta Corp. 09/14/1979
First Atlanta Corp. merged into First Wachovia Corp. 12/05/1985 which name changed to Wachovia Corp. (New) (Ctfs. dated between 05/20/1991 and 09/01/2001) 05/20/1991 which merged into Wachovia Corp. (Ctfs. dated after 09/01/2001) 09/01/2001 which merged into Wells Fargo & Co. (New) 12/31/2008

FIRST NATL HLDG CORP (NV)
Reincorporated 01/28/1994
State of incorporation changed from (DE) to (NV) 01/28/1994
Each share old Common $0.001 par exchanged for (0.004) share new Common $0.001 par 07/01/1994
Name changed to Innovative Weaponry Inc. 09/21/1994
Innovative Weaponry Inc. name changed to 21st Century Technologies Inc. 11/14/1995
(See 21st Century Technologies Inc.)

FIRST NATL HLDG CORP (TN)
Common $10 par changed to $5 par and (1) additional share issued 4/23/70
Name changed to First Tennessee National Corp. 10/27/71
First Tennessee National Corp. name changed to First Horizon National Corp. 4/20/2004

FIRST NATL INVS INC (KS)
Charter forfeited for failure to file annual reports 07/15/1986

FIRST NATL IRON BK NJ (MORRISTOWN, NJ)
Name changed 11/1/71
Stock Dividends - 25% 12/55; 20% 12/22/59; 33-1/3% 3/15/65
Name changed from First National Iron Bank to First National Iron Bank of New Jersey (Morristown, NJ) 12/30/65
Stock Dividend - 10% 3/15/71
Reorganized as Heritage Bancorporation 11/1/71
Each share Capital Stock $10 par exchanged for (1) share Common no par
(See Heritage Bancorporation)

FIRST NATL LEASING CORP (WI)
Completely liquidated 01/28/1972
Each share Common 10¢ par exchanged for first and final distribution of (0.1) share Marshall & Ilsley Corp. (Old) Common $2.50 par
(See Marshall & Ilsley Corp. (Old))

FIRST NATIONAL LIFE INSURANCE CO. (AZ)
Common $4 par changed to $1 par and (1) additional share issued 06/01/1962
Merged into First National Life Insurance Co. (AL) 12/31/1967
Each share Common $1 par exchanged for (1) share Class A Common $1 par
First National Life Insurance Co. (AL) reorganized as First National Corp. (NV) 12/31/1969 which recapitalized as Seal Fleet, Inc. 08/09/1979 which reorganized in Delaware as Seal Holdings Corp. 06/30/1997 which name changed to Le@p Technology, Inc. 07/06/2000

FIRST NATL LIFE INS CO (AL)
Reorganized as First National Corp. (NV) 12/31/69
Each share Class A Common $1 par exchanged for (1) share Class A Common $1 par
First National Corp. (NV) recapitalized as Seal Fleet, Inc. (NV) 8/9/79 which reorganized in Delaware as Seal Holdings Corp. 6/30/97 which name changed to Le@p Technology, Inc. 7/6/2000

FIRST NATL LIFE INS CO (LA)
Merged into Capital Holding Corp. 11/22/1971
Each share Common $2.50 par exchanged for (0.4) share Common $1 par
Capital Holding Corp. name changed to Providian Corp. 05/12/1994 which merged into Aegon N.V. 06/10/1997

FIRST NATL LINCOLN CORP (ME)
Common no par split (4) for (1) by issuance of (3) additional share payable 12/30/1997 to holders of record 12/01/1997
Common no par split (3) for (1) by issuance of (2) additional shares payable 06/01/2004 to holders of record 05/12/2004
Name changed to First Bancorp, Inc. 05/02/2008

FIRST NATL LINCOLN CORP (NE)
Common $10 par changed to $5 par and (1) additional share issued 10/10/1978
Stock Dividends - 10% 09/16/1974; 10% 12/15/1976; 15% 12/15/1981
Merged into FirsTier, Inc. 06/01/1984
Each share Common $5 par exchanged for (0.875) share Common $5 par
FirsTier, Inc. name changed to FirsTier Financial Inc. 05/18/1987 which merged into First Bank System, Inc. 02/16/1996 which name changed to U.S. Bancorp 08/01/1997

FIRST NATIONAL MORTGAGE (1962) CO. LTD. (BC)
Class A no par and Class B no par reclassified as Common no par 04/14/1964
Name changed to Block Bros. Industries Ltd. 05/02/1968
(See Block Bros. Industries Ltd.)

FIRST NATL MTG INVT FD (ON)
Trust terminated 12/22/2017
Each Unit received $9.33 cash

FIRST NATIONAL MUTUAL FUND, INC. (DE)
Name changed to First National Fund, Inc. 12/01/1965
First National Fund, Inc. merged into Standard & Poor's/Intercapital Dynamics Fund, Inc. 10/27/1972 which was acquired by Tudor Hedge Fund 09/30/1975 which name changed to Tudor Fund 06/18/1980 which name changed to WPG Tudor Fund 12/29/1989
(See WPG Tudor Fund)

FIRST NATIONAL OIL & MINERALS CO. (CO)
Merged into Mancos Corp. 7/10/70
Each share Capital Stock no par exchanged for (1) share Capital Stock 1¢ par
Mancos Corp. acquired by Union Oil Co. of California 11/27/78 which reorganized as Unocal Corp. 4/25/83 which merged into Chevron Corp. 8/10/2005

FIRST NATL PA CORP (PA)
Common $12.50 par changed to $4.16-2/3 par and (2) additional shares issued 04/23/1986

FINANCIAL INFORMATION, INC. FIR-FIR

Merged into PNC Financial Corp 07/24/1992
Each share Common $4.16-2/3 par exchanged for (0.81) share Common $5 par
PNC Financial Corp. name changed to PNC Bank Corp. 02/08/1993 which name changed to PNC Financial Services Group, Inc. 03/15/2000

FIRST NATIONAL PETROLEUM TRUST (RI)
Liquidation completed
Each share Common $1 par received initial distribution of $0.05 cash 4/1/64
Each share Common $1 par received second distribution of $0.065 cash 7/1/65
Each share Common $1 par received third and final distribution of $0.075 cash 9/12/68
Certificates were not retired and are now without value

FIRST NATIONAL PICTURES, INC.
Dissolved in 1936

FIRST NATL PWR CORP (DE)
Reorganized under the laws of Nevada as First National Energy Corp. 02/11/2009
Each share Common $0.001 par exchanged for (0.01) share Common $0.001 par

FIRST NATIONAL REAL ESTATE TRUST (MA)
Merged into United National Investors Corp. 10/10/68
Each share Bene. Int. no par exchanged for (1) share 70¢ Conv. Preferred $1 par, (0.2) share Common $1 par and (1/3) Common Stock Purchase Warrant
United National Investors Corp. name changed to United National Corp. (Del.) 7/15/70 which merged into Goldome National Corp. 5/13/83
(See Goldome National Corp.)

FIRST NATL RLTY & CONSTR CORP (NY)
60¢ Conv. Preferred $8 par called for redemption 3/28/69
Name changed to First Phone Corp. 4/6/83
(See First Phone Corp.)

FIRST NATL RLTY ASSOC INC (NV)
Name changed to 1st Realty Investments, Inc. 07/13/2000
1st Realty Investments, Inc. recapitalized as Great Western Land & Recreation, Inc. 02/05/2004
(See Great Western Land & Recreation, Inc.)

FIRST NATL ST BANCORPORATION (NJ)
Name changed to First Fidelity Bancorporation (Old) 05/01/1985
First Fidelity Bancorporation (Old) merged into First Fidelity Bancorporation (New) 02/29/1988 which merged into First Union Corp. 01/01/1996 which name changed to Wachovia Corp. (Ctfs. dated after 09/01/2001) 09/01/2001 which merged into Wells Fargo & Co. (New) 12/31/2008

FIRST NATL ST BK N J (NEWARK, NJ)
Stock Dividend - 10% 02/11/1969
Reorganized as First National State Bancorporation 01/15/1970
Each share Common $6.25 par exchanged for (1) share Common $6.25 par
First National State Bancorporation name changed to First Fidelity Bancorporation (Old) 05/01/1985 which merged into First Fidelity Bancorporation (New) 02/29/1988 which merged into First Union Corp. 01/01/1996 which name changed to Wachovia Corp. (Ctfs. dated after 09/01/2001) 09/01/2001 which merged into Wells Fargo & Co. (New) 12/31/2008

FIRST NATL STORES INC (MA)
Stock Dividend - 100% 07/13/1951
Merged into First National Supermarkets, Inc. 05/25/1978
Each share Common no par exchanged for (0.2208) share Preferred $8 par and (1) share Common 1¢ par
(See First National Supermarkets, Inc.)

FIRST NATL SUPERMARKETS INC (MA)
Each share Preferred $8 par exchanged for (0.664) share Common 1¢ par 09/16/1983
Acquired by a group of investors 09/13/1985
Each share Common 1¢ par exchanged for $24.25 cash

FIRST NATL TR & SVGS BK (LYNCHBURG, VA)
Acquired by United Virginia Bankshares, Inc. 1/10/63
Each share Capital Stock $12.50 par exchanged for (1) share Common $10 par
United Virginia Bankshares, Inc. name changed to Crestar Financial Corp. 9/1/87 which merged into SunTrust Banks, Inc. 12/31/98

FIRST NATIONAL TRUST & SAVINGS BANK (SAN DIEGO, CA)
Common $10 par changed to $5 par and (1) additional share issued 4/21/59
Stock Dividends - 40% 4/21/48; 100% 4/25/56
Name changed to First National Bank (San Diego, CA) 3/1/63
First National Bank (San Diego, CA) name changed to Southern California First National Bank (San Diego, CA) 8/18/67 which reorganized as Southern California First National Corp. 2/28/69
(See Southern California First National Corp.)

FIRST NATL TR BK (SUNBURY, PA)
Common $6.25 par changed to $3.125 par and (1) additional share issued 05/10/1974
Reorganized as FNT Bancorp, Inc. 05/03/1984
Each share Common $3.125 par exchanged for (1) share Common $10 par
FNT Bancorp, Inc. merged into Susquehanna Bancshares, Inc. 10/01/1985 which merged into BB&T Corp. 08/01/2015

FIRST NATL URANIUM MINES LTD (ON)
Capital Stock $1 par changed to no par 07/13/1971
Merged into Groundstar Resources Ltd. (BC) 08/31/1973
Each share Capital Stock no par exchanged for (0.1) share Capital Stock no par
Groundstar Resources Ltd. (BC) reincorporated in Alberta 10/28/2005

FIRST NATL VT CORP (VT)
Name changed to Independent Bankgroup Inc. 4/24/86
(See Independent Bankgroup Inc.)

FIRST NATIONWIDE BK A FED SVGS BK (PLANO, TX)
Under plan of merger each share 11.50% Perpetual Preferred 1¢ par automatically became (1) share California Federal Bank, A Federal Savings Bank (Los Angeles, CA) 11.50% Perpetual Preferred no par 01/03/1997
California Federal Bank, A Federal Savings Bank (Los Angeles, CA) name changed to Citibank (West) FSB (San Francisco, CA) 12/11/2002
(See Citibank (West) FSB (San Francisco, CA))

FIRST NATIONWIDE FINL CORP (DE)
Acquired by Ford Motor Co. 12/16/1985
Each share Common 10¢ par exchanged for $32 cash

1ST NET TECHNOLOGIES INC (CO)
Name changed to VOS International, Inc. 09/23/2005
VOS International, Inc. recapitalized as IdeaEdge, Inc. 10/18/2007 which name changed to Socialwise, Inc. 05/13/2009 which name changed to BillMyParents, Inc. 06/13/2011 which name changed to SpendSmart Payments Co. (CO) 02/28/2013 which reincorporated in Delaware as SpendSmart Networks, Inc. 06/20/2014

FIRST NEW ENG BANKSHARES CORP (MA)
Acquired by Hartford National Corp. 11/14/86
Each share Common $1 par exchanged for (1.512) shares Common $6.25 par
Hartford National Corp. merged into Shawmut National Corp. 2/29/88 which merged into Fleet Financial Group Inc. (New) 11/30/95 which name changed to Fleet Boston Corp. 10/1/99 which name changed to FleetBoston Financial Corp. 4/18/2000 which merged into Bank of America Corp. 4/1/2004

FIRST NEW HAVEN NATL BK (NEW HAVEN, CT)
Common $10 par changed to $5 par and (1) additional share issued 12/30/68
Name changed to First Bank of New Haven (New Haven, CT) 4/1/77
First Bank of New Haven (New Haven, CT) reorganized as FirstBancorp, Inc. (CT) 2/1/79 which merged into Hartford National Corp. 3/30/84 which merged into Shawmut National Corp. 2/29/88 which merged into Fleet Financial Group Inc. (New) 11/30/95 which name changed to Fleet Boston Corp. 10/1/99 which name changed to FleetBoston Financial Corp. 4/18/2000 which merged into Bank of America Corp. 4/1/2004

FIRST NEW MEXICO BANKSHARE CORP (NM)
Common $5 par split (4) for (1) by issuance of (3) additional shares 05/10/1974
Name changed to Sunwest Financial Services, Inc. 07/18/1983
Sunwest Financial Services, Inc. merged into Boatmen's Bancshares, Inc. 10/01/1992 which merged into NationsBank Corp. 01/07/1997 which reincorporated in Delaware as BankAmerica Corp. (Old) 09/25/1998 which merged into BankAmerica Corp. (New) 09/30/1998 which name changed to Bank of America Corp. 04/28/1999

FIRST NEW YORK INVTS INC (FL)
Name changed to Computer Access International, Inc. 01/28/1997
Computer Access International, Inc. recapitalized as Dispatch Auto Parts, Inc. 06/16/2005 which name changed to Environment Ecology Holding Co. of China 11/29/2007

FIRST NEWPORT CORP (CA)
Acquired by Coldwell, Banker & Co. 9/15/81
Each share Common $1 par exchanged for (0.33) share Common no par and $1.24 cash
Coldwell, Banker & Co. merged into Sears, Roebuck & Co. 12/31/81 which merged into Sears Holdings Corp. 3/24/2005

FIRST NEWPORT REALTY INVESTORS (CA)
Name changed to First Newport Corp. and each Share of Bene. Int. $1 par reclassified as Common $1 par 10/31/79
First Newport Corp. acquired by Coldwell, Banker & Co. 9/15/81 which merged into Sears, Roebuck & Co. 12/31/81 which merged into Sears Holdings Corp. 3/24/2005

FIRST NH BKS INC (NH)
Common $1 par split (2) for (1) by issuance of (1) additional share 12/1/83
Each share Conv. Preferred Ser. I no par exchanged for (1.953125) shares Common $1 par 5/3/88
Stock Dividends - 10% 12/1/84; 25% 11/1/85; 25% 10/1/86; 25% 9/1/87
Acquired by Bank of Ireland (US) Holdings Inc. 12/16/88
Each share Common $1 par exchanged for $30.50 cash

FIRST NIAGARA FINL GROUP INC NEW (DE)
Merged into KeyCorp (New) 08/01/2016
Each share Non-Cum. Fixed/Floating Rate Preferred Ser. B 1¢ par exchanged for (1) share Non-Cum. Fixed/Floating Rate Perpetual Preferred Ser. C $1 par
Each share Common 1¢ par exchanged for (0.68) share Common $1 par and $2.30 cash

FIRST NIAGARA FINL GROUP INC OLD (DE)
Merged into First Niagara Financial Group, Inc. (New) 01/17/2003
Each share Common 1¢ par exchanged for (2.58681) shares Common 1¢ par
First Niagara Financial Group, Inc. (New) merged into KeyCorp (New) 08/01/2016

FIRST NICKEL INC (ON)
Discharged from receivership 09/13/2016
No stockholders' equity

FIRST NORDIC EQUITY PARTNERS CORP (DE)
Recapitalized as Nordic Equity Partners Corp. 9/11/95
Each share Common $0.001 par exchanged for (0.001) share Common $0.001 par
(See Nordic Equity Partners Corp.)

FIRST NORTHERN EXPLORATION LTD. (CANADA)
Acquired by Nemco Exploration Ltd. 05/23/1973
Each share Common no par exchanged for (0.25) share Common no par
Nemco Exploration Ltd. name changed to Seaward Resources Ltd. 07/15/1980 which recapitalized as Seaquest Energy Ltd. (BC) 09/10/1982 which reincorporated in Alberta 07/23/1984 which recapitalized as Alta Petroleum Ltd. 01/13/1987 which merged into CanEuro Resources Ltd. 04/04/1989 which merged into Attock Oil Corp. 02/04/1991 which merged into Attock Energy Corp. 08/02/1995
(See Attock Energy Corp.)

FIRST NORTHN BK (DIXON, CA)
Common no par split (2) for (1) by issuance of (1) additional share payable 09/30/1998 to holders of record 08/31/1998
Stock Dividends - 6% payable 03/29/1996 to holders of record 02/29/1996; 5% payable 03/31/1998 to holders of record 02/27/1998; 5% payable 03/31/1999 to holders of record 02/26/1999; 6% payable

03/31/2000 to holders of record 02/29/2000
Under plan of reorganization each share Common no par automatically became (1) share First Northern Community Bancorp Common no par 05/19/2000

FIRST NORTHN CAP CORP (WI)
Common $1 par split (2) for (1) by issuance of (1) additional share payable 08/18/1997 to holders of record 08/01/1997
Merged into Bank Mutual Corp. (USA) 11/01/2000
Each share Common $1 par exchanged for either (0.6) share Common 1¢ par and $9 cash or $15 cash
Note: Holders electing all stock received (1.5) shares for approximately 92.6% of holdings and $15 per share for the balance Non-electing holders received $15 cash per share
Bank Mutual Corp. (USA) reorganized in Wisconsin 10/29/2003 which merged into Associated Banc-Corp 02/01/2018

FIRST NORTHN DEVS INC (BC)
Recapitalized as Consolidated First Northern Developments Inc. 09/20/1993
Each share Common no par exchanged for (0.37735284) share Common no par
Consolidated First Northern Developments Inc. recapitalized as Golden Temple Mining Corp. 03/15/1996 which recapitalized as Amerigo Resources Ltd. 03/08/2002

FIRST NORTHN SVGS BK S A (GREEN BAY, WI)
Name changed 04/26/1989
Common $1 par split (3) for (2) by issuance of (0.5) additional share 12/13/1985
Name changed from First Northern Savings & Loan Association to First Northern Savings Bank, S.A. (Green Bay, WI) 04/26/1989
Common $1 par split (2) for (1) by issuance of (1) additional share 09/18/1992
Under plan of reorganization each share Common $1 par automatically became (1) share First Northern Capital Corp. Common $1 par 12/20/1995
First Northern Capital Corp. merged into Mutual Bank Corp. 11/01/2000 which merged into Associated Banc-Corp 02/01/2018

FIRST NORTHWEST BANCORPORATION (WA)
Merged into KeyCorp (NY) 08/03/1987
Each share Common $10 par exchanged for (1.279) shares Common $5 par
KeyCorp (NY) merged into KeyCorp (New) (OH) 03/01/1994

FIRST NORTHWEST BK (ST. ANN, MO)
Name changed to Landmark Northwest Plaza Bank (St. Ann, MO) 11/1/76
(See Landmark Northwest Plaza Bank (St. Ann, MO))

FIRST NORTHWEST INDS AMER INC (WA)
Common 20¢ par changed to 10¢ par and (1) additional share issued 11/15/79
Reincorporated under the laws of New York as FNI Inc. 5/30/80
FNI Inc. merged into New Century Productions, Ltd. 3/11/85 which name changed to New Century Entertainment Corp. 7/3/86 which name changed to New Visions Entertainment Corp. 8/8/88

(See New Visions Entertainment Corp.)

FIRST NY BK FOR BUSINESS (NEW YORK, NY)
Placed in receivership and FDIC appointed receiver 11/16/1992
No stockholders' equity

FIRST OAK BROOK BANCSHARES INC (DE)
Class A Common $2 par split (3) for (2) by issuance of (0.5) additional share 11/23/1992
Common $2 par split (3) for (2) by issuance of (0.5) additional share 11/23/1992
Class A Common $2 par split (5) for (4) by issuance of (0.25) additional share 12/23/1993
Common $2 par split (5) for (4) by issuance of (0.25) additional share 12/23/93
Class A Common $2 par split (3) for (2) by issuance of (0.5) additional share 09/08/1994
Common $2 par split (3) for (2) by issuance of (0.5) additional share 09/08/1994
Class A Common $2 par split (2) for (1) by issuance of (1) additional share payable 09/03/1998 to holders of record 08/20/1998
Common $2 par split (2) for (1) by issuance of (1) additional share payable 09/03/1998 to holders of record 08/20/1998
Common $2 par reclassified as Class A Common $2 par which was renamed Common $2 par 05/05/1999
Common $2 par split (3) for (2) by issuance of (0.5) additional share payable 08/25/2003 to holders of record 08/11/2003 Ex date - 08/26/2003
Merged into MB Financial, Inc. 08/25/2006
Each share Common $2 par exchanged for (1.0336) shares Common 1¢ par

FIRST OHIO BANCSHARES INC (OH)
Capital Stock $6.25 par split (3) for (2) by issuance of (0.5) additional share 05/20/1983
Capital Stock $6.25 par split (2) for (1) by issuance of (1) additional share 06/25/1985
Stock Dividend - 10% 06/25/1982
Merged into Fifth Third Bancorp 11/30/1989
Each share Capital Stock $6.25 par exchanged for (0.74367) share Common no par

FIRST OHIO INVESTMENT CO.
Business discontinued 00/00/1940
Details not available

FIRST OHIO INVESTMENT GROUP INC. (OH)
Acquired by Care Enterprises 00/00/1985
Each share Class A Common no par exchanged for $12 cash

FIRST OHIO REALTY (OH)
Name changed to Income Realty Shares 04/13/1967
Income Realty Shares name changed to Income Mortgage & Realty Shares 01/18/1972 which name changed to Northern States Mortgage & Realty Investors 11/30/1973 which name changed to Monetary Realty Trust 01/17/1979
(See Monetary Realty Trust)

FIRST OIL & GAS FUND LTD. (AB)
Name changed to Natural Resources Growth Fund Ltd. (AB) 01/14/1966
Natural Resources Growth Fund Ltd. (AB) reincorporated in Canada 02/01/1980 which name changed to All-Canadian Resources Corp. 12/30/1992
(See All-Canadian Resources Corp.)

FIRST OKLA BANCORPORATION INC (DE)
Acquired by Landmark Land Co., Inc. 04/16/1987
Each share 50¢ Preferred $5 par exchanged for $0.02 cash
Each share Common $5 par exchanged for $0.01 cash

FIRST OLYMPIC BANK (SHELTON, CT)
Name changed to Centennial Bank (Olympia, WA) 02/20/1987
(See Centennial Bank (Olympia, WA))

FIRST ONE CAP INC (ON)
Recapitalized as RedCity Search Co. Inc. 09/02/2005
Each share Common no par exchanged for (0.37) share Common no par
RedCity Search Co. Inc. recapitalized as ZipLocal Inc. 03/26/2007
(See ZipLocal Inc.)

FIRST OPPORTUNITY FD INC (MD)
Merged into Boulder Growth & Income Fund, Inc. 03/20/2015
Each share Common $0.001 par exchanged for (1.111719) shares Common 1¢ par

FIRST ORENADA MINES LTD (QC)
Merged into Brominco Inc. 06/01/1976
Each share Common $1 par exchanged for (0.01) share Capital Stock no par
Brominco Inc. merged into Aur Resources Inc. 05/16/1985 which was acquired by Teck Cominco Ltd. 09/28/2007 which name changed to Teck Resources Ltd. 04/27/2009

FIRST OZAUKEE CAP CORP (WI)
Merged into CIB Acquisition Corp. 09/10/1997
Each share Common $1 par exchanged for $15.10 cash

FIRST PA BKG & TR CO (PHILADELPHIA, PA)
Capital Stock $10 par changed to $5 par and (1) additional share issued 11/27/1961
Reorganized as First Pennsylvania Corp. 01/31/1969
Each share Capital Stock $5 par exchanged for (1) share Common $5 par
First Pennsylvania Corp. merged into CoreStates Financial Corp 03/05/1990 which merged into First Union Corp. 04/28/1998 which name changed to Wachovia Corp. (Ctfs. dated after 09/01/2001) 09/01/2001 which merged into Wells Fargo & Co. (New) 12/31/2008

FIRST PA CORP (PA)
Common $5 par changed to $1 par and (1) additional share issued 05/25/1970 (Non-Transferable Ctfs. of Contingent Int. issued on merger of Investors Loan Corp. 06/05/1970) (Ctfs. of Contingent Int. issued thru exchange offer by Associated Mortgage Companies, Inc.)
Each Ctf. of Contingent Interest (Investors Loan Corp.) received initial distribution of (0.33) share Common $1 par 01/31/1971
Each Ctf. of Contingent Interest (Investors Loan Corp.) received second distribution of (0.33) share Common $1 par 01/31/1972
Each Ctf. of Contingent Interest (Investors Loan Corp.) received third and final distribution of (0.4433315) share Common $1 par 01/31/1973
Ctfs. of Contingent Interest (Investors Loan Corp.) were not required to be surrendered and are now valueless
Each Ctf. of Contingent Interest (Associated Mortgage Companies, Inc.) exchanged for first and final distribution of (0.259182) First

Pennsylvania Corp. Common $1 par plus $0.0810502 cash 01/02/1972
$10.50 Conv. Preferred Ser. C no par called for redemption 02/24/1987
Conv. Depositary Preferred no par called for redemption 02/25/1987
6% Preferred Ser. A no par called for redemption 03/01/1987
Merged into CoreStates Financial Corp 03/05/1990
Each share Common $1 par exchanged for (0.4015) share Common $1 par
CoreStates Financial Corp merged into First Union Corp. 04/28/1998 which name changed to Wachovia Corp. (Ctfs. dated after 09/01/2001) 09/01/2001 which merged into Wells Fargo & Co. (New) 12/31/2008

FIRST PA MTG TR (MA)
Shares of Bene. Int. $1 par changed to no par 12/31/1980
Reorganized under the laws of Delaware as Atlantic Metropolitan Corp. and Shares of Bene. Int. no par reclassified as Common 10¢ par 01/29/1982
Atlantic Metropolitan Corp. merged into Hallwood Group Inc. 04/30/1984
(See Hallwood Group Inc.)

FIRST PAC BANCORP INC (DE)
Assets placed in receivership and FDIC appointed receiver 08/10/1990
Stockholders' equity unlikely

FIRST PAC CORP (OR)
Ctfs. dated prior to 06/03/1971
Completely liquidated 06/03/1971
Each share Common $1 par exchanged for first and final distribution of (0.25) share American Guaranty Financial Corp. Common no par
American Guaranty Financial Corp. name changed to Encore Group Inc. 07/18/1990
(See Encore Group Inc.)

FIRST PAC HLDGS LTD (HONG KONG)
Merged into First Pacific Co. Ltd. 09/06/1988
Each ADR for Ordinary HKD $5 par exchanged for $3.736 cash

FIRST PAC INS GROUP (CA)
Charter cancelled for failure to file reports and pay taxes 03/01/1991

FIRST PAC NETWORKS INC (DE)
Assets sold for the benefit of creditors 09/12/1998
Stockholders' equity unlikely

1ST PAC BANCORP (CA)
Company's principal asset placed in receivership 05/07/2010
Stockholders' equity unlikely

1ST PAC BK (SAN DIEGO, CA)
Common no par split (2) for (1) by issuance of (1) additional share payable 06/30/2005 to holders of record 06/15/2005 Ex date - 07/01/2005
Under plan of reorganization each share Common no par automatically became (1) share 1st Pacific Bancorp Common no par 01/30/2007
(See 1st Pacific Bancorp)

FIRST PACIFIC BANK NEW (LOS ANGELES, CA)
Stock Dividend - 15% 11/12/81
Common $2.50 par changed to $1.66 par and (0.5) additional share issued 2/22/82
Reorganized as First Pacific Bancorp, Inc. 10/1/82
Each share Common $1.66 par exchanged for (1) share Common $2.50 par
(See First Pacific Bancorp, Inc.)

FIRST PACIFIC BANK OLD (LOS ANGELES, CA)
Merged into First Pacific Bank (Los Angeles, CA) (New) 10/31/77
Each share Common $5 par exchanged for (2.053) shares Common $2.50 par
First Pacific Bank (Los Angeles, CA) (New) reorganized as First Pacific Bancorp, Inc. 10/1/82
(See First Pacific Bancorp, Inc.)

FIRST PACIFIC CORP. (OR)
Ctfs. dated after 1/22/74
Merged into First Professional Services, Inc. 6/10/85
Each share Common no par exchanged for $5 cash

FIRST PACTRUST BANCORP INC (MD)
Issue Information - 5,290,000 shares COM offered at $12 per share on 08/14/2002
Name changed to Banc of California, Inc. 07/16/2013

FIRST PALM BEACH BANCORP INC (DE)
Merged into Republic Security Financial Corp. 10/29/1998
Each share Common 1¢ par exchanged for (4.194) shares Common 1¢ par
Republic Security Financial Corp. merged into Wachovia Corp. (New) (Ctfs. dated between 05/20/1991 and 09/01/2001) 03/01/2001 which merged into Wachovia Corp. (Ctfs. dated after 09/01/2001) 09/01/2001 which merged into Wells Fargo & Co. (New) 12/31/2008

FIRST PALMETTO FINL CORP (DE)
Non-Voting Preferred 1¢ par called for redemption at $120 on 8/19/2002
(Additional Information in Active)

FIRST PALMETTO STATE BANK & TRUST CO. (COLUMBIA, SC)
Each share Common $10 par exchanged for (2) shares Common $5 par 12/15/84
Acquired by Southern National Corp. 12/3/86
Each share Common $5 par exchanged for (0.644) share Common $5 par
Southern National Corp. name changed to BB&T Corp. 5/19/97

FIRST PARAMOUNT EQUITY CORP (DE)
Merged into Paramount Life Insurance Co. (AR) 8/31/82
Each share Class A Common Ser. II 1¢ par exchanged for (0.1) share Common $2 par
(See Paramount Life Insurance Co.)

FIRST PART FD INC (MD)
Name changed to American General Growth Fund, Inc. 10/05/1970
American General Growth Fund, Inc. name changed to American Capital Growth Fund, Inc. 09/09/1983
(See American Capital Growth Fund, Inc.)

FIRST PASADENA ST BK (PASADENA, TX)
Stock Dividends - 20% 3/31/76; 10% 4/21/78; 10% 4/20/79
Merged into Southwest Bancshares, Inc. 3/29/82
Each share Common $10 par exchanged for (1.2784) shares Common $5 par
Southwest Bancshares, Inc. merged into MCorp 10/11/84
(See MCorp)

FIRST PATRIOT BANKSHARES CORP (VA)
Common $5 par changed to $2.50 par and (1) additional share issued 4/30/93
Merged into United Bankshares, Inc. 8/1/97

Each share Common $2.50 par exchanged for $17 cash

FIRST PELHAM CORP. (NY)
Completely liquidated 3/21/61
Each share Capital Stock $25 par exchanged for (10) shares Sanborn Map Co., Inc. Capital Stock $5 par and $33.26 cash
(See Sanborn Map Co., Inc.)

FIRST PEOPLES BK (JOHNSON CITY, TN)
Name changed to United American Bank (Johnson City, TN) in 1977
United American Bank (Johnson City, TN) name changed to City & County Bank of Washington County (Johnson City, TN) 9/14/82 which name changed to First Peoples Bank of Washington County (Johnson City, TN) 7/25/83
(See First Peoples Bank of Washington County (Johnson City, TN))

FIRST PEOPLES BK N J (WESTMONT, NJ)
Under plan of reorganization each share 9.95% Conv. Preferred $20 par and Common $6 par automatically became (1) share First Peoples Financial Corp. 9.95% Conv. Preferred $20 par and Common $6 par respectively 03/03/1987
First Peoples Financial Corp. merged into CoreStates Financial Corp 09/03/1992 which merged into First Union Corp. 04/28/1998 which name changed to Wachovia Corp. (Ctfs. dated after 09/01/2001) 09/01/2001 which merged into Wells Fargo & Co. (New) 12/31/2008

FIRST PEOPLES BK WASHINGTON CNTY (JOHNSON CITY, TN)
Bank closed 07/29/1983
No stockholders' equity

FIRST PEOPLES FINL CORP (NJ)
9.95% Conv. Preferred $20 par called for redemption 08/27/1987
Merged into CoreStates Financial Corp 09/03/1992
Each share Common $6 par exchanged for (0.935) share Common $1 par
CoreStates Financial Corp merged into First Union Corp. 04/28/1998 which name changed to Wachovia Corp. (Ctfs. dated after 09/01/2001) 09/01/2001 which merged into Wells Fargo & Co. (New) 12/31/2008

FIRST PEOPLES NATIONAL BANK (EDWARDSVILLE, PA)
Acquired by First Fidelity Bancorporation (Old) 03/25/1994
Each share Common $12.50 par exchanged for $465 cash

FIRST PEOPLES NATIONAL BANK OF NEW JERSEY (WESTMONT, NJ)
Common Capital Stock $3.375 par changed to $5 par 03/25/1975
Common Capital Stock $5 par changed to $6 par 04/20/1977
Name changed to First Peoples Bank of New Jersey (Westmont, NJ) 04/20/1978
First Peoples Bank of New Jersey (Westmont, NJ) reorganized as First Peoples Financial Corp. 03/03/1987 which merged into CoreStates Financial Corp 09/03/1992 which merged into First Union Corp. 04/28/1998 which name changed to Wachovia Corp. (Ctfs. dated after 09/01/2001) 09/01/2001 which merged into Wells Fargo & Co. (New) 12/31/2008

FIRST PEORIA CORP (IL)
Merged into Commerce Bancshares, Inc. 06/01/1992
Each share Common $10 par exchanged for either (1.237) shares

Common $5 par, $42.693 cash or a combination thereof

FIRST PERRY BANCORP INC (PA)
Merged into Riverview Financial Corp. (Old) 12/31/2008
Each share Common 25¢ par exchanged for (2.435) shares Common 50¢ par
Riverview Financial Corp. (Old) merged into Riverview Financial Corp. (New) 11/01/2013

FIRST PETE & PIPELINE INC (NY)
Common $0.001 par split (5) for (1) by issuance of (4) additional shares payable 08/15/2005 to holders of record 08/01/2005 Ex date - 08/16/2005
Recapitalized as Luke Entertainment, Inc. 11/15/2007
Each share Common $0.001 par exchanged for (0.0005) share Common 10¢ par
Luke Entertainment, Inc. name changed to Greene Concepts, Inc. 01/14/2011

FIRST PETERBOROUGH BK CORP (DE)
Merged into Granite State Bankshares, Inc. 10/01/1988
Details not available

FIRST PHILADELPHIA CAP CORP (DE)
Name changed to Conservation Anglers Manufacturing, Inc. 11/21/2000
Conservation Anglers Manufacturing, Inc. name changed to Newport International Group Inc. 01/31/2001 which name changed to Spare Backup, Inc. 08/16/2006
(See Spare Backup, Inc.)

FIRST PHILADELPHIA CORP (NY)
Dissolved by proclamation 03/25/1992

FIRST PHILIPPINE FD INC (MD)
Liquidation completed
Each share Common 1¢ par exchanged for initial distribution of $2.52 cash 7/29/2003
Each share Common 1¢ par received second and final distribution of $0.1375 cash payable 10/29/2003 to holders of record 6/18/2003

FIRST PHILSON FINL CORP (DE)
Common $10 par split (4) for (1) by issuance of (3) additional shares payable 11/10/97 to holders of record 10/24/97
Merged into BT Financial Corp. 7/14/99
Each share Common $10 par exchanged for (1.667) shares Common $5 par
BT Financial Corp. name changed to Promistar Financial Corp. 11/15/2000 which merged into F.N.B. Corp. (FL) 1/18/2002

FIRST PHONE CORP (NY)
Dissolved by proclamation 9/28/94

FIRST PIEDMONT BANK & TRUST CO. (GREENVILLE, SC)
Reorganized as First Piedmont Corp. 12/1/69
Each share Common Capital Stock $10 par exchanged for (1) share Common $10 par
First Piedmont Corp. name changed to U.S. Shelter Corp. (SC) 11/16/79 which merged into U.S. Shelter Corp. (DE) 5/31/84
(See U.S. Shelter Corp. (DE))

FIRST PIEDMONT BK (WINDER, GA)
Placed in receivership 07/17/2009
Stockholders' equity unlikely

FIRST PIEDMONT CORP (SC)
Common $10 par changed to $5 par and (1) additional share issued 4/12/72
Common $5 par changed to $2.50 par

and (1) additional share issued 11/5/73
Name changed to U.S. Shelter Corp. (SC) and Common $2.50 par changed to 25¢ par 11/16/79
U.S. Shelter Corp. (SC) merged into U.S. Shelter Corp. (DE) 5/31/84
(See U. S. Shelter Corp. (DE))

FIRST PIONEER BANCORP INC (MA)
Name changed to Pioneer Bancorp, Inc. 11/25/75
Pioneer Bancorp, Inc. merged into T.N.B. Financial Corp. 7/9/79 which merged into New England Merchants Co., Inc. 9/30/81 which name changed to Bank of New England Corp. 5/1/82
(See Bank of New England Corp.)

FIRST PITTSBURGH SMALL BUSINESS INVESTMENT CO. (PA)
Liquidation completed
Each share Common $5 par received initial distribution of $1 cash 4/13/69
Each share Common $5 par received second distribution of $1.20 cash 6/6/69
Each share Common $5 par received third distribution of $1.60 cash 9/19/69
Each share Common $5 par received fourth distribution of $0.75 cash 3/5/70
Each share Common $5 par received fifth distribution of $0.50 cash 7/18/70
Each share Common $5 par received sixth distribution of $0.30 cash 11/18/70
Each share Common $5 par received seventh distribution of $1 cash 10/4/71
Each share Common $5 par received eighth distribution of $2.75 cash 10/19/72
Each share Common $5 par received ninth distribution of $0.75 cash 1/3/74
Each share Common $5 par exchanged for tenth and final distribution of $0.15 cash 8/18/76

FIRST PL FINL CORP (DE)
Chapter 11 bankrupcy proceedings converted to Chapter 7 on 03/25/2013
Stockholders' equity unlikely

FIRST PL FINL CORP (NM)
Common no par split (2) for (1) by issuance of (1) additional share 04/01/1985
Merged into Wells Fargo & Co. (New) 01/18/2000
Each share Common no par exchanged for (2.034708) shares Common $1-2/3 par

FIRST PL TWR INC (ON)
Acquired by O&Y Properties Corp. 09/08/1999
Each share Common no par exchanged for $40 cash

FIRST PLATINUM CARD CORP (NV)
Recapitalized as First Platinum Retail Innovations, Inc. 02/16/2007
Each share Common no par exchanged for (0.2) share Common no par
(See First Platinum Retail Innovations, Inc.)

FIRST PLATINUM RETAIL INNOVATIONS INC (NV)
Charter permanently revoked 06/30/2010

FIRST PT MINERALS CORP (AB)
Name changed from First Point Capital Corp. to First Point Minerals Corp. 01/10
Name changed to FPX Nickel Corp. 08/25/2017

FIRST POLK BANKSHARES INC (GA)
Merged into SouthCrest Financial Group, Inc. 9/30/2004
Each share Common $1 par exchanged for either (1) share Common no par or $16 cash
Note: Option to elect to receive cash expired 11/8/2004

FIRST PORTLAND NATIONAL BANK (PORTLAND, ME)
Capital Stock $25 par changed to $20 par and (0.25) additional share issued 1/31/58
Stock Dividend - 11-1/9% 1/28/55
Name changed to First National Bank (Portland, ME) 4/1/60
First National Bank (Portland, ME) name changed to Maine National Bank (Portland, ME) 8/2/68 which reorganized as Maine National Corp. 2/18/83 which merged into Bank of New England Corp. 12/18/85
(See Bank of New England Corp.)

FIRST POTASH CORP (BC)
Delisted from NEX 09/11/2015

FIRST POTOMAC RLTY TR (MD)
7.75% Perpetual Preferred Ser. A $0.001 par called for redemption at $25 plus $0.269097 accrued dividends on 07/06/2016
Acquired by Government Properties Income Trust 10/02/2017
Each share Common $0.001 par exchanged for $11.15 cash

FIRST PWR & LT INC (FL)
Name changed to Volt Solar Systems, Inc. 05/01/2014
(See Volt Solar Systems, Inc.)

FIRST PRAIRIE DIVERSIFIED ASSET FD (MA)
Ceased operations 12/29/1997
Details not available

FIRST PRAIRIE MONEY MKT FD (MA)
Ceased operations 12/29/1997
Details not available

FIRST PRAIRIE TAX EXEMPT BD FD INC (MD)
Ceased operations 12/29/1997
Details not available

FIRST PRAIRIE TAX EXEMPT MONEY MKT FD (MA)
Ceased operations 12/29/1997
Details not available

FIRST PREF FD INC (UT)
Reincorporated under the laws of Texas as GulfWest Energy, Inc. (Old) 07/22/1992
GulfWest Energy, Inc. (Old) recapitalized as GulfWest Oil Co. 07/30/1992 which name changed to GulfWest Energy, Inc. (New) (TX) 05/21/2001 which reincorporated in Delaware as Crimson Exploration Inc. 06/13/2005 which merged into Contango Oil & Gas Co. 10/02/2013

FIRST PFD CAP TR (DE)
Issue Information - 3,000,000 TRUST PFD SECS 9.25% offered at $25 per share on 01/29/1997
9.25% Trust Preferred Securities called for redemption at $25 on 05/05/2003

FIRST PFD CAP TR II (DE)
10.24% Trust Preferred Securities called for redemption at $25 on 09/30/2005

FIRST PFD CAP TR III (DE)
9% Trust Preferred Securities called for redemption at $25 on 12/31/2006

FIRST PFD CAP TR IV (DE)
8.15% Trust Preferred Securities called for redemption at $25 plus $0.509375 accrued dividends on 12/31/2015

FIRST PFD TR (ON)
Capital Units called for redemption at $25 on 10/12/1990

FIRST PREM INCOME TR (ON)
Each Trust Unit no par received distribution of (1) Warrant expiring 03/31/2010 payable 11/20/2009 to holders of record 11/19/2009
Ex date - 11/17/2009
Merged into Premier Canadian Income Fund 06/30/2010
Each Trust Unit automatically became (2.372708) Trust Units
(See Premier Canadian Income Fund)

FIRST PREM OIL & GAS INCOME TR (ON)
Trust terminated 01/01/2007
Each Trust Unit received first and final distribution of $13.0153 cash

FIRST PREM U S INCOME TR (ON)
Under plan of reorganization each Trust Unit automatically became (0.43514098) share Top 10 Split Trust Preferred and (0.43514098) Capital Unit 12/07/2005

FIRST PRESIDENTIAL SAVINGS & LOAN ASSOCIATION OF FLORIDA (FL)
Each share Capital Stock $10 par exchanged for (4) shares Capital Stock $2.50 par 1/16/84
Merged into Cook Interim Savings & Loan Association 2/1/88
Each share Capital Stock $2.50 par exchanged for $11.70 cash

FIRST PRIORITY BK (MALVERN, PA)
Under plan of reorganization each share Common $1 par automatically became (1) share First Priority Financial Corp. Common $1 par 05/11/2007
First Priority Financial Corp. merged into Mid Penn Bancorp, Inc. 08/01/2018

FIRST PRIORITY FINL CORP (PA)
Merged into Mid Penn Bancorp, Inc. 08/01/2018
Each share Common $1 par exchanged for (0.3481) share Common $1 par

FIRST PRIORITY GROUP INC (NY)
Name changed to Driversshield.com Corp. 11/2/2000
Driversshield.com Corp. name changed to DriverShield Corp. 2/4/2002 which name changed to Accesity Corp. (NY) 1/24/2003
Accesity Corp. (NY) reorganized in Delaware as Pacific Ethanol, Inc. 3/24/2005

FIRST PROJ INC (FL)
Each share old Common $0.0001 par exchanged for (1/3) share new Common $0.0001 par 1/3/97
Recapitalized as Hydrofuser Industries Inc. 6/23/97
Each share new Common $0.0001 par exchanged for (0.5) share Common $0.0001 par

FIRST PROVIDENT GROUP INC (NC)
Administratively dissolved 2/27/95

FIRST PROVIDENT INC (NC)
Under plan of reorganization each share Common $1 par automatically became (1) share Provident Financial Corp. Common $1 par 07/12/1972
Provident Financial Corp. merged into South Carolina National Corp. 08/31/1973 which merged into Wachovia Corp. (New) (Ctfs. dated between 05/20/1991 and 09/01/2001) 12/06/1991 which merged into Wachovia Corp. (Ctfs. dated after 09/01/2001) 09/01/2001 which merged into Wells Fargo & Co. (New) 12/31/2008

FIRST PUB SVGS BK (LOS ANGELES, CA)
Merged into Cathay Bancorp Inc. 11/18/96
Each share Common exchanged for approximately (0.4836) share Common 1¢ par or approximately $7.90 cash
Note: Non-electing holders will receive the final merger allocation as defined in the agreement
Cathay Bancorp Inc. name changed to Cathay General Bancorp 10/20/2003

FIRST PUB SECS TRANSFER CORP (ON)
Name changed to First Canadian American Brokerage Ltd. 10/25/2004

FIRST PURSUIT VENTURES LTD (BC)
Name changed to Silver Pursuit Resources Ltd. 06/03/2011
Silver Pursuit Resources Ltd. name changed to Golden Pursuit Resources Ltd. 06/15/2018

FIRST PYRAMID LIFE INS CO AMER (AR)
Each share Common $8 par exchanged for (4) shares Class V Common $1 par and (4) shares Non-Voting Class N Common $1 par 3/20/64
Class V Common $1 par reclassified as Class V Common $1 par 12/22/77
Non-Voting Class N Common $1 par reclassified as Class N Common $1 par 12/22/77
Class V Common $1 par changed to $1.50 par 4/20/81
Class N Common $1 par changed to $1.50 par 4/20/81
Stock Dividends - paid in Non-Voting Class N Common to Class V Common and Non-Voting Class N Common; 100% 3/1/65; 109.29% 6/9/71; 25% 9/29/72
Acquired by Security Benefit Group, Inc. 11/30/84
Each share Class V Common $1.50 par exchanged for $6.15 cash
Each share Class N Common $1.50 par exchanged for $6.15 cash

FIRST QUALITY CORP (DE)
Charter cancelled and declared inoperative and void for non-payment of taxes 4/15/72

FIRST QUANTUM MINERALS LTD (CANADA)
Reorganized 07/18/1996
Reincorporated 08/11/2003
Reorganized from First Quantum Ventures Ltd. (BC) to First Quantum Minerals Ltd. (Yukon) 07/18/1996
Place of incorporation changed from (Yukon) to (Canada) 08/11/2003
Reincorporated under the laws of British Columbia 06/03/2005

FIRST QUANTUM VENTURES INC (NV)
Each share old Common $0.001 par exchanged for (0.01) share new Common $0.001 par 02/25/2008
Name changed to DiMi Telematics International, Inc. 03/16/2012
DiMi Telematics International, Inc. name changed to Bespoke Extracts, Inc. 03/10/2017

FIRST RR & BKG CO GA (GA)
Class A Common $1 par reclassified as Common $1 par 06/06/1962
Common $1 par changed to 66-2/3¢ par and (0.5) additional share issued 06/05/1970
Common 66-2/3¢ par split (2) for (1) by issuance of (1) additional share 05/15/1986
Acquired by First Union Corp. 11/01/1986
Each share Common 66-2/3¢ par exchanged for (1.08) shares Common $3.33-1/3 par
First Union Corp. name changed to Wachovia Corp. (Ctfs. dated after 09/01/2001) 09/01/2001 which merged into Wells Fargo & Co. (New) 12/31/2008

FIRST RLTY CAP FDS CORP (NY)
Acquired by First Connecticut Small Business Investment Co. 01/25/1971
Details not available

FIRST REALTY CORP. (WA)
Each share Preferred no par exchanged for (1) share Common $1 par in 1936
Liquidation completed 2/28/57

FIRST RLTY FINL INC (NV)
Recapitalized as Hunter Energy Inc. 3/19/92
Each share Common $0.001 par exchanged for (1/3) share Common $0.001 par
(See Hunter Energy Inc.)

FIRST RLTY INVT CORP (DE)
Reincorporated 4/15/71
Place of incorporation changed from (DC) to (DE) 4/15/71
Name changed to Thor Corp. (DE) 6/8/76
Thor Corp. (DE) name changed to Thor Energy Resources, Inc. 7/31/81
(See Thor Energy Resources Inc.)

1ST RLTY INVTS INC (NV)
Recapitalized as Great Western Land & Recreation, Inc. 02/05/2004
Each share Common $0.001 par exchanged for (0.125) share Common $0.001 par
(See Great Western Land & Recreation, Inc.)

FIRST REC CORP (AZ)
Each share Common 50¢ par exchanged for (0.4) share Common $1.25 par 9/11/73
Name changed to Financial Resource Corp. and Common $1.25 par changed to no par 7/24/81
(See Financial Resource Corp.)

FIRST REGL BANCORP (CA)
Common no par split (3) for (1) by issuance of (2) additional shares payable 08/21/2006 to holders of record 07/31/2006 Ex date - 08/22/2006
Plan of reorganization under Chapter 11 Federal Bankruptcy proceedings effective 01/17/2014
Stockholders' equity unlikely

FIRST REGL BANCORP INC (DE)
Common 10¢ par split (3) for (1) by issuance of (2) additional shares 12/1/86
Name changed to First International Bancorp, Inc. 3/26/93
First International Bancorp, Inc. merged into United Parcel Service Inc. 8/7/2001

FIRST REP BANCORP INC (DE)
Name changed to First Republic Bank (San Francisco, CA) 09/12/1997
First Republic Bank (San Francisco, CA) merged into Merrill Lynch & Co., Inc. 09/21/2007 which was acquired by Bank of America Corp. 01/02/2009

FIRST REP BANCORP INC (PA)
Name changed to Republic First Bancorp, Inc. 7/15/97

FIRST REP BK NEW (SAN FRANCISCO, CA)
6.7% Depositary Preferred Ser. A called for redemption at $25 plus $0.139583 accrued dividends on 01/30/2017
6.2% Depositary Preferred Ser. B called for redemption at $25 plus $0.327222 accrued dividends on 06/16/2017

5.625% Depositary Preferred Ser. C called for redemption at $25 plus $0.351563 accrued dividends on 01/02/2018
(Additional Information in Active)

FIRST REP BK OLD (SAN FRANCISCO, CA)
Common 1¢ par split (3) for (2) by issuance of (0.5) additional share payable 03/22/2001 to holders of record 02/28/2001 Ex date - 03/23/2001
Common 1¢ par split (3) for (2) by issuance of (0.5) additional share payable 03/15/2005 to holders of record 03/01/2005 Ex date - 03/16/2005
Merged into Merrill Lynch & Co., Inc. 09/21/2007
Each share Depositary Preferred Ser. A exchanged for (1) share 6.70% Depositary Preferred Ser. 6
Each share Depositary Perpetual Preferred Ser. B exchanged for (1) share 6.25% Depositary Preferred Ser. 7
Each share Common 1¢ par exchanged for (0.7332) share Common $1.33-1/3 par
Merrill Lynch & Co., Inc. acquired by Bank of America Corp. 01/02/2009

FIRST REP PFD CAP CORP (NV)
8.875% Preferred Ser. B 1¢ par called for redemption at $25 plus $0.296 accrued dividends on 11/19/2007
10.50% Non-Cum. Preferred Ser. A 1¢ par called for redemption at $1,021 plus $16.9167 accrued dividends on 02/28/2012
7.25% Non-Cum. Preferred Ser. D 1¢ par redemption at $25 plus $0.453125 accrued dividends on 06/29/2012
Public interest eliminated

FIRST REPUBLICBANK CORP (DE)
Plan of reorganization under Chapter 11 Federal Bankruptcy Code effective 07/15/1991
Each share Adjustable Rate Preferred no par exchanged for $0.0321 cash
Each share Adjustable Rate Preferred Ser. B no par exchanged for $0.0321 cash
Each share Adjustable Rate Preferred Ser. C no par exchanged for $0.0321 cash
Each share $2.125 Conv. Preferred Ser. A no par exchanged for $0.031176 cash
Each share Common $5 par exchanged for $0.02568 cash
Each share Conv. Class A Common $1 par exchanged for $0.02568 cash

FIRST RESH CORP (FL)
Name changed to American & Overseas Corp. 08/07/1967 which name changed back to First Research Corp. 09/09/1968
Assets sold under Charter X bankruptcy reorganization filed 03/02/1970
No stockholders' equity

FIRST RES CORP (NV)
Name changed to Graphite Corp. 06/22/2012

FIRST RESPONDER PRODS INC (DE)
Name changed to GWS Technologies, Inc. 07/07/2008
(See GWS Technologies, Inc.)

FIRST RESPONSE MED INC (FL)
Stock Dividend - 100% 01/17/1990
Recapitalized as RMS Titanic, Inc. 05/19/1993
Each share Common $0.0001 par exchanged for (0.5) share Common $0.0001 par
RMS Titanic, Inc. name changed to Premier Exhibitions, Inc. 10/18/2004

FIRST RESV INC (FL)
Merged into EWM Merger Corp. 07/22/2003

Each share Common no par exchanged for $3 cash

FIRST ROYAL FINL CORP (AB)
Delisted from Alberta Stock Exchange 01/16/1991

FIRST S & L SHS INC (CO)
Stock Dividends - 20% 3/1/71; 20% 3/20/79
Merged into Golden West Financial Corp. 5/28/82
Each share Common $2.50 par exchanged for $15 cash

FIRST SAFE DEPOSIT NATIONAL BANK (NEW BEDFORD, MA)
Name changed to First National Bank (New Bedford, MA) 4/1/66
First National Bank (New Bedford, MA) reorganized as First Melville Bancorp, Inc. 5/10/74 which merged into Shawmut Corp. 10/1/81 which merged into Shawmut National Corp. 2/29/88 which merged into Fleet Financial Group Inc. (New) 11/30/95 which name changed to Fleet Boston Corp. 10/1/99 which name changed to FleetBoston Financial Corp. 4/18/2000 which merged into Bank of America Corp. 4/1/2004

FIRST SAFETY FD NATL BK (FITCHBURG, MA)
Reorganized as Safety Fund Corp. 6/4/74
Each share Common $10 par exchanged for (1) share Common $10 par
Safety Fund Corp. merged into CFX Corp. 7/1/96 which merged into Peoples Heritage Financial Group, Inc. 4/10/98 which name changed to Banknorth Group, Inc. (ME) 5/10/2000 which merged into TD Banknorth Inc. 3/1/2005
(See TD Banknorth Inc.)

FIRST SAHARA ENERGY INC (AB)
Reincorporated 11/26/2014
Place of incorporation changed from (ON) to (AB) 11/26/2014
Name changed to M Pharmaceutical Inc. 01/28/2015
M Pharmaceutical Inc. recapitalized as Callitas Health Inc. 09/20/2017

FIRST SAN FRANCISCO BANK (SAN FRANCISCO, CA)
Acquired by Commonwealth National Bank (San Francisco, CA) 07/26/1968
Each share Capital Stock $20 par exchanged for (0.2) share Morris Plan Co. Capital Stock $5 par and $31.50 cash
Morris Plan Co. name changed to Morlan Pacific Corp. 04/15/1969 which merged into Creditthrift Financial Corp. 11/04/1971 which name changed to American General Finance Corp. 03/20/1989
(See American General Finance Corp.)

FIRST SANLANDO BANK, N.A. (LONGWOOD, FL)
Name changed to First National Bank of Central Florida (Longwood, FL) 6/1/88

FIRST SVGS & LN ASSN (CA)
Under plan of merger each share Common no par exchanged for $32.5152 principal amount of a regular 5-1/2% passbook savings account 11/01/1981

FIRST SVGS & LN ASSN (NEW BRUNSWICK, NJ)
Taken over by New Jersey State Banking Commission and merged into City Federal Savings & Loan Association 1/25/82
Stockholders' equity unlikely

FIRST SAVINGS & LOAN ASSOCIATION OF MIDLAND (TX)
100% acquired by Southern Union

Financial Corp. through purchase offer which Public interest eliminated

FIRST SVGS & LN ASSN S D INC (SD)
Merged into Spectrum Bancorp 3/27/98
Each share Common exchanged for $3.17 cash

FIRST SAVINGS & TRUST CO. (TAMPA, FL)
Name changed to Marine Bank & Trust Co. (Tampa, Fla.) 7/1/49
Marine Bank & Trust Co. (Tampa, Fla.) name changed to Flagship Bank of Tampa (Tampa, Fla.) 11/8/74 which name changed to Sun Bank of Tampa Bay (Tampa, Fla.) 1/1/84

FIRST SVGS ASSN WIS (WI)
Merged into First Financial Corp. (WI) 8/23/85
Each share Common $1 par exchanged for (0.35) share Common $1 par
First Financial Corp. (WI) merged into Associated Banc-Corp 10/29/97

FIRST SVGS BANCORP (OH)
Merged into Tristate Bancorp 9/30/92
Each share Common $1 par exchanged for (1.245) shares Common $1 par
Tristate Bancorp merged into Fifth Third Bancorp 12/22/93

FIRST SVGS BANCORP INC (NC)
Merged into First Bancorp 9/14/2000
Each share Common no par exchanged for (1.2468) shares Common $5 par

FIRST SVGS BK FLA FSB (TARPON SPRINGS, FL)
Merged into Gibraltar Financial Corp. 07/31/1987
Each share Common 1¢ par exchanged for $43 cash

FIRST SVGS BK FSB (CLOVIS, NM)
Common $1 par split (5) for (4) by issuance of (0.25) additional share 05/22/1987
Common $1 par split (6) for (5) by issuance of (0.2) additional share 08/10/1989
Reincorporated under the laws of Delaware as Access Anytime Bancorp, Inc. and Common $1 par changed to 1¢ par 10/21/1996
Access Anytime Bancorp, Inc. merged into First State Bancorporation 01/03/2006
(See First State Bancorporation)

FIRST SVGS BK FSB (GREENVILLE, SC)
Common $1 par split (3) for (2) by issuance of (0.5) additional share 2/23/93
Stock Dividends - 10% 2/15/91; 10% 4/15/92
Merged into Southern National Corp. 1/28/94
Each share Common $1 par exchanged for (0.855) share Common $5 par
Southern National Corp. name changed to BB&T Corp. 5/19/97

FIRST SVGS BK FSB (HICKORY, NC)
Merged into Regency Bancshares Inc. 12/31/1990
Each share Common $1 par exchanged for (1) share Common $1 par
Regency Bancshares Inc. merged into Southern National Corp. 01/31/1994 which name changed to BB&T Corp. 05/19/1997

FIRST SVGS BK NEW JERSEY SLA (BAYONNE, NJ)
Reorganized as Bayonne Bancshares, Inc. 8/21/97
Each share Common 10¢ par exchanged for (0.34094783) share Common 1¢ par

Bayonne Bancshares, Inc. merged into Richmond County Financial Corp. 3/22/99 which merged into New York Community Bancorp, Inc. 7/31/2001

FIRST SVGS BK OF MOORE CNTY (SOUTHERN PINES, NC)
Under plan of reorganization each share Common no par automatically became (1) share First Savings Bancorp, Inc. Common no par 11/1/95
First Savings Bancorp, Inc. merged into First Bancorp 9/14/2000

FIRST SVGS BK SLA (PERTH AMBOY, NJ)
Common 1¢ par split (2) for (1) by issuance of (1) additional share 12/1/94
Stock Dividends - 10% 4/1/94; 10% payable 12/15/96 to holders of record 12/2/96; 10% payable 10/30/97 to holders of record 10/15/97
Reorganized as First Source Bancorp Inc. 4/9/98
Each share Common 1¢ par exchanged for (3.9133) shares Common 10¢ par

FIRST SVGS BK VA (SPRINGFIELD, VA)
Merged into Southern Financial Bancorp, Inc. 09/01/2000
Each share Common exchanged for (0.44) share Common $8 par
Southern Financial Bancorp, Inc. merged into Provident Bankshares Corp. 04/30/2004 which was acquired by M&T Bank Corp. 05/26/2009

FIRST SVGS BK WASH BANCORP INC (DE)
Reincorporated under the laws of Washington as First Washington Bancorp, Inc. 7/24/98
First Washington Bancorp, Inc. name changed to Banner Corp. 10/30/2000

FIRST SVGS FINL CORP (NC)
Merged into FCB Acquisition Corp. 9/26/97
Each share Common $10 par exchanged for $10.75 cash

FIRST SCIENTIFIC INC (DE)
SEC revoked common stock registration 11/18/2005

FIRST SEC BANCORP INC (DE)
Acquired by First Midwest Bancorp, Inc. 01/30/1985
Details not available

FIRST SEC BANCORP INC (KY)
Merged into American Founders Bancorp, Inc. 5/9/2006
Each share Common no par exchanged for $24 cash

FIRST SEC BK (IONIA, MI)
Common $20 par changed to $10 par and (1) additional share issued 02/07/1973
Stock Dividend - 10% 03/08/1973
Reorganized as Independent Bank Corp. 06/01/1974
Each share Common $10 par exchanged for (2) shares Common $1 par

FIRST SEC BK (NEWCASTLE, WY)
Each share old Common exchanged for (0.002) share new Common 10/20/2000
Note: In effect holders received $198.38 cash per share and public interest was eliminated

FIRST SEC BK (ROANOKE, VA)
Bank closed by FDIC 05/24/1991
Stockholders' equity unlikely

FIRST SEC BK LEXINGTON INC (LEXINGTON, KY)
Under plan of reorganization each share Common no par automatically

became (2) shares First Security Bancorp Inc. Common no par 5/31/2000
(See First Security Bancorp Inc.)

FIRST SEC BK OWENSBORO INC (OWENSBORO, KY)
Under plan of reorganization each share Common no par automatically became (1) share First Security Inc. Common no par 8/10/2000

FIRST SEC CORP (BC)
Name changed to Telelink Communications Corp. (Old) 03/08/1993
Telelink Communications Corp. (Old) merged into Telelink Communications Corp. (New) (BC) 08/01/1996 which reorganized in Canada as Ignition Point Technologies Corp. 04/20/2001 which recapitalized as Tilting Capital Corp. 08/24/2009

FIRST SEC CORP (DE)
Each share old Common $2.50 par exchanged for (1) share new Common $2.50 par and (1) share of First Security Investment Co. Common 25¢ par 09/15/1959
(See First Security Investment Co.)
New Common $2.50 par changed to $1.25 par and (1) additional share issued 06/30/1960
Common $1.25 par split (2) for (1) by issuance of (1) additional share 05/27/1972
Common $1.25 par split (2) for (1) by issuance of (1) additional share 05/15/1978
Common $1.25 par split (3) for (2) by issuance of (0.5) additional share 06/03/1991
Common $1.25 par split (3) for (2) by issuance of (0.5) additional share 05/18/1992
Common $1.25 par split (3) for (2) by issuance of (0.5) additional share payable 02/15/1996 to holders of record 02/12/1996
Common $1.25 par split (3) for (2) by issuance of (0.5) additional share payable 05/15/1997 to holders of record 05/12/1997
Common $1.25 par split (3) for (2) by issuance of (0.5) additional share payable 02/24/1998 to holders of record 02/12/1998 Ex date - 02/25/1998
$3.15 Conv. Preferred Ser. A no par called for redemption at $52.50 plus $0.66 accrued dividend on 10/06/2000
Merged into Wells Fargo & Co. (New) 10/26/2000
Each share Common $1.25 par exchanged for (0.355) share Common $1-2/3 par

FIRST SEC CORP KY (KY)
Common $6.25 par split (2) for (1) by issuance of (1) additional share 9/15/81
Common $6.25 par split (3) for (2) by issuance of (0.5) additional share 11/21/83
Common $6.25 par split (3) for (2) by issuance of (0.5) additional share 1/20/86
Common $6.25 par split (3) for (2) by issuance of (0.5) additional share 8/1/86
Common $6.25 par changed to no par 5/19/87
Stock Dividend - 10% 10/1/84
Acquired by Banc One Corp. 8/21/92
Each share Common no par exchanged for (0.553003) share Common no par
Banc One Corp. merged into Bank One Corp. 10/2/98 which merged into J.P. Morgan Chase & Co. 12/31/2000 which name changed to JPMorgan Chase & Co. 7/20/2004

FIRST SEC FINL CORP (NC)
Common $5 par split (3) for (2) by issuance of (0.5) additional share 1/31/86
Common $5 par split (5) for (4) by issuance of (0.25) additional share 1/31/87
Common $5 par split (5) for (4) by issuance of (0.25) additional share 1/29/88
Common $5 par split (5) for (4) by issuance of (0.25) additional share 1/31/91
Stock Dividends - 10% 1/31/85; 25% 1/31/89; 20% 1/31/90
Merged into Security Capital Bancorp 6/30/92
Details not available

FIRST SEC GROUP INC (TN)
Each share old Common 1¢ par exchanged for (0.1) share new Common 1¢ par 09/19/2011
Acquired by Atlantic Capital Bancshares, Inc. 10/31/2015
Each share new Common 1¢ par exchanged for $2.35 cash

FIRST SEC GROWTH FD INC (DE)
Acquired by Mutual of Omaha Growth Fund, Inc. (NE) 12/11/1972
Each share Common $1 par exchanged for (0.8) share Common 1¢ par
Mutual of Omaha Growth Fund, Inc. (NE) reincorporated in Delaware as Pioneer Growth Shares 12/01/1993 which reorganized as Pioneer Independence Fund 12/07/2007

FIRST SEC INC (KY)
Merged into German American Bancorp, Inc. 10/15/2018
Each share Common no par exchanged for (0.7982) share Common no par and $12 cash

FIRST SEC INVT CO (DE)
Merged into First Security Corp. 04/01/1970
Each share Common 25¢ par exchanged for (0.2) share $3.15 Conv. Preferred Ser. A no par
First Security Corp. merged into Wells Fargo & Co. (New) 10/26/2000

FIRST SEC NATL BK & TR CO (LEXINGTON, KY)
Capital Stock $12.50 par split (5) for (4) by issuance of (0.25) additional share 9/4/73
Stock Dividend - 100% 3/3/69
Reorganized as First Security Corp. of Kentucky 10/14/75
Each share Capital Stock $12.50 par exchanged for (2) shares Common $6.25 par
First Security Corp. of Kentucky acquired by Banc One Corp. 8/21/92 which merged into Bank One Corp. 10/2/98 which merged J.P. Morgan Chase & Co. 12/31/2000 which name changed to JPMorgan Chase & Co. 7/20/2004

FIRST SEC NATL BK (BEAUMONT, TX)
Capital Stock $20 par changed to $5 par and (3) additional shares issued 4/24/62
Stock Dividend - 10% 3/27/67
Reorganized as First Security National Corp. 9/30/69
Each share Capital Stock $5 par exchanged for (1) Unit consisting of (1) share First Security National Corp. Common $5 par and (1) share First Beaumont Corp. Common $5 par represented by both names printed on the same certificate
(See each company's listing)

FIRST SEC NATL CORP (TX)
(Stock originally part of a unit with First Beaumont Corp. Common $5 par represented by both names printed on the same certificate)
Under plan of merger each Unit exchanged for (1) share First Security National Corp. Common $5 par 12/06/1971
Common $5 par changed to $2.50 par and (1) additional share issued 02/05/1973
Merged into First City Bancorporation of Texas, Inc. (TX) 12/03/1979
Each share Common $2.50 par exchanged for (0.65) share Common $6.50 par
(See First City Bancorporation of Texas, Inc. (TX))

FIRST SEC TR & SVGS BK (ELMWOOD PARK, IL)
Capital Stock $10 par changed to $15 par 10/26/1965
Capital Stock $15 par changed to $20 par 06/30/1966
Capital Stock $20 par changed to $30 par 11/06/1969
Reorganized as First Security Bancorp, Inc. 10/05/1993
Details not available

FIRST-SECOND NATIONAL BANK & TRUST CO. (CUMBERLAND, MD)
Stock Dividend - 10% 2/10/65
Name changed to First National Bank & Trust Co. of Western Maryland (Cumberland, Md.) 5/1/66
First National Bank & Trust Co. of Western Maryland (Cumberland, Md.) merged into First Maryland Bancorp 9/4/81
(See First Maryland Bancorp)

FIRST SECS CORP SYRACUSE (NY)
Common no par changed to $1 par and $4 cash distributed 00/00/1946
Liquidation completed
Each share Common $1 par exchanged for initial distribution of (0.213835) share First Trust & Deposit Co. (Syracuse, NY) Common $2.50 par 11/15/1967
Each share Common $1 par received second and final distribution of $13 cash 12/13/1967
First Trust & Deposit Co. (Syracuse, NY) reorganized as First Commercial Banks, Inc. 12/31/1971 which name changed to Key Banks Inc. 04/23/1979 which name changed to KeyCorp (NY) 08/28/1985 which merged into KeyCorp (New) (OH) 03/01/1994

FIRST SECURITIES CO. (CA)
Name changed to Assets Corp. 3/15/34
(See Assets Corp.)

FIRST SECURITIES CORP. (PA)
Liquidated 08/28/1959
Details not available

FIRST SECURITY BANK (ADDISON, IL)
Under plan of reorganization each share Common $10 par automatically became (1) share Addison Bancshares, Inc. Common $10 par 11/30/1982
(See Addison Bancshares, Inc.)

FIRST SECURITY BANK (ELK GROVE, CA)
Capital Stock $15 par changed to $7.50 par and (1) additional share issued 10/15/1980
Acquired by RCB Corp. 09/12/1988
Each share Capital Stock $7.50 par exchanged for approximately $33 cash

FIRST SECURITY BANK (MESA, AZ)
Merged into United Bank of Arizona (Phoenix, AZ) 12/31/1967
Each share Common $10 par exchanged for (1.59) shares Common $5 par
United Bank of America (Phoenix, AZ) reorganized as UB Financial Corp. 04/30/1970 which name changed to United Bancorp of Arizona 10/17/1978
(See United Bancorp of Arizona)

FIRST SECURITY CO.
Liquidated 00/00/1934
Details not available

FIRST SECURITY CORP. OF OGDEN
Name changed to First Security Corp. and each share Class A or B Common $10 par exchanged for (4) shares Common $2.50 par in 1951
First Security Corp. merged into Wells Fargo & Co. (New) 10/26/2000

FIRST SECURITY INVESTMENT CORP. (SC)
Name changed to Fripp Island Resort, Inc. 4/6/61
(See Fripp Island Resort, Inc.)

FIRST SECURITY LIFE INSURANCE CO. (MS)
Acquired by Western Reserve Life Assurance Co. of Ohio 2/28/66
Each share Common $1 par exchanged for $13.77 cash

FIRST SECURITY SAVINGS & LOAN ASSOCIATION (CO)
Failed 11/22/1986
No stockholders' equity

FIRST SECURITYFED FINL INC (DE)
Issue Information - 4,118,000 to 5,572,000 shares COM offered at $10 per share on 09/12/1997
Merged into MB Financial, Inc. 6/1/2004
Each share Common 1¢ par exchanged for (0.75452601) share Common 1¢ par and $10.1086425 cash

FIRST SENECA BK & TR CO (OIL CITY, PA)
Stock Dividends - 100% 02/08/1955; 100% 08/26/1963; 100% 06/29/1979
Under plan of reorganization each share Capital Stock $5 par automatically became (1) share First Seneca Corp. Common $5 par 06/01/1982
First Seneca Corp. merged into Pennbancorp 12/31/1983 which merged into Integra Financial Corp. 01/26/1989 which merged into National City Corp. 05/03/1996 which was acquired by PNC Financial Services Group, Inc. 12/31/2008

FIRST SENECA CORP (PA)
Merged into Pennbancorp 12/31/1983
Each share Common $5 par exchanged for (1) share Common $5 par
Pennbancorp merged into Integra Financial Corp. 01/26/1989 which merged into National City Corp. 05/03/1996 which was acquired by PNC Financial Services Group, Inc. 12/31/2008

FIRST SENTINEL BANCORP INC (NJ)
Merged into Provident Financial Services, Inc. 07/15/2004
Each share Common 1¢ par exchanged for (1.092) shares Common 1¢ par

FIRST SENTRY BANCSHARES INC (WV)
Common $1 par split (2) for (1) by issuance of (1) additional share payable 12/31/2003 to holders of record 12/16/2003 Ex date - 01/02/2004
Common $1 par split (2) for (1) by issuance of (1) additional share payable 12/31/2004 to holders of record 12/21/2004 Ex date - 01/03/2005
Merged into WesBanco, Inc. 04/05/2018
Each share Common $1 par exchanged for (1.5869) shares Common $2.0833 par

1ST SVC BK (ARLINGTON, VA)
Merged into Southern National Bancorp of Virginia, Inc. 12/1/2006
Each share Common exchanged for

(0.76092) share Common 1¢ par and $5.26 cash

FIRST SHENANGO BANCORP INC (PA)
Merged into Signal Corp. 06/29/1998
Each share Common 10¢ par exchanged for (1.42875) shares Common $1 par
Signal Corp. merged into FirstMerit Corp. 02/12/1999 which merged into Huntington Bancshares Inc. 08/16/2016

FIRST SHIP LEASE TR (SINGAPORE)
ADR agreement terminated 02/21/2017
Each ADR for Ordinary exchanged for $0.520524 cash

FIRST SHS BANCORP INC (IN)
Common 1¢ par split (3) for (2) by issuance of (0.5) additional share payable 11/27/2002 to holders of record 11/20/2002 Ex date - 11/29/2002
Merged into Lincoln Bancorp 8/2/2004
Each share Common 1¢ par exchanged for $14.80 cash

FIRST SIDNEY BANC CORP (OH)
Acquired by First National Cincinnati Corp. 01/29/1988
Each share Common $5 par exchanged for (1.05) shares Common $5 par
First National Cincinnati Corp. name changed to Star Banc Corp. 04/13/1990 which merged into Firstar Corp. (New) 11/20/1998 which merged into U.S. Bancorp (DE) 02/27/2001

FIRST SIERRA BK (BISHOP, CA)
Closed and liquidated by FDIC 01/23/1987
No stockholders' equity

FIRST SIERRA FD (DE)
Capital Stock $1 par split (7) for (1) by issuance of (6) additional shares 05/14/1971
Merged into Founders Special Fund, Inc. 07/11/1973
Each share Capital Stock $1 par exchanged for (0.349526) share Capital Stock $1 par
Founders Special Fund, Inc. reorganized as Founders Funds, Inc. 08/31/1987 which name changed to Dreyfus Founders Funds, Inc. 12/31/1999 which name changed to Dreyfus Discovery Fund 12/01/2008

FIRST SIERRA FINL INC (DE)
Issue Information - 2,000,000 shares COM offered at $8 per share on 05/15/1997
Name changed to SierraCities.com Inc. 2/1/2000
(See SierraCities.com Inc.)

FIRST SILVER RESV INC (BC)
Merged into First Majestic Resource Corp. 09/18/2006
Each share Common no par exchanged for either (0.5) share Common no par or $2.165 cash
Note: Option to receive cash expired 12/13/2006

FIRST SMALL BUSINESS INVT CORP N J (NJ)
Liquidation completed
Each share Capital Stock $1 par stamped to indicate initial distribution of $2 cash 03/26/1971
Each share Stamped Capital Stock $1 par received second distribution of $1.50 cash 06/15/1971
Each share Stamped Capital Stock $1 par received third distribution of $1.50 cash 12/17/1971
Each share Stamped Capital Stock $1 par received fourth distribution of $1 cash 04/28/1972
Each share Stamped Capital Stock $1 par received fifth distribution of $1 cash 07/14/1972
Each share Stamped Capital Stock $1 par received sixth distribution of $1 cash 12/29/1972
Each share Stamped Capital Stock $1 par received seventh distribution of $2 cash 08/15/1973
Each share Stamped Capital Stock $1 par received eighth distribution of $2.25 cash 01/10/1974
Each share Stamped Capital Stock $1 par received ninth distribution of $0.25 cash 01/20/1976
Each share Stamped Capital Stock $1 par exchanged for tenth and final distribution of $0.50 cash 05/16/1977

FIRST SOCIAL NETWORX CORP (FL)
Name changed to Moxian Group Holdings, Inc. 04/16/2013
Moxian Group Holdings, Inc. recapitalized as Inception Technology Group, Inc. 07/23/2014 which recapitalized as Rebel Group, Inc. 12/05/2014

FIRST SOURCE BANCORP INC (NJ)
Under plan of merger name changed to First Sentinel Bancorp Inc. 12/18/2003
First Sentinel Bancorp Inc. merged into Provident Financial Services, Inc. 7/15/2004

1ST SOURCE CAP TR I (DE)
9% Trust Preferred Securities called for redemption at $25 on 09/16/2004

1ST SOURCE CAP TR II (DE)
Floating Rate Trust Preferred Securities
$25 par called for redemption at $25 on 08/01/2007

1ST SOURCE CORP (IN)
Class B Non-Vtg. Preferred $10 par called for redemption 7/1/89
(Additional Information in Active)

FIRST SOURCE DATA INC (NV)
Common $0.001 par split (4) for (1) by issuance of (3) additional shares payable 06/06/2007 to holders of record 06/05/2007 Ex date - 06/07/2007
Name changed to UOMO Media Inc. 10/30/2007

FIRST SOURCE RES INC (BC)
Recapitalized as CB Gold Inc. 11/02/2010
Each share Common no par exchanged for (0.254512) share Common no par
CB Gold Inc. name changed to Red Eagle Exploration Inc. 03/06/2017 which merged into Red Eagle Mining Corp. 04/25/2018

FIRST SOUTH AFRICA CORP LTD (BERMUDA)
Name changed to Leisureplanet Holdings, Ltd. 05/11/1999
Leisureplanet Holdings, Ltd. name changed to Silverstar Holdings, Ltd. 12/14/2000
(See Silverstar Holdings, Ltd.)

FIRST SOUTH BANCORP INC (VA)
Common 1¢ par split (3) for (2) by issuance of (0.5) additional share payable 04/19/2002 to holders of record 04/08/2002
Common 1¢ par split (3) for (2) by issuance of (0.5) additional share payable 04/23/2004 to holders of record 04/02/2004 Ex date - 04/26/2004
Common 1¢ par split (3) for (2) by issuance of (0.5) additional share payable 05/25/2006 to holders of record 05/04/2006 Ex date - 05/26/2006
Merged into Carolina Financial Corp. (New) 11/01/2017
Each share Common 1¢ par exchanged for (0.5064) share Common 1¢ par

FIRST SOUTH BK (SPARTANBURG, SC)
Under plan of reorganization each share Common no par automatically became (1) share First South Bancorp Inc. Common no par 09/30/1999

FIRST SOUTH BANKCORP (GA)
Merged into First Railroad & Banking Co. of Georgia 12/30/1982
Each share Common $5 par exchanged for $18.75 principal amount of 11% Conv. Promissory Notes due 12/30/1992, (1) share Common 66-2/3¢ par and $23.125 cash
First Railroad & Banking Co. of Georgia acquired by First Union Corp. 11/01/1986 which name changed to Wachovia Corp. (Ctfs. dated after 09/01/2001) 09/01/2001 which merged into Wells Fargo & Co. (New) 12/31/2008

FIRST SOUTHEAST FINL CORP (DE)
Acquired by Carolina First Corp. 11/21/1997
Each share Common 1¢ par exchanged for (0.7971) share Common $1 par
Carolina First Corp. name changed to South Financial Group, Inc. 04/24/2000 which merged into Toronto-Dominion Bank (Toronto, ON) 09/30/2010

FIRST SOUTHERN BANK CORP. (FL)
Merged into Barnett Banks of Florida, Inc. 1/31/84
Each share Common $5 par exchanged for (2) shares $3.88 Conv. Preferred Ser. D 10¢ par
(See Barnett Banks of Florida, Inc.)

FIRST SOUTHERN CO. (NC)
7% Preferred Ser. A $10 par called for redemption 2/1/65
Completely liquidated 6/8/65
Each share Common $1 par exchanged for (1/6) share Liberty Loan Corp. Common $1 par
Liberty Loan Corp. name changed to LLC Corp. 3/14/80 which name changed to Valhi, Inc. 3/10/87

FIRST SOUTHERN MORTGAGE CORP. (GA)
Administratively dissolved 5/13/88

1ST SOUTHN ST BK (AVALON, NJ)
Merged into Covenant Bank for Savings (Haddonfield, NJ) 09/27/1996
Each share Common exchanged for (1.55) shares Common $5 par
Covenant Bank for Savings (Haddonfield, NJ) reorganized as Covenant Bancorp, Inc. 06/13/1997 which merged into First Union Corp. 01/15/1998 which name changed to Wachovia Corp. (Ctfs. dated after 09/01/2001) 09/01/2001 which merged into Wells Fargo & Co. (New) 12/31/2008

FIRST SOUTHN BANCORP INC (FL)
Merged into CenterState Banks, Inc. 06/01/2014
Each share Common 1¢ par exchanged for (0.3) share Common 1¢ par and $3 cash
CenterState Banks, Inc. name changed to CenterState Bank Corp. 09/08/2017

FIRST SOUTHN BANCORP INC (NC)
Merged into Centura Banks, Inc. 6/2/95
Each share Common no par exchanged for (1.125) shares Common no par
Centura Banks, Inc. merged into Royal Bank of Canada (Montreal, QC) 6/5/2001

FIRST SOUTHN BANCSHARES INC (DE)
Each (2,000) shares old Common 1¢ par exchanged for (1) share new Common 1¢ par 1/31/2005
Note: In effect holders received $1.50 cash per share and public interest was eliminated

FIRST SOUTHN CAP CORP (CA)
Acquired by FSCC Merger Corp. 11/01/1984
Each share Common 10¢ par exchanged for $1.92 cash

FIRST SOUTHN FED SVGS & LN ASSN (USA)
Name changed to Altus Bank, A Federal Savings Bank (Mobile, AL) 06/01/1987
(See Altus Bank, A Federal Savings Bank (Mobile, AL))

FIRST SOUTHWEST BANCORP INC (GA)
Merged into First State Bancshares 11/8/96
Each share Common exchanged for $24.25 cash

FIRST SPORTS INTL INC (ON)
Recapitalized as Black Pearl Minerals Inc. 07/21/1995
Each share Common no par exchanged for (0.2) share Common no par
Black Pearl Minerals Inc. recapitalized as Black Pearl Minerals Consolidated Inc. 06/22/2000 which name changed to Canada Lithium Corp. (ON) 01/19/2009 which reorganized in Canada as RB Energy Inc. 02/05/2014

FIRST SPRINGFIELD CORP. (MA)
Liquidation for cash completed 2/11/66

FIRST ST BANCORP (IL)
Reorganized 05/23/1983
Under plan of reorganization each share First State Bank (Princeton, IL) Common $5 par automatically became (1) share First State Bancorp of Princeton Illinois, Inc. Common $5 par 05/23/1983
Acquired by AMCORE Financial, Inc. 08/01/1994
Each share Common $5 par exchanged for 1.835 shares Common $2.02 par
(See AMCORE Financial, Inc.)

FIRST ST BANK (STOCKBRIDGE, GA)
Reorganized as Henry County Bancshares, Inc. 05/00/1983
Each share Common $5 par exchanged for (1) share Common $5 par
(See Henry County Bancshares, Inc.)

FIRST ST CAP FD INC (DE)
All shares redeemed 00/00/1977
Public interest eliminated

FIRST ST CORP (GA)
Common $10 par split (2) for (1) by issuance of (1) additional share 7/15/94
Common $10 par split (3) for (2) by issuance of (0.5) additional share payable 7/1/96 to holders of record 6/15/96
Common $10 par split (3) for (2) by issuance of (0.5) additional share payable 5/20/97 to holders of record 5/10/97
Stock Dividend - 10% 5/3/95
Merged into Regions Financial Corp. (Old) 3/31/98
Each share Common $10 par exchanged for (0.56) share Common $0.625 par
Regions Financial Corp. (Old) merged into Regions Financial Corp. (New) 7/1/2004

FIRST ST FINL CORP (FL)
Issue Information - 2,127,500 shares

COM offered at $12 per share on 12/09/2004
Company's sole asset placed in receivership 08/07/2009
Stockholders' equity unlikely

FIRST ST FINL SVCS INC (DE)
Merged into Sovereign Bancorp, Inc. 02/18/1997
Each share Common 1¢ par exchanged for (1.225) shares Common no par
Sovereign Bancorp, Inc. merged into Banco Santander, S.A. 01/30/2009

FIRST STAMFORD BANK & TRUST CO. (STAMFORD, CT)
Liquidation completed
Each share Common $10 par exchanged for initial distribution of $67 cash 9/15/81
Each share Common $10 par received second distribution of $7 cash 3/30/82
Each share Common $10 par received third distribution of $3 cash 8/23/82
Each share Common $10 par received fourth and final distribution of $1.375 cash 6/28/85

FIRST STANDARD CORP. (DE)
Name changed to Mastercraft Electronics Corp. 1/4/68
(See Mastercraft Electronics Corp.)

FIRST STAR BANCORP INC (PA)
Common $1 par split (2) for (1) by issuance of (1) additional share payable 10/19/2007 to holders of record 10/10/2007 Ex date - 10/22/2007
Stock Dividends - 20% payable 04/14/2000 to holders of record 04/01/2000 Ex date - 04/18/2000; 20% payable 10/15/2003 to holders of record 10/01/2003 Ex date - 10/14/2003
Merged into ESSA Bancorp, Inc. 07/31/2012
Each share Common $1 par exchanged for (0.20120644) share Common 1¢ par and $9.24115664 cash

FIRST STAR CAP CORP (BC)
Name changed 04/03/1990
Name changed from First Star Energy Ltd. to First Star Capital Corp. 04/03/1990
Struck off register and declared dissolved for failure to file returns 07/09/1993

FIRST STAR ENERGY LTD (AB)
Recapitalized as Rosetta Exploration Inc. 07/19/2000
Each share Common no par exchanged for (0.2) share Common no par
Rosetta Exploration Inc. recapitalized as Berkana Energy Corp. 12/11/2006
(See Berkana Energy Corp.)

FIRST STAR INNOVATIONS INC (BC)
Name changed to First Star Resources Inc. 12/16/2003

FIRST STAR SVGS BK (BETHLEHEM, PA)
Under plan of reorganization each share Common $1 par automatically became (1) share First Star Bancorp, Inc. Common $1 par 01/07/1994
First Star Bancorp, Inc. merged into ESSA Bancorp, Inc. 07/31/2012

FIRST ST BANCORP (CA)
Merged into Boston Private Financial Holdings, Inc. 02/17/2004
Each share Common no par exchanged for (0.6757) share Common no par and $2.84265 cash

FIRST ST BANCORP (NJ)
Merged into Staten Island Bancorp, Inc. 01/14/2000

Each share Common no par exchanged for $174.93 cash

1ST ST BANCORP INC (VA)
Merged into Capital Bank Corp. 01/03/2006
Each share Common 1¢ par exchanged for (1.684457) shares Common no par and $11.4486 cash
Capital Bank Corp. merged into Capital Bank Financial Corp. 09/24/2012 which merged into First Horizon National Corp. 11/30/2017

FIRST ST BANCORP INC (WI)
Name changed to First Bancorporation, Inc. 03/19/1997
(See First Bancorporation, Inc.)

FIRST ST BANCORPORATION (NM)
Common no par split (5) for (4) by issuance of (0.25) additional share 11/20/1995
Common no par split (3) for (2) by issuance of (0.5) additional share payable 11/22/1999 to holders of record 11/15/1999
Common no par split (2) for (1) by issuance of (1) additional share payable 03/09/2005 to holders of record 02/09/2005 Ex date - 03/10/2005
Principal asset placed in receivership 01/28/2011
Stockholders' equity unlikely

FIRST ST BANCSHARES CORP (MO)
Name changed to Landmark Bancshares Corp. 09/01/1976
Landmark Bancshares Corp. merged into Magna Group, Inc. 12/20/1991 which merged into Union Planters Corp. 07/01/1998 which merged into Regions Financial Corp. (New) 07/01/2004

FIRST ST BK (CRANFORD, NJ)
Bank closed and FDIC appointed receiver 10/14/2011
Stockholders' equity unlikely

FIRST STATE BANK & TRUST CO. (EUSTIS, FL)
Through voluntary exchange offer 97.4% acquired by Atlantic Bancorporation as of 02/29/1972
Public interest eliminated

FIRST STATE BANK (ARANSAS PASS, TX)
Merged into First City Bancorporation of Texas, Inc. (TX) 12/31/1981
Each share Common $5 par exchanged for (1-1/3) shares Common $3.25 par
(See First City Bancorporation of Texas, Inc. (TX))

FIRST STATE BANK (CORDELE, GA)
Merged into First State Corp. 12/31/84
Each share Common $10 par exchanged for (0.628) share Common $10 par
First State Corp. merged into Regions Financial Corp. (Old) 3/31/98 which merged Regions Financial Corp. (New) 7/1/2004

FIRST STATE BANK (COVINGTON, TN)
Under plan of reorganization each share Common $10 par automatically became (1) share FSB, Inc. Common $10 par 11/3/82
FSB, Inc. merged into Union Planters Corp. 12/31/98 which merged into Regions Financial Corp. (New) 7/1/2004

FIRST STATE BANK (ENCINO, CA)
Common $6 par changed to no par and (1.25) additional shares issued 8/14/79
Name changed to West Coast Bank (Encino, CA) 9/22/80
West Coast Bank (Encino, CA) reorganized as West Coast Bancorp 12/16/81 which reorganized as Genesis Learning Systems, Inc. 5/22/86
(See Genesis Learning Systems, Inc.)

FIRST STATE BANK (MILWAUKIE, OR)
Stock Dividend - 100% 2/1/61
Name changed to First State Bank of Oregon (Milwaukie, OR) 2/3/64
First State Bank of Oregon (Milwaukie, OR) merged into Pacwest Bancorp 12/31/79 which merged into KeyCorp (NY) 11/7/86 which merged into KeyCorp (New) (OH) 3/1/94

FIRST ST BK (ABILENE, TX)
Capital Stock $5 par changed to $2.50 par and (1) additional share issued 02/11/1976
Stock Dividend - 25% 01/16/1980
Reorganized as Independent Bankshares, Inc. 01/01/1981
Each share Capital Stock $2.50 par exchanged for (1) share Common $2.50 par
(See Independent Bankshares, Inc.)

FIRST ST BK & TR CO (WELLSTON, MO)
Name changed to Landmark Central Bank & Trust Co. (Wellston, MO) 11/01/1976
(See Landmark Central Bank & Trust Co. (Wellston, MO))

FIRST ST BK (AUSTIN, TX)
Under plan of merger each share Common $10 par exchanged for $85 cash 06/20/1996

FIRST ST BK (DECATUR, AL)
Stock Dividends - 15% 01/03/1972; 20% 01/03/1973
Merged into FSB Bancorporation 12/31/1982
Each share Common $1 par exchanged for (1) share Common $1 par

FIRST ST BK (DENTON, TX)
Capital Stock $100 par changed to $20 par and (4) additional shares issued 03/13/1961
Capital Stock $20 par changed to $10 par and (1) additional share issued 01/22/1969
Capital Stock $10 par changed to $5 par and (1) additional share issued 03/09/1973
Stock Dividends - 16-2/3% 02/11/1958; 10% 09/11/1959; 25% 02/09/1960; 10% 03/13/1962; 10% 03/04/1971; 10% 03/10/1972; 10% 03/31/1973; 10% 03/22/1974; 10% 04/01/1977; 10% 03/31/1978; 10% 03/05/1979; 10% 03/31/1980; 10% 03/31/1981; 10% 03/31/1982
Acquired by Texas Financial Bancorporation, Inc. 06/15/1992
Details not available

FIRST ST BK (HAWLEY, PA)
Common $5 par changed to $2 par and (2) additional shares issued 01/02/1981
Under plan of reorganization each share Common $2 par automatically became (1) share Number One Bancorp, Inc. Common $2 par 07/28/1983
Number One Bancorp, Inc. merged into Merchants Bancorp, Inc. (PA) 03/01/1985 which was acquired by Fidelcor, Inc. 12/31/1986 which merged into First Fidelity Bancorporation (New) 02/29/1988 which merged into First Union Corp. 01/01/1996 which name changed to Wachovia Corp. (Ctfs. dated after 09/01/2001) 09/01/2001 which merged into Wells Fargo & Co. (New) 12/31/2008

FIRST ST BK (LYNWOOD, CA)
Each share Capital Stock $100 par exchanged for (40) shares Capital Stock $2.50 par 12/21/1961

Stock Dividends - 100% 01/26/1961; 50% 03/01/1962; 100% 07/10/1970
Name changed to First State Bank of Southern California (Lynwood, CA) 09/11/1970
(See First State Bank of Southern California (Lynwood, CA))

FIRST ST BK (MIAMI, FL)
Through voluntary exchange offer over 99.99% acquired by First State Banking Corp. as of 01/01/1979
Public interest eliminated

FIRST ST BK (UNION, NJ)
Capital Stock $10 par changed to $5 par and (1) additional share issued 10/09/1968
Stock Dividends - 10% 07/28/1959; 10% 09/10/1967; 10% 07/10/1969
Name changed to First New Jersey Bank (Union, NJ) 10/14/1969
First New Jersey Bank (Union, NJ) merged into Franklin State Bank (Franklin Township, NJ) 08/17/1973
(See Franklin State Bank (Franklin Township, NJ))

FIRST ST BK (VAN ORIN, IL)
Reorganized as Van Orin Bancorp Inc. 05/31/2000
Each share Common $10 par exchanged for (10) shares Common $10 par

FIRST ST BK CALIF (GRANADA HILLS, CA)
Common no par split (2) for (1) by issuance of (1) additional share payable 05/08/2002 to holders of record 04/17/2002
Under plan of reorganization each share Common no par automatically became (1) share First State Bancorp Common no par 03/10/2003
First State Bancorp merged into Boston Private Financial Holdings, Inc. 02/17/2004

FIRST ST BK HUDSON CNTY (JERSEY CITY, NJ)
Placed in receivership 06/14/1976
Stockholders' equity unlikely

FIRST ST BK OCEAN CNTY (TOMS RIVER, NJ)
Common $2.50 par changed to $2 par and (0.25) additional share issued 02/26/1970
Stock Dividends - 10% 01/15/1970; 10% 01/15/1971; 10% 01/17/1972
Reorganized as American Bancorp 03/31/1972
Each share Common $2 par exchanged for (1) share Common $2 par
(See American Bancorp)

FIRST ST BK ORE (MILWAUKIE, OR)
Capital Stock $100 par changed to $10 par and (9) additional shares issued 09/15/1964
Each share Capital Stock $10 par exchanged for (2) shares Capital Stock $5 par 02/16/1973
Capital Stock $5 par split (3) for (2) by issuance of (0.5) additional share 04/20/1977
Stock Dividends - 20% 02/01/1966; 10% 02/01/1967; 10% 02/03/1969; 10% 04/15/1976; 10% 09/28/1978
Merged into Pacwest Bancorp 12/31/1979
Each share Capital Stock $5 par exchanged for (1) share Common $5 par
Pacwest Bancorp merged into KeyCorp (NY) 11/07/1986 which merged into KeyCorp (New) (OH) 03/01/1994

FIRST ST BK SOUTHN CALIF (LYNWOOD, CA)
Stock Dividend - 100% 03/01/1978
Merged into Popular North America, Inc. 10/31/1998
Each share Common no par exchanged for $60.443 cash

Note: An additional payment of $2.1711 cash per share was made 12/31/1998

FIRST STATE BANK OF THE OAKS (THOUSAND OAKS, CA)
Merged into First Interstate Bank of California (Los Angeles, CA) in 1994
Details not available

FIRST ST BKG CORP (FL)
Merged into Barnett Banks of Florida, Inc. 12/31/1981
Each share Common $5 par exchanged for (1.08) shares $2.375 Conv. Preferred Ser. A 10¢ par
(See Barnett Banks of Florida, Inc.)

FIRST STATE PAWNERS SOCIETY
Liquidation completed in 1950
Details not available

FIRST STATE SAVINGS & LOAN ASSOCIATION, INC. (NC)
Merged into CK Federal Savings Bank (Concord, NC) 10/31/1988
For holdings of (1,000) shares or fewer each share Common 25¢ par exchanged for (0.2384) share Common $1 par and $2.44 cash
For holdings of (1,001) shares or more each share Common 25¢ par exchanged for $5.42 cash
CK Federal Savings Bank (Concord, NC) acquired by SouthTrust Corp. 12/11/1992 which merged into Wachovia Corp. (Ctfs. dated after 09/01/2001) 11/01/2004 which merged into Wells Fargo & Co. (New) 12/31/2008

FIRST STD BK (LOS ANGELES, CA)
Name changed to Open Bank (Los Angeles, CA) 01/12/2011
Open Bank (Los Angeles, CA) reorganized as OP Bancorp 06/29/2016

FIRST STD VENTURES LTD (BC)
Name changed 07/16/1993
Name changed from First Standard Mining Ltd. to First Standard Ventures Ltd. 07/16/1993
Recapitalized as LRG Restaurant Group, Inc. 09/05/1995
Each share Common no par exchanged for (0.1) share Common no par
(See LRG Restaurant Group, Inc.)

FIRST STEP INC (AB)
Name changed to Footsource Inc. 08/29/2001
(See Footsource Inc.)

FIRST STEP VENTURES CORP (BC)
Reorganized under the laws of Ontario as Atikwa Minerals Corp. 07/31/2003
Each share Common no par exchanged for (0.5) share Common no par
Atikwa Minerals Corp. name changed to Atikwa Resources Inc. (ON) 11/18/2009 which reincorporated in Alberta 04/26/2010
(See Atikwa Resources Inc.)

FIRST STERLING BANCSHARES INC (FL)
Name changed to First Commerce Banks of Florida Inc. 08/31/1995
First Commerce Banks of Florida Inc. merged into Colonial BancGroup, Inc. 07/01/1997
(See Colonial BancGroup, Inc.)

FIRST STERLING BKS INC (GA)
Common no par split (2) for (1) by issuance of (1) additional share payable 03/30/1998 to holders of record 03/16/1998
Stock Dividend - 0.2858% payable 04/22/1999 to holders of record 04/22/1999
Name changed to First Sterling Banks, Inc. (New) 05/24/2000
First Sterling Banks, Inc. (New) name changed to Main Street Banks, Inc. (New) 01/02/2001

FIRST STERLING BKS INC NEW (GA)
Name changed to Main Street Banks, Inc. (GA) 01/02/2001
Main Street Banks, Inc. (GA) merged into BB&T Corp. 06/01/2006

FIRST STEUBEN BANCORP INC (OH)
Common $10 par changed to $5 par and (1) additional share issued 04/15/1972
Name changed to Heritage Bancorp, Inc. 04/05/1979
Heritage Bancorp, Inc. merged into Banc One Corp. (DE) 04/01/1983 which reincorporated in Ohio 05/01/1989 which merged into Bank One Corp. 10/02/1998 which merged into J.P. Morgan Chase & Co. 12/31/2000 which name changed to JPMorgan Chase & Co. 07/20/2004

FIRST STOP PROFESSIONAL SVCS INC (DE)
Recapitalized as Continental Ventures, Inc. 02/26/1988
Each share Common $0.0001 par exchanged for (0.02) share Common $0.005 par
Continental Ventures, Inc. reorganized as Unipac Corp. 11/08/1990 which name changed to Hansen Natural Corp. 10/27/1992 which name changed to Monster Beverage Corp. (Old) 01/09/2012 which reorganized as Monster Beverage Corp. (New) 06/15/2015

FIRST STRIKE DIAMONDS INC (ON)
Delisted from NEX 04/20/2004

FIRST STROUDSBURG NATL BK (STROUDSBURG, PA)
Each share Capital Stock $25 par exchanged for (3.75) shares Capital Stock $10 par to effect a (5) for (2) split and a 50% stock dividend 1/30/70
Merged into First National Bank of Eastern Pennsylvania (Wilkes-Barre, PA) 9/10/71
Each share Capital Stock $10 par exchanged for (1.2) shares Common $10 par
First National Bank of Eastern Pennsylvania (Wilkes-Barre, PA) name changed to First Eastern Bank, N.A. (Wilkes-Barre, PA) 11/16/74 which reorganized as First Eastern Corp. 8/2/82
(See First Eastern Corp.)

FIRST SUFFOLK NATIONAL BANK (HUNTINGTON, NY)
Each share Capital Stock $10 par exchanged for (1.25) shares Common $10 par in 1953
Name changed to Security National Bank (Huntington, NY) 11/7/55
Security National Bank (Huntington, NY) name changed to Security National Bank of Long Island (Huntington, NY) 5/26/58 which name changed to Security National Bank (Huntington, NY) 11/12/68 which location changed to (Hempstead, NY) 5/8/72

FIRST SUN SOUTH CORP (SC)
SEC revoked common stock registration 10/11/2013

FIRST SURETY CORP (DE)
Liquidation completed
Each share Capital Stock $1 par exchanged for initial distribution of $16.75 cash 01/02/1979
Each share Capital Stock $1 par received second distribution of $0.45 cash 03/15/1979
Each share Capital Stock $1 par received third and final distribution of $0.177953923 cash 12/29/1981

FIRST SURGICAL PARTNERS INC (DE)
Acquired by First Surgical Partners Holdings Inc. 08/05/2013
Each share Common $0.001 par exchanged for $1.25 cash

FIRST TARGET ACQUISITION INC (NV)
Name changed to Thatlook.com, Inc. 7/26/99
(See Thatlook.com Inc.)

FIRST TEAM SPORTS INC (MN)
Common 1¢ par split (3) for (2) by issuance of (0.5) additional share 2/3/95
Merged into Gen-X Sports Inc. 10/15/2001
Each share Common 1¢ par exchanged for $1.76 cash

FIRST TELECOM CORP (BC)
Recapitalized as Sunorca Development Corp. 03/13/2002
Each share Common no par exchanged for (0.33333333) share Common no par
Sunorca Development Corp. name changed to Wildflower Marijuana Inc. 06/16/2014 which name changed to Wildflower Brands Inc. 05/03/2018

FIRST TENN NATL CORP (TN)
Common $5 par changed to $2.50 par and (1) additional share issued 06/01/1973
Common $2.50 par split (3) for (2) by issuance of (0.5) additional share 11/21/1985
Common $2.50 par split (3) for (2) by issuance of (0.5) additional share 05/22/1992
Common $2.50 par changed to $1.25 par and (1) additional share issued payable 02/16/1996 to holders of record 02/02/1996
Common $2.50 par changed to $0.625 par and (1) additional share issued payable 02/20/1998 to holders of record 02/06/1998
Name changed to First Horizon National Corp. 04/20/2004

FIRST TEX FINL CORP (TX)
Merged into Beneficial Corp. (New) 4/6/79
Each share Common $1 par exchanged for $58.50 cash

FIRST TEXAS FINANCIAL, INC. (TX)
Name changed to Triland, Inc. 7/18/72
(See Triland, Inc.)

1ST TEX NAT GAS CO INC (NV)
Recapitalized as Riverdale Capital Ltd. 08/25/2009
Each share Common $0.001 par exchanged for (0.005) share Common $0.001 par
Riverdale Capital Ltd. name changed to Diversified Energy & Fuel International, Inc. 04/30/2012 which name changed to Zyrox Mining International, Inc. 08/21/2012

FIRST TIFFANY RES CORP (ON)
Delisted from Alberta Stock Exchange 09/21/1988

FIRST TITAN CORP (NV)
Reorganized 06/30/2015
Each share old Common $0.0001 par exchanged for (0.05) share new Common $0.0001 par 08/17/2012
Reorganized from Florida to under the laws of Nevada 06/30/2015
Each share new Common $0.0001 par exchanged for (0.01) share Common $0.001 par
Name changed to AngioSoma, Inc. 06/22/2016

FIRST TOPEKA BANKSHARES INC (KS)
Common $10 par changed to $5 par and (1) additional share issued 7/1/81
Merged into Fourth Financial Corp. 12/17/85
Each share Common $5 par exchanged for (2.38) shares Common $5 par
Fourth Financial Corp. merged into Boatmen's Bancshares, Inc. 1/31/96 which merged into NationsBank Corp. 1/7/97 which reincorporated in Delaware as BankAmerica Corp. (Old) 9/25/98 which merged into BankAmerica Corp. (New) 9/30/98 which name changed to Bank of America Corp. 4/28/99

FIRST TORONTO CAP CORP (ON)
Common no par split (2) for (1) by issuance of (1) additional share 02/24/1987
Merged into First Toronto Mining Corp. 01/01/1989
Each share Common no par exchanged for (1) share Common no par
(See First Toronto Mining Corp.)

FIRST TORONTO MNG CORP (ON)
Declared bankrupt 07/06/1993
No stockholders' equity

FIRST TOWER ENTERPRISES INC (BC)
Recapitalized as eOptimize Advanced Systems Inc. 04/01/2002
Each share Common no par exchanged for (0.5) share Common no par
(See eOptimize Advanced Systems Inc.)

FIRST TRAVEL CORP (CA)
Through purchase offer over 96% acquired by Manlee, Inc. 04/24/1980
Public interest eliminated

FIRST TRENTON NATL BK (TRENTON, NJ)
Common $10 par changed to $5 par and (1) additional share issued 03/12/1965
Stock Dividend - 12-1/2% 01/09/1962
Under plan of merger name changed to New Jersey National Bank (Trenton, NJ) 05/11/1970
New Jersey National Bank (Trenton, NJ) reorganized as NJN Bancorporation 07/01/1971 which name changed to New Jersey National Corp. 03/21/1972 which was acquired by CoreStates Financial Corp 10/30/1986 which merged into First Union Corp. 04/28/1998 which name changed to Wachovia Corp. (Ctfs. dated after 09/01/2001) 09/01/2001 which merged into Wells Fargo & Co. (New) 12/31/2008

FIRST TRIDENT SAVINGS & LOAN CORP. (SC)
Merged into NBSC Corp. 12/21/92
Each share Common $2.66 par exchanged for (0.4844) share Common $5 par
NBSC Corp. merged into Synovus Financial Corp. 2/28/95

FIRST TRIDON INDS INC (BC)
Recapitalized as O.J. Oil & Gas Corp. 07/05/1993
Each share Common no par exchanged for (0.2) share Common no par
O.J. Oil & Gas Corp. name changed to U.S. Oil & Gas Corp. 08/26/1996 which merged into U.S. Oil & Gas Resources Inc. 11/13/1997 which reorganized as Odyssey Petroleum Corp. 08/25/2005 which recapitalized as Petrichor Energy Inc. 03/03/2011

FIRST TRIMARK VENTURES INC (BC)
Recapitalized as Lumina Copper Corp. 05/29/2003
Each share Common no par exchanged for (0.1) share Common no par

(See Lumina Copper Corp.)

FIRST TRITON CAP CORP (CANADA)
Name changed to Executive Inn Group Corp. 07/07/1999
(See Executive Inn Group Corp.)

FIRST TROY NATIONAL BANK & TRUST CO. (TROY, OH)
Capital Stock $100 par changed to $10 par and (9) additional shares issued plus a 33-1/3% stock dividend paid 8/11/45
Stock Dividends - 25% 1/24/55; 30% 1/25/57; 33-1/3% 2/7/63
Name changed to First National Bank & Trust Co. (Troy, OH) 12/15/65
(See First National Bank & Trust Co. (Troy, OH))

FIRST TR / FIDUCIARY ASSET MGMT COVERED CALL FD (MA)
Issue Information - 18,500,000 shares COM offered at $20 per share on 08/26/2004
Name changed to First Trust Enhanced Equity Income Fund 09/30/2007

FIRST TR / FOUR CORNERS SR FLOATING RATE INCOME FD II (MA)
Issue Information - 23,000,000 shares COM offered at $20 per share on 05/25/2004
Auction Market Preferred Ser. A 1¢ par called for redemption at $25,000 on 11/18/2009
Auction Market Preferred Ser. B 1¢ par called for redemption at $25,000 on 11/18/2009
Name changed to First Trust Senior Floating Rate Income Fund II 10/13/2010
(Additional Information in Active)

FIRST TR / FOUR CORNERS SR FLTG RATE INCOME FD (MA)
Money Market Preferred 1¢ par called for redemption at $25,000 on 11/05/2009
Completely liquidated
Each Common Share 1¢ par received first and final distribution of $13.6693 cash payable 10/01/2010 to holders of record 09/30/2010

FIRST TR / GALLATIN SPECIALTY FIN FD (MA)
Issue Information - 12,300,000 shares COM offered at $20 per share on 05/25/2007
Name changed to First Trust Specialty Finance & Financial Opportunities Fund 08/07/2008

FIRST TRUST & DEPOSIT CO. (SYRACUSE, NY)
Each share Class B Preferred $3 par exchanged for (1) share Preferred $2 par and (1) share Common $1 par 00/00/1954
Common $3 par changed to $1 par 00/00/1954
Preferred $2 par changed to $5 par 01/19/1955
Common $1 par changed to $2.50 par 01/19/1955
Preferred $5 par called for redemption 09/15/1961
Reorganized as First Commercial Banks, Inc. 12/31/1971
Each share Common $2.50 par exchanged for (1.2) shares Common $5 par
First Commercial Banks, Inc. name changed to Key Banks Inc. 04/23/1979 which name changed to KeyCorp (NY) 08/28/1985 which merged into KeyCorp (New) (OH) 03/01/1994

FIRST TRUST & SAVINGS BANK (DAVENPORT, IA)
Through exchange offer 100% acquired by Banks of Iowa, Inc. as of 07/25/1977
Public interest eliminated

FIRST TR & SVGS BK (GLENVIEW, IL)
Stock Dividend - 10% 02/02/1970
Name changed to Bank of Northern Illinois (Glenview, IL) 04/10/1989
(See Bank of Northern Illinois (Glenview, IL))

FIRST TR & SVGS BK (KANKAKEE, IL)
Merged into Midwest Financial Group, Inc. 02/08/1983
Each share Common $25 par exchanged for (4.06) shares Common $5 par
Midwest Financial Group, Inc. merged into First of America Bank Corp. 11/01/1989 which merged into National City Corp. 03/31/1998 which was acquired by PNC Financial Services Group, Inc. 12/31/2008

FIRST TR ADVANTAGED SHORT DURATION HIGH YIELD BD FD (ON)
Reorganized as First Trust Short Duration High Yield Bond ETF (CAD-Hedged) 02/01/2016
Each Class A Unit automatically became (0.5) Advisor Class Unit
Each Class F Unit automatically became (0.5) Common Unit

FIRST TR ALPHADEX CDN DIVID ETF (ON)
Name changed 12/24/2015
Name changed from First Trust AlphaDEX Canadian Dividend Plus ETF to First Trust AlphaDEX Canadian Dividend ETF 12/24/2015
Under plan of merger each Common Unit or Advisor Class Unit automatically became (0.60848) First Trust Canadian Capital Capital Strength ETF Common Unit or (0.722499) Advisor Class Unit respectively 10/16/2017

FIRST TR ALPHADEX U S DIVID ETF CAD HEDGED (ON)
Name changed 12/24/2015
Name changed from First Trust AlphaDEX U.S. Dividend Plus ETF (CAD-Hedged) to First Trust AlphaDEX U.S. Dividend ETF (CAD-Hedged) 12/24/2015
Name changed to First Trust Value Line Dividend Index ETF (CAD-Hedged) 11/22/2017

FIRST TR BK (CHARLOTTE, NC)
Stock Dividends - 10% payable 01/15/2002 to holders of record 12/14/2001 Ex date - 12/12/2001; 20% payable 12/04/2002 to holders of record 11/13/2002 Ex date - 11/08/2002; 20% payable 12/04/2003 to holders of record 11/13/2003 Ex date - 11/10/2003; 20% payable 11/17/2004 to holders of record 11/02/2004 Ex date - 10/29/2004; 20% payable 11/29/2005 to holders of record 11/14/2005 Ex date - 11/09/2005; 20% payable 11/27/2006 to holders of record 11/10/2006 Ex date - 11/08/2006; 20% payable 11/28/2007 to holders of record 11/09/2007 Ex date - 11/07/2007
Merged into BNC Bancorp 11/30/2012
Each share Common $2.50 par exchanged for (0.7210702) share Common no par and $1.915552 cash
BNC Bancorp merged into Pinnacle Financial Partners, Inc. 06/16/2017

FIRST TR BK (ONTARIO, CA)
Common $2 par split (2) for (1) by issuance of (1) additional share 5/23/90
Bank closed by California Superintendent of Banks 3/3/95
No stockholders' equity

1ST TRUST BANK FOR SAVINGS (MEMPHIS, TN)
Name changed to Magna Bank (Memphis, TN) 05/14/2007
Magna Bank (Memphis, TN) merged into Pinnacle Financial Partners, Inc. 09/01/2015

FIRST TRUST BANK-STOCK CORP. (DE)
Charter cancelled and declared inoperative and void for non-payment of taxes 4/1/32

FIRST TRUST CO. (ALBANY, NY)
Class B Preferred $50 par called for redemption 9/11/59
Capital Stock $50 par changed to $10 par and (4) additional shares issued 2/28/61
Stock Dividends - 50% 8/14/59; 100% 2/19/65
Acquired by BT New York Corp. 5/31/66
Each share Capital Stock $10 par exchanged for (1.15) shares Common $10 par and $12 principal amount of 4-1/2% 15-year Debentures due 6/1/81
BT New York Corp. name changed to Bankers Trust New York Corp. 9/15/67 which name changed to Bankers Trust Corp. 4/23/98
(See Bankers Trust Corp.)

FIRST TRUST CO. (LINCOLN, NE)
Merged into National Bank of Commerce Trust & Savings Association (Lincoln, NE) 9/8/61
Each share Capital Stock $20 par exchanged for (1-1/3) share Capital Stock $20 par
National Bank of Commerce Trust & Savings Association (Lincoln, NE) reorganized as NBC Co. 3/24/69 which name changed to Commerce Group, Inc. 5/22/78 which merged into First Commerce Bancshares, Inc. 9/30/87 which merged into Wells Fargo & Co. 6/16/2000

FIRST TR CO (JACKSON, MS)
Voluntarily dissolved 5/25/89
Details not available

FIRST TR CO ALLEGANY CNTY (WELLSVILLE, NY)
Under plan of merger name changed to First Trust Union Bank (Wellsville, NY) 12/3/68
First Trust Union Bank (Wellsville, NY) acquired by Security New York State Corp. 7/31/73 which merged into Norstar Bancorp Inc. 5/1/84 which merged into Fleet/ Norstar Financial Group, Inc. 1/1/88 which name changed to Fleet Financial Group, Inc. (New) 4/15/92 which name changed to Fleet Boston Corp. 10/1/99 which name changed to FleetBoston Financial Corp. 4/18/2000 which merged into Bank of America Corp. 4/1/2004

FIRST TR DIVID & INCOME FD (MA)
Name changed 07/01/2013
Name changed from First Trust/Active Dividend Income Fund to First Trust Dividend & Income Fund 07/01/2013
Under plan of merger each Common Share of Bene. Int. 1¢ par automatically became (0.444937) share First Trust Exchange-Traded Fund VI High Income ETF 10/24/2016

FIRST TR DORSEY WRIGHT DYNAMIC U S SECTOR ROTATION INDEX ETF (ON)
Name changed to First Trust Dorsey Wright U.S. Sector Rotation Index ETF (CAD-Hedged) 11/17/2016

FIRST TR DOW JONES STOXX EUROPEAN SELECT DIVID INDEX FD (MA)
Name changed 01/30/2009
Name changed from First Trust DJ STOXX Select Dividend 30 Index Fund to First Trust Dow Jones STOXX European Select Dividend Index Fund 01/30/2009
Name changed to First Trust STOXX European Select Dividend Index Fund 09/24/2010

FIRST TRUST/FIDAC MTG INCOME FD (MA)
Issue Information - 4,000,000 COM SHS offered at $20 per share on 05/25/2005
Name changed to First Trust Mortgage Income Fund 05/02/2011

FIRST TR GLOBAL DIVIDENDSEEKER FD (ON)
Trust terminated 06/08/2016
Each Class A Unit received $6.5385 cash
Each Class F Unit received $8.5796 cash

FIRST TRUST/HIGHLAND CAP FLOATING RATE INCOME FD (ON)
Merged into First Trust/Highland Capital Floating Rate Income Fund II 08/14/2009
Each Unit no par received (0.449719) Unit no par
(See First Trust/Highland Capital Floating Rate Income Fund)

FIRST TR / HIGHLAND CAP FLOATING RATE INCOME FD II (ON)
Liquidation completed
Each Unit received initial distribution of $4 cash payable 12/29/2010 to holders of record 12/20/2010
Ex date - 12/16/2010
Each Unit received second and final distribution of $1.58 cash payable 03/17/2011 to holders of record 03/14/2011

FIRST TR ISE GLOBAL COPPER INDEX FD (MA)
Under plan of reorganization each Common Share of Bene. Int. 1¢ par automatically became (1) First Trust Exchange-Traded Fund II First Trust Indxx Global Natural Resources Income ETF 12/21/2015

FIRST TR ISE GLOBAL PLATINUM INDEX FD (MA)
Under plan of reorganization each Common Share of Bene. Int. 1¢ par automatically became (1) First Trust Exchange-Traded Fund II First Trust Indxx Global Agriculture ETF 12/21/2015

FIRST TR ISE REVERE NAT GAS INDEX FD (MA)
Each Share of Bene. Int. automatically became (0.2) First Trust Exchange-Traded Fund ISE-Revere Natural Gas Index Fund 05/02/2016

FIRST TR LARGE CAP GROWTH OPPORTUNITIES ALPHADEX FD (DE)
Name changed to First Trust Large Cap Growth AlphaDEX Fund 03/25/2011

FIRST TR LARGE CAP VALUE OPPORTUNITIES ALPHADEX FD (DE)
Name changed to First Trust Large Cap Value AlphaDEX Fund 03/25/2011

FIRST TR MONEY MKT FD (MA)
Name changed to Venture Trust Money Market Fund (MA) 02/01/1988
Venture Trust Money Market Fund (MA) reorganized in Maryland as Retirement Planning Funds of America, Inc. 12/31/1989 which name changed to Davis Series, Inc. 10/01/1995

FIRST TR NASDAQ CEA SMART PHONE INDEX FD (MA)
Name changed to First Trust NASDAQ Smartphone Index Fund 12/21/2015

FIRST TRUST SAVINGS BANK, F.S.B. (JACKSONVILLE, FL)
Name changed to Monticello Bank (Jacksonville, FL) in November 1995

FIRST TR SHORT DURATION HIGH YIELD BD ETF (ON)
Merged into First Trust Short Duration High Yield Bond ETF (CAD-Hedged) 02/12/2016
Each Common Unit automatically became (0.83523) Common Unit
Each Advisor Class Unit automatically became (0.929031) Advisor Class Unit

FIRST TR STRATEGIC HIGH INCOME FD (MA)
Issue Information - 8,250,000 COM SHS offered at $20 per share on 07/26/2005
Merged into First Trust Strategic High Income Fund II 10/03/2011
Each share Common 1¢ par exchanged for (0.745047) share Common 1¢ par

FIRST TR STRATEGIC HIGH INCOME FD II (MA)
Each share old Common Share of Bene. Int. 1¢ par exchanged for (0.33333333) share new Common Share of Bene. Int. 1¢ par 10/03/2011
Merged into First Trust High Income Long/Short Fund 06/25/2018
Each share old Common Share of Bene. Int. 1¢ par exchanged for (0.808829) Common Share of Bene. Int. 1¢ par

FIRST TR STRATEGIC HIGH INCOME FD III (MA)
Merged into First Trust Strategic High Income Fund II 10/03/2011
Each share Common Share of Bene. Int. 1¢ par exchanged for (0.870347) Common Share of Bene. Int. 1¢ par
First Trust Strategic High Income Fund II merged into First Trust High Income Long/Short Fund 06/25/2018

FIRST TR TAX-ADVANTAGED PFD INCOME FD (MA)
Auction Preferred Shares Ser. M 1¢ par called for redemption at $25,000 on 06/12/2009
Completely liquidated
Each share Common 1¢ par received first and final distribution of $5.54 cash payable 07/30/2009 to holders of record 07/27/2009
Note: Certificates were not required to be surrendered and are without value

FIRST TR TAX FREE BD FD (MA)
Name changed to Oppenheimer Tax-Exempt Bond Fund, Income Series no par and Insured Series no par reclassified as Intermediate Tax-Exempt Bond Fund and Insured Tax Exempt Bond Fund respectively 7/10/92
Oppenheimer Tax-Exempt Bond Fund name changed to Oppenheimer Municipal Fund 10/10/96

FIRST TR TAX FREE FD (MA)
Name changed to Venture Trust Tax Free Money Market Fund 2/1/88
Venture Trust Tax Free Money Market Fund reorganized as Retirement Planning Funds of America, Inc. 12/31/89 which name changed to Davis Series, Inc. 10/1/95

FIRST TR UN BK (WELLSVILLE, NY)
Acquired by Security New York State Corp. 7/31/73
Each share Common $10 par exchanged for (0.065) share $6 Conv. Preferred Ser. A $5 par and (0.5) share Common $5 par Security New York State Corp. merged into Norstar Bancorp Inc. 5/1/84 which merged into Fleet/Norstar Financial Group, Inc. 1/1/88 which name changed to Fleet Financial Group, Inc. (New) 4/15/92 which name changed to Fleet Boston Corp. 10/1/99 which name changed to FleetBoston Financial Corp. 4/18/2000 which merged into Bank of America Corp. 4/1/2004

FIRST TRUST/VALUE LINE & IBBOTSON EQUITY ALLOCATION FD (MA)
Completely liquidated
Each Common Share of Bene. Int. 1¢ par received first and final distribution of $23.42 cash 11/30/2006

FIRST TR VALUE LINE 100 FD (MA)
Merged into First Trust Value Line 100 Exchange-Traded Fund 06/15/2007
Each Common Share received (1) Common Share

FIRST TR VALUE LINE DIVID FD (MA)
Under plan of merger each Common Share 1¢ par automatically became (1) First Trust Value Line Dividend Index Fund Common Share 1¢ par 12/18/2006

FIRST TR VALUE LINE EQUITY ALLOCATION INDEX FD (MA)
Under plan of reorganization each Share automatically became (1) First Trust Exchange-Traded Fund Total US Market AlphaDEX ETF 01/09/2015

FIRST TUDOR CORP (NY)
Each share old Common $0.0001 par exchanged for (0.05) share new Common $0.0001 par 08/15/1989
Charter cancelled and proclaimed dissolved for failure to pay taxes 09/28/1994

FIRST TULSA BANCORPORATION INC (DE)
Common $10 par split (3) for (2) by issuance of (0.5) additional share 3/16/81
Merged into Banks of Mid-America, Inc. 7/17/84
Each share Common $10 par exchanged for (1.42) shares Common $2.50 Conv. Preferred $1 par
Banks of Mid-America, Inc. reincorporated in Oklahoma as Liberty Bancorp Inc. 5/26/92 which merged into Banc One Corp. 6/1/97 which merged into Bank One Corp. 10/2/98 which merged into J.P. Morgan Chase & Co. 12/31/2000 which name changed to JPMorgan Chase & Co. 7/20/2004

FIRST TUSKALOOSA CORP (AL)
Common $5 par changed to $1 par 4/18/84
Common $1 par split (4) for (3) by issuance of (1/3) additional share 5/21/84
Common $1 par split (2) for (1) by issuance of (1) additional share 8/23/85
Acquired by AmSouth Bancorporation 4/20/87
Each share Common $1 par exchanged for (1.978825) shares Common $1 par
AmSouth Bancorporation merged into Regions Financial Corp. 11/4/2006

FIRST U.S. SOUTHERN CORP. (DE)
Adjudicated bankrupt 4/29/64
No equity for Common stockholders

FIRST ULB CORP (CA)
Merged into BayCom Corp 05/01/2017
Each share Common no par exchanged for (0.9733) share Common no par and $13.50 cash

FIRST UN BANCORPORATION (MO)
Stock Dividends - 50% 11/30/76; 50% 8/31/80
Name changed to Centerre Bancorporation 1/4/82
Centerre Bancorporation acquired by Boatmen's Bancshares, Inc. 12/9/88 which merged into NationsBank Corp. 1/7/97 which reincorporated in Delaware as BankAmerica Corp. (Old) 9/25/98 which merged into BankAmerica Corp. (New) 9/30/98 which name changed to Bank of America Corp. 4/28/99

FIRST UN CORP (NC)
Common $3.33333333 par split (3) for (2) by issuance of (0.5) additional share 06/15/1984
Common $3.33333333 par split (2) for (1) by issuance of (1) additional share 06/13/1986
$2.50 Conv. Preferred Ser. A no par called for redemption 06/18/1993
1990 Adjustable Rate Perpetual Preferred no par called for redemption 03/31/1995
Adjustable Rate Preferred Class A Ser. D no par called for redemption 07/01/1996
10.64% Depositary Preferred called for redemption 07/01/1996
10.64% Preferred Class A Ser. F no par called for redemption 07/01/1996
$2.15 Conv. Preferred Class A Ser. B no par called for redemption at $25 plus $0.26 accrued dividends on 11/15/1996
Common $3.33333333 par split (2) for (1) by issuance of (1) additional share payable 07/31/1997 to holders of record 07/01/1997 Ex date - 08/01/1997
Stock Dividend - 10% 12/15/1978
Name changed to Wachovia Corp. (Ctfs. dated after 09/01/2001) 09/01/2001
Wachovia Corp. (Ctfs. dated after 09/01/2001) merged into Wells Fargo & Co. (New) 12/31/2008

FIRST UN INC (MO)
Name changed to First Union Bancorporation 4/21/76
First Union Bancorporation name changed to Centerre Bancorporation 1/4/82 which was acquired by Boatmen's Bancshares, Inc. 12/9/88 which merged into NationsBank Corp. 1/7/97 which reincorporated in Delaware as BankAmerica Corp. (Old) 9/25/98 which merged into BankAmerica Corp. (New) 9/30/98 which name changed to Bank of America Corp. 4/28/99

FIRST UN NATL BANCORP INC (NC)
Name changed to Cameron Financial Corp. 05/19/1972
Cameron Financial Corp. name changed to First Union Corp. 04/23/1975 which name changed to Wachovia Corp. (Ctfs. dated after 09/01/2001) 09/01/2001 which merged into Wells Fargo & Co. (New) 12/31/2008

FIRST UN NATL BK N C (CHARLOTTE, NC)
Stock Dividend - 100% 08/22/1960
Merged into First Union National Bancorp, Inc. 05/04/1968
Each share Capital Stock $5 par exchanged for (1) share Common $5 par
First Union National Bancorp, Inc. name changed to Cameron Financial Corp. 05/19/1972 which name changed to First Union Corp. 04/23/1975 which name changed to Wachovia Corp. (Ctfs. dated after 09/01/2001) 09/01/2001 which merged into Wells Fargo & Co. (New) 12/31/2008

FIRST UN REAL ESTATE EQUITY & MTG INVTS (OH)
Conv. Preferred $100 par called for redemption 11/01/1982
Shares of Bene. Int. $1 par split (3) for (2) by issuance of (0.5) additional share 04/30/1981
Shares of Bene. Int. $1 par split (3) for (2) by issuance of (0.5) additional share 04/30/1986
Each Share of Bene. Int. $1 par received distribution of (0.05) share Imperial Parking Corp. Common $1 par payable 03/27/2000 to holders of record 03/20/2000 Ex date - 03/28/2000
Name changed to Winthrop Realty Trust 12/01/2005
(See Winthrop Realty Trust)

FIRST UN RLTY (OH)
Name changed to First Union Real Estate Equity & Mortgage Investments 10/1/69
First Union Real Estate Equity & Mortgage Investments name changed to Winthrop Realty Trust 12/1/2005

FIRST UNION BANK, N.A. (BELLAIRE, OH)
Merged into Banc One Corp. (DE) 1/1/86
Each share Common $10 par exchanged for (5.6337) shares Common no par
Banc One Corp. (DE) reincorporated in Ohio 5/1/89 which merged into Bank One Corp. 10/2/98 which merged into J.P. Morgan Chase & Co. 12/31/2000 which name changed to JPMorgan Chase & Co. 7/20/2004

FIRST UNION COMMERCIAL PROPERTIES EXPANSION CO. (DE)
Completely liquidated 05/20/1977
Each share Common 1¢ par received first and final distribution of (0.027566) First Union Real Estate Equity & Mortgage Investments Share of Bene. Int. $1 par
Note: Certificates were not required to be surrendered and are without value
First Union Real Estate Equity & Mortgage Investments name changed to Winthrop Realty Trust 12/01/2005
(See Winthrop Realty Trust)

1ST UTD BANCORP (FL)
Merged into Wachovia Corp. (New) (Ctfs. dated between 05/20/1991 and 09/01/2001) 11/11/1997
Each share Common no par exchanged for (0.3) share Common $5 par
Wachovia Corp. (New) (Ctfs. dated between 05/20/1991 and 09/01/2001) which merged into Wachovia Corp. (Ctfs. dated after 09/01/2001) 09/01/2001 which merged into Wells Fargo & Co. (New) 12/31/2008

FIRST UTD BANCORP INC (AL)
Common $10 par changed to $1 par 5/15/84
Common $1 par changed to 20¢ par and (4) additional shares issued 4/24/87
Merged into SunTrust Banks, Inc. 1/29/93
Each share Common 20¢ par exchanged for (0.9) share Common $1 par

1ST UTD BANCORP INC (FL)
Merged into Valley National Bancorp 11/01/2014
Each share Common 1¢ par exchanged for (0.89) share Common no par

FIRST UTD BANCORPORATION (SC)
- Common $2.50 par split (3) for (2) by issuance of (0.5) additional share 11/22/94
- Common $2.50 par split (3) for (2) by issuance of (0.5) additional share payable 8/29/97 to holders of record 8/15/97
- Stock Dividends - 5% payable 7/15/96 to holders of record 7/1/96; 5% payable 12/13/96 to holders of record 11/29/96
- Merged into Regions Financial Corp. (Old) 3/14/98
- Each share Common $2.50 par exchanged for (0.5173) share Common $0.625 par
- Regions Financial Corp. (Old) merged into Regions Financial Corp. (New) 7/1/2004

FIRST UTD BANCORPORATION INC (TX)
- Stock Dividends - 100% 11/28/75; 15% 3/8/76; 50% 5/29/81
- Merged into InterFirst Corp. 6/28/83
- Each share Common $10 par exchanged for (2.2) shares Common $5 par
- InterFirst Corp. merged into First RepublicBank Corp. 6/6/87
- (See First RepublicBank Corp.)

FIRST UTD BANCSHARES INC (AR)
- Common $1 par split (2) for (1) by issuance of (1) additional share 09/08/1992
- Common $1 par split (3) for (2) by issuance of (0.5) additional share payable 06/28/1996 to holders of record 06/07/1996
- Common $1 par split (2) for (1) by issuance of (1) additional share payable 06/30/1998 to holders of record 06/01/1998
- Merged into BancorpSouth, Inc. 08/31/2000
- Each share Common $1 par exchanged for (1.125) shares Common $2.50 par
- BancorpSouth, Inc. reorganized as BancorpSouth Bank (Tupelo, MS) 11/01/2017

FIRST UTD BK GROUP INC (NM)
- Exchangeable Preferred Ser. B $1 par called for redemption 01/13/1994
- Merged into Norwest Corp. 01/14/1994
- Each share Conv. Exchangeable Preferred Ser. A $1 par exchanged for (2.2) shares Common $1-2/3 par
- Each share Conv. Exchangeable Preferred Ser. C $1 par exchanged for (6.039) shares Common $1-2/3 par
- Each share Common $1 par exchanged for (1.1) shares Common $1-2/3 par
- Norwest Corp. name changed to Wells Fargo & Co. (New) 11/02/1998

FIRST UNITED BANK OF MISSISSIPPI (MERIDIAN, MS)
- Merged into Commonwealth Bank (Meridian, Miss.) 12/31/83
- Each share Common $5 par exchanged for $25 cash

FIRST UTD CAP CORP (ON)
- Cease trade order effective 02/28/1986

FIRST UTD CAPITAL TR (DE)
- 9.375% Preferred Securities called for redemption at $10 on 9/30/2004

FIRST UTD FINL CORP (OH)
- Common $5 par split (2) for (1) by issuance of (1) additional share 12/15/71
- Liquidation completed
- Each share Common $5 par received initial distribution of $5.25 cash 6/12/75
- Final distribution believed to have occurred in 1981; details not available

FIRST UTD FINL SVCS INC (DE)
- Common $5 par split (5) for (2) by issuance of (1.5) additional shares 7/1/86
- Merged into First Chicago Corp. 10/1/87
- Each share Common $5 par exchanged for $20.828 cash

FIRST UTD INC (DE)
- Stock Dividends - 10% 09/01/1979; 10% 05/21/1980
- Merged into Mega Life & Health Insurance Co. 08/10/1992
- Each share Common $1 par exchanged for $0.46 cash

FIRST UTD LIFE INS CO (IN)
- Under plan of reorganization each share Capital Stock $1 par automatically became (1) share First United, Inc. (DE) Common $1 par 02/25/1970
- (See First United, Inc.)

FIRST UTD NATL CORP (IL)
- Class A 45¢ par changed to 40¢ par and (0.05) additional share issued 07/14/1972
- Class A 40¢ par changed to 25¢ par and (0.05) additional share issued 07/30/1976
- Reorganized as United National Financial Corp. 09/01/1977
- Each share Class A 25¢ par exchanged for (0.2) share Common $1 par
- (See United National Financial Corp.)

FIRST UTD SVGS BK F S B (GREENCASTLE, IN)
- Merged into Old National Bancorp 11/3/95
- Each share Common exchanged for (0.8925) share Common no par

FIRST UNITED SECURITY CORP. (IL)
- Class B 50¢ par reclassified as Class A 50¢ par 06/15/1970
- Class A 50¢ par changed to 45¢ par 07/10/1970
- Stock Dividend - 10% 07/10/1970
- Name changed to First United National Corp. 07/07/1971
- First United National Corp. reorganized as United National Financial Corp. 09/01/1977
- (See United National Financial Corp.)

FIRST UNIV CORP (TX)
- Acquired by Compass Bancshares, Inc. 01/29/1998
- Details not available

FIRST URANIUM CORP (ON)
- Reincorporated 07/03/2012
- Place of incorporation changed from (BC) to (ON) and Common no par reclassified as Units 07/03/2012
- Merged into Algold Resources Ltd. 12/20/2013
- Each Unit exchanged for (0.0729849) share Common no par and (0.03649245) Common Stock Purchase Warrant expiring 06/19/2015
- Note: Each Unit consists of (100) Class A Special Shares and (1) share Class B Common

FIRST USA INC (DE)
- Common 1¢ par split (2) for (1) by issuance of (1) additional share 11/11/93
- Common 1¢ par split (2) for (1) by issuance of (1) additional share payable 11/12/96 to holders of record 10/28/96 Ex date - 11/13/96
- 6.250% Increased Dividend Equity Security Preferred 1¢ par called for redemption 5/20/97
- Merged into Banc One Corp. 6/27/97
- Each share Common 1¢ par exchanged for (1.1659) shares Common no par
- Banc One Corp. merged into Bank One Corp. 10/2/98 which merged into J.P. Morgan Chase & Co.

12/31/2000 which name changed to JPMorgan Chase & Co. 7/20/2004

FIRST USA PAYMENTECH INC (DE)
- Name changed to Paymentech, Inc. 10/29/1997
- (See Paymentech, Inc.)

FIRST UTAH CAPITOL CORP. (UT)
- Recapitalized as Natural Energy Systems, Inc. 4/30/76
- Each share Capital Stock 1¢ par exchanged for (0.25) share Capital Stock 1¢ par

FIRST V SHS INC (ON)
- Class I Shares called for redemption 12/31/1993

FIRST VA BKS INC (VA)
- Common $1 par split (3) for (2) by issuance of (0.5) additional share 7/27/92
- Common $1 par split (3) for (2) by issuance of (0.5) additional share payable 9/3/97 to holders of record 8/13/97 Ex date - 9/4/97
- Common $1 par split (2) for (2) by issuance of (0.5) additional share payable 8/16/2002 to holders of record 7/31/2002 Ex date - 8/19/2002
- 5% Conv. Preferred Ser. A $10 par called for redemption at $10 plus $3.78 accrued dividend on 5/1/2003
- 5% Conv. 2nd Preferred Ser. A $10 par called for redemption at $10 plus $3.78 accrued dividend on 5/1/2003
- 5% Conv. 3rd Preferred Ser. A $10 par called for redemption at $10 plus $3.78 accrued dividend on 5/1/2003
- 7% Conv. 1st Preferred Ser. B $10 par called for redemption at $10 plus $3.78 accrued dividend on 5/1/2003
- 7% Conv. 1st Preferred Ser. C $10 par called for redemption at $10 plus $3.02 accrued dividend on 5/1/2003
- 8% Preferred Ser. D $10 par called for redemption at $10 plus $3.78 accrued dividend on 5/1/2003
- Merged into BB&T Corp. 7/1/2003
- Each share Common $1 par exchanged for (1.26) shares Common $5 par

FIRST VA CMNTY BK (FAIRFAX, VA)
- Common $5 par split (5) for (4) by issuance of (0.25) additional share payable 04/30/2015 to holders of record 04/05/2015 Ex date - 05/01/2015
- Under plan of reorganization each share Common $5 par automatically became (1) share FVCBankcorp, Inc. Common 1¢ par 11/02/2015

FIRST VA MTG & REAL ESTATE INVT TR (VA)
- Name changed to Nova Real Estate Investment Trust 03/04/1980
- Nova Real Estate Investment Trust reorganized as Nova Corp. 05/31/1983 which merged into Parkway Co. (TX) 06/30/1983 which reincorporated in Maryland as Parkway Properties, Inc. 08/02/1996 which merged into Cousins Properties Inc. 10/06/2016

FIRST VY BANCORP INC (CT)
- Stock Dividend - 10% payable 01/30/2006 to holders of record 12/30/2005 Ex date - 01/26/2006
- Merged into New England Bancshares, Inc. 07/13/2007
- Each share Common no par exchanged for (0.8907) shares Common 1¢ par and $9 cash
- New England Bancshares, Inc. merged into United Financial Bancorp, Inc. (MD) 11/19/2012 which merged into United Financial Bancorp, Inc. (CT) 05/01/2014

FIRST VY BK (LOMPOC, CA)
- Merged into New Lompac Inc. 3/31/97
- Each share Common $5 par exchanged for $58 cash

FIRST VY CORP (PA)
- Common $1 par split (2) for (1) by issuance of (1) additional share 12/30/71
- Common $1 par split (2) for (1) by issuance of (1) additional share 12/5/83
- Common $1 par split (2) for (1) by issuance of (1) additional share 4/7/86
- Acquired by United Jersey Banks 1/29/88
- Each share Common $1 par exchanged for (1.45) shares Common $2.50 par
- United Jersey Banks name changed to UJB Financial Corp. 6/30/89 which name changed to Summit Bancorp 3/1/96 which merged into FleetBoston Financial Corp. 3/1/2001 which merged into Bank of America Corp. 4/1/2004

FIRST VY NATL BK (LANCASTER, CA)
- Merged into Valencia Bank & Trust (Newhall, CA) 12/01/1999
- Each share Common $5 par exchanged for (0.816) share Common $5 par
- Valencia Bank & Trust (Newhall, CA) merged into UnionBanCal Corp. (CA) 11/01/2002 which reincorporated in Delaware 09/30/2003
- (See UnionBanCal Corp. (DE))

FIRST VARIABLE RATE FD FOR GOVT INCOME INC (MD)
- Capital Stock 1¢ par changed to $0.001 par and (9) additional shares issued 8/27/80
- Reorganized under the laws of Massachusetts as First Variable Rate Fund For Government Income and Capital Stock $0.001 par reclassified as Shares of Bene. Int. no par 4/30/80

FIRST VENTURE CAP CORP (BC)
- Name changed to First Venture Technologies Corp. 11/05/2003
- First Venture Technologies Corp. name changed to Functional Technologies Corp. 05/20/2008
- (See Functional Technologies Corp.)

FIRST VENTURE DEVELOPMENTS LTD (BC)
- Recapitalized as Knightswood Financial Corp. 12/08/1998
- Each share Common no par exchanged for (0.2) share Common no par
- Knightswood Financial Corp. name changed to Cannabis Wheaton Income Corp. 05/08/2017 which name changed to Auxly Cannabis Group Inc. 06/08/2018

FIRST VENTURE TECHNOLOGIES CORP (BC)
- Name changed to Functional Technologies Corp. 05/20/2008
- (See Functional Technologies Corp.)

FIRST VT BK & TR CO (BRATTLEBORO, VT)
- Capital Stock $6 par changed to $3 par and (1) additional share issued 10/04/1973
- Reorganized as First Vermont Financial Corp. 08/31/1982
- Each share Capital Stock $3 par exchanged for (1) share Common $3 par
- First Vermont Financial Corp. name changed to BankNorth Group, Inc. (VT) (New) 05/13/1986 which merged into BankNorth Group, Inc. (DE) 12/01/1989 which merged into BankNorth Group, Inc. (ME) 05/10/2000 which merged into TD Banknorth Inc. 03/01/2005
- (See TD Banknorth Inc.)

FIRST VT FINL CORP (VT)
Name changed to BankNorth Group, Inc. (VT) 05/13/1986
BankNorth Group, Inc. (VT) merged into into BankNorth Group, Inc. (DE) 12/01/1989 which merged into BankNorth Group, Inc. (ME) 05/10/2000 which merged into TD Banknorth Inc. 03/01/2005
(See TD Banknorth Inc.)

FIRST VICTORIA CORP (TX)
Each share Common $5 par received distribution of (1) additional share 6/28/85
Merged into First Victoria National Bank (New) (Victoria, TX) 6/17/91
Each share Common $5 par exchanged for (1) share Common $5 par
First Victoria National Bank (New) (Victoria, TX) reorganized as FVNB Corp. 9/17/98
(See FVNB Corp.)

FIRST VICTORIA NATIONAL BK NEW (VICTORIA, TX)
Common $5 par changed to $2.50 par and (1) additional share issued 1/11/95
Under plan of reorganization each share Common $2.50 par automatically became (1) share FVNB Corp. Common 1¢ par 9/17/98
(See FVNB Corp.)

FIRST VICTORIA NATL BK OLD (VICTORIA, TX)
Capital Stock $20 par changed to $10 par and (1) additional share issued 7/1/71
Stock Dividends - 33-1/3% 3/8/68; 200% 3/3/77
Under plan of reorganization each share Capital Stock $10 par automatically became (1) share First Victoria Corp. Common $5 par 5/31/85
First Victoria Corp. merged into First Victoria National Bank (New) (Victoria, TX) 6/17/91 which reorganized as FVNB Corp. 9/17/98
(See FVNB Corp.)

FIRST VIETNAMESE AMERN BK (WESTMINSTER, CA)
Bank closed and FDIC appointed reciever 11/05/2010
No stockholders' equity

FIRST VIRGINIA BANKSHARES CORP. (VA)
Name changed to First Virginia Banks, Inc. 9/1/78
First Virginia Banks, Inc. merged into BB&T Corp. 7/1/2003

FIRST VIRGINIA CORP. (VA)
Class A and B Common $1 par reclassified as Common $1 par 10/09/1962
Name changed to First Virginia Bankshares Corp. 08/01/1967
First Virginia Bankshares Corp. name changed to First Virginia Banks, Inc. 09/01/1978 which merged into BB&T Corp. 07/01/2003

FIRST VIRTUAL COMMUNICATIONS INC (DE)
Each share old Common $0.001 par exchanged for (0.2) share new Common $0.001 par 6/27/2003
Plan of reorganization under Chapter 11 Federal Bankruptcy Code effective 12/30/2005
No stockholders' equity

FIRST VIRTUAL (DE)
Name changed to FVC.COM, Inc. 07/30/1998
FVC.COM, Inc. name changed to First Virtual Communications, Inc. 02/07/2001
(See First Virtual Communications, Inc.)

FIRST VIRTUAL HLDGS INC (DE)
Name changed to Messagemedia, Inc. 12/16/98
Messagemedia, Inc. merged into DoubleClick Inc. 1/22/2002
(See DoubleClick Inc.)

FIRST VISION BK (TULLAHOMA, TN)
Bank went private 12/00/2007
Details not available

FIRST W VA BANCORP INC (WV)
Common $10 par changed to $5 par and (1) additional share issued 04/25/1994
Common $5 par split (3) for (2) by issuance of (0.5) additional share payable 10/27/1997 to holders of record 10/01/1997 Ex date - 10/28/1997
Stock Dividends - 4% payable 12/16/1996 to holders of record 12/02/1996 Ex date - 11/27/1996; 4% payable 10/26/1998 to holders of record 10/01/1998 Ex date - 09/29/1998; 20% payable 11/18/1999 to holders of record 11/01/1999 Ex date - 11/19/1999; 2% payable 12/15/2000 to holders of record 12/01/2000 Ex date - 11/29/2000; 4% payable 10/16/2008 to holders of record 10/01/2008 Ex date - 09/29/2008; 4% payable 12/27/2010 to holders of record 12/20/2010 Ex date - 12/16/2010; 4% payable 12/27/2012 to holders of record 12/19/2012 Ex date - 12/17/2012
Merged into CB Financial Services Inc. 05/01/2018
Each share Common $5 par exchanged for (0.223473) share Common $0.4167 par and and $21.871473 cash

FIRST WACHOVIA CORP (NC)
Stock Dividend - 20% 08/31/1989
Name changed to Wachovia Corp. (New) (Ctfs. dated between 05/20/1991 and 09/01/2001) 05/20/1991
Wachovia Corp. (New) (Ctfs. dated between 05/20/1991 and 09/01/2001) merged into Wachovia Corp. (Ctfs. dated after 09/01/2001) 09/01/2001 which merged into Wells Fargo & Co. (New) 12/31/2008

FIRST WASH BANCORP INC (WA)
Stock Dividend - 10% payable 8/17/98 to holders of record 8/10/98
Name changed to Banner Corp. 10/30/2000

FIRST WASH FINANCIALCORP (NJ)
Merged into Fulton Financial Corp. 12/31/2004
Each share Common $3.33 par exchanged for (1.35) shares Common $2.50 par

FIRST WASH RLTY TR INC (MD)
Merged into U.S. Retail Partners L.P. 02/28/2001
Each share 9.75% Conv. Participating Preferred Ser. A 144A exchanged for $33.49 cash
Each share 9.75% Accredited Participating Preferred Ser. A exchanged for $33.49 cash
Each share 9.75% Conv. Participating Preferred Ser. A 1¢ par exchanged for $33.49 cash
Each share Common Accredited Investors exchanged for $26.12 cash
Each share 144A Common exchanged for $26.12 cash
Each share Common 1¢ par exchanged for $26.12 cash

FIRST WASH ST BK (WINDSOR, NJ)
Common $5 par changed to $3.33 par and (0.5) additional share issued payable 6/1/98 to holders of record 5/15/98
Stock Dividend - 7% payable 11/3/97 to holders of record 10/6/97

Under plan of reorganization each share Common $3.33 par automatically became (1) share First Washington FinancialCorp Common $3.33 par 10/1/98
First Washington FinancialCorp merged into Fulton Financial Corp. 12/31/2004

1ST WASH BANCORP INC (DE)
Merged into First Maryland Bancorp 8/2/96
Each share Common 1¢ par exchanged for $8.125 cash

FIRST WAVE MARINE INC (DE)
Plan of reorganization under Chapter 11 Federal Bankruptcy Code effective 02/08/2002
In process of liquidation
Each share new Common 1¢ par received initial distribution of $12.35 cash payable 11/15/2004 to holders of record 11/05/2004 Ex date - 11/16/2004
Each share new Common 1¢ par received second distribution of $24.70 cash payable 08/11/2006 to holders of record 11/05/2004 Ex date - 08/14/2006
Each share new Common 1¢ par received third distribution of $7.41 cash payable 12/21/2007 to holders of record 11/05/2004
Note: Number and amount of additional distributions, if any, are not available

FIRST WEST CDA CAP CORP (WY)
Reincorporated 12/20/93
Place of incorporation changed from (BC) to (WY) 12/20/93
Recapitalized as Caring Products International, Inc. 1/14/94
Each share Common no par exchanged for (0.2) share Common no par
Caring Products International, Inc. name changed to US Global Aerospace, Inc. 9/26/2002 which name changed to US Global Nanospace, Inc. 7/24/2003

FIRST WEST CHESTER CORP (PA)
Common $20 par changed to $1 par 04/01/1986
Common $1 par split (4) for (1) by issuance of (3) additional shares 10/15/1986
Stock Dividend - 900% 12/10/1985
Name changed to First Chester County Corp. 06/01/2000
First Chester County Corp. merged into Tower Bancorp, Inc. 12/10/2010
(See Tower Bancorp, Inc.)

FIRST WEST TEXAS CAPITAL CORP. (TX)
Completely liquidated 4/14/72
Each share Common $1 par exchanged for first and final distribution of $4 cash

FIRST WESTCHESTER NATL BK (NEW ROCHELLE, NY)
Common $20 par changed to $10 par and (1) additional share issued in 1954
Common $10 par changed to $5 par and (1) additional share issued 8/2/60
Stock Dividends - 10% 2/18/71; 10% 4/20/72; 10% 3/22/73
Merged into Barclays Bank International Ltd. 5/31/74
Each share Common $5 par exchanged for $65 cash

FIRST WESTERN BANK & TRUST CO. (SAN FRANCISCO, CA)
Stock Dividend - 100% 11/30/54
Merged into United California Bank (Los Angeles, CA) 2/24/61
Each share Common $12.50 par exchanged for (1) share Capital Stock $12.50 par
United California Bank (Los Angeles, CA) merged into Western

Bancorporation 1/16/78 which name changed to First Interstate Bancorp 6/1/81 which merged into Wells Fargo & Co. (Old) 4/1/96 which merged into Wells Fargo & Co. (New) 11/2/98

FIRST WESTERN BANK (BESSEMER, AL)
Through voluntary exchange offer 97.013% held by United Alabama Bancshares Inc. as of 04/17/1975
Public interest eliminated

FIRST WESTERN DEVELOPMENT CO. (CO)
Charter revoked for failure to pay franchise taxes 10/14/65

FIRST WESTERN NATIONAL BANK (MOAB, UT)
Acquired by Zions Bancorporation 06/06/1995
Details not available

FIRST WESTN BANCORP INC (PA)
Common $5 par split (3) for (2) by issuance of (0.5) additional share 11/17/1995
Common $5 par split (3) for (2) by issuance of (0.5) additional share payable 08/15/1997 to holders of record 07/28/1997
Stock Dividends - 300% 04/28/1986; 50% 02/18/1992
Merged into Sky Financial Group, Inc. 08/06/1999
Each share Common $5 par exchanged for (1.211) shares Common no par
Sky Financial Group, Inc. merged into Huntington Bancshares Inc. 07/02/2007

FIRST WESTN BK & TR CO (LOS ANGELES, CA)
Through purchase offer 99.9% acquired by Lloyds First Western Corp. as of 08/15/1974
Public interest eliminated

FIRST WESTN BK (BURNSVILLE, NC)
Merged into MountainBank Financial Corp. 12/31/2001
Each share Common 1¢ par exchanged for (0.5) share Common $4 par
MountainBank Financial Corp. merged into South Financial Group, Inc. 10/3/2003

FIRST WESTN BK (SIMI VALLEY, CA)
Stock Dividends - 5% payable 04/12/1999 to holders of record 03/25/1999; 5% payable 12/01/1999 to holders of record 11/15/1999; 5% payable 04/03/2000 to holders of record 03/15/2000
Merged into UnionBanCal Corp. (CA) 05/13/2002
Each share Common $8 par exchanged for approximately (0.417) share Common no par and $13.308 cash
UnionBanCal Corp. (CA) reincorporated in Delware 09/30/2003
(See UnionBanCal Corp. (DE))

FIRST WESTN BK N A (SAN DIEGO, CA)
Closed by FDIC 4/15/93
Stockholders' equity unlikely

FIRST WESTN COMMUNICATIONS CORP (BC)
Name changed to Galaxy Industries Ltd. 04/28/1988
(See Galaxy Industries Ltd.)

FIRST WESTN CORP (DE)
Name changed to Express America Holdings Corp. 11/04/1993
Express America Holdings Corp. name changed to Pilgrim America Capital Corp. 04/28/1997 which name changed to Pilgrim Capital Corp. 06/21/1999 which merged into

ReliaStar Financial Corp. 10/29/1999
(See ReliaStar Financial Corp.)

FIRST WESTN ENVIRONMENTAL PROTN INC (CANADA)
Dissolved for non-compliance 05/15/2006

FIRST WESTN FINL CORP (DE)
Common $1 par split (2) for (1) by issuance of (1) additional share 09/23/1963
Stock Dividend - 10% 04/06/1983
Merged into AMFED Financial Inc. 10/31/1994
Each share Common $1 par exchanged for (0.45612) share Common 10¢ par
AMFED Financial Inc. merged into Norwest Corp. 01/18/1996 which name changed to Wells Fargo & Co. (New) 11/02/1998

FIRST WESTN FINL VENTURES INC (AB)
Merged into Redcliffe Exploration Inc. 04/03/2009
Each share Common no par exchanged for (0.39) share Class B Common no par
(See Redcliffe Exploration Inc.)

FIRST WESTN INCOME RLTY TR (CA)
Reorganized under the laws of Delaware as Western Real Estate Fund, Inc. 09/30/1987
Each Share of Bene. Int. $10 par exchanged for (0.224) share Common no par
(See Western Real Estate Fund, Inc.)

FIRST WESTN MINERALS INC (BC)
Name changed to Augusta Metals Inc. 07/04/1997
Augusta Metals Inc. name changed to CyberCom Systems Inc. 09/14/2000
(See CyberCom Systems Inc.)

FIRST WESTN PENNBANCORP INC (PA)
Name changed to First Western Bancorp, Inc. 04/08/1985
First Western Bancorp, Inc. merged into Sky Financial Group, Inc. 08/06/1999 which merged into Huntington Bancshares Inc. 07/02/2007

FIRST WESTN RES INC (BC)
Name changed to First Western Communications Corp. 12/10/1984
First Western Communications Corp. name changed to Galaxy Industries Ltd. 04/28/1988
(See Galaxy Industries Ltd.)

FIRST WICHITA BANCSHARES INC (TX)
Common $5 par changed to $2.50 par and (1) additional share issued 4/30/80
Merged into Mercantile Texas Corp. 10/18/83
Each share Common $2.50 par exchanged for (1.143) shares $3.50 Conv. Preferred $1 par
Mercantile Texas Corp. name changed to MCorp 10/11/84
(See MCorp)

FIRST WICHITA NATL BK (WICHITA FALLS, TX)
Stock Dividend - 20.6% 10/20/72
Reorganized as First-Wichita Bancshares, Inc. 10/31/75
Each share Common $10 par exchanged for (1) share Common $5 par
First-Wichita Bancshares, Inc. merged into Mercantile Texas Corp. 10/18/83 which name changed to MCorp 10/11/84
(See MCorp)

FIRST WINSTON CORP. (NC)
Class A Common 1¢ par changed to 10¢ par in October 1980
Each share Class A Common 10¢ par exchanged for (0.01) share Class A Common $10 par 2/26/82
Acquired by a private investor
Details not available

FIRST WIS BANKSHARES CORP (WI)
Common $5 par changed to $2.50 par and (1) additional share issued 05/28/1970
Name changed to First Wisconsin Corp. 03/30/1974
First Wisconsin Corp. name changed to Firstar Corp. (Old) 01/01/1989 which merged into Firstar Corp. (New) 11/20/1998 which merged into U.S. Bancorp (DE) 02/27/2001

FIRST WIS CORP (WI)
Common $2.50 par split (2) for (1) by issuance of (1) additional share 08/12/1983
Common $2.50 par changed to $1.25 par and (1) additional share issued 05/15/1986
$6.25 Preferred Ser. A $1 par called for redemption 06/15/1988
Name changed to Firstar Corp. (Old) 01/01/1989
Firstar Corp. (Old) merged into Firstar Corp. (New) 11/20/1998 which merged into U.S. Bancorp (DE) 02/27/2001

FIRST WIS MTG TR (MA)
Name changed to Novus Property Co. 05/26/1981
Novus Property Co. merged into American Realty Trust (DC) 10/31/1986 which reorganized in Georgia as American Realty Trust, Inc. 06/24/1988 which merged into American Realty Investors Inc. 08/02/2000

FIRST WISCONSIN MORTGAGE INVESTORS (MA)
Name changed to First Wisconsin Mortgage Trust 3/27/73
First Wisconsin Mortgage Trust name changed to Novus Property Co. 5/26/81 which merged into American Realty Trust (D.C.) 10/31/86 which reorganized in Georgia as American Realty Trust, Inc. 6/24/88

FIRST WISCONSIN NATIONAL BANK (FOND DU LAC, WI)
Acquired by Firstar Bank Wisconsin (Madison, WI) 05/13/1996
Details not available

FIRST WISCONSIN NATIONAL BANK (MADISON, WI)
Acquired by Firstar Bank, N.A. (Madison, WI) 09/11/1999
Details not available

FIRST WNB CORP (DE)
Name changed to Abigail Adams National Bancorp, Inc. 06/19/1986
Abigail Adams National Bancorp, Inc. merged into Premier Financial Bancorp, Inc. 10/01/2009

FIRST WOBURN BANCORP INC (DE)
Completely liquidated 5/3/2000
Each share Common received first and final distribution of $1.485265 cash

FIRST WOMEN'S BANK OF MARYLAND (ROCKVILLE, MD)
Under plan of reorganization each share Common $10 par automatically became (1) share FWB Bancorporation Common $10 par 8/9/83
FWB Bancorporation name changed to Grandbanc Inc. 3/10/97 which merged into Century Bancshares, Inc. 3/15/2001 which merged into United Bankshares, Inc. 12/10/2001

FIRST WOMENS BANCORPORATION UTAH (UT)
Name changed to Western Home Financial Corp. 08/18/1979
(See Western Home Financial Corp.)

FIRST WOMENS BK (NEW YORK, NY)
Capital Stock $10 par changed to $5 par 01/29/1980
Under plan of reorganization each share Capital Stock $5 par automatically became (1) share First New York Business Bank Corp. Common 10¢ par 04/06/1989
First New York Business Bank Corp. merged into First New York Bank for Business (New York, NY) 05/21/1992
(See First New York Bank for Business (New York, NY))

FIRST WOMENS FINL CORP (DE)
Name changed to Financial Benefit Group, Inc. and Common 1¢ par reclassified as Class B Common 1¢ par 6/10/86
Financial Benefit Group, Inc. merged into AmVestors Financial Corp. 4/8/96 which merged into AmerUs Life Holdings, Inc. 12/19/97 which name changed to Amerus Group Co. 9/20/2000
(See Amerus Group Co.)

FIRST WORLD CHEESE INC (DE)
Stock Dividend - 50% 3/29/89
Name changed to Alpine Lace Brands, Inc. 6/3/91
(See Alpine Lace Brands, Inc.)

FIRST WORLD CORP (NJ)
Charter revoked for failure to file reports and pay fees 05/31/1994

FIRST WORTH CORP (TX)
Each share Common $10 par exchanged for (2) shares Common $5 par 9/30/68
Recapitalized as Justin Industries Inc. 10/13/72
Each share Common $5 par exchanged for (2) shares Common $2.50 par
(See Justin Industries, Inc.)

FIRST WYO BANCORPORATION (WY)
Merged into KeyCorp (NY) 12/30/1988
Each share Common no par exchanged for (0.765) share Common $5 par
KeyCorp (NY) merged into KeyCorp (New) (OH) 03/01/1994

FIRST YELLOWHEAD EQUITIES INC (AB)
Acquired by 1170552 Alberta Ltd. 07/06/2005
Each share Common no par exchanged for $2.50 cash

FIRST YORK CORP. (DE)
Merged into Equity Corp. 11/3/52
Each share $2 Preferred $1 par exchanged for (1) share $2 Preferred $1 par
Each share Common 10¢ par exchanged for (1.5) shares Common 10¢ par
Equity Corp. name changed to Wheelabrator-Frye Inc. 11/4/71 which merged into Signal Companies, Inc. 2/1/83 which merged into Allied-Signal Inc. 9/19/85 which name changed to AlliedSignal Inc. 4/26/93 which name changed to Honeywell International Inc. 12/1/99

FIRST YRS INC (MA)
Common 10¢ par split (2) for (1) by issuance of (1) additional share 12/29/1995
Common 10¢ par split (2) for (1) by issuance of (1) additional share payable 06/29/1998 to holders of record 05/29/1998
Merged into RC2 Corp. 09/15/2004
Each share Common 10¢ par exchanged for $18.60 cash

FIRST ZENITH MTG CO (CA)
Voluntarily dissolved 12/14/79

Details not available

FIRST ZURICH INVTS INC (FL)
Recapitalized as Terra International Pharmaceuticals Inc. 11/15/1996
Each share Common $0.001 par exchanged for (0.25) share Common $0.001 par
Terra International Pharmaceuticals Inc. recapitalized as Americabilia.Com Inc. (FL) 09/15/1999 which reincorporated in Nevada as Crystalix Group International Inc. 12/06/2002 which recapitalized as Seaena, Inc. 03/31/2006
(See Seaena, Inc.)

FIRSTAMERICA AUTOMOTIVE INC (NV)
Merged into Sonic Automotive, Inc. 12/31/99
Each share Common $0.001 par exchanged for $4.42 cash

FIRSTAMERICA CORP. (DE)
Name changed to Western Bancorporation 4/3/61
Western Bancorporation name changed to First Interstate Bancorp 6/1/81 which merged into Wells Fargo & Co. (Old) 4/1/96 which merged into Wells Fargo & Co. (New) 11/2/98

FIRSTAR CORP (WI)
Incorporated 00/00/1929
Adjustable Rate Preferred Ser. B $1 par called for redemption 12/29/1993
Common $1.25 par split (2) for (1) by issuance of (1) additional share 09/30/1992
Common $1.25 par split (2) for (1) by issuance of (1) additional share payable 02/14/1997 to holders of record 01/27/1997 Ex date - 02/18/1997
Depositary Conv. Preferred Ser. D called for redemption at $25 on 06/10/1998
Merged into Firstar Corp. (New) 11/20/1998
Each share Common $1.25 par exchanged for (0.76) share Common 1¢ par
Firstar Corp. (New) merged into U.S. Bancorp 02/27/2001

FIRSTAR CORP (WI)
Incorporated 04/27/1964
Stock Dividend - 10% 06/30/1983
Merged into Marine Corp. (WI) 09/23/1985
Each share Common $5 par exchanged for (0.801) share Common $5 par
Marine Corp. (WI) merged into Banc One Corp. (DE) 04/01/1988 which reincorporated in Ohio 05/01/1989 which merged into Bank One Corp. 10/02/1998 which merged into J.P. Morgan Chase & Co. 12/31/2000 which name changed to JPMorgan Chase & Co. 07/20/2004

FIRSTAR CORP NEW (WI)
Incorporated 06/18/1998
Common 1¢ par split (3) for (1) by issuance of (2) additional shares payable 04/15/1999 to holders of record 03/31/1999
Merged into U.S. Bancorp 02/27/2001
Each share Common 1¢ par exchanged for (1) share Common 1¢ par

FIRSTAT AMER INC (FL)
Name changed to Nurses Network.com Inc. (FL) 06/17/1999
Nurses Network.com Inc. (FL) reorganized in Delaware as Scandia Inc. 04/29/2008

FIRSTATLANTIC FINL HLDGS INC (FL)
Merged into National Commerce Corp. 01/01/2018
Each share Common 1¢ par

exchanged for (0.44) share Common 1¢ par

FIRSTBANC SVGS ASSN (TX)
Merged into Fort Bend Holding Corp. 08/16/1996
Each share Common exchanged for $13.8625 cash

FIRSTBANCORP INC (CT)
Conv. Preferred no par called for redemption 12/14/83
Merged into Hartford National Corp. 3/30/84
Each share Common $5 par exchanged for (2.93) shares Common $6.25 par
Hartford National Corp. merged into Shawmut National Corp. 2/29/88 which merged into Fleet Financial Group Inc. (New) 11/30/95 which name changed to Fleet Boston Corp. 10/1/99 which name changed to FleetBoston Financial Corp. 4/18/2000 which merged into Bank of America Corp. 4/1/2004

FIRSTBANCORPORATION INC (SC)
Merged into First National Corp. 08/02/1999
Each share Common 1¢ par exchanged for (1.222) shares Common $2.50 par
First National Corp. name changed to SCBT Financial Corp. 02/20/2004 which name changed to First Financial Holdings, Inc. 07/30/2013 which name changed to South State Corp. 06/30/2014

FIRSTBANK CORP (MI)
Common $10 par split (2) for (1) by issuance of (1) additional share 09/15/1993
Common $10 par split (2) for (1) by issuance of (1) additional share payable 04/08/1998 to holders of record 03/30/1998
Stock Dividends - 5% payable 12/28/1995 to holders of record 12/18/1995; 5% payable 12/13/1996 to holders of record 12/04/1996; 5% payable 12/30/1997 to holders of record 12/15/1997; 5% payable 12/31/1998 to holders of record 12/18/1998; 5% payable 12/31/1999 to holders of record 12/16/1999; 5% payable 12/29/2000 to holders of record 12/13/2000 Ex date - 12/11/2000; 5% payable 12/31/2001 to holders of record 12/14/2001 Ex date - 12/12/2001; 5% payable 12/31/2002 to holders of record 12/18/2002; 5% payable 12/31/2003 to holders of record 12/18/2003 Ex date - 12/16/2003; 5% payable 12/31/2004 to holders of record 12/17/2004; 5% payable 12/30/2005 to holders of record 12/16/2005 Ex date - 12/14/2005; 5% payable 12/29/2006 to holders of record 12/15/2006 Ex date - 12/13/2006
Fixed Rate Perpetual Preferred Ser. A no par called for redemption at $1,000 plus $4.027777 accrued dividends on 06/14/2013
Merged into Mercantile Bank Corp. 06/01/2014
Each share Common $10 par exchanged for (1) share Common no par

FIRSTBANK FINL SVCS INC (GA)
Stock Dividends - 10% payable 01/31/2006 to holders of record 11/30/2005 Ex date - 01/25/2006; 20% payable 12/29/2006 to holders of record 12/01/2006 Ex date - 11/29/2006
Chapter 7 bankruptcy proceedings terminated 05/13/2014
Stockholders' equity unlikely

FIRSTBANK GROUP INC (TX)
Merged into Norwest Corp. 12/02/1997
Each share Common exchanged for (3.5741164) shares Common $1-2/3 par
Norwest Corp. name changed to Wells Fargo & Co. (New) 11/02/1998

FIRSTBANK ILL CO (DE)
Common $5 par changed to $2 par and (2) additional shares issued 12/01/1983
Common $2 par changed to $1 par and (1) additional share issued 07/01/1986
Common $1 par split (3) for (2) by issuance of (0.5) additional share 04/01/1995
Common $1 par split (3) for (2) by issuance of (0.5) additional share payable 09/01/1997 to holders of record 08/15/1997
Merged into Mercantile Bancorporation, Inc. 07/01/1998
Each share Common $1 par exchanged for (0.8308) share Common 1¢ par
Mercantile Bancorporation, Inc. merged into Firstar Corp. (New) 09/20/1999 which merged into U.S. Bancorp (DE) 02/27/2001

FIRSTBANK NW CORP (WA)
Name changed 09/01/1999
Name and state of incorporation changed from FirstBank Corp. (DE) to FirstBank NW Corp. (WA) 09/01/1999
Common 1¢ par split (2) for (1) by issuance of (1) additional share payable 02/09/2006 to holders of record 01/26/2006 Ex date - 02/10/2006
Merged into Sterling Financial Corp. 12/01/2006
Each share Common 1¢ par exchanged for (0.789) share Common $1 par and $2.55 cash
Sterling Financial Corp. merged into Umpqua Holdings Corp. 04/18/2014

FIRSTBANK P R (SAN JUAN, PR)
Common 1¢ par split (3) for (2) by issuance of (0.5) additional share 06/09/1995
Common 1¢ par split (2) for (1) by issuance of (1) additional share payable 05/29/1998 to holders of record 05/15/1998 Ex date - 06/01/1998
Under plan of reorganization each share Common 1¢ par automatically became (1) share First Bancorp. Common 1¢ par 10/01/1998

FIRSTBINGO COM (NV)
Each share old Common $0.001 par exchanged for (0.04) share new Common $0.001 par 12/31/2001
New Common $0.001 par split (4) for (1) by issuance of (3) additional shares payable 11/21/2003 to holders of record 11/14/2003 Ex date - 11/24/2003
Recapitalized as South Shore Resources, Inc. 11/01/2006
Each share new Common $0.001 par exchanged for (0.1) share Common $0.001 par
South Shore Resources, Inc. name changed to E-Buy Home Inc. 02/06/2013

FIRSTCITY FINL CORP (DE)
Special Preferred called for redemption at $21 on 09/30/1998
Preferred called for redemption at $21 on 12/30/2004
Acquired by Hotspurs Holdings LLC 05/17/2013
Each share Common 1¢ par exchanged for $10 cash

FIRSTCITY LIQUIDATING TR (DE)
Liquidation completed
Each Ctf. of Bene. Int. Class B received initial distribution of $7 cash payable 1/30/98 to holders of record 1/23/98 Ex date - 1/21/98
Each Ctf. of Bene. Int. Class B received second distribution of $11.50 cash payable 4/15/98 to holders of record 4/1/98 Ex date - 4/16/98
Each Ctf. of Bene. Int. Class B received third distribution of $7 cash payable 7/15/98 to holders of record 7/1/98 Ex date - 7/7/98
Each Ctf. of Bene. Int. Class B received fourth distribution of $2 cash payable 10/15/98
Each Ctf. of Bene. Int. Class B received fifth distribution of $3.50 cash payable 1/25/99 to holders of record 1/15/99 Ex date - 1/19/99
Each Ctf. of Bene. Int. Class B received sixth distribution of $4 cash payable 4/26/99 to holders of record 4/16/99 Ex date - 4/14/99
Each Ctf. of Bene. Int. Class B received seventh distribution of $2 cash payable 7/19/99 to holders of record 7/9/99 Ex date - 7/7/99
Each Ctf. of Bene. Int. Class B received eighth distribution of $1 cash payable 1/10/2000 to holders of record 1/3/2000 Ex date - 12/30/99
Each Ctf. of Bene. Int. Class B received ninth distribution of $1 cash payable 5/19/2000 to holders of record 5/10/2000 Ex date - 5/10/2000
Each Ctf. of Bene. Int. Class B received tenth distribution of $1 cash payable 7/10/2000 to holders of record 7/5/2000 Ex date - 7/5/2000
Each Ctf. of Bene. Int. Class B received eleventh distribution of $1 cash payable 10/20/2000 to holders of record 10/10/2000 Ex date - 10/5/2000
Each Ctf. of Bene. Int. Class B received twelfth distribution of $1 cash payable 3/29/2001 to holders of record 3/19/2001 Ex date - 3/15/2001
Each Ctf. of Bene. Int. Class B received thirteenth distribution of $11 cash payable 7/14/2003 to holders of record 7/7/2003 Ex date - 7/15/2003
Each Ctf. of Bene. Int. Class B received fourteenth distribution of $1 cash payable 12/5/2003 to holders of record 11/21/2003 Ex date - 12/8/2003
Each Ctf. of Bene. Int. Class B received fifteenth and final distribution of (1) share FCLT Loans Asset Corp. Restricted share payable 2/24/2004 to holders of record 1/26/2004 Ex date -1/22/2004
Ctfs. of Bene. Int. Class C received no distribution and are worthless

FIRSTCLASS SYS CORP (AB)
Name changed to Serebra Learning Corp. (AB) 10/01/2001
Serebra Learning Corp. (AB) reorganized in Newfoundland and Labrador as Bluedrop Performance Learning Inc. 01/27/2012

FIRSTCOM CORP (TX)
Merged into AT&T Latin America Corp. 8/29/2000
Each share Common $0.001 par exchanged for (1) share Class A Common $0.0001 par
(See AT&T Latin America Corp.)

FIRSTCORP INC (DE)
Common $1 par reclassified as Class A Common $1 par 10/2/85
Each share Class A Common $1 par received distribution of (1) share Class B Common $1 par 10/10/85
Chapter 11 bankruptcy proceedings converted to Chapter 7 on 1/4/93
No stockholders' equity

FIRSTFED AMER BANCORP INC (DE)
Common 1¢ par split (2) for (1) by issuance of (1) additional share payable 7/17/2003 to holders of record 7/7/2003 Ex date - 7/18/2003
Merged into Webster Financial Corp. 5/14/2004 Each share Common no par exchanged for $24.50 cash

FIRSTFED AMER INC HONOLULU HAWAII (DE)
Merged into Bancorp Hawaii Inc. 7/24/90
Each share Common 1¢ par exchanged for $38.50 cash

FIRSTFED BANCORP INC (DE)
Common 1¢ par split (2) for (1) by issuance of (1) additional share payable 4/16/97 to holders of record 4/1/97
Company went private 12/30/2005
Each share Common 1¢ par exchanged for $11 cash
Note: Holders of (10,000) or more shares will retain their interests

FIRSTFED BANCSHARES INC (DE)
Common 1¢ par split (3) for (2) by issuance of (0.5) additional share payable 05/15/1996 to holders of record 05/01/1996
Name changed to CoVest Bancshares, Inc. 06/02/1997
(See CoVest Bancshares, Inc.)

FIRSTFED FINL CORP (DE)
Common 1¢ par split (3) for (2) by issuance of (0.5) additional share 10/29/1987
Common 1¢ par split (5) for (4) by issuance of (0.25) additional share 11/29/1988
Common 1¢ par split (2) for (1) by issuance of (1) additional share payable 07/30/1998 to holders of record 07/15/1998 Ex date - 07/31/1998
Stock Dividend - 25% 10/30/1991
Plan of reorganization under Chapter 11 Federal Bankruptcy proceedings effective 01/02/2013
No stockholders' equity

FIRSTFED MICH CORP (MI)
Common 1¢ par split (3) for (2) by issuance of (0.5) additional share 09/20/1993
Merged into Charter One Financial, Inc. 10/31/1995
Each share Common 1¢ par exchanged for (1.2) shares Common 1¢ par
(See Charter One Financial, Inc.)

FIRSTFED NORTHN KY BANCORP INC (OH)
Merged into Huntington Bancshares Inc. 12/16/94
Each share Common $1 par exchanged for (2.4965) shares Common no par

FIRSTFEDERAL FINL SVCS CORP (OH)
Common $1 par split (3) for (2) by issuance of (0.5) additional share 05/22/1992
Common $1 par split (3) for (2) by issuance of (0.5) additional share 05/21/1993
Common $1 par split (5) for (4) by issuance of (0.25) additional share 05/20/1994
Common $1 par split (5) for (4) by issuance of (0.25) additional share payable 05/22/1997 to holders of record 05/02/1997
Conv. Preferred Ser. A no par called for redemption 12/16/1997
Conv. Preferred Ser. B no par split (5) for (4) by issuance of (0.25) additional share payable 05/22/1998 to holders of record 05/04/1998
Common $1 par split (5) for (4) by issuance of (0.25) additional share payable 05/22/1998 to holders of record 05/04/1998
Stock Dividends - 10% 05/22/1995;

10% payable 05/22/1996 to holders of record 05/02/1996
Name changed to Signal Corp. 06/16/1998
Signal Corp. merged into FirstMerit Corp. 02/12/1999 which merged into Huntington Bancshares Inc. 08/16/2016

FIRSTFUND CAP 1986 CORP (CANADA)
Recapitalized as Consolidated Firstfund Capital Corp. 10/26/1988
Each share Class A Subordinated no par exchanged for (0.2) share Common no par

FIRSTGOLD CORP (DE)
Chapter 11 bankruptcy proceedings converted to Chapter 7 on 04/10/2012
No stockholders' equity

FIRSTGROWTH CAPITAL INC (BC)
Name changed to FirstGrowth Exploration & Development Services Corp. 08/17/2007
FirstGrowth Exploration & Development Services Corp. name changed to Kinetex Resources Corp. 12/15/2008

FIRSTGROWTH EXPL & DEVELOPMENT SVCS CORP (BC)
Name changed to Kinetex Resources Corp. 12/15/2008

FIRSTGULF BANCORP (DE)
Acquired by AmSouth Bancorporation 8/30/85
Each share Common $4 par exchanged for $47 cash

FIRSTIER CORP (CO)
Merged into Compass Bancshares, Inc. 01/04/2001
Each share Common exchanged for (0.881) share Common $2 par
Compass Bancshares, Inc. merged into Banco Bilbao Vizcaya Argentaria, S.A. 09/07/2007

FIRSTIER FINL INC (NE)
Name changed 05/18/1987
Common $5 par split (2) for (1) by issuance of (1) additional share 06/14/1986
Name changed from FirstTier, Inc. to FirsTier Financial Inc. 05/18/1987
Common $5 par split (2) for (1) by issuance of (1) additional share 06/30/1992
Common $5 par split (3) for (2) by issuance of (0.5) additional share 06/30/1994
Merged into First Bank System, Inc. 02/16/1996
Each share Common $5 par exchanged for (0.8829) share Common $1.25 par
First Bank System, Inc. name changed to U.S. Bancorp 08/01/1997

FIRSTIN WIRELESS TECHNOLOGY INC (NV)
Recapitalized as BioNovelus, Inc. 05/14/2015
Each share Common $0.001 par exchanged for (0.00133333) share Common $0.001 par

FIRSTLAND ENERGY LTD (AB)
Name changed to Traverse Energy Ltd. 06/17/2009

FIRSTLINE ENVIRONMENTAL SOLUTIONS INC (FL)
Name changed to Gemco Minerals, Inc. 04/10/2006

FIRSTLINE POLY PRODS INTL INC (DE)
Each share old Common $0.001 par exchanged for (0.01) share new Common $0.001 par 1/18/2001
Name changed to Arabel Records International, Inc. 9/17/2001
Arabel Records International, Inc. recapitalized as Asia Pacific Engineering Solutions International, Inc. 6/1/2005

FIRSTLINE RECOVERY SYS USA INC (DE)
Common $0.001 par split (3) for (2) by issuance of (0.5) additional share payable 7/6/2000 to holders of record 5/24/2000
Name changed to Firstline Poly Products International, Inc. 5/24/2000
Firstline Poly Products International, Inc. name changed to Arabel Records International, Inc. 9/17/2001 which recapitalized as Asia Pacific Engineering Solutions International, Inc. 6/1/2005

FIRSTLINE VENTURES LTD (BC)
Recapitalized as Aeon Ventures Ltd. 11/18/1999
Each share Common no par exchanged for (0.5) share Common no par
Aeon Ventures Ltd. recapitalized as Statesman Resources Ltd. 06/28/2004

FIRSTLINK COMMUNICATIONS INC (OR)
Name changed to Usol Holdings, Inc. 12/23/1999
(See Usol Holdings, Inc.)

FIRSTMARK CORP (DE)
6% Preferred called for redemption 02/10/1982
Merged into Belmain Realty Inc. 12/31/1982
Each share Common 5¢ par exchanged for $3.50 principal amount of Firstmark Corp. 15% Subordinated Notes due 12/31/1992 and $1.50 cash

FIRSTMARK CORP (ME)
Each share Common 10¢ par exchanged for (0.5) share Common 20¢ par 10/01/1992
Acquired by H-D Advanced Manufacturing Co. 06/30/2015
Each share Common 20¢ par exchanged for $9.66 cash

FIRSTMERIT CORP (OH)
Common no par split (2) for (1) by issuance of (1) additional share payable 09/29/1997 to holders of record 09/02/1997
6.5% Conv. Preferred Ser. B no par called for redemption at $25 on 11/14/2003
Stock Dividend - 0.67% payable 06/15/2009 to holders of record 06/01/2009 Ex date - 05/28/2009
Merged into Huntington Bancshares Inc. 08/16/2016
Each share 5.875% Non-Cum Perpetual Preferred Ser. A 1¢ par exchanged for (1) share 5.875% Non-Cum Perpetual Preferred Ser. C 1¢ par
Each share Common 1¢ par exchanged for (1.72) shares Common no par and $5 cash

FIRSTMERIT FDS (MA)
Merged into Money Market Obligations Trust 08/16/2002
Details not available

FIRSTMISS GOLD INC (NV)
Name changed to Getchell Gold Corp. 06/25/1996
Getchell Gold Corp. merged into Placer Dome Inc. 05/27/1999 which merged into Barrick Gold Corp. 03/08/2006

FIRSTPAC LTD (AUSTRALIA)
Struck off register 10/24/1990
No stockholders' equity

FIRSTPLUS FINL GROUP INC (NV)
Plan of reorganization under Chapter 11 Federal Bankrutpcy proceedings effective 02/22/2012
No stockholders' equity

FIRSTROCK BANCORP INC (DE)
Acquired by First Financial Corp. (WI) 2/28/95
Each share Common 1¢ par exchanged for (1.7893) shares Common $1 par
First Financial Corp. (WI) merged into Associated Banc-Corp 10/29/97

FIRSTRUST BANCSHARES CORP. (IA)
Liquidated 1/15/87
Details not available

FIRSTSERVICE BK (DOYLESTOWN, PA)
Merged into National Penn Bancshares, Inc. 02/25/2003
Each share Common exchanged for (0.5954) share Common $5 par and $3.90 cash
National Penn Bancshares, Inc. merged into BB&T Corp. 04/01/2016

FIRSTSERVICE CORP OLD (ON)
Subordinate Shares no par split (2) for (1) by issuance of (1) additional share payable 12/22/2004 to holders of record 12/15/2004
Each Subordinate Share no par received distribution of (0.2) share 7% Preference Ser. 1 no par payable 08/01/2007 to holders of record 07/25/2007
Each share 7% Preference Ser. 1 no par exchanged for (0.7943) Subordinate Share no par 05/03/2013
Each Subordinate Share no par received distribution of (1) share FirstService Corp. (New) Subordinate Share no par payable 06/01/2015 to holders of record 05/29/2015
Name changed to Colliers International Group Inc. 06/01/2015

FIRSTSHARES TEX INC (TX)
Each share Common $2 par exchanged for (0.499975) share Common $4 par to reflect a (1) for (700) reverse split followed by a (350) for (1) forward split 2/17/95
Merged into Hibernia Corp. 3/16/98
Each share Common $4 par exchanged for (7.15) shares Class A Common no par
Hibernia Corp. merged into Capital One Financial Corp. 11/16/2005

FIRSTSOUTH BANCORP INC (PA)
Merged into BT Financial Corp. 12/10/93
Each share Common 1¢ par exchanged for (0.693) share Common $5 par and $13.50 cash
BT Financial Corp. name changed to Promistar Financial Corp. 11/15/2000 which merged into F.N.B. Corp. (FL) 1/18/2002

FIRSTSOUTH BURLINGTON (BURLINGTON, NC)
Stock Dividend - 10% 10/15/94
Merged into Centura Banks, Inc. 10/25/96
Each share Common $3.33-1/3 par exchanged for (0.55) share Common no par
Centura Banks, Inc. merged into Royal Bank of Canada (Montreal, QC) 6/5/2001

FIRSTSOUTH COML CORP (DE)
Recapitalized as Lonestar Hospitality Corp. 07/20/1994
Each share Common 2¢ par exchanged for (0.5) share Common 2¢ par
Lonestar Hospitality Corp. recapitalized as Citadel Computer Systems Inc. 05/01/1996 which name changed to Citadel Technology Inc. 02/27/1998 which name changed to CT Holdings, Inc. 11/30/1999 which recapitalized as CT Holdings Enterprises, Inc.

02/28/2007 which recapitalized as Xcorporeal, Inc. 10/15/2007

FIRSTSPARTAN FINL CORP (DE)
Merged into BB&T Corp. 3/2/2001
Each share Common 1¢ par exchanged for (1) share Common $5 par

FIRSTWAVE TECHNOLOGIES INC (GA)
Each share old Common no par exchanged for (0.33333333) share new Common no par 09/18/2001
Reorganized under the laws of Nevada as Textmunication Holdings, Inc. 11/15/2013
Each share Common no par exchanged for (0.2) share Common $0.0001 par

FIRSTWAY FINL INC (PA)
Common $5 par split (3) for (1) by issuance of (2) additional shares 8/15/86
Acquired by Financial Trust Corp. 11/2/87
Each share Common $5 par exchanged for (1) share Common $5 par
Financial Trust Corp. merged into Keystone Financial, Inc. 5/30/97 which merged into M&T Bank Corp. 10/6/2000

FIRSTWEB INTERNET SOLUTIONS INC (BC)
Cease trade order effective 03/21/2003
Stockholders' equity unlikely

FIRSTWORLD COMMUNICATIONS INC (DE)
Issue Information - 10,000,000 shares COM SER B offered at $17 per share on 03/07/2000
Name changed to Verado Holdings, Inc. 02/12/2001
(See Verado Holdings, Inc.)

FIRTH BRICK & TILE CO., LTD.
Name changed to Milton Brick (1937), Ltd. in 1937
Milton Brick (1937), Ltd. name changed to Milton Brick Co., Ltd. in 1938 which name changed to Milton Group Ltd. 12/11/72
(See Milton Group Ltd.)

FIRTH CARPET CO. (NY)
Common no par changed to $5 par in 1951
Merged into Mohasco Industries, Inc. 1/31/62
Each share Common $5 par exchanged for (0.666666) share Common $5 par
Mohasco Industries, Inc. name changed to Mohasco Corp. 5/3/74
(See Mohasco Corp.)

FIRTH LOACH METALS INC (PA)
Capital Stock $25 par changed to $5 par and (4) additional shares issued 02/15/1968
Acquired by Howmet Corp. 05/17/1968
Each share Capital Stock $5 par exchanged for (0.488) share Common $1 par
(See Howmet Corp.)

FIRTH STERLING, INC. (PA)
Each share Preferred $100 par exchanged for (9) shares Common $2.50 par 12/11/1967
Completely liquidated 12/21/1967
Each share Common $2.50 par exchanged for first and final distribution of (0.111111) share Teledyne, Inc. Common $1 par
Teledyne, Inc. merged into Allegheny Teledyne Inc. 08/15/1996 which name changed to Allegheny Technologies Inc. 11/29/1999

FIRTH STERLING STEEL & CARBIDE CORP.
Name changed to Firth Sterling, Inc. 00/00/1952

Firth Sterling, Inc. acquired by Teledyne, Inc. 12/21/1967 which merged into Allegheny Teledyne Inc. 08/15/1996 which name changed to Allegheny Technologies Inc. 11/29/1999

FIRTH STERLING STEEL CO.
Name changed to Firth Sterling Steel & Carbide Corp. in 1946
Firth Sterling Steel & Carbide Corp. name changed to Firth Sterling, Inc. in 1952 which was acquired by Teledyne, Inc. 12/21/67 which merged into Allegheny Teledyne Inc. 8/15/96 which name changed to Allegheny Technologies Inc. 11/29/99

FISCAL FUND, INC. (DE)
Liquidation completed
Each Bene. Share Bank Stock Ser. 10¢ par received initial distribution of $1.65 cash in June 1943
Each Bene. Share Insurance Stock 10¢ par received initial distribution of $2.65 cash in June 1943
Each Bene. Share Bank Stock Ser. 10¢ par received second and final distribution of $0.26453 cash in November 1943
Each Bene. Share Insurance Stock Ser. 10¢ par received second and final distribution of $0.31196 cash in November 1943

FISCHBACH & MOORE INC (NY)
Common $1 par split (2) for (1) by issuance of (1) additional share 6/17/69
Reincorporated under the laws of Delaware as Fischbach Corp. 6/16/80
(See Fischbach Corp.)

FISCHBACH CORP (DE)
Merged into American International Group, Inc. 08/24/1990
Each share Common $1 par exchanged for $11 cash

FISCHER & PORTER CO (PA)
Reincorporated 7/1/87
Reincorporated 7/1/90
Each share old Common $1 par exchanged for (1) share Class B Common $1 par 8/16/55
50¢ Part. Preference $1 par called for redemption 10/17/55
5% Preferred $10 par called for redemption 12/31/65
Stock Dividend - 100% 1/15/57
State of incorporation changed from (PA) to (DE) 7/1/87
State of incorporation changed from (DE) back to (PA) 7/1/90
Acquired by Elsag Bailey Process Automation N.V. 8/10/94
Each share Common $1 par exchanged for $24.25 cash

FISCHER IMAGING CORP (DE)
Plan of reorganization under Chapter 11 Federal Bankruptcy Code effective 05/18/2007
No stockholders' equity

FISCHER PACKING CO (KY)
Acquired by Wilson Certified Foods Inc. 07/19/1969
Details not available

FISCHER (HENRY) PACKING CO. (KY)
Name changed to Fischer Packing Co. 2/13/57
(See Fischer Packing Co.)

FISCHER-WATT GOLD INC (NV)
Name changed to Cyclone Uranium Corp. 12/14/2012

FISCHMAN (I.) & SONS
Bankrupt in 1932
Details not available

FISCO INC (PA)
Common 10¢ par split (3) for (2) by issuance of (0.5) additional share 06/25/1971
Common 10¢ par split (5) for (4) by issuance of (0.25) additional share 07/06/1972
Company reported out of business 00/00/1974
Details not available

FISERV INC (DE)
Common 1¢ par split (3) for (2) by issuance of (0.5) additional share 07/01/1991
Reincorporated under the laws of Wisconsin 04/30/1992

FISHER & BURPE LTD. (CANADA)
Name changed to Finlayson Enterprises Ltd. in 1959
(See Finlayson Enterprises Ltd.)

FISHER & PAYKEL APPLIANCES HLDGS LTD (NEW ZEALAND)
ADR agreement terminated 03/14/2014
No ADR's remain outstanding

FISHER & PAYKEL HEALTHCARE CORP LTD (NEW ZEALAND)
Name changed 12/24/2001
Name changed from Fisher & Paykel Industries Ltd. to Fisher & Paykel Healthcare Corp. Ltd. 12/24/2001
ADR agreement terminated 02/28/2003
Each ADR for Ordinary exchanged for $28.34167 cash
(Additional Information in Active)

FISHER-BEER CO., INC. (NY)
Proclaimed dissolved for failure to file reports and pay fees 12/15/69

FISHER BODY OHIO CO.
Acquired by General Motors Corp. 00/00/1927
Details not available

FISHER BRASS CO. (OH)
Charter cancelled for failure to pay taxes 11/15/37

FISHER BROTHERS CO. (OH)
Each share 2nd Preferred no par exchanged for (7.5) shares Common no par in 1945
Common no par exchanged (3) for (1) in 1945
Each share Common no par exchanged for (2) shares Common $2.50 par 5/3/57
Name changed to Fisher Foods, Inc. 4/6/61
Fisher Foods, Inc. merged into Riser Foods, Inc. 6/8/88
(See Riser Foods, Inc.)

FISHER BUSINESS SYS INC (GA)
Each share old Common 1¢ par exchanged for (0.2) share new Common 1¢ par 12/01/1992
Name changed to Halis, Inc. 11/18/1996
Halis, Inc. merged into HealthWatch, Inc. 05/31/2001
(See HealthWatch, Inc.)

FISHER CARL G CORP (FL)
Common $1 par changed to 5¢ par 2/1/60
Name changed to Hemisphere Hotels Corp. 2/19/69
(See Hemisphere Hotels Corp.)

FISHER COMMUNICATIONS INC (WA)
Name changed 03/19/2001
Common $10 par changed to $2.50 par and (3) additional shares issued 05/15/1995
Common $2.50 par split (2) for (1) by issuance of (1) additional share payable 03/06/1998 to holders of record 02/20/1998
Name changed from Fisher Communications, Inc. to Fisher Communications, Inc. 03/19/2001
Acquired by Sinclair Broadcast Group, Inc. 08/08/2013

Each share Common $2.50 par exchanged for $41 cash

FISHER FOODS INC (OH)
Common $2.50 par changed to no par 6/26/65
Stock Dividends - 100% 5/1/68; 100% 2/28/69
Merged into Riser Foods, Inc. 6/8/88
Each share $5 Preferred no par exchanged for (1) share $8 Conv. Preferred Ser. A $100 par
Each share Common no par exchanged for (1) share Class A Common 1¢ par
(See Riser Foods, Inc.)

FISHER GOVERNOR CO. (IA)
Acquired by Monsanto Co. 8/12/69
Each share Common $1 par exchanged for (1) share $2.75 Conv. Preferred no par
Monsanto Co. name changed to Pharmacia Corp. 3/31/2000 which merged into Pfizer Inc. 4/16/2003

FISHER HARRISON CORP (NC)
Merged into PBM Graphics Inc. 12/31/97
Each share Common no par exchanged for $20 cash

FISHER (T.S.), INC (CO)
See - T S Fisher Inc

FISHER OIL & GAS CORP (BC)
Adjudicated bankrupt 09/23/1983
No stockholders' equity

FISHER-PRICE INC (DE)
Common 1¢ par split (2) for (1) by issuance of (1) additional share 06/01/1992
Merged into Mattel, Inc. 11/30/1993
Each share Common 1¢ par exchanged for (1.275) shares Common $1 par

FISHER QUEBEC GOLD MINES LTD.
Bankrupt in 1930

FISHER RESH LAB INC (CA)
Completely liquidated 3/31/67
Details not available

FISHER SCIENTIFIC CO (PA)
Common $5 par changed to $2.50 par and (1) additional share issued 9/29/67
Stock Dividend - 20% 9/10/80
Merged into Allied Corp. 10/27/81
Each share Common $2.50 par exchanged for (0.55) share $12 Conv. Preferred Ser. D no par
Allied Corp. merged into Allied-Signal Inc. 9/19/85 which name changed to AlliedSignal Inc. 4/26/93 which name changed to Honeywell International Inc. 12/1/99

FISHER SCIENTIFIC GROUP INC (DE)
Merged into Henley Group, Inc. (New) 08/24/1989
Each share Common 1¢ par exchanged for $22.25 cash

FISHER SCIENTIFIC INTL INC (DE)
Merged into FSI Merger Corp. 1/21/98
Each share old Common 1¢ par exchanged for either (1) share Fisher Scientific International Inc. new Common 1¢ par or $48.25 cash
Note: Option to receive stock expired 1/14/98
New Common 1¢ par split (5) for (1) by issuance of (4) additional shares payable 4/1/98 to holders of record 3/19/98 Ex date - 4/2/98
Each share new Common 1¢ par received distribution of (1) share ProcureNet Inc. Common 1¢ par payable 4/15/99 to holders of record 3/30/99
Merged into Thermo Fisher Scientific Inc. 11/9/2006
Each share new Common 1¢ par exchanged for (2) shares Common 1¢ par

FISHER TELEVISION CORP (CO)
Recapitalized as MBC Food Corp. 04/15/2002
Each share Common no par exchanged for (0.005) share Common no par
MBC Food Corp. recapitalized as Concorde America, Inc. 06/30/2004

FISHER THOMAS J & CO INC (DC)
Common 33-1/3¢ par changed to 10¢ par 03/12/1965
Name changed to Barnes (James T.) of Washington, D.C., Inc. 11/01/1973
(See Barnes (James T.) of Washington, D.C., Inc.)

FISHER TRANSN SVCS INC (DE)
Recapitalized as Midas Entertainment, Inc. 07/16/2004
Each share Common $0.00001 par exchanged for (0.001) share Common $0.00001 par
Midas Entertainment, Inc. recapitalized as Textechnologies, Inc. 08/01/2006 which name changed to We-R-You Corp. 04/25/2008

FISHKILL NATL BK (BEACON, NY)
Common $10 par changed to $2.50 par and (3) additional shares issued 6/20/74
Reorganized as Fishkill National Corp. 9/27/84
Each share Common $2.50 par exchanged for (1) share Common $2.50 par
Fishkill National Corp. merged into Hudson Chartered Bancorp, Inc. 9/30/94 which name changed to Premier National Bancorp, Inc. 7/17/98 which merged into M&T Bank Corp. 2/9/2001

FISHKILL NATL CORP (NY)
Merged into Hudson Chartered Bancorp, Inc. 9/30/94
Each share Common $2.50 par exchanged for (5.6) shares Common 80¢ par
Hudson Chartered Bancorp, Inc. name changed to Premier National Bancorp, Inc. 7/17/98 which merged into M&T Bank Corp. 2/9/2001

FISHMAN (M.H.) CO., INC. (DE)
Common $1 par split (5) for (4) by issuance of (0.25) additional share 5/14/65
Common $1 par split (2) for (1) by issuance of (1) additional share 7/1/66
Under plan of merger each share Common $1 par exchanged for $3.35 cash 6/29/79

FISHMAN (M.H.) CO., INC. 5¢ TO $1 STORES
Name changed to Fishman (M.H.) Co., Inc. in 1950
Each share Common $1 par exchanged for (2) shares new Common $1 par
(See Fishman (M.H.) Co., Inc.)

FISHTHEWORLD HLDGS INC (FL)
Reincorporated under the laws of Nevada as DDS Technologies USA, Inc. 05/29/2003
(See DDS Technologies USA, Inc.)

FISK REALTY CORP.
Dissolved in 1934
Details not available

FISK RUBBER CO. (MA)
Properties sold to reorganization committee in 1933
Holders received only privilege to purchase common stock of Fisk Rubber Corp.
(See listing for Fisk Rubber Corp.)

FISK RUBBER CO. (NY)
Charter cancelled and proclaimed dissolved for failure to pay taxes 7/15/40

FISK RUBBER CORP. (MA)
Completely liquidated
Each share Common no par exchanged for initial distribution of (0.25) share United States Rubber Co. Common $10 par plus $6 cash in 1940
Each share Common no par received second distribution of $0.60 cash in 1941
Each share Common no par received third and final distribution of $0.065 cash in 1943
United States Rubber Co. name changed to Uniroyal, Inc. 2/28/67
(See Uniroyal, Inc.)

FISONS PLC (UNITED KINGDOM)
ADR's for Ordinary £1 par split (2) for (1) by issuance of (1) additional share 7/16/87
Each Unsponsored ADR for Ordinary £1 par exchanged for (1) Sponsored ADR for Ordinary £1 par 5/23/88
Note: Common Market regulation required all publicly held British companies to replace LTD with PLC in 1982
ADR agreement terminated 1/8/96
Each Sponsored ADR for Ordinary £1 par exchanged for $16.261 cash

FISSION ENERGY CORP (CANADA)
Plan of arrangement effective 04/26/2013
Each share Common no par exchanged for (0.355) share Denison Mines Corp. Common no par, (1) share Fission Uranium Corp. Common no par and $0.0001 cash
(See each company's listing)
Note: Unexchanged certificates will be cancelled and become without value 04/26/2019

FISSION MINES, LTD. (ON)
Charter cancelled and proclaimed dissolved for failure to pay taxes and file returns 03/16/1976

FIT FOR BUSINESS INTL INC (NV)
Recapitalized as Marani Brands, Inc. 03/31/2008
Each share Common $0.001 par exchanged for (0.004) share Common $0.001 par

FITCH (JOHN H.) CO. (OH)
Liquidation completed
Each share Common $100 par exchanged for initial distribution of $80 cash 1/7/66
Each share Common $100 par received second distribution of $20 cash 3/15/66
Each share Common $100 par received third distribution of $5 cash 10/24/66
Each share Common $100 par received fourth and final distribution of $4.50 cash 12/18/67

FITCHBURG GAS & ELEC LT CO (MA)
Each share Common $50 par exchanged for (2) shares Common $25 par 00/00/1929
6-1/4% Preferred $100 par called for redemption 06/01/1966
Common $25 par changed to $10 par and (1.5) additional shares issued 09/04/1973
$4 Preferred $1 par called for redemption 12/28/1987
Merged into UNITIL Corp. 04/28/1992
Each share Common $10 par exchanged for (1) share Common no par

FITCHBURG PAPER CO. (MA)
Acquired by Litton Industries, Inc. 4/6/64
Each share Class A Common $1 par exchanged for (0.2335821) Common $1 par or (0.1705514) share $3 Convertible Preferred Series A $5 par
Option to receive Convertible Preferred expired 3/30/64
(See Litton Industries, Inc.)

FITMEDIA INC (DE)
Name changed to China Runji Cement Inc. 01/22/2008

FITNESS XPRESS SOFTWARE INC (NV)
Reorganized under the laws of Delaware as MSTI Holdings, Inc. 06/01/2007
Each share Common $0.001 par exchanged for (1.05633802) shares Common $0.001 par
(See MSTI Holdings, Inc.)

FITON TECHNOLOGIES CORP (NB)
Each share old Common no par exchanged for (0.05) share new Common no par 02/17/2004
Merged into 615936 N.B. Ltd. 01/07/2005
Each share new Common no par exchanged for $0.0683 cash

FITS MY STYLE INC (NV)
Reorganized under the laws of Delaware as AntriaBio, Inc. 01/10/2013
Each share Common $0.001 par exchanged for (6) shares Common $0.001 par
AntriaBio, Inc. name changed to Rezolute, Inc. 12/19/2017

FITT HWY PRODS INC (NV)
Each share old Common $0.001 par exchanged for (0.01666666) share new Common $0.001 par 02/15/2013
Name changed to Global Future City Holding Inc. 10/29/2014

FITTINGS LTD (CANADA)
Each share Class A no par exchanged for (1) share Common no par 10/01/1966
Common no par reclassified as Conv. Class A Common no par 05/04/1976
Recapitalized as Pedlar Industrial Inc.-Pedlar Industriel Inc. 04/16/1979
Each share Conv. Class A Common no par exchanged for (5) shares Common no par
Each share Conv. Class B Common no par exchanged for (5) shares Common no par
(See Pedlar Industrial Inc.-Pedlar Industriel Inc.)

FITTIPALDI LOGISTICS INC (NV)
Name changed to NuState Energy Holdings, Inc. (NV) 01/08/2008
NuState Energy Holdings, Inc. (NV) reincorporated in Florida 10/28/2015 which recapitalized as Visium Technologies, Inc. 04/25/2018

FITWAYVITAMINS INC (NV)
Common $0.001 par split (14) for (1) by issuance of (13) additional shares payable 03/24/2011 to holders of record 03/22/2011
Ex date - 03/25/2011
Name changed to Zhongbao International, Inc. 04/25/2011

FITZ-SIMMONS & CONNELL DREDGE & DOCK CO. (IL)
Common $20 par changed to no par in 1929
Acquired by Merritt-Chapman & Scott Corp. in 1954
Each share Common no par exchanged for (0.8) share Common $12.50 par
(See Merritt-Chapman & Scott Corp.)

FITZGERALD DEARMAN & ROBERTS INC (DE)
Filed petition under Chapter 7 Federal Bankruptcy Code 6/28/88
Stockholders' equity unlikely

FITZGERALD JAMES W LABS INC (MD)
Name changed to Fitzgerald Laboratories, Inc. 11/5/69
(See Fitzgerald Laboratories, Inc.)

FITZGERALD LABORATORIES, INC. (MD)
Charter annulled for failure to file annual reports 4/18/73

FITZGERALDS GAMING CORP NEW (NV)
Plan of reorganization under Chapter 11 Federal Bankruptcy Code effective 8/27/2003
No stockholders' equity

FITZSIMMONS STORES LTD. (CA)
Name changed to Thriftimart, Inc. 5/28/57
Thriftimart, Inc. name changed to Smart & Final Iris Corp. 7/20/84
(See Smart & Final Iris Corp.)

FIVE BEARS MINING CO. (CA)
Charter suspended for failure to pay taxes 04/01/1952

FIVE DOLLAR COMPUTER SOFTWARE STORE INC (NV)
Name changed to Wiz Technology, Inc. 06/30/1993
Wiz Technology, Inc. recapitalized as Wireless Technologies Inc. 07/21/2005 which name changed to Mattman Specialty Vehicles, Inc. 12/14/2005 which name changed to Remote Surveillance Technologies, Inc. 01/11/2007 which name changed to Stratera, Inc. 07/15/2008 which recapitalized as Gulf West Investment Properties, Inc. 12/16/2009

551 FIFTH AVENUE, INC. (NY)
6% Preferred $100 par changed to $5.40 Preferred $100 par and $10 cash distributed 00/00/1929
$5.40 Preferred $100 par changed to $40 par 11/21/1956
Merged into French (Fred F.) Investing Co., Inc. 10/23/1964
Each share $5.40 Preferred $40 par exchanged for $68 principal amount of 5-1/2% Convertible Subordinated Sinking Fund Debentures Ser. M due 10/01/1979 and $24 cash
Each share Common no par exchanged for $1 cash

5555 EVERET AVENUE BUILDING CORP. (IL)
Common no par changed to $1 par 00/00/1941
Liquidation completed
Each share Common $1 par or VTC for Common $1 par exchanged for initial distribution of $3.14 cash 11/20/1947
Each share Common $1 par or VTC for Common $1 par received second and final distribution of $0.19 cash 05/11/1950

540 CAP CORP (AB)
Name changed to Golden Dory Resources Corp. 12/02/2008
Golden Dory Resources Corp. recapitalized as Sokoman Iron Corp. 10/01/2013

5G WIRELESS COMMUNICATIONS INC (NV)
Each share old Common $0.001 par exchanged for (0.00285714) share new Common $0.001 par 11/23/2005
Each share new Common $0.001 par exchanged for (0.0005) share new Common $0.001 par 08/04/2008
Name changed to Clean Energy & Power, Inc. 06/26/2009
(See Clean Energy & Power, Inc.)

500-R, INC. (DE)
Liquidation completed
Each share Capital Stock $1 par received initial distribution of $368 cash 01/09/1968
Each share Capital Stock $1 par exchanged for second and final distribution of $58.78 cash 10/31/1968

FIVE M RES INC (BC)
Stock Dividends - 10% 11/16/1981; 10% 12/16/1982
Name changed to Leaders Equity Corp. 01/02/1986
(See Leaders Equity Corp.)

FIVE NINES LTD (CO)
Common no par split (2) for (1) by issuance of (1) additional share payable 4/1/2005 to holders of record 4/1/2005
Ex date - 4/6/2005
Name changed to Stem Cell Authority, Ltd. 7/6/2006

FIVE OAKS INVT CORP (MD)
Name changed to Hunt Companies Finance Trust, Inc. 05/29/2018

564 SOUTHN BLVD CORP (DE)
Through purchase offer majority of shares reacquired 00/00/1980
Public interest eliminated

FIVE STAR BROADBAND WIRELESS INC (KS)
Name changed 12/29/1999
Name changed from Five Star Resources, Inc. to Five Star Broadband Wireless, Inc. 12/29/1999
Charter forfeited for failure to file annual reports and pay fees 04/15/2003

FIVE STAR COAL INC (DE)
Name changed to Onyx Hydrocarbon Recovery Corp. 5/25/82
Onyx Hydrocarbon Recovery Corp. name changed to Magna Diversified Inc. 3/22/84 which name changed to Energizer 500 Inc. 6/8/84 which name changed to Opportunity 21 on 6/16/85
(See Opportunity 21)

FIVE STAR ENERGY CORP (CO)
Plan of reorganization confirmed 5/2/83
Each share old Common no par exchanged for (0.1) share new Common no par
Note: Certificates not surrendered by 5/2/88 became valueless
Each (42) shares new Common no par exchanged again for (1) share new Common no par 6/30/88
Name changed to Electronic Publishing Technology Corp. 9/6/88
(See Electronic Publishing Technology Corp.)

5 STAR LIVING ONLINE INC (DE)
Name changed to Viral Genetics, Inc. 11/20/2001
Viral Genetics, Inc. recapitalized as VG Life Sciences Inc. 11/27/2012

FIVE STAR PETE & MINES LTD (AB)
Recapitalized as Consolidated Five Star Resources Ltd. 03/06/1978
Each share Capital Stock no par exchanged for (0.2) share Common no par
Consolidated Five Star Resources Ltd. name changed to CFS International Inc. 12/05/1995
(See CFS International Inc.)

FIVE STAR PRODS INC (DE)
Merged into National Patent Development Corp. 08/28/2008
Each share Common 1¢ par exchanged for $0.40 cash

FIVE STAR QUALITY CARE INC (MD)
Name changed to Five Star Senior Living Inc. 03/08/2017

FIVE STATES URANIUM CORP. (NM)
Dissolved in 1956

535 5TH AVE CORP (PA)
Liquidation completed
Each share Common no par

FINANCIAL INFORMATION, INC.

512-FLA

exchanged for initial distribution of $125 cash 12/15/1970
Each share Common no par received second and final distribution of $24.97527 cash 05/09/1972

512 CORNELIA CORP (IL)
Completely liquidated 06/29/1971
Each share Common no par exchanged for first and final distribution of $215 cash

FIVE YEAR FIXED TRUST SHARES
Trust terminated 00/00/1935
Details not available

5044 SHERIDAN ROAD BUILDING (IL)
Liquidation completed
Each share Common no par stamped to indicate initial distribution of $43 cash 12/02/1948
Each share Stamped Common no par exchanged for second and final distribution of $3.60 cash 11/16/1950

5B TECHNOLOGIES CORP (DE)
Filed a petition under Chapter 7 Federal Bankruptcy Code 07/15/2002
Stockholders' equity unlikely

5BANC SPLIT INC (ON)
Preferred called for redemption at $25 on 12/15/2006
Capital Shares called for redemption at $25 on 12/15/2006
Class B Preferred called for redemption at $10 on 12/15/2011
Each share old Class B Capital Share exchanged for (0.5) share new Class B Capital Share 12/15/2011
Class C Preferred called for redemption at $10 on 12/15/2016
New Class B Capital Shares called for redemption at $27.51 on 12/15/2016

5FIFTY5 COM INC (DE)
Recapitalized as Swap-A-Debt, Inc. 02/26/2008
Each share Common $0.001 par exchanged for (0.05) share Common $0.001 par
Swap-A-Debt, Inc. name changed to WikiLoan Inc. 06/26/2009 which name changed to Wiki Group, Inc. 03/26/2012 which recapitalized as Source Financial, Inc. 03/21/2013 which name changed to Alltemp, Inc. 04/27/2017

5K PETE SVCS INC (CO)
Name changed to USA Fast Lube Systems, Inc. 08/20/1984
(See USA Fast Lube Systems, Inc.)

FIVELAND MINES LTD. (ON)
Charter surrendered 00/00/1953

5TO1 HLDG CORP (DE)
Acquired by Yahoo! Inc. 05/27/2011
Each share Common $0.0001 par exchanged for $0.760759 cash

FIX-A-PIPE INC (MN)
Administratively dissolved 11/29/92

FIX-CORP INTL INC (DE)
Plan of reorganization under Chapter 11 Federal Bankruptcy proceedings confirmed 07/29/2002
No stockholders' equity

FJORDLAND MINERALS LTD (BC)
Recapitalized as Fjordland Exploration Inc. 05/03/2002
Each share Common no par exchanged for (0.5) share Common no par

FKB GROUP PLC (ENGLAND)
Acquired by Carlson Companies 00/00/1990
Details not available

FLABANCO, INC. (FL)
Name changed to Data Lease Financial Corp. 06/13/1968
(See Data Lease Financial Corp.)

FLAG FINL CORP (GA)
Common $1 par split (3) for (2) by issuance of (0.5) additional share payable 6/3/98 to holders of record 5/22/98
Merged into Royal Bank of Canada (Montreal, Que) 12/8/2006
Each share Common $1 par exchanged for $25.50 cash

FLAG HARBOR CORP. (MD)
Dissolved 05/20/1981
No stockholders' equity

FLAG INVS CORPORATE CASH TR (MA)
Trust terminated 12/04/1989
Details not available

FLAG INVS EMERGING GROWTH FD INC (MD)
Name changed to Emerging Growth Fund Inc. (MD) 05/07/2001
Emerging Growth Fund Inc. (MD) reorganized in Delaware as Forum Funds 09/20/2002

FLAG INVS FD INC (MD)
Reorganized as Flag Investors Fund 05/16/1985
Details not available

FLAG INVS INTL TR (MA)
Reorganized as Flag Investors International Fund, Inc. 08/16/1993
Details not available

FLAG OIL CORP. OF DELAWARE (DE)
Common no par changed to $1 par in 1931
Common $1 par changed to 50¢ par 1/1/62
Each share Common 50¢ par exchanged for (0.01) share Common $50 par 6/3/68
Name changed to Flag-Redfern Oil Co. 8/27/70
(See Flag-Redfern Oil Co.)

FLAG OILS LTD (AB)
Name changed to Flag Resources Ltd. 01/04/1982
Flag Resources Ltd. recapitalized as Flag Resources (1985) Ltd. 02/18/1985

FLAG-REDFERN OIL CO. (DE)
Each share Common $50 par exchanged for (10) shares Common $5 par 12/31/72
Common $5 par changed to $2.50 par and (1) additional share issued 12/17/73
Each share Common $2.50 par exchanged for (0.02) share Common $125 par 10/4/77
Acquired by Kerr-McGee Corp. 11/15/88
Each share Common $125 par exchanged for $42.30 cash

FLAG RES LTD (AB)
Recapitalized as Flag Resources (1985) Ltd. 02/18/1985
Each share Class A Common no par exchanged for (0.5) share Class A Common no par

FLAG TELECOM GROUP LTD (BERMUDA)
Acquired by Reliance Gateway Net Ltd. 01/12/2004
Each share Common $1 par exchanged for $97.41 cash

FLAG TELECOM HLDGS LTD (BERMUDA)
Plan of reorganization under Chapter 11 Federal Bankruptcy Code effective 10/09/2002
No stockholders' equity

FLAGG INDS INC (CA)
Merged into National Medical Enterprises, Inc. 01/05/1984
Each share Common 50¢ par exchanged for $15.70 cash

FLAGG RANCH INC. (WY)
Name changed to International Leisure Hosts, Ltd. 7/25/68
International Leisure Hosts, Ltd. merged into Brentwood Industries, Inc. 5/24/71
(See Brentwood Industries, Inc.)

FLAGG-UTICA CORP. (NY)
5% Prior Preferred called for redemption 06/01/1959
Merged into Genesco Inc. 01/02/1965
Each share Common $5 par exchanged for for (0.39) share Common $1 par

FLAGLER BK CORP (FL)
Each share Common 10¢ par exchanged for (0.4) share Class A 10¢ par and (1) share Class B Common 10¢ par 03/13/1984
Merged into SunTrust Banks, Inc. 03/15/1993
Each share Class A Common 10¢ par exchanged for (0.5) share Common $1 par
Each share Class B Common 10¢ par exchanged for (0.5) share Common $1 par

FLAGLER NATIONAL BANK OF THE PALM BEACHES (WEST PALM BEACH, FL)
Reorganized as Flagler Bank Corp. 10/1/83
Each share Common $10 par exchanged for (1) share Common 10¢ par
Flager Bank Corp. merged into SunTrust Banks, Inc. 3/15/93

FLAGRO MINES, LTD. (ON)
Charter cancelled 00/00/1958

FLAGSHIP BK & TR CO (WORCESTER, MA)
Merged into Chittenden Corp. 02/29/1996
Each share Common $5.63 par exchanged for (1.2) shares Common $1 par
(See Chittenden Corp.)

FLAGSHIP BANK OF JACKSONVILLE (JACKSONVILLE, FL)
99.8% held by Flagship Banks Inc. as of 04/26/1980
Public interest eliminated

FLAGSHIP BANK OF ST. PETERSBURG, N.A. (ST. PETERSBURG, FL)
99.18% owned by Holding Co. as of 07/21/1981
Public interest eliminated

FLAGSHIP BANK OF TAMPA-EAST (TAMPA, FL)
Name changed to Sun Bank of Tampa Bay (Tampa, FL) 01/01/1984
(See Sun Bank of Tampa Bay (Tampa, FL))

FLAGSHIP BKS INC (FL)
$2.48 Conv. Preferred no par called for redemption 08/11/1983
Merged into Sun Banks, Inc. 01/01/1984
Each share Common $1 par exchanged for (1.293) shares Common $2.50 par
Sun Banks, Inc. merged into SunTrust Banks, Inc. 07/01/1985

FLAGSHIP ENERGY INC (AB)
Recapitalized as Insignia Energy Ltd. 08/08/2008
Each share Class A Common no par exchanged for (0.01) share Common no par and (0.017694) Common Stock Purchase Warrant expiring 09/04/2008
Each share Class B Common no par exchanged for (0.1) share Common no par and (0.17694) Common Stock Purchase Warrant expiring 09/04/2008
(See Insignia Energy Ltd.)

FLAGSHIP EXPRESS INC (DE)
Charter cancelled and declared inoperative and void for non-payment of taxes 03/01/1992

FLAGSHIP FINL CORP (PA)
Merged into PNC Financial Corp. 11/20/1992
Each share Common 1¢ par exchanged for $13.05 cash

FLAGSHIP FIRST NATIONAL BANK (CORAL GABLES, FL)
Merged into Flagship National Bank of Miami (Miami Beach, FL) 05/01/1978
Each share Common $10 par exchanged for (1.98) shares Common $10 par
Flagship National Bank of Miami (Miami Beach, FL) location changed to (Miami, FL) 03/18/1980 which name changed to Sun Bank/Miami, N.A. (Miami, FL) 04/01/1985 which name changed to SunTrust Bank, Miami, N.A. (Miami, FL) 10/06/1995
(See SunTrust Bank, Miami, N.A. (Miami, FL))

FLAGSHIP FIRST NATIONAL BANK (ORMOND BEACH, FL)
98.65% held by Flagship Banks Inc. as of 06/30/1974
Public interest eliminated

FLAGSHIP GLOBAL HEALTH INC (DE)
Chapter 7 bankruptcy proceedings terminated 09/11/2014
Stockholders' equity unlikely

FLAGSHIP INDS INC (BC)
Reincorporated 12/01/2009
Place of incorporation changed from (ON) to (BC) 12/01/2009
Common no par split (5) for (1) by issuance of (4) additional shares payable 05/08/2007 to holders of record 05/08/2007 Ex date - 05/04/2007
Name changed to Prima Colombia Hardwood Inc. 09/23/2010
Prima Colombia Hardwood Inc. recapitalized as Bravern Ventures Ltd. 01/12/2015

FLAGSHIP NATIONAL BANK (MIAMI, FL)
Merged into Flagship National Bank of Miami (Miami Beach, FL) 05/01/1978
Each share Common $7.50 par exchanged for (0.66) share Common $10 par
Flagship National Bank of Miami (Miami Beach, FL) location changed to (Miami, FL) 03/18/1980 which name changed to Sun Bank/Miami, N.A. (Miami, FL) 04/01/1985 which name changed to SunTrust Bank, Miami, N.A. (Miami, FL) 10/06/1995
(See SunTrust Bank, Miami, N.A. (Miami, FL))

FLAGSHIP NATIONAL BANK OF MIAMI (MIAMI BEACH, FL)
Name changed 05/01/1978
Reorganized 03/18/1980
Name changed from Flagship First National Bank (Miami Beach, FL) to Flagship National Bank of Miami (Miami Beach, FL) 05/01/1978
Location changed from (Miami Beach, FL) to (Miami, FL) 03/18/1980
Name changed to Sun Bank/Miami, N.A. (Miami, FL) 04/01/1985
Sun Bank/Miami, N.A. (Miami, FL) name changed to SunTrust Bank, Miami, N.A. (Miami, FL) 10/06/1995
(See SunTrust Bank, Miami, N.A. (Miami, FL))

FLAGSTAFF ASSOCIATES INC. (AZ)
Charter revoked for failure to file reports and pay fees 12/20/1963

FLAGSTAFF CORP (DE)
Name changed to FSF Industries Inc. 11/27/1978

FSF Industries Inc. name changed to Trafalgar Industries, Inc. 12/17/1979 which merged into Triangle Industries, Inc. (Old) 05/16/1984
(See Triangle Industries, Inc. (Old))

FLAGSTAFF/FLINK CORP. (DE)
Name changed to Flagstaff Corp. 05/11/1972
Flagstaff Corp. name changed to FSF Industries Inc. 11/27/1978 which name changed to Trafalgar Industries, Inc. 12/17/1979 which merged into Triangle Industries, Inc. (Old) 05/16/1984
(See Triangle Industries, Inc. (Old))

FLAGSTAFF RES EXPLS INC (ON)
Recapitalized as Mega-Dial Communications Ltd. 08/13/1985
Each share Common no par exchanged for (0.1) share Common no par
Mega-Dial Communications Ltd. name changed to Faleck & Margolies Ltd. 09/03/1987
(See Faleck & Margolies Ltd.)

FLAGSTAR BANCORP INC (MI)
Issue Information - 13,500,000 shares PERP PFD CONV SER D offered at $20 per share on 10/28/2010
Each share Conv. Perpetual Preferred Ser. D 1¢ par exchanged for (20) shares new Common 1¢ par 12/22/2010
(Additional Information in Active)

FLAGSTAR CAP CORP (MI)
Exchangeable Preferred Ser. A $25 par called for redemption at $25 on 06/30/2003

FLAGSTAR COS INC (DE)
Plan of reorganization under Chapter 11 Federal Bankruptcy Code effective 01/07/1998
No stockholders' equity

FLAGSTAR TR (DE)
9.50% Preferred Securities called for redemption at $25 on 04/30/2004

FLAGSTICK VENTURES INC (DE)
Each share old Common $0.0001 par exchanged for (5) shares new Common $0.0001 par 06/02/2004
Name changed to Diabetic Treatment Centers of America, Inc. 07/01/2004
Diabetic Treatment Centers of America, Inc. recapitalized as Signature Exploration & Production Corp. 05/05/2008 which name changed to GrowBLOX Sciences, Inc. 04/28/2014 which name changed to GB Sciences, Inc. 04/10/2017

FLAGSTONE MINES LTD (BC)
Merged into Grand Prix Resources Ltd. (New) 10/29/1976
Each share Capital Stock no par exchanged for (0.125) share Class A no par or (0.2) share Class B no par
Grand Prix Resources Ltd. (New) recapitalized as Omenica Resources Ltd. 04/08/1980 which recapitalized as Marilyn Resources Inc. 01/30/1984
(See Marilyn Resources Inc.)

FLAGSTONE REINSURANCE HOLDINGS LTD (BERMUDA)
Issue Information - 13,000,000 shares COM offered at $13.50 per share on 03/30/2007
Reincorporated under the laws of Luxembourg as Flagstone Reinsurance Holdings, S.A. 05/17/2010
Flagstone Reinsurance Holdings, S.A. merged into Validus Holdings, Ltd. 11/30/2012

FLAGSTONE REINSURANCE HOLDINGS S A (LUXEMBOURG)
Merged into Validus Holdings, Ltd. 11/30/2012
Each share Common USD $0.01 par exchanged for (0.1935) share Common $0.175 par and $2 cash

FLAH'S OF ALBANY INC. (NY)
Name changed to Flah's, Inc. 05/30/1973
(See Flah's, Inc.)

FLAHERTY & CRUMRINE / CLAYMORE TOTAL RETURN FD INC (MD)
Issue Information - 9,000,000 shares COM offered at $25 per share on 08/26/2003
Auction Market Preferred Ser. T7 1¢ par called for redemption at $25,000 on 06/24/2009
Auction Market Preferred Ser. W28 1¢ par called for redemption at $25,000 on 07/09/2009
Name changed to Flaherty & Crumrine Total Return Fund Inc. 02/22/2013

FLAHERTY & CRUMRINE/CLAYMORE PFD SECS INCOME FD INC (MD)
Auction Rate Preferred Ser. F7 1¢ par called for redemption at $25,000 on 07/13/2009
Auction Rate Preferred Ser. M7 1¢ par called for redemption at $25,000 on 07/14/2009
Auction Rate Preferred Ser. T7 1¢ par called for redemption at $25,000 on 07/15/2009
Auction Rate Preferred Ser. T28 1¢ par called for redemption at $25,000 on 07/15/2009
Auction Rate Preferred Ser. W7 1¢ par called for redemption at $25,000 on 07/16/2009
Auction Rate Preferred Ser. TH7 1¢ par called for redemption at $25,000 on 07/17/2009
Auction Rate Preferred Ser. W28 1¢ par called for redemption at $25,000 on 07/30/2009
Name changed to Flaherty & Crumrine Preferred Securities Income Fund Inc. 02/22/2013

FLAHERTY & CRUMRINE INVT GRADE FIXED INCOME FD (AB)
Each Unit no par received distribution of (1) Warrant expiring 09/15/2009 payable 02/13/2009 to holders of record 02/10/2009 Ex date - 02/06/2009
Each Unit no par received distribution of (0.5) Warrant expiring 06/15/2010 payable 12/16/2009 to holders of record 12/15/2009 Ex date - 12/11/2009
Name changed to Flaherty & Crumrine Investment Grade Preferred Income Fund 09/05/2018

FLAHERTY & CRUMRINE INVT GRADE PFD FD (ON)
Merged into Flaherty & Crumrine Investment Grade Fixed Income Fund 12/31/2008
Each Unit received (1.119448) Unit Flaherty & Crumrine Investment Grade Fixed Income Fund name changed to Flaherty & Crumrine Investment Grade Preferred Income Fund 09/05/2018

FLAHERTY & CRUMRINE PFD INCOME FD INC (MD)
Money Market Auction Preferred 1¢ par called for redemption at $100,000 on 07/14/2009
(Additional Information in Active)

FLAHERTY & CRUMRINE PFD INCOME OPPORTUNITY FD INC (MD)
Auction Preferred 1¢ par called for redemption at $100,000 on 08/04/2009
(Additional Information in Obsolete)

FLAHS INC (NY)
Merged into McCurdy Transition, Inc., 09/28/1984
Each share Common 1¢ par exchanged for $2.426 cash

FLAIR CARDS, INC. (NY)
Adjudicated bankrupt 01/15/1968
No stockholders' equity

FLAIR COMMUNICATIONS INC (DE)
Each share Common $0.0001 par exchanged for (0.025) share Common $0.032 par 11/25/1989
Each share old Common $0.032 par exchanged for (0.125) share new Common $0.032 par 09/08/1994
Name changed to Tier Environmental Services Inc. 10/06/1994
Tier Environmental Services Inc. name changed to Gulfstar Industries, Inc. 01/04/1996 which recapitalized as Media Vision Productions, Inc. 01/05/1999 which name changed to eCONTENT, Inc. 10/01/1999 which name changed to Earthworks Entertainment, Inc. 01/15/2004

FLAIR CORP (DE)
Merged into United Dominion Industries Ltd. 06/09/1995
Each share Common 1¢ par exchanged for $21 cash

FLAIR INC (UT)
Involuntarily dissolved 12/31/1985

FLAIR RES LTD (BC)
Struck off register and declared dissolved for failure to file returns 01/16/1987

FLAKEY JAKES INC (DE)
Filed a petition under Chapter 11 bankruptcy proceedings 10/24/1986
No stockholders' equity

FLAME HEAT TREATING, INC. (MN)
Name changed to Flame Industries, Inc. 10/01/1961
(See Flame Industries, Inc.)

FLAME INDS INC (MN)
Common $2 par changed to 10¢ par 01/08/1965
Common 10¢ par split (2) for (1) by issuance of (1) additional share 07/29/1974
$1.75 Conv. Preferred no par called for redemption 06/01/1977
Common 10¢ par split (3) for (1) by issuance of (2) additional shares 12/30/1977
Reorganized under Chapter 11 Federal Bankruptcy Code 05/29/1985
Each share old Common 10¢ par exchanged for (0.5) share new Common 10¢ par
Statutorily dissolved 06/15/1995

FLAME PETRO-MINERALS CORP (BC)
Name changed to LinuxWizardry Systems, Inc. 03/22/2000
LinuxWizardry Systems, Inc. name changed to Linux Gold Corp. 03/19/2003

FLAMEL TECHNOLOGIES S A (FRANCE)
Each Sponsored ADR for Ordinary exchanged for (1) Avadel Pharmaceuticals PLC Sponsored ADR for Ordinary 01/03/2017

FLAMERET INC (NV)
Reincorporated under the laws of Wyoming and Common $0.001 par changed to $0.0001 par 11/29/2010

FLAMINGO AIR SERVICE, INC.
Bankrupt 00/00/1949
Details not available

FLAMINGO CAP INC (NV)
Name changed to Vision Global, Inc. 2/6/98

FLANAGAN MCADAM RES INC (ON)
Merged into Golden Goose Resources Inc. 09/30/1996
Each share Common no par exchanged for (0.05434782) share Common no par
Golden Goose Resources Inc. merged into Kodiak Exploration Ltd. 12/16/2010 which name changed to Prodigy Gold Inc. 01/04/2011 which merged into Argonaut Gold Inc. 12/11/2012

FLANDERS CORP (NC)
Acquired by Air Acquisition Holdings LLC 05/16/2012
Each share Common $0.001 par exchanged for $4.40 cash

FLANK PETROLEUMS LTD. (AB)
Merged into Consolidated East Crest Oil Co. Ltd. 00/00/1953
Each share Common no par exchanged for (0.3) share Capital Stock no par
Consolidated East Crest Oil Co. Ltd. liquidated for Pan Ocean Oil Corp. 01/01/1972
(See Pan Ocean Oil Corp.)

FLANNER CO.
Liquidated in 1935

FLANNERY MANUFACTURING CO. (DE)
Acquired by Stubnitz Greene Corp. 3/31/58
Details not available

FLAPJACK FOODS INTL INC (MN)
Statutorily dissolved 8/1/97

FLARE INC (TX)
Completely liquidated 9/28/90
Each share Common 1¢ par received first and final distribution of $0.08 cash
Note: Certificates were not required to be surrendered and are now valueless

FLASH AUTOMOTIVE ACCEP CORP (NV)
Each share Common $0.001 par received distribution of (0.108) share Automotive Capital Group Inc. Common $0.001 par payable 6/28/2004 to holders of record 6/23/2004
Name changed to Uniprime Capital Acceptance, Inc. (New) 12/22/2004
Uniprime Capital Acceptance, Inc. (New) name changed to Deep Blue Marine, Inc. 12/20/2005

FLASH PACK LTD (BC)
Recapitalized as Canadian Lynx Petroleum Ltd. (BC) 12/07/1994
Each share Common no par exchanged for (0.2) share Common no par
Canadian Lynx Petroleum Ltd. (BC) reincorporated in Canada as Tanganyika Oil Co. Ltd. 09/19/1995
(See Tanganyika Oil Co. Ltd.)

FLASH READER CORP. (UT)
Proclaimed dissolved for failure to pay taxes 11/9/74

FLASHNET COMMUNICATIONS INC (DE)
Issue Information - 3,000,000 shares COM offered at $17 per share on 03/16/1999
Merged into Prodigy Communications Corp. 5/31/2000
Each share Common no par exchanged for (0.35) share Class A Common 1¢ par
(See Prodigy Communications Corp.)

FLASHPOINT INTL INC (NV)
Name changed to Navitrak International Corp. 05/28/2004
Navitrak International Corp. recapitalized as VECTr Systems, Inc. 05/21/2007
(See VECTr Systems, Inc.)

FLAT TOP BANKSHARES INC (WV)
Merged into FCFT, Inc. 05/09/1990
Each share Common $5 par exchanged for (1.65) shares Common $5 par

FCFT, Inc. reorganized as First Community Bancshares Inc. (NV) 09/30/1997 which reincorporated in Virginia 10/09/2018

FLAT TOP INS AGY (WV)
Acquired by Acordia, Inc. 07/11/1996 Details not available

FLAT TOP NATL BK (BLUEFIELD, WV)
Reorganized as Flat Top Bankshares, Inc. 01/01/1983
Each share Capital Stock $10 par exchanged for (1) share Common $5 par
Flat Top Bankshares, Inc. merged into FCFT, Inc. 05/09/1990 which reorganized as First Community Bancshares Inc. (NV) 09/30/1997 which reincorporated in Virginia 10/09/2018

FLATBUSH FED BANCORP INC (USA)
Stock Dividends - 10% payable 04/25/2005 to holders of record 04/11/2005 Ex date - 04/07/2005; 10% payable 03/29/2006 to holders of record 03/15/2006 Ex date - 03/13/2006
Acquired by Northfield Bancorp, Inc. (USA) 11/02/2012
Each share Common 1¢ par exchanged for (0.4748) share Common 1¢ par
Northfield Bancorp, Inc. (USA) reorganized in Delaware 01/25/2013

FLATLEY RLTY INVS (MA)
Liquidation completed
Each Share of Bene. Int. $1 par exchanged for initial distribution of $9.75 cash 9/1/81
Each Share of Bene. Int. $1 par received second distribution of $0.25 cash 2/9/83
Each Share of Bene. Int. $1 par received third and final distribution of $0.30 cash 12/17/84

FLATO RLTY INVTS (TX)
Charter forfeited for failure to pay taxes 2/15/94

FLAVEX INDS LTD (BC)
Struck off register and declared dissolved for failure to file returns 02/28/1992

FLAVOR BRANDS INC (UT)
Each share old Common $0.001 par exchanged for (0.01) share new Common $0.001 par 10/11/95
Involuntarily dissolved 06/01/1999

FLAVORLAND INDS INC (DE)
Common no par split (2) for (1) by issuance of (1) additional share 08/11/1975
Merged into Foxley & Co. 03/15/1977
Each share Common no par exchanged for $7.50 cash

FLAVOS INTL INC (NY)
Each share Common 5¢ par exchanged for (0.25) share Common 20¢ par 7/30/70
Adjudicated bankrupt 8/9/76
Stockholders' equity unlikely

FLEA FAIR U S A INC (NV)
Charter revoked for failure to file reports and pay fees 04/01/1992

FLECK RES LTD (BC)
Name changed to Polymet Mining Corp. 06/10/1998

FLEER CORP (DE)
Merged into Marvel Entertainment Group, Inc. 10/19/92
Each share Common 1¢ par exchanged for $28 cash

FLEET AEROSPACE INC (DE)
Merged into Fleet Merger Sub 12/23/96
Each share 10% Reset Preferred 1¢ par exchanged for $2.09 cash
Each share Common 1¢ par exchanged for $0.20 cash

FLEET AIRCRAFT, LTD. (CANADA)
Under plan of merger each share exchanged for $9 cash 08/15/1946

FLEET AIRLS INC (MN)
Statutorily dissolved 10/4/91

FLEET BOSTON CORP (RI)
Name changed to FleetBoston Financial Corp. 4/18/2000
FleetBoston Financial Corp. merged into Bank of America Corp. 4/1/2004

FLEET CALL INC (DE)
Name changed to Nextel Communications, Inc. 07/22/1993
Nextel Communications, Inc. merged into Sprint Nextel Corp. 08/12/2005 which merged into Sprint Corp. (DE) 07/10/2013

FLEET CAP TR I (DE)
8% Trust Originated Preferred Securities called for redemption at $25 plus $0.21112 plus accrued dividend on 5/8/2003

FLEET CAP TR III (DE)
7.05% Guaranteed Trust Originated Preferred Securities called for redemption at $25 plus $0.18115 accrued dividend on 5/7/2003

FLEET CAP TR IV (DE)
7.17% Guaranteed Trust Originated Preferred Securities called for redemption at $25 plus $0.18423 accrued dividend on 5/7/2003

FLEET CAP TR VI (DE)
Guaranteed Trust Originated Preferred Securities called for redemption at $25 on 9/30/2005

FLEET CAP TR VII (DE)
7.20% Preferred Securities called for redemption at $25 on 9/29/2006

FLEET CAP TR VIII (DE)
7.20% Preferred Securities called for redemption at $25 plus $0.20 accrued dividends on 07/25/2012

FLEET CAP TR IX (DE)
Issue Information - 7,000,000 TR PFD SECS 6% offered at $25 per share on 07/24/2003
6% Trust Preferred Securities called for redemption at $25 plus $0.35 accrued dividends on 07/25/2012

FLEET CO. (FL)
Recapitalized as Asbury Realty Co. 1/31/69
Each share Common $1 par exchanged for (2) shares Common 50¢ par

FLEET CTL CORP (DE)
Charter cancelled and declared inoperative and void for non-payment of taxes 3/1/76
No stockholders' equity

FLEET FDG CORP (DE)
Money Market Preferred Ser. A called for redemption at $500,000 on 6/19/2006

FLEET FINL GROUP INC NEW (RI)
6.50% Conv. Preferred Ser. II $1 par called for redemption 09/29/1993
12% Conv. Preferred Ser. I $1 par called for redemption 10/01/1993
Preferred $1 par called for redemption 04/01/1994
Preferred $20 par called for redemption 04/01/1994
Common $1 par changed to 1¢ par 11/06/1995
10.12% Depositary Preferred called for redemption 07/31/1996
10.12% Perpetual Preferred Ser. III $1 par called for redemption 07/31/1996
Depositary Preferred Ser. IV called for redemption 12/01/1996
9.375% Perpetual Preferred Ser. IV $1 par called for redemption 12/01/1996
Adjustable Rate Preferred $1 par called for redemption at $50 on 05/05/1997
9.30% Depositary Preferred called for redemption at $25 on 10/15/1997
Common 1¢ par split (2) for (1) by issuance of (1) additional share payable 10/07/1998 to holders of record 09/18/1998 Ex date - 10/08/1998
Under plan of merger name changed to Fleet Boston Corp. 10/01/1999
Fleet Boston Corp. name changed to FleetBoston Financial Corp. 04/18/2000 which merged into Bank of America Corp. 04/01/2004

FLEET FINL GROUP INC OLD (RI)
Common $1 par split (2) for (1) by issuance of (1) additional share 12/31/84
Conv. Preferred Ser. A $1 par called for redemption 10/1/86
Common $1 par split (2) for (1) by issuance of (1) additional share 4/3/87
Under plan of merger name changed to Fleet/Norstar Financial Group, Inc. 1/1/88
Fleet/Norstar Financial Group, Inc. name changed to Fleet Financial Group, Inc. (New) 4/15/92 which name changed to Fleet Boston Corp. 10/1/99 which name changed to FleetBoston Financial Corp. 4/18/2000 which merged into Bank of America Corp. 4/1/2004

FLEET INDS LTD (ON)
Name changed 04/25/1996
Common no par split (2) for (1) by issuance of (1) additional share 10/06/1986
Each share Conv. Preference Ser. 1 no par exchanged for (3.5) shares Ordinary no par 07/27/1992
Each share Common no par exchanged for (1) share Ordinary no par 07/27/1992
Name changed from Fleet Aerospace Corp. to Fleet Industries Ltd. and Ordinary no par reclassified as Common no par 04/25/1996
Recapitalized as Magellan Aerospace Corp. 10/22/1996
Each share Common no par exchanged for (0.2) share Common no par

FLEET MANUFACTURING & AIRCRAFT, LTD. (ON)
Reincorporated 08/20/1946
Place of incorporation changed from (Canada) to (ON) 08/20/1946
Name changed to Fleet Manufacturing, Ltd. 01/31/1948
Fleet Manufacturing, Ltd. name changed to Ronyx Corp. Ltd. 02/14/1973 which name changed to Fleet Aerospace Corp. 03/13/1984 which name changed to Fleet Industries Ltd. 04/25/1996 which recapitalized as Magellan Aerospace Corp. 10/22/1996

FLEET MFG LTD (ON)
Name changed to Ronyx Corp. Ltd. 02/14/1973
Ronyx Corp. Ltd. name changed to Fleet Aerospace Corp. 03/13/1984 which name changed to Fleet Industries Ltd. 04/25/1996 which recapitalized as Magellan Aerospace Corp. 10/22/1996

FLEET MTG GROUP INC (RI)
Merged into Fleet Mortgage Acquisition Co. 5/2/95
Each share Common 1¢ par exchanged for $20 cash

FLEET/NORSTAR FINL GROUP INC (RI)
Name changed to Fleet Financial Group, Inc. (New) 4/15/92
Fleet Financial Group, Inc. (New) name changed to Fleet Boston Corp. 10/1/99 which name changed to FleetBoston Financial Corp. 4/18/2000 which merged into Bank of America Corp. 4/1/2004

FLEETBOSTON FINL CORP (RI)
9.35% Depositary Preferred called for redemption at $25 on 01/15/2000
7.25% Depositary Perpetual Preferred Ser. V called for redemption at $25 on 04/15/2001
Depositary Preferred Ser. VIII called for redemption at $50 on 10/01/2001
Merged into Bank of America Corp. 04/01/2004
Each 6.75% Depositary Preferred Ser. VI exchanged for (1) 6.75% Perpetual Depositary Preferred Ser. VI
Each Depositary Preferred Ser. VII exchanged for (1) Depositary Preferred Ser. VII
Each share Common 1¢ par exchanged for (0.5553) share Common 1¢ par

FLEETCLEAN SYS INC (TX)
Reorganized under the laws of Nevada as ERF Wireless, Inc. 09/20/2004
Each (75) shares Common 1¢ par exchanged for (1) share Common $0.001 par

FLEETCRAFT MARINE CORP (CA)
Charter suspended for failure to file reports and pay fees 07/03/1967

FLEETMATICS GROUP PLC (IRELAND)
Acquired by Verizon Communications Inc. 11/07/2016
Each share Ordinary EUR 0.015 par exchanged for $60 cash

FLEETWOOD CAP TR II (DE)
Each 9.50% Conv. Trust Preferred Security received distribution of (0.02166) share Fleetwood Enterprises, Inc. Common $1 par payable 02/15/2002 to holders of record 01/31/2002
9.50% Conv. Trust Preferred Securities called for redemption at $22 on 06/04/2004

FLEETWOOD CAP TR III (DE)
Each 9.50% Conv. Trust Preferred Security received distribution of (0.0858) share Fleetwood Enterprises, Inc. Common $1 par payable 02/15/2002 to holders of record 01/31/2002
9.50% Conv. Trust Preferred Securities called for redemption at $50 on 04/29/2004

FLEETWOOD CORP (QC)
Acquired by GTE Sylvania Canada Ltd. 10/03/1975
Each share Common $1 par exchanged for $4.50 cash

FLEETWOOD ENTERPRISES INC (DE)
Reincorporated 09/19/1977
Common $1 par split (2) for (1) by issuance of (1) additional share 01/15/1968
Common $1 par split (2) for (1) by issuance of (1) additional share 07/15/1968
Common $1 par split (2) for (1) by issuance of (1) additional share 10/24/1969
Common $1 par split (2) for (1) by issuance of (1) additional share 09/24/1971
State of incorporation changed from (CA) to (DE) 09/19/1977
Common $1 par split (2) for (1) by issuance of (1) additional share 04/01/1983
Common $1 par split (2) for (1) by issuance of (1) additional share 03/01/1993
Plan of reorganization under Chapter 11 Federal Bankruptcy proceedings effective 08/23/2010

No stockholders' equity

FLEETWOOD MINING & EXPLORATION LTD. (ON)
Charter cancelled and company declared dissolved for default in filing returns 05/00/1965

FLEETWOOD MOTEL CORP. (PA)
Adjudged insolvent 02/05/1965
No stockholders' equity

FLEETWOOD PETE CORP (BC)
Recapitalized as Goldie Enterprises Inc. 9/18/95
Each share Common no par exchanged for (0.2) share Common no par
Goldie Enterprises Inc. name changed to MagiCorp Entertainment Inc. (BC) 5/3/2001 which reincorporated in Ontario 7/4/2001 which recapitalized as Lucid Entertainment Inc. 7/5/2004

FLEETWOOD RES LTD (AB)
Struck off register for failure to file annual returns 07/31/1974

FLEETWOOD SECURITIES CORP. OF AMERICA (DE)
Charter cancelled and declared inoperative and void for non-payment of taxes 3/1/74

FLEETWOOD YELLOWKNIFE MINES, LTD. (ON)
Name changed to Fleetwood Mining & Exploration Ltd. 02/00/1957
(See Fleetwood Mining & Exploration Ltd.)

FLEISCHMANN CO.
Merged into Standard Brands, Inc. 00/00/1929
Details not available

FLEMING BERGER FD INC (DE)
Acquired by One Hundred Fund, Inc. 09/30/1975
Each share Common $1 par exchanged for (1.073386) shares Capital Stock 1¢ par
One Hundred Fund, Inc. name changed to Berger Growth Fund, Inc. 01/28/2000 which merged into Janus Investment Fund 04/21/2003

FLEMING CO., INC. (KS)
Each share Common $100 par exchanged for (4) shares Common $25 par 00/00/1946
Each share Common $25 par exchanged for (5) shares Common $5 par 03/01/1957
Common $5 par changed to $2.50 par and (1) additional share issued 03/27/1962
5% Preferred $100 par called for redemption 12/31/1965
Common $2.50 par split (2) for (1) by issuance of (1) additional share 09/10/1968
Stock Dividends - 100% 03/23/1946; 200% 07/10/1951; 100% 05/01/1959
Name changed to Fleming Companies, Inc. (KS) 04/28/1972
Fleming Companies, Inc. (KS) reincorporated in Oklahoma 04/29/1981
(See Fleming Companies, Inc. (OK))

FLEMING COS INC (OK)
Reincorporated 4/29/81
State of incorporation changed from (KS) to (OK) 4/29/81
Common $2.50 par split (2) for (1) by issuance of (1) additional share 4/8/83
Variable Term Preferred Ser. A $10 par called for redemption 7/11/89
Variable Term Preferred Ser. B $10 par called for redemption 1/14/92
Plan of reorganization under Chapter 11 Federal Bankruptcy Code effective 8/23/2004
No stockholders' equity

FLEMING-HALL TOBACCO CO., INC.
Liquidation completed in 1953

FLEMING INVESTMENT CO. (MO)
Charter forfeited for failure to file reports 1/1/36

FLEMING MINES LTD (QC)
Declared dissolved for failure to file reports and pay fees 08/25/1973

FLEMING-WILSON MERCANTILE CO.
Name changed to Fleming Co., Inc. in 1941
Fleming Co., Inc. name changed to Fleming Companies, Inc. (KS) 4/28/72 which reincorporated in Oklahoma 4/29/81
(See Fleming Companies, Inc. (OK))

FLEMINGTON NATL BK & TR CO (FLEMINGTON, NJ)
Common $10 par changed to $5 par and (1.2) additional shares issued to effect a (2) for (1) split and 10% stock dividend 5/1/86
Merged into UJB Financial Corp. 2/23/96
Each share Common $5 par exchanged for (1.3816) shares Common $1.20 par
UJB Financial Corp. name changed to Summit Bancorp 3/1/96 which merged into FleetBoston Financial Corp. 3/1/2001 which merged into Bank of America Corp. 4/1/2004

FLEMINGTON PHARMACEUTICAL CORP (DE)
Reincorporated 01/29/1999
State of incorporation changed from (NJ) to (DE) and Common 1¢ par changed to $0.001 par 01/29/1999
Name changed to NovaDel Pharma Inc. 10/02/2002
(See NovaDel Pharma Inc.)

FLETCHER AMERICAN NATIONAL BANK (INDIANAPOLIS, IN)
Name changed to American National Bank (Indianapolis, IN) 8/23/33
American National Bank (Indianapolis, IN) merged into American Fletcher National Bank & Trust Co. (Indianapolis, IN) 1/1/55 which reorganized as American Fletcher Corp. 12/31/68 which merged into Banc One Corp. (DE) 1/26/87 which reincorporated in Ohio 5/1/89 which merged into Bank One Corp. 10/2/98 which merged into J.P. Morgan Chase & Co. 12/31/2000 which name changed to JPMorgan Chase & Co. 7/20/2004

FLETCHER BLDG LTD (NEW ZEALAND)
ADR agreement terminated 06/14/2002
Each old Sponsored ADR for Ordinary exchanged for $19.0699171 cash (Additional information in Active)

FLETCHER CAP FD INC (DE)
Name changed to Legal List Investments, Inc. 10/28/71
Legal List Investments, Inc. reincorporated in Maryland as American General Total Return Fund, Inc. 1/12/79 which merged into Fund of America, Inc. (NY) 12/31/79 which name changed to American Capital Growth & Income Fund, Inc. (NY) 7/23/90 which reincorporated in Maryland 7/6/93 which reincorporated in Delaware as Van Kampen American Capital Growth & Income Fund 7/31/95 which name changed to Van Kampen Growth & Income Fund 7/14/98

FLETCHER CHALLENGE BLDG DIV (NEW ZEALAND)
Stock Dividend - 4% payable 7/24/97 to holders of record 6/27/97
Reorganized as Fletcher Building Ltd. 3/23/2001
Each Sponsored ADR for Ordinary exchanged for (1) Sponsored ADR for Ordinary
(See Fletcher Building Ltd.)

FLETCHER CHALLENGE CDA LTD (BC)
Name changed to Norske Skog Canada Ltd. (BC) 01/02/2001
Norske Skog Canada Ltd. (BC) reincorporated in Canada 08/27/2001 which name changed to Catalyst Paper Corp. (Old) 10/06/2005
(See Catalyst Paper Corp. (Old))

FLETCHER CHALLENGE ENERGY DIV (NEW ZEALAND)
Stock Dividend - 4% payable 7/24/97 to holders of record 6/27/97
Acquired by Shell Overseas Holdings, Inc. and Apache Corp. 3/23/2001
Each Sponsored ADR for Energy Shares exchanged for (1/7) share Capstone Turbine Corp. Common $0.001 par, (10) shares Rubicon Corp. Ordinary, and $35.50 cash

FLETCHER CHALLENGE FIN CDA INC (CANADA)
8% Retractable Preferred Ser. A no par called for redemption 10/01/1993
7.875% Retractable Preferred Ser. B no par called for redemption 11/30/1993

FLETCHER CHALLENGE FORESTS LTD (NEW ZEALAND)
Name changed 2/2/2001
ADR's for Ordinary N.Z. 50¢ par split (9) for (1) by issuance of (8) additional shares 5/11/87
Each old Sponsored ADR for Ordinary N.Z. 50¢ par exchanged for (0.2) new Sponsored ADR for Ordinary N.Z. 50¢ par 8/1/89
Each new Sponsored ADR for Ordinary N.Z. 50¢ par exchanged for (1) Sponsored ADR for Ordinary N.Z. 40¢ par and (0.25) Sponsored ADR for Forests Division shares N.Z. 40¢ par 12/10/93
Reorganized 3/25/96
Each Sponsored ADR for Ordinary N.Z. 40¢ par exchanged for (0.25) Fletcher Challenge Building Sponsored ADR for Ordinary, (0.25) Fletcher Challenge Energy Sponsored ADR for Ordinary and (0.5) Fletcher Challenge Paper Sponsored ADR for Ordinary
(See each company's listing)
Name changed from Fletcher Challenge Ltd. to Fletcher Challenge Forest Ltd. 2/2/2001
Each old Sponsored ADR for Forest Division Ser. S shares NZ$0.40 par exchanged for (0.2) new Sponsored ADR for Forest Division Ser. S shares NZ$0.40 par 11/29/2002
Each old Sponsored ADR for Forest Division Ser. A shares NZ$0.40 par exchanged for (0.2) new Sponsored ADR for Forest Division Ser. A shares NZ$0.40 par 11/29/2002
Reorganized as Tenon Ltd. 3/31/2004
Each new Sponsored ADR for Forest Division Ser A NZ$0.40 par exchanged for (0.5) share Sponsored ADR for Forest Division and $4.1309434 cash
Each new Sponsored ADR for Forest Division Ser. A NZ$0.40 par exchanged for (0.5) share Sponsored ADR for Forest Division Ser. A and $4.1309434 cash
(See Tenon Ltd.)

FLETCHER CHALLENGE INVTS INC (CANADA)
Name changed 09/14/1988
Name changed from Fletcher Challenge Canada Inc. to Fletcher Challenge Investments Inc. 09/14/1988
Each Exchangeable Share exchanged for (1) Exchangeable Share Ser. 1 or (1) Exchangeable Share Ser. 2 on 07/16/1990
Note: Non-electing holders received Exchangeable Shares Ser. 2
Exchangeable Share Ser. 2 called for redemption 07/16/1993
Each Exchangeable Share Ser. 1 exchanged for (8.2) shares Fletcher Challenge Ltd. Ordinary Stock N.Z. 50¢ par 09/24/1993

FLETCHER CHALLENGE PAPER DIV (NEW ZEALAND)
Merged into Norske Skogindustrier ASA 7/28/2000
Each Sponsored ADR for Ordinary exchanged for $11.3325 cash

FLETCHER FD INC (DE)
Common $1 par split (2) for (1) by issuance of (1) additional share 6/25/69
Merged into Comstock Fund, Inc. (DE) 12/31/77
Each share Common $1 par exchanged for (0.918781) share Common $1 par
Comstock Fund, Inc. (DE) reincorporated in Maryland 12/31/78 which name changed to American General Comstock Fund, Inc. 8/31/79 which name changed to American Capital Comstock Fund, Inc. 9/12/83

FLETCHER-FLORA HEALTH CARE SYS INC (GA)
Merged into a private company 05/21/2010
Details not available

FLETCHER LEISURE GROUP INC (CANADA)
Proposal under Bankruptcy and Insolvency Act effective 03/00/1996
No stockholders' equity

FLETCHER SMITH STUDIOS INC (NY)
Reincorporated under the laws of Delaware as Automated Industries, Inc. 5/1/69
(See Automated Industries, Inc.)

FLETCHER TRUST CO. (INDIANAPOLIS, IN)
Each share Capital Stock $100 par exchanged for (5) shares Capital Stock $20 par and a 33-1/3% stock dividend paid in 1953
Merged into American Fletcher National Bank & Trust Co. (Indianapolis, IN) 1/1/55
Each share Capital Stock $20 par exchanged for (2) shares Common Capital Stock $10 par
American Fletcher National Bank & Trust Co. (Indianapolis, IN) reorganized as American Fletcher Corp. 12/31/68 which merged into Banc One Corp. (DE) 1/26/87 which reincorporated in Ohio 5/1/89 which merged into Bank One Corp. 10/2/98 which merged into J.P. Morgan Chase & Co. 12/31/2000 which name changed JPMorgan Chase & Co. 7/20/2004

FLETCHERS FINE FOODS LTD (CANADA)
Each share old Common no par exchanged for (0.25) share new Common no par 11/29/1996
Name changed to Premium Brands Inc. 06/26/2000
Premium Brands Inc. reorganized as Premium Brands Income Fund 07/27/2005 which merged into Premium Brands Holdings Corp. 07/27/2009

FLEURETTE INC (FL)
Name changed to International Forest Industries Inc. 11/13/1971
International Forest Industries Inc. recapitalized as American Financial Holdings, Inc. 02/16/1979
(See American Financial Holdings, Inc.)

FLEURMONT PLACER DEVELOPMENTS LTD. (BC)
Name changed to Copper-Can Developments Ltd. 6/4/68
Copper-Can Developments Ltd. name changed to S.M.I. Processes Ltd. 12/20/68 which name changed to S.M. Industries Ltd. 3/26/69
(See S.M. Industries Ltd.)

FLEURS DE VIE INC (NV)
Name changed to China Daqing M&H Petroleum, Inc. 10/23/2009

FLEX ELEC PRODS INC (NY)
Name changed to United Flex Corp. 8/18/70
(See United Flex Corp.)

FLEX FUELS ENERGY INC (NV)
Name changed to Bio-AMD, Inc. 05/18/2011

FLEX-I-BRUSH, INC. (DE)
No longer in existence having become inoperative and void for non-payment of taxes 4/1/64

FLEX INDS LTD (INDIA)
Name changed to UFlex Ltd. 04/09/2007
(See UFlex Ltd.)

FLEX RES CO LTD (NV)
Each share old Common $0.001 par exchanged for (11.06) shares new Common $0.001 par 10/03/2008
Name changed to Defense Solutions Holding, Inc. 11/14/2008
Defense Solutions Holding, Inc. recapitalized as Shanrong Biotechnology Corp. 09/25/2017

FLEXCO PHARMACEUTICALS, INC. (CA)
Acquired by Brunswig Drug Co. on a (0.5) for (1) basis 4/13/65
Brunswig Drug Co. merged into Bergen Brunswig Corp. 3/26/69 which merged into AmeriSourceBergen Corp. 8/29/2001

FLEXFRIDGE INC (IL)
Each share old Class A Common $0.0001 par exchanged for (0.002) share new Class A Common $0.0001 par 08/11/2016
Name changed to VW Win Century, Inc. 09/27/2016

FLEXI BUILT MODULAR HSG CORP (FL)
Charter cancelled and proclaimed dissolved for non-payment of taxes 7/28/71

FLEXI VAN CORP (NY)
$2.75 Conv. Preferred $1 par called for redemption 04/12/1984
Merged into Castle & Cooke, Inc. (Old) 07/02/1985
Each share Common 1¢ par exchanged for (1.111) shares 90¢ Conv. Preferred no par and (2.222) shares Common no par
$1.61 Preferred $1 par called for redemption 07/09/1987
Castle & Cooke, Inc. (Old) name changed to Dole Food Co., Inc. (HI) 07/30/1991 which reincorporated in Delaware 07/01/2001
(See Dole Food Co., Inc. (Old) (DE))

FLEXI-VAN CORP NEW (DE)
Merged into FLX Acquisition Corp. 6/1/88
Each share Common 1¢ par exchanged for $38.50 cash

FLEXIBLE BARRICADES INC (DE)
Charter cancelled and declared inoperative and void for non-payment of taxes 3/1/92

FLEXIBLE BD TR INC (MD)
Under plan of reorganization name changed to PaineWebber Classic Flexible Income Fund, Inc. 04/01/1991

(See PaineWebber Classic Flexible Income Fund, Inc.)

FLEXIBLE CIRCUITS INC (PA)
Common no par split (3) for (2) by issuance of (0.5) additional share 12/31/69
Name changed to f c g inc. 5/17/77

FLEXIBLE COMPUTER CORP (DE)
Chapter 11 Federal Bankruptcy Code converted to Chapter 7 on 2/27/90
Stockholders' equity unlikely

FLEXIBLE PRODUCTS, INC. (DE)
Charter cancelled and declared inoperative and void for non-payment of taxes 4/15/72

FLEXIBLE TUBING CORP. (CT)
Stock Dividend - 10% 3/31/58
Merged into Automation Industries, Inc. (CA) 9/30/66
Each share Common $1 par exchanged for (0.5) share Conv. Preferred Ser. B $3 par
(See Automation Industries, Inc. (CA))

FLEXIBLE VACUUM CONTAINER CORP. (NV)
Charter revoked for failure to file reports and pay fees 3/19/69

FLEXICARE INC (FL)
Recapitalized as Pillar Entertainment Group, Inc. 3/15/96
Each share Common 1¢ par exchanged for (0.02) share Common 1¢ par
Pillar Entertainment Group, Inc. name changed to Chrysalis Hotels & Resorts Corp. 11/17/97 which name changed to Cyberecord, Inc. 4/20/99
(See Cyberecord, Inc.)

FLEXPOINT SENSOR SYS INC (DE)
Plan of reorganization under Chapter 11 Federal Bankruptcy Code effective 3/5/2004
Each share old Common $0.001 par received distribution of (1/7) share new Common $0.001 par
(Additional Information in Active)

FLEXSCAN INC (NV)
Name changed to Aperture Health, Inc. 03/03/2008

FLEXTECH HLDGS LTD (SINGAPORE)
Name changed to Dragon Group International Ltd. 01/22/2008
(See Dragon Group International Ltd.)

FLEXTRONICS INC (DE)
Name changed to FI Liquidating Co., Inc. 6/24/92
(See FI Liquidating Co., Inc.)

FLEXTRONICS INTL LTD (SINGAPORE)
Ordinary S$0.01 par split (2) for (1) by issuance of (1) additional share payable 01/11/1999 to holders of record 12/22/1998
Ordinary S$0.01 par split (2) for (1) by issuance of (1) additional share payable 12/22/1999 to holders of record 12/08/1999
Ordinary S$0.01 par split (2) for (1) by issuance of (1) additional share payable 10/16/2000 to holders of record 09/22/2000
Note: Amendment to Companies Act abolished par value 01/30/2006
Name changed to Flex Ltd. 09/28/2016

FLEXWATT CORP (MA)
Common 1¢ par changed to $0.005 par and (1) additional share issued 1/18/85
Company went out of business in December 1995
Details not available

FLEXWEEK INC (NV)
Name changed to Holy Grail Co. 03/24/2017

FLEXWEIGHT CORP (KS)
Each share old Common no par

exchanged for (0.01) share new Common no par 04/20/1998
Merged into Oasis Resorts International, Inc. 11/04/1998
Each share new Common no par exchanged for (1) share Common no par
(See Oasis Resorts International, Inc.)

FLEXWOOD CO. (IL)
Liquidation completed in 1955

FLEXXTECH CORP (NV)
Each share Common no par exchanged for (1.5) shares old Common $0.001 par 03/26/2001
Each share old Common $0.001 par exchanged for (0.005) share new Common $0.001 par 01/17/2003
Name changed to Network Installation Corp. 07/18/2003
Network Installation Corp. name changed to Siena Technologies, Inc. 10/30/2006 which recapitalized as XnE, Inc. 07/01/2009
(See XnE, Inc.)

FLICK REEDY CORP (IL)
Merged into Miller Fluid Power Corp. 06/30/2001
Details not available

FLICKA MINES LTD. (ON)
Charter revoked for failure to file reports and pay fees 11/27/1961

FLICKA RED LAKE MINES LTD. (ON)
Name changed to Flicka Mines Ltd. 00/00/1956
(See Flicka Mines Ltd.)

FLICKERING STAR FINL INC (NV)
Stock Dividend - 20% payable 11/8/2006 to holders of record 11/6/2006 Ex date - 11/2/2006
Name changed to Averox, Inc. 11/15/2006

FLICKINGER S M INC (NY)
Each share Common $100 par exchanged for (19) shares Class A Common $5 par and (1) share Class B Common $5 par 9/30/57
Each share Class A Common $5 par or Class B Common $5 par exchanged for (2) shares Common $2.50 par 7/22/68
Common $2.50 par split (2) for (1) by issuance of (1) additional share 2/15/76
Conv. Preferred no par called for redemption 7/15/81
Common $2.50 par split (3) for (2) by issuance of (0.5) additional share 6/30/83
Stock Dividends - 10% 11/10/77; 10% 10/15/82
Merged into Scrivner, Inc. 12/12/84
Each share Common $2.50 par exchanged for $36 cash

FLICO CORP (UT)
Recapitalized as AutoBale America Corp. 01/18/1972
Each share Capital Stock 1¢ par exchanged for (0.05) share Common no par
(See AutoBale America Corp.)

FLIGHT DYNAMICS, INC. (OK)
Name changed to Platforms International Corp. 7/16/96
Platforms International Corp. name changed to Platforms Wireless International Corp. 2/9/2001

FLIGHT DYNAMICS INC (OR)
Acquired by Inner Pacificorp 6/26/92
Each share Common no par exchanged for $0.30 cash

FLIGHT ENERGY, INC. (UT)
Name changed to Telecake International, Inc. 7/29/83
(See Telecake International, Inc.)

FLIGHT INTL GROUP INC NEW (GA)
Each share Common 1¢ par received distribution of $4.35 cash payable 03/03/2003 to holders of record 02/21/2003

Administratively dissolved 05/16/2008

FLIGHT INTL GROUP INC OLD (GA)
Reorganized as Flight International Group, Inc. (New) 12/20/94
Each share Common 1¢ par received (0.01) share Common 1¢ par
Note: Certificates were not required to be exchanged and are without value

FLIGHT MGMT INTL INC (DE)
Recapitalized as Native American Energy Group, Inc. 11/05/2009
Each share Common $0.001 par exchanged for (0.1) share Common $0.001 par

FLIGHT SAFETY, INC. (DE)
Charter cancelled and declared inoperative and void for non-payment of taxes 4/1/67

FLIGHT SAFETY TECHNOLOGIES INC (NV)
Each share old Common $0.001 par exchanged for (1/3) share new Common $0.001 par 12/31/2003
Name changed to Applied Science Products, Inc. 12/09/2009

FLIGHT TRANSN CORP (MN)
Placed in receivership 6/18/82
No stockholders' equity

FLIGHTSAFETY INTL INC (NY)
Name changed 05/17/1973
Common 10¢ par split (3) for (2) by issuance of (0.5) additional share 06/20/1972
Name changed from Flight Safety, Inc. to FlightSafety International, Inc. 05/17/1973
Common 10¢ par split (2) for (1) by issuance of (1) additional share 05/18/1979
Common 10¢ par split (3) for (2) by issuance of (0.5) additional share 07/17/1980
Common 10¢ par split (3) for (2) by issuance of (0.5) additional share 10/20/1981
Common 10¢ par split (3) for (2) by issuance of (0.5) additional share 05/14/1985
Common 10¢ par split (3) for (2) by issuance of (0.5) additional share 08/05/1988
Stock Dividend - 100% 07/23/1976
Merged into Berkshire Hathaway Inc. 12/23/1996
Each share Common 10¢ par exchanged for (0.043478261) share Class B Common $0.1667 par

FLIGHTSERV COM (DE)
Name changed to eResource Capital Group, Inc. 10/06/2000
eResource Capital Group, Inc. name changed to RCG Companies Inc. 11/14/2003 which name changed to OneTravel Holdings, Inc. 06/08/2005
(See OneTravel Holdings, Inc.)

FLIN FLON MINES LTD (SK)
Placed in receivership 03/26/1985
No stockholders' equity

FLINDERS RES LTD (BC)
Name changed to Leading Edge Materials Corp. 08/26/2016

FLINT CREEK GOLD LTD (BC)
Reincorporated 00/00/1983
Place of incorporation changed from (AB) to (BC) 00/00/1983
Name changed to Calpine Resources Inc. 06/21/1984
Calpine Resources Inc. merged into Prime Resources Group Inc. 04/12/1990 which merged into HomeStake Mining Co. 12/03/1998 which merged into Barrick Gold Corp. 12/14/2001

FLINT ENERGY SVCS LTD (AB)
Common no par split (2) for (1) by issuance of (1) additional share payable 12/27/2006 to holders of record 12/15/2006 Ex date - 12/13/2006

Acquired by URS Corp. 05/14/2012
Each share Common no par exchanged for $25 cash

FLINT HILL BREWING CO.
Dissolved in 1939

FLINT MANUFACTURING CO. (NC)
Acquired by Burlington Mills Corp. 00/00/1946
Details not available

FLINT MEDIA GROUP INC (NV)
Name changed to RiverRun Resources, Inc. 08/29/2008

FLINT MOTOR CO. (MI)
Charter revoked for failure to file reports and pay fees 8/31/32

FLINT ROCK MINES LTD (ON)
Capital Stock $1 par changed to no par 10/05/1970
Merged into Kalrock Resources Ltd. 08/08/1990
Each share Capital Stock no par exchanged for (0.16666666) share Common no par
Kalrock Resources Ltd. merged into Cercal Minerals Corp. 07/09/1993
(See Cercal Minerals Corp.)

FLINT TAVERN HOTEL CO. (MI)
Dissolved 10/31/58

FLINTKOTE CO (MA)
Each share Common no par exchanged for (1) share Class A no par, plus a distribution of (1) additional share as a stock dividend in 1928
Each share Class B no par exchanged for (1) share Class A no par 4/14/36
Class A no par reclassified as Common no par in 1936
Common no par changed to $5 par 3/23/55
Common $5 par split (3) for (2) by issuance of (0.5) additional share 4/22/59
4-1/2% 2nd Conv. Preferred $100 par called for redemption 9/15/72
4% Preferred no par called for redemption 11/13/79
$2.25 2nd Conv. Preferred B no par called for redemption 11/28/79
$4.50 2nd Conv. Preferred A $100 par called for redemption 11/28/79
Merged into Genstar Ltd. 2/8/80
Each share Common $5 par exchanged for $55 cash

FLINTROCK FINL SVCS INC (NV)
Common $0.001 par split (5) for (1) by issuance of (4) additional shares payable 1/21/2000 to holders of record 1/19/2000
Name changed to Auteo Media Inc. 3/22/2000
Auteo Media Inc. name changed to WorldStar Energy, Corp. 4/1/2005

FLIRTY GIRL INTL INC (ANTIGUA)
Ordinary $0.0001 par split (5) for (1) by issuance of (4) additional shares payable 12/27/2005 to holders of record 12/23/2005 Ex date - 12/28/2005
Name changed to PlayStar Corp. (Antigua) (New) 07/27/2006
(See PlayStar Corp. (Antigua) (New))

FLM HLDG CORP (NY)
Common 10¢ par split (2) for (1) by issuance of (1) additional share 01/12/1973
Dissolved by proclamation 03/25/1981

FLO CAP INC (AB)
Name changed to Cancrete Environmental Solutions Inc. 09/11/1996
(See Cancrete Environmental Solutions Inc.)

FLO CORP (DE)
SEC revoked common stock registration 08/20/2013

FLO-MIX FERTILIZERS CORP. (DE)
No longer in existence having become inoperative and void for non-payment of taxes 10/1/59

FLO TEK INC (NJ)
Adjudicated bankrupt 1/13/81
No stockholders' equity

FLO TRONICS INC (MN)
Name changed to Waters Instruments, Inc. 05/01/1970
Waters Instruments, Inc. name changed to Zareba Systems, Inc. 11/01/2005
(See Zareba Systems, Inc.)

FLOAT TO RELAX INC (CO)
Name changed to Hydro-Medical Technology, Inc. 8/15/83
Hydro-Medical Technology, Inc. name changed to Capsule Systems, Inc. 1/31/86
(See Capsule Systems, Inc.)

FLOATING POINT SYS INC (OR)
Common no par split (2) for (1) by issuance of (1) additional share 6/8/81
Chapter 11 Federal Bankruptcy Code converted to Chapter 7 in May 1994
Stockholders' equity unlikely

FLOATING RATE INCOME FD (ON)
Merged into Canoe 'GO CANADA!' Fund Corp. 07/22/2016
Each Unit received (0.87105854) share Floating Rate Income Fund Ser. Z

FLOATING RATE INCOME STRATEGIES FD INC (MD)
Issue Information - 16,125,000 shares COM offered at $20 per share on 10/28/2003
Name changed to BlackRock Floating Rate Income Strategies Fund, Inc. 10/2/2006

FLOATING RATE INCOME STRATEGIES FD II, INC. (MD)
Issue Information - 10,000,000 COM SHS offered at $20 per share on 07/27/2004
Name changed to BlackRock Floating Rate Income Strategies Fund II, Inc. 10/02/2006
BlackRock Floating Rate Income Strategies Fund II, Inc. merged into BlackRock Floating Rate Income Strategies Fund, Inc. 10/08/2012

FLOBEC GOLD MINES, LTD. (ON)
Charter revoked for failure to file reports and pay taxes 00/00/1959

FLOCK BREWING CO.
Out of business in 1952
Details not available

FLOCK GAS & OIL CORP. LTD. (AB)
Common no par changed to 20¢ par 00/00/1952
Completely liquidated 10/14/1966
Each share Common 20¢ par exchanged for first and final distribution of (0.02) share Aldex Drilling & Exploration Ltd. Common 20¢ par

FLOCK INDS INC (NY)
Common 20¢ par split (2) for (1) by issuance of (1) additional share 5/1/72
Each share Common 20¢ par exchanged for (0.2) share Common 1¢ par 2/1/82
Company liquidated in 1991
Details not available

FLOCK RES LTD (AB)
Name changed to Endev Energy Inc. 07/11/2002
Endev Energy Inc. merged into Penn West Energy Trust 07/22/2008 which reorganized as Penn West Petroleum Ltd. (New) 01/03/2011 which name changed to Obsidian Energy Ltd. 06/29/2017

FLOMIC CHIBOUGAMAU MINES LTD. (QC)
Charter annulled for failure to file annual reports 05/25/1974

FLOMORE RES LTD (AB)
Recapitalized as Security Energy Corp. 03/07/1991
Each share Class A Common no par exchanged for (0.5) share Class A Common no par
Security Energy Corp. merged into Clarinet Resources Ltd. 04/03/1995 which recapitalized as Symmetry Resources Inc. 08/16/1996 which merged into Berkley Petroleum Corp. 01/31/2000
(See Berkley Petroleum Corp.)

FLOODSMART INC (NV)
Common $0.001 par split (2) for (1) by issuance of (1) additional share payable 11/17/2005 to holders of record 11/16/2005 Ex date - 11/18/2005
Name changed to Axis Energy Corp. 8/1/2006

FLOOR DECOR INC (DE)
Name changed to Tiger Telematics, Inc. 06/06/2002

FLOORCO LTD (ON)
Company ceased operations 05/00/1995
Plan of reorganization under Bankruptcy and Insolvency Act not approved by Ontario Court of Justice and assets sold 03/00/1996
No stockholders' equity

FLOORING AMER INC (DE)
Plan of reorganization under Chapter 11 Federal Bankruptcy Code effective 06/11/2003
Stockholders' equity unlikely

FLOORING ZONE INC (NV)
Name changed to Profire Energy, Inc. 01/20/2009

FLORA MIR CANDY CORP (NY)
Charter cancelled and proclaimed dissolved for failure to pay taxes and file reports 12/7/76

FLORAFAX INTL INC (DE)
Common 10¢ par changed to $0.06-2/3 par and (0.5) additional share issued 5/30/83
Common $0.06-2/3 par split (5) for (4) by issuance of (0.25) additional share 12/4/84
Name changed to Gerald Stevens Inc. 4/30/99
(See Gerald Stevens Inc.)

FLORAN INTL INC (FL)
Each share old Common no par exchanged for (0.01) share new Common no par 5/10/2001
Recapitalized as FTLA Inc. 10/15/2001
Each share new Common no par exchanged for (0.01) share Common no par
FTLA Inc. name changed to Liska Biometry, Inc. 4/1/2002

FLOREGOLD RED LAKE MINES, LTD. (ON)
Charter surrendered 10/21/1959

FLORENCE GAS & FUEL CO.
Dissolved in 1932

FLORENCE STOVE CO. (MA)
Each share Common $10 par exchanged for (4) shares Common no par and dividend of (1) share Common and (1) share 7% Preferred then paid on each (4) shares new Common in 1927
Common no par changed to $1 par in 1952
Name changed to Roper (Geo. D.) Corp. (MA) 4/4/58
Roper (Geo. D.) Corp. (MA) merged into Roper (Geo. D.) Corp. (DE) 6/30/64 which name changed to Roper Corp. 4/22/68

(See Roper Corp.)

FLORENCE TRUST CO. (FLORENCE, SC)
Dissolved 12/31/78

FLORENTINE MINERAL RES LTD (ON)
Recapitalized as Triangle Multi-Services Corp. 04/05/1995
Each share Common no par exchanged for (0.5) share Common no par
Triangle Multi-Services Corp. name changed to RXT 110 Inc. 04/28/2011 which name changed to BIOSENTA Inc. 06/06/2012

FLORES & RUCKS INC (DE)
Issue Information - 5,750,000 shares COM offered at $10 per share on 11/30/1994
Name changed to Ocean Energy Inc. (Old) 6/17/97
Ocean Energy Inc. (Old) merged into Ocean Energy Inc. (New) 3/27/98 which merged into Ocean Energy, Inc. (TX) 3/30/99 which reincorporated in Delaware 5/9/2001 which merged into Devon Energy Corp. 4/25/2003

FLORES DE NEW MEXICO INC (DE)
Charter cancelled and declared inoperative and void for non-payment of taxes 6/26/90

FLORHAM CONSULTING CORP (DE)
Name changed to Oak Tree Educational Partners, Inc. 10/15/2010

FLORI CORP (DE)
Reincorporated 07/06/1970
State of incorporation changed from (AZ) to (DE) 07/06/1970
Through purchase offer 100% reacquired by by the company as of 09/05/1980
Public interest eliminated

FLORI INVT CO (AZ)
Name changed to Flori Corp. (AZ) 7/21/69
Flori Corp. (AZ) reincorporated under the laws of Delaware 7/6/70
(See Flori Corp. (DE))

FLORIDA AUTOMOTIVE MARKETING CORP (OH)
Liquidation completed
Each share Class A Common $1 par exchanged for initial distribution of $2.82 cash 8/16/84
Each share Class A Common $1 par received second and final distribution of $1.20 cash 9/6/85

FLORIDA BANCGROWTH, INC. (FL)
Merged into Castleton Industries, Inc. 12/29/67
Each share Common $1 par exchanged for (5) shares Common $1 par
(See Castleton Industries, Inc.)

FLORIDA BANCORP INC (FL)
Name changed to Florida Coast Banks, Inc. 12/31/75
(See Florida Coast Banks, Inc.)

FLORIDA BK & TR CO (DAYTONA BEACH, FL)
Through voluntary purchase offer 100% acquired by Florida National Banks of Florida, Inc. 00/00/1974
Public interest eliminated

FLORIDA BANK AT FORT LAUDERDALE (FORT LAUDERDALE, FL)
Through purchase offer 99.9% acquired by Florida National Banks of Florida Inc. as of 12/31/1974
Public interest eliminated

FLORIDA BK GROUP INC (FL)
Merged into IBERIABANK Corp. 02/28/2015
Each share Class A Common 1¢ par exchanged for (0.149) share

Common $1 par and $7.81 cash

FLORIDA BKS INC (FL)
Issue Information - 4,000,000 shares COM offered at $10 per share on 07/29/1998
Merged into South Financial Group, Inc. 07/16/2004
Each share Common 1¢ par exchanged for (0.77) share Common $1 par
South Financial Group, Inc. merged into Toronto-Dominion Bank (Toronto, ON) 09/30/2010

FLORIDA BANKSHARES INC (DE)
Acquired by Flagship Banks Inc. 12/2/80
Each share Common 50¢ par exchanged for $26 cash

FLORIDA BUSINESS BANCGROUP INC (FL)
Merged into Home BancShares, Inc. 10/01/2015
Each share Common 1¢ par exchanged for (0.2662) Common 1¢ par and $2.344 cash

FLORIDA CANADA CORP. (DE)
Name changed to General Development Corp. 4/28/58
General Development Corp. name changed to GDV Inc. 5/23/77
(See GDV Inc.)

FLORIDA CAP CORP (DE)
Reincorporated 4/9/73
State of incorporation changed from (FL) to (DE) 4/9/73
Merged into Alfa-Laval AB 2/22/84
Each share Common $1 par exchanged for $21 cash

FLORIDA CAPITAL BUILDING CORP. (FL)
Recapitalized as Realty Financial Corp. 1/8/65
Each share Common 10¢ par exchanged for (0.1) share Common $1 par
Realty Financial Corp. merged into Roltec, Inc. 4/3/67 which merged into Gould Properties, Inc. 7/24/68 which name changed to Gould Enterprises, Inc. 4/2/69 which merged into Gould Investors Trust 7/1/70 which reorganized in Delaware as Gould Investors L.P. 5/13/86

FLORIDA CHOICE BK (EUSTIS, FL)
Under plan of reorganization each share Common 1¢ par automatically became (1) share Florida Choice Bankshares, Inc. Common $5 par 01/01/2005
Florida Choice Bankshares, Inc. merged into Alabama National BanCorporation (DE) 04/03/2006 which merged into Royal Bank of Canada (Montreal, QUE) 02/22/2008

FLORIDA CHOICE BANKSHARES INC (FL)
Merged into Alabama National BanCorporation (DE) 04/03/2006
Each share Common $5 par exchanged for (0.6079) share Common $1 par
Alabama National BanCorporation (DE) merged into Royal Bank of Canada (Montreal, QUE) 02/22/2008

FLORIDA CITRUS JUICE & SYRUP CO. (DE)
Charter cancelled and declared inoperative and void for non-payment of taxes in 1928

FLORIDA COAST BKS INC (FL)
Conv. Preferred Ser. A no par called for redemption 10/26/83
Acquired by Barnett Banks of Florida, Inc. 6/30/84
Each share Common $1 par exchanged for $27.50 cash

FLORIDA COML BKS INC (FL)
Common $1 par split (3) for (2) by issuance of (0.5) additional share 12/29/1983
Stock Dividend - 50% 11/22/1982
Merged into First Union Corp. 03/01/1988
Each share Common $1 par exchanged for $44 cash

FLORIDA CMNTY BK (IMMOKALEE, FL)
Common $10 par split (6) for (5) by issuance of (0.2) additional share payable 06/01/2000 to holders of record 05/10/2000 Ex date - 05/15/2000
Common $10 par split (6) for (5) by issuance of (0.2) additional share payable 06/01/2001 to holders of record 04/26/2001
Stock Dividend - 10% payable 06/01/1998 to holders of record 05/01/1998
Reorganized as Florida Community Banks, Inc. 04/16/2002
Each share Common $10 par exchanged for (1) share Common $10 par
(See Florida Community Banks, Inc.)

FLORIDA CMNTY BKS INC (FL)
Stock Dividends - 20% payable 12/02/2002 to holders of record 11/12/2002 Ex date - 11/12/2002; 20% payable 12/01/2003 to holders of record 11/03/2003 Ex date - 10/30/2003; 20% payable 12/01/2005 to holders of record 11/03/2005 Ex date - 11/01/2005; 20% payable 12/01/2006 to holders of record 11/03/2006 Ex date - 11/01/2006; 20% payable 12/03/2007 to holders of record 11/02/2007 Ex date - 11/01/2007
Company's principal asset placed in receivership 01/29/2010
Stockholders' equity unlikely

FLORIDA COS (FL)
Merged into Fairfield Communities, Inc. 12/6/83
Each share Common 1¢ par exchanged for (0.25) share Common 10¢ par
(See Fairfield Communities, Inc.)

FLORIDA CYPRESS GARDENS INC (FL)
Acquired by Harcourt Brace Jovanovich, Inc. 8/15/85
Each share Common 25¢ par exchanged for (0.12866) share Common $1 par
Harcourt Brace Jovanovich, Inc. merged into General Cinema Corp. 11/25/91 which name changed to Harcourt General, Inc. 3/15/93
(See Harcourt General, Inc.)

FLORIDA D & M CO (FL)
Class A Common $1.25 par and Class B Common $1.25 par changed to $1 par and (0.25) additional share issued respectively 1/20/69
Recapitalized 7/30/71
Each share Class A Common $1 par exchanged for (1) share Common $1 par
Each share Class B Common $1 par exchanged for (2) shares Common $1 par
Proclaimed dissolved for failure to file reports and pay fees 9/3/76

FLORIDA DEV FD 1995 INC (DE)
Charter revoked 09/21/2001

FLORIDA DIET SVCS INC (FL)
Name changed to www.eBIZnet.com Inc. 12/03/1998
www.eBIZnet.com Inc. name changed to Biznet Group Inc. 06/01/2000 which recapitalized as ProMed Alliance International, Inc. 02/21/2006 which name changed to Biomedtex, Inc. 10/09/2007
(See Biomedtex, Inc.)

FLORIDA DISTRG & MFG CO (FL)
Name changed to Florida D & M Co. 10/3/68
(See Florida D & M Co.)

FLORIDA DOWNS, INC. (FL)
Completely liquidated 11/24/67
Each share Common 5¢ par exchanged for first and final distribution of $2.033 cash

FLORIDA EAST COAST INDS INC (FL)
Common $6.25 par split (4) for (1) by issuance of (3) additional shares payable 06/15/1998 to holders of record 06/01/1998 Ex date - 06/16/1998
Class A Common $6.25 par reclassified as Common $6.25 par 09/22/2003
Class B Common no par reclassified as Common $6.25 par 09/22/2003
Merged into Iron Horse Acquisition Holding LLC 07/26/2007
Each share Common $6.25 par exchanged for $62.50 cash

FLORIDA EAST COAST RY CO (FL)
Capital Stock $25 par changed to $6.25 par and (3) additional shares issued 07/15/1981
Under plan of reorganization each share Capital Stock $6.25 par automatically became (1) share Florida East Coast Industries, Inc. Capital Stock $6.25 par 05/30/1984
(See Florida East Coast Industries, Inc.)

FLORIDA EMPLOYERS INS CO (CAYMAN ISLANDS)
Completely liquidated 6/19/92
Each share Ordinary Stock 1¢ par exchanged for first and final distribution of $16.0743 cash

FLORIDA EQUITY & MTG INVS (FL)
Name changed to Derand Equity Group, Inc. 3/28/80
(See Derand Equity Group, Inc.)

FLORIDA EXPRESS INC (DE)
Acquired by Braniff, Inc. 4/19/88
Each share Common 1¢ par exchanged for (1) share 7% Conv. Preferred Ser. B 50¢ par
(See Braniff, Inc.)

FLORIDA FED SVGS & LN ASSN ST PETERSBURG FLA (USA)
Name changed to Florida Federal Savings Bank (St. Petersburg, FL) 01/01/1989
(See Florida Federal Savings Bank (St. Petersburg, FL))

FLORIDA FED SVGS BK (ST PETERSBURG, FL)
Placed in receivership 11/9/90
No stockholders' equity

FLORIDA FIBER CONTAINERS INC. (FL)
Proclaimed dissolved for failure to file reports and pay fees 9/16/36

FLORIDA FIRST BANCORP INC (FL)
Merged into Regions Financial Corp. (Old) 1/25/97
Each share Common $1 par exchanged for $11.65 cash

FLORIDA FIRST EQUITIES CORP (FL)
Stock Dividend - 20% 12/14/1973
Name changed to Data Imaging Services, Inc. 07/09/1993
(See Data Imaging Services, Inc.)

FLORIDA FIRST FED SVGS BK (PANAMA CITY, FL)
Under plan of reorganization each share Common $1 par automatically became (1) share Florida First Bancorp Inc. Common $1 par 5/1/95
(See Florida First Bancorp Inc.)

FLORIDA 1ST NATL BK (KEY WEST, FL)
Through voluntary exchange offer 98.7% acquired by Florida National Banks of Florida, Inc. as of 02/11/1971
Public interest eliminated

FLORIDA FIRST NATIONAL BANK (BARTOW, FL)
Through voluntary exchange offer Florida National Banks of Florida, Inc. held 98% as of 02/11/1971
Public interest eliminated

FLORIDA FIRST NATIONAL BANK (JACKSONVILLE, FL)
99.819% held by Florida National Banks of Florida, Inc. as of 12/31/1977
Public interest eliminated

FLORIDA FIRST NATIONAL BANK (PORT ST. JOE, FL)
96.3% acquired by Florida National Banks of Florida, Inc. through exchange offer which expired 02/11/1971
Public interest eliminated

FLORIDA FIRST NATIONAL BANK (VERO BEACH, FL)
95.3% acquired by Florida National Banks of Florida, Inc. through exchange offer which expired 02/11/1971
Public interest eliminated

FLORIDA 1ST NATL BK (PENSACOLA, FL)
Through voluntary exchange offer 97.8% acquired by Florida National Banks of Florida, Inc. as of 02/11/1971
Public interest eliminated

FLORIDA FLIGHT ENGINEERING CORP.
Proclaimed dissolved for non-payment of capital stock taxes 4/29/60

FLORIDA FOODS, INC.
Name changed to Vacuum Foods Corp. in 1946 and then to Minute Maid Corp. in 1949 which was merged into Coca Cola Co. 12/30/60

FLORIDA FROZEN FRUITS INC. (FL)
Out of business 00/00/1953
Details not available

FLORIDA FRUIT PRODUCTS CO. INC.
Out of business 00/00/1949
Details not available

FLORIDA GAMING CORP (DE)
Each share Common 10¢ par exchanged for (0.5) share Common 20¢ par 01/27/2003
Plan of reorganization under Chapter 11 Federal Bankruptcy proceedings effective 08/06/2014
No stockholders' equity

FLORIDA GAS CO (FL)
Class A Conv. $1 par reclassified as Common $1 par 5/3/66
Merged into Continental Group, Inc. 8/28/79
Each share 5-1/2% Preferred $100 par exchanged for $101.50 cash
Each share Common $1 par exchanged for (0.35) share $4.50 Preference Ser. C $1 par and $32.50 cash
Continental Group, Inc. merged into KMI Continental Inc. 11/2/84
(See KMI Continental Inc.)

FLORIDA GIFT BASKETS CORP (FL)
Name changed to International Resorts & Entertainment Group Inc. 06/05/1997
International Resorts & Entertainment Group Inc. recapitalized as Raven Moon International, Inc. 12/30/1998 which recapitalized as Raven Moon Entertainment, Inc. 09/01/2001 which recapitalized as Made in America Entertainment, Inc. 08/29/2008

FLORIDA GLASS INDS INC (DE)
Charter cancelled and declared inoperative and void for non-payment of taxes 5/25/95

FLORIDA GROWTH FD INC (FL)
Name changed to Bayrock Growth Fund, Inc. 04/26/1971
Bayrock Growth Fund, Inc. acquired by Affiliated Fund, Inc. (DE) 09/03/1975 which reincorporated in Maryland 11/26/1975 which name changed to Lord Abbett Affiliated Fund, Inc. 03/01/1996

FLORIDA GROWTH INDS INC (UT)
Involuntarily dissolved 07/01/1992

FLORIDA GULF BANCORP INC (FL)
Merged into IBERIABANK Corp. 07/31/2012
Each share Common $5 par exchanged for (0.466) share Common $1 par

FLORIDA GULF RLTY TR (FL)
Shares of Bene. Int. 10¢ par split (2) for (1) by issuance of (1) additional share 3/31/81
Liquidation completed
Each Share of Bene. Int. 10¢ par received initial distribution of $17.75 cash 1/6/86
Each Share of Bene. Int. 10¢ par received second distribution of $0.40 cash 7/31/86
Each Share of Bene. Int. 10¢ par exchanged for third and final distribution of $0.285 cash 11/26/86

FLORIDA HIGHLANDS DEVELOPMENT CORP. (FL)
Charter revoked for failure to file reports and pay fees 6/30/67

FLORIDA HILLSBORO, INC. (DE)
Name changed to Kemline Industries, Inc. 9/12/63
(See Kemline Industries, Inc.)

FLORIDA HOME INSURANCE CO. (FL)
Merged into Guaranty Security Insurance Co. 12/31/62
Holders had three options to exchange each share Common $10 par
First option - (9) shares Common $1 par
Second option - (4) shares $1 Preferred $1 par and (1) share Common $1 par
Third option - (2) shares $1 Preferred $1 par and (5) shares Common $1 par
After 12/28/62 options expired and each share Common $10 par can only be exchanged for (9) shares Common $1 par
Guaranty Security Insurance Co. merged into Diversified Insurers Co. 1/29/68
(See Diversified Insurers Co.)

FLORIDA INCOME FUND III, LIMITED PARTNERSHIP (DE)
Company terminated registration of Units of Limited Partnership and is no longer public as of 12/11/1998
Details not available

FLORIDA INDEX FD INC (FL)
Involuntarily dissolved for failure to file reports and pay fees 10/13/1989

FLORIDA INTERSTATE DEVELOPMENT CO. (FL)
Name changed to Chill Can Industries, Inc. 9/24/69
(See Chill Can Industries, Inc.)

FLORIDA INVT TR (FL)
Merged into Seago Group, Inc. 5/31/78
Each Share of Bene. Int. $5 par exchanged for (0.1) share Conv. Preferred $40 par
(See Seago Group, Inc.)

FLORIDA JAI ALAI INC (FL)
Each share old Common no par exchanged for (0.001) share new Common no par 4/21/82
Note: In effect holders received $11.25 cash per share and public interest was eliminated

FLORIDA LAND CO. (DE)
Name changed to Florida-Patsand Corp. 11/4/59
(See Florida-Patsand Corp.)

FLORIDA LIFE INSURANCE CO. (FL)
Dissolved by court order 11/20/1997
Stockholders' equity unlikely

FLORIDA LIQUID ASSETS CO (MD)
Name changed to Tax Managed Fund for Utilities Shares Inc. 04/03/1978
Tax Managed Fund for Utilities Shares Inc. name changed to ABT Utility Income Fund 12/01/1984
(See ABT Utility Income Fund)

FLORIDA MEDICAL PLAN, INC. (FL)
Charter cancelled and declared inoperative and void for non-payment of taxes 12/11/76

FLORIDA METAL SUPPLY CORP. (FL)
Under plan of merger name changed to Precision Industries, Inc. 03/26/1968
Precision Industries, Inc. name changed to American Imaging, Inc. 04/27/1998 which name changed to Seaescape Entertainment, Inc. 06/12/2000

FLORIDA MICRO INC (NV)
Charter revoked 04/01/2013

FLORIDA MNG & MATLS CORP (FL)
Merged into Moormack Mining, Inc. 12/3/79
Each share Common $1 par exchanged for $48 cash

FLORIDA MUT U S GOVT SECS FD INC (FL)
Voluntarily liquidated 07/10/1980
Each share Portfolio I Common $0.00001 par and Portfolio II Common $0.00001 par exchanged for (1) Pinnacle Government Funds, Inc. (FL) Government Fund Share of Bene. Int. no par
Pinnacle Government Funds, Inc. (FL) reincorporated in Massachusetts as Trinity Liquid Assets Trust 01/31/1990 which name changed to Trinity Assets Trust 11/16/1990
(See Trinity Assets Trust)

FLORIDA MUTUAL FUND, INC. (FL)
Name changed to Citadel Fund, Inc. (FL) 01/26/1966
Citadel Fund, Inc. (FL) reincorporated in Maryland as American National Growth Fund, Inc. 08/01/1968 which name changed to SM&R Growth Fund, Inc. 01/01/1999
(See SM&R Growth Fund, Inc.)

FLORIDA NATIONAL BANK & TRUST CO. (MIAMI, FL)
Stock Dividend - 100% 1/25/65
Thru voluntary exchange offer 99.99736% acquired by Florida National Banks as of July 1977
Public interest eliminated

FLORIDA NATL BK & TR CO (WEST PALM BEACH, FL)
98.7% acquired by Florida National Banks of Florida, Inc. through exchange offer which expired 02/11/1971
Public interest eliminated

FLORIDA NATIONAL BANK (BARTOW, FL)
Name changed to Florida First National Bank (Bartow, FL) 3/31/73
(See Florida First National Bank (Bartow, FL))

FLORIDA NATL BK (CORAL GABLES, FL)
98% acquired by Florida National Banks of Florida, Inc. through exchange offer which expired 02/11/1971
Public interest eliminated

FLORIDA NATL BK (JACKSONVILLE, FL)
Stock Dividends - 233-1/3% 4/9/53; 100% 9/13/60; 25% 3/2/67
Name changed to Florida First National Bank (Jacksonville, FL) 3/1/72
(See Florida First National Bank (Jacksonville, FL))

FLORIDA NATL BK (LAKELAND, FL)
98.9% acquired by Florida National Banks of Florida, Inc. through exchange offer which expired 02/11/1971
Public interest eliminated

FLORIDA NATL BK (ORLANDO, FL)
99.5% acquired by Florida National Banks of Florida, Inc. through exchange offer which expired 02/11/1971
Public interest eliminated

FLORIDA NATIONAL BANK (PENSACOLA, FL)
Name changed to Florida First National Bank (Pensacola, FL) 2/1/66
(See Florida First National Bank (Pensacola, FL))

FLORIDA NATL BK (ST PETERSBURG, FL)
Stock Dividends - 100% 01/01/1941; 150% 01/25/1955; 100% 01/29/1962
99.3% acquired by Florida National Banks of Florida, Inc. through exchange offer which expired 02/11/1971
Public interest eliminated

FLORIDA NATL BKS FLA INC (FL)
Common $12.50 par changed to $8.33-1/3 par and (0.5) additional share issued 06/29/1984
Common $8.33-1/3 par changed to $4.16-2/3 par and (1) additional share issued 06/30/1986
Merged into First Union Corp. 01/29/1990
Each share Common $4.16-2/3 par exchanged for either (0.5425) share Adjustable Rate Perpetual Preferred Ser. 1990 no par, $27.125 cash or a combination thereof
Note: Option to elect to receive cash expired 01/26/1990
(See First Union Corp.)

FLORIDA ONE CAP CORP (FL)
Each share Common $0.0001 par exchanged for (0.1) share Common $0.001 par 07/17/1989
Name changed to Wholesale Optical Club International, Inc. 07/17/1990
Wholesale Optical Club International, Inc. recapitalized as Nu-Vision International, Inc. 12/14/1990 which name changed to Highland Healthcare Corp. 05/31/1991 which recapitalized as Systems Communications Inc. 09/09/1994 which recapitalized as Hitsgalore.com, Inc. 03/19/1999 which name changed to Diamond Hitts Production, Inc. (FL) 05/01/2001 which reincorporated in Nevada 09/04/2001
(See Diamond Hitts Production, Inc.)

FLORIDA PACIFIC CORP. (FL)
Proclaimed dissolved for failure to file reports and pay fees 10/21/74

FLORIDA PACKERS CORP. (FL)
Proclaimed dissolved for failure to file reports and pay fees 9/14/36

FLORIDA PALM AIRE CORP (FL)
Reincorporated under the laws of Delaware as FPA Corp. 10/28/1969
FPA Corp. name changed to Orleans Homebuilders, Inc. 07/14/1998
(See Orleans Homebuilders, Inc.)

FLORIDA PANTHERS HLDGS INC (DE)
Reincorporated 11/19/97
Issue Information - 7,300,000 shares Class A Common offered at $10 per share on 11/13/1996
State of incorporation changed from (FL) to (DE) 11/19/97
Name changed to Boca Resorts Inc. 9/28/99
(See Boca Resorts Inc.)

FLORIDA PAPER MILLS CO. (FL)
Proclaimed dissolved for failure to file reports and pay fees 8/15/44

FLORIDA-PATSAND CORP. (DE)
Each share Common 10¢ par exchanged for (0.1) share Common no par 7/13/62
Assets sold for benefit of creditors in 1966
No stockholders' equity

FLORIDA PEACH CO-OP, INC. (FL)
Name changed to Florida Peach Corp. 11/06/1969
(See Florida Peach Corp.)

FLORIDA PEACH CORP (FL)
Chapter 11 bankruptcy proceedings dismissed 2/22/82
No stockholders' equity

FLORIDA PK BKS INC (FL)
Chapter 11 Federal Bankruptcy Code converted to Chapter 7 in 1987
No stockholders' equity

FLORIDA PORTLAND CEMENT CO.
Merged into General Portland Cement Co. in 1947
Each share Preferred exchanged for (6.4117) shares Common $1 par
Common received two warrants which expired in 1950
General Portland Cement Co. name changed to General Portland Inc. 5/31/72
(See General Portland Inc.)

FLORIDA PWR & LT CO (FL)
Common no par split (2) for (1) by issuance of (1) additional share 06/13/1955
Common no par split (2) for (1) by issuance of (1) additional share 06/01/1959
Common no par split (2) for (1) by issuance of (1) additional share 06/05/1972
Under plan of reorganization each share Common no par automatically became (1) share FPL Group, Inc. Common 1¢ par 12/31/1984
9.25% Preferred Ser. H $100 par called for redemption 04/28/1992
10.08% Preferred Ser. J $100 par called for redemption on 04/01/1993
11.32% Preferred Ser. O $100 par called for redemption 04/01/1993
8.70% Preferred Ser. K $100 par called for redemption 04/16/1993
8.84% Preferred Ser. L $100 par called for redemption 08/02/1993
8.50% Preferred Ser. P $100 par called for redemption 10/08/1993
7.28% Preferred Ser. F $100 par called for redemption 01/26/1996
7.40% Preferred Ser. G $100 par called for redemption 01/26/1996
$2 Preferred Ser. A $100 par called for redemption 03/27/1997
8.625% Preferred Ser. R $100 par called for redemption 04/01/1997
6.84% Preferred Ser. Q $100 par called for redemption at $102.28 on 09/05/1997
4.32% Preferred Ser. D $100 par called for redemption at $103.50 on 11/19/2003
4.35% Preferred Ser. E $100 par called for redemption at $102 on 11/19/2003
4.50% Preferred $100 par called for redemption at $101 on 11/19/2003
4.50% Preferred Ser. B called for redemption at $101 on 11/19/2003

4.50% Preferred Ser. C called for redemption at $103 on 11/19/2003
6.98% Preferred Ser. S called for redemption at $103.49 on 11/19/2003
7.05% Preferred Ser. T called for redemption at $103.52 on 11/19/2003
6.75% Preferred Ser. U called for redemption at $103.37 on 11/19/2003
4.50% Preferred Ser. A $100 par called for redemption at $103.25 on 01/3/2005
FPL Group, Inc. name changed to NextEra Energy, Inc. 05/21/2010

FLORIDA PWR CORP (FL)
Each share old Common no par exchanged for (0.1) share Common $100 par 00/00/1933
Common $100 par changed to new Common no par 00/00/1944
New Common no par changed to $7.50 par 00/00/1945
Common $7.50 par changed to $2.50 par and (2) additional shares issued 11/25/1958
Common $2.50 par changed to no par and (1) additional share issued 05/01/1980
Under plan of reorganization each share Common no par automatically became (1) share Florida Progress Corp. Common no par 03/29/1982
(See Florida Progress Corp.)
10% Preferred $100 par called for redemption 11/15/1986
10.50% Preferred $100 par called for redemption 11/15/1986
13.32% Preferred $100 par called for redemption 08/16/1987
8.80% Preferred $100 par called for redemption 03/12/1993
7.84% Preferred $100 par called for redemption 12/10/1993
7.40% Preferred $100 par called for redemption 06/10/1996
7.76% Preferred $100 par called for redemption 06/10/1996
7.08% Preferred $100 par called for redemption 11/16/1996
4% Preferred $100 par called for redemption at $104.25 plus $0.233 accrued dividends on 03/08/2013
4.40% Preferred $100 par called for redemption at $102 plus $0.257 accrued dividends on 03/08/2013
4.58% Preferred $100 par called for redemption at $101 plus $0.267 accrued dividends on 03/08/2013
4.60% Preferred $100 par called for redemption at $103.25 plus $0.268 accrued dividends on 03/08/2013
4.75% Preferred $100 par called for redemption at $102 plus $0.277 accrued dividends on 03/08/2013

FLORIDA PPTYS INC (DE)
Liquidation completed
Each share Common $10 par received initial distribution of $160 cash 10/18/74
Each share Common $10 par received second distribution of $12.50 cash 10/29/74
Each share Common $10 par received third distribution of $1.85 cash 8/26/75
Each share Common $10 par received fourth and final distribution of $0.61 cash 10/1/79
Certificates were not required to be surrendered and are now without value

FLORIDA PROGRESS CORP (FL)
Common no par split (3) for (2) by issuance of (0.5) additional share 07/29/1992
Each (15) shares Common no par received distribution of (1) share Echelon International Corp. Common 1¢ par payable 12/18/1996 to holders of record 12/05/1996 Ex date - 12/19/1996
Merged into CP&L Energy Inc. 11/30/2000
Each share Common no par exchanged for $54 cash and (1) Contingent Value Obligation

FLORIDA PUB UTILS CO (FL)
Common $5 par changed to $3 par 00/00/1946
Common $3 par changed to $1.50 par and (1) additional share issued 05/01/1984
Common $1.50 par split (3) for (2) by issuance of (0.5) additional share 05/01/1987
$1.12 Conv. Preference $20 par called for redemption 02/01/1988
Common $1.50 par split (2) for (1) by issuance of (1) additional share payable 07/01/1998 to holders of record 06/19/1998
Common $1.50 par split (4) for (3) by issuance of (1/3) additional share payable 07/01/2002 to holders of record 06/14/2002 Ex date - 07/02/2002
Common $1.50 par split (3) for (2) by issuance of (0.5) additional share payable 07/25/2005 to holders of record 07/15/2005 Ex date - 07/26/2005
4.75% Preferred Ser. A $100 par called for redemption at $106 on 09/15/2009
Merged into Chesapeake Utilities Corp. 10/28/2009
Each share Common $1.50 par exchanged for (0.405) share Common 48-2/3¢ par

FLORIDA PUBLIC SERVICE CO.
Merged into Florida Power Corp. 01/14/1944
Details not available

FLORIDA PUBLISHERS INC (NY)
Charter cancelled and proclaimed dissolved for failure to pay taxes 12/29/1982

FLORIDA RAMIE PRODUCTS, INC.
Out of existence in 1948
Details not available

FLORIDA ROCK & TANK LINES INC (FL)
Reorganized as FRP Properties, Inc. 02/02/1989
Each share Common 10¢ par exchanged for (1) share Common 10¢ par
FRP Properties, Inc. name changed to Patriot Transportation Holding, Inc. 03/01/2000 which name changed to FRP Holdings, Inc. 12/05/2014

FLORIDA ROCK INDS INC (FL)
Common 10¢ par split (2) for (1) by issuance of (1) additional share 09/18/1986
Common 10¢ par split (2) for (1) by issuance of (1) additional share payable 10/31/1997 to holders of record 10/15/1997 Ex date - 11/03/1997
Common 10¢ par split (3) for (2) by issuance of (0.5) additional share payable 08/31/2001 to holders of record 08/15/2001 Ex date - 08/22/2001
Common 10¢ par split (3) for (2) by issuance of (0.5) additional share payable 01/16/2004 to holders of record 01/02/2004 Ex date - 01/20/2004
Common 10¢ par split (3) for (2) by issuance of (0.5) additional share payable 07/01/2005 to holders of record 06/15/2005 Ex date - 07/05/2005
Merged into Vulcan Materials Co. 11/16/2007
Each share Common 10¢ par exchanged for (0.63) share Common $1 par

FLORIDA SHS INC (FL)
Voluntarily dissolved 02/19/1982
Details not available

FLORIDA SOUTHERN BANK (PALM SPRINGS, FL)
97.9% acquired by Barnett Banks of Florida, Inc. through exchange offer which expired 11/15/1973
Public interest eliminated

FLORIDA SOUTHERN CORP. (FL)
Adjudged insolvent 8/9/63
No stockholders' equity

FLORIDA-SOUTHERN LAND CORP. (FL)
Name changed to Florida Southern Corp. 4/20/61
(See Florida Southern Corp.)

FLORIDA STATE AIRLINES, INC. (FL)
Charter cancelled and proclaimed dissolved for non-payment of taxes 6/28/71

FLORIDA STATE BANK (HOLIDAY, FL)
Closed by Florida State Commissioner and FDIC appointed receiver 05/24/1991
No stockholders' equity

FLORIDA STL CORP (FL)
Common $1 par split (2) for (1) by issuance of (1) additional share 3/11/80
Common $1 par split (2) for (1) by issuance of (1) additional share 3/11/81
Merged into FLS Holdings Inc. 11/17/88
Each share Common $1 par exchanged for (1) share 17.50% Exchangeable Preferred Ser. A 1¢ par
(See FLS Holdings Inc.)

FLORIDA SUN LIFE INSURANCE CO.
Merged into American Investors Corp. (TN) in 1959
Each share Common $1 par exchanged for (2/3) share Common $1 par
American Investors Corp. (TN) reincorporated in Delaware as AIC Corp. 12/31/64 which name changed to Crutcher Resources Corp. 12/31/68
(See Crutcher Resources Corp.)

FLORIDA SUNCOAST LAND & MINING CO. (FL)
Proclaimed dissolved for non-payment of taxes 6/28/65

FLORIDA SUNSHINE PLTS INC (DE)
Recapitalized as General Growth Industries, Inc. 7/24/79
Each share Common 1¢ par exchanged for (7) shares Common $0.001 par
General Growth Industries, Inc. name changed to Silver Reclamation Industries, Inc. 5/1/80 which recapitalized as Inter America Industries, Inc. 1/28/83 which name changed to Kendee's International Foods, Inc. 11/20/85
(See Kendee's International Foods, Inc.)

FLORIDA TAX-FREE FUND (MA)
Name changed to ABT Southern Master Trust 11/22/1989
(See ABT Southern Master Trust)

FLORIDA TEL CORP (FL)
Each share Common $100 par exchanged for (10) shares Common $10 par 00/00/1946
Common $10 par reclassified as Class A Common $10 par 03/10/1958
Class A Common $10 par changed to $5 par and (1) additional share issued 04/00/1962
Class A Common $5 par changed to $2.50 par and (1) additional share issued 05/01/1966
Acquired by United Telecommunications, Inc. 03/01/1974
Each share Class A Common $2.50 par exchanged for (1.2) shares Common $2.50 par
United Telecommunications, Inc. name changed to Sprint Corp. (KS) 02/26/1992 which name changed to Sprint Nextel Corp. 08/12/2005 which merged into Sprint Corp. (DE) 07/10/2013

FLORIDA TILE INDS INC (FL)
Class A Common $1 par changed to 50¢ par and (1) additional share issued 7/11/68
Name changed to Sikes Corp. 3/1/72
(See Sikes Corp.)

FLORIDA TOWERS CORP. (FL)
Proclaimed dissolved for failure to file reports and pay fees 12/11/76

FLORIDA VENTURE FD INC (WA)
Reincorporated under the laws of Florida as Information-Highway.Com, Inc. 02/23/1999
(See Information-Highway.Com, Inc.)

FLORIDA WEST AIRLS INC (DE)
Charter cancelled and declared inoperative and void for non-payment of taxes 3/1/97

FLORIDA WEST COAST ICE CO.
Acquired by Atlantic Co. in 1936
Details not available

FLORIDA WESTCOAST BKS INC (FL)
Common no par split (2) for (1) by issuance of (1) additional share 9/15/87
Acquired by SBI Subsidiary Corp. 1/21/92
Each share Common no par exchanged for $42 cash

FLORIDA WESTERN OIL CO., INC. (FL)
Declared dissolved for non-payment of taxes 4/24/58

FLORIDA WTR & UTILS CO (FL)
Common $1 par split (5) for (2) by issuance of (1.5) additional shares 03/01/1966
Reincorporated under the laws of Delaware as Helm Resources, Inc. 02/10/1981
Helm Resources, Inc. name changed to Helm Capital Group, Inc. 10/29/1997
(See Helm Capital Group, Inc.)

FLORIDABANK A FEDERAL SVGS BK (JACKSONVILLE, FL)
Common $1 par split (3) for (2) by issuance of (0.5) additional share 06/04/1993
Merged into AmSouth Bancorporation 02/10/1994
Each share Common $1 par exchanged for (0.4902) share Common $1 par
AmSouth Bancorporation merged into Regions Financial Corp. (New) 11/04/2006

FLORIDAFIRST BANCORP (USA)
Reorganized as FloridaFirst Bancorp, Inc. 12/21/2000
Each share Common 10¢ par exchanged for (1.0321) shares Common 10¢ par
FloridaFirst Bancorp, Inc. merged into SouthTrust Corp. 05/14/2004 which merged into Wachovia Corp. (Ctfs. dated after 09/01/2001) 11/01/2004 which merged into Wells Fargo & Co. (New) 12/31/2008

FLORIDAFIRST BANCORP INC (FL)
Merged into SouthTrust Corp. 05/14/2004
Each share Common 10¢ par exchanged for (0.8596) share Common $2.50 par
SouthTrust Corp. merged into

Wachovia Corp. (Ctfs. dated after 09/01/2001) 11/01/2004 which merged into Wells Fargo & Co. (New) 12/31/2008

FLORIDINOS INTL HLDGS INC (FL)
Name changed to Syndicated Food Service International, Inc. 11/27/2001
(See Syndicated Food Service International, Inc.)

FLORIN RES INC (BC)
Merged into Crimsonstar Mining Corp. 06/19/1991
Each share Common no par exchanged for (0.4) share Common no par
Crimsonstar Mining Corp. recapitalized as Mountain View Ventures Inc. 05/21/1993 which recapitalized as Blackrun Ventures Inc. 04/08/1997 which recapitalized as Blackrun Minerals Inc. 06/10/1999 which name changed to Diversified Industries Ltd. 03/29/2000
(See Diversified Industries Ltd.)

FLORON FOOD SVCS LTD (AB)
Acquired by 1049531 Alberta Ltd. 09/02/2003
Each share Common no par exchanged for $1.40 cash

FLOSEAL CORP (DE)
Chapter X Bankruptcy proceedings closed 10/26/1971
No stockholders' equity

FLOTEK INDS INC
Each share Conv. Preferred $0.0001 par exchanged for (434.782) shares Common $0.0001 par 02/03/2011
(Additional Information in Active)

FLOTEK INDS INC (AB)
Reincorporated 09/15/1995
Place of incorporation changed from (BC) to (AB) 09/15/1995
Reorganized under the laws of Delaware 11/05/2001
Each (120) shares Common no par exchanged for (1) share Common no par

FLOTILL PRODUCTS, INC. (CA)
Name changed to Lewis (Tillie) Foods, Inc. 6/22/61
(See Lewis (Tillie) Foods, Inc.)

FLOUR CITY INTL INC (NV)
Each share old Common $0.001 par exchanged for (0.14285714) share new Common $0.001 par 05/19/1998
SEC revoked common stock registration 11/24/2009

FLOUR CITY ORNAMENTAL IRON CO. (MN)
Stock Dividend - 20% 10/5/51
Acquired by Hupp Corp. 12/30/60
Each share Capital Stock $5 par exchanged for (0.875) share Common $1 par
(See Hupp Corp.)

FLOUR MILLS OF AMERICA, INC. (MD)
Common no par changed to $1 par in 1932
Reorganized under the laws of Delaware in 1941
Each share Preferred no par exchanged for (2) shares Common $5 par
Common $1 par stockholders had no equity
(See Flour Mills of America, Inc. (DE))

FLOUR MLS AMER INC (DE)
Common $5 par changed to $1 par 5/11/59
Stock Dividend - 10% 7/15/49
Charter cancelled and declared inoperative and void for non-payment of taxes 6/18/81

FLOW CORP (MA)
Liquidation completed

Each share Common $1 par exchanged for initial distribution of (1.0925) shares C.G.S. Scientific Corp. Common 20¢ par 4/25/69
Each share Common $1 par received second and final distribution of (0.0575) share Common 20¢ par 8/20/70

FLOW ENERGY LTD (BC)
Name changed to Zimtu Capital Corp. 08/11/2008

FLOW GEN INC (DE)
Common 10¢ par split (2) for (1) by issuance of (1) additional share 7/23/80
Common 10¢ par split (3) for (2) by issuance of (0.5) additional share 12/10/80
Name changed to GRC International, Inc. 12/5/89
(See GRC International, Inc.)

FLOW INTL CORP (NV)
Reincorporated 10/01/1998
State of incorporation changed from (DE) to (NV) 10/01/1998
Acquired by Waterjet Holdings, Inc. 01/31/2014
Each share Common 1¢ par exchanged for $4.05 cash

FLOW LABORATORIES, INC. (MD)
Merged into Flow General Inc. 1/3/77
Each share Common 10¢ par exchanged for (1.1) shares Common 10¢ par
Flow General Inc. name changed to GRC International, Inc. 12/5/89
(See GRC International, Inc.)

FLOW LABS INC (DE)
Acquired by General Research Corp. (CA) 8/7/69
Each share Common 10¢ par exchanged for (0.44088) share Common 10¢ par
General Research Corp. (CA) reincorporated in Delaware 3/31/75 which name changed to Flow General Inc. 1/3/77 which name changed to GRC International, Inc. 12/5/89
(See GRC International, Inc.)

FLOW RES LTD (BC)
Delisted from Vancouver Stock Exchange 07/07/1989

FLOW SYS INC (DE)
Reincorporated 10/07/1983
State of incorporation changed from (WA) to (DE) 10/07/1983
Common 5¢ par changed to 1¢ par and (1) additional share issued 10/18/1983
Common 1¢ par split (3) for (2) by issuance of (0.5) additional share 03/22/1985
Common 1¢ par split (3) for (2) by issuance of (0.5) additional share 10/14/1985
Name changed to Flow International Corp. (DE) 03/08/1989
Flow International Corp. (DE) reincorporated in Washington 10/01/1998

FLOW TECH SOLUTIONS INC (NV)
Name changed to World Stevia Corp. 08/15/2013
World Stevia Corp. name changed to Cannabis Capital Corp. 03/04/2014 which name changed to Crown Baus Capital Corp. 07/25/2014

FLOW VENTURES LTD (NV)
Each share old Common $0.001 par exchanged for (0.00025) share new Common $0.001 par 5/5/95
Name changed to Voyager Group Inc. (Old) 7/21/95
Voyager Group Inc. (Old) name changed to Band, Ltd. 3/26/96
(See Band, Ltd.)

FLOWARE WIRELESS SYS LTD (ISRAEL)
Issue Information - 4,500,000 shares

ORD offered at $13 per share on 08/01/2001
Merged into Alvarion Ltd. 08/01/2001
Each share Ordinary ILS 0.01 par exchanged for (0.767) share Ordinary ILS 0.01 par

FLOWER AFFAIRS SYS CORP (AB)
Recapitalized as Canadian Rocky Mountain Properties Inc. (AB) 12/12/2000
Each share Common no par exchanged for (0.2) share Common no par
Canadian Rocky Mountain Properties Inc. (AB) reincorporated in Canada 07/00/2002
(See Canadian Rocky Mountain Properties Inc.)

FLOWER CITY INDUSTRIES, INC. (VIRGIN ISLANDS)
Completely liquidated 8/28/64
Each share Common 1¢ par exchanged for (0.06) share Revlon, Inc. Common $1 par and $0.42 cash
(See Revlon, Inc.)

FLOWER FASHIONS INC (NV)
Reorganized under the laws of Delaware as International Cogeneration Corp. 08/08/1985
Each (42.62) shares Common no par exchanged for (1) share Common 1¢ par
International Cogeneration Corp. name changed to ICC Technologies, Inc. 07/15/1989 which name changed to Rare Medium Group, Inc. 03/16/1999 which name changed to SkyTerra Communications, Inc. 09/26/2003
(See SkyTerra Communications, Inc.)

FLOWER TIME INC (NY)
Stock Dividends - 100% 07/31/1976; 100% 12/15/1979
Merged into General Host Corp. 03/02/1984
Each share Common 10¢ par exchanged for $11 cash

FLOWER VALET (NV)
Name changed to Seaside Exploration, Inc. 12/31/2004
Seaside Exploration, Inc. name changed to Sky Petroleum, Inc. 04/06/2005

FLOWERMAN GROUP INC (ON)
Recapitalized as Nova Growth Corp. 02/12/1996
Each share Common no par exchanged for (0.25) share Common no par
(See Nova Growth Corp.)

FLOWERS INDS INC. (GA)
Reincorporated 12/07/1987
Class A Common $1 par, Class B-1 Common $1 par and Class B-2 Common $1 par changed to 62-1/2¢ par and (0.6) additional share issued respectively 05/15/1969
Each share Class B-1 Common 62-1/2¢ par or Class B-2 Common 62-1/2¢ par exchanged for (1) share Class A Common 62-1/2¢ par 10/07/1970
Class A Common 62-1/2¢ par reclassified as Common 62-1/2¢ par 01/23/1975
Common 62-1/2¢ par split (3) for (2) by issuance of (0.5) additional share 05/20/1977
Common 62-1/2¢ par split (3) for (2) by issuance of (0.5) additional share 08/31/1978
Common 62-1/2¢ par split (3) for (2) by issuance of (0.5) additional share 06/02/1982
Common 62-1/2¢ par split (3) for (2) by issuance of (0.5) additional share 03/31/1983
Common 62-1/2¢ par split (3) for (2) by issuance of (0.5) additional share 10/17/1984
Common 62-1/2¢ par split (3) for (2)
by issuance of (0.5) additional share 11/27/1987
State of incorporation changed from (DE) to (GA) 12/07/1987
Common 62-1/2¢ par split (3) for (2) by issuance of (0.5) additional share 11/17/1995
Common 62-1/2¢ par split (3) for (2) by issuance of (0.5) additional share payable 05/02/1997 to holders of record 04/18/1997 Ex date - 05/05/1997
Secondary Offering - 9,000,000 shares COM offered at $22 per share on 04/21/1998
Each share Common 62-1/2¢ par received distribution of (0.2) share Flowers Foods, Inc. Common 1¢ par payable 04/04/2001 to holders of record 03/26/2001
Merged into Kellogg Co. 03/26/2001
Each share Common 62-1/2¢ par exchanged for $12.50 cash

FLOWING ENERGY CORP (AB)
Merged into Daylight Energy Trust 04/05/2005
Each share Common no par exchanged for (0.07434944) Trust Unit no par
Note: Canadian holders had the option to receive (0.07434944) Daylight Energy Ltd. Exchangeable Share no par
(See Daylight Energy Trust)

FLOWLINE CORP (PA)
Merged into Markovitz Enterprises, Inc. 12/05/1983
Details not available

FLOWMETER CORP. OF AMERICA (NY)
Charter cancelled and proclaimed dissolved for failure to pay taxes 12/15/72

FLOWMOLE CORP (DE)
Name changed to UtiLx Corp. 4/25/91
(See UtiLx Corp.)

FLOWTECH ENERGY CORP (AB)
Name changed to Canadian Chemical Reclaiming Ltd. 06/14/1995
Canadian Chemical Reclaiming Ltd. name changed to CCR Technologies Ltd. 01/21/2000
(See CCR Technologies Ltd.)

FLOWTRON INDS INC (DE)
Stock Dividend - 100% 11/10/72
Merged into Maione-Hirschberg Companies, Inc. 11/24/87
Each share Common 10¢ par exchanged for (0.25) share Common no par
Maione-Hirschberg Companies, Inc. name changed to Maione Companies, Inc. 9/14/88
(See Maione Companies, Inc.)

FLOYD BENNETT STORES, INC. (NY)
Name changed to 300 Sunrise, Inc. 10/4/65
300 Sunrise, Inc. liquidated for Spencer Shoe Corp. which name changed to Spencer Companies, Inc. 9/22/70 which was acquired by Baker (J.), Inc. 4/15/89 which name changed to Casual Male Corp. 2/26/2001
(See Casual Male Corp.)

FLOYD ENTERPRISES INC (FL)
Common $1 par changed to 66-2/3¢ par and (0.5) additional share issued 06/15/1971
Merged into Burnup & Sims Inc. 05/02/1978
Each share Common 66-2/3¢ par exchanged for $15.75 cash

FLOYD INDUSTRIES, INC. (VA)
Charter cancelled and proclaimed dissolved for failure to file reports 9/1/86

FLOYD VALLEY PACKING CO (IA)
Common $5 par reclassified as old Class A Common no par 1/11/71

Each share old Class A Common no par exchanged for (0.001) share new Class A Common no par 12/20/94
Each share old Class B Common no par exchanged for (0.001) share new Class B Common no par 12/20/94
Note: In effect each share Class A Common no par or Class B Common no par exchanged for $0.50 cash and majority interest was eliminated
Completely liquidated 12/17/97
Each share new Class A Common no par exchanged for first and final distribution of $465.64 cash

FLS HLDGS INC (FL)
Acquired by Kyoei Steel Ltd. 12/21/92
Each share 17.50% Exchangeable Preferred Ser. A 1¢ par exchanged for $18.128 cash

FLUGAL FINL SVCS LTD (CANADA)
Name changed to Wierig International Inc. 9/22/2003
Wierig International Inc. recapitalized as SpecOpS Labs Inc. 3/5/2004 which recapitalized as Link Linux Inc. 3/10/2006

FLUID CTLS INC (OH)
Common no par split (5) for (4) by issuance of (0.25) additional share 12/11/78
Merged into Sta-Rite Industries, Inc. 4/1/80
Each share Common no par exchanged for $37 cash

FLUID DYNAMICS, INC. (NY)
Through purchase offer 100% acquired by Brunswick Corp. as of 09/30/1971
Public interest eliminated

FLUID LIFT INTL INC (DE)
Recapitalized as Odessa Foods International, Inc. 01/23/1995
Each share Common 1¢ par exchanged for (0.01470588) share Common 1¢ par
(See Odessa Foods International, Inc.)

FLUID MUSIC CDA INC (CANADA)
Name changed to Mood Media Corp. 07/12/2010
(See Mood Media Corp.)

FLUID POWER PRODUCTS, INC. (CA)
Merged into Fluidgenics 2/28/61
Each share Common $1 par exchanged for (0.094) share Common no par
(See Fluidgenics)

FLUID PWR PUMP CO (DE)
Recapitalized 9/15/81
Each share Common no par exchanged for (1) share Common 10¢ par 10/15/74
Recapitalized as Fluid Corp. 9/15/81
Each share Common 10¢ par exchanged for (0.1) share Common $1 par
Company believed out of business in 1988

FLUID SOLUTIONS INC (NV)
Name changed to Gold Standard Mining Corp. 07/29/2009
Gold Standard Mining Corp. name changed to J.D. Hutt Corp. 11/01/2012 which name changed to Code Green Apparel Corp. 09/09/2015

FLUIDGENICS (CA)
Charter suspended for failure to file reports and pay fees 10/01/1970

FLUIDIC INDS INC (DE)
Name changed to Cooper Energy Inc. 3/11/81
Cooper Energy Inc. name changed to Cooper Resources & Energy, Inc. 8/24/81

(See Cooper Resources & Energy, Inc.)

FLUKE CORP (WA)
Name changed 08/12/1993
Common $1 par changed to 50¢ par and (1) additional share issued 10/23/1961
Common 50¢ par changed to 25¢ par and (1) additional share issued 07/30/1976
Stock Dividend - 100% 03/30/1979
Common 25¢ par split (2) for (1) by issuance of (1) additional share payable 10/15/1997 to holders of record 09/26/1997 Ex date - 10/16/1997
Merged into Danaher Corp. 07/09/1998
Each share Common 25¢ par exchanged for (0.90478) share Common 1¢ par

FLUKONG ENTERPRISE INC (AB)
Recapitalized as Intensity Co. Inc. 02/01/2010
Each share Common no par exchanged for (0.1) share Common no par
Intensity Co. Inc. name changed to LX Ventures Inc. 12/07/2012 which name changed to Mobio Technologies Inc. 07/07/2014

FLUOR CORP OLD (DE)
Reincorporated 07/14/1978
$5.50 Conv. Preferred Ser. A no par called for redemption 01/18/1972
Common $0.625 par split (3) for (2) by issuance of (0.5) additional share 03/11/1974
State of incorporation changed from (CA) to (DE) 07/14/1978
$3 Conv. Preferred Ser. B no par called for redemption 01/18/1980
Common $0.625 par split (3) for (2) by issuance of (0.5) additional share 08/13/1979
Common $0.625 par split (2) for (1) by issuance of (1) additional share 07/18/1980
Name changed to Massey Energy Co. 11/30/2000
Massey Energy Co. merged into Alpha Natural Resources, Inc. 06/01/2011
(See Alpha Natural Resources, Inc.)

FLUOR DANIEL / GTI INC (DE)
Merged into IT Group, Inc. 12/3/98
Each share Common $0.001 par exchanged for $8.25 cash

FLUOR LTD (CA)
Capital Stock $2.50 par changed to $1.25 par and (1) additional share issued 04/18/1966
Capital Stock $1.25 par reclassified as Common $1.25 par 01/06/1967
Common $1.25 par changed to $0.625 par and (1) additional share issued 04/15/1968
Stock Dividend - 20% 08/23/1957
Name changed to Fluor Corp. (CA) 05/22/1969
Fluor Corp. (CA) reincorporated in Delaware 07/14/1978 which name changed to Massey Energy Co. 11/30/2000 which merged into Alpha Natural Resources, Inc. 06/01/2011
(See Alpha Natural Resources, Inc.)

FLUOROCARBON CO (CA)
Common 40¢ par split (2) for (1) by issuance of (1) additional share 5/2/77
Common 40¢ par changed to 20¢ par and (1) additional share issued 10/31/78
Common 20¢ par changed to no par and (0.5) additional share issued 12/31/80
Common no par split (3) for (2) by issuance of (0.5) additional share 7/15/88
Stock Dividend - 50% 4/15/74
Name changed to Furon Co. 1/31/90

(See Furon Co.)

FLUOROSCAN IMAGING SYS INC (DE)
Issue Information - 1,000,000 Units consisting of (1) share COM and (1) WT offered at $7 per Unit on 07/11/1994
Merged into Hologic, Inc. 8/29/96
Each share Common $0.0001 par exchanged for (0.31069) share Common $0.0001 par

FLUORSPAR CORP. OF AMERICA (NV)
Charter revoked for failure to file reports and pay fees 3/4/63

FLURIDA GROUP INC (NV)
Each share old Common $0.001 par exchanged for (0.000002) share new Common $0.001 par 01/18/2018
Note: In effect holders received $0.20 cash per share and public interest was eliminated

FLUSHING NATL BK (FLUSHING, NY)
Name changed to National Bank of New York City (Flushing, NY) 1/1/82
(See National Bank of New York City (Flushing, NY))

FLUX TECHNOLOGIES CORP (NV)
Common $0.001 par split (33.333) for (1) by issuance of (32.333) additional shares payable 01/25/2013 to holders of record 01/22/2013 Ex date - 01/28/2013
Name changed to Brazil Minerals, Inc. 02/01/2013

FLXIBLE CO (OH)
Class B Common Ser. 1 $1 par reclassified as Common $1 par 01/01/1966
Class B Common Ser. 2 $1 par reclassified as Common $1 par 01/01/1967
Class B Common Ser. 3 $1 par reclassified as Common $1 par 01/01/1968
Class B Common Ser. 4 $1 par reclassified as Common $1 par 01/01/1969
Merged into Rohr Corp. 09/15/1970
Each share 7% Class A Preferred $100 par exchanged for (4.722) shares $1.08 Conv. Preferred Ser. A $1 par
Each share 5% Class B Preferred $100 par exchanged for (4.533) shares $1.08 Conv. Preferred Ser. A $1 par
Each share Common no par exchanged for (0.5) share $1.08 Conv. Preferred Ser. A $1 par and (0.385) share Common $1 par
Rohr Corp. name changed to Rohr Industries, Inc. 11/12/1971 which name changed to Rohr, Inc. 12/13/1991 which merged into Goodrich (B.F.) Co. 12/22/1997 which name changed to Goodrich Corp. 06/01/2001
(See Goodrich Corp.)

FLY CLEAN INC (NV)
Company believed out of business 00/00/1987
Details not available

FLY NETWORKS INC (NV)
Name changed to InterCommerceCorp 12/15/2003
InterCommerceCorp recapitalized as CipherPass Corp. 06/06/2005 which recapitalized as Javalon Technology Group, Inc. (NV) 09/06/2007 which reincorporated in British Virgin Islands as WorldVest Equity, Inc. 11/13/2008

FLYCAST COMMUNICATIONS CORP (DE)
Issue Information - 3,000,000 shares COM offered at $25 per share on 05/04/1999

Merged into CMGI Inc. 01/14/2000
Each share Common $0.0001 par exchanged for (0.9476) share Common 1¢ par
CMGI Inc. name changed to ModusLink Global Solutions, Inc. 09/30/2008

FLYER RES LTD (BC)
Recapitalized as International Flyer Resources Ltd. 05/14/1984
Each share Common no par exchanged for (0.25) share Common no par
International Flyer Resources Ltd. name changed to Spectair Industries Inc. 07/30/1987 which recapitalized as International Spectair Resources Inc. 12/01/1989 which name changed to Camden Oil Corp. 11/05/1991 which name changed to Maxwell Resources Inc. 12/02/1992 which name changed to Maxwell Energy Corp. (BC) 05/12/1993 which reincorporated in Alberta 09/12/1996 which recapitalized as Maxwell Oil & Gas Ltd. 11/18/1996
(See Maxwell Oil & Gas Ltd.)

FLYFAIRE INTL INC (DE)
Charter cancelled and declared inoperative and void for non-payment of taxes 03/01/1989

FLYI INC (CA)
Plan of reorganization under Chapter 11 Federal Bankruptcy Code effective 3/30/2007
No stockholders' equity

FLYING CROSS RES LTD (ON)
Reorganized 12/04/1985
Reorganized from Flying Cross Petroleum Corp. to Flying Cross Resources Ltd. 12/04/1985
Each share Capital Stock $1 par exchanged for (0.375) share Common no par
Merged into International Larder Minerals Inc. 05/01/1986
Each share Common no par exchanged for (1) share Common no par
International Larder Minerals Inc. merged into Explorers Alliance Corp. 10/13/2000
(See Explorers Alliance Corp.)

FLYING DIAMOND CORP (UT)
Merged into Flying Diamond Oil Corp. 12/4/74
Each share Capital Stock $1 par exchanged for (0.5) share Common $1 par
(See Flying Diamond Oil Corp.)

FLYING DIAMOND LAND & MINERAL CORP. (UT)
Name changed to Flying Diamond Corp. 10/26/71
Flying Diamond Corp. merged into Flying Diamond Oil Corp. 12/4/74
(See Flying Diamond Oil Corp.)

FLYING DIAMOND OIL CORP (UT)
Merged into Newco Industries Corp. 5/31/78
Each share Common $1 par exchanged for $30 cash

FLYING DISC ENTMT INC (ON)
Name changed to Software Gaming Corp. 03/20/1998
Software Gaming Corp. recapitalized as Xperia Corp. 11/09/2001 which recapitalized as Xgen Ventures Inc. 11/26/2004
(See Xgen Ventures Inc.)

FLYING L SKYTEL (WY)
Charter revoked for failure to pay taxes 03/08/1995

FLYING MACH INTL INC (UT)
Recapitalized as Ucan Corp. (UT) 08/13/1996
Each share Common $0.001 par exchanged for (0.025) share Common $0.001 par
Ucan Corp. (UT) reincorporated in

Florida as Madison Systems, Inc. 10/28/1997

FLYING MONKEY CAP CORP (BC)
Recapitalized as Fabled Copper Corp. 09/27/2018
Each share Common no par exchanged for (0.33333333) share Common no par

FLYING SERVICE OF NEW YORK CITY AIRPORT, INC.
Dissolved in 1931
Details not available

FLYING TIGER CORP (DE)
Common $1 par split (3) for (2) by issuance of (0.5) additional share 2/25/72
$1.20 Conv. Preferred $1 par called for redemption 3/1/73
Name changed to Tiger International, Inc. 7/1/74
(See Tiger International, Inc.)

FLYING TIGER LINE INC (DE)
5% Preferred Ser. A $10 par called for redemption 11/7/66
Old Common $1 par split (2) for (1) by issuance of (1) additional share 3/17/67
Under plan of reorganization name changed to Flying Tiger Corp. 6/30/70
Flying Tiger Corp. name changed to Tiger International, Inc. 7/1/74
(See Tiger International, Inc.)
Merged into FTL Merger Co. 5/25/88
Each share new Common $1 par exchanged for $28 cash

FLYING W AWYS INC (PA)
Adjudicated bankrupt 07/06/1972
Stockholders' equity unlikely

FLYNN-BAR MINES LTD. (ON)
Name changed 01/00/1951
Name changed from Flynn-Bar Gold Mines Ltd. to Flynn-Bar Mines Ltd. 01/00/1951
Charter surrendered 03/03/1960

FLYNN ENERGY CORP (DE)
Merged into Reserve Oil & Gas Co. 12/13/78
Each share Common 10¢ par exchanged for (0.5) Common Stock Purchase Warrant Class D expiring 12/12/83 plus one of the following: $10.15 cash or $9.90 principal amount of 8-1/2% Unsecured Ser. A Promissory Notes and $0.25 cash or $10.15 principal amount of 8-1/2% Unsecured Ser. B Promissory Notes
Note: Options to receive Ser. A Notes and $0.25 cash or Ser. B Notes expired 1/22/79

FM PPTYS INC (DE)
Name changed to Stratus Properties Inc. 5/18/98

FM RES CORP (BC)
Name changed to Strikewell Energy Corp. 09/01/2006

FMC CORP (DE)
3-3/4% Preferred $100 par called for redemption 03/16/1962
3-1/4% Preferred $100 par called for redemption 08/20/1962
$2.25 Conv. Preferred no par called for redemption 05/20/1986
(Additional Information in Active)

FMC GOLD CO (DE)
Merged into Meridian Gold Inc. 07/31/1996
Each share Common 1¢ par exchanged for (1) share Common no par and $0.02 cash
Meridian Gold Inc. merged into Yamana Gold Inc. 12/31/2007

FMC TECHNOLOGIES INC (DE)
Common 1¢ par split (2) for (1) by issuance of (1) additional share payable 08/31/2007 to holders of record 08/17/2007 Ex date - 09/04/2007
Each share Common 1¢ par received distribution of (0.216) share John Bean Technologies Corp. Common 1¢ par payable 07/31/2008 to holders of record 07/22/2008 Ex date - 08/01/2008
Common 1¢ par split (2) for (1) by issuance of (1) additional share payable 03/31/2011 to holders of record 03/14/2011 Ex date - 04/01/2011
Merged into TechnipFMC PLC 01/17/2017
Each share Common 1¢ par exchanged for (1) share Ordinary $1 par

FMG ACQUISITION CORP (DE)
Issue Information - 4,500,000 UNITS consisting of (1) share COM and (1) WT offered at $8 per Unit on 10/04/2007
Name changed to United Insurance Holdings Corp. 09/30/2008

FMG TELECOMPUTER LTD (CANADA)
Common no par split (2) for (1) by issuance of (1) additional share 01/16/1985
Name changed to SOK Properties Ltd. 07/04/1989
SOK Properties Ltd. name changed to Impact Telemedia International Ltd. 08/03/1990 which name changed to UC'NWIN Systems Ltd. (Canada) 07/17/1992 which reincorporated in Delaware as UC'NWIN Systems Corp. 12/11/1995 which recapitalized as Winner's Edge.com, Inc. 10/29/1999 which name changed to Sealant Solutions Inc. 08/06/2001 which name changed to PowerChannel, Inc. 07/28/2003 which recapitalized as Qualibou Energy Inc. 02/05/2008

FMI FINL CORP (FL)
Name changed to Great American Communications Co. (Old) 10/12/87
Great American Communications Co. (Old) reorganized as Great American Communications Co. (New) 12/28/93 which name changed to Citicasters Inc. 6/8/94
(See Citicasters Inc.)

FMI HLDGS LTD (BC)
Completely liquidated
Each share Common no par received first and final distribution of $0.5833 cash payable 01/30/2012 to holders of record 01/18/2012
Note: Certificates were not required to be surrendered and are without value

FMIC CORP (NC)
Name changed to United Guaranty Corp. 12/30/1974
United Guaranty Corp. merged into American International Group, Inc. 10/01/1981

FML EQUITY INCOME FD INC (DE)
Under plan of merger name changed to Combined Shares, Inc. 05/22/1974
Combined Shares, Inc. acquired by Massachusetts Investors Trust 06/05/1975

FML GROWTH FUND, INC. (DE)
Merged into Combined Shares, Inc. 5/22/74
Each share Common $1 par exchanged for (0.6817) share Common $1 par
Combined Shares, Inc. acquired by Massachusetts Investors Trust 6/5/75

FMM CO., INC. (NY)
Completed liquidation
Each share Common 10¢ par exchanged for initial distribution of $14.17 cash 1/18/65
Each share Common 10¢ par received second and final distribution of $0.50 cash 7/2/65

FMS FINL CORP (NJ)
Common 10¢ par split (2) for (1) by issuance of (1) additional share 01/12/1996
Common 10¢ par split (3) for (1) by issuance of (2) additional shares payable 07/14/1998 to holders of record 07/01/1998
Merged into Beneficial Mutual Bancorp, Inc. 07/13/2007
Each share Common 10¢ par exchanged for $28 cash

FMS MGMT SYS INC (MD)
Stock Dividend - 100% 09/07/1978
Reacquired 08/12/1983
Each share Common 25¢ par exchanged for $1.50 cash

FMSA HLDGS INC (DE)
Name changed to Fairmount Santrol Holdings Inc. 07/20/2015
Fairmount Santrol Holdings Inc. merged into Covia Holdings Corp. 06/01/2018

FMX VENTURES INC (ON)
Each share old Common no par exchanged for (0.1) share new Common no par 11/09/2009
Recapitalized as Tolima Gold Inc. 12/12/2011
Each share new Common no par exchanged for (0.5) share Common no par

FN FINL CORP (DE)
Name changed to First Nationwide Financial Corp. 07/11/1983
(See First Nationwide Financial Corp.)

FN NETWORK TAX FREE MONEY MKT FD INC (MD)
Completely liquidated 04/18/1994
Each share Common $0.001 par exchanged for first and final distribution of $1 cash

FNB BANCORP (CA)
Common no par split (3) for (2) by issuance of (0.5) additional share payable 05/26/2017 to holders of record 05/05/2017 Ex date - 05/30/2017
Stock Dividends - 5% payable 12/13/2002 to holders of record 11/29/2002 Ex date - 12/04/2002; 5% payable 12/15/2003 to holders of record 11/28/2003 Ex date - 11/25/2003; 5% payable 12/15/2004 to holders of record 12/01/2004 Ex date - 11/29/2004; 5% payable 12/16/2005 to holders of record 11/30/2005 Ex date - 11/28/2005; 5% payable 12/15/2006 to holders of record 12/01/2006 Ex date - 11/29/2006; 5% payable 12/14/2007 to holders of record 11/30/2007 Ex date - 12/07/2007; 5% payable 12/15/2008 to holders of record 11/28/2008 Ex date - 11/25/2008; 5% payable 12/15/2009 to holders of record 11/30/2009 Ex date - 11/25/2009; 5% payable 12/20/2010 to holders of record 12/03/2010 Ex date - 12/01/2010; 5% payable 12/27/2011 to holders of record 12/12/2011 Ex date - 12/08/2011; 5% payable 12/28/2012 to holders of record 12/14/2012 Ex date - 12/12/2012; 5% payable 12/23/2013 to holders of record 12/02/2013 Ex date - 11/27/2013; 5% payable 01/16/2015 to holders of record 12/15/2014 Ex date - 12/11/2014; 5% payable 12/28/2015 to holders of record 11/25/2015 Ex date - 11/23/2015; 5% payable 12/30/2016 to holders of record 11/30/2016 Ex date - 11/28/2016
Merged into TriCo Bancshares 07/06/2018
Each share Common no par exchanged for (0.98) share Common no par

FNB BANCORP INC (MI)
Completely liquidated 2/27/87
Each share Common $10 par exchanged for first and final distribution of (2.5223) shares Banc One Corp. Common no par
Banc One Corp. merged into Bank One Corp. 10/2/98 which merged into J.P. Morgan Chase & Co. 12/31/2000 which name changed to JPMorgan Chase & Co. 7/20/2004

FNB BANCSHARES INC (SC)
Stock Dividend - 5% payable 04/25/2003 to holders of record 04/11/2003
Merged into American Community Bancshares Inc. 04/21/2004
Each share Common 1¢ par exchanged for $22.64 cash

FNB BANKSHARES (ME)
Common $4 par changed to 80¢ par and (4) additional shares issued 05/10/1994
Common 80¢ par split (3) for (1) by issuance of (2) additional shares payable 04/02/2004 to holders of record 03/22/2004 Ex date - 04/05/2004
Stock Dividend - 5% payable 04/19/2002 to holders of record 04/05/2002 Ex date - 04/03/2002
Merged into First National Lincoln Corp. 01/14/2005
Each share Common 80¢ par exchanged for (2.35) shares Common no par
First National Lincoln Corp. name changed to First Bancorp, Inc. 05/02/2008

FNB BKG CO (GA)
Voluntarily dissolved 12/31/2004
Details not available

FNB DEV CORP (TX)
Name changed to Midland Southwest Corp. 04/05/1977
(See Midland Southwest Corp.)

FNB FINL CORP (MI)
Merged into Southern Michigan Bancorp, Inc. 12/01/2007
Each share Common $1 par exchanged either for (1.87) shares Common $2.50 par, $45.35 or a combination thereof

FNB FINL CORP (OH)
Merged into First Citizens Banc Corp. 10/12/2004
Each share Common $10 par exchanged for (2.0174) shares Common no par and $16.56 cash
First Citizens Banc Corp. name changed to Civista Bancshares, Inc. 05/04/2015

FNB FINL CORP (PA)
Common 63¢ par changed to $0.315 par and (1) additional share issued payable 09/01/2000 to holders of record 09/01/2000
Merged into Tower Bancorp, Inc. 06/01/2006
Each share Common $0.315 par exchanged for (0.8663) share Common $2.50 par
(See Tower Bancorp, Inc.)

FNB FINL SVCS CORP (NC)
Common $1 par split (5) for (4) by issuance of (0.25) additional share payable 03/29/1996 to holders of record 03/08/1996
Common $1 par split (4) for (3) by issuance of (0.33333333) additional share payable 04/30/1997 to holders of record 04/23/1997
Common $1 par split (4) for (3) by issuance of (0.33333333) additional share payable 09/12/1997 to holders of record 09/05/1997
Common $1 par split (5) for (4) by issuance of (0.25) additional share payable 12/26/2003 to holders of record 12/12/2003 Ex date - 12/29/2003
Common $1 par split (5) for (4) by issuance of (0.25) additional share

payable 05/31/2005 to holders of record 05/12/2005 Ex date - 06/01/2005
Merged into NewBridge Bancorp 07/31/2007
Each share Common $1 par exchanged for (1.07) shares Common $5 par
NewBridge Bancorp merged into Yadkin Financial Corp. 03/01/2016 which merged into F.N.B. Corp. 03/11/2017

FNB ROCHESTER CORP (NY)
Merged into M&T Bank Corp. 06/01/1999
Each share Common $1 par exchanged for either (0.06766) share Common $5 par or $33 cash
Note: Electors for stock received 48.10514% of total holdings in stock and the remaining 51.89486% in cash
Option to elect stock expired 05/24/1999

FNB UTD CORP (NC)
Name changed 04/28/2006
Common $2.50 par split (2) for (1) by issuance of (1) additional share payable 03/18/1998 to holders of record 03/04/1998
Stock Dividend - 50% 05/26/1995
Under plan of merger name changed from FNB Corp. to FNB United Corp. 04/28/2006
Each share Common $2.50 par exchanged for (0.01) share Common no par 11/01/2011
Name changed to CommunityOne Bancorp 07/01/2013
CommunityOne Bancorp merged into Capital Bank Financial Corp. 10/26/2016

FNBG BANCSHARES INC (GA)
Merged into GB&T Bancshares, Inc. 03/01/2005
Each share Common $1 par exchanged for either (1.38) shares Common no par or $30 cash
Note: Option to receive cash expired 03/31/2005
GB&T Bancshares, Inc. merged into SunTrust Banks, Inc. 05/01/2008

FNBM FINL CORP (PA)
Merged into GNB Financial Services, Inc. 03/27/2015
Each share Common $5 par exchanged for (3.3448) shares Common $5 par and $82.57 cash

FNBPA BANCORP INC (PA)
Merged into Juniata Valley Financial Corp. 11/30/2015
Each share Common $25 par exchanged for (2.7813) shares Common $1 par

FNC BANCORP INC (GA)
Merged into FNC S-Corp. 12/31/2001
Each share Common $1 par exchanged for $21 cash

FNC RLTY CORP (DE)
Acquired by Kimco Realty Services, Inc. 04/02/2013
Each share Common no par exchanged for $0.73 cash

FNF INDS INC (OH)
Merged into FNF Construction, Inc. 6/6/2006
Each share Common no par exchanged for $0.40 cash

FNH CORP (PA)
Merged into Promistar Financial Corp. 8/14/2001
Each share Common $1 par exchanged for (15) shares Common $5 par
Promistar Financial Corp. merged into F.N.B. Corp. (FL) 1/18/2002

FNI FASHION NETWORK INC (BC)
Recapitalized as Gala-Bari International Inc. 03/22/1994
Each share Common no par exchanged for (0.2) share Common no par
(See Gala-Bari International Inc.)

FNI INC (NY)
Merged into New Century Productions, Ltd. 3/11/85
Each share Common 10¢ par exchanged for (1.15) shares Conv. Preferred Ser. A $0.001 par
New Century Productions, Ltd. name changed to New Century Entertainment Corp. 7/3/86 which name changed to New Visions Entertainment Corp. 8/8/88
(See New Visions Entertainment Corp.)

FNT BANCORP INC (PA)
Common $10 par split (2) for (1) by issuance of (1) additional share 02/22/1985
Merged into Susquehanna Bancshares, Inc. 10/01/1985
Each share Common $10 par exchanged for (0.7) share Common $5 par
Susquehanna Bancshares, Inc. merged into BB&T Corp. 08/01/2015

FNW BANCORP INC (DE)
Common no par split (2) for (1) by issuance of (1) additional share 6/1/87
Common no par split (3) for (2) by issuance of (0.5) additional share 12/28/88
Common no par split (2) for (1) by issuance of (1) additional share 9/15/90
Merged into NBD Bancorp, Inc. 10/1/91
Each share Common no par exchanged for (0.384) share Common $1 par
NBD Bancorp, Inc. name changed to First Chicago NBD Corp. 12/1/95 which merged into Bank One Corp. 10/2/98 which merged into J.P. Morgan Chase & Co. 12/31/2000 which name changed to JPMorgan Chase & Co. 7/20/2004

FNX MNG CO INC (ON)
Merged into Quadra FNX Mining Ltd. 05/27/2010
Each share Common no par exchanged for (0.87) share Common no par and $0.0001 cash
Note: Unexchanged certificates were cancelled and became without value 05/27/2016
(See Quadra FNX Mining Ltd.)

FOA INDS INC (DE)
Name changed to America's Coffee Cup, Inc. 6/19/89
America's Coffee Cup, Inc. name changed to Midland Inc. 2/17/97
(See Midland Inc.)

FOAM-ETTES, INC. (CA)
Charter suspended for failure to pay taxes 05/01/1967

FOAMAT FOODS CORP (OR)
Adjudicated bankrupt 12/1/75
No stockholders' equity

FOAMEX INTL INC (DE)
Each share old Common 1¢ par exchanged for (0.25) share new Common 1¢ par 05/01/2007
Chapter 11 bankruptcy proceedings dismissed 01/20/2010
No stockholders' equity

FOAMITE CHILDS CORP.
Acquired by American-La France & Foamite Corp. 00/00/1927
Details not available

FOAMLAND USA INC (NY)
Merged into Daryl Industries, Inc. 06/15/1971
Each share Common 25¢ par exchanged for (1) share Common 50¢ par
(See Daryl Industries, Inc.)

FOCAL COMMUNICATIONS CORP (DE)
Each share old Common 1¢ par exchanged for (0.02857142) share new Common 1¢ par 03/11/2002
Plan of reorganization under Chapter 11 Federal Bankruptcy Code effective 07/01/2003
No stockholders' equity

FOCAL CORP (UT)
Name changed to Indigenous Global Development Corp. 07/02/2002
(See Indigenous Global Development Corp.)

FOCAL INC (DE)
Issue Information - 2,500,000 shares COM offered at $10 per share on 12/11/1997
Merged into Genzyme Corp. 07/02/2001
Each share Common 1¢ par exchanged for (0.1545) share Common-Biosurgery Division 1¢ par
(See Genzyme Corp.)

FOCAL RES LTD (AB)
Recapitalized as Verdx Minerals Corp. 03/24/2000
Each share Common no par exchanged for (0.2) share Common no par
(See Verdx Minerals Corp.)

FOCAL SURGERY INC (DE)
Name changed to Focus Surgery, Inc. 6/15/94
Focus Surgery, Inc. reorganized as Menlo Acquisition Corp. 1/13/99
(See Menlo Acquisition Corp.)

FOCCINI INTL INC (CANADA)
Name changed to Arch Biopartners Inc. 05/07/2010

FOCH CONSUMER ELECTRS CORP (BC)
Recapitalized as Hawkeye Gold Corp. 1/22/96
Each share Common no par exchanged for (0.2) share Common no par
Hawkeye Gold Corp. recapitalized as Hawkeye Gold International Inc. 12/17/98 which recapitalized as Hawkeye Gold & Diamond Inc. 5/29/2003

FOCUS AFFILIATES INC (DE)
Common 1¢ par changed to $0.001 par 03/16/2007
Recapitalized as Auric Mining Co. 11/12/2009
Each share Common $0.001 par exchanged for (0.001) share Common $0.001 par
Auric Mining Co. recapitalized as Enterra Corp. (Old) 12/18/2013 which name changed to VinCompass Corp. 04/27/2015 which name changed to Enterra Corp. (New) 11/13/2015

FOCUS BUSINESS BK (SAN JOSE, CA)
Stock Dividend - 5% payable 09/27/2013 to holders of record 09/12/2013 Ex date - 09/10/2013
Merged into Heritage Commerce Corp. 08/21/2015
Each share Common no par exchanged for (1.8235) shares Common no par

FOCUS ENERGY TR (AB)
Merged into Enerplus Resources Fund 02/13/2008
Each Trust Unit no par exchanged for (0.425) Trust Unit Ser. G no par
Enerplus Resources Fund reorganized as Enerplus Corp. 01/03/2011

FOCUS ENHANCEMENTS INC (DE)
Plan of reorganization under Chapter 11 Federal Bankruptcy Code effective 05/11/2009
No stockholders' equity

FOCUS ENTMT INTL INC (FL)
Each share old Common $0.001 par exchanged for (0.2) share new Common $0.001 par 07/31/1997
Recapitalized as American Restaurant Holdings, Inc. 06/03/2013
Each share new Common $0.001 par exchanged for (0.02) share Common $0.001 par

FOCUS LTD PARTNERSHIP (AB)
Name changed to Enerplus Exchangeable L.P. 02/13/2008
Enerplus Exchangeable L.P. reorganized as Enerplus Corp. 01/03/2011

FOCUS MEDIA HLDG LTD (CAYMAN ISLANDS)
Issue Information - 10,100,000 Sponsored ADR's offered at $17 per ADR on 07/13/2005
Sponsored ADR's for Ordinary split (2) for (1) by issuance of (1) additional ADR payable 04/10/2007 to holders of record 04/05/2007 Ex date - 04/11/2007
ADR basis changed from (1:10) to (1:5) 04/10/2007
Acquired by Giovanna Parent Ltd. 05/23/2013
Each Sponsored ADR for Ordinary exchanged for $27.45 cash

FOCUS METALS INC (CANADA)
Name changed to Focus Graphite Inc. 05/25/2012

FOCUS NATL MTG CORP (ON)
Merged into Mutual Trust Co. 11/06/1992
Each share Common no par exchanged for $16 cash

FOCUS RES LTD (BC)
Merged into Bluesky Oil & Gas Ltd. (BC) 12/08/1979
Each share Common no par exchanged for (1.817) shares Common no par
Bluesky Oil & Gas Ltd. (BC) reincorporated in Alberta 10/27/1980 which recapitalized as Mark Resources Inc. 11/13/1986 which was acquired by EnerMark Income Fund 04/09/1996 which merged into Enerplus Resources Fund 06/22/2001 which reorganized as Enerplus Corp. 01/03/2011

FOCUS SURGERY INC (DE)
Reorganized under Chapter 11 Federal Bankruptcy Code as Menlo Acquisition Corp. 1/13/99
Each share Common 1¢ par exchanged for (0.01) share Common 1¢ par
(See Menlo Acquisition Corp.)

FOCUS V INC (CO)
Recapitalized as Work Recovery, Inc. (CO) 02/12/1990
Each share Common $0.0001 par exchanged for (0.025) share Common $0.004 par
Work Recovery, Inc. (CO) reorganized under the laws of Delaware 02/11/1997 which recapitalized as Jinhua Marine Biological (USA), Inc. 08/31/2005

FOCUS VENTURES LTD (BC)
Reorganized under the laws of Yukon as CROPS Inc. 04/23/2018
Each share Common no par exchanged for (0.25) share Common no par

FOCUSED CAP CORP (ON)
Recapitalized as Orford Mining Corp. 10/27/2017
Each share Common no par exchanged for (0.42735042) share Common no par

FOCUSED CAP II CORP (ON)
Reorganized under the laws of British Columbia as Fortress Blockchain Corp. 08/22/2018
Each share Common no par

exchanged for (0.30761942) share Common no par

FOCUSED 40 INCOME FD (ON)
Under plan of merger each Unit automatically became IA Clarington Tactical Income Fund Ser. X Units on a net asset basis 06/26/2009

FOCUSED GLOBAL TRENDS FD (ON)
Name changed to Connor, Clark & Lunn Financial Opportunities Fund 10/05/2011
Connor, Clark & Lunn Financial Opportunities Fund merged into Australian Banc Income Fund 06/11/2013 which name changed to Purpose Global Financials Income Fund 06/18/2018

FOCUSSHARES TR (DE)
Trust terminated 10/30/2008
Each share FocusShares ISE-CCM Homeland Security Index Fund no par received $33.75574 cash
Each share FocusShares ISE Homebuilders Index Fund no par received $34.43324 cash
Each share FocusShares ISE SINdex Fund no par received $24.67396 cash
Each share ISE-REVERE Wal-Mart Supplier Index Fund received $37.82554 cash
Trust terminated 08/31/2012
Each share Morningstar Basic Materials Index ETF no par received $21.8960444 cash
Each share Morningstar Communication Services Index ETF no par received $29.5011181 cash
Each share Morningstar Consumer Cyclical Index ETF no par received $28.9941912 cash
Each share Morningstar Consumer Defensive Index ETF no par received $30.04445765 cash
Each share Morningstar Energy Index ETF no par received $23.32672465 cash
Each share Morningstar Financial Services Index ETF no par received $23.47604433 cash
Each share Morningstar Health Care Index ETF no par received $29.66447265 cash
Each share Morningstar Industrials Index ETF no par received $25.0499778 cash
Each share Morningstar Large Cap Index ETF no par received $27.48495964 cash
Each share Morningstar Mid Cap Index ETF no par received $25.57853953 cash
Each share Morningstar Real Estate Index ETF no par received $28.40185013 cash
Each share Morningstar Small Cap Index ETF no par received $25.161438 cash
Each share Morningstar Technology Index ETF no par received $28.34898985 cash
Each share Morningstar U.S. Market Index ETF no par received $26.96542584 cash
Each share Morningstar Utilities Index ETF no par received $29.219462 cash

FOGDOG INC (DE)
Issue Information - 6,000,000 shares COM offered at $11 per share on 12/08/1999
Acquired by Global Sports, Inc. 12/28/2000
Each share Common $0.001 par exchanged for (0.135) share Common 1¢ par
Global Sports, Inc. name changed to GSI Commerce, Inc. 05/24/2002
(See GSI Commerce, Inc.)

FOGO DE CHAO INC (DE)
Acquired by Prime Cut Intermediate Holdings Inc. 04/05/2018
Each share Common 1¢ par exchanged for $15.75 cash

FOHS OIL CO.
Acquired by Texas Gulf Producing Co. on a (0.75) for (1) basis in 1946
(See Texas Gulf Producing Co.)

FOILMARK INC (DE)
Merged into Illinois Tool Works Inc. 05/22/2001
Each share Common 1¢ par exchanged for $6.36 cash

FOILS PACKAGING CORP. (OH)
Charter revoked for failure to file reports and pay fees 8/15/64

FOKKER AIRCRAFT CORP. OF AMERICA (DE)
Incorporated 12/3/27
Name changed to General Aviation Corp. in 1930
(See General Aviation Corp.)

FOLEY SILVER MINES LTD (BC)
Struck off register and declared dissolved for failure to file returns 06/12/1978

FOLIAGE PLUS INC (CO)
Charter suspended for failure to file annual reports 11/01/1993

FOLIO ONE PRODTNS LTD (DE)
Name changed to Ceron Resources Corp. 02/06/1981
Ceron Resources Corp. merged into Wasatch Pharmaceutical Inc. 01/24/1996
(See Wasatch Pharmaceutical Inc.)

FOLIX TECHNOLOGIES INC (NV)
Name changed to Dragon Gold Resources, Inc. 06/14/2004
Dragon Gold Resources, Inc. recapitalized as Edgeline Holdings, Inc. 07/23/2007 which name changed to Oncolin Therapeutics, Inc. 03/24/2008 which recapitalized as Bering Exploration, Inc. 10/14/2010 which name changed to Breitling Energy Corp. 01/22/2014

FOLKESTONE RES LTD (BC)
Recapitalized as Schmitt Industries, Inc. (BC) 04/27/1987
Each share Common no par exchanged for (1/3) share Common no par
Schmitt Industries, Inc. (BC) reincorporated in Oregon 02/16/1996

FOLKS RESTAURANTS INC (GA)
Name changed to FRI Corp. 03/23/1987
FRI Corp. name change to Georgia 400 Industries, Inc. 01/02/1992
(See Georgia 400 Industries, Inc.)

FOLLANSBEE BROTHERS CO.
Reorganized as Follansbee Steel Corp. 00/00/1940
Each share Preferred exchanged for (2.5) shares new Common $10 par
Each share Common exchanged for (0.25) share new Common $10 par
Follansbee Steel Corp. name changed to Union Chemical & Matatterials Corp. 00/00/1954 which merged into Vulcan Materials Co. 12/31/1957

FOLLANSBEE RED LAKE GOLD MINES LTD (ON)
Recapitalized as Alton Corp. 02/27/1984
Each share Common $1 par exchanged for (0.1) share Common no par
Alton Corp. merged into Interquest Resources Corp. 06/13/1985 which name changed to Interquest Technologies Inc. 10/23/1992 which recapitalized as Interquest Inc. 09/30/1995
(See Interquest Inc.)

FOLLANSBEE STEEL CORP. (DE)
Each share 5% Preferred $100 par exchanged for $80 principal amount of 4-1/2% Income Debentures and (2) shares Common $10 par in 1946
Name changed to Union Chemical & Materials Corp. in 1954
Union Chemical & Materials Corp. merged into Vulcan Materials Co. 12/31/57

FOLSOM LAKE BK (FOLSOM, CA)
Merged into Central Valley Community Bancorp 10/01/2017
Each share Common no par exchanged for (0.8) share Common no par

FOLTIS-FISCHER, INC.
Bankrupt in 1934
Details not available

FOMENTO ECONOMICO MEXICANO S A DE C V NEW (MEXICO)
Name changed to Fomento Economico Mexicano, S.A.B. de C.V. 12/7/2006

FOMENTO ECONOMICO MEXICANO S A DE C V OLD (MEXICO)
ADR agreement terminated 11/22/99
Each 144A Sponsored ADR for Ordinary exchanged for $4.28314 cash

FONA INC (NV)
Recapitalized as Evolutionary Genomics, Inc. 10/19/2015
Each share Common $0.001 par exchanged for (0.01642504) share Common $0.001 par

FONCIERE DES REGIONS (FRANCE)
Name changed to Covicio 09/28/2018

FONDA JOHNSTOWN & GLOVERSVILLE RR CO (NY)
Reorganized 06/01/1944
No stockholders' equity
Company became private 00/00/1980
Details not available

FONDEWA GOLD MINES LTD. (ON)
Charter revoked for failure to file reports and pay taxes 00/00/1968

FONDREN SOUTHWEST BANK (HOUSTON, TX)
Acquired by Texas American Bancshares Inc. 10/1/81
Each share Common $5 par exchanged for (1.875) shares Common $5 par
(See Texas American Bancshares Inc.)

FONDS MUTUEL CORP. DE PRET ET REVENU DU CANADA LTEE. (CANADA)
See - Savings & Investment Corp. Mutual Fund of Canada Ltd.

FONE AMER INC (NV)
Each share old Common $0.001 par exchanged for (0.1) share new Common $0.001 par 08/21/1989
Company terminated common stock registration and is no longer public as of 03/09/2007

FONECASH INC (DE)
Recapitalized as TotalMed, Inc. 05/12/2005
Each share Common $0.0001 par exchanged for (0.05) share Common $0.0001 par
TotalMed, Inc. name changed to eNotes Systems, Inc. 06/15/2006 which name changed to Veridigm, Inc. 12/07/2006 which recapitalized as Mobile Media Unlimited Holdings Inc. 02/02/2009 which recapitalized as EnableTS, Inc. 04/18/2011

FONEFRIEND INC (DE)
Name changed to InfiniCall Corp. 10/18/2004
(See InfiniCall Corp.)

FONIX CORP (DE)
Each (90) shares old Common $0.0001 par exchanged for (1) share new Common $0.0001 par 05/18/1994
Each share new Common $0.0001 par exchanged again for (0.025) share new Common $0.0001 par 04/04/2003
Each share new Common $0.0001 par exchanged again for (0.0002) share new Common $0.0001 par 12/26/2008
SEC revoked common stock registration 07/06/2012

FONOROLA INC (CANADA)
Acquired by Call-Net Enterprises Inc. 06/28/1998
Each share Common no par exchanged for either (2.68) shares Common no par and $0.02 cash or $67 cash
Call-Net Enterprises Inc. merged into Rogers Communications Inc. 07/01/2005

FONT EXPLORATIONS LTD. (BC)
Name changed to Mount Leyland Collieries, Ltd. 10/07/1961
(See Mount Leyland Collieries, Ltd.)

FONT PETROLEUMS LTD. (BC)
Recapitalized as Font Explorations Ltd. 11/12/1960
Each share Common no par exchanged for (0.2) share Common 50¢ par
Font Explorations Ltd. name changed to Mount Leyland Collieries, Ltd. 10/07/1961
(See Mount Leyland Collieries, Ltd.)

FONTAINE BROS INC (DE)
Reorganized as a private company 9/8/78
Details not available

FONTAINE CONVERTING WORKS, INC. (VA)
Automatically dissolved for non-payment of registration fees and franchise tax 6/2/59

FONTAINE TR (MA)
Trust terminated 07/13/1998
Details not available

FONTANA FIRST NATIONAL BANK (FONTANA, CA)
Merged into Chino Valley Bank (Ontario, CA) 3/8/93
Each share Common $5 par exchanged for $14.59 cash

FONTANA GOLD MINES LTD. (QC)
Recapitalized as Fontana Mines (1945) 00/00/1945
Each share Capital Stock exchanged for (0.5) share Capital Stock
(See Fontana Mines (1945) Ltd.)

FONTANA MINES 1945 LTD. (QC)
Charter surrendered 01/31/1947

FONTANA RES LTD (BC)
Name changed to Pac Ed Systems Corp. 08/28/1986
Pac Ed Systems Corp. name changed to Autobyte Systems Corp. 04/04/1991
(See Autobyte Systems Corp.)

FONTANA WATER CO.
Merged into Fontana Union Water Co. in 1928
Details not available

FONTENELLE BREWING CO.
Name changed to Metz Brewing Co. in 1939
Metz Brewing Co. name changed to Metz Industries, Inc. 7/9/62 which name changed to Continental Western Corp. 6/24/66
(See Continental Western Corp.)

FOOD & DRUG RESH LABS INC (NY)
Common 50¢ par changed to 25¢ par and (1) additional share issued 05/22/1969
Name changed to Environmental Protection System, Inc. and

Common 25¢ par changed to 1¢ par 09/04/1987
Environmental Protection System, Inc. name changed to Enviro/Analysis Corp. 09/16/1987
(See Enviro/Analysis Corp.)

FOOD CIRCUS SUPER MKTS INC
8% Preferred called for redemption at $27.50 on 1/31/2003

FOOD CONCEPTS INC (NV)
Each share old Common $0.0001 par exchanged for (0.05) share new Common $0.0001 par 11/3/97
Name changed to Viropro Inc. 4/1/98

FOOD CORP. OF AMERICA, INC. (MN)
Merged into Ward Foods, Inc. 3/8/68
Each share Common 10¢ par exchanged for (0.25) share Common $1 par
(See Ward Foods, Inc.)

FOOD CT ENTMT NETWORK INC (DE)
Plan of reorganization under Chapter 11 Federal Bankruptcy Code effective 5/18/99
Each share Ser. A Common 1¢ par exchanged for (0.03565062) share Moro Corp. Common $0.001 par

FOOD DEVICES, INC. (DE)
No longer in existence having become inoperative and void for non-payment of taxes 4/1/59

FOOD DIVIDEND CORP. OF AMERICA (UT)
Name changed to Inairco, Inc. 04/12/1967
Inairco, Inc. name changed to National Sweepstakes Corp. 02/16/1968
(See National Sweepstakes Corp.)

FOOD EXTRUSION INC (NV)
Reincorporated under the laws of Delaware as Ricex Co. 05/19/1998
Ricex Co. merged into NutraCea 10/04/2005 which name changed to RiceBran Technologies 10/26/2012

FOOD FACILITIES, INC. (CA)
Out of business 00/00/1953
Details not available

FOOD FAIR INC (PA)
Reorganized under the laws of Delaware as Pantry Pride, Inc. (Old) and each share $4.20 Preferred $15 par or Common $1 par automatically became (1) share $4.20 Preferred 1951 Ser. $15 par and Common $1 par respectively 7/6/81
Pantry Pride, Inc. (Old) merged into Pantry Pride, Inc. (New) 1/20/83 which name changed to Revlon Group Inc. 4/7/86
(See Revlon Group Inc.)

FOOD FAIR PPTYS INC (DE)
Name changed to Amterre Development Inc. 5/2/72
(See Amterre Development Inc.)

FOOD FAIR STORES INC (PA)
Each share Common $1 par exchanged for (4) shares Common no par in 1946
Common no par changed to $1 par in 1947
$2.50 Preferred called for redemption 2/19/51
Common $1 par split (5) for (4) by issuance of (0.25) additional share in 1954
Common $1 par split (3) for (2) by issuance of (0.5) additional share 8/15/58
Common $1 par split (5) for (4) by issuance of (0.25) additional share 8/14/61
Stock Dividend - 10% 10/31/50
Name changed to Food Fair, Inc. 12/1/76
Food Fair, Inc. reorganized in Delaware as Pantry Pride, Inc. (Old) 7/6/81 which merged into Pantry Pride, Inc. (New) 1/20/83 which name changed to Revlon Group Inc. 4/7/86
(See Revlon Group Inc.)

FOOD FORMULA ONE INC (MN)
Completely liquidated 12/17/90
Each share Common 20¢ par exchanged for first and final distribution of $0.265 cash

FOOD 4 LESS HLDGS INC (DE)
Merged into Meyer (Fred), Inc. (New) 3/10/98
Each share Preferred Ser. A 1¢ par exchanged for (0.59367366) share Common 1¢ par

FOOD GIANT MARKETS, INC. (NJ)
Common $1 par split (3) for (2) by issuance of (0.5) additional share 8/11/61
Merged into Vornado, Inc. (DE) 9/29/67
Each share 4% Preferred $10 par exchanged for (0.45) share Common 4¢ par
Each share Common $1 par exchanged for (0.6) share Common 4¢ par
Vornado, Inc. (DE) reorganized as Vornado Realty Trust (MD) 5/6/93

FOOD HOST U S A INC (NE)
Merged into Kramer Enterprises, Inc. 6/20/80
Each share Common $1 par exchanged for $0.04 cash

FOOD INDS INC (VA)
Assets assigned for the benefit of creditors 12/31/1974
No stockholders' equity
Note: Transfers terminated 00/00/1976

FOOD INTEGRATED TECHNOLOGIES INC (DE)
SEC revoked common stock registration 07/23/2010

FOOD LION INC (NC)
Common 50¢ par reclassified as Class B Common 50¢ par 09/21/1983
Each share Class B Common 50¢ par received distribution of (1) share Class A Common 50¢ par 10/06/1983
Class A Common 50¢ par split (3) for (1) by issuance of (2) additional shares 06/18/1986
Class B Common 50¢ par split (3) for (1) by issuance of (2) additional shares 06/18/1986
Class A Common 50¢ par split (2) for (1) by issuance of (1) additional share 10/29/1987
Class B Common 50¢ par split (2) for (1) by issuance of (1) additional share 10/29/1987
Class A Common 50¢ par split (3) for (2) by issuance of (0.5) additional share 06/08/1992
Class B Common 50¢ par split (3) for (2) by issuance of (0.5) additional share 06/08/1992
Recapitalized as Delhaize America, Inc. 09/09/1999
Each share Class A Common 50¢ par exchanged for (0.33333333) share Class A Common 50¢ par
Each share Class B Common 50¢ par exchanged for (0.33333333) share Class B Common 50¢ par
Delhaize America, Inc. merged into Etablissements Delhaize Freres et Cie Le Lion S.A. 04/25/2001 which merged into Koninklijke Ahold Delhaize N.V. 07/25/2016

FOOD MACHINERY CORP. (DE)
Common no par changed to $10 par and (1) additional share issued 11/18/35
Common $10 par split (2) for (1) by issuance of (1) additional share 1/6/48
Stock Dividend - 25% 6/8/45
Under plan of merger name changed to Food Machinery & Chemical Corp. 9/10/48 which name changed to FMC Corp. 6/30/61

FOOD MACHY & CHEM CORP (DE)
Common $10 par split (2) for (1) by issuance of (1) additional share 11/24/58
Name changed to FMC Corp. 6/30/61

FOOD MARKETING CORP. (IN)
Name changed to Executive Boulevard Corp. 10/16/1963
Executive Boulevard Corp. completed liquidation for Super Valu Stores, Inc. 05/22/1968
(See Super Valu Stores, Inc.)

FOOD MART, INC. (DE)
Common $2 par split (2) for (1) by issuance of (1) additional share 10/8/56
Acquired by Shop Rite Foods, Inc. 10/1/65
Each share Common $2 par exchanged for (0.5) share $2.04 Convertible Preferred $20.50 par
(See Shop Rite Foods, Inc.)

FOOD PRODS CORP (OH)
Reincorporated under the laws of South Carolina as Piemonte Foods, Inc. 10/17/1986
(See Piemonte Foods, Inc.)

FOOD RES INC (DE)
Each share Common 5¢ par exchanged for (0.01) share Common 5¢ par 08/28/1981
Charter cancelled and declared inoperative and void for non-payment of taxes 03/01/1992

FOOD SAFE INTL INC (NV)
Each share old Common 1¢ par exchanged for (0.01) share new Common 1¢ par 01/28/2004
Reorganized under the laws of Colorado as Produce Safety & Security International, Inc. 03/04/2005
Each share Common 1¢ par exchanged for (4) shares Common no par
Produce Safety & Security International, Inc. (CO) reincorporated in Nevada as Eco Green Team Inc. 01/29/2009 which name changed to Champion Investments, Inc. 06/28/2012

FOOD TECHNOLOGY SVC INC (FL)
Each share old Common 1¢ par exchanged for (0.25) share new Common 1¢ par 07/03/2006
Acquired by Sterigenics U.S., LLC 03/06/2014
Each share Common 1¢ par exchanged for $7.23 cash

FOOD TOWN, INC. (DE)
Under plan for reorganization 8% Subordinated Preferred $3 par acquired by Kroger Co. for cash 6/20/60
Holders of Common $1 par had no equity

FOOD TOWN STORES INC (NC)
Common $2.50 par changed to 50¢ par and (4) additional shares issued 02/27/1970
Common 50¢ par split (2) for (1) by issuance of (1) additional share 05/09/1972
Common 50¢ par split (3) for (1) by issuance of (2) additional shares 09/23/1976
Common 50¢ par split (3) for (1) by issuance of (2) additional shares 05/31/1979
Common 50¢ par split (3) for (1) by issuance of (2) additional shares 10/20/1982
Name changed to Food Lion, Inc. 04/21/1983
Food Lion, Inc. recapitalized as Delhaize America, Inc. 09/09/1999 which merged into Etablissements Delhaize Freres et Cie Le Lion S.A. 04/25/2001 which merged into Koninklijke Ahold Delhaize N.V. 07/25/2016

FOOD TRENDS ACQUISITION CORP (DE)
Issue Information - 2,500,000 UNITS consisting of (1) share COM and (2) WTS offered at $6 per Unit on 11/03/1994
Name changed to Silver Diner Development Inc. 03/27/1996
Silver Diner Development Inc. name changed to Silver Diner Inc. 06/25/1996
(See Silver Diner Inc.)

FOODARAMA SUPERMARKETS INC (NJ)
Merged into Saker Holdings Corp. 7/24/2006
Each share Common $1 par exchanged for $53 cash

FOODBRANDS AMER INC (DE)
Merged into IBP, Inc. 05/07/1997
Each share Common 1¢ par exchanged for $23.40 cash

FOODCORP LTD (ON)
Acquired by Cara Operations Ltd. 11/14/1978
Each share Common no par exchanged for $12.50 cash

FOODCRAFT INC (PA)
Merged into UM Acquisition Corp. 12/30/88
Each share Common $1.25 par exchanged for $17 cash

FOODEX INC (CANADA)
Merged into Dexleigh Corp. 06/30/1984
Each share Preference no par exchanged for (1.3) shares Common no par and (1.3) Common Stock Purchase Warrants expiring 12/31/1986
(See Dexleigh Corp.)

FOODEX SYS LTD (CANADA)
Common no par split (3) for (1) by issuance of (2) additional shares 12/15/1972
Merged into Foodex Inc. 06/30/1978
Each share Common no par exchanged for (1) share Preference no par
Foodex Inc. merged into Dexleigh Corp. 06/30/1984
(See Dexleigh Corp.)

FOODMAKER INC (DE)
Ctfs. dated prior to 10/1/70
Merged into Ralston Purina Co. 10/1/70
Each share Common $1 par exchanged for $28 cash

FOODMAKER INC NEW (DE)
Merged into FM Acquisition Corp. 12/8/88
Each share old Common 1¢ par exchanged for $19.425 cash
Name changed to Jack in the Box Inc. 10/4/99

FOODQUEST INC (FL)
Proclaimed dissolved for failure to file reports and pay fees 09/26/1997

FOODQUEST INTL CORP (ON)
Recapitalized 11/30/1994
Recapitalized from Foodquest Corp. to FoodQuest International Corp. 11/30/1994
Each share Common no par exchanged for (0.5) share Common no par
Recapitalized as Dealcheck.com Inc. 01/21/1999
Each share Common no par exchanged for (0.08333333) share Common no par
Dealcheck.com Inc. recapitalized as Bontan Corp. Inc. (ON) 04/17/2003

which reincorporated in British Virgin Islands as Portage Biotech Inc. 08/23/2013

FOODS FOR HEALTH, INC. (CA)
Name changed to Diketan Laboratories, Inc. in February 1958
Diketan Laboratories, Inc. recapitalized as Diketan Inc. 3/4/70 which name changed to Royal American Products Corp. 8/3/78

FOODS PLUS, INC. (DE)
Acquired by APL Corp. on a (0.7) for (1) basis 3/8/65
(See APL Corp.)

FOODVISION COM INC (DE)
Charter forfeited for failure to maintain a registered agent 07/05/2003

FOODWAYS NATL INC (NY)
Stock Dividends - 100% 12/8/76; 25% 8/31/77
Merged into Heinz (H.J.) Co. 6/30/78
Each share Common 25¢ par exchanged for $31 cash

FOOS GAS ENGINE CO.
Assets acquired by Fulton Iron Works Co. in 1928
Details not available

FOOTBALL EQUITIES INC (FL)
Administratively dissolved 09/24/2010

FOOTE & DAVIES, INC. (DE)
Liquidation completed 5/31/63

FOOTE BROTHERS GEAR & MACHINE CO.
Reorganized as Foote Brothers Gear & Machine Corp. in 1936
No stockholders' equity

FOOTE BROTHERS GEAR & MACHINE CORP. (DE)
Each share Common $2 par exchanged for (1) share Class A $5 par and (1) share Class B $5 par 5/8/59
5-3/4% Preferred called for redemption 7/31/59
Stock Dividend - 50% 11/15/51
Merged into Hewitt-Robins, Inc. 9/28/62
Each share Class A $5 par exchanged for (1) share Class A Preferred $10 par
Each share Class B $5 par exchanged for (1/3) share Common $5 par
Hewitt-Robins, Inc. merged into Litton Industries, Inc. 2/24/65
(See Litton Industries, Inc.)

FOOTE-BURT CO. (OH)
Each share Common no par exchanged for (2) shares Common $5 par in 1954
Merged into Curtis Noll Corp. 11/30/65
Each share Common $5 par exchanged for $17 cash

FOOTE BURT MACHINE CO.
Merged into Foote-Burt Co. 00/00/1927
Details not available

FOOTE CONE & BELDING COMMUNICATIONS INC (DE)
Common 33-1/3¢ par split (2) for (1) by issuance of (1) additional share 4/1/88
Name changed to True North Communications, Inc. 12/19/94
True North Communications, Inc. merged into Interpublic Group of Companies, Inc. 6/22/2001

FOOTE CONE & BELDING INC (DE)
Common 33-1/3¢ par split (5) for (4) by issuance of (0.25) additional share 10/30/64
Name changed to Foote, Cone & Belding Communications, Inc. 12/31/69
Foote, Cone & Belding Communications, Inc. name changed to True North Communications, Inc. 12/19/94 which merged into Interpublic Group of Companies, Inc. 6/22/2001

FOOTE MINERAL CO (PA)
Common $2.50 par changed to $1 par and (2) additional shares issued 00/00/1954
$5 Preferred $100 par called for redemption 11/30/1957
Stock Dividends - 100% 04/15/1949; 300% 03/05/1951; 250% 12/16/1974
Merged into Cyprus Minerals Co. 04/13/1988
Each share $2.20 Conv. Preferred $1 par exchanged for $36.153327 cash
Each share Common $1 par exchanged for $10.325922 cash

FOOTHILL COMMUNITY BANK, N.A. (BROWNSVILLE, CA)
Name changed to Gold Country National Bank (Brownsville, CA) 05/17/1993
Gold Country National Bank (Brownsville, CA) name and location changed to Gold Country Bank, N.A. (Marysville, CA) 06/15/2001 which merged into Golden Pacific Bancorp, Inc. 05/03/2010

FOOTHILL GEN CORP (DE)
Name changed to Century General Corp. 6/5/72
(See Century General Corp.)

FOOTHILL GROUP INC (DE)
Reincorporated 06/11/1987
Each share old Common no par exchanged for (0.4) share new Common no par 03/19/1973
New Common no par split (5) for (4) by issuance of (0.25) additional share 05/15/1980
New Common no par reclassified as Class A Common no par 10/08/1980
Class A Common no par split (4) for (3) by issuance of (1/3) additional share 06/12/1981
Class A Common no par split (4) for (3) by issuance of (1/3) additional share 04/12/1982
State of incorporation changed from (CA) to (DE) 06/11/1987
Merged into Norwest Corp. 10/19/1995
Each share Class A Common no par exchanged for (0.92) share Common $1-2/3 par
Norwest Corp. name changed to Wells Fargo & Co. (New) 11/02/1998

FOOTHILL INDEPENDENT BANK (GLENDORA, CA)
Common $10 par changed to no par 00/00/1981
Under plan of reorganization each share Common no par automatically became (1) share Foothill Independent Bancorp (CA) Common no par 11/18/1983
Foothill Independent Bancorp (CA) reincorporated in Delaware 07/18/2000 which merged into First Community Bancorp (CA) 05/10/2006 which reincorporated in Delaware as PacWest Bancorp 05/14/2008

FOOTHILL INDPT BANCORP (DE)
Reincorporated 07/18/2000
State of incorporation changed from (CA) to (DE) 07/18/2000
Common no par split (5) for (4) by issuance of (0.25) additional share payable 05/25/2005 to holders of record 05/10/2005 Ex date - 05/26/2005
Stock Dividends - 10% 05/01/1995; 10% payable 04/05/1996 to holders of record 03/22/1996; 10% payable 06/20/1997 to holders of record 06/06/1997; 15% payable 07/07/1998 to holders of record 06/15/1998; 7% payable 05/29/2001 to holders of record 05/04/2001; 9% payable 01/29/2003 to holders of record 01/08/2003 Ex date - 01/06/2003; 9% payable 01/29/2004 to holders of record 01/08/2004 Ex date - 01/06/2004
Merged into First Community Bancorp (CA) 05/10/2006
Each share Common no par exchanged for (0.4523) share Common no par
First Community Bancorp (CA) reincorporated in Delaware as PacWest Bancorp 05/14/2008

FOOTHILL NATIONAL BANK (GLENDORA, CA)
Name changed to Foothill Independent Bank (Glendora, CA) 07/01/1979
Foothill Independent Bank (Glendora, CA) reorganized as Foothill Independent Bancorp (CA) 11/18/1983 which reincorporated in Delaware 07/18/2000 which merged into First Community Bancorp (CA) 05/10/2006 which reincorporated in Delaware as PacWest Bancorp 05/14/2008

FOOTHILLS CAP INC (CO)
Reorganized under the laws of Nevada as Allied Matrix Corp. 08/21/1997
Each share Common no par exchanged for (0.1058201) share Common no par
(See Allied Matrix Corp.)

FOOTHILLS INDL ESTATES LTD (BC)
Struck off register and declared dissolved for failure to file returns 1/17/77

FOOTHILLS NEWSPAPERS INC (AB)
Name changed to Skylink Communications Inc. 05/01/1991
(See Skylink Communications Inc.)

FOOTHILLS OIL & GAS LTD (AB)
Recapitalized as Midnight Oil & Gas Ltd. 02/10/2003
Each share Common no par exchanged for (0.05555555) share Common no par
(See Midnight Oil & Gas Ltd.)

FOOTHILLS RES INC (NV)
Plan of reorganization under Chapter 11 Federal Bankruptcy Code effective 02/22/2010
Each share Common $0.001 par received initial distribution of $0.004653 cash
Each share Common $0.001 par received second distribution of $0.00343887 cash payable 04/12/2013 to holders of record 02/22/2010
Each share Common $0.001 par received third distribution of $0.00594722 cash payable 07/30/2013 to holders of record 02/22/2010
Each share Common $0.001 par received fourth and final distribution of $0.00040208 cash payable 07/10/2014 to holders of record 02/22/2010

FOOTMAXX HLDGS INC (ON)
Each share old Common no par exchanged for (0.2) share new Common no par 09/05/1996
Name changed to FMX Ventures Inc. 12/07/2007
FMX Ventures Inc. recapitalized as Tolima Gold Inc. 12/12/2011

FOOTSOURCE INC (AB)
Delisted from NEX 12/13/2006

FOOTSTAR INC (DE)
Plan of reorganization under Chapter 11 Federal Bankruptcy Code effective 02/07/2006
Each share old Common 1¢ par exchanged for (1) share new Common 1¢ par
Liquidation completed
Each share new Common 1¢ par received initial distribution of $2 cash payable 05/06/2009 to holders of record 04/30/2009 Ex date - 05/07/2009
Each share new Common 1¢ par received second distribution of $0.40 cash payable 09/10/2009 to holders of record 08/28/2009 Ex date - 09/11/2009
Each share new Common 1¢ par received third distribution of $0.35 cash payable 12/16/2009 to holders of record 12/11/2009 Ex date - 12/17/2009
Each share new Common 1¢ par received fourth distribution of $0.10 cash payable 03/12/2010 to holders of record 03/08/2010 Ex date - 03/19/2010
Each share new Common 1¢ par received fifth distribution of $0.05 cash payable 10/07/2010 to holders of record 10/04/2010 Ex date - 09/30/2010
Each share new Common 1¢ par received sixth and final distribution of (1) share Xstelos Holdings, Inc. Common $0.001 par payable 04/26/2012 to holders of record 04/23/2012
Note: Certificates were not required to be surrendered and are without value

FOOTWALL EXPLS LTD (BC)
Recapitalized as Planet Ventures Inc. (BC) 04/08/1999
Each share Common no par exchanged for (0.1) share Common no par
Planet Ventures Inc. (BC) reincorporated in Alberta as Antares Minerals Inc. 11/25/2004 which merged into First Quantum Minerals Ltd. 12/20/2010

FOR BETTER LIVING INC (DE)
Acquired by Echo Rock Ventures 07/00/1999
Each share Common 5¢ par exchanged for approximately $6.58 cash

FORAN MINES LTD. (QC)
Declared dissolved for failure to file reports and pay fees 00/00/1960

FORAN MNG CORP (SK)
Reincorporated 11/13/2007
Place of incorporation changed from (BC) to (SK) 11/13/2007
Each share old Common no par exchanged for (0.25) share new Common no par 07/06/2010
Reincorporated back under the laws of British Columbia 05/28/2014

FORASOL FORAMER N V (NETHERLANDS)
Completely liquidated 03/03/1997
Each share Common NLG1 par exchanged for first and final distribution of (0.66) share Pride Petroleum Services, Inc. and $3.93 cash
Pride Petroleum Services, Inc. name changed to Pride International, Inc. (LA) 06/27/1997 which merged into Pride International, Inc. (DE) 09/13/2001 which merged into Ensco PLC 06/01/2011

FORATEK INTL INC (QC)
Name changed to F.K.I. International Inc. 09/29/1997

FORBES & MANHATTAN COAL INC (ON)
Name changed to Buffalo Coal Corp. 07/21/2014

FORBES & WALLACE INC (MA)
Assets disposed of 00/00/1980
No stockholders' equity

FORBES ADVERTISING CO (NY)
Assets sold for benefit of creditors 07/23/1974
No stockholders' equity

FORBES ENERGY SVCS LTD (BERMUDA)
Reorganized under the laws of Texas 08/16/2011
Each share Common 1¢ par exchanged for (0.25) share Common 4¢ par
(See Forbes Energy Services Ltd. (TX))

FORBES ENERGY SVCS LTD (TX)
Plan of reorganization under Chapter 11 Federal Bankruptcy proceedings effective 04/13/2017
No stockholders' equity

FORBES MEDI-TECH INC NEW (BC)
Name changed to FMI Holdings Ltd. 04/05/2011
(See FMI Holdings Ltd.)

FORBES MEDI-TECH INC OLD (CANADA)
Reincorporated 04/11/2001
Place of incorporation changed from (BC) to (Canada) 04/11/2001
Reorganized under the laws of British Columbia 02/27/2008
Each share Common no par exchanged for (0.125) share Common no par
Forbes Medi-Tech Inc. (BC) name changed to FMI Holdings Ltd. 04/05/2011
(See FMI Holdings Ltd.)

FORBES RES LTD (BC)
Name changed to Forbes Medi-Tech Inc. (BC) 07/09/1992
Forbes Medi-Tech Inc. (BC) reincorporated in Canada 04/11/2001 which reorganized back in British Columbia 02/27/2008 which name changed to FMI Holdings Ltd. 04/05/2011
(See FMI Holdings Ltd.)

FORBES YELLOWKNIFE GOLD MINES LTD. (ON)
Charter cancelled and company dissolved for default in filing returns in 1955

FORBIDDEN CITY HLDGS INC (NV)
Name changed to Life Industries Inc. 05/26/1995
Life Industries Inc. recapitalized as Quill Industries Inc. 09/19/1997 which recapitalized as Ostrich Products of America, Inc. 06/01/2005 which name changed to PayPro, Inc. 07/11/2005 which name changed to Panamersa Corp. 02/16/2007 which recapitalized as Eagle Worldwide Inc. 01/12/2012

FORCE AIR TECHNOLOGY INC (CA)
Company believed out of business 00/00/1988
Details not available

FORCE CRAG MINES LTD. (ON)
Merged into New Force Crag Mines Ltd. 11/22/1974
Each share Capital Stock $1 par exchanged for (0.22222222) share Common no par
(See New Force Crag Mines Ltd.)

FORCE ENERGY CORP (NV)
Recapitalized as Force Minerals Corp. 06/28/2013
Each share Common no par exchanged for (0.01) share Common no par

FORCE FOUR INC (NV)
Each share old Common $0.0001 par exchanged for (0.04) share new Common $0.0001 par 8/15/86
Each share new Common $0.0001 par exchanged for (0.0625) share Common $0.0025 par 2/7/92
Name changed to Indo Pacific International Corp. 8/3/92
Indo Pacific International Corp. recapitalized as Jurassic Energy U.S.A., Inc. 12/15/95

FORCE FUELS INC (NV)
Name changed to Cafe Serendipity Holdings, Inc. 03/13/2015

FORCE PROTN INC (CO)
Reorganized 02/04/2005
Reorganized from (CO) to under the laws of Nevada 02/04/2005
Each (12) shares Common no par exchanged for (1) share Common $0.001 par
Acquired by General Dynamics Corp. 12/20/2011
Each share Common $0.001 par exchanged for $5.52 cash

FORCE TECHNOLOGIES INC (BC)
Recapitalized 12/05/1994
Recapitalized from Force Resources Ltd. to Force Technologies, Inc. 12/05/1994
Each share Common no par exchanged for (0.2) share Common no par
Reorganized as Glassmaster Industries Inc. 11/03/1997
Each share Common no par exchanged for (2) shares Common no par
Glassmaster Industries Inc. recapitalized as Interlink Systems Inc. 01/19/2000 which recapitalized as iQuest Networks Inc. (BC) 08/14/2000 which reorganized in Wyoming as Quest Ventures Inc. 10/28/2003 which recapitalized as Dorato Resources Inc. (WY) 04/24/2006 which reincorporated in British Columbia 08/21/2006 which recapitalized as Xiana Mining Inc. 10/23/2013

FORCE 10 TRADING INC (NV)
Recapitalized as F10 Oil & Gas Properties, Inc. 12/03/2002
Each (300) shares Common $0.001 par exchanged for (1) share Common $0.001 par
F10 Oil & Gas Properties, Inc. name changed to GFY Foods, Inc. 01/12/2004 which recapitalized as Upturn, Inc. 03/20/2009 which recapitalized as Cityside Tickets Inc. 12/10/2009 which name changed to Causeway Entertainment Co. 10/11/2010 which recapitalized as United Bullion Exchange Inc. 05/10/2011

FORCELOGIX TECHNOLOGIES INC (BC)
Name changed to Courtland Capital Inc. (BC) 03/21/2011
Courtland Capital Inc. (BC) reorganized in Canada as Tree of Knowledge International Corp. 07/09/2018

FORCENERGY INC (DE)
Name changed 05/28/1996
Name changed from Forcenergy Gas Exploration, Inc. to Forcenergy Inc. 05/28/1996
Each share old Common 10¢ par exchanged for approximately (0.0386862) share new Common 10¢ par, (0.0096715) Common Stock Purchase Warrant expiring 2/15/2004, and (0.0096715) Common Stock Purchase Warrant expiring 02/15/2005
Note: Unexchanged certificates were cancelled and became without value 01/19/2001
Merged into Forest Oil Corp. 12/07/2000
Each share Preferred exchanged for (34.30705) shares new Common 10¢ par
Each share new Common 1¢ par exchanged for (0.8) share new Common 10¢ par
Forest Oil Corp. name changed to Sabine Oil & Gas Corp. 01/13/2015
(See Sabine Oil & Gas Corp.)

FORCETEK HLDGS INC (FL)
Recapitalized as Pole Tech International, Inc. 02/04/1998
Each share Common $0.001 par exchanged for (0.1) share Common $0.001 par
Pole Tech International, Inc. name changed to International Construction Products Inc. 08/07/1998 which recapitalized as Construction Products International, Inc. 03/30/1999 which recapitalized as Sports Pouch Beverage Co., Inc. 10/06/2004

FORCITE INC. (NY)
Adjudicated bankrupt 6/20/67
No stockholders' equity

FORD BK GROUP INC (TX)
Merged into First United Bank Group, Inc. 03/26/1993
Each share Common 40¢ par exchanged for (1.7) shares Common $1 par
First United Bank Group, Inc. merged into Norwest Corp. 01/14/1994 which name changed to Wells Fargo & Co. (New) 11/02/1998

FORD CITY BANK & TRUST CO. (CHICAGO, IL)
Name changed 05/13/1977
Common $10 par changed to $5 par and (1) additional share issued plus a 50% stock dividend paid 08/26/1972
Name changed from Ford City Bank (Chicago, IL) to Ford City Bank & Trust Co. (Chicago, IL) 05/13/1977
Acquired by Taylor Capital Group, Inc. 00/00/1984
Details not available

FORD ELECTRONICS CORP. (CA)
Bankrupt 8/1/63
No stockholders' equity

FORD FDG GROUP LTD (NV)
Name changed to Panther Entertainment Inc. 2/12/92

FORD HLDGS INC (DE)
Merged into Ford Holdings Capital Corp. 12/31/95
Each Depositary Preferred Ser. A exchanged for $25 cash
Each share 8% Preferred Ser. A $1 par exchanged for $25 cash
Each Depositary Preferred Ser. B exchanged for $25 cash
Each share Ser. B Preferred $1 par exchanged for $25 cash
Each $1.78 Depositary Preferred Ser. C exchanged for $25 cash
Each share $1.78 Preferred Ser. C $1 par exchanged for $25 cash
Each share Flexible Auction Rate Preferred Ser. A $1 par exchanged for $100,000 cash
Each share Flexible Auction Rate Preferred Ser. B $1 par exchanged for $100,000 cash
Each share Flexible Auction Rate Preferred Ser. C $1 par exchanged for $100,000 cash
Each share Flexible Auction Rate Preferred Ser. D $1 par exchanged for $100,000 cash
Each share Flexible Auction Rate Preferred Ser. E $1 par exchanged for $100,000 cash
Each share Flexible Auction Rate Preferred Ser. F $1 par exchanged for $100,000 cash
Each share Flexible Auction Rate Preferred Ser. G $1 par exchanged for $100,000 cash
Each share Flexible Auction Rate Preferred Ser. H $1 par exchanged for $100,000 cash
Each share Flexible Auction Rate Preferred Ser. I $1 par exchanged for $100,000 cash
Each share Flexible Auction Rate Preferred Ser. J $1 par exchanged for $100,000 cash
Each share Flexible Auction Rate Preferred Ser. K $1 par exchanged for $100,000 cash
Each share Flexible Auction Rate Preferred Ser. L $1 par exchanged for $100,000 cash
Each share Flexible Auction Rate Preferred Ser. M $1 par exchanged for $100,000 cash
Each share Flexible Auction Rate Preferred Ser. N $1 par exchanged for $100,000 cash
Each share Flexible Auction Rate Preferred Ser. O $1 par exchanged for $100,000 cash
Each share Flexible Auction Rate Preferred Ser. P $1 par exchanged for $100,000 cash

FORD MOTOR CO. LTD. (ENGLAND)
Each ADR for Ordinary received (1) additional share 00/00/1953
ADR's for 4-1/2% Preference 16s par called for redemption 07/31/1961
Stock Dividend - 100% 05/27/1955
Acquired by Ford Motor Co. 07/19/1961
Each ADR for Ordinary £1 par exchanged for $19.90 cash

FORD MTR CO CAP TR I (DE)
9% Trust Originated Preferred Securities called for redemption at $25 on 1/2/2004

FORD MTR CO CAP TR II (DE)
6.50% Conv. Trust Preferred Securities called for redemption at $50.33 plus $0.541667 accrued dividends on 03/15/2011

FORD MTR CO (DE)
Common $5 par changed to $2.50 par and (1) additional share issued 07/06/1962
Common $2.50 par changed to $2 par and (0.25) additional share issued 06/24/1977
Common $2 par split (3) for (2) by issuance of (0.5) additional share 12/01/1983
Common $2 par split (3) for (2) by issuance of (0.5) additional share 06/02/1986
Common $2 par split (2) for (1) by issuance of (1) additional share 01/12/1988
Common $2 par split (2) for (1) by issuance of (1) additional share 07/05/1994
Depositary Preferred Ser. A called for redemption at $51.68 on 01/09/1998
Conv. Preferred Ser. A $1 par called for redemption at $51,680 on 01/09/1998
Common $2 par changed to $1 par and (1) additional share issued 01/12/1988
Each share Common $1 par received distribution of (0.262085) share Associates First Capital Corp. Class A Common 1¢ par payable 04/07/1998 to holders of record 03/12/1998
Each share 8.25% Depositary Preferred Ser. B $1 par received distribution of (0.262085) share Associates First Capital Corp. Class A Common 1¢ par payable 04/07/1998 to holders of record 03/12/1998
Each share Common $1 par received distribution of (0.130933) share Visteon Corp. Common no par payable 06/28/2000 to holders of record 06/12/2000 Ex date - 06/29/2000
Plan of recapitalization effective 08/02/2000
Each share Common $1 par exchanged for (1) share Common 1¢ par and either additional Common valued at $20, a combination of stock and cash valued at $20, or $20 cash

Note: Non-electing holders received cash only
8.25% Depositary Preferred Ser. B called for redemption at $25 on 12/01/2002
(Additional Information in Active)

FORD MTR CO CDA LTD (CANADA)
Merged into Ford Motor Co. 10/01/1995
Each share Common no par exchanged for $185 cash

FORD OIL & DEV INC (UT)
Involuntarily dissolved 03/01/1988

FORD SOCIETE ANONYME FRANCAISE (FORD OF FRANCE) (FRANCE)
Merged into Societe Industrielle de Mecanique Carrosserie Automobile 5/3/55
Each ADR for Capital Stock 100 Fcs. par exchanged for (0.086956) American Share $7.14 par
Societe Industrielle de Mecanique Carrosserie Automobile name changed to Simca, S.A. 3/24/59 which reorganized as Simca Automobiles and Simca Industries 5/5/61
(See each company's listing)

FORD-SPOLETI HLDGS INC (NV)
Name changed to Eagle Oil Holding Co., Inc. 07/20/2009

FORD-TRACTOR CO., INC. (DE)
Charter cancelled and declared inoperative and void for non-payment of taxes 01/17/1921

FORDING CDN COAL TR (AB)
Reincorporated 05/02/2006
Trust Units split (3) for (1) by issuance of (2) additional Units payable 09/12/2005 to holders of record 09/02/2005 Ex date - 09/13/2005
Place of incorporation changed from (Canada) to (AB) 05/02/2006
Acquired by Teck Cominco Ltd. 10/30/2008
Each Trust Unit exchanged for (0.245) Class B Subordinate no par and USD$82 cash
Note: Unexchanged certificates were cancelled and became without value 10/30/2014

FORDING INC (CANADA)
Recapitalized as Fording Canadian Coal Trust (Canada) 02/28/2003
Each share Common no par exchanged for (1) Trust Unit
Note: Holders of (20) or fewer shares received $33.33 cash per share
Fording Canadian Coal Trust (Canada) reincorporated in Alberta 05/02/2006 which was acquired by Teck Cominco Ltd. 10/30/2008

FORE SYS INC (DE)
Issue Information - 3,000,000 shares COM offered at $16 per share on 05/23/1994
Common 1¢ par split (2) for (1) by issuance of (1) additional share 2/15/95
Common 1¢ par split (2) for (1) by issuance of (1) additional share payable 6/3/96 to holders of record 5/20/96
Merged into General Electric Co., P.L.C. (New) 6/17/99
Each share Common 1¢ par exchanged for $35 cash

FORECLOSED RLTY EXCHANGE INC (DE)
Name changed to Physical Spa & Fitness, Inc. 10/21/96
Physical Spa & Fitness, Inc. name changed to Physical Property Holdings, Inc. 3/13/2007

FORECLOSURE SOLUTIONS INC (TX)
Name changed to CannaVEST Corp. (TX) 03/28/2013

CannaVEST Corp. (TX) reincorporated in Delaware 08/13/2013 which name changed to CV Sciences, Inc. 06/08/2016

FORECROSS CORP (CA)
Company terminated common stock registration and is no longer public as of 11/30/2004

FOREFRONT GROUP INC (DE)
Merged into CBT Group PLC 05/29/1998
Each share Common 1¢ par exchanged for (0.3137) new Sponsored ADR for Ordinary
CBT Group PLC name changed to SmartForce PLC 02/15/2000 which name changed to SkillSoft PLC 11/19/2002
(See SkillSoft PLC)

FOREFRONT HLDGS INC (FL)
Each share old Common $0.001 par exchanged for (0.2) share new Common $0.001 par 05/28/2008
Administratively dissolved 11/17/2009

FOREFRONT INC (NV)
Old Common $0.001 par split (5) for (1) by issuance of (4) additional shares payable 11/01/2000 to holders of record 10/27/2000
Each share old Common $0.001 par exchanged for (0.2) share new Common $0.001 par 01/10/2001
Charter revoked for failure to file reports and pay fees 07/31/2003

FOREFRONT INDS INC (AB)
Merged into Augen Capital Corp. (AB) 04/16/1997
Each share Common no par exchanged for (0.5) share Common no par
Augen Capital Corp. (AB) reincorporated in Ontario 11/19/2004 which name changed to Gensource Capital Corp. 08/02/2012 which name changed to Gensource Potash Corp. 07/02/2013

FOREFRONT VENTURES LTD (BC)
Recapitalized as First Echelon Ventures, Inc. 02/16/1999
Each share Common no par exchanged for (0.15384615) share Common no par
First Echelon Ventures, Inc. name changed to Aumega Discoveries Ltd. 12/12/2003 which recapitalized as Fortress Base Metals Corp. 01/10/2007 which name changed to Lions Gate Metals Inc. 07/21/2008 which name changed to Block X Capital Corp. 01/25/2018

FOREIGN & COLONIAL EMERGING MIDDLE EAST FD INC (MD)
Liquidation completed
Each share Common $0.001 par exchanged for initial distribution of $11.25 cash 6/26/2000
Each share Common $0.001 par received second and final distribution of $4.4799 cash payable 12/28/2000 to holders of record 6/26/2000

FOREIGN BOND ASSOCIATES, INC.
Name changed to American Foreign Investing Corp. in 1937
American Foreign Investing Corp. name changed to Bowling Green Fund, Inc. in 1947 which name changed to Winfield Growth Industries Fund, Inc. 12/30/57 which name changed to Winfield Growth Fund, Inc. 9/21/66 which name changed to Research Equity Fund, Inc. (DE) 1/26/73 which reincorporated in Maryland 9/9/73 which reincorporated in California as Franklin Equity Fund 10/10/84

FOREIGN CURRENCY EXCHANGE CORP (FL)
Merged into First Rate Enterprises Ltd. 04/30/2003

Each share Common no par exchanged for $3.50 cash

FOREIGN EXPLORATION CORP. LTD. (ON)
Charter cancelled and proclaimed dissolved for failure to pay taxes and file returns 11/25/1970

FOREIGN FD INC (MD)
Name changed to Webs Index Fund, Inc. 01/02/1997
Webs Index Fund, Inc. name changed to iShares Inc. 06/16/2000

FOREIGN LIGHT & POWER CO.
Liquidated in 1951
Details not available

FOREIGN PATENT DEV CORP (NV)
Reorganized under the laws of Delaware as Egan Systems, Inc. 2/1/87
Egan Systems, Inc. (DE) reorganized in Nevada as Goldtech Mining Corp. 11/17/2003 which recapitalized as China Industrial Waste Management, Inc. 5/15/2006

FOREIGN POWER SECURITIES CORP. LTD. (CANADA)
Each share 6% Preferred $100 par exchanged for (1) share new Common no par 00/00/1954
Each share old Common no par exchanged for (0.04) share new Common no par 00/00/1954
Stock Dividend - 900% 04/15/1957
Merged into Warnock Hersey International Ltd. 12/30/1967
Each share new Common no par exchanged for (2) shares Common no par
Warnock Hersey International Ltd. name changed to TIW Industries Ltd.-Les Industries TIW Ltee. 12/31/1977
(See TIW Industries Ltd.-Les Industries TIW Ltee.)

FOREIGNTV COM INC (DE)
Issue Information - 1,700,000 Units consisting of (1) share COM and (1) WT offered at $6 per Unit on 04/13/1999
Name changed to Medium4.com, Inc. 1/1/2000
Medium4.com, Inc. name changed to IA Global, Inc. 1/3/2003

FORELAND CORP (NV)
Each share old Common $0.001 par exchanged for (1/3) share new Common $0.001 par 6/15/96
Plan of reorganization under Chapter 11 Federal Bankruptcy Code effective 12/6/2004
No stockholders' equity

FOREMOST CORP AMER (MI)
Reincorporated 6/30/98
Common $1 par split (3) for (2) by issuance of (0.5) additional share 9/15/83
Common $1 par split (3) for (2) by issuance of (2) additional shares payable 1/20/98 to holders of record 1/5/98 Ex date - 1/21/98
State of incorporation changed from (DE) to (MI) 6/30/98
Merged into Spartan Parent Corp. 3/7/2000
Each share Common $1 par exchanged for $29.25 cash

FOREMOST DAIRIES, INC. (NY)
4% Conv. Preferred called for redemption 10/30/1951
Under plan of merger each share 4-1/2% Preferred $50 par exchanged for (1) share 4-1/2% S.F. Preferred $50 par and each share Common 20¢ par exchanged for (1) share Common $5 par 02/26/1954
6% Preferred called for redemption 03/31/1954
Common $5 par changed to $2 par and (2) additional shares issued 10/00/1954

4-1/2% Preferred called for redemption 09/15/1955
4.50% Preferred called for redemption 09/15/1955
Stock Dividend - 50% 01/02/1950
Merged into Foremost-McKesson, Inc. 07/19/1967
Each share 4-1/2% S.F. Preferred $50 par exchanged for (1) share $2.25 Prior Preferred $50 par
Each share Common $2 par exchanged for (1) share Common $2 par
Foremost-McKesson, Inc. name changed to McKesson Corp. (MD) 07/27/1983 which reincorporated in Delaware 07/31/1987
(See McKesson Corp. (DE))

FOREMOST DAIRIES INC (DE)
Merged into Foremost Dairies, Inc. (NY) on a share for share basis 00/00/1949
Foremost Dairies, Inc. (NY) merged into Foremost-McKesson, Inc. 07/19/1967 which name changed to McKesson Corp. (MD) 07/27/1983 which reincorporated in Delaware 07/31/1987
(See McKesson Corp. (Old) (DE))

FOREMOST DIARY PRODUCTS, INC. (FL)
Certain assets acquired by Foremost Dairies, Inc. (Del.) in 1931
Stockholders only received rights to purchase shares of Foremost Dairies, Inc. (Del.)
Remaining assets sold at foreclosure in 1935
No Conv. Preference or Common stockholders' equity

FOREMOST ENERGY CORP (BC)
Name changed to Fifth Avenue Ventures Corp. 11/17/1988
Fifth Avenue Ventures Corp. recapitalized as Instar Energy Corp. 11/15/1990
(See Instar Energy Corp.)

FOREMOST FINANCE & EQUIPMENT CO. (FL)
Name changed to Astron Industrial Associates, Inc. 5/29/62
(See Astron Industrial Associates, Inc.)

FOREMOST INDS INC (AB)
Merged into Foremost Industries Income Fund 12/27/2002
Each share Common no par exchanged for $4 cash

FOREMOST INDS INC (NY)
Common 50¢ par changed to 25¢ par 5/26/69
Filed a petition under Chapter 7 Federal Bankruptcy Code 6/24/96
Stockholders' equity unlikely

FOREMOST INDS INCOME FD (AB)
Trust Units split (3) for (1) by issuance of (2) additional Units payable 06/29/2005 to holders of record 06/21/2005 Ex date - 06/20/2005
Merged into Foremost Income Fund 01/03/2006
Each Trust Unit exchanged for (1) Trust Unit

FOREMOST INTL INDS LTD (AB)
Recapitalized as Canadian Foremost Ltd. 05/06/1976
Each share Common no par exchanged for (0.1) share Common no par
Canadian Foremost Ltd. name changed to Foremost Industries Inc. 06/01/1994
(See Foremost Industries Inc.)

FOREMOST MCKESSON INC (MD)
$2.25 Prior Preferred $50 par called for redemption 12/31/1979
Name changed to McKesson Corp. (MD) 07/27/1983

McKesson Corp. (MD) reincorporated in Delaware 07/31/1987
(See McKesson Corp. (Old) (DE))

FORENINGSSPARBANKEN AB (SWEDEN)
Sponsored ADR's for Ordinary SKr 20 par split (3) for (2) by issuance of (0.5) additional ADR payable 6/11/99 to holders of record 6/4/99
Name changed to Swedbank AB 10/3/2006

FORENSIC TECHNOLOGIES INTL CORP (MD)
Name changed to FTI Consulting Inc. 6/8/98

FORENT ENERGY INC (AB)
Name changed to Forent Energy Ltd. 03/04/2009

FOREPLAY GOLF & TRAVEL TOURS INC (NV)
Recapitalized as Aladdin Systems Holdings, Inc. 10/26/1999
Each share Common $0.001 par exchanged for (0.45454545) share Common $0.001 par
Aladdin Systems Holdings, Inc. name changed to Monterey Bay Tech, Inc. 11/11/2004 which name changed to SecureLogic Corp. 05/20/2005
(See SecureLogic Corp.)

FORERUNNER ASSOC INC (DE)
Name changed to Aids International Diversified Services Inc. 3/17/89
(See Aids International Diversified Services Inc.)

FORESBEC INC (CANADA)
Acquired by Penrod Canada Ltd. 06/28/1996
Each share Class A Common no par exchanged for $1.17 cash

FORESIGHT CORP. (OH)
Name changed to Globe-American Corp. (OH) 6/1/66
Globe-American Corp. (OH) name changed to Tri-American Corp. 5/19/72
(See Tri-American Corp.)

FORESIGHT COS INC (MN)
Name changed to Century Camera, Inc. 6/1/78
(See Century Camera, Inc.)

FORESIGHT FOUNDATION, INC.
Dissolved in 1948. No equity for Class B stockholders

FORESIGHT SECURITY, INC. (MN)
Name changed to Foresight Companies, Inc. 7/9/74
Foresight Companies, Inc. name changed to Century Camera, Inc. 6/1/78
(See Century Camera, Inc.)

FOREST CITY ENTERPRISES INC (OH)
Common $1 par changed to $0.66666666 par and (0.5) additional share issued 06/02/1972
Conv. Class B Common $1 par changed to $0.66666666 par and (0.5) additional share issued 06/02/1972
Common $0.66666666 par reclassified as Class A Common $0.33333333 par 10/13/1983
Each share Class A Common $0.33333333 par received distribution of (1) share Conv. Class B Common $0.33333333 par 10/21/1983
Class A Common $0.33333333 par split (3) for (2) by issuance of (0.5) additional share payable 02/17/1997 to holders of record 02/03/1997 Ex date - 02/18/1997
Conv. Class B Common $0.33333333 par split (3) for (2) by issuance of (0.5) additional share payable 02/17/1997 to holders of record 02/03/1997 Ex date - 02/18/1997
Class A Common $0.33333333 par split (2) for (1) by issuance of (1) additional share payable 07/16/1998 to holders of record 07/01/1998 Ex date - 07/17/1998
Conv. Class B Common $0.33333333 par split (2) for (1) by issuance of (1) additional share payable 07/16/1998 to holders of record 07/01/1998 Ex date - 07/17/1998
Class A Common $0.33333333 par split (3) for (2) by issuance of (0.5) additional share payable 11/14/2001 to holders of record 10/31/2001 Ex date - 11/15/2001
Conv. Class B Common $0.33333333 par split (3) for (2) by issuance of (0.5) additional share payable 11/14/2001 to holders of record 10/31/2001 Ex date - 11/15/2001
Class A Common $0.33333333 par split (2) for (1) by issuance of (1) additional share payable 07/11/2005 to holders of record 06/27/2005 Ex date - 07/12/2005
Conv. Class B Common $0.33333333 par split (2) for (1) by issuance of (1) additional share payable 07/11/2005 to holders of record 06/27/2005 Ex date - 07/12/2005
Each share 7% 144A Conv. Perpetual Preferred Ser. A no par exchanged for (1) share 7% Conv. Perpetual Preferred Ser. A no par 08/21/2012
7% Conv. Perpetual Preferred Ser. A no par called for redemption at $50 on 03/15/2013
Reincorporated under the laws of Maryland as Forest City Realty Trust, Inc. and Class A Common and Conv. Class B Common $0.33333333 par changed to 1¢ par 01/04/2016

FOREST CITY INDUSTRIES, INC. (OH)
Name changed to Parsons & Co., Inc. 05/10/1957
(See Parsons & Co., Inc.)

FOREST CITY PUBG CO (OH)
6% Preferred $100 par called for redemption 6/23/67
Public interest eliminated

FOREST CLEANERS & DYERS, INC. (MI)
Bankrupt in 1959
Details not available

FOREST COML BK (ASHEVILLE, NC)
Merged into Carolina Alliance Bank (Spartanburg, SC) 04/05/2014
Each share Common exchanged for (0.755) share Common $1 par Carolina Alliance Bank (Spartanburg, SC) reorganized as CAB Financial Corp. 10/23/2017

FOREST GATE RES INC (CANADA)
Issue Information - 6,772,666 shares COM offered at $0.15 per share on 12/03/2002
Each share Common no par received distribution of (0.1168) share Blue Note Metals Inc. Common no par payable 11/16/2005 to holders of record 11/10/2005
Recapitalized as Forest Gate Energy Inc. 06/30/2009
Each share Common no par exchanged for (0.1) share Common no par

FOREST GLADE INTL INC (NV)
Name changed to Fetchomatic Global Internet Inc. 06/02/2000
(See Fetchomatic Global Internet Inc.)

FOREST HILL CAP INC (ON)
Delisted from Canadian Dealer Network 10/13/2000

FOREST HILLS HOTEL, INC.
Liquidated in 1950
Details not available

FOREST INDUSTRIES INSURANCE MANAGEMENT, INC. (OR)
Involuntarily dissolved for failure to file reports and pay fees 10/24/78

FOREST LABS INC (DE)
Capital Stock 10¢ par split (3) for (2) by issuance of (0.5) additional share 12/15/1964
Capital Stock 10¢ par reclassified as Class A Common 10¢ par 12/22/1980
Class A Common 10¢ par split (2) for (1) by issuance of (1) additional share 03/16/1981
Class A Common 10¢ par reclassified as Common 10¢ par 07/27/1981
Common 10¢ par split (2) for (1) by issuance of (1) additional share 01/13/1983
Common 10¢ par split (2) for (1) by issuance of (1) additional share 05/15/1986
Common 10¢ par split (2) for (1) by issuance of (1) additional share 02/28/1991
Common 10¢ par split (2) for (1) by issuance of (1) additional share payable 03/25/1998 to holders of record 03/05/1998 Ex date - 03/26/1998
Common 10¢ par split (2) for (1) by issuance of (1) additional share payable 01/11/2001 to holders of record 12/26/2000 Ex date - 01/12/2001
Common 10¢ par split (2) for (1) by issuance of (1) additional share payable 01/08/2003 to holders of record 12/23/2002 Ex date - 01/09/2003
Merged into Actavis PLC 07/01/2014
Each share Common 10¢ par exchanged for (0.3306) share Ordinary EUR 0.0001 par and $26.04 cash
Actavis PLC name changed to Allergan PLC 06/15/2015

FOREST OIL CORP (NY)
Common $1 par changed to 10¢ par 05/11/1988
Conv. Class B $1 par changed to 10¢ par 05/11/1988
Each share $2.125 Conv. Preferred 1¢ par exchanged for (1) share $0.75 Conv. Preferred 1¢ par 12/04/1991
Each share $15.75 Conv. Preferred 1¢ par exchanged for (7) shares $0.75 Conv. Preferred 1¢ par or $50 principal amount of 12.75% Senior Secured Notes due 06/01/1998 and (1.2) shares $0.75 Conv. Preferred 1¢ par 12/04/1991
Note: Holders' option to elect to receive Notes and stock expired 03/11/1992
Each share Class B Common 10¢ par exchanged for (1.1) shares Common 10¢ par 05/00/1993
Each share old Common 10¢ par exchanged for (0.2) share new Common 10¢ par 01/08/1996
Each share new Conv. Preferred 1¢ par received distribution of (0.068026) share new Common 10¢ par payable 02/01/1996 to holders of record 01/10/1996
Each share new Conv. Preferred 1¢ par received distribution of (0.017863) share new Common 10¢ par payable 05/01/1996 to holders of record 04/10/1996
$0.75 Conv. Preferred 1¢ par called for redemption 02/28/1997
Each share new Common 10¢ par exchanged again for (0.5) share new Common 10¢ par 12/07/2000
Each share new Common 10¢ par received distribution of (0.8093) share Mariner Energy, Inc. Common $0.0001 par payable 03/02/2006 to holders of record 02/21/2006 Ex date - 03/03/2006
Each share new Common 10¢ par received distribution of (0.61248511) share Lone Pine Resources Inc. Common 1¢ par payable 09/30/2011 to holders of record 09/16/2011 Ex date - 10/03/2011
Name changed to Sabine Oil & Gas Corp. 01/13/2015
(See Sabine Oil & Gas Corp.)

FOREST PARK HOTEL CO. (MO)
Liquidation completed 9/22/55
Details not available

FOREST QUEEN COPPER CO. (NM)
Charter forfeited for failure to file reports and pay taxes 7/28/23

FOREST RES MGMT CORP (DE)
Charter cancelled and declared inoperative and void for non-payment of taxes 03/01/2008

FORESTAR GROUP INC (DE)
Each 6% Tangible Equity Unit automatically became (1.3095) share Common $1 par 12/15/2016
(Additional Information in Active)

FORESTAR REAL ESTATE GROUP INC (DE)
Name changed to Forestar Group Inc. 11/21/2008

FORESTER RES INC (BC)
Recapitalized as Tullaree Resources Ltd. 05/11/1995
Each share Common no par exchanged for (0.2) share Common no par
Tullaree Resources Ltd. name changed to Tullaree Capital Inc. 11/09/2000 which recapitalized as Valucap Investments Inc. (Yukon) 12/02/2003 which reincorporated in Ontario 12/15/2008

FORESTER'S SILVIC CORP. (FL)
Proclaimed dissolved for failure to file reports and pay fees 5/24/63

FORESTHILL RES INC (BC)
Recapitalized as Cordex Venture Corp. (BC) 12/12/1995
Each share Common no par exchanged for (0.33333333) share Common no par
Cordex Venture Corp. (BC) reincorporated in Ontario as Brauch Database Systems, Inc. 01/07/2000
(See Brauch Database Systems, Inc.)

FORESTINDUSTRY COM INC (DE)
Each share old Common no par exchanged for (0.1) share new Common no par 06/01/2001
Name changed to Global Golf Holdings, Inc. 01/07/2003
Global Golf Holdings, Inc. recapitalized as Vitasti, Inc. 12/09/2004 which name changed to Welwind Energy International Corp. 10/31/2006
(See Welwind Energy International Corp.)

FORESTRY INTL INC (CO)
Each share Common $0.001 par exchanged for (0.25) share Common $0.0004 03/24/1995
Name changed to Infynia.com Corp. 11/06/2000
(See Infynia.com Corp.)

FOREVER ENTERPRISES INC (TX)
Company terminated common stock registration and is no longer public as of 12/26/2003

FOREVER VALUABLE COLLECTIBLES INC (CO)
Name changed to AEGEA, Inc. 07/22/2013
AEGEA, Inc. recapitalized as FutureLand, Corp. 05/01/2015

FOREVER ZEN LTD (NV)
Name changed to NOWnews Digital Media Technology Co. Ltd. 06/16/2014

FOREWEST INDS LTD (AB)
Merged into Tesco Corp. 12/01/1993
Each share Common no par exchanged for (0.10359473) share Common no par
Tesco Corp. merged into Nabors Industries Ltd. 12/15/2017

FOREX INC (NV)
Name changed to Petrogulf Inc. 03/26/2008
Petrogulf Inc. name changed to Novagant Corp. 01/02/2014

FOREX INTL TRADING CORP (NV)
Each share old Common $0.00001 par exchanged for (0.0001) share new Common $0.00001 par 10/03/2014
Recapitalized as Gopher Protocol Inc. 02/25/2015
Each share Common $0.00001 par exchanged for (0.001) share Common $0.00001 par

FOREX365 INC (NV)
Each share old Common $0.001 par exchanged for (0.015625) share new Common $0.001 par 06/18/2010
Name changed to Fuer International Inc. 08/30/2010
(See Fuer International Inc.)

FORGE INC (DE)
Name changed to Encore Clean Energy, Inc. (DE) 12/19/2003
Encore Clean Energy, Inc. (DE) reincorporated in Nevada 10/21/2005
(See Encore Clean Energy, Inc.)

FORGED STEEL PRODUCTS CO.
Merged into Snap-On Tools Corp. in 1945
Each share Common $100 par exchanged for (12) shares Common $1 par
Snap-On Tools Corp. name changed to Snap-on Inc. 4/22/94

FORGENT NETWORKS INC (DE)
Recapitalized as Asure Software, Inc. 12/29/2009
Each share Common 1¢ par exchanged for (0.1) share Common 1¢ par

FORHAN CO.
Acquired by Zonite Products Corp. in 1929
Details not available

FORK LAKE GOLD MINES LTD. (ON)
Acquired by Wadasa Gold Mines Ltd. on a (1) for (2) basis in 1946
(See Wadasa Gold Mines Ltd.)

FORLARTIC MINES LTD. (ON)
Charter revoked for failure to file reports and pay taxes 06/01/1960

FORLINK SOFTWARE CORP INC (NV)
Each share old Common $0.001 par exchanged for (0.05) share new Common $0.001 par 03/07/2008
Each share new Common $0.001 par exchanged again for (1) share new Common $0.001 par to reflect a (1) for (30,000) reverse split followed by a (30,000) for (1) forward split 08/14/2013
Note: Holders of (29,999) or fewer pre-split shares received $0.26 cash per share
Acquired by Forlink Merger New Co. Ltd. 12/02/2014
Each share new Common $0.001 par exchanged for $0.26 cash

FORM 59 FURNITURE DESIGN INC (CANADA)
Reincorporated under the laws of Nevada as Rio Grana Resources Inc. and (1) additional share issued 10/06/2003
(See Rio Grana Resources Inc.)

FORM HLDGS CORP (DE)
Name changed to XpresSpa Group, Inc. 01/08/2018

FORM MOULDING, INC. (DE)
Class B Common $1 par changed to 10¢ par in 1949
Recapitalized 10/22/54
Class A $1 par changed to Preferred $1 par
Each share Class B 10¢ par exchanged for (0.2) share Common 50¢ par
No longer in existence having become inoperative and void for non-payment of taxes 4/1/62

FORMA SCIENTIFIC INC (OH)
5-3/4% Preferred $25 par called for redemption 12/28/71
Merged into Mallinckrodt, Inc. 8/18/78
Each share Common no par exchanged for $85 cash

FORMAL SYS AMER INC (NV)
Charter revoked for failure to file reports and pay fees 6/1/2000

FORMAN, FORD & CO. (MN)
Stock Dividend - 100% 6/1/59
Merged into Chamberlin Co. of America (DE) 12/12/63
Each share Capital Stock $1 par exchanged for (0.153846) share Common $2.50 par
(See Chamberlin Co. of America (DE))

FORMAN (GEORGE M.) & CO. (DE)
Charter cancelled and declared inoperative and void for non-payment of taxes 4/1/55

FORMAN (GEORGE M.) REALTY TRUST
Reorganized as Forman Realty Corp. in 1946
No stockholders' equity

FORMAQUE GOLD MINES, LTD. (QC)
Acquired by New Formaque Mines, Ltd. 00/00/1948
Each share Capital Stock $1 par exchanged for (1/3) share Capital Stock $1 par
New Formaque Mines, Ltd. recapitalized as Sobiga Mines Ltd.-Les Mines Sobiga Ltee. 01/16/1974
(See Sobiga Mines Ltd.-Les Mines Sobiga Ltee.)

FORMASTER CORP. (CA)
Name changed to Formaster Magnetic Designs Corp. 1/26/87
Formaster Magnetic Designs Corp. name changed to Trace Products 6/1/87
(See Trace Products)

FORMASTER MAGNETIC DESIGNS CORP (CA)
Name changed to Trace Products 6/1/87
(See Trace Products)

FORMAT INC (NV)
Name changed to Power Solutions International, Inc. (NV) 05/13/2011
Power Solutions International, Inc. (NV) reorganized in Delaware 09/01/2011

FORMATION CAP CORP (BC)
Recapitalized as Formation Metals Inc. 11/13/2009
Each share Common no par exchanged for (0.14285714) share Common no par
Formation Metals Inc. name changed to eCobalt Solutions Inc. 08/05/2016

FORMATION FLUID MGMT INC (BC)
Merged into Robix Environmental Technologies, Inc. 10/17/2016
Each share Common no par exchanged for (0.425) share Common no par
Note: Unexchanged certificates will be cancelled and become without value 10/17/2022

FORMATION METALS INC (BC)
Name changed to eCobalt Solutions Inc. 08/05/2016

FORME CAP INC (DE)
Each share old Common $0.001 par exchanged for (0.02857142) share new Common $0.001 par 06/14/2000
New Common $0.001 par split (25) for (1) by issuance of (24) additional shares payable 03/07/2005 to holders of record 02/24/2005
Each share new Common $0.001 par exchanged again for (0.11111111) share new Common $0.001 par 12/13/2007
Name changed to QKL Stores, Inc. 06/19/2008

FORMICA CO. (OH)
Stock Dividend - 100% 6/1/50
Merged into American Cyanamid Co. on a (1.75) for (1) basis 4/16/56
(See American Cyanamid Co.)

FORMICA CORP (DE)
Merged into FM Holdings Inc. 09/11/1989
Each share Common 1¢ par exchanged for $19 cash
Each share Class B Common 1¢ par exchanged for $19 cash

FORMICA INSULATION CO.
Name changed to Formica Co. in 1948
Formica Co. merged into American Cyanamid Co. 4/16/56
(See American Cyanamid Co.)

FORMIGLI CORP (DE)
Merged into High Industries, Inc. 10/22/82
Each share Common 10¢ par exchanged for $6.37 cash

FORMIGLI INC (FL)
Reorganized as Cloudweb, Inc. 12/18/2015
Each share Common no par exchanged for (100) shares Common no par

FORMING MACH CO AMER INC (DE)
Common $1 par split (10) for (1) by issuance of (9) additional shares 8/27/54
Charter cancelled and declared inoperative and void for non-payment of taxes 4/15/72

FORMOSA LIBERTY CORP (DE)
Reorganized under the laws of Wyoming as NanoSave Technologies Inc. 03/28/2016
Each share Common $0.0001 par exchanged for (0.01) share Common $0.0001 par

FORMOSA RES CORP (BC)
Delisted from Vancouver Stock Exchange 3/5/96

FORMQUEST INTL LTD (DE)
Name changed to MegaChain.com, Ltd. 4/9/99
MegaChain.com, Ltd. name changed to Acola Corp. 10/22/2001 which name changed to Teda Travel Group Inc. 4/21/2004 which name changed to Network CN, Inc. 8/15/2006

FORMSPRAG CO (DE)
Reincorporated 03/31/1969
State of incorporation changed from (MI) to (DE) 03/31/1969
Merged into Dana Corp. 08/24/1973
Each share Common $1 par exchanged for (0.75) share Common $1 par
(See Dana Corp.)

FORMULA 409, INC. (MA)
Each share Common no par exchanged for (0.1) share Common $1 par 4/02/1963
Common $1 par split (3) for (1) by issuance of (2) additional shares 12/02/1966

Name changed to Harrell Corp. 03/31/1967
Harrell Corp. name changed to Harrell International, Inc. 04/01/1968 which name changed to Harrell Hospitality Group Inc. 04/01/2000 which name changed to Noram Capital Holdings, Inc. 02/13/2007
(See Noram Capital Holdings, Inc.)

FORMULA FOOTWEAR INC (UT)
Each (533) shares old Common $0.001 par exchanged for (1) share new Common $0.001 par 10/01/1999
Note: No holder of (100) shares or more will receive fewer than (100) post-split shares
Holders of (99) shares or fewer will be rounded up to (100) post-split shares
Each share new Common $0.001 par exchanged again for (0.5) share new Common $0.001 par 11/28/2003
Reincorporated under the laws of Delaware as VSUS Technologies Inc. 06/09/2004
VSUS Technologies Inc. name changed to New Colombia Resources, Inc. 01/24/2013

FORMULA FUND OF BOSTON (MA)
Name changed to Smith (Edson B.) Fund 02/06/1956
Smith (Edson B.) Fund liquidated for Foursquare Fund, Inc. 09/17/1963 which merged into Eaton Vance Investors Fund, Inc. 09/12/1983 which name changed to Eaton Vance Investors Trust 09/29/1993
(See Eaton Vance Investors Trust)

FORMULAB NEURONETICS LTD (AUSTRALIA)
ADR agreement terminated 06/11/2001
Each Sponsored ADR for Ordinary AUD $0.20 par exchanged for $0.0512 cash

FORMULAWON INC (DE)
Common $0.001 par split (3) for (1) by issuance of (2) additional shares payable 09/22/2008 to holders of record 09/12/2008 Ex date - 09/23/2008
Name changed to Reach Messaging Holdings, Inc. 03/05/2010

FORREST CITY FINL CORP (DE)
Acquired by Big Creek Bancshares, Inc. 01/03/2017
Each share Common 1¢ par exchanged for $15.31 cash

FORREST LIFE INS CO (TN)
Reorganized as Synercon Corp. 02/02/1970
Each share Common $1 par exchanged for (1) share Common $1 par
Synercon Corp. acquired by Corroon & Black Corp. 04/30/1976 which merged into Willis Corroon PLC 10/08/1990 which name changed to Willis Corroon Group PLC 01/22/1992
(See Willis Corroon Group PLC)

FORRESTER METALS INC (ON)
Merged into Zinc One Resources Inc. 06/02/2017
Each share Common no par exchanged for (0.18181818) share Common no par
Note: Unexchanged certificates will be cancelled and become without value 06/02/2023

FORSCHNER GROUP INC (DE)
Common 10¢ par split (2) for (1) by issuance of (1) additional share 9/21/87
Name changed to Swiss Army Brands, Inc. 5/21/96
(See Swiss Army Brands, Inc.)

FORSHEIM GROUP INC (DE)
Name changed 12/29/96
Name changed from Florsheim Shoe Co. to Florsheim Group Inc. 12/29/96
Plan of reorganization under Chapter 11 Federal Bankruptcy Code effective 2/13/2006
No stockholders' equity

FORSOFT LTD (ISRAEL)
Acquired by Formula Systems (1985) Ltd. 11/30/2000
Each share Ordinary exchanged for $9 cash

FORST (ALEX) & SONS, INC. (NY)
Completely liquidated for cash 10/25/65

FORST-HUNTER INTL TRADE CORP (CO)
Recapitalized as Equus Resources Inc. 07/17/2004
Each share Common $0.005 par exchanged for (0.005) share Common $0.005 par
Equus Resources Inc. name changed to Quasar Aerospace Industries, Inc. 06/16/2009 which recapitalized as Green Energy Enterprises, Inc. 10/30/2015

FORSTER DRILLING CORP (NV)
SEC revoked common stock registration 01/17/2013

FORSTMANN & CO INC NEW (GA)
Chapter 11 bankruptcy proceedings dismissed 06/28/2002
No stockholders' equity

FORSTMANN & CO INC OLD (GA)
Merged into FI Holdings, Inc. 5/26/89
Each share old Common $0.001 par exchanged for $11.75 cash
Each share new Common $0.001 par exchanged for (0.0004604) share new Common $0.001 par 2/26/92
Plan of reorganization under Chapter 11 Federal Bankruptcy Code effective 7/23/97
Each share 5% Sr. Pay-In-Kind Preferred $1 par exchanged for (0.77158306) Common Stock Purchase Warrant expiring 7/23/99
Each share new Common $0.001 par exchanged for (0.00780914) Common Stock Purchase Warrant expiring 7/23/99

FORSYS CORP (ON)
Recapitalized as Forsys Technologies Inc. 4/16/2003
Each share Common no par exchanged for (1/9) share Common no par
Forsys Technologies Inc. name changed to Forsys Metals Corp. 7/14/2005

FORSYS TECHNOLOGIES INC (ON)
Name changed to Forsys Metals Corp. 7/14/2005

FORSYTH BANK & TRUST CO. (WINSTON-SALEM, NC)
Merged into Southern National Corp. 3/30/82
Each share Common $5 par exchanged for (0.77965024) share Common $5 par
Southern National Corp. name changed to BB&T Corp. 5/19/97

FORSYTH JOHN INC (ON)
Merged into Forsyth Acquisition 11/30/1996
Each share Common no par exchanged for $1.91 cash

FORSYTH MINES LTD. (ON)
Merged into Goldquest Exploration Inc. 08/09/1982
Each share Capital Stock $1 par exchanged for (0.15673981) share Common no par
Goldquest Exploration Inc. merged into Goldcorp Inc. (New) 03/31/1994

FORT ATLANTIC CORP (DE)
Merged out existence 05/29/1998
Details not available

FORT BEND HLDG CORP (DE)
Common 1¢ par split (2) for (1) by issuance of (1) additional share payable 10/01/1997 to holders of record 09/11/1997
Merged into Southwest Bancorporation of Texas, Inc. 04/01/1999
Each share Common 1¢ par exchanged for (1.45) shares Common $1 par
Southwest Bancorporation of Texas, Inc. name changed to Amegy Bancorporation, Inc. 05/05/2005 which merged into Zions Bancorporation 12/03/2005 which merged into Zions Bancorporation, N.A (Salt Lake City, UT) 10/01/2018

FORT BEND NATL BK (RICHMOND, TX)
Merged into First City Bancorporation of Texas, Inc. (TX) 12/1/81
Each share Capital Stock $10 par exchanged for (3) shares Common $3.25 par
(See First City Bancorporation of Texas, Inc. (TX))

FORT BENNING NATL BK (FORT BENNING, GA)
Merged into First National Bank (Columbus, GA) 4/1/82
To holdings of (300) or fewer shares: each share Common $2.50 par exchanged for $20.50 cash
To holdings of (301) or more shares: each share Common $2.50 par exchanged for $15.375 principal amount of 12% promissory notes and $5.125 cash

FORT BRIDGER OIL CO. (WY)
Charter cancelled for non-payment of taxes 7/19/27

FORT BROOKE BANCORPORATION (FL)
Merged into Colonial BancGroup, Inc. 04/22/1997
Each share Common $8 par exchanged for (1.6154) shares Common $2.50 par
(See Colonial BancGroup, Inc.)

FORT BROOKE BK (TAMPA, FL)
Under plan of reorganization each share Common $8 par automatically became (1) share Fort Brooke Bancorporation Common $8 par 07/10/1996
Fort Brooke Bancorporation merged into Colonial BancGroup, Inc. 04/22/1997
(See Colonial BancGroup, Inc.)

FORT CHICAGO ENERGY PARTNERS L P (AB)
Reorganized as Veresen Inc. 01/06/2011
Each Class A Unit of Ltd. Partnership Int. no par exchanged for (1) share Common no par
Note: Unexchanged certificates were cancelled and became without value 01/06/2014
Veresen Inc. merged into Pembina Pipeline Corp. 10/02/2017

FORT COLLINS PRODUCING CORP. (CO)
Capital Stock $25 par changed to $1 par in 1933
Declared defunct and inoperative for failure to pay taxes and file reports 11/3/75

FORT DEARBORN INCOME SECS INC (IL)
Reincorporated 12/31/1991
State of incorporation changed from (DE) to (IL) 12/31/1991
Under plan of reorganization each share Common 1¢ par automatically became (1) share UBS Funds Total Return Bond Fund Class P $0.001 par 05/20/2016

FORT DODGE, DES MOINES & SOUTHERN RAILROAD CO.
Reorganized as Fort Dodge, Des Moines & Southern Railway Co. in 1943
No stockholders' equity

FORT DODGE STREET RAILWAY CO. (ME)
Charter revoked for failure to file reports and pay fees 1/28/30

FORT DRUMMER MILLS
Merged into Berkshire Fine Spinning Associates, Inc. 00/00/1929
Details not available

FORT FAIRFIELD SEWER CO. (ME)
Completely liquidated 1/10/83
Each share Capital Stock $10 par received first and final distribution of $5.80 cash

FORT GARRY BREWING CO LTD NEW (MB)
Merged into Russell Breweries Inc. 10/23/2007
Each share Common no par exchanged for (1) share Common no par

FORT GARRY BREWING CO LTD OLD (MB)
Merged into Fort Garry Brewing Co. Ltd. (New) 05/20/2003
Each share Common no par exchanged for (0.23302) share Common no par
Fort Garry Brewing Co. Ltd. (New) merged into Russell Breweries Inc. 10/23/2007

FORT GEORGE MINES LTD. (ON)
Merged into Jubilant Eagle Holdings & Explorations Ltd. 04/01/1968
Each share Common $1 par exchanged for (0.25) share Capital Stock no par
(See Jubilant Eagle Holdings & Explorations Ltd.)

FORT GEORGE MNG & EXPL LTD (BC)
Struck off register and declared dissolved for failure to file returns 05/20/1980

FORT HLDGS INC (IN)
Liquidation completed
Each share Common no par exchanged for initial distribution of $27.823565 cash 10/15/83
Each share Common no par received second and final distribution of $0.11 cash 3/21/85

FORT HOWARD CORP NEW (DE)
Merged into Fort James Corp. 8/13/97
Each share Common 1¢ par exchanged for (1.375) shares Common 10¢ par
Fort James Corp. merged into Georgia-Pacific Corp. 11/27/2000
(See Georgia-Pacific Corp.)

FORT HOWARD CORP OLD (DE)
Name changed 4/23/87
Common $1 par split (2) for (1) by issuance of (1) additional share 5/22/73
Common $1 par split (2) for (1) by issuance of (1) additional share 1/30/81
Common $1 par split (2) for (1) by issuance of (1) additional share 10/25/85
Name changed from Fort Howard Paper Co. to Fort Howard Corp. 4/23/87
Merged into FH Acquisition Corp. 10/24/88
Each share Common $1 par exchanged for $53 cash
Each share Common $1 par received a settlement distribution of $0.162887 cash 5/12/91

FORT JAMES CORP (VA)
Conv. Exchangeable Preferred Ser. K $10 par called for redemption at $50 on 4/10/98
Depositary Preferred Ser. L called for redemption at $50 on 4/10/98
Preferred Ser. L $10 par called for redemption at $200 on 4/10/98
Merged into Georgia-Pacific Corp. 11/27/2000
Each share Common 10¢ par exchanged for (0.2644) share Common no par and $29.60 cash
(See Georgia-Pacific Corp.)

FORT KNOX GOLD RES INC (ON)
Name changed to FNX Mining Co. Inc. 06/26/2002
FNX Mining Co. Inc. merged into Quadra FNX Mining Ltd. 05/27/2010
(See Quadra FNX Mining Ltd.)

FORT KNOX MINERALS LTD (BC)
Struck off register and declared dissolved for failure to file returns 09/27/1991

FORT KNOX NATL BK (FORT KNOX, KY)
Stock Dividends - 100% 3/31/72; 50% 4/14/78
Reorganized as Investors Services, Inc. 12/16/82
Each share Common $4 par exchanged for (1) share Common $4 par

FORT LAUDERDALE NATL BK (LAUDERDALE, FL)
Stock Dividend - 33-1/3% 1/25/61
Acquired by Broward Bancshares, Inc. 5/28/70
Each share Capital Stock $15 par exchanged for (2.1) shares Common $1 par
Broward Bancshares, Inc. name changed to Century Banks, Inc. 4/8/76 which merged into Sun Banks of Florida, Inc. 7/1/82 which name changed to Sun Banks, Inc. 5/2/83 which merged into SunTrust Banks, Inc. 7/1/85

FT LAUDERDALE RES INC (BC)
Recapitalized as Amcorp Industries Inc. 06/22/1990
Each share Common no par exchanged for (1/3) share Common no par
Amcorp Industries Inc. name changed to Molycor Gold Corp. 05/17/1996 which name changed to Nevada Clean Magnesium Inc. 04/17/2012

FORT MYERS BEACH WATER WORKS, INC. (FL)
Dissolved 9/9/65
Details not available

FORT NECK NATIONAL BANK (SEAFORD, NY)
Each share Capital Stock $100 par exchanged for (5) shares Capital Stock $25 par to effect a (4) for (1) split and 25% stock dividend in 1951
Each share Capital Stock $25 par exchanged for (2) shares Capital Stock $12.50 par in 1954
Capital Stock $12.50 par changed to $5 par and (1.5) additional shares issued 7/13/56
Merged into Security National Bank of Long Island (Huntington, NY) 5/26/58
Each share Capital Stock $5 par exchanged for (1.186) shares Common $5 par
Security National Bank of Long Island (Huntington, NY) name changed to Security National Bank (Huntington, NY) 11/23/68 which changed location to Security National Bank (Hempstead, NY) 5/8/72
(See Security National Bank (Hempstead, NY))

FORT NORMAN EXPLS INC (QC)
Common no par split (2) for (1) by

issuance of (1) additional share 08/18/1977
Name changed to Morgan Hydrocarbons Inc. 12/06/1982
Morgan Hydrocarbons Inc. acquired by Stampeder Exploration Ltd. 10/15/1996 which was acquired by Gulf Canada Resources Ltd. 09/10/1997
(See Gulf Canada Resources Ltd.)

FORT ORANGE FINL CORP (DE)
Stock Dividends - 5% payable 05/30/2008 to holders of record 05/16/2008 Ex date - 05/14/2008; 5% payable 05/14/2010 to holders of record 04/30/2010 Ex date - 05/07/2010
Merged into Chemung Financial Corp. 04/08/2011
Each share Common $4 par exchanged for (0.30126027) share Common 1¢ par and $1.172775 cash

FORT PITT BRDG WKS (PA)
Capital Stock no par changed to $10 par in 1938
Acquired by Magnetics, Inc. 2/1/70
Each share Capital Stock $10 par exchanged for $70.88 cash

FORT PITT BREWING CO. (PA)
Name changed to Fort Pitt Industries, Inc. 10/30/56
Fort Pitt Industries, Inc. name changed to Seeburg Corp. (PA) 4/30/58 which reincorporated in Delaware 3/30/62
(See Seeburg Corp. (DE))

FORT PITT INDUSTRIES, INC. (PA)
Name changed to Seeburg Corp. (PA) 4/30/58
Seeburg Corp. (PA) reincorporated in Delaware 3/30/62
(See Seeburg Corp. (DE))

FORT PITT STEEL CASTING CO.
Acquired by Pittsburgh Steel Foundry Corp. in 1945
Details not available

FORT PLYWOOD & LUMBER LTD. (AB)
100% acquired by Crestbrook Timber Ltd. through purchase offer which expired 10/31/64
Public interest eliminated

FORT POINT RES LTD (BC)
Recapitalized as Osprey Energy Ltd. 09/14/1998
Each share Common no par exchanged for (0.1) share Common no par
(See Osprey Energy Ltd.)

FORT RAE GOLD MINES LTD. (ON)
Completely liquidated 12/18/1962
Each share Capital Stock $1 par exchanged for first and final distribution of (0.1396) share Iron Bay Mines Ltd. Capital Stock $1 par and $0.001 cash
Iron Bay Mines Ltd. recapitalized as Calmor Iron Bay Mines Ltd. 12/14/1966
(See Calmor Iron Bay Mines Ltd.)

FORT RELIANCE MINERALS LTD (ON)
Merged into Nufort Resources Inc. 08/20/1974
Each share Capital Stock no par exchanged for (0.66666666) share Capital Stock no par
Nufort Resources Inc. name changed to Mikotel Networks Inc. 05/09/2000 which recapitalized as Wabi Exploration Inc. 03/04/2005

FORT ST JOHN PETES LTD (BC)
Through purchase offer 100% acquired by Cascade Gas Utilities Ltd. as of 01/14/1980
Public interest eliminated

FORT SAM HOUSTON BANKSHARES INC (TX)
Merged into Republic of Texas Corp. 1/1/81
Each share Common $5 par exchanged for (1.68) shares $2.125 Conv. Preferred Ser. A no par
Republic of Texas Corp. name changed to RepublicBank Corp. 6/30/82 which merged into First RepublicBank Corp. 6/6/87
(See First RepublicBank Corp.)

FORT STOCKTON OIL CO (DE)
Name changed to Western Crude Oil, Inc. 07/07/1972
Western Crude Oil, Inc. merged into Reserve Oil & Gas Co. 04/17/1973
(See Reserve Oil & Gas Co.)

FORT THOMAS FINL CORP (OH)
Merged into Bank of Kentucky Financial Corp. 06/14/2000
Each share Common 1¢ par exchanged for (0.5645) share Common no par
Bank of Kentucky Financial Corp. merged into BB&T Corp. 06/19/2015

FORT WAYNE, VAN WERT & LIMA TRACTION CO.
Reorganized as Fort Wayne & Lima Railroad Co. in 1926
Details not available

FORT WAYNE & JACKSON RR CO (MI & IN)
Merged into Penn Central Corp. 3/17/80
Each share Preferred $100 par exchanged for $22.4121 principal amount of 7% General Mortgage Bonds Ser. A due 12/31/87, $0.9212 principal amount of 7% General Mortgage Bonds Ser. B due 12/31/87, (1.1667) shares Conv. Preference Ser. B $20 par, (0.5259) share Common $1 par and $30 cash
Each share Common $100 par exchanged for (0.5) share Common $1 par
Note: a) distribution is certain only for certificates surrendered prior to 5/1/85 b) distribution may also be made for certificates surrendered between 5/1/85 and 12/31/86 c) no distribution will be made for certificates surrendered after 12/31/86
Penn Central Corp. name changed to American Premier Underwriters, Inc. 3/25/94 which merged into American Premier Group, Inc. 4/3/95 which name changed to American Financial Group, Inc. 6/9/95 which merged into American Financial Group, Inc. (Holding Co.) 12/2/97

FORT WAYNE & LIMA RAILROAD CO.
Property sold in 1933
Details not available

FORT WAYNE CORRUGATED PAPER CO. (IN)
4-1/2% Preferred $25 par called for redemption 03/06/1947
Stock Dividend - 100% 04/01/1952
Merged into Continental Can Co., Inc. 06/15/1959
Each share Common $10 par exchanged for (0.765654) share Common $10 par
Continental Can Co., Inc. name changed to Continental Group, Inc. 04/27/1976
(See Continental Group, Inc.)

FORT WAYNE NATL BK (FORT WAYNE, IN)
Common $20 par changed to $10 par and (1) additional share issued plus a 14-2/7% stock dividend paid 02/10/1960
Stock Dividends - 20% 06/29/1940; 33-1/3% 12/18/1943; 25% 02/05/1953; 40% 02/07/1955; 20% 02/07/1957; (1) for (6.5) 02/07/1962; 19.8083% 02/06/1967; 33-1/3% 02/17/1969; 20% 03/01/1973; 25% 03/05/1975; 20% 04/04/1977; (1) for (9) 04/06/1979
Under plan of reorganization each share Common $10 par automatically became (1) share Fort Wayne National Corp. Common no par 07/20/1982
Fort Wayne National Corp. merged into National City Corp. 03/30/1998 which was acquired by PNC Financial Services Group, Inc. 12/31/2008

FORT WAYNE NATL CORP (IN)
Common no par split (2) for (1) by issuance of (1) additional share 05/22/1985
Common no par split (2) for (1) by issuance of (1) additional share 05/15/1986
Common no par split (3) for (2) by issuance of (0.5) additional share 05/20/1994
Common no par split (3) for (2) by issuance of (0.5) additional share payable 07/15/1997 to holders of record 06/16/1997
Common no par split (3) for (2) by issuance of (0.5) additional share payable 10/01/1997 to holders of record 09/10/1997
Merged into National City Corp. 03/30/1998
Each share 6% Conv. Preferred Class B Ser. I no par exchanged for (1) share 6% Conv. Preferred Ser. 1 no par
Each share Common no par exchanged for (0.75) share Common $4 par
National City Corp. acquired by PNC Financial Services Group, Inc. 12/31/2008

FORT WORTH BANK & TRUST (FORT WORTH, TX)
Name changed to MBank Fort Worth East (Fort Worth, TX) 10/15/1984
(See MBank Fort Worth East (Fort Worth, TX))

FORT WORTH NATL BK (FORT WORTH, TX)
Each share Common Capital Stock $20 par exchanged for (2) shares Common Capital Stock $10 par in 1953
Stock Dividends - 33-1/3% 1/9/40; 25% 1/13/42; 20% 1/3/46; 14-2/7% 1/13/50; 10% 10/12/59; 10% 1/25/62; 10% 11/15/69
Reorganized as Fort Worth National Corp. 4/30/70
Each share Common Capital Stock $10 par exchanged for (1) share Common $10 par
Fort Worth National Corp. name changed to Texas American Bancshares Inc. 4/26/74
(See Texas American Bancshares Inc.)

FORT WORTH NATL CORP (TX)
Common $10 par changed to $5 par and (1) additional share issued 1/15/73
Name changed to Texas American Bancshares Inc. 4/26/74
(See Texas American Bancshares Inc.)

FORT WORTH POWER & LIGHT CO.
Acquired by Texas Electric Service Co. 00/00/1929
Details not available

FORT WORTH STL & MACHY CO (TX)
Stock Dividends - 200% 03/15/1962; 50% 01/16/1976
Merged into Houdaille Industries, Inc. 06/30/1977
Each share Common $1 par exchanged for $19 cash

FORT WORTH STOCK YARDS CO.
Dissolved in 1944
Details not available

FORT WORTH TRANSIT CO., INC. (TX)
Liquidation completed
Each share Capital Stock $10 par received initial distribution of $6 cash 10/4/72
Each share Capital Stock $10 par received second distribution of $5 cash 10/4/73
Each share Capital Stock $10 par received third and final distribution of $1.93 cash 8/15/74
Certificates were not required to be surrendered and are now valueless

FORTE RES INC (AB)
Plan of arrangement effective 07/12/2005
Each share Common no par exchanged for (0.175) Thunder Energy Trust, Trust Unit no par and (0.33333333) share Valiant Energy Ltd. Common no par
(See each company's listing)

FORTE RES INC (BC)
Name changed to Santacruz Silver Mining Ltd. 04/16/2012

FORTE SOFTWARE INC (DE)
Merged into Sun Microsystems, Inc. 10/19/1999
Each share Common 1¢ par exchanged for (0.3) share Common $0.00067 par
(See Sun Microsystems, Inc.)

FORTEGRA FINL CORP (DE)
Acquired by Tiptree Financial Inc. 12/04/2014
Each share Common 1¢ par exchanged for $10 cash

FORTEL INC (CA)
Reorganized under the laws of Delaware as Envit Capital Group, Inc. 08/22/2008
Each share Common no par exchanged for (0.03333333) share Common no par
(See Envit Capital Group, Inc.)

FORTERRA TR (SINGAPORE)
ADR agreement terminated 08/12/2016
No ADR's remain outstanding

FORTERUS INC (NV)
Recapitalized as American Addiction Centers, Inc. 03/20/2013
Each share Common $0.001 par exchanged for (0.01) share Common $0.001 par
American Addiction Centers, Inc. merged into AAC Holdings, Inc. 11/10/2014

FORTICELL BIOSCIENCE INC (DE)
SEC revoked common stock registration 05/30/2013

FORTIFIED HLDGS CORP (NV)
SEC revoked common stock registration 09/07/2011

FORTIFY RES INC (BC)
Each share old Common no par exchanged for (0.28571428) share new Common no par 03/31/2017
Name changed to Crop Infrastructure Corp. 03/13/2018

FORTIS ADVANTAGE PORTFOLIOS INC (MN)
Merged into Fortis Income Portfolios, Inc. 08/23/1994
Government Total Return Portfolio 1¢ par exchanged for U.S. Government Securities Fund on a net asset basis
(See Fortis Income Portfolios, Inc.)
Merged into Hartford Mutual Funds II, Inc. 02/15/2002
Details not available

FORTIS ADVISERS, INC. (MN)
Acquired by Hartford Financial Services Group, Inc. 04/02/2001

Details not available

FORTIS CORP (DE)
Name changed to CorVel Corp.
07/27/1992

FORTIS ENTERPRISES (NV)
Name changed to Renovo Holdings
06/14/2004
Renovo Holdings name changed to
Bebida Beverage Co. (NV)
10/14/2008 which reincorporated in
Wyoming 12/03/2009

FORTIS EQUITY PORTFOLIOS INC (MN)
Merged into Hartford Mutual Funds II
11/30/2001
Details not available

FORTIS FIDUCIARY FD INC (MN)
Merged into Fortis Equity Portfolios
Inc. 10/22/1998
Each share Common 1¢ par
exchanged for (1) share Capital
Fund 1¢ par
(See Fortis Equity Portfolios Inc.)

FORTIS GROWTH FD INC (MN)
Merged into Hartford Mutual Funds II
11/30/2001
Details not available

FORTIS INC (NL)
8.7% Retractable 1st Preference Ser.
A $25 par called for redemption at
$25 plus $0.54375 accrued
dividends on 09/30/1997
5.95% Retractable 1st Preference
Ser. B called for redemption at $25
plus $0.004131 accrued dividends
on 12/02/2002
1st Preference Ser. C no par called
for redemption at $25 plus $0.1456
accrued dividends on 07/10/2013
1st Preference Ser. E no par called
for redemption at $25 plus $0.3063
accrued dividends on 09/01/2016
(Additional Information in Active)

FORTIS INCOME PORTFOLIOS INC (MN)
Merged into Hartford-Fortis Series
Fund, Inc. 11/30/2001
Details not available

FORTIS MONEY PORTFOLIOS INC (MN)
Merged into Hartford Mutual Funds II,
Inc. 02/15/2002
Details not available

FORTIS NL (NETHERLANDS)
Name changed 01/01/1999
Sponsored ADR's for Ordinary split
(5) for (2) by issuance of (1.5)
additional ADR's payable 06/11/1996
to holders of record 06/05/1996
Name changed from Fortis Amev N.V.
to Fortis NL 01/01/1999
Sponsored ADR's for Ordinary split
(2) for (1) by issuance of (1)
additional ADR payable 01/22/1999
to holders of record 01/11/1999
Sponsored ADR's for Ordinary split
(37) for (1) by issuance of (36)
additional ADR's payable
06/26/2000 to holders of record
05/25/2000
Each Sponsored ADR for Ordinary
exchanged for (1) Sponsored ADR
for Equity Units 12/17/2001
Name changed to Ageas 05/14/2010

FORTIS SECS INC (MN)
Reincorporated under the laws of
Maryland as Hartford Income
Shares Fund, Inc. 07/16/2002
Hartford Income Shares Fund, Inc.
merged into Rivus Bond Fund
10/22/2010 which name changed to
Cutwater Select Income Fund
12/09/2011 which name changed to
Insight Select Income Fund
12/29/2016

FORTIS SER FD INC (MN)
Reorganized as Hartford HLS Series
Fund II, Inc. 05/01/2002

Details not available

FORTIS TAX FREE PORTFOLIOS INC (MN)
Merged into Hartford-Fortis Series
Fund, Inc. 11/30/2001
Details not available

FORTIS WORLDWIDE PORTFOLIOS INC (MN)
Merged into Hartford Mutual Funds II,
Inc. 02/15/2002
Details not available

FORTISSIMO ACQUISITION CORP (DE)
Issue Information - 4,000,000 UNITS
consisting of (1) share COM and (2)
WTS offered at $6 per Unit on
10/11/2006
Completely liquidated
Each Unit exchanged for first and
final distribution of $6.18204 cash
payable 10/13/2008 to holders of
record 10/10/2008
Each share Common $0.0001 par
exchanged for first and final
distribution of $6.18204 cash
payable 10/13/2008 to holders of
record 10/10/2008

FORTNEY OIL CO. (MI)
Charter revoked for failure to file
reports and pay fees 3/6/42

FORTRESS ADJUSTABLE RATE U S GOVT FD INC (MD)
Name changed to Federated
Adjustable Rate U.S. Government
Fund Inc. 03/31/1996
Federated Adjustable Rate U.S.
Government Fund Inc. name
changed to Federated Limited
Duration Government Fund, Inc.
09/11/2000 which name changed to
Federated Intermediate Government
Fund, Inc. 04/30/2005

FORTRESS AMER ACQUISITION CORP (DE)
Name changed to Fortress
International Group, Inc. 08/01/2007
Fortress International Group, Inc.
name changed to TSS, Inc.
06/13/2013

FORTRESS BANCSHARES INC (IA)
Common 1¢ par split (2) for (1) by
issuance of (1) additional share
payable 03/09/1998 to holders of
record 02/23/1998
Merged into Merchants &
Manufacturers Bancorporation, Inc.
11/30/2002
Each share Common 1¢ par
exchanged for either (0.81224)
share Common $1 par and $6 cash,
(1.0153) shares Common $1 par, or
$30 cash
Note: Option to receive cash or stock
only expired 12/04/2002
(See Merchants & Manufacturers
Bancorporation, Inc.)

FORTRESS BASE METALS CORP (BC)
Name changed to Lions Gate Metals
Inc. 07/21/2008
Lions Gate Metals Inc. name changed
to Block X Capital Corp. 01/25/2018

FORTRESS ENERGY INC (AB)
Name changed to Alvopetro Inc.
03/11/2013
Alvopetro Inc. name changed to
Fortaleza Energy Inc. 11/19/2013

FORTRESS EXPL INC (NV)
Reincorporated 06/04/2010
State of incorporation changed from
(DE) to (NV) 06/04/2010
Name changed to Greenworld
Development, Inc. 08/20/2010

FORTRESS FINL CORP (BC)
Merged into Berwick Retirement
Communities Ltd. 04/02/2001
Each share Common no par
exchanged for (0.14) share Common
no par

(See Berwick Retirement
Communities Ltd.)

FORTRESS FINL GROUP INC (WY)
Stock Dividend - 25% payable
12/17/2007 to holders of record
12/10/2007 Ex date - 12/18/2007
Each share Common $0.0001 par
received distribution of (0.01189)
share Hunt Gold Corp. Common
$0.0001 par payable 02/15/2008 to
holders of record 11/14/2005
Each share Common $0.0001 par
received distribution of (0.00464)
share Hunt Gold Corp. Common
$0.0001 par payable 02/15/2008 to
holders of record 01/02/2006
Each share Common $0.0001 par
received distribution of (0.0046)
share Hunt Gold Corp. Common
$0.0001 par payable 02/15/2008 to
holders of record 01/04/2006
SEC revoked common stock
registration 12/07/2011

FORTRESS GROUP INC (DE)
Each share old Common 1¢ par
exchanged for (0.25) share new
Common 1¢ par 7/10/2000
Merged into Lennar Corp. 7/26/2002
Each share new Common 1¢ par
exchanged for $3.68 cash

FORTRESS INTL GROUP INC (DE)
Name changed to TSS, Inc.
06/13/2013

FORTRESS INVT GROUP LLC (DE)
Acquired by SoftBank Group Corp.
12/27/2017
Each Class A Share exchanged for
$8.08 cash

FORTRESS IT CORP (CANADA)
Name changed to Fortress Minerals
Corp. 06/28/2004
Fortress Minerals Corp. name
changed to Lundin Gold Inc.
12/18/2014

FORTRESS MINERALS CORP (CANADA)
Each share old Common no par
exchanged for (0.05) share new
Common no par 12/01/2010
Name changed to Lundin Gold Inc.
12/18/2014

FORTRESS MINES & OILS LTD (ON)
Charter cancelled for failure to file
reports and pay taxes 00/00/1956

FORTRESS MUN INCOME FD INC (MD)
Name changed 08/14/1990
Name changed from Fortress High
Yield Tax-Free Fund Inc. to Fortress
Municipal Income Fund Inc.
08/14/1990
Name changed to Federated
Municipal Opportunities Fund, Inc.
03/31/1996
Federated Municipal Opportunities
Fund, Inc. name changed to
Federated Municipal High Yield
Advantage Fund, Inc. 08/01/2004
which merged into Federated
Municipal Securities Income Trust
11/10/2006

FORTRESS PAPER LTD (BC)
Name changed to Fortress Global
Enterprises Inc. 02/01/2018

FORTRESS PETE & RES LTD (BC)
Merged into Tiburon Petroleum Corp.
07/12/1982
Each share Common no par
exchanged for (0.57142857) share
Common no par
Tiburon Petroleum Corp. name
changed to Bristol Trading Co. Ltd.
05/12/1987

FORTRESS RES INC (BC)
Recapitalized as Consolidated
Fortress Resources Inc. (BC)
11/03/1997
Each share Common no par

exchanged for (0.37037037) share
Common no par
Consolidated Fortress Resources Inc.
(BC) reincorporated in Canada as
Fortress IT Corp. 07/31/2002 which
name changed to Fortress Minerals
Corp. 06/28/2004 which name
changed to Lundin Gold Inc.
12/18/2014

FORTRESS TOTAL PERFORMANCE U S TREAS FD INC (MD)
Trust terminated 12/01/1992
Details not available

FORTRESS UTIL FD INC (MD)
Merged into Federated Utility Fund
Inc. (MD) 06/01/1996
Each share Common no par
exchanged for Class A $0.001 par
on a net asset basis
Federated Utility Fund Inc. (MD)
reorganized in Massachusetts as
Federated Capital Income Fund, Inc.
12/20/2002

FORTRIU CAP CORP (BC)
Merged into Terrace Resources Inc.
(New) 06/02/2009
Each share Common no par
exchanged for (0.55099152) share
Common no par
Terrace Resources Inc. (New) name
changed to Terrace Energy Corp.
06/24/2011

FORTSUM BUSINESS SOLUTIONS INC (CANADA)
Merged into GFI Solutions Group Inc.
05/21/2009
Each share Common no par
exchanged for $0.82 cash

FORTUM OPEN JT STK CO (RUSSIA)
ADR agreement terminated
06/20/2013
Each Sponsored 144A GDR for
Ordinary exchanged for $2.7312
cash
Each Sponsored Reg. S GDR for
Ordinary exchanged for $2.7312
cash

FORTUNA CONSOLIDATED MINING CO. (AZ)
Charter expired by time limitation
7/28/42

FORTUNA CORP (NM)
Each share Common 10¢ par
exchanged for (0.25) share Common
40¢ par 08/02/1971
Merged into Kodiak Industries
11/08/1976
Each share Common 40¢ par
exchanged for $3.60 cash

FORTUNA GAMING CORP (NV)
Common $0.001 par split (2) for (1)
by issuance of (1) additional share
payable 09/15/2005 to holders of
record 09/13/2005 Ex date -
09/16/2005
Recapitalized as Principal Capital
Group, Inc. (New) 11/21/2008
Each share Common $0.001 par
exchanged for (0.0004) share
Common $0.001 par
Principal Capital Group, Inc. (New)
name changed to Gazoo Energy
Group, Inc. 09/11/2009
(See Gazoo Energy Group, Inc.)

FORTUNA LAND, OIL & DEVELOPING CO. (DE)
Charter declared void for
non-payment of franchise taxes
3/16/21

FORTUNA VENTURES INC (BC)
Name changed to Fortuna Silver
Mines Inc. 6/29/2005

FORTUNATE SUN MNG CO LTD (BC)
Recapitalized as Sonoma Resources
Inc. 08/29/2013
Each share Common no par
exchanged for (0.125) share new
Common no par
Sonoma Resources Inc. name

FORTUNE BANCORP (FL)
Acquired by AmSouth Bancorporation 6/23/94
Each share 8% Conv. Preferred Ser. A 1¢ par exchanged for either (1.425765) shares Common $1 par and $1.81159 value of Common $1 par or $47.81033 cash
Each share Common 1¢ par exchanged for either (1.0693) shares Common $1 par or $34.49906 cash
Note: Distribution of stock or cash will be made at random
AmSouth Bancorporation merged into Regions Financial Corp. 11/4/2006

FORTUNE BAY CORP OLD (CANADA)
Plan of arrangement effective 07/05/2016
Each share Common no par exchanged for (0.33333333) share kneat.com, inc. Common no par and (0.5) share Fortune Bay Corp. (New) Common no par
(See each company's listing)

FORTUNE BAY RES LTD (NL)
Reincorporated 05/23/1989
Place of incorporation changed from (BC) to (NL) 05/23/1989
Recapitalized as FBA Ventures Ltd. 09/09/1993
Each share Common no par exchanged for (0.2) share Common no par
FBA Ventures Ltd. name changed to Nexstar Automation Inc. 04/15/1994 which merged into Zygo Corp. 09/12/1996
(See Zygo Corp.)

FORTUNE BRANDS INC (DE)
Each share Common $3.125 par received distribution of (0.23148148) share Acco Brands Corp. Common 1¢ par payable 08/16/2005 to holders of record 08/09/2005 Ex date - 08/17/2005
Each share Common $3.125 par received distribution of (1) share Fortune Brands Home & Security, Inc. Common 1¢ par payable 10/03/2011 to holders of record 09/20/2011 Ex date - 10/04/2011
Name changed to Beam Inc. 10/04/2011
(See Beam Inc.)

FORTUNE CHANNEL MINES LTD (BC)
Recapitalized as Consolidated Fortune Channel Mines Ltd. 11/00/1972
Each share Capital Stock no par exchanged for (0.2) share Capital Stock no par
Consolidated Fortune Channel Mines Ltd. recapitalized as United Fortune Channel Mines Ltd. 09/22/1975 which recapitalized as Surewin Resources Corp. 02/07/1984
(See Surewin Resources Corp.)

FORTUNE DIVERSIFIED INDS INC (IN)
Reorganized 06/02/2005
Reorganized from Delaware to under the laws of Indiana 06/02/2005
Each share Common 1¢ par exchanged (0.1) share Common 10¢ par
Name changed to Fortune Industries, Inc. 04/17/2006
(See Fortune Industries, Inc.)

FORTUNE ELECTRS INC (CA)
Name changed to Technical Equities Corp., Inc. 05/15/1969
(See Technical Equities Corp.)

FORTUNE ENERGY INC (AB)
Each share old Common no par exchanged for (0.25) share new Common no par 07/04/1994
Merged into 798374 Alberta Ltd. 12/18/1998
Each share new Common no par exchanged for $0.80 cash

FORTUNE ENTMT CORP (DE)
Each share old Common $0.0001 par exchanged for (0.16666666) share new Common $0.0001 par 02/20/2002
Recapitalized as WT Holdings Corp. 04/03/2006
Each share new Common $0.0001 par exchanged for (0.05) share Common $0.0001 par
WT Holdings Corp. recapitalized as Asiamart, Inc. 12/04/2006
(See Asiamart, Inc.)

FORTUNE EXPL CORP (UT)
Merged into Madrigal Corp. 7/10/74
Each share Common $0.005 par exchanged for (0.1) share Common 1¢ par

FORTUNE FEDERAL SAVINGS & LOAN ASSOCIATION (USA)
Reorganized as Fortune Financial Group, Inc. 02/17/1984
Each share Common 1¢ par exchanged for (1) share Common 1¢ par
Fortune Financial Group, Inc. name changed to Fortune Bancorp 01/18/1992 which was acquired by AmSouth Bancorporation 06/23/1994 which merged into Regions Financial Corp. 11/04/2006

FORTUNE FINL GROUP INC (FL)
Name changed to Fortune Bancorp 1/18/92
Fortune Bancorp acquired by AmSouth Bancorporation 6/23/94 which merged into Regions Financial Corp. 11/4/2006

FORTUNE FINL INC (FL)
Plan of reorganization under Chapter 11 Federal Bankruptcy Code effective 4/6/2004
No stockholders' equity

FORTUNE FINL SYS NEV INC (NV)
Name changed 4/12/99
Name changed from Fortune Financial Systems Inc. to Fortune Financial Systems of Nevada, Inc. 4/12/99
Charter permanently revoked 3/1/2006

FORTUNE 44 CO (DE)
Name changed to Newberry Bancorp, Inc. 3/23/90
Newberry Bancorp, Inc. name changed to University Bancorp, Inc. 6/6/96

FORTUNE GAMING COM (NV)
Name changed to Austin Medical Technologies Inc. 1/30/2002
Austin Medical Technologies Inc. name changed to Las Vegas Central Reservations Corp. 8/3/2006

FORTUNE GRAPHITE INC (DE)
Each share old Common $0.001 par exchanged for (0.01) share new Common $0.001 par 01/27/2007
Reorganized under the laws of British Columbia 05/01/2010
Each share new Common $0.001 par exchanged for (0.01) share Common no par

FORTUNE INDS INC (IN)
Under plan of merger each share Common 10¢ par held by holders of (500) shares or fewer exchanged for $0.61 cash 07/01/2013
Under plan of merger each share Common 10¢ par exchanged for $0.586 cash 11/09/2016

FORTUNE IS MINES LTD (BC)
Merged into Berkley Resources Inc. (New) 08/18/1986
Each share Capital Stock 50¢ par exchanged for (1/6) share Capital Stock no par
Berkley Resources Inc. (New) recapitalized as Berkley Renewables Inc. 04/16/2012

FORTUNE MEDIA INC (DE)
Name changed to Cyberedge Enterprises, Inc. 11/10/2000
Cyberedge Enterprises, Inc. name changed to Wayne's Famous Phillies Inc. 3/10/2003

FORTUNE MINING CO. (ID)
Merged into Northwest Uranium Mines, Inc. on a (1) for (5) basis in 1956

FORTUNE MKT MEDIA INC (NV)
Each share old Common $0.001 par exchanged for (0.001) share new Common $0.001 par 11/05/2008
Charter cancelled 10/31/2013

FORTUNE NAT RES CORP (DE)
Plan of reorganization under Chapter 11 Federal Bankruptcy Code effective 04/21/2006
No stockholders' equity

FORTUNE NATL CORP (PA)
Completely liquidated 08/26/1996
Each share Common $1 par exchanged for first and final distribution of (0.00189393) share Acap Corp. new Common 10¢ par
Acap Corp. merged into UTG, Inc. 11/14/2011

FORTUNE NATL LIFE INS CO (PA)
Acquired by Fortune National Corp. 04/18/1972
Each share Common $1 par exchanged for (1) share Common $1 par
Fortune National Corp. liquidated for Acap Corp. 08/26/1996 which merged into UTG, Inc. 11/14/2011

FORTUNE OIL & GAS INC (NV)
Reorganized under the laws of Wyoming as Manzo Pharmaceuticals, Inc. 09/17/2014
Each share Common $0.001 par exchanged for (0.1) share Common $0.001 par

FORTUNE OIL & GAS LTD (BC)
Merged into Confederation Energy Corp. Ltd. 02/22/1982
Each share Common no par exchanged for (0.1) share Common no par
(See Confederation Energy Corp. Ltd.)

FORTUNE OILS LTD. (AB)
Recapitalized as Canadian Fortune Oil Ltd. and Capital Stock no par changed to 10¢ par 09/30/1955
Canadian Fortune Oil Ltd. merged into Page Petroleum Ltd. 08/13/1971
(See Page Petroleum Ltd.)

FORTUNE 1000 GROUP INC (CANADA)
Name changed to Fortsum Business Solutions Inc. 01/10/2006
(See Fortsum Business Solutions Inc.)

FORTUNE PARTNERS INC (NV)
Common $0.001 par split (3.75) for (1) by issuance of (2.75) additional shares payable 07/20/2005 to holders of record 07/18/2005 Ex date - 07/21/2005
Name changed to Power Air Corp. 12/23/2005
(See Power Air Corp.)

FORTUNE PETE CORP (DE)
Incorporated 05/22/1987
Each share old Common 1¢ par exchanged for (0.25) share new Common 1¢ par 06/16/1993
Name changed to Fortune Natural Resources Corp. 07/03/1997
(See Fortune Natural Resources Corp.)

FORTUNE PETROLEUM CORP. (DE)
Ctfs. dated prior to 10/17/60
Acquired by M J M & M Oil Co. 10/17/60
Each share Common 10¢ par exchanged for (1) share Capital Stock 10¢ par
M J M & M Oil Co. merged into Anza Pacific Corp. 6/12/64
(See Anza Pacific Corp.)

FORTUNE REAL ESTATE DEV CORP (NV)
Recapitalized as Andros Isle Development Corp. 04/18/2005
Each share Common $0.00005 par exchanged for (0.1) share Common $0.00005 par
(See Andros Isle Development Corp.)

FORTUNE RES CORP (CANADA)
Cease trade order effective 04/26/2002
Stockholders' equity unlikely

FORTUNE RIV RESOURCE CORP (BC)
Merged into Bravada Gold Corp. (New) 01/07/2011
Each share Common no par exchanged for (0.85) share Common no par

FORTUNE SYS CORP (DE)
Name changed to Tigera Group Inc. 07/01/1987
Tigera Group Inc. recapitalized as Connectivity Technologies Inc. 12/16/1996
(See Connectivity Technologies Inc.)

FORTUNE URANIUM MINES, INC. (UT)
Merged into Uranium Corp. of America (UT) on a (1) for (20) basis 4/5/55
Uranium Corp. of America (UT) merged into Chemical & Metallurgical Enterprises, Inc. 11/5/56
(See Chemical & Metallurgical Enterprises, Inc.)

FORTUNE VY RES INC (BC)
Merged into Orosur Mining Inc. 01/08/2010
Each share Common no par exchanged for (0.4534) share Common no par and $0.001 cash
Note: Unexchanged certificates were cancelled and became without value 01/08/2016

FORTUNE YELLOWKNIFE MINES, LTD. (ON)
Charter cancelled and declared dissolved for failure to pay taxes and file returns 12/07/1977

FORTUNET INC (NV)
Merged into Yuri Itkis Gaming Trust of 1993 on 03/03/2010
Each share Common $0.001 par exchanged for $2.25 cash

FORTUNISTICS INC (DE)
Recapitalized as Whitestone Industries Inc. (Old) 01/18/1993
Each share Common $0.00001 par exchanged for (1/30) share Common $0.00001 par
Whitestone Industries Inc. (Old) name changed to Entertainment & Gaming International, Inc. 08/03/1994 which name changed to Whitestone Industries Inc. (New) 06/16/1995 which recapitalized as Proformix Systems Inc. 07/15/1997 which name changed to Magnitude Information Systems, Inc. 12/03/1998 which name changed to Kiwibox.Com, Inc. 03/02/2010

40 EAST OAK STREET BUILDING CORP. (IL)
Reorganized as East Oak Street Hotel Co. 00/00/1935
Details not available

4860 SHERIDAN ROAD LIQUIDATION TRUST
Assets liquidated for benefit of creditors 06/00/1947
No stockholders' equity

48TH STREET & LEXINGTON AVE. CORP. (NY)
Liquidation completed 6/1/60

48TH STR REALIZATION CORP (NY)
Liquidation completed
Each share Capital Stock $1 par received initial distribution of $580 cash 07/10/1973
Each share Capital Stock $1 par received second distribution of $30 cash 09/17/1973
Each share Capital Stock $1 par received third distribution of $25 cash 01/07/1974
Each share Capital Stock $1 par received fourth and final distribution of $15 cash 07/02/1974
Note: Certificates were not required to be surrendered and are without value

40 / 86 STRATEGIC INCOME FD (MA)
Name changed to Helios High Yield Fund (MA) 09/08/2009
Helios High Yield Fund (MA) reorganized in Maryland as Brookfield High Income Fund Inc. 03/05/2014 which merged into Brookfield Real Assets Income Fund Inc. 12/05/2016

FORTY EXCHANGE PLACE CORP. (NY)
Liquidation completed
Each share Common $1 par stamped to indicate initial distribution of $85 cash 6/19/61
Each share Stamped Common $1 par exchanged for second distribution of $8 cash 2/27/62
Each share Stamped Common $1 par received third and final distribution of $1.50 cash 7/29/64

41ST STR BLDG CORP (NY)
Liquidation completed
Each share Common $1 par stamped to indicate initial distribution of $90 cash 12/15/72
Each share Stamped Common $1 par stamped to indicate second distribution of $220 cash 2/5/73
Each share Stamped Common $1 par stamped to indicate third distribution of $22 cash 10/25/73
Each share Stamped Common $1 par stamped to indicate fourth distribution of $10 cash 2/8/74
Each share Stamped Common $1 par stamped to indicate fifth distribution of $10 cash 2/28/75
Each share Stamped Common $1 par exchanged for sixth and final distribution of $22.53 cash 10/6/77

4545 BEACON BUILDING
Trust terminated 00/00/1949
Details not available

FORTY FOUR MINES LTD (MB)
Recapitalized as New Forty-Four Mines Ltd. 05/06/1970
Each share Capital Stock $1 par exchanged for (0.4) share Capital Stock no par
New Forty-Four Mines Ltd. merged into Canadian Gold Mines Ltd. 03/24/1986 which merged into Consolidated Canadian Fortune Resources Inc. 12/07/1990 which name changed to Canadian Fortune Resources Inc. (New) 03/15/1993 which merged into Fortune Energy Inc. 09/01/1993
(See Fortune Energy Inc.)

4940 WINTHROP CORP.
Liquidated 00/00/1947
Details not available

49 NORTH RESOURCE FD INC (SK)
Name changed to 49 North Resources Inc. 08/25/2009

49 WEST 37TH STR CORP (NY)
Liquidation completed
Each share Common no par stamped to indicate initial distribution of $58 cash 05/28/1969
Each share Stamped Common no par exchanged for second and final distribution of $3 cash 09/17/1969

FORTY NINER PPTYS LTD (BC)
Recapitalized as Caribbean Resources Corp. 03/20/1986
Each share Common no par exchanged for (0.25) share Common no par
Caribbean Resources Corp. merged into Mishibishu Gold Corp. 10/27/1989 which recapitalized as Messina Minerals Inc. 04/07/2003 which merged into Canadian Zinc Corp. 12/20/2013 which name changed to NorZinc Ltd. 09/11/2018

4145 BROADWAY HOTEL CO.
Reorganized as Buena Park Hotel Corp. in 1951
Each share Common no par exchanged for (1) share Preferred $44 par
(See Buena Park Hotel Corp.)

4737 RAVENSWOOD CORP. (IL)
Liquidation completed 01/11/1961
Details not available

42 PRODS INC (CA)
Stock Dividend - 100% 8/29/69
Merged into Home Fashions Inc. 12/26/85
Each share Class A Common no par exchanged for $3.60 cash

4278 HAZEL BUILDING CORP.
Completely liquidated 05/14/1948
Each share Capital Stock no par exchanged for first and final distribution of $4.40 cash

4207 ADDISON, INC.
Liquidated 00/00/1940
Details not available

FORTY WALL STREET BUILDING, INC. (NY)
Each share Capital Stock 1¢ par exchanged for (0.05) share Capital Stock 1¢ par 4/30/53
Liquidation completed 11/22/61
Details not available

FORUM BK JT STK COML BK (UKRAINE)
GDR agreement terminated 01/17/2017
GDR holders' equity unlikely

FORUM BEVERAGES INC (BC)
Name changed 02/16/1989
Name changed from Forum Resources Inc. to Forum Beverages Inc. 02/16/1989
Struck off register and declared dissolved for failure to file returns 02/07/1992

FORUM CAFETERIAS AMER INC (MO)
Name changed to Forum Restaurants, Inc. 07/01/1969
(See Forum Restaurants, Inc.)

FORUM CAP CORP (CO)
Proclaimed dissolved for failure to file reports and pay fees 5/25/95

FORUM COS INC (DE)
Each share Common $0.001 par exchanged for (0.003636) share Common $0.275 par 02/25/1977
Charter forfeited for failure to maintain a registered agent 02/09/1990

FORUM DEV CORP (BC)
Name changed to Forum Uranium Corp. 06/27/2006
Forum Uranium Corp. name changed to Forum Energy Metals Corp. 02/28/2018

FORUM ENERGY CORP (BC)
Name changed to FEC Resources Inc. 6/9/2005

FORUM GROUP INC (IN)
Common no par split (5) for (4) by issuance of (0.25) additional share 11/27/1981
Common no par split (2) for (1) by issuance of (1) additional share 08/05/1983
Common no par split (5) for (4) by issuance of (0.25) additional share 07/28/1986
Under plan of reorganization each share old Common no par received (0.01600464) share new Common no par 04/02/1992
Note: Certificates were not required to be surrendered and are without value
Stock Dividend - 10% 08/05/1985
Merged into Marriott International, Inc. 06/12/1996
Each share new Common no par exchanged for $13 cash

FORUM INDS INC (NY)
Charter cancelled and proclaimed dissolved for failure to pay taxes 12/24/1991

FORUM MERGER CORP (DE)
Units separated 02/23/2018
Name changed to ConvergeOne Holdings, Inc. and Class A Common $0.0001 par reclassified as Common $0.0001 par 02/23/2018

FORUM OIL & GAS CO (TX)
Voluntarily dissolved 12/27/1999
Details not available

FORUM RE GROUP BERMUDA LTD (BERMUDA)
Struck off register 00/00/1990

FORUM RE GROUP INC (NV)
Name changed to THE Group, Inc. 02/05/1990
(See THE Group, Inc.)

FORUM RESTAURANTS INC (MO)
8% Preferred $100 par called for redemption 04/21/1971
Merged into Star Restaurant Corp. 11/02/1983
Each share Common no par exchanged for $1.50 cash

FORUM RETIREMENT PARTNERS L P (DE)
Common Depositary Units reclassified as Depositary Preferred Units 01/01/1990
Merged into Host Marriott Corp. (New) 03/08/1999
Each Depositary Preferred Unit exchanged for $5.75 cash

FORUM URANIUM CORP (BC)
Each share old Common no par exchanged for (0.06666666) share new Common no par 01/03/2013
Name changed to Forum Energy Metals Corp. 02/28/2018

FORUM VENTURES LTD (BC)
Recapitalized as Forum Development Corp. 10/15/2001
Each share Common no par exchanged for (0.4) share Common no par
Forum Development Corp. name changed to Forum Uranium Corp. 06/27/2006 which name changed to Forum Energy Metals Corp. 02/28/2018

FORWARD INDS INC (FL)
Proclaimed dissolved for failure to file reports and pay fees 07/11/1972

FORWARD RES LTD (CANADA)
Reincorporated 05/23/1984
Place of incorporation changed from (AB) to (Canada) 05/23/1984
Reorganized as Exco Energy Ltd. 12/05/1984
Each share Common no par exchanged for (0.04) share Common no par
(See Exco Energy Ltd.)

FORZA ENVIRONMENTAL BLDG PRODS INC (NV)
SEC revoked common stock registration 12/12/2014

FORZANI GROUP LTD (AB)
Acquired by Canadian Tire Corp., Ltd. 08/18/2011
Each share Class A Common no par exchanged for $26.50 cash

FOSCA OIL CO. LTD. (AB)
Dissolved in 1967
No stockholders' equity

FOSCHINI LTD (SOUTH AFRICA)
Stock Dividend - 2.1043% payable 01/16/2001 to holders of record 11/24/2000 Ex date - 11/21/2000
Name changed to Foschini Group Ltd. 10/04/2010

FOSCO MNG LTD (AB)
Recapitalized as Marbaco Resources Ltd. 07/25/1979
Each share Common no par exchanged for (0.2) share Common no par
(See Marbaco Resources Ltd.)

FOSECO PLC (ENGLAND)
Name changed 08/04/1988
Name changed from Foseco Minsep PLC to Foseco PLC 08/04/1988
Acquired by Burmah Castrol PLC 01/18/1991
Each ADR for Ordinary 25p par exchanged for $5.654 cash

FOSHAY BUILDING CORP.
Property sold to bondholders in 1935

FOSLAKE MINES LTD. (ON)
Charter revoked for failure to file reports and pay taxes 08/01/1961

FOSSIL BAY RES LTD (YT)
Acquired by Terra Energy Corp. 12/31/2004
Each share Common no par exchanged for (0.01) share Common no par
Note: Holders of (9,999) shares or fewer received $0.013 cash per share

FOSSIL GRAPHICS INC (ON)
Reincorporated under the laws of Canada as Wataire Industries Inc. 03/01/2004
Wataire Industries Inc. (Canada) reincorporated in Nevada 08/18/2004 which name changed to Wataire Ecosafe Technologies Inc. 02/14/2007 which name changed to Ecosafe Innotech, Inc. 03/11/2008

FOSSIL INC (DE)
Common 1¢ par split (3) for (2) by issuance of (0.5) additional share payable 04/08/1998 to holders of record 03/25/1998
Common 1¢ par split (3) for (2) by issuance of (0.5) additional share payable 08/17/1999 to holders of record 08/03/1999
Common 1¢ par split (3) for (2) by issuance of (0.5) additional share payable 06/07/2002 to holders of record 05/24/2002 Ex date - 06/10/2002
Common 1¢ par split (3) for (2) by issuance of (0.5) additional share payable 04/08/2004 to holders of record 03/26/2004 Ex date - 04/12/2004
Name changed to Fossil Group, Inc. 06/06/2013

FOSSIL OIL & GAS, INC. (DE)
Merged into Premier Technology Holding, Inc. 5/12/86
Each share Common 10¢ par exchanged for (1/6) share Common $0.001 par
(See Premier Technology Holding, Inc.)

FOSSIL OIL & GAS LTD (AB)
Merged into Elk Point Resources Inc. 12/17/1996
Each share Common no par exchanged for (0.5785) share new Class A Common no par
Elk Point Resources Inc. merged into Acclaim Energy Trust 01/28/2003
(See Acclaim Energy Trust)

FOSTER APARTMENTS LIQUIDATION TRUST
Liquidated in 1952

FOSTER CMNTY INC (FL)
Common no par split (3) for (1) by issuance of (2) additional shares payable 04/29/2003 to holders of record 04/22/2003 Ex date - 04/30/2003
Name changed to GainClients, Inc. 10/31/2003

FOSTER FORBES GLASS CO (IN)
Common $1.50 par split (3) for (2) by issuance of (0.5) additional share 12/31/68
Stock Dividends - 10% 12/26/58; 100% 1/26/59
5-1/2% Preferred Ser. A $50 par called for redemption 1/15/70
Merged into National Can Corp. 6/1/70
Each share Common $1.50 par exchanged for (1) share 60¢ Conv. Preferred Ser. B $10 par and (1.6) share Common $5 par
(See National Can Corp.)

FOSTER GRANT INC (DE)
Each share Common $1 par exchanged for (1) share $1 Special Conv. Part. Preferred $1 par 5/10/74
Merged into American Hoechst Corp. 9/26/75
Each share $1 Special Conv. Part. Preferred $1 par exchanged for $46.20 cash

FOSTER L B CO (DE)
Reincorporated under the laws of Pennsylvania and Class A Common 1¢ par reclassified as Common 1¢ par 05/14/1998

FOSTER LAKE MINES LTD. (ON)
Charter cancelled and declared dissolved for failure to file returns and pay fees 07/27/1976

FOSTER MACHINE CO. (MA)
Acquired by Whitin Machine Works 00/00/1962
Details not available

FOSTER MED CORP (DE)
Common $1 par split (2) for (1) by issuance of (1) additional share 8/1/83
Merged into Avon Products, Inc. 5/30/84
Each share Common $1 par exchanged for (0.745) share Common 50¢ par

FOSTER-OSAGE OIL & GAS CO. (OK)
Charter cancelled for failure to pay taxes 12/15/50

FOSTER WHARF CO. (MA)
Completely liquidated in 1954

FOSTER WHEELER AG (SWITZERLAND)
Merged into Amec Foster Wheeler PLC 01/19/2015
Each Registered Share CHF 3 par exchanged for (0.8998) Sponsored ADR for Ordinary and $16.202455 cash
(See Amec Foster Wheeler PLC)

FOSTER WHEELER CORP (NY)
Common no par changed to $10 par 00/00/1936
Common $10 par changed to $0.33333333 par and (2) additional shares issued 07/15/1966
$1 Conv. Preferred Ser. A no par called for redemption 07/27/1973
Common $0.33333333 par split (2) for (1) by issuance of (1) additional share 03/15/1977
Common $0.33333333 par changed to $1.50 par 04/25/1977
Common $1.50 par changed to $1 par 05/03/1978
Common $1 par split (2) for (1) by issuance of (1) additional share 06/15/1979
Common $1 par split (2) for (1) by issuance of (1) additional share 12/15/1980
Stock Dividends - 100% 04/25/1952; 10% 03/04/1960
Reincorporated under the laws of Bermuda as Foster Wheeler Ltd. 05/25/2001
Foster Wheeler Ltd. (Bermuda) reorganized in Switzerland as Foster Wheeler AG 02/09/2009 which merged into Amec Foster Wheeler PLC 01/19/2015
(See Amec Foster Wheeler PLC)

FOSTER WHEELER LTD (BERMUDA)
Each share Common $1 par exchanged for (0.05) share Common 1¢ par 11/29/2004
Common 1¢ par split (2) for (1) by issuance of (1) additional share payable 01/22/2008 to holders of record 01/08/2008 Ex date - 01/23/2008
Reorganized under the laws of Switzerland as Foster Wheeler AG 02/09/2009
Each share Conv. Preferred Ser. B 1¢ par exchanged for (130) Registered Shares CHF 3 par
Each share Common 1¢ par exchanged for (1) Registered Share CHF 3 par
Foster Wheeler AG merged into Amec Foster Wheeler PLC 01/19/2015
(See Amec Foster Wheeler PLC)

FOSTER WHITNEY, INC. (NV)
Name changed to American International Petroleum Corp. 04/18/1982
(See American International Petroleum Corp.)

FOSTERS BREWING GROUP CDA INC (ON)
7.75% Preferred Ser. A no par called for redemption 12/31/1993
Public interest eliminated

FOSTERS GROUP LTD (AUSTRALIA)
Name changed 07/03/2001
Each Sponsored ADR for Ordinary exchanged for (0.6) Sponsored ADR for Ordinary 11/14/1995
Name changed from Foster's Brewing Group Ltd. to Foster's Group Ltd. 07/03/2001
Each Sponsored ADR for Ordinary received distribution of (0.33333333) Treasury Wine Estates Ltd. Sponsored ADR for Ordinary payable 05/23/2011 to holders of record 05/16/2011 Ex date - 05/12/2011
Acquired by SABMiller PLC 12/16/2011
Each Sponsored ADR for Ordinary exchanged for $5.2987 cash

FOSTERS RES LTD (AB)
Recapitalized as Blue Mountain Resources Ltd. 07/16/2001
Each share Common no par exchanged for (0.25) share Common no par
Blue Mountain Resources Ltd. name changed to Blue Mountain Energy Ltd. 07/18/2002
(See Blue Mountain Energy Ltd.)

FOSTORIA CORP (OH)
Stock Dividends - 10% 3/20/63; 10% 10/28/66
Each share Common $5 par exchanged for (0.005) share Common $1,000 par 3/22/67
Public interest eliminated

FOSTORIA GLASS CO (WV)
Each share Common $100 par exchanged for (10) shares Common $10 par 00/00/1947
Completely liquidated 12/28/1983
Each share Common $10 par exchanged for first and final distribution of (1.2) shares Lancaster Colony Corp. (DE) Common $1 par
Lancaster Colony Corp. (DE) reincorporated in Ohio 01/02/1992

FOSTORIA PRESSED STEEL CORP. (OH)
Each share Common no par exchanged for (2) shares Common $5 par in 1946
Stock Dividend - 10% 11/16/53
Name changed to Fostoria Corp. in 1959
(See Fostoria Corp.)

FOTEK CORP (VA)
Each share old Common $0.00001 par exchanged for (0.01) share new Common $0.00001 par 07/18/1986
Charter cancelled and proclaimed dissolved for failure to file reports 12/31/2004

FOTO MARK INC (MN)
Stock Dividend - 100% 08/21/1981
Merged into F-M Holdings, Inc. 03/26/1985
Each share Common 10¢ par exchanged for $5 cash

FOTO MEM INC (MA)
Stock Dividend - 100% 04/15/1970
Proclaimed dissolved for failure to file reports and pay taxes 12/11/1974

FOTO-VIDEO ELECTRONICS, INC. (NJ)
Adjudicated bankrupt 6/5/62
No stockholders' equity

FOTOBALL USA INC (DE)
Merged into K2 Inc. 01/23/2004
Each share Common 1¢ par exchanged for (0.2757) share Common $1 par
K2 Inc. merged into Jarden Corp. 08/08/2007

FOTOCHROME INC (DE)
Adjudicated bankrupt 12/15/1975
Stockholders' equity unlikely

FOTOMAT CORP (DE)
Reincorporated 07/21/1971
Common no par changed to 10¢ par 07/22/1971
State of incorporation changed from (CA) to (DE) 07/21/1971
Merged into Konishiroku Photo Industry Co. Ltd. 07/08/1986
Each share Common 10¢ par exchanged for $1.70 cash

FOULDS CO.
Merged into Grocery Store Products, Inc. 00/00/1929
Details not available

FOULDS MILLING CO.
Acquired by Grocery Store Products Co. 00/00/1937
Details not available

FOUND LAKE GOLD MINES LTD.
Recapitalized as Consolidated Found Lake Mines Ltd. 00/00/1948
Each share Capital Stock $1 par exchanged for (0.2) share Capital Stock $1 par
(See Consolidated Found Lake Mines Ltd.)

FOUNDATION BANCORP INC (OH)
Acquired by Garfield Acquisition Corp. 08/31/2001
Each share Common no par exchanged for $17.60 cash

FOUNDATION BANCORP INC (WA)
Merged into Pacific Continental Corp. 09/06/2016
Each share Common $1 par exchanged for (0.7911) share Common no par
Pacific Continental Corp. merged into Columbia Banking System, Inc. 11/01/2017

FOUNDATION CO.
Liquidated in 1943
Details not available

FOUNDATION CO. (NY)
Capital Stock no par changed to $1 par in 1937
Adjudicated bankrupt 9/21/64
No stockholders' equity

FOUNDATION CO. OF CANADA, LTD. OLD (CANADA)
Each share 7% 1st and 2nd Preference $100 par exchanged for (6) shares Common no par 00/00/1929
Each share Common $25 par exchanged for (4) shares Common no par 00/00/1929
Common no par exchanged (4) for (1) 00/00/1951
Common no par split (2) for (1) by issuance of (1) additional share 07/15/1958
Acquired by Canadian Foundation Co. Ltd. 02/17/1964
Each share Common no par exchanged for (0.25) share 6% Preferred $20 par and (1) share Common no par
(See Canadian Foundation Co. Ltd.)

FOUNDATION COAL HLDGS INC (DE)
Merged into Alpha Natural Resources, Inc. 07/31/2009
Each share Common 1¢ par exchanged for (1.084) shares Common 1¢ par
(See Alpha Natural Resources, Inc.)

FOUNDATION FINL CORP (NJ)
Charter declared void for non-payment of taxes 6/24/86

FOUNDATION HEALTH CORP (DE)
Common 1¢ par split (3) for (2) by issuance of (0.5) additional share 02/24/1992
Merged into Foundation Health Systems, Inc. 04/01/1997
Each share Common 1¢ par exchanged for (1.3) shares Common $0.001 par
Foundation Health Systems, Inc. name changed to Health Net Inc. 11/06/2000 which merged into Centene Corp. 03/24/2016

FOUNDATION HEALTH SYS INC (DE)
Name changed to Health Net, Inc. 11/06/2000
Health Net, Inc. merged into Centene Corp. 03/24/2016

FOUNDATION HEALTHCARE INC (OK)
Each share old Common $0.0001 par exchanged for (0.1) share new Common $0.0001 par 01/09/2015
Plan of reorganization under Chapter 11 Federal Bankruptcy proceedings effective 10/19/2017
No stockholders' equity

FOUNDATION INDUSTRIAL ENGINEERING CO., INC.
Recapitalized as Stokely Foods, Inc. in 1943
Each share Common 10¢ par exchanged for (0.2) share Common 50¢ par
Stokely Foods, Inc. merged into Stokely- Van Camp, Inc. 5/29/52
(See Stokley-Van Camp, Inc.)

FOUNDATION INVESTMENT CO. (OH)
Common $10 par changed to no par in 1932
Recapitalized in 1936
Each share 6% Preferred $100 par exchanged for (1.1) shares new $5 Preferred $100 par and $5 in cash

Each share Common no par exchanged for (1) share new Common no par
Recapitalized in 1941
$5 Preferred $100 par changed to $25 par
Common no par exchanged for new Common no par
Liquidated in 1955
Details not available

FOUNDATION INVT CORP (GA)
Completely liquidated 10/00/1973
Each share Common $1 par exchanged for first and final distribution of $2.68 cash

FOUNDATION LIFE INS CO (GA)
Under plan of merger each share Common $2.50 par exchanged for (2.5) shares Common $1 par 10/30/62
Acquired by Founders Financial Corp. (FL) 1/28/70
Each share Common $1 par exchanged for (2) shares Common $1 par
Founders Financial Corp. (FL) merged into Laurentian Capital Corp. (FL) 12/1/86 which reincorporated in Delaware 7/24/87
(See Laurentian Capital Corp.)

FOUNDATION LIFE INS CO AMER (NJ)
Under plan of reorganization each share Common 25¢ par automatically became (1) share Foundation Financial Corp. Common 25¢ par 7/31/72
(See Foundation Financial Corp.)

FOUNDATION LIFE INSURANCE SERVICE CO. (GA)
Merged into Foundation Life Insurance Co. 10/30/62
Each share Common 10¢ par exchanged for (0.5) shares Common $1 par
Foundation Life Insurance Co. acquired by Founders Financial Corp. (FL) 1/28/70 which merged into Laurentian Capital Corp. (FL) 12/1/86 which reincorporated in Delaware 7/24/87
(See Laurentian Capital Corp.)

FOUNDATION MEDICINE INC (DE)
Acquired by Roche Holding Ltd. 07/31/2018
Each share Common $0.0001 par exchanged for $137 cash

FOUNDATION MINES LTD (BC)
Charter cancelled 12/11/1982

FOUNDATION PETROLEUMS, LTD.
Merged into Amalgamated Oils, Ltd. 00/00/1941
Details not available

FOUNDATION RLTY FD LTD (FL)
Liquidation completed
Each Unit of Ltd. Partnership Int. I received initial distribution of $260 cash payable in March 2004 to holders of record March 2004
Each Unit of Ltd. Partnership Int. I received second and final distribution of $59 cash payable in July 2004 to holders of record July 2004
Each Unit of Ltd. Partnership Int. II received initial distribution of $500 cash payable 12/24/2004 to holders of record 12/24/2004
Each Unit of Ltd. Partnership Int. II received second and final distribution of $155 cash payable 1/28/2005 to holders of record 1/28/2005
Note: Certificates were not required to be surrendered and are without value

FOUNDATION RES INC (BC)
Recapitalized as Birch Hill Gold Corp. 10/28/2013
Each share Common no par exchanged for (0.1) share Common no par
Birch Hill Gold Corp. merged into Canoe Mining Ventures Corp. 06/04/2014

FOUNDATION RES LTD (YT)
Reincorporated 08/28/1996
Place of incorporation changed from (BC) to (YT) 08/28/1996
Recapitalized as Fury Explorations Ltd. (YT) 08/16/2002
Each share Common no par exchanged for (0.5) share Common no par
Fury Explorations Ltd. (YT) reincorporated in British Columbia 09/21/2006 which merged into Golden Predator Mines Inc. 08/15/2008
(See Golden Predator Mines Inc.)

FOUNDATION SECURITIES CORP.
Dissolved in 1929

FOUNDATION SECURITIES CORP. (AR)
Merged into Pioneer Corp. 8/14/68
Each share Common 5¢ par exchanged for (0.033333) share Common 50¢ par
(See Pioneer Corp.)

FOUNDATION TRUST SHARES, SERIES A (DE)
Trust terminated 12/31/1956
Final liquidating payment 05/03/1957

FOUNDERS ACCEPTANCE CORP. LTD. (MB)
Acquired by Burrard Mortgage & Investments Ltd. 12/31/71
Each VTC's for Common $1 par exchanged for (0.25) share Capital Stock no par
Each share Common $1 par exchanged for (0.25) share Capital Stock no par
Burrard Mortgage & Investments Ltd. name changed to Canlan Investment Corp. 6/26/78 which name changed to Canlan Ice Sports Corp. 6/25/99

FOUNDERS AMERN INVT CORP (MO)
Capital Stock $1 par changed to 50¢ par and (1) additional share issued 12/02/1971
Each (4) shares Capital Stock 50¢ par received (1) share Capital Stock $2 par 11/01/1979
Old certificates were not retired and are now valueless
Merged into Redlaw Industries Inc. 04/29/1986
Each share Capital Stock $2 par exchanged for $2.50 principal amount of 11-1/2% 10-Yr. Debentures due 04/29/1996 and (1) Common Stock Purchase Warrant expiring 04/29/1991
Note: Holdings of (50) or fewer shares received Ser. A Debentures
Holdings of (51) shares or more received Ser. B Debentures

FOUNDERS BANCORP (CA)
Acquired by Heartland Financial USA, Inc. 02/28/2017
Each share Common no par exchanged for $21.87 cash

FOUNDERS BK (BRYN MAWR, PA)
Common $2 par split (6) for (5) by issuance of (0.2) additional share payable 06/14/1996 to holders of record 05/31/1996
Merged into Susquehanna Bancshares, Inc. 07/31/1997
Each share Common $2 par exchanged for (0.566) share Common $2 par
Susquehanna Bancshares, Inc. merged into BB&T Corp. 08/01/2015

FOUNDERS BK (NEW HAVEN, CT)
Common $5 par changed to $1 par 6/6/91
Common $1 par changed to no par 7/26/93
Stock Dividends - 10% 10/13/87; 10% 11/25/88; 10% 12/22/89
Closed by FDIC in July 1995
Stockholders' equity undetermined

FOUNDERS CAP CORP (ON)
Reincorporated 11/21/2000
Place of incorporation changed from (AB) to (ON) 11/21/2000
Name changed to Sentry Select Capital Corp. 01/15/2001
(See Sentry Select Capital Corp.)

FOUNDERS CMNTY BK (SAN LUIS OBISPO, CA)
Reorganized as Founders Bancorp 07/06/2007
Each share Common no par exchanged for (1) share Common no par
(See Founders Bancorp)

FOUNDERS ENERGY LTD (AB)
Each share old Common no par exchanged for (0.25) share new Common no par 02/02/2000
Reorganized as Provident Energy Trust 03/06/2001
Each share new Common no par exchanged for (1/3) Trust Unit no par
Provident Energy Trust reorganized as Provident Energy Ltd. (New) 01/03/2011 which merged into Pembina Pipeline Corp. 04/02/2012

FOUNDERS EQUITABLE CO AMER INC (NV)
Each share Common 20¢ par exchanged for (0.1) share Common $2 par 4/11/83
Name changed to Renaissance Group, Inc. and Common $2 par changed to 1¢ par 11/18/85

FOUNDERS EQUITY CORP (NV)
Charter revoked for failure to file reports and pay fees 03/01/1987

FOUNDERS FDS INC (MD)
Equity Income Fund no par reclassified as Balanced Fund no par 00/00/1994
Blue Chip Fund no par reclassified as Growth & Income Fund no par 04/30/1999
Special Fund no par reclassified as Mid-Cap Growth Fund no par 04/30/1999
Frontier Fund no par reclassified as Discovery Fund no par 08/13/1999
Name changed to Dreyfus Founders Fund, Inc. 12/31/1999

FOUNDERS FINANCIAL CORP. (MI)
Ctfs. dated prior to 05/15/1972
Charter declared inoperative and void for failure to file reports 05/15/1972

FOUNDERS FINL CORP (MD)
Ctfs. dated after 02/03/1998
Merged into Old National Bancorp 01/01/2015
Each share Common no par exchanged for (3.25) shares Common $1 par and $38 cash

FOUNDERS FINL CORP NEW (FL)
Merged into Chase Federal Savings Bank (Miami, FL) 1/12/96
Each share Common $1 par exchanged for (0.96989) share Common 1¢ par
(See Chase Federal Savings Bank (Miami, FL))

FOUNDERS FINL CORP OLD (FL)
Merged into Laurentian Capital Corp. (FL) 12/1/86
Each share Common $1 par exchanged for (0.3575) share Common 5¢ par
Laurentian Capital Corp. (FL) reincorporated in Delaware 7/24/87
(See Laurentian Capital Corp.)

FOUNDERS FINL INC (DE)
Merged into Leasing Credit Corp. (New) 1/1/84
Each share Class A $1 par exchanged for (1.24) shares Common 10¢ par
(See Leasing Credit Corp. (New))

FOUNDERS FIRE & MARINE INSURANCE CO. (CA)
Name changed to Founders Insurance Co. in 1951
Founders Insurance Co. merged into Security Insurance Co. of New Haven 12/31/62 which name changed to Security Insurance Co. of Hartford 1/1/65 which name changed to Security Corp. 6/30/68 which was acquired by Textron Inc. 6/29/73

FOUNDERS FOOD & FIRKINS LTD (MN)
Name changed to Granite City Food & Brewery Ltd. 09/12/2002

FOUNDERS GROWTH FD INC (MD)
Capital Stock $1 par changed to 25¢ par 10/31/1972
Merged into Founders Funds, Inc. 11/30/1987
Details not available

FOUNDERS INCOME FD INC (MD)
Name changed to Founders Equity Income Fund, Inc. 07/23/1986

FOUNDERS INSURANCE CO. (CA)
Merged into Security Insurance Co. of New Haven 12/31/1962
Each share Capital Stock $10 par exchanged for (0.046949) share Common $10 par
Security Insurance Co. of New Haven name changed to Security Insurance Co. of Hartford 01/01/1965 which name changed to Security Corp. 06/30/1968 which was acquired by Textron Inc. 06/29/1973

FOUNDERS LIFE ASSURANCE CO. OF CAROLINA (NC)
Name changed to Life Assurance Co. of Carolina 7/1/66
(See Life Assurance Co. of Carolina)

FOUNDERS LIFE ASSURN CO FLA (FL)
Merged into Founders Financial Corp. (FL) 6/16/69
Each share Capital Stock $1 par exchanged for (1) share Common $1 par
Founders Financial Corp. (FL) merged into Laurentian Capital Corp. (FL) 12/1/86 which reincorporated in Delaware 7/24/87
(See Laurentian Capital Corp.)

FOUNDERS LIFE INS CO (CA)
Common $10 par changed to $1 par and (9) additional shares issued 05/09/1969
Merged into Pinehurst Corp. 01/02/1970
Each share Common $1 par exchanged for (1) share Common 50¢ par
Pinehurst Corp. name changed to Emett & Chandler Companies, Inc. 05/24/1982
(See Emett & Chandler Companies, Inc.)

FOUNDERS MUT DEPOSITOR CORP (CO)
Acquired by Downe Communications, Inc. 8/14/70
Each share Class A Common no par exchanged for (0.656) share Common $1 par
(See Downe Communications, Inc.)

FOUNDERS MUT FD (CO)
Ctfs. of Bene. Int. no par split (2) for (1) by issuance of (1) additional certificate 05/16/1955
Under plan of reorganization each Ctf. of Bene. Int. no par automatically became (1) Founders

Funds, Inc. Equity Income Fund no par 12/01/1987
Founders Funds, Inc. name changed to Dreyfus Founders Funds, Inc. 12/31/1999 which name changed to Dreyfus Discovery Fund 12/01/2008

FOUNDERS NATIONAL BANK (OKLAHOMA CITY, OK)
Name changed to Founders Bank & Trust Co. (Oklahoma City, Okla.) 2/4/70

FOUNDERS PFD LIFE INS CO (TX)
Merged into Citizens Insurance Co. of America 12/31/1980
Each (4.13) shares Common $1 par exchanged for (1) share Class A Common $1 par
Citizens Insurance Co. of America merged into Citizens, Inc. 12/01/1988

FOUNDERS SAVINGS & LOAN ASSOCIATION (CA)
Merged into Columbus-Founders Savings & Loan Assoication 6/30/65
Each share Guarantee Capital Stock $1 par exchanged for (1.6) shares Guarantee Capital Stock $1 par
Columbus-Founders Savings & Loan Association name changed to Columbus Savings & Loan Association (New) 4/10/70 which merged into Imperial Corp. of America (CA) 3/2/72 which reincorporated in Delaware 9/21/87
(See Imperial Corp. of America (DE))

FOUNDERS SPL FD INC (DE)
Capital Stock $1 par split (5) for (1) by issuance of (4) additional shares 08/31/1987
Under plan of reorganization each share Capital Stock $1 par automatically became (1) share Founders Funds, Inc. Special Fund no par 08/31/1987
Founders Funds, Inc. name changed to Dreyfus Founders Funds, Inc. 12/31/1999 which name changed to Dreyfus Discovery Fund 12/01/2008

FOUNDRY HLDGS CORP (BC)
Name changed to Yangtze Telecom Corp. 9/8/2003

FOUNDRY NETWORKS INC (DE)
Common $0.0001 par split (2) for (1) by issuance of (1) additional share payable 01/07/2000 to holders of record 12/29/1999
Merged into Brocade Communications Systems, Inc. 12/18/2008
Each share Common $0.0001 par exchanged for $16.50 cash

FOUNG & FOUNG CHINA CORP (NY)
Name changed to CTS International Ltd. 2/17/88
(See CTS International Ltd.)

FOUNTAIN CITY BANK (KNOXVILLE, TN)
Merged into First Tennessee National Corp. 12/3/73
Each share Capital Stock $20 par exchanged for (6) shares Common $2.50 par
First Tennessee National Corp. name changed to First Horizon National Corp. 4/20/2004

FOUNTAIN COLONY HLDG CORP (CO)
Reincorporated 02/16/1999
State of incorporation changed from (DE) to (CO) 02/16/1999
Name changed to Fountain Colony Ventures Inc. 07/23/1999
Fountain Colony Ventures Inc. recapitalized as SGT Ventures, Inc. 03/20/2006 which name changed to Stronghold Industries, Inc. 07/10/2006 which recapitalized as Image Worldwide, Inc. 11/30/2007 which recapitalized as STL Marketing Group, Inc. 09/03/2009

FOUNTAIN COLONY VENTURES INC (CO)
Common $0.001 par split (4.2) for (1) by issuance of (3.2) additional shares payable 02/11/2000 to holders of record 01/28/2000
Recapitalized as SGT Ventures, Inc. 03/20/2006
Each share Common $0.001 par exchanged for (0.005) share Common $0.001 par
SGT Ventures, Inc. name changed to Stronghold Industries, Inc. 07/10/2006 which recapitalized as Image Worldwide, Inc. 11/30/2007 which recapitalized as STL Marketing Group, Inc. 09/03/2009

FOUNTAIN FRESH INTL (UT)
Each share old Common $0.001 par exchanged for (0.2) share new Common $0.001 par 2/29/96
Name changed to Bevex, Inc. 8/17/98
Bevex, Inc. recapitalized as GTG Ventures, Inc. 11/1/2005

FOUNTAIN HEAD INC (UT)
Recapitalized as Demarco Energy Systems of America, Inc. 11/17/1989
Each share Common $0.001 par exchanged for (0.025) share Common $0.001 par
Demarco Energy Systems of America, Inc. name changed to Energy Vision International, Inc. 03/03/2006
(See Energy Vision International, Inc.)

FOUNTAIN HEALTHY AGING INC (NV)
Common $0.001 par split (2) for (1) by issuance of (1) additional share payable 12/22/2008 to holders of record 12/16/2008 Ex date - 12/23/2008
Charter permanently revoked 03/01/2010

FOUNTAIN HOUSE HLDGS CORP (BC)
Recapitalized as Abbastar Holdings Ltd. 09/18/2002
Each share Common no par exchanged for (0.06666666) share Common no par
Abbastar Holdings Ltd. name changed to Abbastar Uranium Corp. 05/31/2007 which name changed to Abbastar Resources Corp. 07/28/2009 which reorganized as Glenmark Capital Corp. 07/29/2013 which recapitalized as Aldever Resources Inc. 08/05/2015

FOUNTAIN OIL INC (DE)
Recapitalized as CanArgo Energy Corp. 07/15/1998
Each share Common no par exchanged for (0.5) share Common 10¢ par
(See CanArgo Energy Corp.)

FOUNTAIN PHARMACEUTICALS INC (DE)
Each share old Common $0.001 par exchanged for (0.05) share new Common $0.06 par 12/11/1997
Recapitalized as SiriCOMM, Inc. 11/21/2002
Each (60) shares new Common $0.06 par exchanged for (1) share Common $0.001 par
(See SiriCOMM, Inc.)

FOUNTAIN PWR BOAT INDS INC (NV)
Each share old Common 1¢ par exchanged for (0.5) share new Common 1¢ par 02/04/1994
New Common 1¢ par split (3) for (2) by issuance of (0.5) additional share payable 08/14/1997 to holders of record 08/01/1997
Plan of reorganization under Chapter 11 Federal Bankruptcy Code effective 03/01/2010
No stockholders' equity

FOUNTAIN YOUTH INC (UT)
Proclaimed dissolved for failure to pay taxes 3/1/89

FOUNTAIN'S, INC. (DE)
No longer in existence having become inoperative and void for non-payment of taxes 4/1/64

FOUNTAINHEAD PROJS CORP (BC)
Name changed to eMedia Networks International Corp. 10/19/2000
(See eMedia Networks International Corp.)

FOUR CORNERS FINL CORP (NY)
Each share Common 1¢ par exchanged for (0.25) share Common 4¢ par 7/31/92
Each share Common 4¢ par exchanged for (0.01) share new Common $4 par 3/26/99
Note: In effect holders received $12 cash per share and public interest eliminated

FOUR CORNERS OIL & MINERALS CO. (CO)
Completely liquidated 12/07/1967
Each share Common $1 par exchanged for first and final distribution of (0.098039) share Consolidated Oil & Gas, Inc. (CO) Common 20¢ par
Consolidated Oil & Gas, Inc. (CO) acquired by Hugoton Energy Corp. 09/07/1995 which merged into Chesapeake Energy Corp. 03/10/1998

FOUR CORNERS URANIUM CORP. (CO)
Name changed to Four Corners Oil & Minerals Co. 06/00/1959
Four Corners Oil & Minerals Co. acquired by Consolidated Oil & Gas, Inc. (CO) 12/07/1967 which was acquired by Hugoton Energy Corp. 09/07/1995 which merged into Chesapeake Energy Corp. 03/10/1998

FOUR CROWN FOODS INC (CANADA)
Name changed to Universal Domains Inc. 6/5/2000
Universal Domains Inc. recapitalized as Pure Capital Inc. 10/11/2004 which name changed to Tombstone Exploration Corp. 2/12/2007

FOUR CRYSTAL FDG INC (FL)
SEC revoked common stock registration 09/21/2010

4D SEISMIC INC (NV)
SEC revoked common stock registration 08/06/2010

4D VIRTUAL SPACE LTD (BC)
Name changed to Supreme Metals Corp. 12/28/2016

4 F FOODS LTD (BC)
Placed into receivership 03/00/1982
No stockholders' equity

FOUR FLAGS INTERNATIONAL, INC. (MN)
Adjudicated bankrupt 9/10/70

405 FULLERTON PARKWAY BUILDING CORP. (IL)
Liquidation completed 12/30/57
Details not available

444 ST. JAMES LIQUIDATION TRUST
Trust terminated in 1950
Details not available

400 MADISON AVE CORP (NY)
$5 Preferred no par called for redemption 11/01/1964
Liquidation completed
Each share Common $1 par received initial distribution of $360 cash 01/04/1979
Each share Common $1 par received second distribution of $12.50 cash 07/18/1979
Assets transferred from 400 Madison Ave. Corp. to 400 Madison Ave. Corp. Liquidating Trust and Common $1 par reclassified as Shares of Bene. Int. $1 par 08/10/1979
Each Share of Bene. Int. $1 par received first and final distribution of $4.30 cash 12/16/1982
Note: Certificates were not required to be surrendered and are without value

4IMPRINT GROUP PLC (UNITED KINGDOM)
ADR agreement terminated 11/29/2017
Each Sponsored ADR for Ordinary exchanged for (2) shares Ordinary
Note: Unexchanged ADR's will be sold and the proceeds, if any, held for claim after 12/03/2018

4 KIDS ENTMT INC (NY)
Common 1¢ par split (3) for (2) by issuance of (0.5) additional share payable 05/03/1999 to holders of record 04/15/1999
Common 1¢ par split (2) for (1) by issuance of (1) additional share payable 09/13/1999 to holders of record 09/01/1999
Plan of reorganization under Chapter 11 Federal Bankruptcy proceedings effective 12/21/2012
Each share Common 1¢ par exchanged for (1) share 4Licensing Corp. (DE) Common 1¢ par
(See 4Licensing Corp.)

FOUR MEDIA CO (DE)
Issue Information - 5,000,000 shares COM offered at $10 per share on 2/7/97
Merged into AT&T Corp. 4/10/2000
Each share Common 1¢ par exchanged for (0.16129) share Common Liberty Media Group Class A 1¢ par and $6.25 cash
AT&T Corp. merged into AT&T Inc. 11/18/2005

FOUR NINES GOLD INC (CO)
Completely liquidated
Each share Common $0.0001 par received first and final distribution of $0.00076 cash payable 12/28/2007 to holders of record 09/13/2007
Note: Certificates were not required to be surrendered and are without value

FOUR OAKS BK & TR CO (FOUR OAKS, NC)
Under plan of reorganization each share Common $1 par automatically became (1) share Four Oaks Fincorp, Inc. Common $1 par 07/01/1997
Four Oaks Fincorp, Inc. merged into United Community Banks, Inc. 11/01/2017

FOUR OAKS FINCORP INC (NC)
Old Common $1 par split (3) for (2) by issuance of (0.5) additional share payable 07/21/1998 to holders of record 07/06/1998
Old Common $1 par split (3) for (2) by issuance of (0.5) additional share payable 04/07/2000 to holders of record 03/31/2000
Old Common $1 par split (5) for (4) by issuance of (0.25) additional share payable 11/11/2003 to holders of record 11/03/2003 Ex date - 11/12/2003
Old Common $1 par split (5) for (4) by issuance of (0.25) additional share payable 10/29/2004 to holders of record 10/15/2004
Old Common $1 par split (5) for (4) by issuance of (0.25) additional share payable 11/25/2005 to holders of record 11/09/2005 Ex date - 11/28/2005
Old Common $1 par split (5) for (4) by issuance of (0.25) additional share payable 11/10/2006 to holders

of record 10/30/2006 Ex date - 11/13/2006
Each share old Common $1 par (350891 10 7) exchanged for (0.2) share new Common $1 par 03/02/2017
Stock Dividend - 10% payable 11/09/2007 to holders of record 10/30/2007 Ex date - 10/26/2007
Merged into United Community Banks, Inc. 11/01/2017
Each share new Common $1 par exchanged for (0.6178) share new Common $1 par and $1.90 cash

FOUR PHASE SYS INC (DE)
Each share Common 2¢ par exchanged for (0.5) share Common 4¢ par 06/15/1976
Merged into Motorola, Inc. 03/02/1982
Each share Common 4¢ par exchanged for (0.763) share Common $3 par
Motorola, Inc. recapitalized as Motorola Solutions, Inc. 01/04/2011

FOUR POINT MINES LTD. (BC)
Struck off register and declared dissolved for failure to file returns 02/25/1983

FOUR PTS CAP CORP (BC)
Name changed to Yellowhead Mining Inc. 11/17/2010

FOUR RIV VENTURES LTD (BC)
Recapitalized as Canabo Medical Inc. 11/09/2016
Each share Common no par exchanged for (0.5) share Common no par
Canabo Medical Inc. name changed to Aleafia Health Inc. 03/28/2018

FOUR RIVS BIOENERGY INC (NV)
SEC revoked common stock registration 10/01/2013

FOUR SEASONS EQUITY CORP (DE)
Reorganized as ANTA Corp. 07/17/1972
Only holders who suffered losses on purchases on or before 07/22/1970 and who filed claim on or before 07/31/1972 were entitled to participate in the plan There is no equity if the above conditions are not applicable
For each $72.7519 of loss sustained claimants received (1) share ANTA Corp. Common $1 par 02/15/1973
Note: Certificates were not required to be surrendered and are without value
(See ANTA Corp.)

FOUR SEASONS HOTELS INC (ON)
Subordinate Shares no par split (2) for (1) by issuance of (1) additional share 01/09/1990
Subordinate Shares no par reclassified as Limited Shares no par 10/03/1996
Merged into Triple Holdings Ltd. 04/26/2007
Each Limited Share no par exchanged for USD$82 cash

FOUR SEASONS HOTELS LTD (ON)
Common no par split (2) for (1) by issuance of (1) additional share 04/10/1972
6% Conv. 1st Preference Ser. A $10 par reclassified as 8% 1st Preference Ser. A $10 par and conversion privilege expired 02/14/1978
Under plan or reorganization each share Common no par automatically became (1) share 2nd Preference no par 02/14/1978
Note: Prior to 03/01/1978 holders of Common had the option to convert their shares into 3rd Preference no par on a share for share basis
2nd Preference no par called for redemption 03/01/1978
3rd Preference no par called for redemption 03/01/1978
8% 1st Preference Ser. A $10 par called for redemption 10/31/1986

FOUR SEASONS MFG LTD (BC)
Name changed to Renn Industries Inc. 11/29/1974
Renn Industries Inc. name changed to Anthes Industries Inc. 06/04/1981 which name changed to Patheon Inc. 05/12/1993
(See Patheon Inc.)

FOUR SEASONS MINING & RESOURCES LTD. (BC)
Name changed to Four Seasons Manufacturing Ltd. 10/31/1971
Four Seasons Manufacturing Ltd. name changed to Renn Industries Inc. 11/29/1974 which name changed to Anthes Industries Inc. 06/04/1981 which name changed to Patheon Inc. 05/12/1993
(See Patheon Inc.)

FOUR SEASONS NURSING CTRS AMER INC (DE)
Common 50¢ par changed to 25¢ par and (1) additional share issued 03/21/1969
Reorganized as ANTA Corp. 07/17/1972
Only holders who suffered losses on purchases on or before 07/22/1970 and who filed claim on or before 07/31/1972 were entitled to participate in the plan
There was no equity if the above conditions were not applicable
For each $72.7519 of loss sustained claimants received (1) share ANTA Corp. Common $1 par 02/15/1973
(See Anta Corp.)

FOUR SEASONS RECREATION LTD. (BC)
Name changed to Four Seasons Mining & Resources Ltd. 06/04/1970
Four Seasons Mining & Resources Ltd. name changed to Four Seasons Manufacturing Ltd. 10/31/1971 which name changed to Renn Industries Inc. 11/29/1974 which name changed to Anthes Industries Inc. 06/04/1981 which name changed to Patheon Inc. 05/12/1993
(See Patheon Inc.)

FOUR SEASONS RES LTD (BC)
Recapitalized as FSR Industries Inc. 01/31/1991
Each share Common no par exchanged for (0.33333333) share Common no par
FSR Industries Inc. name changed to Syspower Multimedia Industries, Inc. (BC) 06/15/1993 which reincorporated in British Virgin Islands 02/15/1995
(See Syspower Multimedia Industries, Inc.)

4 SPECTRA INC (UT)
Each share Common 1¢ par exchanged for (0.25) share Common 5¢ par 03/10/1972
Name changed to CV 100 Products, Inc. 05/09/1972
CV 100 Products, Inc. merged into American Scientific Industries International 06/19/1972
(See American Scientific Industries International)

FOUR STAR HLDGS INC (FL)
Administratively dissolved 09/23/2011

FOUR STAR INTL INC (CA)
Capital Stock no par reclassified as Common no par 1/5/68
Common no par split (3) for (2) by issuance of (0.5) additional share 3/10/83
Common no par split (3) for (2) by issuance of (0.5) additional share 7/15/83
Merged into Compact Video, Inc. 9/25/86
Each share Common no par exchanged for $6 cash

FOUR STAR TELEVISION (CA)
Name changed to Four Star International Inc. 12/4/67
(See Four Star International Inc.)

4325231 CDA INC (BC)
Name changed to Global Summit Real Estate Inc. 10/17/2007
(See Global Summit Real Estate Inc.)

FOUR WHEEL DRIVE AUTO CO. (WI)
Each share Capital Stock $100 par exchanged for (10) shares Capital Stock $10 par in 1937
Stock Dividend - 50% 3/29/46
Name changed to FWD Corp. and Capital Stock $10 par changed to Common $10 par 1/15/59
(See FWD Corp.)

FOUR WHEEL DRIVE ENGINEERING, INC. (UT)
Name changed to Marathon Energy Inc. 3/29/82

FOURBAR MINES LTD (BC)
Recapitalized as Cloverdale Resources Ltd. 03/00/1973
Each share Common no par exchanged for (0.5) share Common no par
(See Cloverdale Resources Ltd.)

4-D NEUROIMAGING (CA)
Each share old Common no par exchanged for (0.00083333) share new Common no par 03/01/2004
Note: In effect holders received $0.15 cash per share and public interest was eliminated

FOURESS MINES, INC. (WA)
Charter revoked for failure to file reports and pay fees 7/1/66

FOUREYES HLDG INC (UT)
Name changed to New Anaconda Co. 06/07/1999
(See New Anaconda Co.)

4FORGOLF INC (NV)
Reorganized as Tricell, Inc. 07/28/2003
Each share Common $0.001 par exchanged for (20) shares Common $0.001 par
(See Tricell, Inc.)

4FRONT TECHNOLOGIES INC (CO)
Name changed 12/11/97
Name changed from 4Front Software International Inc. to 4Front Technologies Inc. 12/11/97
Merged into NCR Corp. 10/17/2000
Each share Common $0.001 par exchanged for $18.50 cash

4G DATA SYS INC (NY)
Company advised it became private 00/00/1988
Details not available

4HEALTH INC (UT)
Name changed to Irwin Naturals/4Health, Inc. 07/01/1998
Irwin Naturals/4Health, Inc. name changed to Omni Nutraceuticals, Inc. 08/23/1999
(See Omni Nutraceuticals, Inc.)

4LICENSING CORP (DE)
Plan of reorganization under Chapter 11 Federal Bankruptcy proceedings effective 02/03/2017
No stockholders' equity

4NET SOFTWARE INC (DE)
Name changed 03/08/2001
Name changed from 4networld.com, Inc. to 4net Software, Inc. 03/08/2001
Name changed to Regional Brands Inc. 06/01/2016

FOURSQUARE FD INC (MA)
Merged into Eaton Vance Investors Fund, Inc. 09/12/1983
Each share Common $1 par exchanged for (1.37659936) share Common $1 par
Eaton Vance Investors Fund, Inc.
name changed to Eaton Vance Investors Trust 09/29/1993
(See Eaton Vance Investors Trust)

1440 BROADWAY CORP.
Out of business 00/00/1942
Details not available

1425 LIQUIDATION CORP. (CA)
Liquidation completed
Each share Capital Stock no par exchanged for initial distribution of (0.42) share Whittaker Corp. (CA) $1.25 Conv. Preferred Ser. A no par 8/31/67
Each share Capital Stock no par received second and final distribution of (0.08) share Whittaker Corp. (CA) $1.25 Conv. Preferred Ser. A no par 5/21/69
Whittaker Corp. (CA) reincorporated in Delaware 6/16/86
(See Whittaker Corp. (DE))

14-20 NORTH SANGAMON APARTMENTS, INC. (IL)
Completely liquidated 1/5/45
Each Stock Trust Ctf. $5 par exchanged for first and final distribution of $86 cash

1420 WALNUT CORP. (PA)
Declared dissolved by Court Decree 9/8/64
No stockholders' equity

FOURTH & MARKET REALTY CO.
Liquidated in 1948

FOURTH & PINE INVESTMENT CO.
Liquidation completed in 1945

4TH DIMENSION SOFTWARE LTD. (ISRAEL)
Name changed to New Dimension Software Ltd. 11/05/1995
(See New Dimension Software Ltd.)

FOURTH FINL CORP (KS)
Common $5 par split (3) for (2) by issuance of (0.5) additional share 3/1/86
Common $5 par split (5) for (4) by issuance of (0.25) additional share 3/1/90
Stock Dividends - 10% 9/1/80; 10% 9/1/81; 50% 3/1/83
Merged into Boatmen's Bancshares, Inc. 1/31/96
Each 7% Depositary Preferred Class A exchanged for (1) share Common $1 par
Each share 7% Conv. Class A Preferred $100 par exchanged for (1) 7% Conv. Class A Depositary Preferred Share
Each share Common $5 par exchanged for (1) share Common $1 par
Boatmen's Bancshares, Inc. merged into NationsBank Corp. 1/7/97 which reincorporated in Delaware as BankAmerica Corp. (Old) 9/25/98 which merged into BankAmerica Corp. (New) 9/30/98 which name changed to Bank of America Corp. 4/28/99

FOURTH FIRST BANCORP (IN)
Merged into National City Bancshares, Inc. 12/31/1997
Each share Common exchanged for (5.5696) shares Common $3.33-1/3 par
National City Bancshares, Inc. name changed to Integra Bank Corp. 05/22/2000
(See Integra Bank Corp.)

4TH GRADE FILMS INC (UT)
Name changed to Strainwise, Inc. (UT) 09/26/2014
Strainwise, Inc. (UT) reincorporated in Colorado as STWC Holdings, Inc. 11/14/2016

FOURTH JULY SILVER INC (ID)
Name changed to International Basic Resources Inc. 8/12/83
International Basic Resources Inc.

recapitalized as International Resort Developers Inc. (ID) 5/19/97 which reincorporated under the laws of Tennessee as Ameristar International Holdings Corp. 1/22/98
(See Ameristar International Holdings Corp.)

FOURTH NATL BK & TR CO (WICHITA, KS)
Capital Stock $10 par changed to $5 par and (1) additional share issued 06/30/1967
Through exchange offer 98% acquired by Fourth Financial Corp. as of 02/09/1973
Public interest eliminated

FOURTH NATL BK (COLUMBUS, GA)
Name changed to National Bank & Trust Co. (Columbus, GA) 07/01/1974
National Bank & Trust Co. (Columbus, GA) merged into Trust Co. of Georgia 08/17/1978 which merged into SunTrust Banks, Inc. 07/01/1985

FOURTH NATL BK (TULSA, OK)
Each share Common $20 par exchanged for (2) shares Common $10 par in 1953
Stock Dividends - 20% 1/21/52; 33-1/3% 6/30/53; 25% 7/15/55; 25% 7/15/60; 10% 7/31/70
Under plan of reorganization each share Common $10 par automatically became (1) share Fourth National Corp. Common $10 par 11/1/71
Fourth National Corp. merged into Fourth Financial Corp. 12/31/92 which merged into Boatmen's Bancshares, Inc. 1/31/96 which merged into NationsBank Corp. 1/7/97 which reincorporated in Delaware as BankAmerica Corp. (Old) 9/25/98 which merged into BankAmerica Corp. (New) 9/30/98 which name changed to Bank of America Corp. 4/28/99

FOURTH NATIONAL BANK (WICHITA, KS)
Each share Capital Stock $100 par exchanged for (6-2/3) shares Capital Stock $20 par to effect a (5) for (1) split and a 33-1/3% stock dividend 12/16/48
Each share Capital Stock $20 par exchanged for (2.4) shares Capital Stock $10 par to effect a (2) for (1) split and a 20% stock dividend 7/31/59
Stock Dividends - 25% 12/6/43; 20% 5/15/45; 50% 9/23/54; 16-2/3% 2/15/56; 25% 9/23/58
Name changed to Fourth National Bank & Trust Co. (Wichita, KS) 2/4/60
(See Fourth National Bank & Trust Co. (Wichita, KS))

FOURTH NATL CORP (DE)
Merged into Fourth Financial Corp. 12/31/92
Each share Common $10 par exchanged for (0.570554) share Common $5 par
Fourth Financial Corp. merged into Boatmen's Bancshares, Inc. 1/31/96 which merged into NationsBank Corp. 1/7/97 which reincorporated in Delaware as BankAmerica Corp. (Old) 9/25/98 which merged into BankAmerica Corp. (New) 9/30/98 which name changed to Bank of America Corp. 4/28/99

FOURTH NATIONAL INVESTORS CORP.
Merged into National Investors Corp. (Md.) in 1937
Each share Common exchanged for (4.97) shares new Capital Stock $1 par
National Investors Corp. (Md.) name changed to Seligman Growth Fund, Inc. 5/1/82

FOURTH SHIFT CORP (MN)
Merged into AmeriSoft Corp. 04/30/2001
Each share Common 1¢ par exchanged for $3.70 cash

FOURTHSTAGE TECHNOLOGIES INC (DE)
Plan of reorganization under Chapter 11 Federal Bankruptcy Code effective 07/23/2002
No stockholders' equity

FOWLER FARM OIL CORP. (OK)
Charter cancelled for failure to pay taxes 2/23/57

FOWLER HOSIERY CO., INC. (WI)
Liquidating distribution of (1) share Fowler Hosiery Co. (Canada) Ltd. Common no par for each share Common $5 par held paid 06/17/1960
Seven cash distributions were made with the final completing the liquidation 07/20/1962
(See Fowler Hosiery Co. (Canada) Ltd.)

FOWLER HOSIERY CO. (CANADA) LTD. (CANADA)
Completely liquidated for cash in December 1960

FOWLER OIL & GAS CO. (CO)
Charter dissolved for failure to file annual reports 01/01/1927

FOWLER OIL & GAS CORP (DE)
Acquired by FOG Ownership Corp. 01/02/2008
Each share Common 1¢ par exchanged for $0.15 cash

FOWNES BROS & CO INC (NY)
Stock Dividend - 10% 12/24/1951
Merged into Newco, Inc. 01/03/1984
Each share Capital Stock $1 par exchanged for $31.50 cash

FOX & HOUND RESTAURANT GROUP (DE)
Merged into F&H Acquisition Corp. 3/1/2006
Each share Common 1¢ par exchanged for $16.30 cash

FOX (PETER) BREWING CO. (IL)
Each share Common $5 par exchanged for (4) shares Common $1.25 par 7/24/44
Name changed to Fox De Luxe Beer Sales, Inc. 1/31/56
Fox De Luxe Beer Sales, Inc. name changed to Kingsford Co. 6/17/57 which merged into Clorox Co. (Calif.) 3/12/73 which reincorporated in Delaware 10/22/86

FOX CHASE BANCORP INC (MD)
Merged into Univest Corp. of Pennsylvania 07/01/2016
Each share Common 1¢ par exchanged for (0.9731) share Common $5 par

FOX CHASE BANCORP INC (USA)
Reorganized under the laws of Maryland 06/29/2010
Each share Common 1¢ par exchanged for (1.0692) shares Common 1¢ par
Fox Chase Bancorp, Inc. merged into Univest Corp. of Pennsylvania 07/01/2016

FOX DE LUXE BEER SALES, INC. (IL)
Name changed to Kingsford Co. 6/17/57
Kingsford Co. merged into Clorox Co. (Calif.) 3/12/73 which reincorporated in Delaware 10/22/86

FOX DE LUXE BREWING CO. (MI)
Merged into Fox (Peter) Brewing Co. 6/30/52
Each (7.5) shares 5% Preferred $1 par exchanged for (1) share Common $1.25 par
Each share Common $1 par exchanged for (1/3) share Common $1.25 par
Fox (Peter) Brewing name changed to Fox De Luxe Beer Sales, Inc. 1/31/56 which name changed to Kingsford Co. 6/17/57 which merged into Clorox Co. (Calif.) 3/12/73 which reincorporated in Delaware 10/22/86

FOX DE LUXE BREWING CO. OF INDIANA, INC. (IN)
Name changed to Henry (Patrick) Brewing Co., Inc. in July 1951
Henry (Patrick) Brewing Co., Inc. merged into Fox (Peter) Brewing Co. 6/30/52 which name changed to Fox De Luxe Beer Sales, Inc. 1/31/56 which name changed to Kingsford Co. 6/17/57 which merged into Clorox Co. (Calif.) 3/12/73 which reincorporated in Delaware 10/22/86

FOX ENERGY CORP (AB)
Acquired by EOG Resources Canada Inc. 03/14/2002
Each share Common no par exchanged for $0.46 cash

FOX ENTERPRISES INC (DE)
Charter cancelled and declared inoperative and void for non-payment of taxes 3/1/85

FOX ENTMT GROUP INC (DE)
Merged into News Corp. (Old) 03/21/2005
Each share Common 1¢ par exchanged for (2.04) shares Class A Common 1¢ par
News Corp. (Old) name changed to Twenty-First Century Fox, Inc. 07/01/2013

FOX FILM CORP.
Merged into Twentieth Century-Fox Film Corp. (N.Y.) in 1935 which reorganized as Twentieth Century Fox Film Corp. (Del.) and National Theatres, Inc. 9/27/52
(See each company's listing)

FOX HEAD BREWING CO. (WI)
Capital Stock $5 par changed to $1.25 par 06/10/1957
Name changed to Noramco, Inc. 02/01/1962
(See Noramco, Inc.)

FOX HEAD WAUKESHA CORP.
Name changed to Fox Head Brewing Co. 00/00/1946
Fox Head Brewing Co. name changed to Noramco, Inc. 02/01/1962
(See Noramco, Inc.)

FOX LAKE MINES LTD (ON)
Charter cancelled for failure to pay taxes and file returns 03/16/1976

FOX MARKETS, INC. (CA)
Merged into Food Fair Stores, Inc. 9/20/65
Each share Common no par exchanged for (0.2857143) share Common $1 par
Food Fair Stores, Inc. name changed to Food Fair, Inc. 12/1/76 which reorganized in Delaware as Pantry Pride, Inc. (Old) 7/6/81 which merged into Pantry Price, Inc. (New) 1/20/83 which name changed to Revlon Group Inc. 4/7/86
(See Revlon Group Inc.)

FOX METAL PRODUCTS CORP. (CO)
Name changed to Den-Rado Products, Inc. in 1954
(See Den-Rado Products, Inc.)

FOX MTN EXPLORATIONS LTD (ON)
Recapitalized as Migao Corp. 05/25/2006
Each share Common no par exchanged for (0.05882352) share Common no par
(See Migao Corp.)

FOX PAPER CO (OH)
Merged into Olin Corp. 09/24/1971
Each share Common no par exchanged for (0.36) share Common $5 par

FOX PETE INC (NV)
Each share old Common $0.001 par exchanged for (0.2) share new Common $0.001 par 04/21/2008
SEC revoked common stock registration 12/22/2014

FOX PHOTO INC (TX)
Merged into Eastman Kodak Co. 12/23/1986
Each share Common $1 par exchanged for $30 cash

FOX POND RES LTD (BC)
Cease trade order effective 03/01/1991
Stockholders' equity unlikely

FOX RES LTD (BC)
Reincorporated 07/06/2009
Place of incorporation changed from (Canada) to (BC) 07/06/2009
Name changed to Big Sky Petroleum Corp. 12/01/2011

FOX RES LTD (BC)
Name changed to Foxx Industries Inc. 08/24/1988
(See Foxx Industries Inc.)

FOX RIDGE CAP INC (CO)
Name changed to Seahawk Deep Ocean Technology, Inc. 9/12/89
(See Seahawk Deep Ocean Technology, Inc.)

FOX RIV GROUP INC (FL)
Recapitalized as Global Uranium Power, Corp. 03/25/2005
Each share Common $0.0001 par exchanged for (0.01) share Common $0.0001 par
(See Global Uranium Power, Corp.)

FOX RIV HLDGS INC (NV)
Each share old Common $0.001 par exchanged for (0.025) share new Common $0.001 par 12/16/2003
Note: Holders of between (100) and (3,999) shares will receive (100) post-split shares
Holders of (99) shares or fewer were not affected by the reverse split
Name changed to Zynex Medical Holdings, Inc. 12/23/2003
Zynex Medical Holdings, Inc. name changed to Zynex, Inc. 07/08/2008

FOX ST LOUIS PPTYS INC (MO)
Completely liquidated 11/8/86
Each share $3 Preferred no par exchanged for first and final distribution of $3.66 cash
Each share Common no par exchanged for first and final distribution of $3.66 cash

FOX STANLEY PHOTO PRODS INC (TX)
Common $1 par split (4) for (3) by issuance of (1/3) additional share 8/14/68
Common $1 par split (2) for (1) by issuance of (1) additional share 8/14/72
Stock Dividend - 50% 6/1/67
Name changed to Fox Photo, Inc. 9/19/85
(See Fox Photo, Inc.)

FOX TECHNOLOGY INC (DE)
Company believed went private 00/00/1987
Details not available

FOX TELEVISION STAS INC (DE)
Increasing Rate Exchangeable Guaranteed Preferred $1 par called for redemption 07/01/1987
Public interest eliminated

FOX THEATRES CORP.
Dissolved in 1940
No stockholders' equity

FOX WEST COAST THEATRES CORP.
Property sold in 1934

FOXBORO CO (MA)
Each share Common no par exchanged for (16) shares Common $1 par 03/10/1958
Common $1 par split (3) for (2) by issuance of (0.5) additional share 07/20/1965
Common $1 par split (3) for (2) by issuance of (0.5) additional share 12/30/1977
Common $1 par split (3) for (2) by issuance of (0.5) additional share 03/31/1982
Stock Dividend - 100% 04/29/1960
Preferred Stock Purchase Rights declared for Common stockholders of record 04/15/1988 were redeemed at $0.01 per right 08/03/1990 for holders of record 07/27/1990
Merged into FX Acquisition Corp. 09/05/1990
Each share Common $1 par exchanged for $52 cash

FOXBORO NATL BK (FOXBORO, MA)
Merged into Ben Franklin Savings 3/20/98
Each share Common $10 par exchanged for $340 cash

FOXBOROUGH SVGS BK (FOXBORO, MA)
Common $1 par split (2) for (1) by issuance of (1) additional share payable 6/30/96 to holders of record 5/31/96
Acquired by Banknorth Group, Inc. 4/30/2004
Each share Common $1 par exchanged for $100 cash

FOXCO INDS LTD (DE)
Charter forfeited 03/29/1982

FOXCONN INTL HLDGS LTD (CAYMAN ISLANDS)
Name changed to FIH Mobile Ltd. 07/22/2013

FOXHOLLOW TECHNOLOGIES INC (DE)
Issue Information - 4,500,000 shares COM offered at $14 per share on 10/27/2004
Merged into ev3 Inc. 10/04/2007
Each share Common $0.001 par exchanged for (1.45) shares Common 1¢ par and $2.75 cash
(See ev3 Inc.)

FOXMEYER CDA INC (ON)
Name changed to Healthstreams Technology Inc. 10/04/1996
Healthstreams Technology Inc. name changed to MediSolution Ltd. 09/18/1997
(See MediSolution Ltd.)

FOXMEYER CORP NEW (DE)
Merged into FoxMeyer Health Corp. 10/12/1994
Each share Common 1¢ par exchanged for (0.904) share Common $5 par
FoxMeyer Health Corp. name changed to Avatex Corp. 03/07/1997
(See Avatex Corp.)

FOXMEYER CORP OLD (DE)
Acquired by National Intergroup, Inc. 5/2/86
Each share Common 10¢ par exchanged for $35 cash

FOXMEYER HEALTH CORP (DE)
Each share $4.20 Exchangeable Preferred Ser. A no par received distribution of (0.02625) additional share payable 04/15/1996 to holders of record 04/08/1996
Each share $4.20 Exchangeable Preferred Ser. A no par received distribution of (0.02625) additional share payable 07/15/1996 to holders of record 07/08/1996
Each share $4.20 Exchangeable Preferred Ser. A no par received distribution of (0.02625) additional share payable 10/15/1996 to holders of record 10/08/1996
Name changed to Avatex Corp. 03/07/1997
(See Avatex Corp.)

FOXMOOR INDS LTD (DE)
Recapitalized 12/17/1990
Recapitalized from Foxmoor International Films, Ltd. to Foxmoor Industries, Ltd. 12/17/1990
Each share Common 1¢ par exchanged for (0.05) share Common 1¢ par
Charter cancelled and declared inoperative and void for non-payment of taxes 03/01/2001

FOXPOINT CAP CORP (ON)
Name changed to Castle Mountain Mining Co. Ltd. 05/14/2013
Castle Mountain Mining Co. Ltd. name changed to NewCastle Gold Ltd. 06/30/2015 which merged into Equinox Gold Corp. 12/22/2017

FOXPOINT RES LTD (CANADA)
Name changed to Kirkland Lake Gold Inc. 11/18/2002
Kirkland Lake Gold Inc. merged into Kirkland Lake Gold Ltd. 12/06/2016

FOXX INDS LTD (BC)
Struck off register and declared dissolved for failure to file returns 03/20/1992

FOXY JEWELRY INC (NV)
Name changed to PrimePlayer Inc. 11/08/2002
(See PrimePlayer Inc.)

FOY-JOHNSTON INC. (OH)
Company went private 00/00/1990
Details not available

FP BANCORP INC (DE)
Reincorporated 04/11/1995
State of incorporation changed from (CA) to (DE) 04/11/1995
Merged into Zions Bancorporation 05/22/1998
Each share Common $0.001 par exchanged for (0.627) share Common no par
Zions Bancorporation merged into Zions Bancorporation, N.A. (Salt Lake City, UT) 10/01/2018

FP GROUP LTD (CO)
Voluntarily dissolved 05/27/2015
Details not available

FP INDS INC (NV)
Charter revoked for failure to file reports and pay fees 10/01/1993

FP INVESTMENTS, INC. (NV)
Each share Common 1¢ par exchanged for (0.05) share Common 5¢ par 5/31/85
Name changed to FP Industries, Inc. 7/29/85
(See FP Industries, Inc.)

FP NEWSPAPERS INCOME FD (ON)
Under plan of reorganization each Unit no par automatically became (1) share FP Newspapers Inc. (Canada) Common no par 01/07/2011

FP RES LTD (NL)
Under plan of merger each share Common no par exchanged for $17.19 cash 03/19/2008
Note: Unexchanged certificates were cancelled and became without value 03/19/2010

FP TECHNOLOGY INC (DE)
Name changed to Firepond, Inc. 07/12/2007
(See Firepond, Inc.)

FPA CORP (DE)
Common $1 par split (3) for (2) by issuance of (0.5) additional share 07/22/1980
Common $1 par split (3) for (2) by issuance of (0.5) additional share 06/20/1983
Common $1 par changed to 10¢ par 05/29/1992
Name changed to Orleans Homebuilders, Inc. 07/14/1998
(See Orleans Homebuilders, Inc.)

FPA MED MGMT INC (DE)
Stock Dividend - 100% 4/3/95
Plan of reorganization under Chapter 11 Federal Bankruptcy Code effective 7/8/99
No stockholders' equity

FPB BANCORP INC (FL)
Stock Dividends - 5% payable 05/17/2006 to holders of record 05/10/2006 Ex date - 05/08/2006; 5% payable 06/15/2007 to holders of record 05/31/2007 Ex date - 05/29/2007
Principal asset placed in receivership 07/15/2011
Stockholders' equity unlikely

FPC CAP I (DE)
Issue Information - 12,000,000 QUARTERLY INCOME PFD SECS SER 7.10% offered at $25 per share on 04/08/1999
7.10% Quarterly Income Preferred Securities Ser. A called for redemption at $25 plus $0.374722 accrued dividends on 02/01/2013

FPE PIONEER ELEC LTD (MB)
Name changed to Federal Pioneer Ltd. (MB) 12/05/1972
Federal Pioneer Ltd. (MB) reincorporated in Canada 01/27/1978
(See Federal Pioneer Ltd. (Canada))

FPG INC (CO)
Name changed to Tracks International, Inc. 08/28/1986
Tracks International, Inc. recapitalized as Nemdaco, Inc. 12/22/1989
(See Nemdaco, Inc.)

FPI LTD (NL)
Name changed to FP Resources Ltd. 01/08/2008
(See FP Resources Ltd.)

FPI NURSERY PARTNERS 1984-I (HI)
Involuntarily dissolved for failure to file annual reports 12/08/1989

FPIC INS GROUP INC (FL)
Common 10¢ par split (3) for (2) by issuance of (0.5) additional share payable 03/08/2010 to holders of record 02/08/2010 Ex date - 03/09/2010
Acquired by The Doctors Co. 10/19/2011
Each share Common 10¢ par exchanged for $42 cash

FPL GROUP CAP TR I (DE)
5.875% Preferred Trust Securities called for redemption at $25 plus $0.220313 accrued dividends on 11/09/2017

FPL GROUP INC (FL)
Each 8.5% Corporate Unit received (0.8062) share Common 1¢ par 02/16/2005
Common 1¢ par split (2) for (1) by issuance of (1) additional share payable 03/15/2005 to holders of record 03/04/2005 Ex date - 03/16/2005
Each 8% Corporate Unit received (1.4724) shares Common 1¢ par 02/16/2006
Name changed to NextEra Energy, Inc. 05/21/2010

FPS PHARMA INC (BC)
Name changed to Capha Pharmaceuticals Inc. 04/07/2017

FQF TR (DE)
QuantShares U.S. Market Neutral Beta Fund no par reclassified as QuantShares U.S. Market Neutral High Beta Fund no par 10/26/2011
Trust terminated 11/19/2012
Each share QuantShares U.S. Market Neutral Anti-Momentum Fund no par received $21.82 cash
Each share QuantShares U.S. Market Neutral High Beta Fund no par received $24.13 cash
Each share QuantShares U.S. Market Neutral Quality Fund no par received $22.21 cash
Trust terminated 12/12/2017
Each share O'Shares FTSE Asia Pacific Quality Dividend Hedged ETF no par received $29.2564 cash
Each share O'Shares FTSE Europe Quality Dividend Hedged ETF no par received $27.1048 cash
Under plan of reorganization each share O'Shares FTSE Asia Pacific Quality Dividend ETF no par, O'Shares FTSE Europe Quality Dividend ETF no par and O'Shares FTSE U.S. Quality Dividend ETF no par automatically became (1) share OSI ETF Trust O'Shares FTSE Asia Pacific Quality Dividend ETF no par, O'Shares FTSE Europe Quality Dividend ETF no par or O'Shares FTSE U.S. Quality Dividend ETF no par respectively 06/28/2018
(Additional Information in Active)

FR LIQUIDATING GROUP LIQUIDATING TR (PA)
Assets transferred 04/27/1982
Assets transferred from FR Liquidating Group to FR Liquidating Group Liquidating Trust 04/27/1982
Liquidation completed
Each Ctf. of Bene. Int. no par received initial distribution of $3 cash 10/20/1982
Each Ctf. of Bene. Int. no par received second distribution of $3.80 cash 12/08/1982
Each Ctf. of Bene. Int. no par received third distribution of $8.50 cash 03/04/1983
Each Ctf. of Bene. Int. no par received fourth distribution of $3.50 cash 06/14/1983
Each Ctf. of Bene. Int. no par received fifth distribution of $0.50 cash 08/16/1983
Each Ctf. of Bene. Int. no par received sixth distribution of $1 cash 06/27/1984
Each Ctf. of Bene. Int. no par received seventh distribution of $0.25 cash 10/07/1985
Each Ctf. of Bene. Int. no par received eighth distribution of $1 cash 03/10/1986
Each Ctf. of Bene. Int. no par exchanged for ninth distribution of $0.50 cash 01/02/1987
Each Ctf. of Bene. Int. no par received tenth and final distribution of $0.10 cash 12/21/1988

FRAC WTR SYS INC (NV)
Name changed to Cannabis Therapy Corp. 03/24/2014
Cannabis Therapy Corp. name changed to Peak Pharmaceuticals, Inc. 02/05/2015

FRACMASTER LTD (AB)
Each Installment Receipt no par exchanged for (1) share Common no par 09/18/1998
Assets sold for the benefit of creditors 06/28/1999
No stockholders' equity

FRACTAL DESIGN CORP (CA)
Merged into MetaCreations Corp. 05/29/1997
Each share Common $0.001 par exchanged for (0.749) share Common $0.001 par
MetaCreations Corp. name changed to Viewpoint Corp. 12/01/2000 which

name changed to Enliven Marketing Technologies Corp. 01/01/2008 which merged into DG FastChannel, Inc. 10/02/2008 which name changed to Digital Generation, Inc. 11/07/2011 which merged into Sizmek Inc. 02/07/2014
(See Sizmek Inc.)

FRAGMENTED IND EXCHANGE INC (DE)
Name changed to HotApp International, Inc. 12/03/2014
HotApp International, Inc. name changed to HotApp Blockchain Inc. 02/01/2018

FRAGRANCE EXPRESS INC (NV)
Name changed to National Boston Medical, Inc. 10/28/1998
National Boston Medical, Inc. recapitalized as Storage Innovation Technologies, Inc. (NV) 05/21/2004 which reorganized in Florida as Connectyx Technologies Holdings Group, Inc. 10/29/2007

FRALEX THERAPEUTICS INC (ON)
Acquired by Attwell Capital Inc. 06/03/2009
Each share Common no par exchanged for (1) share Common no par and $0.0001 cash
Attwell Capital Inc. recapitalized as Citation Resources Inc. 03/25/2011 which merged into Inlet Resources Ltd. 07/08/2014 which name changed to Guerrero Ventures Inc. 08/19/2014

FRAM CORP. (RI)
Each share Common $5 par exchanged for (1) share $1.375 Preferred $25 par and (30) shares Common 50¢ par in 1946
$1.375 Preferred $25 par called for redemption 7/12/51
Stock Dividends - 50% 8/25/51; 10% 1/15/59; 10% 12/5/59; 10% 12/15/60
Completely liquidated 6/30/67
Each share Common 50¢ par exchanged for first and final distribution of (1) share Bendix Corp. $3 Conv. Preferred Ser. A no par
(See Bendix Corp.)

FRAMATEX CORP (DE)
Voluntarily dissolved 9/17/72
Details not available

FRAME HOUSE GALLERY INC (KY)
Name changed to F.H.G. Liquidating Corp. 9/27/74
(See F.H.G. Liquidating Corp.)

FRAME TECHNOLOGY CORP (CA)
Merged into Adobe Systems Inc. (CA) 10/27/95
Each share Common no par exchanged for (0.52) share Common no par
Adobe Systems Inc. (CA) reincorporated in Delaware 5/30/97

FRAMEWAVES INC (NV)
Name changed to Sigma Labs, Inc. 10/14/2010

FRAMINGHAM FINL CORP (MA)
Completely liquidated 6/21/78
Each share Common $5 par exchanged for first and final distribution of (1) share Framingham Trust Co. (Framingham, MA) (New) Common $2 par
Framingham Trust Co. (Framington, MA) (New) reorganized as Charter Financial Corp. 12/31/83 which merged into Hartford National Corp. 11/19/86 which merged into Shawmut National Corp. 2/29/88 which merged into Fleet Financial Group Inc. (New) 11/30/95 which name changed to Fleet Boston Corp. 10/1/99 which name changed to FleetBoston Financial Corp. 4/18/2000 which merged into Bank of America Corp. 4/1/2004

FRAMINGHAM NATL BK (FRAMINGHAM, MA)
Common $10 par changed to $5 par and (1) additional share issued plus a 5% stock dividend paid 12/29/69
Merged into Community National Bank (Framingham, MA) 12/31/71
Each share Common $5 par exchanged for (1) share Common $5 par
Community National Bank (Framingham, MA) name changed to Shawmut Community Bank, N.A. (Framingham, MA) 4/1/75
(See Shawmut Community Bank, N.A. (Framingham, MA))

FRAMINGHAM SVGS BK (FRAMINGHAM, MA)
Name changed to Metrowest Bank (Framingham, MA) 06/12/1996
(See Metrowest Bank (Framingham, MA))

FRAMINGHAM TRUST CO. OLD (FRAMINGTON, MA)
Each share Capital Stock $50 par exchanged for (2) shares Capital Stock $25 par 6/4/57
Each share Capital Stock $25 par exchanged for (2) shares Capital Stock $12.50 par 2/1/64
Reorganized as Framingham Financial Corp. 5/1/74
Each share Capital Stock $12.50 par exchanged for (3) shares Common $5 par
Framingham Financial Corp. liquidated for Framingham Trust Co. (Framingham, MA) (New) 6/21/78 which reorganized as Charter Financial Corp. 12/31/83 which merged into Hartford National Corp. 11/19/86 which merged into Shawmut National Corp. 2/29/88 which merged into Fleet Financial Group Inc. (New) 11/30/95 which name changed to Fleet Boston Corp. 10/1/99 which name changed to FleetBoston Financial Corp. 4/18/2000 which merged into Bank of America Corp. 4/1/2004

FRAMINGHAM TR CO NEW (FRAMINGHAM, MA)
Reorganized as Charter Financial Corp. 12/31/83
Each share Common $2 par exchanged for (1) share Common $2 par
Charter Financial Corp. merged into Hartford National Corp. 11/19/86 which merged into Shawmut National Corp. 2/29/88 which merged into Fleet Financial Group Inc. (New) 11/30/95 which name changed to Fleet Boston Corp. 10/1/99 which name changed to FleetBoston Financial Corp. 4/18/2000 which merged into Bank of America Corp. 4/1/2004

FRAN TRONICS CORP (DE)
Name changed to Diplomat Industries Corp. and Common 10¢ par reclassified as Class A $0.001 par 2/12/73
(See Diplomat Industries Corp.)

FRANC-OR RES CORP (YT)
Reincorporated 08/25/1997
Place of incorporation changed from (ON) to (YT) 08/25/1997
Recapitalized as Crocodile Gold Corp. (YT) 11/06/2009
Each share Common no par exchanged for (0.15873015) share Common no par
Crocodile Gold Corp. (YT) reincorporated in Ontario 12/04/2009 which merged into Newmarket Gold Inc. (ON) 07/14/2015 which recapitalized as Kirkland Lake Gold Ltd. 12/06/2016

FRANCANA OIL & GAS LTD (CANADA)
5% Preferred $100 par called for redemption 09/30/1971
Acquired by Sceptre Resources Ltd. 05/14/1982
Each share Common no par exchanged for (2.15) shares Common no par
Sceptre Resources Ltd. merged into Canadian Natural Resources Ltd. 08/15/1996

FRANCE FD INC (MD)
Name changed to DR European Equity Fund Inc. 01/10/1990
(See DR European Equity Fund Inc.)

FRANCE GROWTH FD INC (MD)
Completely liquidated 6/23/2004
Each share Common 1¢ par exchanged for first and final distribution of $8.42 cash

FRANCE TELECOM (FRANCE)
Each Sponsored ADR for Contingent Value Rights exchanged for $18.4825 cash 06/29/2004
Name changed to Orange 07/01/2013

FRANCES CREEK MINES LTD (AB)
Recapitalized as Cal-West Petroleums Ltd. 09/11/1975
Each share Common no par exchanged for (0.2) share Common no par
Cal-West Petroleums Ltd. recapitalized as Legacy Petroleum Ltd. 06/26/1985
(See Legacy Petroleum Ltd.)

FRANCES DENNEY COS INC (DE)
Name changed to Trend Laboratories, Inc. 10/1/90
(See Trend Laboratories, Inc.)

FRANCHARD CORP (DE)
Merged into Lee National Corp. 5/29/69
Each share Class A Common $1 par or Class B Common $1 par exchanged for (0.5) share Common $2.50 par
(See Lee National Corp.)

FRANCHISE BANCORP INC (ON)
Acquired by WTF Holdings Inc. 01/23/2017
Each share Common no par exchanged for $2.13 cash

FRANCHISE CAP CORP (NV)
Name changed to Aero Performance Products, Inc. 01/24/2008
(See Aero Performance Products, Inc.)

FRANCHISE DEV CORP (GA)
Proclaimed dissolved for failure to file annual reports 04/29/1988

FRANCHISE DEVELOPMENT CORP. (MN)
Name changed to American Sound Corp. 6/28/72
(See American Sound Corp.)

FRANCHISE FDG INC (AZ)
Name changed to Toltec Agri-Nomics, Inc. 9/21/72
(See Toltec Agri-Nomics, Inc.)

FRANCHISE FIN CORP AMER (MD)
Reincorporated 12/31/2000
State of incorporation changed from (DE) to (MD) 12/31/2000
Merged into GE Capital Commercial Equipment Financing 8/2/2001
Each share Common 1¢ par exchanged for $25 cash

FRANCHISE FING INC (DE)
Name changed to American-Standard Leasing Co. 3/16/72
(See American-Standard Leasing Co.)

FRANCHISE MGMT CORP (NY)
Name changed to P K Management Corp. 8/18/71
(See P K Management Corp.)

FRANCHISE MGMT INTL INC (DE)
Each share old Common $0.001 par exchanged for (0.5) share new Common $0.001 par 04/27/1998
Recapitalized as Flight Management International, Inc. 10/01/2007
Each share new Common $0.001 par exchanged for (0.005) share Common $0.001 par
Flight Management International, Inc. recapitalized as Native American Energy Group, Inc. 11/05/2009

FRANCHISE MGMT SYS INC (MD)
Name changed to FMS Management Systems, Inc. 9/6/72
(See FMS Management Systems, Inc.)

FRANCHISE MTG ACCEP CO (DE)
Merged into Bay View Capital Corp. 11/01/1999
Each share Common $0.001 par exchanged for either (0.5444) share Common 1¢ par, $9.80 cash or a combination thereof
Bay View Capital Corp. name changed to Great Lakes Bancorp, Inc. (New) 05/01/2006 which merged into First Niagara Financial Group, Inc. (New) 02/15/2008 which merged into KeyCorp (New) 08/01/2016

FRANCHISE SVCS NORTH AMER INC (CANADA)
Reincorporated under the laws of Delaware and Common no par changed to $0.001 par 05/03/2013

FRANCHISE UNITS INC (MA)
Name changed to Fiberglass Homes of America, Inc. 9/8/71
(See Fiberglass Homes of America, Inc.)

FRANCHISED FOOD SYS INC (DE)
Name changed to General Restaurants, Inc. 5/18/70
General Restaurants, Inc. name changed to Emersons, Ltd. 2/11/72
(See Emersons, Ltd.)

FRANCHISEIT CORP (DE)
Each share Common $0.001 par exchanged for (0.5) share Common $0.002 par 3/2/87
Name changed to Agrolife Corp. 3/8/90
(See Agrolife Corp.)

FRANCHISEMASTER TECHNOLOGIES INC (CANADA)
Dissolved for non-compliance 11/02/2005

FRANCHISES AMERN INC (KY)
Charter revoked for failure to file annual reports 11/02/1993

FRANCIS CO., INC. (KY)
Charter revoked for failure to file annual reports 10/2/74

FRANCIS OIL & REFINING CO. (OK)
Charter cancelled for failure to pay taxes 12/15/30

FRANCISCO GOLD CORP (BC)
Merged into Glamis Gold Ltd. 07/16/2002
Each share Common no par exchanged for (1) share Common no par, (1) Right expiring 07/14/2003 and (1.55) shares Chesapeake Gold Corp. Common no par
(See each company's listing)

FRANCISCO SUGAR CO (NJ)
Each share Capital Stock $100 par exchanged for (5) shares Capital Stock no par in 1936
Capital Stock no par reclassified as Common 10¢ par 5/21/69
Name changed to Francisco Industries, Inc. 3/4/71

FRANCO NEV MNG LTD NEW (CANADA)
Name changed 09/20/1999
Common no par split (2) for (1) by

issuance of (1) additional share payable 07/11/1996
Common no par split (2) for (1) by issuance of (1) additional share payable 08/14/1997 to holders of record 08/14/1997
Under plan of merger name changed from Franco-Nevada Mining Corp. Ltd. (Old) to Franco-Nevada Mining Corp. Ltd. (New) 09/20/1999
Acquired by Newmont Mining Corp. 02/16/2002
Each share Common no par exchanged for (0.8) share Common $1.60 par

FRANCO OILS LTD. (CANADA)
Acquired by Fargo Oils Ltd. 10/25/1955
Each share Common exchanged for (0.2) share Common $1 par
Fargo Oils Ltd. acquired by Reserve Oil & Gas Co. 06/10/1968
(See Reserve Oil & Gas Co.)

FRANCO WYOMING OIL CO. (DE)
Common $6 par split (2) for (1) by issuance of (1) additional share 5/3/57
In process of liquidation
Each share Common $6 par stamped to indicate initial distribution of $36 cash 5/12/65
Each share Stamped Common $6 par stamped to indicate second distribution of $54 cash 7/2/65
Each share Stamped Common $6 par exchanged for third distribution of $1.91 cash 12/16/65
Each share Stamped Common $6 par received fourth distribution of $0.60 cash 7/10/67
Each share Stamped Common $6 par received fifth distribution of $1.87 cash 6/30/69
Note: Details on subsequent distributions, if any, are not available

FRANCOEUR GOLD MINES LTD. (CANADA)
Name changed to Francoeur Mines Ltd. and Capital Stock no par changed to 20¢ par 08/08/1956
Francoeur Mines Ltd. acquired by Wasamac Mines Ltd. 12/30/1966 which was acquired by Wright-Hargreaves Mines, Ltd. 01/03/1969 which merged into LAC Minerals Ltd. (New) 07/29/1985 which was acquired by American Barrick Resources Corp. 10/17/1994 which name changed to Barrick Gold Corp. 01/18/1995

FRANCOEUR MINES LTD. (CANADA)
Capital Stock 20¢ par changed to no par 09/13/1962
Acquired by Wasamac Mines Ltd. 12/30/1966
Each share Capital Stock no par exchanged for (0.1) share Capital Stock $1 par and (0.05) Stock Purchase Warrant
Wasamac Mines Ltd. acquired by Wright- Hargreaves Mines, Ltd. 01/03/1969 which merged into LAC Minerals Ltd. (New) 07/29/1985 which was acquired by American Barrick Resources Corp. 10/17/1994 which name changed to Barrick Gold Corp. 01/18/1995

FRANCONIA MINERALS CORP (AB)
Merged into Duluth Metals Ltd. 03/09/2011
Each share Common no par exchanged for (0.3179658) share Common no par and $0.0285022 cash
Note: Unexchanged certificates were cancelled and became without value 03/09/2017
(See Duluth Metals Ltd.)

FRANCOR FINANCIAL INC (IN)
Merged into First Merchants Corp. 7/1/2001
Each share Common no par exchanged for (4.32) shares Common no par

FRANK ALBERT GUENTHER LAW INC (NY)
Each share Class A $1 par exchanged for (0.2) share Class A $5 par in 1933
Each share Class B $1 par exchanged for (0.2) share Class B $5 par in 1933
Class A $5 par and Class B $5 par changed to $1 par in 1936
Preferred $5 par changed to $2 par in 1943
Class A $1 par and Class B $1 par reclassified as Common $1 par in 1949
Common $1 par split (10) for (1) by issuance of (9) additional shares 4/4/69
Merged into Foote, Cone & Belding Communications, Inc. 1/5/78
Each share Common $1 par exchanged for (0.417916) share Common 33-1/3¢ par
Foote, Cone & Belding Communications, Inc. name changed to True North Communications, Inc. 12/19/94 which merged into Interpublic Group of Companies, Inc. 6/22/2001

FRANK N STEIN SYS INC (DE)
Name changed to Broome (Gene) Systems, Inc. 3/23/71
(See Broome (Gene) Systems, Inc.)

FRANK'S NURSERY SALES, INC. (MI)
Common $1 par split (2) for (1) by issuance of (1) additional share 05/26/1972
Common $1 par split (3) for (2) by issuance of (0.5) additional share 06/30/1978
Name changed to Frank's Nursery & Crafts, Inc. 08/01/1980
(See Frank's Nursery & Crafts, Inc.)

FRANKEL CAP MGMT INC (FL)
Proclaimed dissolved for failure to file reports and pay fees 10/9/92

FRANKENMUTH BK & TR (FRANKENMUTH, MI)
Merged into Peoples Banking Corp. 7/31/75
Each share Common $12.50 par exchanged for (3.8) shares Common $5 par
Peoples Banking Corp. name changed to NewCentury Bank Corp. 7/1/84 which merged into First of America Bank Corp. 12/31/86 which merged into National City Corp. 3/31/98

FRANKENMUTH BREWING CO. (MI)
Liquidation completed 3/15/60
Details not available

FRANKENMUTH ST BK (FRANKENMUTH, MI)
Common $25 par changed to $12.50 par and (1) additional share issued 1/21/69
Stock Dividends - 25% 1/27/67; 20% 1/19/71
Name changed to Frankenmuth Bank & Trust (Frankenmuth, MI) 6/21/73
Frankenmuth Bank & Trust Co. (Frankenmuth, MI) merged into Peoples Banking Corp. 7/31/75 which name changed to NewCentury Bank Corp. 7/1/84 which merged into First of America Bank Corp. 12/31/86 which merged into National City Corp. 3/31/98

FRANKFIELD CONS CORP (ON)
Recapitalized 08/19/1992
Recapitalized from Frankfield Explorations Ltd. to Frankfield Consolidated Corp. 08/19/1992
Each share Common no par exchanged for (0.33333333) share Common no par

Name changed to Lagasco Corp. (ON) 04/05/1994
Lagasco Corp. (ON) reincorporated in British Columbia as El Condor Minerals Inc. 08/04/2010 which recapitalized as Worldwide Resources Corp. 06/08/2015

FRANKFORD, TACONY & HOLMESBURG STREET RAILWAY CO.
Merged into Philadelphia Rapid Transit Co. in 1926
Details not available

FRANKFORD & SOUTHWARD PHILADELPHIA CITY PASSENGER RAILROAD CO.
Acquired by Philadelphia Transportation Co. in 1940
Each share Common exchanged for $129.67 principal amount of 3%-6% Consolidated Mortgage Bonds and (1.086) shares $1 Part. Preferred $20 par
(See Philadelphia Transportation Co.)

FRANKFORD CORP (PA)
Common $1 par split (3) for (1) by issuance of (2) additional shares 11/3/86
Stock Dividends - 100% 11/1/82; 100% 11/1/84
Merged into Keystone Financial, Inc. 8/1/94
Each share Common $1 par exchanged for (1.333) shares Common $2 par
Keystone Financial, Inc. merged into M&T Bank Corp. 10/6/2000

FRANKFORD TR CO (PHILADELPHIA, PA)
Stock Dividends - 100% 5/5/61; 25% 1/7/66; 20% 1/31/69; 10% 1/31/80
Under plan of reorganization each share Capital Stock $10 par automatically became (1) share Frankford Corp. Common $1 par 7/1/82
Frankford Corp. merged into Keystone Financial, Inc. 8/1/94 which merged into M&T Bank Corp. 10/6/2000

FRANKFORT DISTILLERIES, INC.
Dissolved in 1943
Details not available

FRANKFORT DISTILLERY, INC.
Name changed to Frankfort Distilleries, Inc. in 1934
(See Frankfort Distilleries, Inc.)

FRANKFORT FIRST BANCORP INC (DE)
Each share old Common 1¢ par exchanged for (0.5) share new Common 1¢ par 12/1/97
Merged into Kentucky First Federal Bancorp 3/2/2005
Each share new Common 1¢ par exchanged for $23.50 cash

FRANKFORT KENTUCKY NATURAL GAS CO., INC. (KY)
Acquired by Columbia Gas System, Inc. 5/31/55
Each share Capital Stock $85 par exchanged for (8.25) shares Common no par 5/31/55
Columbia Gas System, Inc. name changed to Columbia Energy Group 1/16/98 which merged into NiSource Inc. 11/1/2000

FRANKFORT TOWER INDS INC (DE)
In process of liquidation
Each share Common 1¢ par received initial distribution of $0.03037264 cash payable 07/17/2009 to holders of record 06/15/2009 Ex date - 07/22/2009
Each share Common 1¢ par received second distribution of $0.0096751 cash payable 01/08/2010 to holders of record 06/15/2009
Each share Common 1¢ par received third distribution of approximately $0.0047 cash payable 04/01/2011 to holders of record 06/15/2009

FRANKIE DOMINION INTL LTD (HONG KONG)
Stock Dividend - 15% payable 06/24/1996 to holders of record 05/07/1996
Name changed to Huscoke Resources Holdings Ltd. 09/12/2008
(See Huscoke Resources Holdings Ltd.)

FRANKLIN-ADAMS CO. (IL)
Liquidation completed 4/20/64
Details not available

FRANKLIN ADVANTAGE REAL ESTATE INCOME FD (CA)
Merged into Franklin Select Realty Trust 05/07/1996
Each share Ser. A Common no par exchanged for (1.2) shares Ser. A Common no par
(See Franklin Select Realty Trust)

FRANKLIN BALANCE SHEET INVT FD (MA)
Name changed to Franklin Value Investors Trust and Shares of Bene. Int. 1¢ par reclassified as Balance Sheet Investment Fund Class A 1¢ par 09/27/1995

FRANKLIN BALMAR CORP (DE)
Merged into Aero-Chatillon Corp. 6/30/68
Each share Capital Stock no par exchanged for $3 cash

FRANKLIN BANCORP (NJ)
Acquired by United Jersey Banks 1/24/86
Each share Common $3.50 par exchanged for (0.825) share Common $2.50 par
United Jersey Banks name changed to UJB Financial Corp. 6/30/89 which name changed to Summit Bancorp 3/1/96 which merged into FleetBoston Financial Corp. 3/1/2001 which merged into Bank of America Corp. 4/1/2004

FRANKLIN BANCORP INC (MI)
Merged into First Place Financial Corp. 05/28/2004
Each share Common $1 par exchanged for either (1.137) shares Common 1¢ par or (0.46413362) share Common 1¢ par and $13.46051966 cash
Note: Option to receive stock and cash expired 07/06/2004
(See First Place Financial Corp.)

FRANKLIN BANCORPORATION INC (DE)
Merged into BB&T Corp. 7/1/98
Each share Common 10¢ par exchanged for (0.35) share Common $5 par

FRANKLIN BK & TR CO (EVANSVILLE, IN)
Merged into Old National Bank (Evansville, IN) 5/1/51
Each share Capital Stock exchanged for (8) shares Common $10 par
Old National Bank (Evansville, IN) reorganized as Old National Bancorp 1/4/83

FRANKLIN BK (HOUSTON, TX)
Placed in receivership 03/24/1975
No stockholders' equity

FRANKLIN BK (PATERSON, NJ)
Capital Stock $10 par changed to $5 par and (1) additional share issued 05/15/1974
Stock Dividend - 11.48% 11/08/1968
Merged into Horizon Bancorp 05/12/1980
Each share Capital Stock $5 par exchanged for $29 cash

FRANKLIN BANK (ST. ALBANS, VT)
Capital Stock $20 par changed to $6.66-2/3 par and (2) additional shares issued 3/19/73

Capital Stock $6.66-2/3 par changed to $7 par 11/13/73
Name changed to Franklin-Lamoille Bank (St. Albans, VT) 3/1/74
Franklin-Lamoille Bank (St. Albans, VT) reorganized as BankNorth Group, Inc. (VT) 10/31/83 which merged into First Vermont Financial Corp. 12/31/85 which name changed to BankNorth Group, Inc. (VT) 5/13/86 which merged into BankNorth Group, Inc. (DE) 12/1/89 which merged into Banknorth Group, Inc. (ME) 5/10/2000 which merged into TD Banknorth Inc. 3/1/2005
(See TD Banknorth Inc.)

FRANKLIN BK CORP (DE)
Chapter 7 bankruptcy proceedings terminated 12/22/2015
No stockholders' equity

FRANKLIN BK N A (SOUTHFIELD, MI)
Conv. Preferred no par called for redemption 10/15/1994
Stock Dividends - 5% payable 01/22/1996 to holders of record 01/05/1996; 5% payable 01/24/1997 to holders of record 01/07/1997; 5% payable 03/02/1998 to holders of record 02/16/1998
Under plan of reorganization each share Common $1 par automatically became (1) share Franklin Bancorp, Inc. Common $1 par 10/23/2002
Franklin Bancorp, Inc. merged into First Place Financial Corp. 5/28/2004
(See First Place Financial Corp.)

FRANKLIN BK SSB (HOUSTON, TX)
Placed in receivership 11/07/2008
Stockholders' equity unlikely

FRANKLIN BROADCASTING CO (MN)
Merged into Pharmacaps, Inc. 8/18/71
Each share Common 10¢ par exchanged for (0.5) share Common 10¢ par
(See Pharmacaps, Inc.)

FRANKLIN BUILDING CO. (NY)
Liquidation completed 12/28/49
Details not available

FRANKLIN CALIF GROWTH FD (DE)
Name changed 07/12/1993
Name changed from Franklin California 250 Growth Fund to Franklin California Growth Fund 07/12/1993
Shares of Bene. Int. 1¢ par reclassified as Shares of Bene. Int. Class I 1¢ par 09/01/1996
Shares of Bene. Int. Class I 1¢ par reclassified as Class A 1¢ par 01/01/1999
Shares of Bene. Int. Class II 1¢ par reclassified as Class C 1¢ par 01/01/1999
Name changed to Franklin Flex Capital Growth Fund 09/01/2002

FRANKLIN CALIF TAX FREE INCOME FD INC (MD)
Reincorporated under the laws of Delaware 08/01/2007

FRANKLIN CALIF TAX FREE TR (MA)
Reincorporated under the laws of Delaware 08/01/2007

FRANKLIN CAP CORP (DE)
Common $1 par split (2) for (1) by issuance of (1) additional share 08/30/1983
Charter cancelled and declared inoperative and void for non-payment of taxes 03/01/1993

FRANKLIN CAP CORP (DE)
Common $1 par split (3) for (2) by issuance of (0.5) additional share payable 06/07/2000 to holders of record 05/15/2000 Ex date - 06/08/2000
Name changed to Patient Safety Technologies, Inc. and Common $1 par changed to 33¢ par 04/04/2005
(See Patient Safety Technologies, Inc.)

FRANKLIN CAPITAL CORP. (NJ)
Capital Stock $10 par changed to no par 00/00/1931
Capital Stock no par changed to 50¢ par 00/00/1937
Acquired by National Newark & Essex Bank (Newark, NJ) 07/01/1966
Each share Capital Stock 50¢ par exchanged for (2/9) share Capital Stock $10 par
National Newark & Essex Bank (Newark, NJ) reorganized as Midlantic Banks Inc. 06/12/1970 which merged into Midlantic Corp. 01/30/1987 which merged into PNC Bank Corp. 12/31/1995 which name changed to PNC Financial Services Group, Inc. 03/15/2000

FRANKLIN CASH MGMT FD (CA)
Name changed to Franklin Federal Tax-Free Income Fund in September 1983

FRANKLIN CLO III LTD (CAYMAN ISLANDS)
144A 3C7 Preferred Shares called for redemption at $74.50 on 01/17/2006

FRANKLIN CLO IV LTD (CAYMAN ISLANDS)
144A 3C7 Preferred called for redemption 09/20/2013

FRANKLIN CO (ME)
In process of liquidation
Each share Capital Stock $100 par received initial distribution of $275 cash 12/15/76
Each share Capital Stock $100 par received second distribution of $177 cash 2/25/77
Note: Details on subsequent distributions, if any, are not available

FRANKLIN COMPUTER CORP (PA)
Name changed to Franklin Electronic Publishers, Inc. 03/02/1990
(See Franklin Electronic Publishers, Inc.)

FRANKLIN CONS MNG INC (DE)
Each share old Common 1¢ par exchanged for (0.04) share new Common 1¢ par 05/26/1998
Name changed to WCM Capital Inc. (DE) 10/14/1998
WCM Capital Inc. (DE) reincorporated in Nevada as Franklin Mining, Inc. 02/09/2004

FRANKLIN CORP. (NY)
Reorganized under the laws of Delaware as Franklin Holding Corp. 10/01/1987
Franklin Holding Corp. (DE) name changed to Franklin Capital Corp. 07/23/1998
Franklin Capital Corp. name changed to Patient Safety Technologies, Inc. 04/04/2005
(See Patient Safety Technologies, Inc.)

FRANKLIN CORP (IN)
Merged into Steak n Shake, Inc. 10/31/1983
Each share Class A Common no par exchanged for (0.69126) share Common no par
Each share Class B Common no par exchanged for (0.69126) share Common no par
Steak n Shake, Inc. reorganized as Consolidated Products, Inc. 05/15/1984 which name changed to Steak n Shake Co. 02/12/2001 which name changed to Biglari Holdings Inc. 04/08/2010

FRANKLIN CORP CASH MGMT FD (CA)
Merged into Franklin Managed Trust (MA) 12/31/1988
Each share Common no par exchanged for (1) Corporate Cash Portfolio Share of Bene. Int. 1¢ par
Franklin Managed Trust (MA) reincorporated in Delaware 08/01/2007

FRANKLIN CNTY TR CO (GREENFIELD, MA)
Each share Common $100 par exchanged for (5) shares Common $20 par in 1946
Acquired by Worcester Bancorp, Inc. 9/26/75
Each share Common $20 par exchanged for (5.5) shares Common $1 par
Worcester Bancorp, Inc. acquired by Shawmut Corp. 5/3/82 which merged into Shawmut National Corp. 2/29/88 which merged into Fleet Financial Group Inc. (New) 11/30/95 which name changed to Fleet Boston Corp. 10/1/99 which name changed to FleetBoston Financial Corp. 4/18/2000 which merged into Bank of America Corp. 4/1/2004

FRANKLIN COVEY CO (UT)
Each share old Ser. A Preferred no par exchanged for (4) shares new Ser. A Preferred no par 3/8/2005
New Ser. A Preferred no par called for redemption at $25 on 4/4/2007
(Additional Information in Active)

FRANKLIN CR HLDG CORP (DE)
Name changed 04/03/2009
Each share old Common 1¢ par exchanged for (0.2) share new Common 1¢ par 12/12/1996
New Common 1¢ par split (4) for (1) by issuance of (3) additional shares payable 09/01/1997 to holders of record 08/20/1997
Name changed from Franklin Credit Management Corp. (Old) to Franklin Credit Holding Corp. 04/03/2009
Plan of reorganization under Chapter 11 Federal Bankruptcy proceedings effective
Each share new Common 1¢ par received distribution of (1) share Franklin Credit Management Corp. (New) Restricted Common 1¢ par payable 08/10/2012 to holders of record 08/02/2012
Note: Certificates were not required to be surrendered and are without value

FRANKLIN ELECTR PUBLISHERS INC (PA)
Common no par changed to 1¢ par 00/00/2003
Acquired by Saunders Acquisition Corp. 02/24/2010
Each share Common 1¢ par exchanged for $2.50 cash

FRANKLIN FIN CORP (MI)
8.75% Exchangeable Preferred Ser. A called for redemption at $10 on 12/31/2002

FRANKLIN FINANCE & LOAN CO. (SC)
Each share Common no par exchanged for (2) shares Common $10 par 3/1/55
Merged into Dealers Discount Corp. 1/31/64
Each share 5% Preferred $10 par and 6% Preferred $10 par exchanged for like share
Each share Common $10 par exchanged for (0.75) share Common $5 par
Dealers Discount Corp. name changed to Develco, Inc. 8/1/68 which name changed to Southern "500" Truck Stops, Inc. 10/31/74
(See Southern "500" Truck Stops, Inc.)

FRANKLIN FINL CORP (CA)
Charter suspended for failure to pay taxes 01/03/1984

FRANKLIN FINL CORP (TN)
Old Common no par split (2) for (1) by issuance of (1) additional share payable 02/17/1998 to holders of record 02/02/1998
Old Common no par split (4) for (1) by issuance of (3) additional shares payable 06/03/1998 to holders of record 05/20/1998
Each share old Common no par exchanged for (0.25) share new Common no par 10/17/2000
Merged into Fifth Third Bancorp 06/11/2004
Each share new Common no par exchanged for (0.5933) share Common no par

FRANKLIN FINL CORP (VA)
Merged into TowneBank (Portsmouth, VA) 01/02/2015
Each share Common 1¢ par exchanged for (1.4) shares Common $1.667 par

FRANKLIN FIRE INSURANCE CO. OF PHILADELPHIA
Merged into Home Insurance Co. in 1948
Each share Capital Stock $5 par exchanged for (0.772) share Common $5 par
(See Home Insurance Co.)

FRANKLIN FIRST FINL CORP (PA)
Common 1¢ par split (3) for (2) by issuance of (0.5) additional share 6/1/92
Acquired by Onbancorp, Inc. 8/31/93
Each share Common 1¢ par exchanged for (0.825) share Common $1 par
Onbancorp, Inc. merged into First Empire State Corp. 4/1/98 which name changed to M&T Bank Corp. 6/1/98

FRANKLIN GOLD FD (CA)
Common 10¢ par reclassified as Class A Shares of Bene. Int. 10¢ par 5/1/95
Reincorporated under the laws of Delaware as Franklin Gold & Precious Metals Fund 4/10/2000

FRANKLIN GOLD MINES (1936) LTD. (ON)
Charter cancelled 00/00/1955

FRANKLIN GOLD MINING CO. LTD. (ON)
Recapitalized as Franklin Gold Mines (1936) Ltd. on a (1) for (5) basis in 1936
(See Franklin Gold Mines (1936) Ltd.)

FRANKLIN HLDG CORP (DE)
Name changed to Franklin Capital Corp. 07/23/1998
Franklin Capital Corp. name changed to Patient Safety Technologies, Inc. 04/04/2005
(See Patient Safety Technologies, Inc.)

FRANKLIN ICE CREAM CO (OH)
Liquidated in November 1964
Details not available

FRANKLIN INDS INC (CA)
Charter cancelled for failure to file reports and pay taxes 08/02/1974

FRANKLIN INTL TR (DE)
Name changed to Franklin Templeton International Trust 2/1/96

FRANKLIN INVS SECS TR (MA)
Reincorporated under the laws of Delaware 08/01/2007

FRANKLIN JOE PRODTNS INC (NV)
Recapitalized as Universal Medical Systems Inc. 10/10/1995
Each (35) shares Common $0.001 par exchanged for (1) share Common $0.001 par
(See Universal Medical Systems Inc.)

FRANKLIN LAKE RES INC (NV)
Recapitalized as Seen On Screen TV Inc. 03/19/2009
Each share Common $0.001 par exchanged for (0.4) share Common $0.001 par

FRANKLIN LAKES NATL BK (FRANKLIN LAKES, NJ)
Name changed to Urban National Bank (Franklin Lakes, NJ) 11/1/71
Urban National Bank (Franklin Lakes, NJ) merged into HUBCO, Inc. 6/30/95 which name changed to Hudson United Bancorp 4/21/99 which merged into TD Banknorth Inc. 1/31/2006
(See TD Banknorth Inc.)

FRANKLIN LAMOILLE BK (ST ALBANS, VT)
Reorganized as BankNorth Group, Inc. (VT) 10/31/1983
Each share Capital Stock $7 par exchanged for (1) share Common $1 par
BankNorth Group, Inc. (VT) merged into First Vermont Financial Corp. 12/31/1985 which name changed to BankNorth Group, Inc. (VT) 05/13/1986 which merged into BankNorth Group, Inc. (DE) 12/01/1989 which merged into Banknorth Group, Inc. (ME) 05/10/2000 which merged into TD Banknorth Inc. 03/01/2005
(See TD Banknorth Inc.)

FRANKLIN LIFE BD FD INC (MD)
Merged into Monthly Income Shares, Inc. 9/27/77
Each share Common $1 par exchanged for (0.633255) share Capital Stock $1 par
Monthly Income Shares, Inc. name changed to Bullock Monthly Income Shares, Inc. 1/14/85 which reorganized as Alliance Bond Fund (MA) 3/13/87 which reorganized in Maryland as Alliance Bond Fund, Inc. 12/7/87 which name changed to AllianceBernstein Bond Fund, Inc. 3/31/2003

FRANKLIN LIFE EQUITY FD INC (MD)
Merged into Bullock Fund, Ltd. 09/27/1977
Each share Common $1 par exchanged for (0.633255) share Capital Stock $1 par
Bullock Fund, Ltd. name changed to Bullock Growth Shares, Inc. 04/08/1985 which merged into Chemical Fund, Inc. 03/13/1987 which name changed to Alliance Fund, Inc. 04/01/1987 which name changed to Alliance Mid-Capital Growth Fund Inc. 02/01/2002 which name changed to AllianceBernstein Mid-Capital Growth Fund, Inc. 03/31/2003

FRANKLIN LIFE INS CO (IL)
Capital Stock $4 par changed to $2 par and (1) additional share issued 04/05/1963
Stock Dividends - 50% 02/07/1944; 25% 02/00/1948; 50% 03/25/1952; 100% 07/15/1953; 50% 08/16/1955; 50% 09/16/1957; 10% 07/01/1959; 25% 08/01/1961; 25% 07/01/1965; 10% 07/01/1968
Under plan of reorganization each share Capital Stock $2 par automatically became (1) share FDS Holding Co. Common $2 par 12/30/1978
FDS Holding Co. merged into American Brands, Inc. (NJ) 02/14/1979 which reincorporated in Delaware 01/01/1986 which name changed to Fortune Brands, Inc. 05/30/1997 which name changed to Beam Inc. 10/04/2011
(See Beam Inc.)

FRANKLIN MANAGED TR (MA)
Corporate Cash Portfolio 1¢ par reclassified as Corporate Qualified Dividend Fund 1¢ par 05/01/1991
Completely liquidated 07/15/1998
Each share Corporate Qualified Dividend Fund 1¢ par received net asset value
Rising Dividends Fund 1¢ par reclassified as Rising Dividends Fund Class A 1¢ par 01/01/1999
Reincorporated under the laws of Delaware 08/01/2007

FRANKLIN (H.H.) MANUFACTURING CO. (NY)
Charter cancelled and proclaimed dissolved for failure to pay taxes 12/15/38

FRANKLIN MARKETING SYS INC (DE)
Name changed to Indy Raceway, Inc. 6/14/75
Indy Raceway, Inc. name changed to Atlantic Gulf Energy, Inc. 11/24/80 which name changed to British American Petroleum Corp. 3/30/83 which name changed to Crest Energy Resources Corp. 7/1/87
(See Crest Energy Resources Corp.)

FRANKLIN MINT, INC. (PA)
Common 10¢ par changed to no par 05/26/1969
Common no par split (2) for (1) by issuance of (1) additional share 08/01/1969
Common no par split (3) for (2) by issuance of (0.5) additional share 12/28/1970
Common no par split (3) for (2) by issuance of (0.5) additional share 01/05/1972
Stock Dividend - 100% 12/16/1968
Name changed to Franklin Mint Corp. 03/29/1972
Franklin Mint Corp. merged into Warner Communications Inc. 03/02/1981 which merged into Time Warner Inc. (Old) 01/10/1990 which merged into AOL Time Warner Inc. 01/11/2001 which name changed to Time Warner Inc. (New) 10/16/2003 which merged into AT&T Inc. 06/15/2018

FRANKLIN MINT CORP (PA)
Common no par split (2) for (1) by issuance of (1) additional share 9/28/72
Merged into Warner Communications Inc. 3/2/81
Each share Common no par exchanged for (0.764) share Common $1 par
Warner Communications Inc. merged into Time Warner Inc. (Old) 1/10/90 which merged into AOL Time Warner Inc. 1/11/2001 which name changed to Time Warner Inc. (New) 10/16/2003

FRANKLIN MONEY FD (CA)
Reincorporated under the laws of Delaware and Common 10¢ par changed to no par 11/01/2007

FRANKLIN MONEY FD II (CA)
Name changed to Franklin Federal Money Fund 03/27/1981

FRANKLIN MULTI-INCOME TR (MA)
Merged into Franklin Custodian Funds, Inc. (MD) 08/04/2005
Each Share of Bene. Int. 1¢ par exchanged for approximately (3.8549) shares Income Ser. Class A 1¢ par
Franklin Custodian Funds, Inc. (MD) reincorporated in Delaware 08/01/2007

FRANKLIN MUT SER FD INC (MD)
Reorganized under the laws of Delaware as Franklin Mutual Series Funds 05/01/2008

FRANKLIN N Y CORP (NY)
Adjudicated bankrupt in 1975
No Preferred or Common stockholders' equity

FRANKLIN N Y TAX FREE INCOME FD INC (NY)
Reincorporated under the laws of Delaware 08/01/2007

FRANKLIN N Y TAX FREE TR (MA)
Reincorporated under the laws of Delaware 08/01/2007

FRANKLIN NATIONAL BANK (FRANKLIN SQUARE, NY)
Each share Common $70 par exchanged for (1.4) shares Common $50 par in 1945
Each share Common $50 par exchanged for (5) shares $10 par in 1947
Common $10 par changed to $5 par and (1) additional share issued in 1955
Stock Dividends - 300% 8/24/42; 100% 7/1/51; (9) for (31) 12/1/53; 28.23% 7/16/56
Under plan of merger name changed to Franklin National Bank of Long Island (Mineola, NY) 10/25/57
Franklin National Bank of Long Island (Mineola, NY) name changed to Franklin National Bank (Mineola, NY) 10/16/62 which reorganized as Franklin New York Corp. 9/22/69
(See Franklin New York Corp.)

FRANKLIN NATL BK (MINEOLA, NY)
Reorganized 9/22/69
Each share $2.45 Conv. Preferred $25 par exchanged for (1) share Franklin New York Corp. $2.45 Conv. Preferred $25 par 9/22/69
Each share Common $5 par exchanged for (1) share Franklin New York Corp. Common $5 par 9/22/69
(See Franklin New York Corp.)

FRANKLIN NATIONAL BANK OF LONG ISLAND (MINEOLA, NY)
Name changed to Franklin National Bank (Mineola, NY) 10/16/62
Franklin National Bank (Mineola, NY) reorganized as Franklin New York Corp. 9/22/69
(See Franklin New York Corp.)

FRANKLIN NATL INVT CORP (IN)
Name changed to Harris Properties, Inc. 12/12/75
(See Harris Properties, Inc.)

FRANKLIN NATL LIFE INS CO (IN)
Common $1 par changed to no par 8/22/80
Stock Dividends - 10% 7/10/68; 10% 9/29/69
Declared insolvent and liquidated 9/24/84
No stockholders' equity

FRANKLIN OIL & GAS CO. (MT)
Charter expired by time limitation 6/9/68

FRANKLIN OIL & GAS CO (OH)
Name changed to Franklin Oil Corp. 10/7/60
(See Franklin Oil Corp.)

FRANKLIN (BEN) OIL & GAS CORP. (DE)
No longer in existence having become inoperative and void for non-payment of taxes 4/1/65

FRANKLIN OIL CORP. (OH)
Merged into Olds (W.J.) Corp. 3/11/77
Each share Common $50 par exchanged for $765 cash

FRANKLIN OPHTHALMIC INSTRS INC (DE)
Filed a petition under Chapter 7 Federal Bankruptcy Code 1/20/2000
Stockholders' equity unlikely

FRANKLIN OPT FD INC (CA)
Name changed in 1983
Name changed from Franklin Option Fund, Inc. (HI) to Franklin Option Fund (CA) and Common 50¢ par changed to no par in 1983
Name changed to Franklin Premier Return Fund 4/12/91

FRANKLIN PLAN CO. OF AMERICA
Merged into Franklin Plan Corp. in 1931
Details not available

FRANKLIN PLAN CORP. (DE)
Bankrupt in 1933
Details not available

FRANKLIN PPTYS INC (NV)
Each share Capital Stock 1¢ par exchanged for (0.2) share Capital Stock par 6/25/71
Charter revoked for failure to file reports and pay fees 3/6/78

FRANKLIN PRESS & OFFSET CO.
Bankrupt in 1933
Details not available

FRANKLIN PROCESS CO. (RI)
Assets sold to Indian Head Mills, Inc. (MA) at $40 per share 1/20/58

FRANKLIN QUEST CO (UT)
Name changed to Franklin Covey Co. 5/30/97

FRANKLIN RAILWAY SUPPLY CO. (DE)
Name changed to Franklin Balmar Corp. 6/30/56
(See Franklin Balmar Corp.)

FRANKLIN RAYON CORP. (RI)
Each share Common no par exchanged for (2) shares Common $1 par 00/00/1936
Name changed to Atlantic Rayon Corp. (RI) 03/24/1939
Atlantic Rayon Corp. (RI) name changed to Textron Inc. (RI) 05/18/1944 which name changed to Textron American, Inc. 02/24/1955 which name changed back to Textron Inc. (RI) 05/15/1956 which reincorporated in Delaware 01/02/1968

FRANKLIN REAL ESTATE INCOME FD (CA)
Merged into Franklin Select Realty Trust 05/07/1996
Each share Ser. A Common no par exchanged for (1.286) shares Ser. A Common no par
(See Franklin Select Realty Trust)

FRANKLIN RLTY GROUP (PA)
Name changed 10/14/1971
Name changed 10/27/1977
Name changed from Franklin Realty to Franklin Realty & Mortgage Trust 10/14/1971
Name changed from Franklin Realty & Mortgage Trust to Franklin Realty Group 10/27/1977
Name changed to FR Liquidating Group 04/28/1981
FR Liquidating Group assets transferred to FR Liquidating Group Liquidating Trust 04/27/1982
(See FR Liquidating Group Liquidating Trust)

FRANKLIN RES LIQUID ASSETS FD (CA)
Name changed to Franklin Money Fund (CA) 02/27/1980
Franklin Money Fund (CA) reincorporated in Delaware 11/01/2007

FRANKLIN RES LTD (BC)
Name changed to European Original New York Seltzer Ltd. 11/12/1986
(See European Original New York Seltzer Ltd.)

FRANKLIN RIVER (BRITISH COLUMBIA) GOLD MINES LTD. (BC)
Charter revoked for failure to file reports and pay fees 1/20/44

FRANKLIN RIVER GOLD MINES LTD. (BC)
Name changed to Franklin River (British Columbia) Gold Mines Ltd. in 1935
(See Franklin River (British Columbia) Gold Mines Ltd.)

FRANKLIN SVGS & LN ASSN SOUTHFIELD (MI)
Under plan of reorganization name changed to Franklin Savings Bank, FSB (Southfield, MI) 10/25/1988
Franklin Savings Bank, FSB (Southfield, MI) name changed to Franklin Bank, N.A. (Southfield, MI) 09/01/1991 which reorganized as Franklin Bancorp, Inc. 10/23/2002 which merged into First Place Financial Corp. 05/28/2004
(See First Place Financial Corp.)

FRANKLIN SVGS ASSN (KS)
Placed in receivership by the Office of Thrift Supervision 7/17/92
Stockholders' equity undetermined

FRANKLIN SVGS BK FSB (SOUTHFIELD, MI)
Common $8 par changed to $1 par 10/25/1988
Name changed to Franklin Bank, N.A. (Southfield, MI) 09/01/1991
Franklin Bank, N.A. (Southfield, MI) reorganized as Franklin Bancorp, Inc. 10/23/2002 which merged into First Place Financial Corp. 05/28/2004
(See First Place Financial Corp.)

FRANKLIN SCIENTIFIC INC (NY)
Dissolved by proclamation 10/26/2011

FRANKLIN SELECT REAL ESTATE INCOME FD (CA)
Under plan of merger name changed to Franklin Select Realty Trust 05/07/1996
(See Franklin Select Realty Trust)

FRANKLIN SELECT RLTY TR (CA)
Liquidation completed
Each share Ser. A Common no par received initial distribution of $7.11 cash payable 03/10/2000 to holders of record 02/29/2000
Each share Ser. A Common no par received second and final distribution of $1.24 cash payable 12/10/2000 to holders of record 12/01/2000
Note: Certificates were not required to be surrendered and are without value

FRANKLIN SHOPS, INC. (NY)
Charter cancelled and proclaimed dissolved for failure to pay taxes and file reports 12/15/65

FRANKLIN SIGNAL CORP (WI)
Administratively dissolved 11/20/92

FRANKLIN SIMON & CO., INC. (NY)
Merged into City Specialty Stores, Inc. 00/00/1953
Each share Common $1 par exchanged for (1) share Common $1 par
City Specialty Stores, Inc. merged into City Stores Co. 01/28/1961 which name changed to CSS Industries, Inc. 09/24/1985

FRANKLIN ST BK SOMERSET N J (FRANKLIN TOWNSHIP, NJ)
Capital Stock $10 par changed to $3.50 par and (2) additional shares issued 2/11/70
Stock Dividends - 10% 12/15/65; 10% 12/27/71; 10% 12/27/72
Through exchange offer majority shares acquired by Franklin Bancorp as of 11/9/82

Note: Shares not tendered exchanged for $28.63 cash

FRANKLIN STORES CORP (DE)
Common $1 par split (3) for (2) by issuance of (0.5) additional share 6/12/67
Stock Dividend - 10% 8/31/66
Name changed to Slater, Walker of America Ltd. 8/6/73
Slater, Walker of America Ltd. name changed to Cornwall Equities, Ltd. 10/17/74
(See Cornwall Equities, Ltd.)

FRANKLIN STR PARTNERS LTD PARTNERSHIP (MA)
Merged into Franklin Street Properties Corp. 1/1/2002
Each Unit of Ltd. Partnership Int. exchanged for (1) share Common $0.0001 par

FRANKLIN SUPPLY CO (AB)
Name changed to CE Franklin Ltd. 12/18/1995
(See CE Franklin Ltd.)

FRANKLIN SURETY CO. OF NEW YORK
Merged into Lloyds Casualty Co. in 1931
Details not available

FRANKLIN TAX FREE INCOME FD INC (MD)
Name changed to Franklin California Tax-Free Income Fund, Inc. (MD) 07/30/1982
Franklin California Tax-Free Income Fund, Inc. (MD) reincorporated in Delaware 08/01/2007

FRANKLIN TAX FREE TR (MA)
Reincorporated under the laws of Delaware 08/01/2007

FRANKLIN TELECOMMUNICATIONS CORP (CA)
Each share old Common no par exchanged for (0.1) share new Common no par 02/01/1994
Reorganized under the laws of Nevada as Franklin Wireless Corp. 01/22/2008
Each (70) shares Common no par exchanged for (1) share Common $0.001 par

FRANKLIN TELEGRAPH CO. (MA)
Dissolved 2/10/59

FRANKLIN/TEMPLETON GLOBAL TR (MA)
Reincorporated under the laws of Delaware 08/01/2007

FRANKLIN TEMPLETON LTD DURATION INCOME TR (DE)
Name changed to Franklin Limited Duration Income Trust 06/30/2014

FRANKLIN THRIFT & LOAN ASSN. OF AMERICA
Acquired by Franklin Plan Corp. in 1931
Details not available

FRANKLIN TILE CO.
Property sold to American Encaustic Tiling Co., Inc. and each share Common no par exchanged for (14) shares Common $1 par in 1948
(See American Encaustic Tiling Co., Inc.)

FRANKLY INC (ON)
Reincorporated under the laws of British Columbia 07/11/2016

FRANKPORT INDIN GOLD MINES LTD. (ON)
Charter revoked for failure to file reports and pay taxes 00/00/1954

FRANKS CORP (AB)
Recapitalized as True North Water Corp. (ALTA) 02/23/1999
Each share Common no par exchanged for (0.25) share Common no par
True North Water Corp. (ALTA) reincorporated in Canada 12/12/2003 which name changed to Watertowne International Inc. 03/19/2004 which recapitalized as Sightus Inc. 03/15/2006
(See Sightus Inc.)

FRANKS NURSERY & CRAFTS INC (DE)
Plan of reorganization under Chapter 11 Federal bankruptcy Code effective 7/27/2005
Each share Common $0.001 par exchanged for $0.75 cash

FRANKS NURSERY & CRAFTS INC (MI)
Merged into General Host Corp. 03/04/1983
Each share Common $1 par exchanged for $19 cash

FRANKSIN MINES LTD. (QC)
Charter suspended 05/01/1959

FRANKVIEW OILS LTD.
Acquired by Apex Consolidated Resources Ltd. 00/00/1946
Each share Capital Stock $1 par exchanged for (0.1) share Capital Stock no par
Apex Consolidated Resources Ltd. recapitalized as Abacus Mines Ltd. 06/01/1959 which name changed to Abacus Mines & Realty Ltd. 00/00/1962 which recapitalized as Abacon Developments Ltd. 03/21/1963
(See Abacon Developments Ltd.)

FRANSACTION INC (CO)
Name changed to H3 Enterprises, Inc. 5/13/2005

FRANSHION PPTYS CHINA LTD (HONG KONG)
Name changed to China Jinmao Holdings Group Ltd. 01/13/2017

FRANTZ INDUSTRIES, INC. (NY)
Adjudicated bankrupt 1/14/67
No stockholders' equity

FRANTZ MFG CO (DE)
Reincorporated 9/11/69
State of incorporation changed from (IL) to (DE) 9/11/69
Common $1 par split (3) for (2) by issuance of (0.5) additional share 7/12/68
Common $1 par split (4) for (3) by issuance of (1/3) additional share 7/1/71
Acquired by S-F Acquisition Co. 3/14/88
Each share Common $1 par exchanged for $60 cash

FRANZIA BROS WINERY (CA)
Acquired by Coca-Cola Bottling Co. of New York, Inc. 12/5/73
Each share Common $1 par exchanged for (1.35) shares Common 25¢ par
(See Coca-Cola Bottling Co. of New York, Inc.)

FRASER COS LTD (CANADA)
Each share Common $100 par exchanged for (3) shares Common no par 00/00/1927
Each share Common no par exchanged for (0.05) share Common no par 00/00/1932
Each share Common no par exchanged for (2) shares Common no par 00/00/1948
Each share Common no par exchanged for (3) shares Common no par 00/00/1952
Common no par reclassified as Conv. Class A Common no par 02/11/1974
Conv. Class A Common no par split (3) for (1) by issuance of (2) additional shares 12/11/1978
Conv. Class B Common no par split (3) for (1) by issuance of (2) additional shares 12/11/1978
Name changed to Fraser Inc. and

Conv. Class A Common no par and Conv. Class B Common no par reclassified as Common no par 07/23/1979
Fraser Inc. merged into Noranda Inc. 06/01/1985 which name changed to Falconbridge Ltd. (New) 2005 on 07/01/2005
(See Falconbridge Ltd. (New) 2005)

FRASER FUND LTD. (ON)
Acquired by Fraser Growth Fund Ltd. 3/28/69
Each share Class A Common 50¢ par exchanged for (2.543859) shares Special Shares 20¢ par
Fraser Growth Fund Ltd. name changed to Industrial Equity Fund Ltd. 8/20/73

FRASER GROWTH FD LTD (ON)
Name changed to Industrial Equity Fund Ltd. 8/20/73

FRASER INC (CANADA)
Merged into Noranda Inc. 06/01/1985
Each share Common no par exchanged for (1) share Fixed/Floating Rate Conv. Retractable Preferred Ser. B no par
(See Noranda Inc.)

FRASER INDS INC (DE)
Name changed to Riverdale Oil & Gas Corp. (DE) 03/12/2007
Riverdale Oil & Gas Corp. (DE) reincorporated in Nevada 07/00/2008

FRASER MTG INVTS (OH)
Reorganized under the laws of Delaware as Fraser Realty Group, Inc. 08/31/1984
Each Share of Bene. Int. no par exchanged for (1) share Common $0.001 par
Fraser Realty Group, Inc. recapitalized as Motorsports USA Inc. 10/24/1999 which name changed to Vast Technologies Holding Corp. 06/02/2000 which name changed to Accelerated Learning Languages Inc. 11/13/2000 which recapitalized as Integrated Enterprises Inc. 06/20/2001 which recapitalized as SeaLife Corp. (DE) 12/20/2002 which reincorporated in Nevada 10/06/2016

FRASER PAPERS INC (CANADA)
Filed a petition under Companies' Creditors Arrangement Act 06/18/2009
Stockholders' equity unlikely

FRASER RLTY GROUP INC (DE)
Recapitalized as Motorsports USA Inc. 10/24/1999
Each share Common $0.001 par exchanged for (0.1) share Common $0.001 par
Motorsports USA Inc. name changed to Vast Technologies Holding Corp. 06/02/2000 which name changed to Accelerated Learning Languages Inc. 11/13/2000 which recapitalized as Integrated Enterprises Inc. 06/20/2001 which recapitalized as SeaLife Corp. (DE) 12/20/2002 which reincorporated in Nevada 10/06/2016

FRASER VALLEY FARMERS, LTD. (BC)
Struck off register and declared dissolved for failure to file returns 5/25/33

FRASERFUND FINL CORP (BC)
Name changed 08/12/1994
Name changed from Fraserfund Venture Capital (VCC) Corp. to Fraserfund Financial Corp. 08/12/1994
Name changed to South Pacific Minerals Corp. 02/09/2005
South Pacific Minerals Corp. recapitalized as Tribune Resources Corp. 07/28/2006 which name

changed to Tribune Uranium Corp. 06/13/2007 which name changed to Tribune Minerals Corp. 07/18/2008 which name changed to Stratton Resources Inc. 09/14/2011 which name changed to Torq Resources Inc. 03/15/2017

FRASURE HULL HLDG CORP (FL)
Recapitalized as South Central Industries Corp. 7/26/71
Each share Common 1¢ par exchanged for (1/15) share Common 15¢ par
(See South Central Industries Corp.)

FRASURE HULL INC (FL)
Each share Common 1¢ par received distribution of (1) share Orlando Harvesting Corp. 05/08/1969
Name changed to La Reina Corp. 10/24/1969
La Reina Corp. merged into Dominion Development Corp. 01/01/1971 which name changed to First Continental Oil & Gas Co. Inc. 05/10/1971 which merged into Continental Resources, International 07/31/1972

FRATERNITY CMNTY BANCORP INC (MD)
Acquired by Hamilton Bancorp, Inc. 05/16/2016
Each share Common 1¢ par exchanged for $19.25 cash

FRAWLEY ENTERPRISES INC (DE)
Under plan of reorganization each (20) shares Common $1 par or multiples thereof exchanged for (20) shares Frawley Corp. Common $1 par 07/01/1977
Note: Holdings not divisible by (20) received scrip certificates expiring 06/30/1983

FRAZIER & JONES CO.
Acquired by Eastern Malleable Iron Co. in 1944 which name was changed to Eastern Co. 2/22/61

FRC RACING PRODS INC (NV)
Recapitalized as Results Technology Group, Corp. 01/22/2001
Each (22) shares Common $0.001 par exchanged for (1) share Common $0.022 par
(See Results Technology Group, Corp.)

FREBERT MINES LTD. (ON)
Acquired by Abcourt Metals Inc. 01/07/1972
Each share Capital Stock $1 par exchanged for (0.05) share Common no par
Abcourt Metals Inc. name changed to Les Mines d'Argent Abcourt Inc. 03/18/1980 which name changed to Abcourt Mines Inc.- Mines Abcourt Inc. 04/23/1985

FREBERT SNOW LAKE MINES LTD. (ON)
Name changed to Frebert Mines Ltd. 00/00/1951
Frebert Mines Ltd. acquired by Abcourt Metals Inc. 01/07/1972 which name changed to Les Mines d'Argent Abcourt Inc. 03/18/1980 which name changed to Abcourt Mines Inc.-Mines Abcourt Inc. 04/23/1985

FRECOM COMMUNICATIONS INC (BC)
Recapitalized as International Frecom Communications Inc. 07/02/1992
Each share Common no par exchanged for (0.33333333) share Common no par
(See International Frecom Communications Inc.)

FREDA CORP (PA)
Common 10¢ par split (3) for (1) by issuance of (2) additional shares 9/7/88
Under plan of liquidation each share Common 10¢ par exchanged for $9.92 cash 4/30/96

FREDERICA BK & TR (ST SIMONS IS, GA)
Merged into Premier Bancshares Inc. (New) 12/17/98
Each share Common no par exchanged for (2.1) shares Common $1 par
Premier Bancshares Inc. (New) merged into BB&T Corp. 1/13/2000

FREDERICK & HERRUD INC (DE)
Stock Dividends - 10% 1/28/77; 25% 7/31/80
Name changed to Thorn Apple Valley, Inc. 10/11/84
(See Thorn Apple Valley, Inc.)

FREDERICK BREWING CO (MD)
Each share old Common $0.0004 par exchanged for (0.1) share new Common $0.0004 par 03/24/1999
SEC revoked common stock registration 01/14/2009

FREDERICK CNTY BK (FREDERICK, MD)
Under plan of reorganization each share Common 1¢ par automatically became (1) share Frederick County Bancorp, Inc. Common 1¢ par 9/30/2003

FREDERICK MINING & DEVELOPMENT LTD. (ON)
Capital Stock $1 par exchanged (5) for (1) in 1953
Merged into Consolidated Frederick Mines Ltd. on a (9) for (4) basis 9/9/57
(See Consolidated Frederick Mines Ltd.)

FREDERICK-WILLYS CO., INC. (MN)
Through purchase offer Stanley Home Products, Inc. held substantially all outstanding shares as of 04/07/1967
Public interest eliminated

FREDERICK YELLOWKNIFE MINES LTD.
Name changed to Frederick Mining & Development Ltd. in 1946
Frederick Mining & Development Ltd. merged into Consolidated Frederick Mines Ltd. 9/9/57
(See Consolidated Frederick Mines Ltd.)

FREDERICKS HOLLYWOOD GROUP INC (NY)
Acquired by FOHG Holdings, LLC 05/30/2014
Each share Common 1¢ par exchanged for $0.27 cash

FREDERICKS HOLLYWOOD INC (DE)
Common $1 par split (3) for (2) by issuance of (0.5) additional share 4/17/89
Common $1 par split (3) for (2) by issuance of (0.5) additional share 9/27/89
Common $1 par split (3) for (2) by issuance of (0.5) additional share 6/15/90
Common $1 par split (3) for (2) by issuance of (0.5) additional share 5/28/91
Each share Common $1 par exchanged for (1/3) share Class A Common $1 par and (2/3) share Class B Common $1 par 10/15/93
Stock Dividends - 100% 11/14/75; 10% 3/29/82
Merged into Royalty Acquisition Corp. 9/29/97
Each share Class A Common $1 par exchanged for $7.75 cash
Each share Class B Common $1 par exchanged for $7.75 cash

FREDERICKSBURG FINANCIAL CORP. (TX)
Merged into Texas American Bancshares Inc. 09/13/1979
Each share Preferred $1 par exchanged for either (1.3585) shares Common $5 par or $36 cash
Each share Common $15 par exchanged for (1.3412) shares Common $5 par
Note: Option to receive cash expired 10/15/1979
(See Texas American Bancshares Inc.)

FREDERICKSBURG NATL BANCORP INC (VA)
Merged into Mercantile Bankshares Corp. 12/01/1994
Each share Common $4 par exchanged for (2.84) shares Common $2 par
Mercantile Bankshares Corp. merged into PNC Financial Services Group, Inc. 03/02/2007

FREDERICKTOWN BK & TR CO (FREDERICK, MD)
Common $20 par changed to $10 par and (1) additional share issued plus a 50% stock dividend paid 04/23/1973
Merged into Mercantile Bankshares Corp. 08/01/1980
Each share Common $10 par exchanged for (3.3) shares Common no par
Mercantile Bankshares Corp. merged into PNC Financial Services Group, Inc. 03/02/2007

FREDONIA BANCSHARES INC (TX)
Merged into First United Bancshares, Inc. 09/02/1997
Each share Common $10 par exchanged for (3.3874) shares Common $1 par
First United Bancshares, Inc. merged into BancorpSouth, Inc. 08/31/2000 which

FREDONIA OIL & GAS LTD (BC)
Recapitalized as Consolidated Fredonia Resources Ltd. 2/25/85
Each share Common no par exchanged for (0.25) share Common no par
Consolidated Fredonia Resources Ltd. name changed to Sun River Gold Corp. 2/20/86 which recapitalized as Yellow Point Mining Corp. 3/11/91 which recapitalized as Desert Sun Mining Corp. (BC) 8/26/94 which reincorporated in Canada 3/20/2003 which was acquired by Yamana Gold Inc. 4/5/2006

FREE CAR WASH INTL INC (AL)
Placed in receivership 9/20/71
No stockholders' equity

FREE DA CONNECTION SVCS INC (TN)
Recapitalized as Earthshine International Ltd. 09/11/2007
Each share Common $0.001 par exchanged for (0.01) share Common $0.001 par

FREE ENERGY INTL INC (BC)
Each share old Common no par exchanged for (0.125) share new Common no par 03/01/2012
Name changed to Darelle Online Solutions Inc. 04/18/2016

FREE ST CONS GOLD MINES LTD (SOUTH AFRICA)
Merged into AngloGold Ltd. 6/29/98
Each ADR for Ordinary Rand-50 par exchanged for (1) Sponsored ADR for Ordinary Rand-50 par
AngloGold Ltd. name changed to AngloGold Ashanti Ltd. 4/26/2004

FREE ST DEV & INVT LTD (SOUTH AFRICA)
Each ADR for Ordinary Rand-50¢ par exchanged for (5) ADR's for Ordinary Rand-10 par 1/24/86
Merged into Randgold & Exploration Co., Ltd. 2/4/2004

Each ADR for Ordinary Rand-10 par exchanged for $0.594353 cash

FREE ST GEDULD MINES LTD (SOUTH AFRICA)
Under plan of merger each ADR for Ordinary Reg. Rand-50¢ par exchanged for ADR's for Ordinary Reg. Rand-50¢ par of FreeState Consolidated Gold Mines Ltd. and Orange Free State Investments Ltd. 3/4/86
(See each company's listing)

FREE STATE SAAIPLAAS GOLD MINING CO. LTD. (SOUTH AFRICA)
Ctfs. dated prior to 01/17/1966
Acquired by President Brand Gold Mining Co. Ltd. 01/17/1966
Each ADR for Ordinary Reg. ZAR 1 exchanged for $0.072 cash

FREE STATE SAAIPLAAS GOLD MINING CO. LTD. (SOUTH AFRICA)
Ctfs. dated after 07/22/1975
Merged into Welkom Gold Mining Co. Ltd. 08/12/1981
Each ADR for Ordinary ZAR 1 par exchanged for (0.5) ADR for Ordinary Reg. Rand ZAR 50 par
Welkom Gold Mining Co. Ltd. name changed to Welkom Gold Holdings Ltd. 02/24/1986 which reorganized into FreeState Consolidated Gold Mines Ltd. 04/19/1994

FREEBUTTON INC (NV)
Name changed to A-1 Group, Inc. 12/01/2014

FREED-EISEMANN RADIO CORP.
Acquired by Freshman (Chas.) Co., Inc. in 1928
Details not available

FREEDCO INTERNATIONAL, INC. (NY)
Name changed to Radon Resources, Inc. 01/19/1983
Radon Resources, Inc. name changed to Industrial Technical Concepts, Inc. 08/25/1983 which name changed to ITC Integrated Systems, Inc. 10/03/1985
(See ITC Integrated Systems, Inc.)

FREEDOM ACQUISITION HLDGS INC (DE)
Issue Information - 48,000,000 UNITS consisting of (1) share COM and (1) WT offered at $10 per Unit on 12/21/2006
Name changed to GLG Partners, Inc. 11/05/2007
(See GLG Partners, Inc.)

FREEDOM BANCSHARES INC (GA)
Company's sole asset placed in receivership 03/06/2009
Stockholders' equity unlikely

FREEDOM BK (BRADENTON, FL)
Bank failed 11/01/2008
No stockholders' equity

FREEDOM COIN CO., INC. (UT)
Company placed in receivership 3/1/90
Details not available

FREEDOM EYE LTD (AUSTRALIA)
Each old Sponsored ADR for Ordinary exchanged for (0.03333333) new Sponsored ADR for Ordinary 04/21/2010
ADR agreement terminated 03/29/2013
Each new Sponsored ADR for Ordinary exchanged for $0.972534 cash

FREEDOM FD INC (MA)
Common $1 par split (2) for (1) by issuance of (1) additional share 7/26/68
Merged into Keystone Custodian Funds 10/24/80
Each share Common $1 par exchanged for (1.3259) shares Keystone Income Fund Ser. K-1 $1 par

(See Keystone Custodian Funds)

FREEDOM FDG INC (CO)
Recapitalized as CBQ Inc. (CO) 12/01/1998
Each share Common $0.0001 par exchanged for (0.25) share Common $0.0001 par
CBQ Inc. (CO) reincorporated in Florida as China Direct Trading Corp. 05/17/2004 which name changed to CHDT Corp. 07/16/2007 which name changed to Capstone Companies, Inc. 07/06/2012

FREEDOM FED SVGS BK (OAK BROOK, IL)
Acquired by Household International, Inc. 8/3/88
Each share Common 1¢ par exchanged for $18.16 cash

FREEDOM FINL GROUP INC (DE)
Liquidation completed
Each share Common no par received initial distribution of $0.17 cash payable 12/21/2009 to holders of record 12/14/2009
Each share Common no par received second and final distribution of $0.03123 cash payable 12/10/2012 to holders of record 12/14/2009

FREEDOM FINL HLDGS INC (MD)
Common $0.0001 par split (40) for (1) by issuance of (39) additional shares payable 05/23/2008 to holders of record 05/20/2008
Ex date - 05/27/2008
Name changed to Freedom Energy Holdings, Inc. 06/07/2010

FREEDOM GOLF CORP (NV)
SEC revoked common stock registration 06/10/2003

FREEDOM GROUP TAX EXEMPT FDS (MA)
California Tax Exempt Money Fund merged into Money Market Obligations Trust 03/08/2002
Details not available
Tax Exempt Money Fund merged into Great Hall Investment Funds, Inc. 03/08/2002
Details not available

FREEDOM HLDG CORP (UT)
Declared dissolved for failure to pay taxes 09/28/1974

FREEDOM INVT TR II (MA)
Name changed to Hancock (John) Investment Trust III and Freedom Global Fund Class B no par and Global Income Fund Class B no par reclassified as Global Fund Class B no par and World Bond Fund Class B no par respectively 03/01/1997
(See Hancock (John) Investment Trust III)

FREEDOM MARINE LTD (BC)
Struck off register and declared dissolved for failure to file returns 08/29/1992

FREEDOM MOTORCYCLES INC (DE)
Recapitalized as Dot1web, Inc. 9/3/2002
Each (19) shares Common 1¢ par exchanged for (1) share Common 1¢ par

FREEDOM NATL BK (NEW YORK, NY)
Common Capital Stock $10 par changed to $2.50 par in 1975
Declared insolvent 11/9/90
No stockholders' equity

FREEDOM NATIONAL LIFE INSURANCE CO. (UT)
Charter revoked for failure to file reports 12/31/1973

FREEDOM PETE INC (NV)
Recapitalized as Steampunk Wizards, Inc. 07/02/2015
Each share Common $0.0001 par exchanged for (0.4) share Common $0.0001 par
Steampunk Wizards, Inc. name changed to Tianci International Inc. 01/31/2017

FREEDOM RES ENTERPRISES INC (NV)
Old Common $0.001 par split (10) for (1) by issuance of (9) additional shares payable 04/05/2005 to holders of record 02/15/2005
Each share old Common $0.001 par exchanged for (0.4) share new Common $0.001 par 11/15/2006
Note: No holder will receive fewer than (100) shares
Each share new Common $0.001 par exchanged again for (0.5) share new Common $0.001 par 11/15/2007
Recapitalized as Colombia Clean Power & Fuels, Inc. (NV) 07/28/2010
Each share new Common $0.001 par exchanged for (0.4) share Common $0.001 par
Colombia Clean Power & Fuels, Inc. (NV) reincorporated in Delaware as Colombia Energy Resources, Inc. 11/04/2011

FREEDOM RES LTD (BC)
Recapitalized as Canadian Trace Minerals Ltd. 07/03/1986
Each share Common no par exchanged for (0.5649717) share Common no par
(See Canadian Trace Minerals Ltd.)

FREEDOM SVGS & LN ASSN TAMPA (FL)
Placed in receivership by Federal Home Loan Bank 7/23/87
No stockholders' equity

FREEDOM SECS CORP (DE)
Issue Information - 7,400,000 shares COM offered at $20 per share on 04/01/1998
Name changed to Tucker Anthony Sutro 4/17/2000
(See Tucker Anthony Sutro)

FREEDOM SURF INC (NV)
Common $0.001 par split (4) for (1) by issuance of (3) additional shares payable 10/11/2000 to holders of record 10/02/2000 Ex date - 10/12/2000
Recapitalized as FreeStar Technologies Inc. 02/23/2001
Each share Common $0.001 par exchanged for (0.25) share Common $0.001 par
FreeStar Technologies Inc. name changed to FreeStar Technology Corp. 02/24/2003 which recapitalized as Rahaxi, Inc. 11/21/2008
(See Rahaxi, Inc.)

FREEDOM SYNTHETIC OIL INC (DE)
Charter cancelled and declared inoperative and void for non-payment of taxes 3/1/84

FREEDOM-VALVOLINE OIL CO. (PA)
Acquired by Ashland Oil & Refining Co. 1/31/50
Each share 6% Preferred $100 par exchanged for (1.2) shares $5 Preferred no par
Each share Common $20 par exchanged for (0.35) share $5 Preferred no par and (0.5) share Common $1 par
Ashland Oil & Refining Co. name changed to Ashland Oil, Inc. 2/2/70 which name changed to Ashland Inc. (Old) 1/27/95
(See Ashland Inc. (Old))

FREEGOLD MINES LTD. (ON)
Recapitalized as Freegold Mining Co. Ltd. on a (1) for (4) basis in 1946
(See Freegold Mining Co., Ltd.)

FREEGOLD MINING CO., LTD. (ON)
Charter cancelled and declared dissolved for failure to file returns and pay fees 11/04/1970

FREEGOLD RECOVERY INC (BC)
Reincorporated 08/21/1991
Place of incorporation changed from (AB) to (BC) 08/21/1991
Recapitalized as International Freegold Mineral Development Inc. 11/25/1993
Each share Common no par exchanged for (0.16666666) share Common no par
International Freegold Mineral Development Inc. recapitalized as Freegold Ventures Ltd. 09/04/2002

FREEGOLFSTATS COM (NV)
Recapitalized as Mobile Nation, Inc. 08/19/2003
Each share Common $0.001 par exchanged for (0.02) share Common $0.001 par
Mobile Nation, Inc. name changed to AuraSource, Inc. 09/09/2008

FREEHAND SYS INTL INC (DE)
SEC revoked common stock registration 08/06/2009

FREEHOLD & JAMESBURG AGRICULTURAL RAILROAD CO. (NJ)
Assets sold to Penndel Co. at $16.50 per share 12/31/57

FREEHOLD GAS & OIL LTD (BC)
Name changed to Westgrowth Petroleums Ltd. (BC) 03/06/1979
Westgrowth Petroleums Ltd. (BC) reincorporated in Alberta 06/06/1980 which recapitalized as Canadian Westgrowth Ltd. 10/14/1986 which merged into Ulster Petroleums Ltd. 10/27/1987 which merged into Anderson Exploration Ltd. 05/23/2000
(See Anderson Exploration Ltd.)

FREEHOLD OIL CORP. LTD. (CANADA)
Merged into Freehold Gas & Oil Ltd. 03/03/1959
Each share Capital Stock no par exchanged for (0.05) share Common no par
Freehold Gas & Oil Ltd. name changed to Westgrowth Petroleums Ltd. (BC) 03/06/1979 which reincorporated in Alberta 06/06/1980 which recapitalized as Canadian Westgrowth Ltd. 10/14/1986 which merged into Ulster Petroleums Ltd. 10/27/1987 which merged into Anderson Exploration Ltd. 05/23/2000
(See Anderson Exploration Ltd.)

FREEHOLD RTY TR (AB)
Reorganized as Freehold Royalties Ltd. 01/07/2011
Each Trust Unit no par exchanged for (1) share Common no par
Note: Unexchanged certificates were cancelled and became without value 01/07/2014

FREEHOLD TRUST CO. (FREEHOLD, NJ)
Capital Stock $25 par changed to $5 par and (4) additional shares issued 08/28/1957
Stock Dividends - 30% 01/26/1949; 15% 12/24/1952
Name changed to Central Jersey Bank & Trust Co. (Freehold, NJ) 02/01/1959
Central Jersey Bank & Trust Co. (Freehold, NJ) reorganized as Central Jersey Bancorp Ctfs. dtd. prior to 01/14/1995 05/31/1985 which merged into National Westminster Bank PLC (London, England) 01/14/1995

FREEMAN CARL M ASSOC INC (MD)
Under plan of merger each share Common $1 par exchanged for $30 cash in 1986

FREEMAN CHEMICAL CORP. (WI)
Acquired by H.H. Robertson Co. on a (2/13) for (1) basis in 1958
H.H. Robertson Co. merged into Robertson- Ceco Corp. 11/8/90

FREEMAN FINL CORP LTD (CAYMAN ISLANDS)
Name changed 05/14/2012
Name changed from Freeman Corp. Ltd. to Freeman Financial Corp. Ltd. 05/14/2012
ADR agreement terminated 02/10/2016
No ADR's remain outstanding

FREEMAN INCOME PLUS, L.P. (DE)
Filed Certificate of Cancellation 12/31/1995
Details not available

FREEMAN MANUFACTURING CO. LTD. (AB)
Out of business in 1958
No stockholders' equity

FREEMARKETS INC (DE)
Issue Information - 3,600,000 shares COM offered at $48 per share on 12/09/1999
Merged into Ariba, Inc. 07/01/2004
Each share Common 1¢ par exchanged for (0.375) share Common 1¢ par and $2 cash
(See Ariba, Inc.)

FREEMONT GOLD CORP (BC)
Delisted from Vancouver Stock Exchange 03/04/1992

FREEPAGES GROUP PLC (ENGLAND & WALES)
Issue Information - 100,000,000 ADR'S offered at $15.39 per ADR on 03/03/1997
Name changed to Scoot.com PLC 02/22/1999
(See Scoot.com PLC)

FREEPCSQUOTE COM INC (NV)
Each share old Common $0.001 par exchanged for (0.1) share new Common $0.001 par 02/03/2003
Reorganized as Digital Learning Management Corp. (NV) 03/19/2004
Each share new Common $0.001 par exchanged for (7.8680269) shares Common $0.001 par
Digital Learning Management Corp. (NV) reincorporated in Delaware 09/23/2004 which recapitalized as Nutradyne Group, Inc. 10/25/2007 which name changed to China Yongxin Pharmaceuticals Inc. 05/15/2008

FREEPORT CAP INC (AB)
Name changed to Hybrid PayTech World Inc. 09/16/2013
Hybrid PayTech World Inc. name changed to Mobi724 Global Solutions Inc. 02/20/2015

FREEPORT LIQUIDATING CO., INC. (DE)
Liquidation completed 12/18/59
Details not available

FREEPORT-MCMORAN COPPER & GOLD INC (DE)
Name changed 01/03/1991
Class A Common 10¢ par split (2) for (1) by issuance of (1) additional share 05/26/1989
Class A Common 10¢ par split (2) for (1) by issuance of (1) additional share 04/02/1990
Name changed from Freeport-McMoRan Copper Inc. to Freeport-McMoRan Copper & Gold Inc. 01/03/1991
Class A Common 10¢ par split (2) for (1) by issuance of (1) additional share 06/15/1992
Issue Information - 4,760,000 DEPOSITARY SH REP 0.025 SILVER PFD DENON offered at $21.01 per share on 07/22/1994
7% Special Depositary Share called for redemption 12/27/1996

FREEPORT MCMORAN INC (DE) (continued)

7% Special Conv. Preference 10¢ par called for redemption 12/27/1996
Class A Common 10¢ par reclassified as Class B Common 10¢ par 05/06/2002
Depositary Gold Shares Preferred 10¢ par called for redemption 08/01/2003
Step-Up Depositary Preferred called for redemption at $25 plus $0.2283 accrued dividend on 12/19/2003
Depositary Gold Denominated Preferred Ser. II 10¢ par called for redemption at $54.892 on 02/01/2006
5.5% 144A Conv. Perpetual Preferred 10¢ par reclassified as 5.5% Conv. Perpetual Preferred 10¢ par 04/07/2006
Depositary Silver Denominated Preferred 10¢ par called for redemption at $5.411 on 08/01/2006
Class B Common 10¢ par reclassified as Common 10¢ par 03/19/2007
5.5% Conv. Perpetual Preferred 10¢ par called for redemption at $1,000 on 09/21/2009
Each share 6.75% Mandatory Conv. Preferred 10¢ par automatically became (1.3716) shares Common 10¢ par 05/01/2010
Common 10¢ par split (2) for (1) by issuance of (1) additional share payable 02/01/2011 to holders of record 01/15/2011 Ex date - 02/02/2011
Name changed to Freeport-McMoRan Inc. 07/14/2014

FREEPORT MCMORAN ENERGY PARTNERS LTD (TX)
Redemption privileges expired and Special Redemption Privilege shares became without value 03/02/1990
Reorganized as Freeport-McMoRan Oil & Gas Co. 03/30/1990
Each Depositary Receipt exchanged for (1) share Common 10¢ par
Freeport-McMoRan Oil & Gas Co. merged into Freeport-McMoRan Inc. 11/15/1990 which merged into IMC Global Inc. 12/22/1997 which merged into Mosaic Co. (Old) 10/22/2004 which merged into Mosaic Co. (New) 05/25/2011

FREEPORT MCMORAN GOLD CO (DE)
Merged into Minorco 03/26/1990
Each share Common 10¢ par exchanged for $17 cash

FREEPORT MCMORAN INC (DE)
Certificates dated prior to 12/22/1997
$1.875 Conv. Exchangeable Preferred $1 par called for redemption 07/11/1994
$4.375 Conv. Exchangeable Preferred $1 par called for redemption at $52.1875 plus $0.3846 accrued dividend on 10/03/1997
Common $1 par split (2) for (1) by issuance of (1) additional share 06/01/1992
Each share Common $1 par exchanged for (0.16666666) share Common 1¢ par 10/20/1995
Each share Common 1¢ par received distribution of (0.2) share Freeport-McMoRan Sulphur Inc. Common $0.001 par payable 12/31/1997 to holders of record 12/22/1997
Merged into IMC Global Inc. 12/22/1997
Each share Common 1¢ par exchanged for (0.9) share Common $1 par and (0.33333333) Common Stock Purchase Warrant expiring 12/22/2000
IMC Global Inc. merged into Mosaic Co. (Old) 10/22/2004 which merged into Mosaic Co. (New) 05/25/2011

FREEPORT MCMORAN OIL & GAS CO (TX)
Merged into Freeport-McMoRan Inc. 11/15/1990
Each share Common 10¢ par exchanged for (0.3119461) share Common $1 par
Freeport-McMoRan Inc. merged into IMC Global Inc. 12/22/1997 which merged into Mosaic Co. (Old) 10/22/2004 which merged into Mosaic Co. (New) 05/25/2011

FREEPORT MCMORAN OIL & GAS RTY TR (TX)
Trust terminated 5/13/2002
No unitholders' equity

FREEPORT MCMORAN RESOURCE PARTNERS L P (DE)
Each Depositary Unit received distribution of (0.1) share Freeport-McMoRan Sulphur Inc. Common $0.001 par payable 12/31/1997 to holders of record 12/22/1997
Name changed to Phosphate Resource Partners L.P. 01/21/1998
Phosphate Resource Partners L.P. merged into IMC Global Inc. 10/19/2004 which merged into Mosaic Co. (Old) 10/22/2004 which merged into Mosaic Co. (New) 05/25/2011

FREEPORT-MCMORAN SULPHUR INC (DE)
Merged into McMoRan Exploration Co. (New) (DE) 11/17/1998
Each share Common $0.001 par exchanged for (0.625) share Common 1¢ par
(See McMoRan Exploration Co. (New))

FREEPORT MINERALS CO (DE)
Common $5 par split (3) for (2) by issuance of (0.5) additional share 06/29/1979
Common $5 par split (3) for (2) by issuance of (0.5) additional share 03/21/1980
Merged into Freeport-McMoRan Inc. 04/07/1981
Each share Common $5 par exchanged for (1.795) shares Common $1 par
Freeport-McMoRan Inc. merged into IMC Global Inc. 12/22/1997 which merged into Mosaic Co. (Old) 10/22/2004 which merged into Mosaic Co. (New) 05/25/2011

FREEPORT SVGS & LN ASSN LTD (BAHAMAS)
Liquidation completed
Each share Common £1 par exchanged for initial distribution of $1 cash 5/1/71
Each share Common £1 par received second distribution of $0.50 cash 8/10/72
Each share Common £1 par received third distribution of $0.10 cash 7/14/75
Each share Common £1 par received fourth and final distribution of $0.01 cash 1/15/85

FREEPORT SULPHUR CO (DE)
Common $10 par split (3) for (1) by issuance of (2) additional shares 05/05/1959
Common $10 par changed to $5 par and (1) additional share issued 05/06/1966
Stock Dividend - 200% 09/22/1951
Name changed to Freeport Minerals Co. 04/26/1971
Freeport Minerals Co. merged into Freeport-McMoRan Inc. 04/07/1981 which merged into IMC Global Inc. 12/22/1997 which merged into Mosaic Co. (Old) 10/22/2004 which merged into Mosaic Co. (New) 05/25/2011

FREEPORT TEXAS CO.
Name changed to Freeport Sulphur Co. 00/00/1936
Freeport Sulphur Co. name changed to Freeport Minerals Co. 04/26/1971 which merged into Freeport-McMoRan Inc. 04/07/1981 which merged into IMC Global Inc. 12/22/1997 which merged into Mosaic Co. (Old) 10/22/2004 which merged into Mosaic Co. (New) 05/25/2011

FREEREALTIME COM INC (DE)
Reincorporated 11/22/1999
State of incorporation changed from (CO) to (DE) and Common no par changed to 1¢ par 11/22/1999
Plan of reorganization under Chapter 11 Federal Bankruptcy proceedings confirmed 01/17/2003
No stockholders' equity

FREESCALE SEMICONDUCTOR INC (DE)
Merged into Firestone Holdings LLC 12/01/2006
Each share Class A Common 1¢ par exchanged for $40 cash
Each share Class B Common 1¢ par exchanged for $40 cash

FREESCALE SEMICONDUCTOR LTD (BERMUDA)
Name changed 05/01/2012
Name changed from Freescale Semiconductor Holdings I, Ltd. to Freescale Semiconductor, Ltd. 05/01/2012
Merged into NXP Semiconductors N.V. 12/07/2015
Each share Common 1¢ par exchanged for (0.3521) share Common EUR 0.20 par and $6.25 cash

FREESE'S INC. (ME)
Liquidated in 1953

FREESERVE P L C (UNITED KINGDOM)
Merged into Wanadoo S.A. 05/07/2001
Each Sponsored ADR for Ordinary exchanged for $11.1035 cash

FREESHOP COM INC (WA)
Name changed to Aptimus, Inc. 10/24/2000
(See Aptimus, Inc.)

FREESOFTWARECLUB COM INC (DE)
SEC revoked common stock registration 07/09/2012

FREESTAR TECHNOLOGIES (NV)
Name changed to FreeStar Technology Corp. 02/24/2003
FreeStar Technology Corp. recapitalized as Rahaxi, Inc. 11/21/2008
(See Rahaxi, Inc.)

FREESTAR TECHNOLOGY CORP (NV)
Each share old Common $0.001 par exchanged for (1/7) share new Common $0.001 par 11/08/2004
Recapitalized as Rahaxi, Inc. 11/21/2008
Each share Common $0.001 par exchanged for (1/3) share Common $0.001 par
(See Rahaxi, Inc.)

FREESTYLE VENTURES INC (DE)
Name changed to Telecash Industries Inc. 11/10/88
(See Telecash Industries Inc.)

FREEWAY RES LTD (BC)
Recapitalized as GRD Industries Ltd. 05/10/1989
Each share Common no par exchanged for (0.5) share Common no par
(See GRD Industries Ltd.)

FREEWEST RES CDA INC (CANADA)
Name changed 10/21/1994
Name changed from Freewest Resources Inc. to Freewest Resources Canada Inc. 10/21/1994
Each share Common no par received distribution of (0.24390243) share Hemlo Gold Mines Inc. Common no par 12/21/1994
Each share Common no par received distribution of (0.04) share Quest Uranium Corp. Common no par payable 12/12/2007 to holders of record 12/10/2007 Ex date - 12/06/2007
Merged into Cliffs Natural Resources Inc. 01/27/2010
Each share Common no par exchanged for (0.02016) share Common $0.125 par
Cliffs Natural Resources Inc. name changed to Cleveland-Cliffs Inc. (New) 08/25/2017

FREEWHEELIN CORP (AB)
Name changed to FW Omnimedia Corp. 07/11/2000
(See FW Omnimedia Corp.)

FREEWILLPC COM INC (NV)
Name changed to American Leisure Holdings, Inc. 6/28/2002

FREEWORLD COATINGS LTD (SOUTH AFRICA)
Acquired by Kansai Paint Co., Ltd. 12/28/2011
Each ADR for Ordinary 1¢ par exchanged for $14.62 cash

FREEZE DRY CORP. OF AMERICA (FL)
Voluntarily dissolved 7/13/72
Details not available

FREFAX INC (FL)
Name changed to China Xin Network Media Corp. 1/4/2002
China Xin Network Media Corp. name changed to Bio-Tracking Security Inc. 6/22/2004 which recapitalized as Nord Oil International Inc. 10/25/2005 which name changed to North West Oil Group, Inc. 11/16/2006

FREIBERG SILVER INC (ID)
Name changed to Inter Stop Travel Centers, Inc. 05/06/1991
(See Inter Stop Travel Centers, Inc.)

FREIGHT CONNECTION INC (DE)
Each (350,000) shares Common $0.001 par exchanged for (1) share Common $200 par 7/18/2001
Note: In effect holders received $0.17 cash per share and public was interest eliminated

FREIGHT MGMT CORP (NV)
Name changed to Genesis Biopharma, Inc. 04/06/2010
Genesis Biopharma, Inc. recapitalized as Lion Biotechnologies, Inc. (NV) 09/26/2013 which reincorporated in Delaware 06/01/2017 which name changed to Iovance Biotherapeutics, Inc. 06/28/2017

FREIGHT SOLUTION INC (NV)
Name changed to Quanta, Inc. 08/16/2018

FREIHEIT PUBLISHING ASSOCIATION, INC. (NY)
Charter cancelled and proclaimed dissolved for failure to pay taxes 12/15/37

FREIHOFER WILLIAM BAKING CO (DE)
Charter cancelled and declared inoperative and void for non-payment of taxes 3/1/74

FREIMAN A J LTD (CANADA)
Common no par split (9) for (1) by issuance of (8) additional shares 05/18/1962
4.5% Preferred called for redemption 08/01/1964

Acquired by Hudson's Bay Co. 07/26/1972
Each share Common no par exchanged for $6 cash

FREMONT BANCORPORATION (CA)
Acquired by Gaslight Leasing Inc. 11/22/2004
Each share Common $20 par exchanged for $2,039 cash

FREMONT CORP (DE)
Each share old Common 1¢ par exchanged for (0.01) share new Common 1¢ par 04/26/1995
Name changed to Wireless Frontier Internet Inc. 09/29/2003
(See Wireless Frontier Internet Inc.)

FREMONT ENERGY CORP (UT)
Reorganized under the laws of Delaware as Fremont Corp. 06/23/1993
Each share Common 1¢ par exchanged for (0.02) share Common 1¢ par
Fremont Corp. (DE) name changed to Wireless Frontier Internet Inc. 09/29/2003
(See Wireless Frontier Internet Inc.)

FREMONT FIRST NATL CO (NE)
Common $5 par changed to $2.50 par and (1) additional share issued 12/11/73
Stock Dividends - 10% 12/28/70; 10% 8/26/74; 10% 9/3/75; 10% 8/31/76
Name changed to Commerce Group National Fremont, Inc. 5/22/78
(See Commerce Group National Fremont, Inc.)

FREMONT FIRST STATE CO. (NE)
Stock Dividend - 10% 12/28/70
Name changed to Commerce Group State Fremont, Inc. 5/22/78
(See Commerce Group State Fremont, Inc.)

FREMONT FUND, INC. (CA)
Charter revoked for failure to file reports and pay fees 8/1/67

FREMONT GEN CORP (NV)
Common $1 par split (2) for (1) by issuance of (1) additional share 10/31/1978
Common $1 par split (3) for (2) by issuance of (0.5) additional share 06/17/1993
Common $1 par split (3) for (2) by issuance of (0.5) additional share payable 02/07/1996 to holders of record 01/08/1996 Ex date - 02/08/1996
Common $1 par split (2) for (1) by issuance of (1) additional share payable 12/10/1998 to holders of record 11/20/1998 Ex date - 12/11/1998
Stock Dividends - 10% 02/29/1980; 50% 02/02/1981; 10% 05/31/1982; 10% 06/15/1995
Name changed to Signature Group Holdings, Inc. (NV) and Common $1 par changed to 1¢ par 06/11/2010
Signature Group Holdings, Inc. (NV) reincorporated in Delaware 01/07/2014 which name changed to Real Industry, Inc. 06/03/2015
(See Real Industry, Inc.)

FREMONT GEN FINL I (DE)
Plan of reorganization under Chapter 11 Federal Bankruptcy proceedings effective 06/11/2010
Each 9% Trust Originated Preferred Security exchanged for approximately (4.887) shares Signature Group Holdings, Inc. Common 1¢ par, $9.076 principal amount of 9% Notes due 12/31/2016 and $10.007 cash

FREMONT GOLD CORP (DE)
Recapitalized as JSDC Inc. 1/28/2002
Each share Common 1¢ par exchanged for (0.005) share Common 1¢ par

JSDC Inc. recapitalized as Housing Solutions Hawaii Inc. 11/25/2002 which name changed Home Solutions Health, Inc. 5/14/2004

FREMONT GOLD MINES, INC. (DE)
No longer in existence and charter revoked for non-payment of taxes 3/1/39

FREMONT METAL & MINING, INC. (WY)
Dissolved 7/1/60

FREMONT MICH INSURACORP INC (MI)
Class A Common no par split (2) for (1) by issuance of (1) additional share payable 11/17/2006 to holders of record 10/31/2006 Ex date - 11/20/2006
Stock Dividend - 3% payable 06/05/2008 to holders of record 05/22/2008 Ex date - 05/20/2008
Acquired by Auto Club Insurance Association 08/01/2011
Each share Class A Common no par exchanged for $36.15 cash

FREMONT PETE CO (WY)
Completely liquidated 01/30/1969
Each share Capital Stock 1¢ par exchanged for first and final distribution of (1.394) shares International Nuclear Corp. Common 2¢ par and (1) Stock Purchase Warrant
International Nuclear Corp. name changed to Inexco Oil Co. 04/06/1970 which merged into Louisiana Land & Exploration Co. 07/22/1986 which merged into Burlington Resources Inc. 10/22/1997 which merged into ConocoPhillips 03/31/2006

FREMONT URANIUM CORP. (CO)
Merged into King Oil, Inc. 09/05/1956
Each share Common exchanged for (10) shares Common
King Oil, Inc. recapitalized as Lane Wood, Inc. 08/10/1964
(See Lane Wood, Inc.)

FREMONT URANIUM CORP (UT)
Recapitalized as Pollution Control & Engineering Corp. 11/10/1970
Each share Common 1¢ par exchanged for (0.037037) share Common 1¢ par
Pollution Control & Engineering Corp. name changed to Fremont Energy Corp. (UT) 09/22/1976 which reorganized in Delaware as Fremont Corp. 06/23/1993 which name changed to Wireless Frontier Internet Inc. 09/29/2003
(See Wireless Frontier Internet Inc.)

FREMONT VALLEY DEVELOPMENT CORP. (CA)
Charter forfeited for non-payment of taxes 5/2/66

FREMONT VALLEY LANDS, INC. (CA)
Acquired by Reserve Oil & Gas Co. 4/27/64
Each share 6% Preferred $10 par exchanged for (1.6) shares Common $1 par
Each share Common no par exchanged for (2) shares Common $1 par
(See Reserve Oil & Gas Co.)

FRENCH & FOREIGN INVESTORS CORP.
Name changed to Fafic Investment Co. Ltd. in 1941
(See Fafic Investment Co.)

FRENCH (FRED F.) OPERATORS, INC. (NY)
Liquidation completed in 1953

FRENCH BAR INDUSTRIES, INC. (CA)
Merged into Paradigm Medical Industries, Inc. (CA) 5/9/93

Each (7.96) shares Common no par exchanged for (1) share Common no par
Paradigm Medical Industries, Inc. (CA) reincorporated in Delaware in February 1996

FRENCH BATTERY CO. (WI)
Name changed to Ray-O-Vac Co. 00/00/1934
Ray-O-Vac Co. merged into Electric Storage Battery Co. 11/20/1957 which reincorporated in Delaware as ESB Inc. 06/30/1967
(See ESB Inc.)

FRENCH F W TUBE CO (CT)
Class A Common $10 par and Class B Common $10 par reclassified as Common $10 par 05/24/1965
Merged into Valley Metallurgical Processing Co., Inc. 09/18/1967
Each share Common $10 par exchanged for (0.15873) share Common no par
Valley Metallurgical Processing Co., Inc. name changed to Gram Industries, Inc. 12/19/1978 which name changed to Transact International Inc. 10/13/1982
(See Transact International Inc.)

FRENCH FRAGRANCES INC (FL)
Name changed to Elizabeth Arden, Inc. 01/25/2001
(See Elizabeth Arden, Inc.)

FRENCH FRED F INVESTING INC (NY)
7% Non-Cum. Preferred $100 par called for redemption 03/16/1981
Merged into FFF Corp. 08/05/1982
For holdings of (999) shares or fewer:
Each share Common no par exchanged for $141.50 cash
For holdings of (1,000) shares or more:
Each share Common no par exchanged for $104 cash
Note: Holdings of (1,000) shares or more will receive in addition $37.50 cash plus 12% interest on or prior to 08/05/1983

FRENCH MKT SHOPPING CTR INC (KS)
Charter cancelled for failure to file reports and pay fees 10/20/71

FRENCH PEAK RES INC (DE)
Recapitalized as Confederate Motors Inc. 12/18/2008
Each share Common $0.001 par exchanged for (0.3157142) share Common $0.001 par
Confederate Motors Inc. name changed to Curtiss Motorcycles Co., Inc. 02/20/2018

FRENCH PETE CO CDA LTD (CANADA)
Preferred $10 par reclassified as Common no par 06/30/1965
Under plan of merger name changed to Total Petroleum (North America) Ltd. and Common no par changed to $1 par 10/02/1970
Total Petroleum (North America) Ltd. merged into Ultramar Diamond Shamrock Corp. 09/25/1997
(See Ultramar Diamond Shamrock Corp.)

FRENCH RIVIERA CAP INC (CANADA)
Name changed to FRV Media Inc. 10/23/2002
FRV Media Inc. recapitalized as Global SeaFarms Corp. 04/03/2012
(See Global SeaFarms Corp.)

FREQUENCY CTL PRODS INC (NY)
Stock Dividend - 100% 07/01/1981
Name changed to FCP Inc. 07/08/1985
(See FCP Inc.)

FREQUENCY SOURCES INC (MA)
Common 10¢ par split (2) for (1) by

issuance of (1) additional share 1/16/78
Stock Dividend - 25% 10/25/78
Merged into Loral Corp. 8/15/80
Each share Common 10¢ par exchanged for (0.75) share Common 25¢ par
(See Loral Corp.)

FRESCA WORLDWIDE TRADING CORP (NV)
Name changed to Go Solar USA, Inc. 04/16/2010

FRESCO DEVS LTD (BC)
Merged into Oromin Explorations Ltd. (New) 02/25/2002
Each share Common no par exchanged for (0.5) share new Common no par
Oromin Explorations Ltd. (New) merged into Teranga Gold Corp. 10/08/2013

FRESENIUS KABI PHARMACEUTICALS HLDG INC (DE)
Contingent Value Rights expired without value 06/30/2011

FRESENIUS MED CARE AG & CO KGAA (GERMANY)
Name changed 02/10/2006
Name changed from Fresenius Medical Care AG to Fresenius Medical Care AG & Co. KGaA 02/10/2006
Sponsored ADR's for Preference basis changed from (3:1) to (1:1) 06/18/2007
Sponsored ADR's for Preference split (2) for (1) by issuance of (1) additional ADR payable 12/03/2012 to holders of record 11/30/2012 Ex date - 12/04/2012
Sponsored ADR's for Preference basis changed from (1:1) to (1:0.5) 12/04/2012
Each Sponsored ADR for Preference exchanged for (1) Sponsored ADR for Ordinary 07/02/2013
(Additional Information in Active)

FRESENIUS MED CARE HLDGS INC (NY)
Name changed 10/01/1996
Name changed from Fresenius National Medical Care Holdings Inc. to Fresenius Medical Care Holdings, Inc. 10/01/1996
Class D Preferred $1 par called for redemption at $0.10 on 03/28/2003
Merged into FMCH Merger Sub 10/30/2007
Each share 6% Preferred $100 par exchanged for $100 cash
Each share 8% Class A Preferred $100 par exchanged for $106.60 cash
Each share 8% Class B Preferred $100 par exchanged for $106.60 cash

FRESENIUS USA INC (MA)
Merged into Fresenius Medical Care AG 9/30/96
Each share Common 1¢ par exchanged for (1.04909) Sponsored ADR for Ordinary DM 5 par
Fresenius Medical Care AG name changed to Fresenius Medical Care AG & Co. KGaA 2/10/2006

FRESH AMER CORP (TX)
Acquired by DiMare Fresh Inc. 01/00/2003
Details not available

FRESH BRANDS INC (WI)
Merged into Certifresh Holdings, Inc. 2/27/2006
Each share Common 5¢ par exchanged for $7.05 cash

FRESH BREATH INDS INC (NV)
Recapitalized as Advanced Interactive Inc. 02/08/2001
Each share Common $0.001 par

exchanged for (0.1) share Common $0.001 par
(See Advanced Interactive Inc.)

FRESH CHOICE INC (DE)
Plan of reorganization under Chapter 11 Federal Bankruptcy Code effective 12/21/2005
No stockholders' equity

FRESH FOODS INC (NC)
Name changed to Pierre Foods Inc. 7/27/2000
(See Pierre Foods Inc.)

FRESH HEALTHY VENDING INTL INC (NV)
Name changed to Generation Next Franchise Brands, Inc. 07/13/2016

FRESH IDEAS FOOD CORP (BC)
Recapitalized as Bobby Cadillac's Food Corp. 09/30/1992
Each share Common no par exchanged for (0.2) share Common no par
Bobby Cadillac's Food Corp. recapitalized as Immune Network Research Ltd. 04/29/1996 which name changed to Immune Network Ltd. 08/16/2000
(See Immune Network Ltd.)

FRESH IDEAS MEDIA INC (NV)
Common $0.001 par split (5) for (1) by issuance of (4) additional shares payable 09/25/2008 to holders of record 09/25/2008
Name changed to China Auto Logistics Inc. 01/29/2009

FRESH JUICE INC (DE)
Common 1¢ par split (2) for (1) by issuance of (1) additional share 8/13/87
Merged into Saratoga Beverage Group, Inc. 1/29/99
Each share Common 1¢ par exchanged for $2.244 cash

FRESH MAID INC (DE)
Filed Chapter 7 on 2/15/90
No stockholders' equity

FRESH MKT INC (DE)
Acquired by Pomegranate Holdings, Inc. 04/27/2016
Each share Common 1¢ par exchanged for $28.50 cash

FRESH N LITE INC (TX)
Reorganized as Restaurant Teams International, Inc. 9/18/98
Each share Common 1¢ par exchanged for (1) share Common 1¢ par and (0.1) Common Stock Purchase Warrant expiring 9/18/2000
Restaurant Teams International, Inc. recapitalized as RTIN Holdings, Inc. 12/14/2001 which name changed to Safescript Pharmacies, Inc. 12/17/2003
(See Safescript Pharmacies, Inc.)

FRESH START PRIVATE HLDGS INC (NV)
Each share old Common $0.001 par exchanged for (0.004) share new Common $0.001 par 05/13/2010
Name changed to Tap Resources, Inc. 08/16/2012

FRESH START PRIVATE MGMT INC (NV)
Name changed to BioCorRx Inc. 02/20/2014

FRESH TRAFFIC GROUP INC (NV)
Recapitalized as Synergetics, Inc. 08/31/2012
Each (75) shares Common $0.001 par exchanged for (1) share Common $0.001 par

FRESH VEG BROKER COM INC (NV)
Each share Common $0.001 par received distribution of (1) share Golden Valley Development, Inc. Common $0.001 par payable 08/26/2004 to holders of record 08/26/2004
Name changed to Tiger Team Technologies, Inc. 08/26/2004
Tiger Team Technologies, Inc. name changed to Physicians Healthcare Management Group, Inc. 07/12/2006

FRESHER COOKER INC (KY)
Under plan of reorganization each share Common no par received distribution of (1) Series 1 Common Stock Purchase Warrant expiring 8/31/86 and (1) Series 2 Common Stock Purchase Warrant expiring 3/31/87 of Cooker Concepts, Inc. 2/14/86
Note: Certificates were not required to be surrendered and are now valueless

FRESHMAN (CHAS.) CO., INC.
Name changed to Earl Radio Corp. 00/00/1929
(See Earl Radio Corp.)

FRESHSTART PPTYS INC (NV)
Name changed to Cascadia Investments Inc. 12/19/2007

FRESHSTART VENTURE CAP CORP (NY)
Merged into Medallion Financial Corp. 10/3/2000
Each share Common exchanged for (0.23865) share Common 1¢ par

FRESHTECH FOOD PROCESSORS LTD (NV)
Reorganized as Extreme Poker, Ltd. 06/17/2004
Each share Common $0.001 par exchanged for (100) shares Common $0.001 par
Extreme Poker, Ltd. recapitalized as China Capital Holdings Corp. 02/28/2006
(See China Capital Holdings Corp.)

FRESHWATER TECHNOLOGIES INC (NV)
Recapitalized as Agent155 Media Corp. 07/27/2011
Each share Common $0.001 par exchanged for (0.00025) share Common $0.001 par

FRESHXTEND TECHNOLOGIES CORP (BC)
Merged into FreshXtend International Pty Ltd. 12/08/2008
Each share Common no par exchanged for $0.03 cash

FRESNILLO CO (NY)
Common no par changed to $1 par 00/00/1949
Merged into Rosario Resources Corp. 09/06/1977
Each share Common $1 par exchanged for (0.9) share Capital Stock $1 par
Rosario Resources Corp. merged into Amax Inc. 04/10/1980 which merged into Cyprus Amax Minerals Co. 11/15/1993 which merged into Phelps Dodge Corp. 12/02/1999 which merged into Freeport-McMoRan Copper & Gold Inc. 03/19/2007 which name changed to Freeport-McMoRan Inc. 07/14/2014

FRESNO BANCORP (CA)
Merged into ValliCorp Holdings, Inc. 11/30/89
Each share Common no par exchanged for (1) share Common no par
ValliCorp Holdings, Inc. merged into Westamerica Bancorporation 4/12/97

FRESNO BANK OF COMMERCE (FRESNO, CA)
Under plan of reorganization each share Common no par automatically became (1) share Western Commercial (CA) Common no par 12/27/82
Western Commercial (CA) reincorporated in Delaware as Western Commercial, Inc. 7/27/87 which merged into ValliCorp Holdings, Inc. 11/30/89 which merged into Westamerica Bancorporation 4/12/97

FRESNO FIRST BK (FRESNO, CA)
Stock Dividends - 5% payable 12/23/2011 to holders of record 12/08/2011 Ex date - 12/06/2011; 5% payable 12/27/2012 to holders of record 12/11/2012 Ex date - 12/07/2012; 5% payable 12/05/2013 to holders of record 11/19/2013 Ex date - 11/15/2013
Under plan of reorganization each share Perpetual Preferred Ser. C $100 par and Common no par automatically became (1) share Communities First Financial Corp. Perpetual Preferred Ser. A $100 par or Common no par respectively 11/10/2014

FRESNO GTEE SVGS & LN ASSN (CA)
Stock Dividends - 100% 12/18/1968; 25% 12/31/1969
100% acquired by Guarantee Financial Corp. of California through exchange offer which expired 07/20/1973 Public interest eliminated

FRESNORE MINES LTD. (ON)
Charter cancelled 04/21/1958

FRETTER INC (MI)
Plan of reorganization under Chapter 11 Federal Bankruptcy Code effective 3/12/99
No stockholders' equity

FREY ASSOC INC (NH)
Charter dissolved for failure to file reports and pay fees 12/1/87

FREYJA RES INC (CANADA)
Name changed to Cyprium Mining Corp. 06/09/2014

FREYMILLER TRUCKING INC (IN)
Liquidating plan of reorganization under Chapter 11 Federal Bankruptcy proceedings confirmed 01/08/1996
No stockholders' equity

FREZER INC (NV)
Each share old Common $0.001 par exchanged for (0.05) share new Common $0.001 par 02/27/2008
Note: Holders of between (101) and (1,999) pre-split shares will receive (100) shares
Recapitalized as BEFUT International Co., Ltd. 06/18/2009
Each share Common $0.001 par exchanged for (0.24570024) share Common $0.001 par
BEFUT International Co., Ltd. name changed to Befut Global, Inc. 10/06/2017

FRI CORP (GA)
Name changed to Georgia 400 Industries, Inc. 01/02/1992
(See Georgia 400 Industries, Inc.)

FRICK CO. (PA)
Each share Common $50 par exchanged for (1) share Preferred $50 par and (1) share Common no par in 1926
Stock Dividends - 50% 6/2/47; 11-1/9% 10/1/50; 200% 12/30/50
Merged into General Waterworks Corp. 10/31/59
Each share Preferred $50 par exchanged for (0.5) share $6 Preferred $100 par
Each share Common no par exchanged for (1) share $2 Conv. 2nd Preferred $1 par
General Waterworks Corp. merged into International Utilities Corp. 3/1/68 which name changed to IU International Corp. 4/27/73
(See IU International Corp.)

FRIDAY CAP INC (ON)
Recapitalized as Hit Technologies Inc. 06/16/2015
Each share Common no par exchanged for (0.44905473) share Common no par

FRIDAY MINES LTD. (BC)
Recapitalized as Polaris Mines Ltd. 04/15/1966
Each share Capital Stock 50¢ par exchanged for (0.33333333) share Capital Stock no par
Polaris Mines Ltd. recapitalized as Titan-Polaris Mines Ltd. 05/28/1973 which recapitalized as Saxton Industries Ltd. 07/28/1975 which name changed to Delbancor Industries Inc. 10/06/1987
(See Delbancor Industries Inc.)

FRIDAY NICKEL MINES LTD. (BC)
Name changed to Friday Mines Ltd. 07/30/1959
Friday Mines Ltd. recapitalized as Polaris Mines Ltd. 04/15/1966 which recapitalized as Titan-Polaris Mines Ltd. 05/28/1973 which recapitalized as Saxton Industries Ltd. 07/28/1975 which name changed to Delbancor Industries Inc. 10/06/1987
(See Delbancor Industries Inc.)

FRIDAY NIGHT INC (AB)
Reincorporated under the laws of British Columbia as 1933 Industries Inc. 10/01/2018

FRIDEN, INC. (CA)
Common $1 par changed to 33-1/3¢ par and (2) additional shares issued 11/16/60
Acquired by Singer Co. 10/14/63
Each share Common 33-1/3¢ par exchanged for (4/7) share Capital Stock $10 par
(See Singer Co.)

FRIDEN CALCULATING MACHINE CO., INC. (CA)
Stock Dividend - 100% 4/22/65
Name changed to Friden, Inc. 11/22/57
Friden, Inc. acquired by Singer Co. 10/14/63
(See Singer Co.)

FRIED & REINEMAN PACKING CO. (PA)
Liquidation completed 7/9/62
Class A Preferred stockholders received an undetermined amount of cash
No Class B Preferred or Common stockholders' equity

FRIEDE GOLDMAN HALTER INC (DE)
Name changed 11/4/99
Common 1¢ par split (2) for (1) by issuance of (1) additional share payable 10/10/97 to holders of record 10/1/97
Under plan of merger name changed from Friede Goldman International, Inc. to Friede Goldman Halter, Inc. 11/4/99
Plan of reorganization under Chapter 11 Federal Bankruptcy Code effective 1/13/2004
No stockholders' equity

FRIEDMAN (LOUIS) REALTY CORP. (DE)
Liquidation completed for cash 10/7/63

FRIEDMAN BILLINGS RAMSEY GROUP INC NEW (VA)
Name changed to Arlington Asset Investment Corp. 06/10/2009

FRIEDMAN BILLINGS RAMSEY GROUP INC OLD (VA)
Issue Information - 11,000,000 shares CL A shares offered at $20 per share on 12/22/1997
Merged into Friedman, Billings,

Ramsey Group Inc. (New) 03/31/2003
Each share Class A Common 1¢ par exchanged for (1) share Class A Common 1¢ par
Each share Class B Common 1¢ par exchanged for (1) share Class A Common 1¢ par
Friedman, Billings, Ramsey Group, Inc. (New) name changed to Arlington Asset Investment Corp. 06/10/2009

FRIEDMANS INC (DE)
Plan of reorganization under Chapter 11 Federal Bankruptcy proceedings effective 12/09/2005
No stockholders' equity

FRIEDRICH TECHNOLOGIES INC (BC)
Name changed to International Prime Technologies Inc. 05/13/1988
(See International Prime Technologies Inc.)

FRIENDFINDER NETWORKS INC (NV)
Issue Information - 5,000,000 shares COM offered at $10 per share on 05/11/2011
Plan of reorganization under Chapter 11 Federal Bankruptcy proceedings effective 12/20/2013
No stockholders' equity

FRIENDLY AUTO DEALERS INC (NV)
Name changed to Therapeutic Solutions International, Inc. 03/18/2011

FRIENDLY ENERGY CORP (NV)
Recapitalized as Friendly Energy Exploration 03/24/2008
Each share Common $0.001 par exchanged for (0.04) share Common $0.001 par
(See Friendly Energy Exploration)

FRIENDLY ENERGY EXPL (NV)
Each share old Common $0.001 par exchanged for (0.05) share new Common $0.001 par 12/17/2012
SEC revoked common stock registration 01/19/2016

FRIENDLY FIN INC (KY)
5-1/2% Conv. Preferred $10 par called for redemption 12/15/72
6% Preferred $10 par called for redemption 12/15/72
Stock Dividend - Common & Class B Common - 20% 11/18/68
Merged into Third National Corp. 12/20/72
Each share Common $1 par or Class B Common $1 par exchanged for (0.50992) share Common $10 par
Third National Corp. merged into SunTrust Banks, Inc. 12/29/86

FRIENDLY FROST INC (NY)
Acquired by Swanton Corp. 1/15/85
Each share Common 10¢ par exchanged for (2.02) shares Common 10¢ par
(See Swanton Corp.)

FRIENDLY ICE CREAM CORP NEW (MA)
Merged into Freeze Operations Holdings Corp. 08/30/2007
Each share Common 1¢ par exchanged for $15.50 cash

FRIENDLY ICE CREAM CORP OLD (MA)
Common $1 par split (2) for (1) by issuance of (1) additional share 09/05/1969
Common $1 par split (2) for (1) by issuance of (1) additional share 03/22/1972
Merged into Hershey Foods Corp. 04/09/1979
Each share Common $1 par exchanged for $23 cash

FRIENDLY NATIONAL BANK OF NEW JERSEY (CINNAMINSON, NJ)
Common Capital Stock $2.50 par changed to $5 par 06/30/1980
Name changed to Eastern National Bank (Cinnaminson, NJ) 04/12/1983
Eastern National Bank (Cinnaminson, NJ) name changed to Cherry Hill National Bank (Medford, NJ) 04/27/1987 which merged into Meridian Bancorp, Inc. 04/16/1993 which merged into CoreStates Financial Corp 04/09/1996 which merged into First Union Corp. 04/28/1998 which name changed to Wachovia Corp. (Ctfs. dated after 09/01/2001) 09/01/2001 which merged into Wells Fargo & Co. (New) 12/31/2008

FRIENDLY PLASTIC LTD (WY)
Reincorporated 8/19/93
State of incorporation changed from (CO) to (WY) 8/19/93
Charter revoked for failure to pay taxes 2/24/97

FRIENDLYWAY CORP (NV)
Name changed to PSI Corp. 10/02/2006
PSI Corp. name changed to Coupon Express, Inc. 01/26/2012

FRIENDS PROVIDENT GROUP P L C (UNITED KINGDOM)
Name changed 06/15/2009
Name changed from Friends Provident PLC to Friends Provident Group PLC 06/15/2009
Each Unsponsored ADR received distribution of $1.057144 cash payable 08/07/2009 to holders of record 07/27/2009
Acquired by Resolution Holdings Ltd. 11/02/2009
Each Unsponsored ADR for Ordinary exchanged for $14.015191 cash

FRIER INDS INC (DE)
Adjudicated bankrupt 11/18/1981
Stockholders' equity unlikely

FRIES ENTMT INC (DE)
Reincorporated 04/23/1987
Common 1¢ par split (3) for (2) by issuance of (0.5) additional share 03/18/1986
State of incorporation changed from (CA) to (DE) 04/23/1987
Plan of reorganization under Chapter 11 Federal Bankruptcy proceedings confirmed 12/01/2004
No stockholders' equity

FRIGIDINNERS, INC. (PA)
Bankrupt in 1953

FRIGIKAR CORP. (DE)
Each share Common $1 par exchanged for (2) shares Common 50¢ par 3/20/56
Liquidation completed
Each share Common 50¢ par exchanged for initial distribution of $15 cash 11/6/64
Each share Common 50¢ par received second distribution of $2.10 cash 8/5/65
Each share Common 50¢ par received third and final distribution of $0.2725 cash 6/21/68

FRIGISTORS LTD. (CANADA)
Name changed to Termo Ltd. 07/29/1967
(See Termo Ltd.)

FRIGITEMP CORP (NY)
Stock Dividend - 33-1/3% 11/29/1974
Adjudicated bankrupt 05/29/1979
Stockholders' equity unlikely

FRIGITRONICS INC (DE)
Common 10¢ par split (4) for (1) by issuance of (3) additional shares 4/18/69
Stock Dividend - 100% 11/28/68
Acquired by Revlon Group Inc. 12/5/86

Each share Common 10¢ par exchanged for $34.50 cash

FRIGOMATIC INC (FL)
Involuntarily dissolved for failure to file reports and pay fees 10/13/89

FRINK CORP. (NY)
Reorganized 1938
Under plan of reorganization state of incorporation changed from (DE) to (NY) in 1938
Merged into Frink Corp. (DE) (New) 10/31/60
Each share Preferred $40 par exchanged for (2) shares Common $1 par
Each share Common $1 par exchanged for (0.1) share Common $1 par
(See Frink Corp. (DE) (New))

FRINK CORP. NEW (DE)
Acquired by Westinghouse Electric Corp. 10/31/68
Each share Common $1 par exchanged for $14 cash

FRIONA INDS INC (TX)
Stock Dividend - 25% 4/13/79
Merged into CHS Partners, Ltd. 6/19/85
Each share Common $1 par exchanged for $19 cash

FRIPP ISLAND RESORT, INC. (SC)
Liquidation completed
Each share Common $1 par exchanged for initial distribution of $1.26 cash 10/31/74
Each share Common $1 par received second and final distribution of $0.08 cash 12/1/76

FRISBY TECHNOLOGIES INC (DE)
Issue Information - 1,600,000 shares COM offered at $7 per share on 04/01/1998
Plan of reorganization under Chapter 11 Federal Bankruptcy Code effective 05/10/2004
No stockholders' equity

FRISCHKORN REAL ESTATE CO.
Dissolved in 1932

FRISCHS RESTAURANTS INC (OH)
Common no par split (2) for (1) by issuance of (1) additional share 11/12/1971
Common no par split (2) for (1) by issuance of (1) additional share 11/16/1984
Stock Dividend - 4% payable 12/27/1996 to holders of record 12/02/1996
Acquired by FRI Holding Co., LLC 08/24/2015
Each share Common no par exchanged for $34 cash

FRISCO BAY INDS LTD (CANADA)
Merged into Stanley Works 03/15/2004
Each share Common no par exchanged for USD$15.25 cash

FRISCO INC (UT)
Recapitalized as Telenet Corp. 11/18/1998
Each share Common $0.001 par exchanged for (0.01) share Common $0.001 par

FRISCO MINES CO. (AZ)
Charter expired by time limitation 1/29/31

FRISCO SILVER LEAD MINING CO. (UT)
Merged into Tintic Lead Co. share for share 12/22/1964
Tintic Lead Co. name changed to Tintic Minerals Resources, Inc. 06/27/1969 which merged into Horn Silver Mines, Inc. 07/20/1983
(See Horn Silver Mines, Inc.)

FRITO CO. (TX)
Common no par changed to $5 par 3/19/56

Common $5 par changed to $2.50 par and (1) additional share issued 3/20/59
Common $2.50 par split (3) for (2) by issuance of (0.5) additional share 4/28/61
Under plan of merger name changed to Frito-Lay, Inc. 9/22/61
Frito-Lay, Inc. merged into PepsiCo, Inc. (Del.) 6/10/65 which reincorporated in North Carolina 12/4/86

FRITO-LAY, INC. (TX)
Merged into PepsiCo, Inc. (Del.) 6/10/65
Each share Common $2.50 par exchanged for (2/3) share Capital Stock 33-1/3¢ par
PepsiCo, Inc. (Del.) reincorporated in North Carolina 12/4/86

FRITZ COS INC (DE)
Common 1¢ par split (2) for (1) by issuance of (1) additional share 10/30/95
Merged into United Parcel Service Inc. 5/25/2001
Each share Common 1¢ par exchanged for (0.2) share Class B 1¢ par

FRITZ W. GLITSCH & SONS, INC. (DE)
See - Glitsch (Fritz W.) & Sons, Inc.

FRITZI CALIF MFG CORP (CA)
Stock Dividends - 125% 6/2/71; 25% 6/27/77
Merged into Benesch Corp. 12/12/90
Each share Common $1 par exchanged for $40 cash

FRM NEXUS INC (DE)
Common 10¢ par split (3) for (2) by issuance of (0.5) additional share payable 07/14/1998 to holders of record 06/24/1998
Name changed to FRMO Corp. and Common 10¢ par changed to $0.001 par 11/29/2000

FROBEX LTD (ON)
Charter cancelled and declared dissolved for failure to pay taxes and file returns 11/08/1977

FROBISHER LTD. (ON)
Name changed 00/00/1947
Name changed from Frobisher Exploration Co. Ltd. to Frobisher Ltd. 00/00/1947
Recapitalized as Frobex Ltd. 10/30/1962
Each share Capital Stock no par exchanged for (0.14285714) share Capital Stock no par
(See Frobex Ltd.)

FROBISHER RES LTD (BC)
Merged into Canadian Frobisher Resources Ltd. 11/21/1991
Each share Common no par exchanged for (1) share Common no par
Canadian Frobisher Resources Ltd. merged into Orbit Oil & Gas Ltd. 08/26/1994
(See Orbit Oil & Gas Ltd.)

FRODAC CONS ENERGY RES LTD (ON)
Recapitalized as Global Aerospace Systems Inc. 9/30/85
Each share Capital Stock no par exchanged for (1/6) share Common no par
Global Aerospace Systems Inc. recapitalized as Venga Aerospace Systems Inc. 11/16/87

FROEDTERT CORP. (WI)
Name changed to Basic Products Corp. 07/31/1957
Basic Products Corp. name changed to Sola Basic Industries, Inc. 10/29/1965 which merged into General Signal Corp. 09/30/1977 which merged into SPX Corp. 10/06/1998

FROEDTERT GRAIN & MALTING CO. INC.
Name changed to Froedtert Corp. 00/00/1951
Froedtert Corp. name changed to Basic Products Corp. 07/31/1957 which name changed to Sola Basic Industries, Inc. 10/29/1965 which merged into General Signal Corp. 09/30/1977 which merged into SPX Corp. 10/06/1998

FROG INDS LTD (NY)
Merged into Chem International Inc. 12/27/1994
Each share Common 1¢ par exchanged for (0.03) share Common 1¢ par
Chem International Inc. name changed to Integrated Health Technologies Inc. 01/05/2001 which name changed to Integrated BioPharma, Inc. 04/15/2003

FROGADS INC (NV)
Voluntarily dissolved 06/07/2013
No stockholders' equity

FROKAR GOLD MINES LTD. (ON)
Charter surrendered 11/30/1955
No stockholders' equity

FRONSAC CAP INC (CANADA)
Reorganized under the laws of Quebec as Fronsac Real Estate Investment Trust 07/04/2011
Each share Common no par exchanged for (1) Trust Unit
Note: Unexchanged certificates will be cancelled and become without value 07/04/2021

FRONT PORCH DIGITAL INC (NV)
Name changed to Incentra Solutions, Inc. 10/29/2004
(See Incentra Solutions, Inc.)

FRONT RANGE CAP TR I (DE)
11% Preferred Securities called for redemption at $8 on 12/28/2005

FRONT RANGE MINES, INC. (CO)
Each share Common $1 par exchanged for (3) shares Common 10¢ par 6/1/55
Defunct 9/1/63; Common stock worthless

FRONT RANGE OIL & URANIUM CO. (CO)
Charter suspended for failure to file corporate reports 09/18/1980

FRONT RANGE RES LTD (AB)
Recapitalized as Arrow Exploration Corp. 10/05/2018
Each share Common no par exchanged for (0.11764705) share Common no par

FRONT RANGE URANIUM MINES, INC. (DE)
No longer in existence having become inoperative and void for non-payment of taxes 4/1/57

FRONT STR U S MLP INCOME FD LTD NEW (CANADA)
Under plan of merger each Equity Share Ser. C and U automatically became (1) Front Street Mutual Funds Ltd. MLP & Infrastructure Income Class MC or MU respectively 01/26/2016

FRONT STR LONG/SHORT INCOME FD II (ON)
Merged into Front Street Long/Short Income Fund 06/02/2006
Each Unit no par received (0.959157) Unit no par
Front Street Long/Short Income Fund name changed to Front Street Yield Opportunities Fund Ltd. 08/09/2007 which merged into Front Street Mutual Funds Ltd. 11/01/2008

FRONT STR MLP INCOME FD LTD (CANADA)
Units separated 01/11/2011
Merged into Front Street U.S. MLP Income Fund Ltd. (Old) 12/17/2012
Each Equity Share received (0.997946) Equity Share Ser. C
Front Street U.S. MLP Income Fund Ltd. (Old) merged into Front Street U.S. MLP Income Fund Ltd. (New) 08/13/2013 which merged into Front Street Mutual Funds Ltd. 01/26/2016

FRONT STR MLP INCOME FD II LTD (CANADA)
Equity Shares reclassified as Equity Shares Series C 10/25/2011
Merged into Front Street U.S. MLP Income Fund Ltd. (Old) 12/17/2012
Each Equity Share Ser. C received (1) Equity Share Ser. C
Each Equity Share Ser. U received (1) Equity Share Ser. U
Front Street U.S. MLP Income Fund Ltd. (Old) merged into Front Street U.S. MLP Income Fund Ltd. (New) 08/13/2013 which merged into Front Street Mutual Funds Ltd. 01/26/2016

FRONT STR PERFORMANCE FD (ON)
Merged into Front Street Performance Fund II 09/01/2006
Each Unit exchanged for (2.8353) Units
Front Street Performance Fund II merged into Front Street Mutual Funds Ltd. 03/02/2009

FRONT STR PERFORMANCE FD II (ON)
Merged into Front Street Mutual Funds Ltd. 03/02/2009
Each Unit exchanged for (1.008616) shares Tactical Equity Class B

FRONT STR RESOURCE PERFORMANCE FD LTD (CANADA)
Under plan of merger each share Common no par automatically became (1) share Front Street Mutual Funds Ltd. Resource Growth & Income Class L 03/01/2010

FRONT STR STRATEGIC YIELD FD LTD (CANADA)
Combined Units separated 06/29/2010
Under plan of merger each Equity Share automatically became (0.455535) Front Street U.S. MLP Income Fund Ltd. (New) Equity Share Ser. C 08/13/2013
Front Street U.S. MLP Income Fund Ltd. (New) merged into Front Street Mutual Funds Ltd. 01/26/2016

FRONT STR U S MLP INCOME FD LTD OLD (CANADA)
Under plan of merger each Equity Share Ser. C and U automatically became (1) Front Street U.S. MLP Income Fund Ltd. (New) Equity Share Ser. C or U respectively 08/13/2013
Front Street U.S. MLP Income Fund Ltd. (New) merged into Front Street Mutual Funds Ltd. 01/26/2016

FRONT STR YIELD OPPORTUNITIES FD LTD (ON)
Name changed 08/09/2007
Name changed from Front Street Long/Short Income Fund to Front Street Yield Opportunities Fund Ltd. 08/09/2007
Merged into Front Street Mutual Funds Ltd. 11/01/2008
Each share Class B no par received shares of Balanced Monthly Income Fund Class B on a net asset basis

FRONTEER DEV FIN INC (DE)
Name changed to eBanker USA.com Inc. 3/31/99

FRONTEER DEV GROUP INC (ON)
Name changed to Fronteer Gold Inc. 05/13/2010
Fronteer Gold Inc. merged into Pilot Gold Inc. 04/08/2011 which name changed to Liberty Gold Corp. 05/12/2017

FRONTEER FINL HLDGS LTD (CO)
Name changed 07/08/1996
Name changed from Fronteer Directory Co., Inc. to Fronteer Financial Holdings Ltd. 07/08/1996
Name changed to eVision USA.Com, Inc. 04/15/1999 eVision USA.Com, Inc. name changed to eVision International, Inc. 02/26/2002
(See eVision International, Inc.)

FRONTEER GOLD INC (ON)
Merged into Pilot Gold Inc. 04/08/2011
Each share Common no par exchanged for (0.25) share Common no par and $14 cash
Pilot Gold Inc. name changed to Liberty Gold Corp. 05/12/2017

FRONTENAC BREWERIES, LTD.
Acquired by National Breweries Ltd. in 1933
Details not available

FRONTENAC MINING CORP. (QC)
Under plan of acquisition name changed to Copperstream-Frontenac Mines Ltd. 2/1/62
(See Copperstream-Frontenac Mines Ltd.)

FRONTENAC OIL REFINERIES, LTD.
Merged into McColl-Frontenac Oil Co., Ltd. 00/00/1927
Details not available

FRONTENAC TRUST SHARES
Liquidated in 1933

FRONTEND INTL TECHNOLOGIES INC (BC)
Struck off register and declared dissolved for failure to file returns 02/26/1993

FRONTEND RES LTD (BC)
Recapitalized as Frontend International Technologies Inc. 07/16/1986
Each share Common no par exchanged for (3) shares Common no par
(See Frontend International Technologies Inc.)

FRONTERA COPPER CORP (CANADA)
Acquired by Invecture Group, S.A. de C.V. 04/01/2009
Each share Common no par exchanged for $0.75 cash

FRONTERA RES CORP (DE)
Reorganized under the laws of Cayman Islands 08/02/2011
Each share Common $0.00004 par exchanged for (1) share Ordinary USD $0.00004 par
Note: Non-Accredited Investors and Accredited Investors who did not surrender their certificates prior to 11/29/2011 will receive $0.065 cash per share

FRONTHAUL GROUP INC (DE)
Name changed to Conversion Solutions Holdings Corp. 08/09/2006
Each share Common $0.001 par exchanged for (1) share Common $0.001 par
(See Conversion Solutions Holdings Corp.)

FRONTIER ACQUISITION CORP (AB)
Recapitalized as Northern Frontier Corp. 02/28/2013
Each (15) shares Common no par exchanged for (1) share Common no par 02/28/2013

FRONTIER ADJUSTERS AMER INC (AZ)
Merged into Merrymeeting, Inc. 10/1/2001
Each share Common 1¢ par exchanged for $1.58 cash

FRONTIER ADJUSTERS INC (CA)
Merged into Frontier Financial Corp. 05/07/1984
Each share Common no par exchanged for (5) shares Common 1¢ par
Frontier Financial Corp. name changed to Frontier Adjusters of America, Inc. 10/17/1986
(See Frontier Adjusters of America, Inc.)

FRONTIER AIRLS HLDGS INC (DE)
Plan of reorganization under Chapter 11 Federal Bankruptcy proceedings effective 10/01/2009
No stockholders' equity

FRONTIER AIRLS INC NEW (CO)
Common no par split (3) for (2) by issuance of (0.5) additional share payable 03/05/2001 to holders of record 02/19/2001 Ex date - 03/06/2001
Reorganized under the laws of Delaware as Frontier Airlines Holdings, Inc. 04/03/2006
Each share Common no par exchanged for (1) share Common $0.001 par
(See Frontier Airlines Holdings, Inc.)

FRONTIER AIRLS INC OLD (NV)
Common $1 par changed to 50¢ par and (1) additional share issued 8/14/67
Conv. Special Preference $25 par called for redemption 12/17/81
Stock Dividend - 25% 12/19/63
Under plan of reorganization each share Common 50¢ par automatically became (1) share Frontier Holdings, Inc. Common 50¢ par 5/6/82
(See Frontier Holdings, Inc.)

FRONTIER BANCORP (CA)
Merged into City Holding Co. 7/1/99
Each share Common no par exchanged for $94.34 cash

FRONTIER BEVERAGE CO INC (NV)
Reorganized under the laws of Wyoming as FBEC Worldwide, Inc. 12/23/2014
Each share Common $0.001 par exchanged for (0.001) share Common $0.001 par

FRONTIER CAP CORP (DE)
Charter cancelled and declared inoperative and void for non-payment of taxes 4/15/72

FRONTIER CHEMICAL CO. (DE)
Merged into Union Chemical & Materials Corp. in 1954
Each share Preferred $10 par exchanged for (0.5) share Common $10 par
Each share Common $1 par exchanged for (0.3) share Common $10 par
Union Chemical & Materials merged into Vulcan Materials Co. 12/31/57

FRONTIER COMMUNICATIONS CORP (DE)
Each share 11.125% Mandatory Conv. Preferred 1¢ par automatically became (1.3333) shares new Common 25¢ par 06/29/2018
(Additional Information in Active)

FRONTIER COMMUNICATIONS NEW YORK INC (NY)
5.875% Preferred Ser. A $100 par called for redemption 1/1/97
Public interest eliminated

FRONTIER CORP (NY)
5% Preferred 2nd Ser. $100 par called for redemption at $101 on 7/1/99
5% Preferred $100 par called for redemption at $101 on 7/1/99
Merged into Global Crossing Ltd. 9/28/99
Each share Common $1 par

exchanged for (2.05) shares Common 1¢ par
(See Global Crossing Ltd.)

FRONTIER ENERGY CORP (UT)
Involuntarily dissolved 11/01/1995

FRONTIER EXPLS LTD (BC)
Recapitalized as New Frontier Exploration Inc. 10/12/76
Each share Capital Stock 50¢ par exchanged for (0.25) share Common no par
New Frontier Exploration Inc. name changed to New Frontier Petroleum, Inc. 4/7/81 which merged into Frontier Petroleum Corp. 1/18/82 which recapitalized as PetroMac Energy Inc. 8/30/85
(See PetroMac Energy Inc.)

FRONTIER FED SVGS & LN ASSN (PONCA CITY, OK)
Declared insolvent 8/31/88
No stockholders' equity

FRONTIER FID SVGS & LN ASSN (NV)
Name changed to Frontier Savings Association 6/30/72
(See Frontier Savings Association)

FRONTIER FINL CORP (AZ)
Stock Dividend - 15% 2/15/85
Name changed to Frontier Adjusters of America, Inc. 10/17/86
(See Frontier Adjusters of America, Inc.)

FRONTIER FINL CORP (WA)
Old Common no par split (2) for (1) by issuance of (1) additional share payable 03/19/1999 to holders of record 03/01/1999
Old Common no par split (3) for (2) by issuance of (0.5) additional share payable 05/16/2005 to holders of record 05/02/2005
Old Common no par split (3) for (2) by issuance of (0.5) additional share payable 09/26/2006 to holders of record 09/12/2006 Ex date - 09/27/2006
Each share old Common no par exchanged for (0.1) share new Common no par 11/25/2009
Principal asset placed into receivership 04/30/2010
Stockholders' equity unlikely

FRONTIER FING TR (DE)
Plan of reorganization under Chapter 11 Federal Bankruptcy Code effective 12/28/2005
Note: Holders are expected to receive net litigation proceeds

FRONTIER GROUP INC. (CA)
Merged into VCNB Merger Co. 10/13/89
Each share Common no par exchanged for $18.87 cash

FRONTIER HLDGS INC (NV)
Merged into People Express, Inc. 11/22/85
Each share Common 50¢ par exchanged for $24 cash

FRONTIER INDUSTRIES, INC. (NY)
Each share Common $1 par exchanged for (2) shares Common 50¢ par in 1948
Stock Dividend - 50% 7/17/53
Merged into Houdaille-Hershey Corp. 6/30/55
Each share Common 50¢ par exchanged for (1.5) shares Common $3 par
Houdaille-Hershey Corp. name changed to Houdaille Industries, Inc. (MI) 11/30/55 which reincorporated under the laws of Delaware 4/1/68
(See Houdaille Industries, Inc. (DE))

FRONTIER INDS INC (CO)
Charter dissolved for failure to file annual reports 1/1/76

FRONTIER INDS INC (UT)
Reorganized under the laws of Nevada 10/15/97
Each share Common $0.001 par exchanged for (1/300) share Common $0.001 par

FRONTIER INS CO (MO)
Reorganized as Washington Security Life Insurance Co. 7/9/97
Each share Common $1 par exchanged for (2/3) share Common $1 par
Note: Holders of (74) shares or fewer received $1.145 cash per share

FRONTIER INS GROUP INC NEW (DE)
Common 1¢ par split (3) for (2) by issuance of (0.5) additional share 06/17/1994
Common 1¢ par split (2) for (1) by issuance of (1) additional share 07/21/1997 to holders of record 06/30/1997 Ex date - 07/22/1997
Stock Dividends - 10% 08/15/1989; 10% 07/16/1990; 10% 09/16/1991; 10% 07/21/1993; 10% payable 07/19/1996 to holders of record 06/28/1996; 10% payable 07/20/1998 to holders of record 07/01/1998
Plan of reorganization under Chapter 11 Federal Bankruptcy proceedings effective 12/28/2005
No stockholders' equity

FRONTIER INVT CORP (SD)
Completely liquidated 9/26/69
Each share Common $1 par exchanged for first and final distribution of (0.94) share Prairie States Life Insurance Co. Common $1 par and $0.325 cash
Prairie States Life Insurance Co. merged into Laurentian Capital Corp. (FL) 2/14/86 which reincorporated in Delaware 7/24/87
(See Laurentian Capital Corp.)

FRONTIER LIFE INSURANCE CO. (MO)
Name changed to Frontier-Tower Life Insurance Co. 10/18/65
Frontier-Tower Life Insurance Co. recapitalized as Frontier Insurance Co. 11/30/73 which reorganized as Washington Security Life Insurance Co. 7/9/97

FRONTIER MINERALS INC (BC)
Delisted from Toronto Venture Stock Exchange 03/13/2003

FRONTIER MNG & OIL CORP (ID)
Charter forfeited for failure to file reports 12/31/90

FRONTIER MINING CO. (CO)
Name changed to Frontier Petroleum Corp. 9/6/60
Frontier Petroleum Corp. name changed to Frontier Industries, Inc. (CO) 2/27/69
(See Frontier Industries, Inc. (CO))

FRONTIER NAT GAS CORP (OK)
Recapitalized as Esenjay Exploration, Inc. 5/14/98
Each share Common 1¢ par exchanged for (1/6) share Common 1¢ par
Note: Preferred not affected except for change of name
(See Esenjay Exploration, Inc.)

FRONTIER NATIONAL CORP.
Merged into Liberty Share Corp. in 1929 which merged into Western New York Fund, Inc. in 1941 which was completely liquidated in 1946

FRONTIER NATL CORP (AL)
Reported out of business 03/08/2013
Stockholders' equity unlikely

FRONTIER OIL & GAS LTD (DE)
Name changed to Alaska Oil & Gas Ltd. 11/16/2004
Alaska Oil & Gas Ltd. name changed to Transworld Oil & Gas, Ltd. 07/29/2005 which recapitalized as Caribbean Exploration Ventures Inc. 01/16/2007 which name changed to Siguiri Basin Mining, Inc. (DE) 03/28/2007 which reorganized in Nevada as Anything Brands Online Inc. 01/17/2008 which name changed to MyFreightWorld Technologies, Inc. 05/13/2010

FRONTIER OIL & MINING CORP. (DE)
Name changed to Frontier Capital Corp. 9/16/69
(See Frontier Capital Corp.)

FRONTIER OIL CORP (WY)
Common no par split (2) for (1) by issuance of (1) additional share payable 06/17/2005 to holders of record 05/23/2005 Ex date - 06/20/2005
Common no par split (2) for (1) by issuance of (1) additional share payable 06/26/2006 to holders of record 06/19/2006 Ex date - 06/27/2006
Merged into HollyFrontier Corp. 07/01/2011
Each share Common no par exchanged for (0.4811) share Common 1¢ par

FRONTIER OIL EXPL CO (NV)
Name changed to FX Energy Inc. 07/23/1996
(See FX Energy, Inc.)

FRONTIER PAC MNG CORP (BC)
Acquired by Eldorado Gold Corp. (New) 07/15/2008
Each share Common no par exchanged for (0.122) share Common no par, (1) Exchange Receipt and $0.0001 cash

FRONTIER PETE CORP (CO)
Name changed to Frontier Industries, Inc. (CO) 2/27/69
(See Frontier Industries, Inc. (CO))

FRONTIER POWER CO. (CO)
Out of business 00/00/1957
Details not available

FRONTIER RED LAKE GOLD MINES LTD.
Acquired by Gold Frontier Mines Ltd. on a (1) for (2) basis in 1939
Gold Frontier Mines Ltd. acquired by Bayview Red Lake Gold Mines Ltd. in 1944 which was acquired by Red Poplar Gold Mines Ltd. in 1947 which recapitalized as Consolidated Red Poplar Minerals Ltd. 3/1/55 which recapitalized as New Dimension Resources Ltd. 11/9/71 which recapitalized as New Dimension Industries Ltd. 9/19/89 which recapitalized as Toxic Disposal Corp. 2/15/94 which recapitalized as Global Disposal Corp. 3/29/96

FRONTIER REFNG CO (WY)
Stock Dividends - 200% 5/1/49; 10% 7/15/52; 10% 7/15/53; 10% 8/2/54; 10% 7/15/55; 10% 7/16/56; 15% 7/15/57; 10% 7/15/58; 10% 7/15/61
Acquired by Husky Oil Canada Ltd. 2/15/68
Each share Common $1 par exchanged for (0.4) share Common $1 par
7% Preferred $100 par called for redemption 6/1/68
Husky Oil Canada Ltd. name changed to Husky Oil Ltd. 9/3/68
(See Husky Oil Ltd.)

FRONTIER RES CORP (NV)
Name changed to Interplex International, Inc. 03/14/1984
Each share Common $0.001 par exchanged for (1) share Common $0.001 par
Interplex International, Inc. recapitalized as Sportsmans Resorts International, Inc. 10/01/1985 which name changed to Business Resources Inc. 06/04/1986
(See Business Resources Inc.)

FRONTIER RES INC (NM)
Merged into Pan Ocean Oil Co. 2/16/77
Each share Common no par exchanged for $7 cash

FRONTIER ROYALTIES, LTD.
Merged into Amalgamated Oils, Ltd. 00/00/1941
Details not available

FRONTIER SVGS & LN ASSN (CA)
Acquired by Gibraltar Financial Corp. of California 9/30/71
Each share Guarantee Stock $1 par exchanged for (2) shares Capital Stock $1 par
Gibraltar Financial Corp. of California name changed to Gibraltar Financial Corp. 5/14/85
(See Gibraltar Financial Corp.)

FRONTIER SVGS ASSN (NV)
Permanent Capital Stock $1 par changed to 80¢ par and (0.25) additional share issued 11/8/78
Declared insolvent and taken over by FDIC in 1990
Stockholders' equity undetermined

FRONTIER SILVER MINES CORP. (ID)
Common 10¢ par changed to 1¢ par 7/14/80
Name changed to Frontier Mining & Oil Corp. 2/27/81
(See Frontier Mining & Oil Corp.)

FRONTIER ST BK (SHOW LOW, AZ)
Merged into Zions Bancorporation 11/25/2002
Each share Common $1 par exchanged for (0.22324) share Common no par
Zions Bancorporation merged into Zions Zions Bancorporation, N.A (Salt Lake City, UT) 10/01/2018

FRONTIER STAFFING INC (NV)
Name changed to Tradestar Services, Inc. 10/11/2005
Tradestar Services, Inc. name changed to Stratum Holdings, Inc. 03/06/2007 name changed to Caprock Oil, Inc. 03/25/2014 which recapitalized as Stack-It Storage, Inc. 07/23/2015 which name changed to Manufactured Housing Properties Inc. 12/08/2017

FRONTIER TEX CORP (DE)
Name changed to IMCO Recycling, Inc. 10/7/88
IMCO Recycling, Inc. name changed to Aleris International, Inc. 12/9/2004
(See Aleris International, Inc.)

FRONTIER TOWER LIFE INS CO (MO)
Recapitalized as Frontier Insurance Co. 11/30/73
Each share Common $1 par exchanged for (0.5) share Common $1 par
Frontier Insurance Co. reorganized as Washington Security Life Insurance Co. 7/9/97

FRONTIER URANIUM CO. (NM)
Dissolved in 1956

FRONTIER VLG (CA)
Liquidation completed
Each share Preferred $5 par exchanged for first and final distribution of $8.56 cash 5/3/73
Each share Common $5 par exchanged for initial distribution of $1.80 cash 1/29/74
Each share Common $5 par received second and final distribution of $0.078 cash 10/1/75

FRONTLINE CAP GROUP (DE)
Plan of reorganization under Chapter 11 Federal Bankruptcy Code effective 09/15/2008
No stockholders' equity

FRONTLINE COMMUNICATIONS CORP (DE)
Each share Conv. Preferred Ser. B exchanged for (6) shares Common 1¢ par 12/19/2003
Name changed to Provo International, Inc. 12/19/2003
Provo International, Inc. recapitalized as Ebenefitsdirect, Inc. 03/23/2007 which recapitalized as Seraph Security, Inc. 12/02/2008 which name changed to Commerce Online, Inc. 06/18/2009 which name changed to Cannabis Medical Solutions, Inc. 03/04/2010 which name changed to MediSwipe Inc. 07/08/2011 which name changed to Agritek Holdings, Inc. 05/20/2014

FRONTLINE LTD (BERMUDA)
ADR agreement terminated 10/05/2001
Each Sponsored ADR for Ordinary $25 par exchanged $6.7634 cash

FRONTLINE TECHNOLOGIES INC (ON)
Filed an assignment in bankruptcy 01/04/2013
No stockholders' equity

FRONTSTEP INC (OH)
Merged into MAPICS, Inc. 2/19/2003
Each share Common no par exchanged for (0.300846) share Common 1¢ par
(See MAPICS, Inc.)

FROOD DEEP NICKEL MINES LTD (ON)
Merged into Hoffman Exploration & Minerals Ltd. 06/29/1981
Each shares Capital Stock no par exchanged for (0.34306611) share Common no par
Hoffman Exploration & Minerals Ltd. merged into Consolidated Thompson-Lundmark Gold Mines Ltd. 01/16/1986 which name changed to Consolidated Thompson Iron Mines Ltd. 08/24/2006
(See Consolidated Thompson Iron Mines Ltd.)

FROSST (CHARLES E.) & CO. (QC)
Acquired by Merck & Co., Inc. 12/10/65
Each share Class A $1 par exchanged for $30 cash

FROST & SULLIVAN INC (ME)
Merged into FAS Acquisition Co. 1/22/88
Each share Common 1¢ par exchanged for $10 cash

FROST & WOOD CO., LTD.
Acquired by Cockshutt Plow Co., Ltd. in 1933
Details not available

FROST BROS INC (TX)
5-1/2% Preferred $100 par called 11/1/69
Acquired by Manhattan Industries, Inc. 12/3/69
Details not available

FROST BROTHERS (TX)
Name changed to Frost Bros., Inc. 3/26/56
(See Frost Bros., Inc.)

FROST GEAR & FORGE CO.
Acquired by Clark Equipment Co. (MI) 00/00/1929
Details not available

FROST HANNA ACQUISITION GROUP INC (FL)
Name changed to Kids Mart Inc. 01/23/1996
(See Kids Mart Inc.)

FROST HANNA CAP GROUP INC (FL)
Name changed to GBI Capital Management Corp. 08/24/1999
GBI Capital Management Corp. name changed to Ladenburg Thalmann Financial Services Inc. 05/08/2001

FROST HANNA HALPRYN CAP GROUP INC (FL)
Name changed to Sterling Healthcare Group, Inc. 6/1/94
Sterling Healthcare Group, Inc. merged into FPA Medical Management Inc. 10/31/96
(See FPA Medical Management Inc.)

FROST HANNA MERGERS GROUP INC (FL)
Name changed to Pan Am Corp. 9/13/96
(See Pan Am Corp. (FL))

FROST LUMBER INDUSTRIES, INC.
Acquired by Olin Industries, Inc. in 1952
Each share Capital Stock $100 par exchanged for (18) shares Common $1 par
Olin Industries, Inc. merged into Olin Mathieson Chemical Corp. in 1954 which name changed to Olin Corp. 9/1/69

FROST NATL BK (SAN ANTONIO, TX)
Common $100 par changed to $10 par and (9) additional shares issued plus a 10% stock dividend paid 02/15/1967
Stock Dividends - 100% 03/04/1969; 200% 04/30/1972
Merged into Frostbank Corp. 05/01/1973
Each share Common $10 par exchanged for (1) share Common $10 par
Frostbank Corp. merged into Cullen/Frost Bankers, Inc. 07/07/1977

FROSTBANK CORP (TX)
Each share Common $10 par exchanged for (2) shares Common $5 par 4/2/74
Merged into Cullen/Frost Bankers, Inc. 7/7/77
Each share Common $5 par exchanged for (1) share Common $5 par

FROSTIE ENTERPRISES (NJ)
Merged into Moxie Enterprises, Inc. 12/31/1979
Each share Common 10¢ par exchanged for $7.50 cash

FROUGE CORP (DE)
Liquidation completed
Each share Common $1 par exchanged for initial distribution of $14 cash 4/18/77
Each share Common $1 par received second distribution of $2.50 cash 1/16/78
Each share Common $1 par received third distribution of $0.50 cash 7/17/78
Each share Common $1 par received fourth distribution of $0.25 cash 9/15/78
Each share Common $1 par received fifth distribution of $1 cash 4/23/79
Each share Common $1 par received sixth distribution of $0.50 cash 10/19/79
Each share Common $1 par received seventh and final distribution of $0.72 cash 3/13/81

FROZEN FOOD EXPRESS INDS INC (TX)
Stock Dividends - 25% 09/16/1983; 25% 09/12/1984; 25% 09/18/1985
Common $1.50 par split (2) for (1) by issuance of (1) additional share 09/14/1988
Common $1.50 par split (3) for (2) by issuance of (0.5) additional share 09/13/1989
Common $1.50 par split (3) for (2) by issuance of (0.5) additional share 03/16/1992
Common $1.50 par split (4) for (3) by issuance of (0.33333333) additional share 10/22/1992
Common $1.50 par split (4) for (3) by issuance of (0.33333333) additional share 11/10/1993
Common $1.50 par split (5) for (4) by issuance of (0.25) additional share 03/03/1995
Acquired by Duff Brothers Capital Corp. 08/20/2013
Each share Common $1.50 par exchanged for $2.10 cash

FROZEN FOOD GIFT GROUP INC (DE)
Name changed to APT Moto Vox Group, Inc. 07/14/2014

FROZYA INDS INC (BC)
Name changed to Canex Resources Corp. 08/31/1994
(See Canex Resources Corp.)

FRP PPTYS INC (FL)
Name changed to Patriot Transportation Holding, Inc. 03/01/2000
Patriot Transportation Holding, Inc. name changed to FRP Holdings, Inc. 12/05/2014

FRUEHAUF CDA INC (CANADA)
Merged into FRH Acquisition Corp. 01/15/1988
Each share Capital Stock no par exchanged for $39 cash

FRUEHAUF CORP (DE)
Name changed to K-H Corp. 8/4/89
K-H Corp. merged into Varity Corp. (Canada) 12/1/89 which reorganized in Delaware 8/1/91 which merged into LucasVarity PLC 9/6/96
(See LucasVarity PLC)

FRUEHAUF CORP (MI)
4% Preferred $100 par called for redemption 6/15/76
Common $1 par split (3) for (2) by issuance of (0.5) additional share 11/1/84
$2 Conv. Preferred no par called for redemption 3/10/86
Each share $2.125 Conv. Exchangeable Preferred no par exchanged for $25 principal amount of 8-1/2% Conv. Subord. Debentures due 4/1/2011 on 10/10/86
Merged into Fruehauf Corp. (DE) 12/23/86
Each share Common $1 par exchanged for (1.746) shares $3.68 Exchangeable Preferred Ser. A 1¢ par and (1) share Class B Common 1¢ par
Fruehauf Corp. (DE) name changed to K-H Corp. 8/4/89 which merged into Varity Corp. (Canada) 12/1/89 which reorganized in Delaware 8/1/91 which merged into LucasVarity PLC 9/6/96
(See LucasVarity PLC)

FRUEHAUF TRAILER CO (MI)
Each share Common no par exchanged for (2) shares Common $1 par in 1937
Stock Dividends - 100% 12/45; 20% 12/28/50; 100% 1/31/56
Name changed to Fruehauf Corp. (MI) 5/9/63
Fruehauf Corp. (MI) merged into Fruehauf Corp. (DE) 12/23/86 which name changed to K-H Corp. 8/4/89 which merged into Varity Corp. (Canada) 12/1/89 which reorganized in Delaware 8/1/91 which merged into LucasVarity PLC 9/6/96
(See LucasVarity PLC)

FRUEHAUF TRAILER CO CDA LTD (CANADA)
Capital Stock no par split (3) for (1) by issuance of (2) additional shares 10/16/1972
Name changed to Fruehauf Canada Inc. 07/25/1979
(See Fruehauf Canada Inc.)

FRUEHAUF TRAILER CORP (DE)
Plan of reorganization under Chapter 11 Federal Bankruptcy Code effective 10/27/98
No stockholders' equity

FRUIT OF THE LOOM, INC. (RI)
Stock Dividend - 20% 5/15/56
Acquired by Philadelphia & Reading Corp. 6/30/64
Each share $3 Preferred $20 par received $55.04 per share and each share Common $1 par received $23 per share
Note: Certificates were not required to surrendered and are now valueless

FRUIT OF THE LOOM, INC. (CAYMAN ISLANDS)
Reincorporated 03/04/1999
13-1/2% Exchangeable Preferred 1¢ par called for redemption 04/09/1987
Place of incoporation changed from (DE) to (Cayman Islands) 03/04/1999
Plan of reorganization under Chapter 11 Federal Bankruptcy Code effective 04/30/2002
No stockholders' equity

FRUND PRODUCTS CO. (DE)
No longer in existence having become inoperative and void for non-payment of taxes 4/1/65

FRV MEDIA INC (CANADA)
Recapitalized as Global SeaFarms Corp. 04/03/2012
Each share Class A no par exchanged for (0.02) share Common no par
(See Global SeaFarms Corp.)

FRY PRODUCTS, INC. (MI)
Out of business in 1956
No stockholders' equity

FRY RED LAKE MINES, LTD. (ON)
Charter cancelled and company declared dissolved for failure to file reports and pay fees 00/00/1953

FRYE INDS INC (DE)
Merged into Wheelabrator-Frye Inc. 11/4/71
Each share Common $2 par exchanged for (1.4) shares Common 10¢ par
Wheelabrator-Frye Inc. merged into Signal Companies, Inc. 2/1/83 which merged into Allied-Signal Inc. 9/19/85 which name changed to AlliedSignal Inc. 4/26/93 which name changed to Honeywell International Inc. 12/1/99

FRYS FOOD STORES INC (CA)
Merged into Dillon Companies, Inc. 11/8/72
Each share Class A Common $1 par exchanged for (0.405515) share Common $1.25 par
Dillon Companies, Inc. merged into Kroger Co. 1/25/83

FSB BANCORP INC (MI)
Stock Dividend - 5% payable 10/15/1999 to holders of record 10/01/1999
Merged into IBT Bancorp Inc. 08/10/2000
Each share Common no par exchanged for (2.1362) shares Common $6 par
IBT Bancorp Inc. name changed to Isabella Bank Corp. 05/14/2008

FSB CMNTY BANKSHARES INC (USA)
Reorganized under the laws of Maryland as FSB Bancorp, Inc. 07/14/2016
Each share Common 10¢ par exchanged for (1.0884) shares Common 1¢ par

FSB FINL CORP (DE)
Issue Information - 920,000 shares COM offered at $10 per share on 05/13/1994

FSB-FUE

Merged into Standard Federal
Bancorporation, Inc. 1/12/96
Each share Common 1¢ par
exchanged for $23.50 cash

FSB INC (TN)
Merged into Union Planters Corp.
12/31/98
Each share Common $10 par
exchanged for (1.61) shares
Common $5 par
Union Planters Corp. merged into
Regions Financial Corp. (New)
7/1/2004

FSBO MEDIA HLDGS INC (NV)
Class A Common $0.0001 par split (2)
for (1) by issuance of (1) additional
share payable 01/30/2006 to holders
of record 01/12/2006 Ex date -
01/31/2006
Class A Common $0.0001 par split
(15) for (1) by issuance of (14)
additional shares payable
05/26/2006 to holders of record
05/19/2006 Ex date - 05/30/2006
Recapitalized as Guard Dog, Inc.
10/28/2008
Each share Class A Common $0.0001
par exchanged for (0.002) share
Class A Common $0.0001 par

FSC CORP (PA)
Reincorporated 10/00/1987
State of incorporation changed from
(DE) to (PA) 10/00/1987
Reorganized as Trilos Corp.
02/24/1989
Each share $1.35 Conv. Preference
Ser. A 1¢ par exchanged for
(0.09956669) share Common 1¢ par
Each share Common 1¢ par
exchanged for (0.01094361) share
Common 1¢ par
Note: Unexchanged certificates were
cancelled and became without
05/15/1990
Trilos Corp. name changed to
Lifetime Products, Inc. 12/17/1990

FSC HLDGS INC (NV)
Name changed to Hyperion
Technologies, Inc. 01/27/1998
Hyperion Technologies, Inc. name
changed Nextpath Technologies Inc.
07/22/1999
(See Nextpath Technologies Inc.)

FSF FINL CORP (MN)
Merged into MidCountry Financial
Corp. 11/1/2004
Each share Common 10¢ par
exchanged for $35 cash

FSF INDS INC (DE)
Name changed to Trafalgar
Industries, Inc. 12/17/79
Trafalgar Industries, Inc. merged into
Triangle Industries, Inc. (Old)
5/16/84
(See Triangle Industries, Inc. (Old))

FSGI CORP (FL)
Name changed to TMANglobal.com,
Inc. (FL) 01/07/1999
TMANglobal.com, Inc. (FL)
reorganized in Nevada as Franchise
Holdings International, Inc.
05/08/2003

FSI ENERGY SVCS INC (AB)
Name changed to FSI Energy Group
Inc. 06/08/2012

FSI INTL INC (MN)
Common no par split (2) for (1) by
issuance of (1) additional share
06/19/1995
Acquired by Tokyo Electron Ltd.
10/11/2012
Each share Common no par
exchanged for $6.20 cash

FSONA SYSTEMS CORP (NV)
Common $0.001 par split (8.23) for
(1) by issuance of (7.23) additional
shares payable 04/19/2007 to
holders of record 04/19/2007
Charter revoked for failure to file
reports and pay taxes 02/26/2010

FSPI TECHNOLOGIES CORP (AB)
Delisted from Canadian Venture
Stock Exchange 05/31/2000

FSR INDS INC (BC)
Name changed to Syspower
Multimedia Industries, Inc. (BC)
06/15/1993
Syspower Multimedia Industries, Inc.
(BC) reincorporated in British Virgin
Islands 02/15/1995
(See Syspower Multimedia Industries,
Inc.)

FSS CONSULTING CORP (DE)
Each share old Common $0.001 par
exchanged for (0.25) share new
Common $0.001 par 12/6/88
Charter cancelled and declared
inoperative and void for
non-payment of taxes 3/1/91

FT CAP LTD (AB)
Wound up and dissolved 06/30/2009
Stockholders' equity unlikely

FT CHIMO MINERALS INC (ON)
Recapitalized as Mag Copper Ltd.
06/15/2011
Each share Common no par
exchanged for (0.2) share Common
no par
Mag Copper Ltd. recapitalized as
Integra Resources Corp. 08/22/2017

FT INDS INC (DE)
Name changed to Claire's Stores, Inc.
(DE) 09/19/1983
Claire's Stores, Inc. (DE)
reincorporated in Florida 06/30/2000
(See Claire's Stores, Inc.)

FT INTL TR (MA)
Reorganized as FT Series Inc.
02/18/1991
Details not available

FTD COM INC (DE)
Issue Information - 4,500,000 shares
CL A offered at $8 per share on
09/28/1999
Merged into FTD, Inc. 6/28/2002
Each share Class A 1¢ par
exchanged for (0.26) share Class A
1¢ par
(See FTD, Inc.)

FTD CORP (DE)
Under plan of merger name changed
to FTD, Inc. 6/28/2002
(See FTD, Inc.)

FTD GROUP INC (DE)
Merged into United Online, Inc.
08/26/2008
Each share Common 1¢ par
exchanged for (0.4087) share
Common $0.001 par and $10.15
cash
(See United Online, Inc.)

FTD INC (DE)
Merged into Nectar Merger Corp.
2/24/2004
Each share Class A Common 1¢ par
exchanged for $24.85 cash
Each share Class B Common 1¢ par
exchanged for $24.85 cash

F 10 OIL & GAS PPTYS INC (NV)
Name changed to GFY Foods, Inc.
01/12/2004
GFY Foods, Inc. recapitalized as
Upturn, Inc. 03/20/2009 which
recapitalized as Cityside Tickets Inc.
12/10/2009 which name changed to
Causeway Entertainment Co.
10/11/2010 which recapitalized as
United Bullion Exchange Inc.
05/10/2011

F3 TECHNOLOGIES INC (DE)
Each share old Common 1¢ par
exchanged for (0.005) share new
Common no par 04/30/2013
Name changed to Here to Serve
Holding Corp. 11/05/2013

FTI FOODTECH INTL INC (BC)
Reincorporated under the laws of
Canada 08/28/2008

FTLA INC (FL)
Name changed to Liska Biometry, Inc.
4/1/2002

FTM INVT CORP (CANADA)
Recapitalized as Cagim Real Estate
Corp. 09/21/2004
Each share Class A no par
exchanged for (0.2) share Class A
no par
(See Cagim Real Estate Corp.)

FTM MEDIA INC (DE)
Reincorporated 01/07/2000
State of incorporation changed from
(CO) to (DE) 01/07/2000
SEC revoked common stock
registration 07/09/2012

FTM RES INC (CANADA)
Recapitalized as First General Mine
Management & Gold Corp.
02/27/1985
Each share Common no par
exchanged for (0.5) share Common
no par
First General Mine Management &
Gold Corp. name changed to Laser
Magic International Inc. 12/21/1989
(See Laser Magic International Inc.)

FTOH CORP (DE)
Name changed to 5to1 Holding Corp.
12/16/2010
(See 5To1 Holding Corp.)

FTP SOFTWARE INC (MA)
Merged into NetManage, Inc.
08/27/1998
Each share Common 1¢ par
exchanged for (0.72767) share
Common 1¢ par
(See NetManage, Inc.)

FTS APPAREL INC (CO)
Reincorporated under the laws of
Nevada as FTS Group, Inc.
01/26/2004
(See FTS Group, Inc.)

FTS GROUP INC (NV)
SEC revoked common stock
registration 06/24/2013

F2 BROADCAST NETWORKS INC (NV)
Each share old Common no par
exchanged for (0.005) share new
Common no par 05/30/2001
Name changed to Strat Petroleum,
Ltd. 07/08/2004
(See Strat Petroleum, Ltd.)

FU JI FOOD & CATERING SVCS HLDGS INC (CAYMAN ISLANDS)
ADR agreement terminated
02/17/2011
Details not available

FUBON INS LTD (TAIWAN)
Stock Dividends - 40% payable
09/24/1998 to holders of record
07/02/1998; 10% payable
09/16/1999 to holders of record
07/02/1999; in 144A GDR's to
holders of 144A GDR's 2% payable
08/25/2000 to holders of record
06/27/2000
Name changed to Fubon Financial
Holding Co., Ltd. 12/19/2001

FUCHS PETROLUB AG (GERMANY)
Name changed to Fuchs Petrolub SE
08/19/2013

FUDDRUCKERS INC (TX)
Merged into Daka International, Inc.
11/23/88
Each share Common 1¢ par
exchanged for (1) share Common
1¢ par
(See Daka International, Inc.)

FUEGO ENTMT INC (NV)
Name changed to Fuego Enterprises,
Inc. 06/09/2009

FUEL AMPLIFIER CORP (DE)
Name changed to Debe Systems
Corp. 1/16/84
(See Debe Systems Corp.)

FUEL CELL TECHNOLOGIES CORP (ON)
Plan of arrangement effective
04/03/2006
Each share Common no par
exchanged for (1) share MP
Western Properties Inc. Class A
Common no par, (0.1) share Class B
Common no par, and (1) share Fuel
Cell Technologies Ltd. Common no
par
(See each company's listing)

FUEL CELL TECHNOLOGIES LTD (ON)
Voluntary dissolution approved
03/22/2007
Any distribution to holders will be
dependent upon amount available
following disposal of remaining
assets

FUEL CORP AMER (NV)
Reincorporated 02/21/1991
State of incorporation changed from
(MN) to (NV) 02/21/1991
Common 1¢ par changed to $0.001
par 04/15/1991
Each (6.5) shares old Common
$0.001 par exchanged for (1) share
new Common $0.001 par
10/07/1993
Each (14) shares new Common
$0.001 par exchanged again for (1)
share new Common $0.001 par
05/16/2005
Name changed to flexSCAN, Inc.
09/20/2005 flexSCAN, Inc. name
changed to Aperture Health, Inc.
03/03/2008

FUEL CTRS INC (NV)
Common $0.001 par split (2.09) for
(1) by issuance of (1.09) additional
shares payable 06/24/2002 to
holders of record 06/21/2002
Ex date - 06/25/2002
Name changed to Fellows Energy
Ltd. 11/14/2003
(See Fellows Energy Ltd.)

FUEL INJECTION CORP.
Acquired by Ex-Cell-O Corp. in
September 1944
Details not available

FUEL OIL MOTORS CORP. (DE)
No longer in existence having
become inoperative and void for
non-payment of taxes 6/1/33

FUEL OIL SUPPLY CO. (DE)
No longer in existence having
become inoperative and void for
non-payment of taxes 4/1/55

FUEL SYS SOLUTIONS INC (DE)
Merged into Westport Fuel Systems
Inc. 06/08/2016
Each share Common $0.001 par
exchanged for (2.4755) shares
Common no par

FUEL-TECH N V (NETHERLANDS ANTILLES)
Reincorporated under the laws of
Delaware as Fuel Tech, Inc.
9/30/2006

FUELCELL ENERGY LTD (AB)
Each Exchangeable Share no par
exchanged for (1) share FuelCell
Energy, Inc. Common $0.0001 par
10/29/2004

FUELCORP INTL INC (BC)
Name changed to Specialty Retail
Concepts Inc. 05/27/1994
Specialty Retail Concepts Inc.
recapitalized as Altoro Gold Corp.
01/09/1997 which merged into
Solitario Resources Corp.
10/18/2000 which name changed to
Solitario Exploration & Royalty Corp.
06/17/2008 which name changed to
Solitario Zinc Corp. 07/18/2017

FUELEX, INC. (UT)
Name changed to Applied Coatings
Technology, Inc. 4/1/82

FUELEX INC
Name changed to Applied Coatings Technology, Inc. 04/01/1982
(See Applied Coatings Technology, Inc.)

FUELNATION INC (FL)
Each share old Common 1¢ par exchanged for (0.00666666) share new Common 1¢ par 01/27/2003
New Common 1¢ par split (10) for (1) by issuance of (9) additional shares payable 06/17/2005 to holders of record 06/03/2005 Ex date - 06/20/2005
Proclaimed dissolved for failure to file reports and pay fees 09/25/2009

FUELTECK CORP (DE)
Charter cancelled and declared inoperative and void for non-payment of taxes 3/1/81

FUER INTL INC (NV)
Acquired by Fuer Merger Newco 07/02/2013
Each share Common $0.001 par exchanged for $1.29 cash

FUFENG GROUP LTD (CAYMAN ISLANDS)
ADR agreement terminated 08/21/2017
Each Sponsored ADR for Ordinary exchanged for $12.412384 cash

FUHUIYUAN INTL HLDGS LTD (NV)
Recapitalized as Wellness Matrix Group, Inc. 09/10/2018
Each share Common $0.0001 par exchanged for (0.05) share Common $0.0001 par

FUISZ TECHNOLOGIES LTD (DE)
Common 1¢ par split (3) for (2) by issuance of (0.5) additional share payable 04/16/1996 to holders of record 04/02/1996
Merged into Biovail Corp. International (New) 11/12/1999
Each share Common 1¢ par exchanged for (0.1197) share Common no par
Biovail Corp. International (New) name changed to Biovail Corp. 02/18/2000 which merged into Valeant Pharmaceuticals International, Inc. (Canada) 09/28/2010 which reincorporated in British Columbia 08/09/2013 which name changed to Bausch Health Companies Inc. 07/16/2018

FUJACORP INDS INC (DE)
Recapitalized as Interactive Multimedia Publishers Inc. 4/12/95
Each share Common $0.00001 par exchanged for (0.01) share Common $0.001 par
(See Interactive Multimedia Publishers Inc.)

FUJI BK (JAPAN)
Merged into Mizuho Holdings, Inc. 9/22/2000
Each ADR for Ordinary 50 Yen par exchanged for $64.259 cash

FUJI CONSTR CO INTL INC (CO)
Name changed to Hokutou Holdings International, Inc. (CO) 11/06/2008
Hokutou Holdings International, Inc. (CO) reincorporated in Nevada 05/23/2014 which name changed to Platinum Pari-Mutuel Holdings, Inc. 12/09/2014 which name changed to Point to Point Methodics, Inc. 04/27/2017

FUJI ELECTROCELL CORP (NV)
Each share old Common $0.001 par exchanged for (0.05) share new Common $0.001 par 06/03/1999
Name changed to Classified Online.com 07/16/1999
Classified Online.com name changed to X-Ramp.com, Inc. 05/26/2000
(See X-Ramp.com, Inc.)

FUJI HEAVY INDS LTD (JAPAN)
ADR's for Common split (5) for (1) by issuance of (4) additional ADR's payable 12/15/2011 to holders of record 12/12/2011 Ex date - 12/16/2011
Basis changed from (1:10) to (1:2) 12/19/2011
ADR's for Common split (4) for (1) by issuance of (3) additional ADR's payable 10/27/2016 to holders of record 10/20/2016 Ex date - 10/28/2016
Basis changed from (1:2) to (1:0.5) 10/28/2016
Name changed to Subaru Corp. 04/03/2017

FUJI INTL FIN BERMUDA TR (JAPAN)
ADR agreement terminated 01/03/2002
Each ADR for Common exchanged for (1) share Common

FUJI PHOTO FILM LTD (JAPAN)
Each old ADR for Common 50 Yen par exchanged for (5) new ADR's for Common 50 Yen par 6/10/82
Stock Dividends - 10% 2/3/83; 10% 12/19/89; 10% 12/19/90; 10% 12/19/91
Name changed to FUJIFILM Holdings Corp. 10/2/2006

FUJI TELEVISION NETWORK INC (JAPAN)
Name changed to Fuji Media Holding, Inc. 11/04/2013

FUJITA CORP (JAPAN)
Each ADR for Common 50 Yen par received distribution of $0.843 cash payable 2/7/2003 to holders of record 1/31/2003
ADR agreement terminated 3/28/2003
Each ADR for Common 50 Yen par exchanged for $0.083 cash

FUJITEC CAP CORP
Auction Preferred Ser. B called for redemption at $1,000,000 on 3/13/2002
Auction Preferred Ser. C called for redemption at $1,000,000 on 3/20/2002
Auction Preferred Ser. A called for redemption at $100,000 on 3/6/2002

FULBRO RED LAKE GOLD MINES LTD.
Recapitalized as Consolidated Fulbro Gold Mines Ltd. 00/00/1946
Each share Capital Stock $1 par exchanged for (0.33333333) share Capital Stock $1 par
Consolidated Fulbro Gold Mines Ltd. recapitalized as Sycon Energy Corp. 01/15/1980 which name changed to Sycon Corp. 11/00/1987
(See Sycon Corp.)

FULCRUM CAP I INC (AB)
Recapitalized as Macro Enterprises Inc. 2/8/2006
Each share Common no par exchanged for (0.2) share Common no par

FULCRUM COMPUTER GROUP INC (MA)
Merged into Adage, Inc. (MA) 10/13/1982
Each share Common 1¢ par exchanged for (0.011076) share Common 10¢ par
Note: An additional (0.032871) share Common 10¢ par has been distributed from escrow fund
Adage, Inc. (MA) reincorporated in Pennsylvania 05/31/1991 which reincorporated in Nevada as RELM Wireless Corp. 01/30/1998 which name changed to BK Technologies, Inc. 06/05/2018

FULCRUM DEVS LTD (BC)
Recapitalized as Wespac Mining Corp. 07/02/1996
Each share Common no par exchanged for (0.33333333) share Common no par
Wespac Mining Corp. name changed to Genesis II Enterprises Ltd. 11/19/1998
(See Genesis II Enterprises Ltd.)

FULCRUM INVT LTD (CANADA)
6% Preferred $50 par changed to $10 par and (4) additional shares issued 07/10/1967
6% Preferred $10 par called for redemption 12/31/1986
Common $25 par changed to $5 par and (4) additional shares issued 07/10/1967
Common $5 par changed to no par 04/17/1973
Stock Dividends - 20% 12/28/1973; 40% 06/09/1982; 12.5% 02/28/1986; 10% 10/31/1986
Company became private 04/29/1987
Details not available

FULCRUM TECHNOLOGIES INC (CANADA)
Common no par split (2) for (1) by issuance of (1) additional share payable 06/19/1996 to holders of record 06/12/1996
Merged into PC Docs Group International Inc. 03/10/1998
Each share Common no par exchanged for (0.2272727) share Common no par
(See PC Docs Group International Inc.)

FULHAM (JOHN) & SONS, INC. (MA)
Voluntarily dissolved 4/13/95
Details not available

FULHAM EXPLS INC (BC)
Delisted from Vancouver Stock Exchange 03/04/1992

FULHAM MALONEY & CO INC (MA)
Name changed to Fulham (John) & Sons, Inc. 12/18/79
(See Fulham (John) & Sons, Inc.)

FULL CIRCLE CAP CORP (MD)
Merged into Great Elm Capital Corp. 11/03/2016
Each share Common 1¢ par exchanged for (0.2219) share Common 1¢ par

FULL CIRCLE IMAGE INC (MN)
Recapitalized as Lecere Corp. 03/11/2009
Each share Common 1¢ par exchanged for (0.05) share Common 1¢ par

FULL CIRCLE INC (UT)
Each share old Common $0.005 par exchanged for (0.5) share new Common $0.005 par 09/01/1993
Reorganized under the laws of Nevada as Hydro Grow Inc. 12/08/1998
Each share new Common $0.005 par exchanged for (0.05) share Common $0.005 par
Hydro Grow Inc. name changed to Asgard Alliance Corp. 09/22/1999 which name changed to Santa Fe Holding Co., Inc. 06/26/2007
(See Santa Fe Holding Co., Inc.)

FULL COLOR CORP (MN)
Name changed to Data Micro Co. 7/24/69
(See Data Micro Co.)

FULL LINE DISTRS INC (GA)
Merged into Broder Bros., Co. 8/20/2001
Each share Common no par exchanged for $2.95 cash

FULL METAL ZINC LTD (BC)
Name changed to Aftermath Silver Ltd. 04/07/2014

FULL MOON UNIVERSE INC (WA)
Involuntarily dissolved 03/09/2004

FULL PWR GROUP INC (FL)
Recapitalized as Biometric Verification Holdings, Inc. 01/22/2001
Each share Common $0.001 par exchanged for (0.1) share Common $0.001 par
Biometric Verification Holdings Inc. name changed to Vadda Energy Corp. 09/02/2003
(See Vadda Energy Corp.)

FULL RICHES INVTS LTD (BC)
Acquired by Medoro Resources Ltd. 03/02/2004
Each share Common no par exchanged for (0.5) share Common no par
Medoro Resources Ltd. merged into Gran Colombia Gold Corp. 06/14/2011

FULL TILT SPORTS INC (CO)
Name changed to FTS Apparel, Inc. 08/23/2000
(See FTS Apparel, Inc.)

FULLCAST CO LTD (JAPAN)
Name changed to Fullcast Holdings Co. Ltd. 10/01/2008

FULLCIRCLE REGISTRY INC (NV)
Recapitalized as Galaxy Next Generation, Inc. 09/18/2018
Each share Common $0.001 par exchanged for (0.00285714) share Common $0.001 par

FULLCOMM TECHNOLOGIES INC (DE)
Recapitalized as Amalgamated Technologies, Inc. 10/08/2002
Each share Common $0.0001 par exchanged for (0.02173913) share new Common $0.0001 par
Amalgamated Technologies, Inc. name changed to ProLink Holdings Corp. 01/26/2006
(See ProLink Holdings Corp.)

FULLER (W.P.) & CO. (CA)
Merged into Hunt Foods & Industries, Inc. on a (0.525) for (1) basis 02/28/1962
Hunt Foods & Industries, Inc. merged into Simon (Norton), Inc. 07/17/1968 which merged into Esmark, Inc. (Inc. 03/14/1969) 09/09/1983
(See Esmark, Inc. (Inc. 03/14/1969))

FULLER (D.B.) & CO., INC. (NY)
Acquired by Stevens (J.P.) & Co., Inc. 06/28/1958
Each share Common 10¢ par exchanged for $3.15 cash

FULLER BKS ENERGY INC (NV)
Recapitalized as Royal Equity Exchange, Inc. 04/13/1987
Each share Common $0.001 par exchanged for (0.01) share Common $0.001 par
Royal Equity Exchange, Inc. name changed to Procare America, Inc. 11/04/1998 which name changed to Indigo-Energy, Inc. 01/20/2006 which name changed to HDIMAX MEDIA, Inc. 12/19/2014 which name changed to Zonzia Media, Inc. 03/09/2015

FULLER BRUSH CO. (CT)
Old Class A Common $5 par changed to $10 par 00/00/1946
Old Class AA Common $20 par changed to $40 par 00/00/1946
Each share Class A Common $10 par exchanged for (10) shares new Class A Common $5 par 01/31/1962
Each share Class AA Common $40 par exchanged for (10) shares new Class AA Common $20 par 01/31/1962
Class A Common $5 par reclassified as Common $5 par 04/03/1967
Each share Class AA Common $20 par exchanged for (4) shares Common $5 par 04/03/1967

Merged into Consolidated Foods Corp. 12/27/1968
Each share Common $5 par exchanged for (0.2621) share $4.50 Conv. Preferred Ser. A no par
(See Consolidated Foods Corp.)

FULLER BUILDING CORP. (NY)
Liquidation completed
Each share Class A $1 par received initial distribution of $20 cash 1/30/61
Each share Class A $1 par received second distribution of $20 cash 3/17/61
Each share Class A $1 par received third distribution of $90 cash 6/1/61
Each share Class A $1 par received fourth distribution of $19 cash 11/30/61
Each share Class A $1 par exchanged for fifth distribution of $4.60 cash 12/31/64
Each share Class A $1 par received sixth and final distribution of $0.825 cash 12/15/67

FULLER CAP CORP (BC)
Issue Information - 3,000,000 shares COM offered at $0.10 per share on 08/27/2010
Name changed to Emerita Gold Corp. 01/11/2013
Emerita Gold Corp. name changed to Emerita Resources Corp. 01/13/2014

FULLER CLEANING & DYEING CO. (OH)
Merged into Universal Fuller Co. 11/4/74
Each share Preferred $25 par exchanged for $1 cash
Each share Common $1 par exchanged for $22.93 cash

FULLER (GEO. A.) CO. (NJ)
Recapitalized in 1938
Each share 6% Prior Preferred no par exchanged for (2/3) share 4% Preferred $100 par and (1/3) share Common $1 par
Each share 6% 2nd Preference no par exchanged for (0.5) share $3 Preferred no par and (0.2) share Common $1 par
Each share Common no par exchanged for (0.2) share Common $1 par
Recapitalized in 1941
Common $1 par exchanged (4) for (1)
Recapitalized in 1947
Each share Common $1 par exchanged for (2) shares Common $5 par
Stock Dividends - 100% 11/17/47; 20% 12/7/59
Name changed to Gafulco Co., Inc. 7/2/65
(See Gafulco Co., Inc.)

FULLER HAMMOND INC (MA)
Merged into Makepeace (A.D.) Co. 11/25/97
Each share Preferred $100 par exchanged for $101.17 cash

FULLER INDS INC (DE)
Liquidation completed
Each share Common 1¢ par received initial distribution of $0.25 cash 8/25/71
Each share Common 1¢ par received second distribution of $0.10 cash 4/7/72
Each share Common 1¢ par received third and final distribution of $0.0925 cash 9/17/74
Certificates were not required to be surrendered and are now valueless

FULLER LABS INC (MN)
Acquired by Warner-Lambert Co. 5/3/74
Each share Common $1 par exchanged for (0.9091) share Common $1 par

Warner-Lambert Co. merged into Pfizer Co. 6/19/2000

FULLER MANUFACTURING CO. (DE)
Stock Dividends - 10% 01/20/1955; 10% 01/20/1956; 10% 01/23/1957; 10% 01/28/1958
Acquired by Eaton Manufacturing Co. 08/15/1958
Each share Common exchanged for (1) share Common $1 par
Eaton Manufacturing Co. name changed to Eaton Yale & Towne Inc. 12/31/1965 which name changed to Eaton Corp. (OH) 04/21/1971 which reincorporated in Ireland as Eaton Corp. PLC 11/30/2012

FULLERTON INC (NV)
Recapitalized as Pacific Power Group, Inc. 10/24/1994
Each share Common $0.001 par exchanged for (0.025) share Common $0.001 par
Pacific Power Group, Inc. name changed to LP Holdings, Inc. 12/20/2005 which name changed to Tanke, Inc. 10/17/2007

FULLERTON PARKWAY CORP. (IL)
Liquidated in 1953
Details not available

FULLERTON PKWY TOWERS BLDG CORP (IL)
Each share Capital Stock 50¢ par exchanged for (0.2) share Capital Stock $2.50 par in 1949
Name changed to Whalen Fullerton Corp. 12/1/68
(See Whalen Fullerton Corp.)

FULLERTON-PORTSMOUTH BRIDGE CO. (KY & OH)
Reorganized 00/00/1940
Each share Preferred $100 par exchanged for (6) shares Common no par
Each share Common $10 par exchanged for (0.4) share Common no par
1st Preferred called for redemption 06/01/1953
2nd Preferred called for redemption 09/17/1957
Liquidation for cash completed 03/19/1958
Details not available

FULLERTON SVGS & LN ASSN (CA)
Each share Guarantee Stock $1 par exchanged for (4) shares Guarantee Stock 25¢ par 06/05/1972
Reorganized as RMG Capital Corp. 03/26/1996
Each share Guarantee Stock 25¢ par exchanged for (2) shares Common no par
(See RMG Capital Corp.)

FULLERTON ZIP NUT INC (UT)
Reincorporated under the laws of Nevada as Fullerton Inc. 02/25/1985
Fullerton Inc. recapitalized as Pacific Power Group, Inc. 10/24/1994 which name changed to LP Holdings, Inc. 12/20/2005 which name changed to Tanke, Inc. 10/17/2007

FULLPLAY MEDIA SYS INC (UT)
Plan of reorganization under Chapter 11 Federal Bankruptcy Code effective 8/26/2003
No stockholders' equity

FULLVIEW INDS INC (DE)
Each share Common 50¢ par exchanged for (1/6) share Common 10¢ par 9/6/66
Recapitalized as Darfield Industries, Inc. 3/9/72
Each share Common 10¢ par exchanged for (0.1) share Common 1¢ par
(See Darfield Industries, Inc.)

FULLVIEW MIRROR CO., INC. (NV)
Charter revoked for failure to file reports and pay fees 3/2/70

FULTON BAG & COTTON MILLS (GA)
Each share Capital Stock $100 par exchanged for (4) shares Capital Stock no par in 1937
Capital Stock no par reduced 50% by payment of $30 in cash 3/25/58
Stock Dividend - 100% 11/22/46
Name changed to Fulton Cotton Mills, Inc. 1/21/59
Fulton Cotton Mills, Inc. name changed to Fulton Industries, Inc. (GA) 5/17/60 which name changed to FII Liquidating Co. 4/30/68
(See FII Liquidating Co.)

FULTON BANCORP INC (DE)
Merged into Central Bancompany, Inc. 12/16/99
Each share Common 1¢ par exchanged for $19.15 cash

FULTON BANCSHARES CORP (PA)
Merged into Franklin Financial Services Corp. 7/1/2006
Each share Common $0.625 par exchanged for either (1.864) shares Common $10 par or $48 cash

FULTON BK (LANCASTER, PA)
Capital Stock $2.50 par split (2) for (1) by issuance of (1) additional share 7/30/74
Stock Dividend - 10% 11/15/78
Under plan of reorganization each share Capital Stock $2.50 par automatically became (1) share Fulton Financial Corp. Common $2.50 par 6/30/82

FULTON-CAROL CO. (IL)
Completely liquidated 8/15/79
Each share Common $1 par exchanged for first and final distribution of $0.50 cash

FULTON COTTON MILLS, INC. (GA)
Name changed to Fulton Industries, Inc. (GA) 5/17/60
Fulton Industries, Inc. (GA) name changed to FII Liquidating Co. 4/30/68
(See FII Liquidating Co.)

FULTON CNTY NATL BK & TR CO (GLOVERSVILLE, NY)
Acquired by Charter New York Corp. 12/03/1969
Each share Capital Stock $14 par exchanged for (1.75) shares Common $10 par
Charter New York Corp. name changed to Irving Bank Corp. 10/17/1979 which merged into Bank of New York Co., Inc. 12/30/1988 which merged into Bank of New York Mellon Corp. 07/01/2007

FULTON FED SVGS BK (ATLANTA, GA)
Name changed 4/24/89
Name changed from Fulton Federal Savings & Loan Association of Atlanta (U.S.A.) to Fulton Federal Savings Bank (Atlanta, GA) 4/24/89
Placed in receivership 2/1/91
Stockholders' equity unlikely

FULTON-FRONT REALTY CORP. (NY)
Proclaimed dissolved for failure to file reports and pay fees 12/16/35

FULTON GROUP OF OIL COMPANIES (DE)
Charter cancelled and declared inoperative and void for non-payment of taxes 1/26/26

FULTON INDUSTRIAL SECURITIES CORP. (DE)
Common no par changed to $1 par 00/00/1936
Completely liquidated 04/27/1959
Details not available

FULTON INDUSTRIES, INC. (DE)
Charter cancelled and declared inoperative and void for non-payment of taxes 4/15/72

FULTON INDUSTRIES, INC. (GA)
Each share Common no par exchanged for (6) shares Common $2 par 09/15/1960
Name changed to FII Liquidating Co. 04/30/1968
(See FII Liquidating Co.)

FULTON INDUSTRIES, INC. (OH)
Merged into Fulton Industries, Inc. (DE) 7/23/70
Each share 6% Preferred $25 par exchanged for (1) share 6% Preferred $25 par
Each share Common no par exchanged for (9) shares Common 10¢ par
(See Fulton Industries, Inc. (DE))

FULTON INVESTMENT CO. (GA)
Merged into Southeastern Capital Corp. (TN) 3/16/65
Each share Common $5 par exchanged for (2) shares Common $1 par
Southeastern Capital Corp. (TN) reincorporated in Georgia 7/31/76
(See Southeastern Capital Corp (GA))

FULTON-IONIA RAMP GARAGE
Dissolved in 1947
Details not available

FULTON IRON WORKS CO. (DE)
Reorganized in 1934
Each share 8% Preferred $100 par exchanged for (1) share Common $1 par
Each (10) shares Common no par exchanged for (1) share new Common $1 par
Recapitalized in 1946
Each share 6% Preferred $10 par exchanged for (1) share Common $5 par
Each share Common $1 par exchanged for (3) shares Common $5 par
Name changed to Fulton Securities Co. 5/21/54
(See Fulton Securities Co.)

FULTON NATL BK (ATLANTA, GA)
Each share Common $100 par exchanged for (10) shares Common $10 par in 1946
Common $10 par changed to $5 par and (1) additional share issued plus a 10% stock dividend paid 2/2/66
Stock Dividends - 12% 4/11/57; 10% 9/15/60; 10.68% 2/17/64; 10% 1/27/65; 10% 1/26/68
Reorganized as Fulton National Corp. 5/1/69
Each share Common $5 par exchanged for (1) share Common $5 par
Fulton National Corp. name changed to Bank South Corp. 5/31/81 which merged into NationsBank Corp. 1/9/96 which reincorporated in Delaware as BankAmerica Corp. (Old) 9/25/98 which merged into BankAmerica Corp. (New) 9/30/98 which name changed to Bank of America Corp. 4/28/99

FULTON NATL BK (LANCASTER, PA)
Capital Stock $20 par changed to $10 par and (1) additional share issued 11/23/66
Capital Stock $10 par changed to $5 par and (1) additional share issued 2/10/71
Stock Dividend - 50% 1/23/51
Name changed to Fulton Bank (Lancaster, PA) and Capital Stock $5 par changed to $2.50 par 7/1/74
Fulton Bank (Lancaster, PA) reorganized as Fulton Financial Corp. 6/30/82

FULTON NATL CORP (GA)
Stock Dividends - 100% 4/1/73; 10% 5/1/80
Name changed to Bank South Corp. 5/31/81
Bank South Corp. merged into

NationsBank Corp. 1/9/96 which reincorporated in Delaware as BankAmerica Corp. (Old) 9/25/98 which merged into BankAmerica Corp. (New) which name changed to Bank of America Corp. 4/28/99

FULTON PETROLEUM CORP. (DE)
Each share old Common $1 par exchanged for (0.5) share new Common $1 par 7/27/39
Liquidation completed 7/5/64
Details not available

FULTON REID & STAPLES FD INC (OH)
Liquidation completed
Each share Common no par held by regular shareholders exchanged for initial distribution of $11.27 cash 5/16/73
Each share Common no par held by regular shareholders received second and final distribution of $0.38 cash 12/28/73
Each share Common no par held by participating shareholders received first and final distribution of $0.24 cash 12/28/73
Note: Regular shareholders are those who did not redeem their shares prior to 2/8/73

FULTON SECURITIES CO. (DE)
Liquidated 7/19/56
Details not available

FULTON SYLPHON CO. (DE)
Under plan of merger name changed to Robertshaw-Fulton Controls Co. 09/24/1947
Robertshaw-Fulton Controls Co. name changed to Robertshaw Controls Co. 04/10/1963
(See Robertshaw Controls Co.)

FULTON VENTURES INC (NV)
Name changed to Triad Warranty Corporation, Inc. 06/16/1990
Triad Warranty Corporation, Inc. name changed to GTM Holdings, Inc. 05/30/2000 which name changed to Asia Premium Television Group, Inc. 09/27/2002 which recapitalized as China Grand Resorts, Inc. 11/17/2009

FUMMERTON MINING & DEVELOPMENT CO. LTD. (ON)
Charter cancelled by the Provincial Secretary of Ontario 03/22/1951

FUN CITY POPCORN INC (NV)
Reincorporated under the laws of Delaware as Lev Pharmaceuticals, Inc. 02/17/2005
Lev Pharmaceuticals, Inc. merged into ViroPharma Inc. 10/21/2008
(See ViroPharma Inc.)

FUN COSMETICS INC (DE)
Recapitalized as Grand Canal Entertainment, Inc. 08/29/2005
Each share Common $0.001 par exchanged for (0.005) share Common $0.001 par 08/29/2005
Grand Canal Entertainment, Inc. name changed to OC Beverages, Inc. 11/25/2008

FUN FOODS INC (DE)
Charter cancelled and declared inoperative and void for non-payment of taxes 3/1/89

FUN KEY STUDIOS INC (CANADA)
Dissolved 06/17/2005
Details not available

FUN TECHNOLOGIES INC (CANADA)
Merged into Liberty Media Corp. 12/24/2007
Each share Common no par exchanged for $3.50 cash

FUN TECHNOLOGIES PLC (ENGLAND & WALES)
Under Scheme of Arrangement each Ordinary Share received (0.5453) share Fun Technologies Inc. Common no par and $3.290824 cash payable 03/13/2006 to holders of record 03/07/2006
Note: Certificates were not required to be surrendered and are without value
(See Fun Technologies Inc.)

FUN TYME CONCEPTS INC (NY)
Reorganized under the laws of Delaware as Diversicon Holdings Corp. 10/28/1998
Each share Common $0.001 par exchanged for (0.25) share Common $0.001 par
(See Diversicon Holdings Corp.)

FUNCO INC (MN)
Merged into Barnes & Noble, Inc. 06/19/2000
Each share Common 1¢ par exchanged for $24.75 cash

FUNCTION X INC (DE)
Recapitalized as Viggle Inc. 06/07/2012
Each share Common $0.001 par exchanged for (0.5) share Common $0.001 par
Viggle Inc. name changed to DraftDay Fantasy Sports, Inc. 01/28/2016 which name changed to Function(x) Inc. 06/13/2016

FUNCTIONAL TECHNOLOGIES CORP (BC)
Filed a petition under Bankruptcy and Insolvency Act 04/25/2013
Company has no funds and all officers and directors have resigned
Stockholders' equity unlikely

FUND ALA INC (DE)
Liquidation completed
Each share Common 1¢ par exchanged for initial distribution of $9.75 cash 8/6/91
Each share Common 1¢ par received second and final distribution of $0.1269 cash 11/8/91

FUND AMER INC (NY)
Reincorporated 10/21/63
State of incorporation changed from (GA) to (NY) 10/21/63
Name changed to American Capital Growth & Income Fund, Inc. (NY) 7/23/90
American Capital Growth & Income Fund, Inc. (NY) reincorporated in Maryland 7/6/93 which reincorporated in Delaware as Van Kampen American Capital Growth & Income Fund 7/31/95 which name changed to Van Kampen Growth & Income Fund 7/14/98

FUND AMERICAN COMPANIES (CA)
Acquired by American Express Co. 10/31/68
Each share 6% Conv. Preferred $25 par exchanged for $28 cash
Each share 4% Conv. Preferred $25 par exchanged for $28 cash
Each share Common $1.25 par exchanged for (0.7) share $2.30 Conv. Preferred $1.66-2/3 par

FUND AMERN ENTERPRISES HLDGS INC (DE)
Name changed 06/19/1992
Plan of partial liquidation completed
Each share Common $1 par received initial distribution of $0.17 cash 03/20/1991
Each share Common $1 par received second distribution of $0.17 cash 06/19/1991
Each share Common $1 par received third distribution of $0.17 cash 08/18/1991
Each share Common $1 par received fourth and final distribution of $0.17 cash 12/18/1991
Name changed from Fund American Companies, Inc. to Fund American Enterprises Holdings, Inc. 06/19/1992
Name changed to White Mountains Insurance Group, Inc. (DE) 06/01/1999
White Mountains Insurance Group, Inc. (DE) reincorporated in Bermuda as White Mountains Insurance Group, Ltd. 10/25/1999

FUND FOR BUSINESS, INC. (NY)
Each share Class A 50¢ par or Class B 50¢ par exchanged for (0.05) share Common 10¢ par in September 1962
Each share Common 10¢ par exchanged for (4) shares Common 2-1/2¢ par 2/21/69
Merged into Royal United Corp. 10/6/69
Each share Class A Preferred 2-1/2¢ par or Common 2-1/2¢ par exchanged for (0.25) share Common 10¢ par
(See Royal United Corp.)

FUND FOR FEDERAL SECURITIES, INC. (MD)
Completely liquidated 4/29/76
Each share Common 10¢ par exchanged for first and final distribution of $9.94 cash

FUND FOR GOVT INVS INC (MD)
Common 1¢ par changed to $0.001 par and (9) additional shares issued 12/31/1975
Name changed to FBR Fund for Government Investors Inc. 04/30/2002
(See FBR Fund for Government Investors Inc.)

FUND FOR INVESTING IN GOVERNMENT SECURITIES, INC. (MD)
Name changed to American Express Government Securities Fund, Inc. 4/16/74
American Express Government Securities Fund, Inc. name changed to American Fund of Government Securities, Inc. 7/25/75

FUND FOR MUTUAL DEPOSITORS INC. (NY)
Acquired by Scudder, Stevens & Clark Common Stock Fund, Inc. 06/30/1977
Each share Common 10¢ par exchanged for (0.8249482) share Capital Stock $1 par
Scudder, Stevens & Clark Common Stock Fund, Inc. name changed to Scudder Common Stock Fund, Inc. 03/07/1979 which name changed to Scudder Growth & Income Fund 12/31/1984
(See Scudder Growth & Income Fund)

FUND OF FUNDS, LTD. (ON)
In process of liquidation
Each share Class A $1 par received initial distribution of $1.50 cash 7/19/77
Each share Class A $1 par received second distribution of $0.75 cash 11/28/79
Each share Class A $1 par received third distribution of $1.25 cash 2/11/81
Each share Class A $1 par received fourth distribution of $2 cash 3/5/82
Each share Class A $1 par received fifth distribution of $2.75 cash 6/24/83
Each share Class A $1 par received sixth distribution of $2.75 cash 7/25/84
Each share Class A $1 par received seventh distribution of $2 cash 7/28/86
Note: Details on subsequent distributions, if any, are not available

FUND OF LETTERS, INC. (DE)
Recapitalized as New America Fund, Inc. 12/17/71
Each share Common $1 par exchanged for (0.3) share Common $1 par
(See New America Fund, Inc.)

FUND OF THE WEST, INC. (WA)
Name changed to Western America Fund, Inc. 9/4/71
(See Western America Fund, Inc.)

FUND SOUTHWEST INC (DE)
Common $1 par split (2) for (1) by issuance of (1) additional share 09/15/1972
Merged into Capstone Series, Inc. 05/12/1992
Each share Common $1 par exchanged for Balanced Fund $1 par on a net asset basis
Capstone Series, Inc. merged into Capstone Growth Fund, Inc. 05/30/1995 which name changed to Capstone Series Fund, Inc. 01/22/2002

FUND U S GOVT SECS INC (MD)
Name changed to Federated Fund for U.S. Government Securities, Inc. 03/31/1996
Federated Fund for U.S. Government Securities, Inc. reorganized as Federated Income Securirties Trust 10/07/2002

FUNDAE ACQUISITION CORP (DE)
Name changed to C Me Run Corp. 02/02/2000
(See C Me Run Corp.)

FUNDAE CORP (FL)
Name changed to cMeRun, Inc. (FL) 12/8/99 cMeRun, Inc. (FL) reorganized in Delaware as Fundae Acquisition Corp. 1/25/2000 which name changed to C Me Run Corp. 2/2/2000
(See C Me Run Corp.)

FUNDAMATIC INVS INC (DE)
Completely liquidated 12/30/75
Each share Common $1 par received first and final distribution of $0.4237 cash
Note: Certificates were not required to be surrendered and are without value

FUNDAMENTAL APPLICATIONS CORP (BC)
Name changed to Global Cannabis Applications Corp. 04/18/2017

FUNDAMENTAL DEVELOPMENT & SECURITIES, INC. (LA)
Name changed to Tidelands Capital Corp. 05/15/1964
Tidelands Capital Corp. merged into Western Preferred Corp. 03/06/1981
(See Western Preferred Corp.)

FUNDAMENTAL FINL CORP (UT)
Each share old Common $0.025 par exchanged for (0.1) share new Common $0.025 par 07/12/1996
Name changed to Ikar Mineral Corp. (UT) 09/22/1997
Ikar Mineral Corp. (UT) reincorporated in Delaware 03/31/1998 which recapitalized as Ethos Capital Inc. 11/02/2000 which name changed to Patriot Energy Corp. 02/04/2002 which name changed to BigBrews Holdings Inc. (DE) 02/18/2003 which reincorporated in Nevada as Patriot Energy Corp. 09/09/2003 which name changed to Healing Hand Network International, Inc. 12/22/2003 which name changed to Patriot Energy Corp. (NV) 10/10/2005
(See Patriot Energy Corp.)

FUNDAMENTAL INVS INC (MD)
Reincorporated 02/01/1990
Each share Capital Stock 25¢ par exchanged for (0.125) share Capital Stock $2 par 00/00/1936
Capital Stock $2 par changed to $1 par and (1) additional share issued 10/26/1959

Stock Dividends - 100% 06/22/1946; 100% 11/28/1954
State of incorporation changed from (DE) to (MD) and Capital Stock $1 par changed to Common $1 par 02/01/1990
Common $1 par reclassified as Class A $1 par 03/15/2000
Class F $1 par reclassified as Class F-1 $1 par 06/16/2008
Under plan of reorganization each share Class A $1 par, Class B $1 par, Class C $1 par, Class F-1 $1 par and Class F-2 $1 par automatically became (1) share Fundamental Investors (DE) Class A $1 par, Class B $1 par, Class C $1 par, Class F-1 $1 par or Class F-2 $1 par respectively 09/01/2010

FUNDAMENTAL TRUST SHARES
Series A Cumulative Type and Series B Disbursement Type trust shares terminated 00/00/1950
Details not available

FUNDED SECURITY CORP. (IL)
Merged into National Industries, Inc. (KY) 06/01/1964
Each share Class A Common $2 par exchanged for (0.33333333) share Common $1 par
National Industries, Inc. (KY) merged into Fuqua Industries, Inc. 01/03/1978 which name changed to Actava Group Inc. 07/21/1993 which name changed to Metromedia International Group, Inc. 11/01/1995
(See Metromedia International Group, Inc.)

FUNDING INC (FL)
Common 1¢ par split (3) for (2) by issuance of (0.5) additional share 10/8/71
Each share Common 1¢ par exchanged for (1/56,500) share Common $1 par 12/22/78
Note: In effect holders received $0.30 cash per share and public interest was eliminated

FUNDING SYS CORP (DE)
Stock Dividends - 50% 1/23/78; 20% 8/31/78
Name changed to FSC Corp. (DE) 5/31/79
FSC Corp. (DE) reincorporated in Pennsylvania in October 1987 which reorganized as Trilos Corp. 2/24/89 which name changed to Lifetime Products, Inc. 12/17/90

FUNDPACK INC (FL)
Completely liquidated 5/21/80
Each share Common 1¢ par exchanged for first and final distribution of $5.06 cash

FUNDS BUSINESS INC (NY)
Each share Class A 50¢ par exchanged for (0.05) share Common 10¢ par 9/4/62
Each share Class B 50¢ par exchanged for (0.05) share Common 10¢ par 9/4/62
Common 10¢ par changed to 2-1/2¢ par and (3) additional shares issued 2/21/69
Merged into Royal United Corp. 10/6/69
Each share Common 2-1/2¢ par exchanged for (0.25) share Common 10¢ par
(See Royal United Corp.)

FUNDS INC (TX)
Merged into Criterion Management Co. 7/14/76
Each share Common $1 par exchanged for $5.15 cash

FUNDS MGMT SYS INC (DE)
Name changed to Bench Group, Inc. 08/25/1987
Bench Group, Inc. name changed to Qualmax, Inc. 12/23/2005 which merged into New World Brands, Inc. 02/20/2009

FUNDSNET INC (DE)
Merged into National Business Systems Inc. 1/27/87
Each share Common 1¢ par exchanged for $6.10 cash

FUNDSTECH CORP (DE)
Common $0.001 par split (2) for (1) by issuance of (1) additional share payable 01/07/2008 to holders of record 12/31/2007 Ex date - 01/08/2008
Name changed to FNDS3000 Corp. 03/28/2008

FUNDTECH LTD (ISRAEL)
Issue Information - 3,000,000 ORD shs. offered at $13 per share on 03/13/1998
Acquired by US FT Parent, Inc. 11/30/2011
Each share Ordinary ILS 0.01 par exchanged for $23.33 cash

FUNDTHATCOMPANY (NV)
Name changed to CLIC Technology, Inc. 07/31/2018

FUNDTRUST TAX FREE TR (MA)
Tax-Free Fund Shares of Bene. Int. $0.001 par redeemed in 1989
Details not available

FUNDY BAY COPPER MINES LTD. (ON)
Recapitalized as Fundy Exploration Ltd. 08/18/1966
Each share Capital Stock $1 par exchanged for (0.2) share Capital Stock $1 par
(See Fundy Exploration Ltd.)

FUNDY CABLE LTD (CANADA)
Name changed to Fundy Communications Inc. 09/08/1997
(See Fundy Communications Inc.)

FUNDY CHEM INTL LTD (NB)
Completely liquidated 12/14/1976
Each share Common no par exchanged for first and final distribution of $1.42 cash

FUNDY CHEMICAL CORP. LTD. (NB)
Merged into Fundy Chemical International Ltd. 03/16/1973
Each share Common no par exchanged for (1.5) shares Common no par
(See Fundy Chemical International Ltd.)

FUNDY COMMUNICATIONS INC (CANADA)
Subordinate no par called for redemption at USD$10.50 on 03/04/1998

FUNDY EXPL LTD (ON)
Charter cancelled for failure to pay taxes and file returns 03/16/1976

FUNERAL HOMES AMER INC (DE)
Name changed to Olympus Service Corp. 8/30/71
Olympus Service Corp. merged into Uniservice Corp. 3/31/76
(See Uniservice Corp.)

FUNIMALS PET ENTERPRISES INC (DE)
Charter cancelled and declared inoperative and void for non-payment of taxes 03/01/1999

FUNK SEEDS INTL INC (DE)
Merged into Ciba-Geigy Corp. 8/2/74
Each share Common 10¢ par exchanged for $17 cash

FUNSCAPE CORP (CO)
Name changed to Titan Energy Corp. (CO) 07/09/1997
Titan Energy Corp. (CO) reincorporated in Nevada as Power Exploration, Inc. 05/31/1998 which name changed to Matrix Energy Services Corp. 05/25/2002 which name changed to Shi Corp. 04/09/2009

FUNSTEN (R.E.) CO. (MO)
Acquired by Pet Milk Co. 10/27/61
Each share Common $1 par exchanged for (0.56) share Common no par
Pet Milk Co. name changed to Pet Inc. 9/1/66
(See Pet Inc.)

FUNTALK CHINA HOLDINGS LTD (CAYMAN ISLANDS)
Units separated 09/27/2010
Acquired by Fortress Group Ltd. 08/25/2011
Each share Orcinary $0.001 par exchanged for $7.20 cash

FUNTASTIC, INC. (VA)
Merged into KMS Industries, Inc. 03/25/1968
Each share Common exchanged for (0.81636) share Common 1¢ par
(See KMS Industries, Inc.)

FUNTIME HOSPITALITY CORP (ON)
Placed in receivership 02/01/2006
Stockholders' equity unlikely

FUNTIME INC (OH)
Common no par split (6) for (5) by issuance of (0.2) additional share 12/16/77
Common no par split (2) for (1) by issuance of (1) additional share 4/25/79
Acquired by Newtime, Inc. 12/31/87
Each share Common no par exchanged for $7 cash

FUQUA ENTERPRISES INC (DE)
Merged into Graham-Field Health Products Inc. 12/30/97
Each share Common $2.50 par exchanged for (2.1) shares Common 2-1/2¢ par
(See Graham-Field Health Products, Inc.)

FUQUA INDS INC (DE)
Reincorporated 05/06/1968
State of incorporation changed from (PA) to (DE) 05/06/1968
Common $5 par changed to $1 par and (1) additional share issued 05/27/1968
$5 Conv. Preferred Ser. A $100 par called for redemption 07/05/1972
$2 Conv. Preferred Ser. B $100 par called for redemption 01/01/1973
60¢ Conv. Preferred Ser. A $1 par called for redemption 11/30/1981
Common $1 par split (2) for (1) by issuance of (1) additional share 07/11/1983
$1.25 Conv. Preferred Ser. B $1 par for redemption 03/11/1985
Common $1 par split (2) for (1) by issuance of (1) additional share 07/02/1986
Name changed to Actava Group Inc. 07/21/1993
Actava Group Inc. name changed to Metromedia International Group, Inc. 11/01/1995
(See Metromedia International Group, Inc.)

FUQUA TELEVISION INC (GA)
Each share Common 10¢ par exchanged for (0.01) share Common $10 par 12/30/74
Merged into FTI, Inc. 5/30/78
Each share Common $10 par exchanged for $700 cash

FUR VAULT INC (DE)
Common 1¢ par split (2) for (1) by issuance of (1) additional share 6/21/85
Common 1¢ par split (3) for (2) by issuance of (0.5) additional share 12/20/85
Name changed to Banyan Corp. 5/25/90
(See Banyan Corp.)

FURA EMERALDS INC (ON)
Name changed to Fura Gems Inc. 04/11/2017

FURIA ORGANIZATION INC (DE)
Name changed 12/12/1986
Name changed from Furia Oringer Productions, Inc. to Furia Organization, Inc. 12/12/1986
Each share Common $0.0001 par exchanged for (0.2) share Common $0.001 par 08/19/2004
Name changed to Fronthaul Group, Inc. 05/01/2006
Fronthaul Group, Inc. name changed to Conversion Solutions Holdings Corp. 08/09/2006
(See Conversion Solutions Holdings Corp.)

FURIEX PHARMACEUTICALS INC (DE)
Acquired by Forest Laboratories, LLC 07/02/2014
Each share Common $0.001 par exchanged for (1) Non-transferable Contingent Value Right and $95 cash

FURIO RES INC (NV)
Reorganized as Aurelio Resource Corp. 06/16/2006
Each share Common $0.001 par exchanged for (6.5) shares Common $0.001 par
(See Aurelio Resource Corp.)

FURLONG PLASTICS LTD (ON)
Acquired by Steeltree Group, Inc. 2/4/71
Each share 6% 1st Preferred $8 par exchanged for (1) share 6% Preference Ser. 1, $7.80 par
Each share Common no par exchanged for (1) share Common 1¢ par

FURMAN-WOLFSON CORP. (NY)
Reorganized as Furman-Wolfson Trust and Common 10¢ par reclassified as Shares of Bene. Int. 10¢ par 5/1/67
(See Furman-Wolfson Trust)

FURMAN WOLFSON TR (NY)
Completely liquidated 4/8/69
Each Share of Bene. Int. 10¢ par exchanged for first and final distribution of $16.4625 cash

FURMANITE CORP (DE)
Merged into Team, Inc. 02/29/2016
Each share Common no par exchanged for (0.215) share Common 30¢ par

FURNESS WITHY & CO LTD (ENGLAND)
ADR agreement terminated 00/00/1980
Details not available

FURNISHING CLUB (NV)
Common $0.001 par split (2) for (1) by issuance of (1) additional share payable 9/30/2002 to holders of record 9/27/2002
Name changed to Rapidtron, Inc. (NV) 10/1/2002
Rapidtron, Inc. (NV) reincorporated in Delaware 5/8/2003

FURNISHINGS 2000 INC (DE)
Plan of reorganization under Chapter 11 Federal Bankruptcy proceedings confirmed 07/23/1991
No stockholders' equity

FURNITURE BRANDS INTL INC (DE)
Each share old Common no par exchanged for (0.14285714) share new Common no par 05/29/2013
Plan of reorganization under Chapter 11 Federal Bankruptcy proceedings effective 08/01/2014
No stockholders' equity

FURNTEC INDS INC (DE)
Merged into Picture Covers, Inc. 12/14/76
Each share Capital Stock 50¢ par exchanged for $0.05 cash

FURON CO (CA)
Common no par split (2) for (1) by

issuance of (1) additional share payable 12/16/97 to holders of record 12/2/97 Ex date - 12/17/97
Merged into Compagnie de Saint-Gobain 11/21/99
Each share Common no par exchanged for $25.50 cash

FURR S CAFETERIAS INC (TX)
Common no par split (2) for (1) by issuance of (1) additional share 8/22/72
Merged into K mart Corp. 5/14/80
Each share Common no par exchanged for $28 cash

FURRS BISHOPS CAFETERIAS L P (DE)
Merged into Furr's/Bishop's Inc. 3/27/91
Each Depositary Preference Unit exchanged for (0.6) share $9 Conv. Preferred Ser. A 1¢ par, (0.25) share Class A Common 1¢ par and $0.75 cash
Furr's/Bishop's Inc. name changed to Furr's Restaurant Group Inc. 2/15/2000
(See Furr's Restaurant Group, Inc.)

FURRS RESTAURANT GROUP INC (DE)
Name changed 2/15/2000
Each share $9 Conv. Preferred Ser. A 1¢ par exchanged for (1.15) shares old Common 1¢ par and (2.04) Common Stock Purchase Warrants expiring 1/2/2001 on 1/2/96
Each share Class A Common 1¢ par exchanged for (1) share old Common 1¢ par and (1.78) Common Stock Purchase Warrants expiring 1/2/2001 on 1/2/96
Each share Class B Common 1¢ par exchanged for (0.95) share old Common 1¢ par and (1.69) Common Stock Purchase Warrants expiring 1/2/2001 on 1/2/96
Each (15) shares old Common 1¢ par exchanged for (1) share new Common 1¢ par 3/22/96
Each share new Common 1¢ par exchanged again for (0.2) share new Common 1¢ par to effect a (1) for (10) reverse split and subsequent (2) for (1) forward split 12/13/99
Name changed from Furr's/Bishop's Inc. to Furr's Restaurant Group, Inc. 2/15/2000
Plan of reorganization under Chapter 11 Federal Bankruptcy Code effective 9/30/2003
No stockholders' equity

FURRY CONCRETE FORMS CO. (OK)
Charter revoked for failure to file reports and pay fees 10/15/23

FURY EXPL LTD (BC)
Ctfs. dated prior to 05/31/1990
Common 50¢ par changed to no par 12/28/1984
Recapitalized as Sundance Resources Ltd. 05/31/1990
Each share Common no par exchanged for (0.33333333) share Common no par
Sundance Resources Ltd. recapitalized as Mammoth Energy Inc. 08/23/1995 which recapitalized as Cierra Pacific Ventures Ltd. 02/25/1998 which recapitalized as Alange Energy Corp. 07/15/2009 which recapitalized as PetroMagdalena Energy Corp. 07/19/2011
(See PetroMagdalena Energy Corp.)

FURY EXPLORATIONS LTD (BC)
Ctfs. dated after 09/21/2006
Reincorporated 09/21/2006
Place of incorporation changed from (Yukon) to (BC) 09/21/2006
Merged into Golden Predator Mines Inc. 08/15/2011
Each share Common no par exchanged for (0.33333333) share Common no par and (0.5) Common Stock Purchase Warrant expiring 08/15/2011
(See Golden Predator Mines Inc.)

FUSA CAP CORP (NV)
Each (1,500) shares old Common $0.0001 par exchanged for (1) share new Common $0.0001 par 09/18/2009
Name changed to Spectral Capital Corp. 09/08/2010

FUSHI COPPERWELD INC (NV)
Acquired by Green Dynasty Ltd. 12/27/2012
Each share Common $0.006 par exchanged for $9.50 cash

FUSHI INTL INC (NV)
Name changed to Fushi Copperweld, Inc. 01/15/2008

FUSION FD INC (DE)
Name changed to Zenascent Inc. 01/08/2001
Zenascent Inc. name changed to Cedric Kushner Promotions Inc. 01/16/2003 which name changed to Ckrush, Inc. 12/27/2005
(See Ckrush, Inc.)

FUSION-IO INC (DE)
Issue Information - 12,300,000 shares COM offered at $19 per share on 06/08/2011
Acquired by SanDisk Corp. 07/23/2014
Each share Common $0.0002 par exchanged for $11.25 cash

FUSION MED TECHNOLOGIES INC (DE)
Merged into Baxter International Inc. 5/3/2002
Each share Common $0.001 par exchanged for (0.1763) share Common $1 par

FUSION NETWORKS HLDGS INC (DE)
Placed in receivership under Chapter 727 Florida Statutes 05/08/2001
Stockholders' equity unlikely

FUSION RD INC (DE)
Name changed to VZillion, Inc. (DE) 09/10/2007
VZillion, Inc. (DE) reincorporated in Nevada 08/25/2008

FUSION RES LTD (AUSTRALIA)
Acquired by Paladin Energy Ltd. 02/16/2009
Each share Common exchanged for (0.16666666) share Ordinary
Note: U.S. holders may receive cash proceeds from the sale of shares
(See Paladin Energy Ltd.)

FUSION SYS CORP (DE)
Issue Information - 4,000,000 shares COM offered at $16 per share on 05/12/1994
Merged into Eaton Corp. 08/05/1997
Each share Common 1¢ par exchanged for $39 cash

FUSION TELECOMMUNICATIONS INTL INC (DE)
Each share old Common 1¢ par exchanged for (0.02) share new Common 1¢ par 05/13/2014
Recapitalized as Fusion Connect, Inc. 05/07/2018
Each share new Common 1¢ par exchanged for (0.66666666) share Common 1¢ par

FUTRONICS, INC. (NC)
Name changed to Investors Equity Corp. (N.C.) and Common 20¢ par reclassified as Capital Stock 20¢ par 12/7/67

FUTTERMAN CORP. (DE)
Name changed to Titan Industries, Inc. and Class A and B $1 par reclassified as Common $1 par 05/23/1966
Titan Industries, Inc. name changed to Titan Group, Inc. 02/23/1967 which name changed to Hanover Companies Inc. 04/29/1985
(See Hanover Companies Inc.)

FUTURA AIRLINES (CA)
Charter revoked for failure to file reports and pay fees 8/1/63

FUTURA AUTOMOTIVE GROUP INC (NV)
Name changed to Spa International Inc. 10/09/1992
(See Spa International Inc.)

FUTURA BANC CORP (OH)
Common no par split (5) for (4) by issuance of (0.25) additional share payable 09/14/1998 to holders of record 09/01/1998
Common no par split (2) for (1) by issuance of (1) additional share payable 09/15/1999 to holders of record 09/01/1999
Stock Dividends - 10% payable 10/01/1996 to holders of record 09/01/1996; 10% payable 09/15/1997 to holders of record 09/02/1997; 10% payable 09/13/2002 to holders of record 09/03/2002 Ex date - 08/29/2002; 10% payable 09/12/2003 to holders of record 09/01/2003 Ex date - 08/27/2003; 20% payable 06/17/2005 to holders of record 06/01/2005 Ex date - 06/03/2005
Merged into First Citizens Banc Corp. 12/17/2007
Each share Common no par exchanged for (1.1726) shares Common no par
First Citizens Banc Corp. name changed to Civista Bancshares, Inc. 05/04/2015

FUTURA ENERGY & RES LTD (BC)
Struck off register and declared dissolved for failure to file returns 11/29/85

FUTURA INDS INC (CA)
Name changed to Surveyor Industries, Inc. 2/5/76
(See Surveyor Industries, Inc.)

FUTURA LOYALTY GROUP INC (CANADA)
Filed a petition under Companies' Creditors Arrangement Act 10/16/2012
No stockholders' equity

FUTURA PICTURES INC (DE)
Name changed to IMK Group, Inc. 03/13/2015

FUTURA WEST INC (AZ)
Merged into Sunbelt Construction Co. 5/23/91
Each share Common 50¢ par exchanged for $0.35 cash

FUTURE AVENIR CORP (ON)
Merged into Ourominas Minerals Inc. 06/28/1996
Each share Class A Common no par exchanged for (0.9) share Common no par
Each share Class B Common no par exchanged for (1) share Common no par
Ourominas Minerals Inc. recapitalized as Thistle Mining Inc. 04/27/1999
(See Thistle Mining Inc.)

FUTURE BEACH CORP (CANADA)
Filed a Notice of Intention to make a proposal under the Bankruptcy and Insolvency Act 01/00/2006
No stockholders' equity

FUTURE CDA CHINA ENVIRONMENT INC (NV)
Common $0.00001 par split (7) for (1) by issuance of (6) additional shares payable 10/09/2008 to holders of record 10/07/2008 Ex date - 10/10/2008
Charter revoked for failure to file reports and pay taxes 02/28/2012

FUTURE CARZ INC (NV)
Name changed 02/05/2001
Name changed from Future Carz.Com, Inc. to Future Carz, Inc. 02/05/2001
Each share old Common $0.001 par exchanged for (0.33333333) share new Common $0.001 par 01/04/2002
SEC revoked common stock registration 07/16/2010

FUTURE CMNTYS INC (CA)
Each share old Common 1¢ par exchanged for (0.181818) share new Common 1¢ par 5/1/73
Privately acquired 3/7/89
Each share new Common 1¢ par exchanged for $8 cash

FUTURE COMMUNICATIONS INC (NJ)
Each share old Common 10¢ par exchanged for (1/3) share new Common 10¢ 5/14/93
Charter revoked for failure to file reports and pay fees 5/7/96

FUTURE EDL SYS INC (NV)
Charter revoked for failure to file reports and pay fees 08/01/2005

FUTURE ENERGY CORP (NV)
Name changed to MarilynJean Interactive Inc. 04/09/2013

FUTURE FDG CORP (DE)
Name changed to Site-Based Media, Inc. 7/2/91
Site-Based Media, Inc. name changed to Site Holdings Inc. 3/8/94
(See Site Holdings Inc.)

FUTURE GERMANY FD INC (MD)
Name changed to Central European Equity Fund, Inc. 06/30/1995
Central European Equity Fund, Inc. name changed to Central Europe & Russia Fund, Inc. 06/25/2003 which name changed to Central Europe, Russia & Turkey Fund, Inc. 04/29/2013 which name changed to Central & Eastern Europe Fund Inc. 08/01/2017

FUTURE GROUP INNOVATIONS INC (BC)
Recapitalized as Interstat Ventures Inc. 01/15/1992
Each share Common no par exchanged for (0.33333333) share Common no par
Interstat Ventures Inc. recapitalized as Consolidated Interstat Ventures Inc. 04/23/1996 which name changed to Diamcor Mining Inc. 11/23/1999

FUTURE HEALTHCARE INC (OH)
Common no par split (2) for (1) by issuance of (1) additional share 12/3/93
Charter cancelled for failure to pay taxes 12/22/98

FUTURE INFORMATION SYS INC (DE)
Name changed to Globalnet Systems Ltd. 04/18/1996

FUTURE LINK SYS INC (WY)
Recapitalized as Cal-Star Inc. 09/28/2001
Each share Common no par exchanged for (0.5) share Common no par
Cal-Star Inc. name changed to Amanta Resources Ltd. (WY) 07/13/2004 which reincorporated in British Columbia 08/31/2004

FUTURE MED PRODS INC (DE)
Name changed to Vasomedical, Inc. 05/15/1995
Vasomedical, Inc. name changed to Vaso Corp. 01/26/2017

FUTURE MED TECHNOLOGIES INTL INC (NV)
Each share old Common $0.001 par

FUT-FUT   FINANCIAL INFORMATION, INC.

exchanged for (0.2) share new Common $0.001 par 05/26/1994
Each share new Common $0.001 par exchanged again for (0.71428571) share new Common $0.001 par 02/22/1995
Name changed to Covalent Group Inc. (NV) 09/20/1996
Covalent Group Inc. (NV) reincorporated in Delaware 07/01/2002 which name changed to Encorium Group, Inc. 10/30/2006
(See Encorium Group, Inc.)

FUTURE MEDIA TECHNOLOGIES CORP (WY)
Reincorporated 01/29/1999
Place of incorporation changed from (BC) to (WY) 01/29/1999
Recapitalized as Future Link Systems Inc. 06/21/1999
Each share Common no par exchanged for (0.1) share Common no par
Future Link Systems Inc. recapitalized as Cal-Star Inc. 09/28/2001 which name changed to Amanta Resources Ltd. (WY) 07/13/2004 which reincorporated in British Columbia 08/31/2004

FUTURE MINERAL CORP (YUKON)
Dissolved and struck off register 01/25/2007

FUTURE NOW GROUP INC (NV)
SEC revoked common stock registration 07/13/2012

FUTURE NOW INC (OH)
Merged into Intelligent Electronics, Inc. 8/18/95
Each share Common no par exchanged for (0.564) share Common 1¢ par
Intelligent Electronics, Inc. acquired by Xerox Corp. 5/20/98

FUTURE PETE CORP (UT)
Reincorporated under the laws of Texas as Bargo Energy Co. 4/29/99
Bargo Energy Co. (TX) merged into Mission Resources Corp. 5/16/2001
(See Mission Resources Corp.)

FUTURE PROJS I CORP (FL)
Name changed to Vactory.com, Inc. 06/22/2000
Vactory.com, Inc. name changed to Vactory, Inc. 08/20/2000 which name changed to Her Personal Feminine Care Products, Inc. 08/06/2001 which recapitalized as OJsys, Inc. 11/07/2006

FUTURE PROJS II CORP (FL)
Name changed to Grand Entertainment & Music Inc. 05/25/2000
(See Grand Entertainment & Music Inc.)

FUTURE PROJS III CORP (FL)
Name changed to Autoleasecheck.com Inc. 09/13/2000
Autoleasecheck.com Inc. name changed to Gatelinx Global Corp. (FL) 03/15/2005 which reincorporated in Nevada as GTX Global Corp. 10/12/2005 which recapitalized as Vision Technology Corp. 07/31/2006

FUTURE PROJS IV CORP (FL)
Reincorporated under the laws of Nevada as Liquidics, Inc. 04/17/2000
Liquidics, Inc. name changed to Global Web TV, Inc. (Old) 12/13/2001 which recapitalized as QOL Holdings, Inc. 12/15/2003 which name changed to Global Web TV, Inc. (New) 10/05/2005 which reorganized as Amore TV, Inc. 01/27/2006 which recapitalized as Rapid Fitness, Inc. 05/11/2007 which name changed to Tri-Star Holdings Inc. 08/27/2008 which recapitalized as Macada Holding, Inc. (NV) 08/20/2009 which reincorporated in Wyoming 02/22/2011 which recapitalized as KMA Holding, Inc. 03/17/2011
(See KMA Holding, Inc.)

FUTURE PROJS V CORP (FL)
Recapitalized as Innovision International Corp. 07/07/2000
Each share Common $0.001 par exchanged for (0.2) share Common $0.001 par
Innovision International Corp. name changed to Tubearoo, Inc. 03/12/2007 which recapitalized as Emerging World Pharma, Inc. 11/24/2009

FUTURE PROJS VI CORP (FL)
Name changed to Buoy Club, Inc. 7/21/2000
Buoy Club, Inc. name changed to Identa Ltd. 1/23/2002 which name changed to Identa Corp. 1/22/2002

FUTURE PROJS VII CORP (FL)
Recapitalized as Berten USA Holdings Inc. 06/02/2000
Each share Common $0.001 par exchanged for (0.2) share Common $0.001 par
Berten USA Holdings Inc. recapitalized as Digitalreach Holdings Inc. 07/13/2001 which name changed to People Dynamics Holdings Inc. 06/10/2003
(See People Dynamics Holdings Inc.)

FUTURE PROJS VIII CORP (FL)
Name changed to American IDC Corp. 7/14/2000
American IDC Corp. name changed to Smart SMS Corp. 11/18/2005

FUTURE QUEST INC (ON)
Each share old Common $0.001 par exchanged for (0.1) share new Common $0.001 par 02/04/2004
Reorganized under the laws of Nevada as Future Quest Nevada, Inc. 03/16/2005
Each share new Common $0.001 par exchanged for (0.05) share Common $0.001 par
Future Quest Nevada, Inc. recapitalized as Intervision Network Corp. 01/28/2008

FUTURE QUEST NEV INC (NV)
Common $0.001 par split (30) for (1) by issuance of (29) additional shares payable 12/19/2005 to holders of record 12/15/2005
Ex date - 12/28/2005
Recapitalized as Intervision Network Corp. 01/28/2008
Each share Common $0.001 par exchanged for (0.02) share Common $0.001 par

FUTURE RESOURCES LTD. (OK)
Merged into Bogert Oil Co. 9/30/81
Each share Common 1¢ par exchanged for (2) shares Common 10¢ par
(See Bogert Oil Co.)

FUTURE SHOP LTD (CANADA)
Common no par split (2) for (1) by issuance of (1) additional share payable 09/11/2000 to holders of record 09/07/2000
Acquired by Best Buy Co., Inc. 11/07/2001
Each share Common no par exchanged for $17 cash

FUTURE SUCCESS SOFTWARE CORP (FL)
Name changed to Fax Utilities Systems & Services Corp. 3/4/98
Fax Utilities Systems & Services Corp. name changed to Netlist Corp. of Florida
(See Netlist Corp. of Florida)

FUTURE SYS INC (NV)
Name changed back to Jefferson Capital Inc. 2/24/92
Jefferson Capital Inc. name changed to Spirit Gaming Group Inc. 1/23/96

FUTURE SYSTEMS, INC. (CA)
Common 50¢ par changed to 33-1/3¢ par and (0.5) additional share issued 11/15/72
Reorganized under the laws of Delaware 7/20/76
Each share Common 33-1/3¢ par exchanged for (1) share Common 1¢ par

FUTURE SYSTEMS, INC. (DE)
Charter cancelled and declared inoperative and void for non-payment of taxes 6/27/74

FUTURE TECHNOLOGIES INC (MN)
Name changed to SE Global Equities Corp. 04/23/2001
SE Global Equities Corp. recapitalized as Sun New Media Inc. (MN) 09/20/2005 which reincorporated in Delaware as NextMart, Inc. 05/08/2007

FUTURE WORLD GROUP INC (NV)
Name changed to Global Entertainment Clubs, Inc. 03/20/2017
Global Entertainment Clubs, Inc. name changed to Wewards, Inc. 01/29/2018

FUTUREBIOTICS INC (DE)
Each share old Common $0.0001 par exchanged for (0.1) share new Common $0.0001 par 12/30/1996
Company terminated registration of common stock and is no longer public as of 01/17/2001
Details not available

FUTUREFUND CAP VCC CORP (BC)
Recapitalized as Pender Growth Fund (VCC) Inc. 08/15/2003
Each share Common no par exchanged for (0.02) share Class A Common Ser. 1 no par

FUTUREIT INC (DE)
SEC revoked common stock registration 06/11/2014

FUTURELINK CORP (DE)
Reincorporated 10/15/1999
Each share old Common $0.0001 par exchanged for (0.2) share new Common $0.0001 par 06/01/1999
Reincorporated from FutureLink Distribution Corp. (CO) to FutureLink Corp. (DE) 10/15/1999
Each share old Common $0.0001 par exchanged for (0.14285714) share new Common $0.0001 par 06/08/2001
Filed a petition under Chapter 11 Federal Bankruptcy Code 08/14/2011
No stockholders' equity

FUTUREMED HEALTHCARE INCOME FD (ON)
Under plan of reorganization each Unit no par automatically became (1) share Futuremed Healthcare Products Corp. Common no par 01/04/2011
(See Futuremed Healthcare Products Corp.)

FUTUREMED HEALTHCARE PRODS CORP (ON)
Acquired by Cardinal Health, Inc. 03/12/2012
Each share Common no par exchanged for $8.15 cash

FUTUREMEDIA PLC (ENGLAND & WALES)
Each old Sponsored ADR for Ordinary exchanged for (0.02) new Sponsored ADR for Ordinary 01/02/2007
Basis changed from (1:1) to (1:50) 01/02/2007
Each new Sponsored ADR for Ordinary exchanged again for (0.05) new Sponsored ADR for Ordinary 12/03/2007
Basis changed from (1:50) to (1:1,000) 12/03/2007
ADR agreement terminated 10/15/2015
No ADR holders' equity

FUTUREONE INC (NV)
Chapter 11 Federal Bankruptcy proceedings converted to Chapter 7 on 9/4/2002
Stockholders' equity unlikely

FUTUREPLAST TECH LTD (AB)
Struck off register and declared dissolved for failure to file returns 03/01/1997

FUTURES EXPANSION FUND LIMITED PARTNERSHIP (DE)
Company terminated registration of Units of Limited Partnership and is no longer public as of 01/23/2004
Details not available

FUTURES FD INC (IA)
Common $1 par changed to 50¢ par and (1) additional share issued 6/15/76
Stock Dividend - 10% 1/31/72
Voluntarily dissolved 6/27/79
Details not available

FUTURESAT INDS INC (NJ)
Recapitalized as Future Communications Inc. 05/01/1990
Each share Common 10¢ par exchanged for (0.25) share Common 10¢ par
(See Future Communications Inc.)

FUTURETRAK INTL INC (FL)
Each share old Common $0.001 par exchanged for (0.25) share new Common $0.001 par 05/13/1999
Name changed to Worldcast Interactive, Inc. (FL) 11/10/1999
Worldcast Interactive, Inc. (FL) reorganized in Delaware as Andorra Capital Corp. 05/28/2008 which recapitalized as Savenergy Holdings, Inc. 08/04/2010

FUTUREVEST INC (NV)
Each share old Common $0.001 par exchanged for (0.622) share new Common $0.001 par 03/14/2006
Name changed to Barotex Technology Corp. 01/09/2008
(See Barotex Technology Corp.)

FUTUREVIEW INC (MB)
Completely liquidated 08/09/2004
Each share Common no par exchanged for first and final distribution of $0.10 cash

FUTUREWORLD ENERGY INC (DE)
Name changed to FutureWorld Corp. 07/17/2014

FUTURIS CORP LTD (AUSTRALIA)
Name changed to Elders Ltd. 06/23/2009

FUTURISTIC INNOVATIONS INC (HI)
Name changed to Asia Pacific Communications Corp. (HI) 05/30/1991
Asia Pacific Communications Corp. (HI) name changed to EIF Holdings Inc. (HI) 12/28/1992 which reorganized in Delaware as U.S. Industrial Services Inc. 05/04/1998 which name changed to Nextgen Communications Corp. 08/07/2001 which name changed to Home Solutions of America, Inc. 12/23/2002
(See Home Solutions of America, Inc.)

FUTURITY OILS LTD (AB)
Merged into Canadian Futurity Oils Ltd. 11/01/1985
Each share Capital Stock no par exchanged for (0.25) share Class A no par
Canadian Futurity Oils Ltd. recapitalized as Baca Resources

Ltd. 08/04/1989 which name changed to CORDEX Petroleums Ltd. 07/11/1994
(See CORDEX Petroleums Ltd.)

FUTURMILL INC (MI)
Stock Dividend - 200% 6/30/66
Completely liquidated 3/31/69
Each share Common $1 par exchanged for first and final distribution of (0.25) share Kysor Industrial Corp. (MI) Common $1 par
Kysor Industrial Corp. (MI) recorporated in Delaware 4/15/70 which incorporated again in Michigan 5/31/85
(See Kysor Industrial Corp. (MI))

FUTURNET INTERNET SVCS INC (NV)
Recapitalized as September Group Inc. 4/27/2001
Each share Common $0.001 par exchanged for (0.1) share Common $0.001 par
September Group Inc. recapitalized as ProSportsBook.Net Inc. 4/10/2002 which recapitalized as Ibises International Inc. 3/27/2003 which recapitalized as Biomag Corp. 3/28/2006 which name changed to Biomagnetics Diagnostics Corp. 12/18/2006

FUTURONICS CORP (NY)
Stock Dividend - 100% 02/24/1972
Merged out of existence 01/31/2003
Details not available

FUTURTEK COMMUNICATIONS INC (BC)
Plan of reorganization under Chapter 11 Federal Bankruptcy proceedings confirmed 01/16/1990
No stockholders' equity

FVC COM INC (DE)
Name changed to First Virtual Communications, Inc. 2/7/2001
(See First Virtual Communications, Inc.)

FVC FIRST VENTURE CAP CORP (BC)
Name changed to Lasik Vision Corp. 4/19/99
Lasik Vision Corp. was acquired by Icon Laser Eye Centers, Inc. 3/13/2001

FVNB CORP (TX)
Merged into FVNB Merger Corp. 8/10/2001
Each share Common 1¢ par exchanged for $45 cash

FW CAP I (DE)
9.325% Guaranteed Preferred Securities called for redemption at $10 on 3/19/2004

FW OMNIMEDIA CORP (AB)
Delisted from Toronto Venture Stock Exchange 06/21/2005

FW PFD CAP TR I (BERMUDA)
9% Preferred Securities Ser. I 1¢ par called for redemption at $25 on 5/26/2006

FWB BANCORPORATION (MD)
Stock Dividend - 10% 5/22/90
Name changed to Grandbanc Inc. 3/10/97
Grandbanc Inc. merged into Century Bancshares, Inc. 3/14/2001 which merged into United Bankshares, Inc. 12/10/2001

FWD CORP (WI)
Common $10 par changed to $1 par and (1) additional share issued 02/08/1966
Merged into Stoarc Corp. 11/05/1982
Each share Common $1 par exchanged for $1.50 cash

FWF HLDGS INC (NV)
Name changed to DOCASA, Inc. 10/03/2016

FX ALLIANCE INC (DE)
Issue Information - 5,200,000 shares COM offered at $12 per share on 02/08/2012
Acquired by Thomson Reuters Corp. 08/23/2012
Each share Common $0.0001 par exchanged for $22 cash

FX ENERGY INC (NV)
Acquired by Polski Koncern Naftowy Orlen S.A. 12/31/2015
Each share Common $0.001 par exchanged for $1.15 cash
9.25% Ser. B Preferred $0.001 par called for redemption at $25 plus $0.61667 accrued dividends on 01/07/2016

FX REAL ESTATE & ENTMT INC (DE)
Name changed to Circle Entertainment Inc. 01/13/2011

FXCM INC (DE)
Each share old Class A Common 1¢ par exchanged for (0.1) share new Class A Common 1¢ par 10/01/2015
Name changed to Global Brokerage, Inc. 02/27/2017

FXR, INC. (NY)
Merged into Amphenol-Borg Electronics Corp. 5/31/61
Each share Common $1 par exchanged for (0.5) share Common $1 par
Amphenol-Borg Electronics Corp. name changed to Amphenol Corp. 5/11/65 which merged into Bunker Ramo Corp. (New) 6/3/68 which merged into Allied Corp. 7/31/81 which merged into Allied- Signal Inc. 9/19/85 which name changed to AlliedSignal Inc. 4/26/93 which name changed to Honeywell International Inc. 12/1/99

FYTOKEM PRODS INC (AB)
Assets sold for the benefit of creditors 11/26/2009
Stockholders' equity unlikely

G

G / O BUSINESS SOLUTIONS INC (CO)
Reorganized under the laws of Nevada as Radiant Oil & Gas Inc. 05/27/2010
Each share Common 1¢ par exchanged for (0.2) share Common 1¢ par

G. & C. MERRIAM CO. (MA)
See - Merriam (G. & C.) Co.

G. & M. PUBLISHING CO. (OH)
Merged into North American Publishing Co. 10/31/77
Each share Common no par exchanged for (0.1) share Common 10¢ par
(See North American Publishing Co.)

G. B. COMPONENTS, INC. (CA)
Charter revoked for failure to file reports and pay fees 5/3/65

G & B AUTOMATED EQUIP LTD (ON)
Common no par split (2) for (1) by issuance of (1) additional share 03/18/1983
Adjudicated bankrupt 00/00/1994
No stockholders' equity

G & F T MFG. CORP. (NV)
Common $5 par changed to 10¢ par 2/16/79
Name changed to G & FT Oil & Gas Corp. 4/30/80
G & FT Oil & Gas Corp. name changed to Yankee Energy Group 1/13/81
(See Yankee Energy Group)

G & FT OIL & GAS CORP. (NV)
Name changed to Yankee Energy Group 1/13/81
(See Yankee Energy Group)

G & G SHOPS INC (DE)
Acquired by Petrie Stores Corp. 7/23/80
Each share Common 10¢ par exchanged for $12.99623 cash

G & H STL INDS LTD (CANADA)
Merged into Harris Steel Group Inc. 05/16/1983
Each share Common no par exchanged for $5.75 cash

G & H TECHNOLOGY, INC. (DE)
Merged into Automation Industries, Inc. (CA) 12/16/75
Each share Capital Stock 10¢ par exchanged for $3 cash

G & K SVCS INC (MN)
Common 50¢ par split (4) for (3) by issuance of (0.33333333) additional share 10/10/1980
Common 50¢ par split (5) for (4) by issuance of (0.25) additional share 10/09/1981
Common 50¢ par split (3) for (2) by issuance of (0.5) additional share 12/03/1984
Common 50¢ par reclassified as Class A Common 50¢ par 06/14/1985
Class A Common 50¢ par split (3) for (2) by issuance of (0.5) additional share 12/29/1986
Class A Common 50¢ par split (3) for (2) by issuance of (0.5) additional share 10/01/1987
Class B Common 50¢ par split (3) for (2) by issuance of (0.5) additional share 10/01/1987
Class A Common 50¢ par split (3) for (2) by issuance of (0.5) additional share 10/02/1989
Class B Common 50¢ par split (3) for (2) by issuance of (0.5) additional share 10/02/1989
Class A Common 50¢ par split (3) for (2) by issuance of (0.5) additional share 01/04/1994
Stock Dividends - 20% 10/31/1979; In Class A Common to holders of Class A Common 10% 07/05/1985
Acquired by Cintas Corp. 03/21/2017
Each share Class A Common 50¢ par exchanged for $97.50 cash

G & L ENERGY INC (UT)
Name changed 06/22/1982
Name changed from G & L Equipment Co. to G & L Energy, Inc. 06/22/1982
Name changed to Diamond Lake Minerals Inc. 12/02/1993

G & R INDS INC (MO)
Adjudicated bankrupt 5/14/79
Stockholders' equity unlikely

G & W LD & DEV CORP (DE)
Name changed to Transnation Development Corp. 1/20/70
(See Transnation Development Corp.)

G A S INVT CORP (UT)
Name changed to Bonniebrook, Inc. 1/16/74
(See Bonniebrook, Inc.)

G ACCION S A DE CV (MEXICO)
ADR agreement terminated 09/01/2005
Each Sponsored Reg. S ADR for Ordinary exchanged for $2.45 cash
Each Sponsored 144A ADR for Ordinary exchanged for $2.45 cash

G B INTL CORP (DE)
Adjudicated bankrupt 10/2/75
Stockholders' equity unlikely

G.B.S. ELECTRICAL CONTROLS LTD. (BC)
Name changed to North American Technology Ltd. 06/27/1975
North American Technology Ltd. name changed to Yalakum Resources Ltd. 02/23/1981
(See Yalakum Resources Ltd.)

G C COMPUTER CORP. (NY)
Name changed to Greyhound Computer Corp. 6/13/68
Greyhound Computer Corp. merged into Greyhound Corp. (DE) 8/31/76 which reincorporated in (AZ) 3/3/78 which name changed to Greyhound Dial Corp. 5/8/90 which name changed to Dial Corp. (AZ) 5/14/91 which reincorporated in (DE) 3/18/92 which name changed to Viad Corp. 8/15/96

G COLLADO S A DE C V (MEXICO)
ADR agreement terminated 04/01/2009
No ADR's remain outstanding

G D M GRAND DEV CORP (BC)
Delisted from Vancouver Stock Exchange 03/05/1996

G.D.W. CORP. (PA)
Completely liquidated 11/00/1968
No stockholders' equity

G E M ENVIRONMENTAL MGMT INC (DE)
Reincorporated 07/13/1990
Place of incorporation changed from (BC) to (DE) 07/13/1990
Merged into Continental Waste Industries, Inc. 06/28/1995
Each share Common no par exchanged for $0.22 cash

G E Q CORP (QC)
Charter cancelled 08/23/1986

G-ESTATE LIQ STORES INC (DE)
Plan of reorganization under Chapter 11 Federal Bankruptcy proceedings effective 11/15/2017
No stockholders' equity

G F A INDS INC (DE)
Charter cancelled and declared inoperative and void for non-payment of taxes 4/15/71

G.F.C. CORP. (IL)
Articles of dissolution filed 5/5/61
Details not available

G F I COMPUTER INDS INC (AZ)
Name changed to First Recreation Corp. 6/27/72
First Recreation Corp. name changed to Financial Resource Corp. 7/24/81
(See Financial Resource Corp.)

G I T INDS INC (DE)
Under plan of merger each share Common $1 par exchanged for $4.90 principal amount 12% Subordinated Debentures due 09/30/2001 on 09/02/1981

G I T RLTY & MTG INVS (MA)
Reorganized as GIT Industries Inc. 03/30/1976
Each Share of Bene. Int. $1 par exchanged for (1) share Common $1 par
(See GIT Industries Inc.)

G K B INC (DE)
Merged into United Industrial Syndicate, Inc. 01/02/1962
Each share Common $1 par exchanged for $3.64 cash

G.L. INDUSTRIES (NJ)
Liquidated 4/2/58
Details not available

G L INDS INC (NJ)
Name changed 11/15/1963
Name changed from G-L Electronics Co., Inc. to G-L Industries, Inc. 11/15/1963
Name changed to SGL Industries, Inc. 12/15/1970
SGL Industries, Inc. name changed to SL Industries, Inc. (NJ) 09/20/1984 which reincorporated in Delaware 06/20/2013
(See SL Industries, Inc.)

G LEARNING CORP (KOREA)
ADR agreement terminated 05/26/2015

G.M.I. LIQUIDATING CORP. (NY)
In process of liquidation
Each share Common 5¢ par exchanged for initial distribution of (0.4165) share Avnet, Inc. $1 Conv. Preferred $1 par 6/28/66
Each share Common 5¢ par received second distribution of (0.052) share Avnet, Inc. $1 Conv. Preferred $1 par 1/27/67
Each share Common 5¢ par received third distribution of (0.052) share Avnet, Inc. $1 Conv. Preferred $1 par 12/15/67
Note: Details on subsequent distributions, if any, are not available

G.M.I. LIQUIDATING CORP. (NY)
In process of liquidation
Each share Common 5¢ par exchanged for initial distribution of (0.4165) share Avnet, Inc. $1 Conv. Preferred $1 par 6/28/66
Each share Common 5¢ par received second distribution of (0.052) share Avnet, Inc. $1 Conv. Preferred $1 par 1/27/67
Each share Common 5¢ par received third distribution of (0.052) share Avnet, Inc. $1 Conv. Preferred $1 par 12/15/67
Note: Details on subsequent distributions, if any, are not available

G.M.P. INTERNATIONAL, INC. (UT)
Proclaimed dissolved for failure to file annual reports 7/1/92

G M RES LTD (CANADA)
Reincorporated 09/08/1982
Place of incorporation changed from (BC) to (Canada) 09/08/1982
Merged into Campbell Resources Inc (New) 06/08/1983
Each share Common no par exchanged for (0.2) share Common no par
(See Campbell Resources Inc. (New))

G M S STORES INC (NY)
Dissolved by proclamation 3/25/92

G O INTL INC (CO)
Each share old Class A Common 1¢ par exchanged for (0.01) share new Class A Common 1¢ par 07/28/1994
Recapitalized as G/O Business Solutions, Inc. (CO) 08/15/2006
Each share new Class A Common 1¢ par exchanged for (0.5) share Common 1¢ par
G/O Business Solutions, Inc. (CO) reorganized in Nevada as Radiant Oil & Gas Inc. 05/27/2010

G P PPTYS INC (NV)
Name changed to Kwikweb.com Inc. 01/11/2000
(See Kwikweb.com Inc.)

G R I CORP (DE)
Reincorporated 6/28/91
Common no par split (3) for (2) by issuance of (0.5) additional share 1/10/69
Common no par split (3) for (2) by issuance of (0.5) additional share 1/22/71
Common no par split (3) for (2) by issuance of (0.5) additional share 1/21/72
Common no par split (3) for (2) by issuance of (0.5) additional share 1/23/73
State of incorporation changed from (IL) to (DE) and Common no par changed to 1¢ par 6/28/91
Filed a petition under Chapter 7 Federal Bankruptcy Code 5/4/92
No stockholders' equity

G R PAC RESOURCE CORP (YUKON)
Reincorporated under the laws of British Columbia as Pacific GeoInfo Corp. 02/03/2003

G REIT INC (MD)
Reincorporated 09/27/2004
State of incorporation changed from (VA) to (MD) 09/27/2004
In process of liquidation
Each share Common 1¢ par received initial distribution of $3.90 cash payable 10/11/2006 to holders of record 09/30/2006
Each share Common 1¢ par received second distribution of $3 cash 04/20/2007
Each share Common 1¢ par received third distribution of $1 cash payable 11/09/2007 to holders of record 11/09/2007
Note: Holders also received monthly distributions totalling $0.79 cash from 04/00/2007 through 12/00/2007
Assets transferred to G REIT Liquidating Trust and Common 1¢ par reclassified as Units of Bene. Int. 01/22/2008

G S B INVTS INC (FL)
Merged into Compass Bancshares, Inc. 01/15/1998
Each share Common exchanged for (2.6224) shares Common $2 par
Compass Bancshares, Inc. merged into Banco Bilbao Vizcaya Argentaria, S.A. 09/07/2007

G.S.T. CORP. (DE)
Liquidation completed 12/23/55
Details not available

G S WENDEY & CO (DE)
Name changed to Sizemore Environmental Group, Inc. 1/27/89
Sizemore Environmental Group, Inc. merged into EnClean, Inc. 6/28/91
(See EnClean, Inc.)

G-VII ENERGY CORP (DE)
Name changed to Nathaniel Energy Corp. (Old) in 07/00/1998
Nathaniel Energy Corp. (Old) reorganized as Nathaniel Energy Corp. (New) in 12/00/1998 which name changed to Vista International Technologies, Inc. 12/20/2007

G T CORP (TN)
Name changed to American Equity Corp. 7/27/73
(See American Equity Corp.)

G T GLOBAL DEVELOPING MKTS FD INC (MD)
Name changed 11/3/97
Name changed from G.T. Global Developing Markets Fund, Inc. to G.T. Global Developing Markets Fund and Common $0.001 par reclassified as Class A $0.001 par 11/3/97
Under plan of reorganization Class A $0.001 par reclassified as Aim Investment Funds Developing Markets Fund Class A 5/29/98

G T MONEY MKT SER INC (MD)
Merged into AIM Investment Portfolios 08/28/1998
Details not available

G V FILMS LTD (INDIA)
Stock Dividend - 248% payable 09/15/2006 to holders of record 09/14/2006
GDR agreement terminated 08/30/2013
No GDR's remain outstanding

G&L RLTY CORP (MD)
Merged into G&L Acquisition, LLC 10/29/2001
Each share Common 1¢ par exchanged for $13 cash
9.8% Preferred Ser. B 1¢ par called for redemption at $25 on 6/8/2006
10.25% Preferred Ser. A 1¢ par called for redemption at $25 on 6/8/2006
Public interest eliminated

GA CAP CORP (ON)
Completely liquidated
Each share Common no par received first and final distribution of (0.4117647) Xtierra Inc. Unit consisting of (1) share Common no par and (0.5) Common Stock Purchase Warrant expiring 04/14/2011 payable 04/16/2010 to holders of record 04/15/2010
Note: Certificates were not required to be surrendered and are without value

GA EXPRESS INC (DE)
Filed a notice of intention to make a proposal under the Bankruptcy and Insolvency Act 08/16/2006
Stockholders' equity unlikely

GA FINL INC (DE)
Merged into First Commonwealth Financial Corp. (PA) 5/24/2004
Each share Common 1¢ par exchanged for (2.752) shares Common $1 par

GAB BANCORP (IN)
Common $10 par split (3) for (2) by issuance of (0.5) additional share 9/10/93
Name changed to German American Bancorp 6/16/95
German American Bancorp name changed to German American Bancorp Inc. 5/22/2006

GABBS RES LTD (BC)
Delisted from Vancouver Stock Exchange 02/01/1991

GABELLI ASSET MGMT INC (NY)
Issue Information - 3,600,000 INCOME PRIDES offered at $25 per Income Pride on 01/31/2002
Each Income Preferred Redeemable Increased Dividend Equity Security received (0.5376) share Class A Common 1¢ par 02/17/2005
Name changed to GAMCO Investors, Inc. (NY) 08/29/2005
GAMCO Investors, Inc. (NY) reincorporated in Delaware 11/22/2013

GABELLI CONVERTIBLE & INCOME SECURITIES FD INC (MD)
Name changed 07/30/2002
Name changed from Gabelli Convertible Securities Fund, Inc. to Gabelli Convertible & Income Securities Fund Inc. 07/30/2002
8% Preferred $0.001 par called for redemption at $25 plus $0.25 accrued dividend on 02/11/2003
Auction Rate Preferred Ser. C $0.001 par called for redemption at $25,000 on 06/25/2008
(Additional Information in Active)

GABELLI EQUITY TR INC (MD)
7.25% Tax Advantaged Preferred called for redemption at $25 plus $0.4078 accrued dividends on 06/17/2003
7.20% Tax Advantaged Preferred Ser. B called for redemption at $25 plus $0.06 accrued dividends on 01/08/2007
6.20% Preferred Ser. F $0.001 par called for redemption at $25 plus $0.185138 accrued dividends on 11/08/2012
(Additional Information in Active)

GABELLI GLOBAL DEAL FD (DE)
Issue Information - 18,750,000 COM SHS BEN INT offered at $20 per share on 01/26/2007
Name changed to GDL Fund 02/10/2011

GABELLI GLOBAL GOLD, NAT RES & INCOME TR (DE)
Name changed to GAMCO Global Gold, Natural Resources & Income Trust by Gabelli 12/19/2011
GAMCO Global Gold, Natural Resources & Income Trust by Gabelli name changed to GAMCO Global Gold, Natural Resources & Income Trust 03/28/2014

GABELLI GLOBAL MULTIMEDIA TR INC (MD)
7.92% Preferred $0.001 par called for redemption at $25 plus $0.033 accrued dividends on 04/02/2003
Name changed to Gabelli Multimedia Trust Inc. 01/27/2012

GABELLI GROWTH FD (MA)
Name changed to GAMCO Growth Fund 12/30/2005

GABELLI INTL GROWTH FD INC (MD)
Name changed to GAMCO International Growth Fund, Inc. 12/23/2005

GABELLI NAT RES GOLD & INCOME TR (DE)
Issue Information - 18,500,000 SH BEN INT offered at $20 per share on 01/26/2011
Name changed to GAMCO Natural Resources, Gold & Income Trust by Gabelli 12/19/2011
GAMCO Natural Resources, Gold & Income Trust by Gabelli name changed to GAMCO Natural Resources, Gold & Income Trust 03/28/2014

GABLE INDS INC (ME)
Name changed to Hajoca Corp. 12/29/1978
(See Hajoca Corp.)

GABLES RESIDENTIAL TR (MD)
Issue Information - 4,000,000 PFD SER A offered at $25 per share on 07/21/1997
8.30% Preferred Ser. A 1¢ par called for redemption at $25 plus $0.31125 accrued dividends on 8/9/2002
Merged into ING Groep N.V. 9/30/2005
Each Share of Bene. Int. 1¢ par exchanged for $43.700833 cash
7.5% Preferred Ser. D 1¢ par called for redemption at $25 plus $0.2343 accrued dividends on 10/31/2005
7.875% Preferred Ser. C-1 1¢ par called for redemption at $25 plus $0.2515 accrued dividends on 10/31/2005

GABRIEL CO (OH)
Each share Class B no par exchanged for (20) shares Class A no par 00/00/1936
Class A no par reclassified as Common $1 par 00/00/1945
5% Preferred $10 par called for redemption 02/28/1962
Stock Dividend - 10% 12/22/1950
Completely liquidated 12/05/1963
Each share Common $1 par exchanged for (0.2) share Maremont Corp. (IL) 4-1/2% Conv. Preferred $100 par and $3 cash
Maremont Corp. (IL) reincorporated in Delaware 04/30/1974
(See Maremont Corp. (DE))

GABRIEL INDS INC (DE)
Common $1 par split (2) for (1) by issuance of (1) additional share 6/17/68
Common $1 par split (5) for (4) by issuance of (0.25) additional share 1/13/78
Merged into CBS Inc. 8/14/78
Each share Common $1 par exchanged for $17.90 cash

GABRIEL RES INC (BC)
Merged into Appian Resources Ltd. 09/06/1989
Each share Common no par exchanged for (0.4209) share Common no par
Appian Resources Ltd. recapitalized as Sultan Minerals Inc. 05/04/1992 which recapitalized as Apex Resources Inc. 07/18/2016

GABRIEL SNUBBER MANUFACTURING CO.
Name changed to Gabriel Co. in 1930

(See Gabriel Co.)

GABRIEL TECHNOLOGIES CORP (DE)
Chapter 11 bankruptcy proceedings converted to Chapter 7 on 07/08/2014
Stockholders' equity unlikely

GABRIELLE MINES LTD.
Assets acquired by San Antonio Gold Mines Ltd. on a (1) for (13) basis in 1935
(See San Antonio Gold Mines Ltd.)

GAC CORP (DE)
Reincorporated 12/20/1973
Each share $1 Preferred no par exchanged for (0.16666666) share $6.50 Preferred no par 08/16/1968
50¢ Conv. Preference no par called for redemption 07/01/1969
State of incorporation changed from (PA) to (DE) and Common $1 par changed to 10¢ par 12/20/1973
Plan of reorganization under Chapter X Federal Bankruptcy Act confirmed 09/12/1980
No stockholders' equity

GAC FIN INC (MN)
Name changed to Finance America Corp. of Minnesota Inc. 10/1/74
(See Finance America Corp. of Minnesota Inc.)

GAC GROWTH FD INC (MD)
Acquired by New York Venture Fund, Inc. 7/24/72
Each share Common 10¢ par exchanged for (0.646) share Capital Stock $1 par
New York Venture Fund, Inc. name changed to Davis New York Venture Fund, Inc. 10/1/95

GAC LIQUIDATING TR (FL)
Liquidation completed
Each Unit of Bene. Int. no par received initial distribution of $1.25 cash 8/28/81
Each Unit of Bene. Int. no par received second distribution of $0.50 cash 3/1/82
Each Unit of Bene. Int. no par received third distribution of $1 cash 8/30/82
Each Unit of Bene. Int. no par received fourth distribution of $0.75 cash 3/31/84
Each Unit of Bene. Int. no par received fifth distribution of $1 cash 3/31/85
Each Unit of Bene. Int. no par received sixth distribution of $1.75 cash 5/15/85
Each Unit of Bene. Int. no par received seventh distribution of $1.75 cash 6/12/86
Each Unit of Bene. Int. no par received eighth distribution of $1 cash 6/1/87
Each Unit of Bene. Int. no par received ninth distribution of $2.75 cash 6/1/88
Each Unit of Bene. Int. no par received tenth and final distribution of $2.465 cash 12/22/88
Note: Units were not required to be surrendered and are now valueless

GADABOUT GADDIS PRODTNS INC (MA)
Name changed to G.G. Communications, Inc. and Common 10¢ par changed to 5¢ par 12/30/70

GADZOOKS INC (TX)
Common 1¢ par split (3) for (2) by issuance of (0.5) additional share payable 5/30/96 to holders of record 5/16/96
Plan of reorganization under Chapter 11 Federal Bankruptcy Code effective 2/17/2006
No stockholders' equity

GADZOOX NETWORKS INC (DE)
Plan of reorganization under Chapter 11 Federal Bankruptcy Code effective 06/23/2003
No stockholders' equity

GAENSEL GOLD MINES INC (NV)
Each share old Common $0.0001 par exchanged for (0.01) share new Common $0.0001 par 01/02/1996
Each share new Common $0.0001 par exchanged again for (0.1) share new Common $0.0001 par 02/28/1997
Name changed to Best Medical Treatment Group Inc. 12/19/1997
Best Medical Treatment Group Inc. name changed to Jenson International Inc. 06/12/1998
(See Jenson International Inc.)

GAENSEL MNG INDS INC (UT)
Each share Common 1¢ par exchanged for (0.01) share Common $1 par 05/01/1983
Name changed to Gaensel Mining & Energy, Inc. 12/15/1987

GAF CORP (DE)
$1.20 Conv. Preferred $1 par called for redemption 5/2/85
Common $1 par split (2) for (1) by issuance of (1) additional share 5/21/86
Merged into Newco Holdings, Inc. 3/29/89
Each share Common $1 par exchanged for $7 principal amount of G-I Holdings Inc. Jr. Subordinated Debentures due 3/29/2005 and $46 cash

GAFFERS & SATTLER CORP. (CA)
Voluntary exchange offer in 1963 by Republic Corp.; held 99.85% as of 7/31/66
Public interest eliminated

GAFFNEY MANUFACTURING CO.
Common $100 par changed to $50 par in 1937
Merged into Pacolet Industries, Inc. on a (13-3/4) for (1) basis 12/3/62
(See Pacolet Industries, Inc.)

GAFULCO CO., INC. (NJ)
Liquidation completed
Each share Common $5 par stamped to indicate initial distribution of $32 cash 7/9/65
Each share Stamped Common $5 par stamped to indicate second distribution of $1 cash 5/9/66
Each share Stamped Common $5 par stamped to indicate third distribution of $5 cash 8/22/79
Each share Stamped Common $5 par exchanged for fourth and final distribution of $1.64 cash 1/20/82

GAGAN GOLD CORP (BC)
Recapitalized as Cachet Enterprises Corp. 11/16/1993
Each share Common no par exchanged for (0.33333333) share Common no par
Cachet Enterprises Corp. name changed to Gold Star Resources Corp. 04/02/2004 which name changed to Simba Energy Inc. 02/19/2010 which name changed to Simba Essel Energy Inc. 04/24/2017

GAGE MINERALS CORP (UT)
Recapitalized as Perfect Golf Inc. 1/23/95
Each share Common $0.001 par exchanged for (0.1) share Common $0.001 par
Perfect Golf Inc. name changed to Golf Star, Inc. 7/14/95 which name changed to Star Entertainment Group, Inc. 8/3/98
(See Star Entertainment Group, Inc.)

GAGER, INC. (MN)
Name changed to Dimensional TEC, Inc. 11/1/89
(See Dimensional TEC, Inc.)

GAIA EXPL INC (NV)
Name changed to EcoMed Corp. 11/21/2000
EcoMed Corp. name changed to Ranger Wireless Corp. 3/30/2005 which name changed to International Ranger Corp. 7/14/2005

GAIA REMEDIES INC (NV)
Name changed to Patriot Berry Farms, Inc. 02/27/2013
Patriot Berry Farms, Inc. name changed to Cyberfort Software, Inc. 11/16/2016

GAIA RES INC (NV)
Recapitalized as Ram Gold & Exploration, Inc. 02/08/2008
Each share Common $0.0001 par exchanged for (0.02) share Common $0.0001 par
Note: No holder will receive fewer than (100) shares
Ram Gold & Exploration, Inc. name changed to DPollution International Inc. 08/31/2010 which recapitalized as Ecrid, Inc. 10/16/2017

GAIAM INC (CO)
Name changed to Gaia, Inc. 07/15/2016

GAIL ROBERTS, INC. (NY)
See - Roberts (Gail), Inc.

GAINER CORP (IN)
Acquired by NBD Bancorp, Inc. 1/23/92
Each share Common no par exchanged for (9.936) shares Common $1 par
NBD Bancorp, Inc. name changed to First Chicago NBD Corp. 12/1/95 which merged into Bank One Corp. 10/2/98 which merged into J.P. Morgan Chase & Co. 12/31/2000 which name changed to JPMorgan Chase & Co. 7/20/2004

GAINER MINERALS LTD (WA)
Under plan of merger name changed to Gold Capital Corp. (WA) 2/29/84
Gold Capital Corp. (WA) merged into Crown Resources Corp. 2/16/89 which was acquired by Kinross Gold Corp. 8/31/2006

GAINESVILLE BK & TR (GAINESVILLE, GA)
Common $5 par split (2) for (1) by issuance of (1) additional share payable 08/15/1997 to holders of record 07/25/1997 Ex date - 08/18/1997
Under plan of reorganization each share Common $5 par automatically became (1) share GB&T Bancshares, Inc. Common $5 par 04/24/1998
GB&T Bancshares, Inc. merged into SunTrust Banks, Inc. 05/01/2008

GAINESVILLE GAS & ELECTRIC CO.
Reorganized as Gainesville Gas Co. in 1935
(See Gainesville Gas Co.)

GAINESVILLE GAS CO.
Assets sold in 1940
Details not available

GAINESVILLE GAS CO (FL)
7% Preferred $100 par called for redemption 05/31/1981
Stock Dividend - 100% 12/30/1980
Acquired by Gainesville Regional Utilities 00/00/1989
Details not available

GAINS GTY CORP (IA)
Liquidation completed
Each share Common $1 par exchanged for initial distribution of (0.08250825) share Life Investors Inc. (IA) 3% Conv. Preferred $25 par 12/02/1968
Each share Common $1 par received second and final distribution of (0.0175467) share Life Investors Inc. (IA) 3% Conv. Preferred $25 par 09/30/1969
(See Life Investors Inc. (IA))

GAINSBORO H T BOSTON INC (MA)
Adjudicated bankrupt 9/7/73
Stockholders' equity unlikely

GAIR (ROBERT) CO.
Reorganized as Gair (Robert) Co., Inc. 00/00/1932
Details not available

GAIR (ROBERT) CO., INC. (DE)
Preferred no par changed to $10 par and Common no par changed to $1 par 00/00/1937
Each share Preferred $10 par exchanged for (1) share Preferred $20 par, (3) shares Common $1 par and $10 principal amount 6% Income Notes due 04/01/1972 00/00/1941
Merged into Continental Can Co., Inc. 10/26/1956
Each share $4.50 Preferred $100 par exchanged for (1) share $4.50 2nd Preferred $100 par
(See Continental Can Co., Inc.)
Each share Common $1 par exchanged for (0.8) share Common $10 par
Continental Can Co., Inc. name changed to Continental Group, Inc. 04/27/1976
(See Continental Group, Inc.)

GAITWIN EXPLS LTD (ON)
Recapitalized as Wingait Diversified Ltd. 02/06/1970
Each share Capital Stock $1 par exchanged for (0.1) share Common no par
Wingait Diversified Ltd. name changed to Aquablast Inc. 07/29/1971
(See Aquablast Inc.)

GAL FRIDAY SVCS INC (DE)
Each share Class B Common 10¢ par exchanged for (0.1) share Common 10¢ par 8/18/68
Adjudicated bankrupt 2/1/71
Stockholders' equity unlikely

GAL-WOOD MINES LTD. (ON)
Charter cancelled and company declared dissolved by default 02/15/1960

GALA-BARI INTL INC (BC)
Cease trade order effective 11/14/2002
Stockholders' equity unlikely

GALA GLOBAL INC (NV)
Old Common $0.001 par split (20) for (1) by issuance of (19) additional shares payable 09/17/2014 to holders of record 09/17/2014
Each share old Common $0.001 par exchanged for (0.01) share new Common $0.001 par 01/31/2017
Name changed to Gala Pharmaceutical, Inc. 01/10/2018

GALA HLDG CORP (FL)
Recapitalized as Global TransNet Corp. 10/14/2003
Each share Common no par exchanged for (0.02) share Common no par
Global TransNet Corp. recapitalized as Legacy Brands Holding, Inc. (FL) 11/19/2009 which reincorporated in British Virgin Islands as Revelation MIS, Inc. 10/22/2010 which reincorporated in Florida as Jolen, Inc. 04/08/2015 which name changed to WOWI, Inc. 06/23/2016

GALA HOSPITALITY CORP (FL)
Each share old Common $0.0001 par exchanged for (0.1) share new Common $0.0001 par 01/31/2002
Name changed to Gala Holding Corp. 09/04/2002
Gala Holding Corp. recapitalized as Global TransNet Corp. 10/14/2003 which recapitalized as Legacy

GAL-GAL — FINANCIAL INFORMATION, INC.

Brands Holding, Inc. (FL) 11/19/2009 which reincorporated in British Virgin Islands as Revelation MIS, Inc. 10/22/2010 which reincorporated in Florida as Jolen, Inc. 04/08/2015 which name changed to WOWI, Inc. 06/23/2016

GALA RES LTD (BC)
Recapitalized as Hydromet-Technologies Ltd. (BC) 03/04/1999
Each share Common no par exchanged for (0.25) share Common no par
Hydromet-Technologies Ltd. (BC) reincorporated in Bermuda as Goldmarca Ltd. 07/02/2003 which name changed to Ecometals Ltd. 10/25/2007

GALACTIC GAMING INC (NV)
Each share Common $0.001 par exchanged for (0.05) share Common $0.0001 par 12/16/2004
Recapitalized as Insight Energy Corp. 11/8/2006
Each share Common $0.0001 par exchanged for (0.0025) share Common $0.0001 par
Insight Energy Corp. recapitalized as Sun Sports & Entertainment, Inc. 3/7/2007

GALACTIC RES LTD (BC)
Common no par split (2) for (1) by issuance of (1) additional share 12/17/1985
Placed in receivership 01/26/1993
No stockholders' equity

GALAGEN INC (DE)
Recapitalized as Let's Talk Recovery, Inc. (DE) 05/04/2006
Each share Common 1¢ par exchanged for (0.001) share Common 1¢ par
Let's Talk Recovery, Inc. (DE) reorganized in Nevada as Columbia Energy Corp. 11/26/2010 which name changed to Cornwall Resources, Inc. 04/16/2012

GALAGRAPH LTD (ISRAEL)
Name changed to TAT Technologies Inc. 05/06/1992

GALAHAD METALS INC (ON)
Each share Common no par received distribution of (0.05) share Red Ore Gold Inc. Common no par payable 12/12/2011 to holders of record 12/09/2011 Ex date - 12/07/2011
Note: Canadian resident holders of (9,999) shares or fewer and all U.S. residents received CAD$0.005 cash per share
Reorganized under the laws of British Columbia as Rosehearty Energy Inc. 07/31/2014
Each share Common no par exchanged for (0.1) share Common no par

GALATEA GOLD MINES, LTD.
Merged into Consolidated Duquesne Mining Co., Ltd. 00/00/1948
Each share Capital Stock no par exchanged for (0.047619) share Capital Stock $1 par
Consolidated Duquesne Mining Co., Ltd. merged into Beattie-Duquesne Mines Ltd. 00/00/1952 which recapitalized as Donchester Duquesne Mines Ltd. 07/11/1972 which merged into Fundy Chemical International Ltd. 10/01/1973
(See Fundy Chemical International Ltd.)

GALAXIE INDS INC (CO)
Merged into Galaxie National Corp. 12/24/1969
Each share Common 25¢ par exchanged for (1) share Common 10¢ par
Galaxie National Corp. reorganized as Marathon Office Supply, Inc. 05/12/1982
(See Marathon Office Supply, Inc.)

GALAXIE MED CTRS INC (CO)
Name changed to Superior Health Services, Inc. 4/13/71
Superior Health Services, Inc. name changed to Wyndon Corp. 2/10/72
(See Wyndon Corp.)

GALAXIE NATL CORP (DE)
Reorganized as Marathon Office Supply, Inc. 5/12/82
Each share Common 10¢ par exchanged for (1/300) share Common 30¢ par
(See Marathon Office Supply, Inc.)

GALAXIWORLD COM LTD (BRITISH VIRGIN ISLANDS)
Acquired by Ostel Management Inc. 12/00/1999
Each share Common no par exchanged for $1.50 cash

GALAXY CAP CORP (BC)
Name changed to Galaxy Graphite Corp. 06/12/2012
Galaxy Graphite Corp. recapitalized as Global Copper Group Inc. 02/26/2015 which name changed to Cobalt Power Group Inc. 10/24/2016

GALAXY CAP LTD (DE)
Charter cancelled and declared inoperative and void for non-payment of taxes 3/1/92

GALAXY CARPET MLS INC (DE)
Common 10¢ par split (3) for (2) by issuance of (0.5) additional share 6/15/73
Common 10¢ par split (5) for (4) by issuance of (0.25) additional share 1/10/83
Stock Dividend - 25% 10/4/78
Merged into Peerless Carpet Corp. 8/31/69
Each share Common 10¢ par exchanged for $14 cash

GALAXY CHAMPIONSHIP WRESTLING INC (NV)
Name changed to FUSA Capital Corp. and Common $0.001 par changed to $0.0001 par 06/17/2004
FUSA Capital Corp. name changed to Spectral Capital Corp. 09/08/2010

GALAXY CHEESE CO (DE)
Name changed to Galaxy Foods Co. 02/24/1992
Galaxy Foods Co. name changed to Galaxy Nutritional Foods Inc. 11/16/2000
(See Galaxy Nutritional Foods Inc.)

GALAXY CITY MINES LTD (BC)
Merged into Moly Mite Resources Inc. 03/16/1982
Each share Common no par exchanged for (1) share Common no par
Moly Mite Resources Inc. recapitalized as Macrotrends Ventures Inc. 07/02/1986 which merged into Macrotrends International Ventures Inc. 08/17/1988 which recapitalized as Global Election Systems Inc. 11/22/1991 which was acquired by Diebold, Inc. 01/22/2002 which name changed to Diebold Nixdorf Inc. 12/12/2016

GALAXY COPPER LTD (BC)
Merged into United Bata Resources Ltd. 03/24/1969
Each share Capital Stock no par exchanged for (0.4) share Common 50¢ par
(See United Bata Resources Ltd.)

GALAXY ENERGY CORP (BC)
Recapitalized as Galaxy Sports Inc. 08/10/2001
Each share Common no par exchanged for (1/3) share Common no par
(See Galaxy Sports Inc.)

GALAXY ENERGY CORP (CO)
Name changed 05/15/2003
Name changed from Galaxy Investments Inc. to Galaxy Energy Corp 05/15/2003
Chapter 11 bankruptcy proceedings converted to Chapter 7 on 01/06/2009
No stockholders' equity

GALAXY ENTERPRISES INC (NV)
Merged into Netgateway, Inc. 06/26/2000
Each share Common $0.007 par exchanged for (0.63217) share Common $0.001 par
Netgateway, Inc. recapitalized as iMergent, Inc. 07/02/2002 which name changed to Crexendo, Inc. (DE) 05/23/2011 which reincorporated in Nevada 12/13/2016

GALAXY ENTMT GROUP LTD (HONG KONG)
ADR agreement terminated 09/24/2015
Each Sponsored ADR for Ordinary exchanged for $36.937497 cash

GALAXY FD (MA)
Trust terminated 11/23/2005
Details not available

GALAXY FD INC (NY)
Dissolved by proclamation 6/24/81

GALAXY FOODS CO (DE)
Each share old Common 1¢ par exchanged for (0.14285714) share new Common 1¢ par 02/12/1999
Name changed to Galaxy Nutritional Foods Inc. 11/16/2000
(See Galaxy Nutritional Foods Inc.)

GALAXY GRAPHITE CORP (BC)
Recapitalized as Global Copper Group Inc. 02/26/2015
Each share Common no par exchanged for (0.25) share Common no par
Global Copper Group Inc. name changed to Cobalt Power Group Inc. 10/24/2016

GALAXY GROUP INC (DE)
Name changed to Quest International Equities, Inc. 10/11/1983
Quest International Equities, Inc. name changed to Agri-Quest Mining, Inc. (DE) 11/27/1990 which reorganized in Nevada as New Century Media, Ltd. 09/01/1994 which name changed to LBU, Inc. 03/24/1995
(See LBU, Inc.)

GALAXY INDS LTD (BC)
Struck off register and declared dissolved for failure to file returns 04/30/1993

GALAXY INVT CORP (CO)
Name changed to Super Struct Building Systems, Inc. 3/2/89

GALAXY MINERALS INC (FL)
Stock Dividend - 20% payable 04/01/2005 to holders of record 03/31/2005 Ex date - 03/29/2005
Chapter 11 bankruptcy petition dismissed 03/01/2007
Stockholders' equity unlikely

GALAXY MINERALS LTD. (BC)
Recapitalized as Galaxy Copper Ltd. 03/20/1964
Each share Capital Stock no par exchanged for (0.5) share Capital Stock no par
Galaxy Copper Ltd. merged into United Bata Resources Ltd. 03/24/1969 which liquidated for Pan Ocean Oil Corp. 02/05/1971
(See Pan Ocean Oil Corp.)

GALAXY NUTRITIONAL FOODS INC (DE)
Merged into MW1 LLC 06/16/2009
Each share Common 1¢ par exchanged for $0.36 cash

GALAXY OIL CO (NV)
Company liquidated 2/13/91
Stockholders are unlikely to receive any liquidating distributions

GALAXY ONLINE INC (YT)
Reincorporated 01/31/2000
Place of incorporation changed from (ON) to (YT) 01/31/2000
Charter dissolved 07/05/2003

GALAXY SPORTS INC (BC)
Delisted from Toronto Venture Stock Exchange 06/20/2003

GALAXY VENTURES INC (DE)
Recapitalized as Minimally Invasive Surgery Corp. 06/23/1998
Each share Common $0.001 par exchanged for (0.0625) share Common $0.001 par
Minimally Invasive Surgery Corp. name changed to eCare Solutions, Inc. 03/23/2000

GALBREATH 1ST MTG INVTS (OH)
Name changed to Nationwide Real Estate Investors 07/24/1974
Nationwide Real Estate Investors acquired by Old Stone Corp. 02/20/1981
(See Old Stone Corp.)

GALCO LEASING SYS (NJ)
Charter declared void for non-payment of taxes 1/5/76

GALCONDA CORP NEW (DE)
Recapitalized as Jax International Inc. 12/3/96
Each share Common 10¢ par exchanged for (0.1) share Common 10¢ par
(See Jax International Inc.)

GALE & CO (MO)
Charter forfeited for failure to file reports 1/1/69

GALE FORCE PETE INC (CANADA)
Each share old Common no par exchanged for (0.02) share new Common no par 02/12/2010
Merged into Montana Exploration Corp. 09/22/2015
Each share new Common no par exchanged for (0.465) share Common no par
Note: Unexchanged certificates were cancelled and became without value 09/21/2018

GALE INDS INC (PA)
Out of business in August 1974
No stockholders' equity

GALEA LIFE SCIENCES INC (FL)
SEC revoked common stock registration 10/10/2008

GALEN HEALTH CARE INC (DE)
Common Stock Purchase Rights declared for Common stockholders were redeemed at $0.01 per right 09/01/1993 for holders of record 08/31/1993
Merged into Columbia Healthcare Corp. 09/01/1993
Each share Common 1¢ par exchanged for (0.775) share Common 1¢ par
Columbia Healthcare Corp. merged into Columbia/HCA Healthcare Corp. 02/10/1994 which name changed to HCA - The Healthcare Co. 05/25/2000 which name changed to HCA Inc. (Ctfs. dated after 06/29/2001) 06/29/2001
(See HCA Inc. (Ctfs. dated after 06/29/2001))

GALEN HLDGS PLC (IRELAND)
Name changed to Warner Chilcott PLC (Old) 06/28/2004
(See Warner Chilcott PLC (Old))

GALENA BIOPHARMA (DE)
Each share old Common $0.0001 par received distribution of (1) share RXi Pharmaceuticals Corp. (New) Common $0.0001 par payable

04/27/2012 to holders of record 04/23/2012
Each share old Common $0.0001 par exchanged for (0.05) share new Common $0.0001 par 11/14/2016
Recapitalized as SELLAS Life Sciences Group, Inc. 01/02/2018
Each share new Common $0.0001 par exchanged for (0.03333333) share Common $0.0001 par

GALENA CAP CORP (BC)
Each share old Common no par exchanged for (0.16666666) share new Common no par 07/18/2011
Recapitalized as Ferro Iron Ore Corp. (BC) 09/26/2012
Each share new Common no par exchanged for (0.25) share Common no par
Ferro Iron Ore Corp. (BC) reorganized in Ontario as Wolf Resource Development Corp. 07/19/2013 which name changed to Fura Emeralds Inc. 03/09/2015 which name changed to Fura Gems Inc. 04/11/2017

GALENA INTL RES LTD (BC)
Name changed to Aurelius Minerals Inc. 01/09/2017

GALENA MINING CO. (DE)
Charter forfeited for failure to maintain a registered agent in 1941

GALENA OIL CORP.
Acquired by Valvoline Oil Co. 00/00/1931
Details not available

GALENA-SIGNAL OIL CO.
Reorganized as Galena Oil Corp. 00/00/1929
Details not available

GALENICA AG (SWITZERLAND)
Name changed to Vifor Pharma AG 06/05/2017

GALES INDS INC (DE)
Name changed to Air Industries Group, Inc. (DE) 07/16/2007
Air Industries Group, Inc. (DE) reincorporated in Nevada 09/03/2013

GALESBURG-COULTER DISK CO.
Merged into Borg-Warner Corp. (IL) in 1928
Details not available

GALEX MINES LTD (ON)
Charter cancelled for failure to pay taxes and file returns 03/07/1977

GALEY & LORD INC (DE)
Plan of reorganization under Chapter 11 Federal Bankruptcy Code effective 03/05/2004
No old Common stockholders' equity
Chapter 11 bankruptcy proceedings converted to Chapter 7 on 11/29/2004
No new Common stockholders' equity

GALICO RES INC (BC)
Name changed to Image Data International Corp. (BC) 01/25/1993
Image Data International Corp. (BC) reincorporated in Ontario 06/10/1993
(See Image Data International Corp.)

GALIGHER CO. (UT)
Acquired by Baker Oil Tools, Inc. 10/01/1969
Details not available

GALILEAN RES CORP (BC)
Recapitalized as New Fibers International Ltd. 07/16/1987
Each share Common no par exchanged for (0.5) share Common no par
(See New Fibers International Ltd.)

GALILEO CORP (DE)
Name changed 9/19/96
Common 1¢ par split (2) for (1) by issuance of (1) additional share 5/15/87
Name changed from Galileo Electro-Optics Corp. to Galileo Corp. 9/19/96
Name changed to Netoptix Corp. 10/1/99
Netoptix Corp. merged into Corning Inc. 5/12/2000

GALILEO INTL INC (DE)
Issue Information - 31,998,000 shares COM offered at $24.50 per share on 07/24/1997
Merged into Cendant Corp. 10/1/2001
Each share Common 1¢ par exchanged for (1.328) shares Common 1¢ par and $4.081097 cash
Cendant Corp. reorganized as Avis Budget Group, Inc. 9/1/2006

GALILEO PETE LTD (BC)
Each share old Common no par exchanged for (0.33333333) share new Common no par 10/20/2014
Name changed to Galileo Exploration Ltd. 12/21/2016

GALILEO TECHNOLOGY LTD (ISRAEL)
Issue Information - 3,000,000 shares ORD offered at $17 per share on 07/28/1997
Ordinary ILS 0.01 par split (2) for (1) by issuance of (1) additional share payable 09/17/1999 to holders of record 09/09/1999
Merged into Marvell Technology Group Ltd. 01/21/2001
Each share Ordinary ILS 0.01 par exchanged for (0.674) share Common $0.002 par

GALIT RESOURCE CORP (BC)
Struck off register and declared dissolved for failure to file returns 06/11/1993

GALKENO MINES LTD. (ON)
Name changed to Canadian Northwest Mines & Oils Ltd. 06/13/1958
(See Canadian Northwest Mines & Oils Ltd.)

GALL R A RLTY INVTS (OH)
Voluntarily dissolved 09/12/1986
Details not available

GALLAGHER & BURTON, INC.
Dissolved in 1942
Details not available

GALLAGHER EXPLS LTD (CANADA)
Reincorporated 11/14/1986
Place of incorporation changed from (BC) to (Canada) 11/14/1986
Name changed to Gunnar Gold Inc. 12/29/1986
Gunnar Gold Inc. recapitalized as Gunnar Gold Mining Corp. 12/14/1988 which recapitalized as ATTN AVECA Entertainment Corp. 02/26/1992 which recapitalized as American Transportation Television Network, Inc. 03/04/1993
(See American Transportation Television Network, Inc.)

GALLAGHER RESH & DEV CO (CO)
Reincorporated under the laws of Nevada as Gallagher Research Corp. and Common $0.0001 par changed to $0.001 par 04/06/1999
Gallagher Research Corp. name changed to Vizario Inc. 05/25/2001
(See Vizario Inc.)

GALLAGHER RESH CORP (NV)
Common $0.001 par split (16) for (1) by issuance of (15) additional shares payable 04/16/1999 to holders of record 04/15/1999
Name changed to Vizario Inc. 05/25/2001
(See Vizario Inc.)

GALLAHAD PETE LTD (BC)
Common no par split (4) for (1) by issuance of (3) additional shares 04/16/1981
Merged into Backer Petroleum Corp. 12/30/1988
Each share Common no par exchanged for (3) shares Class A Common no par
(See Backer Petroleum Corp.)

GALLAHER GROUP PLC (UNITED KINGDOM)
Merged into Japan Tobacco Inc. 4/18/2007
Each Sponsored ADR for Ordinary 10p par exchanged for $90.74856 cash

GALLAHUE NAPLES CORP. (IN)
Name changed to Naples Co., Inc. 8/8/63
(See Naples Co., Inc.)

GALLAND LINEN SERVICE CO.
Merged into National Linen Service Corp. on a (5) for (6) basis in 1948
National Linen Service Corp. name changed to National Service Industries, Inc.
(See National Services Industries, Inc.)

GALLAND MERCANTILE LAUNDRY CO.
Name changed to Galland Linen Service Co. in 1945
Galland Linen Service Co. merged into National Linen Service Corp. in 1948 which name changed to National Service Industries, Inc. 12/14/64
(See National Service Industries, Inc.)

GALLANT GOLD MINES, LTD. (ON)
Charter revoked for failure to file reports and pay fees 12/28/1954

GALLANT GOLD MINES LTD (BC)
Merged into HLX Resources Ltd. 9/1/89
Each share Common no par exchanged for (0.2266) share Common no par
HLX Resources Ltd. recapitalized as Emperor Gold Corp. 3/30/92 which name changed to Emgold Mining Corp. 8/1/97

GALLATIN HOMES CORP (MT)
Merged into Wick Building Systems, Inc. 5/31/80
Each share Common 50¢ par exchanged for $5 cash

GALLATIN NATL BK (UNIONTOWN, PA)
Capital Stock $100 par changed to $10 par and (9) additional shares issued plus a 10% stock dividend paid 01/14/1957
Capital Stock $10 par changed to $20 par 03/02/1964
Capital Stock $20 par changed to $10 par and (1) additional share issued 04/30/1965
Stock Dividend - 50% 05/16/1956
Reorganized as GNB Corp. 02/24/1970
Each share Capital Stock $10 par exchanged for (1) share Common $10 par
GNB Corp. merged into Pennbancorp 12/31/1985 which merged into Integra Financial Corp. 01/26/1989 which merged into National City Corp. 05/03/1996 which was acquired by PNC Financial Services Group, Inc. 12/31/2008

GALLEON ENERGY INC (AB)
Class A Common no par split (3) for (2) by issuance of (0.5) additional share payable 06/23/2006 to holders of record 06/20/2006 Ex date - 06/16/2006
Class B Common no par reclassified as (1.86475) shares Class A Common no par 12/15/2008
Name changed to Guide Exploration Ltd. 11/04/2011
Guide Exploration Ltd. merged into Long Run Exploration Ltd. 10/29/2012
(See Long Run Exploration Ltd.)

GALLEON MNG LTD (BC)
Recapitalized as Pacific Galleon Mining Corp. 08/10/1993
Each share Common no par exchanged for (0.25) share Common no par
Pacific Galleon Mining Corp. recapitalized as Prospector International Resources Inc. 05/29/1998 which recapitalized as Prospector Consolidated Resources Inc. 09/11/2001 which recapitalized as Prospector Resources Corp. (BC) 01/31/2011 which reincorporated in Ontario as Rio2 Ltd. (Old) 04/28/2017 which merged into Rio2 Ltd. (New) 07/27/2018

GALLERIA GROUP, INC. (DE)
Charter cancelled and declared inoperative and void for non-payment of taxes 3/1/92

GALLERIA OPPORTUNITIES INC (AB)
Recapitalized as Galleria Opportunities Ltd. (AB) 04/10/2014
Each share Common no par exchanged for (0.2) share Common no par
Galleria Opportunities Ltd. (AB) reorganized in Ontario as QYOU Media Inc. 03/31/2017

GALLERIA OPPORTUNITIES LTD (AB)
Reorganized under the laws of Ontario as QYOU Media Inc. 03/31/2017
Each share Common no par exchanged for (0.5) share Common no par

GALLERIA RES INC (AB)
Recapitalized as Galleria Opportunities Inc. 11/13/2000
Each share Common no par exchanged for (0.2) share Common no par
Galleria Opportunities Inc. recapitalized as Galleria Opportunities Ltd. (AB) 04/10/2014 which reorganized in Ontario as QYOU Media Inc. 03/31/2017

GALLERY GOLD MINES LTD (AB)
Recapitalized as Gallery Resources Ltd. 06/04/1990
Each share Common no par exchanged for (0.2) share Common no par

GALLERY INVT CORP (DE)
Name changed to Anderson-Cook, Inc. (DE) 3/30/74
Anderson-Cook, Inc. (DE) reincorporated in (MI) 1/1/90
(See Anderson-Cook, Inc.)

GALLERY MGMT HLDG CORP (CO)
Reorganized as T5 Corp. 04/30/2012
Each share Common $0.001 par exchanged for (2) shares Common $0.001 par
(See T5 Corp.)

GALLERY OF HISTORY INC (NV)
Common $0.001 par changed to $0.0005 par and (1) additional share issued payable 01/08/1999 to holders of record 12/24/1998
Merged into New Gallery of History, Inc. 05/14/2010
Each share Common $0.0005 par exchanged for $0.50 cash

GALLERY RODEO INTL INC (CA)
Name changed to Sierra-Rockies Corp. (CA) 11/15/1996
Sierra-Rockies Corp. (CA) reorganized in Nevada as Alpha Nutraceuticals Inc. 01/29/2004 which recapitalized as Alpha Nutra, Inc. 02/08/2005 which name changed to China Broadband, Inc. 05/16/2007 which name changed to

YOU On Demand Holdings, Inc. 04/05/2011 which name changed to Wecast Network, Inc. 11/14/2016 which name changed to Seven Stars Cloud Group, Inc. 07/17/2017

GALLIANO INTL LTD (DE)
Common $0.001 par split (5) for (1) by issuance of (4) additional shares payable 08/02/1999 to holders of record 07/31/1999
Reorganized under the laws of Florida as Resort Clubs International, Inc. 10/27/2004
Each share Common $0.001 par exchanged for (0.002) share Common $0.0001 par
Resort Clubs International, Inc. recapitalized as pH Environmental Inc. 02/27/2012 which name changed to TNI BioTech, Inc. 05/14/2012 which name changed to Immune Therapeutics, Inc. 12/11/2014

GALLIARD RES CORP (BC)
Name changed to Novo Resources Corp. 06/29/2011

GALLIC ENERGY LTD (AB)
Each share old Class A Common no par exchanged for (0.125) share new Class A Common no par 07/29/2009
Merged into Petromanas Energy Inc. 01/04/2013
Each share new Class A Common no par exchanged for (0.3736) share Common no par
Petromanas Energy Inc. recapitalized as PMI Resources Ltd. 06/14/2016 which name changed to PentaNova Energy Corp. 06/05/2017 which recapitalized as CruzSur Energy Corp. 09/04/2018

GALLO ELECTRONICS CORP. (NY)
Adjudicated bankrupt 3/10/65
Common Stock is worthless

GALLO INDS INC (NY)
Completely liquidated 08/29/1969
Each share Common 10¢ par exchanged for first and final distribution of (0.134084) share Di Giorgio Corp. Common $2.50 par
(See Di Giorgio Corp.)

GALLO PET SUPPLIES, INC. (NY)
Charter cancelled and proclaimed dissolved for failure to pay taxes and file reports 12/15/75

GALLOWAY CHIBOUGAMAU MINES LTD. (ON)
Charter cancelled and company declared dissolved for default in filing returns 12/30/1970

GALLOWAY ENERGY INC (NV)
SEC revoked common stock registration 06/14/2011

GALLOWAY OIL & GAS INC (NV)
Name changed to Relay Capital Corp. 12/23/2004
(See Relay Capital Corp.)

GALOOB TOYS INC (DE)
Reincorporated 8/27/87
Name changed 11/6/96
Common no par split (3) for (2) by issuance of (0.5) additional share 6/24/86
State of incorporation changed from (CA) to (DE) 8/27/87
Common no par changed to 1¢ par 8/29/87
Conv. Exchangeable Depositary Preferred called for redemption 6/10/96
Conv. Exchangeable Preferred $1 par called for redemption 6/10/96
Name changed from Galoob Lewis Toys Inc. to Galoob Toys, Inc. 11/6/96
Secondary Offering - 2,392,866 shares COM offered at $28.125 per share on 11/13/1996
Merged into Hasbro Inc. 11/2/98

Each share Common 1¢ par exchanged for $12 cash

GALORE GOLD MINES, LTD. (ON)
Merged into Associated Porcupine Mines Ltd. 11/05/1968
Each share Capital Stock $1 par exchanged for (0.007329) share Capital Stock no par
Associated Porcupine Mines Ltd. merged into American Reserve Mining Corp. 02/27/1989 which recapitalized as AMI Resources Inc. 12/21/1994 which name changed to Ashanti Sankofa Inc. 01/19/2017

GALT & TAGGART CAP (GEORGIA)
Name changed to Liberty Consumer JSC 12/12/2008

GALT FINL CORP (CO)
Recapitalized as Capital Growth Holdings Ltd. 3/3/97
Each share Common $0.0001 par exchanged for (1/60) share Common $0.001 par
Capital Growth Holdings Ltd. name changed to MicroCap Financial Services, Inc. 11/5/98 which name changed to GlobalNet Financial.Com, Inc. 4/16/99
(See GlobalNet Financial.Com, Inc.)

GALT MALLEABLE IRON LTD. (ON)
Common no par split (4) for (1) by issuance of (3) additional shares 02/10/1967
Common no par split (5) for (4) by issuance of (0.25) additional share 06/28/1971
Common no par reclassified as Conv. Class A Common no par 05/30/1975
Name changed to Galtaco Inc. 07/27/1977
Galtaco Inc. recapitalized as Strategic Value Corp. 02/21/1997
(See Strategic Value Corp.)

GALTACO INC (ON)
Conv. Class A Common no par reclassified as Common no par 11/19/1979
Conv. Class B Common no par reclassified as Common no par 11/19/1979
Recapitalized as Strategic Value Corp. 02/21/1997
Each share Common no par exchanged for (0.2) share Common no par
(See Strategic Value Corp.)

GALTECH INC. (UT)
Name changed to Galtech Semiconductor Materials Corp. in June 1994

GALTECH SEMICONDUCTOR MATERIALS CORP (UT)
Each share old Common $0.00025 par exchanged for (0.05) share new Common $0.00025 par 02/24/1995
SEC revoked common stock registration 03/13/2013

GALTON BIOMETRICS INC (DE)
Each share old Common $0.0001 par exchanged for (0.01) share new Common $0.0001 par 11/09/2004
SEC revoked common stock registration 04/01/2013

GALVANIC APPLIED SCIENCES INC (AB)
Acquired by 1756349 Alberta Ltd. 09/20/2013
Each share Common no par exchanged for $1.70 cash

GALVEST INC (NV)
Each share Common $0.001 par exchanged for (0.01) share Common 10¢ par 07/14/1989
Acquired by PrimeEnergy Corp. 01/29/1993
Each share Common 10¢ par exchanged for $0.50 cash

GALVESTON CORP (TX)
Liquidation completed

Each share Common $5 par received initial distribution of $10 cash 03/22/1988
Each share Common $5 par exchanged for second and final distribution of $2.875 cash 10/15/1988

GALVESTON HOUSTON CO (DE)
Each share Common no par exchanged for (5) shares Common $5 par in 1941
Common $5 par changed to $2 par 6/15/66
Common $2 par changed to $1 par 3/28/68
Common $1 par changed to 50¢ par and (1) additional share issued 5/20/76
Common 50¢ par changed to 33-1/3¢ par and (0.5) additional share issued 6/7/78
Common 33-1/3¢ par changed to 25¢ par and (0.5) additional share issued 7/25/80
Stock Dividend - 10% 12/28/51
Merged into GHX Acquisition Co. 2/28/95
Each share Common 25¢ par exchanged for $2.25 cash

GALVESTON HOUSTON ELECTRIC CO.
Reorganized as Galveston-Houston Co. in 1936
Each share Preferred exchanged for (0.25) share Common no par
Each share Common exchanged for (0.01) share Common no par
(See Galveston-Houston Co.)

GALVESTON MINES LTD. (BC)
Capital Stock 50¢ par changed to no par 04/01/1978
Name changed to Galveston Petroleums Ltd. 05/18/1978
Galveston Petroleums Ltd. name changed to Galveston Resources Ltd. 07/29/1986 which merged into Corona Corp. 07/01/1988 which recapitalized as International Corona Corp. 06/11/1991
(See International Corona Corp.)

GALVESTON OIL & GAS INC (DE)
Recapitalized as Topclick International, Inc. 2/5/99
Each share Common $0.001 par exchanged for (0.1) share Common $0.001 par
Topclick International, Inc. recapitalized as Datalogic International Inc. 7/30/2001

GALVESTON PETES LTD (BC)
Under plan of merger name changed to Galveston Resources Ltd. 07/29/1986
Galveston Resources Ltd. merged into Corona Corp. 07/01/1988 which recapitalized as International Corona Corp. 06/11/1991
(See International Corona Corp.)

GALVESTON RES LTD (BC)
Common no par split (3) for (1) by issuance of (2) additional shares 03/27/1987
Each share Common no par exchanged for (0.66666666) share Class A Subordinate no par 11/30/1987
Each share Class A Subordinate no par received distribution of (0.5) share Conv. Class B no par 12/05/1987
Merged into Corona Corp. 07/01/1988
Each share Class A Subordinate no par exchanged for (0.43) share Class A Subordinate no par and (1/23) Class A Subordinate Stock Purchase Warrant expiring 6/30/90
Each share Conv. Class B no par exchanged for (0.43) share Conv. Class B no par and (0.04347826) Class A Subordinate Stock Purchase Warrant expiring 06/30/1990
Corona Corp. recapitalized as International Corona Corp. 06/11/1991
(See International Corona Corp.)

GALVESTON WHARF CO.
Sold to the City of Galveston, Texas in 1940

GALVESTONS STEAKHOUSE CORP (DE)
Name changed to Steakhouse Partners, Inc. 08/09/1999
(See Steakhouse Partners, Inc.)

GALVIN MANUFACTURING CORP. (IL)
Name changed to Motorola, Inc. (IL) 00/00/1947
Motorola, Inc. (IL) reincorporated in Delaware 05/18/1973 which recapitalized as Motorola Solutions, Inc. 01/04/2011

GALWAY GOLD INC (NB)
Reincorporated under the laws of Ontario 08/11/2015

GALWAY METALS INC (NB)
Each share old Common no par exchanged for (0.33333333) share new Common no par 09/16/2013
Reincorporated under the laws of Ontario 07/21/2015

GALWAY RES LTD (BC)
Plan of arrangement effective 12/21/2012
Each share Common no par exchanged for (1) share Galway Gold Inc. Common no par, (1) share Galway Metals Inc. Common no par and $2.05 cash
(See each company's listing)

GALYANS TRADING INC (IN)
Issue Information - 6,500,000 shares COM offered at $19 per share on 06/26/2001
Merged into Dick's Sporting Goods, Inc. 7/29/2004
Each share Common no par exchanged for $16.75 cash

GAM AVALON LANCELOT LLC (DE)
Completely liquidated 05/31/2007
Details not available

GAM RAD INC (MI)
Common $1 par split (2) for (1) by issuance of (1) additional share 04/15/1970
Under plan of merger each share Common 10¢ par held by holders of (2,499) or fewer exchanged for $0.01 cash 09/03/1992
Charter declared inoperative and void for failure to file reports 07/15/2009

GAMA COMPUTER CORP (DE)
Name changed to Bluebook International Holding Co. 11/07/2001
(See Bluebook International Holding Co.)

GAMAR ELECTROMATIC CORP (NY)
Charter cancelled and proclaimed dissolved for failure to pay taxes 03/25/1981

GAMBIER EXPL LTD (BC)
Recapitalized as Breakwater Resources Ltd. (BC) 06/23/1981
Each share Common no par exchanged for (0.5) share Common no par
Breakwater Resources Ltd. (BC) reincorporated in Canada 05/11/1992
(See Breakwater Resources Ltd.)

GAMBINO APPAREL GROUP INC (DE)
Recapitalized as Patient Portal Technologies, Inc. 9/1/2006
Each share Common $0.001 par exchanged for (0.1) share Common $0.001 par

GAMBIT FINL INC (NV)
Each share Common 1¢ par exchanged for (0.5) share Common 2¢ par 4/18/85

Name changed to Worth Corp. (NV) 2/11/87
Worth Corp. (NV) reincorporated in Delaware 7/31/92 which name changed to Krauses Furniture Inc. 12/8/94
(See Krauses Furniture Inc.)

GAMBLE BROS INC (KY)
Common $5 par changed to $2.50 par and (1) additional share issued 9/15/60
Preferred $25 par called for redemption 3/11/66
Stock Dividend - 10% 9/24/57
Merged into Walter (Jim) Corp. 5/10/72
Each share Common $2.50 par exchanged for (1.58) shares Common 16-2/3¢ par
(See Walter (Jim) Corp.)

GAMBLE-ROBINSON CO.
Merged into Pacific Gamble Robinson Co. in 1942
Details not available

GAMBLE SKOGMO INC (DE)
Each share Class A Common no par exchanged for (6) shares Common $5 par 00/00/1946
Each share Class B Common no par exchanged for (6) shares Common $5 par 00/00/1946
5% Preferred $50 par called for redemption 04/30/1960
Merged into Wickes Companies, Inc. 08/13/1980
Each share Common $5 par exchanged for (0.75) share Common $2.50 par and $33 cash
Merged into Wickes Companies, Inc. 01/26/1985
Each share $1.60 Conv. Preferred $5 par exchanged for (4.044723) shares Common 10¢ par
Each share $1.75 Conv. Preferred $40 par exchanged for (4.320054) shares Common 10¢ par
Wickes Companies, Inc. name changed to Collins & Aikman Group Inc. 07/17/1992
(See Collins & Aikman Group Inc.)

GAMBRILL (C.A.) MANUFACTURING CO., INC.
Assets sold in 1926
No stockholders' equity

GAMBRO A B (SWEDEN)
ADR agreement terminated 3/6/98
Each ADR for Ordinary SKr 20 par exchanged for $21.0396 cash

GAMCO GLOBAL GOLD NAT RES & INCOME TR BY GABELLI (DE)
6.625% Preferred Ser. A $0.001 par called for redemption at $25 plus $0.35425 accrued dividends on 06/12/2013
Name changed to GAMCO Global Gold, Natural Resources & Income Trust 03/28/2014

GAMCO INVESTORS INC (NY)
Each share Class A Common $0.001 par received distribution of (0.01493) share Teton Advisors, Inc. Class B Common $0.001 par payable 03/20/2009 to holders of record 03/10/2009
Each share Class A Common $0.001 par received distribution of $3.20 principal amount of 0% Subordinated Debentures due 12/31/2015 and $0.80 cash payable 12/31/2010 to holders of record 12/15/2010
Reincorporated under the laws of Delaware 11/22/2013

GAMCO MATHERS FD (DE)
Trust terminated 08/31/2018
Each share Class AAA $0.001 par received $4.77 cash

GAMCO NAT RES GOLD & INCOME TR BY GABELLI (DE)
Name changed to GAMCO Natural Resources, Gold & Income Trust 03/28/2014

GAME A TRON CORP (DE)
Charter cancelled and declared inoperative and void for non-payment of taxes 6/24/91

GAME FACE GAMING INC (FL)
Name changed to Face Up Entertainment Group, Inc. 04/27/2012

GAME FINL CORP (MN)
Common 1¢ par split (5) for (4) by issuance of (0.25) additional share payable 06/21/1996 to holders of record 06/07/1996
Stock Dividend - 10% 09/26/1995
Merged into Viad Corp. 12/12/1997
Each share Common 1¢ par exchanged for (0.5808) share Common $1.50 par

GAME GROUP PLC (ENGLAND)
ADR agreement terminated 10/05/2015
No ADR's remain outstanding

GAME TECHNOLOGIES INC (NV)
Name changed to digiMedical Solutions, Inc. 7/10/2006

GAME TRADING TECHNOLOGIES INC (DE)
Each share old Common $0.0001 par exchanged for (0.5) share new Common $0.0001 par 02/15/2011
Plan of reorganization under Chapter 11 Federal Bankruptcy proceedings effective 05/03/2012
No stockholders' equity

GAMECOM INC (TX)
Reincorporated 02/04/2000
State of incorporation changed from (NV) to (TX) 02/04/2000
Name changed to VirTra Systems, Inc. (TX) 05/06/2002
VirTra Systems, Inc. (TX) reincorporated in Nevada as VirTra, Inc. 10/07/2016

GAMECORP LTD (ON)
Name changed to DealNet Capital Corp. 09/13/2012

GAMEHOST INCOME FD (AB)
Trust Units split (3) for (1) by issuance of (2) additional Units payable 04/25/2008 to holders of record 04/23/2008 Ex date - 04/21/2008
Reorganized as Gamehost Inc. 01/10/2011
Each Trust Unit exchanged for (1) share Common no par
Note: Unexchanged certificates were cancelled and became without value 01/10/2017

GAMERS GHOST INC (DE)
Name changed to Apparel Manufacturing Associates, Inc. 2/7/2006

GAMES INC (DE)
Each share Common $0.001 par received distribution of (0.25) share Lottery Corp. Restricted Common payable 12/29/2005 to holders of record 12/27/2005
Recapitalized as InQBate Corp. 10/06/2006
Each share Common $0.001 par exchanged for (0.1) share Common $0.001 par
(See InQBate Corp.)

GAMES NETWORK INC (CA)
Charter suspended for failure to file reports and pay fees 03/03/1986

GAMES TRADER INC (CANADA)
Name changed to GTR Group Inc. 6/29/99
GTR Group Inc. name changed to Mad Catz Interactive, Inc. 9/5/2001

GAMESA CORP TECHNOLOGICA S A (SPAIN)
Name changed to Siemens Gamesa Renewable Energy 07/05/2017

GAMESBORO COM INC (DE)
Each share old Common $0.0001 par exchanged for (0.07692307) share new Common $0.0001 par 08/21/2001
Name changed to PLP Holdings Inc. 03/31/2002
PLP Holdings Inc. name changed to Tonogold Resources, Inc. 09/13/2004

GAMESTAR ENTMT INC (NV)
Charter permanently revoked 01/01/2008

GAMESTATE ENTMT INC (NV)
Name changed to Quest Oil Corp. 9/16/2004

GAMESTOP CORP OLD (DE)
Issue Information - 18,055,555 shares CL A offered at $18 per share on 02/12/2002
Under plan of reorganization each share Class A Common $0.001 par and Class B Common $0.001 par automatically became (1) share GameStop Corp. (New) Class A Common $0.001 par or Class B Common $0.001 par respectively 10/08/2005

GAMETECH INTL INC (DE)
Plan of reorganization under Chapter 11 Federal Bankruptcy proceedings effective 12/28/2012
No stockholders' equity

GAMETEK INC (DE)
Chapter 7 bankruptcy proceedings terminated 10/27/2004
Stockholders' equity unlikely

GAMETEK SYS INC (BC)
Delisted from Vancouver Stock Exchange 01/10/1990

GAMETRONICS CORP (NV)
Name changed to Polymer Group Ltd. 02/07/1984

GAMEWEAVER COM INC (NV)
Name changed to Inform Media Group, Inc. 03/15/2002
Inform Media Group, Inc. name changed to Acquisition Media, Inc. 08/12/2002 which name changed to Actionview International, Inc. 08/20/2003 which recapitalized as AVEW Holdings, Inc. 07/31/2015

GAMEWELL CO. (MA)
Stock Dividend - 200% 12/18/44
Acquired by Bliss (E.W.) Co. 12/1/59
Each share Common no par exchanged for (0.5) share $1.80 Conv. Preferred no par and (1) share Common $1 par
Bliss (E.W.) Co. merged into Gulf & Western Industries, Inc. (DE) 1/11/68 which name changed to Gulf + Western Inc. 5/1/86 which name changed to Paramount Communications Inc. 6/5/89 which merged into Viacom Inc. (Old) 7/7/94
(See Viacom Inc. (Old))

GAMEX INDS INC (DE)
Name changed to Global Gaming Technology, Inc. 11/23/1988
Global Gaming Technology, Inc. recapitalized as Left Right Marketing Technology, Inc. 07/30/2003 which name changed to Strategic Gaming Investments, Inc. 04/21/2006 which recapitalized as Amerigo Energy, Inc. 09/11/2008 which name changed to Quest Solution, Inc. 06/10/2014

GAMEZNFLIX INC (NV)
Each share old Common $0.001 par exchanged for (0.001) share new Common $0.001 par 09/06/2007
Each share new Common $0.001 par exchanged again for (0.0001) share new Common $0.001 par 04/09/2009
Name changed to TBC Global News Network, Inc. 07/30/2009
TBC Global News Network, Inc. name changed to InCapta, Inc. 11/10/2015

GAMIN RES INC (BC)
Recapitalized as Mineral Park Mining Corp. 05/24/1989
Each share Common no par exchanged for (0.2) share Common no par
Mineral Park Mining Corp. recapitalized as I.M.P. Industrial Park Mining Corp. 03/02/1994 which name changed to Crystal Graphite Corp. 11/06/2000
(See Crystal Graphite Corp.)

GAMING & ENTMT GROUP INC (UT)
Voluntarily dissolved 12/08/2008
Details not available

GAMING & TECHNOLOGY INC (NV)
Each share old Common 10¢ par exchanged for (0.2) share new Common 10¢ par 04/02/1984
Name changed to United Gaming, Inc. 12/05/1988
United Gaming, Inc. name changed to Alliance Gaming Corp. 12/19/1994 which name changed to Bally Technologies, Inc. 03/08/2006
(See Bally Technologies, Inc.)

GAMING CORP OF AMER (MN)
Merged into Grand Casinos, Inc. 11/30/1995
Each share Common 2¢ par exchanged for (0.19864) share Common 1¢ par
Grand Casinos, Inc. merged into Park Place Entertainment Corp. 12/31/1998 which name changed to Caesars Entertainment, Inc. 01/05/2004
(See Caesars Entertainment, Inc.)

GAMING DEVICES FDG INC (NJ)
Name changed to Capital Gaming International Inc. 03/19/1993
(See Capital Gaming International Inc.)

GAMING LOTTERY CORP LTD (BRITISH VIRGIN ISLANDS)
Reorganized 01/17/1997
Reorganized from Gaming Lottery Corp. (ON) to under the laws of British Virgin Islands as Gaming Lottery Corp. Ltd. 01/17/1997
Each share old Common no par exchanged for (1/7) share new Common no par 07/10/1998
Name changed to GLC Ltd. 09/30/1998
GLC Ltd. name changed to Galaxiworld.com Ltd. 08/30/1999
(See Galaxiworld.com Ltd.)

GAMING NATION INC (ON)
Acquired by OC Special Opportunities Fund, L.P. 11/30/2017
Each share Common no par exchanged for $0.95 cash
Note: Unexchanged certificates will be cancelled and become without value 11/30/2023

GAMING VENTURE CORP U S A NEW (NV)
Recapitalized as Kuhlman Co., Inc. 06/09/2005
Each share Common $0.001 par exchanged for (0.2) share Common $0.001 par
(See Kuhlman Co., Inc.)

GAMING VENTURE CORP U S A OLD (NV)
Name changed to Casino Journal Publishing Group Inc. 04/20/1998
Casino Journal Publishing Group Inc. recapitalized as TableMAX Corp. 08/19/2008

GAMING WORLD INTL LTD (DE)
Charter dissolved 02/09/2004

GAMMA BIOLOGICALS INC (TX)
Common 10¢ par split (4) for (3) by issuance of (1/3) additional share 4/13/81
Common 10¢ par split (3) for (2) by issuance of (0.5) additional share 10/19/82
Merged into Immucor, Inc. 10/30/98
Each share Common 10¢ par exchanged for $5.40 cash

GAMMA INDL SCIENCES LTD (AB)
Struck off register for failure to file annual returns 02/01/1992

GAMMA INTL LTD (DE)
Each share Common 3¢ par exchanged for (0.25) share Common 1¢ par 06/24/1994
Name changed to American Gaming & Entertainment Ltd. 12/12/1994
American Gaming & Entertainment Ltd. recapitalized as Wow Entertainment, Inc. 10/13/2000 which name changed to Fortune Diversified Industries, Inc. (DE) 08/16/2001 which reorganized in Indiana 06/02/2005 which name changed to Fortune Industries, Inc. 04/17/2006
(See Fortune Industries, Inc.)

GAMMA MED PRODS INC (DE)
Charter cancelled and declared inoperative and void for non-payment of taxes 3/1/93

GAMMA PHARMACEUTICALS INC (DE)
SEC revoked common stock registration 10/01/2013

GAMMA PROCESS INC (NY)
Charter cancelled and proclaimed dissolved for failure to pay taxes 3/26/80

GAMMA RES INC (DE)
Name changed to United Medicorp, Inc. 07/10/1989
United Medicorp, Inc. name changed to UMC, Inc. 09/10/2007

GAMMACAN INTL INC (DE)
SEC revoked common stock registration 07/16/2012

GAMMON GOLD INC (QC)
Reincorporated under the laws of Ontario as AuRico Gold Inc. 06/14/2011
AuRico Gold Inc. merged into Alamos Gold Inc. (New) 07/06/2015

GAMMON INDIA LTD (INDIA)
Sponsored Reg. S GDR's for Ordinary split (5) for (1) by issuance of (4) additional GDR's payable 03/29/2005 to holders of record 03/21/2005
GDR agreement terminated 03/27/2015
No GDR's remain outstanding

GAMMON LAKE RES INC (QC)
Name changed to Gammon Gold Inc. (QC) 06/19/2007
Gammon Gold Inc. (QC) reincorporated in Ontario as AuRico Gold Inc. 06/14/2011 which merged into Alamos Gold Inc. (New) 07/06/2015

GAMOGEN INC (NY)
Each share old Common 1¢ par exchanged for (0.5) share new Common 1¢ par 12/15/2000
Name changed to CDMI Productions, Inc. (NY) 09/13/2002
CDMI Productions, Inc. (NY) reincorporated in Delaware as Gener8Xion Entertainment, Inc. 01/14/2005
(See Gener8Xion Entertainment, Inc.)

GAMSAN RES LTD (AB)
Struck off register for failure to file annual returns 01/01/1992

GAMUT AGENCY INC. (NY)
Name changed to Northwood Corp. 3/16/85
Northwood Corp. name changed to Allied Scale Corp. 2/16/86 which name changed to InAmerica Corp. (N.Y.) 11/21/86 which reincorporated in Oklahoma 8/31/88

GAMUT SYS INC (DE)
Acquired by Management Data Corp. 05/05/1970
Each share Common 2¢ par exchanged for (0.145) share Common 50¢ par
Management Data Corp. name changed to MDC Corp. (PA) 03/20/1973 which name changed to Bouton Corp. (PA) 07/14/1982 which reincorporated in Delaware 06/29/1992
(See Bouton Corp.)

GAN COPPER MINES LTD (ON)
Charter cancelled and declared dissolved for failure to file returns and pay fees 07/27/1976

GANAS CORP (DE)
Name changed to Green Automotive Company Corp. (DE) 01/28/2010
Green Automotive Company Corp. (DE) reincorporated in Nevada as Green Automotive Co. 09/30/2011

GANDA SILVER MINES LTD (ON)
Charter cancelled and declared dissolved for failure to file returns and pay fees 03/16/1976

GANDALF TECHNOLOGIES INC (ON)
Plan of Arrangement under Companies' Creditors Arrangement Act effective 01/05/1998
No stockholders' equity

GANDER MTN CO (MN)
Issue Information - 5,725,000 shares COM offered at $16 per share on 04/20/2004
Each share old Common 1¢ par exchanged for (1) share new Common 1¢ par to reflect a (1) for (30,000) reverse split followed by a (30,000) for (1) forward split 01/14/2010
Note: Holders of (29,999) or fewer pre-split shares received $5.15 cash per share
Each share new Common 1¢ par exchanged again for (1) share new Common 1¢ par to reflect a (1) for (500,000) reverse split followed by a (500,000) for (1) forward split 01/25/2011
Note: In effect holders received $5.15 cash per share and public interest was eliminated

GANDER MTN INC (DE)
Stock Dividend - 10% 11/11/91
Plan of reorganization under Chapter 11 Federal Bankruptcy Code effective 2/3/97
Each share Common 1¢ par received $0.1543 cash
Note: Certificates were not required to be surrendered and are now valueless

GANDY BRIDGE CO.
In process of liquidation in 1945
Details not available

GANE ENERGY LTD (AB)
Recapitalized as Northstar Energy Corp. 7/14/86
Each share Common no par exchanged for (0.1) share Common no par
Northstar Energy Corp. merged into Devon Energy Corp. (OK) 12/11/98 which merged into Devon Energy Corp. (New) (DE) 8/17/99

GANE PETE LTD (AB)
Reorganized as Gane Energy Corp. Ltd. 8/25/82
Each share Common no par exchanged for (1) share Common no par
Gane Petroleum Corp. Ltd. recapitalized as Northstar Energy Corp. 7/14/86 which merged into Devon Energy Corp. (OK) 12/11/98 which merged into Devon Energy Corp. (New) (DE) 8/17/99

GANKIT CORP (NV)
Name changed to Nhale Inc. 06/13/2014

GANNAWAY INTERNATIONAL CORP. (NV)
Charter revoked for failure to file reports and pay fees 3/7/60

GANNETT INC OLD (DE)
Reincorporated 05/29/1972
Class B Conv. Preferred no par called for redemption 05/01/1967
Recapitalized 09/05/1967
Each share Part. Preferred exchanged for (20) shares Common $1 par
Each share Class A Common no par or Class B Common no par exchanged for (40) shares Common $1 par
Common $1 par split (3) for (2) by issuance of (0.5) additional share 10/06/1969
Common $1 par split (2) for (1) by issuance of (1) additional share 08/01/1972
Common $1 par split (3) for (2) by issuance of (0.5) additional share 01/05/1981
Common $1 par split (3) for (2) by issuance of (0.5) additional share 01/04/1984
Common $1 par split (2) for (1) by issuance of (1) additional share 01/05/1987
Common $1 par split (2) for (1) by issuance of (1) additional share payable 10/06/1997 to holders of record 09/12/1997 Ex date - 10/07/1997
State of incorporation changed from (NY) to (DE) 05/29/2012
Each share Common $1 par received distribution of (0.5) share Gannett Co., Inc. (New) Common $1 par payable 06/26/2015 to holders of record 06/22/2015 Ex date - 06/29/2015
Name changed to TEGNA Inc. 06/26/2015

GANOT CORP (NY)
Merged into Midbar, Inc. 06/27/1985
Each share Common 10¢ par exchanged for $10.25 cash

GANSCHOW (WILLIAM) CO.
Merged into Gears & Forging, Inc. in 1928
Details not available

GANT (J.W.) FUND, INC. (MD)
Voluntarily dissolved 1/29/93
Details not available

GANTOS INC NEW (MI)
Each share old Common 1¢ par exchanged exchanged for (0.33333333) share new Common 1¢ par 07/21/1999
Reincorporated under the laws of Delaware as Kinder Holding Corp. and Common 1¢ par changed to $0.0001 par 09/26/2008
Kinder Holding Corp. recapitalized as Intiva BioPharma Inc. 11/29/2017 which name changed to Nexien BioPharma Inc. 10/19/2018

GANTOS INC OLD (MI)
Reorganized as Gantos, Inc. (New) (MI) 04/03/1995
Each share Common 1¢ par exchanged for (0.5) share Common 1¢ par
Gantos, Inc. (New) (MI) reincorporated in Delaware as Kinder Holding Corp. 09/26/2008 which recapitalized as Intiva BioPharma Inc. 11/29/2017 which name changed to Nexien BioPharma Inc. 10/19/2018

GAOFENG GOLD CORP (NV)
Each share old Common $0.001 par exchanged for (1.5) shares new Common $0.001 par 06/17/2004
Reorganized as Sun Oil & Gas Corp. 01/03/2005
Each share Common $0.001 par exchanged for (2.6) shares Common $0.001 par
Sun Oil & Gas Corp. recapitalized as China 3C Group 12/20/2005 which recapitalized as Yosen Group, Inc. 12/31/2012

GAP INC (CA)
Common 5¢ par split (2) for (1) by issuance of (1) additional share 01/02/1986
Common 5¢ par split (2) for (1) by issuance of (1) additional share 08/01/1986
Reincorporated under the laws of Delaware 05/31/1988

GAP INSTR CORP (NY)
SEC revoked common stock registration 07/23/2010

GAP STORES INC (CA)
Common 5¢ par split (3) for (2) by issuance of (0.5) additional share 01/31/1983
Name changed to Gap, Inc. (CA) 05/31/1985
Gap, Inc. (CA) reincorporated in Delaware 05/31/1988

GAR LTD (ON)
Reincorporated under the laws of British Columbia as Netcoins Holdings Inc. 08/30/2019

GAR MESA OIL & GAS CORP. (CO)
Charter revoked for failure to file reports and pay fees 10/25/60

GAR WOOD INDS INC (MI)
Each share Common $3 par exchanged for (0.2) share 5% Preferred $10 par and (1) share Common $1 par 00/00/1941
Acquired by Sargent Industries, Inc. (DE) 04/02/1970
Each share 4-1/2% Conv. Preferred $50 par exchanged for (1) share 4-1/2% Conv. Preferred no par
Each share Common $1 par exchanged for (1) share Common no par
(See Sargent Industries, Inc. (DE))

GARAN INC (VA)
Common $1 par split (3) for (2) by issuance of (0.5) additional share 9/12/68
Common $1 par split (9) for (5) by issuance of (0.8) additional share 12/29/71
Common $1 par changed to no par and (1) additional share issued 12/7/92
Stock Dividends - 20% 12/29/72; 20% 12/2/83
Merged into Berkshire Hathaway Inc. 9/4/2002
Each share Common no par exchanged for $60 cash

GARB-OIL CORP. OF AMERICA (UT)
Name changed to Garb Oil & Power Corp. 10/31/1985

GARBALIZER MACHY CORP (UT)
Recapitalized as RecycleNet Corp. 04/01/1999
Each (1.5) shares Common 1¢ par exchanged for (1) share Common 1¢ par
RecycleNet Corp. recapitalized as Maydao Corp. 01/20/2010
(See Maydao Corp.)

GARBELL HLDGS LTD (ON)
10.50% 1st Preference $5 par called for redemption at $5 plus $0.232600 accrued dividends on 12/10/2008

Public interest eliminated

GARBER (A.L.) CO., INC. (DE)
Merged into Wheelabrator-Frye Inc. 9/18/73
Each share Common $1 par exchanged for $8 cash

GARBER (A.L.) CO., INC. (NJ)
Reincorporated under the laws of Delaware and Common $5 par changed to $1 par 5/31/72
Garber (A.L.) Co., Inc. (DE) merged into Wheelabrator-Frye Inc. 9/18/73 which merged into Signal Companies, Inc. 2/1/83 which merged into Allied-Signal Inc. 9/19/85 which name changed to AlliedSignal Inc. 4/26/93 which name changed to Honeywell International Inc. 12/1/99

GARBO INDS LTD (BC)
Reorganized as AISI Research Corp. 03/29/1989
Each share Class A Common no par exchanged for (2) shares Class A Common no par
(See AISI Research Corp.)

GARCIA CORP (NJ)
Name changed to TGC Inc. 12/31/1980
TGC Inc. recapitalized as Equion Corp. 01/31/1985
(See Equion Corp.)

GARCIAS SCOTTSDALE INC (DE)
Name changed to Famous Restaurants Inc. 07/11/1985
(See Famous Restaurants Inc.)

GARCIS U S A INC (CO)
Company reported out of business 05/18/2004
No stockholders' equity

GARDA WORLD SEC CORP (CANADA)
Acquired by Crepax Acquisition Corp. 11/14/2012
Each share Class A no par exchanged for $12 cash

GARDANT PHARMACEUTICALS INC (NV)
Each share Common $0.001 par received distribution of (1.7) Accura Pharma PLC Restricted share payable 05/15/2006 to holders of record 04/21/2006
Acquired by Switch Pharma Ltd. 12/30/2006
Each share Common $0.001 par exchanged for approximately (1) Restricted share

GARDE MNG EXPL INC (CANADA)
Recapitalized as Orezone Resources Inc. 11/29/1996
Each share Class A Common no par exchanged for (0.2) share Class A Common no par
(See Orezone Resources Inc.)

GARDEN BOTANIKA INC (WA)
Assets sold for the benefit of creditors 4/4/2001
No stockholders' equity

GARDEN CITY BUILDING & LOAN ASSOCIATION (KS)
Charter expired by time limitation 7/8/35

GARDEN CITY TR CO (NEWTON, MA)
Merged into University Bank & Trust Co. (Chestnut Hill, MA) 01/01/1974
Each share Common $6 par exchanged for (0.2824) share Common $10 par
(See University Bank & Trust Co. (Chestnut Hill, MA))

GARDEN COM INC (DE)
Issue Information - 4,100,000 shares COM offered at $12 per share on 09/15/1999
Liquidation completed
Each share Common 1¢ par exchanged for initial distribution of $0.20 cash 6/28/2001
Each share Common 1¢ par received second distribution of $0.04 cash payable 12/4/2001 to holders of record 6/28/2001 Ex date - 12/7/2001
Each share Common 1¢ par received third and final distribution of $0.01917028 cash payable 8/6/2004 to holders of record 8/5/2004 Ex date - 8/9/2004

GARDEN FRESH RESTAURANT CORP (DE)
Merged into GF Holdings, Inc. 03/10/2004
Each share Common 1¢ par exchanged for $16.35 cash

GARDEN GROVE COMMUNITY BANK (GARDEN GROVE, CA)
Closed by state banking regulators 6/1/84

GARDEN LAKE RES LTD (ON)
Recapitalized as GAR Ltd. (ON) 09/19/1997
Each share Common no par exchanged for (0.25) share Common no par
GAR Ltd. (ON) reincorporated in British Columbia as Netcoins Holdings Inc. 08/30/2018

GARDEN LD LTD (CA)
Class A no par and Class B no par reclassified as Common $1 par in November 1958
Name changed to Don The Beachcomber Enterprises 2/24/69
Don The Beachcomber Enterprises name changed to Getty Financial Corp. 8/10/72
(See Getty Financial Corp.)

GARDEN RIDGE CORP (DE)
Common 1¢ par split (2) for (1) by issuance of (1) additional share payable 06/28/1996 to holders of record 06/14/1996
Merged into GRDG Holdings LLC 02/02/2000
Each share Common 1¢ par exchanged for $11.50 cash

GARDEN SILK MILLS LTD (INDIA)
GDR agreement terminated 04/04/2011
Unexchanged Reg. S GDR's for Ordinary will be sold and the proceeds, if any, held for claim at an undetermined date

GARDEN ST BANCSHARES INC (NJ)
Common no par split (5) for (4) by issuance of (0.25) additional share 12/15/88
Common no par split (5) for (4) by issuance of (0.25) additional share 12/15/89
Stock Dividend - 12% 1/12/87
Merged into Summit Bancorporation 1/16/96
Each share Common no par exchanged for (1.08) shares Common no par
Summit Bancorporation merged into Summit Bancorp 3/1/96 which merged into FleetBoston Financial Corp. 3/1/2001 which merged into Bank of America Corp. 4/1/2004

GARDEN ST BK (CINNAMINSON, NJ)
Merged into Bank of New Jersey (Camden, NJ) 4/3/70
Each share Capital Stock $25 par exchanged for (2.75) shares Common $5 par
Bank of New Jersey (Camden, NJ) reorganized as Bancshares of New Jersey 12/30/72 which name changed to Northern National Corp. 5/28/81 which merged into Horizon Bancorp 10/1/83
(See Horizon Bancorp)

GARDEN ST INDS INC (DE)
Charter cancelled and declared inoperative and void for non-payment of taxes 3/1/75

GARDEN ST NATL BK (PARAMUS, NJ)
Reorganized 11/15/1974
Under plan of merger each share Common $10 par exchanged for (2.6286) shares Class B Common $5 par 02/01/1971
Location changed from Hackensack, NJ to Paramus, NJ 11/15/1974
Stock Dividend - 10% 04/27/1979
Acquired by Fidelity Union Bancorporation 7/7/80
Each share Class A Common $5 par exchanged for $48 cash
Each share Class B Common $5 par exchanged for $48 cash

GARDEN ST RACING ASSN (NJ)
In process of liquidation
Each share Common no par exchanged for initial distribution of (1) Garden State Racing Association Liquidation Trust Unit and $500 cash 04/10/1978
Note: Details on additional distribution(s), if any, are not available

GARDEN STATE BANK (HAWAIIAN GARDENS, CA)
Name changed to Commercial Bank of California (Hawaiian Gardens, CA) 08/01/1979
Commercial Bank of California (Hawaiian Gardens, CA) location changed to Los Angeles, CA 07/15/1980
(See Commercial Bank of California (Los Angeles, CA))

GARDEN STATE BANK (JACKSON, NJ)
Reorganized as Garden State Bancshares, Inc. 1/16/85
Each share Common $5 par exchanged for (1) share Common no par
Garden State Bancshares, Inc. merged into Summit Bancorporation 1/17/96 which merged into Summit Bancorp 3/1/96 which merged into FleetBoston Financial Corp. 3/1/2001 which merged into Bank of America Corp. 4/1/2004

GARDENAMERICA CORP (DE)
Reincorporated 06/30/1987
State of incorporation changed from (CA) to (DE) 06/30/1987
Merged into Emhart Corp. 11/30/1988
Each share Common no par exchanged for $28.125 cash

GARDENBURGER INC (OR)
Plan of reorganization under Chapter 11 Federal Bankruptcy Code effective 3/30/2006
No stockholders' equity

GARDINER OIL & GAS LTD (AB)
Merged into Poco Petroleums Ltd. 10/10/96
Each share Common no par exchanged for (0.6) share Common no par and $5 cash
Poco Petroleums Ltd. merged into Burlington Resources Inc. 11/18/99 which merged into ConocoPhillips 3/31/2006

GARDINER RES INC (BC)
Struck off register and declared dissolved for failure to file returns 10/24/86

GARDNER & BEEDON CO. (OR)
Merged into Continental Western Industries, Inc. 10/4/72
Each share Common $1 par exchanged for (0.3076) share Common $5 par
Continental Western Industries, Inc. merged into NN Corp. 2/10/78 which merged into Armco Inc. 12/1/80 which merged into AK Steel Holding Corp. 9/30/99

GARDNER DENVER CO (DE)
Each share 7% Preferred $100 par exchanged for (1-2/3) shares $3 Preferred $20 par 00/00/1936
Each share old Common no par exchanged for (3) shares new Common no par 00/00/1937
New Common no par changed to $5 par 00/00/1952
Common $5 par split (2) for (1) by issuance of (1) additional share 09/26/1956
Common $5 par split (3) for (2) by issuance of (0.5) additional share 01/31/1963
4% Preferred $100 par called for redemption 08/01/1963
Common $5 par split (3) for (2) by issuance of (0.5) additional share 05/21/1965
Common $5 par split (3) for (2) by issuance of (0.5) additional share 03/17/1969
Common $5 par split (2) for (1) by issuance of (1) additional share 07/11/1972
Merged into Cooper Industries, Inc. (OH) 04/30/1979
Each share Common $5 par exchanged for (0.5) share $2.90 Conv. Preferred $1 par and (1/3) share Common $5 par
Cooper Industries, Inc. (OH) reincorporated in Bermuda as Cooper Industries, Ltd. 05/22/2002 which reincorporated in Ireland as Cooper Industries PLC 09/08/2009 which merged into Eaton Corp. PLC 11/30/2012

GARDNER DENVER INC (OH)
Name changed 05/05/1998
Common 1¢ par split (2) for (1) by issuance of (1) additional share payable 01/15/1997 to holders of record 12/27/1996
Common 1¢ par split (3) for (2) by issuance of (0.5) additional share payable 12/29/1997 to holders of record 12/08/1997 Ex date - 12/30/1997
Name changed from Gardner Denver Machinery, Inc. to Gardner Denver, Inc. 05/05/1998
Common 1¢ par split (2) for (1) by issuance of (1) additional share payable 06/01/2006 to holders of record 05/11/2006 Ex date - 06/02/2006
Acquired by Renaissance Parent Corp. 07/30/2013
Each share Common 1¢ par exchanged for $76 cash

GARDNER ELECTRIC LIGHT CO.
Merged into Worcester County Electric Co. in 1951
Each share 5% Preferred $100 par exchanged for (1.75) shares Capital Stock $25 par
Each share Common $100 par exchanged for (2) shares Capital Stock $25 par
Worcester County Electric Co. merged into New England Electric System 6/30/59
(See New England Electric System)

GARDNER MACHINE CO.
Assets purchased by Landis Tool Co. in 1949
Details not available

GARDNER MARLOW MAES CORP (WA)
Name changed to Energy Sciences Corp. 9/29/78
(See Energy Sciences Corp.)

GARDNER MOTOR CO.
Liquidated in 1931
Details not available

GARDNER PETROLEUM CO. (DE)
Merged into Goff Oil Co. 4/1/63
Each share 8% Preferred $10 par

exchanged for (75) shares Common 10¢ par
Each share Common $1 par exchanged for (1) share Common 10¢ par
Goff Oil Co. name changed to Reading & Bates Production Co. 8/17/66
(See Reading & Bates Production Co.)

GARFIELD TR CO (GARFIELD, NJ)
Each share Common Capital Stock $50 par exchanged for (5) shares Common Capital Stock $10 par 02/24/1972
Stock Dividend - 10% 12/31/1974
Under plan of reorganization each share Common Capital Stock $10 par automatically became (1) share County Trust Co. (Garfield, NJ) Common Capital Stock $10 par 07/21/1982

GARFINCKEL (JULIUS) & CO., INC. (VA)
Recapitalized in 1946
5-1/2% Preferred $25 par reclassified as 5-1/2% Conv. Preferred $25 par
Each share Common $1 par exchanged for (2) shares Common 50¢ par
4-1/2% Conv. Preferred $25 par called for redemption 4/30/62
Stock Dividends - 100% 12/31/63; 100% 12/5/66
Name changed to Garfinckel, Brooks Brothers, Miller & Rhoads, Inc. 12/5/67
(See Garfinckel, Brooks Brothers, Miller & Rhoads, Inc.)

GARFINCKEL BROOKS BROS MILLER & RHOADS INC (VA)
$5.75 Preference Ser. A $5 par called for redemption 11/04/1981
Merged into Allied Stores Corp. 11/10/1981
Each share Common 50¢ par exchanged for $53 cash

GARFORD MOTOR TRUCK CO. (OH)
Acquired by Relay Motors Corp. 00/00/1927
Details not available

GARGOYLES INC (WA)
Company terminated registration of common stock and is no longer public as of 03/29/2001
Details not available

GARIBALDI GRANITE CORP (AB)
Name changed to Garibaldi Resources Corp. 1/12/2006
Each share Common no par exchanged for (1) share Common no par

GARIBALDI LIFTS LTD (BC)
Acquired by Hastings West Resorts Ltd. 10/28/1980
Each share Common no par exchanged for $938.50 cash
Each share Class A $100 par exchanged for $125 cash

GARLAND BK & TR CO (GARLAND, TX)
Each share Common $20 par exchanged for (2) shares Common $10 par plus a 50% stock dividend paid 1/14/64
Each share Common $10 par exchanged for (2) shares Common $5 par plus a 25% stock dividend paid 1/14/69
Merged into Mercantile Texas Corp. 12/31/81
Each share Common $5 par exchanged for (1.78125) shares Common $5 par
Mercantile Texas Corp. name changed to MCorp 10/11/84
(See MCorp)

GARLAND CORP (MA)
Class A Common $1 par and Class B Common $1 par split (3) for (2) by issuance of (0.5) additional share respectively 4/29/66
Under plan of reorganization each share Class A Common $1 par exchanged for $1 cash 1/13/81

GARLAND KNITTING MILLS (MA)
Name changed to Garland Corp. 4/1/66
(See Garland Corp.)

GARLAND MANUFACTURING CO.
Liquidated in 1944
Details not available

GARLAND MINING & DEVELOPMENT CO LTD. (QC)
Acquired by Amalgamated Mining Development Corp. Ltd. 00/00/1960
Each share Capital Stock $1 par exchanged for (0.125) share Capital Stock $1 par
Amalgamated Mining Development Corp. Ltd. acquired by Amalgamated Mining Western Ltd. 12/20/1984 which name changed to Westall Resources Ltd. 07/12/1994
(See Westall Resources Ltd.)

GARLAND STEAMSHIP CO.
Dissolved in 1927
Details not available

GARLOCK INC (DE)
Reincorporated 05/12/1975
Capital Stock $1 par split (2) for (1) by issuance of (1) additional share 04/22/1964
Capital Stock $1 par split (2) for (1) by issuance of (1) additional share 05/20/1966
Capital Stock $1 par reclassified as Common $1 par 09/28/1967
State of incorporation changed from (NY) to (DE) 05/12/1975
Merged into Colt Industries Inc. (DE) 01/28/1976
Each share Common $1 par exchanged for $35 cash

GARLOCK PACKING CO. (NY)
Each share Common no par exchanged for (2) shares Common $1 par in 1946
Stock Dividend - 10% 10/17/56
Name changed to Garlock, Inc. (N.Y.) 4/25/60
Garlock, Inc. (N.Y.) reincorporated in Delaware 5/12/75
(See Garlock Inc. (Del.))

GARMATEX HLDGS LTD (NV)
Common $0.001 par split (12.5) for (1) by issuance of (11.5) additional share payable 08/15/2016 to holders of record 08/15/2016
Recapitalized as Evolution Blockchain Group Inc. 02/28/2018
Each share Common $0.001 par exchanged for (0.01) share Common $0.001 par

GARMENT CENTER CAPITOL, INC. (NY)
Class A, B and C no par reclassified as Common no par in 1951
Common no par changed to $1 par in 1952
Liquidation completed 12/31/57
Details not available

GARMENT GRAPHICS INC (MN)
Name changed 12/15/1992
Name changed from Garment Graphics International, Inc. to Garment Graphics Inc. 12/15/1992
Company liquidated 00/00/1997
Stockholders' equity unlikely

GARMIN LTD (CAYMAN ISLANDS)
Issue Information - 10,500,000 shares COM offered at $14 per share on 12/08/2000
Common 1¢ par changed to $0.005 par and (1) additional share issued payable 08/15/2006 to holders of record 08/02/2006
Reincorporated under the laws of Switzerland and Common $0.005 par reclassified as Registered Shares CHF 10 par 06/28/2010

GARNEAU INC (AB)
Completely liquidated 09/05/2012
Each share Common no par exchanged for first and final distribution of $0.0312491 cash

GARNER INVTS INC (WY)
Name changed to Hinto Energy, Inc. 08/30/2011

GARNERO GROUP ACQUISITION CO (CAYMAN ISLANDS)
Completely liquidated 07/25/2016
Each Unit exchanged for first and final distribution of $10.05 cash
Each share Ordinary $0.0001 par exchanged for first and final distribution of $10.05 cash

GARNET GOLD MINES LTD. (ON)
Charter surrendered 01/12/1970
No stockholders' equity

GARNET OILS, LTD.
Merged into Calvan Consolidated Oil & Gas Co. Ltd. 00/00/1951
Each share exchanged for (0.5) share Capital Stock $1 par
(See Calvan Consolidated Oil & Gas Co. Ltd.)

GARNET PT RES CORP (BC)
Name changed to Hastings Resources Corp. 02/21/2008
Hastings Resources Corp. recapitalized as Trigen Resources Inc. 09/22/2010 which recapitalized as BlissCo Cannabis Corp. 03/02/2018

GARNET RES CORP (DE)
Merged into Aviva Petroleum Inc. 10/28/98
Each share Common 1¢ par exchanged for (0.1) share Common no par
Note: Holders entitled to (99) or fewer post-merger shares received $0.02 cash per share
(See Aviva Petroleum Inc.)

GARNEY MINES LTD (QC)
Charter surrendered 06/00/1979
No stockholders' equity

GARPA RES INC (NV)
Name changed to Colorado Goldfields, Inc. 06/18/2007

GARRETT CORP (CA)
Common 25¢ par changed to $2 par in 1945
Stock Dividends - 20% 12/31/48; 10% 9/30/53
Merged into Signal Oil & Gas Co. 1/20/64
Each share Common $2 par exchanged for (1) share $2.40 Conv. Preferred no par
Signal Oil & Gas Co. name changed to Signal Companies, Inc. 5/1/68 which merged into Allied-Signal Inc. 9/19/85 which name changed to AlliedSignal Inc. 4/26/93 which name changed to Honeywell International Inc. 12/1/99

GARRETT FREIGHTLINES INC (ID)
Each share Common $10 par exchanged for (6) shares Common $1.66 par 8/1/59
Merged into ANR Freight System, Inc. 12/16/85
Details not available

GARRETT MILLER & CO (DE)
Voluntarily dissolved 12/24/2002
Details not available

GARRETT OIL TOOLS, INC. (TX)
Acquired by U.S. Industries, Inc. 10/3/55
Each share Class A Common $1 par exchanged for (0.5544) share Common $1 par
(See U.S. Industries, Inc.)

GARRISON CREEK CONS MINES LTD (ON)
Stock Dividend - 15% 11/25/1975
Merged into QSR Ltd. 09/07/1993
Each share Common no par exchanged for (0.007) share Common no par
QSR Ltd. name changed to Coniagas Resources Ltd. 06/25/1999 which name changed to Lithium One Inc. 07/23/2009
(See Lithium One Inc.)

GARRISON CREEK MINES LTD. (ON)
Merged into Garrison Creek Consolidated Mines Ltd. 12/09/1954
Each share Common no par exchanged for (0.25) share Common no par
Garrison Creek Consolidated Mines Ltd. merged into QSR Ltd. 09/07/1993 which name changed to Coniagas Resources Ltd. 06/25/1999 which name changed to Lithium One Inc. 07/23/2009
(See Lithium One Inc.)

GARRISON ENTERPRISES INC (BC)
Recapitalized as GNI Petroleum Inc. 4/2/98
Each share Common no par exchanged for (1/3) share Common no par
GNI Petroleum Inc. recapitalized as Logix Enterprises Inc. 10/11/2001 which recapitalized as Transac Enterprise Corp. 11/27/2002 which name changed to Evergreen Gaming Corp. 11/1/2006

GARRISON GROWTH FD (NY)
Completely liquidated 06/28/1973
Details not available

GARRISON-HARBOUR GOLD MINES, LTD. (ON)
Charter cancelled 05/27/1965
No stockholders' equity

GARRISON INTL LTD (ON)
Recapitalized as Desert Eagle Resources Ltd. 01/09/2012
Each share Common no par exchanged for (0.05555555) share Common no par

GARRISON OILS LTD.
Merged into Calvan Consolidated Oil & Gas Co. Ltd. 00/00/1951
Each share Common no par exchanged for (0.5) share Capital Stock $1 par
(See Calvan Consolidated Oil & Gas Co. Ltd.)

GARSITE PRODS INC (NY)
Stock Dividends - 10% 08/11/1969; 75% 07/15/1981
Merged into Thomas Tilling Ltd. 01/29/1982
Each share Common 10¢ par exchanged for $5.714 cash

GARSKIE GOLD MINES, LTD. (ON)
Charter cancelled for failure to pay taxes and file returns 03/16/1976

GARSON GOLD CORP (BC)
Merged into Alexis Minerals Corp. 04/29/2010
Each share Common no par exchanged for (0.29) share Common no par
Alexis Minerals Corp. recapitalized as QMX Gold Corp. 07/05/2012

GARSON RES LTD (BC)
Merged into Garson Gold Corp. 07/04/2007
Each share Common no par exchanged for (0.72500018) share Common no par
Garson Gold Corp. merged into Alexis Minerals Corp. 04/29/2010 which recapitalized as QMX Gold Corp. 07/05/2012

GART SPORTS CO (DE)
Under plan of merger name changed

to Sports Authority, Inc. (New) 8/4/2003
(See Sports Authority, Inc. (New))

GARTHACK MINING CO., LTD. (ON)
Charter revoked for failure to file reports and pay taxes 00/00/1959

GARTLAND SS CO (DE)
Recapitalized under plan of merger 10/8/62
Each share $7 Preferred no par exchanged for (10) shares Common $1 par
Each share Common no par exchanged for (0.02) share Common $1 par
Liquidation completed
Each share Common $1 par exchanged for initial distribution of $9.166 cash 3/29/69
Each share Common $1 par received second and final distribution of $0.03055278 cash 9/1/69

GARTNER GROUP INC (DE)
Merged into Saatchi & Saatchi Co. PLC 07/28/1988
Each share Common 1¢ par exchanged for $22.50 cash

GARTNER GROUP INC NEW (DE)
Class A Common $0.0005 par split (2) for (1) by issuance of (1) additional share 8/26/94
Class A Common $0.0005 par split (2) for (1) by issuance of (1) additional share 6/28/95
Class A Common $0.0005 par split (2) for (1) by issuance of (1) additional share payable 3/29/96 to holders of record 3/16/96
Name changed to Gartner, Inc. 1/3/2001

GARY & INTERURBAN RAILROAD CO. (IN)
Charter revoked for failure to file annual reports in 1975

GARY (THEODORE) & CO. (MO)
Each share Preferred $100 par exchanged for (5) shares new Preferred no par in 1928
Common no par changed to $1 par in 1933
Each share Common $1 par exchanged for (5) shares Common 20¢ par in 1954
Each share Part. Common no par exchanged for (5) shares Part. Common 20¢ par in 1954
Merged into General Telephone Corp. 10/31/55
Each share Part. Common 20¢ par or Common 20¢ par exchanged for (1.5) shares Common $10 par
General Telephone Corp. name changed to General Telephone & Electronics Corp. 3/5/59 which name changed to GTE Corp. 7/1/82 which merged into Verizon Communications Inc. 6/30/2000

GARY ELECTRIC & GAS CO.
Dissolved in 1942
Details not available

GARY HOTEL CORP. (DE)
Capital Stock $20 par changed to $1 par in 1938
Reincorporated under laws of Indiana as Hotel Gary Corp. in 1952
(See Hotel Gary Corp.)

GARY MINES LTD (BC)
Struck off register and declared dissolved for failure to file returns 10/02/1978

GARY NATL BK (GARY, IN)
Common $100 par changed to $10 par 3/19/74
Stock Dividend - 100% 1/27/60
Under plan of reorganization each share Common $10 par automatically became (1) share Gainer Corp. Common no par 1/1/83
Gainer Corp. acquired by NBD Bancorp, Inc. 1/23/92 which name changed to First Chicago NBD Corp. 12/1/95 which merged into Bank One Corp. 10/2/98 which merged into J.P. Morgan Chase & Co. 12/31/2000 which name changed to JPMorgan Chase & Co. 7/20/2004

GARY RAILWAYS CO.
Reorganized as Gary Railways, Inc. in 1943
Each share 7.2% Preferred exchanged for (1) share Common $1 par Old Common had no equity
(See Gary Railways, Inc.)

GARY RYS INC (IN)
Liquidation completed
Each share Common $1 par exchanged for initial liquidating distribution of $24.50 cash 06/30/1975
Each share Common $1 par received second and final distribution of $7.180794 cash 05/28/1980

GARY TRUST & SAVINGS BANK (GARY, IN)
Stock Dividend - 40% 06/21/1962
Name changed to Bank of Indiana (Gary, IN) 11/12/1962
Bank of Indiana (Gary, IN) name changed to Bank of Indiana, N.A. (Gary, IN) 12/24/1964

GARY WHEATON BK (WHEATON, IL)
Under plan of reorganization each share Capital Stock $10 par automatically became (1) share Gary-Wheaton Corp. Common $5 par 03/05/1965
Gary-Wheaton Corp. merged into First Chicago Corp. 08/31/1988 which merged into First Chicago NBD Corp. 12/01/1995 which merged into Bank One Corp. 10/02/1998 which merged into J.P. Morgan Chase & Co. 12/31/2000 which name changed to JPMorgan Chase & Co. 07/20/2004

GARY WHEATON CORP (IL)
Merged into First Chicago Corp. 08/31/1988
Each share Common $5 par exchanged for (2.408) shares Common $5 par
First Chicago Corp. merged into First Chicago NBD Corp. 12/01/1995 which merged into Bank One Corp. 10/02/1998 which merged into J.P. Morgan Chase & Co. 12/31/2000 which name changed to JPMorgan Chase & Co. 07/20/2004

GAS & ELECTRIC CO. OF BERGEN COUNTY
Merged into Public Service Electric & Gas Co. and stock exchanged for a like amount of First and Refunding Mortgage Bonds in 1938

GAS & ELECTRIC PROTECTIVE CO. (ME)
Charter suspended for failure to file annual reports 00/00/1907

GAS AUTH OF INDIA LTD (INDIA)
Name changed to Gail (India) Ltd. 12/6/2002

GAS CO VT INC (VT)
Over 97% owned by the company as of 05/05/1983
Public interest eliminated

GAS CONSUMERS ASSN (CA)
Name changed to GSC Services, Inc. 8/23/78

GAS EXPLORATION CO. OF ALBERTA LTD. (AB)
Recapitalized as New Gas Exploration Co. of Alberta Ltd. 9/26/55
Each (2) shares Capital Stock no par exchanged for (1) share Capital Stock $1 par
New Gas Exploration merged into Medallion Petroleums Ltd. 6/18/58 which merged into Canadian Industrial Gas & Oil Ltd. 3/8/65 which merged into Norcen Energy Resources Ltd. (ALTA) 10/28/75 which reincorporated in Canada 4/15/77 which merged into Union Pacific Resources Group Inc. 4/17/98 which merged into Anadarko Petroleum Corp. 7/14/2000

GAS HILLS URANIUM CO. (CO)
Recapitalized as American Nuclear Corp. 03/10/1967
Each share Common 1¢ par exchanged for (0.25) share Common 4¢ par
(See American Nuclear Corp.)

GAS INDUSTRIES FUND, INC. (DE)
Common $1 par split (2) for (1) by issuance of (1) additional share 07/29/1955
Reincorporated under the laws of Massachusetts as Colonial Energy Shares, Inc. 06/23/1959
Colonial Energy Shares, Inc. name changed to Colonial Growth & Energy Shares, Inc. 06/20/1961 which name changed to Colonial Growth Shares, Inc. 06/20/1967 which reorganized as Colonial Growth Shares Trust 09/02/1986 which reorganized as Colonial Trust III 09/13/1991 which name changed to Liberty Funds Trust III 04/01/1999 which name changed to Columbia Funds Trust III 10/13/2003

GAS LT CO COLUMBUS (GA)
Merged into United Cities Gas Co. 3/30/82
Each share 6% Preferred $50 par exchanged for (0.5) share 6% Preferred 1982 Ser. $100 par
Each share Common $5 par exchanged for (0.3461) share 11-1/2% Conv. Preference $100 par
United Cities Gas Co. merged into Atmos Energy Corp. 7/31/97

GAS MGMT INCOME FD (ON)
Each Instalment Receipt plus final payment of $4 cash received (1) Trust Unit 12/18/1997
Acquired by OPTUS Natural Gas Distribution Income Fund 08/05/1999
Each Trust Unit exchanged for (1) Non-transferable Liability Recovery Right and $4.70 cash

GAS N SAVE IDAHO INC (ID)
Name changed to Classic Financial Corp. 08/16/1979
Classic Financial Corp. name changed to Gourmet General Corp. 10/19/1979 which merged into American General Industries 07/15/1984 which name changed to Pagers Plus 11/18/1987 which name changed to PagePrompt USA 03/09/1994
(See PagePrompt USA)

GAS NAT INC (OH)
Acquired by First Reserve Energy Infrastructure Fund II, L.P. 08/04/2017
Each share Common 15¢ par exchanged for $13.10 cash

GAS NAT SDG S A (SPAIN)
Stock Dividend - 3.57142% payable 07/06/2011 to holders of record 06/14/2011 Ex date - 06/10/2011
Name changed to Naturgy Energy Group, S.A. 08/16/2018

GAS REGISTER CORP. (AZ)
Name changed to National Controls Corp. 4/8/69
(See National Controls Corp.)

GAS SALVAGE CORP (NV)
Reorganized as Pinnacle Energy Corp. 08/14/2008
Each share Common $0.001 par exchanged for (3) shares Common $0.001 par
Pinnacle Energy Corp. name changed to Trans-Pacific Aerospace Co., Inc. (NV) 03/05/2010 reincorporated in Wyoming 01/27/2017

GAS SECURITIES CO.
Liquidated in 1943
Details not available

GAS SVC CO (DE)
Common $10 par changed to $5 par and (1) additional share issued 06/03/1966
Merged into Kansas Power & Light Co. 12/29/1983
Each share Common $5 par exchanged for $16 cash

GAS UTILITIES CO.
Dissolved in 1936
Details not available

GASCARD INC (DE)
Reorganized 9/1/88
Reorganized under Chapter 11 Federal Bankruptcy Code from Gascard Club, Inc. to Gascard Inc. and Common 1¢ par changed to $0.001 par 9/1/88
Merged into Fuelman 10/3/95
Each share Common $0.001 par exchanged for $18.43 cash

GASCO ENERGY INC (NV)
Each share old Common $0.0001 par exchanged for (0.00000001) share new Common $0.0001 par 06/30/2014
Note: In effect holders received $0.00288 cash per share and public interest was eliminated

GASCOME OILS LTD (AB)
Recapitalized as Consolidated Gascome Oils Ltd. 07/13/1982
Each share Common no par exchanged for (0.2) share Common no par
Consolidated Gascome Oils Ltd. name changed to Reef Hydrocarbons Ltd. 10/02/1987 which recapitalized as International Reef Resources Ltd. 09/29/1988 which merged into UTS Energy Corp. 06/30/1998 which merged into SilverBirch Energy Corp. 10/01/2010 which merged into SilverWillow Energy Corp. 04/04/2012
(See SilverWillow Energy Corp.)

GASEL TRANSN LINES INC (OH)
Common no par split (2) for (1) by issuance of (1) additional share payable 05/21/1996 to holders of record 05/15/1996
Common no par split (2) for (1) by issuance of (1) additional share payable 12/01/1998 to holders of record 11/01/1998
Common no par split (2) for (1) by issuance of (1) additional share payable 12/20/1999 to holders of record 12/10/1999
Stock Dividends - 5% payable 06/30/1997 to holders of record 05/30/1997; 5% payable 06/15/1998 to holders of record 05/31/1998
Reincorporated under the laws of Delaware as Precision Aerospace Components, Inc. and Common no par changed to $0.001 par 08/04/2006
Precision Aerospace Components, Inc. name changed to Amerinac Holding Corp. 06/28/2017

GASETERIA, INC. (IN)
Acquired by Standard Oil Co. (NJ) 03/31/1958
Each share Common $10 par exchanged for (2.02) shares Capital Stock $7 par
Standard Oil Co. (NJ) name changed to Exxon Corp. 11/01/1972 which name changed to Exxon Mobil Corp. 11/30/1999

GASFRAC ENERGY SVCS INC (AB)
Plan of arrangement under

Companies Creditors Arrangement Act effective 06/24/2015
No stockholders' equity

GASIFIER MANUFACTURING CO. (DE)
Charter cancelled and declared inoperative and void for non-payment of taxes 4/1/44

GASLIGHT, INC. (UT)
Recapitalized as Lazarus Industries, Inc. 04/18/1988
Each share Common $0.001 par exchanged for (0.04) share Common $0.001 par
Lazarus Industries, Inc. recapitalized as American Dairy, Inc. 05/07/2003 which name changed to Feihe International, Inc. 11/08/2010
(See Feihe International, Inc.)

GASLIGHT CLUB INC (DE)
Reincorporated 2/19/68
State of incorporation changed from (IL) to (DE) 2/19/68
Charter cancelled and declared inoperative and void for non-payment of taxes 3/1/94

GASLITE EQUIPMENT CO., INC. (CO)
Name changed to Astral Industries, Inc. 1/2/69
Astral Industries, Inc. name changed to Pace Industries, Inc. (CO) 2/27/69 which reincorporated in Delaware 5/29/69
(See Pace Industries, Inc. (DE))

GASLITE PETE LTD (AB)
Reincorporated 00/00/1983
Place of incorporation changed from (AB) to (BC) 00/00/1979 and then back to (AB) 00/00/1983
Struck from the register 04/01/1989

GASOIL INC (OH)
Charter cancelled 8/24/92

GASONICS INTL CORP (DE)
Secondary Offering - 2,025,000 shares COM offered at $24.88 per share on 05/19/2000
Common $0.001 par split (3) for (2) by issuance of (0.5) additional share 11/20/1995
Merged into Novellus Systems, Inc. 01/10/2001
Each share Common $0.001 par exchanged for (0.52) share Common no par
Novellus Systems, Inc. merged into Lam Research Corp. 06/04/2012

GASPE COPPER MINES LTD (QC)
Acquired by Noranda Mines Ltd. 8/10/76
Each share Capital Stock $1 par exchanged for $57 cash

GASPE MINERALS LTD (NV)
SEC revoked common stock registration 09/05/2013

GASPE OIL VENTURES LTD. (QC)
Acquired by New Associated Developments Ltd. 04/17/1963
Each share Capital Stock $1 par exchanged for (0.04347826) share Capital Stock $1 par
New Associated Developments Ltd. recapitalized as Consolidated Developments Ltd. 05/10/1971
(See Consolidated Developments Ltd.)

GASPE PK MINES LTD (ON)
Charter cancelled for failure to pay taxes and file returns 03/16/1976

GASPE QUE MINES LTD (QC)
Name changed to G E Q Corp. 08/15/1975
(See G E Q Corp.)

GASPESIE SOCIETE DEXPLORATIONS PETROLIERE ET MINIERE INC (QC)
Name changed to Afcan Mining Corp. 3/6/97
Afcan Mining Corp. merged into Eldorado Gold Corp. (New) 9/13/2005

GASPEX MINES LTD (QC)
Charter annulled for failure to file reports or pay fees 03/22/1975

GAST BREWERY, INC.
Dissolution ordered by Court in 1940
Details not available

GAST PETROLEUM CO. (OK)
Charter cancelled for failure to pay taxes 8/8/21

GASTAR EXPL LTD OLD (DE)
Name changed 11/15/2013
Old Common no par split (4) for (1) by issuance of (3) additional shares payable 07/21/2001 to holders of record 07/16/2001
Each share old Common no par exchanged for (0.2) share new Common no par 08/03/2009
Name and place of incorporation changed from Gastar Exploration, Inc. (AB) to Gastar Exploration Ltd. (Old) (DE) and Common no par changed to $0.001 par 11/15/2013
Under plan of reorganization each share Common $0.001 par automatically became (1) share Gastar Exploration Ltd. (New) Common $0.001 par 02/03/2014

GASTAR EXPL USA INC (DE)
Name changed to Gastar Exploration Inc. 02/03/2014

GASTON FED BANCORP INC (USA)
Name changed to Citizens South Banking Corp. (USA) 05/22/2002
Citizens South Banking Corp. (USA) reorganized in Delaware as Citizens South Banking Corp. 10/01/2002 which merged into Park Sterling Corp. 10/01/2012 which merged into South State Corp. 11/30/2017

GATE CITY BUILDING CORP. (MO)
Charter forfeited for failure to file reports 1/1/32

GATE ENERGY INC (BC)
Name changed to Metahost.net Technologies Inc. 12/06/2000
Metahost.net Technologies Inc. name changed to Network Technology Professionals Inc. 07/30/2001
(See Network Technology Professionals Inc.)

GATE TO WIRE SOLUTIONS INC (NV)
SEC revoked common stock registration 10/25/2012

GATEFIELD CORP (DE)
Each share old Common 10¢ par exchanged for (0.1) share new Common 10¢ par 6/30/99
Merged into Actel Corp. 11/15/2000
Each share new Common 10¢ par exchanged for $5.25 cash

GATEFORD MINES LTD (ON)
Reincorporated under the laws of Canada as Gateford Resources Inc. 07/03/1986
Gateford Resources Inc. merged into Landmark Corp. (New) 01/31/1992 which recapitalized as Landmark Global Financial Corp. 07/05/1996

GATEFORD RES INC (CANADA)
Merged into Landmark Corp. (New) 01/31/1992
Each share Common no par exchanged for (1) share Common no par
Landmark Corp. (New) recapitalized as Landmark Global Financial Corp. 07/05/1996

GATEHOUSE MEDIA INC (DE)
Issue Information - 13,800,000 shares COM offered at $18 per share on 10/24/2006
Under plan of reorganization each share Common 1¢ par automatically became (0.02346) New Media Investment Group Inc. Common Stock Purchase Warrants expiring 11/26/2023 payable 11/29/2013 to holders of record 11/26/2013

GATELINX GLOBAL CORP (FL)
Reincorporated under the laws of Nevada as GTX Global Corp. 10/12/2005
GTX Global Corp. recapitalized as Vision Technology Corp. 07/31/2006
(See Vision Technology Corp.)

GATES AIRCRAFT CORP. (DE)
No longer in existence having become inoperative and void for non-payment of taxes 4/1/32

GATES/FA DISTRG INC (DE)
Each share Common 1¢ par exchanged for (0.125) share Common no par 1/31/92
Acquired by Arrow Electronics, Inc. 8/29/94
Each share new Common no par exchanged for (0.5926) share Common $1 par

GATES LEARJET CORP (DE)
Common $1 par split (2) for (1) by issuance of (1) additional share 12/31/81
Stock Dividends - 10% 3/15/76; 10% 11/15/76; 10% 11/24/78; 10% 12/17/79; 10% 12/16/80
Merged into Integrated Resources, Inc. 10/30/87
Each share Common $1 par exchanged for $7.25 cash

GATEWAY AIRLINES, INC. (DE)
No longer in existence having become inoperative and void for non-payment of taxes 4/1/61

GATEWAY AMERN BANCSHARES INC (FL)
Merged into P.C.B. Bancorp, Inc. 10/1/2002
Each share Common $1 par exchanged for $3.02 cash

GATEWAY AMERN BK (FT LAUDERDALE, FL)
Under plan of reorganization each share Common $1 par automatically became (1) share of Gateway American Bancshares, Inc. Common $1 par 2/8/99
(See Gateway American Bancshares, Inc.)

GATEWAY BANCORP INC (KY)
Merged into Peoples Bancorp Inc. 12/12/1997
Each share Common 1¢ par exchanged for either (0.4978) share Common $1 par, $18.75 cash, or a combination of stock and cash
Note: Option to make a definitive election expired 01/02/1998 after which holders received remaining stock or cash
Note: Holders of (99) shares or fewer received cash

GATEWAY BANCORP INC (NY)
Stock Dividends - 10% 4/29/88; 10% 5/5/89; 10% 4/20/90; 10% 3/17/92
Merged into Staten Island Savings Bank (Staten Island, NY) 8/18/95
Each share Common 50¢ par exchanged for $12.61 cash

GATEWAY BANCSHARES INC (GA)
Under plan of merger each share Common $5 par held by holders of (499) or fewer exchanged for $37 cash 03/16/2005
Acquired by First Volunteer Corp. 04/13/2012
Each share Common $5 par exchanged for $16.12 cash

GATEWAY BANCSHARES INC (WV)
Merged into Commercial Bancshares, Inc. 3/9/98
Each share Common exchanged for (1.742) shares Common $5 par Commercial Bancshares, Inc. merged into WesBanco, Inc. 3/31/98

GATEWAY BK & TR CO (ELIZABETH, NC)
Under plan of reorganization each share Common no par automatically became (1) share Gateway Financial Holdings, Inc. Common no par 10/01/2001
Gateway Financial Holdings, Inc. merged into Hampton Roads Bankshares, Inc. 12/31/2008 which name changed to Xenith Bankshares, Inc. (New) 08/01/2016 which merged into Union Bankshares Corp. 01/01/2018

GATEWAY BANK (GREENSBORO, NC)
Merged into Northwestern Financial Corp. 12/31/1981
Each share Common $6 par exchanged for (1.1875) shares Common $1 par
Northwestern Financial Corp. merged into First Union Corp. 12/02/1985 which name changed to Wachovia Corp. (Ctfs. dated after 09/01/2001) 09/01/2001 which merged into Wells Fargo & Co. (New) 12/31/2008

GATEWAY BK (SOUTH NORWALK, CT)
Common $1 par split (3) for (2) by issuance of (0.5) additional share 6/25/86
Common $1 par split (3) for (2) by issuance of (0.5) additional share 5/27/87
Reorganized under the laws of Delaware as Gateway Financial Corp. 6/30/89
Each share Common $1 par exchanged for (1) share Common 1¢ par
Gateway Financial Corp. merged into Shawmut National Corp. 6/27/94 which merged into Fleet Financial Group Inc. (New) 11/30/95 which name changed to Fleet Boston Corp. 10/1/99 which name changed to FleetBoston Financial Corp. 4/18/2000 which merged into Bank of America Corp. 4/1/2004

GATEWAY BRIDGE CO.
Acquired by Rio Grande Gateway Bridge Corp. in 1934
Details not available

GATEWAY CAP CORP (SK)
Name changed to Sweeprite Mfg. Inc. 02/27/2003
(See Sweeprite Mfg. Inc.)

GATEWAY CASINOS INCOME FD (BC)
Acquired by New World Gaming Partners Ltd. 11/14/2007
Each Unit no par exchanged for $25.26 cash

GATEWAY CERTIFICATIONS INC (NV)
Name changed to American Jianye Greentech Holdings, Ltd. 02/25/2010
American Jianye Greentech Holdings, Ltd. name changed to AJ Greentech Holdings Ltd. 03/13/2014 which name changed to Sino United Worldwide Consolidated Ltd. 07/17/2017

GATEWAY CHEMICALS, INC. (IL)
Common no par split (2) for (1) by issuance of (1) additional share 02/10/1966
Name changed to Gateway Industries, Inc. (IL) 04/27/1966
Gateway Industries, Inc. (IL) reincorporated in Delaware 11/23/1970
(See Gateway Industries, Inc. (DE))

GATEWAY COMMUNICATIONS INC (CA)
Each share old Common no par

FINANCIAL INFORMATION, INC.

exchanged for (0.005) share new Common no par 06/18/1986
Reorganized under the laws of Delaware as Gateway Industries, Inc. 09/22/1994
Each share new Common no par exchanged for (0.2) share Common $0.001 par
Gateway Industries, Inc. recapitalized as Function (x) Inc. 02/16/2011 which recapitalized as Viggle Inc. 06/07/2012 which name changed to DraftDay Fantasy Sports, Inc. 01/28/2016 which name changed to Function(x) Inc. 06/13/2016

GATEWAY DATA SCIENCES CORP (AZ)
Plan of reorganization under Chapter 11 Federal Bankruptcy proceedings confirmed 03/22/2002
Stockholders' equity unlikely

GATEWAY DISTRIPARKS LTD (INDIA)
Sponsored Reg. S GDR's for Ordinary split (5) for (4) by issuance of (0.25) additional GDR payable 10/18/2007 to holders of record 08/02/2007
GDR agreement terminated 8/22/2013
No GDR's remain outstanding

GATEWAY DISTRS LTD (NV)
Each share old Common $0.001 par exchanged for (0.00004) share new Common $0.001 par 11/29/2002
Each share new Common $0.001 par exchanged again for (0.00033333) share new Common $0.001 par 04/16/2003
Each share new Common $0.001 par exchanged again for (0.00111111) share new Common $0.001 par 06/28/2004
Each share new Common $0.001 par exchanged again for (0.001) share new Common $0.001 par 09/03/2004
Each share new Common $0.001 par exchanged again for (0.001) share new Common $0.001 par 12/20/2004
Each share new Common $0.001 par exchanged again for (0.002) share new Common $0.001 par 03/28/2005
Recapitalized as Marshall Holdings International, Inc. 12/04/2006
Each share new Common $0.001 par exchanged for (0.001) share Common $0.001 par
(See Marshall Holdings International, Inc.)

GATEWAY ENERGY CORP (DE)
Each share Common 1¢ par exchanged for (0.04) share Common 25¢ par 03/04/1997
Common 25¢ par changed to 1¢ par 06/01/2011
Acquired by Gateway Energy Holdings LLC 12/31/2013
Each share new Common 1¢ par exchanged for $0.0175 cash

GATEWAY ENTERPRISES LTD (BC)
Name changed to Portal de Oro Resources Ltd. 03/12/2004
Portal de Oro Resources Ltd. name changed to Portal Resources Ltd. 12/21/2004 which recapitalized as Galileo Petroleum Ltd. 04/02/2012 which name changed to Galileo Exploration Ltd. 12/21/2016

GATEWAY FD INC (DE)
Merged into Amcap Fund, Inc. 4/2/75
Each share Common $1 par exchanged for (1.039) shares Capital Stock $1 par

GATEWAY FED CORP (DE)
Merged into PNC Bank Ohio, N.A. (Cincinnati, OH) 11/19/93
Each share Common 1¢ par exchanged for $30.60 cash

GATEWAY FEDERAL SAVINGS & LOAN ASSOCIATION (OH)
Name changed to Gateway Federal Savings Bank (Cincinnati, OH) 12/8/89
Gateway Federal Savings Bank (Cincinnati, OH) reorganized in Delaware as Gateway Fed Corp. 2/1/90
(See Gateway Fed Corp.)

GATEWAY FED SVGS BK (CINCINNATI, OH)
Reorganized under the laws of Delaware as Gateway Fed Corp. 2/1/90
(See Gateway Fed Corp.)

GATEWAY FINL CORP (DE)
Merged into Shawmut National Corp. 6/27/94
Each share Common 1¢ par exchanged for (0.559) share Common 1¢ par
Shawmut National Corp. merged into Fleet Financial Group Inc. (New) 11/30/95 which name changed to Fleet Boston Corp. 10/1/99 which name changed to FleetBoston Financial Corp. 4/18/2000 which merged into Bank of America Corp. 4/1/2004

GATEWAY FINL HLDGS INC (NC)
Stock Dividends - 10% payable 06/05/2002 to holders of record 05/22/2002 Ex date - 05/20/2002; 5% payable 06/12/2003 to holders of record 05/23/2003 Ex date - 05/21/2003; 5% payable 04/08/2004 to holders of record 03/15/2004 Ex date - 03/11/2004; 10% payable 06/20/2005 to holders of record 05/30/2005 Ex date - 05/25/2005; 10% payable 05/15/2006 to holders of record 04/28/2006 Ex date - 04/26/2006
Merged into Hampton Roads Bankshares, Inc. 12/31/2008
Each share Common no par exchanged for (0.67) share Common $0.625 par
Hampton Roads Bankshares, Inc. name changed to Xenith Bankshares, Inc. (New) 08/01/2016 which merged into Union Bankshares Corp. 01/01/2018

GATEWAY GATHERING SYS INC (DE)
Name changed to Gateway Energy Corp. 07/26/1995
(See Gateway Energy Corp.)

GATEWAY GOLD CORP (BC)
Merged into Victoria Gold Corp. 12/18/2008
Each share Common no par exchanged for (0.5) share Common no par

GATEWAY INC (DE)
Common 1¢ par split (2) for (1) by issuance of (1) additional share payable 09/07/1999 to holders of record 08/20/1999 Ex date - 09/08/1999
Merged into Acer Inc. (New) 10/16/2007
Each share Common 1¢ par exchanged for $1.90 cash

GATEWAY INDS INC (DE)
Recapitalized as Function (x) Inc. 02/16/2011
Each share Common $0.001 par exchanged for (0.1) share Common $0.001 par
Function (x) Inc. recapitalized as Viggle Inc. 06/07/2012 which name changed to DraftDay Fantasy Sports, Inc. 01/28/2016 which name changed to Function(x) Inc. 06/13/2016

GATEWAY INDS INC (DE)
Reincorporated 11/23/70
Common no par split (3) for (2) by issuance of (0.5) additional share 12/1/67
State of incorporation changed from (IL) to (DE) and Common no par changed to $1 par 11/23/70
Merged into GATW, Inc. 12/23/81
Each share Common $1 par exchanged for $20.15 cash

GATEWAY INTL HLDGS INC (NV)
Each share old Common $0.001 par exchanged for (2) shares new Common $0.001 par 08/27/2004
Name changed to M Line Holdings, Inc. 03/25/2009

GATEWAY MED SYS INC (DE)
Charter cancelled and declared inoperative and void for non-payment of taxes 3/1/89

GATEWAY NATL BK (EL SEGUNDO, CA)
Acquired by Southern California First National Corp. 6/11/70
Each share Common $6 par exchanged for $20 principal amount of 8-1/2% Conv. Subord. Debentures due 7/1/80 and $5 cash

GATEWAY NATL BK (FORT WORTH, TX)
Merged into First United Bancorporation, Inc. 1/5/76
Each share Common $10 par exchanged for (2) shares Common $10 par
First United Bancorporation, Inc. merged into InterFirst Corp. 6/28/83 which merged into First RepublicBank Corp. 6/6/87
(See First RepublicBank Corp.)

GATEWAY OILS LTD. (AB)
Recapitalized as New Gateway Oils & Minerals Ltd. 01/27/1965
Each share Capital Stock no par exchanged for (0.1) share Capital Stock no par
New Gateway Oils & Minerals Ltd. merged into Killucan Resources Ltd. 09/30/1981 which merged into Skill Resources Ltd. 08/17/1983 which recapitalized as Unicorp Resources Ltd. 06/27/1984 which merged into Asamera Inc. 05/01/1986 which was acquired by Gulf Canada Resources Ltd. 08/04/1988
(See Gulf Canada Resources Ltd.)

GATEWAY SPORTING GOODS CO (DE)
Common $5 par changed to $2.50 par and (1) additional share issued 03/23/1962
Class B Common $2.50 par reclassified as Common $2.50 par 04/01/1967
Common $2.50 par changed to 1¢ par 08/02/1974
Each share Sr. Preferred no par exchanged for (7.5) shares new Common 1¢ par 02/15/1984
Each share old Common 1¢ par exchanged for (0.5) share new Common 1¢ par 02/15/1984
Stock Dividend - 100% 02/14/1969
Name changed to Gateway Gathering Systems, Inc. 09/04/1992
Gateway Gathering Systems, Inc. name changed to Gateway Energy Corp. 07/26/1995
(See Gateway Energy Corp.)

GATEWAY STATE BANK (STATEN ISLAND, NY)
Reorganized as Gateway Bancorp, Inc. (NY) 4/30/85
Each share Common $5 par exchanged for (1) share Common $5 par
(See Gateway Bancorp, Inc. (NY))

GATEWAY TECHNOLOGIES CORP (BC)
Name changed 12/04/1995
Name changed from Gateway Waste Systems Inc. to Gateway Technologies Corp. 12/04/1995
Recapitalized as Trevali Resources Corp. 07/06/2006
Each share Common no par exchanged for (0.5) share Common no par
Trevali Resources Corp. name changed to Trevali Mining Corp. 04/07/2011

GATEWAY 2000 INC (DE)
Common 1¢ par split (2) for (1) by issuance of (1) additional share payable 06/16/1997 to holders of record 06/02/1997 Ex date - 06/17/1997
Name changed to Gateway, Inc. 06/01/1999
(See Gateway, Inc.)

GATEWAY URANIUM CORP. (DE)
Merged into Lisbon Uranium Corp. 10/04/1955
Each share Common $1 par exchanged for (0.13333333) share Common $1 par
(See Lisbon Uranium Corp.)

GATEWAY URANIUM MINES LTD (SK)
Merged into International Gold Resources Corp. 11/15/93
Each share Common no par exchanged for (0.2778) share Common no par
International Gold Resources Corp. merged into Ashanti Goldfields Ltd. 6/17/96 which merged into AngloGold Ashanti Ltd. 4/26/2004

GATEWAY VENTURES INC (AB)
Name changed to Chinook Testing Inc. 12/30/1998
Chinook Testing Inc. recapitalized as Chinook Energy Services Inc. 10/22/2001 which name changed to Deep Resources Ltd. 11/08/2002 which merged into Choice Resources Corp. 08/01/2006 which merged into Buffalo Resources Corp. 08/03/2007 which merged into Twin Butte Energy Ltd. 10/15/2009

GATEWAYS TO SPACE INC (DE)
Recapitalized as eMax Corp. 02/18/2000
Each share Common $0.001 par exchanged for (0.1) share Common $0.001 par
eMax Corp. recapitalized as eMax Holdings Corp. 05/27/2004

GATEX OIL CORP. (DE)
Charter cancelled and declared inoperative and void for non-payment of taxes 3/19/24

GATINEAU POWER CO. (QC)
Name changed to Gatineau Power Co.-Compagnie D'Electricite Gatineau 05/04/1962
(See Gatineau Power Co.-Compagnie D'Electricite Gatineau)

GATINEAU POWER CO.-COMPAGNIE D'ELECTRICITE GATINEAU (QC)
Acquired by Quebec Hydro-Electric Commission 10/01/1963
Each share Common no par exchanged for $35 cash
Each share 5.5% Preferred $100 par exchanged for $100 principal amount of 5.5% 10-year Debentures and $5 cash 11/05/1963
Each share 5% Preferred $100 par exchanged for $100 principal amount of 5% 10-year Debentures and $5 cash 11/05/1963

GATLIN HLDGS INC (NV)
Each share old Common $0.001 par exchanged for (0.04) share new Common $0.001 par 11/05/2001
Recapitalized as Bio Venture Holdings Inc. 06/11/2002
Each (30) shares new Common $0.001 par exchanged for (1) share Common $0.001 par

Bio Venture Holdings Inc. name changed to Midwest Venture Holdings, Inc. 08/16/2002 which name changed to Inspiration Products Group, Inc. 02/03/2003 which name changed to MB-Tech, Inc. 05/18/2003
(See MB-Tech, Inc.)

GATO RIDGE TR (CA)
Completely liquidated 6/9/88
Details not available

GATOR RES CORP (BC)
Recapitalized as EZ Ventures Ltd. 02/11/1986
Each share Common no par exchanged for (0.33333333) share Common no par
EZ Ventures Ltd. name changed to Haglund Industries International Inc. 10/05/1987
(See Haglund Industries International Inc.)

GATORZ INC (CANADA)
Name changed to Pacific Vector Holdings Inc. 06/14/2013
(See Pacific Vector Holdings Inc.)

GATROW RES INC (BC)
Struck off register and declared dissolved for failure to file returns 06/24/1994

GATX CORP (NY)
Adjustable Rate Conv. Preferred $1 par called for redemption 01/15/1987
Preferred Stock Purchase Rights declared for Common stockholders of record 05/30/1986 were redeemed at $0.025 per right 05/15/1994 for holders of record 05/09/1994
$3.875 Conv. Preferred $1 par called for redemption at $51.1625 plus $0.4951 accrued dividends on 06/16/1997
$2.50 Conv. Preferred $1 par called for redemption at $63 plus $0.60 accrued dividends on 06/10/2013
(Additional Information in Active)

GAULEY COAL LD CO (WV)
Liquidation completed
Each share Common $100 par received initial distribution of $250 cash 12/23/70
Each share Common $100 par stamped to indicate second distribution of $250 cash 2/12/71
Each share Stamped Common $100 par exchanged for third distribution of $35 cash 12/3/71
Each share Stamped Common $100 par received fourth distribution of $6 cash 12/20/77
Each share Stamped Common $100 par exchanged for fifth and final distribution of $2.60 cash 12/19/84

GAULEY MOUNTAIN CO (WV)
Voluntarily dissolved 12/10/58
Details not available

GAULEY MOUNTAIN COAL CO. (WV)
Name changed to Gauley Mountain Co. 7/12/56
(See Gauley Mountain Co.)

GAUMONT BRITISH LTD. (ENGLAND)
Merged into Rank Organisation, Ltd. 01/01/1962
Each ADR for (10) shares Class A Ordinary 5s par exchanged for (1.5) shares 6-1/4% Preference £1 par and (6.5) shares Class A Ordinary 5s par
Each ADR for (5) shares Ordinary 10s par exchanged for (1.875) shares 6-1/4% Preference £1 par and (6.5) shares Class A Ordinary 5s par
Note: Holders of the English shares received the Rank shares on the following basis without surrender of certificates which are therefore deemed worthless
For each share 5-1/2% Preference £1 par (0.95) share 6-1/4% Preference £1 par
For each share Class A Ordinary 5s par (0.15) share 6-1/4% Preference £1 par and (0.65) share Class A Ordinary 5s par
For each share Ordinary 10s par (0.375) share 6-1/4% Preference £1 par and (0.325) share Class A Ordinary 5s par
(See Rank Organisation PLC)

GAUMONT-BRITISH PICTURE CORP. LTD. (ENGLAND)
Name changed to Gaumont British Ltd. 11/19/1959
Gaumont British Ltd. merged into Rank Organisation, Ltd. 01/01/1962
(See Rank Organisation PLC)

GAUNTLET ENERGY CORP (AB)
Plan of Compromise and Arrangement under Companies' Creditors Arrangement Act effective 12/08/2003
No stockholders' equity

GAVAN MINES LTD (ON)
Charter cancelled for failure to pay taxes and file returns 07/27/1976

GAVELLA CORP (DE)
Recapitalized as DCI USA, Inc. 12/06/2004
Each share Common $0.001 par exchanged for (0.5) share Common $0.001 par
(See DCI USA, Inc.)

GAVEX A RES CORP (BC)
Recapitalized as Dorchester Hotels, Inc. 05/21/1986
Each share Common no par exchanged for (0.06666666) share Common no par
(See Dorchester Hotels, Inc.)

GAVEX GOLD MINES LTD. (BC)
Name changed to Gavex, A Resource Corporation 06/10/1981
Gavex, A Resource Corporation recapitalized as Dorchester Hotels, Inc. 05/21/1986
(See Dorchester Hotels, Inc.)

GAVWEST RES LTD (BC)
Name changed to Ridgeline Energy Services Inc. 07/21/2006
Ridgeline Energy Services Inc. name changed to RDX Technologies Corp. 08/21/2013

GAY GIBSON INC (DE)
Adjudicated bankrupt 8/19/77
No stockholders' equity

GAY INTL INC (UT)
Name changed to Merit Diversified International, Inc. (UT) 11/28/1988
Merit Diversified International, Inc. (UT) reincorporated in Nevada 08/09/1994 which name changed to Allied Artists Entertainment Group, Inc. 09/15/2000 which recapitalized as International Synergy Holding Co. Ltd. 07/10/2001 which name changed to Along Mobile Technologies, Inc. 12/27/2005
(See Along Mobile Technologies, Inc.)

GAY RIVER LEAD MINES LTD. (ON)
Former transfer agent advised charter was reported cancelled 04/00/1969

GAYLE INDS INC (UT)
Recapitalized as Swing Bike 7/1/77
Each share Common $0.002 par exchanged for (0.5) share Common $0.002 par
Swing Bike recapitalized as Horizon Energy Corp. 12/24/79 which name changed to New Horizon Education, Inc. 6/7/93 which name changed to American Hospital Resources, Inc. 6/26/2002 which name changed to HAPS USA, Inc. 5/12/2005 which name changed to PGMI, Inc. 3/16/2006

GAYLORD CONTAINER CORP. (MD)
Each share Common $5 par exchanged for (3) shares Common $1.66-2/3 par in 1946
Merged into Crown Zellerbach Corp. 11/30/55
Each share Common $1.66-2/3 par exchanged for (1) share Common $5 par
Crown Zellerbach Corp. merged into James River Corp. of Virginia 10/30/86 which name changed to Fort James Corp. 8/13/97 which merged into Georgia-Pacific Corp. 11/27/2000
(See Georgia-Pacific Corp.)

GAYLORD CONTAINER CORP (DE)
Class A Common 1¢ par changed to $0.0001 par 10/16/92
Merged into Temple-Inland Inc. 4/5/2002
Each share Class A Common $0.0001 par exchanged for $1.17 cash

GAYLORD CORP (CO)
Name changed to Benefund Inc. 11/22/1991
(See Benefund Inc.)

GAYLORD COS INC (DE)
Issue Information - 800,000 shares COM offered at $6 per share on 12/12/1994
Name changed to Home Retail Holdings, Inc. 8/12/98
Home Retail Holdings, Inc. name changed to Rolling Pin Kitchen Emporium, Inc. 9/15/98
(See Rolling Pin Kitchen Emporium, Inc.)

GAYLORD ENTMT CO NEW (DE)
Name changed to Ryman Hospitality Properties, Inc. 10/01/2012

GAYLORD ENTMT CO OLD (DE)
Class A Common 1¢ par split (2) for (1) by issuance of (1) additional share 9/13/93
Stock Dividend - 5% payable 6/18/96 to holders of record 6/4/96
Each share Class A Common 1¢ par received distribution of (1/3) share Gaylord Entertainment Co. (New) Common 1¢ par payable 10/7/97 to holders of record 9/30/97
Merged into Westinghouse Electric Corp. 10/1/97
Each share Class A Common 1¢ par exchanged for (0.606) share Common $1 par
Westinghouse Electric Corp. name changed to CBS Corp. 12/1/97 which merged into Viacom Inc. (Old) 5/4/2000
(See Viacom Inc. (Old))

GAYLORD (ROBERT) INC.
Merged into Gaylord Container Corp. in 1937
Details not available

GAYLORD MINES LTD (BC)
Name changed to Moex Industries Ltd. 06/03/1981
(See Moex Industries Ltd.)

GAYLORDS NATL CORP (NY)
Common 10¢ par split (6) for (5) by issuance of (0.2) additional share 5/23/67
Common 10¢ par split (3) for (2) by issuance of (0.5) additional share 12/20/68
Merged into Zayre Sub, Inc. 5/24/85
Each share Common 10¢ par exchanged for $8.50 cash

GAYLORDSVILLE ELECTRIC CO.
Merged into Connecticut Light & Power Co. in 1929
Details not available

GAYMONT MINES LTD. (ON)
Acquired by New Lorie Mines Ltd. 00/00/1952
Each share Capital Stock $1 par exchanged for (0.2) share Capital Stock $1 par
New Lorie Mines Ltd. recapitalized as Lorie Resources Ltd. 03/10/1981 which recapitalized as Theme Restaurants Inc. 12/30/1986
(See Theme Restaurants Inc.)

GAYNOR & CO INC (NY)
Dissolved by proclamation 12/24/91

GAYNOR INDS INC (NY)
Name changed to Gaynor-Stafford Industries, Inc. 11/20/1970
(See Gaynor-Stafford Industries, Inc.)

GAYNOR-STAFFORD INDS INC (NY)
Merged into New Merger Corp. 6/7/85
Each share Common 10¢ par exchanged for $0.20 cash

GAZ METRO LTD PARTNERSHIP (QC)
Name changed 11/18/2003
Name changed from Gaz Metro & Co., Ltd. Partnership to Gaz Metro Limited Partnership 11/18/2003
Reorganized under the laws of Canada as Valener Inc. 10/01/2010
Each Unit exchanged for (1) share Common no par
Note: Unexchanged certificates were cancelled and became without value 10/01/2016

GAZ METROPOLITAIN INC (QC)
Common $1 par changed to no par and (1) additional share issued 12/03/1969
Acquired by Noverco Inc. 08/01/1986
Each share Common no par exchanged for (1) share Common no par
15% 2nd Preferred Ser. B $25 par called for redemption 01/05/1987
2nd Preferred Ser. C $25 par called for redemption 08/09/1991
5.5% Preferred 1966 Ser. $100 par called for redemption 08/09/1991
5.4% Preferred 1965 Ser. $100 par called for redemption 08/09/1991
Public interest eliminated

GAZELLE RES LTD (BC)
Name changed to Pan Oceanic Ventures Inc. 08/29/1990
Pan Oceanic Ventures Inc. recapitalized as Falcon Ventures International Corp. 12/03/1991 which recapitalized as Falcon Ventures Inc. (BC) 12/24/2002 which reincorporated in Alberta as Falcon Ventures International Inc. 06/26/2008 which reorganized in British Columbia as Firebird Resources Inc. 11/05/2009

GAZIT AMER INC (ON)
Merged into First Capital Realty Inc. 08/08/2012
Each share Common no par exchanged for (0.2343) share Common no par and $3.31 cash

GAZOO ENERGY GROUP INC (NV)
SEC revoked common stock registration 04/23/2013

GAZPROM NEFT (RUSSIA)
Name changed to Gazprom Neft PJSC 12/03/2015

GAZPROM O A O (RUSSIA)
Reg. S Sponsored ADR's for Ordinary split (5) for (2) by issuance of (1.5) additional ADR's payable 04/18/2006 to holders of record 04/14/2006 Ex date - 04/19/2006
Reg. S 1999 Sponsored ADR's for Ordinary split (5) for (2) by issuance of (1.5) additional ADR's payable 04/18/2006 to holders of record 04/14/2006 Ex date - 04/19/2006
Basis changed from (1:10) to (1:4) 04/18/2006
Reg. S 1999 Sponsored ADR's for Ordinary reclassified as Sponsored ADR's for Ordinary 05/13/2008
Sponsored ADR's for Ordinary split (2) for (1) by issuance of (1) additional ADR payable 04/21/2011

to holders of record 04/20/2011
Ex date - 04/26/2011
Basis changed from (1:4) to (1:2) 04/21/2011
Name changed to Gazprom PJSC 02/03/2016

GB BANCORPORATION (CA)
Merged into Zions Bancorporation 11/14/1997
Each share Common exchanged for (2.2748) shares Common no par Bancorporation, N.A. (Salt Lake City, UT) 10/01/2018

GB FOODS CORP (DE)
Common 10¢ par split (5) for (4) by issuance of (0.25) additional share 08/28/1991
Name changed to Santa Barbara Restaurant Group, Inc. 09/01/1998
Santa Barbara Restaurant Group, Inc. merged into CKE Restaurants, Inc. 03/01/2002
(See CKE Restaurants, Inc.)

GB HLDGS INC (DE)
Plan of reorganization under Chapter 11 Federal Bankruptcy Code effective 2/9/2007
Holders are expected to receive a cash distribution

GB HLDGS LTD (SINGAPORE)
Sponsored ADR's for Ordinary split (2) for (1) by issuance of (1) additional ADR 11/14/1990
Stock Dividend - 10% 02/24/1993
Name changed to Grand Banks Yachts Ltd. 11/15/2004
(See Grand Banks Yachts Ltd.)

GB MINERALS LTD (BC)
Merged into Itafos 02/28/2018
Each share Common no par exchanged for (0.035714) share Ordinary CAD $0.001 par
Note: Unexchanged certificates will be cancelled and become without value 02/28/2024

GB&T BANCSHARES INC (GA)
Common $5 par split (5) for (4) by issuance of (0.25) additional share payable 09/21/1998 to holders of record 08/31/1998
Common $5 par changed to no par and (0.25) additional share issued payable 06/18/2004 to holders of record 06/01/2004 Ex date - 06/21/2004
Merged into SunTrust Banks, Inc. 05/01/2008
Each share Common no par exchanged for (0.1562) share Common $1 par

GBB CAP I (CA)
Trust Preferred Securities called for redemption at $25 on 07/22/2002

GBB CAP V (DE)
9% Trust Preferred Securities called for redemption at $25 on 8/31/2006

GBC BANCORP (CA)
Common no par split (2) for (1) by issuance of (1) additional share payable 5/15/98 to holders of record 4/30/98
Stock Dividends - 10% 1/16/91; 10% 7/16/92
Merged into Cathay General Bancorp 10/20/2003
Each share Common no par exchanged for (0.09304) share Common no par and $35.55207 cash

GBC CAP LTD (CANADA)
Name changed 04/27/1977
Common $18 par changed to no par and (2) additional shares issued 11/23/1972
Name changed from GBC Capital Ltd. to GBC Capital Ltd.-Capital GBC Ltee. and 5.25% 1st Preferred $50 par reclassified as $2.625 Preferred no par 04/27/1977
Common no par split (27) for (1) by issuance of (26) additional shares 11/30/1984
$2.625 Preferred no par called for redemption 01/15/1988
Name changed to GBC North America Fund Inc. 01/25/1989
GBC North America Fund Inc. name changed to GBC North American Growth Fund Inc. 01/15/1991 which name changed to GBC American Growth Fund Inc. 03/28/2011

GBC NORTH AMERN GROWTH FD INC (CANADA)
Name changed 01/15/1991
Name changed from GBC North America Fund Inc. to GBC North American Growth Fund Inc. 01/15/1991
Name changed to GBC American Growth Fund Inc. 03/28/2011

GBC TECHNOLOGIES INC (NJ)
Merged into Globelle Corp. 01/17/1996
Each share Common 1¢ par exchanged for $9.50 cash

GBCI CAP TR (DE)
8.75% Preferred Securities called for redemption at $25 plus $0.13368 accrued dividend on 4/22/2004

GBCI CAP TR II (DE)
9.12% Guaranteed Preferred Securities called for redemption at $25 on 11/15/2004

GBI CAP MGMT CORP (FL)
Name changed to Ladenburg Thalmann Financial Services Inc. 05/08/2001

GBI INTL INDS INC (NY)
Each share old Common 1¢ par exchanged for (1/3) share new Common 1¢ par 11/6/84
Dissolved by proclamation 9/25/91

GBM EXPLS LTD (BC)
Reorganized as American Biodynamics Inc. (BC) 07/22/1986
Each share Common no par exchanged for (2) shares Common no par
American Biodynamics Inc. (BC) reincorporated in Florida as Biodynamics International, Inc. 06/01/1992 which name changed to Tutogen Medical, Inc. 04/15/1998 which merged into RTI Biologics, Inc. 02/27/2008 which name changed to RTI Surgical, Inc. 07/18/2013

GBO INC (QC)
Deemed to have made an assignment in bankruptcy 10/10/2011
Stockholders' equity unlikely

GBS COM-TECH CORP (DE)
Ceased operations 06/18/1999
Stockholders' equity unlikely

GBS ENTERPRISES INC (NV)
Recapitalized as Marizyme, Inc. 07/27/2018
Each share Common $0.001 par exchanged for (0.03448275) share Common $0.001 par

GBS TECH HLDG CORP (UT)
Merged into International Communications & Technologies Corp. 03/15/1996
Each share Common no par exchanged for (1) share Common $0.0001 par
International Communications & Technologies Corp. recapitalized as GBS Com-Tech Corp. 05/15/1997
(See GBS Com-Tech Corp.)

GBS TECHNOLOGIES CORP (UT)
Recapitalized as GBS Tech Holding Corp. 02/11/1994
Each share Common no par exchanged for (0.1) share Common no par
GBS Tech Holding Corp. merged into International Communications & Technologies Corp. 03/15/1996 which recapitalized as GBS Com-Tech Corp. 05/15/1997
(See GBS Com-Tech Corp.)

GBT BANCORP (MA)
Merged into Andover Bancorp, Inc. 7/1/2000
Each share Common $25 par exchanged for either (0.7543) share Common 10¢ par, $20.50 cash, or a combination thereof
Note: Option to receive stock and cash or cash only expired 7/26/2000
Andover Bancorp, Inc. merged into Banknorth Group, Inc. (ME) 10/31/2001 which merged into TD Banknorth Inc. 3/1/2005
(See TD Banknorth Inc.)

GBX MINES LTD. (BC)
Recapitalized as El Paso Energy Corp. 08/20/1979
Each share Common no par exchanged for (0.33333333) share Common no par
El Paso Energy Corp. recapitalized as E.L.E. Energy Corp. 10/05/1984 which recapitalized as Maple Leaf Springs Water Corp. 11/12/1992 which recapitalized as International Maple Leaf Springs Ltd. 02/24/1998
(See International Maple Leaf Springs Ltd.)

GBX RESOURCE CORP (BC)
Struck off register and declared dissolved for failure to file returns 12/18/1992

GC COS INC (DE)
Plan of reorganization under Chapter 11 bankruptcy proceedings effective 3/29/2002
Each share Common 1¢ par exchanged for $0.86 cash

GC GLOBAL CAP CORP (QC)
Name changed to Fountain Asset Corp. 09/02/2015

GC GREYHAWKE CORP (AB)
Struck off register for failure to file annual returns 12/01/1995

GCA CORP (DE)
Common 60¢ par split (3) for (2) by issuance of (0.5) additional share 3/31/70
Common 60¢ par split (3) for (2) by issuance of (0.5) additional share 12/31/79
Common 60¢ par split (3) for (2) by issuance of (0.5) additional share 9/11/80
Common 60¢ par split (3) for (2) by issuance of (0.5) additional share 5/24/81
Common 60¢ par split (3) for (2) by issuance of (0.5) additional share 8/31/83
Each share Common 60¢ par exchanged for (0.02) share Common 1¢ par 4/23/87
Acquired by General Signal Corp. 6/7/88
Each share Common 1¢ par exchanged for (0.101) share Common $1 par
General Signal Corp. merged into SPX Corp. 10/6/98

GCB BANCORP, INC. (IN)
Acquired by Old National Bancorp 2/28/87
Each share Common no par exchanged for (2.4085) shares Common no par

GCB CAP TR (DE)
Preferred Securitites called for redemption at $25 on 7/8/2002

GCB CAP TR II (DE)
8.45% Trust Preferred Securities called for redemption at $10 on 06/30/2007

GCH CAP PARTNERS INC (BC)
Name changed to Solarvest BioEnergy Inc. 09/19/2008

GCI, INC. (NJ)
Liquidation completed
Each share Common $1 par exchanged for initial distribution of $9.75 cash 11/16/76
Each share Common $1 par received second and final distribution of $0.06612 cash 1/13/78

GCI INDS INC (UT)
Each share old Common 10¢ par exchanged for (0.25) share new Common 10¢ par 8/22/82
Stock Dividend - 100% 8/31/84
Merged into PG Acquisition, Inc. 9/10/90
Each share new Common 10¢ par exchanged for $2.65 cash

GCI INTL INC (NV)
Common $2 par changed to 1¢ par 7/15/83
Name changed to American Dynamics Corp. (NV) 3/15/84
(See American Dynamics Corp.)

GCI LIBERTY INC (AK)
Each share Class A-1 Common no par automatically became (0.2) share Ser. A Preferred and (0.63) share Class A Common no par 03/12/2018
Each share Class B-1 Common no par automatically became (0.2) share Ser. A Preferred and (0.63) share Class A Common no par 03/12/2018
Reincorporated under the laws of Delaware and Ser. A Preferred no par, Class A Common no par and Class B Common no par changed to 1¢ par 05/10/2018

GCL GRAPHIC COMMUNICATIONS LTD (ON)
Ceased operations 12/16/1976
No stockholders' equity

GCP MNG CORP (BC)
Name changed to Kodiak Exploration Ltd. 09/08/2003
Kodiak Exploration Ltd. name changed to Prodigy Gold Inc. 01/04/2011

GCR HLDGS LTD (BERMUDA)
Merged into Exel Ltd. 06/11/1997
Each share Ordinary $10 par exchanged for $27 cash

GCST CORP (FL)
Name changed to RBid.Com Inc. 4/22/99

GDC GROUP INC (CO)
Proclaimed dissolved for failure to file reports 6/1/99

GDF SUEZ (FRANCE)
Name changed to Engie 07/31/2015

GDG DATA SYS INC (NY)
Company reported out of business 00/00/1975
Details not available

GDG ENVIRONMENT GROUP LTD (QC)
Each share old Common no par exchanged for (0.0000025) share new Common no par 02/01/2011
Note: In effect holders received $0.06 cash per share and public interest was eliminated

GDL FD (DE)
8.5% Preferred Ser. A $0.001 par called for redemption at $50 plus $0.7674 accrued dividends on 05/31/2011
Preferred Ser. B $0.001 par called for for redemption at $50 plus $0.2625 accrued dividends on 05/29/2018
(Additional Information in Active)

GDN MGMT LTD (ON)
Name changed to Guardian Capital Group Ltd. 07/18/1973

GDT TEK INC (FL)
Each share old Common $0.001 par exchanged for (0.0001) share new Common $0.001 par 02/29/2012
SEC revoked common stock registration 07/25/2013

GDV INC (DE)
Merged into City Investing Co. 09/12/1983
Each share Common $1 par exchanged for $27.50 cash

GDV RES INC (ON)
Name changed to Cardinal Capital Partners Inc. 09/13/2013

GE CAP PFD ASSET CORP (DE)
Auction Market Preferred Stock Ser. A called for redemption at $100.50 on 6/4/2007
Auction Market Preferred Stock Ser. B called for redemption at $100.50 on 6/4/2007
Auction Market Preferred Stock Ser. C called for redemption at $100.50 on 6/4/2007
Auction Market Preferred Stock Ser. D called for redemption at $100.50 on 6/4/2007
Auction Market Preferred Stock Ser. E called for redemption at $100.50 on 6/4/2007
144A Auction Market Preferred Stock Ser. F called for redemption at $100.50 on 6/4/2007
144A Auction Market Preferred Stock Ser. G called for redemption at $100.50 on 6/4/2007
144A Auction Market Preferred Stock Ser. H called for redemption at $100.50 on 6/4/2007
144A Auction Market Preferred Stock Ser. I called for redemption at $100.50 on 6/4/2007
Auction Market Preferred Stock Ser. J called for redemption at $100.50 on 6/4/2007
Auction Market Preferred Stock Ser. K called for redemption at $100.50 on 6/4/2007
Accredited Investors Auction Market Preferred Stock Ser. L called for redemption at $100.50 on 6/4/2007
Market Preferred Stock called for redemption at $100.50 on 6/4/2007

GEA TECHNOLOGIES LTD (AB)
Name changed to International Cannabrands Inc. 12/05/2017

GEAC COMPUTER LTD (CANADA)
Common no par split (2) for (1) by issuance of (1) additional share payable 11/04/1997 to holders of record 10/31/1997
Merged into Golden Gate Capital 03/15/2006
Each share Common no par exchanged for $11.10 cash

GEAC INC (TX)
Name changed to Golfing Network.com Inc. 08/02/1999
Golfing Network.com Inc. name changed to Netweb Online.com Inc. (TX) 12/14/1999 which reorganized in Florida as Spectrum Brands Corp. 05/16/2001
(See Spectrum Brands Corp.)

GEAR INTL INC (WY)
Reorganized under the laws of Delaware as Matchaah Holdings, Inc. 06/19/2017
Each share Common $0.001 par exchanged for (0.00014066) share Common $0.001 par

GEARHART INDS INC (TX)
Common 50¢ par split (2) for (1) by issuance of (1) additional share 8/15/80
Merged into Halliburton Co. 9/23/88
Each share Common 50¢ par exchanged for (0.02917) share Common $2.50 par

GEARHART-OWEN INDUSTRIES, INC. (TX)
Common 50¢ par split (2) for (1) by issuance of (1) additional share 07/12/1976
Common 50¢ par split (2) for (1) by issuance of (1) additional share 08/15/1978
Name changed to Gearhart Industries, Inc. 06/30/1980
Gearhart Industries, Inc. merged into Halliburton Co. 09/23/1988

GEARKO, INC.
Name changed to Transtates Petroleum, Inc. 00/00/1951
(See Transtates Petroleum, Inc.)

GEARS & FORGING, INC.
Reorganized as Ohio Forge & Machine Corp. in 1934
Details not available

GEARUNLIMITED COM INC (CANADA)
Dissolved for non-compliance 03/12/2007

GECAMEX TECHNOLOGIES INC (CANADA)
Merged into Versatech Group Inc. 06/30/1998
Each share Common no par exchanged for (1.02) shares Common no par
(See Versatech Group Inc.)

GECKOSYSTEMS INC (DC)
Reincorporated under the laws of Wyoming as ImagiTrend, Inc. 08/08/2007
ImagiTrend, Inc. name changed to Castle Technologies, Inc. 04/28/2008 which recapitalized as Hawaiian Hospitality Group, Inc. 08/14/2009

GECKOSYSTEMS INTL CORP (DE)
Reincorporated under the laws of Georgia 08/05/2011

GECO MINES LTD. (ON)
Merged into Noranda Mines Ltd. on a (7/8) for (1) basis 12/15/64
Noranda Mines Ltd. name changed to Noranda Inc. 5/28/84 which name changed to Falconbridge Ltd. (New) 2005 on 7/1/2005
(See Falconbridge Ltd. (New) 2005)

GEDDES RES LTD (ON)
Merged into Royal Oak Mines Inc. 01/15/1996
Each share Common no par exchanged for (0.3) share Common no par
Royal Oak Mines Inc. recapitalized as Royal Oak Ventures Inc. 02/14/2000
(See Royal Oak Ventures Inc.)

GEDEON RICHTER LTD (HUNGARY)
Each Temporary Reg. S GDR for Ordinary exchanged for (1) Reg. S GDR for Ordinary 07/09/1997
(Additional Information in Active)

GEE-TEN VENTURES INC (CANADA)
Reincorporated 07/30/2008
Place of incorporation changed from (BC) to (Canada) 07/30/2008
Each share old Common no par exchanged for (0.1) share new Common no par 06/03/2010
Name changed to Cabia Goldhills Inc. 11/23/2011

GEEKNET INC (DE)
Each share old Common $0.001 par exchanged for (0.1) share new Common $0.001 par 11/10/2010
Acquired by GameStop Corp. (New) 07/17/2015
Each share new Common $0.001 par exchanged for $20 cash

GEERLINGS & WADE INC (MA)
Issue Information - 1,400,000 shares COM offered at $8 per share on 06/17/1994
Filed a petition under Chapter 7 Federal Bankruptcy Code 04/14/2010
No stockholders' equity

GEHL CO (WI)
Common 10¢ par split (3) for (2) by issuance of (0.5) additional share payable 08/24/2005 to holders of record 08/10/2005 Ex date - 08/25/2005
Merged into Manitou BF S.A. 10/27/2008
Each share Common 10¢ par exchanged for $30 cash

GEICO ADJUSTABLE RATE PFD FD (MA)
Name changed to GEICO Qualified Dividend Fund 5/1/87
(See GEICO Qualified Dividend Fund)

GEICO CORP (DE)
$0.736 Conv. Jr. Preferred $1 par called for redemption 11/1/82
Common $1 par split (5) for (1) by issuance of (4) additional shares 6/3/92
Merged into Berkshire Hathaway Inc. 1/2/96
Each share Common $1 par exchanged for $70 cash

GEICO QUALIFIED DIVID FD (MA)
Fund dissolved in 1991
Details not available

G8WAVE HLDGS INC (DE)
Common $0.0000001 par split (32) for (1) by issuance of (31) additional shares payable 08/30/2007 to holders of record 08/30/2007
Name changed to China Gateway Corp. 07/03/2008

GELATECH CORP (CO)
Declared defunct and inoperative for failure to pay taxes and file annual reports 08/01/2000

GELCO CORP (MN)
Common 50¢ par split (2) for (1) by issuance of (1) additional share 8/8/72
Under plan of merger name changed to Gelco-Feld Corp. 10/22/74 which name changed back to Gelco Corp. 12/4/75
Common 50¢ par split (3) for (2) by issuance of (0.5) additional share 10/17/80
Merged into General Electric Capital Corp. 12/17/87
Each share Common 50¢ par exchanged for $35 cash
Class A Preferred Ser. 4 Depositary Receipts called for redemption 12/28/87
Public interest eliminated

GELCO ENTERPRISES, LTD. (CANADA)
Recapitalized 12/28/1965
Each share Common 1¢ par exchanged for $3.25 cash

GELCO FELD CORP (MN)
Name changed back to Gelco Corp. 12/4/75
(See Gelco Corp.)

GELCO-IVM LEASING CO. (MN)
Name changed to Gelco Corp. and Common $1 par changed to 50¢ par 7/18/72
Gelco Corp. name changed to Gelco-Feld Corp. 10/22/74 which name changed back to Gelco Corp. 12/4/75
(See Gelco Corp.)

GELIA GROUP CORP (NV)
Common $0.001 par split (4.2721) for (1) by issuance of (3.272) additional shares payable 11/04/2013 to holders of record 11/04/2013
Ex date - 11/05/2013
Name changed to Starstream Entertainment, Inc. 11/11/2013

GELLIS S & CO INC (DE)
Adjudicated bankrupt 10/30/75
Stockholders' equity unlikely

GELLMAN MANUFACTURING CO. (IL)
Name changed to Amco Industries, Inc. (IL) 3/1/63
Amco Industries, Inc. (IL) reincorporated under the laws of Delaware 6/27/69
(See Amco Industries, Inc. (DE))

GELMAN SCIENCES INC (MI)
Reincorporated 12/31/1969
Name changed 01/05/1979
Reincorporated 01/30/1981
Common no par split (2) for (1) by issuance of (1) additional share 06/01/1966
Common no par split (2) for (1) by issuance of (1) additional share 06/07/1968
State of incorporation changed from (MI) to (DE) and Common no par changed to 10¢ par 12/31/1969
Name changed from Gelman Instrument Co. to Gelman Sciences, Inc. 01/05/1979
Common 10¢ par split (5) for (4) by issuance of (0.25) additional share 02/05/1980
State of incorporation changed from (DE) to (MI) 01/30/1981
Common 10¢ par split (3) for (2) by issuance of (0.5) additional share 12/28/1993
Common 10¢ par split (3) for (2) by issuance of (0.5) additional share 08/12/1994
Stock Dividend - 20% 02/05/1981
Merged into Pall Corp. 03/13/1997
Each share Common 10¢ par exchanged for (1.3047) shares Common 25¢ par
(See Pall Corp.)

GELSENKIRCHENER BERGWERKS A G (GERMANY)
Acquired by Veba AG 00/00/1974
Details not available

GELTEX PHARMACEUTICALS INC (DE)
Merged into Genzyme Corp. 12/14/2000
Each share Common 1¢ par exchanged for $47.50 cash

GELTOLOGY INC (DE)
Recapitalized as General Agriculture Corp. 07/15/2013
Each share Common $0.0001 par exchanged for (0.125) share Common $0.0001 par

GEM EXPLORATIONS LTD. (BC)
Recapitalized as Consolidated Gem Explorations Ltd. 01/08/1968
Each share Capital Stock 50¢ par exchanged for (0.25) share Capital Stock no par
Consolidated Gem Explorations Ltd. recapitalized as Brendon Resources Ltd. 02/13/1973 which recapitalized as Brendex Resources Ltd. 09/10/1976
(See Brendex Resources Ltd.)

GEM INTL INC (CO)
Common $1 par changed to 70¢ par and (0.5) additional share issued 1/23/62
Acquired by Parkview-Gem, Inc. 6/30/66
Each share Common 70¢ par exchanged for (0.25) share Common $1 par
(See Parkview-Gem, Inc.)

GEM LIGOS II LTD (CAYMAN ISLANDS)
144A 3C7 Preferred called for redemption 2/10/2006

GEM RIV CORP (DE)
Company received notice of events of default 07/16/1998
Stockholders' equity unlikely

GEM SOLUTIONS INC (DE)
Each share old Common $0.001 par exchanged for (0.00994367) share new Common $0.001 par 06/02/2008
SEC revoked common stock registration 12/18/2012

GEM SOURCE INC (NV)
Recapitalized as Blue Ridge Energy, Inc. 06/17/1996
Each share Common $0.001 par exchanged for (0.2) share Common $0.005 par
Blue Ridge Energy, Inc. name changed to Bayou City Exploration, Inc. 06/22/2005
(See Bayou City Exploration, Inc.)

GEM ST RES INC (NV)
Name changed to Compliance Recycling Industries, Inc. 5/6/86
Compliance Recycling Industries, Inc. name changed to Enviroserve, Inc. 10/9/92

GEM ST SECS CORP (ID)
Class A Common $1 par reclassified as Common $1 par 04/24/1972
Class B Common $1 par reclassified as Common $1 par 04/24/1972
Common $1 par changed to 50¢ par and (1) additional share issued 06/11/1973
Stock Dividend - 10% 05/19/1972
Merged into Universal Security Life Insurance Co. (WA) 08/05/1982
Each share Common 50¢ par exchanged for (0.2) share Common $1 par
(See Universal Security Life Insurance Co. (WA))

GEM URANIUM & OIL CO (UT)
Recapitalized as Sunbird Technologies, Inc. 11/21/88
Each share Common 1¢ par exchanged for (0.04) share Common 1¢ par
(See Sunbird Technologies, Inc.)

GEMCO, INC. (TX)
Completely liquidated 5/1/66
Each share Capital Stock $1 par exchanged for first and final distribution of $1.50 cash

GEMCO NATL INC (NY)
Reincorporated under the laws of Florida as Investors Insurance Group, Inc. 09/01/1993
(See Investors Insurance Group, Inc.)

GEMCO SHAPER CO (MO)
Completely liquidated 4/10/68
Each share 5% Preferred $10 par exchanged for first and final distribution $2.78 cash
No Common stockholders' equity

GEMCOM SOFTWARE INTL INC (BC)
Acquired by JMI Equity 07/28/2008
Each share Common no par exchanged for $3.05 cash

GEMCRAFT INC (DE)
Merged into FTS Mortgage Corp. 11/4/88
Each share Common 10¢ par exchanged for $1.50 cash

GEMEX MINERALS INC (ON)
Merged into MM-G International Inc. 09/21/1982
Each share Common no par exchanged for (0.1) share Common no par and (0.1) Common Stock Purchase Warrant expiring 09/20/1983
MM-G International Inc. name changed to Stratas Corp. Ltd. 09/30/1983
(See Stratas Corp. Ltd.)

GEMINEX INDS INC (CA)
Charter suspended for failure to pay taxes 4/1/94

GEMINI ACQUISITIONS INC (ON)
Name changed to Silver Shield Resources Corp. 03/12/2008
Silver Shield Resources Corp. name changed to Gunpowder Capital Corp. 05/17/2016

GEMINI ENERGY CORP (BC)
Merged into Bucking Horse Energy Inc. 03/03/2008
Each share Common no par exchanged for $4 cash

GEMINI ENERGY CORP (NV)
Name changed 08/16/1990
Name changed from Gemini Capital Corp to Gemini Energy Corp. 08/16/1990
Name changed to Nerox Energy Corp. 01/28/1994
Nerox Energy Corp. name changed to E*twoMedia.com 12/15/1998 which name changed to Exus Networks, Inc. 12/19/2000 which recapitalized as Exus Global, Inc. 09/12/2003 which recapitalized as StarInvest Group, Inc. 01/14/2005
(See StarInvest Group, Inc.)

GEMINI EXPLORATIONS INC (NV)
Each share old Common $0.001 par exchanged for (10) shares new Common $0.001 par 01/29/2007
Each share new Common $0.001 par exchanged again for (2) shares new Common $0.001 par 07/11/2007
Each share new Common $0.001 par exchanged again for (0.005) share new Common $0.001 par 06/23/2009
SEC revoked common stock registration 07/25/2013

GEMINI FD INC (MD)
Reincorporated 6/1/73
State of incorporation changed from (DE) to (MD) 6/1/73
Income Shares $1 par called for redemption 12/31/84
(Additional Information in Active)

GEMINI FOOD CORP (ON)
Acquired by Prince Edward Island Development Agency 11/29/1988
Each share $10 Conv. Retractable Preferred no par exchanged for $9.50 cash
Each share Common no par exchanged for $0.50 cash

GEMINI GENOMICS PLC (ENGLAND)
Merged into Sequenom, Inc. 09/20/2001
Each Sponsored ADR for Ordinary exchanged for (0.4) share Common $0.001 par
(See Sequenom, Inc.)

GEMINI MARKETING INC (CO)
Recapitalized as Gemini Shareware Inc. 11/21/1990
Each share Common $0.0001 par exchanged for (0.05) share Common $0.0001 par
(See Gemini Shareware Inc.)

GEMINI PAC CORP (NV)
Charter revoked for failure to file reports and pay fees 03/04/1974

GEMINI SHAREWARE INC (CO)
Administratively dissolved 11/02/2002

GEMINI TECHNOLOGY INC (BC)
Recapitalized as International Gemini Technology Inc. 09/23/1993
Each share Common no par exchanged for (0.2) share Common no par
International Gemini Technology Inc. name changed to Widescope Resources Inc. 07/12/2006 which recapitalized as North American Nickel Inc. 07/07/2010

GEMINI II INC (MD)
Income Shares $1 par called for redemption 1/31/97
(Additional Information in Active)

GEMINI VENTURE CORP (UT)
Name changed to A. T. & E. Corp. (UT) 1/1/76
A. T. & E. Corp. (UT) reincorporated in Delaware 6/29/83
(See A.T. & E. Corp.)

GEMINI VENTURES INC (CO)
Recapitalized as Solomon Trading Co. Ltd. 07/17/1989
Each share Common no par exchanged for (0.2) share Common no par
Solomon Trading Co. Ltd. recapitalized as Voyageur First Inc. 11/17/1994 which name changed to North American Resorts Inc. 03/30/1995 which name changed to Immulabs Corp. 09/15/2000 which name changed to Xerion EcoSolutions Group, Inc. (CO) 04/07/2003 which reorganized in Nevada as SINO-American Development Corp. 06/19/2006 which recapitalized as Harvest Bio-Organic International Co., Ltd. 12/07/2010
(See Harvest Bio-Organic International Co., Ltd.)

GEMMER MANUFACTURING CO. (MI)
Recapitalized in 1948
Class A no par changed to $37.50 par
Class B no par changed to $1 par and (1) additional share issued
Recapitalized in 1950
Each share Class A $37.50 par exchanged for (1) share Common $5 par
Each share Class B $1 par exchanged for (1) share Common $5 par
Stock Dividend - 100% 6/25/51
Merged into Ross Gear & Tool Co., Inc. on a (1) for (4.25) basis 8/31/56
Ross Gear & Tool Co., Inc. acquired by Thompson Ramo Wooldridge, Inc. 6/16/64 which name changed to TRW Inc. 4/30/65 which merged into Northrop Grumman Corp. 12/01/2002

GEMMIA OILTECH INDIA LTD (INDIA)
GDR agreement terminated 01/31/2014
Each Reg. S GDR for Ordinary exchanged for (90) shares Ordinary

GEMPLUS INTL S A (LUXEMBOURG)
Acquired by Gemalto N.V. 01/29/2007
Each Sponsored ADR for Ordinary exchanged for approximately $3.375 cash

GEMSTAR COMMUNICATIONS INC (ON)
Acquired by SIRIT Technologies Inc. 09/06/2001
Each share Common no par exchanged for (0.2) share Common no par
SIRIT Technologies Inc. acquired by iTech Capital Corp. 11/01/2002 which name changed to Sirit Inc. 05/05/2003
(See Sirit Inc.)

GEMSTAR ENTERPRISES INC (NV)
Common 2¢ par changed to $0.001 par 03/25/1996
Recapitalized as CGI Holding Corp. 08/04/1997
Each share Common $0.001 par exchanged for (0.2) share Common $0.001 par
CGI Holding Corp. name changed to Think Partnership, Inc. 03/14/2006 which name changed to Kowabunga! Inc. 10/01/2008 which name changed to Inuvo, Inc. 07/30/2009

GEMSTAR INTL GROUP LTD (BRITISH VIRGIN ISLANDS)
Ordinary 1¢ par split (2) for (1) by issuance of (1) additional share payable 12/13/1999 to holders of record 11/29/1999
Reincorporated under the laws of Delaware and Ordinary 1¢ par reclassified as Common 1¢ par 02/09/2000
Gemstar International Group Ltd. (DE) name changed to Gemstar-TV Guide International, Inc. 07/12/2000 which merged into Macrovision Solutions Corp. 05/05/2008 which name changed to Rovi Corp. 07/16/2009 which name changed to TiVo Corp. 09/08/2016

GEMSTAR INTL GROUP LTD (DE)
Name changed to Gemstar-TV Guide International, Inc. 07/12/2000
Gemstar-TV Guide International, Inc. merged into Macrovision Solutions Corp. 05/05/2008 which name changed to Rovi Corp. 07/16/2009 which name changed to TiVo Corp. 09/08/2016

GEMSTAR RES LTD (BC)
Recapitalized as Rouge Resources Ltd. 03/26/2008
Each share Common no par exchanged for (0.1) share Common no par
Rouge Resources Ltd. name changed to Fiore Exploration Ltd. 08/08/2016 which reorganized as Fiore Gold Ltd. 09/26/2017

GEMSTAR-TV GUIDE INTL INC (DE)
Merged into Macrovision Solutions Corp. 05/05/2008
Each share Common 1¢ par exchanged for (0.2548) share Common $0.001 par
Macrovision Solutions Corp. name changed to Rovi Corp. 07/16/2009 which name changed to TiVo Corp. 09/08/2016

GEMTEC CORP (WA)
Liquidation completed
Each share Common $1 par received initial distribution of $4 cash 07/21/1986
Each share Common $1 par received second and final distribution of (1) share Dravon Medical, Inc. Common no par and $0.15 cash 12/22/1986
Note: Certificates were not required to be surrendered and are without value

GEMWOOD PRODUCTIONS INC (NV)
Name changed to Kreido Biofuels, Inc. 11/9/2006

GEN / RX INC (NY)
Ceased operations 00/00/1996
Stockholders' equity unlikely

GEN 11, INC. (UT)
Recapitalized as Data 1, Inc. 08/17/1992
Each (1.75) shares Common $0.001 par exchanged for (1) share Common $0.001 par
Data 1, Inc. name changed to Diversified Resources Group, Inc. 06/06/1999 which name changed to AeroGroup Inc. 07/15/2003
(See AeroGroup Inc.)

GEN-ID LAB SVCS INC (MN)
Common $0.001 par split (2) for (1) by issuance of (1) additional share payable 12/16/2005 to holders of record 12/05/2005 Ex date - 12/20/2005
Recapitalized as Adventura Corp. 11/01/2009
Each share Common $0.001 par exchanged for (0.02) share Common $0.001 par

GEN-PROBE INC (DE)
Merged into Chugai Pharmaceutical Co., Ltd. 12/22/89

Each share Common 1¢ par exchanged for $6.25 cash

GEN-PROBE INC NEW (DE)
Each share Common $0.0001 par received distribution of (0.086) share Chugai Pharmaceutical Co., Ltd. Common payable 09/15/2002 to holders of record 07/31/2002
Common $0.0001 par split (2) for (1) by issuance of (1) additional share payable 09/30/2003 to holders of record 09/16/2003 Ex date - 10/01/2003
Acquired by Hologic Inc. 08/01/2012
Each share Common $0.0001 par exchanged for $82.75 cash

GEN TERM CORP (DE)
Charter cancelled and declared inoperative and void for non-payment of taxes 3/1/90

GENAERA LIQUIDATING TR (DE)
Assets transferred 07/08/2009
Each share old Common $0.002 par exchanged for (0.16666666) share new Common $0.002 par 05/15/2007
Assets transferred from Genaera Corp. to Genaera Liquidating Trust and Common $0.002 par reclassified as Units of Bene. Int. 07/08/2009
Liquidation completed
Each Unit of Bene. Int. received initial distribution of $0.13 cash payable 06/30/2010 to holders of record 06/12/2009
Each Unit of Bene. Int. received second and final distribution of $0.023 cash payable 03/31/2011 to holders of record 06/12/2009
Note: Certificates were not required to be surrendered and are without value

GENAISSANCE PHARMACEUTICALS INC (DE)
Issue Information - 6,000,000 shares COM offered at $13 per share on 08/01/2000
Merged into Clinical Data, Inc. (New) 10/07/2005
Each share Common 1¢ par exchanged for (0.065) share Common 1¢ par
(See Clinical Data, Inc. (New))

GENALTA PETROLEUMS, LTD. (ON)
Charter cancelled and declared dissolved for failure to file returns and pay fees 12/19/1955

GENATRON INC (NV)
Charter revoked for failure to file reports and pay fees 6/1/90

GENBEL SOUTH AFRICA LTD (SOUTH AFRICA)
Name changed 11/24/95
ADR's for Ordinary Rand-1 par changed to Rand-0.001 par and (9) additional ADR's issued 5/25/90
Name changed from Genbel Investments Ltd. to Genbel South Africa Ltd. 11/24/95
Stock Dividends - 2.0795% payable 11/14/97 to holders of record 8/15/97; 3.1324% payable 10/5/98 to holders of record 7/31/98; 4.984% payable 11/19/99 to holders of record 8/27/99; 4.0893% payable 10/24/2000 to holders of record 8/25/2000
ADR agreement terminated 9/12/2002
Each ADR for Ordinary Rand-0.001 par exchanged for $1.341 cash
Note: Due to ADR's being unsponsored exchange rate may vary dependent upon depositary agent

GENCARE HEALTH SYS INC (MO)
Acquired by United HealthCare Corp. 01/03/1995
Each share Common 2¢ par exchanged for $47.50 cash

GENCELL INC (NV)
Name changed to Gene-Cell, Inc. 10/8/97

GENCO INC. (DE)
In process of liquidation
Each share Common no par exchanged for initial distribution of (0.6180) share Foremost-McKesson, Inc. Common $2 par 12/11/78
Further details not available

GENCO INDS INC (BC)
Recapitalized as Consolidated Genco Industries Inc. 05/08/1990
Each share Common no par exchanged for (0.25) share Common no par
(See Consolidated Genco Industries Inc.)

GENCO RES LTD (BC)
Reorganized as Silvermex Resources Inc. 11/16/2010
Each share Common no par exchanged for (1.1) shares Common no par
Silvermex Resources Inc. merged into First Majestic Silver Corp. 07/06/2012

GENCO SHIPPING & TRADING LTD (MARSHALL ISLANDS)
Under Chapter 11 Federal Bankruptcy proceedings each share Common 1¢ par received (0.08860181) Common Stock Purchase Warrant expiring 00/00/2021 payable 07/11/2014 to holders of record 07/09/2014
(Additional Information in Active)

GENCONA MINES LTD (MB)
Recapitalized as Kelly Lake Nickel Mines Ltd. (MB) 09/16/1968
Each share Capital Stock no par exchanged for (0.25) share Capital Stock no par
Kelly Lake Nickel Mines Ltd. (MB) name changed to Albany Oil & Gas Ltd. (MB) 03/22/1971 which reincorporated in Alberta 11/10/1980 which name changed to Albany Corp. 05/17/1988 which merged into LifeSpace Environmental Walls Inc. 08/17/1993 which merged into SMED International Inc. 07/01/1996
(See SMED International Inc.)

GENCOR INVTS LTD (SOUTH AFRICA)
Name changed to Genbel Investments Ltd. 8/13/84
Genbel Investments Ltd. name changed to Genbel South Africa Ltd. 11/24/95
(See Genbel South Africa Ltd.)

GENCOR LTD (SOUTH AFRICA)
Old ADR's for Ordinary Rand-0.04 par split (10) for (1) by issuance of (9) additional ADR's 10/20/89
Each old ADR for Ordinary Rand-0.04 par exchanged for (0.2) new ADR for Ordinary rand-0.04 par 7/28/97
Each new ADR for Ordinary Rand-0.04 par received distribution of (0.75) Billiton PLC ADR for Ordinary payable 8/22/97 to holders of record 7/25/97
Each new ADR for Ordinary Rand-0.04 par received distribution of (0.25) Billiton PLC ADR for Ordinary payable 9/19/97 to holders of record 7/25/97
Company demerged 5/23/2003
Ordinary shares were sold in the local market and each new ADR for Ordinary Rand-0.04 par received $5.6832 cash payable 8/6/2003 to holders of record 7/30/2003
Certificates were not required to be surrendered and are valueless
Note: ADR's were unsponsored and payment rate may vary among agents

GENCORP INC (DE)
Reincorporated 04/14/2014
$5 Preference $100 par called for redemption 01/31/1986
4.75% Preference $100 par called for redemption 01/31/1986
Common 30¢ par changed to 10¢ par and (2) additional shares issued 12/23/1987
Each share Common 10¢ par received distribution of (1) share Omnova Solutions Inc. Common 10¢ par payable 10/01/1999 to holders of record 09/27/1999 Ex date - 10/04/1999
State of incorporation changed from (OH) to (DE) 04/14/2014
Name changed to Aerojet Rocketdyne Holdings, Inc. 04/27/2015

GENDER SCIENCES INC (NJ)
Each share old Common no par exchanged for (0.04) share new Common no par 02/07/2003
Reincorporated under the laws of Delaware as Medical Nutrition USA, Inc. and new Common no par changed to $0.001 par 04/22/2003
(See Medical Nutrition USA, Inc.)

GENDEX CORP (DE)
Common $1 par split (2) for (1) by issuance of (1) additional share 08/21/1992
Name changed to Dentsply International Inc. 06/11/1993
Dentsply International Inc. name changed to DENTSPLY SIRONA Inc. 03/01/2016

GENDIS INC (CANADA)
Conv. Class A Common no par split (4) for (3) by issuance of (0.33333333) additional share 06/15/1983
Conv. Class B Common no par split (4) for (3) by issuance of (0.33333333) additional share 06/15/1983
Conv. Class A Common no par split (2) for (1) by issuance of (1) additional share 05/23/1986
Conv. Class B Common no par split (2) for (1) by issuance of (1) additional share 05/23/1986
Conv. Class A Common no par reclassified as old Common no par 06/29/1999
Each share old Common no par received distribution of (0.5) share Fort Chicago Energy Partners L.P. Class A Unit of Ltd. Partnership Int. no par payable 01/02/2001 to holders of record 12/15/2000
Each share old Common no par exchanged for (0.000002) share new Common no par 04/17/2018
Note: In effect holders received $5.25 cash per share and public interest was eliminated

GENE CELL INC (NV)
Each share old Common $0.001 par exchanged for (0.01538461) share new Common $0.001 par 07/23/2002
Name changed to Redwood Energy Group, Inc. 01/09/2003
Redwood Energy Group, Inc. name changed to Redwood Entertainment Group Inc. 03/03/2003 which recapitalized as SaVi Media Group, Inc. 09/20/2004

GENE LOGIC INC (DE)
Name changed to Ore Pharmaceuticals Inc. 12/14/2007
Ore Pharmaceuticals Inc. reorganized as Ore Pharmaceutical Holdings Inc. 10/21/2009 which reorganized as Ore Holdings Inc. 06/13/2011
(See Ore Holdings Inc.)

GENE SCREEN CORP (AB)
Recapitalized 07/09/1996
Recapitalized from Gene Screen Inc. to Gene Screen Corp. 07/09/1996

Each share Common no par exchanged for (0.5) share Common no par
Name changed to GeneVest Inc. 06/25/1998
GeneVest Inc. merged into Pinetree Capital Corp. 06/01/2004 which recapitalized as Pinetree Capital Ltd. 06/02/2004

GENE SHELLY IMPORTS INC (DE)
Charter cancelled and declared inoperative and void for non-payment of taxes 3/1/74

GENECAN FINL CORP (QC)
Completely liquidated 03/17/1998
No stockholders' equity

GENELABS TECHNOLOGIES INC (CA)
Each share old Common no par exchanged for (0.2) share new Common no par 12/19/2005
Acquired by GlaxoSmithKline PLC 01/07/2009
Each share Common no par exchanged for $1.30 cash

GENELINK INC (PA)
Plan of reorganization under Chapter 11 Federal Bankruptcy proceedings effective 06/25/2015
No stockholders' equity

GENEMAX CORP (NV)
Recapitalized as TapImmune Inc. (NV) 06/28/2007
Each share Common $0.001 par exchanged for (0.4) share Common $0.001 par
TapImmune Inc. (NV) reincorporated in Delaware as Marker Therapeutics, Inc. 10/18/2018

GENEMEDICINE INC (DE)
Merged into Megabios Corp. 03/18/1999
Each share Common $0.001 par exchanged for (0.571) share Common $0.001 par
Megabios Corp. name changed to Valentis, Inc. 05/05/1999 which name changed to Urigen Pharmaceuticals, Inc. 07/30/2007

GENEMEDIX PLC (UNITED KINGDOM)
ADR agreement terminated 10/19/2012
No ADR's remain outstanding

GENENCOR INTL INC (DE)
Issue Information - 7,000,000 shares COM offered at $18 per share on 07/27/2000
Merged into Danisco A/S 4/20/2005
Each share Common 10¢ par exchanged for $19.25 cash

GENENERGY RES LTD (AB)
Merged into American Eagle Petroleums Ltd. (SK) 04/09/1982
Each share Class A Common no par exchanged for (0.73) share Common no par
American Eagle Petroleums Ltd. (SK) reincorporated in Alberta 10/20/1982 which reincorporated in Canada 09/17/1992 which merged into CS Resources Ltd./Les Ressources CS Ltee. 08/01/1993
(See CS Resources Ltd./Les Ressources CS Ltee.)

GENENTECH INC (DE)
Reincorporated 01/28/1987
Old Common 2¢ par split (3) for (2) by issuance of (0.5) additional share 03/30/1983
Old Common 2¢ par split (2) for (1) by issuance of (1) additional share 02/28/1986
State of incorporation changed from (CA) to (DE) 01/28/1987
Old Common 2¢ par split (2) for (1) by issuance of (1) additional share 02/28/1987
Under plan of merger each share old Common 2¢ par exchanged for (0.5)

share Redeemable Common 2¢ par and $18 cash 09/07/1990
Redeemable Common 2¢ par reclassified as Old Common 2¢ par 06/30/1995
Each share old Common 2¢ par exchanged for (1) share Special Common 2¢ par 10/25/1996
Special Common 2¢ par called for redemption at $82.50 on 06/30/1999
Issue Information - 20,000,000 shares COM NEW offered at $97 per share on 07/19/1999
New Common 2¢ par split (2) for (1) by issuance of (1) additional share payable 11/02/1999 to holders of record 10/29/1999 Ex date - 11/03/1999
New Common 2¢ par split (2) for (1) by issuance of (1) additional share payable 10/24/2000 to holders of record 10/17/2000 Ex date - 10/25/2000
New Common 2¢ par split (2) for (1) by issuance of (1) additional share payable 05/12/2004 to holders of record 04/28/2004 Ex date - 05/13/2004
Acquired by Roche Holding Ltd. 03/26/2009
Each share Common 2¢ par exchanged for $95 cash

GENER S A (CHILE)
ADR agreement terminated 8/19/2001
Each Sponsored ADR for Ordinary no par exchanged for $4.380295 cash

GENERAL & TELEPHONE INVESTMENTS, INC. (DE)
Voting Trust Agreement expired 8/10/56
Public interest eliminated

GENERAL ABRASIVE INC (NY)
Common $1 par changed to 50¢ par and (1) additional share issued 4/25/67
Merged into U.S. Industries, Inc. 6/26/69
Each share Common 50¢ par exchanged for (0.125) share Special Conv. Preference Ser. J $2.50 par and (0.236) share Common $1 par
(See U.S. Industries, Inc.)

GENERAL ACCEP CORP (IN)
Issue Information - 1,700,000 shares COM offered at $17 per share on 04/06/1995
Merged into GAC Acquisition Corp. 09/01/1998
Each share Common no par exchanged for $0.30 cash

GENERAL ACCEPTANCE CORP. NEW (PA)
Each share $2.50 Conv. Preference $2.50 par exchanged for (5) shares 50¢ Conv. Preference no par 5/26/65
60¢ Conv. Preference no par called for redemption 10/13/67
Name changed to GAC Corp. (PA) 7/1/68
GAC Corp. (PA) reincorporated in Delaware 12/20/73
(See GAC Corp. (DE))

GENERAL ACCEPTANCE CORP. OLD (PA)
Name changed to General Phoenix Corp. 5/31/44
General Phoenix Corp. name changed to General Acceptance Corp. (New) 7/11/50 which name changed to GAC Corp. (PA) 7/1/68 which reincorporated in Delaware 12/20/73
(See GAC Corp. (DE))

GENERAL AERO PRODS CORP (DE)
Name changed to General Technologies Group Ltd. 3/18/88
(See General Technologies Group Ltd.)

GENERAL AIRCRAFT INC (NV)
Name changed to General Sales & Leasing, Inc. 02/25/2013
General Sales & Leasing, Inc. recapitalized as Xenetic Biosciences, Inc. 01/14/2014

GENERAL ALLIANCE CORP.
Dissolved in 1936
Details not available

GENERAL ALLIED CORP (NY)
Merged into First Computer Fund Inc. 04/01/1968
Each share Common 5¢ par exchanged for (1) share Common 5¢ par
First Computer Fund Inc. name changed to Idex, Inc. 11/21/1978 which name changed to Globus Studios, Inc. 02/03/1988

GENERAL ALLIED OIL & GAS CO (WV)
Recapitalized as Allied Resources Inc. (WV) 1/29/99
Each share Common no par exchanged for (0.2) share Common no par
Allied Resources Inc. (WV) reincorporated in Nevada 4/5/2002

GENERAL ALUM CORP (DE)
Merged into MI Home Products, Inc. 5/26/2000
Each share Common 1¢ par exchanged for $5.639 cash

GENERAL ALUMINUM FABRICATORS, INC. (FL)
Merged into American-International Aluminum Corp. (FL) on a share for share basis 10/25/62
American-International Aluminum Corp. (FL) reincorporated in Delaware as A.I.M. Companies, Inc. 9/6/68
(See A.I.M. Companies, Inc.)

GENERAL AMERICA CORP. (WA)
Each share old Common no par exchanged for (0.1) share new Common no par 00/00/1935
Each share new Common no par exchanged for (4) shares Common $10 par 03/02/1955
Common $10 par changed to $5 par and (1) additional share issued 03/18/1960
Stock Dividends - 10% 04/15/1959; 100% 03/15/1962
Name changed to Safeco Corp. 04/30/1968
(See Safeco Corp.)

GENERAL AMERN CORP (NV)
Each share Common $1 par exchanged for (2) shares Common 50¢ par 10/12/67
Each share Common 50¢ par exchanged for (2) shares Common 25¢ par 8/16/68
Charter revoked for failure to file reports and pay fees 3/3/75

GENERAL AMERICAN INDUSTRIES, INC. (NJ)
Name changed to Tandy Corp. (NJ) 11/14/1960
Tandy Corp. (NJ) reincorporated in Delaware 02/27/1968 which name changed to RadioShack Corp. 05/18/2000 which name changed to RS Legacy Corp. 09/23/2015
(See RS Legacy Corp.)

GENERAL AMERICAN INVESTMENT CORP. (TX)
Charter revoked for failure to file reports and pay fees 4/29/64

GENERAL AMERN INVS INC (DE)
$6 Preferred $100 par changed to no par in 1932
$6 Preferred no par changed to $4.50 Preferred $100 par in 1945
$4.50 Preferred $100 par called for redemption 10/30/81
Issue Information - 6,000,000 TAX ADVANTAGED PFD 7.20% shares offered at $25 per share on 06/16/1998
7.20% Tax Advantaged Preferred $1 par called for redemption at $25 on 9/23/2003
(Additional Information in Active)

GENERAL AMERICAN LIFE INSURANCE CO.
Mutualization completed in 1946

GENERAL AMERN OIL CO TEX (DE)
6% Preferred $10 par called for redemption 05/01/1957
Common $5 par changed to $1 par and (1) additional share issued 12/02/1977
Common $1 par split (3) for (2) by issuance of (0.5) additional share 12/5/1988
Stock Dividends - 100% 12/15/1947; 100% 10/16/1950; 100% 11/16/1956; 10% 10/15/1979
Merged into Phillips Petroleum Co. 03/08/1983
Each share Common $1 par exchanged for $38.1746 cash

GENERAL AMERN RTY INC (DE)
Name changed to World Callnet, Inc. 01/05/1999
(See World Callnet, Inc.)

GENERAL AMERICAN TANK CAR CORP.
Name changed to General American Transportation Corp. and Capital Stock no par changed to $5 par in 1933
General American Transportation Corp. name changed to GATX Corp. 6/27/75

GENERAL AMERN TECHNOLOGIES INC (ON)
Name changed to Kanata Hotels Inc. 1/12/87
Kanata Hotels Inc. recapitalized as Kanata Hotels International Inc. 5/4/87 which merged into Armbro Enterprises Inc. 2/1/90 which name changed to Aecon Group Inc. 6/18/2001

GENERAL AMERN TRANSN CORP (NY)
Common $5 par changed to $2.50 par and (1) additional share issued in 1953
Common $2.50 par changed to $1.25 par and (1) additional share issued 1/23/59
Common $1.25 par changed to 62-1/2¢ par and (1) additional share issued 5/14/65
Name changed to GATX Corp. 6/27/75

GENERAL ANALYTICS CORP (DE)
Completely liquidated in 1971
No stockholders' equity

GENERAL ANESTHETIC EQUIPMENT CO. (IL)
Involuntarily dissolved 11/16/1970
No stockholders' equity

GENERAL ANILINE & FILM CORP (DE)
Recapitalized 11/12/64
Each share Class A Common no par exchanged for (15) shares Common $1 par
Each share Class B Common $1 par exchanged for (1.5) shares Common $1 par
Name changed to GAF Corp. 4/24/68
(See GAF Corp.)

GENERAL APPLIANCE CORP.
Name changed to Holly Corp. in 1952

GENERAL APPLIED SCIENCE LABORATORIES, INC. (NY)
Acquired by Marquardt Corp. 05/27/1965
Each share Common $1 par exchanged for (1.4) shares Capital Stock $1 par
Marquardt Corp. merged into CCI Marquardt Corp. 06/12/1968 which name changed to CCI Corp. 09/26/1969
(See CCI Corp.)

GENERAL ARTISTS CORP (NY)
Name changed to Creative Management Associates, Inc. 4/1/69
(See Creative Management Associates, Inc.)

GENERAL ASBESTOS & RUBBER CO.
Merged into Raybestos-Manhattan, Inc. in 1929
Details not available

GENERAL ASPHALT CO.
Name changed to Barber Co., Inc. 00/00/1936
Barber Co., Inc. name changed to Barber Asphalt Corp. (NJ) 00/00/1938 which reincorporated in Delaware 00/00/1947 which name changed to Barber Oil Corp. 00/00/1948
(See Barber Oil Corp.)

GENERAL ATLANTIC RES INC (DE)
Merged into United Meridian Corp. 11/15/94
Each share Common 1¢ par exchanged for (1.1) shares Common 1¢ par
United Meridian Corp. merged into Ocean Energy Inc. (New) 3/27/98 which merged into Ocean Energy, Inc. (TX) 3/30/99 which reincorporated in Delaware 5/9/2001 which merged into Devon Energy Corp. 4/25/2003

GENERAL ATRONICS CORP (PA)
Completely liquidated 4/25/69
Each share Common no par exchanged for first and final distribution of (0.192307) share Magnavox Co. Common $1 par
(See Magnavox Co.)

GENERAL AUTO PARTS STORES INC (FL)
Merged into Aid Stores, Inc. 5/4/72
Each share Common 1¢ par exchanged for (0.25) share Common 1¢ par
Aid Stores, Inc. recapitalized as Aid Auto Stores, Inc. 11/29/72
(See Aid Auto Stores, Inc.)

GENERAL AUTOMATION CORP (DE)
Reorganized 05/01/1969
Reorganized from (NY) to under the laws of Delaware 05/01/1969
Each share Common 2¢ par exchanged for (0.1) share Common 1¢ par
Merged into A. K. F., Inc. 10/01/1980
Each share Common 1¢ par exchanged for (0.01) share Common $20 par
(See A. K. F., Inc.)

GENERAL AUTOMATION INC (DE)
Reincorporated 00/00/1986
State of incorporation changed from (CA) to (DE) 00/00/1986
Name changed to GA eXpress Inc. 02/06/2001
(See GA eXpress Inc.)

GENERAL AUTOMOTIVE CO (NV)
Name changed to MDCorp 05/26/2017
MDCorp name changed to Qian Yuan Baixing Inc. 05/01/2018

GENERAL AUTOMOTIVE CORP. (UT)
Recapitalized as Simondy Corp. 02/14/1989
Each share Common $0.001 par exchanged for (0.1) share Common no par
Simondy Corp. name changed to Pacific General, Inc. 03/15/1989
(See Pacific General, Inc.)

GENERAL AUTOMOTIVE PARTS CORP (IN)
Common no par split (2) for (1) by

issuance of (1) additional share 5/25/71
Common no par split (3) for (2) by issuance of (0.5) additional share 5/5/78
Merged into Genuine Parts Co. 3/22/82
Each share Common no par exchanged for (2) shares Common $1 par

GENERAL AVIATION CORP. (DE)
Incorporated 12/3/27
Dissolved 12/28/34
Details not available

GENERAL AVIATION CORP. (DE)
Incorporated 5/29/39
No longer in existence having become inoperative and void for non-payment of taxes 4/1/55

GENERAL AVIATION EQUIPMENT CO., INC. (DE)
Name changed to General Aviation Corp. 00/00/1952
(See General Aviation Corp.)

GENERAL BAKERIES LTD (ON)
Common no par split (3) for (1) by issuance of (2) additional shares 07/15/1964
Merged into Dominion Stores Ltd. - Les Supermarches Dominion Ltee. 12/04/1980
Each (3) shares Common no par exchanged for (2) shares Common no par
Dominion Stores Ltd. - Les Supermarches Dominion Ltee. reorganized as Argcen Holdings Inc. 08/30/1984 which merged into Hollinger Inc. 09/17/1985
(See Hollinger Inc.)

GENERAL BAKING CO (NY)
Each share $8 Preferred no par exchanged for (1.35) shares $6 Preferred no par and $24 cash 05/08/1964
Each share $6 Preferred no par exchanged for $100 principal amount of 6% Subord. Income Debentures due 12/01/1990 and $3 cash 11/26/1965
Name changed to General Host Corp. 04/20/1967
(See General Host Corp.)

GENERAL BAKING CORP. (NY)
Name changed to General Baking Co. 00/00/1931
General Baking Co. name changed to General Host Corp. 04/20/1967
(See General Host Corp.)

GENERAL BANCORP (CA)
Voluntarily dissolved 7/14/76
Details not available

GENERAL BANCSHARES CORP (MO)
4-1/2% Conv. Preferred $10 par called for redemption 02/00/1964
Merged into Boatmen's Bancshares, Inc. 03/29/1986
Each share Common $2 par exchanged for (1.75) shares Common $10 par
Boatmen's Bancshares, Inc. merged into NationsBank Corp. (NC) 01/07/1997 which reincorporated in Delaware as BankAmerica Corp. (Old) 09/25/1998 which merged into BankAmerica Corp. (New) 09/30/1998 which name changed to Bank of America Corp. 04/28/1999

GENERAL BANCSHARES CORP IND (IN)
Merged into SummCorp 4/30/87
Each share Common Capital Stock $10 par exchanged for (2.226) shares Common no par
SummCorp merged into NBD Bancorp, Inc. 7/1/92 which name changed to First Chicago NBD Corp. 12/1/95 which merged into Bank One Corp. 10/2/98 which merged into J.P. Morgan Chase & Co. 12/31/2000 which name changed to JPMorgan Chase & Co. 7/20/2004

GENERAL BK & TR CO (NEW HAVEN, CT)
Merged into Hartford National Bank (Hartford, CT) 10/30/70
Each share Common $12.50 par exchanged for (1.5) shares Hartford National Corp. Common $6.25 par
Hartford National Corp. merged into Shawmut National Corp. 2/29/88 which merged into Fleet Financial Group Inc. (New) 11/30/95 which name changed to Fleet Boston Corp. 10/1/99 which name changed to FleetBoston Financial Corp. 4/18/2000 which merged into Bank of America Corp. 4/1/2004

GENERAL BANK OF COMMERCE (LOS ANGELES, CA)
Under plan of reorganization each share Common no par automatically became (1) share GBC Bancorp Common no par 11/25/80
GBC Bancorp merged into Cathay General Bancorp 10/20/2003

GENERAL BANKNOTE CORP.
Bankrupt in 1940
Details not available

GENERAL BANKNOTE ENGINEERING CO., INC.
Merged into General Banknote Corp. in 1937
Details not available

GENERAL BATTERY & CERAMIC CORP. (NY)
Name changed to General Battery Corp. 10/3/69
(See General Battery Corp.)

GENERAL BATTERY & CERAMIC CORP. (PA)
Reorganized under the laws of New York and Common no par changed to $1 par 12/29/61
General Battery & Ceramic Corp. (N.Y.) name changed to General Battery Corp. 10/3/69
(See General Battery Corp.)

GENERAL BATTERY CORP (NY)
Merged into Norbat Corp. 11/22/76
Each share Common 1¢ par exchanged for $34 cash

GENERAL BEARING CORP (DE)
Acquired by SKF AB 08/01/2012
Each share Common 1¢ par exchanged for $23.30682899 cash
Note: Each share Common 1¢ par received an initial additional distribution of $0.6663614 cash from escrow 10/18/2012
Each share Common 1¢ par received a second additional distribution of $0.15442128 cash from escrow 01/08/2013
Each share Common 1¢ par received a third additional distribution of $1.75202 cash from escrow 02/13/2014
Each share Common 1¢ par received a fourth additional distribution of $1.26461748 cash from escrow 04/06/2016

GENERAL BEVERAGES, INC. (TN)
Charter revoked for non-payment of taxes 2/6/57

GENERAL BEVERAGES CO. OF FLORIDA, INC. (FL)
Advised company bankrupt in 1955
Charter cancelled & company proclaimed dissolved for non-payment of taxes 4/25/58

GENERAL BINDING CORP (DE)
Common $1 par changed to no par and (1) additional share issued 10/18/68
Common no par changed to 25¢ par 6/29/70
Common 25¢ par changed to 12-1/2¢ par 5/11/76
Common 12-1/2¢ par split (3) for (2) by issuance of (0.5) additional share 9/24/87
Common 12-1/2¢ par split (3) for (2) by issuance of (0.5) additional share 6/6/88
Common 12-1/2¢ par split (3) for (2) by issuance of (0.5) additional share 8/31/89
Stock Dividends - 100% 9/29/67; 100% 10/11/71
Merged into ACCO Brands Corp. 8/17/2005
Each share Common 12-1/2¢ par exchanged for (1) share Common 1¢ par

GENERAL BIOMETRICS INC (DE)
Recapitalized as Syntello, Inc. 08/10/1993
Each share Common 1¢ par exchanged for (0.04) share Common 1¢ par
Syntello, Inc. reorganized as Maxim Pharmaceuticals, Inc. 10/09/1996 which merged into EpiCept Corp. 01/05/2006 which recapitalized as Immune Pharmaceuticals Inc. 08/21/2013

GENERAL BLDG PRODS CORP (NY)
Charter cancelled and proclaimed dissolved for failure to pay taxes 03/11/1999

GENERAL BLDRS CORP (NY)
Name changed 6/23/58
5% Preferred $1 par called for redemption 8/15/61
Name changed from General Builders Supply Corp. to General Builders Corp. 6/23/58
Dissolved by proclamation 9/23/98

GENERAL BOND & SHARE CORP. (NY)
Acquired by Industrial Realty Shares, Inc. in 1930
Details not available

GENERAL BOTTLERS, INC. (IL)
Stock Dividend - 100% 08/25/1947
Name changed to Pepsi-Cola General Bottlers, Inc. (IL) 00/00/1953
Pepsi-Cola General Bottlers, Inc. (IL) reincorporated in Delaware 04/23/1969 which merged into Illinois Central Industries, Inc. 02/02/1970 which name changed to IC Industries, Inc. 05/21/1975
(See IC Industries, Inc.)

GENERAL BOWLING CORP (NY)
Reorganized under the laws of Delaware as General Leisure, Inc. 10/1/69
Each share Common 10¢ par exchanged for (1) share Common 10¢ par
(See General Leisure, Inc.)

GENERAL BOX CO (DE)
Stock Dividends - 10% 12/21/44; 10% 12/16/67
Merged into Southwest Forest Industries, Inc. 12/28/72
Each share Capital Stock $1 par exchanged for (0.444444) share Common $1 par
(See Southwest Forest Industries, Inc.)

GENERAL BRASS CO.
Liquidation completed in 1943
Details not available

GENERAL BREWING CO (CA)
100% reacquired as of 05/19/1989
Public interest eliminated

GENERAL BREWING CORP. OLD (CA)
Name changed to Lucky Lager Brewing Co. 00/00/1949
Lucky Lager Brewing Co. name changed to General Brewing Corp. (New) 08/02/1963 which name changed to Lucky Breweries Inc. 06/17/1969 which name changed to General Brewing Co. 08/08/1972
(See General Brewing Co.)

GENERAL BREWING CORP NEW (CA)
Voting Trust Agreement terminated 09/06/1963
Each VTC for Common $1 par exchanged for (1) share Common $1 par
Name changed to Lucky Breweries Inc. 06/17/1969
Lucky Breweries Inc. name changed to General Brewing Co. 08/08/1972
(See General Brewing Co.)

GENERAL BROCK HOTEL CO. LTD.
Acquired by Cardy Corp. Ltd. and each share exchanged for (0.4) share Class A, $2.50 in debentures and 30¢ in cash in 1947
Cardy Corp. Ltd. name was changed to Sheraton Ltd. in 1950
(See Sheraton Ltd.)

GENERAL BRONZE CORP (NY)
Common no par changed to $5 par in 1932
Common $5 par changed to $2.50 par and (1) additional share issued 6/28/65
Stock Dividend - 20% 12/28/50
Merged into Allied Products Corp. (DE) 1/31/68
Each share Common $2.50 par exchanged for (0.25) share $3 Conv. Preferred Ser. A no par and (0.1) share Common $5 par
(See Allied Products Corp. (DE))

GENERAL BUSINESS DATA CTRS INC (DE)
Charter cancelled and declared inoperative and void for non-payment of taxes 03/01/1976

GENERAL CABLE CORP (DE)
Merged into General Cable Acquisition Corp. 06/20/1994
Each share Common $1 par exchanged for $6 cash

GENERAL CABLE CORP (NJ)
Each share Class A no par exchanged for (4) shares Common no par 00/00/1946
4% 1st Preferred $100 par called for redemption 01/01/1964
Common no par split (5) for (2) by issuance of (1.5) additional shares 05/20/1964
Common no par changed to $1 par and (1) additional share issued 05/31/1966
Name changed to GK Technologies, Inc. 04/25/1979
(See GK Technologies, Inc.)

GENERAL CABLE CORP NEW (DE)
5.75% Conv. Preferred Ser. A 1¢ par called for redemption at $50 on 11/25/2013
Common 1¢ par split (3) for (2) by issuance of (0.5) additional share payable 05/14/1998 to holders of record 04/28/1998 Ex date - 05/15/1998
Acquired by Prysmian Group 06/06/2018
Each share Common 1¢ par exchanged for $30 cash

GENERAL CABLE PLC (ENGLAND)
Merged into Telewest, PLC 02/16/1999
Each Sponsored ADR £1 par exchanged for (6.215) Sponsored ADR's for Ordinary 10p par and 325 pence cash
Telewest, PLC name changed to Telewest Communications PLC (New) 05/16/1996 which reorganized as Telewest Global Inc. (DE) 07/14/2004 which merged into NTL Inc. (Ctfs. dated after 03/03/2006) 03/03/2006 which name changed to Virgin Media, Inc. 02/06/2007 which

merged into Liberty Global PLC 06/10/2013

GENERAL CALIF TAX EXEMPT MONEY MKT FD (MA)
Name changed to General California Municipal Money Market Fund 03/23/1990

GENERAL CANDY CORP. (IL)
Class A Common $5 par reclassified as Common $5 par in 1942
Acquired by Warner-Lambert Pharmaceutical Co. 3/25/66
Each share Common $5 par exchanged for (0.625) share Common $1 par
Warner-Lambert Pharmaceutical Co. name changed to Warner-Lambert Co. 11/30/70 which merged into Pfizer Co. 6/19/2000

GENERAL CANNABIS INC (NV)
Name changed to SearchCore, Inc. 01/06/2012
SearchCore, Inc. name changed to Wisdom Homes of America, Inc. 03/05/2015

GENERAL CAP CORP (DE)
Certificates dated after 10/19/1972
Charter cancelled and declared inoperative and void for non-payment of taxes 03/01/1984

GENERAL CAPITAL CORP. (DE)
Certificates dated prior to 07/11/1962
Capital Stock no par changed to $1 par 00/00/1942
Capital Stock $1 par split (5) for (1) by issuance of (4) additional shares 09/25/1956
Liquidation completed
Each share Capital Stock $1 par exchanged for initial distribution of (1.2419) shares National Investors Corp. (MD) Capital Stock $1 par 07/11/1962
Each share Capital Stock $1 par received second and final distribution of $0.136 cash 07/08/1963
National Investors Corp. (MD) name changed to Seligman Growth Fund, Inc. 05/01/1982

GENERAL CAPITAL CORP. (OH)
Reincorporated under the laws of Delaware 10/20/1972
(See General Capital Corp. (DE))

GENERAL CAPSULE CORP. (DE)
Each share Class A and/or B Common 10¢ par exchanged for (0.04) share Common 15¢ par 09/23/1960
Name changed to National Brands Inc. 01/04/1965
(See National Brands Inc.)

GENERAL CARBONIC CO.
Acquired by Liquid Carbonic Corp. in 1929
Details not available

GENERAL CARE CORP (TN)
Common 10¢ par split (2) for (1) by issuance of (1) additional share 5/30/75
Common 10¢ par split (4) for (3) by issuance of (1/3) additional share 5/28/76
Common 10¢ par split (5) for (4) by issuance of (0.25) additional share 1/16/79
Stock Dividends - 50% 2/4/77; 50% 1/11/78
Merged into Hospital Corp. of America 9/4/80
Each share Common 10¢ par exchanged for $18 cash

GENERAL CARPET CORP.
Adjudicated bankrupt in 1939
Stockholders' equity unlikely

GENERAL CASSETTE CORP (DE)
Chapter 11 bankruptcy proceedings converted to Chapter 7 on 8/4/87
Stockholders' equity unlikely

GENERAL CASTING CORP (NY)
Merged into Automatic Switch Co. 7/2/75
Each share Common 10¢ par exchanged for $2 cash

GENERAL CELLULAR CORP (DE)
Plan of reorganization under Chapter 11 Federal Bankruptcy proceedings effective 03/17/1992
Each share old Class A Common 1¢ par exchanged for (0.02127659) share new Class A Common 1¢ par
Each share new Class A Common 1¢ par exchanged for (0.01) share Common $1 par 12/30/1994
Voluntarily dissolved 01/25/2001
Details not available

GENERAL CERAMICS INC (NJ)
Common $1 par split (2) for (1) by issuance of (1) additional share 8/30/85
Merged into Tokuyama Soda Co., Ltd. 7/6/89
Each share Common $1 par exchanged for $18 cash

GENERAL CHEM GROUP INC (DE)
Each share old Common 1¢ par received distribution of (.) share GenTek Inc. Common 1¢ par payable 4/30/99 to holders of record 4/16/99 Ex date - 5/3/99
Each share old Common 1¢ par exchanged for (0.1) share new Common 1¢ par 7/13/2001
Plan of reorganization under Chapter 11 Federal Bankruptcy Code effective 3/31/2004
Each share new Common 1¢ par or Class B Common 1¢ par exchanged for approximately (0.0001512) share General Chemical Industrial Products, Inc. Common 1¢ par
Note: The company believes that because fractional shares were dropped the majority of holders will receive no distribution
Note: Unexchanged certificates were cancelled and became without value 3/18/2005

GENERAL CIGAR HLDGS INC (DE)
Merged into Swedish Match AB 05/09/2000
Each share Class A Common 1¢ par exchanged for $15.25 cash
Each share Class B Common 1¢ par exchanged for $15.25 cash

GENERAL CIGAR INC (NY)
Each share Common $100 par exchanged for (2) shares Common no par 00/00/1926
Recapitalized 07/12/1957
Each share 7% Preferred $100 par exchanged for $140 principal amount of 5-1/2% Income Subord. Debentures due 06/01/1987
Common no par changed to $1 par and (2) additional shares issued 05/01/1959
Name changed to Culbro Corp. 06/01/1976
Culbro Corp. merged into General Cigar Holdings, Inc. 08/29/1997
(See General Cigar Holdings, Inc.)

GENERAL CINEMA CORP (DE)
Common no par split (5) for (4) by issuance of (0.25) additional share 10/28/65
Common no par split (5) for (2) by issuance of (1.5) additional shares 9/25/68
Common no par changed to $1 par 4/14/70
Common $1 par split (3) for (2) by issuance of (0.5) additional share 10/8/71
Common $1 par split (2) for (1) by issuance of (1) additional share 4/18/79
Conv. Preferred Ser. A $1 par reclassified as Conv. Ser. A $1 par 3/15/84

Conv. Ser. A $1 par split (2) for (1) by issuance of (1) additional share 10/31/84
Common $1 par split (2) for (1) by issuance of (1) additional share 10/31/84
Conv. Ser. A $1 par split (2) for (1) by issuance of (1) additional share 10/30/87
Common $1 par split (2) for (1) by issuance of (1) additional share 10/30/87
Stock Dividend - to holders of Common (1) share Conv. Preferred Ser. A $1 par 10/29/82
Name changed to Harcourt General, Inc. 3/15/93
(See Harcourt General, Inc.)

GENERAL CLEANING & MAINTENANCE (NV)
Name changed to IPOWorld 04/03/2013

GENERAL COAL INVESTMENTS CORP.
Liquidated in 1948
Details not available

GENERAL COIL PRODUCTS CORP. (NY)
Acquired by Bristol Dynamics, Inc. 9/27/63
Each share Common 10¢ par exchanged for (1) share Common 1¢ par
Bristol Dynamics, Inc. liquidated for Computer Equipment Corp. 12/12/68 which name changed to Cetec Corp. (CA) 5/29/74 which reincorporated in Delaware 5/12/86
(See Cetec Corp. (DE))

GENERAL COLOR GRAPHICS INC (OH)
100% acquired by Colwell Industries Inc. through exchange offer which expired 00/00/1983
Public interest eliminated

GENERAL COMMUNICATION INC (AK)
Name changed to as GCI Liberty, Inc. (AK) and Class A and Class B Common no par reclassified as Class A-1 or Class A-2 Common no par respectively 02/22/2018
GCI Liberty, Inc. (AK) reincorporated in Delaware 05/10/2018

GENERAL COMPONENTS INC (NV)
Old Common $0.001 par split (6.76) for (1) by issuance of (5.76) additional shares payable 09/15/2004 to holders of record 09/13/2004 Ex date - 09/16/2004
Old Common $0.001 par split (2) for (1) by issuance of (1) additional share payable 10/25/2004 to holders of record 10/14/2004 Ex date - 10/26/2004
Each share old Common $0.001 par exchanged for (0.1) share new Common $0.001 par 02/14/2007
Name changed to Hi-Tech Wealth, Inc. 05/02/2007
Hi-Tech Wealth, Inc. name changed to China Mobile Media Technology Inc. 12/27/2007
(See China Mobile Media Technology Inc.)

GENERAL COMPUTER CORP (OH)
Merged into GenCC Holdings Corp. 3/14/95
Each share Common 10¢ par exchanged for $8.75 cash

GENERAL COMPUTER ELECTRONICS CORP. (NJ)
Assets liquidated for benefit of creditors 3/12/65
No stockholders' equity

GENERAL COMPUTER SVCS INC (AL)
Merged into Computerized Automotive Reporting Service, Inc. 6/30/80

Each (15) shares Common 10¢ par exchanged for (1) share Common 66-2/3¢ par
Computerized Automotive Reporting Service, Inc. name changed to Dyatron Corp. 12/1/80 which was acquired by SunGard Data Systems Inc. 11/10/89
(See SunGard Data Systems Inc.)

GENERAL COMPUTER SYS INC (DE)
Name changed to Great Southwest Industries Corp. 6/26/78
(See Great Southwest Industries Corp.)

GENERAL COMPUTING CORP (DE)
Chapter 11 bankruptcy proceedings confirmed 12/5/80
Stockholders' equity undetermined

GENERAL COMPUTING MACHINES CORP. (DE)
Merged into General-Gilbert Corp. 9/13/57
Each share Preferred exchanged for (1) share 5% Non-Cum. Class A Preferred $100 par
Each share Common 1¢ par exchanged for (1) share Common $1 par
(See General-Gilbert Corp.)

GENERAL CONSUMER PRODS INC (FL)
Administratively dissolved for failure to file annual report 10/04/2002

GENERAL CONTRACT CORP. (MO)
Name changed to General Bancshares Corp. 11/6/58
General Bancshares Corp. merged into Boatmen's Bancshares, Inc. 3/29/86 which merged into NationsBank Corp. 1/7/97 which reincorporated in Delaware as BankAmerica Corp. (Old) 9/25/98 which merged into BankAmerica Corp. (New) 9/30/98 which name changed to Bank of America Corp. 4/28/99

GENERAL CONTRACT FINANCE CORP. (MO)
Acquired by Liberty Loan Corp. 1/2/68
Each share 5-1/2% Preferred Ser. A $20 par exchanged for (0.8) share 5-1/2% Conv. Preferred $25 par
Each share Common $2 par exchanged for (0.223713) share $1.25 Conv. Preference $25 par
Liberty Loan Corp. name changed to LLC Corp. 3/14/80 which name changed to Valhi, Inc. 3/10/87

GENERAL CONTRACTING CORP (UT)
Name changed to General International, Inc. and Common no par changed to 10¢ par 8/4/69
(See General International, Inc.)

GENERAL CONTROLS CO. (CA)
Each share Common $10 par exchanged for (2) shares Common $5 par 12/31/46
Stock Dividends - 50% 5/50; 100% 1/26/53; 10% 3/31/60
Merged into International Telephone & Telegraph Corp. (MD) 5/15/63
Each share 6% Preferred $25 par exchanged for (0.25) share 5.25% Preferred Ser. B $100 par
Each share Common $5 par exchanged for (0.1338) share 4% Conv. Preferred Ser. C $100 par and (0.0586) share Capital Stock no par
International Telephone & Telegraph Corp. (MD) reincorporated in Delaware 1/31/68 which name changed to ITT Corp. 12/31/83 which reorganized in Indiana as ITT Industries, Inc. 12/19/95 which name changed to ITT Corp. 7/1/2006

GENERAL CORP OHIO (OH)
Name changed to General Capital Corp. (OH) 5/13/71

General Capital Corp. (OH) reincorporated in Delaware 10/20/72
(See General Capital Corp. (DE))

GENERAL COTTON CORP.
Dissolved 00/00/1941
Details not available

GENERAL CR CORP (NY)
Plan of reorganization under Chapter 11 Federal Bankruptcy Code effective 04/04/2003
No stockholders' equity

GENERAL CREDIT, INC. (DE)
Recapitalized in March 1953
Each share Class A $1 par exchanged for (1) share Part. Preferred $1 par and (1) share Common $1 par
Class B $1 par exchanged for Common $1 par
Recapitalized in October 1953
Each share Common $1 par exchanged for (20) shares Common 5¢ par
Merged into Dalton Finance, Inc. 1/8/60
Each share 6% Preferred $10 par exchanged for $5 in 6% Conv. Notes
Each share Part. Preference $1 par exchanged for 50¢ in 6% Conv. Notes
Each share Common 5¢ par exchanged for (0.1) share Class A Common 50¢ par
(See Dalton Finance, Inc.)

GENERAL CREDIT CORP. (FL)
Charter cancelled and proclaimed dissolved for non-payment of taxes 4/25/58

GENERAL CRUDE OIL CO (DE)
Capital Stock $2.50 par reclassified as Common $2.50 par 10/15/1968
Common $2.50 par changed to $1.25 par and (1) additional share issued 05/01/1969
Common $1.25 par changed to 80¢ par and (1) additional share issued 12/03/1971
Stock Dividends - 10% 12/22/1948; 10% 12/19/1949; 10% 12/20/1950; 10% 09/29/1966
Merged into International Paper Co. 02/10/1975
Each share $4.12 Conv. Preferred Ser. A no par exchanged for either $160 principal amount of IP Petroleum, Inc. 8.5% Guaranteed Notes due 00/00/1982 plus $40.60 cash or $160 principal amount of IP Petroleum, Inc. 8.5% Guaranteed Restricted Notes due 00/00/1980 plus $40.60 cash or $200.60 cash
Each share Common 80¢ par exchanged for either $40 principal amount of IP Petroleum, Inc. 8.5% Guaranteed Notes due 00/00/1982 plus $10 cash or $40 principal amount of IP Petroleum, Inc. 8.5% Guaranteed Restricted Notes due 00/00/1980 plus $10 cash or $50 cash
Note: Above options were available until 02/09/1975 after which holders were entitled to cash only

GENERAL CRUSHED STONE CO (DE)
Merged into Koppers Co., Inc. 12/16/70
Each share Common $50 par exchanged for (10.55125) shares Common $5 par
Each share Common $50 par received additional distribution of (1.17236) shares Common $5 par 12/22/72
(See Koppers Co., Inc.)

GENERAL CYBERNETICS CORP (BC)
Delisted from Vancouver Stock Exchange 10/6/89

GENERAL DATABASE TECHNOLOGY INC (FL)
Merged into GDB Inc. 3/13/86
Details not available

GENERAL DATACOMM INDS INC (DE)
Old Common 10¢ par split (3) for (2) by issuance of (0.5) additional share 08/07/1978
Old Common 10¢ par split (3) for (2) by issuance of (0.5) additional share 02/04/1980
Old Common 10¢ par split (3) for (2) by issuance of (0.5) additional share 11/20/1980
Old Common 10¢ par split (2) for (1) by issuance of (1) additional share 05/24/1984
Plan of reorganization under Chapter 11 Federal Bankruptcy Code effective 09/15/2003
Each share Common 10¢ par exchanged for (0.1) share Common 1¢ par
Each share 144A Common 10¢ par exchanged for (0.1) share Common 1¢ par
Each share Class B Common 10¢ par exchanged for (0.1) share Common 1¢ par
Note: Unexchanged certificates were cancelled and became without value 09/15/2005

GENERAL DEFENSE CORP (PA)
Common 10¢ par split (3) for (2) by issuance of (0.5) additional share 1/16/81
Common 10¢ par split (3) for (2) by issuance of (0.5) additional share 3/15/83
Merged into Clabir Corp. (DE) 7/29/86
Each share Common 10¢ par exchanged for (0.72) share $3.3125 Preferred $1 par and (2) Class B Common Stock Purchase Warrants expiring 7/29/91
Clabir Corp. (DE) merged into Empire of Carolina, Inc. 12/29/89
(See Empire of Carolina, Inc.)

GENERAL DEFENSE SYS INC (NV)
Reorganized 11/06/2003
Reorganized from (FL) to under the laws of Nevada 11/06/2003
Each share old Common $0.001 par exchanged for (0.02) share new Common $0.001 par
Name changed to GenMedx Inc. 03/15/2005
GenMedx Inc. name changed to Pyramidion Technology Group, Inc. 06/19/2013

GENERAL DEV CORP NEW (DE)
Plan of reorganization under Chapter 11 Federal Bankruptcy proceedings confirmed 03/27/1992
No stockholders' equity

GENERAL DEV CORP OLD (DE)
Capital Stock $1 par split (2) for (1) by issuance of (1) additional share plus a 25% stock dividend paid 5/18/59
Under plan of reorganization each share Capital Stock $1 par automatically became (1) share GDV, Inc. Common $1 par 5/23/77
(See GDV, Inc.)

GENERAL DEVICES INC (DE)
Reincorporated 09/08/2000
State of incorporation changed from (NJ) to (DE) 09/08/2000
Each share old Common 1¢ par exchanged for (0.1) share new Common 1¢ par 10/17/2000
Each share new Common 1¢ par exchanged for (0.2) share Common $0.0001 par 12/15/2005
Name changed to Aduromed Industries, Inc. 01/30/2007
Aduromed Industries, Inc. name changed to MedClean Technologies, Inc. 01/26/2009

(See MedClean Technologies, Inc.)

GENERAL DIAMOND CORP (BC)
Recapitalized as Consolidated General Diamond Corp. 09/25/1995
Each share Common no par exchanged for (0.2) share Common no par
Consolidated General Diamond Corp. recapitalized as Exxel Energy Corp. 10/15/2001 which recapitalized as XXL Energy Corp. 05/30/2008

GENERAL DISCOUNT CORP. (GA)
Voluntarily dissolved 9/7/77
Details not available

GENERAL DISCOUNT CORP. (MI)
Each share Class A $3 par exchanged for (1) share Class A $1 par of General Discount Corp. and either (1) share Preferred $1 par or (1) share Common $1 par of Equity Corp. in 1936
Each share Common $1 par exchanged for (0.5) share Class A $1 par in 1937
Name changed to Consolidated Mortgage Corp. 2/15/67
Consolidated Mortgage Corp. name changed to Emil Coolidges Mortgages, Inc. 5/21/83
(See Emil Coolidges Mortgages, Inc.)

GENERAL DISTRIBUTORS, INC. (WV)
Proclaimed dissolved for non-payment of taxes 08/09/1985

GENERAL DISTRS CDA LTD (CANADA)
Common no par split (2) for (1) by issuance of (1) additional share 7/3/73
Common no par reclassified as Conv. Class A Common no par 6/5/75
Name changed to Gendis Inc. 6/8/83

GENERAL DONLEE CDA INC (CANADA)
Common no par split (2) for (1) by issuance of (1) additional share payable 05/31/2011 to holders of record 05/31/2011 Ex date - 05/27/2011
Acquired by Triumph Group, Inc. 10/09/2013
Each share Common no par exchanged for $5.50 cash

GENERAL DONLEE INCOME FD (ON)
Under plan of reorganization each Unit automatically became (1) share General Donlee Canada Inc. Common no par 01/07/2011
(See General Donlee Canada Inc.)

GENERAL DRIVE-IN CORP. (DE)
Name changed to General Cinema Corp. 4/13/64
General Cinema Corp. name changed to Harcourt General, Inc. 3/15/93
(See Harcourt General, Inc.)

GENERAL DRY BATTERIES, INC. (OH)
Merged into Mallory (P.R.) & Co. Inc. 4/26/56
Each share Common $1 par exchanged for (0.2) share 5% Preference Ser. A $50 par and (0.5) share Common $1 par
(See Mallory (P.R.) & Co. Inc.)

GENERAL DYNAMICS CORP (DE)
Conv. Preference Ser. 1963 no par called for redemption 07/30/1965
Conv. Preference Ser. 1964 no par called for redemption 07/30/1965
Conv. Preference Ser. 1965 no par called for redemption 07/30/1965
Conv. Preference no par called for redemption 04/15/1966
$4.25 Conv. Preferred Ser. A $1 par called for redemption 12/30/1983
Common Stock Purchase Rights declared for Common stockholders of record 02/13/1989 were redeemed at $0.01 per right

04/22/1993 for holders of record 04/05/1993
(Additional Information in Active)

GENERAL EASTN CORP (NY)
Stock Dividend - 50% 5/1/69
Merged into Chemical New York Corp. 3/3/72
Each share Common $5 par exchanged for (0.2878) share Common $12 par
Chemical New York Corp. name changed to Chemical Banking Corp. 4/29/88 which name changed to Chase Manhattan Corp. (New) 3/31/96 which name changed to J.P. Morgan Chase & Co. 12/31/2000 which name changed to JPMorgan Chase & Co. 7/20/2004

GENERAL ECONOMICS CORP. (DE)
Common 1¢ par changed to 5¢ par and (2) additional shares issued 1/15/63
Assets liquidated for benefit of creditors 1/6/67
No stockholders' equity

GENERAL ECONOMICS SYNDICATE, INC. (DE)
Name changed to Berel Industries, Inc. 7/8/66
(See Berel Industries, Inc.)

GENERAL EDUCATIONAL SVCS CORP (DE)
Each share Common 10¢ par exchanged for (0.142857) share Common 70¢ par 5/16/75
Name changed to Devon Group, Inc. 7/23/76
(See Devon Group, Inc.)

GENERAL ELEC & ENGLISH ELEC COS LTD (ENGLAND)
Name changed to General Electric Co. PLC (New) 09/18/1970
General Electric Co. PLC (New) name changed to Marconi PLC 11/26/1999 which name changed to M (2003) PLC 01/16/2004
(See M (2003) PLC)

GENERAL ELEC CDA INC (CANADA)
Acquired by G.E. Canada Acquisition Corp. 06/28/1989
Each share Common no par exchanged for $29.50 cash

GENERAL ELEC CAP CORP (DE)
Reincorporated 07/02/2001
State of incorporation changed from (NY) to (DE) 07/02/2001
Variable Preferred Stock Ser. JJ $100 par called for redemption at $100,000 on 09/14/2005
Variable Preferred Stock Ser. X-1 $100 called for redemption at $100,000 on 09/14/2005
Variable Preferred Stock Ser. GG $100 par called for redemption at $100,000 on 09/15/2005
Variable Preferred Stock Ser. HH $100 par called for redemption at $100,000 on 09/15/2005
Variable Preferred Stock Ser. KK $100 par called for redemption at $100,000 on 09/16/2005
Variable Preferred Stock Ser. P $100 par called for redemption at $100,000 on 09/19/2005
Variable Preferred Stock Ser. LL $100 par called for redemption at $100,000 on 09/21/2005
Variable Preferred Stock Ser. D $100 par called for redemption at $100,000 on 09/21/2005
Variable Preferred Stock Ser. AA $100 par called for redemption at $100,000 on 09/22/2005
Variable Preferred Stock Ser. O $100 par called for redemption at $100,000 on 09/22/2005
Variable Preferred Stock Ser. T $100 par called for redemption at $100,000 on 09/22/2005
Variable Preferred Stock Ser. M $100

par called for redemption at $100,000 on 09/26/2005
Variable Preferred Stock Ser. Q $100 par called for redemption at $100,000 on 09/27/2005
Variable Preferred Stock Ser. BB $100 par called for redemption at $100,000 on 09/28/2005
Variable Preferred Stock Ser. R $100 par called for redemption at $100,000 on 09/29/2005
Variable Preferred Stock Ser. E $100 par called for redemption at $100,000 on 09/30/2005
Variable Preferred Stock Ser. DD $100 par called for redemption at $100,000 on 10/03/2005
Variable Preferred Stock Ser. Y-1 $100 called for redemption at $100,000 on 10/03/2005
Variable Preferred Stock Ser. S $100 par called for redemption at $100,000 on 10/04/2005
Variable Preferred Stock Ser. A $100 par called for redemption at $100,000 on 10/05/2005
Variable Preferred Stock Ser. B $100 par called for redemption at $100,000 on 10/07/2005
Variable Preferred Stock Ser. C $100 par called for redemption at $100,000 on 10/07/2005
Variable Preferred Stock Ser. CC $100 par called for redemption at $100,000 on 10/07/2005
Variable Preferred Stock Ser. EE $100 par called for redemption at $100,000 on 10/07/2005
Variable Preferred Stock Ser. F $100 par called for redemption at $100,000 on 10/07/2005
Variable Preferred Stock Ser. FF $100 par called for redemption at $100,000 on 10/07/2005
Variable Preferred Stock Ser. G $100 par called for redemption at $100,000 on 10/07/2005
Variable Preferred Stock Ser. H $100 par called for redemption at $100,000 on 10/07/2005
Variable Preferred Stock Ser. I $100 par called for redemption at $100,000 on 10/07/2005
Variable Preferred Stock Ser. J $100 par called for redemption at $100,000 on 10/07/2005
Variable Preferred Stock Ser. L $100 par called for redemption at $100,000 on 10/07/2005
Variable Preferred Stock Ser. N $100 par called for redemption at $100,000 on 10/07/2005
Variable Preferred Stock Ser. U $100 par called for redemption at $100,000 on 10/07/2005
Variable Preferred Stock Ser. V $100 par called for redemption at $100,000 on 10/07/2005
Variable Preferred Stock Ser. W $100 par called for redemption at $100,000 on 10/07/2005
Variable Preferred Stock Ser. Y $100 par called for redemption at $100,000 on 10/07/2005
Variable Preferred Stock Ser. Z $100 par called for redemption at $100,000 on 10/07/2005
Variable Preferred Stock Ser. II $100 par called for redemption at $103,638 on 12/27/2006
Merged into General Electric Co. 12/03/2015
Each share 5.25% Fixed to Floating Rate Non-Cum Perpetual Preferred Ser. C 1¢ par exchanged for (109.41) shares 4.2% Fixed to Floating Rate Non-Cum Perpetual Preferred Ser. C $1 par
Each share 6.25% Fixed to Floating Rate Non-Cum Perpetual Preferred Ser. B 1¢ par exchanged for (118.43) shares 4.1% Fixed to Floating Rate Non-Cum Perpetual Preferred Ser. B $1 par
Each share 7.125% Fixed to Floating Rate Non-Cum Perpetual Preferred Ser. A 1¢ par exchanged for (123.45) shares 4% Fixed to Floating Rate Non-Cum Perpetual Preferred Ser. A $1 par

GENERAL ELEC LTD (ENGLAND)
Stock Dividends - Ordinary Reg. - 100% 09/26/1952; 10% 10/24/1963; 120% 10/09/1964; ADR's - 100% 10/17/1952; 10% 11/01/1963; 120% 10/23/1964
Merged into General Electric & English Electric Companies Ltd. 12/20/1968
Each ADR for Ordinary Reg. £1 par exchanged for (4) ADR's for Ordinary Reg. 5s par
General Electric & English Electric Companies Ltd. name changed to General Electric Co. PLC (New) 09/18/1970 which name changed to Marconi PLC 11/26/1999 which name changed to M (2003) PLC 01/16/2004
(See M (2003) plc)

GENERAL ELEC PLC NEW (ENGLAND)
ADR's for Ordinary Reg. 5s par changed to 25p par per currency change 02/15/1971
Each ADR for Ordinary Reg. 25p par exchanged for (5) ADR's for Reg. 5p par 10/29/1982
Stock Dividend - 12.5% 11/30/1972
Name changed to Marconi plc 11/26/1999
Marconi plc name changed to M (2003) plc 01/16/2004
(See M (2003) plc)

GENERAL ELECTR LABS INC (DE)
Each share Class A Common 33-1/3¢ par or Class B Common 33-1/3¢ par exchanged for (0.2) share Common no par 1/17/64
Merged into Sippican Corp. 12/31/68
Each share Common no par exchanged for (0.014705) share Common $1 par
Sippican Corp. name changed to TSC Corp. 11/9/81
(See TSC Corp.)

GENERAL ELECTRODYNAMICS CORP (TX)
Each share Common 10¢ par exchanged for (1/300) share Common $30 par in October 1986
Each share Common $30 par exchanged for (1/30) share Common $900 par 1/26/89
Note: Minority holders received an undetermined amount of cash and public interest was eliminated

GENERAL ELECTRONIC CONTROL, INC. (MN)
Class A Common 10¢ par reclassified as Common 10¢ par 12/1/62
Recapitalized as Staco, Inc. (MN) 9/10/65
Each share Common 10¢ par exchanged for (0.125) share Common 50¢ par
Staco, Inc. (MN) reincorporated in Delaware 11/15/73
(See Staco, Inc. (DE))

GENERAL ELECTRONICS CORP. (DE)
No longer in existence having become inoperative and void for non-payment of taxes 6/30/36

GENERAL ELECTRONICS DISTRIBUTORS, INC. (WV)
Name changed to General Distributors, Inc. 11/02/1966
(See General Distributors, Inc.)

GENERAL ELECTRS INC (NJ)
Common 1¢ par exchanged for (0.1) share Class A Common 10¢ par 2/15/60
Company went out of business in 1973

Stockholders' equity undetermined

GENERAL EMPIRE CORP.
Liquidated in 1933
Details not available

GENERAL EMPLOYMENT ENTERPRISES INC (IL)
Old Common no par split (2) for (1) by issuance of (1) additional share 03/08/1968
Old Common no par split (3) for (2) by issuance of (0.5) additional share payable 10/31/1997 to holders of record 10/17/1997 Ex date - 11/03/1997
Each share old Common no par exchanged for (0.1) share new Common no par 10/09/2015
Stock Dividends - 10% 09/11/1980; 10% 08/28/1981; 10% 09/08/1989; 15% 11/16/1994; 15% 11/03/1995; 15% payable 11/01/1996 to holders of record 10/10/1996 Ex date - 10/08/1996; 10% payable 10/30/1998 to holders of record 10/16/1998; 15% payable 10/29/1999 to holders of record 10/15/1999
Name changed to GEE Group Inc. 07/18/2016

GENERAL ENER TECH INC (MT)
Proclaimed dissolved for failure to file annual reports 12/1/89

GENERAL ENERGY AMER CORP (UT)
Proclaimed dissolved for failure to file reports 09/30/1979

GENERAL ENERGY CORP (AZ)
Charter revoked for failure to file reports and pay fees 06/28/1976

GENERAL ENERGY CORP (BC)
Capital Stock no par split (4) for (1) by issuance of (3) additional shares 06/10/1981
Stock Dividend - 10% 05/22/1981
Delisted from Vancouver Stock Exchange 04/07/1986

GENERAL ENERGY CORP (DE)
Merged into Kirby Exploration Co. 07/15/1983
Each share Capital Stock $1 par exchanged for (1.5714) shares Common 10¢ par
Kirby Exploration Co. reorganized as Kirby Exploration Co., Inc. 08/01/1984 which name changed to Kirby Corp. 05/01/1990

GENERAL ENERGY DEV INC (FL)
Reincorporated under the laws of Delaware as Beck Group, Inc. 11/22/82
(See Beck Group, Inc.)

GENERAL ENERGY DEV LTD (TX)
Merged into United Meridian Corp. 5/30/89
Each Depositary Receipt exchanged for $3.25 cash

GENERAL ENERGY OF AMERICA CORP. (UT)
Name changed to Systemeyes International, Inc. 09/12/1986
(See Systemeyes International, Inc.)

GENERAL ENERGY RES & TECHNOLOGY CORP (MI)
Charter declared inoperative and void for failure to file reports 07/15/2002

GENERAL ENGINEERING & MANUFACTURING CO.
Name changed to Gemco Shaper Co. in 1951
(See Gemco Shaper Co.)

GENERAL ENTERPRISES CORP. (DE)
Charter cancelled and declared inoperative and void for non-payment of taxes 3/1/75

GENERAL ENVIRONMENTAL CORP (DE)
Each share old Common $0.001 par exchanged for (1/3) share new Common $0.001 par 12/15/97
Reorganized under the laws of Nevada as NT Technologies, Inc. 3/26/2007
Each share new Common $0.001 par exchanged for (0.05) share Common $0.001 par
NT Technologies, Inc. name changed to NeXplore Corp. 6/5/2007

GENERAL ENVIRONMENTAL EQUIPMENT, INC. (FL)
Proclaimed dissolved for failure to file reports and pay fees 12/11/76

GENERAL ENVIRONMENTAL MGMT INC (NV)
Each share old Common $0.001 par exchanged for (0.03333333) share new Common $0.001 par 02/14/2007
Charter revoked for failure to file reports and pay taxes 03/31/2011

GENERAL ENVIRONMENTS CORP (DE)
Merged into Howell Corp. (TX) 6/28/72
Each share Common 25¢ par exchanged for (0.508388) share Common $1 par
Howell Corp. (TX) reincorporated in Delaware 4/24/84
(See Howell Corp.)

GENERAL EQUITY CORP.
Liquidated in 1938
Details not available

GENERAL EXECUTIVE SVCS INC (DE)
Charter cancelled and declared inoperative and void for non-payment of taxes 03/01/1985

GENERAL EXPLORATION CO. (CA)
Reincorporated under the laws of Delaware 3/25/75
(See General Exploration Co. (DE))

GENERAL EXPLORATION CO. OF CALIFORNIA (CA)
Capital Stock $1 par reclassified as Common $1 par 6/29/65
Name changed to General Exploration Co. 6/24/71
General Exploration Co. reincorporated in Delaware 3/25/75
(See General Exploration Co. (DE))

GENERAL EXPL CO (DE)
Plan of reorganization under Chapter 11 Federal Bankruptcy proceedings confirmed 05/20/1988
No stockholders' equity

GENERAL FABRICS CORP (OH)
Merged out of existence 12/29/86
Details not available

GENERAL FASTENERS INC (AB)
Merged into General Packaging Corp. 08/15/2007
Each share Common no par exchanged for $0.58 cash

GENERAL FELT INDS INC (DE)
Merged into M.C. Corp. 07/25/1974
Each share Common 50¢ par exchanged for $1.50 cash

GENERAL FIN CORP (AZ)
Each share Class A Common no par or Class B Common no par exchanged for (2) shares Common no par 2/17/70
Charter revoked for failure to file reports or pay fees 12/31/75

GENERAL FINANCE CO. (AZ)
Reorganized 3/14/58
Each share Class A Common $1 par exchanged for (1/3) share Class A Common no par and $0.667 principal amount of 8% Debentures due 1998
Each share Class B Common $1 par exchanged for (1/3) share Class B Common no par and $0.667

principal amount of 8% Debentures due 1998
Name changed to General Finance Corp. (AZ) 12/12/69
(See General Finance Co. (AZ))

GENERAL FINANCE CORP. (DE)
Common $1 par split (2) for (1) by issuance of (1) additional share 9/12/63
Merged into General Finance Discount Corp. 12/12/69
Each share Common $1 par exchanged for $30.35 cash

GENERAL FINANCE CORP. (MI)
Recapitalized in 1941
Each share 6% Preferred Ser. A $10 par exchanged for (1) share 6% Preferred Ser. B $10 par
Each share 5% Preferred Ser. B $10 par exchanged for (1) share 5% Preferred Ser. A $10 par
Stock Dividend - 10% 12/22/49
Reincorporated under the laws of Delaware in 1954
(See General Finance Corp. (DE))

GENERAL FINL INDS INC (NV)
Name changed to Monarch Molybdenum & Resources, Inc. (Ctfs. dated prior to 03/07/1988) 09/14/1978
Monarch Molybdenum & Resources, Inc. (Ctfs. dated prior to 03/07/1988) recapitalized as Mediacom Communications, Inc. 03/07/1988 which name changed to Duraco Industries, Inc. 09/15/1990

GENERAL FINL SYS INC (FL)
Name changed to First Marine Banks, Inc. 03/01/1976
(See First Marine Banks, Inc.)

GENERAL FIRE EXTINGUISHER CO.
Name changed to Grinnell Corp. in 1944
Grinnell Corp. merged into International Telephone & Telegraph Corp. (DE) 10/31/69 which name changed to ITT Corp. 12/31/83 which reorganized in Indiana as ITT Industries, Inc. 12/19/95 which name changed to ITT Corp. 7/1/2006

GENERAL FIREPROOFING CO (OH)
Each share old Common no par exchanged for (4) shares new Common no par in 1928
Each share new Common no par exchanged for (2) shares Common $5 par in 1950
Common $5 par split (2) for (1) by issuance of (1) additional share 10/15/65
Common $5 par split (2) for (1) by issuance of (1) additional share 2/2/68
Stock Dividend - 10% 1/3/56
Name changed to GF Business Equipment Inc. 4/27/73
GF Business Equipment Inc. reorganized as GF Corp. 6/6/83
(See GF Corp.)

GENERAL FLOORING CO., INC. (LA)
Adjudicated bankrupt 11/2/62
No stockholders' equity

GENERAL FOAM CORP. (NY)
Completely liquidated 4/7/67
Each share Common $1 par exchanged for first and final distribution of (1) share Tenneco Inc. Common $5 par
Tenneco Inc. merged into El Paso Natural Gas Co. 12/12/96 which reorganized as El Paso Energy Corp. 8/1/98 which name changed to El Paso Corp. 2/5/2001

GENERAL FOODS CORP (DE)
Common no par split (2) for (1) by issuance of (1) additional share 06/05/1956
Common no par split (2) for (1) by issuance of (1) additional share 08/23/1960
Common no par changed to $1 par 07/25/1969
Common $1 par split (2) for (1) by issuance of (1) additional share 03/29/1971
Merged into Morris (Philip) Companies Inc. 11/01/1985
Each share Common $1 par exchanged for $120 cash

GENERAL FORGE CO., INC. (NY)
Charter cancelled and proclaimed dissolved for failure to pay taxes 12/15/51

GENERAL FRIGID TRANSPORTATION CORP.
Out of existence in 1940
Details not available

GENERAL FRUIT CORP.
Name changed to Pacific Fruit & Produce Co. in 1935
Pacific Fruit & Produce Co. merged into Pacific Gamble Robinson Co. in 1942
(See Pacific Gamble Robinson Co.)

GENERAL FUSE CO. (NJ)
Assets sold to pay federal taxes 7/2/59
No stockholders' equity

GENERAL GAS & ELECTRIC CORP. (DE)
Assets distributed to stockholders in 1945
Details not available

GENERAL GAS CORP. (DE)
Common $5 par changed to $2.50 par and (1) additional share issued 5/28/56
Acquired by Standard Oil Co. (Ind.) 7/31/64
Each share Common $2.50 par exchanged for (0.25) share Capital Stock $25 par
Standard Oil Co. (Ind.) name changed to Amoco Corp. 4/23/85

GENERAL GAS CORP (NV)
Each share old Common $0.001 par exchanged for (0.005) share new Common $0.001 par 02/14/2007
Name changed to Advanced Visual Systems, Inc. 08/27/2009
Advanced Visual Systems, Inc. name changed to Visual Management Sciences, Inc. 05/27/2016
(See Visual Management Sciences, Inc.)

GENERAL GENETICS CORP (DE)
Reorganized under the laws of Texas as Note Bankers of America, Inc. 9/15/96
Each share Common $0.001 par exchanged for (0.05) share Common $0.001 par
Note Bankers of America, Inc. (TX) reorganized in Nevada as Facit Group Holdings, Inc. 10/28/98

GENERAL GILBERT CORP (CT)
Adjudicated bankrupt 8/31/70
No stockholders' equity

GENERAL GLAZE CORP. (MD)
Out of business in 1954
Details not available

GENERAL GROCER CO (DE)
Acquired by Wetterau Inc. 00/00/1983
Details not available

GENERAL GROWTH INDS INC (DE)
Name changed to Silver Reclamation Industries, Inc. 5/1/80
Silver Reclamation Industries, Inc. recapitalized as Inter America Industries, Inc. 1/28/83 which name changed to Kendee's International Foods, Inc. 11/20/85
(See Kendee's International Foods, Inc.)

GENERAL GROWTH LTD PARTNERSHIP (DE)
Liquidation completed
Each Depositary Receipt received initial distribution of $150 cash 2/28/86
Each Depositary Receipt received second distribution of $300 cash 9/15/86
Each Depositary Receipt received third distribution of $150 cash 1/15/87
Each Depositary Receipt received fourth distribution of $200 cash 5/29/87
Each Depositary Receipt received fifth distribution of $60 cash 4/15/88
Each Depositary Receipt received sixth distribution of $25 cash 4/11/89
Each Depositary Receipt received seventh distribution of $100 cash 8/1/89
Each Depositary Receipt exchanged for eighth and final distribution of $30.70 cash 10/15/90

GENERAL GROWTH PPTYS (MA)
Units of Bene. Int. $1 par split (2) for (1) by issuance of (1) additional share 8/15/72
Units of Bene. Int. $1 par reclassified as Common Shares of Bene. Int. $1 par 1/29/74
Liquidation completed
Each share $1.90 Conv. Preferred Ser. A $1 par exchanged for first and final distribution of $21 cash 9/30/85
Each (100) Common Shares of Bene. Int. $1 par exchanged for (1) share General Growth Limited Partnership Depositary Receipt 9/30/85
Note: Holdings of (99) or fewer shares of Common exchanged for $6.60 cash per share
(See General Growth Limited Partnership)

GENERAL GROWTH PPTYS INC NEW (DE)
Each share Common 1¢ par received distribution of approximately (0.0375) share Rouse Properties, Inc. Common 1¢ par payable 01/12/2012 to holders of record 12/30/2011 Ex date - 01/13/2012
Name changed to GGP Inc. 01/27/2017

GENERAL GROWTH PPTYS INC OLD (DE)
Each 7.25% Depositary Preferred exchanged for (0.6297) share Common 10¢ par 07/15/2003
Common 10¢ par changed to 1¢ par and (2) additional shares issued payable 12/05/2003 to holders of record 11/20/2003 Ex date - 12/08/2003
Plan of reorganization under Chapter 11 Federal Bankruptcy proceedings effective 11/09/2010
Each share Common 1¢ par exchanged for (1) share General Growth Properties, Inc. (New) Common 1¢ par and (0.098344) share Howard Hughes Corp. Common 1¢ par
General Growth Properties, Inc. (New) name changed to GGP Inc. 01/27/2017

GENERAL HEALTH SVCS INC (DE)
Stock Dividend - 25% 11/23/79
Merged into Hospital Corp. of America 12/30/80
Each share Common $1 par exchanged for $32 cash

GENERAL HOBBIES CORP (PA)
Chapter 11 bankruptcy proceedings converted to Chapter 7 on 12/3/85
Stockholders' equity unlikely

GENERAL HOMES CORP (TX)
Plan of reorganization under Chapter 11 Federal Bankruptcy proceedings confirmed 10/30/1991
No stockholders' equity

GENERAL HOSIERY CO.
Acquired by Gotham Hosiery Co., Inc. 00/00/1944
Details not available

GENERAL HOSIERY MOTOR-MEND CORP. (DE)
No longer in existence having become inoperative and void for non-payment of taxes 4/1/54

GENERAL HOST CORP (NY)
Common $5 par changed to $1 par 03/28/1968
Common $1 par split (2) for (1) by issuance of (1) additional share 02/04/1982
Common $1 par split (5) for (4) by issuance of (0.25) additional share 12/14/1982
Common $1 par split (5) for (4) by issuance of (0.25) additional share 12/16/1983
Common $1 par split (3) for (2) by issuance of (0.5) additional share 03/04/1985
Common $1 par split (3) for (2) by issuance of (0.5) additional share 03/03/1986
Stock Dividends - 5% payable 04/05/1996 to holders of record 03/15/1996; 5% payable 04/04/1997 to holders of record 03/14/1997
Merged into Cyrus Acquisition Corp. 01/07/1998
Each share Common $1 par exchanged for $5.50 cash

GENERAL HOUSEHOLD UTILITIES CO.
Out of business in 1940
Details not available

GENERAL HOUSEWARES CORP (DE)
Merged into Corning Consumer Products 10/21/99
Each share Common 33-1/3¢ par exchanged for $28.75 cash

GENERAL HYDRAULICS CORP. (PA)
Voluntarily dissolved 1/29/81
Details not available

GENERAL HYDROCARBONS INC (MN)
Completely liquidated 5/4/87
Each (296) shares Common 1¢ par received first and final distribution of (1) share Montana Power Co. Common no par
Note: Certificates were not required to be surrendered and are now valueless
Montana Power Co. reorganized under the laws of Delaware as Touch America Holdings, Inc. 2/13/2002
(See Touch America Holdings, Inc.)

GENERAL HYDROCARBONS INC (NV)
Merged into General Hydrocarbons, Inc. (MN) 3/31/83
Each share Common 1¢ par exchanged for (1) share Common 1¢ par
(See General Hydrocarbons, Inc. (MN))

GENERAL ICE CREAM CORP.
Acquired by National Dairy Products Corp. 00/00/1928
Details not available

GENERAL IMPACT EXTRUSIONS LTD. (CANADA)
Acquired by Consumers Glass Co., Ltd. 12/18/70
Each share Common no par exchanged for (0.37) share Common no par and $4.35 cash
Consumers Glass Co., Ltd. name changed to Consumers Packaging Inc./Emballages Consumers Inc. 7/2/86
(See Consumers Packaging Inc./Emballages Consumers Inc.)

GENERAL INDICATOR CORP (DE)
Each share old Common 1¢ par exchanged for (0.1) share new Common 10¢ par 1/31/80

Charter cancelled and declared inoperative and void for non-payment of taxes 6/17/93

GENERAL INDICATOR CORP (NY)
6% Preferred $10 par called for redemption 02/28/1962
Merged into Compudyne Corp. 03/10/1972
Each share Common 1¢ par exchanged for (0.03256) share Common 25¢ par
(See Compudyne Corp.)

GENERAL INDUSTRIAL ALCOHOL CORP.
Merged into American Solvents & Chemical Corp. in 1930
Details not available

GENERAL INDL CONTAINER CORP (PA)
Adjudicated bankrupt 08/02/1967
No stockholders' equity

GENERAL INDUSTRIAL ENTERPRISES, INC. (DE)
Merged into Baldwin Securities Corp. (DE) 09/30/1965
Each share Capital Stock no par exchanged for (4.975869) shares Common 1¢ par
(See Baldwin Securities Corp.)

GENERAL INDUSTRIES CO. (OH)
5% Preferred $100 par called for redemption 6/28/63
Name changed to Elyria Co. 9/25/64
(See Elyria Co.)

GENERAL INDUSTRIES CORP., LTD. (CA)
Liquidation completed
Each share Capital Stock no par exchanged for initial distribution of $2 cash 8/15/67
Each share Capital Stock no par received second and final distribution of 50¢ cash 2/20/70

GENERAL INSTR CORP (DE)
Ctfs. dtd. after 02/02/1998
Merged into Motorola, Inc. 01/05/2000
Each share Common 1¢ par exchanged for (0.575) share Common $3 par
Motorola, Inc. recapitalized as Motorola Solutions, Inc. 01/04/2011

GENERAL INSTR CORP (DE)
Ctfs. dtd. prior to 07/25/1997
Common 1¢ par split (2) for (1) by issuance of (1) additional share 08/08/1994
Each share Common 1¢ par received distribution of (1/3) share CommScope, Inc. Common 1¢ par and (1) share NextLevel Systems, Inc. Common 1¢ par payable 07/28/1997 to holders of record 07/25/1997
Recapitalized as General Semiconductor, Inc. 07/25/1997
Each share Common 1¢ par exchanged for (0.25) share Common 1¢ par
General Semiconductor, Inc. merged into Vishay Intertechnology, Inc. 11/02/2001

GENERAL INSTR CORP (DE)
Incorporated 06/12/1967
Reincorporated 08/31/1967
Common no par changed to $1 par 00/00/1939
Stock Dividend - 100% 10/15/1945
State of incorporation changed from (NJ) to (DE) 08/31/1967
$3 Conv. Preferred Ser. A no par called for redemption 05/29/1981
Common $1 par split (3) for (1) by issuance of (2) additional shares 08/05/1981
Merged into FLGI Acquisition Corp. 08/22/1990
Each share Common $1 par exchanged for $44.50 cash

GENERAL INS INVT CO (TX)
Class A Conv. Preferred Ser. A $1 par called for redemption 4/24/68
Common no par changed to $1 par 11/3/58
In process of liquidation
Each share Common $1 par exchanged for initial distribution of $1 cash 10/6/69
Each share Common $1 par received second distribution of $1 cash 2/3/70
Note: Details on subsequent distributions, if any, are not available

GENERAL INTERIORS CORP (MD)
Completely liquidated 4/17/75
Each share Common 33-1/3¢ par exchanged for first and final distribution of (0.2057) share General Mills, Inc. Common $1.50 par

GENERAL INTL CORP (DE)
Charter cancelled and declared inoperative and void for non-payment of taxes 03/01/1989

GENERAL INTL FILM CORP (NV)
Charter revoked for failure to file reports and pay fees 03/01/1973

GENERAL INTL INC (UT)
Proclaimed dissolved for failure to pay taxes 11/9/74

GENERAL INVESTMENT CORP. (DE)
Merged into Foundation Industrial Engineering Co., Inc. in 1942
Each share $6 Preferred exchanged for (1) share $1.50 Preferred $1 par, (13.5) shares Common 10¢ par and (1) Liquidation Certificate
Each share Class A exchanged for (0.05) share Common 10¢ par
Each share Common $1 par exchanged for (0.05) share Common 10¢ par
Foundation Industrial Engineering Co., Inc. recapitalized as Stokely Foods, Inc. in 1943 which merged into Stokely-Van Camp, Inc. 5/29/52
(See Stokley-Van Camp, Inc.)

GENERAL INVESTMENT CORP. (UT)
Ctfs. dated prior to 11/7/56
Merged into Utah Hydro Corp. on a (1) for (10) basis 11/7/56
Utah Hydro Corp. name changed to Hydro Flame Corp. 6/5/65
(See Hydro Flame Corp.)

GENERAL INVT CORP (UT)
Ctfs. dated after 07/15/1958
Proclaimed dissolved for failure to pay taxes 09/01/1992

GENERAL INVT CORP QUE (QC)
Acquired by the Province of Quebec 08/22/1973
Each share 7% Preferred $10 par exchanged for $10 principal amount of Province of Quebec 7% Debentures due 05/01/1988 (Exchange affected only Preferred holders of (100) shares or multiples thereof; holders of less received $8.78 cash per share)
Each share Common $10 par exchanged for $5 principal amount of Province of Quebec 8% Debentures due 5/1/88 plus $1.57 cash or $10 principal amount of Province of Quebec 6% Debentures due 05/01/1988 (Exchange affected only Common holders of (100) shares or multiples thereof; holders of less received $6.38 cash per share)

GENERAL INVESTMENT TRUST CO.
Succeeded by British Type Investors, Inc. 00/00/1928
Details not available

GENERAL INVESTORS TRUST (MA)
Name changed to Eaton & Howard Income Fund 10/15/1968
Eaton & Howard Income Fund name changed to Eaton Vance High Yield Fund 02/18/1983
(See Eaton Vance High Yield Fund)

GENERAL IRON CORP (NY)
Charter cancelled and proclaimed dissolved for failure to pay taxes 09/27/1995

GENERAL ITALIAN EDISON ELECTRIC CORP. (ITALY)
Deposit Agreement terminated 05/10/1949
Each ADR for Ordinary exchanged for $84.168 cash

GENERAL JEWELERS, INC. (DE)
Proclaimed inoperative and void for non-payment of taxes 4/1/55

GENERAL KINETICS INC (VA)
Common 25¢ par split (2) for (1) by issuance of (1) additional share 03/25/1991
Chapter 11 bankruptcy proceedings terminated 12/29/2008
No stockholders' equity

GENERAL LAB ASSOC INC (NY)
Common $10 par changed to $2.50 par and (2) additional shares issued 7/17/61
Name changed to Simmonds Precision Engine Systems, Inc. 3/18/74
(See Simmonds Precision Engine Systems, Inc.)

GENERAL LAND CORP. (MN)
Merged into Unisource Corp. 3/18/69
Each share Common 10¢ par exchanged for (1) share Common 10¢ par

GENERAL LASER CORP (DE)
Adjudicated bankrupt 12/16/70
Stockholders' equity unlikely
Charter subsequently revoked for failure to file reports or pay taxes 4/15/71

GENERAL LATEX & CHEM CORP (MA)
Merged into GLC Transition Inc. 4/25/2000
Each share Common $2 par exchanged for $383.206 cash
Each share Class A Common $2 par exchanged for $383.206 cash

GENERAL LAUNDRY MACHINERY CORP.
Reorganized as Columbia-Troy Corp. 00/00/1931
No stockholders' equity

GENERAL LEASING CORP. (KS)
Under plan of merger name changed to General United Corp., Inc. 4/26/63
(See General United Corp., Inc.)

GENERAL LEATHER CO.
Property sold for benefit of Bondholders in 1935
No stockholders' equity

GENERAL LEISURE CORP (AB)
Name changed to Westgroup Corporations Inc. 05/13/1991
Westgroup Corporations Inc. recapitalized as Beaumont Select Corporations Inc. 02/28/1995
(See Beaumont Select Corporations Inc.)

GENERAL LEISURE INC (DE)
Under plan of merger each share Common 10¢ par exchanged for $2 cash 1/7/82

GENERAL LEISURE PRODS CORP (NE)
Merged into Arctic Enterprises, Inc. 3/2/71
Each share Common $1 par exchanged for (0.105263) share Common 10¢ par
Arctic Enterprises, Inc. name changed to Minstar Inc. (MN) 12/14/82 which reorganized in Delaware 8/31/85
(See Minstar, Inc. (DE))

GENERAL LIFE INS CORP WIS (WI)
Common 45¢ par changed to $1 par 10/6/61
Each share Common $1 par exchanged for (0.001) share Common $1,000 par 12/14/71
Note: In effect holders received $3.25 cash per share and public interest was eliminated

GENERAL LIFE MO INVT CO (MO)
Merged into Guaranty Corp. 01/17/1974
Each share Class A Common 20¢ par exchanged for (0.083333) share Class AA Common no par

GENERAL LIFE OF IOWA INVESTMENT CO. (IA)
Name changed to General United Group, Inc. 7/10/67
(See General United Group, Inc.)

GENERAL LIFE OF TENNESSEE INSURANCE CO. (TN)
Merged into Guaranty Financial Corp. 12/9/68
Each share Common $1 par exchanged for (0.588235) share Common $1 par
Guaranty Financial Corp. recapitalized as Keymaster Corp. 12/29/69 which merged into Solomon, Inc. 3/8/73
(See Solomon, Inc.)

GENERAL MACHINERY CORP.
Merged into Lima-Hamilton Corp. share for share in 1947
Lima-Hamilton Corp. merged into Baldwin-Lima-Hamilton Corp. in 1950 which was acquired by Armour & Co. (Del.) 7/2/65

GENERAL MAGIC INC (DE)
Each share old Common $0.001 par exchanged for (0.07142857) share new Common $0.001 par 07/15/2002
Plan of reorganization under Chapter 11 Federal Bankruptcy Code effective 04/08/2004
No stockholders' equity

GENERAL MAGNAPLATE CORP (NJ)
Each share Common 50¢ par exchanged for (0.25) share Common $2 par 04/02/1975
Common $2 par changed to no par and (2) additional shares issued 01/16/1981
Common no par split (3) for (1) by issuance of (2) additional shares 10/02/1981
Common no par split (4) for (1) by issuance of (3) additional shares 01/20/1989
Common no par split (2) for (1) by issuance of (1) additional share payable 12/16/1997 to holders of record 12/02/1997
Stock Dividend - 10% 07/29/1966
Reverted to a private company 06/28/2007
Each share Common no par exchanged for $5 cash
Note: Holders of (180,000) shares or more retained their interests

GENERAL MAGNETICS INC. (MN)
Adjudicated bankrupt 6/25/62
No stockholders' equity

GENERAL MANAGEMENT CORP. (IA)
Merged into General Growth Properties 10/13/70
Each share Common $1 par exchanged for (1) Share of Bene. Int. $1 par
(See General Growth Properties)

GENERAL MANIFOLD & PRINTING CO. (PA)
Capital Stock $50 par changed to $10 par in 1933
Each share Capital Stock $10 par exchanged for (5) shares Capital Stock $2 par in 1946

GEN-GEN — FINANCIAL INFORMATION, INC.

Name changed to Arnold Graphic Industries, Inc. 1/6/62
(See Arnold Graphic Industries, Inc.)

GENERAL MARITIME CORP NEW (MARSHALL ISLANDS)
Plan of reorganization under Chapter 11 Federal Bankruptcy proceedings effective 05/17/2012
No stockholders' equity
Name changed to Gener8 Maritime, Inc. 05/07/2015
Gener8 Maritime, Inc. merged into Euronav N.V. 06/12/2018

GENERAL MARITIME CORP OLD (MARSHALL ISLANDS)
Issue Information - 8,000,000 shares COM offered at $18 per share on 06/12/2001
Merged into General Maritime Corp. (New) 12/16/2008
Each share Common 1¢ par exchanged for (1.34) shares Common 1¢ par
(See General Maritime Corp. (New))

GENERAL MARKING SYSTEMS, INC. (CO)
Name changed to Compco General Corp. 8/21/69
(See Compco General Corp.)

GENERAL MED CORP (VA)
Stock Dividends - 50% 12/6/68; 50% 12/30/69
Name changed to GMD Investment Corp. 3/31/80
(See GMD Investment Corp.)

GENERAL MERCHANDISE CO., LTD. (ON)
Completely liquidated 05/00/1969
Each share Class A received $1.75 cash
No stockholders' equity for Class B

GENERAL MERCHANDISE CO. (WI)
Acquired by Penney (J.C.) Co. on a (0.37) for (1) basis 2/21/62
Penney (J.C.) Co. name changed to Penney (J.C.) Co., Inc. 10/17/68

GENERAL METAL & ABRASIVES CO (MI)
Merged into Mid-American Abrasives, Inc. 8/7/91
Each share Common 2¢ par exchanged for $3.35 cash

GENERAL METALCRAFT INC (WA)
Liquidation completed
Each share 6% Preferred $1 par exchanged for initial distribution of $2.33 cash 12/24/86
Each share Common no par exchanged for initial distribution of $2.33 cash 12/24/86
Each share 6% Preferred $1 par received second and final distribution of $0.21 cash 12/24/87
Each share Common no par received second and final distribution of $0.21 cash 12/24/87

GENERAL METALS CORP. (CA)
Merged into Adel Precision Products Corp. for cash 2/17/64

GENERAL METALS CORP. LTD. (CANADA)
Company inactive since 1934 Charter dissolved 12/15/80

GENERAL METALS CORP (DE)
Each share old Common $0.001 par exchanged for (1.1) shares new Common $0.001 par 07/19/2007
Each share new Common $0.001 par exchanged again for (1.1) shares new Common $0.001 par 01/04/2011
Recapitalized as Cibolan Gold Corp. 05/30/2014
Each share new Common $0.001 par exchanged for (0.05) share Common $0.001 par

GENERAL METERS, INC. (CO)
Common $1 par changed to 50¢ par 4/3/63

Merged into Dixson, Inc. 7/1/63
Each share Common 50¢ par exchanged for (0.5) share Common 50¢ par
(See Dixson, Inc.)

GENERAL MICROELECTRONICS CORP (DE)
Name changed to Supercomputing Solutions, Inc. 08/28/1989
(See Supercomputing Solutions, Inc.)

GENERAL MICROWAVE CORP (NY)
Merged into Herley Industries, Inc. 01/06/1999
Each share Common 1¢ par exchanged for (1) Common Stock Purchase Warrant expiring 01/05/2002 and $18 cash

GENERAL MINERALS AMER INC (CO)
Each (7.3) shares old Common no par exchanged for (1) share new Common no par 11/12/1982
Name changed to National Investors Capital, Inc. 05/14/1992

GENERAL MINERALS CORP. (MD)
Acquired by Fargo Oils Ltd. on a (1) for (4.4) basis 9/26/58
Fargo Oils Ltd. acquired by Reserve Oil & Gas Co. 6/10/68
(See Reserve Oil & Gas Co.)

GENERAL MINERALS CORP (CANADA)
Incorporated 08/19/1984
Each share old Common no par exchanged for (0.1) share new Common no par 06/20/2003
Name changed to Sprott Resource Corp. 09/18/2007
Sprott Resource Corp. merged into Sprott Resource Holdings Inc. 02/13/2017

GENERAL MINERALS CORP (CANADA)
Incorporated 09/18/1981
Adjudicated bankrupt 03/08/1990
No stockholders' equity

GENERAL MINERALS CORP (CO)
Common $1 par changed to no par 6/13/69
Proclaimed dissolved for failure to file reports 7/1/99

GENERAL MINES CORP. (DE)
Charter cancelled and declared inoperative and void for non-payment of taxes 04/01/1931

GENERAL MINES CORP. (ID)
Name changed to Idaho General Mines, Inc. (ID) 03/22/1967
Idaho General Mines, Inc. (ID) reincorporated in Delaware as General Moly, Inc. 10/09/2007

GENERAL MINING & FINANCE CORP. LTD. (SOUTH AFRICA)
Each ADR for Ordinary Rand-2 par exchanged for (5) ADR's for Ordinary Rand-0.40 par 12/13/1978
Name changed to General Mining Union Corp. Ltd. 07/09/1980
General Mining Union Corp. Ltd. reorganized as Gencor Ltd. 09/25/1989
(See Gencor Ltd.)

GENERAL MNG UN LTD (SOUTH AFRICA)
Under plan of reorganization name changed to Gencor Ltd. and ADR's for Ordinary Rand-0.40 par changed to Rand-0.04 par 9/25/89
(See Gencor Ltd.)

GENERAL MLS INC (DE)
3-3/8% Conv. Preferred $100 par called for redemption 03/01/1956
5% Preferred $100 par called for redemption 01/01/1965
$1.75 Conv. Preference no par called for redemption 09/28/1973
(Additional Information in Active)

GENERAL MOLDED PLASTICS, INC. (TX)
Charter forfeited for non-payment of franchise taxes 4/29/64

GENERAL MTG CORP (MI)
Each share Class A Common $10 par exchanged for (10) shares Class A Common no par 04/15/1970
Stock Dividend - 10% 03/25/1976
Charter declared inoperative and void for failure to file reports 07/15/2003

GENERAL MTG CORP CDA (CANADA)
Each share $2 Partly Paid Common $10 par exchanged for (0.2) share Fully Paid Common $10 par 07/31/1970
Name changed to Commerce Capital Mortgage Corp.-Societe d'Hypotheque Commerce Capital 12/01/1976
Commerce Capital Mortgage Corp.-Societe d' Hypotheque Commerce Capital name changed to Eaton Bay Mortgage Corp. 09/15/1980 which name changed to Seaway Mortgage Corp.-La Corporation d' Hypotheque Seaway 02/03/1982
(See Seaway Mortgage Corp. -La Corporation d'Hypotheque Seaway)

GENERAL MTG INVTS (MD)
Merged into Goodrich Realty & Development Group, Inc. 01/17/1973
Each Share of Bene. Int. $1 par exchanged for (1/3) share Common 1¢ par and $10 principal amount of 8-1/2% Conv. Subord. Debentures due 01/01/1993
Goodrich Realty & Development Group, Inc. name changed to Midcon Industries Inc. 01/26/1976
(See Midcon Industries Inc.)

GENERAL MORTGAGE SERVICE CORP. OF CANADA (CANADA)
Name changed to General Mortgage Corp. of Canada-Societe Generale d'Hypotheque du Canada 12/14/1966
General Mortgage Corp. of Canada-Societe Generale d'Hypotheque Canada name changed to Commerce Capital Mortgage Corp.-Societe d'Hypotheque Commerce Capital 12/01/1976 which name changed to Eaton Bay Mortgage Corp. 09/15/1980 which name changed to Seaway Mortgage Corp.-La Corporation d'Hypotheque Seaway 02/03/1982
(See Seaway Mortgage Corp. -La Corporation d'Hypotheque Seaway)

GENERAL MTRS CAP TR D (DE)
8.67% Trust Originated Preferred Securities called for redemption at $25 plus $0.01 accrued dividend on 5/2/2000

GENERAL MTRS CO (DE)
Issue Information - 87,000,000 shares JR PFD CONV SER B offered at $50 per share on 11/17/2010
Each share 4.75% Jr. Conv. Preferred Ser. B 1¢ par exchanged for (1.3736) shares Common 1¢ par 11/29/2013
(Additional Information in Active)

GENERAL MTRS CORP (DE)
Each share old Common no par exchanged for (10) shares Common $100 par 03/01/1920
Each share Common $100 par exchanged for (0.25) share new Common no par 09/19/1924
Each share new Common no par exchanged for (2) shares Common $25 par 09/15/1927
Each share Common $25 par exchanged for (2.5) shares Common $10 par 01/07/1929

Each share Common $10 par exchanged for (2) shares Common $5 par 10/03/1950
Common $5 par changed to $1.66666666 par and (2) additional shares issued 11/07/1955
Old Class H Common 10¢ par split (2) for (1) by issuance of (1) additional share 03/07/1988
Class E Common 10¢ par split (2) for (1) by issuance of (1) additional share 06/07/1985
Common $1.66666666 par split (2) for (1) by issuance of (1) additional share 03/28/1989
Class E Common 10¢ par split (2) for (1) by issuance of (1) additional share 03/07/1990
Class E Common 10¢ par split (2) for (1) by issuance of (1) additional share 03/06/1992
Preference Ser. E-I 10¢ par called for redemption 09/15/1993
$3.75 Preferred no par called for redemption 05/01/1993
$5 Preferred no par called for redemption 05/01/1993
Each share $3.31 Preference Equity Stock 10¢ par exchanged for (0.992435) share Common $1.66666666 par and $0.1655 cash 06/18/1994
Depositary Preference Ser. C called for redemption 02/22/1996
Merged into Electronic Data Systems Corp. (DE) 06/07/1996
Each share Class E Common 10¢ par exchanged for (1) share Common 1¢ par
Recapitalized 12/18/1997
Each share old Class H Common 10¢ par exchanged for (1) share new Class H Common 10¢ par and (0.56240) share Raytheon Co. Class A Common $1 par
Each share Common $1.66666666 par received distribution of (0.06377) share Raytheon Co. Class A Common 1¢ par payable 12/18/1997 to holders of record 12/17/1997 Ex date - 12/19/1997
Depositary Preference Ser. B called for redemption at $25 on 04/05/1999
Each share Common $1.66666666 par received distribution of (0.69893) share Delphi Automotive Systems Corp. Common 1¢ par payable 05/28/1999 to holders of record 05/25/1999 Ex date - 05/28/1999
7.92% Depositary Preference Ser. D called for redemption at $25 plus $0.18 accrued dividends on 05/02/2000
New Class H Common 10¢ par split (3) for (1) by issuance of (2) additional shares payable 06/30/2000 to holders of record 06/13/2000 Ex date - 07/03/2000
9.12% Depositary Preference Ser. G called for redemption at $25 plus $0.59 accrued dividends on 04/02/2001
Stock Dividends - Common - 25% 05/01/1920; 50% 09/11/1926
Under plan of recapitalization each share new Class H Common 10¢ par exchanged for (0.8232) share Hughes Electronics Corp. Common 1¢ par and (0.0921) News Corp., Ltd. Sponsored ADR for Ltd. Voting Preferred Ordinary 12/22/2003
(See each company's listing)
Name changed to Motors Liquidation Co. 07/15/2009
(See Motors Liquidation Co.)

GENERAL MUN BD FD INC (MD)
Merged into Dreyfus Premier Municipal Bond Fund 10/13/2004
Details not available

GENERAL N Y TAX EXEMPT MONEY MKT FD (MA)
Name changed to General New York

Municipal Money Market Fund 9/8/95

GENERAL NARROW GAUGE TRUST
Liquidated in 1944
Details not available

GENERAL NUCLEAR (WY)
Name changed to General Mining Co. and Common 1¢ par changed to $0.001 par 6/30/87

GENERAL NUCLEAR INC (TX)
Name changed to Atec, Inc. 7/26/73

GENERAL NUCLEONICS CORP. (DE)
No longer in existence having become inoperative and void for non-payment of taxes 4/1/58

GENERAL NUMISMATICS CORP. (PA)
Name changed to Franklin Mint, Inc. 06/01/1968
Franklin Mint, Inc. name changed to Franklin Mint Corp. 03/29/1972 which merged into Warner Communications Inc. 03/02/1981 which merged into Time Warner Inc. (Old) 01/10/1990 which merged into AOL Time Warner Inc. 01/11/2001 which name changed to Time Warner Inc. (New) 10/16/2003 which merged into AT&T Inc. 06/15/2018

GENERAL NURSING HOMES CORP (PA)
Reported out of business 00/00/1978
No stockholders' equity

GENERAL NUTRITION COS INC (DE)
Common 1¢ par split (2) for (1) by issuance of (1) additional share 10/5/93
Stock Dividend - 100% 10/17/95
Merged into Koninklijke Numico N.V. 8/10/99
Each share Common 1¢ par exchanged for $25 cash

GENERAL NUTRITION INC (PA)
Common no par split (2) for (1) by issuance of (1) additional share 7/21/81
Common no par split (2) for (1) by issuance of (1) additional share 3/15/83
Each share Common no par exchanged for (11.5) shares $0.125 Preferred Ser. A 1¢ par 11/17/89
$0.125 Preferred Ser. A 1¢ par called for redemption 2/12/93
Public interest eliminated

GENERAL OHIO S & L CORP (OH)
Merged into Dana Corp. 12/31/1980
Each share Common 50¢ par exchanged for (0.764) share Common $1 par
(See Dana Corp.)

GENERAL OIL & INDUSTRIES, INC. (NV)
Charter revoked for failure to file reports and pay fees 3/4/63

GENERAL OIL & MINING CORP. (AZ)
Merged into Control Metals Corp. 7/20/71
Each share Capital Stock no par exchanged for (2) shares Capital Stock 1¢ par
(See Controls Metals Corp.)

GENERAL OIL & REFINING CO. (DE)
Charter cancelled for non-payment of taxes in 1925

GENERAL OIL CO. OF OHIO, INC. (OH)
Name changed to General Resources Corp. (OH) 8/30/68
General Resources Corp. (OH) name changed to Graham Stuart Corp. 4/17/69
(See Graham Stuart Corp.)

GENERAL OIL TOOLS, INC. (AZ)
Merged into International Oil Tools, Inc. 01/27/1978
Each share Common $1 par exchanged for (5) shares Capital Stock 1¢ par
(See International Oil Tools, Inc.)

GENERAL OPTICAL CO. (NY)
Liquidation completed 12/21/56
No Common stockholders' equity

GENERAL OUTDOOR ADVERTISING CO., INC. (NJ)
Common no par changed to $15 par 4/9/56
Stock Dividend - 100% 12/9/59
Merged into Gamble-Skogmo, Inc. 10/17/63
Each share Common $15 par exchanged for (1) share $1.75 Convertible Preferred $40 par
Gamble-Skogmo, Inc. merged into Wickes Companies, Inc. 1/26/85 which name changed to Collins & Aikman Group Inc. 7/17/92
(See Collins & Aikman Group Inc.)

GENERAL PACIFIC CORP. (NV)
Liquidation completed 11/17/60
Details not available

GENERAL PACKAGE CORP. (DE)
Each share Common $6 par exchanged for (2) shares Common $3 par 00/00/1954
Merged into Diamond Match Co. 05/31/1955
Each share Common $3 par exchanged for (1) share Common $1 par
Diamond Match Co. name changed to Diamond Gardner Corp. 11/04/1957 which name changed to Diamond National Corp. 09/28/1959 which was changed to Diamond International Corp. 10/29/1964
(See Diamond International Corp.)

GENERAL PAINT CORP. (NV)
Recapitalized in 1936
Each share Class A no par exchanged for (1) share Preferred no par
Each share Class B no par exchanged for (1) share Common no par
Recapitalized in 1945
Each share Preferred no par exchanged for (1) share new 1st Preferred no par and (1) share new 2nd Preferred no par
Name changed to General Pacific Corp. 1/23/59 which was completely liquidated 11/17/60

GENERAL PAINT CORP. OF CANADA LTD. (CANADA)
100% acquired by Canadian Wallpaper Manufacturers Ltd. through voluntary purchase offer at $35 a share as of 09/09/1966
Public interest eliminated

GENERAL PANEL CORP. (NY)
Charter revoked for failure to file reports and pay fees 12/15/52

GENERAL PARAMETRICS CORP (DE)
Name changed to Metal Management, Inc. 04/12/1996
Metal Management, Inc. merged into Sims Group Ltd. 03/14/2008 which name changed to Sims Metal Management Ltd. 11/26/2008

GENERAL PARCEL SVC INC (FL)
Name changed to Transit Group, Inc. 6/30/97
(See Transit Group, Inc.)

GENERAL PETROLEUM CORP.
Acquired by Standard Oil Co. of New York in 1926
Details not available

GENERAL PETROLEUMS, LTD. (AB)
Recapitalized as General Petroleums of Canada, Ltd. in June, 1950
Each share Class A no par exchanged for (0.25) share Class A $1 par
Each share Ordinary no par exchanged for (0.25) share Ordinary $1 par
(See General Petroleums of Canada, Ltd.)

GENERAL PETROLEUMS DRILLING CO. LTD. (AB)
Name changed to Excel Petroleums Ltd. 06/20/1967
(See Excel Petroleums Ltd.)

GENERAL PETROLEUMS DRILLING LTD. (AB)
Under plan of merger each share Common no par exchanged for (1) share 7% Class A Preferred $11.77 par 9/1/69
Merged into Westburne Petroleum & Minerals Ltd. 4/28/70
Each share 7% Class A Preferred $11.77 par automatically became (1) share 7% Preferred Ser. A $11.77 par

GENERAL PETROLEUMS OF CANADA, LTD. (AB)
Reorganized 04/08/1959
Each share Class A or Ordinary $1 par exchanged for (1) share Class A or Ordinary 50¢ par of General Petroleums Drilling Co. Ltd. and (1) share Class A or Ordinary 50¢ par of Eastwood Oil Co. Ltd.
(See each company's listing)

GENERAL PHOENIX CORP. (PA)
Each share Class A Common $5 par exchanged for (3) shares Common $1 par 2/15/47
Each share Common $5 par exchanged for (6) shares Common $1 par 2/15/47
Name changed to General Acceptance Corp. (New) 7/11/50
General Acceptance Corp. (New) name changed to GAC Corp. (PA) 7/1/68 which reincorporated in Delaware 12/20/73
(See GAC Corp. (DE))

GENERAL PHOTOS, INC. (IL)
Completely liquidated 3/31/66
Each share Common 50¢ par exchanged for first and final distribution of (0.75) share Perfect Photo, Inc. Common no par
Perfect Photo, Inc. acquired by United Whelan Corp. 6/30/66 which name changed to Perfect Film & Chemical Corp. 5/31/67 which name changed to Cadence Industries Corp. 10/22/70
(See Cadence Industries Corp.)

GENERAL PHYSICS CORP (DE)
Common $0.025 par split (2) for (1) by issuance of (1) additional share 9/24/91
Merged into National Patent Development Corp. 1/24/97
Each share Common $0.025 par exchanged for (0.6) share new Common 1¢ par
National Patent Development Corp. name changed to GP Strategies Corp. 3/9/98

GENERAL PHYSICS SVCS CORP (DE)
Name changed to GPS Technologies, Inc. 1/4/93
GPS Technologies, Inc. name changed to SGLG, Inc. 8/31/94
(See SGLG, Inc.)

GENERAL PLASTICS, INC.
Merged into Durez Plastics & Chemicals, Inc. on a share for share basis in 1939
Durez Plastics & Chemicals, Inc. merged into Hooker Electrochemical Co. 4/29/55 which name changed to Hooker Chemical Corp. 5/29/58 which was acquired by Occidental Petroleum Corp. (CA) 7/24/68
(See Occidental Petroleum Corp. (CA))

GENERAL PLASTICS CORP. (DE)
Charter cancelled and declared inoperative and void for non-payment of taxes 4/15/72

GENERAL PLASTRONICS, INC. (IA)
Charter revoked for failure to file reports and pay fees 11/23/64

GENERAL PLYWOOD CORP. (DE)
Reincorporated 8/23/72
Each share Common $1 par exchanged for (2) shares Common 50¢ par in 1947
5% Preferred $20 par called for redemption 9/30/57
State of incorporation changed from (KY) to (DE) 8/23/72
Name changed to General Resources Corp. (DE) 10/25/73
(See General Resources Corp. (DE) - Certificates dated after 10/24/73)

GENERAL PORTLAND CEMENT CO. (DE)
Common $1 par split (2) for (1) by issuance of (1) additional share 2/7/55
Common $1 par split (2) for (1) by issuance of (1) additional share 5/1/59
Name changed to General Portland Inc. 5/31/72
(See General Portland Inc.)

GENERAL PORTLAND INC (DE)
Merged into Canada Cement Lafarge Ltd. - Ciments Canada Lafarge Ltee. 01/04/1982
Each share Common $1 par exchanged for $47 cash

GENERAL POWER & LIGHT CO.
Liquidated in 1935
Details not available

GENERAL PRECISION CORP (NY)
Charter cancelled and proclaimed dissolved for failure to pay taxes 12/07/1976

GENERAL PRECISION EQUIPMENT CORP. (DE)
Capital Stock no par reclassified as Common no par 4/28/49
Common no par changed to $1 par 4/30/53
Common $1 par split (2) for (1) by issuance of (1) additional share 2/21/68
Merged into Singer Co. (NJ) 7/11/68
Each share $1.60 Conv. Preference no par exchanged for (0.3167) share $3.50 Conv. Preferred no par and (0.4524) share Common $10 par
Each share Common $1 par exchanged for (0.2375) share $3.50 Conv. Preferred no par and (0.3393) share Common $10 par
$4.75 Preferred no par called for redemption 8/12/68
Singer Co. (NJ) name changed to Bicoastal Corp. 10/16/89
(See Bicoastal Corp.)

GENERAL PRINTING INK CORP.
Name changed to Sun Chemical Corp. 11/28/1945
Sun Chemical Corp. name changed to Sequa Corp. 05/08/1987
(See Sequa Corp.)

GENERAL PRODS HLDGS INC (NV)
Name changed to Diamond Linx Inc. 03/00/1999
Diamond Linx Inc. reorganized back as General Products Holdings Inc. 02/03/2000
Charter permanently revoked 11/01/2005

GENERAL PRODS MFG LTD (ON)
Liquidation completed
Each share Class A Common no par or Class B Common no par received initial distribution of $75 cash 08/24/1972
Each share Class A Common no par or Class B Common no par received

GEN-GEN

second distribution of $10 cash 01/19/1973
Each share Class A Common no par or Class B Common no par exchanged for third and final distribution of $1.30 cash 12/27/1974

GENERAL PRODTN INC (DE)
Acquired by Zapata Exploration Co. 10/20/1983
Each share Common $1 par exchanged for $2.50 cash

GENERAL PPTYS LTD (AB)
Name changed to General Mining Properties Ltd. 10/07/2008

GENERAL PUB UTILS CORP (PA)
Reincorporated 7/1/69
Common $5 par changed to $2.50 par and (1) additional share issued 7/9/59
State of incorporation changed from (NY) to (PA) 7/1/69
Common $2.50 par split (2) for (1) by issuance of (1) additional share 5/29/91
Name changed to GPU, Inc. 8/1/96
(See GPU, Inc.)

GENERAL PUBLIC SERVICE CORP. (DE)
Common no par changed to 10¢ par in 1942
Name changed to Surveyor Fund, Inc. (DE) 3/28/68
Surveyor Fund, Inc. (DE) merged into Surveyor Fund, Inc. (MD) 9/10/73 which name changed to Alliance Global Small Capital Fund, Inc. 9/17/90 which name changed to AllianceBernstein Global Small Capital Fund, Inc. 3/31/2003
(See AllianceBernstein Global Small Capital Fund, Inc.)

GENERAL PUBLIC UTILITIES, INC.
Merged into Southwestern Public Service Co. in 1942
Each share Common no par exchanged for (1.5) shares Common $1 par
Southwestern Public Service Co. merged into New Century Energies, Inc. 8/1/97 which merged into Xcel Energy Inc. 8/18/2000

GENERAL PUBLIC UTILITIES CO.
Reorganized as General Public Utilities Inc. in 1935
Details not available

GENERAL RAILWAY COUPLER CORP. (DE)
Charter cancelled and declared inoperative and void for non-payment of taxes 4/1/33

GENERAL RAILWAY SIGNAL CO. (NY)
Each share 6% Preferred $100 par exchanged for (1.2) shares new 5% Preferred $100 par and (1/3) share Common no par in 1953
Common no par changed to $6.67 par and (2) additional shares issued 11/9/56
Name changed to General Signal Corp. 2/18/63
General Signal Corp. merged into SPX Corp. 10/6/98

GENERAL RE CORP (DE)
Common 50¢ par split (2) for (1) by issuance of (1) additional share 06/07/1982
Common 50¢ par split (2) for (1) by issuance of (1) additional share 06/13/1986
Merged into Berkshire Hathaway Inc. 12/21/1998
Each share Common 50¢ par exchanged for either (0.0035) share Class A Common $5 par or (0.105) share Class B Common $0.1667 par
Note: Option to receive Class A Common expired 03/01/1999

GENERAL REAL ESTATE SHS (MI)
Liquidation completed
Each Share of Bene. Int. $1 par received initial distribution of $24.50 cash 12/15/89
Each Share of Bene. Int. $1 par received second and final distribution of $3.44 cash 12/17/90
Note: Certificates were not required to be surrendered and are without value

GENERAL REALTY & UTILITIES CORP. (DE)
Common no par changed to $1 par in 1932
Recapitalized in 1944
Each share Preferred no par exchanged for $100 principal amount of Debentures and (7) shares Capital Stock 10¢ par
Each share Common $1 par exchanged for (0.5) share Capital Stock 10¢ par
Stock Dividends - 10% 12/15/52; 10% 11/1/55
Liquidation completed 9/19/63

GENERAL REC INC (DE)
Petition filed under Chapter 11 Federal Bankruptcy Code dismissed in March 1987
No stockholders' equity

GENERAL RECORDED TAPE INC (CA)
Name changed to GRT Corp. 3/12/69
(See GRT Corp.)

GENERAL RED INTL INC (TX)
SEC revoked common stock registration 10/09/2012

GENERAL REED CO (DE)
Acquired by Sigma Instruments, Inc. 11/24/69
Each share Common 10¢ par exchanged for (0.5) share Common $1 par
(See Sigma Instruments, Inc.)

GENERAL REFRACTORIES CO (PA)
Common no par changed to $10 par 00/00/1954
Common $10 par changed to $5 par and (1) additional share issued 09/14/1959
Common $5 par changed to 50¢ par 05/25/1983
$5 Conv. 1st Ser. Preferred no par called for redemption 12/31/1984
Stock Dividends - 100% 05/20/1952; 25% 11/29/1955
Acquired by Belmont Industries 12/30/1988
Each share Common 50¢ par exchanged for $22.50 cash

GENERAL REFRIGERATION CORP.
Merged into Yates-American Machine Co. in 1940
Each share 7% Preferred exchanged for (5) shares Common $5 par
(See Yates-American Machine Co.)

GENERAL REINS CORP (DE)
Common $2.66666666 par changed to $2 par and (1) additional share issued 06/04/1973
Common $2 par changed to $1 par and (1) additional share issued 06/18/1979
Common $1 par changed to 50¢ par and (1) additional share issued 07/14/1980
Reorganized as General Re Corp. 10/31/1980
Each share Common 50¢ par exchanged for (1) share Common 50¢ par
General Re Corp. merged into Berkshire Hathaway Inc. 12/21/1999

GENERAL REINS CORP (NY)
Each share Capital Stock $25 par exchanged for (5) shares Capital Stock $5 par in 1936
Each share Capital Stock $5 par exchanged for (1.8) shares Capital Stock $10 par in 1945
Capital Stock $10 par changed to $6.66-2/3 par and (0.5) additional share issued 6/2/69
Capital Stock $6.66-2/3 par changed to $2.66-2/3 par and (1.5) additional shares issued 5/28/71
Stock Dividends - 10% 10/24/52; 20% 6/30/54; 10% 9/30/58
Reincorporated under the laws of Delaware 12/31/72
Each share Capital Stock $2.66-2/3 par exchanged for (1) share Common $2.66-2/3 par
General Reinsurance Corp. (DE) reorganized as General Re Corp. 10/31/80 which merged into Berkshire Hathaway Inc. 12/21/98

GENERAL RESEARCH CORP. (MT)
Dissolved 7/13/65
No stockholders' equity

GENERAL RESH CORP (DE)
Reincorporated 3/31/75
State of incorporation changed from (CA) to (DE) 3/31/75
Under plan of merger name changed from General Research Corp. to Flow General Inc. 1/3/77
Flow General Inc. name changed to GRC International, Inc. 12/5/89
(See GRC International, Inc.)

GENERAL RESIDENTIAL CORP (DE)
Each share Common 5¢ par exchanged for (0.2) share Common 25¢ par 05/30/1972
Common 25¢ par changed to 1¢ par 00/00/1973
Each share Common 1¢ par exchanged for (0.000005) share Common $1 par 07/16/1997
Note: In effect holders received approximately $0.0599 cash per share and public interest was eliminated

GENERAL RESISTANCE INC (NY)
Merged into Chronetics, Inc. 07/30/1968
Each share Common 10¢ par exchanged for (0.25) share Common 10¢ par
(See Chronetics, Inc.)

GENERAL RES CORP (DE)
Ctfs. dated prior to 12/22/72
Name changed to Pizza Corp. of America 12/22/72
Pizza Corp. of America merged into Pizza Hut, Inc. (DE) 9/27/74 which merged into PepsiCo, Inc. (DE) 11/7/77 which reincorporated in North Carolina 12/4/86

GENERAL RES CORP (DE)
Ctfs. dated after 10/24/73
Filed for Chapter XI Federal Bankruptcy Act 10/17/79
No stockholders' equity

GENERAL RES CORP (NV)
Charter revoked for failure to file reports and pay fees 3/4/74

GENERAL RES CORP (OH)
Name changed to Graham Stuart Corp. 4/17/69
(See Graham Stuart Corp.)

GENERAL RESOURCES INC. (DE)
Charter cancelled and declared inoperative and void for non-payment of taxes 4/15/68

GENERAL RESOURCES LTD. (CO)
Merged into Royal Oil & Gas Co. on a (2) for (1) basis in 1956
(See Royal Oil & Gas Co.)

GENERAL RES LTD (BC)
Struck off register and declared dissolved for failure to file returns 2/26/79

GENERAL REST HOMES INC (DE)
Name changed to General Residential Corp. 01/13/1971
(See General Residential Corp.)

GENERAL RESTAURANTS INC (DE)
Name changed to Emersons, Ltd. 2/11/72
(See Emersons, Ltd.)

GENERAL RUBBER PRODUCTS, INC. (TX)
Charter forfeited for failure to pay taxes 4/12/62

GENERAL SALES & LEASING INC (NV)
Common $0.001 par split (10) for (1) by issuance of (9) additional shares payable 02/28/20013 to holders of record 02/25/2013 Ex date - 03/01/2013
Recapitalized as Xenetic Biosciences, Inc. 01/14/2014
Each share Common $0.001 par exchanged for (0.1) share Common $0.001 par

GENERAL SALES CORP (NV)
Each share Common 50¢ par exchanged for (0.5) share Common $1 par 9/26/60
Name changed to United General Corp. 5/21/70
(See United General Corp.)

GENERAL SCANNING INC (MA)
Issue Information - 2,900,000 shares COM offered at $12 per share on 09/21/1995
Merged into GSI Lumonics Inc. 03/22/1999
Each share Common 1¢ par exchanged for (1.347) shares Common 1¢ par
GSI Lumonics Inc. name changed to GSI Group Inc. (Old) 06/06/2005 which reorganized as GSI Group Inc. (New) 07/23/2010

GENERAL SCHUYLER FIRE INSURANCE CO.
Merged into William Penn Fire Insurance Co. on a (1) for (5) basis in 1943

GENERAL SCIENCE CORP (DE)
Merged into J.T.B., Inc. 10/2/72
Each share Common 10¢ par exchanged for $2.30 cash

GENERAL SCIENCES CORP (DE)
Merged into SAIC Acquisition Corp. 8/14/92
Each share Common 1¢ par exchanged for initial payment of $4.49 cash
Each share Common 1¢ par received second and final distribution of $0.7665 cash 12/8/92

GENERAL SCIENTIFIC LABORATORIES, INC. (NV)
Charter revoked for failure to file reports and pay fees 3/5/73

GENERAL SEA HARVEST CORP (BC)
Recapitalized as Consolidated General Sea Harvest Corp. 06/12/1990
Each share Common no par exchanged for (0.2) share Common no par
(See Consolidated General Sea Harvest Corp.)

GENERAL SEC LIFE CO (WA)
Each share Class A Common $2 par exchanged for (0.1) share Common $10 par 10/26/79
Common $10 par changed to $1 par and (9) additional shares issued 5/9/80
Name changed to Life Insurance Co. of America 9/15/82
(See Life Insurance Co. of America)

GENERAL SECS INC (DE)
Dissolved 5/22/36
Details not available

GENERAL SECS INC (MN)
Stock Dividend - 200% 12/20/1955
Merged into Kopp Funds, Inc. 09/30/2004

GENERAL SEMICONDUCTOR INC (DE)
Details not available
Merged into Vishay Intertechnology, Inc. 11/02/2001
Each share Common 1¢ par exchanged for (0.563) share Common 10¢ par

GENERAL SEMICONDUCTOR INDS INC (DE)
Common $1 par changed to 66-2/3¢ par and (0.5) additional share issued 5/20/77
Common 66-2/3¢ par split (3) for (2) by issuance of (0.5) additional share 6/23/78
Common 66-2/3¢ par changed to 10¢ par 3/19/79
Common 10¢ par split (3) for (2) by issuance of (0.5) additional share 6/20/80
Merged into Square D Co. (MI) 1/20/81
Each share Common 10¢ par exchanged for (0.76) share Common $1.66-2/3 par
Square D Co. (MI) reincorporated in Delaware 6/16/89
(See Square D Co. (DE))

GENERAL SVCS LIFE INS CO (DC)
Class A Common $1 par changed to $2 par 7/1/65
Class A Common $2 par changed to $2.50 par 9/24/70
Class A Common $2.50 par changed to $1.25 par and (1) additional share issued 8/15/72
Class A Common $1.25 par changed to $3 par 11/10/77
Stock Dividend - 100% 9/30/75
Each share Class A Common $3 par exchanged for (1/4,000) share Class A Common $12,500 par 7/19/84
In effect holders received $27.50 cash per share and public interest was eliminated

GENERAL SHALE PRODS CORP (DE)
Common no par split (2) for (1) by issuance of (1) additional share 6/10/68
Merged into Marley Acquisition Corp. 6/27/86
Each share Common no par exchanged for $30 cash

GENERAL SHAREHOLDINGS CORP.
Merged into Tri-Continental Corp. in 1948
Each share Preferred exchanged for (0.9) share new Preferred and (1.2) shares new Common
Each share Common exchanged for (0.55) share new Common

GENERAL SHARES, INC. (NY)
Name changed to Allied General Corp. in 1931
(See Allied General Corp.)

GENERAL SHELTER CORP (NY)
Adjudicated bankrupt 6/22/72
No stockholders' equity

GENERAL SHOE CORP. (TN)
Recapitalized in 1937
Each share 8% Preferred $100 par exchanged for (20) shares $0.40 Preferred no par
Each share Class A and B no par exchanged for (4) shares Common $1 par
Recapitalized in 1953
Each share $3.50 Preferred no par exchanged for (1) share new Preference Ser. A no par
Each share $0.40 Preferred no par exchanged for (0.2) share Common $1 par
Recapitalized 3/26/56
Common $1 par split (2) for (1) by issuance of (1) additional share
Name changed to Genesco Inc. 3/2/59

GENERAL SIGNAL CORP (NY)
Common $6.67 par changed to $1 par 04/21/1969
Common $1 par split (2) for (1) by issuance of (1) additional share 01/03/1972
$4 Conv. Preferred Ser. A $5 par called for redemption 12/13/1972
Common $1 par split (2) for (1) by issuance of (1) additional share 07/01/1977
Common $1 par split (2) for (1) by issuance of (1) additional share 07/16/1993
Merged into SPX Corp. 10/06/1998
Each share Common $1 par exchanged for either (0.6977) share Common $10 par, (0.4186) share Common $10 par and $18 cash, or $45 cash
Note: Option to receive stock or cash only expired 10/02/1998

GENERAL SILK CORP. (DE)
No longer in existence having become inoperative and void for non-payment of taxes 4/1/34

GENERAL SPECIFICS INC (NV)
Name changed to Wire Graphics, Inc. 3/28/85
(See Wire Graphics, Inc.)

GENERAL SPORTS AIDES INC (NJ)
Charter declared void for non-payment of taxes 7/31/94

GENERAL SPRAY SERVICE, INC. (NY)
Insolvent and assignment for benefit of creditors made 7/14/65
No stockholders' equity

GENERAL SPRING & BUMPER CORP.
Merged into Houdaille-Hershey Corp. 00/00/1929
Details not available

GENERAL STEEL CASTINGS CORP. (DE)
Common no par changed to $1 par 11/23/55
Common $1 par split (3) for (2) by issuance of (0.5) additional share 11/15/57
Name changed to General Steel Industries, Inc. 5/1/61
(See General Steel Industries, Inc.)

GENERAL STL INDS INC (DE)
Common $1 par split (2) for (1) by issuance of (1) additional share 2/28/63
Stock Dividends - 10% 12/13/78; 20% 7/13/81
Merged into Lukens Steel Co. 3/31/82
Each share Common $1 par exchanged for $16 cash

GENERAL STL WARES LTD (CANADA)
Name changed to GSW Ltd.-GSW Ltee. 01/02/1970
GSW Ltd.-GSW Ltee. name changed to GSW Inc. 10/01/1980
(See GSW Inc.)

GENERAL STOCKYARDS CORP.
Dissolution approved in 1937
Details not available

GENERAL STONE & MATLS CORP (VA)
Name changed to GMC Corp. 4/1/70
(See GMC Corp.)

GENERAL STORES CORP (NY)
Under plan of reorganization each share old Common $1 par exchanged for (1/3) share new Common $1 par 1/14/59
Note: Unexchanged certificates were cancelled are became without value 1/8/69
Reincorporated under the laws of Delaware as GSC Enterprises, Inc. 1/14/69
(See GSC Enterprises, Inc.)

GENERAL STRATEGIES LTD (BC)
Reorganized as Landdrill International Inc. 03/14/2006
Each share Common no par exchanged for (1.5) shares Common no par
(See Landdrill International Inc.)

GENERAL STREET SIGNAL CORP.
Business discontinued in 1951
Details not available

GENERAL SULPHUR CORP.
Acquired by Continental Sulphur & Phosphate Corp. on a (0.5) for (1) basis in 1950
(See Continental Sulphur & Phosphate Corp.)

GENERAL SUPERMARKETS, INC. (NJ)
Common 10¢ par changed to 8¢ par and (0.25) additional share issued 8/21/61
Merged into Supermarkets General Corp. 4/27/66
Each share Common 8¢ par exchanged for (1.5) shares Common $1 par
(See Supermarkets General Corp.)

GENERAL SURETY CO.
Taken over for liquidation by New York State Insurance Dept. in 1933

GENERAL SURGICAL INNOVATIONS INC (CA)
Merged into Tyco International Ltd. (Bermuda) 11/11/1999
Each share Common $0.001 par exchanged for (0.1903) share Common 20¢ par
Tyco International Ltd. (Bermuda) reincorporated in Switzerland 03/17/2009 which merged into Johnson Controls International PLC 09/06/2016

GENERAL SYS RESH INC (AB)
Name changed 02/13/1986
Name changed from General Systems Research Ltd. to General Systems Research Inc. 02/13/1986
Placed in receivership 01/11/1990
No stockholders' equity

GENERAL TAX EXEMPT BD FD INC (MD)
Name changed to General Municipal Bond Fund, Inc. 08/29/1990
(See General Municipal Bond Fund, Inc.)

GENERAL TECHNOLOGIES GROUP LTD (DE)
Each share Common 1¢ par exchanged for (0.25) share Common 4¢ par 9/20/88
Charter cancelled and declared inoperative and void for non-payment of taxes 6/24/92

GENERAL TECHNOLOGY EQUITIES INC (DE)
Merged into Seggos Industries, Inc. 12/31/69
Each share Common 10¢ par exchanged for (0.5) share Common 1¢ par
Seggos Industries, Inc. name changed to Gold'n Treasures Trading Co., Ltd. 4/27/73
(See Gold'N Treasures Trading Co., Ltd.)

GENERAL TEL & ELECTRS CORP (NY)
Common $10 par changed to $3.33333333 par and (2) additional shares issued 05/19/1960
4.25% Conv. Preferred $50 par called for redemption 12/31/1966
4.75% Conv. Preferred $50 par called for redemption 12/31/1966
Name changed to GTE Corp. 07/01/1982
GTE Corp. merged into Verizon Communications Inc. 06/30/2000

GENERAL TEL CO CALIF (CA)
5-1/2% Preferred $20 par called for redemption 8/31/65
Name changed to GTE California Inc. 1/1/88

GENERAL TEL CO FLA (FL)
$1 Preferred $25 par called for redemption 7/1/64
$1.30 Preferred $25 par called for redemption 7/1/64
$1.32 Preferred $25 par called for redemption 7/1/64
Common no par changed to $25 par 1/6/67
Name changed to GTE Florida Inc. 1/1/88
(See GTE Florida Inc.)

GENERAL TEL CO ILL (IL)
Each share $4.75 Preferred no par exchanged for (2) shares $2.375 Preferred no par in 1954
$2.75 Preferred no par called for redemption 8/10/63
Merged into GTE MTO Inc. 3/31/87
Each share $2.30 Preferred no par exchanged for (1) share $2.30 Preferred no par
Each share $2.375 Preferred no par exchanged for (1) share $2.375 Preferred no par
Each share $2.50 Preferred no par exchanged for (1) share $2.50 Preferred no par
GTE MTO Inc. name changed to GTE North Inc. 1/1/88
(See GTE North Inc.)

GENERAL TEL CO IND INC NEW (IN)
Merged into GTE MTO Inc. 3/31/87
Each share $2 Preferred no par exchanged for (1) share $2 Preferred no par
Each share $2.50 Preferred no par exchanged for (1) share $2.50 Preferred no par
Each share $2.50 Preferred Ser. C no par exchanged for (1) share $2.50 Preferred Ser. C no par
Each share $7.60 Preferred no par exchanged for (1) share $7.60 Preferred no par
GTE MTO Inc. name changed to GTE North Inc. 1/1/88
(See GTE North Inc.)

GENERAL TEL CO KY (DE)
Merged into General Telephone Co. of the South 12/31/85
Each share 5% Preferred $50 par exchanged for (1) share 5% Preferred $50 par
Each share 5.16% Preferred $50 par exchanged for (1) share 5.16% Preferred $50 par
Each share 5.2% Preferred $100 par exchanged for (1) share 5.2% Preferred $100 par
Each share $10.48 Preferred no par exchanged for (1) share $10.48 Preferred no par
Each share Common no par exchanged for (0.1) share Common $25 par
General Telephone Co. of the South name changed to GTE South Inc. 1/1/88
(See GTE South Inc.)

GENERAL TEL CO MICH (MI)
$1.35 Preferred $25 par called for redemption 9/14/63
$12.24 Preferred $100 par called for redemption 3/11/78
$7.50 Preference Stock called for redemption 1/1/86
Merged into GTE MTO Inc. 3/31/87
Each share $2.40 Preferred $50 par exchanged for (1) share $2.40 Preferred no par
Each share 4.60% Preferred $50 par exchanged for (1) share 4.60% Preferred no par
Each share 5.16% Preferred $50 par exchanged for (1) share 5.16% Preferred no par

GTE MTO Inc. name changed to GTE North Inc. 1/1/88
(See GTE North Inc.)

GENERAL TEL CO MIDWEST (MO)
$10.50 Preferred no par called for redemption 05/15/1978

GENERAL TEL CO NORTHWEST INC (WA)
Name changed to GTE Northwest Inc. 1/1/88
(See GTE Northwest Inc.)

GENERAL TEL CO OHIO (OH)
$1.32 Preferred no par called for redemption 7/11/63
$1.40 Preferred no par called for redemption 7/11/63
Merged into GTE MTO Inc. 3/31/87
Each share $1.15 Preferred no par exchanged for (1) share $1.15 Preferred no par
Each share $1.25 Preferred no par exchanged for (1) share $1.25 Preferred no par
Each share $2.20 Preferred no par exchanged for (1) share $2.20 Preferred no par
GTE MTO Inc. name changed to GTE North Inc. 1/1/88
(See GTE North Inc.)

GENERAL TEL CO PA (PA)
Merged into GTE MTO Inc. 3/31/87
Each share $2.10 Preferred no par exchanged for (1) share $2.10 Preferred no par
Each share $2.25 Preferred no par exchanged for (1) share $2.25 Preferred no par
GTE MTO Inc. name changed to GTE North Inc. 1/1/88
(See GTE North Inc.)

GENERAL TEL CO SOUTH (VA)
Name changed to GTE South Inc. 1/1/88
(See GTE South Inc.)

GENERAL TEL CO SOUTHWEST (DE)
Each share $5.50 Preferred no par exchanged for (5) shares 5-1/2% Preferred $20 par in 1952
5.6% Preferred $20 par called for redemption 5/31/63
5-1/2% Preferred $20 par called for redemption 5/31/63
Name changed to GTE Southwest Inc. 1/1/88
(See GTE Southwest Inc.)

GENERAL TEL CO WIS (WI)
$10.375 Preferred no par called for redemption 12/2/85
Merged into GTE MTO Inc. 3/31/87
Each share $4.50 Preferred $100 par exchanged for (1) share $4.50 Preferred no par
Each share $5 Preferred $100 par exchanged for (1) share $5 Preferred no par
GTE MTO Inc. name changed to GTE North Inc. 1/1/88
(See GTE North Inc.)

GENERAL TELEPHONE CO. OF INDIANA, INC. OLD (IN)
Merged into General Telephone Co. of Indiana, Inc. (New) 5/5/66
Each share $2 Preferred no par exchanged for (1) share $2 Preferred no par
Each share $2.50 Preferred no par exchanged for (1) share $2.50 Preferred no par
Each share $2.50 Preferred Ser. C no par exchanged for (1) share $2.50 Preferred Ser. C no par
Each share Common no par exchanged for (3) shares $2.50 Preferred no par or $145 cash at stockholders' option
General Telephone Co. of Indiana, Inc. (New) merged into GTE MTO Inc. 3/31/87 which name changed to GTE North Inc. 1/1/88
(See GTE North Inc.)

GENERAL TELEPHONE CO. OF IOWA (IA)
5-1/2% Preferred $25 par called 12/31/63
Public interest eliminated

GENERAL TELEPHONE CO. OF MISSOURI (MO)
6% Conv. Preferred Ser. A $25 par called 12/31/63
Public interest eliminated

GENERAL TELEPHONE CO. OF NEBRASKA (NE)
6% Preferred Ser. A $25 par called 1/31/59
Public interest eliminated

GENERAL TELEPHONE CO. OF THE NORTHWEST (ID)
4.80% Preferred $25 par called 3/15/68
Public interest eliminated

GENERAL TELEPHONE CO. OF THE SOUTHEAST (VA)
5.80% Preferred $25 par called for redemption 4/20/63
Name changed to General Telephone Co. of the South 12/12/85
General Telephone Co. of the South name changed to GTE South Inc. 1/1/88

GENERAL TELEPHONE CORP. (NY)
Common $20 par changed to $10 par 4/21/55
4.40% Preferred $50 par conversion privilege expired 9/30/57
Stock Dividends - 50% 5/15/54; 50% 6/30/55
Under plan of merger name changed to General Telephone & Electronics Corp. 3/5/59
General Telephone & Electronics Corp. name changed to GTE Corp. 7/1/82 which merged into Verizon Communications Inc. 6/30/2000

GENERAL TELEPHONE TRI CORP.
Acquired by General Telephone Corp. on a (2.25) for (1) basis in 1940
General Telephone Corp. name changed to General Telephone & Electronics Corp. 3/5/59 which name changed to GTE Corp. 7/1/82 which merged into Verizon Communications Inc. 6/30/2000

GENERAL TELEPHONY COM INC (NV)
Reincorporated under the laws of Delaware as I.A. Europe Group, Inc. 12/06/2002
I.A. Europe Group, Inc. name changed to Ghost Technology, Inc. 07/15/2008
(See Ghost Technology, Inc.)

GENERAL TELEVISION INC (CO)
Merged into Storer Broadcasting Co. 2/15/79
Each share Common 10¢ par exchanged for $10.50 cash

GENERAL TERM CORP (DE)
Reorganized as Gen Term Corp. 02/20/1986
Each (1.05) shares Common 25¢ par exchanged for (1) share Common 5¢ par, (0.5) share Class A Common Stock Purchase Warrant expiring 01/15/1987, (0.5) share Class B Common Stock Purchase Warrant expiring 01/15/1988, (0.5) share Class C Common Stock Purchase Warrant expiring 01/15/1989, (0.5) share Class D Common Stock Purchase Warrant expiring 01/15/1990, (0.25) share Century Terminals, Inc. Common no par and (0.25) share Terminal Promotions, Inc. Common no par
(See each company's listing)

GENERAL TESTING LABS INC (DE)
Stock Dividend - 10% 10/22/69
Name changed to General Environments Corp. 5/18/70
General Environments Corp. merged into Howell Corp. (TX) 6/28/72 which reincorporated in Delaware 4/24/84
(See Howell Corp. (DE))

GENERAL THEATRES EQUIPMENT, INC. (DE)
Reorganized as General Theatres Equipment Corp. 6/29/36
Holders of Preferred and Common Stock received Common Stock Purchase Warrants which expired 10/1/37
(See General Theatres Equipment Corp.)

GENERAL THEATRES EQUIPMENT CORP. (DE)
Name changed to General Precision Equipment Corp. 5/1/42
General Precision Equipment Corp. merged into Singer Co. (NJ) 7/11/68 which reincorporated in Delaware in 1988 which name changed to Bicoastal Corp. 10/16/89
(See Bicoastal Corp.)

GENERAL THOMAS MINES CO. (NV)
Charter cancelled for failure to file reports and pay fees 3/4/29

GENERAL TIME CORP (DE)
Common no par changed to $10 par 4/3/57
Common $10 par changed to $2.50 par and (3) additional shares issued 5/6/60
Stock Dividends - 10% 1/19/50; 10% 1/19/51; 10% 1/20/55
Merged into Talley Industries, Inc. 5/14/70
Each share Common $2.50 par exchanged for (1) share $1 Conv. Preferred Ser. B $1 par
(See Talley Industries, Inc.)

GENERAL TIME INSTRUMENTS CORP.
Name changed to General Time Corp. in 1949
General Time Corp. merged into Talley Industries, Inc. 5/14/70
(See Talley Industries, Inc.)

GENERAL TIN INVTS LTD (ENGLAND)
Each share Ordinary £1 par exchanged for (5) shares Ordinary 5s par 08/15/1961
Under plan of arrangement each American Certificate 5s par (issued by Southern Maryland Agricultural Association of Prince George's County, Maryland, Inc.) exchanged for $2.1951 cash 11/09/1968

GENERAL TIRE & RUBR CO (OH)
Each share Common $100 par exchanged for (2) shares Common $50 par 00/00/1922
Each share Common $50 par exchanged for (2) shares Common $25 par 00/00/1926
Each share Common $25 par exchanged for (5) shares Common $5 par 00/00/1936
Each share Common $5 par exchanged for (2) shares Common $2.50 par 00/00/1952
5.5% Preferred $100 par and 4.75% Preference $100 par changed to 5.5% Preference $100 par 04/03/1957
5% Preference $100 par and 4.25% Preference $100 par changed to $5 Preference $100 par 04/03/1957
Common $2.50 par changed to $0.83333333 par and (2) additional shares issued 09/26/1957
Common $0.83333333 changed to 30¢ par and (2) additional shares issued 04/27/1962
3.75% Preferred $100 par called for redemption 09/30/1962
4.25% Preferred $100 par called for redemption 09/30/1962
4.5% Preferred $100 par called for redemption 09/30/1962
5.5% Preference $100 par called for redemption 05/27/1965
Stock Dividend - 10% 12/12/1955
Name changed to GenCorp Inc. (OH) 03/30/1984
GenCorp Inc. (OH) reincorporated in Delaware 04/14/2014 which name changed to Aerojet Rocketdyne Holdings, Inc. 04/27/2015

GENERAL TRAINING SVC INC (DE)
Charter cancelled and declared inoperative and void for non-payment of taxes 3/1/75

GENERAL TRANSISTOR CORP. (NY)
Common 25¢ par changed to $1 par and (1) additional share issued 08/07/1959
Merged into General Instrument Corp. (NJ) 08/31/1960
Each share Common $1 par exchanged for (0.7) share Common $1 par
General Instrument Corp. (NJ) reincorporated in Delaware 08/31/1967
(See General Instrument Corp. (Incorporated 06/12/1967))

GENERAL TRANSPORTATION SERVICES, INC. (TN)
Merged into Interstate Corp. 12/10/70
Each share Common $1 par exchanged for (0.5) share Common Capital Stock $1 par
Interstate Corp. merged into Gulf Life Holding Co. 1/30/76 which name changed to Gulf United Corp. 5/16/77
(See Gulf United Corp.)

GENERAL TR CDA (MONTREAL, QC)
Each share Preferred $100 par exchanged for (10) shares Preferred $10 par 03/11/1959
Under plan of merger each (3) shares Preferred $10 par exchanged for (5) shares Common $5 par 01/07/1971
Common $5 par changed to $2.50 par and (1) additional share issued 01/30/1980
$0.935 Conv. Preferred $17 par called for redemption 01/09/1985
Common $2.50 par changed to $0.83333333 par and (2) additional shares issued 08/09/1985
Acquired by General Trustco of Canada Inc. 06/03/1986
Each share Common $0.83333333 par exchanged for (1) share Common no par
General Trustco of Canada Inc. name changed to Genecan Financial Corp. 01/14/1994
(See Genecan Financial Corp.)

GENERAL TRUST CORP. OF CANADA (TORONTO, ON)
Acquired by National Bank of Canada (Montreal, QC) 07/21/1993
Details not available

GENERAL TR CORP (AZ)
Each share Class A Common no par exchanged for (0.2) share Common no par 5/14/65
Reorganized as Building Dynamics, Inc. 9/13/68
Each share Common no par exchanged for (0.666666) share Common $1 par
(See Building Dynamics, Inc.)

GENERAL TRUSTCO OF CANADA INC. (QC)
See - Trustco Gen Cda Inc

GENERAL UNDERWRITERS, INC. (AR)
Charter revoked for non-payment of taxes 2/19/74

GENERAL UNITED CORP., INC. (KS)
Adjudicated bankrupt 6/2/64
No stockholders' equity

GENERAL UTD GROUP INC (IA)
Merged into All American Life & Casualty Co. 5/31/73

Each share Common 25¢ par exchanged for $3.25 cash

GENERAL UNITS INC (ME)
Name changed to Frost & Sullivan, Inc. 2/28/73
(See Frost & Sullivan, Inc.)

GENERAL UTILITIES & INDUSTRIES, INC. (UT)
Reorganized under laws of Florida as General Utilities, Inc. 05/04/1962
Each share Common 5¢ par exchanged for (1.5866) shares Common $1 par
(See General Utilities, Inc.)

GENERAL UTILS INC (FL)
Common $1 par changed to 1¢ par in 1963
Proclaimed dissolved for failure to file reports and pay fees 6/28/65

GENERAL VENDING CORP.
Acquired by Peerless Weighing & Vending Machine Corp. in 1936
Details not available

GENERAL VENTURES INC (NV)
SEC revoked common stock registration 08/08/2008

GENERAL VITAMIN CORP (NY)
Name changed to Alleghany Pharmacal Corp. 11/19/1973
(See Alleghany Pharmacal Corp.)

GENERAL WATER GAS & ELECTRIC CO.
Name changed to International Investment Corp. International Investment Corp. name changed to International Investing Corp. (New) which liquidated 00/00/1946

GENERAL WATER TREATMENT CORP.
Merged into Permutit Co. in 1934
Details not available

GENERAL WATER WORKS & ELECTRIC CORP.
Reorganized as General Water, Gas & Electric Co. in 1933
Details not available

GENERAL WATER WORKS CO.
Name changed to General Water Works & Electric Corp. in 1928
General Water Works & Electric Corp. reorganized as General Water, Gas & Electric Co. in 1933 which name changed to International Investment Corp., then to International Investing Corp. (New) and liquidated in 1946

GENERAL WESTN INDS LTD (BC)
Recapitalized as Consolidated General Western Industries Ltd. 10/23/1986
Each share Common no par exchanged for (0.05) share Common no par
Consolidated General Western Industries Ltd. recapitalized as Danco Industries Ltd. 12/02/1991
(See Danco Industries Ltd.)

GENERAL WIRE & CABLE LTD (ON)
Through purchase offer over 99% acquired by Belden Corp. as of 01/10/1970
Public interest eliminated

GENERAL WTRWKS CORP (DE)
Class B Common $1 par changed to $10 par 00/00/1945
Each share Class B Common $10 par exchanged for (30) shares Common $1 par 00/00/1947
Merged into International Utilities Corp. 03/01/1968
Each share $6 Preferred $100 par exchanged for (1) share $6 Preferred Ser. B no par
Each share 6% Preferred $100 par exchanged for (1) share $6 Preferred Ser. A no par
Each share $5 Preferred $100 par exchanged for (1) share $5 Preferred no par
Each share 5% Preferred $100 par exchanged for (1) share $5 Preferred no par
Each share 5.1% Preferred $100 par exchanged for (1.02) shares $5 Preferred no par
Each share $4.50 Preferred $100 par exchanged for (1) share $4.50 Conv. Preferred no par
Each share $2 2nd Preferred $1 par exchanged for (1) share $2 Conv. Preferred no par
Each share Common $1 par exchanged for (1.875) shares Special Conv. Stock Ser. A no par
International Utilities Corp. name changed to IU International Corp. 04/27/1973
(See IU International Corp.)

GENERATION 5 TECHNOLOGY INC (CO)
Each share old Common $0.001 par exchanged for (0.2) share new Common $0.001 par 1/2/92
Each share new Common $0.001 par exchanged again for (0.2) share new Common $0.001 par 10/28/93
Name changed to China Industrial Group, Inc. 4/6/94
(See China Industrial Group, Inc.)

GENERATION ENTMT CORP (NV)
Recapitalized as Marketing-247, Inc. 7/15/2002
Each share Common $0.001 par exchanged for (0.005) share Common $0.001 par
Marketing-247, Inc. merged into MidAmerica Oil & Gas, Inc. 12/30/2003 which name changed to Sounds 24-7, Inc. 1/15/2004 which recapitalized as Allied Energy Corp. 1/26/2006

GENER8 MARITIME INC (MARSHALL ISLANDS)
Merged into Euronav N.V. 06/12/2018
Each share Common 1¢ par exchanged for (0.7272) share Ordinary no par

GENER8 MEDIA CORP (BC)
Name changed to Eight Solutions Inc. 02/03/2015

GENER8XION ENTMT INC (DE)
SEC revoked common stock registration 05/19/2011

GENEREX BIOTECHNOLOGY CORP (ID)
Reincorporated under the laws of Delaware 4/30/99

GENERIC MARKETING SVCS INC (NV)
Name changed to Total Nutraceutical Solutions 10/21/2008
Total Nutraceutical Solutions recapitalized as Entia Biosciences Inc. 02/15/2012

GENERICS CORP AMER (DE)
Charter cancelled and declared inoperative and void for non-payment of taxes 3/1/80

GENESCO INC (TN)
$3.50 Preferred Ser. A no par called for redemption 07/31/1963
$5 Preferred Ser. B no par called for redemption 07/31/1963
$5 Preferred Ser. D no par called for redemption 08/24/1964
Each share $6 Conv. Preferred Ser. B no par exchanged for (9.5632) shares Common $1 par and $29.20 cash 06/01/1982
Each share $6 Conv. Preferred Ser. C no par exchanged for (9.5632) shares Common $1 par and $29.20 cash 06/01/1982
$2.40 Preferred Ser. 2 no par called for redemption 10/31/1989
$4.50 Conv. Preferred no par called for redemption 12/20/1993
$1.50 Preferred no par called for redemption at $30 on 04/30/2013
$2.30 Preferred Ser. 1 no par called for redemption at $40 plus $0.58 accrued dividends on 04/30/2013
$4.75 Preferred Ser. 3 no par called for redemption at $100 plus $1.19 accrued dividends on 04/30/2013
$4.75 Preferred Ser. 4 no par called for redemption at $100 plus $1.19 accrued dividends on 04/30/2013
(Additional Information in Active)

GENESEE BREWING INC (NY)
Each share Class A no par or Class B no par exchanged for (7) shares Class A Common $1 par or Class B Common $1 par 00/00/1933
Each share Class A Common $1 par exchanged for (1) share Class A Common 50¢ par and (2) shares Class B Common 50¢ par 11/01/1954
Each share Class B Common $1 par exchanged for (3) shares Class B Common 50¢ par 11/01/1954
Stock Dividends - (1) share Class B for each (4) shares Class A or B 01/15/1949; (1) share Class B for each (10) shares Class A or B 08/01/1950; (1) share Class B for each (4) shares Class A or B 02/20/1953; Class A & B respectively - 10% 02/07/1966
Name changed to Genesee Corp. 12/31/1987
(See Genesee Corp.)

GENESEE COMPUTER CTR INC (NY)
Name changed to Genesee Survey Services Inc. 11/04/1994
(See Genesee Survey Services Inc.)

GENESEE CORP (NY)
Liquidation completed
Each share Class A Common 50¢ par received initial distribution of $7.50 cash payable 03/01/2001 to holders of record 02/20/2001
Each share Class B Common 50¢ par received initial distribution of $7.50 cash payable 03/01/2001 to holders of record 02/20/2001
Each share Class A Common 50¢ par received second distribution of $13 cash payable 11/01/2001 to holders of record 10/25/2001 Ex date - 11/02/2001
Each share Class B Common 50¢ par received second distribution of $13 cash payable 11/01/2001 to holders of record 10/25/2001 Ex date - 11/02/2001
Each share Class A Common 50¢ par received third distribution of $5 cash payable 05/17/2002 to holders of record 05/10/2002 Ex date - 05/20/2002
Each share Class B Common 50¢ par received third distribution of $5 cash payable 05/17/2002 to holders of record 05/10/2002 Ex date - 05/20/2002
Each share Class A Common 50¢ par received fourth distribution of $5 cash payable 08/26/2002 to holders of record 08/19/2002 Ex date - 08/27/2002
Each share Class B Common 50¢ par received fourth distribution of $5 cash payable 08/26/2002 to holders of record 08/19/2002 Ex date - 08/27/2002
Each share Class A Common 50¢ par received fifth distribution of $3 cash payable 10/11/2002 to holders of record 10/04/2002 Ex date - 10/15/2002
Each share Class B Common 50¢ par received fifth distribution of $3 cash payable 10/11/2002 to holders of record 10/04/2002 Ex date - 10/15/2002
Each share Class A Common 50¢ par received sixth distribution of $2.50 cash payable 03/17/2003 to holders of record 03/10/2003 Ex date - 03/18/2003
Each share Class B Common 50¢ par received sixth distribution of $2.50 cash payable 03/17/2003 to holders of record 03/10/2003 Ex date - 03/18/2003
Each share Class A Common 50¢ par received seventh distribution of $1.50 cash payable 04/28/2003 to holders of record 04/22/2003 Ex date - 04/29/2003
Each share Class B Common 50¢ par received seventh distribution of $1.50 cash payable 04/28/2003 to holders of record 04/22/2003 Ex date - 04/29/2003
Each share Class A Common 50¢ par received eighth distribution of $1.50 cash payable 06/18/2004 to holders of record 06/11/2004 Ex date - 06/21/2004
Each share Class B Common 50¢ par received eighth distribution of $1.50 cash payable 06/18/2004 to holders of record 06/11/2004 Ex date - 06/21/2004
Each share Class A Common 50¢ par received ninth and final distribution of $2.48 cash payable 08/28/2007 to holders of record 08/20/2007
Each share Class B Common 50¢ par received ninth and final distribution of $2.48 cash payable 08/28/2007 to holders of record 08/20/2007
Note: Certificates were not required to be surrendered and are without value

GENESEE LEASING CORP. (NY)
Liquidation completed
Each share VTC for Common 10¢ par received initial distribution of $27 cash 1/30/59
Each share VTC for Common 10¢ par exchanged for second and final distribution of $40.50 cash 8/3/59

GENESEE MERCHANTS BK & TR CO (FLINT, MI)
Common $10 par changed to $5 par and (1) additional share issued 04/30/1967
Stock Dividends - 20% 02/05/1959; 25% 02/03/1960; 10% 02/14/1961; 10% 01/31/1962; 11-1/9% 04/22/1969
Reorganized as United Michigan Corp. (DE) 05/15/1973
Each share Common $5 par exchanged for (1) share Common $5 par
United Michigan Corp. (DE) reincorporated in Michigan 08/01/1981
(See United Michigan Corp. (MI))

GENESEE PROPERTIES, INC. (NY)
Completely liquidated 8/31/64
Each (1/100th) share VTC for Capital Stock 10¢ par exchanged for $0.165 cash

GENESEE SURVEY SVCS INC (NY)
Merged into CEB 12/22/2008
Each share Common 5¢ par exchanged for $12.75164 cash
Each share Common 5¢ par received an additional distribution of $0.234559 cash from escrow 03/26/2009

GENESEE VALLEY GAS CO., INC. (NY)
Reorganized 7/10/39
No stockholders' equity
Capital Stock no par changed to $1 par 5/28/63
Dissolved 5/27/65

GENESEE VALLEY UNION TRUST CO. (ROCHESTER, NY)
Name changed to Marine Midland Trust Co. (Rochester, NY) 12/2/63
Marine Midland Trust Co. (Rochester, NY) name changed to Marine Midland Bank-Rochester (Rochester, NY) 6/5/70

GEN-GEN

(See Marine Midland Bank-Rochester (Rochester, NY))

GENESIS ADVANTAGE INC (NV)
Each share old Common $0.001 par exchanged for (10) shares new Common $0.001 par 06/05/2006
Charter revoked 09/30/2008

GENESIS BIOPHARMA INC (NV)
Common $0.001 par changed to $0.000041666 par and (23) additional shares issued payable 04/06/2010 to holders of record 04/06/2010
Recapitalized as Lion Biotechnologies, Inc. (NV) 09/26/2013
Each share Common $0.000041666 par exchanged for (0.01) share Common $0.000041666 par
Lion Biotechnologies, Inc. (NV) reincorporated in Delaware 06/01/2017 which name changed to Iovance Biotherapeutics, Inc. 06/28/2017

GENESIS BIOVENTURES INC (NV)
Reincorporated 10/30/2007
State of incorporation changed from (NY) to (NV) 10/30/2007
Name changed to Abviva, Inc. 12/18/2007
(See Abviva, Inc.)

GENESIS CAP CORP (AB)
Name changed to Genesis Land Development Corp. 11/19/1998

GENESIS CAP CORP (CO)
Each share Common $0.001 par exchanged for (0.1) share Common 1¢ par 07/30/1993
Each share Common 1¢ par exchanged for (0.05) share Common $0.001 par 12/08/1997
Reorganized under the laws of Nevada as Genesis Capital Corp. of Nevada 03/09/1999
Each share Common $0.001 par exchanged for (0.0005) share Common $0.001 par
Genesis Capital Corp. of Nevada name changed to Milwaukee Iron Arena Football, Inc. 05/18/2010 which name changed to EV Charging USA, Inc. 12/05/2014

GENESIS CAP CORP (NV)
Charter revoked for failure to file reports and pay fees 03/01/1988

GENESIS CAP CORP OF NEV (NV)
Each share old Common $0.001 par exchanged for (0.01) share new Common $0.001 par 03/29/2007
Each share new Common $0.001 par exchanged again for (0.002) share new Common $0.001 par 05/27/2008
Name changed to Milwaukee Iron Arena Football, Inc. 05/18/2010
Milwaukee Iron Arena Football, Inc. name changed to EV Charging USA, Inc. 12/05/2014

GENESIS DEV & CONSTR LTD (ISRAEL)
Placed in liquidation 08/09/1999
Details not available

GENESIS DIRECT INC (DE)
Issue Information - 11,125,000 shares COM offered at $15 per share on 05/07/1998
Plan of reorganization under Chapter 11 Federal Bankruptcy Code effective 6/5/2000
No stockholders' equity

GENESIS EXPL LTD (AB)
Acquired by Vintage Petroleum, Inc. 05/02/2001
Each share Common no par exchanged for $18.25 cash

GENESIS FINL INC (WA)
Common $0.001 par split (2) for (1) by issuance of (1) additional share payable 01/04/2007 to holders of record 01/02/2007 Ex date - 01/05/2007
Reincorporated under the laws of Wyoming 01/25/2016

GENESIS FLUID SOLUTIONS HLDGS INC (DE)
Reincorporated under the laws of Nevada as Blue Earth, Inc. 10/29/2010
(See Blue Earth, Inc.)

GENESIS GROUP HLDGS INC (DE)
Recapitalized as InterCloud Systems, Inc. 01/14/2013
Each share Common $0.0001 par exchanged for (0.008) share Common $0.0001 par

GENESIS HEALTH VENTURES INC NEW (PA)
Each share Common 2¢ par received distribution of (0.5) share Genesis HealthCare Corp. Common 1¢ par payable 12/1/2003 to holders of record 10/15/2003 Ex date - 12/2/2003
Name changed to NeighborCare, Inc. 12/1/2003
(See NeighborCare, Inc.)

GENESIS HEALTH VENTURES INC OLD (PA)
Common 2¢ par split (3) for (2) by issuance of (0.5) additional share payable 3/29/96 to holders of record 3/15/96
Plan of reorganization under Chapter 11 Federal Bankruptcy Code effective 10/2/2001
No stockholders' equity

GENESIS HEALTHCARE CORP (PA)
Merged into Formation Capital, LLC 07/13/2007
Each share Common 1¢ par exchanged for $69.35 cash

GENESIS HLDGS INC (NV)
Name changed to BioAuthorize Holdings, Inc. 07/16/2008

GENESIS II ENTERPRISES LTD (BC)
Cease trade order effective 05/29/2001
Stockholders' equity unlikely

GENESIS INS & FINL SVCS INC (NV)
Charter revoked for failure to file reports and pay fees 11/1/97

GENESIS INVT GROUP INC (AZ)
Merged into ILX Inc. 11/01/1993
Each (10) shares Common exchanged for (1) Unit consisting of (3) shares Conv. Preferred Ser. C $10 par and (5) shares Common no par
ILX Inc. recapitalized as ILX Resorts Inc. 01/13/1998
(See ILX Resorts Inc.)

GENESIS LEARNING SYS INC (CA)
Charter suspended for failure to file reports and pay fees 01/04/1988

GENESIS LEASE LTD (BERMUDA)
Issue Information - 27,860,000 ADR's offered at $23 per ADR on 12/13/2006
Merged into AerCap Holdings N.V. 03/25/2010
Each ADR for Common $0.001 par exchanged for (1) share Ordinary EUR 0.01 par

GENESIS MEDIA GROUP INC (NJ)
Recapitalized as Open Door Online Inc. (NJ) 08/10/1999
Each (30) shares Common $0.0001 par exchanged for (1) share Common $0.0001 par
Open Door Online Inc. (NJ) reorganized in Delaware as Blue Moon Group, Inc. 11/29/2002 which recapitalized as One Punch Productions, Inc. 12/07/2005 which name changed to Caltas Fitness, Inc. 08/21/2006 which name changed to Cinemaya Media Group, Inc. 02/06/2007 which recapitalized as SNM Global Holdings 11/14/2008

GENESIS MICROCHIP INC (DE)
Merged into STMicroelectronics N.V. 01/25/2008
Each share Common $0.001 par exchanged for $8.65 cash

GENESIS MICROCHIP INC (NS)
Reincorporated 01/20/1999
Issue Information - 2,850,000 shares COM offered at $11.50 per share on 02/23/1998
Place of incorporation changed from (ONT) to (NS) 01/20/1999
Reorganized under the laws of Delaware 02/13/2002
Each share Common no par exchanged for (1) share Common $0.001 par
(See Genesis Microchip (DE))

GENESIS PHARMACEUTICALS ENTERPRISES INC (FL)
Name changed 10/26/2007
Name changed from Genesis Technology Group, Inc. to Genesis Pharmaceuticals Enterprises, Inc. 10/26/2007
Each share old Common $0.001 par exchanged for (0.025) share new Common $0.001 par 09/04/2008
Name changed to Jiangbo Pharmaceuticals, Inc. 05/12/2009
(See Jiangbo Pharmaceuticals, Inc.)

GENESIS RLTY GROUP INC (DE)
Recapitalized as Genesis Group Holdings, Inc. 09/16/2008
Each share Common $0.0001 par exchanged for (0.05) share Common $0.0001 par
Genesis Group Holdings, Inc. recapitalized as InterCloud Systems, Inc. 01/14/2013

GENESIS RES CORP (BC)
Recapitalized as Golden Exodus Ventures Ltd. 05/26/1988
Each share Common no par exchanged for (0.5) share Common no par
Golden Exodus Ventures Ltd. recapitalized as ILM Resources Ltd. 01/16/1990 which recapitalized as Rainier Resources Ltd. 02/11/1993 which recapitalized as Prong Industries Corp. Ltd. (BC) 08/27/1996 which reincorporated in Bermuda 09/03/1996 which name changed to C&C Industries Corp. 11/02/1998 which name changed to Xenex Minerals Ltd. 01/11/2008
(See Xenex Minerals Ltd.)

GENESIS RES LTD (CANADA)
100% acquired by Skywest Resources Corp. through exchange offer which expired 02/24/1986
Public interest eliminated

GENESIS SAFETY SYS INC (NJ)
Recapitalized as Oil Baltija Group Ltd. 1/22/97
Each share Common no par exchanged for (0.1) share Common no par
(See Oil Baltija Group Ltd.)

GENESIS URANIUM CORP (NV)
Common $0.001 par split (3) for (1) by issuance of (2) additional shares payable 02/11/2008 to holders of record 02/11/2008 Ex date - 02/11/2008
Name changed to Vault Technology, Inc. 05/02/2008
Vault Technology, Inc. recapitalized as Modern Renewable Technologies, Inc. 09/17/2009 which name changed to Eco Ventures Group, Inc. 05/16/2011 which recapitalized as Petlife Pharmaceuticals, Inc. (Old) 08/12/2014 which reorganized as Petlife Pharmaceuticals, Inc. (New) 09/12/2016

GENESIS WORLDWIDE INC (CANADA)
Dissolved for non-compliance 05/14/2017

GENESIS WORLDWIDE INC (OH)
Chapter 11 bankruptcy proceedings dismissed 09/27/2007
No stockholders' equity

GENESISINTERMEDIA COM INC (DE)
Issue Information - 2,000,000 shares COM offered at $8.50 per share on 06/14/1999
Stock Dividend - 200% payable 3/21/2001 to holders of record 3/7/2001
Name changed to GenesisIntermedia, Inc. 4/2/2001
(See GenesisIntermedia, Inc.)

GENESISINTERMEDIA INC (DE)
Ceased operations 11/20/2003
No stockholders' equity

GENESYS PHARMA INC (BC)
Merged into Novopharm Biotech Inc. (BC) 08/25/1997
Each share Common no par exchanged for (1.6) shares Common no par
Novopharm Biotech Inc. (BC) name changed to Viventia Biotech Inc. 09/11/2000
(See Viventia Biotech Inc.)

GENESYS S A (FRANCE)
Each old Sponsored ADR for Ordinary exchanged for (0.5) new Sponsored ADR for Ordinary 06/29/2006
Basis changed from (1:0.5) to (1:1) 06/29/2006
Acquired by West Corp. 07/01/2008
Each Sponsored ADR for Ordinary exchanged for $3.93175 cash

GENESYS TELECOMMUNICATIONS LABORATORIES INC (CA)
Merged into Alcatel S.A. 01/21/2000
Each share Common no par exchanged for (1.277) ADR's for Ordinary FF40 par
Alcatel S.A. name changed to Alcatel-Lucent 11/30/2006

GENETHERA INC (FL)
Each share old Common $0.001 par exchanged for (2) shares new Common $0.001 par 09/03/2002
Reincorporated under the laws of Nevada 12/01/2004

GENETIC BREEDING INC (DE)
Recapitalized as Internow Affiliates Inc. 1/31/94
Each share Common $0.0001 par exchanged for (0.002) share Common 1¢ par
Internow Affiliates Inc. name changed to Electronics Communications Corp. in March 1994 which name changed to Northeast Digital Networks Inc. 6/16/98

GENETIC DIAGNOSTICS CORP (NY)
Charter cancelled and proclaimed dissolved for failure to pay taxes 09/28/1994

GENETIC DIAGNOSTICS TECHNOLOGIES CORP (CANADA)
Recapitalized as Polar Star Mining Corp. 08/15/2007
Each share Common no par exchanged for (0.29761904) share Common no par
Polar Star Mining Corp. merged into Revelo Resources Corp. 12/17/2014

GENETIC DYNAMICS CORP (UT)
Involuntarily dissolved for failure to pay taxes 12/31/1986

GENETIC ENGR INC (CO)
Merged into Miller Diversified Corp. 08/06/1992
Each share Common 1¢ par exchanged for (0.5278) share Common $0.001 par
Miller Diversified Corp. recapitalized as Vapor Corp. (NV) 02/10/2010

which reorganized in Delaware 12/27/2013 which name changed to Healthier Choices Management Corp. 03/06/2017

GENETIC LABS INC (MN)
Name changed to BioPlasty Inc. 03/01/1988
(See BioPlasty Inc.)

GENETIC LABS WOUND CARE INC (MN)
Merged into Derma Sciences, Inc. (PA) 10/16/1998
Each share Common 1¢ par exchanged for (0.7) share Common 1¢ par
Derma Sciences, Inc. (PA) reincorporated in Delaware 09/14/2012
(See Derma Sciences, Inc.)

GENETIC RESEARCH LABORATORIES, INC. (DE)
Each share old Common 1¢ par exchanged for (0.1) share new Common 1¢ par 04/01/1987
Merged into Organo Med Products, Ltd. 05/28/1987
Each share new Common 1¢ par exchanged for (1) share Common 1¢ par
(See Organo Med Products, Ltd.)

GENETIC SYS CORP (DE)
Acquired by Bristol-Myers Co. 02/13/1986
Each share Common 1¢ par exchanged for (0.166) share Common $1 par
Bristol-Myers Co. name changed to Bristol-Myers Squibb Co. 10/04/1989

GENETIC THERAPY INC (DE)
Merged into Sandoz Ltd. 8/11/95
Each share Common 1¢ par exchanged for $21 cash

GENETIC VECTORS INC (FL)
Merged into Frontier Resource Corp. 10/20/2008
Details not available

GENETICS INST INC (DE)
Merged into American Home Products Corp. 01/16/1992
Each share Common 1¢ par exchanged for (0.6) Depositary Share and $20 cash
$4 Conv. Exchangeable Preferred $1 par called for redemption 07/15/1993
Merged into American Home Products Corp. 12/31/1996
Each Depositary Share exchanged for $85 cash

GENETRON MARINE INC (BC)
Name changed to Trilogy Entertainment Corp. 03/22/1990
Trilogy Entertainment Corp. recapitalized as Consolidated Trilogy Ventures Ltd. 09/29/1993 which name changed to Thyssen Mining Exploration Inc. 12/22/1998 which name changed to Trilogy Metals Inc. (BC) 12/08/2000 which reincorporated in Canada as NWest Energy Inc. 03/07/2008 which recapitalized as NWest Energy Corp. 11/04/2010 which name changed to Ceylon Graphite Corp. 01/03/2017

GENETRONICS BIOMEDICAL CORP (DE)
Reincorporated 06/21/2001
Name and place of incorporation changed from Genetronics Biomedical Ltd. (BC) to Genetronics Biomedical Corp. (DE) and Common no par changed to $0.001 par 06/21/2001
Each share old Common no par exchanged for (0.25) share new Common no par 09/13/2004
Name changed to Inovio Biomedical Corp. 03/31/2005
Inovio Biomedical Corp. name changed to Inovio Pharmaceuticals, Inc. 05/14/2010

GENEVA ACQUISITION CORP (DE)
Completely liquidated 02/17/2009
Each Unit exchanged for first and final distribution of $5.95865854 cash
Each share Common $0.0001 par exchanged for first and final distribution of $5.95865854 cash

GENEVA AMERN GROUP INC (DE)
Name changed to QRS Music Inc. 07/24/1996
QRS Music Inc. name changed to QRS Music Technologies, Inc. 01/21/1998

GENEVA CAP VENTURES INC (QC)
Completely liquidated 4/14/75
No stockholders' equity

GENEVA FINL CORP (DE)
Company terminated common stock registration and is no longer public as of 08/04/2004

GENEVA FINL CORP (NV)
Company terminated common stock registration and is no longer public as of 08/04/2004

GENEVA GOLD CORP (NV)
Name changed to Geneva Resources, Inc. 03/05/2007
Geneva Resources, Inc. name changed to Sono Resources, Inc. 03/11/2011 which name changed to Alaska Gold Corp. 06/27/2012
(See Alaska Gold Corp.)

GENEVA GOLD MINES LTD.
Merged into Gencona Mines Ltd. 00/00/1944
Each share Capital Stock no par exchanged for (0.09736150) share Capital Stock no par
Gencona Mines Ltd. recapitalized as Kelly Lake Nickel Mines Ltd. 09/16/1968 which name changed to Albany Oil & Gas Ltd. (MB) 03/22/1971 which reincorporated in Alberta 11/10/1980 which name changed to Albany Corp. 05/17/1988 which merged into LifeSpace Environmental Walls Inc. 08/17/1993 which merged into SMED International Inc. 07/01/1996
(See SMED International Inc.)

GENEVA LAKE MINES LTD. (ON)
Recapitalized as Genex Mines Ltd. on 04/12/1956
Each share Capital Stock $1 par exchanged for (0.2) share Capital Stock $1 par
Genex Mines Ltd. recapitalized as Irvington Mining Co. Ltd. 10/17/1966
(See Irvington Mining Co. Ltd.)

GENEVA LAND CO. (DE)
Name changed to Newport Land Co. Inc. 4/3/70
(See Newport Land Co. Inc.)

GENEVA RES INC (NV)
Each share old Common $0.001 par exchanged for (0.25) share new Common $0.001 par 06/18/2010
Name changed to Sono Resources, Inc. 03/11/2011
Sono Resources, Inc. name changed to Alaska Gold Corp. 06/27/2012
(See Alaska Gold Corp.)

GENEVA RESOURCES LTD. (BC)
Name changed to Pacific Jade Industries Inc. 12/00/1973
(See Pacific Jade Industries Inc.)

GENEVA STL CO (UT)
Name changed 3/18/93
Name changed from Geneva Steel to Geneva Steel Co. 3/18/93
Plan of reorganization under Chapter 11 Federal Bankruptcy Code effective 1/3/2001
No stockholders' equity

GENEVA STL HLDGS CORP (UT)
Plan of reorganization under Chapter 11 Federal Bankruptcy Code effective 12/01/2006
Stockholders' equity unlikely

GENEVA TERRACE
Property sold in 1948

GENEVE CAP GROUP INC (DE)
5.5% Conv. Preferred 1st Ser. $10 par called for redemption 03/12/1982
Completely liquidated 08/05/1988
Each share Common 10¢ par exchanged for first and final distribution of (11.674) shares of Stamford Capital Group, Inc. Common $1 par and $21.76 cash
Stamford Capital Group, Inc. name changed to Independence Holding Co. (New) 09/10/1990

GENEVE CORP (DE)
Common 2¢ par reclassified as Class A Common 2¢ par 09/30/1980
Merged into Netter International Ltd. 12/18/1984
Each share Class A Common 20¢ par exchanged for $57.50 cash

GENEVE COSMECEUTICALS INC (BC)
Recapitalized as Pacific Concord Holding (Canada) Ltd. 08/30/1991
Each share Common no par exchanged for (0.2) share Common no par
Pacific Concord Holding (Canada) Ltd. name changed to Pacific Stratus Ventures Ltd. 06/12/1998 which name changed to Pacific Stratus Energy Ltd. 06/14/2005 which merged into Pacific Rubiales Energy Corp. 01/23/2008 which name changed to Pacific Exploration & Production Corp. 08/18/2015 which name changed to Frontera Energy Corp. 06/14/2017

GENEVEST INC (AB)
Merged into Pinetree Capital Corp. 6/1/2004
Each share Common no par exchanged for (2.2) shares Common no par

GENEX CORP (DE)
Reincorporated 7/15/87
State of incorporation changed from (MD) to (DE) 7/15/87
Acquired by Enzon, Inc. 10/31/91
Each share Conv. Preferred Ser. A 60¢ par exchanged for (0.0167801) share Common 1¢ par and (0.0139453) Common Stock Purchase Warrant expiring 10/31/94
Each share Conv. Preferred Ser. B 60¢ par exchanged for (0.2938369) share Common 1¢ par and (0.2441964) Common Stock Purchase Warrant expiring 10/31/94
Each share Common 5¢ par exchanged for (0.0065363) share Common 1¢ par and (0.005432) Common Stock Purchase Warrant expiring 10/31/94
Enzon Corp. name changed to Enzon Pharmaceuticals, Inc. 12/10/2002

GENEX MINES LTD. (ON)
Recapitalized as Irvington Mining Co. Ltd. 10/17/1966
Each share Capital Stock $1 par exchanged for (0.2) share Capital Stock no par
(See Irvington Mining Co. Ltd.)

GENEXUS INTL INC (NV)
Each share Common $0.001 par exchanged for (20) shares old Common $0.0001 par 03/23/1988
Each share old Common $0.0001 par exchanged for (10) shares new Common $0.0001 par 03/23/1988
Each (7,000) shares new Common $0.0001 par exchanged for (1) share Common 1¢ par 12/10/1990

Reorganized as Clearwater Holding Corp. 04/20/1993
Each share Common 1¢ par exchanged for (1.5) shares Common 1¢ par
Clearwater Holding Corp. recapitalized as Cinco Inc. 12/01/1998 which reorganized as Alynx, Co. (NV) 09/21/2006 which reorganized in Florida as MiMedx Group, Inc. 04/02/2008

GENFINITY CORP (DE)
SEC revoked common stock registration 06/18/2008

GENGE INC (CA)
Name changed to Systems Planning Corp. 02/20/1979
Systems Planning Corp. name changed to Greiner Engineering Inc. (CA) 05/11/1984 which reincorporated in Nevada 12/18/1986 which merged into URS Corp. (DE) 03/29/1996 which merged into AECOM Technology Corp. 10/17/2014 which name changed to AECOM 01/06/2015

GENGE INDUSTRIES, INC. (CA)
Common $1 par changed to 50¢ par and (1) additional share issued 01/24/1969
Name changed to Genge Inc. 06/05/1973
Genge Inc. name changed to Systems Planning Corp. 02/20/1979 which name changed to Greiner Engineering Inc. (CA) 05/11/1984 which reincorporated in Nevada 12/18/1986 which merged into URS Corp. (DE) 03/29/1996 which merged into AECOM Technology Corp. 10/17/2014 which name changed to AECOM 01/06/2015

GENICOM CORP (DE)
Plan of reorganization under Chapter 11 Federal Bankruptcy proceedings confirmed 08/03/2001
No stockholders' equity

GENIE OIL & GAS CORP (DE)
Reincorporated under the laws of Oklahoma 09/15/1978

GENIMAR INC (DE)
Under plan of merger each share Common 10¢ par exchanged for $10 cash 00/00/1977

GENIO GROUP INC (DE)
Recapitalized as Millennium Prime, Inc. 10/29/2009
Each share Common $0.0001 par exchanged for (0.0005) share Common $0.0001 par

GENISCO, INC. (CA)
Name changed to Genisco Technology Corp. (Calif.) 12/31/63
Genisco Technology Corp. (Calif.) reincorporated in Delaware 4/9/84

GENISCO TECHNOLOGY CORP (DE)
Reincorporated 04/09/1984
Common $1 par changed to 50¢ par and (1) additional share issued 10/14/1968
Common 50¢ par split (3) for (2) by issuance of (0.5) additional share 03/09/1981
State of incorporation changed from (CA) to (DE) 04/09/1984
Common 50¢ par changed to 1¢ par 12/30/1991
Each share old Common 1¢ par exchanged for (0.1) share new Common 1¢ par 11/21/1994
Plan of reorganization under Chapter 11 Federal Bankruptcy proceedings confirmed 01/21/1997
No stockholders' equity

GENISYS RESERVATION SYS INC (NJ)
Name changed to Netcruise.com, Inc. 10/20/1999
(See Netcruise.com, Inc.)

GENITOPE CORP (DE)
Filed a petition under Chapter 7 Federal Bankruptcy Code 12/31/2014
Stockholders' equity unlikely

GENIUS PPTYS LTD (CANADA)
Each share old Common no par exchanged for (0.2) share new Common no par 02/01/2017
Each share new Common no par received distribution of (0.16666666) share Genius Metals Inc. Common no par payable 08/31/2018 to holders of record 08/30/2018
Name changed to Cerro de Pasco Resources Inc. 10/18/2018

GENIUS PRODS INC (NV)
Each share old Common $0.001 par exchanged (0.25) share new Common $0.001 par 04/10/2001
Reincorporated under the laws of Delaware and Common $0.001 par changed to $0.0001 par 03/02/2005

GENIUS TECHNOLOGIES INC (UT)
Involuntarily dissolved for failure to pay taxes 11/01/1991

GENIUS WORLD INVESTMENTS LTD (CAYMAN ISLANDS)
Name changed to CINS Holding Corp. 09/13/2012
CINS Holding Corp. name changed to Sino Rise Group Holding Corp. 01/29/2016

GENIVAR INC (QC)
Name changed to WSP Global Inc. 01/02/2014

GENIVAR INCOME FD (QC)
Under plan of reorganization each Trust Unit no par automatically became (1) share GENIVAR Inc. Common no par 01/04/2011
GENIVAR Inc. name changed to WSP Global Inc. 01/02/2014

GENLYTE GROUP INC (DE)
Common 1¢ par split (2) for (1) by issuance of (1) additional share payable 05/23/2005 to holders of record 05/09/2005 Ex date - 05/24/2005
Merged into Philips Holding USA Inc. 01/25/2008
Each share Common 1¢ par exchanged for $95.50 cash

GENMAR INDS INC (DE)
Merged into Genac Acquisition Corp. 03/23/1988
Each share Common 1¢ par exchanged for $12.50 cash

GENMED HLDG CORP (NV)
SEC revoked common stock registration 02/16/2016

GENMEDX INC (NV)
Name changed to Pyramidion Technology Group, Inc. 06/19/2013

GENNARO INDS INC (PA)
Under plan of merger name changed to Aeroseal Corp. 12/02/1968

GENNUM CORP (ON)
Common no par split (3) for (1) by issuance of (2) additional shares payable 05/06/1996 to holders of record 04/26/1996
Common no par split (3) for (1) by issuance of (2) additional shares payable 05/10/1999 to holders of record 04/30/1999
Merged into Semtech Corp. 03/20/2012
Each share Common no par exchanged for $13.55 cash

GENOCO ALUMINUM LTD. (ON)
Adjudicated bankrupt 00/00/1963
Stockholders' equity unlikely

GENOME THERAPEUTICS CORP (MA)
Name changed to Oscient Pharmaceuticals Corp. 04/13/2004
(See Oscient Pharmaceuticals Corp.)

GENOMED INC (FL)
Each share old Common 1¢ par exchanged for (50) shares new Common 1¢ par 10/15/2001
SEC revoked common stock registration 04/08/2010
Company may be contacted at: www.genomed.com

GENOMIC SOLUTIONS INC (DE)
Issue Information - 7,000,000 shares COM offered at $8 per share on 05/05/2000
Call Common $0.001 par reclassified as Common $0.001 par 4/18/2001
Merged into Harvard Bioscience, Inc. 10/25/2002
Each share Common $0.001 par exchanged for (0.1017) share Common 1¢ par and $0.2861 cash

GENOMICA CORP (DE)
Issue Information - 6,440,000 shares COM offered at $19 per share on 03/15/2000
Merged into Exelixis, Inc. 1/9/2002
Each share Common $0.001 par exchanged for (0.28309) share Common $0.001 par

GENOMICS ONE CORP (CANADA)
Name changed to Alert B&C Corp. 6/29/2006

GENON ENERGY INC (DE)
Merged into NRG Energy, Inc. 12/14/2012
Each share Common $0.001 par exchanged for (0.1216) share new Common 1¢ par

GENOPTIX INC (DE)
Acquired by Novartis AG 03/07/2011
Each share Common $0.001 par exchanged for $25 cash

GENORAY ADVANCED TECHNOLOGIES LTD (AB)
Cease trade order effective 03/31/2004

GENORAY ADVANCED TECHNOLOGIES LTD (NV)
Recapitalized as Fennel Resources, Inc. 11/07/2005
Each share Common no par exchanged for (0.001) share Common $0.001 par
Fennel Resources, Inc. recapitalized as 3P Networks, Inc. 09/20/2006 which recapitalized as Kender Energy Inc. 10/07/2008 which recapitalized as Bettwork Industries Inc. 07/02/2014

GENOVA BIOTHERAPEUTICS INC (NV)
Common $0.00001 par split (125) for (1) by issuance of (124) additional shares payable 07/13/2009 to holders of record 07/13/2009
SEC revoked common stock registration 10/10/2014

GENOVA INC (MI)
Common $1 par changed to 66-2/3¢ par and (0.5) additional share issued 08/15/1983
Stock Dividends - 20% 10/30/1977; 20% 10/20/1978; 25% 10/01/1979
Merged into Genova Products, Inc. 04/01/1987
Each share Common $1 par exchanged for $5.375 cash

GENOVATION CAP CORP (BC)
Each share old Common no par exchanged for (0.33333333) share new Common no par 11/03/2016
Name changed to Valens Groworks Corp. 11/24/2016

GENOVESE DRUG STORES INC (NY)
Reincorporated 9/12/86
Common $1 par split (2) for (1) by issuance of (1) additional share 10/5/83
Stock Dividends - 50% 2/14/69; 50% 1/30/70; 20% 11/10/76; 20% 1/20/78; 20% 4/15/83
State of incorporation changed from (DE) to (NY) 9/12/86
Each share Common $1 par exchanged for (1) share Class A Common $1 par or (1) share Class B Common $1 par
Note: Option to receive Class B Common expired 11/14/86
Class A Common $1 par split (3) for (2) by issuance of (0.5) additional share 10/6/87
Class B Common $1 par split (3) for (2) by issuance of (0.5) additional share 10/6/87
Stock Dividends - 10% 4/10/89; 10% 7/8/91; 10% 1/5/93; 10% 1/4/94; 10% 1/5/95; 10% payable 1/4/96 to holders of record 12/21/95 Ex date for Class A - 12/19/95; 10% payable 1/14/97 to holders of record 12/26/96; In Class A to holders of Class A 10% payable 1/14/98 to holders of record 12/26/97
Merged into J.C. Penney Co. Inc. 3/1/99
Each share Class A Common $1 par exchanged for (0.6709) share Common 50¢ par
Each share Class B Common $1 par exchanged for (0.6709) share Common 50¢ par

GENOVEVA RESOURCE INC (BC)
Delisted from Vancouver Stock Exchange 3/2/89

GENPROBE TECHNOLOGIES LTD (BC)
Name changed to CBR International Biotechnologies Corp. 11/06/1989
CBR International Biotechnologies Corp. recapitalized as Newen Enterprises Inc. 03/30/1993 which recapitalized as Consolidated Newen Enterprises Inc. 11/02/1998 which recapitalized as North American Gold Inc. 04/07/2003 which name changed to Northland Resources Inc. (BC) 09/07/2005 which reincorporated in Luxembourg as Northland Resources S.A. 06/14/2010

GENRAD INC (MA)
Common $1 par split (3) for (2) by issuance of (0.5) additional share 3/8/83
Stock Dividend - 100% 10/20/80
Merged into Teradyne, Inc. 10/26/2001
Each share Common $1 par exchanged for (0.1733) share Common 12-1/2¢ par

GENROCO INC (WI)
Common $0.001 par split (3) for (1) by issuance of (2) additional shares payable 09/28/1999 to holders of record 09/21/1999
Each share Common $0.001 par received distribution of (1) share VideoPropulsion, Inc. Common 1¢ par payable 07/10/2000 to holders of record 06/30/2000
Common $0.001 par split (2) for (1) by issuance of (1) additional share payable 07/13/2000 to holders of record 07/03/2000
Reorganized as VideoPropulsion Interactive Television, Inc. 05/03/2006
Each share Common $0.001 par held by holders of (10,000) shares or more exchanged for (0.01) share Common $0.001 par
Note: Holders of (9,999) or fewer shares received $0.02 cash per share

GENSCI REGENERATION SCIENCES INC (BC)
Merged into IsoTis S.A. 11/03/2003
Each share Common no par exchanged for (0.475) share Common CHF 1 par and (0.1) share SMC Ventures Inc. Class A Common no par

(See each company's listing)

GENSEL BIOTECHNOLOGIES LTD (ON)
Recapitalized as Greenfield Commercial Credit (Canada) Inc. 01/01/2003
Each share Common no par exchanged for (0.35714285) share Common no par
Greenfield Commercial Credit (Canada) Inc. name changed to Greenfield Financial Group Inc. 08/17/2005 which name changed to Wheels Group Inc. 01/18/2012 which merged into Radiant Logistics, Inc. 04/08/2015

GENSET SA (FRANCE)
ADR agreement terminated 12/27/2002
Each Sponsored ADR for Ordinary FF 17 par exchanged for $3.0589 cash

GENSIA SICOR INC (DE)
Name changed 5/28/93
Name changed 2/28/97
Common 1¢ par split (3) for (2) by issuance of (0.5) additional share 03/02/1992
Name changed from Gensia Pharmaceuticals, to Gensia, Inc. 05/28/1993
Each Contingent Value Right received distribution of (0.375) shares Common 1¢ par payable 01/08/1997 to holders of record 12/31/1996
Name changed from Gensia, Inc. to Gensia Sicor Inc. 02/28/1997
Name changed to Sicor Inc. 06/19/1999
Sicor Inc. merged into Teva Pharmaceutical Industries Ltd. 01/22/2004

GENSOURCE CAP CORP (ON)
Name changed to Gensource Potash Corp. 07/02/2013

GENSPERA INC (DE)
Name changed to Inspyr Therapeutics, Inc. 08/02/2016

GENSTAR CORP (CANADA)
$2.35 Conv. 2nd Preferred Ser. C no par called for redemption 03/17/1986
$1.20 Non-Cum. Conv. Preferred Ser. B $20 par called for redemption 06/30/1986
$1.50 Conv. Preferred Ser. D $20 par called for redemption 06/30/1986
$1.68 Conv. 2nd Preferred Ser. B no par called for redemption 06/30/1986
$1.10 Conv. Preferred Ser. A $20 par called for redemption 06/30/1986
Floating Rate Conv. Retractable 2nd Preferred Ser. D no par called for redemption 07/31/1986
Acquired by Imasco Enterprises Inc. 08/04/1986
Each share Common no par exchanged for $58 cash
$2.375 Retractable 2nd Preferred Ser. E no par called for redemption 09/15/1986
Public interest eliminated

GENSTAR FINL CORP (CANADA)
Name changed to Imasco Financial Corp. 10/23/1987
(See Imasco Financial Corp.)

GENSTAR LTD. (CANADA)
Common no par split (2) for (1) by issuance of (1) additional share 06/08/1979
Name changed to Genstar Corp. 06/15/1981
(See Genstar Corp.)

GENSTAR THERAPEUTICS CORP (DE)
Name changed to CorAutus Genetics, Inc. 02/05/2003
CorAutus Genetics, Inc. recapitalized as VIA Pharmaceuticals, Inc. 06/06/2007

(See VIA Pharmaceuticals, Inc.)

GENSYM CORP (DE)
Merged into Versata Enterprises, Inc. 10/26/2007
Each share Common 1¢ par exchanged for $2.35 cash

GENTA INC (DE)
Each share old Common $0.001 par exchanged for (0.1) share new Common $0.001 par 04/07/1997
Each share new Common $0.001 par exchanged again for (0.16666666) share new Common $0.001 par 07/13/2007
Each share new Common $0.001 par exchanged again for (0.02) share new Common $0.001 par 07/13/2009
Each share new Common $0.001 par exchanged again for (0.01) share new Common $0.001 par 08/02/2010
Each share new Common $0.001 par exchanged again for (0.02) share new Common $0.001 par 02/18/2011
Filed a petition under Chapter 7 Federal Bankruptcy Code 08/03/2012
Stockholders' equity unlikely

GENTECH CAP CORP (BC)
Name changed to CareerExchange Interactive Corp. 08/21/2001
CareerExchange Interactive Corp. name changed to Cytiva Software Inc. 06/21/2005
(See Cytiva Software Inc.)

GENTECH PHARMA INC (FL)
Name changed to Fintech Group, Inc. 09/20/2006
Fintech Group, Inc. name changed to Capital Markets Technologies, Inc. 02/20/2007
(See Capital Markets Technologies, Inc.)

GENTEK INC (DE)
Plan of reorganization under Chapter 11 Federal Bankruptcy Code effective 11/10/2003
No Common 1¢ par stockholders' equity
Merged into ASP GT Holding Corp. 10/29/2009
Each share Common no par exchanged for $38 cash

GENTERRA CAP CORP NEW (BC)
Recapitalized as Genterra Capital Inc. (Old) 06/30/1998
Each share Class A Subordinate no par exchanged for (0.1) share Class A Subordinate no par
Each share Class B Multiple no par exchanged for (0.1) share Class B no par
Preferreds not affected except for change of name
Genterra Capital Inc. (Old) name changed to Genterra Investment Corp. 04/30/1999 which merged into Genterra Inc. 12/31/2003 which merged into Genterra Capital Inc. (New) 05/10/2010 which merged into Gencan Capital Inc. 10/30/2015

GENTERRA CAP CORP OLD (BC)
Merged into Genterra Capital Corp. (New) 02/28/1997
Each share Class A Subordinate no par exchanged for (1) share Class A Subordinate no par
Each share Class B no par exchanged for (1) share Class B Multiple no par
Genterra Capital Corp. (New) recapitalized as Genterra Capital Inc. (Old) 06/30/1998 which name changed to Genterra Investment Corp. 04/30/1999 which merged into Genterra Inc. 12/31/2003 which merged into Genterra Capital Inc. (New) 05/10/2010 which merged into Gencan Capital Inc. 10/30/2015

GENTERRA CAP INC NEW (ON)
Merged into Gencan Capital Inc. 10/30/2015
Each share Common no par exchanged for (2) shares Common no par and $1.96 cash
Note: Holders of (499) or fewer shares received $1.96 cash per share
Class B Preferred no par called for redemption at $0.05 on 11/30/2015

GENTERRA CAP INC OLD (BC)
Under plan of merger name changed to Genterra Investment Corp. 04/30/1999
Genterra Investment Corp. merged into Genterra Inc. 12/31/2003 which merged into Genterra Capital Inc. (New) 05/10/2010 which merged into Gencan Capital Inc. 10/30/2015

GENTERRA INC (ON)
Each share Class C Preferred no par exchanged for (1.667) Class B Preference Shares no par 06/10/2008
Each share Class D Preferred Ser. 1 no par exchanged for (2) Class B Preference Shares no par 06/10/2008
Each share Class D Preferred Ser. 2 no par exchanged for (5.37) Class B Preference Shares no par 06/10/2008
Each share Class E Preferred no par exchanged for (95) Class B Preference Shares no par 06/10/2008
Each share Preferred Ser. 1 no par exchanged for (6.35) Class B Preference Shares no par 06/10/2008
Each Class A Subordinate Participation Share no par exchanged for (1) share Common no par 06/10/2008
Each Class B Multiple Participation Share no par exchanged for (1.25) shares Common no par 06/10/2008
Merged into Genterra Capital Inc. (New) 05/10/2010
Each Class B Preference Share no par exchanged for (1) share Class B Preferred no par
Each share Common no par exchanged for (0.2777) share Common no par
Genterra Capital Inc. (New) merged into Gencan Capital Inc. 10/30/2015

GENTERRA INVT CORP (BC)
Merged into Genterra Inc. 12/31/2003
Each share Class D Preferred Ser. 1 no par exchanged for (1) share Class D Preferred Ser. 1 no par
Each share Class D Preferred Ser. 2 no par exchanged for (1) share Class D Preferred Ser. 2 no par
Each share Class E Preferred no par exchanged for (1) share Class E Preferred no par
Each share Preference Ser. 1 no par exchanged for (1) share Preference Ser. 1 no par
Each Class A Subordinate no par exchanged for (1) share Class A Subordinate no par
Each Class B Multiple no par exchanged for (1) share Class B Multiple no par
Genterra Inc. merged into Genterra Capital Inc. (New) 05/10/2010 which merged into Gencan Capital Inc. 10/30/2015

GENTEX CO., INC. (NY)
Charter cancelled and proclaimed dissolved for failure to pay taxes and file reports 12/15/50

GENTIA SOFTWARE PLC (ENGLAND)
ADR agreement terminated 07/31/2003
No ADR holders' equity

GENTING SINGAPORE PLC (ISLE OF MAN)
Name changed 08/12/2009
Name changed from Genting International PLC to Genting Singapore PLC 08/12/2009
Name changed to Genting Singapore Ltd. 06/14/2018

GENTIUM S P A (ITALY)
ADR agreement terminated 04/13/2014
Each Sponsored ADR for Ordinary exchanged for $56.95 cash

GENTIVA HEALTH SVCS INC (DE)
Each share Common 10¢ par received distribution of (0.19253) share Accredo Health Inc. Common 1¢ par payable 06/26/2002 to holders of record 06/13/2002
Merged into Kindred Healthcare, Inc. 02/02/2015
Each share Common 10¢ par exchanged for (0.257) share Common 25¢ par and $14.50 cash
(See Kindred Healthcare, Inc.)

GENTLE DENTAL SVC CORP (WA)
Issue Information - 1,500,000 shares COM offered at $5 per share on 02/13/1997
Merged into Interdent, Inc. 3/11/99
Each share Common no par automatically became (1) share Common $0.001 par
(See Interdent, Inc.)

GENTNER COMMUNICATIONS CORP (UT)
Name changed to ClearOne Communications, Inc. 01/02/2002
ClearOne Communications, Inc. name changed to ClearOne, Inc. 12/13/2012

GENTNER ELECTRS CO (UT)
Each share old Common $0.001 par exchanged for (0.1) share new Common $0.001 par 01/03/1986
Name changed to Gentner Communications Corp. 07/01/1991
Gentner Communications Corp. name changed to ClearOne Communications, Inc. 01/02/2002 which name changed to ClearOne, Inc. 12/13/2012

GENTOR RES INC (FL)
Reincorporated under the laws of Cayman Islands 02/28/2012

GENTRA INC (CANADA)
Each share Priority Preferred no par exchanged for $27.25 principal amount of 7.5% Jr. Subordinated Debentures due 12/21/2001 on 01/04/1996
Adjustable Dividend Preferred Ser. Q no par called for redemption 10/15/1997
Ser. R Preferred no par called for redemption 10/15/1997
Each share old Common no par exchanged for (0.2) share new Common no par 04/23/1999
Name changed to BPO Properties Ltd. 04/19/2001
(See BPO Properties Ltd.)

GENTRONIX LABS INC (UT)
Merged into Consolidated Holdings Corp. 03/15/1990
Each share Common $0.001 par exchanged for (0.5) share 10% Preferred Ser. A $0.001 par, (0.5) share Preferred Ser. B $0.001 par and (0.1) share Common $0.001 par
Consolidated Holdings Corp. recapitalized as Pacific Diversified Holdings Corp. 03/17/1997 which name changed to Agora Holdings, Inc. 05/01/1998

GENTRY, INC.
Acquired by Consolidated Grocers Corp. 04/30/1951
Each share Capital Stock $1 par exchanged for (0.2) share Common $1.33333333 par
Consolidated Grocers Corp. name changed to Consolidated Foods Corp. 02/24/1954 which name changed to Sara Lee Corp. 04/02/1985 which recapitalized as Hillshire Brands Co. 06/29/2012
(See Hillshire Brands Co.)

GENTRY EQUITIES INC (DE)
Name changed to Drivefone, Inc. 12/10/1988
Drivefone, Inc. name changed to Luxcel Group, Inc. 01/15/1993
(See Luxcel Group, Inc.)

GENTRY MINERAL PRODS INC (NV)
Name changed to Great Western Iron Ore Properties, Inc. 07/27/2009

GENTRY OIL & GAS LTD (BC)
Recapitalized as Laredo Petroleums Ltd. 06/25/1979
Each share Capital Stock 50¢ par exchanged for (0.5) share Capital Stock no par
Laredo Petroleums Ltd. recapitalized as Pedco Energy Ltd. 10/23/1986 which merged into International Pedco Energy Corp. 11/26/1993 which merged into Lateral Vector Resources Inc. 02/29/1996
(See Lateral Vector Resources Inc.)

GENTRY RES LTD (CANADA)
Class B Common no par reclassified as Common no par 06/04/1999
Merged into Crew Energy Inc. 08/22/2008
Each share Common no par exchanged for (0.22) share Common no par

GENTRY STL INC (NV)
Name changed to Gentry Mineral Products, Inc. 01/30/1998
Gentry Mineral Products, Inc. name changed to Great Western Iron Ore Properties, Inc. 07/27/2009

GEN2MEDIA CORP (NV)
Name changed to Vidaroo Corp. 04/26/2010

GENUINE AUTOTRONICS OF CANADA, LTD. (ON)
Adjudicated bankrupt 02/14/1966
No stockholders' equity

GENUITY INC (DE)
Each share old Class A Common 1¢ par exchanged for (0.05) share new Class A Common 1¢ par 05/30/2002
Plan of reorganization under Chapter 11 Federal Bankruptcy Code effective 12/02/2003
No stockholders' equity

GENUNG'S, INC. (NY)
Each share Common no par exchanged for (5.5) shares Common $1 par 8/23/55
5% Preferred $100 par called for redemption 1/28/64
Merged into Supermarkets General Corp. 4/22/68
Each share Common $1 par exchanged for (0.5) share $1.30 Conv. Preferred no par
(See Supermarkets General Corp.)

GENUS EQUITY CORP (ON)
Recapitalized as Golden Hill Mining Co. 09/20/1995
Each share Common no par exchanged for (0.1) share Common no par
Golden Hill Mining Co. acquired by MacDonald Mines Exploration Ltd. (QC) 03/09/1998 which reincorporated in Canada 11/01/2011

GENUS INC (CA)
Merged into Aixtron AG 03/15/2005
Each share Common no par exchanged for (0.51) Sponsored ADR for Ordinary

Aixtron AG name changed to Aixtron S.E. 12/22/2010
(See Aixtron S.E.)

GENUS INTL CORP (WY)
Common $0.001 par split (7.5) for (1) by issuance of (6.5) additional shares payable 10/10/2000 to holders of record 10/02/2000 Ex date - 10/11/2000
Charter dissolved for non-payment of taxes 06/10/2002

GENVEC INC (DE)
Each share old Common $0.001 par exchanged for (0.1) share new Common $0.001 par 04/19/2011
Each share new Common $0.001 par exchanged again for (0.1) share new Common $0.001 par 12/01/2016
Merged into Intrexon Corp. 06/16/2017
Each share new Common $0.001 par exchanged for (0.297) share Common no par and (1) Contingent Value Right

GENVIEW CAP CORP (BC)
Recapitalized as Hempco Food & Fiber Inc. 04/20/2016
Each share Common no par exchanged for (0.5) share Common no par

GENWAY CORP (DE)
Common $1 par changed to 1¢ par 09/01/1972
In process of liquidation
Each share Common 1¢ par received initial distribution of $6.50 cash 12/23/1986
Each share Common 1¢ par received second distribution of $1 cash 10/06/1987
Each share Common 1¢ par received third distribution of $0.55 cash 12/14/1988
Each share Common $1 par received fourth distribution of $0.25 cash 11/02/1989
Each share Common 1¢ par received fifth distribution of $0.65 cash 06/15/1990
Each share Common 1¢ par received sixth distribution of $0.22 cash 11/09/1990
The amount or number of subsequent distributions, if any, are undetermined

GENWORTH FINL INC (DE)
Issue Information - 24,000,000 CORPORATE UNITS offered at $25 per Unit on 05/24/2004
Each Corporate Unit received (1.0623) shares Class A Common $0.001 par 05/16/2007
Issue Information - 2,000,000 shares PFD SER A 5.25% offered at $50 per share on 05/24/2004
5.25% Preferred Ser. A $0.001 par called for redemption at $50 on 06/01/2011
(Additional Information in Active)

GENX RES CORP INC (NV)
Common $0.001 par split (2) for (1) by issuance of (1) additional share payable 07/05/2006 to holders of record 06/22/2006 Ex date - 07/06/2006
Reorganized under the laws of Texas as GenX Corp. 11/06/2008
Each share Common $0.001 par exchanged for (0.001) share Common $0.001 par

GENZYME CORP (MA)
Reincorporated 12/30/1991
State of incorporation changed from (DE) to (MA) 12/30/1991
Common 1¢ par reclassified as Common-General Division 1¢ par 12/23/1994
Each share Common 1¢ par received distribution of (0.135) share Common-Tissue Repair Division 1¢ par 12/23/1994
Common-General Division 1¢ par split (2) for (1) by issuance of (1) additional share payable 07/25/1996 to holders of record 07/11/1996
Each share Common-General Division 1¢ par received distribution of (0.03) share Common-Tissue Repair Division 1¢ par payable 07/22/1997 to holders of record 07/11/1997
Secondary Offering - 4,000,000 shares COM-TISSUE REPAIR offered at $7.75 per share on 11/03/1997
Each share Common-General Division 1¢ par received distribution of (0.11673) share Common-Molecular Oncology Division 1¢ par payable 11/16/1998 to holders of record 11/02/1998
Each share Common-General Division 1¢ par received distribution of (0.17901) share Common-Surgical Products Division 1¢ par payable 06/28/1999 to holders of record 06/14/1999
Each share Common-Tissue Repair 1¢ par exchanged for (0.3352) share Common-Biosurgery Division 1¢ par 12/18/2000
Each share Common-Surgical Products Division 1¢ par exchanged for (0.606) share Biosurgery Division Common 1¢ par 12/18/2000
Each share Common-General Division 1¢ par split (2) for (1) by issuance of (1) additional share payable 06/01/2001 to holders of record 05/24/2001 Ex date - 06/04/2001
Each share Common-Biosurgery Division 1¢ par exchanged for (0.04914) share Common-General Division 1¢ par 06/30/2003
Each share Common-Molecular Oncology Division 1¢ par exchanged for (0.05653) share Common-General Division 1¢ par 06/30/2003
Common-General Products Division 1¢ par reclassified as Common 1¢ par 05/27/2004
Acquired by Sanofi-Aventis 04/08/2011
Each share Common 1¢ par exchanged for (1) Contingent Value Right and $74 cash

GENZYME TRANSGENICS CORP (MA)
Name changed to GTC Biotherapeutics, Inc. 06/03/2002
(See GTC Biotherapeutics, Inc.)

GEO DATA INTL LTD (BC)
Name changed to Trellis Technology Corp. 07/29/1994
(See Trellis Technology Corp.)

GEO DYNE RES LTD (BC)
Recapitalized as Cube Resources Ltd. 11/01/1976
Each share Common no par exchanged for (0.2) share Common no par
(See Cube Resources Ltd.)

GEO ENERGY RES INC (DE)
Each share Common 1¢ par exchanged for (0.1) share Common $0.001 par 8/15/81
Name changed to Guild Mark Industries, Inc. 8/21/87
Guild Mark Industries, Inc. merged into MG Gold Corp. 5/15/97 which name changed to MG Natural Resources Corp. 10/12/98 which name changed to Xenolix Technologies Inc. 6/14/2000 which name changed to Pershing Resources Co., Inc. 4/27/2004

GEO-ENVIRONMENTAL RES INC (UT)
Each share old Common $0.001 par exchanged for (0.1) share new Common $0.001 par 06/30/1992
Name changed to American Absorbents Natural Products, Inc. (UT) 06/05/1995
American Absorbents Natural Products, Inc. (UT) reincorporated in Delaware as Earful of Books, Inc. 08/24/2001
(See Earful of Books, Inc.)

GEO EXPLORATIONS, INC. (NM)
Charter forfeited for non-payment of taxes 10/21/63

GEO GROUP INC OLD (FL)
Common 1¢ par split (3) for (2) by issuance of (0.5) additional share payable 09/29/2006 to holders of record 09/15/2006 Ex date - 10/02/2006
Common 1¢ par split (2) for (1) by issuance of (1) additional share payable 05/31/2007 to holders of record 05/15/2007 Ex date - 06/01/2007
Each share Common 1¢ par received distribution of (0.15200081) share Common 1¢ par and $1.37533705 cash payable 12/31/2012 to holders of record 12/12/2012
Reorganized as GEO Group, Inc. (New) 06/27/2014
Each share Common 1¢ par exchanged for (1) share Common 1¢ par

GEO INTL CORP (DE)
Plan of reorganization under Chapter 11 Federal Bankruptcy Code effective 5/12/95
No stockholders' equity

GEO MINERALS LTD (BC)
Merged into GeoNovus Minerals Corp. 01/02/2012
Each share Common no par exchanged for (0.06666666) share Common no par and $0.16 cash
Note: Unexchanged certificates were cancelled and became without value 01/02/2018
GeoNovus Minerals Corp. name changed to GeoNovus Media Corp. 04/10/2015 which name changed to Imagination Park Entertainment Inc. 05/09/2016

GEO PAX MINES LTD (ON)
Charter cancelled and declared dissolved for failure to file returns and pay fees 03/16/1976

GEO PETE INC (CA)
Ceased operations 07/10/2002
Stockholders' equity unlikely

GEO PIAJA EXPL CORP (AB)
Name changed to Contact Exploration Inc. 05/28/1998
Contact Exploration Inc. merged into Kicking Horse Energy Inc. 12/24/2014
(See Kicking Horse Energy Inc.)

GEO-POINT TECHNOLOGIES INC (NV)
Name changed to Global Resources Technologies, Inc. 09/06/2005
Global Resources Technologies, Inc. name changed to Gold & Onyx Mining Co. 06/10/2009
(See Gold & Onyx Mining Co.)

GEO PT TECHNOLOGIES INC (UT)
Each share old Common $0.001 par received distribution of (1) share Geo Point Resources, Inc. Restricted Common $0.001 par payable 04/22/2013 to holders of record 01/17/2013 Ex date - 01/15/2013
Each share old Common $0.001 par exchanged for (0.33333333) share new Common $0.001 par 05/24/2013
Name changed to RTS Oil Holdings, Inc. 07/02/2013

GEO RECYCLING INC (NV)
Charter permanently revoked 08/01/2004

GEO RESOURCES CORP. (NV)
Merged into GR Resources Corp. (UT) 2/24/2004
Details not available

GEO-SCIENTIFIC PROSPECTORS LTD. (ON)
Acquired by Goldfields Mining Corp. Ltd. on a (3) for (1) basis 02/28/1961
Goldfields Mining Corp. Ltd. liquidated for Copperfields Mining Corp. Ltd. 01/04/1965 which name changed to Copperfields Mining Corp. (ONT) 04/04/1974 which reincorporated in Canada 08/31/1983 which merged into Teck Corp. 09/02/1983 which name changed to Teck Cominco Ltd. 09/12/2001 which name changed to Teck Resources Ltd. 04/27/2009

GEO STAR RES LTD (BC)
Recapitalized as Northern Energy Corp. 05/03/1977
Each share Common no par exchanged for (0.2) share Common no par
Northern Energy Corp. recapitalized as United Northern Petroleum Corp. 03/24/1986 which name changed to UNP Industries Ltd. 11/06/1989 which recapitalized as International UNP Holdings Ltd. 11/29/1990
(See International UNP Holdings Ltd.)

GEO SURVEYS INC (CO)
Charter cancelled for failure to file annual reports 09/30/1984

GEO 2 LTD (AUSTRALIA)
Each old Sponsored ADR for Ordinary exchanged for (0.33333333) new Sponsored ADR for Ordinary 03/02/2000
Each (13) new Sponsored ADR's for Ordinary exchanged again for (2) new Sponsored ADR's for Ordinary 12/03/2002
ADR basis changed from (1:30) to (1:4.61538431) 12/03/2002
ADR agreement terminated 01/21/2003
Each new Sponsored ADR for Ordinary exchanged for $0.0194 cash

GEO VISION INTL GROUP (NV)
Each share old Common $0.001 par exchanged for (0.1) share new Common $0.001 par 05/19/1997
Recapitalized as Kasten, Inc. 10/15/2013
Each share Common $0.001 par exchanged (0.00333333) share Common $0.001 par

GEOALERT INC (NV)
Each share old Common $0.001 par exchanged for (3) shares new Common $0.001 par 11/29/2001
Charter revoked for failure to file reports and pay fees 03/31/2003

GEOASIA ENTERPRISES LTD (NV)
Name changed to Orion Technologies, Inc. 09/05/1997
(See Orion Technologies, Inc.)

GEOCAN ENERGY INC (AB)
Merged into Arsenal Energy Inc. (New) 10/08/2008
Each share Common no par exchanged for either (0.81) share Common no par or $0.70 cash
Note: Option to receive stock expired 10/03/2008
Arsenal Energy Inc. (New) merged into Prairie Provident Resources Inc. 09/16/2016

GEOCHRON LABORATORIES, INC. (DE)
Completely liquidated 2/8/68
Each share Common 1¢ par exchanged for first and final

distribution of (0.2) share Orion Research Inc. Common 10¢ par
(See Orion Research Inc.)

GEOCITIES (DE)
Merged into Yahoo! Inc. 05/28/1999
Each share Common $0.001 par exchanged for (0.6768) share Common $0.001 par
Yahoo! Inc. name changed to Altaba Inc. 06/19/2017

GEOCORE EXPL INC (BC)
Recapitalized as Emerick Resources Corp. 12/31/2007
Each share Common no par exchanged for (1/3) share Common no par
Emerick Resources Corp. name changed to Medgold Resources Corp. 12/17/2012

GEOCRUDE ENERGY INC (CANADA)
Merged into Canada Northwest Energy Ltd. 12/04/1985
Each share Common no par exchanged for (0.07365) share 9% Retractable Preferred Ser. B $25 par, (0.06249) share Common no par, (0.02355) Common Stock Purchase Warrant expiring 12/15/1989 and (0.08372) share PanCana Minerals Ltd. Common no par
(See each company's listing)

GEODATIC (NJ)
Charter declared void for non-payment of taxes 03/31/1974

GEODEX MINERALS LTD (BC)
Each share old Common no par received distribution of (0.145) share Northcliff Resources Ltd. Common no par payable 07/04/2012 to holders of record 06/28/2012
Ex date - 06/26/2012
Each share old Common no par exchanged for (0.1) share new Common no par 09/20/2012
Each share new Common no par exchanged again for (0.1) share new Common no par 02/09/2016
Reincorporated under the laws of Ontario as Intercontinental Gold & Metals Ltd. 11/06/2017

GEODOME PETROLEUM CORP. (BC)
Reincorporated under the laws of Canada 5/1/78
Geodome Petroleum Corp. (Canada) name changed to Geodome Resources Ltd. 11/16/83 which was acquired by CoCa Mines Inc. 5/5/89 which merged into Hecla Mining Co. 6/26/91

GEODOME PETROLEUM CORP. (CANADA)
Name changed to Geodome Resources Ltd. 11/16/83
Geodome Resources Ltd. acquired by CoCa Mines Inc. 5/5/89 which merged into Hecla Mining Co. 6/26/91

GEODOME RES LTD (CANADA)
Acquired by CoCa Mines Inc. 05/05/1989
Each share Common no par exchanged for (0.281) share Common 1¢ par and (0.1275) Common Stock Purchase Warrant expiring 05/05/1994
CoCa Mines Inc. merged into Hecla Mining Co. 06/26/1991

GEODYNAMICS CORP (CA)
Merged into Logicon, Inc. 3/28/96
Each share Common no par exchanged for $10.76 cash

GEODYNE ENERGY INC (AB)
Recapitalized as Ranchgate Energy Inc. 11/14/2002
Each share Common no par exchanged for (0.33333333) share Common no par
Ranchgate Energy Inc. merged into Clear Energy Inc. 08/25/2004
(See Clear Energy Inc.)

GEODYNE ENERGY INCOME LTD PARTNERSHIP (OK)
Completely liquidated
Each Unit of Ltd. Partnership Int. I-D received first and final distribution of $1.83 cash payable 03/28/2008 to holders of record 03/28/2008
Each Unit of Ltd. Partnership Int. I-E received first and final distribution of $1.43 cash payable 03/28/2008 to holders of record 03/28/2008
Each Unit of Ltd. Partnership Int. I-F received first and final distribution of $1.38 cash payable 03/28/2008 to holders of record 03/28/2008
Each Unit of Ltd. Partnership Int. II-A received first and final distribution of $1.46 cash payable 03/28/2008 to holders of record 03/28/2008
Each Unit of Ltd. Partnership Int. II-B received first and final distribution of $1.58 cash payable 03/28/2008 to holders of record 03/28/2008
Each Unit of Ltd. Partnership Int. II-C received first and final distribution of $1.70 cash payable 03/28/2008 to holders of record 03/28/2008
Each Unit of Ltd. Partnership Int. II-D received first and final distribution of $1.44 cash payable 03/28/2008 to holders of record 03/28/2008
Each Unit of Ltd. Partnership Int. II-E received first and final distribution of $1.35 cash payable 03/28/2008 to holders of record 03/28/2008
Each Unit of Ltd. Partnership Int. II-F received first and final distribution of $1.66 cash payable 03/28/2008 to holders of record 03/28/2008
Each Unit of Ltd. Partnership Int. II-G received first and final distribution of $1.65 cash payable 03/28/2008 to holders of record 03/28/2008
Each Unit of Ltd. Partnership Int. II-H received first and final distribution of $1.58 cash payable 03/28/2008 to holders of record 03/28/2008
Each Unit of Ltd. Partnership Int. III-A received first and final distribution of $1.70 cash payable 03/28/2008 to holders of record 03/28/2008
Each Unit of Ltd. Partnership Int. III-B received first and final distribution of $1.72 cash payable 03/28/2008 to holders of record 03/28/2008
Each Unit of Ltd. Partnership Int. III-C received first and final distribution of $3.06 cash payable 03/28/2008 to holders of record 03/28/2008
Each Unit of Ltd. Partnership Int. III-D received first and final distribution of $2.86 cash payable 03/28/2008 to holders of record 03/28/2008
Each Unit of Ltd. Partnership Int. III-E received first and final distribution of $0.74 cash payable 03/28/2008 to holders of record 03/28/2008
Each Unit of Ltd. Partnership Int. III-F received first and final distribution of $0.90 cash payable 03/28/2008 to holders of record 03/28/2008
Each Unit of Ltd. Partnership Int. III-G received first and final distribution of $1 cash payable 03/28/2008 to holders of record 03/28/2008
Note: Certificates were not required to be surrendered and are without value

GEODYNE INSTL/PENSION ENERGY INCOME LTD PARTNERSHIP (OK)
Completely liquidated
Each Unit of Ltd. Partnership Int. P-1 received first and final distribution of $1.70 cash payable 03/28/2008 to holders of record 03/28/2008
Each Unit of Ltd. Partnership Int. P-2 received first and final distribution of $1.61 cash payable 03/28/2008 to holders of record 03/28/2008
Each Unit of Ltd. Partnership Int. P-3 received first and final distribution of $1.60 cash payable 03/28/2008 to holders of record 03/28/2008
Each Unit of Ltd. Partnership Int. P-4 received first and final distribution of $1.71 cash payable 03/28/2008 to holders of record 03/28/2008
Each Unit of Ltd. Partnership Int. P-5 received first and final distribution of $3.82 cash payable 03/28/2008 to holders of record 03/28/2008
Each Unit of Ltd. Partnership Int. P-6 received first and final distribution of $1.67 cash payable 03/28/2008 to holders of record 03/28/2008
Each Unit of Ltd. Partnership Int. P-7 received first and final distribution of $2.63 cash payable 03/28/2008 to holders of record 03/28/2008
Each Unit of Ltd. Partnership Int. P-8 received first and final distribution of $2.77 cash payable 03/28/2008 to holders of record 03/28/2008
Note: Series P-3 through P-8 were incorporated in Texas
Certificates were not required to be surrendered and are without value

GEODYNE RES INC (DE)
Merged into Samson Investment Co. 3/3/93
Each share Common 10¢ par exchanged for $1.22 cash

GEODYNE TECHNOLOGIES INC (AB)
Recapitalized as Geodyne Energy Inc. 12/24/1999
Each share Common no par exchanged for (0.125) share Common no par
Geodyne Energy Inc. recapitalized as Ranchgate Energy Inc. 11/14/2002 which merged into Clear Energy Inc. 08/25/2004
(See Clear Energy Inc.)

GEOEXPLORATIONS, INC. (NM)
Recapitalized as Harold's Coin-O-Matic, Inc. 9/1/61
Each share Common $10 par exchanged for (10) shares Common $1 par
Harold's Coin-O-Matic, Inc. name changed to Harold's Coin-O-Matics, Inc. 11/27/61 which name was changed to Geo Explorations, Inc. 9/25/62
(See Geo Explorations, Inc.)

GEOEYE INC (DE)
Merged into DigitalGlobe, Inc. 02/01/2013
Each share Common 1¢ par exchanged for (1.137) shares Common $0.001 par and $4.10 cash
DigitalGlobe, Inc. merged into MacDonald, Dettwiler & Associates Ltd. 10/05/2017 which name changed to Maxar Technologies Ltd. 10/10/2017

GEOFFRION LECLERC INC (QC)
Merged into National Bank of Canada (Montreal, QC) 07/01/1989
Each share Class B Subordinate no par exchanged for $3.40 cash

GEOGRAPHICS INC (DE)
Reincorporated 10/18/2000
State of incorporation changed from (WY) to (DE) and Common no par changed to $0.001 par 10/18/2000
Reported out of business 09/00/2002
Details not available

GEOIL LTD. (ON)
Charter surrendered and company dissolved 11/22/65
No stockholders' equity

GEOINFORMATICS EXPL INC (YT)
Each share old Common no par exchanged for (0.1) share new Common no par 12/22/2008
Recapitalized as Kiska Metals Corp. 08/05/2009
Each share Common no par exchanged for (0.33333333) share Common no par

Kiska Metals Corp. merged into AuRico Metals Inc. 03/14/2017
(See AuRico Metals Inc.)

GEOKINETICS INC (DE)
Common 20¢ par changed to 10¢ par 00/00/1997
Common 10¢ par changed to 1¢ par 00/00/1998
Each share old Common 1¢ par exchanged for (0.01) share new Common 1¢ par 05/02/2003
Each share new Common 1¢ par exchanged again for (0.1) share new Common 1¢ par 11/06/2006
Plan of reorganization under Chapter 11 bankruptcy proceedings effective 05/10/2013
No stockholders' equity

GEOLECTRIC CORP (NV)
Note: Although it was reported that this company changed its name from Laand Corp. 00/00/1971, and stock certificates were issued under such name, the change in name was subsequently rescinded in that same year and the company is still known as Laand Corp.
(See Laand Corp.)

GEOLOGIX EXPLORATIONS INC (BC)
Recapitalized as ValOro Resources Inc. 06/28/2018
Each share Common no par exchanged for (0.1) share Common no par

GEOMAQUE EXPLS LTD (QC)
Merged into Defiance Mining Corp. 06/25/2003
Each share Common no par exchanged for (0.125) share Common no par
Defiance Mining Corp. merged into Rio Narcea Gold Mines, Ltd. 09/03/2004
(See Rio Narcea Gold Mines, Ltd.)

GEOMARK EXPL LTD (AB)
Merged into Pine Cliff Energy Ltd. 10/19/2012
Each share Common no par exchanged for (1.5) shares Common no par
Note: Unexchanged certificates were cancelled and became without value 10/19/2017

GEOMETAL MINES LTD. (ON)
Charter cancelled 04/09/1969

GEOMETALS N L (AUSTRALIA)
Merged into Resolute Resources Ltd. 05/24/1989
Each ADR for Ordinary AUD $0.50 par exchanged for $0.40 cash

GEOMETRIC STAMPING CO. (OH)
Liquidated in 1959

GEON CO (DE)
Merged into PolyOne Corp. 8/31/2000
Each share Common 10¢ par exchanged for (2) shares Common 1¢ par

GEON INDUSTRIES, INC. (NY)
Common 10¢ par split (3) for (2) by issuance of (0.5) additional share 5/9/72
Name changed to GI Export Corp. 5/23/77
GI Export Corp. name changed to Johnston Industries Inc. 3/22/85 which reincorporated in Delaware 12/31/87
(See Johnston Industries Inc. (DE))

GEONAUTICS, INC. (DE)
Acquired by Computer Sciences Corp. 04/01/1966
Details not available)

GEONEX CORP (MD)
Plan of reorganization under Chapter 11 Federal Bankruptcy proceedings confirmed 12/21/1995
No stockholders' equity

GEONICS INC (CO)
Name changed to Variegate Properties, Inc. 02/13/1979
Variegate Properties, Inc. name changed to Applied Solar Technologies, Inc. 09/21/1981
(See Applied Solar Technologies, Inc.)

GEONOVA EXPLS INC (BC)
Merged into Campbell Resources Inc. (New) 06/30/2001
Each share Common no par exchanged for (0.1) share Common no par
(See Campbell Resources Inc. (New))

GEONOVUS MEDIA CORP (BC)
Each share old Common no par exchanged for (0.1) share new Common no par 07/20/2015
Name changed to Imagination Park Entertainment Inc. 05/09/2016

GEONOVUS MINERALS CORP (BC)
Name changed to GeoNovus Media Corp. 04/10/2015
GeoNovus Media Corp. name changed to Imagination Park Entertainment Inc. 05/09/2016

GEOPHARMA INC (FL)
Plan of reorganization under Chapter 11 Federal Bankruptcy proceedings effective 03/19/2013
No stockholders' equity

GEOPHYSICAL FIELD SURVEYS INC (DE)
Reincorporated 4/28/83
State of incorporation changed from (MS) to (DE) 4/28/83
Merged into Digicon Inc. 4/29/83
Each share Common $1 par exchanged for $8.75 cash

GEOPHYSICAL MICRO COMPUTER APPLICATIONS LTD. (AB)
Name changed to NetDriven Solutions Inc. 03/07/2000
NetDriven Solutions Inc. name changed to NetDriven Storage Solutions Inc. 03/30/2001 which recapitalized as Cervus Financial Group Inc. 07/15/2004
(See Cervus Financial Group Inc.)

GEOPHYSICAL PROSPECTING INC (ON)
Name changed to Revolution Technologies Inc. 03/18/2008

GEOPHYSICAL SYS CORP (CA)
Stock Dividend - 50% 1/29/82
Charter suspended for failure to file reports and pay fees 10/1/93

GEOPHYSICS CORP. OF AMERICA (DE)
Name changed to GCA Corp. 1/20/65
GCA Corp. acquired by General Signal Corp. 6/7/88 which merged into SPX Corp. 10/6/98

GEOQUEST RES LTD (BC)
Recapitalized as Claytron Energy Corp. 12/13/1976
Each share Common 50¢ par exchanged for (0.25) share Common no par
Claytron Energy Corp. merged into International Interlake Industries Inc. 12/31/1986
(See International Interlake Industries Inc.)

GEOR MINE & OIL LTD. (BC)
Name changed to Caprice Resources Inc. 10/26/1976
(See Caprice Resources Inc.)

GEORESEARCH, INC. (DE)
Under plan of merger name changed to Dorchester Gas Producing Co. 1/2/62
Dorchester Gas Producing Co. merged into Panoil Co. 11/26/68 which name changed to Dorchester Gas Corp. 2/1/72
(See Dorchester Gas Corp.)

GEORESOURCES INC (CO)
Merged into Halcon Resources Corp. 08/01/2012
Each share Common 1¢ par exchanged for (1.932) shares Common $0.0001 par and $20 cash

GEORGE DOLLARS (CA)
Merged into Candy Mountain Gold Mines, Ltd. in January 1984
Each share Common 50¢ par exchanged for (10) shares Common $0.001 par
(See Candy Mountain Gold Mines, Ltd.)

GEORGE ENTERPRISE MINING CO. LTD. (BC)
Struck off register and declared dissolved for failure to file returns 06/19/1978

GEORGE GOLD-COPPER MINING CO., LTD. (BC)
Completely liquidated 03/17/1978
Each share Capital Stock $1 par exchanged for first and final distribution of $0.020049 cash

GEORGE MASON BANKSHARES INC (VA)
Common $2.50 par changed to $1.66 par and (0.5) additional share issued 3/20/92
Common $1.66 par split (3) for (2) by issuance of (0.5) additional share payable 2/9/96 to holders of record 1/31/96
Merged into United Bankshares, Inc. 4/3/98
Each share Common $1.66 par exchanged for (1.7) shares Common $2.50 par

GEORGE RESOURCE LTD (BC)
Recapitalized as Rocca Resources Ltd. 5/11/98
Each share Common no par exchanged for (0.1) share Common no par
Rocca Resources Ltd. name changed to Siegesoft Internet Solutions Inc. 3/27/2000 which name changed to Zimtu Technologies Inc. 10/26/2000 which recapitalized as International Zimtu Technologies Inc. (BC) 4/4/2003 which reincorporated in Canada as Petrol One Corp. 9/26/2006

GEORGE WASHINGTON CORP (DE)
Recapitalized as Oxbow Resources Corp. 11/21/2006
Each share Common $1 par exchanged for (0.05) share Common $0.001 par
Oxbow Resources Corp. recapitalized as Texas Sweet Crude Oil Corp. 12/31/2008
(See Texas Sweet Crude Oil Corp.)

GEORGE WASHINGTON LIFE INS CO (WV)
Each share Common $1 exchanged for (0.000379) share Common $2,660 par 03/08/1976
Note: In effect holders received $4.67 cash per share and public interest was eliminated

GEORGETOWN BANCORP INC (MD)
Acquired by Salem Five Bancorp 05/23/2017
Each share Common 1¢ par exchanged for $26 cash

GEORGETOWN BANCORP INC (USA)
Reorganized under the laws of Maryland 07/11/2012
Each share Common 10¢ par exchanged for (0.72014) share Common 1¢ par
(See Georgetown Bancorp, Inc. (MD))

GEORGETOWN CAP CORP (BC)
Name changed to Auryn Resources Inc. 10/15/2013

GEORGETOWN LIFE INS CO (IL)
Under plan of merger each share Common $1 par automatically became (2) shares Exchange Investment Corp. Class A Common 50¢ par 9/30/75
Exchange Investment Corp. merged into Fiduciary & General Corp. 10/22/81
(See Fiduciary & General Corp.)

GEORGETOWN RACING INC (DE)
Assets sold for the benefit of creditors 09/30/1974
No stockholders' equity

GEORGIA BANCSHARES INC (GA)
Ctfs. dated prior to 11/13/84
Merged into Bank South Corp. 11/13/84
Each share Common $8 par exchanged for (1.1) shares Common $5 par
Bank South Corp. merged into NationsBank Corp. 1/9/96 which reincorporated in Delaware as BankAmerica Corp. (Old) 9/25/98 which merged into BankAmerica Corp. (New) 9/30/98 which name changed to Bank of America Corp. 4/28/99

GEORGIA BANCSHARES INC (GA)
Ctfs. dated after 08/05/1995
Common $4 par split (5) for (2) by issuance of (1.5) additional shares payable 09/02/1998 to holders of record 06/23/1998
Merged into First Sterling Banks Inc. (Old) 04/23/1999
Each share Common $4 par exchanged for (1) share Common no par
First Sterling Banks, Inc. (Old) name changed to First Sterling Banks, Inc. (New) 05/24/2000 which name changed to Main Street Banks, Inc. (New) 01/02/2001

GEORGIA BK & TR (CALHOUN, GA)
Merged into Synovus Financial Corp. 12/18/98
Each share Common no par exchanged for (3.4612) shares Common $1 par

GEORGIA BK & TR CO (MACON, GA)
Merged into Georgia Bancshares, Inc. 3/30/79
Each share Capital Stock $8 par exchanged for (1) share Common $8 par
Georgia Bancshares, Inc. merged into Bank South Corp. 11/13/84 which merged into NationsBank Corp. 1/9/96 which reincorporated in Delaware as BankAmerica Corp. (Old) 9/25/98 which merged into BankAmerica Corp. (New) 9/30/98 which name changed to Bank of America Corp. 4/28/99

GEORGIA BK FINL CORP (GA)
Common $1 par split (2) for (1) by issuance of (1) additional share payable 11/21/2003 to holders of record 10/31/2003 Ex date - 11/24/2003
Stock Dividends - 15% payable 08/31/1999 to holders of record 08/06/1999; 15% payable 08/31/2001 to holders of record 08/10/2001; 10% payable 08/29/2003 to holders of record 08/08/2003 Ex date - 08/15/2003
Name changed to Southeastern Bank Financial Corp. 08/01/2005
Southeastern Bank Financial Corp. merged into South State Corp. 01/03/2017

GEORGIA BONDED FIBRES INC (NJ)
Class A Common 10¢ par reclassified as Common 10¢ par 10/31/1967
Class B Common 10¢ par reclassified as Common 10¢ par 10/31/1967
Common 10¢ par split (2) for (1) by issuance of (1) additional share 06/01/1982
Stock Dividends - 50% 03/17/1980; 10% 09/30/1985; 10% 11/30/1988
Reincorporated under the laws of Virginia as Bontex, Inc. 12/16/1996
(See Bontex, Inc.)

GEORGIA CAROLINA BANCSHARES INC (GA)
Common $0.001 par split (2) for (1) by issuance of (1) additional share payable 01/30/2004 to holders of record 01/05/2004 Ex date - 02/02/2004
Common $0.001 par split (5) for (4) by issuance of (0.25) additional share payable 04/01/2005 to holders of record 03/01/2005 Ex date - 04/04/2005
Stock Dividends - 20% payable 12/01/2001 to holders of record 11/15/2001 Ex date - 11/13/2001; 15% payable 12/16/2002 to holders of record 12/02/2002 Ex date - 11/27/2002
Merged into State Bank Financial Corp. 01/01/2015
Each share Common $0.001 par exchanged for (0.794) share Common 1¢ par and $8.85 cash

GEORGIA-CAROLINA BRICK CO.
Reorganized as Georgia Carolina Brick & Tile Co. in 1936
No stockholders' equity

GEORGIA-CAROLINA CHEMICAL CO. (GA)
Liquidated in 1954

GEORGIA CAS & SURETY CO (GA)
Each share Common $10 par exchanged for (2) shares Common $5 par 1/20/56
Each share Common $5 par exchanged for (5) shares Common $1 par 4/15/58
Stock Dividends - 50% 12/20/74; 10% 8/15/78; 100% 11/28/80
Acquired by Atlantic American Corp. in 1981
Details not available

GEORGIA CASH CREDIT CORP.
Merged into Franklin Plan Corp. in 1932
Details not available

GEORGIA CASUALTY CO. (GA)
Merged into Public Indemnity Co. 07/12/1930
Details not available

GEORGIA COMM BANCSHARES INC (GA)
Merged into IBERIABANK Corp. 05/31/2015
Each share Common $1 par exchanged for (0.6134) share Common $1 par

GEORGIA CONTINENTAL TELEPHONE CO. (GA)
6% Preferred $25 par called for redemption 9/12/57

GEORGIA EXPL INC (NV)
Common $0.001 par split (12) for (1) by issuance of (11) additional shares payable 08/21/2006 to holders of record 08/14/2006 Ex date - 08/22/2006
Name changed to Gulf Western Petroleum Corp. 03/08/2007
Gulf Western Petroleum Corp. recapitalized as Wholehealth Products, Inc. 09/17/2012

GEORGIA FACTOR & FINANCE CORP. (GA)
Name changed to Georgia Factors, Inc. 02/14/1968
(See Georgia Factors, Inc.)

GEORGIA FACTORS INC (GA)
Administratively dissolved 06/06/1985

GEORGIA FED BK FSB (ATLANTA, GA)
Merged into Fuqua Industries, Inc. 04/01/1986
Each share Common $1 par exchanged for $27.75 cash

GEORGIA FIRST BANK (GAINESVILLE, GA)
Merged into Dahlonega Bancorp, Inc. 9/11/89
Each share Common $5 par exchanged for (2.894) shares Common $1 par
Dahlonega Bancorp, Inc. recapitalized as Century South Banks, Inc. 11/30/89 which merged into BB&T Corp. 6/7/2001

GEORGIA FIRST SAVINGS & LOAN ASSOCIATION (GA)
Under plan of reorganization each share Common $5 par automatically became (1) share Georgia First Bank (Gainesville, GA) Common $5 par 12/6/85
Georgia First Bank (Gainesville, GA) merged into Dahlonega Bancorp, Inc. 9/11/89 which recapitalized as Century South Banks, Inc. 11/30/89 which merged into BB&T Corp. 6/7/2001

GEORGIA 400 INDS INC (GA)
Proclaimed dissolved for failure to file annual reports 07/09/2005

GEORGIA GULF CORP (DE)
Common 5¢ par split (2) for (1) by issuance of (1) additional share 01/27/1989
Preferred Stock Purchase Rights declared for Common stockholders of record 10/31/1986 were redeemed at $0.01 per right 05/03/1990 for holders of record 04/26/1990
Under plan of reorganization each share Common 5¢ par exchanged for $8.50 principal amount of 15% Sr. Subordinated Notes due 04/15/2000, (1) share old Common 1¢ par and $30 cash 04/27/1990
Each share old Common 1¢ par exchanged for (0.04) share new Common 1¢ par 07/29/2009
Name changed to Axiall Corp. 01/29/2013
(See Axiall Corp.)

GEORGIA HARDWOOD LUMBER CO.
Name changed to Georgia-Pacific Plywood & Lumber Co. 00/00/1948
Georgia-Pacific Plywood & Lumber Co. name changed to Georgia-Pacific Plywood Co. 00/00/1951 which name changed to Georgia-Pacific Corp. 04/27/1956
(See Georgia-Pacific Corp.)

GEORGIA HOME INSURANCE CO.
Merged into Home Insurance Co. in 1948
Each share Capital Stock $10 par exchanged for (1.299) shares Common $5 par
(See Home Insurance Co.)

GEORGIA INTL CORP (GA)
Acquired by Capital Holding Corp. 12/31/72
Each share Common $1 par exchanged for (1) share Common $1 par
Capital Holding Corp. name changed to Providian Corp. 5/12/94 which merged into Aegon N.V. 6/10/97

GEORGIA INTERNATIONAL LIFE INSURANCE CO. (GA)
Common $2.50 par changed to $1 par 04/10/1961
Completely liquidated 12/31/1967
Each share Common $1 par exchanged for first and final distribution of (1) share Georgia International Corp. Common $1 par
Georgia International Corp. acquired by Capital Holding Corp. 12/31/1972 which name changed to Providian Corp. 05/12/1994 which merged into Aegon N.V. 06/10/1997

GEORGIA INTL MNG CORP (NV)
Recapitalized as Jinhao Motor Co. 07/02/2010
Each share Common $0.001 par exchanged for (0.590362) share Common $0.001 par
(See Jinhao Motor Co.)

GEORGIA INVT CORP (AB)
Name changed to Environmental Technologies Inc. 05/28/1990
(See Environmental Technologies Inc.)

GEORGIA INVS INC (GA)
Class A Common $1 par and Class B Common $1 par reclassified as Common $1 par 05/25/1959
Adjudicated bankrupt 03/17/1982
Stockholders' equity unlikely

GEORGIA LAKE LITHIUM MINES LTD. (ON)
Name changed to Georgia Lake Mines Ltd. 08/25/1966
(See Georgia Lake Mines Ltd.)

GEORGIA LAKE MINES LTD (ON)
Charter cancelled for failure to pay taxes and file returns 03/16/1976

GEORGIA LIFE & HEALTH INS CO (GA)
Each share Common $5 par exchanged for (5) shares Common $1 par 1/19/65
Merged into Georgia Investors, Inc. 7/26/71
Each share Common $1 par exchanged for (1.25) shares Common $1 par
(See Georgia Investors, Inc.)

GEORGIA LIGHT, POWER & RAILWAY
Acquired by Georgia Light, Power & Railways, Inc. in 1928
Details not available

GEORGIA LIGHT, POWER & RAILWAYS, INC.
Dissolved in 1931

GEORGIA MARBLE CO (GA)
Each share Common $100 par exchanged for (10) shares Common $10 par in 1946
Stock Dividend - 50% 9/1/54
Merged into Walter (Jim) Corp. 2/21/69
Each share 5% Preferred $100 par exchanged for (0.05) share 3rd Preferred Ser. 4 no par
Each share Common $10 par exchanged for (0.181818) share 3rd Conv. Preferred Ser. 3 no par
(See Walter (Jim) Corp.)

GEORGIA NATL BK (ATHENS, GA)
Merged into SouthTrust Corp. 11/23/1998
Each share Common no par exchanged for (0.6) share Common $2.50 par
SouthTrust Corp. merged into Wachovia Corp. (Ctfs. dated after 09/01/2001) 11/01/2004 which merged into Wells Fargo & Co. (New) 12/31/2008

GEORGIA PAC CORP (GA)
5% Conv. Preferred $100 par called for redemption 3/25/64
5% Conv. Preferred $100 par called for redemption 5/25/64
Common $1 par split (2) for (1) by issuance of (1) additional share 9/28/56
Common $1 par changed to 80¢ par and (0.25) additional share issued 6/25/59
Common 80¢ par split (5) for (4) by issuance of (0.25) additional share 6/19/64
Common 80¢ par split (5) for (4) by issuance of (0.25) additional share 6/23/66
Common 80¢ par split (2) for (1) by issuance of (1) additional share 6/25/69
Common 80¢ par split (3) for (2) by issuance of (0.5) additional share 8/12/76
Common 80¢ par reclassified as Common-Georgia Pacific Group 80¢ par 12/16/97
Common-Georgia Pacific Group 80¢ par received distribution of (1) share Common-Timber Group 80¢ par payable 12/17/97 to holders of record 12/16/97 Ex date - 12/17/97
Common-Georgia Pacific Group 80¢ par split (2) for (1) by issuance of (1) additional share payable 6/4/99 to holders of record 5/14/99 Ex date - 6/4/99
Common-Georgia Pacific Group 80¢ par reclassified as Common 80¢ par 12/21/2001
$1.64 Conv. Preferred no par called for redemption 5/28/71
$1.40 Conv. Preferred no par called for redemption 12/11/72
Adjustable Rate Conv. Preferred Ser. A no par called for redemption 4/15/87
Adjustable Rate Conv. Preferred Ser. B no par called for redemption 4/15/87
Adjustable Rate Conv. Preferred Ser. B 2nd Issue no par called for redemption 4/15/87
Adjustable Rate Conv. Preferred Ser. C no par called for redemption 4/15/87
Merged into Plum Creek Timber Co., Inc. 10/6/2001
Each share Common-Timber Group 80¢ par exchanged for (1.37) shares Common 1¢ par
Each 7.5% Premium Equity Participating Securities Unit exchanged for (1.0554) shares Common 1¢ par 8/16/2002
(See Plum Creek Timber Co., Inc.)
Merged into Koch Industries, Inc. 12/23/2005
Each share Common-Georgia Pacific Group 80¢ par exchanged for $48 cash

GEORGIA-PACIFIC PLYWOOD & LUMBER CO.
Name changed to Georgia-Pacific Plywood Co. in 1951
Georgia-Pacific Plywood Co. name changed to Georgia-Pacific Corp. 4/27/56
(See Georgia-Pacific Corp.)

GEORGIA-PACIFIC PLYWOOD CO. (GA)
Each share $2.25 Preferred no par exchanged for (0.45) share 5% Preferred $100 par 5/5/55
Name changed to Georgia-Pacific Corp. 4/27/56
(See Georgia-Pacific Corp.)

GEORGIA PWR CAP L P (DE)
9% Guaranted Monthly Income Preferred Securities Ser. A called for redemption at $25 on 12/20/99

GEORGIA PWR CAP TR (DE)
Issue Information - 8,000,000 TR IV GTD TR PFD SECS 6.85% offered at $25 per security on 02/17/1999
6.85% Trust IV Guaranteed Preferred Securities called for redemption at $25 on 02/25/2004
Issue Information - 16,000,000 TR V GTD TR PFD SECS 7.125% offered at $25 per security on 06/13/2002
7.125% Trust V Guaranteed Preferred Securities called for redemption at $25 plus $0.400779 accrued dividends on 06/21/2007

GEORGIA PWR CAP TR I (DE)
7.75% Trust Preferred Securities called for redemption at $25 on 07/19/2002

GEORGIA PWR CAP TR II (DE)
Issue Information - 7,000,000 shares TR PFD SECS 7.60% offered at $25 per share on 01/09/1997
7.60% Trust Preferred Securities called for redemption at $25 plus $0.343056 accrued dividends on 12/06/2002

GEORGIA PWR CAP TR III (DE)
7.75% Quarterly Income Preferred Securities called for redemption $25 on 07/19/2002

GEORGIA PWR CAP TR VII (DE)
Issue Information - 8,000,000 TR PFD SECS offered at $25 per share on 01/15/2004
5-7/8% Trust Preferred Securities called for redemption at $25 on 09/23/2011

GEORGIA PWR CO (GA)
$3.76 Class A Preferred no par called for redemption 07/17/1987
$3.44 Class A Preferred no par called for redemption 11/23/1987
$3 Class A Preferred no par called for redemption 04/02/1990
$2.75 Class A Preferred no par called for redemption 11/30/1990
$2.52 Class A Preferred no par called for redemption 12/09/1991
$2.56 Class A Preferred no par called for redemption 12/09/1991
$2.47 Class A Preferred no par called for redemption 03/02/1992
$2.30 Class A Preferred no par called for redemption 08/28/1992
$9.08 Preferred no par called for redemption 08/28/1992
$2.43 Class A Preferred no par called for redemption 07/01/1993
$2.50 Class A Preferred no par called for redemption 07/01/1993
Adjustable Rate Class A 1st Preferred 1984 Ser. no par called for redemption 07/18/1993
$8.20 Preferred no par called for redemption 07/18/1993
$8.76 Preferred no par called for redemption 07/18/1993
Adjustable Rate Class A 1st Preferred 1985 Ser. no par called for redemption 11/20/1993
Adjustable Rate Class A 2nd Preferred 1985 Ser. no par called for redemption 12/02/1993
$7.80 Preferred no par called for redemption 08/02/1996
$2.125 Class A Preferred no par called for redemption 11/02/1996
$1.90 Class A Preferred no par called for redemption 01/02/1997
$7.72 Preferred no par called for redemption 02/10/1997
$1.9875 Class A Preferred no par called for redemption at $25 on 06/02/1997
$1.9375 Class A Preferred no par called for redemption at $25 on 08/18/1997
$1.925 Class A Preferred no par called for redemption at $25 plus $0.32618 accrued dividends on 12/02/1997
Class A Preferred 1993 Ser. no par called for redemption at $25 on 06/02/1998
Class A Preferred 2nd 1993 Ser. no par called for redemption at $25 on 10/02/1998
$4.60 Preferred Ser. 62 no par called for redemption at $102.70 on 01/04/1999
$4.60 Preferred Ser. 63 no par called for redemption at $102.47 on 01/04/1999
$4.60 Preferred Ser. 64 no par called for redemption at $102.70 on 01/04/1999
$4.72 Preferred no par called for

redemption at $102.68 on 01/04/1999
$4.92 Preferred no par called for redemption at $104.50 on 01/04/1999
$4.96 Preferred no par called for redemption at $103.49 on 01/04/1999
$5 Preferred no par called for redemption at $104.50 on 01/04/1999
$5.64 Preferred no par called for redemption at $103.03 on 01/04/1999
$6.48 Preferred no par called for redemption at $103.18 on 01/04/1999
$6.60 Preferred no par called for redemption at $103.19 on 01/04/1999
$4.60 Preferred no par called for redemption at $107 on 01/17/2006
6.125% Class A Preferred $25 par called for redemption at $25 plus $0.09783 accrued dividends on 10/24/2017
6.5% Non-Cum. Preference Ser. 2007 $100 par called for redemption at $100 plus $0.415278 accrued dividends on 10/24/2017
Public interest eliminated

GEORGIA RAILWAY & POWER CO.
Merged into Georgia Power Co. 00/00/1927
Details not available

GEORGIA SVGS BK & TR CO (ATLANTA, GA)
Name changed to Hamilton Bank & Trust Co. (Atlanta, GA) 05/09/1974
(See Hamilton Bank & Trust Co. (Atlanta, GA))

GEORGIA SECURITIES CO.
Liquidated in 1945

GEORGIA SHOE MANUFACTURING CO., INC. (GA)
Completely liquidated 7/13/67
Each share Common $1 par exchanged for first and final distribution of (0.722891) share U.S. Industries, Inc. Common $1 par
(See U.S. Industries, Inc.)

GEORGIA STRAIT RES LTD (BC)
Struck off register and declared dissolved for failure to file returns 05/22/1992

GEORGIA VENTURES INC (BC)
Name changed to Creston Moly Corp. 10/19/2007
Creston Moly Corp. merged into Mercator Minerals Ltd. 06/21/2011

GEORGIAN APARTMENTS
Trust terminated in 1951
Details not available

GEORGIAN BANCORP INC (ON)
Delisted from Canadian Venture Stock Exchange 03/25/2002

GEORGIAN HOTEL CO. (IL)
Liquidation completed 9/27/63

GEORGIAN MINERAL INDUSTRIES LTD. (CANADA)
Assets sold for benefit of debentureholders and dissolved 06/24/1967
No stockholders' equity

GEOROX RES INC (CANADA)
Each share old Common no par exchanged for (0.33333333) share new Common no par 05/02/2016
Name changed to Prospera Energy Inc. 07/19/2018

GEOS COMMUNICATIONS INC (WA)
SEC revoked common stock registration 10/10/2014

GEOS CORP (DE)
Merged into Rodel Inc. 12/28/1983
Each share Common 1¢ par exchanged for $6 cash

GEOSCIENCE CORP (NV)
Merged into Sercel Acquisition Corp. 12/14/99
Each share Common 1¢ par exchanged for $6.71 cash

GEOSCIENCE INSTRS CORP (NY)
Reincorporated under the laws of Delaware as Geos Corp. 07/16/1973
(See Geos Corp.)

GEOSCIENCE TECHNOLOGY SVCS CORP (DE)
Name changed to GTS Corp. 05/12/1981
(See GTS Corp.)

GEOSCIENCES EXPLORATION INC. (UT)
Name changed to Auriga Geosciences, Inc. 04/01/1983
Auriga Geosciences, Inc. recapitalized as Deltek Intertrade Corp. 09/15/1986
(See Deltek Intertrade Corp.)

GEOSCOPIX INC (CO)
Recapitalized as Fight Zone, Inc. 03/03/2008
Each (30) shares Common $0.001 par exchanged for (1) share Common $0.001 par

GEOSEARCH INC (NY)
Class A 3-1/3¢ par reclassified as Common 3-1/3¢ par 8/22/78
Common 3-1/3¢ par changed to 1¢ par and (2) additional shares issued 4/9/80
Dissolved by proclamation 12/24/91

GEOSOURCE INC (DE)
Common $1 par split (2) for (1) by issuance of (1) additional share 12/2/80
Acquired by Aetna Life & Casualty Co. 7/1/82
Each share Common $1 par exchanged for (1.25) shares Common no par
Aetna Life & Casualty Co. name changed to Aetna, Inc. (CT) 7/19/96 which merged ING Groep N.V. 12/13/2000

GEOSPACE TECHNOLOGIES CORP (DE)
Common 1¢ par split (2) for (1) by issuance of (1) additional share payable 10/18/2012 to holders of record 10/15/2012 Ex date - 10/19/2012
Reincorporated under the laws of Texas 04/20/2015

GEOSPATIAL HLDGS INC (NV)
Name changed to Geospatial Corp. 08/18/2015

GEOSTAR METALS INC (BC)
Name changed to Skana Capital Corp. (BC) 11/27/2006
Skana Capital Corp. (BC) reincorporated in Alberta as MENA Hydrocarbons Inc. 06/22/2011

GEOSTAR MINERAL CORP (NV)
Common $0.00001 par split (10) for (1) by issuance of (9) additional shares payable 03/12/2009 to holders of record 02/17/2009 Ex date - 03/13/2009
Name changed to Advanced BioMedical Technologies, Inc. 03/13/2009

GEOSTAR MNG CORP (BC)
Struck off register and declared dissolved for failure to file returns 08/22/1994

GEOTEC INC (FL)
Name changed from Geotec Thermal Generators, Inc. to Geotec, Inc. 06/04/2007
SEC revoked common stock registration 08/27/2010

GEOTECH CAP CORP (BC)
Recapitalized as Vector Venture Corp. 12/31/1991

Each share Common no par exchanged for (0.4) share Common no par
Vector Venture Corp. acquired by Vector Environmental Technologies, Inc. 08/29/1995 which name changed to WaterPur International, Inc. 07/07/1997 which recapitalized as Aquentium, Inc. 05/22/2002

GEOTECH OIL CORP (DE)
Name changed to Walton-Vairex Corp. 12/30/1971
Walton-Vairex Corp. name changed to M.S.E. Cable Systems, Inc. 11/07/1984
(See M.S.E. Cable Systems, Inc.)

GEOTECH RES INC (BC)
Name changed to Sea-1 Aquafarms Ltd. 05/15/1986
Sea-1 Aquafarms Ltd. recapitalized as General Sea Harvest Corp. 11/26/1987 which recapitalized as Consolidated General Sea Harvest Corp. 06/12/1990
(See Consolidated General Sea Harvest Corp.)

GEOTECHNICAL CORP. (DE)
Acquired by Teledyne, Inc. 08/11/1965
Each share Common $1 par exchanged for (0.33333333) share Common $1 par
Teledyne, Inc. merged into Allegheny Teledyne, Inc. 08/15/1996 which name changed to Allegheny Technologies Inc. 11/29/1999

GEOTECHNICS & RESOURCES, INC. (NY)
Under plan of merger each share Capital Stock 25¢ par exchanged for (1) share Class A Common 25¢ par 1/5/62
Adjudicated bankrupt 11/26/63
No stockholders' equity

GEOTECK INTL INC (NV)
Name changed to Marine Shuttle Operations Inc. 06/05/1998
(See Marine Shuttle Operations Inc.)

GEOTEK COMMUNICATIONS INC. (DE)
Name changed 2/16/94
Name changed from Geotek Industries, Inc. to Geotek Communications, Inc. 2/16/94
Liquidating plan of reorganization effective 3/10/2000
No stockholders' equity

GEOTEL COMMUNICATIONS CORP (DE)
Issue Information - 2,200,000 shares COM offered at $12 per share on 11/20/1996
Common 1¢ par split (2) for (1) by issuance of (1) additional share payable 9/22/98 to holders of record 8/31/98
Merged into Cisco Systems, Inc. 6/24/99
Each share Common 1¢ par exchanged for (1.0276) shares Common no par

GEOTEL INC (DE)
Charter cancelled and declared inoperative and void for non-payment of taxes 06/23/1988

GEOTELE COM INC (DE)
Each share old Common 1¢ par exchanged for (0.1) share new Common 1¢ par 11/30/2001
Recapitalized as Anthem Investment Corp. 10/18/2002
Each share Common 1¢ par exchanged for (0.00714285) share Common 1¢ par
Anthem Investment Corp. recapitalized as Wysak Petroleum Inc. 04/24/2003 which name changed to Wild Brush Energy Inc. 04/11/2006

GEOTHERMAL KINETICS, INC. (NV)
Merged into United Siscoe Mines

Inc.-Les Mines United Siscoe Inc. 07/07/1981
Each share Common 1¢ par exchanged for $9.15 cash

GEOTHERMAL RES INTL INC (DE)
Common $1 par changed to 50¢ par 07/05/1967
Each share old Common 50¢ par exchanged for (0.25) share new Common 50¢ par 01/07/1975
Plan of reorganization under Chapter 11 Federal Bankruptcy proceedings confirmed 04/19/1991
No stockholders' equity

GEOTRAQ INC (NV)
Name changed to GoTraq Inc. 11/01/2016
GoTraq Inc. name changed to MJ Venture Partners, Inc. 04/10/2018

GEOVAX LABS INC (IL)
Reincorporated under the laws of Delaware 06/18/2008

GEOVENCAP INC (AB)
Filed a notice under the Bankruptcy and Insolvency Act 11/19/2013
Stockholders' equity unlikely

GEOVEX PETE CORP (ON)
Merged into Flying Cross Resources Ltd. 12/04/1985
Each share Common no par exchanged for (0.25) share Common no par
Flying Cross Resources Ltd. merged into International Larder Minerals Inc. 05/01/1986 which merged into Explorers Alliance Corp. 10/13/2000
(See Explorers Alliance Corp.)

GEOWASTE INC (DE)
Merged into Superior Services Inc. 11/2/98
Each share Common 10¢ par exchanged for (0.0964) share Common $0.001 par

GEOWORKS CORP (DE)
Reincorporated 10/08/1997
Name and state of incorporation changed from Geoworks (CA) to Geoworks Corp. (DE) and Common no par changed to $0.001 par 10/08/1997
Name changed to NCM Services Inc. 05/27/2010

GERA CORP. (DE)
Merged 07/28/1964
6% Preferred no par called for redemption 11/08/1963
Merged from Gera Corp. (NJ) to Gera Corp. (DE) 07/28/1964
Each share Common $100 par exchanged for (1) share Common $100 par
Merged into Glen Alden Corp. 07/24/1972
Each share Common $100 par exchanged for $6,125 cash

GERA MILLS (NJ)
Capital Stock $8.50 par changed to $1 par 00/00/1954
Recapitalized as Gera Corp. (NJ) 00/00/1954
Each share Capital Stock $1 par exchanged for (0.01) share Capital Stock $100 par
Gera Corp. (NJ) merged into Gera Corp. (DE) 07/28/1964
(See Gera Corp. (DE))

GERAGHTY & MILLER INC (DE)
Merged into Heidemij N.V. 12/29/1993
Each share Common 1¢ par exchanged for (1.09) shares Common
Heidemij N.V. name changed to Arcadis N.V. 12/24/1997

GERALD STEVENS INC (DE)
Each share old Common $0.06-2/3 par exchanged for (0.2) share new Common $0.06-2/3 par 11/28/2000
Plan of reorganization under Chapter

11 Federal Bankruptcy Code effective 4/22/2004
No stockholders' equity

GERALDTON LONG LAC GOLD MINES, LTD. (ON)
Charter cancelled 11/05/1956

GERANT INDS INC (NV)
Each share old Common $0.0001 par exchanged for (0.01) share new Common $0.0001 par 3/16/94
Reorganized under Chapter 11 Federal Bankruptcy Code as Xplorer, S.A. 12/16/96
Each share new Common $0.0001 par exchanged for (0.2) share Common $0.001 par and (1) Common Stock Purchase Warrant expiring 8/5/97
Xplorer, S.A. name changed to Netholdings.com Inc. 12/8/99 which name changed to Global Axcess Corp. 5/9/2001

GERARD INDS INTL CORP (FL)
Name changed to Harvey (Walter) Corp. 6/7/72
(See Harvey (Walter) Corp.)

GERBER CHILDRENSWEAR INC (DE)
Issue Information - 3,600,000 shares COM offered at $13 per share on 06/10/1998
Merged into Kellwood Co. 06/26/2002
Each share Common 1¢ par exchanged for (0.11823) share Common 1¢ par and $3.42 cash
(See Kellwood Co.)

GERBER ENERGY INTL INC (CO)
Name changed to Gold King Consolidated, Inc. 06/16/1987
(See Gold King Consolidated, Inc.)

GERBER PRODS CO (MI)
Common $10 par split (2) for (1) by issuance of (1) additional share 00/00/1953
Common $10 par changed to $5 par and (1) additional share issued 05/10/1961
Common $5 par changed to $2.50 par and (1) additional share issued 08/14/1964
Common $2.50 par split (3) for (2) by issuance of (0.5) additional share 07/09/1982
Common $2.50 par split (3) for (2) by issuance of (0.5) additional share 07/06/1984
Common Stock Purchase Rights declared for Common stockholders of record 04/04/1986 were redeemed at $0.05 per right 09/10/1990 for holders of record 08/13/1990
Common $2.50 par split (2) for (1) by issuance of (1) additional share 09/11/1989
Common $2.50 par split (2) for (1) by issuance of (1) additional share 09/10/1992
Stock Dividends - 100% 03/30/1948; 50% 03/09/1955
Merged into SL Sub Corp. 08/26/1994
Each share Common $2.50 par exchanged for $53 cash

GERBER SCIENTIFIC INC (CT)
Name changed 10/04/1978
Common no par changed to $1 par and (1) additional share issued 10/21/68
Name changed from Gerber Scientific Instrument Co. to Gerber Scientific Inc. 10/04/1978
Common $1 par split (3) for (2) by issuance of (0.5) additional share 11/08/1978
Common $1 par split (2) for (1) by issuance of (1) additional share 12/28/1979
Common $1 par split (2) for (1) by issuance of (1) additional share 11/04/1980
Common $1 par split (3) for (2) by issuance of (0.5) additional share 08/08/1983
Common $1 par split (3) for (2) by issuance of (0.5) additional share 09/20/1984
Common $1 par split (3) for (2) by issuance of (0.5) additional share 07/22/1987
Common $1 par changed to 1¢ par 09/22/2004
Acquired by Vector Knife Holdings (Cayman), Ltd. 08/22/2011
Each share Common 1¢ par exchanged for $11 cash and (1) Contingent Value Right

GERBER SYS TECHNOLOGY INC (CT)
Merged into Gerber Scientific Inc. 3/12/87
Each share Common 2¢ par exchanged for $2.25 cash

GERDAU AMERISTEEL CORP (CANADA)
Reincorporated 05/24/2006
Place of incorporation changed from (ON) to (Canada) 05/24/2006
Acquired by Gerdau S.A. 08/30/2010
Each share Common no par exchanged for USD $11 cash
Note: Unexchanged certificates were cancelled and became without value 08/30/2016

GERI CARE NURSING CTRS AMER INC (DE)
Name changed to Lifestyle Companies 2/26/71
(See Lifestyle Companies)

GERIACO INTL INC (DE)
Recapitalized as American Business Financial Services, Inc. 02/12/1993
Each (547.2) shares Common $0.001 par exchanged for (1) share Common $0.001 par
(See American Business Financial Services, Inc.)

GERIATRIC & MED COS INC (DE)
Name changed 12/31/92
Common 10¢ par split (3) for (2) by issuance of (0.5) additional share 8/21/78
Common 10¢ par split (3) for (2) by issuance of (0.5) additional share 12/24/80
Common 10¢ par split (5) for (4) by issuance of (0.25) additional share 5/20/91
Common 10¢ par split (5) for (4) by issuance of (0.25) additional share 4/30/92
Stock Dividends - 10% 11/28/79; 10% 1/31/80; 10% 5/30/80; 10% 8/7/80; 10% 10/27/80; 10% 7/27/81; 30% 5/28/82; 10% 10/27/82; 10% 12/23/82; 25% 7/26/83; 25% 12/19/83; 25% 10/26/84; 25% 10/25/85; 10% 11/3/86
Name changed from Geriatric & Medical Centers, Inc. to Geriatric & Medical Companies, Inc. 12/31/92
Merged into Genesis Health Ventures, Inc. 10/11/96
Each share Common 10¢ par exchanged for $5.75 cash

GERIATRIC PHARMACEUTICAL CORP (NY)
Common 10¢ par split (10) for (1) by issuance of (9) additional shares 10/01/1984
Recapitalized as Pharmaconnect, Inc. 06/16/1999
Each (15.15) shares Common 10¢ par exchanged for (1) share Common 10¢ par
(See Pharmaconnect, Inc.)

GERIATRIC RESEARCH, INC. (IL)
Name changed to G.R.I. Corp. (IL) 4/3/64
G.R.I. Corp. (IL) reincorporated in Delaware 6/28/91
(See G.R.I. Corp. (DE))

GERIATRIC SVCS INC (DE)
Charter cancelled and became inoperative and void for non-payment of taxes 10/1/68

GERIATRICS INC (NV)
Stock Dividend - 10% 12/14/73
Merged into ARA Services, Inc. 8/13/74
Each share Common $1 par exchanged for (0.129) share Common 50¢ par
(See ARA Services, Inc.)

GERIATRX PHARMACEUTICAL CORP (BC)
Recapitalized as Paladin Labs Inc. (BC) 05/10/1996
Each share Common no par exchanged for (0.1) share Common no par
Paladin Labs Inc. (BC) reincorporated in Canada 07/24/1998 which merged into Endo International PLC 03/03/2014

GERIN INC (ON)
7% 1st Preference $10 par called for redemption 05/27/1985
Public interest eliminated

GERIN LTD. (ON)
Name changed to Gerin Inc. 11/04/1981
(See Gerin Inc.)

GERITY-ADRIAN MANUFACTURING CORP.
Merged into Gerity-Michigan Die Casting Co. 03/04/1946
Each share 6% Preferred $100 par exchanged for (1) share Preferred $100 par
Each share Common exchanged for (2.6) shares Common $1 par
Gerity-Michigan Die Casting Co. name changed to Gerity-Michigan Corp. 10/01/1947 which merged into Hoover Ball & Bearing Co. (MI) 12/28/1956 which reincorporated in Delaware 12/31/1968 which reincorporated back in Michigan 08/01/1976 which name changed to Hoover Universal Inc. 01/17/1978 which merged into Johnson Controls, Inc. 05/12/1985 which merged into Johnson Controls International PLC 09/06/2016

GERITY-MICHIGAN CORP. (MI)
Merged into Hoover Ball & Bearing Co. (MI) 12/28/1956
Each (7.5) shares Common $1 par exchanged for (1) share Capital Stock $10 par
Hoover Ball & Bearing Co. (MI) reincorporated in Delaware 12/31/1968 which reincorporated back in Michigan 08/01/1976 which name changed to Hoover Universal Inc. 01/17/1978 which merged into Johnson Controls, Inc. 05/12/1985 which merged into Johnson Controls International PLC 09/06/2016

GERITY-MICHIGAN DIE CASTING CO.
Name changed to Gerity-Michigan Corp. 10/01/1947
Gerity-Michigan Corp. merged into Hoover Ball & Bearing Co. (MI) 12/28/1956 which reincorporated in Delaware 12/31/1968 which reincorporated back to Michigan 08/01/1976 which name changed to Hoover Universal Inc. 01/17/1978 which merged into Johnson Controls, Inc. 05/12/1985 which merged into Johnson Controls International PLC 09/06/2016

GERLACH-BARKLOW CO.
Name changed to United Printers & Publishers, Inc. in 1930 which name was changed to Rust Craft Greeting Cards, Inc. 7/13/62
(See Rust Craft Greeting Cards, Inc.)

GERLE GOLD LTD (BC)
Name changed to GGL Diamond Corp. 06/13/2000
GGL Diamond Corp. name changed to GGL Resources Corp. 09/08/2009

GERLI & CO INC (DE)
Company believed private 00/00/1987
Details not available

GERMAIN INDS LTD (AB)
Name changed to Marquis Resource Corp. 08/02/1989
Marquis Resource Corp. name changed to Panorama Trading Co. Ltd. 10/22/1992 which name changed to Perfect Fry Corp. 05/21/1993 which name changed to Woodrose Corp. (AB) 09/01/2010 which reincorporated in British Columbia as Woodrose Ventures Corp. 11/07/2016 which recapitalized as Novoheart Holdings Inc. 10/03/2017

GERMAN AMERN BANCORP (IN)
Common $10 par changed to no par 4/23/98
Common $10 par split (2) for (1) by issuance of (1) additional share payable 11/1/97 to holders of record 10/15/97 Ex date - 11/3/97
Stock Dividends - 5% payable 12/6/96 to holders of record 11/8/96; 5% payable 12/20/97 to holders of record 11/28/97; 5% payable 12/15/98 to holders of record 11/30/98; 5% payable 12/15/99 to holders of record 11/30/99; 5% payable 12/15/2000 to holders of record 11/30/2000; 5% payable 12/15/2001 to holders of record 11/30/2001 Ex date - 12/28/2001; 5% payable 12/15/2002 to holders of record 11/30/2002; 5% payable 12/15/2002 to holders of record 11/30/2002 Ex date - 11/26/2002; 5% payable 12/15/2003 to holders of record 12/1/2003 Ex date - 11/26/2003
Name changed to German American Bancorp Inc. 5/22/2006

GERMAN CREDIT & INVESTMENT CORP.
Name changed to Credit & Investment Corp. 00/00/1941
(See Credit & Investment Corp.)

GERMAN VLG PRDS INC (OH)
Class A no par reclassified as Common no par 2/28/74
Acquired by Campbell Soup Co. 10/2/79
Each share Common no par exchanged for $3.30 cash

GERMANIA BK A FED SVGS BK (ALTON, IL)
Name changed 05/08/1984
Reorganized 06/01/1987
Name changed from Germania Federal Savings & Loan Association to Germania F.A. (USA) 05/08/1984
Capital Stock 1¢ par split (3) for (2) by issuance of (0.5) additional share 05/15/1986
Under plan of reorganization each share Germania F.A. (USA) Capital Stock 1¢ par automatically became (1) share Germania Bank, A Federal Savings Bank (Alton, IL) Common 1¢ par 06/01/1987
Placed in conservatorship 06/22/1990
No stockholders' equity

GERMANIC FIRE INSURANCE CO.
Merged into American Colony Insurance Co. 00/00/1931
Details not available

GERMANTOWN FIRE INSURANCE CO. (PA)
Capital Stock $20 par changed to $30 par in 1950 and to $40 par 5/5/59
Name changed to Germantown Insurance Co. and each share Capital Stock $40 par exchanged for

(20) shares Capital Stock $2 par 1/22/64
(See Germantown Insurance Co.)

GERMANTOWN INDPT TEL CO (OH)
Acquired by Vincent Acquisition Corp. 11/15/2006
Each share Common $5 par exchanged for $76 cash
Note: Each share Common $5 par received an additional distribution of $3.5457 cash from escrow 03/18/2009

GERMANTOWN INS CO (PA)
Capital Stock $2 par changed to $3 par 4/29/74
Acquired by PC Merger, Inc. 10/20/86
Each share Capital Stock $3 par exchanged for $88.03 cash

GERMANTOWN PASSENGER RWY. CO.
Acquired by Philadelphia Transportation Co. in 1940
Each share Common exchanged for $37.82 of 3%-6% Consolidated Mortgage Bonds and (0.3165) share Part. Preferred $20 par

GERMANTOWN SVGS BK (BALA CYNWYD, PA)
Merged into CoreStates Financial Corp. 12/2/94
Each share Common 10¢ par exchanged for $62 cash

GERMANY FD CDA (ON)
Reorganized as AGF Germany Fund 1/1/95
Each Unit no par exchanged for (1) Series M Unit no par

GERMANY FD INC (MD)
Reincorporated 8/31/90
State of incorporation changed from (DE) to (MD) 8/31/90
Name changed to European Equity Fund, Inc. 10/27/2005

GERO METALLURGICAL CORP (DE)
Voluntarily dissolved 01/02/1987
Details not available

GERONIMO URANIUM MINING CORP. (DE)
Merged into Midwest Consolidated Uranium Corp. 6/10/55
Each share Common exchanged for (0.1) share Common
Midwest Consolidated Uranium Corp. merged into COG Minerals Corp. 5/1/56
(See COG Minerals Corp.)

GEROTOR MAY CORP (MD)
Each share Common $1 par exchanged for (0.25) share Common $4 par in 1954
Acquired by Edy Corp. 1/21/72
Each share Common $4 par exchanged for (1) share Common $4 par
(See Edy Corp.)

GEROVA FINANCIAL GROUP LTD (BERMUDA)
Reincorporated 09/20/2010
Each old Unit exchanged for (1) new Unit 06/08/2010
Place of incorporation changed from (Cayman Islands) to (Bermuda) 09/20/2010
Company terminated registration of Units and Ordinary shares and is no longer public as of 06/15/2011

GERRITY OIL & GAS CORP (DE)
Merged into Patina Oil & Gas Corp. 05/02/1996
Each $12 Conv. Depositary Preferred exchanged for (0.5270) share 7.125% Preferred 1¢ par
Each share Common 1¢ par exchanged for (0.4354) share Common 1¢ par and (0.2177) Common Stock Purchase Warrant expiring 05/02/2001
Patina Oil & Gas Corp. merged into Noble Energy Inc. 05/16/2005

GERTSCH PRODUCTS, INC. (CA)
Completely liquidated 5/1/64
Each share Capital Stock no par exchanged for first and final distribution of $9.81 cash

GESCAR CORP (MA)
Liquidation completed
Each share Class A Common $1 par received initial distribution of $3 cash 2/18/72
Each share Class A Common $1 par received second distribution of $1 cash 5/17/72
Each share Class A Common $1 par received third distribution of $0.38 cash 9/28/73
Each share Class A Common $1 par received fourth and final distribution of $0.2837 cash 12/23/75
Note: Certificates were not required to be surrendered and are without value

GESCO CORP LTD (INDIA)
Name changed to Mahindra Gesco Developers Ltd. 02/20/2003
Mahindra Gesco Developers Ltd. name changed to Mahindra Lifespace Developers Ltd. 10/25/2007

GESCO DISTRIBUTING LTD. (ON)
Name changed to Gesco Industries, Inc. 11/26/1981
(See Gesco Industries, Inc.)

GESCO INDS INC (ON)
Each (63,974) shares old Common no par exchanged for (1) share new Common no par 04/24/2000
Each (86,110) shares old Conv. Class A no par exchanged for (1) share new Conv. Class A no par 04/24/2000
Note: In effect holders received $4 cash per share and public interest was eliminated

GESTALT INTL LTD (CANADA)
Reorganized as Northway-Gestalt Corp. 03/02/1979
Each share 6% Preferred $5 par exchanged for (2) shares Common no par
Each share Common no par exchanged for (0.05) share Common no par
Northway-Gestalt Corp. acquired by Spar Aerospace Ltd. 09/19/1981
(See Spar Aerospace Ltd.)

GESTETNER HLDGS LTD (ENGLAND)
ADR's for Ordinary Reg. 5s par and ADR's for A Ordinary Reg. 5s par changed to 25p par per currency change 02/15/1971
Stock Dividend - Payable in ADR's for A Ordinary - 100% 06/30/1970
Acquired by Ricoh Co., Ltd. 11/08/1995
Each ADR for Ordinary 25p par exchanged for $1.374 cash
Each ADR for Class A 25p par exchanged for $1.374 cash

GESTETNER LTD. (ENGLAND)
Stock Dividends - In ADR's for A Ord. Reg. to holders of ADR's for A Ord. Reg. and holders of ADR's for Ord. Reg. 25% 06/25/1963; 50% 06/23/1964
Name changed to Gestetner (Holdings) PLC 03/01/1966
(See Gestetner (Holdings) PLC)

GESTEVISION TELECINCO SA (SPAIN)
Name changed to Mediaset Espana Communicacion S.A. 01/17/2012

GESTION ALBANEL INC. (CANADA)
Voluntarily dissolved 01/10/1991
Details not available

GETCHELL GOLD CORP (NV)
Merged into Placer Dome Inc. 05/27/1999
Each share Common 1¢ par exchanged for (2.45) shares Common no par
Placer Dome Inc. merged into Barrick Gold Corp. 03/08/2006

GETCHELL MINE, INC. (NV)
Merged into Goldfield Corp. (WY) 9/16/63
Each share Common exchanged for (1.5) share Common
Goldfield Corp. (WY) reincorporated under the laws of Delaware 8/30/68

GETCHELL RES INC (BC)
Name changed to Discovery-Corp Enterprises Inc. 1/31/2000

GETFUGU INC (NV)
Reincorporated under the laws of Delaware and Common $0.001 par changed to $0.0001 par 11/15/2010

GETGO INC (BRITISH VIRGIN ISLANDS)
Name changed 06/29/2001
Name changed from Getgo Mail.com, Inc. to GETGO Inc. 06/29/2001
Struck from register 11/01/2005

GETPOKERRAKEBACK COM (NV)
Name changed to China Skyrise Digital Service Inc. 01/08/2010

GETTHERE INC (DE)
Name changed 7/10/2000
Issue Information - 5,000,000 shares COM offered at $16 per share on 11/22/1999
Name changed from Getthere.Com, Inc. to Getthere Inc. 7/10/2000
Merged into Sabre Holdings Corp. 10/17/2000
Each share Common $0.0001 par exchanged for $17.75 cash

GETTING READY CORP (DE)
Each (15) shares Common $0.001 par exchanged for (1) share Common $0.001 par 12/01/2006
Recapitalized as Winston Pharmaceuticals, Inc. 01/16/2009
Each share Common $0.001 par exchanged for (0.125) share Common $0.001 par

GETTY COMMUNICATIONS P L C (ENGLAND & WALES)
Merged into Getty Images, Inc. 02/10/1998
Each Sponsored ADR for Ordinary 1p par exchanged for (1) share Common 1¢ par
(See Getty Images, Inc.)

GETTY COPPER CORP (CANADA)
Recapitalized as Getty Copper Inc. 3/7/2003
Each share Common no par exchanged for (0.5) share Common no par

GETTY FINL CORP (CA)
Merged into Getty Acquisition Corp. 7/20/78
Each share Common $1 par exchanged for $2.25 cash

GETTY IMAGES INC (DE)
Merged into Abe Investment, L.P. 07/02/2008
Each share Common 1¢ par exchanged for $34 cash

GETTY OIL CO (DE)
4% Preferred $10 par called for redemption 5/29/58
Common $4 par split (5) for (2) by issuance of (1.5) additional shares 5/13/67
Common $4 par changed to no par and (3) additional shares issued 6/30/78
Merged into Texaco Inc. 2/17/84
Each share Common no par exchanged for $128 cash
$1.20 Preferred $25 par called for redemption 3/19/84
Public interest eliminated

GETTY PETE MARKETING INC (MD)
Merged into OAO Lukoil 1/25/2001
Each share Common 1¢ par exchanged for $5 cash

GETTY RLTY CORP (DE)
Name changed 03/31/1997
Common 10¢ par split (4) for (3) by issuance of (1/3) additional share 04/21/1986
Each share Common 10¢ par received distribution of (1) share Getty Petroleum Marketing Inc. Common 1¢ par payable 03/31/1997 to holders of record 03/21/1997
Ex date - 04/01/1997
Name changed from Getty Petroleum Corp. to Getty Realty Corp. 03/31/1997
Merged into Getty Realty Corp. (MD) 01/30/1998
Each share Common 10¢ par exchanged for (1) share Common 1¢ par

GETTY RLTY CORP (MD)
Issue Information - 8,855,000 shares COM 2001 DIVID offered at $16 per share on 08/01/2001
Each share 2001 Dividend Common 1¢ par exchanged for (1) share Common 1¢ par 08/02/2001
Conv. Participating Preferred Ser. A called for redemption at $25 plus $0.27118 accrued dividend on 09/24/2003
(Additional Information in Active)

GETTY RES LTD (CANADA)
Merged into TOTAL Energold Corp. 09/19/1988
Each share Common no par exchanged for (1) share Common no par
(See TOTAL Energold Corp.)

GETTYSBURG & HARRISBURG RAILWAY COMPANY
Merged into Reading Co. 12/31/45
Each share Common $50 par exchanged for (0.32) share Common $50 par
Reading Co. merged into Reading Entertainment Inc. (DE) 10/15/96 which reincorporated in Nevada 12/29/99 which merged into Reading International, Inc. 12/31/2001

GETTYSBURG NATL BK (GETTYSBURG, PA)
Merged into CCNB Corp. 07/09/1986
Each share Capital Stock $5 par exchanged for (2.27) shares Common $1 par or $75 cash
CCNB Corp. merged into PNC Financial Corp. 10/23/1992 which name changed to PNC Bank Corp. 02/08/1993 which name changed to PNC Financial Services Group, Inc. 03/15/2000

GETZ (WILLIAM) CORP. (IL)
Completely liquidated 10/18/1966
Each share Common no par exchanged for first and final distribution of (0.2) share Teledyne, Inc. Common $1 par
Teledyne, Inc. merged into Allegheny Teledyne, Inc. 08/15/1996 which name changed to Allegheny Technologies Inc. 11/29/1999

GEV CORP (DE)
Recapitalized as Pioneer Companies Inc. 04/28/1995
Each share Class A Common 1¢ par exchanged for (0.25) share Common 1¢ par
(See Pioneer Companies Inc.)

GEVAERT PHOTO PRODUCTEN N V (BELGIUM)
ADR's for Ordinary no par split (6) for (1) issuance of (5) additional ADR's 1/5/95
Stock Dividend - 20% 6/14/65
ADR agreement terminated 11/28/97
Each ADR for Ordinary no par exchanged for $87.47412412 cash

GEVALT INC (DE)
Name changed to Ross Anderson Group, Inc. 09/15/1989
Ross Anderson Group, Inc. recapitalized as Makaha, Inc. 06/30/1991 which name changed to TerraCom Inc. 12/24/1993
(See TerraCom Inc.)

GEVITY HR INC (FL)
Merged into TriNet Group, Inc. 06/01/2009
Each share Common 1¢ par exchanged for $4 cash

GEXA CORP (TX)
Reorganized 01/31/2001
Reorganized from Gexa Gold Corp. (NV) to Gexa Corp. (TX) 01/31/2001
Each share Common 1¢ par exchanged for (0.4) share Common 1¢ par
Merged into FPL Group, Inc. 06/17/2005
Each share Common 1¢ par exchanged for (0.1682) share Common 1¢ par
FPL Group, Inc. name changed to NextEra Energy, Inc. 05/21/2010

GEYSER GROUP LTD (NV)
Recapitalized as XStream Beverage Group Ltd. 10/16/2001
Each share Common $0.001 par exchanged for (0.025) share Common $0.001 par
XStream Beverage Group Ltd. name changed to XStream Beverage Network, Inc. 10/06/2004 which name changed to Hull Energy, Inc. 05/12/2008 which name changed to Gemini Group Global Corp. 11/04/2013

GEYSER MINERALS CORP. (NV)
Charter revoked for failure to file reports and pay fees 3/6/78

GEYSERS DEVELOPMENT CO. (CA)
Voluntarily dissolved 1/7/71
Details not available

GF BANCORP INC (DE)
Merged into Camco Financial Corp. 01/08/1998
Each share Common 1¢ par exchanged for (1.32) shares Common $1 par
(See Camco Financial Corp.)

GF BANCSHARES INC (GA)
Merged into Regions Financial Corp. (Old) 12/1/97
Each share Common $1 par exchanged for (0.48) share Common $0.625 par
Regions Financial Corp. (Old) merged into Regions Financial Corp. (New) 7/1/2004

GF BUSINESS EQUIP INC (OH)
Under plan of reorganization each share Conv. Preferred no par and Common $5 par automatically became (1) share GF Corp. Conv. Preferred no par and Common $5 par respectively 6/6/83
(See GF Corp.)

GF CORP (OH)
Common $5 par split (3) for (2) by issuance of (0.5) additional share 9/16/83
Company filed a petition under Chapter 11 Federal Bankruptcy Code 4/18/90
Stockholders' equity unlikely

GF HAYMORE INC (NV)
Name changed to XOZ Entertainment, S.A. 05/24/2001
XOZ Entertainment, S.A. name changed to SMSmobility, Inc. 01/04/2005 which name changed to Star Petroleum Corp. 07/25/2005 which recapitalized as Exact Energy Resources, Inc. 12/11/2007
(See Exact Energy Resources, Inc.)

GF INDS INC (DE)
Reincorporated 07/30/1976
Class A Common $1 par reclassified as Common 25¢ par 03/22/1966
4% Conv. Preferred $2.50 par called for redemption 04/01/1969
State of incorporation changed from (FL) to (DE) 07/30/1976
Each share Common 25¢ par exchanged for (0.0125) share Common 10¢ par
Merged into Swift Ohio Corp. 05/26/1978
Each share Common 10¢ par exchanged for $2 cash

GFC FINL CORP (DE)
Name changed to FINOVA Group Inc. 02/01/1995
(See FINOVA Group Inc.)

GFD, INC. (UT)
Recapitalized as GFD International, Inc. 3/21/86
Each share Common $0.0001 par exchanged for (10) shares Common $0.0001 par
GFD International, Inc. name changed to Prescription Corp. of America (UT) 7/22/86 which reorganized in Delaware 1/5/87 which name changed to CCG Capital Corp. 4/30/92 which recapitalized as Interaxx Technologies Inc. 10/16/97
(See Interaxx Technologies Inc.)

GFD INTERNATIONAL, INC. (UT)
Name changed to Prescription Corp. of America (UT) 7/22/86
Prescription Corp. of America (UT) reorganized in Delaware 1/5/87 which name changed to CCG Capital Corp. 4/30/92 which reorganized as Interaxx Technologies Inc. 10/16/97
(See Interaxx Technologies Inc.)

GFE CAP CORP (BC)
Each share old Common no par exchanged for (0.33333333) share new Common no par 11/09/2009
Name changed to Golden Touch Resources Corp. 10/21/2010
Golden Touch Resources Corp. recapitalized as Arian Resources Corp. 12/19/2012

GFI GROUP INC (DE)
Common 1¢ par split (4) for (1) by issuance of (3) additional shares payable 03/31/2008 to holders of record 03/14/2008 Ex date - 04/01/2008
Acquired by BGC Partners, Inc. 01/12/2016
Each share Common 1¢ par exchanged for $6.10 cash

GFI OIL & GAS CORP (AB)
Merged into Salamander Energy PLC 03/17/2008
Each share Common no par exchanged for either (0.218) share Ordinary or (0.1573) share Ordinary and USD$0.3129 cash

GFK RES INC (BC)
Reincorporated 07/13/2012
Place of incorporation changed from (BC) to (Canada) 07/13/2012
Name changed to Opus One Resources Inc. 07/31/2017

GFM RES LTD (BC)
Reincorporated under the laws of Yukon 07/25/2000

G4G CAPITAL CORP (BC)
Reincorporated under the laws of Ontario as White Gold Corp. 12/23/2016

G4G RES LTD (BC)
Recapitalized as G4G Capital Corp. (BC) 01/23/2015
Each share Common no par exchanged for (0.1) share Common no par
G4G Capital Corp. (BC) reincorporated in Ontario as White Gold Corp. 12/23/2016

GFS BANCORP INC (DE)
Common 1¢ par split (2) for (1) by issuance of (1) additional share payable 04/25/1997 to holders of record 04/11/1997
Merged into First Bankers Trust Co. (Quincy, IL) 03/31/1998
Each share Common 1¢ par exchanged for $17.65 cash

GFSB BANCORP INC (DE)
Common 10¢ par split (3) for (2) by issuance of (0.5) additional share payable 04/20/1998 to holders of record 03/31/1998
Stock Dividend - 25% payable 12/15/2000 to holders of record 12/01/2000 Ex date - 12/18/2000
Merged into First Federal Banc of the Southwest, Inc. 05/31/2005
Each share Common 10¢ par exchanged for (0.82118) share Common 1¢ par and $6.0588 cash
(See First Federal Banc of the Southwest, Inc.)

GFY FOODS INC (NV)
Each share old Common $0.001 par exchanged for (0.004) share new Common $0.001 par 07/01/2004
Each share new Common $0.001 par exchanged again for (0.001) share new Common $0.001 par 10/26/2004
Each share new Common $0.001 par exchanged again for (0.0001) share new Common $0.001 par 02/09/2005
Each share new Common $0.001 par exchanged again for (0.00001) share new Common $0.001 par 05/02/2006
Recapitalized as Upturn, Inc. 03/20/2009
Each (30) shares Common $0.001 par exchanged for (1) share Common $0.001 par
Upturn, Inc. recapitalized as Cityside Tickets Inc. 12/10/2009 which name changed to Causeway Entertainment Co. 10/11/2010 which recapitalized as United Bullion Exchange Inc. 05/10/2011

GGD RES INC (CANADA)
Each share old Common no par exchanged for (0.01) share new Common no par 12/19/2007
Name changed to God's Lake Resources Inc. 06/12/2009

GGL DIAMOND CORP (BC)
Name changed to GGL Resources Corp. 09/08/2009

GGP INC (DE)
Merged into Brookfield Property Partners L.P. 08/28/2018
Each share 6.375% Preferred Ser. A 1¢ par exchanged for (1) share Brookfield Property REIT Inc. 6.375% Preferred Ser. A 1¢ par
Each share Common 1¢ par exchanged for $0.312 cash

GGT GROUP PLC (UNITED KINGDOM)
ADR agreement terminated 11/23/1999
Each Sponsored ADR for Ordinary 5p par exchanged for $16.323 cash

GHANA GOLD CORP (NV)
Name changed to BrightRock Gold Corp. 11/11/2013

GHANA GOLD MINES LTD (AUSTRALIA)
Name changed to Apollo Group Ltd. 09/14/2000
Apollo Group Ltd. name changed to Global Petroleum Ltd. 09/13/2002
(See Global Petroleum Ltd.)

GHANA GOLDFIELDS LTD (BC)
Recapitalized as Icon Industries Ltd. 11/18/1999
Each share Common no par exchanged for (0.05882352) share Common no par
Icon Industries Ltd. name changed to ICN Resources Ltd. 11/16/2009 which merged into Corazon Gold Corp. 10/17/2012 which name changed to NanoSphere Health Sciences Inc. 12/05/2017

GHC INC. (MN)
Statutorily dissolved 10/07/1991

GHG RES LTD (BC)
Name changed to Los Andes Copper Ltd. 03/29/2007

GHI MTG INVS (MB)
Voluntarily dissolved 11/21/1985
Details not available

GHIGLIERI CORP (NV)
Name changed to GRG, Inc. 03/03/1998
GRG, Inc. recapitalized as HumWare Media Corp. 01/11/2005 which recapitalized as EFT Biotech Holdings, Inc. 11/20/2007 which name changed to EFT Holdings, Inc. 05/27/2011

GHISLAU MNG LTD (QC)
Recapitalized as Cedarvale Mines Ltd. 09/13/1971
Each share Capital Stock $1 par exchanged for (0.33333333) share Capital Stock $1 par
(See Cedarvale Mines Ltd.)

GHK RES LTD (BC)
Company went out of business 00/00/1999
No stockholders' equity

GHL ACQUISITION CORP (DE)
Name changed to Iridium Communications Inc. 09/29/2009

GHL TECHNOLOGIES INC (NV)
Recapitalized as NXGen Holdings, Inc. 09/07/2007
Each share Common $0.001 par exchanged for (0.02) share Common $0.001 par
NXGen Holdings, Inc. name changed to Green Bridge Industries, Inc. 08/20/2009

GHOSTMOUNT MINES LTD. (ON)
Charter cancelled for failure to pay taxes and file returns 12/19/1979

GHP EXPL CORP (YT)
Reincorporated 04/30/1997
Place of incorporation changed from (BC) to (YT) 04/30/1997
Merged into TransAtlantic Petroleum Corp. (AB) 12/02/1998
Each share Common no par exchanged for (0.87) share Common no par
TransAtlantic Petroleum Corp. (AB) reincorporated in Bermuda as TransAtlantic Petroleum Ltd. 10/01/2009

GHS INC (DE)
Each share Common 1¢ par received distribution of (1) share U.S. NeuroSurgical, Inc. Common 1¢ par payable 09/17/1999 to holders of record 09/08/1999
Name changed to Dreamlife, Inc. 12/15/1999
Dreamlife, Inc. name changed to EOS International, Inc. 12/31/2001
(See EOS International, Inc.)

GHZ RESOURCE CORP (BC)
Name changed to Canadian Reserve Gold Corp. 6/10/94
Canadian Reserve Gold Corp. recapitalized as Christina Gold Resources Ltd. 4/18/96 which recapitalized as PowerHouse Energy Corp. 12/11/98 which recapitalized as International Powerhouse Energy Corp. 9/18/2001 which name changed to Sea Breeze Power Corp. 7/30/2003

GI EXPT CORP (NY)
Name changed to Johnston Industries Inc. (NY) 03/22/1985
Johnston Industries Inc. (NY) reincorporated in Delaware 12/31/1987
(See Johnston Industries Inc. (DE))

GIANNINI (G.M.) & CO., INC. (NY)
Stock Dividend - 200% 12/01/1956
Name changed to Giannini Controls Corp. 04/14/1959
Giannini Controls Corp. name changed to Conrac Corp. 04/14/1967
(See Conrac Corp.)

GIANNINI CONTROLS CORP. (NY)
5-1/2% Preferred A $20 par called for redemption 07/22/1960
Common $1 par changed to 50¢ par and (1) additional share issued 08/29/1961
5% Conv. Preferred Ser. B $20 par called for redemption 03/01/1966
Name changed to Conrac Corp. 04/14/1967
(See Conrac Corp.)

GIANNINI SCIENTIFIC CORP. (DE)
Name changed to Geotel, Inc. 05/16/1968
(See Geotel, Inc.)

GIANT BACHELOR MINES LTD. (QC)
Charter annulled for failure to file annual reports 02/02/1974

GIANT BAY RES LTD (BC)
Recapitalized as Kafus Capital Corp. 08/29/1995
Each share Common no par exchanged for (0.08333333) share Common no par
Kafus Capital Corp. name changed to Kafus Environmental Industries Ltd. 09/22/1997 which name changed to Kafus Industries Ltd. 06/23/1999
(See Kafus Industries Ltd.)

GIANT CEM HLDG INC (DE)
Issue Information - 10,000,000 shares COM offered at $14 per share on 09/29/1994
Merged into Cementos Portland, S.A. 12/20/99
Each share Common 1¢ par exchanged for $31 cash

GIANT CHIBOUGAMAU MINES LTD. (QC)
Dissolved 06/01/1974
Details not available

GIANT CONS INDS INC (UT)
Name changed to Rando (Joseph), Inc. 1/11/74
Rando (Joseph), Inc. name changed to Rando (Joseph) International 7/3/75
(See Rando (Joseph) International)

GIANT EXPLS LTD (BC)
Merged into Giant Piper Exploration Inc. 11/17/1981
Each share Common no par exchanged for (0.3) share Common no par
Giant Piper Exploration Inc. name changed to Giant Pacific Petroleum Inc. 05/12/1988 which recapitalized as Red Rock Mining Corp. 12/05/1991 which name changed to American Pacific Minerals Ltd. 05/30/1994
(See American Pacific Minerals Ltd.)

GIANT FOOD INC (DE)
Class A Common $1 par split (3) for (2) by issuance of (0.5) additional share 05/17/1979
Class A Common $1 par split (3) for (1) by issuance of (2) additional shares 03/11/1983
Class A Common $1 par split (2) for (1) by issuance of (1) additional share 06/07/1985
Class A Common $1 par split (2) for (1) by issuance of (1) additional share 06/03/1988
Stock Dividend - 100% 11/28/1969
Merged into Koninklijke Ahold N.V. 10/30/1998
Each share Class A Common $1 par exchanged for $43.50 cash

GIANT FOOD PPTYS INC (DE)
Name changed to Giant Food Properties of Maryland, Inc. 2/8/72
(See Giant Food Properties of Maryland, Inc.)

GIANT FOOD PROPERTIES OF MARYLAND, INC. (DE)
Completely liquidated 2/8/72
Each share Common 10¢ par exchanged for first and final distribution of (0.657) share Saul (B.F.) Real Estate Investment Trust Shares of Bene. Int. $10 par
(See Saul (B.F.) Real Estate Investment Trust)

GIANT GROUP LTD (DE)
$25 Conv. Preferred $1 par called for redemption 2/9/87
Common 1¢ par split (3) for (2) by issuance of (0.5) additional share 11/24/92
Each (300) shares old Common 1¢ par exchanged for (1) share new Common 1¢ par 2/1/2005
Note: In effect holders received $1.85 cash per share and public interest was eliminated

GIANT INDS INC (DE)
Acquired by Western Refining, Inc. 05/31/2007
Each share Common 1¢ par exchanged for $77 cash

GIANT INTERACTIVE GROUP INC (CAYMAN ISLANDS)
Acquired by Giant Investment Ltd. 07/18/2014
Each ADR for Ordinary exchanged for $11.95 cash

GIANT JR INVTS CORP (NV)
Each share old Common $0.001 par exchanged for (0.01) share new Common $0.001 par 12/02/2004
Name changed to Financial Media Group, Inc. 09/14/2005
Financial Media Group, Inc. name changed to Clicker Inc. 07/08/2009
(See Clicker Inc.)

GIANT MASCOT MINES LTD (BC)
Capital Stock $1 par changed to no par 02/09/1968
Recapitalized as G M Resources Ltd. (BC) 04/11/1977
Each share Capital Stock no par exchanged for (0.25) share Capital Stock no par
G M Resources Ltd. (BC) reincorporated in Canada 09/08/1982 which merged into Campbell Resources Inc. (New) 06/08/1983
(See Campbell Resources Inc. (New))

GIANT METALLICS MINES LTD (BC)
Recapitalized as Consolidated Giant Metallics Ltd. 07/09/1973
Each share Common 50¢ par exchanged for (0.2) share Common no par
(See Consolidated Giant Metallics Ltd.)

GIANT MINES CORP. OF NEVADA (NV)
Name changed to Giant Resources, Inc. 11/18/56
(See Giant Resources, Inc.)

GIANT NORTH RES LTD (BC)
Name changed to Euromin Canada Ltd. (BC) 11/27/1984
Euromin Canada Ltd. (BC) reincorporated in Canada 04/28/1989 which recapitalized as International Euromin Corp. 06/10/1994 which merged into Eurogas Corp. 06/30/1995 which name changed to Dundee Energy Ltd. 06/22/2011

GIANT OIL & GAS INC (CANADA)
Recapitalized as Giant Resources Inc. 12/13/2011
Each share Common no par exchanged for (0.01) share Common no par
(See Giant Resources Inc.)

GIANT PACIFIC PETES INC (BC)
Recapitalized as Red Rock Mining Corp. 12/05/1991
Each share Common no par exchanged for (0.1) share Common no par
Red Rock Mining Corp. name changed to American Pacific Minerals Ltd. 05/30/1994
(See American Pacific Minerals Ltd.)

GIANT PIPER EXPLORATION INC. (BC)
Name changed to Giant Pacific Petroleum Inc. 05/12/1988
Giant Pacific Petroleum Inc. recapitalized as Red Rock Mining Corp. 12/05/1991 which name changed to American Pacific Minerals Ltd. 05/30/1994
(See American Pacific Minerals Ltd.)

GIANT PORTLAND & MASONRY CEM CO (DE)
Under plan of reorganization each share $25 Conv. Preferred $1 par and Common $1 par automatically became (1) share Giant Group Ltd. $25 Conv. Preferred $1 par and Common 1¢ par respectively 6/7/85
(See Giant Group Ltd.)

GIANT PORTLAND CEMENT CO. (DE)
Each share Preferred $50 par exchanged for (8) shares Common $5 par and a Div. Arrears Unit for $31.67 cash in 1940
Each share Common $50 par exchanged for (1) share Common $5 par in 1940
Common $5 par changed to $1 par in 1944
Common $1 par split (3) for (2) by issuance of (0.5) additional share 9/21/59
Name changed to Giant Portland & Masonry Cement Co. 4/27/77
Giant Portland & Masonry Cement Co. reorganized as Giant Group Ltd. 6/7/85
(See Giant Group Ltd.)

GIANT REEF PETES LTD (AB)
Reincorporated 02/14/1984
Place of incorporation changed from (BC) to (AB) 02/14/1984
Acquired by Numac Oil & Gas Ltd. 12/20/1990
Each share Common no par exchanged for $4.65 cash

GIANT RESOURCES, INC. (NV)
Charter revoked for non-payment of fees 3/4/63

GIANT RES INC (CANADA)
Voluntarily dissolved 12/30/2015
Details not available

GIANT RES LTD (AUSTRALIA)
ADR agreement terminated 03/03/2003
No ADR holders' equity

GIANT STORES CORP (MA)
Common 10¢ par split (5) for (4) by issuance of (0.25) additional share 5/20/71
Reorganized 3/13/74
No stockholders' equity

GIANT STURGEON MINING CORP. LTD. (ON)
Merged into Bayfor Corp. Inc. 05/00/1972
Each share Capital Stock no par exchanged for (0.222222) share Capital Stock no par
(See Bayfor Corp. Inc.)

GIANT TIGER STORES INC (OH)
Completely liquidated 12/6/83
Each share Common no par exchanged for first and final distribution of $0.50 cash

GIANT TIRE & RUBBER CO.
Acquired by Master Tire & Rubber Corp. in 1930 which name was changed to Cooper Tire & Rubber Co. in 1946

GIANT VENTURES DEV LTD (BC)
Recapitalized as Nor-Quest Resources Ltd. 08/10/1977
Each share Capital Stock no par exchanged for (0.25) share Capital Stock no par
Nor-Quest Resources Ltd. recapitalized as Western & Pacific Resources Corp. 04/22/1991 which recapitalized as Consolidated Western & Pacific Resources Corp. 07/05/1994 which name changed to Synergy Resource Technologies Inc. 07/02/1996 which recapitalized as Synergy Renewable Resources Inc. 01/09/1997
(See Synergy Renewable Resources Inc.)

GIANT YELLOWKNIFE GOLD MINES LTD. (ON)
Merged into Giant Yellowknife Mines Ltd. 06/30/1960
Each share Capital Stock no par exchanged for (1) share Capital Stock no par
Giant Yellowknife Mines Ltd. merged into Royal Oak Mines Inc. 07/23/1991 which recapitalized as Royal Oak Ventures Inc. 02/14/2000
(See Royal Oak Ventures Inc.)

GIANT YELLOWKNIFE MINES LTD (ON)
Merged into Royal Oak Mines Inc. 07/23/1991
Each share Capital Stock no par exchanged for (6.5) shares Common no par
Royal Oak Mines Inc. recapitalized as Royal Oak Ventures Inc. 02/14/2000
(See Royal Oak Ventures Inc.)

GIANTSTAR VENTURES INC (BC)
Name changed to Chalk Media Corp. 11/19/2003
(See Chalk Media Corp.)

GIBBEX MINES LTD (BC)
Merged into T.V.S. Industries Ltd. 06/23/1972
Each share Capital Stock 50¢ par exchanged for (0.33333333) share Capital Stock no par
T.V.S. Industries Ltd. name changed to GBX Mines Ltd. 02/11/1974 which recapitalized as El Paso Energy Corp. 08/20/1979 which recapitalized as E.L.E. Energy Corp. 10/05/1984 which recapitalized as Maple Leaf Springs Water Corp. 11/12/1992 which recapitalized as International Maple Leaf Springs Ltd. 02/24/1998
(See International Maple Leaf Springs Ltd.)

GIBBONSVILLE MINING & EXPLORATION CO. (ID)
Charter revoked for failure to file reports and pay fees 11/30/56

GIBBS CONSTR INC (TX)
Common 1¢ par split (2) for (1) by issuance of (1) additional share payable 11/01/1996 to holders of record 10/18/1996
Recapitalized as Acacia Automotive, Inc. 02/20/2007
Each share Common 1¢ par exchanged for (0.125) share Common $0.001 par
Acacia Automotive, Inc. name changed to Acacia Diversified Holdings, Inc. 10/18/2012

GIBCO, INC. (MI)
Liquidation completed
Each share Common $1 par received initial distribution of $1.90 cash 09/29/1961
Each share Common $1 par received second distribution of $3.26 cash 10/31/1961
Each share Common $1 par received third distribution of (0.2547) Preferred and (1.097) share Common of Hupp Corp. 12/22/1961
Each share Common $1 par received fourth and final distribution of $0.74564 cash 06/24/1964
Note: Certificates were not required to be exchanged and are without value

GIBRALTAR EXPL LTD (OK)
Name changed to Hipoint Investments, Ltd. 08/24/1984
(See Hipoint Investments, Ltd.)

GIBRALTAR FINL CORP (DE)
Name changed 05/14/1985
Capital Stock $1 par split (2) for (1) by issuance of (1) additional share 06/15/1976
Capital Stock $1 par split (3) for (2) by issuance of (0.5) additional share 12/15/1978
Name changed from Gibraltar Financial Corp. of California to Gibraltar Financial Corp. 05/14/1985
Plan of reorganization under Chapter 11 Federal Bankruptcy proceedings confirmed 04/20/1993
No stockholders' equity

GIBRALTAR FIRE & CASUALTY CO. (SC)
Name changed to Mt. Vernon Surety Corp. 3/26/65
Mt. Vernon Surety Corp. name changed to Mt. Vernon Insurance Co. 11/10/65 which merged to Triton Insurance Co. 10/3/67 which reorganized as Triton Corp. 3/1/68
(See Triton Corp.)

GIBRALTAR FIRE & MARINE INSURANCE CO.
Merged into Home Insurance Co. in 1948
Each share Capital Stock $10 par exchanged for (0.828) share Common $5 par
(See Home Insurance Co.)

GIBRALTAR GROWTH CORP (ON)
Units separated 11/11/2015
Name changed to LXRandCo, Inc. and Class A Restricted Vtg. Shares reclassified as Class B Shares 06/14/2017

GIBRALTAR GROWTH FD INC (DE)
In process of liquidation
Each share Common $1 par exchanged for initial distribution of (0.36462) share Dreyfus Leverage Fund, Inc. (DE) Capital Stock $1 par 08/07/1972
Note: Details on additional distribution(s), if any, are not available
Dreyfus Leverage Fund, Inc. (DE) reincorporated in Maryland 04/30/1974 which name changed to Dreyfus Capital Growth, Inc. 06/29/1992
(See Dreyfus Capital Growth Fund, Inc.)

GIBRALTAR LIFE INS CO AMER (TX)
Stock Dividend - 10% 3/15/67
Merged into Tidelands Capital Corp. 12/31/77
Each share Capital Stock no par exchanged for (9.3) shares Common no par
Tidelands Capital Corp. merged into Western Preferred Corp. 3/6/81
(See Western Preferred Corp.)

GIBRALTAR MINES LTD (BC)
Acquired by Westmin Resources Ltd. 10/16/1996
Each share Common 50¢ par exchanged for (0.84666) share Common no par and $2.50 cash
Westmin Resources Ltd. merged into Boliden Ltd. (Canada) 02/12/1998 which reorganized in Sweden as Boliden AB 12/07/2001

GIBRALTAR MORTGAGE CO. (FL)
Class B Common 10¢ par changed to $1 par 4/4/56
Class B Common $1 par reclassified as Common $1 par 10/4/60
Each share Common $1 par exchanged for (0.1) share Common 10¢ par 9/13/61
Name changed to United Gibraltar Corp. 10/5/71
United Gibraltar Corp. reorganized in Delaware as United Gibralter Corporation Delaware, Inc. 8/25/86
(See United Gibralter Corporation Delaware, Inc.)

GIBRALTAR PACKAGING GROUP INC (DE)
Merged into Rosmar Packaging Group, Inc. 05/15/2008
Each share Common 1¢ par exchanged for $4.25 cash

GIBRALTAR PARI MUTUEL INC (MD)
Completely liquidated 6/13/85
Each share Capital Stock $1 par exchanged for first and final distribution of $35 cash

GIBRALTAR SAVINGS & LOAN ASSN. OF NORTHERN CALIFORNIA (CA)
100% acquired by Gibraltar Financial Corp. of California through purchase offer which expired 09/29/1972
Public interest eliminated

GIBRALTAR SVGS ASSN HOUSTON TEX (TX)
Merged into First Texas Savings Association 6/29/84
Each share Common $1 par exchanged for $32.275 cash

GIBRALTAR SPRINGS CAP CORP (QC)
Company consented to enforcement of security by secured creditor 12/12/2005
No stockholders' equity

GIBRALTAR STL CORP (DE)
Common 1¢ par split (3) for (2) by issuance of (0.5) additional share payable 10/29/2004 to holders of record 10/15/2004 Ex date - 11/1/2004
Name changed to Gibraltar Industries, Inc. 10/26/2004

GIBRALTER URANIUM CORP. (CO)
Out of business and stock declared worthless in 1958

GIBSON ART CO. (OH)
Common no par changed to $5 par 7/12/55
Name changed to Gibson Greeting Cards, Inc. 6/14/60
(See Gibson Greeting Cards, Inc.)

GIBSON C R CO (DE)
Common $1.25 par split (3) for (2) by issuance of (0.5) additional share 12/31/81
Common $1.25 par split (5) for (4) by issuance of (0.25) additional share 10/31/83
Common $1.25 par changed to 10¢ par 4/13/86
Common 10¢ par split (5) for (4) by issuance of (0.25) additional share 10/31/86
Common 10¢ par split (5) for (4) by issuance of (0.25) additional share 10/30/87
Common 10¢ par split (6) for (5) by issuance of (0.2) additional share 1/31/89
Common 10¢ par split (4) for (3) by issuance of (1/3) additional share 6/29/90
Common 10¢ par split (4) for (3) by issuance of (1/3) additional share 10/31/91
Stock Dividends - 25% 1/31/77; 20% 10/31/78; 10% 1/30/81; 25% 7/31/85
Merged into Nelson (Thomas), Inc. 11/7/95
Each share Common 10¢ par exchanged for $9 cash

GIBSON CHIBOUGAMAU MINES LTD. (ON)
Assets acquired by Gibson Mines Ltd. 00/00/1958
Each share Common exchanged for (0.5) share Common
(See Gibson Mines Ltd.)

GIBSON CNTY BK (PRINCETON, IN)
Under plan of reorganization each share Capital Stock $10 par automatically became (1) share GCB Bancorp, Inc. Common no par 10/3/85
GCB Bancorp, Inc. acquired by Old National Bancorp 2/28/87

GIBSON COUNTY PERPETUAL BUILDING & LOAN ASSOCIATION (IN)
Name changed to Perpetual Savings & Loan Association 1/21/65
(See Perpetual Savings & Loan Association)

GIBSON CRYOGENICS INC (UT)
Petition under Chapter 11 Federal Bankruptcy Code dismissed 4/27/89
No stockholders' equity

GIBSON GIRL MINES LTD. (BC)
Struck off register and declared dissolved for failure to file returns 11/10/1988

GIBSON GREETING CARDS, INC. (OH)
Common $5 par split (3) for (1) by issuance of (2) additional shares 9/1/60
Completely liquidated 3/20/64
Details not available

GIBSON GREETINGS INC (DE)
Merged into American Greetings Corp. 3/9/2000
Each share Common 1¢ par exchanged for $10.25 cash

GIBSON HOMANS CO (OH)
Common no par split (3) for (2) by issuance of (0.5) additional share 7/27/83
Stock Dividends - 50% 1/5/79; 20% 11/14/80
Acquired by Foseco Minsep PLC 1/2/85
Each share Common no par exchanged for $17.50 cash

GIBSON MINES LTD (QC)
Charter annulled for failure to file annual reports 08/05/1982

GIBSON OIL CORP. (DE)
Reincorporated under the laws of Texas in 1938
(See Gibson Oil Corp. (TX))

GIBSON OIL CORP. (TX)
Dissolution completed in 1956
Details not available

GIBSON REFRIGERATOR CO. (MI)
Common $10 par changed to $1 par 00/00/1945
Name changed to Gibco, Inc. 05/04/1956
(See Gibco, Inc.)

GIC GLOBAL INTERTAINMENT CORP (NV)
Recapitalized as Global Networks, Corp. 10/20/2004
Each share Common $0.001 par exchanged for (0.1) share Common $0.001 par
(See Global Networks, Corp.)

GIDDINGS & LEWIS INC NEW (WI)
Common 10¢ par split (2) for (1) by issuance of (1) additional share 05/29/1992
Each Depositary Receipt exchanged for $25 principal amount of 10% Conv. Subordinated Debentures due 10/31/2015 on 06/15/1992
Each share Conv. Sr. Preferred Ser. A $1 par exchanged for $250 principal amount of 10% Conv. Subordinated Debentures due 10/31/2015 on 06/15/1992
Merged into Thyssen A.G. 09/30/1997
Each share Common 10¢ par exchanged for $21 cash

GIDDINGS & LEWIS INC OLD (WI)
Common $2 par split (2) for (1) by issuance of (1) additional share 10/27/1967
Common $2 par split (5) for (4) by issuance of (0.25) additional share 12/28/1978
Common $2 par split (5) for (4) by issuance of (0.25) additional share 03/28/1980
Common $2 par split (3) for (2) by issuance of (0.5) additional share 06/15/1981
Merged into AMCA International Corp. 10/04/1982
Each share Common $2 par exchanged for $30 cash

GIDDINGS & LEWIS MACHINE TOOL CO. (WI)
Recapitalized in 1936
Each share Preferred exchanged for (1) share Common $10 par
Each share Common no par exchanged for (0.25) share Common $10 par
Recapitalized in 1937
Each share Common $10 par exchanged for (4.5) shares Common $2 par
Stock Dividends - 10% 12/3/64; 50% 5/20/66
Name changed to Giddings & Lewis, Inc. 4/26/67
(See Giddings & Lewis, Inc.)

GIDDY UP PRODUCTIONS INC (NV)
Name changed to Branded Beverages, Inc. 12/14/2010
Branded Beverages, Inc. name changed to Raptor Technology Group, Inc. 01/06/2011
(See Raptor Technology Group, Inc.)

GIDEON CAP CORP (ON)
Name changed to Morgan Resources Corp. 01/10/2014
Morgan Resources Corp. name changed to Leviathan Cannabis Group Inc. 04/16/2018

GIELOW (J.J.) & SONS, INC. (MI)
Stock Dividend - 100% 06/15/1948
Name changed to Aunt Jane's Foods, Inc. 03/14/1960
Aunt Jane's Foods Inc. acquired by Borden Co. 04/30/1963 which name changed to Borden, Inc. 04/17/1968 which merged into RJR Nabisco Holdings Corp. 03/14/1995 which name changed to Nabisco Group Holdings Corp. 06/15/1999
(See Nabisco Group Holdings Corp.)

GIENOW WINDOWS & DOORS INCOME FD (AB)
Completely liquidated 11/02/2007
Each Trust Unit received $4.20 cash

GIFFEN INDS INC (FL)
Common $2.50 par changed to $1 par 5/26/58
Common $1 par split (3) for (1) by issuance of (2) additional shares 7/31/68
Name changed to LDB Corp. 3/10/78
LDB Corp. name changed to LDBrinkman Corp. 1/25/83 which recapitalized back as LDB Corp. 2/5/88
(See LDB Corp.)

GIFFORD HILL & CO INC (DE)
Common $2 par split (3) for (2) by issuance of (0.5) additional share 1/16/79

Each (150) shares Common $2 par exchanged for (1) share Common $300 par 12/16/85
Merged into Beazer (C.H.) (Holdings) PLC 1/5/87
Each share Common $300 par exchanged for $4,800 cash

GIFT LIQUIDATORS INC (OK)
Each share old Common 1¢ par exchanged for (0.06666666) share new Common 1¢ par 10/17/2005
Reincorporated under the laws of Maryland as Excellency Investment Realty Trust, Inc. 09/20/2006
(See Excellency Investment Realty Trust, Inc.)

GIGA-BYTE TECHNOLOGY CO LTD (TAIWAN)
Stock Dividends - 25% payable 09/28/2001 to holders of record 07/19/2001 Ex date - 07/17/2001; 15% payable 11/15/2002 to holders of record 09/10/2002 Ex date - 09/06/2002; 5% payable 11/06/2003 to holders of record 08/28/2003; 5% payable 10/28/2004 to holders of record 08/26/2004
GDR agreement terminated 01/31/2013
Each 144A Sponsored GDR for Ordinary exchanged for $3.708076 cash
Each Reg. S Sponsored GDR for Ordinary exchanged for $3.708076 cash

GIGA INFORMATION GROUP INC (DE)
Merged into Forrester Research, Inc. 03/03/2003
Each share Common $0.001 par exchanged for $4.75 cash

GIGABEAM CORP (DE)
Chapter 11 bankruptcy proceedings terminated 01/22/2010
No stockholders' equity

GIGAMON INC (DE)
Acquired by Ginsberg Holdco, Inc. 12/27/2017
Each share Common $0.0001 par exchanged for $38.50 cash

GIGANET LTD (ISRAEL)
Name changed to Ceragon Networks Ltd. 09/06/2000

GIGI RES LTD (BC)
Name changed 10/16/1986
Name changed from Gigi Oil & Gas Ltd. to Gigi Resources Ltd. 10/16/1986
Recapitalized as Rocket Resources Ltd. 10/23/1991
Each share Common no par exchanged for (0.2) share Common no par
Rocket Resources Ltd. name changed to Exeter Oil & Gas Ltd. (BC) 12/11/1997 which reorganized in Alberta as Terradyne Energy Corp. 04/11/2000
(See Terradyne Energy Corp.)

GIGOPTIX INC (DE)
Name changed to GigPeak, Inc. 04/06/2016
(See GigPeak, Inc.)

GIGPEAK INC (DE)
Acquired by Integrated Device Technology, Inc. 04/04/2017
Each share Common $0.001 par exchanged for $3.08 cash

GIGUERE INDS INC (NV)
Recapitalized as Prolong International Corp. 6/21/95
Each share Common 50¢ par exchanged for (0.5) share Common 1¢ par

GIL BERN INDS INC (MA)
Proclaimed dissolved for failure to file reports and pay taxes 1/10/79

GIL DEV CORP (DE)
Charter cancelled and declared inoperative and void for non-payment of taxes 06/30/1981

GILA COMMUNICATIONS, INC. (CO)
Recapitalized as Moya Overview, Inc. 09/11/1987
Each share Common $0.0001 par exchanged for (0.3) share Common $0.0001 par
(See Moya Overview, Inc.)

GILA MINES CORP (CA)
Charter suspended for failure to file reports and pay fees 12/1/83

GILA URANIUM CORP (UT)
Name changed to Continental Dynamics, Inc. (UT) 3/10/69
Continental Dynamics, Inc. (UT) reorganized in Nevada as Continental Dynamics, Ltd. 3/15/71
(See Continental Dynamics, Ltd.)

GILAT COMMUNICATIONS LTD (ISRAEL)
Issue Information - 2,500,000 shs. ORD offered at $8.50 per share on 12/04/1997
Name changed to Mentergy Ltd. 05/21/2001
(See Mentergy Ltd.)

GILAX CORP (NV)
Name changed to ProVest Global Inc. 12/19/2014
ProVest Global Inc. name changed to Imperial Plantation Corp. 05/04/2015

GILBEC MINES LTD. (CANADA)
Reorganized under the laws of Ontario as Pasgil Mines Ltd. 00/00/1941
Each share Common exchanged for (0.2) share Common
(See Pasgil Mines Ltd.)

GILBERT & BENNETT MFG CO (CT)
Each share Common $100 par exchanged for (10) shares Common $10 par 9/24/59
Stock Dividends - 20% 1/15/65; 100% 2/17/67
Merged into JGH Acquisition Corp. 2/22/85
Each share Common $10 par exchanged for $17.85 cash

GILBERT A C CO (MD)
Common no par split (3) for (1) by issuance of (2) additional shares in 1953
Charter annulled for failure to file annual reports and pay taxes 10/7/81

GILBERT ASSOC INC (DE)
Class A Common $1 par split (2) for (1) by issuance of (1) additional share 06/01/1972
Class B Common $1 par split (2) for (1) by issuance of (1) additional share 06/01/1972
Class A Common $1 par split (2) for (1) by issuance of (1) additional share 06/10/1987
Class B Common $1 par split (2) for (1) by issuance of (1) additional share 06/10/1987
Class A Common $1 par split (5) for (4) by issuance of (0.25) additional share 06/10/1988
Class B Common $1 par split (5) for (4) by issuance of (0.25) additional share 06/10/1988
Stock Dividend - 25% 06/11/1990
Name changed to Salient 3 Communications Inc. 05/01/1997

GILBERT (WILLIAM L.) CLOCK CORP. (CT)
Merged into General-Gilbert Corp. 9/13/57
Each share Class B Preferred $20 par exchanged for (1) share 6% Class B Preferred $20 par
Each share Class A Common no par exchanged for (10) shares Common $1 par
Each share Common $1 par exchanged for (0.1) share new Common $1 par
(See General-Gilbert Corp.)

GILBERT COS INC (DE)
Common $1 par changed to 1¢ par 5/30/75
Adjudicated bankrupt 10/26/77
No stockholders' equity

GILBERT DATA SYSTEMS, INC. (NY)
Name changed to Gilbert Systems, Inc. 6/3/64
Gilbert Systems, Inc. name changed to Gilbert Flexi-Van Corp. 6/18/68 which name changed to Flexi-Van Corp. (NY) 6/11/73 which merged into Castle & Cooke, Inc. (Old) 7/2/85 which name changed to Dole Food Co., Inc. (HI) 7/30/91 which reincorporated in Delaware 7/1/2001
(See Dole Food Co., Inc. (DE))

GILBERT FLEXI VAN CORP (NY)
Common 1¢ par split (1.75) for (1) by issuance of (0.75) additional share 7/12/72
Name changed to Flexi-Van Corp. (NY) 6/11/73
Flexi-Van Corp. (NY) merged into Castle & Cooke, Inc. (Old) 7/2/85 which name changed to Dole Food Co., Inc. (HI) 7/30/91 which reincorporated in Delaware 7/1/2001
(See Dole Food Co., Inc. (DE))

GILBERT GOLD MINES, LTD. (ON)
Declared dissolved 01/04/1960
No stockholders' equity

GILBERT LABS (NJ)
Merged into Forest Laboratories, Inc. 05/01/1985
Each share Common no par exchanged for (0.7147) share Common 10¢ par
Note: Additional distribution of stock was made from escrow 00/00/1987
Forest Laboratories, Inc. merged into Actavis PLC 07/01/2014 which name changed to Allergan PLC 06/15/2015

GILBERT MARKETING GROUP INC (NY)
Reverted to private company 9/30/66
Each share Common 50¢ par exchanged for $4.30 cash

GILBERT ROBINSON INC (DE)
Stock Dividend - 20% 04/15/1976
Merged into Grace (W.R.) & Co. (CT) 11/08/1978
Each share Common $1 par exchanged for (0.481885) share Common $1 par
Grace (W.R.) & Co. (CT) reincorporated in New York 05/19/1988
(See Grace (W.R.) & Co.)

GILBERT/ROBINSON RESTAURANTS INC (DE)
Name changed 9/3/93
Name changed from Gilbert/Robinson Parent Corp. to Gilbert/Robinson Restaurants, Inc. 9/3/93
Name changed to Houlihans Restaurants Group, Inc. 3/17/95
(See Houlihans Restaurants Group, Inc.)

GILBERT SHOE STORES INC (OH)
Stock Dividend - 60% 11/27/67
6% Conv. Preferred Ser. A $10 par called for redemption 12/16/68
Reincorporated under the laws of Delaware as Gilbert Companies, Inc. and Class A Common no par and Common no par changed to $1 par 11/10/69
(See Gilbert Companies, Inc.)

GILBERT SYS INC (NY)
Name changed to Gilbert Flexi-Van Corp. 6/18/68
Gilbert Flexi-Van Corp. name changed to Flexi-Van Corp. (NY) 6/11/73 which merged into Castle & Cooke, Inc. (Old) 7/2/85 which name changed to Dole Food Co., Inc. (HI) 7/30/91 which reincorporated in Delaware 7/1/2001
(See Dole Food Co., Inc. (DE))

GILBERT-VARKER, INC. (DE)
No longer in existence having become inoperative and void for non-payment of taxes 4/1/41

GILBERT YOUTH RESEARCH, INC. (NY)
Name changed to Gilbert Marketing Group, Inc. 7/31/62
(See Gilbert Marketing Group, Inc.)

GILCHRIST CO (MA)
Stock Dividends - 20% 3/6/53; 10% 11/7/67
Adjudicated bankrupt 12/17/76
No stockholders' equity

GILCHRIST VENDING LTD (ON)
Liquidation completed
Each share Capital Stock no par exchanged for initial distribution of $5.077 cash 08/02/1968
Each share Capital Stock no par received second and final distribution of $0.56413 cash 08/11/1970

GILDER ENTERPRISES INC (NV)
Name changed to MedaSorb Technologies Corp. 08/07/2006
MedaSorb Technologies Corp. name changed to CytoSorbents Corp. (NV) 05/07/2010 which reorganized in Delaware 12/05/2014

GILFILLAN CORP. (CA)
Acquired by International Telephone & Telegraph Corp. (MD) 1/31/64
Each share Common no par exchanged for (0.068) share 4% Conv. Preferred Ser. E $100 par and (0.1283) share Capital Stock no par
International Telephone & Telegraph Corp. (MD) reincorporated in Delaware 1/31/68 which name changed to ITT Corp. 12/31/83 which reorganized in Indiana as ITT Industries, Inc. 12/19/95 which name changed to ITT Corp. 7/1/2006

GILFORD INDUSTRIES, INC.
Voluntarily dissolved 06/06/1988
Details not available

GILFORD INSTR LABS INC (OH)
Common no par split (2) for (1) by issuance of (1) additional share 8/21/69
Merged into Corning Glass Works 10/22/80
Each share Common no par exchanged for (0.4528) share Common $5 par
Corning Glass Works name changed to Corning Inc. 4/28/89

GILFORD RES LTD (BC)
Merged into American Pyramid Resources Inc. 07/24/1979
Each share Common no par exchanged for (0.5) share Common no par
(See American Pyramid Resources Inc.)

GILGREER MINES LTD. (ON)
Merged into Cobalt Consolidated Mining Corp. Ltd. 00/00/1953
Each (12.5) shares Capital Stock $1 par exchanged for (1) share Capital Stock $1 par
Cobalt Consolidated recapitalized as Agnico Mines Ltd. 10/25/1957 which merged into Agnico-Eagle Mines Ltd. 06/01/1972 which name changed to Agnico Eagle Mines Ltd. 04/30/2013

GILL MINING CORP. (QC)
Charter annulled for failure to file reports 11/09/1974

GILL MOBILE HOMES INC (CA)
Charter suspended for failure to file reports and pay taxes 04/02/1976

GILL URANIUM MINES LTD. (ON)
Charter revoked for failure to file reports and pay taxes 09/00/1960

GILLED INDS INC (NY)
Name changed to Mineral Resources Inc. (NY) 02/26/1974
Mineral Resources Inc. (NY) reorganized in Utah 11/22/1976
(See Mineral Resources Inc. (UT))

GILLETT (E.W.) CO., LTD.
Merged into Standard Brands, Inc. 00/00/1929
Details not available

GILLETT HLDGS INC (DE)
Name changed to Vail Resorts, Inc. 06/03/1996

GILLETTE CO (DE)
Common $1 par split (2) for (1) by issuance of (1) additional share 10/4/55
Common $1 par split (3) for (1) by issuance of (2) additional shares 12/11/61
Common $1 par split (2) for (1) by issuance of (1) additional share 5/23/86
Common $1 par split (2) for (1) by issuance of (1) additional share 5/22/87
Common $1 par split (2) for (1) by issuance of (1) additional share 5/22/91
Common $1 par split (2) for (1) by issuance of (1) additional share 6/22/95
Common $1 par split (2) for (1) by issuance of (1) additional share payable 6/5/98 to holders of record 5/15/98
Ex date - 6/8/98
Merged into Procter & Gamble Co. 10/1/2005
Each share Common $1 par exchanged for (0.975) share Common no par

GILLETTE RUBBER CO.
Dissolution and liquidation approved 00/00/1940
Details not available

GILLETTE SAFETY RAZOR CO.
Each share Common no par exchanged for (2) shares Common $1 par in 1950
Name changed to Gillette Co. in 1952
Gillette Co. merged into Proctor & Gamble Co. 10/1/2005

GILLIES LAKE-PORCUPINE GOLD MINES LTD. (ON)
Recapitalized as Consolidated Gillies Lake Mines Ltd. 00/00/1953
Each share Capital Stock $1 par exchanged for (0.4) share Capital Stock $1 par
Consolidated Gillies Lake Mines Ltd. merged into Associated Porcupine Mines Ltd. 11/05/1968 which merged into American Reserve Mining Corp. 02/27/1989 which recapitalized as AMI Resources Inc. 12/21/1994 which name changed to Ashanti Sankofa Inc. 01/19/2017

GILMAN CIOCIA INC (DE)
Name changed 06/25/1999
Name changed 01/28/2008
Name changed from Gilman & Ciocia, Inc. to Gilman + Ciocia, Inc. 06/25/1999
Name changed from Gilman + Ciocia, Inc. to Gilman Ciocia, Inc. 01/28/2008
Merged into National Holdings Corp. 10/16/2013
Each share Common 1¢ par exchanged for (0.235019) share Common 2¢ par

GILMAN FANFOLD CORP.
Merged into Moore Corp. Ltd. 00/00/1928
Details not available

GILMAN SVCS INC (DE)
Common 10¢ par split (5) for (4) by issuance of (0.25) additional share 04/15/1980
Common 10¢ par split (3) for (2) by issuance of (0.5) additional share 11/10/1980
Plan of liquidation under Chapter 11 Federal Bankruptcy proceedings confirmed 02/10/1987
No stockholders' equity

GILMER (L.H.) CO.
Assets acquired by U.S. Rubber Co. 00/00/1944
Details not available

GILMER FINL SVCS INC (TX)
Merged into East Texas Financial Services Inc. 06/30/2000
Each share Common 1¢ par exchanged for $26.10 cash

GILMORE (FORREST E.) CO.
Dissolved 00/00/1934
Details not available

GILMORE INDS INC (OH)
Stock Dividend - 25% 12/15/1961
Adjudicated bankrupt 02/10/1977
Stockholders' equity unlikely

GILMORE OIL CO., LTD.
Acquired by Socony-Vacuum Oil Co., Inc. 00/00/1945
Details not available

GILPIN EUREKA CONSOLIDATED MINES, INC.
Property sold in 1941
No stockholders' equity

GILPIN HENRY B CO (MD)
Each share Class A Common no par exchanged for (6) shares Common $1 par to effect a (2) for (1) recapitalization and (3) for (1) stock split 1/4/72
Stock Dividend - 100% 6/29/72
Plan of reorganization under Chapter XI Federal Bankruptcy Act confirmed 12/21/81
Attorney opined no stockholders' equity

GILTECH CORP (MN)
Reorganized as Rainville Co., Inc. 02/15/1972
Each share Common 50¢ par exchanged for (1) share Preferred 1¢ par and (1) share Common 1¢ par
Rainville Co., Inc. name changed to Universal Dynamics, Inc. 07/16/1982
(See Universal Dynamics, Inc.)

GIMBEL BROS INC (NY)
Each share 7% Preferred $100 par exchanged for (1.25) shares $6 Preferred no par and $5.625 cash in 1936
Each share $6 Preferred no par exchanged for (1.05) shares $4.50 Preferred no par in 1945
Common no par changed to $5 par in 1946
$4.50 Preferred no par called for redemption 10/25/61
Common $5 par split (2) for (1) by issuance of (1) additional share 3/29/62
Common $5 par split (2) for (1) by issuance of (1) additional share 3/15/67
Stock Dividends - 50% 1/25/46; 33-1/3% 1/14/47
$4.50 Preferred no par called for redemption 10/25/61
Merged into Brown & Williamson Tobacco Corp. 11/9/73
Each share Common $5 par exchanged for $23 cash

GIMBEL INDS INC (DE)
Name changed to UCF Industries Inc. 1/16/75
(See UCF Industries Inc.)

GIMBEL VISION INTL INC (AB)
Name changed to Aris Canada Ltd. 10/16/2002
(See Aris Canada Ltd.)

GIMMEABID COM INC (DE)
SEC revoked common stock registration 05/25/2016

GIMUS RES INC (CANADA)
Name changed to Lamelee Iron Ore Ltd. (Canada) 12/24/2013
Lamelee Iron Ore Ltd. (Canada) reincorporated in Ontario as Aura Health Inc. 08/16/2018

GINCHO INTL VENTURES INC (BC)
Name changed to Banner Mining Corp. 08/09/1994
(See Banner Mining Corp.)

GINGURO EXPL INC (CANADA)
Name changed to Inventus Mining Corp. 05/05/2015

GINN & CO. (MA)
Acquired by Xerox Corp. 7/1/68
Each share Common $1 par exchanged for (0.1525) share Common $1 par

GINN M S & CO (DC)
Stock Dividends - 10% 07/02/1975; 10% 07/15/1976; 10% 07/15/1977; 10% 06/29/1978
Name changed to MSG Investment Co. 02/28/1980

GINOS INC (MD)
Common no par split (2) for (1) by issuance of (1) additional share 05/01/1969
Merged into Marriott Corp. 05/03/1982
Each share Common no par exchanged for $18 cash

GINSENG FST INC (NV)
Name changed to Carroll Shelby International, Inc. 7/28/2003

GINSITE MATLS INC (FL)
Recapitalized as Environmental Construction Products International, Inc. 09/30/1999
Each share Common $0.001 par exchanged for (0.2) share Common $0.001 par
Environmental Construction Products International, Inc. name changed to Empire Film Group, Inc. 11/08/2007 which recapitalized as Tarsin Mobile, Inc. 07/09/2015

GINTEL ERISA FD (MA)
Reincorporated 03/21/1986
Name and place of incorporation changed from Gintel ERISA Fund, Inc. (MD) to Gintel ERISA Fund (MA) 03/21/1986
Merged into Gintel Fund 09/30/1996
Details not available

GINTEL FD (MA)
Reincorporated 09/06/1986
Name and place of incorporation changed from Gintel Fund, Inc. (MD) to Gintel Fund (MA) 09/06/1986
Merged into Tocqueville Trust 10/31/2003
Each share Common 1¢ par exchanged for Tocqueville Fund Class A 1¢ par on a net asset basis

GIORDANO INTL LTD (BERMUDA)
Reorganized 05/29/1995
Reorganized from Giordano Holdings Ltd. (Hong Kong) to Giordano International Ltd. (Bermuda) 05/29/1995
Sponsored ADR's for Ordinary no par split (2) for (1) by issuance of (1) additional share payable 08/16/2000 to holders of record 08/11/2000
Ex date - 08/10/2000
ADR agreement terminated 07/14/2003
Each Sponsored ADR for Ordinary no par exchanged for $5.5445714 cash

GIRARD & CO., INC.
Merged into McKesson & Robbins, Inc. 00/00/1926
Details not available

GIRARD CO (PA)
Common $1 par changed to 50¢ par and (1) additional share issued 07/03/1978
Merged into Mellon National Corp. 04/06/1983
Each share Common 50¢ par exchanged for (0.38) share $2.80 Preferred Ser. A $1 par and (0.95) share Common 50¢ par
Mellon National Corp. name changed to Mellon Bank Corp. 09/30/1984 which name changed to Mellon Financial Corp. 10/17/1999 which merged into Bank of New York Mellon Corp. 07/01/2007

GIRARD INDS CORP (PR)
Adjudicated bankrupt 06/03/1976
Stockholders' equity unlikely

GIRARD INVT CO (DE)
Company believed out of business 00/00/1971
Details not available

GIRARD LAKE MINES LTD. (ON)
Charter cancelled 04/01/1963

GIRARD TR BK (PHILADELPHIA, PA)
Capital Stock $15 par changed to $10 par 03/08/1957
Stock Dividends - 33-1/3% 03/08/1957; 50% 01/21/1966
Reorganized as Girard Co. 06/30/1969
Each share Capital Stock $10 par exchanged for (1) share Common $1 par
Girard Co. merged into Mellon National Corp. 04/06/1983 which name changed to Mellon Bank Corp. 09/30/1984 which name changed to Mellon Financial Corp. 10/17/1999 which merged into Bank of New York Mellon Corp. 07/01/2007

GIRARD TRUST CO. (PHILADELPHIA, PA)
Merged into Girard Trust Corn Exchange Bank (Philadelphia, PA) 06/18/1951
Each share Capital Stock $10 par exchanged for (1) share Capital Stock $15 par
Girard Trust Corn Exchange Bank (Philadelphia, PA) name changed to Girard Trust Bank (Philadelphia, PA) 03/09/1964 which reorganized as Girard Co. 06/30/1969 which merged into Mellon National Corp. 04/06/1983 which name changed to Mellon Bank Corp. 09/30/1984 which name changed to Mellon Financial Corp. 10/17/1999 which merged into Bank of New York Mellon Corp. 07/01/2007

GIRARD TRUST CORN EXCHANGE BANK (PHILADELPHIA, PA)
Capital Stock $15 par changed to $10 par and (0.5) additional share issued 04/01/1957
Name changed to Girard Trust Bank (Philadelphia, PA) 03/09/1964
Girard Trust Bank (Philadelphia, PA) reorganized as Girard Co. 06/30/1969 which merged into Mellon National Corp. 04/06/1983 which name changed to Mellon Bank Corp. 09/30/1984 which name changed to Mellon Financial Corp. 10/17/1999 which merged into Bank of New York Mellon Corp. 07/01/2007

GIRASOLAR INC (DE)
Common 1¢ par split (5) for (2) by issuance of (1.5) additional shares payable 05/02/2006 to holders of record 05/02/2006 Ex date - 05/03/2006
SEC revoked common stock registration 04/11/2014

GIRDLER CORP. (DE)
Common no par changed to $20 par in 1950
Stock Dividend - 25% 12/15/51
Merged into National Cylinder Gas Co. and each share Common $20 par exchanged for (3-1/3) shares Common $1 par in 1953
National Cylinder Gas Co. name was changed to Chemetron Corp. 5/6/58

GIRLTOWN, INC. (MA)
Name changed to M.R.B., Inc. 4/6/67
(See M.R.B., Inc.)

GIS GLOBAL IMAGING SOLUTIONS INC (BC)
Name changed to Segami Images, Inc. 02/05/2001
(See Segami Images, Inc.)

GISH BIOMEDICAL INC (CA)
Common no par split (3) for (2) by issuance of (0.5) additional share 07/05/1990
Merged into CardioTech International, Inc. (MA) 04/08/2003
Each share Common no par exchanged for (1.3422) shares Common 1¢ par
CardioTech International, Inc. (MA) reincorporated in Delaware 10/26/2007 which name changed to AdvanSource Biomaterials Corp. 10/16/2008

GISHOLT CORP. (WI)
Stock Dividend - 10% 02/15/1966
Acquired by Giddings & Lewis Machine Tool Co. 06/30/1966
Each share Common $10 par exchanged for (1) share Common $2 par
Giddings & Lewis Machine Tool Co. name changed to Giddings & Lewis, Inc. (Old) 04/26/1967
(See Giddings & Lewis, Inc. (Old))

GISHOLT MACHINE CO. (WI)
Each share Common $20 par exchanged for (3) shares Common $10 par 00/00/1940
Stock Dividends - 20% 06/01/1951; 16-2/3% 11/30/1953; 10% 02/15/1965
Name changed to Gisholt Corp. 04/14/1965
Gisholt Corp. acquired by Giddings & Lewis Machine Tool Co. 06/30/1966 which name changed to Giddings & Lewis, Inc. (Old) 04/26/1967
(See Giddings & Lewis, Inc. (Old))

GIT TAX FREE TR (MA)
Name changed to Mosaic Tax-Free Trust and Tax Free High Yield Account no par reclassified as Tax-Free National Fund no par 05/12/1997
Mosaic Tax-Free Trust name changed to Madison Mosaic Tax-Free Trust 11/01/2006

GITANO GROUP INC (DE)
Plan of reorganization under Chapter 11 Federal Bankruptcy proceedings confirmed 08/30/1994
No stockholders' equity

GITENNES EXPL INC (ON)
Reincorporated under the laws of British Columbia 02/24/2017

GIVEN IMAGING LTD (ISRAEL)
Acquired by Covidien PLC 02/27/2014
Each share Ordinary ILS 0.05 par exchanged for $30 cash

GIVEN MANUFACTURING CO. (CA)
Stock Dividend - 25% 6/22/53
Name changed to Waste King Corp. 4/18/56
(See Waste King Corp.)

GIYANI GOLD CORP (BC)
Name changed to Giyani Metals Corp. 07/17/2017

GK INTELLIGENT SYS INC (DE)
Each share old Common $0.001 par exchanged for (0.1) share new Common $0.001 par 04/03/2002
Recapitalized as M Power Entertainment, Inc. 05/18/2005
Each share new Common $0.001 par exchanged for (0.005) share Common $0.001 par
M Power Entertainment, Inc. recapitalized as eDoorways Corp., Inc. 09/04/2007 which name changed to eDoorways International Corp. (DE) 09/02/2010 which reincorporated in Nevada 05/06/2013 which recapitalized as Escue Energy, Inc. 06/23/2015

GK TECHNOLOGIES INC (NJ)
Merged into Penn Central Corp. 5/14/81
Each share $1.94 Conv. Preference $25 par exchanged for $59.50 cash
Each share Common $1 par exchanged for $50 cash

GKN HLDG CORP (DE)
Name changed to Research Partners International, Inc. 07/17/1998
Research Partners International, Inc. name changed to Firebrand Financial Group, Inc. 07/27/2000
(See Firebrand Financial Group, Inc.)

GKN PLC (UNITED KINGDOM)
ADR's for Ordinary split (2) for (1) by issuance of (1) additional share payable 06/03/1998 to holders of record 05/26/1998
Each Unsponsored ADR for Ordinary exchanged for (1) Sponsored ADR for Ordinary 08/01/2000
Each Sponsored ADR for Ordinary received distribution of (1) Brambles Industries PLC Ordinary payable 08/07/2001 to holders of record 08/03/2001
ADR agreement terminated 09/06/2018
Each Sponsored ADR for Ordinary exchanged for $5.646068 cash

GL ENERGY & EXPL INC (DE)
Old Common $0.001 par split (3.5) for (1) by issuance of (2.5) additional shares payable 12/05/2001 to holders of record 11/23/2001 Ex date - 12/06/2001
Old Common $0.001 par split (2) for (1) by issuance of (1) additional share payable 07/29/2002 to holders of record 07/26/2002 Ex date - 07/30/2002
Each share old Common $0.001 par exchanged for (0.04545454) share new Common $0.001 par 05/29/2003
Recapitalized as American Southwest Music Distribution, Inc. 08/24/2006
Each share new Common $0.001 par exchanged for (0.01351351) share Common $0.001 par

GL ENTERPRISES INC (NV)
Liquidation completed
Each share Common $1 par exchanged for initial distribution of $3.30 cash 12/23/74
Each share Common $1 par received second distribution of (0.2) share Bankers Mortgage Corp. Common 50¢ par 1/27/75
Each share Common $1 par received third and final distribution of $0.214 cash 12/29/78
Bankers Mortgage Corp. name changed to Bamocor, Inc. 12/21/79 which name changed to Palm Springs Lifestyle, Inc. 5/25/88
(See Palm Springs Lifestyle, Inc.)

GLACIER BANCORP INC (DE)
Common $0.0044 par split (3) for (2) by issuance of (0.5) additional share payable 5/23/97 to holders of record 5/9/97
Stock Dividends - 10% 5/28/92; 10% 5/28/93; 10% 5/26/94; 10% 5/25/95; 10% payable 5/23/96 to holders of record 5/9/96
Under plan of reorganization each share Common $0.0044 par automatically became (1) share Glacier Bancorp, Inc. (New) (DE) Common 1¢ par 7/8/98
Glacier Bancorp, Inc. (New) (DE) reincorporated in Montana 4/30/2004

GLACIER BANCORP INC NEW (DE)
Stock Dividends - 10% payable 10/1/98 to holders of record 9/17/98; 10% payable 5/27/99 to holders of record 5/18/99; 10% payable 5/25/2000 to holders of record 5/16/2000 Ex date - 5/12/2000; 10% payable 5/22/2003 to holders of record 5/13/2003 Ex date - 5/9/2003
Reincorporated under the laws of Montana 4/30/2004

GLACIER CAP TR I (DE)
Trust Preferred Securities called for redemption at $25 on 2/1/2006

GLACIER EXPLORERS LTD. (ON)
Recapitalized as New Glacier Explorers Ltd. 01/10/1967
Each share Capital Stock $1 par exchanged for (0.4) share Capital Stock $1 par
(See New Glacier Explorers Ltd.)

GLACIER HLDGS INC (CO)
Each share old Common no par exchanged for (0.025) share new Common no par 11/26/90
Proclaimed dissolved for failure to file annual reports 9/1/95

GLACIER INVESTMENT CO., INC. (UT)
Reorganized under the laws of Nevada as Chariot Seven Productions 10/22/1990
Each share Common $0.001 par exchanged for (0.1) share Common $0.001 par
Chariot Seven Productions name changed to Upscale Trends Inc. 10/16/1994 which name changed to Electric Entertainment International Inc. 03/07/1997 which recapitalized as Private Media Group Ltd. 12/16/1997
(See Private Media Group Ltd.)

GLACIER MINING LTD. (ON)
Name changed to Glacier Explorers Ltd. 09/25/1957
Glacier Explorers Ltd. recapitalized as New Glacier Explorers Ltd. 01/10/1967
(See New Glacier Explorers Ltd.)

GLACIER RES LTD (BC)
Recapitalized as Bayfield Ventures Corp. 05/18/2001
Each share Common no par exchanged for (0.33333333) share Common no par
Bayfield Ventures Corp. merged into New Gold Inc. 01/02/2015

GLACIER SILVER LEAD MINING CO.
Reorganized as Sunny Peak Mining Co. and stock exchanged on a share for share basis in 1948
(See Sunny Peak Mining Co.)

GLACIER VENTURES INTL CORP NEW (CANADA)
Reincorporated 09/20/1999
Name changed 04/28/2000
Place of incorporation changed from (BC) to (Canada) 09/20/1999
Under plan of merger name changed from Glacier Ventures International Corp. (Old) to Glacier Ventures International Corp. (New) 04/28/2000
Name changed to Glacier Media Inc. 07/01/2008

GLACIER WTR TR I (DE)
9.025% Trust Preferred Securities called for redemption at $25 plus $0.0881 accrued dividends on 06/29/2018

GLACIER WTR SVCS INC (DE)
Merged into Primo Water Corp. 12/12/2016
Each share Common 1¢ par exchanged for (0.252975) share Common $0.001 par, (1) Common Stock Purchase Warrant expiring 12/31/2021 and $12.176087 cash

GLADDEN PRODUCTS CORP. (CA)
Name changed to Buckner Industries, Inc. 3/9/62
(See Buckner Industries, Inc.)

GLADDING, McBEAN & CO. (CA)
Each share old Capital Stock no par exchanged for (4) shares new Capital Stock no par in 1927
New Capital Stock no par changed to $25 par in 1948
Each share Capital Stock $25 par exchanged for (2.5) shares Capital Stock $10 par in 1951
Each share Capital Stock $10 par exchanged for (2) shares Capital Stock $5 par 7/29/57
Stock Dividends - 25% 1/20/56; 20% 7/31/56
Merged into International Pipe & Ceramics Corp. 9/27/62
Each share Capital Stock $5 par exchanged for (0.2) share 5% Conv. Preferred $100 par
International Pipe & Ceramics Corp. name changed to Interpace Corp. 4/25/68 which merged into Clevepak Corp. 8/15/83
(See Clevepak Corp.)

GLADDING CORP (NY)
Common 50¢ par changed to 25¢ par and (1) additional share issued 2/28/69
Merged into Paris Industries Corp. 7/3/84
Holdings of (50) shares or more exchanged for (0.2) share Class A Preferred $3 par and (0.2) share Common no par per share
Holdings of (49) shares or fewer exchanged for $0.85 cash per share
(See Paris Industries Corp.)

GLADDINGS INC (RI)
Company went private 09/01/1972
Public interest eliminated

GLADIATOR MINERALS INC (CANADA)
Issue Information - 2,000,000 shares COM offered at $0.10 per share on 10/29/1997
Recapitalized as Hinterland Metals Inc. 09/25/2002
Each share Common no par exchanged for (0.5) share Common no par

GLADIATOR RESOURCES LTD. (BC)
Incorporated 06/25/1959
Struck off register and declared dissolved for failure to file returns 07/16/1993

GLADIATOR RES LTD (BC)
Incorporated 02/25/1983
Charter cancelled 07/16/1993

GLADSTONE CAP CORP (MD)
7.125% Preferred Ser. 2016 $0.001 par called for redemption at $25.125 plus $0.00989583 accrued dividends on 05/23/2014
6.75% Term Preferred Ser. 2021 $0.001 par called for redemption at $25 plus $0.140625 accrued dividends on 09/29/2017
(Additional Information in Active)

GLADSTONE COML CORP (MD)
7.125% Preferred Ser. C $0.001 par called for redemption at $25 plus $0.09401 accrued dividends on 08/19/2016
(Additional Information in Active)

GLADSTONE ENERGY INC (DE)
Completely liquidated 06/20/2001
Details not available

GLA-GLA

GLADSTONE FARMS, LTD. (BAHAMAS)
Placed in receivership 09/00/2002
Stockholders' equity unlikely

GLADSTONE INVT CORP (DE)
7.125% Term Preferred Ser. A $0.001 par called for redemption at $25 on 09/30/2016
6.5% Term Preferred Ser. C $0.001 par called for redemption at $25 on 08/31/2018
6.75% Term Preferred Ser. B $0.001 par called for redemption at $25 on 08/31/2018
(Additional Information in Active)

GLADSTONE MOUNTAIN MNG CO (WA)
Recapitalized as Gladstone Resources, Inc. (WA) 02/05/1973
Each share Common 10¢ par exchanged for (0.25) share Common no par
Gladstone Resources, Inc. (WA) reorganized in Delaware as Gladstone Energy Inc. 08/11/1999
(See Gladstone Energy Inc.)

GLADSTONE RES INC (WA)
Reorganized under the laws of Delaware as Gladstone Energy Inc. 08/11/1999
Each share Common no par exchanged for (0.2) share Common no par
(See Gladstone Energy Inc.)

GLADSTONE RES LTD (BC)
Reorganized under the laws of Delaware as VAALCO Energy, Inc. 03/01/1989
Each share Common no par exchanged for (1) share Common 10¢ par

GLAGOMA COPPER MINES LTD. (ON)
Charter cancelled and company declared dissolved for default in filing returns 1/6/71

GLAMIS GOLD LTD (BC)
Common no par split (3) for (2) by issuance of (0.5) additional share 01/05/1987
Common no par split (2) for (1) by issuance of (1) additional share 05/20/1987
Merged into Goldcorp Inc. (New) 11/04/2006
Each share Common no par exchanged for (1.69) shares Common no par and $0.0001 cash

GLAMIS RES LTD (AB)
Name changed to Legacy Oil + Gas Inc. 11/12/2009
Legacy Oil + Gas Inc. merged into Crescent Point Energy Corp. 07/06/2015

GLAMORGAN CORP (DE)
Name changed 10/13/1971
Name and state of incorporation changed from Glamorgan Pipe & Foundry Co. (VA) to Glamorgan Corp. (DE) 10/13/1971
Completely liquidated 00/00/1972
Details not available

GLAMOUR VENDING CORP. (CO)
Declared defunct and inoperative by Colorado Secretary of State 10/17/1963

GLAMUR PRODUCTS, INC. (NY)
Each share Common 2¢ par exchanged for (0.25) share Common 8¢ par 09/19/1957
Merged into Wagner (E.R.) Manufacturing Co. 11/14/1962
Each (232) shares Common 8¢ par exchanged for (1) share 6% Preferred 2nd $100 par
(See Wagner (E.R.) Manufacturing Co.)

GLANCE INC (NV)
Common $0.001 par split (3) for (1) by issuance of (2) additional shares payable 03/06/2009 to holders of record 03/06/2009 Ex date - 03/09/2009
Name changed to China Green Creative, Inc. 03/09/2009
China Green Creative, Inc. name changed to China Shianyun Group Corp., Ltd. 08/30/2013

GLAR BAN CORP (NY)
Common $1 par changed to 50¢ par and (1) additional share issued 10/31/1960
Common 50¢ par changed to 10¢ par 10/01/1969
Merged into Mark IV Industries, Inc. 11/30/1977
Each share Common 10¢ par exchanged for $15 cash

GLAS-AIRE INDS GROUP LTD (NV)
Stock Dividends - 2.5% payable 01/14/2000 to holders of record 12/10/1999; 18.5% payable 03/25/2000 to holders of record 03/10/2000; 2.5% payable 06/12/2000 to holders of record 06/12/2000
Recapitalized as Environmental Service Professionals, Inc. 10/10/2006
Each (3.75) shares Common 1¢ par exchanged for (1) share Common $0.001 par

GLASCO INC (IN)
Merged into Universal Match Corp. 10/21/1960
Each share Common $1 par exchanged for (0.66666666) share Common $25 par
Universal Match Corp. name changed to UMC Industries, Inc. 05/17/1966 which name changed to Unidynamics Corp. 04/19/1984
(See Unidynamics Corp.)

GLASCO INC (UT)
Involuntarily dissolved 09/30/1982

GLASFOAM CORP (DE)
No longer in existence having become inoperative and void for non-payment of taxes 04/15/1972

GLASGAL COMMUNICATIONS INC (CA)
Name changed to Datatec Systems Inc. 1/7/98
(See Datatec Systems Inc.)

GLASGOW RAILWAY CO. (KY)
Preferred $100 par called for redemption in 1989
(Additional Information in Active)

GLASROCK MED SVCS CORP (GA)
Common $1 par split (5) for (2) by issuance of (1.5) additional shares 8/22/80
Liquidation completed
Each share Common $1 par received initial distribution of (1) share Porex Technologies Corp. Common 1¢ par and $15 cash 1/20/83
Assets transferred to Glasrock Medical Services Liquidating Corp. 1/2/84
(See Glasrock Medical Services Liquidating Corp.)

GLASROCK MEDICAL SERVICES LIQUIDATING CORP. (GA)
Liquidation completed
Each share Common $1 par received initial distribution of $1.50 cash 1/2/85
Each share Common $1 par received second distribution of $0.93 cash 1/30/86
Each share Common $1 par received third and final distribution of $0.128 cash 3/18/87
Note: Certificates were not required to be surrendered and are without value
(See Glasrock Medical Services Corp. for previous distributions)

GLASROCK PRODUCTS, INC. (GA)
Each share Capital Stock $10 par exchanged for (5) shares Capital Stock $1 par 7/18/61
Capital Stock $1 par reclassified as Common $1 par 2/26/65
Name changed to Glasrock Medical Services Corp. 7/31/80
Glasrock Medical Services Corp. assets transferred to Glasrock Medical Services Liquidating Corp. 1/2/84
(See Glasrock Medical Services Liquidating Corp.)

GLASS, SCOTT & WILCOX, INC. (PA)
Out of existence 04/01/1975
No stockholders' equity

GLASS EARTH GOLD LTD (BC)
Each share old Common no par exchanged for (0.2) share new Common no par 03/18/2010
Recapitalized as Antipodes Gold Ltd. 03/24/2014
Each share new Common no par exchanged for (0.1) share Common no par
Antipodes Gold Ltd. recapitalized as Chatham Rock Phosphate Ltd. 02/24/2017

GLASS EARTH LTD (BC)
Name changed to Glass Earth Gold Ltd. 12/28/2007
Glass Earth Gold Ltd. recapitalized as Antipodes Gold Ltd. 03/24/2014 which recapitalized as Chatham Rock Phosphate Ltd. 02/24/2017

GLASS FIBERS, INC. (OH)
Merged into L-O-F Glass Fibers Co. 3/1/55
Each share Common $1 par exchanged for (1) share Common $5 par
L-O-F Glass Fibers Co. acquired by Johns-Manville Corp. (NY) 12/31/58 which reincorporated in Delaware as Manville Corp. 10/30/81 which name changed to Schuller Corp. 3/29/96 which name changed to Johns-Manville Corp. (New) 5/5/97

GLASS MAGIC BOATS, INC. (TX)
Adjudicated bankrupt 8/17/61
No stockholders' equity

GLASS MARINE INDUSTRIES INC. (DE)
Name changed to Columbia Yacht Corp. 6/28/65
Columbia Yacht Corp. name changed to CYC Corp. 4/13/67 which was acquired by Whittaker Corp. (CA) 4/14/67 which reincorporated in Delaware 6/16/86
(See Whittaker Corp. (DE))

GLASS-TITE INDUSTRIES, INC. (RI)
Common 10¢ par changed to 4¢ par and (1.5) additional shares issued 10/15/59
Name changed to GTI Corp. (RI) 5/13/65
GTI Corp. (RI) reincorporated in Delaware 5/11/87
(See GTI Corp.)

GLASS WAVE ENTERPRISES INC (NV)
Reorganized as Cyplasin Biomedical Ltd. 02/16/2007
Each share Common $0.001 par exchanged for (6.2) shares Common $0.001 par
Cyplasin Biomedical Ltd. name changed to Compass Biotechnologies Inc. 03/29/2011

GLASSCO INSTR CO (CA)
Capital Stock no par split (3) for (1) by issuance of (2) additional shares 08/16/1961
Capital Stock no par split (2) for (1) by issuance of (1) additional share 02/28/1968
Completely liquidated 02/14/1969
Each share Capital Stock no par exchanged for first and final distribution of (1) share Kratos Common no par
Kratos name changed to Kratos, Inc. 08/08/1977 which name changed to Keuffel & Esser Co. (CA) 03/27/1986
(See Keuffel & Esser Co. (CA))

GLASSCOCK (C.G.)-TIDELANDS OIL CO. (DE)
Name changed to Diversa, Inc. 5/1/59
(See Diversa, Inc.)

GLASSESOFF INC (NV)
Each share Common $0.001 par exchanged for (0.1) share new Common $0.001 par 03/31/2015
Name changed to InnoVision Labs, Inc. 01/22/2016

GLASSMASTER CO (SC)
Each share Common 1¢ par exchanged for (0.33333333) share Common 3¢ par 01/28/1983
Chapter 7 bankruptcy proceedings terminated 04/25/2013
No stockholders' equity

GLASSMASTER INDS INC (BC)
Recapitalized as Interlink Systems Inc. 01/19/2000
Each share Common no par exchanged for (0.1) share Common no par
Interlink Systems Inc. recapitalized as iQuest Networks Inc. (BC) 08/14/2000 which reorganized in Wyoming as Quest Ventures Inc. 10/28/2003 which recapitalized as Dorato Resources Inc. (WY) 04/24/2006 which reincorporated in British Columbia 08/21/2006 which recapitalized as Xiana Mining Inc. 10/23/2013

GLASSMASTER PLASTICS CO. (SC)
Common $1 par changed to 25¢ par and (3) additional shares issued 01/03/1967
Common 25¢ par changed to 1¢ par 03/19/1982
Name changed to Glassmaster Co. 04/14/1982
(See Glassmaster Co.)

GLASSPAR CO. (CA)
Capital Stock $1 par changed to 50¢ par and (1) additional share issued 11/13/59
Name changed to 19101 Newport Corp. 10/31/66
19101 Newport Corp. was liquidated by exchange for Larson Industries, Inc. 7/10/67
(See Larson Industries, Inc.)

GLASSTECH INC (DE)
Merged into Glasstech Holdings 06/05/1997
Each share Common 1¢ par exchanged for $57.6875 cash
Each share Common 1¢ par received an initial additional distribution of $0.33983168 cash 10/03/1997
Each share Common 1¢ par received a second additional distribution of $0.09942472 cash 00/00/1998

GLASTONBURY BK & TR CO (GLASTONBURY, CT)
Common $5 par changed to $2.50 par and (1) additional share issued 7/11/80
Common $2.50 par split (2) for (1) by issuance of (1) additional share 7/1/88
Stock Dividends - 100% 6/10/74; 100% 8/1/86
Merged into SIS Bancorp, Inc. 12/17/97
Each share Common $2.50 par exchanged for (0.74) share Common 1¢ par
(See SIS Bancorp, Inc.)

GLASTRON BOAT CO. (TX)
Completely liquidated 4/5/67
Each share Common no par received

first and final distribution of (1) share Conroy, Inc. Common $1 par
Certificates were not retired and are now without value

GLATFELTER P H CO (PA)
Each share Common no par exchanged for (10) shares Common $10 par in 1947
Common $10 par changed to $5 par and (1) additional share issued 5/26/59
Common $5 par split (3) for (2) by issuance of (0.5) additional share 6/29/73
5% Conv Preference $50 par called for redemption 2/20/76
Stock Dividend - 40% 4/9/76
Common $5 par changed to $2.50 par and (1) additional share issued 5/17/77
Common $2.50 par changed to 83-1/3¢ par and (2) additional shares issued 5/15/84
Common 83-1/3¢ par changed to 1¢ par and (1) additional share issued 5/13/86
4-1/2% Preferred $50 par called for redemption 7/25/88
Common 1¢ par split (2) for (1) by issuance of (1) additional share 5/13/92
4.625% Preferred $50 par called for redemption 10/27/93
Name changed to Glatfelter 10/22/2001

GLAXO GROUP LTD (ENGLAND)
Stock Dividends - 25% 12/31/1964; 25% 01/09/1968; 25% 02/27/1970
Merged into Glaxo Holdings Ltd. 06/26/1972
Each ADR for Ordinary 50p par exchanged for (1) ADR for Ordinary 50p par and 60p principal amount of 7-1/2% Conv. Unsecured Loan Stock due 06/30/1985
Note: Above available until 05/11/1973 after which holders were entitled only to $9.596 cash plus accrued dividends per each ADR

GLAXO HLDGS PLC (ENGLAND)
Each ADR for Ordinary 50p par exchanged for (1) Sponsored ADR for Ordinary 50p par 03/15/1987
Sponsored ADR's for Ordinary 50p par split (2) for (1) by issuance of (1) additional ADR 11/24/1989
Sponsored ADR's for Ordinary 50p par changed to 25p par and (1) additional ADR issued 11/08/1991
Stock Dividends - 100% 02/28/1980; 100% 03/04/1983; 100% 02/10/1986
Name changed to Glaxo PLC 01/01/1995
Glaxo PLC name changed to Glaxo Wellcome PLC 04/28/1995 which name changed to GlaxoSmithKline PLC 12/27/2000

GLAXO LABORATORIES, LTD. (ENGLAND)
Stock Dividend - 25% 12/30/1960
Name changed to Glaxo Group Ltd. 12/11/1961
(See Glaxo Group Ltd.)

GLAXO WELLCOME PLC (ENGLAND)
Name changed 04/28/1995
Name changed from Glaxo PLC to Glaxo Wellcome PLC 04/28/1995
Name changed to GlaxoSmithKline PLC 12/27/2000

GLB BANCORP INC (OH)
Issue Information - 1,300,000 shares COM offered at $13 per share on 05/14/1998
Stock Dividend - 10% payable 09/17/2002 to holders of record 09/03/2002 Ex date - 08/29/2002
Merged into Sky Financial Group, Inc. 10/21/2003
Each share Common no par exchanged for (0.74) share Common no par
Sky Financial Group, Inc. merged into Huntington Bancshares Inc. 07/02/2007

GLC LTD (BRITISH VIRGIN ISLANDS)
Name changed to Galaxiworld.com Ltd. 08/30/1999
(See Galaxiworld.com Ltd.)

GLE RES LTD (ON)
Recapitalized as Chelsea Resources Ltd. 01/05/1987
Each share Common no par exchanged for 0.33333333) share Common no par
(See Chelsea Resources Ltd.)

GLEANER COMBINE HARVESTER CORP.
Reorganized as Gleaner Harvester Corp. in 1932
Details not available

GLEANER HARVESTER CORP. (DE)
Each share Common no par exchanged for (2) shares Common $2.50 par 00/00/1937
Stock Dividend - 33-1/3% 11/05/1948
Acquired by Allis-Chalmers Manufacturing Co. 01/31/1955
Each (3.5) shares Common $2.50 par exchanged for (1) share Common $20 par
Allis-Chalmers Manufacturing Co. name changed to Allis-Chalmers Corp. 05/28/1971 which name changed to Allis-Chalmers Energy, Inc. 01/01/2005
(See Allis-Chalmers Energy, Inc.)

GLEASON CORP (DE)
Merged into Torque Acquisition Co., L.L.C. 3/29/2000
Each share Common $1 par exchanged for $23 cash

GLEASON WKS (NY)
Common $2 par changed to $1 par and (1) additional share issued 5/18/70
Reorganized under the laws of Delaware as Gleason Corp. 5/21/84
(See Gleason Corp.)

GLEASONITE PRODUCTS CO.
Name changed to Asbestos & Rubber Products Corp. 00/00/1928
(See Asbestos & Rubber Products Corp.)

GLEEMAR GOLD MINES, LTD. (ON)
Charter revoked for failure to file reports and pay taxes 00/00/1956

GLEEWORKS INC (DE)
Name changed to Capital Art, Inc. 05/09/2011
Capital Art, Inc. name changed to Globe Photos, Inc. 06/25/2018

GLEICHEN RES LTD (BC)
Reincorporated under the laws of Ontario as Torex Gold Resources Inc. 05/04/2010

GLEN ALDEN COAL CO. (PA)
Name changed to Glen Alden Corp. (Pa.) and Common no par changed to $1 par 4/29/55
Glen Alden Corp. (Pa.) reincorporated under the laws of Delaware 5/18/67 which merged into Rapid-American Corp. (Del.) 11/6/72
(See Rapid-American Corp. (Del.))

GLEN ALDEN CORP (DE)
Reincorporated 05/18/1967
Under plan of merger (0.25) additional share Common $1 par distributed 04/21/1959
State of incorporation changed from (PA) to (DE) 05/18/1967
Class C Contingent Preference Ser. 5 no par called for redemption 02/29/1972
$2.25 Senior Conv. Preferred no par called for redemption 07/20/1972
Merged into Rapid-American Corp. (DE) 11/06/1972
Each share $3 Class B Conv. Preferred no par exchanged for $100 principal amount 7% Subord. Deb. due 05/15/1994 plus $25 cash or (1) share $3 Class B Conv. Preferred no par
Note: Option to receive Debs. and cash expired after 12/11/1972
Each share $3.15 Conv. Preferred no par exchanged for $100 principal amount 7% Subord. Deb. due 05/15/1994 plus $30 cash or (1) share $3.15 Conv. Preferred no par
Note: Option to receive Debs. and cash expired after 12/11/1972
Class C Contingent Preference Ser. 6 & 7 no par automatically became same class of new company without exchange of certificates
Each share Common $1 par exchanged for (0.35) share Common $1 par plus (1) Purchase Warrant expiring 05/15/1994
(See Rapid-American Corp. (DE))

GLEN ALSACE WTR CO (PA)
Merged into Citizens Utilities Co. 3/9/83
Each share Capital Stock $10 par exchanged for $17.25 cash

GLEN AUDEN RES LTD (ON)
Recapitalized as Maple Minerals Inc. 06/28/1996
Each share Common no par exchanged for (0.2) share Common no par
Maple Minerals Inc. recapitalized as Maple Minerals Corp. 11/09/2001 which name changed to Mega Uranium Ltd. 10/19/2005

GLEN COPPER MINES LTD (BC)
Recapitalized as Cusac Industries Ltd. 07/04/1974
Each share Common no par exchanged for (0.2) share Common no par
Cusac Industries Ltd. name changed to Cusac Gold Mines Ltd. 08/14/1995 which merged into Hawthorne Gold Corp. (New) 04/15/2008 which name changed to China Minerals Mining Corp. 04/05/2011 which name changed to Wildsky Resources Inc. 08/22/2018

GLEN EXPLS INC (WA)
Charter cancelled and proclaimed dissolved for failure to pay fees 7/1/72

GLEN GERY CORP (OH)
Reincorporated 4/15/74
State of incorporation changed from (PA) to (OH) 4/15/74
Merged into I-J Holdings, Inc. 11/21/79
Each share Common 50¢ par exchanged for $16 cash

GLEN-GERY SHALE BRICK CO.
Reorganized as Glen-Gery Shale Brick Corp. in 1938
Details not available

GLEN-GERY SHALE BRICK CORP. (PA)
Common no par changed to $2 par in 1945
Each share Common $2 par exchanged for (4) shares Common 50¢ par in 1949 6% 1st Preferred called for redemption 12/1/58
Name changed to Glen-Gery Corp. (PA) 4/30/68
Glen-Gery Corp. (PA) reincorporated in Ohio 4/15/74
(See Glen-Gery Corp. (OH))

GLEN GLENN SOUND CO (CA)
Completely liquidated 06/20/1972
Each share Common $1 par exchanged for first and final distribution of (1) share Republic Corp. (DE) Common 50¢ par
Republic Corp. (DE) merged into Triton Group Ltd. 02/15/1985
(See Triton Group Ltd.)

GLEN HAWK MINERALS LTD (BC)
Recapitalized as Oronova Resource Corp. 11/24/2009
Each share Common no par exchanged for (0.25) share Common no par
Oronova Resource Corp. name changed to Oronova Energy Inc. 12/16/2016

GLEN INDS INC (NY)
Adjudicated bankrupt 12/20/1965
No stockholders' equity

GLEN LAKE SILVER MINES LTD (ON)
Into bankruptcy 11/16/1970
No stockholders' equity

GLEN MANOR RES INC (NV)
Name changed to XTX Energy, Inc. 06/01/2006
XTX Energy, Inc. recapitalized as Atomic Guppy, Inc. 06/25/2007 which recapitalized as Quamtel, Inc. 09/09/2009 which name changed to DataJack, Inc. 12/31/2012 which name changed to Unified Signal, Inc. 11/28/2014

GLEN MFG., INC. (WI)
99% acquired by Winter (Jack), Inc. 12/31/1974
Public interest eliminated

GLEN RIDGE TRUST CO (GLEN RIDGE, NJ)
Merged into National Newark & Essex Bank (Newark, NJ) 09/29/1967
Each share Capital Stock $25 par exchanged for (5.775) shares Capital Stock $10 par
National Newark & Essex Bank (Newark, NJ) reorganized as Midlantic Banks Inc. 06/12/1970 which merged into Midlantic Corp. 01/30/1987 which merged into PNC Bank Corp. 12/31/1995 which name changed to PNC Financial Services Group, Inc. 03/15/2000

GLEN ROCK ST BK (GLEN ROCK, PA)
Common $2 par split (2) for (1) by issuance of (1) additional share payable 04/28/1995 to holders of record 04/03/1995
Common $2 par split (2) for (1) by issuance of (1) additional share payable 05/01/1998 to holders of record 04/01/1998
Common $2 par split (2) for (1) by issuance of (1) additional share payable 09/30/1999 to holders of record 08/31/1999
Merged into Community Banks, Inc. 03/30/2001
Each share Common $2 par exchanged for (0.9) share Common $5 par
Community Banks, Inc. merged into Susquehanna Bancshares, Inc. 11/16/2007 which merged into BB&T Corp. 08/01/2015

GLEN ROGER CREDIT, INC. (DE)
Name changed to Prudential Loan Corp. which was acquired by Guardian Consumer Finance Corp. in 1956
Guardian Consumer Finance Corp. merged into Liberty Loan Corp. 4/4/60 which name changed to LLC Corp. 3/14/80 which name changed to Valhi, Inc. 3/10/87

GLENALLAN GOLD MINES LTD. (QC)
Charter abandoned 6/5/58
No stockholders' equity

GLENALLEN CORP. OF NEW YORK (NY)
Charter revoked for failure to file reports and pay fees 12/15/1967

GLENARUM MNG EXPLS LTD (ON)
Charter cancelled for failure to pay taxes and file returns 10/18/1978

GLENAVY INVTS CORP (AB)
Name changed to RHN Recreational Enterprises Ltd. 04/04/2002
(See RHN Recreational Enterprises Ltd.)

GLENAYR KITTEN LTD (ON)
Reincorporated under the laws of Canada 7/10/89

GLENAYRE ELECTRS LTD (CANADA)
Reincorporated 03/09/1989
Place of incorporation changed from (BC) to (Canada) 03/09/1989
Name changed to GLENTEL Inc. 08/05/1993
(See GLENTEL Inc.)

GLENAYRE TECHNOLOGIES INC (DE)
Common 2¢ par split (3) for (2) by issuance of (0.5) additional share 05/14/1993
Common 2¢ par split (2) for (1) by issuance of (1) additional share 11/29/1993
Common 2¢ par split (3) for (2) by issuance of (0.5) additional share 01/05/1995
Common 2¢ par split (3) for (2) by issuance of (0.5) additional share 06/19/1995
Common 2¢ par split (3) for (2) by issuance of (0.5) additional share 12/29/1995
Name changed to Entertainment Distribution Co., Inc. 05/11/2007
Entertainment Distribution Co., Inc. recapitalized as EDCI Holdings, Inc. 08/26/2008
(See EDCI Holdings, Inc.)

GLENBOROUGH RLTY TR INC (MD)
Secondary Offering - 3,500,000 shares Common offered at $13.875 per share on 10/02/1996
7.75% Conv. Preferred Ser. A called for redemption at $25.3875 plus $0.484375 accrued dividends on 11/29/2006
Merged into Gridiron Acquisition LLC 11/29/2006
Each share Common $0.001 par exchanged for $26 cash

GLENBRIAR DEVS LTD (AB)
Name changed to Glenbriar Technologies Inc. 04/02/2001

GLENBURK MINES LTD (ON)
Merged into Glenarum Mining Explorations Ltd. 05/10/1976
Each share Capital Stock $1 par exchanged for (0.25) share Capital Stock no par
(See Glenarum Mining Explorations Ltd.)

GLENCAIR RES INC (ON)
Name changed 02/19/1981
Name changed from Glencair Mining Co., Ltd. to Glencair Resources Inc. 02/19/1981
Cease trade offer effective 09/00/1985
Stockholders' equity unlikely

GLENCAIRN GOLD CORP (CANADA)
Name changed 10/15/2002
Reincorporated 06/08/2005
Name changed from Glencairn Explorations Ltd. to Glencairn Gold Corp. 10/15/2002
Place of incorporation changed from (ON) to (Canada) 06/08/2005
Recapitalized as Central Sun Mining Inc. 12/05/2007
Each share Common no par exchanged for (0.14285714) share Common no par
Note: Unexchanged certificates were cancelled and became without value 12/05/2013
Central Sun Mining Inc. acquired by B2Gold Corp. 03/31/2009

GLENCAR MINING PLC (IRELAND)
Name changed 07/09/1997
Each Unsponsored ADR for Ordinary exchanged for (1) Sponsored ADR for Ordinary 10/10/1987
Each old Sponsored ADR for Ordinary exchanged for (1) new Sponsored ADR for Ordinary 10/25/1996
Each new Sponsored ADR for Ordinary exchanged again for (0.1) new Sponsored ADR for Ordinary 06/13/1997
Name changed from Glencar Explorations PLC to Glencar Mining PLC 07/09/1997
Acquired by Gold Field Metals B.V. 11/09/2009
Each new Sponsored ADR for Ordinary exchanged for $1.391442 cash

GLENCO INTL CORP (DE)
Plan of reorganization under Chapter 11 Federal Bankruptcy proceedings confirmed 07/23/1990
No stockholders' equity

GLENCO SCIENTIFIC INC (TX)
Stock Dividends - 200% 5/2/73; 300% 7/31/75
Merged into Bethesda Research Laboratories, Inc. 9/30/81
Each share Common 10¢ par exchanged for $0.50 cash

GLENCONA EXPLORATION MINING LTD. (QC)
Charter cancelled for failure to file reports and pay fees 09/09/1972

GLENCONA MINING CO., LTD. (ON)
Acquired by Glencona Exploration Mining Ltd. 04/04/1961
Each share Common exchanged for (0.1) share Common
(See Glencona Exploration Mining Ltd.)

GLENCORE INTL PLC (JERSEY)
Name changed to Glencore Xstrata PLC 05/16/2013
Glencore Xstrata PLC name changed to Glencore PLC 05/28/2014

GLENCORE XSTRATA PLC (JERSEY)
Name changed to Glencore PLC 05/28/2014

GLENDALE BANCORPORATION (NJ)
Acquired by Mellon Bank Corp. 9/20/94
Each share Common $2.50 par exchanged for $10.50 cash

GLENDALE CO OPERATIVE BK (EVERETT, MA)
Merged into Massbank Corp. 7/18/97
Each share Common $1 par exchanged for $28 cash

GLENDALE CORP (ON)
Merged into Firan-Glendale Corp. 11/30/1978
Each share Common no par exchanged for (1) share Common no par
Firan-Glendale Corp. name changed to Firan Corp. 07/19/1982 which name changed to Glendale International Corp. 08/31/1999
(See Glendale International Corp.)

GLENDALE FED BK FED SVGS BK (GLENDALE, CA)
Reorganized 12/31/1985
Reorganized 08/26/1993
Glendale Federal Savings & Loan Association (USA) reorganized under the laws of Delaware as GLENFED, Inc. and Common $1 par changed to 1¢ par 12/31/1985
GLENFED, Inc. merged into Glendale Federal Bank, FSB (Glendale, CA) 08/26/1996
Each share Conv. Preferred Ser. D 1¢ par exchanged for (1) share new Common 1¢ par 08/27/1994
Under plan of reorganization each share 8.75% Conv. Preferred Ser. E $1 par and new Common $1 par automatically became (1) share Golden State Bancorp Inc. (DE) 8.75% Conv. Preferred Ser. A $1 par and Common $1 par respectively 07/24/1997
(See Golden State Bancorp Inc.)

GLENDALE INTL CORP (ON)
Filed a petition under Bankruptcy and Insolvency Act 01/19/2010
No stockholders' equity

GLENDALE MOBILE HOMES LTD. (ON)
Name changed to Glendale Corp. 08/15/1973
Glendale Corp. merged into Firan-Glendale Corp. 11/30/1978 which name changed to Firan Corp. 07/19/1982 which name changed to Glendale International Corp. 08/31/1999
(See Glendale International Corp.)

GLENDALE NATIONAL BANK OF NEW JERSEY (VOORHEES TOWNSHIP, NJ)
Reorganized as Atlantic Bancorporation (NJ) 7/1/85
Each share Common $2.50 par exchanged for (1) share Common $2.50 par
Atlantic Bancorporation (NJ) name changed to Glendale Bancorporation 7/28/89
(See Glendale Bancorporation)

GLENDALE RES INC (BC)
Recapitalized as International Glendale Resources Inc. 12/16/1993
Each share Common no par exchanged for (0.25) share Common no par
International Glendale Resources Inc. name changed to Odessa Petroleum Corp. 03/10/1997 which recapitalized as Aquarius Ventures Inc. (BC) 05/12/1999 which reincorporated in Canada as Citotech Systems Inc. 10/30/2000 which recapitalized as SmartCool Systems Inc. 07/21/2004

GLENDORA RES INC (BC)
Name changed to Romulus Resources Ltd. 09/26/1986
Romulus Resources Ltd. merged into Misty Mountain Gold Ltd. 11/07/1995 which recapitalized as Misty Mountain Gold Inc. 11/10/1995 which recapitalized as Continental Minerals Corp. (Incorporated 02/07/1962) 10/18/2001
(See Continental Minerals Corp. (Incorporated 02/07/1962))

GLENEAGLE CAP CORP (CO)
Name changed to Stat-Tech International Corp. 01/30/1989
(See Stat-Tech International Corp.)

GLENEAGLE GRAPHITE MINES LTD. (ON)
Name changed to Silverplace Mines Ltd. 09/30/1964
(See Silverplace Mines Ltd.)

GLENEAGLES PETE INC (BC)
Name changed to Clickhouse.Com Online Inc. 07/29/1999
Clickhouse.Com Online Inc. recapitalized as Windridge Technology Corp. 09/19/2002 which name changed to Dajin Resources Corp. 01/19/2005

GLENEX INDS INC (BC)
Merged into Quest Investment Corp. 07/04/2002
Each share Common no par exchanged for (0.4409171) share Class A Subordinate no par
Quest Investment Corp. merged into Quest Capital Corp. (BC) 06/30/2003 which reincorporated in Canada 05/27/2008 which name changed to Sprott Resource Lending Corp. 09/10/2010 which merged into Sprott Inc. 07/24/2013

GLENFED INC (DE)
Merged into Glendale Federal Bank, FSB (Glendale, CA) 8/26/93
Each share Common 1¢ par exchanged for (0.04) share Common 1¢ par and (0.22) Rights expiring 9/13/93
Glendale Federal Bank, FSB (Glendale, CA) reorganized in Delaware as Golden State Bancorp Inc. 7/24/97
(See Golden State Bancorp Inc.)

GLENGAIR GROUP LTD (ON)
Merged into Jannock Corp. Ltd. 07/04/1973
Each share 6% Non-Cum. Conv. Class B Preference $5 par exchanged for (0.25) share 6% Conv. Class B $20 par
Each share Common no par exchanged for (0.25) share Conv. Special Share no par
Jannock Corp. Ltd. reorganized as Jannock Ltd. 07/05/1977
(See Jannock Ltd.)

GLENGARRY HLDGS LTD (BERMUDA)
Each share Common 5¢ par exchanged for (0.2) share Common 1¢ par 05/31/2002
SEC revoked common stock registration 09/17/2013

GLENGATE APPAREL INC (NJ)
Assets liquidated for benefit of creditors 10/22/98
No stockholders' equity

GLENHAVEN MINERALS INC (BC)
Recapitalized 10/06/1999
Recapitalized from Glenhaven Resources Inc. to Glenhaven Minerals Inc. 10/06/1999
Each share Common no par exchanged for (0.16666666) share Common no par
Recapitalized as Glenhaven Ventures Inc. 01/30/2001
Each share Common no par exchanged for (0.33333333) share Common no par
Glenhaven Ventures Inc. name changed to Red Lake Resources Inc. 07/16/2002 which name changed to Silver Fields Resources Inc. 06/19/2006

GLENHAVEN VENTURES INC (BC)
Name changed to Red Lake Resources Inc. 7/16/2002
Red Lake Resources Inc. name changed to Silver Fields Resources Inc. 6/19/2006

GLENHILLS CORP (UT)
Name changed to Millennium Multi-Media.com Corp. 07/06/2000
Millennium Multi-Media.com Corp. name changed to Voxcorp Inc. 02/13/2002

GLENLIVET GOLD MINES LTD. (ON)
Declared dissolved 03/10/1958
No stockholders' equity

GLENLYON MINES LTD (BC)
Merged into Amca Industries Ltd. 03/18/1974
Each share Capital Stock 50¢ par exchanged for (0.2) share Common no par
Amca Industries Ltd. name changed to Amca Resources Ltd. 12/04/1980
(See Amca Resources Ltd.)

GLENMARK CAP CORP (BC)
Common no par split (4) for (1) by issuance of (3) additional shares payable 07/29/2013 to holders of record 07/29/2013
Recapitalized as Aldever Resources Inc. 08/05/2015
Each share Common no par exchanged for (0.5) share Common no par

GLENMORE DISTILLERIES CO (DE)
Merged into Guinness PLC 08/19/1991
Each share Class A Common $1 par exchanged for $42.50 cash
Each share Class B Common $1 par exchanged for $42.50 cash

GLENMORE HIGHLANDS INC (AB)
Merged into Mountain Province Mining Inc. (New) 06/30/2000
Each share Common no par exchanged for (0.5734) share Common no par
Mountain Province Mining Inc. (New) name changed to Mountain Province Diamonds Inc. 10/16/2000

GLENN EXPLS LTD (ON)
Recapitalized as Camindex Mines Ltd. 04/10/1969
Each share Capital Stock $1 par exchanged for (0.2) share Common $1 par
Camindex Mines Ltd. acquired by MVP Capital Corp. 12/31/1989 which recapitalized as LatinGold Inc. 10/23/1996 which name changed to Travelbyus.Com Ltd. 06/11/1999
(See Travelbyus.Com Ltd.)

GLENN L. MARTIN CO. (MD)
See - Martin (Glenn L.) Co.

GLENN MCCARTHY, INC. (DE)
See - Mccarthy (Glenn), Inc.

GLENN PACIFIC CORP. (CA)
Acquired by Teledyne, Inc. 05/21/1965
Each share Common no par exchanged for (0.1) share Common $1 par
Teledyne, Inc. merged into Allegheny Teledyne, Inc. 08/15/1996 which name changed to Allegheny Technologies Inc. 11/29/1999

GLENN URANIUM MINES LTD. (ON)
Name changed to Glenn Explorations Ltd. 08/18/1964
Glenn Explorations Ltd. recapitalized as Camindex Mines Ltd. 04/10/1969 which was acquired by MVP Capital Corp. 12/31/1989 which recapitalized as LatinGold Inc. 10/23/1996 which name changed to Travelbyus.Com Ltd. 06/11/1999
(See Travelbyus.Com Ltd.)

GLENORA GOLD MINES LTD. (ON)
Recapitalized as Glenn Uranium Mines Ltd. 00/00/1955
Each share Capital Stock $1 par exchanged for (0.2) share Capital Stock $1 par
Glenn Uranium Mines Ltd. name changed to Glenn Explorations Ltd. 08/18/1964 which recapitalized as Camindex Mines Ltd. 04/10/1969 which was acquired by MVP Capital Corp. 12/31/1989 which recapitalized as LatinGold Inc. 10/23/1996 which name changed to Travelbyus.Com Ltd. 06/11/1999
(See Travelbyus.Com Ltd.)

GLENORA RES INC (BC)
Struck off register and declared dissolved for failure to file returns 02/16/1990

GLENROCK GOLD MINES LTD. (ON)
Acquired by Rockdale Mines Ltd. 00/00/1958
Each share Common exchanged for (0.1) share Capital Stock $1 par
Rockdale Mines Ltd. merged into PYX Explorations Ltd. 07/30/1976 which merged into Discovery Mines Ltd. (Canada) 01/15/1982
(See Discovery Mines Ltd. (Canada))

GLENROCK OIL CO.
Out of existence 00/00/1933
Details not available

GLENS FALLS INDEMNITY CO. (NY)
Merged into Glens Falls Insurance Co. 12/31/56
Details not available

GLENS FALLS INS CO (NY)
Capital Stock $10 par changed to $5 par in 1932
Stock Dividend - 100% 1/10/57
Acquired by Continental Corp. (NY) 5/1/70
Each share Capital Stock $5 par exchanged for $65.50 cash

GLENS FALLS NATL BK & TR CO (GLENS FALLS, NY)
Each share Common $100 par exchanged for (4) shares Common $25 par 00/00/1954
Common $25 par changed to $12.50 par and (1) additional share issued 04/02/1963
Common $12.50 par changed to $10 par and (0.25) additional share issued 02/01/1969
Common $10 par changed to $8 par and (0.25) additional share issued 02/13/1974
Stock Dividends - 20% 10/10/1958; 25% 03/01/1971
Under plan of reorganization each share Common $8 par automatically became (1) share Arrow Bank Corp. Common $8 par 09/01/1983
Arrow Bank Corp. name changed to Arrow Financial Corp. 07/02/1990

GLENS FALLS PORTLAND CEMENT CO. (NY)
Each share 6% Preferred $100 par exchanged for (4) shares 6% Preferred $25 par in 1951
Each share Common no par exchanged for (4) shares Common $5 par in 1951
6% Preferred $25 par changed to $5 par and (4) additional shares issued 3/6/56
Common $5 par changed to $3 par and (4) additional shares issued 3/6/56
Each share 6% Preferred $5 par reclassified as (0.55) share Common $3 par 3/7/58
Merged into Flintkote Co. 6/17/59
Each share Common $3 par exchanged for (0.6) share Common $5 par
(See Flintkote Co.)

GLENTEL INC (CANADA)
Common no par split (2) for (1) by issuance of (1) additional share payable 05/30/2011 to holders of record 05/18/2011 Ex date - 05/16/2011
Acquired by BCE Inc. 05/21/2015
Each share Common no par exchanged for $26.50 cash

GLENTHORNE ENTERPRISES INC (BC)
Name changed to Asantae Holdings International Inc. 12/14/2010
Asantae Holdings International Inc. name changed to Avidus Management Group Inc. 05/31/2013

GLENTRONIC INTL INC (BC)
Delisted from Vancouver Stock Exchange 03/02/1991

GLENVET RES LTD (BC)
Recapitalized as Fort Point Resources Ltd. 10/10/1991
Each share Common no par exchanged for (0.33333333) share Common no par
Fort Point Resources Ltd. recapitalized as Osprey Energy Ltd. 09/14/1998
(See Osprey Energy Ltd.)

GLENVIEW METAL PRODUCTS CO. (NJ)
Bankrupt 05/26/1956
Details not available

GLENWAY FINL CORP (DE)
Common 1¢ par split (2) for (1) by issuance of (1) additional share payable 11/17/1997 to holders of record 11/01/1997
Stock Dividend - 5% payable 08/16/1996 to holders of record 08/03/1996
Merged into Fidelity Financial of Ohio, Inc. 03/19/1999
Each share Common 1¢ par exchanged for (1.5) shares Common 10¢ par
Fidelity Financial of Ohio, Inc. merged into Provident Financial Group, Inc. 02/04/2000 which merged into National City Corp. 07/01/2004 which was acquired by PNC Financial Services Group, Inc. 12/31/2008

GLENWOOD APARTMENTS
Liquidated in 1950

GLENWOOD GOLD MINES, LTD. (ON)
Charter revoked for failure to file reports and pay taxes 11/11/57

GLENWOOD VENTURES INC (AB)
Name changed to Toro Energy Inc. 11/29/2001
Toro Energy Inc. recapitalized as Sentra Resources Corp. 9/18/2003 which was acquired by Blue Mountain Energy Ltd. 9/30/2004
(See Blue Mountain Energy Ltd.)

GLF TECHNOLOGIES 1979 LTD (BC)
Recapitalized as Blackberry Gold Resources Inc. 02/24/1986
Each share Common no par exchanged for (0.33333333) share Common no par
(See Blackberry Gold Resources Inc.)

GLG LIFE TECH LTD (BC)
Recapitalized as GLG Life Tech Corp. 03/14/2007
Each share Common no par exchanged for (0.33333333) share Common no par

GLG PARTNERS INC (DE)
Acquired by Man Group PLC 10/14/2010
Each share Common $0.0001 par exchanged for $4.50 cash

GLIATECH INC (DE)
Secondary Offering - 1,500,000 shares COM offered at $12 per share on 06/19/1998
Plan of reorganization under Chapter 11 Federal Bankruptcy proceedings confirmed 04/21/2004
No stockholders' equity

GLICKMAN CORP. (DE)
Name changed to Franchard Corp. 4/29/63
Franchard Corp. merged into Lee National Corp. 5/29/69
(See Lee National Corp.)

GLIDDEN CO (OH)
Common no par split (2) for (1) by issuance of (1) additional share 11/7/47
4-1/4% Preferred $50 par called for redemption 10/1/51
Common no par changed to $10 par 2/11/55
Common $10 par changed to $4 par and (1.5) additional shares issued 8/16/65
$2.125 Conv. Preferred no par called for redemption 6/19/67
Merged into SCM Corp. 9/22/67
Each share Common $4 par exchanged for (0.46) share Common $5 par
(See SCM Corp.)

GLIDE CONTROL CORP. (DE)
No longer in existence having become inoperative and void for non-payment of taxes 4/1/62

GLIDER DEVS INC (BC)
Name changed 11/21/1988
Name changed from Glider Resources Inc. to Glider Developments Inc. 11/21/1988
Recapitalized as Venture Pacific Development Corp. 09/28/1992
Each share Common no par exchanged for (0.16666666) share Common no par
Venture Pacific Development Corp. recapitalized as Pacific Harbour Capital Ltd. 10/21/2002 which name changed to Oceanic Iron Ore Corp. 12/06/2010

GLIMCHER RLTY TR (MD)
9.25% Preferred Shares of Bene. Int. Ser. B 1¢ par called for redemption at $25 plus $0.366146 accrued dividends on 02/27/2004
8.75% Preferred Shares of Bene. Int. Ser. F 1¢ par called for redemption at $25 plus $0.3896 accrued dividends on 09/04/2012
Merged into Washington Prime Group Inc. (Old) 01/16/2015
Each 6.875% Preferred Share of Bene. Int. Ser. I 1¢ par exchanged for (1) share 6.875% Preferred Ser. I $0.0001 par
Each 7.5% Preferred Share of Bene. Int. Ser. H 1¢ par exchanged for (1) share 7.5% Preferred Ser. H $0.0001 par
Each 8.125% Preferred Share of Bene. Int. Ser. G 1¢ par exchanged for (1) share 8.125% Preferred Ser. G $0.0001 par
Each Common Share of Bene. Int. 1¢ par exchanged for (0.1989) share Common 1¢ par and $10.40 cash
Washington Prime Group Inc. (Old) name changed to WP Glimcher Inc. 05/21/2015 which name changed to Washington Prime Group Inc. (New) 08/31/2016

GLIMMER RES INC (ON)
Recapitalized as Baffinland Iron Mines Corp. 01/15/2004
Each share Common no par exchanged for (0.33333333) share Common no par
(See Baffinland Iron Mines Corp.)

GLITSCH (FRITZ W.) & SONS, INC. (DE)
Merged into Foster Wheeler Corp. 11/01/1967
Each share Common $2 par exchanged for (1.7189) shares $1 Conv. Preferred Ser. A no par
(See Foster Wheeler Corp.)

GLITTER GOLD MINES LTD (BC)
Struck off register and declared dissolved for failure to file returns 05/08/1992

GLK STRATEGIES INC (AB)
Recapitalized as Yankee Hat Industries Corp. (ALTA) 02/18/2003
Each share Common no par exchanged for (0.25) share Common no par
Yankee Hat Industries Corp. (ALTA) reincorporated as Yankee Hat Minerals Ltd. in British Columbia 02/09/2005

GLM INDS INC (DE)
Charter cancelled and declared inoperative and void for non-payment of taxes 3/1/75

GLOBA INC (DE)
Charter cancelled and declared inoperative and void for non-payment of taxes 3/1/74

GLOBAL A INC (DE)
SEC revoked common stock registration 10/04/2006

GLOBAL ACCESS PAGERS INC (UT)
Each share old Common $0.001 par exchanged for (0.1) share new Common $0.001 par 06/11/1998
Name changed to Integrated Communication Networks Inc. 01/29/1999

FINANCIAL INFORMATION, INC.

(See Integrated Communication Networks Inc.)

GLOBAL ACQUISITIONS INC (CO)
Each share old Common $0.001 par exchanged for (20) shares new Common $0.001 par 10/12/2001
Name changed to Oak Ridge Micro-Energy, Inc. 02/21/2002
Oak Ridge Micro-Energy, Inc. name changed to Oak Ridge Energy Technologies, Inc. 08/28/2013 which name changed to Oakridge Global Energy Solutions, Inc. 11/07/2014

GLOBAL ADVANCE CORP (DE)
Reorganized as COPsync, Inc. 04/28/2008
Each share Common $0.0001 par exchanged for (15) shares Common $0.0001 par

GLOBAL ADVANTAGED TELECOM & UTILS INCOME FD (ON)
Combined Units separated 04/06/2011
Name changed to Global Telecom & Utilities Income Fund 06/22/2016

GLOBAL AENER / COLOGY CORP (NV)
Charter revoked for failure to file reports and pay fees 06/01/2007

GLOBAL AERIAL SURVEILLANCE (NV)
Each share old Common $0.001 par exchanged for (0.04) share new Common $0.001 par 05/31/2005
Name changed to Klegg Electronics, Inc. 06/24/2005
(See Klegg Electronics, Inc.)

GLOBAL AERIAL SURVEILLANCE INC (DE)
Name changed to Bicoastal Communications Inc. 07/05/2006
(See Bicoastal Communications Inc.)

GLOBAL AEROSPACE SYS INC (ON)
Recapitalized as Venga Aerospace Systems Inc. 11/16/1987
Each share Common no par exchanged for (0.1) share Common no par

GLOBAL AFFILIATE NETWORK INC (NV)
Charter revoked for failure to file reports and pay fees 10/01/2007

GLOBAL AGRI-MED TECHNOLOGIES INC (NJ)
Old Common no par split (2) for (1) by issuance of (1) additional share payable 04/09/2008 to holders of record 04/09/2008
Each share old Common no par exchanged for (0.01) share new Common no par 03/30/2011
Reincorporated under the laws of Nevada as Florida Micro, Inc. and new Common no par changed to $0.001 par 04/29/2011
(See Florida Micro, Inc.)

GLOBAL AGRIBUSINESS TR (ON)
Name changed to Aston Hill Global Agribusiness Fund 01/24/2011
Aston Hill Global Agribusiness Fund name changed to Aston Hill Global Resource & Infrastructure Fund 03/21/2013 which merged into Aston Hill Global Resource Fund (New) 11/06/2015

GLOBAL AIRCRAFT SOLUTIONS INC (NV)
Plan of reorganization under Chapter 11 Federal Bankruptcy proceedings confirmed 11/05/2009
Stockholders' equity unlikely

GLOBAL ALERT SYS CORP (BC)
Recapitalized as Delta Star Resources Inc. (BC) 03/05/1990
Each share Common no par exchanged for (0.33333333) share Common no par
Delta Star Resources Inc. (BC)

reorganized in Ontario as Accord Financial Corp. 04/10/1992

GLOBAL ALLIANCE NETWORKS INC (NJ)
SEC revoked common stock registration 07/31/2009

GLOBAL ALTERNATIVES CORP (DE)
Name changed to Environmental Alternatives Corp. 02/01/1996
Environmental Alternatives Corp. name changed to Healthspan Inc. 03/04/1997 which recapitalized as Riverside Information Technologies, Inc. (DE) 10/10/2006 which reincorporated in Nevada as Clean Coal Technologies, Inc. 10/12/2007

GLOBAL ALUMINA CORP (NB)
Name changed 06/24/2005
Name changed from Global Alumina Products Corp. to Global Alumina Corp. 06/24/2005
Completely liquidated
Each share Common no par received first and final distribution of USD$0.169 cash payable 08/02/2013 to holders of record 07/12/2013

GLOBAL ASSET HLDGS INC (FL)
Name changed to Epixtar Corp. 11/25/2002

GLOBAL ASSETS & SVCS INC (FL)
Recapitalized as Jointland Development, Inc. 12/21/2004
Each share Common $0.001 par exchanged for (0.02) share Common $0.001 par
Jointland Development, Inc. name changed to Gold Royalty Corp. 01/14/2011 which recapitalized as Ally Pharma US, Inc. 12/17/2012 which recapitalized as TPT Global Tech, Inc. 12/02/2014

GLOBAL AXCESS CORP (NV)
Each share old Common $0.001 par exchanged for (0.2) share new Common $0.001 par 04/28/2005
Chapter 11 bankruptcy proceedings terminated 04/30/2014
Stockholders' equity unlikely

GLOBAL BANCORP INC (NV)
Name changed to Voxbox World Telecom, Inc. and (9) additional shares issued 07/06/2005
Voxbox World Telecom, Inc. name changed to Internet Media Technologies, Inc. 11/21/2007 which name changed to Star Entertainment Group, Inc. 01/19/2010

GLOBAL BKS PREM INCOME TR (ON)
Each Trust Unit received distribution of (1) Trust Unit Warrant expiring 07/31/2009 payable 08/15/2008 to holders of record 08/15/2008
Ex date - 08/13/2008
Each Trust Unit received distribution of (1) Trust Unit Warrant expiring 07/30/2010 payable 08/15/2008 to holders of record 08/15/2008
Ex date - 08/13/2008
Under plan of merger each Trust Unit automatically became (0.347759) Portland Global Income Fund Ser. A2 Unit 12/13/2013

GLOBAL BEVERAGE SOLUTIONS INC (NV)
Recapitalized as Real Brands, Inc. 10/22/2013
Each share Common $0.001 par exchanged for (0.00666666) share Common $0.001 par

GLOBAL BEVERAGES INC (NV)
SEC revoked common stock registration 07/24/2013

GLOBAL BIOTECH CORP (DE)
Name changed to Purthanol Resources Ltd. 02/04/2014

GLOBAL BLVD INTL INC (NV)
Each share old Common $0.001 par exchanged for (0.5) share new Common $0.001 par 9/29/2000
Recapitalized as Project Group, Inc. 5/7/2003
Each share new Common $0.001 par exchanged for (0.4) share Common $0.001 par
(See Project Group, Inc.)

GLOBAL BPO SVCS CORP (DE)
Issue Information - 31,250,000 UNITS consisting of (1) share COM and (1) WT offered at $8 per Unit on 10/17/2007
Name changed to Stream Global Services, Inc. 08/02/2008
(See Stream Global Services, Inc.)

GLOBAL BRANDS ACQUISITION CORP (DE)
Liquidation completed
Each Unit received initial distribution of $9.9521739 cash payable 12/22/2009 to holders of record 12/07/2009
Each share Common $0.0001 par received initial distribution of $9.9521739 cash payable 12/22/2009 to holders of record 12/07/2009
Each Unit exchanged for second and final distribution of $0.01682239 cash 12/31/2014
Each share Common $0.0001 par exchanged for second and final distribution of $0.01682239 cash 12/31/2014

GLOBAL BUSINESS INFORMATION DIRECTORY INC (CO)
Recapitalized as Jimmy Vu's Take Out, Inc. 3/4/2005
Each share Common $0.001 par exchanged for (0.005) share Common $0.001 par
(See Jimmy Vu's Take Out, Inc.)

GLOBAL BUSINESS MKTS INC (NV)
Each share old Common $0.001 par exchanged for (0.005) share new Common $0.001 par 11/2/2004
Name changed to GREM USA 3/3/2005

GLOBAL BUSINESS RES INC (DE)
Each share old Common $0.0001 par exchanged for (0.04) share new Common $0.0001 par 08/04/2003
Name changed to Infinium Labs, Inc. 01/08/2004
Infinium Labs, Inc. name changed to Phantom Entertainment, Inc. 07/24/2006
(See Phantom Entertainment, Inc.)

GLOBAL BUSINESS SVCS INC (DE)
Each share old Common 1¢ par exchanged for (0.06666666) share new Common 1¢ par 05/24/2004
Recapitalized as Energetics Holdings, Inc. 11/09/2007
Each share Common 1¢ par exchanged for (0.025) share Common 1¢ par
Note: No holder will receive fewer than (100) post-split shares
Energetics Holdings, Inc. recapitalized as Pavilion Energy Resources, Inc. 07/25/2008 which recapitalized as Matchtrade, Inc. 05/02/2012
(See Matchtrade, Inc.)

GLOBAL CABLE SYS INC (BC)
Recapitalized as Consolidated Global Cable Systems, Inc. 12/19/2000
Each share Common no par exchanged for (0.2) share Common no par
Consolidated Global Cable Systems, Inc. name changed to Chelsea Minerals Corp. 01/20/2010 which merged into Sennen Resources Ltd. 05/13/2011 which name changed to Sennen Potash Corp. 04/15/2013

GLOBAL CAP INDS INC (CO)
Charter suspended for failure to file annual reports 09/30/1989

GLOBAL CAP PARTNERS INC (DE)
Each share old Common 1¢ par exchanged for (0.25) share new Common 1¢ par 07/03/2001
Ceased operations 03/27/2002
Details not available

GLOBAL CAP SECS TR (ON)
Name changed to Redwood Global Financials Income Fund 12/20/2017
(See Redwood Global Financials Income Fund)

GLOBAL CASH ACCESS HLDGS INC (DE)
Name changed to Everi Holdings Inc. 08/24/2015

GLOBAL CASINOS INC (UT)
Each share Common $0.005 par exchanged for (0.1) share Common 5¢ par 11/18/1996
Each share Common 5¢ par received distribution of (0.1) share OnSource Corp. Common $0.0001 par payable 11/23/2003 to holders of record 08/06/2001
Name changed to Global Healthcare REIT, Inc. 10/07/2013

GLOBAL CHAMPIONS SPLIT CORP (ON)
Class A Preferred Ser. 1 no par called for redemption at $25.25 plus $0.1374 accrued dividends on 08/20/2018

GLOBAL CLEAN ENERGY HLDGS INC (UT)
Reincorporated under the laws of Delaware and Common no par changed to $0.001 par 07/19/2010

GLOBAL CLUB INC (NV)
Common $0.001 par split (150) for (1) by issuance of (149) additional shares payable 03/24/2010 to holders of record 03/23/2010
Ex date - 03/25/2010
Recapitalized as Bold Energy Inc. 03/31/2011
Each share Common $0.001 par exchanged for (0.04) share Common $0.001 par
Bold Energy Inc. name changed to Lot78, Inc. 02/07/2013

GLOBAL COGENIX INDL CORP (BC)
Recapitalized as Highwater Power Corp. 07/11/2006
Each share Common no par exchanged for (0.2) share Common no par
(See Highwater Power Corp.)

GLOBAL COMM DEV INC (AB)
Acquired by 1250656 Alberta Ltd. 10/26/2006
Each share Common no par exchanged for $0.20 cash
Note: Unexchanged certificates were cancelled and became without value 10/26/2012

GLOBAL COMMUNICATIONS, INC. (MD)
Name changed to Multi Media Engineering, Inc. 3/7/69

GLOBAL COMMUNICATIONS LTD (CANADA)
Merged into Global Ventures Holdings Ltd. 08/29/1985
Each share Common no par exchanged for $40 cash

GLOBAL CONCEPTS LTD (CO)
SEC revoked common stock registration 09/26/2008

GLOBAL CONDIMENTS INC (NV)
Common $0.001 par changed to $0.0001 par 09/19/2016
Name changed to Restance, Inc. 01/09/2017

GLOBAL CONNECTIONS INC (NV)
Reorganized under the laws of

Oklahoma as Capital Holdings Group, Inc. 08/05/2005
Each (750) shares Common $0.001 par exchanged for (1) share Common $0.001 par
Note: No holder will receive fewer than (100) shares
Capital Holdings Group, Inc. name changed to Avisana Corp. 11/07/2006

GLOBAL CONSTRUCTION DEVICES, INC. (NJ)
Name changed to Global Industries, Inc. 6/23/64
(See Global Industries, Inc.)

GLOBAL CONSUMER ACQUISITION CORP (DE)
Issue Information - 30,000,000 UNITS consisting of (1) share COM and (1) WT offered at $10 per Unit on 11/20/2007
Name changed to Western Liberty Bancorp 10/08/2009
(See Western Liberty Bancorp)

GLOBAL CONSUMER TECHNOLOGIES INC (AB)
Delisted from NEX 06/29/2005

GLOBAL COPPER CORP (BC)
Merged into Teck Cominco Ltd. 08/08/2008
Each share Common no par exchanged for (0.2973) share Class B Subordinate, (1) share Lumina Copper Corp. (New) Common no par and $0.0001 cash
(See Lumina Copper Corp. (New))

GLOBAL COPPER GROUP INC (BC)
Name changed to Cobalt Power Group Inc. 10/24/2016

GLOBAL CORNERSTONE HLDGS LTD (BRITISH VIRGIN ISLANDS)
Issue Information - 8,000,000 UNITS consisting of (1) share ORD and (1) WT offered at $10 per Unit on 04/15/2011
Completely liquidated
Each Unit received first and final distribution of $10 cash payable 01/22/2013 to holders of record 01/20/2013
Each share Ordinary received first and final distribution of $10 cash payable 01/22/2013 to holders of record 01/20/2013

GLOBAL CR PREF CORP (ON)
Preferred no par called for redemption at $8.15 on 06/08/2010

GLOBAL CROSSING HLDGS LTD OLD (BERMUDA)
Stock Dividend - in 10.5% Exchangeable Sr. Preferred to holders of 10.5% Sr. Exchangeable Preferred 5.25% payable 12/1/2001 to holders of record 11/15/2001
Ex date - 11/13/2001
Plan of reorganization under Chapter 11 Federal Bankruptcy Code effective 12/9/2003
No stockholders' equity

GLOBAL CROSSING LTD NEW (BERMUDA)
Merged into Level 3 Communications, Inc. 10/03/2011
Each share Common 1¢ par exchanged for (16) shares Common 1¢ par
Level 3 Communications, Inc. merged into CenturyLink, Inc. 11/01/2017

GLOBAL CROSSING LTD OLD (BERMUDA)
Common 1¢ par split (2) for (1) by issuance of (1) additional share payable 03/09/1999 to holders of record 02/16/1999
Plan of reorganization under Chapter 11 Federal Bankruptcy Code effective 12/09/2003
No stockholders' equity

GLOBAL CT & T TELECOMMUNICATIONS INC (BC)
Delisted from Toronto Venture Stock Exchange 11/09/2001

GLOBAL CYBER SPORTS COM INC (NV)
Recapitalized as International Group Holdings Inc. 04/04/2003
Each share Common no par exchanged for (0.15) share Common no par
International Group Holdings Inc. acquired by Energy Producers Inc. 01/30/2004 which name changed to EGPI Firecreek, Inc. 01/30/2004

GLOBAL DATA SYS CORP (BC)
Recapitalized as Comtron Enterprises Inc. 11/22/1989
Each share Common no par exchanged for (0.33333333) share Common no par
Comtron Enterprises Inc. recapitalized as Olympic Resources Ltd. (BC) 10/21/1993 which reincorporated in Wyoming 01/08/2003 which reorganized in Nevada as Whittier Energy Corp. 01/02/2004
(See Whittier Energy Corp.)

GLOBAL DATATEL INC (NV)
Each share Common $0.001 received distribution of (1) share of DataTel International Restricted Common $0.001 par payable 3/21/2006 to holders of record 7/1/2004
Each share old Common $0.001 par exchanged for (0.002) share new Common $0.001 par
Name changed to Cana Petroleum Corp. 8/30/2006
Cana Petroleum Corp. name changed to XCana Petroleum Corp. 5/22/2007

GLOBAL DEBIT CASH CARD INC (NV)
Each share old Common $0.001 par exchanged for (0.001) share new Common $0.001 par 04/28/2005
Name changed to 1st Global Financial Corp. 03/27/2006 1st Global Financial Corp. recapitalized as Incorporated Productions 08/01/2013

GLOBAL DECS CORP (UT)
Each share old Common $0.001 par exchanged for (0.005) share new Common $0.001 par 11/13/2003
Name changed to Western Sierra Mining Corp. 12/19/2003

GLOBAL DEFENSE & NATL SEC SYS INC (DE)
Common $0.0001 par split (2.06) for (1) by issuance of (0.9433962) additional share payable 11/30/2015 to holders of record 11/23/2015
Ex date - 12/01/2015
Name changed to STG Group, Inc. 12/16/2015

GLOBAL DEFENSE TECHNOLOGY & SYS INC (DE)
Issue Information - 4,600,000 shares COM offered at $13 per share on 11/19/2009
Acquired by Sentinel Acquisition Holdings Inc. 04/04/2011
Each share Common 1¢ par exchanged for $24.25 cash

GLOBAL DEV INC (NEW) (PA)
Reincorporated 6/30/82
State of incorporation changed from (DE) to (PA) 6/30/82
In process of liquidation
Each share Common 5¢ par received initial distribution of $2.80 cash 7/10/86
Assets transferred to Global Development, Inc. Liquidating Trust and Common 5¢ par reclassified as Shares of Bene. Int. 5¢ par 2/2/87

(See Global Development, Inc. Liquidating Trust)

GLOBAL DEV INC OLD (PA)
Each share old Class A Common $1 par exchanged for (1) share Common $1 par or (1) share new Class A Common $1 par 6/4/74
Each share Class B Common no par exchanged for (1) share Common $1 par 6/4/74
Reorganized as Global Real Estate Investment Trust 7/1/75
Each share Common $1 par exchanged for (1) Share of Bene. Int. no par
Each share new Class A Common $1 par exchanged for (1) Share of Bene. Int. no par
Global Real Estate Investment Trust reorganized in Delaware as Global Development, Inc. 10/25/79 which reincorporated in Pennsylvania 6/30/82
(See Global Development, Inc. (New))

GLOBAL DEV RES INC (ON)
Recapitalized as GDV Resources Inc. 12/21/2010
Each share Common no par exchanged for (0.33333333) share Common no par
GDV Resources Inc. name changed to Cardinal Capital Partners Inc. 09/13/2013

GLOBAL DEVELOPMENT, INC. LIQUIDATING TRUST (PA)
Liquidation completed
Each share of Bene. Int. 5¢ par exchanged for second and final distribution of $0.22 cash 10/19/87
(See Global Development, Inc. for previous distribution)

GLOBAL DEVS INC (NV)
Charter permanently revoked 03/31/2010

GLOBAL DIAMOND RESOURCES INC (NV)
Each share Common $0.005 par exchanged for (2) shares Common $0.001 par 12/19/1997
Charter revoked for failure to file reports and pay fees 01/31/2008

GLOBAL DIGITAL INFORMATION INC (UT)
Each (80) shares old Common $0.001 par exchanged for (1) share new Common $0.001 par 06/01/1999
Name changed to Masterpiece Technology Group, Inc. 06/15/1999
(See Masterpiece Technology Group, Inc.)

GLOBAL DIRECTMAIL CORP (DE)
Issue Information - 7,225,000 shares COM offered at $17.50 per share on 06/26/1995
Name changed to Systemax Inc. 5/19/99

GLOBAL DISCOUNTS, INC. (CO)
Adjudicated bankrupt 5/31/63
No stockholders' equity

GLOBAL DISCS TR 2004-1 (ON)
Trust terminated 12/22/2009
Each Trust Unit no par received $25 cash

GLOBAL DISP CORP (WY)
Administratively dissolved 03/14/2009

GLOBAL DIVERSIFIED ACQUISITION CORP (NV)
Name changed to Mailkey Corp. 04/13/2004
Mailkey Corp. name changed to IElement Corp. 08/25/2005
(See IElement Corp.)

GLOBAL DIVERSIFIED INDS INC (NV)
Each share old Common $0.001 par exchanged for (0.05) share new Common $0.001 par 05/21/2008
Each share new Common $0.001 par exchanged again for (1) share new

Common $0.001 par to reflect a (1) for (2,500) reverse split followed by a (2,500) for (1) forward split 08/19/2011
Note: Holders of (2,499) or fewer pre-split shares received $0.03 cash per share
Each share new Common $0.001 par exchanged again for (1) share new Common $0.001 par to reflect a (1) for (1,000,000) reverse split followed by a (1,000,000) for (1) forward split 01/30/2014
Note: In effect holders received $0.0075 cash per share and public interest was eliminated

GLOBAL DIVERSIFIED INVT GRADE INCOME TR (ON)
Trust terminated
Each Fixed/Floating Trust Unit Ser. 2004-1 received initial distribution of $9.55 cash 09/09/2014
Each Fixed/Floating Trust Unit Ser. 2004-1 received second and final distribution of $0.12 cash 12/23/2014

GLOBAL DIVERSIFIED INVT GRADE INCOME TR II (ON)
Trust terminated 02/09/2017
Each Fixed/Resetting Rate Unit Ser. 2005-1 received initial distribution of $0.24 cash
Note: An additional distribution of $0.0128 cash per Unit was paid from escrow 08/18/2017

GLOBAL DIVID FD (ON)
Completely liquidated
Each Unit received initial distribution of $4.10 cash payable 10/25/2016 to holders of record 10/21/2016
Each Unit received second and final distribution of $0.405 cash payable 04/28/2017 to holders of record 03/30/2017

GLOBAL DYNAMICS CORP (DE)
Common $0.0001 par split (100) for (1) by issuance of (99) additional shares payable 09/16/2009 to holders of record 09/09/2009
Ex date - 09/17/2009
Recapitalized as Consumer Products Services Group, Inc. 04/19/2010
Each share Common $0.0001 par exchanged for (0.090009) share Common $0.0001 par

GLOBAL-E INVESTMENTS INC (NV)
Name changed to NowAuto Group, Inc. 09/12/2005
(See NowAuto Group, Inc.)

GLOBAL E TUTOR INC (DE)
Recapitalized as Winning Brands Corp. 11/09/2005
Each share Common $0.001 par exchanged for (0.005) share Common $0.001 par

GLOBAL EAGLE ACQUISITION CORP (DE)
Issue Information - 17,500,000 UNITS consisting of (1) share COM and (1) WT offered at $10 per Unit on 05/12/2011
Combined Units separated 02/01/2013
Name changed to Global Eagle Entertainment Inc. 02/01/2013

GLOBAL EARTH ENERGY INC (NV)
Each share old Common $0.001 par exchanged for (0.01) share new Common $0.001 par 07/17/2009
Each share new Common $0.001 par exchanged again for (0.00066666) share new Common $0.001 par 05/23/2012
SEC revoked common stock registration 01/13/2017

GLOBAL ECO-LOGICAL SVCS INC (FL)
Name changed to Intercontinental Holdings Inc. 3/31/2002

GLOBAL ECOSYSTEMS INC (UT)
Reorganized under the laws of Delaware as Rose International Ltd. 08/07/1995
Each share Common $0.001 par exchanged for (0.0076923) share Common $0.001 par
Rose International Ltd. name changed to Securities Resolution Advisors, Inc. 07/14/1998 which name changed to Sales Online Direct, Inc. 03/16/1999 which name changed to Paid, Inc. 12/08/2003

GLOBAL ED & TECHNOLOGY GROUP LTD (CAYMAN ISLANDS)
Issue Information - 6,375,000 ADS offered at $10.50 per ADS on 10/07/2010
Acquired by Pearson PLC 12/21/2011
Each ADS for Ordinary $0.0001 par exchanged for $11.006 cash

GLOBAL ELECTION SYS INC (BC)
Acquired by Diebold, Inc. 01/22/2002
Each share Common no par exchanged for (0.02421) share Common $1.25 par and $0.227 cash
Diebold, Inc. name changed to Diebold Nixdorf Inc. 12/12/2016

GLOBAL ELECTR RECOVERY CORP (NV)
Common $0.001 par split (22.723829) for (1) by issuance of (21.723829) additional shares payable 10/22/2007 to holders of record 09/27/2007 Ex date - 10/23/2007
Name changed to Marley Coffee Inc. 03/07/2008
Marley Coffee Inc. name changed to Jammin Java Corp. 09/17/2009

GLOBAL ELECTRONICS, INC. (UT)
Charter suspended for failure to pay taxes 3/19/71

GLOBAL ELECTRONICS MFG INC (DE)
Name changed to ECS Industries Inc. 8/19/99
ECS Industries Inc. recapitalized as Infoserve Global Holdings Corp. 2/6/2002

GLOBAL ENERGY CORP (BC)
Recapitalized as United Global Petroleum Inc. 09/13/1985
Each share Capital Stock no par exchanged for (0.33333333) share Common no par
(See United Global Petroleum Inc.)

GLOBAL ENERGY GROUP INC (DE)
SEC revoked common stock registration 05/06/2011

GLOBAL ENERGY HLDGS GROUP INC (DE)
Plan of reorganization under Chapter 11 Federal Bankruptcy proceedings effective 01/24/2011
No stockholders' equity

GLOBAL ENERGY LTD (NV)
Name changed to Global Platinum & Gold Inc. 08/28/1987
Global Platinum & Gold Inc. recapitalized as Bourque Industries, Inc. 02/07/2011

GLOBAL ENERGY RES INC (DE)
Charter cancelled and declared inoperative and void for non-payment of taxes 03/01/2005

GLOBAL ENERGY SVCS LTD (AB)
Name changed to Raise Production Inc. 11/02/2011

GLOBAL ENTERPRISES GROUP INC (NV)
Name changed to Predictive Technology Group, Inc. 07/16/2015

GLOBAL ENTERPRISES INC (NV)
Name changed to Hollywood International Corp. 6/17/70
Hollywood International Corp. merged into Nuclear Dynamics 6/29/70 which name changed to Power Alternatives, Inc. 1/13/78 which name changed to New World Minerals, Inc. 4/15/82

GLOBAL ENTMT ACQUISITION CORP (FL)
Recapitalized as HydroGenetics, Inc. 10/03/2008
Each share Common $0.001 par exchanged for (0.0001) share Common $0.001 par

GLOBAL ENTMT CLUBS INC (NV)
Name changed to Wewards, Inc. 01/29/2018

GLOBAL ENTMT HLDGS / EQUITIES INC (CO)
Old Common $0.001 par split (3) for (1) by issuance of (2) additional shares payable 08/20/1999 to holders of record 08/13/1999
Each share old Common $0.001 par exchanged for (1/3) share new Common $0.001 par 09/26/2006
Placed in receivership 10/15/2007
Details not available

GLOBAL ENTMT LTD (NV)
Recapitalized as American Interactive Media Inc. 03/15/1995
Each share Common $0.001 par exchanged for (0.01) share Common $0.001 par
(See American Interactive Media Inc.)

GLOBAL ENTREPRENEUR A G INC (UT)
Involuntarily dissolved for failure to file annual reports 12/31/86

GLOBAL ENVIRO SOLUTIONS INC (FL)
Name changed back to Green Oasis Environmental, Inc. 01/07/2010

GLOBAL ENVIRONMENTAL, INC. (FL)
Name changed to American Surface Technologies International, Inc. (FL) 10/18/2007
American Surface Technologies International, Inc. (FL) reorganized in Delaware as Ravenwood Bourne, Ltd. 10/30/2008 which name changed to PopBig, Inc. 11/07/2011 which name changed to EMAV Holdings, Inc. 01/03/2014

GLOBAL ENVIRONMENTAL CORP (NY)
Each share Common $0.000001 par exchanged for (0.01) share Common $0.001 par 10/24/89
Name changed to Danzer Corp. (NY) 10/6/99
Danzer Corp. (NY) reincorporated in Delaware as Obsidian Enterprises, Inc. 10/17/2001
(See Obsidian Enterprises, Inc.)

GLOBAL ENVIRONMENTAL ENERGY CORP (DE)
Stock Dividend - 5% payable 1/6/2005 to holders of record 12/10/2004
Reincorporated under the laws of Bahamas 2/25/2005

GLOBAL ENVIRONMENTAL INDS INC (UT)
Involuntarily dissolved 07/01/1998

GLOBAL EQUITIES CORP (DE)
Name changed to Amglobal Corp. 8/19/88
(See Amglobal Corp.)

GLOBAL EQUITY CORP (ON)
Merged into PICO Holdings Inc. (CA) 12/16/1998
Each share Common no par exchanged for (0.4628) share Common $0.001 par
PICO Holdings Inc. (CA) reincorporated in Delaware 05/31/2017

GLOBAL EQUITY FD INC (UT)
Charter expired 06/07/2007

GLOBAL EQUITY INTL INC (NV)
Name changed to Argentum 47, Inc. 04/02/2018

GLOBAL EXPLORATIONS CORP (BC)
Merged into Trincomali, Ltd. 10/15/1999
Each share Common no par exchanged for (1) share Common no par
Trincomali, Ltd. name changed to Global Explorations, Inc. 10/22/1999 which recapitalized as Malers, Inc. 05/17/2005 which name changed to Dot VN, Inc. 08/07/2006

GLOBAL EXPLORATIONS INC (DE)
Each share old Common $0.0001 par exchanged for (0.03333333) share new Common $0.0001 par 03/05/2003
New Common $0.0001 par split (10) for (1) by issuance of (9) additional shares payable 08/27/2004 to holders of record 08/26/2004
Ex date - 08/30/2004
Each share new Common $0.0001 par received distribution of (0.04) share Feinstein Report Inc. Common $0.001 par payable 09/28/2004 to holders of record 09/27/2004
Each share new Common $0.0001 par received distribution of (0.01) share Feinstein Report Inc. Common $0.001 par payable 02/22/2005 to holders of record 02/20/2005
Recapitalized as Malers, Inc. 05/17/2005
Each share new Common $0.0001 par exchanged for (0.001) share Common $0.0001 par
Malers, Inc. name changed to Dot VN, Inc. 08/07/2006

GLOBAL EXPRESS ENERGY INC (AB)
Reincorporated under the laws of Canada as Challenger Energy Corp. 12/12/2005
Challenger Energy Corp. merged into Canadian Superior Energy Inc. 09/24/2009 which recapitalized as Sonde Resources Corp. 06/08/2010
(See Sonde Resources Corp.)

GLOBAL FASHION TECHNOLOGIES INC (NV)
Name changed to Eco Tek 360, Inc. 02/14/2017

GLOBAL FINL GROUP INC (BC)
Name changed to egX Group Inc. 04/17/2007

GLOBAL FOCUS RES LTD (BC)
Delisted from Canadian Dealer Network 06/08/2001

GLOBAL FOODS ONLINE INC (NV)
Name changed to Global Diversified Industries, Inc. 01/03/2002
(See Global Diversified Industries, Inc.)

GLOBAL FORTRESS INC (CANADA)
Reorganized under the laws of Manitoba as Lakeview Hotel Real Estate Investment Trust 04/12/2004
Each share Common no par exchanged for (0.1) Class A Trust Unit
Lakeview Hotel Real Estate Investment Trust (MB) reorganized as Lakeview Hotel Real Investment Trust (Canada) 01/02/2013

GLOBAL 45 SPLIT CORP (ON)
Preferred Shares no par called for redemption at $10 plus $0.13125 accrued dividends on 09/30/2011
Class A Shares no par called for redemption at $4.4827 on 09/30/2011

GLOBAL GAMES CORP (NV)
Recapitalized as Global eScience Corp. 6/8/2001
Each share Common 1¢ par exchanged for (0.2) share Common 1¢ par

GLOBAL GAMES INTL INC (WA)
Charter cancelled and proclaimed dissolved for failure to pay taxes 1/19/88

GLOBAL GAMING NETWORK INC (DE)
Each share old Common $0.0001 par exchanged for (0.01) share new Common $0.0001 par 10/19/2011
Reincorporated under the laws of Washington as Innovativ Media Group, Inc. and new Common $0.0001 par changed to $0.00000001 par 07/27/2015
Innovativ Media Group, Inc. name changed to Demand Brands, Inc. 10/24/2018

GLOBAL GAMING TECHNOLOGY INC (DE)
Recapitalized as Left Right Marketing Technology, Inc. 07/30/2003
Each share Common 1¢ par exchanged for (0.2) share Common 1¢ par
Left Right Marketing Technology, Inc. name changed to Strategic Gaming Investments, Inc. 04/21/2006 which recapitalized as Amerigo Energy, Inc. 09/11/2008 which name changed to Quest Solution, Inc. 06/10/2014

GLOBAL GARDENS GROUP ACQUISITION CORP (BC)
Name changed to Global Gardens Group Inc. 10/05/2015

GLOBAL GAS CORP (NV)
Liquidation completed
Each share Common 5¢ par exchanged for initial distribution of $4 cash 12/17/1979
Each share Common 5¢ par received second and final distribution of $0.58 cash 09/10/1981

GLOBAL GATE PPTY CORP (NV)
SEC revoked common stock registration 07/25/2013

GLOBAL GEN TECHNOLOGIES INC (NV)
Recapitalized as Turbine Aviation, Inc. 12/19/2014
Each share Common $0.001 par exchanged for (0.0001) share Common $0.001 par

GLOBAL GEOPHYSICAL SVCS INC (DE)
Plan of reorganization under Chapter 11 bankruptcy proceedings effective 02/09/2015
No stockholders' equity

GLOBAL GMPC HLDGS INC (QC)
Each share Common no par exchanged for (0.5) Multiple Share no par and (0.5) share Subordinate no par 10/30/2003
Merged into GC-Global Capital Corp. 01/09/2006
Each Multiple Share no par exchanged for (0.3) Multiple Share no par
Each Subordinate Share no par exchanged for (0.3) Subordinate Share no par
GC-Global Capital Corp. name changed to Fountain Asset Corp. 09/02/2015

GLOBAL GOLD CORP (NV)
Each share old Common $0.001 par exchanged for (0.01) share new Common $0.001 par 04/14/2010
Recapitalized as Fernhill Corp. 01/20/2012
Each share new Common $0.001 par exchanged for (0.01) share Common $0.001 par

GLOBAL GOLF HLDGS INC (DE)
Recapitalized as Vitasti, Inc. 12/09/2004
Each share Common $0.001 par exchanged for (0.02941176) share Common $0.0000029 par
Vitasti, Inc. name changed to Welwind Energy International Corp. 10/31/2006
(See Welwind Energy International Corp.)

GLOBAL GOLF HLDGS INC (NV)
Recapitalized as Dino Minichiello Fashions Inc. 11/20/97
Each share Common $0.001 par exchanged for (0.02) share Common $0.001 par
Dino Minichiello Fashions Inc. name changed to Resort World Enterprises, Inc. 6/15/98 which name changed to Remedent USA, Inc. 10/22/98 which recapitalized as Remedent, Inc. 6/6/2005

GLOBAL GOVT PLUS FD INC (MD)
Name changed to Prudential International Bond Fund, Inc. 07/03/1992
Prudential International Bond Fund, Inc. merged into Prudential Global Total Return Fund, Inc. 05/04/2001 which name changed to Dryden Global Total Return Fund, Inc. 07/07/2003

GLOBAL GOVT PLUS FD LTD (BERMUDA)
Completely liquidated 06/17/1994
Each share Common no par exchanged for first and final distribution of CAD$8.84206 cash

GLOBAL GREEN MATRIX CORP (AB)
Name changed to Intercept Energy Services Inc. 09/23/2013

GLOBAL GROUP ENTERPRISES CORP (FL)
Merged into Tyme Technologies, Inc. 09/26/2014
Each share Common $0.0001 par exchanged for (4.3334) shares Common $0.0001 par

GLOBAL GROWTH & INCOME FD INC (MD)
In process of liquidation
Each share Capital Shares $1 par exchanged for initial distribution of $8.6454 cash 8/21/89
Each share Capital Shares $1 par received second distribution of $1.1326 cash 12/13/89
Each share Income Shares $1 par exchanged for first and final distribution of $10.2064 cash 8/21/89
Note: Details on subsequent distribution(s), if any, are not available

GLOBAL GSM SOLUTIONS INC (NV)
Reorganized as Gold & GemStone Mining Inc. 04/30/2012
Each share Common $0.001 par exchanged for (45) shares Common $0.001 par

GLOBAL HEALTH SCIENCES FD (MA)
Name changed to INVESCO Global Health Sciences Fund (MA) 07/01/1997
INVESCO Global Health Sciences Fund (MA) reincorporated in Maryland as INVESCO Advantage Global Health Sciences Fund 05/15/2001
(See INVESCO Advantage Global Health Sciences Fund)

GLOBAL HEALTH SVCS INC (DE)
Name changed to American West Financial, Inc. 5/28/86
(See American West Financial, Inc.)

GLOBAL HEALTH SYS INC (DE)
Name changed to GHS, Inc. 11/15/1988
GHS, Inc. name changed to Dreamlife, Inc. 12/15/1999 which name changed to EOS International, Inc. 12/31/2001
(See EOS International, Inc.)

GLOBAL HEALTH VENTURES INC (NV)
Recapitalized as Kedem Pharmaceuticals Inc. 11/07/2011
Each share Common $0.001 par exchanged for (0.05) share Common $0.0001 par
(See Kedem Pharmaceuticals Inc.)

GLOBAL HEALTHCARE COMMUNICATIONS USA CORP (NEW) (NV)
Recapitalized as Maison Portier Holdings Inc. 10/1/2002
Each share Common $0.001 par exchanged for (0.02) share Common $0.001 par

GLOBAL HEALTHCARE DIVID FD (AB)
Under plan of merger each Trust Unit automatically became (1) share Middlefield Mutual Funds Ltd. Global Healthcare Dividend Fund Ser. A 12/19/2016

GLOBAL HEALTHCARE INCOME & GROWTH FD (ON)
Under plan of reorganization each Unit automatically became (1) Global Healthcare Income & Growth ETF Unit 04/03/2018

GLOBAL HIGH INCOME FD INC (MD)
Name changed 11/07/2006
Name changed from Global High Income Dollar Fund Inc. to Global High Income Fund Inc. 11/07/2006
Trust terminated
Each share Common $0.001 par received first and final distribution of $8.6886 cash payable 04/18/2016 to holders of record 04/11/2016

GLOBAL HLDGS INC (UT)
Name changed to Element Global, Inc. 08/06/2015

GLOBAL HSG GROUP (NV)
Name changed to Global Enterprises Group, Inc. 03/12/2014
Global Enterprises Group, Inc. name changed to Predictive Technology Group, Inc. 07/16/2015

GLOBAL IMAGING SYS INC (DE)
Issue Information - 6,000,000 shares COM offered at $12 per share on 06/17/1998
Common 1¢ par split (2) for (1) by issuance of (1) additional share payable 8/15/2006 to holders of record 8/1/2006 Ex date - 8/16/2006
Merged into Xerox Corp. 5/11/2007
Each share Common 1¢ par exchanged for $29 cash

GLOBAL IMMUNE TECHNOLOGIES INC (BC)
Reincorporated under the laws of Wyoming 5/12/2006

GLOBAL INCOME & CURRENCY FD INC (MD)
Name changed 03/07/2006
Name changed from Global Currency Strategy Income Fund Inc. to Global Income & Currency Fund, Inc. 03/07/2006
Merged into Nuveen Diversified Currency Opportunities Fund 12/10/2012
Each share Common $0.001 par exchanged for (1.00086028) Common Shares of Bene. Int. 1¢ par
Nuveen Diversified Currency Opportunities Fund merged into Nuveen Global High Income Fund 11/24/2014

GLOBAL INCOME FD INC (MD)
Name changed to Self Storage Group, Inc. 11/15/2013
Self Storage Group, Inc. name changed to Global Self Storage, Inc. 01/19/2016

GLOBAL INCOME PLUS FD INC (MD)
Plan of reorganization and liquidation effective 6/30/95
Each share Common $0.001 par with an assigned value of $8.84 exchanged for PaineWebber Investment Series Global Income Fund Class A $0.001 par with an assigned value of $10.18 on a pro rata basis

GLOBAL INDEMNITY PLC (IRELAND)
Reincorporated under the laws of Cayman Islands as Global Indemnity Ltd. 11/07/2016

GLOBAL INDL SVCS INC (NV)
Company terminated common stock registration and is no longer public as of 11/08/2004

GLOBAL INDL TECHNOLOGIES INC (DE)
Merged into RHI AG 12/31/99
Each share Common 25¢ par exchanged for $13 cash

GLOBAL INDS CORP (NV)
Charter permanently revoked 05/02/2011

GLOBAL INDS INC (AB)
Name changed to American Resource Corp. 05/29/1998
(See American Resource Corp.)

GLOBAL INDS INC (NJ)
Adjudicated bankrupt 03/09/1978
Stockholders' equity unlikely

GLOBAL INDS LTD (LA)
Common 1¢ par split (2) for (1) by issuance of (1) additional share payable 01/31/1996 to holders of record 01/24/1996
Common 1¢ par split (2) for (1) by issuance of (1) additional share payable 08/28/1996 to holders of record 08/16/1996
Common 1¢ par split (2) for (1) by issuance of (1) additional share payable 10/27/1997 to holders of record 10/15/1997
Acquired by Technip 12/01/2011
Each share Common 1¢ par exchanged for $8 cash

GLOBAL INFRASTRUCTURE DIVID FD (AB)
Under plan of merger each Trust Unit automatically became (0.78634836) share Middlefield Mutual Funds Ltd. Global Infrastructure Fund Ser. A 08/17/2016

GLOBAL INK SUPPLY CO (DE)
Common $0.0001 par split (14) for (1) by issuance of (13) additional shares payable 08/20/2009 to holders of record 08/20/2009
Name changed to TurkPower Corp. 06/15/2010
TurkPower Corp. recapitalized as Zinco do Brasil, Inc. 12/28/2012

GLOBAL INTELLICOM INC (NV)
Chapter 7 bankruptcy proceedings terminated 05/02/2005
No stockholders' equity

GLOBAL INTL ENERGY INC (ON)
Merged into Equican Ventures Corp. 12/04/1987
Each share Common no par exchanged for (3.125) shares Common no par
Equican Ventures Corp. recapitalized as Equican Capital Corp. 01/27/1988 which name changed to Genterra Capital Corp. (Old) 08/23/1995 which merged into Genterra Capital Corp. (New) 02/28/1997 which recapitalized as Genterra Capital, Inc. 06/30/1998 which name changed to Genterra Investment Corp. 04/30/1999 which merged into Genterra Inc. 12/31/2003

GLOBAL INTL INDEMNITY INC (UT)
Proclaimed dissolved for failure to pay taxes 8/1/93

GLOBAL INTERNET COMMUNICATIONS INC. (NV)
Reincorporated 10/02/2003
Place of incorporation changed from (BC) to (NV) and Common no par changed to $0.00001 par 10/02/2003
Name changed to ProUroCare Medical, Inc. 04/26/2004

GLOBAL INVT FINL GROUP INC (BC)
Name changed 04/04/2001
Name changed from Global Investment.com Financial Inc. to Global Investment Financial Group Inc. 04/04/2001
Recapitalized as Global Financial Group Inc. 03/04/2002
Each share Common no par exchanged for (0.05) share Common no par
Global Financial Group Inc. name changed to egX Group Inc. 04/17/2007

GLOBAL INVT HSE K P S C (KUWAIT)
Name changed 11/24/2014
Each old 144A Sponsored GDR for Ordinary exchanged for (0.404487) new 144A Sponsored GDR for Ordinary 12/10/2012
Each old Reg. S Sponsored GDR for Ordinary exchanged for (0.404487) new Reg. S Sponsored GDR for Ordinary 12/10/2012
Name changed from Global Investment House K.S.C.C. to Global Investment House (K.P.S.C) 11/24/2014
Each old Sponsored 144A GDR for Ordinary exchanged for (0.45769866) new Sponsored 144A GDR for Ordinary 01/06/2015
Each old Sponsored Reg. S GDR for Ordinary exchanged for (0.45769866) new Sponsored Reg. S GDR for Ordinary 01/06/2015
GDR agreement terminated 08/31/2015
Each new Sponsored 144A GDR for Ordinary exchanged for (5) shares Ordinary
Each new Sponsored Reg. S GDR for Ordinary exchanged for (5) shares Ordinary
Note: Unexchanged GDR's will be sold and the proceeds, if any, held for claim after 09/03/2015

GLOBAL INV SVCS INC (NV)
Recapitalized as Investview, Inc. 04/09/2012
Each share Common $0.001 par exchanged for (0.005) share Common $0.001 par

GLOBAL IT HLDGS INC (NV)
Each share old Common $0.001 par exchanged for (0.00285714) share new Common $0.001 par 07/31/2006
Charter revoked for failure to file reports and pay taxes 03/31/2008

GLOBAL ITECHNOLOGY INC (DE)
Company terminated common stock registration and is no longer public as of 10/17/2005

GLOBAL KARAOKE NETWORK INC (DE)
Common $0.00001 par split (90) for (1) by issuance of (89) additional shares payable 08/10/2011 to holders of record 08/08/2011 Ex date - 08/11/2011
Name changed to Anchorage International Holdings Corp. 10/22/2013

GLOBAL LIFE SCIENCES INC (NV)
Each share old Common $0.001 par exchanged for (0.1) share new Common $0.001 par 10/12/2004
Name changed to Nortia Capital Partners, Inc. 11/5/2004

GLOBAL LT TELECOMMUNICATIONS INC (YT)
Filed for protection under Companies' Creditors Arrangement Act 06/28/2002
Stockholders' equity unlikely

GLOBAL LINES INC (NV)
Name changed to Alkaline Water Co. Inc. 05/31/2013

GLOBAL LINK DATA SOLUTIONS LTD (AB)
Name changed to Global Energy Services Inc. 08/16/2005
Global Energy Services Inc. name changed to Raise Production Inc. 11/02/2011

GLOBAL-LINK ENTERPRISES INC (NV)
Name changed to MLM World News Today, Inc. 02/17/2000
MLM World News Today, Inc. name changed to Presidential Air Corp. 08/06/2002 which recapitalized as Safe Travel Care, Inc. 05/02/2003 which recapitalized as Titan Energy Worldwide, Inc. 12/28/2006
(See Titan Energy Worldwide, Inc.)

GLOBAL LINK INTL INC (AB)
Recapitalized as Global Link Data Solutions Ltd. 05/10/2000
Each share Common no par exchanged for (0.25) share Common no par
Global Link Data Solutions Ltd. name changed to Global Energy Services Ltd. 08/16/2005 which name changed to Raise Production Inc. 11/02/2011

GLOBAL LINK TECHNOLOGIES INC (DE)
Each share old Common no par exchanged for (0.002) share new Common no par 05/19/1997
Each share new Common no par exchanged again for (0.025) share new Common no par 12/11/2001
Reorganized under the laws of Wyoming as MutuaLoan Corp. 01/12/2009
Each share Common no par exchanged for (0.0005) share Common no par
MutuaLoan Corp. name changed to Nexus Enterprise Solutions, Inc. 02/27/2012

GLOBAL LINKS CORP OLD (NV)
Each share old Common $0.001 par exchanged for (0.025) share new Common $0.001 par 04/14/2003
Name changed to Global Links Corp. (New) 08/04/2003

GLOBAL LOGISTIC PPTYS LTD (SINGAPORE)
ADR agreement terminated 02/01/2018
Each ADR for Ordinary issued by Bank of New York exchanged for $25.550243 cash

GLOBAL LOGISTICS ACQUISITION CORP (DE)
Name changed to Clark Holdings Inc. 02/14/2008
(See Clark Holdings Inc.)

GLOBAL MAINFRAME CORP (AB)
SEC revoked common stock registration 02/17/2011

GLOBAL MAINTECH CORP NEW (MN)
Filed a petition under Chapter 7 Federal Bankruptcy Code 02/24/2009
No stockholders' equity

GLOBAL MAINTECH CORP OLD (MN)
Each share old Common no par exchanged for (0.2) share new Common no par 11/12/1996
Each share new Common no par exchanged again for (0.2) share new Common no par 09/02/1999
Name changed to Singlepoint Systems Corp. 08/14/2000
Singlepoint Systems Corp. name changed to Global Maintech Corp. (New) 03/07/2001
(See Global Maintech Corp. (New))

GLOBAL MARINE INC (DE)
$5 Conv. Preferred no par called for redemption 11/30/1972
Under plan of reorganization each share $3.50 Conv. Preferred no par exchanged for (0.151) share Common 10¢ par and (0.315) Common Stock Purchase Warrant expiring 03/16/1996 on 03/01/1989
Common 50¢ par split (2) for (1) by issuance of (1) additional share 05/19/1967
Common 50¢ par changed to 25¢ par and (1) additional share issued 06/20/1980
Common 25¢ par changed to 12-1/2¢ par and (1) additional share issued 06/01/1981
Under plan of reorganization each share Common 12-1/2¢ par exchanged for (0.054) share Common 10¢ par and (0.113) Common Stock Purchase Warrant expiring 03/16/1996 on 03/01/1989
Merged into GlobalSantaFe Corp. 11/20/2001
Each share Common 10¢ par exchanged for (0.665) share Ordinary 1¢ par
GlobalSantaFe Corp. merged into Transocean Inc. (New) (Cayman Islands) 11/27/2007 which reorganized in Switzerland as Transocean Ltd. 12/18/2008

GLOBAL MARINE LTD (NV)
SEC revoked common stock registration 07/16/2008

GLOBAL MATLS & SVCS INC (FL)
Each share old Common no par exchanged for (0.001) share new Common no par 03/18/2005
Administratively dissolved 09/14/2007

GLOBAL MATRECHS (DE)
Each share old Common $0.0001 par exchanged for (0.05) share new Common $0.0001 par 05/26/2006
SEC revoked common stock registration 06/19/2009

GLOBAL MED MARKETING INC (FL)
Recapitalized as Virtual Innovations, Inc. 12/30/2005
Each (3.5) shares Common no par exchanged for (1) share Common no par
Virtual Innovations, Inc. name changed to University Health Industries, Inc. 05/09/2008 which name changed to Cognitiv, Inc. 09/19/2012

GLOBAL MED PRODS HLDGS INC (NV)
Company terminated common stock registration and is no longer public as of 03/23/2010

GLOBAL MED TECHNOLOGIES INC (CO)
Issue Information - 1,337,000 UNITS consisting of (2) shares COM and (1) WT CL A offered at $7 per Unit on 02/11/1997
Merged into Haemonetics Corp. 04/13/2010
Each share Common 1¢ par exchanged for $1.22 cash

GLOBAL MEDIA CORP (NV)
Name changed to GlobalMedia.com 04/25/2000
GlobalMedia.com recapitalized as WorldSage, Inc. (NV) 10/27/2006 which reincorporated in Delaware 04/11/2008 which name changed to Career College Holding Co. Inc. 10/29/2008

GLOBAL MET COAL CORP (BC)
Name changed to Minecorp Energy Ltd. 07/15/2014
Minecorp Energy Ltd. name changed to Freedom Energy Inc. 05/29/2017

GLOBAL METALS EXPL NL (AUSTRALIA)
ADR agreement terminated 11/10/2016
No ADR's remain outstanding

GLOBAL MINERAL & CHEM LTD (AB)
Recapitalized as Consolidated Global Minerals Ltd. 01/15/1999
Each share Common no par exchanged for (0.2) share Common no par
Consolidated Global Minerals Ltd. name changed to Global Minerals Ltd. 11/27/2006 which recapitalized as MK2 Ventures Ltd. 06/27/2016

GLOBAL MINERALS LTD (BC)
Each share old Common no par exchanged for (0.08333333) share new Common no par 01/29/2010
Each share new Common no par exchanged again for (0.2) share new Common no par 02/07/2014
Each share new Common no par exchanged again for (0.06666666) share new Common no par 08/06/2015
Recapitalized as MK2 Ventures Ltd. 06/27/2016
Each share new Common no par exchanged for (0.5) share Common no par

GLOBAL MKT INFORMATION INC (DE)
Issue Information - 1,200,000 shares COM offered at $5 per share on 08/11/1994
Name changed to Track Data Corp. 3/31/96

GLOBAL MONITORING SYS INC (FL)
Name changed to Planet Signal, Inc. 11/21/2007
(See Planet Signal, Inc.)

GLOBAL MOTORSPORT GROUP INC (DE)
Merged into Stonington Acquisition Corp. 12/22/1998
Each share Common $0.001 par exchanged for $19.50 cash

GLOBAL MUSIC INTL INC (FL)
Name changed to Global Technologies Group, Inc. 10/15/2008

GLOBAL NAT RES INC (NJ)
Merged into Seagull Energy Corp. 10/03/1996
Each share Common $1 par exchanged for (0.88) share Common 10¢ par
Seagull Energy Corp. name changed to Ocean Energy, Inc. (TX) 03/30/1999 which reincorporated in Delaware 05/09/2001 which merged into Devon Energy Corp. 04/25/2003

GLOBAL NATL COMMUNICATIONS CORP (NV)
Reorganized under the laws of Delaware as GNCC Capital, Inc. 12/01/2008
Each (15) shares Common $0.00001 par exchanged for (1) share Common $0.00001 par

GLOBAL NET ENERGY CORP (NV)
Name changed to Auction Floor, Inc. 01/11/2007
Each share Common $0.001 par exchanged for (1) share Common $0.001 par
(See Auction Floor, Inc.)

GLOBAL NET ENTMT CORP (BC)
Recapitalized as Guildhall Minerals Ltd. 11/17/2006
Each share Common no par exchanged for (0.2) share Common no par
Guildhall Minerals Ltd. name changed to Edge Resources Inc. 07/28/2009
(See Edge Resources Inc.)

GLOBAL NETWORK INC (NV)
Each share old Common $0.001 par exchanged for (0.025) share new Common $0.001 par 05/26/2005
SEC revoked common stock registration 09/08/2008

GLOBAL NETWORKS CORP (NV)
Charter revoked for failure to file reports and pay fees 04/01/2013

GLOBAL NEW ENERGY INDS INC (NV)
Name changed to Coin Citadel 11/06/2014

GLOBAL NICKEL INVTS NL (AUSTRALIA)
Name changed to Global Metals Exploration NL 01/18/2012
(See Global Metals Exploration NL)

GLOBAL NUTECH INC (NV)
Each (300) shares old Common $0.00001 par exchanged for (1) share new Common $0.00001 par 09/14/2011
Note: No holder will receive fewer than (100) shares
Name changed to Texas Gulf Energy, Inc. 03/07/2012

GLOBAL OCEAN CARRIERS LTD (LIBERIA)
Plan of reorganization under Chapter 11 Federal Bankruptcy Code effective 12/29/2000
No old Common stockholders' equity
Merged into Queen Trading Co. 04/30/2002
Each share new Common 1¢ par exchanged for $1 cash

GLOBAL OIL & GOLD CO (UT)
Involuntarily dissolved 03/01/1990

GLOBAL OIL CO (UT)
Name changed to Global Oil & Gold Co. 06/19/1987
(See Global Oil & Gold Co.)

GLOBAL ONE DISTR & MERCHANDISING INC (DE)
Recapitalized as Brite-Strike Tactical Illumination Products, Inc. 07/30/2008
Each share Common 1¢ par exchanged for (0.001) share Common 1¢ par

GLOBAL 1 INVT HLDGS CORP (GA)
SEC revoked common stock registration 04/08/2009

GLOBAL ONLINE INDIA INC (DE)
SEC revoked common stock registration 07/18/2012

GLOBAL OUTDOORS INC (AK)
Name changed 07/23/1996
Each share Common $0.001 par exchanged for (0.05) share Common 2¢ par 03/04/1992
Each share new Common 2¢ par exchanged again for (2) shares new Common 2¢ par 09/12/1994
Stock Dividend - 10% 05/01/1989
Name changed from Global Resources, Inc. to Global Outdoors, Inc. 07/23/1996
Each share 10% Conv. Exchangeable Preferred no par exchanged for (1) share Common 2¢ par 03/22/2002
Name changed to Outdoor Channel Holdings, Inc. (AK) 06/27/2003
Outdoor Channel Holdings, Inc. (AK) reincorporated in Delaware 09/14/2004
(See Outdoor Channel Holdings, Inc. (DE))

GLOBAL PAC FINL CORP (NV)
Name changed to Unitel Corp. 02/10/1992

GLOBAL-PAC MINERALS INC (BC)
Reorganized under the laws of Wyoming as UNIREX Technologies Inc. 04/23/2001
Each share Common no par exchanged for (1) share Common no par and (0.16666666) share Pacific Minerals Inc. Common no par
UNIREX Technologies Inc. recapitalized as UNIREX Corp. 07/19/2001
(See UNIREX Corp.)

GLOBAL PARI-MUTUEL SVCS INC (NV)
Charter revoked for failure to file reports and pay taxes 01/31/2013

GLOBAL PARTNER ACQUISITION CORP (DE)
Units separated 02/05/2018
Name changed to Purple Innovation, Inc. and Common $0.0001 par reclassified as Class A Common $0.0001 par 02/05/2018

GLOBAL PARTNERS INCOME FD INC (MD)
Name changed to Salomon Brothers Global Partners Income Fund Inc. 04/21/2003
Salomon Brothers Global Partners Income Fund Inc. name changed to Western Asset Global Partners Income Fund Inc. 10/09/2006 which merged into Western Asset Global High Income Fund Inc. 08/29/2016

GLOBAL PATH INC (DE)
Each share Class A Common $0.001 par exchanged for (0.01) share Common $0.001 par 12/11/2002
Name changed to Swiss Medica, Inc. 06/27/2003
(See Swiss Medica, Inc.)

GLOBAL PAY SOLUTIONS INC (DE)
Each share old Common 1¢ par exchanged for (0.0005) share new Common 1¢ par 02/21/2008
Recapitalized as China National Appliance of North America Corp. 03/26/2009
Each share Common 1¢ par exchanged for (0.2) share Common 1¢ par

GLOBAL PEOPLELINE TELECOM INC (FL)
SEC revoked common stock registration 03/08/2011

GLOBAL PETE INC (BC)
Name changed to 01/09/1998
Name changed from Global Metals Ltd. to Global Petroleum Inc. 01/09/1998
Recapitalized as Stellar Pacific Ventures Inc. (BC) 06/15/2000
Each share Common no par exchanged for (0.5) share Common no par
Stellar Pacific Ventures Inc. (BC) reincorporated in Canada 04/24/2006 which recapitalized as Stellar AfricaGold Inc. 04/03/2013

GLOBAL PETE LTD (AUSTRALIA)
Each old Sponsored ADR for Ordinary exchanged for (0.04) new Sponsored ADR for Ordinary 12/10/2002
ADR basis changed from (1:5) to (5:1) 12/10/2002
ADR agreement terminated 10/24/2005
Each new Sponsored ADR for Ordinary exchanged for $0.07777 cash

GLOBAL PHARMACEUTICAL CORP (DE)
Name changed to Impax Laboratories, Inc. 12/16/1999
Impax Laboratories, Inc. name changed to Amneal Pharmaceuticals, Inc. 05/07/2018

GLOBAL PLATINUM & GOLD INC (NV)
Each share old Common 1¢ par exchanged for (0.2) share new Common 1¢ par 09/28/1994
Recapitalized as Bourque Industries, Inc. 02/07/2011
Each share new Common 1¢ par exchanged for (0.2) share Common $0.0001 par

GLOBAL PLUS CDN$ INCOME TR (ON)
Name changed to Premier Canadian Income Fund 11/09/2009
(See Premier Canadian Income Fund)

GLOBAL PWR EQUIP GROUP INC (DE)
Under plan of reorganization each share old Common 1¢ par exchanged for (1) share new Common 1¢ par 01/22/2008
Each share new Common 1¢ par exchanged again for (0.11111111) share new Common 1¢ par 07/01/2010
Name changed to Williams Industrial Services Group Inc. 06/29/2018

GLOBAL PRECISION MED INC (WY)
Reincorporated 02/05/2003
Place of incorporation changed from (BC) to Wyoming 02/05/2003
Administratively dissolved for failure to pay taxes 03/14/2009

GLOBAL PFD ADVISORS LTD (NV)
Name changed to Black Sea Prospects, Inc. 03/15/2004

GLOBAL PFD HLDGS INC (DE)
In process of liquidation
Each share Common $0.001 par received initial distribution of approximately (1.07) Aegon N.V. New York Registry Shares EUR 0.12 par payable 07/08/2005 to holders of record 06/01/2005
Each share Common $0.001 par received second distribution of approximately $0.0019051 cash payable 12/28/2005 to holders of record 06/01/2005
Assets transferred to GPH Liquidating Trust and Common $0.001 par reclassified as Shares of Bene. Int. 05/17/2006
(See GPH Liquidating Trust)

GLOBAL PFD SECS TR (ON)
Under plan of merger each Unit no par automatically became (0.713949) Fairway Diversified Income & Growth Trust Unit no par 06/29/2007
Fairway Diversified Income & Growth Trust merged into Crown Hill Fund 01/23/2009 which merged into Citadel Income Fund 12/02/2009

GLOBAL PREMIER INVT GROUP INC (NV)
Charter revoked for failure to file reports and pay fees 11/1/2005

GLOBAL PRESENTATIONS, INC. (DE)
Charter cancelled and declared inoperative and void for non-payment of taxes 4/15/72

GLOBAL PRIVATIZATION FD INC NEW (MD)
Issue Information - 70,000,000 shares COM offered at $15 per share on 03/03/1994
Plan of reorganization and liquidation effective 10/27/95
Each share Common 1¢ par exchanged for (1.3677043) Alliance Worldwide Privatization Fund, Inc. Class A shares
Alliance Worldwide Privatization Fund, Inc. name changed to AllianceBernstein Worldwide Privatization Fund, Inc. 3/31/2003 which name changed to AllianceBernstein International Growth Fund, Inc. 5/16/2005

GLOBAL PRODTNS INC (WA)
Each share old Common no par exchanged for (1/3) share new Common no par 05/09/1994
Recapitalized as Northstar Network Inc. 10/07/1999
Each share new Common no par exchanged for (1/3) share Common no par
(See Northstar Network Inc.)

GLOBAL PROSPECTING VENTURES INC (NV)
Reincorporated 06/04/2004
State of incorporation changed from (FL) to (NV) and Common 4¢ par changed to $0.001 par 06/04/2004
Each share old Common $0.001 par exchanged for (0.25) share new Common $0.001 par 09/01/2004
Name changed to Competitive Games International, Inc. 01/22/2007
Competitive Games International, Inc. recapitalized as PacWest Equities, Inc. 05/07/2010
(See PacWest Equities, Inc.)

GLOBAL RAILWAY INDS LTD (BC)
Reincorporated 04/16/2013
In process of liquidation
Each share Common no par received initial distribution of $1 cash payable 11/02/2011 to holders of record 10/25/2011
Each share Common no par received second distribution of $0.40 cash payable 05/14/2012 to holders of record 05/07/2012 Ex date - 05/03/2012
Note: Certificate of Intent to Dissolve revoked 01/31/2013
Place of incorporation changed from (AB) to (BC) 04/16/2013
Recapitalized as Chinook Tyee Industry Ltd. 08/13/2013
Each share Common no par exchanged for (0.25) share Common no par

GLOBAL REAL ESTATE INVT TR (PA)
Reorganized under the laws of Delaware as Global Development, Inc. 10/25/79
Each Share of Bene. Int. no par exchanged for (1) share Common 5¢ par
Global Development, Inc. reincorporated in Pennsylvania 6/30/82
(See Global Development, Inc. (New))

GLOBAL RLTY MGMT GROUP INC (FL)
Each share old Common $0.001 par exchanged for (0.06775985) share new Common $0.001 par 03/29/2002
Reincorporated under the laws of Delaware as Excalibur Industries, Inc. 06/10/2002
Excalibur Industries, Inc. recapitalized as Shumate Industries, Inc. 10/20/2005 which name changed to Hemiwedge Industries, Inc. 02/19/2009 which name changed to HII Technologies, Inc. 01/17/2012
(See HII Technologies, Inc.)

GLOBAL RECYCLE ENERGY INC (NV)
Name changed to ATI Modular Technology Corp. 06/13/2017
ATI Modular Technology Corp. recapitalized as AmericaTowne Holdings, Inc. 03/08/2018

GLOBAL REIT LEADERS INCOME ETF (ON)
Name changed to Harvest Global REIT Leaders Income ETF 06/19/2018

GLOBAL REMOTE TECHNOLOGIES LTD (BC)
Name changed to Cryptobloc Technologies Corp. 04/09/2018

GLOBAL RES/VENTURES (NV)
Name changed to HelixSphere Technologies Inc. 05/10/1999
HelixSphere Technologies Inc. recapitalized as New China Global, Inc. (NV) 10/02/2013 which reorganized in Wyoming as Globestar Industries 08/07/2014 which name changed to Pineapple Express, Inc. 09/22/2015

GLOBAL RESOURCE SPLIT CORP (ON)
Preferred no par called for redemption at $10 on 06/30/2009
Class A no par called for redemption at approximately $19.6204 on 06/30/2009

GLOBAL RES CORP (NV)
Each share old Common $0.001 par exchanged for (0.01) share new Common $0.001 par 8/14/2006
Charter permanently revoked 06/29/2012

GLOBAL RES TECHNOLOGIES INC (NV)
Name changed to Gold & Onyx Mining Co. 06/10/2009
(See Gold & Onyx Mining Co.)

GLOBAL SATELLITE NETWORK USA INC (NV)
Charter permanently revoked 5/1/2003

GLOBAL SCIENCE CORP (NV)
Each (300) shares old Common $0.001 par exchanged for (1) share new Common $0.001 par 4/7/99
Name changed to Sochrys.Com Inc. 8/25/99
Sochrys.Com Inc. name changed to Validian Corp. 2/6/2003

GLOBAL SEAFARMS CORP (CANADA)
Company received Letter of Demand/Enforcement of Security and all officers and directors have resigned effective 11/02/2015
Stockholders' equity unlikely

GLOBAL SEC & INTELLIGENCE GROUP INC (FL)
Administratively dissolved 09/19/2003

GLOBAL SVCS PARTNERS ACQUISITION CORP (DE)
Name changed to SouthPeak Interactive Corp. 04/25/2008
Each share Class B Common $0.0001 par exchanged for $5.36522 cash 04/28/2008

GLOBAL SIGNAL INC (DE)
Merged into Crown Castle International Corp. (Old) 01/12/2007
Each share Common 1¢ par exchanged for (1.61) shares Common 1¢ par
Crown Castle International Corp. (Old) reorganized as Crown Castle International Corp. (New) 12/16/2014

GLOBAL SMALL CAP FD INC (MD)
Reorganized into PaineWebber Investment Trust 2/15/2000
Each share Common $0.001 par exchanged for (1.38293136) shares PaineWebber Global Equity Fund Class A $0.001 par

GLOBAL SMARTCARDS INC (NV)
Name changed to Global Energy Inc. 4/28/2003

GLOBAL SORTWEB COM INC (BC)
Reorganized as Mantra Mining Inc. 06/12/2006
Each share Common no par exchanged for (2) shares Common no par
Mantra Mining Inc. name changed to

TintinaGold Resources Inc. 09/28/2009 which name changed to Tintina Resources Inc. 05/26/2011 which name changed to Sandfire Resources America Inc. 02/02/2018

GLOBAL SOURCES LTD (BERMUDA)
Stock Dividends - 10% payable 04/01/2004 to holders of record 03/01/2004 Ex date - 02/26/2004; 10% payable 04/01/2005 to holders of record 03/04/2005 Ex date - 03/04/2005; 10% payable 04/17/2006 to holders of record 03/15/2006 Ex date - 03/13/2006; 10% payable 04/16/2007 to holders of record 03/16/2007 Ex date - 03/07/2007; 10% payable 02/01/2008 to holders of record 01/01/2008 Ex date - 12/27/2007; 10% payable 03/31/2009 to holders of record 02/27/2009 Ex date - 02/25/2009
Acquired by Expo Holdings I Ltd. 08/28/2017
Each share Common 1¢ par exchanged for $20 cash

GLOBAL SOURCES LTD (DE)
Charter cancelled and declared inoperative and void for non-payment of taxes 03/01/2001

GLOBAL SPILL MGMT INC (NV)
Each (30) shares old Common $0.001 par exchanged for (1) share new Common $0.001 par 05/15/1996
Name changed to Biofarm, Inc. 10/07/1998
Biofarm, Inc. name changed to friendlyway Corp. 04/22/2005 which name changed to PSI Corp. 10/02/2006 which name changed to Coupon Express, Inc. 01/26/2012

GLOBAL SPORTS & ENTMT INC (DE)
Name changed to GWIN, Inc. 09/24/2002
GWIN, Inc. name changed to Winning Edge International, Inc. 09/27/2006 which assets were transferred to W Technologies, Inc. 10/20/2007

GLOBAL SPORTS INC (DE)
Name changed to GSI Commerce, Inc. 05/24/2002
(See GSI Commerce, Inc.)

GLOBAL SPORTS RETAIL INC (NV)
Name changed to Global Developments, Inc. 03/27/2006
(See Global Developments, Inc.)

GLOBAL SR ENTERPRISES INC (NV)
Recapitalized as World Financial Holding Group 05/01/2018
Each share Common $0.001 par exchanged for (0.1) share Common $0.001 par

GLOBAL STEEL PRODUCTS CORP. (NY)
Whittaker Corp. acquired all but (35) shares through purchase offer as of 10/21/1965
Public interest eliminated

GLOBAL STEVIA CORP (NV)
Each share old Common $0.001 par exchanged for (5) shares new Common $0.001 par 09/11/2012
SEC revoked common stock registration 01/13/2015

GLOBAL STONE CORP (BC)
Acquired by Oglebay Norton Co. 06/22/1998
Each share Common no par exchanged for $7.80 cash

GLOBAL STRATEGY LTD PARTNERSHIP III (ON)
Merged into Global Strategy Master L.P. 01/29/1999
Each Unit of Ltd. Partnership Int. exchanged for (0.93) Unit of Ltd. Partnership
(See Global Strategy Master L.P.)

GLOBAL STRATEGY MASTER LP (ON)
Completely liquidated
Each Unit of Ltd. Partnership received first and final distribution of $0.12 cash payable 11/05/2012 to holders of record 11/05/2012

GLOBAL STRATEGY PARTNERS LP V (ON)
Merged into Global Strategy Master L.P. 01/29/1999
Each Unit of Ltd. Partnership Int. exchanged for (1) Unit of Ltd. Partnership
(See Global Strategy Master L.P.)

GLOBAL STRATEGY PARTNERS L P VI (ON)
Merged into Global Strategy Master L.P. 01/29/1999
Each Unit of Ltd. Partnership Int. exchanged for (1.13) Units of Ltd. Partnership
(See Global Strategy Master L.P.)

GLOBAL SUMMIT REAL ESTATE INC (BC)
Each (8,309,289) shares old Common no par exchanged for (1) share new Common no par 09/06/2013
Note: In effect holders received $0.043 cash per share and public interest was eliminated

GLOBAL SUNRISE INC (CO)
Name changed to Zulu Energy Corp. and Common $0.001 par changed to $0.0001 par 02/09/2007
Zulu Energy Corp. name changed to Vortex Brands Co. 07/03/2014

GLOBAL SYS DESIGNS INC (NV)
Name changed to bBooth, Inc. 10/16/2014
bBooth, Inc. name changed to nFusz, Inc. 04/24/2017

GLOBAL-TECH ADVANCED INNOVATIONS INC (BRITISH VIRGIN ISLANDS)
Recapitalized 12/11/2008
Recapitalized from Global-Tech Appliances Inc. to Global-Tech Advanced Innovations Inc. 12/11/2008
Each share Common 1¢ par exchanged for (0.25) share Ordinary 4¢ par
Acquired by Timely Star Ltd. 03/22/2016
Each share Ordinary 4¢ par exchanged for $8.85 cash

GLOBAL-TECH CAP CORP (NV)
Name changed to Source Direct Holdings, Inc. 10/14/2003
(See Source Direct Holdings, Inc.)

GLOBAL TECHNOLOGIES CORP (DE)
Recapitalized as Avalon GloboCare Corp. 10/18/2016
Each share Common $0.0001 par exchanged for (0.25) share Common $0.0001 par

GLOBAL TECHNOLOGIES INC (BC)
Recapitalized as Consolidated Global Technologies Inc. 12/05/2001
Each share Common no par exchanged for (0.11111111) share Common no par
Consolidated Global Technologies Inc. name changed to Garnet Point Resources Corp. 12/17/2003 which name changed to Hastings Resources Corp. 02/21/2008 which recapitalized as Trigen Resources Inc. 09/22/2010 which recapitalized as BlissCo Cannabis Corp. 03/02/2018

GLOBAL TECHNOVATIONS INC (DE)
Plan of reorganization under Chapter 11 Federal Bankruptcy proceedings confirmed 06/19/2002
No stockholders' equity

GLOBAL TEL & COMMUNICATIONS INC (NV)
Name changed to Viscorp 01/08/1996
Viscorp name changed to U.S. Digital Communications, Inc. 10/29/1997
(See U.S. Digital Communications, Inc.)

GLOBAL TEL COMMUNICATION INC (NV)
Reincorporated 11/24/1998
State of incorporation changed from (UT) to (NV) and Common 2¢ par changed to $0.001 par 11/24/1998
Recapitalized as Spirit Exploration, Inc. 08/14/2006
Each share Common $0.001 par exchanged for (0.00151515) share Common $0.001 par

GLOBAL TELECOM & TECHNOLOGY INC (DE)
Name changed to GTT Communications, Inc. 01/02/2014

GLOBAL TELECOM HLDG S A E (EGYPT)
GDR agreement terminated 04/17/2017
Each 144A GDR for Ordinary exchanged for $1.753314 cash
Each Reg. S GDR for Ordinary exchanged for $1.753314 cash

GLOBAL TELECOM SPLIT SHARE CORP (ON)
Preferred Shares no par called for redemption at $12.4838 plus $0.20625 accrued dividends on 07/02/2008
Class A no par called for redemption 07/02/2008
No stockholders' equity

GLOBAL TELECOMMUNICATION SOLUTIONS INC (DE)
Each share old Common 1¢ par exchanged for (1/3) share new Common 1¢ par 03/25/1997
New Common 1¢ par split (2) for (1) by issuance of (1) additional share payable 05/28/1997 to holders of record 05/12/1997
Name changed to Global iTechnology, Inc. 07/12/2000
(See Global iTechnology, Inc.)

GLOBAL TELEDATA CORP (NV)
SEC revoked common stock registration 06/26/2012

GLOBAL TELEMEDIA INTL INC (DE)
Reincorporated 10/06/1997
State of incorporation changed from (FL) to (DE) 10/06/1997
Each share old Common $0.004 par exchanged for (0.2) share new Common $0.004 par 11/27/2000
Recapitalized as Seacoast Holding Corp. 01/26/2004
Each share new Common $0.004 par exchanged for (0.002) share Common $0.004 par

GLOBAL TELESYSTEMS INC (DE)
Name changed 04/17/2000
Common no par split (2) for (1) by issuance of (1) additional share payable 07/21/1999 to holders of record 07/01/1999
Name changed from Global TeleSystems Group, Inc. to Global TeleSystems, Inc. 04/17/2000
Plan of reorganization under Chapter 11 Federal Bankruptcy Code effective 03/15/2002
No stockholders' equity

GLOBAL THERMOELECTRIC INC (AB)
10% Conv. Preferred Ser. 1 no par called for redemption at USD$2.16 on 08/05/1999
Merged into FuelCell Energy, Inc. 11/03/2003
Each share Common no par exchanged for either (0.279) share Common $0.0001 par or (0.279)

FCE Canada Inc. Exchangeable Share
Note: Option to receive Exchangeable Shares expired 10/31/2003
(See FCE Canada Inc.)

GLOBAL TIMBER CORP (NV)
Each (30) shares old Common $0.001 par exchanged for (1) share new Common $0.001 par 10/23/1996
Charter permanently revoked 01/01/2005

GLOBAL TOTAL RETURN FD INC (MD)
Name changed 12/01/1994
Name changed from Global Yield Fund, Inc. to Global Total Return Fund, Inc. 12/01/1994
Name changed to Prudential Global Total Return Fund, Inc. 08/00/1999
Prudential Global Total Return Fund, Inc. name changed to Dryden Global Total Return Fund, Inc. 07/07/2003

GLOBAL TRADE PORTAL CORP (NV)
Name changed to EXIM Internet Group Inc. 05/23/2005
(See EXIM Internet Group Inc.)

GLOBAL TRAFFIC NETWORK INC (NV)
Reincorporated 02/26/2008
Issue Information - 3,800,000 shares COM offered at $5 per share on 03/23/2006
State of incorporation changed from (DE) to (NV) 02/26/2008
Acquired by GTCR Gridlock Holdings (Cayman), L.P. 09/28/2011
Each share Common $0.001 par exchanged for $14 cash

GLOBAL TRANSNET CORP (FL)
Each share old Common $0.0001 par exchanged for (0.2) share new Common $0.0001 par 02/09/2004
Each share new Common $0.0001 par exchanged again for (5) shares new Common $0.0001 par 09/26/2005
Recapitalized as Legacy Brands Holding, Inc. (FL) 11/19/2009
Each share new Common $0.0001 par exchanged for (0.00333333) share Common $0.0001 par
Legacy Brands Holding, Inc. (FL) reincorporated in British Virgin Islands as Revelation MIS, Inc. 10/22/2010 which reincorporated in Florida as Jolen, Inc. 04/08/2015 which name changed to WOWI, Inc. 06/23/2016

GLOBAL TREE TECHNOLOGIES INC (AB)
Reorganized under the laws of British Columbia as Acadia Resources Corp. 02/07/2011
Each share Common no par exchanged for (0.05) share Common no par
Acadia Resources Corp. (BC) reincorporated in Jersey as Horizon Petroleum PLC 10/08/2013 which reincorporated in Alberta as Horizon Petroleum Ltd. 04/05/2016

GLOBAL TRIAD INC (NV)
Each share old Common 1¢ par exchanged for (0.02) share new Common 1¢ par 12/27/2005
Recapitalized as Miracle Applications Corp. 12/03/2007
Each share Common 1¢ par exchanged for (0.02) share Common 1¢ par
Miracle Applications Corp. name changed to Outfront Companies 01/26/2011
(See Outfront Companies)

GLOBAL-TRON, INC. (DE)
Charter cancelled and declared inoperative and void for non-payment of taxes 3/1/88

GLOBAL URANIUM CORP (BC)
Each share old Common no par exchanged for (0.1) share new Common no par 01/25/2010
Name changed to Global Met Coal Corp. 11/01/2011
Global Met Coal Corp. name changed to Minecorp Energy Ltd. 07/15/2014 which name changed to Freedom Energy Inc. 05/29/2017

GLOBAL URANIUM FD INC (ON)
Name changed to Aston Hill Global Uranium Fund Inc. 09/16/2011
Aston Hill Global Uranium Fund Inc. merged into Aston Hill Global Resource & Infrastructure Fund 04/05/2013 which merged into Aston Hill Global Resource Fund (New) 11/06/2015

GLOBAL URANIUM PWR CORP (FL)
Administratively dissolved 09/15/2006

GLOBAL VACATION GROUP INC (NY)
Issue Information - 3,000,000 shares COM offered at $14 per share on 07/31/1998
Name changed to Classic Vacation Group, Inc. 5/23/2001
Classic Vacation Group, Inc. name changed to Classic Vacation Group Liquidating Trust 3/22/2002
(See Classic Vacation Group Liquidating Trust)

GLOBAL VENTURE FDG INC (CO)
Each share old Common $0.0001 par exchanged for (0.05) share new Common $0.0001 par 08/20/1997
Name changed to U.S. Microbics, Inc. 04/24/1998

GLOBAL VISION HLDGS INC (NV)
Incorporated 08/01/2002
Each share old Common $0.001 par exchanged for (0.025) share new Common $0.001 par 05/17/2004
Recapitalized as Asiana Corp. 01/24/2008
Each share Common $0.001 par exchanged for (0.001) share Common $0.001 par

GLOBAL VISION UNLIMITED INC (UT)
Each share old Common $0.001 par exchanged for (0.1) share new Common $0.001 par 10/20/92
Name changed to DHS Industries Inc. 6/7/96
DHS Industries Inc. name changed to Glenhills Corp. 4/2/98 which name changed to Millennium Multi-Media.com Corp. 7/6/2000 which name changed to Voxcorp Inc. 2/13/2002

GLOBAL VLG COMMUNICATION (DE)
Name changed to OneWorld Systems, Inc. 06/18/1998
(See OneWorld Systems, Inc.)

GLOBAL WATAIRE INC (NV)
Name changed to Global Earth Energy, Inc. 03/10/2008
(See Global Earth Energy, Inc.)

GLOBAL WEAR LTD (DE)
Recapitalized as Sovereign Wealth Corp. 03/12/2008
Each share Common $0.0001 par exchanged for (0.1) share Common $0.0001 par
Sovereign Wealth Corp. name changed to Lenco Mobile Inc. 02/25/2009
(See Lenco Mobile Inc.)

GLOBAL WEB TV INC NEW (NV)
Reorganized as Amore TV, Inc. 01/27/2006
Each share Common $0.001 par exchanged for (22) shares Common $0.001 par
Amore TV, Inc. recapitalized as Rapid Fitness, Inc. 05/11/2007 which name changed to Tri-Star Holdings Inc. 08/27/2008 which recapitalized as Macada Holding, Inc. (NV) 08/20/2009 which reincorporated in Wyoming 02/22/2011 which recapitalized as KMA Holding, Inc. 03/17/2011
(See KMA Holding, Inc.)

GLOBAL WEB TV INC OLD (NV)
Recapitalized as QOL Holdings, Inc. 12/15/2003
Each share Common $0.001 par exchanged for (0.02) share Common $0.001 par
QOL Holdings, Inc. name changed to Global Web TV, Inc. (New) 10/05/2005 which reorganized as Amore TV, Inc. 01/27/2006 which recapitalized as Rapid Fitness, Inc. 05/11/2007 which name changed to Tri-Star Holdings Inc. 08/27/2008 which recapitalized as Macada Holding, Inc. (NV) 08/20/2009 which reincorporated in Wyoming 02/22/2011 which recapitalized as KMA Holding, Inc. 03/17/2011
(See KMA Holding, Inc.)

GLOBAL WEST RES INC (NV)
Name changed to We Save Homes, Inc. 07/30/2009
(See We Save Homes, Inc.)

GLOBAL-WIDE PUBN LTD (NV)
Common $0.001 par split (6) for (1) by issuance of (5) additional shares payable 05/23/2005 to holders of record 05/23/2005
Name changed to VIASPACE Inc. 06/22/2005

GLOBAL WIDE WEB INC (FL)
Name changed to TIE Technologies, Inc. 04/05/2002

GLOBAL WIRELESS & DIGITAL INC (NV)
Name changed to AmerElite Solutions, Inc. 05/18/2005
AmerElite Solutions, Inc. reorganized as RegalWorks Media, Inc. 08/26/2013

GLOBAL WIRELESS SATELLITE NETWORKS USA, INC (DE)
Name changed to Australian Agricultural & Property Development Corp. 11/29/2004
Each share Common $0.001 par exchanged for (1) share Common $0.001 par
Australian Agricultural & Property Development Corp. name changed to Global Realty Development Corp. 07/11/2005

GLOBAL WRESTLING ALLIANCE INC (FL)
Reorganized under the laws of Nevada as Pratt, Wylce & Lords, Ltd. 05/14/1993
Each share Common $0.0001 par exchanged for (0.01) share Common $0.001 par
Pratt, Wylce & Lords, Ltd. name changed to Bionet Technologies, Inc. 11/02/1998
(See Bionet Technologies, Inc.)

GLOBAL WTR ASSET CORP (UT)
Reincorporated under the laws of Delaware 10/26/2010

GLOBAL X FDS (DE)
Trust terminated 02/27/2012
Each share Global X Farming ETF $0.0001 par received $14.628192 cash
Each share Global X Fishing Industry ETF $0.0001 par received $11.066393 cash
Each share Global X Food ETF $0.0001 par received $15.146238 cash
Each share Global X Mexico Small Cap ETF $0.0001 par received $12.80719 cash
Each share Global X Oil Equities ETF $0.0001 par received $15.150424 cash
Each share Global X Russell Emerging Markets Growth ETF $0.0001 par received $22.666974 cash
Each share Global X Russell Emerging Markets Value ETF $0.0001 par received $23.680816 cash
Each share Global X Waste Management ETF $0.0001 par received $12.86112 cash
Global X S&P/TSX Venture 30 Canada ETF $0.0001 par reclassified as Global X Junior Miners ETF $0.0001 par 09/06/2012
Completely liquidated 10/26/2012
Each share Global X Aluminum ETF $0.0001 par received $9.436486 cash
Each share Global X Auto ETF $0.0001 par received $12.967536 cash
Each share Global X NASDAQ 500 ETF $0.0001 par received $29.661268 cash
Each share Global X NASDAQ 400 Mid Cap ETF $0.0001 par received $28.149895 cash
Each share old Global X Junior Miners ETF $0.0001 par exchanged for (0.3333333) share new Global X Junior Miners ETF $0.0001 par 05/16/2013
Each share old Global X Pure Gold Miners ETF $0.0001 par exchanged for (0.5) share new Global X Pure Gold Miners ETF $0.0001 par 05/16/2013
Completely liquidated 10/24/2014
Each share Global X Canada Preferred ETF $0.0001 par received $11.927636 cash
Each share Global X Pure Gold Miners ETF $0.0001 par received $10.15989 cash
Global X GF China Bond ETF $0.0001 par split (2) for (1) by issuance of (1) additional share payable 03/10/2015 to holders of record 03/09/2015 Ex date - 03/11/2015
Trust terminated 10/22/2015
Each share Global X Brazil Financials ETF $0.0001 par received $5.6699 cash
Each share Global X Central Asia & Mongolia Index ETF $0.0001 par received $8.5213 cash
Each share Global X Guru Small Cap Index ETF $0.0001 par received $12.2677 cash
Each share new Global X Junior Miners ETF $0.0001 par received $8.6846 cash
Completely liquidated 04/25/2016
Each share Global X GF China Bond ETF $0.0001 par received $36.517 cash
Trust terminated 10/13/2017
Each share Global X Brazil Consumer ETF $0.0001 par received $17.3624 cash
Each share Global X Brazil Mid Cap ETF $0.0001 par received $11.4671 cash
Each share Global X FTSE Andean 40 ETF $0.0001 par received $9.7258 cash
Each share Global X Guru Activist Index ETF $0.0001 par received $15.8625 cash
Each share Global X Guru International Index ETF $0.0001 par received $15.8302 cash
Each share Global X Junior MLP ETF $0.0001 par received $7.585 cash
Each share Global X Permanent ETF $0.0001 par received $25.7141 cash
(Additional Information in Active)

GLOBAL X-RAY EXCHANGE INC (WY)
Recapitalized as Air to Water Co. 08/15/2007
Each share Common no par exchanged for (0.00001) share Common no par
Note: No holder will receive fewer than (99) shares
Air to Water Co. name changed to New Horizon Group, Inc. 10/15/2008
(See New Horizon Group, Inc.)

GLOBAL YACHT SVCS INC (NV)
Name changed to Halozyme Therapeutics, Inc. (NV) 03/11/2004
Halozyme Therapeutics, Inc. (NV) reincorporated in Delaware 11/15/2007

GLOBALANCE DIVID GROWERS CORP (ON)
Under plan of merger each Equity Share automatically became (1.11019292) MBN Corp. Equity Shares 08/29/2018

GLOBALBANC ADVANTAGED 8 SPLIT CORP (ON)
Preferred Shares called for redemption at $4.58589 on 12/17/2012
Class A Shares called for redemption 12/17/2012
No stockholders' equity

GLOBALCENTER INC
Merged into Frontier Corp. 3/2/98
Each share Common no par exchanged for (0.401) share Common $1 par
Frontier Corp. merged into Global Crossing Ltd. 9/28/99
(See Global Crossing Ltd.)

GLOBALDIGITALCOMMERCE COM INC (DE)
Recapitalized as Dreamfield Holdings Inc. 11/18/2002
Each share Common $0.001 par exchanged for (0.05) share Common $0.001 par
Dreamfield Holdings Inc. changed to Riverside Entertainment Inc. 5/24/2004 which recapitalized as Axis Technologies Group, Inc. 10/20/2006

GLOBALGROUP INV HLDGS INC (NV)
Reincorporated 04/20/2012
State of incorporation changed from (FL) to (NV) 04/20/2012
Each share Common $0.001 par received distribution of (0.02) share Sovereign Oil Inc. Restricted Common payable 09/03/2013 to holders of record 08/31/2013
Name changed to Embarr Downs, Inc. 09/09/2013

GLOBALINK INC (DE)
Merged into Lernout & Hauspie Speech Products N.V. 9/29/98
Each share Common 1¢ par exchanged for (0.12061) share Common 1¢ par
(See Lernout & Hauspie Speech Products N.V.)

GLOBALITE GROUP INC (NV)
Recapitalized as Language 2 Language Universal Holdings, Inc. 11/04/2008
Each (7,000) shares Common $0.001 par exchanged for (1) share Common $0.001 par
(See Language 2 Language Universal Holdings, Inc.)

GLOBALMART. INC. (NY)
Name changed to Globalmart International Inc. 5/20/69
(See Globalmart International Inc.)

GLOBALMART INTL INC (NY)
Each share old Common 1¢ par exchanged for (0.117647) share new Common 1¢ par 03/31/1972

Merged into Jacobson Capital Services, Inc. 05/05/1980
Each share new Common 1¢ par exchanged for $0.82 cash

GLOBALMEDIA COM (NV)
Recapitalized as WorldSage, Inc. (NV) 10/27/2006
Each share Common $0.001 par exchanged for (0.002) share Common $0.001 par
WorldSage, Inc. (NV) reincorporated in Delaware 04/11/2008 which name changed to Career College Holding Co. Inc. 10/29/2008

GLOBALMIN VENTURES INC (NV)
Recapitalized as VetaNova Inc. 06/27/2018
Each share Common $0.0001 par exchanged for (0.001) share Common $0.0001 par

GLOBALNET CORP (NV)
SEC revoked common stock registration 04/30/2010

GLOBALNET EQUITIES INC (NV)
Each share old Common $0.001 par exchanged for (0.1) share new Common $0.001 par 02/01/2001
Recapitalized as Global Net Energy Corp. 10/10/2001
Each share new Common $0.001 par exchanged for (0.1) share Common $0.001 par
Global Net Energy Corp. name changed to Auction Floor, Inc. 01/11/2007
(See Auction Floor, Inc.)

GLOBALNET FINL COM INC (CO)
Each share old Common $0.001 par exchanged for (0.16666666) share new Common $0.001 par 07/06/1999
Merged into NewMedia SPARK PLC 11/14/2001
Each share new Common $0.001 par exchanged for $0.45 cash

GLOBALNET INC (NV)
Merged into Titan Corp. 03/22/2002
Each share Common $0.001 par exchanged for (0.03853) share Common 1¢ par
(See Titan Corp.)

GLOBALNETCARE INC (FL)
Name changed to BusinessWay International Corp. 1/31/2001
BusinessWay International Corp. reorganized as ICBS International Corp. (FL) 12/1/2004 which reorganized in Delaware as Wah King Invest Corp. 6/9/2005 which name changed to Royal Invest International Corp. 3/1/2007

GLOBALOCK CORP (DE)
Each share old Common $0.001 par exchanged for (0.11111111) share new Common $0.001 par 10/25/1999
Name changed to American Inflatables, Inc. 01/06/2000
American Inflatables, Inc. name changed to American Sports Development Group, Inc. 06/18/2002
(See American Sports Development Group, Inc.)

GLOBALONE REAL ESTATE INC (NV)
Name changed to Glow Holdings, Inc. 10/07/2011

GLOBALOPTIONS GROUP INC (DE)
Reincorporated 12/08/2006
State of incorporation changed from (NV) to (DE) 12/08/2006
Each share old Common $0.001 par exchanged for (0.125) share new Common $0.001 par 03/06/2007
Name changed to Patent Properties, Inc. 11/27/2013
Patent Properties, Inc. name changed to Walker Innovation Inc. 08/12/2015

GLOBALSANTAFE CORP (CAYMAN ISLANDS)
Merged into Transocean Inc. (New) (Cayman Islands) 11/27/2007
Each share Ordinary 1¢ par exchanged for (0.4757) share Ordinary 1¢ par and $22.46 cash
Transocean Inc. (New) (Cayman Islands) reorganized in Switzerland as Transocean Ltd. 12/18/2008

GLOBALSTAR TELECOMMUNICATIONS LTD (BERMUDA)
Common $1 par split (2) for (1) by issuance of (1) additional share payable 05/28/1997 to holders of record 05/12/1997
Each share Conv. Equivalent Obligation Preferred exchanged for an undetermined amount of Common $1 par 04/30/1998
Each share 6.50% 144A Equivalent Obligation Conv. Preferred exchanged for an undetermined amount of Common $1 par 04/30/1998
Each share 6.50% Equivalent Obligation Conv. Preferred exchanged for an undetermined amount of Common $1 par 04/30/1998
Common $1 par split (2) for (1) by issuance of (1) additional share payable 06/08/1998 to holders of record 05/29/1998 Ex date - 06/09/1998
Chapter 7 bankruptcy proceedings terminated 12/03/2004
No stockholders' equity

GLOBALSTORE COM INC (BC)
Name changed to GSO Solutions, Inc. 03/24/2000
(See GSO Solutions, Inc.)

GLOBALTEL IP INC (FL)
Name changed to Cleartronic, Inc. 06/20/2008

GLOBALTEL RES INC (WA)
Charter cancelled and proclaimed dissolved for failure to pay fees 02/22/2000

GLOBALTEX INDS INC (BC)
Name changed to Pine Valley Mining Corp. 05/14/2003

GLOBALTRON CORP (FL)
Reincorporated under the laws of Delaware as Phone1 Globalwide Corp. 09/26/2001
Phone1 Globalwide Corp. name changed to Celexpress Inc. 12/10/2007

GLOBALWISE INVTS INC (NV)
Old Common $0.001 par split (2) for (1) by issuance of (1) additional share payable 02/15/2008 to holders of record 02/05/008 Ex date - 02/19/2008
Each share old Common $0.001 par exchanged for (4) shares new Common $0.001 par 12/20/2011
Recapitalized as Intellinetics, Inc. 09/03/2014
Each share new Common $0.001 par exchanged for (0.14285714) share Common $0.001 par

GLOBE & REPUBLIC INSURANCE CO. OF AMERICA (PA)
Merged into American Equitable Assurance Co. of New York on a (1.2) for (1) basis 12/31/62
American Equitable Assurance Co. of New York merged into Reliance Insurance Co. 6/30/65
(See Reliance Insurance Co.)

GLOBE & RUTGERS FIRE INSURANCE CO. (NY)
Common $100 par changed to $25 par 00/00/1932
Common $25 par changed to $15 par 00/00/1934
Each share Common $15 par exchanged for (3) shares Common $5 par 00/00/1949
Merged into American Home Assurance Co. 00/00/1954
Each share old $4.64 Prior Preferred $15 par exchanged for (1) share new $4.64 Prior Preferred $15 par
Each share old Common $5 par exchanged for (1) share new Common $5 par
(See American Home Assurance Co.)

GLOBE AIRCRAFT CORP. (DE)
Bankrupt in 1947
Details not available

GLOBE AIRCRAFT CORP. (TX)
Reorganized as Globe Aircraft Corp. (DE) in 1946
Details not available

GLOBE AMERADA GLASS CO (IL)
Proclaimed dissolved for failure to pay taxes and file reports 07/11/2008

GLOBE AMERICAN CORP. (IN)
Name changed to Vulcan-Hart Corp. 1/12/59
Vulcan-Hart Corp. acquired by Heller (Walter E.) & Co. 12/2/63 which name changed to Heller (Walter E.) International Corp. 7/28/69 which name changed to Amerifin Corp. 1/26/84
(See Amerifin Corp.)

GLOBE AMERN CORP (OH)
Each share Class A Common $100 par exchanged for (10) shares Class A Common $10 par 09/09/1966
Each share Class B Common $1 par exchanged for (10) shares Class B Common 10¢ par 09/09/1966
Class A Common $10 par changed to no par 10/01/1970
Class B Common 10¢ par reclassified as Class A Common no par 12/00/1971
Name changed to Tri-American Corp. and Class A Common no par reclassified as Common no par 05/19/1972
(See Tri-American Corp.)

GLOBE ASSURN CO (OH)
Common $1 par changed to $1.50 par 10/24/66
Stock Dividends - 10% 10/24/66; 10% 11/1/67
Merged into Globe Life Corp. 3/28/68
Each share Common $1.50 par exchanged for (1) share Common no par
Globe Life Corp. name changed to Globe Capital Corp. 5/28/69
(See Globe Capital Corp.)

GLOBE BROADCASTING CO (DE)
Merged into Combined Communications Corp. 4/13/78
Each share Ser. A Common 20¢ par exchanged for $5 cash

GLOBE BUSINESS RES INC (OH)
Merged into Equity Residential Properties Trust 7/11/2000
Each share Common no par exchanged for $13 cash

GLOBE CAP CORP (OH)
Adjudicated bankrupt 03/01/1974
Stockholders' equity unlikely

GLOBE CONSOLIDATED OIL CO. (AZ)
Charter cancelled for non-payment of taxes 3/30/26

GLOBE COTTON OIL MILLS
Merged into Globe Grain & Milling Co. in 1927
Details not available

GLOBE CRUDE OIL CO. (CO)
Declared defunct and inoperative for failure to file reports and pay taxes 10/25/26

GLOBE ENERGY INC (NV)
Charter revoked for failure to file reports and pay fees 07/31/2008

GLOBE ENVELOPES LTD (CANADA)
Class A Common no par split (2) for (1) by issuance of (1) additional share 06/25/1965
Name changed to DRG Ltd. 08/07/1969
DRG Ltd. name changed to DRG Inc. (Canada) 06/23/1981 which reincorporated in British Columbia 00/00/1982
(See DRG Inc.)

GLOBE EXPL & MNG LTD (ON)
Charter cancelled for failure to pay taxes and file returns 03/05/1975

GLOBE FINANCIAL CORP.
Dissolved in 1935

GLOBE GRAIN & MILLING CO.
In process of liquidation in 1940

GLOBE HILL CO (CO)
Name changed to Aadan Corp. 11/1/72
Each share Common 10¢ par exchanged for (1) share Common 10¢ par
(See Aadan Corp.)

GLOBE HILL MINING CO. (CO)
Each share old Common 1¢ par exchanged for (0.1) share new Common 1¢ par 4/16/69
Merged into Globe Hill Co. 9/14/71
Each share Common 1¢ par exchanged for (0.2) share Common 10¢ par
Globe Hill Co. name changed to Aadan Corp. 11/1/72
(See Aadan Corp.)

GLOBE INC (UT)
Proclaimed dissolved for failure to pay taxes 12/31/77

GLOBE INDUSTRIAL LOAN CORP.
Bankrupt in 1943

GLOBE INDUSTRIES, INC. (OH)
Merged into TRW Inc. 6/30/67
Each share Common no par exchanged for (0.0897) share $5 Conv. Preference Ser. B no par
(See TRW Inc.)

GLOBE INDS INC (DE)
Capital Stock $1 par changed to 75¢ par and (0.333) additional share issued 5/3/72
Merged into International Bank (Washington, DC) 12/31/79
Each share Capital Stock 75¢ par exchanged for (1.3) shares Class A Common $1 par
International Bank (Washington, DC) merged into USLICO Corp. 12/31/85 which merged into NWNL Companies, Inc. 1/17/95 which name changed to ReliaStar Financial Corp. 2/13/95
(See ReliaStar Financial Corp.)

GLOBE INSURANCE CO. OF AMERICA (PA)
Merged into Globe & Republic Insurance Co. of America 00/00/1931
Details not available

GLOBE INVESTMENT TRUST PLC (ENGLAND)
Acquired by British Coal Miners Pension Fund 07/00/1990
Details not available

GLOBE KNITTING WORKS (MI)
Acquired by Aetna Industrial Corp. and name changed to Modern Globe, Inc. in 1952

GLOBE LIFE & ACC INS CO (OK)
Reincorporated 12/31/79
Stock Dividends - 25% 11/10/65; 20% 11/10/66; 10% 11/29/67; 10% 11/22/68; 10% 11/24/69; 10% 11/23/70; 15% 5/21/71; 20% 6/30/72; 10% 6/29/73; 20% 7/19/76;

GLO-GLO

20% 7/19/77; 10% 7/7/78; 10% 7/9/79
Place of incorporation changed from (DE) to (OK) 12/31/79
Merged into Liberty National Life Insurance Co. 7/31/80
Each share Common $1 par exchanged for $34.7675 cash

GLOBE LIFE CORP (OH)
Name changed to Globe Capital Corp. 5/28/69
(See Globe Capital Corp.)

GLOBE MACHINE & STAMPING CO.
Acquired by Hupp Motor Car Corp. 07/01/1944
Details not available

GLOBE METALLURGICAL CORP. (OH)
Merged into Interlake Iron Corp. 12/31/56
Each share Common $5 par exchanged for (0.4666-2/3) share Common no par
Interlake Lake Corp. name changed to Interlake Steel Corp. 12/22/64 which reincorporated under the laws of Delaware as Interlake, Inc. 5/15/70 which reorganized as Interlake Corp. 5/29/86
(See Interlake Corp.)

GLOBE MINERALS INC (UT)
Recapitalized as Globe Inc. 10/16/70
Each share Common no par exchanged for (0.2) share Common 25¢ par
(See Globe Inc.)

GLOBE MINES, LTD.
Liquidated in 1949
No stockholders' equity

GLOBE OIL & GAS CORP. (VA)
Charter revoked for failure to file reports and pay fees 6/2/54

GLOBE OIL CO. (DE)
Charter cancelled and declared inoperative and void for non-payment of taxes 01/27/1923

GLOBE OIL CO. LTD.
Merged into Trans Empire Oils Ltd. 00/00/1950
Each share Capital Stock no par exchanged for (0.16666666) share Capital Stock no par
Trans Empire Oils Ltd. name changed to West Canadian Oil & Gas Ltd. 03/10/1958 which merged into Canadian Delhi Oil Ltd. 01/01/1962 which recapitalized as CanDel Oil Ltd. 01/10/1972
(See CanDel Oil Ltd.)

GLOBE OIL CO. (1958) LTD. (AB)
Merged into Trans-Canada Resources Ltd. (New) 11/01/1982
Each share Common no par exchanged for (0.05405405) share Class A Common no par
Trans-Canada Resources Ltd. (New) recapitalized as Consolidated Trans-Canada Resources Ltd. 09/22/1988 which merged into Ranchmen's Resources Ltd. 09/30/1989

GLOBE RLTY LTD (CANADA)
Merged into Royal Bank of Canada 03/04/1981
Each share $1.88 Ser. A Preferred no par exchanged for (1) share $1.88 1st Preferred Ser. A no par
(See Royal Bank of Canada)

GLOBE RES INC (BC)
Recapitalized as Genco Resources Ltd. 03/30/1998
Each share Common no par exchanged for (0.33333333) share Common no par
Genco Resources Ltd. reorganized as Silvermex Resources Inc. 11/16/2010 which merged into First Majestic Silver Corp. 07/06/2012

GLOBE RUBR PRODS CORP (PA)
Name changed to Globe-Superior, Inc. 6/15/71
(See Globe-Superior, Inc.)

GLOBE SEC SYS INC (PA)
Ctfs. dated after 12/28/72
Reincorporated 12/29/72
State of incorporation changed from (DE) to (PA) 12/29/72
Merged into Kidde (Walter) & Co., Inc. (DE) 3/12/75
Each share Common $1 par exchanged for $5 cash

GLOBE SECURITY SYSTEMS, INC. (PA)
Ctfs. dated prior to 5/31/66
Common no par split (5) for (4) by issuance of (0.25) additional share 12/21/61
Common no par split (5) for (4) by issuance of (0.25) additional share 10/15/62
Stock Dividend - 25% 11/2/64
Merged into Kidde (Walter) & Co., Inc. (NY) 5/31/66
Each share Common no par exchanged for (0.25) share $2.20 Conv. Preference Ser. A $1 par
Kidde (Walter) & Co., Inc. (NY) reincorporated in Delaware 7/2/68
(See Kidde (Walter) & Co., Inc. (DE))

GLOBE SOAP CO.
Acquired by Proctor & Gamble Co. in 1928
Details not available

GLOBE SPECIALTY METALS INC (DE)
Merged into Ferroglobe PLC 12/23/2015
Each share Common $0.0001 par exchanged for (1) share Ordinary $7.50 par

GLOBE STEEL TUBES CO. (DE)
Common no par changed to $10 par in 1942
Name changed to G.S.T. Corp. in 1955
(See G.S.T. Corp.)

GLOBE SUPERIOR INC (PA)
Adjudicated bankrupt 6/19/72
No stockholders' equity

GLOBE TICKET CO (PA)
Acquired by International Banknote Co., Inc. 11/1/79
Each share Common no par exchanged for $103.45 cash

GLOBE UN INC (DE)
Capital Stock $5 par split (3) for (2) by issuance of (0.5) additional share 11/06/1962
Capital Stock $5 par reclassified as Common $5 par 04/22/1968
Common $5 par split (3) for (2) by issuance of (0.5) additional share 09/20/1976
Common $5 par split (2) for (1) by issuance of (1) additional share 12/20/1977
Stock Dividend - 100% 12/20/1949
Merged into Johnson Controls, Inc. 10/10/1978
Each share Common $5 par exchanged for (1.333) shares Common $2.50 par
Johnson Controls, Inc. merged into Johnson Controls International PLC 09/06/2016

GLOBE UNDERWRITERS EXCHANGE, INC.
Dissolved in 1936

GLOBE URANIUM, INC. (AZ)
Name changed to Arizona Globe Uranium, Inc. 4/11/55
(See Arizona Globe Uranium, Inc.)

GLOBE-WERNICKE CO. (OH)
Each share Preferred $100 par exchanged for (1) share old Common no par 00/00/1934
Each share old Common no par exchanged for (0.2) share new Common no par
Each share new Common no par exchanged for (5) shares new Common no par 00/00/1941
New Common no par changed to $3.50 par 00/00/1948
Common $3.50 par changed to $7 par 00/00/1952
Name changed to Carthage Corp. 09/01/1955
(See Carthage Corp.)

GLOBE-WERNICKE INDUSTRIES, INC. (OH)
Common $5 par split (3) for (2) by issuance of (0.5) additional share 5/28/65
Merged into Sheller-Globe Corp. 12/30/66
Each share Common $5 par exchanged for (0.425) share $1.35 Conv. Preferred no par and (0.5) share Common no par
(See Sheller-Globe Corp.)

GLOBE-WERNICKE REALTY CO.
In process of liquidation in 1941

GLOBECOMM SYS INC (DE)
Acquired by Wasserstein Cosmos Co-Invest, L.P. 12/11/2013
Each share Common $0.001 par exchanged for $14.15 cash

GLOBEL DIRECT INC (AB)
Placed in receivership and ceased operations 12/12/2007
Stockholders' equity unlikely

GLOBELLE CORP (ON)
Acquired by Tech Data Corp. 10/08/1999
Each share Common no par exchanged for $2.50 cash

GLOBEMIN RES INC (BC)
Name changed to Sutter Gold Mining Inc. 12/29/2004

GLOBENET INTL INC (DE)
Reorganized under the laws of Nevada as Royal Bodycare Inc. 10/19/99
Royal Bodycare Inc. name changed to RBC Life Sciences, Inc. 6/19/2006

GLOBENET RES INC (BC)
Name changed to Terra Nova Gold Corp. 01/28/2003
Terra Nova Gold Corp. name changed to Terra Nova Minerals Inc. (BC) 02/19/2008 which reincorporated in Canada 02/05/2009 which reincorporated in Alberta as Terra Nova Energy Ltd. 08/21/2012 which reincorporated in British Columbia 10/31/2016 which recapitalized as Claren Energy Corp. 11/14/2016

GLOBERIDE INC (JAPAN)
ADR agreement terminated 12/14/2009
Each ADR for Ordinary exchanged for $11.711333 cash

GLOBESAT HLDG CORP (UT)
Each share old Common 1¢ par exchanged for (0.01333333) share new Common 1¢ par 06/30/1995
Involuntarily dissolved 11/30/2000

GLOBESPAN INC (DE)
Issue Information - 3,250,000 shares COM offered at $15 per share on 06/23/1999
Common $0.001 par split (3) for (1) by issuance of (2) additional shares payable 02/25/2000 to holders of record 02/15/2000
Under plan of merger name changed to GlobeSpan Virata, Inc. 12/14/2001
GlobeSpan Virata, Inc. merged into Conexant Systems, Inc. 02/27/2004
(See Conexant Systems, Inc.)

GLOBESPAN TECHNOLOGY PARTNERS INC (DE)
Name changed 2/10/2000
Name changed from GlobSpan Technology Partners, Inc. to GlobeSpan Technology Partners, Inc. 2/10/2000
Name changed to Interactive Gaming & Communications Corp. (New) 9/27/2000
Interactive Gaming & Communications Corp. (New) recapitalized as Great American Financial Corp. 4/1/2003

GLOBESPAN VIRATA INC (DE)
Merged into Conexant Systems, Inc. 02/27/2004
Each share Common $0.001 par exchanged for (1.198) shares Common 1¢ par
(See Conexant Systems, Inc.)

GLOBESTAR INDS (WY)
Name changed to Pineapple Express, Inc. 09/22/2015

GLOBESTAR MNG CORP (CANADA)
Acquired by Perilya Ltd. 01/17/2011
Each share Common no par exchanged for $1.65 cash

GLOBETECH ENVIRONMENTAL INC (NV)
Recapitalized as Global Gold Corp. 03/09/2009
Each share Common $0.001 par exchanged for (0.01) share Common $0.001 par
Global Gold Corp. recapitalized as Fernhill Corp. 01/20/2012

GLOBETEL COMMUNICATIONS CORP (DE)
Each (15) shares old Common $0.00001 par exchanged for (1) share new Common $0.00001 par 05/23/2005
Name changed to Sanswire Corp. 09/24/2008
Sanswire Corp. name changed to World Surveillance Group Inc. 04/27/2011

GLOBETEL COMMUNICATIONS LTD (BC)
Delisted from CNQ 10/13/2000

GLOBETRAC INC (DE)
Recapitalized as Poly Shield Technologies Inc. 07/12/2012
Each share Common $0.001 par exchanged for (0.33333333) share Common $0.001 par
Poly Shield Technologies Inc. name changed to Triton Emission Solutions Inc. 08/25/2014

GLOBETROTTER COMMUNICATIONS INC (DE)
Name changed to Globe Broadcasting Co. 06/22/1976
(See Globe Broadcasting Co.)

GLOBEX BIOTECHNOLOGIES INC (ON)
Recapitalized as MGI Software Inc. 04/30/1996
Each share Common no par exchanged for (0.06666666) share Common no par
MGI Software Inc. merged into Roxio, Inc. 02/01/2002 which name changed to Napster, Inc. 12/23/2004
(See Napster, Inc.)

GLOBEX GROUP INC (NV)
Reorganized as Vertigo Visual System Holdings Inc. 2/23/2000
Each share Common $0.001 par exchanged for (6) shares Common $0.001 par
Vertigo Visual System Holdings Inc. recapitalized as World Poker Stores, Inc. 10/18/2005

GLOBEX INC (NY)
Name changed to UMining Resources Inc. 05/23/2007
UMining Resources Inc. recapitalized

as Stargaze Entertainment Group Inc. 03/12/2015

GLOBEX RES LTD (AB)
Merged into Innova Exploration Ltd. 06/01/2005
Each share Common no par exchanged for (0.75) share Common no par
(See Innova Exploration Ltd.)

GLOBEX UTILIDADES SA (BRAZIL)
Sponsored ADR's for Preferred no par reclassified as Sponsored ADR's for Common no par 02/27/2008
Stock Dividends - 40.3824% payable 03/20/2002 to holders of record 03/15/2002 Ex date - 03/21/2002; 38.31299% payable 02/29/2008 to holders of record 02/28/2008 Ex date - 02/26/2008
Name changed to Via Varejo S.A. 04/26/2012

GLOBIX CORP (DE)
Old Common 1¢ par split (2) for (1) by issuance of (1) additional share payable 12/30/1999 to holders of record 12/20/1999
Old Common 1¢ par split (2) for (1) by issuance of (1) additional share payable 01/31/2000 to holders of record 01/20/2000
Plan of reorganization under Chapter 11 Federal Bankruptcy Code effective 04/25/2002
Each share 6% Conv. Preferred 1¢ par exchanged for approximately (25.76619891) shares new Common 1¢ par
Each share old Common 1¢ par exchanged for approximately (0.00392873) share new Common 1¢ par
Note: Unexchanged certificates were cancelled and became without value 04/25/2004
Name changed to NEON Communications Group, Inc. 03/01/2007
(See NEON Communications Group, Inc.)

GLOBO CABO S A (BRAZIL)
Recapitalized as NET Servicos de Comunicacao S.A. 06/17/2002
Each Sponsored ADR for Preferred no par exchanged for (0.1) Sponsored ADR for Preferred no par
(See NET Servicos de Comunicacao S.A.)

GLOBO PLC (ENGLAND & WALES)
ADR agreement terminated 05/04/2016
No ADR holders' equity

GLOBOTEK HLDGS INC (NV)
Each share old Common $0.001 par exchanged for (0.01724137) share new Common $0.001 par 08/12/2014
Name changed to Itoco Mining Corp. 12/01/2015
Itoco Mining Corp. name changed to Itoco Inc. 05/08/2018

GLOBUS CELLULAR LTD (NV)
Name changed 08/18/1997
Name changed from Globus Cellular & User Protection Ltd. to Globus Cellular Ltd. 08/18/1997
Name changed to Globus Wireless Ltd. 01/10/2000
(See Globus Wireless Ltd.)

GLOBUS FOOD SYS INTL CORP (NY)
Reorganized under the laws of Nevada as Globus International Resources Corp. 10/18/1996
Each share Common $0.001 par exchanged for (0.02) share Common $0.001 par

GLOBUS GROWTH GROUP INC (NY)
Reorganized under the laws of Delaware as China Biopharmaceuticals Holdings, Inc. 08/24/2004
Each share Common 1¢ par exchanged for (0.71428571) share Common 1¢ par
China Biopharmaceuticals Holdings, Inc. merged into NeoStem, Inc. 10/30/2009

GLOBUS WIRELESS LTD (NV)
Charter revoked for failure to file reports and pay fees 06/30/2003

GLOBUSCOPE INC (NY)
Name changed to Globus Growth Group, Inc. (NY) 08/07/1984
Globus Growth Group, Inc. (NY) reorganized in Delaware as China Biopharmaceuticals Holdings, Inc. 08/24/2004 which merged into NeoStem, Inc. 10/30/2009

GLOMAC TECHNOLOGY INC (DE)
Name changed 10/15/2001
Name changed from Glomac Inc. to Glomac Technology, Inc. 10/15/2001
Merged into Glomach Technology Holdings Inc. 10/16/2002
Each share Common exchanged for $0.03 cash

GLORAY KNITTING MLS INC (PA)
Common $1 par split (3) for (2) by issuance of (0.5) additional share 12/6/63
Common $1 par split (4) for (3) by issuance of (1/3) additional share 12/1/64
Common $1 par split (4) for (3) by issuance of (1/3) additional share 12/1/65
Completely liquidated 6/20/68
Each share Common $1 par exchanged for first and final distribution of (0.1362) share U.S. Industries, Inc. Special Conv. Preference Ser. A $2.50 par
(See U.S. Industries, Inc.)

GLORIA GROUP LTD (DE)
Charter cancelled and declared inoperative and void for non-payment of taxes 3/1/78

GLORIA VANDERBILT CORP.
Bankrupt in 1948

GLORIOUS SUN ENTERPRISES LTD (HONG KONG)
ADR agreement terminated 03/14/2016
No ADR's remain outstanding

GLORY EXPL LTD (BC)
Recapitalized as National Fuelcorp Ltd. 07/13/1987
Each share Common no par exchanged for (0.28571428) share Common no par
National Fuelcorp Ltd. recapitalized as Fuelcorp International Ltd. 07/31/1991 which name changed to Specialty Retail Concepts Inc. 05/27/1994 which recapitalized as Altoro Gold Corp. 01/09/1997 which merged into Solitario Resources Corp. 10/18/2000 which name changed to Solitario Exploration & Royalty Corp. 06/17/2008 which name changed to Solitario Zinc Corp. 07/18/2017

GLOSSER BROS INC (PA)
Common no par split (1.2) for (1) by issuance of (0.2) additional share 8/20/76
Common no par split (5) for (4) by issuance of (0.25) additional share 8/18/78
Common no par split (3) for (2) by issuance of (0.5) additional share 8/19/83
Acquired by a group of investors 10/11/85
Each share Common no par exchanged for $20 cash

GLOTECH INDS INC (NV)
Recapitalized as Intra-Asia Entertainment Corp. 01/02/2004
Each (5.37) shares Common $0.001 par exchanged for (1) share Common $0.001 par
Intra-Asia Entertainment Corp. recapitalized as China Transinfo Technology Corp. 08/23/2007
(See China Transinfo Technology Corp.)

GLOUCESTER BK & TR CO (GLOUCESTER, MA)
Under plan of reorganization each share Common $25 par automatically became (1) share GBT Bancorp Common $25 par 8/3/98
GBT Bancorp merged into Andover Bancorp, Inc. 7/1/2000 which merged into Banknorth Group, Inc. (ME) 10/31/2001 which merged into TD Banknorth Inc. 3/1/2005
(See TD Banknorth Inc.)

GLOUCESTER CNTY BANKSHARES INC (NJ)
Merged into Fulton Financial Corp. 2/29/96
Each share Common $5 par exchanged for (1.58) shares Common $2.50 par

GLOUCESTER ELECTRIC CO. (MA)
Under plan of merger each share Capital Stock $25 par exchanged for (3.6) shares
Common $10 par of Essex County Electric Co. in 1953
Essex County Electric Co. merged into Merrimack-Essex Electric Co. 7/30/57 which was acquired by New England Electric System 6/30/59
(See New England Electric System)

GLOUCESTER ENGR INC (MA)
Merged into Battenfeld Massachusetts, Inc. 2/22/78
Each share Common $1 par exchanged for $22 cash

GLOVER INC (NM)
Chapter 11 bankruptcy proceeding converted to Chapter 7 on 3/13/81
Stockholders' equity unlikely

GLOW BENCH SYS INTL INC (DE)
Name changed to Pexcon, Inc. 12/14/2005
Pexcon, Inc. name changed to Tekoil & Gas Corp. 07/18/2005
(See Tekoil & Gas Corp.)

GLOW RES INC (BC)
Name changed to Esstra Industries Corp. 3/24/86
Esstra Industries Corp. name changed to Esstra Industries Inc. 9/11/97

GLP NT CORP (ON)
Acquired by Great Lakes Holdings Inc. 10/03/2006
Each share Non-Vtg. Class A no par exchanged for $8.68 cash

GLR RES INC (CANADA)
Each share Class A Common no par received distribution of (0.397) share Uranium City Resources, Inc. Common no par payable 08/31/2005 to holders of record 08/22/2005 Ex date - 08/18/2005
Recapitalized as Mistango River Resources Inc. 03/21/2011
Each share Class A Common no par exchanged for (0.25) share Class A Common no par

GLS GLOBAL ASSETS LTD (BC)
Name changed 08/27/1992
Name changed from GLS Global Listing Service Ltd. to GLS Global Assets Ltd. 08/27/1992
Name changed to Mobile Lottery Solutions Inc. 02/20/2006
Mobile Lottery Solutions Inc. name changed to NuMedia Games Inc. 09/27/2007 which recapitalized as Brandgamz Marketing Inc. 06/04/2008

GLT, INC. (DE)
Name changed to Intercontinental Men's Apparel, Inc. 8/7/70
Intercontinental Men's Apparel, Inc. name changed to Intercontinental Apparel, Inc. 11/20/72
(See Intercontinental Apparel, Inc.)

GLUCK MILLS
Assets acquired by Wellington Mills, Inc. 00/00/1933
Details not available

GLUCKIN WM LTD (BERMUDA)
Petition under Chapter X proceedings of the Federal Bankruptcy Act filed 2/22/73
No stockholders' equity

GLUV CORP (FL)
Each share old Common no par received distribution of (1) share Homeland Productions, Inc. Common payable 05/23/2005 to holders of record 05/09/2005
Each share old Common no par exchanged for (0.00000015) share new Common no par 05/10/2005
Note: Minority holders received $0.0005 cash per share
New Common no par split (3,000,000) for (1) by issuance of (2,999,999) additional shares payable 05/20/2005 to holders of record 05/13/2005 Ex date - 05/23/2005
Name changed to Media Magic, Inc. 07/08/2005

GLV INC (QC)
Name changed to Ovivo Inc. 12/18/2014
(See Ovivo Inc.)

GLY, INC. (DE)
Merged into Twin Peaks Land & Cattle Co. 2/28/63
Each share Common 30¢ par exchanged for (1) share Common $1 par
(See Twin Peaks Land & Cattle Co.)

GLYCODESIGN INC (ON)
Acquired by Inflazyme Pharmaceuticals Ltd. 06/05/2003
Each share Common no par exchanged for (1.8424) shares Common no par
Inflazyme Pharmaceuticals Ltd. recapitalized as Eacom Timber Corp. 08/26/2008
(See Eacom Timber Corp.)

GLYCOGENESYS INC (ON)
Each share old Common 1¢ par exchanged for (1/6) share new Common 1¢ par 12/21/2004
Chapter 11 bankruptcy proceedings converted to Chapter 7 on 6/1/2006
No stockholders' equity

GLYCOLOGY INC (DE)
Recapitalized as Adoodle, Inc. 06/01/2007
Each share Common $0.001 par exchanged for (0.02) share Common $0.001 par
Adoodle, Inc. named changed to Olfactory Biosciences Corp. 04/20/2010

GLYCOMED INC (CA)
Merged into Ligand Pharmaceuticals Inc. 5/18/95
Each share Common no par exchanged for (0.5301) share Class B $0.001 par

GLYKO BIOMEDICAL LTD (CANADA)
Acquired by BioMarin Pharmaceutical Inc. 08/22/2002
Each share Common no par exchanged for (0.3309) share Common $0.001 par

GM SHARES, INC. (DE)
Merged into General Motors Corp. 12/31/1971
Each share Class A $1 par or Class B $1 par exchanged for (6) shares Common $1-2/3 par

GMA-GOA

General Motors Corp.
Each share Common $1 par exchanged for (5.37) shares Common $1-2/3 par
General Motors Corp. name changed to Motors Liquidation Co. 07/15/2009
(See Motors Liquidation Co.)

GMA COMPUTER CORP (NY)
Charter cancelled and proclaimed dissolved for failure to pay taxes and file reports 12/20/77

GMARKET INC (KOREA)
Name changed to eBay Gmarket Co. Ltd. 07/22/2009
(See eBay Gmarket Co. Ltd.)

GMC CORP. (VA)
In process of liquidation
Each share Common $5 par exchanged for initial distribution of (0.19584) share Medusa Portland Cement Co. Common no par 4/6/70
(See Medusa Portland Cement Co.)
Note: Details on subsequent distributions, if any, are not available

GMC HLDG CORP (FL)
Each share old Common $0.001 par exchanged for (0.1) share new Common $0.001 par 07/20/1998
New Common $0.001 par split (3) for (1) by issuance of (2) additional shares payable 03/28/2002 to holders of record 03/10/2002
Ex date - 04/01/2002
Each share new Common $0.001 par exchanged again for (0.025) share new Common $0.001 par 03/15/2003
SEC revoked common stock registration 04/05/2006

GMD INVT CORP (VA)
Liquidation completed
Each share Common $1 par received initial distribution of $4 cash 1/21/82
Each share Common $1 par received second distribution of $3.50 cash 4/21/82
Each share Common $1 par received third distribution of $6.10 cash 9/13/82
Each share Common $1 par exchanged for fourth and final distribution of $0.0955 cash 10/31/84

GMD RESOURCE CORP (BC)
Recapitalized as Chatworth Resources Inc. 10/14/2004
Each share Common no par exchanged for (0.16666666) share Common no par
Chatworth Resources Inc. merged into ComWest Enterprise Corp. 12/12/2005 which name changed to Unisync Corp. 08/01/2014

GMH CMNTYS TR (MD)
Issue Information - 28,571,429 shares COM offered at $12 per share on 10/28/2004
Merged into American Campus Communities, Inc. 06/11/2008
Each share Common $0.001 par exchanged for (0.07642) share Common 1¢ par and $3.36 cash

GMI GROUP INC (NJ)
Stock Dividend - 20% 2/1/88
Charter revoked for failure to file reports and pay fees 6/30/94

GMINCOME & GROWTH FD (AB)
Combined Units separated 11/16/2010
Under plan of merger each Trust Unit automatically became (0.86725467) COMPASS Income Fund Trust Unit 12/22/2011
COMPASS Income Fund merged into MINT Income Fund 03/21/2017

GMIS INC (DE)
Common 1¢ par split (3) for (2) by issuance of (0.5) additional share 01/31/1993
Merged into HBO & Co. 12/09/1996
Each share Common 1¢ par exchanged for (0.42) share Common 5¢ par
HBO & Co. merged into McKesson HBOC Inc. 01/12/1999 which name changed to McKesson Corp. 07/30/2001

GMM HLDGS INC (NV)
Name changed to Fredericks Entertainment, Inc. 11/1/2005

GMMT INC (NV)
Recapitalized as Latitude Solutions, Inc. 07/09/2009
Each share Common $0.001 par exchanged for (0.04310809) share Common $0.001 par

GMN THE GOSPEL MUSIC NETWORK LTD (BC)
Name changed to Your Host Foods Inc. 05/22/1990
Your Host Foods Inc. name changed to Diaz Resources Ltd. (BC) 06/01/1994 which reincorporated in Alberta 04/14/1998 which merged into Tuscany Energy Ltd. (Old) 07/18/2013 which reorganized as reorganized as Tuscany Energy Ltd. (New) 07/19/2013
(See Tuscany Energy Ltd. (New))

GMO INTERNET INC (JAPAN)
ADR agreement terminated 11/06/2009
No ADR's remain outstanding

GMO PELICAN FD (MD)
Merged into Evergreen Equity Trust 11/08/2002
Details not available

GMP CAP CORP (CANADA)
Merged into GMP Capital Trust 12/01/2005
Each share Common no par exchanged for (2) Trust Units no par and $1 cash
GMP Capital Trust reorganized as GMP Capital Inc. 05/20/2009

GMP CAP TR (ON)
Reorganized as GMP Capital Inc. 05/20/2009
Each Trust Unit no par exchanged for (1) share Common no par

GMR PPTYS (MA)
Merged into Grubb & Ellis Co. 02/28/1981
Each Common Share of Bene. Int. no par exchanged for (1) share Common $1 par
(See Grubb & Ellis Co.)

GMS CAP CORP (FL)
Administratively dissolved 09/25/2015

GMV WIRELESS INC (NV)
Common $0.001 par split (30) for (1) by issuance of (29) additional shares payable 03/09/2011 to holders of record 03/09/2011
Reorganized as HDS International Corp. 06/16/2011
Each share Common $0.001 par exchanged for (12) shares Common $0.001 par
HDS International Corp. name changed to Good Gaming, Inc. 06/30/2016

GMX COMMUNICATIONS INC (FL)
Administratively dissolved 8/13/93

GMX CORP (UT)
Merged into GMX Reorganization Corp. 10/3/97
Each share Common no par exchanged for $95.90 cash

GMX RES INC (OK)
Issue Information - 1,250,000 UNITS consisting of (1) share COM and (1) CL A WT 02/16/2001
Each share old Common $0.001 par exchanged for (0.07692307) share new Common $0.001 par 01/04/2013
Plan of reorganization under Chapter 11 Federal Bankruptcy proceedings effective 02/03/2014
No stockholders' equity

GNB CORP (PA)
Common $10 par changed to $2.50 par and (3) additional shares issued 05/18/1979
Stock Dividend - 100% 06/10/1974
Merged into Pennbancorp 12/31/1985
Each share Common $2.50 par exchanged for (1.2) shares Common $5 par
Pennbancorp merged into Integra Financial Corp. 01/26/1989 which merged into National City Corp. 05/03/1996 which was acquired by PNC Financial Services Group, Inc. 12/31/2008

GNC ENERGY CORP (DE)
SEC revoked common stock registration 01/03/2013

GNI GROUP INC (DE)
Reorganized 10/28/87
Reorganized from GNI, Inc. (TX) to GNI Group, Inc. (DE) and Common no par changed to 1¢ par 10/28/87
Merged into Green 1 Acquisition 7/28/98
Each share Common 1¢ par exchanged for $7 cash

GNI PETE INC (BC)
Recapitalized as Logix Enterprises Inc. 10/11/2001
Each share Common no par exchanged for (0.5) share Common no par
Logix Enterprises Inc. recapitalized as Transac Enterprise Corp. 11/27/2002 which name changed to Evergreen Gaming Corp. 11/01/2006

GNMA MTG BACKED SEC TR (MA)
Trust terminated 2/6/81
Each Unit of Undivided Int. exchanged for $343.94 cash

GNW FINL CORP (DE)
Stock Dividends - 15% 12/28/1990; 15% 06/28/1991
Merged into Washington Mutual Savings Bank (Seattle, WA) 04/01/1992
Each share Common 1¢ par exchanged for (0.589) share Common $1 par and $12.054 cash
(See Washington Mutual, Inc.)

GO CALL INC (DE)
Reorganized under the laws of Nevada as Medical Institutional Services Corp. 10/23/2006
Each share Common $0.001 par exchanged for (0.002) share Common $0.0001 par
Medical Institutional Services Corp. recapitalized as National Pharmaceuticals Corp. 12/04/2009 which recapitalized as Ghana Gold Corp. 07/11/2012 which name changed to BrightRock Gold Corp. 11/11/2013

GO-GAS CO. (DE)
Charter cancelled and declared inoperative and void for non-payment of taxes 4/1/29

GO GREEN DIRECTORIES INC (NV)
Name changed to CrossBox, Inc. 02/04/2014
CrossBox, Inc. name changed to Flikmedia, Inc. 07/31/2014

GO HEALTHY INC (FL)
Name changed to Global Payout, Inc. 12/28/2010

GO INC (TX)
Completely liquidated 4/28/69
Each share Common $1 par exchanged for first and final distribution of (0.263157) share Gearhart-Owens Industries, Inc. Common 50¢ par
Gearhart-Owens Industries, Inc. name changed to Gearhart Industries, Inc. 6/30/80 which merged into Halliburton Co. 9/23/88

GO OIL WELL SERVICES, INC. (TX)
Each share Common $1 par exchanged for (7) shares Common 50¢ par 10/6/59
Name changed to Gearhart-Owen Industries, Inc. 5/13/64
Gearhart-Owen Industries, Inc. name changed to Gearhart Industries, Inc. 6/30/80 which merged into Halliburton Co. 9/23/88

GO ONLINE NETWORKS CORP (DE)
SEC revoked common stock registration 08/21/2006

GO PLC (MALTA)
GDR agreement terminated 05/27/2013
Each Sponsored 144A GDR for Ordinary exchanged for $24.491679 cash
Each Sponsored Reg. S GDR for Ordinary exchanged for $24.491679 cash

GO PUBG INC (NY)
Common 2¢ par changed to 1¢ par 05/00/1970
Dissolved by proclamation 12/24/1991

GO-RACHELS COM CORP (MN)
Name changed to Rachel's Gourmet Snacks Inc. 9/17/2001

GO THINK COM INC (NV)
Recapitalized as Knowledge Transfer Systems Inc. 04/24/2001
Each share Common $0.001 par exchanged for (0.01) share Common $0.001 par
Knowledge Transfer Systems Inc. name changed to Global General Technologies, Inc. 07/08/2005 which recapitalized as Turbine Aviation, Inc. 12/19/2014

GO VIDEO INC (DE)
Reincorporated 08/13/1987
State of incorporation changed from (AZ) to (DE) and Common no par changed to $0.001 par 08/13/1987
Common $0.001 par split (2) for (1) by issuance of (1) additional share 09/24/1987
Name changed to Sensory Science Corp. 03/01/1999
Sensory Science Corp. merged into SONICblue Inc. 06/27/2001
(See SONICblue Inc.)

GO2PHARMACY INC (FL)
Issue Information - 1,000,000 shares COM offered at $7 per share on 11/09/2000
Name changed to Innovative Companies, Inc. 09/06/2002
Each share Common 1¢ par exchanged for (1) share Common 1¢ par
Innovative Companies, Inc. name changed to GeoPharma, Inc. 05/18/2004
(See GeoPharma, Inc.)

GOA SWEET TOURS LTD (DE)
Name changed to Xiangtian (USA) Air Power Co., Ltd. 06/25/2012

GOAL ENERGY INC (AB)
Merged into Tappit Resources Ltd. 08/28/1998
Each share Common no par exchanged for (1) share Common no par
(See Tappit Resources Ltd.)

GOAL SYS INTL INC (OH)
Merged into Legent Corp. 08/03/1992
Each share Common no par exchanged for (0.52356) share Common 1¢ par
(See Legent Corp.)

GOALTIMER INTL INC (CO)
Recapitalized as Pacific Vegas Global Strategies, Inc. 12/19/2002
Each (11) shares Common no par

exchanged for (1) share Common no par
Note: No holder of (100) shares or more will be reversed below (100) shares
Holders of (99) shares or fewer will not be affected by the reverse split

GOAMERICA INC (DE)
Issue Information - 10,000,000 shares COM offered at $16 per share on 04/06/2000
Each share old Common 1¢ par exchanged for (0.1) share new Common 1¢ par 05/14/2004
Each share new Common 1¢ par exchanged again for (0.125) share new Common 1¢ par 10/04/2004
Name changed to Purple Communications, Inc. 02/12/2009
(See Purple Communications, Inc.)

GOANNA RES INC (NV)
Each share old Common $0.001 par exchanged for (0.05) share new Common $0.001 par 3/15/99
Name changed to Fairchild International Corp. 7/8/99
Fairchild International Corp. name changed to Syngas International Corp. 1/9/2006 which recapitalized as Energy Quest Inc. 5/31/2007

GOB SHOPS OF AMERICA, INC. (RI)
Name changed to Sterling Stores of America, Inc. (RI) 07/17/1961
Sterling Stores of America, Inc. (RI) reincorporated in Delaware as Sterling General, Inc. 03/07/1969 which name changed to Carnaby Shops of Florida, Inc. 10/26/1976
(See Carnaby Shops of Florida, Inc.)

GOBABY RACING INC (OK)
Reincorporated under the laws of Nevada as Heartland Energy Group, Inc. 05/15/2006
Heartland Energy Group, Inc. name changed to Tritent International Corp. 01/20/2009

GOBEL (ADOLF), INC. (NY)
Each share old Common no par exchanged for (3) shares new Common no par in 1928
Old Common no par changed to $5 par in 1933
Common $5 par changed to old Common $1 par in 1936
Each share old Common $1 par exchanged for (0.5) share new Common $1 par in 1944
Under plan of merger name changed to Universal Automated Industries, Inc. and new Common $1 par changed to 10¢ par 3/26/63
5% Class A Preferred $2 par called for redemption 5/1/63
Universal Automated Industries, Inc. acquired by Castleton Industries, Inc. 10/11/67
(See Castleton Industries, Inc.)

GOBI GOLD INC (BC)
Reincorporated 09/26/2005
Place of incorporation changed from (YT) to (BC) 09/26/2005
Reorganized as East Energy Corp. 08/29/2006
Each share Common no par exchanged for (2) shares Common no par
East Energy Corp. name changed to Rare Earth Metals Inc. 12/16/2009 which name changed to Canada Rare Earth Corp. 02/08/2013

GOBI OIL & GAS LTD (AB)
Merged into Dominion Explorers Inc. (New) 12/31/1994
Each share Common no par exchanged for (0.18) share Common no par
Dominion Explorers Inc. (New) merged into Neutrino Resources Inc. 02/28/1997
(See Neutrino Resources Inc.)

GOBLE OIL & GAS CO. (OH)
Charter cancelled for failure to pay taxes 10/14/43

GOC FD INC (MD)
Dissolved 06/21/1996
Details not available

GOCITYLINK COM INC (NV)
Recapitalized as Bell AZ Consultants, Inc. 12/08/2003
Each share Common $0.001 par exchanged for (0.1) share Common $0.001 par
Bell AZ Consultants, Inc. name changed to Strategy X, Inc. 03/11/2004 which recapitalized as Alliance Transcription Services, Inc. 08/14/2007
(See Alliance Transcription Services, Inc.)

GOD'S LAKE GOLD MINES LTD. (MB)
Merged into Jowsey (R.J.) Mining Co. Ltd. in 1956
Each (9) shares Capital Stock no par exchanged for (4) shares Capital Stock $1 par
Jowsey (R.J.) Mining Co. Ltd. name changed to Open End Mines Ltd. 8/4/71 which liquidated for New York Oils Ltd. (BC) 4/28/72 which reincorporated in Alberta 7/19/82 which was acquired by Sceptre Resources Ltd. 3/14/89 which merged into Canadian Natural Resources Ltd. 8/15/96

GODCHAUX SUGARS, INC. (NY)
Each share 1st Preferred $100 par exchanged for (1) share 7% Preferred no par and (0.5) share Class A no par in 1929
Class A & B no par changed to $5 par 6/15/55
Name changed to Gulf States Land & Industries, Inc. 7/6/56
Gulf States Land & Industries, Inc. name changed to Landmark Land Co., Inc. 7/10/72 which reincorporated in Delaware 6/26/84

GODDARD, INC. (DE)
Assets sold for benefit of creditors 3/10/66
No stockholders' equity

GODDARD & GODDARD CO. (MI)
Completely liquidated 6/12/68
Each share Common $1 par exchanged for first and final distribution of (0.20856) share Allegheny Ludlum Steel Corp. $2.70 Preferred no par
Allegheny Ludlum Steel Corp. name changed to Allegheny Ludlum Industries, Inc. 4/24/70 which name changed to Allegheny International Inc. 4/29/81
(See Allegheny International Inc.)

GODDARD INDS INC (MA)
Common $1 par changed to 45¢ par 4/5/72
Common 45¢ par split (2) for (1) by issuance of (1) additional share 4/15/85
Common 45¢ par changed to 1¢ par in September 1985
Stock Dividend - 50% 1/12/87
Each share old Common 1¢ par exchanged for (0.002) share new Common 1¢ par 10/28/2003
Note: In effect holders received $0.80 cash per share and public interest was eliminated

GODERICH ELEVATORS LTD (ON)
Name changed 06/27/1978
Name changed from Goderich Elevator & Transit Co. Ltd. to Goderich Elevators Ltd. 06/27/1978
Name changed to Thirdcoast Ltd. 01/01/2011
(See Thirdcoast Ltd.)

GODFATHER MEDIA INC (NV)
Each share old Common $0.001 par exchanged for (0.005) share new Common $0.001 par 12/27/2011
Name changed to Embark Holdings, Inc. 08/20/2012
Embark Holdings, Inc. name changed to Muscle Warfare International, Inc. 06/28/2013 which name changed to Cannabusiness Group, Inc. 02/18/2014

GODFATHERS PIZZA INC (NE)
Under plan of merger name changed to Diversifoods Inc. 12/28/1983
(See Diversifoods Inc.)

GODFREY CO (WI)
Common $5 par split (3) for (2) by issuance of (0.5) additional share 06/30/1971
Common $5 par split (3) for (2) by issuance of (0.5) additional share 11/01/1980
Common $5 par changed to $1 par 05/30/1981
Common $1 par split (3) for (2) by issuance of (0.5) additional share 08/15/1984
Common $1 par split (2) for (1) by issuance of (1) additional share 11/25/1986
Common $1 par changed to 50¢ par 06/12/1987
Stock Dividends - 10% 04/15/1977; 10% 05/01/1979; 10% 05/01/1980; 10% 02/01/1986
Acquired by Fleming Companies, Inc. 11/27/1987
Each share Common 50¢ par exchanged for (0.805461) share Common $2.50 par
(See Fleming Companies, Inc.)

GODFREY REALTY CORP.
Property sold 00/00/1946
Details not available

GODMAN (H.C.) CO. (OH)
Each share 6% 2nd Preferred $100 par exchanged for (6) shares Conv. Preferred $12.50 par and (1) share old Common $1 par 00/00/1938
Each share old Common no par exchanged for (1) share old Common $1 par 00/00/1938
Each share 6% 1st Preferred $100 par exchanged for (4) shares 6% Preferred $25 par and $52.50 cash 00/00/1947
Each share Conv. Preferred $12.50 par exchanged for (0.2) share 6% Preferred $25 par and (1) share new Common $1 par 00/00/1947
Each share old Common $1 par exchanged for (0.2) share new Common $1 par 00/00/1947
New Common $1 par changed to new Common no par 12/15/1958
Name changed to Fulton Industries, Inc. (OH) 04/05/1960
Fulton Industries, Inc. (OH) merged into Fulton Industries, Inc. (DE) 07/23/1970
(See Fulton Industries, Inc.)

GODWIN INDUSTRIES, INC. (IN)
Voluntarily dissolved 12/12/79
Details not available

GOEBEL BREWING CO. (MI)
4-1/2% Preferred $100 par reclassified as 4-1/2% Prior Preferred $100 par in 1954
Adjudicated bankrupt 4/27/64
No stockholders' equity

GOENERGY INC (DE)
Name changed to Wizard World, Inc. 02/18/2011

GOFF OIL CO. (DE)
Name changed to Reading & Bates Production Co. 8/17/66
(See Reading & Bates Production Co.)

GOFRANCHISE COM INC (NV)
Recapitalized as Goldfranchise Corp. 1/2/2003
Each (12) shares Common $0.001 par exchanged for (1) share Common $0.001 par

GOGAMA MINERALS LTD. (ON)
Merged into Coniston Explorations & Holdings Ltd. 02/28/1972
Each share Common no par exchanged for (0.264) share Common no par
(See Coniston Explorations & Holdings Ltd.)

GOGO BABY INC (DE)
Name changed to Alpha Investment Inc. 04/19/2017

GOHEALTH M D INC (NV)
Recapitalized as Tree Top Industries, Inc. 09/18/2006
Each share Common 1¢ par exchanged for (0.01) share Common $0.001 par
Tree Top Industries, Inc. name changed to Global Tech Industries Group, Inc. 07/07/2016

GOLAR LNG ENERGY LTD (BERMUDA)
Acquired by Golar LNG Ltd. 07/12/2011
Each share Common $1 par exchanged for approximately USD $5 cash

GOLCONDA CAP CORP (AB)
Reincorporated under the laws of Ontario as Angus Mining (Namibia) Inc. 09/28/2010
Angus Mining (Namibia) Inc. name changed to Angus Mining Inc. 07/16/2012

GOLCONDA CORP (ID)
Reincorporated under the laws of Delaware as Rego Co. 6/17/77
Rego Co. (DE) name changed to Rego Group, Inc. 2/7/78
(See Rego Group, Inc.)

GOLCONDA EXTENSION MINING CO.
Name changed to United Lead-Zinc Mines Co. in 1938
United Lead-Zinc Mines Co. completely liquidated by exchange for Alice Consolidated Mines Inc. Common 10¢ par

GOLCONDA FINL INC (CA)
Each share old Common no par exchanged for (0.01) share new Common no par 9/1/89
Each share old Common no par exchanged for (0.01) share new Common no par 3/5/93
Name changed to Golden Pacific Holdings International 2/23/95
Golden Pacific Holdings International name changed to Pacrim Information Systems Inc. 2/23/95
(See Pacrim Information Systems Inc.)

GOLCONDA INVS LTD (NY)
Reorganized under the laws of Maryland as Bull & Bear Gold Investors Ltd. 10/26/1987
Each share Common 10¢ par exchanged for (1) share Common 1¢ par
Bull & Bear Gold Investors Ltd. name changed to Midas Investors Ltd. 06/30/1999 which merged into Midas Fund, Inc. (MD) 11/16/2001 which reorganized in Delaware as Midas Series Trust 10/12/2012

GOLCONDA LEAD MINES (ID)
Common $1 par changed to 10¢ par 7/13/56
Name changed to Golconda Mining Corp. 3/23/62
Golconda Mining Corp. name changed to Golconda Corp. 9/15/70 which reincorporated in Delaware as Rego Co. 6/17/77 which name changed to Rego Group, Inc. 2/7/78
(See Rego Group, Inc.)

GOLCONDA MINERALS N L (AUSTRALIA)
ADR agreement terminated 01/22/2003
No ADR holders' equity

GOLCONDA MNG CORP (ID)
Under plan of merger name changed to Golconda Corp. (ID) 9/15/70
Golconda Corp. (ID) reincorporated in Delaware as Rego Co. 6/17/77 which name changed to Rego Group, Inc. 2/7/78
(See Rego Group, Inc.)

GOLCONDA PETROLEUM CORP.
Dissolved and each (10) shares Capital Stock exchanged for (1) share Gato Ridge Trust Capital Stock in 1953

GOLCONDA RES LTD (AB)
Voluntarily dissolved 04/29/2016
No stockholders' equity

GOLD, SILVER & TUNGSTEN, INC.
Charter dissolved for failure to file annual reports 1/1/45

GOLD & MINERALS INC (NV)
Reincorporated 08/30/1999
Each share old Common 1¢ par exchanged for (0.5) share new Common 1¢ par 08/28/1994
State of incorporation changed from (DE) to (NV) and Common 1¢ par changed to $0.001 par 08/30/1999
Merged into El Capitan Precious Metals, Inc. 01/19/2011
Each share Common $0.001 par exchanged for (1.414156) shares Common $0.001 par
Note: Holders entitled to more than (10,000) post merger shares will receive restricted shares for each share above (10,000)

GOLD & ONYX MNG CO (NV)
Charter revoked for failure to file reports and pay fees 09/30/2010

GOLD & SILVER MNG NEV INC (NV)
Each share old Common $0.001 par exchanged for (0.00076923) share new Common $0.001 par 07/22/2015
Note: No holder will receive fewer than (100) post-split shares
Each share new Common $0.001 par exchanged again for (0.0005) share new Common $0.001 par 03/01/2016
Recapitalized as Rainmaker Worldwide Inc. 06/15/2017
Each share new Common $0.001 par exchanged for (0.001) share Common $0.001 par

GOLD & STK TELEG CO (NY)
Merged into Western Union Telegraph Co. (Old) 12/30/1980
Each share Capital Stock $100 par exchanged for $256.97 cash

GOLD AMERN MNG CORP (NV)
Each share old Common $0.00001 par exchanged for (0.005) share new Common $0.00001 par 02/13/2013
Name changed to Inception Mining Inc. 05/17/2013

GOLD ANGEL RES INC (BC)
Recapitalized as Gold-Pan Resources Inc. 01/26/1982
Each share Common no par exchanged for (0.5) share Common no par
(See Gold-Pan Resources Inc.)

GOLD BAG INC (NV)
Name changed to Focus Gold Corp. 06/06/2011

GOLD BANC CORP INC (KS)
Issue Information - 2,000,000 shares COM offered at $8.75 per share on 11/18/1996
Common $1 par split (2) for (1) by issuance of (1) additional share payable 05/18/1998 to holders of record 05/06/1998
Merged into Marshall & Ilsley Corp. (Old) 04/01/2006
Each share Common $1 par exchanged for (0.3576) share Common $1 par and $2.78 cash
(See Marshall & Ilsley Corp. (Old))

GOLD BAR RES INC (CANADA)
Cease trade order effective 5/9/91
Stockholders' equity unlikely

GOLD BAR RES INC (UT)
Common $1 par changed to 1¢ par in April 1973
Reorganized under the laws of Nevada as American Artists, Ltd. 3/16/84
Each share Common 1¢ par exchanged for (1/3) share Common 3¢ par

GOLD BD RES INC (WA)
Name changed 6/8/2000
Name changed from Gold Bond Mining Co. to Gold Bond Resources, Inc. 6/8/2000
Reorganized under the laws of Delaware as EnerTeck Corp. 11/24/2003
Each share Common 5¢ par exchanged for (0.1) share Common 5¢ par

GOLD BEAM CONSOLIDATED MINING & MILLING CO. (AZ)
Charter expired 2/4/33

GOLD BELLE MINES LTD (ON)
Recapitalized as Equus Industries Inc. 04/02/1987
Each share Common no par exchanged for (0.33333333) share Common no par
Equus Industries Inc. recapitalized as Eros Financial Investments Inc. 03/04/1991 which name changed to Eros Entertainment Inc. 06/02/1992 which name changed to Flying Disc Entertainment Inc. 06/28/1994 which name changed to Software Gaming Corp. 03/20/1998 which recapitalized as Xgen Ventures Inc. 11/26/2004
(See Xgen Ventures Inc.)

GOLD BELT MINING CO., LTD.
Acquired by North American Mines, Inc. 00/00/1944
Details not available

GOLD BELT MNG CO (CO)
Common 5¢ par changed to 1¢ par 07/23/1976
Charter suspended for failure to file annual reports 09/30/1984

GOLD BILLION GROUP HLDGS LTD (DE)
Recapitalized as Sky Resort International Ltd. 12/12/2017
Each share Common $0.001 par exchanged for (0.01) share Common $0.001 par

GOLD BRDG DEV CORP (BC)
Recapitalized as Bridge River Development Corp. 05/15/1989
Each share Class A Common no par exchanged for (0.33333333) share Common no par
(See Bridge River Development Corp.)

GOLD BULLION DEV CORP (BC)
Name changed to Granada Gold Mine Inc. 01/16/2017

GOLD BUTTE ENERGY INC (AB)
Name changed to BelAir Energy Corp. 11/26/1997
BelAir Energy Corp. merged into Purcell Energy Ltd. (New) 09/04/2003
(See Purcell Energy Ltd. (New))

GOLD C ENTERPRISES INC (CO)
Liquidation completed
Each share Common no par received initial distribution of $0.074 cash 08/07/1986
Each share Common no par received second and final distribution of $0.004587 cash 07/28/1987

GOLD CACHE INC (ID)
Reorganized under the laws of Delaware as Instracorp 07/11/1988
Each share Common 1¢ par exchanged for (0.05) share Common no par
Instracorp recapitalized as Worldwide Web Networx Corp. 05/18/1998
(See Worldwide Web Networx Corp.)

GOLD CANYON BK (GOLD CANYON, AZ)
Bank closed by Arizona Department of Financial Institutions 04/05/2013
Stockholders' equity unlikely

GOLD CANYON INC (UT)
Name changed to Gold Bug Mining Inc. 12/16/87

GOLD CANYON MINES INC. (CA)
Each share Capital Stock 25¢ par exchanged for (0.125) share Capital Stock $1 par 04/26/1966
Name changed to American Tin Corp. 07/21/1966
American Tin Corp. name changed to Mining & Oil Shale Development Corp. 03/12/1968 which merged into Consolidated General Corp. 04/28/1969 which name changed to Chisholm Resources Inc. (NV) 03/24/1998
(See Chisholm Resources Inc.)

GOLD CANYON MINES INC (BC)
Recapitalized as Island Canyon Mines Inc. 10/02/1984
Each share Common no par exchanged for (0.33333333) share Common no par
Island Canyon Mines Inc. name changed to Access Technologies Inc. 06/26/1987
(See Access Technologies Inc.)

GOLD CANYON MINING CO. (NV)
Name changed to Conglomerates, Inc. (NV) and Common $1 par changed to 1¢ par 11/27/67
Conglomerates, Inc. (NV) merged into Conglomerates, Inc. (DE) 3/18/68 which name changed to National Computer Corp. 8/6/69
(See National Computer Corp.)

GOLD CANYON RES INC (BC)
Merged into First Mining Finance Corp. 11/18/2015
Each share Common no par exchanged for (1) share Common no par and (0.03333) share Irving Resources Inc. Common no par
(See each company's listing)
Note: Unexchanged certificates will be cancelled and become without value 11/18/2021

GOLD CAP CORP (CO)
Merged into Globex Mining Enterprises Inc. 8/29/97
Each share Common $0.0001 par exchanged for (0.276) share Common no par

GOLD CAP CORP (WA)
Merged into Crown Resources Corp. 2/16/89
Each share Common $0.001 par exchanged for (0.18) share Common 1¢ par
Crown Resources Corp. acquired by Kinross Gold Corp. 8/31/2006

GOLD CAPITAL CORP. (TX)
Merged into Gold Capital Corp. (WA) 2/29/84
Each share Common 1¢ par exchanged for (1.2) shares Common $0.001 par
Gold Capital Corp. (WA) merged into Crown Resources Corp. 2/16/89 which was acquired by Kinross Gold Corp. 8/31/2006

GOLD CAR HEATING & LIGHTING CO. (NY)
Capital Stock $100 par changed to no par 00/00/1932
Out of business 00/00/1956
Details not available

GOLD CHAIN INC. (ID)
Name changed to Cimarron Consolidated Mining & Oil Inc. and Common 10¢ par changed to 1¢ par 04/26/1982
(See Cimarron Consolidated Mining & Oil Inc.)

GOLD CHAIN MNG CO (UT)
Name changed to Global DECS Corp. 10/18/2001
Global DECS Corp. name changed to Western Sierra Mining Corp. 12/19/2003

GOLD CHECK SYS INC (NV)
Charter revoked for failure to file reports and pay fees 03/01/1976

GOLD CITY INDS LTD (MB)
Reincorporated 06/21/2005
Place of incorporation changed from (BC) to (MB) 06/21/2005
Merged into San Gold Corp. 06/30/2005
Each share Common no par exchanged for (0.51756228) share Common no par
(See San Gold Corp.)

GOLD CITY MNG CORP (BC)
Recapitalized as Consolidated Gold City Mining Corp. 10/24/1997
Each share Common no par exchanged for (0.33333333) share Common no par
Consolidated Gold City Mining Corp. recapitalized as Gold City Industries Ltd. (BC) 08/26/1998 which reincorporated in Manitoba 06/21/2005 which merged into San Gold Corp. 07/07/2005
(See San Gold Corp.)

GOLD CITY PORCUPINE MINES LTD. (ON)
Charter cancelled and declared dissolved for failure to file returns and pay fees 02/14/1973

GOLD CITY RES INC (CANADA)
Merged into Gold City Mining Corp. 12/07/1994
Each share Common no par exchanged for (1) share Common no par
Gold City Mining Corp. recapitalized as Consolidated Gold City Mining Corp. 10/24/1997 which recapitalized as Gold City Industries Ltd. (BC) 08/26/1998 which reincorporated in Manitoba 06/21/2005 which merged into San Gold Corp. 07/07/2005
(See San Gold Corp.)

GOLD CLOUD CORP (UT)
Recapitalized as Time Wealth Corp. 12/28/72
Each share Common 25¢ par exchanged for (0.5) share Common 5¢ par
(See Time Wealth Corp.)

GOLD CLOUD OIL & MINERALS CO. (UT)
Recapitalized as Gold Cloud Corp. 4/16/68
Each share Capital Stock 5¢ par exchanged for (0.2) share Common 25¢ par
Gold Cloud Corp. recapitalized as Time Wealth Corp. 12/28/72
(See Time Wealth Corp.)

GOLD CLOUD URANIUM CO (UT)
Name changed to Gold Cloud Oil & Minerals Co. 1/25/68
Gold Cloud Oil & Minerals Co. recapitalized as Gold Cloud Corp. 4/16/68 which recapitalized as Time Wealth Corp. 12/28/72
(See Time Wealth Corp.)

GOLD CO OF AMER (CA)
Liquidation completed
Each Depositary Unit received initial distribution of an undetermined amount of gold payable 04/26/1995 to holders of record 04/01/1995
Each Depositary Unit received second and final distribution of approximately $0.26 cash payable 09/30/1995 to holders of record 07/01/1995
Note: Certificates were not required to be surrendered and are without value

GOLD COAST BK (ISLANDIA, NY)
Under plan of reorganization each share Common $4 par automatically became (1) share Gold Coast Bancorp, Inc. Common 1¢ par 08/29/2017

GOLD COAST MINES LTD.
Liquidated 00/00/1952
Details not available

GOLD COAST MNG CORP (DE)
Reincorporated under the laws of Wyoming as Strategic Mining Corp. 12/22/2009

GOLD COAST MNG CORP (FL)
Each share Common 1¢ par received distribution of (0.03333333) share Max Media Group, Inc. Restricted Common $0.001 par payable 09/30/2009 to holders of record 08/31/2009
Name changed to Green Leaf Innovations, Inc. 03/10/2015

GOLD COAST RES INC (NV)
Incorporated 12/05/1996
Reincorporated 12/23/1996
Each share old Common $0.001 par exchanged for (0.004) share new Common $0.001 par 11/25/1996
State of incorporation changed from (UT) to (NV) 12/23/1996
Each share old Common $0.001 par exchanged for (0.005) share new Common $0.001 par 08/18/1998
Recapitalized as Global Datatel Inc. 12/02/1998
Each share new Common $0.001 par exchanged for (0.5) share Common $0.001 par
Global Datatel Inc. name changed to Cana Petroleum Corp. 08/30/2006 which name changed to XCana Petroleum Corp. 05/22/2007

GOLD COIN MINING & LEASING CO. (CO)
Each share old Capital Stock 1¢ par exchanged for (0.1) share new Capital Stock 1¢ par 10/10/1976
Reorganized under the laws of Nevada as Global Energy, Ltd. 09/22/1978
Each share new Capital Stock 1¢ par exchanged for (1) share Common 1¢ par
Global Energy, Ltd. name changed to Global Platinum & Gold Inc. 08/28/1987 which recapitalized as Bourque Industries, Inc. 02/07/2011

GOLD COIN MINING CO.
Inoperative and void in 1932

GOLD COIN MNG INC (WA)
Each share Common $0.001 par exchanged for (0.25) share Common $0.004 par 2/13/90
Each share Common $0.004 par exchanged for (0.08333333) share Common $0.048 par 6/5/91
Merged into Canaveral International Corp. 12/1/92
Each share Common $0.048 par exchanged for (0.4) share Common 50¢ par
Canaveral International Corp. recapitalized as Madison Group Associates Inc. 2/2/93
(See Madison Group Associates Inc.)

GOLD CORAL RES INC (ON)
Name changed to Ca-Network Inc. 07/28/2000

GOLD COUNTRY BANK (GRASS VALLEY, CA)
Merged into Independent Bankshares Corp. 7/31/79
Each share Common $2.50 par exchanged for (1) share Common no par
Independent Bankshares Corp. name changed to Westamerica Bancorporation 7/1/83

GOLD CREEK OIL & REFINING CO. (UT)
Proclaimed dissolved for failure to pay taxes 12/31/74

GOLD CREST MINES INC (NV)
Name changed to Amazing Energy Oil & Gas, Co. 01/21/2015

GOLD CREST PRODS LTD (ON)
Acquired by Canadian Wallpaper Manufacturers Ltd. 06/07/1974
Each share Common no par exchanged for $8.50 cash

GOLD CTRY BK N A (MARYSVILLE, CA)
Name changed 06/15/2001
Name and location changed from Gold Country National Bank (Brownsville, CA) to Gold Country Bank, N.A. (Marysville, CA) 06/15/2001
Merged into Golden Pacific Bancorp, Inc. 05/03/2010
Each share Common exchanged for (1.159) shares Common

GOLD CUP RES LTD (BC)
Cease trade order effective 12/12/1984

GOLD DOME MNG CO (OR)
Name changed to American Development Corp. 4/17/91
(See American Development Corp.)

GOLD DROP MINES LTD. (BC)
Dissolved 00/00/1957
Details not available

GOLD DUST CORP. (NJ)
Name changed to Hecker Products Corp. 00/00/1936
Hecker Products Corp. name changed to Best Foods, Inc. 00/00/1943 which merged into Corn Products Co. (NJ) 09/30/1958 which reincorporated in Delaware 04/30/1959 which name changed to CPC International Inc. 04/23/1969 which name changed to BestFoods (DE) 01/01/1998
(See BestFoods (DE))

GOLD EAGLE CORP (MN)
Statutorily dissolved 10/04/1991

GOLD EAGLE GOLD MINES LTD. (ON)
Recapitalized as Goldray Mines Ltd. 10/19/1959
Each share Capital Stock $1 par exchanged for (0.33333333) share Capital Stock $1 par
Goldray Mines Ltd. merged into Canray Resources Ltd. 12/21/1976 which recapitalized as Exall Resources Ltd. 12/09/1983 which merged into Gold Eagle Mines Ltd. 12/27/2006 which was acquired by Goldcorp Inc. 09/25/2008

GOLD EAGLE MINES, INC. (NV)
Recapitalized as Flowery Gold Mines Co. of Nevada 9/1/77
Each share Common 25¢ par exchanged for (2.5) shares Common 10¢ par

GOLD EAGLE MINES LTD (ON)
Acquired by Goldcorp Inc. 09/25/2008
Each share Common no par exchanged for (0.292) share Common no par and $0.0001 cash

GOLD EAGLE MINING CO. (WA)
Automatically dissolved by State of Washington for non-payment of license fees 7/1/58

GOLD EMPIRE, INC. (CO)
Merged into Crusader Oil & Gas Co. 02/06/1959
Each share Common 1¢ par exchanged for (0.005) share Common 25¢ par
Crusader Oil & Gas Co. merged into Gold Empire Mining Co. 06/15/1968
(See Gold Empire Mining Co.)

GOLD EMPIRE MNG CO (DE)
Charter revoked and proclaimed dissolved for non-payment of taxes 04/15/1971

GOLD ENTMT GROUP INC (FL)
Reincorporated 08/28/2007
Common $0.001 par split (5) for (2) by issuance of (1.5) additional shares payable 10/04/2002 to holders of record 09/26/2002
Ex date - 10/22/2002
Each old Common $0.001 par exchanged exchanged for (0.1) share new Common $0.001 par 02/23/2004
State of incorporation changed from (NV) to (FL) and new Common $0.001 par changed to $0.0001 par 08/28/2007
Administratively dissolved 09/23/2011

GOLD EQUITIES INC (NV)
Reincorporated 1/1/81
State of incorporation changed from (ID) to (NV) 1/1/81
Each share Common 1¢ par exchanged for (0.25) share Common 1¢ par
Name changed to Ameritex, Inc. 7/18/86
(See Ameritex, Inc.)

GOLD EXPRESS COMMUNICATIONS INC (WA)
Reincorporated under the laws of Delaware as Startronix International, Inc. 09/30/1995
(See Startronix International, Inc.)

GOLD EXPRESS CORP (WA)
Each share old Common $0.001 par exchanged for (0.1) share new Common $0.001 par 02/15/1994
Name changed to Gold Express Communications Inc. (WA) 05/17/1995
Gold Express Communications Inc. (WA) reincorporated in Delaware as Startronix International, Inc. 09/30/1995
(See Startronix International, Inc.)

GOLD FEVER INC (WA)
Name changed to Inland Investors Inc. 5/15/87
(See Inland Investors Inc.)

GOLD FIELDS LTD OLD (SOUTH AFRICA)
Merged into Gold Fields Ltd. (New) 05/10/1999
Each Sponsored ADR for Ordinary ZAR 1 par exchanged for (1.55) Sponsored ADR's for Ordinary ZAR 50 par

GOLD FIELDS PPTY LTD (SOUTH AFRICA)
Stock Dividend - 400% payable 06/23/1998 to holders of record 06/05/1998
Name changed to Mawenzi Resources Ltd. 06/08/1998
Mawenzi Resources Ltd. name changed to Zarara Energy Ltd. 10/27/2009
(See Zarara Energy Ltd.)

GOLD FIELDS SOUTH AFRICA LTD (SOUTH AFRICA)
Each ADR for Ordinary Reg. Rand-25 par exchanged for (5) ADR's for Ordinary Reg. Rand-5 par 10/28/1983
Each Unsponsored ADR for Ordinary Reg. Rand-5 par exchanged for (1) Sponsored ADR for Ordinary Reg. Rand-5 par 12/27/1994
ADR agreement terminated 11/02/2000
Each Sponsored ADR for Ordinary Rand-5 par exchanged for $0.0885 cash

GOLD FINDER EXPLORATIONS LTD (BC)
Each share old Common no par exchanged for (0.2) share new Common no par 12/23/2016
Recapitalized as Venzee Technologies Inc. 01/05/2018
Each share new Common no par exchanged for (0.5) share Common no par

GOLD-FINGER INDUSTRIES, INC. (FL)
Proclaimed dissolved for failure to file reports and pay fees 6/28/71

GOLD FRONTIER MINES LTD. (ON)
Acquired by Bayview Red Lake Gold Mines 00/00/1944
Each share Capital Stock $1 par exchanged for (0.5) share Capital Stock $1 par
Bayview Red Lake Gold Mines Ltd. acquired by Red Poplar Gold Mines Ltd. 00/00/1947 which recapitalized as Consolidated Red Poplar Minerals Ltd. 03/01/1955 which recapitalized as New Dimension Resources Ltd. 11/09/1971 which recapitalized as New Dimension Industries Ltd. 09/19/1989 which recapitalized as Toxic Disposal Corp. 02/15/1994 which recapitalized as Global Disposal Corp. 03/29/1996
(See Global Disposal Corp.)

GOLD GENIE WORLDWIDE INC (OR)
Name changed to Products, Services & Technology Corp. (OR) 06/04/1988
Products, Services & Technology Corp. (OR) reorganized in Utah as Wireless Data Solutions, Inc. 06/02/1997 which reorganized in Nevada 08/09/2007

GOLD GIANT MINERALS INC (BC)
Recapitalized as Gold Giant Ventures, Inc. 02/20/2002
Each share Common no par exchanged for (0.1) share Common no par
Gold Giant Ventures, Inc. merged into Cross Lake Minerals Ltd. 12/16/2003 which name changed to 0373849 B.C. Ltd. 06/01/2009
(See 0373849 B.C. Ltd.)

GOLD GIANT VENTURES INC (BC)
Merged into Cross Lake Minerals Ltd. 12/16/2003
Each share Common no par exchanged for (2) shares Common no par
Cross Lake Minerals Ltd. name changed to 0373849 B.C. Ltd. 06/01/2009
(See 0373849 B.C. Ltd.)

GOLD GREENLESS TROTT PLC (UNITED KINGDOM)
Name changed to GGT Group PLC 12/04/1996
(See GGT Group PLC)

GOLD GULCH MINING CO. (ID)
Charter forfeited for failure to file reports 11/30/54

GOLD HAWK EXPL LTD (ON)
Charter cancelled and declared dissolved for default in filing returns 04/09/1975

GOLD HAWK MINES LTD (QC)
Reorganized under the laws of Ontario as Gold Hawk Resources (Ontario) Ltd. 03/10/1980
Each share Capital Stock no par

exchanged for (1) share Common no par
Gold Hawk Resources (Ontario) Ltd. (ON) reorganized in Canada as Consolidated Gold Hawk Resources Inc. 08/26/1986 which name changed to Gold Hawk Resources Inc./Les Ressources Gold Hawk Inc. 05/14/1998 which name changed to Oracle Mining Corp. 08/16/2011

GOLD HAWK RES INC (CANADA)
Each share old Common no par exchanged for (0.04) share new Common no par 12/17/2009
Name changed to Oracle Mining Corp. 08/16/2011

GOLD HAWK RES ONT LTD (ON)
Reorganized under the laws of Canada as Consolidated Gold Hawk Resources Inc. 08/26/1986
Each share Common no par exchanged for (1/3) share Common no par
Consolidated Gold Hawk Resources Inc. name changed to Gold Hawk Resources Inc./ Les Ressources Gold Hawk Inc. 05/14/1998 which name changed to Oracle Mining Corp. 08/16/2011

GOLD HELM MNG CO (WA)
Charter cancelled and proclaimed dissolved for failure to pay fees 7/1/73

GOLD HILL MINES DEVELOPMENT CO. (UT)
Charter revoked for failure to pay taxes 4/2/23

GOLD HILLS MNG LTD (NV)
SEC revoked common stock registration 07/25/2016

GOLD HLDGS CORP (NV)
Name changed to Ocean Electric Inc. 01/27/2012

GOLD HORIZONS INC (UT)
Involuntarily dissolved for failure to file annual reports 12/31/1985

GOLD HORN MINING CO. (AZ)
Charter expired by time limitations 8/19/29

GOLD HORSE INTL INC (FL)
Each share old Common $0.0001 par exchanged for (0.025) share new Common $0.0001 par 09/08/2010
SEC revoked common stock registration 12/08/2014

GOLD ISLAND MINING CO., LTD. (MB)
Charter revoked 12/05/1963

GOLD ISLAND PORCUPINE MINES LTD. (ON)
Name changed to Milmar-Island Mines Ltd. 01/09/1959
Milmar-Island Mines Ltd. name changed to Milmar-Island Metals & Holdings Ltd. 12/22/1980
(See Milmar-Island Metals & Holdings Ltd.)

GOLD JUBILEE CAP CORP (BC)
Name changed to OK2 Minerals Ltd. 09/15/2016

GOLD KEY CAP CORP (BC)
Name changed to Unity Energy Corp. 12/31/2009

GOLD KING CONS INC (CO)
Deliquent for failure to file a Periodic Report or maintain a registered agent 05/01/2006

GOLD KING FROZEN FOODS INC (GA)
Acquired by Seeman Brothers, Inc. 5/23/69
Each share Capital Stock $1 par exchanged for (1/3) share Common $3 par
Seeman Brothers, Inc. name changed to Seabrook Foods, Inc. 7/24/70
(See Seabrook Foods, Inc.)

GOLD KIST INC (DE)
Issue Information - 12,000,000 shares COM offered at $11 per share on 10/06/2004
Merged into Pilgrim's Pride Corp. (Old) 01/09/2007
Each share Common 1¢ par exchanged for $21 cash

GOLD LAKE MINES LTD. (MB)
Name changed to Gold Lake Resources Ltd. 11/24/1972
Gold Lake Resources Ltd. merged into Consolidated Imperial Resources Energy Ltd./Ressources Consolides Imperial Energie Ltee. 12/16/1983 which recapitalized as Consolidated Imperial Resources Inc./Ressources Consolidees Imperial Inc. 04/21/1988
(See Consolidated Imperial Resources Inc./Ressources Consolidees Imperial Inc.)

GOLD LAKE RES LTD (MB)
Merged into Consolidated Imperial Resources Energy Ltd./Ressources Consolides Imperial Energie Ltee. 12/16/1983
Each (10) shares Common no par exchanged for (4) shares Conv. Preferred Ser. A $5 par and (5) shares Common no par
Consolidated Imperial Resources Energy Ltd./ Ressources Consolidees Imperial Energie Ltee. recapitalized as Consolidated Imperial Resources Inc./Ressources Consolidees Imperial Inc. 04/21/1988
(See Consolidated Imperial Resources Inc./Ressources Consolidees Imperial Inc.)

GOLD LEAF VENTURES INC (BC)
Name changed to Tokyo Trading Ltd. 06/16/1992
(See Tokyo Trading Ltd.)

GOLD MEDAL GROUP INC (ON)
Assets sold for the benefit of creditors 12/11/1990
Stockholders' equity unlikely

GOLD MEDAL PACKING CO (NY)
Incorporated in 1958
Proclaimed dissolved for failure to file reports and pay fees 12/16/68

GOLD MEDAL RES LTD (BC)
Recapitalized as Rare Earth Resources Ltd. (BC) 11/27/89
Each share Common no par exchanged for (0.4) share Common no par
Rare Earth Resources Ltd. (BC) reincorporated in Bermuda which name changed to Resource Finance & Investment Ltd. 7/17/97

GOLD MEDALLION CORP (MN)
Stock Dividend - 20% 9/17/79
Completely liquidated 1/8/82
Each share Common 10¢ par exchanged for first and final distribution of (1) share Datron Corp. Common 1¢ par, (0.5) share National Medical Growth Corp. Common 1¢ par, (1) Gold Medallion Corp. Shareholders' Liquidating Trust Unit of Bene. Int. and $4.75 cash
(See each company's listing)

GOLD MEDALLION CORP SHAREHOLDERS LIQUIDATING TR (MN)
In process of liquidation
Each Unit of Bene. Int. received initial distribution of $0.44 cash 7/31/82
Each Unit of Bene. Int. received second distribution of $0.55 cash 1/3/83
Each Unit of Bene. Int. received third distribution of $0.46 cash 7/29/83
Each Unit of Bene. Int. received fourth distribution of $0.46 cash 1/31/84
Note: Details on subsequent distributions, if any, are not available

GOLD MEDALLION NURSING CTRS INC (MN)
Name changed to Gold Medallion Corp. 10/20/70
(See Gold Medallion Corp.)

GOLD METALS CONSOLIDATED MINING CO. (NV)
Each share Capital Stock 10¢ par exchanged for (0.01) share Common $1 par 11/2/67
Name changed to Brown (Tom) Drilling Co., Inc. 2/13/68
Brown (Tom) Drilling Co., Inc. name changed to Brown (Tom), Inc. 9/2/71
(See Brown (Tom), Inc.)

GOLD MINES KALGOORLIE LTD (AUSTRALIA)
Name changed 11/30/1983
Name changed from Gold Mines of Kalgoorlie (Australia) Ltd. to Gold Mines of Kalgoorlie Ltd. 11/30/1983
Each Unsponsored ADR for Ordinary AUD $0.25 par exchanged for (5) Unsponsored ADR's for Ordinary AUD $0.05 par 04/01/1987
Each Unsponsored ADR for Ordinary AUD $0.05 par exchanged for (1) Sponsored ADR for Ordinary AUD $0.05 par 05/12/1989
Merged into Normandy Mining Ltd. 09/11/1996
Each Sponsored ADR for Ordinary AUD $0.05 par exchanged for (0.142) Sponsored ADR for Ordinary AUD $0.20 par
Normandy Mining Ltd. acquired by Newmont Mining Corp. 06/26/2002

GOLD MNG USA INC (FL)
Each share old Common $0.0001 par exchanged for (0.001) share new Common $0.0001 par 12/10/2012
Note: No holder will receive fewer than (100) post-split shares
Name changed to Vita Mobile Systems, Inc. 01/31/2018

GOLD MOUNTAIN MINES, LTD.
Liquidated in 1939

GOLD MTN MNG CORP (BC)
Merged into JDL Gold Corp. 10/07/2016
Each share Common no par exchanged for (0.16) share Common no par
JDL Gold Corp. name changed to Trek Mining Inc. 03/31/2017 which name changed to Equinox Gold Corp. 12/22/2017

GOLD MTN WINERY INC (WY)
Reincorporated 09/15/2006
Each share old Common 1¢ par exchanged for (0.001) share new Common 1¢ par 08/14/2006
State of incorporation changed from (DE) to (WY) 09/15/2006
Name changed to Titan Resources International Corp. 11/17/2006

GOLD ONE INTL LTD (AUSTRALIA)
ADR agreement terminated 03/19/2014
Each ADR for Ordinary exchanged for $2.63944 cash

GOLD ORE LTD CRIPPLE CREEK (CO)
Charter suspended for failure to file annual reports 9/30/84

GOLD ORE MINING CO. (AZ)
Completely liquidated 08/08/1968
Each share Capital Stock $1 par exchanged for first and final distribution of (0.375) share Bagdad Chase, Inc. Common $1 par
(See Bagdad Chase, Inc.)

GOLD-ORE RES LTD (AB)
Merged into Elgin Mining Inc. 05/03/2012
Each share Common no par exchanged for (1) share Common no par and (0.5) Common Stock Purchase Warrant expiring 05/01/2014
Elgin Mining Inc. merged into Mandalay Resources Corp. 09/11/2014

GOLD PAN RES INC (BC)
Struck off register and declared dissolved for failure to file returns 07/23/1993

GOLD PARL RES LTD (BC)
Recapitalized as Canmet Resources Ltd. 09/03/1993
Each share Common no par exchanged for (0.5) share Common no par
Canmet Resources Ltd. name changed to Archangel Diamond Corp. (BC) 06/30/1994 which reincorporated in Yukon 09/16/1996
(See Archangel Diamond Corp.)

GOLD PARTN & INCOME FD (ON)
Combined Units separated 08/26/2009
Name changed to U.S. Tactical Allocation Fund 02/02/2016

GOLD PARTY PAYDAY INC (DE)
Common $0.000001 par split (19.5) for (1) by issuance of (18.5) additional shares payable 10/03/2014 to holders of record 06/30/2014 Ex date - 10/06/2014
Name changed to Canadian Cannabis Corp. 10/15/2014

GOLD PEAK INDS HLDGS LTD (HONG KONG)
ADR agreement terminated 07/06/2017
Each Sponsored ADR for Ordinary exchanged for $1.022167 cash

GOLD PLACERS INC (WA)
Each share old Common no par exchanged for (0.05) share new Common no par 12/1/98
Name changed to Monarch Gold Exploration, Inc. 2/12/2004

GOLD PLATINUM INTL INC (NV)
Name changed to Billington Thermal Sonic Energy Control Corp. 12/22/78
(See Billington Thermal Sonic Energy Control Corp.)

GOLD PLATTER SVCS INC (DE)
Name changed to Hallmark Homes, Inc. 11/30/73
(See Hallmark Homes, Inc.)

GOLD PT ENERGY CORP (BC)
Merged into San Leon Energy PLC 05/28/2009
Each share Common no par exchanged for (0.08335) share Common no par
Note: Each share Common no par received (0.08335) additional share from escrow 05/28/2010

GOLD PT EXPL LTD (BC)
Name changed to Gold Point Energy Corp. 06/22/2005
Gold Point Energy Corp. merged into San Leon Energy PLC 05/28/2009

GOLD POINT RES LTD (BC)
Struck off register and declared dissolved for failure to file returns 07/10/1987

GOLD PORT RES LTD (BC)
Reincorporated 01/15/2007
Place of incorporation changed from (ON) to (BC) 01/15/2007
Recapitalized as Codrington Resource Corp. 10/28/2013
Each share Common no par exchanged for (0.1) share Common no par
Codrington Resource Corp. name changed to NRG Metals Inc. 11/23/2015

GOLD PWR RES CORP (BC)
Recapitalized as Triple Force Industries Inc. 12/06/1991
Each share Ser. A Common no par exchanged for (0.22222222) share Common no par
Triple Force Industries Inc. recapitalized as Petrock Ventures Inc. 01/08/1997 which recapitalized as Croydon Mercantile Corp. 12/31/2002 which name changed to World Mahjong Ltd. 12/01/2015

GOLD PREM INTL CO (FL)
Name changed to GPI, Inc. 3/3/72
(See GPI, Inc.)

GOLD PRODUCERS, INC. (CO)
Declared defunct for failure to pay taxes 10/10/41

GOLD RAPIDS MINES LTD. (ON)
Charter revoked for failure to file reports and pay taxes 00/00/1957

GOLD REACH RES LTD (BC)
Each share old Common no par exchanged for (0.2) share new Common no par 09/19/2008
Each share new Common no par exchanged again for (0.2) share new Common no par 10/05/2009
Name changed to Surge Copper Corp. 02/21/2018

GOLD REEF INC. (UT)
Name changed to Network One, Inc. 05/31/1977
(See Network One, Inc.)

GOLD REEF INTL INC (ON)
Recapitalized as Montana Gold Mining Co. Inc. 01/05/2011
Each share Common no par exchanged for (0.1) share Common no par
Montana Gold Mining Co. Inc. name changed to Peloton Minerals Corp. 07/18/2016

GOLD REEF RES LTD (BC)
Name changed to Venture Gold Corp. 10/28/1986
(See Venture Gold Corp.)

GOLD RESERVE MINING CO. (MT)
Recapitalized as Gold Reserve Corp. 09/05/1973
Each share Common no par exchanged for (0.2) share Common no par
Gold Reserve Corp. merged into Gold Reserve Inc. (YT) 02/04/1999 which reincorporated in Alberta 09/09/2014

GOLD RESV CORP (MT)
Merged into Gold Reserve Inc. (YT) 02/04/1999
Each share Common no par held by Canadian Residents exchanged for (1) share Class A Common no par
Each share Common no par held by U.S. Residents exchanged for either (1) share Class A Common no par or (1) Equity Unit consisting of (1) share Gold Reserve Corp. Class B Common no par and (1) share Gold Reserve Inc. (YT) Class B Common no par
Note: Option to receive Equity Units expired 02/02/1999
Gold Reserve Inc. (YT) reincorporated in Alberta 09/09/2014

GOLD RESV INC (YT)
Reincorporated under the laws of Alberta 09/09/2014

GOLD RIBBON FOODS INC (DE)
Each share old Common no par exchanged for (0.05) share new Common no par 06/30/1977
Charter cancelled and declared inoperative and void for non-payment of taxes 03/01/1989

GOLD RIDGE EXPL CORP (AB)
Recapitalized as GEA Technologies Ltd. 08/08/2016
Each share Common no par exchanged for (0.2) share Common no par
GEA Technologies Ltd. name changed to International Cannabrands Inc. 12/05/2017

GOLD RIDGE MINES INC (ON)
Delisted from Canadian Dealer Network 01/03/1995

GOLD RIDGE RES INC (BC)
Name changed to Cariboo Gold Fields Ltd. 12/09/2005
(See Cariboo Gold Fields Ltd.)

GOLD RIDGE RES INC (NV)
Name changed to CorGreen Technologies Holding Corp. 02/13/2015

GOLD RIV HOTEL & CASINO CORP (DE)
Plan of reorganization under Chapter 11 Federal Bankruptcy proceedings confirmed 03/04/1997
No stockholders' equity

GOLD RIV MINES & ENTERPRISES LTD (BC)
Name changed 07/05/1973
Name changed from Gold River Mines Ltd. to Gold River Mines & Enterprises Ltd. 07/05/1973
Struck off register and declared dissolved for failure to file returns 05/27/1983

GOLD RIVER MINES LTD. (BC)
Ctfs. dated prior to 09/30/1948
Struck off register and declared dissolved for failure to file returns 09/30/1948

GOLD ROCK RES INC (NV)
Each share old Common $0.00001 par exchanged for (10) shares new Common $0.00001 par 07/11/2008
Name changed to RainEarth Inc. 05/21/2009
RainEarth Inc. name changed to CableClix (USA), Inc. 06/16/2015

GOLD ROYALTIES CORP (AB)
Merged into Sandstorm Gold Ltd. 05/05/2015
Each share Common no par exchanged for (0.045) share Common no par
Note: Unexchanged certificates will be cancelled and become without value 05/05/2021

GOLD RTY CORP (FL)
Recapitalized as Ally Pharma US, Inc. 12/17/2012
Each share Common $0.001 par exchanged for (0.01) share Common $0.001 par
Ally Pharma US, Inc. recapitalized as TPT Global Tech, Inc. 12/02/2014

GOLD SEAL DAIRY PRODUCTS CORP. (NY)
Name changed to Gold Seal Products Corp. 5/6/58
Gold Seal Products Corp. name changed to Kulka Electronics Corp. 5/18/61 which name changed to Kulka Smith Electronics Corp. 4/27/62 which merged into Consolidated Electronics Industries Corp. 9/14/64 which name changed to North American Philips Corp. 2/14/69
(See North American Philips Corp.)

GOLD SEAL ELECTRICAL CO., INC.
Adjudicated bankrupt in 1936

GOLD SEAL INTL INC (OK)
Merged into Bonneville Medical Products, Inc. 1/10/73
Each share Common 1¢ par exchanged for (0.005) share Common 10¢ par
Bonneville Medical Products, Inc. recapitalized as Ametex Corp. 2/11/74
(See Ametex Corp.)

GOLD SEAL PRODUCTS CORP. (NY)
Name changed to Kulka Electronics Corp. 5/18/61
Kulka Electronics Corp. name changed to Kulka Smith Electronics Corp. 4/27/62 which merged into Consolidated Electronics Industries Corp. 9/14/64 which name changed to North American Philips Corp. 2/14/69
(See North American Philips Corp.)

GOLD SECS CORP (ID)
Reorganized under the laws of Delaware as Evolutions, Inc. 02/09/1996
Each (30) shares Common no par exchanged for (1) share Common no par
(See Evolutions, Inc.)

GOLD SEEKER RES LTD (BC)
Struck off register and declared dissolved for failure to file returns 03/25/1994

GOLD SHARES, INC. (NV)
Name changed to National Tungsten Corp. in 1955
National Tungsten Corp. recapitalized as Sunburst Petroleum Corp. in 1958 which name changed to Sunburst Industries, Inc. 3/6/70
(See Sunburst Industries, Inc.)

GOLD SHIELD EXPL & DEV INC (AB)
Struck off register for failure to file annual reports 02/01/1990

GOLD SILVER EXPLORATION, INC. (UT)
Name changed to West America Energy, Inc. 6/10/81
(See West America Energy, Inc.)

GOLD STD INC (UT)
Each share old Common $0.001 par exchanged for (0.25) share new Common $0.001 par 04/01/1998
Each share new Common $0.001 par exchanged again for (0.25) share new Common $0.001 par 12/01/1998
Each share new Common $0.001 par exchanged again for (8) shares new Common $0.001 par 05/02/2003
Each share new Common $0.001 par exchanged again for (0.125) share new Common $0.001 par 07/17/2006
Name changed to Chang-On International, Inc. 04/24/2007

GOLD STD MNG CORP (NV)
Common $0.001 par split (3.3) for (1) by issuance of (2.3) additional shares payable 07/30/2009 to holders of record 07/29/2009
Ex date - 07/31/2009
Name changed to J.D. Hutt Corp. 11/01/2012
J.D. Hutt Corp. name changed to Code Green Apparel Corp. 09/09/2015

GOLD STD RES INC (BC)
Reorganized under the laws of Wyoming as Consolidated Gold Standard Resources Inc. 10/09/1986
Each share Common no par exchanged for (0.2) share Common no par
Consolidated Gold Standard Resources Inc. name changed to Strategic Industries Inc. (WY) 01/18/1988 which reincorporated in Delaware 01/22/1990
(See Strategic Industries Inc.)

GOLD STAR ENERGY INC (AB)
Recapitalized as Netherfield Energy Corp. 7/3/98
Each share Common no par exchanged for (1/3) share Common no par
Netherfield Energy Corp. merged into Antrim Energy Inc. 9/29/99

GOLD STAR NORTH AMERN MNG INC (CO)
Name changed to Clearwave Telecommunications, Inc. 08/27/2015

GOLD STAR RES CORP (BC)
Name changed to Simba Energy Inc. 02/19/2010
Simba Energy Inc. name changed to Simba Essel Energy Inc. 04/24/2017

GOLD STAR RES LTD (BC)
Recapitalized as E.E.C. Marketing Corp. 05/02/1990
Each share Common no par exchanged for (0.33333333) share Common no par
E.E.C. Marketing Corp. name changed to Amera Industries Corp. 01/13/1992 which recapitalized as International Amera Industries Corp. 02/10/1995 which recapitalized as IMA Resource Corp. 02/21/1996 which recapitalized as IMA Exploration Inc. 07/07/1998 which recapitalized as Kobex Minerals Inc. 09/30/2009 which name changed to Kobex Capital Corp. 08/29/2014 which name changed to Itasca Capital Ltd. 06/23/2016

GOLD STAR TUTORING SVCS INC (FL)
SEC revoked common stock registration 11/14/2012

GOLD SUMMIT CORP (CANADA)
Each share old Common no par exchanged for (0.1) share new Common no par 04/16/2009
Merged into Crown Gold Corp. 08/31/2010
Each share new Common no par exchanged for (1.65) shares Common no par
Crown Gold Corp. recapitalized as Crown Mining Corp. 06/30/2014

GOLD SUMMIT MINES LTD (ON)
Reincorporated 09/05/2002
Place of incorporation changed from (BC) to (ON) 09/05/2002
Reorganized under the laws of Canada as Gold Summit Corp. 07/10/2003
Each share Common no par exchanged for (0.2) share Common no par, (0.1) Common Stock Purchase Warrant expiring 07/10/2004 and (0.086) share Seafield Resources Inc. Common no par
(See each company's listing)

GOLD SWAP INC (NY)
Reincorporated under the laws of Delaware as Point Capital, Inc. 01/25/2013

GOLD SYNDICATE, INC. (WA)
Charter revoked for failure to file reports and pay fees 7/1/52

GOLD TEX RES LTD (BC)
Acquired by Crown Resources Corp. 12/01/1989
Each share Common no par exchanged for (1.43) shares Common 1¢ par
Crown Resources Corp. acquired by Kinross Gold Corp. 08/31/2006

GOLD TORCH RES LTD (BC)
Common no par split (2) for (1) by issuance of (1) additional share 03/16/1989
Recapitalized as European Ventures Inc. 09/27/1991
Each share Common no par exchanged for (0.5) share Common no par
European Ventures Inc. recapitalized as Cugold Ventures Inc. 12/01/1994 which recapitalized as Firestone Ventures Inc. (BC) 12/05/1999 which reincorporated in Alberta 09/27/2005

GOLD TORRENT INC (NV)
Reincorporated under the laws of

British Columbia as Gold Torrent (Canada) Inc. and Common $0.001 par changed to no par 03/01/2018

GOLD UN INC (DE)
Name changed to Noble Vici Group, Inc. 03/26/2018

GOLD VY INC (WA)
Name changed to Development Bancorp Ltd. 08/12/1993
Development Bancorp Ltd. name changed to Imatel Holdings Inc. 11/24/1997 which recapitalized as Ovvio Better Life, Inc. 03/26/1999 which name changed to Animal Cloning Sciences, Inc. 11/21/2000
(See Animal Cloning Sciences, Inc.)

GOLD VY RES EXPLS LTD (ON)
Recapitalized as R.F. Oil Industries Ltd. 08/26/1983
Each share Common no par exchanged for (0.25) share Common no par
(See R.F. Oil Industries Ltd.)

GOLD VY RES LTD (BC)
Recapitalized as NCA Minerals Corp. 06/06/1977
Each share Capital Stock no par exchanged for (0.2) share Common no par
(See NCA Minerals Corp.)

GOLD VENTURE PLACERS LTD (AB)
Name changed to White Gold Ventures Ltd. 08/29/1990
White Gold Ventures Ltd. name changed to Cash Canada Pawn Corp. 09/25/1992 which recapitalized as Cash Canada Group Ltd. 01/05/1996
(See Cash Canada Group Ltd.)

GOLD VENTURES LTD (BC)
Recapitalized as MBS Software Inc. 03/09/1989
Each share Common no par exchanged for (0.4) share Common no par
(See MBS Software Inc.)

GOLD VESSEL RES INC (CANADA)
Recapitalized as Consolidated Gold Vessel Resources Inc. 03/21/1995
Each share Class A Common no par exchanged for (0.1) share Class A Common no par
Consolidated Gold Vessel Resources Inc. name changed to Golden Bear Minerals Inc. (New) 07/04/1995 which name changed to Augusta Gold Corp. 07/04/1997 which recapitalized as Pulse Data Inc. 10/15/1999 which name changed to Pulse Seismic Inc. 05/28/2009

GOLD WATER INC (UT)
Recapitalized as Sierra Tech, Inc. 6/19/89
Each share Common $0.001 par exchanged for (0.2) share Common $0.001 par
Sierra Tech, Inc. recapitalized as Golf Ventures Inc. 1/6/93 which name changed to Golf Communities of America Inc. 11/19/98
(See Golf Communities of America Inc.)

GOLD WEDGE DIVIDE MINING CO.
Name changed to Eureka Co. in 1948
(See Eureka Co.)

GOLD WHEATON GOLD CORP (BC)
Each share old Common no par exchanged for (0.1) share new Common no par 02/04/2010
Merged into Franco-Nevada Corp. 03/16/2011
Each share new Common no par exchanged for $5.20 cash

GOLD WIN VENTURES INC (BC)
Recapitalized as Consolidated Gold Win Ventures, Inc. 06/17/1998
Each share Common no par exchanged for (0.2) share Common no par
Consolidated Gold Win Ventures, Inc. name changed to Encore Renaissance Resources Corp. 04/09/2009 which recapitalized as WestKam Gold Corp. 05/01/2012

GOLD WORLD RES INC (BC)
Reincorporated under the laws of Ontario 04/18/2007

GOLD ZONE DIVIDE MINING CO. (NV)
Charter cancelled for failure to file reports and pay fees 3/7/38

GOLD ZONE MINING CORP. (NV)
Each share Capital Stock 10¢ par exchanged for (0.1) share Capital Stock $1 par 9/1/61
Name changed to Associated Manufacturers Co., Inc. 12/26/61
Associated Manufacturers Co., Inc. name changed to Armorite, Inc. 3/1/63 which name changed to Coast to Coast Co., Inc. 10/10/63
(See Coast to Coast Co., Inc.)

GOLD'N TREASURES TRADING CO., LTD. (DE)
Charter cancelled and declared inoperative and void for non-payment of taxes 3/1/74

GOLDALE INVTS LTD (ON)
Reincorporated 10/12/1977
Place of incorporation changed from (BC) to (ONT) 10/12/1977
Name changed to Viner (E.A.) Holdings Ltd. 11/14/1986
Viner (E.A.) Holdings Ltd. name changed to Fahnestock Viner Holdings Inc. 06/28/1988 which name changed to Oppenheimer Holdings Inc. (ONT) 09/02/2003 which reincorporated in Canada 05/11/2005 which reincorporated in Delaware 05/11/2009

GOLDALE LTD. (ON)
Recapitalized as Canadian Goldale Corp. Ltd. 06/16/1965
Each share Capital Stock no par exchanged for (0.1) share Common no par
Canadian Goldale Corp. Ltd. name changed to Hambro Canada (1972) Ltd. 01/09/1973 which name changed to Hambro Canada Ltd. 05/28/1974 which name changed to Hatleigh Corp. (Old) 08/03/1978 which merged into Hatleigh Corp. (New) 08/31/1978 which merged into Dexleigh Corp. 06/30/1984
(See Dexleigh Corp.)

GOLDALE MINES LTD. (ON)
Name changed to Goldale Ltd. and Capital Stock $1 par changed to no par 09/17/1962
Goldale Ltd. recapitalized as Canadian Goldale Corp. Ltd. 06/16/1965 which name changed to Hambro Canada (1972) Ltd. 01/09/1973 which name changed to Hambro Canada Ltd. 05/28/1974 which name changed to Hatleigh Corp. (Old) 08/03/1978 which merged into Hatleigh Corp. (New) 08/31/1978 which merged into Dexleigh Corp. 06/30/1984
(See Dexleigh Corp.)

GOLDBANK VENTURES LTD (AB)
Recapitalized as Consolidated Goldbank Ventures Ltd. 09/15/2000
Each share Class A Common no par exchanged for (0.25) share Common no par
Consolidated Goldbank Ventures Ltd. name changed to NEMI Northern Energy & Mining Inc. (AB) 08/13/2003 which reincorporated in British Columbia 04/15/2010
(See NEMI Northern Energy & Mining Inc.)

GOLDBANKS-KIRKLAND MINES LTD.
Succeeded by Goldbanks Mines Ltd. 00/00/1937
Each share Capital Stock exchanged for (0.5) share Capital Stock
(See Goldbanks Mines Ltd.)

GOLDBANKS MINES LTD. (ON)
Charter cancelled 12/18/61
No stockholders' equity

GOLDBARD CAP CORP (ON)
Reorganized under the laws of British Columbia as Eco (Atlantic) Oil & Gas Ltd. 11/29/2011
Each share Common no par exchanged for (0.4) share Common no par

GOLDBEAM MINES LTD (MB)
Charter cancelled and declared dissolved for failure to file returns 03/09/1972

GOLDBEC MINES, LTD. (ON)
Charter revoked for failure to file reports and pay taxes 00/00/1953

GOLDBELT RES LTD (BC)
Recapitalized 07/15/1991
Reorganized 08/27/2001
Reincorporated 02/16/2006
Recapitalized from Goldbelt Mines Inc. to Goldbelt Resources Ltd. 07/15/1991
Each share Common no par exchanged for (0.5) share Common no par
Reorganized from under the laws of (BC) to (Yukon) 08/27/2001
Each share Common no par exchanged for (0.1) share Common no par
Place of incorporation changed from (Yukon) to (BC) 02/16/2006
Acquired by Wega Mining ASA 04/07/2008
Each share Common no par exchanged for $1.55 cash

GOLDBERG PLASTICS INC (CO)
Recapitalized as Pennant Pacific Resources, Inc. 08/10/1982
Each share Common no par exchanged for (8) shares Common 1¢ par
(See Pennant Pacific Resources, Inc.)

GOLDBERG REPORT LTD (ON)
Reorganized under the laws of Delaware as Hee Corp. 12/12/2003
Each share Common no par exchanged for (0.05) share Common no par
Preferred not affected except for change of name
Hee Corp. recapitalized as Preachers Coffee Inc. (DE) 04/11/2008
(See Preachers Coffee Inc. (DE))

GOLDBERG (S.M.) STORES, INC.
Name changed to Grier (S.M.) Stores, Inc. in 1930 which assets were sold in 1933 with no stockholders' equity

GOLDBLATT BROS INC (IL)
Common no par changed to $8 par in 1942
$2.50 Preferred no par called for redemption 1/1/51
Common $8 par changed to $4 par and (1) additional share issued 1/3/67
Common $4 par changed to $2 par and (1) additional share issued 5/26/69
Common $2 par changed to no par 8/30/83
Name changed to JG Industries, Inc. 7/23/85
(See JG Industries, Inc.)

GOLDBOW MINING CO. LTD. (ON)
Name changed to Bowsinque Mines Ltd. 00/00/1950
(See Bowsinque Mines Ltd.)

GOLDBRAE DEVS LTD (BC)
Recapitalized as New Goldbrae Developments Ltd. 06/19/1990
Each share Common no par exchanged for (0.2) share Common no par
(See New Goldbrae Developments Ltd.)

GOLDBROOK EXPLS INC (ON)
Recapitalized as Goldbrook Ventures Inc. (ON) 07/22/2002
Each share Common no par exchanged for (0.33333333) share Common no par
Goldbrook Ventures Inc. (ON) reincorporated in British Columbia 04/14/2003
(See Goldbrook Ventures Inc.)

GOLDBROOK VENTURES INC (BC)
Reincorporated 04/14/2003
Place of incorporation changed from (ON) to (BC) 04/14/2003
Acquired by Jilin Jien Nickel Industry Co., Ltd. 05/28/2012
Each share Common no par exchanged for $0.39 cash

GOLDCAP INC (CANADA)
Reincorporated 09/27/1987
Place of incorporation changed from (AB) to (Canada) 09/27/1987
Recapitalized as Durandel Minerals Corp. 10/26/1994
Each share Common no par exchanged for (0.5) share Common no par
Durandel Minerals Corp. recapitalized as Calliope Metals Corp. (Canada) 07/15/1996 which reincorporated in Yukon 06/17/1997 which merged into Argosy Minerals Inc. (YT) 05/07/1999 which reincorporated in British Columbia 05/26/2005 which reincorporated in Australia as Argosy Minerals Ltd. 03/18/2011

GOLDCO LTD (NV)
Name changed to Resource Ventures, Inc. (NV) 05/18/2000
Resource Ventures, Inc. (NV) reincorporated in British Columbia as New Dawn Mining Corp. 08/22/2006 which reorganized in Canada 11/15/2007
(See New Dawn Mining Corp.)

GOLDCOR INC (DE)
Reincorporated 7/26/84
State of incorporation changed from (UT) to (DE) 7/26/84
Each share Common $0.005 par exchanged for (2) shares Common $0.00025 par 9/15/87
Charter cancelled and declared inoperative and void for non-payment of taxes 3/1/92

GOLDCORE VENTURES LTD. (BC)
Name changed to New Goldcore Ventures Ltd. 12/19/83
New Goldcore Ventures Ltd. recapitalized as Namex Explorations, Inc. 12/8/97

GOLDCORP HLDGS CO (DE)
Name changed to Goldland Holdings, Co. 10/20/2010
Goldland Holdings, Co. name changed to Bravo Multinational Inc. 04/07/2016

GOLDCORP INC NEW (BC)
Class A Subordinate no par split (2) for (1) by issuance of (1) additional share payable 07/12/1996 to holders of record 07/10/1996 Ex date - 07/15/1996
Class B Multiple no par split (2) for (1) by issuance of (1) additional share payable 07/12/1996 to holders of record 07/10/1996 Ex date - 07/15/1996
Each share Class A Subordinate no par exchanged for (1) share Common no par 11/01/2000
Each share Class B Multiple no par

exchanged for (1.25) shares Common no par 11/01/2000 (Additional Information in Active)

GOLDCORP INC OLD (ON)
Name changed 8/30/91
Name changed from Goldcorp Investments Ltd. to Goldcorp Inc. 08/30/1991
Merged into Goldcorp Inc. (New) 03/31/1994
Each share Class A no par exchanged for (1.4) shares Class A Subordinated no par and (0.5) share Lexam Explorations Inc. Common no par
(See each company's listing)

GOLDCREST CORP (DE)
SEC revoked common stock registration 10/01/2008

GOLDCREST MINES, LTD. (ON)
Recapitalized as North Goldcrest Mines Ltd. 07/14/1958
Each share Capital Stock $1 par exchanged for (0.33333333) share Capital Stock $1 par
North Goldcrest Mines Ltd. merged into Crestland Mines Ltd. 05/04/1965 which merged into PYX Explorations Ltd. 07/30/1976 which merged into Discovery Mines Ltd. (Canada) 01/15/1982 which merged into Discovery West Corp. 03/01/1987
(See Discovery West Corp.)

GOLDCREST RES LTD (ON)
Merged into Volta Resources Inc. 03/31/2008
Each share Common no par exchanged for (0.33333333) share Common no par
Volta Resources Inc. merged into B2Gold Corp. 12/27/2013

GOLDEN ADIT RES LTD (BC)
Name changed to First Northern Developments, Inc. 06/08/1990
First Northern Developments, Inc. recapitalized as Consolidated First Developments Inc. 09/20/1993 which recapitalized as Golden Temple Mining Corp. 03/15/1996 which recapitalized as Amerigo Resources Ltd. 03/08/2002

GOLDEN AGE CONVALESCENT CTRS INC (DE)
Name changed to Golden Age Medical Industries, Inc. 7/9/70
Golden Age Medical Industries, Inc. name changed to Arex Industries, Inc. 7/26/73
(See Arex Industries, Inc.)

GOLDEN AGE HOMES INC (NV)
Name changed to American Health Systems Inc. 10/14/1998
(See American Health Systems Inc.)

GOLDEN AGE JUNIOR MINING CO. (ID)
Charter forfeited for failure to file reports and pay taxes 11/30/29

GOLDEN AGE MEDICAL INDS INC (DE)
Name changed to Arex Industries, Inc. 7/26/73
(See Arex Industries, Inc.)

GOLDEN AGE MINES LTD (ON)
Charter cancelled 09/10/1984

GOLDEN AGE RES INC (ON)
Recapitalized as Ottawa Structural Services Ltd. 9/11/91
Each share Common no par exchanged for (0.5) share Common no par
Ottawa Structural Services Ltd. recapitalized as Forsys Corp. 11/12/96 which recapitalized as Forsys Technologies Inc. 4/16/2003 which name changed to Forsys Metals Corp. 7/14/2005

GOLDEN ALGOMA METALS & HLDGS LTD (ON)
Charter cancelled 02/20/1970

GOLDEN ALGOMA MINES LTD (OH)
Name changed to Golden Algoma Metals & Holdings, Ltd. 12/22/1970
(See Golden Algoma Metals & Holdings, Ltd.)

GOLDEN ALLIANCE RES CORP (BC)
Recapitalized as Orovero Resources Corp. 02/14/2013
Each share Common no par exchanged for (0.33333333) share Common no par
Orovero Resources Corp. name changed to Standard Tolling Corp. 03/10/2014
(See Standard Tolling Corp.)

GOLDEN ANCHOR MINING & MILLING CO., CONSOLIDATED, INC. (WA)
Charter cancelled and proclaimed dissolved for failure to pay fees 7/1/66

GOLDEN APPLE ENTERPRISES INC (NV)
Name changed to Diversified Investment Capital 07/12/2006
(See Diversified Investment Capital)

GOLDEN APPLE OIL & GAS INC (NV)
Charter revoked for failure to file reports and pay fees 09/30/2008

GOLDEN ARIA CORP (NV)
Each share old Common $0.001 par exchanged for (0.5) share new Common $0.001 par 09/25/2009
Name changed to Enertopia Corp. 04/07/2010

GOLDEN ARK INC (NV)
Reorganized as Long Distance Direct Holdings Inc. 10/10/1995
Each share Common $0.001 par exchanged for (1.4700477) shares Common $0.001 par
(See Long Distance Direct Holdings Inc.)

GOLDEN ARROW MINES LTD. (ON)
Recapitalized as Consolidated Golden Arrow Mines Ltd. 00/00/1953
Each share Capital Stock $1 par exchanged for (0.25) share Capital Stock $1 par
Consolidated Golden Arrow Mines Ltd. name changed to Canadian Arrow Mines Ltd. 04/13/1970 which merged into Tartisan Resources Corp. 02/02/2018 which name changed to Tartisan Nickel Corp. 03/23/2018

GOLDEN ARROW RES INC (BC)
Merged into Commonwealth Gold Corp. 03/01/1991
Each share Common no par exchanged for (0.33333333) share Common no par
Commonwealth Gold Corp. merged into Aber Resources Ltd. (New) 04/19/1994 which name changed to Aber Diamond Corp. 08/18/2000 which name changed to Harry Winston Diamond Corp. 11/19/2007 which name changed to Dominion Diamond Corp. 03/27/2013
(See Dominion Diamond Corp.)

GOLDEN ARROW SPRAYERS LTD. (AB)
Voluntary dissolved and struck off register 8/31/66

GOLDEN AUTUMN HLDGS INC (NV)
SEC revoked common stock registration 01/17/2013

GOLDEN BAND RES INC (SK)
Reincorporated 07/04/2006
Place of incorporation changed from (BC) to (SK) 07/04/2006
Proposal under the Bankruptcy and Insolvency Act approved 08/12/2016
No stockholders' equity

GOLDEN BEAR GOLF INC (FL)
Each (114,000) shares old Common 1¢ par exchanged for (1) share new Common 1¢ par 07/20/2000
Note: In effect holders received $0.75 cash per share and public interest was eliminated

GOLDEN BEAR MINERALS INC (BC)
Recapitalized as West Coast Forest Products Ltd. 05/21/1993
Each share Common no par exchanged for (0.25) share Common no par

GOLDEN BEAR MINERALS INC NEW (CANADA)
Name changed to Augusta Gold Corp. 07/04/1997
Augusta Gold Corp. recapitalized as Pulse Data Inc. 10/15/1999 which name changed to Pulse Seismic Inc. 05/28/2009

GOLDEN BEAR RES LTD (BC)
Common no par split (2) for (1) by issuance of (1) additional share 11/20/1984
Common no par split (4) for (1) by issuance of (3) additional shares 01/03/1986
Delisted from Vancouver Stock Exchange 02/02/1988

GOLDEN BEVERAGE CO (NV)
Each share old Common $0.001 par exchanged for (0.00080606) share new Common $0.001 par 04/01/1997
Name changed to WorldWater Corp. (NV) 04/24/1997
WorldWater Corp. (NV) reincorporated in Delaware 05/01/2001 which name changed to WorldWater & Power Corp. 08/04/2005 which name changed to WorldWater & Solar Technologies Corp. 10/12/2007 which name changed to Entech Solar, Inc. 01/12/2009
(See Entech Solar, Inc.)

GOLDEN BOOKS FAMILY ENTMT INC (DE)
Plan of reorganization under Chapter 11 Federal Bankruptcy proceedings effective 01/27/2000
Each share old Common 1¢ par exchanged for (0.00571428) Common Stock Purchase Warrant expiring 01/27/2003
Chapter 11 petition dismissed and assets sold for the benefit of creditors 04/03/2002
No stockholders' equity

GOLDEN BRANDS INC (DE)
Charter cancelled and declared inoperative and void for non-payment of taxes 04/15/1972

GOLDEN BRDG DEV CORP (ON)
Recapitalized as CIM International Group Inc. 05/09/2016
Each share Common no par exchanged for (0.2) share Common no par

GOLDEN BRDG MNG CORP (ON)
Name changed to Golden Bridge Development Corp. 09/23/2014
Golden Bridge Development Corp. recapitalized as CIM International Group Inc. 05/09/2016

GOLDEN BRIAR MINES LTD (AB)
Reincorporated 01/01/1980
Place of incorporation changed from (ON) to (AB) 01/01/1980
Delisted from Toronto Venture Stock Exchange 08/26/2005

GOLDEN CADILLAC RES LTD (BC)
Name changed to Seymour-Moss International Ltd. 07/09/1985
(See Seymour-Moss International Ltd.)

GOLDEN CENTER MINES, INC.
Dissolved 00/00/1936

Details not available

GOLDEN CENTY RES LTD (DE)
SEC revoked common stock registration 06/10/2015

GOLDEN CENTY TECHNOLOGIES CORP (DE)
Name changed to Golden Century Resources Ltd. 10/07/2009
(See Golden Century Resources Ltd.)

GOLDEN CHAIN MARKETING INC (CO)
Name changed to Virtual Lender.Com Inc. 02/17/1999
Virtual Lender.Com Inc. name changed to VLDC Technologies, Inc. 10/29/1999 which name changed to JTS International, Inc. 01/24/2006 which recapitalized as Fuji Construction Company International, Inc. 02/08/2008 which name changed to Hokutou Holdings International, Inc. (CO) 11/06/2008 which reincorporated in Nevada 05/23/2014 which name changed to Platinum Pari-Mutuel Holdings, Inc. 12/09/2014 which name changed to Point to Point Methodics, Inc. 04/27/2017

GOLDEN CHALICE RES INC (BC)
Each share Common no par received distribution of (0.33333333) share Chalice Diamond Corp. Common no par payable 12/01/2006 to holders of record 11/22/2006
Recapitalized as Rogue Resources Inc. (Old) 10/15/2010
Each share Common no par exchanged for (0.11111111) share Common no par
Rogue Resources Inc. (Old) name changed to Rogue Iron Ore Corp. 01/23/2012 which reorganized as Rogue Resources Inc. (New) 12/24/2013

GOLDEN CHANCE RES INC (BC)
Common no par split (3) for (1) by issuance of (2) additional shares 11/27/1986
Reorganized under the laws of Yukon as Trimark Resources Ltd. 10/16/1990
Each share Common no par exchanged for (0.11111111) share Common no par
Trimark Resources Ltd. recapitalized as International Trimark Resources Ltd. 12/16/1996 which recapitalized as Trimark Oil & Gas Ltd. 06/17/1997 which recapitalized as Trimark Energy Ltd. 03/21/2002 which name changed to Halo Resources Ltd. (YT) 02/23/2004 which reincorporated in British Columbia 11/16/2004 which merged into Sendero Mining Corp. 07/09/2013

GOLDEN CHARIOT WAR EAGLE MINES CO. (ID)
Charter revoked for failure to file reports and pay fees 11/30/36

GOLDEN CHEST INC (ID)
Each share old Common 10¢ par exchanged for (0.01) share new Common 10¢ par 04/02/1999
Name changed to Senior Care Industries, Inc. (ID) 04/05/1999
Senior Care Industries, Inc. (ID) reincorporated in Nevada 08/26/1999 which name changed to U.S. West Homes Inc. 09/20/2002 which recapitalized as Investco Corp. 05/30/2003
(See Investco Corp.)

GOLDEN CHIEF RES INC (BC)
Reorganized under the laws of Ontario as Roscan Minerals Corp. 11/17/2004
Each share Common no par exchanged for (0.5) share Common no par
Roscan Minerals Corp. name

changed to Roscan Gold Corp. 10/01/2018

GOLDEN CHIEF RES INC (KS)
Each share old Common no par exchanged for (0.1) share new Common no par 12/17/2001
Recapitalized as American Resource Technologies, Inc. 04/23/2007
Each share new Common no par exchanged for (0.02) share Common no par

GOLDEN CHINA RES CORP (CANADA)
Reincorporated 07/01/2005
Place of incorporation changed from (BC) to (Canada) 07/01/2005
Each share old Common no par exchanged for (0.2) share new Common no par 12/12/2006
Merged into Sino Gold Mining Ltd. 12/19/2007
Each share Common no par exchanged for (0.2222) share Ordinary

GOLDEN CHOICE FOODS CORP (NV)
Name changed to International Food Products Group Inc. 04/26/2001
International Food Products Group Inc. name changed to Newport Digital Technologies, Inc. 06/11/2009

GOLDEN COAST ENERGY CORP (BC)
Company announced resignation of Directors and forfeiture of assets to Alberta Energy Regulator 03/24/2016
No stockholders' equity

GOLDEN COAST ENERGY LTD (BC)
Name changed 03/16/1994
Name changed from Golden Coast Minerals Ltd. to Golden Coast Energy Ltd. 03/16/1994
Merged into Founders Energy Ltd. 12/04/1996
Each (1.75) shares Common no par exchanged for (1) share Common no par and (0.25) Common Stock Purchase Warrant expiring 06/04/1998
Founders Energy Ltd. reorganized as Provident Energy Trust 03/06/2001 which reorganized as Provident Energy Ltd. (New) 01/03/2011 which merged into Pembina Pipeline Corp. 04/02/2012

GOLDEN COIN RES LTD (BC)
Common no par split (2) for (1) by issuance of (1) additional share 09/16/1985
Name changed to P.M.C. Technologies Ltd. 11/20/1986
(See P.M.C. Technologies Ltd.)

GOLDEN CONCORD MNG CORP (BC)
Recapitalized as Crossland Industries Corp. 04/18/1985
Each share Common no par exchanged for (0.33333333) share Common no par
(See Crossland Industries Corp.)

GOLDEN CORRAL RLTY CORP (DE)
Name changed to CNL Realty Investors, Inc. 7/17/92
CNL Realty Investors, Inc. name changed to Commercial Net Lease Realty, Inc. (DE) 5/19/93 which reincorporated in Maryland 6/3/94 which name changed to National Retail Properties, Inc. 5/1/2006

GOLDEN CRESCENT CORP (ON)
Recapitalized 05/20/1998
Recapitalized from Golden Crescent Resources Corp. to Golden Crescent Corp. 05/20/1998
Each share old Common no par exchanged for (0.11111111) share new Common no par
Delisted from Canadian Dealer Network 01/03/1995

GOLDEN CREST MINING CO. (SD)
Charter expired by time limitation in 1923

GOLDEN CREST RECORDS INC (NY)
Class A 10¢ par reclassified as Common 5¢ par 7/28/69
Common 5¢ par split (2) for (1) by issuance of (1) additional share 8/11/69
Name changed to Golden Crest Industries, Inc. 3/12/86

GOLDEN CROSS RES INC (BC)
Recapitalized as Blue Gold Water Technologies Ltd. 05/21/2013
Each share Common no par exchanged for (0.5) share Common no par
Blue Gold Water Technologies Ltd. name changed to NanoStruck Technologies Inc. 10/02/2013 which name changed to Fineqia International Inc. 11/01/2016

GOLDEN CROWN MINING CO. (AZ)
Common $1 par changed to 50¢ par 00/00/1951
Merged into Western Gold & Uranium, Inc. on a share for share basis 07/31/1957
Western Gold & Uranium, Inc. name changed to Western Equities, Inc. 12/14/1961 which name changed to Westec Corp. 05/20/1966 which name changed to Tech-Sym Corp. 05/25/1970
(See Tech-Sym Corp.)

GOLDEN CROWN RES LTD (BC)
Struck off register and declared dissolved for failure to file returns 03/03/1995

GOLDEN CYCLE CORP (WV)
Each share Common $1 par exchanged for (0.1) share Common $10 par in 1929
Common $10 par changed to no par and (3) additional shares issued 6/1/65
Reincorporated under the laws of Delaware as ATE Enterprises Inc. and Common no par changed to $1 par 6/21/83
(See ATE Enterprises Inc.)

GOLDEN CYCLE GOLD CORP (CO)
Common no par split (5) for (1) by issuance of (4) additional shares payable 07/13/2004 to holders of record 07/12/2004 Ex date - 07/14/2004
Merged into AngloGold Ashanti Ltd. 07/01/2008
Each share Common no par exchanged for (0.3123) Sponsored ADR for Ordinary Rand-50 par

GOLDEN CYCLE MINING & REDUCTION CO.
Name changed to Golden Cycle Corp. in 1929
Golden Cycle Corp. reincorporated in Delaware as ATE Enterprises Inc. 6/21/83
(See ATE Enterprises Inc.)

GOLDEN DAWN EXPLS LTD (BC)
Name changed to Chuan Hup Canada Ltd. 10/15/1987
Chuan Hup Canada Ltd. recapitalized as IGT International Growth Technologies Inc. 09/25/1992 which name changed to IGT Pharma, Inc. (BC) 02/27/1997 which reincorporated in Canada as Prescient Neuropharma Inc. 02/19/2001 which reincorporated in British Columbia 12/21/2007 which name changed to PNO Resources Ltd. 02/09/2012 which merged into Sandspring Resources Ltd. 09/15/2015

GOLDEN DAY MNG EXPL INC (QC)
Merged into Gothic Resources Inc. (Canada) 09/19/1991
Each share Common no par exchanged for (0.1) share Common no par
Gothic Resources Inc. (Canada) reincorporated in Oklahoma as American Natural Energy Corp. (Ctfs. dtd. after 02/12/2002) 02/12/2002
(See American Natural Energy Corp. (Ctfs. dtd. after 02/12/2002)

GOLDEN DIVID RES CORP (BC)
Recapitalized as Caesar's Gold Ltd. 04/18/1996
Each share Common no par exchanged for (0.2) share Common no par
Caesar's Gold Ltd. recapitalized as Caesar's Explorations Inc. 08/16/1999 which name changed to Great Southern Enterprises Corp. 11/04/2002 which recapitalized as Balmoral Resources Ltd. 03/29/2010

GOLDEN DORY RES CORP (AB)
Recapitalized as Sokoman Iron Corp. 10/01/2013
Each share Common no par exchanged for (0.1) share Common no par

GOLDEN DRAGON HLDGS INC (FL)
Name changed to China Food Services, Corp. (FL) 07/07/2010
China Food Services, Corp. (FL) reorganized in Nevada as California Grapes International, Inc. 11/09/2011

GOLDEN DRAGON HLDG CO (DE)
Name changed to CannaPharmaRx, Inc. 03/23/2015

GOLDEN DRAGON RES LTD (BC)
Ctfs. dated prior to 12/18/1985
Name changed to MDC Financial Inc. 12/18/1985
(See MDC Financial Inc.)

GOLDEN DRAGON RES LTD NEW (BC)
Certificates dated after 02/16/1988
Recapitalized as Canadian Golden Dragon Resources Ltd. 05/16/1994
Each share Common no par exchanged for (0.2) share Common no par
Canadian Golden Dragon Resources Ltd. name changed to Trillium North Minerals Ltd. 11/05/2007 which recapitalized as White Metal Resources Corp. 06/04/2014

GOLDEN DYNASTY RES LTD (BC)
Common no par split (3) for (1) by issuance of (2) additional shares payable 02/01/2005 to holders of record 01/25/2005
Recapitalized as Columbus Energy Ltd. 09/12/2008
Each share Common no par exchanged for (1/6) share Common no par

GOLDEN EAGLE CAP CORP (ON)
Recapitalized as Points North Digital Technologies Inc. 04/04/1996
Each share Common no par exchanged for (0.03333333) share Common no par
Points North Digital Technologies Inc. name changed to Peragis Inc. 01/01/2001
(See Peragis Inc.)

GOLDEN EAGLE FINL CORP (UT)
Involuntarily dissolved for failure to pay taxes 03/31/1986

GOLDEN EAGLE GROUP INC (DE)
Merged into USFreightways Corp. 11/12/1998
Each share Common 1¢ par exchanged for $4.45 cash

GOLDEN EAGLE INTL INC (CO)
Each share old Common $0.0001 par exchanged for (0.002) share new Common $0.0001 par 05/13/2010
Recapitalized as Advantego Corp. 02/22/2018
Each share new Common $0.0001 par exchanged for (0.09090909) share Common $0.0001 par
Note: Holders of (120) or fewer pre-split shares will receive $0.09 cash per share upon written request to company

GOLDEN EAGLE MINING CO. (AZ)
Charter revoked for failure to pay taxes 00/00/1917

GOLDEN EAGLE MINING CO. (OR)
Charter cancelled for failure to pay taxes 00/00/1935

GOLDEN EAGLE RES INC (ON)
Name changed to Golden Eagle Capital Corp. 09/10/1992
Golden Eagle Capital Corp. recapitalized as Points North Digital Technologies Inc. 04/04/1996 which name changed to Peragis Inc. 01/01/2001
(See Peragis Inc.)

GOLDEN EAGLE VENTURES INC (AB)
Recapitalized 11/02/1995
Recapitalized from Golden Eagle Mines Ltd. to Golden Eagle Ventures Inc. 11/02/1995
Each share Common no par exchanged for (0.25) share Common no par
Recapitalized as Alberta Diamondfields Inc. 06/23/1998
Each share Common no par exchanged for (0.5) share Common no par
Alberta Diamondfields Inc. recapitalized as Delray Ventures Inc. (AB) 08/21/2002 which reincorporated in British Columbia as Clydesdale Resources Inc. 08/08/2008

GOLDEN EARTH RES INC (ON)
Merged into Health & Environment Technologies Inc. 05/03/1989
Each share Common no par exchanged for (0.0704837) share Common no par
(See Health & Environment Technologies Inc.)

GOLDEN EDGE ENTMT INC (DE)
Name changed to Luminar Media Group, Inc. 08/26/2016

GOLDEN ELEPHANT GLASS TECHNOLOGY INC (NV)
SEC revoked common stock registration 12/22/2014

GOLDEN ENERGY CORP (NV)
Common $0.002 par changed to $0.001 par and (99) additional shares issued payable 06/16/2009 to holders of record 06/16/2009
Name changed to Golden Grail Technology Corp. 12/31/2014

GOLDEN ENTERPRISES INC (DE)
Class A Common $0.66666666 par reclassified as Common $1 par 10/11/1979
Common $1 par changed to $0.66666666 par and (0.5) additional share issued 10/30/1979
Common $0.66666666 par split (2) for (1) by issuance of (1) additional share 05/25/1983
Common $0.66666666 par split (4) for (3) by issuance of (0.33333333) additional share 10/31/1984
Common $0.66666666 par split (4) for (3) by issuance of (0.33333333) additional share 10/30/1985
Stock Dividends - 50% 10/31/1978; 50% 10/30/1981
Acquired by Utz Quality Foods, Inc. 09/30/2016
Each share Common $0.66666666 par exchanged for $12 cash

GOLDEN EXODUS VENTURES LTD (BC)
Recapitalized as ILM Resources Ltd. 01/16/1990

Each share Common no par exchanged for (0.25) share Common no par
ILM Resources Ltd. recapitalized as Rainier Resources Ltd. 02/11/1993 which recapitalized as Prong Industries Corp. Ltd. (BC) 08/27/1996 which reincorporated in Bermuda 09/03/1996 which name changed to C&C Industries Corp. 11/02/1998 which name changed to Xenex Minerals Ltd. 01/11/2008
(See Xenex Minerals Ltd.)

GOLDEN EYE MINERALS LTD (BC)
Recapitalized as Annex Exploration Corp. 01/31/1991
Each share Common no par exchanged for (0.5) share Common no par
Annex Exploration Corp. recapitalized as Redhawk Resources, Inc. 03/29/1994 which merged into CopperBank Resources Corp. 09/04/2018

GOLDEN FAME RES CORP (BC)
Reorganized as Pan American Fertilizer Corp. (New) 08/07/2013
Each share Common no par exchanged for (0.25) share Common no par

GOLDEN FLAG RES INC (MT)
Each share old Common $0.003125 par exchanged for (0.1) share new Common $0.003125 par 12/21/83
Name changed to Infoserve, Inc. and new Common $0.003125 par reclassified as Class A Common $0.003125 par 11/18/93
Infoserve, Inc. merged into CD-MAX Inc. 4/15/96 which name changed to IMARK Technologies, Inc. 12/31/97 which recapitalized as Pharm Control Ltd. 11/8/2006

GOLDEN FLAKE, INC. (DE)
Name changed to Golden Enterprises, Inc. 01/01/1977
(See Golden Enterprises, Inc.)

GOLDEN FORK CORP (NV)
Common $0.00001 par split (3) for (1) by issuance of (2) additional shares payable 04/16/2012 to holders of record 04/09/2012 Ex date - 04/17/2012
Name changed to Staffing 360 Solutions, Inc. (NV) 04/24/2012
Staffing 360 Solutions, Inc. (NV) reincorporated in Delaware 06/20/2017

GOLDEN FORTUNE INVTS LTD (AB)
Delisted from Toronto Venture Stock Exchange 04/20/2004

GOLDEN GATE BANK (SAN FRANCISCO, CA)
Acquired by a private investor 7/31/84
Each share Common $2.50 par exchanged for $27 cash

GOLDEN GATE CORP. (RI)
Common $1 par changed to 5¢ par 9/17/57
Completely liquidated 3/5/87
Each share 7% Preferred $50 par exchanged for first and final distribution of $2.60 cash
Each share Common 5¢ par exchanged for first and final distribution of $2.60 cash

GOLDEN GATE EXPL LTD (BC)
Common 50¢ par changed to no par 03/09/1988
Recapitalized as Texas Dome Resource Corp. 10/24/1991
Each share Common no par exchanged for (0.33333333) share Common no par
Texas Dome Resource Corp. name changed to Microkey Communications Systems Inc. 06/06/1994
(See Microkey Communications Systems Inc.)

GOLDEN GATE FD INC (CA)
Charter suspended for failure to file reports or pay taxes 04/01/1974

GOLDEN GATE FERRIES, INC.
Merged into Southern Pacific Golden Gate Ferries, Inc. 00/00/1929
Details not available

GOLDEN GATE HOMES INC (DE)
Units separated 04/10/2010
Name changed to Golden Gate Partners, Inc. 01/08/2014

GOLDEN GATE INDS INC (FL)
Proclaimed dissolved for failure to file reports and pay fees 06/28/1971

GOLDEN GATE MINING CO. LTD. (ON)
Succeeded by Kirkland Golden Gate Mines Ltd. on a (1) for (2) basis 00/00/1946
Kirkland Golden Gate Mines Ltd. recapitalized as Gateford Mines Ltd. (ONT) 00/00/1950 which reincorporated in Canada as Gateford Resources Inc. 07/03/1986 which merged into Landmark Corp. (New) 01/31/1992 which recapitalized as Landmark Global Financial Corp. 07/05/1996

GOLDEN GATE NATIONAL BANK (SAN FRANCISCO, CA)
Capital Stock $15 par split (3) for (1) by issuance of (2) additional shares 6/15/62
Merged into Liberty National Bank (San Francisco, CA) 12/15/67
Each share Capital Stock $5 par exchanged for (1) share Common $2 par
(See Liberty National Bank (San Francisco, CA))

GOLDEN GATE RES LTD (YUKON)
Reincorporated 08/26/1998
Place of incorporation changed from (BC) to (Yukon) 08/26/1998
Acquired by Golden Gate Petroleum Ltd. 06/30/2003
Each share Common no par exchanged for (1.6) Ordinary shares

GOLDEN GENESIS CO (DE)
Merged into Kyocera Corp. 8/3/99
Each share Common 10¢ par exchanged for $2.33 cash

GOLDEN GIRL INDS INC (DE)
Each share Common $0.001 par exchanged for (0.1) share Common 1¢ par 7/22/74
Charter cancelled and declared inoperative and void for non-payment of taxes 3/1/77

GOLDEN GLACIER RES INC (BC)
Recapitalized as Exeter Resource Corp. 10/11/2002
Each share Common no par exchanged for (0.1) share Common no par
Exeter Resource Corp. merged into Goldcorp Inc. (New) 08/08/2017

GOLDEN GLORY RES LTD (BC)
Name changed to Shimoda International Systems, Inc. 02/21/1990
(See Shimoda International Systems, Inc.)

GOLDEN GOOSE RESOURCES INC (QC)
Merged into Kodiak Exploration Ltd. 12/16/2010
Each share Common no par exchanged for (1.2) shares Common no par and (0.25) Common Stock Warrant expiring 12/16/2013
Kodiak Exploration Ltd. name changed to Prodigy Gold Inc. 01/04/2011 which merged into Argonaut Gold Corp. 12/11/2012

GOLDEN GRAIL RES INC (BC)
Struck off register and declared dissolved for failure to file returns 04/16/1993

GOLDEN GRAM CAP INC (CANADA)
Name changed 05/10/1999
Name changed from Golden Gram Resources Inc. to Golden Gram Capital Inc. 05/10/1999
Recapitalized as Events International Holding Corp. 10/15/2001
Each share Common no par exchanged for (0.5) share Common no par
Events International Holding Corp. name changed to Dynasty Gaming Inc. 12/09/2005 which recapitalized as Blue Zen Memorial Parks Inc. 01/21/2011

GOLDEN GRANITE MINES LTD (BC)
Out of existence and dissolved 00/00/1979
Details not available

GOLDEN GREEN ENTERPRISES LTD (BRITISH VIRGIN ISLANDS)
Name changed to China Gerui Advanced Materials Group Ltd. 12/14/2009

GOLDEN GROUP EXPL INC (QC)
Merged into Brookline Minerals Inc. 07/26/1991
Each share Common no par exchanged for (0.41666666) share Common no par
Brookline Minerals Inc. name changed to Ventel Inc. 12/15/1995 which name changed to Fifty-Plus.Net International Inc. 07/09/1999 which name changed to ZoomerMedia Ltd. 07/02/2008

GOLDEN HAND RES INC (WA)
Name changed to BrainStorm Cell Therapeutics Inc. (WA) 11/18/2004
BrainStorm Cell Therapeutics Inc. (WA) reincorporated in Delaware 12/21/2006

GOLDEN HARKER EXPLS LTD (ON)
Common $1 par changed to no par 09/17/1981
Each share old Common no par exchanged for (3) shares new Common no par 06/17/2005
Merged into Jubilee Gold Inc. 01/01/2010
Each share new Common no par exchanged for (0.393) share Common no par
Jubilee Gold Inc. merged into Jubilee Gold Exploration Ltd. 01/25/2013

GOLDEN HART EXPL INC (ON)
Recapitalized as Beaufort Hills Resources Inc. 06/30/1999
Each share Common no par exchanged for (0.1) share Common no par
Beaufort Hills Resources Inc. recapitalized as InterRent Properties Ltd. 11/01/1999 which recapitalized as InterRent International Properties Inc. 03/05/2001 which reorganized as InterRent Real Estate Investment Trust 12/07/2006

GOLDEN HARVEST RES INC (UT)
Name changed to Telergy Inc. 7/24/87
(See Telergy Inc.)

GOLDEN HAT RES INC (MB)
Reincorporated 03/28/1984
Place of incorporation changed from (BC) to (MB) 03/28/1984
Reorganized under the laws of British Columbia as Premier Diagnostic Health Services Inc. 10/04/2010
Each share Common no par exchanged for (0.08333333) share Common no par
Premier Diagnostic Health Services Inc. name changed to Premier Diversified Holdings Inc. 04/22/2015

GOLDEN HEALTH HLDGS INC (NV)
SEC revoked common stock registration 09/17/2013

GOLDEN HEMLOCK EXPLS LTD (BC)
Delisted from Toronto Venture Stock Exchange 12/04/2001

GOLDEN HILL MNG CO (ON)
Acquired by MacDonald Mines Exploration Ltd. (QC) 03/09/1998
Each share Common no par exchanged for (0.66) share Common no par and (0.27) Common Stock Purchase Warrant expiring 01/22/1999
MacDonald Mines Exploration Ltd. (QC) reincorporated in Canada 11/01/2011

GOLDEN HIND VENTURES LTD (BC)
Merged into Kam Creed Mines Ltd. 07/13/1988
Each share Common no par exchanged for (1) share Common no par
(See Kam Creed Mines Ltd.)

GOLDEN HOLE INC (NV)
Name changed to IPEC Holdings Inc. 4/15/2002
(See IPEC Holdings Inc.)

GOLDEN HOME HEALTH CARE EQUIP CTRS INC (UT)
Involuntarily dissolved 03/01/1990

GOLDEN HOPE MINING & MILLING CO. (WA)
Charter revoked for failure to file reports and pay fees 7/1/23

GOLDEN HOPE RES CORP (NV)
Reorganized as Eternal Energy Corp. 11/07/2005
Each share Common $0.001 par exchanged for (35) shares Common $0.001 par
Eternal Energy Corp. recapitalized as American Eagle Energy Corp. 12/20/2011
(See American Eagle Energy Corp.)

GOLDEN HOPE RES INC (BC)
Merged into Brookline Minerals Inc. 07/26/1991
Each share Common no par exchanged for (0.5) share Common no par
Brookline Minerals Inc. name changed to Ventel Inc. 12/15/1995 which name changed to Fifty-Plus.Net International Inc. 07/09/1999 which name changed to ZoomerMedia Ltd. 07/02/2008

GOLDEN HORIZON RESOURCE CORP (BC)
Recapitalized as GHZ Resource Corp. 01/02/1990
Each share Common no par exchanged for (0.25) share Common no par
GHZ Resource Corp. name changed to Canadian Reserve Gold Corp. 06/10/1994 which recapitalized as Christina Gold Resources Ltd. 04/18/1996 which recapitalized as PowerHouse Energy Corp. 12/11/1998 which recapitalized as International Powerhouse Energy Corp. 09/18/2001 which name changed to Sea Breeze Power Corp. 07/30/2003

GOLDEN INTST MED MGMT INC (NV)
Each share old Common $0.001 par exchanged for (0.1) share new Common $0.001 par 1/9/96
Charter revoked for failure to file reports and pay fees 5/1/2006

GOLDEN ISKUT RES INC (BC)
Merged into Aegis Resources Ltd. 08/01/1990
Each share Common no par exchanged for (0.125) share Common no par
Aegis Resources Ltd. recapitalized as New Aegis Resources Ltd. 03/17/1993 which was acquired by Norcan Resources Ltd. 08/19/1994 which recapitalized as Odyssey

Exploration Inc. 06/07/2000 which recapitalized as Consolidated Odyssey Exploration Inc. 12/08/2000 which reorganized as Odyssey Petroleum Corp. 08/25/2005 which recapitalized as Petrichor Energy Inc. 03/03/2011

GOLDEN ISLES FINL HLDGS INC (GA)
Merged into ABC Bancorp 07/23/2001
Each share Common exchanged for (0.5) share Common $1 par and $4.13 cash
ABC Bancorp name changed to Ameris Bancorp 12/01/2005

GOLDEN KEY INTL INC (DE)
Common $0.0001 par split (2.44) for (1) by issuance of (1.44) additional shares payable 12/04/2009 to holders of record 12/04/2009
Ex date - 12/07/2009
Name changed to China New Media Corp. 12/28/2009
China New Media Corp. name changed to V Media Corp. 07/24/2012
(See V Media Corp.)

GOLDEN KEY RES LTD (BC)
Recapitalized as Trax Petroleums Ltd. 10/27/1988
Each share Common no par exchanged for (0.2) share Common no par
(See Trax Petroleums Ltd.)

GOLDEN KNIGHT RES INC (BC)
Merged into Repadre Capital Corp. 04/22/1999
For Non-U.S. Residents: Each share Common no par exchanged for either (0.125) share Common no par and CAD$0.33 cash, or (0.2) share Common no par, (0.2) Common Stock Purchase Warrant expiring 00/00/2002, and CAD$0.10 cash
For U.S. Residents: Each share Common no par exchanged for (0.125) share Common no par and CAD$0.33 cash
Repadre Capital Corp. acquired by IAMGold Corp. 01/07/2003

GOLDEN KOOTENAY RES INC (BC)
Recapitalized as Frontier Minerals Inc. 04/18/2000
Each share Common no par exchanged for (0.2) share Common no par
(See Frontier Minerals Inc.)

GOLDEN KRISTY RES LTD (BC)
Name changed to Pan Pacific Gold Corp. 09/23/1994

GOLDEN LAKE RES LTD (BC)
Merged into Ella Resources Inc. 06/01/1993
Each share Common no par exchanged for (0.5) share Common no par
Ella Resources Inc. name changed to Kinetic Energy Inc. 01/25/2001 which recapitalized as Torque Energy Inc. 02/19/2003
(See Torque Energy Inc.)

GOLDEN LEDGE SYNDICATE LTD. (BC)
Defunct; stricken from British Columbia Register of Companies 6/18/59

GOLDEN LION RES LTD (BC)
Common no par split (2) for (1) by issuance of (1) additional share 06/07/1985
Common no par split (2) for (1) by issuance of (1) additional share 08/23/1985
Recapitalized as Consolidated Golden Lion Resources Ltd. 03/08/1989
Each share Common no par exchanged for (0.1) share Common no par
Consolidated Golden Lion Resources Ltd. recapitalized as Americ

Resources Corp. (BC) 09/11/1995 which reincorporated in Canada as Rolland Virtual Business Systems Ltd. 04/27/2001 which name changed to Rolland Energy Inc. 02/16/2007 which recapitalized as Gale Force Petroleum Inc. 06/04/2008 which merged into Montana Exploration Corp. 09/22/2015

GOLDEN LODE, INC. (UT)
Name changed to Chisum Enterprises, Inc. 07/01/1982
Chisum Enterprises, Inc. name changed to Collision Centers International, Inc. 04/11/1988
(See Collision Centers International, Inc.)

GOLDEN LOVE INC (NV)
Name changed to Canada Qatar Oil & Gas Inc. 04/18/1996
Canada Qatar Oil & Gas Inc. recapitalized as Echo Resources Inc. 02/10/1997 which name changed to Big Daddy's BBQ Racing Co. 01/07/1999 which name changed to Ehydrogen Solutions, Inc. 12/14/2009

GOLDEN MAMMOTH MINES, INC. (CO)
Advertised defunct and inoperative for failure to pay taxes 10/16/44

GOLDEN MAMMOUTH RES LTD (BC)
Merged into Canoro Resources Ltd. (BC) 08/11/1995
Each share Common no par exchanged for (0.1) share Common no par
Canoro Resources Ltd. (BC) reincorporated in Alberta 09/21/2001 which reincorporated in British Columbia 03/22/2011

GOLDEN MANITOU MINES LTD. (ON)
Merged into Manitou-Barvue Mines Ltd. 03/23/1959
Each share Capital Stock no par exchanged for (0.2) Capital Stock $1 par
Manitou-Barvue Mines Ltd. name changed to Terratech Resources Inc. 08/31/1983
(See Terratech Resources Inc.)

GOLDEN MAPLE MNG & LEACHING INC (MT)
Each share Common 1¢ par exchanged for (0.04) share Common $0.001 par 08/29/1997
Name changed to Consolidated Medical Management, Inc. 05/23/1998
Consolidated Medical Management, Inc. name changed to Adino Energy Corp. 04/04/2008

GOLDEN MARITIME RES LTD (BC)
Delisted from Toronto Venture Stock Exchange 02/15/2002

GOLDEN MARLIN RES LTD (SK)
Reorganized under the laws of Yukon as Indomin Resources Ltd. 12/06/1995
Each share Class A Common no par exchanged for (0.16666666) share Common no par
Indomin Resources Ltd. name changed to Battlefield Minerals Corp. 06/15/1998 which recapitalized as BM Diamondcorp Inc. 11/21/2001 which name changed to BDI Mining Corp. (Yukon) 07/26/2004 which reincorporated in British Virgin Islands 08/08/2005
(See BDI Mining Corp.)

GOLDEN MEDITECH CO LTD (CAYMAN ISLANDS)
Name changed to Golden Meditech Holdings Ltd. 04/05/2010

GOLDEN MILLER MINES LTD. (ON)
Charter revoked for failure to file reports and pay fees 08/25/1966

GOLDEN MTN (NV)
Reincorporated under the laws of Bermuda as Trevira International Ltd. 1/18/2000

GOLDEN MYRA RES INC (ON)
Delisted from Toronto Stock Exchange 09/23/1991

GOLDEN NEVADA RES INC (BC)
Recapitalized as Goldnev Resources Inc. 06/19/1989
Each share Common no par exchanged for (0.2) share Common no par

GOLDEN NEWS RES INC (BC)
Name changed to Laminco Resources, Inc. (BC) 01/17/1995
Laminco Resources, Inc. (BC) reorganized in Yukon as Zaruma Resources Inc. 11/01/2000 which recapitalized as Red Tiger Mining Inc. 11/08/2011

GOLDEN NORTH RESOURCE CORP (BC)
Merged into Caledonia Mining Corp. (BC) 02/04/1992
Each share Common no par exchanged for (0.71672) share Common no par
Caledonia Mining Corp. (BC) reincorporated in Canada 03/29/1995 which reincorporated in Jersey as Caledonia Mining Corp. PLC 03/24/2016

GOLDEN NUGGET EXPL INC (BC)
Recapitalized as Lucky 1 Enterprises Inc. 05/02/2002
Each share Common no par exchanged for (0.2) share Common no par
Lucky 1 Enterprises Inc. recapitalized as Bronx Ventures Inc. 01/24/2005 which reorganized as ZAB Resources Inc. 03/19/2007 which recapitalized as Kokomo Enterprises Inc. 04/15/2009 which recapitalized as High 5 Ventures Inc. 08/29/2012 which recapitalized as 37 Capital Inc. 07/07/2014

GOLDEN NUGGET INC (NV)
Common $10 par changed to $2.50 par and (3) additional shares issued 01/01/1965
Common $2.50 par changed to $0.8333 par and (2) additional shares issued 02/24/1978
Common $0.8333 par changed to 10¢ par 07/06/1981
Common 10¢ par changed to 2¢ par and (4) additional shares issued 07/15/1983
Stock Dividend - 50% 03/05/1975
Name changed to Mirage Resorts, Inc. 06/03/1991
(See Mirage Resorts, Inc.)

GOLDEN OAK BK (OAKHURST, CA)
Merged into United Security Bank, N.A. (Fresno, CA) 08/12/1995
Each share Common no par exchanged for (3.697) shares Common no par
United Security Bank, N.A. (Fresno, CA) name changed to United Security Bank (Fresno, CA) 02/00/1999 which reorganized as United Security Bancshares 06/12/2001

GOLDEN OASIS EXPL CORP (BC)
Merged into American Consolidated Minerals Corp. 01/30/2009
Each share Common no par exchanged for (1) share Common no par
American Consolidated Minerals Corp. merged into Starcore International Mines Ltd. 12/03/2014

GOLDEN OASIS NEW ENERGY GROUP INC (NV)
Name changed to First America Resources Corp. 08/22/2013

GOLDEN OCEAN GROUP LTD OLD (BERMUDA)
Merged into Golden Ocean Group Ltd. (New) 04/01/2015
Each ADR for Ordinary exchanged for (0.27498) share Common 1¢ par

GOLDEN ODYSSEY MNG INC (CANADA)
Name changed to Deer Horn Metals Inc. 01/27/2011
Deer Horn Metals Inc. name changed to Deer Horn Capital Inc. 10/07/2014

GOLDEN OIL CO (CO)
Merged into Pinnacle Petroleum, Inc. (DE) 09/14/1989
Each share Capital Stock 1¢ par exchanged for (0.3155) share Common 1¢ par
Pinnacle Petroleum, Inc. (DE) name changed to Golden Oil Co. (DE) 02/15/1990
(See Golden Oil Co. (DE))

GOLDEN OIL CO (DE)
Each share old Common $0.001 par exchanged for (0.25) share new Common 1¢ 07/31/1984
Each share new Common 1¢ par exchanged again for (0.02) share new Common 1¢ par 07/14/1993
Plan of reorganization under Chapter 11 Federal Bankruptcy Code effective 10/18/2004
No stockholders' equity

GOLDEN OPPORTUNITIES CORP (DE)
Common $0.001 par changed to $0.00001 par 03/27/2015
Name changed to Umatrin Holding Ltd. 05/06/2015

GOLDEN OPPORTUNITY RES INC (NV)
Common $0.0001 par split (3) for (1) by issuance of (2) additional shares payable 06/01/2004 to holders of record 05/19/2004
Recapitalized as April Energy, Inc. 06/03/2005
Each share Common $0.0001 par exchanged for (0.05) share Common $0.001 par
April Energy, Inc. name changed to AE Holding I, Inc. 01/05/2011

GOLDEN ORE INC (DE)
Recapitalized as Cybersensor International, Inc. 06/29/2004
Each share Common $0.0001 par exchanged for (0.004) share Common $0.0001 par
Cybersensor International, Inc. recapitalized as Angel Telecom Corp. 06/06/2007

GOLDEN PAC AIRLS INC (CA)
Charter suspended for failure to file reports or pay fees 05/01/1973

GOLDEN PAC BK (ONTARIO, CA)
Merged into Network Bank USA (Ontario, CA) 03/21/2000
Each share Common no par exchanged for $2.16 cash

GOLDEN PAC CORP (AB)
Name changed 02/28/1991
Name changed from Golden Pacific Resources Inc. to Golden Pacific Corp. 02/28/1991
Name changed to Pinpoint Retail Solutions Inc. 12/10/1993
(See Pinpoint Retail Solutions Inc.)

GOLDEN PAC HLDGS INTL (CA)
Name changed to Pacrim Information Systems Inc. 02/23/1995
(See Pacrim Information Systems Inc.)

GOLDEN PALM RES LTD (YT)
Reincorporated 12/06/1996
Place of incorporation changed from (BC) to (YT) 12/06/1996
Struck off register and declared

dissolved for failure to file returns 07/05/2003

GOLDEN PANTHER RES LTD (NV)
Name changed to Panther Resources Ltd. 03/13/1998
Panther Resources Ltd. recapitalized as PhantomFilm.Com 06/15/1999 which recapitalized as Komodo, Inc. 10/08/2001
(See Komodo, Inc.)

GOLDEN PATRIOT CORP (NV)
Company terminated common stock registration 03/21/2011

GOLDEN PATRIOT MNG INC (BC)
Name changed to Hana Mining Ltd. (Old) 03/01/2007
(See Hana Mining Ltd. (Old))

GOLDEN PEAK MINERALS INC (BC)
Each share old Common no par exchanged for (0.1) share new Common no par 08/11/2016
Name changed to Bluebird Battery Metals Inc. 04/17/2018

GOLDEN PEAKS RES LTD (BC)
Name changed to Reliance Resources Ltd. 01/12/2012
Reliance Resources Ltd. recapitalized as Resource Capital Gold Corp. 02/29/2016

GOLDEN PHARMACEUTICALS INC (CO)
Recapitalized as docsales.com, inc. 07/12/1999
Each share Common no par exchanged for (0.03125) share Common no par
docsales.com, inc. name changed to Docplanet.com Inc. 10/19/1999
(See Docplanet.com Inc.)

GOLDEN PHEASANT RES LTD (BC)
Struck from the register and dissolved 01/22/1993

GOLDEN PHOENIX, INC. (NV)
Charter revoked for failure to file reports and pay fees 1/1/82

GOLDEN PHOENIX INC (UT)
Name changed to Quantum Energy, Inc. 02/10/1982
Each share Capital Stock $0.005 par exchanged for (1) share Capital Stock $0.005 par
Quantum Energy, Inc. name changed to Western Bell Communications, Inc. 05/20/1985
(See Western Bell Communications, Inc.)

GOLDEN PHOENIX MINERALS INC (MN)
Reincorporated under the laws of Nevada and Common no par changed to $0.001 par 05/30/2008

GOLDEN POINT EXPLS LTD (ON)
Recapitalized as Lombardi (Michael) Publishing Inc. 10/28/1993
Each share Common no par exchanged for (0.2) share Common no par
Lombardi (Michael) Publishing Inc. name changed to Lombardi Media Corp. 11/19/1996
(See Lombardi Media Corp.)

GOLDEN POND HEALTHCARE INC (DE)
Issue Information - 15,625,000 UNITS consisting of (1) share COM and (1) WT offered at $8 per Unit on 11/06/2007
Liquidation completed
Each Unit exchanged for initial distribution of $7.88 cash 11/06/2009
Each share Common $0.001 par exchanged for initial distribution of $7.88 cash 11/06/2009
Each Unit received second distribution of $0.038 cash payable 08/20/2010 to holders of record 11/05/2009
Each share Common $0.001 par received second distribution of $0.038 cash payable 08/20/2010 to holders of record 11/05/2009
Each Unit received third and final distribution of $0.01549864 cash payable 12/12/2012 to holders of record 11/05/2009
Each share Common $0.001 par received third and final distribution of $0.01549864 cash payable 12/12/2012 to holders of record 11/05/2009

GOLDEN POOL RES LTD (AB)
Recapitalized as 1st Century Healthcare International Inc. 01/11/1993
Each share Common no par exchanged for (0.5) share Common no par
1st Century Healthcare International Inc. recapitalized as Pura Vida International Corp. 10/11/1995

GOLDEN POULTRY INC (GA)
Stock Dividends - 25% 5/25/89; 10% 2/25/93; 10% 3/3/94
Merged into Gold Kist Inc. 9/8/97
Each share Common $1 par exchanged for $14.25 cash

GOLDEN PREDATOR CORP (BC)
Name changed to Americas Bullion Royalty Corp. 02/22/2013
Americas Bullion Royalty Corp. merged into Till Capital Ltd. 04/24/2014

GOLDEN PREDATOR MINES INC (BC)
Reorganized as EMC Metals Corp. 03/11/2009
Each share Common no par exchanged for (1) share Common no par and (0.25) share Golden Predator Royalty & Development Corp. Unit consisting of (1) share Common no par and (1) Right expiring 04/01/2009
(See each company's listing)

GOLDEN PREDATOR MNG CORP (AB)
Reincorporated under the laws of British Columbia 10/21/2015

GOLDEN PREDATOR RTY & DEV CORP (BC)
Name changed to Golden Predator Corp. 05/25/2010
Golden Predator Corp. name changed to Americas Bullion Royalty Corp. 02/22/2013 which merged into Till Capital Ltd. 04/24/2014

GOLDEN PRINCESS MNG CORP (BC)
Recapitalized as Pandora Industries Inc. 09/28/1992
Each share Common no par exchanged for (0.2) share Common no par
Pandora Industries Inc. recapitalized as Georgia Ventures Inc. 03/01/2000 which name changed to Creston Moly Corp. 10/19/2007 which merged into Mercator Minerals Ltd. 06/21/2011

GOLDEN PYRAMID RES INC (BC)
Recapitalized as Consolidated Golden Pyramid Resources Inc. 07/06/1992
Each share Common no par exchanged for (0.2) share Common no par
Consolidated Golden Pyramid Resources Inc. name changed to Data Dial International Inc. 12/14/1993 which recapitalized as First Telecom Corp. 05/15/1997 which recapitalized as Sunorca Development Corp. 03/13/2002 which name changed to Wildflower Marijuana Inc. 06/16/2014 which name changed to Wildflower Brands Inc. 05/03/2018

GOLDEN QUAIL RES LTD (BC)
Recapitalized as Consolidated Golden Quail Resources Ltd. 11/24/1997
Each share Common no par exchanged for (0.06666666) share Common no par
(See Consolidated Golden Quail Resources Ltd.)

GOLDEN QUEEN MINING CO. (DE)
Dissolved in December 1953

GOLDEN QUEST INC (NV)
Recapitalized as T-Bay Holdings Inc. 01/23/2002
Each share Common $0.001 par exchanged for (0.0025) share Common $0.001 par
T-Bay Holdings Inc. recapitalized as TOCCA Life Holdings, Inc. 01/12/2015

GOLDEN RAINBOW RES INC (BC)
Name changed to First Silver Reserve Inc. 08/08/1994
First Silver Reserve Inc. merged into First Majestic Resource Corp. 09/18/2006 which name changed to First Majestic Silver Corp. 11/22/2006

GOLDEN REGENT RES LTD (AB)
Recapitalized as Touchstone Petroleum Inc. 06/24/1999
Each share Common no par exchanged for (0.25) share Common no par
Touchstone Petroleum Inc. name changed to Case Resources Inc. 05/17/2001 which merged into Fairborne Energy Ltd. (Old) 07/29/2004
(See Fairborne Energy Ltd. (Old))

GOLDEN REIGN RES LTD (YT)
Reincorporated under the laws of British Columbia 11/14/2007

GOLDEN RES DEV INTL LTD (BERMUDA)
ADR agreement terminated 05/15/2013
No ADR's remain outstanding

GOLDEN RIM RES INC (BC)
Recapitalized as Edge Resources Ltd. 01/26/1990
Each share Common no par exchanged for (0.5) share Common no par
Edge Resources Ltd. merged into Gothic Resources Inc. (BC) 07/09/1991 which reincorporated in Canada 08/01/1991 which reincorporated in Oklahoma as American Natural Energy Corp. (Ctfs. dtd. after 02/12/2002) 02/12/2002
(See American Natural Energy Corp. (Ctfs. dtd. after 02/12/2002))

GOLDEN RING RES LTD (BC)
Recapitalized as Golden Gate Resources Ltd. 06/06/1994
Each share Common no par exchanged for (0.2) share Common no par
Golden Gate Resources Ltd. acquired by Golden Gate Petroleum Ltd. 06/30/2003

GOLDEN RIV RES CORP (DE)
Each share old Common $0.0001 par exchanged for (0.1) share new Common $0.0001 par 11/01/2010
SEC revoked common stock registration 02/15/2018

GOLDEN RIV RES INC (DE)
Recapitalized as Columbus Networks Corp. (Old) 12/08/2000
Each share Common $0.001 par exchanged for (0.25) share Common $0.001 par
Columbus Networks Corp. (Old) name changed to Legacy West Ventures Corp. 08/16/2004 which name changed to Columbus Networks Corp. (New) 01/19/2005
(See Columbus Networks Corp. (New))

GOLDEN ROCK EXPLS INC (QC)
Recapitalized as Gammon Lake Resources Inc. 04/07/1998
Each share Common no par exchanged for (0.06666666) share Common no par
Gammon Lake Resources Inc. name changed to Gammon Gold Inc. (QC) 06/19/2007 which reincorporated in Ontario as AuRico Gold Inc. 06/14/2011 which merged into Alamos Gold Inc. (New) 07/06/2015

GOLDEN ROCK RES LTD (BC)
Recapitalized as Bismillah Ventures Inc. 01/15/1993
Each share Common no par exchanged for (0.41666666) share Common no par
Bismillah Ventures Inc. recapitalized as Royal Rock Ventures Inc. 11/10/1997 which recapitalized as Bi-Optic Ventures Inc. 04/06/2001 which name changed to Arcturus Growthstar Technologies Inc. 02/17/2016 which name changed to Future Farm Technologies Inc. 02/02/2017

GOLDEN ROD MINING & SMELTING CORP.
Merged into Evans-Wallower Lead Co. in 1928
Details not available

GOLDEN RULE RES LTD (AB)
Name changed to CDG Investments Inc. 04/30/2002
CDG Investments Inc. recapitalized as Preo Software Inc. (Old) 07/24/2008 which merged into Preo Software Inc. (New) 08/03/2010
(See Preo Software Inc. (New))

GOLDEN SAND ECO-PROTECTION INC (FL)
Recapitalized as Galaxy Minerals, Inc. 04/15/2004
Each share Common $0.001 par exchanged for (0.25) share Common $0.001 par
(See Galaxy Minerals, Inc.)

GOLDEN SATURN OIL & GAS LTD (ON)
Charter cancelled for failure to file reports and pay taxes 12/10/1994

GOLDEN SCEPTRE RES LTD (BC)
Common no par split (3) for (1) by issuance of (2) additional shares 07/24/1984
Merged into Hemlo Gold Mines Inc. 02/03/1987
Each share Common no par exchanged for (1) share Common no par
Hemlo Gold Mines Inc. merged into Battle Mountain Canada Inc. 07/19/1996 which merged into Newmont Mining Corp. 01/10/2001

GOLDEN SEAL RES LTD (BC)
Name changed to Easton Minerals Ltd. 07/30/1987

GOLDEN SEVEN INDS INC (BC)
Delisted from Vancouver Stock Exchange 03/02/1990

GOLDEN SEVILLE RES LTD (BC)
Struck off register and declared dissolved for failure to file returns 7/5/91

GOLDEN SH MNG CORP NEW (CANADA)
Each share old Common no par exchanged for (0.33333333) share new Common no par 08/13/2015
Name changed to Golden Share Resources Corp. 06/28/2017

GOLDEN SH MNG CORP OLD (CANADA)
Merged into Golden Share Mining Corp. (New) 08/09/2013
Each share Common no par

exchanged for (0.2) share Common no par
Golden Share Mining Corp. (New) name changed to Golden Share Resources Corp. 06/28/2017

GOLDEN SHADOW RES INC (ON)
Recapitalized as Denroy Manufacturing Ltd. 01/21/1991
Each share Capital Stock no par exchanged for (0.10526315) share Common no par
Denroy Manufacturing Ltd. recapitalized as Denroy Resources Corp. (ON) 06/28/2005 which reincorporated in Canada as Nevoro Inc. 05/17/2007 which was acquired by Starfield Resources Inc. 10/08/2009

GOLDEN SHAMROCK RES CORP (BC)
Struck off register and declared dissolved for failure to file returns 07/20/1990

GOLDEN SHAMROCK RES LTD (BC)
Merged into Colt Exploration Ltd. (BC) 07/08/1982
Each share Common no par exchanged for (0.5) share Common no par
Colt Exploration Ltd. (BC) reorganized in Alberta as Colt Exploration (Western) Ltd. 05/17/1983 which recapitalized as Colt Exploration (1988) Ltd. 06/30/1988 which reorganized as Stampede Oils Inc. 12/29/1988
(See Stampede Oils Inc.)

GOLDEN SHEAR MINING CO. (CO)
Charter dissolved for failure to file annual reports 01/01/1919

GOLDEN SHIELD RES LTD (BC)
Assets acquired by a private company through voluntary bankruptcy 03/28/1990
No stockholders' equity

GOLDEN SHORE MINES LTD. (ON)
Charter cancelled for failure to pay taxes and file returns 03/16/1976

GOLDEN SHORES DEVELOPMENT CO. (FL)
Charter proclaimed dissolved for failure to file reports and pay fees 09/03/1976

GOLDEN SIERRA MNG & EXPL CORP (NV)
Reorganized 04/01/1997
Each share old Common $0.001 par exchanged for (0.01) share new Common $0.001 par 11/20/1993
State of incorporation changed from (CO) to (NV) 04/01/1997
Each share new Common $0.001 par exchanged again for (0.5) share new Common $0.001 par
Charter revoked for failure to file reports and pay fees 01/01/2004

GOLDEN SITKA RES INC (BC)
Reorganized under the laws of Yukon as Aurora Platinum Corp. 08/08/2000
Each share Common no par exchanged for (0.25) share Common no par
Aurora Platinum Corp. (YT) reincorporated in British Columbia 06/30/2004 which merged into FNX Mining Co. Inc. 07/01/2005 which merged into Quadra FNX Mining Ltd. 05/27/2010
(See Quadra FNX Mining Ltd.)

GOLDEN SKY VENTURES INTL INC (BC)
Name changed 06/07/1994
Name changed from Golden Sky Resources Inc. to Golden Sky Ventures International Inc. 06/07/1994
Reincorporated under the laws of Canada as iNsu Innovations Group Inc. 07/26/2000 iNsu Innovations Group Inc. name changed to MTY Food Group Inc. 07/08/2003

GOLDEN SLIPPER RES INC (BC)
Name changed to Napa Resources Inc. 11/02/1983
Napa Resources Inc. name changed to Zurfund International Ltd. 12/13/1988 which recapitalized as Atacama Resources Ltd. 02/02/1990 which merged into KAP Resources Ltd. 11/14/1990
(See KAP Resources Ltd.)

GOLDEN SOIL INC (NV)
Each share old Common $0.001 par exchanged for (10) shares new Common $0.001 par 08/09/2000
Name changed to Merilus Inc. 12/29/2000
Merilus Inc. recapitalized as Zendex Holdings, Inc. 06/18/2015 which name changed to Kingsmen Capital Group Ltd. 09/20/2016

GOLDEN SPIKE PETE INC (CO)
Charter suspended for failure to file annual reports 09/30/1982

GOLDEN SPIKE WESTN PETE LTD (AB)
Recapitalized as Oilex Industries Ltd. 09/01/1973
Each share Capital Stock no par exchanged for (0.1) share Capital Stock no par
Oilex Industries Ltd. merged into L.K. Resources Ltd. 10/04/1979 which name changed to XL Food Systems Ltd. 04/21/1986 which name changed to XL Foods Ltd. 06/15/1989 which name changed to Sevenway Capital Corp. 03/09/1999 which merged into Glacier Ventures International Corp. (Canada) (New) 04/28/2000 which name changed to Glacier Media Inc. 07/01/2008

GOLDEN SPIRIT ENTERPRISES LTD (DE)
Name changed to Terralene Fuels Corp. 11/29/2011
Terralene Fuels Corp. recapitalized as Golden Star Enterprises Ltd. 07/16/2013

GOLDEN SPIRIT GAMING LTD (DE)
Recapitalized as Golden Spirit Enterprises Ltd. 06/30/2006
Each shares Common $0.0001 par exchanged for (0.05555555) share Common $0.0001 par
Golden Spirit Enterprises Ltd. name changed to Terralene Fuels Corp. 11/29/2011 which recapitalized as Golden Star Enterprises Ltd. 07/16/2013

GOLDEN SPIRIT MINERALS LTD (DE)
Common $0.0001 par split (3) for (1) by issuance of (2) additional shares payable 10/08/2003 to holders of record 10/07/2003 Ex date - 10/09/2003
Stock Dividend - 10% payable 10/18/2004 to holders of record 09/30/2004 Ex date - 09/28/2004
Name changed to Golden Spirit Mining Ltd. 10/18/2004
Golden Spirit Mining Ltd. name changed to Golden Spirit Gaming Ltd. 07/18/2005 which recapitalized as Golden Spirit Enterprises Ltd. 06/30/2006 which name changed to Terralene Fuels Corp. 11/29/2011 which recapitalized as Golden Star Enterprises Ltd. 07/16/2013

GOLDEN SPIRIT MNG LTD (DE)
Name changed to Golden Spirit Gaming Ltd. 07/18/2005
Golden Spirit Gaming Ltd. recapitalized as Golden Spirit Enterprises Ltd. 06/30/2006 which name changed to Terralene Fuels Corp. 11/29/2011 which recapitalized as Golden Star Enterprises Ltd. 07/16/2013

GOLDEN ST BUSINESS BK (UPLAND, CA)
Under plan of reorganization each share Common no par automatically became (0.05) share Golden State Bancorp no par 11/20/2015

GOLDEN STAR RES LTD (AB)
Merged into Golden Star Resources Ltd. (Canada) 05/20/1992
Each share Common no par exchanged for (0.5) share Common no par

GOLDEN ST BANCORP INC (DE)
Each share Common $1 par received distribution of (1) Litigation Tracking Warrant payable 05/29/1998 to holders of record 05/07/1998
Ex date - 06/01/1998
8.75% Conv. Preferred Ser. A called for redemption at $26.09375 on 10/01/1998
Acquired by Citigroup Inc. 11/07/2002
Each share Common $1 par exchanged for $37.105621 cash

GOLDEN ST BANCORPORATION (CA)
Completely liquidated 02/01/1978
Each share Common Ser. 1 $2.50 par exchanged for $23 cash

GOLDEN ST BK (DOWNEY, CA)
Location changed 04/15/1974
Location changed from (Bell Gardens, CA) to (Downey, CA) 04/15/1974
Merged into Sanwa Bank of California (San Francisco, CA) 01/31/1978
Each share Capital Stock $2.50 par exchanged for $23 cash

GOLDEN ST CAP CORP (DE)
Name changed to Con-Tech Systems, Inc. 09/25/1990
(See Con-Tech Systems, Inc.)

GOLDEN STATE CO. LTD. (DE)
Merged into Foremost Dairies, Inc. (NY) 00/00/1954
Each share 4% Preferred $100 par exchanged for (1) share new 4% Preferred $100 par
Each share Common no par exchanged for (4/50) share new 4-1/2% Preferred $50 par and (1) share Common $5 par
Foremost Dairies, Inc. (NY) merged into Foremost-McKesson, Inc. 07/19/1967 which name changed to McKesson Corp. (MD) 07/27/1983 which reincorporated in Delaware 07/31/1987
(See McKesson Corp. (Old) (DE))

GOLDEN ST FOODS CORP (DE)
Common 10¢ par split (3) for (2) by issuance of (0.5) additional share 07/01/1975
Stock Dividend - 10% 01/21/1980
Merged into GSF Holdings Corp. 09/26/1980
Each share Common 10¢ par exchanged for $27.50 cash

GOLDEN ST HEALTH CTRS INC (CA)
Merged into WK Acquisition Corp. 02/11/1985
Each share Capital Stock 10¢ par exchanged for $13 cash

GOLDEN STATE MILK PRODUCTS CO.
Acquired by Golden State Co. Ltd. in 1930
Details not available

GOLDEN ST RES LTD (BC)
Name changed 04/21/1981
Name changed from Golden Star Mines Ltd. to Golden State Resources Ltd. 04/21/1981
Recapitalized as Golden Maritime Resources Ltd. 05/12/1997
Each share Common no par exchanged for (0.33333333) share Common no par
(See Golden Maritime Resources Ltd.)

GOLDEN ST VINTNERS INC (DE)
Merged into Wine Group LLC 07/14/2004
Each share Class A Common 1¢ par exchanged for $8.25 cash
Each share Class B 1¢ par exchanged for $8.25 cash

GOLDEN STD MINES LTD (BC)
Recapitalized as International Standard Resources Ltd. 02/27/1979
Each share Capital Stock no par exchanged for (0.2) share Capital Stock no par
International Standard Resources Ltd. recapitalized as First Standard Mining Ltd. 03/15/1988 which name changed to First Standard Ventures Ltd. 07/16/1993 which recapitalized as LRG Restaurant Group, Inc. 09/05/1995
(See LRG Restaurant Group, Inc.)

GOLDEN SUN CAP INC (AB)
Recapitalized as Voyageur Minerals Ltd. 03/07/2017
Each share Common no par exchanged for (0.5) share Common no par

GOLDEN SUNSET TRAIL INC (AB)
Company announced resignation of all officers and directors 02/23/2010
Details not available

GOLDEN SYS INC (CA)
Merged into Celetron International, Ltd. 7/31/2001
Each share Common no par exchanged for $0.05 cash

GOLDEN TAG RES LTD (BC)
Reincorporated under the laws of Canada 07/11/1995

GOLDEN TAN INC (NV)
Name changed to Yongye Biotechnology International, Inc. 04/29/2008
Yongye Biotechnology International, Inc. name changed to Yongye International, Inc. 07/27/2009
(See Yongye International, Inc.)

GOLDEN TECH GROUP LTD (NV)
Name changed to Mega Win Investments, Inc. 03/02/2018
Mega Win Investments, Inc. name changed to Invech Holdings, Inc. 08/07/2018

GOLDEN TECH SYS INC (BC)
Name changed 05/07/1987
Name changed from Golden Tech Resources Ltd. to Golden Tech Systems Inc. 05/07/1987
Struck off register and declared dissolved for failure to file reports 07/06/1990

GOLDEN TELECOM INC (DE)
Issue Information - 4,650,000 shares COM offered at $12 per share on 09/30/1999
Merged into VimpelCom Finance B.V. 02/29/2008
Each share Common 1¢ par exchanged for $105 cash

GOLDEN TEMPLE MNG CORP (BC)
Recapitalized as Amerigo Resources Ltd. 03/08/2002
Each share Common no par exchanged for (0.25) share Common no par

GOLDEN TER RES CORP (ON)
Delisted from Toronto Stock Exchange 03/16/1992

GOLDEN THUNDER RES LTD (BC)
Recapitalized as Consolidated Golden Thunder Resources Ltd. 12/04/2000
Each share Common no par exchanged for (0.33333333) share Common no par
Consolidated Golden Thunder Resources Ltd. name changed to GHG Resources Ltd. 05/10/2004 which name changed to Los Andes Copper Ltd. 03/29/2007

GOLDEN TIGER MNG EXPL INC (QC)
Recapitalized as Tiger Resources Inc. 06/23/1988
Each share Common no par exchanged for (0.2) share Class A Common no par
(See Tiger Resources Inc.)

GOLDEN TITAN RES LTD (BC)
Merged into Titan Pacific Resources Ltd. 12/28/1989
Each share Common no par exchanged for (0.2) share Common no par
Titan Pacific Resources Ltd. name changed to Titan Logix Corp. (BC) 06/01/2002 which reincorporated in Alberta 03/27/2013

GOLDEN TONKIN RES LTD (BC)
Struck off register and declared dissolved for failure to file returns 06/17/1994

GOLDEN TOUCH RES CORP (BC)
Recapitalized as Arian Resources Corp. 12/19/2012
Each share Common no par exchanged for (0.2) share Common no par

GOLDEN TREASURE EXPLS LTD (BC)
Recapitalized as Foundry Holdings Corp. 06/21/2001
Each share Common no par exchanged for (0.14285714) share Common no par
Foundry Holdings Corp. name changed to Yangtze Telecom Corp. 09/08/2003

GOLDEN TREND ENERGY LTD (BC)
Recapitalized as World Power Bike Inc. 01/03/1991
Each share Common no par exchanged for (0.33333333) share Common no par
World Power Bike Inc. recapitalized as Parkside 2000 Resources Corp. 03/13/2000 which name changed to Amador Gold Corp. 05/16/2003

GOLDEN TREND PETE LTD (AB)
Discharged from receivership 10/07/2005
No stockholders' equity

GOLDEN TRIANGLE INDUSTRIES, INC. (PA)
Adjudicated bankrupt in August 1964
No stockholders' equity

GOLDEN TRIANGLE INDS INC (CO)
Name changed 5/28/96
Each share old Common $0.001 par exchanged for (0.05) share new Common $0.001 par 7/26/93
Each share new Common $0.001 par exchanged for (0.4) share Common no par 8/2/95
Name changed from Golden Triangle Royalty & Oil Inc. to Golden Triangle Industries Inc. 5/28/96
Name changed to Whitemark Homes, Inc. 6/20/2001

GOLDEN TRIANGLE MNG EXPL INC (CANADA)
Recapitalized as Spectrum Gold Corp. 05/17/1989
Each share Class A Common no par exchanged for (0.125) share Class A Common no par
Spectrum Gold Corp. recapitalized as Scarlett Minerals Inc. 12/30/1991 which name changed to SMI Oil & Gas, Inc. 09/20/1994 which merged into Canadian Leader Energy Inc. 11/02/1995 which merged into Centurion Energy International Inc. 05/20/1997
(See Centurion Energy International Inc.)

GOLDEN TRIO MINERALS LTD (ON)
Recapitalized as PCS Wireless, Inc. 04/11/1994
Each share Common no par exchanged for (0.5) share Common no par
PCS Wireless, Inc. name changed to Unique Broadband Systems Inc. 06/01/1998 which recapitalized as Kure Technologies Inc. 03/20/2017

GOLDEN TRIUMPH RES LTD (BC)
Delisted from Toronto Venture Stock Exchange 06/25/2004

GOLDEN TRUMP RES LTD (BC)
Recapitalized as Golden Triumph Resources Ltd. 09/11/2002
Each share Common no par exchanged for (0.2) share Common no par
(See Golden Triumph Resources Ltd.)

GOLDEN UNICORN MNG CORP (BC)
Recapitalized as Consolidated Golden Unicorn Mining Corp. 03/29/1995
Each share Common no par exchanged for (0.2) share Common no par
Consolidated Golden Unicorn Mining Corp. recapitalized as Kirkstone Ventures Ltd. 12/09/1999 which name changed to Balaton Power Inc. 07/24/2000
(See Balaton Power Inc.)

GOLDEN UTD INVT CO (OH)
Class A $1 par reclassified as Common $1 par 10/21/1971
Name changed to Ilex Corp. 07/20/1973
Ilex Corp. name changed to Financial Industries Corp. (OH) 05/07/1976 which reincorporated in Texas 12/31/1980
(See Financial Industries Corp.)

GOLDEN VALE EXPLS CORP (BC)
Name changed to RFC Resource Finance Corp. 10/21/1987
(See RFC Resource Finance Corp.)

GOLDEN VY MICROWAVE FOODS INC (MN)
Common 1¢ par split (2) for (1) by issuance of (1) additional share 03/16/1987
Common 1¢ par split (3) for (2) by issuance of (0.5) additional share 07/27/1990
Merged into ConAgra, Inc. 07/11/1991
Each share Common 1¢ par exchanged for (0.5676) share Common $5 par
ConAgra, Inc. name changed to ConAgra Foods, Inc. 09/28/2000 which name changed to Conagra Brands, Inc. 11/10/2016

GOLDEN VALLEY MINES LTD. (ON)
Charter revoked for failure to file reports and pay taxes 00/00/1956

GOLDEN VY MINES N L (AUSTRALIA)
Name changed to GVM Metals Ltd. 06/06/2006
GVM Metals Ltd. name changed to Coal of Africa Ltd. 12/04/2007
(See Coal of Africa Ltd.)

GOLDEN VIKING INDS INC (DE)
Proclaimed inoperative and void for non-payment of taxes 4/15/72

GOLDEN VIRTUE RES INC (BC)
Each share old Common no par exchanged for (0.2) share new Common no par 06/06/2014
Name changed to Moseda Technologies, Inc. 04/23/2015
Moseda Technologies, Inc. name changed to Reliq Health Technologies Inc. 05/10/2016

GOLDEN WEST AIRLS INC (CA)
Name changed to Old GWAL, Inc. 6/12/77
(See Old GWAL, Inc.)

GOLDEN WEST BREWING CO INC (DE)
Name changed to Athena Silver Corp. 02/05/2010

GOLDEN WEST CAP INC (CO)
Name changed to Consignee of America, Inc. 03/15/1989
(See Consignee of America, Inc.)

GOLDEN WEST FINL CORP (CA)
6% Preferred $100 par called for redemption 04/26/1971
Common 50¢ par changed to 10¢ par 05/06/1972
Under plan of merger reincorporated under the laws of Delaware and Common 10¢ par changed to $1 par 10/31/1975
Golden West Financial Corp. (DE) merged into Wachovia Corp. (Ctfs. dated after 09/01/2001) 10/02/2006 which merged into Wells Fargo & Co. (New) 12/31/2008

GOLDEN WEST FINL CORP (DE)
Conv. Preferred Ser. A no par called for redemption 10/06/1978
Common $1 par split (2) for (1) by issuance of (1) additional share 11/20/1978
Common $1 par split (3) for (2) by issuance of (0.5) additional share 12/10/1980
Common $1 par changed to 10¢ par 06/01/1981
Common 10¢ par split (3) for (2) by issuance of (0.5) additional share 12/10/1985
Common 10¢ par split (2) for (1) by issuance of (1) additional share 09/08/1989
Common 10¢ par split (3) for (1) by issuance of (2) additional shares payable 12/10/1999 to holders of record 11/15/1999 Ex date - 12/13/1999
Common 10¢ par split (2) for (1) by issuance of (1) additional share payable 12/10/2004 to holders of record 11/15/2004 Ex date - 12/13/2004
Merged into Wachovia Corp. (Ctfs. dated after 09/01/2001) 10/02/2006
Each share Common 10¢ par exchanged for (1.051) shares Common $3.33-1/3 par and $18.6461 cash
Wachovia Corp. (Ctfs. dated after 09/01/2001) merged into Wells Fargo & Co. (New) 12/31/2008

GOLDEN WEST HOMES (CA)
Common no par split (3) for (2) by issuance of (0.5) additional share 2/22/78
Common no par split (3) for (2) by issuance of (0.5) additional share 7/31/81
Merged into Golden Acquisition Corp. 4/23/86
Each share Common no par exchanged for $5 cash

GOLDEN WEST MARKETS, INC. (UT)
Charter suspended for non-payment of corporate taxes 10/14/63

GOLDEN WEST MINES LTD.
Assets acquired by Century Mining Corp. Ltd. 00/00/1946
Details not available

GOLDEN WEST MINES LTD (BC)
Name changed to Golden West Resources Ltd. 07/23/1969
Golden West Resources Ltd. recapitalized as Sachem Exploration Ltd. 03/02/1973 which recapitalized as Brower Exploration Inc. (BC) 08/10/1984 which reincorporated in Wyoming 12/29/1993 which reorganized in Massachusetts as Stocker & Yale, Inc. (New) 05/11/1994 which name changed to StockerYale, Inc. 07/03/2000 which name changed to ProPhotonix Ltd. 07/23/2010

GOLDEN WEST MOBILE HOMES INC (CA)
Common no par split (5) for (4) by issuance of (0.25) additional share 11/14/69
Name changed to Golden West Homes 9/28/77
(See Golden West Homes)

GOLDEN WEST RES LTD (BC)
Recapitalized as Sachem Exploration Ltd. 03/02/1973
Each share Capital Stock no par exchanged for (0.25) share Capital Stock no par
Sachem Exploration Ltd. recapitalized as Brower Exploration Inc. (BC) 08/10/1984 which reincorporated in Wyoming 12/29/1993 which reorganized in Massachusetts as Stocker & Yale, Inc. (New) 05/11/1994 which name changed to StockerYale, Inc. 07/03/2000 which name changed to ProPhotonix Ltd. 07/23/2010

GOLDEN WEST TELEPHONE CO. (CA)
Completely liquidated 8/27/71
Each share 5% Preference $25 par, 5-1/2% Preference $25 par or 6% Preference $25 par exchanged for (1.25) shares Continental Telephone Co. of California 6% Preferred Ser. F $20 par
Each share Common $1 par exchanged for (0.25) share Common $5 par
5-1/8% Preferred $100 par called for redemption 11/3/71
Continental Telephone Co. of California name changed to Contel of California, Inc. 2/19/88
(See Contel of California, Inc.)

GOLDEN WEST TRAILERS INC (CA)
Name changed to Golden West Mobile Homes, Inc. 10/31/69
Golden West Mobile Homes, Inc. name changed to Golden West Homes 9/28/77
(See Golden West Homes)

GOLDEN WINNER RES LTD (ON)
Merged into Castlestar Capital Developments Corp. 03/30/1990
Each share Common no par exchanged for (0.97) share Common no par
Castlestar Capital Developments Corp. recapitalized as Southern Frontier Resources Inc. 11/11/1993
(See Southern Frontier Resources Inc.)

GOLDEN ZONE DEVS LTD (BC)
Reorganized under the laws of Washington as Golden Zone Resources, Inc. 7/1/88
Each share Common no par exchanged for (1) share Common no par

GOLDEN ZONE MINE, INC. (AK)
Charter revoked for failure to file reports and pay fees 1/2/62

GOLDENBANKS COLO INC (DE)
Merged into Norwest Corp. 05/01/1995
Each share Common $1 par exchanged for (1.9876) shares Common $1-2/3 par
Norwest Corp. name changed to Wells Fargo & Co. (New) 11/02/1998

GOLDENBELL RES INC (BC)
Merged into ABM Gold Corp. 03/08/1989
Each share Common no par exchanged for (1/3) share Class A Common no par
ABM Gold Corp. reorganized as NorthWest Gold Corp. 06/01/1990 which merged into Northgate Exploration Ltd. (ON) 06/08/1993 which reincorporated in British Columbia 07/01/2001 which name changed to Northgate Minerals Corp. 05/20/2004 which merged into AuRico Gold Inc. 10/26/2011

GOLDENBERG CO. (MD)
Charter forfeited for failure to file reports and pay fees 10/31/56

GOLDENGOALS COM VENTURES INC (BC)
Recapitalized as General Strategies Ltd. 04/27/2001
Each share Common no par exchanged for (0.1) share Common no par
General Strategies Ltd. reorganized as Landdrill International Inc. 03/14/2006
(See Landdrill International Inc.)

GOLDENLODE RES LTD (BC)
Name changed to Abbey Woods Developments Ltd. 05/11/1987
(See Abbey Woods Developments Ltd.)

GOLDENROD RES & TECHNOLOGY INC (BC)
Recapitalized as Astic Ventures Inc. 03/05/1990
Each share Common no par exchanged for (0.2) share Common no par
(See Astic Ventures Inc.)

GOLDENWEST MINING CORP. (DE)
No longer in existence having become inoperative and void for non-payment of taxes 04/01/1945

GOLDERA RES INC (BC)
Struck off register and declared dissolved for failure to file returns 06/01/1990

GOLDEX INC (WA)
Charter cancelled and proclaimed dissolved for failure to pay taxes 02/10/1986

GOLDEX MINES LTD (ON)
Merged into Agnico-Eagle Mines Ltd. 12/08/1993
Each share Common no par exchanged for (0.36) share Common no par
Agnico-Eagle Mines Ltd. name changed to Agnico Eagle Mines Ltd. 04/30/2013

GOLDEX RES INC (BC)
Recapitalized as Goldmax Resources Inc. (BC) 05/10/1993
Each share Common no par exchanged for (0.4) share Common no par
Goldmax Resources Inc. (BC) reincorporated in Yukon 08/29/1996 which name changed to Aegean Gold Inc. 04/26/1999 which recapitalized as Aegean International Gold Inc. 12/09/1999 which recapitalized as MinRes Resources Inc. 10/20/2003 which name changed to Geoinformatics Exploration Inc. 02/11/2005 which recapitalized as Kiska Metals Corp. 08/05/2009 which merged into AuRico Metals Inc. 03/14/2017
(See AuRico Metals Inc.)

GOLDEYE EXPLORATIONS LTD (ON)
Each share old Common no par exchanged for (0.1) share new Common no par 07/20/2012
Merged into Treasury Metals Inc. 11/28/2016
Each share new Common no par exchanged for (0.1) share Common no par
Note: Unexchanged certificates will be cancelled and become without value 11/28/2022

GOLDEYE USA INC (NV)
Recapitalized as Sierra Diamond International, Inc. 02/10/2004
Each share Common $0.001 par exchanged for (0.005) share Common $0.001 par
Sierra Diamond International, Inc. recapitalized as ITOS, Inc. 04/12/2004 which recapitalized as Satellite Phone Source Inc. (NV) 08/10/2004 which reincorporated in Delaware as Vision Works Media Group, Inc. 04/06/2005 which name changed to Perihelion Global, Inc. (DE) 10/25/2006 which reincorporated in Nevada 04/01/2008 which recapitalized as Nymet Holdings Inc. 04/21/2009

GOLDFARB CORP (ON)
8% Conv. Preferred no par called for redemption 10/01/1993
Each (1,597,578) shares old Class A Subordinate no par exchanged for (1) share new Class A Subordinate no par 07/14/2011
Note: In effect holders received $3.02 cash per share and public interest was eliminated

GOLDFEVER RES LTD (BC)
Struck off register and declared dissolved for failure to file returns 07/31/1992

GOLDFIELD CONSOLIDATED MINES CO. (WY)
Capital Stock $10 par changed to $1 par in 1933
Under plan of merger name changed to Goldfield Corp. (Wyo.) 3/15/63
Goldfield Corp. (Wyo.) reincorporated under the laws of Delaware 8/30/68

GOLDFIELD CORP (WY)
Reincorporated under the laws of Delaware and Capital Stock $1 par reclassified as Common $1 par 8/30/68

GOLDFIELD DEEP MINES CO NEV (NV)
Each share old Capital Stock 5¢ par exchanged for (0.2) share new Capital Stock 5¢ par 5/1/75
Each share new Capital Stock 5¢ par exchanged for (0.05) share Common $2 par 12/31/79
Stock Dividends - Preferred - 10% 5/15/76
Common - 20% 5/15/75; 25% 5/15/76; 10% 6/1/77
Placed in receivership 4/22/83
No stockholders' equity

GOLDFIELD DEVELOPMENT CO. (NV)
Recapitalized as Franklin Properties, Inc. 5/1/70
Each share Capital Stock 5¢ par exchanged for (0.05) share Capital Stock 1¢ par
(See Franklin Properties, Inc.)

GOLDFIELD ENGINEERING ASSOCIATES (NV)
Charter revoked for failure to file reports and pay fees 3/6/61

GOLDFIELD GREAT BEND, LTD. (NV)
Name changed to Siskon Corp. (NV) in 1952
Siskon Corp. (NV) recapitalized under the laws of Delaware 10/1/69
(See Siskon Corp. (DE))

GOLDFIELD JUPITER MINING CO. (WY)
Charter revoked for failure to file reports and pay fees 7/19/27

GOLDFIELD RAND MINES CO. OF NEVADA (NV)
Completely liquidated 11/27/59
Each share Capital Stock $1 par exchanged for (1) share Trans-Union Oil & Mining Co. Capital Stock 50¢ par
Trans-Union Oil & Mining Co. name changed to Water Wonderland Corp. 12/15/60 which name changed to Progressive National Industries, Inc. 8/17/72
(See Progressive National Industries, Inc.)

GOLDFIELDS MINING CORP. LTD. (SK)
Completely liquidated 01/04/1965
Each share Capital Stock $1 par exchanged for (1/3) share Copperfields Mining Corp. Ltd. Common $1 par
Copperfields Mining Corp. Ltd. name changed to Copperfields Mining Corp. (ONT) 04/04/1974 which reincorporated in Canada 08/31/1983 which merged into Teck Corp. 09/02/1983 which name changed to Teck Cominco Ltd. 09/12/2001 which name changed to Teck Resources Ltd. 04/27/2009

GOLDFIELDS URANIUM MINES LTD. (SK)
Capital Stock no par changed to $1 par 00/00/1953
Name changed to Goldfields Mining Corp. Ltd. 09/28/1959
Goldfields Mining Corp. Ltd. liquidated for Copperfields Mining Corp. Ltd. 01/04/1965 which name changed to Copperfields Mining Corp. (ONT) 04/04/1974 which reincorporated in Canada 08/31/1983 which merged into Teck Corp. 09/02/1983 which name changed to Teck Cominco Ltd. 09/12/2001 which name changed to Teck Resources Ltd. 04/27/2009

GOLDFINCH MINES LTD. (QC)
Charter surrendered 6/2/52
No stockholders' equity

GOLDFISH INDS INC (NV)
Name changed to Nutri Berry Industries, Inc. 6/30/2002
(See Nutri Berry Industries, Inc.)

GOLDFUND LTD (CANADA)
Mutual Fund Shares 50¢ par split (3) for (1) by issuance of (2) additional shares 07/10/1980
Voluntarily dissolved 02/28/2003
Details not available

GOLDGROUP MNG INC (QC)
Reincorporated under the laws of British Columbia 07/28/2011

GOLDHAVEN RES LTD (BC)
Reorganized as International Vending Technology Corp. 6/7/85
Each share Common no par exchanged for (4) shares Common no par
International Vending Technology Corp. recapitalized as Universal Movie Butler Inc. 11/12/85 which name changed to Pacific Vending Technology Ltd. 4/15/86 which name changed to Nelson Vending Technology Inc. (BC) 7/10/87 which reincorporated in Canada 7/23/87 which was acquired by Cinram Ltd. 7/31/93 which name changed to Cinram International Inc. 6/12/97 which reorganized as Cinram International Income Fund 5/8/2006

GOLDHAWK PORCUPINE MINES LTD.
Recapitalized as Greyhawk Uranium Mines Ltd. 11/23/1955
Each share Capital Stock exchanged for (0.5) share Capital Stock
(See Greyhawk Uranium Mines Ltd.)

GOLDHILL INDS INC (BC)
Name changed 07/05/1995
Name changed from Goldhill Resource Inc. to Goldhill Industries Inc. 07/05/1995
Acquired by S.G.M. Co. Ltd. 04/23/2001
Each share Common no par exchanged for $0.60 cash

GOLDHUNTER EXPLS INC (ON)
Recapitalized as Tribute Minerals Corp. 01/16/2002
Each share Common no par exchanged for (0.5) share Common no par
Tribute Minerals Corp. recapitalized as AurCrest Gold Inc. 12/03/2010

GOLDHURST RES INC (CANADA)
Reincorporated 12/15/1988
Place of incorporation changed from (BC) to (Canada) 12/15/1988
Merged into Societe d'Exploration Miniere Vior Inc. 08/01/1995
Each share Common no par exchanged for (0.5) share Common no par

GOLDIE ENTERPRISES INC (BC)
Name changed to MagiCorp Entertainment Inc. (BC) 5/3/2001
MagiCorp Entertainment Inc. (BC) reincorporated in Ontario 7/4/2001 which recapitalized as Lucid Entertainment Inc. 7/5/2004

GOLDKING RES INC (NV)
Name changed to Billserv.com, Inc. 12/3/98
Billserv.com, Inc. name changed to Billserv, Inc. 5/24/2001 which name changed to Payment Data Systems, Inc. 8/6/2003

GOLDKNIFE MINES, LTD. (ON)
Charter revoked for failure to file reports and pay taxes 11/27/1961

GOLDLAND HLDGS CO (DE)
Each share old Common $0.0001 par exchanged for (0.1) share new Common $0.0001 par 03/06/2014
Name changed to Bravo Multinational Inc. 04/07/2016

GOLDLEAF FINL SOLUTIONS INC (TN)
Each share old Common no par exchanged for (0.2) share new Common no par 09/08/2006
Merged into Henry (Jack) & Associates, Inc. 10/01/2009
Each share new Common no par exchanged for $0.98 cash

GOLDLINX INTL INC (ON)
Discharged from bankruptcy 01/20/2000
Company is privately held

GOLDLIST PPTYS INC (ON)
Acquired by Acktion Corp. 02/01/2002
Each share Common no par exchanged for $7.25 principal amount of 6% Sr. Notes due 02/01/2006 and $7.25 cash

GOLDLUND MINES LTD (ON)
Merged into Camreco Inc. 12/31/1986
Each share Capital Stock no par exchanged for (0.1) share Capital Stock no par
Camreco Inc. merged into Environmental Technologies International Inc. 11/29/1991 which recapitalized as Eco Technologies International Inc. 04/24/1998
(See Eco Technologies International Inc.)

GOLDMAN SACHS EQUITY PORTFOLIOS INC (MD)
Charter forfeited 10/07/1999

GOLDMAN SACHS GROUP INC (DE)
5.95% Depositary Preferred Ser. I called for redemption at $25 plus $0.028924 accrued dividends on 11/17/2017
(Additional Information in Active)

GOLDMAN SACHS TRADING CORP.
Name changed to Pacific Eastern Corp. in 1933 which merged into Atlas Corp. 10/1/36

GOLDMAN SACHS U S INCOME BLDR TR (ON)
Under plan of merger each Class A and Class U Unit automatically became (0.937273) or (0.926707) Symphony Floating Rate Senior Loan Fund Class A or Class U Unit respectively 02/08/2018

GOLDMAQUE MINES LTD. (ON)
Charter revoked for failure to file reports and pay fees 12/01/1966

GOLDMARCA LTD (BERMUDA)
Name changed to Ecometals Ltd. 10/25/2007

GOLDMARK MINERALS LTD (AB)
Merged into Tuscany Energy Ltd. (Old) 10/07/2009
Each share Common no par exchanged for (0.6) share Common no par
Tuscany Energy Ltd. (Old) reorganized as Tuscany Energy Ltd. (New) 07/19/2013
(See Tuscany Energy Ltd. (New))

GOLDMAX RES INC (YT)
Reincorporated 08/29/1996
Place of incorporation changed from (BC) to (YT) 08/29/1996
Name changed to Aegean Gold Inc. 04/26/1999
Aegean Gold Inc. recapitalized as Aegean International Gold Inc. 12/09/1999 which recapitalized as MinRes Resources Inc. 10/20/2003 which name changed to Geoinformatics Exploration Inc. 02/11/2005 which recapitalized as Kiska Metals Corp. 08/05/2009 which merged into AuRico Metals Inc. 03/14/2017
(See AuRico Metals Inc.)

GOLDMEMBER MINERALS INC (BC)
Name changed to GMV Minerals Inc. 03/13/2008

GOLDMINCO CONSOLIDATED MNG CORP (CANADA)
Recapitalized 12/22/1997
Recapitalized from Goldminco Mining Corp. to Goldminco Consolidated Mining Corp. 12/22/1997
Each share Common no par exchanged for (0.25) share Common no par
Recapitalized as Goldminco Corp. 04/06/2000
Each share Common no par exchanged for (0.25) share Common no par
(See Goldminco Corp.)

GOLDMINCO CORP (CANADA)
Acquired by Straits Resources Ltd. 08/05/2011
Each share Common no par exchanged for $0.10 cash

GOLDMINT EXPS LTD (ON)
Name changed to AXcension Capital Corp. (ONT) 11/06/1998
AXcension Capital Corp. (ONT) reorganized in Bermuda as Caspian Oil Tools Ltd. 08/30/1999
(See Caspian Oil Tools Ltd.)

GOLDMOUNTAIN EXPL CORP (NV)
SEC revoked common stock registration 04/02/2013

GOLDOME (BUFFALO, NY)
Placed in receivership and declared insolvent 5/31/91

GOLDOME FLA FDG CORP (DE)
Dutch Auction Rate Transferable Securities Preferred called for redemption 5/9/90

GOLDOME FLA FDG CORP II (DE)
Dutch Auction Rate Transferable Securities Preferred $1 par called for redemption 5/29/90
Public interest eliminated

GOLDOME NATL CORP (DE)
$2.50 Preferred called for redemption 1/30/85
Public interest eliminated

GOLDOME NEW YORK CAP CORP II (DE)
Exchangeable Auction Preferred Ser. A $1 par called for redemption 5/16/90
Exchangeable Auction Preferred Ser. B $1 par called for redemption 6/6/90
Public interest eliminated

GOLDONLINE INTL INC (DE)
Each share old Common $0.001 par exchanged for (1/6) share new Common $0.001 par 9/3/99
Name changed to SGD Holdings, Ltd. 2/5/2001

GOLDORA MINES LTD. (ON)
Recapitalized as Burchell Lake Mines Ltd. 00/00/1956
Each share Common exchanged for (0.2) share Common
(See Burchell Lake Mines Ltd.)

GOLDPAC INVTS LTD (CANADA)
Reincorporated 07/27/1988
Place of incorporation changed from (BC) to (Canada) 07/27/1988
Recapitalized as Brimstone Gold Corp. 05/19/1994
Each share Common no par exchanged for (0.2) share Common no par
Brimstone Gold Corp. recapitalized as Foxpoint Resources Ltd. 10/21/1999 which name changed to Kirkland Lake Gold Inc. 11/18/2002 which merged into Kirkland Lake Gold Ltd. 12/06/2016

GOLDPARK CHINA LTD (YT)
Name changed 09/28/1994
Reincorporated 12/28/1999
Name changed from Goldpark Mines & Investments Ltd. to Goldpark China Ltd. 09/28/1994
Each share old Common no par exchanged for (0.5) share new Common no par 08/13/1999
Place of incorporation changed from (ON) to (YT) 12/28/1999
Reincorporated under the laws of British Columbia as Bankers Petroleum Ltd. (BC) 06/25/2004
Bankers Petroleum Ltd. (BC) reincorporated in Alberta 03/07/2014
(See Bankers Petroleum Ltd.)

GOLDPLATE HLDGS ENTERPRISES INC (NV)
Recapitalized as Eagletech Communications, Inc. 03/17/1999
Each share Common $0.001 par exchanged for (0.33333333) share Common $0.001 par
(See Eagletech Communications, Inc.)

GOLDPLEX DEV CORP (CANADA)
Involuntarily dissolved for failure to file annual returns 03/03/2003

GOLDPOINT RES INC (NV)
Reincorporated under the laws of Delaware as Island Breeze International, Inc. and Common $0.001 par reclassified as Class A Common $0.001 par 12/14/2009
(See Island Breeze International, Inc.)

GOLDPOST RES INC (ON)
Merged into Antares Mining & Exploration Corp. 09/08/1993
Each share Common no par exchanged for (0.07142857) share Common no par
Antares Mining & Exploration Corp. name changed to Caussa Capital Corp. 09/03/1999 which recapitalized as Rainbow Gold Ltd. 01/20/2003 which recapitalized as Jaguar Mining Inc. 10/16/2003

GOLDQUEST EXPL INC (ON)
Merged into Goldcorp Inc. 03/31/1994
Each share Common no par exchanged for (0.05) share Class A Subordinate no par

GOLDQUEST EXPLORATIONS CORP. (ON)
Merged into Goldquest Exploration Inc. 08/09/1982
Each share Capital Stock no par exchanged for (0.79365079) share Common no par
Goldquest Exploration Inc. merged into Goldcorp Inc. (New) 03/31/1994

GOLDRANGE RES INC (NV)
Each share old Common $0.001 par exchanged for (4) shares new Common $0.001 par 11/30/2006
Name changed to ReoStar Energy Corp. 2/12/2007

GOLDRAY INC (AB)
Delisted from Toronto Venture Stock Exchange 06/25/2004

GOLDRAY MINES LTD (ON)
Capital Stock $1 par changed to no par 09/29/1971
Merged into Canray Resources Ltd. 12/21/1976
Each share Capital Stock no par exchanged for (0.5) share Common no par
Canray Resources Ltd. recapitalized as Exall Resources Ltd. 12/09/1983 which merged into Gold Eagle Mines Ltd. 12/27/2006 which was acquired by Goldcorp Inc. 09/25/2008

GOLDRICH RES INC (BC)
Delisted from Vancouver Stock Exchange 03/01/1989

GOLDRICH YELLOWKNIFE MINES, LTD. (ON)
Charter revoked for failure to file reports and pay taxes 04/00/1958

GOLDRIM MNG LTD (ON)
Charter cancelled and declared dissolved for failure to file returns and pay fees 07/27/1976

GOLDRITE MNG CORP (CANADA)
Recapitalized as Consolidated Goldrite Mining Corp. (Canada) 07/28/1993
Each share Common no par exchanged for (0.2) share Common no par
Consolidated Goldrite Mining Corp. (Canada) reincorporated in Cayman Islands as Bestar International Group Ltd. 04/30/1996
(See Bestar International Group Ltd.)

GOLDROCK MINES CORP (BC)
Merged into Fortuna Silver Mines Inc. 07/28/2016
Each share Common no par exchanged for (0.1331) share Common no par

GOLDRUSH CASINO & MNG CORP (BC)
Name changed 09/10/1992
Name changed from Goldrush Mining Corp. to Goldrush Casino & Mining Corp. 09/10/1992
Name changed to Phoenix Leisure Corp. 07/08/1998
(See Phoenix Leisure Corp.)

GOLDRUSH RES LTD (BC)
Reincorporated 08/10/2006
Place of incorporation changed from (YT) to (BC) 08/10/2006
Merged into First Mining Finance Corp. 01/11/2016
Each share Common no par exchanged for (0.0714) share Common no par
Note: Unexchanged certificates will be cancelled and become without value 01/11/2022
First Mining Finance Corp. name changed to First Mining Gold Corp. 01/11/2018

GOLDSAT MNG INC (CANADA)
Each share old Common no par exchanged for (0.1) share new Common no par 03/22/2005
Name changed to GobiMin Inc. 10/12/2005

GOLDSBOROUGH (F.V.) DISTILLING CORP.
Out of business 00/00/1953
Details not available

GOLDSEARCH CORP (NV)
Recapitalized as KINeSYS Pharmaceuticals, Inc. 04/06/1999
Each share Common $0.00001 par exchanged for (0.04) share Common $0.00001 par
KINeSYS Pharmaceuticals, Inc. recapitalized as Database Solutions Ltd. 03/31/2003 which recapitalized as Blue Data Group, Inc. 10/17/2007 which name changed to Expert Group, Inc. 11/07/2007 which name changed to American Premium Water Corp. 12/19/2013

GOLDSEARCH INC (ON)
Name changed to CSA Minerals Corp. (ON) 05/09/1985
Each share Common no par exchanged for (1) share Common no par
CSA Minerals Corp. (ON) reorganized in Canada as Consolidated CSA Minerals Inc. 01/23/1986 which name changed to Pamorex Minerals Inc. 04/16/1987 which merged into Royal Oak Mines Inc. 07/23/1991 which recapitalized as Royal Oak Ventures Inc. 02/14/2000
(See Royal Oak Ventures Inc.)

GOLDSEARCH LTD. (ON)
Name changed to Goldsearch Inc. 10/13/1981
Goldsearch Inc. name changed to CSA Minerals Corp. (ONT) 05/09/1985 which reorganized in Canada as Consolidated CSA Minerals Inc. 01/23/1986 which name changed to Pamorex Minerals Inc. 04/16/1987 which merged into Royal Oak Mines Inc. 07/23/1991 which recapitalized as Royal Oak Ventures Inc. 02/14/2000
(See Royal Oak Ventures Inc.)

GOLDSEC EXPLS LTD (ON)
Merged into Consolidated Goldsec Explorations Ltd. 12/05/1980
Each share Common no par exchanged for (0.06666666) share Common no par
(See Consolidated Goldsec Explorations Ltd.)

GOLDSHORE HLDGS P L C (UNITED KINGDOM)
Company wound up 04/06/2006
No ADR holders' equity

GOLDSIDE MINING CO. LTD. (ON)
Charter cancelled 00/00/1949

GOLDSIL MNG & MLG INC (CO)
Merged into Cumberland Resources, Inc. 7/30/87
Each share Common 1¢ par exchanged for (0.5) share Common no par
Note: Additional shares may be issued pending certain performance and liquidity requirements

GOLDSIL RES LTD (BC)
Common no par split (2) for (1) by issuance of (1) additional share 12/31/1985
Merged into International Mahogany Corp. 12/10/1990
Each share Common no par exchanged for (0.22) share Class B Subordinate no par
International Mahogany Corp. recapitalized as Reliant Ventures Ltd. 06/06/2000 which name changed to Esperanza Silver Corp. 05/14/2003 which name changed to Esperanza Resources Corp. 07/19/2010

GOLDSMITH BROS (NY)
Stock Dividend - 25% 07/17/1969
Adjudicated bankrupt 04/30/1976
Stockholders' equity unlikely

GOLDSMITH MINERALS LTD (BC)
Recapitalized as Unitec International Controls Corp. 11/09/1993
Each share Common no par exchanged for (0.5) share Common no par
(See Unitec International Controls Corp.)

GOLDSOURCE MINES INC (YUKON)
Reincorporated under the laws of British Columbia 08/03/2005

GOLDSPAN RES INC (NV)
Common $0.001 par split (6.3552) for (1) by issuance of (5.3552) additional shares payable 12/08/2009 to holders of record 12/08/2009
Recapitalized as Walker Lane Exploration, Inc. 10/31/2014
Each share Common $0.001 par exchanged for (0.04) share Common $0.001 par

GOLDSPIKE EXPL INC (ON)
Name changed to Nevada Zinc Corp. 03/06/2015

GOLDSPRING INC (NV)
Reincorporated 11/12/2008
State of incorporation changed from (FL) to (NV) 11/12/2008
Each share old Common $0.000666 par exchanged for (0.005) share new Common $0.000666 par 06/07/2010
Name changed to Comstock Mining Inc. 07/21/2010

GOLDSTACK RES LTD (BC)
Recapitalized as Consolidated Goldstack International Resources Inc. 07/13/1994
Each share Common no par exchanged for (0.2) share Common no par
Consolidated Goldstack International Resources Inc. name changed to Zim-Gold Resources Ltd. 06/30/1995 which name changed to Noise Media Inc. 02/05/2001 which recapitalized as GFK Resources Inc. (BC) 01/17/2008 which reincorporated in Canada 07/13/2012 which name changed to Opus One Resources Inc. 07/31/2017

GOLDSTAR ENTMT MEDIA INC (DE)
Charter cancelled and declared inoperative and void for non-payment of taxes 03/01/1999

GOLDSTAR EXPLORATIONS & INVESTMENTS LTD. (ON)
Charter cancelled for failure to pay taxes and file returns 02/20/1980

GOLDSTAR EXPLORATIONS LTD. (ON)
Name changed to Goldstar Explorations & Investments Ltd. 08/15/1966
(See Goldstar Explorations & Investments Ltd.)

GOLDSTAR VIDEO CORP (UT)
Proclaimed dissolved for failure to file reports 7/1/94

GOLDSTATE CORP (NV)
Each share old Common $0.001 par exchanged for (0.1) share new Common $0.001 par 02/13/2001
Each share new Common $0.001 par exchanged for (0.06666666) share Common $0.001 par 04/24/2003
SEC revoked common stock registration 09/14/2011

GOLDSTONE EXPL LTD (BC)
Recapitalized as INX InSearch Group of Companies Ltd. 10/06/1986
Each share Common no par exchanged for (2.5) shares Common no par
INX Insearch Group of Companies Ltd. recapitalized as Nova Marketing Ltd. 05/02/1988 which recapitalized as National Nova Marketing Inc. 07/24/1992
(See National Nova Marketing Inc.)

GOLDSTONE MINERALS RESOURCE CORP (NV)
Recapitalized as Pacific Petroleums Ltd. 9/28/90
Each share Common 1¢ par exchanged for (0.1) share Common 1¢ par

GOLDSTONE MNG CO (WA)
Name changed to Fire Mountain Beverage Co. and Common 15¢ par changed to $0.0001 par 09/24/2004
Fire Mountain Beverage Co. name changed to FG Fitness & Media Group, Inc. 12/05/2014

GOLDSTONE RES INC (ON)
Merged into Premier Gold Mines Ltd. 08/16/2011
Each share Common no par exchanged for (0.16) share Common no par and $0.0001 cash
Note: Unexchanged certificates will be cancelled and become without value 08/16/2017

GOLDSTRIKE INC (NV)
Common $0.001 par split (3.91304) for (1) by issuance of (2.91304) additional shares payable 09/09/2005 to holders of record 09/09/2005 Ex date - 09/12/2005
Name changed to Gran Tierra Energy Inc. (NV) 11/10/2005
Gran Tierra Energy Inc. (NV) reincorporated in Delaware 10/31/2016

GOLDTECH CORP (NY)
Dissolved by proclamation 9/23/98

GOLDTECH MNG CORP (NV)
Recapitalized as China Industrial Waste Management, Inc. 5/15/2006
Each share Common 5¢ par exchanged for (0.01) share Common 5¢ par

GOLDTECK MINES LTD (ON)
Name changed to Goldpark Mines & Investments Ltd. 08/28/1992
Goldpark Mines & Investments Ltd. name changed to Goldpark China Ltd. (ON) 09/28/1994 which reincorporated in Yukon 12/28/1999 which reorganized in British Columbia as Bankers Petroleum Ltd. 06/25/2004 which reincorporated in Alberta 03/07/2014
(See Bankers Petroleum Ltd.)

GOLDTEX INC (DE)
Merged into Tomen America Inc. 7/8/93
Each share Common 10¢ par exchanged for $6.75 cash

GOLDTEX RES LTD (AB)
Common no par split (5) for (1) by issuance of (4) additional shares payable 04/24/1997 to holders of record 04/23/1997
Under plan of merger name changed to Cantex Mine Development Corp. 04/09/1998

GOLDTOWN INVTS CORP (NV)
Common $0.0001 par split (14) for (1) by issuance of (13) additional shares payable 09/20/2007 to holders of record 09/20/2007
Name changed to Global Health Ventures Inc. 10/24/2008
Global Health Ventures Inc. recapitalized as Kedem Pharmaceuticals Inc. 11/07/2011
(See Kedem Pharmaceuticals Inc.)

GOLDTRAIN RES INC (CANADA)
Each share old Common no par exchanged for (0.05) share new Common no par 05/12/2016
Recapitalized as Idaho Champion Gold Mines Canada Inc. 09/27/2018
Each share new Common no par exchanged for (0.33333333) share Common no par

GOLDUST MINES LTD (AB)
Name changed to Huntington Exploration Inc. 08/19/1997

GOLDVALE RES INC (DE)
Common $0.001 par split (2) for (1) by issuance of (1) additional share payable 11/26/2008 to holders of record 11/26/2008 Ex date - 11/28/2008
Name changed to NXT Nutritionals Holdings, Inc. 01/08/2009

GOLDVUE MINES LTD.
Recapitalized as New Goldvue Mines Ltd. 00/00/1949
Each share Capital Stock $1 par exchanged for (0.25) share Capital Stock $1 par
New Goldvue Mines Ltd. recapitalized as Lava Cap Resources Ltd. 04/06/1979 which name changed to Lava Capital Corp. 11/14/1985 which recapitalized as Samoth Capital Corp. 02/17/1988 which name changed to Sterling Financial Corp. 06/14/2000 which name changed to Sterling Centrecorp Inc. 06/08/2001
(See Sterling Centrecorp Inc.)

GOLDWATER RES LTD (BC)
Name changed to First Goldwater Resources Inc. 12/24/1999
First Goldwater Resources Inc. name changed to Baja Mining Corp. 07/20/2004 which recapitalized as Camrova Resources Inc. 10/17/2016

GOLDWAYS RES INC (BC)
Common no par split (4) for (1) by issuance of (3) additional shares 06/27/1989
Name changed to Inter-Citic Envirotec Inc. 10/01/1993
Inter-Citic Envirotec Inc. name changed to Inter-Citic Mineral Technologies Inc. 10/04/1999 which name changed to Intic-Citic Minerals Inc. 12/19/2003
(See Intic-Citic Minerals Inc.)

GOLDWEST RES LTD (BC)
Recapitalized as Consolidated Goldwest Resources Ltd. 3/3/88
Each share Common no par exchanged for (0.4) share Common no par
Consolidated Goldwest Resources Ltd. recapitalized as Tenby Developments Ltd. 8/6/92 which name changed to Porcher Island Gold Corp. 10/18/96 which recapitalized as Tetra Metals Ltd. 1/8/99 which recapitalized as Palladon Ventures Ltd. 11/2/2000

GOLDWIN EXPLORATION, LTD. (ON)
Merged into Cessland Corp. Ltd. 03/15/1962
Each share Capital Stock $1 par exchanged for (0.54) share Capital Stock no par
(See Cessland Corp. Ltd.)

GOLDWINN RES LTD (BC)
Struck off register and declared dissolved for failure to file returns 07/27/1990

GOLDWYN SAMUEL CO (DE)
Each share Common 1¢ par exchanged for (0.2) share Common 5¢ par 09/16/1992
Each share Common 5¢ par exchanged for (0.25) share Common 20¢ par 05/25/1993
Merged into Metromedia International Group, Inc. 07/02/1996
Each share Common 20¢ par exchanged for (0.3335) share Common $1 par
(See Metromedia International Group, Inc.)

GOLDYKE MINES LTD (ON)
Charter cancelled for failure to pay taxes and file returns 03/16/1976

GOLDYNAMICS (UT)
Name changed to Nugget Gold Mines, Inc. 10/25/1979
(See Nugget Gold Mines, Inc.)

GOLDZONE EXPL INC (BC)
Recapitalized as EnerGulf Resources Inc. (BC) 08/13/2001
Each share Common no par exchanged for (0.33333333) share Common no par
EnerGulf Resources Inc. (BC) reincorporated in Yukon 06/27/2003 which reincorporated in British Columbia 10/05/2004

GOLETA NATL BK (GOLETA, CA)
Under plan of reorganization each share Common $5 par automatically became (1) share Community West Bancshares Common $2.50 par 12/31/97

GOLETA SAVINGS & LOAN ASSOCIATION (CA)
Completely liquidated 12/30/70
Each share Guarantee Stock $10 par exchanged for first and final distribution of (2.125) shares Far West Financial Corp. Common $1 par
Far West Financial Corp. name changed to Westminster Capital, Inc. 7/13/92
(See Westminster Capital, Inc.)

GOLEX RES LTD (AB)
Merged into Kala Exploration Ltd. 09/10/1982
Each share Common no par exchanged for (0.18271514) share Class A Common no par
Kala Exploration Ltd. recapitalized as Kala Feedlots Ltd. 04/06/1987 which name changed to Kala Canada Ltd. 03/27/1989
(See Kala Canada Ltd.)

GOLF ALLIANCE CORP (NV)
Name changed to Silver America, Inc. 03/08/2010
Silver America, Inc. name changed to Gold American Mining Corp. 06/23/2010 which name changed to Inception Mining Inc. 05/17/2013

GOLF CARD INTL INC (UT)
Name changed to GCI Industries Inc. 6/11/82
(See GCI Industries Inc.)

GOLF CMNTYS AMER INC (UT)
Plan of reorganization under Chapter 11 Federal Bankruptcy proceedings confirmed 09/19/2000
No stockholders' equity

GOLF ENTERPRISES INC (DE)
Issue Information - 2,350,000 shares COM offered at $13.50 per share on 07/13/1994
Merged into National Golf Properties, Inc. 7/30/96
Each share Common no par exchanged for (0.23210832) share Common 1¢ par and $6 cash
(See National Golf Properties, Inc.)

GOLF ENTMT INC (DE)
Reincorporated under the laws of Nevada as Contemporary Solutions, Inc. 05/02/2005
(See Contemporary Solutions, Inc.)

GOLF GALAXY INC (MN)
Issue Information - 3,950,000 shares COM offered at $14 per share on 07/29/2005
Merged into Dick's Sporting Goods, Inc. 2/13/2007
Each share Common 1¢ par exchanged for $18.82 cash

GOLF HOSTS INC (FL)
Name changed 01/01/1984
Name changed from Golf Hosts International, Inc. to Golf Hosts, Inc. 01/01/1984
Merged into TM Golf Hosts 06/23/1997
For holdings of (10) shares of fewer each share Common 1¢ par exchanged for $585.3559 cash
For holdings of (11) shares or more each share Common 1¢ par exchanged for $445.8505 cash with possible additional payments to be paid quarterly
Note: An initial additional distribution

of $3.25 cash per share was made 02/05/1998
A second additional distribution of $4.75 cash per share was made 04/24/1998
A third additional distribution of $2 cash per share was made 08/12/1998
A fourth additional distribution of $2.25 cash per share was made 11/25/1998
A fifth additional distribution of $2.75 cash per share was made 03/01/1999
A sixth additional distribution of $2 cash per share was made 05/12/1999
A seventh additional distribution of $2 cash per share was made 09/17/1999
An eighth additional distribution of $1.75 cash per share was made 11/12/1999
A ninth additional distribution of $2.25 cash per share was made 01/26/2000
A tenth additional distribution of $3 cash per share was made 03/07/2000
An eleventh additional distribution of $1.50 cash per share was made 05/09/2000
A twelfth additional distribution of $8.75 cash per share was made 07/26/2000
A thirteenth additional distribution of $1.50 cash per share was made 02/13/2001
A fourteenth additional distribution of $4.75 cash per share was made 03/22/2001
A fifteenth additional distribution of $8 cash per share was made 07/20/2001
A sixteenth additional distribution of $1.25 cash per share was made 11/08/2001
A seventeenth additional distribution of $1.50 cash per share was made 11/27/2001
An eighteenth additional distribution of $31.25 cash per share was made 12/18/2001
A nineteenth additional distribution of $18 cash per share was made 09/13/2004
A twentieth additional distribution of $1.25 cash per share was made 03/28/2005
A twenty-first additional distribution of $1.50 cash per share was made 01/10/2007

GOLF INNOVATIONS CORP (NV)
Each share old Common 1¢ par exchanged for (3) shares new Common 1¢ par 08/13/1998
Name changed to Avid Sportswear & Golf Corp. 05/27/1999
Avid Sportswear & Golf Corp. recapitalized as United Companies Corp. 09/18/2003 which recapitalized as Brownie's Marine Group, Inc. (NV) 08/22/2007 which reincorporated in Florida 12/07/2015

GOLF LINKS LTD (CO)
Recapitalized as American Communications Services Inc. (CO) 9/23/93
Each share Common no par exchanged for (0.01) share Common 1¢ par
American Communications Services Inc. (CO) reincorporated in Delaware 9/29/94 which name changed to e.spire Communications Inc. 4/15/98
(See e.spire Communications Inc.)

GOLF PROD TECHNOLOGIES INC (FL)
Common $0.0001 par split (3) for (1) by issuance of (2) additional shares payable 12/10/2002 to holders of record 12/06/2002 Ex date - 12/11/2002
Name changed to Centurion Gold Holdings, Inc. 03/21/2003
(See Centurion Gold Holdings, Inc.)

GOLF ROUNDS COM INC (DE)
Recapitalized as Fuse Medical, Inc. 05/30/2014
Each share Common 1¢ par exchanged for (0.06839945) share Common 1¢ par

GOLF STAR INC (UT)
Each share old Common $0.001 par exchanged for (0.02) share new Common $0.001 par 4/2/97
Name changed to Star Entertainment Group, Inc. 8/3/98
(See Star Entertainment Group, Inc.)

GOLF-TECHNOLOGY HLDG INC (ID)
Reincorporated under the laws of Delaware as Snake Eyes Golf Clubs, Inc. 12/18/1997
(See Snake Eyes Golf Clubs, Inc.)

GOLF TOWN INCOME FD (ON)
Merged into OMERS Capital Partners Inc. 09/28/2007
Each Trust Unit no par received $17.15 cash

GOLF TRAINING SYS INC (DE)
Each share old Common 1¢ par exchanged for (0.2) share new Common 1¢ par 5/14/98
Chapter 11 bankruptcy proceedings converted to Chapter 7 on 2/26/99
Case subsequently closed 1/22/2003
No stockholders' equity

GOLF TR AMER INC (MD)
Issue Information - 3,400,000 shares COM offered at $21 per share on 02/06/1997
Recapitalized as Pernix Therapeutics Holdings, Inc. 03/10/2010
Each share Common 1¢ par exchanged for (0.5) share Common 1¢ par

GOLF TWO INC (DE)
Common $0.001 par split (3.5) for (1) by issuance of (2.5) additional shares payable 10/20/2005 to holders of record 10/17/2005 Ex date - 10/21/2005
Name changed to Radiant Logistics, Inc. 10/28/2005

GOLF VENTURES INC (UT)
Each share old Common $0.001 par exchanged for (0.2) share new Common $0.001 par 2/1/96
Name changed to Golf Communities of America Inc. 11/19/98
(See Golf Communities of America Inc.)

GOLFBALL WORLD INC (FL)
Recapitalized as Qorus.com, Inc. 05/17/1999
Each share Common $0.001 par exchanged for (1/3) share Common $0.001 par
Qorus.com, Inc. recapitalized as DigitalFX International, Inc. 08/02/2006 which name changed to ComF5 International, Inc. 04/01/2010

GOLFGEAR INTL INC (WY)
Reincorporated 09/16/2010
Each share old Common $0.001 par exchanged for (0.004) share new Common $0.001 par 05/13/2010
State of incorporation changed from (NV) to (WY) 09/16/2010
Name changed to Gear International, Inc. 04/03/2012
Gear International, Inc. reorganized in Delaware as Matchaah Holdings, Inc. 06/19/2017

GOLFING NETWORK COM INC (TX)
Name changed to Netweb Online.com Inc. (TX) 12/14/1999
Netweb Online.com Inc. (TX) reorganized in Florida as Spectrum Brands Corp. 05/16/2001
(See Spectrum Brands Corp.)

GOLFNORTH PPTYS INC (ON)
Acquired by 1458306 Ontario Inc. 05/10/2002
Each share Common no par exchanged for $0.30 cash

GOLFSMART MEDIA INC (NV)
Name changed to Media Awareness International, Inc. (New) 08/29/2008
Media Awareness International, Inc. (New) recapitalized as Cloud Technologies, Inc. 06/17/2009

GOLFSMITH INTL HLDGS INC (DE)
Issue Information - 6,000,000 shares COM offered at $11.50 per share on 06/14/2006
Acquired by Golf Town USA Holdings Inc. 07/24/2012
Each share Common $0.001 par exchanged for $6.10 cash

GOLIATH GOLD MINES LTD (BC)
Common no par split (3) for (1) by issuance of (2) additional shares 7/25/84
Merged into Hemlo Gold Mines Inc. 2/3/87
Each share Common no par exchanged for (1.12495) shares Common no par
Hemlo Gold Mines Inc. merged into Battle Mountain Canada Inc. 7/19/96 which merged into Newmont Mining Corp. 1/10/2001

GOLIATH GOLD MNG LTD (SOUTH AFRICA)
Basis changed from (1:1) to (1:0.1) 05/26/2011
ADR agreement terminated 12/23/2015
Each ADR for Common exchanged for $0.006729 cash

GOLSIL MINES LTD (ON)
Capital Stock no par split (2) for (1) by issuance of (1) additional share 05/01/1967
Recapitalized as Zahavy Mines Ltd. 11/08/1971
Each share Capital Stock no par exchanged for (0.2) share Capital Stock no par
Zahavy Mines Ltd. recapitalized as Xavier Mines Ltd. 02/10/1993 which reorganized in Delaware as Xavier Corp. 07/24/1996
(See Xavier Corp.)

GOMAR MINES LTD. (ON)
Merged into Summit Explorations & Holdings Ltd. 09/19/1969
Each share Capital Stock $1 par exchanged for (0.125) share Capital Stock no par
Summit Explorations & Holdings Ltd. name changed to Summit Diversified Ltd. 03/03/1972 which merged into Sumtra Diversified Inc. 08/30/1978

GOMBOS (JOHN) CO. INC. (NJ)
Name changed to Gombos Microwave Inc. 2/21/62
Gombos Microwave, Inc. reorganized as Biofeedback Management Co. of America, Inc. 2/28/75 which reorganized as TMI Technical Management, Inc. 2/22/78
(See TMI Technical Management, Inc.)

GOMBOS MICROWAVE INC (NJ)
Reorganized under the laws of Florida as Biofeedback Management Co. of America, Inc. 02/28/1975
Each share Common 10¢ par exchanged for (0.2) share Common 1¢ par
Biofeedback Management Co. of America, Inc. reorganized as TMI Technical Management, Inc. 02/22/1978
(See TMI Technical Management, Inc.)

GOME ELECTRICAL APPLIANCES HLDG LTD (BERMUDA)
Name changed to GOME Retail Holdings Ltd. 09/07/2017

GONDAS CORP
Adjudicated bankrupt 02/28/1975
Stockholders' equity unlikely

GONDOLA INC (UT)
Recapitalized as Trafalgar, Inc. (UT) 02/22/1989
Each (14.3468) shares Common $0.001 par exchanged for (1) share Common $0.014 par
Trafalgar, Inc. (UT) reincorporated in Nevada as Atlantic Funding Ltd. 11/13/1989

GONDWANA ENERGY LTD (NV)
Old Common $0.00001 par split (3) for (1) by issuance of (2) additional shares payable 05/26/1999 to holders of record 05/21/1999
Old Common $0.00001 par split (2) for (1) by issuance of (1) additional share payable 10/13/2000 to holders of record 10/10/2000 Ex date - 10/16/2000
Each share old Common $0.00001 par exchanged for (1/6) share new Common $0.00001 par 01/07/2005
Each share new Common $0.00001 par exchanged again for (0.01) share new Common $0.00001 par 03/09/2006
New Common $0.00001 par split (8) for (1) by issuance of (7) additional shares payable 06/13/2006 to holders of record 06/06/2006 Ex date - 06/14/2006
Name changed to FinMetal Mining Ltd. 02/01/2007
FinMetal Mining Ltd. recapitalized as Amazon Goldsands Ltd. 06/09/2008 which name changed to First Colombia Gold Corp. 11/29/2010

GONDWANA GOLD INC (ON)
Name changed to Pan African Oil Ltd. 06/18/2013
Pan African Oil Ltd. merged into Eco (Atlantic) Oil & Gas Ltd. 01/28/2015

GONDWANA OIL CORP (ON)
Name changed to European Metals Corp. 11/07/2014

GONZAGA RES LTD (BC)
Name changed to Osprey Gold Development Ltd. 02/27/2017

GONZALES GOLD MINES LTD (BC)
Name changed 05/03/1983
Name changed from Gonzales Oil Search Inc. to Gonzales Gold Mines Ltd. 05/03/1983
Recapitalized as Osito Ventures Ltd. 10/09/1991
Each (2.6) shares Common no par exchanged for (1) share Common no par
Osito Ventures Ltd. name changed to Sennen Resources Ltd. 08/08/1997 which name changed to Sennen Potash Corp. 04/15/2013

GOOD DEAL SUPER MKTS INC (NJ)
Adjudicated bankrupt 10/00/1973
No stockholders' equity

GOOD GUYS INC (DE)
Reincorporated 3/4/92
Common 1¢ par split (2) for (1) by issuance of (1) additional share 5/20/91
State of incorporation changed from (CA) to (DE) and Common 1¢ par changed to $0.001 par 3/4/92
Merged into CompUSA Inc. 12/19/2003
Each share Common $0.001 par exchanged for $2.05 cash

GOOD HBR PARTNERS ACQUISITION CORP (DE)
Class A Units separated 01/31/2008

Class B Units separated 01/31/2008
Completely liquidated 02/07/2008
Each share Class B Common $0.0001 par received first and final distribution of $5.36 cash
Note: Certificates were not required to be surrendered and are without value
Recapitalized as UAN Cultural & Creative Co., Ltd. 09/02/2010
Each share Class A Common $0.0001 par exchanged for (0.1) share Class A Common $0.0001 par

GOOD HOPE RES LTD (BC)
Merged into Golden North Resource Corp. 10/01/1986
Each share Capital Stock no par exchanged for (1) share Common no par
Golden North Resource Corp. merged into Caledonia Mining Corp. (BC) 02/04/1992 which reincorporated in Canada 03/29/1995 which reincorporated in Jersey as Caledonia Mining Corp. PLC 03/24/2016

GOOD HUMOR CO. OF CALIFORNIA (CA)
Common 50¢ par changed to 10¢ par 6/2/55
Pr. Preferred $5 par called for redemption 4/28/61
Recapitalized as Allstate Industries, Inc 3/7/67
Each share Common 10¢ par exchanged for (0.1) share Common 10¢ par
(See Allstate Industries, Inc.)

GOOD HUMOR CORP. (NY)
Stock Dividend - 10% 12/01/1953
Name changed to Southport Commercial Corp. 05/25/1961
(See Southport Commercial Corp.)

GOOD HUMOR ICE CREAM CO. OF CALIFORNIA
Merged into Good Humor Co. of California in 1947
(See Good Humor Co. of California)

GOOD IDEAS ENTERPRISES INC (DE)
Issue Information - 1,200,000 shares COM offered at $5 per share on 02/17/1994
Merged into Substance Abuse Technologies Inc. 2/17/97
Each share Common $0.001 par exchanged for (0.36) share Common 1¢ par
(See Substance Abuse Technologies Inc.)

GOOD L S & CO (DE)
Stock Dividend - 200% 4/20/71
Filed for Chapter 11 Bankruptcy proceedings 5/27/80 subsequently converted to Chapter 7
No stockholders' equity

GOOD MERGERS INC (NV)
Charter revoked for failure to file reports and pay fees 6/1/93

GOOD ROADS MACHINERY CORP. (PA)
Acquired by Bliss (E.W.) Co. 07/20/1967
Details not available

GOOD SOFTWARE CORP (NM)
Out of business 00/00/1994
Details not available

GOOD TACO CORP (DE)
Name changed to Business Cards Tomorrow, Inc. 2/28/86
Business Cards Tomorrow, Inc. name changed to American Franchise Group, Inc. 10/6/88 which name changed to BCT International, Inc. 7/31/92
(See BCT International, Inc.)

GOOD WTR CO INC (WA)
Name changed to Fusion Interactive Corp. 12/19/2014

GOODALL RUBBER CO. (PA)
Each share Common no par exchanged for (8) shares Common $5 par in 1945
Stock Dividends - 10% 12/15/47; 10% 12/30/48; 10% 3/15/52
Reincorporated under the laws of New Jersey in 1954
(See Goodall Rubber Co. (N.J.))

GOODALL RUBR CO (NJ)
Class A Common $5 par and Common $5 par changed to $1 par 12/29/56
Stock Dividends - Class A Common - 10% 12/15/56; 10% 12/30/48; 10% 3/15/52; 10% 3/15/56; 200% 12/29/56
Acquired by Trelleborg, AB 6/28/88
Each share Class A Common $1 par exchanged for $7 cash
Each share Common $1 par exchanged for $122.50 cash

GOODALL-SANFORD, INC. (ME)
Acquired by Burlington Industries, Inc. 00/00/1959
Details not available

GOODALL SECURITIES CORP.
Liquidated in 1945

GOODALL WORSTED CO.
Merged into Goodall-Sanford, Inc. 00/00/1944
Each share Common exchanged for (3-1/3) shares new Common $10 par
(See Goodall-Sanford, Inc.)

GOODCO INTERNATIONAL LTD. (BC)
Struck off register and declared dissolved for failure to file returns 02/25/1983

GOODE INDS INC (BC)
Reincorporated under the laws of Alberta as Paxton Pacific Resource Products Inc. 09/28/1994
Paxton Pacific Resource Products Inc. recapitalized as Paxton International Resources, Inc. 11/04/1998
(See Paxton International Resources, Inc.)

GOODELL MONORAIL INDS INC (NV)
Charter revoked for failure to file reports and pay fees 3/6/78

GOODELL PRATT CO.
Acquired by Millers Falls Co. in 1930
Details not available

GOODERHAM & WORTS, LTD.
Merged into Walker (Hiram)-Gooderham & Worts Ltd. in 1927
(See Walker (Hiram)-Gooderham & Worts Ltd.)

GOODFELLOW RES LTD (BC)
Name changed to Standard Uranium Inc. 03/29/2005
Standard Uranium Inc. merged into Energy Metals Corp. 03/13/2006 which merged into Uranium One Inc. 08/10/2007
(See Uranium One Inc.)

GOODFISH MINING CO. LTD. (ON)
Recapitalized as Cusco Mines Ltd. 02/04/1955
Each share Capital Stock $1 par exchanged for (0.28571428) share Capital Stock $1 par
Cusco Mines Ltd. recapitalized as Probe Mines Ltd. 03/04/1965 which merged into Goldcorp Inc. 03/17/2015

GOODGOLD RES LTD (BC)
Recapitalized as Classic Gold Resources Ltd. 06/03/1994
Each share Common no par exchanged for (0.2) share Common no par
(See Classic Gold Resources Ltd.)

GOODHEART VENTURES INC (NV)
Recapitalized as Million Dollar Saloon Inc. 11/1/95
Each (12) shares Common $0.001 par exchanged for (1) share Common $0.001 par

GOODHEART WILLCOX INC (DE)
Company terminated registration of securities and is no longer public 8/20/99
Details not available

GOODHOUSE J B INC (MN)
Each share Common no par exchanged for (0.5) share Common 1¢ par 6/20/88
Name changed to Minnesota American, Inc. 11/12/92
Minnesota American, Inc. name changed to Corvu Corp. 1/18/2000
(See Corvu Corp.)

GOODIES GALORE PACKAGING INC (ON)
Reincorporated under the laws of Florida as Sun Rayz Products Inc. 06/04/2004
Sun Rayz Products Inc. name changed to Trivos, Inc. 06/22/2006
(See Trivos, Inc.)

GOODMAN FIELDER LTD (AUSTRALIA)
Acquired by Burns, Philp & Co. Ltd. 08/01/2003
Each Sponsored ADR for Ordinary exchanged for $4.3122 cash
(Additional Information in Active)

GOODMAN GLOBAL INC (DE)
Merged into Chill Holdings, Inc. 02/13/2008
Each share Common 1¢ par exchanged for $25.60 cash

GOODMAN GOLD TR (ON)
Trust terminated 06/23/2016
Each Trust Unit received $3.93858311 cash

GOODMAN MANUFACTURING CO. (IL)
Common $50 par changed to $16.66666666 par and (2) additional shares issued 08/15/1957
Name changed to Mangood Corp. (IL) 09/01/1965
Mangood Corp. (IL) reincorporated in Delaware 04/22/1968 which name changed to Howe Richardson Inc. 12/31/1987
(See Howe Richardson Inc.)

GOODMAN SYS INC (DE)
Charter cancelled and declared inoperative and void for non-payment of taxes 06/26/1985

GOODMARK FOODS INC (NC)
Common 1¢ par split (2) for (1) by issuance of (1) additional share 08/01/1994
Merged into ConAgra, Inc. 07/31/1998
Each share Common 1¢ par exchanged for (1.08108) shares Common $5 par
ConAgra, Inc. name changed to ConAgra Foods, Inc. 09/28/2000 which name changed to Conagra Brands, Inc. 11/10/2016

GOODNOISE CORP (DE)
Name changed to eMusic.com, Inc. 07/22/1999
(See eMusic.com, Inc.)

GOODRICH (WILLIAM O.) CO.
Acquired by Archer-Daniels-Midland Co. 00/00/1928
Details not available

GOODRICH CORP (NY)
Name changed 06/01/2001
Each share 7% Preferred $100 par exchanged for (1.4) shares $5 Preferred no par and (0.5) share Common no par 00/00/1936
Common no par changed to $10 par 00/00/1953
Common $10 par split (2) for (1) by issuance of (1) additional share 00/00/1955
Common $10 par split (3) for (2) by issuance of (0.5) additional share 08/09/1968
Common $10 par changed to $5 par 04/18/1969
$3.125 Conv. Preferred Ser. C $1 par called for redemption 06/10/1983
$0.975 Preferred Ser. B $1 par called for redemption 07/15/1988
$7.85 Preferred Ser. A $1 par called for redemption 08/30/1994
$3.50 Conv. Preferred Ser. D $1 par called for redemption 07/31/1995
Common $5 par split (2) for (1) by issuance of (1) additional share payable 04/01/1996 to holders of record 03/11/1996 Ex date - 04/02/1996
Stock Dividend - 200% 01/19/1951
Name changed from Goodrich (B.F.) Co. to Goodrich Corp. 06/01/2001
Each share Common $5 par received distribution of (0.2) share EnPro Industries, Inc. Common 1¢ par payable 05/31/2002 to holders of record 05/28/2002 Ex date - 06/03/2002
Acquired by United Technologies Corp. 07/26/2012
Each share Common $5 par exchanged for $127.50 cash

GOODRICH INVS GROUP (MA)
Name changed to GIT Realty & Mortgage Investors 07/27/1971
GIT Realty & Mortgage Investors reorganized as GIT Industries Inc. 03/30/1976
(See GIT Industries Inc.)

GOODRICH MINING CO. LTD.
Dissolved 00/00/1950
Details not available

GOODRICH PETE CORP (DE)
Each share old Common 20¢ par exchanged for (0.125) share new Common 20¢ par 03/12/1998
Conv. Preferred Ser. A $1 par called for redemption at $12 plus $0.10667 accrued dividends on 02/17/2016
Plan of reorganization under Chapter 11 Federal Bankruptcy proceedings effective 10/12/2016
No stockholders' equity
(Additional Information in Active)

GOODRICH RLTY & DEV GROUP INC (DE)
Name changed to Midcon Industries Inc. 01/26/1976
(See Midcon Industries Inc.)

GOODROCK GOLD MINES, LTD. (ON)
Charter cancelled 01/16/1961

GOODTIME GOURMET INC (NV)
Name changed to Kimberly Oil & Gas, Inc. 08/24/1979
Kimberly Oil & Gas, Inc. name changed to Resorts International, Ltd. 03/13/1985
(See Resorts International, Ltd.)

GOODWAY COPY CTRS INC (DE)
Charter cancelled and declared inoperative and void for non-payment of taxes 04/15/1972

GOODWAY INC (DE)
Reincorporated 02/28/1969
Capital Stock no par split (3) for (2) by issuance of (0.5) additional share 02/15/1968
State of incorporation changed from (PA) to (DE) and Capital Stock no par reclassified as Common 10¢ par 02/28/1969
Adjudicated bankrupt 03/25/1974
Stockholders' equity unlikely

GOODWAY PRINTING CO., INC. (PA)
Name changed to Goodway, Inc. (PA) 08/11/1967

Goodway, Inc. (PA) reincorporated in Delaware 02/28/1969
(See Goodway, Inc. (DE))

GOODWILL STATIONS, INC. (MI)
Completely liquidated 10/06/1964
Details not available

GOODY PRODS INC (DE)
Common 10¢ par split (2) for (1) by issuance of (1) additional share 10/03/1983
Common 10¢ par split (3) for (2) by issuance of (0.5) additional share 07/01/1986
Merged into Newell Co. 11/09/1993
Each share Common 10¢ par exchanged for $24.75 cash

GOODY SAM INC (NY)
Common $1 par split (2) for (1) by issuance of (1) additional share 12/29/69
Merged into American Can Co. 6/23/78
Each share Common $1 par exchanged for (0.1811) share Common $12.50 par
American Can Co. name changed to Primerica Corp. (NJ) 4/28/87 which was acquired by Primerica Corp. (DE) 12/15/88 which name changed to Travelers Inc. 12/31/93 which name changed to Travelers Group Inc. 4/16/95 which name changed to Citigroup Inc. 10/8/98

GOODYEAR CDA INC (ON)
4% Preferred $50 par called for redemption 07/31/1987
Acquired by Goodyear Tire & Rubber Co. 05/01/1993
Each share Common no par exchanged for $65 cash

GOODYEAR TEXTILE MILLS CO.
Dissolved 00/00/1934
Details not available

GOODYEAR TIRE & RUBR CO (OH)
$5 Preferred called for redemption 09/30/1954
Each share 5.875% Mandatory Conv. Preferred no par exchanged for (2.7574) shares Common no par 04/02/2014
(Additional Information in Active)

GOODYEAR TIRE & RUBR CO CDA LTD (ON)
Each share old Common no par exchanged for (2) shares new Common no par 00/00/1935
Common no par split (10) for (1) by issuance of (9) additional shares 07/30/1973
Name changed to Goodyear Canada Inc. 05/29/1975
(See Goodyear Canada Inc.)

GOODYS FAMILY CLOTHING INC (TN)
Common no par split (3) for (2) by issuance of (0.5) additional share 03/18/1993
Common no par split (2) for (1) by issuance of (1) additional share payable 07/17/1998 to holders of record 07/01/1998
Merged into GF Goods Inc. 01/27/2006
Each share Common no par exchanged for $9.60 cash

GOODYS FOOD SYS INC (NJ)
Merged into MJM Seafoods, Ltd. 09/30/1976
Each share Common 10¢ par exchanged for $1.25 cash

GOODYS INC (NJ)
Name changed to Goody's Food Systems, Inc. 08/27/1969
(See Goody's Food Systems, Inc.)

GOOGLE INC (DE)
Each share Class A Common $0.001 par received distribution of (1) share Class C Non-Vtg. Capital Stock $0.001 par payable 04/02/2014 to holders of record 03/27/2014 Ex date - 04/03/2014
Each share Class C Non-Vtg. Capital Stock $0.001 par received distribution of (0.0027455) additional share payable 05/04/2015 to holders of record 04/02/2015 Ex date - 04/27/2015
Name changed to Alphabet Inc. 10/05/2015

GOOSE RIV CAP INC (AB)
Name changed to Goose River Resources Ltd. 09/14/2001
Goose River Resources Ltd. merged into SignalEnergy Inc. 08/09/2005 which reorganized as Fortress Energy Inc. 02/20/2007 which name changed to Alvopetro Inc. 03/11/2013

GOOSE RIV RES LTD (AB)
Merged into SignalEnergy Inc. 08/09/2005
Each share Common no par exchanged for (0.769216) share Common no par, (0.05) share G2 Resources Inc. Common no par and $0.073234 cash
(See each company's listing)

GOPHER CONTAINER CORP (MN)
Name changed to Simcoa Inc. 02/16/1970
(See Simcoa Inc.)

GOPHER INC (NV)
Name changed to Seaview Underwater Research Inc. 3/30/99
Seaview Underwater Research, Inc. name changed to Seaview Video Technology, Inc. 2/2/2000 which name changed to Powerlinx, Inc. 12/10/2003

GOPHER MEDIA SVCS CORP (CANADA)
Involuntarily dissolved for failure to file annual returns 08/19/2008

GOPHER OIL & GAS LTD (AB)
Recapitalized as Ventus Energy Ltd. 12/31/1998
Each share Common no par exchanged for (0.25) share Common no par
Ventus Energy Ltd. name changed to Navigo Energy Inc. 05/24/2002
(See Navigo Energy Inc.)

GOPUBLICNOW COM INC (DE)
Name changed to GPN Network Inc. 11/08/2000
GPN Network Inc. name changed to IR BioSciences Holdings, Inc. 08/28/2003

GORDMANS STORES INC (DE)
Name changed to G-Estate Liquidation Stores, Inc. 10/24/2017
(See G-Estate Liquidation Stores, Inc.)

GORDON & BREACH SCIENCE PUBLISHERS INC (NY)
Plan of reorganization under Chapter XI Federal Bankruptcy Act confirmed 06/29/1977
Stockholders' equity unlikely

GORDON ELEC MFG INC (NY)
Name changed to Gordon Tube Products Co. 12/17/72
(See Gordon Tube Products Co.)

GORDON FOODS, INC. (GA)
Acquired by Sunshine Biscuits, Inc. 09/26/1956
Each share Common $1 par exchanged for (0.14285714) share Capital Stock $12.50 par
Sunshine Biscuits, Inc. merged into American Tobacco Co. 05/31/1966 which name changed to American Brands, Inc. (NJ) 07/01/1969 which reincorporated in Delaware 01/01/1986 which name changed to Fortune Brands, Inc. 05/30/1997 which name changed to Beam Inc. 10/04/2011
(See Beam Inc.)

GORDON JEWELRY CORP (DE)
Class A $1 par split (2) for (1) by issuance of (1) additional share 3/11/66
Class A $1 par split (2) for (1) by issuance of (1) additional share 12/20/68
Class A $1 par split (3) for (2) by issuance of (0.5) additional share 9/30/81
Class A $1 par split (4) for (3) by issuance of (1/3) additional share 1/24/84
Stock Dividend - 10% 5/19/87
Merged into GJ Acquisition Corp. 7/5/89
Each share Class A $1 par exchanged for $36.75 cash

GORDON LEBEL MINES LTD (ON)
Merged into Hoffman Exploration & Minerals Ltd. 06/29/1981
Each share (12.4545) shares Capital Stock $1 par exchanged for (1) share Common no par
Hoffman Exploration & Minerals Ltd. merged into Consolidated Thompson-Lundmark Gold Mines Ltd. 01/16/1986 which name changed to Consolidated Thompson Iron Mines Ltd. 08/24/2006
(See Consolidated Thompson Iron Mines Ltd.)

GORDON MACKAY & STORES LTD (ON)
Through voluntary exchange offer Peoples Department Stores Ltd. acquired 100% of Class B no par 00/00/1972
Merged into Walkers Holdings Ltd. 06/30/1976
Each share Class A no par exchanged for $8.75 cash

GORDON MANUFACTURING CO. LTD. (ON)
Completely liquidated 12/10/1963
Details not available

GORDON-MILES MNG CO (MN)
Name changed to U.S. Coal Corp. 01/21/1975
(See U.S. Coal Corp.)

GORDON (I.) REALTY CORP. (NY)
Name changed to Gordon (I.) Corp. 8/21/84

GORDON RES LTD (BC)
Recapitalized as Shogun Developments Corp. 01/09/1986
Each share Common no par exchanged for (0.5) Common no par
Shogun Developments Corp. name changed to ESTec Systems Corp. (BC) 05/11/1988 which reincorporated in Alberta 12/19/2005
(See ESTec Systems Corp.)

GORDON RIVER TIMBER CORP.
Dissolved in 1947

GORDON TUBE PRODS INC (NY)
Merged into ATS Acquisition Corp. 1/2/91
Each share Common 1¢ par exchanged for $1.56 cash
Each share Common 1¢ par received an additional payment from escrow of $0.5228 cash 2/5/91

GORDONA MINING CORP., LTD. (ON)
Charter revoked for failure to file reports and pay taxes 00/00/1961

GOREMOTE INTERNET COMMUNICATIONS INC (DE)
Merged into iPass, Inc. 2/15/2006
Each share Common $0.001 par exchanged for $1.71 cash

GOREN FOODS CO (DE)
5% Preference $1 par called for redemption 1/1/71
Public interest eliminated

GORES HLDGS INC (DE)
Units separated 11/03/2016
Name changed to Hostess Brands, Inc. 11/03/2016

GORES HLDGS II INC (DE)
Units separated 10/18/2018
Name changed to Verra Mobility Corp. 10/18/2018

GORHAM, INC. (DE)
Name changed to Black, Starr & Gorham, Inc. in 1951
(See Black, Star & Gorham, Inc.)

GORHAM CORP. (RI)
Completely liquidated 11/8/67
Each share Common $4 par exchanged for first and final distribution of (1.8) shares Textron Inc. (RI) Common 25¢ par
Textron Inc. (RI) reincorporated in Delaware 1/2/68

GORHAM MANUFACTURING CO. (RI)
Common no par changed to $10 par in 1939
Each share Common $10 par exchanged for (2.5) shares Common $4 par in 1950
Name changed to Gorham Corp. 5/4/61
Gorham Corp. liquidated for Textron Inc. (RI) 11/8/67 which reincorporated in Delaware 1/2/68

GORILLA MINERALS CORP (BC)
Common no par split (2) for (1) by issuance of (1) additional share payable 03/30/2018 to holders of record 03/27/2018 Ex date - 03/26/2018
Name changed to Go Cobalt Mining Corp. 06/14/2018

GORILLA RES CORP (BC)
Each share Common no par received distribution of (1) share NU2U Resources Corp. Common no par payable 10/13/2011 to holders of record 09/29/2011
Each share Common no par received distribution of (1.78571428) shares Dizun International Enterprises Inc. Common no par payable 01/17/2012 to holders of record 01/11/2012
Name changed to Winston Resources Inc. 06/25/2012

GORIN STORES INC (DE)
Name changed to Almy Stores Inc. 7/1/77
(See Almy Stores Inc.)

GORINS INC (DE)
Name changed to Gorin Stores Inc. 7/1/70
Gorin Stores Inc. name changed to Almy Stores Inc. 7/1/77
(See Almy Stores Inc.)

GORTDRUM MINES LTD (ON)
Acquired by Northgate Exploration Ltd. (ON) 08/19/1970
Each share Capital Stock $1 par exchanged for (1/3) share Capital Stock $1 par
Northgate Exploration Ltd. (ON) reincorporated in British Columbia 07/01/2001 which name changed to Northgate Minerals Corp. 05/20/2004 which merged into AuRico Gold Inc. 10/26/2011

GORTON CORP. (DE)
Common no par changed to $1 par and (1) additional share issued 7/15/66
Merged into General Mills Inc. 8/16/68
Each share Common $1 par exchanged for (0.714285) share Common $1.50 par

GORTON CORP. (MA)
Reincorporated under the laws of Delaware 7/1/66
Gorton Corp. (Del.) merged into General Mills, Inc. 8/16/68

GOR-GOU

GORTON-PEW FISHERIES CO. LTD. (MA)
Name changed to Gorton's of Gloucester, Inc. 5/16/56
Gorton's of Gloucester, Inc. name changed to Gorton Corp. (MA) 6/14/65 which reincorporated under the laws of Delaware 7/1/66 which merged into General Mills, Inc. 8/16/68

GORTON'S OF GLOUCESTER, INC. (MA)
Common no par split (2) for (1) by issuance of (1) additional share 7/23/59
Stock Dividend - 100% 6/22/62
Name changed to Gorton Corp. (MA) 6/14/65
Gorton Corp. (MA) reincorporated in Delaware 7/1/66 which merged into General Mills, Inc. 8/16/68

GOSNOLD MILLS CO.
Reorganized as Gosnold Mills Corp. in 1929
Details not available

GOSNOLD MILLS CORP.
Acquired by Powdrell & Alexander, Inc. (MA) 00/00/1944
Details not available

GOSS PRINTING PRESS CO. (IL)
Each share Capital Stock $100 par exchanged for (10) shares Capital Stock $10 par 00/00/1949
Under plan of merger each share Capital Stock $10 par exchanged for (2.3) shares Miehle-Goss-Dexter, Inc. Common $7.50 par 01/31/1957
Miehle-Goss-Dexter, Inc. acquired by North American Rockwell Corp. 09/12/1969 which merged into Rockwell International Corp. (Old) 02/16/1973
(See Rockwell International Corp. (Old))

GOSSARD (H.W.) CO. (IL)
Common no par split (2) for (1) by issuance of (1) additional share 04/30/1962
Merged into Wayne-Gossard Corp. 01/31/1967
Each share Common no par exchanged for (1) share $1.60 Conv. Preferred no par
Wayne-Gossard Corp. name changed to Signal Apparel Co., Inc. 02/12/1987
(See Signal Apparel Co., Inc.)

GOSSE PACKING CO. LTD.
Merged into British Columbia Packers Ltd. and liquidated in 1928

GOSSELIN STORES INC (KS)
Merged into Gosselin Merger Co., Inc. 12/29/86
Each share Class A Common $1 par exchanged for $16.76 cash
Each share Class B Common $1 par exchanged for $16.76 cash

GOSSETT MILLS, INC.
Out of existence 00/00/1946
Details not available

GOTAAS LARSEN SHIPPING CORP (LIBERIA)
Acquired by a group of investors 12/15/88
Each share Common $1 par exchanged for $48 cash

GOTHAM APPAREL CORP (NY)
Dissolved by proclamation 09/23/1998

GOTHAM BANK (NEW YORK, NY)
Merged into Royal National Bank (New York, NY) 1/31/63
Each share Capital Stock $10 par exchanged for (2.5) shares Capital Stock $5 par
Royal National Bank (New York, NY) merged into Security National Bank (Hempstead, NY) 5/8/72
(See Security National Bank (Hempstead, NY))

GOTHAM BK NEW YORK (NEW YORK, NY)
Ctfs. dated after 00/00/1980
Acquired by Provident New York Bancorp 08/10/2012
Each share Common $10 par exchanged for $137.08370097 cash

GOTHAM CAP CORP (AB)
Name changed to Long View Resources Corp. 11/26/2004
Long View Resources Corp. merged into Reece Energy Exploration Corp. (New) 05/15/2007 which merged into Penn West Energy Trust 04/30/2009 which reorganized as Penn West Petroleum Ltd. (New) 01/03/2011 which name changed to Obsidian Energy Ltd. 06/29/2017

GOTHAM CAP HLDGS INC (NJ)
Reincorporated under the laws of Nevada as IIOT-OXYS, Inc. 08/16/2017

GOTHAM CR CORP (NY)
Class B $5 par changed to $1 par 00/00/1944
Company became private 00/00/1970
Details not available

GOTHAM HOSIERY CO., INC. (DE)
Merged into Chadbourn Gotham, Inc. 09/30/1955
Each share Common no par exchanged for (1) share Common $1 par
Chadbourn Gotham, Inc. name changed to Chadbourn Inc. 01/31/1969 which reorganized as Stanwood Corp. 06/12/1975 which was acquired by Delta Woodside Industries, Inc. (DE) 09/07/1988 which merged into Delta Woodside Industries, Inc. (SC) 11/15/1989
(See Delta Woodside Industries, Inc. (SC))

GOTHAM KNITBACK MACHINE CORP.
Merged into Gotham Silk Hosiery Co. in 1932
Details not available

GOTHAM PHARMACEUTICAL INC (NY)
Dissolved by proclamation 03/25/1981

GOTHAM SILK HOSIERY CO.
Name changed to Gotham Hosiery Co., Inc. 00/00/1942
Gotham Hosiery Co., Inc. merged into Chadbourn Gotham, Inc. 09/30/1955 which name changed to Chadbourn Inc. 01/31/1969 which reorganized as Stanwood Corp. 06/12/1975 which was acquired by Delta Woodside Industries, Inc. (DE) 09/07/1988 which merged into Delta Woodside Industries, Inc. (SC) 11/15/1989
(See Delta Woodside Industries, Inc. (SC))

GOTHAM YELLOWKNIFE MINES, LTD. (ON)
Charter revoked for failure to file reports and pay taxes 00/00/1960

GOTHIC ENERGY CORP (OK)
Reincorporated 10/11/96
State of incorporation changed from (DE) to (OK) and Common no par changed to 1¢ par 10/11/96
Merged into Chesapeake Energy Corp. 1/16/2001
Each share Common 1¢ par exchanged for (0.1908) share Common 1¢ par

GOTHIC GOLD MINES, LTD. (ON)
Name changed to Gothic Mines & Oils Ltd. 09/00/1953
Gothic Mines & Oils Ltd. merged into Cessland Gas & Oil Corp. Ltd. 07/00/1957 which merged into Cessland Corp. Ltd. 00/00/1962
(See Cessland Corp. Ltd.)

GOTHIC MINES & OILS LTD. (ON)
Merged into Cessland Gas & Oil Corp. Ltd. 07/00/1957
Each share Capital Stock $1 par exchanged for (0.16666666) share Capital Stock $1 par
Cessland Gas & Oil Corp. Ltd. merged into Cessland Corp. Ltd. 03/15/1962
(See Cessland Corp. Ltd.)

GOTHIC RES LTD (CANADA)
Reincorporated 08/01/1991
Place of incorporation changed from (BC) to (Canada) 08/01/1991
Reincorporated under the laws of Oklahoma as American Natural Energy Corp. (Ctfs. dtd. after 02/12/2002) 02/12/2002
(See American Natural Energy Corp. (Ctfs. dtd. after 02/12/2002))

GOTHS RESOURCE INC (CANADA)
Name changed to Diagnos Inc. 09/26/2000

GOTO COM INC (DE)
Name changed to Overture Services, Inc. 10/08/2001
Overture Services, Inc. acquired by Yahoo! Inc. 10/07/2003

GOTRAQ INC (NV)
Each share old Common $0.0001 par exchanged for (0.01) share new Common $0.0001 par 08/25/2017
Name changed to MJ Venture Partners, Inc. 04/10/2018

GOTT CORP (KS)
Common no par split (3) for (2) by issuance of (0.5) additional share 04/01/1983
Merged into Rubbermaid, Inc. 12/20/1985
Each share Common no par exchanged for (0.76731) share Common $1 par
Rubbermaid, Inc. merged into Newell Rubbermaid Inc. 03/24/1999 which name changed to Newell Brands Inc. 04/18/2016

GOTTFRIED BAKING CO., INC. (NY)
Adjudicated bankrupt 8/15/66
No stockholders' equity

GOTTSCHALKS INC (DE)
Common 1¢ par split (2) for (1) by issuance of (1) additional share 04/10/1987
Plan of reorganization under Chapter 11 Federal Bankruptcy proceedings effective 02/28/2011
No stockholders' equity

GO2GREEN LANDSCAPING INC (NV)
Name changed to nDivision Inc. 04/09/2018

GO2NET INC (DE)
Common 1¢ par split (2) for (1) by issuance of (1) additional share payable 02/22/1999 to holders of record 02/05/1999
Common 1¢ par split (2) for (1) by issuance of (1) additional share payable 06/24/1999 to holders of record 05/17/1999
Merged into InfoSpace, Inc. 10/12/2000
Each share Common 1¢ par exchanged for (1.82) shares Common $0.0001 par
InfoSpace, Inc. name changed to Blucora, Inc. 06/07/2012

GOULD & CURRY CO.
Merged into Consolidated Chollar Gould & Savage Mining Co. in 1933
Details not available

GOULD (EDSON) FUND, INC. (MD)
See - Edson Gould Fd Inc

GOULD COUPLER CO.
Reorganized as Symington-Gould Corp. in 1936
Each share Class A exchanged for (0.35) share Common $1 par
Common received nothing but rights to subscribe to new Common
Symington-Gould Corp. name changed to Symington Wayne Corp. 3/12/58 which merged into Dresser Industries, Inc. (New) 4/30/68 which merged into Halliburton Co. 9/29/98

GOULD ENTERPRISES INC (DE)
Merged into Gould Investors Trust (MA) 7/1/70
Each share Class A $1 par exchanged for (1) share of Bene. Int. no par
Gould Investors Trust (MA) reorganized in Delaware as Gould Investors L.P. 5/13/86

GOULD INC (DE)
Common $4 par split (3) for (2) by issuance of (0.5) additional share 3/15/72
Common $4 par split (3) for (2) by issuance of (0.5) additional share 8/20/76
$1.35 Conv. Preferred $1 par called for redemption 7/15/83
Acquired by Nippon Mining Co. 11/1/88
Each share Common $4 par exchanged for $23.25 cash

GOULD INVS TR (MA)
Shares of Bene. Int. no par changed to $1 par 8/27/73
$3.25 Conv. Preferred Ser. B $1 par called for redemption 12/16/85
Reorganized under the laws of Delaware as Gould Investors L.P. 5/13/86
Each Share of Bene. Int. $1 par exchanged for (1) Unit of Ltd. Partnership
Note: Non-voting holders received $31 cash per share

GOULD NATL BATTERIES INC (DE)
Common $4 par split (2) for (1) by issuance of (1) additional share 8/16/60
Stock Dividend - 100% 7/1/54
Under plan of merger name changed to Gould Inc. 7/31/69
(See Gould Inc.)

GOULD PPTYS INC (DE)
Name changed to Gould Enterprises, Inc. 4/2/69
Gould Enterprises, Inc. merged into Gould Investors Trust (MA) 7/1/70 which reorganized in Delaware as Gould Investors L.P. 5/13/86

GOULDS MANUFACTURING CO.
Name changed to Goulds Pumps, Inc. (NY) 00/00/1926
Goulds Pumps, Inc. (NY) reincorporated in Delaware 12/31/1984
(See Goulds Pumps, Inc.)

GOULDS PUMPS INC (DE)
Reincorporated 12/31/1984
Common $100 par changed to $50 par 00/00/1933
Each share 7% Preferred $100 par exchanged for (7) shares 5% Preferred $20 par and (3) shares Common $5 par 00/00/1948
Each share Common $50 par exchanged for (10) shares Common $5 par 00/00/1948
Common $5 par changed to no par and (1) additional share issued 11/23/1959
Common no par split (2) for (1) by issuance of (1) additional share 06/15/1960
5% Preferred $20 par called for redemption 11/30/1964
Common no par split (3) for (1) by issuance of (2) additional share 05/12/1965
Common no par split (2) for (1) by issuance of (1) additional share 05/15/1969
Common no par changed to $1 par

and (0.5) additional share issued 05/10/1972
Common $1 par split (2) for (1) by issuance of (1) additional share 01/14/1976
Common $1 par split (2) for (1) by issuance of (1) additional share 05/15/1978
Common $1 par split (2) for (1) by issuance of (1) additional share 05/15/1981
State of incorporation changed from (NY) to (DE) 12/31/1984
Merged into ITT Industries Inc. 05/27/1997
Each share Common $1 par exchanged for $37 cash

GOUNG HEI INVT LTD (DE)
Name changed to Morgan Cooper Inc. 01/28/2000
(See Morgan Cooper Inc.)

GOURDINE SYS INC (DE)
Assets sold and assigned for benefit of creditors in July 1972
No stockholders' equity

GOURMET CUISINE INTL LTD (NV)
Charter permanently revoked 10/31/1998

GOURMET GEN CORP (ID)
Merged into American General Industries 07/15/1984
Each share Common 1¢ par exchanged for (0.1) share Common no par
American General Industries name changed to Pagers Plus 11/18/1987 which name changed to PagePrompt USA 03/09/1994
(See PagePrompt USA)

GOURMET GIFTS INC (NV)
Each share old Common $0.001 par exchanged for (4) shares new Common $0.001 par 12/07/2001
Name changed to Gateway International Holdings Inc. 01/30/2002
Gateway International Holdings Inc. name changed to M Line Holdings, Inc. 03/25/2009

GOURMET GROUP INC (NV)
Reorganized under the laws of Delaware as Drinks Americas Holdings, Ltd. 6/2/2005
Each share Common $0.001 par exchanged for (0.1) share Common $0.001 par

GOURMET HERB GROWERS INC (NV)
Recapitalized as Hong Kong Winalite Group, Inc. 01/14/2008
Each share Common $0.001 par exchanged for (0.13601036) share Common $0.001 par

GOURMET PRODS INTL CORP (FL)
Proclaimed dissolved for failure to file reports and pay fees 11/14/86

GOURMET RES INTL INC (DE)
Chapter 11 bankruptcy proceedings converted to Chapter 7 on 7/2/86
Stockholders' equity unlikely

GOURMET RESTAURANTS INC (CA)
Liquidation completed
Each share Capital Stock no par exchanged for initial distribution of $1.1989 cash 8/13/68
Each share Capital Stock no par received second distribution of $0.7618 cash 2/1/69
Each share Capital Stock no par received third distribution of $0.7404 cash 8/1/69
Each share Capital Stock no par received fourth distribution of $0.719 2/1/70
Each share Capital Stock no par received fifth distribution of $0.6977 cash 8/1/70
Each share Capital Stock no par received sixth distribution of $0.6763 cash 2/1/71

Each share Capital Stock no par received seventh and final distribution of $0.6549 cash 8/1/71

GOURMET WINES LTD (CA)
Adjudicated bankrupt 05/21/1974
Stockholders' equity unlikely

GOURMETMARKET COM INC (DE)
Recapitalized as TargitInteractive Inc. 08/09/2001
Each share Common $0.001 par exchanged for (0.03333333) share Common $0.001 par
TargitInteractive Inc. recapitalized as NetSpace International Holdings, Inc. 06/11/2007 which recapitalized as Alternative Fuels Americas, Inc. 10/13/2010 which name changed to Kaya Holdings, Inc. 04/07/2015

GOURMETS CHOICE COFFEE INC (NV)
Charter revoked for failure to file reports and pay fees 03/01/2005

GOVERNMENT CONCEPTS INC (UT)
Name changed to Kemgas International Inc. 3/9/84
Kemgas International Inc. (UT) reorganized in British Columbia as Kemgas Holdings Ltd. 6/15/88 which name changed to Envirochem Inc. 11/10/93

GOVERNMENT EMPLOYEES CORP (DE)
Common $5 par changed to $2 par and (1.5) additional shares issued 09/20/1962
Stock Dividend - 10% 04/29/1957
Merged into Government Employees Financial Corp. 04/01/1973
Each share Common $2 par exchanged for (0.525) share $0.84 Conv. Preferred 1973 Ser. $2 par
(See Government Employees Financial Corp.)

GOVERNMENT EMPLOYEES FINL CORP (CO)
Stock Dividend - 10% 11/16/1973
Plan of merger effective 07/27/1983
Each share $0.84 Conv. Preferred 1973 Ser. $2 par exchanged for $22.57 cash
Each share Common $2 par exchanged for $19.72 cash

GOVERNMENT EMPLOYEES INS CO (DC)
Each share Common $100 par exchanged for (25) shares Common $4 par in 1948
Common $4 par split (2) for (1) by issuance of (1) additional share 4/15/54
Common $4 par split (2) for (1) by issuance of (1) additional share 4/30/58
Common $4 par split (3) for (2) by issuance of (0.5) additional share 4/30/60
Common $4 par split (3) for (2) by issuance of (0.5) additional share 3/7/69
Common $4 par split (2) for (1) by issuance of (1) additional share 5/2/72
Common $4 par changed to $1 par 4/2/76
Common $1 par changed to 10¢ par 7/28/76
Common 10¢ par changed to $1 par 4/6/77
Stock Dividends - 66-2/3% 7/30/48; 20% 7/1/49; 16-2/3% 7/1/50; 14-2/7% 7/6/51; 25% 11/7/51; 10% 3/18/53; 50% 5/31/62; 50% 4/29/66
Reincorporated under the laws of Delaware as GEICO Corp. 1/31/79
(See GEICO Corp.)

GOVERNMENT EMPLOYEES LIFE INS CO (DC)
Common $1 par changed to $1.50 par in 1954
Stock Dividends - 100% 8/12/59; 50% 7/31/61; 100% 5/10/63; 100% 6/30/70; 50% 6/7/74
Each share Common $1.50 par exchanged for (1/32,000) share Common $48,000 par 12/22/82
Note: In effect holders received $30.75 cash per share and public interest was eliminated

GOVERNMENT GOLD MNG AREAS CONS LTD (SOUTH AFRICA)
Name changed to Consolidated Modderfontein Mines Ltd. 1/26/81
Consolidated Modderfontein Mines Ltd. merged into Harmony Gold Mining Co. Ltd. 7/31/97

GOVERNMENT GTD SECS TR (MA)
Trust terminated 5/18/89
Details not available

GOVERNMENT PERSONNEL SAVINGS & LOAN ASSOCIATION, INC. (MD)
Charter revoked for failure to file reports and pay fees 11/9/65

GOVERNMENT PPTYS TR INC (MD)
Merged into Record Realty Trust 04/13/2007
Each share Common 1¢ par exchanged for $10.75 cash

GOVERNMENT SVCS SVGS & LN INC (MD)
Each share Guaranty Stock 25¢ par exchanged for (0.25) share Guaranty Stock $1 par 12/28/61
Guaranty Stock $1 par split (4) for (3) by issuance of (1/3) additional share 3/2/72
Guaranty Stock $1 par split (2) for (1) by issuance of (1) additional share 9/13/72
Merged into Chevy Chase Savings & Loan, Inc. 11/1/82
Each share Guaranty Stock $1 par exchanged for $10 cash

GOVERNMENT STRIP BD TR (ON)
Trust terminated
Each Unit received first and final distribution of $26.06 cash payable 01/15/2013 to holders of record 12/31/2012

GOVERNMENT TECHNOLOGY SVCS INC (DE)
Name changed to GTSI Corp. 07/31/2000
(See GTSI Corp.)

GOVERNOR GOLD MINES LTD (ON)
Charter cancelled 04/02/1985

GOVERNORS BK CORP (FL)
Merged into Republic Security Financial Corp. 11/30/1994
Details not available

GOVERNORS COMEDY SHOPS INC (DE)
Recapitalized as American Leisure Entertainment Inc. 11/22/89
Each share Common $0.001 par exchanged for (0.01) share Common $0.001 par
American Leisure Entertainment Inc. recapitalized as National Restaurant Group, Inc. 10/14/94 which name changed to Galconda Corp. (New) 8/2/96 which recapitalized as Jax International Inc. 12/3/96
(See Jax International Inc.)

GOVETT & CO LTD (CHANNEL ISLANDS)
Name changed to London Pacific Group Ltd. 12/29/95
London Pacific Group Ltd. name changed to Berkeley Technology Ltd. 6/25/2003

GOVETT STRATEGIC INVT TR PLC (UNITED KINGDOM)
ADR agreement terminated 08/29/2002
Each ADR for Ordinary 10p par exchanged for $4.8051 cash

GOWE PRTG CO (OH)
Merged into Post Corp. 7/27/78
Each share Common no par exchanged for $11 cash

GOWEST AMAL RES LTD (ON)
Name changed 05/27/1982
Name changed from Gowest Gold Resources Inc. to Gowest Amalgamated Resources Ltd. 05/27/1982
Name changed to Gowest Gold Ltd. 04/13/2011

GOWGANDA RES INC (ON)
Name changed to Calgroup Graphics Corp. Ltd. 02/26/1985
(See Calgroup Graphics Corp. Ltd)

GOWGANDA SILVER MINES LTD. (ON)
Name changed to Gowganda Resources Inc. 03/02/1982
Gowganda Resources Inc. name changed to Calgroup Graphics Corp. Ltd. 02/26/1985
(See Calgroup Graphics Corp. Ltd.)

GOYA MUSIC CORP. (NY)
Completely liquidated 5/26/67
Each share Common 10¢ par exchanged for first and final distribution of (0.2858) share Avnet, Inc. Common $1 par

GOZLAN BROS LTD (ON)
Placed in receivership 07/08/1976
No stockholders' equity

GP FINL CORP (DE)
Name changed to GreenPoint Financial Corp. 5/5/95
GreenPoint Financial Corp. merged into North Fork Bancorporation, Inc. 10/1/2004 which merged into Capital One Financial Corp. 12/1/2006

GP INVESTMENTS ACQUISITION CORP (CAYMAN ISLANDS)
Reincorporated under the laws of Delaware as Rimini Street, Inc. and Ordinary Shares $0.0001 par reclassified as Common $0.0001 par 10/11/2017

GP MFG INC (IL)
Voluntarily dissolved 12/28/2004
Details not available

GPC BIOTECH AG (GERMANY)
ADR agreement terminated 03/31/2009
Each Sponsored ADR for Ordinary exchanged for $1.488562 cash

GPC LTD (CANADA)
Wound up 00/00/1971
No stockholders' equity

GPH LIQUIDATING TRUST (DE)
Liquidation completed
Each Share of Bene. Int. received first and final distribution of $0.20010991 cash payable 04/27/2016 to holders of record 06/01/2005
(See Global Preferred Holdings, Inc. for previous distributions)

GPI INC (FL)
Liquidation completed
Each share Common 10¢ par stamped to indicate initial distribution of $2.25 cash 10/15/73
Each share Stamped Common 10¢ par stamped to indicate second distribution of $0.75 cash 10/31/73
Each share 2nd Stamped Common 10¢ par stamped to indicate third distribution of $1 cash 7/15/74
Each share 3rd Stamped Common 10¢ par stamped to indicate fourth distribution of $0.80 cash 10/9/74
Each share 4th Stamped Common 10¢ par exchanged for fifth and final distribution of $0.0464 cash 4/21/75

GPI INDS LTD (BC)
Acquired by Pattison (Jim) Enterprises Ltd. 00/00/1975
Each share Common no par exchanged for $6.75 cash

GPJ VENTURES LTD (BC)
Name changed to Peak Gold Ltd. 04/04/2007
Peak Gold Ltd. merged into New Gold Inc. 06/30/2008

GPM BALANCED FUND, INC. (MA)
Under plan of merger each share Capital Stock $1 par automatically became (1) share GPM Fund, Inc. Common $1 par 05/19/1978
(See GPM Fund, Inc.)

GPM FD INC (MA)
Voluntarily dissolved 12/21/1990
Details not available

GPN NETWORK INC (DE)
Each share old Common $0.001 par exchanged for (0.05) share new Common $0.001 par 07/01/2003
Name changed to IR BioSciences Holdings, Inc. 08/28/2003

GPS INDS INC (NV)
SEC revoked common stock registration 12/18/2013

GPS INVT CORP (AB)
Name changed to Astrix Networks Inc. 11/01/2013
Astrix Networks Inc. name changed to Memex Inc. 07/22/2015

GPS TECHNOLOGIES INC (DE)
Name changed to SGLG, Inc. 8/31/94
(See SGLG, Inc.)

GPU INC (PA)
Secondary Offering - 6,100,000 shares COM offered at $39.5625 per share on 01/09/1998
Merged into FirstEnergy Corp. 11/7/2001
Each share Common $2.50 par exchanged for $36.50 cash

GR FOODS INC (NY)
Name changed to Ground Round Restaurants, Inc. 6/18/91
(See Ground Round Restaurants, Inc.)

GRABILL BANCORP (IN)
Merged into Independent Alliance Banks, Inc. 05/01/2005
Each share Common exchanged for (116.1) shares Common
Note: Non-Indiana residents or holders of fewer than (5) shares received $7,900 cash per share
Independent Alliance Banks, Inc. merged into First Merchants Corp. 07/14/2017

GRABLER MANUFACTURING CO.
Name changed to Relbarg Liquidating Corp. in 1944
(See Relbarg Liquidating Corp.)

GRABOPLAST RT (HUNGARY)
Acquired by ABC Asset Management 03/31/2002
Each 144A GDR for Ordinary exchanged for $1.0403 cash
Each Reg. S GDR for Ordinary exchanged for $1.0403 cash

GRACE COTTON MILLS CO.
Acquired by Reeves Brothers, Inc. in 1946
Details not available

GRACE DEV INC (CO)
SEC revoked common stock registration 12/21/2016

GRACE ENERGY CORP (DE)
Merged into Grace (W.R.) & Co. 7/14/92
Each share Common $1 par exchanged for $19 cash

GRACE-LARDER GOLD MINES LTD.
Acquired by Mulven Lake Gold Mines Ltd. on a (1) for (10) basis in 1939
(See Mulven Lake Gold Mines Ltd.)

GRACE NATIONAL BANK (NEW YORK, NY)
Stock Dividends - 12-1/2% 9/28/45; 33-1/3% 5/11/51; 50% 1/30/61
Liquidation completed

Each share Capital Stock $100 par received initial distribution of (5) shares Marine Midland Corp. $5.50 Conv. Preferred no par 8/26/65
Each share Capital Stock $100 par received second and final distribution of (0.765) share Marine Midland Corp. $5.50 Conv. Preferred no par 9/15/65
Certificates were not retired and are now without value

GRACE RES INC (AB)
Acquired by Cebanx Investments Inc. 03/13/2001
Each share Common no par exchanged for $1 cash

GRACE W R & CO (DE)
Each share Common 1¢ par received distribution of (1) share Grace (W.R.) & Co. (New) Common 1¢ par payable 4/6/98 to holders of record 3/31/98
Merged into Sealed Air Corp. (New) 3/31/98
Each share Common 1¢ par exchanged for (0.475) share $2 Conv. Preferred Ser. A 10¢ par and (0.536) share Common 10¢ par

GRACE W R & CO (NY)
Reincorporated 05/19/1988
Common $100 par changed to no par 00/00/1929
Each share Common no par exchanged for (2) shares Common no par 00/00/1943
Each share Common no par exchanged for (1.5) shares Common no par 00/00/1945
Each share Common no par exchanged for (3) shares Common no par 00/00/1949
Common no par changed to $1 par 00/00/1954
Common $1 par split (2) for (1) by issuance of (1) additional share 06/01/1962
Common $1 par split (2) for (1) by issuance of (1) additional share 12/10/1987
State of incorporation changed from (CT) to (NY) 05/19/1988
Name changed to Fresenius National Medical Care Holdings, Inc. 09/30/1996
Fresenius National Medical Care Holdings, Inc. name changed to Fresenius Medical Care Holdings Inc. 10/01/1996
(See Fresenius Medical Care Holdings Inc.)
Each share Common $1 par received distribution of (1) share Grace (W.R.) & Co. (DE) payable 10/02/1996 to holders of record 09/25/1996
Merged into Fresenius Medical Care AG 09/30/1996
Each share Common $1 par exchanged for (1.04909) Sponsored ADR's for Bearer Shares DM 5 par and (1) share Fresenius National Medical Care Holdings, Inc. Class D Preferred $1 par
(See each company's listing)

GRACECARE HEALTH SYS INC (DE)
Name changed to Iatros Health Network Inc. 10/25/94
Iatros Health Network Inc. name changed to Phoenix Healthcare Corp. 5/6/99 which name changed to Phoenix Group Corp. 10/10/2000 which name changed to Lighting Science Corp. 12/23/2004

GRACEFIELD CAP LTD (ON)
Name changed 09/01/1989
Reincorporated 10/24/1995
Name changed from Gracefield Explorations Inc. to Gracefield Capital Corp. Ltd. 09/01/1989
Place of incorporation changed from (Canada) to (ON) 10/24/1995

Recapitalized as Southern Reef Ventures Inc. 08/07/1996
Each share Common no par exchanged for (0.05) share Common no par
(See Southern Reef Ventures Inc.)

GRACEY RES INC (BC)
Struck from the register and dissolved 11/6/92

GRACIOUS LIVING, INC. (DE)
Dissolved 4/16/64

GRACKLE GOLD MINES LTD.
Bankrupt in 1952

GRACO OIL & REFINING CO.
Common 10¢ par changed to 1¢ par 09/00/1949
Name changed to Sioux Oil Co. 12/12/1949
Sioux Oil Co. merged into Tesoro Petroleum Corp. (CA) 02/01/1968 which reincorporated in Delaware as Tesoro Petroleum Corp. 03/03/1969 which name changed to Tesoro Corp. 11/08/2004 which name changed to Andeavor 08/01/2017 which merged into Marathon Petroleum Corp. 10/01/2018

GRAD & WALKER ENERGY CORP (AB)
Merged into Crestar Energy Inc. 07/29/1997
Each share Common no par exchanged for either (0.509) share Common no par or $13.50 cash
Crestar Energy Inc. was acquired by Gulf Canada Resources Ltd. 11/13/2000
(See Gulf Canada Resources Ltd.)

GRADALL INDS INC (DE)
Merged into JLG Industries, Inc. 6/18/99
Each share Common $0.001 par exchanged for $20 cash

GRADCO SYS INC (NV)
Reincorporated 04/03/1992
State of incorporation changed from (CA) to (NV) 04/03/1992
Each share old Common no par exchanged for (0.03333333) share new Common no par 10/01/2002
Merged into Gradco Holdings LLC 06/08/2004
Each share new Common no par exchanged for $10 cash

GRADIAZ, ANNIS & CO., INC. (FL)
Merged into General Cigar Co. 5/17/63
Each share Common $1 par exchanged for (0.6) share Common $1 par
General Cigar Co. name changed to Culbro Corp. 6/1/76 which merged into General Cigar Holdings, Inc. 8/29/97
(See General Cigar Holdings, Inc.)

GRADIN EQUITIES INC (NV)
Charter permanently revoked 03/31/2000

GRADIPORE LTD (AUSTRALIA)
Name changed to Life Therapeutics Ltd. 01/21/2005
Life Therapeutics Ltd. recapitalized as Arturus Capital Ltd. 08/14/2012
(See Arturus Capital Ltd.)

GRADISON & CO INC (DE)
Merged into McDonald & Co. Investments, Inc. 10/04/1991
Each share Common 10¢ par had option to receive initial payment of (1.517) shares Common $1 par, $13.8167 cash or a combination thereof
Each share Common 10¢ par had option to receive second payment of (0.1232) share Common $1 par, $1.1217 cash or a combination thereof 12/02/1991
Note: Non-electing holders received

the option elected by the majority of holders
McDonald & Co. Investments, Inc. merged into Keycorp (New) 10/23/1998

GRADISON CASH RESVS TR (MA)
Reorganized 12/29/1981
Under plan of reorganization each share Gradison Cash Reserves Inc. (MD) Common 1¢ par automatically became (1) Gradison Cash Reserves Trust (MA) Share of Bene. Int. 1¢ par 12/29/1981
Merged into Victory Portfolios 04/06/1999
Details not available

GRADISON GROWTH TR (OH)
Merged into Victory Portfolios 04/06/1999
Details not available

GRADISON U S GOVT TR (MA)
Merged into Gradison U.S. Government Reserves 09/27/1993
Details not available

GRADORE MINES LTD (ON)
Charter cancelled for failure to pay taxes and file returns 03/16/1976

GRAFCO INDS INC (NY)
Dissolved by proclamation 03/24/1993

GRAFF PAY-PER-VIEW INC (DE)
Common 1¢ par split (6) for (5) by issuance of (0.2) additional share 03/08/1993
Name changed to Spice Entertainment Inc. 12/02/1996
(See Spice Entertainment Inc.)

GRAFFITI-X INC (DE)
Name changed to Amnis Systems Inc. and (1.82) additional shares issued 08/31/2000
Amnis Systems Inc. name changed to Corridor Communications Corp. 03/31/2004
(See Corridor Communications Corp.)

GRAFIX CORP (NY)
Recapitalized as Player (Gary) Direct Inc. 04/09/1999
Each share Common $0.001 par exchanged for (0.05) share Common $0.001 par
(See Player (Gary) Direct Inc.)

GRAFIX TIME CORP (NY)
Each share old Common $0.001 par exchanged for (0.1) share new Common $0.001 par 05/14/1992
Each share new Common $0.001 par exchanged again for (0.025) share new Common $0.001 par 01/15/1996
Stock Dividend - 40% payable 12/14/1995 to holders of record 12/14/1995
Recapitalized as Grafix Corp. 08/01/1998
Each share new Common $0.001 par exchanged for (0.33333333) share Common $0.001 par
Grafix Corp. recapitalized as Player (Gary) Direct Inc. 04/09/1999
(See Player (Gary) Direct Inc.)

GRAFTECH INTL LTD (DE)
Acquired by BCP IV GrafTech Holdings L.P. 08/17/2015
Each share Common 1¢ par exchanged for $5.05 cash
(Additional Information in Active)

GRAFTON FRASER LTD (ON)
6% Preference called for redemption 03/15/1975
Public interest eliminated

GRAFTON GROUP LTD (ON)
Old Common no par split (3) for (2) by issuance of (0.5) additional share 05/13/1977
Reorganized as Grafton Group Ltd.-Le Groupe Grafton Ltee. 06/05/1979
Each (5) shares old Common no par exchanged for (1) share Preference

Ser. A no par, (8) shares Class A no par and (2) shares new Common no par
Class A no par split (3) for (1) by issuance of (2) additional shares 06/28/1985
New Common no par split (3) for (1) by issuance of (2) additional shares 06/28/1985
Declared bankrupt 04/06/1993
No stockholders' equity

GRAFTONS 1853 LTD. (ON)
Name changed to Grafton-Fraser Ltd. 10/16/1967
(See Grafton-Fraser Ltd.)

GRAHAM BELL LTD. (ON)
Name changed to Cerametal Industries Ltd. 00/00/1959
(See Cerametal Industries Ltd.)

GRAHAM BOUSQUET GOLD MINES LTD. (ON)
Merged into Cadamet Mines Ltd. 11/17/1958
Each share Capital Stock $1 par exchanged for (0.25) share Capital Stock $1 par
Cadamet Mines Ltd. recapitalized as Terrex Mining Co. Ltd. 09/08/1966
(See Terrex Mining Co. Ltd.)

GRAHAM BOUSQUET MINING CORP.
Succeeded by Graham Bousquet Gold Mines Ltd. on a (1) for (2) basis in 1934
Graham Bousquet Gold Mines Ltd. merged into Cadamet Mines Ltd. 11/17/58 which recapitalized as Terrex Mining Co. Ltd. 9/8/66
(See Terrex Mining Co. Ltd.)

GRAHAM CHEMICAL CORP. (NY)
Name changed to Maharg Co., Inc. 3/30/66
Maharg Co., Inc. acquired by Revlon, Inc. 4/8/66
(See Revlon, Inc.)

GRAHAM-FIELD HEALTH PRODS INC (DE)
Chapter 11 bankruptcy proceedings converted to Chapter 7 on 06/20/2003
No stockholders' equity

GRAHAM GOLD MNG CORP (BC)
Name changed to Sense Technologies Inc. (BC) 10/27/1997
Sense Technologies Inc. (BC) reincorporated in Yukon 12/14/2001 which reincorporated back in British Columbia 11/15/2007

GRAHAM MAGNETICS INC (TX)
Merged into Carlisle Corp. 11/29/77
Each share Common 10¢ par exchanged for $18 cash

GRAHAM MFG INC (NY)
Common 10¢ par split (3) for (2) by issuance of (0.5) additional share 6/15/76
Under plan of reorganization each share Common 10¢ par automatically became (1) share Graham Corp. (DE) Common 10¢ par 8/1/83

GRAHAM MCCORMICK OIL & GAS PARTNERSHIP (TX)
Completely liquidated 6/28/88
Each Depositary Receipt for Units of Ltd. Partnership exchanged for (0.02) Preference A Unit of Snyder Oil Partners L.P.
Note: Holdings entitled to fewer than (25) Preference A Units received cash
Depositary Receipts were not required to be surrendered and are now valueless
(See Snyder Oil Partners L.P.)

GRAHAM-NEWMAN CORP. (NY)
Completely liquidated
Each share Capital Stock no par received initial distribution of (10) shares Philadelphia & Reading Corp. Common $1 par and $400 cash 09/19/1956
Note: Holders had the option to receive $220.625 cash in lieu of stock
Each share Capital Stock no par received second distribution of $100 cash 10/25/1956
Each share Capital Stock no par received third distribution of $40 cash 02/11/1957
Each share Capital Stock no par received fourth distribution of $80 cash 05/24/1957
Each share Capital Stock no par received fifth and final distribution of $90.4962 cash 12/09/1960
Note: Certificates were not required to be surrendered and are without value

GRAHAM PACKAGING CO INC (DE)
Issue Information - 16,666,667 shares COM offered at $10 per share on 02/10/2010
Acquired by Reynolds Group Holdings Ltd. 09/08/2011
Each share Common 1¢ par exchanged for $25.50 cash

GRAHAM-PAIGE CORP. (MI)
Common no par changed to $1 par 4/7/59
6% Preferred $10 par reclassified as 60¢ Preferred no par 4/20/60
Name changed to Madison Square Garden Corp. (MI) 4/4/62
(See Madison Square Garden Corp. (MI))

GRAHAM-PAIGE MOTORS CORP. (MI)
Recapitalized as Graham-Paige Corp. and Common $1 par changed to no par 9/18/50
Graham-Paige Corp. name changed to Madison Square Garden Corp. (MI) 4/4/62
(See Madison Square Garden Corp. (MI))

GRAHAM STUART CORP (OH)
Charter cancelled for failure to file reports and pay fees 9/30/71

GRAIL ADVISORS ETF TR (DE)
Trust terminated 08/31/2010
Each RP Financials ETF no par received first and final distribution of $23.18642 cash
Each RP Technology ETF no par received first and final distribution of $27.51981 cash
American Beacon Large Cap Value ETF no par reclassified as Columbia Concentrated Large Cap Value Strategy Fund no par 05/02/2011
Name changed to Columbia ETF Trust and McDonnell Core Taxable Bond ETF no par, McDonnell Intermediate Municipal Bond ETF no par, RP Focused Large Cap Growth ETF no par and RP Growth ETF no par reclassified as Columbia Core Bond Strategy Fund no par, Columbia Intermediate Municipal Bond Strategy Fund no par, Columbia Large-Cap Growth Equity Strategy Fund no par and Columbia Growth Equity Strategy Fund respectively 05/23/2011

GRAIN BELT BREWERIES INC (MN)
Capital Stock $1 par changed to 10¢ par and (1) additional share issued 1/20/70
Name changed to Minneapolis Shareholders Co. 4/5/75
Note: Although name change was effective, certificates under the old name are still being issued
(See Minneapolis Shareholders Co.)

GRAIN ELEVATOR WAREHOUSE CO. (DE)
Merged into National Alfalfa Dehydrating & Milling Co. on a (1.83) for (1) basis 11/1/63
(See National Alfalfa Dehydrating & Milling Co.)

GRALY INC. (NV)
Merged into Genalta, Inc. 09/23/1988
Details not available

GRALY RES INC (NV)
Recapitalized as Graly Inc. 11/10/1986
Each (3,000) shares Common 1¢ par exchanged for (1) share Common 1¢ par
(See Graly Inc.)

GRAM INDS INC (CT)
Name changed to Transact International Inc. 10/13/1982
(See Transact Internatioinal Inc.)

GRAM MINERALS CORP (CANADA)
Charter dissolved for non-compliance 12/05/2003

GRAMAPHONE CO., LTD.
Merged into Electric & Musical Industries Ltd. 04/20/1931
Details not available
(See Electric & Musical Industries Ltd.)

GRAMARA MERCANTILE LTD (BC)
Recapitalized as Groundstar Resources Ltd. (BC) 08/31/1973
Each share Common no par exchanged for (0.2) share Common no par
Groundstar Resources Ltd. (BC) reincorporated in Alberta 10/28/2005

GRAMATAN INC (NY)
Common $1 par changed to $10 par 01/14/1958
Completely liquidated 02/14/1975
Each share Common $10 par exchanged for first and final distribution of $1.20 cash

GRAMATAN REAL ESTATE INVT TR (NY)
Name changed to Home Investors Trust 01/25/1972
(See Home Investors Trust)

GRAMERCY CAP CORP (MD)
Name changed to Gramercy Property Trust Inc. 04/15/2013
Gramercy Property Trust Inc. merged into Gramercy Property Trust 12/17/2015
(See Gramercy Property Trust)

GRAMERCY PARK BLDG CORP (NY)
Liquidation completed
Each share Common no par or VTC's for Common no par stamped to indicate initial distribution of $450 cash 7/15/69
Each share Stamped Common no par or Stamped VTC's for Common no par exchanged for second distribution of $50 cash plus a receipt evidencing right to receive additional distributions 12/5/69
Each receiptholder received third distribution of $20 cash per share 3/2/70
Each receiptholder received fourth distribution of $75 cash per share 7/1/71
Each receiptholder received fifth and final distribution of $6 cash per share 12/15/73

GRAMERCY PPTY TR (MD)
Each old Common Share of Bene. Int. 1¢ par exchanged for (0.33333333) new Common Share of Bene. Int. 1¢ par 01/03/2017
7.125% Preferred Shares of Bene. Int. Ser. A 1¢ par called for redemption at $25.05 on 10/10/2018
Acquired by Blackstone Group L.P. 10/10/2018
Each new Common Share of Bene. Int. 1¢ par exchanged for $27.50 cash

GRAMERCY PPTY TR INC (MD)
8.125% Preferred Ser. A $0.001 par called for redemption at $25 plus $0.32161 accrued dividends on 09/12/2014
Each share old Common $0.001 par exchanged for (0.25) share new Common $0.001 par 03/23/2015
Merged into Gramercy Property Trust 12/17/2015
Each share 7.125% Preferred Ser. B $0.001 par exchanged for (1) 7.125% Preferred Share of Bene. Int. Ser. A 1¢ par
Each share new Common $0.001 par exchanged for (3.1898) Common Shares of Bene. Int. 1¢ par
(See Gramercy Property Trust)

GRAMMES (L.F.) & SONS, INC. (MD)
Adjudicated bankrupt in March 1963
No stockholders' equity

GRAMOTT CORP. (NY)
Charter cancelled and proclaimed dissolved for failure to pay taxes and file reports 12/14/48

GRAN CADENA DE ALMACENES COLOMBIANOS S A (COLOMBIA)
ADR agreement terminated 08/06/2001
Each 144A Sponsored ADR for Ordinary exchanged for $3.1154 cash
Each Sponsored ADR for Class B Preferred exchanged for $3.1154 cash

GRAN COLOMBIA RES INC (BC)
Reincorporated 06/21/1996
Place of incorporation changed from (BC) to (Yukon) 06/21/1996
Name changed to Wavve Telecommunications, Inc. 10/29/1999
(See Wavve Telecommunications, Inc.)

GRAN-MARK INCOME PPTYS LIMITED PARTNERSHIP (MD)
Forfeited for failure to file property returns 10/07/2005

GRAN PRIX ENTERPRISES, INC. (MN)
Statutorily dissolved 11/08/1991

GRAN TIERRA ENERGY INC (NV)
Reincorporated under the laws of Delaware 10/31/2016

GRAN TIERRA EXCHANGECO INC (AB)
Each Exchangeable Share exchanged for (1) share Gran Tierra Energy Inc. Common $0.001 par 07/04/2018
Note: Unexchanged certificates will be cancelled and become without value 07/04/2020

GRANA Y MONTERO S A A (PERU)
ADR agreement terminated 04/26/2013
No ADR's remain outstanding
(Additional Information in Active)

GRANADA BANK (ALHAMBRA, CA)
Merged into California State Bank (Covina, CA) 11/19/85
Each share Common no par exchanged for (1.047) shares Common no par
California State Bank (Covina, CA) merged into First Security Corp. 5/30/98 which merged into Wells Fargo & Co. (New) 10/26/2000

GRANADA CO. (CA)
Dissolved 6/1/61

GRANADA EXPL CORP (BC)
Struck off register and declared dissolved for failure to file returns 07/10/1992

GRANADA MINERAL PRODS INC (NV)
Each share old Common $0.001 par exchanged for (10) shares new Common $0.001 par 04/10/2001
Name changed to Malahat Energy Corp. 05/30/2001

Malahat Energy Corp. name changed to PHC Holdings 12/22/2004 which recapitalized as Rudy 45 on 09/26/2005 which name changed to NMI Group, Inc. 07/13/2007

GRANADA OIL INDUSTRIES INC. (NV)
Charter revoked for failure to file reports and pay fees 3/3/75

GRANAHAN MCCOURT ACQUISITION CORP (DE)
Issue Information - 11,250,000 UNITS consisting of (1) share COM and (1) WT offered at $6 per Unit on 10/18/2006
Completely liquidated 11/18/2008
Each Unit exchanged for first and final distribution of $8.34313854 cash
Each share Common $0.0001 par exchanged for first and final distribution of $8.34313854 cash

GRANATELLI J T LUBRICANTS INC (NV)
Each share old Common $0.001 par exchanged for (0.1) share new Common $0.001 par 7/10/2000
Name changed to Nanotech Fuel Corp. 5/31/2001

GRANBY CONSOLIDATED MINING SMELTING & POWER CO. LTD. (BC)
Capital Stock $100 par changed to $5 par 00/00/1937
Name changed to Granby Mining Co. Ltd. 03/21/1959
Granby Mining Co. Ltd. name changed to Granby Mining Corp. 02/27/1975 which merged into Zapata Granby Corp. 01/01/1979
(See Zapata Granby Corp.)

GRANBY ELASTIC & TEXTILES LTD. (CANADA)
Bankrupt 00/00/1969
No stockholders' equity

GRANBY ELASTIC WEB OF CANADA LTD.
Name changed to Granby Elastic & Textiles Ltd. 00/00/1952
(See Granby Elastic & Textiles Ltd.)

GRANBY INDS INCOME FD (ON)
Acquired by Clarke Inc. 03/04/2008
Each Unit no par received $0.17 cash

GRANBY MINING CO. LTD. (BC)
Common $5 par changed to $1.66666666 par and (2) additional shares issued 05/06/1968
Name changed to Granby Mining Corp. 02/27/1975
Granby Mining Corp. merged into Zapata Granby Corp. 01/01/1979
(See Zapata Granby Corp.)

GRANBY MNG CORP (BC)
Merged into Zapata Granby Corp. 01/01/1979
Each share Common $1.66666666 par exchanged for (2.7) shares $0.40 Conv. Preference no par
(See Zapata Granby Corp.)

GRANBY RES LTD (BC)
Recapitalized as Consolidated Granby Resources Ltd. (BC) 03/17/1995
Each (4.6) shares Common no par exchanged for (1) share Common no par
Consolidated Granby Resources Ltd. (BC) reincorporated in Canada 05/16/1997 which recapitalized as CRA Phase II Ltd. 11/02/2000
(See CRA Phase II Ltd.)

GRANBY SLATE MINING LTD. (QC)
Charter annulled for failure to file reports or pay fees 11/9/74

GRANCAMP RES INC (BC)
Struck off register and declared dissolved for failure to file returns 9/25/90

GRANCARE INC (CA)
Each share Common no par received distribution of (1) share GranCare Inc. (DE) Common $0.001 par payable 2/18/97 to holders of record 2/12/97
Merged into Vitalink Pharmacy Services, Inc. 2/12/97
Each share Common no par exchanged for (0.478) share Common 1¢ par
Vitalink Pharmacy Services, Inc. merged into Genesis Health Ventures, Inc. 8/28/98
(See Genesis Health Ventures, Inc.)

GRANCARE INC (DE)
Merged into Paragon Health Network, Inc. 11/4/97
Each share Common $0.001 par exchanged for (0.2346) share Common 1¢ par
Paragon Health Network, Inc. name changed to Mariner Post-Acute Network, Inc. 7/31/98
(See Mariner Post-Acute Network, Inc.)

GRANCO, INC. (CA)
Class A Common $1 par changed to 50¢ par and (1) additional share issued 4/10/62
Merged into American Vanguard Corp. 2/25/72
Each share Class A Common 50¢ par exchanged for (0.25) share Common 10¢ par

GRANCO PRODUCTS INC. (NY)
Stock Dividend - 10% 07/11/1960
Out of business 11/00/1964
Details not available

GRANCOUR GOLD MINES, LTD. (ON)
Charter revoked for failure to file reports and pay taxes 00/00/1952

GRAND & TOY LTD (ON)
Acquired by T.R. Grand Holdings 09/28/1979
Details not available

GRAND ADVENTURES TOUR & TRAVEL PUBG CORP (DE)
Reincorporated 06/05/2000
Each share old Common $0.0001 par exchanged for (0.14285714) share new Commom $0.0001 par 12/16/1997
State of incorporation changed from (OR) to (DE) 06/05/2000
Company terminated registration of common stock and is no longer public as of 10/30/2008
Details not available

GRAND AMER MINERALS LTD (BC)
Name changed to G.D.M. Grand Development Corp. 04/22/1994
(See G.D.M. Grand Development Corp.)

GRAND AMERN INTL CORP (CO)
Each share old Class A Common $0.003 par exchanged for (0.1) share new Class A Common $0.003 par 4/10/91
Name changed to Continental Wellness Casinos, Inc. 12/23/95
Continental Wellness Casinos, Inc. name changed to Continental Wellness Casinos Trust R.E.I.T. 12/22/97 which name changed to Countryland Wellness Resorts, Inc. 9/22/99 which recapitalized as Minerals Mining Corp. 11/6/2000

GRAND AUTO INC (CA)
Common $1 par changed to no par and (0.5) additional share issued 06/24/1983
Acquired by PACCAR Inc 06/01/1988
Each share Common no par exchanged for $16 cash

GRAND AVE BK & TR CO (KANSAS CITY, MO)
Common Capital Stock $20 par changed to $5 par and (3) additional shares issued 1/21/65
Stock Dividends - 50% 1/18/66; 100% 1/22/74
Name changed to City Bank & Trust Co. (Kansas City, MO) 3/27/78
(See City Bank & Trust Co. (Kansas City, MO))

GRAND AVENUE BANK (KANSAS CITY, MO)
Stock Dividend - 50% 1/18/60
Name changed to Grand Avenue Bank & Trust Co. (Kansas City, MO) 6/4/64
Grand Avenue Bank & Trust Co. (Kansas City, MO) name changed to City Bank & Trust Co. (Kansas City, MO) 3/27/78
(See City Bank & Trust Co. (Kansas City, MO))

GRAND BAHAMA INDUSTRIES LTD. (ON)
Name changed to Bahamas-Caribbean Development Corp. Ltd. 03/31/1966
Bahamas-Caribbean Development Corp. Ltd. recapitalized as Oceanus Industries (Bahamas) Ltd. 03/24/1972
(See Oceanus Industries (Bahamas) Ltd.)

GRAND BANKS ENERGY CORP (AB)
Acquired by Fairborne Energy Ltd. (New) 06/19/2008
Each share Common no par exchanged for $2.90 cash

GRAND BKS YACHTS LTD (SINGAPORE)
ADR agreement terminated 08/25/2017
Each Sponsored ADR for Ordinary exchanged for $1.078 cash

GRAND BAY EXPLS LTD (ON)
Recapitalized as Tropika International Ltd. 05/31/1995
Each share Common no par exchanged for (0.2) share Common no par
(See Tropika International Ltd.)

GRAND CDN MNG LTD (ON)
Charter cancelled for failure to pay taxes and file returns 12/12/1973

GRAND CANAL ENTMT INC (DE)
Stock Dividend - 36.61334% payable 10/10/2008 payable to holders of record 09/29/2008 Ex date - 10/14/2008
Name changed to OC Beverages, Inc. 11/25/2008

GRAND CANYON LIFE INSURANCE CO. (AZ)
Merged into Security National Life Insurance Co. (UT) 12/30/66
Each share Common exchanged for (0.222222) share Class A Common $1.50 par
Security National Life Insurance Co. (UT) merged into S.N.L. Financial Corp. 3/24/80 which name changed to Security National Financial Corp. 12/27/90

GRAND CANYON PUBLICATIONS, INC. (UT)
Proclaimed dissolved for failure to pay taxes 12/31/1983

GRAND CANYON RES INC (BC)
Name changed to T.I. Travel International Inc. 07/10/1986
(See T.I. Travel International Inc.)

GRAND CASINOS INC (MN)
Common 1¢ par split (3) for (2) by issuance of (0.5) additional share 12/28/1995
Each share Common 1¢ par received distribution of (0.25) share Lakes Gaming, Inc. Common 1¢ par payable 12/31/1998 to holders of record 12/23/1998
Stock Dividend - 10% 11/30/1992
Merged into Park Place Entertainment Corp. 12/31/1998

Each share Common 1¢ par exchanged for (0.9699) share Common $2.50 par
Park Place Entertainment Corp. name changed to Caesars Entertainment, Inc. 01/05/2004
(See Caesars Entertainment, Inc.)

GRAND CENT FINL CORP (DE)
Name changed to Central Federal Corp. 4/23/2003

GRAND CENT INC (UT)
Stock Dividends - 20% 11/8/74; 50% 10/15/76
Acquired by Meyer (Fred) Inc., 6/27/84
Each share Common 50¢ par exchanged for $11 cash

GRAND CENT SILVER MINES INC (UT)
Each share old Common $0.001 par exchanged for (0.125) share new Common $0.001 par 01/13/1999
SEC revoked common stock registration 10/24/2007

GRAND CHIBOUGAMAU MINES LTD. (ON)
Merged into Consolidated Federick Mines Ltd. 09/09/1957
Each share Capital Stock no par exchanged for (0.85714285) share Capital Stock no par
(See Consolidated Federick Mines Ltd.)

GRAND CHINA RES LTD (BC)
Recapitalized as New China Resources Ltd. 09/07/1989
Each share Common no par exchanged for (0.2) share Common no par
New China Resources Ltd. name changed to Sino Pac International Investments Inc. 02/06/1991 which recapitalized as Paron Resources Inc. 12/16/1996

GRAND CT LIFESTYLES INC (DE)
Plan of reorganization under Chapter 11 Federal Bankruptcy Code effective 12/19/2002
No stockholders' equity

GRAND DEP MNG CO (NV)
Each share old Capital Stock 5¢ par exchanged for (0.1) share new Capital Stock 5¢ par 3/14/61
Each share new Capital Stock 5¢ par exchanged for (6) shares Capital Stock no par 7/10/64
Charter revoked for failure to file reports and pay fees 3/3/69

GRAND DEPOSIT CONSOLIDATED MINES, INC.
Succeeded by Grand Deposit Mining Co. in 1941
Details not available

GRAND ENTERPRISES INC (DE)
Reorganized as Manhattan Scientifics Inc. 1/8/98
Each share Common $0.001 par exchanged for (11) shares Common $0.001 par

GRAND ENTMT & MUSIC INC (FL)
Each share old Common $0.001 par exchanged for (0.00333333) share new Common $0.001 par 01/30/2006
Administratively dissolved 09/23/2011

GRAND FORKS MINES LTD (BC)
Recapitalized as Attwood Gold Corp. 06/16/1989
Each share Common no par exchanged for (0.2) share Common no par
Attwood Gold Corp. recapitalized as Dynasty Motorcar Corp. (BC) 06/02/2000 which reincorporated in Canada 11/29/2002 which recapitalized as Comwest Capital Corp. 06/29/2004 which merged into ComWest Enterprise Corp.

12/12/2005 which name changed to Unisync Corp. 08/01/2014

GRAND GAMING CORP (MN)
Merged into Grand Casinos, Inc. 11/30/1995
Each share Common 2¢ par exchanged for (0.1397) share Common 1¢ par
Grand Casinos, Inc. merged into Park Place Entertainment Corp. 12/31/1998 which name changed to Caesars Entertainment, Inc. 01/05/2004
(See Caesars Entertainment, Inc.)

GRAND HAVANA ENTERPRISES INC (DE)
Merged into Grand Havana Acquisition Corp. 2/21/2007
Each share Common 1¢ par exchanged for $0.22 cash

GRAND HOTEL HLDGS LTD (HONG KONG)
ADR agreement terminated 03/20/2003
Each Sponsored ADR for Ordinary exchanged $1.1581 cash

GRAND INDUSTRIES, INC. (OH)
Merged into Cleveland Hobbing Machine Co. in 1952
Each share Common $9 par exchanged for (1) share Common $1 par
Cleveland Hobbing Machine Co. acquired by Fanner Manufacturing Co. 8/20/56 which merged into Textron Inc. (R.I.) 1/24/58 which was reincorporated under the laws of Delaware 1/2/68

GRAND IS OVERLAND CO (NE)
Stock Dividends - 10% 05/27/1975; 15% 09/27/1976
Name changed to Commerce Group Grand Island, Inc. 05/22/1978
(See Commerce Group Grand Island, Inc.)

GRAND LUX INC (FL)
Each (900) shares old Common 4¢ par exchanged for (1) share new Common 4¢ par 10/25/2004
Recapitalized as World Hockey Association Corp. 09/23/2005
Each share new Common 4¢ par exchanged for (0.001) share Common 4¢ par

GRAND MANITOU MINES LTD. (QC)
Charter cancelled 07/14/1972

GRAND MESA URANIUM CO. (NV)
Recapitalized as Andy's International, Inc. 11/08/1968
Each share Capital Stock 10¢ par exchanged for (0.05) share Capital Stock $1 par
(See Andy's International, Inc.)

GRAND MET DEL L P (DE)
9.42% Guaranteed Preferred Securities Ser. A called for redemption at $25 plus $0.105 accrued dividend on 11/16/2004

GRAND MET P L C (ENGLAND)
Each Unsponsored ADR for Ordinary 50p par exchanged for (1) Sponsored ADR for Ordinary 50p par 03/28/1988
ADR basis changed from (1:2) to (1:4) 04/15/1992
Stock Dividends - 20% 04/24/1984; 10% 04/22/1986
Merged into Diageo PLC 12/17/1997
Each Sponsored ADR for Ordinary 25p par exchanged for (1) Sponsored ADR for Ordinary 25p par

GRAND METROPOLITAN HOTELS LTD. (ENGLAND)
Name changed to Grand Metropolitan PLC 04/02/1973
Grand Metropolitan PLC merged into Diageo PLC 12/17/1997

GRAND MOTION INC (NV)
Common $0.0001 par split (2) for (1) by issuance of (1) additional share payable 04/02/2008 to holders of record 03/21/2008 Ex date - 04/03/2008
Name changed to OpenCell Biomed Inc. 09/02/2008
OpenCell Biomed Inc. recapitalized as Preferred Commerce Inc. 06/20/2014

GRAND NATL BK (EPHRATA, WA)
Merged into United Security Bancorporation 07/20/1998
Each share Common $25 par exchanged for (14.19) shares Common no par
United Security Bancorporation name changed to AmericanWest Bancorporation 03/05/2001
(See AmericanWest Bancorporation)

GRAND NATIONAL FILMS, INC.
Acquired by Grand National Pictures, Inc. in 1938
Details not available

GRAND NATL RES INC (BC)
Recapitalized as Consolidated Grand National Resources Inc. 3/16/2000
Each share Common no par exchanged for (0.1) share Common no par
Consolidated Grand National Resources Inc. name changed to First Star Innovations Inc. 11/28/2000 which name changed to First Star Resources Inc. 12/16/2003

GRAND OAKES RES CORP (BC)
Acquired by Midlands Minerals Corp. 06/02/2004
Each share Common no par exchanged for (0.22222222) share Common no par
Midlands Minerals Corp. recapitalized as Rosita Mining Corp. 07/28/2015

GRAND OPENING INC (MN)
Adjudicated bankrupt 01/28/1975
Stockholders' equity unlikely

GRAND PACARAIMA GOLD CORP (BC)
Name changed to First Bitcoin Capital Corp. 08/15/2016

GRAND PEAK CAP CORP (YT)
Each share Common no par received distribution of (1.5) shares Lucky Minerals Inc. Common no par payable 06/11/2009 to holders of record 04/09/2009
Reincorporated under the laws of British Columbia 04/27/2010

GRAND PETE INC (AB)
Acquired by Harvest Energy Trust 08/23/2007
Each share Common no par exchanged for $3.84 cash

GRAND PWR LOGISTICS GROUP INC (AB)
Acquired by 2001123 Alberta Ltd. 01/06/2017
Each share Common no par exchanged for $0.09 cash
Note: Unexchanged certificates will be cancelled and become without value 01/06/2019

GRAND PREMIER FINL INC (DE)
Stock Dividend - 10% payable 12/1/98 to holders of record 11/15/98
Merged into Old Kent Financial Corp. 4/3/2000
Each share Perpetual Preferred Ser. B no par exchanged for (1) share Preferred Ser. D no par
Each share Perpetual Preferred Ser. C no par exchanged for (1) share Preferred Ser. E no par
Each share Common no par exchanged for (0.4231) share Common no par
Old Kent Financial Corp. merged into Fifth Third Bancorp 4/2/2001

GRAND PRIX ASSN LONG BEACH (CA)
Merged into Dover Downs Entertainment, Inc. 7/1/98
Each share Common no par exchanged for (0.63) share Common 10¢ par
Dover Downs Entertainment, Inc. name changed to Dover Motorsports, Inc. 3/31/2002

GRAND PRIX RES LTD NEW (BC)
Recapitalized as Omenica Resources Ltd. 04/08/1980
Each share Class A no par exchanged for (0.2) share Class A no par
Each share Class B no par exchanged for (0.2) share Class B no par
Omenica Resources Ltd. recapitalized as Marilyn Resources Inc. 01/30/1984
(See Marilyn Resources Inc.)

GRAND PRIX RES LTD OLD (BC)
Merged into Grand Prix Resources Ltd. (New) 10/29/1976
Each share Capital Stock no par exchanged for (1) share Class A no par
Grand Prix Resources Ltd. (New) recapitalized as Omenica Resources Ltd. 04/08/1980 which recapitalized as Marilyn Resources Inc. 01/30/1984
(See Marilyn Resources Inc.)

GRAND PRIX SPORTS INC (WA)
Recapitalized as Superclick, Inc. 10/10/2003
Each share Common $0.0001 par exchanged for (1/6) share Common $0.0006 par
(See Superclick, Inc.)

GRAND PRODTN CO (DE)
Charter cancelled and declared inoperative and void for non-payment of taxes 03/01/1994

GRAND RAPIDS, GRAND HAVEN & MUSKEGON RAILWAY CO.
Property sold at foreclosure 00/00/1932
No stockholders' equity

GRAND RAPIDS & NORTH WESTERN RAILROAD
Bankrupt 00/00/1929
No stockholders' equity

GRAND RAPIDS BRASS CO.
Dissolved 00/00/1942
Details not available

GRAND RAPIDS BREWING CO.
Liquidated 00/00/1948
Details not available

GRAND RAPIDS METALCRAFT CORP.
Merged into Jacobs (F.L.) Co. on a (1) for (5) basis 00/00/1936
Jacobs (F.L.) Co. name changed to Grand Rapids Metalcraft, Inc. 11/28/1977 which name changed to GRM Industries, Inc. 11/08/1979 which merged into Redlaw Industries Inc. 12/07/1983
(See Redlaw Industries Inc.)

GRAND RAPIDS METALCRAFT INC (MI)
Name changed to GRM Industries, Inc. 11/08/1979
GRM Industries, Inc. merged into Redlaw Industries Inc. 12/07/1983
(See Redlaw Industries Inc.)

GRAND RAPIDS RAILROAD CO.
Dissolved 00/00/1937
Details not available

GRAND RAPIDS RAILWAY CO.
Reorganized as Grand Rapids Railroad Co. 00/00/1927
Details not available

GRAND RAPIDS SHOW CASE CO.
Merged into Grand Rapids Store Equipment Corp. 00/00/1927
Details not available

GRAND RAPIDS STORE EQUIPMENT CO. (MI)
Common no par changed to $5 par 00/00/1937
Dissolution completed 10/31/1960
Details not available

GRAND RAPIDS STORE EQUIPMENT CORP.
Assets sold at auction and company organized as Grand Rapids Store Equipment Co. 00/00/1934
Preferred holders received rights to subscribe to new company's Common
No Common stockholders' equity

GRAND RAPIDS VARNISH CORP. (MI)
Common no par changed to $1 par 04/14/1940
Common $1 par split (5) for (4) by issuance of (0.25) additional share 01/17/1959
Stock Dividends - 50% 11/15/1951; (1) for (3) 01/14/1956; 25% 01/19/1962
Acquired by Guardsman Chemical Coatings, Inc. 01/02/1963
Each share Common $1 par exchanged for (1) share Common $1 par
Guardsman Chemical Coatings, Inc. name changed to Guardsman Chemicals, Inc. 06/01/1975 which name changed to Guardsman Products, Inc. 05/14/1987
(See Guardsman Products, Inc.)

GRAND RESORT INTL LTD (NV)
Charter revoked for failure to file reports and pay fees 07/01/1997

GRAND SAGUENAY MINES & MINERALS LTD (ON)
Name changed to GSM Resource Capital Inc. 2/1/89
GSM Resource Capital Inc. recapitalized as HMH China Investments Ltd. (ONT) 9/18/95 which reincorporated in Bermuda 12/21/95

GRAND SLAM INC (DE)
Charter cancelled and declared inoperative and void for non-payment of taxes 03/01/1974

GRAND SLAM TREASURES INC (NV)
Recapitalized as Asconi Corp. 04/16/2001
Each share Common $0.0001 par exchanged for (0.01) share Common $0.001 par
Note: Holders of (99) or fewer pre-split shares received share for share
Holders of between (100) and (10,000) shares received (100) shares only
(See Asconi Corp.)

GRAND STORES CO. (CA)
Charter revoked for failure to file reports and pay fees 04/01/1958

GRAND TETON INDS INC (BC)
Cease trade order effective 03/18/1992

GRAND TOYS INTL INC (NV)
Each share old Common $0.001 par exchanged for (0.2) share new Common $0.001 par 08/06/1997
Each share new Common $0.001 par exchanged again for (0.25) share new Common $0.001 par 09/04/2001
Merged into Grand Toys International Ltd. (Hong Kong) 08/17/2004
Each share new Common $0.001 par exchanged for (1) Sponsored ADR for Common
(See Grand Toys International Ltd. (Hong Kong))

GRAND TOYS INTL LTD (HONG KONG)
Each old Sponsored ADR for Common exchanged for (0.2) new Sponsored ADR for Common 10/01/2007
ADR basis changed from (1:1) to (1:5) 10/01/2007
ADR agreement terminated 06/01/2009
Each new Sponsored ADR for Common exchanged for (5) shares Common
Note: Unexchanged ADR's will be sold and the proceeds, if any, held for claim after 06/01/2010

GRAND TRAVERSE & ARIZONA MINING CO. (AZ)
Charter expired by time limitation 5/12/28

GRAND TRUNK WAREHOUSE & COLD STORAGE CO. (MI)
Acquired by Beatrice Foods Co. 12/8/60
Each share Common $10 par exchanged for (1.125) shares Common $12.50 par
Beatrice Foods Co. name changed to Beatrice Companies, Inc. 6/5/84
(See Beatrice Companies, Inc.)

GRAND-UINTAH CORP. (UT)
Charter cancelled in December, 1963
Capital Stock worthless

GRAND UN CO NEW (DE)
Old Common no par changed to $1 par in 1933
Each share $3 Preferred no par exchanged for (1) share new Common no par, $2 cash and a Dividend Arrearage Certificate amounting to $5.45 in 1939
Each share Common $1 par exchanged for (1/15) share new Common no par and a warrant to subscribe to (0.1) share Common no par at $10 a share in 1939
New Common no par changed to $10 par and (1.25) additional shares issued in 1948
Common $10 par changed to $5 par and (1) additional share issued 5/31/55
Common $5 par split (3) for (2) by issuance of (0.5) additional share 6/15/59
Stock Dividend - 10% 5/26/50
Each share Common $5 par exchanged for $21 principal amount of Cavenham (USA) Inc. 11-1/2% Sinking Fund Debentures due 12/1/2000 on 7/29/77
4-1/2% Preferred $50 par called for redemption 1/13/84
New Common $1 par changed to 1¢ par 11/7/96
Plan of reorganization under Chapter 11 Federal Bankruptcy Code effective 8/17/98
Each share new Common 1¢ par exchanged for (0.05298) Common Stock Purchase Warrant expiring 8/17/2003
Assets sold for the benefit of creditors 3/4/2001
Stockholders' equity unlikely

GRAND VY GAS CO (UT)
Each share Common $0.005 par exchanged for (0.4) share Common $0.0125 par 10/27/89
Acquired by Associated Natural Gas Corp. 7/1/94
Each share new Common $0.0125 par exchanged for (0.25) share Common 10¢ par
Associated Natural Gas Corp. merged into Panhandle Eastern Corp. 12/15/94 which name changed to Panenergy Corp. 4/26/96 which merged into Duke Energy Corp. (NC) 6/18/97 which merged into Duke Energy Corp. (DE) 4/3/2006

GRAND VALLEY NATIONAL BANK (GRANDVILLE, MI)
Stock Dividend - 10% 03/15/1974
100% acquired by National Detroit Corp. through purchase offer which expired 11/04/1974
Public interest eliminated

GRAND VALLEY OIL CORP. (DE)
Charter cancelled and declared inoperative and void for non-payment of taxes 10/1/56

GRANDBANC INC (MD)
Merged into Century Bancshares, Inc. 3/15/2001
Each share Common $10 par exchanged for (0.3318) share Common $1 par
Century Bancshares, Inc. merged into United Bankshares, Inc. 12/10/2001

GRANDCRU RES CORP (BC)
Merged into Bell Copper Corp. (Old) 05/12/2008
Each share Common no par exchanged for (0.125) share Common no par
Bell Copper Corp. (Old) reorganized as Bell Copper Corp. (New) 07/23/2013

GRANDE CACHE COAL CORP (AB)
Acquired by Marubeni Corp. 03/01/2012
Each share Common no par exchanged for $10 cash

GRANDE PORTAGE RES LTD (YT)
Reincorporated 07/17/1998
Place of incorporation changed from (BC) to (YT) 07/17/1998
Reincorporated back under the laws of British Columbia 05/03/2007

GRANDE PRAIRIE PETROLEUMS LTD.
Acquired by Apex Consolidated Resources Ltd. 00/00/1946
Each share Capital Stock $1 par exchanged for (0.25) share Capital Stock no par
Apex Consolidated Resources Ltd. recapitalized as Abacus Mines Ltd. 06/01/1959 which name changed to Abacus Mines & Realty Ltd. 00/00/1962 which recapitalized as Abacon Development Ltd. 03/21/1963
(See Abacon Development Ltd.)

GRANDE TRUNK RES INC (BC)
Common no par split (5) for (1) by issuance of (4) additional shares 5/31/84
Recapitalized as Erient Resources Inc. 2/3/86
Each share Common no par exchanged for (0.2) share Common no par
Erient Resources Inc. recapitalized as First Idaho Resources Inc. 10/14/87

GRANDEE CORP (DE)
Name changed to Cassco Capital Corp. (Old) 09/01/1987
Cassco Capital Corp. (Old) name changed to International K.C Jakes BBQ & Grill, Inc. 07/20/1992 which name changed to Casso Capital Corp. (New) 07/18/1994 which recapitalized as Diversified Technology Inc. (DE) 06/23/2000 which reincorporated in Nevada 10/04/2000 which reorganized as Diversified Technologies Group, Inc. 01/14/2000 which name changed to X-Change Corp. 07/30/2001 which name changed to Endocan Corp. 11/06/2013

GRANDEN GOLD MINE LTD. (ON)
Merged into Hydra Explorations Ltd. on a (13) for (2) basis 11/16/1959
Hydra Explorations Ltd. name changed to Hydra Capital Corp. 12/30/1992 which name changed to Waterford Capital Management Inc.
11/12/1996 which merged into CPI Plastics Group Ltd. 09/21/1998
(See CPI Plastics Group Ltd.)

GRANDETEL TECHNOLOGIES INC (CANADA)
Reincorporated 09/28/1995
Place of incorporation changed from (BC) to (Canada) 09/28/1995
Struck off register and declared dissolved for failure to file returns 11/02/2005

GRANDEUR BUILDING, INC. (MO)
Liquidation completed 8/2/55

GRANDEUR INC (NV)
Name changed to delSECUR Corp. 05/29/1999
(See delSECUR Corp.)

GRANDEX EXPL & INVT LTD (ON)
Charter cancelled for failure to pay taxes and file returns 03/16/1976

GRANDEX GOLD MINES LTD. (ON)
Name changed to Grandex Exploration & Investment Co. Ltd. 09/19/1968
(See Grandex Exploration & Investment Co. Ltd.)

GRANDEX RES LTD (BC)
Struck off register and declared dissolved for failure to file returns 06/19/1992

GRANDFIELD PAC INC (CANADA)
Each share old Common no par exchanged for (0.1) share new Common no par 06/30/1999
Reincorporated under the laws of British Columbia as Radiant Health Care Inc. 10/21/2016

GRANDINES MINES LTD. (ON)
Recapitalized as Grandroy Mines Ltd. 08/22/1957
Each share Capital Stock no par exchanged for (0.25) share Capital Stock no par
Grandroy Mines Ltd. recapitalized as New Grandroy Resources, Inc. 06/26/1973 which recapitalized as Hillsborough Exploration Ltd. 11/24/1980 which name changed to Hillsborough Resources Ltd. (ON) 03/13/1987 which reincorporated in Canada 11/05/1997
(See Hillsborough Resources Ltd. (Canada))

GRANDMA LEES INC (QC)
Name changed to Heritage Concepts International Inc. 11/14/1997
Heritage Concepts International Inc. name changed to NEXUS Group International Inc. 03/13/2001
(See NEXUS Group International Inc.)

GRANDMAS INC (FL)
Proclaimed dissolved for failure to file reports and pay fees 8/25/95

GRANDMASTER TECHNOLOGIES INC (BC)
Each share Common no par received distribution of (1) share Masterpiece Games Inc. Common no par 08/11/1997
Recapitalized as EM Net Corp. (BC) 08/31/1998
Each share Common no par exchanged for (0.2) share Common no par
EM Net Corp. (BC) reincorporated in Canada as T & E Theatre.com Inc. 11/25/1999 which recapitalized as Manele Bay Ventures Inc. 02/28/2002 which name changed to MBA Gold Corp. 07/15/2003 which name changed to MBA Resources Corp. 10/14/2005 which name changed to Thunderbird Energy Corp. 07/27/2006 which recapitalized as Gordon Creek Energy Inc. 10/24/2013

GRANDORA EXPLS LTD (BC)
Recapitalized as Dora Explorations Ltd. 04/18/1977
Each share Capital Stock 50¢ par exchanged for (0.2) share Capital Stock no par
Dora Explorations Ltd. merged into Meridor Resources Ltd. 04/01/1985 which merged into Hughes Lang Corp. 08/01/1989 which merged into CanGold Resources Inc. (BC) 01/31/1994 which reorganized in Ontario as Amalgamated CanGold Inc. 07/31/1995 which merged into Central Asia Goldfields Corp. 01/08/1996
(See Central Asia Goldfields Corp.)

GRANDORO MINES, LTD. (BC)
Liquidation completed 00/00/1957
Each share Capital Stock no par received third and final distribution of $0.13 cash
Note: Holders previously received two distributions totalling $0.85 per share

GRANDPARENTS COM INC (DE)
Plan of reorganization under Chapter 11 Federal Bankruptcy proceedings effective 09/26/2017
No stockholders' equity

GRANDROY MINES LTD (ON)
Recapitalized as New Grandroy Resources, Inc. 06/26/1973
Each share Capital Stock no par exchanged for (0.2) share Capital Stock no par
New Grandroy Resources, Inc. recapitalized as Hillsborough Exploration Ltd. 11/24/1980 which name changed to Hillsborough Resources Ltd. (ON) 03/13/1987 which reincorporated in Canada 11/05/1997
(See Hillsborough Resources Ltd. (Canada))

GRANDUC MINES LTD (BC)
Merged into Granduc Mining Corp. 11/08/1993
Each share Common $1 par exchanged for (1) share Common no par
Granduc Mining Corp. merged into Black Hawk Mining Inc.-Compagnie Miniere Black Hawk Inc. 07/01/1996 which merged into Glencairn Gold Corp. 10/20/2003 which recapitalized as Central Sun Mining Inc. 12/05/2007 which was acquired by B2Gold Corp. 03/31/2009

GRANDUC MNG CORP (BC)
Merged into Black Hawk Mining Inc.-Compagnie Miniere Black Hawk Inc. 07/01/1996
Each share Common no par exchanged for (1) share Common no par
Black Hawk Mining Inc.-Compagnie Miniere Black Hawk Inc. merged into Glencairn Gold Corp. 10/20/2003 which recapitalized as Central Sun Mining Inc. 12/05/2007 which was acquired by B2Gold Corp. 03/31/2009

GRANDVIEW ENERGY RES INC (ON)
Recapitalized as Consolidated Grandview Inc. 09/22/1983
Each share Common no par exchanged for (0.33333333) share Common no par
Consolidated Grandview Inc. name changed to Grandview Gold Inc. 07/06/2004 which recapitalized as PUDO Inc. 07/13/2015

GRANDVIEW GOLD INC (ON)
Recapitalized as PUDO Inc. 07/13/2015
Each share Common no par exchanged for (0.05) share Common no par

GRANDVIEW MINES INC (WA)
Capital Stock 10¢ par changed to no par 03/03/1982
Name changed to Cimarron Gas & Oil Inc. of Washington 07/11/1990

Cimarron Gas & Oil Inc. of Washington name changed to Cimarron-Grandview Group, Inc. 07/25/1990 which recapitalized as Full Moon Universe, Inc. 01/04/2001
(See Full Moon Universe, Inc.)

GRANDVIEW RACEWAY INC (OH)
Each share Class A Common no par exchanged for (100) shares Class A Common $2.50 par 08/20/1957
Assets transferred to Grandview Raceway, a Limited Partnership 04/10/1969
Each share Class A Common $2.50 par or Class B Common 50¢ par exchanged for (1) Unit of Ltd. Partnership

GRANDVIEW RES INC (BC)
Merged into WMC Acquisition (BC) Corp. 07/22/1988
Each share Common no par exchanged for $9.55 cash

GRANEAGLE HLDGS LTD (BERMUDA)
ADR agreement terminated 06/24/2013
No ADR's remain outstanding

GRANEX RES CORP (BC)
Name changed 04/00/1976
Reincorporated 11/23/1979
Name changed from Granex Mines Ltd. to Granex Resources Corp. 04/00/1976
Place of incorporation changed from (BC) to (Canada) 11/23/1979
Certificate of incorporation cancelled and charter dissolved 10/19/1999

GRANGE GOLD CORP (BC)
Name changed to Lovitt Nutriceutical Corp. 11/25/2005
Lovitt Nutriceutical Corp. name changed to Lovitt Resources Inc. 09/10/2008

GRANGE MINES LTD. (BC)
Struck off register and declared dissolved for failure to file reports 2/17/49

GRANGE NATL BANC CORP (PA)
Common $5 par split (3) for (1) by issuance of (2) additional shares 4/1/94
Common $5 par split (2) for (1) by issuance of (1) additional share payable 8/1/98 to holders of record 7/31/98
Common $5 par split (2) for (1) by issuance of (1) additional share payable 8/15/2002 to holders of record 7/31/2002 Ex date - 8/16/2002
Stock Dividends - 9% payable 12/29/95 to holders of record 12/10/95; 1% payable 12/31/98 to holders of record 12/10/98; 1.5% payable 6/30/2000 to holders of record 6/9/2000; 1% payable 12/29/2000 to holders of record 12/8/2000 Ex date - 12/6/2000
Merged into Community Bank System, Inc. 11/24/2003
Each share Common $5 par exchanged for (0.8463) share Common $5 par and $12.75 cash

GRANGE NATL BK LYCOMING CNTY (HOGHESVILLE, PA)
Merged into Bank of Central Pennsylvania (Montoursville, PA) 12/31/80
Each share Common $25 par exchanged for (1.75) shares Common $5 par
(See Bank of Central Pennsylvania (Montoursville, PA))

GRANGE NATL BK SUSQUEHANNA CNTY (NEW MILFORD, PA)
Acquired by Meridian Bancorp, Inc. 04/25/1994
Each share Common $100 par exchanged for (6.19) shares Common $5 par

Meridian Bancorp, Inc. merged into CoreStates Financial Corp 04/09/1996 which merged into First Union Corp. 04/28/1998 which name changed to Wachovia Corp. (Ctfs. dated after 09/01/2001) 09/01/2001 which merged into Wells Fargo & Co. (New) 12/31/2008

GRANGER ASSOC (CA)
Capital Stock $1 par reclassified as Common no par 01/23/1980
Common no par split (2) for (1) by issuance of (1) additional share 11/08/1982
Common no par split (2) for (1) by issuance of (1) additional share 07/22/1983
Merged into Digital Switch Corp. 06/27/1984
Each share Common no par exchanged for (1.08) shares Common 1¢ par
Digital Switch Corp. name changed to DSC Communications Corp. 04/22/1985 which merged into Alcatel 09/04/1998 which name changed to Alcatel-Lucent 11/30/2006
(See Alcatel-Lucent)

GRANGER DEV CORP (BC)
Name changed 09/07/1990
Name changed from Granger Resources Corp. to Granger Development Corp. 09/07/1990
Delisted from Vancouver Stock Exchange 03/05/1993

GRANGER ENERGY CORP (AB)
Merged into BelAir Energy Corp. 11/01/1998
Each share Class A Common no par exchanged for (2.06) shares Common no par
Each share Non-Vtg. Class B Common no par exchanged for (1.86) shares Common no par
Each share Conv. Class C Ser. 1 no par exchanged for (14.59) shares Common no par
BelAir Energy Corp. merged into Purcell Energy Ltd. (New) 09/04/2003
(See Purcell Energy Ltd. (New))

GRANGER PETROLEUM CORP. (BC)
Name changed to Granger Resources Corp. 05/16/1975
Granger Resources Corp. name changed to Granger Development Corp. 09/07/1990
(See Granger Development Corp.)

GRANGER TRADING CORP. (WA)
Dissolved in 1933

GRANGES EXPLORATION LTD. (BC)
Subordinate Vtg. no par reclassified as Common no par 6/28/85
Reorganized as Granges Inc. (Old) 6/19/89
Each share Common no par exchanged for (1) share Common no par
Granges Inc. (Old) merged into Granges Inc. (New) 5/1/95 which merged into Vista Gold Corp. (BC) 11/1/96 which reincorporated in Yukon 12/27/97

GRANGES INC NEW (BC)
Merged into Vista Gold Corp. (BC) 11/01/1996
Each share Common no par exchanged for (1) share Common no par
Vista Gold Corp. (BC) reincorporated in Yukon 12/27/1997 which reincorporated back in British Columbia 06/12/2013

GRANGES INC OLD (BC)
Subordinate no par reclassified as Common no par 06/28/1985
Reorganized from Granges Exploration Ltd. to Granges Inc. (Old) 06/19/1989
Each share Common no par

exchanged for (1) share Common no par
Merged into Granges Inc. (New) 05/01/1995
Each share Common no par exchanged for (1) share Common no par
Granges Inc. (New) merged into Vista Gold Corp. (BC) 11/01/1996 which reincorporated in Yukon 12/27/1997 which reincorporated back in British Columbia 06/12/2013

GRANGEVILLE GOLD CORP. (WA)
Charter revoked for failure to pay fees 07/01/1941

GRANISLE COPPER LTD (BC)
Merged into Zapata Granby Corp. 01/01/1979
Each share Capital Stock no par exchanged for (1.2) shares $0.40 Conv. Preference no par
(See Zapata Granby Corp.)

GRANITE BANCSHARES INC (CA)
Certificate of dissolution filed 05/06/2011
No stockholders' equity

GRANITE BAY TECHNOLOGIES INC (CA)
Reincorporated 10/31/2000
State of incorporation changed from (OR) to (CA) 10/31/2000
Reincorporated under the laws of Delaware as International DisplayWorks, Inc. 10/11/2001
International DisplayWorks, Inc. merged into Flextronics International Ltd. 11/30/2006 which name changed to Flex Ltd. 09/28/2016

GRANITE-BIMETALLIC CONSOLIDATED MINING CO.
Dissolved in 1932

GRANITE BROADCASTING CORP (DE)
Common 1¢ par split (3) for (2) by issuance of (0.5) additional share 11/05/1991
Stock Dividends - in 12.75% Preferred to holders of 12.75% Preferred 6.375% payable 10/01/1997 to holders of record 09/15/1997; 6.375% payable 10/01/2000 to holders of record 09/15/2000; 6.375% payable 04/2/2001 to holders of record 03/15/2001; 6.375% payable 10/01/2001 to holders of record 09/17/2001 Ex date - 09/20/2001; 6.375% payable 04/01/2002 to holders of record 03/15/2002 Ex date - 03/15/2002
Terminated SEC registration of Conv. Exchangeable Preferred 1¢ par 05/07/2002
Details not available
Plan of reorganization under Chapter 11 Federal Bankruptcy Code effective 06/04/2007
Each share 12.75% Exchangeable Preferred 1¢ par received (0.99812353) share new Common 1¢ par and (2.49530882) Common Stock Purchase Warrant Ser. A expiring 06/04/2012 payable 06/05/2007 to holders of record 03/02/2007 Ex date - 06/06/2007
Each share old Common 1¢ par received (0.00508283) share new Common 1¢ par, (0.01270708) Common Stock Purchase Warrant Ser. A expiring 06/04/2012 and (0.01270708) Common Stock Purchase Warrant Ser. B expiring 06/04/2012 payable 06/05/2007 to holders of record 03/02/2007 Ex date - 06/06/2007
Note: Certificates were not required to be surrendered and are without value
(Additional Information in Active)

GRANITE CITY FOOD & BREWERY LTD (MN)
Each share Conv. Preferred Ser. A exchanged for approximately (63.29) shares Common 1¢ par 11/04/2004
(Additional Information in Active)

GRANITE CITY GENERATING CO. (IL)
In process of liquidation
Each VTC for Common 10¢ par exchanged for initial distribution of $1.32 cash 12/27/1962
Note: Details on subsequent distributions, if any, are not available

GRANITE CITY PIG IRON CO.
Liquidated 00/00/1944
Details not available

GRANITE CITY STL CO (DE)
Each share Common no par exchanged for (2) shares Common $12.50 par 00/00/1951
5-1/2% Conv. Preferred $100 par called for redemption 03/15/1956
Common $12.50 par changed to $6.25 par and (1) additional share issued 02/11/1960
Merged into National Steel Corp. 08/16/1971
Each share Common $6.25 par exchanged for (0.4445) share Capital Stock $5 par
National Steel Corp. reorganized as National Intergroup, Inc. 09/13/1983 which name changed to FoxMeyer Health Corp. 10/12/1994 which name changed to Avatex Corp. 03/07/1997
(See Avatex Corp.)

GRANITE CMNTY BK N A (GRANITE BAY, CA)
Stock Dividend - 5% payable 04/15/2007 to holders of record 03/16/2007 Ex date - 03/14/2007
Under plan of reorganization each share Common $5 par automatically became (1) share Granite Bancshares, Inc. Common $5 par 02/06/2008
(See Granite Bancshares, Inc.)

GRANITE COOP BK (NORTH QUINCY, MA)
Common 10¢ par split (3) for (2) by issuance of (0.5) additional share 6/1/87
Assets sold by FDIC 12/12/91
No stockholders' equity

GRANITE CREEK GOLD LTD (BC)
Each share old Common no par exchanged for (0.25) share new Common no par 12/11/2014
Each share new Common no par exchanged again for (0.33333333) new Common no par 10/17/2018
Name changed to Granite Creek Copper Ltd. 10/17/2018

GRANITE DEV CORP (NV)
Each share Common $0.001 par received distribution of (0.02631578) share Rama Financial Corp. Common $0.001 par payable 8/20/97 to holders of record 6/9/97
Each share old Common $0.001 par exchanged for (0.1) share new Common $0.001 par 12/15/97
Recapitalized as Technology Logistics Systems Inc. 4/15/99
Each share new Common $0.001 par exchanged for (0.1) share Common $0.001 par
Technology Logistics Systems Inc. recapitalized as Interactive Business Development, Inc. (New) 1/3/2006 which name changed to American BioDiesel Fuels Corp. 2/2/2007 which name changed to Planet Resource Recovery, Inc. 3/9/2007

GRANITE ENERGY INC (NV)
Reincorporated 04/11/2006
State of incorporation changed from (FL) to (NV) 04/11/2006

Name changed to Refill Energy, Inc. 11/19/2009
Refill Energy, Inc. name changed to Medical Cannabis Payment Solutions 12/05/2013

GRANITE EQUIP LEASING CORP (NY)
Common 50¢ par split (4) for (3) by issuance of (1/3) additional share 07/12/1968
Name changed to Granite Management Services, Inc. 07/09/1969
Granite Management Services, Inc. name changed to Midland Resources, Inc. 11/10/1975 which name changed to American Midland Corp. 07/06/1984
(See American Midland Corp.)

GRANITE FINL INC (DE)
Issue Information - 1,500,000 shares COM offered at $7.50 per share on 10/25/1996
Merged into Fidelity National Financial, Inc. 2/26/98
Each share Common $0.001 par exchanged for (0.702) share Common $0.0001 par
Fidelity National Financial, Inc. merged into Fidelity National Information Services, Inc. 11/9/2006

GRANITE GOLD MINING CO.
Dissolved in 1936

GRANITE GOLF CORP (DE)
Name changed 07/24/1998
Name and state of incorporation changed from Granite Golf Group Inc. (NV) to Granite Golf Corp. (DE) 07/24/1998
Recapitalized as Beverage Creations, Inc. 01/24/2008
Each share Common $0.001 par exchanged for (0.01) share Common $0.001 par

GRANITE LTD (NV)
Recapitalized as Savon Coffee Inc. 10/27/95
Each share Common $0.0001 par exchanged for (0.1) share Common $0.0001 par
Savon Coffee Inc. name changed to Food Concepts Inc. 3/22/96 which name changed Viropro Inc. 4/1/98

GRANITE MGMT SVCS INC (NY)
Name changed to Midland Resources, Inc. 11/10/1975
Midland Resources, Inc. name changed to American Midland Corp. 07/06/1984
(See American Midland Corp.)

GRANITE MILLS
Acquired by Pepperell Manufacturing Co. (Mass. Voluntary Assn.) 00/00/1929
Details not available

GRANITE MTN MINES LTD (BC)
Recapitalized as Golden Granite Mines Ltd. 04/18/1975
Each share Common no par exchanged for (0.2) share Common no par
(See Golden Granite Mines Ltd.)

GRANITE REAL ESTATE INC (QC)
Plan of arrangement effective 01/03/2013
Each share Common no par exchanged for (1) Granite Real Estate Investment Trust (ON) Stapled Unit

GRANITE ST BK (MONROVIA, CA)
Common no par split (5) for (4) by issuance of (0.25) additional share payable 5/15/2000 to holders of record 5/4/2000 Ex date - 5/16/2000
Common no par split (5) for (4) by issuance of (0.25) additional share payable 6/12/2003 to holders of record 5/30/2003 Ex date - 6/13/2003
Stock Dividends - 20% payable 5/18/98 to holders of record 5/8/98; 20% payable 6/8/2001 to holders of record 5/25/2001 Ex date - 5/23/2001; 25% payable 6/12/2002 to holders of record 5/31/2002
Merged into CVB Financial Corp. 2/25/2005
Each share Common no par exchanged for $19 cash

GRANITE ST BANKSHARES INC (NH)
Each share 7% Conv. Preferred $1 par exchanged for (1) share Common $1 par 10/01/1993
Common $1 par split (3) for (2) by issuance of (0.5) additional share payable 05/09/1997 to holders of record 04/25/1997
Merged into Chittenden Corp. 02/28/2003
Each share Common $1 par exchanged for either (1.64) shares Common $1 par, $46 cash, or (0.82) share Common $1 par and $23 cash
Note: Option to receive stock and cash or cash only expired 03/04/2003
(See Chittenden Corp.)

GRANITE STATE PRODUCTS CO. (MA)
Charter revoked for failure to file reports and pay fees 07/01/1936

GRANITE STATE SPRING WATER CO. (MA)
Name changed to Granite State Products Co. 01/26/1924
(See Granite State Products Co.)

GRANITEVILLE CO (SC)
Each share Capital Stock $100 par exchanged for (5) shares Capital Stock $20 par in 1937
Each share Common $20 par exchanged for (4) shares Common $5 par 2/28/62
Common $5 par split (5) for (4) by issuance of (0.25) additional share 12/8/73
Common $5 par split (2) for (1) by issuance of (1) additional share 12/15/75
Stock Dividends - 100% 4/46; 100% 2/24/48
Merged into Southeastern Public Service Co. 7/24/84
Each share Common $5 par exchanged for $17.50 cash

GRANITEVILLE MANUFACTURING CO.
Name changed to Graniteville Co. in 1937
(See Graniteville Co.)

GRANIZ MONDAL INC (CANADA)
Reincorporated 08/17/2012
Place of incorporation changed from (AB) to (Canada) 08/17/2012
Recapitalized as NanoXplore Inc. 09/08/2017
Each share Common no par exchanged for (0.06666666) share Common no par

GRANJA GOLD INC (BC)
Reincorporated 05/01/2013
Place of incorporation changed from (ON) to (BC) 05/01/2013
Name changed to PDC Diagnostics Corp. 12/31/2013
PDC Diagnostics Corp. name changed to PDC Biological Health Group Corp. 01/25/2014

GRANLEDUC OILS LTD. (ON)
Recapitalized as Paige Petroleum Ltd. on a (1) for (3) basis in 1950
Paige Petroleum Ltd. was acquired by Porcupine Prime Mines Ltd. in April 1960 which name changed to Prime Potash Corp. of Canada Ltd. 12/16/65
(See Prime Potash Corp. of Canada Ltd.)

GRANNING & TREECE FINL CORP (OR)
Common $1 par changed to 1¢ par 3/7/72
Stock Dividend - 50% 3/30/72
Name changed to Grantree Corp. 3/19/73
(See Grantree Corp.)

GRANT ADVERTISING, INC. (TX)
Name changed to Harris-Grant, Inc. 2/21/74
(See Harris-Grant, Inc.)

GRANT BLDG INC (PA)
Each share Preferred $50 par exchanged for (0.6) share Common $1 par 12/31/37
(Additional Information in Active)

GRANT DOUGLAS ACQUISITION CORP (ID)
Recapitalized as Pediatric Prosthetics, Inc. 11/10/2003
Each share Common 5¢ par exchanged for (0.5) share Common $0.001 par
Pediatric Prosthetics, Inc. recapitalized as Marathon Group Corp. (ID) 08/03/2010 which reincorporated in Wyoming 06/02/2011

GRANT ENTERPRISES INC (DE)
Old Common $0.001 par split (5) for (1) by issuance of (4) additional shares payable 03/06/2007 to holders of record 03/05/2007 Ex date - 03/07/2007
Each share old Common $0.001 par exchanged for (0.925) share new Common $0.001 par 08/08/2007
Name changed to KeyOn Communications Holdings, Inc. 08/23/2007
(See KeyOn Communications Holdings, Inc.)

GRANT EXPL LTD (BC)
Recapitalized as Argo Development Corp. 09/28/1984
Each share Common no par exchanged for (0.2) share Common no par
Argo Development Corp. merged into Tymar Resources Inc. 10/31/1989 which recapitalized as Baja Gold, Inc. 01/25/1993 which merged into Viceroy Resource Corp. 05/30/1996 which merged into Quest Capital Corp. (BC) 06/30/2003 which reincorporated in Canada 05/27/2008 which name changed to Sprott Resource Lending Corp. 09/10/2010 which merged into Sprott Inc. 07/24/2013

GRANT FOURTH CORP. (PA)
Merged into Nichols Wire & Aluminum Co. (Del.) 8/17/64
Each share Common $5 par exchanged for (1) share Capital Stock $10 par

GRANT GEOPHYSICAL INC (DE)
Plan of reorganization under Chapter 11 Federal Bankruptcy Code effective 09/30/1997
Holders of $2.4375 Conv. Exchangeable Preferred 1¢ par received an undetermined amount of rights to purchase shares of new Common $0.001 par
Note: Certificates were not required to be surrendered and are without value
No old Common stockholders' equity
Company terminated registration of new Common 01/29/1999
8% Preferred called for redemption at $105.955555 on 12/09/2005
Public interest eliminated

GRANT INDS INC (DE)
Merged into Mobex Corp. 3/23/87
Each share Common 10¢ par exchanged for $7.75 cash

GRANT LEATHER CORP.
Properties sold 00/00/1935
Details not available

GRANT LIFE SCIENCES INC (NV)
Charter revoked for failure to file reports and pay fees 02/01/2010

GRANT-NORPAC INC (DE)
Name changed to Grant Tensor Geophysical Corp. 5/7/91
Grant Tensor Geophysical Corp. name changed to Grant Geophysical Inc. 10/5/93
(See Grant Geophysical Inc.)

GRANT PRIDECO INC (DE)
Merged into National Oilwell Varco, Inc. 04/21/2008
Each share Common 1¢ par exchanged for (0.4498) share Common 1¢ par and $23.20 cash

GRANT RESV CORP (NV)
Common $0.001 par split (2) for (1) by issuance of (1) additional share payable 10/19/1998 to holders of record 10/16/1998
Name changed to InfoCast Corp. 12/29/1998
(See InfoCast Corp.)

GRANT SILVER INC (ID)
Recapitalized as Brewserv Corp. (ID) 09/19/1997
Each share Common no par exchanged for (0.64998375) share Common no par
Brewserv Corp. (ID) reincorporated in Nevada 07/00/2001 which recapitalized as Grant Ventures, Inc. 02/15/2002 which name changed to Grant Life Sciences, Inc. 11/12/2004
(See Grant Life Sciences, Inc.)

GRANT STR NATL BK - LIQ (PITTSBURGH, PA)
Liquidation completed
Each share Common 1¢ par received initial distribution of $0.60 cash 4/22/94
Each share Common 1¢ par exchanged for second and final distribution of $0.343 cash 7/31/95

GRANT TENSOR GEOPHYSICAL CORP (DE)
Name changed to Grant Geophysical Inc. 10/5/93
(See Grant Geophysical Inc.)

GRANT VENTURES INC (NV)
Name changed to Grant Life Sciences, Inc. 11/12/2004
Each share Common no par exchanged for (1) share Common no par
(See Grant Life Sciences, Inc.)

GRANT W 1 CO (DE)
Each share Capital Stock no par exchanged for (0.25) share 5% Preferred $20 par and (1) share Common $10 par in 1937
Each share Common $10 par exchanged for (2) shares Common $5 par in 1945
Common $5 par changed to $2.50 par and (1) additional share issued 5/13/60
Common $2.50 par changed to $1.25 par and (1) additional share issued 5/13/66
Adjudicated bankrupt 4/13/76
Stockholders' equity unlikely

GRANTHAM RES INC (AB)
Delisted from Canadian Dealer Network 08/22/2001

GRANTO INC (NV)
Name changed to Rongfu Aquaculture, Inc. 06/01/2010

GRANTON TECHNOLOGY LTD (NY)
Charter cancelled and proclaimed dissolved for failure to pay taxes 06/24/1992

GRANTREE CORP (OR)
Stock Dividend - 50% 10/23/78

Merged into G Acquisition Corp. 11/10/87
Each share Common 10¢ par exchanged for $11.125 cash

GRANTS PATCH MNG LTD (AUSTRALIA)
ADR agreement terminated 10/31/1992
Each ADR for Ordinary exchanged for $0.978 cash

GRANULES INDIA LTD (INDIA)
GDR agreement terminated 08/14/2017
No GDR's remain outstanding

GRANUM OILS LTD. (AB)
Struck off register and declared dissolved for failure to file returns 08/31/1964

GRANVILLE IS BREWING LTD (BC)
Each share Common no par exchanged for (0.16666666) share Class A Common no par 12/15/1988
Acquired by International Potter Distilling Corp. 08/29/1989
Each share Class A Common no par received (0.1) share Common no par and (0.5) Common Stock Purchase Warrant expiring 04/21/1991
Note: Certificates were not required to be surrendered and are without value
International Potter Distilling Corp. name changed to Cascadia Brands Inc. 03/30/1995
(See Cascadia Brands Inc.)

GRANVILLE LAKE NICKEL MINES LTD. (ON)
Charter surrendered 01/05/1970
No stockholders' equity

GRANVILLE PAC CAP CORP (AB)
Acquired by H&H Total Care Services Inc. 04/11/2013
Each share Common no par exchanged for $0.08 cash
Note: Unexchanged certificates will be cancelled and become without value 04/11/2019

GRANVILLE RES INC (BC)
Struck off register and declared dissolved for failure to file returns 08/09/1991

GRANVILLE UTD BK (OXFORD, NC)
Acquired by Triangle Bancorp Inc. 10/25/96
Each share Common $5 par exchanged for (1.75) shares Common no par
Triangle Bancorp Inc. merged into Centura Banks, Inc. 2/18/2000 which merged into Royal Bank of Canada (Montreal, QC) 6/5/2001

GRANWICK MINES LTD. (ON)
Charter cancelled and company declared dissolved for default in filing returns 12/28/1964

GRAPH MAX INC (ON)
Recapitalized as GRF Technology Inc. 01/30/1996
Each share Common no par exchanged for (0.05) share Common no par
GRF Technology Inc. merged into Mustang Gold Corp. 07/15/1997 which recapitalized as Mustang Minerals Corp. 03/11/1999 which name changed to Grid Metals Corp. 06/08/2018

GRAPHCO HLDGS CORP (DE)
SEC revoked common stock registration 02/03/2010

GRAPHIC ARTS CTR INC (OR)
Acquired by Intermark, Inc. 8/04/1983
Each share Common no par exchanged for $16.45 cash

GRAPHIC ARTS DATA SYS INC (UT)
Name changed to Central States Resources, Inc. 3/9/72
(See Central States Resources, Inc.)

GRAPHIC ARTS PACKAGING CORP (CA)
Merged into Rexham Corp. 12/30/77
Each share Common $1 par exchanged for $5 cash

GRAPHIC ARTS UNLIMITED INC (DE)
Each share Common 1¢ par exchanged for (0.4) share Common 2-1/2¢ par 09/19/1969
Charter forfeited for failure to maintain a registered agent 08/05/1995

GRAPHIC COMMUNICATIONS INC. (UT)
Name changed to Unique Prospects, Inc. 12/18/87
(See Unique Prospects, Inc.)

GRAPHIC CONTROLS CORP. (NY)
Class A $5 par and/or Class B $5 par reclassified as Common $1 par and (0.5) additional share 7/5/66
Stock Dividend - 25% 6/21/76
Merged into T.M.G.C., Inc. 12/31/78
Each share Common $1 par exchanged for $39 cash

GRAPHIC INDS INC (GA)
Common 10¢ par split (3) for (2) by issuance of (0.5) additional share 8/26/85
Common 10¢ par split (3) for (2) by issuance of (0.5) additional share 10/28/97
Merged into Wallace Computer Services, Inc. 12/22/97
Each share Common 10¢ par exchanged for $21.75 cash

GRAPHIC MEDIA INC (NJ)
Common 1¢ par split (3) for (2) by issuance of (0.5) additional share 1/28/83
Stock Dividend - 10% 6/30/86
Name changed to GMI Group Inc. 7/16/87
(See GMI Group Inc.)

GRAPHIC PACKAGING CORP NEW (DE)
Name changed to Graphic Packaging Holding Co. 03/10/2008

GRAPHIC PACKAGING CORP OLD (DE)
Merged into Coors Packaging Co. 11/07/1988
Each share Common 1¢ par exchanged for $16.50 cash

GRAPHIC PACKAGING INTL CORP (CO)
Merged into Graphic Packaging Corp. (New) 08/08/2003
Each share Common 1¢ par exchanged for (1) share Common 1¢ par
Graphic Packaging Corp. (New) name changed to Graphic Packaging Holding Co. 03/10/2008

GRAPHIC SCANNING CORP (DE)
Common 1¢ par split (3) for (2) by issuance of (0.5) additional share 8/28/72
Common 1¢ par split (2) for (1) by issuance of (1) additional share 10/31/83
Stock Dividends - 50% 4/23/81; 150% 10/28/81
Acquired by BellSouth Enterprises 9/17/91
Each share Common 1¢ par exchanged for $5.18 cash
Each share Common 1¢ par received an additional payment of $0.11 cash 8/29/94

GRAPHIC SCIENCES INC (NY)
Stock Dividends - 50% 11/13/69; 25% 5/10/71
Merged into Burroughs Corp. (MI) 2/26/75
Each share Common 50¢ par exchanged for (0.125) share Common $5 par
Burroughs Corp. (MI) reincorporated in Delaware 5/30/84 which name changed to Unisys Corp. 11/13/86

GRAPHIC SERVICE, INC. (MN)
Adjudicated bankrupt 04/13/1977
No stockholders' equity

GRAPHIC SYS INC (MA)
Each share Common 1¢ par exchanged for (0.5) share Common 2¢ par 11/1/71
Name changed to GSI Liquidating Corp. 1/24/79
(See GSI Liquidating Corp.)

GRAPHIC TECHNOLOGY INC (MO)
Common 1¢ par split (3) for (2) by issuance of (0.5) additional share 8/12/87
Merged into GTI Acquisition Corp. 11/9/89
Each share Common 1¢ par exchanged for $18.50 cash

GRAPHICS DIVERSIFIED INC (MN)
Completely liquidated 8/23/84
Each share Common 25¢ par exchanged for first and final distribution of $0.06 cash

GRAPHIDYNE CORP (CA)
Merged into Graphidyne Acquisition, Inc. 12/31/79
Each share Common 10¢ par exchanged for $2.25 cash

GRAPHITE CORP CDA LTD (AB)
Recapitalized as Takla Star Resources Ltd. (AB) 05/09/1991
Each share Common no par exchanged for (0.125) share Common no par
Takla Star Resources Ltd. (AB) reincorporated in Canada as North Group Ltd. 08/30/2002 which reincorporated in British Columbia as North Group Finance Ltd. 12/22/2005 which recapitalized as Peekaboo Beans Inc. 09/29/2016

GRAPHITE ONE RES INC (AB)
Reincorporated under the laws of British Columbia 09/12/2014

GRAPHIX ZONE INC NEW (CA)
Charter forfeited for failure to pay taxes 09/01/2000

GRAPHIX ZONE INC OLD (CA)
Under plan of merger each share Common 1¢ par automatically became (1) share Graphix Zone, Inc. (New) Common 1¢ par 6/28/96
(See Graphix Zone, Inc. (New))

GRAPHON CORP (DE)
Name changed to hopTo Inc. 09/10/2013

GRASON INDS INC (IA)
Recapitalized as ETG International, Inc. (IA) 04/27/1994
Each share Common no par exchanged for (0.08) share Common no par
ETG International, Inc. (IA) reincorporated in Minnesota 01/11/1995 which recapitalized as SolutionNet International, Inc. 03/29/1999
(See SolutionNet International, Inc.)

GRASS-FIBER PULP & PAPER CORP. (DE)
Charter cancelled and declared inoperative and void for non-payment of taxes 4/1/28

GRASS VALLEY BULLION MINES
Property acquired by Idaho Maryland Mines Corp. in 1941 which name was changed to Idaho Maryland Industries, Inc. 7/1/60 which was recapitalized as Allied Equities Corp. 4/1/64

GRASS VALLEY GROUP INC (CA)
Common no par split (2) for (1) by issuance of (1) additional share 04/29/1968
Acquired by Tektronix, Inc. 02/21/1974
Each share Common no par exchanged for (0.311801) share Common no par
(See Tektronix, Inc.)

GRASSELLI CHEMICAL CO.
Acquired by du Pont (E.I.) de Nemours & Co. 00/00/1928
Details not available

GRASSIE LTD (NV)
Charter revoked 07/01/1990

GRASSLANDER (1957) LTD. (ON)
Charter cancelled and company declared dissolved for failure to file returns 4/22/65

GRASSLANDS ENTMT INC (AB)
Reorganized under the laws of Ontario as Lakeside Minerals Inc. 01/04/2012
Each share Common no par exchanged for (0.2) share Common no par
Lakeside Minerals Inc. name changed to Lineage Grow Co. Ltd. 07/25/2017

GRASSO CORP (NV)
Merged into Offshore Logistics, Inc. 9/16/94
Each share Common 1¢ par exchanged for (0.49) share Common 1¢ par
Offshore Logistics, Inc. name changed to Bristow Group, Inc. 2/1/2006

GRASSY CREEK COAL CO (CO)
Voluntarily dissolved 11/09/2004
Details not available

GRATIAM RES INC (BC)
Struck off register and declared dissolved for failure to file returns 05/00/2000

GRATON & KNIGHT CO. (MA)
Name changed to International Packings, Inc. 9/21/56
International Packings, Inc. name changed to International Packings Corp. 3/26/58
(See International Packings Corp.)

GRATON & KNIGHT MANUFACTURING CO.
Succeeded by Graton & Knight Co. in 1926
Details not available

GRATZ NATL BK (GRATZ, PA)
Reorganized as GNB Financial Services, Inc. 10/01/1986
Each share Common $25 par exchanged for (40) shares Common $5 par

GRAUPNER (ROBERT H.), INC.
Dissolved in 1951

GRAVELY FURNITURE INC (VA)
Common $1 par split (4) for (3) by issuance of (1/3) additional share 5/1/72
Merged into Pulaski Furniture Corp. 10/2/85
Each share Common $1 par exchanged for $19.50 cash
(See Pulaski Furniture Corp.)

GRAVES (C.) INC. (FL)
Acquired by Connrex Corp. (Del.) 8/29/69
Each share Common $5 par exchanged for (1.125) shares Common $5 par
Connrex Corp. (Del.) name changed to Chloride Connrex Corp. 8/27/73

GRAVES CORP (MA)
Proclaimed dissolved for failure to file reports and pay fees 10/19/1983

GRAVES TRUCK LINE INC (KS)
Common 50¢ par split (3) for (2) by issuance of (0.5) additional share 7/25/77
Merged into American Natural Resources Co. (MI) 8/30/78
Each share Common 50¢ par

exchanged for (0.3766) share
Common $1 par
American Natural Resources Co. (MI)
reincorporated in Delaware 6/30/83
(See American Natural Resources Co. (DE))

GRAVESEND-SHEEPSHEAD BAY POSTAL STATIONS, INC.
Dissolved in 1956

GRAVIS COMPUTER PERIPHERALS INC (BC)
Recapitalized as International Gravis Computer Technology Inc. 12/11/1985
Each share Common no par exchanged for (0.5) share Common no par
International Gravis Computer Technology Inc. merged into Advanced Gravis Computer Technology Ltd. 04/30/1987
(See Advanced Gravis Computer Technology Ltd.)

GRAVIS ENERGY CORP (BC)
Recapitalized as Biocure Technology Inc. 11/29/2017
Each share Common no par exchanged for (0.16574185) share Common no par

GRAVIS OIL CORP (DE)
Reincorporated 09/11/2012
Place of incorporation changed from (AB) to (DE) and Common no par changed to $0.00001 par 09/11/2012
Name changed to Petro River Oil Corp. 03/20/2013

GRAVITAS INTL INC (FL)
Reorganized under the laws of Nevada as Formcap Corp. 10/12/2007
Each share Common $0.001 par exchanged for (0.005) share Common $0.001 par

GRAVITY SPIN HLDGS INC (NV)
Reorganized as Magnus International Resources Inc. 5/4/2004
Each share Common $0.001 par exchanged for (2) shares Common $0.001 par

GRAVITY WEST MNG CORP (AB)
Recapitalized as Rock Tech Resources Inc. (AB) 03/09/2009
Each share Common no par exchanged for (0.1) share Common no par
Rock Tech Resources Inc. (AB) reincorporated in British Columbia as Rock Tech Lithium Inc. 05/12/2010

GRAY & CO PUB COMMUNICATIONS INTL INC (DE)
Merged into JWT Group, Inc. 10/22/86
Each share Common 1¢ par exchanged for approximately (0.239726) share Common 10¢ par
Note: Exact basis is determined by multiplying the number of shares owned by (8.75) and dividing that amount by (36.50)
(See JWT Group, Inc.)

GRAY (RICHARD) & CO. INC. (NY)
Name changed to Aorec Corp. 5/31/68
Aorec Corp. acquired by BAC Development Corp. (NY) 3/1/69
BAC Development Corp. (NY) reincorporated in Delaware 12/31/70 which liquidated for First Realty Investment Corp. (DE) 6/19/72 which name changed to Thor Corp. (DE) 6/8/76 which name changed to Thor Energy Resources, Inc. 7/31/81
(See Thor Energy Resources, Inc.)

GRAY CABLEVISION INC (GA)
Completely liquidated 12/3/74
Each share Common $1 par exchanged for first and final distribution of $5 cash

GRAY COMMUNICATIONS SYS INC (GA)
Common no par split (10) for (1) by issuance of (9) additional shares 10/15/1991
Common no par split (3) for (2) by issuance of (0.5) additional share 10/02/1995
Common no par split (3) for (2) by issuance of (0.5) additional share payable 09/30/1998 to holders of record 09/16/1998 Ex date - 10/01/1998
Class B Common no par split (3) for (2) by issuance of (0.5) additional share payable 09/30/1998 to holders of record 09/16/1998 Ex date - 10/01/1998
Name changed to Gray Television Inc. 07/25/2002

GRAY DRUG STORES INC (OH)
Common no par changed to $1 par 00/00/1951
Common $1 par split (3) for (1) by issuance of (2) additional shares 10/07/1960
Common $1 par split (3) for (2) by issuance of (0.5) additional share 11/14/1966
Common $1 par split (3) for (2) by issuance of (0.5) additional share 06/30/1978
Stock Dividend - 25% 12/18/1967
Merged into Sherwin-Williams Co. 12/01/1981
Each share Common $1 par exchanged for $21 cash

GRAY EAGLE MINING CORP. (NV)
Charter revoked 3/5/62; stock valueless

GRAY FOX PETE CORP (NV)
Common $0.001 par split (8) for (1) by issuance of (7) additional shares payable 06/20/2013 to holders of record 06/20/2013
Name changed to Grey Fox Holdings Corp. 06/23/2016

GRAY GOOSE AIRWAYS, INC. (NV)
Charter revoked for failure to file reports and pay fees 3/3/41

GRAY INDS INC (DE)
Adjudicated bankrupt 8/20/73

GRAY LINES CORP (NY)
Liquidation completed
Each share Capital Stock $1 par exchanged for initial distribution of $4.89 cash 2/27/73
Each share Capital Stock $1 par received second and final distribution of $1.43 cash 10/30/74

GRAY MANUFACTURING CO. (CT)
Common $10 par changed to $5 par 1/2/42
Stock Dividend - 10% 8/31/73
Adjudicated bankrupt 9/14/76
Stockholders' equity unlikely

GRAY MFG CO (NC)
Merged into Textiles, Inc. 5/29/31
Details not available

GRAY PEAKS INC (DE)
Company announced all board members and officers have resigned and the business is not viable 00/00/2008
Stockholders' equity unlikely

GRAY PUBG & MEDIA INC (CO)
Common $0.001 par split (36.364) for (1) by issuance of (35.364) additional shares payable 11/1/2004 to holders of record 10/29/2004 Ex date - 11/2/2004
Recapitalized as Graystone Park Enterprises Inc. 3/14/2005
Each share Common $0.001 par exchanged for (0.1) share Common $0.001 par

GRAY ROCK MNG CO LTD (BC)
Name changed to Gray Rock Resources Ltd. 04/28/1986

(See Gray Rock Resources Ltd.)

GRAY TELEPHONE PAY STATION CO. (CT)
Name changed to Gray Manufacturing Co. (CT) 2/19/39
(See Gray Manufacturing Co.)

GRAY TOOL CO (TX)
Merged into Combustion Engineering, Inc. 11/30/76
Each share Common $1 par exchanged for $38 cash

GRAY WOLF TECHNOLOGIES INC (NV)
Name changed to Corgenix Medical Corp. 05/14/1998
(See Corgenix Medical Corp.)

GRAY WOLFE CO (DE)
Liquidation completed 1/8/75
Details not available

GRAYCOR LASER SYS INC (AZ)
Charter revoked for failure to file reports and pay fees 11/2/94

GRAYD RES CORP (BC)
Acquired by Agnico-Eagle Mines Ltd. 01/24/2012
Each share Common no par exchanged for (0.01342) share Common no par and $1.89 cash
Agnico-Eagle Mines Ltd. name changed to Agnico Eagle Mines Ltd. 04/30/2013

GRAYDEL MALARTIC GOLD MINES, LTD. (ON)
Charter revoked for failure to file reports and pay taxes 08/06/1957

GRAYHILL EXPL CO (CO)
Each share Common $0.0001 par exchanged for (0.1) share Common $0.001 par 04/16/1984
Merged into U.S. Minerals Exploration Co. (CO) 02/15/1985
Each share Common $0.001 par exchanged for (0.85) share Common no par
U.S. Minerals Exploration Co. (CO) reincorporated in Delaware as USMX Inc. 02/04/1988 which merged into Dakota Mining Corp. 05/29/1997
(See Dakota Mining Corp.)

GRAYHOUND ELECTRS INC (DE)
Charter cancelled and declared inoperative and void for non-payment of taxes 3/1/98

GRAYLUND MINES, LTD. (ON)
Charter cancelled in September 1961

GRAYMAR RES INC (AB)
Name changed to Friendly Fuels Group Inc. 6/13/96

GRAYMARK HEALTHCARE INC (OK)
Name changed 01/07/2008
Name changed from GrayMark Productions, Inc. to Graymark Healthcare, Inc. 01/07/2008
Each share old Common $0.0001 par exchanged for (0.2) share new Common $0.0001 par 04/14/2008
Each share new Common $0.0001 par exchanged again for (0.25) share new Common $0.0001 par 06/03/2011
Name changed to Foundation Healthcare, Inc. 12/12/2013
(See Foundation Healthcare, Inc.)

GRAYMUR CORP.
Acquired by Tri-Continental Corp. 00/00/1933
Details not available

GRAYS HARBOR PULP & PAPER CO.
Merged into Rayonier, Inc. in 1937
Each share $2 Preferred exchanged for (1) share $2 Preferred $25 par and (0.07) share Common $1 par
Each share Common exchanged for (1.07) share Common $1 par
Rayonier, Inc. merged into International Telephone & Telegraph

Corp. (DE) 4/26/68 which name changed to ITT Corp. 12/31/83 which reorganized in Indiana as ITT Industries, Inc. 12/19/95 which name changed to ITT Corp. 7/1/2006

GRAYSON BANKSHARES INC (VA)
Merged into Parkway Acquisition Corp. 07/01/2016
Each share Common $1.25 par exchanged for (1.76) shares Common no par

GRAYSON-ROBINSON STORES, INC. (CA)
Declared a bankrupt 11/9/64
No stockholders' equity

GRAYSON SHOPS, INC.
Name changed to Grayson-Robinson Stores, Inc. 2/14/46
(See Grayson-Robinson Stores Inc.)

GRAYSTONE CORP (AB)
Subordinate no par split (9) for (1) by issuance of (8) additional shares payable 03/24/2004 to holders of record 03/19/2004 Ex date - 03/17/2004
Multiple no par split (9) for (1) by issuance of (8) additional shares payable 03/24/2004 to holders of record 03/19/2004 Ex date - 03/17/2004
Sr. Preferred Ser. A no par called for redemption at $25 on 12/31/2004
Merged into Pyxis Capital Inc. 02/27/2004
Each share Jr. Preferred Ser. A no par exchanged for (1) Non-Vtg. Share no par and (0.38) Dividend Share no par
Each Dividend Share no par exchanged for (1) Dividend Share no par
Each Subordinate Share no par exchanged for (1) share Non-Vtg. Share no par and (0.38) Dividend Share no par
Each Multiple Share no par exchanged for (1) share Common no par and (0.38) Dividend Share no par
(See Pyxis Capital Inc.)

GRAYSTONE FINL SVCS INC (FL)
Each share old Common $0.0001 par exchanged for (0.02) share new Common $0.0001 par 05/01/1990
Reorganized under the laws of Delaware as GS Financial Services, Inc. 12/01/1997
Each share new Common $0.0001 par exchanged for (0.01) share Common $0.0001 par
(See GS Financial Services, Inc.)

GRAYSTONE GOLD MINES, LTD. (ON)
Charter revoked for failure to file reports and pay taxes 12/2/57

GRAYSTONE VENTURES INC (CO)
Name changed to American Jet Holdings, Inc. 12/18/1989
American Jet Holdings, Inc. recapitalized as OTS Holdings Inc. 12/03/1990 which name changed to Thin Film Battery Inc. 04/18/2000 which name changed to Global Acquisition, Inc. 04/17/2001 which name changed to Oak Ridge Micro-Energy, Inc. 02/21/2002 which name changed to Oak Ridge Energy Technologies, Inc. 08/28/2013 which name changed to Oakridge Global Energy Solutions, Inc. 11/07/2014

GRAYTEX OIL & CHEMICAL CO., INC. (NV)
Charter revoked for failure to file reports and pay fees 3/5/56

GRAYWAY PRECISION, INC. (NJ)
Insolvent 11/28/62; stock worthless

GRC HLDGS INC (TX)
Each share old Common $0.0001 par exchanged for (0.5) share new Common $0.0001 par 07/03/2006

Reincorporated under the laws of Delaware as China Biologic Products, Inc. 02/20/2007
China Biologic Products, Inc. (DE) reincorporated in Cayman Islands as China Biologic Products Holdings, Inc. 07/24/2017

GRC INTL INC (DE)
Merged into AT&T Corp. 3/29/2000
Each share Common 10¢ par exchanged for $15 cash

GRD ENTERPRISES INC (AB)
Name changed to Call Genie Inc. 08/17/2004
Call Genie Inc. name changed to VoodooVox Inc. 01/17/2012 which name changed to UpSnap, Inc. 07/25/2014

GRD INDS LTD (BC)
Struck off register and dissolved for failure to file returns 10/14/1994

GREASE 'N GO INTERNATIONAL, INC. (NV)
Name changed to Autocare Corp. 10/18/91
(See Autocare Corp.)

GREASE CREEK PETROLEUMS LTD. (BC)
Recapitalized as Consolidated Grease Creek Petroleums Ltd. 00/00/1954
Each share Capital Stock 50¢ par exchanged for (0.33333333) share Capital Stock 50¢ par
Consolidated Grease Creek Petroleums Ltd. was acquired by Share Oils Ltd. Share Oils Ltd. 00/00/1957 which name changed to Share Mines & Oil Ltd. (AB) 03/01/1965 which reincorporated in Ontario 11/20/1979 which recapitalized as Share Resources Inc. 07/04/1996
(See Share Resources Inc.)

GREASE MONKEY HLDG CORP (UT)
Common $0.001 par split (2) for (1) by issuance of (1) additional share 1/6/81
Each (30) shares Common $0.001 par exchanged for (1) share Common 3¢ par 6/29/92
Merged into QL 3000, Inc. 12/22/99
Each share Preferred Ser. C exchanged for $136.11 cash
Each share Common 3¢ par exchanged for $1 cash

GREAT ALASKA SERVICES CONSOLIDATED LTD. (BC)
Name changed to Vanstates Resources Ltd. 01/09/1980
Vanstates Resources Ltd. recapitalized as Southport Resroces Inc. 07/16/1990 which recapitalized as Olds Industries Inc. 06/03/1992
(See Olds Industries Inc.)

GREAT ALASKA SVCS LTD (BC)
Recapitalized as Great Alaska Services Consolidated Ltd. 07/10/1972
Each share Capital Stock no par exchanged for (0.06666666) share Capital Stock no par
Great Alaska Services Consolidated Ltd. name changed to Vanstates Resources Ltd. 01/09/1980 which recapitalized as Southport Resources Inc. 07/16/1990 which recapitalized as Olds Industries Inc. 06/03/1992
(See Olds Industries Inc.)

GREAT AMERN AUTO LEASING INC (NJ)
Charter declared void for non-payment of taxes 3/1/77

GREAT AMERN BACKRUB STORE INC (NY)
Each share old Common $0.001 par exchanged for (0.125) share new Common $0.001 par 02/23/1995
Reorganized under the laws of Delaware as International Diversified Industries Inc. 08/03/1998
Each share new Common $0.001 par exchanged for (0.25) share Common $0.001 par
(See International Diversified Industries Inc.)

GREAT AMERN BANCORP (CA)
Name changed to First Regional Bancorp 12/09/1987
(See First Regional Bancorp)

GREAT AMERN BK (CENTURY CITY, CA)
Under plan of reorganization each share Common no par automatically became (1) share Great American Bancorp Common no par 03/08/1982
Great American Bancorp name changed to First Regional Bancorp 12/09/1987
(See First Regional Bancorp)

GREAT AMERN BK A FED SVGS BK (SAN DIEGO, CA)
Name changed 6/29/90
Name changed from Great American Bank, SSB (San Diego, CA) to Great American Bank, FSB (San Diego, CA) 6/29/90
Placed in receivership 10/25/91
No stockholders' equity

GREAT AMERICAN BANK OF DADE COUNTY (NORTH MIAMI, FL)
99.01% held by American Bancshares, Inc. as of 03/31/1980
Public interest eliminated

GREAT AMERN BKS INC (FL)
Merged into Barnett Banks of Florida, Inc. 2/22/83
Each share Common $1 par exchanged for $17 principal amount of 10-yr. Promissory Notes due 2/22/93, a combination of cash and Notes or cash only
Note: Option to receive combination of cash and Notes or cash only expired 3/16/83

GREAT AMERN CHEM CORP (DE)
Acquired by Whittaker Corp. 8/11/80
Each share Common $1 par exchanged for $12.90 cash

GREAT AMERN COAL INC (MN)
Statutorily dissolved 7/29/96

GREAT AMERN COMMUNICATIONS CO (FL)
Plan of reorganization under Chapter 11 Federal Bankruptcy Code effective 12/28/93
Each share Common 1¢ par exchanged for (1/300) share Great American Communications Co. (New) Class A Common 1¢ par
Great American Communications Co. (New) name changed to Citicasters Inc. 6/8/94
(See Citicasters Inc.)

GREAT AMERICAN COMMUNICATIONS CO NEW (FL)
Name changed to Citicasters Inc. 6/8/94
(See Citicasters Inc.)

GREAT AMERN CORP (LA)
Each share Common $10 par exchanged for (2) shares Common $5 par 1/15/71
Each share Common $5 par exchanged for (2) shares Common $2.50 par 12/17/71
Stock Dividend - 10% 4/22/77
Charter revoked for failure to file annual reports 2/15/2001

GREAT AMERICAN DEVELOPMENT CO. (TX)
Charter revoked for failure to file reports and pay fees 3/14/63

GREAT AMERN ENERGY INC (DE)
Recapitalized as Sovereign Lithium, Inc. 07/12/2013
Each share Common $0.000001 par exchanged for (0.5) share Common $0.000001 par

GREAT AMERN FAMILY PKS INC (NV)
Name changed to Parks! America, Inc. 06/25/2008

GREAT AMERN FED SVGS BK (SAN DIEGO, CA)
Name changed to Great American First Savings Bank (San Diego, CA) 7/1/84
Great American First Savings Bank (San Diego, CA) name changed to Great American Bank, SSB (San Diego, CA) 7/1/89 which name changed to Great American Bank, FSB (San Diego, CA) 6/29/90
(See Great American Bank, FSB (San Diego, CA))

GREAT AMERN FINL INC (WY)
Each share old Common 1¢ par exchanged for (0.2) share new Common 1¢ par 6/14/83
Charter revoked for failure to file annual reports 2/11/86

GREAT AMERICAN FINL RES INC (DE)
Merged into American Financial Group, Inc. 09/28/2007
Each share Common $1 par exchanged for $24.50 cash

GREAT AMERN FIRST SVGS BK (SAN DIEGO, CA)
Common $1 par split (3) for (2) by issuance of (0.5) additional share 5/30/86
Name changed to Great American Bank, SSB (San Diego, CA) 7/1/89
Great American Bank, SSB (San Diego, CA) name changed to Great American Bank, FSB (San Diego, CA) 6/29/90
(See Great American Bank, FSB (San Diego, CA))

GREAT AMERN GOLD CO (NV)
Each share old Common 1¢ par exchanged for (0.1) share new Common 1¢ par 05/13/1994
Charter revoked for failure to file reports and pay fees 03/31/1999

GREAT AMERN GROUP INC (DE)
Each share old Common $0.0001 par exchanged for (0.05) share new Common $0.0001 par 06/03/2014
Name changed to B. Riley Financial, Inc. 11/07/2014

GREAT AMERN HEALTH & NUTRITION INC (UT)
Proclaimed dissolved for failure to file annual reports 11/1/89

GREAT AMERN HLDG CORP (DE)
Merged into National General Corp. 2/25/69
Each share Common $2.50 par exchanged for (3.5) Common Stock Purchase Warrants which expired 9/30/78

GREAT AMERN HOTELS & RESORTS INC (GA)
SEC revoked common stock registration 10/03/2013

GREAT AMERICAN INDEMNITY CO. (NY)
Capital Stock $10 par changed to $5 par in 1931
Capital Stock $5 par changed to $1 par in 1932
Capital Stock $1 par changed to $2 par 4/3/42
Merged into Great American Insurance Co. 12/31/58
Each share Capital Stock $2 par exchanged for (0.44) share Capital Stock $5 par
Great American Insurance Co. acquired by National General Corp. 11/16/73

GREAT AMERN INDS INC (DE)
Each share Common 10¢ par exchanged for (0.2) share Common 50¢ par 5/21/74
6% Conv. Preferred Ser. B $10 par called for redemption 11/15/84
Merged into PLC Enterprises, Inc. 6/18/85
Each share Common 50¢ par exchanged for $35 cash
6% Preferred Ser. A $10 par called for redemption 11/21/90
Public interest eliminated

GREAT AMERN INS CO (NY)
Each share Capital Stock $100 par exchanged for (10) shares Capital Stock $10 par 00/00/1927
Capital Stock $10 par changed to $5 par 00/00/1932
Under plan of merger each share old Capital Stock $5 par exchanged for (1.28) shares new Capital Stock $5 par 11/22/1953
Stock Dividend - 25% 01/16/1950
Acquired by National General Corp. 11/16/1973
Each share Capital Stock $5 par exchanged for $72 cash

GREAT AMERN INVT NETWORK INC (MS)
Merged into Citizens, Inc. 6/19/97
Each share Class A Common no par exchanged for (7.2) shares Class A Common no par

GREAT AMERICAN LIFE INSURANCE CO. (TX)
Assets acquired by Franklin Life Insurance Co. 00/00/1940
Details not available

GREAT AMERN LIFE INS CO (KS)
Merged out of existence 12/29/1993
Details not available

GREAT AMERICAN LIFE UNDERWRITERS, INC. (TX)
Class A no par split (11) for (1) by issuance of (10) additional shares 10/16/61
Reorganized as Greatamerica Corp. 9/1/62
Each share Class A no par received (10) shares Common $3 par
Note: Certificates were not required to be surrendered and are without value

GREAT AMERN LMBR INC (UT)
Involuntarily dissolved 12/01/1998

GREAT AMERN MGMT & INVT INC (DE)
Reorganized 4/6/79
Reorganized from under the laws of (MA) to (DE) as Great American Management & Investment, Inc. 4/6/79
Each Share of Bene. Int. no par exchanged for (0.25) share Common 1¢ par
Merged into Equity Holding Ltd. 4/26/96
Each share Common 1¢ par exchanged for $50 cash

GREAT AMERN MEDIA CORP (DE)
Charter cancelled and declared inoperative and void for non-payment of taxes 03/01/1993

GREAT AMERN MTG INVS (MA)
Stock Dividend - 100% 2/10/71
Name changed to Great American Management & Investment 11/5/75
Great American Management & Investment reorganized as Great American Management & Investment, Inc. 4/6/79
(See Great American Management & Investment, Inc.)

GREAT AMERN PARTNERS (TX)
Reorganized under Chapter 11 Federal Bankruptcy Code 11/1/89
Each Class A Unit exchanged for (0.0441784) share Eastern Petroleum Co. Class A Common no par
(See Eastern Petroleum Co.)

GREAT AMERICAN PUBLICATIONS, INC. (MD)
Charter annulled for failure to file reports and pay taxes 10/28/60

GREAT AMERN RLTY CORP (NY)
Completely liquidated 09/14/1990
Each share Class A 10¢ par exchanged for first and final distribution of $0.19 cash

GREAT AMERN REC INC (NJ)
Each share old Common 1¢ par exchanged for (0.02) share new Common 1¢ par 01/18/1990
Chapter 11 bankruptcy proceedings closed 03/29/1999
No stockholders' equity

GREAT AMERN RESORTS INC (GA)
Each share old Class A Common no par exchanged for (0.5) share new Class A Common no par 06/18/1993
Each share new Class A Common no par exchanged again for (0.66666666) share new Common no par 06/27/1994
Name changed to Great American Hotels & Resorts, Inc. 05/10/1996
(See Great American Hotels & Resorts, Inc.)

GREAT AMERN RES INC (DE)
Charter cancelled and declared inoperative and void for non-payment of taxes 03/01/1989

GREAT AMERN RESV CORP (TX)
Common $5 par split (3) for (2) by issuance of (0.5) additional share 6/1/70
Acquired by Penney (J.C.) Co., Inc. 12/29/70
Each share Common $5 par exchanged for (0.51) share Common 50¢ par

GREAT AMERN RESV INS CO (TX)
Through voluntary exchange offer 99.99% held by J.C. Penney Co., Inc. as of October 1974
Public interest eliminated

GREAT AMERICAN SEMINOLE BANK (TAMPA, FL)
99.9% held by American Bancshares, Inc. as of 10/15/1973
Public interest eliminated

GREAT AMERN SODA POP & WTR SHOP INC (NV)
Name changed to Casino Players & Travel International, Inc. 01/22/1990
(See Casino Players & Travel International, Inc.)

GREAT ATLANTIC & PAC TEA INC (MD)
Name changed 07/30/1958
Name changed from Great Atlantic & Pacific Tea Co. of America to Great Atlantic & Pacific Tea Co., Inc. 07/30/1958
Each share 7% 1st Preferred $100 par exchanged for (3) shares Common $1 par 12/12/1958
Each share Common no par exchanged for (10) shares Common $1 par 12/12/1958
Plan of reorganization under Chapter 11 Federal Bankruptcy proceedings effective 03/13/2012
No stockholders' equity

GREAT ATLANTIC DEVELOPMENT CORP. (DE)
Common 1¢ par changed to 10¢ par 6/7/65
Completely liquidated 6/9/66
Each share Common 10¢ par exchanged for first and final distribution of (1) share Interamerican Industries Ltd. Capital Stock no par
(See Interamerican Industries Ltd.)

GREAT ATLANTIC LIFE INS CO (PA)
Each share Class A Common $1.50 par or Class B Common $1.50 par exchanged for (1) share Common $1.50 par 8/8/66
Each share Common $1.50 par exchanged for (0.01) share Class B Common $1 par 1/17/74
Class B Common $1 par called for redemption 12/27/76
Public interest eliminated

GREAT AUSTRALIAN RES N L (AUSTRALIA)
Name changed to Trans-Global Resources N.L. 10/13/1988
Trans-Global Resources N.L. name changed to Trans-Global Interactive Ltd. 06/30/1999
(See Trans-Global Interactive Ltd.)

GREAT BASIN FINL CORP (NV)
Common 1¢ par split (2) for (1) by issuance of (1) additional share payable 02/20/2002 to holders of record 01/31/2002 Ex date - 02/21/2002
Common 1¢ par split (4) for (1) by issuance of (3) additional shares payable 05/15/2006 to holders of record 05/01/2006 Ex date - 05/16/2006
Company's sole asset placed in receivership 04/17/2009
Stockholders' equity unlikely

GREAT BASIN GOLD LTD (BC)
Filed a petition under Bankruptcy and Insolvency Act 06/28/2013
Stockholders' equity unlikely

GREAT BASIN LD & LIVESTOCK INC (UT)
Name changed to Uintah Basin Minerals, Inc. 08/15/1991
(See Uintah Basin Minerals, Inc.)

GREAT BASIN METAL MINES LTD (ON)
Charter cancelled for failure to pay taxes and file returns 07/18/1973

GREAT BASIN OIL & LEASING CO. (UT)
Name changed to Great Basin Uranium & Leasing Co. 00/00/1953
(See Great Basin Uranium & Leasing Co.)

GREAT BASIN OIL CO. (AZ)
Out of business in 1928
No stockholders' equity

GREAT BASIN URANIUM & LEASING CO. (UT)
Charter suspended for non-payment of taxes 03/31/1960

GREAT BASIN WTR CO (NV)
Name changed to 37Point9 01/23/2001
37Point9 recapitalized as Global Medical Products Holdings, Inc. 11/25/2002
(See Global Products Medical Holdings, Inc.)

GREAT BASINS PETE CO (CO)
Common no par changed to 20¢ par 11/9/60
Each share Common 20¢ par exchanged for (0.5) share Common 40¢ par 11/18/68
Liquidation completed
Each share Common 40¢ par received initial distribution of $7.70 cash 10/2/81
Each share Common 40¢ par received second distribution off (1) share Columbian Northland Exploration Ltd. Common no par 8/20/82
(See Columbian Northland Exploration Ltd.)
Under plan of liquidation each share Common 40¢ par automatically became (1) share of Bene. Int. 40¢ par of Great Basins Petroleum Co. Liquidating Trust 8/24/82
(See Great Basins Petroleum Co. Liquidating Trust)

GREAT BASINS PETROLEUM CO. LIQUIDATING TRUST (CO)
Liquidation completed
Each Share of Bene. Int. 40¢ par received initial distribution of $0.40 cash 3/19/85
Each share of Bene. Int. 40¢ par received second distribution of $0.42 cash 1/10/86
Each share of Bene. Int. 40¢ par received third distribution of $0.60 cash 12/2/88
Each share of Bene. Int. 40¢ par received fourth distribution of $1.70 cash 6/22/89
Each share of Bene. Int. 40¢ par received fifth distribution of $0.09 cash 9/22/89
Each share of Bene. Int. 40¢ par received sixth and final distribution of $0.04609917 cash 6/28/91

GREAT BAY BANKSHARES INC (NH)
Merged into Bank of Ireland First Holdings, Inc. 3/29/95
Each share Common 10¢ par exchanged for $19.50 cash

GREAT BAY PWR CORP (NH)
Reincorporated under the laws of Delaware as BayCorp Holdings, Ltd. 1/24/97
(See BayCorp Holdings, Ltd.)

GREAT BEAR AUTOMOTIVE CTRS INC (NY)
Charter cancelled and proclaimed dissolved for failure to pay taxes 09/29/1993

GREAT BEAR DEV CORP (BC)
Struck off register and declared dissolved for failure to file returns 06/24/1988

GREAT BEAR DEV CORP (MN)
Recapitalized as Amtron Inc. 1/28/91
Each share Common $0.001 par exchanged for (0.1) share Common $0.001 par
(See Amtron Inc.)

GREAT BEAR INVTS INC (NV)
Recapitalized as Security Biometrics Inc. 09/01/2000
Each share Common $0.001 par exchanged for (4) shares Common $0.001 par
Security Biometrics Inc. name changed to SiVault Systems, Inc. 07/29/2004
(See SiVault Systems, Inc.)

GREAT BEAR MNG LTD (BC)
Recapitalized as Aries Resources Inc. (BC) 05/26/1977
Each share Capital Stock no par exchanged for (0.2) share Capital Stock no par
Aries Resources Inc. (BC) reincorporated in Yukon as Total Global Ventures Inc. 05/19/1999 which recapitalized as JNB Developments Co. Ltd. 10/03/2001 which name changed to Cooper Minerals Inc. (YT) 07/14/2004 which reincorporated in British Columbia as United Coal Holdings Ltd. 05/28/2012

GREAT BEAR RES LTD OLD (BC)
Name changed to Great Bear Uranium Corp. 08/03/2007
Great Bear Uranium Corp. name changed to Great Bear Resources Ltd. (New) 01/29/2010

GREAT BEAR SILVER MINES LTD (ON)
Recapitalized as Frodac Consolidated Energy Resources Ltd. 4/26/79
Each share Capital Stock no par exchanged for (0.1) share Capital Stock no par
Frodac Consolidated Energy Resources Ltd. recapitalized as Global Aerospace Systems Inc. 9/30/85 which recapitalized as Venga Aerospace Systems Inc. 11/16/87

GREAT BEAR SPRING CO (NJ)
Capital Stock no par split (30) for (1) by issuance of (29) additional shares 8/2/72
Merged into Coca-Cola Bottling Co. of Los Angeles 6/5/81
Each share Capital Stock no par exchanged for $65.8378 cash

GREAT BEAR TECHNOLOGY INC (CO)
Merged into Graphix Zone, Inc. (New) 6/28/96
Each share Common no par exchanged for (0.14666) share Common 1¢ par
(See Graphix Zone, Inc. (New))

GREAT BEAR URANIUM CORP (BC)
Name changed to Great Bear Resources Ltd. (New) 01/29/2010

GREAT BEND OILS, LTD. (ON)
Charter cancelled and declared dissolved for failure to file returns and pay fees 01/21/1957

GREAT BEND RESOURCE CORP (CANADA)
Name changed to Rockport Energy Corp. 04/06/1993
Rockport Energy Corp. recapitalized as Liberty Oil & Gas (1998) Ltd. 11/30/1998 which was acquired by Lexxor Energy Inc. 07/23/2002 which reorganized as Find Energy Ltd. 09/05/2003 which was acquired by Shiningbank Energy Income Fund 09/22/2006 which merged into PrimeWest Energy Trust 07/13/2007
(See PrimeWest Energy Trust)

GREAT BRITAIN & CDA INVT CORP (CANADA)
5% Conv. Preferred $100 par changed to $50 par 00/00/1932
Each share Common no par exchanged for (3) shares Common $1 par 04/05/1962
5% Conv. Preferred $50 par called for redemption 05/15/1962
Recapitalized as Great Britain & Canada Investments (1968) Ltd. 12/30/1968
Each share 5% Preferred $50 par exchanged for (1) share 5.25% 1st Preferred $50 par
Each share Common $1 par exchanged for (1) share 1% 2nd Preferred $2 par and (1) share Common $18 par
Great Britain & Canada Investments (1968) Ltd. name changed to Great Britain & Canada Investments Ltd. 09/08/1971 which name changed to GBC Capital Ltd. 11/16/1972 which name changed to GBC Capital Ltd.-Capital GBC Ltee. 04/27/1977 which name changed to GBC North America Fund Inc. 01/25/1989 which name changed to GBC North American Growth Fund Inc. 01/15/1991 which name changed to GBC American Growth Fund Inc. 03/28/2011

GREAT BRITAIN & CDA INVTS LTD (CANADA)
Name changed 09/08/1971
Name changed from Great Britain & Canada Investments (1968) Ltd. to Great Britain & Canada Investments Ltd. 09/08/1971
1% 2nd Preferred $2 par called for redemption 03/31/1972
Name changed to GBC Capital Ltd. 11/16/1972
GBC Capital Ltd. name changed to GBC Capital Ltd.-Capital GBC Ltee. 04/27/1977 which name changed to GBC North America Fund Inc. 01/25/1989 which name changed to GBC North American Growth Fund Inc. 01/15/1991 which name

changed to GBC American Growth Fund Inc. 03/28/2011

GREAT BRITAIN & NORTHN IRELAND (UNITED KINGDOM)
ADR agreement terminated 06/03/2009
Each Sponsored ADR for 3.50% War Loan Stock exchanged for (0.05) share 3.50% War Loan Stock
Note: Unexchanged ADR's will be sold and the proceeds, if any, held for claim after 12/03/2009

GREAT BUFFALO MINING CO. (UT)
Charter expired by time limitation 03/28/1950

GREAT CAMERON LAKE RES INC (ON)
Recapitalized as Cam-Turf Corp. 03/19/1986
Each share Common no par exchanged for (0.5) share Common no par
(See Cam-Turf Corp.)

GREAT CDN CIDER EXPORTERS LTD (BC)
Dissolved and struck from the register 01/15/1993

GREAT CDN OIL SANDS LTD (CANADA)
Merged into Suncor Inc. 08/22/1979
Each share Common no par exchanged for (1) share Conv. Preferred Ser. A no par or $24 cash
Note: Option to receive cash expired 10/12/1979
Suncor Inc. name changed to Suncor Energy Inc. (Old) 04/18/1997
(See Suncor Energy Inc. (Old))

GREAT CENT INS CO (IL)
Common $10 par changed to $3-1/3 par and (2) additional shares issued 1/19/66
Acquired by Teledyne, Inc. 1/1/69
Each share Common $3-1/3 par exchanged for (0.055) share $3.50 Conv. Preferred $1 par
(See Teledyne, Inc.)

GREAT CENT MINES LTD (BC)
Recapitalized as First Canadian Financial Corp. 05/09/1995
Each (60) shares Common no par exchanged for (1) share Class A Common no par
First Canadian Financial Corp. recapitalized as Promax Communications Inc. (BC) 04/03/1997 which reincorporated in Yukon 00/00/1998 which reincorporated in Nevada 04/19/2007 which recapitalized as Sipp Industries, Inc. 08/24/2007

GREAT CENT MINES N L (AUSTRALIA)
Name changed 11/26/1996
Name changed from Great Central Mines N.L. to Great Central Mines Ltd. 11/26/1996
ADR agreement terminated 08/31/1999
Each Sponsored ADR for Ordinary exchanged for $2.7504 cash

GREAT CHIEF URANIUM CO. (NV)
Merged into Columbus-Rexall Oil Co. on a (1) for (200) basis 1/29/57
(See Columbus-Rexall Oil Co.)

GREAT CHINA INTL HLDGS INC (NV)
Name changed to HH Biotechnology Holdings Co. 08/24/2016

GREAT CHINA MANIA HLDGS INC (FL)
Each share old Common 1¢ par exchanged for (0.05) share new Common 1¢ par 01/07/2014
Name changed to GME Innotainment, Inc. 07/07/2015

GREAT CHINA MNG INC (NV)
Merged into Continental Minerals Corp. (Incorporated 02/07/1962) 12/15/2006
Each share Common $0.001 par exchanged for (0.11383946) share Common no par
(See Continental Minerals Corp. (Incorporated 02/07/1962))

GREAT CITIES MEDIA INC (DE)
Company believed out of business 00/00/2008
Details not available

GREAT COLO SILVER VY DEV CO (FL)
Name changed to J.R. Gold Mines, Inc. 10/30/1987
J.R. Gold Mines, Inc. changed to Sarah Acquisition Corp. (FL) 01/16/1996 which reorganized in Nevada as Karts International Inc. 02/23/1996 which name changed to 4D Seismic, Inc. 04/11/2006
(See 4D Seismic, Inc.)

GREAT COLUMBIA CORP. (WA)
Name changed to Chem-Nuclear Systems, Inc. 1/3/73
Chem-Nuclear Systems, Inc. merged into Waste Management, Inc. (Old) 10/28/82 which name changed to WMX Technologies Inc. 5/14/93 which name changed to Waste Management, Inc. (New) 5/12/97 which merged into Waste Management, Inc. 7/16/98

GREAT COMWLTH LIFE INS CO (TX)
Common no par changed to $1 par 12/30/65
Merged into American Commonwealth Financial Corp. 12/31/73
Each share Common $1 par exchanged for (1) share Common $1 par
American Commonwealth Financial Corp. merged into I.C.H. Corp. 10/26/82 which name changed to Southwestern Life Corp. (New) 6/15/94 which name changed to I.C.H. Corp. (New) 10/10/95
(See I.C.H. Corp. (New))

GREAT CTRY BK (ANSONIA, CT)
Merged into Center Financial Corp. 12/15/1995
Each share Common $1 par exchanged for (0.3676) share Common $1 par
Center Financial Corp. merged into First Union Corp. 11/13/1996 which name changed to Wachovia Corp. (Ctfs. dated after 09/01/2001) 09/01/2001 which merged into Wells Fargo & Co. (New) 12/31/2008

GREAT DIVIDE OIL CORP. (NV)
Name changed to American Beryllium & Oil Corp. 07/00/1961

GREAT EAGLE EXPLS & HLDGS LTD (ON)
Merged into Belle Aire Resource Explorations Ltd. 8/29/78
Each share Common no par exchanged for (0.27) share 8% Class A Preference $1 par and (0.1) share Common no par
Belle Aire Resource Explorations Ltd. name changed to Sprint Resources Ltd. 9/23/82 which name changed to Meacon Bay Resources Inc. 3/9/87 which recapitalized as Advantex Marketing International Inc. 9/16/91

GREAT EAGLE HLDGS LTD (HONG KONG)
ADR agreement terminated 06/10/2003
Each Sponsored ADR for Ordinary exchanged for $5.8229565 cash

GREAT EARTH VITAMIN GROUP INC (CO)
Name changed to Kelly's Coffee Group, Inc. (CO) 04/22/1994
Kelly's Coffee Group, Inc. (CO) reincorporated in Nevada 10/10/2000 which name changed to Nexia Holdings Inc. (NV) 03/21/2002 which reincorporated in Utah as Sack Lunch Productions, Inc. 04/20/2015

GREAT EAST BOTTLES & DRINKS CHINA HLDGS INC (FL)
Name changed to Great China Mania Holdings, Inc. 05/12/2011
Great China Mania Holdings, Inc. name changed to GME Innotainment, Inc. 07/07/2015

GREAT EAST ENERGY INC (DE)
Common $0.0001 par split (56) for (1) by issuance of (55) additional shares payable 09/16/2013 to holders of record 09/16/2013
Name changed to GASE Energy, Inc. 06/13/2014

GREAT EASTERN NATURAL GAS CO., INC. (DE)
Charter cancelled and declared inoperative and void for non-payment of taxes 4/1/37

GREAT EASTERN STORES
Acquired by Grand Union Co. on a (12.3151) for (1) basis in 1951
(See Grand Union Co.)

GREAT EASTN ENERGY & DEV CORP (VA)
Merged into Caprito Gas Corp. 10/3/97
Each share Common 10¢ par exchanged for $0.22 cash

GREAT EASTN ENERGY CORP (DE)
Name changed to Great Eastern International Inc. 06/19/1984
Great Eastern International Inc. recapitalized as Cable Car Beverage Corp. 07/20/1989 which merged into Triarc Companies, Inc. 11/25/1997 which name changed to Wendy's/Arby's Group, Inc. 09/29/2008 which name changed to Wendy's Co. 07/11/2011

GREAT EASTN FINL MGMT CDA LTD (CANADA)
Recapitalized as Greatok Group Ltd. 08/17/1984
Each share Common no par exchanged for (0.25) share Common no par
(See Greatok Group Ltd.)

GREAT EASTN INS CO (NY)
Common $2 par changed to $1 par 10/26/1966
99.97% acquired by Great Eastern Insurance Co. through exchange offer which expired 08/10/1973
Public interest eliminated

GREAT EASTN INTL INC (DE)
Recapitalized as Cable Car Beverage Corp. 07/20/1989
Each share Common 1¢ par exchanged for (1/3) share Common 1¢ par
Cable Car Beverage Corp. merged into Triarc Companies, Inc. 11/25/1997 which name changed to Wendy's/Arby's Group, Inc. 09/29/2008 which name changed to Wendy's Co. 07/11/2011

GREAT EASTN LTD (PE)
4.50% Preferred $10 par called for redemption at $10 on 11/03/2009
5.50% Preferred $10 par called for redemption at $10 on 11/03/2009

GREAT EASTN MGMT CORP (NY)
Common $1 par changed to 50¢ par and (1) additional share issued 05/29/1969
Stock Dividend - 10% 02/08/1968
Name changed to Gemco National, Inc. (NY) 06/05/1979
Gemco National, Inc. (NY) reincorporated in Florida as Investors Insurance Group, Inc. 09/01/1993

GREAT EASTN RES CDA LTD (CANADA)
Merged into Great Eastern Financial Management of Canada Ltd. 03/06/1975
Each share Capital Stock no par exchanged for (0.1) share Common no par
Great Eastern Financial Management of Canada Ltd. recapitalized as Greatok Group Ltd. 08/17/1984
(See Greatok Group Ltd.)

GREAT EASTN SHIPPING LTD (INDIA)
Each old Sponsored 144A GDR for Ordinary exchanged for (0.9) new Sponsored 144A GDR for Ordinary 03/21/2000
Each old Sponsored Reg. S GDR for Ordinary exchanged for (0.8) new Sponsored Reg. S GDR for Ordinary 12/27/2006
Each new Sponsored 144A GDR for Ordinary exchanged again for (0.8) new Sponsored 144A GDR for Ordinary 12/27/2006
GDR agreement terminated 11/20/2017
Each new Sponsored 144A GDR for Ordinary exchanged for $17.438673 cash
Each new Sponsored 144A GDR for Ordinary exchanged for $17.438673 cash

GREAT ENTMT & SPORTS INC (NV)
Name changed to Rockit!, Inc. 06/11/2007
(See Rockit!, Inc.)

GREAT EQUITY FINANCIAL CORP. (DE)
Name changed to Ryan Insurance Group, Inc. 1/21/76
(See Ryan Insurance Group, Inc.)

GREAT EQUITY LIFE INS CO (IL)
Reorganized under the laws of Delaware as Great Equity Financial Corp. 2/25/71
Each share Common 58¢ par exchanged for (0.5) share Common $1 par
Great Equity Financial Corp. name changed to Ryan Insurance Group, Inc. 1/21/76
(See Ryan Insurance Group, Inc.)

GREAT EXPECTATIONS & ASSOC INC (CO)
Name changed to Advaxis, Inc. (CO) and Common no par changed to $0.001 par 12/28/2004
Advaxis, Inc. (CO) reincorporated in Delaware 06/20/2006

GREAT FALLS BANCORP (NJ)
Stock Dividends - 10% 08/01/1989; 10% 08/01/1990; 10% 09/30/1992; 10% 07/31/1994; 10% 07/31/1995
Name changed to Greater Community Bancorp 07/01/1996
Greater Community Bancorp merged into Valley National Bancorp 07/02/2008

GREAT FALLS BREWERIES INC (MT)
Merged into Blitz-Weinhard Co. 1/31/69
Each share Common $1 par exchanged for $1.50 cash

GREAT FALLS CAP CORP (MT)
Involuntarily dissolved 12/1/97

GREAT FALLS GAS CO (MT)
Common $1.50 par changed to 15¢ par and (9) additional shares issued 06/29/1984
Name changed to Energy West Inc. 11/18/1993
Energy West Inc. name changed to Energy, Inc. (MT) 08/04/2009 which reincorporated in Ohio as Gas Natural Inc. 07/09/2010
(See Gas Natural Inc.)

GREAT FALLS MANUFACTURING CO.
Dissolved in 1933
No stockholders' equity

GREAT FALLS MINING & SMELTING LTD. (MB)
Property sold to Stanmore Mining & Smelting Co. Ltd. 00/00/1953
Details not available

GREAT FALLS POWER CO.
Merged into Duke Power Co. 00/00/1928
Details not available

GREAT FID LIFE INS CO (IN)
Merged into Mutual Security Life Insurance Co. 08/14/1989
Each share Capital Stock $1 par exchanged for $1.30 cash

GREAT FINL CORP (DE)
Merged into Star Banc Corp. 02/06/1998
Each share Common no par exchanged for $44 cash

GREAT FINGALL MNG N L (AUSTRALIA)
Each old Sponsored ADR for Ordinary exchanged for (0.1) new Sponsored ADR for Ordinary 10/01/1990
ADR agreement terminated 10/26/2015
Each new Sponsored ADR for Ordinary exchanged for (30) shares Ordinary
Note: Unexchanged ADR's will be sold and the proceeds, if any, held for claim after 04/26/2016

GREAT FLA BK (MIAMI LAKES, FL)
Acquired by Bond Street Holdings 01/31/2014
Each share Class A Common $5 par exchanged for $3.24 cash
Each share Class B Common $5 par exchanged for $3.24 cash

GREAT FRONTIER MINING CORP. (UT)
Merged into Frontier Oil & Mining Corp. in 1958
Each share Common 5¢ par exchanged for (1) share Common 5¢ par
Frontier Oil & Mining Corp. name changed to Frontier Capital Corp. 9/16/69
(See Frontier Capital Corp.)

GREAT HERCULES RES INC (BC)
Name changed to Pacific Coast Funding & Resources Inc. 09/26/1979
Pacific Coast Funding & Resources Inc. name changed to Alliance Resources Ltd. 04/23/1987 which recapitalized as Acrex Ventures Ltd. 10/19/1993 which recapitalized as Alba Minerals Ltd. 07/10/2014

GREAT HERITAGE LIFE INS CO (MO)
Common $2 par changed to $1 par 12/28/66
Merged into Equity Educators Assurance Co. 12/31/69
Each share Common $1 par exchanged for (0.44) share Common $1 par
(See Equity Educators Assurance Co.)

GREAT HORN INC (DE)
Recapitalized 02/18/1983
Name changed 10/05/1987
Recapitalized from Great Horn Mining Syndicate, Inc. to Great Horn Mining, Inc. 02/18/1983
Each share Common 1¢ par exchanged for (0.33333333) share Common 3¢ par
Each share Common 3¢ par exchanged for (0.25) share Common 12¢ par 12/30/1985
Name changed from Great Horn Mining, Inc. to Great Horn, Inc. 10/05/1987
Under plan of merger each share Common 12¢ par exchanged for $0.432 cash 10/01/2014

GREAT ICELANDIC WTR CORP (CANADA)
Reincorporated 10/28/1992
Place of incorporation changed from (BC) to (Canada) 10/28/1992
Struck off register and declared dissolved for failure to file returns 06/10/2004

GREAT INDIAN EXPLS LTD (ON)
Merged into Staple Mining Co. Ltd. 8/11/72
Each share Capital Stock no par exchanged for (0.142857) share Capital Stock no par
Staple Mining Co. Ltd. merged into Gerrard Realty Inc. 1/28/76

GREAT LAKES ACQUISITION INC (NV)
Reincorporated 12/31/2003
State of incorporation changed from (TX) to (NV) 12/31/2003
Recapitalized as Integrated Parking Solutions, Inc. 03/31/2006
Each share Common $0.001 par exchanged for (0.1) share Common $0.001 par
Integrated Parking Solutions, Inc. name changed to Integrated Cannabis Solutions, Inc. 04/21/2014

GREAT LAKES BANCORP A FED SVGS BK ANN ARBOR MICH (USA)
Non-Cum. Perpetual Preferred Ser. A no par split (10) for (1) by issuance of (9) additional shares 08/15/1991
Merged into TCF Financial Corp. 02/08/1995
Each share Non-Cum Perpetual Preferred Ser. A no par exchanged for (1) share Preferred Ser. A 1¢ par
Each share Common 1¢ par exchanged for (0.72259) share Common 1¢ par

GREAT LAKES BANCORP INC NEW (DE)
Merged into First Niagara Financial Group, Inc. (New) 02/15/2008
Each share Common $0.001 par exchanged for either (0.993) share Common 1¢ par or $14 cash
First Niagara Financial Group, Inc. (New) merged into KeyCorp (New) 08/01/2016

GREAT LAKES BANCORP INC OLD (DE)
Merged into Great Lakes Bancorp, Inc. (New) 05/01/2006
Each share Common $0.001 par exchanged for (1.0873) shares Common $0.001 par
Great Lakes Bancorp, Inc. (New) merged into First Niagara Financial Group, Inc. (New) 02/15/2008 which merged into KeyCorp (New) 08/01/2016

GREAT LAKES BANCSHARES, INC. (OH)
Voluntarily dissolved 04/01/1977
No stockholders' equity

GREAT LAKES BIOGAS TECHNOLOGIES INC (NV)
Merged into American Great Lakes Corp. 05/01/2009
Each share Common $0.001 par exchanged for (0.33333333) share Common $0.001 par
American Great Lakes Corp. recapitalized as Unique Transportation Solutions, Inc. 12/02/2009
(See Unique Transportation Solutions, Inc.)

GREAT LAKES CARBON INCOME FD (ON)
Completely liquidated
Each share Common no par received first and final distribution of $14 cash payable 05/10/2007 to holders of record 05/10/2007

GREAT LAKES CHEM CORP (DE)
Reincorporated 09/16/1970
State of incorporation changed from (MI) to (DE) 09/16/1970
Common $1 par split (2) for (1) by issuance of (1) additional share 10/27/1978
Common $1 par split (2) for (1) by issuance of (1) additional share 10/31/1983
Common $1 par split (2) for (1) by issuance of (1) additional share 10/31/1989
Common $1 par split (2) for (1) by issuance of (1) additional share 01/30/1992
Each share Common $1 par received distribution of (0.25) share Octel Corp. Common 1¢ par payable 05/22/1998 to holders of record 05/15/1998 Ex date - 05/26/1998
Preferred Stock Purchase Rights declared for Common stockholders of record 02/15/1999 were redeemed at $0.01 per right 04/30/2002 to holders of record 04/01/2002
Merged into Chemtura Corp. 07/01/2005
Each share Common $1 par exchanged for (2.2232) shares Common 1¢ par
(See Chemtura Corp.)

GREAT LAKES CHEMICAL CORP. (MI)
Incorporated 7/13/36
Dissolved in 1957
Details not available

GREAT LAKES DETROIT TERMINAL CO.
Liquidated in 1935

GREAT LAKES DREDGE & DOCK CO (NJ)
Each share Common $100 par exchanged for (8) shares Common no par in 1930
Common no par split (2) for (1) by issuance of (1) additional share 4/18/69
Common no par split (2) for (1) by issuance of (1) additional share 12/2/77
Reorganized as Great Lakes International, Inc. 7/2/79
Each (2) shares Common no par exchanged for (3) shares Common no par
(See Great Lakes International, Inc.)

GREAT LAKES ENGINEERING WORKS (MI)
Liquidation completed 3/16/62

GREAT LAKES FD INC (MI)
Auction Market Preferred Ser. C called for redemption at $100,000 on 11/3/98
Auction Market Preferred Ser. E called for redemption at $100,000 on 11/10/98
Auction Market Preferred Ser. F called for redemption at $100,000 on 11/17/98
144A Auction Market Preferred Ser. A called for redemption at $100,000 on 11/24/98
144A Auction Market Preferred Ser. B called for redemption at $100,000 on 12/1/98

GREAT LAKES FED SVGS & LN ASSN ANN ARBOR MICH (USA)
Stock Dividend - 20% 01/10/1986
Name changed to Great Lakes Bancorp, A Federal Savings Bank 05/26/1987
Great Lakes Bancorp, A Federal Savings Bank merged into TCF Financial Corp. 02/08/1995

GREAT LAKES FINL CORP (DE)
Stock Dividend - 10% 2/12/81
Name changed to Union Bancorp, Inc. (DE) 5/18/81
Union Bancorp, Inc. (DE) reincorporated in Michigan 10/1/82
(See Union Bancorp, Inc. (MI))

GREAT LAKES FINL RES INC (DE)
Merged into First Midwest Bancorp, Inc. 12/08/2014
Each share Common $12.50 par exchanged for (15.737) shares Common 1¢ par and $112.50 cash

GREAT LAKES FOREST PRODS LTD (ON)
Common no par split (4) for (1) by issuance of (3) additional shares 05/15/1985
Name changed to Canadian Pacific Forest Products Ltd. (ON) 06/02/1988
Canadian Pacific Forest Products Ltd. (ON) reincorporated in Canada 01/01/1989 which name changed to Avenor Inc. 03/21/1994
(See Avenor Inc.)

GREAT LAKES FUNDING, INC. (UT)
Recapitalized as Energroup Technologies Corp. (UT) 01/15/1986
Each share Common $0.001 par exchanged for (0.1) share Common $0.001 par
Energroup Technologies Corp. (UT) reorganized in Nevada as Energroup Holdings Corp. 08/21/2007

GREAT LAKES GROUP INC (ON)
Name changed to Great Lakes Power Inc. 06/01/1992
Great Lakes Power Inc. merged into Brascan Corp. 03/02/2001 which name changed to Brookfield Asset Management, Inc. 11/10/2005

GREAT LAKES HOMES INC (WI)
Adjudicated bankrupt 11/01/1966
No stockholders' equity

GREAT LAKES HYDRO INCOME FD (QC)
Name changed to Brookfield Renewable Power Fund (QC) 09/02/2009
Brookfield Renewable Power Fund reorganized in Bermuda as Brookfield Renewable Energy Partners L.P. 11/30/2011 which name changed to Brookfield Renewable Partners L.P. 05/10/2016

GREAT LAKES INDS INC (IL)
Common $1 par changed to no par 11/30/60
Completely liquidated 9/30/68
Each share Common no par exchanged for first and final distribution of $1.02 cash

GREAT LAKES INS CORP WIS (WI)
Each share Common 50¢ par exchanged for (0.1) share Common $2 par 3/8/67
Name changed to American Interstate Insurance Corp. of Wisconsin 12/18/76
(See American Interstate Insurance Corp. of Wisconsin)

GREAT LAKES INTL INC (DE)
Merged into Itel Corp. 11/27/85
Each share Common no par exchanged for $62.50 cash

GREAT LAKES IRON MINES LTD. (ON)
Charter revoked for failure to file reports and pay taxes 00/00/1956

GREAT LAKES MANAGEMENT CO., INC. (WI)
Common $1 par changed to 50¢ par 4/27/62
Completely liquidated 8/17/72
Each share Common 50¢ par received first and final distribution of (0.1904) share Great Lakes Insurance Corp. of Wisconsin Common $2 par
Certificates were not required to be surrendered and are now valueless

GREAT LAKES MEDICO PRODS INC (NY)
Charter cancelled and proclaimed dissolved for failure to pay taxes 9/26/79

GREAT LAKES MINERALS INC (ON)
Each (32.448792) shares Common no par received distribution of (1) share Newmex Mining Co., Ltd. Common no par payable 02/28/1997 to holders of record 02/10/1997
Recapitalized as Communicorp Corp. 01/30/1998
Each share Common no par exchanged for (0.05) share Common no par
(See Communicorp Corp.)

GREAT LAKES MONEY FUND, INC. (MI)
Reorganized under the laws of Indiana as Liquid Green Tax-Free Trust and Common no par reclassified as Units of Bene. Int. 08/30/1983
(See Liquid Green Tax-Free Trust)

GREAT LAKES NAT GAS CORP (DE)
Completely liquidated 5/7/73
Each share Common 50¢ par exchanged for first and final distribution of $2.25 cash

GREAT LAKES NICKEL CORP. LTD. (ON)
Merged into Great Lakes Nickel Ltd. 08/29/1969
Each share Common $1 par exchanged for (1) share Common $1 par
(See Great Lakes Nickel Ltd.)

GREAT LAKES NICKEL LTD (ON)
Delisted from Toronto Venture Stock Exchange 06/20/2003

GREAT LAKES OIL & CHEMICAL CO. (MI)
Name changed to Great Lakes Chemical Corp. (MI) 05/12/1960
Great Lakes Chemical Corp. (MI) reincorporated in Delaware 09/16/1970 which merged into Chemtura Corp. 07/01/2005
(See Chemtura Corp.)

GREAT LAKES PAPER LTD (ON)
Each share old Class A Preference no par exchanged for (1) share Class A Preference no par and (2) shares Common no par 00/00/1947
Each share old Common no par exchanged for (2) shares new Common no par 00/00/1947
Each share new Common no par exchanged again for (3) shares new Common no par 00/00/1951
New Common no par split (3) for (1) by issuance of (2) additional shares 05/26/1961
Name changed to Great Lakes Forest Products Ltd. 01/01/1979
Great Lakes Forest Products Ltd. name changed to Canadian Pacific Forest Products Ltd. (ONT) 06/02/1988 which reincorporated in Canada 01/01/1989 which name changed to Avenor Inc. 03/21/1994
(See Avenor Inc.)

GREAT LAKES PLATING CO.
Name changed to Great Lakes Industries, Inc. in 1948
(See Great Lake Industries, Inc.)

GREAT LAKES POWER CORP. LTD. (ON)
5% Preference 1st Ser. $25 par called for redemption 06/30/1961
Common no par split (5) for (2) by issuance of (1.5) additional shares 11/13/1961
Merged into Brascan Ltd. 01/01/1981
Each (100) shares Common no par exchanged for (231) shares Conv. Class A Ordinary no par
Brascan Ltd. merged into EdperBrascan Corp. 08/01/1997 which name changed to Brascan Corp. 04/28/2000 which name changed to Brookfield Asset Management, Inc. 11/10/2005

GREAT LAKES PWR INC (ON)
Common no par split (2) for (1) by issuance of (1) additional share payable 3/16/98 to holders of record 3/2/98
Merged into Brascan Corp. 3/2/2001
Each share Common no par exchanged for (0.905) share Class A Common no par
Brascan Corp. name changed to Brookfield Asset Management, Inc. 11/10/2005

GREAT LAKES REAL ESTATE TRUST (MI)
Majority owned by Care Corp. 00/00/1968
Public interest eliminated

GREAT LAKES REIT INC (MD)
Name changed 7/27/98
Issue Information - 5,700,000 shares COM offered at $15.50 per share on 05/08/1997
Under plan of reorganization name changed from Great Lakes REIT, Inc. to Great Lakes REIT 7/27/98
9.75% Preferred Shares of Bene. Int. Ser. A called for redemption at $25 on 4/27/2004
Merged into Transwestern Superior Acquisition, LLC 4/27/2004
Each share Common 1¢ par exchanged for $15.44 cash

GREAT LAKES SHARE CORP.
Acquired by Liberty Share Corp. in 1930
Details not available

GREAT LAKES SILVER HLDGS LTD (CANADA)
Name changed 06/13/1974
Reincorporated 03/20/1981
Name changed from Great Lakes Silver Mines Ltd. to Great Lakes Silver Holdings Ltd. 06/13/1974
Place of incorporation changed from (ON) to (Canada) 03/20/1981
Name changed to Springlake Resources Ltd. 12/22/1982
Springlake Resources Ltd. recapitalized as Savoy Minerals Ltd. 12/08/1988
(See Savoy Minerals Ltd.)

GREAT LAKES STEAMSHIP CO. INC. (DE)
Each share Common no par exchanged for (0.25) share 4-1/2% Preferred $100 par and (1.5) shares new Common no par in 1948
Liquidation completed 2/3/58

GREAT LAKES STEEL CORP.
Merged into National Steel Corp. 00/00/1929
Details not available

GREAT LAKES TERM WHSE CO (OH)
Common no par changed to $1 par in 1941
Name changed to Higginson Capital Management Inc. and Common $1 par changed to 10¢ par 12/1/70
(See Higginson Capital Management Inc.)

GREAT LAKES TERMINAL WAREHOUSE CO. OF TOLEDO
Reorganized as Great Lakes Terminal Warehouse Co. in 1935
(See Great Lakes Terminal Warehouse Co.)

GREAT LAKES TOWING CO (NJ)
Each share Common $100 par exchanged for (2) shares Common no par in 1952
Common no par split (2) for (1) by issuance of (1) additional share 5/21/56
7% Preferred $100 par called for redemption 5/12/69
Stock Dividend - 50% 8/31/49
Acquired by American Ship Building Co. 6/20/72
Each share Common no par exchanged for (1.57647) shares 5% Conv. Preferred Ser. A $1 par
(See American Ship Building Co.)

GREAT LAKES TRANSIT CORP.
Liquidated in 1950

GREAT LAKES UTILITIES CO.
Dissolved in 1947

GREAT LAKES UTILITIES CORP.
Reorganized as Great Lakes Utilities Co. in 1937 which dissolved in 1947

GREAT LARDER GOLD MINES LTD. (ON)
Charter revoked for failure to file reports and pay fees 11/10/1966

GREAT LAURIER URANIUM MINES LTD (QC)
Charter cancelled 03/16/1976

GREAT MANHATTAN GOLD CORP (BC)
Dissolved 10/07/1983

GREAT MARKWESTERN PACKING CO (MI)
Adjudicated bankrupt 09/22/1972
Stockholders' equity unlikely

GREAT MIDWEST CORP (DE)
Merged into Newsub, Inc. 4/30/80
Each share Common 10¢ par exchanged for $13.50 cash

GREAT MIDWEST LIFE INSURANCE CO. (OK)
Merged into United Investors, Inc. 04/09/1969
Each share Common 10¢ par exchanged for (0.25) share 6% Class A Preferential Common 50¢ par
(See United Investors Inc.)

GREAT MISSOURI LIFE INSURANCE CO. (MO)
Merged into Modern Security Life Insurance Co. 8/3/70
Each share Common $1 par exchanged for (1) share Common $1 par
Modern Security Life Insurance Co. merged into I.C.H. Corp. 11/4/82 which name changed to Southwestern Life Corp. (New) 6/15/94 which name changed to I.C.H. Corp. (New) 10/10/95
(See I.C.H. Corp. (New))

GREAT MOLLY EXPLORATIONS & ENTERPRISES LTD. (ON)
Merged into Great Eagle Explorations & Holdings Ltd. 7/7/69
Each share Common no par exchanged for (1) share Common no par
Great Eagle Explorations & Holdings Ltd. merged into Belle Aire Resource Explorations Ltd. 8/29/78 which name changed to Sprint Resources Ltd. 9/23/82 which name changed to Meacon Bay Resources Inc. 3/9/87 which recapitalized as Advantex Marketing International Inc. 9/16/91

GREAT MOLLY EXPLORATIONS LTD. (ON)
Merged into Great Molly Explorations & Enterprises Ltd. 01/29/1968
Each share Common no par exchanged for (0.33333333) share Common no par
Great Molly Explorations & Enterprises Ltd. merged into Great Eagle Explorations & Holdings Ltd. 07/07/1969 which merged into Belle Aire Resource Explorations Ltd. 08/29/1978 which name changed to Sprint Resources Ltd. 09/23/1982 which name changed to Meacon Bay Resources Inc. 03/09/1987 which recapitalized as Advantex Marketing International Inc. 09/16/1991

GREAT NATL CORP (DE)
Stock Dividend - 50% 09/15/1980
Name changed to GNC Energy Corp. 08/05/1981
(See GNC Energy Corp.)

GREAT NATL LD & INVT CORP (BC)
Recapitalized as Great National Investments Ltd. 11/23/87
Each share Class A Common no par exchanged for (1) share Common no par
Each share Class B Common no par exchanged for (1) share Common no par

GREAT NATIONAL LIFE INSURANCE CO. (TX)
Completely liquidated 11/27/68
Each share Common $2 par exchanged for first and final distribution of (1) share USLIFE Holding Corp. Common $2 par
USLIFE Holding Corp. name changed to USLIFE Corp. 5/22/70 which merged into American General Corp. 6/17/97 which merged into American International Group, Inc. 8/29/2001

GREAT NORTHERN BUILDING & LOAN CO. (OH)
Recapitalized as Great Northern Savings Co. 02/27/1973
Each share Permanent Capital Stock $100 par exchanged for (4) shares Permanent Capital Stock $25 par
Great Northern Savings Co. reorganized as Great Northern Financial Corp. 12/31/1985 which was acquired by First Bancorporation of Ohio, Inc. 04/22/1994 which name changed to FirstMerit Corp. 12/26/1994 which merged into Huntington Bancshares Inc. 08/16/2016

GREAT NORTHERN CAPITAL CO., LTD. (CANADA)
$2.50 Preferred $50 par called for redemption 08/07/1964
$2.80 Preferred 1957 Ser. $50 par called for redemption 08/07/1964
Liquidation completed 05/21/1965
Each share Common $1 par exchanged for initial distribution of (1) share Great Northern Capital Corp. Ltd. Common no par, (0.26) share Lakeland Natural Gas Ltd. Common $1 par, $2.20 cash and a deposit receipt for further liquidating payments 08/21/1964
Deposit receipts exchanged for second and final distribution of $0.153666 cash 05/21/1965
(See each company's listing)

GREAT NORTHERN DISTILLERIES, INC.
Dissolved in 1934

GREAT NORTHERN FINANCIAL CORP. (OH)
Acquired by First Bancorporation of Ohio, Inc. 04/22/1994
Each share Common no par exchanged for (3.746) shares Common $3.33333333 par
First Bancorporation of Ohio, Inc. name changed to FirstMerit Corp. 12/26/1994 which merged into Huntington Bancshares Inc. 08/16/2016

GREAT NORTHERN GAS UTILITIES LTD. (CANADA)
Incorporated 07/04/1950
Name changed to Great Northern Capital Co., Ltd. 05/08/1962
(See Great Northern Capital Co., Ltd.)

GREAT NORTHERN GOLD MINES, INC. (DE)
No longer in existence having become inoperative and void for non-payment of taxes 4/1/40

GREAT NORTHERN INVESTMENTS, INC. (DE)
Dissolved 6/1/59

GREAT NORTHERN LIFE INSURANCE CO. (IN)
Acquired by Midwestern United Life Insurance Co. 07/26/1965
Each share Common $1 par exchanged for (0.2380952) share Common $1 par
(See Midwestern United Life Insurance Co.)

GREAT NORTHERN MORTGAGE CO. (OH)
Charter cancelled for failure to pay franchise taxes 2/15/27

GREAT NORTHERN SAVINGS CO. (OH)
Under plan of reorganization each share Permanent Capital Stock $25 par automatically became (1) share Great Northern Financial Corp. Common no par 12/31/1985
Great Northern Financial Corp. acquired by First Bancorporation of Ohio, Inc. 04/22/1994 which name changed to FirstMerit Corp. 12/26/1994 which merged into Huntington Bancshares Inc. 08/16/2016

GREAT NORTHLAND DEVELOPMENT LTD. (SK)
Company struck from Provincial Register 10/2/59

GREAT NORTHN CAP LTD (ON)
Merged into Abbey Glen Property Corp. 5/8/74
Each share Common no par exchanged for (1.5) shares Common no par
(See Abbey Glen Property Corp.)

GREAT NORTHN EXPL LTD (AB)
Acquired by APF Energy Trust 06/04/2004
Each share Common no par exchanged for either (0.414614) Trust Unit no par or (0.285447) Trust Unit no par and $1.573252 cash
Note: Option to receive Units and cash expired 07/02/2004
(See APF Energy Trust)

GREAT NORTHN FINL CORP (ON)
Under plan of reorganization each share Common no par automatically became (1) share Embassy Resources Ltd. Common no par 8/12/83
Embassy Resources Ltd. merged into Unicorp Canada Corp. 3/2/84 which recapitalized as Unicorp Energy Corp. 6/25/91 which name changed to Unicorp Inc. 5/28/99 which name changed to Wilmington Capital Management Inc. 3/8/2002

GREAT NORTHN GAS CO (CO)
Merged into St. Francis Resources, Inc. 8/27/2001
Each share Common 1¢ par exchanged for $1.50 cash

GREAT NORTHN GAS UTILS LTD (CANADA)
Incorporated 03/19/1962
Name changed to ICG Utilities Ltd. 07/07/1980
ICG Utilities Ltd. name changed to ICG Utility Investments Ltd. 10/25/1984
(See ICG Utility Investments Ltd.)

GREAT NORTHN GOLD EXPL CORP (BC)
Reorganized under the laws of Ontario as Poydras Gaming Finance Corp. 05/08/2014
Each share Common no par exchanged for (0.5) share Common no par
Poydras Gaming Finance Corp. (ON) reincorporated in British Columbia 11/12/2015 which name changed to Integrity Gaming Corp. 01/02/2018

GREAT NORTHN GOLD INC (AB)
Merged into Ascentex Energy, Inc. 12/24/91
Each share Common no par exchanged for (0.062344) share Common no par
Ascentex Energy, Inc. recapitalized as Bonavista Petroleum Ltd. 3/3/97
(See Bonavista Petroleum Ltd.)

GREAT NORTHN INC (UT)
Common 1¢ par split (5) for (1) by issuance of (4) additional shares 09/01/1972
Common 1¢ par split (3) for (1) by issuance of (2) additional shares 12/01/1972
Proclaimed dissolved for failure to file annual report 12/31/1977

GREAT NORTHN IRON ORE PPTYS (MN)
Liquidation completed
Each Ctf. of Bene. Int. received initial distribution of $6.71 cash payable 02/02/2017 to holders of record 04/06/2015
Each Ctf. of Bene. Int. received second and final distribution of $0.581556 cash payable 06/09/2017 to holders of record 04/06/2015
Note: A Letter of Transmittal was sent to holders of record requesting surrender of certificate(s) in exchange for future final distribution 04/10/2015

GREAT NORTHN NEKOOSA CAP CORP (DE)
Merged into Great Northern Nekoosa Corp. 4/6/83
Each share $4.75 Conv. Exchangeable Preferred $10 par exchanged for (1) share $4.75 Conv. Exchangeable Preferred no par
(See Great Northern Nekoosa Corp.)

GREAT NORTHN NEKOOSA CORP (ME)
Conv. Preferred Ser. A no par called for redemption 3/9/72
Conv. Preferred Ser. C no par called for redemption 6/7/72
Common $10 par split (5) for (4) by issuance of (0.25) additional share 12/31/74
Conv. Preferred Ser. D no par called for redemption 3/9/76
Conv. Preferred Ser. B no par called for redemption 4/9/76
Common $10 par changed to $5 par and (1) additional share issued 5/26/76
Common $5 par split (3) for (2) by issuance of (0.5) additional share 12/31/83
Each share $4.75 Conv. Exchangeable Preferred no par exchanged for $50 principal amount of 9-1/2% Conv. Subord. Debs. due 3/31/2013 on 3/31/85
Common $5 par changed to $2.50 par and (1) additional share issued 5/19/87
Merged into NM Acquisition Corp. 6/26/90
Each share Common $2.50 par exchanged for $65.75 cash

GREAT NORTHN OILSANDS INC (NV)
Each share old Common $0.0001 par exchanged for (50) shares new Common $0.0001 par 04/16/2007
Reorganized under the laws of Florida as New Asia Gold Corp. 06/05/2008
Each share Common $0.0001 par exchanged for (0.001) share Common $0.0001 par
New Asia Gold Corp. recapitalized as New World Gold Corp. 05/08/2009

GREAT NORTHN PAPER CO (ME)
Each share Capital Stock $100 par exchanged for (4) shares Capital Stock $25 par in 1927
4.40% Preferred Ser. A $100 par called for redemption 12/15/58
Capital Stock $25 par reclassified as Common $10 par and (1.5) additional shares issued 10/22/65
Under plan of merger name changed to Great Northern Nekoosa Corp. 4/1/70
(See Great Northern Nekoosa Corp.)

GREAT NORTHN PETE & MINES LTD (BC)
Recapitalized as GNP Oil & Gas Ltd. 3/5/91
Each share Common 50¢ par exchanged for (0.2) share Common no par

GREAT NORTHN RY CO (MN)
Preferred $100 par changed to no par 00/00/1936
Each share Preferred no par exchanged for (2) shares Common no par 00/00/1954
Merged into Burlington Northern Inc. 03/02/1970
Each share Common no par exchanged for (0.5) share 5-1/2% Preferred $10 par and (1) share Common no par
Burlington Northern Inc. name changed to Burlington Northern Santa Fe Corp. 09/22/1995
(See Burlington Northern Santa Fe Corp.)

GREAT NORTHWEST LIFE INSURANCE CO. (WA)
Merged into Sunset Life Insurance Co. of America on a (1) for (0.75) basis 12/31/64

GREAT NORTHWEST RES CORP (BC)
Name changed to Quadrant Financial Corp. 08/05/1993
Quadrant Financial Corp. acquired by Walker's Hook International, Ltd. 10/28/1999 which name changed to Quadrant Resources Corp. 11/08/1999 which recapitalized as Pinnacle Transportation Inc. 05/27/2003 which name changed to ZYTO Corp. 09/19/2006 which name changed to Global Unicorn Holdings, Inc. 05/02/2018

GREAT OAKS FINL CORP (DE)
Charter cancelled and declared inoperative and void for non-payment of taxes 3/1/93

GREAT OUTDOOR AMERN ADVENTURE INC (WA)
Name changed to American Adventure, Inc. (WA) 3/26/84
American Adventure, Inc. (WA) reorganized in Delaware 3/27/87
(See American Adventure, Inc. (DE))

GREAT OUTDOORS INC (NV)
Name changed to Pivotal Technology, Inc. 8/21/2006
Pivotal Technology, Inc. name changed to Somatic Systems, Inc. 8/28/2006

GREAT PAC ENTERPRISES INC (BC)
Merged into Jim Pattison Industries Ltd. 07/29/1997
Each share Common no par exchanged for $80 cash

GREAT PAC FD LTD (CANADA)
Merged into Cambridge Growth Fund 12/20/1974
Each Mutual Fund Share no par exchanged for (0.5713065) Share of Bene. Int. no par
Note: Cambridge Growth Fund is privately held

GREAT PAC INDS INC (BC)
Merged into Pattison (Jim) International Ltd. 04/25/1990
Each share Common no par exchanged for $47 cash

GREAT PAC INDS LTD (BC)
Recapitalized as G.P.I. Industries Ltd. 03/20/1975
Each share Common no par exchanged for (0.25) share Common no par
(See G.P.I. Industries Ltd.)

GREAT PAC INTL INC (AB)
Recapitalized as WesCan Energy Corp. 10/04/2012
Each share Common no par exchanged for (0.05) share Common no par

GREAT PAC RES INC (BC)
Recapitalized as Micro Minerals Resources Inc. 11/17/94
Each (6.5) shares Common no par exchanged for (1) share Common no par

GREAT PANTHER INC (YT)
Recapitalized as Great Panther Resources Ltd. (YT) 10/02/2003
Each share Common no par exchanged for (0.1) share Common no par
Great Panther Resources Ltd. (YT) reincorporated in British Columbia 07/14/2004 which name changed to Great Panther Silver Ltd. 01/12/2010

GREAT PANTHER RES LTD (BC)
Reincorporated 07/14/2004
Place of incorporation changed from (YT) to (BC) 07/14/2004
Name changed to Great Panther Silver Ltd. 01/12/2010

GREAT PEE DEE BANCORP INC (DE)
Stock Dividend - 10% payable 11/09/2001 to holders of record 10/30/2001
Merged into First Bancorp 04/01/2008
Each share Common 1¢ par exchanged for (1.15) shares Common no par

GREAT PINE MINES LTD (ON)
Capital Stock $1 par changed to no par 01/20/1972
Charter cancelled for failure to pay taxes and file returns 03/16/1976

GREAT PINES WTR INC (TX)
Merged into Suntory Water Co. 6/6/99
Each share Common 1¢ par exchanged for $5.87 cash
Note: An additional escrow payment of $0.1525 cash per share was made in September 2002

GREAT PLAINS DEV CO CDA LTD (CANADA)
Acquired by Burmah Oil Canada Ltd. 10/11/1974
Each share Capital Stock $1 par exchanged for $40 cash

GREAT PLAINS ENERGY INC (MO)
Each Income Pride automatically became (0.79152748) share Common no par 02/16/2007
Each Corporate Unit automatically became (2.9762) shares Common no par 06/15/2012
3.8% Preferred $100 par called for redemption at $103.70 plus $0.75 accrued dividends on 08/10/2016
4.2% Preferred $100 par called for redemption at $102 plus $0.83 accrued dividends on 08/10/2016
4.35% Preferred $100 par called for redemption at $101 plus $0.86 accrued dividends on 08/10/2016
4.5% Preferred $100 par called for redemption at $101 plus $0.89 accrued dividends on 08/10/2016
7% Depositary Preferred Ser. B called for redemption at $56.12056 on 08/17/2017
Merged into Evergy, Inc. 06/05/2018
Each share Common no par exchanged for (0.5981) share Common no par

GREAT PLAINS EXPL INC NEW (AB)
Reincorporated 01/01/2009
Place of incorporation changed from (Canada) to (AB) 01/01/2009
Merged into Avenir Diversified Income Trust 11/10/2010
Each share Common no par exchanged for either (0.088) Trust Unit or (0.088) Avenir Exchange Corp. Exchangeable Share
Note: Canadian residents option to receive Exchangeable Shares expired 11/02/2010
Unexchanged certificates will be cancelled and become without value 11/10/2020
Avenir Diversified Income Trust reorganized as AvenEx Energy Corp. 01/07/2011 which merged into Spyglass Resources Corp. 04/04/2013

GREAT PLAINS EXPL INC OLD (CANADA)
Merged into Great Plains Exploration Inc. (New) (Canada) 07/29/2005
Each share Common no par exchanged for (0.46948356) share Common no par
Great Plains Exploration Inc. (New) (Canada) reincorporated in Alberta 01/01/2009 which merged into Avenir Diversified Income Trust 11/10/2010 which reorganized as AvenEx Energy Corp. 01/07/2011 which merged into Spyglass Resources Corp. 04/04/2013

GREAT PLAINS HLDGS INC (NV)
Each share old Common $0.001 par exchanged for (0.18181818) share new Common $0.001 par 11/25/2015
Name changed to Jerrick Media Holdings, Inc. 03/04/2016

GREAT PLAINS LIFE INSURANCE CO., INC. (KS)
Acquired by Pacific Western Corp. 3/27/72
Each share Common $1 par exchanged for (0.8) share Common 10¢ par
(See Pacific Western Corp.)

GREAT PLAINS LIFE INSURANCE CO. (TX)
Acquired by American Educational Life Insurance Co. 10/31/64
Each share Preferred $50 par exchanged for (100) shares Class A Common $1 par
Each share Common no par exchanged for (0.6) share Class B Common $1 par
American Educational Life Insurance Co. declared insolvent 1/13/67

GREAT PLAINS LIFE INSURANCE CO. OF WYOMING (WY)
Name changed to Great Plains Life Insurance Co. 02/23/1965
Great Plains Life Insurance Co. acquired by Mid-America Great Plains Financial Corp. 01/02/1969 which name changed to Mid-America/Great Plains Corp. 12/16/1981
(See Mid-America/Great Plains Corp.)

GREAT PLAINS LIFE INS CO (WY)
Completely liquidated 01/02/1969
Each share Common $1 par exchanged for first and final distribution of (1) share Mid-America Great Plains Financial Corp. Common no par
Mid-America Great Plains Financial Corp. name changed to Mid-America/Great Plains Corp. 12/16/1981
(See Mid-America/Great Plains Corp.)

GREAT PLAINS NAT GAS CO (MN)
Merged into Great Plains Energy Corp. 3/1/83
Each share Class A $1 par exchanged for $12 cash

GREAT PLAINS PETE CORP (WA)
Capital Stock 5¢ par changed to no par 12/1/78
Recapitalized as Great Plains Corp. 2/25/97
Each share Common no par exchanged for (0.02) share Common no par

GREAT PLAINS SOFTWARE INC (MN)
Issue Information - 3,000,000 shares COM offered at $16 per share on 06/19/1997
Merged into Microsoft Corp. 4/5/2001
Each share Common 1¢ par exchanged for (1.1) shares Common $0.0000125 par

GREAT QUEST METALS LTD (BC)
Name changed to Great Quest Fertilizer Ltd. 06/09/2014

GREAT REP CORP (WA)
Common $1 par changed to 25¢ par and (3) additional shares issued 9/17/69
Out of business in July 1971
No stockholders' equity

GREAT REP GROWTH FD INC (WA)
Name changed to Commodore Growth Fund, Inc. 11/5/71
(See Commodore Growth Fund, Inc.)

GREAT REP HLDG CORP (GA)
Merged into Atlantic American Corp. 5/31/78
Each share Class A Common 25¢ par exchanged for $1.25 cash

GREAT RIV FINL GROUP INC (IA)
Name changed to Two Rivers Financial Group, Inc. 02/05/2008

GREAT ROCK DEV CORP (FL)
Recapitalized as Comepay, Inc. 03/01/2018
Each share Common $0.001 par exchanged for (0.01) share Common $0.001 par

GREAT SAN FRANCISCO SEAFOOD INC (MN)
Statutorily dissolved 10/7/91

GREAT SCOTT SUPER MKTS INC (MI)
Stock Dividends - 10% 05/06/1975; 10% 05/21/1976
Merged into Allied Supermarkets, Inc. (MI) 06/15/1976
Each share Common $1 par exchanged for $4.32 cash

GREAT SHIELD URANIUM MINES LTD. (ON)
Charter revoked for failure to file reports and pay fees 12/10/1962

GREAT SLAVE MINES LTD. (BC)
Recapitalized as Alaska Kenai Oils Ltd. 04/06/1972
Each share Capital Stock $1 par exchanged for (0.1) share Capital Stock no par
Alaska Kenai Oils Ltd. recapitalized as Kenai Oils Ltd. 03/01/1976

GREAT SOUTHERN BOX CO., INC. (LA)
Acquired by Gair (Robert) Co., Inc. 05/16/1955
Each share 1st Preferred $100 par or 2nd Preferred $100 par exchanged for (1) share $4.50 Preferred $100 par
Each share Common $12.50 par exchanged for (0.25) share $4.50 Preferred $100 par and (2/3) share Common $1 par
(See Gair (Robert) Co., Inc.)

GREAT SOUTHN CAP TR I (DE)
9% Trust Preferred Securities called for redemption at $10 on 11/21/2006

GREAT SOUTHERN LAND & PAPER CO. (GA)
Each share Class A 50¢ par exchanged for (0.1) share Class A $5 par 7/6/64
Acquired by Great Northern Paper Co. 10/1/65
Each share Class A $5 par exchanged for (1) share Conv. Preferred Ser. A no par
Great Northern Paper Co. merged into Great Northern Nekoosa Corp. 4/1/70
(See Great Northern Nekoosa Corp.)

GREAT SOUTHERN LUMBER CO. (LA)
Liquidated in 1939

GREAT SOUTHERN LUMBER CO. (PA)
Acquired by Gaylord Container Corp. and Great Southern Lumber Co. (LA) in 1937
Each share Common exchanged for (0.52) share 5-1/2% Preferred and (2.38) shares Common of Gaylord Container plus (1) share Common of Great Southern Lumber Co. (LA)
(See each company's listing)

GREAT SOUTHERN SULPHUR CO. (AZ)
Charter expired 11/16/42

GREAT SOUTHN BANCORP (FL)
Merged into Colonial BancGroup, Inc. 07/01/1997
Each share Common 1¢ par exchanged for (0.5359) share Common $2.50 par
(See Colonial BancGroup, Inc.)

GREAT SOUTHN BANCORP INC (DE)
Common 1¢ par split (3) for (1) by issuance of (2) additional shares 7/25/94
Common 1¢ par split (2) for (1) by issuance of (1) additional share payable 10/21/96 to holders of record 10/11/96
Common 1¢ par split (2) for (1) by issuance of (1) additional share payable 6/1/2004 to holders of record 5/17/2004 Ex date - 6/2/2004
Reincorporated under the laws of Maryland 5/18/2004

GREAT SOUTHN BK (LANTANA, FL)
Under plan of reorganization each share Common $5 par automatically became (1) share Great Southern Bancorp Common 1¢ par 01/01/1996
Great Southern Bancorp merged into Colonial BancGroup, Inc. 07/01/1997
(See Colonial BancGroup, Inc.)

GREAT SOUTHN CORP (DE)
Merged into NLT Corp. 2/27/79
Each share Common $2 par exchanged for $58 cash

GREAT SOUTHN ENTERPRISES CORP (BC)
Each share old Common no par exchanged for (0.14285714) share new Common no par 01/28/2004
Recapitalized as Balmoral Resources Ltd. 03/29/2010
Each share new Common no par exchanged for (0.06666666) share Common no par

GREAT SOUTHN ENTERPRISES INC (GA)
Merged into ARC Boulevard Inc. 4/20/93
Each share Common $1 par exchanged for $19 cash

GREAT SOUTHN FED SVGS BK (SAVANNAH, GA)
Placed in conservatorship 6/22/89
No stockholders' equity

GREAT SOUTHN FINL CORP (FL)
Common $1 par changed to 80¢ par and (0.25) additional share issued 4/30/65
Proclaimed dissolved for failure to file reports and pay fees 12/14/82

GREAT SOUTHN INVT CORP (AL)
Declared a legal bankrupt 02/22/1971

Stockholders' equity unlikely

GREAT SOUTHN LIFE INS CO (TX)
Common $10 par changed to $2 par and (4) additional shares issued plus an 11-1/9% stock dividend paid 12/29/67
Stock Dividends - 6-2/3% 12/10/53; 66-2/3% 5/31/65
Merged into Great Southern Corp. 5/31/72
Each share Common $2 par exchanged for (1) share Common $2 par
(See Great Southern Corp.)

GREAT SOUTHN REAL ESTATE TR (GA)
Merged into Great Southern Enterprises, Inc. 04/20/1971
Each Share of Bene. Int. no par exchanged for (1) share Common $1 par
(See Great Southern Enterprises, Inc.)

GREAT SOUTHWEST CORP. (TX)
Common $1 par changed to 10¢ par and (9) additional shares issued 4/25/69
Reincorporated under the laws of Delaware 12/31/72
(See Great Southwest Corp. (DE))

GREAT SOUTHWEST CORP (DE)
Each share Common 10¢ par exchanged for (0.05) share Common $2 par 6/24/76
Merged into Pennsylvania Co. 12/22/78
Each share Common $2 par exchanged for $19 cash

GREAT SOUTHWEST FIRE INS CO (AZ)
Each share Common $1 par exchanged for (0.001) share Common $1000 par 9/7/72
Note: In effect holders received $4 cash per share and public interest was eliminated

GREAT SOUTHWEST INDS CORP (DE)
Common 1¢ par changed to 10¢ par 3/22/79
Charter cancelled and declared inoperative and void for non-payment of taxes 3/1/87

GREAT SOUTHWEST INVESTMENT CO., INC. (AZ)
Charter revoked for failure to file reports and pay fees in December 1963

GREAT SOUTHWEST LIFE INS CO (TX)
Closed by the State Insurance Tax Department 2/2/95
Stockholders' equity unlikely

GREAT SOUTHWESTN INDS INC (DE)
Name changed to New American Video, Inc. 2/20/81
New American Video, Inc. recapitalized as Tropicana, Inc. 6/18/83

GREAT SPIRITS INC (CO)
SEC revoked commmon stock registration 02/19/2014

GREAT ST BK (WILKESBORO, NC)
Merged into Parkway Acquisition Corp. 07/01/2018
Each share Common $5 par exchanged for (1.21) shares Common no par

GREAT STS LIFE INS CO (IL)
Merged into State Security Life Insurance Co. 11/24/68
Each share Common 25¢ par exchanged for (2/3) share Common 50¢ par

GREAT SWEET GRASS OILS LTD. (ON)
Capital Stock 20¢ par changed to no par 08/04/1961
Recapitalized as Kardar Canadian Oils Ltd. 06/29/1962
Each share Capital Stock no par exchanged for (0.5) share Capital Stock no par
(See Kardar Canadian Oils Ltd.)

GREAT TRAIN STORE CO (DE)
Plan of reorganization under Chapter 11 Federal Bankruptcy code effective 08/15/2000
Stockholders' equity unlikely

GREAT UNVL STORES PLC (ENGLAND)
ADR's for Ordinary Reg. 5s par and ADR's for Class A Ordinary Reg. 5s par changed to 25p par per currency change 02/15/1971
ADR's for Ordinary Reg. 25p par split (4) for (1) by issuance of (3) additional shares 10/26/1993
ADR's for Ordinary Class A Reg. 25p par reclassified as Unsponsored ADR's for Ordinary 25p par 10/25/1993
Each Unsponsored ADR for Ordinary 25p par exchanged for (1) Sponsored ADR for Ordinary 25p par 12/10/1999
Stock Dividends - 100% 06/18/1958; 10% in ADR's for Class A Ordinary Reg. 11/20/1959; 10% in ADR's for Class A Ordinary Reg. to holders of ADR's for Class A Ordinary Reg. or ADR's for Ordinary Reg. 11/09/1964
Name changed to GUS PLC 07/25/2001
GUS PLC merged into Experian Group Ltd. 10/11/2006 which name changed to Experian PLC 07/21/2008
Note: Common Market regulation required all publicly held British companies to replace LTD with PLC 00/00/1982

GREAT VY BK (CERES, CA)
Merged into Union Safe Deposit Bank (San Francisco, CA) 6/28/96
Each share Common $2 par exchanged for $8.712 cash

GREAT VALLEY EXPLORATION & MINING LTD. (QC)
Merged into Resource Exploration & Development Co. Ltd. 06/11/1968
Each share Capital Stock $1 par exchanged for (0.421940) share Capital Stock no par
(See Resource Exploration & Development Co. Ltd.)

GREAT WALL ACQUISITION CORP (DE)
Name changed to ChinaCast Education Corp. 2/9/2007

GREAT WALL CYBERTECH LTD (HONG KONG)
Name changed 04/03/2000
Each old Sponsored ADR for Ordinary exchanged for (0.5) new Sponsored ADR for Ordinary 01/09/1998
Name changed from Great Wall Electronic International Ltd. to Great Wall Cybertech Ltd. 04/03/2000
Name changed to EPI Holdings Ltd. 10/31/2006
(See EPI Holdings Ltd.)

GREAT WALL FOOD & BEVERAGE CORP (FL)
Reorganized as DuraVest, Inc. 12/7/2001
Each share Common $0.0001 par exchanged for (10) shares Common $0.0001 par

GREAT WALL PAN ASIA HLDGS LTD (BERMUDA)
ADR agreement terminated 06/05/2017
Each Sponsored ADR for Ordinary exchanged for $0.801038 cash

GREAT WEST COAL CO., LTD. (CANADA)
Each share Common no par exchanged for (2) shares Class A no par and (2) shares Class B no par 00/00/1951
Acquired by Loram Coal Ltd. 03/15/1965
Each share Class A no par exchanged for $5.85 cash
Each share Class B no par exchanged for $5.85 cash

GREAT WEST CORP. (UT)
Charter suspended for failure to pay taxes 9/28/73

GREAT WEST GOLD & SILVER INC (DE)
Each share old Common $0.001 par exchanged for (0.05) share new Common $0.001 par 5/7/87
Charter cancelled and declared inoperative and void for non-payment of taxes 5/30/96

GREAT WEST GOLD INC (WY)
Old Common $0.0001 par split (2) for (1) by issuance of (1) additional share payable 10/09/2006 to holders of record 10/05/2006 Ex date - 10/10/2006
Old Common $0.0001 par split (2) for (1) by issuance of (1) additional share payable 02/13/2007 to holders of record 02/08/2007 Ex date - 02/14/2007
Each share old Common $0.0001 par exchanged for (0.0005) share new Common $0.0001 par 05/14/2007
Stock Dividends - 25% payable 03/17/2005 to holders of record 03/16/2005 Ex date - 03/18/2005; 25% payable 08/08/2005 to holders of record 08/01/2005 Ex date - 08/09/2005; 25% payable 02/07/2006 to holders of record 01/06/2006 Ex date - 02/08/2006; 30% payable 09/08/2006 to holders of record 08/28/2006 Ex date - 09/11/2006
Name changed to Fortress Financial Group, Inc. 10/08/2007
(See Fortress Financial Group, Inc.)

GREAT WEST INTL EQUITIES LTD (CANADA)
Acquired by Trizec Corp. Ltd. 10/28/71
Each share Common no par exchanged for $2 principal amount of Trizec Corp. Ltd. 7% Conv. Notes due 12/31/90, $1.35 principal amount of Triton Centres Ltd. 7% Notes due 6/30/76, (1) share Trizec Corp. Ltd. Common no par and $2.50 cash
Trizec Corp. Ltd. name changed to Trizec Corp. Ltd./La Corporation Trizec Ltee. 4/1/77 recapitalized as Trizec Ltd. (New) 7/25/94 which merged into Trizec Hahn Corp. 11/2/96 which was acquired by Trizec Canada Inc. 5/8/2002
(See Trizec Canada Inc.)

GREAT-WEST LIFE & ANNUITY INS CAP I (DE)
Issue Information - $175,000,000 principal amount of GTD SUB CAP INCOME SECS 7.25% offered at $25 per security on 04/29/1999
7.25% Guaranteed Subordinated Capital Income Securities called for redemption at $25 on 12/16/2004

GREAT WEST LIFE ASSURN CO (CANADA)
Each share Common $100 par exchanged for (10) shares Common $10 par 00/00/1953
Each share Common $10 par exchanged for (10) shares Common $1 par 06/01/1965
Common $1 par split (2) for (1) by issuance of (1) additional share 07/01/1970
Acquired by Great-West Lifeco Inc. 01/14/2000
Each share Common $1 par exchanged for $5,200 cash
7.80% Preferred Ser. B $25 par called for redemption 12/31/1992
7.7% Preferred Ser. A $25 par called for redemption at $25 on 09/30/1997
Preferred Ser. L called for redemption at $25 on 10/31/2007
5.55% Non-Cum. Preferred Ser. O called for redemption at $25 on 10/31/2010
Public interest eliminated

GREAT WEST LIFECO INC (CANADA)
7.50% 1st Preferred Ser. A called for redemption at $25 on 04/01/1999
7.45% 1st Preferred Ser. B called for redemption at $25 on 12/31/2002
7.75% 1st Preferred Ser. C no par called for redemption at $25.50 on 09/30/2003
5% Class A Preferred Ser. 1 no par called for redemption at $25 on 10/31/2004
4.8% 1st Preferred Ser. E $25 par called for redemption at $26 on 12/31/2009
4.70% 1st Preferred Ser. D no par called for redemption at $25.25 on 03/31/2010
Non-Cum. 5-Yr. Rate Reset 1st Preferred Ser. J no par called for redemption at $25 plus $0.375 accrued dividends on 12/31/2013
(Additional Information in Active)

GREAT WEST MNG & SMLT LTD (ON)
Capital Stock $1 par changed to no par 12/29/1970
Charter cancelled for failure to pay taxes and file returns 03/16/1976

GREAT WEST MINING CORP. LTD. (BC)
Recapitalized as Four Seasons Recreation Ltd. 02/13/1970
Each share Capital Stock 50¢ par exchanged for (0.1) share Capital Stock no par
Four Seasons Recreation Ltd. name changed to Four Seasons Mining & Resources Ltd. 06/04/1970 which name changed to Four Seasons Manufacturing Ltd. 10/31/1971 which name changed to Renn Industries Inc. 11/29/1974 which name changed to Anthes Industries Inc. 06/04/1981 which name changed to Patheon Inc. 05/12/1993
(See Patheon Inc.)

GREAT WEST RES INC (NV)
Name changed to Orbital Tracking Corp. 02/20/2015

GREAT WEST SADDLERY LTD (CANADA)
Name changed 02/01/1969
Reorganized 00/00/1937
Each share 1st Preferred $100 par exchanged for (1) share 1st Preferred $50 par and (3) shares new Common no par
Each share 2nd Preferred $100 par exchanged for (0.8) share 2nd Preferred $50 par and (2) shares new Common no par
Each share old Common no par exchanged for (0.4) share new Common no par
Under plan of merger name changed from Great West Saddlery Co. Ltd. to Great West Saddlery Ltd. and each share Common no par exchanged for (1) share Common no par 02/01/1969
Name changed to Great West International Equities Ltd. 05/27/1970
Great West International Equities Ltd. acquired by Trizec Corp. Ltd.

10/28/1971 which name changed to Trizec Corp. Ltd./ La Corporation Trizec Ltee. 04/01/1977 which recapitalized as Trizec Ltd. (New) 07/25/1994 which merged into Trizec Hahn Corp. 11/01/1996 which was acquired by Trizec Canada Inc. 05/08/2002
(See Trizec Canada Inc.)

GREAT WEST STL INDS LTD (BC)
Common no par reclassified as Class A Common no par 1/30/81
Class A Common no par reclassified as Common no par 6/17/87
Name changed to GWIL Industries Inc. 4/18/88
(See GWIL Industries Inc.)

GREAT WEST URANIUM MINES LTD. (SK)
Charter revoked for failure to file reports and pay fees 09/27/1963

GREAT WESTERN ASSURANCE CO. (NM)
Name changed to Cibola Life Insurance Co. 05/15/1975
(See Cibola Life Insurance Co.)

GREAT WESTERN BISCUIT CO.
Bankrupt 00/00/1949
Details not available

GREAT WESTERN CONTAINER, INC. (CA)
Name changed to Great Western General, Inc. and Common $1 par changed to $0.025 par 6/1/66
Great Western General, Inc. recapitalized as Ropak West Inc. 12/21/81 which name changed to Ropak Corp. 5/17/85
(See Ropak Corp.)

GREAT WESTERN CORP. (DE)
Ctfs. dated prior to 05/17/1956
Name changed to Great Western Financial Corp. 05/17/1956
Great Western Financial Corp. merged into Washington Mutual Inc. 07/01/1997
(See Washington Mutual, Inc.)

GREAT WESTERN ELECTROCHEMICAL CO.
Merged into Dow Chemical Co. 00/00/1939
Each share 6% Preferred $20 par exchanged for (0.1875) share Common no par
Each share Common no par exchanged for (1) share Common no par
Dow Chemical Co. merged into DowDuPont Inc. 09/01/2017

GREAT WESTN FINL TR I (DE)
8.25% Trust Originated Preferred Securities called for redemption at $25 on 11/29/2002

GREAT WESTERN GARMENT CO. LTD. (AB)
6% Preferred $10 par called 6/30/65

GREAT WESTERN GENERAL, INC. (CA)
Recapitalized as Ropak West Inc. 12/21/81
Each share Common $0.025 par exchanged for (0.05) share Common no par
Ropak West Inc. name changed to Ropak Corp. 5/17/85
(See Ropak Corp.)

GREAT WESTERN INVESTMENT TRUST (OK)
Liquidation completed
Each share Common $5 par exchanged for $5.66 cash
Note: Above amount represents payments made periodically from October 1974 thru 5/15/81

GREAT WESTERN LIFE INSURANCE CO. (OK)
Merged into American Preferred Corp. on a (0.2) for (1) basis 04/28/1961
American Preferred Corp. acquired by

Kennesaw Life & Accident Insurance Co. 08/12/1965 which merged into Lykes-Youngstown Financial Corp. 11/14/1969 which name changed to LifeSurance Co. 05/10/1971 which merged into Regan Holding Corp. 10/31/1991
(See Regan Holding Corp.)

GREAT WESTERN MINES CO. (UT)
Name changed to Bates-Great Western Energy, Inc. 10/15/82
(See Bates-Great Western Energy, Inc.)

GREAT WESTERN MINING CO., LTD. (ID)
Charter revoked for failure to file reports and pay fees 11/30/65

GREAT WESTERN OIL CO. (CO)
Charter suspended for failure to file annual reports 9/30/55

GREAT WESTERN OIL CO. (NV)
Charter revoked for failure to file reports and pay fees 3/5/62

GREAT WESTERN PETROLEUM CO. (CO)
Declared defunct and inoperative by State of Colorado for non-payment of taxes 9/23/57

GREAT WESTERN PETROLEUM CORP. (NV)
Dissolved 12/8/59
Common stock declared worthless

GREAT WESTERN POWER CO. OF CALIFORNIA
Dissolved in 1936

GREAT WESTERN PRODUCERS, INC. (MD)
6% Preferred Ser. A $30 par called for redemption 6/30/65
Stock Dividend - 10% 12/31/59
Liquidation completed
Each share Common 60¢ par received initial distribution of (0.166666) share Taylor Wine Co., Inc. Common $2 par 7/20/66
Each share Common 60¢ par exchanged for second and final distribution of $0.96 cash 11/30/66
Taylor Wine Co., Inc. merged into Coca-Cola Co. 1/21/77

GREAT WESTERN SAVINGS & LOAN ASSOCIATION OF SOUTHERN CALIFORNIA (CA)
99.68% acquired by Great Western Financial Corp. through exchange offer which expired 08/28/1970
Public interest eliminated

GREAT WESTERN SUGAR CO. (NJ)
Each share Common $25 par exchanged for (3) shares Common no par in 1927
Merged into Great Western United Corp. 1/15/68
Each share Preferred $100 par exchanged for $190 principal amount of 6% Debentures due 5/1/87
Each share Common no par exchanged for (1) share $1.88 Preferred no par and (1/3) share Common $1 par
Great Western United Corp. reorganized as Hunt International Resources Corp. 2/22/78
(See Hunt International Resources Corp.)

GREAT WESTERN URANIUM CORP. (DE)
Recapitalized as Great Western Consolidated, Inc. 1/21/70
Each share Common 10¢ par received (0.2) share Common 1¢ par
Certificates were not required to be surrendered and are now valueless

GREAT WESTN AIRLS INC (DE)
Recapitalized as United States Barium Corp. 4/17/87
Each share Common 10¢ par exchanged for (0.05) share Common 2¢ par

GREAT WESTN BK & TR CO (TUCSON, AZ)
Merged into Patagonia Corp. 6/22/70
Each share Common $10 par exchanged for (3.824) shares Common $1 par
(See Patagonia Corp.)

GREAT WESTN CONS INC (DE)
Adjudicated bankrupt 04/10/1972
Stockholders' equity unlikely

GREAT WESTN CORP (DE)
Ctfs. dated after 10/24/68
Stock Dividend - 100% 12/31/69
Name changed to Patagonia Corp. 6/9/70
(See Patagonia Corp.)

GREAT WESTN CORP (TX)
Name changed to Terramar Corp. 12/18/72

GREAT WESTN DIAMONDS CORP (CANADA)
Merged into Vaaldiam Resources Ltd. 03/11/2008
Each share Common no par exchanged for (0.45) share Common no par
Vaaldiam Resources Ltd. merged into Vaaldiam Mining Inc. 03/26/2010
(See Vaaldiam Mining Inc.)

GREAT WESTN EQUITIES GROUP INC (NV)
Name changed to American International Marketing, Inc. 9/21/89

GREAT WESTN EXPL (UT)
Involuntarily dissolved 1/1/96

GREAT WESTN FED SVGS BK (BELLEVUE, WA)
Stock Dividend - 10% 05/31/1985
Name changed to Great Western Savings Bank (Bellevue, WA) 07/18/1985
Great Western Savings Bank (Bellevue, WA) acquired by Great Western Financial Corp. 02/25/1988 which merged into Washington Mutual, Inc. 07/01/1997
(See Washington Mutual, Inc.)

GREAT WESTN FINL CORP (DE)
Capital Stock $1 par split (5) for (2) by issuance of (1.5) additional shares 01/20/1959
Capital Stock $1 par split (2) for (1) by issuance of (1) additional share 08/01/1960
Capital Stock $1 par split (3) for (2) by issuance of (0.5) additional share 01/12/1962
Capital Stock $1 par split (3) for (2) by issuance of (0.5) additional share 03/16/1979
Capital Stock $1 par reclassified as Common $1 par 05/15/1979
Common $1 par split (5) for (2) by issuance of (1.5) additional shares 05/28/1987
8.75% Conv. Depositary Preferred called for redemption 09/16/1996
8.75% Conv. Preferred $1 par called for redemption 09/16/1996
Merged into Washington Mutual, Inc. 07/01/1997
Each 8.3% Depositary Share exchanged for (1) 8.3% Depositary Share Ser. F
Each share Common $1 par exchanged for (0.9) share Common no par
(See Washington Mutual, Inc.)

GREAT WESTN GOLD CORP (BC)
Name changed to Great Western Minerals Group Ltd. (BC) 08/14/2002
Great Western Minerals Group Ltd. (BC) reincorporated in Canada 12/12/2007
(See Great Western Minerals Group Ltd.)

GREAT WESTN LD & REC INC (NV)
SEC revoked common stock registration 05/13/2011

GREAT WESTN MINERALS GROUP LTD (CANADA)
Reincorporated 12/12/2007
Place of incorporation changed from (BC) to (Canada) 12/12/2007
Filed an assignment in bankruptcy 12/03/2015
Stockholders' equity unlikely

GREAT WESTN NATL BK (PORTLAND, OR)
Merged into First State Bank of Oregon (Milwaukie, OR) 8/21/75
Each share Common $5 par exchanged for (0.54265) share Capital Stock $5 par
First State Bank of Oregon (Milwaukie, OR) merged into Pacwest Bancorp 12/31/79 which merged into Keycorp. (NY) 11/7/86 which merged into KeyCorp. (New) (OH) 3/1/94

GREAT WESTN OIL & GAS CO (DE)
Charter cancelled and declared inoperative and void for non-payment of taxes 4/1/64

GREAT WESTN PETE CORP (BC)
Recapitalized as Cassidy Resources Ltd. 08/19/1985
Each share Common no par exchanged for (0.33333333) share Common no par
Cassidy Resources Ltd. recapitalized as Massif Minerals Corp. 11/03/1989 which merged into World Wide Oil & Gas Inc. 06/25/1991
(See World Wide Oil & Gas Inc.)

GREAT WESTN SVGS BK (BELLEVUE, WA)
Acquired by Great Western Financial Corp. 02/25/1988
Each share Common 1¢ par exchanged for (1.25) shares Common $1 par
Great Western Financial Corp. merged into Washington Mutual, Inc. 07/01/1997
(See Washington Mutual, Inc.)

GREAT WESTN SUBDIVS INC (DE)
Name changed to Bates Financial Corp. 8/18/72
(See Bates Financial Corp.)

GREAT WESTN SYS INC (PA)
Plan of reorganization under Chapter 11 Federal Bankruptcy proceedings confirmed 02/00/1993
No stockholders' equity

GREAT WESTN UTD CORP (DE)
Common $1 par split (2) for (1) by issuance of (1) additional share 1/10/69
Reorganized as Hunt International Resources Corp. 2/22/78
Each share $1.88 Preferred no par exchanged for (1) share $1.88 Preferred no par or $21.05 principal amount of 9-7/8% Subord. Debentures Ser. A due 12/31/2004 and (0.12) share Common $1 par
Each share $3 Conv. Preferred no par exchanged for (1) share $3 Conv. Preferred no par or $30.50 principal amount of 9-7/8% Subord. Debentures Ser. A due 12/31/04 and (0.55) share Common $1 par
Each share Common $1 par exchanged for (2) shares Common $1 par
Note: Option to receive new Preferred stock expired 1/27/78
(See Hunt International Resources Corp.)

GREAT WHITE MARINE & REC INC (NV)
Charter revoked for failure to file reports and pay fees 07/01/2000

GREAT WOLF RESORTS INC (DE)
Issue Information - 14,000,000 shares COM offered at $17 per share on 12/14/2004
Acquired by K-9 Holdings, Inc. 05/04/2012
Each share Common 1¢ par exchanged for $7.85 cash

GREAT WORLD RES LTD (BC)
Struck off register and declared dissolved for failure to file returns 07/10/1992

GREAT YELLOWKNIFE MINES, LTD. (ON)
Charter revoked for failure to file reports and pay taxes 00/00/1952

GREAT YELLOWSTONE CORP (NV)
Common $1 par changed to 50¢ par 3/24/77
Name changed to Dalco Petroleum Corp. and Common 50¢ par changed to 10¢ par 2/13/79
(See Dalco Petroleum Corp.)

GREAT YELLOWSTONE URANIUM CO. (NV)
Recapitalized as Great Yellowstone Corp. 07/29/1960
Each share Common 10¢ par exchanged for (0.1) share Common $1 par
Great Yellowstone Corp. name changed to Dalco Petroleum Corp. 02/13/1979
(See Dalco Petroleum Corp.)

GREAT YUKON MINES LTD. (ON)
Merged into Great Molly Explorations & Enterprises Ltd. 01/29/1968
Each share Common no par exchanged for (0.25) share Common no par
Great Molly Explorations & Enterprises Ltd. merged into Great Eagle Explorations & Holdings Ltd. 07/07/1969 which merged into Belle Aire Resource Explorations Ltd. 08/29/1978 which name changed to Sprint Resources Ltd. 09/23/1982 which name changed to Meacon Bay Resources Inc. 03/09/1987 which recapitalized as Advantex Marketing International Inc. 09/16/1991

GREATAMERICA CORP. (NV)
Common $3 par changed to $2.50 par and (0.2) additional share issued 6/19/64
Completely liquidated 11/8/68
Each share Common $2.50 par received first and final distribution of $30 principal amount of Ling-Temco-Vought, Inc. 5% Conv. Subord. Debentures due 1/15/88 and (0.1) Common Stock Purchase Warrant
Certificates were not retired and are now without value

GREATBANC INC (IL)
Old Common 1¢ par split (2) for (1) by issuance of (1) additional share 7/17/86
Each share old Common 1¢ par received distribution of (1) share Conv. Class B 1¢ par 7/17/86
Each share old Common 1¢ par exchanged for (0.002) share new Common 1¢ par 3/15/2002
Note: In effect holders received $20 cash per share and public interest was eliminated

GREATBATCH INC (DE)
Each share Common $0.001 par received distribution of (0.33333333) share Nuvectra Corp. Common $0.001 par payable 03/14/2016 to holders of record 03/07/2016
Ex date - 03/14/2016
Name changed to Integer Holdings Corp. 07/01/2016

GREATBIO TECHNOLOGIES INC (NV)
Name changed to Biophan Technologies, Inc. 7/19/2001

GREATE BAY CASINO CORP (DE)
Plan of reorganization under Chapter 11 Federal Bankruptcy Code effective 07/23/2002
No stockholders' equity

GREATE BAY CASINO CORP (NJ)
Merged into Pratt Hotels Corp. 04/17/1985
Each share Class A Common 25¢ par exchanged for $17 cash

GREATEASTERN FUND OF BOSTON, INC. (MA)
Completely liquidated 4/29/77
Each share Common $1 par received first and final distribution of $2.863 cash
Certificates were not required to be surrendered and are now valueless

GREATER ALA CORP (AL)
Adjudicated bankrupt 09/06/1968
No stockholders' equity

GREATER ALL AMERICAN MARKETS, INC. (CA)
Merged into Albertson's Inc. (NV) 07/23/1964
Each share Common $1 par exchanged for (10/49) share Common $1 par
Albertson's, Inc. (NV) reincorporated in Delaware 08/01/1969 which merged into Supervalu Inc. 06/02/2006
(See Supervalu Inc.)

GREATER ARIZONA INVESTMENT CO., INC. (AZ)
Charter revoked for failure to file reports or pay fees 12/31/75

GREATER ARIZONA MORTGAGE CO. (AZ)
Merged into Space Financial Corp. on a (2) for (1) basis 12/14/62
Space Financial Corp. name changed to Western Energy Corp. 6/21/67 which recapitalized as United Western Energy Corp. 11/29/78
(See United Western Energy Corp.)

GREATER ATLANTIC FINL CORP (DE)
Issue Information - 2,000,000 shares COM offered at $9.50 per share on 06/24/1999
Company's sole asset placed in receivership 12/04/2009
Stockholders' equity unlikely

GREATER BAY BANCORP (CA)
Common no par split (2) for (1) by issuance of (1) additional share payable 05/15/1998 to holders of record 04/30/1998
Common no par split (2) for (1) by issuance of (1) additional share payable 10/18/2000 to holders of record 10/04/2000 Ex date - 10/19/2000
Preferred Stock Purchase Rights declared for Common stockholders of record 11/30/1998 were redeemed at $0.001 per right 04/30/2007 for holders of record 04/13/2007
7.25% Conv. Preferred Ser. B called for redemption at $50 on 07/02/2007
Merged into Wells Fargo & Co. (New) 10/01/2007
Each share Common no par exchanged for (0.7867) share Common $1-2/3 par

GREATER BETHLEHEM SVGS & LN ASSN (PA)
Name changed to First Star Savings Bank (Bethlehem, PA) 07/27/1993
First Star Savings Bank (Bethlehem, PA) reorganized as First Star Bancorp, Inc. 01/07/1994 which merged into ESSA Bancorp, Inc. 07/31/2012

GREATER BUFFALO THEATRES, INC.
Acquired by Midland Properties, Inc. 00/00/1933

Details not available

GREATER CANADA MINES CORP. LTD.
Acquired by Maralgo Mines Ltd. (ON) 00/00/1937
Each share Common no par exchanged for (0.1) share Common no par
Maralgo Mines Ltd. (ON) reincorporated in British Columbia 06/06/1984 which recapitalized as Rich Coast Sulphur Ltd. 03/13/1986 which recapitalized as Consolidated Rich Coast Sulphur Ltd. 06/19/1991 which merged into Rich Coast Resources Ltd. (BC) 01/25/1993 which reincorporated in Delaware as Rich Coast Inc. 09/16/1996 which reincorporated in Nevada 07/14/1998 which recapitalized as Media Pal Holdings, Corp. 03/16/2010

GREATER CAROLINAS CORP (SC)
Common 20¢ par split (3) for (1) by issuance of (2) additional shares 09/18/1987
Name changed to First Sun South Corp. 04/26/1988
(See First Sun South Corp.)

GREATER CHINA CAP INC (ON)
Name changed to Golden Bridge Mining Corp. 07/09/2012
Golden Bridge Mining Corp. name changed to Golden Bridge Development Corp. 09/23/2014 which recapitalized as CIM International Group Inc. 05/09/2016

GREATER CHINA CORP (DE)
SEC revoked common stock registration 02/19/2008

GREATER CHINA FD INC (MD)
Name changed to Aberdeen Greater China Fund, Inc. 12/02/2013
Aberdeen Greater China Fund, Inc. reorganized as Aberdeen Emerging Markets Equity Income Fund, Inc. 04/30/2018

GREATER CHINA TECHNOLOGY GROUP LTD (HONG KONG)
ADR agreement terminated 10/21/2013
No ADR's remain outstanding

GREATER COLUMBIA BANCSHARES INC (WI)
Merged into Associated Banc-Corp 4/5/96
Each share Common exchanged for (1.0665) shares Common 1¢ par

GREATER CMNTY BANCORP (NJ)
Common $1 par changed to 50¢ par and (1) additional share issued payable 07/31/1998 to holders of record 07/15/1998
Stock Dividends - 10% payable 07/31/1996 to holders of record 07/15/1996; 5% payable 09/15/1999 to holders of record 09/01/1999; 10% payable 07/31/2000 to holders of record 07/14/2000; 5% payable 07/31/2001 to holders of record 07/13/2001 Ex date - 07/11/2001; 5% payable 07/31/2002 to holders of record 07/12/2002 Ex date - 07/10/2002; 2.5% payable 07/31/2003 to holders of record 07/15/2003 Ex date - 07/11/2003; 2.5% payable 07/31/2004 to holders of record 07/15/2004; 2.5% payable 07/29/2005 to holders of record 07/15/2005 Ex date - 07/13/2005; 2.5% payable 07/31/2006 to holders of record 07/14/2006 Ex date - 07/12/2006; 2.5% payable 09/28/2007 to holders of record 09/14/2007 Ex date - 09/12/2007
Merged into Valley National Bancorp 07/02/2008
Each share Common 50¢ par exchanged for (0.9975) share Common no par and (0.105)

Common Stock Purchase Warrant expiring 06/30/2015

GREATER CONTL CORP (DE)
Charter cancelled and declared inoperative and void for non-payment of taxes 3/1/75

GREATER DEL VY SVGS BK (BROOMALL, PA)
Stock Dividend - 5% payable 05/04/2001 to holders of record 04/20/2001 Ex date - 04/18/2001
Merged into Alliance Bancorp, Inc. of Pennsylvania (USA) 01/30/2007
Each share Common 1¢ par exchanged for (2.09945) shares Common 1¢ par
Alliance Bancorp, Inc. of Pennsylvania (USA) reorganized in Pennsylvania 01/18/2011

GREATER HERITAGE CORP (IL)
Merged out of existence in 1994
Details not available

GREATER HOUSTON BK (HOUSTON, TX)
Acquired by Bantex Bancshares Inc. 07/02/1981
Details not available

GREATER HUDSON BANK N A (MIDDLETOWN, NY)
Name changed to Greater Hudson Bank (Middletown, NY) 07/07/2015

GREATER IDAHO CORP. (ID)
Name changed to Tiara Corp. 03/05/1980
(See Tiara Corp.)

GREATER IOWA CORP (IA)
Name changed to Dico Corp. 1/7/69
Dico Corp. name changed to First Main Corp. 10/31/78
(See First Main Corp.)

GREATER JERSEY BANCORPORATION (NJ)
Merged into Midlantic Banks Inc. 08/12/1983
Each share Common $5.50 par exchanged for (0.9646) share Common $6-2/3 par or cash
Midlantic Banks Inc. merged into Midlantic Corp. 01/30/1987 which merged into PNC Bank Corp. 12/31/1995 which name changed to PNC Financial Services Group, Inc. 03/15/2000

GREATER LENORA RES CORP (CANADA)
Reincorporated 05/03/2001
Place of incorporation changed from (ON) to (Canada) 05/03/2001
Plan of arrangement effective 07/24/2001
Each share Common no par exchanged for (1) share GLR Resources Inc. Common no par and (1) share GVIC Communications Inc. Class A Common no par and (1) share Non-Vtg. Class B no par
(See each company's listing)

GREATER NEB CORP (NE)
Recapitalized as First Greatwest Corp. 12/8/72
Each share Common $1 par exchanged for (0.25) share Common $4 par
(See First Greatwest Corp.)

GREATER NEW YORK BREWERY, INC. (NY)
Name changed to Greater New York Industries, Inc. 12/19/44
(See Greater New York Industries, Inc.)

GREATER NEW YORK INDUSTRIES, INC. (NY)
Proclaimed dissolved by the Secretary of State of New York 12/16/63

GREATER NEW YORK SVGS BK (NEW YORK, NY)
Merged into Astoria Financial Corp. 09/30/1997
Each share 12% Perpetual Preferred Ser. B $1 par exchanged for (1) share 12% Perpetual Preferred Ser. B 1¢ par
Each share Common $1 par exchanged for either (0.5) share Common 1¢ par, $19 cash, or a combination thereof

GREATER NEW YORK SUFFOLK TITLE & GUARANTEE CO.
Insolvent 00/00/1935
Stockholders' equity unlikely

GREATER NORTHWEST RESH & DEV GROUP INC (FL)
SEC revoked common stock registration 10/31/2002

GREATER OHIO CORP (OH)
Merged into Diamond Financial Holdings, Inc. 9/29/89
Each share Common no par exchanged for $0.90 cash
Note: Each share Common no par received an additional and final escrow payment of $0.214161 cash 10/31/91

GREATER PA CORP (PA)
Merged into 20th Century Corp. 07/01/1971
Each share Common 10¢ par exchanged for (0.45) share Common no par
20th Century Corp. name changed to Consumers Financial Corp. (PA) 05/30/1980 which reincorporated in Nevada 02/26/2008
(See Consumers Financial Corp.)

GREATER PACIFIC BANK (ALBANY, OR)
Merged into Western Security Financial Corp. 3/1/85
Each share Common no par exchanged for initial distribution of (0.1293) share Common $2 par 3/1/85
Each share Common no par received second and final distribution of (0.55) share Common $2 par 3/1/87
Western Security Financial Corp. acquired by KeyCorp (NY) 12/31/87 which merged into KeyCorp (New) (OH) 3/1/94

GREATER POTTSVILLE FED SVGS & LN ASSN (PA)
Name changed to Liberty Savings Bank F.S.B. (Pottsville, PA) 02/05/1996
Liberty Savings Bank F.S.B. (Pottsville, PA) reorganized as Liberty Centre Bancorp, Inc. 08/13/1999
(See Liberty Centre Bancorp, Inc.)

GREATER PROVIDENCE DEP CORP (RI)
Merged into Capital Investors Inc. 11/6/86
Each share Capital Stock $1 par exchanged for $35 cash

GREATER ROME BANCSHARES INC (GA)
Each share old Common exchanged for (0.0005) share new Common 12/30/2002
Note: In effect holders received $18 cash per share and public interest was eliminated

GREATER SACRAMENTO BANCORP (CA)
Common no par split (3) for (2) by issuance of (0.5) additional share payable 08/22/2006 to holders of record 06/09/2006 Ex date - 08/23/2006
Stock Dividends - 4% payable 05/28/2004 to holders of record 04/28/2004 Ex date - 04/26/2004; 4% payable 04/11/2005 to holders of

record 03/10/2005 Ex date - 03/08/2005; 5% payable 03/23/2006 to holders of record 03/09/2006 Ex date - 03/07/2006; 5% payable 09/21/2007 to holders of record 09/07/2007 Ex date - 09/05/2007
Acquired by Starbuck Bancshares, Inc. 02/02/2015
Each share Common no par exchanged for $22.05 cash

GREATER SOONER HLDGS INC (NV)
Recapitalized as Dovarri Inc. 01/07/2008
Each share Common $0.001 par exchanged for (0.00666666) share Common $0.001 par
(See Dovarri Inc.)

GREATER TEMAGAMI MINES LTD (BC)
Name changed to Max Communications Corp. 1/28/94
Max Communications Corp. name changed to Speyside Ventures Inc. 9/29/95 which name changed to Trandirect.com Technologies Inc. 7/19/99 which recapitalized as Consolidated Trandirect.com Technologies Inc. 8/14/2000 which name changed to International Samuel Exploration Corp. 6/20/2001

GREATER TENN CORP (TN)
Recapitalized as G T Corp. 6/22/67
Each share Common $1 par exchanged for (0.1) share Capital Stock $10 par
G T Corp. name changed to American Equity Corp. 7/27/73
(See American Equity Corp.)

GREATER WASHINGTON INDUSTRIAL INVESTMENTS, INC. (DC)
Name changed to Greater Washington Investors, Inc. (DC) 7/1/68
Greater Washington Investors, Inc. (DC) reincorporated in Delaware 12/31/87 which recapitalized as Jupiter Industries, Inc. 6/3/91 which name changed to Jupiter National, Inc. 8/25/92

GREATER WASHINGTON INVS INC (DE)
Reincorporated 12/31/87
Common $1 par split (3) for (2) by issuance of (0.5) additional share 4/25/69
Common $1 par changed to 10¢ par 6/30/78
Stock Dividend - 10% 8/8/68
State of incorporation changed from (DC) to (DE) 12/31/87
Recapitalized as Jupiter Industries, Inc. 6/3/91
Each share Common 10¢ par exchanged for (0.25) share Common 40¢ par
Jupiter Industries, Inc. name changed to Jupiter National, Inc. 8/25/92
(See Jupiter National, Inc.)

GREATER WESTERN CORP. (WA)
Merged into Greater Western Real Estate Investment Trust 3/29/72
Each share Common 5¢ par exchanged for (1) Share of Bene. Int. no par

GREATER WESTERN HOME MANUFACTURERS (CA)
Merged into Greater Western Corp. 2/29/72
Each share Common $5 par exchanged for (1) share Common 5¢ par

GREATER WESTERN REAL ESTATE INVESTMENT TRUST (WA)
Charter cancelled and proclaimed dissolved for failure to pay fees 7/2/81

GREATER WINNIPEG GAS CO (MB)
Voting Trust Agreement terminated 12/01/1963
Each VTC for Common no par exchanged for (1) share Common no par
Name changed to ICG Utilities (Manitoba) Ltd. 11/30/1989
ICG Utilities (Manitoba) Ltd. name changed to Centra Gas Manitoba Inc. 01/21/1991
(See Centra Gas Manitoba Inc.)

GREATER WINNIPEG TRANSIT CO. (MB)
Certificates of Interest in Common redeemed in 1953

GREATESTESCAPES COM INC (NV)
Recapitalized as American Ammunition Inc. (Ctfs. dated prior to 10/03/2001) 07/17/2001
Each share Common $0.001 par exchanged for (0.005) share Common $0.001 par
American Ammunition Inc. (Ctfs. dated prior to 10/03/2001) name changed to American Recreational Enterprises, Inc. 10/03/2001 which name changed to Bidville, Inc. 12/11/2003 which name changed to PrimEdge, Inc. 08/17/2006
(See PrimEdge, Inc.)

GREATLAKES COPPER MINES LTD. (ON)
Merged into Andover Mining & Exploration Ltd. 09/19/1958
Each share Capital Stock exchanged for (0.25) share Capital Stock 25¢ par
Andover Mining & Exploration Ltd. recapitalized as Andover Resources Ltd. 05/31/1971 which name changed to Andover Telecommunications Inc. 10/02/1986 which name changed to Kennecom Inc. 06/02/1989 which recapitalized as Deltona Industries Inc. 01/25/1995
(See Deltona Industries Inc.)

GREATMAT TECHNOLOGY CORP (NV)
Reincorporated under the laws of Cayman Islands and Common $0.001 par reclassified as Ordinary USD $0.001 par 10/27/2011

GREATOK GROUP LTD (CANADA)
Certification of incorporation cancelled and charter dissolved 08/27/1997

GREATWEIGHS INDS INC (BC)
Delisted from Vancouver Stock Exchange 01/09/1989

GREATWEST HOSPS INC (DE)
Stock Dividend - 50% 1/15/82
Name changed to HealthCare USA Inc. 4/22/85
(See HealthCare USA Inc.)

GREB INDS LTD (ON)
Each share Common no par exchanged for (1) share Part. Class B no par 03/20/1972
100% acquired by Warrington Products Ltd. through purchase offer which expired 09/16/1974
Public interest eliminated

GREEK CANADIAN MINES LTD. (NV)
Recapitalized as BioGenetic Technologies Inc. 10/17/1997
Each share Common no par exchanged for (0.5) share Common no par
(See BioGenetic Technologies Inc.)

GREEKTOWN SUPERHOLDINGS INC (DE)
Each share old Common Ser. A-1 1¢ par exchanged for (0.00000956) share new Common Ser. A-1 1¢ par 01/13/2014
Note: In effect holders received $90 cash per share and public interest was eliminated

GREELEY GAS CO (CO)
6-1/2% Preferred Ser. B $100 par called for redemption 3/1/82
5-1/2% Preferred Ser. A $100 par called for redemption 10/1/83
Merged into Atmos Energy Corp. 12/23/93
Each share Common exchanged for (14.916) shares Common no par
Public interest eliminated

GREELEY NATL BK (GREELEY, CO)
Each share Capital Stock $100 par exchanged for (10) shares Capital Stock $10 par 01/20/1953
Stock Dividends - 25% 01/23/1958; 20% 01/28/1959; 33-1/3% 02/07/1963; 25% 01/28/1966
100% acquired by Affiliated Bankshares of Colorado, Inc. through exchange offer which expired 07/24/1970
Public interest eliminated

GREELEY SQUARE BUILDING CORP. (NY)
Capital Stock $50 par changed to $25 par in 1948
Liquidation completed 3/7/62

GREEN & COATES ST. PASSENGER RAILWAY CO.
Acquired by Philadelphia Transportation Co. in 1940
Each share Common exchanged for $43.23 of 3%-6% Consolidated Mortgage Bonds and (0.362) share Part. Preferred $20 par

GREEN & QUALITY HOME LIFE INC (NV)
Name changed to American Graphite Technologies Inc. 07/18/2012

GREEN A L LTD (QC)
Acquired by Metropolitan Stores of Canada Ltd. 03/31/1976
Each share Common no par exchanged for $1.75 cash

GREEN A P INDS INC (DE)
Common $1 par split (3) for (2) by issuance of (0.5) additional share 12/10/93
Common $1 par split (2) for (1) by issuance of (1) additional share payable 9/20/96 to holders of record 9/6/96
Merged into Global Industrial Technologies, Inc. 7/1/98
Each share Common $1 par exchanged for $22 cash

GREEN ACQUISITION CO (DE)
Name changed to Cherokee Inc. (Old) 6/4/90
Cherokee Inc. (Old) reorganized as Cherokee Inc. (New) (Ctfs. dated prior to 12/22/94) 5/28/93 which reorganized as Cherokee Inc. (New) (Ctfs. dated after 12/23/94) 12/23/94

GREEN AMER LD HLDGS (WY)
Name changed to Green Card Capital Corp. 03/10/2009
Green Card Capital Corp. name changed to CUBA Beverage Co. 09/27/2010

GREEN AUTOMOTIVE CO (DE)
Reincorporated under the laws of Nevada as Green Automotive Co. 09/30/2011

GREEN BANKSHARES INC (TN)
Name changed 05/18/2007
Common $10 par split (3) for (1) by issuance of (2) additional shares payable 10/03/1997 to holders of record 09/19/1997
Common $10 par split (5) for (1) by issuance of (4) additional shares payable 05/29/2001 to holders of record 05/15/2001 Ex date - 05/30/2001
Each share Common $10 par exchanged for (1) share Common $2 par 05/06/2002
Under plan of merger name changed from Greene County Bancshares Inc. to Green Bankshares, Inc. 05/18/2007
Common $2 par changed to 1¢ par 09/07/2011
Stock Dividend - 0.9254% payable 12/29/2008 to holders of record 12/13/2008 Ex date - 12/10/2008
Merged into Capital Bank Financial Corp. 09/20/2012
Each share Common 1¢ par exchanged for (0.0915) share Class A Common 1¢ par
Capital Bank Financial Corp. merged into First Horizon National Corp. 11/30/2017

GREEN BAY & MISS CANAL CO (WI)
Completely liquidated and dissolved 12/19/74
Details not available

GREEN BAY & WESTN RR CO (WI)
Merged into Itel Corp. 11/11/78
Each share Common $100 par exchanged for $330 cash

GREEN BAY MNG & EXPL LTD (AB)
Each share Capital Stock 30¢ par exchanged for (0.1) share Capital Stock no par 03/16/1960
Struck off register and declared dissolved for failure to file returns 08/31/1974

GREEN BERET HLDG CORP (VA)
Involuntarily dissolved for failure to file reports 4/12/72

GREEN BIKES RENTAL CORP (NV)
Name changed to Affinity Mediaworks Corp. (NV) 01/30/2009
Affinity Mediaworks Corp. (NV) reorganized in Maryland as American Housing Income Trust, Inc. 06/10/2015 which reincorporated in Wyoming as Corix Bioscience, Inc. 08/02/2017

GREEN BLDRS INC (TX)
Each share old Common $0.001 par exchanged for (1) share new Common $0.001 par to reflect a (1) for (500) reverse split followed by a (500) for (1) forward split 03/31/2010
Note: Holders of (499) or fewer pre-split shares will receive $0.26 cash per share
Plan of reorganization under Chapter 11 Federal Bankruptcy proceedings effective 02/10/2012
No stockholders' equity

GREEN BLUFF COPPER MINES LTD (BC)
Delisted from Vancouver Stock Exchange 11/06/1987

GREEN BRDG TECHNOLOGIES INTL INC (FL)
Recapitalized as Paradise Ridge Hydrocarbons, Inc. 08/20/2012
Each share Common no par exchanged for (0.0001) share Common no par
Paradise Ridge Hydrocarbons, Inc. name changed to Grupo Resilient International, Inc. 08/10/2017

GREEN BRIAR APARTMENTS
Trust terminated in 1950
Details not available

GREEN BROS. PUBLISHING CO., INC. (NY)
Charter cancelled and proclaimed dissolved for failure to pay taxes and file reports 12/15/61

GREEN BROS INDS INC (CO)
In process of liquidation
Each share Common 10¢ par received initial distribution of $0.20 cash 9/15/75
Each share Common 10¢ par received second distribution of $0.05 cash 6/15/76
Each share Common 10¢ par exchanged for third distribution of $0.95 cash 11/15/77
Further details not available

GREEN BROTHERS CO.
Name changed to Tastyeast, Inc. (MA) 00/00/1933
(See Tastyeast, Inc. (MA))

GREEN CAP GROUP INC (NV)
Charter revoked for failure to file reports and pay fees 12/31/2004

GREEN CARD CAP CORP (WY)
Name changed to CUBA Beverage Co. 09/27/2010

GREEN (H.L.) CHAIN STORES, INC. (NY)
Name changed to Green (H.L.) Co., Inc. 00/00/1937
Green (H.L.) Co., Inc. merged into McCrory Corp. 06/21/1961 which merged into Rapid-American Corp. 03/12/1976
(See Rapid-American Corp.)

GREEN COAST RES LTD (QC)
Recapitalized as Ridgepoint Resources Ltd. 06/15/1988
Each share Common no par exchanged for (0.33333333) share Common no par
Ridgepoint Resources Ltd. recapitalized as Ridgepoint Mineral Corp. 10/31/1997 which name changed to Jet Drill Canada Inc. 09/15/2000
(See Jet Drill Canada Inc.)

GREEN (H.L.) CO., INC. (NY)
Each share Common $3 par exchanged for (3) shares Common $1 par 00/00/1935
Stock Dividend - 100% 07/03/1947
Merged into McCrory Corp. 06/21/1961
Each share Common $1 par exchanged for (0.2) share 4-1/2% Conv. Preference Ser. B $100 par and (1.5) Warrants to purchase Common 50¢ par
(See McCrory Corp.)

GREEN CONSOLIDATED GOLD CO. (WV)
Dissolved 12/31/1918
Details not available

GREEN CROSS INDS INC (MO)
Charter forfeited for failure to file reports 1/1/75

GREEN DANIEL CO (MA)
Each share Common no par exchanged for (3) shares Common $10 par 12/1/61
Common $10 par changed to $5 par and (1.5) additional shares issued 12/14/66
Common $5 par changed to $2.50 par and (1) additional share issued 7/27/84
Stock Dividend - 200% 11/13/46
Reincorporated under the laws of Delaware as Phoenix Footwear Group, Inc. and Common $2.50 par changed to 1¢ par 5/10/2002

GREEN DIAMOND OIL CORP (ON)
Recapitalized as Can-Med Technology Inc. 11/18/1991
Each share Common no par exchanged for (0.16666666) share Common no par
(See Can-Med Technology Inc.)

GREEN DLR FUTURES INC (IA)
Charter cancelled for failure to file annual reports 11/21/77

GREEN DLR NURSERIES (CA)
Name changed to National Mobile Industries, Inc. 10/13/70
(See National Mobile Industries, Inc.)

GREEN DOLPHIN SYS CORP (DE)
Each (12) shares old Common 1¢ par exchanged for (1) share new Common 1¢ par 10/03/2006
Name changed to Gold Coast Mining Corp. (DE) 01/24/2007
Gold Coast Mining Corp. (DE) reincorporated in Wyoming as Strategic Mining Corp. 12/22/2009

GREEN DOLPHIN SYS CORP (NV)
Name changed to Home/Office Express, Inc. 02/25/2000
Home/Office Express, Inc. changed to IAMG Holdings, Inc. 04/27/2000 which name changed to Curv Entertainment Group, Inc. 11/26/2007 which name changed to SuperBox, Inc. 09/01/2011

GREEN DRAGON WOOD PRODS INC (FL)
Each share old Common $0.001 par exchanged for (0.05) share new Common $0.001 par 12/16/2009
Name changed to Zeecol International, Inc. 04/06/2017

GREEN EAGLE MINES LTD (BC)
Recapitalized as Northern Eagle Mines Ltd. (BC) 03/16/1976
Each share Capital Stock 50¢ par exchanged for (1/3) share Common no par
Northern Eagle Mines Ltd. (BC) recapitalized as Bentley Resources Ltd. 07/19/1985
(See Bentley Resources Ltd.)

GREEN ENDEAVORS LTD (DE)
Name changed to Green Endeavors Inc. 08/30/2010

GREEN ENERGY HLDG CORP (NV)
Reincorporated 01/16/2007
Reincorporated from Green Energy Corp. (CO) to under the laws of Nevada as Green Energy Holding Corp. 01/16/2007
Each (5.1) shares old Common $0.001 par exchanged for (1) share new Common $0.001 par 06/18/2007
Name changed to Energy Holdings International, Inc. 05/22/2009

GREEN ENERGY RENEWABLE SOLUTIONS INC (FL)
Stock Dividend - 100% payable 07/30/2012 to holders of record 06/29/2012 Ex date - 07/31/2012
Name changed to Cirque Energy, Inc. 07/01/2015

GREEN EQUITY HLDGS INC (NV)
Recapitalized as Holdings Energy, Inc. 04/25/2012
Each share Common $0.0001 par exchanged for (0.005) share Common $0.0001 par
Holdings Energy, Inc. name changed to Grillit, Inc. 04/22/2013

GREEN (DANIEL) FELT SHOE CO. (MA)
Name changed to Green (Daniel) Co. (MA) in 1930
Green (Daniel) Co. (MA) reincorporated in Delaware as Phoenix Footwear Group, Inc. 5/10/2002

GREEN (A.P.) FIRE BRICK CO. (MO)
Name changed to Green (A.P.) Refractories Co. 10/29/65
Green (A.P.) Refractories Co. merged into United States Gypsum Co. (Del.) 12/29/67 which reorganized as USG Corp. 1/1/85

GREEN FOREST LMBR CORP (ON)
Merged into MacMillan Bloedel Ltd. 01/20/1995
Each share Subordinate no par exchanged for $12.50 cash

GREEN 4 MEDIA INC (NV)
Common $0.001 par split (11.671652) for (1) by issuance of (10.671652) additional shares payable 08/12/2013 to holders of record 07/29/2013 Ex date - 08/13/2013
Name changed to Fresh Healthy Vending International, Inc. 09/19/2013
Fresh Healthy Vending International, Inc. name changed to Generation Next Franchise Brands, Inc. 07/13/2016

GREEN FUSION CORP (NV)
Common $0.001 par split (3) for (1) by issuance of (2) additional shares payable 09/04/2001 to holders of record 08/31/2001 Ex date - 09/05/2001
Recapitalized as House of Brussels Chocolates Inc. 03/04/2003
Each share Common $0.001 par exchanged for (0.2) share Common $0.001 par
(See House of Brussels Chocolates Inc.)

GREEN GIANT CO. (DE)
Acquired by Pillsbury Co. 3/9/79
Each share $1.76 Conv. Preference Ser. D $1 par exchanged for (1.1654) shares Common no par
Each share 5% Preferred $100 par exchanged for (2.4581) shares Common no par
Each share Common no par exchanged for (0.8324) share Common no par
(See Pillsbury Co.)

GREEN GIANT CO. (MN)
Each share Class A Common no par exchanged for (20) shares Common no par 7/15/60
Each share Class B Common no par exchanged for (2) shares Common no par 7/15/60
Common no par split (2) for (1) by issuance of (1) additional share 4/30/65
Reincorporated under the laws of Delaware 11/1/73
Green Giant Co. (DE) was acquired by Pillsbury Co. 3/9/79
(See Pillsbury Co.)

GREEN GLOBAL INVTS INC (FL)
Name changed to LivingVentures, Inc. 02/06/2013

GREEN GOLD INC (NV)
Name changed to Exterra Energy, Inc. 08/09/2007
(See Exterra Energy, Inc.)

GREEN ICE CORP (BC)
Recapitalized as International Green Ice Inc. (BC) 7/21/99
Each share Common no par exchanged for (0.2) share Common no par
International Green Ice Inc. (BC) reincorporated in Yukon Territory 3/3/2000 which reincorporated in British Columbia 7/21/2004

GREEN IRONS HLDGS CORP (NV)
Name changed to Alamo Energy Corp. 12/16/2009

GREEN ISLE ENVIRONMENTAL SVCS INC (MN)
Name changed to Reuter Manufacturing, Inc. 8/25/95
Reuter Manufacturing, Inc. name changed to MagStar Technologies, Inc. 2/12/2001

GREEN LIVING CONCEPTS INC (NV)
Name changed to CES Synergies, Inc. 11/08/2013

GREEN MAPLE ENERGY INC (AB)
Name changed to Overlord Financial Inc. 11/29/2001
Overlord Financial Inc. name changed to Aston Hill Financial Inc. 06/05/2007 which name changed to LOGiQ Asset Management Inc. 12/16/2016

GREEN MEADOW PRODS INC (WY)
Name changed to Optec International, Inc. 08/31/2017

GREEN MOUNTAIN HERBS LTD NEW (CO)
Each share old Common no par exchanged for (0.1339) share new Common no par 7/24/86
Name changed to United Financial Operations, Inc. 1/25/88
(See United Financial Operations, Inc.)

GREEN MOUNTAIN MEADOWS INC. OF VERMONT (VT)
Charter revoked for failure to file annual reports 12/30/77

GREEN MOUNTAIN PWR CORP (VT)
Each share $6 Preferred no par exchanged for (3) shares Common $10 par 00/00/1951
Common $10 par changed to $5 par and (1) additional share issued 06/18/1956
Common $5 par changed to $3.33-1/3 par and (0.5) additional share issued 06/15/1961
5% Preferred Ser. A $100 par called for redemption 00/00/1991
Merged into Gaz Metro Limited Partnership 04/12/2007
Each share Common $3.33-1/3 par exchanged for $35 cash

GREEN MOUNTAIN RESOURCES, INC. (MT)
Recapitalized as Golden Flag Resources, Inc. in March 1983
Each share Common $0.003125 par exchanged for (0.5) share Common $0.003125 par
Golden Flag Resources, Inc. name changed to Infoserve, Inc. 11/18/93 which merged into CD-MAX Inc. 4/15/96 which name changed to IMARK Technologies, Inc. 12/31/97 which recapitalized as Pharm Control Ltd. 11/8/2006

GREEN MOUNTAIN URANIUM CORP. (DE)
Class A 1¢ par and Class B 1¢ par reclassified as Common 1¢ par 02/19/1963
Completely liquidated 08/23/1968
Each share Common 1¢ par received first and final distribution of $0.0141977 cash
Note: Certificates were not required to be surrendered and are without value

GREEN MT LABS INC (NV)
Common $0.001 par split (3.8) for (1) by issuance of (2.8) additional shares payable 08/17/2005 to holders of record 08/16/2005 Ex date - 08/18/2005
Name changed to Hydrogen Engine Center, Inc. 08/30/2005

GREEN MT P S INC (ID)
Name changed to Generex Biotechnology Corp. (ID) in January 1998
Generex Biotechnology Corp. (ID) reincorporated in Delaware 4/30/99

GREEN MTN CAP INC (NV)
Reincorporated 7/12/2005
State of incorporation changed from (NH) to (NV) 7/12/2005
Each share old Common $0.0001 par exchanged for (0.001) share new Common $0.0001 par 1/12/2006
Name changed to IT Group Holdings, Inc. 2/26/2007

GREEN MTN COFFEE ROASTERS INC (DE)
Name changed 01/02/2003
Common 10¢ par split (2) for (1) by issuance of (1) additional share payable 01/11/2001 to holders of record 12/28/2000 Ex date - 01/12/2001
Name changed from Green Mountain Coffee, Inc. to Green Mountain Coffee Roasters, Inc. 01/02/2003
Common 10¢ par split (3) for (1) by issuance of (2) additional shares payable 07/27/2007 to holders of record 07/17/2007 Ex date - 07/30/2007
Common 10¢ par split (3) for (2) by issuance of (0.5) additional share payable 06/08/2009 to holders of

record 05/29/2009 Ex date - 06/09/2009
Common 10¢ par split (3) for (1) by issuance of (2) additional shares payable 05/17/2010 to holders of record 05/10/2010 Ex date - 05/18/2010
Name changed to Keurig Green Mountain, Inc. 03/11/2014
(See Keurig Green Mountain, Inc.)

GREEN MTN RECOVERY INC (DE)
Name changed to Masterbeat Corp. 03/22/2010

GREEN MTN VENTURE CORP (NV)
Common $0.001 par split (2) for (1) by issuance of (1) additional share 3/28/87
Name changed to Sherwood Financial Ltd. 3/30/87
Sherwood Financial Ltd. recapitalized as Max, Inc 10/19/87
(See Max, Inc.)

GREEN OASIS ENVIRONMENTAL INC (FL)
Name changed to Global Enviro Solutions, Inc. 07/10/2009 which name changed back to Green Oasis Environmental, Inc. 01/07/2010

GREEN OIL LTD (AB)
Name changed to Koval Resources Ltd. 09/20/1990
Koval Resources Ltd. recapitalized as Ironwood Petroleum Ltd. 01/17/1994
(See Ironwood Petroleum Ltd.)

GREEN PALMS INSURANCE CORP. (CA)
Charter suspended for failure to file reports and pay fees 12/1/69

GREEN PK CAP CORP (BC)
Recapitalized as Josephine Mining Corp. 03/29/2011
Each share Common no par exchanged for (0.2) share Common no par

GREEN PLAINS RENEWABLE ENERGY INC (IA)
Name changed to Green Plains Inc. 05/19/2014

GREEN POINT MINES LTD (ON)
Capital Stock $1 par changed to no par 03/25/1971
Charter cancelled for failure to pay taxes and file returns 03/16/1976

GREEN PWR ENERGY HLDGS CORP (DE)
Reorganized under the laws of Nevada as Axiom Management Inc. 06/15/2007
Each share Common $0.001 par exchanged for (0.002) share Common $0.001 par
Note: No holder will receive fewer than (100) shares
Axiom Management Inc. name changed to Potential Holdings, Inc. 07/24/2007 which name changed to RightSmile, Inc. 08/28/2009

GREEN PROCESSING TECHNOLOGIES INC (DE)
Recapitalized as Umbra Applied Technologies Group, Inc. 01/13/2014
Each share Common $0.001 par exchanged for (0.04) share Common $0.001 par

GREEN PT RES INC (BC)
Recapitalized as Wildcard Wireless Solutions Inc. (BC) 10/18/2000
Each share Common no par exchanged for (0.5) share Common no par
Wildcard Wireless Solutions Inc. (BC) reincorporated in Alberta 06/30/2001 which name changed to TransAKT Corp. 07/02/2003 which recapitalized as TransAKT Ltd. (AB) 08/04/2006 which reincorporated in Nevada 12/15/2010

GREEN (A.P.) REFRACTORIES CO. (MO)
Common $5 par split (4) for (3) by issuance of (1/3) additional share 11/18/65
Merged into United States Gypsum Co. (DE) 12/29/67
Each share 5% Conv. Preferred $100 par exchanged for (2.78) shares $1.80 Conv. Preferred $1 par
Each share Common $5 par exchanged for (1) share $1.80 Conv. Preferred $1 par
United States Gypsum Co. (DE) reorganized as USG Corp. 1/1/85

GREEN RES INC (NV)
Name changed to Eclectix, Inc. 6/23/86
Eclectix, Inc. name changed to Loch Harris, Inc. 9/27/88
(See Loch Harris, Inc.)

GREEN RIV HLDGS INC (AB)
Recapitalized as Netco Energy Inc. 10/03/2000
Each share Common no par exchanged for (0.5) share Common no par
Netco Energy Inc. name changed to Netco Silver Inc. (AB) 07/14/2011 which reincorporated in British Columbia as Brisio Innovations Inc. 02/12/2014

GREEN RIV PETE INC (AB)
Recapitalized as Green River Holdings Inc. 07/06/1999
Each share Common no par exchanged for (0.2) share Common no par
Green River Holdings Inc. recapitalized as Netco Energy Inc. 10/03/2000 which name changed to Netco Silver Inc. (AB) 07/14/2011 which reincorporated in British Columbia as Brisio Innovations Inc. 02/12/2014

GREEN RIV RES LTD (BC)
Name changed to Canus Laboratories Ltd. 09/11/1986
(See Canus Laboratories Ltd.)

GREEN RIVER OIL & URANIUM CO. (UT)
Merged into Gold Bar Resources, Inc. 8/30/62
Each (20) shares Common 1¢ par exchanged for (1) share Common 1¢ par
Gold Bar Resources, Inc. reorganized in Nevada as American Artists, Ltd. 3/16/84

GREEN RIVER STL CORP (KY)
Acquired by Jessop Steel Co. 05/01/1957
Each share Common 1¢ par exchanged for (0.066666) share Common $1 par
Jessop Steel Co. merged into Athlone Industries, Inc. 05/08/1969 which merged into Allegheny Ludlum Corp. 11/10/1993 which merged into Allegheny Teledyne Inc. 08/15/1996 which name changed to Allegheny Technologies Inc. 11/29/1999

GREEN SHIELD PLAN, INC. (CO)
Acquired by Consumers National Life Insurance Co. 12/27/1963
Each share Common 25¢ par exchanged for (0.344827) share Common Capital Stock $1 par
Consumers National Life Insurance Co. reorganized as Consumers National Corp. 02/01/1972
(See Consumers National Corp.)

GREEN SHOE MFG CO (MA)
Common $3 par changed to $1 par 03/26/1969
Name changed to Stride Rite Corp. 03/24/1972
(See Stride Rite Corp.)

GREEN SHORES INC (DE)
Name changed to Pacific Shore Holdings, Inc. 10/12/2010

GREEN SPIRIT INDS INC (NV)
Name changed to GSRX Industries Inc. 07/16/2018

GREEN STAR ALTERNATIVE ENERGY INC (NV)
Each share old Common $0.001 par exchanged for (1.75) shares new Common $0.001 par 01/29/2010
Recapitalized as Gold Hill Resources, Inc. 11/09/2012
Each share new Common $0.001 par exchanged for (0.01) share Common $0.001 par

GREEN STAR ENERGIES INC (NV)
Recapitalized as Rock Ridge Resources, Inc. 12/08/2011
Each share Common $0.0001 par exchanged for (0.001) share Common $0.0001 par

GREEN STAR MNG CORP (DE)
Common $0.0001 par split (5) for (1) by issuance of (4) additional shares payable 12/08/2009 to holders of record 12/07/2009 Ex date - 12/09/2009
Name changed to HQ Global Education Inc. 03/22/2010

GREEN STD TECHNOLOGIES INC (NV)
Name changed to ZZLL Information Technology, Inc. 06/02/2016

GREEN STR FINL CORP (NC)
Merged into NewSouth Bancorp, Inc. 12/01/1999
Each share Common no par exchanged for $15.25 cash

GREEN SWAN CAP CORP (CANADA)
Each share Common no par received distribution of (0.05) share Tempus Capital Inc. Common no par payable 08/05/2015 to holders of record 07/31/2015 Ex date - 07/29/2015
Name changed to CBLT Inc. 06/12/2017

GREEN TECHNOLOGY SOLUTIONS INC (DE)
Each share old Common $0.001 par exchanged for (0.00333333) share new Common $0.001 par 01/10/2012
Reorganized under the laws of Nevada 09/02/2014
Each share new Common $0.001 par exchanged for (0.00333333) share Common $0.001 par
Note: No holder will receive fewer than (5) shares

GREEN TREE FINL CORP (DE)
Name changed 5/27/92
Reincorporated 6/30/95
Common 1¢ par split (2) for (1) by issuance of (1) additional share 6/30/86
Name changed from Green Tree Acceptance, Inc. to Green Tree Financial Corp. 5/27/92
Common 1¢ par split (2) for (1) by issuance of (1) additional share 1/29/93
Common 1¢ par split (2) for (1) by issuance of (1) additional share 6/30/94
State of incorporation changed from (MN) to (DE) 6/30/95
Common 1¢ par split (2) for (1) by issuance of (1) additional share 10/16/95
Merged into Conseco, Inc. 6/30/98
Each share Common 1¢ par exchanged for (0.9165) share Common no par
(See Conseco, Inc.)

GREEN VY MINE INC (BC)
Each share old Common no par exchanged for (0.22222222) share new Common no par 05/05/2017

Name changed to Skychain Technologies Inc. 09/26/2018

GREEN VALLEY MINES LTD. (ON)
Merged into Alchib Developments Ltd. 07/10/1969
Each share Capital Stock no par exchanged for (0.29) share Capital Stock no par
Alchib Developments Ltd. merged into Kalrock Developments Ltd. 10/23/1978 which merged into Kalrock Resources Ltd. 08/08/1980 which merged into Cercal Minerals Corp. 07/09/1993
(See Cercal Minerals Corp.)

GREEN'S READY-BUILT HOMES, INC. (IL)
Adjudicated bankrupt in 1948
No stockholders' equity

GREENACRES INC (WA)
Acquired by Audiscan, Inc. 1/31/74
Each share Common $2 par exchanged for $8 cash

GREENANGEL ENERGY CORP (BC)
Name changed to TIMIA Capital Corp. 09/24/2015

GREENBANK GOLD MINING CO. LTD. (ON)
Recapitalized as Jellicoe Mines (1939) Ltd. on a (1) for (6) basis in 1939
Jellicoe Mines (1939) Ltd. recapitalized as Jelex Mines Ltd. 10/1/63 which recapitalized as Key Lake Explorations Ltd. 6/21/78
(See Key Lake Explorations Ltd.)

GREENBELT CONSUMER SVCS INC (MD)
Name changed to Greenbelt Cooperative, Inc. and Class A Common $10 par and Class B Common $10 par reclassified as Common $10 par 06/03/1979
(See Greenbelt Cooperative, Inc.)

GREENBELT COOP INC (MD)
Charter annulled for failure to file annual reports 11/13/1991

GREENBERG STORES LTD (CANADA)
Acquired by Metropolitan Stores of Canada Ltd. 04/00/1970
Each share Common no par exchanged for $8 cash

GREENBERG WM JR DESSERTS & CAFES INC (NY)
Name changed to Creative Bakeries, Inc. 07/30/1997
Creative Bakeries, Inc. name changed to Brooklyn Cheesecake & Desserts Co., Inc. 02/18/2005 which name changed to Meridian Waste Solutions, Inc. 04/16/2015 which name changed to Attis Industries Inc. 05/01/2018

GREENBRIAR CORP (NV)
Each share old Common 1¢ par exchanged for (0.04) share new Common 1¢ par 12/01/2001
New Common 1¢ par split (2) for (1) by issuance of (1) additional share payable 10/28/2003 to holders of record 10/20/2003
Stock Dividend - 25% payable 02/04/2002 to holders of record 01/25/2002 Ex date - 02/05/2002
Name changed to CabelTel International Corp. 02/10/2005
CabelTel International Corp. name changed to New Concept Energy, Inc. 06/03/2008

GREENBRIDGE TECHNOLOGY INC (CA)
Completely liquidated 02/15/2012
Each share Common no par exchanged for first and final distribution of $0.17 cash

GREENBRIER COS INC (DE)
Reincorporated under the laws of

Oregon and Common $0.001 par changed to no par 02/28/2006

GREENBRIER EQUIPMENT FUND I (FL)
Voluntarily dissolved 12/11/1991
Details not available

GREENCHOICE INTL INC (NV)
Name changed to Bison Petroleum Corp. 06/19/2013
Bison Petroleum Corp. recapitalized as Yinhang Internet Technologies Development, Inc. 09/01/2015

GREENDALE PRODUCTS CO.
Operations discontinued 00/00/1936
Details not available

GREENE, STABELL MINES LTD.
Reorganized as Jacola Mines Ltd. on a (1) for (3) basis in 1937
(See Jacola Mines Ltd.)

GREENE (M.J.) CO. (PA)
Name changed to Kincaid Industries, Inc. 11/1/64
Kincaid Industries, Inc. recapitalized as Drinks By The Case on 10/11/85 which name changed to Acustar Corp. 12/1/86

GREENE CANANEA COPPER CO (MN)
Merged into Anaconda Minerals Co. 7/30/81
Each share Capital Stock $100 par exchanged for $144 cash

GREENE CNTY BANCORP INC (DE)
Issue Information - 1,096,958 shares COM offered at $10 per share on 11/12/1998
Stock Dividend - 10% payable 08/09/1999 to holders of record 07/26/1999
Reincorporated under the laws of United States of America 04/02/2001

GREENE KING PLC (UNITED KINGDOM)
ADR agreement terminated 03/11/2010
No ADR's were outstanding
(Additional Information in Active)

GREENEBAUM INVESTMENT CO. (IL)
Liquidation completed 2/1/60

GREENEBAUM SONS INVESTMENT CO. (IL)
Reorganized as Greenebaum Investment Co. on a (1) for (25) basis in 1937 which completed liquidation 2/1/60

GREENERY REHABILITATION GROUP INC (DE)
Common 1¢ par split (3) for (2) by issuance of (0.5) additional share 07/21/1986
Merged into Horizon Healthcare Corp. 02/11/1994
Each share Common 1¢ par exchanged for (0.25) share Common $0.001 par
Horizon Healthcare Corp. name changed to Horizon/CMS Healthcare Corp. 07/10/1995 which merged into HealthSouth Corp. 10/29/1997 which name changed to Encompass Health Corp. 01/02/2018

GREENESTONE HEALTHCARE CORP (CO)
Name changed to Ethema Health Corp. 07/12/2017

GREENFAB BUILD SYS INC (BC)
Reorganized under the laws of Canada as MOAG Copper Gold Resources Inc. 01/09/2012
Each share Common no par exchanged for (0.25) share Common no par

GREENFIELD (ALBERT M.) & CO. (DE)
Name changed to Elizabeth Realty Co. 8/5/57

GREENFIELD COML CR CDA INC (ON)
Name changed to Greenfield Financial Group Inc. 08/17/2005
Greenfield Financial Group Inc. name changed to Wheels Group Inc. 01/18/2012 which merged into Radiant Logistics, Inc. 04/08/2015

GREENFIELD ELECTRS INC (NY)
Charter cancelled and proclaimed dissolved for failure to pay taxes 12/15/1973

GREENFIELD FD INC (NY)
Charter cancelled and proclaimed dissolved for failure to pay taxes 09/23/1998

GREENFIELD FINL CORP (UT)
Recapitalized as Technology Transfer Inc. 7/12/91
Each (30) shares Common $0.001 par exchanged for (1) share Common $0.001 par

GREENFIELD FINL GROUP INC (ON)
Each share old Common no par exchanged for (0.1) share new Common no par 08/16/2010
Name changed to Wheels Group Inc. 01/18/2012
Wheels Group Inc. merged into Radiant Logistics, Inc. 04/08/2015

GREENFIELD INDS INC (DE)
Merged into Kennametal Inc. 11/18/97
Each share Common 1¢ par exchanged for $38 cash

GREENFIELD ONLINE INC (DE)
Issue Information - 5,000,000 shares COM offered at $13 per share on 07/15/2004
Merged into Microsoft Corp. 10/15/2008
Each share Common $0.0001 par exchanged for $17.50 cash

GREENFIELD REAL ESTATE INVT TR (PA)
Name changed to Greit Realty Trust 3/4/71
Greit Realty Trust merged into Unicorp American Corp. (Old) 10/29/81 which merged into Unicorp American Corp. (New) 2/15/84 which recapitalized as Lincorp Holdings Inc. 9/15/92
(See Lincorp Holdings Inc.)

GREENFIELD SAMUEL FD INC (NY)
Name changed to Greenfield Fund, Inc. 08/12/1981
(See Greenfield Fund, Inc.)

GREENFIELD TAP & DIE CORP. (MA)
Common no par split (2) for (1) by issuance of (1) additional share 10/26/56
Stock Dividend - 25% 9/17/51
Merged into United-Greenfield Corp. 2/14/58
Each share Common no par exchanged for (1.15) shares Common $10 par
United-Greenfield Corp. merged into TRW Inc. 9/20/68 which merged into Northrop Grumman Corp. 12/11/2002

GREENFIELDS DEV LTD (BC)
Struck off register and declared dissolved for failure to file returns 11/15/1976

GREENFIELDS INDS INC (BC)
Recapitalized as Oracle Minerals Inc. 12/06/1993
Each share Common no par exchanged for (0.5) share Common no par
Oracle Minerals Inc. recapitalized as Prophet Minerals Corp. 05/02/1997 which name changed to Meridex Network Corp. 12/21/1999 which recapitalized as Meridex Software Corp. 02/13/2003 which name changed to Cannabis Technologies Inc. 05/21/2014 which name changed to InMed Pharmaceuticals Inc. 10/21/2014

GREENFIELDS PETE CORP (DE)
Issue Information - 4,235,000 shares COM offered at $8.50 per share on 11/03/2010
Reincorporated under the laws of Cayman Islands 08/18/2011

GREENFIRE URANIUM CORP. (UT)
Merged into Republic Oil & Mining Corp. share for share in 1957
Republic Oil & Mining Corp. merged into Entrada Corp. 1/17/58 which recapitalized as Pacific Energy Corp. 1/14/76 which name changed to Aimco, Inc. 9/1/77 which recapitalized as Colt Technology, Inc. 3/31/83

GREENFLAG VENTURES INC (BC)
Recapitalized as Prosalutis Holdings Inc. 05/02/2016
Each share Common no par exchanged for (0.001) share Common no par

GREENGOLD RAY ENERGIES INC (TN)
Reincorporated 12/17/2013
Common 10¢ par changed to $0.00000001 par 01/25/2011
State of incorporation changed from (TX) to (TN) 12/17/2013
Reorganized under the laws of South Africa as Au Min Africa Pty Ltd. 08/27/2014
Each share Common $0.00000001 par exchanged for (1) share Common USD$0.10 par
Note: Holders of (3,999) or fewer shares received (4,000) shares

GREENHAVEN COAL FD (DE)
Name changed to WisdomTree Coal Fund 01/04/2016
(See WisdomTree Coal Fund)

GREENHAVEN CONTINUOUS COMMODITY INDEX FD (DE)
Name changed to WisdomTree Continuous Commodity Index Fund 01/04/2016

GREENHOLD GROUP INC (FL)
Recapitalized as Datrek Miller International, Inc. 11/15/2004
Each (35) shares Common $0.001 par exchanged for (1) share Common $0.001 par
Datrek Miller International, Inc. name changed to ForeFront Holdings, Inc. 07/28/2006
(See ForeFront Holdings, Inc.)

GREENHOPE RES INC (CANADA)
Name changed to Head4 Solutions Inc. 06/29/2000
Head4 Solutions Inc. recapitalized as Saratoga Electronic Solutions Inc. 01/25/2005 which name changed to Abba Medix Group Inc. 05/14/2015 which recapitalized as Canada House Wellness Group Inc. 11/09/2016

GREENHOUSE HLDGS INC (NV)
Common $0.001 par split (5) for (1) by issuance of (4) additional shares payable 02/26/2010 to holders of record 02/22/2010 Ex date - 03/01/2010
Merged into Premier Alliance Group, Inc. 03/05/2012
Each share Common $0.001 par exchanged for (0.13954) share Common $0.001 par
Note: Approximately (0.026178) share will be held in escrow for possible future distribution
Premier Alliance Group, Inc. name changed to root9B Technologies, Inc. 12/01/2014 which recapitalized as root9B Holdings, Inc. 12/05/2016

GREENHUNTER RES INC (DE)
Name changed 05/28/2013
Name changed from GreenHunter Energy, Inc. to GreenHunter Resources, Inc. 05/28/2013
Plan of reorganization under Chapter 11 Federal Bankruptcy proceedings effective 10/02/2017
No stockholders' equity

GREENING INDUSTRIES, LTD. (CANADA)
Acquired by Donald Ropes & Wire Cloth Ltd. 07/26/1964
Each share Common no par exchanged for $4 cash

GREENING (B.) WIRE CO., LTD. (CANADA)
Common no par exchanged (8) for (1) in 1937 and (3) for (1) in 1945
Name changed to Greening Industries Ltd. 12/20/61
(See Greening Industries Ltd.)

GREENLAND CORP (NV)
Each share old Common $0.001 par exchanged for (0.1) share new Common $0.001 par 07/02/1998
Each share new Common $0.001 par exchanged again for (0.02) share new Common $0.001 par 10/28/2002
SEC revoked common stock registration 04/30/2010

GREENLAND EXPL LTD (AB)
Recapitalized as Pac-West Industries Ltd. 02/18/1980
Each share Common no par exchanged for (1/3) share Common no par
(See Pac-West Industries Ltd.)

GREENLAW GOLD MINES LTD.
Merged into Greenlee Mines Ltd. 00/00/1938
Each share Capital Stock exchanged for (1/3) share Capital Stock
Greenlee Mines Ltd. acquired by New Athona Mines Ltd. 00/00/1954 which recapitalized as Lakota Resources Inc. 11/21/1994 which recapitalized as Tembo Gold Corp. 09/26/2011

GREENLEAF FST PRODS INC (NV)
Reorganized under the laws of Delaware as Halcyon Jets Holdings, Inc. 09/06/2007
Each share Common $0.001 par exchanged for (4.8295454) shares Common $0.001 par
Halcyon Jets Holdings, Inc. recapitalized as Alliance Network Communications Holdings, Inc. 09/02/2009 which name changed to BioCube, Inc. 01/05/2011

GREENLEAF TECHNOLOGIES CORP (DE)
Name changed 12/3/97
Name changed from GreenLeaf Capital Corp. to GreenLeaf Technologies Corp. 12/3/97
Charter cancelled and declared inoperative and void for non-payment of taxes 3/1/2002

GREENLEE MINES LTD. (ON)
Acquired by New Athona Mines Ltd. 00/00/1954
Each share Capital Stock exchanged for (0.125) share Capital Stock $1 par
New Athona Mines Ltd. recapitalized as Lakota Resources Inc. 11/21/1994 which recapitalized as Tembo Gold Corp. 09/26/2011

GREENLIGHT COMMUNICATIONS INC (ON)
Each share old Common no par exchanged for (0.2) share new Common no par 05/26/1997
Delisted from Canadian Stock Exchange 10/31/2000

GREENLIGHT RES INC (BC)
Name changed to Great Atlantic Resources Corp. 06/19/2012

GREENMAN BROS INC (NY)
Common 10¢ par split (2) for (1) by

issuance of (1) additional share 1/20/70
Common 10¢ par split (5) for (4) by issuance of (0.25) additional share 5/27/82
Common 10¢ par split (3) for (2) by issuance of (0.5) additional share 5/27/83
Common 10¢ par split (5) for (4) by issuance of (0.25) additional share 8/20/84
Common 10¢ par split (4) for (3) by issuance of (1/3) additional share 12/28/84
Common 10¢ par split (5) for (4) by issuance of (0.25) additional share 8/29/86
Name changed to Noodle Kidoodle Inc. (NY) 12/14/95
Noodle Kidoodle Inc. (NY) reincorporated in Delaware 1/22/96 which recapitalized as Zany Brainy, Inc. 7/27/2000
(See Zany Brainy, Inc.)

GREENMAN TECHNOLOGIES INC (DE)
Each share old Common 1¢ par exchanged for (0.2) share new Common 1¢ par 03/23/1998
Name changed to American Power Group Corp. 08/07/2012

GREENOAKS MINES LTD. (ON)
Charter cancelled for failure to pay taxes and file returns 11/28/1973

GREENOCK RES INC (ON)
Each share old Common no par exchanged for (0.03333333) share new Common no par 03/12/2014
Each share new Common no par exchanged again for (0.57142857) share new Common no par 01/25/2016
Name changed to BeWhere Holdings Inc. 02/03/2016

GREENPOINT FINL CORP (DE)
Common 1¢ par split (2) for (1) by issuance of (1) additional share payable 3/4/98 to holders of record 2/20/98 Ex date - 3/5/98
Common 1¢ par split (3) for (2) by issuance of (0.5) additional share payable 8/20/2003 to holders of record 8/8/2003 Ex date - 8/21/2003
Merged into North Fork Bancorporation, Inc. 10/1/2004
Each share Common 1¢ par exchanged for (1.0514) shares Common 1¢ par
North Fork Bancorporation, Inc. merged into Capital One Financial Corp. 12/1/2006

GREENPRO INC (NV)
Name changed to Greenpro Capital Corp. 06/01/2015

GREENRAY INDS INC (PA)
Stock Dividend - 100% 4/25/68
Merged into Greenray Acquisition 8/16/95
Each share Common $1 par exchanged for $4.35 cash

GREENS WORLDWIDE INC (FL)
Reincorporated 12/03/2008
Each share old Common no par exchanged for (0.03333333) share new Common no par 01/24/2005
State of incorporation changed from (AZ) to (FL) and Common no par changed to $0.0001 par 12/03/2008
Recapitalized as Black Castle Developments, Inc. (FL) 03/03/2011
Each share Common $0.0001 par exchanged for (0.001) share Common $0.0001 par
Black Castle Developments, Inc. (FL) reincorporated in Nevada 06/01/2011 which name changed to Black Castle Developments Holdings, Inc. 08/02/2011 which recapitalized as ingXabo Corp. 01/28/2015
(See ingXabo Corp.)

GREENSBORO NATL BK (GREENSBORO, NC)
Merged into Mutual Community Savings Bank Inc. SSB 9/29/95
Each share Common $4 par exchanged for $11.50 cash

GREENSCAPE CAP GROUP INC (BC)
Recapitalized as Parkit Enterprise Inc. 09/11/2013
Each share Common no par exchanged for (0.1) share Common no par

GREENSCAPE LABORATORIES INC (NV)
Recapitalized as Ultrack Systems, Inc. 04/11/2016
Each share Common $0.001 par exchanged for (0.01) share Common $0.001 par

GREENSHIELD EXPLORATIONS LTD (ON)
Reincorporated under the laws of British Columbia 10/19/2007

GREENSHIELD RES INC (ON)
Acquired by Greenshield Resources Ltd. 11/11/2002
Each share Common no par exchanged for (1) share Common no par
Greenshield Resources Ltd. recapitalized as Greenshield Explorations Ltd. (ON) 06/13/2006 which reincorporated in British Columbia 10/19/2007

GREENSHIELD RES LTD (ON)
Recapitalized as Greenshield Explorations Ltd. (ON) 06/13/2006
Each share Common no par exchanged for (0.05) share Common no par
Greenshield Explorations Ltd. (ON) reincorporated in British Columbia 10/19/2007

GREENSHIFT CORP (DE)
Recapitalized as Carbonics Capital Corp. 02/12/2008
Each share Common $0.001 par exchanged for (0.05) share Common $0.001 par
Carbonics Capital Corp. recapitalized as Westport Energy Holdings Inc. 12/03/2012

GREENSTAR TELECOMMUNICATIONS LTD (CANADA)
Name changed 03/09/1993
Name changed from Greenstar Resources Ltd. to Greenstar Telecommunications Ltd. 03/09/1993
Name changed to GST Telecommunciations, Inc. 03/09/1995
(See GST Telecommunications, Inc.)

GREENSTONE HLDGS INC (FL)
Each share old Common $0.0001 par exchanged for (0.04) share new Common $0.0001 par 09/19/2007
Administratively dissolved 09/23/2011

GREENSTONE INDS INC (DE)
Issue Information - 925,000 Units consisting of (2) shares COM and (1) WT offered at $10.125 per Unit on 07/20/1994
Merged into Louisiana-Pacific Corp. 1/2/97
Each share Common $0.001 par exchanged for $5.25 cash

GREENSTONE RES LTD (BC)
Filed a petition under Bankruptcy and Insolvency Act on 10/26/2000
Stockholders' equity unlikely

GREENSTONE ROBERTS ADVERTISING INC (NY)
Name changed 04/05/1991
Name changed from Greenstone Rabasca Roberts, Inc. to Greenstone Roberts Advertising, Inc. 04/05/1991

Each share old Common 1¢ par exchanged for (0.1) share new Common 1¢ par 07/29/1997
Name changed to Kupper Parker Communications, Inc. 10/10/2000
Kupper Parker Communications, Inc. recapitalized as Principal Solar, Inc. (NY) 05/25/2011 which reincorporated in Delaware 10/24/2012

GREENSTRIKE GOLD CORP (ON)
Merged into IATCO Industries Inc. 11/7/89
Each share Common no par exchanged for (1) share Common no par
IATCO Industries Inc. name changed to AirBoss of America Corp. 5/2/94

GREENSWAN VENTURES INC (BC)
Name changed to Canbras Communications Corp. 02/23/1995
(See Canbras Communications Corp.)

GREENTECH USA INC (FL)
SEC revoked common stock registration 05/27/2005

GREENTEK CORP (UT)
SEC revoked common stock registration 11/19/2014

GREENTREE ENERGY INC (BC)
Recapitalized as STS Power Pedal Corp. 12/28/1990
Each share Common no par exchanged for (0.33333333) share Common no par
STS Power Pedal Corp. recapitalized as Mark-Can Investment Corp. 01/31/2001 which recapitalized as Yale Resources Ltd. 09/30/2003 which recapitalized as Alta Vista Ventures Ltd. 05/29/2013 which name changed to Global UAV Technologies Ltd. 05/17/2017

GREENTREE GAS & OIL LTD (ON)
Assets sold for the benefit of creditors 04/15/2011
Stockholders' equity unlikely

GREENTREE SOFTWARE INC (NY)
Each share Common 1¢ par exchanged for (0.25) share Common 4¢ par 04/28/1994
Each share Common 4¢ par exchanged for (1/6) share Common 1¢ par 07/21/1997
Reincorporated under the laws of Delaware as PurchaseSoft, Inc. 11/20/1998
(See PurchaseSoft, Inc.)

GREENVALE ENERGY NL (AUSTRALIA)
Name changed 08/17/2015
Name changed from Greenvale Mining N.L. to Greenvale Energy NL 08/17/2015
Name changed to Greenvale Energy Ltd. 12/15/2015

GREENVILLE & NORTHERN RAILWAY CO. (SC)
Acquired by Pinsly (S.M.) Co. 00/00/1957
Details not available

GREENVILLE AVENUE BANK & TRUST (DALLAS, TX)
Merged into Republic of Texas Corp. 08/28/1978
Each share Common $3.33333333 par exchanged for $21 cash

GREENVILLE FINL CORP (SC)
Common no par split (2) for (1) by issuance of (1) additional share 8/16/96
Merged into Regions Financial Corp. (Old) 2/12/98
Each share Common no par exchanged for (1.2) shares Common $0.625 par
Regions Financial Corp. (Old) merged into Regions Financial Corp. (New) 7/1/2004

GREENVILLE FIRST BANCSHARES INC (SC)
Common 1¢ par split (3) for (2) by issuance of (0.5) additional share payable 11/17/2003 to holders of record 11/17/2003
Stock Dividend - 10% payable 08/14/2006 to holders of record 07/24/2006 Ex date - 07/20/2006
Name changed to Southern First Bancshares, Inc. 07/02/2007

GREENVILLE INDS INC (DE)
Common no par changed to 10¢ par 06/00/1967
Charter cancelled and declared inoperative and void for non-payment of taxes 03/01/1984

GREENVILLE NATIONAL EXCHANGE BANK (GREENVILLE, TX)
Name changed to First Greenville National Bank (Greenville, TX) 10/01/1962
First Greenville National Bank (Greenville, TX) reorganized as First Greenville Bancshares Inc. 07/25/1980
(See First Greenville Bancshares Inc.)

GREENVILLE SALES, INC. (DE)
Name changed to Greenville Industries, Inc. 11/14/1966
(See Greenville Industries, Inc.)

GREENVOLT PWR CORP (NV)
Recapitalized as Satellite Enterprises Corp. 09/15/2002
Each share Common $0.001 par exchanged for (0.01) share Common $0.001 par
Satellite Enterprises Corp. name changed to Satellite Newspapers Corp. 11/30/2005 which recapitalized as Genmed Holding Corp. 01/28/2008
(See Genmed Holding Corp.)

GREENWATER RED BOY COPPER CO. (WY)
Charter revoked for failure to file reports and pay fees 07/19/1927

GREENWATER SARATOGA COPPER CO. (WY)
Charter revoked for failure to file reports and pay fees 07/19/1927

GREENWAY APARTMENT CO. (MD)
Completely liquidated 10/15/1963
Each share Common $1 par and VTC's for Common $1 par exchanged for an undetermined amount of cash

GREENWAY DESIGN GROUP INC (DE)
Recapitalized as Redwood Scientific Technologies, Inc. 02/14/2018
Each share Common $0.001 par exchanged for (0.00066666) share Common $0.001 par

GREENWAY ENERGY (NV)
Name changed to Greenway Technology 09/19/2008

GREENWAY ENVIRONMENTAL SVCS INC (NV)
Charter delinquent for failure to file annual reports 07/01/1995

GREENWAY ENVIRONMENTAL SYS INC (NV)
Recapitalized as Travel Dynamics, Inc. 01/13/1999
Each (19.5) shares Common $0.001 par exchanged for (1) share Common $0.001 par
Travel Dynamics, Inc. name changed to TRU Dynamics International, Inc. 02/14/2001
(See TRU Dynamics International, Inc.)

GREENWAY FD INC (MD)
Name changed to Sigma Value Shares, Inc. 06/10/1988
Sigma Value Shares, Inc. name changed to ProvidentMutual Value Shares, Inc. 03/01/1990

(See ProvidentMutual Value Shares, Inc.)

GREENWAY MED TECHNOLOGIES INC (DE)
Issue Information - 6,666,667 shares COM offered at $10 per share on 02/01/2012
Acquired by VCG Holdings, LLC 11/04/2013
Each share Common $0.0001 par exchanged for $20.35 cash

GREENWELL RES CORP (BC)
Cease trade order effective 12/22/1997
Stockholders' equity unlikely

GREENWICH AIR SVCS INC (DE)
Common 1¢ par reclassified as Class A Common 1¢ par 3/11/96
Each share Class A Common 1¢ par received distribution of (1) share Class B Common 1¢ par payable 5/8/96 to holders of record 4/18/96
Merged into General Electric Co. 9/2/97
Each share Class A Common 1¢ par exchanged for either (0.4792) share Common 16¢ par or $31 cash
Each share Class B Common 1¢ par exchanged for either (0.4792) share Common 16¢ par or $31 cash
Note: Non-electors received (0.3738) share Class A Common 1¢ par and $6.82 cash

GREENWICH BK & TR CO (GREENWICH, CT)
Reorganized as Associated Community Bancorp, Inc. (DE) 2/25/2000
Each share Common 1¢ par exchanged for (1.075) shares Common 1¢ par

GREENWICH FINL CORP (DE)
Stock Dividend - 10% 7/19/93
Merged into First Fidelity Bancorporation (New) 1/31/94
Each share Common 1¢ par exchanged for $16 cash

GREENWICH GAS CO (CT)
$1.25 Part. Preferred no par reclassified as $1.50 Preferred no par in March 1951
Merged into Connecticut Natural Gas Corp. 8/30/74
Each share $1.50 Preferred no par exchanged for (0.25) share 6% Preferred Ser. B $100 par
Each share Common no par exchanged for (0.6667) share Common $12.50 par

GREENWICH GLOBAL CAP INC (ON)
Recapitalized as Xinergy Ltd. 12/24/2009
Each share Common no par exchanged for (0.0502008) share Common no par
(See Xinergy Ltd.)

GREENWICH LAKE EXPLS LTD (ON)
Name changed to G.L.E. Resources Ltd. 03/21/1983
G.L.E. Resources Ltd. recapitalized as Chelsea Resources Ltd. 01/05/1987
(See Chelsea Resources Ltd.)

GREENWICH PHARMACEUTICALS INC (DE)
Name changed to Boston Life Sciences, Inc. and Common 10¢ par changed to 1¢ par 06/15/1995
Boston Life Sciences, Inc. name changed to Alseres Pharmaceuticals, Inc. 06/11/2007

GREENWICH REAL ESTATE CO.
Liquidated 00/00/1951
Details not available

GREENWICH RES INC (BC)
Merged into Greenwich Resources PLC 03/28/1985
Each share Common no par exchanged for (1) share Ordinary Stock no par

GREENWICH STR CALIF MUN FD INC (MD)
Completely liquidated 01/18/2002
Each share Common $0.001 par received first and final distribution of Smith Barney California Municipals Fund Inc. Class A 1¢ par on a net asset basis
Note: Certificates were not required to be surrendered and are without value
Smith Barney California Municipals Fund Inc. name changed to Legg Mason Partners California Municipals Fund, Inc. 04/07/2006 which name changed to Legg Mason Partners Income Trust 04/16/2007

GREENWICH STR N Y MUN FD INC (MD)
Charter forfeited for failure to file reports 10/04/1996

GREENWICH WATER & GAS CO.
Name changed to Greenwich Water & Gas System, Inc. 00/00/1929
Greenwich Water & Gas System, Inc. name changed to Greenwich Water System, Inc. 00/00/1939
(See Greenwich Water Systems, Inc.)

GREENWICH WATER & GAS SYSTEM, INC.
Name changed to Greenwich Water System, Inc. 00/00/1939
(See Greenwich Water System, Inc.)

GREENWICH WATER SYSTEM, INC. (DE)
6% Preferred $100 called for redemption 01/01/1954

GREENWIND NRG INC (NV)
Common $0.001 par split (4) for (1) by issuance of (3) additional shares payable 09/19/2016 to holders of record 09/19/2016
Name changed to NewGen BioPharma Corp. 11/18/2016

GREENWIND PWR CORP USA (NV)
Each share old Common $0.001 par exchanged for (0.33333333) share new Common $0.001 par 08/13/2004
Recapitalized as HD Retail Solutions Inc. 07/07/2009
Each share new Common $0.001 par exchanged for (0.05) share Common $0.001 par
HD Retail Solutions Inc. name changed to Greenscape Laboratories, Inc. 06/10/2014 which recapitalized as Ultrack Systems, Inc. 04/11/2016

GREENWOOD BK BETHEL INC (BETHEL, CT)
Closed by the Connecticut Banking Commissioner and placed in receivership 11/6/92
Stockholders' equity undetermined

GREENWOOD ENVIRONMENTAL INC (CANADA)
Dissolved 01/02/2003

GREENWOOD EXPLS LTD (BC)
Each share old Common no par exchanged for (3) shares new Common no par 01/28/1981
Recapitalized as United Greenwood Explorations Ltd. 04/04/1983
Each share new Common no par exchanged for (0.2) share Common no par
United Greenwood Explorations Ltd. name changed to Elektra Power Inc. 03/15/1985
(See Elektra Power Inc.)

GREENWOOD GOLD RES INC (NV)
Old Common $0.001 par split (20) for (1) by issuance of (19) additional shares payable 02/14/2011 to holders of record 02/07/2011
Ex date - 02/15/2011
Each share old Common $0.001 par exchanged for (0.002) share new Common $0.001 par 03/23/2012
Name changed to Bluforest Inc. 06/05/2012

GREENWOOD HLDGS INC (CO)
Each share old Common 1¢ par exchanged for (0.5) share new Common 1¢ par 10/28/92
Name changed to Packaging Research Corp. 2/3/93

GREENWOOD NATL BANCORPORATION (SC)
Name changed to Community Capital Corp. 05/16/1994
Community Capital Corp. merged into Park Sterling Corp. 11/01/2011 which merged into South State Corp. 11/30/2017

GREENWOOD RES INC (CO)
Recapitalized as Greenwood Holdings, Inc. 8/13/87
Each share 80¢ Conv. Preferred $1 par exchanged for (0.5) share Common 1¢ par
Each share Common 1¢ par exchanged for (0.6) share Common 1¢ par
Greenwood Holdings, Inc. name changed to Packaging Research Corp. 2/3/93

GREENWOOD RES LTD (DE)
Reincorporated under the laws of Colorado as Greenwood Resources Inc. 12/8/83
Greenwood Resources Inc. recapitalized as Greenwood Holdings, Inc. 8/13/87 which name changed to Packaging Research Corp. 2/3/93

GREENWOOD VENTURES CORP (BC)
Recapitalized as Norwich Ventures Ltd. 08/30/1991
Each share Common no par exchanged for (0.2) share Common no par
(See Norwich Ventures Ltd.)

GREENWORKS CORP (DE)
Name changed to GreenShift Corp. 05/17/2005
GreenShift Corp. recapitalized as Carbonics Capital Corp. 02/12/2008 which recapitalized as Westport Energy Holdings Inc. 12/03/2012

GREENZAP INC (NV)
Each share old Common $0.001 par exchanged for (0.01) share new Common $0.001 par 05/23/2008
Name changed to Blue Star Opportunities Corp. 07/28/2008

GREER BANCSHARES INC (SC)
Common $5 par split (3) for (2) by issuance of (0.5) additional share payable 03/15/2004 to holders of record 03/01/2004 Ex date - 03/16/2004
Stock Dividends - 5% payable 09/04/2001 to holders of record 08/15/2001 Ex date - 08/13/2001; 2.5% payable 05/30/2002 to holders of record 05/17/2002 Ex date - 06/06/2002
Merged into Carolina Financial Corp. (New) 03/18/2017
Each share Common $5 par exchanged for (0.385008) share Common 1¢ par and $9.137912 cash

GREER HYDRAULICS, INC. (NY)
Ctfs. dated after 12/26/79
Merged into Greer Hydraulics of California, Inc. 1/1/82
Each share Common 25¢ par exchanged for $5 cash

GREER HYDRAULICS INC (NY)
Ctfs. dated prior to 3/5/79
Capital Stock 50¢ par changed to 25¢ par and (1) additional share issued 2/28/73
Merged into Liquidonics Industries, Inc. 3/5/79
Each share Capital Stock 25¢ par exchanged for $18 cash

GREER SOFTWARE ASSOC INC (NY)
Proclaimed dissolved 9/28/94

GREER ST BK (GREER, SC)
Stock Dividend - 5% payable 06/01/1998 to holders of record 05/15/1998
Under plan of reorganization each share Common $5 par automatically became (1) share Greer Bancshares Inc. Common $5 par 07/20/2001
Greer Bancshares Inc. merged into Carolina Financial Corp. (New) 03/18/2017

GREGGS FOOD PRODS INC (OR)
Merged into Staley (A.E.) Manufacturing Co. 11/1/76
Each share Common no par exchanged for (0.254000) share Common no par
Staley (A.E.) Manufacturing Co. reorganized as Staley Continental, Inc. 2/12/85
(See Staley Continental, Inc.)

GREGOR GOLDFIELDS CORP (ON)
Recapitalized as Aavdex Corp. 02/24/1998
Each share Common no par exchanged for (0.125) share Common no par
Aavdex Corp. name changed to Richmond Minerals Inc. 11/17/2005

GREGORY EXPL LTD (AB)
Name changed to Global Mineral & Chemical Ltd. 03/04/1992
Global Mineral & Chemical Ltd. recapitalized as Consolidated Global Minerals Ltd. 01/15/1999 which name changed to Global Minerals Ltd. 11/27/2006 which recapitalized as MK2 Ventures Ltd. 06/27/2016

GREGORY INDS INC (MI)
Common $1 par changed to 66-2/3¢ par and (0.5) additional share issued 9/2/65
Stock Dividend - 10% 10/9/53
Merged into TRW Inc. 1/31/69
Each share Common 66-2/3¢ par exchanged for (0.12) share $4.50 Conv. Preference II Ser. 3 no par and (0.48) share Common $1.25 par
TRW Inc. merged into Northrop Grumman Corp. 12/11/2002

GREGORY INDS LTD (BC)
Name changed to Primex Forest Industries Ltd. 05/23/1986
Primex Forest Industries Ltd. name changed to Primex Forest Products, Ltd. 01/12/1990
(See Primex Forest Products, Ltd.)

GREIF BROS COOPERAGE CORP (DE)
Name changed to Greif Bros. Corp. 3/3/69
Greif Bros. Corp. name changed to Greif, Inc. 3/28/2003

GREIF BROS CORP (DE)
Class A Common no par and Class B Common no par split (5) for (1) by issuance of (4) additional shares respectively 9/11/69
Class A Common no par and Class B Common no par split (2) for (1) by issuance of (1) additional share respectively 11/21/72
Class A Common no par and Class B Common no par split (2) for (1) by issuance of (1) additional share respectively 11/28/78
Class A Common no par and Class B Common no par split (2) for (1) by issuance of (1) additional share respectively 11/28/79
Class A Common no par split (2) for

(1) by issuance of (1) additional share 3/10/95
Class B Common no par split (2) for (1) by issuance of (1) additional share 3/10/95
Name changed to Greif, Inc. 3/28/2003

GREINER ENGR INC (NV)
Reincorporated 12/18/1986
Stock Dividend - 10% 11/01/1985
State of incorporation changed from (CA) to (NV) 12/18/1986
Common 50¢ par split (5) for (4) by issuance of (0.25) additional share 12/02/1988
Common 50¢ par split (5) for (4) by issuance of (0.25) additional share 06/02/1989
Common 50¢ par split (4) for (3) by issuance of (0.33333333) additional share 02/16/1990
Merged into URS Corp. (DE) 03/29/1996
Each share Common 50¢ par exchanged for (0.298) share Common 1¢ par and $13.50 cash
URS Corp. (DE) merged into AECOM Technology Corp. 10/17/2014 which name changed to AECOM 01/06/2015

GREIT RLTY TR (PA)
Merged into Unicorp American Corp. (Old) 10/29/81
Each Share of Bene. Int. no par exchanged for (1) share Common 10¢ par
Unicorp American Corp. (Old) merged into Unicorp American Corp. (New) 2/15/84 which recapitalized as Lincorp Holdings Inc. 9/15/92
(See Lincorp Holdings Inc.)

GREKA ENERGY CORP (CO)
Stock Dividend - 5% payable 1/29/2001 to holders of record 12/31/2000 Ex date - 12/27/2000
Merged into Alexi Holdings Ltd. 8/19/2003
Each share Common no par exchanged for $6.25 cash

GREMAR, INC. (MA)
Completely liquidated 12/20/68
Each share Common no par exchanged for first and final distribution of (0.17) share International Telephone & Telegraph Corp. (DE) Common $1 par
International Telephone & Telegraph Corp. (DE) name changed to ITT Corp. 12/31/83 which reorganized in Indiana as ITT Industries, Inc. 12/19/95 which name changed to ITT Corp. 7/1/2006

GREMAR MFG INC (MA)
Name changed to Gremar, Inc. 6/28/68
Gremar, Inc. acquired by International Telephone & Telegraph Corp. (DE) 12/20/68 which name changed to ITT Corp. 12/31/83 which reorganized in Indiana as ITT Industries, Inc. 12/19/95 which name changed to ITT Corp. 7/1/2006

GREMOR MTR INNS INC (DE)
Charter cancelled and declared inoperative and void for non-payment of taxes 03/01/1990

GRENACHE INC (QC)
Each share Class A no par or Class B no par exchanged for (1) share Common no par 11/05/1971
6% Preference $100 par called for redemption 10/31/1972
Acquired by Quebec-Lait, Inc. 11/19/1973
Each share Common no par exchanged for $7.97 cash

GRENADA BK (GRENADA, MS)
Each share Capital Stock $100 par exchanged for (14) shares Capital Stock $10 par to effect a (10) for (1) split and a 40% stock dividend 1/11/66
Capital Stock $10 par changed to $5 par and (1) additional share issued 7/20/85
Capital Stock $5 par changed to $2.50 par and (1) additional share issued 4/15/86
Stock Dividends - 20% 1/14/58; 25% 1/10/61; 33-1/3% 7/9/63; 25% 3/1/69; 20% 3/1/71; 20% 4/2/73; 50% 11/15/74; 10% 9/30/76; 10% 7/15/78; 10% 11/8/83
Reincorporated under the laws of Delaware as Grenada Sunburst System Corp. and Capital Stock $2.50 par reclassified as Common $1 par 5/20/86
Grenada Sunburst System Corp. merged into Union Planters Corp. 12/30/94 which merged into Regions Financial Corp. (New) 7/1/2004

GRENADA SUNBURST SYS CORP (DE)
Stock Dividend - 100% 10/8/86
Merged into Union Planters Corp. 12/30/94
Each share Common $1 par exchanged for (1.453) shares Common $5 par
Union Planters Corp. merged into Regions Financial Corp. (New) 7/1/2004

GRENADIER GOLD MINES, LTD. (ON)
Charter revoked for failure to file reports and pay taxes 7/11/60

GRENADIER RESOURCE CORP (BC)
Name changed to Laguna Blends Inc. 09/23/2015
Laguna Blends Inc. name changed to Isodiol International Inc. 06/09/2017

GRENDALE MINING SYNDICATE LTD.
Acquired by Buckhorn Mines Ltd. on a (5) for (1) basis in 1942
(See Buckhorn Mines Ltd.)

GRENELL BUILDING CORP. (IL)
Completely liquidated 9/16/43
Each Trust Ctf. no par exchanged for first and final distribution of $42 cash

GRENFELL ACQUISITIONS INC (CANADA)
Recapitalized as International Grenfell Acquisitions Inc. 01/20/1994
Each share Common no par exchanged for (0.2) share Common no par
International Grenfell Acquisitions Inc. name changed to Worldwide Ginseng Corp. 07/21/1995
(See Worldwide Ginseng Corp.)

GRENFELL-KIRKLAND GOLD MINES LTD. (ON)
Acquired by Grengold Mines Ltd. 00/00/1946
Each share Common exchanged for (0.5) share Common
(See Grengold Mines Ltd.)

GRENGOLD MINES LTD. (ON)
Charter cancelled 12/10/1962

GRENLOCH ENERGY INC (BC)
Struck off register and declared dissolved for failure to file returns 01/14/1994

GRENMAC SILVER MINES LTD. (BC)
Recapitalized as Buckeye Explorations Ltd. 06/16/1971
Each share Common no par exchanged for (0.33333333) share Common no par
(See Buckeye Explorations Ltd.)

GRENNAN BROS. PIE CO.
Name changed to Orchard Farm Pie Co. in 1930 which name was then changed to Orchard Farm Baking Co. in 1945 which merged into Jersey Farm Baking Co. (Del.) in 1947 which name was changed to Farm Crest Bakeries, Inc. 3/8/65
Farm Crest Bakeries, Inc. merged into Ward Foods, Inc. 12/25/65
(See Ward Foods, Inc.)

GRENOBLE ENERGY LTD (BC)
Recapitalized as Grenloch Energy Inc. 10/30/1984
Each share Common no par exchanged for (0.2) share Common no par
(See Grenloch Energy Inc.)

GRENVIEW CORP (AB)
Name changed to Linmor Inc. 01/09/1997
Linmor Inc. merged into NUVO Network Management Inc. 05/21/2004
(See NUVO Network Management Inc.)

GRENVILLE GOLD CORP OLD (BC)
Reincorporated 06/09/2009
Place of incorporation changed from (ON) to (BC) 06/09/2009
Recapitalized as Grenville Gold Corp. (New) 12/24/2010
Each share Common no par exchanged for (0.1) share Common no par

GRENVILLE STRATEGIC RTY CORP (ON)
Merged into LOGiQ Asset Management Inc. (AB) 06/07/2018
Each share Common no par exchanged for (6.25) shares Common no par
Note: Unexchanged certificates will be cancelled and become without value 06/07/2021
LOGiQ Asset Management Inc. (AB) reorganized in British Columbia as Flow Capital Corp. 06/11/2018

GRESCHNER INVESTMENT CORP. (CA)
Name changed to Fremont Fund, Inc. 1/5/65
(See Fremont Fund, Inc.)

GRESHAM HOTEL GROUP PLC (ENGLAND)
Acquired by Precinct Investments Ltd. 00/00/2004
Each ADR for Ordinary 5p par exchanged for approximately $2.98544 cash

GRESHAM RES INC (BC)
Acquired by True Energy Inc. 07/31/2002
Each share Common no par exchanged for (1.4) shares Common no par
(See True Energy Inc.)

GRETA OIL CORP.
Assets acquired by Barnsdall Oil Co. in 1938
Details not available

GREW VENTURES INC (NB)
Cease trade order effective 02/24/2004
Stockholders' equity unlikely

GREY ADVERTISING INC (DE)
Reincorporated 06/26/1974
State of incorporation changed from (NY) to (DE) 06/26/1974
Each share Common $1 par received distribution of (1) share Limited Duration Conv. Class B Common $1 par 04/30/1986
Name changed to Grey Global Group Inc. 07/20/2000
(See Grey Global Group Inc.)

GREY EAGLE EXPL INC (ID)
Charter forfeited 12/02/1996

GREY EAGLE FRACTION MINING & LEASING CO. (NV)
Charter revoked for failure to file reports and pay fees 3/3/24

GREY GLOBAL GROUP INC (DE)
Merged into WPP Group PLC (Old) 03/08/2005
Each share Common $1 par exchanged for $1,005 cash
Each share Limited Duration Class B $1 par exchanged for $1,005 cash

GREY GOOSE LTD (CANADA)
Reincorporated 01/15/1980
Common no par reclassified as Conv. Class A Common no par 06/13/1975
Conv. Class A Common no par reclassified as Common no par 09/28/1979
Conv. Class B Common no par reclassified as Common no par 09/28/1979
Common no par split (2) for (1) by issuance of (1) additional share 10/01/1979
Place of incorporation changed from (ON) to (Canada) 01/15/1980
9.75% First Preference Ser. A $10 par called for redemption 02/28/1985
Reacquired 06/24/1985
Each share Common no par exchanged for $30 cash

GREY HORSE CAP CORP (CANADA)
Name changed to Grey Horse Corp. 06/25/2007
Grey Horse Corp. name changed to Equity Financial Holdings Inc. 12/21/2010
(See Equity Financial Holdings Inc.)

GREY HORSE CORP (CANADA)
Name changed to Equity Financial Holdings Inc. 12/21/2010
(See Equity Financial Holdings Inc.)

GREY IS SYS INTL INC (AB)
Merged into Webtech Wireless Inc. 10/28/2009
Each share Common no par exchanged for (0.35) share Common no par
Webtech Wireless Inc. merged into BSM Technologies Inc. 10/05/2015

GREY WOLF EXPL INC NEW (AB)
Merged into Insignia Energy Ltd. 07/24/2009
Each share Common no par exchanged for (0.34) share Common no par
(See Insignia Energy Ltd.)

GREY WOLF EXPL INC OLD (AB)
Each share old Common no par exchanged for (0.1) share new Common no par 06/15/1999
Acquired by Abraxas Petroleum Corp. 10/05/2001
Each share new Common no par exchanged for (0.6) share Common 1¢ par

GREY WOLF INC (TX)
Acquired by Precision Drilling Trust 12/23/2008
Each share Common 10¢ par exchanged for (0.4225) Trust Unit no par
Precision Drilling Trust reorganized as Precision Drilling Corp. 06/03/2010

GREYFIELD CAP INC (NV)
Reincorporated 06/14/2005
State of incorporation changed from (NV) to (OR) 06/14/2005
Involuntarily dissolved for failure to file reports and pay fees 08/11/2006
Note: Actions taken after company's identity was misappropriated 04/15/2005
Legitimate officers have abandoned plans for the corporate shell
No stockholders' equity

GREYHAWK OIL & GAS INC (AB)
Acquired by Braegan Energy Ltd. 03/05/1999
Each share Common no par exchanged for (0.27548) share Common no par
(See Braegan Energy Ltd.)

GREYHAWK RES LTD (BC)
Recapitalized as GHK Resources Ltd. 08/17/1992
Each share Common no par exchanged for (0.2) share Common no par
(See GHK Resources Ltd.)

GREYHAWK STAINED GLASS INC (NV)
Stock Dividend - 15% payable 11/19/1997 to holders of record 11/12/1997
Name changed to R & R Resources Inc. 11/00/1997
R & R Resources Inc. name changed to Centenary International Corp. 12/22/1998

GREYHAWK URANIUM MINES LTD. (ON)
Charter cancelled 00/00/1962
No stockholders' equity

GREYHOUND CDA TRANSN CORP (CANADA)
Merged into Laidlaw Inc. 10/14/1997
Each share Common no par exchanged for $5.50 cash

GREYHOUND COMMISSARY INC (NV)
Recapitalized as Tanke Biosciences Corp. 02/10/2011
Each share Common $0.001 par exchanged for (0.1174812) share Common $0.001 par

GREYHOUND COMMUNICATIONS LTD (BC)
Name changed to Eastmin Resources Inc. 01/07/1991
(See Eastmin Resources Inc.)

GREYHOUND COMPUTER CDA LTD (CANADA)
Name changed to Greyvest Financial Services Inc. 11/11/1987
Greyvest Financial Services Inc. name changed to Greyvest Capital Inc. 11/24/1994
(See Greyvest Capital Inc.)

GREYHOUND COMPUTER CORP (NY)
Merged into Greyhound Corp. (DE) 8/31/76
Each share Common $1 par exchanged for (0.5) share Common $1.50 par
Greyhound Corp. (DE) reincorporated in Arizona 3/3/78 which name changed to Greyhound Dial Corp. 5/8/90 which name changed to Dial Corp. (AZ) 5/14/91 which reincorporated in (DE) 3/18/92 which name changed to Viad Corp. 8/15/96

GREYHOUND CORP. (AZ)
3% 2nd Conv. Preference $100 par called for redemption 9/30/82
Name changed to Greyhound Dial Corp. 5/8/90
Greyhound Dial Corp. name changed to Dial Corp. (AZ) 5/14/91 which reincorporated in (DE) 3/18/92 which name changed to Viad Corp. 8/15/96

GREYHOUND CORP. (DE)
Each share $8 Preference no par exchanged for (5) shares Common $5 par in 1933
Each share Common no par exchanged for (0.05) share Common $5 par in 1933
Each share Common $5 par exchanged for (4) shares Common no par in 1936
Common no par changed to $3 par in 1947
5% Preferred 1954 Ser. $100 par called for redemption 10/31/60
4-1/4% Preferred $100 par called for redemption 10/31/62
Common $3 par changed to $1.50 par and (1) additional share issued 7/10/64
4-1/2% Conv. Preference $50 par called for redemption 7/1/68
Stock Dividends - 200% 6/17/47; 10% 10/24/60
Reincorporated under the laws of Arizona 3/3/78
Greyhound Corp. (AZ) name changed to Greyhound Dial Corp. 5/8/90 which name changed to Dial Corp. (AZ) 5/14/91 which reincorporated in (DE) 3/18/92 which name changed to Viad Corp. 8/15/96

GREYHOUND DIAL CORP (AZ)
Name changed to Dial Corp. (AZ) 5/14/91
Dial Corp. (AZ) reincorporated in (DE) 3/18/92 which name changed to Viad Corp. 8/15/96

GREYHOUND LINES CDA LTD (CANADA)
Common no par split (2) for (1) by issuance of (1) additional share 08/20/1963
Common no par split (2) for (1) by issuance of (1) additional share 07/26/1967
Common no par split (2) for (1) by issuance of (1) additional share 06/16/1980
Reorganized as Greyhound Canada Transportation Corp. 05/31/1996
Each share Common no par exchanged for (3.1775) shares Common no par
(See Greyhound Canada Transportation Corp.)

GREYHOUND LINES INC (DE)
Secondary Offering - 10,004,144 shares COM offered at $4.125 per share on 09/28/1995
Merged into Laidlaw Inc. 03/16/1999
Each share Common 1¢ par exchanged for $6.50 cash
Each share 8.5% Accredited Investors Conv. Exchangeable Preferred received $33.33 cash upon conversion
8.5% Conv. 144A Exchangeable Preferred called for redemption at $26.7425 on 04/30/2001
8.50% Conv. Exchangeable Preferred called for redemption at $26.7425 on 04/30/2001

GREYLOCK MILLS
Merged into Berkshire Fine Spinning Associates, Inc. 00/00/1929
Details not available

GREYMANTLE INDS LTD (AB)
Name changed to Newhaven Media Inc. 03/17/1997
(See Newhaven Media Inc.)

GREYSTAR RES LTD NEW (BC)
Each share old Common no par exchanged for (0.2) share new Common no par 06/25/2002
Name changed to Eco Oro Minerals Corp. 08/19/2011

GREYSTAR RES LTD OLD (BC)
Merged into Greystar Resources Ltd. (New) 08/15/1997
Each share Common no par exchanged for (1) share Common no par
Greystar Resources Ltd. (New) name changed to Eco Oro Minerals Corp. 08/19/2011

GREYSTOKE EXPLS LTD (BC)
Struck off register and declared dissolved for failure to file returns 08/14/1992

GREYSTONE RESH CORP (CANADA)
Acquired by Javelin Capital Corp. 08/04/2005
Each share Common no par exchanged for (0.285) share Common no par
Javelin Capital Corp. recapitalized as Javelin Energy Inc. 03/30/2006
(See Javelin Energy Inc.)

GREYSTONE TECHNOLOGY INC (DE)
Merged into Greystone Technology, Inc. 12/29/99
Each share Common exchanged for (1) share Common $0.001 par

GREYVEST CAP INC (CANADA)
Name changed 11/24/1994
Common no par split (2) for (1) by issuance of (1) additional share 11/25/1987
Common no par split (5) for (4) by issuance of (0.25) additional share 12/13/1993
Name changed from Greyvest Financial Services Inc. to Greyvest Capital Inc. 11/24/1994
Common no par split (5) for (4) by issuance of (0.25) additional share payable 07/05/1996 to holders of record 06/17/1996
Assets foreclosed upon 05/16/2002
No stockholders' equity

GREYWACKE EXPL LTD (CANADA)
Name changed to Green River Gold Corp. 09/08/2017

GRF TECHNOLOGY INC (ON)
Merged into Mustang Gold Corp. 07/15/1997
Each share Common no par exchanged for (0.2) share Common no par
Mustang Gold Corp. recapitalized as Mustang Minerals Corp. 03/11/1999 which name changed to Grid Metals Corp. 06/08/2018

GRG INC (NV)
Recapitalized as HumWare Media Corp. 01/11/2005
Each share Common $0.001 par exchanged for (0.02) share Common $0.001 par
HumWare Media Corp. recapitalized as EFT Biotech Holdings, Inc. 11/20/2007 which name changed to EFT Holdings, Inc. 05/27/2011

GRI COMPUTER CORP (MA)
Name changed to Fulcrum Computer Group Inc. 05/01/1981
Fulcrum Computer Group Inc. merged into Adage, Inc. (MA) 10/13/1982 which reincorporated in Pennsylvania 05/31/1991 which reincorporated in Nevada as RELM Wireless Corp. 01/30/1998 which name changed to BK Technologies, Inc. 06/05/2018

GRIC COMMUNICATIONS INC (DE)
Name changed to GoRemote Internet Communications, Inc. 5/19/2004
(See GoRemote Internet Communications, Inc.)

GRID CAP CORP (CANADA)
Recapitalized as Lornex Capital Inc. (Canada) 09/22/2008
Each share Common no par exchanged for (0.33333333) share Common no par
Lornex Capital Inc. (Canada) reincorporated in British Columbia as Norsemont Capital Inc. 02/16/2016

GRID CLOUD SOLUTIONS INC (FL)
Recapitalized as Great Rock Development Corp. 02/29/2012
Each share Common $0.001 par exchanged for (0.02) share Common $0.001 par Great Rock Development Corp. recapitalized as Comepay, Inc. 03/01/2018

GRID PETE CORP (NV)
Each share Common $0.001 par exchanged for (0.001) share Common $0.00001 par 09/04/2015
Name changed to Simlatus Corp. 04/26/2016

GRID RES LTD (BC)
Name changed to F M Resources Ltd. 3/15/85
F M Resources Ltd. name changed to Designed Data (Canada) Inc. 10/20/87 which recapitalized as Pier Mac Environment Management Inc. 5/3/90 which recapitalized as Ebony Gold & Gas Inc. 4/7/95 which recapitalized as Running Foxes Petroleum Corp. 12/9/98 which recapitalized as Running Fox Resource Corp. 10/17/2000

GRIDCOMM INC (DE)
Common 1¢ par split (2) for (1) by issuance of (1) additional share 3/31/86
Chapter 11 Federal Bankruptcy Code converted to Chapter 7 on 11/29/89
Stockholders' equity unlikely

GRIDIRON RES LTD (BC)
Cease trade order effective 03/30/1990
Stockholders' equity unlikely

GRIDOIL FREEHOLD LEASES LTD. (AB)
Each share Capital Stock no par exchanged for (5) shares Capital Stock 9¢ par 00/00/1952
Merged into Canadian Gridoil Ltd. 02/18/1966
Each share Capital Stock 9¢ par exchanged for (0.2) share Capital Stock 45¢ par
Canadian Gridoil Ltd. merged into Ashland Oil Canada Ltd. 09/14/1970 which name changed to Kaiser Petroleum Ltd. 03/23/1979
(See Kaiser Petroleum Ltd.)

GRIDSENSE SYS INC (BC)
Recapitalized as Viridis Energy Inc. 07/17/2009
Each share Common no par exchanged for (0.1) share Common no par
Viridis Energy Inc. name changed to Viridis Holdings Corp. 08/14/2018

GRIER (S.M.) STORES, INC.
Assets sold in 1933
No stockholders' equity

GRIESEDIECK CO (IL)
Under plan of merger each share Common $2 par exchanged for (1.525) shares Common $1 par 9/15/55
Liquidation completed
Each share Common $1 par exchanged for (1) Non-Negotiable Receipt and $16.50 cash 7/1/76
Each Non-Negotiable Receipt received second distribution of $1.85 cash 2/15/77
Each Non-Negotiable Receipt received third and final distribution of $0.108 cash 12/28/77

GRIESEDIECK WESTERN BREWERY CO. (IL)
Common no par changed to $6 par in 1947
Each share Common $6 par exchanged for (3) shares Common $2 par in 1948
Name changed to Griesedieck Co. in 1954
(See Griesedieck Co.)

GRIESS PFLEGER TANNING CO (OH)
Each share Preferred $100 par exchanged for (3.75) shares Common $1 par in 1939
Each share Common no par exchanged for (0.222222) share Common $1 par in 1939
Common $1 par changed to $5 par in 1948
Voluntarily dissolved 12/31/74
Details not available

GRIFCO INTL INC (NV)
Each share Common no par received distribution of (1.89) shares Coil Tubing Technology, Inc. Restricted Common $0.001 par payable 08/07/2007 to holders of record 05/01/2006

Charter permanently revoked 02/28/2011

GRIFF MINES, INC. (NV)
Charter revoked for failure to file reports and pay fees 4/11/57

GRIFFIN CAP INC (CO)
Name changed to National Resource Recovery Systems Inc. 3/15/90

GRIFFIN CORP (ON)
Merged into Zayma Realty Holdings Inc. 01/22/2008
Each share Common no par exchanged for $0.08 cash
Note: Unexchanged certificates were cancelled and became without value 01/22/2014

GRIFFIN GAMING & ENTMT INC (DE)
Merged into Sun International Hotels Ltd. 12/16/96
Each share Common 1¢ par exchanged for (0.4324) share Ordinary Stock $0.001 par
Each share Class B Common 1¢ par exchanged for (0.1928) share Ordinary Stock $0.001 par
Sun International Hotels Ltd. name changed to Kerzner International Ltd. 7/1/2002
(See Kerzner International Ltd.)

GRIFFIN GROUP PLC (UNITED KINGDOM)
ADR agreement terminated 01/15/2009
No ADR's remain outstanding

GRIFFIN INDS INC (MD)
Recapitalized as Perfisans Holdings, Inc. 12/16/2003
Each (30) shares Common $0.001 par exchanged for (1) share Common $0.001 par
Holders of between (101) and (3,000) shares received (100) shares only
Note: Holders of (99) or fewer pre-split shares were not affected by reverse split
Perfisans Holdings, Inc. name changed to Aspire International Inc. 12/18/2007

GRIFFIN LD & NURSERIES INC (DE)
Name changed to Griffin Industrial Realty, Inc. 05/18/2015

GRIFFIN PETE CORP (CO)
Merged into MGF Oil Corp. 04/01/1982
Each (4.27) shares Common no par exchanged for (1) share Capital Stock $1 par
(See MGF Oil Corp.)

GRIFFIN REAL ESTATE FD LTD PARTNERSHIP (MN)
Unit of Limited Partnership Int. VI trust terminated 12/31/1996
Details not available
Unit of Ltd. Partnership Int. IV trust terminated 12/29/1998
Details not available
Unit of Ltd. Partnership Int. II trust terminated 12/31/1998
Details not available
Unit of Ltd. Partnership Int. V trust terminated 12/31/1998
Details not available

GRIFFIN SKYE CORP (ON)
Recapitalized as ANB Canada Inc. 10/01/2016
Each share Class A no par exchanged for (0.5) share Class A no par

GRIFFIN STL & SUPPLY CO (CA)
Name changed to Oilfield Steel Supply 3/17/80
(See Oilfield Steel Supply)

GRIFFIN TECHNOLOGY INC (NY)
Common 5¢ par split (3) for (1) by issuance of (2) additional shares 07/01/1983
Merged into Diebold, Inc. 12/07/1995
Each share Common 5¢ par exchanged for $7.75 cash

GRIFFITH CONSUMERS CO (MD)
Merged into Griffith Holding Inc. 12/15/94
Each share Common 1¢ par exchanged for $23 cash

GRIFFITH (D.W.) INC. (MD)
Charter forfeited for failure to file annual reports 2/15/35

GRIFFITHS ELECTRONICS, INC. (NJ)
Adjudicated bankrupt 11/18/74
No stockholders' equity

GRIFFON CORP (DE)
2nd Preferred Ser. I 25¢ par called for redemption 03/10/1997
(Additional Information in Active)

GRIFFON PETE LTD (AB)
Recapitalized as High Plains Energy Inc. 04/08/1997
Each share Common no par exchanged for (0.25) share Common no par
High Plains Energy Inc. recapitalized as Action Energy Inc. 11/27/2006
(See Action Energy Inc.)

GRIGGS, COOPER & CO.
Each share Common no par exchanged for (3) shares Common $1 par 00/00/1946
5% 1st Preferred $100 par called for redemption 05/18/1953
Acquired by Consolidated Grocers Corp. 05/29/1953
Each share Common $1 par exchanged for (1.2203) shares Common $1.33333333 par
Consolidated Grocers Corp. name changed to Consolidated Foods Corp. 02/24/1954 which name changed to Sara Lee Corp. 04/02/1985 which recapitalized as Hillshire Brands Co. 06/29/2012
(See Hillshire Brands Co.)

GRIGGS EQUIPMENT, INC. (DE)
Each share Common 50¢ par exchanged for (1/3) share Common $1.50 par 5/6/75
Name changed to Griggs International, Inc. 4/29/79
Griggs International, Inc. name changed to Auric International, Inc. 12/11/81
(See Auric International, Inc.)

GRIGGS INTL INC (DE)
Each share Common 50¢ par exchanged for (0.33333333) share Common $1.50 par 05/00/1975
Name changed to Auric International, Inc. 12/11/1981
(See Auric International, Inc.)

GRIGSBY-GRUNOW CO.
Bankrupt 00/00/1934
No stockholders' equity

GRILL CONCEPTS INC (NV)
Reincorporated 08/03/2011
Each share Common $0.001 par exchanged for (0.25) share old Common $0.00004 par 08/09/1999
Each share old Common $0.00004 par exchanged for (1) share new Common $0.00004 par to reflect a (1) for (35) reverse split followed by a (35) for (1) forward split 03/25/2009
Note: Holders of (34) or fewer pre-split shares received $1.50 cash per share
State of incorporation changed from (DE) to (NV) 08/03/2011
Each share new Common $0.00004 par exchanged for (0.00000111) share Common $0.0000000004 par 11/25/2013
Note: In effect holders received $0.30 cash per share and public interest was eliminated

GRILLI PPTY GROUP INC (QC)
Acquired by 9145-2276 Quebec Inc. 10/21/2004
Each share Common no par exchanged for $3.82 cash

GRIME BUSTERS INC (DE)
Name changed to G B International, Corp. 12/6/72
(See G B International, Corp.)

GRIMES CONS INC (NV)
Each share Capital Stock 10¢ par exchanged for (0.05) share Capital Stock $2 par 10/13/1970
Name changed to GCI International, Inc. 12/01/1972
(See GCI International, Inc.)

GRIMES DIVIDE MINING CO. (NV)
Name changed to Grimes Consolidated, Inc. 1/22/69
Grimes Consolidated, Inc. name changed to GCI International, Inc. 12/1/72
(See GCI International, Inc.)

GRIMM & DAVIS INC (NY)
Name changed to Eicon Group, Inc. 01/13/1994
(See Eicon Group, Inc.)

GRINNELL BROTHERS, INC. (MI)
Common $100 par changed to no par 00/00/1932
Acquired by American Music Stores, Inc. (MI) 00/00/1965
Details not available

GRINNELL CORP (DE)
Common no par split (2) for (1) by issuance of (1) additional share 7/25/62
Merged into International Telephone & Telegraph Corp. (DE) 10/31/69
Each share Common no par exchanged for (1.2) shares $4 Conv. Preferred Ser. K no par and (1.1) shares Common $1 par
International Telephone & Telegraph Corp. name changed to ITT Corp. 12/31/83 which reorganized in Indiana as ITT Industries, Inc. 12/19/95 which name changed to ITT Corp. 7/1/2006

GRINNELL MANUFACTURING CORP.
Liquidated in 1937

GRIP TECHNOLOGIES INC (CA)
Chapter 11 bankruptcy proceedings converted to Chapter 7 on 11/1/99
No stockholders' equity

GRISSOL FOODS LTD (ON)
99.90% of 1% Conv. Preference and 99.95% of Common held by Imasco Ltd. as of 09/30/1972
Public interest eliminated

GRIST ML CO (DE)
Common 10¢ par split (5) for (1) by issuance of (4) additional shares 03/25/1985
Each share old Common 10¢ par exchanged for (0.4) share new Common 10¢ par 11/04/1985
New Common 10¢ par split (3) for (2) by issuance of (0.5) additional shares 11/16/1992
Merged into International Home Foods, Inc. 04/17/1998
Each share new Common 10¢ par exchanged for $14.50 cash

GRISTEDES FOODS INC (NY)
Name changed 10/21/99
Name changed from Gristede's Sloan's, Inc. to Gristede's Foods, Inc. 10/21/99
Acquired by Gristedes Acquisition Corp. 11/19/2004
Each share Common 2¢ par exchanged for $0.87 cash

GRISWOLD BUILDING, INC. (MI)
Liquidation completed for cash 9/20/65
Certificates were not retired and are now without value

GRISWOLD OIL CORP. (DE)
Charter declared void for non-payment of franchise taxes 4/1/28

GRIT INTL GROUPS INC (NV)
Recapitalized as GRIT International Inc. 12/23/2008
Each share Common $0.001 par exchanged for (0.05) share Common $0.001 par

GRIT RES INC (BC)
Name changed to Canamera Explorations Inc. 06/11/1985
Canamera Explorations Inc. recapitalized as Wind River Resources Ltd. 05/03/1988 which recapitalized as Richlode Investments Corp. 05/03/1993 which recapitalized as Thundelarra Exploration Ltd. (BC) 07/30/1998 which reincorporated in Yukon 01/23/2001 which reincorporated in Western Australia 09/08/2003 which name changed to Thundelarra Ltd. 03/21/2013

GRIZZLY CAP INC (CO)
Recapitalized as Plants for Tomorrow, Inc. 08/01/1990
Each share Common no par exchanged for (0.1) share Common no par
Plants for Tomorrow, Inc. name changed to Optimax Industries Inc. 01/11/1995 which name changed to Electric Motors Corp. 04/09/2009

GRIZZLY CREEK RES LTD (BC)
Name changed to Luzon Minerals Ltd. 07/14/1993
Luzon Minerals Ltd. recapitalized as Black Isle Resources Corp. 01/14/2010

GRIZZLY DIAMONDS LTD (AB)
Name changed to Grizzly Discoveries Inc. 01/12/2010

GRIZZLY INC. & BEOWULF (UT)
Merged into Mandrake Food & Ale 04/12/1978
Each share Common 1¢ par exchanged for (0.16666666) share Common 1¢ par
Mandrake Food & Ale recapitalized as International Leisure & Casino Inc. 08/06/1979
(See International Leisure & Casino Inc.)

GRIZZLY VALLEY GAS & OIL CO. LTD. (BC)
Acquired by T.C. Explorations Ltd. 11/19/65
Each share Capital Stock no par exchanged for (0.256339) share Common no par
T.C. Explorations Ltd. recapitalized as Decca Resources Ltd. 10/20/70 which name changed to Sceptre Resources Ltd. (BC) 12/27/77 which reincorporated in Canada 10/31/79 which merged into Canadian Natural Resources Ltd. 8/15/96

GRJ INDS INC (NJ)
Charter revoked for failure to file reports and pay fees 7/8/95

GRM INDS INC (MI)
Merged into Redlaw Industries Inc. 12/07/1983
Each share Common $1 par exchanged for (1.875) shares Common no par
(See Redlaw Industries Inc.)

GRO-CORD RUBBER CO. (OH)
Adjudicated bankrupt 10/24/63
Common stock worthless

GRO PLT INDS INC (FL)
Determined to be insolvent per Chapter X bankruptcy proceedings 00/00/1974
No stockholders' equity

GRO-RITE SHOE CO., INC. (NC)
Common $1 par changed to no par 7/19/62
Name changed to McRae Shoe, Inc. 1/29/64
McRae Shoe, Inc. name changed to

McRae Industries, Inc. (N.C.) 7/14/69 which reincorporated in Delaware 9/23/83

GROCERETTE VENDING MACHINES, INC. (CO)
Name changed to Automation International, Inc. 2/28/69
(See Automation International, Inc.)

GROCERY CTR INC (IL)
Ceased operations and subsequently dissolved 11/26/1974
No stockholders' equity

GROCERY STORE PRODS CO (DE)
Capital Stock 25¢ par changed to $5 par 05/00/1951
Capital Stock $5 par changed to $2.50 par and (1) additional share issued 08/10/1964
Completely liquidated 04/01/1971
Each share Capital Stock $2.50 par received first and final distribution of (1.25) shares Clorox Co. (OH) Common $1 par
Note: Certificates were not required to be surrendered and are without value
Clorox Co. (OH) reincorporated in California 03/12/1973 which reincorporated in Delaware 10/22/1986

GROCERY STORE PRODUCTS, INC. (DE)
Reorganized as Grocery Store Products Co. in 1935
(See Grocery Store Products Co.)

GROEP COLRUYT (BELGIUM)
Name changed to Colruyt S.A. 08/20/2009

GROFEED INC (NV)
Reincorporated 09/27/2005
Place of incorporation changed from (ON) to (NV) and Common no par changed to $0.001 par 09/27/2005
Recapitalized as Rima International Holdings Inc. 12/21/2007
Each share Common $0.001 par exchanged for (0.02173913) share Class A Common $0.001 par
(See Rima International Holdings Inc.)

GROFF INDS INC (FL)
Common 50¢ par split (2) for (1) by issuance of (1) additional share 8/2/85
Merged into Metals International B.V. 11/9/88
Each share Common 50¢ par exchanged for $21 cash

GROLIER INC (DE)
Common $1 par changed to 50¢ par and (1) additional share issued 08/07/1969
75¢ Conv. Preferred Ser. B $1 par called for redemption 02/28/1986
Merged into Hachette S.A. 05/18/1988
Each share Common 50¢ par exchanged for $24.25 cash

GROLIER SOCIETY INC. (DE)
Common and Class B Common $1 par split (3) for (1) by the issuance of (2) additional shares 4/25/57
Stock Dividend - 50% 2/24/55
Name changed to Grolier Inc. 1/4/60
(See Grolier Inc.)

GROM RES INC (BC)
Common no par split (3) for (1) by issuance of (2) additional shares 04/10/1986
Name changed to Micro-Phonics Technology International Corp. 06/12/1986
Micro-Phonics Technology International Corp. recapitalized as Var Computer Solutions Corp. 05/24/1989 which name changed to Econ Ventures Ltd. 06/05/1995 which recapitalized as Richcor Resources Ltd. (BC) 09/12/2000 which reincorporated in Canada 07/24/2001 which name changed to Bioxel Pharma Inc. 08/13/2001
(See Bioxel Pharma Inc.)

GROMAN CORP (DE)
Acquired by Talley Industries, Inc. 07/16/1985
Each share Common $1 par exchanged for $14 cash

GROMPO RED LAKE MINES LTD. (ON)
Name changed to Deermont Oil & Gas Co., Ltd. 00/00/1952
(See Deermont Oil & Gas Co. Ltd.)

GRONARTIC RES INC (CANADA)
Recapitalized 12/10/1997
Recapitalized from gronArctic Energy Inc. to gronArctic Resources Inc. 12/10/1997
Each share Common no par exchanged for (0.1) share Class A Common no par
Merged into Kicking Horse Resources Ltd. 08/13/1999
Each share Class A Common no par exchanged for (0.0167203) and (0.5) Common Stock Purchase Warrant expiring 08/13/2000
Kicking Horse Resources Ltd. name changed to Launch Resources Inc. 10/02/2003
(See Launch Resources Inc.)

GROOS BK N A (SAN ANTONIO, TX)
Name changed 04/19/1982
Each share Common $100 par exchanged for (10) shares Common $10 par 01/12/1954
Name changed from Groos National Bank (San Antonio, TX) to Groos Bank, N.A. (San Antonio, TX) 04/19/1982
Name changed to Norwest Bank Texas, South, N.A. (San Antonio, TX) 06/17/1996
(See Norwest Bank Texas, South, N.A. (San Antonio, TX))

GROOTVLEI PROPRIETARY MINES LTD (SOUTH AFRICA)
ADR's for Stock Units Rand-35 par changed to Rand-30¢ par 6/29/73
Each Unsponsored ADR for Stock Units Rand-30 par exchanged for (0.5) Sponsored ADR for Stock Units Rand-30 par 8/12/96
Merged into Harmony Gold Mining Co. Ltd. 6/9/97
Each Sponsored ADR for Stock Units Rand-30 par exchanged for (0.6) Sponsored ADR for Ordinary Rand-50 par

GROOVER-STEWARD DRUG CO.
Acquired by McKesson & Robbins, Inc. 00/00/1928
Details not available

GROSBEAK GOLD MINES LTD.
Bankrupt in 1952

GROSMONT RES LTD (AB)
Merged into Paramount Resources Ltd. 01/01/1992
Each share Capital Stock no par exchanged for $2.60 cash

GROSS ENERGY INC (UT)
Name changed to Wichita Petroleum Corp. 11/18/85
(See Wichita Petroleum Corp.)

GROSS TELECASTING INC (MI)
Class B Common $1 par split (2) for (1) by issuance of (1) additional share 4/16/69
Common $1 par split (2) for (1) by issuance of (1) additional share 4/16/69
Liquidation completed
Each share Class B Common $1 par received initial distribution of $50 cash 10/15/84
Each share Common $1 par received initial distribution of $50 cash 10/15/84
Each share Class B Common $1 par received second distribution of $12.55 cash 5/16/85
Each share Common $1 par received second distribution of $12.55 cash 5/16/85
Each share Class B Common $1 par exchanged for third and final distribution of $15 cash 5/30/85
Each share Common $1 par exchanged for third distribution of $15 cash 5/30/85
Assets transferred to Gross Telecasting Liquidating Trust 5/30/85
(See Gross Telecasting Liquidating Trust)

GROSS TELECASTING LIQUIDATING TRUST (MI)
Liquidation completed
Each Share of Bene. Int. received fourth distribution of $2.008 cash 7/20/87
Each Share of Bene. Int. received fifth distribution of $1.65 cash 12/28/89
Each Share of Bene. Int. received sixth distribution of $1 cash 8/20/90
Each Share of Bene. Int. received seventh distribution of $0.70 cash 11/27/91
Each Share of Bene. Int. received eighth and final distribution of $0.82 cash 6/26/92
(See Gross Telecasting Inc. for previous distributions)

GROSSBARD SECS CORP (NY)
Name changed to L. G. Industries, Inc. 2/14/79
L. G. Industries, Inc. name changed to Sunbelt Airlines, Inc. 7/9/79 which recapitalized as Florida Publishers, Inc. 10/15/80
(See Florida Publishers, Inc.)

GROSSE POINTE EXPLORATION CO. LTD. (ON)
Charter cancelled 12/23/1965

GROSSER INC (DE)
Name changed to IMAR Corp. 4/11/89
(See IMAR Corp.)

GROSSET & DUNLAP INC (NY)
Merged into NGC Publishing Corp. 08/16/1968
Each share Common $1 par exchanged for $41 cash

GROSSMANS INC (DE)
Plan of reorganization under Chapter 11 Federal Bankruptcy Code effective 12/22/97
No stockholders' equity

GROSSMOM BK (LA MESA, CA)
Acquired by Bancomer, S.A. 04/13/1982
Each share Common $3 par exchanged for $24.52 cash

GROSVENOR EXPLORATIONS INC (NV)
Each share old Common $0.001 par exchanged for (7) shares new Common $0.001 par 03/15/2007
New Common $0.001 par split (6) for (1) by issuance of (5) additional shares payable 01/18/2008 to holders of record 01/17/2008
Ex date - 01/22/2008
Name changed to South American Gold Corp. 10/18/2010

GROSVENOR INTL HLDGS LTD (BC)
Under plan of merger each share Common no par exchanged for $25 cash 03/02/1978

GROTE MOLEN INC (NV)
Name changed to Blackridge Technology International, Inc. 06/15/2017

GROTON MINERALS LTD (BC)
Cease trade order effective 03/01/1991
Stockholders' equity unlikely

GROUND DATA CORP (FL)
Proclaimed dissolved for failure to file reports and pay fees 12/16/1981

GROUND GRIPPER SHOE CO., INC.
Assets sold to Orthopedic Shoes, Inc. in 1932
Details not available

GROUND OWNERSHIP ANNUITY TRUST
All outstanding shares were purchased by an individual prior to dissolution which was effected 10/31/63

GROUND ROUND RESTAURANTS INC (NY)
Merged into GRR Holdings, LLC 12/02/1997
Each share Common $0.16666666 par exchanged for $1.65 cash

GROUND WTR INDS INC (DE)
Common $1 par split (2) for (1) by issuance of (1) additional share 3/10/72
Acquired by New GWI Corp. 5/23/85
Each share Common $1 par exchanged for $10 cash

GROUNDHOG GOLD MINES LTD. (ON)
Charter cancelled and company declared dissolved for default in filing returns 11/30/1964

GROUNDSTAR RES LTD (BC)
Reincorporated under the laws of Alberta 10/28/2005

GROUNDWATER TECHNOLOGY INC (DE)
Common 1¢ par split (3) for (2) by issuance of (0.5) additional share 6/30/87
Merged into Fluor Daniel/GTI, Inc. 5/10/96
Each share Common 1¢ par exchanged for (0.5274) share Common $0.001 par and $8.62 cash
(See Fluor Daniel/GTI, Inc.)

GROUP ASSETS, INC.
Merged into Distributors Group, Inc. 00/00/1936
Details not available

GROUP CORP.
Liquidation completed 00/00/1947
Details not available

GROUP ECONOMICS FOR MEDICINE LTD (NY)
Name changed to Scorpion Systems, Inc. 12/2/84
(See Scorpion Systems, Inc.)

GROUP FIVE EQUITY & MORTGAGE PARTNERS I (MO)
Partnership term expired 08/28/2009
Details not available

GROUP FIVE WKS (WY)
Name changed to Advanced Lighting Solutions Inc. 12/22/95

GROUP LONG DISTANCE INC (FL)
Administratively dissolved 09/14/2007

GROUP MAINTENANCE AMER CORP (TX)
Under plan of merger name changed to Encompass Services Corp. 02/22/2000
(See Encompass Services Corp.)

GROUP MGMT CORP (DE)
Reincorporated under the laws of Georgia as Silver Screen Studios, Inc. 09/05/2003
Silver Screen Studios, Inc. name changed to Global 1 Investment Holdings Corp. 11/13/2006
(See Global 1 Investment Holdings Corp.)

GROUP NINE FINL CORP (TX)
Charter forfeited for failure to pay taxes 11/20/89

GROUP NO. 1 OIL CORP.
Merged into Continental Oil Co. (DE) in 1948
Each share Capital Stock no par exchanged for (82.2) shares Capital Stock $5 par
Continental Oil Co. (DE) name changed to Conoco Inc. 7/2/79 which was acquired by Du Pont (E.I.) De Nemours & Co. 9/30/81

GROUP NO. 2 OIL CORP.
Merged into Continental Oil Co. (DE) in 1948
Each share Capital Stock 50¢ par exchanged for (0.06) share Capital Stock $5 par
Continental Oil Co. (DE) name changed to Conoco Inc. 7/2/79 which was acquired by Du Pont (E.I.) De Nemours & Co. 9/30/81

GROUP 1 SOFTWARE INC OLD (DE)
Stock Dividend - 25% 11/7/88
Merged into Group 1 Software, Inc. (New) (MD) 9/28/98
Each share Common 1¢ par exchanged for (1.15) shares Common 1¢ par
(See Group 1 Software, Inc. (New))

GROUP 1 SOFTWARE INC NEW (MD)
Common 1¢ par split (3) for (2) by issuance of (0.5) additional share payable 03/02/2000 to holders of record 02/17/2000
Common 1¢ par split (2) for (1) by issuance of (1) additional share payable 12/02/2002 to holders of record 11/15/2002 Ex date - 12/03/2002
Merged into Pitney Bowes Inc. 07/20/2004
Each share Common 1¢ par exchanged for $23 cash

GROUP SEVEN COMMUNICATIONS INC (NV)
Recapitalized as Zcom Networks, Inc. 03/12/2007
Each share Common $0.005 par exchanged for (0.005) share Common $0.001 par
Zcom Networks, Inc. recapitalized as Global Gateway Media & Communications, Inc. 12/02/2009

GROUP TECHNOLOGIES CORP (FL)
Issue Information - 2,000,000 shares COM offered at $10 per share on 05/18/1994
Reorganized under the laws of Delaware as Sypris Solutions, Inc. 3/30/98
Each share Common 1¢ par exchanged for (0.25) share Common 1¢ par

GROUP V CORP (DE)
Name changed to TotalAxcess.com, Inc. 05/17/1999
(See TotalAxcess.com, Inc.)

GROUP WEST SYS LTD (BC)
Merged into Appareo Software Inc. (New) 03/14/2001
Each share Common no par exchanged for (0.3) share Common no par
Appareo Software Inc. (New) name changed to Cellstop Systems Inc. 09/29/2004

GROUPE AB SA (FRANCE)
ADR agreement terminated 9/13/2001
Each Sponsored ADR for Ordinary exchanged for $4.8825 cash

GROUPE AEROPLAN INC (CANADA)
Name changed to Aimia Inc. 05/09/2012

GROUPE BIKINI VLG INC (CANADA)
Each share old Common no par exchanged for (0.008) share new Common no par 09/30/2010
Proposal in bankruptcy approved 05/14/2015
No stockholders' equity

GROUPE BOCENOR INC (QC)
Each share old Common no par exchanged for (0.25) share new Common no par 12/15/2004
Name changed to GBO Inc. 09/04/2007
(See GBO Inc.)

GROUPE CANTREX INC (QC)
Merged into Transamerica Acquisition Corp. 10/18/1999
Each share Common no par exchanged for $7 cash

GROUPE COVITEC INC (QC)
Merged into Carlton Communications PLC 11/29/2000
Each share Common no par exchanged for $0.88 cash

GROUPE DANONE (FRANCE)
Sponsored ADR's for Ordinary FF 10 par split (2) for (1) by issuance of (1) additional ADR payable 06/05/2000 to holders of record 06/02/2000 Ex date - 06/06/2000
Sponsored ADR's for Ordinary EUR 10 par changed to EUR 1 par due to currency change 01/01/2002
Sponsored ADR's for Ordinary EUR 1 par split (2) for (1) by issuance of (1) additional ADR payable 06/22/2004 to holders of record 06/14/2004 Ex date - 06/23/2004
Sponsored ADR's for Ordinary EUR 1 par split (2) for (1) by issuance of (1) additional ADR payable 06/06/2007 to holders of record 05/31/2007 Ex date - 06/07/2007
Name changed to Danone 05/01/2009

GROUPE EUROTUNNEL SA (FRANCE)
Name changed to Getlink S.E. 05/04/2018

GROUPE FOREX INC (QC)
Merged into Louisiana-Pacific Corp. 09/15/1999
Each share Class A Preferred no par exchanged for $33 cash
Each share Common no par exchanged for $33 cash

GROUPE GORGE (FRANCE)
ADR agreement terminated 11/20/2017
Each Sponsored ADR for Ordinary exchanged for $18.403333 cash

GROUPE LAPERRIERE & VERREAULT INC (QC)
Class B Multiple no par split (2) for (1) by issuance of (1) additional share payable 03/24/2005 to holders of record 03/24/2005
Class A Subordinate no par split (2) for (1) by issuance of (1) additional share payable 03/24/2005 to holders of record 03/24/2005
Plan of Arrangement effective 08/13/2007
Each share Class B Multiple no par par exchanged for (1) share GLV Inc. Class B Multiple no par and $33 cash
Each share Class A Subordinate no par exchanged for (1) share Class A Subordinate no par and $33 cash
GLV Inc. name changed to Ovivo Inc. 12/18/2014
(See Ovivo Inc.)

GROUPE LES AILES DE LA MODE INC (CANADA)
Name changed to Groupe Bikini Village Inc. 01/24/2006
(See Groupe Bikini Village Inc.)

GROUPE OPUS COMMUNICATIONS INC (BC)
Struck from the register and dissolved 08/25/1989

GROUPE T C G QUE INC (QC)
Name changed to Autostock Inc. 05/25/1990
(See Autostock Inc.)

GROUPE TRANSAT A T INC (CANADA)
Name changed to Transat A.T. Inc. 08/03/1993

GROUPE VAL ROYAL INC (QC)
Name changed to Reno-Depot Inc. 6/6/95
(See Reno-Depot Inc.)

GROUPED INCOME SHARES, SERIES A
Trust expired 05/31/1951
Details not available

GROUPED INCOME SHS LTD (CANADA)
Each share Common $1 par and Special $1 par exchanged for (2) shares Common 50¢ par respectively 00/00/1955
Common 50¢ par reclassified as Mutual Fund Shares no par 07/27/1983
Merged into Guardian Growth Fund Ltd. 04/26/1984
Each Mutual Fund Share no par exchanged for (0.20197) Mutual Fund Share 20¢ par
Guardian Growth Fund Ltd. reorganized as Guardian Group of Funds Ltd. 06/00/1998

GROUPMED INTL INC (NV)
Each share old Common $0.001 par exchanged for (0.1) share new Common $0.001 par 8/28/97
Recapitalized as Sun Cut Floral Network, Inc. 2/9/98
Each share new Common $0.001 par exchanged for (0.1) share Common $0.001 par
Sun Cut Floral Network, Inc. recapitalized as Avis Financial Corp. 12/9/2005

GROUPWORKS FINL CORP (ON)
Name changed to People Corp. 10/03/2011

GROUSE CREEK MINES LTD. (BC)
Recapitalized as New Grouse Creek Mines Ltd. 04/00/1971
Each share Capital Stock no par exchanged for (0.005) share Capital Stock no par
(See New Grouse Creek Mines Ltd.)

GROUSE MOUNTAIN RESORTS LTD (BC)
Each share 6% Conv. 1st Preference $10 par exchanged for (4) shares 6% Conv. 1st Preference $2.35 par plus $0.60 cash 11/04/1968
Acquired by Western Delta Lands Inc. 03/15/1989
Details not available

GROVE BK (BRIGHTON, MA)
Name changed 5/27/91
Name changed from Grove Bank for Savings (Brighton, MA) to Grove Bank (Brighton, MA) 5/27/91
Merged into Citizens Financial Group, Inc. 3/4/97
Each share Common 10¢ par exchanged for $51 cash

GROVE CAP CORP (FL)
Name changed to Valco Communications Inc. 04/24/1989
(See Valco Communications Inc.)

GROVE DOWLING HARDWOOD CO.
Sold under foreclosure in 1930

GROVE ENERGY LTD (BC)
Reincorporated 06/02/2005
Place of incorporation changed from (YT) to (BC) 06/02/2005
Acquired by Stratic Energy Corp. 04/24/2007
Each share Common no par exchanged for (0.61879) share Common no par
Note: Unexchanged certificates were cancelled and became without value 04/24/2013
(See Stratic Energy Corp.)

GROVE EXPLS LTD (BC)
Merged into Golden North Resource Corp. 08/30/1984
Each share Common 50¢ par exchanged for (0.33333333) share Common no par
Golden North Resource Corp. merged into Caledonia Mining Corp. (BC) 02/04/1992 which reincorporated in Canada 03/29/1995 which reincorporated in Jersey as Caledonia Mining Corp. PLC 03/24/2016

GROVE FARM CO., LTD. (HI)
Name changed to Grove Farm Co., Inc. 4/23/62

GROVE FOODS INC (CO)
Proclaimed dissolved for failure to file reports and pay fees 1/1/87

GROVE HALL SVGS BK (BRIGHTON, MA)
Name changed to Grove Bank For Savings (Brighton, MA) 5/16/87
Grove Bank For Savings (Brighton, MA) name changed to Grove Bank (Brighton, MA) 5/27/91
(See Grove Bank (Brighton, MA))

GROVE INVS INC (DE)
Acquired by Manitowoc Co., Inc. 8/8/2002
Each share Common exchanged for (0.4329) share Common 1¢ par

GROVE MANUFACTURING CO. (PA)
Each share Capital Stock $5 par exchanged for (3) shares Capital Stock $1.60 par 09/07/1966
Completely liquidated 11/24/1967
Each share Capital Stock $1.60 par exchanged for first and final distribution of (0.04546) share Kidde (Walter) & Co., Inc. (NY) $2.20 Conv. Preference Ser. A $1 par and (0.29894) share Common $2.50 par
Kidde (Walter) & Co., Inc. (NY) reincorporated in Delaware 07/02/1968 which name changed to Kidde, Inc. 04/18/1980 which merged into Hanson Trust PLC 12/31/1987 which name changed to Hanson PLC (Old) 01/29/1988 which reorganized as Hanson PLC (New) 10/15/2003

GROVE-PORTOLA SAVINGS & LOAN ASSOCIATION (CA)
Acquired by Golden West Financial Corp. (CA) 04/17/1970
Each share Guarantee Stock no par exchanged for (2.7149) shares Common 50¢ par
Golden West Financial Corp. (CA) reincorporated in Delaware 10/31/1975 which merged into Wachovia Corp. (Ctfs. dated after 09/01/2001) 10/02/2006 which merged into Wells Fargo & Co. (New) 12/31/2008

GROVE PRESS INC (NY)
Merged into GPI Acquisition Corp. 07/22/1985
Each share Common 50¢ par exchanged for $1.45 cash

GROVE PPTY TR (MD)
Name changed 3/12/97
Name changed from Grove Real Estate Asset Trust to Grove Properties Trust 3/12/97
Shares of Bene. Int. 1¢ par split (9) for (8) by issuance of (0.125) additional Share payable 3/28/97 to holders of record 3/10/97 Ex date - 3/13/97
Stock Dividend - 5% payable 3/28/97 to holders of record 3/10/97 Ex date - 3/13/97
Merged into Equity Residential Properties Trust 11/1/2000
Each share Common 1¢ par exchanged for $17 cash

GROVEWARE TECHNOLOGIES LTD (NV)
Each share old Common $0.001 par exchanged for (0.2) share new Common $0.001 par 09/28/2012
SEC revoked common stock registration 08/08/2016

GROW BIZ INTL INC (MN)
Name changed to Winmark Corp. 11/19/2001

GROW CORP. (NY)
Name changed to Grow Chemical Corp. 10/19/64
Grow Chemical Corp. name changed to Grow Group, Inc. 4/20/79
(See Grow Group, Inc.)

GROW GROUP INC (NY)
Name changed 04/20/1979
Name changed from Grow Chemical Corp. to Grow Group, Inc. 04/20/1979
Common 10¢ par split (5) for (4) by issuance of (0.25) additional share 01/30/1981
Common 10¢ par split (3) for (2) by issuance of (0.5) additional share 01/31/1985
Merged into Imperial Chemical Industries PLC 06/14/1995
Each share Common 10¢ par exchanged for $22 cash

GROW RITE CORP (NY)
Proclaimed dissolved for failure to file reports and pay taxes 12/15/1970

GROW VENTURES CORP (DE)
Name changed to GVC Venture Corp. 12/19/1989
GVC Venture Corp. recapitalized as Halo Labs, Inc. 02/25/2010

GROWBLOX SCIENCES INC (DE)
Name changed to GB Sciences, Inc. 04/10/2017

GROWERS DIRECT COFFEE CO INC (NV)
Chapter 7 bankruptcy proceedings terminated 07/29/2013
Stockholders' equity unlikely

GROWERS EXPRESS INC (NY)
Each share old Common 1¢ par exchanged for (1/3) share new Common 1¢ par 3/28/94
Name changed to Nuko Information Systems Inc. (NY) 5/27/94
Nuko Information Systems Inc. (NY) reincorporated in Delaware 1/8/97
(See Nuko Information Systems Inc.)

GROWERS FINANCE CORP. (IN)
Company liquidated in 1988
Details not available

GROWLNOLA INC (NV)
Petition under Chapter 11 Federal Bankruptcy Code dismissed 11/15/90
Stockholders' equity unlikely

GROWPROS CANNABIS VENTURES INC (CANADA)
Name changed to Tetra Bio-Pharma Inc. 09/28/2016

GROWTH CANADIAN, INC. (DE)
Name changed to Growth Energy Inc. 5/20/75
Growth Energy Inc. name changed to Dalco Liquids, Inc. 1/10/80 which name changed to International Drilling & Energy Corp. 11/10/80
(See International Drilling & Energy Corp.)

GROWTH CAPITAL, INC. (OH)
Completely liquidated 4/1/67
Each share Common $1 par exchanged for first and final distribution of (1) share Growth International, Inc. Common $1 par
Note: On 3/15/68 the above distribution was made to the remaining holders of record and therefore all unsurrendered certificates are now valueless

Growth International, Inc. name changed to Park-Ohio Industries, Inc. (DE) 6/1/72 which reorganized as Park-Ohio Industries, Inc. (OH) (New) 1/23/85 which name changed to Park-Ohio Holdings Corp. 6/16/98

GROWTH COMPANIES, INC. (DE)
Merged into Philadelphia Fund, Inc. (DE) share for share 00/00/1954
Philadelphia Fund, Inc. (DE) reincorporated in Maryland 11/30/1984 which merged into Advisors' Inner Circle Fund 11/13/2009

GROWTH DEV CORP (DE)
Plan of reorganization under Chapter 11 Federal Bankruptcy Code filed 12/24/91 and subsequently changed to Liquidating Chapter 11
No stockholders' equity

GROWTH ENERGY INC (DE)
Name changed to Dalco Liquids, Inc. 1/10/80
Dalco Liquids, Inc. name changed to International Drilling & Energy Corp. 11/10/80
(See International Drilling & Energy Corp.)

GROWTH ENVIRONMENTAL INC (IL)
Each share old Common no par exchanged for (0.5) share new Common no par 7/9/93
Plan of reorganization under Chapter 11 Federal Bankruptcy Code effective 7/29/96
No stockholders' equity

GROWTH EQUITIES CORP. (FL)
Bankrupt April 1962; stock worthless

GROWTH FD AMER INC (MD)
Stock Dividends - 10% 10/04/1980; 20% 09/29/1981
State of incorporation changedd from (DE) to (MD) 09/22/1983
Common 10¢ par reclassified as Class A $0.001 par 01/03/2000
Under plan of reorganization each share Class A, B and C $0.001 par automatically became (1) share Growth Fund of America (DE) Class A, B or C $0.001 par respectively 05/01/2013

GROWTH FD FLA INC (FL)
Liquidation completed
Each share Common $0.001 par exchanged for initial distribution of $5.71907 cash 12/21/1987
Each share Common $0.001 par received second didtribution of $0.12 cash 12/19/1988
Each share Common $0.001 par received third and final distribution of $0.1616 cash 06/09/1989

GROWTH FD SPAIN INC (MD)
Reorganized as Kemper Global/International Series Inc. 12/11/1998
Each share Common 1¢ par exchanged for (1) share Growth Fund Spain Class A 1¢ par
Kemper Global/International Series Inc. name changed to Scudder International Research Fund Inc. 05/25/2001
(See Scudder International Research Fund Inc.)

GROWTH FINL CORP (NJ)
Merged into HUBCO, Inc. 01/12/1996
Each share Common $1 par exchanged for (0.69) share Common no par
HUBCO, Inc. name changed to Hudson United Bancorp 04/21/1999 which merged TD Banknorth Inc. 01/31/2006
(See TD Banknorth Inc.)

GROWTH HOLDING CO. (IL)
Recapitalized as Growth Environmental Inc. 08/12/1991
Each share Common no par exchanged for (0.5) share Common no par
(See Growth Environmental Inc.)

GROWTH INC (UT)
Recapitalized as Westland Resources, Inc. 05/05/1980
Each share Common 1¢ par exchanged for (10) shares Common $0.001 par
(See Westland Resources, Inc.)

GROWTH INCOME PROPERTIES LTD. (AB)
Name changed to Centron Equity Corp. Ltd. 08/13/1969
(See Centron Equity Corp. Ltd.)

GROWTH INDS INC (NV)
Charter revoked for failure to maintain a resident agent 09/01/1989

GROWTH INSURORS HLDG CORP (IL)
Class A 75¢ par changed to no par and (1) additional share issued 3/17/66
Each share Class B no par exchanged for (2) shares Class A no par 10/20/66
Recapitalized as Progressive National Corp. 9/15/71
Each share Class A no par exchanged for (0.2) share Common no par
Progressive National Corp. merged into I.C.H. Corp. 11/14/79 which name changed to Southwestern Life Corp. (New) 6/15/94 which name changed to I.C.H. Corp. (New) 10/10/95
(See I.C.H. Corp. (New))

GROWTH INTL INC (DE)
Stock Dividend - 50% 5/31/68
Name changed to Park-Ohio Industries, Inc. (DE) 6/1/72
Park-Ohio Industries, Inc. (DE) reorganized as Park-Ohio Industries, Inc. (OH) (New) 1/23/85 which name changed to Park-Ohio Holdings Corp. 6/16/98

GROWTH INVT CORP (BC)
Liquidation completed
Each share Common 1¢ par received initial distribution of $11.45 cash 10/00/1992
Each share Common 1¢ par received second distribution of $11.50 cash 12/30/1992
Each share Common 1¢ par received third distribution of $0.82 cash 12/30/1993
Each share Common 1¢ par received fourth and final distribution of $0.0216 cash 11/16/1994

GROWTH MGMT INC (KY)
Administratively dissolved 08/29/1980

GROWTH OIL & MINERALS INC (UT)
Proclaimed dissolved for failure to pay taxes 03/29/1975

GROWTH RLTY COS (CA)
Name changed to British Land of America (CA) 11/17/1983
British Land of America (CA) reincorporated in Delaware as British Land of America, Inc. 12/15/1986 which merged into Medical Management of America, Inc. 09/23/1988
(See Medical Management of America, Inc.)

GROWTH REALTY INVESTORS (CA)
Under plan of reorganization each Share of Bene. Int. $1 par automatically became (1) share Growth Realty Companies Common $1 par 2/9/79
Growth Realty Companies name changed to British Land of America (Calif.) 11/17/83 which reincorporated in Delaware as British Land of America Inc. 12/15/86 which merged into Medical Management of America, Inc. 9/23/88
(See Medical Management of America, Inc.)

GROWTH SCIENCES INC (DE)
Merged into Data-Link Corp. 09/26/1972
Each share Common 1¢ par exchanged for (0.125) share Common $1 par

GROWTH STK OUTLOOK TR INC (MD)
Name changed to Allmon (Charles) Trust, Inc. 06/03/1991
Allmon (Charles) Trust, Inc. name changed to Liberty All-Star Growth Fund, Inc. 11/07/1995

GROWTH SYS GROUP INC (PA)
Acquired by Deco Industries, Inc. 08/24/1970
Each share Capital Stock no par exchanged for (0.5) share Common 5¢ par
Deco Industries, Inc. name changed to First Estate Group Ltd. (PA) 06/01/1985 which reincorporated in Colorado as Companies West Group Inc. 10/09/1986

GROWTH TECHNOLOGIES INTL INC (FL)
Recapitalized as Alternafuels, Inc. 03/18/2011
Each share Common $0.001 par exchanged for (0.01) share Common $0.001 par
(See Alternafuels, Inc.)

GROWTHGEN EQUITY II INC (ON)
Name changed to GuestLogix Inc. 08/08/2007
(See GuestLogix Inc.)

GROWTHGEN EQUITY INC (ON)
Name changed to Tarquin Group Inc. 04/04/2007
(See Tarquin Group Inc.)

GROWTHLOGIC INC (NV)
Name changed to Sunburst Alliance, Inc. 01/31/2005
(See Sunburst Alliance, Inc.)

GRT CORP (CA)
Capital Stock $2 par reclassified as Common no par and (3) additional shares issued 02/12/1969
Common no par changed to 50¢ par 12/15/1972
Adjudicated bankrupt 11/28/1979
Stockholders' equity unlikely

GRUBB & ELLIS CO (DE)
Preferred Stock Purchase Rights declared for Common stockholders of record 05/24/1989 were redeemed at $0.01 per right for holders of record 01/29/1993
Each share Common $1 par exchanged for (0.2) share Common 1¢ par 01/29/1993
Plan of reorganization under Chapter 11 Federal Bankruptcy proceedings effective 04/01/2013
No stockholders' equity

GRUBB & ELLIS RLTY ADVISORS INC (DE)
Issue Information - 20,833,334 UNITS consisting of (1) share COM and (2) WTS offered at $6 per Unit on 02/27/2006
Completely liquidated
Each share Common $0.0001 par received first and final distribution of $6.08929094 cash payable 04/18/2008 to holders of record 04/17/2008
Note: Certificates were not required to be surrendered and are without value

GRUBB & ELLIS RLTY INCOME LIQUDATING TR (CA)
Name changed 5/14/92
Liquidation completed
Each share Common no par received

initial distribution of $1.50 cash 6/29/90
Each share Common no par received second distribution of $0.26 cash 5/31/91
Each share Common no par received third distribution of $0.10 cash 8/16/91
Each share Common no par received fourth distribution of $0.82 cash 10/15/91
Each share Common no par received fifth distribution of $0.07 cash 12/13/91
Each share Common no par received sixth distribution of $0.50 cash 2/21/92
Each share Common no par received seventh distribution of $0.07 cash 5/14/92
Assets transferred from Grubb & Ellis Realty Income Trust to Grubb & Ellis Realty Income Trust Liquidating Trust 5/14/92
Each share Common no par received eighth distribution of $0.07 cash 8/14/92
Each share Common no par received ninth distribution of $0.07 cash 12/11/92
Each share Common no par received tenth distribution of $0.07 cash 2/27/93
Each share Common no par received eleventh distribution of $0.05 cash 5/20/93
Each share Common no par received twelfth distribution of $1.95 cash 4/14/94
Each share Common no par received thirteenth distribution of $0.58 cash 10/28/96
Each share Common no par received fourteenth distribution and final distribution of $0.025 cash 9/27/97
Note: Certificates were not required to be surrendered and are without value

GRUDGE MUSIC GROUP INC (NY)
Name changed to Echo Springs Water Co., Inc. 9/21/93
(See Echo Springs Water Co., Inc.)

GRUEN INDS INC (DE)
Reincorporated 08/01/1968
State of incorporation changed from (OH) to (DE) 08/01/1968
Merged into Jewelcor, Inc. 10/31/1985
Each share Common $1 par exchanged for $0.75 cash

GRUEN MKTG CORP (DE)
Acquired by S.H. Holdings Inc. 12/06/1988
Each share Common 1¢ par exchanged for $11.75 cash

GRUEN WATCH CO. (OH)
Each share Class C Preferred $25 par exchanged for (1) share 5% Preferred $25 par and (0.5) share Common $1 par in 1941
Name changed to Gruen Industries, Inc. (OH) in 1956
Gruen Industries, Inc. (OH) reincorporated in Delaware 8/1/68
(See Gruen Industries, Inc. (DE))

GRUENE INC (CA)
Common no par split (3) for (2) by issuance of (0.5) additional share 7/5/88
Common no par split (3) for (2) by issuance of (0.5) additional share 3/8/89
Common no par split (4) for (3) by issuance of (1/3) additional share 6/12/89
Charter suspended for failure to file reports and pay fees 9/4/90

GRUMA S A B DE C V (MEXICO)
Name changed 06/22/2007
Stock Dividends - 2% payable 05/23/1997 to holders of record 05/07/1997; 1.66666666% payable 05/20/1998 to holders of record 05/07/1998
ADR agreement terminated 04/01/1999
Each Sponsored 144A ADR for Class B exchanged for approximately $4.38 cash
Name changed from Gruma, S.A. de C.V. to Gruma, S.A.B. de C.V. 06/22/2007
ADR agreement terminated 09/08/2015
Each Sponsored ADR for Class B exchanged for $58.616461 cash

GRUMMAN AIRCRAFT ENGR CORP (NY)
Each share Common $5 par exchanged for (5) shares Common $1 par in 1937
Common $1 par split (2) for (1) by issuance of (1) additional share 6/4/65
Common $1 par split (3) for (2) by issuance of (0.5) additional share 3/30/67
Stock Dividends - 100% 6/29/48; 100% 11/30/50; 10% 12/29/55
Name changed to Grumman Corp. 7/23/69
(See Grumman Corp.)

GRUMMAN ALLIED INDS INC (NY)
Merged into Grumman Corp. 04/30/1974
Each share Capital Stock $1 par exchanged for (1) share 80¢ Conv. Preferred $1 par
(See Grumman Corp.)

GRUMMAN CORP (NY)
Common $1 par split (2) for (1) by issuance of (1) additional share 8/19/83
$2.80 Preferred $1 par called for redemption 7/30/92
80¢ Conv. Preferred $1 par called for redemption 11/30/92
Stock Dividend - 10% 1/30/76
Merged into Northrop Acquisition Inc. 5/18/94
Each share Common $1 par exchanged for $62 cash

GRUNTAL FINL CORP (DE)
Merged into Home Group, Inc. 08/19/1987
Each share Common 10¢ par exchanged for $9.50 cash

GRUPA ADV S A (POLAND)
Name changed to SMT S.A. 02/09/2016
SMT S.A. name changed to iAlbatros Group S.A. 08/18/2016

GRUPE S A DE C V (MEXICO)
ADR agreement terminated 06/26/2009
No ADR's remain outstanding

GRUPO AEROPORTUARIO DEL PACIFICO S A DE C V (MEXICO)
Issue Information - 290,256,520 SPONSORED ADR'S offered at $21 per ADR on 2/23/2006
Name changed to Grupo Aeroportuario del Pacifico, S.A.B. de C.V. 10/27/2007

GRUPO AEROPORTUARIO DEL SURESTE S A DE C V (MEXICO)
Name changed to Grupo Aeroportuario del Sureste, S.A.B. de C.V. 4/14/2007

GRUPO CASA SABA S A DE C V (MEXICO)
Name changed 05/19/2000
Name changed from Grupo Casa Autrey, S.A. de C.V. to Grupo Casa Saba, S.A. de C.V. 05/19/2000
ADR agreement terminated 03/13/2013
Each Sponsored ADR for Ordinary exchanged for (10) shares Ordinary
Note: Unexchanged ADR's were sold and the proceeds, if any, held for claim after 03/13/2014

GRUPO CATALANA OCCIDENTE S A (SPAIN)
ADR agreement terminated 08/06/2018
No ADR's remain outstanding

GRUPO CONTL S A (MEXICO)
Sponsored ADR's for Ordinary MXN 10 par split (2) for (1) by issuance of (1) additional ADR payable 05/24/1999 to holders of record 05/21/1999
Merged into Embotelladoras Arca S.A. 06/01/2011
Each Sponsored ADR for Ordinary MXN 10 par exchanged for $39.079912 cash

GRUPO DATAFLUX S A DE C V (MEXICO)
ADR agreement terminated 12/18/2007
Each Sponsored ADR for Ser. B shares exchanged for $1.598152 cash

GRUPO ELEKTRA S A DE C V (MEXICO)
GDR's for Ordinary Participation Ctfs. split (2) for (1) by issuance of (1) additional GDR payable 01/12/1998 to holders of record 01/09/1998 Ex date - 01/13/1998
Each GDR for Ordinary Participation Ctfs. exchanged for (0.5) Sponsored ADR for Common 09/09/2002
GDR agreement terminated 08/01/2005
Each Sponsored ADR for Common exchanged for $28.90514 cash

GRUPO EMBOTELLADOR DE MEXICO S A DE C V (MEXICO)
Issue Information - 2,950,000 GLOBAL DEP RCPT REP ORD PARTN offered at $31 per Receipt on 03/29/1994
Global Depositary Receipts for Ordinary no par split (3) for (1) by issuance of (2) additional Receipts payable 10/20/95 to holders of record 10/17/95
Name changed to Pepsi-Gemex, S.A. de C.V. 3/13/97
(See Pepsi-Gemex, S.A. de C.V.)

GRUPO FERROVIAL S A (SPAIN)
Merged into Cintra Concesiones de Infraestructuras de Transporte, S.A. 01/25/2010
Each ADR for Common exchanged for (4) ADR's for Ordinary
Cintra Concesiones de Infraestructuras de Transporte, S.A. name changed to Ferrovial S.A. 01/29/2010

GRUPO FINANCIERO BANCOMER S A DE C V (MEXICO)
Name changed to Grupo Financiero BBVA Bancomer and Sponsored ADR's for C Shares reclassified as Sponsored ADR's for O Shares 7/1/2000
(See Grupo Financiero BBVA Bancomer)

GRUPO FINANCIERO BBVA BANCOMER (MEXICO)
Sponsored ADR's for O Shares reclassified as Sponsored ADR's for B Shares 08/16/2002
ADR agreement terminated 12/23/2004
Each 144A Sponsored ADR for Ser. B Share exchanged for $9.011619 cash
Each Sponsored ADR for Ser. B Share exchanged for $9.011619 cash

GRUPO FINANCIERO BITAL S A DE C V (MEXICO)
ADR agreement terminated 02/26/2007
Each Sponsored ADR for Ser. L Ordinary no par exchanged for (10) Ser. L shs.
Note: Unexchanged ADR's will be sold and proceeds, if any, held for claim after 02/25/2008

GRUPO FINANCIERO GBM ATLANTICO S A DE C V (MEXICO)
Each old Sponsored 144A ADR for Class L exchanged for (1) new Sponsored 144A ADR for Class L 10/21/2001
ADR agreement terminated 09/01/2004
Each new Sponsored 144A ADR for Class L exchanged for $8.43525 cash
Each Sponsored Reg. S GDR for Class L exchanged for $8.43525 cash
ADR agreement terminated 09/01/2004
Details not available

GRUPO FINANCIERO SANTANDER MEXICANO (MEXICO)
Each old Sponsored ADR for Class B New exchanged for (0.778051) new Sponsored ADR for Class B New 5/27/2003
Stock Dividend - 68.49314% payable 3/6/2003 to holders of record 2/28/2003 Ex date - 2/26/2003
ADR agreement terminated 9/14/2005
Each new Sponsored ADR for new Class B exchanged for $8.2726 cash

GRUPO FINANCIERO SANTANDER MEXICO S A B DE C V (MEXICO)
Merged into Banco Santander (Mexico), S.A. 01/29/2018
Each Sponsored ADR for Ser. B Shares exchanged for (1) Sponsored ADR for Ser. B Shares

GRUPO FINANCIERO SERFIN S A (MEXICO)
Name changed 04/17/1995
Name changed from Grupo Financiero Serfin, S.A. de C.V. to Grupo Financiero Serfin, S.A. 04/17/1995
ADR agreement terminated 09/28/1999
No stockholders' equity

GRUPO GIGANTE S A B DE C V (MEXICO)
Name changed 09/24/2007
Each old 144A Sponsored ADR for B Shares exchanged for (0.33333333) new 144A Sponsored ADR for B Shares 05/15/2000
Name changed from Grupo Gigante S.A. de C.V. to Grupo Gigante S.A.B. de C.V. 09/24/2007
ADR agreement terminated 09/29/2017
Each Sponsored ADR for B Shares exchanged for (10) B Shares
Note: Unexchanged ADR's will be sold and the proceeds, if any, held for claim after 10/04/2018
ADR agreement terminated 11/28/2017
Each 144A Sponsored ADR for B Shares exchanged for $15.921786 cash

GRUPO HERDEZ S A B DE C V (MEXICO)
Name changed 08/24/2015
Sponsored ADR's for B Shares split (6.25) for (1) by issuance of (5.25) additional ADR's payable 08/27/2013 to holders of record 08/26/2013 Ex date - 08/28/2013
Basis changed from (1:25) to (1:4) 08/28/2013
Stock Dividend - 2.5% payable 05/20/2015 to holders of record 05/11/2015 Ex date - 05/07/2015
Name changed from Grupo Herdez S.A. de C.V. to Grupo Herdez S.A.B. de C.V. 08/24/2015
ADR agreement terminated 11/20/2017

GRU-GSC   **FINANCIAL INFORMATION, INC.**

Each Sponsored ADR for B Shares exchanged for (4) B Shares
Note: Unexchanged ADR's will be sold and the proceeds, if any, held for claim after 11/23/2018

GRUPO IMSA S A DE C V (MEXICO)
Issue Information - 5,500,000 ADR's offered at $19 per ADR on 12/10/1996
ADR agreement terminated 04/07/2005
Each ADR for Equity Units no par exchanged for $30.14739 cash

GRUPO INDL DURANGO S A DE C V (MEXICO)
Name changed to Corporacion Durango, S.A. de C.V. 02/12/2002
Corporacion Durango, S.A. de C.V. name changed to Corporacion Durango, S.A.B. de C.V. 04/13/2007 which name changed to Bio Pappel S.A.B. de C.V. 05/19/2014
(See Bio Pappel S.A.B. de C.V.)

GRUPO INDL MASECA S A DE C V (MEXICO)
ADR agreement terminated 11/15/2005
Each ADR for Ser. A no par exchanged for $5.686358 cash
Each new Sponsored ADR for Ordinary no par exchanged for $8.549536 cash

GRUPO IUSACELL S A DE C V NEW (MEXICO)
Each old Sponsored ADR for Ser. V no par exchanged for (0.1) new Sponsored ADR for Ser. V no par 5/9/2003
Each new Sponsored ADR for Ser. V no par exchanged for (0.05) new Sponsored ADR for Common no par 12/17/2003
ADR agreement terminated 9/19/2005
Each new Sponsored ADR for Ser. V no par exchanged for $11.87833 cash

GRUPO IUSACELL S A DE C V OLD (MEXICO)
Issue Information - 571,542 Units consisting of (3) SPONSORED ADR's REPSTG 10 SER D SHS AND (7) SPONSORED ADR's REPSTG 10 SER L SHS offered at $272.50 per Unit on 06/14/1994
ADR agreement terminated 02/29/2000
Each Sponsored ADR for Ser. D exchanged for $17.462 cash
Each Sponsored ADR for Ser. L exchanged for $17.462 cash

GRUPO MELO S A (PANAMA)
ADR agreement terminated 1/06/2010
No ADR's remain outstanding

GRUPO MEXICANO DE DESARROLLO S A (MEXICO)
Sponsored ADR's for Ser. L no par reclassified as Sponsored ADR's for Ser. B no par 5/30/2001
ADR agreement terminated 12/14/2005
Each Sponsored ADR for Ser. B no par exchanged for $2.3658 cash

GRUPO MINSA S A DE C V (MEXICO)
ADR agreement terminated 10/18/2005
Each 144A Sponsored ADR for Ser. C exchanged for (10) Ser. C shares
Each Reg. S Sponsored ADR for Ser. C exchanged for (10) Ser. C shares
Note: Unexchanged ADR's will be sold and the proceeds, if any, held for claim after 4/15/2006

GRUPO MODELO S A DE C V (MEXICO)
ADR agreement terminated 10/25/2013
Each Sponsored ADR for Ser. C exchanged for $90.926729 cash

GRUPO NACIONAL DE CHOCOLATES SA (COLOMBIA)
Name changed to Grupo Nutresa S.A. 06/28/2011

GRUPO PARANAPANEMA S A (BRAZIL)
ADR basis changed from (1:4,000) to (1:2) 06/09/2005
Sponsored ADR's for Preferred reclassified as Sponsored ADR's for Common 11/01/2010
ADR agreement terminated 10/03/2014
Each Sponsored ADR for Common exchanged for $1.53378 cash

GRUPO POSADAS S A B DE C V (MEXICO)
GDR agreement terminated 05/16/2013
Each 144A GDR for Ser. L exchanged for $35.63585 cash
GDR agreement terminated 10/27/2017
Each 144A GDR for Common exchanged for (20) shares Common
Note: Unexchanged GDR's will be sold and the proceeds, if any, held for claim after 11/01/2018

GRUPO PROFESIONAL PLANEACION Y PROYECTOS S A DE C V (MEXICO)
ADR agreement terminated 11/13/2008
Each Sponsored ADR for Ordinary exchanged for (2) shares Ordinary
Note: Unexchanged ADR's will be sold and the proceeds, if any, held for claim after 05/13/2009

GRUPO QUMMA S A DE C V (MEXICO)
ADR agreement terminated 03/27/2013
No ADR's remain outstanding

GRUPO RADIO CENTRO S A B DE C V (MEXICO)
Name changed 07/31/2006
Name changed from Grupo Radio Centro, S.A. de C.V. to Grupo Radio Centro, S.A.B. de C.V. 07/31/2006
ADR agreement terminated 01/28/2013
Each ADR for Ordinary Participation Certificates exchanged for $10.446201 cash

GRUPO SIDEK S A DE C V (MEXICO)
Assets sold for the benefit of creditors in 2002
Details not available

GRUPO SIMEC S A DE C V (MEXICO)
Name changed to Grupo Simec, S.A.B. de C.V. 10/29/2006

GRUPO SITUR S A DE C V (MEXICO)
ADR agreement terminated 12/07/2006
No ADR's remain outstanding

GRUPO SYNKRO S A DE C V (MEXICO)
ADR agreement terminated 1/17/2000
No ADR holder's equity

GRUPO TELEVISA S A (MEXICO)
Sponsored ADR's for Ordinary no par split (4) for (1) by issuance of (3) additional ADR's payable 03/21/2006 to holders of record 02/27/2006 Ex date - 03/22/2006
Name changed to Grupo Televisa, S.A.B. 07/23/2007

GRUPO TMM S A (MEXICO)
Name changed 10/15/2002
Each Sponsored ADR for Ser. L exchanged for (1) ADR for Ser. A no par 09/13/2002
Name changed from Grupo TMM, S.A. DE C.V. to Grupo TMM, S.A. 10/15/2002
Name changed to Grupo TMM, S.A.B. 06/19/2007

GRUPO TRIBASA S A DE C V (MEXICO)
Each old Sponsored ADR for Ordinary no par exchanged for (0.1) new Sponsored ADR for Ordinary no par 5/30/2000
Name changed to Promotora y Operadora de Infraestructura S.A. 4/6/2006

GRUSS MINING CO. (CA)
Name changed to Vivian Mining Co., Inc. 00/00/1941
Vivian Mining Co., Inc. (CA) reincorporated in Nevada 03/15/1956 which name changed to Vivian Consolidated Ltd. 05/26/1956 which merged into Entrada Corp. 05/14/1957 which recapitalized as Pacific Energy Corp. 01/14/1976 which name changed to Aimco, Inc. 09/01/1977 which recapitalized as Colt Technology, Inc. 03/31/1983

GRYPHON FD INC (MD)
Name changed to Founders Growth Fund, Inc. 11/09/1970
(See Founders Growth Fund, Inc.)

GRYPHON HLDGS INC (DE)
Merged into Markel Corp. 2/17/99
Each share Common 1¢ par exchanged for $19 cash

GRYPHON PETROLEUM CORP. (BC)
Merged into Interaction Resources Ltd. (BC) 12/22/1982
Each share Common no par exchanged for (0.66666666) share Common no par
Interaction Resources Ltd. (BC) reincorporated in Alberta 04/28/1994 which recapitalized as Ketch Energy Ltd. 06/16/2000 which merged into Acclaim Energy Trust 10/01/2002
(See Acclaim Energy Trust)

GRYPHON RES INC (NV)
Common $0.001 par split (19.5) for (1) by issuance of (18.5) additional shares payable 07/07/2008 to holders of record 07/03/2008 Ex date - 07/08/2008
Voluntarily dissolved 05/04/2012
Details not available

GS AGRIFUELS CORP (DE)
Completely liquidated
Each share Common $0.0001 par received first and final distribution of $0.50 cash payable 03/27/2008 to holders of record 02/29/2008
Note: Certificates were not required to be surrendered and are without value

GS CAP GROWTH FD INC (MD)
Name changed to Goldman Sachs Equity Portfolios, Inc. 05/14/1991
(See Goldman Sachs Equity Portfolios, Inc.)

GS CARBON CORP (DE)
Name changed to Seaway Valley Capital Corp. 08/17/2007

GS CLEANTECH CORP (DE)
Each share old Common $0.001 par exchanged for (0.02) share new Common $0.001 par 12/12/2007
Name changed to GreenShift Corp. 02/13/2008

GS ENERGY CORP (DE)
Recapitalized as EcoSystem Corp. 02/12/2008
Each share Common $0.001 par exchanged for (0.002) share Common $0.001 par
EcoSystem Corp. recapitalized as Adarna Energy Corp. 07/07/2011
(See Adarna Energy Corp.)

GS ENVIROSERVICES INC (DE)
SEC revoked common stock registration 10/04/2017

GS FINL CORP (LA)
Acquired by Home Bancorp, Inc. 07/15/2011

Each share Common 1¢ par exchanged for $21 cash

GS FINL SVCS INC (DE)
Each share Common $0.0001 par received distribution of (0.9) share Agri Bio-Sciences Inc. Common $0.001 par payable 11/03/1999 to holders of record 06/01/1999
Company terminated registration of common stock and is no longer public as of 01/26/2005

GS GLOBAL FDG INC (DE)
144A 3C7 Resettable Rate Preferred Ser. A called for redemption at $100,000 on 4/15/2007

GS INTL TECHNOLOGIES INC (NV)
Recapitalized as Protective Technologies International Marketing Inc. 11/15/96
Each share Common $0.001 par exchanged for (0.2) share Common $0.001 par
Protective Technologies International Marketing Inc. recapitalized as Armed Alert Security Inc. 6/4/99 which recapitalized as Acquired Sales Corp. 3/1/2006

GS TELECOM LTD (CO)
SEC revoked common stock registration 09/26/2005

GS VALET INC (NV)
Name changed to International Metals Streaming Corp. 09/26/2013
International Metals Streaming Corp. name changed to Environmental Packaging Technologies Holdings, Inc. 02/28/2017

GSA INC (CA)
Each share old Common $0.001 par exchanged for (0.1) share new Common $0.001 par 5/20/94
Recapitalized as Spintek Gaming Technologies, Inc. (CA) 9/29/95
Each share Common $0.001 par exchanged for (0.5) share Common $0.001 par
Spintek Gaming Technologies, Inc. (CA) reincorporated in Nevada 8/24/98
(See Spintek Gaming Technologies, Inc.)

GSB FINL CORP (DE)
Merged into Berkshire Bancorp, Inc. 3/30/2001
Each share Common 1¢ par exchanged for (0.6027) share Common 10¢ par

GSB FINL SVCS INC (DE)
Recapitalized as Nationwide Delivery Inc. 07/29/2008
Each share Common $0.0001 par exchanged for (0.01) share Common $0.0001 par

GSC ACQUISITION CO (DE)
Completely liquidated 06/26/2009
Each Unit exchanged for first and final distribution of $9.832212 cash
Each share Common $0.001 par exchanged for first and final distribution of $9.832212 cash

GSC ENTERPRISES INC (DE)
Common $1 par changed to 10¢ par 1/17/75
Under plan of partial liquidation each share Common 10¢ par received distribution of $0.42 cash 1/31/75
Merged into Lincolnwood Bancorporation, Inc. 10/24/77
Each share Common 10¢ par exchanged for $1.15 face value of Bank of Lincolnwood (Lincolnwood, IL) 8-1/2% Capital Notes due 1989 or $1.15 cash
Note: Unexchanged shares became valueless 10/24/81

GSC INVT CORP (MD)
Each share Common $0.001 par received distribution of (1.209) additional shares payable

12/31/2009 to holders of record 11/25/2009 Ex date - 11/23/2009
Name changed to Saratoga Investment Corp. 08/03/2010

GSC PERFORMANCE FD INC (GA)
Name changed to Interstate Capital Growth Fund Inc. 5/6/86
(See Interstate Capital Growth Fund Inc.)

GSE HLDG INC (DE)
Plan of reorganization under Chapter 11 Federal Bankruptcy proceedings effective 08/11/2014
No stockholders' equity

GSF PRODTNS INC (DE)
Charter cancelled and declared inoperative and void for non-payment of taxes 3/1/75

GSI COMM INC (DE)
Acquired by eBay Inc. 06/17/2011
Each share Common 1¢ par exchanged for $29.58 cash

GSI COMPUTER INC (NY)
Name changed to Hidoc International, Inc. 10/17/69
Hidoc International, Inc. merged into Graphic Sciences, Inc. 8/31/72 which merged into Burroughs Corp. (MI) 2/26/75 which reincorporated in Delaware 5/30/84 which name changed to Unisys Corp. 11/13/86

GSI GROUP INC NEW (NB)
Each share old Common no par exchanged for (0.33333333) share new Common no par 12/29/2010
Name changed to Novanta Inc. 05/12/2016

GSI GROUP INC OLD (NB)
Plan of reorganization under Chapter 11 Federal Bankruptcy Code effective 07/23/2010
Each share Common no par exchanged for initial distribution of (0.93835) share GSI Group Inc. (New) Common no par
Each share Common no par received second and final distribution of (0.02055) share GSI Group Inc. (New) Common no par payable 03/04/2011 to holders of record 07/23/2010
GSI Group Inc. (New) name changed to Novanta Inc. 05/12/2016

GSI LIQUIDATING CORP. (MA)
Liquidation completed
Each share Common 2¢ par received initial distribution of $0.45 cash 2/1/79
Each share Common 2¢ par received second and final distribution of $0.028 cash 4/2/79
Note: Certificates were not required to be surrendered and are now valueless

GSI SECURITIZATION INC (NV)
SEC revoked common stock registration 07/14/2008

GSI SECURITIZATION LTD (CAYMAN ISLANDS)
Reincorporated under the laws of Nevada as GSI Securitization Inc. and Ordinary 2¢ par reclassified as Common $0.001 par 10/18/2007
(See GSI Securitization Inc.)

GSI TECHNOLOGIES USA INC (DE)
Company terminated common stock registration and is no longer public as of 03/11/2004

GSL GROUP INC (BRITISH VIRGIN ISLANDS)
SEC revoked common stock registration 08/30/2007

GSM FD GROUP INC (NV)
Charter revoked 08/31/2016

GSM RESOURCE CAP INC (ON)
Recapitalized as HMH China Investments Ltd. (ON) 09/18/1995
Each share Common no par exchanged for (0.2) share Common no par
HMH China Investments Ltd. (ON) reincorporated in Bermuda 12/21/1995

GSME ACQUISITION PARTNERS I (CAYMAN ISLANDS)
Issue Information - 3,600,000 UNITS consisting of (1) share ORD and (1) WT offered at $10 per Unit on 11/19/2009
Combined Units separated 12/14/2009
Name changed to Plastec Technologies, Ltd. 02/04/2011

GSO SOLUTIONS INC (NS)
Cease trade order effective 03/28/2001

GSOCIETY INC (FL)
SEC revoked common stock registration 02/20/2007

GSP-2 INC (NV)
SEC revoked common stock registration 09/10/2015

GSR GOLDSEARCH RES INC (BC)
Name changed to Goldrush Mining Corp. 09/24/1991
Goldrush Mining Corp. name changed to to Goldrush Casino & Mining Corp. 09/10/1992 which name changed to Phoenix Leisure Corp. 07/10/1998
(See Phoenix Leisure Corp.)

GSS VENTURE CAP CORP (UT)
Proclaimed dissolved for failure to file reports 2/28/91

GST GLOBAL TELECOMMUNICATIONS INC (YT)
Name changed to Global Light Telecommunications Inc. 10/28/1998
(See Global Light Telecommunications Inc.)

GST LABS INC (DE)
Charter cancelled and declared inoperative and void for non-payment of taxes 3/1/88

GST TELECOMMUNICATIONS INC (CANADA)
Plan of reorganization under Chapter 11 Federal Bankruptcy Code effective 04/30/2002
No stockholders' equity

GSW INC (CANADA)
Name changed 10/01/1980
Each share Common no par exchanged for (1) share Conv. Class A Common no par and (2) shares Conv. Class B Common no par 07/01/1970
Conv. Class A Common no par and Conv. Class B Common no par split (2) for (1) by issuance of (1) additional share respectively 05/29/1973
5% Preference $100 par called for redemption 03/09/1979
Name changed from GSW Ltd.-GSW Ltee. to GSW Inc. and Conv. Class C Common no par reclassified as Conv. Class A Common no par and Conv. Class D Common no par reclassified as Conv. Class B Common no no par 10/01/1980
Acquired by Smith (A. O.) Corp. 04/06/2006
Each share Class A Common no par exchanged for $115 cash
Each share Conv. Class B Common no par exchanged for $115 cash

GT ADVANCED TECHNOLOGIES INC (DE)
Plan of reorganization under Chapter 11 Federal Bankruptcy proceedings effective 03/17/2016
No stockholders' equity

GT BICYCLES INC (CA)
Merged into Schwinn Holdings Corp. 10/2/98
Each share Common $0.001 par exchanged for $8 cash

GT CDA CAP CORP (CANADA)
Name changed to GT Canada Medical Properties Inc. (Canada) 03/29/2010
GT Canada Medical Properties Inc. (Canada) reorganized in Ontario as GT Canada Medical Properties REIT 01/04/2011 which name changed to NorthWest International Healthcare Properties REIT 11/02/2012 which merged into NorthWest Healthcare Properties REIT 05/19/2015

GT CDA MED PPTYS INC (CANADA)
Reorganized under the laws of Ontario as GT Canada Medical Properties REIT 01/04/2011
Each share Common no par exchanged for (0.1) Trust Unit
Note: Unexchanged certificates were cancelled and became without value 01/04/2017
GT Canada Medical Properties REIT name changed to NorthWest International Healthcare Properties REIT 11/02/2012 which merged into NorthWest Healthcare Properties REIT 05/19/2015

GT CDA MED PPTYS REAL ESTATE INVT TR (ON)
Name changed to NorthWest International Healthcare Properties REIT 11/02/2012
NorthWest International Healthcare Properties REIT merged into NorthWest Healthcare Properties REIT 05/19/2015

G T 5-LIMITED (NV)
Name changed to CryoPort, Inc. 3/16/2005

GT GLOBAL FLOATING RATE FD INC (MD)
Under plan of reorganization each share Common automatically became (1) share AIM Floating Rate Fund (DE) Class B Common 03/31/2000
(See AIM Floating Rate Fund)

GT GROUP TELECOM INC (CANADA)
Assets sold for the benefit of creditors 02/04/2003
No stockholders' equity

GT INTERACTIVE SOFTWARE CORP (DE)
Recapitalized as Infogrames Inc. 06/27/2000
Each share Common 1¢ par exchanged for (0.2) share Common 1¢ par
Infogrames Inc. name changed to Atari, Inc. 05/06/2003
(See Atari, Inc.)

GT SOLAR INTL INC (DE)
Name changed to GT Advanced Technologies Inc. 08/08/2011
(See GT Advanced Technologies Inc.)

GTA CORPFIN CAP INC (ON)
Name changed to GTA Resources & Mining Inc. 07/26/2010

GTC BIOTHERAPEUTICS INC (MA)
Each share old Common 1¢ par exchanged for (0.1) share new Common 1¢ par 05/27/2009
Merged into LFB Biotechnologies S.A.S. 12/02/2010
Each share new Common 1¢ par exchanged for $0.30 cash

GTC TELECOM CORP (NV)
Charter revoked for failure to file reports and pay fees 05/30/2008

GTC TRCNTNTL GROUP LTD (CANADA)
Common no par split (2) for (1) by issuance of (1) additional share 05/22/1986
Common no par reclassified as Class B no par 07/25/1988
1st Preferred Ser. C no par called for redemption at $25 plus $0.55537 accrued dividends on 11/01/1999
Name changed to Transcontinental Inc. 03/27/2003

GTDATA CORP (NV)
Each share old Common $0.001 par exchanged for (0.05) share new Common $0.001 par 2/10/2003
Each share new Common $0.001 par exchanged again for (0.1) share new Common $0.001 par 1/6/2005
Recapitalized as Frontier Energy Corp. 9/28/2005
Each share new Common $0.001 par exchanged for (0.025) share Common $0.001 par

GTE CALIF INC (CA)
8.8% Preferred $100 par called for redemption 08/01/1986
11% Preferred $100 par called for redemption 08/01/1986
8.375% Preferred $100 par called for redemption 01/22/1990
7.48% Preferred $100 par called for redemption 07/04/1997
4.5% Preferred 1945 Ser. $20 par called for redemption at $23.50 on 03/15/2000
4.5% Preferred 1956 Ser. $20 par called for redemption at $22 on 03/15/2000
5% Preferred $20 par called for redemption at $22 on 03/15/2000
Public interest eliminated

GTE CORP (NY)
11.25% Preferred $50 par called for redemption 10/01/1986
Common $3.33333333 par changed to 10¢ par and (0.5) additional share issued 02/12/1987
Conv. Adjustable Rate Preferred no par called for redemption 07/01/1989
Conv. Adj. Rate Preferred Ser. B no par called for redemption 07/01/1989
Common 10¢ par changed to 5¢ par and (1) additional share issued 06/22/1990
$1,000 Auction Preferred Ser. A no par called for redemption 00/00/1992
$1,000 Auction Preferred Ser. B no par called for redemption 00/00/1992
1000 Shs Auction Preferred Ser. C no par called for redemption 00/00/1992
1000 Shs Auction Preferred Ser. D no par called for redemption 00/00/1992
1000 Shs Auction Preferred Ser. E no par called for redemption 00/00/1992
$2.475 Preferred no par called for redemption 04/20/1994
4.4% Preferred $50 par called for redemption 12/11/1995
$2 Conv. Preferred no par called for redemption 12/26/1995
4% Conv. Preferred $50 par called for redemption 12/26/1995
4.36% Conv. Preferred $50 par called for redemption 12/26/1995
4.75% Conv. Preferred $50 par called for redemption 12/26/1995
5% Conv. Preferred $50 par called for redemption 12/26/1995
5.05% Conv. Preferred $50 par called for redemption 12/26/1995
5.28% Conv. Preferred $50 par called for redemption 12/26/1995
5.35% Conv. Preferred $50 par called for redemption 12/26/1995
5.5% Conv. Preferred $50 par called for redemption 12/26/1995
Merged into Verizon Communications Inc. 06/30/2000
Each share Common 5¢ par exchanged for (1.22) shares Common $1 par

GTE DEL L P (DE)
9.25% Guaranteed Monthly Income Preferred Securities A called for redemption at $25 on 10/17/99
8.750% Guaranteed Monthly Income Preferred Securities B called for redemption at $25 on 3/6/2000

GTE FLA INC (FL)
10.85% Preferred $100 par called for redemption 5/27/86
8.16% Preferred $100 par called for redemption at $102.04 on 5/1/97
$1.25 Preferred $25 par called for redemption at $25.50 25 on 3/15/2000
$1.30 Preferred Ser. B $25 par called for redemption at $26.25 30 on 3/15/2000
Public interest eliminated

GTE MTO INC. (WI)
Name changed to GTE North Inc. 1/1/88
(See GTE North Inc.)

GTE NORTH INC (WI)
$7.60 Preferred no par called for redemption at $100.65 on 5/1/97
$1.15 Preferred no par called for redemption at $25.25 on 3/31/98
$1.25 Preferred no par called for redemption at $25.75 on 3/31/98
$2.30 Preferred no par called for redemption at $50.50 on 3/31/98
$2.40 Preferred no par called for redemption at $51.50 on 3/31/98
$2.50 Preferred no par called for redemption at $51.50 on 3/31/98
$2.50 Preferred no par called for redemption at $51 on 3/31/98
$2.50 Preferred Ser. C no par called for redemption at $52.50 on 3/31/98
4.60% Preferred no par called for redemption at $50.50 on 3/31/98
5.16% Preferred no par called for redemption at $52.50 on 3/31/98
$2 Preferred no par called for redemption at $51.50 on 3/15/2000
$2.20 Preferred no par called for redemption at $52.50 on 3/15/2000
$2.375 Preferred no par called for redemption at $52.375 on 3/15/2000
$4.50 Preferred no par called for redemption at $101 on 3/15/2000
$5 Preferred no par called for redemption at $110 on 3/15/2000
$2.10 Preferred no par called for redemption at $56.60 on 3/15/2000
$2.25 Preferred no par called for redemption at $51.50 on 3/15/2000
Public interest eliminated

GTE NORTHWEST INC (WA)
$8.16 Preferred no par called for redemption 8/1/95
Public interest eliminated

GTE SOUTH INC (VA)
5% Preferred $50 par called for redemption at $51.50 on 3/31/98
5.20% Preferred $100 par called for redemption at $110 on 3/15/2000
Public interest eliminated

GTE SOUTHWEST INC (DE)
$9.72 Preferred no par called for redemption 11/1/86
$9.52 Preferred no par called for redemption 12/1/86
$2.20 Preferred no par called for redemption at $51.50 on 3/15/2000
5.10% Preferred $20 par called for redemption at $22 on 3/15/2000

GTECH CORP (DE)
Merged into GTEK Acquisition Corp. 02/01/1990
Each share Common 1¢ par exchanged for $16.625 cash

GTECH HLDGS CORP (DE)
Common 1¢ par split (2) for (1) by issuance of (1) additional share payable 5/23/2002 to holders of record 5/16/2002 Ex date - 5/24/2002
Common 1¢ par split (2) for (1) by issuance of (1) additional share payable 7/30/2004 to holders of record 7/1/2004 Ex date - 8/2/2004
Merged into Lottomatica SPA 8/29/2006
Each share Common 1¢ par exchanged for $35 cash

GTECH INTL RES LTD (YUKON)
Reorganized under the laws of British Columbia as Simavita Ltd. 12/06/2013
Each share Common no par exchanged for (0.33333333) share Common no par

GTECH S P A (ITALY)
Merged into International Game Technology PLC 04/07/2015
Each Sponsored ADR for Ordinary exchanged for (1) share Ordinary USD $0.10 par

GTI CORP (DE)
Reincorporated 05/11/1987
State of incorporation changed from (RI) to (DE) 05/11/1987
Merged into Technitrol, Inc. 11/16/1998
Each share Common 4¢ par exchanged for $3.10 cash

GTM CAP CORP (AB)
Reorganized under the laws of Ontario as Feronia Inc. 09/09/2010
Each share Common no par exchanged for (0.28571428) share Common no par

GTM HLDGS INC (NV)
Old Common $0.001 par split (13) for (1) by issuance of (12) additional shares payable 06/13/2001 to holders of record 06/12/2001 Ex date - 06/14/2001
Each share old Common $0.001 par exchanged for (0.05) share new Common $0.001 par 09/20/2001
Name changed to Asia Premium Television Group, Inc. 09/27/2002
Asia Premium Television Group, Inc. recapitalized as China Grand Resorts, Inc. 11/17/2009

GTO RES INC (BC)
Incorporated 04/26/1984
Recapitalized as Ram Power, Corp. 10/20/2009
Each share Common no par exchanged for (0.1) share Common no par
Ram Power, Corp. recapitalized as Polaris Infrastructure Inc. 05/19/2015

GTO RES INC (BC)
Incorporated 05/10/2011
Name changed to Velocity Data Inc. 08/14/2014

GTP123 INC (NV)
Each share old Common $0.001 par exchanged for (2,000,000) shares new Common $0.001 par to reflect a (1) for (1,000,000) reverse split followed by a (2,000,000,000,000) for (1) forward split 12/20/2007
Note: Holders of (999,999) or fewer pre-split shares were not affected and also received an additional 15% in restricted shares
Name changed to Dream Factory, Inc. 01/25/2008

GTR GROUP INC (CANADA)
Name changed to Mad Catz Interactive, Inc. 09/05/2001

GTRADE NETWORK INC (DE)
Name changed to VS2, Inc. 01/12/2001
VS2, Inc. recapitalized as EuroWork Global, Ltd. 11/08/2004 which name changed to Quintessence Holdings, Inc. 07/25/2007 which name changed to Terminus Energy, Inc. 12/04/2009

GTREX CAP INC (DE)
Name changed 03/07/2005
Name changed from GTREX, Inc. to GTREX Capital, Inc. 03/07/2005
Recapitalized as Green Globe International, Inc. 03/10/2008
Each share Common $0.0001 par exchanged for (0.01) share Common $0.0001 par

GTS CORP (DE)
Reincorporated 8/14/74
Reincorporated from under the laws of (LA) to (DE) as Geoscience Technology Services Corp. and Common no par changed to 1¢ par 8/14/74
Geoscience Technology Services Corp. name changed to GTS Corp. 5/12/81
Stock Dividends - 15% 8/15/83; 30% 3/15/84
Liquidating Plan of Reorganization under Chapter 11 Federal Bankruptcy Code effective 6/28/93
No stockholders' equity

GTS DURATEK INC (NY)
Name changed to Duratek Inc. 1/22/2001
(See Duratek Inc.)

GTSI CORP (DE)
Acquired by UNICOM Systems, Inc. 06/20/2012
Each share Common $0.005 par exchanged for $7.75 cash

G2 RES INC (AB)
Merged into Regal Energy Ltd. 07/10/2008
Each share Class A Common no par exchanged for (0.66666666) share Common no par
Regal Energy Ltd. recapitalized as Novus Energy Inc. 08/05/2009
(See Novus Energy Inc.)

G2 VENTURES INC (TX)
Reincorporated under the laws of Nevada as Joway Health Industries Group Inc. 12/28/2010

GTX GLOBAL CORP (NV)
Recapitalized as Vision Technology Corp. 07/31/2006
Each share Common $0.001 par exchanged for (0.5) share Common $0.001 par
(See Vision Technology Corp.)

GUANGDONG INVT LTD (HONG KONG)
ADR agreement terminated 02/24/2003
Each Sponsored ADR for Ordinary exchanged for $1.79048 cash
(Additional Information in Active)

GUANGNAN HLDGS LTD (HONG KONG)
Each old Sponsored ADR for Ordinary exchanged for (0.1) new Sponsored ADR for Ordinary 05/02/2006
ADR agreement terminated 03/09/2017
Each new Sponsored ADR for Ordinary exchanged for $0.4579 cash

GUANGZHOU BAIYUNSHAN PHARMACEUTICAL HLDGS LTD (CHINA)
ADR agreement terminated 11/28/2017
Each Sponsored ADR for Ordinary exchanged for (20) shares Ordinary
Note: Unexchanged ADR's will be sold and the proceeds, if any, held for claim after 12/03/2018

GUANGZHOU GLOBAL TELECOM INC (FL)
Each share old Common 1¢ par exchanged for (0.1) share new Common 1¢ par 02/16/2012
Name changed to China Teletech Holding, Inc. 03/20/2012

GUANGZHOU INVT LTD (HONG KONG)
Each Sponsored ADR for Ordinary received distribution of $0.01487 cash payable 07/07/2006 to holders of record 06/27/2006 Ex date - 06/23/2006
Name changed to Yuexiu Property Co., Ltd. 10/07/2011
(See Yuexiu Property Co., Ltd.)

GUANGZHOU PHARMACEUTICAL LTD (CHINA)
Name changed to Guangzhou Baiyunshan Pharmaceutical Holdings Co. Ltd. 04/30/2015
(See Guangzhou Baiyunshan Pharmaceutical Holdings Co. Ltd.)

GUANGZHOU SHIPYARD INTL LTD (CHINA)
ADR agreement terminated 05/25/2017
No ADR's remain outstanding

GUANTANAMO & WESTN RR CO (ME)
Charter suspended for non-payment of franchise taxes 12/1/61
Note: Property reported seized by Cuban Government in 1960

GUARANTEE BANCORP INC (NJ)
Merged into First Jersey National Corp. 1/17/84
Each share Common $1 par exchanged for (0.274381) share $2.88 Conv. Preferred Ser. B $1 par or $8.75 cash
(See First Jersey National Corp.)

GUARANTEE BANK & TRUST CO. (ATLANTIC CITY, NJ)
Capital Stock $100 par changed to $1 par in 1946
Stock Dividends - 10% 5/1/59; 10% 5/1/61; 10% 5/2/66; 10% 5/1/67; 10% 5/1/68; 10% 1/17/69; 10% 1/16/70; 10% 1/15/71
Name changed to Guarantee Bank (Atlantic City, NJ) 5/11/71
Guarantee Bank (Atlantic City, NJ) reorganized as Guarantee Bancorp Inc. 1/2/81 which merged into First Jersey National Corp. 1/17/84
(See First Jersey National Corp.)

GUARANTEE BK (ATLANTIC CITY, NJ)
Stock Dividends - 10% 1/14/74; 10% 1/13/75; 10% 1/9/78; 10% 1/30/79; 10% 1/7/80
Reorganized as Guarantee Bancorp Inc. 1/2/81
Each share Capital Stock $1 par exchanged for (1) share Common $1 par
Guarantee Bancorp Inc. merged into First Jersey National Corp. 1/17/84
(See First Jersey National Corp.)

GUARANTEE FINL CORP CALIF (CA)
Capital Stock $2 par split (5) for (4) by issuance of (0.25) additional share 7/27/79
Capital Stock $2 par changed to no par and (1) additional share issued 6/3/83
Merged into GLENFED, Inc. 10/31/87
Each share Capital Stock no par exchanged for (1.1828) shares Common 1¢ par
GLENFED, Inc. merged into Glendale Federal Bank, FSB (Glendale, CA) 8/26/93 which reorganized in Delaware as Golden State Bancorp Inc. 7/24/97
(See Golden State Bancorp Inc.)

GUARANTEE LIFE COS INC (DE)
Merged into Jefferson-Pilot Corp. 12/31/99
Each share Common 1¢ par exchanged for $32 cash

GUARANTEE RESERVE LIFE INSURANCE CO. (CO)
Declared insolvent by the State of

Colorado Insurance Department 12/31/57
No stockholders' equity

GUARANTEE TR & SAFE DEP CO (SHAMOKIN, PA)
Merged into Northern Central Bank (Williamsport, PA) 9/30/77
Each share Common $20 par exchanged for (7.5) shares Common $5 par
Northern Central Bank (Williamsport, PA) merged into NCB Financial Corp. 7/29/83 which merged into Keystone Financial, Inc. 12/31/84 which merged into M&T Bank Corp. 10/6/2000

GUARANTEED MORTGAGE CO. OF NEW YORK
Taken over for liquidation by New York State Superintendent of Insurance in 1934
Details not available

GUARANTEED TITLE CO. (NY)
Merged into American Title Insurance Co. 6/5/63
Each share Common $4 par exchanged for $7.33 cash

GUARANTEED TUNE UP INC (DE)
Recapitalized as Advanced Orbital Services, Inc. 10/1/2001
Each (15) shares Common $0.001 par exchanged for (1) share Common $0.001 par
Advanced Orbital Services, Inc. name changed to Sea Star Group Inc. 12/18/2006

GUARANTY BANCSHARES CORP (PA)
Under plan of reorganization each share Common no par exchanged for $8.75 cash 12/29/97

GUARANTY BANCSHARES HLDG CORP (LA)
Merged into MC Bancshares Inc. 11/30/97
Each share $2.70 Preferred exchanged for $27.60 cash
Each share Common exchanged for $1.183 cash
Each share Class B exchanged for $1.183 cash

GUARANTY BANCSHARES INC (LA)
Merged into Louisiana Bancshares, Inc. 7/31/85
Each share Common $1 par exchanged for (0.50505) share Common no par
Louisiana Bancshares, Inc. name changed to Premier Bancorp, Inc. 4/15/87 which merged into Banc One Corp. 1/2/96 which merged into Bank One Corp. 10/2/98 which merged into J.P. Morgan Chase & Co. 12/31/2000 which name changed to JPMorgan Chase & Co. 7/20/2004

GUARANTY BANK & TRUST CO. (GREENVILLE, NC)
Each share Common $100 par exchanged for (10) shares Common $10 par 01/16/1951
Stock Dividends - 25% 11/30/1945; 10% 01/17/1951; 16.66666666% 01/00/1954; (1) for (7) 01/00/1955; 12.5% 01/05/1956
Merged into Wachovia Bank & Trust Co. (Winston-Salem, NC) 00/00/1960
Details not available

GUARANTY BK & TR CO (ALEXANDRIA, LA)
Common $10 par changed to $5 par and (1) additional share issued 01/11/1966
Common $5 par changed to $2.50 par and (1) additional share issued plus a 50% stock dividend paid 03/08/1971
Reorganized as Guaranty Commerce Corp. 06/07/1982

Each share Common $2.50 par exchanged for (1) share Common $10 par
(See Guaranty Commerce Corp.)

GUARANTY BK & TR CO (CEDAR RAPIDS, IA)
Under plan of reorganization each share Common $5 par automatically became (1) share Guaranty Bankshares, Ltd. Common no par 12/22/1983
(See Guaranty Bankshares, Ltd.)

GUARANTY BK & TR CO (CHICAGO, IL)
Declared insolvent and receiver appointed 7/14/79
No stockholders' equity

GUARANTY BK & TR CO (FAIRFAX, VA)
Common $5 par changed to $2.50 par and (1) additional share issued 5/23/74
Stock Dividends - 10% 2/27/70; 10% 2/11/71; 10% 2/10/72; 10% 3/1/73; 10% 3/8/74; 10% 3/28/75; 10% 3/20/76; 10% 5/6/77; 10% 5/5/78; 10% 5/6/80; 10% 5/8/81; 10% 5/7/82; 10% 5/6/83; 10% 5/4/84
Acquired by Riggs National Corp. 12/8/86
Each share Common $2.50 par exchanged for $31.50 cash

GUARANTY BK & TR CO (HARTFORD, CT)
Acquired by Connecticut BancFederation, Inc. 12/28/73
Each share Common $10 par exchanged for (2.1212) shares Common $10 par
(See Connecticut BancFederation, Inc.)

GUARANTY BK & TR CO (LAFAYETTE, LA)
Capital Stock $10 par changed to $5 par and (1) additional share issued plus a 20% stock dividend paid 3/9/77
Reorganized as Guaranty Bancshares, Inc. 8/1/82
Each share Capital Stock $5 par exchanged for (5) shares Common $1 par
Guaranty Bancshares, Inc. merged into Louisiana Bancshares, Inc. 7/31/85 which name changed to Premier Bancorp, Inc. 4/15/87 which merged into Banc One Corp. 1/2/96 which merged into Bank One Corp. 10/2/98 which merged into J.P. Morgan Chase & Co. 12/31/2000 which name changed to JPMorgan Chase & Co. 7/20/2004

GUARANTY BK & TR CO (VENICE, FL)
Merged into F.N.B. Corp. 01/12/1999
Each share Common $8 par exchanged for $43 cash

GUARANTY BK & TR CO (WORCESTER, MA)
Acquired by Conifer Group Inc. (Old) 09/29/1973
Each share Capital Stock $10 par exchanged for (1.1) shares Common $1 par
Conifer Group Inc. (Old) merged into Conifer/Essex Group, Inc. 02/17/1983 which name changed back to Conifer Group Inc. (New) 01/01/1985 which merged into Bank of New England Corp. 04/22/1987
(See Bank of New England Corp.)

GUARANTY BK (MILWAUKEE, WI)
Name changed 06/00/2002
Name changed from Guaranty Bank S.S.B (Milwaukee, WI) to Guaranty Bank (Milwaukee, WI) 06/00/2002
Under plan of reorganization each share Common $10 par automatically became (1) share

Guaranty Financial Corp. Common $10 par 08/08/2003

GUARANTY BK (PHOENIX, AZ)
Each share Common $10 par exchanged for (2) shares Common $5 par 4/6/62
Under plan of merger name changed to United Bank of Arizona (Phoenix, AZ) 12/31/67
United Bank of Arizona (Phoenix, AZ) reorganized as UB Financial Corp. 4/30/70 which name changed to United Bancorp of Arizona 10/17/78
(See United Bancorp of Arizona)

GUARANTY BK SOUTHWEST (VENICE, FL)
Merged into F.N.B. Corp. (PA) 1/12/99
Each share Common $2 par exchanged for (1.536) shares Common $2 par
F.N.B. Corp. (PA) reincorporated in Florida 6/13/2001

GUARANTY BANKSHARES, LTD. (IA)
Merged into QCR Holdings, Inc. 10/02/2017
Details not available

GUARANTY BD & FIN CO (LA)
Reorganized as Guaranty Corp. 10/31/69
Each share Preferred $10 par exchanged for $15 principal amount of 8% Conv. Subord. Debentures due 1/1/89
Each share Class B Common $1 par exchanged for $1.50 principal amount of 8% Conv. Subord. Debentures due 1/1/89
Each share Class A Common no par exchanged for (1) share Class A Common no par

GUARANTY CO. OF NEW JERSEY
Liquidation completed in 1954
Details not available

GUARANTY COMM CORP (LA)
Common $10 par split (2) for (1) by issuance of (1) additional share 6/8/83
Common $10 par split (3) for (2) by issuance of (0.5) additional share 5/1/84
Merged into Hibernia Corp. 8/1/85
Each share Common $10 par exchanged for $25.78254 cash

GUARANTY FED SVGS BK (CLARKSVILLE, TN)
Merged into Peoples First Corp. 8/30/96
Each share Common no par exchanged for (2.6316) shares Common no par
Peoples First Corp. merged into Union Planters Corp. 7/1/98 which merged into Regions Financial Corp. (New) 7/1/2004

GUARANTY FED SVGS BK (SPRINGFIELD, MO)
Reorganized as Guaranty Federal Bancshares Inc. 12/31/97
Each share Common $1 par exchanged for (1.931) shares Common 10¢ par

GUARANTY FINANCE CO., INC. (IN)
Charter revoked for failure to file reports and pay fees 12/5/46

GUARANTY FINL CORP (AR)
Recapitalized as Keymaster Corp. 12/29/69
Each share 8% Non-Cum. Preferred $5 par exchanged for (1) share 8% Non-Cum. Preferred $5 par
Each share Common $1 par exchanged for (1) share Common $1 par
Keymaster Corp. merged into Solomon, Inc. 3/8/73
(See Solomon, Inc.)

GUARANTY FINL CORP (VA)
Common $2.50 par split (2) for (1) by issuance of (1) additional share

payable 01/31/1996 to holders of record 01/15/1996
Merged into Union Bankshares Corp. 05/01/2004
Each share Common $2.50 par exchanged for (0.1684) share Common $2 par and $22.40 cash
Union Bankshares Corp. name changed to Union First Market Bankshares Corp. 02/01/2010 which name changed to Union Bankshares Corp. 04/28/2014

GUARANTY FINL GROUP INC (DE)
Plan of reorganization under Chapter 11 bankruptcy proceedings effective 05/13/2011
No stockholders' equity

GUARANTY FIRE INSURANCE CO.
Merged into Merchants Insurance Co. of Providence in 1932
Details not available

GUARANTY FIRST MORTGAGE CO. (TX)
Charter revoked for failure to file reports and pay fees 6/20/66

GUARANTY FIRST NATL BK (FORT LAUDERDALE, FL)
98.75% acquired by Landmark Banking Corp. of Florida 07/16/1973
Public interest eliminated
qualifying shares - See Our Card

GUARANTY FIRST TR CO (WALTHAM, MA)
Reorganized as New England Bancorp, Inc. 11/1/73
Each share Common $4 par exchanged for (1) share Common $1 par
(See New England Bancorp, Inc.)

GUARANTY FOUNDERS TRUST
Liquidated in 1930
Details not available

GUARANTY INCOME LIFE INS CO (LA)
Capital Stock $10 par changed to $1 par in 1956
Merged into Guaranty Corp. 11/3/78
Each (3.5) shares Capital Stock $1 par exchanged for (1) share Class A Common no par

GUARANTY INS TR (SC)
Completely liquidated 12/28/67
Each share Common $1 par exchanged for first and final distribution of (0.07) share Mortgage Guaranty Insurance Corp. Common $1 par
(See Mortgage Guaranty Insurance Corp.)

GUARANTY LIFE INSURANCE CO. OF AMERICA (DC)
Acquired by Chesapeake Life Insurance Co. 7/6/64
Each share Class A Common $1.80 par or Class B Common 20¢ par exchanged for (0.4) share Class A $1 par
Chesapeake Life Insurance Co. (MD) recapitalized under the laws of Oklahoma 9/27/93
(See Chesapeake Life Insurance Co.)

GUARANTY LIFE INSURANCE CO. OF NEW YORK
Liquidated in 1935
Details not available

GUARANTY LIFE INS CO FLA (FL)
Over 93% Non-Vtg. Common $1 par and over 99% Vtg. Common $1 par acquired by Security Life Insurance Co. as of 08/04/1981
Public interest eliminated

GUARANTY NATIONAL BANK & TRUST (CORPUS CHRISTI, TX)
Merged into Texas Commerce Bancshares, Inc. 07/26/1974
Each share Capital Stock $10 par exchanged for (2.04591) shares Common $4 par
Texas Commerce Bancshares, Inc.

acquired by Chemical New York Corp. 05/01/1987 which name changed to Chemical Banking Corp. 04/29/1988 which name changed to Chase Manhattan Corp. (New) 03/31/1996 which name changed to J.P. Morgan Chase & Co. 12/31/2000 which name changed to JPMorgan Chase & Co. 07/20/2004

GUARANTY NATL BK (FORT LAUDERDALE, FL)
Name changed to Guaranty First National Bank (Fort Lauderdale, FL) 07/06/1970
(See Guaranty First National Bank (Fort Lauderdale, FL))

GUARANTY NATL BK (HUNTINGTON, WV)
Reorganized as GuarantyShares of West Virginia, Inc. 08/31/1984
Each share Capital Stock $6.25 par exchanged for (5) shares Common $1.25 par
GuarantyShares of West Virginia, Inc. acquired by National Banc of Commerce Co. 02/15/1989 which name changed to Commerce Banc Corp. 04/21/1992 which merged into Huntington Bancshares Inc. 09/24/1993

GUARANTY NATL CORP NEW (CO)
Merged into Orion Capital Corp. 12/16/97
Each share Common $1 par exchanged for $36 cash

GUARANTY NATL CORP OLD (CO)
Common $1 par split (3) for (2) by issuance of (0.5) additional share 5/31/78
Common $1 par split (4) for (3) by issuance of (1/3) additional share 8/24/79
Common $1 par split (4) for (3) by issuance of (1/3) additional share 8/22/80
Common $1 par split (4) for (3) by issuance of (1/3) additional share 8/28/81
Stock Dividends - 30% 12/3/76; 50% 5/31/77
Merged into Orion Capital Corp. 11/1/88
Each share Common $1 par exchanged for $8.75 cash

GUARANTY NATIONAL INSURANCE CO. (CO)
Name changed to Guaranty National Corp. (Old) and Common 50¢ par changed to $1 par 3/20/73
(See Guaranty National Corp. (Old))

GUARANTY NATIONAL TRUST (IN)
In process of liquidation
Each Share of Bene. Int. no par exchanged for initial distribution of $1.04 cash 1/18/79
Note: Details on subsequent distributions, if any, are not available

GUARANTY SVGS & LN ASSN INC (NC)
Each share old Common $1 par exchanged for (0.00025) share new Common $1 par 2/27/85
Note: In effect holders received $16.20 cash per share and public interest was eliminated

GUARANTY SVGS & LN F A (VA)
Name changed to Guaranty Financial Corp. 01/15/1996
Guaranty Financial Corp. merged into Union Bankshares Corp. 05/01/2004 which name changed to Union First Market Bankshares Corp. 02/01/2010 which name changed to Union Bankshares Corp. 04/28/2014

GUARANTY SVGS LIFE INS CO (AL)
Completely liquidated 5/8/69
Each share Common $1 par received first and final distribution of (0.9) share United Security Life Co. Common 25¢ par

Note: Certificates were not required to be surrendered and are without value

GUARANTY SEC INS CO (MN)
Under plan of merger 12/31/62 holders had option to exchange each share Capital Stock $5 par for (5.5) shares old Common $1 par or for (2) shares $1 Preferred $1 par and (1.5) shares old Common $1 par or for (1) share $1 Preferred $1 par and (3.5) shares old Common $1 par
After 12/28/62 options expired and each share Capital Stock $5 par can only be exchanged for (5.5) shares old Common $1 par
Each share old Common $1 par exchanged for (0.5) share new Common $1 par 1/26/68
Merged into Diversified Insurers Co. 1/29/68
Each share new Common $1 par exchanged for (0.11) share Common $1 par
(See Diversified Insurers Co.)

GUARANTY SILK CORP.
Acquired by Duplan Silk Corp. in 1928
Details not available

GUARANTY ST BANCORP (NC)
Merged into Triangle Bancorp Inc. 4/16/98
Each share Common $1 par exchanged for (1.41) shares Common no par
Triangle Bancorp Inc. merged into Centura Banks, Inc. 2/18/2000 which merged into Royal Bank of Canada (Montreal, QC) 6/5/2001

GUARANTY ST BK (DURHAM, NC)
Under plan of reorganization each share Common $5 par automatically became (1) share Guaranty State Bancorp Common $1 par 9/20/93
Guaranty State Bancorp merged into Triangle Bancorp Inc. 4/16/98 which merged into Centura Banks, Inc. 2/18/2000 which merged into Royal Bank of Canada (Montreal, QC) 6/5/2001

GUARANTY TRUST CO. (NEW YORK, NY)
Each share Capital Stock $100 par exchanged for (5) shares Capital Stock $20 par 1/21/53
Stock Dividends - 11-1/9% 2/15/47; 20% 2/21/57
Merged into Morgan Guaranty Trust Co. (New York, NY) 4/24/59
Each share Capital Stock $20 par exchanged for (1) share Capital Stock $25 par
Morgan Guaranty Trust Co. (New York, NY) reorganized as Morgan (J.P.) & Co. Inc. (DE) 4/1/66 which merged into J.P. Morgan Chase & Co. 12/31/2000 which name changed to JPMorgan Chase & Co. 7/20/2004

GUARANTY TR CO (WALTHAM, MA)
Under plan of merger name changed to Guaranty-First Trust Co. (Waltham, MA) 1/1/73
Guaranty-First Trust Co. (Waltham, MA) reorganized as New England Bancorp, Inc. 11/1/73
(See New England Bancorp, Inc.)

GUARANTY TRUSTCO LTD (ON)
Name changed to Central Guaranty Trustco Ltd. 05/10/1988
(See Central Guaranty Trustco Ltd.)

GUARANTY UNION CORP. (AZ)
Charter revoked for failure to file reports and pay fees 9/5/74

GUARANTYSHARES W VA INC (WV)
Acquired by National Banc of Commerce Co. 02/15/1989
Each share Common $1.25 par

exchanged for (2.05) shares Common $1 par and $2 cash
National Banc of Commerce Co. name changed to Commerce Banc Corp. 04/21/1992 which merged into Huntington Bancshares Inc. 09/24/1993

GUARD CORP (IN)
Administratively dissolved 12/31/1987

GUARD INC (ON)
Cease trade order effective 05/23/2002
Stockholders' equity unlikely

GUARDCOR INVTS INC (QC)
Merged into Guardian Trustco Inc. 06/28/1991
Each share Common no par exchanged for $10 cash

GUARDIAN ANGEL GROUP INC (NV)
Recapitalized as Ree International, Inc. 06/29/2011
Each share Common $0.001 par exchanged for (0.002) share Common $0.001 par

GUARDIAN BANCORP LOS ANGELES CALIF (CA)
Common no par split (5) for (4) by issuance of (0.25) additional share 7/29/88
Common no par split (3) for (2) by issuance of (0.5) additional share 5/24/89
Common no par split (5) for (4) by issuance of (0.25) additional share 12/24/90
Taken over by the FDIC 1/20/95
Stockholders' equity undetermined

GUARDIAN BANCORP LTD (AB)
Issue Information - 1,000,000 shares COM offered at $0.20 per share on 04/07/1997
Acquired by Infiniti Resources International Ltd. 10/16/2000
Each share Common no par exchanged for (0.75) share Common no par
Infiniti Resources International Ltd. acquired by Welton Energy Corp. (New) 08/04/2005 which merged into Churchill Energy Inc. 02/13/2009 which merged into Zargon Energy Trust 09/23/2009 which reorganized as Zargon Oil & Gas Ltd. (New) 01/07/2011

GUARDIAN BANK (LOS ANGELES, CA)
Merged into Manufacturers Bank (Los Angeles, CA) 7/2/65
Each share Common $10 par or VTC therefor exchanged for (0.375) share Capital Stock $3.75 par
(See Manufacturers Bank (Los Angeles, CA))

GUARDIAN BK N A (HEMPSTEAD, NY)
Placed in receivership and FDIC appointed receiver 06/21/1989
No stockholders' equity

GUARDIAN CDN FD (ON)
Under plan of reorganization each Mutual Fund Share no par automatically became (1) Guardian Group of Funds Ltd. Growth Equity Fund Class B no par in December 1994

GUARDIAN CARE CORP. (KY)
Name changed to Excepticon, Inc. 08/31/1971
Excepticon, Inc. merged into Forum Group, Inc. 09/08/1981
(See Forum Group, Inc.)

GUARDIAN CARE INC (VA)
Reincorporated under the laws of North Carolina as Guardian Corp. 03/03/1972
(See Guardian Corp.)

GUARDIAN CASUALTY CO. (NY)
Taken over and liquidated by

Insurance Department of New York in 1933
Details not available

GUARDIAN CENTRAL TRUST, INC. (TN)
Name changed to Memphis Trust Co. 10/24/68
(See Memphis Trust Co.)

GUARDIAN CHEM CORP (DE)
Merged into United-Guardian, Inc. 2/16/82
Each share Common 10¢ par exchanged for (0.58) share Common 10¢ par

GUARDIAN COAL & OIL CO. (WV)
Name changed to Guardian Coal Co. 11/25/38
(See Guardian Coal Co.)

GUARDIAN COAL CO. (WV)
Proclaimed dissolved for non-payment of taxes 5/13/40

GUARDIAN COML CORP (DE)
Each share Class A Common $10 par exchanged for (5) shares Class A Common $1 par 4/20/66
Acquired by First Jersey National Corp. 6/30/70
Each share 6% Preferred $10 exchanged for $10 principal amount of 6% Subord. Debentures due 5/1/80
Each share Class A Common $1 par exchanged for $3.50 principal amount 7% Subord. Notes due 5/1/72

GUARDIAN COMMUNICATIONS INDS INC (BC)
Name changed to Guardian Enterprises Ltd. 02/11/1994
Guardian Enterprises Ltd. recapitalized as Interactive Enterprises Inc. 12/07/1999 which name changed to Interactive Exploration Inc. 02/16/2004 which name changed to Anglo-Canadian Uranium Corp. 08/22/2005 which name changed to Anglo-Canadian Mining Corp. 08/29/2011 which name changed to Canada One Mining Corp. 08/30/2017

GUARDIAN CONSULTANTS & MGMT INC (NV)
Charter revoked for failure to file reports and pay fees 3/6/72

GUARDIAN CONSUMER FINANCE CORP. (DE)
Merged into Liberty Loan Corp. 4/4/60
Each share 60¢ Preferred $10 par exchanged for (0.4) share 5-3/4% Preference 1960 Ser. $25 par
Each share Class A Common $1 par exchanged for (0.27) share 5-3/4% Preference 1960 Series $25 par
Liberty Loan Corp. name changed to LLC Corp. 3/14/80 which name changed to Valhi, Inc. 3/10/87

GUARDIAN CORP (NC)
Common 10¢ par changed to no par 03/01/1973
Stock Dividend - 15% 12/21/1973
Majority shares acquired by Hillhaven Corp. (NV) through purchase offer which expired 11/30/1981
Public interest eliminated

GUARDIAN DEPOSITORS CORP.
Liquidation completed in 1944
Details not available

GUARDIAN DEV CORP (NY)
Merged into GDC Merging Corp. 6/7/85
Each share Common 25¢ par exchanged for $1 cash

GUARDIAN DEV INC (WA)
Name changed to Churchill Companies, Inc. 8/28/90

GUARDIAN DIVERSIFIED FUND (ON)
Under plan of reorganization each Mutual Fund Unit automatically

became (1) share Guardian Group of Funds Ltd. International Balanced Fund Class B no par 9/14/93

GUARDIAN ENTERPRISE FD CDA (ON)
Recapitalized as Guardian Enterprise Fund in 1988
Each Mutual Fund Share no par exchanged for (0.1) Mutual Fund Share no par

GUARDIAN ENTERPRISES LTD (BC)
Recapitalized as Interactive Enterprises Inc. 12/07/1999
Each share Common no par exchanged for (0.2) share Common no par
Interactive Enterprises Inc. name changed to Interactive Exploration Inc. 02/17/2004 which name changed to Anglo-Canadian Uranium Corp. 08/22/2005 which name changed to Anglo-Canadian Mining Corp. 08/29/2011 which name changed to Canada One Mining Corp. 08/30/2017

GUARDIAN EQUITY FD (ON)
Name changed to Guardian World Equity Fund 11/1/73
Guardian World Equity Fund reorganized as Guardian Group of Funds Ltd. Global Equity Fund in June 1988

GUARDIAN EXPLORATIONS LTD. (ON)
Charter cancelled and declared dissolved by default 08/09/1972

GUARDIAN FIRE ASSURANCE CORP. OF NEW YORK
Merged into American Equitable Assurance Co. of New York in 1931
Details not available

GUARDIAN GROSS PROT SYS INC (RI)
Name changed to Colbert's Security Services Inc. 01/23/1973
(See Colbert's Security Services Inc.)

GUARDIAN GROWTH FD LTD (ON)
Preference 20¢ par reclassified as Mutual Fund Shares 04/26/1984
Common 20¢ par reclassified as Mutual Fund Shares 04/26/1984
Under plan of reorganization each Mutual Fund Share 20¢ par automatically became (1) share Guardian Group of Funds Ltd. American Equity Fund 06/00/1998

GUARDIAN HLDGS INC (OH)
Merged into Meridian Reserve, Inc. 12/20/1985
Each share Common no par exchanged for (6) shares Common 1¢ par
(See Meridian Reserve, Inc.)

GUARDIAN INDS CORP (DE)
Common $1 par split (3) for (1) by issuance of (2) additional shares 06/16/1972
Common $1 par split (3) for (2) by issuance of (0.5) additional share 07/25/1979
Common $1 par split (3) for (2) by issuance of (0.5) additional share 07/15/1981
Common $1 par split (3) for (2) by issuance of (0.5) additional share 07/14/1983
Stock Dividends - 50% 07/15/1969; 25% 08/01/1977
Merged into GDC Transition Co. 02/22/1985
Each share Common $1 par exchanged for $24 cash

GUARDIAN INS & FINL SVCS INC (NV)
Name changed to Genesis Insurance & Financial Services, Inc. 6/7/96
(See Genesis Insurance & Financial Services, Inc.)

GUARDIAN INTL INC (NV)
Merged into Devcon International Corp. 03/06/2006
Each share Common $0.001 par exchanged for $2.6196 cash
Note: Each share Common $0.001 par received an initial distribution of $0.1674548 cash from escrow 07/18/2006
Each share Common $0.001 par received second and final distribution of $0.03438 cash from escrow 10/03/2007

GUARDIAN INVESTMENT TRUST
Liquidation completed 8/11/55
Details not available

GUARDIAN INVESTORS CORP.
Reorganized 7/30/42
No stockholders' equity

GUARDIAN MINES LTD (QC)
Recapitalized as Green Coast Resources Ltd. 07/20/1971
Each share Common no par exchanged for (0.1) share Common no par
Green Coast Resources Ltd. recapitalized as Ridgepoint Resources Ltd. 06/15/1988 which recapitalized as Ridgepoint Mineral Corp. 10/31/1997 which name changed to Jet Drill Canada Inc. 09/15/2000
(See Jet Drill Canada Inc.)

GUARDIAN MTG INVS (MA)
Reorganized under the laws of Florida as Florida Cos. 2/18/81
Each Share of Bene. Int. no par exchanged for (1) share Common 1¢ par
Florida Cos. merged into Fairfield Communities, Inc. 12/6/83
(See Fairfield Communities, Inc.)

GUARDIAN MORTON SHULMAN PRECIOUS METALS INC (BC)
Name changed to FCMI Precious Metals Fund Inc. and Participating Partially Voting Special Share 1¢ par reclassified as Class A Mutual Fund Share 1¢ par 06/04/1990
(See FCMI Precious Metals Fund Inc.)

GUARDIAN NORTH AMERN FD (ON)
Reincorporated in 1973
Place of incorporation changed from (BC) to (ONT) in 1973
Under plan of reorganization each Mutual Fund Share no par automatically became (1) Guardian Group of Funds Ltd. American Equity Fund no par in July 1994

GUARDIAN OIL CO., INC. (DE)
Merged into Consolidated Rimrock Oil Corp. on a (0.875) for (1) basis 10/01/1956
Consolidated Rimrock Oil Corp. merged into Consolidated Oil & Gas, Inc. (CO) 04/30/1958 which was acquired by Hugoton Energy Corp. 09/07/1995 which merged into Chesapeake Energy Corp. 03/10/1998

GUARDIAN PACKAGING CORP (CA)
Common 50¢ par changed to 34¢ par and (0.5) additional share issued 5/1/73
Common 34¢ par split (4) for (3) by issuance of (1/3) additional share 3/1/77
Common 34¢ par changed to 26¢ par and (1/3) additional share issued 10/15/85
Common 26¢ par split (3) for (2) by issuance of (0.5) additional share 6/1/87
Merged into Triangle Industries, Inc. 2/29/88
Each share Common 26¢ par exchanged for $31.50 cash

GUARDIAN PAPER CO. (CA)
Common $1 par changed to 50¢ par and (1) additional share issued 3/24/62
Stock Dividend - 100% 9/1/59
Name changed to Guardian Packaging Corp. 4/2/63
(See Guardian Packaging Corp.)

GUARDIAN PK AVE FD INC (DE)
Under plan of reorganization each share Common $1 par automatically became (1) Park Avenue Portfolio Guardian Park Avenue Fund Class A share 2/15/93

GUARDIAN PUBLIC UTILITIES INVESTMENT TRUST (CT)
Liquidated in 1954
Details not available

GUARDIAN REALTY CO. OF CANADA LTD. (ON)
Liquidation completed 12/5/56
Details not available

GUARDIAN RES CORP (BC)
Name changed to Guardian Communication Industries Inc. 04/08/1991
Guardian Communication Industries Inc. name changed to Guardian Enterprises Inc. 02/11/1994 which recapitalized as Interactive Enterprises Inc. 12/07/1999 which name changed to Interactive Exploration Inc. 02/16/2004 which name changed to Anglo-Canadian Uranium Corp. 08/22/2005 which name changed to Anglo-Canadian Mining Corp. 08/29/2011 Corp. 08/30/2017

GUARDIAN SAFE DEPOSIT CO. (NY)
Dissolved in 1951
Details not available

GUARDIAN SECURITIES, LTD. (IA)
Completely liquidated 11/20/67
Each share Common Capital Stock $7.50 par exchanged for first and final distribution of shares of Security State Trust & Savings Bank (Bettendorf, IA) Common $20 par and shares of Steel Valley, Inc. Common Capital Stock no par
(See each company's listing)

GUARDIAN SHORT TERM MONEY FD (ON)
Reincorporated in 1973
Name changed 7/3/81
Place of incorporation changed from (BC) to (ONT) in 1973
Name changed from Guardian Security Income Fund to Guardian Short Term Money Fund 7/3/81
Under plan of reorganization each Unit no par automatically became (1) Guardian Group of Funds Ltd. Canadian Money Market Fund no par in September 1993

GUARDIAN TECHNOLOGIES INTL INC (DE)
Each share old Common $0.001 par exchanged for (1/3) share new Common $0.001 par 05/23/1997
New Common $0.001 par split (2) for (1) by issuance of (1) additional share payable 04/01/2000 to holders of record 03/15/2000
Each share new Common $0.001 par exchanged again for (0.2) share new Common $0.001 par 07/05/2002
Name changed to Applied Visual Sciences, Inc. 07/16/2010

GUARDIAN TILDEN CORP. (DE)
Name changed to Guardian Commercial Corp. 5/27/65
(See Guardian Commercial Corp.)

GUARDIAN TRUSTCO INC (QC)
Common no par split (3) for (1) by issuance of (2) additional shares 09/09/1987
Liquidated by Court Order 05/26/1992
No stockholders' equity

GUARDIAN VANTAGE BALANCED FUND (ON)
Name changed to Guardian Diversified Fund 1/1/91
Guardian Diversified Fund reorganized as Guardian Group of Funds Ltd. International Balanced Fund Class B 9/14/93

GUARDIAN WORLD EQUITY FD (ON)
Under plan of reorganization each Mutual Fund Share automatically became (1) share Guardian Group of Funds Ltd. Global Equity Fund no par in June 1988

GUARDSMAN CHEMICAL COATINGS, INC. (DE)
Name changed to Guardsman Chemicals, Inc. 06/01/1975
Guardsman Chemicals, Inc. name changed to Guardsman Products, Inc. 05/14/1987
(See Guardsman Products, Inc.)

GUARDSMAN CHEMS INC (DE)
Common $1 par split (5) for (4) by issuance of (0.25) additional share 12/20/1983
Common $1 par split (5) for (4) by issuance of (0.25) additional share 12/16/1986
Stock Dividends - 10% 09/28/1976; 10% 03/29/1979; 10% 03/25/1980; 10% 09/22/1981; 10% 12/18/1984; 10% 12/17/1985
Name changed to Guardsman Products, Inc. 05/14/1987
(See Guardsman Products, Inc.)

GUARDSMAN INS INVS INC (IA)
Liquidation completed
Each share Common no par exchanged for initial distribution of $4.40 cash 1/23/76
Each share Common no par received second and final distribution of $0.59112 cash 9/10/76

GUARDSMAN LEASE PLAN INC (NY)
Merged into MLP Capital Corp. 1/30/79
Each share Common 1¢ par exchanged for $18.60 cash

GUARDSMAN PRODS INC (DE)
Common $1 par split (5) for (4) by issuance of (0.25) additional share 12/22/1989
Stock Dividend - 10% 12/21/1988
Merged into Lilly Industries, Inc. 04/08/1996
Each share Common $1 par exchanged for $23 cash

GUARDSMARK INC (TN)
Reorganized under the laws of Delaware as Guardsmark, Inc. 3/6/79
Each share Class A Common 1¢ par exchanged for $5 principal amount of 11.25% Subord. Debentures due 3/1/94

GUARNACCIO GOLD MINES LTD. (ON)
Name changed to Kent Mines Ltd. 01/20/1955
(See Kent Mines Ltd.)

GUATE TOURISM INC (NV)
Name changed to Agro Capital Management Corp. 12/11/2015

GUAYACO CORP (PR)
Adjudicated a bankrupt 05/17/1963
No stockholders' equity

GUAYAQUIL & QUITO RAILWAY CO. (DE)
No longer in existence having become inoperative and void for non-payment of taxes 4/1/60

GUAYAQUIL & QUITO RAILWAY CO. (NJ)
Merged into Guayaquil & Quito Railway Co. (DE) on a share for share basis in 1940

GUB-GUI

GUBER-PETERS ENTMT CO (DE)
Merged into Sony USA Inc. 11/9/89
Each share Common 50¢ par exchanged for $17.50 cash

GUCCI GROUP N V (NETHERLANDS)
Acquired by Pinault-Printemps-Redoute S.A. 05/04/2004
Each share Common EUR 1.02 par exchanged for $85.52 cash
Note: Minority shares received $179.43609 cash per share through squeeze-out proceedings 07/10/2012

GUENTHER (RUDOLPH)-RUSSELL LAW, INC.
Merged into Frank (Albert)-Guenther Law, Inc. of 1932
Details not available

GUENTHER SYS INC (NY)
Dissolved by proclamation 12/24/1991

GUERDON INDS INC (DE)
Class A Common no par reclassified as Common no par 6/19/62
Merged into City Investing Co. 9/29/72
Each share Common no par exchanged for $30 principal amount of 8-1/8% Subord. Debenture due 7/15/91

GUERIN MILLS, INC. (RI)
Liquidated in 1954
Details not available

GUERNSEY BK A FED SAVING BK (CAMBRIDGE, OH)
Each (15,000) shares old Common exchanged for (1) share new Common 6/12/97
Note: In effect holders received $54.04 cash per share and public interest was eliminated

GUESS CAP CORP (AB)
Name changed to Helix Hearing Care of America Corp. 05/16/1997
(See Helix Hearing Care of America Corp.)

GUEST KEEN & NETTLEFOLDS PLC (UNITED KINGDOM)
Name changed to GKN PLC 06/02/1986
(See GKN PLC)

GUEST SUPPLY INC (NJ)
Common no par split (3) for (2) by issuance of (0.5) additional share 10/24/95
Merged into Sysco Corp. 3/15/2001
Each share Common no par exchanged for (0.9564) share Common $1 par

GUEST-TEK INTERACTIVE ENTMT LTD (AB)
Acquired by 1456537 Alberta Inc. 12/02/2009
Each share Common no par exchanged for $0.50 cash

GUESTLOGIX INC (ON)
Plan of arrangement under Companies Creditors Arrangement Act effective 09/21/2016
No stockholders' equity

GUESTMETRICS INC (FL)
Each share Common $0.001 par received distribution of (2/3) share Shot Spirits Corp. Common $0.001 par payable 02/15/2010 to holders of record 01/15/2010
Name changed to Cloud Centric Systems, Inc. 03/26/2010
Cloud Centric Systems, Inc. reorganized as Cloud Centric, Inc. 08/15/2011

GUGGENHEIM BUILD AMER BDS MANAGED DURATION TR (DE)
Name changed to Guggenheim Taxable Municipal Managed Duration Trust 07/26/2016

GUGGENHEIM ENHANCED EQUITY INCOME FD (MA)
Reincorporated under the laws of Delaware 03/20/2017

GUGGENHEIM ENHANCED EQUITY STRATEGY FD (DE)
Under plan of merger each Common Share of Bene. Int. 1¢ par automatically became (2.13281431) Guggenheim Enhanced Equity Income Fund Common Shares of Bene. Int. 1¢ par 03/20/2017

GUGGENHEIM EQUAL WEIGHT ENHANCED EQUITY INCOME FD (DE)
Under plan of merger each Common Share of Bene. Int. 1¢ par automatically became (2.08664173) Guggenheim Enhanced Equity Income Fund Common Shares of Bene. Int. 1¢ par 03/20/2017

GUGOL SCIENCE CORP (NY)
Name changed 10/7/70
Name changed from Gugol Clini-Tex, Inc. to Gugol Science Corp. 10/7/70
Assets sold for the benefit of creditors 10/25/77
No stockholders' equity

GUI-POR GOLD MINES LTD. (ON)
Name changed to Gui-Por Uranium Mines & Metals Ltd. 00/00/1953
Gui-Por Uranium Mines & Metals Ltd. acquired by Indian Mountain Metal Mines Ltd. 07/31/1975 which merged into Initiative Explorations Inc. 02/13/1980 which merged into Canhorn Chemical Corp. 04/26/1995 which merged into Nayarit Gold Inc. 05/02/2005 which merged into Capital Gold Corp. 08/02/2010 which merged into Gammon Gold Inc. (QC) 04/08/2011 which reincorporated in Ontario as AuRico Gold Inc. 06/14/2011 which merged into Alamos Gold Inc. (New) 07/06/2015

GUI POR URANIUM MINES & METALS LTD (ON)
Acquired by Indian Mountain Metal Mines Ltd. 07/31/1975
Each share Capital Stock $1 par exchanged for (0.03174603) share Capital Stock $1 par
Indian Mountain Metal Mines Ltd. merged into Initiative Explorations Inc. 02/13/1980 which merged into Canhorn Chemical Corp. 04/26/1995 which merged into Nayarit Gold Inc. 05/02/2005 which merged into Capital Gold Corp. 08/02/2010 which merged into Gammon Gold Inc. (QC) 04/08/2011 which reincorporated in Ontario as AuRico Gold Inc. 06/14/2011 which merged into Alamos Gold Inc. (New) 07/06/2015

GUICHON MINE LTD (BC)
Struck off register and declared dissolved for failure to file returns 08/06/1976

GUIDANCE SOFTWARE INC (DE)
Acquired by Open Text Corp. 09/14/2017
Each share Common $0.001 par exchanged for $7.10 cash

GUIDANCE TECHNOLOGY INC (CA)
Each share Capital Stock 10¢ par exchanged for (0.05) share Common no par 8/4/67
Common no par changed to 10¢ par 4/25/75
Stock Dividends - (14) shares Common no par for each share 7% Conv. Preferred Ser. A $10 par, (35) shares Common no par for each share $1.75 Conv. Preferred Ser. B $10 par 8/30/74
Merged into Rospatch Corp. (DE) 11/5/85
Each share 7% Conv. Preferred Ser. A $10 par exchanged for (1) share Common $5 par
Each share $1.75 Conv. Preferred Ser. B $10 par exchanged for (1.5) shares Common $5 par
Each share Common 10¢ par exchanged for (0.0151515) share Common $5 par
Rospatch Corp. (DE) reincorporated in Michigan 6/3/85 which name changed to Ameriwood Industries International Corp. 12/13/91
(See Ameriwood Industries International Corp.)

GUIDANT CORP (IN)
Common no par split (2) for (1) by issuance of (1) additional share payable 09/16/1997 to holders of record 09/02/1997 Ex date - 09/17/1997
Common no par split (2) for (1) by issuance of (1) additional share payable 01/27/1999 to holders of record 01/13/1999 Ex date - 01/28/1999
Merged into Boston Scientific Corp. 04/21/2006
Each share Common no par exchanged for (1.6799) shares Common 1¢ par and $42.28 cash

GUIDE ENERGY INC (CO)
Charter suspended for failure to maintain a resident agent 9/9/90

GUIDE EXPL LTD (AB)
Class A no par reclassified as Common no par 06/14/2012
Merged into Long Run Exploration Ltd. 10/29/2012
Each share Common no par exchanged for (0.4167) share Common no par
(See Long Run Exploration Ltd.)

GUIDE HLDGS INC (UT)
Each share old Common $0.001 par exchanged for (0.33333333) share new Common $0.001 par 02/22/2011
Name changed to Talon Real Estate Holding Corp. 06/17/2013

GUIDE PUBLISHING CO., INC. (VA)
Charter revoked for failure to file reports 6/1/91

GUIDE SCIENTIFIC INDS INC (CA)
Name changed to SaCom 7/11/72
(See SaCom)

GUIDELINE INC (NY)
Merged into infoUSA Inc. 08/23/2007
Each share Common $0.0001 par exchanged for $1.35 cash

GUIDELOCATOR COM INC (TX)
Reincorporated under the laws of Delaware as Decorize, Inc. 07/05/2001
Decorize, Inc. recapitalized as GuildMaster, Inc. 11/04/2009
(See GuildMaster, Inc.)

GUIJARRAL SERVICE CO. (CA)
Completely liquidated 7/6/71
Each share Capital Stock $1 par exchanged for first and final distribution of $4.6875 cash

GUILD FILMS CO., INC. (CO)
Adjudicated bankrupt 12/23/60
No stockholders' equity

GUILD MARK INDS INC (DE)
Merged into MG Gold Corp. 5/15/97
Each share Common $0.001 par exchanged for (0.04) share Common $0.0001 par
MG Gold Corp. name changed to MG Natural Resources Corp. 10/12/98 which name changed to Xenolix Technologies Inc. 6/14/2000 name changed to Pershing Resources Co., Inc. 4/27/2004

GUILD MASTER INC (DE)
Plan of reorganization under Chapter 11 Federal Bankruptcy proceedings effective 10/11/2013
No stockholders' equity

GUILD MTG INVTS INC (MD)
Merged into M.D.C. Asset Investors, Inc. 07/01/1988
Each share Common 1¢ par exchanged for (0.407) share Common 1¢ par
M.D.C. Asset Investors, Inc. name changed to Asset Investors Corp. (MD) 01/01/1989 which reincorporated under the laws of Delaware 05/25/1999 which name changed to American Land Lease, Inc. 08/11/2000
(See American Land Lease, Inc.)

GUILD MUSICAL INSTRUMENT CORP. (NY)
Stock Dividend - 25% 2/1/66
Name changed to G.M.I. Liquidating Corp. 6/28/66
(See G.M.I. Liquidating Corp.)

GUILDHALL MINERALS LTD (BC)
Reincorporated under the laws of Alberta as Edge Resources Inc. 07/28/2009
(See Edge Resources Inc.)

GUILFORD ACQUISITIONS INC (CANADA)
Recapitalized as Wildcat Acquisitions Inc. 02/01/1991
Each share Common no par exchanged for (0.16666666) share Common no par
Wildcat Acquisitions Inc. name changed to Condor Gold Fields Inc. 04/08/1997 which recapitalized as Cloudbreak Resources Ltd. (Canada) 11/08/2002 which reorganized in British Columbia 04/26/2010 which name changed to Petro One Energy Corp. 12/14/2010 which merged into Goldstrike Resources Ltd. 02/29/2016

GUILFORD-CHESTER WATER CO. (CT)
Merged into Connecticut Water Co. 7/24/56
Each share Capital Stock no par exchanged for (2) shares Common no par
Connecticut Water Co. merged into Connecticut Water Service, Inc. 4/10/75

GUILFORD INDUSTRIES, INC. (ME)
Became private 00/00/1980
Details not available

GUILFORD INDS INC (DE)
Common 1¢ par split (2) for (1) by issuance of (1) additional share 09/30/1983
Merged into Debron Investments PLC 01/30/1987
Each share Common 1¢ par exchanged for $17.25 cash

GUILFORD MILLS INC (DE)
Common 5¢ par changed to 2-1/2¢ par and (1) additional share issued 12/07/1979
Common 2-1/2¢ par changed to 2¢ par and (0.25) additional share issued 12/12/1980
Old Common 2¢ par split (3) for (2) by issuance of (0.5) additional share 06/23/1983
Old Common 2¢ par split (5) for (4) by issuance of (0.25) additional share 07/03/1986
Old Common 2¢ par split (3) for (2) by issuance of (0.5) additional share 01/17/1992
Old Common 2¢ par split (3) for (2) by issuance of (0.5) additional share payable 05/06/1997 to holders of record 05/01/1997 Ex date - 05/07/1997
Plan of reorganization under Chapter 11 Federal Bankruptcy Code effective 10/04/2002
Each share old Common 2¢ par

received distribution of (0.02875518) share new Common 2¢ par
Note: Certificates were not required to be surrendered and are without value
Merged into GMI Holding Corp. 04/26/2004
Each share new Common 2¢ par exchanged for $19 cash

GUILFORD NATIONAL BANK (GREENSBORO, NC)
Stock Dividend - 100% 1/22/58
Merged into Security National Bank (Greensboro, NC) 4/8/60
Each share Capital Stock $5 par exchanged for (1) share Capital Stock $5 par
Security National Bank (Greensboro, NC) merged into North Carolina National Bank (Charlotte, NC) 6/30/60 which reorganized as NCNB Corp. 11/4/68 which name changed to NationsBank Corp. 12/31/91 which reincorporated in Delaware as BankAmerica Corp. (Old) 9/25/98 which merged into BankAmerica Corp. (New) 9/30/98 which name changed to Bank of America Corp. 4/28/99

GUILFORD PHARMACEUTICALS INC (DE)
Issue Information - 1,875,000 shares COM offered at $8 per share on 06/17/1994
Merged into MGI Pharma, Inc. 10/03/2005
Each share Common 1¢ par exchanged for (0.1103) share Common 1¢ par and $1.125 cash
(See MGI Pharma, Inc.)

GUILFORD TRUST CO. (GUILFORD, CT)
Merged into Second National Bank (New Haven, CT) 11/16/64
Each share Capital Stock $10 par exchanged for (1.833334) shares Common $12.50 par
Second National Bank (New Haven, CT) name changed to Second New Haven Bank (New Haven, CT) 9/1/72 which was acquired by Colonial Bancorp, Inc. (CT) 4/12/75 which merged into Bank of Boston Corp. 6/20/85 which name changed to BankBoston Corp. 4/25/97 which merged into Fleet Boston Corp. 10/1/99 which name changed to FleetBoston Financial Corp. 4/18/2000 which merged into Bank of America Corp. 4/1/2004

GUILFORD WOOLEN MILLS, INC. (ME)
Name changed to Guilford Industries, Inc. 09/13/1962
(See Guilford Industries, Inc.)

GUILIN PAPER INC (NV)
SEC revoked common stock registration 06/03/2013

GUILLEVIN INTL INC (CANADA)
Acquired by Consolidated Electrical Distributors Inc. 04/28/1995
Each share Class A no par exchanged for $10.25 cash

GUILT-FREE GOODIES LTD (BC)
Name changed to Epicure Food Products, Inc. 06/06/1990
(See Epicure Food Products, Inc.)

GUINESS CAP FDG INC (FL)
Involuntarily dissolved for failure to file annual reports 11/22/89

GUINNESS GOLD RES LTD (ON)
Recapitalized as Roycefield Resources Ltd. 10/28/1991
Each share Common no par exchanged for (0.14285714) share Common no par
(See Roycefield Resources Ltd.)

GUINNESS PEAT GROUP PLC (ENGLAND)
Stock Dividend - 10% payable 06/08/2009 to holders of record 05/29/2009 Ex date - 05/27/2009
Name changed to Coats Group PLC 02/24/2016

GUINNESS PLC (ENGLAND)
Sponsored ADR's for Ordinary 25p par split (2) for (1) by issuance of (1) additional ADR 11/12/1991
Under plan of merger name changed to Diageo PLC 12/17/1997

GUINNESS (ARTHUR) SON & CO. PLC (ENGLAND)
Recapitalized as Guinness PLC 12/01/1986
Each ADR for Ordinary 25p par exchanged for (1) Sponsored ADR for Ordinary 25p par
Guinness PLC name changed to Diageo PLC 12/17/1997

GUINNESS TELLI PHONE CORP (UT)
SEC revoked common stock registration 04/22/2010

GUINOR GOLD CORP (YT)
Merged into Crew Gold Corp. 02/06/2006
Each share Common no par exchanged for $1.50 cash

GUITAR CTR INC (DE)
Issue Information - 6,750,000 shares COM offered at $15 per share on 03/13/1997
Merged into VH AcquisitionCo., Inc. 10/09/2007
Each share Common 1¢ par exchanged for $63 cash

GUJARAT AMBUJA CEMENTS LTD (INDIA)
144A GDR's for Ordinary split (2) for (1) by issuance of (1) additional GDR payable 3/22/2000 to holders of record 1/3/2000
144A GDR's for Ordinary split (5) for (1) by issuance of (4) additional GDR's payable 6/28/2005 to holders of record 6/24/2005
Stock Dividend - 50% payable 7/29/2005 to holders of record 6/24/2005
Name changed to Ambuja Cements Ltd. 5/10/2007

GULCH RES LTD (ON)
Recapitalized 08/14/1974
Reorganized 08/31/1978
Recapitalized from Gulch Mines Ltd. to Gulch Mines Inc. 08/14/1974
Each share Capital Stock $1 par exchanged for (0.2) share Capital Stock no par
Reorganized from Gulch Mines Inc. to Gulch Resources Ltd. 08/31/1978
Each share Capital Stock no par exchanged for (0.25) share Common no par
Merged into Camel Oil & Gas Ltd. 10/21/1982
Each share Common no par exchanged for (0.39215686) share Common no par
Camel Oil & Gas Ltd. merged into Trans-Canada Resources Ltd. (New) 11/01/1985 which recapitalized as Consolidated Trans-Canada Resources Ltd. 09/22/1988 which merged into Ranchmen's Resources Ltd. 09/30/1989 which merged into Crestar Energy Inc. 10/11/1995 which was acquired by Gulf Canada Resources Ltd. 11/13/2000
(See Gulf Canada Resources Ltd.)

GULD RES CORP (BC)
Name changed to Medsource Systems Inc. 12/24/1986
Medsource Systems Inc. recapitalized as Inter-Med Technologies Inc. 10/03/1995 which recapitalized as Botex Industries Corp. 08/07/1998 which name changed to Radical Elastomers Inc. 08/02/2001
(See Radical Elastomers Inc.)

GULDERAND MNG CORP (BC)
Cease trade order effective 02/16/1993
Stockholders' equity unlikely

GULF, MOBILE & NORTHERN RAILROAD CO. (MS)
Merged into Gulf, Mobile & Ohio Railroad Co. 09/13/1940
Each share Preferred exchanged for (1) share $5 Preferred no par and (1.5) shares Common no par
Each share Common exchanged for (0.75) share Common no par
Gulf, Mobile & Ohio Railroad Co. merged into Illinois Central Industries, Inc. 08/10/1972 which name changed to IC Industries, Inc. 05/21/1975
(See IC Industries, Inc.)

GULF & MISSISSIPPI CORP (DE)
Merged into Cryenco Sciences Inc. 2/11/92
Each share Common $1 par exchanged for (1) share Common 1¢ par
(See Cryenco Sciences Inc.)

GULF & SOUTHN FINL CORP (FL)
Merged into Southtrust Acquisition Co. 12/30/93
Each share Class A Common 10¢ par exchanged for $11 cash

GULF & WESTERN CORP. (MI)
Name changed to Gulf & Western Industries, Inc. (MI) 8/2/60
Gulf & Western Industries, Inc. (MI) reincorporated under the laws of Delaware 7/12/67 which name changed to Gulf + Western Inc. 5/1/86 which name changed to Paramount Communications Inc. 6/5/89 which merged into Viacom Inc. (Old) 7/7/94
(See Viacom Inc. (Old))

GULF AEROSPACE CORP (DE)
Adjudicated bankrupt 01/08/1973
Stockholders' equity unlikely

GULF AMERN CORP (FL)
Merged into GAC Corp. (PA) 2/24/69
Each share Common $1 par exchanged for (0.416) share Common $1 par
GAC Corp. (PA) reincorporated under the laws of Delaware 12/20/73
(See GAC Corp. (DE))

GULF AMERN FIRE & CAS CO (AL)
Stock Dividend - 10% 03/11/1976
99.9% acquired by American States Insurance Co. through purchase offer which expired 01/15/1978
Public interest eliminated

GULF AMERICAN LAND CORP. (FL)
Common $1 par split (4) for (1) by issuance of (3) additional shares 3/19/62
Name changed to Gulf American Corp. 12/20/66
Gulf American Corp. merged into GAC Corp. (PA) 2/24/69 which reincorporated in Delaware 12/20/73
(See GAC Corp. (DE))

GULF + WESTN INC (DE)
Reincorporated 07/12/1967
Name changed 05/01/1986
Common $1 par split (3) for (1) by issuance of (2) additional shares 07/01/1966
State of incorporation changed from (MI) to (DE) 07/12/1967
$1.75 Conv. Preferred Ser. A $2.50 par called for redemption 04/01/1974
$3.50 Conv. Preferred Ser. B $2.50 par called for redemption 04/01/1974
Common $1 par split (2) for (1) by issuance of (1) additional share 08/22/1975
Common $1 par split (5) for (4) by issuance of (0.25) additional share 07/30/1976
Common $1 par split (5) for (4) by issuance of (0.25) additional share 04/29/1980
$2.50 Conv. Preferred Ser. D $2.50 par called for redemption 04/29/1983
$3.875 Conv. Preferred Ser. C $2.50 par called for redemption 04/29/1983
Name changed from Gulf & Western Industries, Inc. to Gulf + Western Inc. 05/01/1986
Common $1 par split (2) for (1) by issuance of (1) additional share 05/02/1988
Stock Dividend - 10% 02/13/1980
Name changed to Paramount Communications Inc. 06/05/1989
Paramount Communications Inc. merged into Viacom Inc. (Old) 07/07/1994
(See Viacom Inc. (Old))

GULF APPLIED TECHNOLOGIES INC (DE)
Name changed to Gulfmark International Inc. 03/29/1991
Gulfmark International Inc. merged into Energy Ventures, Inc. 05/01/1997 which name changed to EVI, Inc. 05/06/1997 which name changed to EVI Weatherford, Inc. 05/27/1998 which name changed to Weatherford International Inc. (New) (DE) 09/21/1998 which reincorporated in Bermuda as Weatherford International Ltd. 06/26/2002 which reincorporated in Switzerland 02/25/2009 which reincorporated in Ireland as Weatherford International PLC 06/18/2014

GULF ATLANTIC TRANSPORTATION CO. (FL)
Common $1 par changed to 25¢ par in 1949
Liquidated 1/31/56
Details not available

GULF ATLANTIC UTILITIES, INC. (FL)
Completely liquidated 6/29/66
Each share Common 50¢ par received first and final distribution of (0.133333) share General Waterworks Corp. $4.50 Preferred $100 par
Note: Certificates were not required to be surrendered and are without value
General Waterworks Corp. merged into International Utilities Corp. 3/1/68
(See International Utilities Corp.)

GULF BAY MINES LTD. (ON)
Merged into Alchib Developments Ltd. 07/10/1969
Each share Capital Stock $1 par exchanged for (0.22) share Capital Stock no par
Alchib Developments Ltd. merged into Kalrock Developments Ltd. 10/23/1978 which merged into Kalrock Resources Ltd. 08/08/1990 which merged into Cercal Minerals Corp. 07/09/1993
(See Cercal Minerals Corp.)

GULF BIOMEDICAL CORP (TX)
Name changed to Southern Star Energy Corp. 10/22/2007

GULF BROADCAST CO. LIQUIDATING TRUST (NV)
Liquidation completed
Each share Common 10¢ par received initial distribution of $12 cash 8/26/85
Each share Common 10¢ par received second distribution of $3 cash 9/30/85
Each share Common 10¢ par received third distribution of $0.60 cash 4/15/86
Assets transferred from Gulf Broadcast Co. to Gulf Broadcast Co.

Liquidating Trust and Common 10¢ par reclassified as Shares of Ben. Int. 10¢ par 5/13/86
Each Share of Bene. Int. 10¢ par exchanged for fourth distribution of $0.10 cash 1/31/87
Each Share of Bene. Int. 10¢ par received fifth distribution of $0.04 cash 2/29/88
Each Share of Bene. Int. 10¢ par received sixth and final distribution of $0.05 cash 2/14/89

GULF CDA LTD (CANADA)
Common no par split (5) for (1) by issuance of (4) additional shares 05/27/1980
Acquired by Gulf Canada Corp. 02/10/1986
Each share Common no par exchanged for (1) share Fixed/Adjustable Rate Sr. Preference Ser. 1 no par and (1) share Common no par
Gulf Canada Corp. reorganized as Gulf Canada Resources Ltd. 07/01/1987
(See Gulf Canada Resources Ltd.)

GULF CDA RES LTD (CANADA)
Reorganized 07/01/1987
Reorganized from Gulf Canada Corp. to Gulf Canada Resources Ltd. 07/01/1987
Each share Fixed/Adjustable Rate Sr. Preference Ser. 1 no par automatically became (1) share Fixed/Adjustable Rate Sr. Preference Ser. 1 no par
Each share Common no par exchanged for (0.66) share Gulf Canada Resources Ltd. Ordinary Stock no par, (0.29) share Abitibi-Price Inc. Common no par and (0.2) share GW Utilities Ltd. Common no par
(See each company's listing)
Merged into Conoco Inc. 07/17/2001
Each share Ordinary no par exchanged for $12.40 cash
Name changed to Conoco Canada Resources Ltd. 08/24/2001
(See Conoco Canada Resources Ltd.)

GULF CITIES GAS CORP (FL)
Each share Class A Common $1 par exchanged for (0.01) share Class A Common $100 par 07/31/1978
Acquired by Cities Corp. 11/02/1981
Each share Class A Common $100 par exchanged for $450 cash

GULF COAST DRILLING & EXPLORATION INC. (DE)
Recapitalized 1/20/64
Each share Class A Preferred $10 par exchanged for (5.26) shares Common 1¢ par and $2.25 principal amount of 6% Subord. Income Debentures
Name changed to America Southwest Corp. 11/13/64
America Southwest Corp. name changed to U.S. Energy Search, Inc. 11/4/77 which name changed to Espero Energy Corp. 5/15/89
(See Espero Energy Corp.)

GULF COAST LEASEHOLDS, INC. (DE)
Name changed to Coronet Petroleum Corp. 09/04/1964
Coronet Petroleum Corp. liquidated for Texstar Corp. 04/15/1965
(See Texstar Corp.)

GULF COAST NATL BK (HOUSTON, TX)
Merged into Southwest Bancshares, Inc. 2/13/73
Each share Common $10 par exchanged for (0.892) share Common $5 par
Southwest Bancshares, Inc. merged into MCorp 10/11/84
(See MCorp)

GULF COAST RICE FARMS, INC. (TX)
Name changed to Gulfco Corp. in 1958
(See Gulfco Corp.)

GULF COAST WATER CO. (TX)
Common no par changed to $5 par in 1946
Name changed to Gulf Coast Rice Farms, Inc. in 1952
Gulf Coast Rice Farms, Inc. name changed to Gulfco Corp. in 1958
(See Gulfco Corp.)

GULF COAST WESTERN OIL CO. (AZ)
Common $1 par changed to 5¢ par 7/7/65
Common 5¢ par changed to 10¢ par 1/13/66
Recapitalized as General Energy Corp. (AZ) 1/8/68
Each share Common 10¢ par exchanged for (0.1) share Common 50¢ par
(See General Energy Corp. (AZ))

GULF CONTL INC (NV)
Charter revoked for failure to file reports and pay fees 7/1/82

GULF CORP (DE)
Merged into Standard Oil Co. of California 6/15/84
Each share Common $1 par exchanged for $80 cash

GULF CORPORATE FUND, INC. (FL)
Proclaimed dissolved for failure to file reports and pay fees 11/04/1988

GULF ENERGY & DEV CORP (DE)
Common 10¢ par split (5) for (4) by issuance of (0.25) additional share 9/2/75
Common 10¢ par split (5) for (4) by issuance of (0.25) additional share 1/12/78
Common 10¢ par split (4) for (3) by issuance of (1/3) additional share 8/6/79
Common 10¢ par split (2) for (1) by issuance of (1) additional share 3/26/80
Stock Dividends - 10% 6/14/74; 10% 1/31/75; 10% 10/22/76; 10% 1/15/79; 10% 10/6/81; 10% 12/27/82
Merged into Penn Central Corp. 8/24/83
Each share Common 10¢ par exchanged for $15 cash

GULF ENERGY CORP (CO)
Name changed to Indie Ranch Media Inc. 11/19/2007

GULF ETHANOL CORP (OK)
Recapitalized as Gulf Alternative Energy Corp. 03/24/2009
Each share Common $0.0001 par exchanged for (0.05) share Common $0.0001 par

GULF EXPL CONSULTANTS INC (DE)
Charter cancelled and declared inoperative and void for non-payment of taxes 02/25/1998

GULF FIN HSE B S C (BAHRAIN)
144A Sponsored GDR's for Ordinary split (5) for (2) by issuance of (1.5) additional GDR's payable 04/01/2011 to holders of record 03/25/2011
Reg. S Sponsored GDR's for Ordinary split (5) for (2) by issuance of (1.5) additional GDR's payable 04/01/2011 to holders of record 03/25/2011
GDR basis changed from (1:10) to (1:1) 04/01/2011
GDR agreement terminated 07/28/2014
Each 144A Sponsored GDR for Ordinary exchanged for (1) share Ordinary
Each Reg. S Sponsored GDR for Ordinary exchanged for (1) share Ordinary

GULF FINANCE & SECURITIES CO.
Liquidation completed in 1939
No Common stockholders' equity

GULF FREEWAY NATL BK (HOUSTON, TX)
Acquired by Southwest Bancshares, Inc. 3/29/79
Each share Common $10 par exchanged for (1.14) shares Common $5 par
Southwest Bancshares, Inc. merged into MCorp 10/11/84
(See MCorp)

GULF GUARANTY LAND & TITLE CO. (FL)
Name changed to Gulf American Land Corp. 5/8/61
Gulf American Land Corp. name changed to Gulf American Corp. 12/20/66 which merged into GAC Corp. (PA) 2/24/69 which reincorporated in Delaware 12/20/73
(See GAC Corp. (DE))

GULF INDONESIA RES LTD (NB)
Merged into Conoco Inc. 07/31/2002
Each share Common 1¢ par exchanged for $13.25 cash

GULF INSURANCE CO. (TX)
Each share Common $100 par exchanged for (5) shares Common $10 par 00/00/1932
Common $10 par changed to $5 par and (1) additional share issued 03/10/1960
Common $5 par changed to $2.50 par and (1) additional share issued 04/06/1965
Stock Dividends - 11.11111111% 05/12/1953; 10% 02/23/1954; 11.11111111% 03/05/1955; 10% 03/05/1956; 16.66666666% 03/09/1959; 12.5% 03/13/1964; 20% 06/02/1967
Completely liquidated 01/07/1969
Each share Common $2.50 par exchanged for first and final distribution of (0.55) share University Computing Co. (TX) Common no par
University Computing Co. (TX) reincorporated in Delaware 06/30/1972 which name changed to Wyly Corp. 05/25/1973 which name changed to Uccel Corp. 05/22/1984 which merged into Computer Associates International, Inc. 08/19/1987 which name changed to CA, Inc. 02/01/2006

GULF INTL MINERALS LTD (YUKON)
Reincorporated under the laws of Yukon 8/14/2002 which reincorporated back in British Columbia 6/17/2004

GULF INTERSTATE GAS CO. (DE)
Assets sold to Columbia Gas System, Inc. on a (0.79375) for (1) basis 12/30/58
Columbia Gas System, Inc. name changed to Columbia Energy Group 1/16/98 which merged into NiSource Inc. 11/1/2000

GULF INTST CO (DE)
Common $1 par split (2) for (1) by issuance of (1) additional share 10/14/1980
Stock Dividends - 100% 03/15/1960; 25% 09/01/1962
Name changed to Gulf Applied Technologies, Inc. 09/28/1983
Gulf Applied Technologies, Inc. name changed to Gulfmark International Inc. 03/29/1991 which merged into Energy Ventures, Inc. 05/01/1997 which name changed to EVI, Inc. 05/06/1997 which name changed to EVI Weatherford, Inc. 05/27/1998 which name changed to Weatherford International Inc. (New) (DE) 09/21/1998 which reincorporated in Bermuda as Weatherford International Ltd. 06/26/2002 which reincorporated in Switzerland 02/25/2009 which reincorporated in Ireland as Weatherford International PLC 06/18/2014

GULF LEAD MINES LTD (ON)
Common $1 par changed to no par 08/11/1971
Charter cancelled for failure to pay taxes and file returns 03/16/1976

GULF LEASING CORP (FL)
Proclaimed dissolved for failure to file reports and pay fees 11/21/84

GULF LIFE HLDG CO (FL)
Common $2.50 par changed to $1 par and (2) additional shares issued 01/02/1974
Name changed to Gulf United Corp. 05/16/1977
(See Gulf United Corp.)

GULF LIFE INS CO (FL)
Each share Common $10 par exchanged for (8) shares Common $2.50 par to effect a (4) for (1) split and a 100% stock dividend in 1953
Each share Common $2.50 par exchanged for (0.025) share Common $100 par 2/15/72
Stock Dividends - 10% 4/15/57; 10% 11/16/62
Merged into Interstate Life & Accident Insurance Co. 7/7/80
Each share Common $100 par exchanged for $2,000 cash

GULF MOBILE & OHIO RR CO (MS)
Merged into Illinois Central Industries, Inc. 08/10/1972
Each share Common no par exchanged for (0.75) share $6 Conv. 1st Preferred Ser. A no par
$5 Preferred no par called for redemption 09/11/1972
Illinois Central Industries, Inc. name changed to IC Industries, Inc. 05/21/1975
(See IC Industries, Inc.)

GULF MTG & RLTY INVTS (MA)
Shares of Bene. Int. no par reclassified as Common Shares of Bene. Int. no par 6/27/74
Name changed to GMR Properties 7/5/77
GMR Properties merged into Grubb & Ellis Co. 2/28/81

GULF NAT GAS CORP (LA)
Completely liquidated 5/30/72
Each share Common $1 par exchanged for first and final distribution of $5 cash

GULF NATL BK (GULFPORT, MS)
Common $10 par changed to $5 par and (1) additional share issued 02/01/1974
Acquired by Peoples Bank of Biloxi (Biloxi, MS) 08/20/1988
Details not available

GULF NUCLEAR INC (TX)
Name changed to GNI, Inc. (TX) 10/27/84
GNI, Inc. (TX) reorganized in Delaware as GNI Group, Inc. 10/28/87
(See GNI Group, Inc.)

GULF OIL CDA LTD (CANADA)
Each share old Common no par exchanged for (2) shares new Common no par 04/01/1969
Name changed to Gulf Canada Ltd.-Gulf Canada Ltee. 06/02/1978
Gulf Canada Ltd.-Gulf Canada Ltee. acquired by Gulf Canada Corp. 02/10/1986 which reorganized as Gulf Canada Resources Ltd. 07/01/1987
(See Gulf Canada Resources Ltd.)

GULF OIL CORP. OF PENNSYLVANIA (PA)
Name changed to Gulf Oil Corp. in 1936

Gulf Oil Corp. reorganized in Delaware as Gulf Corp. 1/18/84
(See Gulf Corp.)

GULF OIL CORP (PA)
Capital Stock $25 par changed to $8.33-1/3 par and (2) additional shares issued 12/30/59
Capital Stock $8.33-1/3 par changed to no par and (1) additional share issued 10/25/68
Capital Stock no par reclassified as Common no par 4/29/80
Stock Dividend - 100% 7/16/51
Reorganized under the laws of Delaware as Gulf Corp. and Common no par changed to $1 par 1/18/84
(See Gulf Corp.)

GULF ONSHORE INC (NV)
Name changed to Cannabis Science, Inc. 05/07/2009

GULF PETE EXCHANGE INC (LA)
Recapitalized as Software Effective Solutions Corp. 11/14/2006
Each share Common no par exchanged for (0.002) share Common no par

GULF PETROLEUM CO. (NV)
Name changed to Wesco General Corp. 2/19/69
Wesco General Corp. name changed to International Leisure Time & Development Corp. 12/20/71 which recapitalized as G & F T Mfg. Corp. 8/25/75 which name changed to G & FT Oil & Gas Corp. 4/30/80 which name changed to Yankee Energy Group 1/13/81
(See Yankee Energy Group)

GULF PWR CAP TR I (DE)
7.625% Quarterly Income Preferred Securities called for redemption at $25 on 01/15/2003

GULF PWR CAP TR II (DE)
7% Quarterly Income Preferred Securities called for redemption at $25 on 10/17/2003

GULF PWR CAP TR III (DE)
7.375% Trust Preferred Securities called for redemption at $25 on 12/18/2006

GULF PWR CO (ME)
Reincorporated 11/02/2005
9.52% Preferred $100 par called for redemption 02/24/1992
10.40% Preferred $100 par called for redemption 02/24/1992
8.28% Preferred $100 par called for redemption 10/29/1993
8.52% Preferred $100 par called for redemption 10/29/1993
11.36% Preferred $100 par called for redemption 02/01/1995
7% Class A Preferred $100 par called for redemption 03/03/1997
7.52% Preferred $100 par called for redemption 03/03/1997
7.88% Preferred $100 par called for redemption 03/03/1997
7.30% Class A Preferred $100 par called for redemption at $25 on 08/04/1997
6.72% Class A Preferred $100 par called for redemption at $25 on 09/02/1998
Adjustable Rate Class A Preferred $100 par called for redemption at $25 on 11/02/1998
4.64% Preferred $100 par called for redemption at $105 on 10/17/2005
5.16% Preferred $100 par called for redemption at $103.468 on 10/17/2005
5.44% Preferred $100 par called for redemption at $103.06 on 10/17/2005
State of incorporation changed from (ME) to (FL) 11/02/2005

GULF PUBLIC SERVICE CO., INC.
Merged into Central Louisiana Electric Co., Inc. in 1951
Each share Common $4 par exchanged for (0.4) share Common $10 par and (0.04) share 4.5% Preferred $100 par
(See Central Louisiana Electric Co., Inc.)

GULF REP FINL CORP (TX)
Stock Dividend - 100% 11/25/77
Merged into GRFC, Inc. 7/12/78
Each share Common 50¢ par exchanged for $13 cash

GULF RES & CHEM CORP (DE)
$1.60 Conv. Preferred Ser. C $1 par called for redemption 10/30/80
Name changed to Gulf USA Corp. 5/1/92
(See Gulf USA Corp.)

GULF RES INC (DE)
Common $0.001 par changed to $0.0005 par and (1) additional share issued payable 11/28/2007 to holders of record 11/28/2007
Each share old Common $0.0005 par exchanged for (0.25) share new Common $0.0005 par 10/12/2009
Reincorporated under the laws of Nevada 12/10/2015

GULF RES INC (DE)
Name changed to Gulf Energy & Development Corp. 5/14/70
(See Gulf Energy & Development Corp.)

GULF RES INC (NV)
Charter revoked for failure to file reports and pay fees 07/01/1985

GULF SHIPBUILDING, INC. (AL)
Completely liquidated 8/27/58
Each share $5 Preferred $10 par received first and final distribution of $100 cash
Each share Common 1¢ par received first and final distribution of $0.00755 cash
Surrender of certificates was not required and are now valueless

GULF SHORES INVTS INC (NV)
Reincorporated under the laws of Delaware as UAN Power Corp. 11/28/2011

GULF SHORES RES LTD (BC)
Each share old Common no par exchanged for (0.03333333) share new Common no par 06/20/2014
Each share new Common no par exchanged again for (0.5) share new Common no par 06/27/2016
Name changed to Ashanti Gold Corp. 08/15/2016

GULF SOUTH BK & TR CO (GRETNA, LA)
Acquired by Regions Financial Corp. 04/12/1997
Details not available

GULF SOUTH CORP (OK)
Pursuant to Chapter X bankruptcy proceedings stock declared worthless 09/23/1977

GULF SOUTH MED SUPPLY INC (DE)
Common 1¢ par split (2) for (1) by issuance of (1) additional share 05/25/1995
Merged into PSS World Medical, Inc. 03/27/1998
Each share Common 1¢ par exchanged for (1.75) shares Common 1¢ par
(See PSS World Medical, Inc.)

GULF SOUTH MTG INVS (MA)
Name changed to Tierco (MA) 11/07/1975
Tierco (MA) reorganized in Delaware as Tierco Group, Inc. 06/04/1981 which name changed to Premier Parks Inc. 10/13/1994 which name changed to Six Flags, Inc. 06/30/2000

(See Six Flags, Inc.)

GULF SOUTHWEST BANCORP INC (TX)
Name changed to Merchants Bancshares, Inc. 6/13/96
Merchants Bancshares, Inc. merged into Union Planters Corp. 7/31/98 which merged into Regions Financial Corp. (New) 7/1/2004

GULF-SOUTHWEST CAPITAL CORP. (TX)
Liquidation completed
Each share Common $1 par stamped to indicate initial distribution of $8.02 cash 4/12/65
Each share Stamped Common $1 par exchanged for second and final distribution of $0.70 cash 11/26/73

GULF STATES INDUSTRIES, INC. (DE)
Charter cancelled and declared inoperative and void for non-payment of taxes 4/1/67

GULF STATES LIFE INSURANCE CO.
Merged into Southland Life Insurance Co. 00/00/1938
Details not available

GULF STATES LIFE INSURANCE CO. (GA)
Common $1 par changed to 50¢ par 12/01/1959
Acquired by Kentucky Central Life & Accident Insurance Co. 10/17/1962
Each (3.56) shares Common 50¢ par exchanged for (1) share Class A Common $1 par
Kentucky Central Life & Accident name changed to Kentucky Central Life Insurance Co. 03/08/1963
(See Kentucky Central Life Insurance Co.)

GULF STATES OIL CO.
Name changed to Western Natural Gas Co. in 1947
(See Western Natural Gas Co.)

GULF STATES SECURITY LIFE INSURANCE CO.
Name changed to Gulf Life Insurance Co. in 1936
(See Gulf Life Insurance Co.)

GULF STATES STEEL CO.
Merged into Republic Steel Corp. on a (2-1/3) for (1) basis in 1937
Republic Steel Corp. merged into LTV Corp. (Old) 6/29/84 which reorganized as LTV Corp. (New) 6/28/93
(See LTV Corp. (New))

GULF STS LD & INDS INC (NY)
Class A $5 par called for redemption 1/11/57
Class B $5 par changed to $1 par 2/5/57
Class B $1 par reclassified as Common $1 par 7/29/57
Each share Common $1 par exchanged for (10) shares Common 50¢ par 12/30/57
$4.50 Prior Preferred no par called for redemption 1/1/67
Name changed to Landmark Land Co., Inc. (NY) 7/10/72
Landmark Land Co., Inc. (NY) reincorporated in Delaware 6/26/84

GULF STS UTILS CO (TX)
$6 Preferred called for redemption 11/09/1944
$5.50 Preferred called for redemption 11/09/1944
Common no par split (2) for (1) by issuance of (1) additional share 06/24/1959
Common no par split (2) for (1) by issuance of (1) additional share 06/18/1965
$3.85 Preference no par called for redemption 06/04/1992
$4.40 Preference no par called for redemption 06/04/1992

$13.64 Preferred $100 par called for redemption 11/15/1992
$11.48 Preferred $100 par called for redemption 07/06/1993
$11.50 Preferred $100 par called for redemption 07/06/1993
$12.92 Preferred $100 par called for redemption 07/06/1993
Stock Dividend - 25% 05/15/1953
Merged into Entergy Corp. (DE) 12/31/1993
Each share Common no par exchanged for (0.558) share Common 1¢ par
(See Entergy Corp. (DE))
Depositary Preferred Shares called for redemption 03/15/1996
$9.75 Preferred $100 par called for redemption 03/15/1996
Name changed to Entergy Gulf States, Inc. 04/22/1996
(See Entergy Gulf States, Inc.)

GULF SULPHUR CORP. (DE)
Each share Preferred 10¢ par exchanged for (4) shares Common 1¢ par 03/01/1961
Class B Common 10¢ par reclassified as Common 1¢ par 03/01/1961
Common 10¢ par changed to 1¢ par 03/01/1961
Each share Common 1¢ par exchanged for (0.1) share Capital Stock 10¢ par 12/28/1962
Capital Stock 10¢ par reclassified as Common 10¢ par 11/01/1966
Under plan of merger name changed to Gulf Resources & Chemical Corp. 06/19/1967
Gulf Resources & Chemical Corp. name changed to Gulf USA Corp. 05/01/1992
(See Gulf USA Corp.)

GULF SUPER MARKETS, INC. (FL)
Name changed to Star Super Markets, Inc. in 1959
Star Super Markets, Inc. name changed to United Star Companies, Inc. 1/15/62
(See United Star Companies, Inc.)

GULF TITANIUM LTD (BC)
Struck off register and declared dissolved for failure to file returns 10/28/1994

GULF UN CORP (LA)
Plan of reorganization under Chapter X Federal Bankruptcy Act confirmed 5/24/80
No stockholders' equity

GULF UTD CORP (FL)
Completely liquidated 2/6/84
Each share $1.20 Conv. Preferred Ser. A $2.50 par exchanged for first and final distribution of $30.42 cash
Each share $3.78 Conv. Preferred Ser. B $2.50 par exchanged for first and final distribution of $51.32 cash
Each share Common $1 par exchanged for first and final distribution of (0.5) share American General Corp. $2.64 Conv. Preferred $1.50 par, (1) share Gulf Broadcast Co. Common 10¢ par and (0.25) American General Corp. Common Stock Purchase Warrant expiring 1/4/89
(See each company's listing)

GULF URANIUM & DEVELOPMENT CO. (NM)
Dissolved 00/00/1956
Details not available

GULF USA CORP (DE)
Plan of reorganization under Chapter 11 Federal Bankruptcy Code effective 8/9/95
No stockholders' equity

GULF WEST BKS INC (FL)
Stock Dividends - 10% payable 3/16/98 to holders of record 2/16/98; 10% payable 12/15/98 to holders of record 11/30/98; 5% payable 11/15/99 to holders of record

GUL-GUN

11/1/99; 5% payable 10/20/2000 to holders of record 10/6/2000
Ex date - 10/4/2000; 5% payable 10/19/2001 to holders of record 10/5/2001
Merged into South Financial Group, Inc. 8/31/2002
Each share Common $1 par exchanged for (0.4893147) share Common $1 par and $4.0417006 cash

GULF WEST PPTY INC (NV)
Each share old Common $0.0001 par exchanged for (0.01) share new Common $0.0001 par 09/30/2005
Reincorporated under the laws of Colorado as Titan Global Entertainment, Inc. and Common $0.0001 par changed to $0.001 par 11/10/2005
Titan Global Entertainment, Inc. recapitalized as Sunset Island Group, Inc. 05/30/2008

GULF WESTN PETE CORP (NV)
Recapitalized as Wholehealth Products, Inc. 09/17/2012
Each share Common $0.001 par exchanged for (0.0076923) share Common $0.001 par

GULFBOARD OIL CORP.
Merged into Salt Dome Oil Corp. on a (1) for (3.75) basis in 1943
(See Salt Dome Oil Corp.)

GULFCO CORP. (TX)
Voluntarily dissolved 3/13/69
Details not available

GULFCO INVT GROUP INC (LA)
Each share Common 10¢ par exchanged for (0.05) share Common $2 par 1/24/69
Name changed to Gulfco Investment, Inc. and Common $2 par changed to no par 5/20/75
(See Gulfco Investment, Inc.)

GULFCO INVT INC (LA)
Merged into Independent Insurance Group, Inc. 10/31/83
Each share Common no par exchanged for $40 cash

GULFMARK ENERGY INC (NV)
Name changed to Gambit Energy, Inc. 11/08/2011

GULFMARK INTL INC (DE)
Each share Common $1 par received distribution of (2) shares GulfMark Offshore, Inc. Common 1¢ par payable 04/30/1997 to holders of record 03/17/1997
Merged into Energy Ventures, Inc. 05/01/1997
Each share Common $1 par exchanged for (0.6693) share Common $1 par
Energy Ventures, Inc. name changed to EVI, Inc. 05/06/1997 which name changed to EVI Weatherford, Inc. 05/27/1998 which name changed to Weatherford International Inc. (New) (DE) 09/21/1998 which reincorporated in Bermuda as Weatherford International Ltd. 06/26/2002 which reincorporated in Switzerland 02/25/2009 which reincorporated in Ireland as Weatherford International PLC 06/18/2014

GULFPORT OIL & DEVELOPMENT CO. (DE)
Charter cancelled and declared inoperative and void for non-payment of taxes 3/18/25

GULFSIDE INDS LTD (BC)
Recapitalized as Consolidated Gulfside Resources Inc. 01/13/1998
Each share Common no par exchanged for (0.2) share Common no par
Consolidated Gulfside Resources Inc. name changed to Gulfside Minerals Ltd. 04/11/2007 which name changed to Arrowstar Resources Ltd. 03/07/2012

GULFSIDE MINERALS LTD (BC)
Name changed to Arrowstar Resources Ltd. 03/07/2012

GULFSTAR INDS INC (DE)
Recapitalized as Media Vision Productions, Inc. 01/05/1999
Each share Common $0.032 par exchanged for (0.04) share Common 8¢ par
Media Vision Productions, Inc. name changed to eCONTENT, Inc. 10/01/1999 which name changed to Earthworks Entertainment, Inc. 01/15/2004

GULFSTREAM AEROSPACE CORP (NEW) (DE)
Merged into General Dynamics Corp. 07/30/1999
Each share Common 1¢ par exchanged for (1) share Common $1 par

GULFSTREAM AEROSPACE CORP OLD (DE)
Merged into Chrysler Corp. 08/16/1985
Each share Common 10¢ par exchanged for $19 cash

GULFSTREAM BANCSHARES INC (FL)
Merged into CenterState Banks, Inc. 01/17/2014
Each share Common 1¢ par exchanged for (3.012) shares Common $1 par and 14.65 cash
CenterState Banks, Inc. name changed to CenterState Bank Corp. 09/08/2017

GULFSTREAM BKS INC (FL)
Merged into NCNB Corp. 9/3/82
Each share Common $1 par exchanged for $17.50 cash

GULFSTREAM INDS INC (FL)
Recapitalized as Single Source Investment Group, Inc. 01/03/2006
Each share Common 1¢ par exchanged for (0.05) share Common 1¢ par
(See Single Source Investment Group, Inc.)

GULFSTREAM INTL GROUP INC (DE)
Plan of reorganization under Chapter 11 Federal Bankruptcy proceedings effective 09/29/2011
Stockholders' equity unlikely

GULFSTREAM LD & DEV CORP (DE)
Class A Common 10¢ par split (2) for (1) by issuance of (1) additional share 6/9/72
Class A Common 10¢ par reclassified as Common 10¢ par 7/1/73
Merged into KMG Acquisition Corp. 1/23/86
Each share Common 10¢ par exchanged for $37 cash

GULFSTREAM RES CDA LTD (ON)
Acquired by Anadarko Petroleum Corp. 08/15/2001
Each share Common no par exchanged for $2.65 cash

GULFTERRA ENERGY PARTNERS LP (DE)
Merged into Enterprise Products Partners L.P. 9/30/2004
Each Common Unit exchanged for (1.81) Common Units

GULFTEX ENERGY CORP (TX)
Name changed to Gulftex Partners, Inc. 09/09/2003
(See Gulftex Partners, Inc.)

GULFTEX PARTNERS INC (TX)
Each share old Common $0.001 par exchanged for (0.01603592) share new Common $0.001 par 09/18/2003
SEC revoked common stock registration 07/15/2013

GULFWEST ENERGY INC NEW (TX)
Name changed 05/21/2001
Name changed from GulfWest Oil Co. to GulfWest Energy Inc. (New) 05/21/2001
Reincorporated under the laws of Delaware as Crimson Exploration Inc. 06/13/2005
Crimson Exploration Inc. merged into Contango Oil & Gas Co. 10/02/2013

GULFWEST ENERGY INC OLD (TX)
Recapitalized as GulfWest Oil Co. 07/30/1992
Each share Common $0.001 par exchanged for (0.01) share Common $0.001 par
GulfWest Oil Co. name changed to GulfWest Energy, Inc. (New) (TX) 05/21/2001 which reincorporated in Delaware as Crimson Exploration Inc. 06/13/2005 which merged into Contango Oil & Gas Co. 10/02/2013

GULL INC (DE)
Acquired by Parker-Hannifin Corp. 02/19/1988
Each share Common 10¢ par exchanged for (0.55) share Common 50¢ par

GULL KIRKLAND MINES LTD.
Acquired by Kirkland Eastern Gold Mines Ltd. on a (1) for (7) basis in 1945

GULL LABS INC (UT)
Each share old Common $0.001 par exchanged for (1/6) share new Common $0.001 par 12/16/1987
Merged into Meridian Diagnostics, Inc. 11/05/1998
Each share new Common $0.001 par exchanged for $2.25 cash

GULL LAKE ENERGY RES LTD (ON)
Name changed 08/11/1977
Name changed from Gull Lake Iron Mines Ltd. to Gull Lake Energy Resources Ltd. and Capital Stock $1 par changed to no par 08/11/1977
Merged into Petroflo Petroleum Corp. 08/18/1980
Each (0.28571428) shares Capital Stock no par exchanged for (1) share Capital Stock no par
Petroflo Petroleum Corp. merged into Flying Cross Resources Ltd. 12/04/1985 which merged into International Larder Minerals Inc. 05/01/1986 which merged into Explorers Alliance Corp. 10/13/2000
(See Explorers Alliance Corp.)

GULTON INDS INC (DE)
Reincorporated 06/28/1968
Common $1 par split (2) for (1) by issuance of (1) additional share 07/19/1967
$2 Conv. Preferred Ser. A $50 par changed to $10 par 06/00/1968
State of incorporation changed from (NJ) to (DE) 06/28/1968
Merged into Mark IV Industries, Inc. 05/13/1986
Each share Common $1 par exchanged for $34 cash
$2 Conv. Preferred Ser. A $10 par called for redemption 10/31/1996
Public interest eliminated

GUM PRODS INC (MA)
Each share Class A $5 par exchanged for $3 principal amount of 5% Income Debentures due 5/15/68 and (1) share Non-Voting Common no par in 1953
Each share Common $1 par exchanged for (0.5) share Class B Common no par in 1953
Non-Voting Common no par and Class B Common no par reclassified as Common no par 4/10/57
Stock Dividend - 10% 5/16/60
Merged into Moxie-Monarch-NuGrape Co. 12/27/71
Each share Common no par exchanged for (0.2083) share Comon $1 par
Moxie-Monarch-NuGrape Co. name changed to Moxie Industries, Inc. 5/19/72 which merged into SPI Acquisition Corp. 8/11/88
(See SPI Acquisition Corp.)

GUM TECH INTL INC (UT)
Reincorporated under the laws of Delaware as Matrixx Initiatives, Inc. and Common no par changed to $0.001 par 06/18/2002
(See Matrixx Initiatives, Inc.)

GUMP & CO INC (DE)
Each share old Common 1¢ par exchanged for (0.1) share new Common 1¢ par 4/16/2001
Name changed to CRD Holdings Inc. 6/24/2002

GUNDAKER / JORDAN AMERN HOLDINGS INC (FL)
Administratively dissolved 09/23/2016

GUNDLE / SLT ENVIRONMENTAL INC (DE)
Merged into GEO Holdings Corp. 5/18/2004
Each share Common 1¢ par exchanged for $18.50 cash

GUNDLE ENVIRONMENTAL SYS INC (DE)
Common 1¢ par split (5) for (4) by issuance of (0.25) additional share 4/19/88
Common 1¢ par split (3) for (2) by issuance of (0.5) additional share 3/29/89
Name changed to Gundle/SLT Environmental, Inc. 7/27/95
(See Gundle/SLT Environmental, Inc.)

GUNFLINT RES LTD (BC)
Recapitalized as Advent Communications Corp. 05/06/1992
Each share Common no par exchanged for (0.5) share Common no par
Advent Communications Corp. recapitalized as Advent Wireless Inc. 08/19/2003 which name changed to Advent-AWI Holdings Inc. 03/23/2017

GUNN MINES LTD (BC)
Recapitalized as United Gunn Resources Ltd. 01/19/1977
Each share Common 50¢ par exchanged for (0.2) share Common no par
(See United Gunn Resources Ltd.)

GUNNAR GOLD MINES LTD. (ON)
Name changed to Gunnar Mines Ltd. 00/00/1954
Gunnar Mines Ltd. merged into Gunnar Mining Ltd. 11/30/1960 which name changed to Bovis Corp. Ltd. 02/16/1971
(See Bovis Corp. Ltd.)

GUNNAR GOLD MINING CORP (CANADA)
Recapitalized 12/14/1988
Recapitalized from Gunnar Gold Inc. to Gunnar Gold Mining Corp. 12/14/1988
Each share Common no par exchanged for (0.1) share Common no par
Recapitalized as ATTN AVECA Entertainment Corp. 02/26/1992
Each share Common no par exchanged for (0.1) share Common no par
ATTN AVECA Entertainment Corp. recapitalized as American Transportation Television Network, Inc. 03/04/1993
(See American Transportation Television Network, Inc.)

GUNNAR MINES LTD. (ON)
Merged into Gunnar Mining Ltd. 11/30/1960
Each share Capital Stock $1 par

exchanged for (1) share Capital Stock $1 par
Gunnar Mining Ltd. name changed to Bovis Corp. Ltd. 02/16/1971
(See Bovis Corp. Ltd.)

GUNNAR MNG LTD (ON)
Capital Stock $1 par changed to no par 09/14/1970
Name changed to Bovis Corp. Ltd. 02/16/1971
(See Bovis Corp. Ltd.)

GUNNER ENERGY CORP (UT)
Each share old Common $0.001 par exchanged for (0.01) share new Common $0.001 par 07/31/1998
Reincorporated under the laws of Nevada as Generation Entertainment Corp. 08/17/1998
Generation Entertainment Corp. recapitalized as Marketing-247, Inc. 07/15/2002 which merged into MidAmerica Oil & Gas, Inc. 12/30/2003 which name changed to Sounds 24-7, Inc. 01/15/2004 which recapitalized as Allied Energy Corp. 01/26/2006

GUNNISON OIL CO. (UT)
Completely liquidated 3/19/69
Each share Common 10¢ par exchanged for first and final distribution of (0.5) share Mitre Industries, Inc. Common 5¢ par
(See Mitre Industries, Inc.)

GUNNS LTD (AUSTRALIA)
ADR agreement terminated 03/20/2014
No ADR's remain outstanding

GUNSITE BUTTE URANIUM CORP. (UT)
Each share Capital Stock 1¢ par exchanged for (0.2) share Capital Stock 5¢ par 05/09/1955
Name changed to Gunsite Oil & Gas Corp. 09/18/1959
(See Gunsite Oil & Gas Corp.)

GUNSITE OIL & GAS CORP (UT)
Each share Capital Stock 5¢ par exchanged for (0.5) share Capital Stock no par 05/20/1968
Involuntarily dissolved 01/01/1993

GUNSLINGER RECORDS INC (FL)
Reincorporated 11/05/2009
State of incorporation changed from (AZ) to (FL) 11/05/2009
Name changed to Kinbasha Gaming International, Inc. 06/20/2011

GUNSMITHCENTRAL COM INC (NV)
Reincorporated 6/28/2004
State of incorporation changed from (CO) to (NV) 6/28/2004
Name changed to AD Capital U.S., Inc. 12/8/2004

GUNSTEEL RES INC (BC)
Cease trade order effective 05/29/2001
Stockholders' equity unlikely

GUOCOLEISURE LTD (NEW ZEALAND)
Reincorporated under the laws of Bermuda as GL Ltd. 11/18/2015

GUODONG CAP CORP (AB)
Name changed to Cosmo Capital Corp. 08/28/2003
Cosmo Capital Corp. name changed to Reco International Group Inc. (Old) 12/17/2004 which reorganized as Reco International Group Inc. (New) 04/08/2015

GUPTA CORP (CA)
Name changed to Centura Software Corp. (CA) 10/4/96
Centura Software Corp. (CA) reincorporated in Delaware 2/16/99
(See Centura Software Corp.)

GURATA GOLD INC (NV)
Name changed to Forza Environmental Building Products, Inc. 07/30/2010
(See Forza Environmental Building Products, Inc.)

GURD (CHAS.) & CO., LTD.
Liquidated in 1947
Details not available

GURNEY ELEVATOR CO.
Merged into Atlantic Elevator Co. in 1938
Details not available

GURNEY PRODS LTD (CANADA)
Name changed to Tappan-Gurnery Ltd. 05/15/1961
(See Tappan-Gurnery Ltd.)

GURNEY REFRIGERATOR CO.
Bankrupt in 1934

GURNEY'S INN CORP. (NY)
Charter cancelled and proclaimed dissolved for failure to pay taxes 09/25/1991

GURU HEALTH INC (NV)
Reorganized as Global Stevia Corp. 06/18/2012
Each share Common $0.001 par exchanged for (13) shares Common $0.001 par
(See Global Stevia Corp.)

GURUNET CORP (DE)
Issue Information - 2,350,000 shares COM offered at $5 per share on 10/13/2004
Name changed to Answers Corp. 10/18/2005
(See Answers Corp.)

GUS PLC (ENGLAND)
Each old Sponsored ADR for Ordinary 29-3/43p par exchanged for (0.86) new Sponsored ADR for Ordinary 29-3/43p par and $2.17501 cash 12/13/2005
Merged into Experian Group Ltd. 10/11/2006
Each new Sponsored ADR for Ordinary 29-3/43p par exchanged for (1) ADR for Ordinary and $7.6431 cash
Experian Group Ltd. name changed to Experian PLC 07/21/2008

GUSANA EXPLORATIONS INC (NV)
Each share old Common $0.00001 par exchanged for (12) shares new Common $0.00001 par 05/27/2003
Name changed to True Religion Apparel, Inc. (NV) 08/18/2003
True Religion Apparel, Inc. (NV) reincorporated in Delaware 08/19/2005
(See True Religion Apparel, Inc.)

GUSHAN ENVIRONMENTAL ENERGY LTD (CAYMAN ISLANDS)
Issue Information - 18,000,000 SPONSORED ADRS offered at $9.60 per ADR on 12/18/2007
Each old Sponsored ADR for Ordinary HKD $0.00001 par exchanged for (0.2) new Sponsored ADR for Ordinary HKD $0.00001 par 11/12/2010
Acquired by Trillion Energy Holdings Ltd. 10/17/2012
Each new Sponsored ADR for Ordinary HKD $0.00001 par exchanged for $1.60 cash

GUSTIN-BACON MANUFACTURING CO. (DE)
Merged into Certain-Teed Products Corp. 7/1/66
Each share Common $2.50 par exchanged for (1) share Conv. Preferred Ser. A $1 par
(See Certain-Teed Products Corp.)

GUSTIN-BACON MANUFACTURING CO. (MO)
Each share Common $20 par exchanged for (4) shares Common $5 par plus a 150% stock dividend paid in 1952
Each share Common $5 par exchanged for (2) shares Common $2.50 par 12/12/56
Under plan of merger reincorporated under the laws of Delaware 2/14/62
Gustin-Bacon Manufacturing Co. (Del.) merged into Certain-Teed Products Corp. 7/1/66 which name changed to Certain-Teed Corp. 5/28/76
(See Certain-Teed Corp.)

GUSTO MINES LTD. (ON)
Charter cancelled in June, 1960

GUTHRIE SVGS INC (OK)
Merged into Local Oklahoma Bank, N.A. (Oklahoma City, OK) 10/15/99
Each share Common 1¢ par exchanged for $22.25 cash

GUWENHUA INTL CO (NV)
Name changed to Tyin Group Holdings Ltd. 01/29/2014

GUWO HLDGS INC (NY)
Name changed to QED Connect, Inc. 07/23/2007

GUY F. ATKINSON CO. OF CALIFORNIA (CA)
See - Atkinson Guy F Co Calif

GUY P. HARVEY & SON CORP. (MA)
See - Harvey (Guy P.) & Son Corp.

GUYANA GOLD CORP (BC)
Name changed to Beringer Gold Corp. 11/18/1996
Beringer Gold Corp. merged into Lions Gate Entertainment Corp. 11/13/1997

GUYANA GOLDFIELDS INC (QC)
Each share old Common no par exchanged for (3) shares new Common no par 8/19/97
Reorganized under the laws of Canada 5/26/2005
Each share new Common no par exchanged for (1) share Common no par

GUYANA MINES LTD. (ON)
Recapitalized as Consolidated Guyana Mines Ltd. 00/00/1952
Each share Capital Stock $1 par exchanged for (0.5) share Common 50¢ par
Consolidated Guyana Mines Ltd. recapitalized as Latin American Mines Ltd. 12/09/1957
(See Latin American Mines Ltd.)

GUYANA PRECIOUS METALS INC (ON)
Each share old Common no par exchanged for (0.5) share new Common no par 07/27/2011
Name changed to GPM Metals Inc. 08/29/2013

GUYANOR RESSOURCES S A (FRANCE)
Name changed to EURO Ressources S.A. 07/19/2005

GUYER OIL CO (NV)
Merged into Great Basins Petroleum Co. 5/8/70
Each share Capital Stock 10¢ par exchanged for (1.00784) shares Common 40¢ par
(See Great Basins Petroleum Co.)

GUYS FOODS INC (MO)
Common $2 par split (2) for (1) by issuance of (1) additional share 6/20/69
Merged into Degrem Inc. 8/30/79
Each share Common $2 par exchanged for $13.55 cash

GV MEDICAL INC (MN)
Name changed to SpectraScience, Inc. 10/16/1992

GVC CORP (TAIWAN)
Each old Sponsored Reg. S GDR for Common exchanged for (0.65) new Sponsored Reg. S GDR for Common 01/03/2001
Each old Sponsored 144A GDR for Common exchanged for (0.65) new Sponsored 144A GDR for Common 01/03/2001
Stock Dividends - 45% 09/16/1995; 35% payable 08/24/1996 to holders of record 06/17/1996; 35% payable 08/21/1997 to holders of record 05/30/1997; 20% payable 08/19/1998 to holders of record 06/09/1998; 5% payable 10/07/1999 to holders of record 07/30/1999
Merged into Lite-On Technology Corp. 11/06/2002
Each new Sponsored Reg. S GDR for Common exchanged for (0.19379845) Reg. S GDR for Ordinary
Each new Sponsored 144A GDR for Common exchanged for (0.19379845) 144A GDR for Ordinary

GVC VENTURE CORP (DE)
Common 10¢ par changed to 1¢ par 06/30/2004
Recapitalized as Halo Companies, Inc. 02/25/2010
Each share Common 1¢ par exchanged for (0.13210039) share Common 1¢ par

GVCL VENTURES INC (DE)
Recapitalized as Rain Forest International, Inc. 05/22/2018
Each share Common $0.001 par exchanged for (0.005) share Common $0.001 par

GVI SEC SOLUTIONS INC (DE)
Each share old Common $0.001 par exchanged for (0.02) share new Common $0.001 par 11/28/2006
Merged into GenNx360 GVI Holding, Inc. 12/11/2009
Each share new Common $0.001 par exchanged for $0.3875 cash

GVIC COMMUNICATIONS INC (CANADA)
Acquired by Glacier Ventures International Corp. (New) 12/28/2006
Each share Class A no par exchanged for (0.0429) share Common no par
Each share Non-Vtg. Class B no par exchanged for (0.0429) share Common no par
Glacier Ventures International Corp. (New) name changed to Glacier Media Inc. 07/01/2008

GVIC PUBLICATIONS LTD (CANADA)
Reincorporated 05/04/2006
Place of incorporation changed from (Yukon) to (Canada) 05/04/2006
Recapitalized as GVIC Communications Corp. 05/18/2007
Each (30) shares Class B Common no par exchanged for (1) share Class B Common no par
Each (30) shares Non-Vtg. Class C Common no par exchanged for (1) share Non-Vtg. Class C Common no par

GVM METALS LTD (AUSTRALIA)
Name changed to Coal of Africa Ltd. 12/04/2007
(See Coal of Africa Ltd.)

GVS MED INC (DE)
Charter cancelled and declared inoperative and void for non-payment of taxes 03/01/1993

GW UTILS LTD (ON)
Plan of Arrangement effective 03/30/1993
Each share Common no par exchanged for (0.4112) share Home Oil Co. Ltd. (New) Common no par
Home Oil Co. Ltd. (New) merged into Anderson Exploration Ltd. 09/07/1995
(See Anderson Exploration Ltd.)

GWA INTL INC (AUSTRALIA)
Name changed to GWA Group Ltd. 03/27/2012

GWA-H & FINANCIAL INFORMATION, INC.

GWALIA RES INTL LTD (AUSTRALIA)
Scheme of Arrangement effective 09/27/1990
Details not available

GWALTNEY INC (VA)
Each share Common $10 par exchanged for (5) shares Common $2 par 03/10/1967
Stock Dividend - 50% 11/20/1968
Acquired by International Telephone & Telegraph Corp. 08/28/1970
Each share Common $2 par exchanged for (0.988) share Common $1 par
International Telephone & Telegraph Corp. name changed to ITT Corp. (DE) 12/31/1983 which reorganized in Indiana as ITT Industries, Inc. 12/19/1995 which name changed to ITT Corp. 07/01/2006

GWALTNEY (P.D.), JR. & CO., INC. (VA)
Name changed to Gwaltney, Inc. 07/15/1957
Gwaltney, Inc. acquired by International Telephone & Telegraph Corp. 08/28/1970 which name changed to ITT Corp. (DE) 12/31/1983 which reorganized in Indiana as ITT Industries, Inc. 12/19/1995 which name changed to ITT Corp. 07/01/2006

GWB CAP TR I (DE)
10% Preferred Securities called for redemption at $10 on 8/18/2004

GWB CAP TR II (DE)
Preferred Securities called for redemption at $10 on 3/20/2006

GWC CORP (DE)
Merged into United Water Resources Inc. 4/22/94
Each share 7.625% Preferred Ser. A 1¢ par exchanged for (1) share 7.625% Preferred Ser. B no par
Each share Common 1¢ par exchanged for (1.2) shares Common no par and $13.794 cash

GWIL INDS INC (BC)
Merged into GII Acquisition Corp. 12/02/1999
Each share Common no par exchanged for $5.65 cash

GWILLIM LAKE GOLD MINES LTD. (ON)
Charter revoked for failure to file reports and pay fees 12/08/1966

GWIN INC (DE)
Name changed to Winning Edge International, Inc. 09/27/2006
Winning Edge International, Inc. assets transferred to W Technologies, Inc. 10/20/2007

GWINNETT BANCORP INC (GA)
Merged into Century South Banks Inc. 4/14/95
Each share Common $1 par exchanged for (1.173) shares Common $1 par
Century South Banks, Inc. merged into BB&T Corp. 6/7/2001

GWINNETT BANCSHARES INC (GA)
Common $1 par split (3) for (2) by issuance of (0.5) additional share 11/15/93
Merged into Bank South Corp. 2/17/95
Each share Common $1 par exchanged for (1.75) shares Common $5 par
Bank South Corp. merged into NationsBank Corp. (NC) 1/9/96 which reincorporated in Delaware as BankAmerica Corp. (Old) 9/25/98 which merged into BankAmerica Corp. (New) 9/30/98 which name changed to Bank of America Corp. 4/28/99

GWR GLOBAL WTR RES CORP (BC)
Merged into Global Water Resources, Inc. 05/03/2016
Each share Common no par exchanged for (1) share Common 1¢ par
Note: Unexchanged certificates were cancelled and became without value 05/03/2018

GWR RES INC (BC)
Name changed 03/23/2007
Name changed from G W R Resources Inc. to GWR Resources Inc. 03/23/2007
Name changed to Engold Mines Ltd. 05/16/2016

GWS TECHNOLOGIES INC (DE)
Each share old Common $0.001 par exchanged for (0.05) share new Common $0.001 par 10/31/2008
SEC revoked common stock registration 09/22/2014

GYK VENTURES INC (NV)
Name changed to Diatom Corp. 08/08/2005
Diatom Corp. reorganized as Planktos Corp. (NV) 03/08/2007 which reincorporated in Delaware as Planktos Merger Co. 05/06/2014 which name changed to Solar Gold Ltd. 06/24/2014

GYM PLASTICS CORP. (DE)
Name changed to Gym Toys, Inc. 12/14/61
(See Gym Toys, Inc.)

GYM TOYS, INC. (DE)
No longer in existence having become inoperative and void for non-payment of taxes 4/1/65

GYMBOREE CORP (DE)
Common $0.001 par split (2) for (1) by issuance of (1) additional share 08/23/1994
Merged into Giraffe Holding, Inc. 11/23/2010
Each share Common $0.001 par exchanged for $65.40 cash

GYNECARE INC (DE)
Merged into Johnson & Johnson 11/19/97
Each share Common no par exchanged for (0.1426) share Common $1 par

GYNEX PHARMACEUTICALS INC (NV)
Name changed 11/11/1991
Name changed from Gynex Inc. to Gynex Pharmaceuticals Inc. 11/11/1991
Merged into Bio-Technology General Corp. 08/06/1993
Each share Common 3¢ par exchanged for (0.61) share Common 1¢ par
Bio-Technology General Corp. name changed to Savient Pharmaceuticals, Inc. 06/23/2003
(See Savient Pharmaceuticals, Inc.)

GYPSUM LIME & ALABASTINE CANADA, LTD. (CANADA)
Common no par exchanged (4) for (1) 00/00/1929
Each share old Common no par exchanged for (2) shares new Common no par 06/01/1956
Assets sold to Dominion Tar & Chemical Co. Ltd. 02/23/1959
Each share Common no par exchanged for (2) shares Common no par and $14.50 cash
Dominion Tar & Chemical Co. Ltd. name changed to Domtar Ltd. 07/01/1965 which name changed to Domtar Ltd.-Domtar Ltee. 01/13/1972 which name changed to Domtar Inc. 02/23/1978 which reorganized as Domtar Corp. (DE) 03/07/2007

GYPSY BLAIR MINING & MILLING CO. (UT)
Charter expired by time limitation 10/14/49

GYPSY BLAIR MINING & OIL CO. (UT)
Proclaimed dissolved for failure to file reports 12/31/74

GYPSY BLAIR MINING CO. (UT)
Name changed to Gypsy Blair Mining & Oil Co. and Common 50¢ par changed to 1¢ par 1/4/69
(See Gypsy Blair Mining & Oil Co.)

GYPSY RES LTD (BC)
Common no par split (2) for (1) by issuance of (1) additional share 07/27/1989
Name changed to Pacific Century Explorations Ltd. 02/05/1990
Pacific Century Explorations Ltd. recapitalized as Goldwater Resources Ltd. 06/10/1994 which name changed to First Goldwater Resources Inc. 12/24/1999 which name changed to Baja Mining Corp. 07/20/2004 which recapitalized as Camrova Resources Inc. 10/17/2016

GYREX INC (NJ)
Assets sold for benefit of creditors 7/29/70
No stockholders' equity

GYRO DYNAMICS CORP (DE)
Reorganized as I.A.F.A., Inc. 2/16/84
Each share Preferred 1¢ par exchanged for (0.2) share Common $0.0025 par
(See I.A.F.A., Inc.)

GYRO ENERGY & MINERALS CORP (BC)
Recapitalized as Dimension House International, Inc. 03/23/1987
Each share Common no par exchanged for (1) share Common no par
Dimension House International, Inc. name changed to PII Photovision International, Inc. 09/04/1990
(See PII Photovision International, Inc.)

GYRO SENSORS INTL INC (UT)
Involuntarily dissolved 05/01/1988

GYRODYNE CO AMER INC (NY)
Each share Class A Common $1 par or Class B Common 10¢ par exchanged for (5) shares Common 10¢ par 00/00/1953
Each share Common 10¢ par exchanged for (0.1) share Common $1 par 07/23/1957
5% Preferred $4 par called for redemption 01/15/1962
6% Preferred $4 par called for redemption 01/15/1962
Stock Dividends - 10% 08/19/1966; 10% 08/31/1967; 10% payable 05/15/2002 to holders of record 05/01/2002
Merged into Gyrodyne, LLC 08/31/2015
Each share Common $1 par exchanged for (0.0904) Common Share

GYSAN HLDGS INC (NV)
Name changed to Dino Energy Corp. 07/11/2013

GYZER CAP INC (CANADA)
Name changed to Manicouagan Minerals Inc. 11/19/2004
Manicouagan Minerals Inc. recapitalized as Murchison Minerals Ltd. 06/05/2014

GZA GEOENVIRONMENTAL TECHNOLOGIES INC (DE)
Merged into Futureco Environmental, Inc. 11/21/2000
Each share Common 1¢ par exchanged for $6.40 cash

GZITIC HUALING HLDGS LTD (HONG KONG)
Name changed to Hualing Holdings Ltd. 07/11/2003
Hualing Holdings Ltd. name changed to Welling Holding Ltd. 07/14/2008
(See Welling Holding Ltd.)

H

H., L. & L. DEVELOPMENT CO. (MO)
Charter forfeited for failure to file reports 1/1/52

H. & C. SHARES, INC. (NY)
Dissolved 10/29/40

H. & G. PROPERTIES, INC. (DE)
Liquidation completed 8/22/62
Details not available

H & B AMER CORP (NY)
Merged into Teleprompter Corp. 9/17/70
Each share Common 10¢ par exchanged for (0.32) share Common $1 par
(See Teleprompter Corp.)

H & B AMERICAN MACHINE CO., INC. (NY)
Name changed to H & B American Corp. 7/23/59
H & B American Corp. merged into Teleprompter Corp. 9/17/70
(See Teleprompter Corp.)

H & B AMERICAN MACHINE CO. (ME)
Recapitalized in 1947
Each share Preferred $10 par exchanged for (0.75) share Common no par
Each share Common $10 par exchanged for (0.1) share Common no par
Recapitalized in 1950
Common no par changed to $1 par
Recapitalized in 1952
Common $1 par changed to 25¢ par
Merged into H & B American Machine Co., Inc. 3/31/54
Each share Common 25¢ par exchanged for (1.75) shares Common 10¢ par and $7.30 principal amount of 3% 10-Year Notes
H & B American Machine Co., Inc. name changed to H & B American Corp. 7/23/59 which merged into Teleprompter Corp. 9/17/70
(See Teleprompter Corp.)

H & B CARRIERS (UT)
Involuntarily dissolved 09/01/1988

H & CB (KOREA)
Stock Dividend - 9.5656% payable 04/20/2001 to holders of record 12/29/2000
Merged into Kookmin Bank (New) 11/01/2001
Each Sponsored ADR for Ordinary exchanged for (0.5) Sponsored ADR for Common
Kookmin Bank (New) merged into KB Financial Group Inc. 09/29/2008

H & H IMPORTS INC (FL)
Recapitalized as As Seen On TV, Inc. 10/27/2011
Each share Common $0.0001 par exchanged for (0.05) share Common $0.0001 par

H & H OIL TOOL INC (DE)
Reincorporated 06/04/1987
State of Incorporation changed from (CA) to (DE) 06/04/1987
Merged into Weatherford International Inc. (Old) 09/01/1994
Each share Common no par exchanged for (0.789) share Common 10¢ par
Weatherford International Inc. (Old) recapitalized as Weatherford Enterra, Inc. 10/05/1995 which merged into EVI Weatherford, Inc.

05/27/1998 which name changed to Weatherford International Inc. (New) (DE) 09/21/1998 which reincorporated in Bermuda as Weatherford International Ltd. 06/26/2002 which reincorporated in Switzerland 02/25/2009 which reincorporated in Ireland as Weatherford International PLC 06/18/2014

H & L INVTS INC (NV)
Name changed to Asia4sale.com, Inc. 12/29/99
Asia4sale.com, Inc. recapitalized as Asia8, Inc. 4/27/2007

H & M TAXSAVERS LTD. (CANADA)
Ceased operations 00/00/1972
Details not available

H & Q HEALTHCARE INVS (MA)
Stock Dividends - 17.82% payable 09/28/2004 to holders of record 08/20/2004 Ex date - 08/18/2004; 0.0180972% payable 09/30/2013 to holders of record 08/29/2013 Ex date - 08/27/2013
Name changed to Tekla Healthcare Investors 10/20/2014

H & Q LIFE SCIENCES INVS (MA)
Stock Dividend - 0.0180972% payable 09/30/2013 to holders of record 08/29/2013 Ex date - 08/27/2013
Name changed to Tekla Life Sciences Investors 10/20/2014

H & S TREAT & RELEASE INC (NY)
Each share old Common $0.001 par exchanged for (0.2) share new Common $0.001 par 7/8/92
Reincorporated under the laws of Delaware as Home Theatre Products International Inc. 2/11/94
(See Home Theatre Products International Inc.)

H A S ANTIQUE MART INC (NY)
Reincorporated under the laws of Delaware as Ponderosa Industries Inc. 1/17/72
(See Ponderosa Industries Inc.)

H.D. VEST INC (TX)
Merged into Wells Fargo & Co. 07/02/2001
Each share Common 5¢ par exchanged for $21.03 cash

H E C HITECK ENTMT CORP (BC)
Name changed to Gleneagles Petroleum Corp. 02/03/1997
Gleneagles Petroleum Corp. name changed to Clickhouse.Com Online Inc. 07/29/1999 which recapitalized as Windridge Technology Corp. 09/19/2002 which name changed to Dajin Resources Corp. 01/19/2005

H E R O INDS LTD (BC)
Reincorporated under the laws of Ontario as Middlefield Bancorp Ltd. 04/25/1997
Middlefield Bancorp Ltd. merged into Middlefield Tactical Energy Corp. 02/23/2012 which name changed to MBN Corp. 02/27/2012

H E VENTURES INC (MN)
Common 1¢ par changed to $0.005 par and (1) additional share issued 3/27/86
Statutorily dissolved 12/31/93

H-ENTERTAINMENT INC (NV)
SEC revoked common stock registration 07/14/2009

H F IMAGE SYS INC (CA)
Name changed to Image Systems, Inc. (CA) 12/28/69
Image Systems, Inc. (CA) reincorporated in Delaware 8/29/74
(See Image Systems, Inc. (DE))

H.G.R. CORP. (MI)
Liquidation completed 10/18/1963
Details not available

H H R FOOD INDS INC (NY)
Dissolved by proclamation 9/28/94

H I S A INVTS LTD (BC)
Struck off register and declared dissolved for failure to file returns 06/11/1993

H J FST PRODS INC (AB)
Name changed to Bradstone Equity Partners, Inc. 07/31/1997
Bradstone Equity Partners, Inc. merged into Quest Investment Corp. 07/04/2002 which merged into Quest Capital Corp. (BC) 06/30/2003 which reincorporated in Canada 05/27/2008 which name changed to Sprott Resource Lending Corp. 09/10/2010 which merged into Sprott Inc. 07/24/2013

H K S CORP. (DE)
Liquidation completed
Each share Common $5.50 par stamped to indicate initial distribution of $185 cash 12/22/69
Each share Stamped Common $5.50 par stamped to indicate second and final distribution of $40.10 cash 9/9/70

H-L CORP (NV)
Common $0.001 par split (5) for (1) by issuance of (4) additional shares 12/1/94
Common $0.001 par split (10) for (1) by issuance of (9) additional shares 7/10/95
Name changed to Indocan Resources Inc. 3/25/96

H L INTL INC (AB)
Name changed to Maple Mark International Inc. 04/17/1996
Maple Mark International Inc. name changed to Linear Resources Inc. 10/15/1999 which name changed to Linear Gold Corp. (AB) 11/24/2003 which reincorporated in Canada 11/10/2004 which merged into Brigus Gold Corp. (YT) 06/25/2010 which reincorporated in Canada 06/09/2011
(See Brigus Gold Corp.)

H.M. LIQUIDATION CORP. (MI)
Under plan of liquidation each share Common $10 par exchanged for initial distribution of (0.343642) share Hercules Powder Co. Common $2-1/12 par 04/24/1957
(See Hercules Powder Co.)
Each share Common $10 par received a second and final distribution of an undetermined amount of cash from escrow 03/16/1962

H M INDS INC (NY)
Reorganized under the laws of Delaware as LaTouraine Foods, Inc. 5/31/70
Each share Common 5¢ par exchanged for (1) share Common 5¢ par
LaTouraine Foods, Inc. merged into LaTouraine-Bickford's Foods, Inc. 11/30/70 which name changed to Bickford Corp. 5/2/78
(See Bickford Corp.)

H M S S INC (DE)
Merged into Secomerica, Inc. 11/3/89
Each share Common 1¢ par exchanged for $50 cash

H-NET NET INC (CO)
Name changed 8/1/2000
Common $0.0001 par split (2) for (1) by issuance of (1) additional share payable 4/17/2000 to holders of record 4/3/2000
Name changed from H-Net.com, Inc. to H-Net.Net Inc. 8/1/2000
Each share old Common $0.0001 par exchanged for (0.1) share new Common $0.0001 par 9/10/2001
Each share new Common $0.0001 par exchanged for (0.05) share old Common $0.001 par 11/30/2001
Each share old Common $0.001 par received distribution of (0.01) share Career Worth, Inc. Common $0.001 par payable 4/25/2002 to holders of record 4/3/2002
Each share old Common $0.001 par exchanged for (0.03125) share new Common $0.001 par 1/26/2004
Reincorporated under the laws of Nevada as DONOBi, Inc. 7/21/2004
DONOBi, Inc. recapitalized as Gottaplay Interactive, Inc. 7/25/2006

H O FINL LTD (ON)
Common no par reclassified as old Class A Common no par 12/03/1982
Each share old Conv. Class A Common no par exchanged for (0.2) share new Conv. Class A Common no par 08/25/1986
Each share old Conv. Class B Common no par exchanged for (0.2) share new Common no par 08/25/1986
Each share new Conv. Class A Common no par received distribution of (0.4) share Perle Systems Ltd. Common no par payable 05/31/1996 to holders of record 05/10/1996
Each share new Class B Common no par received distribution of (0.4) share Perle Systems Ltd. Common no par payable 05/31/1996 to holders of record 05/10/1995
Each share new Conv. Class A Common no par exchanged for (4) shares new Common no par 09/09/1996
Each share new Class B Common no par exchanged for (4) shares new Common no par 09/09/1996
Merged into Mandukwe Inc. 02/28/2007
Each share new Common no par exchanged for $1.03 cash

H.P. CAMPBELL INC. (TX)
Voluntarily dissolved 3/28/86
Details not available

H PWR CORP (DE)
Issue Information - 7,000,000 shares COM offered at $16 per share on 08/09/2000
Each share old Common $0.001 par exchanged for (0.2) share new Common $0.001 par 10/16/2002
Merged into Plug Power, Inc. 3/25/2003
Each share new Common $0.001 par exchanged for (0.8305) share Common 1¢ par

H Q MINERALS LTD (BC)
Struck off register and declared dissolved for failure to file returns 06/05/1992

H QUOTIENT INC (VA)
Each share Common $0.0001 par received distribution of (0.005) share Healthnostics, Inc. Common $0.0001 par payable 08/31/2004 to holders of record 07/30/2004
Stock Dividend - 0.5% payable 08/31/2004 to holders of record 07/30/2004
SEC revoked common stock registration 10/31/2006

H R S INDS INC (BC)
Class A Common no par split (3) for (1) by issuance of (2) additional shares 03/31/1983
Class B Common no par split (3) for (1) by issuance of (2) additional shares 03/31/1983
Merged into International H.R.S. Industries Inc. 05/15/1984
Each share Class A Common no par exchanged for (1) share Common no par
Each share Class B Common no par exchanged for (0.25) share Common no par

International H.R.S. Industries Inc. name changed to Glenex Industries Inc. 05/25/1987 which merged into Quest Investment Corp. 07/04/2002 which merged into Quest Capital Corp. (BC) 06/30/2003 which reincorporated in Canada 05/27/2008 which name changed to Sprott Resource Lending Corp. 09/10/2010 which merged into Sprott Inc. 07/24/2013

H-S ROYALTY, LTD. (OK)
Voluntarily dissolved 05/31/2000
Details not available

H.S.S., INC. (IN)
Liquidation completed for cash 3/10/66
Details not available

H T E INC (FL)
Common 1¢ par split (2) for (1) by issuance of (1) additional share payable 6/18/98 to holders of record 6/8/98
Merged into SunGard Data Systems Inc. 3/19/2003
Each share Common 1¢ par exchanged for $7 cash

H T PRODS CORP (NY)
Completely liquidated 3/6/73
Each share Class A 20¢ par exchanged for first and final distribution of $3 cash
Each share Class B 20¢ par exchanged for $3 cash

H T R INDS INC (BC)
Common no par split (2) for (1) by issuance of (1) additional share 04/11/1986
Recapitalized as Lazer Maze Industries Inc. 06/02/1989
Each share Common no par exchanged for (0.25) share Common no par
(See Lazer Maze Industries Inc.)

H T V SYS INC (NY)
Merged into Magnavox Co. 4/22/71
Each share Common 5¢ par exchanged for (0.0077248) share Common $1 par
(See Magnavox Co.)

H-TECH CORP. (UT)
Name changed to Sooner Grant Corp. 4/24/85

H W I INDS INC (ON)
Charter cancelled 05/23/1988

H&A BRUSH CORP. (CA)
Liquidation completed
Each share Common 25¢ par exchanged for initial distribution of (1) Ctf. of Right to Receive Contingent Payment plus first Contingent payment of $0.32 cash; (1) Ctf. of Bene. Int. in Litigated Claim and $6.12 cash 7/10/69
Holders of Certificates of Rights to Receive Contingent Payment received second distribution of $0.335 cash 10/8/70
Holders of Certificates of Rights to Receive Contingent Payment received third and final distribution of $0.35 cash 9/28/71
Certificates were not required to be surrendered and are now valueless
Holders of Certificates of Bene. Int. in Litigated Claim received first and final distribution of $0.16 cash 4/1/71
Certificates were not required to be surrendered and are now valueless

H&A INDUSTRIES (OH)
Name changed to Bolen Holding Co. 8/2/84
(See Bolen Holding Co.)

H&D LTD (DE)
Name changed to Exclusive Incentives Inc. 05/17/1991
(See Exclusive Incentives Inc.)

H&R-HAC   FINANCIAL INFORMATION, INC.

H&R REAL ESTATE INVT TR/H&R FIN TR (ON)
Units unstapled 09/10/2018
Each Stapled Unit exchanged for (1) H&R Real Estate Investment Trust new Unit
Note: Each Unit consisted of (1) H&R REIT Trust Unit and (1) H&R Finance Trust Unit

H&R REAL ESTATE INVT TR (ON)
Reorganized as H&R Real Estate Investment Trust/H&R Finance Trust 10/03/2008
Each Unit no par exchanged for (1) Stapled Unit no par and $0.00019408 cash
(Additional Information in Active)

HA-LO INDS INC (IL)
Reincorporated 8/31/2000
Common no par split (3) for (2) by issuance of (0.5) additional share payable 6/3/96 to holders of record 5/17/96
Common no par split (5) for (4) by issuance of (0.25) additional share payable 12/11/96 to holders of record 11/21/96 Ex date - 12/12/96
Common no par split (3) for (2) by issuance of (0.5) additional share payable 2/19/99 to holders of record 2/5/99 Ex date - 2/22/99
State of incorporation changed from (IL) to (DE) and Common no par changed to $0.001 par 8/31/2000
Plan of reorganization under Chapter 11 Federal Bankruptcy Code effective 2/10/2004
Stockholders' equity unlikely

HAAG DRUG INC (IN)
Common $1 par split (2) for (1) by issuance of (1) additional share 3/15/61
Merged into Peoples Drug Stores, Inc. 2/13/81
Each share Common $1 par exchanged for $19 cash

HAAGEN ALEXANDER PPTYS INC (MD)
Name changed to CenterTrust Retail Properties, Inc. 8/28/98
CenterTrust Retail Properties, Inc. name changed to Center Trust, Inc. 7/21/99 which merged into Pan Pacific Retail Properties, Inc. 1/17/2003 which merged into Kimco Realty Corp. 10/31/2006

HAAS NEVEUX & CO (CO)
Recapitalized as Century Milestone S & T Co. Ltd. 7/21/2000
Each share Common $0.0001 par exchanged for (0.1) share Common $0.0001 par
Century Milestone S & T Co. Ltd. recapitalized as Sino Real Property Development Corp. 10/21/2003

HABANERO CORP (DE)
Name changed to Terra Linda Corp. 6/10/88
(See Terra Linda Corp.)

HABANERO LUMBER CO. (NJ)
Under plan of merger name changed to Habanero Corp. and state of incorporation changed to Delaware 12/27/71
Habanero Corp. name changed to Terra Linda Corp. 6/10/88
(See Terra Linda Corp.)

HABANERO RES INC (BC)
Recapitalized as Sienna Resources Inc. 01/24/2014
Each share Common no par exchanged for (0.1) share Common no par

HABEN INDS INC (DE)
Each share old Common $0.001 par exchanged for (0.1) share new Common $0.001 par 02/26/1991
Recapitalized as Embrace Systems Corp. 04/29/1992
Each share new Common $0.001 par exchanged for (0.2) share Common $0.001 par
(See Embrace Systems Corp.)

HABER INC (DE)
Name changed 04/01/1980
Name and place of incorporation changed from Haber Instruments, Inc. (NY) to Haber, Inc. (DE) and Common 10¢ par changed to 1¢ par 04/01/1980
Common 1¢ par split (2) for (1) by issuance of (1) additional share 09/26/1980
Common 1¢ par split (2) for (1) by issuance of (1) additional share 01/16/1981
Special Vtg. Common 1¢ par reclassified as Common 1¢ par 12/01/1982
Common 1¢ par split (7) for (5) by issuance of (0.4) additional share 10/15/1985
Stock Dividends - In Special Vtg. Common to holders of Common 12.5% 01/15/1982
In Common to holders of Common 20% 07/09/1984
SEC revoked preferred and common stock registration 07/22/2011

HABERCO, INC. (MN)
100% reacquired through purchase offer which expired 03/21/1980

HABERSHAM ENERGY CO (OK)
Recapitalized as Trinity Companies Inc. (OK) 03/15/2002
Each share Common 10¢ par exchanged for (0.01) share Common $0.001 par
Trinity Companies Inc. (OK) reincorporated in Utah 05/07/2002 which name changed to Trinity Learning Corp. 03/31/2003 which name changed to TWL Corp. (UT) 10/13/2006 which reorganized in Nevada 12/12/2007
(See TWL Corp.)

HABIBI RES CORP (BC)
Recapitalized as One World Investments Inc. 10/07/2009
Each share Common no par exchanged for (0.125) share Common no par
One World Investments Inc. name changed to One World Minerals Inc. 02/28/2017 which name changed to One World Lithium Inc. 01/19/2018

HABICO INDS INC (DE)
Charter cancelled and declared inoperative and void for non-payment of taxes 03/01/1976

HABITANT GOLD MINES, LTD. (ON)
Charter cancelled for failure to file reports and pay taxes 02/00/1958

HABITEX INDS INC (OK)
Recapitalized as Oklahoma Land & Exploration Co. 12/15/80
Each share Common 10¢ par exchanged for (4) shares Common $0.025 par
Oklahoma Land & Exploration Co. name changed to Leadership Properties, Inc. 11/7/83
(See Leadership Properties, Inc.)

HABSBURG RES INC (ON)
Name changed to Dome Mountain Resources Ltd. 09/14/1994
Dome Mountain Resources Ltd. recapitalized as DMR Resources Ltd. 11/06/1996
(See DMR Resources Ltd.)

HACH CO (DE)
Name changed 09/24/1980
Common $1 par split (5) for (4) by issuance of (0.25) additional share 11/04/1971
Stock Dividend - 100% 01/20/1970
Name changed from Hach Chemical Co. to Hach Co. 09/24/1980
Common $1 par split (2) for (1) by issuance of (1) additional share 01/13/1986
Common $1 par split (5) for (4) by issuance of (0.25) additional share 10/13/1988
Common $1 par split (5) for (4) by issuance of (0.25) additional share 01/10/1990
Common $1 par split (5) for (4) by issuance of (0.25) additional share 04/10/1991
Common $1 par split (3) for (2) by issuance of (0.5) additional share 06/04/1992
Common $1 par split (5) for (4) by issuance of (0.25) additional share 04/08/1994
Each share Common $1 par received distribution of (1) share Class A Common $1 par payable 10/02/1997 to holders of record 09/22/1997
Merged into Danaher Corp. 07/14/1999
Each share Common $1 par exchanged for (0.2987) share Common 1¢ par
Each share Class A Common $1 par exchanged for (0.2987) share Common 1¢ par

HACHMEISTER-LIND CO.
Bankrupt in 1935
Details not available

HACI OMER SABANCI HLDG S A (TURKEY)
Each Temporary Sponsored ADR for Ordinary exchanged for (1) 144A Sponsored ADR for Ordinary 04/06/2001
Each Temporary 2001 Sponsored ADR for Ordinary exchanged for (1) Reg. S Sponsored ADR for Ordinary 04/06/2001
Each 144A Sponsored ADR for Ordinary received distribution of (0.25) 144A Temporary Bonus Sponsored ADR for Ordinary payable 03/20/2003 to holders of record 02/27/2003 Ex date - 02/25/2003
Each Reg. S Sponsored ADR for Ordinary received distribution of (0.25) Reg. S Temporary Bonus Sponsored ADR for Ordinary payable 03/20/2003 to holders of record 02/27/2003 Ex date - 02/25/2003
Each Temporary Bonus 144A Sponsored ADR for Ordinary exchanged for (1) 144A Sponsored ADR for Ordinary 04/14/2003
Each Temporary Bonus Reg. S Sponsored ADR for Ordinary exchanged for (1) Reg. S Sponsored ADR for Ordinary 04/14/2003
(Additional Information in Active)

HACIENDA BK (SANTA MARIA, CA)
Name changed 12/12/1997
Name changed from Hacienda National Bank (Santa Maria, CA) to Hacienda Bank (Santa Maria, CA) 12/12/1997
Merged into Heritage Oaks Bancorp 10/31/2003
Each share Common $5 par exchanged for either (0.5208) share Common no par or $6.75 cash
Note: Option to receive stock expired 10/27/2003
Heritage Oaks Bancorp merged into Pacific Premier Bancorp, Inc. 03/31/2017

HACIENDA RESORTS INC (NV)
Name changed to Sahara Resorts 2/6/84
Sahara Resorts merged into Sahara Gaming Corp. 9/30/93 which name changed to Santa Fe Gaming Corp. 2/21/96 which name changed to Archon Corp. 5/11/2001

HACKENSACK TRUST CO. (HACKENSACK, NJ)
Common $25 par changed to $10 par and (4.5) additional shares issued 03/02/1962
Name changed to Hackensack Trust Co., N.A. (Hackensack, NJ) 01/19/1966
Hackensack Trust Co., N.A. (Hackensack, NJ) name changed to Garden State National Bank (Hackensack, NJ) 05/05/1970 which changed location to Paramus, NJ 11/15/1974
(See Garden State National Bank (Paramus, NJ))

HACKENSACK TR CO N A (HACKENSACK, NJ)
Stock Dividend - 10% 3/13/68
Name changed to Garden State National Bank (Hackensack, NJ) 5/5/70
Garden State National Bank (Hackensack, NJ) location changed to Garden State National Bank (Paramus, NJ) 11/15/74
(See Garden State National Bank (Paramus, NJ))

HACKENSACK WTR CO (NJ)
Common $25 par changed to $12.50 par and (1) additional share issued 05/25/1962
4-1/2% Preferred $100 par changed to no par 05/09/1977
5% Preferred $100 par changed to no par 05/09/1977
10-3/4% Preferred $100 par changed to no par 05/09/1977
Common $12.50 par changed to $6.25 par and (1) additional share issued 09/01/1979
Common $6.25 par changed to $5 par and (0.5) additional share issued 09/01/1982
Stock Dividend - 25% 03/01/1950
Under plan of reorganization each share Common $5 par automatically became (1) share United Water Resources Inc. Common $5 par 08/16/1983
(See United Water Resources Inc.)
Name changed to United Water New Jersey 01/00/1995
(See United Water New Jersey)

HACKER ATOMPOWER MINES LTD. (ON)
Charter revoked for failure to file reports and pay fees 04/15/1965

HACKER BOAT CO. (MI)
Liquidation completed
Each share Common $1 par exchanged for initial distribution of $1 cash 8/23/67
Each share Common $1 par received second and final distribution of $0.08 cash 8/15/68

HACKERPROOF LTD (DE)
Name changed to Alcard Chemicals Group, Inc. 03/14/2006
Alcard Chemicals Group, Inc. name changed to Alcar Chemicals Group, Inc. 04/03/2006

HACKETT, GATES HURTY CO.
Liquidated 00/00/1931
Details not available

HACKETTS STORES INC (FL)
Each share old Common $0.0001 par exchanged for (0.02) share new Common $0.0001 par 10/27/2009
Recapitalized as WiseBuys, Inc. 06/17/2010
Each (35) shares new Common $0.0001 par exchanged for (1) share Common $0.0001 par
WiseBuys, Inc. name changed to Empire Pizza Holdings, Inc. 04/20/2011 which recapitalized as Vestiage, Inc. 03/22/2013

HACKLEY UN NATL BK & TR CO (MUSKEGON, MI)
Common $10 par changed to $5 par and (1) additional share issued 2/1/66
Stock Dividends - 33-1/3% 1/15/51;

20% 2/2/59; 10% 3/8/63; 10% 1/24/64; 10% 1/19/65; 10% 2/8/67; 10% 2/7/68; 20% 1/28/69; 50% 2/10/70; 33-1/3% 2/6/71
Reorganized under the laws of Delaware as Lake Shore Financial Corp. 7/2/73
Each share Common $5 par exchanged for (1) share Common $5 par
(See Lake Shore Financial Corp.)

HACKNEY CORP (DE)
Acquired by Merchants Inc. 12/17/73
Each share Common 50¢ par exchanged for $7 cash

HADA ENTERPRISES LTD (DE)
Adjudicated bankrupt 02/23/1976
Stockholders' equity unlikely

HADCO CORP (MA)
Secondary Offering - 2,300,000 shares COM offered at $56.875 per share on 06/05/1997
Merged into Sanmina Corp. 06/23/2000
Each share Common 50¢ par exchanged for (1.4) shares Common 1¢ par
Sanmina Corp. name changed to Sanmina-SCI Corp. 12/10/2001 which name changed back to Sanmina Corp. 11/15/2012

HADDEN SAFETY INDS INC (PA)
Out of business 1/31/81
Details not available

HADDINGTON INTL RES LTD (YT)
Reorganized 05/20/1999
Reincorporated 06/23/2000
Reorganized from Haddington Resources Ltd. (BC) to Haddington International Reources (Yukon) 05/20/1999
Each share old Common no par exchanged for (1/6) share new Common no par
Place of incorporation changed from (Yukon) to (Australia) 06/23/2000
Name changed back to Haddington Resources Ltd. 01/16/2003

HADDON HALL APARTMENTS LIQUIDATION TRUST
Liquidation completed in 1950

HADDONFIELD NATIONAL BANK (HADDONFIELD, NJ)
Stock Dividends - 10% 03/01/1965; 10% 03/01/1966; 10% 03/01/1967
Name changed to Colonial National Bank (Haddonfield, NJ) 09/07/1967
Colonial National Bank (Haddonfield, NJ) acquired by Midlantic Banks Inc. 08/31/1972 which merged into Midlantic Corp. 01/30/1987 which merged into PNC Bank Corp. 12/31/1995 which name changed to PNC Financial Services Group, Inc. 03/15/2000

HADFIELD PENFIELD STEEL CO.
Property sold 00/00/1927
Details not available

HADLEY FALLS TRUST CO. (HOLYOKE, MA)
Merged into Safe Deposit Bank & Trust Co. (Springfield, Mass.) 3/5/62
Each share Common $50 par exchanged for (6.25) shares Capital Stock $10 par
Safe Deposit Bank & Trust Co. (Springfield, Mass.) name changed to First Bank & Trust Co. of Hampden County (Springfield, Mass.) 5/6/68 which name changed to Shawmut First Bank & Trust Co. (Springfield, Mass.) 4/1/75

HADLEY MNG INC (ON)
Each share old Common no par exchanged for (0.08333333) share new Common no par 02/21/2017
Name changed to SpeakEasy Cannabis Club Ltd. 04/04/2018

HADRO RES INC (NV)
Recapitalized as Petrogen Corp. 02/12/2003
Each share Common $0.001 par exchanged for (0.05) share Common $0.001 par
Petrogen Corp. recapitalized as Pluris Energy Group Inc. 09/12/2006 which name changed to Nationwide Utilities Corp. 12/02/2009

HADRON INC (NY)
Each share old Common 2¢ par exchanged for (0.1) share new Common 2¢ par 8/13/93
Reincorporated under the laws of Delaware as Analex Corp. 7/1/2002
(See Analex Corp.)

HADSON CORP NEW (DE)
Merged into LG&E Energy Corp. 5/15/95
Each share Common 1¢ par exchanged for $2.75 cash
Each share Automatically Conv. Jr. Exercisable Preferred Ser. B 1¢ par exchanged for $0.00275 cash 12/14/95
Public interest eliminated

HADSON CORP OLD (DE)
Reincorporated 3/3/80
Name changed 6/10/86
State of incorporation changed from (OH) to (DE) and Common no par changed to 10¢ par 3/3/80
Stock Dividend - 50% 4/3/80
Common no par split (3) for (1) by issuance of (2) additional shares 2/18/81
Name changed from Hadson Petroleum Corp. to Hadson Corp. (Old) 6/10/86
Common 10¢ par changed to 1¢ par 12/16/92
Merged into Hadson Corp. (New) 12/14/93
Each share 8% Jr. Conv. Preferred Ser. B 1¢ par exchanged for (1.09667) shares Jr. Preferred Ser. B 1¢ par and (1.50733) shares Common 1¢ par
Each share Common 1¢ par exchanged for (0.01667) share Jr. Conv. Preferred Ser. B 1¢ par and (0.06667) share Common 1¢ par
(See Hadson Corp. (New))

HADSON ENERGY RES CORP (DE)
Merged into Apache Corp. 11/12/93
Each share Common 10¢ par exchanged for either (0.574) share Common $1.25 par or $15 cash
Note: Option to receive stock expired 2/1/94

HADSON EUROPE INC (DE)
Name changed to Midwest Energy Companies, Inc. and Common 10¢ par changed to $0.001 par 12/20/91

HADSON OHIO OIL CO. (OH)
Name changed to Hadson Petroleum Corp. (OH) 6/7/79
Hadson Petroleum Corp. (OH) reincorporated in Delaware 3/3/80 which name changed to Hadson Corp. (Old) 6/10/86 which merged into Hadson Corp. (New) 12/14/93
(See Hadson Corp. (New))

HAELAN LABORATORIES, INC. (PA)
Recapitalized as Connelly Containers, Inc. 4/29/55
Each share Common $1 par exchanged for (0.5) share Common 50¢ par and (0.25) share 40¢ Preferred $1 par
(See Connelly Containers, Inc.)

HAEMACURE CORP (CANADA)
Chapter 11 bankruptcy proceedings confirmed 06/18/2010
Stockholders' equity unlikely

HAEMONETICS CORP (DE)
Merged into American Hospital Supply Corp. 8/30/83
Each share Common $1 par exchanged for (0.6383) share Common no par
American Hospital Supply Corp. merged into Baxter Travenol Laboratories, Inc. 11/25/85 which name changed to Baxter International Inc. 5/18/88

HAFNER FABRICS CDA LTD (CANADA)
Name changed 08/02/1958
Name changed from Hafner Fabrics of Canada (1954) Ltd. to Hafner Fabrics of Canada Ltd. 08/02/1958
Voting Trust Agreement terminated 04/01/1960
Each VTC for Common no par exchanged for (1) share Common no par
Company went private 05/25/1990
Details not available

HAFSLUND ASA (NORWAY)
Name changed 5/14/96
Each Sponsored ADR for A Shares NOK 5 par received distribution of (1) Nycomed ASA Sponsored ADR for Class A payable 5/21/96 to holders of record 5/13/96
Each Sponsored ADR for Non-Voting B Shares NOK 5 par received distribution of (1) Nycomed ASA Sponsored ADR for Class B payable 5/21/96 to holders of record 5/13/96
Name changed from Hafslund Nycomed AS to Hafslund ASA 5/14/96
ADR agreement terminated 6/14/96
Each Sponsored ADR for A Shares NOK 5 par exchanged for $7.12214 cash
Each Sponsored ADR for Non-Voting B Shares NOK 5 par exchanged for $6.37547 cash

HAGAN CHEMICALS & CONTROLS, INC. (PA)
Common $1 par split (5) for (2) by issuance of (1.5) additional shares 02/25/1959
Name changed to Calgon Corp. 04/17/1963
Calgon Corp. merged into Merck & Co., Inc. (Old) 01/31/1968 which merged into Merck & Co., Inc. (New) 11/03/2009

HAGAN CORP. (PA)
Name changed to Hagan Chemicals & Controls, Inc. 01/01/1957
Hagan Chemicals & Controls, Inc. name changed to Calgon Corp. 04/17/1963 which merged into Merck & Co., Inc. (Old) 01/31/1968 which merged into Merck & Co., Inc. (New) 11/03/2009

HAGANAH LTD (DE)
Name changed to I.M.T., Inc. 04/02/1986
(See I.M.T., Inc.)

HAGENSBORG RES LTD (BC)
Struck off register and declared dissolved for failure to file returns 01/06/1995

HAGER INC (CT)
Common no par changed to 10¢ par 9/30/74
Merged into GCMC Holding Corp. 5/11/81
Each share Common 10¢ par exchanged for $0.50 cash

HAGERSTOWN GAS CO. (MD)
Common $1.25 par changed to 62-1/2¢ par and (1) additional share issued 12/20/61
Acquired by Columbia Gas System, Inc. 3/29/68
Each share 5% Preferred $100 par exchanged for (4.057971) shares Common $10 par
Each share Common 62-1/2¢ par exchanged for (0.667) share Common $10 par
Columbia Gas System, Inc. name changed to Columbia Energy Group 1/16/98 which merged into NiSource Inc. 11/1/2000

HAGERSTOWN TR CO (HAGERSTOWN, MD)
Reorganized as Mid-Atlantic Bankcorp 6/2/85
Each share Capital Stock $10 par exchanged for (2) shares Common $5 par
Mid-Atlantic Bankcorp merged into Fulton Financial Corp. 7/29/94

HAGGAR CORP (NV)
Merged into Texas Clothing Holding Corp. 11/1/2005
Each share Common 10¢ par exchanged for $29 cash

HAGLER BAILLY INC (DE)
Issue Information - 3,150,000 shares COM offered at $14 per share on 07/03/1997
Merged into PA Consulting Group 10/27/2000
Each share Common 1¢ par exchanged for $5.32 cash

HAGLUND INDS INTL INC (BC)
Cease trade order effective 02/20/1992
Stockholders' equity unlikely

HAGUE CORP (NV)
Name changed to Quantum Materials Corp. 04/13/2010

HAHN AUTOMOTIVE WHSE INC (NY)
Each share old Common 1¢ par exchanged for (1/3) share new Common 1¢ par 5/11/2001
Stock Dividends - 4% payable 5/1/96 to holders of record 4/10/96; 4% payable 5/1/97 to holders of record 4/10/97
Merged into HAW Acquisition, Inc. 9/21/2001
Each share new Common 1¢ par exchanged for $3 cash

HAHN BRASS CO., LTD. (ON)
Recapitalized as Hahn Brass Ltd. (ON) 09/25/1950
Each share $1 Preference no par exchanged for (2) shares Class A no par
Each share Common no par exchanged for (2) shares Common no par
Hahn Brass Ltd. (ON) reincorporated in Canada 12/17/1976
(See Hahn Brass Ltd.)

HAHN BRASS LTD (CANADA)
Reincorporated 12/17/1976
Each share Class A no par received (1) share 5% 1st Preference $18 par 01/21/1959
Note: Class A certificates were not retired and are now without value
Common no par split (2) for (1) by issuance of (1) additional share 12/17/1959
5% 2nd Preference $10 par called for redemption 02/15/1960
5% 1st Preference $18 par called for redemption 10/22/1971
Place of incorporation changed from (ON) to (Canada) 12/17/1976
Acquired by Stanley Works Ltd. 01/02/1977
Details not available

HAHN DEPARTMENT STORES, INC.
Name changed to Allied Stores Corp. in 1935
(See Allied Stores Corp.)

HAHN ERNEST W INC (CA)
Common $1 par changed to 66-2/3¢ par and (0.5) additional share issued 4/5/73
Merged into Trizec Corp. Ltd. 11/17/80
Each share Common 66-2/3¢ par exchanged for $54.42 cash

HAI SUN HUP GROUP LTD (SINGAPORE)
Name changed to Stamford Land Corp. Ltd. 09/05/2001
(See Stamford Land Corp. Ltd.)

HAI VENTURE LTD (NV)
Name changed to Arkam Gold, Inc. 1/19/88
Arkam Gold, Inc. recapitalized as Silver State Mining & Exploration, Inc. 4/4/94 which recapitalized as Trivest Equities Ltd. 11/24/2004 which name changed to MCN Multicast Networks, Inc. 2/11/2005 which name changed to Downtown America Funding Corp. 9/8/2005 which name changed to Savior Energy Corp. 12/22/2006

HAI XIA HLDGS LTD (BERMUDA)
Name changed to China Gas Holdings Ltd. 08/02/2002
(See China Gas Holdings Ltd.)

HAIKU FRUIT & PACKING CO.
Merged into Haiku Pineapple Co. Ltd. in 1928
Details not available

HAIKU PINEAPPLE CO. LTD.
Assets sold and name changed to Island Pineapple Co. Ltd. 00/00/1935
(See Island Pineapple Co. Ltd.)

HAILE GOLD MINES, INC. (DE)
Name changed to Haile Mines, Inc. in 1945
Haile Mines, Inc. merged into Howe Sound Co. (DE) 6/30/58 which name changed to Howmet Corp. 11/26/65
(See Howmet Corp.)

HAILE MINES, INC. (DE)
Merged into Howe Sound Co. (DE) 6/30/58
Each share Capital Stock 25¢ par exchanged for (0.4) share Common $1 par
Howe Sound Co. (DE) name changed to Howmet Corp. 11/26/65
(See Howmet Corp.)

HAILEY ENERGY CORP (UT)
Each share Common $0.005 par exchanged for (0.03333333) share Common 15¢ par 11/15/1990
Name changed to Cytoprobe Corp. 12/01/1992
Cytoprobe Corp. name changed to Medical Device Technologies, Inc. 04/20/1995 which name changed to Miracor Diagnostics Inc. 10/12/1999
(See Miracor Diagnostics Inc.)

HAIN FOOD GROUP INC (DE)
Under plan of merger name changed to Hain Celestial Group, Inc. 5/30/2000

HAINES GYPSUM INC (BC)
Cease trade order effective 10/25/1988
Stockholders' equity unlikely

HAIR ANALYSIS INC (MT)
Recapitalized as OTC Stock Journal, Inc. 3/16/83
Each share Common $0.001 par exchanged for (3) shares Common $0.001 par
(See OTC Stock Journal, Inc.)

HAIR EXTN CTR INC (NY)
Name changed to Kennington Corp. 2/8/71
(See Kennington Corp.)

HAIR-STRATE, INC. (IN)
Name changed to Summit Laboratories, Inc. 5/28/62

HAIRMAX INTL INC (NV)
Each share old Common $0.001 par exchanged for (0.01) share new Common $0.001 par 01/10/2005
Name changed to China Digital Media Corp. 03/31/2005
(See China Digital Media Corp.)

HAITEX OIL CORP. (DE)
Charter cancelled and declared inoperative and void for non-payment of taxes 4/15/70

HAITIAN-AMERICAN MINERALS CORP. (DE)
Dissolved 8/31/56

HAITIAN COPPER CORP. LTD. (ON)
Charter cancelled 1/7/65

HAJECATE OIL CO. (TX)
Reincorporated 02/10/1983
State of incorporation changed from (UT) to (TX) 02/10/1983
Charter forfeited for failure to pay taxes 01/09/1989

HAJOCA CORP (DE)
Each share 7% Preferred $100 par exchanged for (1) share Common $1 par 00/00/1936
Each share Common no par exchanged for (0.05) share Common $1 par 00/00/1936
Stock Dividends - 50% 12/01/1947; 10% 12/30/1948; 10% 12/01/1950
100% acquired by Gable Industries, Inc. through purchase offer which expired 03/01/1972
Public interest eliminated

HAJOCA CORP (ME)
Merged into Panda Star Acquisition Corp. 02/17/1982
Each share Common $1 par exchanged for $7.25 cash

HAKALAU PLANTATION CO (CA)
Reincorporated under the laws of Hawaii as Hakalau Sugar Co. Ltd. in 1956
Hakalau Sugar Co. Ltd. merged into Pepeekeo Sugar Co. 12/31/62 which merged into Brewer (C.) & Co. Ltd. which merged into IU International Corp. 8/14/78
(See IU International Corp.)

HAKALAU SUGAR CO. LTD. (HI)
Common $100 par changed to $20 par in 1959
Merged into Pepeekeo Sugar Co. 12/31/62
Each share Common $20 par exchanged for (0.4) share Common $20 par
Pepeekeo Sugar Co. merged into Brewer (C.) & Co., Ltd. 4/25/73 which merged into IU International Corp. 8/14/78
(See IU International Corp.)

HAKO MINUTEMAN INC (IL)
Name changed to Minuteman International Inc. 4/18/94
(See Minuteman International Inc.)

HAL CONCEPTS LTD (YT)
Name changed to Halmont Properties Corp. (YT) 02/27/2007
Each share Common no par exchanged for (1) share Class A Common no par 02/27/2007
Halmont Properties Corp. (YT) reincorporated in Ontario 02/18/2009

HAL INC (HI)
Plan of reorganization under Chapter 11 Federal Bankruptcy Code effective 09/12/1994
No stockholders' equity

HAL ROACH STUDIOS, INC. (DE)
See - Roach (Hal) Studios, Inc.

HAL ROACH STUDIOS, INC. (NY)
See - Roach (Hal) Studios, Inc.

HALBERN INDS INC (NY)
Dissolved by proclamation 09/26/1979

HALCO CHEMICAL CO. (NJ)
Name changed to Halco Products Corp. (NJ) 2/5/73
Halco Products Corp. (NJ) merged into Halco Products Corp. (NY) 3/14/74 which merged into Tobin Packing Co., Inc. 11/2/79
(See Tobin Packing Co., Inc.)

HALCO PRODS CORP (NJ)
Merged into Halco Products Corp. (NY) 3/14/74
Each share Common 10¢ par exchanged for (1) share Common $1 par
Halco Products Corp. (NY) merged into Tobin Packing Co., Inc. 11/2/79
(See Tobin Packing Co., Inc.)

HALCO PRODS CORP (NY)
Merged into Tobin Packing Co., Inc. 11/2/79
Each share Common $1 par exchanged for (0.2488) share Common $3 par
(See Tobin Packing Co., Inc.)

HALCON INTERNATIONAL, INC. (DE)
Acquired by Texas Eastern Corp. 00/00/1982
Details not available

HALCON RES CORP (DE)
Each share 5.75% Conv. Perpetual Preferred Ser. A $0.0001 par received distribution of (3.448948) shares old Common $0.0001 payable 12/02/2013 to holders of record 11/15/2013 Ex date - 11/13/2013
Each share 5.75% Conv. Perpetual Preferred Ser. A $0.0001 par received distribution of (4.040258) shares old Common $0.0001 par payable 03/03/2014 to holders of record 02/14/2014 Ex date - 02/12/2014
Each share 5.75% Conv. Perpetual Preferred Ser. A $0.0001 par received distribution of (2.625096) shares old Common $0.0001 par payable 06/02/2014 to holders of record 05/15/2014 Ex date - 05/13/2014
Each share 5.75% Conv. Perpetual Preferred Ser. A $0.0001 par received distribution of (2.78851) shares old Common $0.0001 par payable 09/02/2014 to holders of record 08/15/2014 Ex date - 08/13/2014
Each share 5.75% Conv. Perpetual Preferred Ser. A $0.0001 par received distribution of (7.415257) shares old Common $0.0001 par payable 03/02/2015 to holders of record 02/13/2015 Ex date - 02/11/2015
Each share 5.75% Conv. Perpetual Preferred Ser. A $0.0001 par received distribution of (12.437594) shares old Common $0.0001 par payable 06/01/2015 to holders of record 05/15/2015 Ex date - 05/13/2015
Plan of reorganization under Chapter 11 Federal Bankruptcy proceedings effective 09/09/2016
Each share 5.75% Conv. Perpetual Preferred Ser. A $0.0001 par exchanged for $49.897956 cash
(Additional Information in Active)

HALCROW SWAYZE MINES LTD.
Recapitalized as Halcrow Swayze Mining Co. Ltd. 00/00/1941
Each share Capital Stock $1 par exchanged for (0.2) share Capital Stock $1 par
Halcrow Swayze Mining Co. Ltd. recapitalized as Landover Oils & Mines 00/00/1952 which recapitalized as Belcher Mining Corp. Ltd. 00/00/1954 which merged into Little Long Lac Mines Ltd. (Old) 01/08/1971 which name changed to Little Long Lac Gold Mines Ltd. (New) 07/03/1975 which merged into LAC Minerals Ltd. (New) 07/29/1985 which was acquired by American Barrick Resources Corp. 10/17/1994 which name changed to Barrick Gold Corp. 01/18/1995

HALCROW SWAYZE MINING CO. LTD.
Recapitalized as Landover Oils & Mines Ltd. 00/00/1952
Each share Capital Stock $1 par exchanged for (0.25) share Capital Stock $1 par
Landover Oils & Mines Ltd. recapitalized as Belcher Mining Corp. Ltd. 00/00/1954 which merged into Little Long Lac Mines Ltd. 01/08/1971 which name changed to Little Long Lac Gold Mines Ltd. (New) 07/03/1975 which merged into LAC Minerals Ltd. (New) 07/29/1985 which was acquired by American Barrick Resources Corp. 10/17/1994 which name changed to Barrick Gold Corp. 01/18/1995

HALCYON JETS HLDGS INC (DE)
Recapitalized as Alliance Network Communications Holdings, Inc. 09/02/2009
Each (15) shares Common $0.001 par exchanged for (1) share Common $0.001 par
Alliance Network Communications Holdings, Inc. name changed to BioCube, Inc. 01/05/2011

HALCYON RES LTD (BC)
Struck off register and declared dissolved for failure to file returns 06/09/1995

HALDEN RED LAKE MINES, LTD. (ON)
Charter surrendered 05/19/1958

HALE & KILBURN CORP.
Dissolved 00/00/1938
Details not available

HALE (NATHAN) LIFE INSURANCE CO. OF NEW YORK (NY)
See - Nathan Hale Life Ins Co NY (NY)

HALE BROS ASSOC INC (DE)
Name changed to Hale Technology Corp. 09/01/1981
(See Hale Technology Corp.)

HALE BROTHERS STORES, INC.
Acquired (over 99%) by (1-3/4) for (1) exchange offer in 1950 and subsequently merged into Broadway Department Store Inc. 4/20/51
Broadway Department Store Inc. name changed to Broadway-Hale Stores, Inc. (DE) 5/15/51 which merged into Broadway- Hale Stores, Inc. (CA) 8/27/70 which name changed to Carter Hawley Hale Stores Inc. (CA) 5/30/74 which reincorporated in Delaware 7/26/84 which name changed to Broadway Stores, Inc. 6/17/94 which merged into Federated Department Stores, Inc. 10/11/95 which name changed to Macy's, Inc. 6/1/2007

HALE DESK CO. (NY)
Proclaimed dissolved for failure to file reports and pay fees 12/15/51

HALE (NATHAN) LIFE INSURANCE CO. (IL)
Each share Common 35¢ par exchanged for (5) shares Common 7¢ par 10/10/1963
Merged into Hale (Nathan) Investment Corp. 03/26/1968
Each share Common 7¢ par exchanged for (0.2) share Class A Common $1 par
(See Hale (Nathan) Investment Corp.)

HALE RES LTD (BC)
Recapitalized as Consolidated Hale Resources Ltd. 07/12/1993
Each share Common no par exchanged for (0.33333333) share Common no par
Consolidated Hale Resources Ltd. name changed to Richco Investors Inc. (BC) 03/22/1994 which reincorporated in Ontario 08/16/1994

HALE TECHNOLOGY CORP. (DE)
Company believed out of business 00/00/1985
Details not available

HALEY INDS LTD (ON)
Common no par split (2) for (1) by issuance of (1) additional share 03/09/1987
Acquired by Magellan Aerospace Corp. 12/01/2002
Each share Common no par exchanged for (0.45) share Common no par

HALF DLR TR & SVGS BK (WHEELING, WV)
Capital Stock $25 par changed to $6.25 par and (3) additional shares issued 3/16/77
Merged into Intermountain Bankshares Inc. 6/12/85
Each share Capital Stock $6.25 par exchanged for (0.7) share Common $1 par
Intermountain Bankshares Inc. merged into United Bankshares, Inc. 7/1/86

HALI CAP CORP (AB)
Reorganized as Athabasca Minerals Inc. 01/08/2007
Each share Common no par exchanged for (0.4) share Common no par and (0.2) Common Stock Purchase Warrant expiring 09/30/2010

HALIFAX CORP VA (VA)
Name changed 08/07/2007
Common 35¢ par changed to 24¢ par and (0.5) additional share issued payable 12/27/1996 to holders of record 12/13/1996
Name changed from Halifax Corp. to Halifax Corp. of Virginia 08/07/2007
Acquired by Global Iron Holdings, LLC 03/05/2010
Each share Common 24¢ par exchanged for $1.20 cash

HALIFAX DEVS LTD (NS)
Common no par split (3) for (1) by issuance of (2) additional shares 10/13/87
Acquired by Empire Co. Ltd. 9/17/93
Each share Common no par exchanged for $1.50 cash

HALIFAX ENGR INC (VA)
Name changed to Halifax Corp. 09/06/1991
Halifax Corp. name changed to Halifax Corp. of Virginia 08/07/2007
(See Halifax Corp. of Virginia)

HALIFAX GROUP PLC (UNITED KINGDOM)
Merged into HBOS PLC 09/10/2001
Each Sponsored ADR for Ordinary exchanged for (1) Sponsored ADR for Ordinary
HBOS PLC merged into Lloyds Banking Group PLC 01/20/2009

HALIFAX NATL BK (HALIFAX, PA)
Common $1 par split (10) for (1) by issuance of (9) additional shares payable 05/03/1999 to holders of record 03/15/1999
Common $1 par split (25) for (1) by issuance of (24) additional shares payable 05/03/2004 to holders of record 05/03/2004
Reorganized as HNB Bancorp, Inc. 08/31/2007
Each share Common $1 par exchanged for (1) share Common 8¢ par
HNB Bancorp, Inc. merged into Riverview Financial Corp. (Old) 12/31/2008 which merged into Riverview Financial Corp. (New) 11/01/2013

HALIFAX TONOPAH MINING CO. (UT)
Charter suspended for failure to pay taxes 03/11/1949

HALIS INC (GA)
Merged into HealthWatch, Inc. 05/31/2001
Each share Common 1¢ par exchanged for (0.05) share Common 5¢ par
(See HealthWatch, Inc.)

HALITEC INDS CORP (BC)
Name changed to Senco Sensors Inc. 08/09/1996
(See Senco Sensors Inc.)

HALKIN MINES LTD. (ON)
Charter revoked for failure to file reports and pay fees 04/29/1965

HALL AEROPLANE CO. (CA)
Charter cancelled for failure to pay taxes in 1925

HALL C M LAMP CO (MI)
Each share Common no par exchanged for (0.5) share Common $5 par and $0.50 cash in 1939
Common $5 par changed to $2 par in 1954
Stock Dividend - 50% 10/30/47
Reincorporated under the laws of Delaware as Leader International Industries, Inc. 6/24/69
(See Leader International Industries, Inc.)

HALL FINL GROUP INC (DE)
Merged into HFGI Acquisition Corp. 2/10/94
Each share Common 5¢ par exchanged for $0.31 cash

HALL FRANK B & CO INC (DE)
Common 50¢ par split (2) for (1) by issuance of (1) additional share 6/9/72
Merged into Reliance Group Holdings, Inc. 11/2/92
Each share Common 50¢ par exchanged for (0.625) share Common 10¢ par
$4 Conv. Preferred Ser. B 10¢ par called for redemption 12/31/92
(See Reliance Group Holdings, Inc.)

HALL KINION & ASSOCS INC (DE)
Merged into Kforce Inc. 6/7/2004
Each share Common $0.001 par exchanged for (0.45) share Common 1¢ par

HALL MARK ELECTRS CORP (TX)
Acquired by Tyler Corp. (Old) 10/2/81
Each share Common 10¢ par exchanged for $100.52 cash

HALL MARK ELECTRS CORP NEW (DE)
Merged into Avnet, Inc. 7/1/93
Each share Common 1¢ par exchanged for (0.45) share Common $1 par amd $20 cash

HALL MOUNTAIN SILVER MINES, INC. (ID)
Name changed to Network Videotex Systems, Inc. 05/00/1989
Network Videotex Systems, Inc. name changed to Wessex International, Inc. 11/06/1989 which name changed to Ocean Express Lines, Inc. (ID) 05/00/1991 which reincorporated in Nevada 03/02/2000 which name changed to American Thorium, Inc. 07/29/2003 which recapitalized as Cementitious Materials, Inc. 10/21/2003 which name changed to NaturalNano, Inc. 12/02/2005 which name changed to Omni Shrimp, Inc. 05/03/2017

HALL (W.F.) PRINTING CO. (DE)
Reincorporated 7/6/71
Each share Common $10 par exchanged for (2) shares Common $5 par in 1946
State of incorporation changed from (IL) to (DE) 7/6/71
Common $5 par changed to $2.50 par and (1) additional share issued 7/3/72
Stock Dividend - 25% 12/29/45

Merged into Mobil Corp. 2/20/79
Each share Common $2.50 par exchanged for $27.50 cash

HALL-SCOTT, INC. (DE)
Merged into DuBois Chemicals, Inc. on a (0.85) for (1) basis 04/29/1960
DuBois Chemicals, Inc. acquired by Grace (W.R.) & Co. (CT) 05/06/1964 which reincorporated in New York 05/19/1988
(See Grace (W.R.) & Co.)

HALL-SCOTT MOTORS CO. (DE)
Name changed to Hall-Scott, Inc. 03/26/1956
Hall-Scott, Inc. merged into DuBois Chemicals, Inc. 04/29/1960 which was acquired by Grace (W.R.) & Co. (CT) 05/06/1964 which reincorporated in New York 05/19/1988
(See Grace (W.R.) & Co.)

HALL TRAIN ENTMT INC (CANADA)
Merged into GoldTrain Resources Inc. 04/27/2009
Each share Common no par exchanged for (0.06666666) share Common no par and (0.01666666) Common Stock Purchase Warrant expiring 08/10/2009
GoldTrain Resources Inc. recapitalized as Idaho Champion Gold Mines Canada Inc. 09/27/2018

HALL (H.E.) VOTING TRUST, INC. (KY)
Trust terminated 4/13/74
Each Trust Ctf. no par exchanged for (1) share Mammoth Life & Accident Insurance Co. Capital Stock $10 par
(See Mammoth Life & Accident Insurance Co.)

HALLADOR PETE CO (CO)
Each share old Common 1¢ par exchanged for (0.1) share new Common 1¢ par 01/02/1991
Each share new Common 1¢ par exchanged again for (0.01) share new Common 1¢ par 05/29/1996
New Common 1¢ par split (10) for (1) by issuance of (9) additional shares payable 05/30/1996 to holders of record 05/30/1996
Name changed to Hallador Energy Co. 03/17/2010

HALLAMORE CORP (DE)
Charter cancelled and declared inoperative and void for non-payment of taxes 6/17/93

HALLAMORE HOMES, INC. (CA)
Name changed to Hallamore, Inc. 1/7/74

HALLAMORE INC (CA)
Charter suspended for failure to file reports and pay fees 03/02/1981

HALLCRAFT HOMES INC (AZ)
Merged into Nu-West Development Corp. of Arizona 4/30/78
Each share Common no par exchanged for (1/3) share Common no par
Nu-West Development Corp. of Arizona name changed to Nu-West Arizona, Inc. 6/27/80 which name changed to Nu-West, Inc. 12/31/80
(See Nu-West, Inc.)

HALLE BROS CO (OH)
Common $10 par changed to $5 par in 1933
Stock Dividends - 10% 5/15/56; 10% 5/15/57; 10% 5/15/58; 10% 5/15/59; 10% 5/16/60
Merged into Field (Marshall) & Co. 11/30/70
Each share $2.40 1st Preferred $50 par exchanged for (1) share $2.40 Preferred Ser. A $1 par
Each share Common $5 par exchanged for (1) share Common $1 par
(See Field (Marshall) & Co.)

HALLEY RES LTD (BC)
Recapitalized as Rugby Resources Ltd. 09/13/1991
Each share Common no par exchanged for (0.11111111) share Common no par
Rugby Resources Ltd. name changed to Euro-Ad Systems, Inc. 04/30/1993 which recapitalized as Sun Devil Gold Corp. 07/03/1997 which name changed to Cardero Resource Corp. 05/13/1999

HALLIBURTON OIL WELL CEMENTING CO. (DE)
Common $5 par split (2) for (1) by issuance of (1) additional share in 1953
Common $5 par split (5) for (4) by issuance of (0.25) additional share 8/4/55
Name changed to Halliburton Co. 7/5/60

HALLICRAFTERS CO. (DE)
Stock Dividend - 100% 6/5/61
Completely liquidated 12/20/66
Each share Capital Stock $1 par exchanged for (0.17857) share Northrop Corp. (Calif.) $1.45 Preferred $1 par
(See Northrop Corp. (Calif.))

HALLICRAFTERS CO. (IL)
Merged into Penn-Texas Corp. on a (1) for (2.5) basis 3/19/56
Penn-Texas Corp. name changed to Fairbanks Whitney Corp. 5/29/59 which recapitalized as Colt Industries Inc. (Pa.) 5/15/64 which reincorporated in Delaware 10/17/68 then reincorporated in Pennsylvania 5/6/76
(See Colt Industries Inc. (Pa.))

HALLICRAFTERS COMMUNICATIONS INTL LTD (BC)
Name changed to Johnston & Frye Securities Ltd. 12/01/1987
(See Johnston & Frye Securities Ltd.)

HALLIDAY CRAFTSMEN LTD. (NS)
6% Preference $10 par called for redemption 1/31/70

HALLIDAY LITHOGRAPH CORP (MA)
Common $1 par split (4) for (3) by issuance of (1/3) additional share 10/28/66
Merged into Arcata National Corp. 6/24/69
Each share Common $1 par exchanged for (0.6) share Common 25¢ par
Arcata National Corp. name changed to Arcata Corp. 11/30/78 which name changed to Atacra Liquidating Corp. 6/4/82
(See Atacra Liquidating Corp.)

HALLIWELL GOLD MINES LTD. (QC)
Recapitalized as Consolidated Halliwell Ltd. 00/00/1954
Each share Capital Stock $1 par exchanged for (0.25) share Capital Stock $1 par
Consolidated Halliwell Ltd. recapitalized as International Halliwell Mines Ltd. 10/02/1969
(See International Halliwell Mines Ltd.)

HALLMAC MINES LTD (BC)
Reorganized under the laws of Alberta as Royal Oak Resources Ltd. 07/14/1986
Each share Common 50¢ par exchanged for (0.33333333) share Common no par
Royal Oak Resources Ltd. merged into Royal Oak Mines Inc. 07/23/1991 which recapitalized as Royal Oak Ventures Inc. 02/14/2000
(See Royal Oak Ventures Inc.)

HALLMARK BK & TR CO (SPRINGFIELD, VA)
Merged into F & M National Corp. 07/01/1994

HALLMARK CAP CORP (WI)
(continued from previous column)
Each share Common $2.50 par exchanged for (0.6406) share Common $2 par
F & M National Corp. merged into BB&T Corp. 08/09/2001

HALLMARK CAP CORP (WI)
Common $1 par split (2) for (1) by issuance of (1) additional share payable 11/24/97 to holders of record 11/10/97
Name changed to Ledger Capital Corp. 10/27/2000
Ledger Capital Corp. merged into Anchor BanCorp Wisconsin Inc. 11/9/2001

HALLMARK CO., INC. (NY)
Voluntarily dissolved 2/16/37
Details not available

HALLMARK COMMUNICATIONS INC (NY)
Name changed to Hallmark Group Companies, Inc. 4/10/72
Hallmark Group Companies, Inc. name changed to Western America Energy Corp. 3/18/76
(See Western America Energy Corp.)

HALLMARK DATA SYS INC (DE)
Reincorporated 6/8/70
State of incorporation changed from (IL) to (DE) and Common no par changed to 1¢ par 6/8/70
Acquired by Century Communications, Inc. 1/1/92
Each share Common 1¢ par exchanged for (0.3043) share Common 1¢ par
Note: Century Communications, Inc. is privately held

HALLMARK GROUP COS INC (NY)
Each share Common 1¢ par exchanged for (0.5) share Common 2¢ par 12/29/72
Name changed to Western America Energy Corp. 3/18/76
Each share Common 2¢ par exchanged for (1) share Common 2¢ par
(See Western America Energy Corp.)

HALLMARK HEALTHCARE CORP (DE)
Each share 25% Conv. Participating Preferred $1 par exchanged for (0.2) share 25% Conv. Participating Preferred $5 par 11/10/92
Each share Common 1¢ par exchanged for (0.2) share Common 5¢ par 11/10/92
Merged into Community Health Systems Inc. 10/5/94
Each share 25% Conv. Participating Preferred $5 par exchanged for (5.4) shares Common 1¢ par
Each share Common 5¢ par exchanged for (0.97) share Common 1¢ par
(See Community Health Systems Inc.)

HALLMARK HOMES INC (DE)
Adjudicated bankrupt 03/28/1974
Stockholders' equity unlikely

HALLMARK INSURANCE CO., INC. (WI)
Common $2 par changed to $1.80 par 04/10/1967
Stock Dividend - 25% 02/15/1966
95% acquired by CIC Financial Corp. through purchase offer which expired 08/22/1977
Public interest eliminated

HALLMARK LIFE ASSURANCE CO. (NM)
Merged into Great Western Assurance Co. 04/24/1967
Each share Common $1 par or VTC for Common $1 par exchanged for (0.5) share Common Capital Stock $1 par
Great Western Assurance Co. name changed to Cibola Life Insurance Co. 05/15/1975
(See Cibola Life Insurance Co.)

HALLMARK PPTYS INC (CO)
Name changed to Norton Motorcycles, Inc. 04/23/1999
(See Norton Motorcycles, Inc.)

HALLMARK RESH CORP (NV)
Charter revoked for failure to file reports and pay fees 2/1/2000

HALLMARK RES LTD (BC)
Struck off register and declared dissolved for failure to file returns 01/13/1995

HALLMARK TECHNOLOGIES INC (ON)
Merged into HTI Acquisition Inc. 12/29/2000
Each share Common no par exchanged for $4 cash

HALLMARK YELLOWKNIFE GOLD MINES, LTD. (ON)
Charter surrendered 01/21/1957

HALLNOR MINES LTD (ON)
Completely liquidated 05/03/1974
Each share Capital Stock $1 par exchanged for first and final distribution of $0.32814 cash

HALLS CREEK PARTNERS INC (NV)
Common $0.001 par split (5) for (1) by issuance of (4) additional shares payable 8/4/2006 to holders of record 8/3/2006 Ex date - 8/7/2006
Name changed to Clearvision International, Inc. 8/7/2006

HALLS MTR TRAN CO (PA)
Common no par split (2) for (1) by issuance of (1) additional share 6/23/72
Merged into Tiger International, Inc. 1/24/80
Each share Common no par exchanged for (1) share Common $1 par
(See Tiger International, Inc.)

HALLWOOD CONS RES CORP (DE)
Each share old Common 1¢ par exchanged for (0.1) share new Common 1¢ par 11/9/95
New Common 1¢ par split (3) for (1) by issuance of (2) additional shares payable 8/11/97 to holders of record 8/4/97
Reorganized as Hallwood Energy Corp. 6/8/99
Each share new Common 1¢ par exchanged for (1.5918) shares Common 1¢ par
(See Hallwood Energy Corp.)

HALLWOOD ENERGY CORP (DE)
Merged into Pure Resources, Inc. 5/31/2001
Each share Preferred 1¢ par exchanged for $10.84 cash
Each share Common 1¢ par exchanged for $12.50 cash

HALLWOOD ENERGY CORP (TX)
Each share old Common 1¢ par exchanged for (0.02) share new Common 1¢ par 10/26/1990
Merged into Hallwood Group Inc. 11/27/1996
Each share new Common 1¢ par exchanged for $19.50 cash

HALLWOOD ENERGY PARTNERS L P (DE)
Each Depository Receipt exchanged for (0.05) Unit of Ltd. Partnership Int. 5/10/90
Each Unit of Ltd. Partnership Inc. received distribution of (0.0666666) Class C Unit of Ltd. Partnership Int. payable 1/19/96 to holders of record 12/18/95 Ex date - 1/22/96
Reorganized as Hallwood Energy Corp. 6/8/99
Each Unit of Ltd. Partnership Int. exchanged for (0.7417) share Common 1¢ par
Each Class C Unit of Ltd. Partnership Int. exchanged for (1) share Preferred 1¢ par
(See Hallwood Energy Corp.)

HALLWOOD GROUP INC (DE)
Each share 7% Part. Conv. Preferred $8 par exchanged for (0.5) share new Common 10¢ par 02/18/1986
Each share old Common 10¢ par exchanged for (0.07142857) share new Common 10¢ par 02/18/1986
Each share new Common 10¢ par exchanged again for (0.25) share new Common 10¢ par 06/29/1995
New Common 10¢ par split (3) for (2) by issuance of (0.5) additional share payable 11/05/1999 to holders of record 10/28/1999 Ex date - 11/08/1999
Each share new Common 10¢ par received distribution of $37.70 cash payable 05/27/2005 to holders of record 05/20/2005
Each share new Common 10¢ par received distribution of $6.17 cash payable 08/18/2005 to holders of record 05/12/2005
Ser. B Preferred 10¢ par called for redemption at $4 on 07/20/2010
Acquired by Hallwood Financial Ltd. 05/16/2014
Each share new Common 10¢ par exchanged for $12.39 cash

HALLWOOD HLDGS INC (DE)
Name changed to Oakhurst Capital, Inc. 07/16/1993
Oakhurst Capital, Inc. name changed to Oakhurst Co., Inc. 08/23/1995 which name changed to Sterling Construction Co., Inc. 11/13/2001

HALLWOOD INDS INC (DE)
Under plan of reorganization each share Common $1 par exchanged for (1) share Common 1¢ par and (1) share Hallwood Holdings Inc. Common 1¢ par 07/05/1991
(See Hallwood Holdings Inc.)
Name changed to Steel City Products, Inc. 01/13/1993
(See Steel City Products, Inc.)

HALLWOOD RLTY PARTNERS L P (DE)
Each old Depositary Unit exchanged for (0.2) new Depositary Unit 03/03/1995
Merged into HRPT Properties Trust 07/16/2004
Each new Depositary Unit exchanged for $136.5675 cash
Note: An additional $0.31 per Unit was placed in escrow for possible future distribution
Each new Depositary Unit received initial distribution of $0.1775 cash 02/09/2005

HALMA PLC (ENGLAND & WALES)
Each Unsponsored ADR for Ordinary exchanged for (1) Sponsored ADR for Ordinary 06/02/2010
Sponsored ADR's for Ordinary split (5) for (3) by issuance of (0.66666666) additional ADR payable 06/23/2013 to holders of record 06/21/2010 Ex date - 06/24/2010
Basis changed from (1:5) to (1:3) 06/21/2010
ADR agreement terminated 05/11/2016
Each Sponsored ADR for Ordinary exchanged for $37.54467 cash
(Additional Information in Active)

HALMI ROBERT INC (NY)
Merged into HRI Group, Inc. 4/8/88
Each (2.5) shares Common 1¢ par exchanged for (1) share Common 1¢ par
HRI Group, Inc. name changed to Qintex Entertainment Inc. 12/9/88
(See Qintex Entertainment Inc.)

HALMON MNG & PROCESSING LTD (ON)
Charter cancelled for failure to pay taxes and file returns 12/20/1978

HALMONT PPTYS CORP (YT)
Reincorporated under the laws of Ontario 02/18/2009

HALO GAMING CORP (BC)
Cease trade order effective 06/03/1994
Stockholders' equity unlikely

HALO HLDGS NEV INC (NV)
Name changed to A1 Internet.com, Inc. 07/09/1999
A1 Internet.com, Inc. name changed to WorldTeq Group International, Inc. 10/19/2001 which name changed to China Printing, Inc. 04/19/2005 which name changed to CYIOS Corp. 11/07/2005

HALO LIGHTING, INC. (IL)
Completely liquidated 6/30/67
Each share Common no par exchanged for first and final distribution of (0.4347) share McGraw-Edison Co. Common $1 par
(See McGraw-Edison Co.)

HALO OIL PRODUCERS, INC. (CA)
Dissolved 02/04/1970
No stockholders' equity

HALO RES LTD (BC)
Reincorporated 11/16/2004
Place of incorporation changed from (YT) to (BC) 11/16/2004
Each share old Common no par exchanged for (0.689553) share new Common no par 09/07/2010
Merged into Sendero Mining Corp. 07/09/2013
Each share Common exchanged for (0.689553) share Common no par and (0.689553) share Common Stock Purchase Warrant expiring 07/09/2014

HALO TECHNOLOGY HLDGS INC (NV)
Plan of reorganization under Chapter 11 Federal Bankruptcy Code effective 12/28/2009
No stockholders' equity

HALO URANIUM MINES LTD. (ON)
Merged into Amalgamated Rare Earth Mines Ltd. 05/27/1957
Each share Capital Stock $1 par exchanged for (0.095) share Common $1 par and (0.15) share Consolidated Halo Uranium Mines Ltd. Capital Stock $1 par
(See each company's listing)

HALOGEN SOFTWARE INC (ON)
Acquired by Saba Software, Inc. 05/03/2017
Each share Common no par exchanged for $12.50 cash
Note: Unexchanged certificates will be cancelled and become without value 05/03/2023

HALOID CO. (NY)
Each share Common no par exchanged for (3) shares Common $5 par 00/00/1936
Common $5 par split (3) for (1) by issuance of (2) additional shares 04/20/1955
Name changed to Haloid Xerox, Inc. 04/16/1958
Haloid Xerox, Inc. name changed to Xerox Corp. 06/01/1961

HALOID XEROX, INC. (NY)
Common $5 par changed to $1.25 par and (3) additional shares issued 12/11/1959
Name changed to Xerox Corp. 06/01/1961

HALOZONE TECHNOLOGIES INC (ON)
Cease trade order effective 05/17/1996
Stockholders' equity unlikely

HALOZYME THERAPEUTICS INC (NV)
Reincorporated under the laws of Delaware 11/15/2007

HALPORT MINES LTD. (ON)
Charter cancelled for failure to pay taxes and file returns 03/16/1976

HALREN MINES LTD (ON)
Charter cancelled for failure to pay taxes and file returns 03/16/1976

HALS-DEVELOPMENT PJSC (RUSSIA)
Name changed
Name changed from HALS-Development JSC to HALS-Development PJSC 08/31/2015
GDR agreement terminated 12/21/2017
Each 144A Sponsored GDR for Ordinary exchanged for $0.55 cash
Each Reg. S Sponsored GDR for Ordinary exchanged for $0.55 cash

HALSEY DRUG INC (NY)
Common 10¢ par changed to 5¢ par and (1) additional share issued 4/2/84
Common 5¢ par changed to 1¢ par and (4) additional shares issued 2/19/86
Name changed to Acura Pharmaceuticals, Inc. 8/13/2004

HALSTEAD ENERGY CORP (NV)
Each share old Common $0.001 par exchanged for (0.5) share new Common $0.001 par 10/22/1998
Recapitalized as Native American Energy Group, Inc. (NV) 02/07/2005
Each share Common $0.001 par exchanged for (0.005) share Common $0.001 par
Native American Energy Group, Inc. (NV) merged into Native American Energy Group, Inc. (DE) 12/18/2009

HALSTEAD INDS INC (PA)
Merged into Mueller Industries, Inc. 11/20/98
Details not available

HALTER MARINE GROUP INC (DE)
Common 1¢ par split (3) for (2) by issuance of (0.5) additional share payable 10/31/97 to holders of record 10/15/97 Ex date - 11/3/97
Merged into Friede Goldman Halter, Inc. 11/3/99
Each share Common 1¢ par exchanged for (0.57) share Common 1¢ par
(See Friede Goldman Halter, Inc.)

HALTER VENTURE CORP (TX)
Name changed 07/25/1988
Name changed from Halter Racing Stables Inc. to Halter Venture Corp. 07/25/1988
Each share old Common no par exchanged for (0.1) share new Common no par 03/28/1989
Each share new Common no par exchanged again for (0.025) share new Common no par 06/10/1991
Reincorporated under the laws of Nevada as Reynolds (Debbie) Hotel & Casino, Inc. and new Common no par changed to $0.001 par 11/30/1994
(See Reynolds (Debbie) Hotel & Casino, Inc.)

HALTERM INCOME FD (NS)
Each Installment Receipt plus final payment of $4 cash received (1) Trust Unit prior to 05/13/1998
Fund terminated
Each Trust Unit received first and final distribution of $19.08 cash payable 01/19/2007 to holders of record 01/19/2007

HALTON & PEEL TR & SVGS CO (OAKVILLE, ON)
100% acquired by Canhuron Investments Ltd. through exchange offer which expired 10/25/1968
Public interest eliminated

HALTON REINS LTD (BERMUDA)
Name changed to Alexander Touche Insurance Inc. 05/08/1995
(See Alexander Touche Insurance Inc.)

HALTON UNVL BRANDS INC (NV)
Name changed to World Media & Technology Corp. 12/22/2014
World Media & Technology Corp. name changed to World Technology Corp. 12/04/2017

HALTONE RENT CORP (NY)
Charter cancelled and proclaimed dissolved for failure to pay taxes and file reports 12/15/70

HALVEN OIL LTD. (BC)
Merged into Deex Resources Corp. 5/5/83
Each (3.6256) shares Common no par exchanged for (1) share Common no par
Deex Resources Corp. recapitalized as Seam Resources Corp. 5/22/87

HALYARD HEALTH INC (DE)
Name changed to Avanos Medical, Inc. 07/02/2018

HALYX DEV INC (DE)
Recapitalized as EFI Electronics Corp. 6/26/87
Each share Common $0.0001 par exchanged for (0.05) share Common $0.0001 par
(See EFI Electronics Corp.)

HAMAKUA MILL CO. (HI)
Acquired by Laupahoehoe Sugar Co. 1/1/74
Each share Common $20 par exchanged for $55 cash

HAMBLETON CORP.
Liquidated in 1937

HAMBRECHT & QUIST GROUP (DE)
Merged into Chase Manhattan Corp. 12/10/99
Each share Common no par exchanged for $50 cash

HAMBRECHT ASIA ACQUISITION CORP (CAYMAN ISLANDS)
Name changed to SGOCO Technology, Ltd. 03/11/2010
SGOCO Technology, Ltd. name changed to SGOCO Group, Ltd. 11/17/2010

HAMBRO CDA LTD (ON)
Name changed 05/28/1974
Name changed from Hambro Canada (1972) Ltd. to Hambro Canada Ltd. 05/28/1974
Preference no par called for redemption 05/21/1978
Name changed to Hatleigh Corp. (Old) 08/03/1978
Hatleigh Corp. (Old) merged into Hatleigh Corp. (New) 08/31/1978 which merged into Dexleigh Corp. 06/30/1984
(See Dexleigh Corp.)

HAMBRO CORP CDA LTD (QC)
Acquired by Hambro Canada (1972) Ltd. 05/16/1973
Each share Common $5 par exchanged for (4.25) shares Common no par
Hambro Canada (1972) Ltd. name changed to Hambro Canada Ltd. 05/28/1974 which merged into Hatleigh Corp. (Old) 08/03/1978 which merged into Hatleigh Corp. (New) 08/31/1978 which merged into Dexleigh Corp. 06/30/1984
(See Dexleigh Corp.)

HAMBRO RES INC (BC)
Recapitalized as Richwell Resources Ltd. 04/29/1987
Each share Common no par exchanged for (0.33333333) share Common no par
(See Richwell Resources Ltd.)

HAMBURG GAS & ELECTRIC CO.
Merged into Metropolitan Edison Co. in 1928
Details not available

HAMBURG INDS INC (PA)
Name changed 11/04/1996
Class B $1 par split (5) for (2) by issuance of (1.5) additional shares 07/15/1987
Name changed from Hamburg Broom Works to Hamburg Industries, Inc. 11/04/1996
Each share old Class B 20¢ par exchanged for (0.004) share new Class B 20¢ par 07/21/2000
Note: Holders of (249) or fewer pre-split shares received $5 cash per share
Assets sold and business closed 09/00/2011
Details not available

HAMBURGER DENS INC (CA)
Name changed to Burlingame Foods 9/4/70
Burlingame Foods name changed to Burlingame-Western 6/7/71
(See Burlingame-Western)

HAMBURGER HAMLET RESTAURANTS INC (DE)
Chapter 11 bankruptcy proceedings terminated 01/23/2001
No stockholders' equity

HAMBURGER HAMLETS INC (CA)
Common $1 par split (4) for (3) by issuance of (1/3) additional share 6/20/69
Common $1 par split (5) for (4) by issuance of (0.25) additional share 1/27/70
Common $1 par split (4) for (1) by issuance of (3) additional shares 7/8/86
Stock Dividends - 10% 6/26/86
Merged into Weatherly Restaurant Group Ltd. 5/12/88
Each share Common $1 par exchanged for $9.20 cash

HAMCO MACH & ELECTRS CORP (NY)
Name changed to Kayex Corp. 1/27/70
Kayex Corp. acquired by General Signal Corp. 8/19/80 which merged into SPX Corp. 10/6/98

HAMCO OIL & DRILLING, INC. (TX)
Charter forfeited for failure to pay taxes 2/24/61

HAMDEN NATL BK (HAMDEN, CT)
Name changed to American National Bank (Hamden, CT) 7/1/73
American National Bank (Hamden, CT) reorganized as American Bancorp, Inc. (CT) 8/30/85 which merged into Constitution Bancorp of New England, Inc. 5/31/88 which name changed to Lafayette American Bancorp, Inc. 5/21/91 which reorganized as Lafayette American Bank & Trust Co. (Hamden, CT) 2/23/94 which merged into HUBCO, Inc. 7/1/96 which name changed to Hudson United Bancorp 4/21/99 which merged into TD Banknorth Inc. 1/31/2006
(See TD Banknorth Inc.)

HAMERSLEY PAPER MLS INC (NJ)
Adjudicated bankrupt 5/11/68
No stockholders' equity

HAMIL SILVER LEAD MINES LTD. (BC)
Recapitalized as New Hamil Silver-Lead Mines Ltd. 01/06/1958
Each share Common 50¢ par exchanged for (0.2) share Ordinary no par
(See New Hamil Silver-Lead Mines Ltd.)

HAMILTON (W.C.) & SONS (PA)
Recapitalized as Hamilton Paper Co. and Capital Stock $10 par changed to $5 par through the issuance of (1) additional share 10/31/56
Hamilton Paper Co. was acquired by Weyerhaeuser Co. 4/30/61

HAMILTON BANCORP INC (DE)
Merged into New York Bancorp Inc. 01/27/1995
Each share Common 1¢ par exchanged for (1.705) shares Common 1¢ par
New York Bancorp Inc. merged into North Fork Bancorporation, Inc. 03/27/1998 which merged into Capital One Financial Corp. 12/01/2006

HAMILTON BANCORP INC (FL)
Administratively dissolved 09/14/2007

HAMILTON BANCSHARES INC (TN)
Common no par split (2) for (1) by issuance of (1) additional share 5/31/73
Adjudicated bankrupt 3/26/76
Stockholders' equity unlikely

HAMILTON BANK & TRUST CO. (ATLANTA, GA)
Declared insolvent 10/08/1976
Stockholders' equity unlikely

HAMILTON BK & TR CO (BAILEY'S CROSSROADS, VA)
Common $10 par changed to $2 par and (4) additional shares issued 05/14/1969
Reorganized as Northern Virginia Bankshares Inc. 07/01/1971
Each share Common $2 par exchanged for (1) share Common $1 par
Northern Virginia Bankshares Inc. liquidated for Central National Corp. (VA) 01/02/1975 which merged into Commonwealth Banks, Inc. 12/31/1978 which name changed to Central Fidelity Banks, Inc. 06/01/1979 which merged into Wachovia Corp. (New) (Ctfs. dated between 05/20/1991 and 09/01/2001) 12/15/1997 which merged into Wachovia Corp. (Ctfs. dated after 09/01/2001) 09/01/2001 which merged into Wells Fargo & Co. (New) 12/31/2008

HAMILTON BANK (JOHNSON CITY, TN)
Merged into Hamilton Bancshares, Inc. 11/15/1972
Each share Capital Stock $10 par exchanged for (2.3) shares Common no par
(See Hamilton Bancshares, Inc.)

HAMILTON BK (MORRISTOWN, TN)
Name changed 11/01/1972
Stock Dividend - 66-2/3% 11/15/1965
Name changed from Hamilton National Bank (Morristown, TN) to Hamilton Bank (Morristown, TN) 11/01/1972
99% acquired by Hamilton Bancshares, Inc. through exchange offer which expired 02/28/1974
Public interest eliminated

HAMILTON-BIOPHILE COS (NV)
Reincorporated 11/26/2001
State of incorporation changed from (DE) to (NV) 11/26/2001
Each share old Common 1¢ par exchanged for (0.125) share new Common 1¢ par 03/01/2002
Recapitalized as Brampton Crest International, Inc. 10/04/2004
Each share new Common 1¢ par exchanged for (0.1) share Common $0.001 par

HAMILTON BREWING ASSN., LTD.
Merged into Brewing Corp. of Canada Ltd. 00/00/1930

HAM-HAM FINANCIAL INFORMATION, INC.

Details not available

HAMILTON BRIDGE CO. LTD. (CANADA)
Recapitalized 00/00/1939
Each share 6.5% 1st Preferred $100 par exchanged for (10) shares Common no par
Each share Common no par exchanged for (1) share Common no par
Liquidated 00/00/1954
Details not available

HAMILTON BROS EXPL CO (DE)
Merged into Hamilton Brothers Petroleum Corp. 10/15/1979
Each share Common $1 par exchanged for $25 cash

HAMILTON BROS PETE CORP (DE)
Under plan of recapitalization Common $1 par changed to 25¢ par and (0.33333333) share $1.95 Preference $1 par issued 10/20/1978
Stock Dividends - 50% 03/31/1980; 50% 01/15/1981
Merged into Hamilton Oil Corp. 03/30/1984
Each share $1.95 Preference $1 par exchanged for (1) share $1.95 Preference Ser. A $1 par
Each share Common 25¢ par exchanged for (1) share Common 25¢ par
(See Hamilton Oil Corp.)

HAMILTON-BROWN SHOE CO.
Adjudicated bankrupt in 1939

HAMILTON CAP CDN BK DYNAMIC WEIGHT ETF (ON)
Name changed to Hamilton Capital Canadian Bank Variable-Weight ETF 10/16/2018

HAMILTON CAP TR I (DE)
Underlying debentures became worthless as a result of receivership 01/11/2002
No stockholders' equity

HAMILTON (S. WARD) CO.
Bankrupt in 1935

HAMILTON CORP. (NV)
Charter revoked for failure to file reports and pay fees 3/2/70

HAMILTON (ALEXANDER) CORP. (MI)
Merged into Hamilton International Corp. 4/17/67
Each share Common $1 par exchanged for (1) share Common $1 par
(See Hamilton International Corp.)

HAMILTON (R.G.) CORP., LTD.
Liquidated in 1946

HAMILTON COSCO INC (IN)
Common no par split (2) for (1) by issuance of (1) additional share 5/1/59
Common no par split (3) for (2) by issuance of (0.5) additional share 5/9/60
Stock Dividend - 10% 2/2/59
Name changed to Cosco, Inc. 1/1/74
(See Cosco, Inc.)

HAMILTON COTTON LTD (CANADA)
Each share Common $30 par exchanged for (2) shares Common no par 00/00/1943
Recapitalized as Hamilton Group Ltd. 06/11/1970
Each share Common no par exchanged for (5) shares Common no par
Preferreds not affected except for change of name
(See Hamilton Group Ltd.)

HAMILTON DAIRIES, LTD.
Acquired by Borden Co. 00/00/1930
Details not available

HAMILTON DIGITAL CTLS INC (NY)
Common 5¢ par changed to 2-1/2¢ par and (1) additional share issued 11/29/1971
Operations ceased and assets sold for benefit of creditors 08/09/1995
Stockholders' equity unlikely

HAMILTON ELECTRO CORP. (CA)
Acquired by Avnet Electronics Corp. on a (0.5) for (1) basis 11/20/62 which name changed to Avnet, Inc. 12/2/64

HAMILTON EXPL INC (UT)
Each (1,500) shares old Common $0.0001 par exchanged for (1) share new Common $0.0001 par 5/22/95
Name changed to Eurotronics Holdings Inc. 12/20/95
Eurotronics Holdings Inc. name changed to Legalopinion.com 8/16/99 which recapitalized as Drayton Richdale Corp. 4/14/2004

HAMILTON FDS INC (MD)
Reincorporated 12/22/80
Ser. H-C7 Shares merged into Ser. H-DA Shares 10/30/63
Each Ser. H-C7 Shares Capital Stock 10¢ par reclassified as Ser. H-DA Shares Capital Stock 10¢ par on a share for share basis and (0.02089) additional Ser. H-DA Shares Capital Stock 10¢ par issued
State of incorporation changed from (DE) to (MD) 12/22/80
Name changed to Oppenheimer Total Return Fund, Inc. 5/1/87
Oppenheimer Total Return Fund, Inc. name changed to Oppenheimer Equity Fund, Inc. 8/29/2003

HAMILTON FINL SVCS CORP (DE)
Merged into Harbor Financial Group Inc. 05/15/1996
Each share Common no par exchanged for $0.61 cash

HAMILTON GAS CO.
Reorganized as Hamilton Gas Corp. in 1939
No stockholders' equity

HAMILTON GAS CORP. (DE)
Merged into Southeastern Gas Co. and each share Common $1 par exchanged for (1) share 5% Preferred $40 par 9/6/55

HAMILTON GAS CORP. (WV)
Reincorporated under laws of Delaware 5/16/55
Hamilton Gas Corp. (DE) merged into Southeastern Gas Co. 9/6/55

HAMILTON GROUP HLDGS INC (DE)
Reincorporated 2/3/87
State of incorporation changed from (UT) to (DE) 2/3/87
Charter cancelled and declared inoperative and void for non-payment of taxes 3/1/89

HAMILTON GROUP LTD (CANADA)
5% Preference Ser. A $100 par called for redemption 10/29/1975
Merged into General Electric Capital Canada Inc. 09/30/1993
Each share Conv. Class A Common no par exchanged for $13.75 cash
Each share Conv. Class B Common no par exchanged for $13.75 cash

HAMILTON GROWTH FD INC (MD)
Reincorporated 12/22/80
State of incorporation changed from (DE) to (MD) 12/22/80
Name changed to Centennial Growth Fund Inc. 9/1/81

HAMILTON HASTING LTD (ON)
Charter cancelled for failure to pay taxes and file returns 3/16/76

HAMILTON INCOME FD INC (MD)
Reincorporated 12/22/80
State of Incorporation changed from (DE) to (MD) 12/22/80
Name changed to Centennial Equity Income Fund Inc. 9/1/81
Centennial Equity Income Fund Inc. name changed to Oppenheimer Equity Income Fund, Inc. 3/31/83 which reincorporated in Massachusetts as Oppenheimer Equity Income Fund 11/1/86

HAMILTON INTL CORP (DE)
Each share Class C Conv. Common 10¢ par exchanged for (0.01) share Common $1 par 8/16/76
Merged into Household Finance Corp. 3/11/77
Each share Class B Conv. Preferred 10¢ par exchanged for $1 cash
Each share 4% Conv. Preferred $20 par exchanged for $20 cash
Each share Common $1 par exchanged for $4 cash

HAMILTON INVT TR (MA)
Name changed to Johnstown American Companies 3/15/83
Johnstown American Companies name changed to Consolidated Companies 11/28/88
(See Consolidated Companies)

HAMILTON LIFE INS CO N Y (NY)
Capital Stock $2 par changed to $1 par 10/25/66
Capital Stock $1 par changed to 50¢ par 8/15/67
Stock Dividend - 30% 4/6/64
Company liquidated under Article 16 of the New York Insurance Law 9/30/70
Capital Stock 50¢ par was cancelled

HAMILTON (ALEXANDER) LIFE INSURANCE CO. (MI)
Name changed to Hamilton (Alexander) Life Insurance Co. of America 7/9/65
Hamilton (Alexander) Life Insurance Co. of America merged into Hamilton International Corp. 8/15/69
(See Hamilton International Corp.)

HAMILTON (ALEXANDER) LIFE INSURANCE CO. OF AMERICA (MI)
Class A Common $1 par reclassified as Common $1 par 4/28/67
Merged into Hamilton International Corp. 8/15/69
Each share Common $1 par exchanged for (1) share Common $1 par
(See Hamilton International Corp.)

HAMILTON (HARVEY) LTD. (BC)
Name changed to Vantage Group Ltd. 6/19/72
Vantage Group Ltd. name changed to Barron Hunter Hargrave Strategic Resources Inc. 3/14/85
(See Barron Hunter Hargrave Strategic Resources Inc.)

HAMILTON MANAGEMENT CORP. (DE)
Recapitalized 3/21/60
Each share Class A no par exchanged for (120) shares Class A Common 10¢ par
Each share Class B no par exchanged for (269) shares Class A Common 10¢ par and (68) shares Class B Common 10¢ par
Completely liquidated 12/21/65
Each share Class A Common 10¢ par or Class B Common 10¢ par exchanged for first and final distribution of (0.3494) share International Telephone & Telegraph Corp. (MD) Common no par
International Telephone & Telegraph Corp. (MD) reincorporated in Delaware 1/31/68 which name changed to ITT Corp. 12/31/83 which reorganized in Indiana as ITT Industries, Inc. 12/19/95 which name changed to ITT Corp. 7/1/2006

HAMILTON MFG CO (WI)
Each share 7% 1st Preferred $100 par exchanged for (7) shares Part. Class A Preferred $10 par in 1933
Each share Common $70 par exchanged for (3-1/3) shares Common $10 par in 1933
Each share Common $10 par exchanged for (2) shares Common $5 par in 1946
Stock Dividends - 100% 3/15/50; 10% 12/26/56
Completely liquidated 4/1/68
Each share Common $5 par exchanged for first and final distribution of (0.715) share American Hospital Supply Corp. Common no par
American Hospital Supply Corp. merged into Baxter Travenol Laboratories, Inc. 11/25/85 which name changed to Baxter International Inc. 5/18/88

HAMILTON MANUFACTURING CORP. (IN)
Each share Common $1 par exchanged for (5) shares Common no par 12/18/53
Stock Dividends - 20% 2/1/57; 10% 1/2/58
Name changed to Hamilton Cosco, Inc. 1/1/59
Hamilton Cosco, Inc. name changed to Cosco, Inc. 1/1/74
(See Cosco, Inc.)

HAMILTON MINES CORP (NV)
Name changed to Target Petroleum Corp. of Nevada 4/20/82

HAMILTON NATIONAL ACCEPTANCE CORP. (IN)
Liquidation completed
Each share Common no par received initial distribution of $5 cash 9/5/76
Each share Common no par received second and final distribution of $0.45 cash 2/19/77
Certificates were not required to be surrendered and are now valueless

HAMILTON NATL ASSOC INC (TN)
Common $25 par changed to no par in 1937
Common no par split (2) for (1) by issuance of (1) additional share 3/25/70
Stock Dividend - 33-1/3% 7/16/65
Name changed to Hamilton Bancshares, Inc. 3/16/71
(See Hamilton Bancshares, Inc.)

HAMILTON NATL BK (JOHNSON CITY, TN)
Each share Capital Stock $40 par exchanged for (2) shares Capital Stock $25 par to effect a (1.6) for (1) split and a 25% stock dividend 1/13/59
Each share Capital Stock $25 par exchanged for (3-1/3) shares Capital Stock $10 par to effect a (2.5) for (1) split and a 33-1/3% stock dividend 1/14/66
Stock Dividends - 50% 8/1/50; 33-1/3% 2/1/52; 20% 1/17/62; 25% 1/24/64; 25% 1/24/70
Name changed to Hamilton Bank (Johnson City, TN) 2/1/73
Hamilton Bank (Johnson City, TN) merged into Hamilton Bancshares, Inc. 11/15/73
(See Hamilton Bancshares, Inc.)

HAMILTON NATL BK (KNOXVILLE, TN)
Common $100 par changed to $50 par and (1) additional share issued 01/23/1968
Common $50 par changed to $5 par 03/18/1975
Stock Dividends - 100% 12/31/1945; 50% 01/31/1950; 33-1/3% 01/19/1954; 25% 01/29/1958; 20% 01/31/1961; 20% 01/29/1965; 11-1/9% 01/16/1968
Name changed to United American Bank, N.A. (Knoxville, TN) 12/31/1975
United American Bank, N.A. (Knoxville, TN) name changed to United American Bank in Knoxville (Knoxville, TN) 11/01/1976

(See United American Bank in Knoxville (Knoxville, TN))

HAMILTON NATL LIFE INS CO (IN)
Stock Dividends - 10% 04/20/1962; 10% 03/08/1963; 10% 06/20/1966
Merged into National Western Life Insurance Co. (CO) 05/20/1977
Each share Common $1 par exchanged for (0.66666666) share Class A Common $1 par
National Western Life Insurance Co. (CO) reincorporated in Delaware as National Western Life Group, Inc. 10/02/2015

HAMILTON OIL & GAS CORP. (CO)
Declared defunct and inoperative for non-payment of franchise taxes 10/11/61

HAMILTON OIL CORP (CO)
$1.95 Preference Ser. A $1 par called for redemption 07/01/1991
Merged into Broken Hill Proprietary Co. Ltd. 07/02/1991
Each share Common 25¢ par exchanged for $40 cash

HAMILTON PAPER CO. (PA)
Acquired by Weyerhaeuser Co. on a (0.9) for (1) basis 4/30/61

HAMILTON RADIO CORP. (NY)
Name changed to Olympic Radio & Television, Inc. in August 1946
Olympic Radio & Television, Inc. name changed to Unitronics Corp. 8/6/56 which merged into Siegler Corp. 9/13/57 which name changed to Lear Siegler, Inc. 6/5/62
(See Lear Siegler, Inc.)

HAMILTON RES INC (DE)
Name changed to Lyntex Resources, Inc. 8/18/84
Lyntex Resources, Inc. name changed to Lyntex International, Inc. 3/29/85
(See Lyntex International, Inc.)

HAMILTON ST BANCSHARES INC (GA)
Merged into Ameris Bancorp 06/29/2018
Each share Common 1¢ par exchanged for (0.16) share Common $1 par and $0.93 cash

HAMILTON TECHNOLOGY INC (DE)
Merged into General Defense Corp. 2/22/85
Each share Common 10¢ par exchanged for (0.275) share Common 10¢ par and $3.60 cash
General Defense Corp. merged into Clabir Corp. (DE) 7/29/86 which merged into Empire of Carolina, Inc. 12/29/89
(See Empire of Carolina, Inc.)

HAMILTON TR & SVGS CORP (HAMILTON, ON)
Common $10 par and VTC's for Common $10 par changed to $5 par and (1) additional share issued respectively 12/03/1971
Voting Trust terminated and each VTC for Common $5 par exchanged for (1) share Common $5 par 09/05/1973
Merged into Canada Permanent Trust Co. (Toronto, ON) 01/01/1978
Each share 7% Conv. 1st Preference Ser. A $10 par exchanged for (1.6) shares 8% Preference Ser. B $25 par
Each share Common $5 par exchanged for (0.884956) share 8% Preference Ser. B $25 par

HAMILTON UNITED THEATRES LTD.
Acquired by Theatre Properties (Hamilton) Ltd. 00/00/1944
Each share Preferred exchanged for either $100 principal amount of 5% bonds and $26.50 cash
Each share Common exchanged for (1) share Common no par or $1 cash

(See Theatre Properties (Hamilton) Ltd.)

HAMILTON WATCH CO (PA)
Each share Common $25 par exchanged for (2) shares Common no par in 1930
Common no par changed to $1 par 5/11/56
Voting Trust Agreement expired 12/1/60
Common $1 par split (2) for (1) by issuance of (1) additional share 3/12/65
4% Conv. Preferred $100 par called for redemption 4/9/65
Common $1 par split (2) for (1) by issuance of (1) additional share 9/14/66
Name changed to HMW Industries, Inc. 6/2/72
(See HMW Industries, Inc.)

HAMILTON WOOLEN CO.
Liquidated in 1935

HAMLET-DEXTER MINES CORP. (CO)
Charter dissolved for failure to file annual reports 1/1/44

HAMLIN MOTOR CO. (DE)
Incorporated 8/29/19
Charter cancelled and declared inoperative and void for non-payment of taxes 4/1/28

HAMLIN MOTOR CO. (DE)
Incorporated 8/3/27
Charter cancelled and declared inoperative and void for non-payment of taxes 4/1/31

HAMMELITE PRODUCTS CORP. (CA)
Charter suspended for failure to file reports and pay taxes 08/03/1964

HAMMER-BRAY CO., LTD.
Name changed to Spark Stoves Co., Inc. in 1948
(See Spark Stoves Co., Inc.)

HAMMER COMPUTER SYS INC (CO)
Name changed to Tridon Corp. 10/13/1989
Tridon Corp. recapitalized as Tridon Enterprises Inc. 04/19/1996 which name changed to Alpha Spacecom, Inc. (CO) 08/01/2002 which reorganized in Nevada 06/30/2005 which name changed to Beicang Iron & Steel, Inc. 10/31/2006
(See Beicang Iron & Steel, Inc.)

HAMMER DRY PLATE & FILM CO. (DE)
Common 50¢ par changed to 10¢ par in 1949
Name changed to Consolidated Hammer Dry Plate & Film Co. in 1952
Consolidated Hammer Dry Plate & Film Co. name changed to Consolidated International Corp. 1/1/70
(See Consolidated International Corp.)

HAMMER HANDLE ENTERPRISES INC (NV)
Common $0.001 par split (10) for (1) by issuance of (9) additional shares payable 07/10/2009 to holders of record 06/03/2009 Ex date - 07/13/2009
Name changed to Shentang International, Inc. 07/24/2009

HAMMER TECHNOLOGIES INC (CO)
Common $0.001 par split (3) for (2) by issuance of (0.5) additional share 5/6/86
Name changed to Vintage Group, Inc. 1/5/87

HAMMERMILL PAPER CO (PA)
Each share Common $10 par exchanged for (2) shares Common $5 par 00/00/1948
Each share Common $5 par exchanged for (2) shares Common $2.50 par 00/00/1952
Common $2.50 par changed to $1.25 par and (1) additional share issued 06/08/1966
4.5% Preferred $100 par called for redemption 10/01/1981
Common $1.25 par split (3) for (2) by issuance of (0.5) additional share 02/21/1985
2nd Preferred Ser. B $50 par called for redemption 10/16/1986
4.25% Preferred $100 par called for redemption 10/16/1986
Merged into International Paper Co. 11/10/1986
Each share Common $1.25 par exchanged for $64.50 cash

HAMMERS PLASTIC RECYCLING CORP (NY)
Name changed to Plastic Recycling Inc. 09/14/1995
(See Plastic Recycling Inc.)

HAMMERSON CDA INC (ON)
9.12% Retractable Preferred Ser. A no par called for redemption 01/19/1990
9% Retractable Preferred Ser. B no par called for redemption 06/30/1990
Public interest eliminated

HAMMERTIME HLDGS INC (NV)
Name changed to VR Systems, Inc. 12/10/2003
VR Systems, Inc. name changed to Hansen Gray & Co., Inc. 03/29/2004 which recapitalized as AMF Capital, Inc. 06/22/2007 which name changed to Pro Motors Group Corp. 10/29/2007 which recapitalized as Hydrogen Hybrid Corp. 11/25/2008 which name changed to Get Real USA Inc. 01/12/2011

HAMMETT J L CO (MA)
Involuntarily dissolved 06/18/2012

HAMMOND & LITTLE RIVER REDWOOD CO., LTD.
Name changed to Hammond Redwood Co. in 1936
(See Hammond Redwood Co.)

HAMMOND CLOCK CO. (DE)
Recapitalized as Hammond Instrument Co. and each share Common $5 par exchanged for (4) shares Common $1 par in 1937
Hammond Instrument Co. name changed to Hammond Organ Co. 8/25/53 which name changed to Hammond Corp. 4/6/67
(See Hammond Corp.)

HAMMOND CO. (CT)
Dissolved by forfeiture for failure to file statutory reports 12/12/47

HAMMOND CO (CA)
Merged into Western Financial Savings Bank (Irvine, CA) 1/31/96
Each share Common no par exchanged for $4.2928 cash

HAMMOND CORP (DE)
Merged into Cerro-Marmon Corp. 1/26/77
Each share $5 Conv. Preferred no par exchanged for $75 cash
Each share Common $1 par exchanged for $7.75 cash
(See Cerro-Marmon Corp.)

HAMMOND INSTRUMENT CO. (DE)
Name changed to Hammond Organ Co. 8/25/53 which name changed to Hammond Corp. 4/6/67
(See Hammond Corp.)

HAMMOND LUMBER CO. (DE)
Each share Common $100 par exchanged for (5) shares Common $20 par in 1948
Assets sold and company liquidated 10/22/56
Details not available

HAMMOND ORGAN CO. (DE)
Common $1 par split (2) for (1) by issuance of (1) additional share 6/9/60
Stock Dividends - 100% 9/10/53; 100% 11/25/55
Name changed to Hammond Corp. 4/6/67
(See Hammond Corp.)

HAMMOND REDWOOD CO.
Merged into Hammond Lumber Co. in 1942
Details not available

HAMMOND STANDISH & CO. (MI)
Common $10 par changed to $5 par in 1950
Recapitalized 6/30/52
Each share 6% Prior Preferred $10 par exchanged for (1) share Common $1 par
Common $5 par changed to $1 par
Adjudicated a bankrupt 9/21/59
Charter subsequently cancelled for failure to pay taxes and file reports in 1961

HAMMONDS INDS INC (NV)
Recapitalized as Delta Seaboard International, Inc. 06/10/2010
Each share Common $0.0001 par exchanged for (0.1) share Common $0.0001 par
Delta Seaboard International, Inc. recapitalized as American International Holdings Corp. 08/13/2012

HAMMONS JOHN Q HOTELS INC (DE)
Merged into JHQ Merger Corp. 9/16/2005
Each share Common 1¢ par exchanged for $24 cash

HAMNER ELECTRS CO (NJ)
Dissolved 08/04/1969
No stockholders' equity

HAMPDEN BANCORP INC (DE)
Merged into Berkshire Hills Bancorp, Inc. 04/17/2015
Each share Common 1¢ par exchanged for (0.81) share Common 1¢ par

HAMPDEN FD INC (OH)
Name changed to Fulton Reid & Staples Fund, Inc. 3/30/70
(See Fulton Reid & Staples Fund, Inc.)

HAMPDEN GROUP INC (NV)
Each share old Common 1¢ par exchanged for (0.01) share new Common 1¢ par 10/06/2004
Recapitalized as myPhotoPipe.com, Inc. 10/06/2006
Each share new Common 1¢ par exchanged for (0.1) share Common $0.001 par
(See myPhotoPipe.com, Inc.)

HAMPSHIRE DESIGNERS INC (DE)
Name changed to HDI Investment Corp. 08/01/1977
(See HDI Investment Corp.)

HAMPSHIRE FIRST BK (MANCHESTER, NH)
Acquired by NBT Bancorp Inc. 06/08/2012
Each share Common $1 par exchanged for (0.456235) share Common 1¢ par and $5.25 cash

HAMPSHIRE GROUP LTD (DE)
Common 10¢ par split (2) for (1) by issuance of (1) additional share payable 06/28/2005 to holders of record 05/31/2005 Ex date - 06/29/2005
Plan of reorganization under Chapter 11.Federal Bankruptcy proceedings effective 10/05/2017
No stockholders' equity

HAMPSHIRE MINES LTD. (ON)
Name changed 07/29/1959
Name changed from Hampshire

Nickel Mines Ltd. to Hampshire Mines Ltd. 07/29/1959
Name changed to Kaiser Mines of Canada Ltd. 06/25/1965
Kaiser Mines of Canada Ltd. acquired by Mission Financial Corp. Ltd. 05/09/1968 which merged into H.R.S. Industries, Inc. 05/21/1982 which merged into International H.R.S. Industries Inc. 05/15/1984 which name changed to Glenex Industries Inc. 05/25/1987 which merged into Quest Investment Corp. 07/04/2002 which merged into Quest Capital Corp. (BC) 06/30/2003 which reincorporated in Canada 05/27/2008 which name changed to Sprott Resource Lending Corp. 09/10/2010 which merged into Sprott Inc. 07/24/2013

HAMPSON INDS PLC (UNITED KINGDOM)
ADR agreement terminated 03/19/2014
No ADR's remain outstanding

HAMPTON BK (ST LOUIS, MO)
Name changed to Hampton Metro Bank (St. Louis, MO) 04/26/1979
Hampton Metro Bank (St. Louis, MO) name changed to Metro Bank (St. Louis, MO) 06/01/1982
(See Metro Bank (St. Louis, MO))

HAMPTON BANKSHARES CORP (MO)
Merged into Metro Bancholding Corp. 09/02/1980
Each share 5% Preferred 1st Ser. $10 par exchanged for (1) share 8% Preferred Ser. A $10 par
Each share Common $1 par exchanged for (3.8) shares Common $1 par
(See Metro Bancholding Corp.)

HAMPTON BERKSHIRE INS & FINL CO (NV)
Recapitalized as Innovate Oncology, Inc. 10/05/2004
Each (3.8) shares Common $0.001 par exchanged for (1) share Common $0.001 par
Innovate Oncology, Inc. name changed to Avantogen Oncology, Inc. 07/03/2006
(See Avantogen Oncology, Inc.)

HAMPTON CONSULTING CORP (UT)
SEC revoked common stock registration 08/27/2010

HAMPTON COOP BK (HAMPTON, NH)
Acquired by Mid Maine Savings Bank, F.S.B. (Auburn, ME) 01/04/1989
Each share Common $1 par exchanged for $53.50 cash

HAMPTON COURT RES INC (AB)
Issue Information - 3,500,000 shares COM offered at $0.10 per share on 10/07/1993
Cease trade order effective 06/18/2004
Stockholders' equity unlikely

HAMPTON FARMS CORP. (NJ)
Charter cancelled for failure to pay taxes in 1930

HAMPTON HEALTHCARE INC (DE)
Plan of reorganization under Chapter 11 Federal Bankruptcy proceedings confirmed 12/31/1991
Each share Common 10¢ par exchanged for (0.076) share Hampton Resources Corp. Common 10¢ par
Hampton Resources Corp. merged into Bellwether Exploration Co. 03/01/1995 which name changed to Mission Resources Corp. 05/06/2001
(See Mission Resources Corp.)

HAMPTON INDS INC (NC)
Stock Dividends - 10% 7/2/79; 10% 7/1/80; 10% 7/1/81; 10% 7/1/82; 10% 7/15/83; 10% 7/23/84; 10% 7/23/85; 10% 7/23/86; 10% 7/23/87; 10% 7/28/89; 10% 7/9/92; 10% 7/9/93; 10% payable 7/2/98 to holders of record 6/2/98; 10% payable 7/2/99 to holders of record 6/2/99
Liquidation completed
Each share Common $1 par received initial distribution of $0.60 cash payable 9/29/2004 to holders of record 8/27/2004
Each share Common $1 par received second and final distribution of $0.1225 cash payable 4/4/2007 to holders of record 9/29/2004
Ex date - 4/5/2007
Note: Certificates were not required to be surrendered and are without value

HAMPTON METRO BK (ST. LOUIS, MO)
Name changed to Metro Bank (St. Louis, MO) 06/01/1982
(See Metro Bank (St. Louis, MO))

HAMPTON RDS BANKSHARES INC (VA)
Common $0.625 par changed to 1¢ par 09/28/2010
Each share old Common 1¢ par exchanged for (0.04) share new Common 1¢ par 04/28/2011
Under plan of merger name changed to Xenith Bankshares, Inc. (New) 08/01/2016
Xenith Bankshares, Inc. (New) merged into Union Bankshares Corp. 01/01/2018

HAMPTON RES CORP (DE)
Merged into Bellwether Exploration Co. 3/1/95
Each share Common 10¢ par exchanged for $6.75 cash

HAMPTON SALES CO., INC. (NY)
Merged into Bell Television, Inc. 08/14/1969
Each share Common 10¢ par exchanged for (0.285714) share Common 10¢ par
Bell Television, Inc. name changed to Holmes Protection Services Corp. 01/07/1972 which merged into National Kinney Corp. 10/13/1972 which name changed to Andal Corp. 11/07/1983
(See Andal Corp.)

HAMPTON SHIRT INC (NC)
Name changed to Hampton Industries, Inc. 5/18/73
(See Hampton Industries, Inc.)

HAMPTON ST BK (MILWAUKEE, WI)
Acquired by Mid-Continental Holdings, Inc. 06/16/1987
Details not available

HAMPTON UTILS TR (MA)
$4 Preferred 1¢ par called for redemption 1/18/57
Trust terminated 10/3/94
Details not available

HAMPTONS BANCSHARES INC (NY)
Common $4 par split (2) for (1) by issuance of (1) additional share 11/13/1987
Merged into Suffolk Bancorp 04/11/1994
Each share Common $4 par exchanged for either (0.6744) share Common $5 par, $14.50 cash or a combination thereof
Suffolk Bancorp merged into People's United Financial, Inc. 04/01/2017

HAMPTONS EXTREME INC (DE)
Name changed to China Polypeptide Group, Inc. 12/24/2009

HAMPTONS LUXURY HOMES INC (DE)
Acquired by Porver Holdings, LLC 05/25/2017
Each share Common $0.0001 par exchanged for $0.006 cash

HAMRICK MILLS
Acquired by Lowenstein (M.) & Sons, Inc. in 1947
Details not available

HAN LOGISTICS INC (NV)
Each share old Common $0.001 par exchanged for (5) shares new Common $0.001 par 06/28/2011
Name changed to Eason Education Kingdom Holdings, Inc. 08/28/2015

HANA BK NEW (KOREA)
GDR agreement terminated 12/1/2005
Each Reg. S GDR for Ordinary exchanged for $45.793474 cash

HANA BK OLD (KOREA)
Stock Dividend - 4% payable 4/4/2002 to holders of record 12/31/2001 Ex date - 12/27/2001
Merged into Hana Bank (New) 12/1/2002
Each GDR for Ordinary Reg. S exchanged for (1) GDR for Ordinary Reg. S
(See Hana Bank (New))

HANA BIOLOGICS INC (DE)
Recapitalized as Somatix Therapy Corp. 03/15/1991
Each share Common 1¢ par exchanged for (0.25) share Common 1¢ par
Somatix Therapy Corp. merged into Cell Genesys, Inc. 05/30/1997 which merged into BioSante Pharmaceuticals, Inc. 10/14/2009 which recapitalized as ANI Pharmaceuticals, Inc. 07/18/2013

HANA BIOSCIENCES INC (DE)
Each share old Common $0.001 par exchanged for (0.25) share new Common $0.001 par 09/13/2010
Name changed to Talon Therapeutics, Inc. 12/02/2010
(See Talon Therapeutics, Inc.)

HANA MICROELECTRONICS PUB LTD (THAILAND)
Sponsored ADR's for Ordinary THB 10 par changed to THB 5 par and (1) additional ADR issued payable 10/02/2000 to holders of record 09/19/2000 Ex date - 09/20/2000
Sponsored ADR's for Ordinary THB 5 par changed to THB 1 par and (4) additional ADR issued payable 07/13/2004 to holders of record 07/12/2004
Stock Dividend - 82.629% payable 04/08/1998 to holders of record 10/31/1997
ADR agreement terminated 10/26/2012
Each Sponsored ADR for Ordinary THB 1 par exchanged for $1.170237 cash

HANA MNG LTD NEW (BC)
Acquired by Cupric Canyon Capital LP 02/20/2013
Each share Common no par exchanged for $0.82 cash
Note: Unexchanged certificates will be cancelled and become without value 02/20/2019

HANA MNG LTD OLD (BC)
Each share old Common no par exchanged for (0.33333333) share new Common no par 04/13/2009
Reorganized as Hana Mining Ltd. (New) 11/26/2010
Each share new Common no par exchanged for (1) share Common no par and (0.25) share New Hana Copper Mining Ltd. Common no par
(See each company's listing)

HANAROTELECOM INCORPORATED (KOREA)
Name changed 12/16/2004
Issue Information - 24,000,000 ADR'S offered at $15.51 per ADR on 03/29/2000
Name changed from Hanaro Telecom, Inc. to Hanarotelecom Inc. 12/16/2004
Each old Sponsored ADR for Common W5,000 par exchanged for (0.5) new Sponsored ADR for Common W5,000 par 05/18/2006
ADR agreement terminated 06/27/2008
Each new Sponsored ADR for Common W5,000 par exchanged for $4.4581 cash

HANCO FOODS INC (AB)
Name changed to Continental Fashion Group Inc. (AB) 08/31/1994
Continental Fashion Group Inc. (AB) reorganized in Canada as Genoil Inc. 08/07/1996

HANCOCK ACCEPTANCE CORP. (PA)
Acquired by National Banner Corp. 9/15/65
Each share Common 10¢ par exchanged for (0.6) share Common 50¢ par
National Banner Corp. name changed to Turbo Cast Industries, Inc. 7/20/67
(See Turbo Cast Industries, Inc.)

HANCOCK BANCSHARES CORP. (IN)
Merged into Merchants National Corp. 04/18/1986
Each share Common no par exchanged for (1.863) shares Common no par
Merchants National Corp. merged into National City Corp. 05/02/1992 which was acquired by PNC Financial Services Group, Inc. 12/31/2008

HANCOCK BK & TR CO (QUINCY, MA)
Reorganized as Hancock Group Inc. 4/19/74
Each share Common $5 par exchanged for (1) share Common $5 par
(See Hancock Group Inc.)

HANCOCK BK (GULFPORT, MS)
Reorganized as Hancock Holding Co. 09/06/1984
Each share Common $10 par exchanged for (1) share Common $10 par
Hancock Holding Co. name changed to Hancock Whitney Corp. 05/25/2018

HANCOCK FABRICS INC (DE)
Common 1¢ par split (2) for (1) by issuance of (1) additional share 04/15/1991
Plan of reorganization under Chapter 11 Federal Bankruptcy proceedings effective 07/28/2017
No stockholders' equity

HANCOCK GROUP INC (MA)
Acquired by Bank of New England Corp. 12/2/82
Each share Common $5 par exchanged for $52.50 cash

HANCOCK HLDG CO (MS)
Common $10 par split (2) for (1) by issuance of (1) additional share 09/25/1985
Common $10 par changed to $3.33 par and (2) additional shares issued 05/09/1988
Common $3.33 par split (2) for (1) by issuance of (1) additional share 11/04/1991
Common $3.33 par split (3) for (2) by issuance of (0.5) additional share payable 08/05/2002 to holders of record 07/23/2002 Ex date - 08/06/2002
Common $3.33 par split (2) for (1) by issuance of (1) additional share payable 03/18/2004 to holders of record 03/08/2004 Ex date - 03/19/2004
Stock Dividend - 15% payable

12/16/1996 to holders of record 12/05/1996
Name changed to Hancock Whitney Corp. 05/25/2018

HANCOCK HLDG CO (MS)
8% Conv. Preferred Ser. A $20 par called for redemption at $20.1511 on 2/4/2004
(Additional Information in Active)

HANCOCK INDS INC (MI)
Merged into International Telephone & Telegraph Corp. 5/23/72
Each share Common $1 par exchanged for (0.388) share Common $1 par
International Telephone & Telegraph Corp. name changed to ITT Corp. 12/31/83 which reorganized in Indiana as ITT Industries, Inc. 12/19/95 which name changed to ITT Corp. 7/1/2006

HANCOCK J W INC (DE)
Merged into Hanko Properties, Inc. 9/6/68
Each share 6% Preferred $2 par exchanged for (0.8) share Common 1¢ par
Each share Common 10¢ par exchanged for (0.6) share Common 1¢ par
(See Hanko Properties, Inc.)

HANCOCK JOHN BALANCED FD INC (DE)
Name changed to Hancock (John) U.S. Government Securities Fund, Inc. (DE) 11/18/1981
Hancock (John) U.S. Government Securities Fund, Inc. (DE) reorganized in Massachusetts as Hancock (John) U.S. Government Securities Trust 12/31/1984 which name changed to Hancock (John) U.S. Government Securities Fund 05/01/1991 which name changed to Hancock (John) Limited Term Government Fund 07/01/1993
(See Hancock (John) Limited Term

HANCOCK JOHN BK & THRIFT OPPORTUNITY FD (MA)
Issue Information - 22,500,000 SHS BEN INT offered at $20 per share on 08/16/1994
Old Shares of Bene. Int. no par split (4) for (1) by issuance of (3) additional shares payable 12/01/1997 to holders of record 11/17/1997 Ex date - 12/02/1997
Each old Share of Bene. Int. no par exchanged for (0.25) new Share of Bene. Int. no par 12/30/2008
Name changed to Hancock (John) Financial Opportunities Fund 12/14/2012

HANCOCK JOHN BD FD INC (MD)
Reorganized under the laws of Massachusetts as Hancock (John) Bond Trust and Capital Stock $1 par reclassified as Shares of Bene. Int. no par 12/31/84
Hancock (John) Bond Trust name changed to Hancock (John) Sovereign Bond Fund 6/1/92

HANCOCK JOHN BD TR (MA)
Name changed to Hancock (John) Sovereign Bond Fund 6/1/92

HANCOCK JOHN CAP GROWTH FD (MA)
Merged into Hancock (John) Capital Series 09/15/1995
Details not available

HANCOCK JOHN CASH MGMT FD (MA)
Merged into John Hancock Current Interest 11/16/1995
Each Share of Bene. Int. no par exchanged for (1) share Money Market Fund Class A
Each Class B Share of Bene. Int. no par exchanged for (1) share Money Market Fund Class B

HANCOCK JOHN CASH MGMT TR II (MA)
Name changed to Hancock (John) U.S. Government Guaranteed Mortgages Trust 08/02/1984
Hancock (John) U.S. Government Guaranteed Mortgages Trust name changed to Hancock (John) Government Spectrum Fund 12/10/1990
(See Hancock (John) Government Spectrum Fund)

HANCOCK JOHN FINL SVCS INC (DE)
Issue Information - 102,000,000 shares COM offered at $17 per share on 01/26/2000
Merged into Manulife Financial Corp. 4/28/2004
Each share Common 1¢ par exchanged for (1.1853) shares Common 1¢ par

HANCOCK JOHN FINL TRENDS FD INC (MD)
Name changed to Financial Trends Fund, Inc. 11/20/2007
Financial Trends Fund, Inc. name changed to Diamond Hill Financial Trends Fund, Inc. 01/15/2008
(See Diamond Hill Financial Trends Fund, Inc.)

HANCOCK JOHN GLOBAL FD (MA)
Name changed 03/01/1991
Name changed from Hancock (John) Global Trust to Hancock (John) Global Fund 03/01/1991
Trust terminated 09/25/1992
Details not available

HANCOCK JOHN GOVT SPECTRUM FD (MA)
Trust terminated 09/25/1992
Details not available

HANCOCK JOHN GROWTH FD (MA)
Name changed 05/01/1991
Name changed from Hancock (John) Growth Trust to Hancock (John) Growth Fund 05/01/1991
Reorganized as Hancock (John) Capital Series 10/01/1993
Details not available

HANCOCK JOHN GROWTH FD INC (DE)
Reorganized under the laws of Massachusetts as Hancock (John) Growth Trust and Capital Stock $1 par reclassified as Shares of Bene. Int. no par 12/31/1984
Hancock (John) Growth Trust name changed to Hancock (John) Growth Fund 05/01/1991
(See Hancock (John) Growth Fund)

HANCOCK JOHN INCOME SECS CORP (MD)
Reorganized under the laws of Massachusetts as Hancock (John) Income Securities Trust and Capital Stock $1 par reclassified as Shares of Bene. Int. no par 12/31/84

HANCOCK JOHN INCOME SECS TR (MA)
Auction Preferred Ser. A no par called for redemption at $25,000 on 06/26/2008
Auction Preferred Ser. B no par called for redemption at $25,000 on 06/26/2008
(Additional Information in Active)

HANCOCK JOHN INVT TR III (MA)
World Bond Fund Class B completely liquidated 02/19/1999
Details not available
Global Bond Fund Class B no par reclassified as International Fund Class B no par 04/16/2003
International Fund Class B abolished 05/25/2007
Details not available

HANCOCK JOHN INVS INC (DE)
Reorganized under the laws of Massachusetts as Hancock (John) Investors Trust and Capital Stock $1 par reclassified as Shares of Bene. Int. $1 par 12/31/84

HANCOCK JOHN INVS TR (MA)
Auction Rate Preferred Ser. A called for redemption 06/11/2008
Auction Rate Preferred Ser. B called for redemption 06/12/2008
(Additional Information in Active)

HANCOCK JOHN LTD TERM GOVT FD (MA)
Trust terminated 12/05/1997
Details not available

HANCOCK JOHN PATRIOT GLOBAL DIVID FD (MA)
Merged into Hancock (John) Patriot Premium Dividend Fund II 06/04/2007
Each share Dutch Auction Rate Transferable Securities Preferred no par exchanged for Dividend Fund II Ser. F no par on a net asset basis
Each share Common no par exchanged for (1.12386918) Common Shares of Bene. Int. no par
Hancock (John) Patriot Premium Dividend Fund II name changed to Hancock (John) Premium Dividend Fund 10/18/2010

HANCOCK JOHN PATRIOT PFD DIVID FD (MA)
Merged into Hancock (John) Patriot Premium Dividend Fund II 05/29/2007
Each share Dutch Auction Rate Transferable Securities Preferred Ser. A no par exchanged for Dividend Fund II Preferred Ser. E no par on a net asset basis
Each Common no par exchanged for (1.06840725) Common Shares of Bene. Int. no par
Hancock (John) Patriot Premium Dividend Fund II name changed to Hancock (John) Premium Dividend Fund 10/18/2010

HANCOCK JOHN PATRIOT PREM DIVID FD I (MA)
Merged into Hancock (John) Patriot Premium Dividend Fund II 06/25/2007
Each share Dutch Auction Rate Preferred Ser. A 1¢ par exchanged for (1) share Dividend Fund II Ser. C no par
Each share Common 1¢ par exchanged for (0.78846147) Common Share of Bene. Int. no par
Hancock (John) Patriot Premium Dividend Fund II name changed to Hancock (John) Premium Dividend Fund 10/18/2010

HANCOCK JOHN PATRIOT PREM DIVID FD II (MA)
Dividend Fund Ser. C no par called for redemption at $100,000 on 06/02/2008
Dividend Fund Ser. D no par called for redemption at $100,000 on 06/11/2008
Dividend Fund Ser. E no par called for redemption 06/24/2008
Dutch Auction Rate Preferred Ser. A no par called for redemption 06/26/2008
Dividend Fund Ser. F no par called for redemption 06/30/2008
Dutch Auction Rate Preferred Ser. B no par called for redemption 07/03/2008
Name changed to Hancock (John) Premium Dividend Fund 10/18/2010

HANCOCK JOHN PATRIOT SELECT DIVID TR (MA)
Merged into Hancock (John) Patriot Premium Dividend Fund II 10/10/2007
Each share Auction Market Preferred Ser. A exchanged for (1) share Dividend Fund II Ser. D no par
Each share Auction Market Preferred Ser. B exchanged for (1) share Dividend Fund II Ser. D no par
Each share Common no par exchanged for (1.19743657) Common Shares of Ben. Int. no par
Hancock (John) Patriot Premium Dividend Fund II name changed to Hancock (John) Premium Dividend Fund 10/18/2010

HANCOCK JOHN PFD INCOME FD (MA)
Name changed 08/22/2002
Name changed from Hancock (John) Preferred Equity Income Fund to Hancock (John) Preferred Income Fund 08/22/2002
Auction Rate Preferred Ser. W called for redemption at $25,000 on 05/22/2008
Auction Rate Preferred Ser. TH called for redemption at $25,000 on 05/23/2008
Auction Rate Preferred Ser. F called for redemption at $25,000 on 05/27/2008
Auction Rate Preferred Ser. M called for redemption at $25,000 on 05/27/2008
Auction Rate Preferred Ser. T called for redemption at $25,000 on 05/28/2008
(Additional Information in Active)

HANCOCK JOHN PFD INCOME FD II (MA)
Auction Preferred Ser. W called for redemption at $25,000 on 05/22/2008
Auction Preferred Ser. TH called for redemption at $25,000 on 05/23/2008
Auction Preferred Ser. F called for redemption at $25,000 on 05/27/2008
Auction Preferred Ser. M called for redemption at $25,000 on 05/27/2008
Auction Preferred Ser. T called for redemption at $25,000 on 05/28/2008
(Additional Information in Active)

HANCOCK JOHN PFD INCOME FD III (MA)
Auction Preferred Ser. W called for redemption at $25,000 on 05/22/2008
Auction Preferred Ser. TH called for redemption at $25,000 on 05/23/2008
Auction Preferred Ser. F called for redemption at $25,000 on 05/27/2008
Auction Preferred Ser. M called for redemption at $25,000 on 05/27/2008
Auction Preferred Ser. T called for redemption at $25,000 on 05/28/2008
(Additional Information in Active)

HANCOCK JOHN SIGNATURE FD INC (DE)
Name changed to Hancock (John) Balanced Fund, Inc. 04/15/1976
Hancock (John) Balanced Fund, Inc. name changed to Hancock (John) U.S. Government Securities Fund, Inc. (DE) 11/18/1981 which reorganized in Massachusetts as Hancock (John) U.S. Government Securities Trust 12/31/1984 which name changed to Hancock (John) U.S. Government Securities Fund 05/01/1991 which name changed to Hancock (John) Limited Term Government Fund 07/01/1993
(See Hancock (John) Limited Term Government Fund)

HAN-HAN   FINANCIAL INFORMATION, INC.

HANCOCK JOHN TAX-ADVANTAGED DIVID INCOME FD (MA)
Auction Preferred Ser. W called for redemption at $25,000 on 05/22/2008
Auction Preferred Ser. TH called for redemption at $25,000 on 05/23/2008
Auction Preferred Ser. F called for redemption at $25,000 on 05/27/2008
Auction Preferred Ser. M called for redemption at $25,000 on 05/27/2008
(Additional Information in Active)

HANCOCK JOHN TAX EXEMPT INCOME TR (MA)
Name changed 05/01/1991
Name changed from Hancock (John) Tax-Exempt Income Trust to Hancock (John) Tax-Exempt Income Fund 05/01/1991
Trust terminated 05/03/1996
Details not available

HANCOCK JOHN TAX EXEMPT SER TR (MA)
Name changed 10/23/1990
Name changed from Hancock (John) Tax-Exempt Series Trust to Hancock (John) Tax-Exempt Series Fund 10/23/1990
Merged into Hancock (John) California Tax-Free Fund 09/15/1995
Details not available
Merged into Hancock (John) Municipal Securities Trust 02/13/2015
Details not available

HANCOCK JOHN TECHNOLOGY SER INC (MD)
Merged into Hancock (John) Series Trust 03/11/1997
Details not available

HANCOCK JOHN U S GOVT GTD MTGS TR (MA)
Name changed to Hancock (John) Government Spectrum Fund 12/10/1990
(See Hancock (John) Government Spectrum Fund)

HANCOCK JOHN U S GOVT SECS FD (MA)
Name changed 05/01/1991
Name changed from Hancock (John) U.S. Government Securities Trust to Hancock (John) U.S. Government Securities Fund 05/01/1991
Name changed to Hancock (John) Limited Term Government Fund 07/01/1993
(See Hancock (John) Limited Term Government Fund)

HANCOCK JOHN U S GOVT SECS FD INC (DE)
Reorganized under the laws of Massachusetts as Hancock (John) U.S. Government Securities Trust and Capital Stock $1 par reclassified as Shares of Bene. Int. no par 12/31/1984
Hancock (John) U.S. Government Securities Trust name changed to Hancock (John) U.S. Government Securities Fund 05/01/1991 which name changed to Hancock (John) Limited Term Government Fund 07/01/1993
(See Hancock (John) Limited Term Government Fund)

HANCOCK JOHN WORLD FD (MA)
Name changed 01/01/1991
Name changed from Hancock (John) World Trust to Hancock (John) World Fund 01/01/1991
Trust terminated 12/31/2003
Details not available

HANCOCK MANUFACTURING CO. (TX)
Completely liquidated 8/1/66
Each share Common $1 par or Class A Common $1 par exchanged for first and final distribution of (0.75) share Clark Equipment Co. (MI) Common $7.50 par
Clark Equipment Co. (MI) reincorporated under the laws of Delaware 7/1/68
(See Clark Equipment Co. (DE))

HANCOCK OIL CO. (DE)
Merged into Signal Oil & Gas Co. 12/31/58
Each share 5% Preferred $25 par exchanged for (1) share 5% Preferred $25 par
Each share Class A Common $1 par exchanged for (1) share Class A Common $2 par
Each share Class B Common $1 par exchanged for (1) share Class B Common $2 par
Signal Oil & Gas Co. name changed to Signal Companies, Inc. 5/1/68 which merged into Allied-Signal Inc. 9/19/85 which name changed to AlliedSignal Inc. 4/26/93 which name changed to Honeywell International Inc. 12/1/99

HANCOCK OIL CO. OF CALIFORNIA
Recapitalized as Hancock Oil Co. in 1952
Each share Class A Common no par exchanged for (10) shares Class A Common $1 par
Each share Class B Common no par exchanged for (10) shares Class B Common $1 par
Hancock Oil Co. merged into Signal Oil & Gas Co. 12/31/58 which name changed to Signal Companies, Inc. 5/1/68 which merged into Allied-Signal Inc. 9/19/85 which name changed to AlliedSignal Inc. 4/26/93 which name changed to Honeywell International Inc. 12/1/99

HANCOCK SVGS BK (LOS ANGELES, CA)
Name changed in March 1990
Guarantee Stock $8 par changed to $6.40 par in 1986
Name changed from Hancock Savings & Loan Association to Hancock Savings Bank (Los Angeles, CA) in March 1990
Stock Dividends - 10% 3/20/89; 10% 4/2/91; 10% 3/31/92
Merged into Bank Plus Corp. 7/29/97
Each share Common $6.40 par exchanged for (0.8125) share Common $1 par
(See Bank Plus Corp.)

HAND BRAND DISTR INC (FL)
Each share old Common $0.001 par exchanged for (0.5) share new Common $0.001 par 02/01/1997
Each share new Common $0.001 par exchanged again for (0.125) share new Common $0.001 par 01/15/2002
Name changed to GeneThera, Inc. (FL) 06/10/2003
GeneThera, Inc. (FL) reincorporated in Nevada 12/01/2007

HAND CHEM INDS LTD (CANADA)
Each share Class A Conv. Stock no par exchanged for (2) shares Preferred no par 09/02/1969
Name changed to HCI Holdings Ltd. 03/22/1977
HCI Holdings Ltd. recapitalized as Consolidated HCI Holdings Corp. 12/31/1986

HANDA COPPER CORP (BC)
Each share old Common no par exchanged for (0.2) share new Common no par 08/15/2014
Name changed to Handa Mining Corp. 06/13/2018

HANDELL-GRAFF INC (NV)
Name changed to Healthcomp Evaluation Services Corp. 3/17/99
Healthcomp Evaluation Services Corp. name changed to Exemplar International Inc. 12/12/2002 which recapitalized as Now Corp. 12/4/2006

HANDEX CORP (DE)
Name changed 05/09/1995
Common 1¢ par split (5) for (4) by issuance of (0.25) additional share 03/25/1991
Name changed from Handex Environmental Recovery, Inc. to Handex Corp. 05/09/1995
Name changed to New Horizons Worldwide, Inc. 01/02/1997
(See New Horizons Worldwide, Inc.)

HANDHELD ENTMT INC (DE)
Each share old Common $0.0001 par exchanged for (0.68965517) share new Common $0.0001 par 08/15/2006
Name changed to ZVUE Corp. 11/02/2007
(See ZVUE Corp.)

HANDLEMAN CO (MI)
Reincorporated under the laws of Delaware 10/24/1969 which reincorporated back under the laws of Michigan 12/31/1979
Common $1 par and Class B Common $1 par split (3) for (2) respectively by issuance of (0.5) additional share 08/19/1966
Common $1 par and Class B Common $1 par split (2) for (1) respectively by issuance of (1) additional share 02/21/1968
Common $1 par and Class B Common $1 par split (4) for (3) respectively by issuance of (0.33333333) additional share 07/31/1969
Common $1 par split (3) for (2) by issuance of (0.5) additional share 01/30/1984
Common $1 par split (2) for (1) by issuance of (1) additional share 05/10/1985
Common $1 par changed to 1¢ par 09/07/1988
Common 1¢ par split (3) for (2) by issuance of (0.5) additional share 11/10/1988
Common 1¢ par split (3) for (2) by issuance of (0.5) additional share 08/10/1989
Liquidation completed
Each share Common 1¢ par received first and final distribution of $0.367898 cash payable 01/16/2013 to holders of record 06/20/2009
Note: Holders may receive an additional distribution following the settlement of a remaining tax claim

HANDMACHER VOGEL INC (NY)
Stock Dividend - 50% 05/22/1961
Name changed to Country Miss, Inc. 10/02/1972
(See Country Miss, Inc.)

HANDSCHY INDS INC (IL)
Name changed 08/02/1977
Stock Dividends - 10% 09/30/1972; 15% 08/30/1974; 15% 08/15/1975; 10% 12/03/1976; 10% 08/14/1978
Name changed from Handschy Chemical Co. to Handschy Industries, Inc. 08/02/1977
Company advised privately held as of 00/00/1991

HANDSPRING INC (DE)
Merged into palmOne, Inc. 10/29/2003
Each share Common no par exchanged for (0.09) share Common $0.001 par palmOne, Inc. name changed to Palm, Inc. (New) 07/14/2005
(See Palm, Inc. (New))

HANDY & HARMAN (NY)
5% Preferred $100 par called for redemption 03/01/1966
Common $1 par split (3) for (2) by issuance of (0.5) additional share 12/01/1976
Common $1 par split (2) for (1) by issuance of (1) additional share 12/01/1978
Common $1 par split (2) for (1) by issuance of (1) additional share 11/28/1980
Merged into WHX Corp. 04/13/1998
Each share Common $1 par exchanged for $35.25 cash

HANDY & HARMAN LTD (DE)
Merged into Steel Partners Holdings L.P. 10/12/2017
Each share Common 1¢ par exchanged for (1.484) 6% Preferred Units Ser. A no par

HANDY ANDY AUTO CTRS INC (QC)
Name changed 07/24/1978
Name changed 07/10/1982
Name changed from Handy Andy Co. to Handy Andy Inc. 07/24/1978
Name changed from Handy Andy Inc. to Handy Andy Auto-Centres Inc./Centres-Auto Handy Andy Inc. 07/10/1982
Acquired by UAP Inc. 04/16/1984
Each share Common $1 par exchanged for $8.53 cash

HANDY ANDY MERCHANDISING CORP. (EASTERN) LTD. (ON)
$2.80 1st Preference Stock $50 par called for redemption and company dissolved 11/03/1976

HANDY DAN HOME IMPT CTRS INC (DE)
Merged into Daylin, Inc. (DE) 01/08/1978
Each share Common $1 par exchanged for $25.50 cash

HANDYMAN CORP. LIQUIDATING TRUST (NV)
In process of liquidation
Each Share of Bene. Int. $1 par received initial distribution of $22 cash 12/26/1986
Each Share of Bene. Int. $1 par exchanged for second distribution of $9 cash 04/03/1987
Each Share of Bene. Int. $1 par received third distribution of $9 cash 09/11/1987
Each Share of Bene. Int. $1 par received fourth distribution of $5 cash 03/23/1988
Each Share of Bene. Int. $1 par received fifth distribution of $2.25 cash 03/20/1989
Details on subsequent distributions, if any, are not available

HANDYMAN CORP (NV)
Assets transferred to Handyman Corp. Liquidating Trust and Common $1 par reclassified as Shares of Bene. Int. $1 par 12/22/1987
(See Handyman Corp. Liquidating Trust)

HANES CORP (NC)
Merged into Consolidated Foods Corp. 01/30/1979
Each share Common $1 par exchanged for $61 cash

HANES (P.H.) KNITTING CO. (NC)
Common and Class B Common $10 par changed to $5 par 00/00/1933
Preferred $100 par called for redemption 04/01/1962
Common and Class B Common $5 par changed to $2 par and (2) additional shares issued respectively 05/31/1963
Merged into Hanes Corp. 02/26/1965
Each share Common $2 par exchanged for (1.5) shares Common $1 par
Each share Class B Common $2 par exchanged for (1.5) shares Common $1 par
(See Hanes Corp.)

HANFENG EVERGREEN INC (ON)
Each Class A Special Share no par automatically became (1) share McVicar Resources Inc. Common no par 04/19/2004
(See McVicar Resources Inc.)
(Additional Information in Active)

HANFORD SILVER INC (UT)
Merged into First Midwest Financial Corp. 12/10/1982
Each (112) shares Common $0.001 par exchanged for (1) share Common $0.001 par
(See First Midwest Financial Corp.)

HANG LUNG DEV LTD (HONG KONG)
Each Unsponsored ADR for Ordinary HKD $1 par exchanged for (2) Sponsored ADR's for Ordinary HKD $1 par 02/17/1993
Stock Dividend - 100% 10/15/1987
Name changed to Hang Lung Group Ltd. 01/10/2002

HANGER ORTHOPEDIC GROUP INC (DE)
Each share old Common 1¢ par exchanged for (0.25) share new Common 1¢ par 12/31/1990
Name changed to Hanger, Inc. 06/11/2012

HANGMAN PRODUCTIONS INC (UT)
Each share old Common 1¢ par exchanged for (2) shares new Common 1¢ par 12/21/2009
Name changed to LYFE Communications, Inc. 05/14/2010

HANIFEN IMHOFF COLO BONDSHARES -A TAX EXEMPT FD (MA)
Name changed to Colorado BondShares-A Tax-Exempt Fund 12/01/1994

HANKERSEN INTL CORP (DE)
Name changed to Asia Cork, Inc. 07/28/2008
(See Asia Cork, Inc.)

HANKIN WATER TECHNOLOGIES LTD (CANADA)
Name changed 03/26/1999
Name changed from Hankin Atlas Industries Ltd. to Hankin Water Technologies Ltd. 03/26/1999
Cease trade order effective 02/25/2002
Stockholders' equity unlikely

HANKO PPTYS INC (DE)
Charter cancelled and declared inoperative and void for non-payment of taxes 3/1/76

HANKS SEAFOOD INC (MD)
Merged into HSC Acquisition Corp. 3/8/96
Each share Common 2¢ par exchanged for $1.25 cash

HANKUK GLASS INDS INC (KOREA)
GDR agreement terminated 08/07/2003
Each 144A GDR for Common exchanged for $5.4450871 cash

HANLEY (JAMES) CO. (RI)
Name changed to Golden Gate Corp. 6/17/57
(See Golden Gate Corp.)

HANLEY CONS INC (FL)
Proclaimed dissolved for failure to file reports and pay fees 10/21/1974
No stockholders' equity

HANMI BK (LOS ANGELES, CA)
Stock Dividends - 8% payable 04/23/1996 to holders of record 04/01/1996; 9% payable 04/08/1998 to holders of record 03/20/1998; 11% payable 05/03/1999 to holders of record 04/26/1999; 11% payable 04/03/2000 to holders of record 03/01/2000
Under plan of reorganization each share Common no par automatically became (1) share Hanmi Financial Corp. (DE) Common $0.001 par 06/09/2000

HANNA (M.A.) CO. OLD (DE)
Each share Common no par exchanged for (2) shares Class A $10 par and (1) share Class B $10 par 00/00/1952
Each share Class A $10 par exchanged for (4) shares Common $2.50 par 10/31/1961
Each share Class B $10 par exchanged for (4) shares Common $2.50 par 10/31/1961
Liquidation completed
Each share Common $2.50 par received initial distribution of (0.0232) share Algoma Steel Corp., Ltd. Capital Stock no par; (0.1259) share Consolidation Coal Co. Common $1 par; (0.0066) share General Reinsurance Corp. (NY) Capital Stock $10 par; (0.1663) share Hanna Mining Co. Common $1 par; (0.0220) share McDermott (J.Ray) & Co., Inc. Common $1 par; (0.0088) share National City Bank (Cleveland, OH) Common $8 par; (0.2004) share National Steel Corp. Capital Stock $5 par; (0.0067) share Phelps Dodge Corp. Capital Stock $12.50 par; (0.0417) share Standard Oil Co. (NJ) Capital Stock $7 par; (0.0342) share Texaco Inc. Capital Stock $12.50 par; $4.17 principal amount of Hanna Mining Co. 4.75% Debentures due 12/15/1990 and $10 cash 12/27/1965
Each share Common $2.50 par exchanged for second distribution of $1.70 cash 08/26/1966
Each share Common $2.50 par received third and final distribution of $0.16455 cash 12/23/1968
(See each company's listing)

HANNA ACCEP CORP (OR)
Involuntarily dissolved for failure to file reports and pay fees 09/19/1996

HANNA CHEM COATINGS CORP (OH)
Stock Dividend - 100% 12/31/1970
Merged into Tyler Corp. (Old) 03/01/1985
Each share Common $5 par exchanged for $54.30 cash

HANNA FURNACE CO.
Acquired by National Steel Corp. 00/00/1929
Details not available

HANNA GOLD MINES LTD. (BC)
Name changed to Dorchester Resources Ltd. 05/17/1972
Dorchester Resources Ltd. recapitalized as Taurus Resources Ltd. 12/22/1976 which recapitalized as International Taurus Resources Inc. 11/24/1988 which merged into American Bonanza Gold Corp 03/31/2005 which merged into Kerr Mines Inc. 07/07/2014

HANNA M A CO NEW (DE)
Name changed 05/03/1985
Common $1 par split (3) for (1) by issuance of (2) additional shares 05/20/1964
Common $1 par split (2) for (1) by issuance of (1) additional share 05/02/1969
Name changed from Hanna Mining Co. to Hanna (M.A.) Co. (New) 05/03/1985
Common $1 par split (3) for (2) by issuance of (0.5) additional share 10/31/1988
$2.125 Conv. Exchangeable Preferred no par called for redemption 06/15/1989
Common $1 par split (3) for (2) by issuance of (0.5) additional share 06/15/1994
Common $1 par split (3) for (2) by issuance of (0.5) additional share payable 06/17/1996 to holders of record 05/24/1996 Ex date - 06/18/1996
Merged into PolyOne Corp. 08/31/2000
Each share Common $1 par exchanged for (1) share Common 1¢ par

HANNA PACIFIC STL LTD (BC)
Recapitalized as Foch Consumer Electronics Corp. 03/05/1993
Each share Common no par exchanged for (0.2) share Common no par
Foch Consumer Electronics Corp. recapitalized as Hawkeye Gold Corp. 01/22/1996 which recapitalized as Hawkeye Gold International Inc. 12/17/1998 which recapitalized as Hawkeye Gold & Diamond Inc. 05/29/2003

HANNA PAINT MFG CO INC (OH)
Name changed to Hanna Chemical Coatings Corp. 11/13/1969
(See Hanna Chemical Coatings Corp.)

HANNA PETROLEUMS, LTD. (AB)
Acquired by Edoran Oil Corp. Ltd. in 1953
Each share Common no par exchanged for (0.1) share Common no par
Edoran Oil Corp. was recapitalized as Kamalta Exploration Ltd. 7/26/65 which became bankrupt 9/9/70

HANNAFORD BROS CO (ME)
Common $1 par changed to 75¢ par and (0.33333333) additional share issued 06/08/1976
Common 75¢ par split (2) for (1) by issuance of (1) additional share 02/28/1983
Common 75¢ par split (2) for (1) by issuance of (0.5) additional share 02/26/1985
Common 75¢ par split (2) for (2) by issuance of (0.5) additional share 08/30/1985
Common 75¢ par split (2) for (1) by issuance of (1) additional share 02/28/1989
Common 75¢ par split (2) for (1) by issuance of (1) additional share 03/10/1992
Merged into Delhaize America, Inc. 07/31/2000
Each share Common 75¢ par exchanged for (2.9259) shares Class A Common 50¢ par
Delhaize America, Inc. merged into Etablissements Delhaize Freres et Cie Le Lion S.A. 04/25/2001 which merged into Koninklijke Ahold Delhaize N.V. 07/25/2016

HANNIBAL BRIDGE CO.
Dissolved in 1937

HANNIBAL LTD (UT)
Each share old Common $0.001 par exchanged for (0.1) share new Common $0.001 par 10/1/96
Each share new Common $0.001 par exchanged for (0.05) share Common $0.0001 par 11/22/99
Reincorporated under the laws of Nevada as Jarvis Entertainment Group, Inc. 2/1/2001
Jarvis Entertainment Group, Inc. name changed to Westlin Corp. 11/17/2003

HANNIBAL MO BOTTLING CO (GA)
Company no longer public as of 00/00/1975
Details not available

HANNOVER RUECKVERSICHERUNG AG (GERMANY)
Name changed 10/16/2000
Name changed from Hannover Reinsurance Corp. to Hannover Rueckversicherung AG 10/16/2000
Name changed to Hannover Rueckversicherung SE 03/26/2013

HANOVER BANCORP INC (PA)
Common $2.50 par split (2) for (1) by issuance of (1) additional share 06/16/1986
Common $2.50 par split (3) for (2) by issuance of (0.5) additional share 05/15/1993
Common $2.50 par split (3) for (2) by issuance of (0.5) additional share 04/01/1995
Stock Dividends - 10% 06/01/1984; 10% 08/01/1989; 10% 07/17/1992
Merged into Sterling Financial Corp. 07/27/2000
Each share Common $2.50 par exchanged for (0.93) share Common $5 par
(See Sterling Financial Corp.)

HANOVER BANK & TRUST CO. (HANOVER, NH)
Under plan of reorganization each share Capital Stock $1 par automatically became (1) share United Banks Corp. Common $2 par 12/14/1977
United Banks Corp. merged into BankEast Corp. 02/27/1987
(See BankEast Corp.)

HANOVER BANK (NEW YORK, NY)
Each share Capital Stock $20 par exchanged for (2) shares Capital Stock $10 par in 1955
Stock Dividends - 14-2/7% 2/15/51; 12-1/2% 2/15/54; 11-1/9% 2/15/55; 20% 8/31/56; 33-1/3% 2/2/59
Merged into Manufacturers Hanover Trust Co. (New York, NY) 9/8/61
Each share Capital Stock $10 par exchanged for (1) share Capital Stock $15 par
Manufacturers Hanover Trust Co. (New York, NY) reorganized in Delaware as Manufacturers Hanover Corp. 4/28/69 which merged into Chemical Banking Corp. 12/31/91

HANOVER BANK (WILMINGTON, NC)
Merged into Planters National Bank & Trust Co. (Rocky Mount, NC) 7/9/76
Each share Common $5 par exchanged for (0.6) share Capital Stock $5 par
Planters National Bank & Trust Co. (Rocky Mount, NC) reorganized as Planters Corp. 3/8/83 which merged into Centura Banks, Inc. 11/5/90 which merged into Royal Bank of Canada (Montreal, QC) 6/5/2001

HANOVER BK PA (WILKES BARRE, PA)
Common $20 par changed to $5 par and (3) additional shares issued 09/28/1984
Merged into First Valley Corp. 06/30/1985
Each share Common $5 par exchanged for $68.65 cash

HANOVER BK VA (MECHANICSVILLE, VA)
Merged into MainStreet BankGroup Inc. 11/13/96
Each share Common no par exchanged for either (0.884) share Common $5 par or $15.25 cash
MainStreet BankGroup Inc. name changed to MainStreet Financial Corp. 6/1/98 which merged into BB&T Corp. 3/8/99

HANOVER CAP MTG HLDGS INC (MD)
Merged into Walter Investment Management Corp. 04/20/2009
Each share Common 1¢ par exchanged for (0.02) share Common 1¢ par
(See Walter Investment Management Corp.)

HANOVER CMNTY BK (GARDEN CITY PARK, NY)
Under plan of reorganization each

share Common 1¢ par automatically became (1) share Hanover Bancorp Inc. Common 1¢ par 08/10/2016

HANOVER COMPRESSOR CAP TR (DE)
7.25% Conv. Preferred Securities 1¢ par called for redemption at $50 plus $0.755175 accrued dividends on 5/31/2007

144A 7.25% Conv. Preferred Securities 1¢ par called for redemption at $50 plus $0.755175 accrued dividends on 5/31/2007

HANOVER COMPRESSOR CO (DE)
Common $0.001 par split (2) for (1) by issuance of (1) additional share payable 06/13/2000 to holders of record 05/30/2000 Ex date - 06/14/2000

Merged into Exterran Holdings, Inc. 08/20/2007

Each share Common $0.001 par exchanged for (0.325) share Common 1¢ par

Exterran Holdings, Inc. name changed to Archrock, Inc. 11/04/2015

HANOVER COS INC (DE)
Charter cancelled and declared inoperative and void for non-payment of taxes 3/1/88

HANOVER DIRECT INC (DE)
Each share 7.50% Preferred 1¢ par converted into (4) shares Common 66-2/3¢ par in December 1993

Each share Common 66-2/3¢ par exchanged for (0.1) share Common 1¢ par 9/23/2004

Merged into Chelsey Direct, LLC 4/12/2007

Each share new Common 1¢ par exchanged for $0.25 cash

HANOVER EQUITIES CORP. (DE)
Acquired by Rapid-American Corp. (Ohio) 6/10/66

Each share Class A $1 par or Class B 10¢ par exchanged for (1/3) share 75¢ Conv. Preferred $1 par

Rapid-American Corp. (Ohio) merged into Rapid-American Corp. (Del.) 11/6/72

(See Rapid-American Corp. (Del.))

HANOVER FD (NV)
Recapitalized as F-D Capital Fund 04/00/1970

Each Share of Bene. Int. no par exchanged for (0.2) Share of Bene. Int. no par

F-D Capital Fund merged into Pine Tree Fund, Inc. 11/27/1972

(See Pine Tree Fund, Inc.)

HANOVER GOLD INC (DE)
Each share old Common $0.0001 par exchanged for (0.25) share new Common $0.0001 par 05/05/1998

Recapitalized as Rock Energy Resources, Inc. 02/19/2008

Each share Common $0.0001 par exchanged for (0.125) share Common $0.0001 par

HANOVER GTY INC (CO)
Charter suspended for failure to file annual reports 09/30/1987

HANOVER INS CO (NH)
Name changed 1/2/58
Reincorporated 1/1/73

Each share Capital Stock $50 par exchanged for (5) shares Capital Stock $10 par in 1928

Name changed from Hanover Fire Insurance Co. (NY) to Hanover Insurance Co. 1/2/58

State of incorporation changed from (NY) to (NH) 1/1/73

Capital Stock $10 par changed to $2 par and (1) additional share issued 4/27/73

Capital Stock $2 par changed to $1.33-1/3 par and (0.5) additional share issued 4/30/81

Capital Stock $1.33-1/3 par changed to $1 par and (1) additional share issued 5/3/84

Capital Stock $1 par split (2) for (1) by issuance of (1) additional share 4/30/87

Merged into Allmerica Property & Casualty Companies, Inc. 12/11/92

Each share Capital Stock $1 par exchanged for (1) share Common $1 par

Allmerica Property & Casualty Companies, Inc. merged into Allmerica Financial Corp. 7/16/97 which name changed to Hanover Insurance Group, Inc. 12/1/2005

HANOVER LAMONT CORP (GA)
Name changed to Warren, Gorham & Lamont, Inc. 10/18/72

(See Warren, Gorham & Lamont, Inc.)

HANOVER LEASE INCOME LTD PARTNERSHIP (MA)
Filed Certificate of Cancellation 12/30/1998

Details not available

HANOVER LIFE INS CO (NJ)
Acquired by State Mutual Life Assurance Co. 12/15/72

Each share Common $5 par exchanged for $13.46 cash

HANOVER MFG CO (OH)
Merged into Cummings & Co., The International Sign Service, Inc. 4/2/70

Each share Common no par exchanged for (1.38) shares Common $1 par

Each share Common no par received an additional (0.074583) share Common $1 par upon completion of escrow agreement 5/14/73

Cummings & Co., The International Sign Service, Inc. name changed to Cummings Inc., The International Sign Service 11/15/74

(See Cummings Inc., The International Sign Service)

HANOVER MORTGAGE CO. (OH)
Charter revoked for failure to file reports and pay fees 11/15/32

HANOVER NATL BK (WILKES-BARRE, PA)
Name changed to Hanover Bank of Pennsylvania (Wilkes-Barre, PA) 4/18/77

(See Hanover Bank of Pennsylvania (Wilkes-Barre, PA))

HANOVER PETE CORP (DE)
Merged into Total Petroleum (North America) Ltd. 4/30/76

Each share Common 20¢ par exchanged for $6.40 principal amount of 11-1/2% Guaranteed Debentures due 12/31/90, (0.6) Common Stock Purchase Warrant expiring 12/31/80, $6.40 cash and (1) Non-Transferable Unit of Bene. Int. or an additional $1.25 cash

Note: In the absence of an election holders received all of the above except the Non-Transferable Unit of Bene. Int.

(See Total Petroleum (North America) Ltd.)

HANOVER PLANNING CO., INC. (DE)
Name changed to Hanover Petroleum Corp. 11/21/74

(See Hanover Petroleum Corp.)

HANOVER PORTFOLIO ACQUISITIONS INC (DE)
Name changed to Endonovo Therapeutics, Inc. 05/05/2014

HANOVER RAILWAY CO.
Out of existence 00/00/1934
Details not available

HANOVER SHOE INC (PA)
Each share Common $1 par exchanged for (2) shares Common 50¢ par 05/10/1971

Name changed to Shepmyers Investment Co. 12/29/1977

Shepmyers Investment Co. merged into Smith Barney Muni Bond Funds 04/20/2000 which name changed to Smith Barney Muni Funds 05/25/1994 which name changed to Legg Mason Partners Municipal Funds 04/07/2006

(See Legg Mason Partners Municipal Funds)

HANOVER SQUARE RLTY INVS (MA)
Merged into Pearce, Urstadt, Mayer & Greer, Inc. 11/20/1980

Each Share of Bene. Int. no par exchanged for (1) share Common $1 par

(See Pearce, Urstadt, Mayer & Greer, Inc.)

HANSA CORP (AB)
Name changed to Azteca Gold Corp. 12/28/2006

HANSA INTL RES LTD (BC)
Struck off register and declared dissolved for failure to file returns 01/21/1994

HANSA.NET GLOBAL COMM INC (ANGUILLA)
Name changed to KMT-Hansa Corp. 09/27/2013

HANSA PETE CORP (BC)
Merged into Orbit Oil & Gas Ltd. 01/22/1982

Each share Common no par exchanged for (0.125) share Common no par

(See Orbit Oil & Gas Ltd.)

HANSEN GRAY & CO INC (NV)
Each share old Common $0.001 par exchanged for (2) shares new Common $0.001 par 08/28/2004

Recapitalized as AMF Capital, Inc. 06/22/2007

Each share Common $0.001 par exchanged for (0.05) share Common $0.001 par

AMF Capital, Inc. name changed to Pro Motors Group Corp. 10/29/2007 which recapitalized as Hydrogen Hybrid Corp. 11/25/2008 which name changed to Get Real USA Inc. 01/12/2011

HANSEN MFG CO (OH)
Stock Dividends - 25% 12/15/1957; 100% 03/15/1960

Merged into Tuthill Corp. 01/03/1980

Each share Common $1 par exchanged for $37 cash

HANSEN MED INC (DE)
Each share old Common $0.0001 par exchanged for (0.1) share new Common $0.0001 par 09/23/2015

Acquired by Auris Surgical Robotics, Inc. 07/27/2016

Each share new Common $0.0001 par exchanged for $4 cash

HANSEN NAT CORP (DE)
Common $0.005 par split (2) for (1) by issuance of (1) additional share payable 08/08/2005 to holders of record 08/01/2005 Ex date - 08/09/2005

Common $0.005 par split (4) for (1) by issuance of (3) additional shares payable 07/07/2006 to holders of record 06/30/2006 Ex date - 07/10/2006

Name changed to Monster Beverage Corp. (Old) 01/09/2012

Monster Beverage Corp. (Old) reorganized as Monster Beverage Corp. (New) 06/15/2015

HANSEN TRANSMISSIONS INTL NV (BELGIUM)
Acquired by ZF Friedrichshafen AG 11/29/2011

Each ADR for Common exchanged for $2.013159 cash

HANSOL PAPER LTD (KOREA)
Stock Dividends - 4% payable 05/06/1998 to holders of record 12/30/1997; 4% payable 04/28/1999 to holders of record 12/30/1998

GDR agreement terminated 03/05/2008

Each Sponsored Reg. S GDR for Common exchanged for $6.762289 cash

Each Sponsored 144A GDR for Common exchanged for $6.762289 cash

HANSOM EASTN HLDGS LTD (CAYMAN ISLANDS)
Name changed to Inner Mongolia Development (Holdings) Ltd. 09/15/2005

Inner Mongolia Development (Holdings) Ltd. name changed to Freeman Corp., Ltd. 07/06/2006 which name changed to Freeman Financial Corp. Ltd. 05/14/2012

(See Freeman Financial Corp. Ltd.)

HANSON JOHN BANCORP INC (MD)
Taken over by Office of Thrift Supervision 4/26/91
No stockholders' equity

HANSON JOHN SVGS BK F S B (BELTSVILLE, MD)
Under plan of reorganization each share Common $1 par automatically became (1) share Hanson (John) Bancorp, Inc. Common $1 par 10/31/90

(See Hanson (John) Bancorp, Inc.)

HANSON MINERAL EXPL LTD (ON)
Merged into McNickel Inc. 03/21/1989

Each share Common no par exchanged for (0.2) share Common no par

McNickel Inc. recapitalized as Sahelian Goldfields Inc. 09/09/1996 which recapitalized as Sage Gold Inc. 03/03/2005

HANSON MINES LTD. (ON)
Each share Common $1 par exchanged for (1) share Common 95¢ par and (0.2) share of Share Mines & Oils Ltd. Common no par 12/01/1965

Each share Common 95¢ par exchanged for (1) share Common 90¢ par and (0.1) share of Share Mines & Oils Ltd. Common no par 04/07/1966

(See Share Mines & Oils Ltd.)

Recapitalized as Hanson Mineral Exploration Ltd. 09/04/1980

Each share Common 90¢ par exchanged for (0.33333333) share Common no par

Hanson Mineral Exploration Ltd. merged into McNickel Inc. 03/21/1989 which recapitalized as Sahelian Goldfields Inc. 09/09/1996 which recapitalized as Sage Gold Inc. 03/03/2005

HANSON (HERMAN) OIL SYNDICATE (ND)
Charter revoked for failure to file reports and pay fees 12/27/61

HANSON PLC NEW (ENGLAND)
Acquired by HeidelbergCement AG 08/24/2007

Each Sponsored ADR for Ordinary 25p par exchanged for $110.2415 cash

HANSON PLC OLD (ENGLAND)
Each Sponsored ADR for Ordinary 25p par received distribution of (0.07142857) share Millennium Chemicals Inc. Common 1¢ par and (0.25) Imperial Tobacco Group PLC Sponsored ADR for Ordinary 10p par payable 10/01/1996 to holders of record 09/30/1996 Ex date - 10/02/1996

Each old Sponsored ADR for Ordinary 25p par exchanged for (0.125) new

Sponsored ADR for Ordinary 25p par 02/21/1997
Each new Sponsored ADR for Ordinary 25p par received distribution of (0.125) Energy Group PLC Sponsored ADR for Ordinary payable 02/24/1997 to holders of record 02/23/1997
Scheme of arrangement effective 10/15/2003
Each Sponsored ADR for Ordinary 25p par exchanged for (1) Hanson PLC (New) Sponsored ADR for Ordinary 25p par
(See Hanson PLC (New))

HANSON (JOHN) SAVINGS & LOAN, INC. (MD)
Name changed to Hanson (John) Savings Bank FSB (Beltsville, MD) 09/01/1986
Hanson (John) Savings Bank FSB (Beltsville, Md.) reorganized as Hanson (John) Bancorp, Inc. 10/31/1990
(See Hanson (John) Bancorp, Inc.)

HANSON TRUST P.L.C. (ENGLAND)
Each Unsponsored ADR for Ordinary 25p par exchanged for (1) Sponsored ADR for Ordinary 25p par 11/13/1986
Sponsored ADR's for Ordinary 25p par split (4) for (3) by issuance of (1/3) additional ADR 01/26/1987
Stock Dividends - 50% 03/25/1983; 50% 02/29/1984; 50% 02/27/1985; 33-1/3% 02/25/1986
Note: Common Market regulation required all publicly held British companies to replace LTD with PLC 00/00/1982
Name changed to Hanson PLC (Old) 01/29/1988
Hanson PLC (Old) reorganized as Hanson PLC (New) 10/15/2003
(See Hanson PLC (New))

HANSON-VAN WINKLE-MUNNING CO. (NJ)
Stock Dividends - 10% 12/22/50; 10% 12/21/51; 15% 12/31/53
Acquired by American Can Co. 9/25/64
Each share Common $3.50 par exchanged for (0.465) share Common $12.50 par
American Can Co. name changed to Primerica Corp. (NJ) 4/28/87 which was acquired by Primerica Corp. (DE) 12/15/88 which name changed to Travelers Inc. 12/31/93 which name changed to Travelers Group Inc. 4/16/95 which name changed to Citigroup Inc. 10/8/98

HANVIT BK (KOREA)
ADR agreement terminated 12/18/2000
Each 144A Sponsored GDR for Ordinary exchanged for $0.51258 cash

HANWHA SOLARONE CO LTD (CAYMAN ISLANDS)
Name changed to Hanwha Q CELLS Co., Ltd. 02/09/2015

HAOMA NORTHWEST N L (AUSTRALIA)
Name changed 07/01/1982
Name changed from Haoma Gold Mines NL to Haoma North West NL 07/01/1982
Name changed to Haoma Mining NL 07/12/1994

HAPC INC (DE)
Name changed to InfuSystem Holdings, Inc. 10/26/2007

HAPMAN CORP (MI)
Name changed 10/01/1959
Name changed from Hapman-Conveyors, Inc. to Hapman Corp. 10/01/1959
Each share Common $1 par exchanged for (0.2) share Common no par 07/07/1971
Adjudicated bankrupt 03/14/1972
No stockholders' equity

HAPMAN-DUTTON CO. (MI)
Name changed to Hapman Conveyors, Inc. 05/01/1958
Hapman Conveyors, Inc. name changed to Hapman Corp. 10/01/1959
(See Hapman Corp.)

HAPPINESS CANDY STORES, INC.
Liquidated 00/00/1948
Details not available

HAPPINESS EXPRESS INC (DE)
Charter cancelled and declared inoperative and void for non-payment of taxes 3/1/96

HAPPY FOOD CORP (OK)
Reorganized as Laser Energetics, Inc. 08/01/2005
Each share Class A Common $0.001 par exchanged for (3.40184265) shares Class A Common $0.001 par

HAPPY KIDS INC (NY)
Issue Information - 2,200,000 shares COM offered at $10 per share on 04/02/1998
Merged into HIG Capital LLC 12/20/99
Each share Common 1¢ par exchanged for $12 cash

HAPPY RES LTD (BC)
Common no par split (3) for (1) by issuance of (2) additional shares 04/03/1986
Name changed to HPY Industries Ltd. 02/25/1987
(See HPY Industries Ltd.)

HAPPY VY ENTERPRISES INC (DE)
Name changed to Travelmax International, Inc. (DE) 10/8/87
(See Travelmax International, Inc. (DE))

HAPS USA INC (UT)
Name changed to PGMI, Inc. 03/16/2006
(See PGMI, Inc.)

HAPYKIDZ COM INC (NV)
Common $0.001 par split (25) for (1) by issuance of (24) additional shares payable 09/18/2013 to holders of record 09/16/2013
Ex date - 09/19/2013
Name changed to Symbid Corp. 09/25/2013
Symbid Corp. recapitalized as Sincerity Applied Materials Holdings Corp. 06/14/2017

HARAMBEE MNG CORP (BC)
Recapitalized as Neuer Kapital Corp. 01/03/2002
Each share Common no par exchanged for (0.33333333) share Common no par
Neuer Kapital Corp. name changed to Crescent Resources Corp. 08/03/2005 which recapitalized as Coventry Resources Inc. 01/09/2013
(See Coventry Resources Inc.)

HARATINE GAS & OIL CO., INC. (DE)
No longer in existence having become inoperative and void for non-payment of taxes 4/1/65

HARBEN INDS LTD (BC)
Name changed to Merit Industries Inc. 07/19/2000
Merit Industries Inc. recapitalized as Ialta Industries Ltd. 07/02/2002
(See Ialta Industries Ltd.)

HARBIN ELEC INC (NV)
Acquired by Tech Full Electric Co., Ltd. 11/01/2011
Each share Common $0.00001 par exchanged for $24 cash

HARBIN PWR EQUIP LTD (CHINA)
ADR agreement terminated 09/20/2013
No ADR's remain outstanding

HARBINGER CORP (GA)
Common $0.0001 par split (3) for (2) by issuance of (0.5) additional share payable 01/31/1997 to holders of record 01/17/1997
Common $0.0001 par split (3) for (2) by issuance of (0.5) additional share payable 05/15/1998 to holders of record 05/01/1998
Merged into Peregrine Systems, Inc. 06/19/2000
Each share Common $0.0001 par exchanged for (0.75) share Common $0.001 par
(See Peregrine Systems, Inc.)

HARBINGER GROUP INC (DE)
Name changed to HRG Group, Inc. 03/11/2015
HRG Group, Inc. recapitalized as Spectrum Brands Holdings, Inc. (New) 07/16/2018

HARBISON-WALKER REFRACTORIES CO. (PA)
Each share Common $100 par exchanged for (4) share Common no par in 1928
Common no par changed to $15 par in 1953
Common $15 par changed to $7.50 par and (1) additional share issued 5/21/57
Merged into Dresser Industries, Inc. (New) 10/26/67
Each share 6% Preferred $100 par exchanged for (3.4) shares $2.20 Conv. Preferred Ser. A no par
Each share Common $7.50 par exchanged for (1.1) shares $2.20 Conv. Preferred Ser. A no par
Dresser Industries, Inc. (New) merged into Halliburton Co. 9/29/98

HARBOR ACQUISITION CORP (DE)
Issue Information - 10,000,000 UNITS consisting of (1) share COM and (2) WTS offered at $6 per Unit on 04/26/2006
Completely liquidated 06/09/2008
Each share Common $0.0001 par exchanged for first and final distribution of $5.92052485 cash

HARBOR AMERN HEALTH CARE TR INC (MD)
Name changed to Healthcare Investors of America, Inc. 12/27/1996
Healthcare Investors of America, Inc. name changed to REIT Americas, Inc. 06/25/2004
(See REIT Americas, Inc.)

HARBOR BANCORP (CA)
Acquired by City National Corp. 1/20/98
Each share Common $2.50 par exchanged for either (0.7517) share Common $1 par, $24.10 cash, or a combination thereof subject to proration

HARBOR BANCORP INC (WA)
Merged into Pacific Financial Corp. 12/15/1999
Each share Common no par exchanged for (0.785) share Common $1 par

HARBOR BK (LONG BEACH, CA)
Common $5 par changed to $2.50 par and (1) additional share issued 8/11/78
Under plan of reorganization each share Common $2.50 par automatically became (1) share Harbor Bancorp Common $2.50 par 5/5/83
Harbor Bancorp acquired by City National Corp. 1/20/98

HARBOR BK (NEWPORT NEWS, VA)
Stock Dividend - 5% payable 05/25/2001 to holders of record 04/18/2001 Ex date - 06/06/2001
No ADR's remain outstanding
Merged into TowneBank (Portsmouth, VA) 03/22/2004
Each share Common $5 par exchanged for (2) shares Common $2.50 par

HARBOR BK GROUP INC (SC)
Merged into BNC Bancorp 12/01/2014
Each share Common $1 par exchanged for (0.95) share Common no par
BNC Bancorp merged into Pinnacle Financial Partners, Inc. 06/16/2017

HARBOR BIOSCIENCES INC (DE)
Each share old Common 1¢ par exchanged for (1) share new Common 1¢ par to reflect a (1) for (1,000) reverse split followed by a (1,000) for (1) forward split 11/02/2011
Note: Holders of (999) or fewer pre-split shares received $0.142 cash per share
Name changed to Harbor Diversified, Inc. 02/28/2012

HARBOR BREWING CO INC (FL)
Each share old Common $0.0001 par exchanged for (0.0004) share new Common $0.0001 par 01/19/2011
Name changed to CTGX Mining, Inc. 02/28/2013

HARBOR CAP CORP (NV)
Name changed to Divide Drives, Inc. 08/24/1989

HARBOR CMNTY BK (RAYMOND, WA)
Acquired by Security State Corp. 12/06/2004
Details not available

HARBOR FD INC (MD)
Reincorporated 12/31/1978
State of incorporation changed from (DE) to (MD) 12/31/1978
Name changed to American General Harbor Fund, Inc. 12/10/1980
American General Harbor Fund, Inc. name changed to American Capital Harbor Fund, Inc. (MD) 09/12/1983 which reincorporated in Delaware as Van Kampen American Capital Harbor Fund 08/19/1995 which name changed to Van Kampen Harbor Fund 07/14/1998

HARBOR FED BANCORP INC (MD)
Stock Dividend - 10% payable 08/10/1998 to holders of record 07/31/1998
Merged into Provident Bankshares Corp. 08/31/2000
Each share Common 1¢ par exchanged for (1.256) shares Common $1 par
Provident Bankshares Corp. acquired by M&T Bank Corp. 05/26/2009

HARBOR FLA BANCORP INC (DE)
Reorganized 06/16/1997
Under plan of reorganization each share Harbor Federal Savings Bank of Florida (Fort Pierce, FL) Common $1 par automatically became (1) share Harbor Florida Bancorp, Inc. Common 1¢ par 06/16/1997
Reorganized as Harbor Florida Bancshares Inc. 03/06/1998
Each share Common 1¢ par exchanged for (6.0094) shares Common 10¢ par
Harbor Florida Bancshares Inc. merged into National City Corp. 12/01/2006 which was acquired by PNC Financial Services Group, Inc. 12/31/2008

HARBOR FLA BANCSHARES INC (DE)
Merged into National City Corp. 12/01/2006
Each share Common 10¢ par exchanged for (1.2206) shares Common $4 par
National City Corp. acquired by PNC

Financial Services Group, Inc. 12/31/2008

HARBOR GLOBAL CO LTD (BERMUDA)
Acquired by Isvias Trading Ltd. 11/29/2006
Each share Common $0.0025 par exchanged for $11.5663 cash

HARBOR GROWTH FD (MA)
Under plan of reorganization each Share of Bene. Int. 1¢ par automatically became (1) Harbor Fund Growth Fund Share of Bene. Int. 1¢ par 12/29/87

HARBOR INS CO (CA)
Each share Capital Stock $10 par exchanged for (2) shares Capital Stock $5 par in 1950
Stock Dividend - 10% 3/15/55
Merged into Union Bancorp 4/18/69
Each share Capital Stock $5 par exchanged for (0.433135) share Common $10 par
Union Bancorp name changed to Unionamerica, Inc. (CA) 5/9/69
(See Unionamerica, Inc. (CA))

HARBOR INVT CORP (MD)
Merged into FCNB Corp. 4/30/96
Each share Common 1¢ par exchanged for $69.08 cash

HARBOR IS DEV CORP (NV)
Common $0.001 par split (200) for (1) by issuance of (199) additional shares payable 10/12/2012 to holders of record 10/12/2012
SEC revoked common stock registration 07/25/2016

HARBOR NATIONAL BANK (BOSTON, MA)
Merged into Patriot Bancorporation 12/5/80
Each share Common $10 par exchanged for (1) share Common $10 par
Patriot Bancorporation acquired by Conifer Group Inc. (Old) 7/10/86 which merged into Conifer/Essex Group, Inc. 2/17/83 which name changed back to Conifer Group Inc. (New) 1/1/85 which merged into Bank of New England Corp. 4/22/87
(See Bank of New England Corp.)

HARBOR NATL BK (BRANFORD, CT)
Bank was closed and the FDIC was appointed receiver 10/4/91
Stockholders' equity undetermined

HARBOR NATL BK (DANA POINT, CA)
Merged into First Community Bancorp 04/16/2004
Each share Common $2.50 par exchanged for $13.28 cash

HARBOR PLAZA SHOPPING CENTER (CA)
Liquidation completed
Each share Capital Stock $1 par exchanged for initial distribution of $25 principal amount of Security Investment Co. 4% 3-Year Self Liquidating Debentures and $65 cash 7/24/64
Each share Capital Stock $1 par received second and final distribution of $5.80 cash 4/29/68

HARBOR PLYWOOD CORP. (DE)
Each share $2 Preference no par exchanged for (2) shares Capital Stock no par 00/00/1944
Each share Common no par exchanged for (0.1) share Capital Stock no par 00/00/1944
Each share Capital Stock no par exchanged for (2) shares Capital Stock $1 par 00/00/1947
Merged into Hunt Foods & Industries, Inc. on a (0.72188) for (1) basis 03/05/1962
Hunt Foods & Industries, Inc. merged into Simon (Norton), Inc. 07/17/1968 which merged into Esmark, Inc. (Inc. 03/14/1969) 09/09/1983
(See Esmark, Inc. (Inc. 03/14/1969))

HARBOR RES INC (NV)
Common $1 par changed to no par 10/3/72
Name changed to Western Smelting & Refining Inc. 2/12/79
(See Western Smelting & Refining Inc.)

HARBORSIDE HEALTHCARE CORP (DE)
Acquired by Investcorp 08/11/1998
Each share Common 1¢ par exchanged for either (1) share Class A Common 1¢ par or $25 cash
Note: Option to retain shares expired 08/07/1998
Stock Dividends - in 13.5% Exchangeable Preferred to holders of 13.5% Exchangeable Preferred 3.375% payable 08/01/1999 to holders of record 07/15/1999; 3.375% payable 11/01/1999 to holders of record 10/15/1999; 3.375% payable 02/01/2000 to holders of record 01/15/2000; 3.375% payable 05/01/2001 to holders of record 04/15/2001
100% of 13.5% Exchangeable Preferred 1¢ par acquired by company through exchange offer which expired 05/09/2001
Acquired by Sun Healthcare Group, Inc. (Old) 04/26/2007
Each share Class A Common 1¢ par exchanged for $13.60 cash

HARBORSIDE VENTURES INC (NV)
Reorganized as Impala Mineral Exploration Corp. 09/19/2008
Each share Common $0.001 par exchanged for (10) shares Common $0.001 par
(See Impala Mineral Exploration Corp.)

HARBOUR CAP CORP (DE)
Common $0.00001 par split (7) for (1) by issuance of (6) additional shares payable 09/17/1997 to holders of record 09/16/1997
Name changed to SuperPro Vending Group, Inc. 09/06/2006
SuperPro Vending Group, Inc. name changed to AFA Music Group Ltd. (DE) 10/08/2007 which reincorporated in Florida as AFA Music Group, Inc. 01/17/2008 which name changed to 3D Eye Solutions, Inc. 09/16/2008

HARBOUR COS INC (DE)
Each share old Common $0.001 par exchanged for (0.1) share new Common $0.001 par 10/9/90
Name changed to Castle Court Development Corp. 12/12/96

HARBOUR FRONT HLDGS INC (NV)
Recapitalized as American Eagle Manufacturing Co. 10/20/2003
Each share Common $0.001 par exchanged for (0.005) share Common $0.001 par
American Eagle Manufacturing Co. name changed to No Borders, Inc. 10/27/2004

HARBOUR INTERMODAL LTD (DE)
Each share Common $0.001 par exchanged for (0.1) share Common 1¢ par 03/05/1996
SEC revoked common stock registration 07/10/2008

HARBOUR PAC OIL & GAS LTD (BC)
Recapitalized as Harbour Minerals Inc. 8/30/2005
Each share Common no par exchanged for (0.1) share Common no par

HARBOUR PETE LTD (AB)
Recapitalized as Boundary Creek Resources Ltd. 08/09/1999
Each share Common no par exchanged for (0.2) share Common no par
Boundary Creek Resources Ltd. acquired by Bow Valley Energy Ltd. 08/30/2002
(See Bow Valley Energy Ltd.)

HARBOURTON FINL CORP (DE)
Recapitalized as Harbourton Capital Group, Inc. 4/15/2005
Each share Common no par exchanged for (1/3) share new Common no par

HARBOURTON FINL SVCS L P (DE)
Completely liquidated 12/15/97
Each Preferred Unit of Limited Partnership exchanged for first and final distribution of $1.03 cash 12/15/97

HARCOM PRODUCTIONS INC (OK)
Name changed to US Highland, Inc. (OK) 03/31/2010
US Highland, Inc. (OK) reincorporated in Nevada as Cruzani, Inc. 10/02/2018

HARCOR ENERGY INC (DE)
Each share Common 1¢ par exchanged for (0.1) share Common 10¢ par 4/9/91
Merged into National Fuel Gas Co. 5/15/98
Each share Common 10¢ par exchanged for $2 cash

HARCOURT, BRACE & CO., INC. (NY)
Under plan of merger name changed to Harcourt, Brace & World, Inc. 12/13/60
Harcourt, Brace & World, Inc. name changed to Harcourt Brace Jovanovich, Inc. 6/2/70 which merged into General Cinema Corp. 11/25/91 which name changed to Harcourt General, Inc. 3/15/93
(See Harcourt General, Inc.)

HARCOURT BRACE & WORLD INC (NY)
Name changed to Harcourt Brace Jovanovich, Inc. 6/2/70
Harcourt Brace Jovanovich, Inc. merged into General Cinema Corp. 11/25/91 which name changed to Harcourt General, Inc. 3/15/93
(See Harcourt General, Inc.)

HARCOURT BRACE JOVANOVICH INC (NY)
Common $1 par split (2) for (1) by issuance of (1) additional share 5/7/81
Common $1 par split (3) for (1) by issuance of (2) additional shares 6/23/86
Under plan of recapitalization each share Common $1 par received distribution of (1) share 12% Exchangeable Preferred $1 par and $40 cash 7/27/87
Stock Dividend - 12% Exchangeable Preferred 12% 9/30/87
Merged into General Cinema Corp. 11/25/91
Each share 12% Exchangeable Preferred $1 par exchanged for (0.0395) share Common $1 par
Each share Common $1 par exchanged for (0.0395) share Common $1 par
General Cinema Corp. name changed to Harcourt General, Inc. 3/15/93
(See Harcourt General, Inc.)

HARCOURT GEN INC (DE)
Each share Common $1 par received distribution of (0.1) share GC Companies, Inc. Common 1¢ par payable 12/15/93 to holders of record 12/10/93 Ex date - 12/16/93
Each share Common $1 par received distribution of (0.3013) share Neiman Marcus Group, Inc. Class B Common 1¢ par payable 10/22/99 to holders of record 10/12/99 Ex date - 10/25/99
Merged into Reed Elsevier Inc. 7/13/2001
Each share $0.59 Conv. Ser. A $1 par exchanged for $77.29 cash
Each share Class B Common exchanged for $59 cash
Each share Common $1 par exchanged for $59 cash

HARCOURT-SYMES LTD (OR)
Each share old Common no par exchanged for (0.01) share new Common no par 06/03/1997
Reincorporated under the laws of Nevada as Nordic American Inc. 06/09/1997
Nordic American Inc. (NV) reorganized in Delaware as Stark Beneficial, Inc. 02/08/2008 which name changed to China Greenstar Corp. 01/22/2015

HARD CREEK NICKEL CORP (BC)
Each share old Common no par exchanged for (0.2) share new Common no par 07/14/2015
Recapitalized as Giga Metals Corp. 08/28/2017
Each share new Common no par exchanged for (0.5) share Common no par

HARD FDG INC (NV)
Name changed to Marinex Multimedia Corp. 2/12/96
Marinex Multimedia Corp. name changed to Texas Equipment Corp. 10/2/96
(See Texas Equipment Corp.)

HARD MANUFACTURING CO. (NY)
Name changed to Abino Co., Inc. 6/30/67
(See Abino Co., Inc.)

HARD ROCK GOLD MINES LTD. (ON)
Merged into MacLeod Mosher Gold Mines Ltd. 06/15/1967
Each share Capital Stock $1 par exchanged for (0.1) share Common no par
MacLeod Mosher Gold Mines Ltd. acquired by Lake Shore Mines Ltd. 12/31/1968 which merged into LAC Minerals Ltd. (New) 07/29/1985 which was acquired by American Barrick Resources Corp. 10/17/1994 which name changed to Barrick Gold Corp. 01/18/1995

HARD ROCK INTL PLC (UNITED KINGDOM)
Name changed 10/27/1987
Name changed from Hard Rock Cafe PLC to Hard Rock International PLC 10/27/1987
Became a private company 00/00/1988
Details not available

HARD SUITS INC (BC)
Merged into American Oilfield Divers, Inc. 06/30/1997
Each share Common no par exchanged for $1.65 cash

HARDAN LIQUIDATING CO. (DE)
Liquidation completed
Immediate Redemption Plan: Each share Common $1 par exchanged for first and final distribution of (0.174) share Beatrice Foods Co. Common no par and $0.40 cash 01/29/1965
Deferred Redemption Plan: Each share Common $1 par exchanged for initial distribution of (0.164) share Beatrice Foods Co. Common no par 01/29/1965
Each share Common $1 par received second distribution of (0.01622) share Beatrice Foods Co. Common no par and $0.04 cash 07/01/1967
Each share Common $1 par received third and final distribution of $0.13511 cash 08/09/1968

HARDBOARD FABRICATORS CORP (NJ)
Name changed to GRJ Industries Inc. 1/15/73
(See GRJ Industries Inc.)

HARDEE FARMS INTL LTD (ON)
Reincorporated 12/16/1978
Each share Preferred Ser. A $100 par exchanged for $75 principal amount of 6% Conv. Promissory Notes due 12/31/1976 and (50) shares Common no par 01/19/1973
Place of incorporation changed from (Canada) to (ON) 12/16/1978
Name changed to Cobi Foods Inc. 05/15/1986
(See Cobi Foods Inc.)

HARDEES FOOD SYS INC (NC)
Common 33-1/3¢ par changed to no par and (1) additional share issued 6/12/67
Common no par split (2) for (1) by issuance of (1) additional share 7/10/69
Merged into Imasco Ltd.-Imasco Ltee. 1/29/81
Each share Common no par exchanged for $28 cash

HARDEES LEASE PARTNERS LTD PARTNERSHIP (DE)
Merged into Franchise Finance Corp. of America (DE) 6/1/94
Each Unit of Ltd. Partnership Int. 1980 Ser. exchanged for (19.523665) shares Common 1¢ par Franchise Finance Corp. of America (DE) reincorporated in Maryland 12/31/2000
(See Franchise Corp. of America)

HARDEMAN (PAUL), INC. (DE)
Merged into Hardeman (Paul), Inc. (MI) on a (2/3) for (1) basis 4/30/64
(See Hardeman (Paul), Inc. (MI))

HARDEMAN PAUL INC (MI)
Charter declared inoperative and void for failure to file reports 5/15/74

HARDIE MFG CO (PA)
Completely liquidated 03/06/1962
Each share Common 50¢ par exchanged for first and final distribution of $5.57 cash

HARDIMAN BAY MINES LTD. (ON)
Charter cancelled for failure to pay taxes and file returns 03/16/1976

HARDIN BANCORP INC (DE)
Merged into Dickinson Financial Corp. 2/16/2001
Each share Common 1¢ par exchanged for $21.75 cash

HARDING ASSOC INC (DE)
Common 1¢ par split (3) for (2) by issuance of (0.5) additional share 7/18/89
Name changed to Harding Lawson Associates Group Inc. 11/3/95
(See Harding Lawson Associates Group Inc.)

HARDING CARPETS LTD (ON)
Each share Preferred $100 par exchanged for (20) shares new Common no par 00/00/1934
Each share old Common no par exchanged for (1) share new Common no par 00/00/1934
5.75% Preference $25 par called for redemption 02/17/1964
Each share new Common no par received (2) shares Class A $1 par 03/27/1964
Common no par split (2) for (1) by issuance of (1) additional share 02/20/1967
Class A $1 par changed to 50¢ par and (1) additional share issued 02/20/1967
Common no par split (3) for (1) by issuance of (2) additional shares 03/06/1973
Class A 50¢ par changed to $0.16666666 par and (2) additional shares issued 03/06/1973
Each share Common no par exchanged for (1) share Conv. Class C no par or Conv. Class D no par 11/05/1973
Each share Class A $0.16666666 par exchanged for (1) share Conv. Class A $0.16666666 par or Conv. Class B $0.16666666 par 11/05/1973
Conv. Class A $0.16666666 par and Conv. Class B $0.16666666 par changed to no par respectively 01/12/1979
Recapitalized as New Harding Group Inc. 01/07/1987
Each share Conv. Class A no par exchanged for (0.25) share Subordinate no par
Each share Conv. Class B no par exchanged for (0.25) share Subordinate no par
Each share Conv. Class C no par exchanged for (0.25) share Conv. Multiple no par
Each share Conv. Class D no par exchanged for (0.25) share Conv. Multiple no par
New Harding Group Inc. name changed to Clarus Corp. 06/19/1989
(See Clarus Corp.)

HARDING GLASS INDUSTRIES, INC. (MO)
Each share Common $5 par exchanged for (1) share Common $1 par 01/31/1973
Merged into Sun Co., Inc. 08/08/1980
Each share Common $1 par exchanged for (0.281759) share Common $1 par
Note: An additional (0.031306) escrowed share Common $1 par was distributed 08/29/1983
Sun Co., Inc. name changed to Sunoco, Inc. 11/06/1998 which merged into Energy Transfer Partners, L.P. (Old) 10/05/2012 which merged into Energy Transfer Partners, L.P. (New) 05/01/2017 which merged into Energy Transfer L.P. 10/19/2018

HARDING LAWSON ASSOCS GROUP INC (DE)
Merged into MACTEC Inc. 6/2/2000
Each share Common 1¢ par exchanged for $11.50 cash

HARDINGE INC (NY)
Name changed 05/17/1995
Class A Common $5 par split (3) for (1) by issuance of (2) additional shares 03/25/1988
Class B Common $5 par split (3) for (1) by issuance of (2) additional shares 03/25/1988
Name changed from Hardinge Brothers, Inc. to Hardinge Inc. 05/17/1995
Each share Class A Common $5 par exchanged for (2) shares Common 1¢ par 05/24/1995
Each share Class B Common $5 par exchanged for (2.05) shares Common 1¢ par 05/24/1995
Common 1¢ par split (3) for (2) by issuance of (0.5) additional share payable 05/29/1998 to holders of record 05/08/1998
Acquired by Privet Fund Management LLC 05/25/2018
Each share Common 1¢ par exchanged for $18.50 cash

HARDLINES DISTRIBUTORS, INC. (DE)
Acquired by Zayre Corp. 8/2/66
Each share Common 50¢ par exchanged for (1) share Conv. Preferred Ser. A $1 par
Zayre Corp. name changed to TJX Companies, Inc. 6/20/89

HARDMAN RES N L (AUSTRALIA)
ADR agreement terminated 01/23/1998
Each Sponsored ADR for Ordinary exchanged for (10) shares Ordinary
Note: Unexchanged ADR's will be sold and the proceeds, if any, held for claim after 07/23/1998

HARDROCK EXTN INC (ON)
Cease trade order effective 09/08/1999
Stockholders' equity unlikely

HARDWICK & WOODBURY RAILROAD
Out of business 00/00/1938
Details not available

HARDWICK HLDG CO (GA)
Merged into BB&T Corp. 6/13/2000
Each share Common 50¢ par exchanged for (0.932) share Common $5 par

HARDWICKE COS INC (DE)
Plan of reorganization under Chapter 11 Federal Bankruptcy proceedings confirmed 02/28/1985
No stockholders' equity

HARDWICKE INVT LTD (BC)
Struck off register and declared dissolved for failure to file returns 07/31/1978

HARDWIRED INTERACTIVE INC (NV)
Recapitalized as iGlue, Inc. 01/27/2012
Each share Common $0.001 par exchanged for (0.0090909) share Common $0.001 par
iGlue, Inc. recapitalized as AC Partners Inc. 02/05/2018

HARDWOOD LAKE NICKEL MINES LTD. (ON)
Charter revoked for failure to file reports and pay fees 06/17/1965

HARDWOOD PPTYS LTD (AB)
In process of liquidation
Each share Common no par received initial distribution of $0.30 cash payable 9/26/2002 to holders of record 9/25/2002 Ex date - 9/23/2002
Each share Common no par received second distribution of $0.07 cash payable 1/24/2003 to holders of record 1/24/2003
Note: Number and amount of subsequent distribution(s), if any, are not available

HARDWOOD TIMBER CO.
Liquidation completed in 1943

HARDWOODS DISTR INCOME FD (BC)
Issue Information 14,410,000 UNITS offered at $10 per Unit on 03/12/2004
Under plan of reorganization each Unit automatically became (1) share Hardwoods Distribution Inc. (Canada) Common no par 07/11/2011

HARDY COAL CO.
Dissolved in 1935

HARDY-GRIFFIN ENGINEERING CORP. (TX)
Acquired by Atlas Pipe, Inc. on a (1) for (9.3597) basis 12/16/57
Atlas Pipe, Inc. name changed to Atlas Bradford Co. in 1960 which was liquidated by Rucker Co. 4/15/69 which merged into N L Industries, Inc. 1/21/77

HARDY INTL DEVS INC (BC)
Recapitalized as Unisave Energy Ltd. 11/6/86
Each (3.5) shares Common no par exchanged for (1) share Common no par
Unisave Energy Ltd. recapitalized as U.C. Valve Corp. 4/26/89 which reorganized as Blackbridge Capital Corp. 12/1/89 which name changed to Rupert Resources Ltd. 11/1/94

HARFORD NATL BK (ABERDEEN, MD)
Stock Dividends - 20% payable 12/25/98 to holders of record 12/4/98; 5% payable 12/24/99 to holders of record 12/3/99; 5% payable 12/22/2000 to holders of record 12/1/2000 Ex date - 12/12/2000
Name changed to Harford Bank (Aberdeen, MD) 7/1/2001

HARFORD PURE RYE DISTILLERS, INC. (MD)
Property sold 00/00/1937
Details not available

HARGAL OILS, LTD. (CANADA)
Merged into Freehold Gas & Oil Ltd. 03/03/1959
Each share Common no par exchanged for (0.1) share Common no par
Freehold Gas & Oil Ltd. name changed to Westgrowth Petroleums Ltd. (BC) 03/06/1979 which reincorporated in Alberta 06/06/1980 which recapitalized as Canadian Westgrowth Ltd. 10/14/1986 which merged into Ulster Petroleums Ltd. 10/27/1987 which merged into Anderson Exploration Ltd. 05/23/2000
(See Anderson Exploration Ltd.)

HARGO WOOLEN MLS INC (DE)
Adjudicated bankrupt 03/09/1970
No stockholders' equity

HARGOR RES INC (BC)
Name changed to Harken Technologies Inc. 06/09/1986
(See Harken Technologies Inc.)

HARGRAVE SILVER MINES, LTD. (ON)
Charter revoked for failure to file reports and pay fees 1/21/57

HARGRAVES ELECTRS CORP (AZ)
Recapitalized as Western International Industries, Inc. 4/11/68
Each share Capital Stock 20¢ par exchanged for (0.2) share Capital Stock $1 par
(See Western International Industries, Inc.)

HARGROM SVCS CORP (DE)
Each share Common 1¢ par exchanged for (0.25) share Common 4¢ par 2/14/73
Each (15) shares Common 4¢ par exchanged for (1) share Common 60¢ par 2/9/84
Each share Common 60¢ par exchanged for (0.1) share Common $6 par 10/1/85
Merged into Groman Mortuary, Inc. 8/22/95
Each share Common $6 par exchanged for $1.36 cash

HARICO MINING & DEVELOPMENT CO. LTD. (ON)
Charter cancelled 07/00/1963
No stockholders' equity

HARISTON CORP (CANADA)
Recapitalized as Midland Holland Inc. (Canada) 02/10/1999
Each share Common no par exchanged for (0.2) share Common no par
Midland Holland Inc. (Canada) reincorporated in Yukon 03/11/1999 which name changed to Mercury Partners & Co. Inc. 02/22/2000 which name changed to Black Mountain Capital Corp. 05/02/2005 which recapitalized as Grand Peak Capital Corp. (YT) 11/20/2007 which reincorporated in British Columbia 04/27/2010

HARKEMA INDS LTD (ON)
Name changed to Acuma International Inc. 06/14/1990
(See Acuma International Inc.)

HARKEN ENERGY CORP (DE)
Name changed 1/1/89
Name changed from Harken Oil & Gas, Inc. to Harken Energy Corp. 1/1/89
Common $1 par changed to 1¢ par 2/19/91
Each share old Common 1¢ par exchanged for (0.1) share new Common 1¢ par 11/8/2000
Recapitalized as HKN, Inc. 6/6/2007
Each (22.4) shares new Common 1¢ par exchanged for (1) share Common 1¢ par

HARKEN TECHNOLOGIES INC (BC)
Cease trade order effective 02/03/1988
Stockholders' equity unlikely

HARKER GOLD MINES LTD. (ON)
Recapitalized as Golden Harker Explorations Ltd. 08/09/1955
Each share Common no par exchanged for (0.2) share Common no par
Golden Harker Explorations Ltd. merged into Jubilee Gold Inc. 01/01/2010 which merged into Jubilee Gold Exploration Ltd. 01/25/2013

HARLAKE CAP GROUP INC (QC)
Name changed to Madison Grant Resources Inc. (QC) 10/11/1990
Madison Grant Resources Inc. (QC) reorganized in Canada as Banro International Capital Inc. 03/02/1995 which name changed to Banro Resources Corp. (Canada) 05/06/1996 which reincorporated in Ontario 10/24/1996 which recapitalized as Banro Corp. (ON) 01/22/2001 which reincorporated in Canada 04/02/2004

HARLAND JOHN H CO (GA)
Common $10 par changed to $1 par and (7) additional shares issued 09/05/1969
Common $1 par split (2) for (1) by issuance of (1) additional share 03/10/1972
Common $1 par split (3) for (2) by issuance of (0.5) additional share 03/07/1980
Common $1 par split (2) for (1) by issuance of (1) additional share 06/01/1981
Common $1 par split (2) for (1) by issuance of (1) additional share 03/01/1985
Common $1 par split (2) for (1) by issuance of (1) additional share 03/02/1987
Merged into M & F Worldwide Corp. 05/01/2007
Each share Common $1 par exchanged for $52.75 cash

HARLEQUIN ENTERPRISES LTD (CANADA)
Common no par split (3) for (1) by issuance of (2) additional shares 07/08/1975
Common no par split (3) for (1) by issuance of (2) additional shares 02/10/1978
Common no par reclassified as Conv. Class A Common no par 11/03/1980
100% acquired by Torstar Corp. through purchase offer which expired 06/19/1981
Public interest eliminated

HARLEY CORP (SC)
Common 50¢ par changed to 25¢ par and (1) additional share issued 10/24/1975
In process of liquidation
Each share Common 25¢ par received initial distribution of $15.26 cash 04/09/1982
Each share Common 25¢ par received second distribution of $3.76 cash 06/30/1982
Each share Common 25¢ par exchanged for third distribution of $0.17 cash 09/30/1982
Assets transferred to HC Liquidation Trust 10/01/1982
(See HC Liquidation Trust)

HARLEY DAVIDSON INC (DE)
Common 1¢ par split (2) for (1) by issuance of (1) additional share 06/15/1990
Preferred Stock Purchase Rights declared for Common stockholders of record 05/23/1988 were redeemed at $0.005 per right 08/31/1990 for holders of record 08/20/1990
Reincorporated under the laws of Wisconsin 06/28/1991

HARLEY-DAVIDSON MOTOR CO. (WI)
Common $20 par changed to $5 par and (1) additional share issued 4/16/65
Merged into American Machine & Foundry Co. 1/8/69
Each share Common $5 par exchanged for (1.5) shares Common $1.75 par
American Machine & Foundry Co. name changed to AMF Inc. 4/30/70
(See AMF Inc.)

HARLEY PATENTS, INC. (NY)
Proclaimed dissolved and charter forfeited for failure to file reports and pay taxes 12/15/61

HARLEY STR CLINICS INC (NV)
Name changed to Nutribrands, Inc. 10/05/2004
Nutribrands, Inc. name changed to St. James Capital Holdings, Inc. 04/25/2005
(See St. James Capital Holdings, Inc.)

HARLEY STR SOFTWARE LTD (BC)
Recapitalized as Cardiocomm Solutions Inc. 12/07/1998
Each share Common no par exchanged for (1/3) share Common no par
Cardiocomm Solutions Inc. name changed to Cardiocomm Solutions, Inc. 11/26/2007

HARLEYSVILLE GROUP INC (DE)
Common $1 par split (3) for (2) by issuance of (0.5) additional share 11/04/1991
Common $1 par split (2) for (1) by issuance of (1) additional share payable 10/06/1997 to holders of record 09/15/1997
Acquired by Nationwide Mutual Insurance Co. 05/01/2012
Each share Common $1 par exchanged for $60 cash

HARLEYSVILLE LIFE INS CO (PA)
Acquired by Harleysville Mutual Insurance Co. 05/14/1980
Each share Capital Stock $5 par exchanged for $25 cash

HARLEYSVILLE NATL CORP (PA)
Common $1 par split (2) for (1) by issuance of (1) additional share 12/29/1989
Common $1 par split (2) for (1) by issuance of (1) additional share 12/31/1993
Common $1 par split (2) for (1) by issuance of (1) additional share payable 08/10/2001 to holders of record 07/27/2001 Ex date - 08/13/2001
Common $1 par split (5) for (4) by issuance of (0.25) additional share payable 09/15/2003 to holders of record 09/02/2003 Ex date - 09/16/2003
Stock Dividends - 5% payable 06/28/1996 to holders of record 06/14/1996; 5% payable 06/30/1997 to holders of record 06/13/1997; 5% payable 09/30/1999 to holders of record 09/17/1999; 5% payable 11/09/2000 to holders of record 10/26/2000; 5% payable 09/16/2002 to holders of record 09/03/2002 Ex date - 08/29/2002; 5% payable 09/15/2004 to holders of record 08/30/2004; 5% payable 09/15/2005 to holders of record 09/01/2005 Ex date - 08/30/2005; 5% payable 09/15/2006 to holders of record 09/01/2006 Ex date - 08/30/2006
Merged into First Niagara Financial Group, Inc. (New) 04/09/2010
Each share Common $1 par exchanged for (0.474) share Common 1¢ par
First Niagara Financial Group, Inc. (New) merged into KeyCorp (New) 08/01/2016

HARLEYSVILLE SVGS BK (HARLEYSVILLE, PA)
Name changed 06/05/1991
Name changed from Harleysville Savings Association (Harleysville, PA) to Harleysville Savings Bank (Harleysville, PA) 06/05/1991
Common $1 par split (3) for (2) by issuance of (0.5) additional share 02/24/1993
Common $1 par split (3) for (2) by issuance of (0.5) additional share 02/22/1995
Common $1 par split (5) for (4) by issuance of (0.25) additional share payable 02/19/1997 to holders of record 02/05/1997
Common $1 par split (4) for (3) by issuance of (0.33333333) additional share payable 02/24/1999 to holders of record 02/10/1999
Stock Dividend - 10% 11/14/1991
Under plan of reorganization each share Common $1 par automatically became (1) share Harleysville Savings Financial Corp. Common 1¢ par 02/25/2000
Harleysville Savings Financial Corp. name changed to Harleysville Financial Corp. 05/26/2017

HARLEYSVILLE SVGS FINL CORP (PA)
Common 1¢ par split (5) for (3) by issuance of (0.66666666) additional share payable 02/23/2005 to holders of record 02/09/2005 Ex date - 02/24/2005
Name changed to Harleysville Financial Corp. 05/26/2017

HARLIGHT GOLD MINES LTD. (ON)
Charter cancelled 01/28/1954

HARLIN RES LTD (BC)
Recapitalized as Consolidated Harlin Resources Ltd. 03/15/1989
Each share Common no par exchanged for (0.33333333) share Common no par
(See Consolidated Harlin Resources Ltd.)

HARLOFF MANUFACTURING CO. (CO)
100% reacquired through purchase offer 00/00/1972
Public interest eliminated

HARLOW AIRCRAFT CO. (CA)
Liquidation completed 12/11/57

HARLOW RES LTD (BC)
Recapitalized as American Daleco Technologies Corp. (BC) 10/14/1986
Each share Common no par exchanged for (3) shares Common no par
American Daleco Technologies Corp. (BC) reorganized in California as International Daleco Technologies Corp. 10/20/1987 which recapitalized as International Daleco Corp. 06/21/1990

HARLOW VENTURES INC (BC)
Recapitalized as International LMM Ventures Corp. 07/19/2007
Each share Common no par exchanged for (0.5) share Common no par
International LMM Ventures Corp. name changed to US Oil Sands Inc. (BC) 04/20/2011 which reincorporated in Alberta 05/09/2011

HARLYN PRODS INC (CA)
Common 10¢ par split (3) for (2) by issuance of (0.5) additional share 03/15/1985
Common 10¢ par split (5) for (4) by issuance of (0.25) additional share 04/17/1989
Common 10¢ par split (5) for (4) by issuance of (0.25) additional share 05/17/1991
Stock Dividends - 30% 07/21/1975; 30% 06/22/1976; 30% 01/30/1978; 25% 02/04/1986; 10% 06/30/1988
Chapter 11 bankruptcy proceedings converted to Chapter 7 on 06/02/1997
No stockholders' equity

HARMAC PAC INC (BC)
Merged into Pope & Talbot Inc. 11/8/99
Each share Common no par exchanged for (0.21255758) share Common $1 par and $5.094501 cash

HARMAN (WM. H.) CORP.
Bankrupt in 1948

HARMAN INTL INDS INC (MI)
Stock Dividends - 10% 01/25/1974; 10% 02/05/1975; 10% 02/05/1976; 10% 02/04/1977
Merged into Beatrice Foods Co. 08/01/1977
Each share Common $1 par exchanged for (1.42857) shares Common no par
Beatrice Foods Co. name changed to Beatrice Companies, Inc. 06/05/1984
(See Beatrice Companies, Inc.)

HARMAN INTL INDS INC NEW (DE)
Common 1¢ par split (2) for (1) by issuance of (1) additional share payable 09/19/2000 to holders of record 08/28/2000 Ex date - 09/20/2000
Common 1¢ par split (2) for (1) by issuance of (1) additional share payable 12/04/2003 to holders of record 11/24/2003 Ex date - 12/05/2003
Acquired by Samsung Electronics Co., Ltd. 03/10/2017
Each share Common 1¢ par split exchanged for $112 cash

HARMAN-KARDON, INC. (NY)
Acquired by Jerrold Electronics Corp. 03/01/1961
Each share Common par exchanged for (0.551854) share Common 10¢ par
Jerrold Electronics Corp. name changed to Jerrold Corp. 06/30/1962 which merged into General Instrument Corp. (Incorporated 06/12/1967) 12/21/1967
(See General Instrument Corp. (Incorporated 06/12/1967))

HARMAN OILS & MINERALS LTD.
Acquired by Sapphire Petroleums Ltd. 00/00/1952
Each share Common no par exchanged for (0.9) share Capital Stock $1 par
Sapphire Petroleums Ltd. recapitalized as Cabol Enterprises, Ltd. 01/19/1962
(See Cabol Enterprises, Ltd.)

HARMAT ORGANIZATION INC (DE)
Name changed to Barpoint.com, Inc. 06/18/1999
Barpoint.com, Inc. name changed to LoyaltyPoint, Inc. 04/21/2004
(See LoyaltyPoint, Inc.)

HARMON (WM. E.) & CO. INC. (NY)
Dissolved 5/14/43

HARMON COLOR WORKS, INC.
Acquired by American Home Products Corp. 11/30/1942
Details not available

HARMON (GEORGE) CO. INC. (NV)
Charter revoked for failure to file reports and pay fees 3/4/63

HARMON GLASS CO., INC. (MN)
Name changed to Apogee Enterprises, Inc. 3/4/68

HARMON INDS INC NEW (MO)
Name changed to SAB Harmon Industries, Inc. 2/8/78 which name changed back to Harmon Industries, Inc. 5/9/86
Common 25¢ par split (3) for (2) by issuance of (0.5) additional share payable 2/27/98 to holders of record 2/13/98
Merged into General Electric Co. 9/1/2000
Each share Common 25¢ par exchanged for (0.527) share Common 16¢ par

HARMONEY STR CAP INC (DE)
Recapitalized as Network Long Distance Inc. 8/30/91
Each share Common $0.0001 par exchanged for (0.1) share Common $0.0001 par
Network Long Distance Inc. merged into IXC Communications Inc. 6/3/98 which merged into Cincinnati Bell Inc. (Old) 11/9/99 which name changed to Broadwing Inc. 11/15/99 which name changed to Cincinnati Bell Inc. (New) 5/16/2003

HARMONIA BANCORP INC (DE)
Merged into Sovereign Bancorp, Inc. 01/15/1993
Each share Common 1¢ par exchanged for (1.7325) share Common no par and $2.50 cash
Sovereign Bancorp, Inc. merged into Banco Santander, S.A. 01/30/2009

HARMONIA FIRE INSURANCE CO.
Name changed to Revere (Paul) Fire Insurance Co. in 1937
Revere (Paul) Fire Insurance Co. merged into Home Insurance Co. in 1948
(See Home Insurance Co.)

HARMONIC ENERGY INC (NV)
Old Common $0.001 par split (5) for (1) by issuance of (4) additional shares payable 03/12/2012 to holders of record 03/12/2012 Ex date - 03/13/2012
Each share old Common $0.001 par exchanged for (0.07142857) share new Common $0.001 par 06/10/2016
Name changed to THC Therapeutics, Inc. 02/07/2017
THC Therapeutics, Inc. name changed to Millennium BlockChain, Inc. 02/07/2018

HARMONIC LIGHTWAVES INC (DE)
Issue Information - 2,600,000 shares COM offered at $13.50 per share on 05/22/1995
Name changed to Harmonic Inc. 3/23/99

HARMONIC REED CORP (DE)
Name changed to Reed Toys Inc. 02/03/1971
(See Reed Toys Inc.)

HARMONY ASSET LTD (CAYMAN ISLANDS)
Shares transferred to Hong Kong register 08/21/2013

HARMONY BK (JACKSON, NJ)
Stock Dividends - 5% payable 08/29/2012 to holders of record 08/15/2012 Ex date - 08/13/2012; 5% payable 09/20/2013 to holders of record 09/06/2013 Ex date - 09/04/2013
Merged into Lakeland Bancorp, Inc. 07/01/2016
Each share Common $5 par exchanged for (1.25) shares Common no par

HARMONY BROOK INC (MN)
Merged into Culligan International Corp. 3/19/98
Each share Common no par exchanged for $0.545 cash

HARMONY GOLD CORP (BC)
Name changed to Pure Energy Minerals Ltd. 10/22/2012

HARMONY GOLD MINES, LTD. (ON)
Charter cancelled for failure to file reports and pay taxes 00/00/1955

HARMONY GROUP LTD (DE)
Charter cancelled and declared inoperative and void for non-payment of taxes 03/01/1994

HARMONY HLDGS INC (DE)
Merged into INTELEFILM Corp. 05/14/2001
Each share Common 1¢ par exchanged for (0.07272727) share Common 2¢ par
(See INTELEFILM Corp.)

HARMONY INC (WI)
Merged into Isle Resources Inc. 04/19/1982
Each share Common $1 par exchanged for (0.5365) share Common 40¢ par
(See Isle Resources Inc.)

HARMONY INTEGRATED SOLUTIONS INC (CANADA)
Dissolved for non-compliance 09/19/2005

HARMONY MERGER CORP (DE)
Units separated 07/25/2017
Name changed to NextDecade Corp. 07/25/2017

HARMONY MILLS
Liquidation completed in 1940

HARMONY PRODS INC (VA)
Each share old Common no par exchanged for (0.25) share new Common no par 5/6/96
Merged into Environmental Fert 12/31/96
Each share new Common no par exchanged for $2 cash

HARMONY TRADING CORP (NY)
Common $0.001 par split (3) for (1) by issuance of (2) additional shares payable 12/4/2000 to holders of record 11/20/2000 Ex date - 12/5/2000
Name changed to Vitalstate, Inc. 6/7/2002

HARN CORP (OH)
Common $1 par changed to 5¢ par 07/05/1966
Adjudicated bankrupt 08/07/1967
No stockholders' equity

HARNISCHFEGER CORP (DE)
Reincorporated 01/25/1972
Common no par changed to $10 par 00/00/1935
5% 1st Preferred $100 par called for redemption 11/00/1955
6% Conv. Preferred $100 par called for redemption 02/17/1966
Stock Dividend - 100% 07/25/1952
State of incorporation changed from (WI) to (DE) 01/25/1972
Common $10 par split (7) for (4) by issuance of (0.75) additional share 06/30/1975
Common $10 par changed to $1 par 01/30/1976
Common $1 par split (2) for (1) by issuance of (1) additional share 07/01/1976
Under plan of reorganization name changed to Harnischfeger Industries, Inc. 10/31/1986
(See Harnischfeger Industries, Inc.)

HARNISCHFEGER INDS INC (DE)
Depositary Preferred Ser. C called for redemption 12/26/1986
Depositary Preferred Ser. B called for redemption 02/12/1987
$3.402 S.F. Exchangeable Pfd. Ser. B $100 par called for redemption 02/12/1987
Plan of reorganization under Chapter 11 Federal Bankruptcy Code effective 07/12/2001
No stockholders' equity

HAROLD'S COIN-O-MATIC, INC. (NM)
Name changed to Harold's Coin-O-Matics, Inc. 11/27/61
Harold's Coin-O-Matics, Inc. name changed to Geo Explorations, Inc. 9/25/62
(See Geo Explorations, Inc.)

HAROLD'S COIN-O-MATICS, INC. (NM)
Name changed to Geo Explorations, Inc. 9/25/62
(See Geo Explorations, Inc.)

HAROLDS STORES INC (OK)
Reincorporated 08/29/1994
Stock Dividends - 10% 01/15/1993; 10% 01/19/1994; 10% 01/18/1995; 5% payable 02/02/1996 to holders of record 01/19/1996; 5% payable 01/31/1997 to holders of record 01/17/1997; 5% payable 01/30/1998 to holders of record 01/16/1998 Ex date - 01/14/1998
State of incorporation changed from (DE) to (OK) 08/29/1994
Each share old Common 1¢ par exchanged for (1) share new Common 1¢ par to reflect a (1) for (1,000) reverse split followed by a (1,000) for (1) forward split 12/06/2007
Note: Holders of (999) or fewer pre-split shares received $0.30 cash per share
Chapter 7 bankruptcy proceedings terminated 01/28/2016
No stockholders' equity

HARPER & BROTHERS (NY)
Merged into Harper & Row, Publishers, Inc. (Ill.) on a (22) for (1) basis 5/1/62
Harper & Row, Publishers, Inc. (Ill.) reincorporated under the laws of Delaware 9/5/69
(See Harper & Row, Publishers, Inc. (Del.))

HARPER & ROW PUBLISHERS INC (DE)
Reincorporated 09/05/1969
Common no par split (2) for (1) by issuance of (1) additional share 02/28/1969
Stock Dividend - 10% 01/20/1967
State of incorporation changed from (IL) to (DE) and Common no par changed to 10¢ par 09/05/1969
Common 10¢ par split (3) for (2) by issuance of (0.5) additional share 09/04/1985
Merged into Harper Acquisition, Inc. 05/08/1987
Each share Common 10¢ par exchanged for $65 cash

HARPER (H.M.) CO. (DE)
Reincorporated 3/31/67
State of incorporation changed from (IL) to (DE) 3/31/67
Common $1 par split (2) for (1) by issuance of (1) additional share 6/30/61
Merged into International Telephone & Telegraph Corp. 3/3/71
Each share Common $1 par exchanged for (0.188) share $4 Conv. Preferred Ser. K no par
International Telephone & Telegraph Corp. name changed to ITT Corp. 12/31/83 which reorganized under the laws of Indiana as ITT Industries, Inc. 12/19/95 which name changed to ITT Corp. 7/1/2006

HARPER GROUP INC (DE)
Reincorporated in 1987
Common no par split (2) for (1) by issuance of (1) additional share 9/18/80
Common no par split (3) for (2) by issuance of (0.5) additional share 6/28/85
Common no par split (3) for (2) by issuance of (0.5) additional share 1/5/87
Reincorporated from Harper Group (CA) to Harper Group, Inc. (DE) in 1987
Common no par split (3) for (2) by issuance of (0.5) additional share 3/20/92
Name changed to Circle International Group Inc. 5/14/97
Circle International Group Inc. merged into EGL, Inc. 10/2/2000

HARPER INTL INC (DE)
Name changed to Reco International, Inc. 08/18/1987
(See Reco International, Inc.)

HARPER INVESTMENT CORP. (UT)
Recapitalized as Gold Lake Mines Inc. 9/14/80
Each share Common 1¢ par exchanged for (5) shares Common $0.002 par

HARPER TERRACE CO. (IL)
Liquidation completed
Each share Common $5 par exchanged for initial distribution of $85 cash 1/4/66
Each share Common $5 par received second and final distribution of $2.90 cash 9/30/66

HARPER UTD CORP (NY)
Charter cancelled and proclaimed dissolved for failure to pay taxes 12/20/1977

HARPER VENDING INC (NY)
Name changed to Dakar Enterprises Inc. 12/22/1969
(See Dakar Enterprises Inc.)

HARPERS MALARTIC GOLD MINES LTD. (ON)
Acquired by Consolidated Harpers Malartic Gold Mines Ltd. and Capital Stock $1 par exchanged (1) for (5) in 1949
(See Consolidated Harpers Malartic Gold Mines Ltd.)

HARRAHS (NV)
Common $1 par changed to 50¢ par and (1) additional share issued 07/21/1972
Merged into Holiday Inns, Inc. 02/28/1980
Each share Common 50¢ par exchanged for $17.75 principal amount of 9-5/8% Conv. Subordinated Debentures due 04/01/2005 and $17.75 cash

HARRAHS ENTMT INC (DE)
Merged into Hamlet Holdings LLC 01/28/2008
Each share Common 10¢ par exchanged for $90 cash

HARREL INC (DE)
Acquired by Davis-Standard, LLC 11/19/2010
Details not available

HARRELL CORP. (MA)
Name changed to Harrell International, Inc. 04/01/1968
Harrell International, Inc. name changed to Harrell Hospitality Group Inc. 04/01/2000 which name changed to Noram Capital Holdings, Inc. 02/13/2007
(See Noram Capital Holdings, Inc.)

HARRELL HOSPITALITY GROUP INC (DE)
Reincorporated 03/00/1987
Name changed 04/01/2000
Each share old Common $1 par exchanged for (0.2) share new Common $1 par 11/06/1978
New Common $1 par reclassified as Class A Common 1¢ par 08/28/1990
Class A Common $1 par changed to $0.002 par and (4) additional shares issued payable 11/15/2000 to holders of record 09/01/2000
Ex date - 11/16/2000
Each share old Class A Common $0.002 par exchanged for (0.1) share new Class A Common $0.002 par 10/19/2006
State of incorporation changed from (MA) to (DE) 03/00/1987
Stock Dividend - 15% 12/30/1970
Name changed from Harrell International, Inc. to Harrell Hospitality Group Inc. 04/01/2000
Name changed to Noram Capital Holdings, Inc. 02/13/2007
(See Noram Capital Holdings, Inc.)

HARRELSON RUBR CO (DE)
Name changed to HRUB Corp. 03/11/1983
(See HRUB Corp.)

HARRICANA AMALGAMATED GOLD MINES, INC.
Name changed to Harricana Gold Mine, Inc. (1939) 00/00/1939
Harricana Gold Mine, Inc. (1939) recapitalized as New Harricana Mines Ltd. 00/00/1953
(See New Harricana Mines Ltd.)

HARRICANA GOLD MINE, INC. (1939) (QC)
Recapitalized as New Harricana Mines Ltd. 00/00/1953
Each share Common exchanged for (0.25) share Common
(See New Harricana Mines Ltd.)

HARRIER CAP CORP (AB)
Name changed to e-Manufacturing Networks Inc. 01/31/2000
(See e-Manufacturing Networks Inc.)

HARRIER INC (DE)
Each share old Common $0.001 par exchanged for (0.02) share new Common $0.001 par 12/29/86
New Common $0.001 par split (3) for (2) by issuance of (0.5) additional share 7/18/88
State of incorporation changed from (UT) to (DE) 6/15/90
Recapitalized as Cope, Inc. 9/25/98
Each (58) shares new Common $0.001 par exchanged for (1) share Common $0.001 par
Cope, Inc. name changed to Mount10, Inc. 10/20/2001
(See Mount10, Inc.)

HARRIES ELECTRONICS CORP. (DE)
Ceased operations in 1960
Company without funds

HARRIET & HENDERSON YARNS INC (NC)
Capital Stock $50 par split (5) for (1) by issuance of (4) additional shares 05/31/1978
Plan of liquidation under Chapter 11 Federal Bankruptcy proceedings confirmed 05/12/2004
No stockholders' equity

HARRIET COTTON MLS (NC)
Name changed to Harriet & Henderson Yarns, Inc. 07/29/1977
(See Harriet & Henderson Yarns, Inc.)

HARRINGTON & RICHARDSON, INC. (MA)
Stock Dividends - 100% 8/21/61; 10% 1/30/62
Acquired by Kidde (Walter) & Co., Inc. (DE) 8/8/68
Each share Common $1 par exchanged for (0.25) share Common $2.50 par
Kidde (Walter) & Co., Inc. (DE) name changed to Kidde, Inc. 4/18/80 which merged into Hanson Trust p.l.c. 12/31/87 which name changed to Hanson plc (Old) 1/29/88 which reorganized as Hanson plc (New) 10/15/2003

HARRINGTON & RICHARDSON ARMS CO. (MA)
Name changed to Harrington & Richardson, Inc. in 1954
Harrington & Richardson, Inc. acquired by Kidde (Walter) & Co., Inc. (DE) 8/8/68 which name changed to Kidde, Inc. 4/18/80 which merged into Hanson Trust p.l.c. 12/31/87 which name changed to Hanson plc (Old) 1/29/88 which reorganized as Hanson PLC (New) 10/15/2003

HARRINGTON FINL GROUP INC (IN)
Merged into Hasten Bancshares 01/22/2002
Each share Common $0.125 par exchanged for $12.4916 cash

HARRINGTON FINL INC (ON)
Reorganized under the laws of Yukon Territory as TecnoPetrol Inc. 06/16/1997
Each share Common no par exchanged for (0.06666666) share Common no par
TecnoPetrol Inc. (Yukon) name changed to Bolivar Gold Corp. 01/24/2003
(See Bolivar Gold Corp.)

HARRINGTON RESH CORP (DE)
Charter cancelled and declared inoperative and void for non-payment of taxes 03/01/1978

HARRINGTON WEST FINL GROUP INC (DE)
Stock Dividend - 20% payable 03/11/2004 to holders of record 02/25/2004
Chapter 7 bankruptcy proceedings terminated 04/26/2017
No stockholders' equity

HARRIS, HALL & CO. (DE)
Liquidation completed 05/14/1957
Details not available

HARRIS & HARRIS GROUP INC (NY)
Name changed to 180 Degree Capital Corp. 03/27/2017

HARRIS & PAULSON INC (CO)
Stock Dividend - 25% 10/29/1984
Each share old Common 1¢ par exchanged for (0.00001) share new Common 1¢ par 04/20/1989
Note: Fractional shares issued as a result of the reverse split became without value 08/08/1989
Public interest eliminated

HARRIS AUTOMATIC PRESS CO.
Succeeded by Harris-Seybold-Potter Co. in 1926
Harris-Seybold-Potter Co. name changed to Harris-Seybold Co. in 1946 which name changed to Harris-Intertype Corp. 6/27/57 which name changed to Harris Corp. 5/15/74

HARRIS BANKCORP INC (DE)
Common $16 par changed to $8 par and (1) additional share issued 7/15/75
Merged into Bank of Montreal (Montreal, Que.) 9/4/84
Each share Common $8 par exchanged for $82 cash

HARRIS CALORIFIC CO (OH)
Acquired by Emerson Electric Co. 8/29/73
Each share Common no par exchanged for (4.2429) shares Common $1 par

HARRIS COMPUTER SYS CORP (FL)
Common 1¢ par split (3) for (1) by issuance of (2) additional shares payable 03/29/1996 to holders of record 03/18/1996
Name changed to CyberGuard Corp. 06/27/1996
CyberGuard Corp. merged into Secure Computing Corp. 01/12/2006

HARRIS CONSTRUCTION CO.
Name changed to Harris (B.T.) Corp. in 1927
(See Harris (B.T.) Corp.)

HARRIS CORP (TX)
Completely liquidated
Each share Common no par exchanged for first and final distribution of $6.0525 cash 01/08/1975

HARRIS (B.T.) CORP. (DE)
Completely liquidated 03/09/1965
Details not available

HARRIS ENERGY CORP. (CO)
Merged into Energy Capital Development Corp. (DE) 12/31/80
Each share Common 1¢ par exchanged for (0.231428) share Common 1¢ par plus (1) Common Stock Purchase Warrant expiring 9/30/84 for each (5) shares Common 1¢ par
Energy Capital Development Corp. (DE) name changed to ENERCAP Corp. 3/13/89
(See ENERCAP Corp.)

HARRIS EXPL INC (NV)
Each share old Common $0.001 par exchanged for (0.001) share new Common $0.001 par 01/17/2006
Charter revoked for failure to file reports and pay fees 03/31/2009

HARRIS FINL INC (PA)
Common 1¢ par split (3) for (1) by issuance of (2) additional shares payable 11/18/97 to holders of record 11/4/97
Stock Dividend - 5% payable 2/16/2000 to holders of record 2/2/2000
Merged into Waypoint Financial Corp. 10/17/2000
Each share Common 1¢ par exchanged for (0.7667) share Common 1¢ par
(See Waypoint Financial Corp.)

HARRIS-GRANT, INC. (TX)
Charter forfeited for failure to pay taxes 3/15/76

HARRIS GRAPHICS CORP (DE)
Merged into AM International, Inc. 6/24/86
Each share Common 1¢ par exchanged for $22 cash
Each share Class B Common 1¢ par exchanged for $22 cash

HARRIS INTERACTIVE INC (DE)
Acquired by Nielsen Holdings N.V. 02/03/2014
Each share Common $0.001 par exchanged for $2.04 cash

HARRIS INTERTYPE CORP (DE)
Common $1 par split (2) for (1) by issuance of (0.5) additional share 9/14/60
Common $1 par split (2) for (1) by issuance of (1) additional share 9/24/64
Stock Dividend - 10% 9/28/62
Name changed to Harris Corp. 5/15/74

HARRIS J & SONS LTD (ON)
Common no par split (3) for (2) by issuance of (2) additional shares 06/19/1974
Common no par reclassified as Conv. Class A Common no par 10/29/1976
Recapitalized as Harris Steel Group Inc. 11/06/1979
Each share Conv. Class A Common no par exchanged for (1) share Class A Common no par and (0.5) share Class B Common no par
Each share Conv. Class B Common no par exchanged for (1) share Class A Common no par and (0.5) Class B Common no par
(See Harris Steel Group Inc.)

HARRIS KAYOT INC (MN)
Merged into HK Investment Corp. 12/3/86
Each share Common 10¢ par exchanged for $1.08 cash

HARRIS MANUFACTURING CO. (CA)
Each share Class A Common $2 par exchanged for (0.4) share Class A Common $5 par in 1944
Class A Common $5 par and Class B Common $2 par changed to 10¢ par 4/10/62
Class A Common 10¢ par & Class B Common 10¢ par called for redemption 7/14/65

HARRIS PFD CAP CORP (MD)
7.375% Exchangeable Preferred Ser. A $1 par called for redemption at $25 plus $0.1536 accrued dividends on 04/30/2013

HARRIS PPTYS INC (IN)
Each (300) shares old Common no par exchanged for (1) share new Common no par 12/17/77
Administratively dissolved 12/31/87

HARRIS SVGS BK (HARRISBURG, PA)
Under plan of reorganization each share Common 1¢ par automatically became (1) share Harris Financial, Inc. Common 1¢ par 9/17/97
Harris Financial, Inc. merged into Waypoint Financial Corp. 10/17/2000
(See Waypoint Financial Corp.)

HARRIS-SEYBOLD CO. (DE)
Common $1 par split (3) for (2) by issuance of (0.5) additional share in 1955
Stock Dividends - 10% 12/28/48; 10% 3/31/50; 20% 12/22/50; 15% 12/21/51
Under plan of merger name changed to Harris-Intertype Corp. 6/27/57
Harris-Intertype Corp. name changed to Harris Corp. 5/15/74

HARRIS-SEYBOLD-POTTER CO.
Name changed to Harris-Seybold Co. in 1946
Harris-Seybold Co. name changed to Harris-Intertype Corp. 6/27/57 which name changed to Harris Corp. 5/15/74

HARRIS SILK HOSIERY CO.
Liquidation ordered by Court in 1939

HARRIS STL GROUP INC (ON)
Class A Common no par split (2) for (1) by issuance of (1) additional share 04/16/1985
Class B Common no par split (2) for (1) by issuance of (1) additional share 04/16/1985
Each share Class A Common no par exchanged for (4) shares Common no par 07/07/2004
Each share Class B Common no par exchanged for (4) shares Common no par 07/07/2004
Acquired by Nucor Corp. 03/13/2007
Each share Common no par exchanged for $46.25 cash

HARRIS STRATEX NETWORKS INC (DE)
Class A Common 1¢ par reclassified as Common 1¢ par 10/19/2009
Name changed to Aviat Networks, Inc. 01/27/2010

HARRIS TEETER PPTYS INC (NC)
Merged into IRT Property Co. 12/31/1987
Each share Common 10¢ par

exchanged for (0.595) share
Common $1 par
IRT Property Co. merged into Equity
One, Inc. 02/13/2003 which merged
into Regency Centers Corp.
03/01/2017

HARRIS TEETER SUPER MKTS INC OLD (NC)
Common $5 par changed to $2.50 par
and (1) additional share issued
09/01/1965
Acquired by Ruddick Corp.
09/16/1969
Each share Common $2.50 par
exchanged for (1.3) shares 56¢
Conv. Preference $5 par and (0.56)
share Common $1 par
Ruddick Corp. name changed to
Harris Teeter Supermarkets, Inc.
(New) 04/02/2012
(See Harris Teeter Supermarkets, Inc. (New))

HARRIS TEETER SUPERMARKETS INC NEW (NC)
Acquired by Kroger Co. 01/28/2014
Each share Common no par
exchanged for $49.38 cash

HARRIS TR & SVGS BK (CHICAGO, IL)
Each share Capital Stock $100 par
exchanged for (5) shares Capital
Stock $20 par 1/9/58
Capital Stock $20 par changed to $16
par and (0.25) additional share
issued plus a 25% stock dividend
paid 4/5/66
Stock Dividends - 33-1/3% 12/18/44;
25% 7/20/50; 20% 1/29/53; 25%
2/1/56; 33-1/3% 2/2/59; 10% 2/1/60;
17.2161% 2/14/64; 25% 4/15/71
Reorganized under the laws of
Delaware as Harris Bankcorp, Inc.
4/3/72
Each share Capital Stock $16 par
exchanged for (1) share Common
$16 par
(See Harris Bankcorp, Inc.)

HARRISBURG BANCSHARES INC (TX)
Merged into Cullen/Frost Bankers,
Inc. 1/2/98
Each share Common $10 par
exchanged for $258.34 cash

HARRISBURG BK (HOUSTON, TX)
Stock Dividends - 33-1/3% 1/28/74;
20% 3/15/78; 25% 3/6/85
Reorganized as Harrisburg
Bancshares, Inc. 4/25/86
Each share Common $10 par held by
Texas residents exchanged for (1)
share Common $10 par
Each share Common $10 par held by
non- Texas residents exchanged for
$60 cash
(See Harrisburg Bancshares, Inc.)

HARRISBURG BRIDGE CO.
Sold to the Commonwealth of
Pennsylvania in 1949
Details not available

HARRISBURG-DAYTON RESOURCE CORP (BC)
Recapitalized as San Fernando
Mining Co. Ltd. (BC) 11/05/1991
Each share Common no par
exchanged for (0.33333333) share
Common no par
San Fernando Mining Ltd. (BC)
reincorporated in Canada as
KeyWest Energy Corp. 05/14/1998
(See KeyWest Energy Corp.)

HARRISBURG FINANCE CO. (PA)
Liquidation completed
Each share Common $50 par
received initial distribution of $60
cash 9/30/74
Each share Common $50 par
received second distribution of $55
cash 6/30/75
Each share Common $50 par
exchanged for third and final
distribution of $18.57 cash 11/4/76

HARRISBURG GAS CO. (PA)
Merged into United Gas Improvement
Co. in 1952
Each share Common no par
exchanged for (4) shares Common
$13.50 par
United Gas Improvement Co. name
changed to UGI Corp. (Old) 7/1/68
which reorganized as UGI Corp.
(New) 4/10/92

HARRISBURG NATL BK & TR CO (HARRISBURG, PA)
Capital Stock $25 par changed to
$12.50 par and (1) additional share
issued 11/24/65
Stock Dividend - 15% 6/30/67
Merged into Commonwealth National
Bank (Harrisburg, PA) 1/1/70
Each share Capital Stock $12.50 par
exchanged for (1.25) shares
Common $10 par
Commonwealth National Bank
(Harrisburg, PA) reorganized as
Commonwealth National Financial
Corp. 3/5/82
(See Commonwealth National Financial Corp.)

HARRISBURG PIPE & PIPE BENDING CO. (PA)
Name changed to Harrisburg Steel
Corp. 5/16/35, which was
reincorporated under the laws of
Delaware as Harsco Corp. 5/1/56

HARRISBURG STEEL CORP. (PA)
Each share Capital Stock $50 par
exchanged for (10) shares new
Capital Stock $5 par in 1937
Each share Common $5 par or Class
B Common $5 par exchanged for (2)
shares Common $2.50 par or Class
B Common $2.50 par in 1953
Each share Class B Common $2.50
par exchanged for (1) share
Common $2.50 par 4/26/55
Stock Dividends - 10% Common
1/5/55; 10% Class B Common
1/12/55
Reincorporated under the laws of
Delaware as Harsco Corp. 5/1/56

HARRISON B M ELECTROSONICS INC (MA)
Reincorporated under the laws of
Delaware as Trans American
Funding Corp. and Common no par
changed to 10¢ par 11/1/68
Trans American Funding Corp. name
changed to Hooker American Inc.
3/4/69 which name changed to
Curtis-Hooker Corp. 9/23/70 which
name changed back to Hooker
American Inc. 5/5/75
(See Hooker American Inc.)

HARRISON DEV INC (CO)
Reincorporated under the laws of
Delaware as TJ Systems Corp.
11/27/1989
TJ Systems Corp. name changed to
Leasing Edge Corp. 07/01/1995
which name changed to LEC
Technologies, Inc. 03/20/1997 which
name changed to Golf
Entertainment, Inc. (DE) 02/18/1999
which reincorporated in Nevada as
Contemporary Solutions, Inc.
05/02/2005
(See Contemporary Solutions, Inc.)

HARRISON DIGICOM INC (NV)
Each share old Common $0.001 par
exchanged for (0.25) share new
Common $0.001 par 5/27/99
Name changed to Infinite Networks
Corp. (Old) 2/8/2000
Infinite Networks Corp. (Old) name
changed to Infinite Coffee Co.
11/18/2003 which reorganized as
Infinite Networks Corp. (New)
12/21/2004

HARRISON HIBBERT MINES LTD. (ON)
Recapitalized as Harrison Minerals,
Ltd. 04/20/1955

Each share Capital Stock $1 par
exchanged for (0.2) share Capital
Stock $1 par
Harrison Minerals, Ltd. recapitalized
as Cantri Mines Ltd. 12/14/1964
which merged into Can-Con
Enterprises & Explorations Ltd.
11/30/1970 which name changed to
Aubet Resources Inc. 09/08/1981
which recapitalized as Aubet
Explorations Ltd. 09/30/1998 which
name changed to Visa Gold
Explorations Inc. 08/25/1999
(See Visa Gold Explorations Inc.)

HARRISON HLDGS INC (DE)
Name changed to Intelligent Motor
Cars Group, Inc. 02/05/2003
Intelligent Motor Cars Group, Inc.
name changed to Selective Brands
Holdings Inc. 05/16/2007 which
recapitalized as East Morgan
Holdings Inc. 02/28/2008

HARRISON MINERALS, LTD. (ON)
Recapitalized as Cantri Mines Ltd.
12/14/1964
Each share Capital Stock $1 par
exchanged for (0.25) share Capital
Stock $1 par
Cantri Mines Ltd. merged into
Can-Con Enterprises & Explorations
Ltd. 11/30/1970 which name
changed to Aubet Resources Inc.
09/08/1981 which recapitalized as
Aubet Explorations Ltd. 09/30/1998
which name changed to Visa Gold
Explorations Inc. 08/25/1999
(See Visa Gold Explorations Inc.)

HARRISON PIERCE PHARMACEUTICALS (UT)
Proclaimed dissolved for failure to
pay taxes 12/31/74

HARRISON WHOLESALE CO. (IL)
Name changed to
Luminator-Harrison, Inc. in 1949
Luminator-Harrison, Inc. name
changed to Luminator, Inc. 5/8/67
which merged into Gulton Industries,
Inc. (Del.) 1/2/69
(See Gulton Industries, Inc. (Del.))

HARRISONBURG TEL CO (VA)
Common $10 par split (3) for (2) by
issuance of (0.5) additional share
4/14/67
Stock Dividend - 50% 4/1/63
Merged into Continental Telephone
Corp. 2/27/70
Each share Common $10 par
exchanged for (1.5) shares $1 Conv.
Preferred Ser. D no par
Continental Telephone Corp. name
changed to Continental Telecom Inc.
5/6/82 which name changed to
Contel Corp. 5/1/86 which merged
into GTE Corp. 3/14/91 which
merged into Verizon
Communications Inc. 6/30/2000

HARRODSBURG FIRST FINL BANCORP INC (DE)
Name changed to 1st Independence
Financial Group, Inc. 07/09/2004
1st Independence Financial Group,
Inc. merged into MainSource
Financial Group, Inc. 08/29/2008
which merged into First Financial
Bancorp 04/02/2018

HARROUN MOTORS CORP. (DE)
Charter cancelled and declared
inoperative and void for
non-payment of taxes 03/22/1922

HARROW INDS INC (CO)
Recapitalized as Stone Media Corp.
3/7/94
Each share Common $0.001 par
exchanged for (0.25) share Common
$0.001 par

HARROW INDS INC (DE)
Merged into Ingersoll-Rand Co. (NJ)
03/29/1999
Each share Common 1¢ par
exchanged for $155.2489 cash

HARROWSTON CORP (CANADA)
Name changed to Harrowston Inc.
04/05/1993
Note: U.S. shareholders must
exchange their stock for legended
certificates
(See Harrowston Inc.)

HARROWSTON INC (CANADA)
Each share old Class A no par
exchanged for (0.05) share new
Class A no par 10/04/1993
Acquired by 1479523 Ontario Inc.
07/27/2001
Each share new Class A no par
exchanged for $7.35 cash

HARRY & DAVID HLDGS INC (DE)
Acquired by 1-800-FLOWERS.COM,
Inc. 09/30/2014
Each share Common 1¢ par
exchanged for $143.260583 cash

HARRY WINSTON DIAMOND CORP (CANADA)
Name changed to Dominion Diamond
Corp. 03/27/2013
(See Dominion Diamond Corp.)

HARRYS FMRS MKT INC (GA)
Name changed to Hurry Inc.
11/14/2001
(See Hurry Inc.)

HARRYS TRUCKING INC (DE)
Name changed to Premier Power
Renewable Energy, Inc. 09/08/2008

HARS SYS INC (BC)
Acquired by Trimin Capital Corp.
08/22/2002
Each share Common no par
exchanged for $0.62 cash

HARSHAW CHEM CO (OH)
Common no par changed to $10 par
in 1948
Common $10 par changed to $5 par
and (1) additional share issued
1/12/56
Stock Dividend - 25% 10/1/54
Merged into Kewanee Oil Co. 12/9/66
Each share Common $5 par
exchanged for (1) share $2 Conv.
Preferred Ser. A no par
Kewanee Oil Co. name changed to
Kewanee Industries, Inc. 7/1/75
(See Kewanee Industries, Inc.)

HART & COOLEY CO., INC. (CT)
Each share Common $25 par
exchanged for (2.5) shares Common
$10 par and subsequent dividend of
100% paid in 1947
Merged into Fafnir Bearing Co. on a
share for share basis in 1954
Fafnir Bearing Co. acquired by
Textron Inc. (Del.) 1/4/68

HART & COOLEY MANUFACTURING CO. (DE)
Merged into Allied Thermal Corp. on a
(1.1) for (1) basis 6/30/64
(See Allied Thermal Corp.)

HART & CROUSE CO., INC. (NY)
Name changed to H. & C. Shares,
Inc. 2/17/38
(See H. & C. Shares, Inc.)

HART & HEGEMAN MANUFACTURING CO.
Merged into Arrow-Hart & Hegeman
Electric Co. 00/00/1928
Details not available

HART ALFRED CO (CA)
Capital Stock $1 par split (5) for (4)
by issuance of (0.25) additional
share 9/29/65
Name changed to Harucal, Inc.
1/31/74
(See Harucal, Inc.)

HART BATTERY CO. LTD. (CANADA)
Charter surrendered and assets
distributed in 1957

HART BATTERY CO. (1957) LTD. (CANADA)
Name changed to Associated
Batteries (Canada) Ltd. 07/22/1963

Associated Batteries (Canada) Ltd. name changed to Associated Landterre Ltd. 09/04/1964
(See Associated Landterre Ltd.)

HART BREWING INC (WA)
Name changed to Pyramid Breweries Inc. 07/01/1996
(See Pyramid Breweries Inc.)

HART CARTER CO (DE)
Common no par changed to $1 par in 1941
Common $1 par split (5) for (2) by issuance of (1.5) additional shares 6/30/65
Stock Dividend - 25% 9/29/72
Merged into Combustion Equipment Associates, Inc. 2/28/73
Each share Common $1 par exchanged for (0.553) share Common 1¢ par
(See Combustion Equipment Associates, Inc.)

HART EXPL & PRODTN CO (CO)
Merged into Brock Acquisition Corp. 9/10/85
Each share Common 1¢ par exchanged for $0.01 cash

HART GRAIN WEIGHER CO.
Acquired by Hart-Carter Co. in 1928
Details not available

HART HLDG INC (DE)
Each (600) shares Common 1¢ par exchanged for (1) share Common $1 par 08/16/1994
Note: In effect holders received $2.25 cash per share and public interest was eliminated

HART INDS INC (NV)
Reorganized 03/08/1994
Each share Common $0.001 par exchanged for (0.1) share Common 1¢ par 04/03/1991
Reorganized from under the laws of (UT) to Nevada 03/08/1994
Each share Common 1¢ par exchanged for (0.05) share old Common 1¢ par
Each share old Common 1¢ par exchanged for (0.04) share new Common $0.001 par 10/16/2000
Each share new Common 1¢ par exchanged again for (5) shares new Common 1¢ par 06/20/2001
Name changed to H-Entertainment, Inc. 08/24/2001
(See H-Entertainment, Inc.)

HART LABS INC (PA)
Partial liquidation and name changed to Extar Co. effected by exchange of each share Common no par for (0.6) share Extar Co. Common no par, (0.8) share Nutrion Corp. $1 Conv. Preferred Ser. A $1 par and 20¢ cash 4/22/68

HART-PARR CO.
Merged into Oliver Farm Equipment Co. in 1929
Details not available

HART RIV MINES LTD (BC)
Recapitalized as North Hart Resources Ltd. 07/16/1976
Each share Capital Stock 50¢ par exchanged for (0.2) share Capital Stock no par
North Hart Resources Ltd. recapitalized as Calypso Developments Ltd. 08/20/1984 which recapitalized as Calypso Acquisition Corp. 11/18/2002 which name changed to Calypso Uranium Corp. 09/24/2007 which merged into U308 Corp. 05/15/2013

HART-ROSS COAL CO. (DE)
Liquidation completed in 1953

HART SCHAFFNER & MARX (NY)
Common $100 par changed to $20 par 00/00/1935
Each share Common $20 par exchanged for (2.5) shares Common $10 par 00/00/1944
Common $10 par changed to $5 par and (1) additional share issued 04/14/1960
Common $5 par changed to $2.50 par and (1) additional share issued 04/15/1965
Common $2.50 par split (3) for (2) by issuance of (0.5) additional share 02/04/1966
Common $2.50 par split (3) for (2) by issuance of (0.5) additional share 02/17/1969
Stock Dividends - 25% 04/16/1956; 25% 02/07/1963
Reorganized as Hartmarx Corp. 04/13/1983
Each share Common $2.50 par exchanged for (1.5) shares Common $2.50 par
(See Hartmarx Corp.)

HART STORES INC (CANADA)
Acquired by 9102221 Canada Inc. 02/19/2015
Each share Common no par exchanged for $0.20 cash
Note: Unexchanged certificates will be cancelled and become without value 02/19/2021

HART TECHNOLOGIES INC (DE)
Name changed to Lifschultz Industries Inc. 02/01/1991
(See Lifschultz Industries Inc.)

HARTALEGA HLDGS BERHAD (MALAYSIA)
ADR's for Ordinary split (2) for (1) by issuance of (1) additional ADR payable 09/30/2015 to holders of record 09/21/2015 Ex date - 10/01/2015
ADR agreement terminated 10/16/2017
Each ADR for Ordinary exchanged for $29.395049 cash

HARTCO CORP (CANADA)
Reorganized as Hartco Income Fund 08/31/2005
Each share Common no par exchanged for (1) Trust Unit
Hartco Income Fund reorganized as Hartco Inc. 04/20/2009
(See Hartco Inc.)

HARTCO ENTERPRISES INC (CANADA)
Common no par split (4) for (3) by issuance of (0.33333333) additional share 07/14/1989
Common no par split (2) for (1) by issuance of (1) additional share 07/19/1993
Stock Dividend - 20% 07/15/1988
Name changed to Hart Stores Inc. and each share Common no par received distribution of (1) share Hartco Corp. Common no par 07/14/2000
(See Hart Stores Inc.)

HARTCO INC (CANADA)
Acquired by H&N Family Subco Inc. 07/03/2015
Each share Common no par exchanged for $3.40 cash

HARTCO INCOME FD (CANADA)
Reorganized as Hartco Inc. 04/20/2009
Each Trust Unit exchanged for (1) share Common no par
Note: Unexchanged certificates were cancelled and became without value 04/20/2015
(See Hartco Inc.)

HARTCO LTD (NV)
Name changed to Exo-Web.Com 8/26/99
Exo-Web.Com recapitalized as Pan American Gold Resources Corp. 5/24/2004 which name changed to Dragon Venture 4/18/2005 which name changed to Dragon Capital Group Corp. 12/13/2005

HARTCOURT COS INC (UT)
Each share Common $0.001 par exchanged for (0.2) share new Common $0.001 par 08/01/1996
Stock Dividend - 3% payable 08/10/1996 to holders of record 07/31/1996
Each share new Common $0.001 par received distribution of (1) share Financial Telecom Ltd. (USA), Inc. Common $0.001 par payable 11/01/2004 to holders of record 10/25/2004
SEC revoked common stock registration 01/18/2013

HARTCOURT INVTS USA INC (UT)
Recapitalized as Hartcourt Companies, Inc. 10/6/95
Each share Common $0.001 par exchanged for (5/7) share Common $0.001 par

HARTE HANKS COMMUNICATIONS INC (DE)
Common $1 par split (2) for (1) by issuance of (1) additional share 8/21/78
Common $1 par split (2) for (1) by issuance of (1) additional share 7/8/83
Acquired by HH Acquiring Corp. 9/11/84
Each share Common $1 par exchanged for $13 principal amount of 16% Jr. Subord. Discount Debentures due 12/31/2004 and $27 cash

HARTE-HANKS COMMUNICATIONS INC NEW (DE)
Common $1 par split (3) for (2) by issuance of (0.5) additional share 12/15/1995
Common $1 par split (2) for (1) by issuance of (1) additional share payable 03/16/1998 to holders of record 03/02/1998 Ex date - 03/17/1998
Name changed to Harte-Hanks, Inc. 05/05/1998

HARTE-HANKS NEWSPAPERS, INC. (DE)
Name changed to Harte-Hanks Communications, Inc. 9/1/77
(See Harte-Hanks Communications, Inc.)

HARTE RES CORP (ON)
Name changed to Harte Gold Corp. 12/15/2003

HARTEBEESTFONTEIN GOLD MNG LTD (SOUTH AFRICA)
Each old ADR for Ordinary exchanged for (10) new ADR's for Ordinary 08/01/1984
Each new ADR for Ordinary exchanged for (0.0887255) Avgold Ltd. ADR for Ordinary 01/03/1997
(See Avgold Ltd.)

HARTER (GEO. D.) BANK (CANTON, OH)
Capital Stock $50 par changed to $20 par and (1.5) additional shares issued plus a 20% stock dividend paid 5/9/42
Name changed to Harter Bank & Trust Co. (Canton, OH) 2/1/43
Harter Bank & Trust Co. (Canton, OH) reorganized as Harter BanCorp 2/28/75 which was acquired by Society Corp. 7/9/79 which merged into KeyCorp (New) 3/1/94

HARTER BANCORP (OH)
Stock Dividend - 25% 9/2/75
Acquired by Society Corp. 7/9/79
Each share Common no par exchanged for (2) shares Common $1 par
Society Corp. merged into KeyCorp (New) 3/1/94

HARTER BK & TR CO (CANTON, OH)
Each share Capital Stock $20 par exchanged for (2) shares Capital Stock $15 par 07/20/1961
Capital Stock $15 par changed to $7.50 par and (1) additional share issued 04/21/1970
Stock Dividends - 66-2/3% 07/03/1946; 100% 06/25/1957; 20% 02/11/1964; 15% 02/28/1967; 10% 04/23/1973
Reorganized as Harter BanCorp 02/28/1975
Each share Capital Stock $7.50 par exchanged for (1) share Common no par
Harter BanCorp acquired by Society Corp. 07/09/1979 which merged into KeyCorp (New) 03/01/1994

HARTER FINANCIAL INC (NY)
SEC revoked common stock registration 10/04/2007

HARTFIELD STORES, INC. (DE)
Name changed to Hartfield-Zodys, Inc. 5/17/67
Hartfield-Zodys, Inc. reorganized as HRT Industries, Inc. 12/22/81
(See HRT Industries, Inc.)

HARTFIELD ZODYS INC (DE)
Common $1 par split (4) for (3) by issuance of (1/3) additional share 6/14/68
Each share $1.20 Preferred no par exchanged for (2) shares Common $1 par 7/19/76
Stock Dividend - 10% 7/6/79
Under plan of reorganization each share Common $1 par automatically became (1) share HRT Industries, Inc. Common $1 par 12/22/81
(See HRT Industries, Inc.)

HARTFORD & CONNECTICUT WESTERN RAILROAD CO.
Merged into New York, New Haven & Hartford Railroad Co. under plan of reorganization on basis of (1) share Common no par for each $100 of allowed claims 5/26/48
(See New York, New Haven & Hartford Railroad Co.)

HARTFORD AETNA REALTY CORP.
Liquidated in 1944

HARTFORD CAP I (DE)
Quarterly Income Preferred Securities called for redemption at $25 plus $0.48125 accrued dividend on 9/30/2003

HARTFORD CAP II (DE)
8.35% Quarterly Income Preferred Securities called for redemption at $25 on 12/31/2001

HARTFORD CAP III (DE)
7.45% Trust Originated Preferred Securities called for redemption at $25 on 11/17/2006

HARTFORD CITY GAS LIGHT CO.
Name changed to Hartford Gas Co. in 1927
Hartford Gas Co. merged into Connecticut Natural Gas Corp. 8/30/68

HARTFORD-CONNECTICUT CO.
Dissolved in 1934

HARTFORD-CONNECTICUT TRUST CO. (HARTFORD, CT)
Merged into Connecticut Bank & Trust Co. (Hartford, CT) 7/1/54
Each share Capital Stock $25 par exchanged for (1.2) shares Capital Stock $25 par
Connecticut Bank & Trust Co. (Hartford, CT) reorganized as CBT Corp. 2/27/70 which merged into Bank of New England Corp. 6/14/85
(See Bank of New England Corp.)

HARTFORD COURANT CO. (CT)
VTC's for Common $10 par changed to $1 par and (9) additional share issued 4/15/77
Merged into Times Mirror Co. (Old) 10/11/79

Holdings of (5) shares or fewer exchanged for $200 cash per share
Holdings of more than (5) shares exchanged for $200 principal amount of 9% Installment Notes due from 1980 thru 1994 per share

HARTFORD ELEC LT CO (CT)
Each share Common $100 par exchanged for (4) shares Common $25 par 00/00/1928
Common $25 par changed to $12.50 par and (1) additional share issued 12/20/1962
Each share Common $12.50 par exchanged for (2.9) shares Northeast Utilities Common $5 par 12/26/1967
(See Northeast Utilities)
Note: Unexchanged certificates were cancelled and became without value 12/27/1972
Under plan of merger each share 3.90% Preferred 1949 Ser. $50 par, 4.50% Preferred 1956 Ser. $50 par, 4.50% Preferred 1963 Ser. $50 par, 4.96% Preferred 1958 Ser. $50 par, 5.28% Preferred 1967 Ser. $50 par, 6.56% Preferred 1968 Ser. $50 par, 7.60% Preferred 1971 Ser. $50 par, 9.36% Preferred 1970 Ser. $50 par, 9.60% Preferred 1974 Ser. $50 par, 10.48% Preferred 1980 Ser. $50 par and 11.52% Preferred 1975 Ser. $50 par automatically became (1) share Connecticut Light & Power Co.
3.90% Preferred 1949 Ser. $50 par, 4.50% Preferred 1956 Ser. $50 par, 4.50% Preferred 1963 Ser. $50 par, 4.96% Preferred 1958 Ser. $50 par, 5.28% Preferred 1967 Ser. $50 par, 6.56% Preferred 1968 Ser. $50 par, 7.60% Preferred 1971 Ser. $50 par, 9.36% Preferred 1970 Ser. $50 par, 9.60% Preferred 1974 Ser. $50 par, 10.48% Preferred 1980 Ser. $50 par and 11.52% Preferred 1975 Ser. $50 par respectively 06/30/1982

HARTFORD EMPIRE CO. (DE)
Name changed to Emhart Manufacturing Co. 3/9/51
Emhart Manufacturing Co. merged into Emhart Corp. (Conn.) 6/30/64 which reincorporated in Virginia 5/4/76
(See Emhart Corp. (Va.))

HARTFORD FDS EXCHANGE TRADED TR (DE)
Trust termination 09/21/2018
Each Corporate Bond ETF received $48.87 cash
Each Quality Bond ETF received $48.81 cash
(Additional Information in Active)

HARTFORD FINL SVCS GROUP INC (DE)
Each 7% Normal Unit received (0.8791) share Common 1¢ par 08/16/2006
Each 6% Equity Unit received (0.8674) share Common 1¢ par 11/16/2006
Each share 7.25% Mandatory Conv. Depositary Preferred 1¢ par exchanged for (0.9208) share Common 1¢ par 04/01/2013
(Additional Information in Active)

HARTFORD FIRE INS CO (CT)
Each share Common $100 par exchanged for (10) shares Common $10 par 00/00/1930
Common $10 par changed to $5 par and (1) additional share issued plus a 100% stock dividend paid 04/01/1960
Common $5 par changed to $2.50 par and (1) additional share issued 04/14/1967
Through exchange offer majority of Common $2.50 par acquired by International Telephone & Telegraph Corp. on the basis of (1) share $2.25 Conv. Preferred no par for each share Common 00/00/1970
(See International Telephone & Telegraph Corp.)
Stock Dividends - 33-1/3% 11/01/1949; 25% 04/23/1954; 25% 04/22/1955
10% Class A Preferred Ser. 1 $50 par called for redemption 07/15/1987
8.95% Class A Preferred Ser. 3 $50 par called for redemption 09/18/1987
7.50% Class C Preferred Ser. 1 $50 par called for redemption 06/30/1994
Floating Rate Preferred Class A Ser. 2 $50 par called for redemption 11/15/1995

HARTFORD GAS CO. (CT)
Preferred $25 par and Common $25 par changed to $12.50 par respectively and (1) additional share issued 4/19/63
Under plan of merger name changed to Connecticut Natural Gas Corp. 8/30/68

HARTFORD HEAT TREATING CORP.
Liquidated in 1950
No stockholders' equity

HARTFORD INCOME SHS FD INC (MD)
Merged into Rivus Bond Fund 10/22/2010
Each share Common $0.001 par exchanged for (0.3176) Share of Bene. Int. 1¢ par
Rivus Bond Fund name changed to Cutwater Select Income Fund 12/09/2011 which name changed to Insight Select Income Fund 12/29/2016

HARTFORD LIFE CAP I (DE)
7.20% Trust Preferred Securities Ser. A called for redemption at $25 plus $0.30 accrued dividend on 3/15/2004

HARTFORD LIFE CAP II (DE)
7.625% Trust Preferred Securities Ser. B called for redemption at $25 on 7/14/2006

HARTFORD LIFE INC (DE)
Issue Information - 23,000,000 shares CL A offered at $28.25 per share on 05/21/1997
Merged into Hartford Financial Services Group, Inc. 6/27/2000
Each share Class A Common 1¢ par exchanged for $50.50 cash

HARTFORD LIFE INSURANCE CO. (MA)
Each share Capital Stock $20 par exchanged for (0.0004) share Capital Stock $50,000 par 02/05/1971
Acquired by Hartford Fire Insurance Co. 08/08/1974
Each (0.0004) share Capital Stock $50,000 par exchanged for $400 cash

HARTFORD NATL BK & TR CO (HARTFORD, CT)
Common $10 par changed to $6.25 par and (0.6) additional share issued 2/8/66
Stock Dividends - 10% 8/25/67; 10% 8/26/68
Reorganized under the laws of Delaware as Hartford National Corp. 4/30/69
Each share Common $6.25 par exchanged for (1) share Common $6.25 par
Hartford National Corp. merged into Shawmut National Corp. 2/29/88 which merged into Fleet Financial Group Inc. (New) 11/30/95 which name changed to Fleet Boston Corp. 10/1/99 which name changed to FleetBoston Financial Corp. 4/18/2000 which merged into Bank of America Corp. 4/1/04

HARTFORD NATL CORP (DE)
Common $6.25 par split (3) for (2) by issuance of (0.5) additional share 01/20/1984
Common $6.25 par split (3) for (2) by issuance of (0.5) additional share 10/20/1986
Merged into Shawmut National Corp. 02/29/1988
Each share Adjustable Rate Preferred no par exchanged for (1) share Adjustable Rate Preferred no par
Each share Common $6.25 par exchanged for (1) share Common 1¢ par
Shawmut National Corp. merged into Fleet Financial Group Inc. (New) 11/30/1995 which name changed to Fleet Boston Corp. 10/01/1999 which name changed to FleetBoston Financial Corp. 04/18/2000 which merged into Bank of America Corp. 04/01/2004

HARTFORD RAYON CORP.
Acquired by Bigelow-Sanford Carpet Co., Inc. (DE) in 1951
Each share Common $1 par exchanged for (0.166666) share Common $5 par
Bigelow-Sanford Carpet Co., Inc. (DE) name changed to Bigelow-Sanford, Inc. 5/4/60
(See Bigelow-Sanford, Inc.)

HARTFORD RETIREMENT NETWORK CORP (NV)
Name changed to HQDA Elderly Life Network Corp. 06/07/2018

HARTFORD SPL INC (CT)
Name changed 12/31/1979
Each share Capital Stock $100 par exchanged for (5) shares Capital Stock $20 par 00/00/1951
Name changed from Hartford Special Machinery Co. to Hartford Special, Inc. and Capital Stock $20 par changed to no par 12/31/1979
Dissolved 08/08/1983
Details not available

HARTFORD STEAM BOILER INSPECTION & INS CO (CT)
Each share Common $100 par exchanged for (10) shares Common $10 par in 1930
Common $10 par changed to $5 par and (1) additional share issued plus a 25% stock dividend paid 4/1/66
Common $5 par changed to $2.50 par and (1) additional share issued 5/20/85
Common $2.50 par changed to no par 4/15/86
Common no par split (2) for (1) by issuance of (1) additional share 7/31/86
Common no par split (2) for (1) by issuance of (1) additional share 4/30/87
Stock Dividends - 33-1/3% 3/12/59; 100% 11/20/69; 100% 4/30/79
Under plan of reorganization each share Common no par automatically became (1) share HSB Group, Inc. Common no par 6/24/97
HSB Group, Inc. merged into American International Group, Inc. 11/22/2000

HARTFORD TIMES INC (MD)
99.9% acquired by Gannett Co., Inc. through purchase offer which expired 04/21/1972
Public interest eliminated

HARTFORD ZINC CO. (DE)
Charter cancelled and declared inoperative and void for non-payment of taxes in January 1904

HARTLAND, INC. OF DELAWARE (DE)
Charter cancelled and declared inoperative and void for non-payment of taxes 4/15/70

HARTLAND MINES LTD. (QC)
Charter cancelled 06/00/1979

HARTLAND PIPELINE SVCS LTD (AB)
Placed in receivership 11/25/1999
No stockholders' equity

HARTLEY OILS LTD. (AB)
Struck from Alberta Registrar of Companies and proclaimed dissolved 1/15/63

HARTLINE BLOTTER PEN CO. (FL)
Proclaimed dissolved for failure to file reports and pay fees 12/23/36

HARTMAN CORP. (VA)
Charter revoked for failure to file reports and pay fees 5/31/35

HARTMAN ELECTRICAL MANUFACTURING CO. (OH)
Merged into Mid-Continent Manufacturing Co. (OH) 01/01/1966
Each share Common no par exchanged for (1.2) shares Common $1 par
Mid-Continent Manufacturing Co. (OH) reincorporated in Delaware as Mid-Con Inc. 10/31/1968 which merged into A-T-O Inc. 10/29/1969 which name changed to Figgie International Inc. (OH) 06/01/1981 which reorganized in Delaware as Figgie International Holdings Inc. 07/18/1983 which name changed to Figgie International Inc. 12/31/1986 which name changed to Scott Technologies, Inc. 05/20/1998 which merged into Tyco International Ltd. (Bermuda) 05/03/2001 which reincorporated in Switzerland 03/17/2009 which merged into Johnson Controls International PLC 09/06/2016

HARTMAN MARINE INC (NJ)
Charter declared void for non-payment of taxes 1/5/76

HARTMAN REALTY TRUST
Reorganized as Terminal Properties, Inc. in 1935
Details not available

HARTMAN TOB CO (CT)
Common $10 par changed to no par in 1933
Each share 6-1/2% 1st Preferred $100 par exchanged for (1) share $4 Prior Preference no par, (1) share $3 Non-Cum. Preference no par, (2) shares Common no par and $4 cash in 1937
Common no par changed to $1 par in 1950
$4 Prior Preference no par called for for redemption in June 1986
In process of liquidation
Each share Common $1 par exchanged for initial distribution of $7 cash 6/25/86
Assets transferred to Hartman Tobacco Liquidating Trust 12/30/86
Each share Common $1 par received second distribution of (1) Ctf. of Bene. Int. and $21 cash
(See Hartman Tobacco Liquidating Trust)

HARTMAN TOBACCO LIQUIDATING TRUST (CT)
Liquidation completed
Each Ctf. of Bene. Int. received third distribution of $2.75 cash 12/21/87
Each Ctf. of Bene. Int. received fourth distribution of $2.75 cash 12/14/88
Each Ctf. of Bene. Int. received fifth and final distribution of $2.18 cash 1/16/90 (For previous distributions see Hartman Tobacco Co.)

HARTMARX CORP (DE)
Common $2.50 par split (3) for (2) by issuance of (0.5) additional share 05/15/1986
Plan of reorganization under Chapter 11 Federal Bankruptcy proceedings effective 06/01/2014

No stockholders' equity
HARTNEY INDL SVCS CORP
Merged into Serv-Tech Inc.
06/13/1994
Details not available
HARTOGEN ENERGY LTD (AUSTRALIA)
Liquidated 11/10/1995
No stockholders' equity
HARTSFIELD CO., INC.
Merged into General Phoenix Corp. 00/00/1945
Each share Class A exchanged for (1.375) shares Preferred
Each share Class B exchanged for (2.5) shares Class A Common $5 par
General Phoenix Corp. name changed to General Acceptance Corp. (New) 07/11/1950 which name changed to GAC Corp. (PA) 07/01/1968 which reincorporated in Delaware 12/20/1973
(See GAC Corp. (DE))
HARTSTONE GROUP PLC (ENGLAND)
Each old Sponsored ADR for Ordinary 10p par exchanged for (0.5) new Sponsored ADR for Ordinary 10p par 04/07/1997
ADR agreement terminated 02/14/2003
Each new Sponsored ADR for Ordinary 10p par exchanged for $0.1732 cash
HARTUNG DEVELOPMENT CO. (PA)
Merged into Marlin Investment Co. 5/7/71
Each share Capital Stock 1¢ par exchanged for (10) shares Common no par
HARTVILLE GROUP INC (NV)
Old Common $0.001 par split (4) for (1) by issuance of (3) additional shares payable 09/13/2002 to holders of record 09/11/2002
Each share old Common $0.001 par exchanged for (0.06666666) share new Common $0.001 par 11/21/2007
Acquired by Fairfax Financial Holdings Ltd. 07/03/2013
Each share new Common $0.001 par exchanged for $2.38876809 cash
HARTWELL & CAMPBELL FD INC (NY)
Name changed to Hartwell Growth Fund, Inc. (NY) 1/10/74
Hartwell Growth Fund, Inc. (NY) reorganized in Massachusetts as Keystone America Hartwell Growth Fund Inc. 1/1/93 which merged into Keystone America Omega Fund, Inc. (MA) 4/1/96 which reincorporated in Delaware as Evergreen Omega Fund 10/31/97
HARTWELL & CAMPBELL LEVERAGE FD INC (NY)
Name changed to Hartwell Leverage Fund, Inc. 01/10/1974
Hartwell Leverage Fund, Inc. name changed to Hartwell Emerging Growth Fund, Inc. 10/08/1987 which reorganized as Keystone America Hartwell Emerging Growth Fund Inc. 01/01/1993 which merged into Evergreen Trust 08/01/1997
(See Evergreen Trust)
HARTWELL EMERGING GROWTH FD INC (NY)
Reorganized under the laws of Massachusetts as Keystone America Hartwell Emerging Growth Fund Inc. 01/01/1993
Each share Common $1 par exchanged for (1) share Class A Common no par
Keystone America Hartwell Emerging Growth Fund Inc. merged into Evergreen Trust 08/01/1997

(See Evergreen Trust)
HARTWELL GROWTH FD INC (NY)
Reorganized under the laws of Massachusetts as Keystone America Hartwell Growth Fund Inc. 1/1/93
Each share Common $1 par exchanged for (1) share Class A Common no par
Keystone America Hartwell Growth Fund Inc. merged into Keystone America Omega Fund, Inc. (MA) 4/1/96 which reincorporated in Delaware as Evergreen Omega Fund 10/31/97
HARTWELL LEVERAGE FD INC (NY)
Common $1 par split (2) for (1) by issuance of (1) additional share 12/08/1983
Stock Dividend - 50% 09/23/1976
Name changed to Hartwell Emerging Growth Fund, Inc. 10/08/1987
Hartwell Emerging Growth Fund, Inc. reorganized as Keystone America Hartwell Emerging Growth Fund Inc. 01/01/1993 which merged into Evergreen Trust 08/01/1997
(See Evergreen Trust)
HARTWELL MLS INC (GA)
Merged out of existence 06/04/1990
Details not available
HARTWELL PETES LTD (AB)
Merged into CrownJoule Exploration Ltd. 02/11/1997
Each share Common no par exchanged for $1.667 cash
HARTZ MOUNTAIN PET FOODS, INC. (NJ)
Under plan of merger name changed to Hartz Mountain Corp. 5/31/73
(See Hartz Mountain Corp.)
HARTZ MTN CORP (NJ)
Merged into Hartz Mountain Industries Inc. 2/13/79
Each share Common 1¢ par exchanged for $14 cash
HARTZ RESTAURANTS INC (WA)
Reincorporated 4/13/89
State of incorporation changed from (WA) to (DE) 4/13/89
Name changed to Hartz Restaurants International Inc. 2/16/96
HARUCAL INC (CA)
Completely liquidated 6/3/74
Each share Capital Stock $1 par exchanged for first and final distribution of $17.56 cash
HARVARD APPARATUS REGENERATIVE TECHNOLOGY INC (DE)
Name changed to Biostage, Inc. 04/01/2016
HARVARD BREWING CO. (DE)
Name changed to Harvard Investors, Inc. 2/22/57
Harvard Investors, Inc. name changed to Harvard Industries, Inc. 4/23/59
(See Harvard Industries, Inc.)
HARVARD CAP CORP (BC)
Recapitalized as Harvard International Technologies Ltd. 2/16/93
Each share Common no par exchanged for (0.2) share Common no par
(See Harvard International Technologies Ltd.)
HARVARD FINL SVCS CORP (DE)
Recapitalized as e*machinery.net, inc. 02/09/2000
Each share Common $0.0001 par exchanged for (0.1) share Common $0.0001 par
HARVARD HOUSING TRUST (MA)
Liquidation completed
Each share Preferred no par exchanged for first and final distribution of $169 cash 1/15/63

Each Common Trust Share no par exchanged for initial distribution of $180 cash 3/29/63
Each Common Trust Share no par exchanged for second and final distribution of $19.67 cash 12/19/63
HARVARD INDS INC (DE)
Each share $2 Conv. Preferred Ser. A $10 par exchanged for (5.25) shares Common $1 par 09/05/1984
Common $1 par changed to 10¢ par 04/11/1985
Common 10¢ par split (3) for (1) by issuance of (2) additional shares 04/30/1985
Common 10¢ par split (2) for (1) by issuance of (1) additional share 05/28/1987
Acquired by Harvard Acquisition Corp. 11/18/1988
Each share Common 10¢ par exchanged for $13 cash
Class B Common 1¢ par reclassified as Common 1¢ par 03/14/1995
Each share 14.25% Exchangeable Pay-In-Kind Preferred 1¢ par received distribution of (0.1425) additional share payable 09/30/1996 to holders of record 08/28/1996
Plan of reorganization under Chapter 11 Federal Bankruptcy proceedings confirmed 11/24/1998
Each share 14.25% Exchangeable Pay-In-Kind Preferred 1¢ par exchanged for (0.09133) Common Stock Purchase Warrant expiring 11/23/2003 on 11/24/1998
Each share old Common 1¢ par exchanged for (0.02996) Common Stock Purchase Warrant expiring 11/23/2003 on 11/24/1998
Plan of reorganization under Chapter 11 Federal Bankruptcy proceedings effective 03/17/2004
No stockholders' equity
HARVARD INTL TECHNOLOGIES LTD (BC)
Discharged from receivership 10/25/2005
Stockholders' equity unlikely
HARVARD INVESTORS, INC. (DE)
Name changed to Harvard Industries, Inc. 4/23/59
(See Harvard Industries, Inc.)
HARVARD KNITWEAR INC (NY)
Chapter 11 bankruptcy proceedings converted to Chapter 7 on 3/7/90
No stockholders' equity
HARVARD LEARNING CTRS INC (FL)
Name changed to Americas Learning Centers, Inc. 09/25/2007
Americas Learning Centers, Inc. recapitalized as Hackett's Stores, Inc. 01/26/2009 which recapitalized as WiseBuys, Inc. 06/17/2010 which name changed to Empire Pizza Holdings, Inc. 04/20/2011 which recapitalized as Vestiage, Inc. 03/22/2013
HARVARD MINES LTD. (ON)
Charter cancelled and company declared dissolved for failure to file returns 06/24/1965
HARVARD RES I LTD (DE)
Name changed to AET, Inc. 2/7/89
(See AET, Inc.)
HARVARD SCIENTIFIC CORP (NV)
Each share old Common $0.001 par exchanged for (0.25) share new Common $0.001 par in November 1994
Each share new Common $0.001 par exchanged for (0.1) share Common 1¢ par 1/2/98
Chapter 11 Federal Bankruptcy proceedings converted to Chapter 7 on 1/23/2002 was dismissed 5/29/2002
No stockholders' equity

HARVARD TR CO (CAMBRIDGE, MA)
Each share Capital Stock $20 par exchanged for (2) shares Capital Stock $10 par in 1947
Stock Dividends - 10% 4/1/52; 36% 2/7/56; 100% 2/10/64
Name changed to BayBank Harvard Trust Co. (Cambridge, MA) 2/2/76
(See BayBank Harvard Trust Co. (Cambridge, MA))
HARVARD URANIUM MINES LTD. (ON)
Name changed to Harvard Mines Ltd. 01/00/1956
(See Harvard Mines Ltd.)
HARVEL INDS CORP (NJ)
Merged into Fill-Mor Holding, Inc. 3/27/85
Each share Common 8¢ par exchanged for $17.50 cash
HARVEST ACQUISITION CORP (AB)
Recapitalized as Helin Industries Inc. 11/25/1997
Each share Common no par exchanged for (0.2) share Common no par
Helin Industries Inc. name changed to Second Chance Corp. 07/25/2001
(See Second Chance Corp.)
HARVEST BIO-ORGANIC INTL CO LTD (NV)
Charter revoked for failure to file reports and pay taxes 12/30/2011
HARVEST BRAND INC (KS)
Reorganized under the laws of Delaware as Harvest Industries, Inc. and Common 10¢ par changed to no par 6/30/69
(See Harvest Industries, Inc.)
HARVEST CAP CORP (DE)
Recapitalized as New Harvest Capital Corp. 08/09/2005
Each (1,370) shares Common $0.0001 par exchanged for (1) share Common $0.0001 par
New Harvest Capital Corp. name changed to Azur Holdings, Inc. 01/23/2006
(See Azur Holdings, Inc.)
HARVEST ENERGY TR (AB)
Stock Dividend - 1.098% payable 04/15/2005 to holders of record 03/31/2005 Ex date - 03/29/2005
Acquired by Korea National Oil Corp. 12/22/2009
Each Trust Unit no par exchanged for $10 cash
HARVEST FARMS INC (CA)
Adjudicated bankrupt 10/10/1973
Stockholders' equity unlikely
HARVEST FINL CORP (IA)
Common $1 par split (2) for (1) by issuance of (1) additional share 06/15/1993
Stock Dividends - 10% 11/29/1991; 30% 08/27/1992
Merged into Firstar Corp. (Old) 01/26/1996
Each share Common $1 par exchanged for (0.708) share Common $1.25 par
Firstar Corp. (Old) merged into Firstar Corp. (New) 11/20/1998 which merged into U.S. Bancorp (DE) 02/27/2001
HARVEST HOME FINL CORP (OH)
Merged into Peoples Community Bancorp, Inc. 04/01/2000
Each share Common 1¢ par exchanged for (0.9) share Common 1¢ par and $9 cash
(See Peoples Community Bancorp, Inc.)
HARVEST INDS INC (DE)
Common no par changed to 10¢ par 5/31/72
Each share Common 10¢ par exchanged for (0.005) share Common $20 par 7/16/85

Stock Dividend - 10% 9/20/76
Each (300) shares old Common $20 par exchanged for (1) share new Common $20 par 5/27/87
Note: In effect holders received $600 cash per share and public interest was eliminated

HARVEST MKTS INC (NY)
Adjudicated bankrupt 02/25/1974
Stockholders' equity unlikely

HARVEST ONE CAP INC (BC)
Recapitalized as Harvest One Cannabis Inc. 04/28/2017
Each share Common no par exchanged for (0.55865921) share Common no par

HARVEST REC VEHS INC (CA)
Each share old Common no par exchanged for (0.2) share new Common no par 12/8/93
Name changed to Grip Technologies, Inc. 2/15/94
(See Grip Technologies, Inc.)

HARVEST RESTAURANT GROUP INC (TX)
Name changed to Tanner's Restaurant Group, Inc. 03/12/1999
Tanner's Restaurant Group, Inc. name changed to Corzon Inc. 09/18/2000 which recapitalized as LecStar Corp. 03/29/2001
(See LecStar Corp.)

HARVEST SPRING NUTRITIONAL SYS 1981 CORP (BC)
Recapitalized as Xemac Resources Inc. 05/28/1996
Each share Common no par exchanged for (0.2) share Common no par
Xemac Resources Inc. recapitalized as Abitex Resources Inc. 03/26/2004 which recapitalized as ABE Resources Inc. 04/16/2013 which name changed to Vision Lithium Inc. 03/27/2018

HARVEST SUSTAINABLE INCOME FD (ON)
Units reclassified as Ser. R Units 12/12/2012
Merged into Harvest Canadian Income & Growth Fund 11/06/2013
Each Ser. A Unit received net asset value
Each Ser. F Unit received net asset value
Each Ser. R Unit received net asset value

HARVEY (FRED) (NJ)
Completely liquidated 7/22/68
Each share Common $2 par exchanged for first and final distribution of (1.1) shares Amfac, Inc. Common Capital Stock $10 par
(See Amfac, Inc.)

HARVEY (GUY P.) & SON CORP. (MA)
Became bankrupt in 1963
No stockholders' equity

HARVEY ALUM INC (INC.) (CA)
Class A Common $1 par reclassified as Common $1 par 02/18/1970
Name changed to Martin Marietta Aluminum Inc. 04/18/1972
Martin Marietta Aluminum Inc. merged into Martin Marietta Corp. (Old) 06/27/1974 which merged into Martin Marietta Corp. (New) 04/02/1993 which merged into Lockheed Martin Corp. 03/15/1995

HARVEY BOAT WORKS, INC. (OR)
Name changed to Harvey Corp. 12/22/60

HARVEY COMICS ENTMT INC (CA)
Name changed to Harvey Entertainment Co. 06/01/1994
Harvey Entertainment Co. name changed to Sunland Entertainment Co., Inc. (CA) 06/22/2001 which reorganized in Delaware 08/09/2002 which name changed to Trestle Holdings, Inc. 09/17/2003 which recapitalized as MoqiZone Holding Corp. 08/31/2009 which name changed to Balincan USA, Inc. 09/30/2015

HARVEY CREEK GOLD PLACERS LTD (BC)
Name changed to New Millennium Metals Corp. 03/23/1999
New Millennium Metals Corp. merged into Platinum Group Metals Ltd. 02/19/2002

HARVEY CRUDE OIL CO. (DE)
No longer in existence having become inoperative and void for non-payment of taxes 3/21/23

HARVEY ELECTRONICS INC (NY)
Each share old Common 1¢ par exchanged for (0.25) share new Common 1¢ par 1/10/2006
Chapter 11 bankruptcy proceedings dismissed 12/16/2008
No stockholders' equity

HARVEY ENTMT CO (CA)
Name changed to Sunland Entertainment Co., Inc. (CA) 06/22/2001
Sunland Entertainment Co., Inc. (CA) reorganized in Delaware 08/09/2002 which name changed to Trestle Holdings, Inc. 09/17/2003 which recapitalized as MoqiZone Holding Corp. 08/31/2009 which name changed to Balincan USA, Inc. 09/30/2015

HARVEY GROUP INC (NY)
Reorganized under Chapter 11 Federal Bankruptcy Code as Harvey Electronics, Inc. 12/26/96
Each share Common $1 par received (0.00635) share Common 1¢ par
Note: Certificates not required to be surrendered and are without value

HARVEY HAMILTON LTD. (BC)
See - Hamilton (Harvey) Ltd.

HARVEY HOUSE INC (NY)
Dissolved 10/08/1996
Details not available

HARVEY HUBBELL, INC. (CT)
See - Hubbell (Harvey), Inc.

HARVEY R J INSTR CORP (NJ)
Common 1¢ par split (4) for (1) by issuance of (3) additional shares 08/20/1971
Company advised private 00/00/1977
Details not available

HARVEY RADIO INC (NY)
Name changed to Harvey Group Inc. 6/27/69
Harvey Group Inc. reorganized as Harvey Electronics, Inc. 12/26/96

HARVEY UNVL INC (DE)
Charter declared void for non-payment of franchise taxes 3/1/98

HARVEY WALTER CORP (FL)
Proclaimed dissolved for failure to file reports and pay fees 12/11/1976

HARVEY-WELLS CORP. (NJ)
Name changed to Dage-Bell Corp. 6/19/64
(See Dage-Bell Corp.)

HARVEY WOODS LTD (ON)
Each share Class B no par exchanged for (6) shares Common no par 07/02/1975
Each share Class A no par exchanged for (1) share Common no par 07/02/1975
Under plan of merger each share Common no par received $3.30 cash 02/11/1985
Note: Certificates were not required to be surrendered and are without value

HARVEYS CASINO RESORTS (NV)
Merged into Harveys Acquisition Corp. 2/2/99
Each share Common 1¢ par exchanged for $28.73 cash

HARVEYS FOODS LTD (ON)
Common no par split (3) for (1) by issuance of (2) additional shares 01/20/1969
Merged into Foodcorp Ltd. 01/15/1974
Each share Common no par exchanged for (1) share Common no par
(See Foodcorp Ltd.)

HARVEYS STORES INC (DE)
Reincorporated 06/30/1971
Class A $1 par reclassified as Common $1 par 06/01/1967
State of incorporation changed from (NY) to (DE) 06/30/1971
Common $1 par split (2) for (1) by issuance of (1) additional share 03/20/1972
Under plan of merger name changed to Nexus Industries, Inc. 03/04/1975
Nexus Industries, Inc. reorganized as Shirt Shed, Inc. 12/19/1986 which merged into Signal Apparel Co., Inc. 07/22/1992
(See Signal Apparel Co., Inc.)

HARVILL AIRCRAFT DIE CASTING CORP.
Name changed to Harvill Corp. in 1942
(See Harvill Corp.)

HARVILL CORP. (CA)
Assets liquidated for benefit of creditors 2/22/67
No stockholders' equity

HARWILL, INC. (MI)
100% acquired by Browning Arms Co. through purchase offer which expired 06/30/1969
Public interest eliminated

HARWIN EXPL & DEV INC (BC)
Struck off register and declared dissolved for failure to file returns 06/23/1995

HARWOOD COS INC (NY)
Merged into MR Acquisition Corp. 6/9/83
Each share Common 1¢ par exchanged for $2.60 cash

HARWYN INDS CORP (NY)
Class A Common 10¢ par reclassified as Common 10¢ par 1/1/68
Common 10¢ par split (2) for (1) by issuance of (1) additional share 11/19/79
Common 10¢ par split (3) for (2) by issuance of (0.5) additional share 10/14/80
Out of Business in 1986
Details not available

HARWYN PUBLISHING CORP. (NY)
Name changed to Harwyn Industries Corp. 9/7/65
(See Harwyn Industries Corp.)

HARZFELDS INC (MO)
Name changed to FLM Industries, Inc. 4/1/72

HASAGA GOLD MINES LTD. (ON)
Merged into Little Long Lac Gold Mines Ltd. (The) 04/27/1967
Each share Capital Stock $1 par exchanged for (0.05) share Capital Stock no par
Little Long Lac Gold Mines Ltd. (The) merged into Little Long Lac Mines Ltd. 01/08/1971 which name changed to Little Long Lac Gold Mines Ltd. (New) 07/03/1975 which merged into LAC Minerals Ltd. (New) 07/29/1985 which was acquired by American Barrick Resources Corp. 10/17/1994 which name changed to Barrick Gold Corp. 01/18/1995

HASBRO BRADLEY, INC. (RI)
Common 50¢ par split (5) for (2) by issuance of (1.5) additional shares 1/25/85
Name changed to Hasbro Inc. 6/6/85

HASBRO INC (RI)
8% Conv. Preference $2.50 par called for redemption 09/15/1989
(Additional Information in Active)

HASBRO INDUSTRIES, INC. (RI)
Common 50¢ par split (3) for (2) by issuance of (0.5) additional share 8/19/82
Common 50¢ par split (3) for (2) by issuance of (0.5) additional share 2/18/83
Common 50¢ par split (3) for (2) by issuance of (0.5) additional share 8/19/83
Stock Dividend - 10% 5/27/81
Under plan of merger name changed to Hasbro Bradley, Inc. 9/10/84
Hasbro Bradley, Inc. name changed to Hasbro Inc. 6/6/85

HASCO MED INC (FL)
Acquired by WMK, Inc. 10/28/2015
Each share Common $0.001 par exchanged for $0.0233 cash

HASHINGSPACE CORP (NV)
Common $0.001 par split (30) for (1) by issuance of (29) additional shares payable 06/15/2015 to holders of record 06/15/2015
SEC revoked common stock registration 10/06/2017

HASINA RES CORP (BC)
Recapitalized as Bradbury International Equities Ltd. 11/05/1987
Each share Common no par exchanged for (0.5) share Common no par
Bradbury International Equities Ltd. recapitalized as Consolidated Bradbury International Equities Ltd. 10/05/1998 which recapitalized as Talus Ventures Corp. 04/17/2001 which name changed to SolutionInc Technologies Ltd. (BC) 06/26/2002 which reincorporated in Nova Scotia 02/24/2004

HASKEL INTL INC (CA)
Merged into HI Holdings Inc. 4/23/99
Each share Common no par exchanged for $12.90 cash

HASKELITE MANUFACTURING CORP. (NY)
Each share 8% Preferred $100 par exchanged for (2) shares $7 Preferred no par in 1930
Each share $7 Preferred no par exchanged for (4) shares Common $5 par in 1936
Each share Common no par exchanged for (1) share Common $5 par in 1936
Merged into Evans Products Co. 2/20/57
Each share Common $5 par exchanged for (1/3) share Common $5 par
(See Evans Products Co.)

HASKELL TELEPHONE CO.
Acquired by Southwestern Associated Telephone Co. in 1940
Details not available

HASKELL WM H MFG CO (RI)
Name changed to Commerce Corp. 10/23/68
(See Commerce Corp.)

HASTINGS CORP (NV)
Recapitalized as Anodyne Corp. 5/8/92
Each share Common $0.001 par exchanged for (0.1) share Common $0.001 par

HASTINGS ENTMT INC (TX)
Acquired by Draw Another Circle, LLC 07/15/2014
Each share Common 1¢ par exchanged for $3 cash

HASTINGS FINL CORP (MI)
Merged into First Financial Bancorp 1/1/97
Each share Common $1 par exchanged for (4.006632) shares Common 10¢ par

HASTINGS INDS INC (DE)
Charter cancelled and declared inoperative and void for non-payment of taxes 3/1/80

HASTINGS MFG CO (MI)
Common $2 par split (2) for (1) by issuance of (1) additional share payable 03/23/1998 to holders of record 03/02/1998
Stock Dividends - 100% 12/20/1943; 50% 10/15/1946
Chapter 11 bankruptcy proceedings converted to Chapter 7 on 04/18/2006
Stockholders' equity unlikely

HASTINGS MNG & DEV LTD (QC)
Completely liquidated 03/17/1969
Each share Capital Stock $1 par exchanged for first and final distribution of (0.16) share Sullivan Mines Ltd. Common no par
Sullivan Mines Ltd. merged into Sullivan Mining Group Ltd. 09/02/1969 which merged into Sullivan Mines Inc.-Mines Sullivan Inc. 07/01/1983
(See Sullivan Mines Inc.-Mines Sullivan Inc.)

HASTINGS RAYDIST INC (VA)
Acquired by Teledyne, Inc. 04/09/1968
Each share Capital Stock $1 par exchanged for (0.345639) share Common $1 par
Teledyne, Inc. merged into Allegheny Teledyne, Inc. 08/15/1996 which name changed to Allegheny Technologies Inc. 11/29/1999

HASTINGS RES CORP (BC)
Recapitalized as Trigen Resources Inc. 09/22/2010
Each share Common no par exchanged for (0.2) share Common no par
Trigen Resources Inc. recapitalized as BlissCo Cannabis Corp. 03/02/2018

HASTINGS SQUARE HOTEL CO (NJ)
Liquidation completed
Each share Capital Stock $100 par received first distribution of $300 cash 4/2/73
Each share Capital Stock $100 par received second distribution of $234 cash 11/15/73
Each share Capital Stock $100 par received third distribution of $20 cash 7/8/74
Each share Capital Stock $100 par received fourth distribution of $200 cash 1/3/77
Each share Capital Stock $100 par exchanged for fifth and final distribution of $52.65 cash 3/28/77

HAT CORP AMER (DE)
Each share 6-1/2% Preferred $100 par exchanged for (1) share 4-1/2% Preferred $100 par and $2.50 cash in 1945
Class A Common $1 par and Class B Common $1 par reclassified as Common $1 par in 1949
Each share 4-1/2% Preferred $100 par exchanged for (2) shares 4-1/2% Preferred $50 par in 1952
4-1/2% Preferred $50 par reclassified as 5% Preferred $50 par 2/24/61
Recapitalized 2/27/69
Each share 5% Preferred $50 par exchanged for (2.75) shares Common $3 par
Common $1 par changed to $3 par
Stock Dividends - 16-2/3% 11/22/48; 20% 11/29/49
Name changed to HCA Industries, Inc. 4/30/70
HCA Industries, Inc. name changed to HCA-Martin, Inc. 5/11/73 which name changed to Martin Processing, Inc. 5/16/75
(See Martin Processing, Inc.)

HAT CREEK ENERGY CORP (BC)
Recapitalized as Fairchild Resources Inc. 07/17/1986
Each share Capital Stock no par exchanged for (0.33333333) share Capital Stock no par
Fairchild Resources Inc. name changed to Fairchild Gold Corp. 11/18/1988 which recapitalized as First International Metals Corp. 12/07/1990 which recapitalized as Mill Bay Ventures Inc. 07/17/2000 which recapitalized as Great Thunder Gold Corp. 04/16/2013

HATCH INTL TECHNOLOGIES CORP (BC)
Name changed to Fandom Sports Media Corp. 08/03/2016

HATCO CAP INC (BC)
Name changed to SoftQuad International Inc. (BC) 12/07/1992
SoftQuad International Inc. (BC) reincorporated in Ontario 08/31/1994 which reincorporated in New Brunswick 09/18/1998 which name changed to NewKidco International Inc. 01/28/1999
(See NewKidco International Inc.)

HATCO HLDGS LTD (OR)
SEC revoked common stock registration 01/11/1997

HATFIELD-CAMPBELL CREEK COAL CO. (OH)
Each share 8% Preferred $100 par exchanged for (1) share Prior Preferred $12 par and (1) share Part. Preferred $100 par in 1934
Each share Common no par exchanged for (2/3) share new Common no par in 1934 5% Prior Preferred called for redemption 4/1/44
Part. Preferred called for redemption 7/1/52
Merged into Amherst Coal Co. 12/31/52
Each share Common no par exchanged for (0.025) share Common no par
Amherst Coal Co. merged into Diamond Shamrock Corp. 8/4/81 which name changed to Maxus Energy Corp. 4/30/87
(See Maxus Energy Corp.)

HATFIELD RELIANCE COAL CO.
Name changed to Hatfield-Campbell Creek Coal Co. in 1928
Hatfield-Campbell Creek Coal Co. merged into Amherst Coal Co. 12/31/52 which merged into Diamond Shamrock Corp. 8/4/81 which name changed to Maxus Energy Corp. 4/30/87
(See Maxus Energy Corp.)

HATHAWAY BAKERIES, INC. (DE)
Name changed to Hathaway Industries, Inc. 5/1/58
Hathaway Industries, Inc. name changed to Seaboard Allied Milling Corp. 10/12/59 which name changed to Seaboard Corp. (Incorporated 7/24/46) 1/29/82

HATHAWAY BAKERIES, INC. (MA)
Recapitalized under the laws of Delaware in 1946
Each share $7 Preferred no par exchanged for (5) shares Common $1 par and $100 in new Debentures
Each share Class A no par exchanged for (5) shares Common $1 par and $21.85 in new Debentures
Each share Class B Common no par exchanged for (1/3) share Common $1 par
Hathaway Bakeries, Inc. (DE) name changed to Hathaway Industries, Inc. 5/1/58 which name changed to Seaboard Allied Milling Corp. 10/12/59 which name changed to Seaboard Corp. (Incorporated 7/24/46) 1/29/82

HATHAWAY BAKING CO.
Merged into Hathaway Bakeries, Inc. (MA) in 1928
Details not available

HATHAWAY (C.F.) CO. (ME)
Liquidation completed 11/30/60
Details not available

HATHAWAY CORP (CO)
Name changed 9/16/82
Common 50¢ par changed to no par 8/19/82
Name changed from Hathaway Instruments, Inc. to Hathaway Corp. 9/16/82
Common no par split (3) for (2) by issuance of (0.5) additional share 4/11/85
Stock Dividends - 25% 12/11/81; 100% 10/29/82
Name changed to Allied Motion Technologies Inc. 10/25/2002

HATHAWAY INC (DE)
Each share Common $0.0001 par received distribution of (0.5) share OptiCon Systems, Inc. Common $0.001 par payable 08/31/2007 to holders of record 02/19/2007
Ex date - 08/13/2007
Recapitalized as Isys Medical Inc. 05/29/2008
Each share Common $0.0001 par exchanged for (0.05) share Common $0.0001 par
Isys Medical Inc. name changed to FutureWorld Energy, Inc. 04/06/2009 which name changed to FutureWorld Corp. 07/17/2014

HATHAWAY INDUSTRIES, INC. (DE)
Name changed to Seaboard Allied Milling Corp. 8/12/59
Seaboard Allied Milling Corp. name changed to Seaboard Corp. (Incorporated 7/24/46) 1/29/82

HATHAWAY INSTRUMENTS, INC. (DE)
Merged into Lionel Corp. 11/3/61
Each share Common $1 par exchanged for (1/3) share 3-3/4% Preferred $20 par
(See Lionel Corp.)

HATHAWAY MANUFACTURING CO. (MA)
Capital Stock $100 par changed to $25 par and (3) additional shares issued in 1948
Stock Dividend - 100% 12/20/47
Merged into Berkshire Hathaway Inc. (MA) 3/14/55
Each share Capital Stock $25 par exchanged for (4) shares Common $5 par
Berkshire Hathaway Inc. (MA) reincorporated in Delaware 8/27/73

HATHAWAY METAL MINES LTD (ON)
Charter cancelled for failure to pay taxes and file returns 03/16/1976

HATHOR EXPL LTD (CANADA)
Acquired by Rio Tinto PLC 01/11/2012
Each share Common no par exchanged for $4.70 cash

HATLEIGH CORP NEW (ON)
Name changed 08/31/1978
Under plan of merger name changed from Hatleigh Corp. (Old) to Hatleigh Corp. (New) and each (5) shares no par exchanged for (2) Class A Special shares $7 par and (3) Class B Special shares $7 par 08/31/1978
Merged into Dexleigh Corp. 06/30/1984
Each Class A Special Share $7 par exchanged for (1) share Common no par and (1) Common Stock Purchase Warrant expiring 12/31/1986
(See Dexleigh Corp.)

HATTERAS FINL CORP (MD)
Merged into Annaly Capital Management, Inc. 07/12/2016
Each share 7.625% Preferred Ser. A $0.001 par exchanged for (1) share 7.625% Preferred Ser. E 1¢ par
Each share Common $0.001 par exchanged for (0.9894) share Common 1¢ par and $5.55 cash

HATTERAS INCOME SECS INC (NC)
Completely liquidated
Each share Common $1 par received first and final distribution of $14.823604 cash payable 3/7/2005 to holders of record 3/7/2005
Note: Certificates were not required to be surrendered and are without value

HATTERAS YACHT CO. (NC)
Completely liquidated 5/14/68
Each share Capital Stock 33-1/3¢ par exchanged for first and final distribution of (0.113586) share North American Rockwell Corp. $4.75 Conv. Preferred Ser. A no par
North American Rockwell Corp. merged into Rockwell International Corp. (Old) 2/16/73 which merged into Boeing Co. 12/6/96

HATTHAWAY MATHESON ENTERPRISES INC (BC)
Name changed to Innovis Corp. (BC) 10/08/1993
Innovis Corp. (BC) reincorporated in Wyoming 10/15/1993
(See Innovis Corp. (WY))

HATTIE CARNEGIE JEWELRY ENTERPRISES LTD (NY)
Name changed to Carnegie Industries, Inc. 12/20/76
(See Carnegie Industries, Inc.)

HATTON CAP CORP (CANADA)
Issue Information - 800,000 shares COM offered at $0.25 per share on 05/07/2004
Name changed to Nevgold Resource Corp. 12/29/2006
Nevgold Resource Corp. merged into Silver Predator Corp. 02/28/2012

HAUGHTON ELEVATOR CO. (OH)
Merged into Toledo Scale Corp. share for share 11/19/57
Toledo Scale Corp. merged into Reliance Electric & Engineering Co. 12/29/67 which reincorporated in Delaware as Reliance Electric Co. 2/28/69
(See Reliance Electric Co.)

HAULTAIN RES LTD (BC)
Name changed to Canasia Industries Corp. 09/19/1986
Canasia Industries Corp. recapitalized as Makena Resources Inc. 01/23/2013

HAUSER INC (DE)
Reincorporated 12/3/96
Reincorporated 12/9/99
Each share old Common $0.001 par exchanged for (0.1) share new Common $0.001 par 2/21/90
Name and place of incorporation changed from Hauser Chemical Research Inc. (DE) to Hauser Inc. (CO) 12/3/96
Each share old Common $0.001 par exchanged for (0.2) share new Common $0.001 par 6/11/99
State of incorporation changed from (CO) to (DE) 12/9/99
Plan of reorganization under Chapter 11 Federal Bankruptcy Code effective 1/12/2005
Holders are expected to receive an undetermined amount of cash

HAUSERMAN E F CO (OH)
Name changed to Hauserman, Inc. 6/3/70
(See Hauserman, Inc.)

HAUSERMAN INC (OH)
Common $1 par split (3) for (2) by issuance of (0.5) additional share 06/25/1982
Stock Dividend - 100% 10/01/1976
Plan of reorganization under Chapter 11 Bankruptcy proceedings confirmed 04/12/1999
No stockholders' equity

HAUSMAN CORP (OH)
Voting Trust Agreement terminated 7/14/67
$1.14 Conv. Preferred $5 par called for redemption 10/22/74
$1.50 Preferred called for redemption 10/22/74
Each VTC for Common $5 par exchanged for (1) share Common $5 par
Merged into Penn-Dixie Steel Corp. 11/23/74
Each share Common $5 par exchanged for $26 cash

HAUSMAN STEEL CO. (OH)
Name changed to Hausman Corp. 4/26/65
(See Hausman Corp.)

HAV INFO COMPUTERS INC (BC)
Recapitalized as National Hav-Info Communications Inc. (BC) 08/14/1989
Each share Common no par exchanged for (0.2) share Common no par
National Hav-Info Communications Inc. (BC) reincorporated in Canada 08/13/1993 which name changed to NHC Communications Inc. 02/02/1995
(See NHC Communications Inc.)

HAVA JAVA CATERERS OF COLORADO, INC. (CO)
Adjudicated bankrupt 04/03/1963
Stockholders' equity unlikely

HAVANA DOCKS CORP (DE)
Common no par changed to $40 par in 1946
Common $40 par changed to $5 par 9/17/63
Under plan of partial liquidation Common $5 par changed to no par and each share received distribution of $15 cash 5/9/72
Note: Additional distributions are dependant upon collection from Cuban government

HAVANA ELECTRIC & UTILITIES CO.
Dissolved in 1951
Details not available

HAVANA ELECTRIC RAILWAY CO. (ME)
Out of business 6/8/53
Details not available

HAVANA FURNISHINGS INC (NV)
Name changed to NuZee, Inc. 05/15/2013

HAVANA GROUP INC (DE)
Name changed to Surge Global Energy, Inc. 10/12/2004

HAVANA NATL BK (HAVANA, IL)
Merged into Community Investment Group Ltd. 7/25/2000
Each share Common exchanged for (5) shares Common $4 par

HAVANA RACING CO., INC. (DE)
No longer in existence having become inoperative and void for non-payment of taxes 4/1/60

HAVANA REP INC (CO)
Reincorporated under the laws of Florida 11/25/1997
Havana Republic Inc. (FL) name changed to Delek Resources, Inc. 09/27/2004
(See Delek Resources, Inc.)

HAVANA REP INC (FL)
Each (300) shares old Common no par exchanged for (1) share new Common no par 07/24/2003
Name changed to Delek Resources, Inc. 09/27/2004
(See Delek Resources, Inc.)

HAVARI VENDING CORP (NJ)
Charter declared void for non-payment of taxes 1/16/80

HAVAS (FRANCE)
Acquired by Vivendi Universal 00/00/1999
Details not available

HAVAS S A (FRANCE)
Name changed 05/24/2002
Name changed from Havas Advertising S.A. to Havas S.A. 05/24/2002
ADR agreement terminated 07/28/2006
Each Sponsored ADR for Ordinary exchanged for $4.42687 cash
ADR agreement terminated 10/10/2018
No ADR's remain outstanding

HAVATAMPA CIGAR CORP. (FL)
Each share Common $1 par exchanged for (2/15) share Common $7.50 par 6/29/66
Stock Dividend - 10% 12/17/74
Name changed to Havatampa Corp. 7/28/75
Havatampa Corp. name changed to Eli Securities Co. 7/29/77
(See Eli Securities Co.)

HAVATAMPA CORP (FL)
Name changed to Eli Securities Co. and Common $7.50 par changed to 10¢ par 7/29/77
(See Eli Securities Co.)

HAVE GUN WILL TRAVEL ENTMT INC (NV)
Name changed to Image Chain Group Ltd., Inc. 06/11/2015

HAVEG INDUSTRIES, INC. (DE)
Each share Capital Stock $5 par received (0.9) share Budd Co. Common $5 par 10/17/1955
Each share Capital Stock $5 par exchanged for (3) shares Common $1 par 04/24/1958
Common $1 par changed to 40¢ par and (1.5) additional shares issued 05/24/1961
Acquired by Hercules Powder Co. 07/31/1964
Each share Common 40¢ par exchanged for (0.4) share $1.65 Conv. Class A no par
Hercules Powder Co. name changed to Hercules Inc. 04/29/1966
(See Hercules Inc.)

HAVELOCK ENERGY & RES INC (ON)
Recapitalized as Municipal Ticket Corp. 03/04/1994
Each share Common no par exchanged for (1/3) share Common no par
Municipal Ticket Corp. recapitalized as I.D. Investments Inc. 11/18/1994 which recapitalized as BioLink Corp. 03/12/1997 which recapitalized as First Empire Entertainment.com Inc. 03/31/2000 which recapitalized as First Empire Corp. 08/14/2003 which reorganized as Noble House Entertainment Inc. (ON) 11/01/2004 which reincorporated in Canada as LiveReel Media Corp. 12/01/2006

HAVELOCK RESOURCES INTERNATIONAL, INC. (CO)
Charter suspended for failure to file annual reports 9/30/83

HAVEMEYERS & ELDER, INC. (NY)
Liquidation completed 1/11/60
Each share Capital Stock $100 par exchanged for (1) share Capital Stock $30 par and $59.07895 1st Mortgage Bonds of Brooklyn Eastern District Terminal

HAVEN BANCORP INC (DE)
Common 1¢ par split (2) for (1) by issuance of (1) additional share payable 11/28/97 to holders of record 10/31/97
Merged into New York Community Bancorp, Inc. 11/30/2000
Each share Common 1¢ par exchanged for (1.04) shares Common 1¢ par

HAVEN FEDERAL SAVINGS & LOAN ASSOCIATION (USA)
Merged into Admiral Financial Corp. 06/16/1988
Each share Common 10¢ par exchanged for (1.3325359) shares Common $0.001 par
(See Admiral Financial Corp.)

HAVEN FINL INC (DE)
Recapitalized as Asia-Pacific Group, Inc. 2/9/99
Each share Common $0.001 par exchanged for (0.05) share Common $0.001 par
Asia-Pacific Group, Inc. name changed to IVAT Industries Inc. 9/13/2001

HAVEN HOMES INC (DE)
Recapitalized as Haven Financial, Inc. 6/15/98
Each share Common $0.001 par exchanged for (0.01) share Common $0.001 par
Haven Financial, Inc. recapitalized as Asia-Pacific Group, Inc. 2/9/99 which name changed to IVAT Industries Inc. 9/13/2001

HAVEN INDS INC (DE)
Each share Common 10¢ par exchanged for (0.25) share Common 1¢ par 4/19/68
Name changed to Federated Communications Corp. 4/29/75
(See Federated Communications Corp.)

HAVEN INTL PICTURES INC (NY)
Name changed to Kundan Investment Corp. 01/26/1989
Kundan Investment Corp. name changed to Silent Partner Body Armor, Inc. 01/26/1989
(See Silent Partner Body Armor, Inc.)

HAVEN LIFE INSURANCE CO. (FL)
Merged into George Washington Life Insurance Co. 03/07/1966
Each share Common $2 par exchanged for (2) shares Common $1 par
(See George Washington Life Insurance Co.)

HAVENWOOD VENTURES INC (DE)
Recapitalized as Boots & Coots International Well Control, Inc. 07/29/1997
Each (135) shares Common $0.00001 par exchanged for (1) share Common $0.00001 par
Note: No holder will receive fewer than (100) post-split shares
Boots & Coots International Well Control, Inc. name changed to Boots & Coots, Inc. 06/23/2009 which merged into Halliburton Co. 09/17/2010

HAVERFIELD CORP (OH)
Stock Dividends - 10% 10/1/93; 10% 10/1/95
Merged into Charter One Financial, Inc. 9/19/97
Each share Common 1¢ par exchanged for (0.4952) share Common 1¢ par
(See Charter One Financial, Inc.)

HAVERHILL ELECTRIC CO. (MA)
Merged into Merrimack-Essex Electric Co. on a (1.875) for (1) basis 7/30/57 which Common was acquired by New England Electric System 6/30/59
(See New England Electric System)

HAVERHILL GAS CO (MA)
Common $25 par changed to $10 par and (1.5) additional shares issued 6/11/56
Common $10 par changed to $5 par and (1) additional share issued 6/30/81
Name changed to Essex County Gas Co. 1/18/83
Essex County Gas Co. merged into Eastern Enterprises 9/30/98
(See Eastern Enterprises)

HAVERHILL GAS LIGHT CO. (MA)
Name changed to Haverhill Gas Co. 4/11/55
Haverhill Gas Co. name changed to Essex County Gas Co. 1/18/83 which merged into Eastern Enterprises 9/30/98
(See Eastern Enterprises)

HAWAII BANCORPORATION INC (HI)
Stock Dividend - 10% 3/10/78
Name changed to Bancorp Hawaii, Inc. 1/2/80
Bancorp Hawaii, Inc. name changed to Pacific Century Financial Corp. (HI) 4/25/97 which reincorporated in Delaware 4/24/98 which name changed to Bank of Hawaii Corp. 4/26/2002

HAWAII CLAY PRODUCTS, INC. (HI)
Proclaimed dissolved for failure to file annual reports 2/10/69

HAWAII CONSOLIDATED RWY. LTD.
Dissolved in 1947
Details not available

HAWAII CORP (HI)
Reorganized under Chapter X bankruptcy proceedings 12/30/80
No stockholders' equity

HAWAII FURNITURE LEASE (UT)
Each share Common $0.005 par exchanged for (0.05) share Common 10¢ par 1/29/73
Name changed to Metals Research Corp. of America 3/5/85
Metals Research Corp. of America name changed to Metals Research Group Corp. 12/15/97

HAWAII LD & FARMING CO (DE)
Merged into HLFC Acquisition Inc. 3/28/2000
Each share Class A Common 1¢ par exchanged for $0.50 cash
Each share Class B Common 1¢ par exchanged for $0.50 cash

HAWAII LD CORP (DE)
Charter cancelled and declared inoperative and void for non-payment of taxes 3/1/81

HAWAII PAC GROWTH FD INC (DE)
Charter cancelled and declared inoperative and void for non-payment of taxes 3/1/83

HAWAII THERMAL POWER CO. (DE)
Name changed to Geothermal Resources International, Inc. 10/22/65
(See Geothermal Resources International, Inc.)

HAWAII VENTURES INC (UT)
Recapitalized as Infinity Worldwide Inc. 8/10/92
Each (35) shares Common $0.001 par exchanged for (1) share Common $0.001 par

HAWAIIAN AGRIC CO (HI)
Common $20 par changed to $6-2/3 par and (2) additional shares issued 8/23/65
Merged into Ka'u Sugar Co., Inc. 12/29/72
Each share Common $6-2/3 par

exchanged for (1) share Common $10 par
(See Ka'u Sugar Co., Inc.)

HAWAIIAN AIRLINES, LTD. (HI)
Each share Capital Stock $10 par exchanged for (2) shares Capital Stock $5 par in 1950
Capital Stock $5 par changed to $3 par 4/22/55
Name changed to Hawaiian Airlines, Inc. (Old) 4/28/60
Hawaiian Airlines, Inc. (Old) reorganized as HAL, Inc. 1/1/85
(See HAL, Inc.)

HAWAIIAN AIRLS INC NEW (HI)
Class A Common 1¢ par reclassified as Common 1¢ par 07/15/1996
Reincorporated under the laws of Delaware as Hawaiian Holdings, Inc. 08/29/2002

HAWAIIAN AIRLS INC OLD (HI)
Stock Dividends - 10% 12/30/65; 50% 5/18/67; 10% 12/20/74
Under plan of reorganization each share Capital Stock $3 par automatically became (1) share HAL, Inc. Capital Stock $3 par 1/1/85
(See HAL, Inc.)

HAWAIIAN CANNERIES CO. LTD. (HI)
Liquidation completed
Each share Capital Stock $20 par exchanged for initial distribution of $30 cash 9/15/66
Each share Capital Stock $20 par received second and final distribution of $3.082 cash 10/4/66

HAWAIIAN COMMERCIAL & SUGAR CO., LTD. (HI)
Each share Common $25 par exchanged for (4) shares Common $10 par 00/00/1948
Merged into Alexander & Baldwin Inc. (Old) on a (0.6) for (1) basis 01/01/1962
Alexander & Baldwin Inc. (Old) name changed to Alexander & Baldwin Holdings, Inc. 06/06/2012 which name changed to Matson, Inc. 06/29/2012

HAWAIIAN ELEC INC (HI)
$1.44 Conv. Preferred Ser. L $20 par called for redemption 4/15/85
Under plan of reorganization each share Common $6-2/3 par automatically became (1) share Hawaiian Electric Industries, Inc. Common $6-2/3 par 7/1/83
8.05% Preferred Ser. M $100 par called for redemption at $101 on 1/15/99
7.68% Preferred Ser. Q $100 par called for redemption at $108.56 on 1/15/99
8.75% Preferred Ser. R $100 par called for redemption at $103.50 on 1/15/99
(Additional Information in Active)

HAWAIIAN ELEC INDS CAP TR I (DE)
8.36% Trust Originated Preferred Securities called for redemption at $25 on 04/16/2004

HAWAIIAN ELECTRIC CO. LTD. (HI)
5% Preferred Ser. B called for redemption 1/15/62
Common $20 par changed to $6-2/3 par and (2) additional shares issued 3/9/62
5-1/2% Preferred Ser. F $20 par called for redemption 7/1/63
5-3/4% Preferred Ser. G $20 par called for redemption 1/15/64
Stock Dividend - 10% 4/30/56
Name changed to Hawaiian Electric Co., Inc. 3/16/64

HAWAIIAN INTERNATIONAL FINANCES INC. (HI)
Name changed to United Hawaiian Investment Corp. 04/30/1966

(See United Hawaiian Investment Corp.)

HAWAIIAN LANES, INC. (HI)
Foreclosed in July 1967
No stockholders' equity

HAWAIIAN LEGEND INC (DE)
Name changed to Liberty International Entertainment Inc. 1/9/2002

HAWAIIAN NAT WTR INC (HI)
Issue Information - 2,000,000 Units consisting of (1) share COM and (1) WT offered at $4 per Unit on 05/14/1997
Merged into Amcon Distributing Co. 12/17/2001
Each share Common no par exchanged for (0.052) share Common 1¢ par

HAWAIIAN PAC INDS INC (HI)
Acquired by Lone Star Cement Corp. (DE) 3/12/70
Each share Common no par exchanged for (0.75) share Common $1 par
Lone Star Cement Corp. (DE) name changed to Lone Star Industries, Inc. 5/20/71
(See Lone Star Industries, Inc.)

HAWAIIAN PALISADE HOMES INC (NV)
Name changed to AAA Manufacturing, Inc. 09/27/2004
AAA Manufacturing, Inc. recapitalized as Gulf West Property, Inc. (NV) 03/10/2005 which reincorporated in Colorado as Titan Global Entertainment, Inc. 11/10/2005 which recapitalized as Sunset Island Group, Inc. 05/30/2008

HAWAIIAN PHILIPPINE CO (PHILIPPINES)
7% Preferred P10 par called for redemption 06/01/1969
Stock Dividends - 20% 09/20/1962; 36.05852% 03/29/1974; 88.34% 05/22/1975; 20% 08/06/1976; 20% 05/04/1977
Acquired by Silay-Saravia Railways Cooperative 00/00/2005
Details not available

HAWAIIAN PINEAPPLE CO. LTD. (HI)
Common $5 par changed to no par in 1937 and to $7.50 par 11/28/55
Name changed to Dole Corp. 9/30/60
Dole Corp. merged into Castle & Cooke, Inc. (Old) 6/1/61 which name changed to Dole Food Co., Inc. (HI) 7/30/91 which reincorporated in Delaware 7/1/2001
(See Dole Food Co., Inc. (DE))

HAWAIIAN RANCH CO., INC. (HI)
Merged into Brewer (C.) & Co., Ltd. 6/16/64
Each share Common no par exchanged for (0.548) share Common no par
Brewer (C.) & Co., Ltd. merged into IU International Corp. 8/14/78
(See IU International Corp.)

HAWAIIAN SUGAR CO.
In process of dissolution in 1941
Details not available

HAWAIIAN SUGAR TECHNOLOGIES INC (NY)
Recapitalized as Entertainment Inns of America, Inc. 10/21/1983
Each share Common 1¢ par exchanged for (0.25) share Common 1¢ par
Entertainment Inns of America, Inc. name changed to Tiger Marketing, Inc. 11/08/1984 which recapitalized as U.S. Health Services, Inc. 04/08/1986 which name changed to Diamond Trade Center, Inc. 10/30/1990
(See Diamond Trade Center, Inc.)

HAWAIIAN SUMATRA PLANTATIONS, LTD. (HI)
Capital Stock $15 par changed to $10 par 00/00/1934
Name changed to American-Hawaii Ventures, Inc. 01/08/1963
(See American-Hawaii Ventures, Inc.)

HAWAIIAN TELCOM HOLDCO INC (DE)
Merged into Cincinnati Bell, Inc. (New) 07/02/2018
Each share Common 1¢ par exchanged for (0.6522) share new Common 1¢ par and $18.45 cash

HAWAIIAN TELEPHONE CO. (HI)
Common $10 par changed to $5 par and (1) additional share issued 5/1/61
5-1/2% Preferred Ser. D $10 par called for redemption 6/12/63
5.30% Preferred Ser. E $10 par called for redemption 6/12/63
5% Preferred Ser. B $10 par called for redemption 3/12/65
Merged into General Telephone & Electronics Corp. 5/17/67
Each share 4.8% Preferred Ser. A $10 par exchanged for (0.2) share 5.05% Conv. Preferred $50 par
Each share 5.1% Preferred Ser. C $10 par exchanged for (0.2) share 5.35% Conv. Preferred $50 par
Each share 5.25% Preferred Ser. F $10 par exchanged for (0.2) share 5.50% Conv. Preferred $50 par
Each share 4.5% Preferred Ser. G $10 par exchanged for (0.2) share 4.75% Conv. Preferred $50 par
Each share Common $5 par exchanged for (1) share Common $3.33-1/3 par
General Telephone & Electronics Corp. name changed to GTE Corp. 7/1/82 which merged into Verizon Communications Inc. 6/30/2000

HAWAIIAN TR LTD (HONOLULU, HI)
Each share Capital Stock $100 par exchanged for (5) shares Capital Stock $20 par in 1944
Capital Stock $20 par changed to $10 par and (1) additional share issued 8/31/62
Stock Dividends - 18% 1/15/69; 11-1/9% 12/16/63
Acquired by Bancorp Hawaii, Inc. 2/8/85
Each share Capital Stock $10 par exchanged for $101.29 cash
Each share Capital Stock $10 par received an additional and final distribution of $1.61 cash 1/31/90

HAWAIIAN VINTAGE CHOCOLATE CO (HI)
Company terminated common stock registration and is no longer public as of 10/12/2004

HAWAIIAN WESTN STL LTD (DE)
Charter cancelled and declared inoperative and void for non-payment of taxes 03/24/1998

HAWAIIAN WINES INC (WV)
Name changed to River View Vintners, Inc. 3/1/72
(See River View Vintners, Inc.)

HAWAIILOVE COM INC (DE)
Name changed to Ornate Solutions Inc. 8/2/2001
Ornate Solutions Inc. recapitalized as Ornate Holdings Inc. 9/20/2001 which name changed to Absolute Health & Fitness, Inc. 5/14/2004

HAWK CORP (DE)
Acquired by Carlisle Companies Inc. 12/01/2010
Each share Class A Common 1¢ par exchanged for $50 cash

HAWK ENERGY CORP (AB)
Acquired by Flagship Energy Inc. 05/17/2006
Each share Class A Common no par exchanged for (1.5566) shares Class A no par
Each share Class B Common no par exchanged for (1.8868) shares Class A no par
Flagship Energy Inc. recapitalized as Insignia Energy Ltd. 08/08/2008
(See Insignia Energy Ltd.)

HAWK ENTERPRISES INC (UT)
Recapitalized as Amco Energy Corp. 12/16/1974
Each share Common no par exchanged for (0.16666666) share Common no par
Amco Energy Corp. name changed to Amcole Energy Corp. 07/12/1978
(See Amcole Energy Corp.)

HAWK EXPL LTD (AB)
Each share Class B no par exchanged for (10) shares Class A Common no par 07/31/2014
Acquired by Kaisen Energy Corp. 07/18/2016
Each share Class A Common no par exchanged for $0.08 cash
Note: Unexchanged certificates will be cancelled and become without value 07/17/2019

HAWK INTL INC (UT)
Each share old Common 1¢ par exchanged for (0.1) share new Common 1¢ par 07/31/1997
Name changed to Beverly Hills Country Club Inc. 02/26/1998
Beverly Hills Country Club Inc. name changed to Beverly Hills Inc. 08/14/1998 which name changed to Aladdin Trading & Co. (UT) 08/01/2006 which reincorporated in Florida as Caribbean Casino & Gaming Corp. 05/15/2009 which recapitalized as Caribbean International Holdings, Inc. 01/17/2013

HAWK-JEN MINING CORP. LTD. (SK)
Struck off Saskatchewan register for non-payment of fees 09/27/1963

HAWK MFG INC (NY)
Completely liquidated 2/16/73
Each share Common 1¢ par exchanged for first and final distribution of (0.5) share National Recycled Containers Corp. Common 1¢ par
National Recycled Containers Corp. name changed to Natcontainer Corp. 12/1/74
(See Natcontainer Corp.)

HAWK MARINE PWR INC (FL)
Reincorporated 08/25/1989
State of incorporation changed from (UT) to (FL) 08/25/1989
Each (12) shares Common $0.001 par exchanged for (1) share Common $0.001 par
Recapitalized as Alchemy Holdings Inc. 05/20/1997
Each share new Common $0.001 par exchanged for (0.0125) share Common $0.001 par
(See Alchemy Holdings Inc.)

HAWK OIL INC (AB)
Each share Class B Subordinate no par exchanged for (3.315) shares Class A Common no par 07/13/2001
Acquired by APF Energy Trust 02/06/2003
Each share Class A Common no par exchanged for (0.5079365) Trust Unit no par
(See APF Energy Trust)

HAWK RES INC (BC)
Recapitalized as Zicor Mining Inc. (BC) 08/02/1995
Each share Common no par exchanged for (0.25) share Common no par
Zicor Mining Inc. (BC) reincorporated in Yukon 00/00/1996 which name changed to Mano River Resources Inc. (YT) 09/18/1998 which

reincorporated in British Columbia 07/19/2004 which recapitalized as African Aura Mining Inc. 10/14/2009
(See African Aura Mining Inc.)

HAWK URANIUM INC (ON)
Name changed 04/02/2007
Name changed from Hawk Precious Minerals Inc. to Hawk Uranium Inc. 04/02/2007
Name changed to Ring of Fire Resources Inc. 07/30/2010
Ring of Fire Resources Inc. name changed to Noble Mineral Exploration Inc. 03/07/2012

HAWKER INDUSTRIES LTD. (CANADA)
Merged into Hawker Siddeley Canada Ltd. 10/02/1978
Each share Common no par exchanged for (2) shares Conv. Class A Common no par
Hawker Siddeley Canada Ltd. name changed to Hawker Siddeley Canada Inc. 07/29/1980 which was acquired by Glacier Ventures International Corp. (Canada) (New) 09/12/2001 which name changed to Glacier Media Inc. 07/01/2008

HAWKER PAC AEROSPACE (CA)
Issue Information - 2,766,667 shares COM offered at $8 per share on 01/29/1998
Merged into Lufthansa Technik AG 4/15/2002
Each share Common no par exchanged for $3.25 cash

HAWKER RES INC (AB)
Name changed to Iteration Energy Ltd. 07/11/2005
Iteration Energy Ltd. merged into Chinook Energy Inc. (Old) 07/05/2010
(See Chinook Energy Inc. (Old))

HAWKER SIDDELEY CDA INC (CANADA)
Name changed 07/29/1980
Common no par reclassified as Conv. Class A Common no par 11/03/1976
Conv. Class A Common no par reclassified as Common no par 07/06/1979
Conv. Class B Common no par reclassified as Common no par 07/06/1979
Name changed from Hawker Siddeley Canada Ltd. to Hawker Siddeley Canada Inc. 07/29/1980
5.75% Preferred $100 par called for redemption 08/15/1996
Acquired by Glacier Ventures International Corp. (Canada) (New) 09/12/2001
Each share Common no par exchanged for (0.63) share Common no par or $0.77 cash
Note: Non-electing and U.S. holders received cash only
Glacier Ventures International Corp. (Canada) (New) name changed to Glacier Media Inc. 07/01/2008

HAWKER SIDDELEY GROUP PLC (ENGLAND)
Ordinary Registered Stock £1 par changed to 25p par and (3) additional shares issued 07/08/1977
Acquired by BTR PLC 11/00/1991
Details not available

HAWKER URANIUM MINES LTD. (AB)
Merged into Inland Resources Corp. on 08/08/1956
Each share Common no par exchanged for (0.25) share Common 2¢ par
Inland Resources Corp. merged into Universal Major Corp. 10/10/1966 which name changed to Universal Major Industries Corp. 12/19/1966
(See Universal Major Industries Corp.)

HAWKEYE BANCORPORATION (IA)
Class A $3 par reclassified as Common $3 par 04/01/1974
Stock Dividend - 10% 07/15/1978
Merged into Mercantile Bancorporation, Inc. 01/02/1996
Each share Common $3 par exchanged for (0.585) share Common $5 par
Mercantile Bancorporation, Inc. merged into Firstar Corp. (New) 09/20/1999 which merged into U.S. Bancorp (DE) 02/27/2001

HAWKEYE BANK & TRUST CO. (BURLINGTON, IA)
Acquired by Two Rivers Bank & Trust (Burlington, IA) 07/01/2009
Details not available

HAWKEYE CASUALTY CO.
Name changed to Hawkeye-Security Insurance Co. in 1950
(See Hawkeye-Security Insurance Co.)

HAWKEYE COMMUNICATIONS INC (IA)
Name changed to Heritage Communications, Inc. 4/16/73
Heritage Communications, Inc. acquired by Tele-Communications, Inc. (Old) 8/11/87 which merged into Tele-Communications, Inc. (New) 8/5/94 which merged into AT&T Corp. 3/9/99 which merged into AT&T Inc. 11/18/2005

HAWKEYE DEVS LTD (BC)
Name changed to Western Garnet Co., Ltd. 06/22/1992
Western Garnet Co., Ltd. name changed to Western Garnet International Ltd. 07/05/1996 which name changed to WGI Heavy Minerals, Inc. 11/27/2002
(See WGI Heavy Minerals, Inc.)

HAWKEYE GOLD CORP (BC)
Recapitalized as Hawkeye Gold International Inc. 12/17/1998
Each share Common no par exchanged for (0.25) share Common no par
Hawkeye Gold International Inc. recapitalized as Hawkeye Gold & Diamond Inc. 05/29/2003

HAWKEYE GOLD INTL INC (BC)
Recapitalized as Hawkeye Gold & Diamond Inc. 05/29/2003
Each share Common no par exchanged for (0.25) share Common no par

HAWKEYE INDS INC (UT)
Proclaimed dissolved for failure to file reports 12/31/86

HAWKEYE NATL INVT CO (IA)
Completely liquidated 12/22/78
Each (7.6) shares Common $1 par exchanged for first and final distribution of (1) share Hawkeye National Life Insurance Co. Common $1 par
(See Hawkeye National Life Insurance Co.)

HAWKEYE NATL LIFE INS CO (IA)
100% acquired by GAN Vie through purchase offer which expired 02/25/1982

HAWKEYE PORTLAND CEMENT CO.
Dissolved in 1940

HAWKEYE PRODUCING & REFINING CO. (IA)
Charter revoked for failure to file reports and pay fees 4/17/22

HAWKEYE SEC INS CO (IA)
Each share Common $10 par exchanged for (10) shares Common $1 par 04/22/1966
Under plan of merger each share Common $1 par exchanged for $42 cash 02/01/1978
Preferred $50 par called for redemption at $50 on 07/15/2008

HAWKEYE VENTURES INC (AB)
Name changed to Puma Exploration Inc. 07/16/2003

HAWKINS CHEM INC (MN)
Common 10¢ par changed to 5¢ par 02/17/1983
Common 5¢ par split (2) for (1) by issuance of (1) additional share 04/21/1989
Stock Dividends - 50% 01/17/1975; 20% 04/15/1976; 30% 03/24/1977; 30% 03/31/1978; 30% 03/23/1979; 15% 03/21/1980; 15% 03/20/1981; 15% 04/02/1982; 15% 03/31/1983; 10% 03/30/1984; 10% 04/19/1985; 10% 03/14/1986; 10% 04/24/1987; 10% 04/22/1988; 10% 04/12/1995; 5% payable 04/12/1996 to holders of record 03/29/1996; 5% payable 04/11/1997 to holders of record 03/28/1997
Name changed to Hawkins, Inc. 03/13/2001

HAWKINS ENERGY CORP (OK)
Name changed to Equity Compression Services Corp. 12/19/1996
Equity Compression Services Corp. name changed to OEC Compression Corp. 04/15/1998 which merged into Hanover Compressor Co. 03/19/2001 which merged into Exterran Holdings, Inc. 08/20/2007 which name changed to Archrock, Inc. 11/04/2015

HAWKINS EXPLORATION 1985 LIMITED PARTNERSHIP (OK)
Through exchange offer 100% acquired by Hawkins Energy Corp. as of 12/20/1989
Public interest eliminated

HAWKPOINT GOLD MINES LTD. (ON)
Charter surrendered 01/16/1962

HAWKS INDS INC (NV)
Reorganized 02/02/1998
Reincorporated 02/18/2000
Reorganized from under the laws of (DE) to (WY) 02/02/1998
Each share Common 1¢ par exchanged for (0.05) share Common 1¢ par
State of incorporation changed from (WY) to (NV) 02/18/2000
Stock Dividend - 7.5% payable 06/01/2000 to holders of record 05/01/2000
Name changed to Emex Corp. 02/20/2001
(See Emex Corp.)

HAWKSBILL RES INC (BC)
Delisted from Vancouver Stock Exchange 04/07/1986

HAWKSDALE FINL VISIONS INC (NV)
Name changed to Advanced Medical Institute, Inc. 10/15/2005
(See Advanced Medical Institute, Inc.)

HAWKSTONE ENERGY CORP (BC)
Name changed to Range Energy Resources Inc. (New) 11/17/2011

HAWKWOOD INDS INC (AB)
Name changed 09/21/1989
Name changed from Hawkwood Energy Ltd. to Hawkwood Industries Inc. 09/21/1989
Recapitalized as Environmental Containment Systems Ltd. 08/24/1992
Each share Common no par exchanged for (0.2) share Common no par
Environmental Containment Systems Ltd. recapitalized as ATC Environmental Group Inc. 01/20/1994 which name changed to ATC Petroleum Services International Inc. 09/25/2001 which recapitalized as Tiger Pacific Mining Corp. (AB) 02/03/2004 which reincorporated in British Columbia

07/29/2004 which recapitalized as Chantrell Ventures Corp. 08/31/2010

HAWLEY PRODUCTS CO. (DE)
Stock Dividend - 10% 1/31/67
Completely liquidated 9/18/67
Each share Common $5 par exchanged for first and final distribution of (1) share Hitco Conv. Preferred Ser. A no par
Hitco merged into Armco Steel Corp. 12/31/69 which name changed to Armco Inc. 7/1/78 which merged into AK Steel Holding Corp. 9/30/99

HAWLEY PULP & PAPER CO. (DE)
Voluntarily dissolved and liquidated 8/3/48
Details not available

HAWTHORN-MELLODY, INC. (DE)
Merged into National Industries, Inc. (KY) 11/01/1968
Each share Common $6 par exchanged for (0.93) share Common $1 par and (1) Common Stock Purchase Warrant
National Industries, Inc. (KY) merged into Fuqua Industries, Inc. 01/03/1978 which name changed to Actava Group Inc. 07/21/1993 which name changed to Metromedia International Group, Inc. 11/01/1995
(See Metromedia International Group, Inc.)

HAWTHORNE FINL CORP (DE)
Capital Stock $1 par split (3) for (1) by issuance of (2) additional shares 06/01/1986
Capital Stock $1 par changed to 1¢ par 00/00/1995
Capital Stock $1 par split (3) for (2) by issuance of (0.5) additional share payable 10/27/2003 to holders of record 10/06/2003 Ex date 10/28/2003
Merged into Commercial Capital Bancorp, Inc. 06/04/2004
Each share Common 1¢ par exchanged for (1.9333) shares Common 1¢ par
(See Commercial Capital Bancorp, Inc.)

HAWTHORNE GOLD CORP NEW (BC)
Name changed to China Minerals Mining Corp. 04/05/2011
China Minerals Mining Corp. name changed to Wildsky Resources Inc. 08/22/2018

HAWTHORNE GOLD CORP OLD (BC)
Merged into Eureka Resources Inc. 03/30/1990
Each share Capital Stock no par exchanged for (0.2) share Common no par

HAY GOLD MINES LTD. (ON)
Charter cancelled for failure to pay taxes and file returns 11/9/81

HAYAKAWA ELEC LTD (JAPAN)
Name changed to Sharp Corp. 1/1/70

HAYDEN FRANCHISE CORP (MN)
Name changed to Norco Oil Corp. 8/26/69
(See Norco Oil Corp.)

HAYDEN ISLAND INC (OR)
Common 25¢ par changed to 12-1/2¢ par and (1) additional share issued 12/1/72
Name changed to Island Properties, Inc. 9/20/77
(See Island Properties, Inc.)

HAYDEN PUBG INC (DE)
Reincorporated 7/1/71
State of incorporation changed from (NY) to (DE) 7/1/71
Under plan of merger each share Common 1¢ par exchanged for $15 cash 3/1/83

HAYDEN RES LTD (BC)
Recapitalized as Austin Developments Corp. 03/14/2000

Each share Common no par exchanged for (0.25) share Common no par
Austin Developments Corp. recapitalized as Universal Wing Technologies Inc. 12/11/2009 which recapitalized as Red Oak Mining Corp. 03/21/2014

HAYDEN STONE INC (DE)
Name changed to Shearson Hayden Stone Inc. 9/26/74
Shearson Hayden Stone Inc. name changed to Shearson Loeb Rhoades, Inc. 12/19/79 which merged into American Express Co. 6/29/81

HAYDOCK FUND, INC. (OH)
Capital Stock no par exchanged (6) for (1) 00/00/1948
Merged into Scudder, Stevens & Clark Fund, Inc. 12/31/1962
Each share Capital Stock no par exchanged for (1.4254966) shares Capital Stock $1 par
Scudder, Stevens & Clark Fund, Inc. name changed to Scudder, Stevens & Clark Balanced Fund, Inc. 03/08/1963 which name changed to Scudder Income Fund, Inc. 03/02/1977 which name changed to Scudder Income Fund 12/31/1984
(See Scudder Income Fund)

HAYDOCK-LAMSON FUND, INC.
Dissolved in 1947

HAYDON SWITCH & INSTR INC (DE)
Reincorporated 11/29/68
Common no par split (2) for (1) by issuance of (1) additional share 10/6/67
Under plan of merger state of incorporation changed from (CA) to (DE) and each share Common no par exchanged for (1) share Common $1 par 11/29/68
Merged into Tri-Tech, Inc. 8/29/80
Each share Common $1 par exchanged for $1.05 cash

HAYDU ELECTRONIC PRODUCTS, INC. (NJ)
Name changed to Haydu Industries, Inc. 4/15/59
(See Haydu Industries, Inc.)

HAYDU INDUSTRIES, INC. (NJ)
Adjudicated bankrupt 6/3/60

HAYES AIRCRAFT CORP. (DE)
Recapitalized as Hayes Corp. 9/1/60
Each share Common $10 par exchanged for (4) shares Common $2.50 par
Hayes Corp. name changed to Hayes International Corp. 2/28/62 which name changed to Hayes Holding Co. 11/17/66 which merged into City Investing Co. (NY) 3/15/67 which reincorporated in Delaware 2/9/68
(See City Investing Co. (DE))

HAYES ALBION CORP (MI)
Reincorporated 12/11/68
Common $5 par changed to $2.50 par and (1) additional share issued 5/15/68
State of incorporation changed from (MI) to (DE) and Common $2.50 par changed to $1 par 12/11/68
Stock Dividend - 10% 7/29/76
State of incorporation changed from (DE) back to (MI) 12/31/79
Merged into Harvard Industries, Inc. 3/24/87
Each share Common $1 par exchanged for $13 cash

HAYES BODY CORP. (MI)
Name changed to Hayes Manufacturing Corp. 12/26/1939
Hayes Manufacturing Corp. name changed to to United Industrial Corp. (MI) 10/20/1955 which merged into United Industrial Corp. (DE) 12/31/1959
(See United Industrial Corp.)

HAYES-CADILLAC GOLD MINES, LTD. (ON)
Charter cancelled 00/00/1955

HAYES CORP. (DE)
Name changed to Hayes International Corp. 2/28/62
Hayes International Corp. name changed to Hayes Holding Co. 11/17/66 which merged into City Investing Co. (NY) 3/15/67 which reincorporated in Delaware 2/9/68
(See City Investing Co. (DE))

HAYES CORP (DE)
Each share old Common 1¢ par exchanged for (1/3) share new Common 1¢ par 02/26/1998
Chapter 11 bankruptcy proceedings converted to Chapter 7 on 03/17/2000
Stockholders' equity unlikely

HAYES DANA INC (CANADA)
Name changed 11/30/1979
Common no par split (2) for (1) by issuance of (1) additional share 12/01/1972
Common no par reclassified as Conv. Class A Common no par 12/10/1973
Conv. Class A Common no par and Conv. Class B Common no par reclassified as Common no par respectively 01/30/1979
Name changed from Hayes-Dana Ltd. to Hayes-Dana Inc. 11/30/1979
Common no par split (2) for (1) by issuance of (1) additional share 04/11/1985
Acquired by Dana Canada Acquisition Inc. 05/05/1995
Each share Common no par exchanged for $18.50 cash

HAYES HOLDING CO. (DE)
Merged into City Investing Co. (NY) 3/15/67
Each share Common $2.50 par exchanged for (0.285714) share Common $5 par plus a Ctf. of Contingent Interest
City Investing Co. (NY) reincorporated in Delaware 2/9/68
(See City Investing Co. (DE))

HAYES HOTEL CORP. (IL)
In process of liquidation in 1953

HAYES INDUSTRIES, INC. (MI)
Common $1 par changed to $5 par 10/23/56
Common $5 par split (3) for (2) by issuance of (0.5) additional share 4/1/63
Stock Dividends - 10% 12/10/53; 10% 2/10/56; 10% 3/31/64; 10% 6/30/65; 10% 7/20/66; 10% 7/20/67
Under plan of merger name changed to Hayes-Albion Corp. (MI) 8/14/67
Hayes-Albion Corp. (MI) reincorporated in Delaware 12/11/68 which reincorporated back to Michigan 12/31/79
(See Hayes-Albion Corp. (MI))

HAYES INTERNATIONAL CORP. (DE)
Name changed to Hayes Holding Co. 11/17/66
Hayes Holding Co. merged into City Investing Co. (NY) 3/15/67 which reincorporated in Delaware 2/9/68
(See City Investing Co. (DE))

HAYES IONA (MI)
Name changed to Hayes Body Corp. 00/00/1927
Hayes Body Corp. name changed to Hayes Manufacturing Corp. 12/26/1939 which name changed to United Industrial Corp. (MI) 10/20/1955 which merged into United Industrial Corp. (DE) 12/31/1959
(See United Industrial Corp.)

HAYES-JACKSON CORP.
Dissolved in 1936

HAYES LEMMERZ INTL INC (DE)
Plan of reorganization under Chapter 11 Federal Bankruptcy Code effective 06/03/2003
No old Common stockholders' equity
Plan of reorganization under Chapter 11 Federal Bankruptcy Code effective 12/21/2009
No new Common stockholders' equity

HAYES MANUFACTURING CO. LTD. (BC)
Name changed to Hayes Trucks Ltd. 11/30/71
(See Hayes Trucks Ltd.)

HAYES MANUFACTURING CORP. (MI)
Name changed to United Industrial Corp. (MI) 10/20/1955
United Industrial Corp. (MI) merged into United Industrial Corp. (DE) 12/31/1959
(See United Industrial Corp.)

HAYES MFG. CO., INC. (NY)
Proclaimed dissolved for failure to file reports and pay fees 12/15/36

HAYES-SAMMONS CHEMICAL CO. (TX)
Name changed to Mission Chemical Co. 5/7/66
Mission Chemical Co. name changed to Tex-Ag Co. 7/9/69 which merged into Tanger Industries 6/30/71 which name changed to Verit Industries (CA) 4/2/73 which reincorporated in Delaware as Verit Industries, Inc. 1/2/92
(See Verit Industries, Inc.)

HAYES STEEL PRODUCTS LTD. (CANADA)
Each share old Common no par exchanged for (3) shares new Common no par 00/00/1940
New Common no par split (3) for (1) by issuance of (2) additional shares 08/03/1962
New Common no par split (2) for (1) by issuance of (1) additional share 07/11/1963
New Common no par split (2) for (1) by issuance of (1) additional share 04/15/1966
Name changed to Hayes-Dana Ltd. 10/28/1966
Hayes-Dana Ltd. name changed to Hayes-Dana Inc. 11/27/1979
(See Hayes-Dana Inc.)

HAYES TRUCKS LTD (BC)
Acquired by Gearmatic Co. Ltd. 02/11/1974
Each share Common no par exchanged for $7.04 cash
Details on 4.5% Preferred not available

HAYES WHEEL CO.
Merged into Kelsey-Hayes Wheel Corp. 00/00/1927
Details not available

HAYES WHEELS & FORGINGS LTD.
Reorganized as Hayes Steel Products Ltd. 00/00/1936
Each share Preferred exchanged for (3) shares Common no par
Each share Common exchanged for (0.1) share Common no par
Hayes Steel Products Ltd. name changed to Hayes-Dana Ltd. 10/28/1966 which name changed to Hayes-Dana Inc. 11/27/1979
(See Hayes-Dana Inc.)

HAYES WHEELS INTL INC NEW (DE)
Common 1¢ par split (2) for (1) by issuance of (1) additional share payable 01/06/1997 to holders of record 12/20/1996
Name changed to Hayes Lemmerz International, Inc. 10/20/1997
(See Hayes Lemmerz International, Inc.)

HAYES WHEELS INTL INC OLD (DE)
Merged into Hayes Wheels International, Inc. (New) 07/02/1996
Each share Common 1¢ par exchanged for (0.1) share Common 1¢ par and $28.80 cash
Hayes Wheels International, Inc. (New) name changed to Hayes Lemmerz International, Inc. 10/20/1997
(See Hayes Lemmerz International, Inc.)

HAYGART CORP.
Acquired by Adams Express Co. 00/00/1930
Details not available

HAYMARKET CO OPERATIVE BK (BOSTON, MA)
Merged into Century Bank & Trust Co. (Somerville, MA) 6/11/98
Each share Common $1 par exchanged for $117.80 cash
Each share Common $1 par received a second and final distribution of $1.32 cash per share 1/16/2004

HAYS CORP (IN)
5% Preferred $100 par called for redemption 2/1/65
Acquired by Milton Roy Co. 12/8/69
Each share Common $5 par exchanged for (2.16574) shares Common no par
(See Milton Roy Co.)

HAYSE CORP (DE)
Charter cancelled and declared inoperative and void for non-payment of taxes 03/01/2009

HAYSTAR SVCS & TECHNOLOGY INC (NV)
Name changed to DIBZ International, Inc. 09/14/2007
DIBZ International, Inc. name changed to Turbo Global Partners, Inc. 05/02/2017

HAYTIAN CORP. OF AMERICA
Liquidated in 1949

HAYWARD INDS INC (NJ)
Name changed 10/28/1981
Common 10¢ par split (5) for (4) by issuance of (0.25) additional share 12/06/1973
Name changed from Hayward Manufacturing Co., Inc. to Hayward Industries, Inc. 10/28/1981
Acquired by a group of investors 08/04/2017
Each share Common 10¢ par exchanged for approximately $1,588.65 cash

HAYWARD NATL BK (HAYWARD, CA)
Merged into First National Bank San Jose, CA) 7/31/74
Each share Common $10 par exchanged for (2.25) shares Capital Stock $5 par
First National Bank (San Jose, CA) reorganized as First National Bancshares Inc. 6/16/76 which name changed to Bancwest Corp. 3/15/79 which name changed to BWC Liquidating Corp. 3/18/80
(See BWC Liquidating Corp.)

HAYWOOD BANCSHARES INC (NC)
Merged into Century South Banks, Inc. 2/15/2000
Each share Common $1 par exchanged for either (0.9984) share Common $1 par or $21.30 cash
Note: Holders of (99) shares or fewer received cash only
Century South Banks, Inc. merged into BB&T Corp. 6/7/2001

HAYWOOD SVGS BK SSB (WAYNESVILLE, NC)
Name changed 12/1/92
Name changed from Haywood Savings & Loan Association, Inc. to Haywood Savings Bank SSB (Waynesville, NC) 12/1/92
Common $1 par split (2) for (1) by issuance of (1) additional share 12/17/93
Under plan of reorganization each

share Common $1 par automatically became (1) share Haywood Bancshares Inc. Common $1 par 7/1/95
Haywood Bancshares Inc. merged into Century South Banks, Inc. 2/15/2000 which merged into BB&T Corp. 6/7/2001

HAZ HLDGS INC (TX)
Reincorporated under the laws of Delaware 3/15/2007

HAZARDOUS WASTE SOLUTIONS CORP (FL)
Common $0.0002 par split (4) for (1) by issuance of (3) additional shares 07/01/1987
Common $0.0002 par split (2) for (1) by issuance of (1) additional share 03/16/1988
Proclaimed dissolved for failure to file reports and pay fees 10/09/1992

HAZEL ATLAS GLASS CO. (WV)
Each share Capital Stock $25 par exchanged for (5) shares Capital Stock $5 par 00/00/1946
Merged into Continental Can Co., Inc. 09/21/1956
Each share Capital Stock $5 par exchanged for (0.46) share Common $20 par
Continental Can Co., Inc. name changed to Continental Group, Inc. 04/27/1976
(See Continental Group, Inc.)

HAZEL KIRK GOLD MINING CO. (WA)
Charter revoked for failure to file reports and pay fees 7/1/23

HAZEL PARK RACING ASSN INC (MI)
Each share Common $10 par exchanged for (10) shares Common $1 par in 1951
Voting Trust Agreement expired 1/31/68
Each 1968 Ser. VTC for Common $1 par exchanged for (1) share Common $1 par
Name changed to HPRA, Inc. 9/26/72
(See HPRA, Inc.)

HAZELTINE & PERKINS DRUG CO. (MI)
Merged into Brunswig Drug Co. on a (1.85) for (1) basis 3/2/64
Brunswig Drug Co. merged into Bergen Brunswig Corp. 3/26/69 which merged into AmeriSourceBergen Corp. 8/29/2001

HAZELTINE AVENUE REALTY CORP. (NY)
Proclaimed dissolved for failure to pay taxes 10/15/50

HAZELTINE CORP (DE)
Capital Stock no par split (2) for (1) by issuance of (1) additional share 7/3/59
Capital Stock no par split (3) for (1) by issuance of (2) additional shares 5/31/83
Stock Dividends - 100% 12/45; 100% 9/5/52; 25% 7/18/69
Merged into Emerson Electric Co. 12/12/86
Each share Capital Stock no par exchanged for $30 cash

HAZELTON OIL & GAS CO (UT)
Recapitalized as Microcap Inc. 3/30/84
Each share Common $0.001 par exchanged for (0.01) share Common $0.001 par
(See Microcap Inc.)

HAZELWOOD VENTURES INC (NV)
Name changed to Monarch Molybdenum & Resources, Inc. 07/13/2007
Monarch Molybdenum & Resources, Inc. name changed to Thorium Energy, Inc. 01/07/2008 which name

cahaged to Monolith Ventures, Inc. 04/28/2008 which name changed to Zero Gravity Solutions, Inc. 03/13/2013

HAZEUR CHIBOUGAMAU MINES LTD. (ON)
Charter cancelled and company declared dissolved for default in filing returns 11/30/1964

HAZLETON LABS CORP (WA)
Merged into Corning Glass Works 4/2/87
Each share Common 10¢ par exchanged for (0.5165) share Common $5 par
Corning Glass Works name changed to Corning Inc. 4/28/89

HAZLETON NATL BK (HAZLETON, PA)
Common $100 par changed to $10 par and (9) additional shares issued 11/12/68
Common $10 par changed to $5 par and (1) additional share issued 5/31/76
Common $5 par changed to $2.50 par (1) additional share issued 5/26/82
Stock Dividend - 50% 11/16/59
Merged into First Valley Corp. 9/30/84
Each share Common $2.50 par exchanged for (3.2) shares Common $1 par
First Valley Corp. acquired by United Jersey Banks 1/29/88 which name changed to UJB Financial Corp. 6/30/89 which name changed to Summit Bancorp 3/1/96 which merged into FleetBoston Corp. 3/1/2001 which merged into Bank of America Corp. 4/1/2004

HAZLO TECHNOLOGIES INC (NV)
Name changed to China Liaoning Dingxu Ecological Agriculture Development, Inc. 12/06/2011

HBANC CAP SECS TR (ON)
Merged into Global Capital Securities Trust 02/04/2016
Each Class A Ser. 1 Unit automatically became (0.949297) Class A Unit
Each Class A Ser. 2 Unit automatically became (0.968918) Class A Unit
Global Capital Securities Trust name changed to Redwood Global Financials Income Fund 12/20/2017
(See Redwood Global Financials Income Fund)

HBANCORPORATION INC (DE)
Merged into Newco Inc. 07/17/2001
Each share Common 1¢ par exchanged for $19.44 cash

HBL - HADASIT BIO-HLDGS LTD (ISRAEL)
Each old Sponsored ADR for Ordinary exchanged for (0.2) new Sponsored ADR for Ordinary 06/29/2015
ADR agreement terminated 07/18/2016
Each new Sponsored ADR for Ordinary exchanged for $1.241564 cash

HBO & CO (DE)
Common 5¢ par split (3) for (2) by issuance of (0.5) additional share 04/20/1984
Common 5¢ par split (2) for (1) by issuance of (1) additional share 03/28/1994
Common 5¢ par split (2) for (1) by issuance of (1) additional share payable 06/10/1996 to holders of record 05/27/1996
Common 5¢ par split (2) for (1) by issuance of (1) additional share payable 09/09/1997 to holders of record 08/25/1997
Common 5¢ par split (2) for (1) by issuance of (1) additional share payable 06/09/1998 to holders of record 05/27/1998

Stock Dividends - 50% 04/20/1982; 50% 04/20/1983
Merged into McKesson HBOC Inc. 01/12/1999
Each share Common 5¢ par exchanged for (0.37) share Common 1¢ par
McKesson HBOC Inc. name changed to McKesson Corp. 07/30/2001

HBOA HLDGS INC (FL)
Common $0.001 par split (2) for (1) by issuance of (1) additional share payable 02/19/2001 to holders of record 02/14/2001 Ex date - 02/21/2001
Name changed to Kirshner Entertainment & Technologies, Inc. 07/17/2003
Kirshner Entertainment & Technologies, Inc. name changed to Linkwell Corp. 08/17/2005
(See Linkwell Corp.)

HBOS PLC (UNITED KINGDOM)
Sponsored ADR's for Ordinary split (3) for (1) by issuance of (2) additional ADR's payable 10/26/2006 to holders of record 10/25/2006 Ex date - 10/27/2006
Stock Dividend - 2.61637% payable 10/07/2008 to holders of record 10/03/2008 Ex date - 10/01/2008
Merged into Lloyds Banking Group PLC 01/20/2009
Each Sponsored ADR for Ordinary exchanged for (0.15125) Sponsored ADR for Ordinary 25p par

HC INNOVATIONS INC (DE)
Chapter 11 bankruptcy proceedings dismissed 02/17/2012
No stockholders' equity

HC LIQUIDATION TRUST (SC)
Liquidation completed
Each Unit of Bene. Int. received fourth distribution of $0.07 cash 1/12/83
Each Unit of Bene. Int. received fifth distribution of $0.17 cash 3/31/83
Each Unit of Bene. Int. received sixth distribution of $1.13 cash 7/15/83
Each Unit of Bene. Int. received seventh distribution of $0.17 cash 9/30/83
Each Unit of Bene. Int. received eighth distribution of $0.34 cash 12/31/83
Each Unit of Bene. Int. received ninth and final distribution of $1.04 cash 4/10/84
(See Harley Corp. for previous distribution)

HC&D LTD. (HI)
Thru purchase offer 100% acquired by Ameron, Inc. as of 1967
Public interest eliminated

HCA HLDGS INC (DE)
Name changed to HCA Healthcare, Inc. 05/08/2017

HCA HOSP CORP AMER (DE)
Recapitalized 4/1/91
Each share $4.375 Exchangeable Preferred 1¢ par exchanged for $25 principal amount of 17.5% Jr. Subordinated Exchangeable Debentures Ser. A due 7/1/2005
Merged into Columbia/HCA Healthcare Corp. 2/10/94
Each share Class A Common 1¢ par exchanged for (1.05) shares Common 1¢ par
Columbia/HCA Healthcare Corp. name changed to HCA - The Healthcare Co. 5/25/2000 which name changed to HCA Inc. (Ctfs. dated after 6/29/2001) 6/29/2001
(See HCA Inc. (Ctfs. dated after 6/29/2001))

HCA INC (DE)
Ctfs. dated prior to 10/14/82
Stock Dividend - 200% 5/20/81
Merged into I.C.H. Corp. 10/14/82
Each share Common $1 par

exchanged for (0.6705) share Common $1 par
I.C.H. Corp. name changed to Southwestern Life Corp. (New) 6/15/94 which name changed to I.C.H. Corp. (New) 10/10/95
(See I.C.H. Corp. (New))

HCA INC (DE)
Ctfs. dated after 06/29/2001
Name changed 06/29/2001
Name changed from HCA - The Healthcare Co. to HCA Inc. 06/29/2001
Merged into Hercules Holdings II, LLC 11/17/2006
Each share Common 1¢ par exchanged for $51 cash

HCA INDUSTRIES, INC. (DE)
Name changed to HCA-Martin, Inc. 5/11/73
HCA-Martin, Inc. name changed to Martin Processing, Inc. 5/16/75
(See Martin Processing, Inc.)

HCA MARTIN INC (DE)
Name changed to Martin Processing, Inc. 05/16/1975
(See Martin Processing, Inc.)

HCB BANCORP (IN)
Merged into First Capital, Inc. 01/12/2000
Each share Common no par exchanged for (15.5) shares Common 1¢ par

HCB BANCSHARES INC (OK)
Acquired by Rock Bancshares, Inc. 8/26/2004
Each share Common 1¢ par exchanged for $18.63 cash

HCC INDUSTRIES (CA)
Common no par split (2) for (1) by issuance of (1) additional share 8/17/79
Name changed to HCC Industries Inc. 9/16/86
(See HCC Industries Inc.)

HCC INDS INC (CA)
Merged into HCC Merger Corp. 12/5/89
Each share Common no par exchanged for $9 cash

HCC INS HLDGS INC (DE)
Common $1 par split (3) for (2) by issuance of (0.5) additional share 03/31/1994
Common $1 par split (5) for (2) by issuance of (1.5) additional shares payable 05/15/1996 to holders of record 04/30/1996
Common $1 par split (3) for (2) by issuance of (0.5) additional share payable 07/15/2005 to holders of record 07/01/2005 Ex date - 07/18/2005
Acquired by Tokio Marine Holdings, Ltd. 10/28/2015
Each share Common $1 par exchanged for $78 cash

HCI GROUP INC (FL)
7% Preferred Ser. A no par called for redemption at $10 plus $0.05833 accrued dividends on 06/02/2014
(Additional Information in Active)

HCI HLDGS LTD (CANADA)
Each share Preferred no par exchanged for (3) Common Stock Purchase Warrants expiring 9/30/80 and (3) shares new Common no par 9/21/77
Each share old Common no par exchanged for (3) shares new Common no par 9/21/77
New Common no par reclassified as Conv. Class B no par and (1/3) share Class A Non-Vtg. no par distributed 5/26/80
Class A Non-Vtg. no par split (3) for (1) by issuance of (2) additional shares 1/19/81
Conv. Class B no par split (3) for (1)

by issuance of (2) additional shares 1/19/81
Recapitalized as Consolidated HCI Holdings Corp. 12/30/86
Each share Class A Non-Vtg. no par exchanged for (1/7) share Class A Non-Vtg. no par
Each share Conv. Class B no par exchanged for (1/7) share Conv. Class B no par

HCI VIOCARE (NV)
Common $0.0001 par split (7) for (1) by issuance of (6) additional shares payable 08/07/2015 to holders of record 08/07/2015
Recapitalized as Rafina Innovations Inc. 07/09/2018
Each share Common $0.0001 par exchanged for (0.05) share Common $0.001 par

HCIA INC (MD)
Merged into VS&A Communications Partners III, L.P. 11/24/1999
Each share Common 1¢ par exchanged for $11 cash

HCO ENERGY LTD (CANADA)
Recapitalized as Consolidated HCO Energy Ltd. 04/12/1989
Each share Common no par exchanged for (0.1) share Common no par
Consolidated HCO Energy Ltd. name changed to HCO Energy Ltd. 06/18/1993 which merged into Pinnacle Resources Ltd. (New) 10/20/1997 which merged into Renaissance Energy Ltd. 07/16/1998 which merged into Husky Energy Inc. 08/25/2000

HCO ENERGY LTD (CANADA)
Each share old Common no par exchanged for (0.25) share new Common no par 07/11/1997
Merged into Pinnacle Resources Ltd. (New) 10/20/1997
Each share 7% Conv. 1st Preferred Ser. A no par exchanged for $10 cash
Each share 1st Preferred Ser. B no par exchanged for $10 cash
Each share new Common no par exchanged for either (0.4819) share Common no par, (0.1525657) share Common no par and $6.8340805 cash, or $10 cash
Note: Option to receive stock or cash and stock expired 11/17/1998
Pinnacle Resources Ltd. (New) merged into Renaissance Energy Ltd. 07/16/1998 which merged into Husky Energy Inc. 08/25/2000

HCP INC (MD)
7.1% Preferred Ser. F $1 par called for redemption at $25 on 04/23/2012
7.25% Preferred Ser. E $1 par called for redemption at $25 on 04/23/2012
(Additional Information in Active)

HCR MANOR CARE INC (DE)
Name changed to Manor Care, Inc. (New) 09/30/1999
(See Manor Care, Inc. (New))

HCS INTL (NV)
Name changed to Standard Pacific Financial Corp. 5/30/90
Standard Pacific Financial Corp. recapitalized as Standard General Group 9/11/90

HCSB FINL CORP (SC)
Common 1¢ par split (2) for (1) by issuance of (1) additional share payable 02/13/2007 to holders of record 01/30/2007 Ex date - 02/14/2007
Stock Dividends - 5% payable 03/20/2002 to holders of record 02/22/2002 Ex date - 03/21/2002; 5% payable 03/21/2003 to holders of record 02/28/2003 Ex date - 03/20/2003; 7.5% payable 03/12/2004 to holders of record 02/13/2004 Ex date - 02/11/2004;
3% payable 03/10/2005 to holders of record 02/11/2005 Ex date - 02/09/2005; 3% payable 03/03/2006 to holders of record 02/10/2006 Ex date - 02/27/2006; 3% payable 02/15/2008 to holders of record 02/05/2008 Ex date - 02/01/2008; 3% payable 02/20/2009 to holders of record 02/06/2009 Ex date - 02/04/2009
Merged into United Community Banks, Inc. 07/31/2017
Each share Common 1¢ par exchanged for (0.005) share new Common $1 par

HCW INC (DE)
Merged into Southmark Corp. 02/06/1986
Each share Common 10¢ par exchanged for $6.40 cash

HCW OIL & GAS, INC. (DE)
Name changed to HCW Inc. 10/14/84
(See HCW Inc.)

HCW OIL INCOME FUND (MA)
Filed Certificate of Cancellation 05/15/1989
Details not available

HD PARTNERS ACQUISITION CORP (DE)
Issue Information - 18,750,000 UNITS consisting of (1) share COM and (1) WT offered at $8 per Unit on 06/01/2006
Completely liquidated 05/05/2008
Each Unit exchanged for first and final distribution of $7.97989 cash
Each share Common $0.001 par exchanged for first and final distribution of $7.97989 cash

HD RETAIL SOLUTIONS INC (NV)
Name changed to Greenscape Laboratories, Inc. 06/10/2014
Greenscape Laboratories, Inc. recapitalized as Ultrack Systems, Inc. 04/11/2016

HDH INDS INC (NV)
Name changed to Las Vegas Resorts Corp. 09/14/1987
Las Vegas Resorts Corp. name changed to Winner Medical Group, Inc. 03/06/2006
(See Winner Medical Group, Inc.)

HDI INVT CORP (DE)
Each share old Common $1 par exchanged for (0.00066666) share new Common $1 par 12/02/1977
Note: In effect holders received $8.45 cash per share plus an additional $0.38 cash per share 09/26/1978 and public interest was eliminated

HDIMAX MEDIA INC (NV)
Name changed to Zonzia Media, Inc. 03/09/2015

HDL COMMUNICATIONS (CA)
Each share old Common no par exchanged for (0.00073349) share new Common no par 03/10/1995
Name changed to Bikers Dream Inc. 03/30/1995
Bikers Dream Inc. name changed to Ultra Motorcycle Co. (CA) 01/17/2001 which reincorporated in Delaware as New Dover Capital Corp. 08/02/2007

HDR PWR SYS INC (DE)
Merged into SolidState Controls 8/27/93
Each share Common 1¢ par exchanged for $3.25 cash

HDS INTL CORP (NV)
Name changed to Good Gaming, Inc. 06/30/2016

HDS NETWORK SYS INC (DE)
Name changed to Neoware Systems, Inc. 08/01/1997
Neoware Systems, Inc. name changed to Neoware, Inc. 12/01/2005
(See Neoware, Inc.)

HE-5 RES CORP (NV)
Old Common $0.001 par split (5) for (1) by issuance of (4) additional shares payable 06/15/2006 to holders of record 06/09/2006 Ex date - 06/16/2006
Each share old Common $0.001 par exchanged for (0.005) share new Common $0.001 par 10/20/2006
Recapitalized as Fansfrenzy Corp. 12/05/2017
Each share new Common $0.001 par exchanged for (0.01) share Common $0.001 par

HE-RO GRP LTD (DE)
Name changed to Nahdree Group, Ltd. 06/09/1998
(See Nahdree Group, Ltd.)

HEAD N V (NETHERLANDS)
New York Registry Shares EUR 0.2 par changed to EUR 0.01 par 05/30/2007
Each New York Registry Share EUR 0.01 par exchanged for $0.74123 cash 12/04/2015

HEAD OF THE LAKES IRON LTD. (ON)
Recapitalized as Lakehead Mines Ltd. 07/25/1963
Each share Common exchanged for (0.5) share Common
Lakehead Mines Ltd. merged into Parlake Resources Ltd. 06/18/1979 which name changed to Concord Capital Corp. 07/23/1991
(See Concord Capital Corp.)

HEAD SKI INC (DE)
Common $1.50 par changed to 50¢ par and (2) additional shares issued 7/20/64
Common 50¢ par split (2) for (1) by issuance of (1) additional share 9/29/65
Merged into AMF Inc. 5/3/71
Each share Common 50¢ par exchanged for $13.50 cash

HEAD4 SOLUTIONS INC (CANADA)
Recapitalized as Saratoga Electronic Solutions Inc. 01/25/2005
Each share Common no par exchanged for (0.25) share Common no par
Saratoga Electronic Solutions Inc. name changed to Abba Medix Group Inc. 05/14/2015 which recapitalized as Canada House Wellness Group Inc. 11/09/2016

HEADGATE LAND CO. (CA)
In process of liquidation
Each share Capital Stock no par received initial distribution of $64 cash 11/1/77
Note: Details on subsequent distributions, if any, are not available

HEADHUNTER NET INC (GA)
Issue Information - 3,000,000 shares COM offered at $10 per share on 08/19/1999
Merged into Career Holdings, Inc. 11/8/2001
Each share Common 1¢ par exchanged for $9.25 cash

HEADLANDS MTG CO (DE)
Issue Information - 8,000,000 shares COM offered at $12 per share on 02/04/1998
Merged into GreenPoint Financial Corp. 3/31/99
Each share Common no par exchanged for (0.62) share Common 1¢ par
GreenPoint Financial Corp. merged into North Fork Bancorporation, Inc. 10/1/2004 which merged into Capital One Financial Corp. 12/1/2006

HEADLINE MEDIA GROUP INC (CANADA)
Name changed to Score Media Inc. 02/23/2005
Score Media Inc. reorganized as theScore, Inc. 10/19/2012

HEADLINERS ENTMT GROUP INC (DE)
Each share old Common $0.0001 par exchanged for (0.001) share new Common $0.001 par 03/17/2005
Chapter 11 bankruptcy proceedings converted to Chapter 7 on 06/12/2007
Stockholders' equity unlikely

HEADVUE MINES LTD (ON)
Charter cancelled for failure to pay taxes and file returns 03/16/1976

HEADWATER MINES LTD (ON)
Charter cancelled and declared dissolved for failure to pay taxes and file returns 12/07/1977

HEADWATERS INC (DE)
Acquired by Boral Ltd. (New) 05/08/2017
Each share Common $0.001 par exchanged for $24.25 cash

HEADWAY CORPORATE RES INC (DE)
Plan of reorganization under Chapter 11 Federal Bankruptcy Code effective 9/19/2003
No stockholders' equity

HEADWAY LTD (ON)
Capital Stock no par reclassified as Conv. Class A Capital Stock no par 05/31/1976
Acquired by Nu-West Group Ltd. (AB) 10/15/1980
Each share Conv. Class A Capital Stock no par exchanged for (0.25) share Conv. Class A Common no par
Each share Conv. Class B Capital Stock no par exchanged for (0.25) share Conv. Class B Common no par
Nu-West Group Ltd. (AB) reincorporated in Delaware 01/29/1988 which recapitalized as N-W Group, Inc. 02/24/1988 which name changed to Glenayre Technologies, Inc. 11/10/1992 which name changed to Entertainment Distribution Co. 05/11/2007 which recapitalized as EDCI Holdings, Inc. 08/26/2008
(See EDCI Holdings, Inc.)

HEADWAY RED LAKE GOLD MINES LTD (ON)
Each share old Capital Stock $1 par exchanged for (0.05) share new Capital Stock $1 par 02/10/1977
Merged into Wayfair Explorations Ltd. 11/00/1980
Each share new Capital Stock $1 par exchanged for (1) share Common no par
(See Wayfair Explorations Ltd.)

HEALEY CAP CORP (AB)
Name changed to Run of River Power Inc. (AB) 07/04/2005
Run of River Power Inc. (AB) reincorporated in British Columbia 09/13/2006
(See Run of River Power Inc.)

HEALING HAND NETWORK INTL INC (NV)
Name changed to Patriot Energy Corp. (NV) 10/10/2005
(See Patriot Energy Corp.)

HEALTH & ATHLETIC SPAS INC (DE)
Common 1¢ par split (3) for (1) by issuance of (2) additional shares 9/21/72
Name changed to Repadco Industries Inc. 12/13/72
(See Repadco Industries Inc.)

HEALTH & ENVIRONMENT TECHNOLOGIES INC (ON)
Charter cancelled for failure to file reports and pay taxes 8/30/96

HEALTH & FITNESS RETREATS INC (UT)
Name changed to Ormc Laboratories, Inc. 1/11/85
(See Ormc Laboratories, Inc.)

HEALTH & LEISURE INC (UT)
Each share Common $0.001 par exchanged for (0.1) share Common 1¢ par 05/12/1988
Recapitalized as Marketshare Recovery, Inc. 08/22/2003
Each share Common 1¢ par exchanged for (0.1) share Common 1¢ par
Marketshare Recovery, Inc. name changed to bioMETRX, Inc. 10/10/2005
(See bioMETRX, Inc.)

HEALTH & NUTRITION SYS INTL INC (FL)
Each share old Common $0.001 par exchanged for (0.5) share new Common $0.001 par 08/01/2000
Name changed to Ashlin Development Corp. (FL) 03/14/2005
Ashlin Development Corp. (FL) reincorporated in Delaware as Gales Industries Inc. 02/15/2006 which name changed to Air Industries Group, Inc. (DE) 07/16/2007 which reincorporated in Nevada 09/03/2013

HEALTH & RETIREMENT PPTYS TR (MD)
Name changed 07/01/1994
Common Shares of Bene. Int. 1¢ par split (2) for (1) by issuance of (1) additional share 08/31/1987
Name changed from Health & Rehabilitation Properties Trust to Health & Retirement Properties Trust 07/01/1994
Name changed to HRPT Properties Trust 07/01/1998
HRPT Properties Trust recapitalized as CommonWealth REIT 07/01/2010 which name changed to Equity Commonwealth 08/01/2014

HEALTH & WEALTH INC (UT)
Recapitalized as Twenty First Century Health Inc. 05/23/1995
Each share Common $0.001 par exchanged for (0.02) share Common $0.001 par
Twenty First Century Health Inc. name changed to Bio-Tech Industries Inc. 05/21/1997
(See Bio-Tech Industries Inc.)

HEALTH ACCOUNTING SVC (OR)
Name changed to First Pacific Corp. 01/23/1974
(See First Pacific Corp.)

HEALTH ADVANCEMENT INC (DE)
Charter cancelled and declared inoperative and void for non-payment of taxes 6/27/84

HEALTH ADVANCEMENT SVCS INC (DE)
Each share old Common $0.001 par exchanged for (0.33333333) share new Common $0.001 par 01/20/1992
Each share old Common $0.001 par exchanged for (0.03333333) share new Common $0.001 par 08/25/1995
Charter cancelled and declared inoperative and void for non-payment of taxes 03/01/1997

HEALTH ANTI-AGING LIFESTYLE OPTS INC (UT)
Each share old Common $0.001 par exchanged for (0.02) share new Common $0.001 par 10/04/2010
Name changed to Previsto International Holdings, Inc. 12/07/2010

HEALTH BENEFITS DIRECT CORP (DE)
Name changed to InsPro Technologies Corp. 12/06/2010

HEALTH BUILDERS INTL INC (DE)
Reorganized as MCY.Com Inc. 8/2/99
Each share Common $0.001 par exchanged for (2) shares Common $0.001 par

HEALTH CARE & BIOTECHNOLOGY VENTURE FD (ON)
Liquidation completed
Each Trust Unit received initial distribution of $2.042 cash payable 02/27/1996 to holders of record 02/27/1996
Each Trust Unit received second distribution of $1.0851 cash payable 02/18/1997 to holders of record 02/18/1997
Each Trust Unit received third distribution of $0.2310 cash payable 02/17/1998 to holders of record 02/17/1998
Each Trust Unit received fourth distribution of $4 cash payable 02/15/2001 to holders of record 02/15/2001
Each Trust Unit received fifth distribution of $3 cash payable 02/14/2002 holders of record 02/14/2002
Each Trust Unit received sixth distribution of $1 cash payable 06/28/2002 to holders of record 06/28/2002
Each Trust Unit received seventh distribution of $0.80 cash payable 02/12/2003 to holders of record 02/12/2003
Each Trust Unit received eighth distribution of $1.06 cash payable 02/25/2004 to holders of record 02/25/2004
Each Trust Unit received ninth and final distribution of $0.3319 cash payable 05/03/2005 to holders of record 08/04/2004

HEALTH CARE & RETIREMENT CORP (DE)
Common 1¢ par split (2) for (1) by issuance of (1) additional share 03/05/1993
Common 1¢ par split (3) for (2) by issuance of (0.5) additional share payable 06/05/1996 to holders of record 06/21/1996
Under plan of merger name changed to HCR Manor Care, Inc. 09/25/1998
HCR Manor Care, Inc. name changed to Manor Care, Inc. (New) 09/30/1999
(See Manor Care, Inc. (New))

HEALTH CARE & RETIREMENT CORP AMER (OH)
Common 10¢ par split (6) for (5) by issuance of (0.2) additional share 1/6/84
Acquired by Owens-Illinois, Inc. 12/3/84
Each share Common 10¢ par exchanged for $22 cash

HEALTH CARE CTRS AMER INC (NV)
Each share Common 2¢ par exchanged for (0.001) share Common $0.001 par 06/30/1998
Name changed to Hexagon Consolidated Companies of America Inc. 08/31/1999
Hexagon Consolidated Companies of America Inc. name changed to NMC Inc. 09/09/2003

HEALTH CARE FD (OH)
Reorganized under the laws of Delaware as Health Care REIT Inc. and Shares of Bene. Int. $1 par changed to Common $1 par 07/01/1985
Health Care REIT Inc. name changed to Welltower 09/30/2015

HEALTH CARE GROUP LABS (UT)
Reincorporated 07/02/1981
State of incorporation changed from (IL) to (UT) 07/02/1981
Each share Common $0.001 par exchanged for (0.25) share Common $0.004 par 01/10/1983
Reorganized under the laws of Delaware as Healthtek Inc. 07/10/1987
Each share Common $0.004 par exchanged for (0.25) share Common 1¢ par
Healthtek Inc. recapitalized as C'Watre International, Inc. 06/26/2007 which recapitalized as Biomimix, Inc. 04/13/2009

HEALTH CARE INC (TN)
Merged into Hospital Affiliates, Inc. 7/22/71
Each share Common 50¢ par exchanged for $3 principal amount of 4% Sub. Conv. Income Debentures due 7/22/91

HEALTH CARE PRODS INC (ON)
Recapitalized as Celltech Media Inc. 03/31/1994
Each share Subordinate Class A no par exchanged for (0.1) share Subordinate Class A no par
Celltech Media Inc. recapitalized as Smartel Communications Corp. 06/21/1995 which name changed to Intasys Corp. 07/29/1996 which name changed to Mamma.com Inc. 01/12/2004 which name changed to Copernic Inc. 06/21/2007 which merged into Comamtech Inc. (ON) 11/04/2010 which reincorporated in Delaware as DecisionPoint Systems, Inc. (New) 06/22/2011

HEALTH CARE PPTY INVS INC (MD)
Depositary Preferred Ser. C called for redemption at $25 on 05/02/2003
7.875% Preferred Ser. A $1 par called for redemption at $25 on 09/10/2003
8.70% Preferred Ser. B $1 par called for redemption at $25 plus $0.00604 accrued dividend on 10/01/2003
Common $1 par split (2) for (1) by issuance of (1) additional share 05/20/1992
Common $1 par split (2) for (1) by issuance of (1) additional share payable 03/01/2004 to holders of record 02/04/2004 Ex date - 03/02/2004
Name changed to HCP, Inc. 09/07/2007

HEALTH CARE REIT INC (DE)
Common $1 par split (3) for (2) by issuance of (0.5) additional share 09/03/1985
8.875% Preferred Ser. B $1 par called for redemption at $25 plus $0.0924 accrued dividends on 07/15/2003
7.5% Preferred Ser. G $1 par called for redemption at $25 plus $0.46875 accrued dividends on 09/30/2010
7.625% Preferred Ser. F $1 par called for redemption at $25 plus $0.47656 accrued dividends on 04/02/2012
7.875% Preferred Ser. D $1 par called for redemption at $25 plus $0.49219 accrued dividends on 04/02/2012
Name changed to Welltower Inc. 09/30/2015

HEALTH-CHEM CORP (DE)
Common 1¢ par split (4) for (3) by issuance of (1/3) additional share 01/14/1980
Common 1¢ par split (4) for (3) by issuance of (0.33333333) additional share 10/15/1980
Stock Dividends - 50% 03/31/1976; 40% 06/30/1978
Charter declared void for non-payment of franchise taxes 03/01/2002

HEALTH CLUB TELEVISION NETWORK INC (NY)
Dissolved by proclamation 12/27/1995

HEALTH CONCEPTS IV INC (DE)
Filed Chapter 11 Federal Bankruptcy Code 01/27/1992
Stockholders' equity unlikely

HEALTH CORP AMER (DE)
Charter cancelled and declared void for failure to pay franchise taxes 03/01/1992
Attorney advised stock is worthless

HEALTH DELIVERY SYS INC (NY)
Common 1¢ par split (2) for (1) by issuance of (1) additional share 02/05/1973
Name changed to Quality Care, Inc. 06/22/1978
(See Quality Care, Inc.)

HEALTH DEV SVCS INC (CANADA)
Reincorporated under the laws of Ontario as Spinnaker Development Corp. 10/30/1990
(See Spinnaker Development Corp.)

HEALTH DIRECTORY INC (NV)
Reorganized as Sollensys Corp. 08/27/2012
Each share Common $0.001 par exchanged for (131.69) shares Common $0.001 par

HEALTH DISCOVERY CORP (TX)
Reincorporated under the laws of Georgia 07/12/2007

HEALTH EMPORIUM INC (DE)
Name changed to Pacific Engineering Systems, Inc. 5/5/98
Pacific Engineering Systems, Inc. recapitalized as Royal Pet Meals, Inc. 3/28/2005 which recapitalized as Kodiak Gaming, Inc. 5/10/2006 which name changed to Straight Up Brands, Inc. 8/7/2006

HEALTH ENHANCEMENT PRODS INC (NV)
Name changed to Zivo Bioscience, Inc. 11/10/2014

HEALTH EQUITIES INC (NV)
Name changed to Waste Conversion Systems, Inc. 6/18/87
Waste Conversion Systems, Inc. name changed to Urban Television Network Corp. 6/10/2002

HEALTH EQUITY PPTYS INC (NC)
Reincorporated 6/3/91
State of incorporation changed from (DE) to (NC) 6/3/91
Merged into Omega Healthcare Investors, Inc. 9/30/94
Each share Common 1¢ par exchanged for (0.393) share Common 10¢ par

HEALTH EVALUATION SYS INC (DE)
Charter cancelled and declared inoperative and void for non-payment of taxes 4/15/72

HEALTH EXPRESS USA INC (FL)
Name changed to CSI Business Finance, Inc. (FL) 10/10/2005
CSI Business Finance, Inc. (FL) reincorporated in Nevada as Natural Nutrition, Inc. 11/03/2006 which recapitalized as AppTech Corp. 11/16/2009

HEALTH EXTN SVCS INC (NY)
Stock Dividend - 100% 9/15/80
Name changed to Professional Care, Inc. (NY) 2/26/86
Professional Care, Inc. (NY) reorganized in Delaware as Health Professionals, Inc. 11/26/91
(See Health Professionals, Inc.)

HEALTH FITNESS CORP (MN)
Name changed 06/09/1997
Name changed from Health Fitness Physical Therapy, Inc. to Health Fitness Corp. 06/09/1997
Each share old Common 1¢ par

exchanged for (0.5) share new
Common 1¢ par 10/07/2008
Acquired by Trustmark Mutual
Holding Co. 02/26/2010
Each share new Common 1¢ par
exchanged for $8.78 cash

HEALTH FOOD CTRS INC (OH)
Completely liquidated 10/31/77
Each share Common $1 par
exchanged for $1 cash

HEALTH GRADES INC (DE)
Acquired by Mountain Acquisition
Corp. 10/07/2010
Each share Common $0.001 par
exchanged for $8.20 cash

HEALTH IMAGE MEDIA INC (DE)
Name changed to Inmark Enterprises
Inc. 09/29/1995
Inmark Enterprises Inc. name
changed to CoActive Marketing
Group, Inc. 10/01/1999 which name
changed to mktg, inc. 09/18/2008
(See mktg, inc.)

HEALTH IMAGES INC (DE)
Reincorporated 06/29/1989
State of incorporation changed from
(FL) to (DE) 06/29/1989
10% Conv. Preferred Ser. A 1¢ par
called for redemption 07/01/1989
Preferred Stock Purchase Rights
redeemed at $0.01 per right
03/03/1997 for holders of record
03/03/1997
Merged into HealthSouth Corp.
03/03/1997
Each share Common 1¢ par
exchanged for (0.446) share
Common 1¢ par
HealthSouth Corp. name changed to
Encompass Health Corp.
01/02/2018

HEALTH IN HARMONY INC (NV)
Common $0.001 par split (2) for (1)
by issuance of (1) additional share
payable 03/25/2013 to holders of
record 03/13/2013 Ex date -
03/26/2013
Name changed to Life Care Medical
Devices Ltd. 04/18/2013

HEALTH INDS INC (UT)
Merged into Health Industries
Acquisition Co. 2/16/84
Each share Capital Stock 1¢ par
exchanged for $0.85 cash

HEALTH INFORMATION SYS INC 1978 (NY)
Incorporated 07/19/1978
Stock Dividend - 100% 05/08/1981
Common 1¢ par split (3) for (2) by
issuance of (0.5) additional share
12/06/1982
Name changed to AME - HIS, Inc.
11/14/1988
(See AME - HIS, Inc.)

HEALTH INFORMATION SYSTEMS, INC. (NY)
Incorporated 09/30/1968
Out of business 00/00/1973
No stockholders' equity

HEALTH INS VT INC (VT)
Common Capital Stock $1 par
changed to $1.20 par 5/20/65
Common Capital Stock $1.20 par
changed to $1.375 par 6/25/79
Common Capital Stock $1.375 par
changed to $2 par 8/2/83
Common Capital Stock $2 par
changed to $3 par 8/1/89
Stock Dividends - 10% 1/13/86; 15%
1/12/87
Merged into Penn Treaty American
Corp. 8/30/96
Each share Common $3 par
exchanged for (0.85920456) share
Common 10¢ par and $4 cash

HEALTH INTL INC (DE)
Merged into Sykes HealthPlan
Services, Inc. 3/31/98
Each share Common 10¢ par
exchanged for $8 cash

HEALTH MGMT ASSOC INC NEW (DE)
Class A Common 1¢ par split (3) for
(2) by issuance of (0.5) additional
share 04/09/1992
Class A Common 1¢ par split (3) for
(2) by issuance of (0.5) additional
share 11/03/1993
Class A Common 1¢ par split (3) for
(2) by issuance of (0.5) additional
share 06/17/1994
Class A Common 1¢ par split (3) for
(2) by issuance of (0.5) additional
share 10/20/1995
Class A Common 1¢ par split (3) for
(2) by issuance of (0.5) additional
share payable 06/14/1996 to holders
of record 05/31/1996
Class A Common 1¢ par split (3) for
(2) by issuance of (0.5) additional
share payable 10/23/1997 to holders
of record 10/06/1997 Ex date -
10/24/1997
Class A Common 1¢ par split (3) for
(2) by issuance of (0.5) additional
share payable 07/17/1998 to holders
of record 06/30/1998 Ex date -
07/20/1998
Merged into Community Health
Systems, Inc. 01/27/2014
Each share Class A Common 1¢ par
exchanged for (0.06942) share
Common 1¢ par, (1) Contingent
Value Right and $10.50 cash

HEALTH MGMT ASSOC INC OLD (DE)
Merged into HMA Holding Corp.
9/12/88
Each share Common 20¢ par
exchanged for $14.75 cash

HEALTH MGMT INC (DE)
Merged into Transworld Health
10/01/1997
Each share Common 3¢ par
exchanged for $0.30 cash

HEALTH MGMT INC (FL)
Merged into Nouveau International
Inc. 1/16/96
Each share Common $0.001 par
exchanged for (0.65768734) share
Common $0.001 par
Nouveau International Inc.
reorganized as My Screen Mobile,
Inc. 5/23/2007

HEALTH MGMT INTL INC (DE)
Name changed to TDX Corp.
01/05/1993
(See TDX Corp.)

HEALTH MGMT SVCS INC (IA)
Each share Common $1 par
exchanged for (0.00002) share
Common $1 par 10/19/1976
Note: In effect holders received $1.36
cash per share and public interest
was eliminated

HEALTH MGMT SYS INC (NY)
Common 1¢ par split (3) for (2) by
issuance of (0.5) additional share
03/31/1995
Common 1¢ par split (3) for (2) by
issuance of (0.5) additional share
12/29/1995
Under plan of reorganization each
share Common 1¢ par automatically
became (1) share HMS Holdings
Corp. (NY) Common 1¢ par
03/03/2003
HMS Holdings Corp. (NY)
reincorporated in Delaware
07/23/2013

HEALTH MOR INC (DE)
Common $1 par split (2) for (1) by
issuance of (1) additional share
10/13/78
Common $1 par split (3) for (2) by
issuance of (0.5) additional share
9/22/92
Common $1 par split (3) for (2) by
issuance of (0.5) additional share
2/25/94
Name changed to HMI Industries Inc.
1/20/95
(See HMI Industries Inc.)

HEALTH NET INC (DE)
Class A Common $0.001 par
reclassified as Common $0.001 par
06/04/2004
Merged into Centene Corp.
03/24/2016
Each share Common $0.001 par
exchanged for (0.622) share
Common $0.001 par and $28.25
cash

HEALTH O METER PRODS INC (DE)
Name changed to Signature Brands
USA, Inc. 4/1/97
(See Signature Brands USA, Inc.)

HEALTH OUTCOMES MGMT INC (MN)
Reorganized under the laws of
Delaware as Hudson Holding Corp.
09/07/2005
Each share Common 1¢ par
exchanged for (0.125) share
Common $0.001 par
Hudson Holding Corp. merged into
Rodman & Renshaw Capital Group,
Inc. 04/08/2011 which name
changed to Direct Markets Holdings
Corp. 06/01/2012
(See Direct Markets Holdings Corp.)

HEALTH PAK INC (DE)
Each share old Common $0.002 par
exchanged for (0.06666666) share
new Common $0.002 par
01/08/1999
Name changed to Life Energy &
Technology Holdings, Inc. (DE)
12/19/2000
Life Energy & Technology Holdings,
Inc. (DE) reincorporated in Bahamas
as Global Environmental Energy
Corp. 08/30/2004

HEALTH PARTNERSHIP INC (CO)
Name changed to Naerodynamics,
Inc. 04/17/2008

HEALTH PWR INC (DE)
Issue Information - 900,000 shares
COM offered at $11 per share on
03/03/1994
Merged into Security Capital Corp.
12/21/2000
Each share Common 1¢ par
exchanged for $6.94 cash

HEALTH PROFESSIONALS INC (DE)
Old Common 2¢ par split (2) for (1)
by issuance of (1) additional share
03/06/1992
Each share old Common 2¢ par
exchanged for (0.1) share new
Common 2¢ par 04/26/1996
SEC revoked common stock
registration 06/02/2008

HEALTH RESH LTD (NV)
Name changed to TransAmerican
Holdings, Inc. 11/15/1999
TransAmerican Holdings, Inc. name
changed to American Holding
Investments, Inc. 10/14/2004
(See American Holding Investments, Inc.)

HEALTH RES CORP AMER (DE)
Merged into Republic Health Corp.
12/31/1984
Each share Common 1¢ par
exchanged for (1) share Common
5¢ par
(See Republic Health Corp.)

HEALTH RESTORATION RES INC (NY)
Dissolved by proclamation 6/23/93

HEALTH RISK MGMT INC (MN)
Chapter 11 bankruptcy proceedings
converted to Chapter 7 on 3/13/2002
Stockholders' equity unlikely

HEALTH SCIENCES GROUP INC (DE)
Reincorporated 07/14/2005
State of incorporation changed from
(CO) to (DE) 07/14/2005

Reincorporated under the laws of
Florida and Common $0.001 par
changed to $0.0001 par 02/09/2009

HEALTH SYS DESIGN CORP (DE)
Acquired by Perot Systems Corp.
12/15/2000
Each share Common $0.001 par
exchanged for $2 cash

HEALTH SYS INTL INC (DE)
Under plan of merger name changed
to Foundation Health Systems, Inc.
04/01/1997
Foundation Health Systems, Inc.
name changed to Health Net, Inc.
11/06/2000 which merged into
Centene Corp. 03/24/2016

HEALTH SYS SOLUTIONS INC (DE)
Reincorporated 02/19/2009
Each share old Common $0.001 par
exchanged for (0.5) share new
Common $0.001 par 07/08/2004
Each share new Common $0.001 par
exchanged again for (0.5) share new
Common $0.001 par 02/24/2006
State of incorporation changed from
(NV) to (DE) 02/19/2009 Shares
reacquired 12/09/2009
Each share Common $0.001 par
exchanged for $0.07 cash

HEALTH TECHNOLOGIES INTL INC (DE)
Charter cancelled and declared
inoperative and void for
non-payment of taxes 03/01/1991

HEALTH TEX INC (NY)
Acquired by Chesebrough-Pond's,
Inc. 5/17/73
Each share Common $1 par
exchanged for (0.65) share Common
$1 par
(See Chesebrough-Pond's, Inc.)

HEALTHAMERICA CORP (DE)
Common 1¢ par split (5) for (2) by
issuance of (1.5) additional shares
7/9/84
Acquired by Maxicare Health Plans,
Inc. 11/1/86
Each share Common 1¢ par
exchanged for $16.50 cash

HEALTHAXIS COM INC (PA)
Merged into HealthAxis Inc.
01/26/2001
Each share Common 10¢ par
exchanged for (1.334) shares
Common 10¢ par
HealthAxis Inc. name changed to
BPO Management Services, Inc.
12/30/2008
(See BPO Management Services, Inc.)

HEALTHAXIS INC (PA)
Each share old Common 10¢ par
exchanged for (0.1) share new
Common 10¢ par 08/21/2003
Under plan of merger name changed
to BPO Management Services, Inc.
12/30/2008
(See BPO Management Services, Inc.)

HEALTHBRIDGE INC (TX)
Each share old Common $0.0001 par
exchanged for (0.05) share new
Common $0.0001 par 7/22/2003
Name changed to Providence
Resources, Inc. 10/9/2006

HEALTHCARE ACQUISITION CORP NEW (DE)
Units separated 10/06/2005
Name changed to PharmAthene, Inc.
08/03/2007
PharmAthene, Inc. recapitalized as
Altimmune, Inc. 05/05/2017

HEALTHCARE ACQUISITION CORP OLD (DE)
Name changed to Encore Medical
Corp. 3/26/97
(See Encore Medical Corp.)

HEALTHCARE ACQUISITION PARTNERS CORP (DE)
Name changed to HAPC, Inc. 04/25/2006
HAPC, Inc. name changed to InfuSystem Holdings, Inc. 10/26/2007

HEALTHCARE AFFILIATES INC (DE)
Charter cancelled and declared inoperative and void for non-payment of taxes 3/1/88

HEALTHCARE AMER INC (DE)
Plan of reorganization under Chapter 11 Federal Bankruptcy Code effective 5/13/96
Each share Common received first and final distribution of $0.047543 cash payable 6/5/2003 to holders of record 5/2/96
Note: Transfer books closed 4/29/96; stockholders did not receive any equity interest in the reorganized company
Certificates were not required to be surrendered and without value

HEALTHCARE BUSINESS SVCS GROUPS INC (NV)
Recapitalized as PPJ Enterprise (NV) 04/24/2008
Each share Common $0.001 par exchanged for (0.0025) share Common $0.001 par
PPJ Enterprise (NV) reorganized in Florida as PPJ Healthcare Enterprises, Inc. 12/01/2014

HEALTHCARE CAP CORP (AB)
Recapitalized as Sonus Corp. 02/09/1998
Each share Common no par exchanged for (0.2) share Common no par
(See Sonus Corp.)

HEALTHCARE COM CORP (GA)
Merged into XCare.net, Inc. 08/13/2001
Each share Common 1¢ par exchanged for (0.375) share Common 1¢ par
XCare.net, Inc. name changed to Quovadx, Inc. 10/01/2001
(See Quovadx, Inc.)

HEALTHCARE COMPARE CORP (DE)
Common 1¢ par split (2) for (1) by issuance of (1) additional share 12/17/1990
Common 1¢ par split (2) for (1) by issuance of (1) additional share 06/25/1991
Name changed to First Health Group Corp. 01/01/1998
First Health Group Corp. merged into Conventry Health Care, Inc. 01/28/2005 which merged into Aetna, Inc. 05/07/2013

HEALTHCARE FINL PARTNERS INC (DE)
Issue Information - 2,100,000 shares Common offered at $12.50 per share on 11/21/1996
Merged into Heller Financial, Inc. 7/28/99
Each share Common 1¢ par exchanged for either (1.2975) shares Class A Common $0.25 par, $35 cash, or a combination thereof
Note: Cash electors received cash for 86% of their holdings with the balance issued in stock

HEALTHCARE INTEGRATED SVCS INC (DE)
Name changed 8/1/99
Name changed from Healthcare Imaging Services, Inc. to Healthcare Intergrated Services, Inc. 8/1/99
Each share old Common 1¢ par exchanged for (0.1) share new Common 1¢ par 1/20/2000
Plan of reorganization under Chapter 11 Federal Bankruptcy Code effective 2/1/2005

No stockholders' equity

HEALTHCARE INTL INC (TX)
Plan of reorganization under Chapter 11 Federal Bankruptcy proceedings confirmed 03/00/1992
Details not available

HEALTHCARE INVS OF AMER INC (MD)
Name changed to REIT Americas, Inc. 06/25/2004
(See REIT Americas, Inc.)

HEALTHCARE LEADERS INCOME ETF (ON)
Name changed to Harvest Healthcare Leaders Income ETF 06/19/2018

HEALTHCARE LEADERS INCOME FD (ON)
Under plan of reorganization each Unit automatically became (1) Healthcare Leaders Income ETF Class A Unit 10/24/2016
Healthcare Leaders Income ETF name changed to Harvest Healthcare Leaders Income ETF 06/19/2018

HEALTHCARE NETWORK SOLUTIONS INC (DE)
Recapitalized as Nova BioGenetics, Inc. 08/14/2003
Each (8.9) shares Common $0.0001 par exchanged for (1) share Common $0.0001 par
(See Nova Biogenetics, Inc.)

HEALTHCARE PROVIDERS DIRECT INC (NV)
Chapter 11 bankruptcy proceedings dismissed 10/29/2010
No stockholders' equity

HEALTHCARE RLTY TR (MD)
8.875% Preferred Ser. A 1¢ par called for redemption at $25 on 09/30/2002
(Additional Information in Active)

HEALTHCARE RECOVERIES INC (DE)
Issue Information - 9,800,000 shares COM offered at $14 per share on 05/21/1997
Name changed to Trover Solutions Inc. 1/17/2003
(See Trover Solutions Inc.)

HEALTHCARE RES MGMT INC (NV)
Recapitalized as Triad Industries, Inc. 3/25/99
Each share Common $0.001 par exchanged for (0.1) share Common $0.001 par
Triad Industries, Inc. name changed to Direct Equity International, Inc. 5/12/2006

HEALTHCARE REV MGMT INC (NV)
Merged into HRM Acquisition Corp. 11/12/97
Each share Common $0.001 par exchanged for $0.1990354 cash

HEALTHCARE SVCS AMER INC (DE)
Name changed to Ramsay Health Care Inc. 11/3/88
Ramsay Health Care Inc. name changed to Ramsay Youth Services Inc. 1/1/99
(See Ramsay Youth Services Inc.)

HEALTHCARE TECHNOLOGIES LTD (ISRAEL)
Name changed to Nexgen Biofuels Ltd. 02/21/2008

HEALTHCARE USA INC (DE)
Acquired by Maxicare Health Plans, Inc. 10/1/86
Each share Common 1¢ par exchanged for $13.55 cash

HEALTHCENTRAL COM (DE)
Issue Information - 7,500,000 shares COM offered at $11 per share on 12/07/1999
Each share old Common $0.001 par exchanged for (0.02) share new Common $0.001 par 6/28/2001

Assets sold for the benefit of creditors 12/6/2001
Stockholders' equity unlikely

HEALTHCO, INC. (DE)
Name changed to Healthco International, Inc. 8/30/84
(See Healthco International, Inc.)

HEALTHCO INTL INC (DE)
Common 5¢ par split (5) for (4) by issuance of (0.25) additional share 10/5/87
Merged into HMD Acquisition Corp. 5/22/91
Each share Common 5¢ par exchanged for $15 cash

HEALTHCOMP EVALUATION SVCS CORP (NV)
Name changed to Exemplar International Inc. 12/31/2002
Exemplar International Inc. recapitalized as Now Corp. 12/4/2006

HEALTHCOR HLDGS INC (DE)
Plan of reorganization under Chapter 11 Federal Bankruptcy Code confirmed 03/03/2000
No stockholders' equity

HEALTHCORE MED SOLUTIONS INC (DE)
Issue Information - 1,760,000 UNITS consisting of (1) share CL A and (1) WT offered at $5 per Unit on 10/14/1997
Name changed to Adatom.com, Inc. (DE) 10/13/1999
Adatom.com, Inc. (DE) reincorporated in Ontario as First Canadian American Holding Corp. 09/19/2002 which reincorporated in Wyoming 12/05/2004 which name changed to Blackout Media Corp. 01/09/2006

HEALTHDATA INTERNATIONAL, INC. (DE)
Voluntarily dissolved 12/21/84
Details not available

HEALTHDESK CORP (CA)
Issue Information - 1,700,000 shares COM and 1,700,000 WTS offered at $5 per COM and 10¢ per WT on 01/16/1997
Name changed to MC Informatics, Inc. 03/29/1999
(See MC Informatics, Inc.)

HEALTHDYNE INC (GA)
Common 1¢ par split (3) for (2) by issuance of (0.5) additional share 05/25/1983
Stock Dividend - 100% 07/19/1982
Merged into Matria Healthcare, Inc. 03/08/1996
Each share Common 1¢ par exchanged for (1) share Common 1¢ par
Matria Healthcare, Inc. merged into Inverness Medical Innovations, Inc. 05/09/2008 which name changed to Alere Inc. 07/14/2010
(See Alere Inc.)

HEALTHDYNE INFORMATION ENTERPRISES INC (GA)
Secondary Offering - 2,750,000 shares COM offered at $4.25 per share on 10/30/1996
Name changed to Hie Inc 02/24/1999
Hie Inc. name changed to Healthcare.com Corp. 04/10/2000 which merged into XCare.net, Inc. 08/13/2001 which name changed to Quovadx, Inc. 10/01/2001
(See Quovadx, Inc.)

HEALTHDYNE TECHNOLOGIES INC (GA)
Common 1¢ par split (4) for (3) by issuance of (1/3) additional share 09/14/1994
Merged into Respironics, Inc. 02/11/1998
Each share Common 1¢ par exchanged for (0.922) share Common 1¢ par

(See Respironics, Inc.)

HEALTHEON WEBMD CORP (DE)
Name changed 11/11/1999
Under plan of merger name changed from Healtheon Corp. to Healtheon/WebMD Corp. 11/11/1999
Under plan of merger name changed to WebMD Corp. 09/12/2000
WebMD Corp. name changed to Emdeon Corp. 10/17/2005 which name changed to HLTH Corp. 05/21/2007 which merged into WebMD Health Corp. 10/23/2009
(See WebMD Health Corp.)

HEALTHETECH INC (DE)
Issue Information - 4,000,000 shares COM offered at $7.50 per share on 07/12/2002
Each share old Common $0.001 par exchanged for (0.2) share new Common $0.001 par 01/02/2004
Liquidation completed
Each share new Common $0.001 par received initial distribution of $0.27 cash payable 12/19/2007 to holders of record 12/17/2007 Ex date - 01/07/2008
Each share new Common $0.001 par received second and final distribution of $0.14464 cash payable 08/29/2011 to holders of record 08/29/2011
Note: Certificates were not required to be surrendered and are without value

HEALTHEXTRAS INC (DE)
Name changed to Catalyst Health Solutions, Inc. 09/29/2008
Catalyst Health Solutions, Inc. merged into SXC Health Solutions Corp. 07/03/2012 which name changed to Catamaran Corp. 07/11/2012
(See Catamaran Corp.)

HEALTHGARDE CORP (UT)
Name changed to Allscope Resources International, Inc. 04/09/1982
(See Allscope Resources International, Inc.)

HEALTHGATE DATA CORP (DE)
Each share old Common 1¢ par exchanged for (0.33333333) share new Common 1¢ par 07/01/2001
Company terminated common stock registration and is no longer public as 05/26/2005

HEALTHGRADES COM INC (DE)
Name changed to Health Grades Inc. 11/21/2000
(See Health Grades Inc.)

HEALTHGROUP INTL (CA)
Merged into Hospital Corp. of America 7/17/85
Each share Common no par exchanged for $10 cash

HEALTHIENT INC (NV)
Each share old Common $0.001 par exchanged for (0.02) share new Common $0.001 par 10/01/2012
Recapitalized as SnackHealthy, Inc. 10/28/2013
Each share Common $0.001 par exchanged for (0.01) share Common no par
SnackHealthy, Inc. name changed to Amaize Beverage Corp. 08/19/2015 which name changed to Curative Biosciences, Inc. 03/14/2018

HEALTHINFUSION INC (FL)
Common 1¢ par split (3) for (2) by issuance of (0.5) additional share 12/16/91
Merged into Coram Healthcare Corp. 7/8/94
Each share Common 1¢ par exchanged for (0.447) share Common $0.001 par
(See Coram Healthcare Corp.)

HEALTHLEASE PPTYS REAL ESTATE INVT TR (ON)
Acquired by Health Care REIT, Inc. 11/24/2014
Each Unit exchanged for $14.20 cash
Note: Unexchanged certificates will be cancelled and become without value 11/24/2020

HEALTHMATE INC (DE)
Under plan of reorganization each share Common 1¢ par exchanged for $0.03 cash 6/15/91

HEALTHNET INTL INC (CO)
Name changed to General Oil & Gas, Inc. 8/4/2006

HEALTHNOSTICS INC (DE)
Each share old Common $0.0001 par exchanged for (1) share new Common $0.0001 par to reflect a (1) for (100) reverse split followed by a (100) for (1) forward split 03/15/2007
Note: Holders of (99) or fewer pre-split shares received $0.026 cash per share
Each share new Common $0.0001 par exchanged again for (0.01) share new Common $0.0001 par 01/30/2009
Each share new Common $0.0001 par exchanged for (0.00066666) share old Common $0.00001 par 07/31/2013
Each share old Common $0.00001 par exchanged for (0.005) share new Common $0.00001 par 05/20/2015
Recapitalized as EnviroTechnologies International, Inc. 09/08/2016
Each share new Common $0.00001 par exchanged for (0.0001) share Common $0.00001 par

HEALTHPLACE CORP (NV)
Name changed to China Packaging Group, Inc. 08/13/2010
China Packaging Group, Inc. name changed to China Shengda Packaging Group, Inc. 12/09/2010
(See China Shengda Packaging Group, Inc.)

HEALTHPLAN SVCS CORP (DE)
Name changed to PlanVista Corp. 04/12/2001
PlanVista Corp. merged into ProxyMed, Inc 03/02/2004
(See ProxyMed, Inc.)

HEALTHPLEX INC (DE)
Merged into Dent Acquisition Inc. 3/9/2000
Each share Common $0.001 par exchanged for $2.75 cash

HEALTHPRICER INTERACTIVE LTD (CANADA)
Recapitalized as Disani Capital Corp. (Canada) 03/18/2013
Each share Common no par exchanged for (0.03333333) share Common no par
Disani Capital Corp. (Canada) reorganized in British Columbia as NeutriSci International Inc. 12/04/2014

HEALTHRENU MED INC (NV)
SEC revoked common stock registration 12/21/2016

HEALTHRIDER INC (UT)
Recapitalized as Parkside Industries, Inc. (UT) 4/29/93
Each share Common no par exchanged for (0.25) share Common no par
Parkside Industries, Inc. (UT) reorganized in Nevada as Labco Pharmaceuticals Corp. 4/23/96 which recapitalized as Checkpoint Genetics Pharmaceuticals Inc. 8/15/2000 which recapitalized as InterNatural Pharmaceuticals Inc. 7/13/2001

HEALTHRITE INC (DE)
Name changed to Medifast, Inc. 02/05/2001

HEALTHSCREEN SOLUTIONS INC (BC)
Filed a petition under Bankruptcy and Insolvency Act 09/02/2011
Stockholders' equity unlikely

HEALTHSHARES INC (MD)
Completely liquidated 09/30/2008
Each share Autoimmune-Inflamation ETF $0.0001 par received approximately $20.97 cash
Each share Cardio Devices ETF $0.0001 par received approximately $26.49 cash
Each share Cardiology ETF $0.0001 par received approximately $23.10 cash
Each share Composite ETF $0.0001 par received approximately $23.37 cash
Each share Dermatolgy & Wound Care ETF $0.0001 par received approximately $20.61 cash
Each share Emerging Cancer ETF $0.0001 par received approximately $14.69 cash
Each share European Medical Products & Devices ETF $0.0001 par received approximately $17.42 cash
Each share GI/Gender Health ETF $0.0001 par received approximately $17.68 cash
Each share Infectious Disease ETF $0.0001 par received approximately $20.38 cash
Each share Metabolic-Endocrine Disorders ETF $0.0001 par received approximately $14.09 cash
Each share Neuroscience ETF $0.0001 par received approximately $21.58 cash
Each share Ophthalmology ETF $0.0001 par received approximately $14.49 cash
Each share Orthopedic Repair ETF $0.0001 par received approximately $21.93 cash
Each share Patient Care Services ETF $0.0001 par received approximately $20.96 cash
Each share Respiratory/Pulmonary ETF $0.0001 par received approximately $18.63 cash
Completely liquidated 12/31/2008
Each share Cancer ETF $0.0001 par received approximately $25.98 cash
Each share Diagnostics ETF $0.0001 par received approximately $21.17 cash
Each share Drug Discovery Tools ETF $0.0001 par received approximately $24.64 cash
Each share European Drugs ETF $0.0001 par received approximately $15.76 cash

HEALTHSONIX INC (NV)
Charter revoked 03/31/2009

HEALTHSOURCE INC (NH)
Common 10¢ par split (3) for (2) by issuance of (0.5) additional share 12/15/92
Common 10¢ par split (2) for (1) by issuance of (1) additional share 3/14/94
Common 10¢ par split (2) for (1) by issuance of (1) additional share 12/15/95
Merged into CIGNA Corp. 7/31/97
Each share Common 10¢ par exchanged for $21.75 cash

HEALTHSOUTH CORP (DE)
Name changed 12/30/1994
Common 1¢ par split (3) for (2) by issuance of (0.5) additional share 12/31/1991
Name changed from HealthSouth Rehabilitation Corp. to HealthSouth Corp. 12/30/1994
Old Common 1¢ par split (2) for (1) by issuance of (1) additional share 04/17/1995
Old Common 1¢ par split (2) for (1) by issuance of (1) additional share payable 03/17/1997 to holders of record 03/13/1997
Each share old Common 1¢ par exchanged for (0.2) share new Common 1¢ par 10/26/2006
Each share 6.5% Conv. Perpetual Preferred Ser. A 10¢ par exchanged for (33.9905) shares new Common 1¢ par 04/23/2015
Each share 144A 6.5% Conv. Perpetual Preferred Ser. A 10¢ par exchanged for (33.9905) shares new Common 1¢ par 04/23/2015
Name changed to Encompass Health Corp. 01/02/2018

HEALTHSPAN INC (DE)
Recapitalized as Riverside Information Technologies, Inc. (DE) 10/10/2006
Each (300) shares Common $0.00001 par exchanged for (1) share Common $0.00001 par
Riverside Information Technologies, Inc. (DE) reincorporated in Nevada as Clean Coal Technologies, Inc. 10/12/2007

HEALTHSPORT INC (DE)
Chapter 11 bankruptcy proceedings dismissed 09/04/2013
No stockholders' equity

HEALTHSPRING INC (DE)
Acquired by Cigna Corp. 01/31/2012
Each share Common 1¢ par exchanged for $55 cash

HEALTHSTAR CORP (DE)
Name changed to BlueStone Holding Corp. 09/05/2001
(See BlueStone Holding Corp.)

HEALTHSTREAMS TECHNOLOGY INC (ON)
Name changed to MediSolution Ltd. 09/18/1997
(See MediSolution Ltd.)

HEALTHTALK LIVE INC (NV)
Name changed to Right On Brands, Inc. 08/31/2017

HEALTHTECH INTL INC (NV)
Charter permanently revoked 02/28/2001

HEALTHTEK INC (DE)
Each share Common 1¢ par exchanged for (0.2) share Common 5¢ par 02/09/1990
Recapitalized as C'Watre International, Inc. 06/26/2007
Each share Common 5¢ par exchanged for (0.01) share Common 5¢ par
C'Watre International, Inc. recapitalized as Biomimix, Inc. 04/13/2009

HEALTHTRAC INC (CANADA)
Dissolved for non-compliance 11/09/2012

HEALTHTRONICS INC (GA)
Name changed 6/7/2001
Name changed 11/10/2004
Name changed from HealthTronics, Inc. to HealthTronics Surgical Services Inc. 06/07/2001 which name changed back to HealthTronics, Inc. 11/10/2004
Acquired by Endo Pharmaceuticals Holdings Inc. 07/12/2010
Each share Common no par exchanged for $4.85 cash

HEALTHTRUST INC-THE HOSPITAL CO (DE)
Merged into Columbia/HCA Healthcare Corp. 04/24/1995
Each share Common $0.001 par exchanged for (0.88) shares Common 1¢ par
Columbia/HCA Healthcare Corp. name changed to HCA - The Healthcare Co. 05/25/2000 which name changed to HCA Inc. (Ctfs. dated after 06/29/2001) 06/29/2001
(See HCA Inc. (Ctfs. dated after 06/29/2001))

HEALTHVEST (MD)
Acquired by Healthcare America, Inc. 12/31/93
Each Share of Bene. Int. no par exchanged for (1) share Common 1¢ par

HEALTHWATCH INC (MN)
Each share old Common no par exchanged for (0.1) share new Common no par 10/22/1987
Each share new Common no par exchanged for (0.25) share Common 1¢ par 01/12/1994
Each share Common 1¢ par exchanged for (0.14285714) share old Common 7¢ par 05/13/1996
Each share old Common 7¢ par exchanged again for (0.2) share new Common 7¢ par 02/23/1998
Each share new Common 7¢ par exchanged for (0.2) share Common 5¢ par 12/22/1999
SEC revoked common stock registration 12/02/2004

HEALTHWAYS INC (DE)
Name changed to Tivity Health, Inc. 01/11/2017

HEALTHWAYS SYS INC (DE)
Merged into Aetna Life Insurance Co. 6/27/89
Each share Common 1¢ par exchanged for $7 cash

HEALTHWISE AMER INC (DE)
Common 25¢ par split (3) for (2) by issuance of (0.5) additional share 05/26/1994
Merged into United HealthCare Corp. 04/12/1996
Each share Common 25¢ par exchanged for (0.6475) share Common 1¢ par
United HealthCare Corp. name changed to UnitedHealth Group Inc. (MN) 03/01/2000 which reincorporated in Delaware 07/01/2015

HEALTHWORLD CORP (DE)
Issue Information - 2,100,000 shares COM offered at $9 per share on 11/21/1997
Merged into Cordiant Communications Group PLC 03/02/2000
Each share Common 1¢ par exchanged for (0.8664) new Sponsored ADR for Ordinary 25p par
Cordiant Communications Group PLC merged into WPP Group PLC (United Kingdom) 08/01/2003 which reorganized in Jersey as WPP PLC (Old) 11/20/2008 which reorganized as WPP PLC (New) 01/02/2013

HEALTHY CHOICE CORP (NV)
Name changed to Imagin Net Inc. 10/28/98
Imagin Net Inc. name changed to Virtual Games, Inc. 4/23/99 which recapitalized as MidAmerica Oil & Gas Inc. 8/13/2002 which name changed to Sounds 24-7, Inc. 1/15/2004 which recapitalized as Allied Energy Corp. 1/26/2006

HEALTHY EATING INC (AB)
Name changed to Humpty's Restaurants International Inc. 09/12/1991
(See Humpty's Restaurants International Inc.)

HEALTHY FAST FOOD INC (NV)
Units separated 04/18/2008
Units separated 11/22/2010
Name changed to U-Swirl, Inc. 05/16/2011

HEALTHY PLANET PRODS INC (DE)
Assets assigned for the benefit of creditors 02/24/2003
Stockholders' equity unlikely

HEALTHZONE LTD (AUSTRALIA)
Each old Sponsored ADR for Ordinary exchanged for (0.5) new Sponsored ADR for Ordinary 11/01/2010
ADR basis changed from (1:10) to (1:20) on 11/01/2010
ADR agreement terminated 02/28/2012
No ADR holders' equity

HEARME (DE)
Liquidation completed
Each share Common $0.00005 par received initial distribution of $0.18 cash payable 3/12/2002 to holders of record 11/26/2001
Each share Common $0.00005 par received second distribution of $0.0467 cash payable 12/17/2004 to holders of record 11/26/2001
Ex date - 12/20/2004
Each share Common $0.00005 par received third and final distribution of $0.009977 cash payable 8/30/2005 to holders of record 11/26/2001
Note: Certificates were not required to be surrendered and are without value

HEARN DEPARTMENT STORES, INC. (NY)
Common $5 par changed to 1¢ par 8/15/56
Name changed to Specialty Stores Co., Inc. 10/30/56
Specialty Stores Co., Inc. name changed Diversified Specialty Stores Corp. 5/27/58 which name changed to Diversified Stores Corp. 1/9/59 which merged into City Stores Co. 1/30/60 which name changed to CSS Industries, Inc. 9/24/85

HEARNE COPPERMINE EXPLS LTD (BC)
Recapitalized as United Hearne Resources Ltd. (BC) 10/25/1973
Each share Common 50¢ par exchanged for (0.5) share Common $1 par
United Hearne Resources Ltd. (BC) reincorporated in Canada 11/17/1986
(See United Hearne Resources Ltd.)

HEARST-ARGYLE TELEVISION INC (DE)
Acquired by Hearst Corp. 06/04/2009
Each share Common 1¢ par exchanged for $4.50 cash

HEARST CONS PUBNS INC (DE)
Each share Class A $25 par exchanged for $30 cash 12/15/1964

HEARST LARDER MINES LTD. (ON)
Charter revoked for failure to file reports and pay fees 09/29/1966

HEART AMER GROWTH FD INC (DE)
Ceased operations 01/22/1981
Details not available

HEART FED SVGS & LN ASSN AUBURN (CA)
Common $1 par changed to 50¢ par and (1) additional share issued 4/30/87
Reorganized under the laws of Delaware as Heartfed Financial Corp. and Common 50¢ par changed to 1¢ par 12/22/89
Heartfed Financial Corp. merged into U.S. Bancorp (OR) 3/28/91 which merged into U.S. Bancorp (Old) (DE) 8/1/97 which merged into U.S. Bancorp (New) 2/27/2001

HEART HEALTH INC (DE)
Each share old Common $0.001 par exchanged for (0.005) share new Common $0.001 par 06/19/2008
Reincorporated under the laws of Nevada as Blue Gold Beverages, Inc. 06/15/2010
Blue Gold Beverages, Inc. recapitalized as Dragon Polymers Inc. 04/27/2012 which name changed to Hitec Corp. 11/04/2015 which recapitalized as Lead Innovation Corp. 03/27/2018

HEART LABS AMER INC (FL)
Name changed to Medical Industries of America, Inc. 10/30/1996
Medical Industries of America, Inc. reorganized as Cyber-Care, Inc. 08/26/1999 which name changed to CyberCare, Inc. 06/26/2001
(See CyberCare, Inc.)

HEART MINERALS LTD (BC)
Name changed to SRO Entertainment International Inc. 06/27/1984
SRO Entertainment International Inc. recapitalized as PacRim Entertainment Group Inc. 01/30/1990 which name changed to Evergreen International Technology Inc. 01/09/1991 which name changed to Jot-It! Software Corp. 02/01/1997 which name changed to Sideware Systems Inc. (BC) 02/18/1998 which reincorporated in Yukon 01/02/2002 which reincorporated in Delaware as Knowledgemax, Inc. 05/21/2002
(See Knowledgemax, Inc.)

HEART TECHNOLOGY INC (DE)
Merged into Boston Scientific Corp. 12/29/95
Each share Common 1¢ par exchanged for (0.675) share Common 1¢ par

HEARTFED FINL CORP (DE)
Merged into U.S. Bancorp (OR) 03/28/1991
Each share Common 1¢ par exchanged for (0.975) share Common $5 par
U.S. Bancorp (OR) merged into U.S. Bancorp 08/01/1997

HEARTHBRITE INDS INC (NJ)
Charter revoked for failure to file annual reports 3/5/96

HEARTLAND BANCORP (IA)
Reincorporated under the laws of Delaware as Heartland Financial USA Inc. 5/8/91

HEARTLAND BANCSHARES INC (IL)
Merged into Banterra Acquisition 6/1/99
Each share Common $1 par exchanged for $15.75 cash

HEARTLAND BANCSHARES INC (IN)
Stock Dividends - 5% payable 10/20/2000 to holders of record 10/06/2000 Ex date - 10/04/2000; 5% payable 11/19/2001 to holders of record 11/05/2001 Ex date - 11/01/2001
Merged into Horizon Bancorp 07/17/2012
Each share Common no par exchanged for (0.54) share Common no par
Horizon Bancorp name changed to Horizon Bancorp, Inc. 05/08/2018

HEARTLAND BRDG CAP INC (DE)
Name changed to InterCore Energy, Inc. 05/16/2012
InterCore Energy, Inc. recapitalized as InterCore, Inc. 12/31/2013

HEARTLAND DEV CORP (NY)
5% Conv. Preferred $12 par called for redemption 05/01/1964
Merged into Wytex Corp. 04/30/1971
Each share Common $1 par exchanged for (0.1) share Conv. Preference $25 par
(See Wytex Corp.)

HEARTLAND ENERGY GROUP INC (NV)
Name changed to Tritent International Corp. 01/20/2009

HEARTLAND FINL INC (NV)
Charter revoked for failure to file reports and pay fees 06/01/1990

HEARTLAND GROUP COS INC (FL)
Name changed to Banc Stock Group, Inc. 6/19/97
Banc Stock Group, Inc. name changed to Diamond Hill Investment Group, Inc. (FL) 4/27/2001 which reincorporated in Ohio 5/6/2002

HEARTLAND GROUP INC (MD)
U.S. Government Fund $0.001 par reclassified as U.S. Government Securities Fund $0.001 par 04/26/1994
U.S. Government Securities Fund $0.001 par reclassified as Government Fund $0.001 par 05/01/1999
Completely liquidated 08/09/2000
Each share Government Fund $0.001 par received net asset value
(Additional Information in Active)

HEARTLAND HOLDING CORP. (NY)
Name changed to Heartland Development Corp. 2/18/58
Heartland Development Corp. merged into Wytex Corp. 4/30/71
(See Wytex Corp.)

HEARTLAND INC (NV)
Name changed to California Venture Group. 8/18/98
(See California Venture Group.)

HEARTLAND OIL & GAS CORP (BC)
Merged into American Energy Corp. 08/03/1982
Each share Common no par exchanged for (0.5) share Common no par
American Energy Corp. recapitalized as Nickling Resources Inc. 06/05/1984 which recapitalized as Florin Resources Inc. 05/09/1989 which merged into Crimsonstar Mining Corp. 06/19/1991 which recapitalized as Mountain View Ventures Inc. 05/21/1993 which recapitalized as Blackrun Ventures Inc. 04/08/1997 which recapitalized as Blackrun Minerals Inc. 08/10/1999 which name changed to Diversified Industries Ltd. 03/29/2000
(See Diversified Industries Ltd.)

HEARTLAND OIL & GAS CORP (NV)
Each share old Common $0.001 par exchanged for (0.1) share new Common $0.001 par 07/25/2007
SEC revoked common stock registration 01/18/2013

HEARTLAND PARTNERS L P (DE)
Plan of reorganization under Chapter 11 Federal Bankruptcy Code effective 11/7/2006
No stockholders' equity

HEARTLAND PMT SYS INC (DE)
Merged into Global Payments Inc. 04/25/2016
Each share Common $0.001 par exchanged for (0.6687) share Common no par and $53.28 cash

HEARTLAND RES INC (ON)
Name changed to Ryland Oil Corp. 09/10/2007
Ryland Oil Corp. merged into Crescent Point Energy Corp. 08/23/2010

HEARTLAND TECHNOLOGY INC (DE)
Plan of reorganization under Chapter 11 Federal Bankruptcy Code effective 11/15/2005
No stockholders' equity

HEARTLAND WIRELESS COMMUNICATIONS INC (DE)
Issue Information - 2,100,000 shares COM offered at $10.50 per share on 04/21/1994
Reorganized under Chapter 11 Federal Bankruptcy Code as Nucentrix Broadband Networks, Inc. 04/01/1999
Each share Common received (0.013) Common Stock Purchase Warrant expiring 10/01/2007 payable 05/15/2002 to holders of record 03/05/1999
Note: Certificates were not required to be surrendered and are without value
Holders of (71) or fewer shares received no distribution
(See Nucentrix Broadband Networks, Inc.)

HEARTPORT INC (DE)
Merged into Johnson & Johnson 4/18/2001
Each share Common $0.001 par exchanged for (0.0307) share Common $1 par

HEARTSTAT TECHNOLOGY INC (DE)
Name changed to Verdant Technology Corp. 03/01/2006
(See Verdant Technology Corp.)

HEARTSTREAM INC (DE)
Merged into Hewlett-Packard Co. (CA) 03/26/1998
Each share Common no par exchanged for (0.173433) share Common $1 par
Hewlett-Packard Co. (CA) reincorporated in Delaware 05/20/1998 which name changed to HP Inc. 11/02/2015

HEARTWARE INTL INC (DE)
Acquired by Medtronic PLC 08/23/2016
Each share Common $0.001 par exchanged for $58 cash

HEARTWOOD CAP CORP (AB)
Name changed to Neo Alliance Minerals Inc. 04/10/2006
Neo Alliance Minerals Inc. name changed to Synergy Acquisition Corp. (AB) 12/20/2010 reincorporated in Canada as Genius Properties Ltd. 02/13/2014 which name changed to Cerro de Pasco Resources Inc. 10/18/2018

HEARX CANADA INC (CANADA)
Each Exchangeable Share no par exchanged for (1) share HearUSA, Inc. Common 10¢ par 12/29/2009

HEARX LTD (DE)
Each share old Common 10¢ par exchanged for (0.1) share new Common 10¢ par 6/30/99
Name changed to HearUSA, Inc. 7/8/2002

HEASTON RES LTD (BC)
Name changed to W.H. Helijet Airways Inc. 06/16/1987
W.H. Helijet Airways Inc. name changed to Helijet International Inc. 02/14/2000

HEAT-TIMER CORP. (NY)
Name changed to Standard Instrument Corp. 7/8/60
Standard Instrument Corp. name changed to H-T Products Corp. 7/12/67
(See H-T Products Corp.)

HEATH (D.C.) & CO. (ME)
Acquired by Raytheon Co. 7/22/66
Each share Common $5 par exchanged for (0.75) share Common $5 par

HEATH GOLD MINES LTD (ON)
Charter cancelled for failure to pay taxes and file returns 03/16/1976

HEATH TECNA CORP (WA)
Common no par split (2) for (1) by

issuance of (1) additional share 08/22/1967
Common no par split (2) for (1) by issuance of (1) additional share 05/06/1968
Each share old Common no par exchanged for (0.1) share new Common no par 03/11/1975
New Common no par split (3) for (1) by issuance of (2) additional shares 06/16/1977
New Common no par split (5) for (4) by issuance of (0.5) additional share 08/31/1979
Name changed to Criton Corp. 07/01/1980
(See Criton Corp.)

HEATH TECNA-PLASTICS, INC. (WA)
Name changed to Heath Tecna Corp. 07/22/1965
Heath Tecna Corp. name changed to Criton Corp. 07/01/1980
(See Criton Corp.)

HEATHERCLIFF GROUP INC (NV)
Name changed to StarMed Group Inc. 07/27/2001
StarMed Group Inc. name changed to Westmoore Holdings, Inc. 01/28/2008 which name changed to Rockwall Holdings, Inc. 04/22/2010
(See Rockwall Holdings, Inc.)

HEATHRIDGE MINES LTD. (ON)
Charter cancelled for failure to pay taxes and file returns 04/09/1975

HEATING OIL PARTNERS INCOME FD (ON)
Subsidiaries plan of reorganization recognized and implemented in the Ontario Superior Court of Justice 06/26/2006
No Unitholders' equity

HEATMASTERS INC. (MD)
Charter forfeited 10/31/1952

HEATWURX INC (DE)
Recapitalized as Processa Pharmaceuticals, Inc. 12/08/2017
Each share Common $0.0001 par exchanged for (0.14285714) share Common $0.0001 par

HEAVENEXPRESS COM INC (FL)
Name changed to Golden Sand Eco-Protection, Inc. 09/02/2003
Golden Sand Eco-Protection, Inc. recapitalized as Galaxy Minerals, Inc. 04/15/2004
(See Galaxy Minerals, Inc.)

HEAVENLY HOT DOGS INC (NV)
Reincorporated 07/13/2000
State of incorporation changed from (DE) to (NV) 07/13/2000
Each share old Common $0.001 par exchanged for (0.0001) share new Common $0.001 par 04/04/2001
Note: No holder will receive fewer than (100) post-split shares
Name changed to B4MC Gold Mines, Inc. 11/12/2013
B4MC Gold Mines, Inc. name changed to RocketFuel Blockchain, Inc. 09/28/2018

HEAVENLY SLENDER FOODS INC (DE)
Recapitalized 03/07/1994
Recapitalized from Heavenly Slender Sweets, Inc. to Heavenly Slender Foods Inc. 03/07/1994
Each share Common $0.001 par exchanged for (0.1) share Common $0.001 par
Name changed to Pacific Pharmaceuticals I, Inc. 06/17/1994
Pacific Pharmaceuticals I, Inc. recapitalized as Sunmark Industries I, Inc. 06/27/1994 name changed to Mark I Industries, Inc. 05/14/1998 which name changed to Foodvision.com Inc. 06/00/1999
(See Foodvision.com Inc.)

HEAVENLYDOOR COM INC (DE)
Name changed to Paligent Inc. 12/31/2000
Paligent Inc. recapitalized as International Fight League, Inc. 11/29/2006 which recapitalized as IFLI Acquisition Corp. 07/08/2010 which name changed to SimplePons, Inc. 12/27/2011 which recapitalized as Eco-Shift Power Corp. 11/26/2013

HEAVENS DOOR CORP (DE)
Merged into Procept, Inc. 01/28/2000
Each share Common $0.001 par exchanged for (0.8381) share Common $0.001 par
Procept, Inc. name changed to HeavenlyDoor.com, Inc. 01/31/2000 which name changed to Paligent Inc. 12/31/2000 which recapitalized as International Fight League, Inc. 11/29/2006 which recapitalized as IFLI Acquisition Corp. 07/08/2010 which name changed to SimplePons, Inc. 12/27/2011 which recapitalized as Eco-Shift Power Corp. 11/26/2013

HEAVY DUTY AIR INC (MN)
Assets sold in 1991
Details not available

HEAVY METAL INC (NV)
Name changed to Options Media Group Holdings, Inc. 07/10/2008

HEAVY METAL TECHNOLOGY CORP. (CA)
Name changed to Vanderbilt Gold Corp. (CA) 05/24/1971
Vanderbilt Gold Corp. (CA) reincorporated in Delaware 04/24/1987
(See Vanderbilt Gold Corp.)

HEBECOURT GOLD MINES, LTD. (QC)
Charter annulled for failure to file reports 5/11/74

HEBREW NATL KOSHER FOODS INC (NY)
Merged into Riviana Foods, Inc. (Old) 4/3/69
Each share Common 50¢ par exchanged for (0.445) share Common $3.50 par
Riviana Foods, Inc. (Old) acquired by Colgate-Palmolive Co. 6/14/76

HEBRON BAY RES LTD (AB)
Cease trade order effective 02/04/2000
Stockholders' equity unlikely

HEBRON BRICK CO
5% Preferred called for redemption at $100 on 10/17/2000

HEBRON FJORD RES INC (CANADA)
Name changed to H2O Innovation (2000) Inc. 12/01/2000
H2O Innovation (2000) Inc. name changed to H2O Innovation Inc. 12/04/2008

HEBRON SVGS BK (HEBRON, MD)
Under plan of reorganization each share Common 1¢ par automatically became (1) share HSB Bancorp Inc. Common 1¢ par 2/29/2000
(See HSB Bancorp Inc.)

HEC INVTS LTD (AB)
Name changed to Humboldt Capital Corp. 08/29/1994
(See Humboldt Capital Corp.)

HECATE GOLD CORP (BC)
Merged into Host Ventures Ltd. 06/29/1982
Each share Capital Stock no par exchanged for (1) share Common no par
Host Ventures Ltd. recapitalized as Hot Resources Ltd. 04/30/1984 which name changed to Inter-Globe Resources Ltd. 04/16/1985
(See Inter-Globe Resources Ltd.)

HECHINGER CO (DE)
Reincorporated 1/30/87
Common 10¢ par split (3) for (2) by issuance of (0.5) additional share 5/22/81
Common 10¢ par split (5) for (4) by issuance of (0.25) additional share 9/10/82
Common 10¢ par reclassified as Conv. Class B Common 10¢ par 10/14/83
Each share Conv. Class B Common 10¢ par received distribution of (0.25) share Class A Common 10¢ par 10/31/83
Class A Common 10¢ par split (5) for (4) by issuance of (0.25) additional share 6/17/85
Conv. Class B Common 10¢ par split (5) for (4) by issuance of (0.25) additional share 6/17/85
Class A Common 10¢ par split (5) for (4) by issuance of (0.25) additional share 6/20/86
Conv. Class B Common 10¢ par split (5) for (4) by issuance of (0.25) additional share 6/20/86
Stock Dividends - 20% 8/24/79; 20% 5/30/80
State of incorporation changed from (DC) to (DE) 1/30/87
Merged into Green Equity Investors II, L.P. 9/25/97
Each share Class A Common 10¢ par exchanged for $2.375 cash
Each share Conv. Class B Common 10¢ par exchanged for $2.375 cash

HECHT CO. (MD)
Merged into May Department Stores Co. 2/2/59
Each share 3-3/4% Preferred $100 par exchanged for (1) share new 3-3/4% Preferred $100 par
Each share Common $15 par exchanged for (0.925) share Common $5 par
May Department Stores Co. merged into Federated Department Stores, Inc. 8/30/2005 which name changed to Macy's, Inc. 6/1/2007

HECKER PRODUCTS CORP. (NJ)
Name changed to Best Foods, Inc. 00/00/1943
Best Foods, Inc. merged into Corn Products Co. (NJ) 09/30/1958 which reincorporated in Delaware 04/30/1959 which name changed to CPC International Inc. 04/23/1969 which name changed to BestFoods (DE) 01/01/1998
(See BestFoods (DE))

HECKMANN CORP (DE)
Units separated 11/09/2011
Name changed to Nuverra Environmental Solutions, Inc. 05/20/2013
(See Nuverra Environmental Solutions, Inc.)

HECKS INC (WV)
Class A Common 10¢ par reclassified as Common 10¢ par 05/25/1970
Common 10¢ par split (3) for (2) by issuance of (0.5) additional share 07/02/1970
Common 10¢ par split (2) for (1) by issuance of (1) additional share 05/07/1971
Common 10¢ par split (2) for (1) by issuance of (1) additional share 05/14/1976
Common 10¢ par split (3) for (2) by issuance of (0.5) additional share 05/28/1981
Reorganized under Chapter 11 Federal Bankruptcy Code 09/28/1989
Each share Common 10¢ par exchanged for (0.0225325) share Common $1 par and (0.0067597) Common Stock Purchase Warrant expiring 09/28/1994
Reincorporated under the laws of Delaware as Hallwood Industries Inc. 07/02/1990
Hallwood Industries Inc. name changed to Steel City Products, Inc. 01/13/1993
(See Steel City Products, Inc.)

HECLA-CHECKMATE MINING & DEVELOPMENT CO. (NV)
Charter revoked for failure to file reports and pay fees 3/4/74

HECLA COAL & COKE CO.
Liquidated in 1953

HECLA MNG CO (DE)
Reincorporated 06/06/1983
Capital Stock 25¢ par split (2) for (1) by issuance of (1) additional share 06/07/1968
Capital Stock 25¢ par reclassified as Common 25¢ par 01/16/1976
Common 25¢ par split (3) for (2) by issuance of (0.5) additional share 03/24/1981
State of incorporation changed from (WA) to (DE) 06/06/1983
Issue Information - 1,750,000 shares PFD CONV 6.5% offered at $100 per share on 12/12/2007
Each share 6.5% Conv. Preferred 25¢ par exchanged for (9.3773) shares Common 25¢ par 01/01/2011
(Additional Information in Active)

HECO CAP TR I (DE)
8.05% Quarterly Income Preferred Securities called for redemption at $25 on 4/19/2004

HECO CAP TR II (DE)
7.30% Quarterly Income Preferred Securities called for redemption at $25 on 4/19/2004

HECO LIQUIDATING CORP. (CA)
Liquidation completed 4/7/64

HECTOR COMMUNICATIONS CORP (MN)
Merged into Alltel Corp. 11/03/2006
Each share Conv. Preferred Ser. A $1 par exchanged for $36.40 cash
Each share Common 1¢ par exchanged for $36.40 cash

HECTOR REALTY CO. INC. (NY)
Proclaimed dissolved for failure to file reports and pay taxes 12/15/39

HECTOR RES INC (BC)
Recapitalized as Abacus Minerals Corp. 03/12/1993
Each share Common no par exchanged for (0.25) share Common no par
Abacus Minerals Corp. recapitalized as Abacus Mining & Exploration Corp. 04/23/2001

HEDBERG & GORDON FD INC (PA)
Name changed to Plitrend Fund, Inc. 02/20/1974
Plitrend Fund, Inc. name changed to U.S. Trend Fund, Inc. (PA) 02/00/1986 which reincorporated in Maryland as Capstone U.S. Trend Fund, Inc. 05/11/1992 which name changed to Capstone Growth Fund, Inc. 08/26/1994 which name changed to Capstone Series Fund, Inc. 01/22/2002

HEDBERG & GORDON LEVERAGE FD (PA)
Completely liquidated 12/13/73
Each share Common $1 par received first and final distribution of $801.36 cash

HEDGE FD AMER INC (DE)
Acquired by Oppenheimer A.I.M. Fund, Inc. 8/13/75
Each share Common $1 par exchanged for (0.7299216) share Capital Stock $1 par
Oppenheimer A.I.M. Fund, Inc. name changed to Oppenheimer Global Fund 2/1/87

HEDGEHOG MINES, LTD. (ON)
Charter cancelled for failure to file reports and pay taxes 00/00/1955

HEDGER CAP INC (BC)
Name changed to Pinestar Gold Inc. 02/03/2010

HEDGES DIESEL, INC. (NJ)
Charter voided for non-payment of taxes 02/05/1963

HEDLEY AMALGAMATED GOLD MINES, LTD. (BC)
Struck off register and declared dissolved for failure to file returns 06/21/1956

HEDLEY GOLD HILL MINING CO. LTD.
Dissolved 00/00/1948
Details not available

HEDLEY GOLD MINING CO., LTD.
Dissolved 00/00/1935
Details not available

HEDLEY MASCOT GOLD MINES LTD.
Acquired by Giant Mascot Mines Ltd. on a (0.55) for (1) basis 00/00/1951
Giant Mascot Mines Ltd. recapitalized as G M Resources Ltd. (BC) 04/11/1977 which reincorporated in Canada 09/08/1982 which merged into Campbell Resources Inc. (New) 06/08/1983
(See Campbell Resources Inc. (New))

HEDLEY MONARCH GOLD MINES LTD. (BC)
Merged into Friday Mines Ltd. 05/00/1961
Each share Capital Stock 50¢ par exchanged for (0.1) share Capital Stock 50¢ par
Friday Mines Ltd. recapitalized as Polaris Mines Ltd. 04/15/1966 which recapitalized as Titan-Polaris Mines Ltd. 05/28/1973 which recapitalized as Saxton Industries Ltd. 07/28/1975 which name changed to Delbancor Industries Ltd. 10/06/1987
(See Delbancor Industries Ltd.)

HEDLEY SHAMROCK GOLD MINES LTD.
Acquired by Canty Gold Mines (Hedley) Ltd. 00/00/1937
Each share Common exchanged for (0.4) share Common
Canty Gold Mines (Hedley) Ltd. was succeeded by Canty Gold Mines (1945) Ltd. 00/00/1945 which liquidated for Nighthawk Gold Mines Ltd. 00/00/1954 which recapitalized as High Point Mines Ltd. 03/07/1966 which recapitalized as Highhawk Mines Ltd. 05/18/1972 which recapitalized as Newhawk Gold Mines Ltd. 03/12/1979 which merged into Silver Standard Resources Inc. 09/30/1999

HEDLEY STERLING EXPLS INC (AB)
Recapitalized as Western Envirotech Inc. 03/05/1991
Each share Common no par exchanged for (0.25) share Common no par
Western Envirotech Inc. name changed to Aquasol International Group Inc. 10/31/1995
(See Aquasol International Group Inc.)

HEDLEY TECHNOLOGIES INC (CANADA)
Name changed 08/21/1992
Name changed 07/16/1996
Reincorporated 05/19/1999
Name changed from Hedley Pacific Mining Corp. Ltd. to Hedley Pacific Ventures Ltd. 08/21/1992
Name changed from Hedley Pacific Ventures Ltd. to Hedley Technologies Inc. 07/16/1996
Place of incorporation changed from (BC) to (Canada) 05/19/1999

Name changed to BioSyent Inc. 06/13/2006

HEDMAN MINES LTD (ON)
Name changed to Hedman Resources Ltd. and Common $1 par changed to no par 9/3/82

HEDONG ENERGY INC (CANADA)
Recapitalized as Benchmark Energy Corp. 02/09/2004
Each share Common no par exchanged for (0.33333333) share Common no par
Benchmark Energy Corp. name changed to Bolivar Energy Corp. (Canada) 10/29/2010 which reorganized in Alberta as Anatolia Energy Corp. 12/13/2011 which merged into Cub Energy Inc. 07/01/2013

HEDSTROM HLDGS INC (DE)
Plan of reorganization under Chapter 11 Federal Bankruptcy Code effective 8/1/2001
No stockholders' equity

HEE CORP
Each share Common no par received distribution of (1) share Preferred no par payable 09/15/2004 to holders of record 09/06/2004 Ex date - 09/01/2004
Recapitalized as Preachers Coffee Inc. (DE) 04/11/2008
Each (101) shares Common no par exchanged for (1) share Common $0.00000001 par and (1) share Preferred $0.000001 par
Preferred not affected except for change of name and no par changed to $0.000001 par
(See Preachers Coffee Inc. (DE))

HEEKIN CAN CO. (OH)
Ctfs. dated prior to 4/23/65
Liquidation completed
Each share Capital Stock no par exchanged for initial distribution of (1.823264) shares Diamond International Corp. Common 50¢ par 4/23/65
Each share Capital Stock no par received second and final distribution of (0.076745) share Diamond International Corp. Common 50¢ par 10/21/68
(See Diamond International Corp.)

HEEKIN CAN INC (OH)
Ctfs. dated after 9/13/85
Merged into Ball Corp. 3/19/93
Each share Common 1¢ par exchanged for (0.769) share Common no par

HEELYS INC (DE)
Issue Information - 6,425,000 shares COM offered at $21 per share on 12/07/2006
Acquired by Sequential Brands Group, Inc. 01/24/2013
Each share Common $0.001 par exchanged for $2.25 cash

HEENAN PETE LTD (CANADA)
Merged into Heenan Senlac Resources Ltd. 08/07/1986
Each share Capital Stock no par exchanged for (1.5) shares Common no par
Heenan Senlac Resources Ltd. merged into Mining & Allied Supplies (Canada) Ltd. 08/25/1992 which name changed to Bearing Power (Canada) Ltd. 03/28/1994
(See Bearing Power (Canada) Ltd.)

HEENAN SENLAC RES LTD (ON)
Merged into Mining & Allied Supplies (Canada) Ltd. 8/25/92
Each share Common no par exchanged for (0.4) share Common no par and (0.04) Common Stock Purchase Warrant expiring 6/30/94
Mining & Allied Supplies (Canada) Ltd. name changed to Bearing Power (Canada) Ltd. 3/28/94

(See Bearing Power (Canada) Ltd.)

HEERMANCE STORAGE & REFRIGERATING CO. CO. (NY)
Dissolved in 1951

HEES (GEO. H.) CO. LTD. (CANADA)
Recapitalized as National Hees Industries Ltd. 6/25/63
Each share 6% 1st Preferred $100 par exchanged for (2.5) shares 6% Conv. 1st Preferred 1963 Ser. $10 par
Each share Common no par exchanged for (1/3) share Common no par
National Hees Industries Ltd. name changed to EHN Industries Ltd. 6/28/72

HEES INTL BANCORP INC (ON)
Under plan of merged name changed to Edper Group Ltd. (New) 01/01/1997
Edper Group Ltd. (New) merged into EdperBrascan Corp. 08/01/1997 which name changed to Brascan Corp. 04/28/2000 which name changed to Brookfield Asset Management, Inc. 11/10/2005

HEES INTERNATIONAL CORP. (ON)
Floating Rate Class A Preference Ser. F $25 par reclassified as Floating Rate Class A Preference Ser. E $25 par 6/9/86
Common no par split (3) for (2) by issuance of (0.5) additional share 6/1/87
Name changed to Hees International Bancorp Inc. 5/6/88
Hees International Bancorp Inc. name changed to Edper Group Ltd. (New) 1/1/97 which merged into EdperBrascan Corp. 8/1/97 which name changed to Brascan Corp. 4/28/2000 which name changed to Brookfield Asset Management, Inc. 11/10/2005

HEFTEL BROADCASTING CORP (DE)
Class A Common $0.001 par split (2) for (1) by issuance of (1) additional share payable 12/01/1997 to holders of record 11/18/1997
Name changed to Hispanic Broadcasting Corp. 06/08/1999
Hispanic Broadcasting Corp. merged into Univision Communications, Inc. 09/22/2003
(See Univision Communications, Inc.)

HEGCO CDA INC (AB)
Delisted from Toronto Venture Stock Exchange 06/20/2003

HEGWER DRILLING CO., INC. (CO)
Recapitalized as National Energy Corp. (CO) 07/14/1967
Each share Common 1¢ par exchanged for (0.05) share Common 20¢ par
National Energy Corp. (CO) reincorporated in Tennessee as Aaminex Gold Corp. 04/01/1975 which reincorporated in Nevada 01/29/1981 which name changed to Aaminex Capital Corp. 12/23/1986
(See Aaminex Capital Corp.)

HEI CORP (NV)
Merged into Columbia/HEI Acquisition Corp. 7/31/90
Each share Common 10¢ par exchanged for $4.50 cash

HEI INC (MN)
Common 5¢ par split (6) for (5) by issuance of (0.2) additional share 01/12/1983
Plan of reorganization under Chapter 11 bankruptcy proceedings effective 10/08/2015
No stockholders' equity

HEICAROMAT OF INDIANA, INC. (IN)
Adjudicated bankrupt 2/17/67
No stockholders' equity

HEICO CORP (FL)
Common 16-2/3¢ par split (3) for (2) by issuance of (0.5) additional share 01/31/1989
Reorganized as HEICO Corp. (New) 04/28/1993
Each share Common 16-2/3¢ par exchanged for (1) share Common 1¢ par

HEIDE HENRY INC (NY)
Acquired by Hershey Foods Corp. 12/13/95
Details not available

HEIDELBERG BREWING CO. (KY)
Property sold and name changed to Heidelberg Co. in 1950 which name was changed to Kentucky Co. in 1952

HEIDELBERG BREWING CO. (WA)
Assets sold and name changed to Brewery Liquidation Co. 12/31/58
(See Brewery Liquidation Co.)

HEIDELBERG CO. (KY)
Name changed to Kentucky Co. in 1952

HEIDEMIJ N V (NETHERLANDS)
Name changed to Arcadis N.V. 12/24/1997

HEIDIS FLA INC (FL)
Name changed 8/6/87
Name changed from Heidis Frogen Yozurt Shoppes Florida, Inc. to Heidis of Florida, Inc. 8/6/87
Involuntarily dissolved 11/4/98

HEIDIS FROGEN YOZURT SHOPPES INC (FL)
Administratively dissolved 8/26/94

HEIDLER CORP (DE)
Adjudicated bankrupt 12/12/1972
Stockholders' equity unlikely

HEIGHTS FIN CORP (DE)
Stock Dividends - 10% 12/8/78; 10% 3/23/83
Merged into United Savings of America 3/30/84
Each share Common $1-2/3 par exchanged for $27.75 cash
Name changed to USA Financial Services Inc. 7/31/86
(See USA Financial Services Inc.)

HEIGHTS ST BK (HOUSTON, TX)
Common $25 par changed to $10 par and (1.5) additional shares issued 4/15/67
Stock Dividends - 50% 7/1/50; 50% 4/8/55; 33-1/3% 4/9/62; 25% 6/24/64; 10% 2/9/65; 33-1/3% 9/30/69; 25% 1/31/71; 20% 4/16/73; 16.66% 2/15/74; 14.28% 2/15/75; 12.5% 2/22/77; 11.11% 1/21/78; 10% 2/14/79; 12.72% 2/21/80
Merged into National Bancshares Corp. of Texas 11/28/83
Each share Common $10 par exchanged for (4.187572) shares Common $5 par
(See National Bancshares Corp. of Texas)

HEIJN ALBERT N V (NETHERLANDS)
Stock Dividends - 10% 07/14/1966; 10% 09/01/1967
Name changed to Ahold N.V. 09/10/1973
Ahold N.V. reorganized as Koninklijke Ahold N.V. 10/11/1989 which name changed to Koninklijke Ahold Delhaize N.V. 07/25/2016

HEILEMAN (G.) BREWING CO. (DE)
Stock Dividend - 50% 9/10/48
Merged into Heileman (G.) Brewing Co. Inc. (WI) 12/31/62
Each share Common exchanged for (1) share Common $1 par
(See Heileman (G.) Brewing Co., Inc. (WI))

HEILEMAN G BREWING INC (WI)
Common $1 par split (2) for (1) by

issuance of (1) additional share 4/30/68
Common $1 par split (4) for (1) by issuance of (3) additional shares 3/9/70
Common $1 par split (3) for (2) by issuance of (0.5) additional share 3/5/79
Common $1 par split (3) for (2) by issuance of (0.5) additional share 9/7/79
Common $1 par split (3) for (2) by issuance of (0.5) additional share 6/8/81
Common $1 par split (2) for (1) by issuance of (1) additional share 6/6/83
Each share Common $1 par exchanged for (0.0000001) share Common $10,000,000 par 3/3/88
Note: In effect holders received $40.75 cash per Common $1 par held and public interest was eliminated

HEILIG MEYERS CO (VA)
Common $2 par split (3) for (2) by issuance of (0.5) additional share 12/2/83
Common $2 par split (3) for (2) by issuance of (0.5) additional share 3/7/86
Common $2 par split (3) for (2) by issuance of (0.5) additional share 1/8/92
Common $2 par split (3) for (2) by issuance of (0.5) additional share 11/18/92
Common $2 par split (3) for (2) by issuance of (0.5) additional share 7/27/93
Stock Dividends - 10% 6/13/77; 10% 6/2/78; 10% 7/27/79; 10% 6/6/80; 10% 1/12/82
Plan of reorganization under Chapter 11 Federal Bankruptcy Code effective 2/17/2006
No stockholders' equity

HEIN WERNER CORP (WI)
Common $3 par changed to $1 par and (2) additional shares issued 4/19/68
Stock Dividends - 10% 11/30/64; 5% payable 1/26/96 to holders of record 1/5/96; 5% payable 1/24/97 to holders of record 1/3/97; 5% payable 1/23/98 to holders of record 1/2/98
Merged into Snap-On Inc. 7/17/98
Each share Common $1 par exchanged for $12.60 cash

HEIN-WERNER MOTOR PARTS CORP.
Name changed to Hein-Werner Corp. and 100% stock dividend paid in 1947
(See Hein-Werner Corp.)

HEINE BOILER CO.
Sold to Superheater Co. 00/00/1934
Details not available

HEINICKE INSTRS CO (FL)
Common 50¢ par changed to 16-2/3¢ par and (2) additional shares issued 06/26/1961
Stock Dividend - 25% 07/31/1962
Name changed to HEICO Corp. (Old) 03/18/1986
HEICO Corp. (Old) reorganized as HEICO Corp. (New) 04/28/1993

HEINZ H J CO (PA)
Common $25 par changed to $8.33-1/3 par and (2) additional shares issued 02/17/1961
Common $8.33-1/3 par changed to $4.16-2/3 par and (1) additional share issued 03/11/1969
$3.50 2nd Preferred 2nd Ser. $18.50 par conversion privilege expired 01/31/1976
Common $4.16-2/3 par changed to $3 par and (0.5) additional share issued 10/04/1976
$3.50 2nd Preferred 1st Ser. $18.50

par called for redemption 09/01/1980
Common $3 par changed to $1.50 par and (1) additional share issued 10/10/1981
Common $1.50 par changed to $1 par and (0.5) additional share issued 10/07/1983
Common $1 par changed to 50¢ par and (1) additional share issued 10/10/1985
3.65% Preferred $100 par called for redemption 01/01/1986
$3.50 2nd Preferred 2nd Ser. $18.50 par called for redemption 01/01/1986
Common 50¢ par changed to 25¢ par 09/12/1986
Common 25¢ par split (2) for (1) by issuance of (1) additional share 10/23/1989
Common 25¢ par split (3) for (2) by issuance of (0.5) additional share 11/09/1995
Each share Common 25¢ par received distribution of (0.4466) share Del Monte Foods Co. Common 1¢ par payable 12/20/2002 to holders of record 12/19/2002 Ex date - 12/23/2002
$1.70 3rd Preferred 1st Ser. $10 par called for redemption at $28.50 plus $0.53 accrued dividends on 04/08/2013
Stock Dividend - 20% 10/18/1951
Acquired by Hawk Acquisition Holding Corp. 06/07/2013
Each share Common 25¢ par exchanged for $72.50 cash

HEIST C H CORP (NY)
Common 5¢ par split (5) for (4) by issuance of (0.25) additional share 10/12/90
Common 5¢ par split (3) for (2) by issuance of (0.5) additional share 10/14/91
Stock Dividends - 10% 10/15/75; 10% 10/16/78; 10% 10/14/88
Reincorporated under the laws of Delaware as Ablest Inc. 3/13/2000
(See Ablest Inc.)

HEITMAN CDN RLTY INVS (ON)
Name changed to Canadian Realty Investors 07/25/1977
(See Canadian Realty Investors)

HEITMAN MTG INVS (MA)
Name changed to Regency Investors (MA) 8/31/82
Regency Investors (MA) reorganized in Delaware as Regency Equities Corp. 4/26/84
(See Regency Equities Corp.)

HEIZER CORP (DE)
Liquidation completed
Each share Common 1¢ par received initial distribution of $9 cash 8/2/84
Each share Common 1¢ par received second distribution of (0.1198) share Computer Consoles, Inc. Common 10¢ par, (0.2498) share Material Sciences Corp. Common 2¢ par and (0.077) share Paradyne Corp. Common 10¢ par 12/7/84
Each share Common 1¢ par received third distribution of (0.2436) share Commodore Corp. Common 5¢ par, (0.1258) share Fotomat Corp. Common 10¢ par and (0.0279) share International Capital Equipment Ltd. Common 5¢ par 12/21/84
Each share Common 1¢ par received (0.1418) share IDC Services Inc. Common 1¢ par distributed 1/24/85
Each share Common 1¢ par received $0.812 cash distributed 2/20/85
Each share Common 1¢ par exchanged for fourth distribution of $0.75 cash 2/25/85
Assets transferred to Heizer Corp. Stockholders' Liquidating Trust 2/26/85

Note: Details on subsequent distributions, if any, are not available

HELDOR ELECTRS MFG CORP (NJ)
Under plan of merger each share Common 10¢ par automatically became (1) share Heldor Industries, Inc. Common 1¢ par 3/13/70
Heldor Industries, Inc. name changed to Intertec-National Inc. 6/8/70
(See Intertec-National Inc.)

HELDOR INDUSTRIES, INC. (DE)
Name changed to Intertec-National Inc. 6/8/70
(See Intertec-National Inc.)

HELDOR INDS INC (CT)
Orderly Liquidation Plan of Reorganization confirmed 1/4/94
No stockholders' equity

HELEMANO CO. LTD. (HI)
Merged into Castle & Cooke, Inc. (Old) share for share 5/29/58
Castle & Cooke, Inc. (Old) name changed to Dole Food Co., Inc. (HI) 7/30/91 which reincorporated in Delaware 7/1/2012
(See Dole Food Co., Inc. (DE))

HELEN OF TROY CORP (TX)
Common 10¢ par split (3) for (2) by issuance of (0.5) additional share 10/01/1992
Stock Dividend - 100% 09/26/1983
Reincorporated under the laws of Bermuda as Helen of Troy Ltd. 02/16/1994

HELENA GAS & ELECTRIC CO.
Acquired by American Power & Light Co. 00/00/1928
Details not available

HELENA GOLD MINES LTD.
Struck off register 00/00/1948

HELENA LIGHT & RAILWAY CO.
Succeeded by Helena Gas & Electric Co. in 1927
Details not available

HELENA RES LTD (YT)
Name changed to THEMAC Resources Group Ltd. 03/05/2007

HELENA RUBINSTEIN INC (NY)
Recapitalized 00/00/1936
Each share $3 Preference no par exchanged for (1) share Class A no par and (1) share new Common no par
Each share old Common no par exchanged for (0.2) share new Common no par
New Common no par changed to $1 par 06/12/1969
Common $1 par split (2) for (1) by issuance of (1) additional share 02/05/1970
Stock Dividends - 50% 08/19/1955; 10% 10/08/1956; 10% 10/08/1957; 10% 10/14/1959; 60% 10/19/1960; 10% 04/15/1966
Merged into Colgate-Palmolive Co. 09/05/1973
Each share Common $1 par exchanged for (1.5) shares Common $1 par

HELENA SILVER MINES INC (MT)
Each share old Common 5¢ par exchanged for (0.125) share new Common 5¢ par 12/12/2003
Name changed to Consolidated Goldfields Corp. and Common 5¢ par changed to $0.001 par 07/28/2006
Consolidated Goldfields Corp. recapitalized as Brilliant Sands Inc. 03/16/2015 which name changed to NexGen Mining, Inc. 01/18/2018

HELENE CURTIS INDS INC (DE)
Reincorporated 7/26/84
50¢ Conv. Preferred A $5 par redesignated as 50¢ S.F. Preferred $5 par 4/26/55
Each share old Common $1 par exchanged for (0.6) share Class A

$1 par and (0.4) share Class A $1 par 4/4/56
50¢ S.F. Preferred $5 par called for redemption 3/9/61
Class A $1 par and Class B $1 par reclassified as new Common $1 par 6/1/62
New Common $1 par split (2) for (1) by issuance of (1) additional share 2/2/84
State of incorporation changed from (IL) to (DE) 7/26/84
Common $1 par changed to 50¢ par and (1) additional share issued 8/1/89
Merged into Unilever N.V. 3/19/96
Each share Common 50¢ par exchanged for $70 cash

HELENITA MINES, LTD. (CANADA)
Declared dissolved for failure to file annual reports 12/16/1980

HELGENA MINES LTD (BC)
Name changed to Strategic Metals Corp. 06/24/1981
Strategic Metals Corp. merged into Consolidated Strategic Metals Inc. 03/29/1982 which merged into New Strategic Metals Inc. 05/25/1983 which name changed to P.S.M. Technologies Inc. 12/29/1986
(See P.S.M. Technologies Inc.)

HELI COIL CORP (DE)
Common $1 par changed to no par and (1) additional share issued 12/29/59
Common no par split (2) for (1) by issuance of (1) additional share 10/11/66
Merged into Mite Corp. 5/21/70
Each share Common no par exchanged for (2.5) shares Common $1 par
(See Mite Corp.)

HELI ELECTRONICS CORP (NV)
Each share Common $0.00001 par exchanged for (0.02) share Common $0.0005 par 11/30/2010
SEC revoked common stock registration 03/02/2012

HELIAN HEALTH GROUP INC (DE)
Merged into TheraTx, Inc. 12/28/95
Each share Common 1¢ par exchanged for (0.4486) share Common $0.001 par
(See TheraTx, Inc.)

HELICOPTER AIR SERVICE, INC. (DE)
Common no par changed to $1 par 12/21/55
Name changed to Chicago Helicopter Airways, Inc. 8/20/56
Chicago Helicopter Airways, Inc. name changed to Chicago Helicopter Industries, Inc. 5/12/69 which name changed to D.M. Holdings, Inc. 10/20/81
(See D.M. Holdings, Inc.)

HELICOPTER CORP. OF AMERICA (MD)
Charter revoked for failure to file reports and pay fees 12/14/61

HELICOPTERS, INC. (CO)
Charter revoked for failure to file reports and pay fees 10/13/66

HELICOPTERS, INC. (DE)
Assets sold at auction 9/7/49
No stockholders' equity

HELICOPTERS FOR INDUSTRY, INC. (NY)
Proclaimed dissolved for failure to file reports and pay fees 12/15/59

HELICOS BIOSCIENCES CORP (DE)
Plan of reorganization under Chapter 11 Federal Bankruptcy proceedings effective 02/05/2014
No stockholders' equity

HELIKOPTER SVC A S (NORWAY)
ADR agreement terminated 04/15/2009

No ADR's remain outstanding

HELILA LIQUIDATING CORP. (DE)
Liquidation for cash completed 9/8/65

HELIN INDS INC (AB)
Name changed to Second Chance Corp. 07/25/2001
(See Second Chance Corp.)

HELIO AIRCRAFT CORP (DE)
Name changed to General Aircraft Corp. 04/28/1969

HELIO CAP CORP (BC)
Name changed to Helio Resource Corp. 11/04/2004

HELIOGEN PRODUCTS, INC. (DE)
Charter cancelled for non-payment of taxes 04/01/1962

HELIONETICS INC (CA)
Reorganized under Chapter 11 Federal Bankruptcy Code 03/15/1989
Each share Common 10¢ par exchanged for (0.1) share Common no par and (0.2) Conv. Preferred Stock Purchase Warrant expiring 06/15/1989
Each share new Common no par exchanged again for (0.1) share new Common no par 04/01/1996
Charter suspended for failure to file reports and pay fees 09/17/1998

HELIOS & MATHESON INFORMATION TECHNOLOGY INC (DE)
Reincorporated 11/20/2009
Recapitalized 06/27/2011
State of incorporation changed from (NY) to (DE) 11/20/2009
Recapitalized from Helios & Matheson North America Inc. to Helios & Matheson Information Technology Inc. 06/27/2011
Each share Common 1¢ par exchanged for (0.4) share Common 1¢ par
Name changed to Helios & Matheson Analytics Inc. 05/06/2013

HELIOS ADVANTAGE INCOME FD INC (MD)
Each share old Common $0.0001 par exchanged for (0.2) share new Common $0.0001 par 09/01/2009
Merged into Brookfield High Income Fund Inc. 08/13/2014
Each share Common $0.0001 par exchanged for (0.89548712) share Common $0.001 par
Brookfield High Income Fund Inc. merged into Brookfield Real Assets Income Fund Inc. 12/05/2016

HELIOS HIGH INCOME FD INC (MD)
Each share old Common $0.0001 par exchanged for (0.2) share new Common $0.0001 par 09/01/2009
Merged into Brookfield High Income Fund Inc. 08/13/2014
Each share Common $0.0001 par exchanged for (0.85513247) share Common $0.001 par
Brookfield High Income Fund Inc. merged into Brookfield Real Assets Income Fund Inc. 12/05/2016

HELIOS HIGH YIELD FD (MA)
Under plan of reorganization each Common Share of Bene. Inc. $0.001 par automatically became (1) share Brookfield Brookfield High Income Fund Inc. (MD) Common $0.001 par 03/05/2014
Brookfield High Income Fund Inc. merged into Brookfield Real Assets Income Fund Inc. 12/05/2016

HELIOS MULTI-SECTOR HIGH INCOME FD INC (MD)
Each share old Common $0.0001 par exchanged for (0.2) share new Common $0.0001 par 09/01/2009
Merged into Brookfield High Income Fund Inc. 08/13/2014
Each share Common $0.0001 par exchanged for (0.61277401) share Common $0.001 par
Brookfield High Income Fund Inc. merged into Brookfield Real Assets Income Fund Inc. 12/05/2016

HELIOS SELECT FD INC (MD)
Completely liquidated 06/16/2009
Each share Short Term Bond Fund Class A received net asset value
Each share Short Term Bond Fund Class C received net asset value
Completely liquidated 06/17/2009
Each share High Income Fund Class A received net asset value
Each share High Income Fund Class C received net asset value
Completely liquidated 06/18/2009
Each share Intermediate Bond Fund Class A received net asset value
Each share Intermediate Bond Fund Class C received net asset value

HELIOS STRATEGIC INCOME FD INC (MD)
Each share old Common $0.0001 par exchanged for (0.2) share new Common $0.0001 par 09/01/2009
Merged into Brookfield High Income Fund Inc. 08/13/2014
Each share Common $0.0001 par exchanged for (0.6752608) share Common $0.001 par
Brookfield High Income Fund Inc. merged into Brookfield Real Assets Income Fund Inc. 12/05/2016

HELIOS STRATEGIC MTG INCOME FD INC (MD)
Merged into Helios Total Return Fund, Inc. 04/02/2012
Each share Common 1¢ par exchanged for (1.06571093) shares Common 1¢ par
Helios Total Return Fund, Inc. name changed to Brookfield Total Return Fund Inc. 03/13/2013 which merged into Brookfield Real Assets Income Fund Inc. 12/05/2016

HELIOS TOTAL RETURN FD INC (MD)
Each share old Common 1¢ par exchanged for (0.25) share new Common 1¢ par 08/22/2012
Name changed to Brookfield Total Return Fund Inc. 03/13/2013
Brookfield Total Return Fund Inc. merged into Brookfield Real Assets Income Fund Inc. 12/05/2016

HELIOSCIENCE INC (NY)
Each share old Common 1¢ par exchanged for (0.2) share new Common 1¢ par 5/22/81
Name changed to H.H.R. Food Industries, Inc. 8/4/86
(See H.H.R. Food Industries, Inc.)

HELISYS INC (DE)
Recapitalized as Fraser Industries Inc. 07/20/2006
Each share Common $0.001 par exchanged for (0.01) share Common $0.001 par
Fraser Industries Inc. name changed to Riverdale Oil & Gas Corp. (DE) 03/12/2007 which reincorporated in Nevada 07/00/2008

HELIUM CORP. OF AMERICA (DE)
Acquired by International Helium Co. Ltd. 12/03/1962
Each share Capital Stock no par exchanged for (0.33333333) share Capital Stock no par
International Helium Co. recapitalized as Mineral Resources International Ltd. 12/22/1970 which merged into Conwest Exploration Co. Ltd. (Old) 06/01/1990 which merged into Conwest Exploration Co. Ltd. (New) (AB) 09/01/1993 which merged into Alberta Energy Co. Ltd. 01/31/1996 which merged into EnCana Corp. 01/03/2003

HELIX BIOCORE INC (MN)
Name changed to ATS Medical, Inc. 05/22/1992
(See ATS Medical, Inc.)

HELIX BIOMEDIX INC (CO)
Each share old Common no par exchanged for (0.002) share new Common no par 12/30/93
Reincorporated under the laws of Delaware and Common no par changed to $0.001 par 12/29/2000

HELIX BIOTECH CORP (BC)
Recapitalized as International Helix Biotechnologies Inc. 10/22/1993
Each share Common no par exchanged for (0.5) share Common no par
International Helix Biotechnologies Inc. merged into Helix BioPharma Corp. 08/15/1995

HELIX CIRCUITS INC (CANADA)
Name changed to Circuit World Corp. 08/14/1995
Circuit World Corp. name changed to Firan Technology Group Corp. 05/18/2004

HELIX HEARING CARE AMER CORP (CANADA)
Reincorporated 07/09/1999
Place of incorporation changed from (AB) to (Canada) 07/09/1999
Merged into HearUSA, Inc. 07/11/2002
Each share Common no par held by Non-Canadian residents exchanged for (0.3537) share Common 10¢ par
Each share Common no par held by Canadian residents exchanged for (0.3537) HEARx Canada Inc. Exchangeable Share no par
(See each company's listing)

HELIX MARKETING CORP (DE)
Adjudicated bankrupt 10/28/1976
Stockholders' equity unlikely

HELIX SYS LTD (BC)
Struck off register and declared dissolved for failure to file returns 04/28/1989

HELIX TECHNOLOGY CORP (DE)
Common $1 par split (2) for (1) by issuance of (1) additional share 11/11/93
Common $1 par split (2) for (1) by issuance of (1) additional share 11/15/94
Common $1 par split (2) for (1) by issuance of (1) additional share payable 11/13/97 to holders of record 10/30/97
Merged into Brooks Automation, Inc. 10/26/2005
Each share Common $1 par exchanged for (1.11) shares Common 1¢ par

HELIXSPHERE TECHNOLOGIES INC (NV)
Recapitalized as New China Global, Inc. (NV) 10/02/2013
Each share Common $0.001 par exchanged for (0.01) share Common $0.001 par
New China Global, Inc. (NV) reorganized in Wyoming as Globestar Industries 08/07/2014 which name changed to Pineapple Express, Inc. 09/22/2015

HELLA KGAA HUECK & CO (GERMANY)
Name changed to HELLA GmbH & Co. KGaA 10/27/2017

HELLABY HLDGS LTD (NEW ZEALAND)
ADR agreement terminated 03/31/2017
Each ADR for Common exchanged for $24.800769 cash

HELLENIC RES INC (BC)
Recapitalized as U.S. Grant Gold Mining Co. Ltd. 09/17/1987
Each share Common no par exchanged for (0.25) share Common no par
U.S. Grant Gold Mining Co. Ltd. recapitalized as Atrium Resources Ltd. 08/13/1990 which name changed to McCulloch's Canadian Beverages Ltd. 07/08/1992 which recapitalized as MCB Investments Corp. 10/06/1994
(See MCB Investments Corp.)

HELLENIC TELECOMMUNICATIONS ORGANIZATION S A (GREECE)
GDR agreement terminated 04/05/2002
Each 144A GDR for Ordinary exchanged for $7.4005 cash
(Additional Information in Active)

HELLENS MINING & REDUCTION CO., LTD. (ON)
Merged into Cobalt Consolidated Mining Corp. Ltd. 00/00/1953
Each share Capital Stock $1 par exchanged for (1/3) share Capital Stock $1 par
Cobalt Consolidated Mining Corp. Ltd. recapitalized as Agnico Mines Ltd. 10/25/1957 which merged into Agnico-Eagle Mines Ltd. 06/01/1972 which name changed to Agnico Eagle Mines Ltd. 04/30/2013

HELLER FINL INC (DE)
Dutch Auction Rate Transferable Securities Preferred Ser. D no par called for redemption 02/19/1991
8.125% Sr. Perpetual Preferred Ser. A no par called for redemption at $25 on 05/15/2001
Merged into General Electric Capital Corp. 10/25/2001
Each share Class A Common 25¢ par exchanged for $53.75 cash
6.687% Sr. Perpetual Preferred Ser. C 1¢ par called for redemption at $100 on 11/15/2011
6.95% Sr. Perpetual Preferred Ser. D 1¢ par called for redemption at $100 on 11/15/2011

HELLER-MARK & CO (CO)
Name changed to Bankers National Service Corp. 03/23/1983
Bankers National Service Corp. name changed to Red Carpet Financial Corp. 08/22/1984 which name changed back to Bankers National Service Corp. 07/12/1985
(See Bankers National Service Corp.)

HELLER WALTER E & CO (DE)
Common no par changed to $4 par in 1934
Each share Common $4 par exchanged for (2) shares Common $2 par in 1935
7% Preferred called for redemption 9/30/44
Stock Dividends - 10% 7/10/50; 20% 1/10/52
Common $2 par changed to $1 par and (1) additional share issued 9/9/55
Common $1 par changed to 25¢ par and (3) additional shares issued 4/30/62
$6.50 Conv. Preferred Ser. A no par (issued in 1981) called for redemption 2/16/84
Reorganized as Heller (Walter E.) International Corp. 7/28/69
Each share 5-1/2% Preferred $100 par exchanged for (1) share 5-1/2% Preferred $100 par
Each share 4% Preferred $100 par exchanged for (1) share 4% Preferred $100 par
Each share $4.07 Conv. Preferred no par exchanged for (1) share $4.07 Conv. Preferred no par
Each share Common 25¢ par exchanged for (1) share Common 25¢ par
Heller (Walter E.) International Corp.

name changed to Amerifin Corp.
1/26/84
(See Amerifin Corp.)
HELLER WALTER E INTL CORP (DE)
Name changed to Amerifin Corp.
1/26/84
(See Amerifin Corp.)
HELLERS BROTHERS CO. (NJ)
Acquired by Simonds Saw & Steel Co. 9/1/55
Details not available
HELLMAN (RICHARD) INC.
Acquired by Postum Cereal Co., Inc. 3/23/27
Details not available
HELLO CHANNEL INC (AB)
Struck off register for failure to file annual returns 11/01/1992
HELLO DIRECT INC (DE)
Merged into GN Great Nordic Ltd. 11/10/2000
Each share Common no par exchanged for $16.40 cash
HELLROARING SILVER LEAD LTD. (BC)
Name changed to St. Mary's Mines Ltd. 4/19/68
Each share Capital Stock 50¢ par exchanged for (1) share Capital Stock 50¢ par
St. Mary's Mines Ltd. recapitalized as Can-Base Industries Ltd. 3/15/71
(See Can-Base Industries Ltd.)
HELM CAP GROUP INC (DE)
SEC revoked common stock registration 06/19/2009
HELM LTD (AUSTRALIA)
ADR agreement terminated 11/13/2002
ADR holders' equity unlikely
HELM RES INC (DE)
Each share Common 10¢ par exchanged for (0.06666666) share Common 1¢ par 12/17/1993
Name changed to Helm Capital Group, Inc. 10/29/1997
(See Helm Capital Group, Inc.)
HELME (GEORGE W.) CO. (NJ)
Recapitalized in 1948
Each share 7% Preferred $100 par exchanged for (4) shares 7% Preferred $25 par
Each share Common $25 par exchanged for (2.5) shares Common $10 par
Name changed to Helme Products, Inc. (NJ) 4/15/64
Helme Products, Inc. (NJ) reincorporated in Delaware 6/1/67
(See Helme Products, Inc. (DE))
HELME PRODS INC (DE)
Reincorporated 06/01/1967
Common $10 par changed to $5 par and (1) additional share issued 05/01/1964
Recapitalized 04/12/1966
Each share 7% Preferred $25 par exchanged for $41 cash or at option of holder $41 principal amount of 5.35% Subord. Debentures due 04/01/1986
Option to receive Debentures expired 05/20/1966
State of incorporation changed from (NJ) to (DE) 06/01/1967
Merged into General Cigar Co., Inc. 11/10/1975
Each share Common $5 par exchanged for $15 principal amount 11-1/2% Subord. Debentures due 04/01/2005
HELMET PETE CORP (CA)
Merged into Arapaho Petroleum, Inc. 2/22/79
Each share Common 1¢ par exchanged for (0.285714) share Common no par and (1) Common Stock Purchase Warrant expiring 2/21/82

(See Arapaho Petroleum, Inc.)
HELMS EXPRESS INC (DE)
Completely liquidated 5/29/71
Each share Class A Common $1 par exchanged for first and final distribution of $11.50 cash
HELMSTAR GROUP INC (DE)
Name changed to CareerEngine Network, Inc. 3/28/2000
CareerEngine Network, Inc. name changed to CNE Group, Inc. 6/9/2003 which name changed to Arrow Resources Development, Inc. 12/20/2005
HELP AT HOME INC (DE)
Petition under Chapter 11 bankruptcy proceedings dismissed 3/1/2005
Stockholders' equity unlikely
HELP/SYSTEMS, INC. (MN)
Acquired by Help Acquisition Corp. 9/13/90
Each share Common no par exchanged for $0.50 cash
HELP/38 SYS INC (MN)
Name changed to Help/Systems, Inc. 03/09/1989
(See Help/Systems, Inc.)
HELPMATE ROBOTICS INC (CT)
Each share old Common no par exchanged for (0.04506534) share new Common no par 03/18/2002
Reincorporated under the laws of Florida as PainCare Holdings, Inc. and Common no par changed to $0.0001 par 12/13/2002
(See PainCare Holdings, Inc.)
HELSINKI CAP PARTNERS INC (DE)
Name changed to Skyframes, Inc. 10/22/2002
HELVETIA COAL MINING CO.
Merged into Rochester & Pittsburgh Coal Co. in 1938
Details not available
HELVETIA COPPER CO.
Dissolved in 1932
HELVETIA FD INC (DE)
Name changed to Swiss Helvetia Fund, Inc. 05/29/1990
HELVETIA OIL CO.
Liquidated in 1943
HELVETIA PHARMACEUTICALS INC (DE)
Reorganized back as Delta Mutual, Inc. 02/06/2003
Each share Common $0.0001 par exchanged for (10) shares Common $0.0001 par
Delta Mutual, Inc. name changed to Delta International Oil & Gas Inc. 11/27/2013
HEMAGOLD MINES LTD. (ON)
Name changed to Northern Nuclear Mines Ltd. 00/00/1968
Northern Nuclear Mines Ltd. reincorporated in Alberta as Northern Nuclear Energy Ltd. 10/03/1977 which recapitalized as Gaslite Petroleum Ltd. (AB) 01/28/1980 which reincorporated in British Columbia 00/00/1979 which reincorporated back in Alberta 00/00/1983
(See Gaslite Petroleum Ltd.)
HEMASURE INC (DE)
Name changed to HMSR Inc. 05/29/2001
HMSR Inc. recapitalized as Point Therapeutics Inc. 03/15/2002 which recapitalized as DARA BioSciences, Inc. 02/13/2008 which merged into Midatech Pharma PLC 12/04/2015
HEMCARE HEALTH SVCS INC (NV)
Recapitalized as DLT Resolution Inc. 12/20/2017
Each share Common $0.001 par exchanged for (0.1) share Common $0.001 par

HEMCURE INC (NV)
Reincorporated 09/22/2006
State of incorporation changed from (MN) to (NV) 09/22/2006
Each (17.5) shares Common 1¢ par exchanged for (1) share Common 1¢ par
Name changed to AuraSound, Inc. 02/27/2008
HEMDALE COMMUNICATIONS INC (DE)
Reincorporated 08/00/1992
State of incorporation changed from (FL) to (DE) 08/00/1992
SEC revoked common stock registration 08/25/2009
HEMDALE ENTERPRISES INC (DE)
Name changed to Redlaw Enterprises Inc. 12/18/1975
Redlaw Enterprises Inc. name changed to Redlaw, Inc. 08/29/1977 which merged into Redlaw Industries Inc. 07/13/1979
(See Redlaw Industries Inc.)
HEMERDON MNG & SMLT LTD (BAHAMAS)
Completely liquidated 02/28/1987
Each share Common 10¢ par received first and final distribution of (0.05) share of Amax Inc. Common $1 par
Note: Certificates were not required to be surrendered and are without value
HEMET BANCORP (CA)
Merged into Hemet Financial Group 9/5/2002
Each share Common no par exchanged for $54 cash
HEMGOLD RES LTD (BC)
Name changed to Hydro Home Appliances Ltd. 11/15/1985
Hydro Home Appliances Ltd. name changed to Santa Marina Gold Ltd. 12/16/1987 which merged into Akiko-Lori Gold Resources Ltd. 01/16/1991 which merged into Akiko Gold Resources Ltd. (BC) 11/09/1992 which reincorporated in Yukon as Prospex Mining Inc. 07/30/1997 which merged into Semafo Inc. 06/30/1999
HEMINGWAY TRANS INC (MA)
Involuntarily dissolved for failure to file reports and pay taxes 12/31/90
HEMIS CORP (NV)
Recapitalized as Modern Cinema Group, Inc. 09/14/2015
Each share Common $0.001 par exchanged for (0.004) share Common $0.001 par
HEMISPHERE DEV CORP (BC)
Recapitalized as Northern Hemisphere Development Corp. 01/14/2000
Each share Common no par exchanged for (0.2) share Common no par
Northern Hemisphere Development Corp. recapitalized as Hemisphere Energy Corp. 04/27/2009
HEMISPHERE GOLD INC (NV)
Charter revoked for failure to file reports and pay taxes 03/31/2009
HEMISPHERE GPS INC (AB)
Name changed to AgJunction Inc. 05/29/2013
HEMISPHERE HOTELS CORP (FL)
Adjudicated bankrupt 09/18/1971
Petition for reorganization denied and assets sold for benefit of creditors
No stockholders' equity
HEMISPHERE LTD (UT)
Name changed to Biologix International Ltd. (UT) 4/21/93
Biologix International Ltd. (UT) reincorporated in Nevada as Axess Media Group, Ltd. 3/31/2001 which

recapitalized as MEDIA GLOBO Corp. 3/12/2007
HEMISPHERE MINERALS (OK)
Charter cancelled and proclaimed dissolved for failure to file reports and pay fees 02/14/1973
HEMISPHERE NATIONAL BANK (WASHINGTON, DC)
Name changed to Capital Bank, N.A. (Washington, DC) 5/17/82
(See Capital Bank, N.A. (Washington, DC))
HEMISPHERE TRADING CO., INC.
Name changed to Hemisphere International Corp. in 1948
HEMISPHERES FDG CORP
1994 Ser. A Preferred 144A called for redemption at $1,000 on 11/26/2001
1995 Ser. A Preferred 144A called for redemption at $1,000 on 7/17/2002
1996 Ser. A Preferred 144A called for redemption at $1,000 on 3/12/2003
HEMIWEDGE INDS INC (DE)
Name changed to HII Technologies, Inc. 01/17/2012
(See HII Technologies, Inc.)
HEMKAT SPORTS INTL CORP (NV)
Name changed to Market Basket Enterprises, Inc. 12/28/95
Market Basket Enterprises, Inc. reorganized as J.T.'s Restaurants, Inc. 11/12/96 which name changed to National Integrated Food Service Corp. 12/10/98
(See National Integrated Food Service Corp.)
HEMLO EXPLS LTD (BC)
Name changed to Akiko-Lori Gold Resources Ltd. 05/20/1988
Akiko-Lori Gold Resources Ltd. merged into Akiko Gold Resources Ltd. (BC) 11/09/1992 which reincorporated in Yukon as Prospex Mining Inc. 07/30/1997 which merged into Semafo Inc. 06/30/1999
HEMLO GOLD MINES INC (ON)
Merged into Battle Mountain Canada Inc. 07/19/1996
Each share Common no par exchanged for (1.48) Exchangeable Shares no par
Battle Mountain Canada Inc. merged into Newmont Mining Corp. 01/10/2001
HEMLOCK FED FINL CORP (DE)
Issue Information - 2,076,000 shares COM offered at $10 per share on 04/02/1997
Each share old Common 1¢ par exchanged for (0.01) share new Common 1¢ par 7/21/2004
Merged into Marquette National Corp. 4/3/2006
Each share new Common 1¢ par exchanged for $55.50 cash
HEMMETER CIGAR CO.
Liquidated in 1947
HEMOCARE INC (NY)
Each share Common 1¢ par exchanged for (0.125) share old Common 8¢ par 05/22/1990
Each share old Common 8¢ par exchanged for (0.8) share new Common 8¢ par 08/06/1991
Name changed to Mediware Information Systems, Inc. 05/00/1991
(See Mediware Information Systems, Inc.)
HEMODYNAMICS INC (DE)
Common 1¢ par split (3) for (2) by issuance of (0.5) additional share 09/01/1988
Name changed to Thunder Group Inc. 07/20/1992
(See Thunder Group Inc.)

HEMOKINETICS INC (DC)
SEC revoked common stock registration 08/25/2009

HEMOSENSE INC (DE)
Merged into Inverness Medical Innovations, Inc. 11/07/2007
Each share Common $0.001 par exchanged for (0.274192) share Common $0.001 par
Inverness Medical Innovations, Inc. name changed to Alere Inc. 07/14/2010
(See Alere Inc.)

HEMOSOL CORP (ON)
Each share old Common no par exchanged for (0.25) share new Common no par 06/10/2005
Name changed to 1608557 Ontario Inc. 08/07/2007

HEMOSOL INC (ON)
Each share Common no par received distribution of (1) share Hemosol Corp. Common no par payable 05/07/2004 to holders of record 05/07/2004
Name changed to Hemosol Corp. 05/07/2004

HEMOTEC INC (CO)
Common 1¢ par changed to $0.00667 par and (0.5) additional share issued 06/07/1982
Merged into Bio-Medicus, Inc. 08/29/1989
Each share Common 1¢ par exchanged for (0.61) share Common 1¢ par
Bio-Medicus, Inc. merged into Medtronic, Inc. (MN) 09/21/1990 which reincorporated in Ireland as Medtronic PLC 01/27/2015

HEMOXYMED INC (DE)
Name changed to Applied NeuroSolutions, Inc. 10/30/2003
(See Applied NeuroSolutions, Inc.)

HEMPSTEAD BK (HEMPSTEAD, NY)
Capital Stock $10 par changed to $5 par and (1) additional share issued plus a 11-1/9% stock dividend paid 02/02/1959
Stock Dividends - 20% 03/01/1961; 11-1/9% 03/15/1963; 25% 03/12/1965; 20% 01/03/1967; 31.58% 04/01/1971
Merged into United Bank Corp. of New York 09/30/1977
Each share Capital Stock $5 par exchanged for (1) share Conv. Preferred Ser. C $20 par
Note: Holders had the option to receive $32 cash per share prior to 09/12/1977
United Bank Corp. of New York name changed to Norstar Bancorp Inc. 01/04/1982
(See Norstar Bancorp Inc.)

HEMPTECH CORP (NV)
Name changed to Nuvus Gro Corp. and Common $0.0001 par changed to $0.001 par 04/12/2018

HEMPTOWN CLOTHING INC (BC)
Name changed to Naturally Advanced Technologies Inc. 03/23/2006
Naturally Advanced Technologies Inc. name changed to Crailar Technologies Inc. 10/31/2012

HENDERSHOT (G.W.) CORRUGATED PAPER CO., LTD.
Acquired by Hendershot Paper Products Ltd. in 1946
Details not available

HENDERSHOT PAPER PRODS LTD (ON)
5% Preference $100 par reclassified as 6% Preference $100 par 06/28/1956
Each share old Common no par exchanged for (4) shares new Common no par 06/28/1956
100% acquired through purchase offer by Canadian International Paper Co. as of 05/00/1966
6% Preference $100 par called for redemption 05/15/1970
Public interest eliminated

HENDERSON CTZNS BANCSHARES INC (TX)
Merged into HCB Merger Corp. 8/14/2003
Each share Common $5 par exchanged for $32 cash
Note: Holders of (500) or more shares will retain their interests

HENDERSON ENGR CO (IL)
Each share old Common no par exchanged for (0.00004) share new Common no par 01/06/1992
Note: In effect holders received $0.10 cash and public interest was eliminated

HENDERSON NATL BK (HUNTSVILLE, AL)
Merged into First Bancgroup-Alabama, Inc. 11/30/1973
Each share Common $5 par exchanged for (1.39) shares Common $4 par
First Bancgroup-Alabama, Inc. name changed to Firstgulf Bancorp 03/30/1984
(See Firstgulf Bancorp)

HENDERSON OIL HOLDINGS LTD. (AB)
Merged into Medallion Petroleums Ltd. 4/20/59
Each share Capital Stock no par exchanged for (0.02) share Common $1.25 par
Medallion Petroleums Ltd. merged into Canadian Industrial Gas & Oil Ltd. 3/8/65 which merged into Norcen Energy Resources Ltd. (ALTA) 10/28/75 which reincorporated in Canada 4/15/77 which merged into Union Pacific Resources Group Inc. 4/17/98 which merged ino Anadarko Petroleum Corp. 7/14/2000

HENDERSON PETE CORP (NV)
Recapitalized as Burkhart Petroleum Corp. 12/31/1985
Each share Common 1¢ par exchanged for (0.25) share Common 1¢ par
Burkhart Petroleum Corp. merged into ZG Energy Corp. (DE) 06/29/1987 which reorganized in Oklahoma as Vantage Point Energy, Inc. 04/30/1990
(See Vantage Point Energy, Inc.)

HENDERSON'S PORTION PAK, INC. (FL)
Completely liquidated 10/22/1965
Each share Common $1 par exchanged for first and final distribution of (0.3543) share Borden Co. Capital Stock $3.75 par
Borden Co. name changed to Borden, Inc. 04/17/1968 which merged into RJR Nabisco Holdings Corp. 03/14/1995 which name changed to Nabsico Group Holdings Corp. 06/15/1999
(See Nabisco Group Holdings Corp.)

HENDEY CORP. (CT)
Liquidation completed in 1954

HENDEY MACHINE CO. (CT)
Name changed to Hendey Corp. in 1952
(See Hendey Corp.)

HENDLER CREAMERY CO., INC.
Acquired by Borden Co. 00/00/1929
Details not available

HENDON EXPL INC (TX)
Name changed to U.S. Energy Corp. of America, Inc. 11/3/89

HENDRICK RANCH RLTYS INC (TX)
Name changed 04/30/1976
Common no par changed to $1 par 00/00/1937
Name changed from Hendrick Ranch Royalties to Hendrick Ranch Royalties, Inc. 04/30/1976
Liquidation completed
Each share Common $1 par exchanged for initial distribution of $80 cash 01/00/2002
Each share Common $1 par received second distribution of $18 cash 07/00/2002
Each share Common $1 par received third distribution of $5 cash 08/00/2003
Each share Common $1 par received fourth distribution of $8 cash 09/00/2004
Each share Common $1 par received fifth distribution of $1.50 cash 08/00/2005
Each share Common $1 par received sixth and final distribution of approximately $0.41 cash 08/08/2006

HENDRICKS MINERALS CDA LTD (ON)
Recapitalized as MCK Mining Corp. 05/06/1997
Each share Class A Subordinate no par exchanged for (0.4) share Common no par
MCK Mining Corp. name changed to PhosCan Chemical Corp. (ON) 08/01/2006 which reincorporated in Canada 10/19/2006
(See PhosCan Chemical Corp.)

HENG FAI CHINA INDS INC (DE)
Name changed to Powersoft Technologies Inc. (DE) 04/03/1998
Powersoft Technologies Inc. (DE) reorganized in Colorado as Asia Supernet Corp. 12/22/1999
(See Asia Supernet Corp.)

HENG FAI ENTERPRISES LTD (HONG KONG)
ADR agreement terminated 11/30/2015
Each Sponsored ADR for Ordinary exchanged for $5.809292 cash

HENG FUNG HLDGS CO LTD (HONG KONG)
Each old Sponsored ADR for Ordinary exchanged for (0.1) new Sponsored ADR for Ordinary 10/19/1998
Name changed to Online Credit International Ltd. 12/27/1999
Online Credit International Ltd. name changed to Heng Fung Holdings Ltd. 11/16/2001 which name changed to China Credit Holdings Ltd. 02/01/2005 which name changed to Xpress Group Ltd. 06/13/2007 which name changed to Heng Fai Enterprises Ltd. 10/22/2013
(See Heng Fai Enterprises Ltd.)

HENG FUNG HLDGS LTD (HONG KONG)
Each Sponsored ADR for Ordinary received distribution of $0.2458 cash payable 02/09/2005 to holders of record 02/01/2005
Name changed to China Credit Holdings Ltd. 02/01/2005
China Credit Holdings Ltd. name changed to Xpress Group Ltd. 06/13/2007 which name changed to Heng Fai Enterprises Ltd. 10/22/2013
(See Heng Fai Enterprises Ltd.)

HENIX RES INC (NV)
Reorganized as China Forest Energy Corp. 12/29/2010
Each share Common $0.00001 par exchanged for (9) shares Common $0.00001 par
China Forest Energy Corp. reorganized as Narnia Corp.

01/25/2012 which name changed to Neologic Animation Inc. 05/11/2012
(See Neologic Animation Inc.)

HENKE & PILLOT, INC. (TX)
Stock Dividends - 13% 4/15/50; 10% 7/15/50; 10% 10/15/50; 10% 1/15/51; 10% 3/15/51; 10% 6/30/51; 10% 9/29/51
Liquidated in 1956

HENKE & PILLOT REALTY CO. (TX)
Name changed to Sutherland Properties, Inc. 03/26/1958
(See Sutherland Properties, Inc.)

HENKEL-CLAUSS CO. (OH)
Name changed to Clauss Cutlery Co. 05/10/1954
Clauss Cutlery Co. merged into Alco Standard Corp. 10/13/1967 which name changed to IKON Office Solutions, Inc. 01/24/1997
(See IKON Office Solutions, Inc.)

HENKEL KGAA (GERMANY)
Sponsored ADR's for Preferred DM 5 par changed to EUR 1 par and (2) additional ADR's issued payable 06/19/2007 to holders of record 06/15/2007 Ex date - 06/20/2007
Sponsored ADR's for Ordinary DM 5 par changed to EUR 1 par and (2) additional ADR's issued payable 06/19/2007 to holders of record 06/15/2007 Ex date - 06/20/2007
Name changed to Henkel AG & Co. KGaA 05/01/2008

HENLEY GROUP INC (DE)
Merged into Bolsa Chica Co. 07/16/1992
Each share Common 1¢ par exchanged for (2) shares Conv. Preferred Ser. A 1¢ par and (1) share Class A Common 5¢ par
Bolsa Chica Co. name changed to Koll Real Estate Group Inc. 09/30/1993 which name changed to California Coastal Communities, Inc. 05/29/1998
(See California Coastal Communities, Inc.)

HENLEY GROUP INC (FL)
Name changed to CIS.com, Inc. 05/27/1999
CIS.com, Inc. name changed to InterAmerican Resources, Inc. 08/13/2001 which name changed to Allixon Corp. 06/04/2004 which recapitalized as Simcoe Mining Resources Corp. 01/16/2008

HENLEY GROUP INC NEW (DE)
Name changed to Henley Properties, Inc. 12/31/1989
Henley Properties, Inc. name changed to Bolsa Chica Co. 07/16/1992 which name changed to Koll Real Estate Group Inc. 09/30/1993 which name changed to California Coastal Communities Inc. 05/29/1998
(See California Coastal Communities Inc.)

HENLEY GROUP INC OLD (DE)
Each share Common 1¢ par received distribution of (0.225) share Henley Group, Inc. (New) Class A Common 5¢ par 12/31/88
Name changed to Wheelabrator Group Inc. 12/31/88
Wheelabrator Group Inc. recapitalized as Wheelabrator Technologies Inc. (New) 8/24/89
(See Wheelabrator Technologies Inc. (New))

HENLEY HEALTHCARE INC (TX)
Filed a petition under Chapter 7 Federal Bankruptcy Code 10/19/2001
No stockholders' equity

HENLEY INTL INC (TX)
Name changed to Maxxim Medical, Inc. 3/8/93
(See Maxxim Medical, Inc.)

HENLEY LTD PARTNERSHIP (DE)
Merged into Castle Creek Partnership GP, Inc. 04/28/2003
Each Unit of Ltd. Partnership exchanged for $27 cash
Each Unit of Ltd. Partnership received first and final distribution of $5.35 cash from escrow 06/09/2008

HENLEY MFG CORP (DE)
Merged into New Hampshire Oak, Inc. 1/19/89
Each share Common 1¢ par exchanged for $90 cash

HENLEY PPTYS INC (DE)
Each share Class A Common 5¢ par received distribution of (1) share Henley Group, Inc. (The) Common 1¢ par 12/31/1989
Name changed to Bolsa Chica Co. 07/16/1992
Bolsa Chica Co. name changed to Koll Real Estate Group Inc. 09/30/1993 name changed to California Coastal Communities Inc. 05/29/1998
(See California Coastal Communities Inc.)

HENLEY VENTURES INC (NV)
Each share old Common $0.001 par exchanged for (9) shares new Common $0.001 par 03/06/2007
Name changed to South Sea Energy Corp. and (2.6) additional shares issued 07/02/2007
South Sea Energy Corp. name changed to Ameriwest Energy Corp. 09/11/2007
(See Ameriwest Energy Corp.)

HENLYS GROUP LTD (CANADA)
Name changed to Sechura Inc. (Canada) 10/05/1989
Sechura Inc. (Canada) reincorporated in Bermuda as Aaxis Ltd. 08/30/1996 which was acquired by BHI Corp. 03/31/1998 which name changed to Carlisle Holdings Ltd. 06/02/1999 which name changed to BB Holdings Ltd. 08/18/2005
(See BB Holdings Ltd.)

HENLYS GROUP PLC (UNITED KINGDOM)
ADR agreement terminated 11/15/2004
No ADR holders' equity

HENNESSY CAP ACQUISITION CORP (DE)
Units separated 02/25/2015
Name changed to Blue Bird Corp. 02/25/2015

HENNESSY CAP ACQUISITION CORP II (DE)
Units separated 02/28/2017
Name changed to Daseke, Inc. 02/28/2017

HENNESSY CAP ACQUISITION CORP III (DE)
Units separated 10/18/2018
Name changed to NRC Group Holdings Corp. 10/18/2018

HENNESSY RESOURCE CORP (BC)
Name changed to Fastlane International Enterprises Inc. (BC) 05/20/1992
Fastlane International Enterprises Inc. (BC) reincorporated in Wyoming 05/10/1993
(See Fastlane International Enterprises Inc.)

HENNEY MOTOR CO.
Name changed to Allied Motor Industries, Inc. 00/00/1928
(See Allied Motor Industries, Inc.)

HENNINGER BREWERY ONT LTD (ON)
Name changed to H.O. Financial Ltd. 08/26/1981
(See H.O. Financial Ltd.)

HENREDON FURNITURE INDS INC (NC)
Common $2 par split (2) for (1) by issuance of (1) additional share 10/15/74
Stock Dividend - 100% 11/3/80
Merged into Masco Corp. 9/9/86
Each share Common $2 par exchanged for $58 cash

HENRIETTA MILLS (NC)
Name changed to Trimil Corp. which completed liquidation 05/02/1960

HENRIETTA MINES LTD (BC)
Recapitalized as Caledonia Resources Ltd. 02/22/1978
Each share Common 50¢ par exchanged for (0.4) share Common no par
Caledonia Resources Ltd. recapitalized as Aston Resources Ltd. (New) 02/03/1988 which recapitalized as Consolidated Aston Resources Ltd. 06/13/1996
(See Consolidated Aston Resources Ltd.)

HENROSCO-LARDER MINES LTD. (ON)
Charter cancelled and company declared dissolved by default 02/15/1960

HENRY B. GILPIN CO. (MD)
See - Gilpin (Henry B.) Co.

HENRY (PATRICK) BREWING CO., INC. (IN)
Merged into Fox (Peter) Brewing Co. 6/30/52
Each share Common $1 par exchanged for (0.5) share Common $1.25 par
Fox (Peter) Brewing Co. name changed to Fox De Luxe Beer Sales, Inc. 1/31/56 which name changed to Kingsford Co. 6/17/57 which merged into Clorox Co. (Calif.) 3/12/73 which reincorporated in Delaware 10/22/86

HENRY BROS ELECTRONICS INC (DE)
Acquired by Kratos Defense & Security Solutions, Inc. 12/15/2010
Each share Common 1¢ par exchanged for $8.20 cash

HENRY CLAY HOTEL CO. OF LOUISVILLE (KY)
In liquidation in 1952

HENRY CNTY BANCSHARES INC (GA)
Common $5 par changed to $2.50 par and (1) additional share issued payable 01/11/2001 to holders of record 01/11/2001
Common $2.50 par split (2) for (1) by issuance of (1) additional share payable 12/14/2006 to holders of record 12/14/2006
Common $2.50 par changed to 10¢ par 05/18/2010
Principal asset placed in receivership 01/20/2012
Stockholders equity unlikely

HENRY CNTY BK (NAPOLEON, OH)
Under plan of reorganization each share Common $2.50 par automatically became (1) share Comunibanc Corp. Common $2.50 par 6/3/97

HENRY CNTY PLYWOOD CORP (NV)
Reincorporated 03/18/2008
Each share Common $5 par exchanged for (5) shares Common $1 par 07/31/1972
State of incorporation changed from (VA) to (NV) and Common $1 par changed to $0.001 par 03/17/2008
Stock Dividends - 20% 10/01/1964; 10% 04/16/1968; 10% 01/03/1972
Name changed to Sino Green Land Corp. 03/17/2009

HENRY EDITH SHOES INC (PA)
Common 20¢ par changed to 10¢ par and (1) additional share issued 08/01/1969
Merged into New Laribee, Inc. 09/28/1979
Each share Common 10¢ par exchanged for $0.05 cash

HENRY ENERGY CORP (DE)
Recapitalized as Kimco Energy Corp. 1/1/88
Each share Common 1¢ par exchanged for (0.1) share Common 1¢ par
(See Kimco Energy Corp.)

HENRY ENGR CO (CA)
Assets sold for the benefit of creditors 12/30/1974
No stockholders' equity

HENRY FIELD CO. (DE)
Charter cancelled and declared inoperative and void for non-payment of taxes 4/1/38

HENRY FISCHER PACKING CO. (KY)
See - Fischer (Henry) Packing Co.

HENRY HOLT & CO., INC. (DE)
See - Holt (Henry) & Co., Inc.

HENRY (PATRICK) HOTEL, INC. (VA)
Assets sold 03/18/1968
No stockholders' equity

HENRY HUDSON HOTEL CORP (NY)
$4 Preferred no par and Common no par changed to $1 par 00/00/1949
Assets sold for the benefit of creditors 03/00/1967
No stockholders' equity

HENRY LIKLY & CO., INC. (NY)
See - Likly (Henry) & Co., Inc.

HENRY MANDEL ASSOCIATES, INC. (NY)
See - Mandel (Henry) Associates, Inc.

HENRY MOUNTAINS URANIUM CORP.
Merged into Midwest Consolidated Uranium Corp. on a (0.01) for (1) basis 6/10/55
Midwest Consolidated Uranium Corp. merged into COG Minerals Corp. 5/1/56 which was acquired by Colorado Oil & Gas Corp. for cash 12/31/60

HENRY (MIKE) OIL CO. (WY)
Charter revoked for failure to pay taxes 6/18/31

HENRY PATRICK NATL BK (BASSETT, VA)
Stock Dividends - 10% payable 07/31/2000 to holders of record 06/30/2000 Ex date - 08/15/2000; 10% payable 07/31/2001 to holders of record 06/30/2001 Ex date - 07/20/2001; 10% payable 07/31/2002 to holders of record 06/28/2002 Ex date - 07/29/2002; 10% payable 10/31/2003 to holders of record 09/30/2003 Ex date - 11/03/2003
Merged into Carter Bank & Trust (Martinsville, VA) 12/29/2006
Each share Common $1.25 par exchanged for (1.112) shares Common

HENRY'S SYSTEM NORTHWEST INC. (MN)
Name changed to Northwest Systems Corp. 02/12/1964
(See Northwest Systems Corp.)

HENRYS DRIVE IN INC (IL)
Name changed to Amfood Industries, Inc. 09/04/1974
(See Amfood Industries, Inc.)

HENSBERRY & CO INC (FL)
Each share old Common $0.001 par exchanged for (0.01) share new Common $0.001 par 7/18/97
Recapitalized as Renaissance Eastern Holdings Corp. 12/1/97
Each share new Common $0.001 par exchanged for (0.2) share Common $0.001 par

HENYA FOOD CORP (DE)
Each share old Common $0.001 par exchanged for (0.001) share new Common $0.001 par 07/02/2009
Name changed to Foodfest International 2000 Inc. 04/01/2010

HEPALIFE TECHNOLOGIES INC (FL)
Name changed to Alliqua, Inc. (FL) 01/05/2011
Alliqua, Inc. (FL) reincorporated in Delaware as Alliqua BioMedical, Inc. 06/06/2014

HER MAJESTY INDS INC (SC)
Merged into Gulf & Western Industries, Inc. 1/25/77
Each share Class A Common $1 par exchanged for $18.75 cash

HER PERS FEMININE CARE PRODS INC (FL)
Recapitalized as OJsys, Inc. 11/07/2006
Each share Common $0.001 par exchanged for (0.05) share Common $0.001 par

HERA RES INC (BC)
Recapitalized as Medallion Resources Ltd. 02/10/1998
Each share Common no par exchanged for (0.2) share Common no par

HERALD NATL BK (NEW YORK, NY)
Merged into BankUnited, Inc. 02/29/2012
Each share Common $1 par exchanged for (0.036087) share Common 1¢ par and $2.817199 cash

HERALD RES LTD (AUSTRALIA)
Acquired by PT Bumi Resources Tbk 12/16/2009
Each share Ordinary exchanged for $0.93 cash
ADR agreement terminated 09/30/2011
No ADR's remain outstanding

HERB LAKE MINING & EXPLORATION LTD. (ON)
Recapitalized as Big Herb Lake Mining & Exploration Ltd. 02/01/1957
Each share Common exchanged for (0.33333333) share Common
(See Big Herd Lake Mining & Exploration Ltd.)

HERBAL CLONE BK CDA INC (BC)
Name changed to High Hampton Holdings Corp. 06/18/2015

HERBAL SCIENCE INTL INC (NV)
Dissolved 06/15/2004
Details not available

HERBAL SCIENCE INTL INC (UT)
Reincorporated under the laws of Nevada 09/10/1996
(See Herbal Science International, Inc. (NV))

HERBALIFE INTL INC (NV)
Each share Common 1¢ par exchanged for (0.33333333) share Class A Common 1¢ par and (0.66666666) share Class B Common 1¢ par 12/12/1997
Merged into WH Holdings (Cayman Islands) Ltd. 07/31/2002
Each share Class A Common 1¢ par exchanged for $19.50 cash
Each share Class B Common 1¢ par exchanged for $19.50 cash

HERBALIFE LTD (CAYMAN ISLANDS)
Common $0.002 par changed to $0.001 par and (1) additional share issued payable 05/17/2011 to holders of record 05/10/2011
Ex date - 05/18/2011

Name changed to Herbalife Nutrition Ltd. 04/25/2018

HERBALORGANICS COM (NV)
Each share old Common $0.001 par exchanged for (10) shares new Common $0.001 par 09/22/2003
Name changed to Teleplus Enterprises, Inc. and (1.375) additional shares issued 10/22/2003
Teleplus Enterprises, Inc. name changed to Teleplus World, Corp. 10/30/2006
(See Teleplus World, Corp.)

HERBALPHARM HLDGS INC (FL)
Name changed to MitoPharm Corp. 3/9/2007

HERBALPHARM INC (FL)
Reorganized as Herbalpharm Holdings, Inc. 2/22/2007
Each share Common $0.001 par exchanged for (2) shares Common $0.001 par
Herbalpharm Holdings, Inc. name changed to MitoPharm Corp. 3/9/2007

HERBDIX GOLD MINES, LTD. (ON)
Charter revoked for failure to file reports and pay fees 00/00/1961

HERBEL INDS INC (NY)
Dissolved by proclamation 12/15/1975

HERBERT ARTHUR MORRIS ADVERTISING INC (NY)
Assets assigned for benefit of creditors 08/28/1973
No stockholders' equity

HERBRAND CO.
Plan of reorganization effective 01/01/1935
No stockholders' equity

HERBRAND CORP. (OH)
Common $1 par split (20) for (1) by issuance of (19) additional shares 03/02/1937
Common $1 par changed to $3 par 06/22/1943
Stock Dividend - 100% 07/20/1943
Merged into Bingham Stamping Co. 07/01/1947
Each share Common $3 par exchanged for (1) share Common $1 par
Bingham Stamping Co. name changed to Bingham-Herbrand Corp. 08/21/1947 which was acquired by Van Norman Industries, Inc. 12/05/1956 which merged into Universal American Corp. (DE) (Ctfs. dated prior to 01/12/1968) 01/31/1962 which merged into Gulf & Western Industries, Inc. (DE) 01/12/1968
(See Gulf & Western Industries, Inc. (DE))

HERBS OF CHINA LTD (CO)
Name changed to Bioenergy Nutrients, Inc. 10/18/1988
Bioenergy Nutrients, Inc. name changed to Amrion Inc. 03/26/1993 which merged into Whole Foods Market, Inc. 09/11/1997
(See Whole Foods Market, Inc.)

HERBTECH INC (AB)
Merged into CV Technologies Inc. (New) 07/01/1998
Each share Common no par exchanged for (0.896) share Common no par
CV Technologies Inc. (New) name changed to Afexa Life Sciences Inc. 04/03/2009
(See Afexa Life Sciences Inc.)

HERCON ELECTRONICS CORP. (NJ)
Name changed to Harvey-Wells Corp. 10/3/60
Harvey-Wells Corp. name changed to Dage-Bell Corp. 6/19/64 which was acquired by Raytheon Co. 8/6/65

HERCON PETROLEUMS LTD. (AB)
Reorganized under the laws of British Columbia as Hercon Resources Ltd. 11/22/73
Each share Capital Stock no par exchanged for (0.2) share Capital Stock no par
Hercon Resources Ltd. reorganized as Chilco Resources Ltd. 4/1/80
(See Chilco Resources Ltd.)

HERCON RES LTD (BC)
Reorganized as Chilco Resources Ltd. 04/01/1980
Each share Capital Stock no par exchanged for (1) share Common no par
(See Chilco Resources Ltd.)

HERCULES CEMENT CORP. (PA)
Common no par exchanged (2) for (1) in 1947
Each share Common no par exchanged for (3) shares Common $10 par in 1951
Each share Common $10 par exchanged for (3) shares Common $1 par 10/1/56
Merged into American Cement Corp. 12/31/57
Each share Common $1 par exchanged for (1.145) shares Common $5 par
American Cement Corp. name changed to Amcord, Inc. 5/2/73
(See Amcord, Inc.)

HERCULES CORP.
Name changed to Servel Corp. 00/00/1926
(See Servel Corp.)

HERCULES DEV GROUP INC (CO)
Common $0.0001 par split (10) for (1) by issuance of (9) additional shares payable 03/15/2001 to holders of record 03/14/2001
Name changed to Astralis Pharmaceuticals, Ltd. (CO) 11/01/2001
Astralis Pharmaceuticals, Ltd. (CO) reincorporated in Delaware as Astralis, Ltd. 12/10/2001
(See Astralis, Ltd.)

HERCULES DIVERSIFIED INC (DE)
Charter cancelled and declared inoperative and void for non-payment of taxes 3/1/75

HERCULES EXTN INC (ID)
Charter forfeited for failure to file reports 12/01/1969

HERCULES GALION PRODS INC (DE)
6% Conv. Preferred Ser. B $20 par called for redemption 03/02/1964
Name changed to Peabody Galion Corp. 12/11/1969
Peabody Galion Corp. name changed to Peabody International Corp. 11/19/1976 which merged into Pullman-Peabody Co. 10/24/1985 which name changed back to Pullman Co. 02/12/1987
(See Pullman Co.)

HERCULES INC (DE)
$1.65 Conv. Class A no par called for redemption 03/15/1972
Common $1.04166666 par changed to no par and (1) additional share issued 05/04/1973
Common no par split (3) for (1) by issuance of (2) additional shares 01/30/1995
Acquired by Ashland Inc. (New) (KY) 11/13/2008
Each share Common no par exchanged for (0.093) share Common $1 par and $18.60 cash Ashland Inc. (New) (KY) reincorporated in Delaware as Ashland Global Holdings Inc. 09/20/2016

HERCULES INVESTMENT CORP. (UT)
Name changed to Southern California Land Development Corp. 7/21/58
(See Southern California Land Development Corp.)

HERCULES MINES CO NEV (NV)
Common 10¢ par changed to 2¢ par 3/16/64
Merged into Ranrex, Inc. 8/16/71
Each share Common 2¢ par exchanged for (0.5) share Common 5¢ par
Ranrex, Inc. merged into Argus Resources, Inc. (NV) 12/27/72 which reincorporated in Delaware as 1st Global Petroleum Group, Inc. 3/31/2005 which name changed to Commonwealth American Financial Group, Inc. 5/13/2005 which name changed to James Monroe Capital Corp. 5/30/2006

HERCULES MOTORS CORP. (OH)
Stock Dividend - 20% 3/21/50
Acquired by Hupp Corp. 10/2/61
Each share Common no par exchanged for (2.5) shares Common $1 par
(See Hupp Corp.)

HERCULES OFFSHORE INC (DE)
Plan of reorganization under Chapter 11 Federal Bankruptcy proceedings effective 11/06/2015
Each share old Common 1¢ par exchanged for (0.0037212) share new Common 1¢ par and (0.03000969) Common Stock Purchase Warrant expiring 11/08/2021
Plan of reorganization under Chapter 11 Federal Bankruptcy proceedings effective 12/02/2016
Assets transferred to HERO Liquidating Trust
(See HERO Liquidating Trust)

HERCULES PLASTICS CORP. (DE)
Name changed to Hercules Diversified, Inc. and Common 25¢ par changed to 3¢ par 9/6/66
(See Hercules Diversified, Inc.)

HERCULES POWDER CO. (DE)
Each share Common $100 par exchanged for (4) shares Common no par 00/00/1929
7% Preferred $100 par reclassified as 6% Preferred $100 par 00/00/1936
6% Preferred $100 par reclassified as 5% Preferred $100 par 00/00/1945
Common no par split (2) for (1) by issuance of (1) additional share 04/15/1946
Common no par changed to $2-1/12 par and (2) additional shares issued 04/30/1956
Common $2-1/12 par changed to $1-1/24 par and (1) additional share issued 04/30/1962
5% Preferred $100 par called for redemption 11/15/1964
$2 Conv. Class A no par called for redemption 04/01/1965
Name changed to Hercules Inc. 04/29/1966
Hercules Inc. acquired by Ashland Inc. (New) 11/13/2008

HERCULES STEEL PRODUCTS CORP. (DE)
Under plan of merger name changed to Hercules Galion Products, Inc. 08/31/1955
Hercules Galion Products, Inc. name changed to Peabody Galion Corp. 12/11/1969 which name changed to Peabody International Corp. 11/19/1976 which merged into Pullman-Peabody Co. 10/24/1985 which name changed back to Pullman Co. 02/12/1987
(See Pullman Co.)

HERCULES TECHNOLOGY GROWTH CAP INC (MD)
Each share Common $0.001 par received distribution of approximately (0.05600806) share Common $0.001 par and $0.0422 cash payable 03/30/2009 to holders of record 02/23/2009 Ex date - 02/19/2009
Common Accredited Investors $0.001 par reclassified as Common $0.001 par 06/11/2012
Name changed to Hercules Capital, Inc. 02/25/2016

HERCULES TR I (DE)
9.42% Guaranteed Trust Originated Preferred Securities called for redemption at $25 on 5/10/2004

HERCULES URANIUM CO. (UT)
Name changed to Hercules Investment Corp. 02/14/1958
Hercules Investment Corp. name changed to Southern California Land Development Corp. 07/21/1958
(See Southern California Land Development Corp.)

HERCULES URANIUM MINES LTD. (ON)
Charter cancelled for failure to pay taxes and file returns 03/16/1976

HERCULES VENTURES INC (BC)
Recapitalized as Tucan Ventures Inc. 05/07/1993
Each share Common no par exchanged for (0.4) share Common no par
Tucan Ventures Inc. name changed to Sandhurst Resource Ltd. 10/15/1996
(See Sandhurst Resource Ltd.)

HERDIS INTL CDA INC (BC)
Name changed to Deep Shaft Technology International Inc. 02/11/1987
Deep Shaft Technology International Inc. name changed to Noram Environmental Solutions Inc. (BC) 11/10/1988 which reincorporated in Alberta 02/27/1997 which name changed to Alternative Fuel Systems Inc. 07/07/1997
(See Alternative Fuel Systems Inc.)

HERDRON CAP CORP (CANADA)
Name changed to El Tigre Silver Corp. (Canada) 03/09/2010
El Tigre Silver Corp. (Canada) reincorporated in British Columbia 07/09/2013 which merged into Oceanus Resources Corp. 11/24/2015

HERE COMES GRANDMA INC (FL)
Name changed to GMC Holding Corp. 12/10/1997
(See GMC Holding Corp.)

HERE ENTERPRISES INC (NV)
Common $0.001 par split (100) for (1) by issuance of (99) additional shares payable 11/19/2010 to holders of record 11/18/2010 Ex date - 11/22/2010
SEC revoked common stock registration 11/06/2014

HEREFORD CORP.
Dissolved in 1943

HEREFORD RAILWAY
Road abondoned 00/00/1930
Stockholders' equity unlikely

HEREUARE INC (DE)
SEC revoked common stock registration 04/09/2012

HERFF JONES CO (IN)
Each share Class A Preference $1 par exchanged for (2) shares Common no par 4/11/62
Common no par split (6) for (5) by issuance of (0.2) additional share 8/1/71
Common no par split (3) for (2) by issuance of (0.5) additional share 8/1/72
Stock Dividend - 10% 11/2/70
Acquired by Carnation Co. 11/8/73
Each share Common no par exchanged for (0.1845) share Common $2 par
(See Carnation Co.)

HERGET NATIONAL BANK (PEKIN, IL)
Stock Dividend - 20% 1/23/62
Reorganized as Herget Financial Corp. 11/14/78
Each share Capital Stock $25 par exchanged for (5) shares Common $5 par

HERINGRAT 478 INC (DE)
Name changed to United Music & Media Group, Inc. 06/23/2010
United Music & Media Group, Inc. recapitalized as New Generation Consumer Group, Inc. 10/07/2014

HERITAGE AMERN RESOURCE CORP (BC)
Recapitalized as Heritage Explorations Ltd. 09/17/2001
Each share Common no par exchanged for (0.25) share Common no par
Heritage Explorations Ltd. merged into St Andrew Goldfields Ltd. 08/22/2005 which merged into Kirkland Lake Gold Inc. 01/29/2016 which merged into Kirkland Lake Gold Ltd. 12/06/2016

HERITAGE BANCORP (CA)
Common no par split (2) for (1) by issuance of (1) additional share 2/15/82
Out of business in 1984
No stockholders' equity

HERITAGE BANCORP INC (DE)
Charter cancelled and declared inoperative and void for non-payment of taxes 5/25/94

HERITAGE BANCORP INC (OH)
Merged into Banc One Corp. (DE) 04/01/1983
Each share Common $5 par exchanged for (1.03125) shares Common no par
Banc One Corp. (DE) reincorporated in Ohio 05/01/1989 which merged into Bank One Corp. 10/02/1998 which merged into J.P. Morgan Chase & Co. 12/31/2000 which name changed to JPMorgan Chase & Co. 07/20/2004

HERITAGE BANCORP INC (PA)
Common $5 par split (2) for (1) by isssuance of (1) additional share payable 05/23/1997 to holders of record 05/14/1997
Stock Dividend - 25% payable 05/24/1996 to holders of record 05/10/1996
Merged into Main Street Bancorp, Inc. 05/01/1998
Each share Common $5 par exchanged for (1.05) shares Common $1 par
Main Street Bancorp, Inc. merged into Sovereign Bancorp, Inc. 03/08/2002 which merged into Banco Santander, S.A. 01/30/2009

HERITAGE BANCORP INC (VA)
Merged into Cardinal Financial Corp. 09/01/2000
Each share Common no par exchanged for (1.2) shares Common $1 par and $6 cash
Cardinal Financial Corp. merged into United Bankshares, Inc. 04/24/2017

HERITAGE BANCORP INC NEW (DE)
Merged into SouthBanc Shares, Inc. 7/31/2000
Each share Common 1¢ par exchanged for (0.992) share Common 1¢ par
SouthBanc Shares, Inc. merged into National Commerce Financial Corp. 11/19/2001 which merged into SunTrust Banks, Inc. 10/1/2004

HERITAGE BANCORPORATION (NJ)
Common no par split (2) for (1) by issuance of (1) additional share 10/2/72
Merged into Midlantic Banks Inc. 5/1/85
Each share Common no par exchanged for $47 cash

HERITAGE BANCSHARES INC (DE)
Merged into HGroup Acquisition Co. 6/28/2004
Each share Common 1¢ par exchanged for $26.25 cash

HERITAGE BANCSHARES INC (FL)
Acquired by Southtrust of Florida, Inc. 09/30/1996
Details not available

HERITAGE BK (ANAHEIM, CA)
Stock Dividend - 20% 01/30/1981
Under plan of reorganization each share Common no par automatically became (1) share Heritage Bancorp Common no par 12/28/1981
(See Heritage Bancorp)

HERITAGE BK (DECATUR, AL)
Common 1¢ par split (2) for (1) by issuance of (1) additional share payable 12/17/99 to holders of record 11/8/99
Under plan of reorganization each share Common 1¢ par automatically became (1) share Heritage Financial Holding Corp. Common 1¢ par 10/10/2000
Heritage Financial Holding Corp. merged into Peoples Holding Co. 1/3/2005 which name changed to Renasant Corp. 4/19/2005

HERITAGE BK (MCLEAN, VA)
Name changed to Heritage Bancorp Inc. 10/01/1998
Heritage Bancorp Inc. merged into Cardinal Financial Corp. 09/01/2000 which merged into United Bankshares, Inc. 04/24/2017

HERITAGE BK (RENO, NV)
Common 1¢ par split (2) for (1) by issuance of (1) additional share payable 8/15/99 to holders of record 8/15/99
Under plan of reorganization each share Common 1¢ par automatically became (1) share Heritage Bancorp Common 1¢ par 3/28/2003

HERITAGE BK (WATERTOWN, CT)
Merged into Center Financial Corp. 04/12/1996
Each share Common $1 par exchanged for (0.6938) share Common $1 par
Center Financial Corp. merged into First Union Corp. 11/13/1996 which name changed to Wachovia Corp. (Ctfs. dated after 09/01/2001) 09/01/2001 which merged into Wells Fargo & Co. (New) 12/31/2008

HERITAGE BK (WHARTON, TX)
Acquired by Commercial Bancshares, Inc. 12/20/1999
Details not available

HERITAGE BK COMM (SAN JOSE, CA)
Common no par split (3) for (2) by issuance of (0.5) additional share payable 8/15/97 to holders of record 8/1/97 Ex date - 8/18/97
Under plan of reorganization each share Common no par automatically became (1) share Heritage Commerce Corp. Common no par 2/17/98

HERITAGE BK HARRISON CNTY INC (CLARKSBURG, WV)
Merged into Wesbanco, Inc. 4/30/99
Each share Common no par exchanged for (1.76639) shares Common $2.0833 par

HERITAGE BK WHITEFISH BAY (MILWAUKEE, WI)
Acquired by Heritage Bank-Mayfair (Milwaukee, WI) 12/31/82
Each share Capital Stock $10 par exchanged for and undetermined amount of cash

HERITAGE BANKCORP INC (DE)
Common 1¢ par split (3) for (2) by issuance of (0.5) additional share 5/15/92
Merged into Standard Federal Bank (Troy, MI) 12/4/93
Each share Common 1¢ par exchanged for $33.25 cash

HERITAGE BANKS INC. (NH)
Merged into BankEast Corp. 03/01/1982
Each share $2.70 Conv. Preferred $20 par exchanged for (3) shares Common $5 par
Each share Common $10 par exchanged for (3) shares Common $5 par
(See BankEast Corp.)

HERITAGE BANKSHARES INC (VA)
Common $5 par split (2) for (1) by issuance of (1) additional share payable 09/30/2004 to holders of record 09/15/2004
Acquired by Southern BancShares (N.C.), Inc. 02/01/2016
Each share Common $5 par exchanged for $21.05 cash

HERITAGE CAP CR CORP (FL)
Recapitalized as Protective Capital Structures Corp. 12/11/2008
Each share Common $0.001 par exchanged for (0.00001) share Common $0.001 par

HERITAGE COLLECTION INC (DE)
Common $0.001 par split (10) for (1) by issuance of (9) additional shares payable 6/21/2004 to holders of record 6/7/2004 Ex date - 6/22/2004
Name changed to Sakha Resource Technologies Corp. in July 2004
Sakha Resource Technologies Corp. name changed to Canary Resources Inc. 1/31/2005

HERITAGE COMM CORP (CA)
Preferred Stock Purchase Rights declared for Common stockholders of record 11/12/2001 were redeemed at $0.001 per right 03/14/2005 to holders of record 03/07/2005
(Additional Information in Active)

HERITAGE COMMUNICATIONS INC (IA)
Common $1 par changed to 50¢ par and (1) additional share issued 6/18/79
Common 50¢ par split (3) for (2) by issuance of (0.5) additional share 4/18/85
$1.50 Conv. Preferred Ser. B no par called for redemption 3/3/86
Merged into Tele-Communications, Inc. (Old) 8/11/87
Each share Common 50¢ par exchanged for (0.311486) share Class A Common $1 par and $26 cash
Tele-Communications, Inc. (Old) merged into Tele-Communications, Inc. (New) 8/5/94 which merged into AT&T Corp. 3/9/99 which merged into AT&T Inc. 11/18/2005

HERITAGE CMNTY BANCORPORATION INC (IL)
Company's sole asset placed in receivership 02/27/2009
Stockholders' equity unlikely

HERITAGE CMNTY BK (DANVILLE, KY)
Merged into Community Trust Bancorp, Inc. 6/10/2005
Each share Common $5 par exchanged for $25.75 cash

HERITAGE CONCEPTS INTL INC (QC)
Name changed to NEXUS Group International Inc. 03/13/2001
(See NEXUS Group International Inc.)

HERITAGE CONV INCOME GROWTH TR (MA)
Name changed to Heritage Income-Growth Trust 02/01/1990
Heritage Income-Growth Trust name changed to Heritage Growth & Income Trust 07/02/2001

HERITAGE CORP N Y (NY)
Liquidation completed
Each share Common 10¢ par received initial distribution of $5 cash 11/10/1973
Each share Common 10¢ par received second distribution of (2.18) shares Applied Concepts, Inc. Common 1¢ par, (2.08) shares Educational Horizons, Inc. Capital Stock 5¢ par and (2.08) shares SSA, Inc. Common 1¢ par 12/03/1973
Each share Common 10¢ par received third distribution of $5 cash 02/28/1974
Each share Common 10¢ par received fourth distribution of $1.50 cash 07/01/1974
Each share Common 10¢ par received fifth distribution of (0.52) share Common no par and (0.26) share Common Stock Purchase Warrant expiring 07/31/1979 of University Patents, Inc. 05/12/1975
Each share Common 10¢ par received sixth distribution of $1.2431 cash 12/28/1977
Each share Common 10¢ par received seventh and final distribution of $0.3417 cash 10/12/1978
Note: Certificates were not required to be surrendered and are without value

HERITAGE COS INC (NV)
Each share old Common $0.001 par exchanged for (0.16666666) share new Common $0.001 par 08/16/2002
Name changed to Songzai International Holding Group, Inc. 11/10/2003
Songzai International Holding Group, Inc. name changed to U.S. China Mining Group, Inc. 07/27/2010

HERITAGE CNTY BK & TR CO (BLUE ISLAND, IL)
Acquired by First Midwest Bancorp, Inc. 10/24/1998
Details not available

HERITAGE ENTERPRISES, INC. (NY)
Name changed to Heritage Entertainment, Inc. (NY) 03/05/1985
Heritage Entertainment, Inc. (NY) reincorporated in Delaware 6/25/1986 which reorganized as Goldwyn (Samuel) Co. 12/06/1991 which merged into Metromedia International Group, Inc. 07/02/1996
(See Metromedia International Group, Inc.)

HERITAGE ENTMT INC (DE)
Reincorporated 06/25/1986
12-1/2% Conv. Preferred Class A $5 par called for redemption 06/30/1986
State of incorporation changed from (NY) to (DE) 06/25/1986
Reorganized under Chapter 11 Federal Bankruptcy Code 12/06/1991
Each share Common 1¢ par exchanged for (0.8602) share Goldwyn (Samuel) Co. Common 1¢ par, (0.2245) share Common Stock Purchase Warrant, Class A expiring 12/06/1993 and (0.8112) Common Stock Purchase Warrant, Class B expiring 12/06/1994
Goldwyn (Samuel) Co. merged into Metromedia International Group, Inc. 07/02/1996
(See Metromedia International Group, Inc.)

HERITAGE EXPLORATIONS INC (NV)
Each share old Common $0.001 par exchanged for (6) shares new Common $0.001 par 04/16/2008
Name changed to USR Technology, Inc. 06/26/2008
USR Technology, Inc. recapitalized as Ecologic Transportation, Inc. 06/11/2009 which recapitalized as Peartrack Security Systems, Inc. 10/17/2014

HERITAGE EXPLORATIONS LTD (BC)
Merged into St Andrew Goldfields Ltd. 08/22/2005
Each share Common no par exchanged for (1.2) shares new Common no par
St Andrew Goldfields Ltd. merged into Kirkland Lake Gold Inc. 01/29/2016 which merged into Kirkland Lake Gold Ltd. 12/06/2016

HERITAGE FD INC (NY)
Name changed to American Heritage Fund, Inc. 08/30/1976
(See American Heritage Fund, Inc.)

HERITAGE FED BANCSHARES INC (TN)
Common $1 par split (3) for (2) by issuance of (0.5) additional share 9/30/93
Common $1 par split (4) for (3) by issuance of (1/3) additional share 8/26/94
Merged into First American Corp. (TN) 11/1/95
Each share Common $1 par exchanged for (0.8116) share Common $5 par
First American Corp. (TN) merged into AmSouth Bancorporation 10/1/99 which merged into Regions Financial Corp. 11/4/2006

HERITAGE FED SVGS & LN ASSN DAYTONA BEACH FLA (USA)
Merged into American Pioneer Savings Bank (Orlando, FL) 07/31/1986
Each share Common 1¢ par exchanged for $23.51 cash

HERITAGE FINL CORP (DE)
Name changed to HBancorporation, Inc. 12/4/96
(See HBancorporation, Inc.)

HERITAGE FINL CORP (VA)
Common 33-1/3¢ par split (3) for (1) by issuance of (2) additional shares 07/31/1978
Stock Dividend - 10% 04/16/1981
Charter cancelled and proclaimed dissolved for failure to file reports 08/05/1991

HERITAGE FINL GROUP (USA)
Reorganized under the laws of Maryland as Heritage Financial Group, Inc. 11/30/2010
Each share Common 1¢ par exchanged for (0.8377) share Common 1¢ par
Heritage Financial Group, Inc. merged into Renasant Corp. 06/30/2015

HERITAGE FINL GROUP INC (MD)
Merged into Renasant Corp. 06/30/2015
Each share Common 1¢ par exchanged for (0.9266) share Common $5 par

HERITAGE FINL HLDG CORP (AL)
Merged into Peoples Holding Co. 1/1/2005
Each share Common 1¢ par exchanged for (0.12) share Common $5 par and $2.50 cash
Peoples Holding Co. name changed to Renasant Corp. 4/19/2005

HERITAGE FINL LTD (IA)
Merged into Commercial Federal Corp. 10/1/96
Each share Common $1 par exchanged for (2.4985) shares Common 1¢ par and $18.73 cash
Note: An additional distribution of $2.8263146 cash per share was made 9/1/97
(See Commercial Federal Corp.)

HERITAGE FINL SVCS CORP (PA)
Merged into Omega Financial Corp. 12/31/86
Each share Common $5 par exchanged for $50 cash

HERITAGE FINL SVCS INC (IL)
Common $1.25 par split (5) for (4) by issuance of (0.25) additional share 07/14/1989
Common $1.25 par changed to $0.625 par and (1) additional share issued 05/15/1992
Common $0.625 par split (3) for (2) by issuance of (0.5) additional share payable 06/13/1997 to holders of record 05/27/1997
Merged into First Midwest Bancorp, Inc. 07/01/1998
Each share Common $0.625 par exchanged for (0.7695) share Common 1¢ par

HERITAGE FOODS INC (DE)
Charter cancelled and declared inoperative and void for non-payment of taxes 3/1/78

HERITAGE FUNERAL SERVICES, INC. (KS)
Name changed to Heritage Services, Inc. 7/20/73
Heritage Services, Inc. name changed to Farmers Group Purchasing, Inc. 2/4/74
(See Farmers Group Purchasing, Inc.)

HERITAGE GROUP INC (ON)
Name changed back to Schneider Corp. (New) 06/26/1986
Schneider Corp. (New) merged into Smithfield Foods Inc. 12/21/1998

HERITAGE INCOME GROWTH TR (MA)
Name changed to Heritage Growth & Income Trust 07/02/2001

HERITAGE INDUSTRIAL CORP. (NY)
Stock Dividends - 100% 8/16/67; 20% 10/13/67; 10% 2/1/68
Reincorporated under the laws of Delaware as National Hospital Corp. and Common $1 par changed to 25¢ par 9/5/68
(See National Hospital Corp.)

HERITAGE INDS INC (NV)
Charter revoked for failure to file reports and pay fees 03/04/1974

HERITAGE MGMT INC (NV)
Name changed to Edgewater Foods International, Inc. 08/30/2005
Edgewater Foods International, Inc. name changed to Ocean Smart, Inc. 03/03/2009

HERITAGE MEDIA CORP (DE)
Reincorporated 07/15/1996
Each share old Common 1¢ par exchanged for (0.25) share new Common 1¢ par 03/30/1992
State of incorporation changed from (IA) to (DE) 07/15/1996
Merged into News Corp., Ltd. 08/20/1997
Each share Class A Common 1¢ par exchanged for (1.3825) Sponsored ADR's for Ltd. Voting Preferred Ordinary AUD $0.50 par
News Corp., Ltd. reorganized as News Corp. (Old) 11/03/2004 which name changed to Twenty-First Century Fox, Inc. 07/01/2013

HERITAGE MEDIA CORP (NV)
Recapitalized as Oliveda International, Inc. 03/24/2017
Each share Common $0.001 par exchanged for (0.002) share Common $0.001 par

HERITAGE MINES LTD (CO)
Reincorporated under the laws of Nevada as Southern Cosmetics, Inc. and Common no par changed to $0.001 par 07/20/2005
Southern Cosmetics, Inc. name changed to Revenge Designs, Inc. 12/18/2007 which name changed to Cartel Blue, Inc. 09/18/2015

HERITAGE NATIONAL BANK (LOS ANGELES, CA)
Under plan of merger name changed to Heritage-Wilshire National Bank (Los Angeles, CA) 10/15/65
Heritage-Wilshire National Bank (Los Angeles, CA) merged into Southern California First National Bank (San Diego, CA) 10/6/67 which reorganized as Southern California First National Corp. 2/28/69
(See Southern California First National Corp.)

HERITAGE NIS BK FOR SVGS (NORTHAMPTON, MA)
Reorganized under the laws of Delaware as Heritage Bancorp, Inc. 9/15/88
Heritage Bancorp, Inc. merged into Main Street Bancorp, Inc. 5/1/98 which merged into Sovereign Bancorp, Inc. 3/8/2002

HERITAGE NURSING CTRS INC (DE)
Name changed to Heritage Rembrandt Corp. 1/23/70
Heritage Rembrandt Corp. name changed to Rembrandt Enterprises, Inc. 1/31/72
(See Rembrandt Enterprises, Inc.)

HERITAGE OAKS BANCORP (CA)
Common no par split (3) for (2) by issuance of (0.5) additional share payable 11/05/1997 to holders of record 10/15/1997
Common no par split (2) for (1) by issuance of (1) additional share payable 08/15/2002 to holders of record 08/02/2002 Ex date - 08/16/2002
Common no par split (3) for (2) by issuance of (0.5) additional share payable 12/02/2005 to holders of record 11/10/2005 Ex date - 12/05/2005
Stock Dividends - 4% payable 02/26/1999 to holders of record 02/15/1999; 5% payable 04/17/2000 to holders of record 04/03/2000; 5% payable 03/30/2001 to holders of record 03/16/2001 Ex date - 04/05/2001; 5% payable 03/29/2002 to holders of record 03/08/2002 Ex date - 03/14/2002; 5% payable 03/28/2003 to holders of record 03/14/2003 Ex date - 03/12/2003; 5% payable 04/23/2004 to holders of record 04/09/2004 Ex date - 04/06/2004; 5% payable 04/22/2005 to holders of record 04/08/2005 Ex date - 04/06/2005; 5% payable 05/16/2008 to holders of record 05/02/2008 Ex date - 04/30/2008
Merged into Pacific Premier Bancorp, Inc. 03/31/2017
Each share Common no par exchanged for (0.3471) share Common 1¢ par

HERITAGE OAKS BK (PASO ROBLES, CA)
Under plan of reorganization each share Common no par automatically became (1) share Heritage Oaks Bancorp Common no par 03/00/1994
Heritage Oaks Bancorp merged into Pacific Premier Bancorp, Inc. 03/31/2017

HERITAGE OIL CORP (AB)
Class A Common no par reclassified as Common no par 07/16/2004
Reorganized as Heritage Oil PLC 04/03/2008
Each share Common no par exchanged for either (10) shares Ordinary or (10) Heritage Oil Corp. Exchangeable Shares
Note: Option to receive Exchangeable Shares expired 03/18/2008
Each Exchangeable Share exchanged for (1) share Heritage Oil PLC Ordinary 05/16/2014

HERITAGE OLYMPIA BK (CHICAGO HEIGHTS, IL)
Acquired by Olympia Bancorporation, Inc. 10/17/1995
Details not available

HERITAGE PETES INC (BC)
Merged into Heritage American Resource Corp. 07/25/1994
Each share Common no par exchanged for (0.14285714) share Common no par
Heritage American Resource Corp. recapitalized as Heritage Explorations Ltd. 09/17/2001 which merged into St Andrew Goldfields Ltd. 08/22/2005 which merged into Kirkland Lake Gold Inc. 01/29/2016 which merged into Kirkland Lake Gold Ltd. 12/06/2016

HERITAGE PETROLEUM CORP. (DE)
Common $1 par changed to no par and (2) additional shares issued 06/02/1959
Acquired by Landa Oil Co. (Old) 11/16/1965
Each share Common no par exchanged for (0.074635) share Common 10¢ par
Landa Oil Co. (Old) name changed to Landa Industries, Inc. 04/07/1967 which recapitalized as Surveyor Companies, Inc. 11/12/1971 which name changed to Forum Companies, Inc. 09/23/1974
(See Forum Companies, Inc.)

HERITAGE PRINTING TECHNOLOGY CORP (FL)
Name changed 06/28/2016
Name changed from Heritage Action Corp. to Heritage Printing Technology Corp. 06/28/2016
Recapitalized as Comerton Corp. 11/07/2017
Each share Common $0.001 par exchanged for (0.02) share Common $0.001 par

HERITAGE PRODUCTIONS INC (LA)
Reincorporated under the laws of Delaware as Heritage Worldwide Inc. and Common no par changed to $0.001 par 08/24/2001
(See Heritage Worldwide Inc.)

HERITAGE PROPANE PARTNERS L P (DE)
Name changed to Energy Transfer Partners, L.P. (Old) 02/10/2004
Energy Transfer Partners, L.P. (Old) merged into Energy Transfer Partners, L.P. (New) 05/01/2017 which merged into Energy Transfer L.P. 10/19/2018

HERITAGE PPTY INVT TR INC (MD)
Issue Information - 18,000,000 shares COM offered at $25 per share on 04/23/2002
Merged into Centro Properties Group 10/5/2006
Each share Common $0.001 par exchanged for $36.675 cash

HERITAGE PULLMAN BK & TR CO (CHICAGO, IL)
Merged into Pullman Bank of Commerce & Industry (Chicago, IL) 1/31/97
Each share Common $10 par exchanged for $28 cash

HERITAGE QUILTS INC (DE)
Common 50¢ par changed to 40¢ par and (0.25) additional share issued 11/07/1979

HER-HER   **FINANCIAL INFORMATION, INC.**

Chapter 11 converted to Chapter 7 bankruptcy proceedings 05/17/1982
No stockholders' equity

HERITAGE REMBRANDT CORP (DE)
Name changed to Rembrandt Enterprises, Inc. 1/31/72
(See Rembrandt Enterprises, Inc.)

HERITAGE SAVINGS & LOAN ASSOCIATION (CA)
Liquidation completed
Each Guarantee Stock $8 par received initial distribution of $27.50 cash 12/10/1976
Each Guarantee Stock $8 par exchanged for second and final distribution of $23.50 cash 01/14/1977

HERITAGE SVGS & LN ASSN (VA)
Guarantee Stock $10 par changed to $2.50 par and (3) additional shares issued 10/03/1972
Guarantee Stock $2.50 par reclassified as Capital Stock $1.25 par and (1) additional share issued 03/07/1973
Capital Stock $1.25 par changed to $1 par and (0.25) additional share issued 08/15/1975
Under plan of reorganization each share Capital Stock $1 par automatically became (1) share Heritage Financial Corp. Common $0.33333333 par 07/03/1978
(See Heritage Financial Corp.)

HERITAGE SAVINGS & TRUST CO. (EDMONTON, AB)
Merged into North West Trust Co. (Edmonton, AB) 03/13/1987
Details not available

HERITAGE SVGS BK (OLYMPIA, WA)
Reorganized as Heritage Financial Corp. 01/08/1998
Each share Common $1 par exchanged for (5.1492) shares Common no par

HERITAGE SCHOLASTIC CORP (NV)
Common $0.001 par split (4) for (1) by issuance of (3) additional shares payable 02/07/2005 to holders of record 02/07/2005 Ex date - 02/08/2005
Name changed to Nano Chemical Systems Holdings, Inc. 03/01/2005
Nano Chemical Systems Holdings, Inc. recapitalized as PanGenex Corp. 04/08/2008 which recapitalized as Virtual Sourcing, Inc. 08/31/2012

HERITAGE SERVICES, INC. (KS)
Name changed to Farmers Group Purchasing, Inc. and Common no par changed to 10¢ par 02/04/1974
(See Farmers Group Purchasing, Inc.)

HERITAGE STD BK & TR CO (CHICAGO, IL)
Reorganized as Standard Bancshares, Inc. 11/14/1984
Each share Capital Stock $10 par exchanged for (1) share Common $10 par
Standard Bancshares, Inc. merged into First Midwest Bancorp, Inc. 12/06/2016

HERITAGE U S GOVT INCOME FD (MA)
Under plan of reorganization Shares of Bene. Int. no par automatically became Heritage Income Trust Intermediate Government Fund Class A no par on a net asset value basis 10/15/99

HERITAGE WILSHIRE NATL BK (LOS ANGELES, CA)
Merged into Southern California First National Bank (San Diego, CA) 10/06/1967
Each share Common $10 par exchanged for (0.503498) share Common $5 par

Southern California First National Bank (San Diego, CA) reorganized as Southern California First National Corp. 02/28/1969
(See Southern California First National Corp.)

HERITAGE WIS CORP (WI)
Stock Dividends - 10% 01/25/1979; 10% 10/25/1979
Merged into Marshall & Ilsley Corp. 07/09/1985
Each share Common $1 par exchanged for $23 cash

HERITAGE WORLDWIDE INC (DE)
SEC revoked common stock registration 01/21/2014

HERKIMER CNTY TR CO (LITTLE FALLS, NY)
Under plan of reorganization each share Common $100 par automatically became (1) share Herkimer TrustCorporation, Inc. Common $100 par 3/18/83
(See Herkimer TrustCorporation, Inc.)

HERKIMER TRUSTCORPORATION INC (DE)
Acquired by Partners Trust Financial Group, Inc. (USA) 12/27/2002
Each share Common $1 par exchanged for approximately $18,566 cash

HERKY PACKING CO (MN)
Name changed to H.P.C., Inc. (MN) 07/05/1972
H.P.C., Inc. (MN) reincorporated in Nevada as HPC Acquisitions, Inc. 08/07/2006 which name changed to Vegalab, Inc. 11/13/2017

HERLEY INDS INC (DE)
Name changed 10/01/1983
Reincorporated 06/00/1986
Name changed 12/19/1989
Common 10¢ par split (3) for (1) by issuance of (2) additional shares 08/14/1983
Name changed from Herley Industries, Inc. to Herley Microwave Systems, Inc. 10/01/1983
State of incorporation changed from (NY) to (DE) 06/00/1986
Name changed from Herley Microwave Systems, Inc. to Herley Industries, Inc. 12/19/1989
Common 10¢ par split (4) for (3) by issuance of (1/3) additional share payable 09/29/1997 to holders of record 09/15/1997
Common 10¢ par split (3) for (2) by issuance of (0.5) additional share payable 09/10/2001 to holders of record 08/28/2001 Ex date - 09/11/2001
Acquired by Kratos Defense & Security Solutions, Inc. 03/30/2011
Each share Common 10¢ par exchanged for $19 cash

HERMAN & APPLEY INC (DE)
Name changed to Coliseum Properties, Inc. 1/29/70
(See Coliseum Properties, Inc.)

HERMAN HANSON OIL SYNDICATE (ND)
See - Hanson (Herman) Oil Syndicate

HERMAN LAKE GOLD MINES LTD.
Name changed to Apex Oils & Mines Ltd. in 1943
Apex Oils & Mines Ltd. acquired by Apex Consolidated Resources Ltd. in 1946 which recapitalized as Abacus Mines Ltd. 6/1/59 which name changed to Abacus Mines & Realty Ltd. in 1962 which was recapitalized as Abacon Developments Ltd. 3/21/63
(See Abacon Developments Ltd.)

HERMAN NELSON CORP.
See - Nelson (Herman) Corp.

HERMANS SPORTING GOODS INC (DE)
Merged into HSG Holdings, Inc. 4/18/86
Each share Common 1¢ par exchanged for $35.25 cash

HERMANS SPORTING GOODS INC NEW (DE)
Each share old Common 1¢ par exchanged for (0.0008) share new Common 1¢ par 5/23/95
Filed petition under Chapter 11 Federal Bankruptcy Code effective 4/26/96
No stockholders' equity

HERMATON CO (DE)
Name changed to Las Vegas Airlines, Inc. 04/00/1998
Las Vegas Airlines, Inc. recapitalized as LASV Enterprises, Inc. 05/18/2000
(See LASV Enterprises, Inc.)

HERMES ELECTRONICS CO. (DE)
Merged into Itek Corp. (Del.) on a (1) for (4.75) basis 7/26/60
(See Itek Corp. (Del.))

HERMES JETS INC (NV)
Recapitalized as Continental Beverage Brands Corp. 02/25/2015
Each share Common $0.001 par exchanged for (0.1) share Common $0.001 par

HERMES VENTURES LTD (BC)
Recapitalized as Profile Ventures Ltd. 09/26/1994
Each share Common no par exchanged for (0.33333333) share Common no par
Profile Ventures Ltd. name changed to Multivision Communications Corp. (BC) 12/21/1995 which reincorporated in Yukon 10/02/2000 which reorganized in British Columbia 01/24/2011 which name changed to ZoomAway Travel Inc. 10/05/2016

HERMETIC SEAL CORP. (NJ)
Completely liquidated 5/10/68
Each share Class A 10¢ par or Class B 10¢ par exchanged for first and final distribution of (0.1666) share Sterling Electronics Corp. Common 50¢ par
(See Sterling Electronics Corp.)

HERMETIC SEAL CORP (CA)
Common 10¢ par changed to no par and (1) additional share issued 2/15/78
Name changed to HCC Industries 7/19/79
HCC Industries name changed to HCC Industries Inc. 9/16/86
(See HCC Industries Inc.)

HERMETITE CORP (MA)
Merged into HCC Industries 03/27/1986
Each share Common no par exchanged for $5.50 cash

HERMINE OPERATING CO. (DE)
No longer in existence having become inoperative and void for non-payment of taxes 03/17/1920

HERMIT LAKE COPPER CO. (ME)
Voluntarily dissolved in 1901
Details not available

HERMITAGE CORP (TN)
Placed in receivership 10/31/1986
No stockholders' equity

HERMITAGE PORTLAND CEMENT CO.
Acquired by Marquette Cement Manufacturing Co. (IL) 00/00/1947
Details not available

HERMOSA-REDONDO WATER CO.
Merged into California Water Service Co. (CA) in 1926
Details not available

HEROES INC (NV)
Chapter 7 bankruptcy proceedings dismissed 05/20/2003
Stockholders' equity unlikely

HEROLD FD INC (MD)
Name changed to Bruce Fund, Inc. 10/17/1983

HEROLD RADIO & ELECTRONICS CORP. (NY)
Liquidation completed 4/14/61
No stockholders' equity

HERON EXPL INC (QC)
Cease trade order effective 05/29/2002

HERON RES LTD (AUSTRALIA)
Each share old Ordinary exchanged for (0.1) share new Ordinary 12/14/2017
Shares transferred to Australian share register 09/28/2018

HERON RES LTD (BC)
Recapitalized as Consolidated Heron Resources Ltd. 08/18/1988
Each share Common no par exchanged for (0.2) share Common no par
Consolidated Heron Resources Ltd. recapitalized as Fintra Ventures Ltd. 02/08/1993 which name changed to U.S. Diamond Corp. 06/21/1996
(See U.S. Diamond Corp.)

HEROUX INC (QC)
Name changed to Heroux-Devtek Inc. 09/25/2000

HERRIMEN OIL & GAS INC (NV)
Recapitalized as Boundaries Capital Inc. 03/24/2003
Each share Common $0.001 par exchanged for (0.00666666) share Common $0.001 par
Boundaries Capital Inc. name changed to Golden Patriot Corp. 09/29/2003
(See Golden Patriot Corp.)

HERRONA SA-FUEL PRODUCTS, INC. (CT)
Out of business 09/00/1968
No stockholders' equity

HERS APPAREL INDS INC (DE)
Charter cancelled and declared inoperative and void for non-payment of taxes 03/01/1989

HERSEY MANUFACTURING CO. (MA)
Each share Common $100 par exchanged for (5) shares Common $20 par in 1950
Name changed to Hershey-Sparling Meter Co. 12/31/59
Hersey-Sparling Meter Co. name changed to Hersey Products Inc. 6/1/71
(See Hersey Products Inc.)

HERSEY PRODS INC (MA)
Merged out of existence 12/17/87
Details not available

HERSEY SPARLING METER CO (MA)
Common $20 par changed to $4 par and (4) additional shares issued 8/3/65
Common $4 par changed to $1.33-1/3 par and (2) additional shares issued 5/4/70
Common $1.33-1/3 par changed to $1 par 5/24/71
Name changed to Hersey Products Inc. 6/1/71
(See Hersey Products Inc.)

HERSHA HOSPITALITY TR (MD)
8% Preferred Shares of Bene. Int. Ser. A 1¢ par called for redemption at $25 plus $0.4056 accrued dividends on 03/28/2013
8% Preferred Shares of Bene. Int. Ser. B 1¢ par called for redemption at $25 plus $0.3722 accrued dividends on 06/08/2016
(Additional Information in Active)

HERSHBERGER ENTERPRISES INC (DE)
Adjudicated bankrupt 11/15/1974
Stockholders' equity unlikely

HERSHBERGER EXPLORATIONS, INC. (DE)
Name changed to Hershberger Enterprises, Inc. 4/18/73
(See Hershberger Enterprises, Inc.)

HERSHEY CHOCOLATE CO.
Succeeded by Hershey Chocolate Corp. in 1927
Details not available

HERSHEY CHOCOLATE CORP. (DE)
Each share $4 Preference no par exchanged for (1) share 4-1/4% Preferred Ser. A $50 par, (1) share 4-1/2% Preferred Ser. B $50 par and (1) share Common no par in 1949
Common no par split (5) for (1) by issuance of (4) additional shares 4/17/62
Stock Dividend - 200% 9/18/47
Name changed to Hershey Foods Corp. 2/19/68
Hershey Foods Corp. name changed to Hershey Co. 4/19/2005

HERSHEY CORP.
Merged into Houdaille-Hershey Corp. in 1929
Houdaille-Hershey Corp. name changed to Houdaille Industries, Inc. (Mich.) 11/30/55 which reincorporated under the laws of Delaware 4/1/68
(See Houdaille Industries, Inc. (Del.))

HERSHEY FD INC (MD)
Completely liquidated 06/01/1973
Each share Common 50¢ par exchanged for first and final distribution of $3.371 cash

HERSHEY FOODS CORP (DE)
Common no par split (2) for (1) by issuance of (1) additional share 9/15/83
Common no par changed to $1 par 10/9/84
Common $1 par split (3) for (1) by issuance of (2) additional shares 9/15/86
Common $1 par split (2) for (1) by issuance of (1) additional share payable 9/13/96 to holders of record 8/23/96 Ex date - 9/16/96
Common $1 par split (2) for (1) by issuance of (1) additional share payable 6/15/2004 to holders of record 5/25/2004 Ex date - 6/16/2004
Name changed to Hershey Co. 4/19/2005

HERSHEY OIL CORP (CA)
Merged into American Exploration Co. 08/29/1990
Each share Common 10¢ par exchanged for (1.611) shares Common 5¢ par
American Exploration Co. merged into Louis Dreyfus Natural Gas Corp. 10/14/1997 which merged into Dominion Resources, Inc. (New) 11/01/2001 which name changed to Dominion Energy, Inc. 05/11/2017

HERTS-LION INTERNATIONAL (CA)
Out of existence 00/00/1965
No stockholders' equity

HERTZ CORP (DE)
Common $6 par changed to $1 par 05/24/1955
Common $1 par split (2) for (1) by issuance of (1) additional share 10/06/1955
Common $1 par split (3) for (2) by issuance of (0.5) additional share 12/31/1958
Merged into Radio Corp. of America 05/11/1967
Each share $2 Conv. Part. Preferred Ser. B no par exchanged for (0.52) share $4 1st Conv. Preferred no par

Each share Common $1 par exchanged for (0.25) share $4 1st Conv. Preferred no par and (0.5) share Common no par
Radio Corp. of America name changed to RCA Corp. 05/09/1969
(See RCA Corp.)
Merged into Ford Motor Co. 03/09/2001
Each share Class A Common 1¢ par exchanged for $35.50 cash

HERTZ GLOBAL HLDGS INC OLD (DE)
Each share Common 1¢ par received distribution of (0.2) share Hertz Global Holdings, Inc. (New) Common 1¢ par payable 06/30/2016 to holders of record 06/22/2016
Ex date - 07/01/2016
Recapitalized as Herc Holdings Inc. 07/01/2016
Each share Common 1¢ par exchanged for (0.06666666) share Common 1¢ par

HERTZ INDS LTD (BC)
Common $1 par changed to no par 08/17/1971
Struck off register and declared dissolved for failure to file returns 05/02/1986

HERTZ TECHNOLOGY GROUP INC (DE)
Each share old Common $0.001 par exchanged for (1/3) share new Common $0.001 par 11/02/1998
New Common $0.001 par split (2) for (1) by issuance of (1) additional share payable 05/18/1999 to holders of record 04/29/1999
Name changed to Return Assured Inc. 10/17/2000
(See Return Assured Inc.)

HERZING INSTS INC (WI)
Each share old Common 10¢ par exchanged for (0.00005) share new Common 10¢ par 09/03/1980
Note: In effect holders received $1.25 cash per share and public interest was eliminated
Certificates were not required to be surrendered and are now without value

HERZOG INTL HLDGS INC (NV)
SEC revoked common stock registration 07/19/2012

HESCA RES LTD (BC)
Acquired by T.R.V. Minerals Corp. 05/01/1981
Each share Common 50¢ par exchanged for (2/7) share Common no par
(See T.R.V. Minerals Corp.)

HESCO, INC. (WI)
Involuntarily dissolved 02/16/2007

HESPERIA HLDGS INC (NV)
Recapitalized as Max Media Group, Inc. 08/10/2009
Each share Common $0.001 par exchanged for (0.005) share Common $0.001 par
Max Media Group, Inc. name changed to Altavoz Entertainment, Inc. 04/20/2016

HESS CORP (DE)
Each Automatic Common Exchange Security received (2.4915) shares Common $1 par 12/01/2006
(Additional Information in Active)

HESS-IVES CORP.
Dissolved in 1948

HESS OIL & CHEM CORP (DE)
Class A Common 50¢ par reclassified as Common 50¢ par 1/1/65
Merged into Amerada Hess Corp. 6/20/69
Each share Common 50¢ par exchanged for (1) share Common $1 par

Amerada Hess Corp. name changed to Hess Corp. 5/3/2006

HESS S INC (PA)
99.9% acquired by Crown American Corp. 11/30/1979
Public interest eliminated

HESSTON CORP (KS)
Stock Dividend - 50% 11/13/1972
Merged into Fiat S.p.A. 05/20/1987
Each share Common $2 par exchanged for $4 cash
Merged into M.M.S.-Marketing & Management Services Corp. 07/18/1989
Each share $1.60 Conv. Preferred $2 par exchanged for $12.50 cash
Public interest eliminated

HESTONVILLE, MANTUA & FAIRMOUNT PASSENGER RAILROAD CO.
Acquired in reorganization by Philadelphia Transportation Co. in 1940
Each share Preferred exchanged for $12.65 of 3%-6% Consolidated Mortgage Bonds and (0.3115) share Part. Preferred $20 par
Each share Common exchanged for $8.42 of 3%-6% Consolidated Mortgage Bonds and (0.207) share Part. Preferred $20 par

HETRA COMPUTER & COMMUNICATIONS INDS INC (DE)
Merged into Extel Acquisition, Inc. 12/30/88
Each share Common 1¢ par exchanged for $0.93 cash

HEUBLEIN INC (CT)
Common $5 par changed to $1 par and (2) additional shares issued 11/02/1961
Common $1 par changed to no par and (1) additional share issued 11/02/1967
Conv. Preferred Ser. A no par called for redemption 09/30/1982
Conv. Preferred Ser. B-1 thru B-5 no par called for redemption 09/30/1982
Merged into Reynolds (R.J.) Industries, Inc. 10/13/1982
Each share Common no par exchanged for (0.25) share $11.50 Preferred Ser. B no par
Reynolds (R.J.) Industries, Inc. name changed to RJR Nabisco, Inc. 04/25/1986 which merged into RJR Holdings Group, Inc. 04/28/1989
(See RJR Holdings Group, Inc.)

HEURISTIC CONCEPTS INC (NY)
Adjudicated bankrupt 06/16/1972
Stockholders' equity unlikely

HEURISTIC DEVELOPMENT GROUP INC (DE)
Issue Information - 1,200,000 UNITS consisting of (1) share COM and (1) WT CL A and (1) WT CL B offered at $5 per Unit on 02/11/1997
Name changed to Virtual Communities Inc. 10/29/1999
(See Virtual Communities Inc.)

HEVA-CADILLAC GOLD MINES LTD.
Reorganized as Heva Gold Mines Ltd. on a (0.5) for (1) basis 00/00/1946
Heva Gold Mines Ltd. name changed to Heva Mines Ltd. 00/00/1956 which merged into Hydra Explorations Ltd. 11/16/1959 which name changed to Hydra Capital Corp. 12/30/1992 which name changed to Waterford Capital Management Inc. 11/12/1996 which merged into CPI Plastics Group Ltd. 09/21/1998
(See CPI Plastics Group Ltd.)

HEVA GOLD MINES LTD. (ON)
Name changed to Heva Mines Ltd. 00/00/1956
Heva Mines Ltd. merged into Hydra Explorations Ltd. 11/16/1959 which

name changed to Hydra Capital Corp. 12/30/1992 which name changed to Waterford Capital Management Inc. 11/12/1996 which merged into CPI Plastics Group Ltd. 09/21/1998
(See CPI Plastics Group Ltd.)

HEVA MINES LTD. (ON)
Merged into Hydra Explorations Ltd. on a (0.04) for (1) basis 11/16/1959
Hydra Explorations Ltd. name changed to Hydra Capital Corp. 12/30/1992 which name changed to Waterford Capital Management Inc. 11/12/1996 which merged CPI Plastics Group Ltd. 09/21/1998
(See CPI Plastics Group Ltd.)

HEVI-DUTY ELECTRIC CO. (WI)
Merged into Basic Products Corp. share for share 6/15/59
Basic Products Corp. name changed to Sola Basic Industries, Inc. 10/29/65 which merged into General Signal Corp. 9/30/77 which merged into SPX Corp. 10/6/98

HEWBET MINES LTD (ON)
Reincorporated under the laws of Canada as Sundance Energy Resources Ltd. 09/20/1979
Sundance Energy Resources Ltd. name changed to Sunmist Energy Resources Ltd. 03/25/1980 which recapitalized as Sunmist Energy '84 Inc. 06/04/1984 which name changed to Sunmist Energy '86 Inc. 03/05/1987
(See Sunmist Energy '86 Inc.)

HEWFRAN GOLD MINES LTD. (ON)
Charter cancelled for failure to pay taxes and file returns 04/00/1975

HEWITT ASSOCS INC (DE)
Issue Information - 11,150,000 shares COM offered at $19 on 06/26/2002
Merged into Aon Corp. (DE) 10/01/2010
Each share Class A Common 1¢ par exchanged for (0.6362) share Common $1 par and $25.61 cash
Aon Corp. (DE) reorganized in England & Wales as Aon PLC 04/02/2012

HEWITT-GUTTA PERCHA RUBBER CORP.
Name changed to Hewitt Rubber Corp. in 1933
Hewitt Rubber Corp. name changed to Hewitt-Robins, Inc. in 1946 which merged into Litton Industries, Inc. 2/24/65
(See Litton Industries, Inc.)

HEWITT-ROBINS, INC. (NY)
Merged into Litton Industries, Inc. 2/24/65
Each share Class A Preferred $10 par exchanged for (0.09822) share $3 Series A Convertible Preferred $5 par
Each share Common $5 par exchanged for (0.35359) share $3 Series A Convertible Preferred $5 par
(See Litton Industries, Inc.)

HEWITT RUBBER CO.
Succeeded by Hewitt-Gutta Percha Rubber Corp. in 1928
(See Hewitt-Gutta Percha Rubber Corp.)

HEWITT RUBBER CORP.
Name changed to Hewitt-Robins, Inc. in 1946
Hewett-Robins, Inc. merged into Litton Industries, Inc. 2/24/65
(See Litton Industries, Inc.)

HEWLETT PACKARD CO (DE)
Reincorporated 05/20/1998
Capital Stock $1 par reclassified as Common $1 par 08/30/1961
90¢ Conv. Preferred $1 par called for redemption 09/01/1965
Common $1 par split (2) for (1) by

issuance of (1) additional share 03/18/1970
Common $1 par split (2) for (1) by issuance of (1) additional share 07/30/1979
Common $1 par split (2) for (1) by issuance of (1) additional share 07/17/1981
Common $1 par split (2) for (1) by issuance of (1) additional share 08/25/1983
Common $1 par split (2) for (1) by issuance of (1) additional share 04/13/1995
Common $1 par split (2) for (1) by issuance of (1) additional share payable 07/15/1996 to holders of record 06/21/1996
Stock Dividend - 200% 09/15/1960
State of incorporation changed from (CA) to (DE) and Common $1 par changed to 1¢ par 05/20/1998
Each share Common 1¢ par received distribution of (0.3814) share Agilent Technologies Inc. Common 1¢ par payable 06/02/2000 to holders of record 05/02/2000 Ex date - 06/05/2000
Common 1¢ par split (2) for (1) by issuance of (1) additional share payable 10/27/2000 to holders of record 09/27/2000 Ex date - 10/30/2000
Each share Common 1¢ par received distribution of (1) share Hewlett Packard Enterprise Co. Common 1¢ par payable 11/01/2015 to holders of record 10/21/2015 Ex date - 11/02/2015
Name changed to HP Inc. 11/02/2015

HEWLYN CORP (AB)
Struck off register for failure to file annual returns 08/01/1992

HEWS STAR RES LTD (BC)
Name changed to Arch Global Technologies Inc. 04/26/1989
(See Arch Global Technologies Inc.)

HEXAGON CONS COS AMER INC (NV)
Name changed to NMC Inc. 9/9/2003

HEXAGON LABS INC (NY)
Merged into New Hexagon Laboratories, Inc. 07/31/1975
Each share Common $1 par exchanged for $6.60 cash

HEXAWARE TECHNOLOGIES LTD (INDIA)
144A GDR's for Equity Shares split (2) for (1) by issuance of (1) additional GDR payable 03/14/2011 to holders of record 02/28/2011 Ex date - 03/15/2011
Reg. S GDR's for Equity Shares split (2) for (1) by issuance of (1) additional GDR payable 03/14/2011 to holders of record 02/28/2011 Ex date - 03/15/2011
GDR agreement terminated 09/22/2017
Each 144A GDR for Equity Shares exchanged for (0.5) Equity Share
Each Reg. S GDR for Equity Shares exchanged for (0.5) Equity Share
Note: Unexchanged GDR's will be sold and the proceeds, if any, held for claim after 09/24/2018

HEXCEL CORP OLD (DE)
Reincorporated 4/29/83
Common $1 par split (2) for (1) by issuance of (1) additional share 10/30/67
Common $1 par split (5) for (4) by issuance of (0.25) additional share 7/30/76
Common $1 par changed to no par in 1977
Stock Dividend - 33.3% 11/28/78
State of incorporation changed from (CA) to (DE) 4/29/83
Common no par changed to 1¢ par in May 1987
Common 1¢ par split (3) for (2) by issuance of (0.5) additional share 5/20/88
Reorganized as Hexcel Corp. (New) 2/9/95
Each share Common 1¢ par exchanged for (1) share Common 1¢ par and 1.21273)
Common Stock Purchase Rights expiring 3/27/95

HEXCEL PRODUCTS INC. (CA)
Capital Stock $1 par split (6) for (5) by issuance of (0.2) additional share 2/15/65
Capital Stock $1 par split (5) for (4) by issuance of (0.25) additional share 4/20/66
Capital Stock $1 par split (5) for (4) by issuance of (0.25) additional share 4/15/67
Name changed to Hexcel Corp. (CA) 4/17/67
Hexcel Corp. (CA) reincorporated in Delaware 4/29/83 which reorganized as Hexcel Corp. (New) 2/9/95

HEYDEN CHEMICAL CORP. (DE)
Reorganized 3/31/43
Reorganized from (NY) to under the laws of (DE) 3/31/43
Each share 4-1/4% Ser. A Preferred $100 par exchanged for (1) share 4-1/4% Preference $100 par
Each share Common $10 par exchanged for (4) shares Common $2.50 par
Each share Common $2.50 par exchanged for (2.5) shares Common $1 par 5/6/46
Under plan of merger name changed to Heyden Newport Chemical Corp. 1/9/57
Heyden Newport Chemical Corp. acquired by Tennessee Gas Transmission Co. 10/4/63 which name changed to Tenneco Inc. 4/11/66 which merged into El Paso Natural Gas Co. 12/12/96 which reorganized as El Paso Energy Corp. 8/1/98 which name changed to El Paso Corp. 2/5/2001

HEYDEN NEWPORT CHEMICAL CORP. (DE)
$4-3/8 2nd Preferred no par called for redemption 10/3/63
3-1/2% Preferred Ser. A $100 par called for redemption 10/3/63
Acquired by Tennessee Gas Transmission Co. on a (1.11) for (1) basis 10/4/63
Tennessee Gas Transmission Co. name changed to Tenneco Inc. 4/11/66 which merged into El Paso Natural Gas Co. 12/12/96 which reorganized as El Paso Energy Corp. 8/1/98 which name changed to El Paso Corp. 2/5/2001

HEYSON RED LAKE GOLD MINES, LTD. (ON)
Charter cancelled and company declared dissolved for default in filing returns 12/23/1965

HEYWOOD STARTER CORP.
Merged into Sky Specialties Corp. in 1929
Details not available

HEYWOOD WAKEFIELD CO (MA)
Common $100 par changed to $25 par in 1933
Each share Common $25 par exchanged for (2) shares Common $12.50 par in 1948 5% 1st Preferred Ser. B $25 par reclassified as 5% Preferred $25 par 2/7/72
Common $12.50 par changed to $1 par 5/3/73
Chapter 11 bankruptcy proceedings converted to Chapter 7 on 8/6/85
Stockholders' equity unlikely

HF BANCORP INC (DE)
Merged into Temple-Inland Inc. 6/29/99
Each share Common 1¢ par exchanged for $18.50 cash

HF CAP CORP (AB)
Name changed to MicroPlanet Technology Corp. 05/06/2005
Each share Common no par exchanged for (1) share new Common no par

HF FINL CORP (DE)
Common 1¢ par split (2) for (1) by issuance of (1) additional share payable 01/31/1996 to holders of record 01/10/1996
Common 1¢ par split (3) for (2) by issuance of (0.5) additional share payable 05/29/1998 to holders of record 05/08/1998
Stock Dividends - 10% payable 12/31/2003 to holders of record 12/03/2003 Ex date - 12/01/2003; 10% payable 04/24/2006 to holders of record 04/10/2006 Ex date - 04/06/2006
Acquired by Great Western Bancorp, Inc. 05/16/2016
Each share Common 1¢ par exchanged for (0.30108949) share Common 1¢ par and $10.4673153 cash

HFB FINL CORP (TN)
Common $1 par split (5) for (3) by issuance of (2/3) additional share payable 6/30/97 to holders of record 6/15/97
Stock Dividend - 20% payable 6/19/2000 to holders of record 6/5/2000
Merged into HFB Merger Corp. 2/26/2004
Each share Common $1 par exchanged for $22.75 cash

HFG HLDGS INC (AB)
Acquired by Cequence Energy Ltd. 11/13/2009
Each share Common no par exchanged for (0.04) share Common no par

HFI FLOORING INC (AB)
Assets sold for the benefit of creditors 03/23/2001
Stockholders' equity unlikely

HFNC FINL CORP (NC)
Merged into First Charter Corp. 10/01/1998
Each share Common 1¢ par exchanged for (0.57) share Common no par
First Charter Corp. merged into Fifth Third Bancorp 06/06/2008

HFS BK F S B (HOBART, IN)
Common $1 par split (2) for (1) by issuance of (1) additional share payable 04/15/1999 to holders of record 03/31/1999
Merged into MainSource Financial Group, Inc. 05/24/2006
Each share Common $1 par exchanged for (1.1231) shares Common no par
MainSource Financial Group, Inc. merged into First Financial Bancorp 04/02/2018

HFS INC (DE)
Secondary Offering - 2,786,000 shares COM offered at $49.875 per share on 09/18/1995
Common 1¢ par split (2) for (1) by issuance of (1) additional share payable 2/14/96 to holders of record 1/30/96 Ex date - 2/15/96
Merged into Cendant Corp. 12/17/97
Each share Common 1¢ par exchanged for (2.4031) shares Common 1¢ par
Cendant Corp. reorganized as Avis Budget Group, Inc. 9/1/2006

HF2 FINL MGMT INC (DE)
Name changed to ZAIS Group Holdings, Inc. 03/18/2015
(See ZAIS Group Holdings, Inc.)

HGI RLTY INC (MI)
Name changed to Horizon Group, Inc. 6/14/96
Horizon Group, Inc. merged into Prime Retail, Inc. 6/15/98
(See Prime Retail, Inc.)

HGIC CORP (VA)
Merged into Kansa Corp., Ltd. 12/28/84
Each share Capital Stock $1 par exchanged for $4.50 cash

HHB SYS INC (DE)
Acquired by Cadnetix Corp. 11/8/88
Each share Common 1¢ par exchanged for (1.5) shares Common 1¢ par
(See Cadnetix Corp.)

HHGREGG INC (DE)
Reincorporated under the laws of Indiana 09/01/2015

HHH ENTMT INC (NV)
Name changed to Advanced Medical Isotope Corp. 06/12/2006
Advanced Medical Isotope Corp. name changed to Vivos Inc. 01/02/2018

HHHP INC (FL)
Name changed to WCollect.com, Inc. 02/15/1999
W Collect.com, Inc. recapitalized as Granite Energy Inc. (FL) 12/23/2005 which reincorporated in Nevada 04/11/2006 which name changed to Refill Energy, Inc. 11/19/2009 which name changed to Medical Cannabis Payment Solutions 12/05/2013

HHT INVTS INC (ON)
Reorganized as Boulevard Industrial Real Estate Investment Trust 04/04/2014
Each share Common no par exchanged for (1) Trust Unit
Boulevard Industrial Real Estate Investment Trust reorganized as PRO Real Estate Investment Trust 10/02/2015

HI / FN INC (DE)
Acquired by Exar Corp. 04/03/2009
Each share Common $0.001 par exchanged for (0.3529) share Common $0.0001 par and $1.60 cash
(See Exar Corp.)

HI-ALTA CAP INC (AB)
Each share old Common no par exchanged for (0.25) share new Common no par 06/26/1998
Name changed to Western Financial Group Inc. (Old) 05/27/2002
(See Western Financial Group Inc. (Old))

HI-CARBON & CHEMICAL CO. (WA)
Charter revoked for failure to file reports and pay fees 7/1/66

HI COR RES LTD (BC)
Recapitalized as International Burgers Now Ltd. 12/05/1986
Each share Common no par exchanged for (0.33333333) share Common no par
(See International Burgers Now Ltd.)

HI-DEF ENTERPRISES INC (FL)
Each share old Common $0.001 par exchanged for (1/15) share new Common $0.001 par 2/14/96
Administratively dissolved 9/24/99

HI G INC (CT)
Stock Dividend - 25% 07/11/1967
Name changed to Tridex Corp. (CT) 08/27/1984
Tridex Corp. (CT) reorganized under the laws of Delaware as Progressive Software Holding Inc. 08/06/2002
(See Progressive Software Holding Inc.)

HI HO SILVER & GOLD CORP (UT)
Name changed to Trident Resources Corp. 9/22/72

(See Trident Resources Corp.)

HI LITE URANIUM EXPL LTD (ON)
Charter cancelled for failure to pay taxes and file returns 02/28/1973

HI-LO AUTOMOTIVE INC (DE)
Merged into O'Reilly Automotive, Inc. (Old) 01/30/1998
Each share Common 1¢ par exchanged for $4.35 cash

HI-LO-NO INC (CO)
Name changed to Colorado Royal Casinos Ltd. 12/05/1990

HI PEG RES LTD (BC)
Name changed to Elegance Business Corp. Ltd. 02/02/1987
(See Elegance Business Corp. Ltd.)

HI PLAINS ENTERPRISES INC (DE)
Charter cancelled and declared inoperative and void for non-payment of taxes 4/15/72

HI PLAINS ENTERPRISES INC (KS)
Stock Dividend - 50% 4/7/70
In process of liquidation
Each share Common 50¢ par exchanged for initial distribution of $1.35 cash 12/13/78
Note: Details on subsequent distributions, if any, are not available

HI PORT INDS INC (TX)
Common 5¢ par split (2) for (1) by issuance of (1) additional share 09/10/1987
Stock Dividend - 10% 04/27/1983
Merged into CCL Industries Inc. 11/03/1989
Each share Common 5¢ par exchanged for $12.50 cash

HI-PRESS AIR CONDITIONING OF AMERICA, INC. (NY)
Adjudicated bankrupt 1/15/64

HI-RISE RECYCLING SYS INC (FL)
Chapter 11 bankruptcy proceedings dismissed 04/10/2002
Stockholders' equity unlikely

HI SCORE CORP (DE)
Each share old Common $0.0001 par exchanged for (0.001) share new Common $0.0001 par 08/27/2009
Reincorporated under the laws of Florida 07/01/2010

HI SHEAR CORP (CA)
Capital Stock no par reclassified as Common no par 7/20/67
Common no par split (2) for (1) by issuance of (1) additional share 8/7/67
Stock Dividend - 100% 1/31/75
Merged into Hi-Shear Industries, Inc. 1/28/77
Each share Common no par exchanged for (1) share Common 10¢ par
(See Hi-Shear Industries, Inc.)

HI SHEAR INDS INC (DE)
Common 10¢ par split (5) for (4) by issuance of (0.25) additional share 4/28/86
Stock Dividend - 20% 3/31/80
Liquidation completed
Each share Common 10¢ par exchanged for first and final distribution of $4 cash 8/1/96

HI SHEAR TECHNOLOGY CORP (DE)
Acquired by Chemring Group PLC 11/25/2009
Each share Common $0.001 par exchanged for $19.18 cash

HI-TEC MINERAL RECOVERY INC (UT)
Involuntarily dissolved for failure to file annual reports 9/1/92

HI-TECH COMPUTER PRODS INC (DE)
Charter cancelled and declared inoperative and void for non-payment of taxes 3/1/94

HI TECH CORP (UT)
Reorganized under the laws of Delaware as Hi-Tech Ventures, Inc. 6/1/90
Each share Common 1¢ par exchanged for (0.2) share Common $0.001 par
Hi-Tech Ventures, Inc. recapitalized as Rubicon Medical Corp. 11/16/2000
(See Rubicon Medical Corp.)

HI TECH CRIME SOLUTIONS (OK)
Name changed to Montague International Holding Ltd. 07/20/2012

HI TECH INDS INC (NY)
Each share Common 5¢ par exchanged for (0.8) share Common 6¢ par 3/18/70
Dissolved by proclamation 9/25/90

HI TECH LEASING & CELLULAR COMMUNICATIONS INC (DE)
Name changed to First Financial of Broward, Inc. 09/04/1985
(See First Financial of Broward, Inc.)

HI-TECH PHARMACAL INC (DE)
Reincorporated 10/09/1996
Common 1¢ par split (3) for (2) by issuance of (0.5) additional share 11/01/1993
State of incorporation changed from (NY) to (DE) 10/09/1996
Common 1¢ par split (3) for (2) by issuance of (0.5) additional share payable 01/17/2003 to holders of record 12/30/2002 Ex date - 01/21/2003
Common 1¢ par split (3) for (2) by issuance of (0.5) additional share payable 01/11/2006 to holders of record 12/30/2005 Ex date - 01/12/2006
Acquired by Akorn, Inc. 04/17/2014
Each share Common 1¢ par exchanged for $43.50 cash

HI TECH ROBOTICS LTD (DE)
Charter forfeited for failure to maintain a registered agent 10/29/91

HI-TECH VENTURES, INC. (DE)
Recapitalized as Rubicon Medical Corp. 11/16/2000
Each share Common $0.001 par exchanged for (0.05) share Common $0.001 par
(See Rubicon Medical Corp.)

HI TECH VENTURES INC (BC)
Recapitalized as Pro-Tech Venture Corp. 09/07/1993
Each share Common no par exchanged for (0.2) share Common no par
(See Pro-Tech Venture Corp.)

HI-TECH WEALTH INC (NV)
Name changed to China Mobile Media Technology Inc. 12/27/2007
(See China Mobile Media Technology Inc.)

HI TIGER INTL INC (UT)
Each (12) shares old Common $0.001 par exchanged for (1) share new Common $0.001 par 12/2/87
Name changed to Avtel Communications, Inc. (UT) 11/6/96
Avtel Communications, Inc. (UT) reorganized in Delaware 12/1/97 which name changed to Netjolix Communications Inc. 9/15/99
(See Netloix Communications Inc.)

HI-TOWER DRILLING CO. LTD. (AB)
Name changed to Bow Valley Industries Ltd. 06/01/1962
Bow Valley Industries Ltd. name changed to Bow Valley Energy Inc. 06/07/1993 which was acquired by Talisman Energy Inc. 08/11/1994
(See Talisman Energy Inc.)

HIA INC (NY)
Each (45,000) shares old Common 1¢ par exchanged for (1) share new Common 1¢ par 02/16/2006
Note: In effect holders received $0.60 cash per share and public interest was eliminated

HIALEAH MIAMI SPRINGS BK (HIALEAH, FL)
Name changed to Hialeah-Miami Springs First State Bank (Hialeah, FL) 03/01/1970
(See Hialeah-Miami Springs First State Bank (Hialeah, FL))

HIALEAH MIAMI SPRINGS FIRST ST BK (HIALEAH, FL)
98.41% acquired by First State Banking Corp. through exchange offer which expired 08/31/1972
Public interest eliminated

HIALEAH RACE COURSE, INC. (FL)
Liquidation completed
Each share Common $1 par exchanged for initial distribution of $100 cash 3/30/73
Each share Common $1 par received second distribution of $100 cash 7/9/73
Each share Common $1 par received third and final distribution of $45 cash 11/9/73
Name changed to Hialeah Race Course Inc. Liquidation Trust and Common $1 par reclassified as Shares of Bene. Int. $1 par 12/13/73
(See Hialeah Race Course Inc.-Liquidation Trust)

HIALEAH RACE COURSE INC.-LIQUIDATION TRUST (FL)
Liquidation completed
Each share of Bene. Int. $1 par received initial distribution of $4.75 cash 1/20/75
Each share of Bene. Int. $1 par received second distribution of $9 cash 10/2/75
Each share of Bene. Int. $1 par received third distribution of $7.75 cash 5/6/76
Each share of Bene. Int. $1 par exchanged for fourth and final distribution of $2.67 cash 6/30/77

HIAWATHA GOLD MINES, LTD. (ON)
Charter cancelled 12/00/1965

HIAWATHA INDUSTRY INTERNET CORP (DE)
Name changed to Centacom Technologies Inc. 10/16/2001
Centacom Technologies Inc. recapitalized as Insight Medical Group, Inc. 04/10/2008
(See Insight Medical Group, Inc.)

HIAWATHA OIL & GAS CO. (DE)
Each share 7% Preferred $5 par exchanged for (1) share 5% Class A Preferred $10 par and $0.55 cash 00/00/1939
Common $5 par changed to $1 par 00/00/1939
5% Conv. Preferred Class A $10 par reclassified as 5% Conv. Preferred $10 par 06/07/1955
5% Conv. Preferred $10 par called for redemption 10/15/1964
Completely liquidated 06/15/1965
Details not available

HIAWATHA OIL & GAS CORP. (DE)
Incorporated 09/22/1995
Recapitalized as Community Equities Inc. 10/30/1995
Each share Common $0.002 par exchanged for (0.0000333) share Common $0.002 par
(See Community Equities Inc.)

HIAWATHA OIL & GAS CORP (DE)
Incorporated 03/20/1980
Each share old Common $0.001 par received distribution of (0.0004415) share Castle Energy Corp. Common 50¢ par 01/15/1990
Each (155) shares old Common $0.001 par exchanged for (1) share new Common $0.001 par 01/15/1996
Each (3.25) shares new Common $0.001 par exchanged again for (1) share new Common $0.001 par 03/14/1996
Name changed to Hiawatha Industry Internet Corp. 06/21/1996
Hiawatha Industry Internet Corp. name changed to Centacom Technologies Inc. 10/16/2001 which recapitalized as Insight Medical Group, Inc. 04/10/2008
(See Insight Medical Group, Inc.)

HIBACHI HOUSE INC (DE)
Name changed to Dynasty Oil Corp. 07/22/1980
(See Dynasty Oil Corp.)

HIBBARD, SPENCER, BARTLETT & CO. (IL)
Reorganized as Hibbard, Spencer, Bartlett Trust 1/31/64
Each share Common $25 par exchanged for (1) Share of Bene. Int. $25 par
(See Hibbard, Spencer, Bartlett Trust)

HIBBARD SPENCER BARTLETT TR (IL)
Shares of Bene. Int. $25 par split (8) for (1) by issuance of (7) additional shares 11/01/1964
Liquidation completed
Each Share of Bene. Int. $25 par exchanged for initial distribution of $1.52 cash 04/04/1984
Each Share of Bene. Int. $25 par received second distribution of $20.65 cash 05/01/1984
Each Share of Bene. Int. $25 par received third distribution of $0.75 cash 07/20/1984
Each Share of Bene. Int. $25 par received fourth distribution of $1.50 cash 11/16/1984
Each Share of Bene. Int. $25 par received fifth and final distribution of $3.65 cash 03/15/1985

HIBBETT SPORTING GOODS INC (DE)
Common 1¢ par split (3) for (2) by issuance of (0.5) additional share payable 2/19/2002 to holders of record 2/1/2002 Ex date - 2/20/2002
Common 1¢ par split (3) for (2) by issuance of (0.5) additional share payable 7/15/2003 to holders of record 6/27/2003 Ex date - 7/16/2003
Common 1¢ par split (3) for (2) by issuance of (0.5) additional share payable 4/16/2004 to holders of record 4/1/2004 Ex date - 4/19/2004
Common 1¢ par split (3) for (2) by issuance of (0.5) additional share payable 9/27/2005 to holders of record 9/9/2005 Ex date - 9/28/2005
Name changed to Hibbett Sports, Inc. 2/10/2007

HIBERNIA BANCORP INC (LA)
Name changed 06/29/2011
Name changed from Hibernia Homestead Bancorp, Inc. to Hibernia Bancorp, Inc. 06/29/2011
Acquired by Union Savings & Loan Association 07/02/2018
Each share Common 1¢ par exchanged for $32 cash

HIBERNIA BANCSHARES CORP (CA)
Merged into First Pacific Corp. 12/31/1982
Each share Common $6.25 par exchanged for $55.029 cash

HIBERNIA BK (SAN FRANCISCO, CA)
Common $25 par and VTC's for Common $25 par changed to $12.50 par and (1) additional share issued plus a 10% stock dividend paid respectively 07/10/1969
Voting Trust Agreement terminated 08/01/1969

Each VTC for Common $12.50 par exchanged for (1) share Common $12.50 par
Common $12.50 par changed to $6.25 par and (1) additional share issued 04/13/1979
Under plan of reorganization each share Common $6.25 par automatically became (1) share Hibernia Bancshares Corp. Common $6.25 par 07/01/1980
(See Hibernia Bancshares Corp.)

HIBERNIA CORP (LA)
Common no par split (2) for (1) by issuance of (1) additional share 10/26/78
Common no par reclassified as Class A Common no par 5/3/82
Class A Common no par split (5) for (4) by issuance of (0.25) additional share 5/27/83
Class A Common no par split (4) for (3) by issuance of (1/3) additional share 5/24/84
Class A Common no par split (5) for (4) by issuance of (0.25) additional share 6/9/86
Class A Common no par split (5) for (4) by issuance of (0.25) additional share 5/25/89
Adjustable Fixed Rate Preferred Ser. A no par called for redemption at $50 plus $0.8265 accrued dividend on 10/1/2001
Stock Dividends - 15% 3/15/77; 10% 10/19/79; 15% 5/20/80; 20% 5/29/81; 10% 11/23/82; 10% 3/15/85; 10% 5/20/87
Merged into Capital One Financial Corp. 11/16/2005
Each share Class A Common no par exchanged for either (0.3792) share Common 1¢ par or $30.46 cash
Note: Holders making a valid election received (0.3792) share for approximately 79.77% of holdings and $30.46 cash for the balance
Stock election expired 11/11/2005

HIBERNIA FOODS PLC (IRELAND)
ADR agreement terminated 06/30/2004
No ADR holders' equity

HIBERNIA MINE RAILROAD
Merged into Central Railroad Co. of New Jersey in 1930
Details not available

HIBERNIA MNG LTD (BC)
Name changed to Great World Resources Ltd. 11/20/1972
Each share Common no par exchanged for (1) share Common no par
(See Great World Resources Ltd.)

HIBERNIA NATL BK (NEW ORLEANS, LA)
Common $20 par changed to $10 par and (1) additional share issued 2/15/62
Stock Dividends - 33-1/3% 1/17/42; 20% 2/2/56; 20% 11/20/57; 11-1/9% 2/15/62; 25% 2/25/66; 20% 2/28/67; 33-1/3% 3/21/69; 12-1/2% 10/25/72
Reorganized as Hibernia Corp. 4/24/73
Each share Common $10 par exchanged for (1) share Common no par
Hibernia Corp. merged into Capital One Financial Corp. 11/16/2005

HIBERNIA SVGS BK (BOSTON, MA)
Common $1 par split (3) for (2) by issuance of (0.5) additional share 2/1/95
Under plan of reorganization each share Common $1 par automatically became (1) share Emerald Isle Bancorp, Inc. Common $1 par 10/1/96
(See Emerald Isle Bancorp, Inc.)

HIBERNIAN INTL DEV LTD (BC)
Struck off register and declared dissolved for failure to file returns 06/30/1980

HIBISCUS DEVS LTD (CANADA)
Name changed to Mongowin-Sudbury Explorations Ltd. 06/02/1976
Mongowin-Sudbury Explorations Ltd. liquidated for Natural Resources Guardianship International, Inc. 05/19/1978 which name changed to XRG International, Inc. 11/13/1978
(See XRG International Inc.)

HIBRIGHT MINERALS INC (BC)
Name changed to Frontier Pacific Mining Corp. 10/25/1996
Frontier Pacific Mining Corp. acquired by Eldorado Gold Corp. (New) 07/15/2008

HIBU PLC (UNITED KINGDOM)
ADR agreement terminated 11/30/2017
No ADR's remain outstanding

HIBURD PPTYS INC (BC)
Struck off register and declared dissolved for failure to file returns 01/15/1993

HICCO ENERGY INC (AB)
Name changed to Intersoft Technologies Inc. 10/26/1989
(See Intersoft Technologies Inc.)

HICKAM DOW B INC (TX)
Acquired by Mylan Laboratories Inc. 10/30/1991
Each share Common 1¢ par exchanged for (0.85524) share Common 50¢ par
Mylan Laboratories Inc. name changed to Mylan Inc. 10/02/2007 which merged into Mylan N.V. 02/27/2015

HICKOK ELECTRICAL INSTR CO (OH)
Name changed to Hickok Inc. 2/23/95

HICKOK OIL CORP.
Acquired by Pure Oil Co. and each (5.5) shares Class A $1 par exchanged for (1) share Common no par in 1952
Pure Oil Co. merged into Union Oil Co. of California 7/16/65
(See Union Oil Co. of California)

HICKOK PRODUCING CO.
Succeeded by Hickok Oil Corp. in 1928
Details not available

HICKORY FARMS OHIO INC (OH)
Common no par split (5) for (2) by issuance of (1.5) additional shares 05/21/1973
99.6% acquired by General Host Corp. through purchase offer which expired 09/09/1980
Public interest eliminated

HICKORY FURNITURE CO (DE)
Stock Dividend - 10% 05/14/1976
Charter cancelled and declared inoperative and void for non-payment of taxes 03/01/2009

HICKORY TECH CORP (MN)
Common no par split (2) for (1) by issuance of (1) additional share 07/15/1987
Common no par split (2) for (1) by issuance of (1) additional share 02/10/1989
Common no par split (3) for (1) by issuance of (2) additional shares 02/12/1990
Common no par split (3) for (1) by issuance of (2) additional shares payable 08/17/1998 to holders of record 08/03/1998
Name changed to Enventis Corp. 05/08/2014
Enventis Corp. merged into Consolidated Communications Holdings, Inc. 10/16/2014

HICKS ACQUISITION CO I INC (DE)
Issue Information - 48,000,000 UNITS consisting of (1) share COM and (1) WT offered at $10 per Unit on 10/03/2007
Merged into Resolute Energy Corp. 09/25/2009
Each Unit exchanged for (1) share Common $0.0001 par
Each share Common $0.0001 par exchanged for (1) share Common $0.0001 par

HICKS ACQUISITION CO II INC (DE)
Issue Information - 15,000,000 UNITS consisting of (1) share COM and (1) WT offered at $10 per share on 10/08/2010
Completely liquidated 07/20/2012
Each Unit exchanged for first and final distribution of $9.95 cash
Each share Common $0.0001 par exchanged for first and final distribution of $9.95 cash

HICKS PONDER CO (TX)
Acquired by Blue Bell, Inc. (DE) 03/31/1969
Each share Common $1 par or Class B Common $1 par exchanged for (0.2712) share Common $5 par
(See Blue Bell, Inc. (DE))

HICO CORP AMER (NY)
Class A $1 par and Class B $1 par reclassified as Common $1 par 12/29/1960
Common $1 par changed to 50¢ par 06/18/1965
Each share Common 50¢ par exchanged for (0.25) share Common $2 par 06/30/1972
Adjudicated bankrupt 07/01/1981
Stockholders' equity unlikely

HIDALGO MNG INTL (DE)
Reincorporated 01/05/2010
Common $0.0001 par changed to $0.001 par and (3) additional shares issued payable 05/05/2007 to holders of record 04/27/2007
Ex date - 05/07/2007
State of incorporation changed from (NV) to (DE) 01/05/2010
Common $0.001 par changed to $0.0001 par 02/19/2010
Name changed to Verde Media Group Inc. 09/15/2010

HIDDEN LADDER INC (FL)
Common $0.0001 par split (12) for (1) by issuance of (11) additional shares payable 06/21/2011 to holders of record 06/20/2011 Ex date - 06/22/2011
Name changed to Elite Nutritional Brands, Inc. (FL) 06/27/2011
Elite Nutritional Brands, Inc. (FL) reorganized in Delaware as Aspen Group, Inc. 03/05/2012

HIDDEN LAKE GOLD MINES LTD (BC)
Cease trade order effective 04/29/1992
Stockholders' equity unlikely

HIDDEN SPLENDOR MINING CO. (DE)
6% Preferred $11 par called for redemption 09/17/1962
Merged into Atlas Corp. 08/17/1962
Each share Common 50¢ par exchanged for $6 principal amount of 5% Conv. Sub. Debentures

HIDDEN SPLENDOR MINING CO. (UT)
Merged into Trans Pacific Enterprises, Inc. 1/29/69
Each share Capital Stock 1¢ par exchanged for (0.2) share Common no par

HIDDEN VALLEY MINES INC (AB)
Recapitalized as Blis International Inc. 09/14/1993
Each share Common no par exchanged for (0.33333333) share Common no par
Blis International Inc. name changed to Millennia Foods Inc. 10/01/1994
(See Millennia Foods Inc.)

HIDENET SECURE ARCHITECTURES INC (NJ)
Recapitalized as Bio Nitrogen Corp. 11/08/2011
Each share Common $0.025 par exchanged for (0.00333333) share Common $0.025 par
Bio Nitrogen Corp. name changed to BioNitrogen Holdings Corp. 10/15/2013

HIDOC INTL INC (NY)
Merged into Graphic Sciences, Inc. 08/31/1972
Each share Common 75¢ par exchanged for (0.32) share Common 50¢ par
Graphic Sciences, Inc. merged into Burroughs Corp. (MI) 02/26/1975 which reincorporated in Delaware 05/30/1984 which name changed to Unisys Corp. 11/13/1986

HIE INC (GA)
Name changed to Healthcare.com Corp. 04/10/2000
Healthcare.com Corp. merged into XCare.net, Inc. 08/13/2001 which name changed to Quovadx, Inc. 10/01/2001
(See Quovadx, Inc.)

HIENERGY TECHNOLOGIES INC (DE)
Reincorporated 10/16/2002
State of incorporation changed from (WA) to (DE) and Common $0.0001 par changed to $0.001 par 10/16/2002
Chapter 7 bankruptcy proceedings terminated 06/11/2013
No stockholders' equity

HIEX DEV U S A INC (NV)
Charter revoked for failure to file reports and pay fees 12/1/90

HIGBEE CO (DE)
Reorganized 00/00/1942
Each share 7% 1st Preferred $100 par exchanged for (1.241788) shares Preferred $100 par and (0.483576) share Common $1 par
Each share 8% 2nd Preferred $100 par exchanged for (1.822609) shares Common $1 par Old Common stock had no equity
Each share Common $1 par exchanged for (5) shares Common $1 par 00/00/1945
Each share Common $1 par exchanged for (4) shares Common $1 par 00/00/1946
Preferred $100 par called for redemption 11/01/1955
Common $1 par split (3) for (2) by issuance of (0.5) additional share 06/15/1967
Merged into Industrial Equity (Pacific) Ltd. 10/24/1984
Each share Common $1 par exchanged for $50 cash

HIGBIE MFG CO (MI)
5% Conv. Preferred called for redemption 02/14/1956
Common $1 par split (5) for (4) by issuance of (0.25) additional share 07/15/1964
Common $1 par split (5) for (4) by issuance of (0.25) additional share 07/20/1965
Common $1 par split (2) for (1) by issuance of (1) additional share 04/19/1968
Stock Dividend - 25% 10/15/1959
Merged into International Telephone & Telegraph Corp. 03/02/1972
Each share Common $1 par exchanged for (0.566) share Common $1 par
International Telephone & Telegraph Corp. name changed to ITT Corp. (DE) 12/31/1983 which reorganized

in Indiana as ITT Industries Inc. 12/19/1995 which name changed to ITT Corp. 07/01/2006

HIGBYS J INC (NV)
Acquired by American Confectionery Corp. 3/9/90
Each share Common 1¢ par exchanged for (0.00523225) share Conv. Preferred Ser. B 50¢ par, (0.0020929) Series A Common Stock Purchase Warrant which expired 6/7/90 and (0.0020929) Series B Common Stock Purchase Warrant which expired 9/5/90
(See American Confectionery Corp.)

HIGCO INC (LA)
Assets liquidated for benefit of creditor 03/23/1966
No stockholders' equity

HIGGINS, INC. (LA)
Name changed to Higco, Inc.
(See Higco, Inc.)

HIGGINS INDUSTRIES INC.
In liquidation in 1946

HIGGINSON CAP MGMT INC (OH)
Charter cancelled for failure to maintain a statutory agent 07/14/1978

HIGH AMERN GOLD INC (ON)
Reorganized under the laws of Alberta as Antioquia Gold Inc. 07/29/2008
Each share Common no par exchanged for (0.1) share Common no par
Antioquia Gold Inc. (AB) reincorporated in British Columbia 03/24/2016

HIGH ARCTIC ENERGY SVCS TR (AB)
Reorganized as High Arctic Energy Services Inc. 06/29/2007
Each Trust Unit no par exchanged for (1) share Common no par
Note: Unexchanged certificates were cancelled and became without value 06/29/2013

HIGH BULLEN RES LTD (AB)
Merged into Highridge Exploration Ltd. 07/31/1996
Each share Common no par exchanged for (0.0357142) share Class A Common no par
Note: Holders of fewer than (2,799) shares will receive $0.10 cash
Highridge Exploration Ltd. merged into Talisman Energy Inc. 08/05/1999
(See Talisman Energy Inc.)

HIGH CLIMBERS INC (FL)
Name changed to Hydrogiene Corp. 10/30/98
Hydrogiene Corp. name changed to Synergie Holdings Ltd., Inc 9/4/2002 which name changed to Synergie Wellness Products, Inc. 3/15/2004

HIGH CREST OILS LTD. (AB)
Recapitalized as Canadian High Crest Oils Ltd. 6/11/57
Each share Common 20¢ par exchanged for (0.25) share Common 20¢ par
Canadian High Crest Oils Ltd. recapitalized as Canadian Tricentrol Oils Ltd. 6/1/66 which name changed to Tricentrol Canada Ltd. (Alta.) 5/5/72 which reincorporated under the laws of Ontario (Old) 11/28/72 which merged into Tricentrol Canada Ltd. (Ont.) (New) 12/28/72

HIGH CTRY BK (BOONE, NC)
Stock Dividend - 20% payable 08/14/2000 to holders of record 07/31/2000
Under plan of reorganization each share Common no par automatically became (1) share High Country Financial Corp. Common no par 07/01/2002
High Country Financial Corp. merged into Yadkin Valley Bank & Trust Co. (Elkin, NC) 01/02/2004 which reorganized as Yadkin Valley Financial Corp. 07/01/2006 which recapitalized as Yadkin Financial Corp. 05/28/2013 which merged into F.N.B. Corp. 03/11/2017

HIGH CTRY FINL CORP (NC)
Merged into Yadkin Valley Bank & Trust Co. (Elkin, NC) 01/02/2004
Each share Common no par exchanged for (1.3345) shares Common $5 par
Yadkin Valley Bank & Trust Co. (Elkin, NC) reorganized as Yadkin Valley Financial Corp. 07/01/2006 which recapitalized as Yadkin Financial Corp. 05/28/2013 which merged into F.N.B. Corp. 03/11/2017

HIGH CTRY OIL & GAS (UT)
Merged into First Midwest Financial Corp. 12/10/1982
Each (2,063) shares Common $0.001 par exchanged for (1) share Common $0.001 par
(See First Midwest Financial Corp.)

HIGH CTRY VENTURES INC (MN)
Name changed to Spiderboy International Inc. (MN) 10/13/2000
Spiderboy International Inc. (MN) reorganized in Delaware as Charys Holding Co., Inc. 07/20/2004
(See Charys Holding Co., Inc.)

HIGH DESERT ASSETS INC (CO)
Name changed to New Asia Energy, Inc. 08/12/2015
New Asia Energy, Inc. recapitalized as LNPR Group Inc. 01/17/2018

HIGH DESERT GOLD CORP (CANADA)
Issue Information - 30,000,000 UNITS consisting of (1) share COM and (1) WT offered at $0.50 per Unit on 10/09/2007
Merged into South American Silver Corp. 12/24/2013
Each share Common no par exchanged for (0.275) share Common no par
Note: Unexchanged certificates will be cancelled and become without value 12/24/2019
South American Silver Corp. name changed to TriMetals Mining Inc. 03/19/2014

HIGH DESERT MINERAL RES INC (BC)
Merged into Royal Gold, Inc. 12/16/2002
Each share Common no par exchanged for $0.572 cash

HIGH EFFICIENCY MTRS INC (NV)
Recapitalized as International Equestrian Development Corp. 08/11/1986
Each share Common 1¢ par exchanged for (0.5) share Common 1¢ par

HIGH END VENTURES INC (CO)
Common $0.001 par split (5) for (1) by issuance of (4) additional shares payable 09/27/2006 to holders of record 09/27/2006
SEC revoked common stock registration 01/21/2014

HIGH ENERGY PROCESSING CORP (NY)
Under plan of reorganization each share old Common 1¢ par exchanged for (1) share new Common 1¢ par to effect a (1/3) for (1) split and a subsequent (3) for (1) split 12/21/1971
Charter cancelled and proclaimed dissolved for failure to pay taxes 09/29/1982

HIGH ENERGY VENTURES INC (AB)
Ceased to be a reporting issuer 09/21/2004
Details not available

HIGH EQUITY PARTNERS L P (DE)
Under plan of merger each Unit of Ltd. Partnership Ser. 86 automatically became (2) shares Shelbourne Properties II, Inc. Common 1¢ par 04/17/2001
(See Shelbourne Properties II, Inc.)

HIGH FIVE OILFIELD SVCS LTD (AB)
Name changed to Patch Safety Services Ltd. 09/08/2000
Patch Safety Services Ltd. recapitalized as HSE Integrated Ltd. 09/01/2004
(See HSE Integrated Ltd.)

HIGH 5 VENTURES INC (BC)
Recapitalized as 37 Capital Inc. 07/07/2014
Each share Common no par exchanged for (0.16666666) share Common no par

HIGH FRONTIER RES LTD (BC)
Cease trade order effective 07/29/2004
Stockholders' equity unlikely

HIGH GOLD INC (NV)
Charter revoked for failure to file reports and pay fees 12/1/88

HIGH GRADE MNG CORP (NV)
Common no par split (4) for (1) by issuance of (1) additional share payable 12/13/2005 to holders of record 12/9/2005 Ex date - 12/14/2005
Name changed to Global Green Solutions, Inc. 3/24/2006

HIGH GRAVITY OIL CO. (DE)
No longer in existence having become inoperative and void for non-payment of taxes 3/17/26

HIGH GROUND CAP CORP (CANADA)
Merged into Algonquin Power Income Fund 08/11/2008
Each share Common no par exchanged for (0.9749) Trust Unit Algonquin Power Income Fund merged into Algonquin Power & Utilities Corp. 10/27/2009

HIGH HOPES INC (NV)
Each share old Common $0.001 par exchanged for (0.01) share new Common $0.001 par 11/1/95
Each share new Common $0.001 par exchanged again for (1/3) share new Common $0.001 par 12/28/95
Name changed to Medtech Inc. 1/4/99
Medtech Inc. name changed to e-MedSoft.com 2/16/99 which name changed to Med Diversified, Inc. 1/9/2002
(See Med Diversified, Inc.)

HIGH INCOME ADVANTAGE TR (MA)
Under plan of merger name changed to Morgan Stanley Dean Witter 12/21/1998
Morgan Stanley Dean Witter name changed to Morgan Stanley Trusts 12/20/2001
(See Morgan Stanley Trusts)

HIGH INCOME ADVANTAGE TR II (MA)
Under plan of merger name changed to Morgan Stanley Dean Witter 12/21/1998
Morgan Stanley Dean Witter name changed to Morgan Stanley Trusts 12/20/2001
(See Morgan Stanley Trusts)

HIGH INCOME ADVANTAGE TR III (MA)
Under plan of merger name changed to Morgan Stanley Dean Witter 12/21/1998
Morgan Stanley Dean Witter name changed to Morgan Stanley Trusts 12/20/2001
(See Morgan Stanley Trusts)

HIGH INCOME OPPORTUNITY FD INC (MD)
Name changed to Western Asset High Income Opportunity Fund Inc. 10/9/2006

HIGH INCOME PFD SHS CORP (CANADA)
Preferred Shares Ser. 1 called for redemption at $25 plus $2.80 accrued dividends on 03/12/2010
Preferred Shares Ser. 2 called for redemption at $14.70 plus $1.76 accrued dividends on 03/12/2010

HIGH INCOME PRIN & YIELD SECS CORP (ON)
Preferred Shares no par called for redemption at $25 on 08/08/2008
Equity Shares no par called for redemption at $11.49 on 08/08/2008

HIGH INCOME SHS INC (MD)
Name changed to Bullock High Income Shares, Inc. 1/14/85
Bullock High Income Shares merged into Alliance Bond Fund, Inc. 3/13/87 which name changed to AllianceBernstein Bond Fund, Inc. 3/31/2003

HIGH LEVEL DESIGN SYS (DE)
Merged into Cadence Design Systems, Inc. 12/18/1996
Each share Common $0.001 par exchanged for (0.22) share Common 1¢ par

HIGH LEVEL RES LTD (BC)
Recapitalized as Colorfax International Inc. 11/23/1990
Each share Common no par exchanged for (0.25) share Common no par
(See Colorfax International Inc.)

HIGH LINE INVT & DEV CO (UT)
Reorganized as Gayle Industries, Inc. 5/18/77
Each share Common 1¢ par exchanged for (5) shares Common $0.002 par
Gayle Industries, Inc. recapitalized as Swing Bike 7/1/77 which recapitalized as Horizon Energy Corp. 12/24/79 which name changed to New Horizon Education, Inc. 6/1/93 which name changed to American Hospital Resources, Inc. 6/26/2002 which name changed to HAPS USA, Inc. 5/12/2005 which name changed to PGMI, Inc. 3/16/2006

HIGH LINER FOODS INC (NS)
5.5% Conv. Preference Ser. C no par called for redemption at $5 on 12/15/2003
5.5% Conv. Preference Ser. D no par called for redemption at $5 on 12/15/2003
Each Non-Voting Equity Share exchanged for (1) share Common no par 12/17/2012
(Additional Information in Active)

HIGH NORTH RES INC (ON)
Recapitalized as HNR Ventures Inc. 06/30/2000
Each share Common no par exchanged for (0.25) share Common no par
HNR Ventures Inc. recapitalized as RMM Ventures Inc. (ON) 06/06/2006 which reorganized in Alberta as PowerComm Inc. 12/31/2006 which name changed to PetroCorp Group Inc. 12/23/2009

HIGH NORTH RES LTD (BC)
Assets sold for the benefit of creditors 12/14/2016
No stockholders' equity

HIGH PLAINS CORP (KS)
Common 10¢ par split (6) for (5) by

issuance of (0.2) additional share 2/18/94
Common 10¢ par split (6) for (5) by issuance of (0.2) additional share 5/27/94
Common 10¢ par split (3) for (2) by issuance of (0.5) additional share 8/19/94
Common 10¢ par split (4) for (3) by issuance of (1/3) additional share 2/22/95
Merged into Abengoa, S.A. 2/13/2002
Each share Common 10¢ par exchanged for $5.6358 cash

HIGH PLAINS ENERGY INC (AB)
Recapitalized as Action Energy Inc. 11/27/2006
Each share Common no par exchanged for (0.2) share Common no par
(See Action Energy Inc.)

HIGH PLAINS GAS INC (NV)
Common $0.001 par split (2) for (1) by issuance of (1) additional share payable 12/16/2010 to holders of record 12/02/2010 Ex date - 12/17/2010
SEC revoked common stock registration 01/09/2015

HIGH PLAINS GENETICS INC (CO)
Each share old Common 1¢ par exchanged for (0.1) share new Common 1¢ par 6/28/85
Company advised went private in 1993
Details not available

HIGH PLAINS OIL CORP (DE)
Stock Dividend - 10% 9/12/84
Merged into Adobe Resources Corp. 5/29/87
Each share Common 10¢ par exchanged for (1.12) shares Common 1¢ par
Adobe Resources Corp. merged into Santa Fe Energy Resources, Inc. 5/19/92 which name changed to Santa Fe Snyder Corp. 5/5/99 which merged into Devon Energy Corp. (New) 8/29/2000

HIGH PLAINS URANIUM INC (NB)
Acquired by Energy Metals Corp. 01/19/2007
Each share Common no par exchanged for (0.16129032) share Common no par
Energy Metals Corp. merged into Uranium One Inc. 08/10/2007
(See Uranium One Inc.)

HIGH POINT BK & TR CO (HIGH POINT, NC)
Under plan of reorganization each share Common $5 par automatically became (1) share High Point Bank Corp. Common $5 par 04/01/1990
High Point Bank Corp. merged into BNC Bancorp 11/01/2016 which merged into Pinnacle Financial Partners, Inc. 06/16/2017

HIGH POINT BK CORP (DE)
Merged into BNC Bancorp 11/01/2016
Each share Common $5 par exchanged for (12.1611) shares Common no par and $1.96 cash
BNC Bancorp merged into Pinnacle Financial Partners, Inc. 06/16/2017

HIGH POINT CHEMICAL CO., INC. (NY)
Proclaimed dissolved for failure to file reports and pay fees 12/16/1968

HIGH POINT FINL CORP (NJ)
Merged into Lakeland Bancorp, Inc. 07/15/1999
Each share Common no par exchanged for (1.2) shares Common no par

HIGH POINT INDUSTRIES, INC. (NY)
Name changed to High Point Chemical Co., Inc. 1/8/59
(See High Point Chemical Co., Inc.)

HIGH POINT MINES LTD. (BC)
Recapitalized as Highhawk Mines Ltd. 05/18/1972
Each share Common no par exchanged for (0.33333333) share Common no par
Highhawk Mines Ltd. recapitalized as Newhawk Gold Mines Ltd. 03/12/1979 which merged into Silver Standard Resources Inc. 09/30/1999 which name changed to SSR Mining Inc. 08/03/2017

HIGH POINT OVERALL CO.
Name changed to Anvil Brand, Inc. in 1948
Anvil Brand, Inc. acquired by B.V.D. Co., Inc. 2/1/66 which was acquired by Glen Alden Corp. (Del.) 5/19/67 which merged into Rapid-American Corp. (Del.) 11/6/72
(See Rapid-American Corp. (Del.))

HIGH POINT VENTURES INC (DE)
Name changed to Aviation Education Systems, Inc. 8/26/87
Aviation Education Systems, Inc. name changed to Setech, Inc. 2/6/97
(See Setech, Inc.)

HIGH PRESSURE EQUIP INC (PA)
Completely liquidated 11/13/1980
Each share Common $1 par exchanged for first and final distribution of $0.80 cash

HIGH PT ENERGY CORP (AB)
Class A Common no par reclassified as Common no par 04/15/2002
Reorganized as High Point Resources Inc. 06/19/2002
Each share Common no par exchanged for (0.33333333) share Common no par
High Point Resources Inc. merged into Enterra Energy Trust 08/17/2005 which reorganized as Equal Energy Ltd. 06/03/2010
(See Equal Energy Ltd.)

HIGH PT RES INC (AB)
Merged into Enterra Energy Trust 08/17/2005
Each share Common no par exchanged for (0.105) Trust Unit
Enterra Energy Trust reorganized as Equal Energy Ltd. 06/03/2010
(See Equal Energy Ltd.)

HIGH RAIL OIL & GAS, INC. (UT)
Merged into Trancor Industries, Inc. 9/28/84
Details not available

HIGH RESOLUTION SCIENCES INC (DE)
Charter cancelled and declared inoperative and void for non-payment of taxes 6/17/93

HIGH RESV RES LTD (BC)
Struck off register and declared dissolved for failure to file returns 07/09/1993

HIGH RIDER CAP INC (BC)
Name changed to Sirona Biochem Corp. 05/04/2009

HIGH RIDGE RES INC (BC)
Recapitalized as New High Ridge Resources Inc. 01/04/2010
Each share Common no par exchanged for (0.25) share Common no par
New High Ridge Resources Inc. name changed to Newton Gold Corp. 02/07/2011 which recapitalized as Chlormet Technologies Inc. 11/07/2013 which name changed to PUF Ventures Inc. 11/13/2015

HIGH RISE RES INC (BC)
Struck off register and declared dissolved for failure to file returns 12/28/1990

HIGH RIV GOLD MINES LTD (YT)
Reincorporated 02/02/2011
Place of incorporation changed from (Canada) to (YT) 02/02/2011
Merged into Nord Gold N.V. 03/12/2013
Each share Common no par exchanged for $1.40 cash
Note: Unexchanged certificates will be cancelled and become without value 03/12/2019

HIGH RIV RES LTD (BC)
Merged into High River Gold Mines Ltd. (Canada) 12/08/1988
Each share Common no par exchanged for (1) share Common no par
High River Gold Mines Ltd. (Canada) reincorporated in Yukon 02/02/2011
(See High River Gold Mines Ltd.)

HIGH ROAD INTL INC (NV)
Name changed to Global IT Holdings, Inc. 07/05/2005
(See Global IT Holdings, Inc.)

HIGH ROCK CDN HIGH YIELD BD FD (ON)
Trust terminated 12/30/2016
Each Class A Unit received $8.11 cash

HIGH SIERRA ACQUISITIONS INC (CO)
Name changed to Passage Home Communications Inc. 05/06/1988
(See Passage Home Communications, Inc.)

HIGH SIERRA ACQUISITIONS INC (NV)
Name changed to Anasazi Energy Corp. 11/20/2014
Anasazi Energy Corp. name changed to Solar Quartz Technologies, Inc. 12/19/2016

HIGH SPEED ACCESS CORP (DE)
Issue Information - 13,000,000 shares COM offered at $13 per share on 06/04/1999
Liquidation completed
Each share Common 1¢ par received initial distribution of $1.40 cash payable 5/30/2003 to holders of record 5/23/2003 Ex date - 6/2/2003
Each share Common 1¢ par received second distribution of $0.17 cash payable 8/29/2003 to holders of record 8/22/2003 Ex date - 9/2/2003
Each share Common 1¢ par received third distribution of $0.0287 cash payable 12/31/2003 to holders of record 12/31/2003
Assets transferred to High Speed Access Corp. Liquidating Trust 12/31/2003
Each share Common 1¢ par received fourth and final distribution of $0.042 cash payable 12/28/2005 to holders of record 12/28/2005
Note: Certificates were not required to be surrendered and are without value

HIGH SPEED NET SOLUTIONS INC (FL)
Name changed to Summus, Inc. (FL) 02/27/2002
Summus, Inc. (FL) reorganized in Delaware 03/16/2005 which name changed to Oasys Mobile, Inc. 02/06/2006
(See Oasys Mobile, Inc.)

HIGH STOY TECHNOLOGICAL CORP (DE)
Assets foreclosed 10/07/1982
No stockholders' equity

HIGH STR BKG CO (ASHEVILLE, NC)
Under plan of reorganization each share Common $5 par automatically became (1) share High Street Corp. Common no par 11/1/2001
High Street Corp. merged into Capital Bank Corp. 12/4/2002

HIGH STR CORP (NC)
Merged into Capital Bank Corp. 12/4/2002
Each share Common no par exchanged for (0.747) share Common no par

HIGH STREET INVESTMENT FUND, INC. (RI)
Liquidation completed
Each share Common $10 par exchanged for initial distribution of (4.667849) shares of Broad Street Investing Fund, Inc. Common 50¢ par 6/30/64
Common holders received second and final distribution of $2.1577 cash 11/29/65

HIGH SUMMIT OIL & GAS INC (UT)
Involuntarily dissolved 08/01/1988

HIGH TECH COMPUTER CORP (TAIWAN)
Stock Dividends - In 144A GDR's for Common to holders of 144A GDR's for Common 20% payable 08/24/2006 to holders of record 07/26/2006
In Reg. S GDR's for Common to holders of Reg. S GDR's for Common 20% payable 10/14/2004 to holders of record 08/12/2004; 20% payable 10/07/2005 to holders of record 08/04/2005 Ex date - 08/02/2005; 20% payable 08/24/2006 to holders of record 07/26/2006; 30% payable 08/19/2008 to holders of record 07/15/2008
Name changed to HTC Corp. 04/02/2009

HIGH TECHNOLOGY CAP CORP (DE)
Recapitalized as HITK Corp. 12/02/1986
Each share Common $0.001 par exchanged for (0.25) share Common $0.001 par
(See HITK Corp.)

HIGH TECHNOLOGY INVESTMENTS, INC. (DE)
Merged into Reed Industries, Inc. (New) 9/30/74
Each share Common $1 par exchanged for (0.083963) share Common 10¢ par

HIGH TIDE VENTURES INC (NV)
Name changed to MMC Energy, Inc. (NV) 05/12/2006
MMC Energy, Inc. (NV) reincorporated in Delaware 09/22/2006
(See MMC Energy, Inc.)

HIGH VACUUM PROCESSES, INC. (PA)
Liquidation completed 12/27/61
Preferred holders received 65¢ per share No distribution paid on Common

HIGH VELOCITY ALTERNATIVE ENERGY CORP (NV)
Each share old Common $0.001 par exchanged for (0.02) share new Common $0.001 par 11/01/2007
Note: No holder will receive fewer than (100) post-split shares
New Common $0.001 par split (4) for (1) by issuance of (3) additional shares payable 10/21/2008 to holders of record 10/21/2008
Name changed to Reflectkote, Inc. 07/31/2009

HIGH VELOCITY ENTERPRISES INC (NV)
Reorganized as NanoTech Gaming, Inc. 04/23/2015
Each share Common $0.0001 par exchanged for (10) shares Common $0.0001 par

HIGH VOLTAGE ENGR CORP NEW (MA)
Stock Dividends - 6.25% payable 2/15/2000 to holders of record

2/1/2000; 6.25% payable 8/15/2000 to holders of record 8/1/2000; 6.25% payable 2/15/2001 to holders of record 2/1/2001; 6.25% payable 8/15/2001 to holders of record 8/1/2001; 7% payable 2/15/2002 to holders of record 2/1/2002 Ex date - 1/30/2002; 7.25% payable 8/15/2002 to holders of record 8/1/2002 Ex date - 8/8/2002
Plan of reorganization under Chapter 11 Federal Bankruptcy Code effective 8/10/2004
Each share 12.5% Ser. A Exchange Preferred exchanged for (9.033448) Common Stock Purchase Warrants
Plan of reorganization under Chapter 11 Federal Bankruptcy Code effective 8/1/2006
HVE Liquidating Trust was formed for possible future distribution

HIGH VOLTAGE ENGR CORP OLD (MA)
Common $1 par split (5) for (1) by issuance of (4) additional shares 12/1/61
Merged into Natalie Acquisition Corp. 8/18/88
Each share Common $1 par exchanged for $18 cash

HIGH YIELD & MTG PLUS TR (ON)
Trust terminated 12/31/2014
Each Unit received $12.399 cash

HIGH YIELD INCOME FD INC (MD)
Merged into Dryden High Yield Fund, Inc. 06/19/2009
Each share Common 1¢ par exchanged for (0.9042567) share Class A 1¢ par

HIGH YIELD PLUS FD INC (MD)
Merged into Dryden High Yield Fund, Inc. 06/19/2009
Each share Common 1¢ par exchanged for (0.6420778) share Class A 1¢ par

HIGHBOURNE CAP CORP (CANADA)
Recapitalized as A&E Capital Funding Corp. 08/12/1996
Each share Common no par exchanged for (0.1) share Common no par
A&E Capital Funding Corp. recapitalized as E & E Capital Funding Inc. 10/18/2005 which merged into GC-Global Capital Corp. 01/09/2006 which name changed to Fountain Asset Corp. 09/02/2015

HIGHBOURNE EXPLS LTD (ON)
Recapitalized as Universal Genetics Corp. Ltd. 09/10/1987
Each share Common no par exchanged for (0.2) share Common no par
Universal Genetics Corp. merged into Starbright Venture Capital Inc. 11/18/1997 which merged into Grasslands Entertainment Inc. (AB) 07/11/2001 which reorganized in Ontario as Lakeside Minerals Inc. 01/04/2012 which name changed to Lineage Grow Co. Ltd. 07/25/2017

HIGHBURY FINL INC (DE)
Merged into Affiliated Managers Group, Inc. 04/15/2010
Each share Common $0.0001 par exchanged for (0.07595179) share Common $0.0001 par

HIGHER ONE HLDGS INC (DE)
Acquired by Winchester Acquisition Holdings Corp. 08/04/2016
Each share Common $0.001 par exchanged for $5.15 cash

HIGHFIELD PPTY INVTS LTD (AB)
Common no par reclassified as Class A Common no par 10/20/1980
Recapitalized as HPIL Resources Ltd. 12/05/1985
Each share Class A Common no par exchanged for (0.1) share Class A Common no par
Each share Class B Common no par exchanged for (0.1) share Class B Common no par
(See HPIL Resources Ltd.)

HIGHGRADE VENTURES LTD (BC)
Under plan of merger name changed to Brasilca Mining Corp. 04/03/2000
(See Brasilca Mining Corp.)

HIGHHAWK MINES LTD (BC)
Recapitalized as Newhawk Gold Mines Ltd. 03/12/1979
Each share Common no par exchanged for (0.2) share Common no par
Newhawk Gold Mines Ltd. merged into Silver Standard Resources Inc. 09/30/1999 which name changed to SSR Mining Inc. 08/03/2017

HIGHLAND APTS CORP (NY)
Charter cancelled and proclaimed dissolved for failure to pay taxes 7/17/87

HIGHLAND BANCORP INC (DE)
Common 1¢ par split (2) for (1) by issuance of (1) additional share payable 5/14/99 to holders of record 5/3/99
Merged into Jackson Federal Bank (San Bernardino, CA) 9/29/2000
Each share Common 1¢ par exchanged for $25.45 cash

HIGHLAND BELL LTD (BC)
Completely liquidated 04/30/1971
Each share Capital Stock $1 par exchanged for first and final distribution of (0.66666666) share Teck Corp. Ltd. Class B Common no par
Teck Corp. Ltd. name changed to Teck Corp. 11/21/1978 which name changed to Teck Cominco Ltd. 09/12/2001 which name changed to Teck Resources Ltd. 04/27/2009

HIGHLAND BUSINESS SVCS INC (NV)
Each share old Common $0.001 par exchanged for (6) shares new Common $0.001 par 02/28/2011
Name changed to Elevate, Inc. 11/09/2011

HIGHLAND CAP CORP (DE)
Liquidation completed
Each share Common $1 par received initial distribution of $3 cash 4/10/84
Each share Common $1 par received second distribution of (0.049) share Caesars World, Inc. Common 10¢ par, (0.182) share First Executive Corp. Common $2 par, (0.15) share Genesco Inc. Common $1 par, (0.024) share Resorts International, Inc. Class A Common $1 par and $2 cash 8/27/84
Each share Common $1 par received third distribution of (0.141) share Leisure Technology, Inc. (Old) Common 10¢ par and $0.98 cash 11/13/84
(See each company's Listing)
Assets transferred to Highland Capital Liquidating Trust 11/13/84
Each share Common $1 par exchanged for (1) Unit of Bene. Int.
(See Highland Capital Liquidating Trust)

HIGHLAND CAP INC (DE)
Recapitalized as Y&A Group, Inc. 06/30/1989
Each share Common $0.00001 par exchanged for (0.004) share Common $0.0025 par
(See Y&A Group, Inc.)

HIGHLAND CAPITAL LIQUIDATING TRUST (DE)
Liquidation completed
Each Unit of Bene. Int. exchanged for fourth distribution of $0.15 cash 2/28/90
Each Unit of Bene. Int. received fifth and final distribution of $0.0385 cash 3/26/93 (For previous distributions see Highland Capital Corp.)

HIGHLAND CHIEF MINES LTD (BC)
Recapitalized as New Chief Mines Ltd. 09/10/1973
Each share Capital Stock no par exchanged for (0.4) share Capital Stock no par
New Chief Mines Ltd. recapitalized as Sydney Development Corp. (BC) 05/10/1978 which reorganized in Canada as SDC Sydney Development Corp. 09/18/1986
(See SDC Sydney Development Corp.)

HIGHLAND CLAN CREATIONS CORP (NV)
Each share old Common $0.001 par exchanged for (14) shares new Common $0.001 par 04/04/2006
Reincorporated under the laws of Delaware as Raptor Pharmaceuticals Corp. 06/09/2006
Raptor Pharmaceuticals Corp. merged into Raptor Pharmaceutical Corp. 09/29/2009
(See Raptor Pharmaceutical Corp.)

HIGHLAND COAL CO.
In process of liquidation in 1939

HIGHLAND CR STRATEGIES FD (DE)
Name changed to Pyxis Credit Strategies Fund 01/11/2012
Pyxis Credit Strategies Fund name changed to NexPoint Credit Strategies Fund 06/25/2012 which name changed to NexPoint Strategic Opportunities Fund 03/19/2018

HIGHLAND CROW RES LTD (BC)
Merged into Noramco Mining Corp. 01/01/1988
Each share Capital Stock no par exchanged for (1) share Common no par
Noramco Mining Corp. name changed to Quest Capital Corp. 01/03/1995 which name changed to Quest Oil & Gas Inc. 11/15/1996 which merged into EnerMark Income Fund 04/18/1997 which merged into Enerplus Resources Fund 06/22/2001 which reorganized as Enerplus Corp. 01/03/2011

HIGHLAND DAIRY, LTD. (ON)
7% Preferred $100 par changed to 5% Preferred $100 par 00/00/1938
Liquidation completed
Each share 5% Preferred $100 par received initial distribution of $110 cash 04/08/1965
Each share 5% Preferred $100 par received final distribution of $10 cash 10/21/1965
No Common stockholders' equity
Note: Certificates were not required to be surrendered and are without value

HIGHLAND DISTRESSED OPPORTUNITIES INC (DE)
Merged into Highland Credit Strategies Fund 06/12/2009
Each share Common $0.001 par exchanged for approximately (0.46133) share Common $0.001 par
Highland Credit Strategies Fund name changed to Pyxis Credit Strategies Fund 01/11/2012 which name changed to NexPoint Credit Strategies Fund 06/25/2012 which name changed to NexPoint Strategic Opportunities Fund 03/19/2018

HIGHLAND ENERGY INC (AB)
Merged into Interaction Resources Ltd. 05/30/2000
Each share Common no par exchanged for (0.96) share Common no par
Interaction Resources Ltd. recapitalized as Ketch Energy Ltd. 06/16/2000 which merged into Acclaim Energy Trust 10/01/2002
(See Acclaim Energy Trust)

HIGHLAND FED BK FSB (LOS ANGELES, CA)
Name changed 12/21/89
Name changed from Highland Federal Savings & Loan Association of Los Angeles to Highland Federal Bank, F.S.B. (Los Angeles, CA) 12/21/89
Under plan of reorganization each share Common no par automatically became (1) share Highland Bancorp, Inc. Common 1¢ par 12/16/97
(See Highland Bancorp, Inc.)

HIGHLAND FEDERAL SAVINGS BANK (CINCINNATI, OH)
Merged into First Financial Bancorp 02/01/1994
Each share Common $1 par exchanged for (1.048) shares Common 10¢ par

HIGHLAND FLOATING RATE OPPORTUNITIES FD II (MA)
Reorganized as Highland Floating Rate Opportunities Fund 11/06/2017
Each Class A Share exchanged for (0.48482497) Common Share of Bene. Int.
Each Class C Share exchanged for (0.48459003) Common Share of Bene. Int.
Each Class Z Share exchanged for (0.48437878) Common Share of Bene. Int.

HIGHLAND HEALTHCARE CORP (FL)
Recapitalized as Systems Communications Inc. 09/09/1994
Each share Common $0.001 par exchanged for (0.2) share Common $0.001 par
Systems Communications Inc. recapitalized as Hitsgalore.com, Inc. 03/19/1999 which name changed to Diamond Hitts Production, Inc. (FL) 05/01/2001 which reincorporated in Nevada 09/04/2001
(See Diamond Hitts Production, Inc.)

HIGHLAND HLDGS INTL INC (DE)
Each share old Common $0.001 par exchanged for (0.14285714) share new Common $0.001 par 07/21/1998
Each share new Common $0.001 par exchanged for (0.06666666) share Common no par 01/10/2001
Reorganized under the laws of Nevada as Bio-Clean International, Inc. 11/13/2007
Each share Common no par exchanged for (0.025) share Common no par

HIGHLAND HOMES UTICA INC (NY)
Adjudicated bankrupt 08/30/1973
Stockholders' equity unlikely

HIGHLAND HOSPITALITY CORP (MD)
Issue Information - 34,500,000 shares COM offered at $10 per share on 12/16/2003
Merged into JER Partners Acquisitions IV, LLC 07/17/2007
Each share Ser. A Preferred 1¢ par exchanged for $25 cash
Each share Common 1¢ par exchanged for $19.50 cash

HIGHLAND INNS CORP (TN)
Stock Dividend - 200% 7/1/76
Name changed to Advantage Companies, Inc. 4/28/80
Advantage Companies, Inc. merged into LDDS Communications, Inc. (DE) 8/11/89 which merged into Resurgens Communications Group, Inc. 9/15/93 which name changed to LDDS Communications, Inc. (GA) 9/15/93 which name changed to WorldCom, Inc. 5/26/95 which name changed to MCI WorldCom, Inc.

9/14/98 which name changed to WorldCom Inc. (New) 5/1/2000
(See WorldCom Inc. (New))

HIGHLAND LASS LTD.
Acquired by Highland-Bell Ltd. on approximately (2) for (1) basis 00/00/1936
Highland-Bell Ltd. liquidated for Teck Corp. Ltd. 04/30/1971 which name changed to Teck Corp. 11/21/1978 which name changed to Teck Cominco Ltd. 09/12/2001 which name changed to Teck Resources Ltd. 04/27/2009

HIGHLAND LEASEHOLDS LTD. (AB)
Charter revoked for failure to file reports and pay fees 4/15/57

HIGHLAND LODE MINES LTD (BC)
Recapitalized as CDR Resources Inc. 03/01/1977
Each share Common 50¢ par exchanged for (0.33333333) share Common no par
(See CDR Resources Inc.)

HIGHLAND MFG INC (NV)
Name changed to FRC Racing Products Inc. 04/18/1995
FRC Racing Products Inc. recapitalized as Results Technology Group, Corp. 01/22/2001
(See Results Technology Group, Corp.)

HIGHLAND MERCURY MINES LTD (BC)
Merged into Highland-Crow Resources Ltd. 09/25/1978
Each share Capital Stock no par exchanged for (0.2) share Capital Stock no par
Highland-Crow Resources Ltd. merged into Noramco Mining Corp. 01/01/1988 which name changed to Quest Capital Corp. 01/03/1995 which name changed to Quest Oil & Gas Inc. 11/15/1996 which merged into EnerMark Income Fund 04/18/1997 which merged into Enerplus Resources Fund 06/22/2001 which reorganized as Enerplus Corp. 01/03/2011

HIGHLAND NATL BK (NEWBURGH, NY)
Capital Stock $50 par changed to $25 par and (1) additional share issued 1/12/60
Stock Dividends - 12.5% 1/18/44; 50% 1/18/56; 20% 2/24/70
Acquired by United Bank Corp. of New York 12/1/72
Each share Capital Stock $25 par exchanged for (5.75) shares Common $5 par

HIGHLAND PARK MFG CO (NC)
Voluntarily dissolved 6/8/72
Details not available

HIGHLAND PARK ST BK (SAN ANTONIO, TX)
Stock Dividends - 11.11111111% 02/19/1970; 10% 01/29/1971
Merged into Texas Commerce Bancshares, Inc. 10/10/1974
Each share Common $4 par exchanged for (0.722222) share Common $4 par
Texas Commerce Bancshares, Inc. acquired by Chemical New York Corp. 05/01/1987 which name changed to Chemical Banking Corp. 04/29/1988 which name changed to Chase Manhattan Corp. (New) 03/31/1996 which name changed to J.P. Morgan Chase &Co. 12/31/2000 which name changed to JPMorgan Chase & Co. 07/20/2004

HIGHLAND QUEEN MINES LTD (BC)
Struck off register and declared dissolved for failure to file returns 04/10/1992

HIGHLAND QUEEN SPORTSWEAR LTD (ON)
Common no par reclassified as Conv. Class A no par in 1973
Conv. Class A no par called for redemption 1/12/87
Conv. Class B no par called for redemption 1/12/87
Public interest eliminated

HIGHLAND RES INC (BC)
Recapitalized as Highland Copper Co. Inc. 11/01/2012
Each share Common no par exchanged for (0.2) share Common no par

HIGHLAND RES INC (DE)
Name changed to Highland Holdings International Inc. (DE) 11/12/1997
Highland Holdings International Inc. (DE) reorganized in Nevada as Bio-Clean International, Inc. 11/13/2007

HIGHLAND RES INC (WA)
Charter cancelled and proclaimed dissolved for failure to pay fees 09/18/1989

HIGHLAND RIDGE INC (DE)
Name changed to TEC Technology, Inc. (DE) 07/15/2010
TEC Technology, Inc. (DE) reincorporated in Nevada 06/30/2012

HIGHLAND STAR MINES LTD (BC)
Recapitalized as Pembroke Star Resources Ltd. 03/09/1977
Each share Common no par exchanged for (0.5) share Common no par
Pembroke Star Resources Ltd. name changed to Eskimo Resources Ltd. 06/25/1980 which name changed to Ft. Lauderdale Resources Inc. 01/05/1987 which recapitalized as Amcorp Industries Inc. 06/22/1990 which name changed to Molycor Gold Corp. 05/17/1996 which name changed to Nevada Clean Magnesium Inc. 04/17/2012

HIGHLAND SUPERSTORES INC (MI)
Chapter 11 bankruptcy proceedings converted to Chapter 7 on 3/18/93
No stockholders' equity

HIGHLAND TEL CO (NY)
Common no par changed to $4.50 par and (2) additional shares issued 8/17/70
Under plan of merger each share Common $4.50 par exchanged for (1.336) shares Rochester Telephone Corp. Common $2.50 par 3/31/76
Rochester Telephone Corp. name changed to Frontier Corp. 1/1/95 which merged into Global Crossing Ltd. 9/28/99
(See Global Crossing Ltd.)
5% Preferred $100 par reclassified as 5-7/8% Preferred Ser. A $100 par 2/1/72
Name changed to Frontier Communications of New York, Inc. 1/1/95
(See Frontier Communications of New York, Inc.)

HIGHLAND URANIUM, INC. (WY)
Charter revoked for non-payment of corporate license taxes 2/19/60

HIGHLAND VY MINES LTD (BC)
Recapitalized as New Highland Valley Mines Ltd. 07/10/1973
Each share Capital Stock no par exchanged for (0.4) share Capital Stock no par
New Highland Valley Mines Ltd. merged into Great Manhattan Gold Corp. 08/21/1975
(See Great Manhattan Gold Corp.)

HIGHLAND VALLEY MINING CORP. LTD. (BC)
Recapitalized as Highland Valley Mines Ltd. 10/25/1968 (Holders were notified 04/07/1969)
Each share Capital Stock $1 par exchanged for (0.05) share Capital Stock no par
Highland Valley Mines Ltd. recapitalized as New Highland Valley Mines Ltd. 07/10/1973 which merged into Great Manhattan Gold Corp. 08/21/1975
(See Great Manhattan Gold Corp.)

HIGHLAND VY RES LTD (BC)
Name changed to Loki Gold Corp. 05/20/1988
Loki Gold Corp. merged into Viceroy Resource Corp. 05/30/1996 which merged into Quest Capital Corp. (BC) 06/30/2003 which reincorporated in Canada 05/27/2008 which name changed to Sprott Resource Lending Corp. 09/10/2010 which merged into Sprott Inc. 07/24/2013

HIGHLANDER INCOME FD INC (MN)
Merged into First American Investment Funds Inc. 7/31/98
Each share Common 1¢ par exchanged for (1.4537094) shares Strategic Income Fund Retail Class A $0.0001 par

HIGHLANDER INTL CORP (NJ)
Name changed to Worldwide Collections Fund, Inc. 09/25/1991
(See Worldwide Collections Fund, Inc.)

HIGHLANDS ACQUISITION CORP (DE)
Completely liquidated 10/05/2009
Each Unit exchanged for first and final distribution of $9.85008524 cash
Each share Common $0.0001 par exchanged for first and final distribution of $9.85008524 cash

HIGHLANDS CAP TR I (DE)
9.25% Capital Securities called for redemption at $25.4625 on 07/15/2014

HIGHLANDS COAL & CHEM CORP (DE)
Name changed to Rio Verde Energy Corp. 05/07/1981
(See Rio Verde Energy Corp.)

HIGHLANDS INDPT BK (SEBRING, FL)
Reorganized as Highlands Independent Bancshares, Inc. 4/1/98
Each share Common $5 par exchanged for (2) shares Common 1¢ par

HIGHLANDS INS GROUP INC (DE)
Plan of reorganization under Chapter 11 Federal Bankruptcy Code effective 3/31/2003
No stockholders' equity

HIGHLANDS NATL INC (DE)
Merged into Parkway Co. (TX) 04/30/1986
Each share Common $1 par exchanged for (0.15873015) share Common $1 par
Parkway Co. (TX) reincorporated in Maryland as Parkway Properties, Inc. 08/02/1996 which merged into Cousins Properties Inc. 10/06/2016

HIGHLANDS ST BK (HIGHLANDS, TX)
Under plan of reorganization each share Common no par automatically became (1) share HB Financial Corp. Common no par 07/31/1998

HIGHLANDS ST BK (VERNON, NJ)
Reorganized as Highlands Bancorp, Inc. 08/31/2010
Each share Common $5 par exchanged for (1) share Common no par

HIGHLANDS TRUST
Liquidated in 1947

HIGHLANDS UNION BANK (ABINGDON, VA)
Reorganized as Highlands Bankshares, Inc. 12/29/95
Each share Common $2.50 par exchanged for (1) share Common $2.50 par

HIGHLIGHT NETWORKS INC (NV)
Name changed to Xiamen Lutong International Travel Agency Co., Ltd. 05/14/2018

HIGHLINE INDS INC (NV)
Charter revoked for failure to file reports and pay fees 12/1/94

HIGHLINE TECHNICAL INNOVATIONS INC (ID)
Name changed to SPO Networks, Inc. 01/12/2017

HIGHMARK MARKETING CORP (BC)
Common no par split (4) for (1) by issuance of (3) additional shares payable 12/04/2014 to holders of record 12/01/2014
Each share Common no par received distribution of (0.25) share Highmark Technologies Corp. Common no par payable 01/28/2015 to holders of record 01/12/2015
Each share Common no par received distribution of (0.25) share MJ Bioscience Corp. Common no par payable 01/28/2015 to holders of record 01/12/2015
Name changed to Lightning Ventures Inc. 06/20/2016

HIGHMARK RES LTD (BC)
Struck off register and declared dissolved for failure to file returns 12/28/1990

HIGHMONT MNG CORP (BC)
Merged into Teck Corp. 09/28/1979
Each share Common no par exchanged for (0.6) share Class B Common no par or $16.66 cash
Note: Option to receive cash expired 10/28/1979
Teck Corp. name changed to Teck Cominco Ltd. 09/12/2001 which name changed to Teck Resources Ltd. 04/27/2009

HIGHMONT MNG LTD (BC)
Merged into Highmont Mining Corp. 07/04/1977
Each share Common 50¢ par exchanged for (1) share Common no par
Highmont Mining Corp. merged into Teck Corp. 09/28/1979 which name changed to Teck Cominco Ltd. 09/12/2001 which name changed to Teck Resources Ltd. 04/27/2009

HIGHMONT RESOURCES LTD. (BC)
Acquired by Torwest Resources (1962) Ltd. on a (0.5) for (1) basis 02/08/1962
Torwest Resources (1962) Ltd. merged into Highmont Mining Corp. 07/04/1977 which merged into Teck Corp. 09/28/1979 which name changed to Teck Cominco Ltd. 09/12/2001 which name changed to Teck Resources Ltd. 04/27/2009

HIGHPINE OIL & GAS LTD (AB)
Merged into Daylight Resources Trust 10/08/2009
Each share Common no par exchanged for (0.85) Trust Unit no par
Daylight Resources Trust reorganized as Daylight Energy Ltd. 05/12/2010
(See Daylight Energy Ltd.)

HIGHPOINT TECHNOLOGY INC (CO)
Recapitalized as Renaissance Entertainment Corp. 4/21/93
Each share Common $0.0001 par exchanged for (0.01) share Common $0.0001 par
(See Renaissance Entertainment Corp.)

HIGHPOINT TELECOMMUNICATIONS INC (YT)
Name changed 07/27/1998
Reincorporated 07/29/1998
Name changed from Highpoint Capital Corp. to Highpoint Telecommunications Inc. (AB) 07/27/1998
Place of incorporation changed from (AB) to (YT) 07/29/1998
Dissolved and struck off register 05/19/2005

HIGHPOINTE EXPL INC (BC)
Recapitalized as Oxford Resources Inc. 11/08/2013
Each share Common no par exchanged for (0.2) share Common no par

HIGHRIDGE EXPL LTD (AB)
Class A Common no par reclassified as Common no par 07/08/1993
Merged into Talisman Energy Inc. 08/05/1999
Each share Common no par exchanged for (0.11) share Common no par
(See Talisman Energy Inc.)

HIGHRIDGE MINING CO. LTD.
Recapitalized as New Highridge Mining Co. Ltd. 00/00/1952
Each share Capital Stock no par exchanged for (0.33333333) share Capital Stock no par
New Highridge Mining Co. Ltd. recapitalized as Combined Metal Mines Ltd. 06/25/1958 which recapitalized as CME Resources Inc. 11/15/1979 which name changed to CME Capital Inc. 10/15/1986
(See CME Capital Inc.)

HIGHSEAS ENTMT & CASINO LTD (NV)
Name changed to Phoenix Media Group Ltd. 03/24/1994
Phoenix Media Group Ltd. recapitalized as TecScan International, Inc. 06/23/2003 which name changed to Bio-Labs, Inc. 05/19/2004
(See Bio-Life Labs, Inc.)

HIGHSTAKE MINES LTD. (ON)
Charter cancelled for failure to pay taxes and file returns 4/3/68

HIGHTEC INC (DE)
SEC revoked common stock registration 07/19/2002
No stockholders' equity

HIGHTIDE INC (NV)
Recapitalized as Total Medical, Elective Care Clinics Inc. 05/22/2000
Each share Common $0.001 par exchanged for (0.2) share Common $0.001 par
(See Total Medical, Elective Care Clinic Inc.)

HIGHTOWER PETROLEUM CORP. (CO)
Charter revoked for failure to file reports and pay fees 9/14/51

HIGHTOWERS PETE HLDGS LTD (NV)
Name changed to International Oil & Gas Holdings Corp. 07/19/2006
International Oil & Gas Holdings Corp. name changed to Inscor, Inc. 05/26/2011 which recapitalized as Oicintra, Inc. 01/14/2016

HIGHVELD STL & VANADIUM LTD (SOUTH AFRICA)
Unsponsored ADR's for Ordinary reclassified as Sponsored ADR's for Ordinary 08/31/2009
Stock Dividends - 2.2137% payable 04/26/1996 to holders of record 03/01/1996; 0.8576% payable 10/18/1996 to holders of record 08/23/1996; 1.1394% payable 05/09/1997 to holders of record 03/14/1997; 0.9664% payable 10/22/1997 to holders of record 08/22/1997
Name changed to Evraz Highveld Steel & Vanadium Ltd. 07/26/2010
(See Evraz Highveld Steel & Vanadium Ltd.)

HIGHVIEW RES LTD (AB)
Recapitalized as Paris Energy Inc. 07/06/2007
Each share Common no par exchanged for (0.1) share Common no par
Paris Energy Inc. recapitalized as Mapan Energy Ltd. 09/10/2014 which merged into Tourmaline Oil Corp. 08/17/2015

HIGHWATER PWR CORP (BC)
Acquired by Taylor NGL Limited Partnership 08/28/2007
Each share Common no par exchanged for $1.50 cash

HIGHWATER RES LTD (BC)
Cease trade order effective 07/29/1993
Stockholders' equity unlikely

HIGHWAY CRUISERS INC (CA)
Name changed to Macro Synetic Systems, Inc. 09/09/1970
(See Macro Synetic Systems, Inc.)

HIGHWAY ONE-OWEB INC (UT)
Name changed to Michelex Corp. 9/29/2003

HIGHWAY PRODUCTS, INC. (DE)
Charter forfeited for failure to maintain a registered agent 02/21/1978

HIGHWAY SAFETY APPLIANCES, INC. (MN)
Acquired by Napco Industries, Inc. 06/00/1955
Details not available

HIGHWAY TRAILER CO. (DE)
Name changed to Trailco Corp. 11/06/1957
(See Trailco Corp.)

HIGHWAY TRAILER CO. (WI)
Reincorporated under the laws of Delaware 00/00/1946
Highway Trailer Co. (DE) name changed to Trailco Corp. 11/06/1957
(See Trailco Corp.)

HIGHWAY TRAILER INDS INC (DE)
7.5% Preferred $10 par reclassified as 5% Preferred $10 par 06/05/1959
Each share Common 25¢ par exchanged for (0.2) share Common $1.25 par 09/07/1962
Merged into Highway Industries Inc. 12/31/1969
Each share 5% Conv. Preferred $10 par exchanged for $19.81 cash
Each share Common $1.25 par exchanged for $19.75 cash

HIGHWAYMASTER COMMUNICATIONS INC (DE)
Name changed to @Track Communications, Inc. 04/11/2000
@Track Communications, Inc. name changed to Minorplanet Systems USA, Inc. 07/23/2002 which reorganized as Remote Dynamics, Inc. 07/02/2004

HIGHWIRE ENTMT GROUP INC (AB)
Recapitalized as Creation Ventures Inc. 05/21/2002
Each share Common no par exchanged for (0.1) share Common no par
Creation Ventures Inc. name changed to Creation Casinos Inc. (AB) 11/28/2003 which reincorporated in British Columbia 12/16/2004 which recapitalized as Orca Power Corp. (BC) 07/22/2008 which reorganized in Canada as AFG Flameguard Ltd. 04/11/2012

HIGHWOOD DISTILLERS LTD (AB)
Reacquired 02/14/2001

Each share Common no par exchanged for $0.20 cash

HIGHWOOD RES LTD (AB)
Acquired by Beta Minerals Inc. 11/29/2002
Each share Common no par exchanged for (1) share Common no par
Beta Minerals Inc. name changed to Advanced Primary Minerals Corp. (ON) 03/06/2009 which reincorporated in Canada 07/18/2012 which recapitalized as Morien Resources Corp. 11/09/2012

HIGHWOOD SARCEE OILS LTD. (CANADA)
Capital Stock no par changed to 20¢ par 07/23/1956
Merged into Sarcee Petroleums Ltd. 03/09/1959
Each share Capital Stock 20¢ par exchanged for (0.25) share Capital Stock no par
(See Sarcee Petroleums Ltd.)

HIGHWOODS PPTYS INC (MD)
Issue Information - 4,000,000 DEPOSITARY SHS REPSTG 1/10 PFD SER D 8% offered at $25 per share on 04/16/1998
8% Depositary Preferred Ser. D 1¢ par called for redemption at $25 on 08/22/2005
8% Preferred Ser. B 1¢ par called for redemption at $25 on 06/24/2011 (Additional Information in Active)

HII TECHNOLOGIES INC (DE)
Plan of reorganization under Chapter 11 Federal Bankruptcy proceedings effective 05/20/2016
No stockholders' equity

HIKING ADVENTURES INC (NV)
Each share old Common $0.001 par exchanged for (12.5) shares new Common $0.001 par 03/02/2000
Name changed to iQrom Communications, Inc. 04/10/2000
(See iQrom Communications, Inc.)

HIKO BELL MNG & OIL CO (UT)
Each share old Common 1¢ par exchanged for (0.25) share new Common 1¢ par 07/28/1978
Name changed to Hiko Energy Corp. 02/02/2011
(See Hiko Energy Corp.)

HIKO ENERGY CORP (UT)
SEC revoked common stock registration 01/28/2013

HIKU BRANDS CO LTD (BC)
Merged into Canopy Growth Corp. 09/06/2018
Each share Common no par exchanged for (0.046) share Common no par
Note: Unexchanged certificates will be cancelled and become without value 09/06/2024

HIL LTD (CANADA)
Merged into Hees International Bancorp Inc. 11/30/1995
Each share Class A Subordinate no par exchanged for (0.4) share Common no par
Hees International Bancorp Inc. name changed to Edper Group Ltd. (New) 01/01/1997 which merged into EdperBrascan Corp. 08/01/1997 which name changed to Brascan Corp. 04/28/2000 which name changed to Brookfield Asset Management, Inc. 11/10/2005

HILAND HLDGS GP LP (DE)
Acquired by HH GP Holding, LLC 12/04/2009
Each Unit of Ltd. Partnership Int. exchanged for $3.20 cash

HILAND PARTNERS L P (DE)
Issue Information - 2,000,000 UNITS LTD PARTNERSHIP INT offered at $22.50 per Unit on 02/10/2005

Acquired by HH GP Holding, LLC 12/04/2009
Each Unit of Ltd. Partnership Int. exchanged for $10 cash

HILASAL MEXICANA S A DE C V (MEXICO)
ADR agreement terminated 12/18/2017
Each Sponsored ADR for Common exchanged for (20) shares Common
Note: Unexchanged ADR's will be sold and the proceeds, if any, held for claim after 12/21/2018

HILB ROGAL & HOBBS CO (VA)
Name changed 05/04/2004
Common no par split (5) for (4) by issuance of (0.25) additional share 12/29/1989
Common no par split (2) for (1) by issuance of (1) additional share payable 12/31/2001 to holders of record 12/14/2001 Ex date - 01/02/2002
Stock Dividend - 10% 02/14/1989
Name changed from Hilb, Rogal & Hamilton Co. to Hilb Rogal & Hobbs Co. 05/04/2004
Acquired by Willis Group Holdings Ltd. (Bermuda) 10/01/2008
Each share Common no par exchanged for (1.451) shares Common $0.000115 par
Willis Group Holdings Ltd. (Bermuda) reincorporated in Ireland as Willis Group Holdings PLC 12/31/2009 which reorganized in Bermuda as Willis Towers Watson PLC 01/05/2016

HILCOAST DEV CORP (DE)
Merged into a private company 2/12/97
Each share Common 1¢ par exchanged for $6 cash

HILDICK PRODUCTS CORP.
Liquidated 00/00/1942
Details not available

HILDON MNG EXPLS LTD (BC)
Cease trade order effective 12/21/1995
Stockholders' equity unlikely

HILITE INDUSTRIES INC (DE)
Merged into Hilite Mergerco, Inc. 7/26/99
Each share Common 1¢ par exchanged for $14.25 cash

HILL BROS INC (FL)
Merged into HB Acquisition, Inc. 11/08/1984
Each share Common 5¢ par exchanged for $1.40 cash

HILL CORP. (DE)
Merged into American Hardware Corp. 7/26/63
Each share Common $5 par exchanged for (0.25) share Common $12.50 par
American Hardware Corp. merged into Emhart Corp. (Conn.) 6/30/64 which reincorporated in Virginia 5/4/76
(See Emhart Corp. (Va.))

HILL DIESEL ENGINE CO. (MI)
Merged into Indian Motocycle Co. 02/28/1947
Each share Common $1 par exchanged for (0.33333333) share Common $1 par
Indian Motorcycle Co. recapitalized as Titeflex, Inc. 00/00/1951 which merged into Atlas Corp. 08/17/1962
(See Atlas Corp.)

HILL (FANNY) ENTERPRISES, INC (NY)
See - Fanny Hill Enterprises Inc

HILL (TOM) GOLF CO. (OR)
Assets transferred for the benefit of creditors 00/00/1974
No stockholders' equity

HILL (R.H.), INC. (IN)
Charter revoked for failure to file reports and pay fees 8/28/66

HILL INDUSTRIES, INC. (TX)
Common $1 par changed to 1¢ par 1/31/75
Name changed to Hillcrest Carpets, Inc. 12/3/75
(See Hillcrest Carpets, Inc.)

HILL MANUFACTURING CO.
Acquired by Bates Manufacturing Co. 00/00/1946
Details not available

HILL MINING & MILLING CO. (ID)
Merged into Yreka United, Inc. (ID) 06/07/1957
Each share Common exchanged for (0.5) share Common 50¢ par
Yreka United, Inc. (ID) reorganized in Nevada as Southern Home Medical Equipment, Inc. 10/23/2006 which name changed to Southern Home Medical, Inc. 07/27/2012

HILL PACKING CO. (KS)
Recapitalized 1/1/55
Each share Preferred $5 par exchanged for (0.06) share 6% Preferred $100 par
Each share Common no par exchanged for (2.5) shares Common $1 par
Merged into Riviana Foods Inc. (Old) 9/25/68
Each share 6% Preferred $100 par exchanged for (1.923080) shares $2.60 Conv. Preferred no par
Each share Common $1 par exchanged for (0.057179) shares $2.60 Conv. Preferred no par and (0.115432) share Common $3.50 par
Riviana Foods, Inc. (Old) acquired by Colgate-Palmolive Co. 6/14/76

HILL PUBLISHING CO., INC. (MA)
Each share Class A Common no par and Class B Common no par exchanged for (29) shares Common no par 03/25/1970
Voluntarily dissolved 03/14/1974
No stockholders' equity

HILL TOP GOLD MINES CO., LTD. (ON)
Charter cancelled in 1944
No stockholders' equity

HILL TOP RES CORP (BC)
Name changed to Tanzania Minerals Corp. 09/07/2010

HILL'S SUPERMARKETS, INC. (NY)
Merged into Korvette (E.J.), Inc. 02/01/1965
Each share Class A 50¢ par exchanged for (1) share 4% Conv. Preferred $10 par and (0.6) share Common $1 par
Each share Class B 50¢ par exchanged for (0.8) share Common $1 par
Korvette (E.J.), Inc. merged into Spartans Industries, Inc. (NY) 09/25/1966 which merged into Arlen Realty & Development Corp. 02/26/1971 which name changed to Arlen Corp. 10/16/1985
(See Arlen Corp.)

HILLCREST CARPETS INC (TX)
Charter forfeited for failure to pay taxes 06/25/1984

HILLCREST COLLIERIES LTD (CANADA)
Recapitalized 00/00/1942
Each share Preferred $100 par exchanged for (20) shares Common no par
Each share Common $100 par exchanged for (1) share Common no par
Liquidated 11/00/1960
Each share Common no par exchanged for (1) share Hillcrest Collieries Ltd. (Bahamas) Capital Stock $1 par

HILLCREST NATURAL GAS CO.
Merged into Northeastern Oil & Gas Co. in 1936
Details not available

HILLCREST RES LTD (AB)
Acquired by Mark Resources Inc. 05/09/1995
Each share Common no par exchanged for (0.8) share Common no par
Mark Resources Inc. acquired by EnerMark Income Fund 04/09/1996 which merged into Enerplus Resources Fund 06/22/2001 which reorganized as Enerplus Corp. 01/03/2011

HILLCREST RES LTD (BC)
Name changed to Hillcrest Petroleum Ltd. 03/11/2015

HILLCREST STATE BANK OF UNIVERSITY PARK (DALLAS, TX)
Common $20 par changed to $5 par and (3) additional shares issued 08/13/1979
Merged into Texas Commerce Bancshares, Inc. 12/04/1981
Each share Common $5 par exchanged for (0.807745) share Common $4 par
Texas Commerce Bancshares, Inc. acquired by Chemical New York Corp. 05/01/1987 which name changed to Chemical Banking Corp. 04/29/1988 which name changed to Chase Manhattan Corp. (New) 03/31/1996 which name changed to J.P. Morgan Chase & Co. 12/31/2000 which name changed to JPMorgan Chase & Co. 07/20/2004

HILLDALE EXPLS CORP (ON)
Name changed 09/18/1995
Name changed from Hilldale Holdings Inc. to Hilldale Explorations Corp. 09/18/1995
Merged into Oro Blanco Resources Corp. 08/26/1996
Each share Common no par exchanged for (0.2) share Common no par
Oro Blanco Resources Corp. merged into Minpro International Ltd. 03/06/1998

HILLENBRAND INDS INC (IN)
Common no par split (2) for (1) by issuance of (1) additional share 03/02/1973
Common no par split (2) for (1) by issuance of (1) additional share 02/25/1982
Common no par split (2) for (1) by issuance of (1) additional share 02/24/1984
Common no par split (2) for (1) by issuance of (1) additional share 02/27/1987
Common no par split (2) for (1) by issuance of (1) additional share 02/28/1992
Each share Common no par received distribution of (1) share Hillenbrand, Inc. Common no par payable 03/31/2008 to holders of record 03/24/2008 Ex date - 04/01/2008
Name changed to Hill-Rom Holdings, Inc. 03/31/2008

HILLER AIRCRAFT CORP. (CA)
Name changed to Hiller Realization Corp. 11/30/60 which was liquidated 1/25/61
(See Hiller Realization Corp.)

HILLER AVIATION INC (CA)
Common $1 par split (3) for (2) by issuance of (0.5) additional share 10/31/1980
Stock Dividend - 10% 08/30/1982
Plan of reorganization under Chapter 11 bankruptcy proceedings confirmed 04/11/1985
No stockholders' equity

HILLER HELICOPTERS, INC. (CA)
Name changed to Hiller Aircraft Corp. 7/11/58 which name was changed to Hiller Realization Corp. 11/30/60 which was liquidated 1/25/61
(See Hiller Realization Corp.)

HILLER REALIZATION CORP. (CA)
Completely liquidated 01/25/1961
Each (4.25) shares Capital Stock $1 par held by holders of record 01/25/1961 received (1) share Electric Auto-Lite Co. Common $5 par
Note: Certificates were not required to be exchanged and are without value

HILLHAVEN CORP (NV)
Each share Common 15¢ par exchanged for (0.2) share Common 75¢ par 11/01/1993
Merged into Vencor Inc. (Old) 09/28/1995
Each share Common 75¢ par exchanged for (0.935) share Common 25¢ par
Vencor Inc. (Old) name changed to Ventas, Inc. 05/01/1998

HILLHAVEN CORP (TN)
Merged into National Medical Enterprises, Inc. 01/02/1980
Each share Common $1 par exchanged for $25 cash

HILLHAVEN INC (DE)
Reincorporated 10/7/74
Stock Dividend - 200% 7/26/68
State of incorporation changed from (WA) to (DE) 10/7/74
Under plan of merger each share Common 16-2/3¢ par automatically became (1) share Hillhaven Corp. Common $1 par 3/31/78
(See Hillhaven Corp.)

HILLIARD CORP (NY)
Each share Prior Preferred $100 par exchanged for (3) shares Common $20 par 5/18/68
Each share Preferred $100 par exchanged for (3) shares Common $20 par 5/18/68
(Additional Information in Active)

HILLIARD OIL & GAS, INC. (NV)
100% acquired by Tidewater Marine Service, Inc. through exchange offer which expired 06/30/1977
Public interest eliminated

HILLMAN COAL & COKE CO. (PA)
Liquidated 11/00/1954
Details not available

HILLS DEPT STORES INC (DE)
Reorganized under Chapter 11 Federal Bankruptcy Code 10/4/93
Each share Common 1¢ par exchanged for (0.0219) Hills Stores Co. (New) Common Stock Purchase Warrant expiring 10/4/2000
(See Hills Stores Co. (New))

HILLS STORES CO NEW (DE)
Merged into Ames Department Stores, Inc. 3/19/99
Each share Conv. Preferred 1¢ par exchanged for $1.50 cash
Each share Common 1¢ par exchanged for $1.50 cash

HILLS STORES CO OLD (DE)
Adjustable Rate Exchangeable Preferred Ser. B no par called for redemption 7/24/87
Public interest eliminated

HILLSBORO ASSOCIATION, INC. (DE)
Each share Capital Stock no par exchanged for (0.01) share Capital Stock no par 2/5/80
Note: In effect holders received $153 cash per share and public interest was eliminated

HILLSBORO GROUP INC (FL)
Name changed to CapTech Financial Group, Inc. 07/28/2004
CapTech Financial Group, Inc. name changed to Boo Koo Holdings, Inc. (FL) 08/13/2007 which reincorporated in Delaware 12/17/2007 which name changed to Performing Brands, Inc. 08/19/2008
(See Performing Brands, Inc.)

HILLSBOROUGH EXPL LTD (ON)
Name changed to Hillsborough Resources Ltd. (ON) 03/13/1987
Hillsborough Resources Ltd. (ON) reincorporated in Canada 11/05/1997
(See Hillsborough Resources Ltd. (Canada))

HILLSBOROUGH NATL BK (BELLE MEAD, NJ)
Acquired by United Jersey Banks 01/16/1988
Details not available

HILLSBOROUGH RES LTD (CANADA)
Reincorporated 11/05/1997
Place of incorporation changed from (ON) to (Canada) 11/05/1997
Merged into Vitol Group 12/21/2009
Each share Common no par exchanged for $0.50 cash
Note: Unexchanged certificates were cancelled and became without value 12/21/2015

HILLSDALE CNTY NATL BK (HILLSDALE, MI)
Common split (2) for (1) by issuance of (1) additional share payable 03/31/2000 to holders of record 03/08/2000
Reorganized as CNB Community Bancorp, Inc. 08/16/2005
Each share Common exchanged for (1) share Common

HILLSDALE STATE BANK (MADISON, WI)
Through voluntary exchange offer of (5) shares Affiliated Bank Corp. Common $5 par for each share Common $20 par, 100% was acquired as of 03/31/1970
Affiliated Bank Corp. merged into Marshall & Ilsley Corp. (Old) 12/31/1980
(See Marshall & Ilsley Corp. (Old))

HILLSDOWN HLDGS PLC (UNITED KINGDOM)
Acquired by Hicks, Muse, Tate & Furst Inc. 07/27/1999
Each new Sponsored ADR for Ordinary exchanged for $9.4238 cash

HILLSHIRE BRANDS CO (MD)
Acquired by Tyson Foods, Inc. 08/28/2014
Each share Common 1¢ par exchanged for $63 cash

HILLSIDE BEDDING INC (DE)
Each share old Conv. Preferred Ser. A 1¢ par exchanged for (0.1) share new Conv. Preferred Ser. A 1¢ par 09/09/1994
Each share old Common 1¢ par exchanged for (0.1) share new Common 1¢ par 09/09/1994
Name changed to ATEC Group Inc. 12/14/1995
ATEC Group Inc. name changed to Interpharm Holdings, Inc. 06/02/2003
(See Interpharm Holdings, Inc.)

HILLSIDE COTTON MILLS
Merged into Callaway Mills 00/00/1932
Details not available

HILLSIDE ENERGY CORP (BC)
Recapitalized as Charter Minerals Inc. 04/11/1989
Each share Common no par exchanged for (0.4) share Common no par
Charter Minerals Inc. recapitalized as New Charter Minerals Inc. 05/21/1991 which name changed to

Cambridge BioChemics Inc. 04/23/1992 which name changed to Cambridge Softek Inc. 06/23/1993 which recapitalized as Alantra Venture Corp. 11/21/1994
(See Alantra Venture Corp.)

HILLSIDE METAL PRODS INC (NY)
Name changed to Art Metal-U.S.A., Inc. 08/03/1973
(See Art Metal-U.S.A., Inc.)

HILLSIDE NATIONAL BANK (HILLSIDE, NJ)
Stock Dividend - 100% 02/01/1961
Merged into National State Bank (Elizabeth, NJ) 09/09/1962
Each share Common $50 par exchanged for (7.8) shares Common $10 par
National State Bank (Elizabeth, NJ) reorganized as Constellation Bancorp 03/08/1985 which merged into CoreStates Financial Corp 03/16/1994 which merged into First Union Corp. 04/28/1998 which name changed to Wachovia Corp. (Ctfs. dated after 09/01/2001) 09/01/2001 which merged into Wells Fargo & Co. (New) 12/31/2008

HILLTOP ACQUISITION HLDG CORP (TX)
Recapitalized as Alford Refrigerated Warehouses, Inc. 12/15/1998
Each share Common 1¢ par exchanged for (0.625) share Common 1¢ par
(See Alford Refrigerated Warehouses, Inc.)

HILLTOP CMNTY BANCORP INC (NJ)
Stock Dividends - 5% payable 12/22/2004 to holders of record 12/06/2004 Ex date - 12/02/2004; 5% payable 12/22/2005 to holders of record 12/06/2005 Ex date - 12/02/2005; 5% payable 12/22/2006 to holders of record 12/12/2006 Ex date - 12/08/2006; 5% payable 12/21/2007 to holders of record 12/10/2007 Ex date - 12/06/2007; 5% payable 12/26/2008 to holders of record 12/12/2008 Ex date - 12/11/2008; 5% payable 12/24/2009 to holders of record 12/10/2009 Ex date - 12/08/2009; 5% payable 12/24/2010 to holders of record 12/13/2010 Ex date - 12/09/2010
Acquired by Haven Bancorp, Inc. 11/08/2013
Each share Common no par exchanged for $9.42 cash

HILLTOP CMNTY BK (SUMMIT, NJ)
Stock Dividend - 5% payable 12/22/2003 to holders of record 12/05/2003 Ex date - 12/03/2003
Under plan of reorganization each share Common $5 par automatically became (1) share Hilltop Community Bancorp, Inc. Common no par 10/01/2004
(See Hilltop Community Bancorp, Inc.)

HILLTOP MINERALS LTD (ON)
Charter cancelled for failure to pay taxes and file returns 04/29/1985

HILLTOP PRODS INC (DE)
Recapitalized as Demark Financial Corp. 8/30/92
Each (60) shares Common no par exchanged for (1) share Common no par
Demark Financial Corp. name changed to Home Lending Associates, Inc. 8/2/93 which name changed to Microsure Inc. 11/27/96 which recapitalized as 9A Investment Holding Corp. 8/31/2001 which name changed to Viking Power Services, Inc. 7/3/2006

HILLTOWN RES INC (BC)
Recapitalized as Anexco Resources Ltd. 06/19/2013
Each share Common no par exchanged for (0.2) share Common no par
Anexco Resources Ltd. name changed to Kaneh Bosm Biotechnology Inc. 11/05/2014 which name changed to ICC International Cannabis Corp. (New) 09/20/2018

HILO ELEC LT LTD (HI)
Common $20 par changed to $10 par and (1) additional share issued 12/01/1961
Stock Dividend - 10% 12/15/1960
Merged into Hawaiian Electric Co., Inc. 02/01/1970
Each share Common $10 par exchanged for (1.0072) shares Common $6-2/3 par

HILO SUGAR CO. LTD. (HI)
Merged into Mauna Kea Sugar Co., Inc. 7/26/65
Each share Common $20 par exchanged for (1/6) share Common $10 par
Mauna Kea Sugar Co., Inc. merged into Brewer (C.) & Co., Ltd. 4/25/73 which merged into IU International Corp. 8/14/78
(See IU International Corp.)

HILSEWECK MINERALS CORP. (DE)
Name changed to Mid-America Minerals, Inc. 02/05/1958
Mid-America Minerals, Inc. merged into Calvert Exploration Co. 12/31/1964 which merged into Sun Oil Co. (PA) 07/31/1974 which name changed to Sun Co., Inc. 04/27/1976 which name changed to Sunoco, Inc. 11/06/1998 which merged into Energy Transfer Partners, L.P. (Old) 10/05/2012 which merged into Energy Transfer Partners, L.P. (New) 05/01/2017 which merged into Energy Transfer L.P. 10/19/2018

HILSTAR CAP CORP (AB)
Recapitalized as Kinesys Pharmaceutical Inc. 12/13/1995
Each share Common no par exchanged for (0.33333333) share Common no par
Kinesys Pharmaceutical Inc. name changed to Green River Petroleum Inc. 08/20/1997 which recapitalized as Green River Holdings Inc. 07/06/1999 which recapitalized as Netco Energy Inc. 10/03/2000 which name changed to Netco Silver Inc. (AB) 07/14/2011 which reincorporated in British Columbia as Brisio Innovations Inc. 02/12/2014

HILTON CR CORP (DE)
Merged into Carte Blanche Corp. 12/31/1965
Each share Common $1 par exchanged for (1) share Class A $1 par plus $4 principal amount of 4% 3-year Notes
(See Carte Blanche Corp.)

HILTON-DAVIS CHEMICAL CO.
Acquired by Sterling Drug Inc. 00/00/1945
Details not available

HILTON GROUP PLC (ENGLAND & WALES)
Recapitalized as Ladbrokes PLC 04/17/2006
Each Sponsored ADR for Ordinary exchanged for (0.70588235) Sponsored ADR for Ordinary
Ladbrokes PLC name changed to Ladbrokes Coral Group PLC 11/03/2016
(See Ladbrokes Coral Group PLC)

HILTON HOTELS CORP (DE)
Common $5 par changed to $2.50 par and (1) additional share issued 09/28/1916
5-1/2% Conv. Preferred A $25 par called for redemption 10/08/1962
Common $2.50 par split (2) for (1) by issuance of (1) additional share 10/07/1968
Common $2.50 par split (2) for (1) by issuance of (1) additional share 03/19/1976
Common $2.50 par split (2) for (1) by issuance of (1) additional share 12/22/1978
Common $2.50 par split (2) for (1) by issuance of (1) additional share 06/17/1988
Common $2.50 par split (4) for (1) by issuance of (3) additional shares payable 09/25/1996 to holders of record 09/19/1996 Ex date - 09/26/1996
8% Conv. Preferred Increased Dividend Equity Security no par called for redemption at (0.92) share Common $2.50 par plus $0.2225 accrued dividend on 10/03/1998
Each share Common $2.50 par received distribution of (1) share Park Place Entertainment Corp. Common $2.50 par payable 12/31/1998 to holders of record 12/23/1998 Ex date - 01/04/1999
Merged into Blackstone Group L.P. 10/24/2007
Each share Common $2.50 par exchanged for $47.50 cash

HILTON INTERNATIONAL CO. (DE)
Merged into Trans World Airlines, Inc. 05/10/1967
Each share Common no par exchanged for (0.275) share Common $5 par and (0.5) share $2 Conv. Preferred Ser. A no par
Trans World Airlines, Inc. name changed to Trans World Corp. (DE) 01/01/1979 which name changed to Transworld Corp. (DE) 04/25/1984 which assets were transferred to Transworld Corp. Liquidating Trust 12/31/1986
(See Transworld Corp. Liquidating Trust)

HILTON PETE LTD (YT)
Reincorporated 04/01/1999
Place of incorporation changed from (BC) to (YT) 04/01/1999
Each share old Common no par exchanged for (0.1) share new Common no par 12/30/2002
Name changed to Hilton Resources Ltd. (YT) 03/02/2004
Hilton Resources Ltd. (YT) reincorporated in British Columbia 11/23/2004 which recapitalized as Rochester Resources Ltd. 08/26/2005

HILTON RESOURCE CORP (BC)
Recapitalized as North Slope Minerals Inc. 06/13/1991
Each share Common no par exchanged for (0.28571428) share Common no par
North Slope Minerals Inc. recapitalized as Sino Pacific Development Ltd. 01/18/1995 which name changed to Prominex Resource Corp. 11/17/2005

HILTON RES LTD (BC)
Reincorporated 11/23/2004
Place of incorporation changed from (YT) to (BC) 11/23/2004
Recapitalized as Rochester Resources Ltd. 08/26/2005
Each share Common no par exchanged for (0.1) share Common no par

HIMAC RES LTD (BC)
Recapitalized as O T Industries Inc. 07/05/1985
Each share Common no par exchanged for (0.5) share Common no par
O T Industries Inc. name changed to Golden Princess Mining Corp. 03/12/1987 which recapitalized as Pandora Industries Inc. 09/28/1992 which recapitalized as Georgia Ventures Inc. 03/01/2000 which name changed to Creston Moly Corp. 10/19/2007 which merged into Mercator Minerals Ltd. 06/21/2011

HIMACHAL FUTURISTIC COMMUNICATIONS LTD (INDIA)
GDR agreement terminated 12/22/2013
Each 144A GDR for Equity Shares exchanged for $0.264422 cash
Each Reg. S GDR for Equity Shares exchanged for $0.264422 cash

HIMALAYAN CAP CORP (AB)
Name changed to Azul Ventures Inc. 05/04/2012
Azul Ventures Inc. recapitalized as Austin Resources Ltd. 09/24/2014

HIMATSINGKA SEIDE LTD (INDIA)
GDR agreement terminated 04/23/2015
No GDR's remain outstanding

HIMEDICS INC (FL)
Name changed to Pharmasciences, Inc. 2/26/93
(See Pharmasciences, Inc.)

HIMONT INC (DE)
Merged into Montedison S.p.A. 2/20/90
Each share Common $1 par exchanged for $51 cash

HINDE & DAUCH LTD (ON)
99.9% held by St. Lawrence Corp. Ltd. as of 05/01/1974
Public interest eliminated

HINDE & DAUCH PAPER CO. (OH)
Each share Common $100 par exchanged for (10) shares Common $10 par 00/00/1936
Acquired by West Virginia Pulp & Paper Co. 00/00/1953
Each share Common $10 par exchanged for (1.33333333) shares Common $5 par
West Virginia Pulp & Paper Co. name changed to Westvaco Corp. 03/03/1969 which merged into MeadWestvaco Corp. 01/29/2002 which merged into WestRock Co. 07/01/2015

HINDE & DAUCH PAPER CO. OF CANADA LTD. (ON)
Stock Dividend - 100% 04/29/1949
Name changed to Hinde & Dauch Ltd. 04/22/1960
(See Hinde & Dauch Ltd.)

HINDERLITER INDS INC (DE)
Name changed 10/12/82
Under plan of merger name changed from Hinderliter Energy Equipment Corp. to Hinderliter Industries, Inc. 10/12/82
Filed Chapter 11 Federal Bankruptcy 8/14/92 which was subsequently converted to a Chapter 7 proceeding
No stockholders' equity

HINDUSTAN DEV LTD (INDIA)
Scheme of arrangement effective 08/27/2001
Each GDR for Reg. S Ordinary exchanged for (0.778) Malanpur Steel Ltd. Sponsored GDR for Reg. S Ordinary and (0.222) Hindustan Engineering & Industries Ltd. GDR for Reg. S Ordinary 08/27/2001
Each GDR for 144A Ordinary exchanged for (0.778) Malanpur Steel Ltd. Sponsored GDR for 144A Ordinary and (0.222) Hindustan Engineering & Industries Ltd. GDR for Reg. S Ordinary 08/27/2001

HINES EDWARD LMBR CO (DE)
Liquidation completed
Each share Common $10 par received initial distribution of $20 cash 11/26/1985
Each share Common $10 par received second distribution of $5 cash 02/04/1986
Each share Common $10 par

HINES HORTICULTURE INC (DE) (continued from previous entry)
received third distribution of (1.27) shares Southern Mineral Corp. Common 1¢ par 03/17/1986
(See Southern Mineral Corp.)
Each share Common $10 par received fourth distribution of $9 cash 06/12/1986
Each share Common $10 par received fifth distribution of $2 cash 06/24/1988
Stock Dividends - 50% 12/15/1950; 33-1/3% 12/15/1954; 25% 01/02/1974; 100% 07/10/1979
Assets transferred to EHLCO Liquidating Trust and Common $10 par reclassified as Shares of Bene. Int. $10 par 01/30/1989
Each Share of Bene. Int. $10 par received sixth and final distribution of $1 cash payable 09/30/2003 to holders of record 09/15/2003
Ex date - 10/09/2003
Note: Certificates were not required to be surrendered and are without value

HINES HORTICULTURE INC (DE)
Issue Information - 5,100,000 shares COM offered at $11 per share on 06/22/1998
Plan of reorganization under Chapter 11 Federal Bankruptcy proceedings effective 04/10/2009
No stockholders' equity

HINES LAND & TIMBER CO.
Name changed to Hines (Edward) Lumber Co. in 1937
(See Hines (Edward) Lumber Co.)

HINES REAL ESTATE INVT TR INC (MD)
Liquidation completed
Each share Common $0.001 par received initial distribution of $6.20 cash payable 12/23/2016 to holders of record 12/07/2016
Each share Common $0.001 par received second distribution of $0.30 cash payable 04/18/2017 to holders of record 04/17/2017
Each share Common $0.001 par received third and final distribution of $0.08 cash payable 07/26/2018 to holders of record 07/10/2018

HINGELINE OVERTHRUST OIL & GAS INC (UT)
Merged into Whiting Petroleum Corp. 12/16/83
Each share Common $0.001 par exchanged for (0.25134) share Common 1¢ par
Whiting Petroleum Corp. acquired by IES Industries Inc. 2/18/92 which merged into Interstate Energy Corp. 4/21/98 which name changed to Alliant Energy Corp. 5/19/99

HINKLE & LAMEAR, INC. (OR)
Name changed 5/27/83
Name changed from Hinkle Northwest, Inc. to Hinkle & Lamear, Inc. 5/27/83
Name changed to L & H Capital Services Corp. 6/18/84
(See L & H Capital Services Corp.)

HINSDALE BANCORP INC (IL)
Merged into Wintrust Financial Corp. 9/1/96
Each share Common no par exchanged for (6.03398) shares Common no par

HINSDALE FINL CORP (DE)
Common 1¢ par split (5) for (4) by issuance of (0.25) additional share 11/13/95
Under plan of merger name changed to Alliance Bancorp 2/10/97
Alliance Bancorp merged into Charter One Financial, Inc. 7/2/2001
(See Charter One Financial, Inc.)

HINSDALE RACEWAY INC (NH)
Company went private in November 1987
Details not available

HIP CUISINE INC. (FL)
Name changed to Nature's Best Brands, Inc. 06/06/2018

HIP ENERGY CORP (BC)
SEC revoked common stock registration 04/05/2016

HIP INTERACTIVE CORP (ON)
Filed an assignment under the Bankruptcy and Insolvency Act 07/11/2005
Stockholders' equity unlikely

HIPCRICKET INC (DE)
Plan of reorganization under Chapter 11 Federal Bankruptcy proceedings effective 05/15/2015
No stockholders' equity

HIPEAK INTL CORP (CO)
Name changed to SSF Inc. (CO) 08/12/1987
SSF Inc. (CO) reorganized in Pennsylvania as Micro Diagnostics Corp. 07/31/1989

HIPOINT INVESTMENTS, LTD. (OK)
Company reported out of business 03/23/2001
Details not available

HIPOTRONICS INC (DE)
Common 10¢ par split (2) for (1) by issuance of (1) additional share 9/21/81
Common 10¢ par split (3) for (2) by issuance of (0.5) additional share 7/10/88
Acquired by Hubbell Inc. 11/20/92
Each share Common 10¢ par exchanged for $22.21 cash

HIPP INTL INC (UT)
Name changed to Assembly & Maunufacturing Systems Corp. 04/12/1995
Assembly & Manufacturing Systems Corp. recapitalized as American Ship Inc. 09/05/1997 which name changed to Petshealth, Inc. 05/20/1998
(See Petshealth, Inc.)

HIPSO MULTIMEDIA INC (FL)
Recapitalized as Buildablock Corp. 03/07/2012
Each share Common $0.00001 par exchanged for (0.125) share Common $0.00001 par

HIPSTYLE COM INC (FL)
Name changed to Security Intelligence Technologies, Inc. 03/26/2002
(See Security Intelligence Technologies, Inc.)

HIRAM WALKER-CONSUMERS HOME LTD. (ON)
See - Walker (Hiram)-Consumers Home Ltd.

HIRAM WALKER-GOODERHAM & WORTS LTD. (CANADA)
See - Walker (Hiram)-Gooderham & Worts Ltd.

HIRAM WALKER RESOURCES LTD. (ON)
See - Walker (Hiram) Resources Ltd.

HIRAM WALKER'S LTD.
See - Walker's (Hiram), Ltd.

HIRE INTL INC (DE)
Recapitalized as TruLan Resources Inc. 11/20/2012
Each share Common $0.001 par exchanged for (0.001) share Common $0.001 par
TruLan Resources Inc. recapitalized as Trinity Resources Inc. 09/18/2015

HIREL HLDGS INC (FL)
Recapitalized as Accel Energy Group Inc. 05/02/2005
Each share Common $0.001 par exchanged for (0.002) share Common $0.001 par
Accel Energy Group Inc. recapitalized as Power-Save Energy Corp.
01/09/2006 which name changed to Disability Access Corp. (DE) 11/01/2006 which reorganized in Nevada 11/30/2006
(See Disability Access Corp. (NV))

HIRERIGHT INC (DE)
Merged into US Investigations Services, LLC 08/21/2008
Each share Common 1¢ par exchanged for $19.75 cash

HIRES (CHARLES E.) CO. (DE)
Each share Class B Common no par exchanged for (3) shares Capital Stock $1 par in 1940
Assets sold and liquidation completed 11/1/60

HIROSE GROUP LTD (MB)
Cease trade order effective 08/01/1991
Stockholders' equity unlikely

HIRSCH (P.N.) & CO. (MO)
Thru voluntary exchange offer 99.65070% acquired by Interco, Inc. as of 1965
Public interest eliminated

HIRSCH CHEMIE LTD (VA)
Charter cancelled and proclaimed dissolved for failure to file reports 12/31/2003

HIRSCH INTL CORP (DE)
Class A Common 1¢ par split (5) for (4) by issuance of (0.25) additional share 07/24/1995
Class A Common 1¢ par split (5) for (4) by issuance of (0.25) additional share payable 07/22/1996 to holders of record 07/08/1996
Merged into Hirsch Holdings, Inc. 10/29/2009
Each share Class A Common 1¢ par exchanged for $0.31 cash

HIRSCHHORN DON INC (NY)
Stock Dividend - 150% 05/03/1971
Name changed to Enco Products Inc. 04/13/1979

HIRTS AL SANDWICH SALOONS INC (TN)
Name changed to Carolingian Corp. 10/28/1970

HISKERR GOLD MINES, LTD. (ON)
Charter cancelled for default in filing returns 04/11/1973

HISLOP GOLD MINES LTD.
Recapitalized as Hislop Mines Ltd. 00/00/1944
Each share Capital Stock exchanged for (0.33333333) share Capital Stock
(See Hislop Mines Ltd.)

HISLOP MINES LTD. (ON)
Charter surrendered 00/00/1960
No stockholders' equity

HISOFT TECHNOLOGY INTL LTD (CAYMAN ISLANDS)
Stock Dividend - 36.22% payable 11/09/2012 to holders of record 11/08/2012
Under plan of merger name changed to Pactera Technology International Ltd. 11/13/2012
(See Pactera Technology International Ltd.)

HISPANIC BROADCASTING CORP (DE)
Common $0.001 par split (2) for (1) by issuance of (1) additional share payable 6/15/2000 to holders of record 6/5/2000
Merged into Univision Communications, Inc. 9/22/2003
Each share Common $0.001 par exchanged for (0.85) share Class A Common 1¢ par
(See Univision Communications, Inc.)

HISPANIC EXPRESS INC (DE)
Company terminated common stock registration and is no longer public as of 09/11/2002

HISPANIC TELEVISION NETWORK INC (DE)
Plan of reorganization under Chapter 11 Federal Bankruptcy Code effective 7/7/2003
No stockholders' equity

HISPANICA INTL DELIGHTS AMER INC (DE)
Name changed to Life on Earth, Inc. 02/20/2018

HISTORIC GEORGETOWN, INC. (DE)
Charter cancelled and declared inoperative and void for non-payment of taxes 03/01/1984

HISTORIC HARDER HALL INC (FL)
Recapitalized as Historic Hotel Holding Inc. 02/10/1997
Each share Common $0.001 par exchanged for (0.01) share Common $0.001 par
Historic Hotel Holding Inc. name changed to Windfall Ventures of Nevis, Inc. 07/18/2002
(See Windfall Ventures of Nevis, Inc.)

HISTORIC HOTEL HLDG INC (FL)
Name changed to Windfall Ventures of Nevis, Inc. 07/18/2002
(See Windfall Ventures of Nevis, Inc.)

HISTORIC HOUSING FOR SENIORS II LIMITED PARTNERSHIP (DE)
Filed Certificate of Cancellation 06/01/2002
Details not available

HISTORIC PRESERVATION PPTYS L P TAX CR FD (DE)
Completely liquidated 12/31/1999
Details not available

HISTORIC PRESERVATION PPTYS LTD PARTNERSHIP (DE)
Completely liquidated 09/00/2006
Details not available

HISTORIC SMITHVILLE INNS INC (NJ)
Stock Dividend - 100% 4/13/73
Name changed to Smithville Liquidating Corp. 8/30/74
(See Smithville Liquidating Corp.)

HISTORICAL AUTOGRAPHS U S A INC (DE)
Common $0.001 par split (2) for (1) by issuance of (1) additional share payable 10/13/2003 to holders of record 10/6/2003 Ex date - 10/21/2003
Name changed to Arbios Systems, Inc. (NV) 10/30/2003
Arbios Systems, Inc. (NV) reincorporated in Delaware 7/25/2005

HISWAY RES CORP (BC)
Recapitalized as International Bioremediation Services Inc. 05/21/1993
Each share Common no par exchanged for (0.33333333) share Common no par
International Bioremediation Services Inc. recapitalized as IBIS Ventures Inc. 02/24/2000 which name changed to Tranzcom Security Networks Inc. 12/12/2001 which name changed to Tranzcom China Security Networks Inc. 06/25/2004 which recapitalized as Pacific Link Mining Corp. 09/12/2007

HITACHI CABLE LTD (JAPAN)
Merged into Hitachi Metals, Ltd. 07/01/2013
Each ADR for Ordinary exchanged for (0.17) ADR for Ordinary

HITACHI KOKUSAI ELEC INC (JAPAN)
ADR agreement terminated 07/05/2018
Each ADR for Ordinary exchanged for $56.77148 cash

FINANCIAL INFORMATION, INC.

HITCO (CA)
Merged into Armco Steel Corp.
12/31/1969
Each share Conv. Preferred Ser. A no par exchanged for (0.9) share $2.10 Conv. Preferred no par
Each share Common no par exchanged for (1) share $2.10 Conv. Preferred no par
Armco Steel Corp. name changed to Armco Inc. 07/01/1978 which merged into AK Steel Holding Corp. 09/30/1999

HITCOM CORP (DE)
Each share Common $0.001 par exchanged for (0.25) share Common $0.004 par 01/24/1997
Charter cancelled and declared inoperative and void for non-payment of taxes 03/01/2002

HITEC CORP (NV)
Recapitalized as Lead Innovation Corp. 03/27/2018
Each share Common $0.001 par exchanged for (0.00125) share Common $0.001 par

HITEC DEV CORP (BC)
Struck off register and declared dissolved for failure to file returns 00/00/1982

HITECH ENGR CO (DE)
Reorganized 12/15/87
Reorganized from (CO) to under the laws of (DE) 12/15/87
Each share Common $0.001 par exchanged for (0.1) share Common $0.001 par
Charter cancelled and declared inoperative and void for non-payment of taxes 6/24/92

HITECH INVT INC (DE)
Name changed to 5 Star Living Online, Inc. 04/02/1999
5 Star Living Online, Inc. name changed to Viral Genetics, Inc. 11/20/2001 which recapitalized as VG Life Sciences Inc. 11/27/2012

HITECH RES CORP (DE)
Each share old Common $0.0001 par exchanged for (20) shares new Common $0.0001 par 09/02/2000
Recapitalized as Billy Martin's USA Inc. 11/01/2001
Each share new Common $0.0001 par exchanged for (0.02) share Common $0.0001 par
Billy Martin's USA Inc. name changed to Real American Brands, Inc. 01/14/2008 which recapitalized as Real American Capital Corp. 06/17/2011

HITK CORP (DE)
Charter cancelled and declared inoperative and void for non-payment of franchise taxes 3/1/2000

HITOX CORP AMER (DE)
Name changed to TOR Minerals International Inc. 5/10/2000

HITSGALORE COM INC (FL)
Name changed to Diamond Hitts Production, Inc. (FL) 05/01/2001
Diamond Hitts Production, Inc. (FL) reincorporated in Nevada 09/04/2001
(See Diamond Hitts Production, Inc.)

HITTITE MICROWAVE CORP (DE)
Acquired by Analog Devices, Inc. 07/22/2014
Each share Common 1¢ par exchanged for $78 cash

HITTMAN ASSOC INC (DE)
Name changed to Hittman Corp. 04/25/1970
Hittman Corp. assets transferred to Hittman Corp. Liquidation Trust 11/21/1983
(See Hittman Corp. Liquidation Trust)

HITTMAN CORP. LIQUIDATION TRUST (DE)
Liquidation completed
Each Unit of Bene. Int. received third distribution of $2.10 cash 12/5/83
Each Unit of Bene. Int. received fourth and final distribution of $1.938056 cash 2/22/85
(See Hittman Corp. for previous distributions)

HITTMAN CORP (DE)
Common 10¢ par split (3) for (2) by issuance of (0.5) additional share 5/15/81
In process of liquidation
Each share Common 10¢ par received initial distribution of $11 cash 1/5/83
Each share Common 10¢ par received second distribution of $0.90 cash 7/15/83
Assets transferred to Hittman Corp. Liquidation Trust 11/21/83
Certificates requested to be surrendered 3/15/84
(See Hittman Corp. Liquidation Trust)

HIV-VAC INC (NV)
Each share old Common no par exchanged for (0.01) share new Common no par 07/24/2001
Name changed to Grupo International, Inc. 10/28/2010

HIXON GOLD RES INC (AB)
Name changed to Aloak Corp. 03/15/2001
Aloak Corp. name changed to Okalla Corp. 06/27/2006 which recapitalized as SportsClick Inc. 07/10/2008

HIXON PLACERS, INC. (WA)
Charter cancelled and proclaimed dissolved for failure to pay fees 7/1/75

HIXON-QUESNELLE PLACER LTD.
Dissolved 00/00/1948
Details not available

HJSI BOZEMAN I LLC (FL)
Accredited Investors Class A Equity Units called for redemption at $3,288.429033 on 09/23/2013

HK INTL GROUP INC (NV)
Name changed to Hygeialand Biomedical Corp. 07/11/2013
Hygeialand Biomedical Corp. name changed to Angstron Holdings Corp. 08/19/2013 which name changed to HK Graphene Technology Corp. 07/31/2015

HK-TVB LTD (HONG KONG)
Name changed to TVE (Holdings) Ltd. 05/30/1989
(See TVE (Holdings) Ltd.)

HL VENTURES INC (NV)
Name changed to Urban Barns Foods Inc. 08/19/2009

HL&P CAP TR I (DE)
Issue Information - 10,000,000 TR PFD SECS SER A 8.125% offered at $25 per share on 1/30/97
8.125% Trust Preferred Securities Ser. A called for redemption at $25 on 1/20/2004

HLH PETE CORP (TX)
Each share Capital Stock 1¢ par exchanged for (1/3) share Capital Stock 3¢ par 11/10/80
Merged out of existence 12/14/89
Details not available

HLHK WORLD GROUP INC (NV)
Name changed to TrimFast Group, Inc. 09/04/1998
TrimFast Group, Inc. recapitalized as eDollars Inc. 11/21/2006 which recapitalized as Forex Inc. 06/18/2007 which name changed to Petrogulf Inc. 03/26/2008 which name changed to Novagant Corp. 01/02/2014

HLI CORP. (NJ)
Liquidation completed
Each share Common 25¢ par stamped to indicate initial distribution of (0.1557) share Air Reduction Co., Inc. Common no par 03/24/1964
Each share Common 25¢ (Stamped) exchanged for second and final distribitition of (0.0245) share Air Reduction Co., Inc. Common $1 par 06/06/1967
Air Reduction Co., Inc. name changed to Airco, Inc. (NY) 10/01/1971 which reincorporated in Delaware 08/03/1977
(See Airco, Inc. (DE))

HLM DESIGN INC (DE)
Issue Information - 1,200,000 shares COM offered at $6 per share on 06/16/98
Plan of reorganization under Chapter 11 Federal Bankruptcy Code effective 1/4/2006
No stockholders' equity

HLS INDS (CA)
Common no par split (2) for (1) by issuance of (1) additional share payable 10/01/1976
Charter suspended for failure to file reports and pay fees 09/01/1978

**HLS SYS INTL, LTD.
(BRITISH VIRGIN ISLANDS)**
Name changed to Hollysys Automation Technologies, Ltd. 07/17/2009

HLT ENERGIES INC (CANADA)
Voluntary assignment of assets made to creditors 09/17/2009
Details not available

HLT ENERGIES 2006 INC (CANADA)
Name changed to HLT Energies Inc. 02/28/2007
(See HLT Energies Inc.)

HLTH CORP (DE)
Merged into WebMD Health Corp. 10/23/2009
Each share Common $0.0001 par exchanged for (0.4444) share Common 1¢ par
(See WebMD Health Corp.)

HLV TRADING CORP (WY)
Each share old Common $0.0001 par exchanged for (42) shares new Common $0.0001 par 02/15/2005
Name changed to X-tra Petroleum 08/30/2006
X-tra Petroleum recapitalized as Xtra Energy Corp. 11/05/2010

HLX RES LTD (BC)
Recapitalized as Emperor Gold Corp. 03/30/1992
Each share Common no par exchanged for (0.2) share Common no par
Emperor Gold Corp. name changed to Emgold Mining Corp. 08/01/1997

HMC HEALTHGARD MARKETING CORP (BC)
Recapitalized as Reward Mining Corp. 08/07/1996
Each share Common no par exchanged for (0.2) share Common no par
Reward Mining Corp. name changed to Riverdance Resources Corp. 03/11/1998 which recapitalized as Luminex Ventures Inc. 05/26/1999 which recapitalized as Lateegra Resources Corp. 06/12/2002 which recapitalized as Lateegra Gold Corp. 01/12/2006 which merged into Excellon Resources Inc. (BC) 08/05/2011 which reincorporated in Ontario 06/05/2012

HMD, INC. (TX)
Charter forfeited for failure to pay taxes 2/22/82

HMG DIGITAL TECHNOLOGIES CORP (DE)
Name changed to Allied Digital Technologies Corp. 1/11/95
(See Allied Digital Technologies Corp.)

HMG PPTY INVS INC (DE)
Name changed to HMG/Courtland Properties, Inc. 09/01/1987

HMG WORLDWIDE CORP (DE)
Chapter 11 Bankruptcy proceedings dismissed 08/28/2003
No stockholders' equity

HMH CHINA INVTS LTD (ON)
Reincorporated under the laws of Bermuda 12/21/95

HMI INDS INC (DE)
Merged into Ace Distribution Ltd. 11/21/2006
Each share Common $1 par exchanged for $0.54 cash

HMK BETA LTD (NY)
Adjudicated bankrupt 10/17/78
Stockholders' equity unlikely

HMM INVT GROUP INC (NV)
Name changed to Infrastructure Technologies, Inc. 04/27/1998
Infrastructure Technologies, Inc. name changed to @tventureworks Inc. 04/03/2000 which name changed to Underground Solutions, Inc. 01/30/2001
(See Underground Solutions, Inc.)

HMO AMER INC (NV)
Merged into United HealthCare Corp. 08/31/1993
Each share Common 1¢ par exchanged for (0.64) share Common 1¢ par
United HealthCare Corp. name changed to UnitedHealth Group Inc. (MN) 03/01/2000 which reincorporated in Delaware 07/01/2015

HMO INTL (CA)
Merged into INA Corp. 12/19/78
Each share Common 10¢ par exchanged for (4/9) share $1.90 Conv. Preferred Ser. C $1 par or (0.23) share Common $1 par
INA Corp. merged into Cigna Corp. 4/1/82

HMR WORLD ENTERPRISES INC (BC)
Struck off register and declared dissolved for failure to file returns 06/17/1994

HMS HLDGS CORP (NY)
Common 1¢ par split (3) for (1) by issuance of (2) additional shares payable 08/16/2011 to holders of record 07/22/2011 Ex date - 08/17/2011
Reincorporated under the laws of Delaware 07/23/2013

HMSR INC (DE)
Recapitalized as Point Therapeutics Inc. 03/15/2002
Each share Common 1¢ par exchanged for (0.1) share Common 1¢ par
Point Therapeutics Inc. recapitalized as DARA BioSciences, Inc. 02/13/2008 which merged into Midatech Pharma PLC 12/04/2015

HMT TECHNOLOGY CORP (DE)
Merged into Komag, Inc. 10/2/2000
Each share Common $0.001 par exchanged for (0.9094) share Common 1¢ par
(See Komag, Inc.)

HMV GROUP PLC
12.875% Preference called for redemption at $1,898.05 on 6/28/2002

HMW INDS INC (PA)
Merged into Clabir Corp. 3/7/84
Each share Common $1 par

exchanged for $47 principal amount of 14-1/2% Subordinated Debentures due 3/1/2004

HMZ METALS INC (CANADA)
Each share old Common no par exchanged for (0.2) share new Common no par 09/01/2009
Dissolved for non-compliance 05/17/2012

HNB BANCORP INC (PA)
Merged into Riverview Financial Corp. (Old) 12/31/2008
Each share Common 8¢ par exchanged for (2.52) shares Common 50¢ par
Riverview Financial Corp. (Old) merged into Riverview Financial Corp. (New) 11/01/2013

HNB CORP. (LA)
Acquired by Premier Bancorp, Inc. 11/30/95
Each share Common no par exchanged for (13.61386) shares Common no par and $178.07 cash
Premier Bancorp, Inc. merged into Banc One Corp. 1/2/96 which merged into Bank One Corp. 10/2/98 which merged into J.P. Morgan Chase & Co. 12/31/2000 which name changed to JPMorgan Chase & Co. 7/20/2004

HNB FINL GROUP (CA)
Merged into First Bank of St. Louis (St. Louis, MO) 4/28/95
Each share Common $5 par exchanged for $10.90 cash

HNC MTG & RLTY INVS (MA)
Name changed to Westport Co. 10/18/77
Westport Co. name changed to CenTrust Trust 7/17/84
(See CenTrust Trust)

HNC SOFTWARE INC (DE)
Common no par split (2) for (1) by issuance of (1) additional share payable 04/03/1996 to holders of record 03/18/1996
Each share Common no par received distribution of (1.465) shares Retek Inc. Common no par payable 09/29/2000 to holders of record 09/15/2000
Merged into Fair, Isaac & Co., Inc. 08/05/2002
Each share Common no par exchanged for (0.519) share Common 1¢ par
Fair, Isaac & Co., Inc. name changed to Fair Isaac Corporation 04/01/2003

HNR VENTURES INC (ON)
Recapitalized as RMM Ventures Inc. (ON) 06/06/2006
Each share Common no par exchanged for (0.1) share Common no par
RMM Ventures Inc. (ON) reorganized in Alberta as PowerComm Inc. 12/31/2006 which name changed to PetroCorp Group Inc. 12/23/2009

HNZ GROUP INC (CANADA)
Common reclassified as Common & Variable Vtg. Shares 05/19/2016
Variable Vtg. Shares reclassified as Common & Variable Vtg. Shares 05/19/2016
Note: Non-Canadian holders hold Variable Vtg. Shares
Acquired by 2075568 Alberta ULC 01/03/2018
Each Common & Variable Vtg. Share exchanged for $18.70 cash
Note: Unexchanged certificates will be cancelled and become without value 01/03/2024

HOAN PRODS LTD (NY)
Common 1¢ par changed to $0.005 par and (1) additional share issued 01/07/1981
Common $0.005 par split (2) for (1) by issuance of (1) additional share 07/22/1983
Merged into Lifetime-Hoan Inc. 09/05/1990
Each share Common $0.005 par exchanged for $1.25 cash

HOBAM INC (NY)
Merged into 40 Anderson Road, Inc. 02/04/1981
Each share Class A 6¢ par exchanged for $2.50 cash

HOBART CORP (OH)
Merged into Dart & Kraft, Inc. 04/29/1981
Each share Common no par exchanged for $40 cash

HOBART FED SVGS & LN ASSN (IN)
Name changed to HFS Bank, F.S.B. (Hobart, IN) 07/14/1993
HFS Bank, F.S.B. (Hobart, IN) merged into MainSource Financial Group, Inc. 05/24/2006 which merged into First Financial Bancorp 04/02/2018

HOBART MANUFACTURING CO. (OH)
Common no par changed to Class A no par in 1934
Each share Class A no par exchanged for (3) shares Common $10 par in 1947
Common $10 par changed to no par and (1) additional share issued 5/25/62
Common no par split (2) for (1) by issuance of (1) additional share 11/30/66
Common no par split (2) for (1) by issuance of (1) additional share 12/15/72
Stock Dividend - 100% 8/15/57
Name changed to Hobart Corp. 4/29/74
(See Hobart Corp.)

HOBBS-WALL & CO.
Liquidation completed in 1944

HOBE SOUND NATL BK (HOBE SOUND, FL)
Merged into Barnett Banks of Florida, Inc. 5/13/81
Each share Common Capital Stock $10 par exchanged for $36.01 cash

HOBERG PAPER & FIBRE CO.
Name changed to Hoberg Paper Mills, Inc. 00/00/1936
Hoberg Paper Mills, Inc. name changed to Charmin Paper Mills, Inc. 00/00/1953 which merged into Procter & Gamble Co. 01/17/1957

HOBERG PAPER MILLS, INC. (WI)
Each share old Common no par exchanged for (5) shares new Common no par 00/00/1937
Each share new Common no par exchanged for (2) shares Common $5 par 00/00/1952
Name changed to Charmin Paper Mills, Inc. 00/00/1953
Charmin Paper Mills, Inc. merged into Procter & Gamble Co. 01/17/1957

HOBO CREEK COPPERMINES LTD (BC)
Name changed to Storm Cloud Development Corp. 02/01/1977
(See Storm Cloud Development Corp.)

HOBOKEN LAND & IMPROVEMENT CO.
Dissolved in 1946

HOBOKEN RAILROAD & TERMINAL CO.
Property sold 00/00/1931
Details not available

HOBROUGH LTD (CANADA)
Name changed to Gestalt International Ltd. 04/19/1974
Gestalt International Ltd. reorganized as Northway-Gestalt Corp.

03/02/1979 which was acquired by Spar Aerospace Ltd. 09/19/1981
(See Spar Aerospace Ltd.)

HOBSON OIL CO INC (CA)
Recapitalized as Arthritis Clinics International, Inc. 6/2/72
Each share Capital Stock 10¢ par exchanged for (0.2) share Capital Stock 5¢ par
(See Arthritis Clinics International, Inc.)

HOCHENG CORP (TAIWAN)
Stock Dividends - 15% payable 10/19/1996 to holders of record 07/19/1996; 5% payable 11/04/1997 to holders of record 07/29/1997
GDR agreement terminated 11/22/2002
Each 144A GDR for Common exchanged for $1.106334 cash

HOCKANNUS MILLS
Reorganized as Greendale Products Co. in 1927
Details not available

HOCKEY CO (DE)
Under plan of merger each share Common 1¢ par exchanged for (1) share Non-Vtg. Exchangeable Common 1¢ par 06/11/2003
Acquired by Reebok International Ltd. 06/23/2004
Each share Non-Vtg. Exchangeable Common 1¢ par exchanged for CAD $21.25 cash

HOCKEY CO HLDGS INC (CANADA)
Acquired by Reebok International Ltd. 06/23/2004
Each share Common no par exchanged for $21.25 cash

HOCKEY HOSE ATHLETIC INC (AB)
Recapitalized as Tri-Northern Pacific Resources Ltd. 10/4/93
Each share Common no par exchanged for (0.5) share Common no par

HOCKING GLASS CO.
Assets acquired by Anchor Hocking Glass Corp. 12/31/1937
Details not available

HOCKING VALLEY OIL CO. (OH)
Charter revoked for failure to file reports and pay fees 08/27/1914

HOCKING VALLEY PRODUCTS CO.
Reorganized as Greendale Products Co. in 1927
Details not available

HOCKING VALLEY RAILWAY
Acquired by Chesapeake & Ohio Railway Co. in 1930
Details not available

HODGDON SHOOTING RANGES, INC. (KS)
Voluntarily dissolved 11/14/72
Details not available

HODGES WILLIAM & CO INC (PA)
Merged into Falcon Products, Inc. (DE) 2/1/75
Each share Common 10¢ par exchanged for $4 cash

HODGINS AUCTIONEERS INC (AB)
Each share old Common no par exchanged for (0.5) share new Common no par 07/02/2015
Each share new Common no par exchanged again for (0.25) share new Common no par 10/02/2015
Went private 01/18/2016
Each share new Common no par exchanged for $0.0001 cash
Note: Holdings of (249,999) or fewer shares were cancelled and are without value

HODGMAN RUBBER CO. (MA)
Name changed to HRC Inc. 10/16/69

HODGSON BLDG CORP (MN)
Completely liquidated 12/31/1969
Each share Capital Stock no par exchanged for first and final distribution of $192 cash

HODGSON HOUSES INC (MA)
Each share Preferred no par exchanged for (60) shares Common $1 par 11/19/64
Out of business in 1991
Details not available

HODY'S RESTAURANTS, INC. (CA)
Assets sold for benefit of creditors 02/00/1970
No stockholders' equity

HOE R & CO INC. (NY)
Each share Class A $10 par exchanged for (1) share Class A $10 par and (4) shares Class B 10¢ par 00/00/1947
Each 144A GDR for Class A $10 par exchanged for (4) shares Class A $2.50 par and (2) shares Common $1 par 00/00/1950
Each share Class B 10¢ par exchanged for (0.5) share Class A $2.50 par, (1) share Common $1 par and $3 cash 00/00/1950
Each share Common $1 par exchanged for (1) share Common $1 par 00/00/1950
Common $1 par split (3) for (1) by issuance of (2) additional shares 05/15/1968
Reorganized under Chapter X Federal Bankruptcy Act 03/31/1978
Each (1.2) shares Class A $2.50 par exchanged for (1) share old Common 1¢ par
No Common $1 par stockholders' equity
Acquired by Pacific Saw & Knife Co. 00/00/1984
Details not available

HOECHST A G (GERMANY)
Each old ADR for Common Capital Stock DM50 par exchanged for (2) new ADR's for Common Capital DM50 par 02/09/1984
Note: Unexchanged shares will receive cash upon surrender after 12/09/1984
Each ADR for Ordinary DM50 par exchanged for (1) Sponsored ADR for Ordinary DM50 par 09/24/1997
Each Sponsored ADR for Ordinary DM50 par received distribution of (0.1) Celanese AG Registered Share no par payable 10/25/1999 to holders of record 10/22/1999
Ex date - 10/26/1999
Stock Dividend - 400% payable 06/18/1996 to holders of record 06/07/1996
Merged into Aventis 12/15/1999
Each Sponsored ADR for Ordinary DM50 par exchanged for (1.333) Sponsored ADR's for Ordinary Fr 25 par
Aventis merged into Sanofi-Aventis 01/03/2005

HOENIG GROUP INC (DE)
Merged into Investment Technology Group, Inc. (New) 09/03/2002
Each share Common 1¢ par exchanged for $11.35 cash and a Contingent Payment Right
Note: Each share Common 1¢ par received initial escrow payment of $0.373711 cash 12/00/2004
Each share Common 1¢ par received second and final escrow payment of $0.07644303 cash 02/08/2007

HOERNER BOXES, INC. (DE)
Common and Class B Common $1 par changed to 50¢ par and (1) additional share issued 3/11/65
Merged into Hoerner Waldorf Corp. 5/17/66
Each share Common 50¢ par exchanged for (1) share Common 50¢ par
Each share Class B Common 50¢ par exchanged for (1) share Common 50¢ par

Hoerner Waldorf Corp. merged into Champion International Corp. 2/24/77 which merged into International Paper Co. 6/20/2000

HOERNER BOXES OF SAND SPRINGS, INC. (DE)
Merged into Hoerner Boxes, Inc. 11/01/1954
Details not available

HOERNER WALDORF CORP (DE)
Common 50¢ par changed to 25¢ par and (1) additional share issued 4/8/74
Merged into Champion International Corp. 2/24/77
Each share Common 25¢ par exchanged for (0.95) share Common 50¢ par
$4 Conv. Preferred Ser. A $1.50 par called for redemption 3/31/77
Public interest eliminated

HOESCH AKTIENGESELLSCHAFT (GERMANY)
ADR agreement terminated 6/20/96
Each ADR for Ordinary DM50 par exchanged for $195.63 cash

HOESCH WERKE A.G. (GERMANY)
Name changed to Hoesch Aktiengesellschaft 4/29/59
(See Hoesch Aktiengesellschaft)

HOFFMAN ELECTRS CORP (CA)
Common 50¢ par split (2) for (1) by issuance of (1) additional share 6/25/59
Merged into Gould Inc. 1/27/78
Each share Common 50¢ par exchanged for (0.28) share Common $4 par
(See Gould Inc.)

HOFFMAN EXPL & MINERALS LTD (ON)
Merged into Consolidated Thompson-Lundmark Gold Mines Ltd. 01/16/1986
Each share Common no par exchanged for (0.31454651) share Common no par
Consolidated Thompson-Lundmark Gold Mines Ltd. name changed to Consolidated Thompson Iron Mines Ltd. 08/24/2006
(See Consolidated Thompson Iron Mines Ltd.)

HOFFMAN INTERNATIONAL CORP. (DE)
Common $1 par changed to 50¢ par and (1) additional share issued 07/29/1960
Common 50¢ par changed to 40¢ par and (0.25) additional share issued 07/31/1962
Name changed to Brewster Industries, Inc. 10/02/1967
(See Brewster Industries, Inc.)

HOFFMAN LEASING & SVC CORP (NY)
Name changed to Interallied Resources Corp. 5/27/71
Interallied Resources Corp. recapitalized as Tri Tec Plastics Corp. 2/24/84 which merged into Secom General Corp. 12/17/91
(See Secom General Corp.)

HOFFMAN PRODS INC (NJ)
Adjudicated bankrupt 07/31/1973
Stockholders' equity unlikely

HOFFMAN RADIO CORP. (CA)
Each share Common $1 par exchanged for (1.5) shares Common 66-2/3¢ par in March 1950
Each share Common 66-2/3¢ par exchanged for (1-1/3) shares Common 50¢ par in September 1950
Name changed to Hoffman Electronics Corp. in 1954
Hoffman Electronics Corp. merged into Gould Inc. 1/27/78
(See Gould Inc.)

HOFFMAN RES CORP (CO)
Name changed to Alasco Gold & Oil Corp. 4/23/74
Alasco Gold & Oil Corp. reorganized as Talkeetna Gold Exploration Ltd. 8/15/75 which recapitalized as Founders Equity Corp. 1/8/86
(See Founders Equity Corp.)

HOFFMAN ROSNER CORP (DE)
Merged into Hoffman Group, Inc. 05/27/1976
Each share Common $1 par exchanged for $4 cash

HOFFMAN-TAFF, INC. (MO)
Name changed to Hoffman-Taff Holding Co. 12/12/69
Hoffman-Taff Holding Co. liquidated for Syntex Corp. 1/21/71
(See Syntex Corp.)

HOFFMAN-TAFF HOLDING CO. (MO)
Liquidation completed
Each share Common $1 par exchanged for initial distribution of (0.106791) share Syntex Corp. Common $1 par 12/12/69
Each share Common $1 par received second and final distribution of (0.004545) share Syntex Corp. Common $1 par 1/21/71
(See Syntex Corp.)

HOFMAN LABORATORIES, INC. (NJ)
Name changed to HLI Corp. 3/24/64
HLI Corp. completely liquidated for Air Reduction Co., Inc. Common $1 par 6/6/67
Air Reduction Co., Inc. name changed to Airco, Inc. (N.Y.) 10/1/71 which reincorporated in Delaware 8/3/77
(See Airco, Inc. (Del.))

HOGAN FAXIMILE CORP (DE)
Each share Common 10¢ par exchanged for (0.01) share Common $10 par 07/13/1970
Merged into Telautograph Corp. 09/05/1980
Each share Common $10 par exchanged for $323.98 cash

HOGAN MINES LTD (BC)
Recapitalized as Bow River Resources Ltd. 02/09/1972
Each share Common no par exchanged for (0.2) share Common no par
Bow River Resources Ltd. recapitalized as Suneva Resources Ltd. 04/06/1979 which recapitalized as International Suneva Resources Ltd. 01/20/1989 which recapitalized as Nevsun Resources Ltd. 12/19/1991

HOGAN SYS INC (CA)
Common no par split (2) for (1) by issuance of (1) additional share 12/2/83
Merged into Continuum Co., Inc. 3/15/96
Each share Common 1¢ par exchanged for (0.315) share Common 10¢ par
Continuum Co., Inc. merged into Computer Sciences Corp. 8/1/96

HOGUET REAL ESTATE CORP. (NY)
Dissolved 11/24/58

HOH CORP (HI)
Name changed to Kuan Corp. 10/4/82
(See Kuan Corp.)

HOH WTR TECHNOLOGY CORP (CA)
Recapitalized as Electropure, Inc. 7/25/96
Each share Common 1¢ par exchanged for (0.1) share Common 1¢ par
Electropure, Inc. name chanhed to Micro Imaging Technology, Inc. 3/14/2006

HOJO HLDGS INC (DE)
Name changed to Senticore, Inc. 6/17/2003
Senticore, Inc. name changed to Integrative Health Technologies, Inc. 8/1/2006

HOKO EXPLS LTD (BC)
Name changed to ABDA International Holdings Corp. 02/26/1988
(See ABDA International Holdings Corp.)

HOKU SCIENTIFIC INC (DE)
Issue Information - 3,500,000 shares COM offered at $6 per share on 08/05/2005
Name changed to Hoku Corp. 03/25/2010

HOKURIKU BK LTD (JAPAN)
ADR agreement terminated 4/5/2004
Each ADR for Ordinary 50 Yen par exchanged for $13.574 cash
Note: Due to ADR's being unsponsored exchange rate may vary dependent upon depositary agent

HOKUTOU HLDGS INTL INC (NV)
Reincorporated 05/23/2014
Each share old Common $0.001 par exchanged for (0.00094073) share new Common $0.001 par 10/25/2013
State of incorporation changed from (CO) to (NV) 05/23/2014
Name changed to Platinum Pari-Mutuel Holdings, Inc. 12/09/2014
Platinum Pari-Mutuel Holdings, Inc. name changed to Point to Point Methodics, Inc. 04/27/2017

HOL-LAC GOLDMINES LTD (ON)
Name changed to Augusta Resource Corp. (ON) 07/04/1997
Augusta Resource Corp. (ON) reincorporated in Canada 06/28/1999 which merged into HudBay Minerals Inc. 09/23/2014

HOLA COMMUNICATIONS INC (NV)
Reorganized as Tamm Oil & Gas Corp. 11/13/2007
Each share Common $0.001 par exchanged for (15) shares Common $0.001 par

HOLAN (J.H.) CORP. (OH)
Merged into Ohio Brass Co. 11/17/58
Each share Common $1 par exchanged for (0.4487) share Common $1 par
Ohio Brass Co. merged into Hubbell (Harvey), Inc. 8/25/78 which name changed to Hubbell Inc. 5/12/86

HOLBERG MINES LTD (BC)
Recapitalized as World Cement Industries Inc. 10/02/1978
Each share Capital Stock $1 par exchanged for (1) share Capital Stock no par
World Cement Industries Inc. recapitalized as Topper Gold Corp. 07/05/1989 which recapitalized as Consolidated Topper Gold Corp. 04/13/2000 which name changed to Topper Resources Inc. (BC) 02/06/2002 which reincorporated in Alberta 05/03/2006 which name changed to Century Energy Ltd. (AB) 05/19/2006 which reincorporated in British Columbia 10/20/2016

HOLBOROUGH INVESTMENTS LTD. (CANADA)
Recapitalized as MICC Investments Ltd. 05/04/1972
Each share Common no par exchanged for (0.5) share Common no par
(See MICC Investments Ltd.)

HOLCIM ECUADOR S A (ECUADOR)
GDR agreement terminated 06/25/2007
Each 144A GDR for Ordinary exchanged for $55.7777 cash
Each Reg. S GDR for Ordinary exchanged for $55.7777 cash

HOLCIM LTD (SWITZERLAND)
ADR agreement terminated 04/27/2005
Each Sponsored ADR for Ordinary exchanged for $42.46964 cash
Stock Dividend - 5% payable 05/26/2009 to holders of record 05/11/2009 Ex date - 05/07/2009
Basis changed from 1:0.02 to 1:0.1 05/23/2001
Basis changed from 1:0.1 to 1:0.5 06/10/2003
Name changed to LafargeHolcim Ltd. 07/27/2015

HOLCO SECD MTG INVT III (CA)
Liquidation completed
Each Ltd. Partnership Int. exchanged for initial distribution of $0.97 cash 03/15/1990
Each Ltd. Partnership Int. received second distribution of $0.46 cash 07/16/1990
Each Ltd. Partnership Int. received third and final distribution of $3.80 cash 02/28/1992

HOLCOT CAP CORP (BC)
Name changed to Goldmember Minerals Inc. 07/21/2015
Goldmember Minerals Inc. name changed to GMV Minerals Inc. 03/13/2008

HOLDEN DAY INC (CA)
Assets transferred to Holden Day Liquidating Trust 4/15/92
(See Holden Day Liquidating Trust)

HOLDEN DAY LIQUIDATING TRUST (CA)
In process of liquidation
Each share Capital Stock $1 par exchanged for initial distribution of $0.20 cash 5/15/92
Note: Details on subsequent distribution(s), if any, are not available

HOLDEN-LEONARD CO., INC.
In process of dissolution in 1940

HOLDEN MANUFACTURING CO., LTD. (ON)
Name changed to Woods (S.E.)-Holden Ltd.-Woods (S.E.)-Holden Ltee. 05/17/1967
Woods (S.E.)-Holden Ltd.-Woods (S.E.)- Holden Ltee. name changed to Cantrend Industries Ltd.-Les Industries Cantrend Ltee. 05/28/1968
(See Cantrend Industries Ltd.-Les Industries Cantrend Ltee.)

HOLDER COMMUNICATIONS CORP (FL)
Name changed to GMX Communications Inc. 6/30/87
(See GMX Communications Inc.)

HOLDER INTL INDS INC (DE)
Chapter 11 bankruptcy proceedings converted to Chapter 7 on 03/29/1989
Stockholders' equity unlikely

HOLDERBANK FINANCIERE GLARIS LTD (SWITZERLAND)
Name changed to Holcim Ltd. 05/23/2001
(See Holcim Ltd.)

HOLDFAST NAT RES LTD (BC)
Completely liquidated 09/20/1972
No stockholders' equity

HOLDING CO FINL INVTS LAKAH GROUP S A E (EGYPT)
GDR agreement terminated 07/30/2009
Each Reg. S GDR for Ordinary exchanged for $0.552692 cash
Each 144A GDR for Ordinary exchanged for $0.552692 cash

HOLDING CONSOLIDATED GOLD MINES LTD.
Bankrupt in 1933

HOL-HOL FINANCIAL INFORMATION, INC.

HOLDING CORP. OF AMERICAN LITHOGRAPHIC CO., INC.
Name changed to Publication Corp. 00/00/1929
Publication Corp. merged into Crowell Collier & Macmillan, Inc. 05/31/1968 which name changed to Macmillan, Inc. 01/01/1973
(See Macmillan, Inc.)

HOLDING CORP AMER (IL)
Each share Class A Common $1 par exchanged for (0.2) share Class A Common $5 par 9/15/72
Reorganized under the laws of Delaware as HCA, Inc. and Class A Common $5 par reclassified as Common $1 par 12/21/78
HCA, Inc. (DE) merged into I.C.H. Corp. 10/14/82 which name changed to Southwestern Life Corp. (New) 6/15/94 which name changed to I.C.H. Corp. (New) 10/10/95
(See I.C.H. Corp. (New))

HOLDING MRSK JT STK CO (RUSSIA)
Name changed to Interregional Distribution Grid Companies Holding JSC 09/11/2009
Interregional Distribution Grid Companies Holding JSC name changed to JCS Russian Grids 05/07/2013 which name changed to JSC Rosseti 08/22/2014 which name changed to PJSC Rosseti 09/15/2015

HOLDINGS ENERGY INC (NV)
Name changed to Grillit, Inc. 04/22/2013

HOLDINGS OF U S GOVT SECS INC (FL)
Proclaimed dissolved for failure to file reports and pay fees 11/10/83

HOLDINGS US INC (DE)
Name changed to California Style Palms, Inc. 09/25/2013

HOLDMAR RED LAKE GOLD MINES, LTD. (ON)
Charter cancelled by default 08/18/1958

HOLEPROOF HOSIERY CO. (WI)
Each share 7% Preferred $100 par exchanged for (1) share 6-2/3% Preferred $60 par in 1933
Each share Common no par exchanged for (7.5) shares Common $5 par in September 1950
Name changed to Fowler Hosiery Co., Inc. 9/23/55
(See Fowler Hosiery Co., Inc.)

HOLFAST RUBBER CO., INC. (NY)
Liquidation completed 10/29/54

HOLIDAY AIRLS INC (CA)
Recapitalized as Holiday Resources, Inc. 05/30/1972
Each share Capital Stock $1 par exchanged for (0.25) share Common $1 par
(See Holiday Resources, Inc.)

HOLIDAY BANK (HOLIDAY, FL)
Name changed to Florida State Bank (Holiday, FL) 02/21/1989
(See Florida State Bank (Holiday, FL))

HOLIDAY BRANDS, INC. (DE)
Name changed to Holiday Coffee Corp. 00/00/1955
Holiday Coffee Corp. merged into Schroeder Industries, Inc. 05/11/1959 which name changed to Gold Ribbon Foods, Inc. 06/22/1966
(See Gold Ribbon Foods, Inc.)

HOLIDAY COFFEE CORP. (DE)
Merged into Schroeder Industries, Inc. on a (0.1) for (1) basis 05/11/1959
Schroeder Industries, Inc. name changed to Gold Ribbon Foods Inc. 06/22/1966
(See Gold Ribbon Foods Inc.)

HOLIDAY CORP (DE)
Conv. Special Stock Ser. A $1.12-1/2 par called for redemption 01/13/1987
Merged into Bass PLC 02/07/1990
Each share Common $1.50 par exchanged for (0.26626) Sponsored ADR for Ordinary 25p par and $30 cash
Bass PLC name changed to Six Continents PLC 07/31/2001
(See Six Continents PLC)

HOLIDAY GULF HOMES INC (MN)
Company terminated common stock registration and is no longer public as of 05/29/2002

HOLIDAY INDUSTRIES (UT)
Charter suspended for failure to pay taxes 09/30/1977

HOLIDAY INDS INC (TX)
Charter forfeited for failure to pay taxes 12/02/1985

HOLIDAY INNS INC (TN)
Common $1.50 par split (2) for (1) by issuance of (1) additional share 06/03/1969
Reincorporated under the laws of Delaware as Holiday Corp. 05/15/1985
Holiday Corp. merged into Bass PLC 02/07/1990 which name changed to Six Continents PLC 07/31/2001
(See Six Continents PLC)

HOLIDAY INNS OF AMERICA, INC. (TN)
Common $1.50 par split (3) for (2) by issuance of (0.5) additional share 4/10/61
Common $1.50 par split (2) for (1) by issuance of (1) additional share 11/17/61
Class A Common $1.50 par split (2) for (1) by issuance of (1) additional share 11/17/61
Common $1.50 par split (6) for (5) by issuance of (0.2) additional share 11/30/62
Class A Common $1.50 par split (6) for (5) by issuance of (0.2) additional share 11/30/62
Class A Common $1.50 par reclassified as Common $1.50 par 3/4/63
Common $1.50 par split (2) for (1) by issuance of (1) additional share 9/15/67
Name changed to Holiday Inns, Inc. 5/22/69
Holiday Inns, Inc. reorganized in Delaware as Holiday Corp. 5/15/85 which merged into Bass PLC 2/7/90 which name changed to Six Continents PLC 7/31/2001

HOLIDAY MINES, INC. (WA)
Charter revoked for failure to file reports and pay fees 7/1/61

HOLIDAY OIL & GAS CORP. (DE)
Name changed to White Star Oil Co. in 1957
(See White Star Oil Co.)

HOLIDAY ON LAKE LANIER (GA)
Involuntarily dissolved for failure to file annual reports 5/13/88

HOLIDAY PLASTICS, INC. (MO)
Adjudicated bankrupt and charter forfeited for failure to comply with corporation laws 1/1/61

HOLIDAY PRODUCTIONS (UT)
Reincorporated under the laws of Nevada as $5 Computer Software Store, Inc. 08/13/1992
$5 Computer Software Store, Inc. name changed to Wiz Technology, Inc. 06/30/1993 which recapitalized as Wireless Technologies Inc. 07/21/2005 which name changed to Mattman Specialty Vehicles, Inc. 12/14/2005 which name changed to Remote Surveillance Technologies, Inc. 01/11/2007 which name changed to Stratera, Inc. 07/15/2008 which recapitalized as Gulf West Investment Properties, Inc. 12/16/2009

HOLIDAY RESORTS INTL INC (OK)
Name changed to Rendezvous Trails of America, Inc. 06/29/1972
Rendezvous Trails of America, Inc. recapitalized as Rain Forest-Moose Ltd. 02/23/1996 which name changed to Aarow Environmental Group, Inc. 06/13/1997 which name changed to Aaro Broadband Wireless Communications, Inc. 09/25/2000
(See Aaro Broadband Wireless Communications, Inc.)

HOLIDAY RES INC (CA)
Plan of reorganization under Chapter 11 Federal Bankruptcy proceedings confirmed 07/09/1988
No stockholders' equity

HOLIDAY RV SUPERSTORES INC (FL)
Each share old Common 1¢ par exchanged for (0.1) share new Common 1¢ par 08/07/2002
Plan of reorganization under Chapter 11 Federal Bankruptcy Code effective 10/11/2004
No stockholders' equity

HOLIDAY SVCS INC (UT)
Involuntarily dissolved 08/01/1992

HOLIDAY SPORTSWEAR, INC. (KS)
Name changed to King Louie International, Inc. 3/21/62
(See King Louie International, Inc.)

HOLIDAY THEATRES INC (FL)
Merged into D&W Theatres, Inc. 03/03/1981
Each share Common 1¢ par exchanged for $0.11645 cash

HOLIDAY TRAILER LODGES OF OREGON, INC. (OR)
Name changed to Trailer Host of America, Inc. and Capital Stock $1 par changed to $2 par 08/01/1968
(See Trailer Host of America, Inc.)

HOLIDAY UNVL INC (MD)
Reorganized under the laws of Delaware as U.S. Health & Recreation, Inc. 05/31/1979
Each share Common $1 par exchanged for (4) shares Common 25¢ par
U.S. Health & Recreation, inc. name changed to U.S. Health Inc. 12/23/1981
(See U.S. Health Inc.)

HOLIDAY VEGAS INC (NV)
Name changed to Ark Energy Co., Inc. 9/2/82
(See Ark Energy Co., Inc.)

HOLISTIC SVCS CORP (FL)
Stock Dividend - 500% 6/4/81
Name changed to International Media Corp. 10/5/88
(See International Media Corp.)

HOLLAND CUSTARD & ICE CREAM, INC. (IN)
Name changed to Holland Dairies, Inc. 7/1/69
(See Holland Dairies, Inc.)

HOLLAND DAIRIES, INC. (IN)
Common no par and Class A Common no par split (3) for (1) by issuance of (2) additional shares respectively 9/1/69
Company went private 1/5/88
Details not available

HOLLAND FURNACE CO. (DE)
Reorganized 00/00/1939
Reorganized from (MI) to under the laws of (DE) 00/00/1939
Each share Preferred no par exchanged for (1) share Preferred $98 par
Each share Common no par exchanged for (1) share Common $10 par
Each share Common $10 par exchanged for (2) shares Common $5 par 00/00/1946
Common $5 par changed to 10¢ par 12/01/1965
Name changed to Athlone Industries, Inc. 05/24/1966
Athlone Industries, Inc. merged into Allegheny Ludlum Corp. 11/10/1993 which merged into Allegheny Teledyne Inc. 08/15/1996 which name changed to Allegheny Technologies Inc. 11/29/1999

HOLLAND-GASPE MINES LTD. (ON)
Charter surrendered 11/00/1973
No stockholders' equity

HOLLAND GLOBAL CAP CORP (ON)
Reorganized as Maplewood International Real Estate Investment Trust 09/23/2013
Each share Common no par exchanged for (0.125) Trust Unit
Note: Unexchanged certificates will be cancelled and become without value 09/23/2019

HOLLAND INDS INC (NV)
Name changed to U.S. Transportation Systems, Inc. 10/01/1990
U.S. Transportation Systems, Inc. name changed to Transportation Equities, Inc. 03/31/1998
(See Transportation Equities, Inc.)

HOLLAND LAKE SILVER MINES LTD. (ON)
Charter cancelled for failure to file reports and pay taxes 00/00/1969

HOLLAND LAND CO.
Liquidation completed in 1942

HOLLAND'S FAR EAST TEA, COFFEE & COCOA CO. (MA)
Charter cancelled for non-payment of taxes in 1933

HOLLANDER A & SON INC (DE)
Capital Stock no par changed to $5 par in 1933
Name changed to Philips Electronics, Inc. (DE) and Capital Stock $5 par reclassified as Common $5 par 7/31/57
Philips Electronics, Inc. (DE) reincorporated in Maryland as Philips Electronics & Pharmaceutical Industries Corp. 10/19/59 which name changed to Pepi, Inc. 2/17/69 which merged into North American Philips Corp. 10/31/73
(See North American Philips Corp.)

HOLLIDAYSBURG TR CO (HOLLIDAYSBURG, PA)
Merged into Penn Central Bancorp, Inc. 08/16/1985
Each share Common $2.50 par exchanged for (1) share Common $2.50 par
Penn Central Bancorp, Inc. merged into Omega Financial Corp. 01/28/1994 which merged into F.N.B. Corp. 04/01/2008

HOLLINGER ARGUS LTD (ON)
Conv. Class A Common no par reclassified as Common no par 01/23/1981
Conv. Class B Common no par reclassified as Common no par 01/23/1981
Merged into Hollinger Inc. 09/17/1985
Each share Common no par exchanged for (2.5) shares Common no par
(See Hollinger Inc.)

HOLLINGER CDN NEWSPAPERS LTD PARTNERSHIP (ON)
Each (25,000,000) old Units of Ltd. Partnership no par exchanged for (1) new Unit of Ltd. Partnership no par 03/17/2006
Note: In effect holders received

HOLLINGER CDN PUBG HLDGS INC (AB)
$0.737 cash per Unit and public interest was eliminated
Acquired by Hollinger International, Inc. 06/26/2000
Each Non-Vtg. Special Share no par exchanged for USD$8.88 cash

HOLLINGER CONSOLIDATED GOLD MINES, LTD. (ON)
Name changed to Hollinger Mines Ltd. 06/29/1968
Hollinger Mines Ltd. name changed to Hollinger Argus Ltd. 01/21/1980 which merged into Hollinger Inc. 09/17/1985
(See Hollinger Inc.)

HOLLINGER EASTN PUBG INC (AB)
Name changed to Hollinger Canadian Publishing Holdings Inc. 06/19/1997
(See Hollinger Canadian Publishing Holdings Inc.)

HOLLINGER INC (CANADA)
Common no par split (4) for (1) by issuance of (3) additional shares 05/22/1987
Each share Common no par exchanged for (1) Equity Unit 09/12/1997
Each Equity Unit exchanged for (1) share Retractable Common no par 06/01/1998
Non-Voting Exchangeable Preference Ser. 1 no par called for redemption at $4 plus $0.02 accrued dividends on 06/05/1998
Non-Voting Exchangeable Preference Ser. 3 no par called for redemption at $10 plus $0.419 accrued dividends on 06/11/2004
Filed petition under Companies' Creditors Arrangement Act 08/01/2007
Stockholders' equity unlikely

HOLLINGER INTL INC (DE)
9.75% Conv. Preferred Ser. B 1¢ par called for redemption at (1.6878) shares Class A Common 1¢ par on 01/03/2000
9.75% Preferred Increased Dividend Equity Security 1¢ par called for redemption at (0.84397) share Class A Common 1¢ par on 01/03/2000
Name changed to Sun-Times Media Group, Inc. 07/14/2006
(See Sun-Times Media Group, Inc.)

HOLLINGER MINES LTD. (ON)
Common $5 par reclassified as Conv. Class A Common no par 07/11/1974
Name changed to Hollinger Argus Ltd. 01/21/1980
Hollinger Argus Ltd. merged into Hollinger Inc. 09/17/1985
(See Hollinger Inc.)

HOLLINGFIELD CAP CORP (BC)
Name changed to PKI Innovations (Canada) Inc. 08/29/2001
PKI Innovations (Canada) Inc. recapitalized as Newton Ventures Inc. 06/07/2005 which recapitalized as Rusoro Mining Ltd. 11/09/2006

HOLLINGPORT VENTURE INC (BC)
Name changed to Changyu MedTech Ltd. 05/05/2009

HOLLINGSHEAD (R.M.) CO.
Merged into Hollingshead (R.M.) Corp. 00/00/1937
Details not available

HOLLINGSHEAD R M CORP (NJ)
Stock Dividend - 100% 05/31/1951
Acquired by Dayco Corp. (DE) 10/31/1969
Each share Common $1 par exchanged for $35 principal amount of 5-3/4% Conv. Subord. Debentures due 01/01/1994

HOLLINGSWORTH & WHITNEY CO. (MA)
Common no par exchanged (2) for (1) 00/00/1946
Merged into Scott Paper Co. 00/00/1954
Each share Common no par exchanged for (1.4) shares new Common no par
Scott Paper Co. merged into Kimberly-Clark Corp. 12/12/1995

HOLLIS-EDEN PHARMACEUTICALS INC (DE)
Name changed to Harbor BioSciences, Inc. 02/18/2010
Harbor BioSciences, Inc. name changed to Harbor Diversified, Inc. 02/28/2012

HOLLISTER TECHNOLOGIES INC (UT)
Proclaimed dissolved for failure to pay taxes 3/1/89

HOLLOWAY CAP CORP (CANADA)
Reorganized under the laws of Ontario as Holloway Lodging Real Estate Investment Trust 06/07/2006
Each share Common no par exchanged for (0.2) Unit
Holloway Lodging Real Estate Investment Trust reorganized as Holloway Lodging Corp. 12/31/2012

HOLLOWAY LODGING REAL ESTATE INVT TR (ON)
Each old Unit exchanged for (0.025) new Unit 04/02/2012
Reorganized as Holloway Lodging Corp. 12/31/2012
Each new Unit exchanged for (1) share Common no par

HOLLOWAY OUTDOOR ADVERTISING, INC. (CA)
Name changed to Holloway Western Corp. 7/30/70
(See Holloway Western Corp.)

HOLLOWAY WESTN CORP (CA)
Charter suspended for failure to file reports and pay fees 04/01/1977

HOLLUND INDL INC (WA)
Common 1¢ par split (17) for (1) by issuance of (16) additional shares payable 11/20/2007 to holders of record 11/20/2007
Name changed to Hollund Industrial Marine, Inc. 08/18/2008

HOLLY CORP (DE)
Each share Common 10¢ par exchanged for (1/6) share Common 60¢ par 00/00/1953
Each share Common 60¢ par exchanged for (0.25) share Common 50¢ par 06/30/1960
Each share Common 50¢ par exchanged for (0.46) share Common $1 par and $6.07 cash 07/19/1984
Each share Common $1 par exchanged for (0.864) share Common 1¢ par and $13.35 cash 12/06/1985
Common 1¢ par split (2) for (1) by issuance of (1) additional share 07/20/1988
Common 1¢ par split (2) for (1) by issuance of (1) additional share payable 07/06/2001 to holders of record 06/22/2001 Ex date - 07/09/2001
Common 1¢ par split (2) for (1) by issuance of (1) additional share payable 08/30/2004 to holders of record 08/16/2004 Ex date - 08/31/2004
Common 1¢ par split (2) for (1) by issuance of (1) additional share payable 06/01/2006 to holders of record 05/22/2006 Ex date - 06/02/2006
Under plan of merger name changed to HollyFrontier Corp. 07/01/2011

HOLLY DEVELOPMENT CO. (CA)
Merged into Holly Oil Co. on a (1/3) for (1) basis 7/7/60
Holly Oil Co. name changed to Holly Resources Corp. 11/1/68
(See Holly Resources Corp.)

HOLLY FARMS CORP (DE)
Merged into Holly Acquisition Corp. 08/09/1989
Each share Common $12 par exchanged for $70 cash

HOLLY GRILLS INC (MI)
Name changed to Holly's Inc. 05/15/1970
(See Holly's Inc.)

HOLLY HLDGS INC (NJ)
Operations discontinued in 1998
Stockholders' equity unlikely

HOLLY MINERALS CORP. (DE)
Acquired by Holly Corp. 02/13/1957
Each share Common exchanged for (0.5) share Common 60¢ par
Holly Corp. name changed to HollyFrontier Corp. 07/01/2011

HOLLY OIL CO. (CO)
Capital Stock $5 par changed to $1 par 00/00/1936
Name changed to Holly Resources Corp. 11/01/1968
(See Holly Resources Corp.)

HOLLY PRODS INC (NJ)
Recapitalized as Holly Holdings, Inc. 12/26/96
Each share Common no par exchanged for (0.1) share Common no par
Preferred not affected except for change of name
(See Holly Holdings, Inc.)

HOLLY RESIDENTIAL PPTYS INC (WA)
Merged into Wellsford Residential Property Trust 12/14/94
Each share Common 1¢ par exchanged for (0.75) Common Share of Bene. Int. 1¢ par
Wellsford Residential Property Trust merged into Equity Residential Properties Trust 5/30/97 which name changed to Equity Residential 5/15/2002

HOLLY RES CORP (CO)
Completely liquidated 10/01/1979
Each share Capital Stock $1 par exchanged for first and final distribution of $3.02 cash

HOLLY-STONINGTON TELEPHONE (CO)
Declared defunct and inoperative for failure to pay taxes and file annual reports 4/21/26

HOLLY STORES, INC. (NY)
5% Conv. Preferred $25 par called for redemption 12/22/64
Acquired by Kresge (S.S.) Co. 2/1/65
Each share Common $1 par exchanged for (0.470588) share Common $10 par
Kresge (S.S.) Co. name changed to K mart Corp. 5/17/77
(See K mart Corp.)

HOLLY SUGAR CORP (NY)
Common no par exchanged (5) for (1) 00/00/1935
5% Preferred $30 par called for redemption 02/01/1963
Common no par changed to $10 par 00/00/1946
Common $10 par changed to $5 par and (1) additional share issued 08/01/1966
Stock Dividend - 25% 01/31/1955
Merged into Imperial Holly Corp. 04/26/1988
Each share Common $5 par exchanged for (3) shares Common no par
Imperial Holly Corp. name changed to Imperial Sugar Co. (New) 02/09/1999
(See Imperial Sugar Co. (New))

HOLLY URANIUM CORP. (DE)
Name changed to Holly Minerals Corp. 05/10/1956
Holly Minerals Corp. acquired by Holly Corp. 02/13/1957 which name changed to HollyFrontier Corp. 07/01/2011

HOLLYCROFT RESOURCE CORP (BC)
Recapitalized as Beretta Resource Corp. 06/14/1990
Each share Common no par exchanged for (0.2) share Common no par
Beretta Resource Corp. name changed to Optimark Data Systems, Inc. 04/24/1992
(See Optimark Data Systems, Inc.)

HOLLYMATIC CORP (DE)
Common no par split (5) for (4) by issuance of (0.25) additional share 5/15/70
Name changed to Bomarko, Inc. 10/15/82
(See Bomarko, Inc.)

HOLLYS INC (MI)
Merged into OSKR XXI, Ltd. 12/17/1986
Each share Common $2 par exchanged for $40.18 cash
Each share Common $2 par received initial additional payment of $1.05 cash 05/29/1987
Each share Common $2 par received second additional payment of $1.35 cash 06/03/1988
Each share Common $2 par received third additional payment of $1.05 cash 08/12/1988
Each share Common $2 par received fourth and final additional distribution of $1.45 cash 12/23/1988

HOLLYWOOD ANGELS, INC. (NV)
Charter revoked for failure to file reports and pay fees 3/5/56

HOLLYWOOD BK & TR CO (HOLLYWOOD, FL)
99.8% acquired by Barnett Banks of Florida, Inc. through exchange offer which expired 06/30/1971
Public interest eliminated

HOLLYWOOD BEAUTY CORP (DE)
Recapitalized as World Internet Technologies Inc. 10/9/2000
Each share Common $0.001 par exchanged for (0.02) share Common $0.001 par
World Internet Technologies Inc. recapitalized as Soundworks Entertainment Inc. 6/11/2002 which recapitalized as Data Evolution Holdings, Inc. 4/12/2004

HOLLYWOOD BROADCASTING CO. (FL)
Name changed to Rand Broadcasting Co. 12/24/56
(See Rand Broadcasting Co.)

HOLLYWOOD BUILDING TRUST
Liquidated in 1947

HOLLYWOOD CASINO CORP (DE)
Each share Class A Common $0.0001 par received distribution of (0.167852) share Greate Bay Casino Corp. Common 10¢ par payable 12/31/96 to holders of record 12/24/96 Ex date - 12/20/96
Merged into Penn National Gaming, Inc. 3/3/2003
Each share Class A Common $0.0001 par exchanged for $12.75 cash

HOLLYWOOD COLOR LABS INC (NY)
Dissolved by proclamation 09/25/1991

HOL-HOL   FINANCIAL INFORMATION, INC.

HOLLYWOOD COLORFILM CORP.
Charter revoked for failure to file reports and pay fees 10/5/50

HOLLYWOOD COM INC (FL)
Name changed to Hollywood Media Corp. 12/18/2000
Hollywood Media Corp. name changed to NovelStem International Corp. 09/26/2018

HOLLYWOOD ENTMT CORP (OR)
Common no par split (3) for (2) by issuance of (0.5) additional share 7/26/94
Common no par split (2) for (1) by issuance of (1) additional share 7/28/95
Merged into Movie Gallery, Inc. 4/28/2005
Each share Common no par exchanged for $13.25 cash

HOLLYWOOD ENTMT NETWORK INC (NV)
Common $0.001 par split (3) for (1) by issuance of (2) additional shares payable 05/19/2000 to holders of record 05/19/2000 Ex date - 05/22/2000
Name changed to Cyber Group Network Corp. 06/02/2000
Cyber Group Network Corp. recapitalized as Skystar Bio-Pharmaceutical Co. 02/16/2006

HOLLYWOOD INS PL INC (FL)
Recapitalized as New Millennium Communications Corp. 11/17/1997
Each share Common $0.001 par exchanged for (0.5) share Common $0.001 par
(See New Millennium Communications Corp.)

HOLLYWOOD INTL CORP (NV)
Merged into Nuclear Dynamics 6/29/70
Each share Common Capital Stock $0.001 par exchanged for (1) share Common $0.025 par
Nuclear Dynamics name changed to Power Alternatives, Inc. 1/13/78 which name changed to New World Minerals, Inc. 4/15/82

HOLLYWOOD INTL STUDIOS (UT)
Recapitalized as Utah Libra Corp. 12/24/1972
Each share Common 1¢ par exchanged for (0.05) share Common 1¢ par
(See Utah Libra Corp.)

HOLLYWOOD INVT CORP (BC)
Name changed to Walking Stick Oil & Gas Corp. 06/07/1990
Walking Stick Oil & Gas Corp. merged into Ascentex Energy Inc. 02/25/1994 which recapitalized as Bonavista Petroleum Ltd. 03/03/1997
(See Bonavista Petroleum Ltd.)

HOLLYWOOD KNICKERBOCKER (CA)
Charter revoked for failure to file reports and pay fees 2/1/66

HOLLYWOOD MEDIA CORP (FL)
Name changed to NovelStem International Corp. 09/26/2018

HOLLYWOOD NATL BK (LOS ANGELES, CA)
Common $10 par changed to $5 par 9/14/67
Merged into United States National Bank (San Diego, CA) 6/25/71
Each share Common $5 par exchanged for (0.8) share Capital Stock $10 par
(See United States National Bank (San Diego, CA))

HOLLYWOOD PAPER BOX CORP.
Dissolved in 1941

HOLLYWOOD PK INC OLD (DE)
Common $1 par changed to 80¢ par and (0.25) additional share issued 11/25/1980
Under plan of reorganization each share Common 80¢ par exchanged for (1) Non-Separable Unit consisting of (1) share Hollywood Park Realty Enterprises, Inc. Common 10¢ par and (1) share Hollywood Park Operating Co. Common 10¢ par 04/13/1982
(See each company's listing)

HOLLYWOOD PK INC NEW (DE)
Common 10¢ par split (5) for (4) by issuance of (0.25) additional share 06/01/1993
Each share Depositary Preferred exchanged for (0.8333) share Common 10¢ par 08/28/1997
Name changed to Pinnacle Entertainment, Inc. (Old) 02/23/2000
Pinnacle Entertainment, Inc. (Old) merged into Gaming & Leisure Properties, Inc. 04/28/2016

HOLLYWOOD PARK OPERATING CO. (DE)
See - Hollywood Pk Rlty Enterprises Inc

HOLLYWOOD PK RLTY ENTERPRISES INC. (DE)
(Issued and transferred only in Non-Separable Units of (1) share Hollywood Park Realty Enterprises, Inc. Common 10¢ par and (1) share Hollywood Park Operating Co. Common 10¢ par) Units split (5) for (4) by issuance of (0.25) additional Unit 11/18/1983
Each share Hollywood Park Operating Co. Common 10¢ par received an additional (1.33333333) share Hollywood Park, Inc. (New) Common 10¢ par for each share to reflect (4) for (3) stock dividend declared 09/30/1991
Paired certificates separated by exchange 01/02/1992
Hollywood Park Realty Enterprises, Inc. name changed to Hollywood Park, Inc. (New)
Hollywood Park Inc. (New) name changed to Pinnacle Entertainment, Inc. (Old) 02/23/2000 which merged into Gaming & Leisure Properties, Inc. 04/28/2016

HOLLYWOOD PARTNERS COM INC (DE)
Recapitalized as Universal Guardian Holdings Inc. 12/12/2002
Each share Common $0.001 par exchanged for (0.05) share Common $0.001 par
(See Universal Guardian Holdings Inc.)

HOLLYWOOD PRODUCTIONS INC (DE)
Each share old Common $0.001 par exchanged for (1/3) share new Common $0.001 par 02/05/1998
New Common $0.001 par split (2) for (1) by issuance of (1) additional share payable 02/05/1999 to holders of record 01/29/1999
Name changed to Shopnet.Com Inc. 05/10/1999
(See Shopnet.Com Inc.)

HOLLYWOOD SECURITIES CORP. (FL)
Liquidation completed
Each share Common 1¢ par received initial distribution of $4.25 cash 09/04/1970
Each share Common 1¢ par received second distribution of $3.20 cash 12/08/1970
Each share Common 1¢ par received third distribution of $0.04 cash 05/05/1972
Each share Common 1¢ par received fourth distribution of $0.024502 cash 05/04/1973
Each share Common 1¢ par exchanged for fifth and final distribution of $0.7751914 cash 10/03/1973

HOLLYWOOD SHOWCASE TELEVISION NETWORK INC (NJ)
Name changed to Genesis Media Group, Inc. 02/17/1998
Genesis Media Group, Inc. recapitalized as Open Door Online Inc. (NJ) 08/10/1999 which reorganized in Delaware as Blue Moon Group, Inc. 11/29/2002 which recapitalized as One Punch Productions, Inc. 12/07/2005 which name changed to Caltas Fitness, Inc. 08/21/2006 which name changed to Cinemaya Media Group, Inc. 02/06/2007 which recapitalized as SNM Global Holdings 11/14/2008

HOLLYWOOD TRENZ INC (DE)
Each share old Common $0.0001 par exchanged for (0.1) share new Common $0.0001 par 10/14/1994
SEC revoked common stock registration 12/02/2005

HOLLYWOOD TURF CLUB (CA)
Capital Stock $100 par changed to $40 par and (1.5) additional shares issued 09/18/1962
Capital Stock $40 par changed to $20 par and (1) additional share issued 10/02/1964
Capital Stock $20 par changed to $10 par and (1) additional share issued 06/28/1965
Capital Stock $10 par changed to $3.3333333 par and (2) additional shares issued 11/26/1969
Capital Stock $3.33333333 par reclassified as Common $1 par and (1) additional share issued 12/17/1971
Reincorporated under the laws of Delaware as Hollywood Park, Inc. (Old) 01/31/1974
Hollywood Park, Inc. (Old) reorganized as Hollywood Park Realty Enterprises, Inc. 04/13/1982 which reorganized as Hollywood Park, Inc. (New) 01/02/1992 which name changed to Pinnacle Entertainment, Inc. (Old) 02/23/2000 which merged into Gaming & Leisure Properties, Inc. 04/28/2016

HOLLYWOODMOVIECLUB COM INC (NV)
Charter permanently revoked 05/01/2007

HOLMER GOLD MINES LTD (ON)
Merged into Lake Shore Gold Corp. (BC) 12/31/2004
Each share Common no par exchanged for (0.66666666) share Common no par
Lake Shore Gold Corp. (BC) reincorporated in Canada 07/18/2008 which merged into Tahoe Resources Inc. 04/07/2016

HOLMES (THOMAS) CORP. (DE)
See - Thomas Holmes Corp

HOLMES BIOPHARMA INC (NV)
Recapitalized as Swiftsure International, Inc. 09/08/2010
Each share Common $0.001 par exchanged for (0.005) share Common $0.001 par

HOLMES D H LTD (LA)
Each share Common $100 par exchanged for (5) shares Common $20 par in 1945
Common $20 par split (6) for (5) by issuance of (0.2) additional share 12/15/66
Common $20 par changed to $5 par and (0.5) additional share issued 11/26/68
Common $5 par split (5) for (4) by issuance of (0.25) additional share 1/31/76
Common $5 par split (5) for (4) by issuance of (0.25) additional share 9/1/78
Common $5 par changed to $2.50 par and (1) additional share issued 6/1/83
Stock Dividends - 20% 1/14/49; 10% 11/1/67; 20% 1/15/72; 20% 2/23/73
Acquired by Dillard Department Stores, Inc. 5/9/89
Each share Common $2.50 par exchanged for (0.244445) share Class A Common no par
Dillard Department Stores, Inc. name changed to Dillard's Inc. 5/19/97

HOLMES ELEC PROT CO (NY)
Name changed to Holmes Protection, Inc. 8/11/70
Holmes Protection, Inc. merged into National Kinney Corp. 10/13/72 which name changed to Andal Corp. 11/7/83
(See Andal Corp.)

HOLMES EUREKA LUMBER CO. (CA)
Liquidation completed 8/15/60

HOLMES HERBS INC (NV)
Each share old Common $0.001 par exchanged for (0.04) share new Common $0.001 par 10/22/2004
Reorganized as Holmes Biopharma, Inc. 07/21/2006
Each share new Common $0.001 par exchanged for (3) shares Common $0.001 par
Holmes Biopharma, Inc. recapitalized as Swiftsure International, Inc. 09/08/2010

HOLMES MANUFACTURING CO.
Property sold 00/00/1934
Details not available

HOLMES MICROSYSTEMS INC (TX)
Each share old Common $0.0001 par exchanged for (0.01) share new Common $0.0001 par 01/04/2000
New Common $0.0001 par split (1.7) for (1) by issuance of (0.7) additional share payable 02/26/2001 to holders of record 02/23/2001 Ex date - 02/27/2001
Name changed to Gosun Communications Ltd. Inc. and Common $0.0001 par changed to $0.001 par 03/27/2001

HOLMES PROTN GROUP INC (DE)
Merged into Tyco International Ltd. (Bermuda) 02/09/1998
Each share Common 1¢ par exchanged for $17 cash

HOLMES PROTN INC (NY)
Common $50 par changed to $5 par 12/15/67
Common $5 par changed to $1 par 4/24/69
Merged into National Kinney Corp. 10/13/72
Each share Common $1 par exchanged for (2.223) shares Common $1 par
National Kinney Corp. name changed to Andal Corp. 11/7/83
(See Andal Corp.)

HOLMES PROTN SVCS CORP (NY)
Merged into National Kinney Corp. 10/13/1972
Each share Common 10¢ par exchanged for (0.129) share Common $1 par
National Kinney Corp. name changed to Andal Corp. 11/07/1983
(See Andal Corp.)

HOLNAM INC (DE)
Common no par changed to 1¢ par 12/31/90
Acquired by Holderbank Financiere Glaris, Ltd. 2/22/94
Each share Common 1¢ par exchanged for $7.65 cash

HOLO-DECK ADVENTURES INC (DE)
Charter cancelled and declared

inoperative and void for non-payment of taxes 03/01/2000

HOLOFILE TECHNOLOGY INC (CANADA)
Reincorporated 10/08/1976
Place of incorporation changed from (ON) to (Canada) 10/08/1976
Dissolved for non-compliance 08/10/1984

HOLOGRAPH CORP (DE)
Name changed to TeleConcepts Corp. 5/25/76
TeleConcepts Corp. name changed to Virology Testing Sciences, Inc. 10/7/92 which name changed to Viral Testing Systems Corp. 12/31/92
(See Viral Testing Systems Corp.)

HOLOGRAPHIC DEV CORP AMER (UT)
Involuntarily dissolved 01/08/1982

HOLOGRAPHIC DIMENSIONS INC (CO)
Recapitalized as Creston Resources, Ltd. 8/24/2004
Each share Common $0.001 par exchanged for (0.005) share Common $0.001 par

HOLOGRAPHIC STORAGE LTD (DE)
Charter cancelled and declared inoperative and void for non-payment of taxes 03/01/2008

HOLOGRAPHIC SYS INC (NV)
Reorganized 2/7/2000
Each share old Common $0.0001 par exchanged for (0.05) share new Common $0.0001 par 8/10/90
Reorganized from Colorado to under the laws of Nevada 2/7/2000
Each share new Common $0.0001 par exchanged for (0.05) share Common $0.001 par 2/7/2000
Name changed to Emission Control Devices Inc. 1/25/2001

HOLOMETRIX INC (DE)
Recapitalized as Metrisa Inc. 5/1/98
Each share Common 1¢ par exchanged for (0.02) share Common 50¢ par
Metrisa Inc. name changed to P.A. Instruments Inc. 10/27/2003

HOLOPAK TECHNOLOGIES INC (DE)
Merged into Foilmark, Inc. 04/23/1999
Each share Common 1¢ par exchanged for (1.11) shares Common 1¢ par and $1.42 cash
(See Foilmark, Inc.)

HOLOPHANE CORP (DE)
Common 1¢ par split (3) for (2) by issuance of (0.5) additional share 12/15/95
Merged into National Service Industries, Inc. 7/29/99
Each share Common 1¢ par exchanged for $38.50 cash

HOLOPHANE INC (DE)
Common no par split (2) for (1) by issuance of (1) additional share 1/3/61
Common no par split (2) for (1) by issuance of (1) additional share 11/16/65
Stock Dividends - 100% 6/1/51; 100% 6/30/52
Merged into Johns-Manville Corp. (NY) 12/15/71
Each share Common no par exchanged for (1) share Common $2.50 par
Johns-Manville Corp. (NY) reincorporated in Delaware as Manville Corp. 10/30/81
(See Manville Corp.)

HOLOVISION SYS INC (UT)
Involuntarily dissolved 07/11/2001
Details not available

HOLSON BURNES GROUP INC (DE)
Merged into Newell Co. 1/22/96

Each share Common 1¢ par exchanged for $5.50 cash

HOLT, RINEHART & WINSTON, INC. (DE)
Common $1 par split (3) for (2) by issuance of (0.5) additional share 6/14/61
Merged into Columbia Broadcasting System, Inc. 8/1/67
Each share Common $1 par exchanged for (1) share $1 Conv. Preference Ser. A $1 par and (0.5) share Common $2.50 par
Columbia Broadcasting System, Inc. name changed to CBS Inc. 4/18/74
(See CBS Inc.)

HOLT (HENRY) & CO., INC. (DE)
Recapitalized in 1944 $1.80 Class A no par not exchanged for Debentures changed to $1 Class A no par
Each share Class B no par exchanged for (0.5) share Common $1 par
Under plan of merger each share Class A no par exchanged for (2.5) shares 5-1/2% Preferred $10 par in 1951
Each share 5% Cum. Conv. Preferred and 5-1/2% Cum. Preferred $10 par exchanged for (1) share new 5-1/2% S.F. Preferred $10 par in 1954
5-1/2% Preferred $10 par called for redemption 2/25/55
Common $1 par split (3) for (1) by issuance of (2) additional shares 11/20/57
Common $1 par split (3) for (2) by issuance of (0.5) additional share 11/5/59
Name changed to Holt, Rinehart & Winston, Inc. 3/1/60
Holt, Rinehart & Winston, Inc. merged into Columbia Broadcasting System, Inc. 8/1/67 which name changed to CBS Inc. 4/18/74
(See CBS Inc.)

HOLT INTL INVTS LTD (BC)
Name changed to Argent Resources Ltd. 11/04/1998
Argent Resources Ltd. recapitalized as Argent Mining Corp. 04/07/2006 which recapitalized as Avion Resources Corp. 06/21/2007 which name changed to Avion Gold Corp. (BC) 06/05/2009 which reincorporated in Ontario 06/14/2011 which merged into Endeavour Mining Corp. 10/18/2012

HOLT RENFREW & CO LTD (QC)
Each share 7% Preferred $100 par exchanged for (1) share $5 1st Preferred $50 par, (1) share $5 Conv. 2nd Preferred $50 par and $10.25 cash in 1953 $5 Conv. 2nd Preferred $50 par converted into Common by 12/18/58
$5 1st Preferred $50 par called for redemption 12/1/59
Each share Common $100 par exchanged for (10) shares Common $5 par 12/18/58
Common $5 par changed to $2.50 par and (1) additional share issued 6/30/64
Acquired by Canadian Acceptance Corp. Ltd. 12/7/65
Each share Common $2.50 par exchanged for $20 cash

HOLT T J & CO INC (NY)
Charter cancelled and proclaimed dissolved for failure to pay taxes 06/26/1996

HOLTER TECHNOLOGIES HLDG AG (NV)
Recapitalized as International Consortium Corp. 06/17/2008
Each (15) shares Common $0.001 par exchanged for (1) share Common $0.001 par
(See International Consortium Corp.)

HOLTS CIGAR HLDGS INC (DE)
Stock Dividends - 2% payable 12/23/1998 to holders of record 11/24/1998; 2% payable 03/23/1999 to holders of record 02/23/1999; 2% payable 09/22/1999 to holders of record 09/01/1999
Merged into HCH Acquisition Corp. 01/17/2001
Each share Common $0.001 par exchanged for $5.50 cash

HOLY CROSS MTN MINES LTD (BC)
Name changed to Camero Resource Industries Ltd. 01/14/1974
Camero Resource Industries Ltd. recapitalized as International Camero Resources Ltd. 10/03/1983 which name changed to International Pharmadyne Ltd. 03/05/1985
(See International Pharmadyne Ltd.)

HOLY SMOKE CAP CORP (AB)
Name changed to Anterra Corp. 11/08/2002
Anterra Corp. merged into Anterra Energy Inc. 05/08/2007

HOLYOKE NATL BK (HOLYOKE, MA)
Capital Stock $50 par changed to $10 par and (4) additional shares issued 02/20/1963
Stock Dividends - 10% 02/01/1940; 10% 02/01/1941; 20% 02/01/1943
Acquired by First National Boston Corp. 12/03/1973
Each share Capital Stock $10 par exchanged for (1.5) shares Common $6.25 par
First National Boston Corp. name changed to Bank of Boston Corp. 04/01/1983 which name changed to BankBoston Corp. 04/25/1997 which merged into Fleet Boston Corp. 10/01/1999 which name changed to FleetBoston Financial Corp. 04/18/2000 which merged into Bank of America Corp. 04/01/2004

HOLYOKE SHARES, INC. (DE)
Common $5 par changed to $1.65-2/3 par and (2) additional shares issued 1/10/64
Liquidation completed
Each Ctf. of Participation stamped to indicate initial distribution of $5 cash 12/30/64
Each stamped Ctf. of Participation stamped to indicate second distribution of $2.50 cash 5/20/66
Each share Common $1.66-2/3 par stamped to indicate initial distribution $14 cash 8/22/67
Each Stamped Ctf. of Participation exchanged for third and final distribution of $1.96 cash 10/16/67
Each Stamped Common $1.66-2/3 par exchanged for second and final distribution of $1.10 cash 7/27/70

HOLYOKE WTR PWR CO (MA)
Each share Capital Stock $100 par exchanged for (10) shares Capital Stock $10 par 00/00/1938
Capital Stock $10 par changed to $5 par and (1) additional share issued 12/21/1963
Acquired by Northeast Utilities 10/31/1969
Each share Capital Stock $5 par exchanged for (2.25) shares Common $5 par
Note: After 10/31/1974 and until 10/31/1984 each share Capital Stock $5 par could only be exchanged for cash
Unexchanged certificates became worthless 11/01/1984
Northeast Utilities name changed to Eversource Energy 02/19/2015

HOLZGANG J G INC (CA)
Charter suspended for failure to file reports or pay fees 03/03/1975

HOM CORP (GA)
Name changed to R Wireless Inc. 1/22/2003
R Wireless Inc. name changed to TX Holdings, Inc. 9/19/2005

HOMA OIL & GAS CO (NV)
Liquidation completed
Each share Common no par exchanged for initial distribution of (0.2) share Maynard Oil Co. Common 50¢ par 9/30/71
Each share Common no par received second and final distribution of $0.05 cash 7/2/73
(See Maynard Oil Co.)

HOMAC-BARNES, INC. (DE)
Name changed to Homac Inc. 04/10/1981
Homac Inc. name changed to Oxidyne Group, Inc. 05/27/1988
(See Oxidyne Group, Inc.)

HOMAC INC (DE)
Name changed to Oxidyne Group, Inc. 05/27/1988
(See Oxidyne Group, Inc.)

HOMAOKLA OIL CO.
Acquired by Sunray Oil Corp. 00/00/1930
Details not available

HOMASOTE CO (NJ)
Preferred $10 par called for redemption 6/15/65
5% Preferred Ser. B $10 par called for redemption 9/15/66
(Additional Information in Active)

HOMASSIST CORP (NV)
Common $0.001 par split (26) for (1) by issuance of (26) additional shares payable 8/3/2006 to holders of record 8/1/2006 Ex date - 8/4/2006
Name changed to DigitalPost Interactive, Inc. 1/26/2007

HOMBRE CAP INC (AB)
Name changed to NovaTeqni Corp. 03/30/2015

HOMBURG CDA REAL ESTATE INVT TR (QC)
Name changed to CANMARC Real Estate Investment Trust 10/13/2011
(See CANMARC Real Estate Investment Trust)

HOMBURG INVEST INC (AB)
Each share Common no par exchanged for (0.5) share old Class B Multiple no par and (0.5) share old Class A Subordinate no par 04/05/2005
Each share old Class B Multiple no par received distribution of (0.06877) share old Class A Subordinate no par payable 09/30/2008 to holders of record 09/19/2008 Ex date - 09/17/2008
Each share old Class A Subordinate no par exchanged for (0.1) share new Class A Subordinate no par 12/16/2008
Each share old Class B Multiple no par exchanged for (0.1) share new Class B Multiple no par 12/16/2008
Stock Dividend - In Class A Subordinate to holders of Class A Subordinate 6.877% payable 09/30/2008 to holders of record 09/19/2008 Ex date - 09/17/2008 03/27/2014
Plan of arrangement under Companies' Creditors Arrangement Act effective 03/27/2014
No stockholders' equity

HOMCO INDS LTD (SK)
Common no par reclassified as Conv. Class A Common no par 08/23/1974
Struck off register for failure to file annual returns 09/29/1978

HOME & CITY SVGS BK (ALBANY, NY)
Merged into TrustCo Bank Corp NY 09/30/1991
Each share Common $1 par exchanged for (0.5) share Common $2 par and $10 cash

HOME & FOREIGN SECURITIES CORP. (MD)
Recapitalized in 1932
Preferred no par changed to $10 par
Common no par changed to 10¢ par
Merged into Chesapeake Industries, Inc. 2/14/55
Each share $3 Preferred $10 par exchanged for (1-1/3) shares $4 Preferred $10 par and (5.5) shares Common $1 par
Each share Common 10¢ par exchanged for (0.75) share Common $1 par
Chesapeake Industries, Inc. name changed to America Corp. (OH) 8/10/59 which recapitalized as America Corp. (DE) 12/31/63 which name changed to Pathe Industries, Inc. (DE) 11/20/64
(See Pathe Industries, Inc. (DE))

HOME BANCORP (IN)
Merged into Old Kent Financial Corp. 10/13/2000
Each share Common no par exchanged for (0.6945) share Common no par
Old Kent Financial Corp. merged into Fifth Third Bancorp 4/2/2001

HOME BANCORP ELGIN INC (DE)
Merged into State Financial Services Corp. 12/15/98
Each share Common 1¢ par exchanged for (0.914) share Class A Common 10¢ par
State Financial Services Corp. merged into Associated Banc-Corp 10/3/2005

HOME BANK & TRUST CO. (HENDERSONVILLE, NC)
Merged into Financial Corp. 8/29/69
Each share Common $5 par exchanged for (0.75) share Common $5 par
Financial Corp. name changed to Bancshares of North Carolina, Inc. 3/10/71 which merged into NCNB Corp. 12/23/82 which name changed to NationsBank Corp. 12/31/91 which reincorporated in Delaware as BankAmerica Corp. (Old) 9/25/98 which merged into BankAmerica Corp. (New) 9/30/98 which name changed to Bank of America Corp. 4/28/99

HOME BK & TR CO (MERIDEN, CT)
Capital Stock $10 par changed to $5 par and (1) additional share issued 4/15/82
Stock Dividend - 10% 10/1/82
Acquired by Shawmut Corp. 7/1/86
Each share Capital Stock $5 par exchanged for (2.5) shares Common $5 par
Shawmut Corp. merged into Shawmut National Corp. 2/29/88 which merged into Fleet Financial Group Inc. (New) 11/30/95 which name changed to Fleet Boston Corp. 10/1/99 which name changed to FleetBoston Financial Corp. 4/18/2000 which merged into Bank of America Corp. 4/1/2004

HOME BANK (MILWAUKEE, WI)
Merged into Midland National Bank (Milwaukee, WI) 09/01/1970
Each share Common $10 par exchanged for (1) share Common $7.50 par
(See Midland National Bank (Milwaukee, WI))

HOME BK (SIGNAL HILL, CA)
Common $2.40 par split (5) for (1) by issuance of (4) additional shares 2/1/72
Common $2.40 par split (5) for (1) by issuance of (4) additional shares 7/1/73
Common $2.40 par changed to $1.20 par and (1) additional share issued 9/2/77
Common $1.20 par changed to 40¢ par and (2) additional shares issued 12/15/80
Stock Dividend - 100% 10/28/58
Under plan of reorganization each share Common 40¢ par automatically became (1) share Home Interstate Bancorp. Common no par 9/7/82
Home Interstate Bancorp. merged into CU Bancorp 8/9/96
(See CU Bancorp)

HOME BEN CORP (VA)
Class A Common $2.50 par changed to $1.25 par and (1) additional share issued 5/2/78
Class B Common $2.50 par changed to $1.25 par and (1) additional share issued 5/2/78
Class A Common $1.25 par changed to 62-1/2¢ par and (1) additional share issued 5/1/84
Class B Common $1.25 par changed to 62-1/2¢ par and (1) additional share issued 5/1/84
Class A Common 62-1/2¢ par changed to $0.3125 and (1) additional share issued 12/31/91
Class B Common 62-1/2¢ par changed to $0.3125 and (1) additional share issued 12/31/91
Merged into American General Corp. 4/16/97
Each share Class A Common $0.3125 par exchanged for either (0.967) share Common 50¢ par or $39 cash
Each share Class B Common $0.3125 par exchanged for either (0.967) share Common 50¢ par or $39 cash
Note: Option to receive stock expired 4/11/97
American General Corp. merged into American International Group, Inc. 8/29/2001

HOME BEN LIFE INS CO (VA)
Under plan of reorganization each share Class A $2.50 par or Class B $2.50 par automatically became (1) share Home Beneficial Corp. Class A Common $2.50 par or Class B Common $2.50 par 12/31/70
Home Beneficial Corp. merged into American General Corp. 4/16/97 which merged into American International Group, Inc. 8/29/2001

HOME BLDG BANCORP INC (DE)
Merged into First Bancorp Indiana, Inc. (New) 10/2/2006
Each share Common 1¢ par exchanged for (1.5366) shares Common 1¢ par and $14.49 cash

HOME BUILDERS ACCEPTANCE CORP. (CO)
Name changed to Riley Aeronautics International Corp. 7/21/67
Riley Aeronautics International Corp. name changed to Riley International Corp. 8/11/67
(See Riley International Corp.)

HOME BUILDERS OF AMERICA, INC. (MN)
Statutorily dissolved 10/07/1991

HOME CAP GROUP INC (CANADA)
Reincorporated under the laws of Ontario 07/18/1988

HOME CAPITAL INVT CORP (NV)
Each share old Common 1¢ par exchanged for (0.2) share new Common 1¢ par 10/19/1998
Charter revoked for failure to file reports and pay fees 10/31/2000

HOME CARE AMER INC (NV)
Name changed to Bizrocket.com, Inc. 5/27/99

HOME CENTERS (DIY) LTD (ISRAEL)
Acquired by Bilu Enterprises (H.C.) Ltd. 12/00/2000
Each share Ordinary ILS 1 par exchanged for $9.4814 cash

HOME CHOICE HLDGS INC (DE)
Merged into Rent-Way, Inc. 12/10/98
Each share Common 1¢ par exchanged for (0.588) share Common no par
(See Rent-Way, Inc.)

HOME CTRS AMER INC (DE)
Merged into K mart Corp. 9/27/84
Each share Common 1¢ par exchanged for $11 cash

HOME CTRS INC (OH)
Charter cancelled by operation of law 6/28/93

HOME CTRY FURNITURE INC (NY)
Out of business 06/06/1975
No stockholders' equity

HOME DAIRY INC (MI)
Recapitalized 00/00/1943
Each share Class A no par exchanged for (1) share Preferred no par and (2) shares Common $10 par
Each share Class B no par exchanged for (0.5) share Common $10 par
Completely liquidated 02/16/1970
Each share Preferred no par exchanged for first and final distribution of (0.2) share O'Connor Drug Co. Preferred $100 par
Each share Common $10 par exchanged for first and final distribution of $0.25 cash
(See O'Connor Drug Co.)

HOME DIAGNOSTICS INC (DE)
Issue Information - 6,599,487 shares COM offered at $12 per share on 09/20/2006
Acquired by Nipro Corp. 03/15/2010
Each share Common 1¢ par exchanged for $11.50 cash

HOME DIRECTOR INC (DE)
Plan of reorganization under Chapter 11 Federal Bankruptcy Code effective 10/23/2006
No stockholders' equity

HOME DISH SATELLITE NETWORKS INC (NV)
Company reported out of business 00/00/1990
No stockholders' equity

HOME EQUITY INCOME TR (ON)
Under plan of reorganization each Unit no par automatically became (1) share HOMEQ Corp. Common no par 07/03/2009
(See HOMEQ Corp.)

HOME FED BANCORP (IN)
Common 1¢ par changed to no par and (0.5) additional share issued 09/17/1993
Common no par split (3) for (2) by issuance of (0.5) additional share payable 12/20/1996 to holders of record 12/06/1996
Common no par split (3) for (2) by issuance of (0.5) additional share payable 11/24/1997 to holders of record 11/10/1997
Name changed to Indiana Community Bancorp 05/01/2008
Indiana Community Bancorp merged into Old National Bancorp 09/17/2012

HOME FED BANCORP INC (MD)
Merged into Cascade Bancorp 05/16/2014
Each share Common 1¢ par exchanged for (1.6772) shares new Common no par and $8.4285961 cash
Cascade Bancorp merged into First Interstate BancSystem, Inc. 05/30/2017

HOME FED BANCORP INC LA (USA)
Reorganized under the laws of Louisiana 12/22/2010
Each share Common 1¢ par exchanged for (0.911) share Common 1¢ par

HOME FED BANCORP MO INC (MO)
Common $1 par split (3) for (2) by issuance of (0.5) additional share 03/15/1993
Merged into Roosevelt Financial Group, Inc. 04/22/1994
Each share Common $1 par exchanged for (0.4945) share Common 1¢ par and $7.50 cash
Roosevelt Financial Group, Inc. merged into Mercantile Bancorporation, Inc. 07/01/1997 which merged into Firstar Corp. (New) 09/20/1999 which merged into U.S. Bancorp (DE) 02/27/2001

HOME FED BK FLA F S B (ST. PETERSBURG, FL)
Merged into Barnett Banks, Inc. 7/26/87
Each share Common 1¢ par exchanged for (1.095) shares Common $2 par
Barnett Banks, Inc. merged into NationsBank Corp. 1/9/98 which reincorporated in Delaware as BankAmerica Corp. (Old) 9/25/98 which merged into BankAmerica Corp. (New) 9/30/98 which name changed to Bank of America Corp. 4/28/99

HOME FED CORP (MD)
Reincorporated 07/31/1989
State of incorporation changed from (DE) to (MD) 07/31/1989
Merged into F&M Bancorp 11/15/1996
Each share Common $1 par exchanged for (0.49535) share Common $5 par
F&M Bancorp merged into Mercantile Bankshares Corp. 08/12/2003 which merged into PNC Financial Services Group, Inc. 03/02/2007

HOME FED FINL CORP (CA)
Stock Dividends - 10% 03/15/1993; 10% 11/15/1993; 10% 10/15/1994
Acquired by First Nationwide Bank (San Francisco, CA) 05/31/1996
Each share Common 1¢ par exchanged for $18.50 cash

HOME FED SVGS & LN ASSN ATLANTA (GA)
Common $1 par split (2) for (1) by issuance of (1) additional share 2/14/86
Acquired by Southeast Financial Corp. 12/29/86
Each share Common $1 par exchanged for $16.295 cash

HOME FED SVGS & LN ASSN MERIDIAN MISS (MS)
Under plan of reorganization each share Common 1¢ par automatically became (1) share Common 1¢ par Home Savings Bank, S.S.B. (Meridian, MS) 05/31/1993
(See Home Savings Bank, S.S.B. (Meridian, MS))

HOME FED SVGS & LN ASSN PALM BEACH FLA (USA)
Merged into City Federal Savings & Loan Association 06/30/1983
Each share Common 1¢ par exchanged for $35 cash

HOME FED SVGS & LN ASSN ROCKIES FT COLLINS COLO (USA)
Name changed to Home Federal Savings Bank (Fort Collins, CO) 06/14/1990
Home Federal Savings Bank (Fort Collins, CO) acquired by KeyCorp

(NY) 06/30/1993 which merged into KeyCorp (New) (OH) 03/01/1994

HOME FED SVGS & LN ASSN SAN DIEGO CALIF (USA)
Incorporated 00/00/1934
Reorganized under the laws of Delaware as HomeFed Corp. 12/30/1988

HOME FED SVGS & LN ASSN SAN FRANCISCO (CA)
Stock Dividend - 20% 01/31/1987
Under plan of reorganization each share Common $1 par automatically became (1) share Home Federal Financial Corp. Common 1¢ par 08/31/1990
(See Home Federal Financial Corp.)

HOME FED SVGS & LN ASSN TUCSON ARIZ (USA)
Incorporated 00/00/1937
Merged into Great American First Savings Bank (San Diego, CA) 03/21/1986
Each share Common 1¢ par exchanged for $36.71 cash

HOME FED SVGS BK (CARBONDALE, IL)
Merged into Charter Financial, Inc. 1/15/97
Each share Common $1 par exchanged for $21 cash

HOME FED SVGS BK (CHARLESTON, SC)
Reorganized under the laws of Delaware as Carolina Financial Corp. 02/19/1991
Each share Common $1 par exchanged for (1) share Common 1¢ par
Carolina Financial Corp. acquired by SouthTrust Corp. 10/23/1992 which merged into Wachovia Corp. (Ctfs. dated after 09/01/2001) 11/01/2004 which merged into Wells Fargo & Co. (New) 12/31/2008

HOME FED SVGS BK (FORT COLLINS, CO)
Acquired by KeyCorp (NY) 6/30/93
Each share Common $1 par exchanged for (0.848) share Common $5 par
KeyCorp (NY) merged into KeyCorp (New) (OH) 3/1/94

HOME FED SVGS BK (HAGERSTOWN, MD)
Under plan of reorganization each share Common $1 par automatically became (1) share Home Federal Corp. (DE) Common $1 par 12/18/1987
Home Federal Corp. (DE) reincorporated in Maryland 07/31/1989 which merged into F&M Bancorp 11/15/1996 which merged into Mercantile Bankshares Corp. 08/12/2003 which merged into PNC Financial Services Group, Inc. 03/02/2007

HOME FED SVGS BK (SEYMOUR, IN)
Common 1¢ par split (3) for (2) by issuance of (0.5) additional share 08/24/1992
Reorganized as Home Federal Bancorp 03/01/1993
Each share Common 1¢ par exchanged for (1) share Common 1¢ par
Home Federal Bancorp name changed to Indiana Community Bancorp 05/01/2008 which merged into Old National Bancorp 09/17/2012

HOME FED SVGS BK (WASHINGTON, DC)
Stock Dividend - 10% 01/31/1994
Acquired by First Union Corp. 11/01/1994
Each share Common 1¢ par exchanged for (0.4835) share Common $3.33-1/3 par
First Union Corp. name changed to Wachovia Corp. (Ctfs. dated after 09/01/2001) 09/01/2001 which merged into Wells Fargo & Co. (New) 12/31/2008

HOME FED SVGS BK (WORCESTER, MA)
Acquired by American Heritage Bancorp 6/13/86
Each share Common 1¢ par exchanged for $7.50 cash

HOME FEDERAL SAVINGS BANK (XENIA, OH)
Under plan of reorganization each share Common 1¢ par automatically became (1) share Ultra Bancorp Common 1¢ par 08/03/1990
Ultra Bancorp merged into Mid Am, Inc. 12/31/1992 which merged into Sky Financial Group, Inc. 10/02/1998 which merged into Huntington Bancshares Inc. 07/02/2007

HOME FED SVGS BK ALA (LAFAYETTE, AL)
Merged into Colonial BancGroup, Inc. 03/17/1993
Each share Common 1¢ par exchanged for (0.879) share Class A Common $2.50 par
(See Colonial BancGroup, Inc.)

HOME FED SVGS BK GA (GAINESVILLE, GA)
Under plan of reorganization name changed to HomeTrust Bank (Gainesville, GA) 11/1/91
HomeTrust Bank (Gainesville, GA) acquired by SunTrust Banks, Inc. 1/1/93

HOME FED SVGS BK MO (ST LOUIS, MO)
Under plan of reorganization name changed to Home Federal Bancorp of Missouri, Inc. 11/18/92
Home Federal Bancorp of Missouri, Inc. merged into Roosevelt Financial Group, Inc. 4/22/94 which merged into Mercantile Bancorporation, Inc. 7/1/97 which merged into Firstar Corp. (New) 9/20/99 which merged into U.S. Bancorp (New) 2/27/2001

HOME FED SVGS BK NORTHN OHIO (LAKEWOOD, OH)
Common 1¢ par split (2) for (1) by issuance of (1) additional share 6/16/86
Under plan of reorganization each share Common 1¢ par automatically became (1) share Haverfield Corp. Common 1¢ par 8/23/89
Haverfield Corp. merged into Charter One Financial, Inc. 9/19/97
(See Charter One Financial, Inc.)

HOME FEDERAL SAVINGS BANK OF EASTERN NORTH CAROLINA (GREENVILLE, NC)
Merged into United Carolina Bancshares Corp. 11/12/93
Each share Common $1 par exchanged for $40 cash

HOME FINANCE GROUP, INC. (NC)
Stock Dividends - 100% 7/24/52; 25% 6/1/53; 25% 3/31/60
Under plan of merger name changed to American Credit Corp. 12/31/64
American Credit Corp. merged into Wachovia Corp. 7/1/70
(See Wachovia Corp.)

HOME FINL CORP (DE)
Merged into First Tennessee National Corp. 12/14/1992
Each share Common 1¢ par exchanged for (0.981) share Common $2.50 par
First Tennessee National Corp. name changed to First Horizon National Corp. 04/20/2004

HOME FINL CORP DEL HOLLYWOOD FL (DE)
Merged into First Union Corp. 11/25/1996
Each share Common $1 par exchanged for (0.2257) share Common $3.33-1/3 par
First Union Corp. name changed to Wachovia Corp. (Ctfs. dated after 09/01/2001) 09/01/2001 which merged into Wells Fargo & Co. (New) 12/31/2008

HOME FING CTRS INC (NV)
Each share old Common $0.001 par exchanged for (0.125) share new Common $0.001 par 11/21/2001
Recapitalized as WorldWide Indoor Karting, Inc. 07/23/2003
Each share new Common $0.001 par exchanged for (0.0005) share Common $0.001 par
WorldWide Indoor Karting, Inc. name changed to Vault Financial Services Inc. 10/08/2003 which name changed to Prime Restaurants, Inc. 04/18/2007 which name changed to BIH Corp. 03/19/2008
(See BIH Corp.)

HOME FIRE SECURITY CORP. (NY)
Capital Stock became valueless in 1942 and the company was dissolved by proclamation of the New York Secretary of State 12/16/46

HOME FURNACE CO (MI)
Acquired by Lear Siegler, Inc. 12/9/66
Each share Common no par exchanged for (1.1) shares Common $1 par
(See Lear Siegler, Inc.)

HOME GROUP INC (DE)
$1.10 Preferred Ser. A $1 par called for redemption 06/01/1986
Name changed to AmBase Corp. 05/19/1989

HOME HEALTH CARE AMER INC (DE)
Name changed to Caremark, Inc. 4/15/85
Caremark, Inc. acquired by Baxter Travenol Laboratories, Inc. 8/3/87 which name changed to Baxter International Inc. 5/18/88

HOME HEALTH CARE OF AMERICA, INC. (CA)
Common no par split (2) for (1) by issuance of (1) additional share 12/15/82
Reincorporated under the laws of Delaware 1/1/85
Home Health Care of America, Inc. (DE) name changed to Caremark, Inc. 4/15/85 which was acquired by Baxter Travenol Laboratories, Inc. 8/3/87 which name changed to Baxter International Inc. 5/18/88

HOME HEALTH CORP AMER INC (PA)
Plan of reorganization under Chapter 11 Federal Bankruptcy Code effective 1/7/2002
No stockholders' equity

HOME HEALTH INTL INC (NV)
Recapitalized as American Transportation Holdings, Inc. 04/29/2014
Each share Common $0.0001 par exchanged for (0.00041666) share Common $0.0001 par

HOME HLDGS INC (DE)
Plan of reorganization under Chapter 11 Federal Bankruptcy Code effective 7/29/98
No stockholders' equity

HOME IMPROVEMENT FINANCING CORP. (DE)
Incorporated 03/20/1925
No longer in existence having become inoperative and void for non-payment of taxes 04/01/1937

HOME IMPT FING CORP (DE)
Incorporated 01/30/1953
Charter cancelled and declared inoperative and void for non-payment of taxes 03/01/1974

HOME INNS & HOTELS MGMT INC (CAYMAN ISLANDS)
Name changed to Homeinns Hotel Group 12/18/2014
(See Homeinns Hotel Group)

HOME INSURANCE CO. OF HAWAII LTD. (HI)
Capital Stock $20 par changed to $8 par and (1.5) additional shares issued 3/1/56
Name changed to First Insurance Co. of Hawaii, Ltd. 8/11/61
(See First Insurance Co. of Hawaii, Ltd.)

HOME INS CO (NH)
$2.95 Preferred Ser. A $1 par called for redemption 12/1/91
Public interest eliminated

HOME INS CO (NY)
Each share Common $100 par exchanged for (10) shares Common $10 par 00/00/1929
Common $10 par changed to $5 par 00/00/1932
Common $5 par changed to $2.50 par and (1) additional share issued 05/12/1967
Stock Dividend - 10% 05/05/1961
Reacquired 06/30/1970
Each share Common $2.50 par exchanged for $35 cash

HOME INTENSIVE CARE INC (FL)
Conv. Preferred 1¢ par called for redemption 6/15/87
Common 1¢ par split (2) for (1) by issuance of (1) additional share 8/21/87
Merged into Grace H Acquisition Corp. 7/16/93
Each share Common 1¢ par exchanged for $6.60 cash

HOME INTST BANCORP (CA)
Merged into CU Bancorp 8/9/96
Each share Common no par exchanged for (1.409) shares Common no par
(See CU Bancorp)

HOME INVS TR (NY)
Completely liquidated 2/14/75
Each Share of Bene. Int. 1¢ par received first and final distribution of $1.20 cash
Note: Certificates were not required to be surrendered and are without value

HOME LAKE RES LTD (ON)
Recapitalized as Dovetec Corp. 06/11/1992
Each share Common no par exchanged for (0.5) share Common no par

HOME LENDING ASSOC INC (DE)
Each share old Common 1¢ par exchanged for (0.33333333) share new Common 1¢ par 09/16/1996
Name changed to Microsure Inc. 11/27/1996
Microsure Inc. recapitalized as 9A Investment Holding Corp. 08/31/2001 which name changed to Viking Power Services, Inc. 07/03/2006

HOME LIFE INS CO AMER (DE)
Over 99.9% held by Peoples Life Insurance Co. (DC) as of 07/01/1981
Public interest eliminated

HOME LN & SECS CORP (OH)
Charter cancelled for non-payment of taxes 07/24/1987

HOME LN SERVICING SOLUTIONS LTD (CAYMAN ISLANDS)
Each share Ordinary 1¢ par received partial liquidating distribution of

$16.613 cash payable 04/27/2015 to holders of record 04/20/2015
Ex date - 04/28/2015
Acquired by New Residential Investment Corp. 10/23/2015
Each share Ordinary 1¢ par exchanged for $0.704059 cash

HOME LT & PWR CO (CO)
Common $25 par changed to $6.25 par and (3) additional shares issued 05/17/1971
4-1/2% Preferred $100 par called for redemption 04/01/1977
Stock Dividends - 10% 07/02/1955; 10% 10/05/1964; 10% 10/03/1966; 10% 10/03/1968; 10% 10/02/1970; 10% 07/20/1972
Through exchange offer 99.5% acquired by Public Service Co. of Colorado as of 07/29/1977
Public interest eliminated

HOME-MAKER STORES, INC. (MN)
Adjudicated bankrupt 12/18/64
No stockholders' equity

HOME MEDIA CORP (AB)
Merged into IVRnet Inc. (New) 07/31/2003
Each share Common no par exchanged for (0.19888623) share Common no par

HOME MINING DEVELOPMENTS LTD. (ON)
Merged into New Force Crag Mines Ltd. 11/22/1974
Each share Capital Stock $1 par exchanged for (0.14285714) share Common no par
(See New Force Crag Mines Ltd.)

HOME MTG & INVT INC (TX)
Name changed to Great American Reserve Corp. 5/27/68
Great American Reserve Corp. acquired by Penney (J.C.) Co., Inc. 12/29/70

HOME NATL BK & TR CO (MERIDEN, CT)
Stock Dividend - 11.76% 3/15/67
Name changed to Home Bank & Trust Co. (Meriden, CT) 3/27/73
Home Bank & Trust Co. (Meriden, CT) acquired by Shawmut Corp. 7/1/86 which merged into Shawmut National Corp. 2/29/88 which merged into Fleet Financial Group Inc. (New) 11/30/95 which name changed to Fleet Boston Corp. 10/1/99 which name changed to FleetBoston Financial Corp. 4/18/2000 which merged into Bank of America Corp. 4/1/2004

HOME NATIONAL BANK (BROCKTON, MA)
Stock Dividend - 10% 1/18/54
Merged into Plymouth-Home National Bank (Brockton, Mass.) 4/18/63
Each share Capital Stock $50 par exchanged for (5.1515) shares Capital Stock $10 par

HOME NATIONAL BANK (MERIDEN, CT)
Each share Capital Stock $100 par exchanged for (4) shares Capital Stock $25 par 3/11/29
Recapitalized as Home National Bank & Trust Co. (Meriden, CT) 1/14/47
Each share Capital Stock $25 par exchanged for (2.5) shares Capital Stock $10 par
Home National Bank & Trust Co. (Meriden, CT) name changed to Home Bank & Trust Co. (Meriden, CT) 3/27/73 which was acquired by Shawmut Corp. 7/1/86 which merged into Shawmut National Corp. 2/29/88 which merged into Fleet Financial Group Inc. (New) 11/30/95 which name changed to Fleet Boston Corp. 10/1/99 which name changed to FleetBoston Financial Corp. 4/18/2000 which merged into Bank of America Corp. 4/1/2004

HOME NATL CORP (MA)
Common $2.50 par changed to 50¢ par and (4) additional shares issued 06/20/1986
Common 50¢ par split (3) for (1) by issuance of (2) additional shares 06/19/1987
Stock Dividend - 5% 01/11/1988
Involuntarily dissolved 08/31/1998
Stockholders' equity unlikely

HOME NUTRITIONAL SVCS INC (NJ)
Merged into Grace (W.R.) & Co. 4/6/94
Each share Common no par exchanged for $7.85 cash

HOME-O-NIZE CO. (IA)
Name changed to HON Industries Inc. 4/24/68
HON Industries Inc. name changed to HNI Corp. 5/4/2004

HOME/OFFICE EXPRESS INC (NV)
Name changed to IAMG Holdings, Inc. 04/27/2000
IAMG Holdings, Inc. name changed to Curv Entertainment Group, Inc. 11/26/2007 which name changed to SuperBox, Inc. 09/01/2011

HOME OFFICE REFERENCE LAB INC (DE)
Name changed to LabOne, Inc. (Old) 2/22/94
LabOne, Inc. (Old) merged into LabOne, Inc. (New) 8/10/99
(See LabOne, Inc. (New))

HOME OIL LTD NEW (CANADA)
Merged into Anderson Exploration Ltd. 09/07/1995
Each share Common no par exchanged for (1.38) shares Common no par
(See Anderson Exploration Ltd.)

HOME OIL LTD OLD (CANADA)
Common $1 par changed to no par 00/00/1930
Common no par reclassified as Class B no par 00/00/1955
Stock Dividend - Class A & B - 10% in Class A 07/01/1963
Merged into Consumers' Gas Co. (ON) 12/21/1979
Each share Class A no par exchanged for $95 cash
Each share Class B no par exchanged for $95 cash

HOME OWNERS FED SVGS & LN ASSN BOSTON MASS (USA)
Common 1¢ par split (3) for (2) by issuance of (0.5) additional share 01/16/1986
Common 1¢ par split (3) for (2) by issuance of (0.5) additional share 03/26/1986
Common 1¢ par split (3) for (2) by issuance of (0.5) additional share 09/16/1986
Name changed to Home Owners Savings Bank, F.S.B. (Boston, MA) 04/03/1989
(See Home Owners Savings Bank, F.S.B. (Boston, MA))

HOME OWNERS INS CO (IL)
Common $1.50 par changed to Common $1.60 par 12/27/63
Insolvent and ordered into liquidation 4/8/71
No stockholders' equity

HOME OWNERS LIFE INSURANCE CO. (FL)
Merged into Pioneer Home Owners Life Insurance Co. on a (2/3) for (1) basis 1/1/62
Pioneer Home Owners Life Insurance Co. merged into American Life Insurance Co. 12/31/63 which name changed to American-Amicable Life Insurance Co. 3/1/65
(See American-Amicable Life Insurance Co.)

HOME OWNERS SVGS BK F S B (BOSTON, MA)
Taken over by FDIC 4/27/90
No stockholders' equity

HOME PORT BANCORP INC (DE)
Merged into Seacoast Financial Services Corp. 12/31/2000
Each share Common 1¢ par exchanged for $37 cash

HOME PPTYS INC (MD)
Name changed 09/24/2003
Name changed from Home Properties of New York, Inc. to Home Properties, Inc. 09/24/2003
9% Preferred Ser. F 1¢ par called for redemption at $25 on 03/26/2007
Acquired by Lone Star Real Estate Fund IV (U.S.) L.P. 10/07/2015
Each share Common 1¢ par exchanged for $75.23 cash

HOME PRODS INC (BC)
Each share Preference Ser. 4 no par exchanged for (4.166) shares Common no par 04/21/1997
Delisted from Canadian Dealer Network 01/14/2000

HOME PRODS INTL INC (DE)
92.9% acquired by purchase offer which expired 12/13/2004
Plan of reorganization under Chapter 11 Federal Bankruptcy Code effective 03/20/2007
Each share Common 1¢ par exchanged for $0.01721 cash

HOME PROT CO (PA)
Completely liquidated 5/21/76
Each share Common 10¢ par exchanged for first and final distribution of $220 cash

HOME RETAIL GROUP (UNITED KINGDOM)
Each Unsponsored ADR for Ordinary exchanged for (1) Sponsored ADR for Ordinary 10/01/2009

HOME RETAIL GROUP PLC (ENGLAND & WALES)
ADR agreement terminated 09/02/2016
Each Sponsored ADR for Ordinary exchanged for $8.389989 cash

HOME RETAIL HOLDINGS, INC. (DE)
Name changed to Rolling Pin Kitchen Emporium, Inc. 9/15/98
(See Rolling Pin Kitchen Emporium, Inc.)

HOME SAVINGS & LOAN ASSOCIATION (NV)
Name changed to Home Savings Association 3/8/71
(See Home Savings Association)

HOME SVGS & LN ASSN DURHAM (NC)
Stock Dividend - 20% 4/28/87
Merged into BB&T Financial Corp. 3/15/91
Each share Common $1 par exchanged for (0.4686) share Common $2.50 par and $8.33 cash
BB&T Financial Corp. merged into Southern National Corp. 2/28/95 which name changed to BB&T Corp. 5/19/97

HOME SVGS & LN ASSN LAWTON (OK)
Placed in receivership 8/31/88
No stockholders' equity

HOME SVGS & LN ASSN ROCKY MT (NC)
Common $1 par split (3) for (2) by issuance of (0.5) additional share 11/19/85
Name changed to Pioneer Savings Bank, Inc. 3/1/86
Pioneer Savings Bank, Inc. reorganized as Pioneer Bancorp, Inc. 12/28/88
(See Pioneer Bancorp, Inc.)

HOME SAVINGS ASSOCIATION (NV)
Merged into United States Leasing International, Inc. 2/1/79
Each share Capital Stock $1 par exchanged for $15.70 cash

HOME SVGS ASSN PENNA TAMAQUA (PA)
Name changed to American Savings Bank (Tamaqua, PA) 10/1/90
(See American Savings Bank (Tamaqua, PA))

HOME SAVINGS BANK, S.S.B. (MERIDIAN, MS)
Merged into Bancplus Corp. 5/17/96
Each share Common 1¢ par exchanged for $25 cash

HOME SVGS BK (BROOKLYN, NY)
Acquired by Ahmanson (H.F.) & Co. 11/19/1990
Each share Common $1 par exchanged for (1.3889) shares Common 1¢ par
Ahmanson (H.F.) & Co. merged into Washington Mutual, Inc. 10/01/1998
(See Washington Mutual, Inc.)

HOME SVGS BK F S B (HOLLYWOOD, FL)
Common $1 par split (2) for (1) by issuance of (1) additional share 06/03/1994
Stock Dividend - 10% 09/29/1993
Reorganized as Home Financial Corp. (DE) 10/24/1994
Each share Common $1 par exchanged for (1.331878) shares Common $1 par
Home Financial Corp. (DE) merged into First Union Corp. 11/25/1996 which name changed to Wachovia Corp. (Ctfs. dated after 09/01/2001) 09/01/2001 which merged into Wells Fargo & Co. (New) 12/31/2008

HOME SVGS BK SILER CITY INC SSB (NC)
Merged into Capital Bank Corp. 03/31/1999
Each share Common $11 par exchanged for (1.28) shares Common $5 par
Capital Bank Corp. merged into Capital Bank Financial Corp. 09/24/2012 which merged into First Horizon National Corp. 11/30/2017

HOME SEC INTL INC (DE)
Company terminated registration of common stock and is no longer public as of 05/15/2001
Details not available

HOME SEC LIFE INS CO (NC)
Each share Capital Stock $100 par exchanged for (30) shares Capital Stock $5 par 9/30/65
Stock Dividends - 25% 5/25/71; 33-1/3% 1/25/73
Acquired by Capital Holding Corp. 12/28/73
Each share Capital Stock $5 par exchanged for (1.5) shares Common $1 par
Capital Holding Corp. name changed to Providian Corp. 5/12/94 which merged into Aegon N.V. 6/10/97

HOME SECURITY SAVINGS & LOAN ASSOCIATION, INC. (ID)
Completely liquidated 12/31/73
Each share Savings Account Stock $125 par or Permanent Guarantee $12.50 par exchanged for first and final distribution of $6 cash

HOME SERVICE CO. (NV)
Reorganized as Home Service Corp. in 1937
Preferred exchanged share for share
Common remained unchanged

HOME SVCS INTL INC (NV)
Name changed to Internal Hydro International, Inc. (NV) 01/02/2004
Internal Hydro International, Inc. (NV) reincorporated in Florida 02/04/2004 which name changed to Renewable

Energy Resources, Inc. 02/20/2007 which name changed to New Green Technologies, Inc. 07/03/2008 which recapitalized as Spur Ranch, Inc. 08/25/2010 which name changed to Rounder, Inc. 01/24/2012 which name changed to Fortitude Group, Inc. 01/08/2013

HOME SHOPPING LATINO INC (DE)
Each share old Common $0.001 par exchanged for (0.00666666) share new Common $0.001 par 02/25/2009
Name changed to OrgHarvest, Inc. 07/03/2018

HOME SHOPPING NETWORK INC (DE)
Common 1¢ par split (3) for (1) by issuance of (2) additional shares 09/05/1986
Common 1¢ par split (2) for (1) by issuance of (1) additional share 01/16/1987
Merged into HSN, Inc. (Old) 12/20/1996
Each share Common 1¢ par exchanged for (0.45) share Common 1¢ par
HSN, Inc. (Old) name changed to USA Networks, Inc. 02/17/1998 which name changed to USA Interactive 05/09/2002 which name changed to InterActiveCorp 06/23/2003 which name changed to IAC/InterActiveCorp 07/14/2004

HOME SMITH INTL LTD (ON)
99.97% acquired by Great Northern Capital Corp. Ltd. through exchange offer which expired 04/24/1972
Public interest eliminated

HOME SOLUTIONS AMER INC (DE)
SEC revoked common stock registration 01/05/2010

HOME ST HLDGS INC (DE)
Plan of reorganization under Chapter 11 Federal Bankruptcy Code effective 12/4/2000
No stockholders' equity

HOME STAKE OIL & GAS CO (OK)
Merged into Cortez Oil & Gas, Inc. 12/12/2000
Each share Common 1¢ par exchanged for $11 cash

HOME STAKE PRODTN CO (OK)
Reorganized under Chapter X bankruptcy proceedings 10/14/82
No stockholders' equity

HOME STAKE RTY CORP (OK)
Stock Dividends - 100% 5/6/74; 100% 5/5/78
Merged into Home-Stake Oil & Gas Co. 12/31/97
Each share Common $40 par exchanged for (48.66) shares Common 1¢ par
(See Home-Stake Oil & Gas Co.)

HOME STATE BANK (TEANECK, NJ)
Merged into First Jersey National Corp. 8/15/80
Each share Capital Stock $10 par exchanged for (1.32) shares Common $5 par and $5.50 cash
(See First Jersey National Corp.)

HOME TELEPHONE & TELEGRAPH CO. (IN)
Each share Common $50 par exchanged for (3) shares Common no par in 1951
5% Preferred Ser. A $50 par called for redemption 10/26/56
Merged into General Telephone Co. of Indiana, Inc. (Old) 12/11/56
Each share Common no par exchanged for (1.1) shares Common no par
General Telephone Co. of Indiana, Inc. (Old) merged into General Telephone Co. of Indiana, Inc. (New) 5/5/66 which merged into GTE MTO

Inc. 3/31/87 which name changed to GTE North Inc. 1/1/88
(See GTE North Inc.)

HOME TELEPHONE & TELEGRAPH CO. OF VIRGINIA (VA)
Merged into Continental Telephone Corp. 8/5/68
Each share Capital Stock $5 par exchanged for (1) share Common $1 par
Continental Telephone Corp. name changed to Continental Telecom Inc. 5/6/82 which name changed to Contel Corp. 5/1/86 which merged into GTE Corp. 3/14/91 which merged into Verizon Communications Inc. 6/30/2000

HOME TELEPHONE CO. OF RIDGWAY (PA)
Merged into Mid-Continent Telephone Corp. 07/31/1968
Each share 5% Preferred $50 par exchanged for (2) shares 5-1/2% Preferred Ser. F $25 par
Each share Common $50 par exchanged for (12) shares Common no par
Note: Until 07/31/1970 unexchanged ctfs. could be exchanged for stock; after that date and until 07/31/1972 unexchanged ctfs. could be exchanged for cash and after 07/31/1972 unexchanged ctfs. became void
Mid-Continent Telephone Corp. name changed to Alltel Corp. (OH) 10/25/1983 which reincorporated in Delaware 05/15/1990
(See Alltel Corp.)

HOME THEATRE PRODS INTL INC (DE)
Plan of reorganization under Chapter 11 Federal Bankruptcy proceedings confirmed 01/28/1998
No stockholders' equity

HOME TICKET NETWORK CORP (AB)
Name changed to Applause Corp. 09/18/2001
(See Applause Corp.)

HOME TITLE GUARANTY CO. (NY)
Merged into Chicago Title Insurance Co. for cash 9/9/63

HOME TITLE INSURANCE CO. (NY)
Reorganized as Home Title Guaranty Co. in 1940. Stockholders received short-term Warrants only

HOME TOUCH HLDG CO (NV)
Each share old Common $0.001 par exchanged for (0.05) share new Common $0.001 par 09/03/2010
Name changed to Prime Global Capital Group Inc. 02/03/2011

HOME UNITY SVGS BK PASA (LAFAYETTE HILL, PA)
Name changed 01/01/1987
Name changed from Home Unity Savings & Loan Association to Home Unity Savings Bank, PaSA (Lafayette Hill, PA) 01/01/1987
Stock Dividend - 10% 05/15/1987
Placed in receivership by Office of Thrift Supervision 06/04/1992
No stockholders' equity

HOME VY BANCORP INC (OR)
Common $3 par split (2) for (1) by issuance of (1) additional share payable 12/15/2000 to holders of record 12/15/2000 Ex date - 01/12/2001
Common $3 par split (2) for (1) by issuance of (1) additional share payable 05/16/2005 to holders of record 04/19/2005
Stock Dividends - 3.2841% payable 12/01/2001 to holders of record 09/12/2001; 5% payable 12/02/2003 to holders of record 10/15/2003 Ex date - 11/12/2003; 5% payable 12/01/2004 to holders of record

10/29/2004 Ex date - 12/15/2004; 5% payable 12/08/2005 to holders of record 10/28/2005 Ex date - 11/01/2005; 5% payable 12/05/2006 to holders of record 10/30/2006 Ex date - 10/27/2006; 5% payable 12/10/2007 to holders of record 10/31/2007 Ex date - 11/13/2007; 5% payable 11/17/2008 to holders of record 10/31/2008 Ex date - 11/06/2008
Chapter 7 bankruptcy proceedings terminated 12/08/2017
No stockholders' equity

HOME VY BK (CAVE JUNCTION, OR)
Under plan of reorganization each share Common $3 par automatically became (1) share Home Valley Bancorp Inc. Common $3 par 05/09/1998
(See Home Valley Bancorp Inc.)

HOME VENTURES LTD (BC)
Recapitalized as Buck Lake Ventures Ltd. 02/15/2000
Each share Common no par exchanged for (0.33333333) share Common no par
Buck Lake Ventures Ltd. recapitalized as Ultra Uranium Corp. 05/11/2006 which recapitalized as Ultra Resources Corp. 11/14/2012 which recapitalized as Empire Rock Minerals Inc. 10/22/2015 which name changed to Empire Metals Corp. 02/02/2017

HOME WARRANTY SVCS AMER INC (NV)
Each share old Common $0.001 par exchanged for (0.02) share new Common $0.001 par 09/06/2005
Name changed to Golden Apple Oil & Gas, Inc. 10/31/2005
(See Golden Apple Oil & Gas, Inc.)

HOME WEB INC (NV)
Common $0.001 par split (2.2) for (1) by issuance of (1.2) additional shares payable 02/23/2000 to holders of record 02/22/2000
Name changed to Duro Enzyme Products Inc. 02/06/2001
Duro Enzyme Products Inc. recapitalized as EAPI Entertainment, Inc. 05/27/2003 which name changed to Organic Recycling Technologies, Inc. 07/11/2005 which name changed to Global 8 Environmental Technologies, Inc. 05/15/2008

HOME WTR CO (PA)
Merged into Citizens Utilities Co. 12/30/1970
Each share Capital Stock $25 par exchanged for (2.692875) shares Ser. A Common $1 par
Citizens Utilities Co. name changed to Citizens Communications Co. 05/18/2000 which name changed to Frontier Communications Corp. 07/31/2008

HOMEAWAY INC (DE)
Merged into Expedia, Inc. 12/15/2015
Each share Common $0.0001 par exchanged for (0.2065) share Common $0.0001 par and $10.15 cash
Expedia, Inc. name changed to Expedia Group, Inc. 03/27/2018

HOMEBANC CORP (AL)
Merged into BancorpSouth Inc. 02/26/1999
Each share Common no par exchanged for (1.5747417) shares Common no par
BancorpSouth Inc. reorganized as BancorpSouth Bank (Tupelo, MS) 11/01/2017

HOMEBANC CORP (GA)
Issue Information - 34,250,000 shares COM offered at $7.50 per share on 07/13/2004
Chapter 11 bankruptcy proceedings

converted to Chapter 7 on 02/24/2009
Stockholders equity unlikely

HOMEBANK TECHNOLOGIES INC (QC)
Name changed to Selient Inc. 06/15/2005
(See Selient Inc.)

HOMEBASE INC (DE)
Name changed to House2Home, Inc. 9/8/2001
(See House2Home, Inc.)

HOMECALL INC (MD)
Each share Common $0.001 par exchanged for (0.1) share Common 1¢ par 02/20/1992
Merged into Mid Atlantic Medical Services, Inc. 10/07/1994
Each share Common 1¢ par exchanged for $3.10 cash

HOMECARE MGMT INC (DE)
Each share Common 1¢ par exchanged for (1/3) share Common 3¢ par 3/31/92
Name changed to Health Management Inc. 10/28/94
(See Health Management Inc.)

HOMECARE UTD INC (DE)
Name changed to Oasis Holdings Inc. 2/8/2000

HOMECLUB INC (DE)
Merged into Zayre Corp. 1/9/86
Each share Common no par exchanged for (0.2373) share Common $1 par
Zayre Corp. name changed to TJX Companies, Inc. 6/20/89

HOMECO LIFE INS INC (WI)
Name changed to Secura Life Insurance Co. 9/11/86
(See Secura Life Insurance Co.)

HOMECOM COMMUNICATIONS INC (DE)
Name changed to Global Matrechs, Inc. 05/31/2004
(See Global Matrechs, Inc.)

HOMECORP INC (DE)
Common 1¢ par split (3) for (2) by issuance of (0.5) additional share 03/31/1993
Common 1¢ par split (3) for (2) by issuance of (0.5) additional share payable 05/30/1997 to holders of record 05/09/1997
Merged into Mercantile Bancorporation, Inc. 03/02/1998
Each share Common 1¢ par exchanged for (0.4968) share Common $5 par
Mercantile Bancorporation, Inc. merged into Firstar Corp. (New) 09/20/1999 which merged into U.S. Bancorp (DE) 02/27/2001

HOMECRAFTERS WHSE INC (DE)
Plan of reorganization under Chapter 11 Federal Bankruptcy proceedings confirmed 11/06/1986
Each share Common 1¢ par exchanged for (0.02) share of Wickes Companies, Inc. Common 10¢ par
Wickes Companies, Inc. name changed to Collins & Aikman Group Inc. 07/17/1992
(See Collins & Aikman Group Inc.)

HOMEDCO GROUP INC (DE)
Merged into Apria Healthcare Group Inc. 06/28/1995
Each share Common 1¢ par exchanged for (2) shares Common 1¢ par
(See Apria Healthcare Group Inc.)

HOMEFED CORP (DE)
Plan of reorganization under Chapter 11 Federal Bankruptcy Code effective 7/13/95
Each share old Common 1¢ par exchanged for (0.269964) share new Common 1¢ par

HOM-HOM

(Additional Information in Active)

HOMEFOODCLUB COM INC (NV)
Reincorporated under the laws of Delaware as iKarma Inc. and Common $0.001 par changed to $0.0000001 par 02/02/2006
iKarma Inc. recapitalized as Medtino, Inc. 10/12/2010 which name changed to IntelaKare Marketing, Inc. 03/01/2011

HOMEFREE VLG RESORTS INC (DE)
Reorganized 6/15/88
Each share Common $0.001 par exchanged for (1) Non-Separable Unit consisting of (1) share Homefree Village Resorts, Inc. Common $0.001 par and (1) Homefree Investors L.P. Assignee Limited Partnership Int.
Each share old Paired Certificate exchanged for (0.00001) share new Paired Certificate 3/28/97
Note: In effect holders received $0.05 cash per Paired Certificate and public interest was eliminated

HOMEFRONT SAFETY SVCS NEV INC (NV)
Name changed to Litewave Corp. 05/10/1999

HOMEGATE CORP (DE)
Recapitalized as Covenant Financial Corp. 04/04/2002
Each share Common $0.001 par exchanged for (0.1) share Common $0.001 par
Covenant Financial Corp. name changed to Air-Q Wi-Fi Corp. 06/30/2003 which name changed to AirRover Wi-Fi Corp. 06/04/2004 which name changed to Diamond I, Inc. 01/28/2005 which recapitalized as ubroadcast, inc. 02/09/2009 which name changed to Santeon Group Inc. 06/11/2010

HOMEGATE HOSPITALITY INC (DE)
Merged into Prime Hospitality Corp. 12/01/1997
Each share Common 1¢ par exchanged for (0.6073) share Common 1¢ par
(See Prime Hospitality Corp.)

HOMEGOLD FINL INC (SC)
Plan of reorganization under Chapter 11 Federal Bankruptcy Code effective 10/16/2003
No stockholders' equity

HOMEGROCER COM INC (WA)
Merged into Webvan Group, Inc. 09/05/2000
Each share Common no par exchanged for (1.07605) shares Common $0.0001 par
(See Webvan Group, Inc.)

HOMEINNS HOTEL GROUP (CAYMAN ISLANDS)
Acquired by BTG Hotels Group (HONGKONG) Holdings Co., Ltd. 04/06/2016
Each Sponsored ADR for Ordinary exchanged for $35.75 cash

HOMELAND BANKSHARES CORP (IA)
Merged into Magna Group, Inc. 03/01/1997
Each share Common $12.50 par exchanged for $42.80 cash

HOMELAND ENERGY GROUP LTD (CANADA)
Reorganized under the laws of British Columbia as Sixonine Ventures Corp. 03/22/2017
Each share Common no par exchanged for (0.01333333) share Common no par

HOMELAND HLDG CORP NEW (DE)
Plan of reorganization under Chapter 11 Federal Bankruptcy Code effective 09/07/2002
No stockholders' equity

HOMELAND HLDG CORP OLD (DE)
Reorganized under Chapter 11 Federal Bankruptcy Code as Homeland Holding Corp. (New) 08/02/1996
Each share Class A Common 1¢ par exchanged for (0.773) share Common 1¢ par and (0.814) Common Stock Purchase Warrant expiring 08/02/2001
(See Homeland Holding Corp. (New))

HOMELAND INTEGRATED SEC SYS INC (FL)
Each share old Common $0.00001 par exchanged for (0.0025) share new Common $0.00001 par 10/24/2007
Recapitalized as DirectView Technology Group, Inc. 12/01/2010
Each share Common $0.00001 par exchanged for (0.0001) share Common $0.00001 par
DirectView Technology Group, Inc. name changed to Green Bridge Technologies International, Inc. 08/25/2019 which recapitalized as Paradise Ridge Hydrocarbons, Inc. 08/20/2012 which name changed to Grupo Resilient International, Inc. 08/10/2017

HOMELAND PRECIOUS METALS CORP (AB)
Reorganized 06/08/2009
Old Common no par split (3) for (1) by issuance of (2) additional shares payable 02/14/2005 to holders of record 02/14/2005
Reorganized from (BC) to under the laws of Alberta 06/08/2009
Each share Common no par exchanged for (0.01) share Common no par
SEC revoked common stock registration 09/22/2014

HOMELAND SEC CAP CORP (DE)
Each share old Common $0.001 par exchanged for (0.01) share new Common $0.001 par 08/01/2007
Recapitalized as Timios National Corp. 08/29/2012
Each share new Common $0.001 par exchanged for (0.002) share Common $0.001 par
(See Timios National Corp.)

HOMELAND SEC GROUP INTL INC (FL)
Recapitalized as Domestic Energy Corp. 04/07/2008
Each share Common $0.001 par exchanged for (0.001) share Common $0.001 par
(See Domestic Energy Corp.)

HOMELAND SEC NETWORK INC (NV)
Name changed to Global Ecology Corp. 01/05/2010

HOMELAND SEC TECHNOLOGY INC (NV)
Merged into Amnis Energy Inc. 03/15/2005
Each share Common $0.001 par exchanged for (1) share Common $0.001 par
Amnis Energy Inc. name changed to Homeland Security Group International, Inc. 10/10/2005 which recapitalized as Domestic Energy Corp. 04/07/2008
(See Domestic Energy Corp.)

HOMELAND URANIUM INC (ON)
Recapitalized as Western Uranium Corp. 12/16/2014
Each share Common no par exchanged for (0.00125) share Common no par
Western Uranium Corp. name changed to Western Uranium & Vanadium Corp. 10/04/2018

HOMELIFE INC (NV)
Each share old Common $0.001 par exchanged for (0.04545454) share new Common $0.001 par 02/04/2008
Name changed to Moneylogix Group, Inc. 02/08/2008
Moneylogix Group, Inc. name changed to Panacea Global, Inc. 06/16/2011

HOMEOWNERS CHOICE INC (FL)
Issue Information - 1,666,668 UNITS consisting of (1) share COM and (1) WT offered at $7 per Unit on 07/24/2008
Name changed to HCI Group, Inc. 06/19/2013

HOMEOWNERS GROUP INC (DE)
Merged into HAC Inc. 3/12/98
Each share Common 1¢ par exchanged for $0.55 cash
Note: An additional payment of $1.44 cash per share was made from escrow 10/27/98

HOMEOWNUSA (NV)
Name changed to SeD Intelligent Home Inc. 12/13/2017

HOMEPLEX MTG INVTS CORP (MD)
Recapitalized as Monterey Homes Corp. 12/31/96
Each share Common 1¢ par exchanged for (1/3) share Common 1¢ par
Monterey Homes Corp. name changed to Meritage Corp. 9/16/98 which name changed to Meritage Homes Corp. 9/14/2004

HOMEPROJECT COM INC (CANADA)
Dissolved 10/04/2005

HOMEQ CORP (ON)
Acquired by Monaco Acquisition Inc. 11/30/2012
Each share Common no par exchanged for $9.50 cash
Note: Unexchanged certificates will be cancelled and become without value 11/30/2018

HOMEQUEST INC (NV)
Recapitalized as WarpRadio.com Inc. 10/04/1999
Each share Common $0.001 par exchanged for (0.13888888) share Common $0.001 par
(See WarpRadio.com Inc.)

HOMER NATIONAL BANK (HOMER, LA)
Merged into Premier Bancorp, Inc. 11/30/95
Each share Common $25 par exchanged for (14.65048) shares Common no par and $191.67 cash
Premier Bancorp, Inc. merged into Banc One Corp. 1/2/96 which merged into Bank One Corp. 10/2/98 which merged into J.P. Morgan Chase & Co. 12/31/2000 which name changed to JPMorgan Chase & Co. 7/20/2004

HOMER YELLOWKNIFE MINES LTD. (ON)
Recapitalized as Desmont Mining Corp. Ltd. 10/28/1955
Each share Capital Stock no par exchanged for (0.2) share Capital Stock no par
(See Desmont Mining Corp.)

HOMESEEKERS COM INC (NV)
Plan of reorganization under Chapter 11 Federal Bankruptcy Code effective 8/11/2004
No stockholders' equity

HOMESERVE TECHNOLOGIES INC (ON)
Merged into Brookfield Asset Management Inc. 07/29/2011
Each share Common no par exchanged for $2.75 cash
Note: Unexchanged certificates were cancelled and became without value 07/28/2017

HOMESERVICES COM INC (DE)
Merged into MidAmerican Energy Holdings Co. 9/26/2001
Each share Common 1¢ par exchanged for $17 cash

HOMESIDE INC (DE)
Issue Information - 7,350,000 shares COM offered at $15 per share on 01/30/1997
Merged into National Australia Bank Ltd. 2/10/98
Each share Common 1¢ par exchanged for $27.825 cash

HOMESKILLS INC NEW (CO)
Name changed to Curve Wireless Corp. 1/12/2006
Curve Wireless Corp. name changed to OTC Wireless, Inc. 8/7/2006

HOMESKILLS INC OLD (CO)
Name changed to Pegasus Wireless Corp. 12/14/2004
Pegasus Wireless Corp. name changed to Homeskills, Inc. (New) 5/31/2005 which name changed to Curve Wireless Corp. 1/12/2006 which name changed to OTC Wireless, Inc. 8/7/2006

HOMESMART COM INC (CO)
Reorganized under the laws of Nevada as Smart Truck Systems, Inc. 03/28/2005
Each share Common no par exchanged for (0.01) share Common $0.001 par
Smart Truck Systems, Inc. recapitalized as Speechphone, Inc. 05/20/2008 which name changed to Hallmark Venture Group, Inc. 08/12/2008

HOMESTAKE CDA INC (ON)
Name changed to Barrick Gold Inc. (ONT) 06/27/2003
Barrick Gold Inc. (ONT) reincorporated in Alberta 05/09/2006 which was exchanged for Barrick Gold Corp. 03/02/2009

HOMESTAKE EXPLS LTD (MB)
Capital Stock $1 par reclassified as Common no par 04/29/1983
Name changed to HSK Minerals Ltd. 10/24/1986
HSK Minerals Ltd. merged into Queenston Mining Inc. 01/02/1990 which merged into Osisko Mining Corp. 01/02/2013
(See Osisko Mining Corp.)

HOMESTAKE MNG CO. (DE)
Reincorporated 05/08/1984
Each share Capital Stock $100 par exchanged for (8) shares Capital Stock $12.50 par 00/00/1937
Capital Stock $12.50 par changed to $1 par and (1) additional share issued 10/04/1968
Capital Stock $1 par reclassified as Common $1 par and (1) additional share issued 06/06/1974
Common $1 par split (3) for (2) by issuance of (0.5) additional share 09/26/1980
Common $1 par split (2) for (1) by issuance of (1) additional share 03/14/1983
State of incorporation changed from (CA) to Delaware 05/08/1984
Common $1 par split (2) for (1) by issuance of (1) additional share 11/16/1987
Merged into Barrick Gold Corp. 12/14/2001
Each share Common $1 par exchanged for (0.53) share Common no par

HOMESTAKE OIL & GAS CO (OK)
Common $100 par changed to $20 par 11/28/88
Stock Dividends - 100% 5/5/67; 300% 6/13/80
Merged into Home-Stake Oil & Gas Co. 12/31/97
Each share Common $20 par

exchanged for (30) shares Common 1¢ par
(See Home-Stake Oil & Gas Co.)

HOMESTAKE RESOURCE CORP (BC)
Merged into Auryn Resources Inc. 09/07/2016
Each share Common no par exchanged for (0.0588) share Common no par
Note: Unexchanged certificates will be cancelled and become without value 09/07/2022

HOMESTAKE SILVER LTD (BC)
Recapitalized as Northern Homestake Mines Ltd. 08/06/1971
Each share Capital Stock no par exchanged for (0.2) share Capital Stock no par
Northern Homestake Mines Ltd. recapitalized as Thunderwood Explorations Ltd. 05/31/1976 which recapitalized as International Thunderwood Explorations Ltd. (BC) 07/14/1983 which reincorporated in Canada 04/27/1987 which reorganized in Ontario as Thunderwood Resources Inc.-Les Ressources Thunderwood Inc. 06/01/1989 which merged into Thundermin Resources Inc. 11/01/1998 which merged into Rambler Metals & Mining PLC 01/12/2016

HOMESTEAD BANCORP INC (LA)
Acquired by First Guaranty Bank (Hammond, LA) 07/31/2007
Each share Common 1¢ par exchanged for $17.60 cash

HOMESTEAD BK (SUWANEE, GA)
Merged into Security Bank Corp. 07/31/2006
Each share Common exchanged for (1.0443) shares Common $1 par
(See Security Bank Corp.)

HOMESTEAD CONSOLIDATED OIL CO., LTD. (AB)
Name changed to Consolidated Homestead Oil Co., Ltd. 00/00/1948
Consolidated Homestead Oil Co., Ltd. recapitalized as Western Homestead Oils Ltd. 08/00/1950 which recapitalized as Canadian Homestead Oils Ltd. 03/01/1954 which merged into Inter-City Gas Corp. (MB) 04/14/1980 which reorganized as Inter-City Products Corp. 04/18/1990

HOMESTEAD CORP. (UT)
Name changed to Homestead Oil Corp. 07/11/1961
Homestead Oil Corp. name changed to Homestead Minerals Corp. (UT) 04/15/1968 which reincorporated in Nevada 08/18/1988
(See Homestead Minerals Corp.)

HOMESTEAD FINL CORP (DE)
Reincorporated 12/15/86
Common 75¢ par changed to $0.375 par and (1) additional share issued 3/29/83
Common $0.375 par split (5) for (4) by issuance of (0.25) additional share 4/7/86
State of incorporation changed from (CA) to (DE) and Common $0.375 par reclassified as Class A Common 1¢ par 12/15/86
Each share Class A Common 1¢ par received distribution of (1) share Conv. Class B Common 1¢ par 1/14/87
Stock Dividends - 25% 3/1/72; 25% 1/30/73; 25% 3/31/76; 50% 4/25/78; 50% 3/15/79
Recapitalized as Dover Investments Corp. 5/17/93
Each share Class A Common 1¢ par exchanged for (0.1) share Class A Common 1¢ par
Each share Class B Common 1¢ par exchanged for (0.1) share Class B Common Common 1¢ par

HOMESTEAD FIRE INSURANCE CO.
Merged into Home Insurance Co. in 1948
Each share Common $10 par exchanged for (0.747) share Common $5 par
(See listing for Home Insurance Co.)

HOMESTEAD GOLD EXPL CORP (CA)
Charter revoked for failure to file reports and pay fees 07/01/1969

HOMESTEAD INDS INC (PA)
Common $2 par changed to $1 par and (1) additional share issued 05/01/1969
Filed a petition under Chapter 11 Federal Bankruptcy Code 11/26/1990
Stockholders' equity unlikely

HOMESTEAD INTL INC (AR)
Reincorporated under the laws of Delaware as Candler Co. 04/16/1973
(See Candler Co.)

HOMESTEAD MINERALS CORP (NV)
Reincorporated 08/18/1988
Each share Common 1¢ par exchanged for (0.1) share Common 10¢ par 05/20/1985
State of incorporation changed from (UT) to (NV) 08/18/1988
Each share Common 10¢ par exchanged for (1/3) share Common 10¢ par
Chapter 7 bankruptcy proceedings terminated 01/16/2001
Stockholders' equity unlikely

HOMESTEAD NURSING CTRS AMER (AR)
Each share Common 10¢ par exchanged for (0.1) share Common $1 par 02/12/1969
Name changed to Homestead International Inc. (AR) 12/23/1969
Homestead International Inc. (AR) reincorporated in Delaware as Candler Co. 04/16/1973
(See Candler Co.)

HOMESTEAD OIL & GAS LTD. (AB)
Recapitalized as Homestead Consolidated Oil Co. Ltd. 07/00/1947
Each share Capital Stock no par exchanged for (0.25) share Capital Stock no par
Homestead Consolidated Oil Co. Ltd. name changed to Consolidated Homestead Oil Co. Ltd. 00/00/1948 which recapitalized as Western Homestead Oils Ltd. 08/00/1950 which recapitalized as Canadian Homestead oils Ltd. 03/01/1954 which merged into Inter-City Gas Corp. (MB) 04/14/1980 which reorganized as Inter-City Products Corp. 04/18/1990

HOMESTEAD OIL & URANIUM CO. (CO)
Merged into Texas Adams Oil Co., Inc. 03/11/1956
Details not available

HOMESTEAD OIL CORP. (UT)
Name changed to Homestead Minerals Corp. (UT) 04/15/1968
Homestead Minerals Corp. (UT) reincorporated in Nevada 08/18/1988
(See Homestead Minerals Corp.)

HOMESTEAD OIL INC (NV)
Recapitalized as Hallmark Investment Corp. 1/13/89
Each share Common $0.001 par exchanged for (0.1) share Common $0.001 par

HOMESTEAD OILS, LTD. (CANADA)
Dissolution approved and assets sold in 1936

No stockholders' equity

HOMESTEAD RES INC (BC)
Recapitalized as International Homestead Resources Inc. 05/13/1993
Each share Common no par exchanged for (0.33333333) share Common no par
International Homestead Resources Inc. name changed to Novawest Resources Inc. 09/11/1996 which name changed to Apella Resources Inc. 04/02/2008 which name changed to PacificOre Mining Corp. 05/28/2012 which name changed to Vanadiumcorp Resource Inc. 11/22/2013

HOMESTEAD SVGS BK F S B (PORTSMOUTH, PA)
Merged into Cenit Bancorp, Inc. 4/1/94
Each share Common no par exchanged for $17.08 cash

HOMESTEAD URANIUM CORP. (UT)
Name changed to Homestead Corp. 07/13/1957
Homestead Corp. name changed to Homestead Oil Corp. 07/11/1961 which name changed to Homestead Minerals Corp. 04/15/1968 which reincorporated in Nevada 08/18/1988
(See Homestead Minerals Corp.)

HOMESTEAD VALVE MFG CO (PA)
Each share Common $50 par exchanged for (25) shares Common $2 par 11/21/47
Name changed to Homestead Industries Inc. 3/7/69

HOMESTEAD VLG INC (MD)
Name changed 8/2/96
Name changed from Homestead Village Properiettes Inc. to Homestead Village Inc. 8/2/96
Merged into Security Capital Group Inc. 6/8/2000
Each share Common 1¢ par exchanged for $4.10 cash

HOMESTOCK RES LTD (BC)
Recapitalized as International Homestock Resources Ltd. 05/16/1986
Each share Common no par exchanged for (0.5) share Common no par
International Homestock Resources Ltd. name changed to Coscient Group Inc. 02/14/1989 which name changed to Motion International Inc. 01/25/2000
(See Motion International Inc.)

HOMESTORE INC (DE)
Name changed 05/22/2002
Name changed from Homestore.com, Inc. to Homestore, Inc. 05/22/2002
Name changed to Move, Inc. 06/23/2006
(See Move, Inc.)

HOMESTYLE BUFFET INC (FL)
Stock Dividends - 10% 05/08/1989; 15% 03/30/1990
Name changed to Stacey's Buffet, Inc. 12/13/1993
(See Stacey's Buffet, Inc.)

HOMESTYLE HARMONY INC (UT)
Name changed to Catalyst Communications Inc. 12/31/1996
Catalyst Communications Inc. name changed to DNAPrint Genomics, Inc. 07/07/2000
(See DNAPrint Genomics, Inc.)

HOMETOWN AUTO RETAILERS INC (DE)
Merged into Hometown Acquisition I Corp. 01/31/2007
Each share Class A Common $0.001 par exchanged for $2.30 cash

HOMETOWN BANCORP INC (USA)
Acquired by Wallkill Valley Federal Savings & Loan Association 08/11/2017
Each share Common $0.001 par exchanged for $3.01 cash

HOMETOWN BANCORPORATION INC (DE)
Merged into HUBCO, Inc. 08/30/1996
Each share Common $1 par exchanged for $17.75 cash

HOMETOWN BANCSHARES INC (TX)
Merged into Sterling Bancshares, Inc. 11/20/1998
Each share Common exchanged for (0.423438) share Common $1 par
Sterling Bancshares, Inc. merged into Comerica, Inc. 07/28/2011

HOMETOWN BK (MOODUS, CT)
Merged into Liberty Bank (Middletown, CT) 06/29/2001
Each share Common $1 par exchanged for $33.06 cash

HOMETOWN BK (ROANOKE, VA)
Under plan of reorganization each share Common $5 par automatically became (1) share HomeTown Bankshares Corp. Common $5 par 09/04/2009

HOMETOWN BUFFET INC (DE)
Common 1¢ par split (3) for (2) by issuance of (0.5) additional share 3/7/94
Merged into Buffets, Inc. 9/20/96
Each share Common 1¢ par exchanged for (1.17) shares Common 1¢ par
(See Buffets, Inc.)

HOMETREND INC (NV)
Charter revoked 01/31/2010

HOMETRUST BK (GAINESVILLE, GA)
Acquired by SunTrust Banks, Inc. 1/1/93
Each share Common $1 par exchanged for (0.38) share Common $1 par

HOMETRUST CORP., INC. (AL)
In receivership since 1962
Receiver advises Common Stock assumed valueless in 1963

HOMEUSA INC (DE)
Issue Information - 5,000,000 shares COM offered at $8 per share on 11/21/1997
Merged into Fleetwood Enterprises, Inc. 08/10/1998
Each share Common 1¢ par exchanged for (0.2779) share Common $1 par
(See Fleetwood Enterprises, Inc.)

HOMEWOOD CORP (ON)
Acquired by RBJ Schlegel Holdings Inc. 01/14/2011
Each share Common no par exchanged for $68 cash

HOMEWOOD FINL CORP (DE)
Exchangeable Auction Market Preferred no par called for redemption 7/11/89
Public interest eliminated

HOMEWOOD HOLDING CO. (MD)
Proclaimed dissolved for failure to file annual reports 10/30/86

HOMEZIPR CORP (CO)
Reorganized under the laws of Delaware as Advansys Companies, Inc. 12/28/2006
Each share Common no par exchanged for (0.02) share Common no par

HOMIE RECIPES INC (NV)
Name changed to Stevva Corp. 10/04/2017

HON INDS INC (IA)
Common $2 par split (3) for (1) by issuance of (2) additional shares 06/01/1968
Common $2 par changed to $1 par

and (1) additional share issued 05/17/1969
Common $1 par split (2) for (1) by issuance of (1) additional share 06/01/1973
Common $1 par split (2) for (1) by issuance of (1) additional share 06/26/1987
Common $1 par split (2) for (1) by issuance of (1) additional share 07/02/1990
Common $1 par split (2) for (1) by issuance of (1) additional share payable 03/27/1998 to holders of record 03/06/1998
Stock Dividends - 50% 05/20/1977; 100% 04/09/1979
Name changed to HNI Corp. 05/04/2004

HONCHO GOLD MINES INC (BC)
Reorganized under the laws of Canada as Takla Gold Mines Ltd. 08/09/1988
Each share Common no par exchanged for (0.2) share Common no par
Takla Gold Mines Ltd. recapitalized as Canard Resources Ltd. 01/24/1994
(See Canard Resources Ltd.)

HONDO OIL & GAS CO (DE)
Merged into Lonrho PLC 12/23/98
Each share Common $1 par exchanged for $0.05 cash

HONDURAS CONSOLIDATED MINES, LTD. (ON)
Charter cancelled for failure to file reports and pay taxes 2/6/56

HONEGGERS & CO INC (DE)
Reincorporated 1/8/76
Common no par split (2) for (1) by issuance of (1) additional share 3/19/59
State of incorporation changed from (IL) to (DE) and Common no par changed to 10¢ par 1/8/76
Merged into Honehe, Inc. 1/12/77
Each share Common 10¢ par exchanged for $4.32 cash

HONESDALE NATL BK (HONESDALE, PA)
Common $50 par changed to $12.50 par and (3) additional shares issued 1/25/72
Stock Dividend - 100% 7/27/45
Reorganized as Honat Bancorp, Inc. 7/29/87
Each share Common $12.50 par exchanged for (1) share Common $1.25 par

HONEY BEE GOLD MINES LTD. (ON)
Name changed to Peak Oils Ltd. 00/00/1951
Peak Oils Ltd. recapitalized as Consolidated Peak Oils Ltd. 00/00/1953 which was acquired by Western Allenbee Oil & Gas Co. Ltd. 06/20/1960 which name changed to Convoy Capital Corp. 04/28/1989 which recapitalized as Hariston Corp. 09/25/1992 which recapitalized as Midland Holland Inc. (Canada) 02/10/1999 which reincorporated in Yukon 03/11/1999 which name changed to Mercury Partners & Co. Inc. 02/22/2000 which name changed to Black Mountain Capital Corp. 05/02/2005 which recapitalized as Grand Peak Capital Corp. (YT) 11/20/2007 which reincorporated in British Columbia 04/27/2010

HONEY DEW, LTD. (ON)
Name changed to Canadian Food Products, Ltd. 00/00/1943
(See Canadian Food Products, Ltd.)

HONEY DEW FOOD STORES, INC. (DE)
No longer in existence having become inoperative and void for non-payment of taxes 4/1/64

HONEYBEE INC (MO)
Acquired by Spiegel, Inc. 8/23/88
Each share Common no par exchanged for $11.18 cash

HONEYBEE TECHNOLOGY INC (CANADA)
Delisted from Toronto Venture Stock Exchange 06/27/2006

HONEYCOMB PRODS INC (OH)
Reincorporated under the laws of Nevada as Orbitex, Inc. and Common no par changed to 1¢ par 12/2/70
Orbitex, Inc. recapitalized as OTX, Inc. 8/15/74 which name changed to Mills-Jennings Co. 6/4/81
(See Mills-Jennings Co.)

HONEYCOMB SYS INC (FL)
Common 10¢ par changed to 2¢ par and (4) additional shares issued 12/6/68
Name changed to Decraform, Inc. 1/6/72
(See Decraform, Inc.)

HONEYMEAD PRODUCTS CO. (IA)
Name changed to Interoceanic Industries, Inc. 8/25/60
Interoceanic Industries, Inc. name changed to First Interoceanic Corp. 5/18/64 which was acquired by Archer-Daniels-Midland Co. in November 1969

HONEYWELL INC (DE)
3% Conv. Preference $100 par called for redemption 08/01/1968
Common $1.50 par split (2) for (1) by issuance of (1) additional share 01/15/1965
Common $1.50 par split (2) for (1) by issuance of (1) additional share 02/06/1984
Common $1.50 par split (2) for (1) by issuance of (1) additional share 12/24/1990
Common $1.50 par split (2) for (1) by issuance of (1) additional share 12/18/1992
Merged into Honeywell International Inc. 12/01/1999
Each share Common $1.50 par exchanged for (1.875) shares Common $1 par

HONG KONG AIRCRAFT ENGR LTD (HONG KONG)
ADR agreement terminated 10/28/2015
Each Sponsored ADR for Ordinary exchanged for $6.998159 cash

HONG KONG CONSTR HLDGS LTD (HONG KONG)
Sponsored ADR's for Ordinary HKD $1 par changed to HKD $0.01 par 10/05/2005
ADR agreement terminated 11/05/2007
No ADR's remain outstanding

HONG KONG DAILY NEWS HLDGS LTD (HONG KONG)
Name changed to Graneagle Holdings Ltd. 01/11/2000
(See Graneagle Holdings Ltd.)

HONG KONG GOLD CORP (BC)
Name changed to Inovision Technologies Inc. 09/28/1993
Inovision Technologies Inc. recapitalized as Inovision Solutions Inc. 05/15/2001 which name changed to Sierra Geothermal Power Corp. 05/16/2006 which merged into Ram Power, Corp. 09/02/2010 which recapitalized as Polaris Infrastructure Inc. 05/19/2015

HONG KONG HEALTH CHECK & LABORATORY HOLDINGS CO LTD (BERMUDA)
Name changed to China Gogreen Assets Investment Ltd. 09/02/2011
(See China Gogreen Assets Investment Ltd.)

HONG KONG HIGHPOWER TECHNOLOGY INC (DE)
Issue Information - 525,000 shares COM offered at $3.25 per share on 06/19/2008
Each share old Common $0.0001 par exchanged for (0.625) share new Common $0.0001 par 06/19/2008
Name changed to Highpower International Inc. 10/21/2010

HONG KONG TELECOMMUNICATIONS LTD (HONG KONG)
Sponsored ADR's for Ordinary split (3) for (1) by issuance of (2) additional ADR's payable 06/13/1994 to holders of record 06/10/1994
Stock Dividends - 5% payable 01/09/1998 to holders of record 11/26/1997; 0.466% payable 08/14/1998 to holders of record 06/12/1998
Name changed to Cable & Wireless HKT 07/20/1999
Cable & Wireless HKT merged into Pacific Century CyberWorks Ltd. 08/17/2000 which name changed to PCCW Ltd. 08/09/2002

HONGKONG & KOWLOON WHARF & GODOWN LTD (HONG KONG)
Stock Dividend - 10% 07/28/1982
Name changed to Wharf Holdings Ltd. 10/06/1986
(See Wharf Holdings Ltd.)

HONGKONG & SHANGHAI BKG CORP (HONG KONG)
Each share Ordinary HK$125 par exchanged for (5) shares Ordinary HK$25 par 03/12/1961
Each share Ordinary HK$25 par exchanged for (10) shares Ordinary HK$2.50 par 07/00/1973
Ordinary Stock HK$2.50 par split (4) for (3) by issuance of (1/3) additional share 05/14/1982
ADR's for Ordinary HK$2.50 par split (4) for (3) by issuance of (1/3) additional share 06/14/1982
Stock Dividends - In ADR's for Ordinary to holders of ADR's for Ordinary 25% 03/12/1955; 100% 08/09/1957; 100% 03/12/1965; 10% 03/18/1966; 10% 04/08/1969; 100% 04/15/1970; 10% 04/16/1971; 10% 04/20/1972; 20% 04/19/1973; 20% 05/01/1974; 10% 06/09/1978; 50% 05/18/1979; 60% 06/13/1980; 25% 05/26/1981; 10% 07/05/1983; 25% 06/06/1984; 10% 06/14/1985; 12-1/2% 06/19/1987; 10% 05/25/1988; 10% 05/24/1989; 10% 06/12/1990
In Ordinary to holders of Ordinary 25% 03/27/1975; 10% 03/26/1976; 10% 04/15/1977; 60% 04/25/1980; 25% 05/15/1981; 10% 07/05/1983; 25% 06/06/1984; 20% 06/17/1986; 12-1/2% 06/19/1987
Reorganized under the laws of England as HSBC Holdings plc 04/08/1991
Each share Ordinary HK$2.50 par exchanged for (0.25) share Ordinary
Each ADR for Ordinary HK$2.50 par exchanged for (0.25) ADR for Ordinary

HONGKONG ELEC HLDGS LTD (HONG KONG)
Unsponsored ADR's for Ordinary HKD $2 par split (7) for (5) by issuance of (0.4) additional share 08/08/1981
Each Unsponsored ADR for Ordinary HKD $2 par exchanged for (1) Sponsored ADR for Ordinary HKD $2 08/01/1996
Stock Dividends - 10% 06/07/1984; 10% 05/29/1990
Name changed to Power Assets Holdings Ltd. 03/01/2011

HONGKONG LD HLDGS LTD (BERMUDA)
ADR agreement terminated 05/28/2004
Each Sponsored ADR for Ordinary USD $0.10 par exchanged for $14.17568 cash
(Additional Information in Active)

HONGKONG LD LTD (HONG KONG)
Each ADR for Ordinary HKD 5 par exchanged for (2) ADR's for Ordinary HKD 2.50 par 02/02/1981
Stock Dividends - 10% 06/12/1979; 10% 06/26/1980; 25% 08/25/1981
Scheme of Arrangement approved 06/09/1989
Each ADR for Ordinary HKD 2.50 par exchanged for $2.58 cash

HONIGS PKWY INC (NY)
Administratively dissolved 12/23/1992

HONOKAA SUGAR CO (HI)
Merged into Davies (Theo. H.) & Co., Ltd. 5/31/79
Each share Common $20 par exchanged for $100 cash

HONOLULU CONSOLIDATED OIL CO.
Succeeded by Honolulu Oil Corp. Ltd. in 1930
Honolulu Oil Corp. Ltd. name changed to Honolulu Oil Corp. in 1937 which completed liquidation 3/25/68

HONOLULU CONSTRUCTION & DRAYING CO., LTD. (HI)
Name changed to HC&D Ltd. 3/19/63
(See HC&D Ltd.)

HONOLULU FINANCE & THRIFT CO. LTD. (HI)
Acquired by Seaboard Finance Co. 3/31/56
Each share Capital Stock $20 par exchanged for (1.666666) shares Common $1 par
(See listing for Seaboard Finance Co.)

HONOLULU GAS CO., LTD. (HI)
Each share Capital Stock $20 par exchanged for (2) shares Common $10 par in 1953
6% Preferred $20 par called for redemption in May 1963
Common $10 par changed to $6-2/3 par and (0.5) additional share issued 7/15/70
Under plan of reorganization each share Common $6-2/3 par automatically became (1) share Pacific Resources, Inc. (Hawaii) Common $6-2/3 par 4/1/71
(See Pacific Resources, Inc. (Hawaii))

HONOLULU IRON WORKS CO. (HI)
Each share Common $100 par exchanged for (5) shares Common $20 par in 1956
Thru voluntary exchange offer 100% acquired by Ward Foods, Inc. as of 1967

HONOLULU OIL CORP. (DE)
Capital Stock no par changed to $10 par and (1) additional share issued 10/6/55
Stock Dividend - 100% 12/15/50
Liquidation completed
Each share Capital Stock $10 par stamped to indicate initial distribution of $95 cash 10/25/61
Each share Stamped Capital Stock $10 par stamped to indicate second distribution of $3.50 cash 12/26/61
Each share Stamped Capital Stock $10 par stamped to indicate third distribution of $1.60 cash 4/4/62
Each share Stamped Capital Stock $10 par exchanged for fourth distribution of $0.75 cash 1/20/64
Each share Stamped Capital Stock $10 par received fifth distribution of $0.50 cash 12/4/67
Each share Stamped Capital Stock

$10 par received sixth and final distribution of $0.0725 cash 3/25/68

HONOLULU OIL CORP. LTD.
Name changed to Honolulu Oil Corp. in 1937
Honolulu Oil Corp. completed liquidation 3/25/68

HONOLULU PAPER CO. LTD. (HI)
Acquired by Boise Cascade Corp. 06/30/1964
Each share Capital Stock $10 par exchanged for (0.25) share Common $5 par
Boise Cascade Corp. name changed to OfficeMax Inc. 11/01/2004 which merged into Office Depot, Inc. 11/05/2013

HONOLULU PLANTATION CO.
Liquidation completed in 1951

HONOLULU RAPID TRAN LTD (HI)
Common $20 par changed to $10 par in 1941
Common $10 par changed to $5 par and (1) additional share issued 3/12/63
Name changed to HRT, Ltd. 3/17/72
(See HRT, Ltd.)

HONOMU SUGAR CO.
Merged into Pepeekeo Sugar Co. in 1946
Each share Capital Stock $20 par exchanged for (0.5) share Capital Stock $100 par
Pepeekeo Sugar Co. merged into Brewer (C.) & Co., Ltd. 4/25/73 which merged into IU International Corp. 8/14/78
(See IU International Corp.)

HONOR ONE CORP (NV)
Name changed to AlphaTrade.com 01/04/1999
(See AlphaTrade.com)

HOOD CANAL STATE BANK (HOODSPORT, WA)
Location changed to Hood Canal State Bank (Shelton, Wash.) 10/20/78

HOOD CANAL STATE BANK (SHELTON, WA)
Name changed to First Olympic Bank (Shelton, WA) 2/20/87
First Olympic Bank (Shelton, WA) name changed to Centennial Bank (Olympia, WA) 3/9/90
(See Centennial Bank (Olympia, WA))

HOOD CHEMICAL CO., INC. (NY)
Acquired by Texize Chemicals, Inc. (DE) on a (10/33) for (1) basis 8/31/61
Texize Chemicals, Inc. (DE) merged into Norwich Pharmacal Co. 12/6/67 which merged into Morton-Norwich Products, Inc. (NY) 4/25/69 which reincorporated in Delaware 11/28/69 which merged into Morton Thiokol, Inc. 9/24/82 which reorganized as Thiokol Corp. (DE) (New) 7/1/89 which name changed to Cordant Technologies Inc. 5/7/98
(See Cordant Techologies Inc.)

HOOD H P INC (MA)
Plan of merger effective 9/10/97
Each share $2.60 Preferred exchanged for either $43.75 principal amount Subordinated Notes due 3/1/2001, $38.75 cash, or a combination of Notes and cash
Each share 6% Preferred no par exchanged for either $43.75 principal amount Subordinated Notes due 3/1/2001, $38.75 cash, or a combination of Notes and cash
Note: Option to make an election expired 10/30/97

HOOD INDS INC (MS)
Acquired by Masonite Corp. 6/16/70
Each share Capital Stock $1 par exchanged for (0.071942) share Common no par
(See Masonite Corp.)

HOOD RUBBER CO.
Acquired by Goodrich (B.F.) Co. 00/00/1929
Details not available

HOOD RUBBER PRODUCTS CO.
Acquired by Goodrich (B.F.) Co. 00/00/1929
Details not available

HOODIA INTL INC (NV)
Recapitalized as Oceanic Research & Recovery, Inc. 04/22/2008
Each share Common $0.001 par exchanged for (0.00285714) share Common $0.001 par
Oceanic Research & Recovery, Inc. name changed to McCusker Holdings Corp. 11/13/2017

HOODOO HYDROCARBONS LTD (AB)
Name changed to Cruiser Oil & Gas Ltd. 07/28/2005
Cruiser Oil & Gas Ltd. merged into One Exploration Inc. 11/21/2008 which recapitalized as TriOil Resources Ltd. 04/07/2010
(See TriOil Resources Ltd.)

HOODOO LAKE MINES, LTD. (ON)
Name changed to Dunvegan Mines Ltd. 00/00/1950
(See Dunvegan Mines Ltd.)

HOOGOVENS EN STAALFABRIEKEN N V (NETHERLANDS)
Stock Dividends - 10% 05/20/1970; 10% 07/10/1974
Name changed to Koninklijke Hoogovens N.V. 07/17/1995
(See Koninklijke Hoogovens N.V.)

HOOK DRUG CO.
Succeeded by Hook Drugs, Inc. in 1930
(See Hook Drugs, Inc.)

HOOK DRUGS INC (IN)
Common no par split (2) for (1) by issuance of (1) additional share 6/11/65
Common no par split (2) for (1) by issuance of (1) additional share 6/20/68
Common no par split (2) for (1) by issuance of (1) additional share 5/10/72
Common no par split (5) for (2) by issuance of (1.5) additional shares 8/30/72
Common no par split (3) for (2) by issuance of (0.5) additional shares 5/13/83
Merged into Kroger Co. 5/28/85
Each share Common no par exchanged for $37 cash

HOOK-SUPERX INC (DE)
Merged into Revco D.S., Inc. 7/15/94
Each share Common 1¢ par exchanged for $13.75 cash

HOOKER AMERN INC (DE)
Name changed to Curtis-Hooker Corp. 9/23/70 which name changed back to Hooker American, Inc. 5/5/75
Each share Common 10¢ par exchanged for (0.1) share Common $1 par 10/17/78
Charter cancelled and declared inoperative and void for non-payment of taxes 3/1/86

HOOKER CHEM CORP (NY)
Acquired by Occidental Petroleum Corp. (Calif.) 7/24/68
Each share $2.16 Conv. Preference $1 par exchanged for (1) share $2.16 Conv. Preferred $1 par
Each share Common $5 par exchanged for (0.5) share $3.60 Conv. Preferred $1 par
$4.25 Preferred no par called for redemption 8/23/68
$5 2nd Preferred Ser. C no par called for redemption 8/23/68
Public interest eliminated

HOOKER ELECTROCHEMICAL CO. (NY)
Each share Common $100 par exchanged for (10) shares Common $10 par in 1940
Each share Common $10 par exchanged for (2) shares Common $5 par in 1947
Common $5 par split (3) for (1) by issuance of (2) additional shares in 1954
Under plan of reorganization name changed to Hooker Chemical Corp. 5/29/58
(See Hooker Chemical Corp.)

HOOKER ENTERPRISES INC (TN)
Administratively dissolved 08/17/2001

HOOKLESS FASTENER CO.
Name changed to Talon, Inc. in 1937
Talon, Inc. acquired by Textron Inc. (Del.) 7/15/68

HOOKUP COMMUNICATION CORP (ON)
Name changed to PC Chips Corp. 05/12/1999
(See PC Chips Corp.)

HOOPSOFT DEV CORP (NV)
Name changed to Yellowcake Mining Inc. and (29) additional shares issued 01/23/2007
Yellowcake Mining Inc. recapitalized as SKY Digital Stores Corp. 04/20/2011 which recapitalized as Qualis Innovations, Inc. 02/14/2018

HOOSAC COTTON MILLS
Acquired by Hoosac Mills Corp. in 1931
Details not available

HOOSAC MILLS CORP. (MA)
Acquired by Indian Head Mills, Inc. for cash 3/7/56

HOOSAC TUNNEL & MINING CO. (CO)
Charter revoked for failure to file reports and pay fees 9/21/21

HOOSIER AIR FREIGHT CORP.
Name changed to Air-Borne Cargo Lines, Inc. in August 1946
(See Air-Borne Cargo Lines, Inc.)

HOOSIER ENGR CO (DE)
Merged into Myers (L.E.) Co. (Old) 8/31/77
Each share Common $1 par exchanged for (0.286) share Common $1 par
(See Myers (L.E.) Co. (Old))

HOOSIER SOIL SERVICE, INC. (IN)
Name changed to H.S.S., Inc. 3/12/65
(See H.S.S., Inc.)

HOOVEN & ALLISON CO (OH)
Each share Common $100 par exchanged for (0.5) share Common $100 par in 1933
Each share Common $100 par exchanged for (2) shares Common $100 par 10/1/53
Each share Common $100 par exchanged for (10) shares Common $10 par 2/23/60
Name changed to H&A Industries 2/3/83
H&A Industries name changed to Bolen Holding Co. 8/2/84
(See Bolen Holding Co.)

HOOVEN AUTOMATIC TYPEWRITER CORP. (NY)
Each share Capital Stock $10 par exchanged for (5) shares Capital Stock $1 par in 1933
Charter revoked for failure to file reports and pay fees 12/15/51

HOOVENS-OWENS RENTSCHLER CO.
Acquired by General Machinery Corp. in 1928
Details not available

HOOVER BALL & BEARING CO. (MI)
Reincorporated 12/31/1968
Reincorporated 08/01/1976
Common $10 par changed to $5 par and (1) additional share issued 12/21/1959
Common $5 par changed to $2.50 par and (1) additional share issued 07/31/1963
Common $2.50 par changed to $2 par and (0.25) additional share issued 03/31/1966
Stock Dividend - 25% 12/22/1947
State of incorporation changed from (MI) to (DE) 12/31/1968
Common $2 par changed to $1 par 11/18/75
State of incorporation changed from (DE) to (MI) 08/01/1976
Common $1 par split (3) for (2) by issuance of (0.5) additional share 08/02/1976
Common $1 par split (3) for (2) by issuance of (0.5) additional share 07/08/1977
Name changed to Hoover Universal Inc. 01/17/1978
Hoover Universal Inc. merged into Johnson Controls, Inc. 05/12/1985 which merged into Johnson Controls International PLC 09/06/2016

HOOVER CO (DE)
Reincorporated 10/29/65
Each share Common $5 par exchanged for (2) shares Common $2.50 par in 1946
Each share Common $2.50 par exchanged for (0.8) share Class A Common $2.50 par and (0.2) share Class B Common $2.50 par in 1954
4-1/2% Preferred $100 par called for redemption 6/30/65
State of incorporation changed from (OH) to (DE) 10/29/65
Class A Common $2.50 par and Class B Common $2.50 par reclassified as Common $2.50 par 10/2/67
Common $2.50 par split (2) for (1) by issuance of (1) additional share 5/19/72
Stock Dividends - In Class A Common to Class A and/or B Common - 100% 1/28/58; 100% 11/30/59; 100% 5/29/64
Merged into Chicago Pacific Corp. 11/20/85
Each share Common $2.50 par exchanged for $43 cash

HOOVER MINING & EXPLORATION LTD. (SK)
Charter revoked for failure to file reports and pay fees 10/2/59

HOOVER STEEL BALL CO.
Name changed to Hoover Ball & Bearing Co. (MI) 3/10/36
Hoover Ball & Bearing Co. (MI) reincorporated in Delaware 12/31/68 which reincorporated back in Michigan 8/1/76
Name changed to Hoover Universal Inc. 1/17/78
Hoover Universal Inc. merged into Johnson Controls, Inc. 5/12/85

HOOVER TRANSMISSION CO., INC. (MA)
Charter revoked for failure to file reports and pay fees 11/21/62

HOOVER UNVL INC (MI)
Common $1 par split (3) for (2) by issuance of (0.5) additional shares 08/01/1983
Merged into Johnson Controls, Inc. 05/12/1985
Each share Common $1 par exchanged for (0.8381) share Common 50¢ par
Johnson Controls, Inc. merged into Johnson Controls International PLC 09/06/2016

HOO-HOR   FINANCIAL INFORMATION, INC.

HOOVERS INC (DE)
Merged into Dun & Bradstreet Corp. 03/03/2003
Each share Common 1¢ par exchanged for $7 cash

HOP IN FOOD STORES INC (VA)
Common $2.50 par changed to $1.25 par and (1) additional share issued 11/27/78
Merged into Silverwood Industries Ltd. 6/25/82
Each share Common $1.25 par exchanged for $17 cash

HOP-ON COM (NV)
Recapitalized as Hop-On, Inc. 5/18/2005
Each share Common $0.001 par exchanged for (0.0005) share Common $0.001 par

HOPE BAY GOLD INC (QC)
Merged into Miramar Mining Corp. 05/23/2002
Each share Common no par exchanged for (0.263) share Common no par and (0.1) Ariane Gold Corp. Special Common Stock Purchase Warrant
(See Miramar Mining Corp.)

HOPE BROOK GOLD INC (ON)
Acquired by BP Canada Inc. 06/27/1991
Each share Common no par exchanged for $1.20 cash

HOPE PRINCETON MINES LTD. (BC)
Charter cancelled for failure to file reports and pay taxes in 1968

HOPE SILVER LEAD MINES INC (ID)
Voluntarily dissolved 5/19/78
No stockholders' equity

HOPE TECHNOLOGIES INC (NV)
Name changed to Lithium Technology Corp. (NV) 12/05/1994
Lithium Technology Corp. (NV) reorganized in Delaware 12/05/1994
(See Lithium Technology Corp.)

HOPEWELL VY CMNTY BK (PENNINGTON, NJ)
Common $5 par split (6) for (5) by issuance of (0.2) additional share payable 02/18/2005 to holders of record 02/04/2005 Ex date - 02/02/2005
Stock Dividends - 5% payable 03/11/2002 to holders of record 02/28/2002 Ex date - 04/02/2002; 5% payable 01/31/2003 to holders of record 01/15/2003 Ex date - 01/31/2003; 5% payable 01/16/2004 to holders of record 12/31/2003 Ex date - 01/29/2004; 10% payable 03/06/2009 to holders of record 02/17/2009 Ex date - 02/12/2009; 5% payable 03/08/2010 to holders of record 02/16/2010 Ex date - 02/11/2010; 5% payable 10/10/2014 to holders of record 09/10/2014 Ex date - 09/08/2014
Acquired by Northfield Bancorp, Inc. 01/08/2016
Each share Common $5 par exchanged for $14.50 cash

HOPI MINING CO. (MO)
Charter forfeited for failure to file reports 1/1/50

HOPKINS & ELLIS, INC. (MA)
Charter revoked for failure to file reports and pay fees 3/31/26

HOPKINS COUNTY BROADCASTING CO. (TX)
Reacquired in June, 1974
Each share Preferred $10 par exchanged for 7-1/2% Subordinated Debentures due 10/1/83

HOPPER SOLIDAY CORP (MD)
Merged into H.S. Acquisition Corp. 9/6/91
Each share Common $0.001 par exchanged for $1.25 cash

HOPPI-COPTERS, INC. (WA)
Each share Common $1 par exchanged for (70) shares Common 10¢ par to effect a (10) for (1) split and a 600% stock dividend in 1948
Charter revoked for failure to file reports and pay fees 7/1/63

HOPPIE ELECTRICAL APPLIANCE CO. (UT)
Proclaimed dissolved for failure to pay taxes 11/9/74

HOPPY TAW CORP. (UT)
Charter suspended for failure to pay taxes 09/30/1967

HORACE MANN EDUCATORS CORP OLD (DE)
Stock Dividend - 100% 11/17/69
Merged into INA Corp. 1/27/75
Each share Common $1 par exchanged for $10 cash

HORACE MANN FD INC (MD)
Name changed to Horace Mann Growth Fund, Inc. 10/31/83

HORACE MANN LIFE INS CO (IL)
Stock Dividend - 10% 6/1/66
Reorganized as Horace Mann Educators Corp. 10/3/68
Each share Common $1 par exchanged for (1) share Common $1 par
Horace Mann Educators Corp. merged into INA Corp. 1/27/75

HORACE SMALL APPAREL PLC (UNITED KINGDOM)
Name changed to Redbus Interhouse PLC 4/5/2000
(See Redbus Interhouse PLC)

HORDER'S INC. (IL)
Common $10 par changed to no par 00/00/1929
Name changed to Associated Stationers Supply Co., Inc. 11/05/1958
Associated Stationers Supply Co., Inc. was acquired by Boise Cascade Corp. 09/30/1964 which name changed to OfficeMax Inc. 11/01/2004 which merged into Office Depot, Inc. 11/05/2013

HORIYOSHI WORLDWIDE INC (NV)
Each share old Common $0.001 par exchanged for (0.1) share new Common $0.001 par 01/27/2012
Each share new Common $0.001 par exchanged again for (0.08333333) share new Common $0.001 par 04/03/2013
Name changed to HW Holdings, Inc. 03/02/2015

HORIZON ACQUISITIONS INC (CO)
Charter suspended for failure to file annual reports 09/30/1987

HORIZON AIR INDS INC (WA)
Acquired by Alaska Air Group, Inc. 7/1/87
Each share $1.20 Conv. Exchangeable Preferred 2¢ par exchanged for $12.34 cash
Each share Common 2¢ par exchanged for $9.50 cash

HORIZON BANCORP (IN)
Common no par split (3) for (2) by issuance of (0.5) additional share payable 11/16/2001 to holders of record 10/31/2001 Ex date - 11/19/2001
Common no par split (3) for (2) by issuance of (0.5) additional share payable 11/17/2003 to holders of record 11/03/2003 Ex date - 11/18/2003
Common no par split (3) for (2) by issuance of (0.5) additional share payable 12/09/2011 to holders of record 11/28/2011 Ex date - 12/12/2011
Common no par split (3) for (2) by issuance of (0.5) additional share payable 11/09/2012 to holders of record 10/29/2012 Ex date - 11/13/2012
Common no par split (3) for (2) by issuance of (0.5) additional share payable 11/14/2016 to holders of record 10/31/2016 Ex date - 11/15/2016
Name changed to Horizon Bancorp, Inc. 05/08/2018

HORIZON BANCORP (NJ)
$3 Conv. Preferred no par called for redemption 04/29/1983
Common $4 par split (3) for (2) by issuance of (0.5) additional share 02/01/1984
Adjustable Rate Preferred no par called for redemption 10/03/1988
Stock Dividend - 10% 03/01/1978
Merged into Chemical Banking Corp. 01/03/1989
Each share Common $4 par exchanged for $75.12 cash

HORIZON BANCORP INC (TX)
Merged into Compass Bancshares, Inc. 03/12/1997
Each share Common 1¢ par exchanged for (0.5629) share Common $2 par
Compass Bancshares, Inc. merged into Banco Bilbao Vizcaya Argentaria, S.A. 09/07/2007

HORIZON BANCORP INC (WV)
Common $1 par split (2) for (1) by issuance of (1) additional share payable 12/15/1996 to holders of record 12/01/1996
Merged into City Holding Co. 12/31/1998
Each share Common $1 par exchanged for (1.111) shares Common $2.50 par

HORIZON BANCORPORATION INC (FL)
Name changed to Manasota Group, Inc. 12/09/2015

HORIZON BK & TR CO (BRAINTREE, MA)
Merged into South Shore Savings Bank (South Weymouth, MA) 2/19/2004
Each share Common exchanged for $16.75 cash

HORIZON BK (BELLINGHAM, WA)
Common $1 par split (3) for (2) by issuance of (0.5) additional share 04/21/1987
Common $1 par split (4) for (3) by issuance of (1/3) additional share 08/22/1989
Common $1 par split (5) for (4) by issuance of (0.25) additional share 08/05/1992
Stock Dividends - 10% 01/24/1989; 10% 05/16/1991; 15% 05/25/1993; 10% 08/25/1994
Under plan of reorganization each share Common $1 par automatically became (1) share Horizon Financial Corp. (WA) Common $1 par 10/13/1995
(See Horizon Financial Corp. (WA))

HORIZON BK (FAIRFAX, VA)
Common $2.50 par split (2) for (1) by issuance of (1) additional share payable 05/30/1996 to holders of record 04/30/1996
Stock Dividends - 10% payable 02/15/1996 to holders of record 01/15/1996; 5% payable 03/16/1998 to holders of record 03/02/1998
Merged into Southern Financial Bancorp, Inc. 10/01/1999
Each share Common $2.50 par exchanged for (0.63) share Common 1¢ par
Southern Financial Bancorp, Inc. merged into Provident Bankshares Corp. 04/30/2004 which was acquired by M&T Bank Corp. 05/26/2009

HORIZON BKS INC (NH)
Merged into Peterborough Savings Bank (Peterborough, NH) 4/15/95
Each share Class A 10¢ par exchanged for (0.03567) share Common 1¢ par

HORIZON CAP CORP (DE)
Recapitalized as Reconversion Technologies Inc. 10/15/1992
Each share Common $0.0001 par exchanged for (0.02052979) share Common $0.0001 par
Reconversion Technologies Inc. name changed to Logisoft Corp. 04/28/2000 which name changed to Team Sports Entertainment, Inc. 05/18/2001 which name changed to Idea Sports Entertainment Group, Inc. 11/09/2004 which recapitalized as HealthSport, Inc. 05/16/2006
(See HealthSport, Inc.)

HORIZON CAP INC (AB)
Name changed to Altachem Pharma Ltd. 11/25/1998
Altachem Pharma Ltd. name changed to Quest PharmaTech Inc. 10/06/2005

HORIZON/CMS HEALTHCARE CORP (DE)
Merged into HealthSouth Corp. 10/29/1997
Each share Common $0.001 par exchanged for (0.84338) share Common 1¢ par
HealthSouth Corp. name changed to Encompass Health Corp. 01/02/2018

HORIZON CORP (DE)
Common 1¢ par split (3) for (2) by issuance of (0.5) additional share 3/29/72
Merged into Horizon Acquisition Corp. 12/28/89
Each share Common 1¢ par exchanged for $2.50 cash

HORIZON ENERGY CORP (UT)
Each share old Common 1¢ par exchanged for (0.000625) share new Common 1¢ par 05/09/1991
Name changed to New Horizon Education, Inc. 06/01/1993
New Horizon Education, Inc. name changed to American Hospital Resources, Inc. 06/26/2002 which name changed to HAPS USA, Inc. 05/12/2005 which name changed to PGMI, Inc. 03/16/2006

HORIZON ENERGY CORP (WY)
Recapitalized as Technovative Group, Inc. 03/02/2015
Each share Common $0.001 par exchanged for (0.05) share Common $0.001 par

HORIZON FDS (MA)
Fund terminated 12/26/1990
Details not available

HORIZON FINL CORP (UT)
Name changed to Assurance Network, Inc. 06/06/1991
Assurance Network, Inc. recapitalized as Ult-I-Med Health Centers, Inc. (UT) 12/22/1993 which reincorporated in Delaware as Youthline USA, Inc. 08/17/1999
(See Youthline USA, Inc.)

HORIZON FINL CORP (WA)
Common $1 par split (5) for (4) by issuance of (0.25) additional share payable 10/23/2006 to holders of record 10/06/2006 Ex date - 10/24/2006
Stock Dividends - 15% payable 05/29/1997 to holders of record 05/08/1997; 15% payable 06/04/2001 to holders of record 05/11/2001 Ex date - 05/09/2001; 25% payable 07/23/2002 to holders of record 07/11/2002 Ex date - 07/24/2002
Completely liquidated

Each share Common $1 par received first and final distribution of $0.0385 cash payable 11/21/2014 to holders of record 07/17/2014

HORIZON FINL SVCS CORP (DE)
Common 1¢ par split (2) for (1) by issuance of (1) additional share payable 11/10/1997 to holders of record 10/20/1997
Liquidation completed
Each share Common 1¢ par exchanged for initial distribution of $1.66 cash 12/15/2008
Each share Common 1¢ par received second and final distribution of $0.29 cash payable 02/01/2012 to holders of record 07/31/2008

HORIZON FINL SVCS INC (DE)
Merged into Republic Bancorp Inc. 06/30/1993
Each share Common $1 par exchanged for (2) shares Common $5 par
Republic Bancorp Inc. merged into Citizens Banking Corp. 12/29/2006 which name changed to Citizens Republic Bancorp, Inc. 04/26/2007 which merged into FirstMerit Corp. 04/12/2013 which merged into Huntington Bancshares Inc. 08/16/2016

HORIZON GOLD CORP (CO)
Name changed 08/28/1990
Preferred Ser. B $10 par called for redemption 06/30/1987
Name changed from Horizon Gold Shares, Inc. to Horizon Gold Corp. 08/28/1990
Reorganized as Horizon Resources Corp. 09/17/1992
Each share Common 1¢ par exchanged for (0.125) share Common 8¢ par
(See Horizon Resources Corp.)

HORIZON GROUP INC (MI)
Merged into Prime Retail, Inc. 6/15/98
Each share Common 1¢ par exchanged for (0.2) share 8.50% Conv. Preferred Ser. B 1¢ par and (0.597) share Common 1¢ par
(See Prime Retail, Inc.)

HORIZON HEALTH CORP (DE)
Ctfs. dated prior to 03/05/1984
Merged into Republic Health Corp. 03/05/1984
Each share Common 10¢ par exchanged for (0.83) share Common 5¢ par
(See Republic Health Corp.)

HORIZON HEALTH CORP (DE)
Ctfs. dtd. after 8/11/97
Common 1¢ par split (2) for (1) by issuance of (1) additional share payable 6/15/2005 to holders of record 5/31/2005 Ex date - 6/16/2013
Merged into Psychiatric Solutions, Inc. 5/31/2007
Each share Common 1¢ par exchanged for $20 cash

HORIZON HEALTH INTL CORP (DE)
Each share old Common 1¢ par exchanged for (0.005) share new Common 1¢ par 12/16/2010
Name changed to Horizons Holdings International, Corp. 04/16/2013

HORIZON HEALTHCARE CORP (DE)
Under plan of merger name changed to Horizon/CMS Healthcare Corp. 07/10/1995
Horizon/CMS Healthcare Corp. merged into HealthSouth Corp. 10/29/1997 which name changed to Encompass Health Corp. 01/02/2018

HORIZON HLDG CORP (DE)
Name changed to Inverted Paradigms Corp. 05/12/2006
Inverted Paradigms Corp. recapitalized as Transfer Technology International Corp. 12/07/2007 which name changed to Enviro-Serv, Inc. 04/23/2013

HORIZON INDS INC (GA)
Merged into Mohawk Industries, Inc. 10/23/1992
Each share Common no par exchanged for (0.309) share Common 1¢ par and $11.095 cash

HORIZON INDS LTD (BC)
Recapitalized as Petro Horizon Energy Corp. 02/13/2009
Each share Common no par exchanged for (0.125) share Common no par
Petro Horizon Energy Corp. name changed to Greenlight Resources Inc. 08/13/2010 which name changed to Great Atlantic Resources Corp. 06/19/2012

HORIZON INDS LTD (NY)
Charter cancelled and proclaimed dissolved for failure to pay taxes 03/31/1982

HORIZON LAND CORP. (DE)
Stock Dividend - 10% 2/28/63
Name changed to Horizon Corp. 3/4/68
(See Horizon Corp.)

HORIZON LINES INC (DE)
Each share old Common 1¢ par exchanged for (0.04) share new Common 1¢ par 12/20/2011
Acquired by Matson, Inc. 05/29/2015
Each share Common 1¢ par exchanged for $0.72 cash

HORIZON MED PRODS INC (GA)
Issue Information - 3,473,000 shares COM offered at $14.50 per share on 04/14/1998
Merged into RITA Medical Systems, Inc. 7/30/2004
Each share Common $0.001 par exchanged for (0.4212) share Common $0.001 par
RITA Medical Systems, Inc. merged into AngioDynamics, Inc. 1/29/2007

HORIZON MENTAL HEALTH MGMT INC (DE)
Common 1¢ par split (3) for (2) by issuance of (0.5) additional share payable 1/31/97 to holders of record 1/22/97
Name changed to Horizon Health Corp. (Ctfs. dtd. after 8/11/97) 8/11/97
(See Horizon Health Corp. (Ctfs. dtd. after 8/11/97))

HORIZON NETWORKS INC (NV)
Name changed to Espion International, Inc. 7/28/2005

HORIZON OFFSHORE INC (DE)
Issue Information - 5,000,000 shares COM offered at $13 per share on 04/01/1998
Common $1 par changed to $0.001 par 09/13/2005
Common $0.001 par changed to $0.00001 par 12/12/2005
Each share old Common $0.00001 par exchanged for (0.04) share new Common $0.00001 par 4/13/2006
Merged into Cal Dive International, Inc. 12/10/2007
Each share Common $0.00001 par exchanged for (0.625) share Common 1¢ par and $9.25 cash

HORIZON ORGANIC HLDG CORP (DE)
Merged into Dean Foods Co. (New) 01/05/2004
Each share Common $0.001 par exchanged for $24 cash

HORIZON OUTLET CTRS INC (MI)
Name changed to HGI Realty, Inc. 7/14/95
HGI Realty, Inc. name changed to Horizon Group, Inc. 6/14/96 which merged into Prime Retail, Inc. 6/15/98
(See Prime Retail, Inc.)

HORIZON PCS INC (DE)
Merged into iPCS, Inc. 07/01/2005
Each share new Class A Common 1¢ par exchanged for (0.7725) share Common 1¢ par
(See iPCS, Inc.)

HORIZON PETE PLC (JERSEY)
Reincorporated under the laws of Alberta as Horizon Petroleum Ltd. 04/05/2016

HORIZON PHARMA INC (DE)
Merged into Horizon Pharma PLC 09/19/2014
Each share Common $0.0001 par exchanged for (1) share Ordinary $0.0001 par

HORIZON PHARMACIES INC (DE)
Reincorporated 6/30/98
Common 1¢ par split (3) for (2) by issuance of (0.5) additional share payable 11/24/97 to holders of record 11/21/97 Ex date - 11/25/97
State of incorporation changed from (TX) to (DE) 6/30/98
Plan of reorganization under Chapter 11 Federal Bankruptcy Code effective 5/24/2002
No stockholders' equity

HORIZON RES CORP (CO)
Administratively dissolved 01/01/2004

HORIZON SOLAR CORP. (CO)
Name changed to Horizon Technology, Inc. 12/31/79
(See Horizon Technology, Inc.)

HORIZON TECHNOLOGY CORP (CO)
Charter suspended for failure to file annual reports 09/30/1985

HORIZON TELCOM INC (OH)
Common no par reclassified as Class A Common no par 10/00/1999
Each share Class A Common no par received distribution of (3) shares Class B Common no par payable 12/15/1999 to holders of record 11/01/1999
Each share old Non-Vtg. Class B Common no par exchanged for (1) share new Non-Vtg. Class B Common no par to reflect a (1) for (125) reverse split followed by a (125) for (1) forward split 03/28/2005
Note: Holders of (124) or fewer pre-split shares received $165 cash per share
Acquired by Novacap TMT 09/13/2018
Each share Class A Common no par exchanged for $341.27 cash
Each share new Non-Vtg. Class B Common no par exchanged for $341.27 cash

HORIZON TOTAL RETURN FD (ON)
Name changed to HTR Total Return Fund 12/28/2006
HTR Total Return Fund merged into INDEXPLUS Income Fund 05/26/2008 which reorganized as Middlefield Mutual Funds Ltd. 06/05/2017

HORIZON VILLAGE CORP CDA (CANADA)
Recapitalized as Roxbury Capital Corp. 09/01/1993
Each share Common no par exchanged for (0.2) share Common no par
Roxbury Capital Corp. merged into Optima Petroleum Corp. (BC) 09/19/1995 which reincorporated in Delaware as Petroquest Energy Inc. 09/01/1998

HORIZON WIMBA INC (DE)
Name changed to Hayse Corp. 09/08/2006
(See Hayse Corp.)

HORIZONS ACTIVE ADVANTAGE YIELD ETF (ON)
Name changed to Horizons Active Yield Matched Duration ETF 09/17/2013
Horizons Active Yield Matched Duration ETF name changed to Horizons Active Global Fixed Income ETF 02/02/2015

HORIZONS ACTIVE BALANCED ETF (ON)
Name changed to Horizons Active Diversified Income ETF 01/30/2013
(See Horizons Active Diversified Income ETF)

HORIZONS ACTIVE DIVERSIFIED INCOME ETF (ON)
Trust terminated 02/26/2016
Each Class E Unit received $10.205808 cash
Each Advisor Class Unit received $10.206237 cash

HORIZONS ACTIVE INCOME PLUS ETF (ON)
Trust terminated 03/22/2013
Each Advisor Class Unit received $8.815652 cash
Each Class E Unit received $8.786368 cash

HORIZONS ACTIVE NORTH AMERN GROWTH ETF (ON)
Trust terminated 06/28/2013
Each Class E Unit received $13.802028 cash

HORIZONS ACTIVE NORTH AMERN VALUE ETF (ON)
Trust terminated 03/22/2013
Each Advisor Class Unit received $12.163918 cash
Each Class E Unit received $11.708721 cash

HORIZONS ACTIVE S&P 60 INDEX COVERED CALL ETF (ON)
Trust terminated 02/06/2015
Each Class E Unit received $10.37767 cash
Each Advisor Class Unit received $10.365366 cash

HORIZONS ACTIVE YIELD MATCHED DURATION ETF (ON)
Name changed to Horizons Active Global Fixed Income ETF 02/02/2015

HORIZONS ALPHAPRO BALANCED ETF (ON)
Name changed to Horizons Balanced ETF 10/11/2011
Horizons Balanced ETF name changed to Horizons Active Balanced ETF 11/01/2012 which name changed to Horizons Active Diversified Income ETF 01/30/2013
(See Horizons Active Diversified Income ETF)

HORIZONS ALPHAPRO CORPORATE BD ETF (ON)
Name changed to Horizons Corporate Bond ETF 10/11/2011
Horizons Corporate Bond ETF name changed to Horizons Active Corporate Bond ETF 11/01/2012

HORIZONS ALPHAPRO DIVID ETF (ON)
Name changed to Horizons Dividend ETF 10/11/2011
Horizons Dividend ETF name changed to Horizons Active Canadian Dividend ETF 11/01/2012

HORIZONS ALPHAPRO ENHANCED INCOME ENERGY ETF (ON)
Name changed to Horizons Enhanced Income Energy ETF 09/09/2011

HORIZONS ALPHAPRO ENHANCED INCOME EQUITY ETF (ON)
Name changed to Horizons Enhanced Income Equity ETF 09/09/2011

HORIZONS ALPHAPRO ENHANCED INCOME FINANCIALS ETF (ON)
Name changed to Horizons Enhanced Income Financials ETF 09/09/2011

HORIZONS ALPHAPRO ENHANCED INCOME GOLD PRODUCERS ETF (ON)
Name changed to Horizons Enhanced Income Gold Producers ETF 09/09/2011

HORIZONS ALPHAPRO FIERA TACTICAL BOND FUND (ON)
Reorganized as Horizons AlphaPro Tactical Bond ETF 01/04/2011
Each Class A Unit no par automatically became (1) Class E Unit
Each Class F Unit no par automatically became (1.04398) Class E Units
Horizons AlphaPro Tactical Bond ETF name changed to Horizons Tactical Bond ETF 09/27/2011 which name changed to Horizons Active Advantage Yield ETF 10/02/2012 which name changed to Horizons Active Yield Matched Duration ETF 09/17/2013 which name changed to Horizons Active Global Fixed Income ETF 02/02/2015

HORIZONS ALPHAPRO FLOATING RATE BD ETF (ON)
Name changed to Horizons Floating Rate Bond ETF 10/11/2011
Horizons Floating Rate Bond ETF name changed to Horizons Active Floating Rate Bond ETF 11/01/2012

HORIZONS ALPHAPRO GARTMAN FD (ON)
Each Class A Unit no par automatically became (1) Class E Unit no par 11/19/2009
Each Class F Unit no par automatically became (1.0318) Class E Units no par 11/19/2009
Name changed to Horizons Gartman ETF 10/25/2011
(See Horizons Gartman ETF)

HORIZONS ALPHAPRO GLOBAL DIVID ETF (ON)
Name changed to Horizons Global Dividend ETF 10/11/2011
Horizons Global Dividend ETF name changed to Horizons Active Global Dividend ETF 11/01/2012

HORIZONS ALPHAPRO INCOME PLUS FD (ON)
Combined Units separated 12/23/2009
Class A Trust Units reclassified as Class E Trust Units 05/09/2011
Name changed to Horizons Income Plus ETF 09/27/2011
Horizons Income Plus ETF name changed to Horizons Active Income Plus ETF 10/02/2012
(See Horizons Active Income Plus ETF)

HORIZONS ALPHAPRO NORTH AMERN GROWTH ETF (ON)
Name changed to Horizons North American Growth ETF 10/11/2011
Horizons North American Growth ETF name changed to Horizons Active North American Growth ETF 11/01/2012
(See Horizons Active North American Growth ETF)

HORIZONS ALPHAPRO NORTH AMERN VALUE ETF (ON)
Name changed to Horizons North American Value ETF 10/11/2011
Horizons North American Value ETF name changed to Horizons Active North American Value ETF 11/01/2012
(See Horizons Active North American Value ETF)

HORIZONS ALPHAPRO PFD SH ETF (ON)
Name changed to Horizons Preferred Share ETF 10/11/2011
Horizons Preferred Share ETF name changed to Horizons Active Preferred Share ETF 11/01/2012

HORIZONS ALPHAPRO S&P/TSX 60 130/30 ETF (ON)
Name changed to Horizons S&P/TSX 60 130/30™ Index ETF 02/18/2011
(See Horizons S&P/TSX 60 130/30™ Index ETF)

HORIZONS ALPHAPRO S&P/TSX 60 EQUAL WEIGHT INDEX ETF (ON)
Name changed to Horizons S&P/TSX 60 Equal Weight Index ETF 10/11/2011

HORIZONS ALPHAPRO S&P/TSX 60 ETF (ON)
Merged into Horizons AlphaPro S&P/TSX 60 Equal Weight Index ETF 06/30/2011
Each Class E Unit no par automatically became (1.018419) Class E Units no par
Horizons AlphaPro S&P/TSX 60 Equal Weight Index ETF name changed to Horizons S&P/TSX 60 Equal Weight Index ETF 10/11/2011

HORIZONS ALPHAPRO SEASONAL ROTATION ETF (ON)
Name changed to Horizons Seasonal Rotation ETF 10/25/2011

HORIZONS ALPHAPRO TACTICAL BD ETF (ON)
Name changed to Horizons Tactical Bond ETF 09/27/2011
Horizons Tactical Bond ETF name changed to Horizons Active Advantage Yield ETF 10/02/2012 which name changed to Horizons Active Yield Matched Duration ETF 09/17/2013 which name changed to Horizons Active Global Fixed Income ETF 02/02/2015

HORIZONS AUSPICE BROAD COMMODITY INDEX ETF (ON)
Trust terminated 06/30/2015
Each Advisor Class Unit received $7.727145 cash
Each Class E Unit received $7.882718 cash

HORIZONS AUSPICE MANAGED FUTURES INDEX ETF (ON)
Each Advisor Class Unit automatically became (0.956829) Class E Unit 04/28/2017
Trust terminated 03/28/2018
Each Class E Unit received $8.257626 cash

HORIZONS AUSTRALIAN DLR CURRENCY ETF (ON)
Trust terminated 01/31/2014
Each Class A Unit received $9.781083 cash

HORIZONS BALANCED ETF (ON)
Name changed to Horizons Active Balanced ETF 11/01/2012
Horizons Active Balanced ETF name changed to Horizons Active Diversified Income ETF 01/30/2013
(See Horizons Active Diversified Income ETF)

HORIZONS BETAPRO COMEX COPPER BEAR PLUS ETF (ON)
Trust terminated 01/31/2014
Each Class A Unit received $10.215396 cash

HORIZONS BETAPRO COMEX COPPER BULL PLUS ETF (ON)
Class A Units split (2) for (1) by issuance of (1) additional Unit payable 03/18/2011 to holders of record 03/18/2011 Ex date - 03/16/2011
Trust terminated 01/31/2014
Each Class A Unit received $7.255932 cash

HORIZONS BETAPRO COMEX COPPER ETF (ON)
Name changed to Horizons COMEX Copper ETF 06/24/2011
(See Horizons COMEX Copper ETF)

HORIZONS BETAPRO COMEX GOLD BULLION BEAR PLUS ETF (ON)
Each old Class A Unit automatically became (0.25) new Class A Unit 09/19/2011
Name changed to BetaPro Gold Bullion -2x Daily Bear ETF 01/03/2017

HORIZONS BETAPRO COMEX GOLD BULLION BULL PLUS ETF (ON)
Class A Units split (2) for (1) by issuance of (1) additional unit payable 03/18/2011 to holders of record 03/18/2011 Ex date - 03/16/2011
Name changed to BetaPro Gold Bullion 2x Daily Bull ETF 01/03/2017

HORIZONS BETAPRO COMEX GOLD ETF (ON)
Name changed to Horizons COMEX Gold ETF 06/24/2011
Horizons COMEX Gold ETF name changed to Horizons Gold ETF 01/03/2017

HORIZONS BETAPRO COMEX GOLD INVERSE ETF (ON)
Completely liquidated 06/29/2012
Each Class A Unit received first and final distribution of $9.278875 cash

HORIZONS BETAPRO COMEX LONG GOLD/SHORT SILVER SPREAD ETF (ON)
Completely liquidated 06/29/2012
Each Class A Unit received first and final distribution of $11.869672 cash

HORIZONS BETAPRO COMEX LONG SILVER/SHORT GOLD SPREAD ETF (ON)
Completely liquidated 06/29/2012
Each Class A Unit received first and final distribution of $7.713175 cash

HORIZONS BETAPRO COMEX SILVER (ON)
Name changed to Horizons COMEX Silver ETF 06/24/2011
Horizons COMEX Silver ETF name changed to Horizons Silver ETF 01/03/2017

HORIZONS BETAPRO COMEX SILVER BEAR PLUS ETF (ON)
Each old Class A Unit automatically became (0.25) new Class A Unit 03/16/2011
Name changed to BetaPro Silver -2x Daily Bear ETF 01/03/2017

HORIZONS BETAPRO COMEX SILVER BULL PLUS ETF (ON)
Old Class A Units split (3) for (1) by issuance of (2) additional Units payable 11/10/2010 to holders of record 11/10/2010 Ex date - 11/08/2010
Old Class A Units split (3) for (1) by issuance of (2) additional Units payable 05/12/2011 to holders of record 05/12/2011 Ex date - 05/10/2011
Each old Class A Unit automatically became (0.25) new Class A Unit 05/06/2013
Each new Class A Unit automatically became (0.2) new Class A Unit 11/26/2015
Name changed to BetaPro Silver 2x Daily Bull ETF 01/03/2017

HORIZONS BETAPRO COMEX SILVER INVERSE ETF (ON)
Completely liquidated 06/29/2012
Each Class A Unit received first and final distribution of $11.119748 cash

HORIZONS BETAPRO DJ AIGSM AGRICULTURAL GRAINS BEAR PLUS ETF (ON)
Common no par split (2) for (1) by issuance of (1) additional share payable 12/22/2008 to holders of record 12/22/2008 Ex date - 12/18/2008
Name changed to Horizons BetaPro S&P Agribusiness North American Bear Plus ETF 08/25/2009
(See Horizons BetaPro S&P Agribusiness North American Bear Plus ETF)

HORIZONS BETAPRO DJ AIGSM AGRICULTURAL GRAINS BULL PLUS ETF (ON)
Each old Class A Unit no par automatically became (0.25) new Class A Unit no par 12/18/2008
Name changed to Horizons BetaPro S&P Agribusiness North American Bull Plus ETF 08/25/2009
(See Horizons BetaPro S&P Agribusiness North American Bull Plus ETF)

HORIZONS BETAPRO MSCI EMERGING MARKETS BEAR PLUS ETF (ON)
Each old Class A Unit automatically became (0.25) new Class A Unit 10/27/2009
Trust terminated 03/13/2015
Each new Class A Unit received $6.150981 cash

HORIZONS BETAPRO MSCI EMERGING MARKETS BULL PLUS ETF (ON)
Each old Class A Unit automatically became (0.2) new Class A Unit 12/18/2008
New Class A Units split (3) for (1) by issuance of (2) additional Units payable 10/29/2009 to holders of record 10/29/2009
Trust terminated 03/13/2015
Each new Class A Unit received $8.749179 cash

HORIZONS BETAPRO MSCI JAPAN BEAR PLUS ETF (ON)
Trust terminated 03/13/2015
Each Class A Unit received $17.385586 cash

HORIZONS BETAPRO MSCI JAPAN BULL PLUS ETF (ON)
Trust terminated 03/13/2015
Each Class A Unit received $19.75268 cash

HORIZONS BETAPRO NASDAQ 100 BEAR PLUS ETF (ON)
Each old Class A Unit automatically became (0.25) new Class A Unit 11/18/2013
Each new Class A Unit automatically became (0.2) new Class A Unit 11/26/2015
Name changed to BetaPro NASDAQ-100 -2x Daily Bear ETF 01/03/2017

HORIZONS BETAPRO NASDAQ 100 BULL PLUS ETF (ON)
Class A Units split (2) for (1) by issuance of (1) additional Unit payable 06/23/2014 to holders of record 06/20/2014 Ex date - 06/24/2014
Name changed to BetaPro NASDAQ-100 2x Daily Bull ETF 01/03/2017
BetaPro NASDAQ-100 2x Daily Bull ETF

HORIZONS BETAPRO NYMEX CRUDE OIL BEAR PLUS ETF (ON)
Class A Units split (2) for (1) by issuance of (1) additional Unit payable 01/06/2009 to holders of record 01/06/2009 Ex date - 01/02/2009
Name changed to BetaPro Crude Oil -2x Daily Bear ETF 01/03/2017

HORIZONS BETAPRO NYMEX CRUDE OIL BULL PLUS ETF (ON)
Each old Class A Unit automatically

became (0.2) new Class A Unit 01/02/2009
Each new Class A Unit automatically became (0.5) new Class A Unit 11/24/2014
Each new Class A Unit automatically became (0.25) new Class A Unit 01/16/2015
Each new Class A Unit automatically became (0.5) new Class A Unit 11/26/2015
Each new Class A Unit automatically became (0.5) new Class A Unit 05/30/2016
Name changed to BetaPro Crude Oil 2x Daily Bull ETF 01/03/2017

HORIZONS BETAPRO NYMEX CRUDE OIL INVERSE ETF (ON)
Trust terminated 10/12/2012
Each Class A Unit received $8.773586 cash

HORIZONS BETAPRO NYMEX LONG CRUDE OIL / SHORT NAT GAS SPREAD ETF (ON)
Trust terminated 10/12/2012
Each Class A Unit received $13.983911 cash

HORIZONS BETAPRO NYMEX LONG NAT GAS / SHORT CRUDE OIL SPREAD ETF (ON)
Each old Class A Unit automatically became (0.25) new Class A Unit 04/13/2012
Trust terminated 10/12/2012
Each new Class A Unit received $15.328559 cash

HORIZONS BETAPRO NYMEX NAT GAS BEAR PLUS ETF (ON)
Old Class A Units split (5) for (1) by issuance of (4) additional Units payable 04/17/2009 to holders of record 04/17/2009 Ex date - 04/15/2009
Old Class A Units split (2) for (1) by issuance of (1) additional Unit payable 09/18/2009 to holders of record 09/18/2009 Ex date - 09/16/2009
Old Class A Units split (4) for (1) by issuance of (3) additional Units payable 05/09/2012 to holders of record 05/09/2012 Ex date - 05/07/2012
Each old Class A Unit automatically became (0.5) new Class A Unit 04/05/2013
Each new Class A Unit automatically became (0.5) new Class A Unit 02/14/2014
Name changed to BetaPro Natural Gas -2x Daily Bear ETF 01/03/2017

HORIZONS BETAPRO NYMEX NAT GAS BULL PLUS ETF (ON)
Each old Class A Unit automatically became (0.25) new Class A Unit 04/15/2009
Each new Class A Unit automatically became (0.2) new Class A Unit 09/16/2009
Each new Class A Unit automatically became (0.5) new Class A Unit 11/08/2010
Each new Class A Unit automatically became (0.25) new Class A Unit 11/23/2011
Each new Class A Unit automatically became (0.25) new Class A Unit 04/13/2012
Each new Class A Unit automatically became (0.1) new Class A Unit 11/26/2015
Name changed to BetaPro Natural Gas 2x Daily Bull ETF 01/03/2017

HORIZONS BETAPRO NYMEX NAT GAS INVERSE ETF (ON)
Class A Units split (4) for (1) by issuance of (3) additional Units payable 05/09/2012 to holders of record 05/09/2012 Ex date - 05/07/2012
Trust terminated 10/12/2012
Each Class A Unit received $5.320379 cash

HORIZONS BETAPRO S&P / TSX 60 INDEX ETF (ON)
Name changed to Horizons S&P/TSX 60 Index ETF 02/23/2011

HORIZONS BETAPRO S&P 500 BEAR PLUS ETF (ON)
Each old Class A Unit automatically became (0.25) new Class A Unit 06/19/2014
Name changed to BetaPro S&P 500 -2x Daily Bear ETF 01/03/2017

HORIZONS BETAPRO S&P 500 BULL PLUS ETF (ON)
Name changed to BetaPro S&P 500 2x Daily Bull ETF 01/03/2017

HORIZONS BETAPRO S&P 500 INVERSE ETF (ON)
Each old Class A Unit automatically became (0.1) new Class A Unit 11/26/2015
Name changed to BetaPro S&P 500 Daily Inverse ETF 01/03/2017

HORIZONS BETAPRO S&P 500 VIX SHORT TERM FUTURES BULL PLUS ETF (ON)
Each old Class A Unit automatically became (0.1) new Class A Unit 07/20/2012
Each new Class A Unit automatically became (0.25) new Class A Unit 03/13/2013
Each new Class A Unit automatically became (0.25) new Class A Unit 11/18/2013
Each new Class A Unit automatically became (0.2) new Class A Unit 07/31/2014
Each new Class A Unit automatically became (0.1) new Class A Unit 08/24/2015
Each new Class A Unit automatically became (0.1) new Class A Unit 11/24/2016
Name changed to BetaPro S&P 500 VIX Short-Term Futures 2x Daily Bull ETF 01/03/2017
(See BetaPro S&P 500 VIX Short-Term Futures 2x Daily Bull ETF)

HORIZONS BETAPRO S&P 500 VIX SHORT TERM FUTURES ETF (ON)
Each old Class A Unit automatically became (0.25) new Class A Unit 04/05/2013
Each new Class A Unit automatically became (0.1) new Class A Unit 08/24/2015
Name changed to BetaPro S&P 500 VIX Short-Term Futures ETF 01/03/2017

HORIZONS BETAPRO S&P 500 VIX SHORT-TERM FUTURES INVERSE ETF (ON)
Class A Units split (2) for (1) by issuance of (1) additional Unit payable 08/24/2015 to holders of record 08/21/2015 Ex date - 08/25/2015
Name changed to BetaPro S&P 500 VIX Short-Term Futures Daily Inverse ETF 01/03/2017
(See BetaPro S&P 500 VIX Short-Term Futures Daily Inverse ETF)

HORIZONS BETAPRO S&P AGRIBUSINESS NORTH AMERN BEAR PLUS ETF (ON)
Trust terminated 08/20/2010
Each Class A Unit received first and final distribution of $15.61 cash

HORIZONS BETAPRO S&P AGRIBUSINESS NORTH AMERN BULL PLUS ETF (ON)
Trust terminated 08/20/2010
Each Class A Unit received first and final distribution of $19.25 cash

HORIZONS BETAPRO S&P/TSX 60 BEAR PLUS ETF (ON)
Each old Class A Unit automatically became (0.5) new Class A Unit 11/26/2015
Name changed to BetaPro Canadian S&P/TSX 60 -2x Daily Bear ETF 01/03/2017

HORIZONS BETAPRO S&P/TSX 60 BULL PLUS ETF (ON)
Name changed to BetaPro S&P/TSX 60 2x Daily Bull ETF 01/03/2017

HORIZONS BETAPRO S&P/TSX 60 INVERSE ETF (ON)
Name changed to BetaPro S&P/TSX 60 Daily Inverse ETF 01/03/2017

HORIZONS BETAPRO S&P/TSX CAPPED ENERGY BEAR PLUS ETF (ON)
Each old Class A Unit automatically became (0.25) new Class A Unit 06/19/2014
Name changed to BetaPro S&P/TSX Capped Energy -2x Daily Bear ETF 01/03/2017

HORIZONS BETAPRO S&P/TSX CAPPED ENERGY BULL PLUS ETF (ON)
Each old Class A Unit automatically became (0.25) new Class A Unit 08/24/2015
Name changed to BetaPro S&P/TSX Capped Energy 2x Daily Bull ETF 01/03/2017

HORIZONS BETAPRO S&P TSX CAPPED ENERGY INVERSE ETF (ON)
Trust terminated 01/15/2013
Each Class A Unit received first and final distribution of $10.76215 cash

HORIZONS BETAPRO S&P/TSX CAPPED FINANCIALS BEAR PLUS ETF (ON)
Each old Class A Unit automatically became (0.25) new Class A Unit 06/19/2014
Name changed to BetaPro S&P/TSX Capped Financials -2x Daily Bear ETF 01/03/2017

HORIZONS BETAPRO S&P/TSX CAPPED FINANCIALS BULL PLUS ETF (ON)
Name changed to BetaPro S&P/TSX Capped Financials 2x Daily Bull ETF 01/03/2017

HORIZONS BETAPRO S&P/TSX CAPPED FINANCIALS INVERSE ETF (ON)
Trust terminated 01/15/2013
Each Class A Unit received first and final distribution of $7.306227 cash

HORIZONS BETAPRO S&P/TSX GLOBAL BASE METALS BEAR PLUS ETF (ON)
Each old Class A Unit automatically became (0.25) new Class A Unit 10/27/2009
Trust terminated 06/12/2015
Each new Class A Unit received $4.476497 cash

HORIZONS BETAPRO S&P/TSX GLOBAL BASE METALS BULL PLUS ETF (ON)
Class A Units split (3) for (1) by issuance of (2) additional Units payable 10/29/2009 to holders of record 10/29/2009
Trust terminated 06/12/2015
Each Class A Unit received $6.192322 cash

HORIZONS BETAPRO S&P/TSX GLOBAL GOLD BEAR PLUS ETF (ON)
Each old Class A Unit automatically became (0.2) new Class A Unit 01/02/2009
Each new Class A Unit automatically became (0.25) new Class A Unit 06/03/2010
Each new Class A Unit automatically became (0.25) new Class A Unit 05/30/2016
Name changed to BetaPro Canadian Gold Miners -2x Daily Bear ETF 01/03/2017

HORIZONS BETAPRO S&P/TSX GLOBAL GOLD BULL PLUS ETF (ON)
Each old Class A Unit automatically became (0.25) new Class A Unit 05/06/2013
Each new Class A Unit automatically became (0.2) new Class A Unit 11/26/2015
New Class A Units split (2) for (1) by issuance of (1) additional Unit payable 05/27/2016 to holders of record 05/26/2016 Ex date - 05/30/2016
Name changed to BetaPro Canadian Gold Miners 2x Daily Bull ETF 01/03/2017

HORIZONS BETAPRO S&P TSX GLOBAL GOLD INVERSE ETF (ON)
Trust terminated 01/15/2013
Each Class A Unit received $12.198764 cash

HORIZONS BETAPRO S&P/TSX GLOBAL MNG BEAR PLUS ETF (ON)
Name changed to Horizons BetaPro S&P/TSX Global Base Metals Bear Plus ETF 08/25/2009
(See Horizons BetaPro S&P/TSX Global Base Metals Bear Plus ETF)

HORIZONS BETAPRO S&P/TSX GLOBAL MNG BULL PLUS ETF (ON)
Each old Class A Unit no par exchanged for (0.25) new Class A Unit no par 12/18/2008
Name changed to Horizons BetaPro S&P/TSX Global Base Metals Bull Plus ETF 08/25/2009
(See Horizons BetaPro S&P/TSX Global Base Metals Bull Plus ETF)

HORIZONS BETAPRO S&P 500 INDEX C$ HEDGED ETF (ON)
Name changed to Horizons S&P 500 Index (C$ Hedged) ETF 02/23/2011
Horizons S&P 500 Index (C$ Hedged) ETF name changed to Horizons S&P 500 Index ETF 04/01/2013

HORIZONS BETAPRO US 30 YR BD BEAR PLUS ETF (ON)
Each old Class A Unit automatically became (0.5) new Class A Unit 05/30/2016
Name changed to BetaPro US 30-year Bond -2x Daily Bear ETF 01/03/2017
(See BetaPro US 30-year Bond -2x Daily Bear ETF)

HORIZONS BETAPRO US 30 YR BD BULL PLUS ETF (ON)
Completely liquidated 06/29/2012
Each Class A Unit received first and final distribution of $42.71203 cash

HORIZONS BETAPRO US DLR BEAR PLUS ETF (ON)
Trust terminated 05/31/2013
Each Class A Unit received $16.163326 cash

HORIZONS BETAPRO US DLR BULL PLUS ETF (ON)
Trust terminated 05/31/2013
Each Class A Unit received $17.360463 cash

HORIZONS BETAPRO WINTER TERM NYMEX CRUDE OIL ETF (ON)
Name changed to Horizons Winter-Term NYMEX Crude Oil ETF 11/14/2011
Horizons Winter-Term NYMEX Crude Oil ETF name changed to Horizons NYMEX Crude Oil ETF 12/27/2012 which name changed to Horizons Crude Oil ETF 01/03/2017

HORIZONS CDN BLACK SWAN ETF (ON)
Name changed to Horizons Cdn Equity Managed Risk ETF 11/13/2014
(See Horizons Cdn Equity Managed Risk ETF)

HORIZONS CDN EQUITY MANAGED RISK ETF (ON)
Trust terminated 09/09/2016
Each Advisor Class Unit received $9.187319 cash
Each Class E Unit received $9.196283 cash

HORIZONS CAP CORP (DE)
Recapitalized as Interference Control Technologies, Inc. 07/12/1985
Each share Common $0.001 par exchanged for (1/3) share Common $0.0001 par
(See Interference Control Technologies, Inc.)

HORIZONS COMEX COPPER ETF (ON)
Trust terminated 01/15/2013
Each Class A Unit received first and and final distribution of $7.3692 cash

HORIZONS COMEX GOLD ETF (ON)
Name changed to Horizons Gold ETF 01/03/2017

HORIZONS COMEX SILVER ETF (ON)
Name changed to Horizons Silver ETF 01/03/2017

HORIZONS CORPORATE BD ETF (ON)
Name changed to Horizons Active Corporate Bond ETF 11/01/2012

HORIZONS CRUDE OIL YIELD ETF (ON)
Trust terminated 01/10/2014
Each Advisor Class Unit received $7.347615 cash
Each Class E Unit received $7.348748 cash

HORIZONS DIVID ETF (ON)
Name changed to Horizons Active Canadian Dividend ETF 11/01/2012

HORIZONS ENHANCED U S EQUITY INCOME ETF (ON)
Merged into Horizons Enhanced Income US Equity (USD) ETF 03/14/2014
Each Advisor Class Unit received (0.750113) Advisor Class Unit
Each Class E Unit received (0.750218) Class E Unit

HORIZONS ENHANCED US EQUITY INCOME FD (ON)
Name changed to Horizons Enhanced U.S. Equity Income ETF and Class A Units reclassified as Class E Units 09/04/2012
Horizons Enhanced U.S. Equity Income ETF merged into Horizons Enhanced Income US Equity (USD) ETF 03/14/2014

HORIZONS ETF TR (DE)
Trust terminated 05/05/2016
Each share Korea KOSPI 200 ETF received $31.3142 cash

HORIZONS ETF TR I (DE)
Trust terminated 09/08/2017
Each share Horizons USA Managed Risk ETF received $26.1725 cash
Trust terminated 10/16/2017
Each share BullMark LatAm Select Leaders ETF received $34.6852 cash
(Additional Information in Active)

HORIZONS FLOATING RATE BD ETF (ON)
Name changed to Horizons Active Floating Rate Bond ETF 11/01/2012

HORIZONS GARTMAN ETF (ON)
Trust terminated 03/22/2013
Each Advisor Class Unit received $7.793321 cash
Each Class E Unit received $7.884547 cash

HORIZONS GLOBAL DIVID ETF (ON)
Name changed to Horizons Active Global Dividend ETF 11/01/2012

HORIZONS GMP JR OIL & GAS INDEX ETF (ON)
Completely liquidated
Each Class A Unit received first and final distribution of $2.9621349 cash payable 08/10/2012 to holders of record 08/10/2012

HORIZONS GOLD YIELD FD (ON)
Name changed to Horizons Gold Yield ETF and Class A Units reclassified as Class E Units 02/28/2012

HORIZONS HIGH YIELD BD ETF (ON)
Name changed to Horizons Active High Yield Bond ETF 11/01/2012

HORIZONS INCOME PLUS ETF (ON)
Name changed to Horizons Active Income Plus ETF 10/02/2012
(See Horizons Active Income Plus ETF)

HORIZONS MANAGED MULTI-ASSET MOMENTUM ETF (ON)
Each Advisor Class Unit automatically became (0.988591) Class E Unit 04/28/2017
Trust terminated 08/18/2017
Each Class E Unit received $10.345195 cash

HORIZONS MED MARIJUANA LIFE SCIENCES ETF (ON)
Name changed to Horizons Marijuana Life Sciences Index ETF 06/19/2017

HORIZONS NORTH AMERN GROWTH ETF (ON)
Name changed to Horizons Active North American Growth ETF 11/01/2012
(See Horizons Active North American Growth ETF)

HORIZONS NORTH AMERN VALUE ETF (ON)
Name changed to Horizons Active North American Value ETF 11/01/2012
(See Horizons Active North American Value ETF)

HORIZONS NYMEX CRUDE OIL ETF (ON)
Each old Class A Unit automatically became (0.5) new Class A Unit 05/30/2016
Name changed to Horizons Crude Oil ETF 01/03/2017

HORIZONS NYMEX NAT GAS ETF (ON)
Name changed to Horizons Natural Gas ETF 01/03/2017

HORIZONS PFD SH ETF (ON)
Name changed to Horizons Active Preferred Share ETF 11/01/2012

HORIZONS RESH INC (OH)
Acquired by a group of investors 2/11/88
Each share 2¢ Conv. Preferred Ser. A no par exchanged for $0.20 cash
Each share Common no par exchanged for $4 cash

HORIZONS S&P / TSX 60 130/30 INDEX ETF (ON)
Trust terminated 8/21/2013
Each Advisor Class Unit received $12.203025 cash
Each Class E Unit received $12.351012 cash

HORIZONS S&P 500 INDEX C$ HEDGED ETF (ON)
Name changed to Horizons S&P 500 Index ETF 04/01/2013

HORIZONS SILVER YIELD ETF (ON)
Trust terminated 01/10/2014
Each Class E Unit received $5.041451 cash

Each Advisor Class Unit received $5.040321 cash

HORIZONS TACTICAL BD ETF (ON)
Name changed to Horizons Active Advantage Yield ETF 10/02/2012
Horizons Active Advantage Yield ETF name changed to Horizons Active Yield Matched Duration ETF 09/17/2013 which name changed to Horizons Active Global Fixed Income ETF 02/02/2015

HORIZONS TITANIUM CORP. (NJ)
Charter voided for non-payment of taxes 2/3/64

HORIZONS U S DLR CURRENCY ETF (ON)
Each old Class A Unit automatically became (0.99049128) new Class A Unit 01/07/2013
Each new Class A Unit automatically became (0.99464977) new Class A Unit 12/23/2013
Under plan of reorganization each new A Unit automatically became (0.9940842) Horizons US Dollar Currency ETF new Class A Unit 01/14/2015

HORIZONS U S FLOATING RATE BD ETF (ON)
Name changed to Horizons Active U.S. Floating Rate Bond (USD) ETF 11/01/2012

HORIZONS UNIVERSA CDN BLACK SWAN ETF (ON)
Name changed to Horizons Canadian Black Swan ETF 05/22/2014
Horizons Canadian Black Swan ETF name changed to Horizons Cdn Equity Managed Risk ETF 11/13/2014
(See Horizons Cdn Equity Managed Risk ETF)

HORIZONS UNIVERSA US BLACK SWAN ETF (ON)
Name changed to Horizons US Black Swan ETF 05/22/2014
Horizons US Black Swan ETF name changed to Horizons US Equity Managed Risk ETF 11/13/2014
(See Horizons US Equity Managed Risk ETF)

HORIZONS UNLIMITED (AZ)
Dissolved 11/8/56

HORIZONS US BLACK SWAN ETF (ON)
Name changed to Horizons US Equity Managed Risk ETF 11/13/2014
(See Horizons US Equity Managed Risk ETF)

HORIZONS US EQUITY MANAGED RISK ETF (ON)
Trust terminated 09/09/2016
Each Advisor Class Unit received USD$11.481075 cash
Each Class E Unit received USD$11.494924 cash

HORIZONS WINTER TERM NYMEX CRUDE OIL ETF (ON)
Name changed to Horizons NYMEX Crude Oil ETF 12/27/2012
Horizons NYMEX Crude Oil ETF name changed to Horizons Crude Oil ETF 01/03/2017

HORIZONS WINTER TERM NYMEX NAT GAS ETF (ON)
Each old Class A Unit no par automatically became (0.25) new Class A Unit no par 04/13/2012
Name changed to Horizons NYMEX Natural Gas ETF 12/27/2012
Horizons NYMEX Natural Gas ETF name changed to Horizons Natural Gas ETF 01/03/2017

HORIZONTAL PETE EXPLS LTD (ON)
Company believed out of business 00/00/1992
Details not available

HORIZONTAL VENTURES INC (CO)
Under plan of merger name changed to GREKA Energy Corp. 3/24/99
(See GREKA Energy Corp.)

HORMEL GEO A & CO (DE)
Each share Common no par exchanged for (1.1) shares Common $15 par 00/00/1949
Common $15 par changed to $7.50 par and (1) additional share issued 02/11/1960
6% Preferred Ser. A $100 par called for redemption 02/15/1960
Common $7.50 par changed to $3.75 par and (1) additional share issued 02/23/1968
Common $3.75 par changed to $1.875 par and (1) additional share issued 12/14/1971
Common $1.875 par changed to $0.9375 par and (1) additional share issued 02/20/1980
Common $0.9375 par changed to $0.4688 par and (1) additional share issued 09/03/1985
Common $0.4688 par changed to $0.2344 par and (1) additional share issued 06/01/1987
Common $0.2344 par changed to $0.1172 par and (1) additional share issued 02/20/1990
Stock Dividend - 10% 01/25/1957
Name changed to Hormel Foods Corp. 02/01/1995

HORN & HARDART BAKING CO (NJ)
Capital Stock no par reclassified as Common $1 par 4/28/67
Each share Conv. Preferred $1 par exchanged for (5) shares Common $1 par 5/1/86
Charter revoked for failure to file reports and pay fees 8/31/94

HORN & HARDART CO (NV)
Reincorporated 10/24/1980
Each share 7% Preferred $100 par exchanged for (1) share 5% Preferred $100 par 00/00/1936
Common no par changed to $1 par 08/19/1969
Common $1 par split (2) for (1) by issuance of (1) additional share 03/07/1980
State of incorporation changed from (NY) to (NV) 10/24/1980
Recapitalized 02/27/1981
Each share 5% Preferred $100 par exchanged for $80 principal amount 10% 5-Yr. Conv. Notes due 02/26/1986
Common $1 par changed to 66-2/3¢ par and (0.5) additional share issued 07/11/1983
Stock Dividends - 10% 01/29/1982; 10% 10/15/1982
Reincorporated under the laws of Delaware as Hanover Direct, Inc. 09/07/1993
(See Hanover Direct, Inc.)

HORN (A.C.) CO.
Acquired by General Printing Ink Corp. 00/00/1945
Details not available

HORN PETE CORP (BC)
Name changed to Africa Energy Corp. 03/12/2015

HORN SILVER MINES CO (UT)
Name changed to McMoRan Exploration Co. (UT) and Common $1 par changed to no par 12/05/1969
McMoRan Exploration Co. (UT) reincorporated in Delaware 03/31/1978 which name changed to McMoRan Oil & Gas Co. (Old) 01/31/1979 which merged into Freeport-McMoRan Inc. 04/07/1981 which merged into IMC Global Inc. 12/22/1997 which merged into Mosaic Co. (Old) 10/22/2004 which merged into Mosaic Co. (New) 05/25/2011

HORN SILVER MINES INC (UT)
Each share Common no par exchanged for (0.05) share Common $0.001 par 04/10/1997
SEC revoked common stock registration 04/22/2009

HORNBECK OFFSHORE SVCS INC OLD (DE)
Merged into Tidewater Inc. (Old) 03/13/1996
Each share Common 10¢ par exchanged for (0.628) share Common 10¢ par
Tidewater Inc. (Old) reorganized as Tidewater Inc. (New) 07/31/2017

HORNBY BAY EXPL LTD (ON)
Name changed to Unor Inc. 05/01/2006
Unor Inc. recapitalized as Hornby Bay Mineral Exploration Ltd. 04/12/2010

HORNE & PITFIELD FOODS LTD (AB)
Under plan of amalgamation each share Capital Stock 20¢ par exchanged for $15.50 cash 11/24/1978

HORNE (LENA) BEAUTY PRODUCTS, INC. (DE)
Charter revoked for non-payment of taxes 10/1/63

HORNE FAULT MINES LTD (QC)
Recapitalized 07/21/1976
Recapitalized from Horne Fault Mines Ltd. to Horne Fault Mines Ltd.-Les Mines de la Faille Horne Ltee. 07/21/1976
Each share Common $1 par exchanged for (0.2) share Common no par
Liquidation completed
Each share Common no par received initial distribution of (0.25) share Spider Resources Inc. Common no par 10/22/1992
Each share Common no par received second and final distribution of (0.75) share Spider Resources Inc. Common no par 11/00/1992
(See Spider Resources Inc.)

HORNE INTL INC (DE)
SEC revoked common stock registration 10/11/2017

HORNER (FRANK W.) LTD. (CANADA)
Acquired by Carter Products, Inc. in February 1962
Each share Class A no par exchanged for $40 cash

HORNES ENTERPRISES INC (FL)
99.77% acquired by Greyhound Corp. (DE) through exchange offer which expired 11/19/1969
Public interest eliminated

HORNET ENERGY LTD (AB)
Acquired by Compton Petroleum Corp. 07/25/2001
Each share Common no par exchanged for $2 cash

HORNI SIGNAL MANUFACTURING CORP.
Assets sold in 1947
No stockholders' equity

HORRY CNTY ST BK (LORIS, SC)
Under plan of reorganization each share Common 1¢ par automatically became (1) share HCSB Financial Corp. Common 1¢ par 06/10/1999
HCSB Financial Corp. merged into United Community Banks, Inc. 07/31/2017

HORSE CANYON URANIUM INC (UT)
Recapitalized as Major D Corp. (UT) 11/21/69
Each share Common 1¢ par exchanged for (0.01) share Common no par
Major D Corp. (UT) reincorporated under the laws of California 3/27/70
(See Major D Corp. (CA))

HORSE THIEF PETROLEUM, INC. (WA)
Charter cancelled and proclaimed dissolved for failure to pay fees 7/1/37

HORSEHEAD HLDG CORP (DE)
Plan of reorganization under Chapter 11 Federal Bankrutpcy proceedings effective 09/30/2016
No stockholders' equity

HORSEHEAD RESOURCE DEV INC (DE)
Each share old Common 1¢ par exchanged for (0.00000016) share new Common 1¢ par 4/2/97
Note: In effect holders received $2.50 cash per share and public interest was eliminated

HORSESHOE BEND URANIUM CO. (NV)
Merged into Century Mining & Development Corp. on a (2) for (1) basis 07/09/1956
Century Mining & Development Corp. name changed to Century Industries, Inc. 12/17/1959 which recapitalized as 20th Century Industries, Inc. 10/11/1961
(See 20th Century Industries, Inc.)

HORSESHOE GOLD MNG INC (BC)
Reincorporated 07/27/2007
Place of incorporation changed from (AB) to (BC) 07/27/2007
Recapitalized as Cosigo Resources Ltd. 04/26/2011
Each share Common no par exchanged for (1/3) share Common no par

HORSESHOE MINES, LTD. (ON)
Charter cancelled for failure to file reports and pay taxes 12/00/1957

HORSETHIEF CANYON URANIUM, INC. (UT)
Name changed to Consolidated Resources, Inc. 12/6/68

HORSHAM CORP (QC)
Reincorporated under the laws of Ontario as Trizec Hahn Corp. 11/01/1996
Trizec Hahn Corp. was acquired by Trizec Canada Inc. 05/08/2002
(See Trizec Canada Inc.)

HORTI TECH INC (UT)
Charter suspended for failure to file annual reports 08/01/1986

HORTITECH INC (UT)
Each share old Common $0.001 par exchanged for (0.02) share new Common $0.001 par 08/23/1996
Name changed to Microaccel, Inc. 02/02/2000
Microaccel, Inc. name changed to Health Anti-Aging Lifestyle Options, Inc. 03/18/2002 which name changed to Previsto International Holdings, Inc. 12/07/2010

HORTMAN SALMEN CO., INC. (LA)
Liquidation completed 11/10/60

HORTON & CONVERSE (CA)
Charter suspended for failure to file reports or pay taxes 03/18/1971

HORTON HYDROCARBONS INC (BC)
Name changed to Pencrude Resources Inc. 10/25/1985
(See Pencrude Resources Inc.)

HORTON TECHNOLOGIES LTD (BC)
Cease trade order effective 10/25/1988
Stockholders' equity unlikely

HORUFF SHOE CORP.
Assets sold in 1932
No stockholders' equity

HOSAT INC (FL)
Name changed to First Atlantic Enterprises, Inc. 11/26/84
(See First Atlantic Enterprises, Inc.)

HOSCO GOLD MINES LTD. (ON)
Recapitalized as New Hosco Mines Ltd. 00/00/1954
Each share Common $1 par exchanged for (0.25) share Common $1 par
(See New Hosco Mines Ltd.)

HOSCO INC (DC)
Merged into CHS, Inc. 07/20/1979
Each share Common 1¢ par exchanged for $0.85 cash

HOSKINS MFG CO (MI)
Each share Common no par exchanged for (4) shares Common $2.50 par in 1937
Common $2.50 par split (3) for (1) by issuance of (2) additional shares 6/10/66
Merged into Armada Corp. 6/3/74
Each share Common $2.50 par exchanged for (1.27) shares Common $1 par

HOSOI GARDEN MORTUARY INC (HI)
SEC revoked common stock registration 04/15/2005

HOSPIRA INC (DE)
Acquired by Pfizer Inc. 09/03/2015
Each share Common 1¢ par exchanged for $90 cash

HOSPITAL AFFILIATES, INC. (TN)
Reincorporated under the laws of Delaware as Hospital Affiliates International, Inc. 4/30/75
Hospital Affiliates International, Inc. merged into INA Corp. 10/18/77 which merged into Cigna Corp. 4/1/82

HOSPITAL AFFILIATES INTL INC (DE)
Common 40¢ par split (3) for (2) by issuance of (0.5) additional share 6/15/77
Merged into INA Corp. 10/18/77
Each share Common 40¢ par exchanged for (0.425) share Common $1 par
INA Corp. merged into Cigna Corp. 4/1/82

HOSPITAL CORP AMER (TN)
Common $1 par split (5) for (4) by issuance of (0.25) additional share 6/22/72
Common $1 par split (5) for (4) by issuance of (0.25) additional share 10/28/77
Common $1 par split (4) for (3) by issuance of (1/3) additional share 9/11/78
Common $1 par split (3) for (2) by issuance of (0.5) additional share 6/2/80
Common $1 par split (3) for (2) by issuance of (0.5) additional share 3/27/81
Common $1 par split (4) for (3) by issuance of (1/3) additional share 1/17/83
Acquired by HCA-Hospital Corp. of America 3/16/89
Each share Common $1 par exchanged for $6 principal amount of 15.75% Subordinated Discount Debentures due 7/1/2003, (1/6) share Exchangeable Preferred 1¢ par and $43 cash
(See HCA-Hospital Corp. of America)

HOSPITAL FINL CORP (DE)
Merged into Wilken Transitory Corp. 9/30/81
Each share Common $1 par exchanged for $1.35 cash

HOSPITAL GREETINGS CORP (AB)
Recapitalized as Culane Energy Corp. 05/14/2003
Each share Common no par exchanged for (0.13793103) share Common no par
(See Culane Energy Corp.)

HOSPITAL INVS (MD)
Name changed to Atlanta National Real Estate Trust 5/21/73
Atlanta National Real Estate Trust reorganized as Anret, Inc. 10/15/79 which name changed to Sunlite Inc. 12/13/83
(See Sunlite Inc.)

HOSPITAL MORTGAGE GROUP (MA)
Reorganized under the laws of Delaware as Hospital Mortgage Group Inc. 07/31/1979
Each Share of Bene. Int. $1 par exchanged for (1) share Common $1 par
Hospital Mortgage Group Inc. name changed to HMG Property Investors Inc. 06/02/1981 which name changed to HMG/Courtland Properties, Inc. 09/01/1987

HOSPITAL MTG GROUP INC (DE)
Name changed to HMG Property Investors Inc. 06/02/1981
HMG Property Investors Inc. name changed to HMG/Courtland Properties, Inc. 09/01/1987

HOSPITAL NEWSPAPERS GROUP INC (NY)
Dissolved by proclamation 3/20/96

HOSPITAL SOFTWARE AMER INC (DE)
Recapitalized as New Health Technologies Inc. 1/23/96
Each share Common $0.00001 par exchanged for (0.0001) share Common 5¢ par
New Health Technologies Inc. name changed to Pubbs Worldwide, Inc. 8/28/96 which recapitalized as Chasen's International Inc. 5/25/99 which name changed to Tril-Medianet.Com, Inc. 7/6/99 which name changed to TecFactory.Net 11/28/2000

HOSPITAL STAFFING SVCS INC (FL)
Administratively dissolved for failure to file annual reports 09/24/1999

HOSPITAL TR CORP (RI)
Name changed to RIHT Financial Corp. 04/20/1983
RIHT Financial Corp. merged into Bank of Boston Corp. 11/14/1985 which name changed to BankBoston Corp. 04/25/1997
(See BankBoston Corp.)

HOSPITALITY CAP CORP (AZ)
Each share old Common no par exchanged for (0.5) share new Common no par 06/12/1987
Name changed to International Environmental Corp. 07/02/1991
International Environmental Corp. recapitalized as International Fibercom, Inc. 06/06/1994
(See International Fibercom, Inc.)

HOSPITALITY CONCEPTS INC (DE)
Name changed to Sunlite Technologies Corp. 01/06/1990
Sunlite Technologies Corp. recapitalized as Discover Capital Holdings Corp. 09/24/2001 which name changed to FSBO Media Holdings, Inc. 11/04/2005 which recapitalized as Guard Dog, Inc. 10/28/2008

HOSPITALITY FRANCHISE SYS INC (DE)
Common 1¢ par split (2) for (1) by issuance of (1) additional share 4/4/94
Name changed to HFS Inc. 8/31/95
HFS Inc. merged into Cendant Corp. 12/17/97 which reorganized as Avis Budget Group, Inc. 9/1/2006

HOSPITALITY HEALTH CARE, INC. (DE)
Merged into PMG, Inc. 8/29/80
Each share Common 1¢ par exchanged for $0.40 cash

HOSPITALITY INTL INC (MA)
Voluntarily dissolved 11/12/86
Details not available

HOSPITALITY MTR INNS INC (OH)
Merged into Helmsley Enterprises, Inc. 3/23/79
Each share Common no par exchanged for $25 cash

HOSPITALITY PLUS INC (DE)
Charter cancelled and declared inoperative and void for non-payment of taxes 3/1/90

HOSPITALITY PPTYS TR (MD)
9.5% Preferred Ser. A no par called for redemption at $25 plus $0.059375 accrued dividends on 04/12/2004
8.875% Preferred Ser. B no par called for redemption at $25 on 02/13/2012
7% Preferred Ser. C no par called for redemption at $25 plus $0.223611 accrued dividends on 07/01/2013
7.125% Preferred Ser. D no par called for redemption at $25 plus $0.123697 accrued dividends on 02/10/2017
(Additional Information in Active)

HOSPITALITY WORLDWIDE SVCS INC (NY)
Name changed to Hotelworks.com, Inc. 12/23/1999
(See Hotelworks.com, Inc.)

HOSPLEX SYS INC (DE)
Charter cancelled and declared inoperative and void for non-payment of taxes 3/1/90

HOSPOSABLE PRODS INC (NY)
Name changed to Wyant Corp. 3/19/97
(See Wyant Corp.)

HOST AMER CORP (CO)
Reincorporated 04/30/1999
State of incorporation changed from (DE) to (CO) 04/30/1999
Name changed to EnerLume Energy Management Corp. 11/01/2007

HOST ENTERPRISES INC (DE)
Merged into Westinghouse Electric Corp. 8/7/72
Each share Common $1 par exchanged for (0.17349) share Common $3.12-1/2 par
Westinghouse Electric Corp. name changed to CBS Corp. 12/1/97 which merged into Viacom Inc. (Old) 5/4/2000
(See Viacom Inc. (Old))

HOST FDG INC (MD)
SEC revoked common stock registration 02/15/2006

HOST HOTELS & RESORTS INC (MD)
Name changed 04/17/2006
Stock Dividend - 8.7% payable 01/27/1999 to holders of record 12/28/1998 Ex date - 12/23/1998
10% Preferred Class A called for redemption at $25 plus $0.125 accrued dividends on 08/03/2004
10% Preferred Class B called for redemption at $25 plus $0.2431 accrued dividends on 05/20/2005
Name changed from Host Marriott Corp. to Host Hotels & Resorts, Inc. 04/17/2006
10% Preferred Class C called for redemption at $25 plus $0.2361 accrued dividends on 05/19/2006
8.875% Preferred Class E 1¢ par called for redemption at $25 plus $0.394444 accrued dividends on 06/18/2010
(Additional Information in Active)

HOST INTL HLDGS INC (BC)
Cease trade order effective 09/06/2005
Stockholders' equity unlikely

HOST INTL INC (DE)
Common $2.50 par split (2) for (1) by issuance of (1) additional share 10/11/1968
Merged into Marriott Corp. 03/03/1982
Each share Common $2.50 par exchanged for $31 cash

HOST MARRIOTT CORP (DE)
Each share Common $1 par received distribution of (0.2) share Host Marriott Services Corp. Common no par payable 12/29/1995 to holders of record 12/22/1995
4.125% Depositary Preferred called for redemption 01/15/1996
4.125% Conv. Preferred Ser. A no par called for redemption 01/15/1996
Each share Common $1 par received distribution of (1) share Crestline Capital Corp. Common 1¢ par payable 12/29/1998 to holders of record 12/28/1998
Reorganized under the laws of Maryland 12/29/1998
Each share Common $1 par exchanged for (1) share Common $1 par
Host Marriott Corp. (MD) name changed to Host Hotels & Resorts, Inc. 04/17/2006

HOST MARRIOTT FINL TR (MD)
6.75% Quarterly Income Conv. Preferred called for redemption at $100.675 on 4/5/2006

HOST MARRIOTT SVCS CORP (DE)
Merged into Autogrill S.p.A. 9/1/99
Each share Common no par exchanged for $15.75 cash

HOST VENTURES INC (NV)
Reorganized as Sun Cal Energy, Inc. 11/06/2006
Each share Common $0.001 par exchanged for (10) shares Common $0.001 par
(See Sun Cal Energy, Inc.)

HOST VENTURES LTD. (BC)
Recapitalized as Hot Resources Ltd. 04/30/1984
Each share Common no par exchanged for (0.2) share Common no par
Hot Resources Ltd. name changed to Inter-Globe Resources Ltd. 04/16/1985
(See Inter-Globe Resources Ltd.)

HOSTED DATA TRANSACTION SOLUTIONS INC (ON)
Name changed to Posera-HDX Inc. (ON) 10/07/2010
Posera-HDX Inc. (ON) reincorporated in Alberta as Posera-HDX Ltd. 10/12/2011 which name changed to Posera Ltd. 04/14/2016

HOSTEE MINES LTD. (ON)
Charter cancelled for failure to file reports and pay taxes 00/00/1957

HOSTING SITE NETWORK INC (DE)
Recapitalized as Single Touch Systems, Inc. 05/15/2008
Each share Common $0.001 par exchanged for (0.4347826) share Common $0.001 par
Single Touch Systems, Inc. name changed to SITO Mobile, Ltd. 10/07/2014

HOSTNYC INC (FL)
Recapitalized as Lumiere International Corp. 12/31/2001
Each share Common $0.001 par exchanged for (0.1) share Common $0.001 par
Lumiere International Corp. name changed to Air Temp North America, Inc. 01/30/2007
(See Air Temp North America, Inc.)

HOSTOPIA.COM INC (DE)
Merged into Deluxe Corp. 08/06/2008
Each share Common $0.0001 par exchanged for CAD$10.55 cash

HOT BRANDS INC (NV)
Each (600) shares old Common $0.0001 par exchanged for (1) share new Common $0.001 par 7/20/2006
Note: No holder will receive fewer than (100) shares
Name changed to G&S Minerals, Inc. 10/9/2006

HOT HSE GROWERS INCOME FD (CANADA)
Name changed to Village Farms Income Fund 11/01/2006
Village Farms Income Fund reorganized as Village Farms International, Inc. 12/31/2009

HOT PRODS INC COM (AZ)
Each share old Common 1¢ par exchanged for (0.01) share new Common 1¢ par 03/13/2006
Reorganized under the laws of Washington as B-Teller, Inc. 04/03/2006
Each share new Common 1¢ par exchanged for (2.5) shares Common 1¢ par
B-Teller, Inc. name changed to Congo Crest Mineral Corp. 08/01/2006 which reorganized as New Wave Mobile, Inc. 11/22/2006 which name changed to New Wave Media, Inc. 03/26/2007 which name changed to CA Goldfields, Inc. 04/08/2008
(See CA Goldfields, Inc.)

HOT RES LTD (BC)
Name changed to Inter-Globe Resources Ltd. 04/16/1985
Each share Common no par exchanged for (1) share Common no par
(See Inter-Globe Resources Ltd.)

HOT SHOPPES, INC. (DE)
Stock Dividend - 100% 12/22/60
Name changed to Marriott-Hot Shoppes, Inc. 11/10/64
Marriott-Hot Shoppes, Inc. name changed to Marriott Corp. 11/21/67 which name changed to Host Marriott Corp. (DE) 10/8/93 which reorganized in Maryland 12/29/98

HOT SPRINGS COPPER CO. (OR)
Charter revoked for failure to file reports and pay fees 01/05/1914

HOT TOPIC INC (CA)
Common no par split (2) for (1) by issuance of (1) additional share payable 12/27/1999 to holders of record 12/13/1999
Common no par split (2) for (1) by issuance of (1) additional share payable 12/27/2000 to holders of record 12/14/2000 Ex date - 12/28/2000
Common no par split (3) for (2) by issuance of (0.5) additional share payable 02/06/2002 to holders of record 01/23/2002 Ex date - 02/07/2002
Common no par split (3) for (2) by issuance of (0.5) additional share payable 09/02/2003 to holders of record 08/21/2003 Ex date - 09/03/2003
Acquired by Sycamore Partners Management, LLC 06/12/2013
Each share Common no par exchanged for $14 cash

HOT WEB INC (FL)
Name changed to Gold Coast Mining Corp. 07/02/2009
Gold Coast Mining Corp. name changed to Green Leaf Innovations, Inc. 03/10/2015

HOTAPP INTL INC (DE)
Name changed to HotApp Blockchain Inc. 02/01/2018

HOTCLOUD MOBILE INC (NV)
SEC revoked common stock registration 12/12/2014

HOTEI INC (DE)
Class A Common 1¢ par reclassified as Common 1¢ par in December 1969
Charter cancelled and declared inoperative and void for non-payment of taxes 4/15/72

HOTEL ALCAZAR, INC.
Liquidated in 1945

HOTEL ALMS CO.
Reorganized as Alms Hotel Corp. in 1935, which merged into Sheraton Louisiana Corp. 4/30/56
Sheraton Louisiana Corp. liquidation completed 7/27/59

HOTEL BARBIZON, INC. LIQUIDATING TRUST (NY)
Completely liquidated
Each Share of Bene. Int. no par received first and final distribution of $51.39 cash
Note: Certificates were not required to be surrendered and are now valueless

HOTEL BARBIZON INC (NY)
Liquidation completed
Each share Common no par received initial distribution of $1,500 cash 2/14/79
Each share Common no par received second distribution of $625 cash 7/2/79
Each share Common no par received third distribution of $370 cash 1/3/80
Assets transferred to Hotel Barbizon, Inc. Liquidating Trust and Common no par reclassified as Shares of Bene. Int. no par 1/3/80
(See Hotel Barbizon, Inc. Liquidating Trust)

HOTEL CHARLES CO. (MA)
Liquidation completed 6/19/54
No Common stockholders' equity

HOTEL CORP AMER (NY)
Name changed to Sonesta International Hotels Corp. 06/01/1970
(See Sonesta International Hotels Corp.)

HOTEL CORP ISRAEL (DE)
Common $5 par changed to $3 par and (0.66666666) additional share issued 12/22/61
Voluntarily dissolved 03/13/1979
Details not available

HOTEL DE LA SALLE, INC. (QC)
Dissolved 04/25/1962
No stockholders' equity

HOTEL DISCOVERY INC (DE)
Name changed to Cafe Odyssey Inc. 05/21/1998
Cafe Odyssey Inc. name changed to Popmail.Com, Inc. 09/16/1999
(See Popmail.Com, Inc.)

HOTEL DRAKE CORP. (NY)
Common no par changed to $5 par in 1953
Liquidation completed 3/10/59

HOTEL EQUITIES CORP (CA)
Each share Capital Stock $1 par exchanged for (0.2) share Capital Stock $5 par 10/02/1967
Merged into H.E. Corp. 12/02/1968
Each share Capital Stock $5 par exchanged for $25 cash

HOTEL FORT SUMTER, INC. (SC)
Dissolved in 1967

HOTEL FOURTEEN, INC. (NY)
Charter cancelled and proclaimed dissolved for failure to pay taxes and file reports 11/19/70

HOTEL GARY CORP. (IN)
Charter revoked for failure to file reports and pay fees 6/1/70

HOTEL GIBSON CO.
Reorganized as Hotel Gibson Corp.
(See Hotel Gibson Corp.)

HOTEL GIBSON CORP. (OH)
Name changed to Sheraton Gibson Corp. 9/4/53
(See Sheraton Gibson Corp.)

HOTEL GOVERNOR CLINTON, INC.
Reorganized in 1937
No stockholders' equity

HOTEL HALWOOD, INC. (DE)
Completely liquidated 9/25/40
Each Capital Trust Ctf. no par exchanged for first and final distribution of $42.69 cash

HOTEL INVESTORS CORP. (MD)
See - Hotel Invs Tr

HOTEL INVS TR (MD)
Reorganized 06/26/1980
Reorganized from Hotel Investors to Hotel Investors Trust 06/26/1980
Each Share of Bene. Int. $1 par exchanged for (1) Non-Separable Unit of (1) Hotel Investors Trust Share of Bene. Int. $1 par and (1) share Hotel Investors Corp. Common 10¢ par
Units split (3) for (2) by issuance of (0.5) additional Unit 11/01/1985
Recapitalized as Starwood Lodging Trust 02/01/1995
Each Combined Certificate representing (0.14285714) Hotel Investors Trust Share of Bene. Int. $1 par and (1) share Hotel Investors Corp. Common 10¢ par exchanged for (1) Combined Certificate representing (1) Starwood Lodging Trust Share of Bene. Int. 1¢ par and (1) share Starwood Lodging Trust Common 10¢ par
Starwood Lodging Trust name changed to Starwood Hotels & Resorts Trust 01/02/1998 which name changed to Starwood Hotels & Resorts 02/24/1998 which reorganized as Starwood Hotels & Resorts Worldwide, Inc. 01/06/1999 which merged into Marriott International, Inc. (New) 09/23/2016

HOTEL LANCASTER CO. (OH)
Charter cancelled for failure to pay taxes 5/30/75

HOTEL LASALLE CO.
Property and assets sold 00/00/1935
Details not available

HOTEL LEXINGTON, INC. (NY)
Name changed to 48th Street & Lexington Ave. Corp. 05/02/1955
(See 48th Street & Lexington Ave. Corp.)

HOTEL MGMT SYS INC (NV)
Common $0.001 par split (8.6) for (1) by issuance of (7.6) additional shares payable 04/05/2010 to holders of record 04/05/2010
Ex date - 04/06/2010
Name changed to TouchIT Technologies, Inc. 07/14/2010
TouchIT Technologies, Inc. recapitalized as Bitcoin Shop Inc. 02/05/2014 which name changed to BTCS Inc. 08/03/2015

HOTEL OLCOTT, INC. (NY)
Liquidation completed in 1950

HOTEL 128 DEDHAM INC (MA)
Adjudicated bankrupt 05/04/1971
Stockholders' equity unlikely

HOTEL OUTSOURCE MGMT INTL INC (DE)
Each share old Common $0.001 par exchanged for (0.01) share new Common $0.001 par 01/28/2013
Recapitalized as Gold Billion Group Holdings Ltd. 08/28/2015
Each share new Common $0.001 par exchanged for (0.02) share Common $0.001 par
Gold Billion Group Holdings Ltd. recapitalized as Sky Resort International Ltd. 12/12/2017

HOTEL PPTYS INC (DE)
Merged into Hotel Investors Trust 09/16/1986
Each share Class A Common $1 par exchanged for (1) Unit of Hotel Investors Trust consisting of (1) Hotel Investors Trust Non-Separable Share of Bene. Int. $1 par and (1) share Hotel Investors Corp. Common 10¢ par
Hotel Investors Trust recapitalized as Starwood Lodging Trust 02/01/1995 which name changed to Starwood Hotels & Resorts Trust 01/02/1998 which name changed to Starwood Hotels & Resorts 02/24/1998 which reorganized as Starwood Hotels & Resorts Worldwide, Inc. 01/06/1999 which merged into Marriott International, Inc. (New) 09/23/2016

HOTEL RENT A CAR SYS INC (CO)
Name changed to Red Carpet Inns International, Inc. 06/22/1979
(See Red Carpet Inns International, Inc.)

HOTEL RESERVATIONS NETWORK INC (DE)
Issue Information - 5,400,000 shares CL A offered at $16 per share on 02/25/2000
Name changed to Hotels.com 4/25/2002
Hotels.com merged into InterActiveCorp 6/23/2003 which name changed to IAC/InterActiveCorp 7/14/2004

HOTEL SHERMAN, INC. (DE)
Common no par changed to $1 par 00/00/1942
Acquired by Webb & Knapp, Inc. 02/05/1960
Details not available

HOTEL SYLVANIA CO.
Property acquired by bondholders protective committee in 1947
No stockholders' equity

HOTEL TAFT CORP. (NY)
Dissolved in 1958

HOTEL WALDORF-ASTORIA CORP. (NY)
Capital Stock no par changed to $1 par 00/00/1936
Merged into Hilton Hotels Corp. 00/00/1953
Each share Capital Stock $1 par exchanged for (1.25) shares Capital Stock $5 par
(See Hilton Hotels Corp.)

HOTELECOPY INC (FL)
Name changed to EDD Helms Group Inc. 7/30/99

HOTELPLACE INC (NV)
Reorganized as Rarus Minerals, Inc. 07/08/2011
Each share Common $0.001 par exchanged for (50) shares Common $0.001 par
Rarus Minerals, Inc. name changed to Rarus Technologies Inc. 02/08/2012

HOTELS COM (DE)
Merged into InterActiveCorp 6/23/2003
Each share Class A 1¢ par exchanged for (2.4) shares Common 1¢ par
InterActiveCorp name changed to IAC/InterActiveCorp 7/14/2004

HOTELS STATLER CO., INC. (NY)
Each share Common no par exchanged for (5) shares Common $10 par in 1943
Stock Dividend - 100% 11/15/46
Liquidated in 1954

HOTELWORKS COM INC (NY)
SEC revoked common stock registration 02/07/2013

HOTGATE TECHNOLOGY INC (NV)
Each (12) shares old Common $0.0001 par exchanged for (1) share new Common $0.0001 par 08/30/2010
Name changed to REDtone Asia, Inc. 03/14/2011

HOTJOBS COM LTD (DE)
Merged into Yahoo! Inc. 02/12/2002
Each share Common 1¢ par exchanged for (0.3045) share Common $0.001 par and $5.25 cash
Yahoo! Inc. name changed to Altaba Inc. 06/19/2017

HOTSTONE GOLD MINES LTD. (ON)
Recapitalized as Hotstone Minerals Ltd. 09/28/1955
Each share Capital Stock $1 par exchanged for (0.3) share Capital Stock $1 par
(See Hotstone Minerals Ltd.)

HOTSTONE MINERALS LTD (ON)
Charter cancelled for failure to pay taxes and file returns 02/14/1978

HOTSY CORP (FL)
Each share Common 5¢ par exchanged for (0.0025) share Common $20 par 4/7/78
Merged into Hotsy Holding Co. 11/5/86
Each share Common $20 par exchanged for $949.03 cash

HOTYELLOW 98 COM INC (NV)
Recapitalized as Azur International, Inc. 02/09/2004
Each share Common $0.001 par exchanged for (0.01) share Common $0.001 par
(See Azur International, Inc.)

HOUDAILLE CORP.
Merged into Houdaille-Hershey Corp. in 1929
Details not available

HOUDAILLE-HERSHEY CORP. (MI)
Class B no par reclassified as Common no par in 1945
Common no par changed to $3 par in 1951
Name changed to Houdaille Industries, Inc. (MI) 11/30/55
Houdaille Industries, Inc. (MI) reincorporated in Delaware 4/1/68
(See Houdaille Industries, Inc. (DE))

HOUDAILLE INDS INC (DE)
Reincorporated 4/1/68
$2.25 Preferred $50 par redesignated as $2.25 Prior Preferred $50 par 10/25/65
Common $3 par changed to $1.50 par and (1) additional share issued 7/15/66
State of incorporation changed from (MI) to (DE) 4/1/68
Common $1.50 par changed to 75¢ par and (1) additional share issued 8/15/68
4-1/2% Conv. Preferred Ser. A $25 par called for redemption 10/2/72
$2.25 Prior Preferred $50 par called for redemption 5/2/79
Acquired by Kohlberg, Kravis, Roberts & Co. 5/4/79
Each share Common 75¢ par exchanged for $40 cash

HOUDINI PICTURE CORP. (NY)
Charter revoked for failure to file reports and pay fees 12/15/36

HOUDRY PROCESS CORP. (DE)
Merged into Air Products & Chemicals, Inc. on a share for share basis 1/25/62

HOUGHTEN PHARMACEUTICALS INC (DE)
Name changed to Trega Biosciences Inc. 5/1/97
Trega Biosciences Inc. merged into LION Bioscience A.G. 3/14/2001
(See LION Bioscience A.G.)

HOUGHTON & DUTTON BLDG., INC.
Dissolved by Court order in 1942
No stockholders' equity

HOUGHTON & DUTTON BLDG. TRUST
Trust terminated in 1936
No stockholders' equity

HOUGHTON FINANCIAL, INC. (MI)
Merged into Michigan Financial Corp. 4/1/94
Each share Common 10¢ par exchanged for (3.47) shares Common no par
Michigan Financial Corp. merged into Wells Fargo & Co. 3/30/2000

HOUGHTON MIFFLIN CO (MA)
Each Stock Appreciation Income Linked Security exchanged for (2) shares Inso Corp. Common 1¢ par 8/2/99
Each share Common $100 par exchanged for (40) shares Common $1 par 5/2/67
Common $1 par split (2) for (1) by issuance of (1) additional share 8/3/83
Common $1 par split (2) for (1) by issuance of (1) additional share 9/10/86
Common $1 par split (2) for (1) by issuance of (1) additional share payable 7/25/97 to holders of record 7/11/97 Ex date - 7/28/97
Merged into Vivendi Universal 8/2/2001
Each share Common $1 par exchanged for $60 cash

HOUGHTON NATL BK (HOUGHTON, MI)
Capital Stock $50 par changed to $12.50 par and (4) additional shares issued plus a 25% stock dividend paid 3/15/77
Stock Dividend - 100% 3/16/70
Reorganized as Houghton Financial, Inc. 5/31/87
Each share Capital Stock $12.50 par exchanged for (1) share Common 10¢ par
Houghton Financial, Inc. merged into Michigan Financial Corp. 4/1/94 which merged into Wells Fargo & Co. 3/30/2000

HOULIHANS RESTAURANT GROUP INC (DE)
Merged into New HRG Inc. 6/25/98
Each share Common 1¢ par exchanged for $8 cash

HOUSATONIC BK & TR CO
Declared insolvent and taken over by FDIC 7/26/91
Stockholders' equity unlikely

HOUSATONIC PUBLIC SERVICE CO. (CT)
Merged into Connecticut Light & Power Co. 05/01/1961
Each share Common $15 par exchanged for (1.4) shares Common no par
(See Connecticut Light & Power Co.)

HOUSE ADLER INC (CO)
Each share old Common no par exchanged for (0.00038461) share new Common no par 12/21/1990
Note: In effect holders received $3 cash per share and public interest was eliminated

HOUSE BRAEMORE FURNITURE LTD (ON)
Under plan of merger each share Common no par exchanged for $6.32 cash 12/29/1979

HOUSE CHROME INC (NY)
Charter cancelled and proclaimed dissolved for failure to pay taxes 3/31/82

HOUSE FLY RENTALS INC (NV)
Name changed to Octavian Global Technologies, Inc. 11/17/2008

HOUSE FRASER LTD (UNITED KINGDOM)
ADR agreement terminated 00/00/1985
Details not available
Note: Common Market regulation required all publicly held British companies to replace LTD with PLC 00/00/1982

HOUSE IN THE PINES-CATONSVILLE, INC. (MD)
Merged into Convalescent Care Centers, Inc. 9/26/68
Each share Common $1 par automatically became (1) share Common 25¢ par
Convalescent Care Centers, Inc. name changed to Medical Services Corp. 12/5/69
(See Medical Services Corp.)

HOUSE IN THE PINES-EASTON, INC. (MD)
Merged into Convalescent Care Centers, Inc. 9/26/68
Each share Common $1 par automatically became (1) share Common 25¢ par
Convalescent Care Centers, Inc. name changed to Medical Services Corp. 12/5/69
(See Medical Services Corp.)

HOUSE KNITTING INC (NY)
Stock Dividends - 10% 11/06/1970; 100% 04/30/1971
Dissolved by proclamation 01/25/2012

HOUSE OF BETTER VISION, INC. (FL)
Name changed to Miracle Mile Opticians, Inc. 05/06/1955
(See Miracle Mile Opticians, Inc.)

HOUSE OF BRUSSELS CHOCOLATES INC (NV)
All officers resigned and company ceased operations 01/17/2007
Stockholders' equity unlikely

HOUSE OF FABRICS INC NEW (DE)
Merged into Fabri-Centers of America, Inc. 04/21/1998
Each share Common 10¢ par exchanged for $4.25 cash

HOUSE OF FABRICS INC OLD (DE)
Reincorporated 12/31/1979
Common no par split (3) for (2) by issuance of (0.5) additional share 07/29/1968
Common no par split (3) for (2) by issuance of (0.5) additional share 07/11/1969
Common no par split (3) for (2) by issuance of (0.5) additional share 12/28/1970
Common no par split (2) for (1) by issuance of (1) additional share 05/12/1972
State of incorporation changed from (CA) to (DE) and Common no par changed to 10¢ par 12/31/1979
Common 10¢ par split (5) for (4) by issuance of (0.25) additional share 01/21/1983
Common 10¢ par split (2) for (1) by issuance of (1) additional share 04/30/1991
Reorganized as House of Fabrics, Inc. (New) 07/31/1996
Each share Common 10¢ par exchanged for (0.00751879) share Common 10¢ par and (53.413654) Common Stock Purchase Warrants Class A expiring 00/00/1997
(See House of Fabrics, Inc. (New))

HOUSE OF MANN, INC. (KY)
Name changed to National Chemical Corp. 04/01/1968
National Chemical Corp. name changed to Orbit Gas Co. 11/01/1974 which name changed to Orco, Inc. 04/13/1992
(See Orco, Inc.)

HOUSE OF TAYLOR JEWELRY INC (NV)
Company executed a peaceful possession of collateral with secured lender 06/24/2008
Stockholders' equity unlikely

HOUSE RONNIE INC (NY)
Common 10¢ par split (5) for (4) by issuance of (0.25) additional share 9/8/71
Common 10¢ par split (4) for (3) by issuance of (1/3) additional share 9/14/72
Common 10¢ par split (5) for (4) by issuance of (0.25) additional share 7/1/80
Stock Dividends - 10% 9/8/70; 10% 6/29/79; 10% 1/2/81
Completely liquidated 8/11/81
Each share Common 10¢ par exchanged for first and final distribution of $14 cash

HOUSE STEIN ELECTRS LTD (BC)
Name changed to Steintron International Electronics Ltd. 1/25/71
(See Steintron International Electronics Ltd.)

HOUSE VISION INC (DE)
Common $1 par split (3) for (2) by issuance of (0.5) additional share 3/26/71
Stock Dividend - 100% 3/30/66
Merged into Frigitronics, Inc. 3/23/82
Each share Common $1 par exchanged for (0.08) share Common 10¢ par
(See Frigitronics, Inc.)

HOUSE WESTMORE INC (NY)
Common 10¢ par changed to 5¢ par and (1) additional share issued 5/6/66
Merged into Syntex Corp. 10/27/78
Each share Common 5¢ par exchanged for (0.11026) share Class A Conv. Preferred no par
(See Syntex Corp.)

HOUSECALL MED RES INC (DE)
Merged into Adventist Health 7/31/98
Each share Common 1¢ par exchanged for $1.50 cash

HOUSEHOLD CAP TR I (DE)
8.25% Trust Originated Preferred Securities called for redemption at $25 on 8/15/2003

HOUSEHOLD CAP TR II (DE)
8.70% Trust Preferred Securities called for redemption at $25 on 12/21/2001

HOUSEHOLD CAP TR IV (DE)
Issue Information - 8,000,000 TR PFD SECS 7.25% offered at $25 per share on 03/12/1998
7.25% Trust Preferred Securities called for redemption at $25 on 8/15/2003

HOUSEHOLD CAP TR V (DE)
10% Trust Preferred Securities called for redemption at $25 on 6/8/2005

HOUSEHOLD CAP TR VI (DE)
8.25% Guaranteed Trust Preferred Securities called for redemption at $25 on 3/13/2006

HOUSEHOLD CAP TR VII (DE)
Issue Information - 8,000,000 GTD TR PFD SECS 7.5% offered at $25 per share on 11/01/2001
7.5% Guaranteed Trust Preferred Securities called for redemption at $25 on 11/8/2006

HOUSEHOLD DIRECT INC (DE)
Name changed 01/22/2002
Name changed from Household Direct.com, Inc. to Household Direct Inc. 01/22/2002
SEC revoked common stock registration 01/19/2005

HOUSEHOLD FIN CORP (DE)
Common no par split (2) for (1) by issuance of (1) additional share 00/00/1954
3.75% Preferred $100 par called for redemption 09/17/1965
4% Preferred $100 par called for redemption 09/17/1965
4.4% Preferred $100 par called for redemption 09/17/1965
Common no par split (2) for (1) by issuance of (1) additional share 04/29/1966
$4.40 Conv. Preferred no par called for redemption 08/25/1972
Common no par changed to $1 par and (0.5) additional share issued 09/18/1972
Stock Dividends - 200% 03/27/1945; 10% 12/16/1949; 10% 03/13/1953; 10% 11/05/1954
Under plan of reorganization each share $2.375 Conv. Preferred no par, $2.50 Conv. Preferred no par and Common $1 par automatically became (1) share Household International, Inc. $2.375 Conv. Preferred no par, $2.50 Conv. Preferred no par and Common $1 par respectively 06/26/1981
7.25% Depositary Preferred Ser. A called for redemption at $100 on 08/15/1997
Household International, Inc. merged into HSBC Holdings PLC 03/28/2003

HOUSEHOLD FINANCE CO.
All stock acquired by Household Finance Corp. 00/00/1939
Details not available

HOUSEHOLD GAS SERVICE, INC. (NY)
Liquidation completed
Each share Preferred $25 par exchanged for first and final distribution of $25 cash 11/20/64
Each share Common $10 par received initial distribution of $12 cash 12/23/64
Each share Common $10 par received second distribution of $2 cash 10/15/65
Each share Common $10 par exchanged for third and final distribution of $1.203191764 cash 10/1/66

HOUSEHOLD INTL INC (DE)
$2.375 Conv. Preferred no par called for redemption 03/10/1989
$2.50 Conv. Preferred no par called for redemption 03/10/1989
Flexible Auction Rate Preferred Ser. A no par called for redemption 07/13/1993
11-1/4% Enhanced Rate Preferred no par called for redemption 10/01/1993
Depositary Enhanced Preferred called for redemption 10/01/1993
$6.25 Conv. Preferred no par called for redemption 06/28/1995
Flexible Auction Rate Preferred Ser. B no par called for redemption 07/13/1995
Depositary Preferred Ser. 1989-A no par called for redemption 07/27/1995
9.50% Preferred Ser. 1989-A no par called for redemption 07/27/1995
9.5% Depositary Preferred Ser. 91-A no par called for redemption 01/23/1997
9.5% Preferred Ser. 91-A no par called for redemption 01/23/1997
7.35% Depositary Preferred Ser. 93-A called for redemption at $25 plus $0.071458 accrued dividends on 10/15/1999
$4.30 Preferred no par called for redemption at $100 on 04/28/2003
$4.50 Preferred no par called for redemption at $103 on 04/28/2003
5% Preferred no par called for redemption at $50 on 04/28/2003
Common $1 par split (2) for (1) by issuance of (1) additional share 10/15/1993
Common $1 par split (3) for (1) by issuance of (2) additional shares payable 06/01/1998 to holders of record 05/14/1998 Ex date - 06/02/1998
Merged into HSBC Holdings PLC 03/28/2003
Each share Preferred Ser. A 1992 exchanged for $1,000 cash
Each Depositary Preferred 2001-A exchanged for $25 cash
Each 7.60% Depositary Preferred 2002-A exchanged for $25 cash
Each Depositary Preferred 2002-B exchanged for $25 cash
Each Depositary Preferred exchanged for $25 cash
Each share Common $1 par exchanged for either (2.675) Ordinary Shares or (0.535) new Sponsored ADR for Ordinary
Note: Option to receive new Sponsored ADR's for Ordinary expired 09/26/2003

HOUSEHOLD PRODUCTS, INC.
Acquired by Drug, Inc. in 1930
Details not available

HOUSERAISING INC (NC)
Filed a petition under Chapter 7 Federal Bankruptcy Code 03/31/2008
Stockholders' equity unlikely

HOUSE2HOME INC (DE)
Plan of reorganization under Chapter 11 Federal Bankruptcy Code effective 10/06/2003
No stockholders' equity

HOUSEVALUES INC (WA)
Name changed to Market Leader, Inc. 11/10/2008
Market Leader, Inc. merged into Trulia, Inc. 08/20/2013 which merged into Zillow Group, Inc. 02/18/2015

HOUSING & COML BK (KOREA)
Name changed to H & CB 06/23/2000
H & CB merged into Kookmin Bank (New) 11/01/2001 which merged into KB Financial Group Inc. 09/29/2008

HOUSING BK FOR TRADE & FINANCE (JORDAN)
Name changed 04/24/2000
Name changed from Housing Bank to Housing Bank for Trade & Finance 04/24/2000
ADR agreement terminated 05/01/2017
No ADR's remain outstanding

HOUSING DYNAMICS INC (PA)
Completely liquidated in June 1987
Each share Common no par exchanged for first and final distribution of $2.70 cash

HOUSING INDS AMER INC (NY)
Name changed to HIA, Inc. 09/19/1985
(See HIA, Inc.)

HOUSING SOLUTIONS HAWAII INC (DE)
Name changed to Home Solutions Health, Inc. 5/14/2004

HOUSING SYS INC (GA)
Stock Dividend - 20% 9/20/72
Merged into HSI Acquisition Corp. 5/3/88
Each share Common 1¢ par exchanged for $8 cash

HOUSLEY FLUE CONNECTION CORP. (CA)
Charter revoked for failure to file reports and pay fees in 1933

HOUSTON A-1 CAR STEREO PLUS INC (CO)
Administratively dissolved 07/01/2003

HOUSTON AMERICAN LIFE INSURANCECO. (TX)
Merged into Guaranty Income Life Insurance Co. 12/31/65

Each share Capital Stock $1 par exchanged for (0.037037) share Capital Stock $1 par
Guaranty Income Life Insurance Co. merged into Guaranty Corp. 11/3/78

HOUSTON BK & TR CO (HOUSTON, TX)
Each share Capital Stock $100 par exchanged for (5) shares Capital Stock $20 par 02/22/1956
Each share Capital Stock $20 par exchanged for (2) shares Capital Stock $10 par 01/19/1965
Stock Dividends - 15% 01/20/1960; 14% 03/11/1964
Merged into Houston-Citizens Bank & Trust Co. (Houston, TX) 11/01/1970
Each share Capital Stock $10 par exchanged for (1) share Common $10 par
Houston-Citizens Bank & Trust Co. (Houston, TX) reorganized as First International Bancshares, Inc. 12/31/1972 which name changed to InterFirst Corp. 12/31/1981 which merged into First RepublicBank Corp. 06/06/1987
(See First RepublicBank Corp.)

HOUSTON BIOMEDICAL INC (DE)
Common $0.001 par split (3) for (1) by issuance of (2) additional shares 5/16/88
Recapitalized as Andromeda I Inc. 12/11/95
Each share Common $0.001 par exchanged for (0.001) share Common $0.001 par
Andromeda I Inc. recapitalized as Sin Jin Technology, Inc. 1/30/96
(See Sin Jin Technology, Inc.)

HOUSTON BIOTECHNOLOGY INC (DE)
Merged into Medarex, Inc. 02/28/1997
Each share Common 1¢ par exchanged for (0.182) share Common 1¢ par
(See Medarex, Inc.)

HOUSTON CTZNS BK & TR CO (HOUSTON, TX)
Reorganized as First International Bancshares, Inc. 12/31/72
Each share Common $10 par exchanged for (1.8) shares Common $5 par
First International Bancshares, Inc. name changed to InterFirst Corp. 12/31/81 which merged into First RepublicBank Corp. 6/6/87
(See First RepublicBank Corp.)

HOUSTON COMPLEX INC (DE)
Charter cancelled and declared inoperative and void for non-payment of taxes 03/01/1981

HOUSTON CORP. (FL)
Under plan of merger name changed to Florida Gas Co. 5/31/62
Florida Gas Co. merged into Continental Group, Inc. 8/28/79

HOUSTON EXPL CO (DE)
Merged into Forest Oil Corp. 06/06/2007
Each share Common 1¢ par exchanged for $60.0239 cash

HOUSTON FARMS DEV CO (TX)
Merged into General Crude Oil Co. 10/15/1968
Each share Common no par exchanged for (0.48) share $4.12 Conv. Preferred Ser. A no par and (0.175) share Common $2.50 par
(See General Crude Oil Co.)

HOUSTON FEARLESS CORP (CA)
Merged into Image Systems, Inc. (CA) 4/20/70
Each share Common $1 par exchanged for (0.1) share Ser. B Common $1 par and (0.00775) share Common $1 par
Image Systems, Inc. (CA) reincorporated in Delaware 8/29/74
(See Image Systems, Inc. (DE))

HOUSTON FINL CORP (TX)
Reorganized as Houston First Corp. 12/15/69
Each share Common $10 par exchanged for (2.88889) shares Common $1 par
Houston First Corp. name changed to Houston First Financial Group, Inc. 4/17/70 which name changed to M.A.G. Liquidating Corp. 6/30/78
(See M.A.G. Liquidating Corp.)

HOUSTON 1ST CORP (TX)
Name changed to Houston First Financial Group, Inc. 4/17/70
Houston First Financial Group, Inc. name changed to M.A.G. Liquidating Corp. 6/30/78
(See M.A.G. Liquidating Corp.)

HOUSTON FIRST FINL GROUP INC (TX)
Name changed to M.A.G. Liquidating Corp. 6/30/78
(See M.A.G. Liquidating Corp.)

HOUSTON FIRST SVGS ASSN (TX)
Each share Permanent Reserve Fund Stock $10 par exchanged for (5) shares Permanent Reserve Fund Stock $2 par 11/4/64
Under plan of recapitalization each share Permanent Reserve Fund Stock $2 par exchanged for $64 cash 11/16/70
Public interest eliminated

HOUSTON GULF GAS CO.
Acquired by United Gas Corp. 00/00/1930
Details not available

HOUSTON INDS INC (TX)
Common no par split (3) for (2) by issuance of (0.5) additional share 06/12/1981
Common no par split (2) for (1) by issuance of (1) additional share 12/08/1995
Name changed to Reliant Energy Inc. 02/08/1999
Each Automatic Common Exchangeable Security exchanged for (1.6528) shares Time Warner Inc. Common 1¢ par 07/03/2000
(See each company's listing)

HOUSTON LAKE MNG INC (AB)
Name changed to Frontier Lithium Inc. 07/11/2016

HOUSTON (SAM) LIFE INSURANCE CO. (TX)
See - Sam Houston Life Ins Co

HOUSTON LTG & PWR CO (TX)
$6 Preferred called for redemption 3/25/44
7% Preferred called for redemption 3/25/44
Common no par split (3) for (1) by issuance of (2) additional shares 5/17/63
Stock Dividends - 100% 5/19/47; 200% 4/19/51
Under plan of reorganization each share Common no par automatically became (1) share Houston Industries, Inc. Common no par 1/14/77
(See Houston Industries, Inc.)
$9.04 Preferred no par called for redemption 11/12/91
$9.08 Preferred no par called for redemption 11/12/91
$9.52 Preferred no par called for redemption 11/12/91
Adjustable Rate Preferred Ser. A no par called for redemption 10/28/92
Adjustable Rate Preferred Ser. B no par called for redemption 10/28/92
$8.50 Preferred no par called for redemption 6/1/95
Variable Term Preferred Ser. D no par called for redemption 11/27/96
Variable Term Preferred Ser. A no par called for redemption 12/11/96
Variable Term Preferred Ser. B no par called for redemption 12/18/96
Variable Term Preferred Ser. C no par called for redemption 12/26/96
$6.72 Preferred no par called for redemption 2/25/97
$7.52 Preferred no par called for redemption 2/25/97
$8.12 Preferred no par called for redemption 2/25/97
$4 Preferred no par called for redemption at $105 on 12/14/2001

HOUSTON METALS CORP (BC)
Recapitalized as Pacific Houston Resources, Inc. 03/30/1989
Each share Common no par exchanged for (0.2) share Common no par
(See Pacific Houston Resources, Inc.)

HOUSTON NAT GAS CORP (TX)
Reincorporated 05/29/1940
State of incorporation changed from (DE) to (TX) 05/26/1940
7% Preferred called for redemption 03/31/1943
Common no par split (3) for (1) by issuance of (2) additional shares 01/31/1948
Common no par changed to $5 par and (1) additional share issued 04/22/1958
Common $5 par split (5) for (4) by issuance of (0.25) additional share 09/30/1960
Common $5 par split (5) for (4) by issuance of (0.25) additional share 03/30/1963
4.65% Preference $100 par called for redemption 11/27/1964
5% Preferred $25 par called for redemption 11/27/1964
5% Preferred $50 par called for redemption 11/27/64
5-1/4% Conv. Preferred $100 par called for redemption 11/27/1964
Common $5 par and Class B Common $5 par changed to no par 11/30/1964
Common no par and Class B Common no par split (5) for (4) by issuance of (0.25) additional share respectively 12/28/1964
Class B Common no par reclassified as Common no par 11/15/1965
Common no par split (5) for (4) by issuance of (0.25) additional share 01/31/1967
Common no par changed to $1 par 01/31/1969
Common $1 par split (5) for (4) by issuance of (0.25) additional share 07/30/1971
Common no par split (2) for (1) by issuance of (1) additional share 04/30/1973
$2.50 Conv. Preference Ser. A $1 par called for redemption 04/10/1975
Common $1 par split (2) for (1) by issuance of (1) additional share 04/16/1976
Merged into InterNorth, Inc. 07/16/1985
Each share Common $1 par exchanged for $70 cash
4.65% Preferred $100 par called for redemption 09/16/1985
Public interest eliminated

HOUSTON NATL BK (HOUSTON, TX)
Each share Common $20 par exchanged for (2) shares Common $10 par in 1954
Common $10 par changed to $5 par and (1) additional share issued 10/16/64
Stock Dividend - 10% 12/12/67
Reorganized as Houston National Co. 3/27/69
Each share Common $5 par exchanged for (1) share Common $5 par
Houston National Co. merged into Republic of Texas Corp. 4/23/75 which name changed to RepublicBank Corp. 6/30/82 which merged into First RepublicBank Corp. 6/6/87
(See First RepublicBank Corp.)

HOUSTON NATL CO (DE)
Common $5 par reclassified as Class A Common $5 par 6/26/69
Merged into Republic of Texas Corp. 4/23/75
Each share Class A Common $5 par exchanged for (1.0738) shares Common $5 par
Republic of Texas Corp. name changed to RepublicBank Corp. 6/30/82 which merged into First RepublicBank Corp. 6/6/87
(See First RepublicBank Corp.)

HOUSTON OIL & ENERGY INC (NV)
Acquired by Golden Triangle Royalty & Oil Inc. 7/29/92
Each share Common $0.0025 par exchanged for (0.32) share Common $0.001 par
Golden Triangle Royalty & Oil Inc. name changed to Golden Triangle Industries Inc. 5/28/96 which name changed to Whitemark Homes, Inc. 6/20/2001

HOUSTON OIL & MINERALS CORP (NV)
Common 10¢ par split (4) for (3) by issuance of (0.333) additional share 1/15/73
Common 10¢ par split (2) for (1) by issuance of (1) additional share 10/15/73
Common 10¢ par split (2) for (1) by issuance of (1) additional share 6/28/74
Common 10¢ par split (2) for (1) by issuance of (1) additional share 11/17/76
Common 10¢ par split (3) for (2) by issuance of (0.5) additional share 6/30/77
Conv. Preferred $1 par called for redemption 6/15/78
$1.69 Conv. Preferred $1 par called for redemption 1/28/81
Stock Dividend - 25% 3/31/76
Merged into Tenneco Inc. 4/24/81
Each share Common 10¢ par exchanged for (0.31) share Common $5 par
Tenneco Inc. merged into El Paso Natural Gas Co. 12/12/96 which reorganized as El Paso Energy Corp. 8/1/98 which name changed to El Paso Corp. 2/5/2001

HOUSTON OIL CO. OF TEXAS (DE)
Recapitalized in 1930
Each share Preferred $100 par exchanged for (4) shares Preferred $25 par
Each share Common $100 par exchanged for (4) shares Common $25 par
Reincorporated under the laws of Delaware in 1950
Stock Dividend - 20% 6/16/52
Liquidation completed 4/9/57
Details not available

HOUSTON OIL FIELD MATERIAL CO., INC. (DE)
Stock Dividend - 100% 2/28/57
Name changed to International Systems & Controls Corp. 7/24/67

HOUSTON OIL FIELDS CO (DE)
Merged into Plains Resources Inc. 04/22/1987
Each share Common 10¢ par exchanged for (0.15) share Common 2¢ par
(See Plains Resources Inc.)

HOUSTON OIL FIELDS CO (TX)
Merged into Houston Oil Fields Co. (DE) 06/24/1983
Each share Common $10 par exchanged for (45) shares Common 10¢ par
Houston Oil Fields Co. (DE) merged

into Plains Resources Inc. 04/22/1987
(See Plains Resources Inc.)

HOUSTON OIL RTY TR (TX)
Completely liquidated 12/20/91
Each Unit of Bene. Int. no par received first and final distribution of $0.128 cash
Note: Certificates were not required to be surrendered and are without value

HOUSTON OIL TR (TX)
Trust terminated 12/19/89
Each Unit of Bene. Int. exchanged for first and final distribution of $1.996 cash

HOUSTON OILS LTD (AB)
Recapitalized as Bridger Petroleum Corp. Ltd. 10/09/1975
Each share Capital Stock no par exchanged for (0.5) share Capital Stock no par
(See Bridger Petroleum Corp. Ltd.)

HOUSTON OPER CO (DE)
Name changed to NetFabric Holdings, Inc. 04/19/2005
NetFabric Holdings, Inc. name changed to XCel Brands, Inc. 10/28/2011

HOUSTON ROYALTY CO. (TX)
Class B no par reclassified as Common no par 3/12/64
Merged into Houston Royalty Co. (NV) 7/5/66
Each share Common no par exchanged for (2) shares Common 10¢ par
Houston Royalty Co. (NV) name changed to Houston Oil & Minerals Corp. 12/20/68 which merged into Tenneco Inc. 4/24/81 which merged into El Paso Natural Gas Co. 12/12/96 which reorganized as El Paso Energy Corp. 8/1/98 which name changed to El Paso Corp. 2/5/2001

HOUSTON RTY CO (NV)
Name changed to Houston Oil & Minerals Corp. 12/20/68
Houston Oil & Minerals Corp. merged into Tenneco Inc. 4/24/81 which merged into El Paso Natural Gas Co. 12/12/96 which reorganized as El Paso Energy Corp. 8/1/98 which name changed to El Paso Corp. 2/5/2001

HOUSTON SALT CORP (TX)
Company became private 00/00/1979
Details not available

HOUSTON SCIENTIFIC INDS INC (DE)
Name changed to Texas Scientific Industries, Inc. 10/27/83
Texas Scientific Industries, Inc. name changed to Bridgestone Capital Corp. 1/6/88 which name changed to Imagetrust Inc. 10/13/92
(See Imagetrust Inc.)

HOUSTON UTD BK (HOUSTON, TX)
Reorganized as Houston United Bancshares, Inc. 11/20/80
Each share Capital Stock $10 par held by Texas residents exchanged for $44 principal amount of 9% Debentures due 11/20/95
Each share Capital Stock $10 par held by Non-Texas residents exchanged for $46.75 cash

HOUSTRON CORP (FL)
Proclaimed dissolved for failure to file reports and pay fees 11/21/1984

HOVIK MED CORP (BC)
Recapitalized as Globetel Communications Ltd. 07/14/1993
Each share Common no par exchanged for (0.33333333) share Common no par
(See Globetel Communications Ltd.)

HOVING CORP. (DE)
Name changed to 721 Corp. 6/13/61
721 Corp. merged into Genesco Inc. 9/23/66

HOW TO GO PUB INC (NV)
Name changed to Medex Inc. 11/23/2009
(See Medex Inc.)

HOWARD AIRCRAFT CORP.
Name changed to Howard Industries, Inc. in 1946
Howard Industries, Inc. merged into MSL Industries, Inc. (MN) 9/1/65 which reincorporated in Delaware 6/1/73
(See MSL Industries, Inc. (DE))

HOWARD BANCORP (VT)
Capital Stock $5 par split (3) for (2) by issuance of (0.5) additional share 10/28/1988
Merged into BankNorth Group, Inc. (DE) 12/01/1989
Each share Capital Stock $5 par exchanged for (1) share Common $1 par
BankNorth Group, Inc. (DE) merged into Banknorth Group, Inc. (ME) 05/10/2000 which merged into TD Banknorth Inc. 03/01/2005
(See TD Banknorth Inc.)

HOWARD BK (BURLINGTON, VT)
Each share Capital Stock $25 par exchanged for (5) shares Capital Stock $5 par 07/01/1972
Under plan of reorganization each share Capital Stock $5 par automatically became (1) share Howard Bancorp Capital Stock $5 par 01/01/1984
Howard Bancorp merged into BankNorth Group, Inc. (Old) (DE) 12/01/1989 which merged into Banknorth Group, Inc. (DE) 05/10/2000 which merged into TD Banknorth Inc. 03/01/2005
(See TD Banknorth Inc.)

HOWARD-BOSWORTH BUILDING CORP.
Liquidation completed in 1949

HOWARD BROS DISC STORES INC (LA)
Stock Dividend - 25% 7/15/70
Acquired by Gamble-Skogmo, Inc. 7/21/78
Each share Common $1 par exchanged for $15 cash

HOWARD CORP ORE (OR)
Name changed to Bio-Pure, Inc. 10/29/74

HOWARD DISC CTRS INC (DE)
Merged into Aurora Street Corp. 11/7/77
Each share Common $1 par exchanged for $4.07 cash

HOWARD EQUITY FD (DE)
Name changed to Howard Capital Appreciation Fund 4/16/2003

HOWARD-GIBCO CORP. (DE)
Name changed to Howard Discount Centers, Inc. 10/9/73
(See Howard Discount Centers, Inc.)

HOWARD INDUSTRIES, INC. (IL)
Merged into MSL Industries, Inc. (Minn.) 9/1/65
Each share Common $1 par exchanged for (0.4) share Common no par
MSL Industries, Inc. (Minn.) reincorporated under the laws of Delaware 6/1/73
(See MSL Industries, Inc. (Del.))

HOWARD INTL CORP (DE)
Under plan of merger each share Common 1¢ par exchanged for $9.625 cash 9/13/79

HOWARD JOHNSON CO (MD)
Common $1 par and Class B Common $1 par split (2) for (1) by issuance of (1) additional share respectively 5/19/66
Class B Common $1 par reclassified as Common $1 par in 1967
Common $1 par split (2) for (1) by issuance of (1) additional share 5/19/69
Common $1 par split (2) for (1) by issuance of (1) additional share 8/7/72
Acquired by Imperial Group Ltd. 6/17/80
Each share Common $1 par exchanged for $28 cash

HOWARD NATL BK & TR CO (BURLINGTON, VT)
Each share Capital Stock $100 par exchanged for (4) shares Capital Stock $25 par 01/25/1955
Stock Dividend - 10% 06/01/1970
Name changed to Howard Bank (Burlington, VT) 01/01/1972
Howard Bank (Burlington, VT) reorganized as Howard Bancorp 01/01/1984 which merged into BankNorth Group, Inc. (DE) 12/01/1989 which merged into Banknorth Group, Inc. (ME) 05/10/2000 which merged into TD Banknorth Inc. 03/01/2005
(See TD Banknorth Inc.)

HOWARD SVGS BK (NEWARK, NJ)
Common $2 par split (2) for (1) by issuance of (1) additional share 02/19/1987
Placed in receivership and FDIC appointed receiver 10/02/1992
Stockholders' equity unlikely

HOWARD SMITH PAPERS MLS LTD (CANADA)
Common no par exchanged (4) for (1) 00/00/1951
Acquired by Dominion Tar & Chemical Co., Ltd. 09/00/1961
Each share Common no par exchanged for (2.5) shares Common no par
(See Dominion Tar & Chemical Co., Ltd.)
Merged into Domtar Ltd.-Domtar Ltee. 01/13/1972
Each share $2 Preferred $50 par exchanged for (2) shares $1 Preference $23.50 par
Domtar Ltd.-Domtar Ltee. name changed to Domtar Inc. 02/23/1978
(See Domtar Inc.)

HOWARD STORES CORP (NY)
Dissolved by proclamation 12/23/92

HOWDEN D H & CO LTD (ON)
5-1/2% Part. 1st Preference $50 par called for redemption 10/14/77
Acquired by Sodisco Inc. 7/31/87
Each share Common no par exchanged for (1) share Common no par and $46 cash
(See Sodisco Inc.)

HOWE CAVERNS INC (NY)
Acquired by Wright-Galasso Inc. 4/19/2007
Each share Common no par exchanged for $228.30 cash

HOWE LUMBER CO.
Bankrupt in 1931

HOWE PLAN FUND, INC. (MD)
Acquired by Whitehall Fund, Inc. 00/00/1953
Each share Common $1 par exchanged for (0.239816) share Capital Stock $1 par
Whitehall Fund, Inc. name changed to Union Income Fund, Inc. 05/01/1974 which name changed to Seligman Income Fund, Inc. 05/01/1982 which name changed to Seligman Income & Growth Fund, Inc. 11/06/2002

HOWE PLASTICS & CHEM INC (NY)
Dissolved by proclamation 12/24/1991

HOWE RICHARDSON INC (DE)
Merged into Staveley Industries plc 4/26/90
Each share Common no par exchanged for $11.50 cash

HOWE SCALE CO. (VT)
Common no par changed to $5 par and (1) additional share issued 00/00/1948
Stock Dividend - 1,100% 07/00/1948
Liquidated 00/00/1954
Details not available

HOWE SOUND CO. (DE)
Name changed to Howmet Corp. 11/26/1965
(See Howmet Corp.)

HOWE SOUND CO. (ME)
Capital Stock no par changed to $5 par in 1932 and redesignated as Common $5 par in 1950
Common $5 par changed to $1 par and (2) additional shares distributed in 1952
Merged into Howe Sound Co. (Del.) 6/30/58
Each share Common $1 par exchanged for (1) share Common $1 par
Howe Sound Co. (Del.) name changed to Howmet Corp. 11/26/65
(See Howmet Corp.)

HOWELL CORP (DE)
Reincorporated 4/24/84
Common $1 par split (2) for (1) by issuance of (1) additional share 8/26/75
Common $1 par split (3) for (2) by issuance of (0.5) additional share 3/20/80
State of incorporation changed from (TX) to (DE) 4/24/84
Stock Dividends - 50% 4/18/74; 10% payable 3/22/2001 to holders of record 3/8/2001; 10% payable 3/21/2002 to holders of record 3/7/2002
Merged into Anadarko Petroleum Corp. 12/6/2002
Each share $3.50 Conv. Preferred Ser. A $1 par exchanged for $76.15 cash
Each share Common $1 par exchanged for $20.75 cash

HOWELL ELEC MTRS CO (MI)
Each share Class A no par exchanged for (3) shares Common $1 par 00/00/1936
Each share Class B no par exchanged for (1) share Common $1 par 00/00/1936
Name changed to Howell International, Inc. (MI) 11/01/1966
Howell International, Inc. (MI) reincorporated in Delaware as Butler Aviation International, Inc. 06/01/1968 which name changed to Butler International, Inc. (DE) 06/20/1974 which merged into North American Ventures, Inc. 02/02/1987 which recapitalized as Butler International Inc. (MD) 06/29/1992
(See Butler International Inc. (MD))

HOWELL INDS INC (MI)
Merged into Oxford Automotive 8/13/97
Each share Common no par exchanged for $37 cash

HOWELL INSTRS INC (TX)
Capital Stock no par changed to $1 par 3/16/62
Stock Dividend - 200% 12/3/65
Merged into Howell Enterprises, Inc. 7/5/77
Each share Capital Stock $1 par exchanged for $6.25 cash

HOWELL INTERNATIONAL, INC. (MI)
Reincorporated under the laws of Delaware as Butler Aviation International, Inc. 06/01/1968
Butler Aviation International, Inc. name changed to Butler

International, Inc. (DE) 06/20/1974 which merged into North American Ventures, Inc. 02/02/1987 which recapitalized as Butler International Inc. (MD) 06/29/1992
(See Butler International Inc. (MD))

HOWELL MINING CO. (UT)
Merged into Federal Uranium Corp. (NV) on a (1) for (25) basis 04/28/1955
Federal Uranium Corp. merged into Federal Resources Corp. 05/02/1960
(See Federal Resources Corp.)

HOWELL PETE CORP (DE)
Merged into Howell Corp. 3/30/84
Each share Common $1 par exchanged for $30 cash

HOWELL STATE BANK (HOWELL TOWNSHIP, NJ)
Stock Dividends - 10% 2/15/80; 12% 5/27/81
Reorganized as First State Bancorp 9/30/84
Each share Common $5 par exchanged for (1) share Common no par
(See First State Bancorp)

HOWEY CONSOLIDATED MINES LTD. (ON)
Merged into Teck Corp. Ltd. 09/11/1963
Each share Capital Stock $1 par exchanged for (0.8) share Teck Corp. Ltd. Capital Stock no par, (1) share Goldfields Mining Corp. Ltd. Capital Stock $1 par and (0.05) share Geco Mines Ltd. Capital Stock $1 par
(See each company's listing)

HOWEY GOLD MINES, LTD. (ON)
Recapitalized as Consolidated Howey Gold Mines, Ltd. 00/00/1949
Each share Capital Stock $1 par exchanged for (0.4) share Capital Stock $1 par and $0.10 cash
Consolidated Howey Gold Mines, Ltd. name changed to Howey Consolidated Mines Ltd. 04/08/1960
(See Howey Consolidated Mines Ltd.)

HOWMEDICA INC (DE)
Merged into Pfizer, Inc. 10/30/72
Each share Common $1 par exchanged for (0.925) share Common 11-1/9¢ par

HOWMET CORP (DE)
$5.50 Conv. Preferred called for redemption 2/4/66
Common $1 par split (2) for (1) by issuance of (1) additional share 1/18/68
Merged into Pechiney Enterprises Housing Corp. 8/8/75
Each share Common $1 par exchanged for $19 cash

HOWMET INTL INC (DE)
Merged into Alcoa Inc. 06/20/2000
Each share Common 1¢ par exchanged for $21 cash

HOWTEK INC (DE)
Name changed to iCAD, Inc. 06/28/2002

HOYLE GOLD MINES, LTD.
Reorganized as Hoyle Mining Co., Ltd. 00/00/1944
Details not available

HOYLE MINES LTD. (ON)
Succeeded by Hoyle Gold Mines Ltd. on a (0.32848) for (1) basis in 1938
Hoyle Gold Mines Ltd. reorganized as Hoyle Mining Co. Ltd. in 1944
(See Hoyle Mining Co. Ltd.)

HOYLE MINING CO., LTD. (ON)
5.75% Preference $100 par called for redemption 00/00/1960
Dissolved 11/18/1960
Each share Capital Stock no par exchanged for (0.66666666) share Opemiska Copper Mines (Quebec) Ltd. Common $1 par, (1) share Onaping Mines Ltd. Common, (0.06666666) share United Keno Hills Mines Ltd. Common no par and $0.35 cash
(See each company's listing)

HOYLE RES INC (BC)
Recapitalized as Westate Energy Inc. 03/27/1992
Each share Common no par exchanged for (0.4) share Common no par
(See Westate Energy Inc.)

HPB INVTS INC (ON)
Reorganized as Bradstone Capital Corp. 12/30/2015
Each share Common no par exchanged for (0.08333333) Subordinate Share

HPC ACQUISITIONS INC (NV)
Name changed to Vegalab, Inc. 11/13/2017

HPC INC (MN)
Reincorporated under the laws of Nevada as HPC Acquisitions, Inc. 08/07/2006
HPC Acquisitions, Inc. name changed to Vegalab, Inc. 11/13/2017

HPC POS SYS CORP (NV)
Each share old Common $0.001 par exchanged for (1) share new Common $0.001 par 02/19/2013
Name changed to Interactive Health Network 04/28/2014

HPEV INC (NV)
Name changed to Cool Technologies, Inc. 04/12/2016

HPI RECYCLING INC (NV)
Recapitalized 05/31/1994
Recapitalized from H.P. Industries to HPI Recycling, Inc. 05/31/1994
Each share Common 2¢ par exchanged for (0.5) share Common 2¢ par
Name changed to HP Capital Corp. 10/19/1994 which name changed back to HPI Recycling, Inc. 02/24/1995
Recapitalized as Araldica Wineries Ltd. 08/08/1996
Each share Common 2¢ par exchanged for (0.1) share Common $0.001 par
Araldica Wineries Ltd. recapitalized as Interactive Solutions Corp. (NV) 02/14/2000 which reorganized in Wyoming as MyMedicalCD, Ltd. 11/24/2004 which recapitalized as United Treatment Centers, Inc. 01/30/2009 which name changed to PotNetwork Holdings, Inc. (WY) 07/24/2015 which reincorporated in Colorado 03/03/2017

HPIL RES LTD (AB)
Struck off register for failure to file annual returns 06/01/1993

HPL TECHNOLOGIES INC (DE)
Issue Information - 6,000,000 shares COM offered at $11 per share on 07/30/2001
Merged into Synopsys, Inc. 12/7/2005
Each share Common $0.001 par exchanged for $0.30 cash

HPM CORP (OH)
Merged into Stadco, Inc. 4/15/96
Each share Common no par exchanged for $40.06 cash

HPR INC (DE)
Common 1¢ par split (2) for (1) by issuance of (1) additional share payable 05/06/1996 to holders of record 04/26/1996
Merged into HBO & Co. 12/23/1997
Each share Common 1¢ par exchanged for (0.6) share Common 5¢ par
HBO & Co. merged into McKesson HBOC Inc. 01/12/1999 which name changed to McKesson Corp. 07/30/2001

HPRA, INC. (MI)
In process of liquidation
Each share Common $1 par exchanged for initial distribution of $6 cash 12/20/72
Note: Details on subsequent distributions, if any, are not available

HPSC INC (DE)
Merged into General Electric Co. 1/12/2004
Each share Common 1¢ par exchanged for (0.464) share Common 16¢ par

HPVC INC (CANADA)
Plan of arrangement effective 10/03/2006
Each share Common no par exchanged for (0.1) Temple Real Estate Investment Trust Unit
Temple Real Estate Investment Trust reorganized as Temple Hotels Inc. 12/31/2012

HPY INDS LTD (BC)
Delisted from Vancouver Stock Exchange 1/31/91

HQ OFFICE INTL INC (DE)
Name changed to New World Capital Advisors Inc. 10/23/92
(See New World Capital Advisors Inc.)

HQ OFFICE SUPPLIES WHSE INC (DE)
Charter cancelled and declared inoperative and void for non-payment of taxes 3/1/95

HQ SUSTAINABLE MARITIME INDS INC (DE)
Each share old Common $0.001 par exchanged for (0.05) share new Common $0.001 par 01/31/2007
Note: No holder will receive fewer than (100) post-split shares
SEC revoked common stock registration 04/10/2012
No stockholders' equity

HRC DEV CORP (CANADA)
Reincorporated 07/01/1996
Place of incorporation changed from (BC) to Canada 07/01/1996
Merged into Eldorado Gold Corp. (New) 11/19/1996
Each share Common no par exchanged for (0.5) share Common no par and (1) Common Stock Purchase Warrant expiring 11/19/1998

HRC INC. (MA)
Voluntarily dissolved 12/31/1986
Details not available

HRE PPTYS INC (MD)
Reincorporated 03/13/1997
State of incorporation and name changed from HRE Properties (MA) to HRE Properties, Inc. (MD) 03/13/1997
Name changed to Urstadt Biddle Properties Inc. 03/12/1998

HRG GROUP INC (DE)
Recapitalized as Spectrum Brands Holdings, Inc. (New) 07/16/2018
Each share Common 1¢ par exchanged for (0.16125488) share Common 1¢ par

HRI GROUP INC (DE)
Name changed to Qintex Entertainment Inc. 12/9/88
(See Qintex Entertainment Inc.)

HRPT PPTYS TR (MD)
Each Common Share of Bene. Int. 1¢ par received distribution of (0.1) share Senior Housing Properties Trust Common Share of Bene. Int. 1¢ par payable 10/12/1999 to holders of record 10/08/1999
Ex date - 10/13/1999
Each Common Share of Bene. 1¢ par received distribution of (0.01) share Five Star Quality Care, Inc. Common 1¢ par payable 12/31/2001 to holders of record 12/17/2001
Ex date - 01/02/2002
9.875% Preferred Shares Ser. A called for redemption at $25 on 03/02/2006
Recapitalized as CommonWealth REIT 07/01/2010
Each Common Share of Bene. Int. 1¢ par exchanged for (0.25) Common Share of Bene. Int. 1¢ par
Preferreds not affected except for change of name
CommonWealth REIT name changed to Equity Commonwealth 08/01/2014

HRT INDS INC (DE)
Each share old Common $1 par exchanged for (0.25) share new Common $1 par 3/13/84
Merged into McCrory Corp. 4/19/85
Each share new Common 1¢ par exchanged for $6 principal amount of 14-1/2% Subord. Notes due 5/31/88

HRT LTD (HI)
Merged into TRH Ltd. in 1987
Each share 5% Preferred $10 par exchanged for $10 cash
Each share Common $5 par exchanged for $118 cash

HRT PARTICIPACOES EM PETROLEO S A (BRAZIL)
Basis changed from (1:0.01) to (1:0.5) 06/01/2012
Each old Sponsored GDR for Common exchanged for (0.1) new Sponsored GDR for Common 08/05/2014
Name changed to Petro Rio S.A. 07/07/2015
(See Petro Rio S.A.)

HRUB CORP (DE)
Liquidation completed
Each share Common $1 par received initial distribution of $1.30 cash 4/29/83
Each share Common $1 par received second distribution of $1.20 cash 5/27/86
Each share Common $1 par exchanged for third and final distribution of $2 cash 7/18/88

HRVATSKE TELEKOMUNIKACIJE D D (CROATIA)
Name changed to Hrvatski Telekom D.D. 10/28/2010
(See Hrvatski Telekom D.D.)

HRVATSKI TELEKOM D D (CROATIA)
GDR agreement terminated 10/01/2014
Each 144A GDR for Ordinary exchanged for $22.978344 cash
Each Reg. S GDR for Ordinary exchanged for $22.978344 cash

HS GROUP INC. LIQUIDATING TRUST (DE)
Liquidation completed
Each share Common 50¢ par exchanged for initial distribution of (1.5) shares Monterey Farming Corp. Common no par 10/7/85
Each share Common 50¢ par received second and final distribution of $2 cash 12/6/85
(See Monterey Farming Corp.)

HS GROUP INC (DE)
In process of liquidation
Each share Common 50¢ par received initial distribution of $7 cash 7/26/85
Assets transferred to HS Group Inc. Liquidating Trust and Common 50¢ par reclassified as Shares of Bene. Int. 50¢ par 8/23/85
(See HS Group Inc. Liquidating Trust)

HS RES INC (DE)
Merged into Kerr-McGee Corp. 8/1/2001
Each share Common $0.001 par exchanged for either (0.9404) share Common $1 par or (0.27) share Common $1 par and $46.86 cash
Note: Option to receive stock only expired 8/29/2001

HSB BANCORP INC (MD)
Each share old Common 1¢ par exchanged for (0.00333333) share new Common 1¢ par 11/18/2004
Note: In effect holders received $38 cash per share and public interest was eliminated

HSB GROUP INC (CT)
Common no par split (3) for (2) by issuance of (0.5) additional share payable 5/22/98 to holders of record 5/1/98 Ex date - 5/26/98
Merged into American International Group, Inc. 11/22/2000
Each share Common no par exchanged for (0.4178) share Common $2.50 par

HSBC AMERS INC (DE)
Adjustable Rate Preferred Ser. A $1 par called for redemption 3/31/97
$5.50 Conv. Preferred no par called for redemption 3/31/97
Public interest eliminated

HSBC BK CDA (VANCOUVER, BC)
Class 1 Preferred Ser. A called for redemption at $25 on 09/30/2005
Class 1 5-Yr. Rate Reset Preferred Ser. E called for redemption at $25 on 06/30/2014
Non-Cum. Class 1 Preferred Ser. C called for redemption at $25 on 01/02/2018
Class 1 Preferred Ser. D called for redemption at $25 on 01/02/2018

HSBC BK PLC (ENGLAND & WALES)
Sponsored ADR's for B1 & B2 called for redemption at $25 plus $1.0256 accrued dividends on 7/25/2001
Sponsored ADR's for Ser. D called for redemption at $25 plus $1.0256 accrued dividends on 7/25/2001
Sponsored ADR's for A1 & A2 called for redemption at $25 plus $0.044375 accrued dividends on 10/29/2001
Sponsored ADR's for C1 & C2 called for redemption at $25 plus $0.9125 accrued dividends on 10/29/2001

HSBC CAP FDG DLR 2 L P (JERSEY)
4.61% 144A Step-up Perpetual Preferred called for redemption at $1,000 on 06/27/2013
4.61% Reg. S Step-up Perpetual Preferred called for redemption at $1,000 on 06/27/2013

HSBC EUROPEAN ABSOLUTE LTD (UNITED KINGDOM)
Each old Sponsored EDR for Ordinary exchanged for (0.1) new Sponsored EDR for Ordinary 2/11/2002
EDR agreement terminated 6/29/2005
Each new Sponsored EDR for Ordinary exchanged for (10) Ordinary shares

HSBC FIN CORP (DE)
6.36% Depositary Preferred Ser. B called for redemption at $25 plus 0.06625 accrued dividends on 06/30/2016

HSBC USA INC (MD)
$1.8125 Preferred called for redemption at $25 on 12/15/2005
Dutch Auction Rate Preferred Ser. A called for redemption at $100,000 on 11/14/2007
Dutch Auction Rate Preferred Ser. B called for redemption at $100,000 on 11/20/2007
Depositary Preferred Ser. D called for redemption at $25 plus $0.265624 accrued dividends on 06/26/2015
$2.8575 Preferred no par called for redemption at $50 plus $0.674687 accrued dividends on 06/26/2015
Floating Rate Non-Cum. Preferred Ser. F no par called for redemption at $25 plus $0.21875 accrued dividends on 06/30/2016
Depositary Preferred Ser. G called for redemption at $25 plus $0.25 accrued dividends on 06/30/2016
6.5% Depositary Preferred Ser. H called for redemption at $25 plus $0.401736 accrued dividends on 06/30/2016
New York Corp. 01/04/2000

HSC SVCS INC (CO)
Declared defunct and inoperative for failure to pay taxes and file annual reports 01/01/1993

HSE INTEGRATED LTD (AB)
Acquired by DXP Enterprises, Inc. 07/12/2018
Each share Common no par exchanged for $1.80 cash
Note: Unexchanged certificates were cancelled and became without value 07/12/2018

HSF CAP CORP (BC)
Name changed to China Keli Electric Co. Ltd. 05/05/2010

HSI HYDROSYSTEMS INTL INC (BC)
Recapitalized as R.W. Gas Group Inc. 05/09/1994
Each Share of Bene. Int. no par exchanged for (0.25) share Common no par
R.W. Gas Group Inc. recapitalized as Anglo-Canadian Gas Corp. 10/28/1996 which recapitalized as Jager Metal Corp. 01/20/2011 which name changed to Jagercor Energy Corp. 01/27/2014

HSK MINERALS LTD (MB)
Merged into Queenston Mining Inc. 01/02/1990
Each share Common no par exchanged for (0.434) share Common no par
Queenston Mining Inc. merged into Osisko Mining Corp. 01/02/2013
(See Osisko Mining Corp.)

HSM HLDGS INC (NV)
Name changed to Custom Coals Corp. 05/22/1996
(See Custom Coals Corp.)

HSN INC NEW (DE)
Merged into Liberty Interactive Corp. 12/29/2017
Each share Common 1¢ par exchanged for (1.65) shares QVC Group Common Ser. A 1¢ par
Liberty Interactive Corp. name changed to Qurate Retail, Inc. 04/10/2018

HSN INC OLD (DE)
Name changed to USA Networks, Inc. 02/17/1998
USA Networks, Inc. name changed to USA Interactive 05/09/2002 which name changed to InterActiveCorp 06/23/2003 which name changed to IAC/InterActiveCorp 07/14/2004

HSW INTL INC (DE)
Each share old Common $0.001 par exchanged for (0.1) share new Common $0.001 par 02/17/2010
Name changed to Remark Media, Inc. 01/03/2012
Remark Media, Inc. name changed to Remark Holdings, Inc. 04/11/2017

HT CAP INC (BC)
Name changed to Asia Packaging Group Inc. 07/13/2011
(See Asia Packaging Group Inc.)

HT INSIGHT FDS INC (MD)
Name changed to Phoenix Insight Funds Trust 05/15/2006
(See Phoenix Insight Funds Trust)

HTC HYDROGEN TECHNOLOGIES CORP (AB)
Name changed to HTC Purenergy Inc. 02/21/2008

HTI VENTURES CORP (CANADA)
Each share old Common no par exchanged for (0.33333333) share new Common no par 12/02/2003
Each share new Common no par exchanged again for (0.1) share new Common no par 06/01/2012
New Common no par split (3) for (2) by issuance of (0.5) additional share payable 06/28/2016 to holders of record 06/23/2016 Ex date - 06/29/2016
Reincorporated under the laws of British Columbia as Leagold Mining Corp. 08/31/2016

HTN INC (AB)
Reincorporated under the laws of Ontario as Internet of Things Inc. 05/14/2015

HTR TOTAL RETURN FD (ON)
Merged into INDEXPLUS Income Fund 05/26/2008
Each Trust Unit exchanged for (0.74976784) Unit
INDEXPLUS Income Fund reorganized as Middlefield Mutual Funds Ltd. 06/05/2017

HTS LTD (AB)
Name changed to Prism Petroleum Ltd. (Old) 02/21/1996
Prism Petroleum Ltd. (Old) recapitalized as Prism Petroleum Ltd. (New) 09/01/1996 which recapitalized as Prism Petroleum Inc. 06/08/2000 which was acquired by Real Resources Inc. 09/11/2000 which merged into TriStar Oil & Gas Ltd. (New) 08/16/2007 which merged into PetroBakken Energy Ltd. (Old) 10/05/2009 which reorganized as PetroBakken Energy Ltd. (New) 01/07/2013 which name changed to Lightstream Resources Ltd. 05/28/2013

HTTL ENTERPRISES INC. (ON)
Merged into Unisphere Satellite Corp. 11/03/1989
Details not available

HTTP TECHNOLOGY INC (DE)
Reincorporated 12/19/2000
State of incorporation changed from (UT) to (DE) and Common 1¢ par changed to $0.001 par 12/19/2000
Common $0.001 par split (2) for (1) by issuance of (1) additional share payable 2/5/2001 to holders of record 1/22/2001 Ex date - 2/6/2001
Name changed to Medicsight, Inc. 10/28/2002
Medicsight, Inc. name changed to MGT Capital Investments, Inc. 1/24/2007

H2DIESEL HLDGS INC (FL)
Name changed to New Generation Biofuels Holdings, Inc. 04/16/2008
(See New Generation Biofuels Holdings, Inc.)

H2O ENTMT CORP (BC)
Recapitalized as Consolidated H2O Entertainment Corp. 07/14/2005
Each share Common no par exchanged for (0.1) share Common no par
Consolidated H2O Entertainment Corp. name changed to Tri-River Ventures, Inc. 07/30/2007

H2O INNOVATION 2000 INC (CANADA)
Each share old Common no par exchanged for (0.1) share new Common no par 03/01/2006
Name changed to H2O Innovation Inc. 12/04/2008

HUADING FINL NETWORKS INC (NV)
Charter revoked for failure to file reports and pay fees 11/1/2004

HUAKAN INTL MNG INC (BC)
Acquired by Hong Kong Huakan Investment Co., Ltd. 04/28/2014
Each share Common no par exchanged for $0.50 cash

HUALING HLDGS LTD (HONG KONG)
Name changed to Welling Holding Ltd. 07/14/2008
(See Welling Holding Ltd.)

HUAYANG INTL HLDGS INC (NV)
Recapitalized as China Energy & Carbon Black Holdings, Inc. 10/25/2004
Each share Common 2¢ par exchanged for (1/6) share Common 2¢ par
China Energy & Carbon Black Holdings, Inc. recapitalized as CO2 Tech Ltd. 1/9/2007

HUAYUE ELECTRONICS INC (DE)
Name changed to Tarsier Ltd. 12/11/2015

HUB, HENRY C. LYTTON & CO.
Name changed to Lytton's, Henry C. Lytton & Co. in 1946
(See Lytton's, Henry C. Lytton & Co.)

HUB AIRLS INC (IN)
Declared insolvent 12/19/73
Details not available

HUB FINANCIAL CORP.
Dissolved in 1931

HUB GROUP LTD (ON)
Name changed to Hub International Ltd. (ON) 09/14/2000
Hub International Ltd. (ON) reincorporated in Canada 05/18/2004
(See Hub International Ltd.)

HUB INTL LTD (CANADA)
Reincorporated 5/18/2004
Place of incorporation changed from (ON) to Canada 05/18/2004
Merged into Maple Tree Acquisition Corp. 06/13/2007
Each share Common no par exchanged for $41.50 cash

HUB LOAN CO. (NJ)
Each share Preferred and Common $10 par exchanged for (3-1/3) shares Preferred $2 par in 1950
Class A Common $1 par changed to 25¢ par 1/14/51
Charter voided for failure to pay taxes 2/3/64

HUB MNG & EXPLS LTD (BC)
Recapitalized as Senator Minerals Corp. 08/02/1978
Each share Common 50¢ par exchanged for (0.25) share Common no par
(See Senator Minerals Corp.)

HUB-WYOMING OIL CO. (CO)
Charter dissolved for failure to file annual reports 1/1/35

HUB YELLOWKNIFE MINES, LTD. (ON)
Charter cancelled for failure to file reports and pay taxes 03/21/1956

HUBBARD & CO. (PA)
5-1/2% Preferred $20 par called for redemption 12/12/60

HUBBARD DYERS INC (QC)
Name changed to Hubbard Holding Inc. 03/01/1991
(See Hubbard Holding Inc.)

HUBBARD DYERS LTD (CANADA)
Each share Class A no par exchanged for (1.75) shares $1 Preferred no par and (0.133333) share Common no par 02/16/1967
Each share Class B no par exchanged for (1.75) shares $1 Preferred no par 02/16/1967

FINANCIAL INFORMATION, INC.   HUB-HUD

Each share Common no par exchanged for (1.75) shares Common no par 02/16/1967
Each share old Common no par exchanged for (5) shares new Common no par 02/09/1972
Acquired by Dominion Textile Ltd.- Dominion Textile Ltee. 12/09/1972
Each share $1 Preferred no par exchanged for $14 cash
Each share new Common no par exchanged for $12.50 cash

HUBBARD ENGINE CO.
Acquired by General Motors Corp. 00/00/1930
Details not available

HUBBARD FELT CO. LTD. (CANADA)
Name changed to Hubbard Dyers Ltd. 03/30/1965
(See Hubbard Dyers Ltd.)

HUBBARD HLDG INC (QC)
Delisted from Toronto Venture Stock Exchange 6/20/2003

HUBBARD M M ASSOC INC (MA)
Each share Capital Stock $1 par exchanged for (300) shares Capital Stock 10¢ par 10/21/1966
Proclaimed dissolved for failure to file reports and pay taxes 10/19/1983

HUBBARD REAL ESTATE INVTS (MA)
Shares of Bene. Int. no par reclassified as Common no par 4/9/74
Name changed to HRE Properties (MA) 2/1/86
HRE Properties (MA) reincorporated in Maryland as HRE Properties, Inc. 3/13/97 which name changed to Urstadt Biddle Properties Inc. 3/12/98

HUBBARD STATE BANK (BAD AXE, MI)
Name changed to Community Bank (Bad Axe, MI) 07/01/1969
(See Community Bank (Bad Axe, MI))

HUBBARD STEEL FOUNDRY CO.
Merged into Continental Roll & Steel Foundry Co. in 1930 which name was changed to Continental Foundry & Machine Co. in 1944 which completed liquidation 11/25/58
(See Continental Foundry & Machine Co.)

HUBBARDS CUPBOARD INC (NJ)
Merged into HubCup Enterprises, Inc. 7/6/82
Each share Common 1¢ par exchanged for $5.25 cash

HUBBELL INC (CT)
Name changed 05/12/1986
Common $5 par changed to Class A Common $5 par and (1) additional share Class A Common $5 par and (2) shares Class B Common $5 par issued 04/29/1960
Class A Common $5 par and Class B Common $5 par split (5) for (4) respectively by issuance of (0.25) additional share 04/21/1966
Class A Common $5 par and Class B Common $5 par split (4) for (3) respectively by issuance of (1/3) additional share 07/21/1969
Class A Common $5 par and Class B Common $5 par split (4) for (3) respectively by issuance of (1/3) additional share 08/05/1977
$1.75 Conv. Preferred Ser. B no par called for redemption 02/28/1978
$1.75 Conv. Preferred Ser. A no par called for redemption 11/30/1978
Class A Common $5 par and Class B Common $5 par split (2) for (1) respectively by issuance of (1) additional share 02/10/1981
Class A Common $5 par split (2) for (1) by issuance of (1) additional share 08/09/1985
Class B Common $5 par split (2) for (1) by issuance of (1) additional share 08/09/1985
Name changed from Hubbell (Harvey), Inc. to Hubbell Inc. 05/12/1986
$2.06 Conv. Preferred Ser. C no par called for redemption 09/01/1988

HUBBLE CAP INC (QC)
Name changed to Bigknowledge Enterprises Inc. 6/23/2005

HUBCO INC (NJ)
Common no par split (3) for (2) by issuance of (0.5) additional share 12/15/1983
Common no par split (2) for (1) by issuance of (1) additional share 08/01/1986
Common no par split (3) for (2) by issuance of (0.5) additional share 01/14/1995
Preferred Ser. A no par called for redemption 07/01/1995
Stock Dividends - 10% 11/20/1987; 10% 11/15/1991; 10% 06/01/1993; 3% payable 11/15/1996 to holders of record 11/04/1996; 3% payable 12/01/1997 to holders of record 11/13/1997; 3% payable 09/01/1998 to holders of record 08/14/1998
Name changed to Hudson United Bancorp 04/21/1999
Hudson United Bancorp which merged into merged into TD Banknorth Inc. 01/31/2006
(See TD Banknorth Inc.)

HUBEI PHARMACEUTICAL GROUP LTD (NV)
Name changed to Amersin Life Sciences Corp. 01/14/2005
Amersin Life Sciences Corp. recapitalized as Golden Tech Group, Ltd. 05/21/2007 which name changed to Mega Win Investments, Inc. 03/02/2018 which name changed to Invech Holdings, Inc. 08/07/2018

HUBER CORP. (OH)
$1.25 Conv. Preferred no par called for redemption 08/21/1967
Merged into Mid-Continent Manufacturing Co. (OH) 09/25/1967
Each share Common $1 par exchanged for (2.25) shares Common $1 par
Mid-Continent Manufacturing Co. (OH) reincorporated in Delaware as Mid-Con Inc. 10/31/1968 which merged into A-T-O Inc. 10/29/1969 which name changed to Figgie International Inc. (OH) 06/01/1981 which reorganized in Delaware as Figgie International Holdings Inc. 07/18/1983 which name changed to Figgie International Inc. 12/31/1986 which name changed to Scott Technologies, Inc. 05/20/1998 which merged into Tyco International Ltd. (Bermuda) 05/03/2001 which reincorporated in Switzerland 03/17/2009 which merged into Johnson Controls International PLC 09/06/2016

HUBER MANUFACTURING CO. (OH)
Each share 6% Preferred exchanged for (5) shares $1.25 Preferred no par and $1 cash 00/00/1943
Name changed to Huber-Warco Co. 12/07/1954
Huber-Warco Co. name changed to Huber Corp. 11/13/1964 which merged into Mid-Continent Manufacturing Co. (OH) 09/25/1967 which reincorporated in Delaware as Mid-Con Inc. 10/31/1968 which merged into A-T-O Inc. 10/29/1969 which name changed to Figgie International Inc. (OH) 06/01/1981 which reorganized in Delaware as Figgie International Holdings Inc. 07/18/1983 which name changed to Figgie International Inc. 12/31/1986 which name changed to Scott Technologies, Inc. 05/20/1998 which merged into Tyco International Ltd. (Bermuda) 05/03/2001 which reincorporated in Switzerland 03/17/2009 which merged into Johnson Controls International PLC 09/06/2016

HUBER WARCO CO (OH)
Each share Common $100 par exchanged for (8) shares Common $1 par 01/12/1955
Name changed to Huber Corp. 11/13/1964
Huber Corp. merged into Mid-Continent Manufacturing Co. (OH) 09/25/1967 which reincorporated in Delaware as Mid-Con Inc. 10/31/1968 which merged into A-T-O Inc. 10/29/1969 which name changed to Figgie International Inc. (OH) 06/01/1981 which reorganized in Delaware as Figgie International Holdings Inc. 07/18/1983 which name changed to Figgie International Inc. 12/31/1986 which name changed to Scott Technologies, Inc. 05/20/1998 which merged into Tyco International Ltd. (Bermuda) 05/03/2001 which reincorporated in Switzerland 03/17/2009 which merged into Johnson Controls International PLC 09/06/2016

HUBERT LAKE UNGAVA NICKEL MINES LTD (QC)
Recapitalized as Superior Financial Holdings, Inc. 01/15/1990
Each share Capital Stock $1 par exchanged for (0.33333333) share Common $1 par
Superior Financial Holdings, Inc. recapitalized as Superior Capital Inc. 12/23/1991 which name changed to Emerging Africa Gold EAG Inc. 06/27/1996 which merged into Diagem International Resources Corp. (BC) 05/31/2002 which reincorporated in Canada as Diagem Inc. 11/18/2004
(See Diagem Inc.)

HUBINGER CO (IA)
Common $2.50 par changed to $1.25 par and (1) additional share issued 04/017/1961
Stock Dividends - 50% 02/28/1951; 10% 12/10/1954
Merged into Heinz (H.J.) Co. 02/17/1975
Each share Common $1.25 par exchanged for (2) shares $1.70 3rd Conv. Preferred $10 par
(See Heinz (H.J.) Co.)

HUBOREX MINES LTD. (ON)
Charter cancelled for failure to file reports and pay taxes in 1970

HUBSHMAN FACTORS CORP. (NY)
Completely liquidated 1/18/65
Each share Class A $1 par exchanged for first and final distribution of $12.6481 cash

HUBSHMAN FD INC (NY)
Name changed to Sagittarius Fund Inc. 5/11/71

HUCK FINN INC (MN)
Common 10¢ par changed to 3-1/3¢ par and (2) additional shares issued 5/30/72
Common 3-1/3¢ par changed to 1-2/3¢ par and (1) additional share issued 10/25/72
Assets seized for the benefit of creditors 12/8/75
No stockholders' equity

HUCK MFG CO (MI)
Merged into Federal-Mogul Corp. 09/09/1980
Each share Common $1 par exchanged for $41 cash

HUCLIF PORCUPINE MINES LTD (ON)
Charter cancelled for failure to pay taxes and file returns 03/16/1976

HUDBAY MINERALS INC (ON)
Reincorporated under the laws of Canada 10/25/2005

HUDCO TELECOMMUNICATIONS, INC. (UT)
Name changed to Centauri Communications, Inc. and Common $0.001 par changed to no par 10/18/1982
(See Centauri Communications, Inc.)

HUDSON & MANHATTAN CORP (NJ & NY)
Liquidation completed
Each share Class A $10 par stamped to indicate initial distribution of $32.30 cash 9/1/71
Each share Class B $10 par stamped to indicate initial distribution of $372.59 cash 9/1/71
Each share Stamped Class A $10 par received second distribution of $12.82 cash 12/30/71
Each share Stamped Class B $10 par received second distribution of $66.77 cash 12/30/71
Each share Stamped Class A $10 par received third distribution of $2.20 cash 5/15/72
Each share Stamped Class B $10 par received third distribution of $20.50 cash 5/15/72
Each share Stamped Class A $10 par received fourth distribution of $3.35 cash 3/6/73
Each share Stamped Class B $10 par received fourth distribution of $25.32 cash 3/6/73
Each share Stamped Class A $10 par received fifth distribution of $5.09 cash 4/16/73
Each share Stamped Class B $10 par received fifth distribution of $43.62 cash 4/16/73
Each share Stamped Class A $10 par exchanged for sixth distribution of $1 cash and a Non-Transferable Registered Receipt 10/15/73
Each share Stamped Class B $10 par exchanged for sixth distribution of $2.80 cash and a Non-Transferable Registered Receipt 10/15/73
Each Non-Transferable Registered Receipt received seventh and final distribution of $0.162 cash 12/30/74
Note: Non-Transferable Registered Receipts were not required to be surrendered and are now without value

HUDSON & MANHATTAN RAILROAD CO. (NJ & NY)
Reorganized 12/31/1961
No stockholders' equity

HUDSON BAY DIECASTING LTD (ON)
Discharged from bankruptcy 06/00/2004
No stockholders' equity

HUDSON BAY MINES LTD (ON)
Capital Stock $5 par changed to $1 par 00/00/1952
Name changed to T & H Resources Ltd. (ON) and Capital Stock $1 par changed to Common no par 09/26/1984
T & H Resources Ltd. (ON) reorganized in Canada as LAB International Inc. 05/16/2002 which name changed to Akela Pharma Inc. 07/13/2007
(See Akela Pharma Inc.)

HUDSON BAY MNG & SMLT LTD (CANADA)
Capital Stock no par split (3) for (1) by issuance of (2) additional shares 05/02/1970
Capital Stock no par reclassified as Conv. Class A Common no par 05/27/1974

Conv. Class A Common no par reclassified as Common no par 01/03/1979
Conv. Class B Common no par reclassified as Common no par 01/03/1979
Under plan of reorganization each share Common no par exchanged for (1.1) Hudson Bay Mining & Smelting Co. Ltd. Exchangeable Special Shares no par or (1.15) shares Inspiration Resources Corp. Common no par 07/06/1983
Note: Non-electing Non-Canadian residents received Inspiration Resources Corp. and Canadian residents received Hudson Bay Mining & Smelting Co. Ltd.
Each Special Share no par exchanged for (1) share Terra Industries Inc. Common no par 07/06/1993
(See each company's listing)

HUDSON BAY MTN SILVER MINES LTD (BC)
Struck off register and declared dissolved for failure to file returns 10/30/1978

HUDSON CASUALTY INSURANCE CO.
Merged into Public Indemnity Co. in 1930
Details not available

HUDSON CHARTERED BANCORP INC (NY)
Conv. Preferred Ser. B 1¢ par called for redemption 4/15/96
Common 80¢ par split (3) for (2) by issuance of (0.5) additional share payable 10/31/97 to holders of record 10/16/97 Ex date - 11/3/97
Stock Dividends - 10% payable 1/31/96 to holders of record 1/8/96; 10% payable 1/15/97 to holders of record 12/31/96
Under plan of merger name changed to Premier National Bancorp, Inc. 7/17/98
Premier National Bancorp, Inc. merged into M&T Bank Corp. 2/9/2001

HUDSON CHIBOUGAMAU MINES LTD. (ON)
Charter cancelled in September 1960

HUDSON CITY BANCORP INC (DE)
Common 1¢ par split (2) for (1) by issuance of (1) additional share payable 06/17/2002 to holders of record 05/24/2002 Ex date - 06/17/2002
Common 1¢ par split (3.206) for (1) by issuance of (2.206) additional shares payable 06/07/2005 to holders of record 06/06/2005
Acquired by M&T Bank Corp. 10/30/2015
Each share Common 1¢ par exchanged for $10.062172 cash

HUDSON CLEANERS, INC. (NV)
Charter revoked for non-payment of filing fees and penalties 3/2/64

HUDSON COUNTIES TITLE & MORTGAGE CO. (NEWBURGH, NY)
Insolvent 00/00/1936
No stockholders' equity

HUDSON COUNTY GAS CO.
Merged into Public Service Electric & Gas Co. in 1939
Details not available

HUDSON CNTY NATL BK (JERSEY CITY, NJ)
Common $25 par changed to $30 par in January 1945
Common $30 par changed to $32.50 par in May 1945
Common $32.50 par changed to $35 par in October 1945
Common $35 par changed to $50 par in November 1952

Each share Common $50 par exchanged for (2) shares Common $25 par 1/22/57
Common $25 par changed to $10 par and (1.5) additional shares issued 11/15/60
Stock Dividends - 20% 2/14/58; 10% 2/15/60; 11.38% 2/15/63; 11% 2/23/65; 20% 4/15/66; 10% 3/14/69
Name changed to North Jersey National Bank (Jersey City, NJ) 7/15/69
North Jersey National Bank (Jersey City, NJ) merged into Garden State National Bank (Hackensack, NJ) 2/1/71 which changed location to (Paramus, NJ) 11/15/74
(See Garden State National Bank (Paramus, NJ))

HUDSON FOODS INC (DE)
Common 1¢ par reclassified as Class A Common 1¢ par 2/6/87
Class A Common 1¢ par split (3) for (2) by issuance of (0.5) additional share 3/27/95
Merged into Tyson Foods, Inc. 1/9/98
Each share Class A Common 1¢ par exchanged for (0.6) share Class A Common 10¢ par and $8.40 cash
Each share Class B Common 1¢ par exchanged for (0.6) share Class A Common 10¢ par and $8.40 cash

HUDSON FUND, INC. (MD)
Capital Stock $1 par split (2) for (1) by issuance of (1) additional share in 1953
Name changed to Fiduciary Mutual Investing Co., Inc. 3/1/57
Fiduciary Mutual Investing Co., Inc. acquired by Steadman Fiduciary Investment Fund, Inc. 11/2/67 which merged into Steadman Investment Fund, Inc. (New) 1/25/73 which name changed to Ameritor Investment Fund 9/23/98

HUDSON GEN CORP (DE)
Merged into Deutsche Lufthansa AG 3/29/99
Each share Common $1 par exchanged for $76 cash

HUDSON-HARLEM VALLEY CORP.
Dissolved in 1947

HUDSON HIGHLAND GROUP INC (DE)
Common $0.001 par split (2) for (1) by issuance of (1) additional share payable 02/25/2005 to holders of record 02/14/2005 Ex date - 02/28/2005
Name changed to Hudson Global, Inc. 04/30/2012

HUDSON HLDG CORP (DE)
Merged into Rodman & Renshaw Capital Group, Inc. 04/08/2011
Each share Common $0.001 par exchanged for approximately (0.0332) share Common $0.001 par
Rodman & Renshaw Capital Group, Inc. name changed to Direct Markets Holdings Corp. 06/01/2012
(See Direct Markets Holdings Corp.)

HUDSON HOTELS CORP (NY)
Each share old Common $0.001 par exchanged for (0.33333333) share new Common $0.001 par 09/18/2000
Plan of reorganization under Chapter 11 Federal Bankruptcy Code effective 10/02/2004
No stockholders' equity

HUDSON LEASING CORP (DE)
4% Preferred 1966 Ser. $50 par called for redemption in July 1969
$2.75 Conv. Preferred Ser. A $1 par called for redemption 11/1/70
Name changed to Hudson General Corp. 11/23/71
(See Hudson General Corp.)

HUDSON MOTOR CAR CO. (MI)
Capital Stock no par changed to $12.50 par 00/00/1949
Merged into American Motors Corp. 00/00/1954
Each share Capital Stock $12.50 par exchanged for (0.66666666) shares Capital Stock $5 par
American Motors Corp. merged into Chrysler Corp. 08/05/1987 which merged into DaimlerChrysler AG 11/12/1998 which name changed to Daimler AG 10/19/2007

HUDSON NATIONAL, INC. (DE)
Acquired by United Whelan Corp. 6/30/66
Each share Common $1 par exchanged for (0.475) share Common $1.20 par
United Whelan Corp. name changed to Perfect Film & Chemical Corp. 5/31/67 which name changed to Cadence Industries Corp. 10/22/70
(See Cadence Industries Corp.)

HUDSON NAVIGATION CO.
Acquired by Hudson River Navigation Corp. in 1926
Details not available

HUDSON OIL CO. (DE)
Charter cancelled and declared inoperative and void for non-payment of taxes 3/17/26

HUDSON PAC PPTYS INC (MD)
8.375% Preferred Ser. B 1¢ par called for redemption at $25 plus $0.401302 accrued dividends on 12/10/2015
(Additional Information in Active)

HUDSON-PATRICIA GOLD MINES LTD.
Bankrupt 00/00/1937
Details not available 00/00/1934)

HUDSON PETE LTD (BC)
Name changed to Hudson Resources Ltd. 03/09/1984
Hudson Resources Ltd. recapitalized as United Hudson Resources Inc. 03/22/1989 which recapitalized as Northrich Pacific Ventures Inc. 02/17/1993
(See Northrich Pacific Ventures Inc.)

HUDSON PHARMACEUTICAL CORP (DE)
Merged into Hudpharmco Inc. 12/31/1976
Each share Class A Common 10¢ par exchanged for $1.50 cash

HUDSON PULP & PAPER CORP (ME)
Class A Common $1 par and Class B Common $1 par reclassified as Common $1 par 04/19/1972
Common $1 par split (2) for (1) by issuance of (1) additional share 07/19/1974
5.12% Preferred Ser. B $25 par called for redemption 04/20/1976
5% Preferred Ser. A $25 par called for redemption 07/15/1977
Merged into Georgia-Pacific Corp. 01/19/1979
Each share Common $1 par exchanged for (1.76207) share Conv. Preferred Ser. A no par 01/19/1979
$1.41 2nd Preferred $24.50 par called for redemption 02/18/1979
(See Georgia-Pacific Corp.)

HUDSON RADIO & TELEVISION CORP. (NY)
Merged into Terminal-Hudson Electronics, Inc. 09/30/1960
Each share Capital Stock 25¢ par exchanged for (1) share Capital Stock 25¢ par
Terminal-Hudson Electronics, Inc. name changed to Terminal-Hudson Corp. (NY) 05/05/1971 which reincorporated in Nevada as Titmus Optical Corp. 07/10/1972 which

name changed to King Optical Corp. 05/17/1974
(See King Optical Corp.)

HUDSON RAND GOLD MINES LTD. (ON)
Name changed to Hudson Rand Mines Ltd. 06/13/1956
Hudson Rand Mines Ltd. recapitalized as Canorama Explorations Ltd. 12/02/1957 which recapitalized as Consolidated Canorama Explorations Ltd. 10/08/1963
(See Canorama Explorations Ltd.)

HUDSON RAND MINES LTD. (ON)
Recapitalized as Canorama Explorations Ltd. 12/02/1957
Each share Capital Stock $1 par exchanged for (0.2) share Capital Stock $1 par
Canorama Explorations Ltd. recapitalized as Consolidated Canorama Explorations Ltd. 10/08/1963
(See Consolidated Canorama Explorations Ltd.)

HUDSON RES LTD (BC)
Recapitalized as United Hudson Resources Inc. 03/22/1989
Each share Common no par exchanged for (0.125) share Common no par
United Hudson Resources Inc. recapitalized as Northrich Pacific Ventures Inc. 02/17/1993
(See Northrich Pacific Ventures Inc.)

HUDSON RIV BANCORP INC (DE)
Merged into First Niagara Financial Group, Inc. (New) 01/14/2005
Each share Common 1¢ par exchanged for (0.3544) share Common 1¢ par and $14.33 cash
First Niagara Financial Group, Inc. (New) merged into KeyCorp (New) 08/01/2016

HUDSON RIVER DAY LINE
Name changed to Indian Point Corp. 00/00/1949
(See Indian Point Corp.)

HUDSON RIVER NAVIGATION CORP.
Bankrupt 00/00/1936
Details not available

HUDSON TRUST CO. (UNION CITY, NJ)
Common $6 par changed to $8 par 04/01/1952
Stock Dividends - 33.33333333% 06/16/1944; 25% 10/15/1945; 20% 05/31/1946; 16.66666666% 12/19/1947; 14.28571428% 05/02/1949; 12.5% 02/20/1952; 10% 02/10/1961; 10% 01/31/1969; 50% 08/02/1971
Under plan of merger name changed to Hudson United Bank (Union City, NJ) 06/30/1972
Hudson United Bank (Union City, NJ) reorganized as HUBCO, Inc. 10/01/1982 which name changed to Hudson United Bancorp 04/21/1999 which merged into TD Banknorth Inc. 01/31/2006
(See TD Banknorth Inc.)

HUDSON-UNGAVA NICKEL MINES LTD. (ON)
Liquidation completed 11/18/1960
Each share Capital Stock exchanged for $0.049 cash

HUDSON UTD BANCORP (NJ)
Stock Dividends - 3% payable 12/01/1999 to holders of record 11/26/1999; 10% payable 12/01/2000 to holders of record 11/20/2000
Merged into TD Banknorth Inc. 01/31/2006
Each share Common no par exchanged for (1.2426) shares Common 1¢ par and $5.81 cash
(See TD Banknorth Inc.)

HUDSON UTD BK (UNION CITY, NJ)
Stock Dividend - 15% 12/1/79
Reorganized as HUBCO, Inc. 10/1/82
Each share Common $8 par exchanged for (1) share Common no par
HUBCO, Inc. name changed to Hudson United Bancorp 4/21/99 which merged into TD Banknorth Inc. 1/31/2006
(See TD Banknorth Inc.)

HUDSON VALLEY COKE & PRODUCTS CORP.
Sold to Niagara Hudson Power Corp. in 1929
Details not available

HUDSON VY HLDG CORP (NY)
Stock Dividends - 10% payable 12/20/1996 to holders of record 12/06/1996; 10% payable 12/15/2000 to holders of record 12/04/2000 Ex date - 12/04/2000; 10% payable 12/14/2001 to holders of record 12/03/2001 Ex date - 11/29/2001; 10% payable 12/13/2002 to holders of record 12/02/2002; 10% payable 12/17/2003 to holders of record 12/10/2003 Ex date - 12/08/2003; 10% payable 12/17/2004 to holders of record 12/10/2004; 10% payable 12/19/2005 to holders of record 12/09/2005 Ex date - 12/07/2005; 10% payable 12/15/2006 to holders of record 12/08/2006 Ex date - 12/06/2006; 10% payable 12/14/2007 to holders of record 12/07/2007 Ex date - 12/05/2007; 10% payable 12/19/2008 to holders of record 12/12/2008 Ex date - 12/10/2008; 10% payable 12/17/2009 to holders of record 12/07/2009 Ex date - 12/03/2009; 10% payable 12/10/2010 to holders of record 11/29/2010 Ex date - 11/24/2010; 10% payable 12/05/2011 to holders of record 11/23/2011 Ex date - 11/21/2011
Merged into Sterling Bancorp 06/30/2015
Each share Common 20¢ par exchanged for (1.92) shares Common 1¢ par

HUDSON VY INDS INC (DE)
Name changed to Centrack International Inc. 04/02/1999
(See Centrack International Inc.)

HUDSON VALLEY NATIONAL BANK (YONKERS, NY)
Reorganized as Hudson Valley Holding Corp. 12/31/1983
Each share Capital Stock $4 par exchanged for (0.5) share Common $4 par or $13 cash
Note: Option for holdings of (100) or more shares to receive stock expired 02/29/1984
Hudson Valley Holding Corp. merged into Sterling Bancorp 06/30/2015

HUDSON VY PATROL INC (NY)
Charter cancelled and proclaimed dissolved for failure to pay taxes 12/28/94

HUDSON VITAMIN PRODUCTS, INC. (DE)
Common $1 par split (5) for (4) by issuance of (0.25) additional share 5/31/61
Name changed to Hudson National, Inc. 10/26/64
Hudson National, Inc. acquired by United Whelan Corp. 6/30/66 which name changed to Perfect Film & Chemical Corp. 5/31/67 which name changed to Cadence Industries Corp. 10/22/70
(See Cadence Industries Corp.)

HUDSON WHOLESALE GROCERIES, INC. (DE)
Name changed to Filigree Foods, Inc. 10/27/1964

(See Filigree Foods, Inc.)

HUDSON-YUKON MINING CO. LTD. (CANADA)
Merged into All-North Resources Ltd. 08/08/1988
Each share Capital Stock no par exchanged for (2.55) shares Common no par
All-North Resources Ltd. recapitalized as International All-North Resources Ltd. 07/10/1996 which recapitalized as Kaieteur Resource Corp. 04/14/1999 which name changed to Samba Gold Inc. 03/22/2005 which recapitalized as Caerus Resource Corp. 02/26/2009 which name changed to Angel Gold Corp. 10/04/2012

HUDSONS BAY CO OLD (CANADA)
Reincorporated 05/29/1970
Stock Dividends - 100% 01/09/1953; 100% 08/18/1961
Place of incorporation changed from (England) to (Canada) and each share Ordinary 1¢ par exchanged for (1) share Ordinary no par 05/29/1970
$2.25 Exchangeable Preferred Ser. F no par called for redemption 05/30/1986
$1.512 Preferred Ser. D no par called for redemption 06/30/1988
$1.875 Conv. Preferred Ser. H no par called for redemption 10/31/1989
$1.80 Preferred Ser. A no par called for redemption 01/17/1992
Variable Rate Preferred Ser. C no par called for redemption 03/15/1992
Merged into Maple Leaf Heritage Investments Acquisition Corp. 03/16/2006
Each share Ordinary no par exchanged for $15.25 cash
Note: Although the complete name of this company is Governor & Company of Adventurers of England Trading Into Hudson's Bay, it is more widely known and traded as Hudson's Bay Co.

HUDSONS BAY OIL & GAS LTD (CANADA)
Capital Stock $2.50 par reclassified as Common $2.50 par 09/12/1967
5% Preference Ser. A $50 par called for redemption 10/15/1979
Common $2.50 par split (4) for (1) by issuance of (3) additional shares 05/26/1980
Merged into Dome Petroleum Ltd. 03/10/1982
Each share Common $2.50 par exchanged for (1) share Dome Resources Ltd. $5.75 Preferred Class A Retractable no par and (1.33333333) Dome Petroleum Ltd. Common Stock Purchase Warrant expiring 12/31/1984
(See Dome Resources Ltd.)

HUDSONS GRILL AMER INC (CA)
Stock Dividend - 10% 07/15/1991
Each share Common no par received distribution of (1) share Hudson's Grill International, Inc. Class A Common no par payable 08/15/2000 to holders of record 05/15/2000
Company ceased operations 00/00/2000
Details not available

HUDSONS GRILL INTL INC (TX)
Reorganized under the laws of Nevada as Lansdowne Security, Inc. 08/02/2010
Each share Class A Common no par exchanged for (0.02) share Common $0.001 par
(See Lansdowne Security, Inc.)

HUESTIS MINING CORP. LTD. (BC)
Completely liquidated 09/15/1965
Each share Common 50¢ par exchanged for first and final distribution of (0.5) share Bethex Explorations Ltd. Capital Stock 50¢ par
(See Bethex Explorations Ltd.)

HUFFMAN KOOS INC (DE)
Merged into Breuner's Home Furnishings Corp. 10/27/95
Each share Common 1¢ par exchanged for $9.375 cash

HUFFMAN MFG CO (OH)
Common $1 par split (3) for (2) by issuance of (0.5) additional share 8/22/68
Name changed to Huffy Corp. 10/19/77
(See Huffy Corp.)

HUFFY CORP (OH)
Common $1 par split (4) for (3) by issuance of (1/3) additional share 10/11/78
Common $1 par split (5) for (4) by issuance of (0.25) additional share 12/10/79
Common $1 par split (4) for (3) by issuance of (1/3) additional share 10/15/80
Common $1 par split (3) for (2) by issuance of (0.5) additional share 7/1/88
Plan of reorganization under Chapter 11 Federal Bankruptcy Code effective 10/14/2005
No stockholders' equity

HUGH KEITH MOBILE ENTERPRISES, LTD. (DE)
See - Keith (Hugh) Mobile Enterprises, Ltd.

HUGH MALARTIC MINES LTD.
Recapitalized as New Hugh Malartic Mines Ltd. 00/00/1950
Each share Capital Stock $1 par exchanged for (0.25) share Capital Stock $1 par
New Hugh Malartic Mines Ltd. recapitalized as Alba Explorations Ltd. 08/12/1955 which recapitalized as Accra Explorations Ltd. 12/21/1962 which merged into Xtra Developments Inc. 05/25/1972 which merged into in Sumtra Diversified Inc. 08/30/1978

HUGH PAM PORCUPINE MINES LTD (ON)
Capital Stock $1 par changed to no par 06/12/1975
Merged into Broulan Resources Inc. 04/26/1983
Each share Capital Stock no par exchanged for (1/3) share Common no par
Broulan Resources Inc. merged into Cabre Exploration Ltd. 11/24/1989 which was acquired by EnerMark Income Fund 01/10/2001 which merged into Enerplus Resources Fund 06/22/2001 which reorganized as Enerplus Corp. 01/03/2011

HUGH RUSSEL & SONS LTD. (CANADA)
See - Russel (Hugh) & Sons Ltd.

HUGH RUSSEL INC. (CANADA)
See - Russel (Hugh) Inc.

HUGH RUSSEL LTD. (CANADA)
See - Russel (Hugh) Ltd.

HUGH W. LONG & CO., INC. (DE)
See - Long (Hugh W.) & Co., Inc.

HUGHES & HATCHER INC (NY)
Capital Stock $1 par split (3) for (2) by issuance of (0.5) additional share 2/26/65
Capital Stock $1 par split (3) for (2) by issuance of (0.5) additional share 1/12/66
Capital Stock $1 par split (5) for (4) by issuance of (0.25) additional share 12/20/68
Capital Stock $1 par reclassified as Common $1 par 5/14/70
Stock Dividend - 10% 1/17/64

Name changed to Widener Place Fund, Inc. 9/28/77
Widener Place Fund, Inc. liquidated for Dreyfus Tax Exempt Bond Fund, Inc. 7/16/81 which name changed to Dreyfus Municipal Bond Fund Inc. 2/9/93

HUGHES CAP CORP (FL)
Proclaimed dissolved for failure to file reports and pay fees 11/04/1988

HUGHES CAP CORP (UT)
Each share Common 1¢ par exchanged for (10) shares Common $0.001 par 12/01/1979
Name changed to Affiliated Capital Corp. 07/27/1984
(See Affiliated Capital Corp.)

HUGHES COMMUNICATIONS INC (DE)
Acquired by EchoStar Corp. 06/08/2011
Each share Common $0.001 par exchanged for $60.70 cash

HUGHES (K.A.) CO. (ME)
Charter suspended for non-payment of franchise taxes 12/01/1964

HUGHES ELECTRONICS CORP (DE)
Name changed to DIRECTV Group, Inc. 03/16/2004
DIRECTV Group, Inc. merged into DIRECTV 11/20/2009 which merged into AT&T Inc. 07/24/2015

HUGHES HOMES INC (WA)
Stock Dividend - 10% 12/30/88
Charter cancelled and proclaimed dissolved for failure to pay fees 8/23/93

HUGHES INDUSTRIES, INC. (NV)
Charter revoked for failure to file reports and pay fees 3/4/74

HUGHES LANG CORP (BC)
Merged into CanGold Resources Inc. (BC) 01/31/1994
Each share Class B Subordinate no par exchanged for (1) share Common no par
CanGold Resources Inc. (BC) reorganized in Ontario as Amalgamated CanGold Inc. 07/31/1995 which merged into Central Asia Goldfields Corp. 01/08/1996
(See Central Asia Goldfields Corp.)

HUGHES OWENS LTD (CANADA)
Each share Class A Common no par exchanged for (1) share Class B Common no par 07/15/1968
Acquired by Ozalid Group Holdings Ltd. 03/26/1973
Each share Class B Common no par exchanged for $20 cash
$6.40 Preferred $25 par called for redemption 12/31/1975
Public interest eliminated

HUGHES PHARMACEUTICAL CORP (DE)
Recapitalized as First National Holding Corp. (DE) 11/06/1991
Each share Common $0.001 par exchanged for (0.1) share Common $0.001 par
First National Holding Corp. (DE) reincorporated in Nevada 01/28/1994 which name changed to Innovative Weaponry Inc. 09/21/1994 which name changed to 21st Century Technologies Inc. 11/14/1995
(See 21st Century Technologies Inc.)

HUGHES RES INC (CO)
Each (1.88) shares old Common $0.0001 par exchanged for (1) share new Common $0.0001 par 12/03/1991
Each share new Common $0.0001 par exchanged for (0.1) share Common $0.001 par 07/31/1995
Reincorporated under the laws of

Nevada as Phoenix Resources Technologies, Inc. 02/29/1996
(See Phoenix Resources Technologies, Inc.)

HUGHES SUPPLY INC (FL)
Common $2 par changed to $1 par and (1) additional share issued 2/29/72
Common $1 par split (3) for (2) by issuance of (0.5) additional share 6/15/79
Common $1 par split (3) for (2) by issuance of (0.5) additional share 6/15/88
Common $1 par split (3) for (2) by issuance of (0.5) additional share payable 7/17/97 to holders of record 7/10/97 Ex date - 7/18/97
Common $1 par split (2) for (1) by issuance of (1) additional share payable 9/22/2004 to holders of record 9/15/2004 Ex date - 9/23/2004
Stock Dividend - 50% 2/25/83
Merged into Home Depot, Inc. 3/30/2006
Each share Common $1 par exchanged for $46.50 cash

HUGHES TELEMATICS INC (DE)
Units separated 01/25/2012
Acquired by Verizon Communications Inc. 07/26/2012
Each share Common $0.0001 par exchanged for $12 cash

HUGHES TEX PETE CORP (NY)
Dissolved by proclamation 09/28/1997

HUGHES TOOL CO (DE)
Common $1 par split (2) for (1) by issuance of (1) additional share 08/29/1975
Common $1 par split (3) for (2) by issuance of (0.5) additional share 08/31/1979
Common $1 par split (2) for (1) by issuance of (1) additional share 06/01/1981
Merged into Baker Hughes Inc. 04/03/1987
Each share Common $1 par exchanged for (0.8) share Common $1 par
Baker Hughes Inc. merged into Baker Hughes, a GE company 07/05/2017

HUGO INTL TELECOM INC (DE)
Each share old Common $0.0001 par exchanged for (0.001) share new Common $0.0001 par 05/19/2006
Name changed to GS AgriFuels Corp. 07/28/2006
(See GS AgriFuels Corp.)

HUGO STINNES CORP. (MD)
Capital Stock no par changed to $5 par 00/00/1935
Reorganized 08/25/1961
Each share Capital Stock $5 par exchanged for DM100 par amount of Hugo Stinnes A.G. Bearer Capital Stock
Each share Capital Stock $5 par received an additional (0.006436) share Hugo Stinnes A.G. Bearer Capital Stock as a pro rata distribution of Hugo Stinnes A.G. shares set aside for unexchanged Hugo Stinnes Corp. shares 05/31/1973
Note: Unexchanged shares are without value

HUGOTON ENERGY CORP (KS)
Merged into Chesapeake Energy Corp. 03/10/1998
Each share Common no par exchanged for (1.3) shares Common 10¢ par

HUGOTON PRODTN CO (DE)
Common $1 par split (2) for (1) by issuance of (1) additional share 4/19/62
Merged into Mesa Petroleum Co. 4/30/69
Each share Common $1 par exchanged for (1) share $2.20 Conv. Sr. Preferred $1 par
(See Mesa Petroleum Co.)

HUHILL YELLOWKNIFE MINES, LTD. (ON)
Dissolved 01/01/1959
Details not available

HUHTAMAKI OY (FINLAND)
ADR agreement terminated 10/03/2002
Each 144A Sponsored ADR for Ser. I exchanged for $43.7126 cash

HUI YING TECHNOLOGY & MEDIA GROUP HLDG CO (NV)
Class A Common $0.001 par split (30) for (1) by issuance of (29) additional shares payable 12/26/2013 to holders of record 12/17/2013 Ex date - 12/27/2013
Name changed to Andalusian Resorts & Spas, Inc. 03/06/2014

HUIHENG MEDICAL INC (NV)
Shares reacquired 04/27/2015
Each share Common $0.001 par exchanged for $0.95 cash

HUILE OIL & GAS INC (NV)
Common $0.001 par split (9) for (1) by issuance of (8) additional shares payable 11/26/2002 to holders of record 11/24/2002 Ex date - 11/27/2002
Name changed to C&D Production, Inc. 07/23/2003
C&D Production, Inc. name changed to Planet Nutrition Holdings, Inc. 07/30/2007 which recapitalized as GT Legend Automotive Holdings, Inc. 11/26/2008

HULDRA SILVER INC (BC)
Each share old Common no par exchanged for (0.5) share new Common no par 07/17/2014
Recapitalized as Nicola Mining Inc. 06/01/2015
Each share Common no par exchanged for (0.2) share Common no par

HULL CO OPERATIVE BK (HULL, MA)
Merged into Abington Savings Bank (Abington, MA) (Old) 6/3/94
Each share Common $1 par exchanged for $22 cash

HULL ENERGY INC (NV)
Each share old Common $0.001 par exchanged for (0.1) share new Common $0.001 par 01/14/2013
Name changed to Gemini Group Global Corp. 11/04/2013

HULL ENTERPRISES INC (UT)
Involuntarily dissolved 02/01/1995

HULL EXPLS LTD (ON)
Merged into Belle Aire Resource Explorations Ltd. 08/29/1978
Each share Common no par exchanged for (0.11) share Common no par
Belle Aire Resource Explorations Ltd. name changed to Sprint Resources Ltd. 09/23/1982 which name changed to Meacon Bay Resources Inc. 03/09/1987 which recapitalized as Advantex Marketing International Inc. 09/16/1991

HULL IRON MINES LTD. (QC)
Acquired by Corgemines Ltd. 01/19/1965
Each share Capital Stock $1 par exchanged for (0.52) share Common $1 par
(See Corgemines Ltd.)

HUMAGEN INC (DE)
Name changed to First Medical International, Inc. 08/29/1990
(See First Medical International, Inc.)

HUMAN & ENVIRONMENTAL RES CORP (CO)
Name changed to Videocomm, Inc. 9/7/88
Videocomm, Inc. name changed to Vanguard Environmental Solutions, Inc. 9/28/93

HUMAN BIOSYSTEMS (CA)
Each share old Common no par exchanged for (0.0125) share new Common no par 03/04/2009
Name changed to San West, Inc. (CA) 09/28/2009
San West, Inc. (CA) reincorporated in Nevada 09/13/2011 which recapitalized as AppSwarm, Inc. 09/25/2015

HUMAN GENOME SCIENCES INC (DE)
Common 1¢ par split (2) for (1) by issuance of (1) additional share payable 01/28/2000 to holders of record 01/14/2000
Common 1¢ par split (2) for (1) by issuance of (1) additional share payable 10/05/2000 to holders of record 09/28/2000 Ex date - 10/06/2000
Acquired by GlaxoSmithKline PLC 08/03/2012
Each share Common 1¢ par exchanged for $14.25 cash

HUMAN RES FOR GROWTH INC (ON)
Name changed to IBI Corp. 12/12/1994

HUMAN SCIENCE SYS INC (NV)
Recapitalized as Nutralogix Laboratories, Inc. 11/14/2005
Each share Common $0.0001 par exchanged for (0.01) share Common $0.001 par
Nutralogix Laboratories, Inc. recapitalized as Matrix Denture Systems International, Inc. 10/09/2007

HUMAN TECHNOLOGIES CAP CORP (NY)
Dissolved by proclamation 9/29/93

HUMANA INC (DE)
$2.50 Preferred $1 par called for redemption 5/1/84
(Additional Information in Active)

HUMANA TRANS SVCS HLDG CORP (DE)
Name changed to Accountabilities, Inc. 12/06/2005
Accountabilities, Inc. name changed to Corporate Resource Services, Inc. 04/21/2010

HUMANICS INC (DE)
Name changed to IMC International, Inc. 6/3/71
(See IMC International, Inc.)

HUMANTICS B C LTD (BC)
Cease trade order effective 05/15/1991
Stockholders' equity unlikely

HUMAR CORP. LTD. (ON)
Completely liquidated 09/15/1970
Each share Capital Stock no par exchanged for first and final distribution of $0.057 cash

HUMASCAN INC (DE)
Recapitalized as Cell Tech International Inc. 08/18/1999
Each share Common 1¢ par exchanged for (0.09214812) share Common 1¢ par
(See Cell Tech International Inc.)

HUMASON MANUFACTURING CO.
Acquired by Stanley Works 00/00/1950
Each share Common exchanged for (1) share Common $25 par
Stanley Works name changed to Stanley Black & Decker, Inc. 03/12/2010

HUMBER AMUSEMENT PIER LTD (ON)
Completely liquidated 12/29/1966
Each share Capital Stock no par received first and final distribution of $1 cash

HUMBER CAP CORP (CANADA)
Name changed to Rocky Mountain Liquor Inc. 09/21/2009

HUMBER OILS LTD. (ON)
Completely liquidated 00/00/1958
Each share Capital Stock $1 par exchanged for first and final distribution of $1.82 cash

HUMBERSTONE SHOE CO., LTD. (ON)
Under plan of merger each share Common no par exchanged for $17.50 cash 05/00/1961

HUMBLE OIL & REFINING CO. (TX)
Each share Capital Stock $25 par exchanged for (3) shares Capital Stock no par 00/00/1933
Capital Stock no par exchanged (2) for (1) 00/00/1943
Capital Stock no par split (2) for (1) by issuance of (1) additional share 06/21/1957
Stock Dividend - 100% 12/21/1951
Merged into Standard Oil Co. (NJ) 12/02/1959
Each share Capital Stock no par exchanged for (1.25) shares Capital Stock $7 par
Standard Oil Co. (NJ) name changed to Exxon Corp. 11/01/1972 which name changed to Exxon Mobil Corp. 11/30/1999

HUMBLE PETE CORP (DE)
Name changed to Maxxim International Corp. 05/00/1993
Maxxim International Corp. name changed to Global Link Technologies, Inc. (DE) 05/00/1995 which reorganized in Wyoming as MutuaLoan Corp. 01/12/2009 which name changed to Nexus Enterprise Solutions, Inc. 02/27/2012

HUMBLEFORD EXPLORATION & INVESTMENTS LTD. (ON)
Charter cancelled for failure to pay taxes and file returns 02/20/1980

HUMBLEFORD EXPLORATION LTD. (ON)
Name changed to Humbleford Exploration & Investments Ltd. and Common $1 par changed to no par 11/28/1969
(See Humbleford Exploration & Investments Ltd.)

HUMBOLDT BANCORP (CA)
Common no par split (5) for (2) by issuance of (1.5) additional shares payable 06/30/1999 to holders of record 06/01/1999
Common no par split (6) for (5) by issuance of (0.2) additional share payable 08/19/2002 to holders of record 08/05/2002 Ex date - 08/01/2002
Stock Dividends - 10% payable 05/31/1996 to holders of record 04/30/1996; 10% payable 05/30/1997 to holders of record 04/30/1997; 10% payable 06/30/1998 to holders of record 05/29/1998; 10% payable 02/07/2000 to holders of record 01/28/2000; 10% payable 06/15/2001 to holders of record 06/01/2001 Ex date - 05/30/2001
Merged into Umpqua Holdings Corp. 07/10/2004
Each share Common no par exchanged for (1) share Common no par

HUMBOLDT BK (EUREKA, CA)
Under plan of reorganization each share Common no par automatically became (1) share Humboldt

Bancorp Common no par 01/02/1996
Humboldt Bancorp merged into Umpqua Holdings Corp. 07/10/2004

HUMBOLDT CAP CORP (AB)
Each share Common no par exchanged for (1) Subordinate Share no par and (1) Multiple Share no par 07/17/1997
Each share Multiple no par exchanged for (1) share Common no par 06/06/2003
Each share Subordinate no par exchanged for (1) share Common no par 06/06/2003
Merged into Lamond Investments Ltd. 06/28/2016
Each share Common no par exchanged for (1.4074) shares Tuscany Energy Ltd. (New) Common no par and $1.075 cash
(See Tuscany Energy Ltd. (New))
Note: Unexchanged certificates will be cancelled and become without value 06/27/2019

HUMBOLDT ENERGY CORP (AB)
Reincorporated 06/20/1984
Each share Common no par exchanged for (1) share Subordinate no par 07/16/1982
Place of incorporation changed from (BC) to (AB) 06/20/1984
Subordinate no par reclassified as Common no par 08/26/1988
Recapitalized as HEC Investments Ltd. 08/04/1989
Each share Common no par exchanged for (0.1) share Common no par
HEC Investments Ltd. name changed to Humboldt Capital Corp. 08/29/1994
(See Humboldt Capital Corp.)

HUMBOLDT FLOUR MLS INC (CANADA)
Merged into Saskatchewan Wheat Pool 05/29/1998
Each share Common no par exchanged for $1.20 cash

HUMBOLDT GRAIN & MLG INC (CANADA)
Name changed to Humboldt Flour Mills Inc. 03/26/1993
(See Humboldt Flour Mills Inc.)

HUMBOLDT MALT & BREWING CO.
Bankrupt in 1940

HUMBOLDT NATIONAL BANK (EUREKA, CA)
Merged into Security Pacific National Bank (Los Angeles, CA) 01/02/1979
Each share Capital Stock $10 par exchanged for $66 cash

HUMEDATECH INTL INC (CANADA)
Recapitalized as Feathertouch E-Comm Inc. 11/10/1999
Each share Common no par exchanged for (0.1) share Common no par
(See Feathertouch E-Comm Inc.)

HUMITECH INC (NV)
Recapitalized as Humitech International Group Inc. 11/11/2004
Each share Common $0.001 par exchanged for (0.1) share Common $0.001 par

HUMLIN RED LAKE MINES LTD (ON)
Merged into Pan African Resources Corp. 02/06/1996
Each share Common no par exchanged for (0.2) share Common no par
Pan African Resources Corp. merged into Golden Star Resources Ltd. 04/21/1998

HUMMEL-ROSS FIBRE CORP.
Acquired by Continental Can Co., Inc. on a (0.75) for (1) basis in 1947

HUMMINGBIRD LTD (CANADA)
Name changed 04/25/2000
Common no par split (2) for (1) by issuance of (1) additional share payable 04/24/2000 to holders of record 04/17/2000
Name changed from Hummingbird Communications Ltd. to Hummingbird Ltd. 04/25/2000
Merged into Open Text Corp. 10/02/2006
Each share Common no par exchanged for USD$27.85 cash

HUMMINGBIRD RES LTD (BC)
Name changed 03/01/1982
Name changed from Hummingbird Mines Ltd. to Hummingbird Resources Ltd. 03/01/1982
Struck off register and declared dissolved for failure to file returns 06/22/1990

HUMPHREY HOSPITALITY TR (VA)
Name changed to Supertel Hospitality, Inc. (VA) 05/27/2005
Supertel Hospitality, Inc. (VA) reincorporated in Maryland 11/20/2014 which name changed to Condor Hospitality Trust, Inc. 07/21/2015

HUMPHREY INC (CA)
Capital Stock $1 par split (4) for (1) by issuance of (3) additional shares 03/17/1980
Capital Stock $1 par changed to no par 11/25/1980
Capital Stock no par split (2) for (1) by issuance of (1) additional share 04/18/1983
Merged into REMEC, Inc. 01/18/1994
Each share Common 1¢ par exchanged for $6 cash

HUMPHREYS CORP.
Liquidation completed in 1932

HUMPHREYS OIL CO.
Acquired by Pure Oil Co. in 1927
Details not available

HUMPHRYES MANUFACTURING CO. (OH)
Each share 8% Preferred $25 par exchanged for (0.25) share 6% Preferred $100 par and (0.083333) share new Common no par in 1936
Each share old Common no par exchanged for (1) share new Common no par in 1936
New Common no par changed to $10 par in 1940
Stock Dividend - 20% 12/31/48
Merged into Borg-Warner Corp. (Ill.) on a (0.8) for (1) basis 8/21/56
Borg-Warner Corp. (Ill.) reincorporated under the laws of Delaware 10/31/67
(See Borg-Warner Corp. (Del.))

HUMPTY DUMPTY SNACK FOODS INC (ON)
Merged into HD Snax Ltd. 05/18/2006
Each share Common no par exchanged for $2.85 cash

HUMPTYS RESTAURANTS INTL INC (AB)
Acquired by 823533 Alberta Ltd. 10/01/2009
Each share Common no par exchanged for $0.26 cash

HUMWARE MEDIA CORP (NV)
Recapitalized as EFT Biotech Holdings, Inc. 11/20/2007
Each share Common $0.001 par exchanged for (0.00005) share Common $0.001 par
EFT Biotech Holdings, Inc. name changed to EFT Holdings, Inc. 05/27/2011

HUNAPU INC (NV)
Name changed to InforMedix Holdings, Inc. 05/08/2003
(See InforMedix Holdings, Inc.)

HUNCH MINES LTD (ON)
Charter cancelled and declared dissolved for failure to file returns and pay fees 11/09/1976

HUNDRED MILE PLUS LTD (FL)
Each share old Common no par exchanged for (0.01) share new Common no par 12/30/2002
Recapitalized as Ultra Pure Water Technologies, Inc. 05/24/2004
Each share new Common no par exchanged for (0.03272251) share Common no par

HUNGARIAN BROADCASTING CORP (DE)
Each share Common $0.001 par received distribution of (1) share Central European Satellite Corp. Common payable 03/31/1998 to holders of record 12/31/1997
Each share Accredited Investor Conv. Preferred Ser. A $0.001 par received distribution of (1) share Common $0.001 par payable 09/15/1998 to holders of record 09/12/1998
Charter cancelled and declared inoperative and void for non-payment of taxes 03/01/2002

HUNGARIAN GENERAL SAVINGS BANK LTD. (HUNGARY)
Merged into Hungarian General Creditbank 01/07/1939
Each American Share 50 Pengoe par exchanged for (0.2) share Bearer Stock

HUNGARIAN TEL & CABLE CORP (DE)
Reorganized under the laws of Denmark as Invitel Holdings A/S 02/27/2009
Each share Common $0.001 par exchanged for (1) Sponsored ADR for Ordinary
(See Invitel Holdings A/S)

HUNGARIAN TELECONSTRUCT CORP (DE)
Name changed to EuroWeb International Corp. 07/17/1997
EuroWeb International Corp. name changed to EMVELCO Corp. 01/08/2007 which name changed to Vortex Resources Corp. 09/02/2008 which name changed to Yasheng Eco-Trade Corp. 07/15/2009 which recapitalized as Eco-Trade Corp. 12/09/2010

HUNGERFORD PLASTICS CORP. (NJ)
Merged into Air Reduction Co., Inc. 5/31/62
Each share Capital Stock 25¢ par exchanged for (0.058256) share Common no par
Air Reduction Co., Inc. name changed to Airco, Inc. (N.Y.) 10/1/71 which reincorporated in Delaware 8/3/77
(See Airco, Inc. (Del.))

HUNGRY MINDS INC (DE)
Merged into Wiley (John) & Sons, Inc. 09/26/2001
Each share Class A Common $0.001 par exchanged for $6.09 cash

HUNGRY TIGER INC (CA)
Capital Stock 5¢ par split (3) for (2) by issuance of (1/3) additional share 05/09/1980
Capital Stock 5¢ par split (4) for (3) by issuance of (1/3) additional share 08/21/1981
Stock Dividend - 50% 11/12/1982
Merged into Grace (W.R.) & Co. (CT) 11/27/1985
Each share Capital Stock 5¢ par exchanged for (0.17012) share Common $1 par
Grace (W.R.) & Co. (CT) reincorporated in New York 05/19/1988
(See Grace (W.R.) & Co.)

HUNNO TECHNOLOGIES INC (DE)
Name changed to Abazias, Inc. 10/08/2003
Abazias, Inc. acquired by OmniReliant Holdings, Inc. 08/27/2009

HUNSAKER (S.V.) & SONS (CA)
Name changed to SVH Liquidating Corp. 7/22/64
SVH Liquidating Corp. liquidated for Occidental Petroleum Corp. (Calif.) 8/14/64 which reincorporated in Delaware 5/21/86

HUNT BLDG CORP (DE)
Reincorporated 4/24/72
State of incorporation changed from (TX) to (DE) 4/24/72
Each share Common 15¢ par exchanged for (0.002) share Class A Common $75 par 2/16/78
Note: In effect holders received $4 cash per share and public interest was eliminated

HUNT BROTHERS PACKING CO.
Recapitalized as Hunt Foods, Inc. 00/00/1945
Each share Common $10 par exchanged for (2/3) share Common $6.66-2/3 par
Hunt Foods, Inc. merged into Hunt Foods & Industries, Inc. 12/05/1958 which merged into Simon (Norton), Inc. 07/17/1968 which merged into Esmark, Inc. (Inc. 03/14/1969) 09/09/1983
(See Esmark, Inc. (Inc. 03/14/1969))

HUNT BUILDING MARTS, INC. (TX)
Name changed to Hunt Building Corp. (TX) 1/17/72
Hunt Building Corp. (TX) reincorporated in Delaware 4/24/72
(See Hunt Building Corp. (DE))

HUNT CORP (PA)
Merged into FAC Holding Corp. 12/19/2002
Each share Common 10¢ par exchanged for $12.50 cash

HUNT FOODS, INC. (DE)
Merged into Hunt Foods & Industries, Inc. 12/05/1958
Each share 5% Preference Ser. A $10 par or 5% Preferred $10 par exchanged for (0.1) share 5% Preferred Ser. A $100 par
Each share Common $6.66-2/3 par exchanged for (2.2) shares Common $5 par
Hunt Foods & Industries, Inc. merged into Simon (Norton), Inc. 07/17/1968 which merged into Esmark, Inc. (Inc. 03/14/1969) 09/09/1983
(See Esmark, Inc. (Inc. 03/14/1969))

HUNT FOODS & INDS INC (DE)
Merged into Simon (Norton), Inc. 07/17/1968
Each share 5% Preferred Ser. A $100 par or 5% Preferred Ser. B $100 par exchanged for $100 principal amount of 6% Subord. Debentures due 07/01/1998
Each share Common $5 par exchanged for (0.2976) share $1.60 Conv. Preferred Ser. A $5 par and (1.1905) shares Common $1 par
Simon (Norton), Inc. merged into Esmark, Inc. (Inc. 03/14/1969) 09/09/1983
(See Esmark, Inc. (Inc. 03/14/1969))

HUNT FOR TRAVEL INC (NV)
Name changed to Praco Corp. 03/09/2012
Praco Corp. name changed to Arista Financial Corp. 02/09/2018

HUNT GLOBAL RES INC (CO)
SEC revoked common stock registration 09/30/2014

HUNT GOLD CORP (FL)
Administratively dissolved 09/24/2010

HUNT INTL RES CORP (DE)
Under plan of merger each share Common $1 par exchanged for $16 cash 10/2/79
$1.88 Preferred no par called for redemption 11/20/79
$3 Conv. Preferred no par called for redemption 11/20/79
Public interest eliminated

HUNT MFG CO (PA)
Common 10¢ par split (5) for (4) by issuance of (0.25) additional share 2/27/77
Common 10¢ par split (5) for (4) by issuance of (0.25) additional share 2/28/79
Common 10¢ par split (2) for (1) by issuance of (1) additional share 11/25/80
Common 10¢ par split (3) for (2) by issuance of (0.5) additional share 3/1/82
Common 10¢ par split (3) for (2) by issuance of (0.5) additional share 1/9/86
Common 10¢ par split (3) for (2) by issuance of (0.5) additional share 10/23/87
Common 10¢ par split (3) for (2) by issuance of (0.5) additional share 5/8/89
Name changed to Hunt Corp. 10/10/97
(See Hunt Corp.)

HUNT MNG CORP (AB)
Reincorporated under the laws of British Columbia 11/06/2013

HUNT PHILIP A CHEM CORP (DE)
Class A Common $1 par split (3) for (2) by issuance of (0.5) additional share 07/07/1967
Class A Common $1 par split (3) for (2) by issuance of (0.5) additional share 01/23/1969
Class A Common no par reclassified as Common $1 par and (1) additional share issued 05/15/1970
Stock Dividend - 25% 04/15/1965
Merged into Olin Corp. 07/05/1984
Each share Common $1 par exchanged for $20 cash

HUNT-PIERCE CORP. (CT)
Voluntarily dissolved 11/5/82
Details not available

HUNTCO INC (MO)
Plan of reorganization under Chapter 11 Bankruptcy proceedings confirmed 03/16/2004
No stockholders' equity

HUNTER AIRCRAFT CORP (NV)
Each share old Common 2¢ par exchanged for (0.03333333) share new Common 2¢ par 10/15/1996
Recapitalized as Prepaid Depot Inc. 08/18/2001
Each share Common 2¢ par exchanged for (0.05) share Common 2¢ par
Prepaid Depot Inc. recapitalized as Reed Holdings Corp. 07/30/2002 which name changed to Ostara Corp., Inc. 03/12/2004 which name changed to Rheologics Technologies, Inc. 10/18/2005 which name changed to KKS Venture Management, Inc. 07/24/2007 which recapitalized as Codima, Inc. 06/09/2008
(See Codima, Inc.)

HUNTER ARMS CO., INC.
Acquired by Marlin Firearms Co. 00/00/1945
Each share Common exchanged for $80 cash

HUNTER BASIN MINES LTD (BC)
Struck off register and declared dissolved for failure to file returns 05/28/1979

HUNTER-BRISTOL CORP. (DE)
Name changed to Emilie Corp. 3/10/58
(See Emilie Corp.)

HUNTER DOUGLAS CDA LTD (MB)
100% acquired by Hunter Douglas N.V. through purchase offer which expired 07/18/1980
Public interest eliminated

HUNTER DOUGLAS LTD (QC)
Completely liquidated 11/3/71
Each share Common 35¢ par received (1) share Hunter Douglas N.V. Common 1 Fl. par
Certificates were not required to be surrendered and are now valueless

HUNTER DOUGLAS N V (NETHERLANDS ANTILLES)
ADR agreement terminated 12/31/2002
Each Sponsored ADR for Common 1 Fl par exchanged for $12.1282 cash

HUNTER ENERGY INC (NV)
Each (7.3) shares old Common $0.001 par exchanged for (1) share new Common $0.001 par 8/6/92
Charter revoked for failure to file reports and pay fees 1/1/94

HUNTER ENGINEERING CO. (CA)
Name changed to Heco Liquidating Corp. 5/15/63
6% Conv. Preferred $25 par called for redemption 6/21/63
(See Heco Liquidating Corp.)

HUNTER ENVIRONMENTAL SVCS INC (DE)
Charter cancelled and declared inoperative and void for non-payment of taxes 03/01/2001

HUNTER FINL GROUP LTD (AB)
Cease trade order effective 06/10/1999
Stockholders' equity unlikely

HUNTER MACHINERY CO.
Liquidated in 1934

HUNTER MANUFACTURING & COMMISSION CO.
Liquidation completed in 1941

HUNTER MANUFACTURING CORP. (DE)
Name changed to Hunter-Bristol Corp. 10/26/56
Hunter-Bristol Corp. name changed to Emilie Corp. 3/10/58
(See Emilie Corp.)

HUNTER MFG CORP (NY)
Merged into Globalcraft Inc. 12/16/99
Each share Common 1¢ par exchanged for $24 cash

HUNTER-MELNOR INC (DE)
Merged into HM Merger Corp. 9/30/88
Each share Common 1¢ par exchanged for $15.50 cash

HUNTER PACKING CO. (IL)
Reorganized 00/00/1939
Each share 8% 1st Preferred $100 par exchanged for (1) share 5% 1st Prior Preferred $100 par, (2) shares Common $10 par and $6 in cash
Each share 8% 2nd Preferred $100 par exchanged for (1) share 5% 2nd Prior Preferred $100 par, (2) shares Common $10 par and $6 in cash
Name changed to Paco, Inc. (IL) 11/28/1959
(See Paco, Inc.)

HUNTER PETE CORP (CO)
Charter suspended for failure to file annual reports 09/30/1984

HUNTER PUBLISHING INC. (NC)
Merged into Jostens, Inc. 10/26/88
Each share Capital Stock $1 par exchanged for $33.55 cash

HUNTER RES INC (PA)
Plan of reorganization and liquidation effective 11/01/1996
Each (3.916) shares Common 10¢ par exchanged for (1) share Magnum Petroleum, Inc. Common $0.002 par
Magnum Petroleum, Inc. name changed to Magnum Hunter Resources, Inc. 03/18/1997 which merged into Cimarex Energy Co. 06/07/2005

HUNTER STEEL CO.
Dissolved in 1941

HUNTERDON CNTY NATL BK (FLEMINGTON, NJ)
Capital Stock $20 par changed to $5 par and (3) additional shares issued plus a 4% stock dividend paid 06/10/1958
Stock Dividend - 400% 00/00/1947
Merged into First National State Bancorporation 12/31/1982
Each share Capital Stock $5 par exchanged for (1.273216) shares Common $6.75 par
First National State Bancorporation name changed to First Fidelity Bancorporation (Old) 05/01/1985 which merged into First Fidelity Bancorporation (New) 02/29/1988 which merged into First Union Corp. 01/01/1996 which name changed to Wachovia Corp. (Ctfs. dated after 09/01/2001) 09/01/2001 which merged into Wells Fargo & Co. (New) 12/31/2008

HUNTINGDON & BROAD TOP MOUNTAIN RAILROAD & COAL CO. (PA)
Assets liquidated for benefit of creditors 2/7/57
No stockholders' equity

HUNTINGDON CAP CORP (BC)
Acquired by Slate Properties Inc. 11/07/2014
Each share Common no par exchanged for $13.25 cash
Note: Unexchanged certificates will be cancelled and become without value 11/07/2020

HUNTINGDON CAP INC (CANADA)
Recapitalized as MetroBridge Networks International Inc. 07/30/2007
Each share Common no par exchanged for (0.784) share Common no par
MetroBridge Networks International Inc. name changed to Clemson Resources Corp. (Canada) 12/06/2011 which reincorporated British Columbia 10/22/2012 which name changed to Oyster Oil & Gas Ltd. 04/16/2013

HUNTINGDON LIFE SCIENCES GROUP PLC (ENGLAND)
Name changed 04/04/1997
ADR's for Ordinary 10p par split (2) for (1) by issuance of (1) additional ADR 03/13/1987
ADR's for Ordinary 10p par split (2) for (1) by issuance of (1) additional ADR 06/08/1989
Name changed from Huntingdon International Holdings PLC to Huntingdon Life Sciences Group PLC 04/04/1997
Each ADR for Ordinary 10p par exchanged for (0.2) ADR for Ordinary 5p par 07/10/2000
Merged into Life Sciences Research, Inc. 03/21/2002
Each share Ordinary 5p par exchanged for (0.02) share Common 1¢ par
Each ADR for Ordinary 5p par exchanged for (0.5) share Common 1¢ par
(See Life Sciences Research, Inc.)

HUNTINGDON REAL ESTATE INVT TR (MB)
Each old Trust Unit exchanged for (0.11111111) new Trust Unit 02/16/2010
Under plan of reorganization each new Trust Unit automatically became (1) share Huntingdon Capital Corp. (BC) Common no par 01/05/2012
(See Huntingdon Capital Corp.)

HUNTINGDON RESH CENTRE PLC (ENGLAND)
Name changed to Huntingdon International Holdings PLC 06/28/1985
Huntingdon International Holdings PLC name changed to Huntingdon Life Sciences Group PLC 04/04/1997 which merged into Life Sciences Research, Inc. 03/21/2002
(See Life Sciences Research, Inc.)

HUNTINGTON BANCSHARES INC (MD)
Multiple Adjustable Rate Preferred Ser. A no par called for redemption 05/27/1986
$2.25 Preferred no par called for redemption 08/01/1987
Each share 8.5% Non-Cum. Conv. Perpetual Preferred 1¢ par automatically became (83.668) shares Common no par 02/22/2018
(Additional Information in Active)

HUNTINGTON BANK (ARCADIA, CA)
Merged into CVB Financial Corp. 5/15/87
Each share Common no par exchanged for $5.80 cash

HUNTINGTON BEACH CO (CA)
Merged into Chevron Corp. 2/10/87
Each share Capital Stock $1 par exchanged for (14.7727) shares Common $3 par
Chevron Corp. name changed to ChevronTexaco Corp. 10/9/2001 which name changed back to Chevron Corp. 5/9/2005

HUNTINGTON CHAMBERS TRUST
Liquidated in 1948

HUNTINGTON FDS (MA)
Name changed to Franklin/Templeton Global Trust (MA) 11/16/1993
Franklin/Templeton Global Trust (MA) reincorporated in Delaware 08/01/2007

HUNTINGTON FIRST NATIONAL BANK (LIMA, OH)
Merged into Huntington Bancshares Inc. 12/31/79
Each share Capital Stock $10 par exchanged for (1.523728) shares Common no par

HUNTINGTON HALL CORP. (PA)
Voting Trust Agreement terminated 6/28/55
Each VTC for Capital Stock no par exchanged for (1) share Capital Stock 5¢ par
Liquidation completed
Each share Capital Stock 5¢ par exchanged for initial distribution of $52 cash 6/2/71
Each share Capital Stock 5¢ par received second distribution of $12 cash 10/27/71
Each share Capital Stock 5¢ par received third and final distribution of $1.69 cash 5/21/73

HUNTINGTON HEALTH SVCS INC (DE)
Acquired by American Health Care Management Inc. 12/1/83
Each share Common 20¢ par exchanged for $18.05 cash

HUNTINGTON INVT TR (MA)
Trust terminated 09/29/1993
Details not available

HUNTINGTON LAGONDA NATIONAL BANK (SPRINGFIELD, OH)
Merged into Huntington Bancshares Inc. 12/31/79
Each share Common $12.50 par

exchanged for (2.1) shares Common no par

HUNTINGTON NATL BK (COLUMBUS, OH)
Each share Common $100 par exchanged for (5) shares Common $20 par 00/00/1952
Common $20 par changed to $10 par and (1) additional share issued plus a 10% stock dividend paid 07/22/1964
Stock Dividends - 20% 01/25/1957; 11-1/9% 01/17/1961
100% acquired by Huntington Bancshares, Inc. through exchange offer which expired 12/31/1979

HUNTINGTON NATIONAL BANK (HUNTINGTON BEACH, CA)
Under plan of reorganization each share Common $5 par automatically became (1) share HNB Financial Group Common $5 par 7/12/84
HNB Financial Group merged into First Bank of St. Louis 4/28/95

HUNTINGTON PFD CAP INC (OH)
7.875% Non-Cum. Exchangeable Perpetual Preferred Class C $25 par called for redemption at $25 on 12/31/2013

HUNTINGTON RES INC (BC)
Recapitalized as Vulcan Ventures Corp. 10/20/1999
Each share Common no par exchanged for (0.2) share Common no par
Vulcan Ventures Corp. name changed to VVC Exploration Corp. (BC) 10/01/2001 which reincorporated in Canada 09/25/2003

HUNTINGTON RHODES INC (ON)
Cease trade order effective 05/17/2006

HUNTINGTON-ROCKFORD CORP. LTD. (ON)
Adjudicated bankrupt 03/12/1971
No stockholders' equity

HUNTINGTON SVGS & LN ASSN (CA)
99.9% acquired by Acvo Corp. through purchase offer which expired 10/02/1970
Public interest eliminated

HUNTINGTON STRATEGY SHS (DE)
Name changed to Strategy Shares 02/22/2016

HUNTINGTON TR & SVGS BK (HUNTINGTON, WV)
Common $12.50 par changed to $6.25 par and (1) additional share issued 00/00/1976
Acquired by Key Bancshares of West Virginia, Inc. 08/24/1985
Details not available

HUNTINGTON WATER WORKS CO.
Merged into New York Water Service Corp. in 1927
New York Water Service Corp. name changed to Utilities & Industries Corp. (N.Y.) 5/19/60 which merged into Carter Group Inc. 11/19/74 which name changed to Utilities & Industries Corp. (Del.) 11/20/74
(See Utilities & Industries Corp. (Del.))

HUNTLEY OF YORK LTD (NC)
Common $1 par split (3) for (2) by issuance of (0.5) additional share 5/28/72
Merged into Quality Mills, Inc. 1/1/79
Each share Common $1 par exchanged for $0.50 cash

HUNTMOUNTAIN RES (NV)
Reincorporated under the laws of Washington as HuntMountain Resources Ltd. 08/19/2008

HUNTON KIRKLAND GOLD MINES LTD.
Succeeded by Kirkland Hunton Mines Ltd. on a (0.5) for (1) basis 00/00/1926
Kirkland Hunton Mines Ltd. merged into Amalgamated Kirkland Mines Ltd. 00/00/1939 which merged into Mayfield Explorations & Developments Ltd. 06/21/1971 which merged into Microsolve Computer Capital Inc. 02/11/1998 which name changed to Homebank Technologies Inc. 12/20/2000 which name changed to Selient Inc. 06/15/2005
(See Selient Inc.)

HUNTS, LTD. (ON)
Class A and B no par exchanged (4) for (1) 00/00/1946
Acquired by Canadian Food Products Ltd. 00/00/1954
Each share Class A exchanged for $11.50 cash
Each share Class B exchanged for $11.50 cash

HUNTS THEATRES INC (DE)
8% Preferred $10 par called for redemption 01/12/1978

HUNTSMAN CORP (DE)
Each share 5% Mandatory Conv. Preferred 1¢ par received approximately (2.1) shares Common 1¢ par 02/19/2008
(Additional Information in Active)

HUNTWAY PARTNERS L P (DE)
Each Preference Unit of Ltd. Partnership Int. no par exchanged for (1) Common Unit of Ltd. Partnership Int. no par 12/30/96
Reorganized as Huntway Refining Co. 6/1/98
Each Common Unit of Ltd. Partnership Int. no par exchanged for (1) share Common 1¢ par
(See Huntway Refining Co.)

HUNTWAY REFNG CO (DE)
Merged into Valero Energy Corp. 6/1/2001
Each share Common 1¢ par exchanged for $1.90 cash

HUP INDS INC (DE)
Charter cancelled and declared inoperative and void for non-payment of taxes 03/01/1974

HUPP CORP (VA)
Merged into White Consolidated Industries, Inc. 10/23/67
Each share 5% Preferred Ser. A $50 par exchanged for (1) share $2.75 Class B Preferred $50 par
Each share Common $1 par exchanged for $7.692307 principal amount of 5-1/2% Conv. Subord. Debentures due 10/23/92
(See White Consolidated Industries, Inc.)

HUPP MOTOR CAR CORP. (VA)
Name changed to Hupp Corp. 6/25/46
(See Hupp Corp.)

HUPP SYSTEMS, INC. (FL)
Reincorporated under the laws of Delaware as Dart National Corp. 5/8/63
(See Dart National Corp.)

HURCO MFG INC (IN)
Name changed to Hurco Companies, Inc. 3/14/85

HURD COAL & IRON CO. (OH)
Charter cancelled for failure to pay taxes 7/9/57

HURD LOCK & MANUFACTURING CO. (MI)
Each share Common $1 par exchanged for (0.2) share Common $5 par 10/26/44
Name changed to Avis Industrial Corp. (MI) 4/22/60
Avis Industrial Corp. (MI) reincorporated in Delaware 6/5/61 which merged into International General Industries, Inc. 4/6/71 which merged into into International Bank (Washington, DC) 12/31/79 which merged into USLICO Corp. 12/31/85 which merged into NWNL Companies, Inc. 1/17/95 which name changed to ReliaStar Financial Corp. 2/13/95
(See ReliaStar Financial Corp.)

HURLETRON INC (DE)
Name changed to Altair Corp. 4/19/72

HURLEY EXPL INC (DE)
Recapitalized as China Clean Energy Inc. 10/23/2006
Each share Common $0.001 par exchanged for (0.44211106) share Common $0.001 par

HURLEY MACHINE CO.
Name changed to Electric Household Utilities Corp. in 1926
Electric Household Utilities Corp. name changed to Thor Corp. (Ill.) in 1947 which name changed to Allied Paper Corp. 10/5/56 which liquidated for SCM Corp. 12/31/67
(See SCM Corp.)

HURLEY RIV GOLD CORP (YT)
Reincorporated 12/17/1997
Place of incorporation changed from (BC) to (YT) 12/17/1997
Recapitalized as Ouro Brasil Ltd. 03/20/1998
Each share Common no par exchanged for (0.5) share Common no par
Ouro Brasil Ltd. recapitalized as Consolidated Ouro Brasil Ltd. 02/18/2000 which name changed to Superior Diamonds Inc. (YT) 09/03/2002 which reincorporated in British Columbia 06/30/2004 which name changed to Northern Superior Resources Inc. 04/15/2008

HURLEY RIVER MINES LTD. (BC)
Recapitalized as Hurley Uranium Ltd. 11/01/1967
Each share Capital Stock $1 par exchanged for (0.1) share Capital Stock no par
Hurley Uranium Ltd. name changed to New Cinch Uranium Ltd. 04/09/1968
(See New Cinch Uranium Ltd.)

HURLEY URANIUM LTD. (BC)
Name changed to New Cinch Uranium Ltd. 04/09/1968
(See New Cinch Uranium Ltd.)

HURLKAPP, INC. (MA)
Liquidation completed
Each share Common $5 par exchanged for initial distribution of $5.25 cash 2/18/70
Each share Common $5 par received second and final distribution of $1.16 cash 10/9/70

HURON & ERIE MTG CORP (CANADA)
Each share Capital Stock $100 par exchanged for (5) shares Capital Stock $20 par 03/25/1955
Each share Capital Stock $20 par exchanged for (2) shares Capital Stock $10 par 04/14/1961
Each share Capital Stock $10 par exchanged for (5) shares Capital Stock $2 par 10/04/1965
Capital Stock $2 par reclassified as Common $2 par 09/30/1974
Common $2 par reclassified as Conv. Class A Common $2 par 12/29/1975
Name changed to Canada Trustco Mortgage Co. 05/03/1976
Canada Trustco Mortgage Co. reorganized as CT Financial Services Inc. 11/25/1997
(See CT Financial Services Inc.)

HURON BRUCE MINES LTD (ON)
Charter cancelled for failure to file reports and pay taxes 06/12/1989

HURON CORP (NV)
Name changed to Wallfrin Industries Inc. 06/18/1987
(See Wallfrin Industries Inc.)

HURON COUNTY BANKING CO. (NORWALK, OH)
Stock Dividends - 11-1/9% 3/1/71; 100% 4/1/78
Name changed to Huron County Banking Co., N.A. (Norwalk, Ohio) 12/31/74
(See Huron County Banking Co., N.A. (Norwalk, Ohio))

HURON CNTY BKG CO N A (NORWALK, OH)
Acquired by National City Corp. 4/30/79
Each share Capital Stock $25 par exchanged for $45 cash

HURON HOLDING CORP. (NY)
Liquidation completed
Each share Common 10¢ par exchanged for initial distribution of $0.45 cash 6/30/54
Each share Common 10¢ par received second and final distribution of $0.1475 cash 7/5/55

HURON INVT FD INC
Auction Market Preferred Ser. A called for redemption at $100,000 on 10/22/97
Auction Market Preferred Ser. B called for redemption at $100,000 on 10/22/97
Auction Market Preferred Ser. C called for redemption at $100,000 on 10/29/97
Auction Market Preferred Ser. D called for redemption at $100,000 on 11/5/97
Auction Market Preferred Ser. E called for redemption at $100,000 on 11/12/97

HURON MILLING CO. (MI)
Name changed to H.M. Liquidation Corp. 12/3/56
(See H.M. Liquidation Corp.)

HURON STAR RES LTD (ON)
Name changed to Triangle Capital Energy Corp. 07/07/1993
Triangle Capital Energy Corp. recapitalized as Black Mountain Minerals Inc. 05/07/1997 which recapitalized as Augustine Ventures Inc. 11/30/2006 which merged into Red Pine Exploration Inc. 02/06/2017

HURON VALLEY NATL BK (ANN ARBOR, MI)
Common $15 par changed to $7.50 par and (1) additional share issued 1/21/70
Stock Dividends - 10% 1/18/67; 10% 2/15/68; 10% 2/28/69; 20% 3/22/72; 20% 10/15/73; 20% 6/26/76; 10% 4/21/80
Merged into Detroitbank Corp. 5/1/82
Each share Common $7.50 par exchanged for (0.75) share Common $5 par
Detroitbank Corp. name changed to Comerica, Inc. 7/1/82

HURON VY ST BK (MILFORD, MI)
Under plan of reorganization each share Common no par automatically became (1) share Huron Valley Bancorp, Inc. Common no par 09/02/2015

HURON VENTURES INC (DE)
Name changed to Cano Petroleum, Inc. 06/01/2004
(See Cano Petroleum, Inc.)

HURONIAN MINES LTD (ON)
Merged into Far East Gold Inc. 12/14/1995
Each share Common no par exchanged for (0.1) share Common no par
Far East Gold Inc. merged into KWG Resources Inc. 03/31/1997

HURONIAN MINING & FINANCING CO., LTD.
Merged into Anglo-Huronian Ltd. 00/00/1933
Each share Capital Stock exchanged for (0.2) share Capital Stock
Anglo-Huronian Ltd. merged into Kerr Addison Mines Ltd. 11/18/1963 which merged into Noranda Inc. 04/11/1996 which name changed to Falconbridge Ltd. (New) 2005 on 07/01/2005
(See Falconbridge Ltd. (New) 2005)

HURRAY HLDG CO LTD (CAYMAN ISLANDS)
Name changed to Ku6 Media Co., Ltd. 08/17/2010
(See Ku6 Media Co., Ltd.)

HURRICANE HYDROCARBONS LTD (AB)
Name changed to PetroKazakhstan Inc. 06/02/2003
(See PetroKazakhstan Inc.)

HURRICANE OIL PRODS O J S C (KAZAKHSTAN)
Name changed to PetroKazakhstan Oil Products OJSC 7/24/2003
(See PetroKazakhstan Oil Products OJSC)

HURRICANE RESCUE CRAFT INC (BC)
Name changed to Zodiac Hurricane Marine Ltd. 10/09/1987
Zodiac Hurricane Marine Ltd. recapitalized as Zodiac Hurricane Marine (Consolidated) Inc. 06/28/1989 which name changed to Zodiac Hurricane Technologies Inc. 04/05/1990
(See Zodiac Hurricane Technologies Inc.)

HURRY INC (GA)
Liquidation completed
Each share Class A Common no par received initial distribution of $0.11 cash payable 12/02/2002 to holders of record 11/29/2002 Ex date - 12/03/2002
Each share Class A Common no par received second distribution of $0.06 cash payable 08/26/2003 to holders of record 08/25/2003 Ex date - 08/21/2003
Each share Class A Common no par received third and final distribution of $0.032 cash payable 02/18/2004 to holders of record 02/17/2004 Ex date - 02/19/2004
Note: Certificates were not required to be surrendered and are without value

HURST HARRY JR INC (DE)
Reorganized under the laws of Nevada as Golfgear International, Inc. 12/10/1997
Each share Common $0.001 par exchanged for (0.5) share Common $0.001 par
Golfgear International, Inc. (NV) reincorporated in Wyoming 09/16/2010 which name changed to Gear International, Inc. 04/03/2012 which reorganized in Delaware as Matchaah Holdings, Inc. 06/19/2017

HURST PERFORMANCE INC (PA)
Merged into Sunbeam Corp. (Old) 6/22/76
Each share Common 10¢ par exchanged for $8 cash

HUSCOKE RES HLDGS LTD (HONG KONG)
ADR agreement terminated 07/27/2009
Each Sponsored ADR for Ordinary HKD 0.10 par exchanged for $0.943565 cash

HUSKY DEVS LTD (UT)
Involuntarily dissolved 03/01/1990

HUSKY INJECTION MOLDING SYS LTD (ON)
Merged into Onex Partners II, LP 12/13/2007
Each share Common no par exchanged for $8.235 cash

HUSKY OIL CDA LTD (CANADA)
5.75% Conv. Preferred Ser. C $50 par called for redemption 01/24/1968
Name changed to Husky Oil Ltd. 09/03/1968
(See Husky Oil Ltd.)

HUSKY OIL CO (DE)
6% 1st Preferred $100 par reclassified as 6-1/2% 1st Preferred $100 par 1/1/61
Each share Common $1 par exchanged for (0.15) share 6-1/2% 1st Preferred $100 par 12/31/64
Stock Dividend - 25% 11/30/55
6-1/2% 1st Preferred $100 par called for redemption 4/1/72
Public interest eliminated

HUSKY OIL LTD (CANADA)
Common no par split (7) for (1) by issuance of (6) additional shares 05/30/1980
6% Preferred Ser. A no par called for redemption 06/25/1982
6% Preferred Ser. B no par called for redemption 06/25/1982
13% Conv. Preferred Ser. A no par called for redemption 07/02/1985
Merged into UFSC Holdings Inc. 04/30/1987
Each share Common no par exchanged for USD$8.85 to U.S. shareholders or CAD$11.80 to Canadian shareholders

HUSKY REFINING CO. (DE)
Merged into Husky Oil Co. on a (1163) for (1) basis in 1950

HUSSMANN INTL INC (DE)
Merged into Ingersoll-Rand Co. (NJ) 6/16/2000
Each share Common $0.001 par exchanged for $29 cash

HUSSMANN-LIGONIER CO. (DE)
Recapitalized as Hussmann Refrigerator Co. 7/21/47
Each share $2.25 Preferred exchanged for (1) share $2.25 Preferred which was immediately called for redemption
Each share Common no par exchanged for (2) shares Common no par
Hussmann Refrigerator Co. merged into Pet Milk Co. 2/18/66
Pet Milk Co. name changed to Pet Inc. 9/1/66
(See Pet Inc.)

HUSSMANN REFRIGERATOR CO. (DE)
$2.25 Preferred called for redemption 7/21/47
Common no par changed to $5 par and a 50% stock dividend paid in 1954
Common $5 par split (2) for (1) by issuance of (1) additional share 10/10/56
Merged into Pet Milk Co. 2/18/66
Each share Common $5 par exchanged for (1) share 80¢ Conv. Preference no par
Pet Milk Co. name changed to Pet Inc. 9/1/66
(See Pet Inc.)

HUSSMANN (HARRY L.) REFRIGERATOR CO. (DE)
Merged into Hussmann-Ligonier Co. 02/13/1929
Details not available

HUSTLER INC (ID)
Charter forfeited for failure to file returns and pay fees 11/30/1970

HUSTON (T.A.) & CO.
Acquired by National Biscuit Co. 00/00/1931
Details not available

HUSTON (TOM) PEANUT CO. (GA)
Common Capital Stock no par split (5) for (1) by issuance of (4) additional shares 12/15/62
Stock Dividends - 100% 10/10/46; 20% 11/14/59
Acquired by General Mills, Inc. 8/27/66
Each share Common Capital Stock no par exchanged for (1) share $1.75 Conv. Preference no par

HUSTON RED LAKE RESOURCES LTD. (ON)
Dissolved 09/03/1994
Details not available

HUSZAGH-SHERIDAN PROPERTY, INC. (IL)
Liquidated in 1956

HUTCH APPAREL LTD (BC)
Name changed to Cherry Lane Fashion Group (North America) Ltd. 06/29/1988
Cherry Lane Fashion Group (North America) Ltd. name changed to Maracote International Resources, Inc. 07/08/1998 which recapitalized as Lund Ventures Ltd. 05/28/2001 which recapitalized as Lund Gold Ltd. 07/10/2003 which recapitalized as Lund Enterprises Corp. 12/19/2013

HUTCHINGS-SEALY NATIONAL BANK (GALVESTON, TX)
Name changed to First Hutchings-Sealy National Bank (Galveston, Tex.) 6/27/58
First Hutchings-Sealy National Bank (Galveston, Tex.) merged into First International Bancshares, Inc. 12/31/73 which name changed to InterFirst Corp. 12/31/81 which merged into First RepublicBank Corp. 6/6/87
(See First RepublicBank Corp.)

HUTCHINS/DARCY INC. (NY)
Merged out of existence 12/19/1977
Details not available

HUTCHINS INVESTING CORP.
Liquidation completed in 1951

HUTCHINSON (W.H.) & SON, INC. (IL)
Stock Dividend - 10% 10/25/57
Name changed to W.H.S., Inc. 10/9/62 which completed liquidation 9/11/63

HUTCHINSON LUMBER CO. OF CALIF.
Property sold 00/00/1928
Details not available

HUTCHINSON NATL BK & TR CO (HUTCHINSON, KS)
Capital Stock $20 par changed to $10 par and (1) additional share issued plus a 16-2/3% stock dividend paid 2/4/60
Stock Dividends - 12-1/2% 12/4/63; 25% 9/9/66
Reorganized as United Financial Corp. 2/15/72
Each share Capital Stock $10 par exchanged for (1) share Common $10 par
United Financial Corp. name changed to Polaris Financial Corp. 3/13/73
(See Polaris Financial Corp.)

HUTCHINSON SUGAR LTD (HI)
Merged into Ka'u Sugar Co., Inc. 12/29/72
Each share Capital Stock $15 par exchanged for (0.325782) share Common $10 par

HUTCHINSON SUGAR PLANTATION CO. (CA)
Reincorporated under the laws of Hawaii as Hutchinson Sugar Co. Ltd. 12/31/55
Hutchinson Sugar Co. Ltd. merged into Ka'u Sugar Co., Inc. 12/29/72

HUTCHINSON TECHNOLOGY INC (MN)
Common 2¢ par split (3) for (1) by issuance of (2) additional shares payable 02/11/1997 to holders of record 01/31/1997
Acquired by TDK Corp. 10/05/2016
Each share Common 2¢ par exchanged for $4 cash

HUTCHISON LAKE GOLD MINES LTD.
Succeeded by Maylac Gold Mines Ltd. on a (1) for (4) basis in 1946

HUTCHISON TELECOMMUNICATIONS INTL LTD (CAYMAN ISLANDS)
Each Sponsored ADR for Ordinary received distribution of (1) Hutchison Telecommunications Hong Kong Holdings Ltd. Sponsored ADR for Ordinary payable 05/08/2009 to holders of record 04/30/2009 Ex date - 05/11/2009
Acquired by Hutchison Whampoa Ltd. 05/24/2010
Each Sponsored ADR for Ordinary exchanged for $4.178113 cash

HUTCHISON WHAMPOA LTD (CAYMAN ISLANDS)
ADR's for Ordinary split (5) for (4) by issuance of (0.25) additional ADR 06/12/1987
ADR's for Ordinary split (5) for (2) by issuance of (1.5) additional ADR's payable 07/06/2011 to holders of record 07/01/2011 Ex date - 07/07/2011
ADR basis changed from (1:5) to (1:2) 07/07/2011
Stock Dividends - 10% 06/20/1980; 10% payable 06/01/2000 to holders of record 05/16/2000 Ex date - 05/12/2000
Scheme of Arrangement effective 06/19/2015
Each ADR for Ordinary exchanged for (1.368) CK Hutchison Holdings Ltd. ADR's for Ordinary

HUTTIG SASH & DOOR CO (DE)
Each share old Preferred $100 par exchanged for (1) share new Preferred $100 par, (4.5) shares Common $5 par and $2.25 cash in 1936
Each share Common no par exchanged for (1) share Common $5 par in 1936
Common $5 par changed to $10 par and (1) additional share issued in 1950
5% Preferred $100 par called for redemption 3/31/68
Stock Dividend - 50% 4/10/50
Merged into Crane Co. 9/9/87
Each share Common $10 par exchanged for $770 cash

HUTTON E F & CO (DE)
Under plan of reorganization each share Common $1 par automatically became (1) share Hutton (E.F.) Group Inc. Common $1 par 12/31/73
(See Hutton (E.F.) Group Inc.)

HUTTON E F GROUP INC (DE)
Common $1 par split (5) for (4) by issuance of (0.25) additional share 3/29/76
Common $1 par split (5) for (4) by issuance of (0.25) additional share 1/28/80
Common $1 par split (5) for (4) by issuance of (0.25) additional share 8/13/80
Common $1 par split (5) for (4) by issuance of (0.25) additional share 11/21/80
Common $1 par split (5) for (4) by issuance of (0.25) additional share 6/29/81
Common $1 par split (5) for (4) by issuance of (0.25) additional share 4/22/83

Merged into Shearson Lehman Brothers Holdings Inc. 4/29/88
Each share Common $1 par exchanged for $29.25 principal amount of 10-3/4% Sr. Subordinated Notes due 4/29/96

HUTTON HLDGS CORP (NV)
Name changed to China Bottles Inc. 05/08/2008

HUTZLER BROTHERS CO. (MD)
Common $100 par reclassified as Class A Common $75 par 3/30/70
Class A Common $75 par split (4) for (1) by issuance of (3) additional shares plus a 200% stock dividend paid in Class B Common $75 par 5/11/70
Charter forfeited for failure to file reports 10/3/91

HUYCK (F.C.) & SONS (NY)
Common $5 par split (2) for (1) by issuance of (1) additional share in 1952
Reorganized as Huyck Corp. and Common $5 par changed to no par and (2) additional shares issued 12/23/59
(See Huyck Corp.)

HUYCK CORP (NY)
4-1/2% Conv. Prior Preferred Ser. I $100 par called for redemption 12/6/66
Common no par changed to $1 par and (1) additional share issued 7/19/68
Common $1 par split (3) for (2) by issuance of (0.5) additional share 6/5/69
Common $1 par split (2) for (1) by issuance of (1) additional share 6/30/72
$2.75 Class A Preferred $50 par called for redemption 8/17/77
Merged into BTR Ltd. 10/24/80
Each share Common $1 par exchanged for $25.125 cash

HUYLER'S
Insolvent in 1952
No stockholders' equity

HUYLERS OF DELAWARE, INC.
Reorganized as Huyler's 00/00/1940 which became insolvent 00/00/1952

HVIDE MARINE INC (DE)
Name changed to Seabulk International, Inc. 3/19/2001
Seabulk International Inc. merged into SEACOR Holdings Inc. 7/1/2005

HVIDE MARINE INC (FL)
Reorganized under Chapter 11 Federal Bankruptcy Code as HVIDE Marine Inc. (DE) 12/15/99
Each share Common $0.001 par received distribution of (0.0080363) Common Stock Purchase Warrant, Class A expiring 12/14/2003
Note: Certificates were not required to be exchanged and are without value
HVIDE Marine Inc. (DE) name changed to Seabulk International, Inc. 3/19/2001 which merged into SEACOR Holdings Inc. 7/1/2005

HWC DISTR CORP (DE)
Acquired by Alltel Corp. (OH) 4/14/89
Each share Common 1¢ par exchanged for $26.05 cash

HWI GLOBAL INC (NV)
Common $0.0001 par changed to $0.001 par and (6) additional shares issued payable 06/01/2011 to holders of record 05/26/2011 Ex date - 06/02/2011
Filed a petition under Chapter 7 Federal Bankruptcy Code 06/12/2012
Stockholders' equity unlikely

HXT HLDGS INC (DE)
Name changed to Huayue Electronics, Inc. 11/03/2011

Huayue Electronics, Inc. name changed to Tarsier Ltd. 12/11/2015

HY & ZELS INC (ON)
Merged into 2012413 Ontario Inc. 12/17/2003
Each share Common no par exchanged for $2.25 cash

HY-CHARGER PETROLEUMS LTD. (ON)
Recapitalized as Vandoo Consolidated Explorations Ltd. 03/16/1956
Each share Capital Stock $1 par exchanged for (0.2) share Capital Stock $1 par
(See Vandoo Consolidated Explorations Ltd.)

HY-DRIVE TECHNOLOGIES LTD (AB)
Name changed to blutip Power Technologies Ltd. 06/01/2011
(See blutip Power Technologies Ltd.)

HY-DYNAMIC CO. (IL)
Merged into Bucyrus-Erie Co. (Old) 08/10/1971
Each share Common $10 par exchanged for (4) shares Common $5 par
Bucyrus-Erie Co. (Old) name changed to Becor Western Inc. 04/30/1985 which was acquired by B-E Holdings, Inc. 02/04/1988 which reorganized as Bucyrus-Erie Co. (New) 12/14/1994 which name changed to Bucyrus International Inc. (Old) 05/24/1996
(See Bucyrus International Inc. (Old))

HY-FLO PETROLEUMS LTD.
Acquired by Ellesmere Oil & Development Ltd. 00/00/1952
Each share Capital Stock no par exchanged for (0.1) share Capital Stock no par
Ellesmere Oil & Development Ltd. merged into New Concord Development Corp. Ltd. 00/00/1952
(See New Concord Development Corp. Ltd.)

HY-GAIN ELECTRONICS CORP. (DE)
Common 25¢ par split (3) for (1) by issuance of (2) additional shares 09/10/1975
Common 25¢ par split (2) for (1) by issuance of (1) additional share 12/31/1975
Stock Dividend - 10% 01/28/1977
Adjudicated bankrupt 04/04/1978
Stockholders' equity unlikely

HY-GAIN ELECTRONICS CORP. (NE)
Reincorporated under the laws of Delaware and Common $1 par changed to 25¢ par 8/29/75
(See Hy-Gain Electronics Corp. (DE))

HY-LAB INDS LTD (BC)
Cease trade order effective 08/12/1991
Stockholders' equity unlikely

HY LAKE GOLD INC (ON)
Name changed to West Red Lake Gold Mines Inc. 06/29/2012

HY LOND ENTERPRISES (CA)
Each share Common $1 par exchanged for (0.25) share Common $4 par 12/7/71
Name changed to Consolidated Liberty Inc. 1/30/79
Consolidated Liberty Inc. merged into Beverly Enterprises (CA) 3/12/81 which reorganized in Delaware as Beverly Enterprises, Inc. 7/31/87
(See Beverly Enterprises, Inc.)

HY POLL TECHNOLOGY INC (DE)
Recapitalized as Universal Turf Inc. 08/31/1995
Each share Common $0.0001 par exchanged for (0.1) share Common $0.0001 par
Universal Turf Inc. name changed to Universal Media Holdings, Inc. 12/03/1999 which recapitalized as

National Management Consulting Inc. 11/12/2002 which name changed to Genio Group, Inc. 09/11/2003 which recapitalized as Millennium Prime, Inc. 10/29/2009

HY-TECH TECHNOLOGY GROUP INC (DE)
Name changed to Innova Holdings, Inc. 07/29/2004
Innova Holdings, Inc. recapitalized as Innova Robotics & Automation, Inc. 11/20/2006 which name changed to CoroWare, Inc. 05/12/2008

HYAK SKIING CORP (WA)
Common $10 par changed to no par 10/06/1961
Charter cancelled and proclaimed dissolved for failure to pay fees 07/01/1979

HYAL PHARMACEUTICAL CORP (ON)
Reorganized under the laws of Yukon as Cade Struktur Corp. 07/27/2001
Each share Common no par exchanged for (0.1) share Common no par
Cade Struktur Corp. acquired by KHD Humboldt Wedag International Ltd. 10/23/2006 which reorganized as Terra Nova Royalty Corp. 03/30/2010 which name changed to MFC Industrial Ltd. 09/30/2011 which name changed to MFC Bancorp Ltd. (BC) 02/16/2016
(See MFC Bancorp Ltd. (BC))

HYATON ORGANICS INC (NV)
Name changed to Sun Power Corp. 11/01/2001
Sun Power Corp. recapitalized as Cardinal Minerals, Inc. 01/16/2004 which recapitalized as Universal Food & Beverage Co. 03/04/2005
(See Universal Food & Beverage Co.)

HYATT CORP. OF AMERICA (CA)
Name changed to Hotel Equities Corp. 9/1/67
(See Hotel Equities Corp.)

HYATT CORP (DE)
Capital Stock $1 par changed to 50¢ par and (1) additional share issued 6/28/68
Capital Stock 50¢ par reclassified as Common 50¢ par 8/24/70
Common 50¢ par split (3) for (2) by issuance of (0.5) additional share 5/16/72
Stock Dividend - 100% 12/18/68
Merged into Elsinore Corp. 2/5/79
Each share Common 50¢ par exchanged for (1.12) shares Common no par and $13 cash
(See Elsimore Corp.)

HYATT INTL CORP (DE)
Merged into Anartic Investment Co. 2/12/82
Each share Class A Common 10¢ par exchanged for $25 cash

HYBERLAB TEKNOLOGIES CORP (ON)
Delisted from Canadian Dealer Network 10/13/2000

HYBRED INTL INC (CO)
Recapitalized as All Grade Mining, Inc. 11/23/2011
Each share Common $0.001 par exchanged for (0.002) share Common $0.001 par

HYBRID DYNAMICS CORP (NV)
Each share old Common $0.00015 par exchanged for (0.01) share new Common $0.00015 par 08/14/2007
Note: No holder will receive fewer than (100) post-split shares
Recapitalized as DAM Holdings, Inc. 09/24/2009
Each share Common $0.00015 par exchanged for (0.005) share Common $0.00015 par
DAM Holdings, Inc. name changed to

Premier Beverage Group Corp. 11/25/2011

HYBRID FUEL SYS INC (GA)
Name changed to US Energy Initiatives Corp. (GA) 06/05/2006
US Energy Initiatives Corp. (GA) reincorporated in Delaware 05/26/2008
US Energy Initiatives Corp. (DE) reincorporated in Nevada as U.S. Energy Initiatives Corporation 04/03/2013

HYBRID FUELS INC (NV)
Name changed to Nouveau Life Pharmaceuticals, Inc. 05/22/2012

HYBRID NETWORKS INC (DE)
Issue Information - 2,700,000 shares COM offered at $14 per share on 11/12/1997
Business operations terminated and assets sold in foreclosure 05/31/2002
No stockholders' equity

HYBRID PAYTECH WORLD INC (AB)
Name changed to Mobi724 Global Solutions Inc. 02/20/2015

HYBRID TECHNOLOGIES INC (NV)
Each share old Common $0.001 par exchanged for (0.14285714) share new Common $0.001 par 01/17/2008
Stock Dividends - 5% payable 06/17/2005 to holders of record 06/15/2005 Ex date - 06/13/2005; 5% payable 09/02/2005 to holders of record 08/31/2005 Ex date - 08/29/2005; 5% payable 12/05/2005 to holders of record 11/30/2005 Ex date - 11/28/2005; 10% payable 03/03/2006 to holders of record 02/28/2006 Ex date - 02/24/2006; 5% payable 04/03/2006 to holders of record 03/31/2006 Ex date - 03/29/2006; 5% payable 06/02/2006 to holders of record 05/31/2006 Ex date - 05/26/2006; 10% payable 12/04/2006 to holders of record 11/30/2006 Ex date - 11/28/2006; 5% payable 02/05/2007 to holders of record 01/31/2007 Ex date - 01/29/2007; 5% payable 04/05/2007 to holders of record 03/30/2007 Ex date - 03/28/2007; 10% payable 06/05/2007 to holders of record 05/31/2007 Ex date - 05/29/2007
Recapitalized as EV Innovations, Inc. 02/19/2009
Each share Common $0.001 par exchanged for (0.33333333) share Common $0.001 par
EV Innovations, Inc. recapitalized as Li-ion Motors Corp. 02/01/2010 which recapitalized as Terra Inventions Corp. 12/21/2012
(See Terra Inventions Corp.)

HYBRIDOMA SCIENCES INC (DE)
Name changed to Hycor Biomedical Inc. 7/1/86
Hycor Biomedical Inc. merged into Stratagene Corp. 6/2/2004
(See Stratagene Corp.)

HYBRIDON INC (DE)
Each share old Common $0.001 par exchanged for (0.2) share new Common $0.001 par 12/10/97
Name changed to Idera Pharmaceuticals, Inc. 9/12/2005

HYBRILONICS INC (DE)
Each share Common $0.0001 par exchanged for (0.01) share Common 1¢ par 02/20/1992
Charter cancelled and declared inoperative and void for non-payment of taxes 03/01/2006

HYBRIT INTL INC (NV)
Recapitalized as First Fitness Inc. 03/21/1991
Each (70) shares Common $0.001 par exchanged for (1) share Common $0.001 par

(See First Fitness Inc.)

HYBRITECH INC (CA)
Acquired by Lilly (Eli) & Co. 03/18/1986
Each share Common no par exchanged for $22 principal amount of 6.75% 10-Yr. Conv. Notes due 03/31/1996, $22 cash or a combination thereof plus (1.4) Common Stock Purchase Warrant expiring 03/31/1991 and (1) Contingent Payment Unit
Note: Option to elect to receive Notes, cash or a combination thereof expired 06/16/1986

HYBROOK RES CORP (NV)
Name changed to Best Energy Services, Inc. 02/25/2008
(See Best Energy Services, Inc.)

HYCALOG, INC. (DE)
Each share Common no par exchanged for (2) shares Common $1 par 4/16/57
Completely liquidated 11/30/66
Each share Common $1 par exchanged for first and final distribution of (0.2) share Rucker Co. Common no par
Rucker Co. merged into N L Industries, Inc. 1/21/77

HYCEL INC (DE)
Common 50¢ par split (2) for (1) by issuance of (1) additional share 9/22/69
Common 50¢ par changed to 25¢ par and (1) additional share issued 3/9/70
Merged into Boehringer Mannheim Corp. 6/12/79
Each share Common 25¢ par exchanged for $5 cash

HYCOMP INC (MA)
Reincorporated under the laws of Delaware as eieiHome.com Inc. and Common 1¢ par changed to $0.001 par 03/06/2000
eieiHome.com Inc. name changed to Wireless Ventures, Inc. 09/25/2000 which name changed to Pivotal Self-Service Technologies Inc. 10/02/2001 which name changed to Phantom Fiber Corp. 07/21/2004 which recapitalized as Accelerated Technologies Holding Corp. 09/18/2017

HYCON MFG CO (DE)
Each share Common 10¢ par exchanged for (0.2) share Common $2.50 par 4/24/64
Acquired by McDonnell Douglas Corp. 5/28/71
Each share 5-1/2% Preferred $10 par exchanged for $10.25 cash
Each share Common $2.50 par exchanged for (0.19) share Common $1.25 par

HYCOR BIOMEDICAL INC (DE)
Merged into Stratagene Corp. 06/02/2004
Each share Common 1¢ par exchanged for (0.6158) share Common $0.0001 par
(See Stratagene Corp.)

HYCOR INC (MA)
Each share Common 1¢ par exchanged for (0.00025) share Common 1¢ par 2/14/80
Note: In effect holders received $5 cash per share and public interest was eliminated

HYCROFT RES & DEV CORP (BC)
Merged into Granges Inc. (New) 05/01/1995
Each share Common no par exchanged for (0.88) share Common no par
Granges Inc. (New) merged into Vista Gold Corp. (BC) 11/01/1996 which reincorporated in Yukon 12/27/1997

which reincorporated back in British Columbia 06/12/2013

HYDE ATHLETIC INDS INC (MA)
Common $1 par changed to 33-1/3¢ par and (2) additional shares issued 6/10/83
Common 33-1/3¢ par reclassified as Class A Common 33-1/3¢ par 5/16/93
Each share Class A Common 33-1/3¢ par received distribution of (1) share Class B Common 33-1/3¢ par 5/25/93
Name changed to Saucony, Inc. 5/22/98
(See Saucony, Inc.)

HYDE CREEK MINES LTD. (BC)
Charter cancelled for failure to file returns in 1968

HYDE PK ACQUISITION CORP (DE)
Issue Information - 11,250,000 UNITS consisting of (1) share COM and (1) WT offered at $8 per Unit on 03/05/2007
Name changed to Essex Rental Corp. 05/28/2009

HYDE PK ACQUISITION CORP II (DE)
Issue Information - 7,500,000 shares COM offered at $10 per share on 08/01/2012
Completely liquidated 05/06/2014
Each share Common $0.0001 par exchanged for first and final distribution of $10.5002469 cash

HYDE PARK BREWERIES ASSN., INC.
Merged into Griesedieck Western Brewery Co. on a (0.8) for (1) basis in 1948
Griesedieck Western Brewery Co. name changed to Griesedieck Co. in 1954
(See Griesedieck Co.)

HYDER GOLD INC (BC)
Recapitalized as Gleichen Resources Ltd. (BC) 08/03/2006
Each share Common no par exchanged for (0.5) share Common no par
Gleichen Resources Ltd. (BC) reincorporated in Ontario as Torex Gold Resources Inc. 05/04/2010

HYDER JUMBO MINING CO. (AK)
Proclaimed dissolved for failure to file reports and pay fees 7/2/29

HYDER MINES, INC. (WA)
Charter cancelled and proclaimed dissolved for failure to pay fees 07/01/1978

HYDER SKOOKUM MINING CO. (AK)
Proclaimed dissolved for failure to file reports and pay fees 7/2/29

HYDRA CAP CORP (ON)
Name changed 12/30/1992
Capital Stock $1 par changed to no par 02/11/1972
Name changed from Hydra Explorations Ltd. to Hydra Capital Corp. 12/30/1992
Name changed to Waterford Capital Management Inc. 11/12/1996
Waterford Capital Management Inc. merged into CPI Plastics Group Ltd. 09/21/1998
(See CPI Plastics Group Ltd.)

HYDRA INDS ACQUISITION CORP (DE)
Merged into Inspired Entertainment, Inc. 12/28/2016
Each Unit exchanged for (1.1) shares Common $0.0001 par and (1) Common Stock Purchase Warrant expiring 12/20/2021
Each share Common $0.0001 par exchanged for (1) share Common $0.0001 par

HYDRA PWR CORP (NY)
Acquired by Teledyne, Inc. 01/28/1966

Each share Common 10¢ par exchanged for (0.277777) share Common $1 par
Teledyne, Inc. merged into Allegheny Teledyne, Inc. 08/15/1996 which name changed to Allegheny Technologies Inc. 11/29/1999

HYDRAMOTIVE CORP. (OK)
Charter revoked for failure to file reports and pay fees 3/21/67

HYDRATRON SYS INC (NY)
Dissolved by proclamation 12/23/92

HYDRAULIC BRAKE ASSOCIATES LTD.
Acquired by Bendix Aviation Corp. 00/00/1930
Details not available

HYDRAULIC BRAKE CO.
Acquired by Bendix Aviation Corp. 00/00/1930
Details not available

HYDRAULIC CO (DE)
Common $10 par changed to no par 4/22/75
Common no par split (3) for (2) by issuance of (0.5) additional share 4/30/87
Name changed to Aquarion Co. 4/23/91
(See Aquarion Co.)

HYDRAULIC DIAMOND DRILL & PRODUCTS CO., LTD. (ON)
Charter revoked for failure to file reports and pay fees 8/10/59

HYDRAULIC MACHINERY, INC.
Insolvent 00/00/1949
No stockholders' equity

HYDRAULIC PRESS BRICK CO (MO)
Merged into HPB Acquisition Co. 4/20/2000
Each share Common $1 par exchanged for $51.50 cash

HYDRAULIC PRESS MANUFACTURING CO. (OH)
Stock Dividends - 10% 12/14/51; 10% 12/19/52; 10% 12/18/53
Merged into Koehring Co. 6/23/56
Each share Common $5 par exchanged for (0.2) share 5% Conv. Preferred Ser. A $50 par and (2/3) share Common $5 par
(See Koehring Co.)

HYDRAULIC STEEL CO.
Acquired by Truscon Steel Co. in 1929
Details not available

HYDRIL CO (DE)
Merged into Tenaris S.A. 05/08/2007
Each share Common 50¢ par exchanged for $97 cash

HYDRO ELECTRS CORP (NY)
Merged into Borne Chemical Co., Inc. (New) 05/28/1974
Each share Common 1¢ par exchanged for (1) share Common 10¢ par
(See Borne Chemical Co., Inc. (New))

HYDRO ENVIRONMENTAL RES INC (NV)
Reorganized as Global Trade Portal Corp. 01/24/2005
Each share Common $0.001 par exchanged for (0.001) share Common $0.001 par
Global Trade Portal Corp. name changed to EXIM Internet Group Inc. 05/23/2005
(See EXIM Internet Group Inc.)

HYDRO ENVIRONMENTAL RES INC (OK)
Reorganized under the laws of Nevada 08/20/2001
Each share Common $0.001 par exchanged for (0.2) share Common $0.001 par
Hydo Environmental Resources, Inc. (NV) reorganized as Global Trade Portal Corp. 01/24/2005 which name

changed to EXIM Internet Group Inc. 05/23/2005
(See EXIM Internet Group Inc.)

HYDRO FLAME CORP (UT)
Merged into Atwood Acquisition Corp. 2/19/93
Each share Common $1 par exchanged for $10.50 cash

HYDRO HOME APPLIANCES LTD (BC)
Reincorporated 00/00/1985
Place of incorporation changed from (BC) to (ON) 00/00/1985
Name changed to Santa Marina Gold Ltd. 12/16/1987
Santa Marina Gold Ltd. merged into Akiko-Lori Gold Resources Ltd. 01/16/1991 which merged into Akiko Gold Resources Ltd. (BC) 11/09/1992 which reincorporated in Yukon as Prospex Mining Inc. 07/30/1997 which merged into Semafo Inc. 06/30/1999

HYDRO MAID INTL INC (NV)
SEC revoked common stock registration 10/25/2007

HYDRO MED SCIENCES INC (DE)
Merged into National Patent Development Corp. 12/31/74
Each share Common 1¢ par exchanged for (0.5) share Common 1¢ par
National Patent Development Corp. name changed to GP Strategies Corp. 3/9/98

HYDRO MED TECHNOLOGY INC (CO)
Name changed to Capsule Systems, Inc. 1/31/86
(See Capsule Systems, Inc.)

HYDRO NUCLEAR CORP (NM)
Name changed to Cobb Nuclear Corp. 06/29/1977
Cobb Nuclear Corp. name changed to Cobb Resources Corp. 01/02/1981 which name changed to Family Room Entertainment Corp. 04/26/2000

HYDRO OPTICS INC (DE)
Stock Dividend - 10% 08/01/1983
Recapitalized as NexiaSoft, Inc. 05/31/2006
Each share Common $0.001 par exchanged for (0.01) share Common $0.001 par
NexiaSoft, Inc. recapitalized as SPI Worldwide, Inc. 04/18/2008 which name changed to Talent Alliance, Inc. 06/30/2008 which name changed to Hire International, Inc. 09/24/2010 which recapitalized as TruLan Resources Inc. 11/20/2012 which recapitalized as Trinity Resources Inc. 09/18/2015

HYDRO PWR DEV INC (CO)
Reorganized as American Capital Group, Ltd. 07/08/1988
Each share Common no par exchanged for (0.1) share Common no par

HYDRO SEEK INC (CO)
Name changed to Accelr8 Technology Corp. (CO) 07/05/1988
Accelr8 Technology Corp. (CO) reincorporated in Delaware as Accelerate Diagnostics, Inc. 12/26/2012

HYDRO SKI INTL CORP (DE)
Charter cancelled and declared inoperative and void for non-payment of taxes 3/1/75

HYDRO SPACE SYS CORP (IA)
Out of business 04/00/1970
No stockholders' equity

HYDRO-SPACE TECHNOLOGY, INC. (DE)
Liquidated 05/08/1963
Each (3.913) shares Common 50¢

par exchanged for (1) share Imperial 400 National, Inc. Common 50¢ par
(See Imperial 400 National, Inc.)

HYDRO TECHNICS LABORATORIES INC. (NY)
Charter cancelled and proclaimed dissolved for failure to pay taxes and file reports 12/15/67

HYDRO-UNITED TIRE CO. (DE)
Charter cancelled and declared inoperative and void for non-payment of taxes 3/18/25

HYDROCAP EASTERN INC. (DE)
No longer in existence having become inoperative and void for non-payment of taxes 4/1/56

HYDROCARBON CHEMICALS, INC. (NJ)
Reorganized as Transcoastal Industries Corp. 7/12/67
Each share Common $1 par exchanged for (0.155233) share Common $1 par
(See Transcoastal Industries Corp.)

HYDROCARBON TECHNOLOGIES CORP (ID)
Charter forfeited for failure to file reports 12/02/1991

HYDROCRAFT, INC. (CA)
Charter suspended for failure to pay franchise and license taxes 10/01/1963

HYDRODYNE INDS INC (NY)
Each share old Common 1¢ par exchanged for (0.25) share new Common 1¢ par 12/19/1983
Dissolved by proclamation 10/26/2011

HYDROFLO INC (NC)
Name changed to SolarBrook Water & Power Corp. 12/20/2007
(See SolarBrook Water & Power Corp.)

HYDROGEN CORP (NV)
SEC revoked common stock registration 10/09/2013

HYDROGEN ENERGY CORP (UT)
Charter expired 04/27/1999

HYDROGEN HYBRID CORP (NV)
Name changed to Get Real USA Inc. 01/12/2011

HYDROGEN PWR INC (DE)
Name changed 12/26/2006
Name changed from Hydrogen Power International, Inc. to Hydrogen Power, Inc. 12/26/2006
SEC revoked common stock registration 05/20/2011

HYDROGENICS CORP OLD (CANADA)
Under plan of reorganization each share Common no par automatically became (1) share Hydrogenics Corp. (New) Common no par 10/27/2009

HYDROGIENE CORP (FL)
Name changed to Synergie Holdings Ltd., Inc. 09/04/2002
Synergie Holdings Ltd., Inc. name changed to Synergie Wellness Products, Inc. 03/15/2004

HYDROGROW INC (NV)
Name changed to Asgard Alliance Corp. 09/22/1999
Asgard Alliance Corp. name changed to Santa Fe Holding Co., Inc. 06/26/2007
(See Santa Fe Holding Co., Inc.)

HYDROIL, INC. (TX)
Acquired by Petrosur Oil Corp. share for share 8/15/58
Petrosur Oil Corp. merged into Techtro-Matic Corp. 8/24/61
(See Techtro-Matic Corp.)

HYDROMATICS INC (NJ)
Name changed to Computer Machining Technology Corp. 04/29/1970

Computer Machining Technology Corp. name changed to CMT Industries, Inc. 03/25/1974 which name changed to Matrix Corp. (NJ) 01/12/1979 which reincorporated in Delaware 04/19/1988
(See Matrix Corp. (DE))

HYDROMATION FILTER CO (MI)
Completely liquidated 7/8/75
Each share Common $1 par exchanged for first and final distribution of $5 cash

HYDROMEDIX GROUP INC (FL)
Common 1¢ par split (4) for (1) by issuance of (3) additional shares payable 11/30/2006 to holders of record 11/30/2006 Ex date - 12/01/2006
Administratively dissolved 09/26/2008

HYDROMET ENVIRONMENTAL RECOVERY LTD (AB)
Each share old Class A Common no par exchanged for (0.16666666) share new Class A Common no par 11/20/2003
Cease trade order effective 06/30/2004

HYDROMET LTD (AUSTRALIA)
ADR agreement terminated 09/07/2012
Each Sponsored ADR for Ordinary exchanged for $0.198976 cash

HYDROMET TECHNOLOGIES LTD (BC)
Reincorporated under the laws of Bermuda as Goldmarca Ltd. 07/02/2003
Goldmarca Ltd. name changed to Ecometals Ltd. 10/25/2007

HYDROMETALS INC (IL)
60¢ Conv. Preferred no par called for redemption 7/1/77
Merged into Wallace-Murray Corp. 10/16/78
Each share Common $2.50 par exchanged for $20.50 principal amount of 9% Senior Promissory Note due 10/16/83

HYDRON EUROPE INC (DE)
Merged into National Patent Development Corp. 12/31/74
Each share Common 1¢ par exchanged for (0.5) share Common 1¢ par
National Patent Development Corp. name changed to GP Strategies Corp. 3/9/98

HYDRON INTERNATIONAL, LTD. (DE)
Name changed to Hydron Pacific, Ltd. and Common 5¢ par changed to $0.025 par 7/30/71
Hydron Pacific, Ltd. merged into National Patent Development Corp. 12/31/74 which name changed to GP Strategies Corp. 3/9/98

HYDRON PAC LTD (DE)
Common $0.025 par split (2) for (1) by issuance of (1) additional share 8/20/71
Merged into National Patent Development Corp. 12/31/74
Each share Common $0.025 par exchanged for (0.5) share Common 1¢ par
National Patent Development Corp. name changed to GP Strategies Corp. 3/9/98

HYDRONIC INDS INC (NY)
Adjudicated bankrupt 12/15/71
Trustee's attorney advises there is no stockholders' equity

HYDROPHILICS INTERNATIONAL, INC. (DE)
Name changed to Sun Equities Corp. 6/6/80
(See Sun Equities Corp.)

HYDROPLEX CORP (NY)
Charter cancelled and proclaimed dissolved for failure to pay taxes and file reports 12/15/75

HYDROPONICS INC. (IN)
Administratively dissolved 7/31/89

HYDROPOTHECARY CORP (ON)
Name changed to HEXO Corp. 09/05/2018

HYDROTECH CORP (FL)
Recapitalized as Hanley Consolidated, Inc. 7/20/71
Each share Common 10¢ par exchanged for (0.1) share Common 10¢ par
(See Hanley Consolidated, Inc.)

HYDROTEX SYSTEMS, INC. (MN)
Name changed to Agri-Quip Manufacturing, Inc. and Common 10¢ par changed to 1¢ par 9/17/73
(See Agri-Quip Manufacturing, Inc.)

HYDUKE RES LTD (AB)
Name changed 10/22/1998
Name changed from Hyduke Capital Resources Ltd. to Hyduke Resources Ltd. 10/22/1998
Name changed to Hyduke Energy Services Inc. 01/22/2002

HYENA CAP INC (NV)
Reorganized as Advanced Lumitech Inc. 8/14/98
Each share Common $0.001 par exchanged for (5) shares Common $0.001 par
Advanced Lumitech Inc. name changed to Brightec, Inc. 11/13/2006

HYGEIA HLDGS LTD (DE)
Name changed to Novopharm Biotech Inc. (DE) 07/28/1995
Novopharm Biotech Inc. (DE) merged into Novopharm Biotech Inc. (BC) 08/25/1997 which name changed to Viventia Biotech Inc. 09/11/2000
(See Viventia Biotech Inc.)

HYGEIA SCIENCES INC (DE)
Merged into Tambrands Inc. 02/25/1987
Each share Common 1¢ par exchanged for $14.50 cash

HYGEIALAND BIOMEDICAL CORP (NV)
Name changed to Angstron Holdings Corp. 08/19/2013
Angstron Holdings Corp. name changed to HK Graphene Technology Corp. 07/31/2015

HYGIENE INDUSTRIES, INC. (NY)
Completely liquidated 5/27/65
Each share Common $1 par exchanged for first and final distribution of (1) Ctf. of Bene. Int. no par of Hyndus Co., Inc. and $7.27 cash
(See Hyndus Co., Inc.)

HYGOLD MINES LTD. (ON)
Charter revoked for failure to file reports and pay fees 04/17/1968

HYGRADE ASBESTOS MINING CORP LTD. (ON)
Charter cancelled for failure to file reports and pay taxes in 1969

HYGRADE BUSINESS SYS INC (NY)
Adjudicated bankrupt 1/28/69
No stockholders' equity

HYGRADE FOOD PRODS CORP (NY)
Common no par changed to $5 par in 1933
Under plan of merger each share Common $5 par exchanged for $31 cash 3/9/77
5% Preferred Ser. B $100 par called for redemption 12/1/79
$4 Conv. Preference Ser. A $1 par called for redemption 7/1/86
Stock Dividend - 100% 10/29/73
4% Preferred Ser. A $100 par called for redemption 12/1/86
Public interest eliminated

HYGRADE LAMP CO.
Merged into Hygrade Sylvania Corp. in 1931
Details not available

HYGRADE PACKAGING CORP (NY)
Adjudicated bankrupt 1/28/69
No stockholders' equity

HYGRADE SYLVANIA CORP.
Name changed to Sylvania Electric Products, Inc. in 1942
Sylvania Electric Products, Inc. merged into General Telephone & Electronics Corp. 3/5/59 which name changed to GTE Corp. 7/1/82 which merged into Verizon Communications Inc. 6/30/2000

HYLAND BASIN GOLD MINES LTD.
Dissolved in 1948

HYLAND MFG INC (IA)
Bankruptcy proceedings closed 4/25/78
No stockholders' equity

HYLAND OIL CO. INC. (TX)
Charter forfeited for failure to pay taxes 4/10/51

HYLAND PARK ESTATES LTD. (BC)
Struck off register and declared dissolved 2/8/72

HYLSAMEX S A DE C V (MEXICO)
ADR agreement terminated 11/16/2005
Each Reg. S Sponsored ADR for B Share no par exchanged for $15.57943 cash

HYMEX DIAMOND CORP (YT)
Reincorporated 09/04/1996
Place of incorporation changed from (BC) to (YT) 09/04/1996
Struck off register 05/31/2005

HYNAUTIC INC (FL)
Merged into Fluid Controls, Inc. 7/1/76
Each share Common no par exchanged for $0.10 cash

HYNDUS CO., INC. (NY)
Liquidation completed
Each Ctf. of Bene. Int. no par received initial distribution of $0.209267 cash per share 7/8/66
Each Ctf. of Bene. Int. no par received second distribution of $0.2504145 cash per share 6/26/67
Each Ctf. of Bene. Int. no par exchanged for third and final distribution of $0.3612155 cash per share 12/27/67

HYNIX SEMICONDUCTOR INC (KOREA)
Each old Sponsored 144A GDR for Common exchanged for (0.04761904) new Sponsored 144A GDR for Common 03/31/2003
Each new Sponsored 144A GDR for Common exchanged again for (5) new Sponsored 144A GDR's for Common 10/31/2005
Name changed to SK Hynix, Inc. 04/09/2012

HYPAZ TECHNOLOGY CORP (BC)
Name changed to Calibre Technologies Corp. 09/12/1994
(See Calibre Technologies Corp.)

HYPERBARIC OXYGENATION CORP (NV)
Name changed to Building Turbines, Inc. 02/04/2011
Building Turbines, Inc. recapitalized as HempTech Corp. 03/31/2016 which name changed to Nuvus Gro Corp. 04/12/2018

HYPERBARIC SYS (CA)
Name changed to Human BioSystems 11/13/2002
Human BioSystems name changed to San West, Inc. (CA) 09/28/2009 which reincorporated in Nevada 09/13/2011 which recapitalized as AppSwarm, Inc. 09/25/2015

HYPERCOM CORP (DE)
Merged into VeriFone Systems, Inc. 08/04/2011
Each share Common $0.001 par exchanged for (0.23) share Common 1¢ par
(See VeriFone Systems, Inc.)

HYPERERA INC (NV)
Recapitalized as Life's Time Capsule Services, Inc. 03/13/2017
Each share Common $0.001 par exchanged for (0.01) share Common $0.001 par

HYPERFEED TECHNOLOGIES INC (DE)
Each share old Common $0.001 par exchanged for (0.1) share new Common $0.001 par 8/13/2003
Filed a plan of liquidation under Chapter 7 Federal Bankruptcy Code 11/29/2006
Stockholders' equity unlikely

HYPERION 2005 INVT GRADE OPPORTUNITY TERM TR INC (MD)
Trust terminated 11/30/2005
Each share Common 1¢ par exchanged for approximately $9.98 cash

HYPERION BROOKFIELD COLLATERALIZED SECURITIES FUND, INC. (MD)
Name changed 05/08/2007
Name changed from Hyperion Collateralized Securities Fund, Inc. to Hyperion Brookfield Collateralized Securities Fund, Inc. 05/08/2007
Completely liquidated 08/06/2010
Each Common Share of Bene. Int. 1¢ par received net asset value

HYPERION BROOKFIELD STRATEGIC MTG INCOME FD INC (MD)
Name changed 05/08/2007
Name changed from Hyperion Strategic Mortgage Income Fund, Inc. to Hyperion Brookfield Strategic Mortgage Income Fund, Inc. 05/08/2007
Name changed to Helios Strategic Mortgage Income Fund, Inc. 12/29/2008
Helios Strategic Mortgage Income Fund, Inc. merged into Helios Total Return Fund, Inc. 04/02/2012 which name changed to Brookfield Total Return Fund Inc. 03/13/2013 which merged into Brookfield Real Assets Income Fund Inc. 12/05/2016

HYPERION BROOKFIELD TOTAL RETURN FD INC (MD)
Name changed 10/10/2007
Name changed from Hyperion Total Return Fund, Inc. to Hyperion Brookfield Total Return Fund, Inc. 10/10/2007
Name changed to Helios Total Return Fund, Inc. 12/29/2008
Helios Total Return Fund, Inc. name changed to Brookfield Total Return Fund Inc. 03/13/2013 which merged into Brookfield Real Assets Income Fund Inc. 12/05/2016

HYPERION EXPL CORP (AB)
Acquired by Tri-Win International Investment Group Inc. 01/13/2015
Each share Common no par exchanged for $0.14 cash
Note: Unexchanged certificates were cancelled and became without value 01/12/2018

HYPERION FD INC (DE)
Acquired by First Multifund of America Inc. 06/04/1974
Each share Capital Stock 10¢ par exchanged for (1.1765) shares Common 1¢ par
First Multifund of America Inc. acquired by Oppenheimer Special Fund, Inc. (MD) 11/20/1979 which reincorporated in Massachusetts as Oppenheimer Special Fund 11/01/1985 which name changed to Oppenheimer Growth Fund 12/21/1994 which merged into Oppenheimer Capital Appreciation Fund 11/08/2007

HYPERION INDS LTD (NV)
Charter revoked for failure to file reports and pay fees 10/1/2000

HYPERION 1999 TERM TR INC (MD)
Trust terminated 11/30/99
Each share Common 1¢ par exchanged for first and final distribution of $7.273376 cash

HYPERION 1997 TERM TR INC (MD)
Called for redemption 12/1/97
Public interest eliminated

HYPERION RES CORP (YT)
Recapitalized as Chariot Resources Ltd. (YT) 02/21/2002
Each share Common no par exchanged for (0.2) share Common no par
Chariot Resources Ltd. (YT) reincorporated in British Columbia 10/28/2004
(See Chariot Resources Ltd.)

HYPERION RES LTD (BC)
Recapitalized as First Security Corp. 09/20/1989
Each share Common no par exchanged for (0.5) share Common no par
First Security Corp. name changed to Telelink Communications Corp. (Old) 03/08/1993 which merged into Telelink Communications Corp. (BC) (New) 08/01/1996 which reorganized in Canada as Ignition Point Technologies Corp. 04/20/2001 which recapitalized as Tilting Capital Corp. 08/24/2009

HYPERION SOFTWARE CORP (DE)
Common 1¢ par split (2) for (1) by issuance of (1) additional share 12/15/95
Merged into Hyperion Solutions Corp. 8/24/98
Each share Common 1¢ par exchanged for (0.95) share Common $0.001 par
(See Hyperion Solutions Corp.)

HYPERION SOLUTIONS CORP (DE)
Common $0.001 par split (3) for (2) by issuance of (0.5) additional share payable 12/19/2005 to holders of record 12/01/2005 Ex date - 12/20/2005
Merged into Oracle Corp. 04/19/2007
Each share Common $0.001 par exchanged for $52 cash

HYPERION TECHNOLOGIES INC (NV)
Name changed to Nextpath Technologies Inc. 07/22/1999
(See Nextpath Technologies Inc.)

HYPERION TELECOMMUNICATIONS INC (DE)
Issue Information - 12,500,000 shares CL A offered at $16 per share on 05/04/1998
Stock Dividend - in Preferred to holders of Preferred 3.21875% payable 10/15/99 to holders of record 10/1/99
Name changed to Adelphia Business Solutions Inc. 10/27/99
(See Adelphia Business Solutions Inc.)

HYPERION THERAPEUTICS INC (DE)
Acquired by Horizon Pharma PLC 05/07/2015
Each share Common $0.0001 par exchanged for $46 cash

HYPERION 2002 TERM TR INC (MD)
Trust terminated 11/29/2002
Each share Common 1¢ par exchanged for net asset value

HYPERMARCAS S A (BRAZIL)
Name changed to Hypera S.A. 02/23/2018

HYPERMEDIA COMMUNICATIONS INC (CA)
Reincorporated under the laws of Florida as Univercell Holdings, Inc. 10/02/2001
(See Univercell Holdings, Inc.)

HYPERSPACE COMMUNICATIONS INC (CO)
Issue Information - 1,800,000 UNITS consisting of (1) share COM and (2) WTS offered at $5.50 per Unit on 09/30/2004
Name changed to MPC Corp. 01/08/2007
(See MPC Corp.)

HYPERTENSION DIAGNOSTICS INC (MN)
Assets sold 08/00/2011
Details not available

HYPO REAL ESTATE HLDG AG (GERMANY)
ADR agreement terminated 06/01/2009
Each Sponsored ADR for Ordinary exchanged for $1.891307 cash

HYPONEX CORP (DE)
Acquired by Scott (O.M.) & Sons Co. 11/10/88
Each share Common 10¢ par exchanged for $14 cash

HYPOTHEEK MINING & MILLING CO. (ID)
Charter forfeited for failure to file reports and pay taxes 12/1/59

HYS CDA LTD (BC)
100% acquired by Prime Food Systems Ltd. through purchase offer which expired 07/14/1979
Public interest eliminated

HYSEQ INC (NV)
Issue Information - 3,000,000 shares COM offered at $14 per share on 08/07/1997
Under plan of merger name changed to Nuvelo, Inc. (NV) 01/31/2003
Nuvelo, Inc. (NV) reorganized in Delaware 02/23/2004 which recapitalized as ARCA biopharma, Inc. 01/28/2009

HYSTAR AEROSPACE CORP (BC)
Delisted from Vancouver Stock Exchange 5/11/93

HYSTAR AEROSPACE CORP (NV)
Common $0.001 par split (6) for (1) by issuance of (5) additional shares payable 11/07/2000 to holders of record 11/05/2000
Name changed to Angus Energy Corp. 06/19/2003
(See Angus Energy Corp.)

HYSTAR WORLDNET, INC. (NV)
Name changed to VIP Worldnet, Inc. 10/28/1988
(See VIP Worldnet, Inc.)

HYSTER CO (NV)
Each share Class A 50¢ par exchanged for (0.75) share Common 50¢ par 05/06/1968
Stock Dividends - Class A & Common - 100% 07/10/1965 - Common 100% 01/22/1973
Merged into Esco Corp. 02/16/1984
Each share Common 50¢ par exchanged for $69 cash

HYTEC FLOW SYS INC (BC)
Delisted from Canadian Dealer Network 03/22/2001

HYTEK INTL CORP (DE)
Charter cancelled and declared inoperative and void for non-payment of taxes 04/19/1989

HYTEK MICROSYSTEMS INC (CA)
Merged into Natel Engineering Co., Inc. 6/1/2005
Each share Common no par exchanged for $2 cash

HYTHIAM INC (DE)
Name changed to Catasys, Inc. 03/17/2011

HYTK INDS INC (NV)
Each (140) shares old Common $0.001 par exchanged for (1) share new Common $0.001 par 09/01/1991
Each share new Common $0.001 par exchanged again for (0.025) share new Common $0.001 par 10/31/1995
Name changed to Quest Resource Corp. 06/25/2000
Quest Resource Corp. merged into PostRock Energy Corp. 03/05/2010

HYTRON RADIO & ELECTRONICS CORP.
Acquired by Columbia Broadcasting System, Inc. in 1951
Each share Common $1 par exchanged for (0.155) share Class A $2.50 par and (0.155) share Class B $2.50 par
Columbia Broadcasting System, Inc. name changed to CBS Inc. 4/18/74
(See CBS Inc.)

HYUNDAI ELECTRONICS INDS LTD (KOREA)
Name changed to Hynix Semiconductor Inc. 05/14/2001
Hynix Semiconductor Inc. name changed to SK Hynix, Inc. 04/09/2012

HYUNDAI ENGR & CONSTR LTD (KOREA)
Each old Reg. S GDR for Common exchanged for (0.1) new Reg. S GDR for Common 04/11/2000
Each old 144A GDR for Common exchanged for (0.1) GDR for Common 04/11/2000
Each new Reg. S GDR for Common exchanged for (0.16945) GDR for Preferred 06/20/2001
Each new 144A GDR for Common exchanged for (0.16945) GDR for Ordinary 06/20/2001
GDR agreement terminated 01/30/2004
Each GDR for Preferred exchanged for $8.501156 cash
Each GDR for Ordinary exchanged for $4.75171 cash

HYWY CORP (ON)
Name changed 05/18/2000
Name changed from HYWY.Com Corp. to HYWY Corp. 05/18/2000
Recapitalized as HY Lake Gold Inc. 03/30/2006
Each share Common no par exchanged for (0.1) share Common no par
HY Lake Gold Inc. name changed to West Red Lake Gold Mines Inc. 06/29/2012

I

I A EUROPE GROUP INC (DE)
Name changed to Ghost Technology, Inc. 07/15/2008
(See Ghost Technology, Inc.)

I A F A INC (DE)
Charter cancelled and declared inoperative and void for non-payment of taxes 3/1/86

I A LIQUIDATING CORP (NY)
Liquidation completed
Each share Common 5¢ par exchanged for initial distribution of (1) share Empire Petroleum Co. Common $1 par 3/31/70
Empire Petroleum Co. name changed to Empire International, Inc. 7/15/70
Each share Common 5¢ par received second and final distribution of (2)

shares Empire International, Inc. 8/5/70
(See Empire Internarional, Inc.)

I A N MARINE CORP (DE)
Charter cancelled and declared inoperative and void for non-payment of taxes 04/15/1972

I-AEROBIDS COM INC (DE)
Name changed to Schoolwurks, Inc. 09/04/2001
(See Schoolwurks, Inc.)

I-ANTIQUEAUCTION COM INC (DE)
Recapitalized as Photo America Inc. 03/07/2001
Each share Common $0.0001 par exchanged for (0.30303030) share Common $0.0001 par
Photo America Inc. name changed to Concept Digital, Inc. 07/19/2001
(See Concept Digital, Inc.)

I B FINL CORP (CA)
Merged into Halifax Financial Holdings, Inc. 01/08/1980
Each share Common $2 par exchanged for $15.96 cash

I B I SEC SVC INC (NY)
Common 10¢ par reclassified as Class A 10¢ par 4/11/72
Chapter 7 bankruptcy case closed 11/27/2001
No stockholders' equity

I B NET LTD (DE)
Charter cancelled and declared inoperative and void for non-payment of taxes 03/01/2007

I.C.C. LOAN CO. (PA)
Acquired by General Acceptance Corp. (New) 11/01/1962
Each share 6% Preferred $100 par exchanged for (10) shares 60¢ Vtg. Conv. Preference no par
General Acceptance Corp. (New) name changed to GAC Corp. (PA) 07/01/1968 which reincorporated in Delaware 12/20/1973
(See GAC Corp. (DE))

I C E ICE FACTORY INC (BC)
Struck off register and declared dissolved for failure to file returns 04/16/1992

I C H CORP NEW (DE)
Reorganized under Chapter 11 Federal Bankruptcy Code 2/19/97
Each share $1.75 Exchangeable Preferred Ser. 1986 A no par exchanged for (0.2) share new Common $1 par or $0.36 cash
Each share Common $1 par exchanged for (0.0269) share new Common $1 par or $0.05 cash
Note: Option to receive cash expired 3/31/97; maximum cash payments were $234 for $1.75 Exchangeable Preferred Ser. 1986 A holders and $250 for Common holders
Holders of less than (14) shares $1.75 Exchangeable Preferred Ser. 1986 A or less than (101) shares Common were not entitled to the distribution; shares were cancelled and are valueless
Plan of reorganization under Chapter 11 Federal Bankruptcy Code effective 12/27/2002
No stockholders' equity

I C H CORP OLD (DE)
Reincorporated 08/15/1977
Stock Dividend - 10% 05/31/1972
State of incorporation changed from (MO) to (DE) 08/15/1977
Common $1 par split (2) for (1) by issuance of (1) additional share 07/22/1985
Common $1 par split (3) for (1) by issuance of (2) additional shares 05/19/1986
Name changed to Southwestern Life Corp. (New) 06/15/1994
Southwestern Life Corp. (New) name changed to I.C.H. Corp. (New) 10/10/1995
(See I.C.H. Corp. (New))

I C LIQUIDATING CORP (CA)
Merged into Pacific Standard Life Co. (AZ) 12/23/1970
Each share Common $4 par exchanged for (2.5) shares Common $1 par
Pacific Standard Life Co. (AZ) reincorporated in Delaware 05/13/1974 which merged into Southmark Corp. 08/30/1983

I C T CORP. (TX)
Name changed to Unitex Industries, Inc. 7/20/57
Unitex Industries, Inc. acquired by Texstar Corp. 12/19/66
(See Texstar Corp.)

I C T DISCOUNT CORP (TX)
Name changed to I C T Corp. 7/15/52
I C T Corp. name changed to Unitex Industries, Inc. 7/20/57 which was acquired by Texstar Corp. 12/19/66
(See Texstar Corp.)

I C W INDS INC (DE)
Charter cancelled and declared inoperative and void for non-payment of taxes 03/01/1991

I-CARAUCTION COM INC (DE)
Each share old Common $0.0001 par exchanged for (0.02) share new Common $0.0001 par 10/10/2001
SEC revoked common stock registration 06/10/2009

I.D. INVESTMENTS INC. (ON)
Recapitalized as BioLink Corp. 03/12/1997
Each share Common no par exchanged for (0.25) share Common no par
BioLink Corp. recapitalized as First Empire Entertainment.com Inc. 03/31/2000 which recapitalized as First Empire Corp. 08/14/2003 which reorganized as Noble House Entertainment Inc. (ON) 11/01/2004 which reincorporated in Canada as LiveReel Media Corp. 12/01/2006

I D INTERNET DIRECT LTD (BC)
Merged into Look Communications Inc. 10/31/1999
Each share Common no par exchanged for (1) share Class A Limited Vtg. no par
Look Communications Inc. name changed to ONEnergy Inc. 07/12/2013

I D PACKING INC (IA)
Liquidation completed
Each share Common $1 par exchanged for initial distribution of $6.80 cash 12/03/1971
Each share Common $1 par received second distribution of $1.20 cash 01/06/1972
Each share Common $1 par received third and final distribution of $0.77 cash 08/25/1972

I D PRECISION COMPONENTS CORP (NY)
Adjudicated bankrupt 07/09/1973
Stockholders' equity unlikely

I-D SYSTEMS, INC. (NY)
Merged into R.D. Products, Inc. 6/15/72
Each share Common 2-1/2¢ par exchanged for (4/9) share Common 5¢ par
R.D. Products, Inc. name changed to Griffin Technology Inc. 6/29/82
(See Griffin Technology Inc.)

I.E.B. CORP. (IL)
Liquidation completed
Each share Common $10 par stamped to indicate initial distribution of $75 cash 01/04/1968
Each share Stamped Common $10 par stamped to indicate second distribution of $10 cash 07/19/1968
Each share Stamped Common $10 par exchanged for third distribution of $5 cash 10/25/1968
Each share Stamped Common $10 par received fourth and final distribution of $5.3812142 cash 10/25/1968

I E L S INC (NV)
Name changed to Miracom Corp. 09/29/1998
Miracom Corp. name changed to Parts.com, Inc. 01/05/2000
(See Parts.com, Inc.)

I E S TECHNOLOGIES CORP (BC)
Delisted from Vancouver Stock Exchange 03/04/1992

I-FLOW CORP (DE)
Reincorporated 07/30/2001
Each share old Common no par exchanged for (0.2) share new Common no par 05/11/1992
State of incorporation changed from (CA) to (DE) and new Common no par changed to $0.001 par 07/30/2001
Merged into Kimberly-Clark Corp. 11/24/2009
Each share Common $0.001 par exchanged for $12.65 cash

I G E INC (MA)
Each share old Common 1¢ par exchanged for (0.1) share new Common 1¢ par 11/01/1977
Recapitalized as Life Partners Holdings Inc. (MA) 02/09/2000
Each share new Common 1¢ par exchanged for (0.5) share Common 1¢ par
Life Partners Holdings Inc. (MA) reincorporated in Texas 02/19/2003
(See Life Partners Holdings Inc.)

I.H.L. CORP. (DE)
Liquidated 10/1/59

I H V CORP (CA)
Name changed to California Beach Restaurants, Inc. 07/10/1990

I I B LTD (DE)
Each share Common 1¢ par exchanged for (0.1) share Common 10¢ par 1/2/79
Recapitalized as Sparkling Water of Austria, Inc. 12/22/80
Each share Common 10¢ par exchanged for (0.25) share Common 1¢ par
Sparkling Water of Austria, Inc. recapitalized as Dairy Whey Foods Corp. 7/27/83 which name changed to Novar International Corp. 6/8/84
(See Novar International Corp.)

I I INC (AZ)
Name changed to Unico, Inc. 12/04/1979

I I S INTELLIGENT INFORMATION SYS LTD (ISRAEL)
Ordinary IS 1 par split (3) for (1) by issuance of (2) additional shares 02/19/1993
Each share Ordinary IS 1 par exchanged for (0.33333333) share Ordinary NIS 0.003 par 05/08/1998
Company ceased operations 12/24/2008
Stockholders' equity unlikely

I IN THE SKY INC (NV)
Name changed to Asia Equity Exchange Group, Inc. 08/11/2015

I-INCUBATOR COM INC (FL)
Each share old Common $0.0001 par received distribution of (0.4111) share i-Aerobids.com, Inc. Common $0.0001 par payable 02/23/2001 to holders of record 02/13/2001 Ex date - 02/26/2001
Each share old Common $0.0001 par received distribution of (0.4111) share i-AntiqueAuction.com, Inc. Common $0.0001 par payable 02/23/2001 to holders of record 02/13/2001 Ex date - 02/26/2001
Each share old Common $0.0001 par received distribution of (0.4111) share i-CarAuction.com, Inc. Common $0.0001 par payable 02/23/2001 to holders of record 02/13/2001 Ex date - 02/26/2001
Each share old Common $0.0001 par received distribution of (0.1439) share i-RealtyAuction.com, Inc. Common $0.0001 par payable 02/23/2001 to holders of record 02/13/2001 Ex date - 02/26/2001
Each share old Common $0.0001 par received distributon of (0.781) share I-Teleco.com, Inc. Common $0.0001 par payable 02/23/2001 to holders of record 02/13/2001 Ex date - 02/26/2001
Each share old Common $0.0001 par received distribution of (0.062) share WealthHound.com, Inc. Common $0.0001 par payable 02/23/2001 to holders of record 02/13/2001 Ex date - 02/26/2001
Each share old Common $0.0001 par exchanged for (0.01728907) share new Common $0.0001 par 04/01/2002
Proclaimed dissolved for failure to file reports and pay fees 09/26/2008

I.L.I. CORP. (NY)
Completely liquidated 9/19/66
Each share Common no par exchanged for first and final distribution of $36 cash

I-LEVEL MEDIA GROUP INC (NV)
Each share old Common $0.001 par exchanged for (0.01428571) share new Common $0.001 par 07/07/2011
Name changed to Telupay International Inc. 10/22/2013

I-LINK INC (FL)
Recapitalized as Acceris Communications Inc. 11/30/2003
Each share Common $0.007 par exchanged for (0.05) share Common 1¢ par
Acceris Communications Inc. name changed to C2 Global Technologies Inc. 08/15/2005 which name changed to Counsel RB Capital Inc. 02/04/2011 which name changed to Heritage Global Inc. 08/29/2013

I LOVE PIZZA INC (NV)
Recapitalized as Revenge Marine, Inc. 02/19/1998
Each share Common $0.001 par exchanged for (0.1) share Common $0.001 par
Revenge Marine, Inc. name changed to eTravelServe.com, Inc. 01/28/2000
(See eTravelServe.com, Inc.)

I LOVE YOGURT CORP (UT)
Each share old Common $0.001 par received distribution of $0.0236 cash 04/15/1992
Each share old Common $0.001 par exchanged for (0.1) share new Common $0.001 par 04/20/1992
Name changed to Chelsea Street Financial Holding Corp. 06/26/1992
Chelsea Street Financial Holding Corp. name changed to Wexford Technology Inc. 12/03/1993 which name changed to sureBET Casinos, Inc. 06/24/1999
(See sureBET Casinos, Inc.)

I M A FD INC (OH)
Completely liquidated 03/21/1974
Each share Common no par exchanged for first and final distrubution of $3.89 cash

I M P A C T MINERALS LTD (BC)
Recapitalized as IMPACT Minerals International Inc. 8/20/99
Each share Common no par

FINANCIAL INFORMATION, INC.

exchanged for (0.2) share Common no par
IMPACT Minerals International Inc. name changed to IMPACT Silver Corp. 8/18/2005

I M P INDL MINERAL PK MNG CORP (BC)
Name changed to Crystal Graphite Corp. 11/06/2000
(See Crystal Graphite Corp.)

I M S INTL INC (DE)
Common 1¢ par split (2) for (1) by issuance of (1) additional share 03/29/1985
Common 1¢ par split (2) for (1) by issuance of (1) additional share 03/28/1986
Stock Dividend - 100% 03/27/1980
Merged into Dun & Bradstreet Corp. 05/26/1988
Each share Common 1¢ par exchanged for (0.801) share Common $1 par
Dun & Bradstreet Corp. name changed to R.H. Donnelley Corp. 07/01/1998
(See R.H. Donnelley Corp.)

I M TECHNOLOGIES INC (BC)
Cease trade order effective 02/12/1999
Stockholders' equity unlikely

I MANY INC (DE)
Issue Information - 7,500,000 shares COM offered at $9 per share on 07/13/2000
Merged into LLR Equity Partners III, L.P. 06/25/2009
Each share Common $0.0001 par exchanged for $0.61472 cash

I-MINERALS INC (CANADA)
Name changed to I-Minerals Inc. 12/15/2011

I/NET INC (DE)
Recapitalized as Ardmore Holding Corp. 06/11/2007
Each share Common $0.001 par exchanged for (0.005) share Common $0.001 par
Ardmore Holding Corp. name changed to Yayi International Inc. 09/25/2008
(See Yayi International Inc.)

I O A DATA CORP (NY)
Merged into International Office Appliances, Inc. 02/11/1980
Each share Common 10¢ par exchanged for $2.25 cash

I O DEVICES INC (DE)
Recapitalized as Medcomp Technologies, Inc. 04/27/1983
Each share Common 1¢ par exchanged for (0.004) share Common 1¢ par

I O S LTD (CANADA)
In process of liquidation
Each share Common U.S. 25¢ par exchanged for initial distribution of $0.075 cash 9/24/85
Note: Details on subsequent distributions, if any, are not available

I O SVCS INC (CO)
Recapitalized as Sabre Industries, Inc. 05/05/1988
Each share Common $0.0001 par exchanged for (0.2) share Common $0.0001 par
(See Sabre Industries, Inc.)

I O SYS INC (MA)
Out of business and liquidated 12/31/1972
No stockholders' equity

I-ONE NET INTL LTD (SINGAPORE)
Name changed to Xpress Holdings Ltd. 3/1/2002

I Q BIOMETRIX INC (DE)
Each share old Common no par exchanged for (0.25) share new Common no par 11/29/2004

Name changed to Wherify Wireless, Inc. 08/05/2005
(See Wherify Wireless, Inc.)

I R ASSOC INC (DE)
Recapitalized as Epcom, Inc. 06/25/1980
Each share Common 10¢ par exchanged for (1/3) share Common 10¢ par
(See Epcom, Inc.)

I.R.E. FLORIDA INCOME PARTNERS, LTD. (FL)
Charter revoked 11/02/1984

I.R.E. REAL ESTATE PARTNERS LTD. (FL)
Reorganized as I.R.E. Series III, Inc. 2/1/78
Each Unit of Ltd. Partnership exchanged for (50) shares Preferred Ser. A $1 par and (50) shares Common $1 par
I.R.E. Series III, Inc. merged into I.R.E. Financial Corp. in August 1980 which name changed to BankAtlantic Financial Corp. 1/4/88 which name changed to BFC Financial Corp. 3/27/92

I R E FINL CORP (FL)
Each share Conv. Preferred Ser. A $1 par exchanged for (1) share old Common 1¢ par 10/23/1981
Each share old Common 1¢ par exchanged for (0.33333333) share new Common 1¢ par 03/04/1986
Name changed to BankAtlantic Financial Corp. 01/04/1988
BankAtlantic Financial Corp. name changed to BFC Financial Corp. 03/27/1992 which name changed to BBX Capital Corp. (New) 02/03/2017

I R E INVS CORP (NY)
Dissolved by proclamation 12/7/76

I R E REAL ESTATE FD LTD SER 25 LP (FL)
Voluntarily dissolved 03/01/1991
Details not available

I-REALTYAUCTION COM INC (DE)
Recapitalized as Genesis Realty Group, Inc. 09/06/2001
Each share Common $0.0001 par exchanged for (0.5) share Common $0.0001 par
Genesis Realty Group, Inc. recapitalized as Genesis Group Holdings, Inc. 09/16/2008 which recapitalized as InterCloud Systems, Inc. 01/14/2013

I-ROCK INDS INC (DE)
Name changed to IR Operating Corp. 04/26/1999
IR Operating Corp. name changed to Digi Link Technologies, Inc. 02/12/2001
(See Digi Link Technologies, Inc.)

I S B C CORP (DE)
Name changed to Coral Companies, Inc. (DE) 6/27/88
Coral Companies, Inc. (DE) reorganized in Nevada as CNH Holdings Co. 5/31/96 which name changed to Cistera Networks, Inc. 9/27/2005

I S I S INS CO (IL)
Liquidation completed
Each share Common $1 par exchanged for initial distribution of $3.59 cash 11/01/1977
Each share Common $1 par received second and final distribution of $0.05 cash 08/01/1978

I S INDS LTD (DE)
Charter cancelled and declared inoperative and void for non-payment of taxes 3/1/75

I S M CORP (MA)
Completely liquidated 11/2/73
Each share Common 5¢ par exchanged for first and final distribution of (0.097427) share Minnesota Mining & Manufacturing Co. Common no par
Minnesota Mining & Manufacturing Co. name changed to 3M Co. 4/8/2002

I-SECTOR CORP (DE)
Name changed to INX Inc. 01/03/2006
(See INX Inc.)

I SIM INTL INC (DE)
Name changed back to Life Medical Technologies Inc. 01/26/2000
Life Medical Technologies Inc. name changed to iBonZai.com, Inc. 05/12/2000 which name changed to IbonZi.com, Inc. (DE) 01/10/2002 which reorganized in Nevada as China Global Development, Inc. 01/23/2002 which recapitalized as Arizona Ventures, Inc. 11/18/2002 which name changed to Fox River Holdings, Inc. 10/13/2003 which name changed to Zynex Medical Holdings, Inc. 12/23/2003 which name changed to Zynex, Inc. 07/08/2008

I-STAT CORP (DE)
Merged into Abbott Laboratories 1/29/2004
Each share Common 15¢ par exchanged for $15.35 cash

I-STORM INC (NV)
SEC revoked common stock registration 06/01/2009

I.T.C. CORP.
Liquidation completed in 1949

I T C MICROCOMPONENTS INC (BC)
Name changed to Intrinsyc Software Inc. (BC) 06/16/1997
Intrinsyc Software Inc. (BC) reincorporated in Canada as Intrinsyc Software International, Inc. 05/01/2003 which recapitalized as Intrinsyc Technologies Corp. 06/20/2014

I T D INTL TECHNOLOGY DEV INC (CANADA)
Certificate of incorporation cancelled and dissolved 10/19/1999

I T E CIRCUIT BREAKER CO (PA)
Each share Common $50 par exchanged for (5) shares Common $10 par in 1947
Each share Common $10 par exchanged for (2) shares Common $5 par in 1953
Common $5 par changed to $3.33-1/3 par and (0.5) additional share issued 5/9/66
Stock Dividend - 10% 12/18/50
Merged into I-T-E Imperial Corp. 4/30/68
Each share 4.60% Preferred $50 par exchanged for (1) share 4.60% Preferred $50 par
Each share Common $3.33-1/3 par exchanged for (2) shares Common $1 par
(See I-T-E Imperial Corp.)

I T E IMPERIAL CORP (DE)
4.60% Preferred $50 par called for redemption 11/3/75
Merged into Gould Inc. 4/30/76
Each share Common $1 par exchanged for (0.83) share Common $4 par
(See Gould Inc.)

I T FINL (CA)
Name changed to First Investors Bancorp 12/31/1982

I T I ELECTRS INC (NJ)
Name changed to Bala Cynwyd Corp. 04/21/1983
(See Bala Cynwyd Corp.)

I T L INDS LTD (ON)
Common no par split (3) for (1) by issuance of (2) additional shares 11/14/1967

Each share 6.5% Preference Ser. A $25 par exchanged for (1) share 2nd Preference Ser. 1 no par 03/04/1985
Stock Dividend - In Common to holders of 2nd Preference Ser. 1 - 300% 03/06/1985
$0.755 Conv. 1st Preference 1 no par reclassified as Non-Cum. Conv. 1st Preference no par 04/13/1988
2nd Preference Ser. 1 no par reclassified as Non-Cum. Conv. 2nd Preference Ser. I no par 04/13/1988
Name changed to Ventra Group Inc. 05/04/1989
(See Ventra Group Inc.)

I T TECHNOLOGY INC (DE)
Each (5) shares old Common $0.0002 par exchanged for (1) share new Common $0.0002 par 11/06/2000
Name changed to Avenue Group, Inc. 01/31/2003
(See Avenue Group, Inc.)

I-TECH HLDGS GROUP INC (CO)
Name changed to Stockgroup.com Holdings, Inc. 05/18/1999
Stockgroup.com Holdings, Inc. name changed to Stockgroup Information Systems, Inc. 09/20/2001 which name changed to Stockhouse, Inc. 07/21/2008 which name changed to Invictus Financial Inc. 04/01/2010

I-TELECO COM INC (FL)
Name changed to Skyway Communications Holding Corp. 4/17/2003
(See Skyway Communications Holding Corp.)

I-TRACK INC (NV)
Each share old Common $0.001 par exchanged for (0.05) share new Common $0.001 par 11/30/2002
Name changed to China Wireless Communications Inc. 03/31/2003
China Wireless Communications Inc. recapitalized as Media Exchange Group, Inc. 05/06/2011 which name changed to Intellicell Biosciences, Inc. 07/07/2011
(See Intellicell Biosciences, Inc.)

I-TRANSACTION NET INC (NJ)
Each share old Common $0.001 par exchanged for (0.02) share new Common $0.001 par 10/11/2001
Name changed to Global Alliance Networks 10/11/2005
(See Global Alliance Networks Inc.)

I-TRAX INC (DE)
Reorganized 02/05/2001
Reorganized from I-Trax.com Inc. to I-Trax, Inc. 02/05/2001
Each share old Common $0.001 par exchanged for (0.2) share new Common $0.001 par 01/03/2003
Merged into Walgreen Co. 05/01/2008
Each share Common $0.001 par exchanged for $5.40 cash

I U INDLS INC (NJ)
Merged into IUI Inc. 12/01/1970
Each share Common $1 par exchanged for $10 cash

I-WEB MEDIA INC (DE)
Name changed to Heartland Bridge Capital, Inc. 12/29/2010
Heartland Bridge Capital, Inc. name changed to InterCore Energy, Inc. 05/16/2012 which recapitalized as InterCore, Inc. 12/31/2013

I X L MINING CO. (PHILIPPINES)
Each share P10 par exchanged for (100) shares 10 Centavos par 00/00/1935
Merged into Atlas Consolidated Mining & Development Corp. 00/00/1953
Each share Ordinary P0.10 par exchanged for (0.825) share Capital Stock P0.10 par

IA CLARINGTON ASTON HILL TACTICAL YIELD FD (ON)
Combined Units separated 04/30/2010
Under plan of merger each Trust Unit automatically became IA Clarington Tactical Income Fund Ser. X Units on a net asset basis 04/30/2012

IA CORP I (DE)
Issue Information - 2,525,000 shares COM offered at $6 per share on 11/08/1996
Name changed to Alysis Technologies Inc. 9/13/99
(See Alysis Technologies Inc.)

IA HLDGS CORP (PA)
Acquired by IA Construction Corp. 6/30/86
Details not available

IAA TR GROWTH FD INC (MD)
Name changed to COUNTRY Growth Fund, Inc. (MD) 09/28/1992
COUNTRY Growth Fund, Inc. (MD) reincorporated in Delaware as COUNTRY Mutual Funds Trust 11/01/2001

IAA TR TAX EXEMPT BD FD INC (MD)
Name changed to COUNTRY Tax-Exempt Bond Fund, Inc. (MD) 09/25/2000
COUNTRY Tax-Exempt Bond Fund, Inc. (MD) reincorporated in Delaware as COUNTRY Mutual Funds Trust 11/01/2001

IAC / INTERACTIVECORP (DE)
Reorganized 08/09/2005
Each share Conv. Preferred Ser. A 1¢ par exchanged for $50 cash
Conv. Preferred Ser. B 1¢ par called for redemption at $27.77 on 08/11/2008
(Additional Information in Active)

IAC CAP TR (DE)
Issue Information - 6,000,000 TR ORIG PFD SECS SER A 8-1/4% offered at $25 per share on 01/14/1998
8-1/4% Trust Originated Preferred Securities called for redemption at $25 plus $0.515625 accrued dividends on 12/31/2002

IAC COMPUTER SYS CORP (NY)
Name changed to Players Group Companies, Inc. 11/20/72
(See Players Group Companies, Inc.)

IAC INC (NV)
Each share old Common $0.001 par exchanged for (0.25) share new Common $0.001 par 08/14/1998
Name changed to Eagle Capital International, Ltd. 11/05/1998
Eagle Capital International, Ltd. name changed to Eagle Building Technologies, Inc. 05/14/2001
(See Eagle Building Technologies, Inc.)

IAC LTD (CANADA)
Name changed to Continental Bank of Canada (Toronto, ON) 11/09/1981
Continental Bank of Canada (Toronto, ON) name changed to CBOC Continental Inc. 10/22/1996 which reorganized as Coastal Group Inc. 04/17/2001 which merged into Continental (CBOC) Corp. 08/30/2002 which name changed to Stonington Capital Corp. 06/22/2004 which merged into Pyxis Capital Inc. 02/27/2006
(See Pyxis Capital Inc.)

IAE HONG KONG EQUITIES INC (AB)
Struck off register and declared dissolved for failure to file returns 05/02/2002

IAF BIOCHEM INTL INC (QC)
Common no par split (2) for (1) by issuance of (1) additional share 06/04/1990
Common no par split (2) for (1) by issuance of (1) additional share 11/04/1991
Name changed to BioChem Pharma Inc. 02/19/1992
BioChem Pharma Inc. merged into Shire Pharmaceuticals Group PLC 05/11/2001 which name changed to Shire PLC (England & Wales) 11/25/2005 which reincorporated in Channel Islands as Shire Ltd. 05/23/2008 which name changed to Shire PLC 10/01/2008

IAI APOLLO FD INC (MN)
Reorganized as IAI Investment Funds VIII, Inc. 06/25/1993
Details not available

IAI BD FD INC (MN)
Reorganized as IAI Investment Funds I, Inc. 06/25/1993
Details not available

IAI INTL FD INC (MN)
Reorganized as IAI Investment Funds III, Inc. 07/26/1993
Details not available

IAI REGL FD INC (MN)
Reorganized as IAI Investment Funds IV, Inc. 07/03/1992
Details not available

IAI RESV FD INC (MN)
Reorganized as IAI Investment Funds V, Inc. 07/03/1992
Details not available

IAI STK FD INC (MN)
Reorganized as IAI Investment Funds VII, Inc. 06/25/1993
Details not available

IALTA INDS LTD (BC)
Cease trade order effective 08/02/2007
Stockholders' equity unlikely

IAMG HLDGS INC (NV)
Each share old Common $0.001 par exchanged for (0.02) share new Common $0.001 par 06/06/2001
Name changed to Curv Entertainment Group, Inc. 11/26/2007
Curv Entertainment Group, Inc. name changed to SuperBox, Inc. 09/01/2011

IAMGOLD INTL AFRICAN MNG GOLD CORP (CANADA)
Name changed to IAMGOLD Corp. 06/27/1997

IANETT INTL SYS LTD (BC)
Name changed to Data Fortress Systems Group Ltd. 09/03/2002
(See Data Fortress Systems Group Ltd.)

IAO KUN GROUP HLDG CO LTD (CAYMAN ISLANDS)
Name changed to LiNiu Technology Group 04/27/2017

IAS COMMUNICATIONS INC (OR)
Name changed to IAS Energy, Inc. 06/25/2007

IASIAWORKS INC (DE)
Issue Information - 9,000,000 shares COM offered at $13 per share on 08/08/2000
Voluntarily dissolved 03/07/2002
No stockholders' equity

IAT AIR CARGO FAC INCOME FD (BC)
Each Installment Receipt plus final payment of $4 cash received (1) Trust Unit prior to 06/12/1998
Merged into Huntingdon Real Estate Investment Trust (MB) 01/01/2010
Each Trust Unit exchanged for (9.75) Trust Units
Note: Unqualified U.S. holders received cash from the sale of Units
Huntingdon Real Estate Investment Trust (MB) reorganized as Huntingdon Capital Corp. (BC) 01/05/2012
(See Huntingdon Capital Corp.)

IAT MULTIMEDIA INC (DE)
Issue Information - 3,350,000 shares COM offered at $6 per share on 03/26/1997
Name changed to Spigadoro, Inc. 01/12/2000
(See Spigadoro, Inc.)

IAT RES CORP (DE)
Each share 8.50% Preferred Ser. A $0.001 par received distribution of (0.04823) share Common $0.001 par payable 10/26/1999 to holders of record 10/04/1999
Each share 8.50% Preferred Ser. A $0.001 par received distribution of (0.04823) share Common $0.001 par payable 12/17/1999 to holders of record 12/02/1999
Stock Dividend - 4.823% payable 12/17/1999 to holders of record 12/02/1999
Name changed to NetCurrents, Inc. 01/04/2000
NetCurrents, Inc. reorganized as NetCurrents Information Services, Inc. 08/30/2001
(See NetCurrents Information Services, Inc.)

IATCO INDS INC (ON)
Name changed to AirBoss of America Corp. 05/02/1994

IATRIC CORP (AZ)
Name changed to FCS Industries, Inc. 11/03/1981
FCS Industries, Inc. name changed to FCS Laboratories, Inc. 10/24/1985
(See FCS Laboratories, Inc.)

IATROS HEALTH NETWORK INC (DE)
Name changed to Phoenix Healthcare Corp. 5/6/99
Phoenix Healthcare Corp. name changed to Phoenix Group Corp. 10/10/2000 which name changed to Lighting Science Corp. 12/23/2004

IB & T CORP (ID)
Merged into KeyCorp (NY) 10/3/88
For holdings of (167) shares or fewer each share Common $5 par exchanged for $22.816 cash
For holdings of (168) shares or more each share Common $5 par exchanged for (0.5953) share Common $5 par and $10.267 cash
KeyCorp (NY) merged into KeyCorp (New) (OH) 3/1/94

IBA INC (WI)
Merged into BT of Milwaukee, Ltd. 4/29/88
Each share Common 30¢ par exchanged for $0.075 cash

IBA LTD (BELIZE)
Reorganized under the laws of Wyoming as Avalon Partners Holdings, Inc. 02/07/2006
Each share Ordinary $1 par exchanged for (80) shares Common $1 par
Avalon Partners Holdings, Inc. name changed to Vision Airships, Inc. 10/02/2006

IBAC CORP (DE)
Each share old Common $0.001 par exchanged for (0.0125) share new Common $0.001 par 03/10/2006
Stock Dividends - 10% payable 02/01/2005 to holders of record 01/07/2005 Ex date - 01/05/2005; 15% payable 05/15/2005 to holders of record 05/01/2005 Ex date - 04/27/2005; 15% payable 03/31/2006 to holders of record 03/24/2006 Ex date - 03/22/2006; 25% payable 12/15/2006 to holders of record 12/01/2006 Ex date - 12/18/2006
Recapitalized as Three Sixty, Inc. 05/17/2007
Each share new Common $0.001 par exchanged for (0.001) share Common $0.001 par
Three Sixty, Inc. name changed to IAHL Corp. 11/30/2007

IBAH INC (DE)
Merged into Omnicare, Inc. 06/29/1998
Each share Common 1¢ par exchanged for (0.1638) share Common $1 par
(See Omnicare, Inc.)

IBASIS INC (DE)
Each share old Common $0.001 par exchanged for (1/3) share new Common $0.001 par 05/03/2006
Merged into Koninklijke KPN N.V. 12/31/2009
Each share new Common $0.001 par exchanged for $3 cash

IBC / INTEGRATED BUSINESS COMPUTERS INC (WA)
Involuntarily dissolved 01/31/2001

IBC CAP FIN II (DE)
8.25% Trust Preferred Securities called for redemption at $25 on 10/11/2013

IBC INDS INC (DE)
Charter cancelled and declared inoperative and void for non-payment of taxes 3/1/77

IBC INDS INC (NY)
Charter cancelled and proclaimed dissolved for failure to pay taxes 9/26/79

IBEAM BROADCASTING CORP (DE)
Issue Information - 11,000,000 shares COM offered at $10 per share on 05/17/2000
Each share old Common $0.0001 par exchanged for (0.1) share new Common $0.0001 par 9/18/2001
Plan of reorganization under Chapter 11 Federal Bankruptcy Code effective 4/1/2002
No stockholders' equity

IBERDROLA RENOVABLES S A (SPAIN)
ADR agreement terminated 05/23/2011
Each Sponsored ADR for Ordinary exchanged for $21.948146 cash

IBERDROLA RENOVABLES S A UNIPERSONAL (SPAIN)
Recapitalized as Iberdrola Renovables, S.A. 06/04/2009
Each Unsponsored ADR for Ordinary exchanged for (0.4) Sponsored ADR for Ordinary
(See Iberdrola Renovables, S.A.)

IBERIA INTL BRANDS INC (NY)
Charter cancelled and proclaimed dissolved for failure to pay taxes 9/30/81

IBERIA LINEAS AEREAS DE ESPANA SA (SPAIN)
Merged into International Consolidated Airlines Group S.A. 01/21/2011
Each ADR for Common exchanged for (1.0205) Sponsored ADR's for Ordinary

IBERIAN MINERALS CORP. (SWITZERLAND)
Acquired by Trafigura Beheer B.V. 02/06/2013
Each share Common CHF 0.05 par exchanged for CAD$1.10 cash

IBERIAN MINERALS CORP (CANADA)
Reincorporated under the laws of Switzerland and Common no par changed to CHF 0.05 par 06/15/2009
(See Iberian Minerals Corp. (Switzerland))

IBERIAN MINERALS LTD (AB)
Each share Common no par received distribution of (0.09393) share EnviroLeach Technologies Inc.

Common no par payable 03/28/2017 to holders of record 03/21/2017
Name changed to Mineworx Technologies Ltd. 06/06/2017

IBERO-AMERICA FD INC (MD)
Completely liquidated
Each share Common 1¢ par received first and final distribution of $5.6969 cash payable 09/30/2011 to holders of record 08/31/2011
Note: Certificates were not required to be surrendered and are without value

IBEX ADVANCED MTG TECHNOLOGY INC (FL)
Administratively dissolved 09/25/2015

IBEX MINERALS INC (WA)
Each share old Common no par exchanged for (3) shares new Common no par 10/15/1978
Charter cancelled and proclaimed dissolved for failure to file annual reports and pay fees 05/10/1985

IBEX OIL LTD (CANADA)
Recapitalized as Dalier Resources Ltd. 07/02/1982
Each share Common no par exchanged for (0.33333333) share Common par
Dalier Resources Ltd. name changed to Vescan Equities Inc. 12/15/1999 which recapitalized as Inouye Technologies (Canada) Inc. 01/26/2000
(See Inouye Technologies (Canada) Inc.)

IBEX RES CORP (NV)
Name changed to Source Gold Corp. 10/14/2009
Source Gold Corp. recapitalized as Golden Matrix Group, Inc. 04/07/2016

IBEX TECHNOLOGIES INC (CANADA)
Subordinated Class A no par reclassified as Common no par 02/26/1996
Multiple Class B no par reclassified as Common no par 02/26/1996
(Additional Information in Active)

IBF 1 CORP (CANADA)
Name changed to Gatorz Inc. 07/13/2007
Gatorz Inc. name changed to Pacific Vector Holdings Inc. 06/14/2013
(See Pacific Vector Holdings Inc.)

IBI INCOME FD (ON)
Under plan of reorganization each Trust Unit no par automatically became (1) share IBI Group Inc. (Canada) Common no par 01/04/2011

IBIOPHARMA INC (DE)
Name changed to iBio, Inc. 09/24/2010

IBIS TECHNOLOGY CORP (MA)
Issue Information - 1,200,000 shares COM offered at $7 per share on 03/17/1997
Liquidation completed
Each share Common $0.008 par received initial distribution of $0.07 cash payable 02/25/2009 to holders of record 02/23/2009 Ex date - 02/26/2009
Each share Common $0.008 par received second and final distribution of $0.02 cash payable 05/01/2012 to holders of record 02/23/2009
Note: Certificates were not required to be surrendered and are without value

IBIS VENTURES INC (BC)
Name changed to Tranzcom Security Networks Inc. 12/12/2001
Tranzcom Security Networks Inc. name changed to Tranzcom China Security Networks Inc. 06/25/2004
which recapitalized as Pacific Link Mining Corp. 09/12/2007

IBISES INTL INC (NV)
Recapitalized as Biomag Corp. 3/28/2006
Each share Common $0.001 par exchanged for (0.004) share Common $0.001 par
Biomag Corp. name changed to Biomagnetics Diagnostics Corp. 12/18/2006

IBIZ TECHNOLOGY CORP (FL)
Each share old Common $0.001 par exchanged for (0.1) share new Common $0.001 par 10/03/2002
SEC revoked common stock registration 07/11/2006

IBL BANCORP INC (LA)
Merged into Shay Investment Services, Inc. 3/3/2003
Each share Common 1¢ par exchanged for $24 cash

IBL EQUITIES LTD (BC)
Recapitalized as Serena Resources Ltd. 01/03/1996
Each share Common no par exchanged for (0.2) share Common no par
Serena Resources Ltd. recapitalized as Consolidated Serena Resources Ltd. 05/17/2001 which name changed to Capstone Gold Corp. 03/07/2003 which name changed to Capstone Mining Corp. 02/13/2006

IBONZI COM INC (DE)
Name changed 01/10/2002
Name changed from iBonZai.com, Inc. to IbonZi.com, Inc. 01/10/2002
Reorganized under the laws of Nevada as China Global Development, Inc. 01/23/2002
Each share Common no par exchanged for (0.04) share Common $0.001 par
China Global Development, Inc. recapitalized as Arizona Ventures, Inc. 11/18/2002 which name changed to Fox River Holdings, Inc. 10/13/2003 which name changed to Zynex Medical Holdings, Inc. 12/23/2003 which name changed to Zynex, Inc. 07/08/2008

IBOS INC (DE)
Name changed to Liberty Gold Corp. 05/19/2011
(See Liberty Gold Corp.)

IBP INC (DE)
Common 5¢ par split (2) for (1) by issuance of (1) additional share payable 01/19/1996 to holders of record 12/28/1995
Merged into Tyson Foods, Inc. 09/28/2001
Each share Common 50¢ par exchanged for (2.381) shares Common 10¢ par

IBS AUTO IMPORTERS INC (DE)
Name changed to Unicap International Inc. 5/20/80
(See Unicap International Inc.)

IBS COMPUTER CORP (DE)
Charter cancelled and declared inoperative and void for non-payment of taxes 03/01/1991

IBS FINL CORP (NJ)
Stock Dividends - 10% payable 03/15/1996 to holders of record 02/22/1996; 15% payable 05/06/1997 to holders of record 04/21/1997
Merged into HUBCO, Inc. 08/14/1998
Each share Common 1¢ par exchanged for (0.534) share Common no par
HUBCO, Inc. name changed to Hudson United Bancorp 04/21/1999 which merged into TD Banknorth Inc. 01/31/2006
(See TD Banknorth Inc.)

IBS GROUP HLDG LTD (RUSSIA)
Scheme of arrangement effective 11/07/2014
Each Sponsored Reg. S GDR for Ordinary exchanged for (0.95) share Luxoft Holding, Inc. Class A Ordinary no par

IBS INTERACTIVE INC (DE)
Issue Information - 1,200,000 shares COM offered at $6 per share on 05/14/1998
Name changed to Digital Fusion, Inc. 11/15/2001
Digital Fusion, Inc. merged into Kratos Defense & Security Solutions, Inc. 12/24/2008

IBS TECHNOLOGIES LTD (BC)
Each share old Common no par exchanged for (0.125) share new Common no par 09/04/1987
Struck off register and declared dissolved for failure to file returns 02/26/1993

IBSEN COBALT SILVER MINES LTD (ON)
Merged into Mayfair Resources & Developments Ltd. 04/12/1978
Each share Capital Stock $1 par exchanged for (0.04) share Common no par
(See Mayfair Resources & Developments Ltd.)

IBSTONE PETROLEUMS, LTD. (CANADA)
Recapitalized as Swiss Oils of Canada (1959) Ltd. on a (1) for (10) basis 00/00/1959

IBT BANCORP INC (MI)
Common $6 par changed to no par 06/21/1999
Common no par split (3.3) for (1) by issuance of (2.3) additional shares payable 02/18/2000 to holders of record 01/03/2000
Stock Dividends - 10% payable 03/02/1998 to holders of record 02/02/1998; 10% payable 02/28/2002 to holders of record 01/01/2002; 10% payable 02/19/2004 to holders of record 01/01/2004 Ex date - 01/29/2004; 10% payable 02/15/2006 to holders of record 01/03/2006 Ex date - 03/02/2006; 10% payable 02/29/2008 to holders of record 01/02/2008 Ex date - 03/11/2008
Name changed to Isabella Bank Corp. 05/14/2008

IBT BANCORP INC (PA)
Common $1.25 par split (3) for (1) by issuance of (2) additional shares payable 01/31/1999 to holders of record 01/06/1999
Common $1.25 par split (2) for (1) by issuance of (1) additional share payable 11/16/2006 to holders of record 10/27/2006 Ex date - 11/17/2006
Stock Dividend - 5% payable 02/02/1998 to holders of record 01/15/1998
Merged into S&T Bancorp, Inc. 06/09/2008
Each share Common $1.25 par exchanged for either (0.93) share Common $2.50 par, $31 cash or a combination thereof

IB3 NETWORKS INC (NV)
SEC revoked common stock registration 01/17/2013

IBX GROUP INC (FL)
Administratively dissolved 09/14/2007

IC INDS INC (DE)
$6 Conv. 1st Preferred Ser. A no par called for redemption 09/30/1977
Common no par split (2) for (1) by issuance of (1) additional share 06/29/1984
$3.50 Conv. 2nd Preferred Ser. 1 no par called for redemption 03/05/1985
Common no par split (2) for (1) by issuance of (1) additional share 07/01/1986
Name changed to Whitman Corp. (Old) 12/01/1988
Whitman Corp. (Old) name changed to Whitman Corp. (New) 11/30/2000 which name changed to PepsiAmericas, Inc. (DE) 01/24/2001 which merged into PepsiCo, Inc. 02/26/2010

IC PLS INC (DE)
Each share Common $0.0001 par exchanged for (0.1) share old Common $0.00001 par 05/22/2007
Each share old Common $0.00001 par exchanged for (0.03333333) share new Common $0.00001 par 07/07/2010
Name changed to IC Punch Media, Inc. 12/06/2012
IC Punch Media, Inc. recapitalized back as IC Places, Inc. 03/27/2014 which recapitalized as Imagination TV, Inc. 10/20/2014

IC PLS INC (DE)
Recapitalized as Imagination TV, Inc. 10/20/2014
Each share Common $0.00001 par exchanged for (0.00333333) share Common $0.00001 par

IC POTASH CORP (CANADA)
Name changed to Belgravia Capital International Inc. 11/23/2017

IC PUNCH MEDIA INC (DE)
Recapitalized back as IC Places, Inc. 03/27/2014
Each share Common $0.00001 par exchanged for (0.01) share Common $0.00001 par
IC Places, Inc. recapitalized as Imagination TV, Inc. 10/20/2014

ICAGEN INC OLD (DE)
Each share old Common $0.001 par exchanged for (0.125) share new Common $0.001 par 09/22/2010
Acquired by Pfizer Inc. 10/28/2011
Each share new Common $0.001 par exchanged for $6 cash

ICAHN ENTERPRISES L P (DE)
Each 5% Pay-in-Kind Conv. Preferred Unit exchanged for (0.22451258) Depositary Unit 03/31/2010
(Additional Information in Active)

ICAN MINERALS LTD (AB)
Reincorporated 12/02/1992
Place of incorporation changed from (BC) to (AB) 12/02/1992
Recapitalized as Net Resources Inc. 12/17/1998
Each share Common no par exchanged for (0.16666666) share Common no par
Net Resources Inc. name changed to BakBone Software Inc. (AB) 03/13/2000 which reincorporated in Canada 08/11/2003
(See BakBone Software Inc.)

ICAN RES LTD (BC)
Merged into Ican Minerals Ltd. (BC) 12/18/1986
Each share Common no par exchanged for (1) share Common no par
Ican Minerals Ltd. (BC) reincorporated in Alberta 12/02/1992 which recapitalized as Net Resources Inc. 12/17/1998 which name changed to Bakbone Software Inc. (AB) 03/13/2000 which reincorporated in Canada 08/11/2003
(See BakBone Software Inc.)

ICAP P L C (UNITED KINGDOM)
Each share ADR for Ordinary exchanged for (1) NEX Group PLC Sponsored ADR for Ordinary 12/15/2016

ICARBON CORP (NV)
SEC revoked common stock registration 03/30/2011

ICB CORP (LA)
Common $5 par changed to $4 par and (0.25) additional share issued 08/06/1973
Articles of dissolution filed 05/08/1987
Details not available

ICB FINL (CA)
Acquired by Starbuck Bancshares, Inc. 11/01/2012
Each share Common $1 par exchanged for $4.6395 cash

ICBS INTL CORP (FL)
Reorganized under the laws of Delaware as Wah King Invest Corp. 6/9/2005
Each share Common $0.001 par exchanged for (0.1) share Common $0.001 par
Wah King Invest Corp. name changed to Royal Invest International Corp. 3/1/2007

ICC ENTERPRISES, INC. (IL)
Liquidation completed
Each share Common $2 par received initial distribution of $1 cash 12/21/1967
Each share Common $2 par received second distribution of $3.55 principal amount of Mercantile Industries, Inc. 7% Conv. Debentures due 06/01/1979 on 03/16/1968
Each share Common $2 par received third and final distribution of $0.35 cash 08/15/1968
Each share Common $2 par became (1) ICC Enterprises Liquidating Trust Unit of Bene. Int. $2 par 08/15/1968
(See ICC Enterprises Liquidating Trust)

ICC ENTERPRISES LIQUIDATING TRUST (IL)
Completely liquidated 07/08/1971
Each Unit of Bene. Int. $2 par received first and final distribution of $0.36 cash

ICC INTL CANNABIS CORP OLD (BC)
Name changed to ICC Labs Inc. 12/21/2017

ICC TECHNOLOGIES INC (DE)
Each share old Common 1¢ par exchanged for (0.2) share new Common 1¢ par 06/18/1990
Name changed to Rare Medium Group, Inc. 03/16/1999
Rare Medium Group, Inc. name changed to SkyTerra Communications, Inc. 09/26/2003
(See SkyTerra Communications, Inc.)

ICC WORLDWIDE INC (DE)
SEC revoked common stock registration 02/06/2014

ICCI INTEGRATED CR & COMM INC (BC)
Cease trade order effective 10/29/1997
Stockholders' equity unlikely

ICE AGE ENTMT INC (NV)
Recapitalized as Janus International, Inc. 06/19/1998
Each share Common $0.001 par exchanged for (0.2) share Common $0.001 par
Janus International, Inc. recapitalized as Diamond Worldwide, Inc. 08/19/2002 which name changed to FutureVest, Inc. 12/07/2004 which name changed to Barotex Technology Corp. 01/09/2008
(See Barotex Technology Corp.)

ICE BAN AMER INC (NV)
Name changed to Natural Solutions Corp. 11/12/1998
(See Natural Solutions Corp.)

ICE DREAM INTL INC (FL)
Name changed to Wispy International, Inc. 11/3/92
(See Wispy International, Inc.)

ICE DRILLING ENTERPRISES INC (AB)
Delisted from Toronto Venture Stock Exchange 05/31/2001

ICE-FLO CORP.
Bankrupt in 1950

ICE HLDGS INC (DE)
Each share old Common 3¢ par exchanged for (0.004) share new Common 3¢ par 10/15/1996
Each share new Common 3¢ par exchanged again for (0.002) share new Common 3¢ par 03/24/1999
Reorganized under the laws of Nevada as Gaia Resources, Inc. 10/20/2006
Each share new Common 3¢ par exchanged for (1.01) shares Common $0.0001 par
Note: No holder will receive fewer than (100) shares
Gaia Resources, Inc. recapitalized as Ram Gold & Exploration, Inc. 02/08/2008 which name changed to DPollution International Inc. 08/31/2010 which recapitalized as Ecrid, Inc. 10/16/2017

ICE SERVICE CO INC
Acquired by Rubel Coal & Ice Corp. in 1927
Details not available

ICE STA RES LTD (BC)
Struck off register and declared dissolved for failure to file returns 07/23/1993

ICEBERG BRANDS CORP (NV)
Recapitalized as Avalon Gold Corp. 09/08/2003
Each share Common $0.001 par exchanged for (0.25) share Common $0.001 par
Avalon Gold Corp. name changed to Avalon Energy Corp. 03/22/2005 which recapitalized as Shotgun Energy Corp. 09/25/2007 which name changed to Organa Gardens International Inc. 04/07/2009 which recapitalized as Bravo Enterprises Ltd. 06/08/2012

ICEBERG CORP AMER (NV)
Recapitalized as Royal Alliance Entertainment, Inc. 08/07/2006
Each share Common $0.0001 par exchanged for (0.01) share Common $0.0001 par
Royal Alliance Entertainment, Inc. name changed to Infinity Medical Group, Inc. 06/06/2007
(See Infinity Medical Group, Inc.)

ICEBERG MEDIA COM INC (ON)
Merged into Slaight Broadcasting Corp. Ltd. 09/01/2002
Each share Common no par exchanged for $0.05 cash

ICEE USA CORP (DE)
Reincorporated 10/21/1987
State of incorporation changed from (CA) to (DE) 10/21/1987
Acquired by J & J Snack Foods Corp. 05/12/1988
Each (3.27) shares Common $0.025 par exchanged for (1) share Common no par

ICEFLOE TECHNOLOGIES INC (ON)
Filed an assignment in bankruptcy 01/31/2008
Stockholders' equity unlikely

ICELANDIC GOLD CORP (NB)
Recapitalized as PGM Ventures Corp. (NB) 11/03/2000
Each share Common no par exchanged for (0.1) share Common no par
PGM Ventures Corp. (NB) reincorporated in Canada 10/05/2005 which name changed to Iberian Minerals Corp. (Canada) 07/25/2006 which reincorporated in Switzerland 06/15/2009
(See Iberian Minerals Corp. (Switzerland))

ICEWEB INC (DE)
Old Common $0.001 par split (10) for (1) by issuance of (9) additional shares payable 10/12/2004 to holders of record 09/30/2004
Each share old Common $0.001 par exchanged for (0.0125) share new Common $0.001 par 04/27/2005
Recapitalized as UnifiedOnline, Inc. 01/05/2015
Each share new Common $0.001 par exchanged for (0.0025) share Common $0.001 par

ICF CORP (DE)
SEC revoked common stock registration 08/12/2013

ICF KAISER INTL INC (DE)
Name changed 6/29/92
Class A Common 1¢ par reclassified as Common 1¢ par 6/29/92
Name changed from ICF International Inc. to ICF Kaiser International, Inc. 6/26/93
Recapitalized as Kaiser Group International, Inc. 12/27/99
Each (4.77) shares Common 1¢ par exchanged for (1) share Common 1¢ par
Kaiser Group International, Inc. reorganized as Kaiser Group Holdings, Inc. 12/18/2000

ICG COMMUNICATIONS INC (DE)
Plan of reorganization under Chapter 11 Federal Bankruptcy Code effective 10/10/2002
No stockholders' equity
Merged into MCCC ICG Holdings LLC 10/18/2004
Each share new Common 1¢ par exchanged for $0.75 cash

ICG FDG LLC (DE)
Plan of reorganization under Chapter 11 Federal Bankruptcy Code effective 10/10/2002
No stockholders' equity

ICG GROUP INC (DE)
Name changed to Actua Corp. 09/03/2014

ICG HLDGS INC (DE)
Stock Dividends - 3.5% payable 9/15/97 to holders of record 9/1/97; 3.5% payable 9/15/99 to holders of record 9/1/99
Plan of reorganization under Chapter 11 Federal Bankruptcy Code effective 10/10/2002
No stockholders' equity

ICG INC (DE)
Name changed to International Coal Group, Inc. (New) 11/21/2005
(See International Coal Group, Inc. (New))

ICG UTIL INVTS LTD (CANADA)
Name changed 10/25/84
Name changed from ICG Utilities Ltd. to ICG Utility Investments Ltd. 10/25/84
6% Preferred Ser. A $25 par called for redemption 12/31/87
Public interest eliminated

ICG UTILITIES (MANITOBA) LTD. (MB)
Name changed to Centra Gas Manitoba Inc. 01/21/1991
(See Centra Gas Manitoba Inc.)

ICG UTILS ONT LTD (ON)
Name changed to Centra Gas Ontario Inc. 01/21/1991
(See Centra Gas Ontario Inc.)

ICHANCE INTL INC (NV)
Recapitalized as AngelCiti Entertainment, Inc. 01/20/2003
Each share Common $0.001 par exchanged for (0.25) share Common $0.001 par
(See AngelCiti Entertainment, Inc.)

ICHARGEIT INC (DE)
Reincorporated 11/12/1999
State of incorporation changed from (TX) to (DE) 11/12/1999
Reincorporated under the laws of Nevada as Freestone Resources, Inc. 08/15/2006

ICHOR CORP (DE)
Name changed to Mymetics Corp. 7/31/2001

ICI HLDG INC (NY)
Dissolved by proclamation 3/24/93

ICI INDL MINERALS LTD (ON)
Name changed to Commercial Industrial Minerals Ltd. 07/12/1985
Commercial Industrial Minerals Ltd. recapitalized as ICV Integrated Commercial Ventures Inc. 10/31/1994 which recapitalized as Blue Gold International, Inc. 12/23/1997
(See Blue Gold International, Inc.)

ICICI LTD (INDIA)
Merged into ICICI Bank Ltd. 05/03/2002
Each Sponsored ADR for Equity Rs. 10 par exchanged for (1.25) Sponsored ADR's for Equity

ICIENA VENTURES INC (BC)
Each share old Common no par exchanged for (0.33333333) share new Common no par 04/23/2009
Recapitalized as Barksdale Capital Corp. 02/08/2013
Each share new Common no par exchanged for (0.025) share Common no par

ICIS MGMT GROUP INC (FL)
SEC revoked common stock registration 06/10/2009

ICL P L C (ENGLAND)
Each ADR for Ordinary Reg. exchanged for (4) ADR's for Ordinary Reg. 02/20/1980
Acquired by STC PLC 05/16/1986
Each ADR for Ordinary Reg. exchanged for (0.33333333) share Ordinary 25p par
(See STC PLC)

ICM EQUITY FD INC (DE)
Acquired by MagnaCap Fund Inc. 12/21/1971
Each share Common $1 par exchanged for (0.37) share Capital Stock 10¢ par
MagnaCap Fund Inc. name changed to Pilgrim Magnacap Fund, Inc. 06/20/1985

ICM FINL FD INC (MD)
Acquired by Pilgrim Fund, Inc. 12/21/1971
Each share Common $1 par exchanged for (0.7637) share Common $1 par
Pilgrim Fund, Inc. merged into Pilgrim Magnacap Fund, Inc. 06/20/1985

ICM PPTY INVS INC (DE)
Reincorporated under the laws of Maryland as Bedford Property Investors, Inc. 7/1/93
(See Bedford Property Investors, Inc.)

ICM RLTY (MD)
Name changed to Eastgroup Properties 04/22/1983
Eastgroup Properties reorganized as Eastgroup Properties, Inc. 06/05/1997

ICM TELECOMMUNICATIONS INC (NV)
Each share Common $0.001 par received distribution of (0.02) share Legendary Superstars Inc. Common $0.001 par payable 04/23/2002 to holders of record 04/16/2002
Each share Common $0.001 par

received distribution of (0.02) share Canyon Mountain Theaters Inc. Common 1¢ par payable 08/08/2002 to holders of record 07/31/2002 Ex date - 07/29/2002
Each share Common $0.001 par received distribution of (0.0025) share Extreme Media, Inc. Common no par payable 02/01/2003 to holders of record 01/29/2003 Ex date - 01/27/2003
Recapitalized as eHolding Technologies, Inc. 05/26/2006
Each (700) shares Common $0.001 par exchanged for (1) share Common $0.001 par
eHolding Technologies, Inc. recapitalized as Pine Ridge Holdings, Inc. 03/10/2008 which name changed to Mike the Pike Productions, Inc. (NV) 08/05/2009 which reorganized in Wyoming 03/03/2011

ICM VENTURES INC (BC)
Name changed to RMS Medical Systems Inc. 04/30/1996
RMS Medical Systems Inc. recapitalized as Pacific Genesis Technologies Inc. (BC) 12/21/1999 which reincorporated in Alberta as Ware Solutions Corp. 10/01/2001
(See Ware Solutions Corp.)

ICN BIOMEDICALS INC (DE)
Stock Dividend - 20% 07/31/1989
Merged into ICN Pharmaceuticals, Inc. (New) 11/10/1994
Each share Common 1¢ par exchanged for (0.197) share Common 1¢ par
ICN Pharmaceuticals, Inc. (New) name changed to Valeant Pharmaceuticals International 11/12/2003 which merged into Valeant Pharmaceuticals International, Inc. (Canada) 09/28/2010 which reincorporated in British Columbia 08/09/2013

ICN PHARMACEUTICALS, INC. SHAREHOLDERS' TRUST (CA)
Liquidation completed
Each Non-Transferable Trust Ctf. received initial distribution of $0.48 cash 2/28/86
Each Non-Transferable Trust Ctf. received second and final distribution of $0.10 cash 4/11/86

ICN PHARMACEUTICALS INC NEW (DE)
Common 1¢ par split (3) for (2) by issuance of (0.5) additional share payable 03/16/1998 to holders of record 02/17/1998 Ex date - 03/17/1998
Name changed to Valeant Pharmaceuticals International 11/12/2003
Valeant Pharmaceuticals International merged into Valeant Pharmaceuticals International, Inc. (Canada) 09/28/2010 which reincorporated in British Columbia 08/09/2013

ICN PHARMACEUTICALS INC OLD (DE)
Reincorporated 10/03/1986
Each share Common $1 par received distribution of (1) ICN Pharmaceuticals, Inc. Shareholders' Trust Non-Transferable Trust Ctf. 07/15/1983
$2.70 Conv. Exchangeable Preferred $1 par called for redemption 09/05/1986
State of incorporation changed from (CA) to (DE) 10/03/1986
Merged into ICN Pharmaceuticals, Inc. (New) 11/10/1994
Each share Common $1 par exchanged for (0.512) share Common 1¢ par
ICN Pharmaceuticals, Inc. (New) name changed to Valeant Pharmaceuticals International 11/12/2003 which merged into Valeant Pharmaceuticals International, Inc. (Canada) 09/28/2010 which reincorporated in British Columbia 08/09/2013

ICN RES LTD (BC)
Merged into Corazon Gold Corp. 10/17/2012
Each share Common no par exchanged for (1) share Common no par
Note: Unexchanged certificates were cancelled and became without value 10/17/2015
Corazon Gold Corp. name changed to NanoSphere Health Sciences Inc. 12/05/2017

ICNB FINL CORP (MI)
Common $1 par split (3) for (1) by issuance of (2) additional shares payable 06/08/1998 to holders of record 05/11/1998
Stock Dividends - 5% payable 01/15/2003 to holders of record 12/20/2002 Ex date - 12/18/2002; 5% payable 12/19/2003 to holders of record 10/31/2003 Ex date - 10/29/2003; 5% payable 12/20/2004 to holders of record 11/01/2004; 5% payable 11/30/2005 to holders of record 10/25/2005 Ex date - 10/21/2005; 5% payable 11/30/2006 to holders of record 10/23/2006 Ex date - 10/19/2006
Merged into Firstbank Corp. 07/01/2007
Each share Common $1 par exchanged for (1.407) shares Common $10 par
Firstbank Corp. merged into Mercantile Bank Corp. 06/01/2014

ICO CORP. (IA)
Charter cancelled for failure to file annual reports 11/21/79

ICO GLOBAL COMMUNICATIONS (HOLDINGS) LTD (BERMUDA)
Issue Information - 10,000,000 shares ORD offered at $12 per share on 07/31/1998
Plan of reorganization under Chapter 11 Federal Bankruptcy Code effective 05/17/2000
Each share Ordinary 1¢ par received distribution of (0.00961538) share ICO Global Communications Holdings Ltd. (DE) Class A 1¢ par and (0.07142857) Class A Purchase Warrant expiring 5/16/2006
Note: Certificates were not required to be exchanged and are without value

ICO GLOBAL COMMUNICATIONS HLDGS LTD (DE)
Name changed to Pendrell Corp. (DE) 07/21/2011
Pendrell Corp. (DE) reincorporated in Washington 11/19/2012

ICO GLOBAL COMMUNICATIONS HLDGS LTD NEW (DE)
Name changed to ICO Global Communications (Holdings) Ltd. 12/05/2001
ICO Global Communications (Holdings) Ltd. name changed to Pendrell Corp. (DE) which reincorporated in Washington 11/19/2012

ICO INC NEW TX
$6.75 Depositary Preferred no par called for redemption at $25 plus $0.164063 accrued dividends on 11/05/2007
Merged into Schulman (A.), Inc. 04/30/2010
Each share Common no par exchanged for (0.181816) share Common $1 par and $3.64 cash
(See Schulman (A.), Inc.)

ICO INC OLD (TX)
Each share old Common no par exchanged for (0.2) share new Common no par 06/15/1993
Under plan of reorganization each share Depositary Conv. Preferred and new Common no par automatically became (1) share ICO, Inc. (New) $6.75 Depositary Conv. Preferred or Common no par respectively 04/01/1998
ICO, Inc. (New) merged into Schulman (A.), Inc. 04/30/2010
(See Schulman (A.), Inc.)

ICOA LIFE INSURANCE CO. (OR)
Completely liquidated 1/19/68
Each share Common 25¢ par exchanged for first and final distribution of (0.111111) share First Executive Corp. (Calif.) Common $2 par
First Executive Corp. (Calif.) reincorporated under the laws of Delaware 4/22/70

ICOMMERCE GROUP INC (DE)
SEC revoked common stock registration 06/10/2009

ICON CAP CORP (AB)
Name changed to Extreme Energy Corp. 10/09/1997
Extreme Energy Corp. merged into C1 Energy Ltd. 12/16/2004 which merged into Penn West Energy Trust 09/25/2007 which reorganized as Penn West Petroleum Ltd. (New) 01/03/2011

ICON CMT CORP (DE)
Issue Information - 3,850,000 shares COM offered at $10 per share on 02/12/1998
Merged into Qwest Communications International 01/04/1999
Each share Common $0.001 par exchanged for (0.32) share Common 1¢ par
Qwest Communications International Inc. merged into CenturyLink, Inc. 04/01/2011

ICON ENERGY LTD (AB)
Recapitalized 11/29/1994
Recapitalized from Icon Resources Ltd. to Icon Energy Ltd. 11/29/1994
Each share old Common no par exchanged for (0.4) share new Common no par
Merged into Lexxor Energy Inc. 04/03/2000
Each share Common no par exchanged for (0.25) share Class A Common no par and (0.125) Common Stock Purchase Warrant expiring 06/15/2000
Lexxor Energy Inc. reorganized as Find Energy Ltd. 09/05/2003 which was acquired by Shiningbank Energy Income Fund 09/22/2006 which merged into PrimeWest Energy Trust 07/13/2007
(See PrimeWest Energy Trust)

ICON FINL INC (NV)
Name changed to International Gaming Group, Inc. 06/04/1999
International Gaminig Group, Inc. name changed to American Standard Energy Inc. 04/16/2002 which name changed to Sports Wheels, Inc. 04/17/2003 which recapitalized as Automotive Specialty Concepts, Inc. 02/01/2005 which name changed to Drake Gold Resources, Inc. 02/13/2006 which name changed to Universal Apparel & Textile Co. 04/27/2015

ICON INDS LTD (BC)
Name changed to ICN Resources Ltd. 11/16/2009
ICN Resources Ltd. merged into Corazon Gold Corp. 10/17/2012 which name changed to NanoSphere Health Sciences Inc. 12/05/2017

ICON INTL HLDGS INC (FL)
SEC revoked common stock registration 02/22/2007

ICON LASER EYE CTRS INC (BC)
Delisted from Toronto Venture Stock Exchange 06/05/2002

ICON PLC (IRELAND)
Issue Information - 3,500,000 ADR'S offered at $18 per ADR on 05/14/1998
Sponsored ADR's for Ordinary split (2) for (1) by issuance of (1) additional ADR payable 10/23/2006 to holders of record 10/13/2006 Ex date - 10/24/2006
Sponsored ADR's for Ordinary split (2) for (1) by issuance of (1) additional ADR payable 08/12/2008 to holders of record 08/08/2008 Ex date - 08/13/2008
Each Sponsored ADR for Ordinary exchanged for (1) share Ordinary EUR 0.06 par 02/04/2013
(Additional Information in Active)

ICON SYS INC (NV)
Each share old Common $0.001 par exchanged for (0.02) share new Common $0.001 par 12/28/1998
Recapitalized as Advanced Wound Technologies - MidAtlantic Inc. 05/29/2007
Each (15) shares new Common $0.001 par exchanged for (1) share Common $0.001 par
Advanced Wound Technologies - MidAtlantic Inc. recapitalized as American CryoStem Corp. (Old) 02/03/2009 which name changed to ACS Global, Inc. 06/15/2011

ICONET INC (NV)
Each share old Common $0.001 par exchanged for (0.006993) share new Common $0.001 par 07/31/2003
Name changed to Anglotajik Minerals, Inc. 09/10/2003
Anglotajik Minerals, Inc. name changed to Intercontinental Resources, Inc. 05/31/2006 which name changed to China Valves Technology, Inc. 01/09/2008

ICONFIDENTIAL INC (NY)
Recapitalized as Quality of Life Health Corp. 3/4/2003
Each share Common $0.001 par exchanged for (0.01) share Common $0.001 par
Quality of Life Health Corp. recapitalized as LifeHouse Retirement Properties, Inc. 7/14/2005

ICOP DIGITAL INC (CO)
Each share old Common no par exchanged for (0.1) share new Common no par 03/16/2005
Each share new Common no par exchanged again for (0.1) share new Common no par 06/22/2010
Plan of reorganization under Chapter 11 Federal Bankruptcy proceedings effective 07/24/2012
No stockholders' equity

ICOR OIL & GAS LTD (AB)
Assets sold for benefit of creditors 00/00/1992
No stockholders' equity

ICORIA INC (DE)
Merged into Clinical Data, Inc. (New) 12/20/2005
Each share Common 1¢ par exchanged for (0.01552) shares Common 1¢ par
(See Clinical Data, Inc. (New))

ICOS CORP (WA)
Reincorporated 09/27/2005
State of incorporation changed from (DE) to (WA) 09/27/2005
Merged into Lilly (Eli) & Co. 01/29/2007

Each share Common 1¢ par exchanged for $34 cash

ICOS VISION SYSTEMS CORP N V (BELGIUM)
Issue Information - 2,250,000 shares COM offered at $10 per share on 12/09/1997
Acquired by KLA-Tencor Corp. 06/17/2008
Each share Common no par exchanged for EUR 36.50 cash

ICOT CORP (DE)
Name changed to Amati Communications Corp. 11/28/95
(See Amati Communications Corp.)

ICOWORKS INC (NV)
Common $0.001 par split (2) for (1) by issuance of (1) additional share payable 12/05/2002 to holders of record 12/05/2002
Recapitalized as Bioquest Technologies, Inc. 11/09/2006
Each share Common $0.001 par exchanged for (0.00666666) share Common $0.001 par
Bioquest Technologies, Inc. name changed to Texas Hill Country Barbecue Inc. 06/28/2010 which name changed to South American Properties, Inc. 04/10/2013 which name changed to USA Restaurant Funding Inc. 11/17/2014 which name changed to Chron Organization, Inc. 03/24/2016 which name changed to Zenergy Brands, Inc. 12/01/2017

ICP INC (IL)
Reincorporated under the laws of Delaware as Oce-Industries Inc. 04/26/1973
(See Oce-Industries Inc.)

ICP SOLAR TECHNOLOGIES INC (NV)
SEC revoked common stock registration 01/30/2013

ICR SYS INC (NV)
Each share old Common $0.001 par exchanged for (3) shares new Common $0.001 par 04/21/2004
Each share new Common $0.001 par exchanged again for (0.05) share new Common $0.001 par 08/08/2005
Name changed to Redux Holdings, Inc. 05/30/2006

ICRON SYS INC (CANADA)
Recapitalized as Icron Technologies Corp. 07/10/2001
Each share Common no par exchanged for (0.14285714) share Common no par
(See Icron Technologies Corp.)

ICRON TECHNOLOGIES CORP (CANADA)
Merged into Pender Financial Group Corp. 08/29/2011
Each share Common no par exchanged for $0.53 cash
Note: Unexchanged certificates were cancelled and became without value 08/29/2017

ICRYSTAL INC (DE)
Name changed 06/15/2000
Each share old Common 1¢ par exchanged for (0.05882352) share new Common 1¢ par 09/10/2004
Name changed from I Crystal, Inc. to ICrystal, Inc. 06/15/2000
Name changed to ALL Fuels & Energy Co. 05/07/2007
ALL Fuels & Energy Co. recapitalized as All Energy Corp. 01/17/2012

ICS COPPER SYS LTD (BC)
Recapitalized as Nubian Resources Ltd. 02/09/2011
Each share Common no par exchanged for (0.2) share Common no par

ICS 9612 INC (NV)
Name changed to Lion Industries USA Inc. 3/11/97
Lion Industries USA Inc. name changed to Sedona Horizons Corp. 7/3/2002 which name changed to Sedona Horizons Corp. 7/3/2002 which name changed to Cornerstone Entertainment, Inc. 7/21/2003 which name changed to Beverly Hills Film Studios, Inc. 10/28/2003 which name changed to Big Screen Entertainment Group, Inc. 4/1/2005

ICT GROUP INC (PA)
Issue Information - 2,500,000 shares COM offered at $16 per share on 06/14/1996
Merged into Sykes Enterprises, Inc. 02/02/2010
Each share Common 1¢ par exchanged for (0.3423) share Common 1¢ par and $7.69 cash

ICT INSURANCE CO. (TX)
Assets sold for benefit of creditors 03/05/1957
No stockholders' equity

ICT TECHNOLOGIES INC (DE)
Reincorporated 05/27/1999
State of incorporation changed from (NY) to (DE) 05/27/1999
Name changed to Euro Group of Companies, Inc. 11/09/2007
(See Euro Group of Companies, Inc.)

ICTC GROUP INC (DE)
Acquired by BEK Communications Cooperative 10/19/2018
Each share Class A Common $0.0001 par exchanged for $65.251322 cash

ICURIE INC (NV)
Name changed to Celsia Technologies, Inc. 10/09/2006
(See Celsia Technologies, Inc.)

ICV INC (DE)
Charter cancelled and declared inoperative and void for non-payment of taxes 4/15/72

ICV INTEGRATED COML VENTURES INC (ON)
Recapitalized as Blue Gold International, Inc. 12/23/1997
Each share Common no par exchanged for (0.66666666) share Common no par
(See Blue Gold International, Inc.)

ICX TECHNOLOGIES INC (DE)
Issue Information - 5,000,000 shares COM offered at $16 per share on 11/07/2007
Merged into FLIR Systems, Inc. 10/04/2010
Each share Common $0.001 par exchanged for $7.55 cash

ID BIOMEDICAL CORP (BC)
Common no par split (2) for (1) by issuance of (1) additional share 08/15/1995
Merged into GlaxoSmithKline PLC 12/08/2005
Each share Common no par exchanged for $35 cash

ID-CONFIRM INC (NV)
SEC revoked common stock registration 05/13/2011

ID FOUR LTD (NV)
Each share old Common $0.001 par received distribution of (0.02) share Cyberfast Systems Inc. Common 1¢ par payable 01/07/2002 to holders of record 12/10/2001
Each share old Common $0.001 par exchanged for (0.01) share new Common $0.001 par 06/23/2002
Name changed to Swung, Inc. 08/06/2002
Swung, Inc. name changed to American Capital Holdings 11/15/2002 which name changed to Symphony Investments, Inc. 05/09/2003 which name changed to International Pharmacy Outlets Inc. 09/29/2003 which name changed to Bionic Products, Inc. 12/11/2006 which recapitalized as Texas Oil & Minerals Inc. 02/01/2012

ID GLOBAL SOLUTIONS CORP (DE)
Name changed to Ipsidy Inc. 11/17/2017

ID WATCHDOG INC (CAYMAN ISLANDS)
Acquired by Equifax, Inc. 08/10/2017
Each share Ordinary no par exchanged for USD$0.40 cash

IDA MAY RES LTD (BC)
Name changed to Limoges Porcelaines Ltd. 10/09/1985
Limoges Porcelaines Ltd. recapitalized as Boch & Limoges Ltd. 10/20/1988 which recapitalized as Vannessa Ventures Ltd. 07/21/1994 which name changed to Infinito Gold Ltd. 05/28/2008

IDAHO ALTA METALS CORP. (DE)
No longer in existence having become inoperative and void for non-payment of taxes 4/1/61

IDAHO BANCORP (ID)
Common $5 par split (2) for (1) by issuance of (1) additional share payable 12/28/2004 to holders of record 12/14/2004 Ex date - 12/29/2004
Plan of reorganization under Chapter 11 Federal Bankruptcy proceedings effective 11/25/2014
No stockholders' equity

IDAHO BK & TR CO (POCATELLO, ID)
Each share Common $100 par exchanged for (5) shares Common $20 par 02/01/1938
Stock Dividends - 13.61% 06/30/1939; 10% 07/01/1940; 33-1/3% 01/01/1946; 25% 08/24/1946; 25% 05/15/1948; 35.71% 09/15/1951; 100% 07/25/1957; 50% 12/21/1959; 33-1/3% 09/15/1964; 25% 12/03/1965; 20% 01/28/1970
Reorganized as IB&T Corp. 12/30/1974
Each share Common $20 par exchanged for (4) shares Common $5 par
IB&T Corp. merged into KeyCorp (NY) 10/03/1988 which merged into KeyCorp (OH) 03/01/1994

IDAHO BIRTHDAY MINES CO. (ID)
Charter cancelled for failure to file reports and pay taxes 3/22/57

IDAHO BKG CO (ID)
Under plan of reorganization each share Common $5 par automatically became (1) share Idaho Bancorp Common $5 par 12/14/2004
(See Idaho Bancorp)

IDAHO CIBOLA MINES, INC. (ID)
Voluntarily dissolved 4/19/82
Details not available

IDAHO CONS METALS CORP (YT)
Reincorporated 08/17/2001
Place of incorporation changed from (BC) to (YT) 08/17/2001
Name changed to Beartooth Platinum Corp. (YT) 07/24/2002
Beartooth Platinum Corp. (YT) reincorporated in Ontario 08/11/2004 which recapitalized as Kria Resources Ltd. 07/24/2009 which merged into Trevali Mining Corp. 04/07/2011

IDAHO CONS MINES INC (WA)
Charter cancelled and proclaimed dissolved for failure to pay fees 1/31/99

IDAHO CONTINENTAL MINING CO. (MN)
Charter expired by time limitation 10/25/31

IDAHO COPPER CO.
Bankrupt 00/00/1937
No stockholders' equity

IDAHO CORP. (ID)
Charter forfeited for failure to file reports 12/2/85

IDAHO CUSTER MINES, INC. (ID)
Acquired by Idaho Custer Silver-Lead Mines, Inc. share for share 6/1/56

IDAHO FARMS CO (DE)
Completely liquidated 09/07/1973
Each share Common $45 par exchanged for first and final distribution of $152.58 cash

IDAHO 1ST NATL BK (BOISE, ID)
Each share Capital Stock $100 par exchanged for (10) shares Capital Stock $10 par in 1950
Capital Stock $10 par changed to $5 par and (1) additional share issued 2/12/65
Capital Stock $5 par changed to $2.50 par and (1) additional share issued 3/24/78
Stock Dividends - 66-2/3% 10/11/33; 20% 1/30/37; 25% 1/20/39; 33-1/3% 1/25/41; 50% 12/28/43; 20% 12/28/44; 50% 1/13/50; 20% 1/25/55; 25% 3/3/68; 10% 2/5/71; 10% 1/18/73; 10% 3/21/80
Under plan of reorganization each share Capital Stock $2.50 par automatically became (1) share Moore Financial Group Inc. Common $1 par 8/14/81
Moore Financial Group Inc. name changed to West One Bancorp 4/21/89 which merged into U.S. Bancorp (OR) 12/26/95 which merged into U.S. Bancorp (Old) (DE) 8/1/97 which merged into U.S. Bancorp (New) 2/27/2001

IDAHO GEN MINES INC (ID)
Class A Common 10¢ par and Class B Common 10¢ par reclassified as Common 10¢ par 03/18/1967
Common 10¢ par changed to $0.001 par 11/16/2004
Reincorporated under the laws of Delaware as General Moly, Inc. 10/09/2007

IDAHO GOLD CORP. (NV)
Charter revoked for failure to file reports and pay fees 3/2/31

IDAHO INVT CORP (ID)
Merged into Greater Idaho Corp. 12/29/1972
Details not available

IDAHO LAKEVIEW MINES CO (ID)
Voluntarily dissolved 8/5/76
Details not available

IDAHO LEADVILLE MINES CO (WA)
Recapitalized as Tamboril Cigar Co. (WA) 11/06/1996
Each share Common 5¢ par exchanged for (0.05) share Common $0.001 par
Tamboril Cigar Co. (WA) reincorporated in Delaware 01/15/1997 which reorganized as Axion Power International, Inc. 06/07/2004

IDAHO LIVE STOCK LANDS, INC.
Liquidated in 1945

IDAHO MANUFACTURING CO., INC. (ID)
Charter revoked for failure to file reports and pay fees 12/1/59

IDAHO MARYLAND CONSOLIDATED MINES, INC.
Merged into Idaho Maryland Mines Corp. in 1935 which name was changed to Idaho Maryland Industries, Inc. 7/1/60 which was recapitalized as Allied Equities Corp. 4/1/64

IDAHO MARYLAND INDUSTRIES, INC. (NV)
Recapitalized as Allied Equities Corp. 4/1/64
Each share Common 50¢ par exchanged for (0.05) share Common $1 par

IDAHO MARYLAND MINES CO.
Merged into Idaho Maryland Mines Corp. in 1935 which name was changed to Idaho Maryland Industries, Inc. 7/1/60 which was recapitalized as Allied Equities Corp. 4/1/64

IDAHO MARYLAND MINES CORP. (NV)
Common $1 par changed to 50¢ par 10/25/57
Name changed to Idaho Maryland Industries, Inc. 7/1/60
Idaho Maryland Industries, Inc. recapitalized as Allied Equities Corp. 4/1/64 which name changed to Precision Technologies 9/23/83

IDAHO-MD MNG CORP (BC)
Common no par split (2) for (1) by issuance of (1) additional share 06/11/1991
Recapitalized as HMC Healthgard Marketing Corp. 06/23/1993
Each share Common no par exchanged for (0.5) share Common no par
HMC Healthgard Marketing Corp. recapitalized as Reward Mining Corp. 08/07/1996 which name changed to Riverdance Resources Corp. 03/11/1998 which recapitalized as Luminex Ventures Inc. 05/26/1999 which recapitalized as Lateegra Resources Corp. 06/12/2002 which recapitalized as Lateegra Gold Corp. 01/12/2006 which merged into Excellon Resources Inc. 08/05/2011

IDAHO MINERALS CO. (ID)
Charter forfeited for failure to file reports 12/02/1991

IDAHO MINING & MILLING, INC. (ID)
Charter revoked for failure to file reports and pay fees 11/30/67

IDAHO MINING CO. (ID)
Charter revoked for failure to file reports and pay fees 11/30/56

IDAHO MONT SILVER INC (ID)
Each share old Common 5¢ par exchanged for (0.01818181) share new Common 5¢ par 03/14/2000
Recapitalized as Grant Douglas Acquisition Inc. 03/09/2001
Each share new Common 5¢ par exchanged for (0.025) share Common 5¢ par
Grant Douglas Acquisition Inc. recapitalized as Pediatric Prosthetics, Inc. 11/10/2003 which recapitalized as Marathon Group Corp. (ID) 08/03/2010 which reincorporated in Wyoming 06/02/2011

IDAHO-MONTANA PULP & PAPER CO. (MT)
Completely liquidated for cash 10/29/52

IDAHO NAT RES CORP (AB)
Creditor enforced its security over assets 11/13/2012
Stockholders' equity unlikely

IDAHO-NEVADA EXPLORATION CO., LTD. (ID)
Charter forfeited for failure to file reports 12/1/21

IDAHO PWR CO (ID)
Reincorporated 06/30/1989
6% Preferred called for redemption 08/01/1944
7% Preferred called for redemption 08/01/1944
Common $20 par changed to $10 par and (1) additional share issued 05/11/1955
Common $10 par changed to $5 par and (1) additional share issued 05/24/1961
Common $5 par changed to $2.50 par and (1) additional share issued 06/06/1985
State of incorporation changed from (ME) to (ID) 06/30/1989
9.50% Preferred no par called for redemption 11/01/1991
8.375% Preferred no par called for redemption 11/07/1996
Under plan of reorganization each share Common $2.50 par automatically became (1) share IDACORP, Inc. Common no par 10/01/1998
Flexible Auction Preferred Ser. A no par called for redemption at $100,000 on 08/15/2002
4% Preferred $100 par called for redemption at $104 plus $0.548 accrued dividends on 09/20/2004
7.07% Preferred no par called for redemption at $103.182 plus $0.6005 accrued dividends on 09/20/2004
7.68% 1st Ser. Preferred $100 par called for redemption at $102.97 plus $1.0521 accrued dividends on 09/20/2004

IDAHO RAILWAY, LIGHT & POWER CO. (ME)
Charter suspended for non-payment of taxes 00/00/1916

IDAHO SILVER CORP. (ID)
Acquired by Silver Mountain Lead Mines, Inc. in 1952
Each (3.4) shares Common 10¢ par exchanged for (1) share Capital Stock 10¢ par
Silver Mountain Lead Mines, Inc. name changed to Silver Syndicate Mining Corp. 10/19/2004 which name changed to 99 Dollar Stores, Inc. 8/17/2005 which name changed to InvestSource Communications, Inc. 1/17/2006 which name changed to United Resource Holdings Group, Inc. 2/5/2007

IDAHO SILVER INC (ID)
Recapitalized as Enviro Voraxial Technology Inc. 05/28/1996
Each share Common 10¢ par exchanged for (0.1) share Common $0.001 par
Enviro Voraxial Technology Inc. name changed to Enviro Technologies, Inc. 11/14/2017

IDAHO TECHNICAL INC (NV)
Name changed to Greatbio Technologies, Inc. 12/4/2000
Greatbio Technologies, Inc. name changed to Biophan Technologies, Inc. 7/19/2001

IDAMONT OIL & MINING CO. (ID)
Charter forfeited for failure to file reports 11/30/70

IDAN SOFTWARE INDS - I S I LTD (ISRAEL)
Each (15) shares old Ordinary Stock ILS 0.01 par exchanged for (1) share new new Ordinary Stock ILS 0.01 par 06/10/1997
Name changed to ForSoft Ltd. 09/30/1997
(See ForSoft Ltd.)

IDANT CORP (NY)
Name changed to Daxor Corp. 04/26/1973

IDB BANKHOLDING LTD (ISRAEL)
ADR's for Conv. Preference I£20 par split (1.4) for (1) by issuance of (0.4) additional share 3/7/80
ADR's for Conv. Preference I£20 par, changed to IS2 par per currency change in 1980
ADR's for Ordinary I£20 par and ADR's for B I!20 par changed to IS2 par per currency change in 1980
Each ADR for Ordinary IS2 par exchanged for (0.02) ADR for Ordinary IS100 par 8/1/83
ADR's for Conv. Preference IS2 par called for redemption 3/30/84
ADR's for Ordinary IS100 par changed to NIS0.01 par per currency change 1/1/86
Stock Dividends - 20% 7/31/73; 25% 10/11/74; 25% 8/19/77; 25% 8/25/78; 100% 3/31/83
ADR's for Ordinary NIS0.01 par called for redemption in 1991

IDB COMMUNICATIONS GROUP INC (DE)
Common 1¢ par split (3.15) for (1) by issuance of (2.15) additional shares 2/4/94
Merged into LDDS Communications, Inc. 12/30/94
Each share Common 1¢ par exchanged for (0.476879) share Common 1¢ par

IDC HLDGS LTD (NV)
Chapter 7 bankruptcy proceedings dismissed 02/22/1996
No stockholders' equity

IDC SVCS INC (DE)
Acquired by Apollo Partners Ltd. 02/29/1988
Each share Common 1¢ par exchanged for $16 cash

IDC TECHNOLOGIES INC (NV)
Each share old Common $0.001 par exchanged for (0.2) share new Common $0.001 par 02/28/2002
Name changed to Jill Kelly Productions Holding, Inc. 08/20/2003
Jill Kelly Productions Holding, Inc. name changed to eWorldCompanies, Inc. 03/13/2007

IDCENTRIX INC (NV)
Each share old Common $0.00001 par exchanged for (0.003521113) share new Common $0.00001 par 06/04/2010
Name changed to North China Horticulture, Inc. 09/01/2010
(See North China Horticulture, Inc.)

IDE (GEORGE P.) & CO., INC.
Liquidated in 1933

IDEA SPORTS ENTMT GROUP INC (DE)
Recapitalized as HealthSport, Inc. 05/16/2006
Each share Common $0.0001 par exchanged for (0.005) share Common $0.0001 par
(See HealthSport, Inc.)

IDEAEDGE INC (CO)
Common $0.001 par split (3) for (1) by issuance of (2) additional shares payable 03/12/2008 to holders of record 03/12/2008
Name changed to Socialwise, Inc. 05/13/2009
Socialwise, Inc. name changed to BillMyParents, Inc. 06/13/2011 which name changed to SpendSmart Payments Co. (CO) 02/28/2013 which reincorporated in Delaware as SpendSmart Networks, Inc. 06/20/2014

IDEAL ACCENTS INC (FL)
Recapitalized as IEG Holdings Corp. 03/11/2013
Each share Common $0.001 par exchanged for (0.16666666) share Common $0.001 par
IEG Holdings Corp. name changed to Mr. Amazing Loans Corp. 04/30/2018

IDEAL AEROSMITH INC (CA)
Completely liquidated 02/05/1960
Each share Capital Stock $1 par exchanged for first and final distribution of $1.3144 cash

IDEAL AEROSMITH INC (WY)
Charter dissolved for failure to file reports and pay fees 08/30/1984

IDEAL BASIC INDS INC (DE)
Reincorporated 05/15/1987
4-3/4% Conv. Preferred $100 par called for redemption 06/29/1981
Common $5 par changed to no par 00/00/1986
State of incorporation changed from (CO) to (DE) and Common no par changed to 1¢ par 05/15/1987
Merged into Holnam Inc. 03/08/1990
Each share Common 1¢ par exchanged for (0.25) share Common no par
(See Holnam Inc.)

IDEAL BAY EXPL LTD (ON)
Charter cancelled for failure to pay taxes and file returns 07/27/1976

IDEAL BRUSHES INC (CA)
Name changed to H&A Brush Corp. 07/10/1969
(See H&A Brush Corp.)

IDEAL CEMENT CO. (CO)
Each share old Capital Stock no par exchanged for (2) shares new Capital Stock no par in 1928
Each share new Capital Stock no par exchanged for (3) shares Capital Stock $10 par in 1937
Capital Stock $10 par changed to $5 par and (2) additional shares issued 1/30/59
Stock Dividend - 100% 10/15/54
Under plan of merger name changed to Ideal Basic Industries, Inc. (CO) and Capital Stock $5 par changed to Common $5 par 12/31/67
Ideal Basic Industries, Inc. (CO) reincorporated in Delaware 5/15/87 which merged into Holnam Inc. 3/8/90
(See Holnam Inc.)

IDEAL FINL SOLUTIONS INC (NV)
Each share old Common $0.001 par exchanged for (0.005) share new Common $0.001 par 01/06/2011
Court appointed permanent receiver suspended operations, froze assets and laid off all employees 02/15/2013
Stockholders' equity unlikely

IDEAL FINANCING ASSOCIATION, INC.
Merged into American Investment Co. of Illinois in 1938
Each share Preferred exchanged for (4) shares $2 Cumulative Preferred $25 par
Each share Convertible Preferred exchanged for (1) share $2 Preference no par
Each (6) shares Class A Common exchanged for (1) share $2 Preference no par and (1) share Common no par
American Investment Co. of Illinois name changed to American Investment Co. 11/30/63

IDEAL GROUP COS INC (CANADA)
Acquired by Waxman Acquisition Inc. 05/26/1989
Each share Class A Subordinate no par exchanged for $10 cash

IDEAL INS CORP AMER (WY)
Name changed to Remington Financial Group, Inc. 4/8/92

IDEAL METAL INC (QC)
Merged into Atlas Alloys Inc. 06/17/1998
Each share Common no par exchanged for $5.75 cash

IDEAL NATL INS CO (UT)
Common $10 par changed to $2.50 par and (3) additional shares issued 4/15/63
Common $2.50 par changed to $2 par and (0.25) additional shares issued 6/15/66

Merged into First Continental Life Group, Inc. 9/15/78
Each share Common $2 par exchanged for (1) share Part. Preferred Ser. A $1 par
(See First Continental Life Group, Inc.)

IDEAL PRECISION METER INC (NY)
Name changed to IPM Technology, Inc. 8/20/69
IPM Technology, Inc. name changed to Mercury Air Group, Inc. (NY) 12/21/89 which reincorporated in Delaware 3/1/2001
(See Mercury Air Group, Inc.)

IDEAL SCH SUPPLY CORP (DE)
Acquired by ISSC Holdings, Inc. 06/29/1988
Each share Common 1¢ par exchanged for $12 cash

IDEAL TOY CORP (DE)
Reincorporated 6/9/72
Common $1 par split (2) for (1) by issuance of (1) additional share 1/30/70
State of incorporation changed from (NY) to (DE) 6/9/72
Merged into CBS Inc. 8/17/82
Each share Common $1 par exchanged for $14.85 cash

IDEALISTICS INC (DE)
Name changed to American West Aircraft Corp. 10/20/1988

IDEAMALL INC (CA)
Name changed to PC Mall, Inc. 06/19/2001
PC Mall, Inc. name changed to PCM, Inc. 01/02/2013

IDEARC INC (DE)
Plan of reorganization under Chapter 11 Federal Bankruptcy proceedings effective 12/31/2009
No stockholders' equity

IDEATION ACQUISITION CORP (DE)
Units separated 10/29/2009
Reincorporated under the laws of Cayman Islands as SearchMedia Holdings Ltd. and Common $0.0001 par reclassified as Ordinary USD$0.0001 par 10/29/2009
SearchMedia Holdings Ltd. name changed to Tiger Media, Inc. (Cayman Islands) 12/18/2012 which reincorporated in Delaware 03/20/2015 which name changed to IDI, Inc. 05/04/2015 which name changed to Cogint, Inc. 09/26/2016 which name changed to Fluent, Inc. 04/16/2018

IDEC PHARMACEUTICALS CORP (DE)
Reincorporated 06/02/1997
State of incorporation changed from (CA) to (DE) and Common no par changed to $0.0005 par 06/02/1997
Common $0.0005 par split (2) for (1) by issuance of (1) additional share payable 12/20/1999 to holders of record 12/01/1999
Common $0.0005 par split (3) for (1) by issuance of (2) additional shares payable 01/17/2001 to holders of record 12/26/2000 Ex date - 01/18/2001
Under plan of merger name changed to Biogen Idec Inc. 11/13/2003
Biogen Idec Inc. name changed to Biogen Inc. (DE) 03/24/2015

IDENIX PHARMACEUTICALS INC (DE)
Acquired by Merck & Co., Inc. (New) 08/05/2014
Each share Common $0.001 par exchanged for $24.50 cash

IDENTA LTD (FL)
Name changed to Identa Corp. 01/22/2002

IDENTCORPORATION INC (NY)
Charter cancelled and proclaimed dissolved for failure to pay taxes 12/20/1977

IDENTICON CORP (MA)
Merged into NEI Canada Ltd. 06/27/1984
Each share Common $0.0091 par exchanged for $0.01 cash

IDENTIMATION CORP (DE)
Charter cancelled and declared inoperative and void for non-payment of taxes 3/1/94

IDENTIPHI INC (DE)
Chapter 11 bankruptcy proceedings terminated 03/29/2010
No stockholders' equity

IDENTIVE GROUP INC (DE)
Recapitalized as Identive, Inc. 05/27/2014
Each share Common $0.001 par exchanged for (0.1) share Common $0.001 par

IDENTIX INC (DE)
Reincorporated 12/16/1998
State of incorporation changed from (CA) to (DE) and Common no par changed to 1¢ par 12/16/1998
Merged into L-1 Identity Solutions, Inc. 08/30/2006
Each share Common 1¢ par exchanged for (0.473) share Common $0.001 par
(See L-1 Identity Solutions, Inc.)

IDEON GROUP INC (DE)
Merged into CUC International Inc. 08/07/1996
Each share Common 1¢ par exchanged for (0.3944) share Common 1¢ par
CUC International Inc. name changed to Cendant Corp. 12/17/1997 which reorganized as Avis Budget Group, Inc. 09/01/2006

IDEX CORP (DE)
Sr. Adjustable Rate Exchangeable Preferred 1¢ par called for redemption 7/10/89
(Additional Information in Active)

IDEX INC (DE)
Name changed to Globus Studios, Inc. 02/03/1988

IDEX TOTAL INCOME TR (MA)
Acquired by IDEX II Series Fund 10/01/1993
Details not available

IDF INTL INC (NY)
Recapitalized as Compliance Resource Group, Inc. (NY) 02/15/2007
Each share Common $0.001 par exchanged for (0.01) share Common $0.001 par
Compliance Resource Group, Inc. (NY) reincorporated in Nevada as EnerBrite Technologies Group, Inc. 06/15/2007 which recapitalized as Limitless Venture Group Inc. 02/04/2013

IDG BOOKS WORLDWIDE INC (DE)
Issue Information - 3,180,000 shares CL A COM offered at $15.50 per share on 07/27/1998
Name changed to Hungry Minds Inc. 11/14/2000
(See Hungry Minds Inc.)

IDI GLOBAL INC (NV)
SEC revoked common stock registration 05/07/2014

IDI INC (DE)
Name changed to Cogint, Inc. 09/26/2016
Cogint, Inc. name changed to Fluent, Inc. 04/16/2018

IDIAL NETWORKS INC (NV)
Common $0.0001 par split (2) for (1) by issuance of (1) additional share payable 12/01/2000 to holders of record 11/15/2000 Ex date - 12/04/2000

Name changed to GlobalNet Corp. 12/19/2003
(See GlobalNet Corp.)

IDICO INC (UT)
Each (15) shares old Common no par exchanged for (1) share new Common no par 06/13/1983
Charter suspended for failure to pay taxes 12/31/1985

IDINE REWARDS NETWORK INC (DE)
Each share Conv. Preferred Ser. A 10¢ par exchanged for (1.19316) shares Common 2¢ par 01/23/2003
Name changed to Rewards Network Inc. 12/09/2003
(See Rewards Network Inc.)

IDLE WILD FOODS INC (DE)
Common $1 par split (3) for (2) by issuance of (0.5) additional share 11/20/78
Acquired by Union Holdings Inc. 8/29/86
Each share Common $1 par exchanged for $40.475 cash

IDLEAIRE TECHNOLOGIES CORP (DE)
Chapter 7 bankruptcy proceedings terminated 01/18/2017
No stockholders' equity

IDM ENVIRONMENTAL CORP (NJ)
Each share old Common $0.001 par exchanged for (0.1) share new Common $0.001 par 04/16/1999
Merged into Fusion Networks Holdings, Inc. 04/13/2000
Each share new Common $0.001 par exchanged for (1) share Common $0.00001 par
(See Fusion Networks Holdings, Inc.)

IDM INTL LTD (AUSTRALIA)
Basis changed from (1:20) to (1:0.8) 02/24/2017
ADR agreement terminated 03/22/2017
Each Sponsored ADR for Ordinary exchanged for (0.8) share Ordinary
Note: Due to delisting, sale of underlying shares may not be possible ADR's surrendered for Ordinary shares until 03/26/2018

IDM PHARMA INC (DE)
Merged into Takeda Pharmaceutical Co. Ltd. 06/24/2009
Each share Common 1¢ par exchanged for $2.64 cash

IDMEDICAL COM INC (CO)
Name changed to Opus Media Group, Inc. 09/25/2002
Opus Media Group, Inc. recapitalized as Opus Resource Group, Inc. 09/29/2003 which recapitalized as BlastGard International, Inc. 03/31/2004 which name changed to HighCom Global Security, Inc. 08/03/2017

IDNA INC (DE)
SEC revoked common stock registration 01/30/2013

IDOLEYEZ CORP (WY)
SEC revoked common stock registration 09/30/2005

IDORA SILVER MINES INC (ID)
Each share old Common 10¢ par exchanged for (1/6) share new Common 10¢ par 09/14/1998
Recapitalized as American Health Providers Corp. 11/13/1998
Each share new Common 10¢ par exchanged for (0.5) share Common 10¢ par
American Health Providers Corp. name changed to Bitterroot Mountain Mining Corp. 11/11/1999 which recapitalized as Advanced Process Technologies Inc. 09/20/2000 which name changed to Integrated Pharmaceuticals, Inc. 12/12/2000

(See Integrated Pharmaceuticals, Inc.)

IDP LIQUIDATING CORP. (DE)
Voluntarily dissolved 12/4/97
Details not available

IDREAMSKY TECHNOLOGY LTD (CAYMAN ISLANDS)
Acquired by Dream Investment Holdings Ltd. 09/09/2016
Each Sponsored ADS for Class A Ordinary exchanged for $13.93 cash

IDREX INC (DE)
Company believed out of business 08/31/1990
Details not available

IDS INDS INC (NV)
Name changed to Aja Cannafacturing, Inc. 08/11/2014

IDS NUVEEN INCOME TR (IL)
Trust terminated 12/06/1993
Details not available

IDS RLTY TR (MA)
Shares of Bene. Int. $1 par reclassified as Common $1 par 06/07/1974
Merged into Boothe Financial Corp. (DE) 01/31/1980
Each share Common $1 par exchanged for (0.2) share Common $1 par
Boothe Financial Corp. (DE) name changed to Robert Half International Inc. 06/17/1987

IDS SOLAR TECHNOLOGIES INC (NV)
Common $0.001 par split (12) for (1) by issuance of (11) additional shares payable 02/07/2013 to holders of record 02/07/2013 Ex date - 02/08/2013
Name changed to IDS Industries, Inc. 06/10/2013
IDS Industries, Inc. name changed to Aja Cannafacturing, Inc. 08/11/2014

IDS WORLDWIDE INC (DE)
Reincorporated under the laws of Nevada as Avalon Technology Group, Inc. and Common 10¢ par changed to $0.0001 par 06/16/2008

IDS WORLDWIDE SOLUTIONS INC (DE)
Name changed to IDS Worldwide, Inc. (DE) 10/19/2005
IDS Worldwide, Inc. (DE) reincorporated in Nevada as Avalon Technology Group, Inc. 06/16/2008
(See Avalon Technology Group, Inc.)

IDT HLDGS SINGAPORE LTD (SINGAPORE)
ADR agreement terminated 09/17/2003
Details not available

IDT INTL LTD (BERMUDA)
ADR agreement terminated 07/17/2003
Details not available

IDX SYS CORP (VT)
Merged into General Electric Co. 1/4/2006
Each share Common 1¢ par exchanged for $44 cash

IDYIA INNOVATIONS INC (MB)
Company's principal asset filed a notice of intention to make a proposal under the Bankruptcy and Insolvency Act 12/30/1995
Stockholders' equity unlikely

IE INDS INC (IA)
Under plan of merger name changed to IES Industries Inc. 07/01/1991
IES Industries Inc. merged into Interstate Energy Corp. 04/21/1998 which name changed to Alliant Energy Corp. 05/19/1999

IEA CORP. (DE)
Charter cancelled and declared

IEA CORP (FL)
inoperative and void for non-payment of taxes 3/1/74
Reincorporated under the laws of Delaware 6/21/71
(See IEA Corp. (DE))

IEA INCOME FUND L P (CA)
Completely liquidated
Each Unit of Ltd. Partnership Int. VI received first and final distribution of approximately $31 cash payable 12/31/2000 to holders of record 12/31/2000
Each Unit of Ltd. Partnership Int. VII received first and final distribution of approximately $75 cash payable 13/31/2000 to holders of record 12/31/2000
Each Unit of Ltd. Partnership Int. VIII received initial distribution of approximately $11.80 cash payable 09/30/2005 to holders of record 09/01/2005
Each Unit of Ltd. Partnership Int. IX received initial distribution of approximately $17.89 cash payable 09/30/2005 to holders of record 09/01/2005
Each Unit of Ltd. Partnership Int. X received initial distribution of approximately $13.03 cash payable 09/30/2005 to holders of record 09/01/2005
Each Unit of Ltd. Partnership Int. XI received initial distribution of approximately $0.52 cash payable 02/28/2006 to holders of record 02/01/2006
Each Unit of Ltd. Partnership Int. XII received initial distribution of approximately $1.19 cash payable 11/30/2007 to holders of record 11/01/2007
Note: Amount of second and final distributions are not available

IEC ELECTRS CORP (NY)
Acquired by DFT Holdings Corp. 09/23/1988
Each share Common 5¢ par exchanged for $11.25 cash

IEG HLDGS CORP (FL)
Each share old Common $0.001 par exchanged for (0.01) share new Common $0.001 par 06/17/2015
Each share new Common $0.001 par exchanged again for (1) share new Common $0.001 par to reflect a (1) for (100) reverse split followed by a (100) for (1) forward split 04/01/2016
Note: Holders of (99) or fewer pre-split shares received $7.20 cash per share
Each share new Common $0.001 par exchanged again for (0.001) share new Common $0.001 par to reflect a (1) for (1,000) reverse split followed by a (100) for (1) forward split 10/27/2016
Note: Holders of (999) or fewer pre-split shares received $0.6045333 cash per share
Name changed to Mr. Amazing Loans Corp. 04/30/2018

IEI ENERGY INC (AB)
Under plan of merger name changed to Rider Resources Ltd. 02/21/2003
Rider Resources Ltd. merged into NuVista Energy Ltd. 03/04/2008

IELEMENT CORP (NV)
Each share old Common $0.001 par exchanged for (0.0625) share new Common $0.001 par 01/11/2008
SEC revoked common stock registration 01/29/2014

IEM S A (MEXICO)
Acquired by Grupo Condumex, S.A. de C.V. 00/00/1977
Details not available

IEMI (NV)
SEC revoked common stock registration 07/22/2005

Stockholders' equity unlikely

IES INDS INC (IA)
Merged into Interstate Energy Corp. 4/21/98
Each share Common no par exchanged for (1.14) shares Common no par
Interstate Energy Corp. name changed to Alliant Energy Corp. 5/19/99

IES UTILS INC (IA)
Name changed to Interstate Power & Light Co. and 4.30% Preferred $50 par, 4.80% Preferred $50 par and 6.10% Preferred $50 par reclassified as 4.30% Class A Preferred $50 par, 4.80% Class A Preferred $50 par and 6.10% Class A Preferred $50 par respectively 1/1/2002
(See Interstate Power & Light Co.)

IESI BFC LTD (ON)
Name changed to Progressive Waste Solutions Ltd. 05/11/2011
Progressive Waste Solutions Ltd. recapitalized as Waste Connections, Inc. 06/01/2016

IFB CORP (FL)
Name changed to ePHONE Telecom, Inc. 04/04/1999
(See ePHONE Telecom, Inc.)

IFC CAP TR I (DE)
Issue Information - 1,750,000 TR PFD SECS 9.25% offered at $25 per security on 01/13/1997
9.25% Trust Preferred Securities called for redemption at $25 on 12/15/2003

IFC CAP TR III (DE)
Issue Information - 1,800,000 GTD TR CONV PFD SECS 8.75% offered at $25 per share on 11/16/2000
8.75% Guaranteed Trust Conv. Preferred Securities called for redemption at $25 plus $0.394965 accrued dividends on 3/6/2006

IFC CAP TR VI (DE)
Guarantor filed a petition under Chapter 7 Federal Bankruptcy Code 09/18/2009

IFC CAP TR II (DE)
Issue Information - 1,800,000 GTD TR PFD SECS 10.50% offered at $25 per share on 11/16/2000
10.50% Guaranteed Trust Preferred Securities called for redemption at $25 on 9/30/2005

IFCO SYS N V (NETHERLANDS)
Each share Ordinary EUR 2 par exchanged for (0.1) share Ordinary EUR 0.01 par 12/16/2002
Acquired by Brambles Investment Ltd. 04/19/2013
Each share Ordinary EUR 0.01 par exchanged for $18.6909 cash

IFEX INC (DE)
Acquired by FSS Consulting Corp. 6/22/88
Each share Common 1¢ par exchanged for (1) share Common $0.001 par
(See FSS Consulting Corp.)

IFH PERU LTD (PERU)
Stock Dividends - in Reg. S ADR's to holders of Reg. S ADR's 32.6615% payable 06/07/2004 to holders of record 05/11/2004; 21% payable 06/10/2005 to holders of record 05/31/2005; 12.68% payable 01/05/2006 to holders of record 12/21/2005
Name changed to Intercorp Peru Ltd. 06/26/2012

IFL INVT FNDTN CDA LTD (CANADA)
Conv. Class A Common no par reclassified as Common no par 05/09/1990
Conv. Class B Common no par reclassified as Common no par 05/09/1990

Completely liquidated
Each share Common no par received first and final distribution of $192.90 cash payable 03/30/2012 to holders of record 03/06/2012

IFLI ACQUISITION CORP (DE)
Common 1¢ par split (2) for (1) by issuance of (1) additional share payable 12/16/2011 to holders of record 12/12/2011 Ex date - 12/19/2011
Name changed to SimplePons, Inc. 12/27/2011
SimplePons, Inc. recapitalized as Eco-Shift Power Corp. 11/26/2013

IFM FOOD MGMT LTD (ON)
Name changed to Air Systems Plus Corp. 02/25/1992
Air Systems Plus Corp. name changed to Sales Initiatives International Inc. 06/01/1993 which name changed to Greenlight Communications Inc. 06/14/1994
(See Greenlight Communications Inc.)

IFM INVTS LTD (CAYMAN ISLANDS)
Each old ADS for Class A Ordinary exchanged for (0.33333333) new ADS for Class A Ordinary 04/16/2012
Basis changed from (1:15) to (1:45) 04/16/2012
ADS agreement terminated 09/16/2016
Each new ADS for Class A Ordinary exchanged for $0.18 cash

IFORUM FINL NETWORK INC (CANADA)
Filed a Notice of Intention pursuant to the Bankruptcy and Insolvency Act 03/14/2006
Stockholders' equity unlikely

IFR SYS INC (DE)
Common 1¢ par split (3) for (2) by issuance of (0.5) additional share payable 12/5/97 to holders of record 11/21/97
Merged into Aeroflex Inc. 6/19/2002
Each share Common 1¢ par exchanged for $1.35 cash

IFS CATSKILL L.L.C.
Liquidation completed
Each Share of Bene. Int. received initial distribution of $35 cash payable 4/7/95 to holders of record 3/31/95
Each Share of Bene. Int. received second distribution of $120 cash payable 8/22/95 to holders of record 6/30/95
Each Share of Bene. Int. received third distribution of $52 cash payable 10/11/95 to holders of record 9/30/95
Each Share of Bene. Int. received fourth and final distribution of $95 cash payable 1/15/96 to holders of record 12/31/95
Note: Certificates were not required to be exchanged and are without value

IFS INDS INC (IA)
Merged into Service Corp. International 12/10/81
Each share Common 50¢ par exchanged for (2/3) share Common $1 par

IFS INTL HLDGS INC (DE)
Name changed 07/03/1992
Name changed 03/17/1999
Name changed 11/16/2000
Name changed from IFS International Inc. to IFS Holdings, Inc. 07/03/1992
Each share old Common $0.001 par exchanged for (0.1) share new Common $0.001 par 11/08/1996
Name changed from IFS Holdings, Inc. to IFS International, Inc. 03/17/1999
Each share Conv. Preferred Ser. A $0.001 par exchanged for (1.1) shares Common 03/31/1999
Name changed from IFS

International, Inc. to IFS International Holdings, Inc. 11/16/2000
Charter cancelled and declared inoperative and void for non-payment of taxes 03/01/2005

IFSA STRONGMAN INC (DE)
Each share old Common $0.001 par exchanged for (0.1) share new Common 0.001 par 11/19/2007
Company terminated common stock registration and is no longer public as of 11/03/2009

IFT CORP (DE)
Name changed to Lapolla Industries, Inc. 11/08/2005
(See Lapolla Industries, Inc.)

IFT FING I
6.50% Conv. Trust Preferred Securities called for redemption at $50 on 1/11/2005
6.50% Conv. Trust Preferred Securities 144A called for redemption at $50 on 1/11/2005

IFTH ACQUISITION CORP (DE)
Name changed to Steel Vault Corp. 03/18/2009
Steel Vault Corp. merged into PositiveID Corp. 11/10/2009

IFUTURE COM INC (ON)
Name changed 10/09/2000
Name changed from iFuture Inc. to iFuture.com Inc. 10/09/2000
Merged into Red Dragon Resources Corp. (ON) 05/20/2005
Each share Common no par exchanged for (1) share Common no par
Red Dragon Resources Corp. (ON) reincorporated in British Columbia 08/23/2007 which name changed to Brazilian Gold Corp. 01/06/2010 which merged into Brazil Resources Inc. (BC) 11/22/2013 which reincorporated in Canada as GoldMining Inc. 12/07/2016

IFX CORP (DE)
Each share Common $0.004 par exchanged for (0.2) share Common 2¢ par 01/12/1998
Each share old Common 2¢ par exchanged for (0.00333333) share new Common 2¢ par 08/08/2003
Note: In effect holders received $0.12 cash per share and public interest was eliminated

IG LABS INC (DE)
Merged into Genzyme Corp. 10/02/1995
Each share Common 1¢ par exchanged for (0.1201) share Common 1¢ par
(See Genzyme Corp.)

IGAMES ENTMT INC (NV)
Each share Common $0.001 par exchanged for (0.25) share Common $0.004 par 12/10/2003
Merged into Money Centers of America, Inc. 10/19/2004
Each share Common $0.004 par exchanged for (1) share Common $0.001 par
(See Money Centers of America, Inc.)

IGAMING CORP (ON)
Name changed to Big Stick Media Corp. 06/29/2007
(See Big Stick Media Corp.)

IGATE COMPUTER SYS LTD (INDIA)
ADR agreement terminated 01/14/2013
Each Sponsored ADR for Equity Shares exchanged for $10.911498 cash

IGATE CORP (PA)
Name changed 03/25/2002
Name changed from iGate Capital Corp. to iGate Corp. 03/25/2002
Each share Common 1¢ par received distribution of (0.06666666) share

Mastech Holdings, Inc. Common 1¢ par payable 09/30/2008 to holders of record 09/16/2008 Ex date - 09/17/2008
Acquired by Capgemini North America, Inc. 07/01/2015
Each share Common 1¢ par exchanged for $48 cash

IGC INC (NY)
Merged into ElectroSound Group, Inc. 12/28/1984
Each (13.125) shares Common 1¢ par exchanged for (1) share Common 1¢ par
(See ElectroSound Group, Inc.)

IGC INTL GOLF CORP (BC)
Recapitalized as Medilase Industries Inc. 03/02/1992
Each share Common no par exchanged for (0.5) share Common no par
(See Medilase Industries Inc.)

IGC INTERNET GAMING CORP (BC)
Name changed to IGN Internet Global Network Inc. 11/20/1996
IGN Internet Global Network Inc. recapitalized as AssistGlobal Technologies Corp. 09/23/2003 which recapitalized as Bassett Ventures Inc. 07/08/2005 which name changed to Arris Resources Inc. 06/25/2007 which name changed to RTN Stealth Software Inc. 01/08/2010 which name changed to Quantitative Alpha Trading Inc. (BC) 04/29/2011 which reincorporated in Ontario 12/09/2011
(See Quantitative Alpha Trading Inc.)

IGEN INTL INC (DE)
Name changed 11/08/1996
Name changed from Igen, Inc. to Igen International, Inc. and state of incorporation changed from (CA) to (DE) 11/08/1996
Merged into Roche Holding Ltd. 02/13/2004
Each share Common $0.001 par exchanged for (1) share BioVeris Corp. Common $0.001 par and $47.25 cash
(See BioVeris Corp.)

IGF METALS INC (CANADA)
Name changed to Independent Growth Finders Inc. 07/10/1998

IGG INTL INC (NV)
Name changed to Safescience, Inc. 1/21/98
Safescience, Inc. name changed to GlycoGenesys, Inc. 11/7/2001
(See GlycoGenesys, Inc.)

IGI LABS INC (DE)
Name changed 05/08/2008
Name changed from IGI, Inc. to IGI Laboratories, Inc. 05/08/2008
Name changed to Teligent, Inc. 10/26/2015

IGLEHEART BROTHERS, INC.
Merged into General Foods Corp. in 1949
Details not available

IGLOO CORP (TX)
Common 20¢ par split (3) for (2) by issuance of (0.5) additional share 8/23/72
Merged into Coca-Cola Bottling Co. of New York, Inc. 12/21/72
Each share Common 20¢ par exchanged for (1) share Common 25¢ par
(See Coca-Cola Bottling Co. of New York, Inc.)

IGLOO VIKSKI INC (CANADA)
Acquired by Lanctot Licensing Inc. 02/13/2007
Each share Common no par exchanged for $1.10 cash

IGLUE INC (NV)
Recapitalized as AC Partners, Inc. 02/05/2018
Each share Common $0.001 par exchanged for (0.004) share Common $0.001 par

IGM FINL INC (CANADA)
1st Preferred Ser. A no par called for for redemption at $26 plus $0.359375 accrued dividends on 12/31/2009
(Additional Information in Active)

IGN ENTMT INC (DE)
Merged into Great Hill Partners, LLC 8/28/2003
Each share Common $0.001 par exchanged for $12 cash

IGN INTERNET GLOBAL NETWORK INC (BC)
Recapitalized as AssistGlobal Technologies Corp. 09/23/2003
Each share Common no par exchanged for (1/3) share Common no par
AssistGlobal Technologies Corp. recapitalized as Bassett Ventures Inc. 07/08/2005 which name changed to Arris Resources Inc. 06/25/2007 which name changed to RTN Stealth Software Inc. 01/08/2010 which name changed to Quantitative Alpha Trading Inc. (BC) 04/29/2011 which reincorporated in Ontario 12/09/2011
(See Quantitative Alpha Trading Inc.)

IGNACIO OIL & GAS INC (CO)
Name changed to American Gaming Enterprises, Inc. and Common no par changed to $0.001 par 11/3/87

IGNITE RESTAURANT GROUP INC (DE)
Plan of reorganization under Chapter 11 Federal Bankruptcy proceedings effective 12/19/2017
No stockholders' equity

IGNITION PT TECHNOLOGIES CORP (CANADA)
Recapitalized as Tilting Capital Corp. 08/24/2009
Each share Common no par exchanged for (0.33333333) share Common no par

IGNYTA INC (NV)
Reincorporated 06/17/2014
State of incorporation changed from (NV) to (DE) and Common $0.00001 par changed to $0.0001 par 06/17/2014
Acquired by Roche Holding Ltd. 02/08/2018
Each share Common $0.0001 par exchanged for $27 cash

IGO CORP (DE)
Issue Information - 5,000,000 shares COM offered at $12 per share on 10/13/1999
Merged into Mobility Electronics, Inc. 9/3/2002
Each share Common $0.001 par exchanged for (0.11859) share Common 1¢ par and $0.14824 cash

IGOHEALTHY COM INC (CO)
Name changed to Health Sciences Group, Inc. (CO) 09/10/2001
Health Sciences Group, Inc. (CO) reincorporated in Delaware 07/14/2005 which reincorporated in Florida 02/09/2009

IGSM GROUP INC (NV)
Each share old Common $0.001 par exchanged for (0.004) share new Common $0.001 par 09/27/2011
Recapitalized as Continental Rail Corp. 08/09/2013
Each share Common $0.001 par exchanged for (0.005) share Common $0.001 par
Continental Rail Corp. recapitalized as MediXall Group, Inc. 11/22/2016

IGT PHARMA INC (BC)
Name changed 02/27/1997
Name changed from IGT International Growth Technologies Inc. to IGT Pharma, Inc. 02/27/1997
Reincorporated under the laws of Canada as Prescient Neuropharma Inc. 02/19/2001
Prescient Neuropharma Inc. (Canada) reincorporated in British Columbia 12/21/2007 which name changed to PNO Resources Ltd. 02/09/2012 which merged into Sandspring Resources Ltd. 09/15/2015

IGUANA VENTURES LTD (NV)
Reorganized as Integrated Security Technologies, Inc. 06/14/2004
Each share Common $0.001 par exchanged for (3.3) shares Common $0.001 par
Integrated Security Technologies, Inc. name changed to Oramed Pharmaceuticals, Inc. (NV) 04/10/2006 which reincorporated in Delaware 03/11/2011

IHA, INC. (NH)
Adjudicated bankrupt 8/23/76

IHC INC (OH)
Common $1 par changed to 66-2/3¢ par and (0.5) additional share issued 06/20/1969
Name changed to Portage Industries Corp. 07/23/1973
Portage Industries Corp. name changed to Sweitzer Holdings, Inc. 03/18/1976
(See Sweitzer Holdings, Inc.)

IHC LIQUIDATION CO. (MN)
Liquidation completed
Each share Common 10¢ par exchanged for initial distribution of $1 cash 1/20/66
Each share Common 10¢ par received second and final distribution of $0.107 cash 11/10/66

IHO-AGRO INTL INC (NV)
Recapitalized as Grandwon Corp. 01/18/2018
Each share Common $0.0001 par exchanged for (0.05) share Common $0.0001 par

IHOOKUP SOCIAL INC (NV)
Each share old Common $0.0001 par exchanged for (0.01) share new Common $0.0001 par 03/19/2015
Name changed to Friendable, Inc. 10/27/2015

IHOP CORP NEW (DE)
Name changed to DineEquity, Inc. 05/28/2008
DineEquity, Inc. name changed to Dine Brands Global, Inc. 03/01/2018

IHOP CORP OLD (DE)
Merged into Wienerwald Holding AG 10/16/1981
Each share Common $1 par exchanged for $2.60 cash

IHS INC (DE)
Merged into IHS Markit Ltd. 07/13/2016
Each share Class A Common 1¢ par exchanged for (3.5566) shares Common 1¢ par

IIBA HLDGS INC (UT)
Involuntarily dissolved for failure to file annual reports 05/01/1990

IIC INDS INC (DE)
Common $1 par changed to 25¢ par and (3) additional shares issued payable 3/16/98 to holders of record 3/3/98
Merged into CP Holdings Ltd. 4/10/2002
Each share Common 25¢ par exchanged for $10.50 cash

II GROUP INC (DE)
Name changed to Travlang, Inc. 04/26/2001
(See Travlang, Inc.)

IITC HLDGS LTD (CANADA)
Liquidation completed
Each share Common no par received initial distribution of $8 cash 11/17/95
Each share Common no par received second distribution of $2 cash 12/9/96
Each share Common no par received third distribution of (4) shares Intermap Technologies Ltd. Class A no par 3/12/97
Each share Common no par received fourth distribution of (1) share Intermap Technologies Ltd. Class A no par and $1.35 cash 8/20/97
Each share Common no par received fifth distribution of $0.60 cash payable 4/21/98 to holders of record 4/7/98
Each share Common no par received sixth distribution of (2) shares Intermap Technologies Ltd. Class A no par payable 9/30/98 to holders of record 9/21/98
Each share Common no par received seventh distribution of $0.35 cash payable 5/30/2001 to holders of record 5/18/2001
Each share Common no par received eighth and final distribution of (0.039) share Intermap Technologies Ltd. Class A no par payable 7/14/2004 to holders of record 6/11/2004
Note: Certificates were not required to be surrendered and are without value

IJC VENTURES CORP (FL)
Name changed to Uncommon Media Group, Inc. 12/12/2000
(See Uncommon Media Group, Inc.)

IJNT NET INC (DE)
Name changed to Universal Broadband Networks Inc. 7/25/2000
(See Universal Broadband Networks Inc.)

IJOIN SYS INC (DE)
SEC revoked common stock registration 07/31/2009

IKANOS COMMUNICATIONS INC (DE)
Each share old Common $0.001 par exchanged for (0.1) share new Common $0.001 par 02/17/2015
Acquired by Qualcomm Inc. 09/28/2015
Each share new Common $0.001 par exchanged for $2.75 cash

IKAR MINERAL CORP (DE)
Recapitalized as Ethos Capital Inc. 11/02/2000
Each share Common $0.001 par exchanged for (0.005) share Common no par
Ethos Capital Inc. name changed to Patriot Energy Corp. 02/04/2002 which name changed to BigBrews Holdings Inc. (DE) 02/18/2003 which reincorporated in Nevada as Patriot Energy Corp. 09/09/2003 which name changed to Healing Hand Network International, Inc. 12/22/2003 which name changed to Patriot Energy Corp. (NV) 10/10/2005

IKAR MINERAL CORP (UT)
Reincorporated under the laws of Delaware and Common $0.025 par changed to $0.001 par 03/31/1998
Ikar Mineral Corp. (DE) recapitalized as Ethos Capital Inc. 11/02/2000 which name changed to Patriot Energy Corp. 02/04/2002 which name changed to BigBrews Holdings Inc. (DE) 02/18/2003 which reincorporated in Nevada as Patriot Energy Corp. 09/09/2003 which name changed to Healing Hand Network International, Inc. 12/22/2003 which name changed to Patriot Energy Corp. (NV) 10/10/2005
(See Patriot Energy Corp.)

IKARMA INC (DE)
Recapitalized as Medtino, Inc. 10/12/2010
Each share Common $0.0000001 par exchanged for (0.04) share Common $0.0000001 par
Medtino, Inc. name changed to IntelaKare Marketing, Inc. 03/01/2011

IKON OFFICE SOLUTIONS INC (OH)
Each 2.05% Depositary Preferred Ser. BB exchanged for (2.4972) shares Common no par 10/01/1998
Merged into Ricoh Co., Ltd. 10/31/2008
Each share Common no par exchanged for $17.25 cash

IKON VENTURES INC (NV)
Each share old Common $0.001 par exchanged for (0.01) share new Common $0.001 par 02/23/2001
Name changed to Sutton Trading Solutions Inc. 10/31/2001
Sutton Trading Solutions Inc. recapitalized as Global Diversified Acquisition Corp. 04/24/2003 which name changed to MailKey Corp. 04/13/2004 which name changed to IElement Corp. 08/25/2005
(See IElement Corp.)

IKOR INC (DE)
Adjudicated bankrupt 04/08/1976
Stockholders' equity unlikely

IKOS SYS INC (DE)
Each share old Common 1¢ par exchanged for (0.5) share new Common 1¢ par 04/27/1995
Merged into Mentor Graphics Corp. 04/26/2002
Each share new Common 1¢ par exchanged for $11 cash

IKS CORP (DE)
Acquired by Simonds Industries Inc. 10/31/2003
Each share Common exchanged for (0.494244) share Class A and $0.02 cash

IL FORNAIO AMER CORP (DE)
Issue Information - 1,500,000 shares COM offered at $11 per share on 09/18/1997
Merged into Bruckmann, Rosser, Sherrill & Co. II, L.P. 7/18/2001
Each share Common $0.001 par exchanged for $12 cash

IL INTL INC (DE)
Completely liquidated 8/14/98
Each share Common 1¢ par exchanged for first and final distribution of $0.02 cash

IL&FS INVESTSMART LTD (INDIA)
ADR agreement terminated 06/16/2009
No ADR's remain outstanding

ILC INDS INC (DE)
Merged into Lanlin, Inc. 03/04/1982
Each share Common $1 par exchanged for $10 cash

ILC PRODS INC (DE)
Merged into Patrick Industries, Inc. 12/31/1980
Each share Common 10¢ par exchanged for (0.8) share Common no par

ILC TECHNOLOGY INC (CA)
Common no par split (2) for (1) by issuance of (1) additional share 3/8/91
Merged into Lumen Technologies, Inc. 3/12/98
Each share Common no par exchanged for (2.2042) shares Common 1¢ par
(See Lumen Technologies, Inc.)

ILEX CORP (OH)
Name changed to Financial Industries Corp. (OH) 05/07/1976
Financial Industries Corp. (OH) reincorporated in Texas 12/31/1980
(See Financial Industries Corp.)

ILEX ONCOLOGY INC (DE)
Merged into Genzyme Corp. 12/21/2004
Each share Common 1¢ par exchanged for (0.4682) share Common 1¢ par
(See Genzyme Corp.)

ILG INC (DE)
Merged into Marriott Vacations Worldwide Corp. 09/04/2018
Each share Common 1¢ par exchanged for (0.165) share Common 1¢ par and $14.75 cash

ILG INDS INC (DE)
Merged into Carrier Corp. 02/23/1973
Each share Common no par exchanged for (4) shares Common $2.50 par
Carrier Corp. acquired by United Technologies Corp. 07/06/1979

ILI TECH CORP (AB)
Name changed 05/06/1999
Name changed from ILI Technologies Group Inc. to ILI Technologies Corp. 05/06/1999
Recapitalized as ILI Technologies (2002) Corp. 02/03/2003
Each share Common no par exchanged for (0.33333333) share Common no par
ILI Technologies (2002) Corp. name changed to Cdn Oilfield Technologies & Solutions Corp. 09/15/2011 which name changed to Canadian Oilfield Solutions Corp. 10/17/2012 which name changed to Divergent Energy Services Corp. 06/09/2014

ILI TECHNOLOGIES 2002 CORP (AB)
Name changed to Cdn Oilfield Technologies & Solutions Corp. 09/15/2011
Cdn Oilfield Technologies & Solutions Corp. name changed to Canadian Oilfield Solutions Corp. 10/17/2012 which name changed to Divergent Energy Services Corp. 06/09/2014

ILIFE COM INC (FL)
Name changed to Bankrate, Inc. 09/18/2000
(See Bankrate, Inc.)

ILIKON CORP (DE)
Each share Common 10¢ par exchanged for (0.2) share Common 50¢ par 5/21/76
Stock Dividend - 100% 6/30/64
Charter cancelled and declared inoperative and void for non-payment of taxes 3/1/80

ILINC COMMUNICATIONS INC (DE)
Acquired by BroadSoft, Inc. 10/03/2011
Each share Common $0.001 par exchanged for $0.044 cash
Note: An additional $0.02891327 cash per share was distributed from escrow 01/15/2013

ILINK TELECOM INC (NV)
Name changed to 9278 Communications Inc. (NV) 12/29/99
9278 Communications Inc. reincorporated in Delaware 4/24/2000
(See 9278 Communications Inc.)

ILIO INC (NY)
Common 1¢ par split (4) for (3) by issuance of (1/3) additional share 5/16/90
Proclaimed dissolved 9/24/97

ILIVE INC (NV)
Each share old Common $0.001 par exchanged for (0.1) share new Common $0.001 par 05/31/2002
Company terminated common stock registration and is no longer public as of 08/27/2007

ILLEGAL RESTAURANT GROUP INC (NV)
Name changed back to Nexus Energy Services, Inc. 08/13/2015

ILLINI BEEF PACKERS INC (DE)
Reincorporated 9/7/73
State of incorporation changed from (IL) to (DE) 9/7/73
Name changed to Imark Industries, Inc. 10/28/81
(See Imark Industries, Inc.)

ILLINI CMNTY BANCORP INC (IL)
Name changed to Illini Corp. 04/21/1994
(See Illini Corp.)

ILLINI CORP (IL)
Common $10 par changed to 1¢ par 03/21/2002
Each share Common 1¢ par exchanged for (1) share new Common 1¢ par 02/27/2006
Note: Holders of (199) shares or fewer received $40.50 cash per share
Acquired by United Community Bancorp 11/16/2016
Each share new Common 1¢ par exchanged for $67 cash

ILLINOIS AMERN WTR CO (IL)
6% 1st Preferred $100 par called for redemption at $105 on 06/30/2002

ILLINOIS BANKERS LIFE ASSURANCE CO.
Acquired by Central Standard Life Insurance Co. in 1951
Stockholders received $5 in cash plus Certificate of Obligation for ten annual payments of $1 each
Central Standard Life Insurance Co. name changed to Reliance Standard Life Insurance Co. 8/9/65
(See Reliance Standard Life Insurance Co.)

ILLINOIS BELL TEL CO (IL)
Common $100 par changed to $20 par and (4) additional shares issued 4/8/60
Merged into American Telephone & Telegraph Co. 4/5/74
Each share Common $20 par exchanged for (0.9) share Common $16-2/3 par
American Telephone & Telegraph Co. name changed to AT&T Corp. 4/20/94 which merged into AT&T Inc. 11/18/2005

ILLINOIS BRICK CO (IL)
Capital Stock $25 par changed to $10 par 00/00/1936
Merged into Old Fort Industries, Inc. 12/29/1972
Each share Capital Stock $10 par exchanged for $25 principal amount of 9-1/4% Installment Debentures due 09/30/1987

ILLINOIS CAP INVT CORP (IL)
Declared insolvent by Court Order 06/27/1973
No stockholders' equity

ILLINOIS CASH CREDIT CORP. OF N.J.
Merged into Franklin Plan Corp. in 1932
Details not available

ILLINOIS CASUALTY CO.
Merged into Hawkeye Casualty Co. 00/00/1942
Details not available

ILLINOIS CENT CORP (DE)
Ser. A Common $0.001 par split (3) for (2) by issuance of (0.5) additional share 2/28/92
Ser. A Common $0.001 par split (3) for (2) by issuance of (0.5) additional share payable 3/14/96 to holders of record 2/14/96 Ex date - 3/15/96
Merged into Canadian National Railway Co. 6/4/98
Each share Ser. A Common $0.001 par exchanged for (0.633) share Common no par

ILLINOIS CENT INDS INC (DE)
Common no par split (2) for (1) by issuance of (1) additional share 04/21/1967
Common no par split (3) for (2) by issuance of (0.5) additional share 10/01/1969
Name changed to IC Industries, Inc. 05/21/1975
IC Industries, Inc. name changed to Whitman Corp. (Old) 12/01/1988 which name changed to Whitman Corp. (New) 11/30/2000 which name changed to PepsiAmericas, Inc. (DE) 01/24/2001 which merged into PepsiCo, Inc. 02/26/2010

ILLINOIS CENT RR CO (IL)
Recapitalized 00/00/1954
6% Preferred Ser. A $100 par changed to $50 par and (1) additional share issued which was subsequently called for redemption
Common $100 par changed to no par and (1) additional share issued
Merged into Illinois Central Industries, Inc. 08/10/1972
Each share Common no par exchanged for (3) shares Common no par
Illinois Central Industries, Inc. name changed to IC Industries, Inc. 05/21/1975 which name changed to Whitman Corp. (Old) 12/01/1988 which name changed to Whitman Corp. (New) 11/30/2000 which name changed to PepsiAmericas, Inc. (DE) 01/24/2001 which merged into PepsiCo, Inc. 02/26/2010

ILLINOIS CENT TRANSN CO (DE)
Merged into Prospect Group, Inc. 7/31/89
Each share Common 1¢ par exchanged for $20 cash

ILLINOIS CLAY PRODUCTS CO. (IL)
Preferred $100 par called for redemption 10/25/56
Acquired by Green (A.P.) Fire Brick Co. 1/22/63
Each share Common $5 par exchanged for (3.4) shares Common $5 par
Green (A.P.) Fire Brick Co. name changed to Green (A.P.) Refractories Co. 10/29/65 which merged into United States Gypsum Co. (Del.) 12/29/67 which reorganized as USG Corp. 1/1/85

ILLINOIS COAL CORP.
Property acquired by Bondholders' Committee in 1934
No stockholders' equity

ILLINOIS COMMERCIAL TELEPHONE CO.
Name changed to General Telephone Co. of Illinois in 1952
General Telephone Co. of Illinois merged into GTE MTO Inc. 3/31/87 which name changed to GTE North Inc. 1/1/88
(See GTE North Inc.)

ILLINOIS CMNTY BANCORP INC (IL)
Merged into Centrue Financial Corp. (New) 04/08/2005
Each share Common $1 par exchanged for approximately either (0.05749) share Common 1¢ par and $5.7336 cash or (0.264) share Common 1¢ par
Note: Option to receive stock only expired 05/27/2005
Centrue Financial Corp. (New) merged into Midland States Bancorp, Inc. 06/09/2017

ILLINOIS CONS TEL CO (IL)
Each share 4-1/2% Preferred Ser. A $100 par exchanged for (2) shares 4-1/2% Preferred Ser. A $50 par 7/1/63

4.50% Preferred $50 par called for redemption 11/5/92
5% Preferred Series B $50 par called for redemption 11/5/92
7-7/8% Preferred Ser. A $100 par called for redemption 11/5/92
(Additional Information in Active)

ILLINOIS GLASS CO.
Merged into Owens-Illinois Glass Co. in 1929
Details not available

ILLINOIS GTEE SVGS BK FSB (EFFINGHAM, IL)
Under plan of reorganization each share Common $1 par automatically became (1) share Illinois Community Bancorp, Inc. Common $1 par 08/27/1996
Illinois Community Bancorp, Inc. merged into Centrue Financial Corp. (New) 04/08/2005 which merged into Midland States Bancorp, Inc. 06/09/2017

ILLINOIS INDS INC (NV)
Reincorporated in 1969
State of incorporation changed from (UT) to (NV) in 1969
Name changed to Trans Atlantic Resource Corp. 9/26/83
(See Trans Atlantic Resource Corp.)

ILLINOIS IOWA POWER CO. (IL)
Name changed to Illinois Power Co. (New) 11/01/1943
(See Illinois Power Co. (New))

ILLINOIS IRON & BOLT CO (IL)
Acquired by Ilinco, Inc. 00/00/1961
Details not available

ILLINOIS KELLOGG CO.
Merged into International Telephone & Telegraph Corp. (MD) on a (1.44) for (1) basis in 1952
International Telephone & Telegraph Corp. (MD) reincorporated under the laws of Delaware 1/31/68 which name changed to ITT Corp. 12/31/83 which reorganized in Indiana as ITT Industries Inc. 12/19/95 which name changed to ITT Corp. 7/1/2006

ILLINOIS-KENTUCKY BRIDGE
Reorganized as Paducah-Ohio River Bridge Co. in 1933
Details not available

ILLINOIS MARINE BANCORP INC (DE)
Common $10 par split (2.75) for (1) by issuance of (1.75) additional shares 10/01/1985
Name changed to Illinois Regional Bancorp, Inc. 01/30/1987
(See Illinois Regional Bancorp, Inc.)

ILLINOIS MID-CONTINENT LIFE INSURANCE CO. (IL)
Common $0.175 par changed to 50¢ par 08/11/1961
Merged into National Western Life Insurance Co. (CO) 03/29/1965
Each share Common 50¢ par exchanged for (0.8) share Common 10¢ par
National Western Life Insurance Co. (CO) reincorporated in Delaware as National Western Life Group, Inc. 10/02/2015

ILLINOIS NATL BANCORP INC (DE)
Merged into Midwest Financial Group, Inc. 02/08/1983
Each share Common $5 par exchanged for (1.05) shares Common $5 par
Midwest Financial Group, Inc. merged into First of America Bank Corp. 11/01/1989 which merged into National City Corp. 03/31/1998 which was acquired by PNC Financial Services Group, Inc. 12/31/2008

ILLINOIS NATL BK & TR CO (ROCKFORD, IL)
Each share Capital Stock $100 par exchanged for (25) shares Capital Stock $20 par to effect a (5) for (1) split and a 400% stock dividend 01/11/1955
Each share Capital Stock $20 par exchanged for (2.25) shares Capital Stock $15 par to effect a (3) for (2) split and a 50% stock dividend 11/09/1955
Capital Stock $15 par changed to $20 par 12/18/1958
Capital Stock $20 par split (3) for (2) by issuance of (0.5) additional share 04/12/1971
Merged into Americorp Financial Inc. 11/18/1985
Each share Capital Stock $20 par exchanged for (1) share Common $1 par and $132 cash
Americorp Financial Inc. name changed to AMCORE Financial, Inc. 11/26/1985
(See AMCORE Financial, Inc.)

ILLINOIS NATL BK (SPRINGFIELD, IL)
Each share Capital Stock $100 par exchanged for (8-1/3) shares Capital Stock $20 par to effect a (5) for (1) split and 66-2/3% stock dividend 08/00/1953
Capital Stock $20 par changed to $10 par and (1) additional share issued plus a 20% stock dividend paid 01/08/1957
Capital Stock $10 par changed to $5 par and (1) additional share issued plus a 10% stock dividend paid 03/29/1974
Stock Dividends - 10% 02/24/1959; 10% 06/07/1961; 10% 04/24/1967; 25% 03/24/1969
Reorganized as Illinois National Bancorp, Inc. 12/31/1976
Each share Capital Stock $5 par exchanged for (1) share Common $5 par
Illinois National Bancorp, Inc. merged into Midwest Financial Group, Inc. 02/08/1983 which merged into First of America Bank Corp. 11/01/1989 which merged into National City Corp. 03/31/1998 which was acquired by PNC Financial Services Group, Inc. 12/31/2008

ILLINOIS NATIONWIDE ART CTRS INC (DE)
Name changed to Inter-Continental Management Co. 12/16/70
(See Inter-Continental Management Co.)

ILLINOIS OIL CO.
In process of liquidation in 1945

ILLINOIS POWER & LIGHT CORP. (IL)
Recapitalized as Illinois Iowa Power Co. 05/01/1937
Each share $6 Preferred and 6% Preferred exchanged for (1) share 5% Preferred $50 par
Illinois Iowa Power Co. name changed to Illinois Power Co. (New) 11/01/1943
(See Illinois Power Co. (New))

ILLINOIS POWER CO. OLD (IL)
Acquired by Central Illinois Light Co. 7/1/33
Details not available

ILLINOIS PWR CO NEW (IL)
5% Preferred $50 par called for redemption 09/17/1948
Common no par changed to $15 par and (1) additional share issued 04/30/1957
Common $15 par changed to no par and (1) additional share issued 04/30/1962
11.66% Preferred $50 par called for redemption 02/01/1987
11.75% Preferred no par called for redemption 02/15/1991
8.94% Preferred $50 par called for redemption 07/12/1993
8.52% Preferred $50 par called for redemption 07/30/1993
Under plan of reorganization each share Common no par automatically became (1) share Illinova Corp. Common no par 05/31/1994
(See Illinova Corp.)
8% Preferred Ser. 1986 no par called for redemption 05/01/1995
7.56% Preferred $50 par called for redemption 12/01/1995
8% Preferred $50 par called for redemption 12/01/1995
Adjustable Rate Preferred Ser. B no par called for redemption 05/15/1996
8.24% Preferred $50 par called for redemption 12/01/1995
Adjustable Rate Preferred Ser. A no par called for redemption 11/01/1997
Merged into Ameren Illinois Co. 10/01/2010
Each share 4.08% Preferred $50 par exchanged for (0.5) share 4.08% Preferred $100 par
Each share 4.2% Preferred $50 par exchanged for (0.5) share 4.2% Preferred $100 par
Each share 4.26% Preferred $50 par exchanged for (0.5) share 4.26% Preferred $100 par
Each share 4.42% Preferred $50 par exchanged for (0.5) share 4.42% Preferred $100 par
Each share 4.7% Preferred $50 par exchanged for (0.5) share 4.7% Preferred $100 par
Each share 7.75% Preferred $50 par exchanged for (0.5) share 7.75% Preferred $100 par

ILLINOIS PWR FING I
8% Trust Originated Preferred Securities called for redemption at $25 on 9/30/2001

ILLINOIS REGL BANCORP INC (DE)
Merged into Old Kent Financial Corp. 12/28/87
Each share Common $10 par exchanged for $48 cash

ILLINOIS ST BANCORP INC (DE)
Merged into First Midwest Corp. of Delaware 09/29/1986
Details not available

ILLINOIS ST BK (CHICAGO, IL)
Stock Dividends - 10% 02/01/1966; 15% 01/27/1967; 10% 03/03/1969
Reorganized as Illinois State Bancorp, Inc. 07/01/1980
Each share Common Capital Stock $10 par exchanged for (1) share Common Capital $10 par
(See Illinois State Bancorp, Inc.)

ILLINOIS STATE TRUST CO. (EAST ST. LOUIS, IL)
Stock Dividend - 100% 2/15/54
Merged into First Bancorp of Belleville, Inc. 12/31/75
Each share Common $12.50 par exchanged for (0.9) share Common $12.50 par
First Bancorp of Belleville, Inc. name changed to Magna Group, Inc. 4/26/83 which merged into Union Planters Corp. 7/1/98 which merged into Regions Financial Corp. (New) 7/1/2004

ILLINOIS SUPERCONDUCTOR CORP (DE)
Name changed to ISCO International, Inc. 06/22/2001
(See ISCO International, Inc.)

ILLINOIS TERM RR CO (IL)
Completely liquidated 6/15/56
Each share Common $5 par exchanged for first and final distribution of $17.16716 cash

ILLINOIS TRACTION CO.
Liquidated in 1944

ILLINOIS WIRE & CABLE CO.
Merged into Inland Wire & Cable Co. 00/00/1927
Details not available

ILLINOIS ZINC CO. (IL)
Each share Capital Stock $100 par exchanged for (2) shares Capital Stock no par in 1935
Capital Stock no par changed to $5 par 1/19/55
Capital Stock $5 par changed to $2.50 par and (1) additional share issued 4/12/55
Stock Dividend - 100% 10/31/46
Name changed to Hydrometals, Inc. 6/20/56
(See Hydrometals, Inc.)

ILLINOVA CORP (IL)
Under plan of merger name changed to Dynegy Inc. (IL) 02/01/2000
Dynegy Inc. (IL) merged into Dynegy Inc. (DE) (Old) 04/02/2007 which reorganized as Dynegy Inc. (DE) (New) 10/01/2012 which merged into Vistra Energy Corp. 04/09/2018

ILLIUM CORP. (DE)
Name changed to Burco, Inc. in 1954 which was liquidated 3/31/55

ILLUMICELL CORP (AB)
Name changed to Multiplied Media Corp. 08/16/2007
Multiplied Media Corp. name changed to Poynt Corp. 10/27/2010
(See Poynt Corp.)

ILLUMINATING & POWER SECURITIES CORP.
Dissolved in 1941

ILLUMINATING SHARES CO.
Liquidation completed in 1942

ILLUMINATION AMER INC (FL)
Name changed to Grom Social Enterprises, Inc. 09/07/2017

ILLUMINET HLDGS INC (DE)
Issue Information - 3,900,000 shares CDT-COM offered at $19 per share on 10/07/1999
Merged into VeriSign, Inc. 12/12/2001
Each share Common 1¢ par exchanged for (0.93) share Common $0.001 par

ILLUMINO DEVICES INC (NY)
Charter cancelled and proclaimed dissolved for failure to pay taxes 09/30/1981

ILLUMITRY CORP (NV)
Name changed to Huale Acoustics Corp. 11/07/2017

ILLUSION SYS INC (DE)
Reincorporated 02/27/2001
Place of incorporation changed from (BC) to (DE) 02/27/2001
Delisted from Toronto Venture Stock Exchange 06/20/2003

ILLUSTRATED WORLD ENCYCLOPEDIA INC (NY)
Dissolved by proclamation 10/28/2009

ILLUSTRIOUS MERGERS INC (NV)
Name changed to Allied Devices Corp. 6/18/91
Allied Devices Corp. reorganized as Deep Well Oil & Gas, Inc. 9/23/2003

ILM RES LTD (BC)
Recapitalized as Rainier Resources Ltd. 02/11/1993
Each share Common no par exchanged for (0.2857142) share Common no par
Rainier Resources Ltd. recapitalized as Prong Industries Corp. Ltd. (BC) 08/27/1996 which reincorporated in Bermuda 09/03/1996 which name changed to C&C Industries Corp. 11/02/1998 which name changed to Xenex Minerals Ltd. 01/11/2008
(See Xenex Minerals Ltd.)

ILOG S A (FRANCE)
Issue Information - 2,500,000 SPONSORED ADR'S offered at $11 per ADR on 02/14/1997
Sponsored ADR's for Ordinary FF 4 par changed to Euro 0.61 par 09/07/2001
Sponsored ADR's for Ordinary Euro. 0.61 par changed to Euro 1 par 09/27/2005
Acquired by International Business Machines Corp. 01/06/2009
Each Sponsored ADR for Ordinary Euro 1 par exchanged for $13.042 cash

ILOVETV ENTMT INC (BC)
Delisted from Toronto Venture Stock Exchange 06/30/2005

ILSEDER HUETTE (GERMANY)
Name changed to Stahlwerke Peine Salzgitter A.G. 10/01/1970
(See Stahlwerke Peine Salzgitter A.G.)

ILX RESORTS INC (AZ)
Recapitalized 01/13/1998
Recapitalized from ILX Inc. to ILX Resorts Inc. 01/13/1998
Each share Common no par exchanged for (0.2) share Common no par
Each share Common no par received distribution of (0.862942) share Sedona Worldwide Inc. Common no par payable 01/12/2000 to holders of record 12/21/1999
Plan of reorganization under Chapter 11 Federal Bankruptcy proceedings effective 09/01/2010
Each share Preferred Ser. A $10 par exchanged for $2 cash
Each share Preferred Ser. C $10 par exchanged for $2 cash
Each share Common no par exchanged for $0.88 cash
Each share Common no par received an initial additional distribution of $0.27 cash payable 03/31/2011 to holders of record 09/01/2010
Each share Common no par received a second and final distribution of $0.06148 cash payable 11/08/2012 to holders of record 09/01/2010
Note: Unexchanged certificates were cancelled and remaining funds distributed to holders who exchanged their certificates prior to 09/01/2011

IMA EXPL INC (BC)
Each share Class A Common no par received distribution of (0.3368) share Viceroy Resource Corp. Common no par 07/07/1998
Class A Common no par reclassified as Common no par 07/15/1999
Each share Common no par received distribution of (0.1) share Golden Arrow Resources Corp. Common no par payable 07/07/2004 to holders of record 07/07/2004
Recapitalized as Kobex Minerals Inc. 09/30/2009
Each share Common no par exchanged for (0.41666666) share Common no par
Kobex Minerals Inc. name changed to Kobex Capital Corp. 08/29/2014 which name changed to Itasca Capital Ltd. 06/23/2016

IMA-GRAPHICS INC (DE)
Recapitalized as Southeastern Control Systems, Inc. 06/09/1989
Each share Common $0.001 par exchanged for (1/3) share Common $0.001 par
(See Southeastern Control Systems, Inc.)

IMA RESOURCE CORP (BC)
Recapitalized as IMA Exploration Inc. 07/07/1998
Each share Common no par exchanged for (0.25) share Common no par
IMA Exploration Inc. recapitalized as Kobex Minerals Inc. 09/30/2009 which name changed to Kobex Capital Corp. 08/29/2014 which name changed to Itasca Capital Ltd. 06/23/2016

IMABV LTD (UT)
Involuntarily dissolved for failure to file annual reports 5/1/90

IMAC FOOD SYS INC (RI)
Name changed to Intercontinental Mining & Abrasives, Inc. and Common no par changed to 1¢ par 5/19/71
(See Intercontinental Mining & Abrasives, Inc.)

IMAG GROUP INC (FL)
Administratively dissolved 09/27/2013

IMAGE BK INC (NY)
Merged into J.S. Acquisition Co. 11/06/1991
Each share Common 1¢ par exchanged for $6.75 cash

IMAGE BUSINESS SYS CORP (DE)
Charter cancelled and declared inoperative and void for non-payment of taxes 3/1/96

IMAGE DATA INTL CORP (ON)
Reincorporated 06/10/1993
Place of incorporation changed from (BC) to (ON) 06/10/1993
Delisted from Vancouver Stock Exchange 03/05/1996

IMAGE ENTMT INC (DE)
Reincorporated 06/19/1990
Reincorporated 09/09/2005
State of incorporation changed from (CO) to (CA) 06/19/1990
Each share old Common no par exchanged for (0.06730769) share new Common no par 02/08/1991
Stock Dividend - 10% 05/31/1985
State of incorporation changed from (CA) to (DE) and Common no par changed to $0.0001 par 09/09/2005
Merged into RLJ Entertainment, Inc. 10/03/2012
Each share Common $0.0001 par exchanged for (0.00972) share Common $0.001 par

IMAGE GUIDED TECHNOLOGIES INC (CO)
Merged into Stryker Corp. 8/16/2000
Each share Common no par exchanged for (0.04947) share Common 10¢ par

IMAGE INDS INC (DE)
Merged into Maxim Group, Inc. 8/30/96
Each share Common 1¢ par exchanged for (1) share Common $0.001 par
Maxim Group, Inc. name changed to Flooring America, Inc. 1/1/2000
(See Flooring America, Inc.)

IMAGE INNOVATIONS HLDGS INC (NV)
Plan of reorganization under Chapter 11 Federal Bankruptcy Code effective 09/01/2007
No stockholders' equity

IMAGE INSTRUMENTS, INC. (DE)
Each share Class A exchanged for (1) share Common $1 par 10/01/1964
Each share Class B exchanged for (1) share Common $1 par 10/01/1964
Common $1 par changed to 25¢ par 07/20/1965
Completely liquidated 02/14/1967
Each share Common 25¢ par exchanged for first and final distribution of (0.25) share Dasa Corp. Common $1 par
(See Dasa Corp.)

IMAGE MGMT SYS INC (RI)
Charter cancelled and declared inoperative and void for non-payment of taxes 9/21/89

IMAGE-PHOTO SYS INC (MN)
Each share old Common $0.001 par exchanged for (0.1) share new Common $0.001 par 06/25/1999
Name changed to e-bidd.com, Inc. 09/08/1999
e-bidd.com, Inc. name changed to xraymedia.com, Inc. 06/28/2000 which name changed to Xraymedia, Inc. 12/04/2003 which recapitalized as T.W. Christian, Inc. 08/14/2007
(See T.W. Christian, Inc.)

IMAGE PROCESSING SYS INC (ON)
Acquired by Photon Dynamics, Inc. 12/22/2000
Each share Common no par exchanged for either (0.0447) share Image Processing Systems Inc. Common no par or (0.0447) Exchangeable Share no par 12/22/2000
Note: U.S. residents received Common
Each Exchangeable Share no par exchanged for (1) share Photon Dynamics, Inc. Common no par 12/19/2005
(See Photon Dynamics, Inc.)

IMAGE PRODUCTIONS INC (WA)
Each share old Common $0.0001 par exchanged for (0.05) share new Common $0.0001 par 11/01/1985
Name changed to A G Holdings, Inc. 08/04/1994
A G Holdings, Inc. recapitalized as Bahui USA, Inc. 12/03/1997 which name changed back to A G Holdings, Inc. 04/06/1998 which name changed to Wasatch Interactive Learning Corp. 01/20/2000 which merged into Plato Learning, Inc. 04/05/2001
(See Plato Learning, Inc.)

IMAGE RES & SYS LTD (BC)
Recapitalized as Big M Petroleum Inc. 07/17/1985
Each share Common no par exchanged for (0.2) share Common no par
Big M Petroleum Inc. name changed to Big M Resources Ltd. 08/17/1990 which recapitalized as Nickelodeon Minerals Inc. 07/17/1992 which name changed to Strongbow Resources Inc. (BC) 08/18/2000 which reorganized in Canada as Strongbow Exploration Inc. 05/03/2004

IMAGE RETAILING GROUP INC (MN)
Name changed to Audio King Corp. 3/5/92
Audio King Corp. merged into Ultimate Electronics, Inc. 6/27/97
(See Ultimate Electronics, Inc.)

IMAGE SCULPTING INTL INC (AB)
Delisted from Toronto Venture Stock Exchange 06/30/2003

IMAGE SOFTWARE INC (CO)
Company terminated common stock registration and is no longer public as of 11/01/2005

IMAGE SYS CORP (MN)
Merged into Communications Systems, Inc. 3/24/2004
Each share Common no par exchanged for $0.643 cash

IMAGE SYS INC (DE)
Reincorporated 8/29/74
State of incorporation changed from (CA) to (DE) 8/29/74
Common $1 par changed to 10¢ par and Ser. B Common $1 par reclassified as Common 10¢ par 8/9/78
Charter cancelled and declared inoperative and void for non-payment of taxes 3/1/89

IMAGE TECHNOLOGY LABORATORIES INC (DE)
Name changed to Image Protect, Inc. 12/09/2016

IMAGE WORLD MEDIA INC (CO)
SEC revoked common stock registration 09/05/2006

IMAGE WORLDWIDE INC (CO)
Recapitalized as STL Marketing Group, Inc. 09/03/2009
Each share Common $0.001 par exchanged for (0.002) share Common $0.001 par

IMAGEAMERICA INC (TN)
Name changed to MedAlliance, Inc. 6/1/94
(See MedAlliance, Inc.)

IMAGEMATRIX CORP (CO)
Company terminated common stock registration and is no longer public as of 02/20/2007

IMAGEMAX INC (PA)
Issue Information - 3,100,000 shares COM offered at $12 per share on 12/03/1997
Acquired by DataBank IMX 12/12/2005
Details not available

IMAGENET SYS INC (CO)
Recapitalized as Phoenix Metals U.S.A. II, Inc. 07/12/1993
Each share Common $0.0001 par exchanged for (0.01) share Common $0.0001 par
Phoenix Metals U.S.A. II, Inc. (CO) reincorporated in Nevada 03/01/2000 which reorganized as TM Media Group, Inc. 09/22/2006
(See TM Media Group, Inc.)

IMAGES LIFE INC (NV)
Recapitalized as Geo-Point Technologies, Inc. 06/22/2005
Each share Common $0.001 par exchanged for (0.005) share Common $0.001 par
Geo-Point Technologies, Inc. name changed to Global Resources Technologies, Inc. 09/06/2005 which name changed to Gold & Onyx Mining Co. 06/10/2009
(See Gold & Onyx Mining Co.)

IMAGETRUST INC (DE)
Each share old Common 5¢ par exchanged for (0.2) share new Common 5¢ par 05/28/1993
Charter cancelled and declared inoperative and void for non-payment of taxes 03/01/1997

IMAGEWARE INTL INC (DE)
Recapitalized as Pearce Systems International, Inc. 01/08/1993
Each share Common 1¢ par exchanged for (0.01) share Common $0.0005 par
(See Pearce Systems International, Inc.)

IMAGEWARE SYS INC (CA)
Issue Information - 1,875,000 Units consisting of (1) share COM and (1) WT offered at $8 per Unit on 03/30/2000
Reincorporated under the laws of Delaware 1/20/2006

IMAGEX INC (WA)
Name changed 10/21/2001
Issue Information - 5,000,000 shares COM offered at $23 per share on 02/11/2000
Name changed from Imagex.com, Inc. to ImageX, Inc. 10/22/2001
Merged into Kinko's, Inc. 5/13/2003
Each share Common 1¢ par exchanged for $0.512 cash

IMAGEX SVCS INC (NV)
Recapitalized as InterSecurity Holdings Corp. 05/27/2005
Each share Common $0.001 par exchanged for (0.0025) share Common $0.001 par

InterSecurity Holdings Corp. recapitalized as Founders Bay Holdings 04/25/2017

IMAGEXPRESS INC (CO)
Name changed to Imagexpres Corp. 10/01/2003

IMAGI INTL HLDGS LTD (BERMUDA)
Basis changed from (1:100) to (1:10) 04/19/2010
Basis changed from (1:10) to (1:2) 05/31/2016
ADR agreement terminated 07/20/2016
Each ADR for Ordinary exchanged for $0.027988 cash

IMAGICA ENTMT INC (FL)
Each share old Common 2¢ par exchanged for (0.1) share new Common 2¢ par 11/11/97
Recapitalized as Broadcast Marketing Group, Inc. 5/27/2005
Each share new Common $0.001 par exchanged for (0.005) share Common $0.001 par

IMAGICTV INC (CANADA)
Acquired by Alcatel 04/30/2003
Each share Common no par exchanged for (0.158517) Sponsored ADR for Class A Common
Alcatel name changed to Alcatel-Lucent 11/30/2006
(See Alcatel-Lucent)

IMAGIN MOLECULAR CORP (DE)
SEC revoked common stock registration 08/13/2014

IMAGIN NET INC (NV)
Name changed to Virtual Games, Inc. 4/23/99
Virtual Games, Inc. recapitalized as MidAmerica Oil & Gas Inc. 8/13/2002 which name changed to Sounds 24-7, Inc. 1/15/2004 which recapitalized as Allied Energy Corp. 1/26/2006

IMAGINAMICS INC (ON)
Name changed to Bynamics Inc. 03/26/1984
(See Bynamics Inc.)

IMAGINATION TECHNOLOGIES GROUP (UNITED KINGDOM)
ADR agreement terminated 11/29/2017
Each ADR for Ordinary exchanged for $4.798 cash

IMAGINE AMER INC (NJ)
Name changed to Charter Financial Network Inc. 07/19/1993
Charter Financial Network Inc. name changed to Imagine America, Inc. (New) 08/10/1995

IMAGINE FILMS ENTMT INC (DE)
Merged into IFE Acquisition Co., Inc. 3/29/93
Each share Common 1¢ par exchanged for $9 cash

IMAGINE HLDG CORP (NV)
Name changed to DNA Beverage Corp. (NV) 09/18/2007
DNA Beverage Corp. (NV) reorganized in Oklahoma as Digital Caddies, Inc. 11/14/2011 which name changed to IZON Network, Inc. 09/19/2017

IMAGINE MEDIA LTD (DE)
Name changed to TransBiotec, Inc. 02/15/2012

IMAGING CTR INC (MD)
Voluntarily dissolved 12/27/2006
Details not available

IMAGING DIAGNOSTIC SYS INC (FL)
Reincorporated 07/01/1995
State of incorporation changed from (NJ) to (FL) 07/01/1995
Each share old Common no par exchanged for (0.002) share new Common no par 12/10/2012

SEC revoked common stock registration 09/25/2014

IMAGING DYNAMICS CORP (AB)
Recapitalized as Imaging Dynamics Co. Ltd. 11/05/2001
Each share Common no par exchanged for (0.2) share Common no par

IMAGING MGMT ASSOC INC (CO)
Recapitalized as Gulf Energy Corp. 07/23/2007
Each share Common no par exchanged for (0.01) share Common no par
Gulf Energy Corp. name changed to Indie Ranch Media Inc. 11/19/2007

IMAGING SCIENCE TECHNOLOGIES INFRARED IMAGING DIV INC (DE)
Charter forfeited for failure to maintain a registered agent 10/21/95

IMAGING SCIENCE TECHNOLOGIES RADIATION BLOCKING DIVISION INC (DE)
Charter forfeited for failure to maintain a registered agent 11/15/94

IMAGING TECHNOLOGIES CORP (DE)
Each share old Common $0.005 par exchanged for (0.05) share new Common $0.005 par 8/9/2002
Name changed to Dalrada Financial Corp. 3/8/2004
Each share 5% Conv. Preferred $0.005 par exchanged for (1) share 5% Conv. Preferred $0.005 par
Each share new Common $0.005 par exchanged for (1) share Common $0.005 par

IMAGING3 INC NEW (CA)
Reorganized under the laws of Delaware 03/16/2018
Each share Common no par exchanged for (0.05) share Common no par

IMAGING3 INC OLD (CA)
Under plan of reorganization each share Common no par received distribution of (0.01503759) share Imaging3, Inc. (New) (CA) Common no par payable 09/09/2013 to holders of record 07/31/2013
Imaging3, Inc. (New) (CA) reorganized in Delaware 03/16/2018

IMAGIS TECHNOLOGIES INC (BC)
Each share old Common no par exchanged for (0.22222222) share new Common no par 11/25/2003
Reincorporated under the laws of Canada as Visiphor Corp. 07/07/2005

IMAGISTICS INTL INC (DE)
Merged into Oce N.V. 10/31/2005
Each share Common 1¢ par exchanged for $42 cash

IMAGITREND INC (WY)
Name changed to Castle Technologies, Inc. 04/28/2008
Castle Technologies, Inc. recapitalized as Hawaiian Hospitality Group, Inc. 08/14/2009

IMAGYN MED INC (DE)
Merged into Imagyn Medical Technologies, Inc. 09/29/1997
Each share Common $0.001 par exchanged for (1.4) shares Common no par
(See Imagyn Medical Technologies, Inc.)

IMAGYN MED TECHNOLOGIES INC (DE)
Plan of reorganization under Chapter 11 Federal Bankruptcy Code effective 10/08/1999
No stockholders' equity

IMALL INC (NV)
Each share old Common $0.001 par exchanged for (3) shares new Common $0.001 par 5/21/96

Each share new Common $0.001 par exchanged again for (0.125) share new Common $0.001 par 2/10/98
Merged into At Home Corp. 10/27/99
Each share new Common $0.001 par exchanged for (0.46) share Common 1¢ par
(See At Home Corp.)

IMANAGE INC (DE)
Merged into Interwoven, Inc. 11/18/2003
Each share Common $0.001 par exchanged for (0.523575) share new Common $0.001 par and $1.20 cash
(See Interwoven, Inc.)

IMAR CORP (DE)
Charter cancelled and declared inoperative and void for non-payment of taxes 3/1/92

IMARK CORP (ON)
Merged into Maxim Atlantic Corp. 08/19/2003
Each share Common no par exchanged for (0.19751759) share Common no par

IMARK INDS INC (DE)
Stock Dividend - 100% 5/14/92
Liquidation completed
Each share Common no par received initial distribution of $3.20 cash 2/26/88
Each share Common no par received second distribution of $1 cash 7/15/89
Each share Common no par exchanged for third distribution of $1.30 cash 3/16/90
Each share Common no par received fourth and final distribution of $0.2241 cash 5/28/93

IMARK TECHNOLOGIES INC (DE)
Each share old Common 1¢ par exchanged for (0.1) share new Common 1¢ par 03/03/1999
Recapitalized as Pharm Control Ltd. 11/08/2006
Each share new Common 1¢ par exchanged for (0.001) share Common 1¢ par
(See Pharm Control Ltd.)

IMARKETING SOLUTIONS GROUP INC (AB)
Discharged from receivership 02/02/2015
No stockholders' equity

IMARX THERAPEUTICS INC (DE)
Issue Information - 3,000,000 shares COM offered at $5 per share on 07/25/2007
Reincorporated under the laws of Nevada as Sycamore Entertainment Group Inc. and Common $0.0001 par changed to $0.001 par 11/29/2010

IMASCO FINL CORP (CANADA)
$2.25 Retractable 1st Preferred Ser. A no par called for redemption 10/22/1990

IMASCO LTD (CANADA)
Common no par reclassified as Conv. Class A Common no par 06/20/1974
Conv. Class A Common no par reclassified as Common no par 01/01/1979
Conv. Class B Common no par reclassified as Common no par 01/01/1979
Conv. Preference Ser. A no par called for redemption 07/19/1979
Common no par split (2) for (1) by issuance of (1) additional share 08/11/1980
Common no par split (2) for (1) by issuance of (1) additional share 11/30/1982
$3.06 Conv. Preference Ser. B no par called for redemption 03/30/1984
Common no par split (2) for (1) by

issuance of (1) additional share 03/31/1985
7.375% 1st Preference Ser. C no par called for redemption 07/17/1993
Common no par split (2) for (1) by issuance of (1) additional share 05/23/1995
Common no par split (2) for (1) by issuance of (1) additional share payable 06/30/1998 to holders of record 05/29/1998
6% Preference $4.86666666 par called for redemption 06/00/1999
Merged into British American Tobacco PLC 02/01/2000
Each share new Common no par exchanged for $41.60 cash

IMATEC LTD (DE)
Common $0.0001 par split (2) for (1) by issuance of (1) additional share payable 11/17/2000 to holders of record 10/2/2000 Ex date - 11/20/2000
Name changed to Sequel Technology Corp. 11/27/2000
(See Sequel Technology Corp.)

IMATEL HLDGS INC (WA)
Recapitalized as Ovvio Better Life, Inc. 03/26/1999
Each share Common no par exchanged for (0.25) share Common no par
Ovvio Better Life, Inc. name changed to Animal Cloning Sciences, Inc. 11/21/2000
(See Animal Cloning Sciences, Inc.)

IMATION CORP (DE)
Recapitalized as GlassBridge Enterprises, Inc. 02/22/2017
Each share Common 1¢ par exchanged for (0.1) share Common 1¢ par

IMATRON INC (NJ)
Merged into General Electric Co. 12/19/2001
Each share Common no par exchanged for (0.05) share Common 16¢ par

IMATTERS COM INC (NV)
Name changed to Iweb Corp. 06/01/1999
Iweb Corp. reorganized as National Health Scan Inc. 05/09/2002 which name changed to Gaensel Energy Group, Inc. 02/24/2015

IMB GROUP (UKRAINE)
Name changed to PT Platinum Public Ltd. 03/10/2010
(See PT Platinum Public Ltd.)

IMBREX LTD (CANADA)
Acquired by Neon Products of Canada Ltd. 02/19/1969
Each share Common no par exchanged for (0.461539) share Common no par
Neon Products of Canada Ltd. name changed to Neonex International Ltd. 03/24/1969
(See Neonex International Ltd.)

IMC GLOBAL INC (DE)
Name changed 10/21/1994
Name changed from IMC Fertilizer Group, Inc. to IMC Global Inc. 10/21/1994
Common $1 par split (2) for (1) by issuance of (1) additional share 11/30/1995
Merged into Mosaic Co. (Old) 10/22/2004
Each Mandatory Conv. Preferred Share exchanged for (1) share 7.50% Mandatory Conv. Preferred 1¢ par
Each share Common $1 par exchanged for (1) share Common 1¢ par
Mosaic Co. (Old) merged into Mosaic Co. (New) 05/25/2011

IMC INTEGRATED MARKETING COMMUNICATIONS INC (ON)
Charter cancelled for failure to file reports and pay taxes 8/7/95

IMC INTL INC (DE)
Charter cancelled and declared inoperative and void for non-payment of taxes 04/15/1973

IMC MAGNETICS CORP (NY)
Merged into Minebea Co. Ltd. 02/10/1984
Each share Common $0.33333333 exchanged for $24 cash

IMC MTG CO (FL)
Common 1¢ par split (2) for (1) by issuance of (1) additional share payable 2/13/97 to holders of record 2/6/97
Ceased operations 7/13/2001
No stockholders' equity

IMC VENTURES INC (BC)
Reincorporated under the laws of Yukon Territory as Triumph Gold Corp. 03/29/2004
Triumph Gold Corp. (YT) reincorporated in British Columbia 08/26/2004 which recapitalized as Kenai Resources Ltd. 05/01/2007 which merged into Serabi Gold PLC 07/22/2013

IMCERA GROUP INC (NY)
Common $5 par changed to $1 par 10/00/1991
Common $1 par split (3) for (1) by issuance of (2) additional shares 11/12/1991
Name changed to Mallinckrodt Group Inc. 03/15/1994
Mallinckrodt Group Inc. name changed to Mallinckrodt Inc. 10/16/1996 which merged into Tyco International Inc. (Bermuda) 10/17/2000 which reincorporated in Switzerland 03/17/2009 which merged into Johnson Controls International PLC 09/06/2016

IMCLONE SYS INC (DE)
Common $0.001 par split (2) for (1) by issuance of (1) additional share payable 10/13/2000 to holders of record 09/29/2000 Ex date - 10/16/2000
Merged into Lilly (Eli) & Co. 11/24/2008
Each share Common $0.001 par exchanged for $70 cash

IMCO RECYCLING INC (DE)
Under plan of merger name changed to Aleris International, Inc. 12/9/2004
(See Aleris International, Inc.)

IMCO RES LTD (QC)
Recapitalized as Meridian Peak Resources Corp. (QC) 07/18/1995
Each share Common no par exchanged for (0.28571428) share Common no par
Meridian Peak Resources Corp. (QC) reincorporated in Canada 05/12/1997 which reorganized as Meridian Peak Resources Corp. (New) (Canada) 06/23/1999 which reincorporated in Yukon 10/04/1999 which name changed to Arcata Resources Corp. 09/26/2001 which recapitalized as Goldrush Resources Ltd. (YT) 05/14/2003 which reincorporated in British Columbia 08/10/2006 which merged into First Mining Finance Corp. 01/11/2016 which name changed to First Mining Gold Corp. 01/11/2018

IMCOR PHARMACEUTICAL CO (NV)
Each share old Common $0.001 par exchanged for (0.05) share new Common $0.001 par 03/04/2005
Each share new Common $0.001 par exchanged again for (0.00000087) share new Common $0.0001 par 07/30/2009
Note: In effect holders received $0.01 cash per share and public interest was eliminated

IMC2 CORP (AB)
Name changed to Aztek Energy Ltd. 10/05/2005
Aztek Energy Ltd. merged into Spartan Exploration Ltd. 01/18/2010 which merged into Spartan Oil Corp. 06/03/2011 which merged into Bonterra Energy Corp. (New) 01/29/2013

IMERGENT INC (DE)
Name changed to Crexendo, Inc. (DE) 05/23/2011
Crexendo, Inc. (DE) reincorporated in Nevada 12/13/2016

IMETRIK M2M SOLUTIONS INC (NV)
Common $0.00001 par split (10) for (1) by issuance of (9) additional shares payable 09/27/2010 to holders of record 08/18/2010 Ex date - 09/28/2010
Name changed to Wiless Controls Inc. 02/28/2013
Wiless Controls Inc. name changed to Next Galaxy Corp. 08/19/2014

IMEX CORP (DE)
Merged into OC Acquisition Corp. 11/01/1991
Each share Common 10¢ par exchanged for $0.08 cash

IMEX MED SYS INC (CO)
Merged into Nicolet Biomedical Inc. 8/22/97
Each share Common $0.001 par exchanged for $1.34875 cash
Each share Common $0.001 par received an additional and final distribution of $0.0076 cash per share 8/5/98

IMG LATIN AMER INC (NV)
Name changed to International Healthcare Holdings Inc. 4/1/99

IMGE INC (DE)
Name changed to nStor Technologies, Inc. 11/15/1996
(See nStor Technologies, Inc.)

IMH COML HLDGS INC (MD)
Issue Information - 5,500,000 shares COM offered at $15 per share on 08/05/1997
Name changed to Impac Commercial Holdings, Inc. 2/2/98

IMI INTL MED INNOVATIONS INC (CANADA)
Name changed to PreMD Inc. 09/30/2005

IMI SCIENTIFIC INC (CO)
Charter suspended for failure to file annual report 10/01/1991

IMM ENERGY SVCS & TECHNOLOGY INC (DE)
Common no par split (4) for (3) by issuance of (1/3) additional share 02/19/1982
Recapitalized as Crestek, Inc. (DE) 12/24/1984
Each share Common no par exchanged for (0.2) share Common no par
(See Crestek, Inc. (DE))

IMMEDIA INFOMATIC CORP (CANADA)
Recapitalized 12/16/1991
Recapitalized from Immedia Infomatic International Inc. to Immedia Infomatic Corp. 12/16/1991
Each share Class A Common no par exchanged for (0.1) share Common no par
Name changed to MPACT Immedia Corp. 01/18/1994
MPACT Immedia Corp. name changed to BCE Emergis Inc. 01/21/1999 which name changed to Emergis Inc. 12/01/2004
(See Emergis Inc.)

IMMEDIATE ENTMT GROUP INC (NV)
Recapitalized as Strategic Growth Ventures, Inc. 01/31/2005
Each share Common $0.001 par exchanged for (0.004) share Common $0.001 par
Strategic Growth Ventures, Inc. recapitalized as Beere Financial Group, Inc. 05/31/2006 which recapitalized as Steadfast Holdings Group, Inc. 10/01/2007 which recapitalized as Scorpex, Inc. 05/20/2011

IMMEDIENT CORP (DE)
Reacquired 06/19/2003
Each share Common 1¢ par exchanged for $0.04 cash

IMMERSIVE MEDIA CORP (AB)
Name changed to EmberClear Inc. 05/05/2010
EmberClear Inc. name changed to EmberClear Corp. 12/29/2010
(See EmberClear Corp.)

IMMIGRANT RES INC (AB)
Name changed to Alta Natural Herbs & Supplements Ltd. 05/21/1996

IMMO-FIN CORP (DE)
Common $0.001 par split (4) for (3) by issuance of (0.33333333) additional share 12/18/1995
Name changed to BioCoral Inc. 12/30/1995
(See BioCoral Inc.)

IMMS INC (NV)
Name changed to EV Transportation, Inc. 08/25/2008

IMMTECH PHARMACEUTICALS INC (DE)
Name changed 03/22/2006
Name changed from Immtech International, Inc. to Immtech Pharmaceuticals, Inc. 03/22/2006
SEC revoked common stock registration 01/21/2014

IMMUCOR INC (GA)
Common 10¢ par split (5) for (4) by issuance of (0.25) additional share 04/15/1987
Common 10¢ par split (5) for (4) by issuance of (0.25) additional share 07/24/1990
Common 10¢ par split (3) for (2) by issuance of (0.5) additional share 07/19/1991
Common 10¢ par split (3) for (2) by issuance of (0.5) additional share payable 09/13/2002 to holders of record 08/26/2002 Ex date - 09/16/2002
Common 10¢ par split (3) for (2) by issuance of (0.5) additional share payable 11/14/2003 to holders of record 10/24/2003 Ex date - 11/17/2003
Common 10¢ par split (3) for (2) by issuance of (0.5) additional share payable 07/16/2004 to holders of record 06/30/2004 Ex date - 07/19/2004
Common 10¢ par split (3) for (2) by issuance of (0.5) additional share payable 12/13/2004 to holders of record 11/22/2004
Common 10¢ par split (3) for (2) by issuance of (0.5) additional share payable 05/15/2006 to holders of record 04/24/2006 Ex date - 05/16/2006
Acquired by IVD Holdings Inc. 08/19/2011
Each share Common 10¢ par exchanged for $27 cash

IMMUDYNE INC (DE)
Reincorporated 06/30/1994
State of incorporation changed from (WY) to (DE) 06/30/1994
Name changed to Conversion Labs, Inc. 06/22/2018

IMMULABS CORP (CO)
Old Common $0.001 par split (4) for (1) by issuance of (3) addtional shares payable 11/01/2000 to holders of record 10/31/2000 Ex date - 11/02/2000
Each share old Common $0.001 par exchanged for (0.01) share new Common $0.001 par 12/06/2002
Name changed to Xerion EcoSolutions Group, Inc. (CO) 04/07/2003
Xerion EcoSolutions Group, Inc. (CO) reorganized in Nevada as SINO-American Development Corp. 06/19/2006 which recapitalized as Harvest Bio-Organic International Co., Ltd. 12/07/2010
(See Harvest Bio-Organic International Co., Ltd.)

IMMULOGIC PHARMACEUTICAL CORP (DE)
Liquidation completed
Each share Common 1¢ par received initial distribution of $1.94 cash payable 9/1/99 to holders of record 8/25/99
Each share Common 1¢ par received second distribution of $0.47 cash payable 9/1/2000 to holders of record 8/25/2000
Each share Common 1¢ par received third distribution of $0.09 cash payable 12/2/2000 to holders of record 11/3/2000
Each share Common 1¢ par received fourth distribution of $0.05 cash payable 12/21/2001 to holders of record 12/13/2001 Ex date - 12/24/2001
Each share Common 1¢ par received fifth and final distribution of $0.07125 cash payable 12/22/2003 to holders of record 8/30/2002 Ex date - 12/23/2003
Note: Certificates were not required to be surrendered and are without value

IMMUNALL SCIENCE INC NEW (BC)
Reincorporated 06/30/2016
Place of incorporation changed from (AB) to (BC) 06/30/2016
Recapitalized as AREV Nutrition Sciences Inc. 01/23/2017
Each share Common no par exchanged for (0.03030303) share Common no par
AREV Nutrition Sciences Inc. name changed to AREV Brands International Ltd. 09/12/2018

IMMUNALL SCIENCE INC OLD (AB)
Reorganized as Immunall Science Inc. (New) (AB) 03/31/2011
Each share Common no par exchanged for (1) share Common no par, (0.025) share Aileron Ventures Ltd. Common no par and (0.025) share Nautor Progressive Corp. Common no par
(See each company's listing)
Note: Unexchanged certificates will be cancelled and become without value 03/31/2013
Immunall Science Inc. (New) (AB) reincorporated in British Columbia 06/30/2016 which recapitalized as AREV Nutrition Sciences Inc. 01/23/2017 which name changed to AREV Brands International Ltd. 09/12/2018

IMMUNE AMER INC (NV)
Each (120) shares old Common $0.001 par exchanged for (1) share new Common $0.001 par 11/8/96
Name changed to King Power International Group Ltd. 6/13/97
(See King Power International Group Ltd.)

IMMUNE NETWORK LTD (BC)
Name changed 08/16/2000
Name changed from Immune Network Research Ltd. to Immune Network Ltd. 08/16/2000
Each share old Common no par

exchanged for (0.1) share new Common no par 07/29/2002
Delisted from Canadian Venture Exchange 01/23/2002

IMMUNE RESPONSE CORP (DE)
Each share old Common $0.0025 par exchanged for (0.25) share new Common $0.0025 par 10/09/2002
Each share new Common $0.0025 par exchanged again for (0.01) share new Common $0.0025 par 12/20/2006
Name changed to Orchestra Therapeutics, Inc. 04/16/2007
(See Orchestra Therapeutics, Inc.)

IMMUNE RESPONSE INC (CO)
Old Common $0.0001 par split (100) for (1) by issuance of (99) additional shares 9/13/88
Each share old Common $0.0001 par exchanged for (0.01) share new Common $0.0001 par 3/3/97
Each share new Common $0.0001 par exchanged again for (1/3) share new Common $0.0001 par 2/1/2000
Reincorporated under the laws of Delaware as Opticon Medical, Inc. 7/27/2000
Opticon Medical, Inc. name changed to Nextelligence, Inc. 6/9/2004

IMMUNEX CORP (DE)
Reincorporated 7/23/87
State of incorporation changed from (WA) to (DE) 7/23/87
Merged into Immunex Corp. (New) 6/1/93
Each share Common 1¢ par exchanged for (1) share Common 1¢ par and $21 cash
Immunex Corp. (New) merged into Amgen Inc. 7/16/2002

IMMUNEX CORP NEW (DE)
Common 1¢ par split (2) for (1) by issuance of (1) additional share payable 3/25/99 to holders of record 3/11/99
Common 1¢ par split (2) for (1) by issuance of (1) additional share payable 8/26/99 to holders of record 8/12/99
Common 1¢ par split (3) for (1) by issuance of (2) additional shares payable 3/20/2000 to holders of record 3/6/2000
Merged into Amgen Inc. 7/16/2002
Each share Common 1¢ par exchanged for (0.44) share Common $0.0001 par and $4.50 cash

IMMUNICON CORP (DE)
In process of liquidation
Each share Common $0.001 par received inital distribution of $0.04 cash payable 08/17/2009 to holders of record 08/29/2008 Ex date - 08/18/2009
Note: Information on additional distribution(s), if any, are not available

IMMUNIS CORP (DE)
Recapitalized as Star8 Corp. 09/28/2010
Each share Common 1¢ par exchanged for (0.01) share Common 1¢ par

IMMUNO NUCLEAR CORP (MN)
Stock Dividend - 100% 1/15/82
Name changed to Incstar Corp. 12/13/86
(See Incstar Corp.)

IMMUNO RESH INC (BC)
Name changed to IRI Separation Technologies Inc. 08/14/2006

IMMUNO SCIENCE CORP (CA)
Stock Dividend - 100% 04/28/1972
Merged into Johnson & Johnson 01/28/1977
Each share Common 12-1/2¢ par exchanged for (0.1348) share Common $2.50 par

IMMUNOCLIN INTL INC (UT)
Name changed to Pacific Health Care Organization, Inc. 01/31/2001

IMMUNOGENETICS INC (DE)
Name changed to IGI, Inc. 05/21/1987
IGI, Inc. name changed to IGI Laboratories, Inc. 05/08/2008 which name changed to Teligent, Inc. 10/26/2015

IMMUNOSYN CORP (DE)
SEC revoked common stock registration 07/10/2015

IMMUNOTEC INC (CANADA)
Acquired by Immuno Holding S.A. de C.V. 05/23/2017
Each share Common no par exchanged for $0.485 cash
Note: Unexchanged certificates will be cancelled and become without value 05/22/2020

IMMUNOTECHNOLOGY CORP (DE)
Each share old Common $0.00001 par exchanged for (0.1) share new Common $0.00001 par 01/26/1998
New Common $0.00001 par split (5) for (1) by issuance of (4) additional shares payable 05/27/2003 to holders of record 05/23/2003 Ex date - 05/28/2003
Each share new Common $0.00001 par exchanged again for (0.1) share new Common $0.00001 par 03/16/2005
Recapitalized as Petals Decorative Accents, Inc. 09/21/2006
Each share new Common $0.00001 par exchanged for (1/3) share Common $0.00001 par
(See Petals Decorative Accents, Inc.)

IMMUNOTHERAPEUTICS INC (DE)
Each share old Common 1¢ par exchanged for (0.1) share new Common 1¢ par 02/28/1992
Name changed to Endorex Corp. 08/15/1996
Endorex Corp. name changed to DOR BioPharma, Inc. 12/03/2001 which name changed to Soligenix, Inc. 09/30/2009

IMMUNOVACCINE INC (CANADA)
Recapitalized as IMV Inc. 05/10/2018
Each share Common no par exchanged for (0.3125) share Common no par

IMMUNOVATIVE INC (FL)
Name changed to Tauriga Sciences, Inc. 04/09/2013

IMMUREBOOST INC (NV)
Name changed to Fountain Healthy Aging, Inc. 10/09/2008
(See Fountain Healthy Aging, Inc.)

IMMUTRON INC (CA)
Name changed to Spectrum Laboratories, Inc. (CA) 11/15/82
Spectrum Laboratories, Inc. (CA) reincorporated in Delaware 9/30/98 (Spectrum Laboratories, Inc. (DE))

IMN EQUITIES INC (NY)
Merged into IMN Financial Corp. 05/05/1997
Each share Common $0.0001 par exchanged for (0.25) share Common $0.001 par
IMN Financial Corp. name changed to AppOnline.com, Inc. 05/11/1999
(See AppOnline.com, Inc.)

IMN FINL CORP (DE)
Name changed to AppOnline.com, Inc. 05/11/1999
(See AppOnline.com, Inc.)

IMNET INC (DE)
Name changed to IMGE, Inc. 10/07/1992
IMGE, Inc. name changed to nStor Technologies, Inc. 11/15/1996
(See nStor Technologies, Inc.)

IMNET SYS INC (DE)
Issue Information - 3,000,000 shares COM offered at $12 per share on 07/20/1995
Merged into HBO & Co. 10/30/1998
Each share Common 1¢ par exchanged for (0.945) share Common 5¢ par
HBO & Co. merged into McKesson HBOC Inc. 01/12/1999 which name changed to McKesson Corp. 07/30/2001

IMO DELAVAL INC. (DE)
Common $1 par split (2) for (1) by issuance of (1) additional share 5/9/88
Name changed to IMO Industries Inc. 3/10/89
(See IMO Industries Inc.)

IMO INDS INC (DE)
Merged into II Acquisition Corp. 7/2/98
Each share Common $1 par exchanged for $7.05 cash

IMOBOLIS INC (NV)
Common $0.001 par split (5) for (1) by issuance of (4) additional shares payable 11/11/2011 to holders of record 10/12/2011 Ex date - 11/14/2011
Name changed to FrogAds, Inc. 11/22/2011
(See FrogAds, Inc.)

IMOCO GATEWAY CORP (DE)
Stock Dividends - 10% 9/2/69; 10% 9/2/70
In process of liquidation
Each share Common $1 par exchanged for initial distribution of (0.298568) share Air Wisconsin, Inc. Common 25¢ par and $10 cash 9/15/80
Note: Details on subsequent distributions, if any, are not available

IMODCO INC (DE)
Merged into Amtel, Inc. 02/26/1977
Each share Common 10¢ par exchanged for $15 cash

IMP CORP. (MI)
Completely liquidated 9/10/62
Each share Common $1 par exchanged for first and final distribution of $3.69 cash

IMP INC (DE)
Each share old Common $0.001 par exchanged for (0.1) share new Common $0.001 par 01/13/1999
Each share new Common $0.001 par exchanged for (0.2) share Common 1¢ par 10/03/2001
Chapter 11 barkruptcy proceedings converted to Chapter 7 on 04/07/2005
Stockholders' equity unlikely

IMPAC COML HLDGS INC (MD)
Merged into Fortress Investment Corp. 11/22/2000
Each share Common 1¢ par exchanged for $7.55 cash

IMPAC MED SYS INC (DE)
Issue Information - 2,187,500 shares COM offered at $15 per share on 11/19/2002
Merged into Elekta AB 4/4/2005
Each share Common $0.001 par exchanged for $24 cash

IMPACT CAP LTD (AUSTRALIA)
Name changed to Ask Funding Ltd. 07/02/2010
(See Ask Funding Ltd.)

IMPACT E-SOLUTIONS CORP (NV)
Charter permanently revoked 06/01/2009

IMPACT ENERGY INC (CO)
Reincorporated under the laws of Texas as Colonial Industries, Inc. 04/23/1998
(See Colonial Industries, Inc.)

IMPACT ENERGY INC CDA (AB)
Merged into Thunder Energy Inc. 04/30/2004
Each share Common no par exchanged for (0.22222222) share Common no par
(See Thunder Energy Inc.)

IMPACT EXPLORATIONS INC (NV)
Name changed to Americas Diamond Corp. 10/15/2012
Americas Diamond Corp. name changed to Midwest Oil & Gas Inc. 06/12/2014

IMPACT FD INC (TX)
Merged into Commerce Income Shares, Inc. (TX) 05/31/1979
Each share Common $1 par exchanged for (0.986) share Common $1 par
Commerce Income Shares, Inc. (TX) reorganized in Massachusetts as Commerce Income Shares 08/26/1985

IMPACT INCOME INVTS INC (CO)
Name changed to Financial Freedom Enterprises Inc. 06/24/1996
Financial Freedom Enterprises Inc. name changed to Cambridge Universal Corp. (CO) 07/15/1997 which reorganized in Florida as Whitehall Limited, Inc. 06/23/1999
(See Whitehall Limited, Inc.)

IMPACT INTL INC (DE)
Charter cancelled and declared inoperative and void for non-payment of taxes 3/1/90

IMPACT MED SOLUTIONS INC (DE)
Name changed to iTech Medical, Inc. 06/17/2010

IMPACT MINERALS INTL INC (BC)
Name changed to IMPACT Silver Corp. 08/18/2005

IMPACT RESOURCES, INC. (NV)
Recapitalized as Dyna-Seal Corp. 09/11/1989
Each (28) shares Common $0.001 par exchanged for (1) share Common $0.028 par
Dyna-Seal Corp. name changed to Interactive Buyers Network International Ltd. 07/21/1995 which name changed to Vsource, Inc. (NV) 12/03/1999 which reincorporated in Delaware 11/08/2000 which name changed to Tri-Isthmus Group, Inc. 12/30/2005 which name changed to First Physicians Capital Group, Inc. 01/08/2010

IMPACT RES INC (BC)
Recapitalized as New Impact Resources Inc. 10/27/1986
Each share Common no par exchanged for (0.25) share Common no par
New Impact Resources Inc. recapitalized as Consolidated Impact Resources Inc. 08/22/1989 which name changed to InContext Systems Inc. 07/22/1992 which merged into EveryWare Development Canada Inc. 06/30/1997
(See EveryWare Development Canada Inc.)

IMPACT SYS INC (CA)
Merged into Voith Sulzer Acquisition Corp. 2/12/98
Each share Common no par exchanged for $2.75 cash

IMPACT TELEMEDIA INTL LTD (CANADA)
Name changed to UC'NWIN Systems Ltd. (Canada) 07/17/1992
UC'NWIN Systems Ltd. (Canada) reincorporated in Delaware as UC'NWIN Systems Corp. 12/11/1995 which recapitalized as Winner's Edge.com, Inc. 10/29/1999 which name changed to Sealant Solutions Inc. 08/06/2001 which name

changed to PowerChannel, Inc. 07/28/2003 which recapitalized as Qualibou Energy Inc. 02/05/2008

IMPACT TRAVEL TECHNOLOGY INC (BC)
Recapitalized as MCF Enterprises, Inc. 03/12/1999
Each share Common no par exchanged for (0.5) share Common no par
MCF Enterprises, Inc. name changed to Online Consortium Corp. 02/09/2001 which name changed to Equicap Financial Corp. 07/10/2003 which name changed to Zecotek Medical Systems, Inc. 02/10/2005 which name changed to Zecotek Photonics Inc. 11/26/2007

IMPACTOR ENVIRONMENTAL PRODS INC (NV)
Each share old Common $0.001 par exchanged for (0.25) share new Common $0.001 par 10/2/96
Recapitalized as New Thought Broadcasting Inc. 3/27/2003
Each share new Common $0.001 par exchanged for (0.02) share Common $0.001 par
New Thought Broadcasting Inc. name changed to Mundus Environmental Products Inc. 8/16/2004 which name changed to Mundus Group Inc. 8/28/2006

IMPALA MINERAL EXPL CORP (NV)
SEC revoked common stock registration 01/21/2014

IMPALA MINES LTD. (ON)
Merged into Nordev Resources Ltd. 03/24/1972
Each share Capital Stock $1 par exchanged for (0.1) share Common no par
Nordev Resources Ltd. recapitalized as Vedron Ltd. 06/05/1979 which recapitalized as Vedron Gold Inc. 01/04/1995 which name changed to VG Gold Corp. 08/07/2007 which merged into Lexam VG Gold Inc. 01/04/2011 which merged into McEwen Mining Inc. 05/01/2017

IMPALA RES LTD (BC)
Common no par split (3) for (1) by issuance of (2) additional shares 05/17/1983
Recapitalized as International Impala Resources Ltd. 08/26/1987
Each share Common no par exchanged for (0.2) share Common no par
International Impala Resources Ltd. recapitalized as Tapestry Ventures Ltd. 11/13/1992 which recapitalized as Tapestry Resource Corp. 12/23/2004 which name changed to Gran Colombia Gold Corp. 08/24/2010

IMPART MEDIA GROUP INC (NV)
Plan of reorganization under Chapter 11 Federal Bankruptcy proceedings effective 02/11/2009
No stockholders' equity

IMPATH INC (DE)
Common $0.005 par split (2) for (1) by issuance of (1) additional share payable 08/28/2000 to holders of record 08/16/2000
Assets transferred to IMPATH Bankruptcy Liquidating Trust 07/22/2005
(See IMPATH Bankruptcy Liquidating Trust)

IMPATH LIQUIDATING TR (DE)
Liquidation completed
Each Class A Bene. Int. received initial distribution of $2.55 cash payable 08/12/2005 to holders of record 08/05/2005 Ex date - 08/15/2005
Each Class A Bene. Int. received second distribution of $1.36 cash payable 01/10/2007 to holders of record 12/29/2006 Ex date - 01/16/2007
Each Class A Bene. Int. received third distribution of $1.73 cash payable 06/03/2008 to holders of record 05/23/2008 Ex date - 06/04/2008
Each Class A Bene. Int. received fourth distribution of $0.31 cash payable 10/22/2010 to holders of record 10/12/2010 Ex date - 10/25/2010
Each Class A Bene. Int. received fifth and final distribution of $0.096 cash payable 02/10/2011 to holders of record 02/04/2011

IMPATICA COM INC (ON)
Name changed to Impatica Inc. 11/29/2001

IMPAX ENERGY SVCS INCOME TR (ON)
Monitor discharged 10/29/2010
Unitholders' equity unlikely

IMPAX LABORATORIES INC (DE)
Name changed to Amneal Pharmaceuticals, Inc. and Common 1¢ par reclassified as Class A Common 1¢ par 05/07/2018

IMPCO TECHNOLOGIES INC (DE)
Each share Common $0.001 par received distribution of (1) share Quantum Fuel Systems Technologies Worldwide, Inc. Common $0.001 par payable 07/23/2002 to holders of record 07/05/2002
Recapitalized as Fuel Systems Solutions, Inc. 08/25/2006
Each share Common $0.001 par exchanged for (0.5) share Common $0.001 par
Fuel Systems Solutions, Inc. merged into Westport Fuel Systems Inc. 06/08/2016

IMPELL CORP (DE)
Stock Dividends - 50% 09/15/1977; 25% 03/15/1979; 25% 03/14/1980; 50% 03/13/1981
Merged into Combustion Engineering, Inc. 07/12/1984
Each share Common 2¢ par exchanged for $24.50 cash

IMPERIA ENTMT INC (NV)
Reincorporated 08/28/2006
State of incorporation changed from (CA) to (NV) and Common $0.001 par changed to $0.0001 par 08/28/2006
Each share old Common $0.0001 par exchanged for (0.002) share new Common $0.0001 par 10/10/2006
Each share new Common $0.0001 par exchanged again for (0.0005) share new Common $0.0001 par 01/31/2008
Recapitalized as Viratech Corp. 10/11/2011
Each share new Common $0.0001 par exchanged for (0.01) share Common $0.0001 par

IMPERIAL AMERN ENERGY INC (CO)
Completely liquidated 05/10/1978
Each share Common no par exchanged for first and final distribution of $21 cash

IMPERIAL BANCORP (CA)
Common $10 par changed to $4 par and (2) additional shares issued 6/15/73
Common $4 par changed to no par 2/22/77
Common no par split (2) for (1) by issuance of (1) additional share 4/18/80
Common no par split (2) for (1) by issuance of (1) additional share 4/25/81
Common no par split (3) for (2) by issuance of (0.5) additional share payable 10/18/96 to holders of record 10/11/96
Common no par split (3) for (2) by issuance of (0.5) additional share payable 2/6/98 to holders of record 2/2/98 Ex date - 2/9/98
Stock Dividends - 10% 6/15/78; 15% 4/15/79; 15% 5/15/80; 15% 5/5/81; 10% 5/7/82; 8% payable 2/23/96 to holders of record 2/15/96; 10% payable 2/24/97 to holders of record 2/17/97; 8% payable 3/5/99 to holders of record 2/19/99; 8% payable 2/18/2000 to holders of record 2/4/2000
Merged into Comerica, Inc. 1/29/2001
Each share Common no par exchanged for (0.46) share Common $5 par

IMPERIAL BK (LOS ANGELES, CA)
Each share Common $10 par exchanged for (0.006667) share Common $1,500 par 12/29/1970
Note: In effect holders received $44.44 cash per share and public interest was eliminated

IMPERIAL BANK OF COMMERCE (TORONTO, ONT)
Each share Capital Stock $100 par exchanged for (10) shares Capital Stock $10 par 00/00/1944
Merged into Canadian Imperial Bank of Commerce (Toronto, ON) 06/01/1961
Each share Capital Stock $10 par exchanged for (1.66666666) shares Capital Stock $10 par

IMPERIAL CAP BANCORP INC (DE)
Plan of reorganization under Chapter 11 Federal Bankruptcy proceedings effective 06/08/2012
No stockholders' equity

IMPERIAL CAP FD INC (MN)
Name changed to St. Paul Capital Fund, Inc. 03/30/1977
St. Paul Capital Fund, Inc. name changed to AMEV Capital Fund, Inc. 05/01/1985 which reorganized as Fortis Equity Portfolios Inc. 02/22/1992
(See Fortis Equity Portfolios Inc.)

IMPERIAL CHEM INDS PLC (ENGLAND)
7% Preference £1 par reclassified as 5% Preference £1 par and a 40% stock dividend paid 07/16/1954
5% Preference £1 par called for redemption 11/17/1986
Each old ADR for Ordinary Reg. £1 par exchanged for (0.25) new ADR for Ordinary Reg. £1 par 10/24/1993
Each new ADR for Ordinary Reg. £1 par received distribution of (1.333) Zeneca Group PLC Sponsored ADR for Ordinary 06/01/1993
Stock Dividends - in Ordinary 100% 07/16/1954; 50% 06/30/1958; 50% 01/24/1964 in ADR's - 50% 02/07/1964
Acquired by Akzo Nobel N.V. 01/02/2008
Each share Ordinary £1 par exchanged for 670p cash
Each new ADR for Ordinary exchanged for $52.349631 cash

MPERIAL COLOR CHEMICAL & PAPER CORP. (NY)
Capital Stock $10 par changed to $5 par and (1) additional share issued 10/15/1959
Acquired by Hercules Powder Co. 04/01/1960
Each share Capital Stock $5 par exchanged for (0.5) share $2 Conv. Class A no par
(See Hercules Powder Co.)

IMPERIAL CONSOLIDATED MINING CO. (AZ)
Charter expired by time limitation 4/29/38

IMPERIAL CORP AMER (DE)
Reincorporated 09/21/1987
State of incorporation changed from (CA) to (DE) and Common $1 par changed to 1¢ par 09/21/1987
Plan of reorganization under Chapter 11 Federal Bankruptcy proceedings confirmed 09/28/1990
Stockholders' equity unlikely

IMPERIAL CR COML HLDGS INC (MD)
Name changed to IMH Commercial Holdings, Inc. 6/30/97
IMH Commercial Holdings, Inc. name changed to Impac Commercial Holdings, Inc. 2/2/98

IMPERIAL CR COML MTG INVT CORP (MD)
Merged into Imperial Credit Industries Inc. 3/28/2000
Each share Common $0.0001 par exchanged for $11.5753246 cash

IMPERIAL CR INDS INC (CA)
Common no par split (3) for (2) by issuance of (0.5) additional share 10/24/1995
Common no par split (2) for (1) by issuance of (1) additional share payable 10/22/1996 to holders of record 10/15/1996
Stock Dividends - 10% 12/30/1993; 10% payable 02/26/1996 to holders of record 02/12/1996
Charter suspended for failure to file reports and pay fees 11/09/2004

IMPERIAL CR MTG HLDGS INC (MD)
Common 1¢ par split (3) for (2) by issuance of (0.5) additional share payable 11/24/1997 to holders of record 11/03/1997 Ex date - 11/25/1997
Name changed to Impac Mortgage Holdings, Inc. 02/02/1998

IMPERIAL DEVELOPMENT CO. (NV)
Capital Stock 25¢ par changed to 10¢ par 4/8/55
Stock Dividend - 10% 9/7/59
Name changed to Imperial-Western 2/2/60
Imperial-Western name changed to Royal Properties, Inc. 7/15/63
(See Royal Properties, Inc.)

IMPERIAL DIVERSIFIED INDS INC (NV)
Charter revoked for failure to file reports and pay fees 03/03/1975

IMPERIAL-EASTMAN CORP. (IL)
Common $20 par changed to $8 par and (2) additional shares issued 5/2/66
Common $8 par changed to $4 par and (1) additional share issued 12/29/67
Merged into I-T-E Imperial Corp. 4/30/68
Each share Common $4 par exchanged for (0.86) share Common $1 par
I-T-E Imperial Corp. merged into Gould Inc. 4/30/76
(See Gould Inc.)

IMPERIAL ENERGY CORP (CO)
Each share Common no par exchanged for (0.01) share Common 2¢ par 12/20/1983
Name changed to Funscape Corp. 10/08/1996
Funscape Corp. name changed to Titan Energy Corp. (CO) 07/09/1997 which reincorporated in Nevada as Power Exploration, Inc. 05/31/1998 which name changed to Matrix Energy Services Corp. 05/25/2002 which name changed to Shi Corp. 04/09/2009

IMPERIAL EQUITY CORP. (MN)
Liquidation completed
Each share Common 1¢ par received initial distribution of $0.85 cash 6/30/65
Each share Common 1¢ par received second distribution of $1.25 cash 6/30/66

Each share Common 1¢ par received third distribution of $0.25 cash 5/28/67
Each share Common 1¢ par received fourth distribution of $0.40 cash 10/20/69
Each share Common 1¢ par received fifth distribution of $0.21 cash 10/30/70
Note: At time of above liquidating payments holder had option to receive dollar amount in Imperial Growth Fund, Inc. Common 1¢ par; option was not applicable to sixth and final distribution
Each share Common 1¢ par exchanged for sixth and final distribution of $0.016 cash 6/15/71

IMPERIAL FINL SVCS INC (MN)
Name changed to Imperial Investment Management Co. 04/02/1969
Imperial Investment Management Co. name changed to St. Paul Advisors, Inc. 11/01/1976 which name changed to AMEV Advisers, Inc. 04/01/1985 which name changed to Fortis Advisers, Inc. 02/22/1992
(See Fortis Advisers, Inc.)

IMPERIAL FLO-GLAZE PAINTS LTD. (ON)
$1.50 Preference called for redemption 01/31/1959
Name changed to Morse Paint Manufacturing Ltd. 05/26/1964
(See Morse Paint Manufacturing Ltd.)

IMPERIAL 400 NATL INC (DE)
Each share 6.60% Preferred $100 par exchanged for (37) shares Common $1 par and $2.20 cash 04/30/1976
Each share Common 50¢ par exchanged for (1/3) share Common $1 par 04/30/1976
Merged into Interpart S.A. 12/20/1988
Details not available

IMPERIAL FUND, INC. (MN)
Name changed to Imperial Growth Fund, Inc. 02/25/1966
Imperial Growth Fund, Inc. name changed to St. Paul Growth Fund, Inc. 03/30/1977 which name changed to AMEV Growth Fund, Inc. 05/01/1985 which name changed to Fortis Growth Fund, Inc. 02/22/1992
(See Fortis Growth Fund, Inc.)

IMPERIAL GEN PPTYS LTD (ON)
Merged into Abacus Cities Ltd. 07/13/1979
Each share Common no par exchanged for either (1) share Class A Special Stock $1 par, (1) share Class B Special Stock $1 par or (1) share Common no par
Note: Option to receive Class B Special or Common $1 par expired 07/27/1979
Class A Preference $25 par called for redemption 01/08/1982
Class B Preference $1 par called for redemption 01/08/1982
(See Abacus Cities Ltd.)

IMPERIAL GINSENG PRODS LTD (BC)
Each share old Conv. Preference Ser. A no par exchanged for (0.05) share new Conv. Preference Ser. A no par 02/11/2011
Each share new Conv. Preference Ser. A no par exchanged for (1.11) shares new Common no par 06/23/2015
(Additional Information in Active)

IMPERIAL GROUP LTD (GA)
Name changed to Cindy's Inc. (GA) 9/7/77
Cindy's Inc. (GA) reincorporated in Delaware 3/5/82 which merged into Prime Motor Inns Inc. 3/6/84 which reorganized as Prime Hospitality Corp. 7/31/92
(See Prime Hospitality Corp.)

IMPERIAL GROUP 1 LTD (DE)
Name changed to Ancona Group, Ltd. 02/25/1991
Ancona Group, Ltd. name changed to American Home Alliance Corp. 10/08/1993

IMPERIAL GROUP PLC (ENGLAND)
Ordinary £1 par changed to 5s par and (3) additional shares issued plus a 50% stock dividend paid 02/07/1969
Each ADR for Ordinary £1 par exchanged for (6) ADR's for Ordinary 5s par 02/28/1969
Ordinary 5s par and ADR's for Ordinary 5s par changed to 25p par per currency change 02/15/1971
Acquired by Hanson Trust PLC 11/26/1986
Each share Ordinary 25p par exchanged for (1) share Ordinary 25p par and 153p cash
Each ADR for Ordinary 25p par exchanged for $4.91 cash

IMPERIAL GROWTH FD INC (MN)
Name changed to St. Paul Growth Fund, Inc. 03/30/1977
St. Paul Growth Fund, Inc. name changed to AMEV Growth Fund, Inc. 05/01/1985 which name changed to Fortis Growth Fund, Inc. 02/22/1992
(See Fortis Growth Fund, Inc.)

IMPERIAL HLDGS INC (FL)
Name changed to Emergent Capital, Inc. 09/01/2015

IMPERIAL HOLLY CORP (TX)
Common no par split (3) for (2) by issuance of (0.5) additional share 04/17/1989
Common no par split (3) for (2) by issuance of (0.5) additional share 04/17/1990
Name changed to Imperial Sugar Co. (New) 02/09/1999
(See Imperial Sugar Co. (New))

IMPERIAL HOME BLDRS INC (ME)
Charter suspended for failure to file annual reports 12/06/1976

IMPERIAL INCOME FD INC (MN)
Name changed to St. Paul Income Fund, Inc. 11/30/1976
St. Paul Income Fund, Inc. name changed to AMEV U.S. Government Securities Fund, Inc. 05/01/1985 which name changed to Fortis Income Portfolios, Inc. 02/22/1992
(See Fortis Income Portfolios, Inc.)

IMPERIAL INDS INC (DE)
Common 10¢ par split (3) for (2) by issuance of (0.5) additional share 08/27/1979
Common 10¢ par split (2) for (1) by issuance of (1) additional share 02/28/1980
Common 10¢ par changed to 1¢ par 12/31/1998
Each share $1.10 Conv. Preferred $1 par exchanged for either $8 principal amount of Subordinated Debentures due 12/31/2001, (5) shares old Common 1¢ par and $2.25 cash or (10) shares old Common 1¢ par and $4.75 cash 12/31/1998
Note: Option to receive stock and cash only expired 03/01/1999
Each share old Common 1¢ par exchanged for (0.25) share new Common 1¢ par 03/23/2005
Acquired by Q.E.P. Co., Inc. 10/17/2012
Each share new Common 1¢ par exchanged for $0.30 cash

IMPERIAL INNS OF AMERICA (MS)
Liquidation completed
Each share Common $5 par recevied initial distribution of $1.70 cash in August 1970
Each share Common $5 par received second and final distribution of $1.11 cash in November 1972
Certificates were not required to be surrendered and are now valueless

IMPERIAL INTL CORP (MN)
Charter revoked for failure to file reports and pay fees 10/19/79

IMPERIAL INVESTMENT CORP. LTD. (BC)
Class A and B Common no par split (2) for (1) by issuance of (1) additional share respectively 12/31/1957
Name changed to Laurentide Financial Corp., Ltd. (BC) 09/01/1961
Laurentide Financial Corp., Ltd. (BC) reorganized in Canada as Laurentide Financial Corp. Ltd.-Le Financier Laurentide Ltee. 02/12/1979
(See Laurentide Financial Corp. Ltd.-Le Financier Laurentide Ltee.)

IMPERIAL INVT CORP (CO)
Declared defunct and inoperative for failure to pay taxes 10/16/1970

IMPERIAL INVESTMENT MANAGEMENT CO. (MN)
Name changed to St. Paul Advisers, Inc. 11/01/1976
St. Paul Advisers, Inc. name changed to AMEV Advisers, Inc. 04/01/1985 which name changed to Fortis Advisers, Inc. 02/22/1992
(See Fortis Advisers, Inc.)

IMPERIAL LD INVT CO (GA)
Stock Dividend - 100% 10/2/72
Name changed to Imperial Group, Ltd. (GA) 8/1/73
Imperial Group, Ltd. (GA) name changed to Cindy's Inc. (GA) 9/7/77 which reincorporated in Delaware 3/5/82 which merged into Prime Motor Inns Inc. 3/6/84 which reorganized as Prime Hospitality Corp. 7/31/92
(See Prime Hospitality Corp.)

IMPERIAL LIFE ASSURN CO CDA (CANADA)
Each share Capital Stock $100 par exchanged for (10) shares Capital Stock $10 par 00/00/1951
Each share Capital Stock $10 par exchanged for (2) shares Capital Stock $5 par 04/17/1972
Each share Capital Stock $5 par exchanged for (5) shares Capital Stock $1 par 04/02/1979
Capital Stock $1 par reclassified as Common $1 par 00/00/1981
$3.0625 Preferred Ser. A $25 par called for redemption 07/18/1986
$2.25 Retractable 2nd Preferred Ser. 2 $25 par reclassified as Class 1 Preferred Ser. 2 $25 par 11/09/1992
7.375% Retractable 2nd Preferred Ser. 3 $25 par reclassified as 7.375% Class 1 Preferred Ser. 3 $25 par 11/09/1992
7.375% Retractable Preferred Class 1 Ser. 2 $25 par called for redemption 01/15/1993
7.375% Class 1 Preferred Ser. 3 $25 par called for redemption 01/15/1993
99.9% acquired by Desjardins Laurentian Financial Corp. through purchase offer which expired 05/20/1977
Class 1 2nd Preferred Ser. I $25 par called for redemption at $25 on 01/15/1998
Class II Preferred Ser. I $25 par called for redemption at $25 plus $0.53125 accrued dividend on 01/15/1998
Public interest eliminated

IMPERIAL MARINE INDS LTD (BC)
Acquired by Rivtow Straits Ltd. 00/00/1976
Each share Common no par exchanged for $0.07 cash

IMPERIAL METAL & CHEMICAL CO. (PA)
Completely liquidated 02/21/1969
Each share Capital Stock $2.50 par exchanged for first and final distribution of (0.127401) share Richardson Co. Conv. Preferred Ser. E no par

IMPERIAL METALS & PWR LTD (BC)
Merged into Imperial Metals Corp. (Old) 12/01/1981
Each share Common no par exchanged for (0.5) share Common no par
Imperial Metals Corp. (Old) reorganized as Imperial Metals Corp. (New) 04/30/2002

IMPERIAL METALS CORP OLD (BC)
Each share 6% Conv. Preferred Class A $5 par exchanged for (0.25) share Common no par 04/28/1987
Plan of arrangement effective 04/30/2002
Each share Common no par exchanged for (0.1) share Imperial Metals Corp. (New) Common no par and (0.1) share IEI Energy Inc. Common no par
(See each company's listing)

IMPERIAL MINERALS (QC)
Recapitalized as Consolidated Imperial Minerals Ltd. 03/04/1971
Each share Capital Stock $1 par exchanged for (0.5) share Capital Stock no par
Consolidated Imperial Minerals Ltd. recapitalized as Consolidated Imperial Resources Ltd.-Ressources Consolidees Imperial Ltee. 11/15/1979 which recapitalized as Consolidated Imperial Resources Energy Ltd./Ressources Consolidees Imperial Energie Ltee. 03/22/1983 which recapitalized as Consolidated Imperial Resources Inc./Ressources Consolidees Imperial Inc. 04/21/1988
(See Consolidated Imperial Resources Inc./Ressources Consolidees Imperial Inc.)

IMPERIAL MINES & METALS LTD. (AB)
Recapitalized as New Imperial Mines Ltd. 00/00/1957
Each share Capital Stock no par exchanged for (0.25) share Capital Stock no par
New Imperial Mines Ltd. recapitalized as Whitehorse Copper Mines Ltd. 09/08/1971
(See Whitehorse Copper Mines Ltd.)

IMPERIAL MNG NL (AUSTRALIA)
Name changed to Imperial One International Ltd. 04/19/2000
Imperial One International Ltd. name changed to Imperial One Ltd. 05/30/2000 which name changed to Empire Energy Group Ltd. 07/12/2011

IMPERIAL MODULAR INDS LTD (BC)
Struck off register and declared dissolved for failure to file returns 03/03/1978

IMPERIAL NATURAL GAS CO. (SD)
Charter cancelled for failure to file annual reports 7/1/70

IMPERIAL OIL CO. (CO)
Charter revoked for failure to file reports and pay fees 10/11/30

IMPERIAL OIL CO CALIF (CA)
Acquired by IOC Acquisition 12/15/94
Each share Common 50¢ par exchanged for $24 cash

IMPERIAL OIL LTD (CANADA)
Each share old Capital Stock no par exchanged for (4) shares new Capital Stock no par 00/00/1929
New Capital Stock no par split (4) for (1) by issuance of (3) additional shares 02/10/1969

IMPERIAL ONE LTD (AUSTRALIA)
Name changed 05/30/2000
Name changed from Imperial One International Ltd. to Imperial One Ltd. 05/30/2000
Name changed to Empire Energy Group Ltd. 07/12/2011

IMPERIAL PACKING CORP (DE)
Name changed to Alison International, Inc. 9/12/69
(See Alison International, Inc.)

IMPERIAL PAPER & COLOR CORP. (NY)
Each share Capital Stock $100 par exchanged for (4) shares Capital Stock $25 par and (1) additional share distributed 00/00/1937
Each share Capital Stock $25 par exchanged for (2.5) shares Capital Stock $10 par and (1) additional share distributed 00/00/1947
Name changed to Imperial Color Chemical & Paper Corp. 01/12/1959
Imperial Color Chemical & Paper Corp. acquired by Hercules Powder Co. 04/01/1960
(See Imperial Color Chemical & Paper Corp.)

IMPERIAL PAPER CO (OH)
Common no par changed to $1 par 6/30/69
Common $1 par split (3) for (2) by issuance of (0.5) additional share 5/14/71
Merged into Collins & Aikman Corp. 10/22/71
Each share Common $1 par exchanged for (0.75) share Common no par
(See Collins & Aikman Corp.)

IMPERIAL PETE RECOVERY CORP (NV)
Chapter 7 bankruptcy proceedings terminated 04/18/2016
No stockholders' equity

IMPERIAL PETROLEUM CO. (NV)
Charter revoked for failure to file reports and pay fees 3/6/61

IMPERIAL PKG CORP (DE)
Merged into Imperial Parking Management, LLC 5/4/2004
Each share Common $1 par exchanged for $26.015834 cash

IMPERIAL PKG LTD (BC)
Acquired by Vencap Acquisition 05/02/1996
Each share Common no par exchanged for $5 cash

IMPERIAL PLASTECH INC (ON)
Each share old Common no par exchanged for (0.33333333) share new Common no par 02/05/2004
Reincorporated under the laws of British Columbia as GPJ Ventures Ltd. 11/13/2006
GPJ Ventures Ltd. name changed to Peak Gold Ltd. 04/04/2007 which merged into New Gold Inc. 06/30/2008

IMPERIAL RAYON CORP.
In process of liquidation in 1945

IMPERIAL ROYALTIES CO. (CANADA)
Reorganized as Toklan Royalty Corp. 00/00/1940
Details not available

IMPERIAL SUGAR CO NEW (TX)
Plan of reorganization under Chapter 11 Federal Bankruptcy Code effective 08/29/2001
Each share old Common no par received (0.00617) share new Common no par and (0.03428046) New Capital Stock no par reclassified as Conv. Class A Common no par 05/01/1974
Name changed to Imperial Oil Ltd.-Compagnie Petroliere Imperial Ltee. 04/29/1976
Common Stock Purchase Warrant expiring 08/29/2008
Note: Above distribution applies only to holdings of (82) or more shares
Holders of (30) to (81) shares will only receive Warrants
Holders of (29) shares or fewer will not receive any distribution
Note: Certificates were not required to be surrendered and are without value
Each share new Common no par received distribution of (0.35) additional share payable 02/21/2002 to holders of record 09/26/2001
Acquired by LD Commodities Sugar Holdings L.L.C. 06/21/2012
Each share new Common no par exchanged for $6.35 cash

IMPERIAL SUGAR CO OLD (TX)
Each share Common $100 par exchanged for (4) shares Common no par 00/00/1929
Stock Dividend - 200% 12/17/1956
Recapitalized as Imperial Holly Corp. 04/26/1988
Each share Common no par exchanged for (14.63184) shares Common no par
Imperial Holly Corp. name changed to Imperial Sugar Co. (New) 02/09/1999
(See Imperial Sugar Co. (New))

IMPERIAL SYS INC (DE)
Charter cancelled and declared inoperative and void for non-payment of taxes 3/1/77

IMPERIAL THERMAL SYSTEMS, INC. (CA)
Acquired by Teledyne, Inc. 10/31/1963
Each share Common no par exchanged for (0.27753878) share Common $1 par
Teledyne, Inc. merged into Allegheny Teledyne, Inc. 08/15/1996 which name changed to Allegheny Technologies Inc. 11/29/1999

IMPERIAL THRIFT & LN ASSOC (CA)
Recapitalized as ITLA Capital Corp. 10/01/1996
Each share Common no par exchanged for (1) share Common 1¢ par
ITLA Capital Corp. name changed to Imperial Capital Bancorp, Inc. 08/03/2007
(See Imperial Capital Bancorp, Inc.)

IMPERIAL TOB CO CDA LTD (CANADA)
Name changed 4/15/66
Common $5 par changed to no par 05/01/1962
Name changed from Imperial Tobacco Co. of Canada, Ltd. to Imperial Tobacco Co. of Canada Ltd.-Imperial Tobacco du Canada Ltee. 04/15/1966
Name changed to Imasco Ltd.-Imasco Ltee. 12/01/1970
(See Imasco Ltd. - Imasco Ltee.)

IMPERIAL TOB GROUP LTD (ENGLAND)
Name changed to Imperial Group PLC 04/01/1973
(See Imperial Group PLC)

IMPERIAL TOB GROUP PLC (UNITED KINGDOM)
Name changed to Imperial Brands PLC 02/08/2016

IMPERIAL TOBACCO CO. (OF GREAT BRITAIN & IRELAND), LTD. (ENGLAND)
Stock Dividends - ADR's - 60% 09/16/1952; 50% 09/11/1963
Stock Dividend - Ordinary - 50% 09/07/1963
Name changed to Imperial Tobacco Group, Ltd. 01/27/1969
Imperial Tobacco Group, Ltd. name changed to Imperial Group PLC 04/01/1973
(See Imperial Group PLC)

IMPERIAL URANIUM CO. (UT)
Recapitalized as Duraco Industries, Inc. 04/20/1970
Each share Common 1¢ par exchanged for (0.5) share Common 1¢ par
(See Duraco Industries, Inc.)

IMPERIAL VALLEY NATL BK (EL CENTRO, CA)
Completely liquidated 04/01/1974
Each share Common $10 par exchanged for first and final distribution of $47 cash

IMPERIAL VARNISH & COLOUR CO. LTD. (ON)
Name changed to Imperial Flo-Glaze Paints Ltd. 00/00/1955
Imperial Flo-Glaze Paints Ltd. name changed to Morse Paint Manufacturing Ltd. 05/26/1964
(See Morse Paint Manufacturing Ltd.)

IMPERIAL VENDING CO. (CA)
Charter suspended for non-payment of taxes 01/02/1964

IMPERIAL-WESTERN (NV)
Each share Capital Stock 10¢ par exchanged for (0.2) share Capital Stock 50¢ par 10/01/1962
Name changed to Royal Properties, Inc. 07/15/1963
(See Royal Properties, Inc.)

IMPERUS TECHNOLOGIES CORP (BC)
Name changed to Tangelo Games Corp. 06/28/2016
(See Tangelo Games Corp.)

IMPLANT SCIENCES CORP (MA)
Common 10¢ par changed to $0.001 par 01/17/2013
Name changed to Secure Point Technologies Inc. 02/23/2017

IMPLANT TECHNOLOGIES INC (MN)
Recapitalized as Oasis Online Technologies Corp. 09/26/2007
Each share Common 1¢ par exchanged for (0.125) share Common 1¢ par
Oasis Online Technologies Corp. name changed to Capital Group Holdings, Inc. 11/01/2010

IMPLANT TECHNOLOGY INC (NJ)
Recapitalized as Osteoimplant Technology, Inc. 12/09/1992
Each share Common 1¢ par exchanged for (0.0230644) share Common 1¢ par
(See Osteoimplant Technology, Inc.)

IMPLANTABLE VISION INC (UT)
Name changed to Arcland Energy Corp. 09/11/2008
(See Arcland Energy Corp.)

IMPLEX CORP (NV)
Name changed to Consorteum Holdings, Inc. 06/09/2009

IMPOREX INVTS CORP (NV)
Name changed to Pervasys Inc. 05/02/2001
Pervasys Inc. name changed to Film & Music Entertainment, Inc. 05/28/2003
(See Film & Music Entertainment, Inc.)

IMPORT DYNAMICS INC (NV)
Recapitalized as Peak Performance Products, Inc. 6/13/85
Each share Common $0.00001 par exchanged for (0.2) share Common $0.001 par
Peak Performance Products, Inc. recapitalized as Lumalure Manufacturing, Inc. 5/1/86 which recapitalized as Sairam Technologies Inc. 12/29/89 which name changed to Balanced Environmental Services Technology Inc. 4/5/91 which recapitalized as United States Imdemnity & Casualty, Inc. 7/8/93 which name changed to Birch Financial, Inc. 1/20/2000

IMPORT MTR PARTS CO (FL)
Acquired by Beck/Arnley Corp. 04/05/1973
Each share Common 10¢ par exchanged for $1.75 cash

IMPORTERS & EXPORTERS INSURANCE CO.
Merged into Importers & Exporters Insurance Co. of New York in 1935
Details not available

IMPORTERS & EXPORTERS INSURANCE CO. OF NEW YORK
Merged into Merchants & Manufacturers Insurance Co. of New York in 1939
Each share Capital Stock $5 par exchanged for (1.25) shares Capital Stock $4 par
Merchants & Manufacturers Insurance Co. of New York merged into American Equitable Assurance Co. of New York 12/31/60 which merged into Reliance Insurance Co. 6/30/65
(See Reliance Insurance Co.)

IMPREGILO SPA (ITALY)
Name changed to Salini Impregilo S.p.A. 05/16/2014

IMPRESO COM INC (DE)
Name changed to Impreso, Inc. 04/18/2001

IMPRESSION DELIVERY CORP (NV)
Name changed to IDC Holdings, Ltd. 09/02/1993
(See IDC Holdings, Ltd.)

IMPRESSIVE VENTURES LTD (NV)
Each share old Common $0.001 par exchanged for (0.05) share new Common $0.001 par 6/7/94
Recapitalized as Wealth International Inc. 8/27/96
Each share new Common $0.001 par exchanged for (0.004) share Common $0.001 par 8/27/96
Wealth International Inc. name changed to World Internetworks Inc. 4/13/98 which name changed to GTDATA Corp. 12/3/2001 which recapitalized as Frontier Energy Corp. 9/28/2005

IMPRINT PRODS INC (NY)
Merged into Imprint Holdings Inc. 07/10/1985
Each share Common 1¢ par exchanged for $1.50 cash

IMPRINT RECORDS INC (TN)
Administratively dissolved for failure to file reports 10/20/2000

IMPRIVATA INC (DE)
Acquired by Imprivata Intermediate Holdings, Inc. 09/16/2016
Each share Common $0.001 par exchanged for $19.25 cash

IMPRO, INC. (TX)
Charter revoked for failure to file reports and pay fees 8/12/64

IMPROCOM INC (NV)
Each share old Common $0.001 par exchanged for (0.33333333) share new Common $0.001 par 11/30/1989
Name changed to InVision Technology, Inc. 03/15/1996
InVision Technology, Inc. name changed to Shepherd Surveillance Solutions, Inc. 05/22/1996
(See Shepherd Surveillance Solutions, Inc.)

IMPROVENET INC (DE)
Issue Information - 2,760,000 shares COM offered at $16 per share on 03/15/2000
Merged into ServiceMagic, Inc. 8/10/2005

Each share Common $0.001 par exchanged for $0.12 cash

IMPSAT FIBER NETWORKS INC (DE)
Plan of reorganization under Chapter 11 Federal Bankruptcy Code effective 03/25/2003
No old Common stockholders' equity
Merged into Global Crossing Ltd. (New) 05/09/2007
Each share new Common 1¢ par exchanged for $9.32 cash

IMPTRON CORP (NY)
Recapitalized as Rex Mining USA, Inc. 06/05/1989
Each share Common $0.001 par exchanged for (0.2) share Common $0.001 par
(See Rex Mining USA, Inc.)

IMPULSE ENERGY SYS INC (UT)
Involuntarily dissolved 05/01/1992

IMPULSE MEDIA TECHNOLOGIES INC (CO)
Name changed to Napoli Enterprises, Inc. 11/25/2002
Napoli Enterprises, Inc. name changed to Lion-Gri International, Inc. 10/20/2004 which recapitalized as Promotora Valle Hermoso, Inc. 07/24/2006 which name changed to UNR Holdings, Inc. 10/15/2009

IMRE CORP (DE)
Each share Common 1¢ par exchanged for (0.5) share Common 2¢ par 06/10/1991
Name changed to Cypress Bioscience, Inc. 05/21/1996
(See Cypress Bioscience, Inc.)

IMREG INC (DE)
Class A Common no par changed to 10¢ par 12/07/1984
Class B Common no par changed to 10¢ par 12/07/1984
Class A Common 10¢ par changed to 5¢ par and (1) additional share issued 02/28/1986
Conv. Class B Common 10¢ par changed to 5¢ par and (1) additional share issued 02/28/1986
Class B Common 5¢ par reclassified as Class A Common 5¢ par 01/01/1989
Assets sold for the benefit of creditors 04/00/1998
No stockholders' equity

IMRGLOBAL CORP (FL)
Merged into Groupe CGI Inc. 7/27/2001
Each share Common 10¢ par exchanged for (1.5974) shares Class A Subordinate no par

IMRS INC (DE)
Name changed to Hyperion Software Corp. 2/14/95
Hyperion Software Corp. merged into Hyperion Solutions Corp. 8/24/98
(See Hyperion Solutions Corp.)

IMS HEALTH HLDGS INC (DE)
Merged into Quintiles IMS Holdings, Inc. 10/03/2016
Each share Common 1¢ par exchanged for (0.384) share Common 1¢ par
Quintiles IMS Holdings, Inc. name changed to IQVIA Holdings Inc. 11/15/2017

IMS HEALTH INC (DE)
Common 1¢ par split (2) for (1) by issuance of (1) additional share payable 01/15/1999 to holders of record 12/29/1998 Ex date - 01/19/1999
Each share Common 1¢ par received distribution of (0.1302) share Gartner Group Inc. (New) Class B Common $0.0005 par payable 07/26/1999 to holders of record 07/17/1999
Each share Common 1¢ par received distribution of (0.05) share Synavant Inc. Common 1¢ par payable 08/31/2000 to holders of record 07/28/2000 Ex date - 09/01/2000
Merged into Healthcare Technology Holdings, Inc. 02/26/2010
Each share Common 1¢ par exchanged for $22 cash

IMS INC (NV)
Reorganized under the laws of Massachusetts as IMSCO, Inc. 07/01/1987
Each share Common $0.001 par exchanged for (0.05) share Common $0.001 par
IMSCO, Inc. (MA) reincorporated in Delaware as IMSCO Technologies, Inc. 09/19/1996 which recapitalized as Global Sports & Entertainment Inc. 08/28/2001 which name changed to GWIN, Inc. 09/24/2002 which name changed to Winning Edge International, Inc. 09/27/2006 which assets were transferred to W Technologies, Inc. 10/20/2007

IMS PETE INC (AB)
Recapitalized as Pocaterra Energy Inc. 01/14/2005
Each share Common no par exchanged for (0.125) share Common no par
Pocaterra Energy Inc. acquired by Buffalo Oil Corp. 01/01/2007 which name changed to Buffalo Resources Corp. 08/03/2007 which merged into Twin Butte Energy Ltd. 10/15/2009

IMSCO TECHNOLOGIES INC (DE)
Reincorporated 09/19/1996
Name changed and state of incorporation changed from IMSCO, Inc. (MA) to IMSCO Technologies, Inc. 09/19/1996
Recapitalized as Global Sports & Entertainment Inc. 08/28/2001
Each share Common $0.001 par exchanged for (0.25) share Common $0.001 par
Global Sports & Entertainment Inc. name changed to GWIN, Inc. 09/24/2002 which name changed to Winning Edge International, Inc. 09/27/2006 which assets were transferred to W Technologies, Inc. 10/20/2007

IMSURE NETWORK INC (NV)
Charter revoked for failure to file reports and pay fees 5/1/2004

IMT INC (DE)
Charter cancelled and declared inoperative and void for non-payment of taxes 03/01/1992

IMT MOBILE MED TECHNOLOGIES LTD (BC)
Struck off register and declared dissolved for failure to file returns 03/26/1993

IMTEC INC (DE)
Merged into Brady Corp. 03/22/2000
Each share Common 1¢ par exchanged for $12 cash

IMTEK OFFICE SOLUTIONS INC (DE)
Company terminated registration of common stock and is no longer public as of 08/31/2000
Details not available

IMTREX INDS & RECYCLING INC (BC)
Struck off register and declared dissolved for failure to file returns 06/17/1994

IMUMED INTL LTD (BERMUDA)
Each share old Common $0.001 par exchanged for (1/3) share new Common $0.001 par 10/11/2001
Each share new Common $0.001 par exchanged for (0.2) share new Common $0.001 par 05/07/2002
Name changed to Ashby Corp. Ltd. 05/13/2002

IMUTEC PHARMA INC (ON)
Name changed 11/27/1996
Name changed from Imutec Corp. to Imutec Pharma Inc. 11/27/1996
Name changed to Lorus Therapeutics Inc. (ON) 11/19/1998
(See Lorus Therapeutics Inc. (ON))

IMVESCOR RESTAURANT GROUP INC (CANADA)
Merged into MTY Food Group Inc. 03/01/2018
Each share Common no par exchanged for (0.0785) share Common no par for 79.86% of holdings and $4.10 cash for remaining 20.14%
Note: Unexchanged certificates will be cancelled and become without value 03/01/2024

IMX PHARMACEUTICALS INC (UT)
Name changed 07/14/1997
Each share old Common $0.001 par exchanged for (0.25) share new Common $0.001 par 11/21/1995
Name changed from IMX Corp. to IMX Pharmaceuticals Inc. 07/14/1997
Each share old Common $0.001 par exchanged for (0.05) share new Common $0.001 par 12/11/2001
Reincorporated under the laws of Delaware as Dialog Group, Inc. 11/15/2002
(See Dialog Group, Inc.)

IMX RESOURCES LTD (AUSTRALIA)
Shares transferred to Australian share register 09/15/2015

IN CTL SEC INC (NV)
Recapitalized as Envirotek 10/28/2009
Each share Common $0.001 par exchanged for (0.001) share Common $0.001 par
Envirotek name changed to Suffer 06/21/2010 which recapitalized as Ophir Resources Co. 01/23/2013
(See Ophir Resources Co.)

IN-FAL MINES LTD. (ON)
Charter revoked for failure to file reports and pay fees 09/23/1954

IN-FLIGHT PHONE CDA INC (ON)
Name changed to Normex Technologies Corp. 09/30/1996
Normex Technologies Corp. recapitalized as Cygnal Technologies Corp. 04/07/1998
(See Cygnal Technologies Corp.)

IN FOCUS SYS INC (OR)
Common no par split (2) for (1) by issuance of (1) additional share payable 02/27/1998 to holders of record 02/10/1998
Name changed to InFocus Corp. 06/02/2000
(See InFocus Corp.)

IN FULL AFFECT INC (NV)
Name changed to Western Transitions, Inc. 05/05/2005
Western Transitions, Inc. name changed to KAT Exploration, Inc. 05/15/2009

IN HOME HEALTH INC (MN)
Each share Common 1¢ par exchanged for (1/3) share Common 3¢ par 11/30/98
Merged into ManorCare Health Services, Inc. 12/28/2000
Each share Common 3¢ par exchanged for $3.70 cash

IN-HOUSE REHAB CORP (CO)
Name changed to Perennial Health Systems, Inc. 11/16/1998
(See Perennial Health Systems, Inc.)

IN MARK LTD (ON)
Name changed to Gemini Food Corp. 03/30/1984
(See Gemini Food Corp.)

IN PLACE ELECTRS LTD (ON)
Charter cancelled for failure to pay taxes and file returns 04/09/1975

IN-SPORTS INTL INC (DE)
Each share Common $0.001 par received distribution of (0.1) share Perma Grass Corp. Common payable 01/10/2001 to holders of record 12/01/2000
Name changed to Avery Sports Turf, Inc. 08/30/2002
Avery Sports Turf, Inc. name changed to ECash, Inc. 05/15/2006 which recapitalized as Pacific Green Technologies Inc. 06/13/2012

IN-STORE ADVERTISING INC (DE)
Plan of reorganization under Chapter 11 Federal Bankruptcy proceedings confirmed 08/06/1993
No stockholders' equity

IN STORE MEDIA SYS INC (NV)
Reorganized under Chapter 11 Federal Bankruptcy Code as AFG Enterprises, Inc. 01/31/2005
Each share Common $0.001 par exchanged for (0.00626291) share Common $0.001 par
Note: Unexchanged certificates were cancelled and became without value 06/30/2005
AFG Enterprises, Inc. name changed to AFG Enterprises USA, Inc. (NV) 08/24/2005 which reincorporated in Delaware as FP Technology, Inc. 07/06/2006 which name changed to Firepond, Inc. 07/12/2007
(See Firepond, Inc.)

IN SYNC INDS INC (BC)
Name changed to Jet Gold Corp. 05/27/2003
Jet Gold Corp. recapitalized as Deep-South Resources Inc. 11/16/2016

IN TEC INTL USA INC (UT)
Reincorporated under the laws of Delaware as Seed Products International, Inc. 6/25/87

IN-TOUCH INTERACTIVE MULTIMEDIA INC (UT)
Recapitalized as Synaptx Worldwide Inc. (UT) 02/24/1997
Each (1.75) shares Common $0.00004 par exchanged for (1) share Common $0.00004 par
Synaptx Worldwide Inc. (UT) reincorporated in Delaware as Paladyne Corp. 03/05/1999 which reorganized as Market Central, Inc. 02/05/2003 which name changed to Scientigo, Inc. 02/17/2006 which recapitalized as Incumaker, Inc. 06/01/2011

IN TOUCH MEDIA GROUP INC (FL)
SEC revoked common stock registration 08/20/2013

IN-TOUCH SURVEY SYS LTD (CANADA)
Each share old Common $0.001 par exchanged for (0.2) share new Common $0.001 par 10/24/2005
Name changed to Intouch Insight Ltd. 07/15/2016

IN VITRO CARE INC (DE)
Name changed to IVCI Corp. 8/8/89
(See IVCI Corp.)

IN VIVO MED DIAGNOSTICS INC (CO)
Name changed to In Veritas Medical Diagnostics, Inc. 4/8/2005

INA CASH FD INC (MD)
Name changed to Parkway Cash Fund, Inc. 08/13/1982
(See Parkway Cash Fund, Inc.)

INA CORP (PA)
Common $1 par split (3) for (2) by issuance of (0.5) additional share 2/14/80
$1.90 Conv. Preferred Ser. C $1 par called for redemption 1/25/82

INA-INC FINANCIAL INFORMATION, INC.

Merged into Cigna Corp. 4/1/82
Each share Common $1 par exchanged for (0.158) share $2.75 Conv. Preferred Ser. A $1 par and (0.8534) share Common $1 par

INA HIGH YIELD FD INC (MD)
Name changed to CIGNA High Yield Fund, Inc. (MD) 04/22/1983
CIGNA High Yield Fund, Inc. (MD) reorganized in Massachusetts as CIGNA Funds Group High Yield Fund 04/30/1985 which reincorporated in Delaware as AIM Funds Group 06/30/1992

INA TAX FREE RESV FD INC (MD)
Name changed to Parkway Tax-Free Reserve Fund, Inc. 8/23/82
(See Parkway Tax-Free Reserve Fund, Inc.)

INACOM CORP (VA)
Plan of reorganization under Chapter 11 Federal Bankruptcy Code effective 6/9/2003
No stockholders' equity

INACOMP COMPUTER CTRS INC (MI)
Merged into InaCom Corp. 8/6/91
Each share Common 5¢ par exchanged for (0.5609) share Common 10¢ par and $1 cash
(See InaCom Corp.)

INAIRCO, INC. (UT)
Name changed to National Sweepstakes Corp. 2/16/68
(See National Sweepstakes Corp.)

INAMED CORP (DE)
Reincorporated 12/28/1998
State of incorporation changed from (FL) to (DE) 12/28/1998
Common 1¢ par split (3) for (2) by issuance of (0.5) additional share payable 12/15/2003 to holders of record 12/01/2003 Ex date - 12/16/2003
Merged into Allergan, Inc. 03/23/2006
Each share Common 1¢ par exchanged for (0.46825) share Common 1¢ par and $37.71 cash
Allergan, Inc. merged into Actavis PLC 03/17/2015 which name changed to Allergan PLC 06/15/2015

INAMERICA CORP (NY)
Reincorporated under the laws of Oklahoma and Common 1¢ par changed to no par 08/31/1988

INAPA-INVESTIMENTOS PARTICIPACOES E GESTAO S A (PORTUGAL)
ADR agreement terminated 02/08/2018
No ADR's remain outstanding

INARCO CORP (OH)
Class A Common no par and Class B Common no par reclassified as Common no par 02/29/1968
Stock Dividend - 20% 07/15/1971
Name changed back to International Artware Corp. 04/29/1982
(See International Artware Corp.)

INAV TRAVEL CORP (CO)
Name changed to MB Software Corp. (CO) 06/18/1996
MB Software Corp. (CO) reorganized in Texas 6/24/2002 which name changed to Wound Management Technologies, Inc. 06/12/2008

INB FINL CORP (IN)
Merged into NBD Bancorp, Inc. 10/15/92
Each share Common no par exchanged for (1.6) shares Common $1 par
NBD Bancorp, Inc. name changed to First Chicago NBD Corp. 12/1/95 which merged into Bank One Corp. 10/2/98 which merged into J.P. Morgan Chase & Co. 12/31/2000 which name changed to JPMorgan Chase & Co. 7/20/2004

INBA LIQUIDATING TRUST (CA)
Each Uncertificated Unit of Bene. Int. received initial distribution of $0.15 cash 3/15/92
Each Uncertificated Unit of Bene. Int. received second distribution of $0.05 cash 3/15/93
Note: Details on subsequent distribution(s), if any, are not available

INBANCSHARES (CA)
Stock Dividends - 10% 5/23/88; 10% 2/23/89
Acquired by Comerica, Inc. 6/28/91
Each share Common no par exchanged for $17.041 cash
Note: Upon surrender each share Common no par became representative of (1) INBA Liquidating Trust Uncertificated Unit of Bene. Int.
(See INBA Liquidating Trust)

INBRAND CORP (GA)
Common 10¢ par split (3) for (2) by issuance of (0.5) additional share 06/29/1994
Common 10¢ par split (3) for (2) by issuance of (0.5) additional share payable 11/22/1996 to holders of record 11/08/1996
Merged into Tyco International Ltd. (Bermuda) 08/27/1997
Each share Common 10¢ par exchanged for (0.43) share Common 20¢ par
Tyco International Ltd. (Bermuda) reincorporated in Switzerland 03/17/2009 which merged into Johnson Controls International PLC 09/06/2016

INBUSINESS SOLUTIONS INC (CANADA)
Merged into TrekLogic Technologies Inc. 02/27/2004
Each share Common no par exchanged for $0.15 cash

INC RESH HLDGS INC (DE)
Name changed to Syneos Health, Inc. 01/08/2018

INC UBATOR CAP INC (DE)
Name changed to Emergent Financial Group, Inc. 07/23/2001
Emergent Financial Group, Inc. recapitalized as EGX Funds Transfer, Inc. 06/14/2002
(See EGX Funds Transfer, Inc.)

INCA ENTERPRISES CORP (CO)
Name changed to Velocity International Corp. (CO) 05/10/2004
Velocity International Corp. (CO) reincorporated in Nevada as Deep Blue, Inc. 03/13/2006 which recapitalized as Bell Rose Capital, Inc. 03/05/2014

INCA GOLD CORP (UT)
Name changed to G.M.P. International, Inc. 4/3/91
G.M.P. International, Inc. charter dissolved 7/1/92

INCA GOLD INC (BC)
Name changed to AirPro Industries Inc. 12/10/1992
AirPro Industries Inc. recapitalized as Camelot Industries Inc. 05/08/1995 which merged into DC Diagnosticare, Inc. 07/15/1996
(See DC Diagnosticare, Inc.)

INCA MNG CORP (AB)
Recapitalized as Graniz Mondal Inc. (AB) 07/18/2000
Each share Common no par exchanged for (0.2) share Common no par
Graniz Mondal Inc. (AB) reincorporated in Canada 08/17/2012 which recapitalized as NanoXplore Inc. 09/08/2017

INCA ONE METALS CORP (CANADA)
Name changed to Inca One Resources Inc. 10/26/2011
Inca One Resources Inc. name changed to Inca One Gold Corp. 09/17/2014

INCA ONE RES CORP (CANADA)
Name changed to Inca One Gold Corp. 09/17/2014

INCA PAC RES INC (BC)
Each share old Common no par exchanged for (0.1) share new Common no par 11/08/2004
Merged into Compania Minera Milpo S.A.A. 10/26/2011
Each share new Common no par exchanged for $0.61 cash

INCA RES INC (BC)
Merged into ABM Gold Corp. 11/17/1989
Each (15) shares Common no par exchanged for (1) share Common no par
ABM Gold Corp. reorganized as NorthWest Gold Corp. 06/01/1990 which merged into Northgate Exploration Ltd. (ON) 06/08/1993 which reincorporated in British Columbia 07/01/2001 which name changed to Northgate Minerals Corp. 05/20/2004 which merged into AuRico Gold Inc. 10/26/2011

INCALL SYS INC (NV)
Name changed 02/01/2002
Name changed from iCall Systems, Inc. to inCall Systems, Inc. 02/01/2002
Common $0.001 par split (2) for (1) by issuance of (1) additional share payable 04/09/2002 to holders of record 04/02/2002 Ex date - 04/10/2002
Recapitalized as West Point Capital, Inc. 06/21/2006
Each share Common $0.001 par exchanged for (0.001) share Common $0.001 par
West Point West Capital, Inc. name changed to Intelective Communications, Inc. 10/02/2007 which name changed to Beacon Redevelopment Industrial Corp. 07/09/2008

INCAM AG (GERMANY)
ADR agreement terminated 11/09/2009
Each Sponsored ADR for Ordinary no par exchanged for (0.025) share Ordinary no par
Note: Unexchanged ADR's will be sold and the proceeds, if any, held for claim after 11/09/2010

INCANA INVTS INC (BC)
Name changed to EasyMed Services Inc. 02/22/2010
EasyMed Services Inc. recapitalized as EasyMed Technologies Inc. 10/21/2013 which recapitalized as Easy Technologies Inc. 02/05/2016

INCARA PHARMACEUTICALS CORP NEW (DE)
Recapitalized as Aeolus Pharmaceuticals, Inc. 7/16/2004
Each share Common $0.001 par exchanged for (0.1) share Common $0.001 par

INCARA PHARMACEUTICALS CORP OLD (DE)
Under plan of merger name changed to Incara Pharmaceuticals Corp. (New) 11/21/2003
Incara Pharmaceuticals Corp. (New) recapitalized as Aeolus Pharmaceuticals, Inc. 7/16/2004

INCE IV INC (CO)
Each (137) shares old Common no par exchanged for (1) share new Common no par 10/27/92
Name changed to Pontus Industries Inc. 12/7/92

Pontus Industries Inc. recapitalized as Continental Orinoco Co., Inc. 5/14/96

INCE II INC (CO)
Recapitalized as Blue Willow Holdings, Inc. (CO) 04/22/1987
Each share Common no par exchanged for (0.01) share Common no par
Blue Willow Holdings, Inc. (CO) reincorporated in Delaware as Americana Gold & Diamond Holdings, Inc. 02/02/1993 which recapitalized as MineCore International, Inc. (DE) 06/29/2004 which reincorporated in Nevada 04/09/2008
(See MineCore International, Inc.)

INCE INC (CO)
Recapitalized as Foliage Plus Inc. 03/24/1986
Each share Common no par exchanged for (0.01) share Common no par
(See Foliage Plus Inc.)

INCENTIVE DESIGN GROUP LTD (BC)
Recapitalized as Envoy Communications Group Inc. (BC) 01/22/1996
Each share Common no par exchanged for (0.2) share Common no par
Envoy Communications Group Inc. (BC) reincorporated in Ontario 12/05/1997 which name changed to Envoy Capital Group Inc. 04/05/2007 which merged into Merus Labs International Inc. (New) 12/22/2011
(See Merus Labs International Inc. (New))

INCENTIVE FD INC (DE)
Name changed to Cumulo Fund, Inc. 09/28/1971
(See Cumulo Fund, Inc.)

INCENTRA SOLUTIONS INC (NV)
Each share old Common $0.001 par exchanged for (0.1) share new Common $0.001 par 06/09/2005
Chapter 11 bankruptcy proceedings converted to Chapter 7 on 11/03/2010
Stockholders' equity unlikely

INCEPTION TECHNOLOGY GROUP INC (FL)
Recapitalized as Rebel Group, Inc. 12/05/2014
Each share Common $0.0001 par exchanged for (0.05) share Common $0.0001 par

INCHCAPE MTRS LTD (SINGAPORE)
Name changed 1/6/98
Stock Dividend - 100% payable 1/27/98 to holders of record 12/24/97
Name changed from Inchcape Berhad to Inchcape Motors Ltd. 1/6/98
ADR agreement terminated 7/12/2002
Each ADR for Ordinary S$1 par exchanged for $1.506448 cash

INCHORUS COM
Recapitalized as Lifestyle Enhancement Systems Inc. 09/12/2002
Each share Common $0.001 par exchanged for (0.005) share Common $0.001 par
Lifestyle Enhancement Systems Inc. name changed to Australian Agricultural & Property Development Inc. 12/08/2003 which name changed to WorldSource, Inc. 06/21/2005
(See WorldSource, Inc.)

INCITATIONS INC (NV)
Common 1¢ par changed to $0.0002 par and (3) additional shares issued payable 11/14/2000 to holders of

record 10/23/2000 Ex date - 02/08/2001
Recapitalized as Osprey Gold Corp. 05/16/2003
Each share Common $0.0002 par exchanged for (0.02) share Common $0.0002 par
Osprey Gold Corp. recapitalized as Gilla Inc. 03/30/2007

INCO HOMES CORP (DE)
Each share old Common 1¢ par exchanged for (0.16666666) share new Common 1¢ 01/16/1997
Filed a petition under Chapter 11 Federal Bankruptcy Code 10/15/1999
Stockholders' equity unknown

INCO LTD (CANADA)
Conv. Class A Common no par reclassified as Common no par 01/01/1979
Conv. Class B Common no par reclassified as Common no par 01/01/1979
Floating Rate Preferred Ser. A $25 par called for redemption 11/03/1986
10% Commodity-Indexed Preferred Ser. C $25 par called for redemption 08/01/1989
7.85% Preferred Ser. B $25 par called for redemption 03/30/1995
Class VBN shares called for redemption at $7.50 cash and (0.45) Common Stock Purchase Warrant expiring 08/21/2006 on 12/14/2000
5.50% Conv. Preferred Ser. E no par called for redemption at $51.10 on 05/01/2003
Merged into Companhia Vale do Rio Doce 01/05/2007
Each share Common no par exchanged for $86 cash

INCODE TECHNOLOGIES CORP (NV)
Reincorporated under the laws of Delaware as Inseq Corp. 07/13/2005
Inseq Corp. name changed to GS Energy Corp. 07/19/2006 which recapitalized as EcoSystem Corp. 02/12/2008 which recapitalized as Adarna Energy Corp. 07/07/2011
(See Adarna Energy Corp.)

INCOME & CAP SHS INC (MA)
Income Shares $1 par called for redemption 03/31/1982
Name changed to P-C Capital Fund Inc. 03/31/1982
P-C Capital Fund Inc. name changed to Phoenix Total Return Fund Inc. 07/09/1986 which name changed to Phoenix Strategic Allocation Fund, Inc. 07/03/1992 which name changed to Phoenix-Oakhurst Strategic Allocation Fund, Inc. (MA) 10/29/1999 which reincorporated in Delaware as Phoenix-Oakhurst Strategic Allocation Fund 00/00/2001 which name changed to Phoenix Strategic Allocation Fund 01/01/2005
(See Phoenix Strategic Allocation Fund)

INCOME & EQUITY INDEX PARTN FD (AB)
Merged into CGF Mutual Funds Corp. 02/27/2009
Each Trust Unit received (1) share Income & Equity Class A
(See CGF Mutual Funds Corp.)

INCOME & GROWTH SPLIT TR (ON)
Under plan of merger name changed to Faircourt Income & Growth Split Trust 01/31/2007
Faircourt Income & Growth Split Trust merged into Faircourt Split Trust 09/30/2010

INCOME DISABILITY & REINSURANCE CO. OF CANADA NEW (ON)
Voting Trust terminated 07/12/1972
Each VTC for Common $5 par exchanged for (1) share Common $5 par
Name changed to Canadian General Life Insurance Co. 11/01/1973
(See Canadian General Life Insurance Co.)

INCOME DISABILITY & REINSURANCE CO. OF CANADA OLD (ON)
Name changed to Executive Life & Disability Co. of Canada 05/01/1967
Executive Life & Disability Co. of Canada acquired by Income Disability & Reinsurance Co. of Canada (New) 01/13/1968 which name changed to Canadian General Life Insurance Co. 11/01/1973
(See Canadian General Life Insurance Co.)

INCOME FD AMER INC (MD)
Reincorporated 09/22/1983
Capital Stock $1 par split (2) for (1) by issuance of (1) additional share 02/10/1978
State of incorporation changed from (DE) to (MD) and Capital Stock $1 par reclassified as Common $1 par 09/22/1983
Common $1 par reclassified as Class A $0.001 par 03/15/2000
Under plan of reorganization each share Class A, Class B and Class C $0.001 par automatically became (1) share Income Fund of America (DE) Class A, Class B or Class C $0.001 par respectively 10/01/2010

INCOME FD BOSTON INC (MA)
Merged into Oppenheimer Income Fund of Boston, Inc. 12/7/76
Each share Capital Stock $1 par exchanged for (0.7043506) share Common Capital Stock $1 par
Oppenheimer Income Fund of Boston, Inc. name changed to Eaton Vance Income Fund of Boston, Inc. 11/16/82 which name changed to Eaton Vance Series Trust II 10/3/2003

INCOME FINL PLUS TR (ON)
Merged into Income Financial Trust 03/01/2006
Each Unit exchanged for (0.74373548) Trust Unit

INCOME FNDTN FD INC (MD)
Each share Capital Stock 10¢ par exchanged for (0.2) share Capital Stock 50¢ par 03/31/1966
Name changed to Boston Foundation Fund Inc. 09/22/1969
Boston Foundation Fund Inc. name changed to Federated Stock & Bond Fund, Inc. (Old) 01/01/1985 which name changed to Stock & Bond Fund, Inc. 04/17/1993 which name changed to Federated Stock & Bond Fund, Inc. (New) (MD) 03/31/1996 which reincorporated in Massachusetts as Federated Stock & Bond Fund 09/05/2008

INCOME LIFE INSURANCE CO. OF CANADA (ON)
Name changed to Abbey Life Insurance Co. of Canada 12/21/67

INCOME MTG & RLTY SHS (OH)
Name changed to Northern States Mortgage & Realty Investors 11/30/1973
Northern States Mortgage & Realty Investors name changed to Monetary Realty Trust 01/17/1979
(See Monetary Realty Trust)

INCOME NOW CONSULTING (NV)
Common $0.0001 par split (18.66) for (1) by issuance of (17.66) additional shares payable 03/22/2012 to holders of record 03/09/2012 Ex date - 03/23/2012
Name changed to ACM Corp. 03/30/2012
(See ACM Corp.)

INCOME OPPORTUNITIES FD 1999 INC (MD)
Completely liquidated
Each share Common 10¢ par exchanged for first and final distribution of $10.01 cash payable 12/17/1999 to holders of record 12/15/1999

INCOME OPPORTUNITIES FD 2000 INC (MD)
Completely liquidated
Each share Common 10¢ par exchanged for first and final distribution of $10.13 cash payable 12/27/2000 to holders of record 12/27/2000

INCOME OPPORTUNITY RLTY TR (CA)
Each old Share of Bene. Int. no par exchanged for (0.25) new Share of Bene. Int. no par 09/09/1991
Reorganized under the laws of Nevada as Income Opportunity Realty Investors, Inc. 03/15/1996
Each new Share of Bene. Int. no par exchanged for (1) share Common 1¢ par

INCOME PLANNING CORP. (PA)
Voluntarily dissolved 04/05/1972
No stockholders' equity

INCOME PPTYS INC (NY)
Name changed to National Showmanship Services, Inc. and Class A 50¢ par and Class B no par reclassified as Common 50¢ par 5/19/69
(See National Showmanship Services, Inc.)

INCOME RLTY SHS (OH)
Name changed to Income Mortgage & Realty Shares 01/18/1972
Income Mortgage & Realty Shares name changed to Northern States Mortgage & Realty Investors 11/30/1973 which name changed to Monetary Realty Trust 01/17/1979
(See Monetary Realty Trust)

INCOME SHARES CORP.
Name changed to Aberdeen Petroleum Corp. in 1946
(See Aberdeen Petroleum Corp.)

INCOME STREAMS III CORP (ON)
Issue Information - 7,500,000 CAP YIELD SHS offered at $25 per share on 06/27/2001
Issue Information - 7,500,000 EQUITY DIVIDEND SHS offered at $15 per share on 06/27/2001
Merged into Dividend 15 Split Corp. 12/01/2013
Each Capital Yield Share exchanged for (1.22352296) Preferred Shares no par and (1.22352296) Class A Shares no par
Each Equity Dividend Share exchanged for (0.3682901) Preferred Share no par and (0.37682901) Class A Share no par

INCOME TR FOR U S GOVT GTD SECS (PA)
Name changed to Kemper Government Guaranteed Securities Fund 10/01/1979

INCOME TRUST SHARES
Trust terminated 00/00/1933
Details not available

INCOMEALTA CORP (AB)
Each share old Common no par exchanged for (1) share new Common no par, (1) share Pinnacle Resources Ltd. (New) Common no par and $1.125 cash 09/03/1991
Acquired by 622305 Alberta Ltd. 07/05/1995
Each share Common no par exchanged for $6.50 cash

INCOMEALTA II CORP (AB)
Common no par split (5) for (1) by issuance of (4) additional shares 10/13/1992
Name changed to Pacific Mercantile Co. Ltd. 07/23/1996
Pacific Mercantile Co. Ltd. merged into Mercury Partners & Co. Inc. 09/28/2001 which name changed to Black Mountain Capital Corp. 05/02/2005 which recapitalized as Grand Peak Capital Corp. (YT) 11/20/2007 which reincorporated in British Columbia 04/27/2010

INCOMED CORP (DE)
Each share old Common $0.001 par exchanged for (0.25) share new Common $0.001 par 01/03/1994
Recapitalized as International Ally Group, Inc. 03/14/2007
Each share Common $0.001 par exchanged for (0.04) share Common $0.001 par
International Ally Group, Inc. recapitalized as Green Shores Inc. 07/27/2009 which name changed to Pacific Shore Holdings, Inc. 10/12/2010

INCOMNET INC (CA)
Each share old Common no par exchanged for (0.5) share new Common no par 6/1/89
Plan of reorganization Chapter 11 Federal Bankruptcy Code effective 5/2/2000
No stockholders' equity

INCONTACT INC (DE)
Acquired by NICE Ltd. 11/14/2016
Each share Common $0.0001 par exchanged for $14 cash

INCONTEXT SYS INC (BC)
Merged into EveryWare Development Canada Inc. 06/30/1997
Each share Common no par exchanged for (0.035) share Common no par and (0.05) Common Stock Purchase Warrant expiring 11/07/1997
(See EveryWare Development Canada Inc.)

INCONTROL INC (DE)
Merged into Guidant Corp. 09/15/1998
Each share Common 1¢ par exchanged for $6 cash

INCORP INC (UT)
Name changed to Customer Sports, Inc. 01/15/1997
(See Customer Sports, Inc.)

INCORPORATED CARRIERS LTD (TX)
Merged into Microtron Industries, Inc. 4/20/81
Each share Common no par exchanged for $2 cash

INCORPORATED EQUITIES
Merged into Incorporated Investors Equities in 1930
Details not available

INCORPORATED INCOME FUND (MA)
Name changed to Putnam Income Fund, Inc. 4/6/66
Putnam Income Fund, Inc. name changed to Putnam Income Fund (New) 11/8/82

INCORPORATED INVESTORS (MA)
Capital Stock no par changed to $5 par in 1932
Capital Stock $5 par changed to $1 par and (2) additional shares issued in 1952
Capital Stock $1 par split (2) for (1) by issuance of (1) additional share 6/25/65
Name changed to Putnam Investors Fund, Inc. 4/6/66

INCORPORATED INVESTORS EQUITIES
Name changed to Consolidated Equities, Inc. in 1932

(See Consolidated Equities, Inc.)

INCORPORATED OZONE (UT)
Name changed to Landmark Publishers Corp. 6/3/77
(See Landmark Publishers Corp.)

INCOTEL LTD (NY)
Assets transferred to Incotel Liquidating Corp. 07/29/1977
Liquidation completed
Each share Common 1¢ par exchanged for initial distribution of $6 cash 08/01/1977
Each share Common 1¢ par received second distribution of $2 cash 12/22/1977
Each share Common 1¢ par received third and final distribution of $1.239 cash 12/31/1979

INCOTERM CORP (MA)
Merged into Honeywell Inc. 1/24/78
Each share Class A Common $1 par exchanged for (0.42) share Common $1.50 par
Honeywell Inc. merged into Honeywell International Inc. 12/1/99

INCREDIMAIL LTD (ISRAEL)
Issue Information - 2,500,000 ORD shares offered at $7.50 per share on 01/30/2006
Name changed to Perion Network Ltd. 11/10/2011

INCREMENTAL DATA INC (NV)
Recapitalized as Golden Age Homes Inc. 09/15/1997
Each shares Common $0.001 par exchanged for (0.03333333) share Common $0.001 par
Golden Age Homes Inc. name changed to American Health Systems Inc. 10/14/1998
(See American Health Systems Inc.)

INCSTAR CORP (MN)
Merged into American Standard Co. 6/30/97
Each share Common 1¢ par exchanged for $6.32 cash

INCUBATE THIS INC (DE)
Reincorporated 01/16/2001
State of incorporation changed from (CO) to (DE) 01/16/2001
Name changed to OrganiTECH USA Inc. 03/20/2001
(See OrganiTECH USA Inc.)

INCYTE GENOMICS INC (DE)
Name changed 6/5/2000
Common $0.001 par split (2) for (1) by issuance of (1) additional share payable 11/7/97 to holders of record 10/17/97
Name changed from Incyte Pharmaceuticals, Inc. to Incyte Genomics, Inc. 6/5/2000
Common $0.001 par split (2) for (1) by issuance of (1) additional share payable 8/31/2000 to holders of record 8/7/2000
Name changed to Incyte Corp. 3/15/2003

IND DAIRYTECH LTD (CAYMAN ISLANDS)
Each share old Common no par exchanged for (0.0000005) share new Common no par 08/03/2011
Note: In effect holders received CAD $0.50 cash per share and public interest was eliminated

INDAL CANADA LTD. (CANADA)
Name changed to Indal Ltd.-Indal Ltee. 08/07/1975
(See Indal Ltd.-Indal Ltee.)

INDAL LTD (CANADA)
Common no par split (2) for (1) by issuance of (1) additional share 06/08/1977
6% Preferred Ser. A $10 par called for redemption 03/03/1978
6% Preferred Ser. B $100 par called for redemption 03/03/1978
Common no par split (2) for (1) by issuance of (1) additional share 06/07/1983
Common no par split (2) for (1) by issuance of (1) additional share 06/06/1986
Reacquired 01/09/1989
Each share Common no par exchanged for $15 cash

INDE INC (NV)
Name changed to Growth Industries, Inc. 7/22/88
(See Growth Industries, Inc.)

INDEBANCORP (OH)
Merged into Croghan Bancshares, Inc. 12/06/2013
Each share Common 1¢ par exchanged for either (1.63) shares Common $12.50 par or $55 cash

INDECON INC (IL)
Each share Common 1¢ par exchanged for (0.00004) share Common $1 par 12/19/1980
Note: In effect holders received $3.50 cash per share and public interest was eliminated

INDEFINITELY CAP CORP (BC)
Name changed to Spearmint Resources Inc. 02/07/2012

INDEMNITY HLDGS INC (CO)
Name changed to Star Casinos International, Inc. 3/1/94
(See Star Casinos International, Inc.)

INDEMNITY INSURANCE CO. OF NORTH AMERICA (PA)
Merged into Insurance Co. of North America 1/1/61
Insurance Co. of North America acquired by INA Corp. 5/29/68 which merged into Cigna Corp. 4/1/82

INDENET INC (DE)
Recapitalized as Enterprise Software, Inc. 07/15/1998
Each share Common $0.0001 par exchanged for (0.25) share Common $0.0001 par
(See Enterprise Software, Inc.)

INDEPENDENCE BANCORP INC (NJ)
Common $6.67 par changed to $3.335 par and (1) additional share issued 09/01/1984
Common $3.335 par changed to $1.667 par and (1) additional share issued 00/00/1987
9% Conv. Preferred Ser. A $1 par called for redemption 09/06/1996
Merged into Commerce Bancorp, Inc. 01/21/1997
Each share Common $1.667 par exchanged for (0.98175) share Common $1.5625 par
Commerce Bancorp, Inc. merged into Toronto-Dominion Bank (Toronto, ONT) 03/31/2008

INDEPENDENCE BANCORP INC (PA)
Common $2.50 par split (2) for (1) by issuance of (1) additional share 06/10/1986
Merged into CoreStates Financial Corp 06/27/1994
Each share Common $2.50 par exchanged for (1.5) shares Common $1 par
CoreStates Financial Corp merged into First Union Corp. 04/28/1998 which name changed to Wachovia Corp. (Ctfs. dated after 09/01/2001) 09/01/2001 which merged into Wells Fargo & Co. (New) 12/31/2008

INDEPENDENCE BANCSHARES INC (SC)
Acquired by First Reliance Bancshares, Inc. 01/23/2018
Each share Common 1¢ par exchanged for $0.125 cash

INDEPENDENCE BK (CANOGA PARK, CA)
100% acquired by I.B. Financial Corp. through exchange offer which expired 12/19/1969

INDEPENDENCE BANK (INDEPENDENCE, OH)
Through exchange offer 100% acquired by Independence Bancorp as of 08/15/1982
Public interest eliminated

INDEPENDENCE BK (NEWPORT BEACH, CA)
Merged into Pacific Premier Bancorp, Inc. 01/26/2015
Each share Common no par exchanged for (0.84821004) share Common 1¢ par and $1.15 cash

INDEPENDENCE BK GROUP INC (WI)
Common $8.33-1/3 par split (3) for (2) by issuance of (0.5) additional share 09/01/1983
Stock Dividend - 100% 12/05/1980
Merged into Marine Corp. (WI) 03/14/1985
Each share Common $8.33-1/3 par exchanged for $33 cash

INDEPENDENCE BANK OF NEW JERSEY (ALLENDALE, NJ)
Reorganized as Independence Bancorp, Inc. 06/28/1984
Each share Common $6.67 par exchanged for (1) share Common $6.67 par
Independence Bancorp, Inc. merged into Commerce Bancorp, Inc. 01/21/1997 which merged into Toronto-Dominion Bank (Toronto, ONT) 03/31/2008

INDEPENDENCE BREWING CO (PA)
Issue Information - 900,000 shares COM and 4,000,000 WTS offered at $5 per share and $0.50 per WT on 02/11/1997
SEC revoked common stock registration 07/07/2011

INDEPENDENCE CMNTY BK CORP (DE)
Merged into Sovereign Bancorp, Inc. 06/01/2006
Each share Common 1¢ par exchanged for $42 cash

INDEPENDENCE FD INC (MA)
Merged into Keystone Custodian Funds 12/23/80
Each share Common $1 par exchanged for (1.5858) shares Keystone Growth Fund Ser. K-2 $1 par
(See Keystone Custodian Funds)

INDEPENDENCE FED SVGS BK (WASHINGTON, DC)
Common 1¢ par split (2) for (1) by issuance of (1) additional share 03/18/1987
Stock Dividends - 10% payable 05/28/2002 to holders of record 05/17/2002; 10% payable 06/06/2003 to holders of record 06/02/2003 Ex date - 05/29/2003
Under plan of merger each share Common 1¢ par automatically became (1) share Colombo Bank (Rockville, MD) Common 1¢ par 12/04/2013
Colombo Bank (Rockville, MD) merged into FVCBankcorp, Inc. 10/15/2018

INDEPENDENCE FIRE INSURANCE CO. OF PHILADELPHIA
Merged into American Equitable Assurance Co. of New York in 1931
Details not available

INDEPENDENCE FIRE INSURANCE SECURITY CO.
Liquidation completed in 1945

INDEPENDENCE FUND OF NORTH AMERICA, INC.
Name changed to National Securities & Research Corp. in 1940
(See National Securities & Research Corp.)

INDEPENDENCE HEALTH PLAN INC (MI)
Merged into HealthCare USA Inc. 05/06/1985
Each share Common 1¢ par exchanged for $26 cash

INDEPENDENCE HLDG CO OLD (DE)
Under plan of merger name changed to Stamford Capital Group, Inc. and each share Common $1 par received distribution of (1.322) shares Common $1 par 11/4/87
Note: Option to receive either an additional (0.5) share or $5 cash expired 12/2/87
Non-electing holders received stock 1/2/88
Stamford Capital Group, Inc. name changed to Independence Holding Co. (New) 9/10/90

INDEPENDENCE INDEMNITY CO. (PA)
Acquired by International Re-Insurance Corp. (DE) 11/01/1932
Details not available

INDEPENDENCE LEAD MINES CO (AZ)
Class A Common $1 par and Class B Common $1 par reclassified as Common $1 par 05/24/1968
Common $1 par changed to 10¢ par 09/23/2005
Each share old Common 10¢ par exchanged for (1.1) shares new Common 10¢ par 07/11/2007
Completely liquidated
Each share new Common 10¢ par received first and final distribution of (1.2) shares Hecla Mining Co. Common 25¢ par payable 12/01/2008 to holders of record 11/17/2008 Ex date - 12/02/2008
Note: Certificates were not required to be surrendered and are without value

INDEPENDENCE LIFE INSURANCE CO. (NC)
Name changed to Skyland Life Insurance Co. 2/28/56
Skyland Liie Insurance Co. merged into Guaranty Savings Life Insurance Co. in 1960
(See Guaranty Savings Life Insurance Co.)

INDEPENDENCE LIFE INS CO AMER (CA)
Stock Dividend - 20% 5/1/64
Merged into USLIFE Holding Corp. 9/28/67
Each share Capital Stock $1.50 par exchanged for (0.609756) share Capital Stock $2 par
USLIFE Holding Corp. name changed to USLIFE Corp. 5/22/70 which merged into American General Corp. 6/17/97 which merged into American International Group, Inc. 8/29/2001

INDEPENDENCE MGMT CORP (DE)
Completely liquidated 03/04/1997
Each share Common $1 par exchanged for first and final distribution of $0.14375458 cash

INDEPENDENCE MINING CO., LTD. (BC)
Charter revoked for failure to file reports and pay fees 12/07/1961

INDEPENDENCE MTG TR (GA)
Under plan of reorganization each Share of Bene. Int. $1 par automatically became (1) share Independence Holding Co. (Old) Common $1 par 12/31/80
Independence Holding Co. (Old) name changed to Stamford Capital Group, Inc. 11/4/87 which name changed to Independence Holding Co. (New) 9/10/90

INDEPENDENCE NATL BK (GASTONIA, NC)
Stock Dividend - 10% 6/1/77

Merged into Branch Corp. 10/5/81
Each share Common $2.50 par exchanged for (2) shares Common $2.50 par
Branch Corp. name changed to BB&T Financial Corp. 5/10/88 which name changed to Southern National Corp. 2/28/95 which name changed to BB&T Corp. 5/19/97

INDEPENDENCE NATIONAL CORP. (OH)
Merged into Independence National Corp. (DE) 12/7/76
Each (3.75) shares Class A no par exchanged for (1) share Class A no par
Independence National Corp. (DE) merged into I.C.H. Corp. 4/18/85 which name changed to Southwestern Life Corp. (New) 6/15/94 which name changed to I.C.H. Corp. (New) 10/10/95
(See I.C.H. Corp. (New))

INDEPENDENCE NATL CORP (DE)
Merged into I.C.H. Corp. 4/18/85
Each share Class A no par exchanged for (0.67) share Common $1 par
Each share Class B no par exchanged for (0.67) share Common $1 par
I.C.H. Corp. name changed to Southwestern Life Corp. (New) 6/15/94 which name changed to I.C.H. Corp. (New) 10/10/95
(See I.C.H. Corp. (New))

INDEPENDENCE PETES INC (BC)
Assets acquired by Tren Exploration, Inc. 08/25/1997
Details not available

INDEPENDENCE RES INC (BC)
Name changed to iLoveTV Entertainment Inc. 01/15/2002
(See iLoveTV Entertainment Inc.)

INDEPENDENCE RES PLC (ENGLAND)
ADR agreement terminated 01/22/2016
Depositary advised that due to their inability to establish contact with the company they will neither be able to sell or receive any value for the shares

INDEPENDENCE TRUST SHARES (PA)
Trust terminated and liquidated 00/00/1954
Details not available

INDEPENDENT AIR HLDGS INC (CO)
Filed a petition under Chapter 11 Federal Bankruptcy Code 4/1/91
Details not available

INDEPENDENT ALLIANCE BKS INC (IN)
Common no par split (3) for (1) by issuance of (2) additional shares payable 06/03/2013 to holders of record 06/01/2013 Ex date - 06/04/2013
Merged into First Merchants Corp. 07/14/2017
Each share Common no par exchanged for (1.653) shares Common no par

INDEPENDENT AMERN LIFE INS CO (TX)
Merged into American Commonwealth Financial Corp. 12/31/73
Each share Common no par exchanged for (0.8) share Common $1 par
American Commonwealth Financial Corp. merged into I.C.H. Corp. 10/26/82 which name changed to Southwestern Life Corp. (New) 6/15/94 which name changed to I.C.H. Corp. (New) 10/10/95
(See I.C.H. Corp. (New))

INDEPENDENT BANCORP ARIZ INC (DE)
Merged into Norwest Corp. 02/15/1995
Each share Common 1¢ par exchanged for $23.67 cash

INDEPENDENT BANCSHARES INC (FL)
Stock Dividends - 5% payable 03/31/2001 to holders of record 03/15/2001 Ex date - 04/05/2001; 5% payable 03/29/2002 to holders of record 03/15/2002; 5% payable 03/30/2007 to holders of record 03/15/2007 Ex date - 03/28/2007
Common $2 par changed to $1 par 11/03/2009
Common holders of (399) shares or fewer reclassified as Ser. A Preferred no par 02/22/2010
Company's principal asset placed in receivership 08/20/2010
Stockholders' equity unlikely

INDEPENDENT BANCSHARES INC (GA)
Merged into United Community Banks, Inc. 7/26/2000
Each share Common $1 par exchanged for (0.4211) share Common $1 par

INDEPENDENT BANK & TRUST CO. (WILLIMANTIC, CT)
Merged into First Connecticut Bancorp, Inc. 10/31/83
Each share Common $5 par exchanged for (3.25) share Common $10 par
First Connecticut Bancorp, Inc. merged into Fleet Financial Group, Inc. (Old) 3/17/86 which merged into Fleet/Norstar Financial Group, Inc. 1/1/88 which name changed to Fleet Financial Group, Inc. (New) 4/15/92 which name changed to Fleet Boston Corp. 10/1/99 which name changed to FirstBoston Financial Corp. 4/18/2000 which merged into Bank of America Corp. 4/1/2004

INDEPENDENT BK & TR CO (WEST TRENTON, NJ)
Stock Dividend - 10% 9/3/79
Merged into Franklin Bancorp 9/30/83
Each share Capital Stock $2 par exchanged for (0.8334) share Common $3.50 par
Franklin Bancorp acquired by United Jersey Banks 1/24/86 which name changed to UJB Financial Corp. 6/30/89 which name changed to Summit Bancorp 3/1/96 which merged into FleetBoston Financial Corp. 3/1/2001 which merged into Bank of America Corp. 4/1/2004

INDEPENDENT BANK (MANASSAS, VA)
Each share Common $6 par exchanged for (3) shares Common $2 par 01/20/1982
Merged into Crestar Financial Corp. 01/20/1995
Each share Common $2 par exchanged for either (0.03063) share Common $5 par or $12.25 cash

INDEPENDENT BK CORP (MI)
$2.75 Conv. Preferred Ser. A no par called for redemption 12/1/91
Trust Preferred Securities called for redemption at $25 on 4/21/2003
(Additional Information in Active)

INDEPENDENT BANKGROUP INC (VT)
Plan of reorganization under Chapter 11 Federal Bankruptcy proceedings effective 07/31/1995
No stockholders' equity

INDEPENDENT BKS VA INC (VA)
Under plan of reorganization each share Common $5 par automatically became (1) share Heritage Bankshares, Inc. Common $5 par 08/00/1992
(See Heritage Bankshares, Inc.)

INDEPENDENT BANKSHARES CORP (CA)
Common $5 par changed to no par and (1) additional share issued 04/28/1978
Stock Dividend - 10% 02/28/1979
Name changed to Westamerica Bancorporation 07/01/1983

INDEPENDENT BANKSHARES CORP (TN)
Stock Dividends - 3% payable 02/15/1999 to holders of record 12/31/1998; 3% payable 01/28/2000 to holders of record 01/18/2000; 3% payable 03/01/2001 to holders of record 01/23/2001 Ex date - 03/14/2001; 3% payable 02/26/2002 to holders of record 01/24/2002 Ex date - 03/19/2002
Merged into Greene County Bancshares, Inc. 11/21/2003
Each share Capital Stock exchanged for (0.339682) share Common $2 par and $36.45 cash
Greene County Bancshares Inc. name changed to Green Bankshares, Inc. 05/18/2007 which merged into Capital Bank Financial Corp. 09/20/2012 which merged into Capital Bank Financial Corp. 11/30/2017

INDEPENDENT BANKSHARES INC (TX)
Each share Common $1.25 par exchanged for (0.125) share Common 25¢ par 05/31/1991
Common 25¢ par split (4) for (3) by issuance of (1/3) additional share 05/31/1995
Common 25¢ par split (5) for (4) by issuance of (0.25) additional share payable 05/30/1997 to holders of record 05/15/1997
Merged into State National Bankshares, Inc. 08/11/2000
Each share Common 25¢ par exchanged for $20.0165 cash

INDEPENDENT BISCUIT CO.
Acquired by Weston (George) Ltd. in 1931
Details not available

INDEPENDENT BONDING & CASUALTY INSURANCE CO.
Receiver appointed for purpose of liquidation in 1930
Details not available

INDEPENDENT BREWERIES CO.
Discontinued operations 00/00/1930
Stockholders' equity unlikely

INDEPENDENT BREWING CO. OF PITTSBURGH
Dissolved in 1936

INDEPENDENT BUSINESS ALLIANCE INC (DE)
Each share Common $0.001 par exchanged for (0.005) share Common 2¢ par 06/28/1991
Name changed to I.C.W. Industries, Inc. 07/28/1991
(See I.C.W. Industries, Inc.)

INDEPENDENT CAP TR (DE)
8.50% Guaranteed Trust Preferred Securities called for redemption at $10 on 9/22/2003

INDEPENDENT CAP TR I (DE)
9.28% Trust Preferred Securities called for redemption at $25 on 05/20/2002

INDEPENDENT CAP TR II (DE)
Trust Preferred Securitites called for redemption at $25 on 01/31/2002

INDEPENDENT CAP TR III (DE)
8.625% Trust Preferred Securities called for redemption at $25 on 12/31/2006

INDEPENDENT CAP TR IV (DE)
8.375% Trust Preferred Securities called for redemption at $25 plus $0.162845 accrued dividends on 4/30/2007

INDEPENDENT CHEMICAL, INC. (DE)
Liquidation completed 7/5/61
Holders of 7% Preferred $100 par stock only received cash
No funds available for 2nd Preferred and Common

INDEPENDENT COAL & COKE CO. (WY)
Name changed to 706 Judge Building Corp. 1/2/68
(See 706 Judge Building Corp.)

INDEPENDENT CMNTY BANKSHARES INC (VA)
Common $5 par split (2) for (1) by issuance of (1) additional share payable 11/24/1997 to holders of record 11/24/1997
Name changed to Middleburg Financial Corp. 05/15/2002
Middleburg Financial Corp. merged into Access National Corp. 03/31/2017

INDEPENDENT CONSUMER ACCEP CO (MI)
Charter declared inoperative and void for failure to file reports 05/15/1977

INDEPENDENT COS AMER INC (DE)
Name changed to I.I.B. Ltd. 10/19/77
I.I.B. Ltd. recapitalized as Sparkling Water of Austria, Inc. 12/22/80 which recapitalized as Dairy Whey Foods Corp. 7/27/83 which name changed to Novar International Corp. 6/8/84
(See Novar International Corp.)

INDEPENDENT DISTILLERS OF KENTUCKY, INC.
Bankrupt in 1938

INDEPENDENT EASTERN TORPEDO CO. (OH)
Name changed to Chemical Process Co. (OH) 12/31/54
Chemical Process Co. (OH) was acquired by Borg-Warner Corp. (IL) 10/21/57 which reincorporated in Delaware 10/31/67
(See Borg-Warner Corp. (DE))

INDEPENDENT ENERGY HLDGS PLC (ENGLAND & WALES)
Placed in liquidation 09/00/2000
No ADR holders' equity

INDEPENDENT ENERGY INC (AB)
Acquired by Stampeder Exploration Ltd. 03/20/1996
Each share Class A Common no par exchanged for $4 cash

INDEPENDENT ENTERPRISES INC (ON)
Name changed to Becker Gold Mines Ltd. (ON) and (3) additional shares issued 01/09/2003
Becker Gold Mines Ltd. (ON) reincorporated in British Columbia 01/15/2007 which name changed to Sonoro Metals Corp. 01/09/2012

INDEPENDENT ENTMT GROUP INC (CO)
Each (150) shares old Common $0.0001 par exchanged for (1) share new Common $0.0001 par 10/23/89
Each share new Common $0.0001 par exchanged again for (0.1) share new Common $0.0001 par 9/21/92
Name changed to Independent TeleMedia Group Inc. (CO) 7/7/93
Independent Telemedia Group Inc. (CO) reorganized in Delaware as IndeNet, Inc. 6/28/95 which recapitalized as Enterprise Software, Inc. 7/15/98
(See Enterprise Software, Inc.)

INDEPENDENT EXPLORATION CO.
Name changed to Intex Oil Co. 00/00/1952
Intex Oil Co. merged into Tesoro

IND-IND   **FINANCIAL INFORMATION, INC.**

Petroleum Corp. (CA) 02/01/1968 which reincorporated in Delaware as Tesoro Petroleum Corp. 03/03/1969 which name changed to Tesoro Corp. 11/08/2004 which name changed to Andeavor 08/01/2017 which merged into Marathon Petroleum Corp. 10/01/2018

INDEPENDENT FINL NETWORK INC (OR)
Stock Dividends - 5% payable 8/16/2000 to holders of record 8/2/2000 Ex date - 7/31/2000; 5% payable 3/16/2001 to holders of record 3/2/2001
Merged into Umpqua Holdings Corp. 12/31/2001
Each share Common $5 par exchanged for (0.8) share Common 83-1/3¢ par

INDEPENDENT FINANCIAL SERVICES, INC. (ID)
Merged into Independent Tax Corp. 08/29/1978
Each share Preferred $1 par exchanged for (1) share Common no par
Each share Common 10¢ par exchanged for (1) share Common no par
(See Independent Tax Corp.)

INDEPENDENT GROWTH FINDERS INC (CANADA)
Dissolved for non-compliance 03/12/2007

INDEPENDENT HARVESTER CO. (ME)
Dissolved 08/06/1918
No stockholders' equity

INDEPENDENT INS GROUP INC (FL)
Non-Vtg. Common $1 par split (2) for (1) by issuance of (1) additional share 6/8/90
Merged into American General Corp. 2/29/96
Each share Common $1 par exchanged for (0.748) Common $1 par and $27.50 cash
Each share Non-Vtg. Common $1 par exchanged for (0.748) share Common $1 par and $27.50 cash
American General Corp. merged into American International Group, Inc. 8/29/2001

INDEPENDENT INVT CORP (KS)
Merged into Londen Insurance Group, Inc. 01/01/1988
Each share Common 10¢ par exchanged for $1.60 cash

INDEPENDENT LIBERTY LIFE INS CO (MI)
Each share Common $1 par exchanged for (0.01) share Common $12.50 par 11/30/1982
Liquidated by Court Order 08/30/1985
No stockholders' equity

INDEPENDENT LIFE & ACC INS CO (FL)
Stock Dividend - Common & Non-Vtg. Common - 100% 6/7/73
Reorganized as Independent Insurance Group, Inc. 1/1/81
Each share Common $1 par exchanged for (1) share Common $1 par
Each share Non-Vtg. Common $1 par exchanged for (1) share Non-Vtg. Common $1 par
Independent Insurance Group, Inc. merged into American General Corp. 2/29/96 which merged into American International Group, Inc. 8/29/2001

INDEPENDENT LIFE INSURANCE CO. (MD)
Acquired by North American Equitable Life Assurance Co. 03/17/1960
Details not available

INDEPENDENT MNG LTD (ON)
Recapitalized as Independent Enterprises Inc. 08/17/2000
Each share Common no par exchanged for (0.25) share Common no par
Independent Enterprises Inc. name changed to Becker Gold Mines Ltd. (ON) 01/09/2003 which reincorporated in British Columbia 01/15/2007 which name changed to Sonoro Metals Corp. 01/09/2012

INDEPENDENT MUSIC GROUP INC (DE)
Name changed to Falcon Entertainment Corp. 12/14/1999
(See Falcon Entertainment Corp.)

INDEPENDENT NICKEL CORP (ON)
Reincorporated 09/11/2007
Place of incorporation changed from (BC) to (ONT) 09/11/2007
Merged into Victory Nickel Inc. 01/05/2009
Each share Common no par exchanged for (1.1) shares Common no par

INDEPENDENT OIL & GAS CO.
Acquired by Phillips Petroleum Co. in 1930
Details not available

INDEPENDENT PLOW, INC. (KS)
Each share Common $1 par exchanged for (2) shares Common 50¢ par in 1952
Charter cancelled for failure to file reports and pay franchise fees 12/31/54

INDEPENDENT PNEUMATIC TOOL CO. (DE)
Stock Dividend - 100% 06/00/1946
Name changed to Thor Power Tool Co. 00/00/1953
(See Thor Power Tool Co.)

INDEPENDENT REALTY & INVESTMENT CO.
Liquidated in 1937

INDEPENDENT REFINING CO.
Liquidated in 1943

INDEPENDENT RES LTD (AUSTRALIA)
Struck off register 12/01/2004
No ADR holders' equity

INDEPENDENT SECURITY LIFE INSURANCE CO. (MI)
Merged into Independent Liberty Life Insurance Co. 03/30/1966
Each share Common $1 par exchanged for (0.415) share Common $1 par
(See Independent Liberty Life Insurance Co.)

INDEPENDENT SHOE DISCOUNTERS ASSOCIATION, INC. (OK)
Name changed to International Sales Development Association, Inc. and Common $1 par changed to 10¢ par 11/10/69
International Sales Development Association, Inc. name changed to Aardvark, Inc. 4/7/70
(See Aardvark, Inc.)

INDEPENDENT TAX CORP. (CA)
Merged out of existence 00/00/1980
Details not available

INDEPENDENT TELEMEDIA GROUP INC (CO)
Reincorporated under the laws of Delaware as IndeNet, Inc. 06/28/1995
IndeNet, Inc. recapitalized as Enterprise Software, Inc. 07/15/1998
(See Enterprise Software, Inc.)

INDEPENDENT TELEPHONE CORP. (NY)
Merged into Continental Independent Telephone Corp. 3/31/64
Each share 5% Conv. Preferred Series A, B or D $10 par or 4% Conv. Preferred Series C $10 par exchanged for (0.4) share 5% Conv. Preferred $25 par
Each share Common $1 par exchanged for (0.825) share Common $1 par
Continental Independent Telephone Corp. name changed to Continental Telephone Corp. 5/11/65 which name changed to Continental Telecom Inc. 5/6/82 which name changed to Contel Corp. 5/1/86 which merged into GTE Corp. 3/14/91 which merged into Verizon Communications Inc. 6/30/2000

INDEPTH DATA INC (DE)
Merged into TLR Administration Inc. 3/12/99
Details not available

INDESCOR HYDRODYNAMICS INC (BC)
Recapitalized as Consolidated Indescor Corp. 12/11/1985
Each share Common no par exchanged for (0.33333333) share Common no par
(See Consolidated Indescor Corp.)

INDESTRUCTIBLE I INC (DE)
Name changed to Dongsheng Pharmaceutical International Co. Ltd. 05/26/2010

INDEVUS PHARMACEUTICALS INC (DE)
Merged into Endo Pharmaceuticals Holdings Inc. 03/23/2009
Each share Common $0.001 par exchanged for $4.50 cash

INDEX CORP. (OR)
Charter cancelled and declared dissolved for failure to file reports and pay fees 2/15/72

INDEX DEV PARTNERS INC (DE)
Name changed to WisdomTree Investments, Inc. 9/22/2005

INDEX FD BOSTON INC (MA)
Name changed to Index Fund Inc. 01/01/1970
Index Fund Inc. acquired by Pilgrim Fund, Inc. 12/15/1972 which merged into Pilgrim Magnacap Fund, Inc. 06/20/1985

INDEX FUND INC. (MA)
Acquired by Pilgrim Fund, Inc. 12/15/72
Each share Common 10¢ par exchanged for (0.5520) share Common $1 par
Pilgrim Fund, Inc. merged into Pilgrim Magnacap Fund, Inc. 6/20/85

INDEX INC (TX)
Recapitalized as DXP Enterprises, Inc. 5/12/97
Each share Common 1¢ par exchanged for (0.5) share Common 1¢ par

INDEX OIL & GAS INC (NV)
Charter revoked 03/30/2012

INDEX TECHNOLOGY CORP (MA)
Merged into Intersolv, Inc. 03/19/1991
Each share Common 10¢ par exchanged for (1.059) shares Common 1¢ par
Intersolv, Inc. merged into Micro Focus Group PLC 09/15/1998 which name changed to Merant PLC 02/16/1999 which was acquired by Serena Software, Inc. 06/30/2004
(See Serena Software, Inc.)

INDEXIQ ETF TR (DE)
Trust terminated 12/30/2011
Each IQ Hong Kong Small Cap ETF no par received $13.3196 cash
Each IQ Japan Mid Cap ETF no par received $18.2965 cash
Each IQ Taiwan Small Cap ETF no par received $21.2132 cash
Trust terminated 08/17/2012
Each IQ South Korea Small Cap ETF no par received $23.43 cash
Trust terminated 12/17/2012
Each IQ Emerging Markets Mid Cap ETF no par received $17.31 cash
Trust terminated 03/23/2018
Each share IQ Australia Small Cap ETF no par received $19.55563 cash
Each share IQ Canada Small Cap ETF no par received $17.15503 cash
Each share IQ Global Oil Small Cap ETF no par received $10.41831 cash
(Additional Information in Active)

INDEXONLY TECHNOLOGIES INC (NV)
Name changed to Nutrifeeds Technologies Inc. 5/5/2003
Nutrifeeds Technologies Inc. name changed to Advanced Solutions & Technologies, Inc. 1/16/2004
(See Advanced Solutions & Technologies, Inc.)

INDEXPLUS DIVID FD (AB)
Merged into INDEXPLUS Income Fund 12/19/2012
Each Trust Unit received (0.7702396) Unit
INDEXPLUS Income Fund reorganized as Middlefield Mutual Funds Ltd. 06/05/2017

INDEXPLUS INCOME FD (ON)
Under plan of reorganization each Trust Unit automatically became (1) share Middlefield Mutual Funds Ltd. INDEXPLUS Income Fund Ser. F 06/05/2017
Note: U.S. holders were redeemed for cash

INDEXPLUS 2 INCOME FD (AB)
Merged into INDEXPLUS Income Fund 04/25/2006
Each Trust Unit exchanged for (0.8969775) Trust Unit
INDEXPLUS Income Fund reorganized as Middlefield Mutual Funds Ltd. 06/05/2017

INDIA CORP. (MA)
Liquidation completed 02/28/1963
Details not available

INDIA ECOMMERCE CORP (NV)
Recapitalized as Ystrategies Corp. 06/03/2016
Each share Common $0.001 par exchanged for (0.1) share Common $0.001 par

INDIA GROWTH FD INC (MD)
Completely liquidated 5/30/2003
Each share Common 1¢ par exchanged for first and final distribution of approximately $9.9388 cash

INDIA TIRE & RUBBER CO.
Acquired by India Tire Co. in 1934 which liquidated in 1936

INDIA TIRE CO.
Liquidated in 1936

INDIA TYRE & RUBBER CO.
Acquired by Dunlop Rubber Co. Ltd. 00/00/1936
Details not available

INDIABULLS FINL SVCS LTD (INDIA)
Each Reg. S GDR for Ordinary received distribution of (1) Indiabulls Securities Ltd. Reg. S Sponsored GDR for Ordinary payable 04/14/2008 to holders of record 01/08/2008
Each 144A GDR for Ordinary received distribution of (1) Indiabulls Securities Ltd. 144A Sponsored GDR for Ordinary payable 04/14/2008 to holders of record 01/08/2008
Merged into Indiabulls Housing Finance Ltd. 09/12/2013
Each Reg. S GDR for Ordinary exchanged for (1) Reg. S Sponsored GDR for Ordinary
Each 144A GDR for Ordinary

exchanged for (1) Reg. S Sponsored GDR for Ordinary

INDIABULLS SECS LTD (INDIA)
Name changed to Indiabulls Ventures Ltd. 04/01/2015

INDIAN ALUMINIUM LTD (INDIA)
GDR agreement terminated 06/22/2004
Each 144A GDR for Ordinary exchanged for $2.4012 cash

INDIAN CREEK URANIUM & OIL CORP. (UT)
Completely liquidated 10/23/70
Each share Common 10¢ par exchanged for first and final distribution of (1) share Pan American Energy, Inc. (NV) Common 1¢ par
Pan American Energy, Inc. (NV) merged into Colorado River & Eagle Co. 7/1/81
(See Colorado River & Eagle Co.)

INDIAN FIN CORP (IN)
Merged into ISC Industries Inc. 1/5/70
Each share 5.8% Preferred Ser. A or Ser. B $20 par exchanged for (1) share 5.80% Preferred $20 par
Each share Common $1 par exchanged for (0.5) share Conv. Jr. Preferred no par
ISC Industries Inc. name changed to ISC Financial Corp. 9/26/74
(See ISC Financial Corp.)

INDIAN GOLD RES LTD (BC)
Name changed to Advanced Aero-Wing Systems Corp. 06/04/1985
(See Advanced Aero-Wing Systems Corp.)

INDIAN HEAD ASSOC INC (NH)
Name changed to IHA, Inc. 5/7/73
(See IHA, Inc.)

INDIAN HEAD BKS INC (NH)
Common $5 par split (5) for (4) by issuance of (0.25) additional share 10/15/86
Stock Dividends - 100% 4/21/80; 25% 12/22/83; 10% 1/13/86
Acquired by Fleet/Norstar Financial Group, Inc. 12/21/88
Each share 12% Conv. Preferred Ser. I $100 par exchanged for (1) share 12% Conv. Preferred Ser. I $1 par
Each share Common $5 par exchanged for (1.775) shares Common $1 par
Fleet/Norstar Financial Group, Inc. name changed to Fleet Financial Group, Inc. (New) 4/15/92 which name changed to Fleet Boston Corp. 10/1/99 which name changed to FleetBoston Financial Corp. 4/18/2000 which merged into Bank of America Corp. 4/1/2004

INDIAN HEAD INC (DE)
$4.50 Conv. Preferred Ser. A no par called for redemption 10/11/1976
Merged into Thyssen-Boremisza Holdings Ltd. 11/30/1976
Each share Common $1 par exchanged for $32 cash

INDIAN HEAD MILLS, INC. (MA)
Reincorporated 02/18/1955
State of incorporation changed from (RI) to (MA) 02/18/1955
Common $1 par split (2) for (1) by issuance of (1) additional share 03/02/1959
Common $1 par split (2) for (1) by issuance of (1) additional share 10/20/1961
$1.25 Preferred $20 par called for redemption 06/30/1965
$1.50 Preferred $20 par called for redemption 06/30/1965
Stock Dividends - 10% 11/23/1959; 50% 07/30/1963
Reincorporated under the laws of Delaware as Indian Head Inc. 06/08/1966
(See Indian Head Inc.)

INDIAN HEAD NATL BK (CLAREMONT, NH)
Merged into Indian Head Banks, Inc. 8/31/84
Each share Common $20 par exchanged for (7.5) shares Common $5 par
Indian Head Banks, Inc. acquired by Fleet/Norstar Financial Group, Inc. 12/21/88 which name changed to Fleet Financial Group, Inc. (New) 4/15/92 which name changed to Fleet Boston Corp. 10/1/99 which name changed to FleetBoston Financial Corp. 4/18/2000 which merged into Bank of America Corp. 4/1/2004

INDIAN HEAD NATIONAL BANK (CONCORD, NH)
Merged into Indian Head Banks, Inc. 8/31/84
Each share Common $5 par exchanged for (1) share Common $5 par
Indian Head Banks, Inc. acquired by Fleet/Norstar Financial Group, Inc. 12/21/88 which name changed to Fleet Financial Group, Inc. (New) 4/15/92 which name changed to Fleet Boston Corp. 10/1/99 which name changed to FleetBoston Financial Corp. 4/18/2000 which merged into Bank of America Corp. 4/1/2004

INDIAN HEAD NATIONAL BANK (MANCHESTER, NH)
Merged into Indian Head Banks, Inc. 11/30/74
Each share Common $50 par exchanged for (2) shares Common $5 par
Indian Head Banks, Inc. acquired by Fleet/Norstar Financial Group, Inc. 12/21/88 which name changed to Fleet Financial Group, Inc. (New) 4/15/92 which name changed to Fleet Boston Corp. 10/1/99 which name changed to FleetBoston Financial Corp. 4/18/2000 which merged into Bank of America Corp. 4/1/2004

INDIAN HEAD NATL BK (NASHUA, NH)
Capital Stock $100 par changed to $75 par and (0.333) additional share issued 7/31/56
Capital Stock $75 par changed to $25 par and (2) additional shares issued 11/10/60
Stock Dividend - 66-2/3% 2/13/63
Merged into Indian Head Banks, Inc. 11/30/74
Each share Capital Stock $25 par exchanged for (6) shares Common $5 par
Indian Head Banks, Inc. acquired by Fleet/Norstar Financial Group, Inc. 12/21/88 which name changed to Fleet Financial Group, Inc. (New) 4/15/92 which name changed to Fleet Boston Corp. 10/1/99 which name changed to FleetBoston Financial Corp. 4/18/2000 which merged into Bank of America Corp. 4/1/2004

INDIAN HOTELS LTD (INDIA)
GDR agreement terminated 09/07/2015
Each 144A GDR for Equity Shares exchanged for $0.73375737 cash

INDIAN LAKE GOLD MINES LTD. (ON)
Name changed to Indian Lake Mines Ltd. 12/23/1955
Indian Lake Mines Ltd. merged into Hydra Explorations Ltd. 11/16/1959 which name changed to Hydra Capital Corp. 12/30/1992 which name changed to Waterford Capital Management Inc. 11/12/1996 which merged into CPI Plastics Group Ltd. 09/21/1998
(See CPI Plastics Group Ltd.)

INDIAN LAKE MINES LTD. (ON)
Merged into Hydra Explorations Ltd. 11/16/1959
Each share Capital Stock $1 par exchanged for (0.05) share Capital Stock $1 par
Hydra Explorations Ltd. name changed to Hydra Capital Corp. 12/30/1992 which name changed to Waterford Capital Management Inc. 11/12/1996 which merged into CPI Plastics Group Ltd. 09/21/1998
(See CPI Plastics Group Ltd.)

INDIAN MINES (1946) LTD. (BC)
Recapitalized as New Indian Mines Ltd. 05/10/1957
Each share Capital Stock 50¢ par exchanged for (0.2) share Capital Stock no par
New Indian Mines Ltd. recapitalized as Azure Resources Ltd. 05/11/1972 which recapitalized as Consolidated Azure Resources Ltd. 04/23/1987 which name changed to Caltech Data Ltd. 02/05/1988 which recapitalized as Roraima Gold Corp. 09/14/1994 which recapitalized as International Roraima Gold Corp. 06/13/1996
(See International Roraima Gold Corp.)

INDIAN MINES CORP. LTD.
Acquired by Indian Mines (1946) Ltd. 00/00/1946
Each share Capital Stock exchanged for (0.25) share Capital Stock 50¢ par
Indian Mines (1946) Ltd. recapitalized as New Indian Mines Ltd. 05/10/1957 which recapitalized as Azure Resources Ltd. 05/11/1972 which recapitalized as Consolidated Azure Resources Ltd. 04/23/1987 which name changed to Caltech Data Ltd. 02/05/1988 which recapitalized as Roraima Gold Corp. 09/14/1994 which recapitalized as International Roraima Gold Corp. 06/13/1996
(See International Roraima Gold Corp.)

INDIAN MOTOCYCLE CO. (MA)
Each share 7% Preferred $100 par exchanged for (1) share 6% Preferred $10 par 00/00/1933
Each share Common no par exchanged for (0.1) share new Common no par 00/00/1933
Common no par changed to $1 par 01/00/194 01/00/1947
Common $1 par changed to no par 08/00/1947
Recapitalized as Titeflex, Inc. 00/00/1951
Each share $0.50 Preferred no par exchanged for (0.4) share new Common $1 par
Each share Common no par exchanged for (0.1) share Common $1 par
Titeflex, Inc. merged into Atlas Corp. 08/17/1962
(See Atlas Corp.)

INDIAN MTN METAL MINES LTD (ON)
Merged into Initiative Explorations Inc. 02/13/1980
Each share Capital Stock $1 par exchanged for (0.12903225) share Capital Stock no par
Initiative Explorations Inc. merged into Canhorn Chemical Corp. 04/26/1995 which merged into Nayarit Gold Inc. 05/02/2005 which merged into Capital Gold Corp. 08/02/2010 which merged into Gammon Gold Inc. (QC) 04/08/2011 which reincorporated in Ontario as AuRico Gold Inc. 06/14/2011 which merged into Alamos Gold Inc. (New) 07/06/2015

INDIAN PETROCHEMICALS LTD (INDIA)
Merged into Reliance Industries Ltd. 11/19/2007
Each 144A GDR for Equity shares exchanged for (0.6) Sponsored 144A GDR for Equity shares

INDIAN POINT CORP. (NY)
Liquidation completed in 1953

INDIAN QUEEN CONSOLIDATED MINING CO. (UT)
Recapitalized as Delta Oil Co. of Utah 06/15/1957
Each share Capital Stock 10¢ par exchanged for (0.01) share Common $1 par
Delta Oil Co. of Utah liquidated for Bloomfield Royalty Corp. 04/19/1963 which name changed to Financial Technology, Inc. 12/29/1969 which name changed to Texon Energy Corp. 05/14/1974
(See Texon Energy Corp.)

INDIAN RAYON & INDS INC (INDIA)
144A GDR's for Ordinary split (3) for (2) by issuance of (0.5) additional GDR payable 01/05/1998 to holders of record 09/03/1997
Stock Dividend - 9.1774% payable 10/01/1999 to holders of record 07/29/1999
Name changed to Aditya Birla Nuvo Ltd. 11/23/2005
(See Aditya Birla Nuvo Ltd.)

INDIAN REFINING CO.
Liquidated 4/24/43
Each share Common $10 par exchanged for (0.25) share Texas Co. (New) Common $25 par
Texas Co. (New) name changed to Texaco, Inc. 5/1/59 which merged into ChevronTexaco Corp. 10/9/2001 which name changed to Chevron Corp. 5/9/2005

INDIAN RIV BKG CO (FL)
Common $1 par split (2) for (1) by issuance of (1) additional share payable 4/5/2000 to holders of record 3/15/2000
Stock Dividends - 10% payable 4/30/96 to holders of record 3/25/96; 10% payable 4/7/99 to holders of record 1/14/99; 10% payable 1/10/2000 to holders of record 1/3/2000; 10% payable 4/4/2001 to holders of record 2/14/2001 Ex date - 4/25/2001; 10% payable 1/24/2002 to holders of record 1/9/2002; 10% payable 2/14/2003 to holders of record 1/31/2003 Ex date - 1/29/2003
Merged into Alabama National BanCorporation 2/27/2004
Each share Common $1 par exchanged for (0.9408) share Common $1 par

INDIAN RIV RES INC (BC)
Reorganized as Mainfort Marine International Corp. 03/17/1989
Each share Common no par exchanged for (1) share Common no par
(See Mainfort Marine International Corp.)

INDIAN RIVER CITRUS BK (VERO BEACH, FL)
99.9% acquired by First National Bankshares of Florida, Inc. through exchange offer which expired 07/31/1973
Public interest eliminated

INDIAN RIVER CITRUS FRUITS INC (PA)
Liquidation completed
Each share Common $2 par exchanged for initial distribution of $5.50 cash 03/27/1974
Each share Common $2 par received

second distribution of $1.50 cash 08/09/1974
Each share Common $2 par received third distribution of $0.35 cash 11/27/1974
Each share Common $2 par received fourth and final distribution of $0.04 cash 12/23/1976

INDIAN RIVER FEDERAL SAVINGS BANK (VERO BEACH, FL)
Acquired by PNC Bank Corp. 1/16/95
Each share Common $1 par exchanged for $18.25 cash

INDIAN ROCKS ST BK (LARGO, FL)
Merged into F.N.B. Corp. (PA) 10/17/97
Each share Common $4 par exchanged for (1.8) shares Common $2 par
F.N.B. Corp. (PA) reincorporated in Florida 6/13/2001

INDIAN TERRITORY ILLUMINATING OIL CO.
In process of liquidation in 1942

INDIAN TRAIL RANCH INC (FL)
Voluntarily dissolved 11/6/74
Details not available

INDIAN VILLAGE MANOR CO (MI)
Each share Common $1 par stamped to indicate distribution of (2) shares 6% Conv. Preferred $1 par 00/00/1953
Completely liquidated 07/07/1968
Each share Common $1 par stamped exchanged for first and final distribution of $10 cash

INDIAN VLG BANCORP INC (PA)
Stock Dividend - 10% payable 01/06/2005 to holders of record 12/20/2004 Ex date - 12/16/2004
Merged into CSB Bancorp, Inc. 10/31/2008
Each share Common 1¢ par exchanged for (0.7611) share Common $6.25 par and $4.375 cash

INDIAN WELLS ACQUISITIONS LTD (NV)
Name changed to Nitro Lube, Inc. 11/25/2005
Nitro Lube, Inc. name changed to Uranium City Mining Corp. 11/14/2007 which name changed to U.S. Mine Makers, Inc. (NV) 01/28/2008 which reincorporated in Wyoming as Vid3G, Inc. 02/13/2014 which recapitalized as Argus Worldwide Corp. 11/14/2016

INDIAN WELLS WTR INC (CA)
Each share old Common $0.001 par exchanged for (0.06666666) share new Common $0.001 par 03/30/1999
Filed a petition under Chapter 11 Federal Bankruptcy Code 08/16/1999
Stockholders' equity unlikely

INDIANA & ILLINOIS COAL CORP.
Liquidated in 1941

INDIANA & MICH ELEC CO (IN)
$3.63 Preferred $25 par called for redemption 04/01/1987
Name changed to Indiana Michigan Power Co. 09/09/1987
(See Indiana Michigan Power Co.)

INDIANA ASSD TEL CORP (IN)
Name changed to General Telephone Co. of Indiana, Inc. (Old) 5/5/52
General Telephone Co. of Indiana, Inc. (Old) merged into General Telephone Co. of Indiana, Inc. (New) 5/5/66 which merged into GTE MTO Inc. 3/31/87 which name changed to GTE North Inc. 1/1/88
(See GTE North Inc.)

INDIANA BANCORP INC (IN)
Stock Dividend - 10% 11/26/80
Merged into Summit Bancorp 12/31/83
Each share Common $10 par exchanged for (1.6604623) shares Common no par
Under plan of merger each share Conv. Preferred $10 par automatically became (1) share Summcorp Conv. Preferred $10 par 4/24/84
(See each company's listing)

INDIANA BANCSHARES INC (IN)
Merged into CNB Bancshares Inc. 5/1/92
Each share Common no par exchanged for (1.25) shares Common no par
CNB Bancshares Inc. merged into Fifth Third Bancorp 10/29/99

INDIANA BANK & TRUST CO. (FORT WAYNE, IN)
Stock Dividends - 25% 3/15/63; 10% 3/23/68; 33-1/3% 3/24/75; 20% 3/31/77; 10% 11/17/80
Under plan of reorganization each share Conv. Preferred $10 par automatically became (1) share Indiana Bancorp, Inc. Conv. Preferred $10 par and each share Common $10 par automatically became (1) share Indiana Bancorp, Inc. Common $10 par 11/10/80
(See Indiana Bancorp, Inc.)

INDIANA BONDING & SURETY CO (IN)
Name changed to Indiana National Marketing Corp. 5/19/78
(See Indiana National Marketing Corp.)

INDIANA BROADCASTING CORP. (DE)
5% Preferred $100 par called for redemption 12/01/1960
Public interest eliminated

INDIANA BUSINESS BANCORP (IN)
Stock Dividends - 5% payable 03/10/2014 to holders of record 02/28/2014 Ex date - 02/26/2014; 5% payable 02/20/2015 to holders of record 02/09/2015 Ex date - 02/05/2015
Acquired by Lizton Financial Corp. 10/21/2016
Each share Common $1 par exchanged for $7.25 cash

INDIANA BUSINESS BK (INDIANAPOLIS, IN)
Under plan of reorganization each share Common $1 par automatically became (1) share Indiana Business Bancorp Common $1 par 07/03/2006
(See Indiana Business Bancorp)

INDIANA CENTRAL TELEPHONE CO.
Acquired by General Telephone Tri Corp. 00/00/1938
Details not available

INDIANA COKE & GAS CO.
Taken over by Indiana Consumers Gas Products Co. in 1926
Details not available

INDIANA COLUMBUS & EASTERN TRACTION CO
Acquired by Cincinnati, Hamilton & Dayton Railway Co. in 1929
Details not available

INDIANA CMNTY BANCORP (IN)
Merged into Old National Bancorp 09/17/2012
Each share Common no par exchanged for (1.9455) shares Common no par

INDIANA CMNTY BK SB (LEBANON, IN)
Merged into Union Federal Savings Bank (Indianapolis, IN) 4/29/98
Each share Common no par exchanged for $21.65 cash

INDIANA CONSUMERS GAS & BYPRODUCTS CO.
Reorganized as Indiana Gas & Chemical Corp. 00/00/1935
Details not available

INDIANA ENERGY INC (IN)
Common no par split (2) for (1) by issuance of (1) additional share 02/02/1989
Common no par split (3) for (2) by issuance of (0.5) additional share 10/01/1993
Common no par split (4) for (3) by issuance of (1/3) additional share payable 10/02/1998 to holders of record 09/18/1998 Ex date - 10/05/1998
Merged into Vectren Corp. 03/31/2000
Each share Common no par exchanged for (1) share Common no par

INDIANA FED CORP (DE)
Reincorporated 11/30/88
Place of incorporation changed from (USA) to (DE) 11/30/88
Common 1¢ par split (4) for (3) issuance of (1/3) additional share 2/26/93
Common 1¢ par split (3) for (2) by issuance of (0.5) additional share 5/31/94
Merged into Pinnacle Financial Services, Inc. 8/1/97
Each share Common 1¢ par exchanged for (1) share Common no par
Pinnacle Financial Services, Inc. merged into CNB Bancshares Inc. 4/17/98 which merged into Fifth Third Bancorp 10/29/99

INDIANA FLOORING CO.
Property acquired by Bondholders Committee in 1930

INDIANA FLORIDA RLTY TR (IN)
Name changed to National Financial Realty Trust 9/1/87
(See National Financial Realty Trust)

INDIANA GAS & CHEM CORP (IN)
Each share $6 Preferred no par exchanged for (2) shares $3 Preferred no par 00/00/1938
Each share Common $5 par exchanged for (10) shares Common 50¢ par 00/00/1938
$3 Preferred no par called for redemption 07/02/1951
Merged into Indiana Energy, Inc. 07/31/1990
Each share Common 50¢ par exchanged for (8.38323) shares Common no par
Note: Additional shares and cash will be held in an escrow fund for possible future distribution
Indiana Energy, Inc. merged into Vectren Corp. 03/31/2000

INDIANA GAS & WTR INC (IN)
Common $10 par changed to no par and (1) additional share issued 00/00/1954
Name changed to Indiana Gas Co., Inc. 09/01/1967
Indiana Gas Co., Inc. reorganized as Indiana Energy, Inc. 03/03/1986 which merged into Vectren Corp. 03/31/2000

INDIANA GAS INC (IN)
Common no par split (2) for (1) by issuance of (1) additional share 10/19/1984
10% Preferred $100 par called for redemption 09/30/1985
Reorganized as Indiana Energy, Inc. 03/03/1986
Each share Common no par exchanged for (1) share Common no par
Indiana Energy, Inc. merged into Vectren Corp. 03/31/2000

INDIANA GEAR WORKS, INC. (IN)
Name changed to Buehler Corp. and each share Common no par split (2) for (1) by issuance of (1) additional share 12/12/60
Buehler Corp. merged into Maul Technology Corp. 9/30/77
(See Maul Technology Corp.)

INDIANA GEN CORP (DE)
Reincorporated 06/03/1968
Common $1 par split (2) for (1) by issuance of (1) additional share 06/10/1960
Stock Dividend - 10% 02/10/1967
State of incorporation changed from (IN) to (DE) 06/03/1968
Merged into Electronic Memories & Magnetics Corp. 07/11/1969
Each share Common $1 par exchanged for (1) share $1 Conv. Preferred $1 par and (0.75) share Common $1 par
Electronics Memories & Magnetics Corp. name changed to Titan Corp. 05/30/1985
(See Titan Corp.)

INDIANA GROUP INC (IN)
Common $1.25 par changed to 83-1/3¢ par and (0.5) additional share issued 06/10/1977
Acquired by National Distillers & Chemical Corp. 04/23/1979
Each share Common 83-1/3¢ par exchanged for (2) shares Common $2.50 par
National Distillers & Chemical Corp. name changed to Quantum Chemical Corp. 01/04/1988 which merged into Hanson PLC (Old) 10/01/1993 which reorganized as Hanson PLC (New) 10/15/2003
(See Hanson PLC (New))

INDIANA HYDRO-ELECTRIC POWER CO.
Merged into Northern Indiana Public Service Co. in 1944
Each share 7% Preferred exchanged for (2/3) share 5% Preferred $100 par
(See Northern Indiana Public Service Co.)

INDIANA INDS INC (IN)
Name changed to Bankshares of Indiana, Inc. 05/04/1972
Bankshares of Indiana, Inc. name changed to Money Management Corp. 12/31/1975 which merged into Banc One Corp. (DE) 07/01/1986 which reincorporated in Ohio 05/01/1989 which merged into Bank One Corp. 10/02/1998 which merged into J.P. Morgan Chase & Co. 12/31/2000 which name changed to JPMorgan Chase & Co. 07/20/2004

INDIANA INS CO (IN)
Class A Common $2.50 par and Class B Common $2.50 par reclassified as Common $2.50 par 01/02/1968
Common $2.50 par changed to $1.25 par and (1) additional share issued 10/29/1971
Stock Dividend - 25% 02/16/1970
Under plan of reorganization each share Common $1.25 par automatically became (1) share Indiana Group, Inc. Common $1.25 par 01/11/1972
Indiana Group, Inc. acquired by National Distillers & Chemical Corp. 04/23/1979 which name changed to Quantum Chemical Corp. 01/04/1988 which merged into Hanson PLC (Old) 10/01/1993 which reorganized as Hanson PLC (New) 10/15/2003
(See Hanson PLC (New))

INDIANA LIMESTONE CO.
Reorganized as Indiana Limestone Corp. in 1933
Details not available

INDIANA LIMESTONE CORP.
Reorganized as Indiana Limestone Co., Inc. 7/31/45. No stockholders' equity

INDIANA MICH PWR CO (IN)
$2.75 Preferred $25 par called for redemption 02/01/1990
12% Preferred $100 par called for redemption 02/01/1990
$2.25 Preferred $25 par called for redemption 03/01/1993
$2.15 Preferred $25 par called for redemption 11/14/1993
8.68% Preferred $100 par called for redemption 12/19/1993
7.76% Preferred $100 par called for redemption 02/13/1994
7.08% Preferred $100 par called for redemption 04/01/1996
5.90% Preferred called for redemption at $100 on 01/01/2005
6.25% Preferred called for redemption at $100 on 01/01/2005
6.30% Preferred called for redemption at $100 on 01/01/2005
6.875% Preferred called for redemption at $100 on 01/01/2005
4.12% Preferred $100 par called for redemption at $102.728 on 12/01/2011
4.125% Preferred $100 par called for redemption at $106.125 plus $0.6875 accrued dividends on 12/01/2011
4.56% Preferred called for redemption at $102 on 12/01/2011

INDIANA MTG & RLTY INVS (MD)
Reincorporated under the laws of Indiana as Indiana Financial Investors, Inc. and Shares of Bene. Int. $1 par reclassified as Common no par 06/30/1979

INDIANA NAT GAS CORP (IN)
Acquired by Midwest Natural Gas Corp. 05/01/2015
Each share Common no par exchanged for $152.48 cash

INDIANA NATIONAL BANK (INDIANAPOLIS, IN)
Under plan of merger each share Capital Stock exchanged for (1.3160) shares new Capital Stock $100 par in 1950
Capital Stock $100 par changed to $20 par and (4) additional shares issued 8/24/56
Capital Stock $20 par changed to $10 par and (1) additional share issued 2/10/65
Stock Dividends - (7) for (13) 6/30/54; 10% 1/24/62; 10% 9/16/68
Reorganized as Indiana National Corp. 5/12/69
Each share Capital Stock $10 par exchanged for (1) share Common no par
Indiana National Corp. name changed to INB Financial Corp. 4/26/89 which merged into NBD Bancorp, Inc. 10/15/92 which name changed to First Chicago NBD Corp. 12/1/95 which merged into Bank One Corp. 10/2/98 which merged into J.P. Morgan Chase & Co. 12/31/2000 which name changed to JPMorgan Chase & Co. 7/20/2004

INDIANA NATL CORP (IN)
Common no par split (3) for (1) by issuance of (2) additional shares 04/03/1972
Common no par split (3) for (2) by issuance of (0.5) additional share 02/14/1986
Depositary Preferred 1984 Ser. called for redemption 06/13/1986
Common no par split (4) for (3) by issuance of (0.33333333) additional share 08/19/1988
Stock Dividends - 10% 08/24/1984; 10% 08/15/1986
Name changed to INB Financial Corp. 04/26/1989
INB Financial Corp. merged into NBD Bancorp, Inc. 10/15/1992 which name changed to First Chicago NBD Corp. 12/01/1995 which merged into Bank One Corp. 10/02/1998 which merged into J.P. Morgan Chase & Co. 12/31/2000 which name changed to JPMorgan Chase & Co. 07/20/2004

INDIANA NATL MARKETING CORP (IN)
Administratively dissolved 7/11/88

INDIANA PIPE LINE CO.
Merged into Buckeye Pipe Line Co. and each share Common exchanged for (0.4) share Common no par and $2.50 in cash in 1943
Buckeye Pipe Line Co. was acquired by Pennsylvania Co. 7/24/64
(See Pennsylvania Co.)

INDIANA SERVICE CORP. (IN)
Merged into Indiana & Michigan Electric Co. on a (1) for (2) basis in 1948
Indiana & Michigan Electric Co. name changed to Indiana Michigan Power Co. 9/9/87

INDIANA SOUTHWESTERN GAS & UTILITIES CORP.
Reorganized in 1937
No stockholders' equity

INDIANA STEEL PRODUCTS CO. (IN)
Common $1 par split (2) for (1) by issuance of (1) additional share 03/10/1955
Name changed to Indiana General Corp. (IN) 11/16/1959
Indiana General Corp. (IN) reincorporated in Delaware 06/03/1968 which merged into Electronic Memories & Magnetics Corp. 07/11/1969 which name changed to Titan Corp. 05/30/1985
(See Titan Corp.)

INDIANA TEL CORP (IN)
Each share Common $100 par exchanged for (4) shares Common $50 par in 1950
Each share Common $50 par exchanged for (7) shares Common no par 12/30/54
Common no par split (2) for (1) by issuance of (1) additional share 1/26/70
4.80% Preferred 1950 Ser. $100 par called for redemption 3/24/78
4.80% Preferred 1951 Ser. $100 par called for redemption 3/24/78
5% Preferred 1956 Ser. $100 par called for redemption 3/24/78
5-1/4% Preferred 1954 Ser. $100 par called for redemption 3/24/78
6-1/8% Preferred 1967 Ser. $100 par called for redemption 3/24/78
Merged into Continental Telephone Corp. 6/2/78
Each share Common no par exchanged for (6.75) shares Common $1 par
Continental Telephone Corp. name changed to Continental Telecom Inc. 5/6/82 which name changed to Contel Corp. 5/1/86 which merged into GTE Corp. 3/14/91 which merged into Verizon Communications Inc. 6/30/2000

INDIANA TRUCK CORP.
Merged into Brockway Motor Truck Corp. in 1928
Details not available

INDIANA TRUST CO. (INDIANAPOLIS, IN)
Each share Capital Stock $100 par exchanged for (10) shares Capital Stock $10 par 00/00/1950
Merged into Merchants National Bank & Trust Co. (Indianapolis, IN) 09/30/1953
Each share Capital Stock $10 par exchanged for (1) share Capital Stock $10 par
Merchants National Bank & Trust Co. (Indianapolis, IN) reorganized as Merchants National Corp. 01/03/1972 which merged into National City Corp. 05/02/1992 which was acquired by PNC Financial Services Group, Inc. 12/31/2008

INDIANA UTD BANCORP (IN)
Stock Dividends - 10% 12/30/1994; 5% payable 01/19/2001 to holders of record 12/29/2000 Ex date - 12/27/2000; 5% payable 01/25/2002 to holders of record 12/31/2001
Name changed to MainSource Financial Group, Inc. 05/01/2002
MainSource Financial Group, Inc. merged into First Financial Bancorp 04/02/2018

INDIANAPOLIS & CINCINNATI TRACTION CO.
Property sold 00/00/1926
Details not available

INDIANAPOLIS & NORTHWESTERN TRACTION CO.
Property sold 00/00/1932
Details not available

INDIANAPOLIS ATHLETIC CLUB REALTY CO.
Bankrupt in 1938

INDIANAPOLIS GAS CO.
Sold to the City of Indianapolis 00/00/1942
Details not available

INDIANAPOLIS POWER & LIGHT CORP.
Liquidated in 1929

INDIANAPOLIS PWR & LT CO (IN)
5-1/4% Preferred $100 par called for redemption 6/10/46
5% Preferred $100 par called for redemption 9/25/50
Common no par split (2) for (1) by issuance of (1) additional share in 1954
5.65% Preferred $100 par called for redemption 7/31/61
Common no par split (2) for (1) by issuance of (1) additional share 5/16/62
6-1/4% Conv. Preferred $100 par called for redemption 9/30/83
Reorganized as IPALCO Enterprises, Inc. 12/31/83
Each share Common no par exchanged for (1) share Common no par
7-3/8% Preferred $100 par called for redemption 1/3/89
10.40% Preferred $100 par called for redemption 11/1/90
6% Preferred $100 par called for redemption at $102 plus $1.23 accrued dividend 12/15/97
8.20% Preferred $100 par called for redemption at $101 plus $1.69 accrued dividend 12/15/97
Ipalco Enterprises, Inc. merged into AES Corp. 3/27/2001
(Additional Information in Active)

INDIANAPOLIS RACEWAY PK INC (IN)
Common $10 par changed to $1 par 12/27/1961
Liquidation completed 12/00/1989
Details not available

INDIANAPOLIS RAILWAYS, INC. (IN)
Name changed to Indianapolis Transit System, Inc. in 1954

INDIANAPOLIS ST. RAILWAY CO.
Reorganized as Indianapolis Railways, Inc. in 1930 which name was changed to Indianapolis Transit System, Inc. in 1954

INDIANAPOLIS STKYDS INC (IN)
Recapitalized 12/16/1966
Preferred $50 par changed to no par
Common $50 par changed to no par
Acquired by Lilly (Eli) & Co. 04/12/1968
Each share Preferred no par exchanged for (0.44) share Common $2.50 par
Each share Common no par exchanged for (0.33) share Common $2.50 par

INDIANAPOLIS TRANS SYS INC (IN)
In process of liquidation
Each share Common no par exchanged for initial distribution of $40 cash 03/07/1975
Each share Common no par received second distribution of $15 cash 04/21/1975
Each share Common no par received third distribution of $15 cash 06/24/1975
Each share Common no par received fourth distribution of $6 cash 10/28/1975
Details on subsequent distributions, if any, are not available

INDIANAPOLIS WTR CO (IN)
Class A Common $10.50 par changed to no par in 1942
Each share Class A Common no par exchanged for (2.15) shares Common $10 par 11/9/56
Each share Class B Common no par exchanged for (2.1) shares Common $10 par 11/9/56
Common $10 par changed to $7.50 par and (1) additional share issued 6/1/56
Under plan of reorganization each share Common $7.50 par automatically became (2) shares IWC Resources Corp. Common no par 7/1/86
IWC Resources Corp. merged into NIPSCO Industries, Inc. 3/25/97
4% Class C Preferred $100 par called for redemption at $100 on 4/30/2002
4.25% Preferred Ser. B called for redemption at $100 on 4/30/2002
4.50% Preferred Ser. D called for redemption at $105 on 4/30/2003
5% Preferred Ser. A called for redemption at $103 on 4/30/2002

INDIANOLA OIL CO. (KY)
Dissolved 7/1/41

INDIAPORTS INC (NY)
Charter cancelled and proclaimed dissolved for failure to pay taxes 12/20/1977

INDICATOR MINERALS INC (BC)
Reincorporated 06/13/2005
Place of incorporation changed from (AB) to (BC) 06/13/2005
Recapitalized as Bluestone Resources Inc. 01/11/2012
Each share Common no par exchanged for (0.05) share Common no par

INDICO RES LTD (BERMUDA)
Reincorporated under the laws of British Columbia 10/15/2009

INDICO TECHNOLOGIES CORP (BERMUDA)
Reincorporated 04/12/2002
Reincorporated 10/15/2009
Place of incorporation changed from (AB) to (Bermuda) 04/12/2002
Name changed to Indigo Technologies Ltd. 05/23/2002
Each share old Common no par exchanged for (0.1) share new Common no par 11/28/2005
Name changed to Indico Resources Ltd. (Bermuda) 04/27/2007
Indico Resources Ltd. (Bermuda) reincorporated in British Columbia 10/15/2009

INDIE GROWERS ASSN (NV)
Recapitalized as Nexgen Applied Solutions Inc. 04/04/2016
Each share Common $0.001 par exchanged for (0.01) share Common $0.001 par
Nexgen Applied Solutions Inc. name changed to Bingo Nation, Inc. 11/08/2016

INDIGENOUS GLOBAL DEV CORP (UT)
SEC revoked common stock registration 02/13/2007

INDIGINET INC (FL)
Each share old Common $0.001 par exchanged for (0.004) share new Common no par 07/10/2003
Each share new Common no par exchanged again for (0.004) share new Common no par 08/17/2004
Each share new Common no par exchanged again for (0.001) share new Common no par 12/01/2004
Recapitalized as Winsted Holdings, Inc. 03/07/2005
Each share Common no par exchanged for (0.001) share Common no par
Winsted Holdings, Inc. recapitalized as Aventura Equities, Inc. 11/03/2008

INDIGO AVIATION AB (SWEDEN)
ADR agreement terminated 01/21/2000
Each ADR for Ordinary exchanged for $15.556 cash

INDIGO CONSOLIDATED GOLD MINES LTD. (ON)
Acquired by Nationwide Minerals Ltd. 00/00/1952
Each share Common exchanged for (0.5) share Common

INDIGO ENERGY INC (DE)
Recapitalized as Global Wireless Satellite Networks (USA), Inc. 09/15/2003
Each share Common $0.001 par exchanged for (0.1) share Common $0.001 par
Global Wireless Satellite Networks (USA), Inc. name changed to Australian Agricultural & Property Development Corp. 11/29/2004 which name changed to Global Realty Development Corp. 07/11/2005

INDIGO-ENERGY INC (NV)
Each share old Common $0.001 par exchanged for (0.02272727) share new Common $0.001 par 11/12/2014
Name changed to HDIMAX MEDIA, Inc. 12/19/2014
HDIMAX MEDIA, Inc. name changed to Zonzia Media, Inc. 03/09/2015

INDIGO GOLD MINES INC (AB)
Recapitalized as New Indigo Resources Inc. 10/05/1992
Each share Common no par exchanged for (0.2) share Common no par
New Indigo Resources Inc. merged into Tahera Corp. 03/01/1999 which name changed to Tahera Diamond Corp. 06/23/2004
(See Tahera Diamond Corp.)

INDIGO INTL CORP (NV)
Name changed to Berkshire Homes, Inc. 12/14/2012

INDIGO N V (NETHERLANDS)
96% acquired through offer by Hewlett-Packard Co. as of 03/25/2002
Each share Common NLG 0.04 par exchanged for either (0.3759) share Common 1¢ par or (0.3008) share Common 1¢ par and (1) Contingent Value Right
Minority holders received approximately $6.48 cash in a compulsory acquisition 09/10/2008
Public interest eliminated

INDIGO SKY CAP CORP (BC)
Name changed to Gatekeeper Systems Inc. 05/31/2013

INDIGO TECHNOLOGIES INC (BC)
Name changed to Robop Tek (Canada), Inc. 07/31/1987
(See Robop Tek (Canada), Inc.)

INDIGO TECHNOLOGIES INC (NV)
Name changed to China Shoe Holdings, Inc. 06/21/2007

INDIN GOLD LTD (BC)
Merged into Lintex Minerals Ltd. 06/01/1983
Each share Common no par exchanged for (1) share Common no par
Lintex Minerals Ltd. recapitalized as New Lintex Minerals Ltd. 12/07/1987 which merged into Globaltex Industries Inc. 03/05/1993 which name changed to Pine Valley Mining Corp. 05/14/2003

INDIO HACIENDA INC (CA)
Charter suspended for failure to pay taxes 08/01/1972

INDIO VENTURES INC (AB)
Name changed to Reliance Services Group Ltd. 08/21/1998
Reliance Services Group Ltd. merged into Integrated Production Services Ltd. 03/31/2000
(See Integrated Production Services Ltd.)

INDIVIDUAL DRINKING CUP CO., INC.
Merged into Dixie-Vortex Co. in 1936
Each share Common exchanged for (217.3) shares Class A no par and (202.916) shares Common no par
Dixie-Vortex Co. name changed to Dixie Cup Co. in 1943 which merged into American Can Co. 6/26/57 which name changed to Primerica Corp. (NJ) 4/28/87 which was acquired by Primerica Corp. (DE) 12/15/88 which name changed to Travelers Inc. 12/31/93 which name changed to Travelers Group Inc. 4/16/95 which name changed to Citigroup Inc. 10/8/98

INDIVIDUAL INC (DE)
Merged into NewsEdge Corp. 2/24/98
Each share Common 1¢ par exchanged for (0.5) share Common 1¢ par
(See Newsedge Corp.)

INDIVIDUAL INV GROUP INC (DE)
Name changed to Index Development Partners, Inc. 6/18/2002
Index Development Partners, Inc. name changed to WisdomTree Investments, Inc. 9/22/2005

INDO GULF CORP LTD (INDIA)
Name changed 08/21/1998
Name changed from Indo Gulf Fertilisers & Chemicals Ltd. to Indo Gulf Corp. Ltd. 08/21/1998
Under plan of merger each 144A GDR for Ordinary exchanged for (0.08333333) Hidalco Industries Ltd. 144A GDR for Ordinary, (0.2) Indo Gulf Fertilisers Ltd. 144A GDR for Ordinary, or $0.14414138 cash 02/13/2003
Note: Option to receive GDR's expired 03/21/2003
(See each company's listing)

INDO GULF FERTILISERS LTD (INDIA)
Merged into Aditya Birla Nuvo Ltd. 04/12/2006
Each Sponsored 144A GDR for Ordinary exchanged for (0.33333333) 144A GDR for Ordinary
(See Aditya Birla Nuvo Ltd.)

INDO METALS LTD (BC)
Recapitalized as Blue Lagoon Ventures Inc. 03/14/2001
Each share Common no par exchanged for (0.1) share Common no par
Blue Lagoon Ventures Inc. recapitalized as VMX Resources Inc. 12/08/2004 which name changed to Monster Uranium Corp. 09/07/2007

INDO PAC INTL CORP (NV)
Recapitalized as Jurassic Energy U.S.A., Inc. 12/15/95
Each share Common $0.0025 par exchanged for (1/3) share Common $0.0025 par

INDO PAC RES LTD (AB)
Delisted from Toronto Venture Stock Exchange 02/25/2003

INDO-PACIFIC ENERGY LTD (YT)
Reincorporated 10/15/1997
Old Common no par split (3) for (2) by issuance of (0.5) additional share payable 04/15/1996 to holders of record 04/15/1996
Old Common no par split (2) for (1) by issuance of (1) additional share payable 06/03/1996 to holders of record 05/31/1996
Each share old Common no par exchanged for (0.2) share new Common no par 07/23/2001
Place of incorporation changed from (BC) to (YT) 10/15/1997
Name changed to Austral Pacific Energy Ltd. (YT) 01/02/2004
Austral Pacific Energy Ltd. (YT) reincorporated in British Columbia 10/16/2006
(See Austral Pacific Energy Ltd.)

INDO RAMA SYNTHETICS INDIA LTD (INDIA)
Basis changed from (1:10) to (1:8) 09/17/2003
Each 144A GDR for Equity Shares received distribution of $0.9167 cash payable 12/22/2003 to holders of record 12/12/2003
Each Reg. S GDR for Equity Shares received distribution of $0.9167 cash payable 12/22/2003 to holders of record 12/12/2003
GDR agreement terminated 10/11/2017
Each 144A GDR for Equity Shares exchanged for $2.308214 cash
Each Reg. S GDR for Equity Shares exchanged for $2.308214 cash

INDOCHINA GOLDFIELDS LTD (CANADA)
Name changed to Ivanhoe Mines Ltd. 07/05/1999
Ivanhoe Mines Ltd. name changed to Turquoise Hill Resources Ltd. 08/08/2012

INDOMIN RES LTD (YT)
Name changed to Battlefield Minerals Corp. 06/15/1998
Battlefield Minerals Corp. recapitalized as BM Diamondcorp Inc. 11/21/2001 which name changed to BDI Mining Corp (Yukon) 07/26/2004 which reincorporated in British Virgin Islands 08/08/2005
(See BDI Mining Corp.)

INDONESIA FD INC (MD)
Name changed to Aberdeen Indonesia Fund, Inc. 03/26/2010
Aberdeen Indonesia Fund, Inc. reorganized as Aberdeen Emerging Markets Equity Income Fund, Inc. 04/30/2018

INDONESIAN DIAMOND LTD (AUSTRALIA)
Each Unsponsored ADR for Ordinary A$0.20 par exchanged for (1) Sponsored ADR for Ordinary A$0.20 par 2/19/91
ADR agreement terminated 2/12/2007
No ADR holders' equity

INDOOR ADVERTISING, INC. (DE)
No longer in existence having become inoperative and void for non-payment of taxes 4/1/61

INDOSTAR GOLD CORP (CANADA)
Name changed to Petroflow Energy Ltd. 10/28/1997

INDOSUEZ HLDGS S C A (LUXEMBOURG)
ADR agreement terminated 12/20/2001
Each 144A Sponsored ADR for Preference Ser. A exchanged for approximately $25.50 cash

INDRESCO INC (DE)
Under plan of reorganization each share Common 25¢ par automatically became (1) share Global Industrial Technologies, Inc. Common 25¢ par 11/01/1995
(See Global Industrial Technologies, Inc.)

INDTECH CORP (DE)
Charter cancelled and declared inoperative and void for non-payment of taxes 03/31/1990

INDUCON FDG CORP (UT)
Name changed to U.S. International Group, Ltd. 2/11/93

INDUCTION MOTORS CORP. (NY)
Stock Dividend - 10% 08/15/1956
Reorganized as IMC Magnetics Corp. 07/10/1959
Each share Common $1 par exchanged for (3) shares Common $0.33333333 par
(See IMC Magnetics Corp.)

INDUS GROUP INC (CA)
Merged into Indus International, Inc. 8/25/97
Each share Common no par exchanged for (1) share Common $0.001 par
(See Indus International, Inc.)

INDUS INTL INC (DE)
Merged into Fortezza Iridium Holdings 1/5/2007
Each share Common $0.001 par exchanged for $3.85 cash

INDUSMIN ENERGY CORP (BC)
Name changed to Transeuro Energy Corp. 10/07/2004

INDUSMIN LTD (CANADA)
Merged into Falconbridge Ltd. 10/23/84
Each share Capital Stock no par exchanged for $35 cash

INDUSTRA SVC CORP (BC)
Merged into American Eco Corp. 01/02/1997
Each share Common no par exchanged for (0.425) share Common no par
(See American Eco Corp.)

INDUSTRALEASE CORP (NY)
Merged into Elms Leasing Inc. 03/26/1982
Each share Common 10¢ par exchanged for $6 cash

INDUSTREA LTD (AUSTRALIA)
Each (1.2) old Sponsored ADR's for Ordinary exchanged for (1) new Sponsored ADR for Ordinary 11/29/2010
ADR basis changed from (1:50) to (1:20) 11/29/2010
ADR agreement terminated 01/04/2013
Each new Sponsored ADR for Ordinary exchanged for $26.478253 cash

INDUSTRI-MATEMATIK INTL CORP (DE)
Merged into STG OMS Ireland Ltd. 1/21/2003
Each share Common 1¢ par exchanged for $0.35 cash

INDUSTRIA ELECTRICA DE MEXICO S A (MEXICO)
Recapitalized 11/21/1955
Each American Share $100 par exchanged for (0.8) share American Share 1955 Ser. $100 par
Each share 6% Preferred $100 par

exchanged for (1) share new
Common $100 par
Each Special Share $5 par
exchanged for (0.075002) share
new Common P100 par
Each share old Common $100 par
exchanged for (0.8) share new
Common $100 par
American Shares 1955 Ser. $100 par
reclassified as American Shares
1969 Ser. (Unstamped) $100 par
06/13/1969
American Shares 1969 Ser. $100 par
stamped (Dividend Restrictions)
reclassified as American Shares
1969 Ser. $100 par (Unstamped)
11/20/1970
Name changed to IEM, S.A.
08/22/1973
(See IEM, S.A.)

INDUSTRIAL & ENVIRONMENTAL SVCS LTD (BERMUDA)
Name changed to Trask Corp.
01/10/1994
Trask Corp. name changed to Med
Net International Ltd. 01/08/1996
(See Med Net International Ltd.)

INDUSTRIAL & GENERAL TRUST, LTD. (ENGLAND)
Ordinary 5s par changed to 25p par
per currency change 02/15/1971
Company reported out of business
00/00/1985
Details not available

INDUSTRIAL & PETROLEUM, INC. (NV)
Name changed to Pershing Gold and
Common $1 par changed to 10¢ par
07/27/1987
Pershing Gold recapitalized as
Pershing Products Inc. 05/31/1996
which recapitalized as Royal
American Mining Properties Ltd.
07/25/1997 which recapitalized as
Capita Research Group, Inc.
01/30/1998
(See Capita Research Group, Inc.)

INDUSTRIAL & POWER SECURITIES CO.
Name changed to Wellington Fund,
Inc. (DE) 00/00/1935
Wellington Fund, Inc. (DE)
reincorporated in Maryland
04/01/1973 which name changed to
Vanguard/Wellington Fund, Inc.
(MD) 03/17/1993 which reorganized
in Delaware as Vanguard Wellington
Fund 05/29/1998

INDUSTRIAL ACCEP LTD (CANADA)
Each share Class A Common no par
exchanged for (2) shares Common
no par 00/00/1948
Each share Common no par
exchanged for (2) shares Common
no par 00/00/1952
Each share Common no par
exchanged for (2) shares Common
no par 09/24/1956
Common no par split (2) for (1) by
issuance of (1) additional share
10/12/1961
5-1/2% Preferred $50 par called for
redemption 02/28/1963
4-1/2% Preferred $50 par called for
redemption 03/30/1964
Common no par split (2) for (1) by
issuance of (1) additional share
05/15/1969
Name changed to IAC Ltd.-IAC Ltee.
11/25/1970
IAC Ltd.-IAC Ltee. name changed to
Continental Bank of Canada
(Toronto, ON) 11/09/1981 which
name changed to CBOC Continental
Inc. 10/22/1996 which reorganized
as Coastal Group Inc. 04/17/2001
which merged into Continental
(CBOC) Corp. 08/30/2002 which
name changed to Stonington Capital
Corp. 06/22/2004 which merged into
Pyxis Capital Inc. 02/27/2006
(See Pyxis Capital Inc.)

INDUSTRIAL ACCEPTANCE CORP.
Dissolved in 1942

INDUSTRIAL ACOUSTICS INC (NY)
Merged into IAC Holdings Corp.
10/29/98
Each share Common 10¢ par
exchanged for $11 cash

INDUSTRIAL ADHESIVES LTD (CANADA)
Acquired by Chromasco Ltd.
07/19/1977
Each share Common no par
exchanged for $23 cash

INDUSTRIAL AIR PRODS CO (OR)
Merged into Liquid Air Inc. 11/15/73
Each share Common $1 par
exchanged for $13.52 cash

INDUSTRIAL AIRCRAFT DEVELOPMENT, INC. (DE)
Charter cancelled and declared
inoperative and void for
non-payment of taxes 4/1/55

INDUSTRIAL-ALLIANCE INS & FINL SVCS INC (QC)
Name changed 06/11/2003
Name changed from
Industrial-Alliance Life Insurance Co.
to Industrial Alliance Insurance &
Financial Services 06/11/2003
Non-Cum. Class A 5-Yr. Rate Reset
Preferred Ser. C no par called for
redemption at $25 plus $0.3875
accrued dividends on 12/31/2013
6% Non-Cum. Class A Preferred Ser.
E no par called for redemption at
$26 on 12/31/2014
5.9% Non-Cum. Class A Preferred
Ser F no par called for redemption
at $26 on 03/31/2015
(Additional Information in Active)

INDUSTRIAL AMER CORP (FL)
Filed petition under Chapter 7 Federal
Bankruptcy Code 11/30/84
No stockholders' equity

INDUSTRIAL BANCORP INC (DE)
Common $1 par split (3) for (1) by
issuance of (2) additional shares
05/15/1969
Reincorporated under the laws of
Rhode Island as Industrial National
Corp. 04/29/1970
Industrial National Corp. name
changed to Fleet Financial Group,
Inc. (Old) 04/14/1982 which merged
into Fleet/Norstar Financial Group,
Inc. 01/01/1988 which name
changed to Fleet Financial Group,
Inc. (New) 04/15/1992 which name
changed to Fleet Boston Corp.
10/01/1999 which name changed to
FleetBoston Financial Corp.
04/18/2000 which merged into Bank
of America Corp. 04/01/2004

INDUSTRIAL BANCORP INC (OH)
Merged into United Community
Financial Corp. 7/2/2001
Each share Common no par
exchanged for $20.375 cash

INDUSTRIAL BANCSHARES CORP. (MO)
Recapitalized as General Contract
Corp. in 1950
Common $4 par changed to $2 par
and 100% stock dividend distributed
General Contract Corp. name
changed to General Bancshares
Corp. 11/6/58 which merged into
Boatmen's Bancshares, Inc. 3/29/86
which merged into NationsBank
Corp. 1/7/97 which reincorporated in
Delaware as BankAmerica Corp.
(Old) 9/25/98 which merged into
BankAmerica Corp. (New) 9/30/98
which name changed to Bank of
America Corp. 4/28/99

INDUSTRIAL BANK & TRUST CO. (EVERETT, MA)
Merged into Coolidge Bank & Trust
Co. (Watertown, MA) 4/1/71
Each share Common Capital Stock
$10 par exchanged for (0.2) share
Common 60¢ par
Coolidge Bank & Trust Co.
(Watertown, MA) reorganized as
First Coolidge Corp. 6/1/72
(See First Coolidge Corp.)

INDUSTRIAL BK (GLENDALE, CA)
Merged into Washington Mutual, Inc.
12/31/1998
Each share Common no par
exchanged for $7.98 cash

INDUSTRIAL BK (VAN NUYS, CA)
Merged into Washington Mutual Bank
(Van Nuys, CA) 12/31/1998
Each share Common no par
exchanged for $7.98 cash

INDUSTRIAL BK JAPAN LTD (JAPAN)
ADR agreement terminated
01/00/2001
Each ADR for Ordinary exchanged for
approximately $58 cash

INDUSTRIAL BANK OF COMMERCE (NEW YORK, NY)
Name changed to Bank of Commerce
(New York, NY) 6/30/61
(See Bank of Commerce (New York, NY))

INDUSTRIAL BANKERS OF AMERICA, INC.
Merged into Beneficial Industrial Loan
Corp. in 1929
Details not available

INDUSTRIAL BANKING CORP. OF AMERICA
Dissolution approved in 1934
Details not available

INDUSTRIAL BIOTECHNOLOGY CORP (WA)
Each share old Common $0.001 par
exchanged for (0.000249) share
new Common $0.001 par
12/17/2007
Name changed to Renewable Corp.
11/20/2008

INDUSTRIAL BROWNHOIST CORP. (OH)
Reorganized in 1935
Each share Preferred $100 par
exchanged for (10) shares new
Common no par
Each share old Common no par
exchanged for (0.5) share new
Common no par
Recapitalized in 1941
1st Preferred no par and 2nd
Preferred no par changed to $10 par
New Common no par changed to $1
par
Acquired by Penn-Texas Corp. share
for share in 1954
Penn-Texas Corp. name changed to
Fairbanks Whitney Corp. 5/29/59
which recapitalized as Colt
Industries Inc. (PA) 5/15/64 which
reincorporated in Delaware 10/17/68
which reincorporated in
Pennsylvania 5/6/76
(See Colt Industries Inc. (PA))

INDUSTRIAL BUILDING CO. OF BALTIMORE (MD)
Liquidation completed
Each share Common no par stamped
to indicate initial distribution of $50
cash 11/6/61
Each share Stamped Common no par
stamped to indicate second
distribution of $25 cash 6/27/62
Each share Stamped Common no par
exchanged for third and final
distribution of $0.56 cash 11/12/65

INDUSTRIAL BUILDINGS CO.
In process of liquidation in 1946
Details not available

INDUSTRIAL CAPITAL CORP. (CA)
Completely liquidated for cash
3/23/65
Surrender of certificates was not
required and are now without value

INDUSTRIAL CAPITAL OF WISCONSIN, INC. (WI)
Completely liquidated 12/21/62
Each share Common $1 par
exchanged for first and final
distribution of $74.80 cash

INDUSTRIAL CO.
Dissolved in 1937
Details not available

INDUSTRIAL COMPONENTS INC (MN)
Merged into D & M Electronic
Components, Inc. 3/25/83
Each share Common 10¢ par
exchanged for $4.75 cash

INDUSTRIAL CONCEPTS CORP (NM)
Each share Common $1 par
exchanged for (3) shares Common
33-1/3¢ par 05/10/1971
Charter revoked for failure to file
reports and pay fees 09/27/1997

INDUSTRIAL CONTROL PRODUCTS, INC. (NJ)
Declared bankrupt 3/6/63
No stockholders' equity

INDUSTRIAL CR & INVT CORP INDIA LTD (INDIA)
Each 144A GDR for Equity
exchanged for (1) ICICI Ltd.
Sponsored ADR for Equity Rs. 10
par 10/29/1999
Each Reg. S GDR for Equity
exchanged for (1) ICICI Ltd.
Sponsored ADR for Equity Rs. 10
par 10/29/1999
ICICI Ltd. merged into ICICI Bank Ltd.
05/03/2002

INDUSTRIAL CREDIT CORP. OF NEW ENGLAND (MA)
Liquidation completed in 1958
Details not available

INDUSTRIAL CREDIT GUARANTY CORP. (MS)
Charter suspended for failure to file
reports 5/29/63

INDUSTRIAL DATA SYS CORP (NV)
Name changed to ENGlobal Corp.
6/6/2002

INDUSTRIAL DEV BK ISRAEL LTD (ISRAEL)
Shares reacquired 12/22/2009
Each share 6% Participating
Preference Ser. C NIS 0.00018 par
exchanged for USD $1.4458 cash
Each share 6% Participating
Preference Ser. CC NIS0.003 par
exchanged for USD $14.5892 cash
Each share 7.5% Preference Ser. D
NIS 0.03 par exchanged for USD
$161.671 cash
Each share 7.5% Preference Ser. DD
NIS 2.1 par exchanged for USD
$1,560.46 cash

INDUSTRIAL DEVELOPMENT CORP. (IL)
Liquidation completed 06/13/1958
Details not available

INDUSTRIAL DISTR GROUP INC (DE)
Merged into Eiger Holdco, LLC
08/06/2008
Each share Common 1¢ par
exchanged for $12.10 cash

INDUSTRIAL DOMINION INC (WA)
Charter cancelled and proclaimed
dissolved for failure to file annual
report 11/30/1995

INDUSTRIAL DYNAMICS CORP. (DE)
Preference $10 par changed to 10¢
par 01/10/1962
Special Voting Preferred $10 par
changed to 10¢ par 01/10/1962
Common $1 par changed to 1¢ par
01/10/1962
Charter declared inoperative and void
for non-payment of taxes
04/01/1966

INDUSTRIAL DYNAMICS INC (NV)
Each share old Capital Stock 10¢ par

exchanged for (1/3) share new Capital Stock 10¢ par 3/21/70
Charter revoked for failure to file reports and pay fees 3/1/71

INDUSTRIAL ECOSYSTEMS INC (UT)
Each share old Common $0.001 par exchanged for (2/3) share new Common $0.001 par 4/30/98
Each (40,000) shares new Common $0.001 par exchanged again for (1) share new Common $0.001 par 9/3/2002
Note: In effect holders received $0.0175 cash per share and public interest was eliminated

INDUSTRIAL ELEC SVCS INC (FL)
Name changed to China Organic Agriculture, Inc. 07/05/2007
(See China Organic Agriculture, Inc.)

INDUSTRIAL ELECTR HARDWARE CORP (NY)
Common 50¢ par split (2) for (1) by issuance of (1) additional share 7/15/81
Name changed to IEH Corp. 9/9/88

INDUSTRIAL ELECTRS ASSOC INC (FL)
Name changed to IEA Corp. (FL) 5/22/70
IEA Corp. (FL) reincorporated in Delaware 6/21/71
(See IEA Corp. (DE))

INDUSTRIAL ENGRAVERS INC (NY)
Adjudicated bankrupt 2/22/71
No stockholders' equity

INDUSTRIAL ENTERPRISES, INC. (NV)
Name changed to International Postal Systems, Inc. 08/31/1971
(See International Postal Systems, Inc.)

INDUSTRIAL ENTERPRISES, INC. (NY)
Common no par changed to $1 par 06/26/1956
Common $1 par split (5) for (2) by issuance of (1.5) additional shares 09/17/1956
Name changed to Novo Industrial Corp. 04/28/1960
Novo Industrial Corp. name changed to Novo Corp. 05/05/1969
(See Novo Corp.)

INDUSTRIAL ENTERPRISES AMER INC (NV)
Each share old Common $0.001 par exchanged for (0.1) share new Common $0.001 par 06/05/2006
Plan of reorganization under Chapter 11 Federal Bankruptcy proceedings effective 05/31/2016
No stockholders' equity

INDUSTRIAL EQUITY LTD (AUSTRALIA)
Stock Dividends - 20% 01/30/1987; 20% 03/01/1988
Merged into Dextran Pty Ltd. 09/07/1990
Each ADR for Ordinary AUD $0.50 par exchanged for $1.73 cash

INDUSTRIAL EQUITY PAC LTD (HONG KONG)
Stock Dividends - 25% 12/31/1987; 20% 11/04/1988; 20% 11/21/1989
Acquired by Brierley Investments Ltd. 07/17/1991
Details not available

INDUSTRIAL FASTENERS, INC. (CA)
Adjudicated bankrupt 4/20/64
No stockholders' equity

INDUSTRIAL FDG CORP (OR)
Completely liquidated 10/9/97
Each share Class A Common no par exchanged for first and final distribution of $0.065 cash

INDUSTRIAL FIBRE CORP. OF AMERICA
Acquired by Industrial Rayon Corp. in 1928
Details not available

INDUSTRIAL FINANCE CORP. (VA)
Common $10 par changed to $1 par in 1932
Merged into Morris Plan Corp. of America in 10/30/45
Each share 7% Preferred $100 par exchanged for (12.5) shares Common 10¢ par
Each share Common $1 par or VTC's for Common $1 par exchanged for (0.25) share Common 10¢ par
Morris Plan Corp. of America name changed to Financial General Corp. 4/25/56 which name changed to Financial General Bankshares, Inc. 4/29/70 which name changed to First American Bankshares, Inc. 8/12/82
(See First American Bankshares, Inc.)

INDUSTRIAL FIRE & CASUALTY INSURANCE CO. (IL)
Declared insolvent by the Illinois Department of Insurance 03/07/1991
No stockholders' equity

INDUSTRIAL FIRE & SAFETY INC
Completely liquidated
Each share Common received initial distribution of $1.50 cash payable 06/05/2007 to holders of record 06/04/2007
Each share Common exchanged for second and final distribution of $1.46 cash 04/02/2008

INDUSTRIAL FIRE INSURANCE CO.
Merged into Stuyvesant Insurance Co. in 1933
Each share Capital Stock $25 par exchanged for (1.82052) shares Capital Stock $10 par
(See Stuyvesant Insurance Co.)

INDUSTRIAL FLEXIBLE MATLS INC (NY)
Dissolved by proclamation 12/26/2001

INDUSTRIAL FUELS CORP (MI)
Stock Dividends - 10% 9/12/74; 20% 8/16/77
Merged into Peoples Gas Co. 10/1/78
Each share Common $1 par exchanged for $25 cash

INDUSTRIAL GAS CO., INC. (NV)
Charter revoked for failure to file reports and pay fees 3/7/77

INDUSTRIAL GROWTH INCOME CORP (CANADA)
Recapitalized as PyroGenesis Canada Inc. 07/20/2011
Each share Common no par exchanged for (0.32298) share Common no par

INDUSTRIAL HARDWARE MANUFACTURING CO. INC. (NY)
Name changed to Industrial Electronic Hardware Corp. 6/30/59
Industrial Electronic Hardware Corp. name changed to IEH Corp. 9/9/88

INDUSTRIAL HLDGS INC (TX)
Reorganized under the laws of Delaware as T-3 Energy Services, Inc. 12/17/2001
Each share Common 1¢ par exchanged for (0.1) share Common $0.001 par
T-3 Energy Services, Inc. merged into Robbins & Myers, Inc. 01/10/2011
(See Robbins & Myers, Inc.)

INDUSTRIAL HOSE & RUBBER CO., INC. (FL)
Name changed to Perma Vinyl Corp. 5/25/62
Perma Vinyl Corp. name changed to Dade Plastics Corp. 12/15/64 which was acquired by United States Pipe & Foundry Co. 4/22/65 which

merged into Walter (Jim) Corp. 8/30/69
(See Walter (Jim) Corp.)

INDUSTRIAL INCOME TR INC (MD)
Each share Common 1¢ par received distribution of (1) DC Industrial Liquidating Trust Non-Transferrable Unit of Bene. Int. and $0.26 cash payable 11/04/2015 to holders of record 10/21/2015
Acquired by Global Logistic Properties Ltd. 11/04/2015
Each share Common 1¢ par exchanged for $10.30 cash

INDUSTRIAL INSTR CORP (TX)
Adjudicated bankrupt 02/17/1970
No stockholders' equity

INDUSTRIAL INSTRUMENTS, INC. (NJ)
Acquired by Beckman Instruments, Inc. 12/2/65
Each share Common 50¢ par exchanged for (0.2117522) share Common $1 par
Beckman Instruments, Inc. merged into SmithKline Beckman Corp. 3/4/82 which merged into SmithKline Beecham p.l.c. 7/26/89 which merged into GlaxoSmithKline PLC 12/27/2000

INDUSTRIAL INVT CORP (OR)
Common $1 par changed to no par 3/24/70
Name changed to Book Centers Inc. 10/21/90
(See Book Centers Inc.)

INDUSTRIAL LABORATORIES CORP. (MA)
Charter revoked for failure to file reports and pay fees 12/21/28

INDUSTRIAL LEASING CORP (OH)
99% acquired by Leaseway Transportation Corp. through purchase offer which expred 11/07/1973
Public interest eliminated

INDUSTRIAL LEASING CORP (OR)
Merged into Peabody Galion Corp. 09/28/1971
Each share Common $1 par exchanged for (0.28017) share Common 10¢ par
Peabody Galion Corp. name changed to Peabody International Corp. 11/19/1976 which merged into Pullman-Peabody Co. 10/24/1985 which name changed to Pullman Co. 02/12/1987
(See Pullman Co.)

INDUSTRIAL LIFE INSURANCE CO. (PA)
Name changed to American Industrial Life Insurance Co. 11/15/1961
American Industrial Life Insurance Co. merged into Chesapeake Life Insurance Co. (MD) 10/31/1966 which recapitalized in Oklahoma 09/27/1993
(See Chesapeake Life Insurance Co.)

INDUSTRIAL LIFE INSURANCE CO. (QC)
Deposit Agreement terminated 12/31/1965
Each Depositary Receipt for Capital Stock $5 par exchanged for (1) share Capital Stock $5 par
Capital Stock $5 par changed to $1 par and (4) additional shares issued 04/28/1966
Stock Dividends - Capital Stock - 50% 03/01/1963; 25% 02/01/1965
Stock Dividend - Depositary Receipts for Capital Stock - 25% 02/01/1965
Mutualized 11/04/1969
Each share Capital Stock $1 par exchanged for $43 cash

INDUSTRIAL LIMEROCK, INC. (DE)
Name changed to Fuller Industries Inc. 7/3/61
(See Fuller Industries Inc.)

INDUSTRIAL LN CORP (PA)
Acquired by Citizens Consumer Discount Co. 5/31/83
Details not available

INDUSTRIAL LOAN SOCIETY, INC.
Name changed to Merchants Acceptance Corp. (MA) 00/00/1926
Merchants Acceptance Corp. (MA) acquired by Transamerica Financial Corp. 11/04/1968 which was acquired by Transamerica Corp. 08/03/1961
(See Transamerica Corp.)

INDUSTRIAL LUMBER CO., INC. (LA)
Each share Capital Stock $15 par exchanged for (4) shares Capital Stock $10 par 3/28/63
Acquired by Boise Cascade Co. 6/1/66
Details not available

INDUSTRIAL MACHINE CORP.
Liquidation completed in 1942
Details not available

INDUSTRIAL MACHINE PRODUCTS, INC. (MI)
Name changed to IMP Corp. 3/23/62
(See IMP Corp.)

INDUSTRIAL MINERALS CORP LTD (AUSTRALIA)
Name changed to IDM International Ltd. 01/03/2012
(See IDM International Ltd.)

INDUSTRIAL MINERALS INC (DE)
Each share old Common $0.001 par exchanged for (2) shares new Common $0.001 par 06/13/2003
Each share new Common $0.001 par exchanged for (1.5) shares Common $0.0001 par 09/27/2004
Recapitalized as Mindesta Inc. 07/26/2011
Each share Common $0.0001 par exchanged for (0.05) share Common $0.0001 par
Mindesta Inc. recapitalized as CTT Pharmaceutical Holdings, Inc. 08/28/2015

INDUSTRIAL MINERALS INC (OR)
Name changed to Danbourne Corp. 6/25/71
(See Danbourne Corp.)

INDUSTRIAL MINERALS OF CANADA LTD. (ON)
Merged into Indusmin Ltd. 11/06/1968
Each share Capital Stock no par exchanged for (1) share Capital Stock no par
(See Indusmin Ltd.)

INDUSTRIAL MTG & TR CO (SARNIA, ON)
98% acquired by Royal Trust Co. (Montreal, QC) through exchange offer which expired 00/00/1969
Public interest eliminated

INDUSTRIAL NATIONAL BANK (PROVIDENCE, RI)
Each share Common $20 par exchanged for (2) shares Common $10 par 10/24/56
Stock Dividend - 10% 11/9/56
Name changed to Industrial National Bank of Rhode Island (Providence, RI) 10/3/61
Industrial National Bank of Rhode Island (Providence, RI) merged into Industrial Bancorp, Inc. 9/18/68 which reincorporated in Rhode Island as as Industrial National Corp. 4/29/70 which name changed to Fleet Financial Group, Inc. (Old) 4/14/82 which merged into Fleet/Norstar Financial Group, Inc. 1/1/88 which name changed to Fleet Financial Group, Inc. (New) 4/15/92 which name changed to Fleet Boston Corp. 10/1/99 which name changed to FleetBoston Financial Corp. 4/18/2000 which merged into Bank of America Corp. 4/1/2004

INDUSTRIAL NATL BK R I (PROVIDENCE, RI)
Stock Dividends - 10% 10/21/66; 10% 10/18/67
Merged into Industrial Bancorp, Inc. 9/18/68
Each share Common $10 par exchanged for (1) share Common $1 par
Industrial Bancorp, Inc. reincorporated in Rhode Island as Industrial National Corp. 4/29/70 which name changed to Fleet Financial Group, Inc. (Old) 4/14/82 which merged into Fleet/Norstar Financial Group, Inc. 1/1/88 which name changed to Fleet Financial Group, Inc. (New) 4/15/92 which name changed to Fleet Boston Corp. 10/1/99 which name changed to FleetBoston Financial Corp. 4/18/2000 which merged into Bank of America Corp. 4/1/2004

INDUSTRIAL NATL CORP (RI)
Name changed to Fleet Financial Group, Inc. (Old) 4/14/82
Fleet Financial Group, Inc. (Old) merged into Fleet/Norstar Financial Group, Inc. 1/1/88 which name changed to Fleet Financial Group, Inc. (New) 4/15/92 which name changed to Fleet Boston Corp. 10/1/99 which name changed to FleetBoston Financial Corp. 4/18/2000 which merged into Bank of America Corp. 4/1/2004

INDUSTRIAL NUCLEONICS CORP (DE)
Common no par changed to $1 par 4/21/72
Name changed to AccuRay Corp. 7/2/79
(See AccuRay Corp.)

INDUSTRIAL OFFICE BUILDING CO.
Reorganized as Industrial Office Building Corp. 00/00/1933
Details not available

INDUSTRIAL OFFICE BUILDING CORP.
Liquidated in 1950
No stockholders' equity

INDUSTRIAL OIL & REFINING CO. (DE)
No longer in existence having become inoperative and void for non-payment of taxes 3/18/25

INDUSTRIAL PHOSPHATE MINES LTD. (ON)
Charter cancelled 11/05/1962
No stockholders' equity

INDUSTRIAL PLYWOOD CO., INC. (NY)
Name changed to Ply-Gem Industries, Inc. (NY) 07/01/1968
Ply-Gem Industries, Inc. (NY) reincorporated in Delaware 06/02/1970
(See Ply-Gem Industries, Inc. (DE))

INDUSTRIAL PROPERTIES, INC. (OH)
Liquidated in 1948
Details not available

INDUSTRIAL PROPERTIES (IL)
Liquidation completed
Each Capital Trust Ctfs. no par exchanged for initial distribution of $40 cash 9/8/44
Each Capital Trust Ctfs. no par received second and final distribution of $3.92 cash 3/13/46

INDUSTRIAL RAYON CORP. (DE)
Each share Class A and B no par exchanged for (0.2) shares Capital Stock no par in 1928
Capital Stock no par exchanged (3) for (1) in 1934
Capital Stock no par changed to Common no par in 1944
Each share Common no par exchanged for (2) shares Common $1 par in 1946
Merged into Midland-Ross Corp. 4/28/61
Each share Common $1 par exchanged for (2/5) share Common $5 par
(See Midland-Ross Corp.)

INDUSTRIAL REALTY SHARES, INC. (DE)
No longer in existence having become inoperative and void for non-payment of taxes 4/1/36

INDUSTRIAL RESEARCH, INC. (FL)
Common $1 par changed to 10¢ par in 1954
Charter cancelled and company declared dissolved for non-payment of taxes 4/18/61

INDUSTRIAL RES INC (UT)
Name changed to NaTec Resources, Inc. 10/31/89
(See NaTec Resources, Inc.)

INDUSTRIAL RUBR INNOVATIONS INC (FL)
Each share old Common $0.001 par exchanged for (0.01) share new Common $0.001 par 10/09/2000
SEC revoked common stock registration 08/30/2007

INDUSTRIAL RUBR PRODS INC (MN)
Issue Information - 1,260,000 shares COM offered at $5 per share on 04/24/1998
Merged into Lime Rock Partners 09/16/2008
Each share Common $0.001 par exchanged for $15.6095 cash
Note: An additional $0.89 cash per share is being held in escrow for possible future distribution

INDUSTRIAL SALES & MARKETING CORP (UT)
Name changed to Oneida General Corp. 2/16/79
Oneida General Corp. name changed to Communitronics of America, Inc. (UT) 10/26/98 which reorganized in Nevada as RPM Advantage, Inc. 4/12/2006

INDUSTRIAL SALVAGE CO.
Dissolved in 1926
Details not available

INDUSTRIAL SCIENCE CORP. (PA)
Bankrupt 7/11/63; no stockholders' equity

INDUSTRIAL SCIENTIFIC CORP (PA)
Acquired by ISC Acquisition Corp. 05/21/1999
Each share Common 1¢ par exchanged for $28.50 cash

INDUSTRIAL SECURITIES CO. (DE)
Charter cancelled for non-payment of taxes 1/23/22

INDUSTRIAL SECURITIES CORP.
Acquired by Standard Factors Corp. through exchange of $28 of Debentures for each share Preferred and $3.30 of Debentures for each share Common in 1943

INDUSTRIAL SVCS AMER INC (KY)
Merged into Mobile Waste Controls, Inc. (DE) 9/29/72
Each share Common no par exchanged for (0.666666) share Common 50¢ par
Mobile Waste Controls, Inc. (DE) merged into SCA Services, Inc. 10/26/73
(See SCA Services, Inc.)

INDUSTRIAL SHOE MACHY CORP (MA)
Name changed to ISM Corp. 7/15/70
(See ISM Corp.)

INDUSTRIAL SILICA CORP. (OH)
Each share 6-1/2% Preferred $100 par exchanged for (10) shares 6-1/2% Preferred $10 par in 1946
Each share Common no par exchanged for (1) share Common $1 par in 1946
Acquired by Pennsylvania Glass Sand Corp. on a (1) for (2.75) basis 12/15/58
Pennsylvania Glass Sand Corp. merged into International Telephone & Telegraph Corp. (DE) 6/27/68 which name changed to ITT Corp. 12/31/83 which reorganized in Indiana as ITT Industries Inc. 12/19/95 which name changed to ITT Corp. 7/1/2006

INDUSTRIAL ST BK & TR CO (KALAMAZOO, MI)
Capital Stock $25 par changed to $16-2/3 par and (0.5) additional share issued 04/10/1967
Capital Stock $16-2/3 par changed to $12.50 par and (1/3) additional share issued 03/01/1968
Capital Stock $12.50 par changed to $10 par and (0.25) additional share issued 03/21/1969
96.7% acquired by ISB Financial Corp. as of 00/00/1980
Public interest eliminated

INDUSTRIAL STAMPING & MANUFACTURING CO.
Merged into Vinco Corp. in 1952
Each (30) shares Common $1 par exchanged for (1) share new Preferred $12.50 par and (2) shares new Common $1 par
(See Vinco Corp.)

INDUSTRIAL STATE BANK (KALAMAZOO, MI)
Each share Capital Stock $100 par exanged for (4) shares Capital Stock $25 par plus a 25% stock dividend paid in 1950
Name changed to Industrial State Bank & Trust Co. (Kalamazoo, MI) 6/1/66
Each share Capital Stock $25 par exchanged for (2) share Capital Stock $25 par
(See Industrial State Bank & Trust Co. (Kalamazoo, MI))

INDUSTRIAL TECH INC (UT)
Charter suspended for failure to file annual reports 12/31/1985

INDUSTRIAL TECHNICAL CONCEPTS INC (NY)
Name changed to ITC Integrated Systems, Inc. 10/03/1985
(See ITC Integrated Systems, Inc.)

INDUSTRIAL TECHNOLOGIES INC (DE)
Company terminated common stock registration and is no longer public as of 05/21/2001

INDUSTRIAL TELEVISION, INC. (NJ)
Name changed to ITI Electronics, Inc. 05/01/1959
ITI Electronics, Inc. name changed to Bala Cynwyd Corp. 04/21/1983
(See Bala Cynwyd Corp.)

INDUSTRIAL TIMER CORP. (DE)
Acquired by Vapor Corp. on a (1) for (4.25) basis 4/22/65
Vapor Corp. merged into Amercon Corp. 3/17/66 which was acquired by General Precision Equipment Corp. 3/27/67 which merged into Singer Co. (NJ) 7/11/68 which reincorporated in Delaware in 1988 which name changed to Bicoastal Corp. 10/16/89
(See Bicoastal Corp.)

INDUSTRIAL TRAINING CORP (MD)
Common 10¢ par split (2) for (1) by issuance of (1) additional share 02/22/1992
Name changed to ITC Learning Corp. 05/09/1997
(See ITC Learning Corp.)

INDUSTRIAL TRAINING SYS CORP (NJ)
Merged into Westcott Communications, Inc. 6/2/93
Each share Common 1¢ par exchanged for $3 cash

INDUSTRIAL TR & SVGS BK (MUNCIE, IN)
Stock Dividends - 16-2/3% 2/29/68; 14.3% 2/28/69; 18.2% 2/26/71; 16-2/3% 2/28/73; 14.3% 4/2/75; 25% 2/28/78; 25% 3/31/81
Acquired by SummCorp 12/11/86
Each share 10% Conv. Preferred $16 par exchanged for (1.55) shares Common no par
Each share Common $10 par exchanged for (1.55) shares Common no par
SummCorp merged into NBD Bancorp, Inc. 7/1/92 which name changed to First Chicago NBD Corp. 12/1/95 which merged into Bank One Corp. 10/2/98 which merged into J.P. Morgan Chase & Co. 12/31/2000 which name changed to JPMorgan Chase & Co. 7/20/2004

INDUSTRIAL TRUST CO. (PROVIDENCE, RI)
Each share Capital Stock $100 par exchanged for (5) shares Capital Stock $20 par in 1945
Merged into Industrial National Bank (Providence, RI) 2/1/54
Each share Capital Stock $20 par exchanged for (1.22) shares Common $20 par
Industrial National Bank (Providence, RI) name changed to Industrial National Bank of Rhode Island (Providence, RI) 10/3/61 which merged into Industrial Bancorp, Inc. 9/18/68 which reincorporated under the laws of Rhode Island as Industrial National Corp. Island as Industrial National Corp. Financial Group, Inc. (Old) 4/14/82 which merged into Fleet/Norstar Financial Group, Inc. 1/1/88 which name changed to Fleet Financial Group, Inc. (New) 4/15/92 which name changed to Fleet Boston Corp. 10/1/99 which name changed to FleetBoston Financial Corp. 4/18/2000 which merged into Bank of America Corp. 4/1/2004

INDUSTRIAL TRUSTEE SHARES
Trust terminated 00/00/1929
Details not available

INDUSTRIAL VALLEY BK & TR CO (JENKINTOWN, PA)
Under plan of reorganization each share Common $5 par automatically became (1) share IVB Financial Corp. 1/1/84
(See IVB Financial Corp.)

INDUSTRIAL VALLEY TITLE INS CO (PA)
Merged into Industrial Valley Bank & Trust Co. (Jenkintown, PA) 12/31/1973
Each share Capital Stock $1 par exchanged for (1/3) share Common $5 par
Industrial Valley Bank & Trust Co. (Jenkintown, PA) reorganized as IVB Financial Corp. 01/01/1984
(See IVB Financial Corp.)

INDUSTRIAL VINYLS INC (FL)
Involuntarily dissolved 12/5/79

INDUSTRIAL WASTE PROCESSING INC (DE)
Recapitalized as Whitney American Corp. (New) 02/20/1997
Each share Common $0.00001 par exchanged for (0.01) share Common $0.00001 par
(See Whitney American Corp. (New))

INDUSTRIAL WIRE & CABLE LTD (ON)
Name changed to IWC Industries, Ltd. 04/25/1969
IWC Industries, Ltd. name changed to IWC Communications Ltd. 12/05/1972 which recapitalized as Radio IWC Ltd. 04/07/1978
(See Radio IWC Ltd.)

INDUSTRIAL WIRE CLOTH PRODUCTS CORP. (MI)
Stock Dividend - 100% 7/15/47
Acquired by Purolator Products, Inc. on a (1) for (3) basis 1/30/56
Purolator Products, Inc. name changed to Puralator, Inc. (DE) 4/16/68 which reincorporated in New York as Purolator Courier Corp. 7/1/84
(See Purolator Courier Corp. (NY))

INDUSTRIAL WORKS
Reorganized as Industrial Brownhoist Corp. in 1927
Details not available

INDUSTRIALISTICS INC (DE)
Recapitalized as Crown Laboratories, Inc. 12/2/91
Each share Common $0.00001 par exchanged for (0.3125) share Common $0.00001 par
(See Crown Laboratories, Inc.)

INDUSTRIAS BACHOCO S A DE C V (MEXICO)
Issue Information - 3,750,000 ADR'S offered at $17 per ADR on 09/18/1997
Sponsored ADR's for Units reclassified as Sponsored ADR's for Ser. B 9/26/2006
Name changed to Industrias Bachoco, S.A.B. de C.V. 4/13/2007

INDUSTRIAS DE PAPEL SIMAO S A (BRAZIL)
Name changed to Votorantim Celulose e Papel S.A. 01/30/1995
Votorantim Celulose e Papel S.A. name changed to Fibria Celulose S.A. 11/18/2009

INDUSTRIAS KLABIN DE PAPEL E CELULOSE S A (BRAZIL)
Name changed to Klabin S.A. 01/02/2002

INDUSTRIE NATUZZI S P A (ITALY)
ADR's for Ordinary 250 Lire par changed to 125 Lire par and (1) additional ADR issued payable 12/23/1996 to holders of record 12/20/1996 Ex date - 12/24/1996
ADR's for Ordinary 125 Lire par changed to EUR 1 par 12/00/2001
Name changed to Natuzzi S.p.A. 05/01/2002

INDUSTRIES, INC. (VA)
Liquidation completed
Each share Common $10 par received initial distribution of $9 cash 3/28/67
Each share Common $10 par exchanged for second and final distribution of $1.63 cash 10/21/67

INDUSTRIES & MINES, INC. (UT)
Merged into General Utilities & Industries, Inc. (UT) 08/29/1960
Each share Common 5¢ par exchanged for (0.2) share Common 5¢ par
General Utilities & Industries, Inc. (UT) reorganized in Florida as General Utilities, Inc. 05/04/1962
(See General Utilities, Inc.)

INDUSTRIES AMISCO LTEE (QC)
Merged into Gestion Martin Poitras Inc. 03/03/2009
Each share Common no par exchanged for $1.75 cash
Note: Unexchanged certificates were cancelled and became without value 03/03/2015

INDUSTRIES COVER INC (QC)
Acquired by 2750-7268 Quebec Inc. 06/21/1990
Each share Common no par exchanged for $2.91 cash

INDUSTRIES EXCHANGE FD INC (TX)
Acquired by Commerce Fund, Inc. (TX) 4/2/73
Each share Common $1 par exchanged for (1.555) shares Common $1 par
Commerce Fund, Inc. (TX) name changed to Commerce Income Shares, Inc. (TX) 10/14/77 which reorganized in Massachusetts as Commerce Income Shares 8/26/85

INDUSTRIES INTL INC (DE)
Charter cancelled and declared inoperative and void for non-payment of taxes 3/1/75

INDUSTRIES INTL INC (NV)
Each share old Common 1¢ par exchanged for (0.25) share new Common 1¢ par 6/3/2003
Recapitalized as SIPP International Industries, Inc. 5/24/2007
Each share new Common 1¢ par exchanged for (0.001) share Common 1¢ par

INDUSTRIES TREND FUND INC. (TX)
Merged into Pilot Fund, Inc. 05/01/1981
Each share Common $1 par exchanged for (1.399) shares Common $1 par
Pilot Fund, Inc. name changed to Transamerica Technology Fund 06/23/1989 which name changed to Transamerica Capital Appreciation Fund 04/19/1991 which merged into Hancock (John) Capital Growth Fund 12/22/1994
(See Hancock (John) Capital Growth Fund)

INDUSTRIFORVALTNINGS AB KINNEVIK (SWEDEN)
Each Sponsored ADR for Class A received distribution of (0.2) Transcom Worldwide S.A. Sponsored ADR for Class A payable 9/11/2001 to holders of record 9/4/2001
Each Sponsored ADR for Class B received distribution of (0.07) Transcom Worldwide S.A. Sponsored ADR for Class A and (0.13) Class B Sponsored ADR payable 9/11/2001 to holders of record 9/4/2001
ADR agreement terminated 6/20/2003
Each Sponsored ADR for Class A exchanged for $31.7295 cash
Each Sponsored ADR for Class B exchanged for $32.3374 cash

INDUSTRIONICS CDA LTD (ON)
Charter cancelled 10/11/1982

INDUSTRO TRANSISTOR CORP (NY)
Charter cancelled and proclaimed dissolved for failure to pay taxes 9/24/80

INDUSTRON CORP. (MA)
Completely liquidated 04/30/1968
Each share Class A Common $1 par exchanged for first and final distribution of (0.344827) share Seaboard Plywood & Lumber Corp. Common $1 par
Seaboard Plywood & Lumber Corp. merged into North American Development Corp. 10/20/1972 which name changed to Scotts Seaboard Corp. 07/03/1980
(See Scotts Seaboard Corp.)

INDUSTRONICS INC (DE)
Stock Dividends - 10% 10/30/74; 10% 10/30/75; 10% 12/23/76
Acquired by Spencer Turbine Co. 9/27/84
Each share Common 1¢ par exchanged for $3.50 cash

INDUSTRY CONCEPT HLDGS INC (CO)
SEC revoked common stock registration 02/20/2014

INDUSTRY FD AMER INC (NV)
Fund terminated 12/31/1986
Details not available

INDWEST INC (UT)
Name changed to Medi-Hut Co., Inc. (UT) 1/28/98
Medi-Hut Co., Inc. (UT) reincorporated in Delaware 2/27/98 which reincorporated in Nevada 10/31/2001 which name changed to Scivanta Medical Corp. 1/4/2007

INDY RACEWAYS INC (DE)
Name changed to Atlantic Gulf Energy, Inc. and Common 5¢ par changed to 1¢ par 11/24/80
Atlantic Gulf Energy, Inc. name changed to British American Petroleum Corp. 3/30/83 which name changed to Crest Energy Resources Corp. 7/1/87
(See Crest Energy Resources Corp.)

INDYKE GOLD MINES, LTD. (ON)
Charter cancelled and company declared dissolved for default in filing returns 12/30/1970

INDYMAC BANCORP INC (DE)
Name changed 07/03/2000
Name changed from IndyMac Mortgage Holdings, Inc. to IndyMac Bancorp, Inc. 07/03/2000
Filed a petition under Chapter 7 Federal Code 07/31/2008
Stockholders' equity unlikely

INEDCO LTD (DE)
Charter cancelled and declared inoperative and void for non-payment of taxes 3/1/84

INEI CORP (DE)
Liquidation completed
Each share Common 4¢ par received initial distribution of $1 cash payable 11/01/2004 to holders of record 10/15/2004 Ex date - 11/02/2004
Each share Class B Common 4¢ par received initial distribution of $1 cash payable 11/01/2004 to holders of record 10/15/2004 Ex date - 11/02/2004
Each share Common 4¢ par received second distribution of $0.15 cash payable 5/16/2005 to holders of record 04/29/2005 Ex date - 05/17/2005
Each share Class B Common 4¢ par received second distribution of $0.15 cash payable 05/16/2005 to holders of record 04/29/2005
Each share Common 4¢ par received third distribution of $0.20 cash payable 01/17/2006 to holders of record 01/03/2006 Ex date - 01/18/2006
Each share Class B Common 4¢ par received third distribution of $0.20 cash payable 01/17/2006 to holders of record 01/03/2006
Each share Common 4¢ par received fourth distribution of $0.08 cash payable 10/31/2006 to holders of record 10/13/2006 Ex date - 11/01/2006
Each share Class B Common 4¢ par received fourth distribution of $0.08 cash payable 10/31/2006 to holders of record 10/13/2006
Each share Common 4¢ par received fifth and final distribution of $0.07 cash payable 06/29/2007 to holders of record 06/14/2007 Ex date - 07/02/2007
Each share Class B Common 4¢ par received fifth and final distribution of $0.07 cash payable 06/29/2007 to holders of record 06/14/2007
Note: Certificates were not required to be surrendered and are without value

INEL RES LTD (BC)
Merged into Gulf International Minerals Ltd. (BC) 04/09/1990
Each share Common no par exchanged for (0.4) share Common no par
Gulf International Minerals Ltd. (BC) reincorporated in Yukon 08/14/2002 which reincorporated back in British Columbia 06/17/2004

INELCO CORP (NV)
SEC revoked common stock registration 02/17/2016

INERGY HLDGS L P (DE)
Issue Information - 3,910,000 COM UNITS offered at $22.50 per Unit on 06/24/2005
Common Units split (3) for (1) by issuance of (2) additional Units payable 06/01/2010 to holders of record 05/24/2010 Ex date - 06/02/2010
Merged into Inergy L.P. 11/05/2010
Each Common Unit exchanged for (0.77) Unit of Ltd. Partnership Int.
Inergy L.P. name changed to Crestwood Equity Partners L.P. 10/08/2013

INERGY L P (DE)
Issue Information - 1,600,000 UNITS LTD PARTNERSHIP INT offered at $22 per Unit 07/25/2001
Units of Ltd. Partnership Int. split (2) for (1) by issuance of (1) additional Unit payable 01/12/2004 to holders of record 01/02/2004 Ex date - 01/13/2004
Each Unit of Ltd. Partnership Int. received distribution of (0.108011) Suburban Propane Partners, L.P. Unit of Ltd. Partnership Int. payable 09/14/2012 to holders of record 08/29/2012 Ex date - 09/17/2012
Each Unit of Ltd. Partnership Int. received distribution of (0.4321) Inergy Midstream, L.P. Unit of Ltd. Partnership Int. payable 06/18/2013 to holders of record 06/14/2013 Ex date - 06/19/2013
Name changed to Crestwood Equity Partners L.P. 10/08/2013

INERGY MIDSTREAM LP (DE)
Under plan of merger name changed to Crestwood Midstream Partners L.P. (New) 10/08/2013
Crestwood Midstream Partners L.P. (New) merged into Crestwood Equity Partners L.P. 09/30/2015

INERTIA DYNAMICS CORP (DE)
Common 1¢ par split (3) for (2) by issuance of (0.5) additional share 8/27/84
Common 1¢ par split (3) for (2) by issuance of (0.5) additional share 11/26/86
Common 1¢ par split (3) for (2) by issuance of (0.5) additional share 5/1/87
Merged into Ryobi Merger Corp. 3/15/90
Each share Common 1¢ par exchanged for $15.25 cash

INERTIA-MATIC, INC. (DE)
No longer in existence having become inoperative and void for non-payment of taxes 4/1/66

INERTIAL MTRS CORP (DE)
Reincorporated 12/1/82
Stock Dividends - 10% 6/27/78; 10% 7/16/79; 10% 7/16/80
State of incorporation changed from (PA) to (DE) 12/1/82
Liquidation completed
Each share Common 1¢ par received initial distribution of $0.07 cash 10/24/95
Each share Common 1¢ par received second and final distribution of $0.14 cash in November 1996

FINANCIAL INFORMATION, INC.

Note: Certificates were not required to be exchanged and are without value

INET COMM CONDUIT CORP (FL)
Name changed to SBS Interactive, Co. 07/30/2002
(See SBS Interactive, Co.)

INET TECHNOLOGIES INC (DE)
Merged into Tektronix, Inc. 09/30/2004
Each share Common $0.001 par exchanged for (0.192) share Common no par and $6.25 cash
(See Tektronix, Inc.)

INETEVENTS INC (DE)
Recapitalized as International Card Establishment, Inc. 10/29/2003
Each share Common $0.001 par exchanged for (0.5) share Common $0.001 par

INETVISIONZ COM INC (DE)
Ceased operations 05/29/2001
Stockholders' equity unlikely

INEX PHARMACEUTICALS CORP (AB)
Reorganized 04/30/2007
Reorganized from (BC) to under the laws of Alberta 04/30/2007
Each share Common no par exchanged for (0.5) share Class A Common no par and (0.5) share Tekmira Pharmaceuticals Corp. Common no par
Merged into Primary Corp. 08/05/2008
Each share Class A Common no par exchanged for (0.05) share Common no par
Primary Corp. name changed to Marret Resource Corp. 07/06/2012

INEXCO MNG CORP (BC)
Name changed to Worldwide Marijuana Inc. 03/30/2015

INEXCO NORTHN EXPL CO (DE)
Merged into Inexco Oil Co. 4/11/74
Each share Common $1 par exchanged for (0.78) share Common 2¢ par
Inexco Oil Co. merged into Louisiana Land & Exploration Co. 7/22/86 which merged into Burlington Resources Inc. 10/22/97 which merged into ConocoPhillips 3/31/2006

INEXCO OIL CO (DE)
Common 2¢ par split (2) for (1) by issuance of (1) additional share 12/30/1980
Merged into Louisiana Land & Exploration Co. 07/22/1986
Each share Common 2¢ par exchanged for (0.171) share Capital Stock 15¢ par and $0.247 cash
Louisiana Land & Exploration Co. merged into Burlington Resources Inc. 10/22/1997 which merged into ConocoPhillips 03/31/2006

INFANTLY AVAILABLE INC (NV)
Reorganized as IFAN Financial, Inc. 09/03/2014
Each share Common $0.001 par exchanged for (140) shares Common $0.001 par

INFE-HUMAN RES INC (NV)
Each share Common $0.001 par received distribution of (0.01) share Daniels Corporate Advisory Co., Inc. Common $0.001 par payable 06/22/2010 to holders of record 06/22/2010
Recapitalized as Rhino Human Resources, Inc. 08/25/2010
Each share Common $0.001 par exchanged for (0.01) share Common $0.001 par
Rhino Human Resources, Inc. recapitalized as Rhino Novi, Inc. 07/23/2018

INFE INC (FL)
Recapitalized 8/17/2001
Recapitalized from INFE.com, Inc. to INFE Inc. 8/17/2001
Each share Common $0.0001 par exchanged for (0.25) share Common $0.0001 par
Common $0.0001 par split (2) for (1) by issuance of (1) additional share payable 7/31/2002 to holders of record 7/10/2002 Ex date - 8/1/2002
Name changed to Pacer Health Corp. 2/19/2004

INFERENCE CORP (CA)
Merged into eGain Communications Corp. 06/29/2000
Each share Class A Common no par exchanged for (0.7362) share Common $0.001 par
eGain Communications Corp. name changed to eGain Corp. 11/13/2012

INFERGENE CO (DE)
Recapitalized as Zaxis International Inc. 08/25/1995
Each share Common 1¢ par exchanged for (0.02) share Common 1¢ par
Zaxis International Inc. name changed to Emerald Medical Applications Corp. 10/06/2015 which name changed to Virtual Crypto Technologies Inc. 03/07/2018

INFERNO SNUFFERS INC (DE)
Charter cancelled and declared inoperative and void for non payment of taxes 3/1/93

INFERTEK INC (WA)
Name changed to Metarunner, Inc. 06/15/2004
(See Metarunner, Inc.)

INFERX CORP (DE)
Each share old Common $0.0001 par exchanged for (0.05) share new Common $0.0001 par 07/27/2009
SEC revoked common stock registration 08/07/2015

INFICON HLDG A G (SWITZERLAND)
Issue Information - 1,736,000 Sponsored ADR's offered at $11.77 per ADR on 11/08/2000
ADR agreement terminated 3/27/2005
Each Sponsored ADR for Ordinary CHF10 par exchanged for $8.7485 cash

INFINICALL CORP (DE)
SEC revoked common stock registration 01/14/2009

INFINIS ENERGY PLC (ENGLAND & WALES)
ADR agreement terminated 01/22/2016
Each ADR for Ordinary exchanged for $10.882019 cash

INFINITE COFFEE CO (NV)
Reorganized as Infinite Networks Corp. (New) 12/21/2004
Each share Common $0.001 par exchanged for (5) shares Common $0.001 par

INFINITE HLDGS GROUP INC (TX)
Each share old Common $0.001 par exchanged for (40) shares new Common $0.001 par 10/25/2007
SEC revoked common stock registration 03/01/2011

INFINITE MACHS CORP (DE)
Name changed to Infinite Group, Inc. 01/08/1998

INFINITE NETWORKS CORP OLD (NV)
Each share old Common $0.001 par exchanged for (0.1) share new Common $0.001 par 11/21/2000
Name changed to Infinite Coffee Co. 8/29/2002
Infinite Coffee Co. reorganized as Infinite Networks Corp. (New) 12/21/2004

INFINITE RESH INC (DE)
Charter cancelled and declared inoperative and void for non-payment of taxes 3/1/94

INFINITE TECHNOLOGY CORP (NV)
Recapitalized as Flexxtech Corp. 05/12/2000
Each share Common no par exchanged for (0.33333333) share new Common no par
Flexxtech Corp. name changed to Network Installation Corp. 07/18/2003 which name changed to Siena Technologies, Inc. 10/30/2006 which recapitalized as XnE, Inc. 07/01/2009
(See XnE, Inc.)

INFINITI RES INTL LTD (AB)
Acquired by Welton Energy Corp. (New) 08/04/2005
Each share Common no par exchanged for (0.2) share Common no par and (0.05) Common Stock Purchase Warrant expiring 08/04/2007
Welton Energy Corp. (New) merged into Churchill Energy Inc. 02/13/2009 which merged into Zargon Energy Trust 09/23/2009 which reorganized as Zargon Oil & Gas Ltd. (New) 01/07/2011

INFINITY ALLIANCE VENTURES INC (BC)
Name changed to CBM Asia Development Corp. 11/18/2008

INFINITY AUGMENTED REALITY INC (NV)
Each share old Common $0.00001 par exchanged for (1) share new Common $0.00001 par to reflect a (1) for (101) reverse split followed by a (101) for (1) forward split 11/06/2015
Note: Holders of (101) or fewer pre-split shares received $0.15 cash per share
Acquired by IAR Merger Sub Inc. 09/23/2016
Each share new Common $0.00001 par exchanged for $0.063451 cash

INFINITY BROADCASTING CORP. (DE)
Ctfs. dated prior to 6/10/86
Merged into WCK Acquisition Corp. 8/4/88
Each share Class A Common 1¢ par exchanged for $30.25 cash

INFINITY BROADCASTING CORP NEW (DE)
Merged into Viacom Inc. (Old) 02/21/2001
Each share Class A Common 1¢ par exchanged for (0.592) share Class B Common 1¢ par
(See Viacom Inc. (Old))

INFINITY BROADCASTING CORP OLD (DE)
Class A Common $0.002 par split (3) for (2) by issuance of (0.5) additional share 08/16/1993
Class A Common $0.002 par split (3) for (2) by issuance of (0.5) additional share 11/19/1993
Class A Common $0.002 par split (3) for (2) by issuance of (0.5) additional share 05/19/1995
Class A Common $0.002 par split (3) for (2) by issuance of (0.5) additional share payable 04/11/1996 to holders of record 03/28/1996 Ex date - 04/12/1996
Merged into Westinghouse Electric Corp. 12/31/1996
Each share Class A Common $0.002 par exchanged for (1.71) shares Common $1 par
Westinghouse Electric Corp. name changed to CBS Corp. 12/01/1997 which merged into Viacom Inc. (Old) 05/04/2000
(See Viacom Inc. (Old))

INFINITY CAP GROUP INC (MD)
Name changed to 30DC, Inc. 12/09/2010

INFINITY CROSS BORDER ACQUISITION CORP (BRITISH VIRGIN ISLANDS)
Issue Information - 5,000,000 UNITS consisting of (1) share ORD and (1) WT offered at $8 per Unit on 07/19/2012
Units separated 04/15/2014
Reincorporated under the laws of Delaware as Glori Energy Inc. and Ordinary no par reclassified as Common $0.0001 par 04/15/2014

INFINITY FDS INC (MD)
Merged into Amsouth Funds 03/13/2000
Details not available

INFINITY FINL TECHNOLOGY INC (DE)
Merged into SunGard Data Systems Inc. 1/2/98
Each share Common 1¢ par exchanged for (0.68) share Common 1¢ par
(See SunGard Data Systems Inc.)

INFINITY INC (CO)
Each (12) shares old Common $0.0001 par exchanged for (1) share new Common $0.0001 par 11/30/93
Each share new Common $0.0001 par exchanged again for (0.25) share new Common $0.0001 par 3/24/99
New Common $0.0001 par split (2) for (1) by issuance of (1) additional share payable 5/13/2002 to holders of record 5/6/2002 Ex date - 5/14/2002
Reincorporated under the laws of Delaware as Infinity Energy Resources, Inc. 9/13/2005

INFINITY MED GROUP INC (NV)
Charter revoked for failure to file reports and pay fees 08/01/2011

INFINITY MINERALS CORP (BC)
Name changed to Herbal Clone Bank Canada Inc. 09/08/2014
Herbal Clone Bank Canada Inc. name changed to High Hampton Holdings Corp. 06/18/2015

INFINITY MUSIC CO (NV)
Name changed to Infinity Acquisition Corp. 12/1/2005

INFINITY OIL & GAS CO (NV)
Recapitalized as Ignyta, Inc. (NV) 11/01/2013
Each share Common $0.00001 par exchanged for (0.01) share Common $0.00001 par
Ignyta, Inc. (NV) reincorporated in Delaware 06/17/2014
(See Ignyta, Inc.)

INFINITY PETE CORP (FL)
Proclaimed dissolved for failure to file reports and pay fees 08/26/1994

INFINITY PPTY & CAS CORP (OH)
Merged into Kemper Corp. (New) 07/02/2018
Each share Common no par exchanged for (1.2019) shares Common 10¢ par and $51.60 cash

INFINITY RES HLDGS CORP (NV)
Name changed to Quest Resource Holding Corp. 10/28/2013

INFINITY SPECULATIVE FD INC (CO)
Name changed to Redwood Microcap Fund, Inc. 7/26/91
(See Redwood Microcap Fund, Inc.)

INFINIUM LABS INC (DE)
Common $0.0001 par split (5) for (1) by issuance of (4) additional shares payable 01/20/2004 to holders of record 01/19/2004 Ex date - 01/21/2004
Common $0.0001 par split (4) for (1) by issuance of (3) additional shares

INF-INF FINANCIAL INFORMATION, INC.

payable 05/10/2004 to holders of record 05/05/2004 Ex date - 05/11/2004
Name changed to Phantom Entertainment, Inc. 07/24/2006
(See Phantom Entertainment, Inc.)

INFINIUM SOFTWARE INC (MA)
Merged into SSA Global Technologies, Inc. 12/23/2002
Each share Common 1¢ par exchanged for $7 cash
(See SSA Global Technologies, Inc.)

INFINTY ACQUISITION CORP (NV)
Name changed to Younger America, Inc. 5/14/2007

INFLAZYME PHARMACEUTICALS LTD (BC)
Recapitalized as Eacom Timber Corp. 08/26/2008
Each share Common no par exchanged for (0.25) share Common no par
(See Eacom Timber Corp.)

INFLIGHT SVCS INC (DE)
Name changed 5/10/73
Name changed from Inflight Motion Pictures, Inc. to Inflight Services, Inc. 05/10/1973
Common $1 par changed to 50¢ par 04/04/1978
Chapter 11 Federal Bankruptcy Code converted to Chapter 7 on 01/08/1987
Stockholders' equity unlikely

INFLO SYS INC (DE)
Charter cancelled and declared inoperative and void for non-payment of taxes 3/1/80

INFLOT HLDGS CORP (FL)
Recapitalized as iTrackr Technologies, Inc. 05/21/2009
Each share Common no par exchanged for (0.001) share Common no par
iTrackr Technologies, Inc. name changed to Delivery Technology Solutions, Inc. 03/16/2010

INFO CTR INTL INC (NV)
Name changed to Budgethotels.com, Inc. 03/09/1999
Budgethotels.com, Inc. name changed to Budgethotels Network Inc. 08/14/2001 which recapitalized as Edentify, Inc. 07/19/2005
(See Edentify, Inc.)

INFO DATA INC (DE)
Charter cancelled and declared inoperative and void for non-payment of taxes 3/1/90

INFO DESIGNS INC (MI)
Involuntarily dissolved by court order 2/22/89

INFO INVS INC (DE)
Name changed to Pure Earth, Inc. 2/6/2006

INFO MED DATASOFT INC (DE)
Name changed to Elliott Technologies Inc. 01/06/1986
Elliott Technologies Inc. name changed to Elliot-Murdoch, Inc. 11/14/1986
(See Elliot-Murdoch, Inc.)

INFO-PAC INC (DE)
Name changed to Digital Armor Inc. 9/3/98

INFO STOP COMMUNICATIONS INC (BC)
Name changed to Alpha Gold Corp. 09/20/1990
Alpha Gold Corp. recapitalized as ALQ Gold Corp. 08/20/2013

INFO TOUCH TECHNOLOGIES CORP (BC)
Name changed to TIO Networks Corp. 04/11/2006
(See TIO Networks Corp.)

INFOAMERICA INC (CO)
Name changed to Las Americas Broadband Inc. 02/16/2001
(See Las Americas Broadband Inc.)

INFOBLOX INC (DE)
Acquired by Delta Holdco, LLC 11/07/2016
Each share Common $0.0001 par exchanged for $26.50 cash

INFOBOOTH INC (DE)
Name changed to RedCell Power Corp. 05/23/2002
(See RedCell Power Corp.)

INFOCALL COMMUNICATIONS CORP (FL)
Name changed to INFE.com, Inc. 3/17/2000
INFE.com, Inc. recapitalized as INFE Inc. 8/17/2001 which name changed to Pacer Health Corp. 2/19/2004

INFOCAST CORP (NV)
SEC revoked common stock registration 02/11/2013

INFOCODE INC (DE)
Charter cancelled and declared inoperative and void for non-payment of taxes 3/1/86

INFOCORP, INC. (MN)
Merged into Computer Graphic in 1984
Details not available

INFOCROSSING INC (NY)
Merged into Wipro Ltd. 09/20/2007
Each share Common 1¢ par exchanged for $18.70 cash

INFOCURE CORP (DE)
Issue Information - 1,400,000 shares COM offered at $5.50 per share on 07/10/1997
Common $0.001 par split (2) for (1) by issuance of (1) additional share payable 08/19/1999 to holders of record 08/05/1999
Each share Common $0.001 par received distribution of (0.25) share PracticeWorks Inc. Common 1¢ par payable 03/05/2001 to holders of record 02/21/2001
Name changed to VitalWorks, Inc. 08/06/2001
VitalWorks, Inc. name changed to AMICAS, Inc. 01/03/2005
(See AMICAS, Inc.)

INFOCUS CORP (OR)
Acquired by Image Holdings Corp. 05/28/2009
Each share Common no par exchanged for $0.95 cash

INFODATA SYS INC (VA)
Reincorporated 6/2/95
Each share old Common 1¢ par exchanged for (1/3) share new Common 3¢ par 4/27/94
State of incorporation changed from (NY) to (VA) 6/2/95
New Common 3¢ par split (2) for (1) by issuance of (1) additional share payable 8/26/96 to holders of record 8/12/96
Stock Dividends - 50% 3/14/80; 50% 7/27/81; 16.67% payable 5/17/96 to holders of record 4/17/96
Merged into McDonald Bradley, Inc. 8/30/2005
Each share new Common 3¢ par exchanged for $1.09 cash

INFODEX INC (DE)
Name changed to Midwest Venture Group, Inc. 03/21/2005
Midwest Venture Group, Inc. recapitalized as Automated Vending Technologies, Inc. (DE) 09/28/2005 which reorganized in Nevada as AVT, Inc. 01/17/2008
(See AVT, Inc.)

INFODYNAMX CORP (NV)
Name changed to Worldwide Golf Resources, Inc. 09/30/1994
(See Worldwide Golf Resources, Inc.)

INFOGRAMES INC (DE)
Name changed to Atari, Inc. 05/06/2003
(See Atari, Inc.)

INFOGROUP INC (DE)
Acquired by Omaha Holdco Inc. 07/01/2010
Each share Common $0.0025 par exchanged for $8 cash

INFOIMAGING TECHNOLOGIES INC (NV)
Name changed to Intacta Technologies Inc. 08/17/1999
(See Intacta Technologies Inc.)

INFOINTERACTIVE INC (AB)
Acquired by AOL Time Warner Inc. 07/19/2001
Each share Common no par exchanged for $1.42 cash

INFOLIFE INC (TX)
Recapitalized as China Marketing Media Holdings, Inc. 02/10/2006
Each share Common $0.001 par exchanged for (0.1) share Common $0.001 par
(See China Marketing Media Holdings, Inc.)

INFOLINE INC (NY)
Name changed to International Information Network Inc. (NY) 6/20/85
International Information Network Inc. (NY) reincorporated in Nevada as Megaphone International, Inc. 6/5/86 which reincorporated in (DE) 1/15/87 which was acquired by Votrax, Inc. 1/19/89
(See Votrax, Inc.)

INFOLINK TECHNOLOGIES LTD (ON)
Acquired by 2153357 Ontario Inc. 12/11/2007
Each share Common no par exchanged for $0.0472 cash

INFOLINX COMMUNICATIONS LTD (BC)
Reincorporated under the laws of Nevada and Common no par changed to $0.001 par 11/30/2006
InfoLinx Communications Ltd. (NV) recapitalized as GSM Fund Group, Inc. 11/21/2014
(See GSM Fund Group, Inc.)

INFOLINX COMMUNICATIONS LTD (NV)
Recapitalized as GSM Fund Group, Inc. 11/21/2014
Each share Common $0.001 par exchanged for (0.01) share Common $0.001 par
(See GSM Fund Group, Inc.)

INFOLOGIX INC (DE)
Each share old Common $0.00001 par exchanged for (0.04) share new Common $0.00001 par 01/06/2010
Acquired by Stanley Black & Decker, Inc. 01/18/2011
Each share new Common $0.00001 par exchanged for $4.75 cash

INFOMAX CORP (MN)
Statutorily dissolved 12/31/1992

INFOMED HLDGS INC (DE)
Name changed to Simione Central Holdings, Inc. 12/19/96
Simione Central Holdings, Inc. name changed to CareCentric Inc. 1/31/2001
(See CareCentric Inc.)

INFOMETRICS INC (CA)
Name changed to Envirocon Manufacturing Co. 04/04/1973
Envirocon Manufacturing Co. name changed to Traditional Industries, Inc. 07/09/1982
(See Traditional Industries, Inc.)

INFONATIONAL INC (NY)
Completely liquidated 04/30/1977
Each share Common 10¢ par received first and final distribution of $0.1066 cash

INFONAUTICS CORP (PA)
Name changed to Tucows Inc. 8/28/2001

INFONET SVCS CORP (DE)
Merged into BT Group plc 2/25/2005
Each share Class B Common 1¢ par exchanged for $2.06 cash

INFONICS INC (CA)
Common 10¢ par split (2) for (1) by issuance of (1) additional share 12/10/1969
Merged into Electronic Associates, Inc. 11/24/1972
Each share Common 10¢ par exchanged for (0.11765) share Common $1 par
Electronic Associates, Inc. name changed to EA Industries, Inc. 10/25/1995
(See EA Industries, Inc.)

INFOPAC SYS INC (MN)
Name changed to Inter-Con/PC, Inc. 06/08/1999
(See Inter-Con/PC, Inc.)

INFOPAGE INC (DE)
Recapitalized as Tamija Gold & Diamond Exploration, Inc. 07/31/2006
Each share Common 1¢ par exchanged for (0.001) share Common 1¢ par
(See Tamija Gold & Diamond Exploration, Inc.)

INFOR ACQUISITION CORP (ON)
Units separated 07/06/2015
Completely liquidated 05/04/2017
Each Class A Restricted Vtg. Share received $10.04 cash

INFORETECH WIRELESS TECHNOLOGY INC (NV)
Name changed to GPS Industries, Inc. 10/01/2003
(See GPS Industries, Inc.)

INFOREX INC (DE)
Common 25¢ par split (4) for (3) by issuance of (1/3) additional share 09/08/1972
Acquired by Datapoint Corp. 09/26/1980
Each share Common 25¢ par exchanged for (0.006523) share Common 25¢ par
Datapoint Corp. name changed to Dynacore Holdings Corp. 05/08/2000 which name changed to CattleSale Co. 02/25/2003
(See CattleSale Co.)

INFORM EXPL CORP (BC)
Recapitalized as OrganiGram Holdings Inc. 08/25/2014
Each share Common no par exchanged for (0.88360475) share Common no par

INFORM MEDIA GROUP, INC. (NV)
Name changed to Acquisition Media, Inc. 08/12/2002
Acquisition Media, Inc. name changed to Actionview International, Inc. 08/20/2003 which recapitalized as AVEW Holdings, Inc. 07/31/2015

INFORM WORLDWIDE HLDGS INC (FL)
Reincorporated 02/21/2005
State of incorporation changed from (CO) to (FL) 02/21/2005
Each share old Common no par exchanged for (0.01) share new Common no par 03/01/2005
Each share new Common no par exchanged again for (0.00066666) share new Common no par 08/29/2005
SEC revoked common stock registration 05/07/2014

INFORMA PLC (JERSEY)
Each Unsponsored ADR for Ordinary

exchanged for (1) Sponsored ADR for Ordinary 07/01/2013
Reorganized under the laws of England & Wales 05/30/2014
Each Sponsored ADR for Ordinary exchanged for (1) Sponsored ADR for Ordinary

INFORMATICA CORP (DE)
Common $0.001 par split (2) for (1) by issuance of (1) additional share payable 03/06/2000 to holders of record 02/18/2000
Common $0.001 par split (2) for (1) by issuance of (1) additional share payable 12/13/2000 to holders of record 11/29/2000 Ex date - 12/14/2000
Acquired by Italics Inc. 08/06/2015
Each share Common $0.001 par exchanged for $48.75 cash

INFORMATICS, INC. (DE)
Ctfs. dated prior to 2/28/74
Common 10¢ par split (2) for (1) by issuance of (1) additional share 1/16/69
State of incorporation changed from (CA) to (DE) 7/25/69
Merged into Equitable Life Assurance Society of the United States 2/28/74
Each share Common 10¢ par exchanged for $7 cash

INFORMATICS GEN CORP (DE)
Merged into Sterling Software, Inc. 09/12/1985
Each share Common 15¢ par exchanged for $27 cash

INFORMATICS INC. (DE)
Name changed to Informatics General Corp. 05/04/1982
(See Informatics General Corp.)

INFORMATION & COMPUTING CTRS CORP (TX)
Assets sold for benefit of creditors 7/3/73
No stockholders' equity

INFORMATION ADVANTAGE INC (DE)
Merged into Sterling Software, Inc. 8/31/99
Each share Common 1¢ par exchanged for $6.50 cash

INFORMATION AMER INC (GA)
Merged into Lohengrin Enterprises, Inc. 11/14/94
Each share Common 1¢ par exchanged for $6 cash

INFORMATION BUR INC (DE)
Name changed to Central Corporate Reports Services, Inc. 8/25/89
Central Corporate Reports Services, Inc. name changed to Combined Assets Inc. 6/6/90 which name changed to Environmental Products & Technologies Corp. 1/13/95
(See Environmental Products & Technologies Corp.)

INFORMATION CONCEPTS INC. (NY)
Common $1 par changed to 4¢ par and (24) additional shares issued 07/29/1968
Common 4¢ par changed to 2¢ par and (1) additional share issued 03/12/1969
Dissolved by proclamation 01/25/2012

INFORMATION DIALOGUES INC (MN)
Name changed to GHC Inc. 1/24/77
(See GHC Inc.)

INFORMATION DISPLAY TECHNOLOGY INC (NY)
Recapitalized as Polyvision Corp. 5/25/95
Each (15) shares Common $0.001 par exchanged for (1) share Common $0.001 par
(See Polyvision Corp.)

INFORMATION DISPLAYS INC (NY)
Each share Common 10¢ par exchanged for (0.2) share Common 50¢ par 10/16/78
Chapter 11 Bankruptcy proceedings converted to Chapter 7 on 3/13/85
Stockholders' equity unlikely

INFORMATION DYNAMICS INC (CA)
Name changed to Infonics Inc. 09/22/1969
Infonics, Inc. merged into Electronic Associates, Inc. 11/24/1972 which name changed to EA Industries, Inc. 10/25/1995
(See EA Industries, Inc.)

INFORMATION DYNAMICS INC (DE)
Charter cancelled and declared inoperative and void for non-payment of taxes 3/1/75

INFORMATION FOR INDS INC (DC)
Completely liquidated 12/29/67
Each share Common 25¢ par exchanged for first and final distribution of (0.025) share Plenum Publishing Corp. (NY) Common 10¢ par
Plenum Publishing Corp. (NY) reincorporated in Delaware 3/23/87
(See Plenum Publishing Corp.)

INFORMATION HLDGS INC (DE)
Issue Information - 4,250,000 shares COM offered at $12 per share on 08/06/1998
Merged into Thomson Corp. 11/30/2004
Each share Common 1¢ par exchanged for $28 cash

INFORMATION HWY COM INC (FL)
SEC revoked common stock registration 06/16/2008

INFORMATION INDS INC (PA)
Recapitalized as Moyco Industries, Inc. 5/27/75
Each share Common $0.005 par exchanged for (0.2) share Common $0.025 par
Moyco Industries, Inc. name changed to Moyco Technologies Inc. 12/6/95
(See Moyco Technologies Inc.)

INFORMATION INTL INC (MA)
Common 25¢ par split (3) for (1) by issuance of (2) additional shares 10/21/68
Name changed to Autologic Information International, Inc. 1/31/96
(See Autologic Information International, Inc.)

INFORMATION MACHS CORP (CA)
Common no par split (2) for (1) by issuance of (1) additional share 5/15/70
Common no par split (2) for (1) by issuance of (1) additional share 1/25/71
Adjudicated bankrupt 6/21/73
Attorneys opined no stockholders' equity

INFORMATION MAGNETICS CORP (CA)
Reincorporated under the laws of Delaware as Computer & Communications Technology Corp. 11/2/79
Computer & Communications Technology Corp. name changed to Sunward Technologies, Inc. 8/31/90 which merged into Read-Rite Corp. 8/22/94
(See Read-Rite Corp.)

INFORMATION MGMT ASSOC INC (CT)
Issue Information - 3,900,000 shares COM offered at $13 per share on 07/30/1997
Plan of reorganization under Chapter 11 Federal Bankruptcy Code effective 1/8/2002
Each share Common no par exchanged for initial distribution of $0.13 cash
Each share Common no par received a second and final distribution of $0.187 cash 1/8/2002

INFORMATION MGMT CORP (FL)
Recapitalized as Atlas Healthcare Inc. 04/12/1999
Each share Common $0.0001 par exchanged for (0.33333333) share Common $0.0001 par
Atlas Healthcare Inc. recapitalized as MyGlobal Concierge.com, Inc. (FL) 10/02/2000 which reincorporated in Delaware 08/21/2008

INFORMATION MGMT RES INC (FL)
Issue Information - 3,500,000 shares Common offered at $14 per share on 11/07/1996
Common 10¢ par split (3) for (2) by issuance of (0.5) additional share payable 7/10/97 to holders of record 6/26/97
Common 10¢ par split (3) for (2) by issuance of (0.5) additional share payable 4/3/98 to holders of record 3/20/98 Ex date - 4/6/98
Name changed to IMRGlobal Corp. 11/17/98
IMRGlobal Corp. merged into Groupe CGI Inc. 7/27/2001

INFORMATION MGMT TECHNOLOGIES CORP (DE)
Each share Class A 1¢ par exchanged for (0.25) share Class A 4¢ par 06/14/1995
Charter forfeited for failure to maintain a registered agent 08/27/2000

INFORMATION PROCESSING SYS INC (DE)
Common $0.025 par split (2) for (1) by issuance of (1) additional share 5/20/85
Common $0.025 par split (3) for (2) by issuance of (0.5) additional share 8/8/86
Merged into IPS Acquisition Corp. 12/15/88
Each share Common $0.025 par exchanged for $14.15 cash

INFORMATION RESOURCE ENGR INC (DE)
9% Conv. Preferred 1¢ par called for redemption 06/30/1995
Each share Common $0.001 par exchanged for (0.1) share Common 1¢ par 10/15/1992
Common 1¢ par split (2) for (1) by issuance of (1) additional share 07/07/1995
Name changed to SafeNet, Inc. 11/01/2000
(See SafeNet, Inc.)

INFORMATION RES INC (DE)
Common 1¢ par split (2) for (1) by issuance of (1) additional share 08/05/1983
Common 1¢ par split (3) for (2) by issuance of (0.5) additional share 06/10/1986
Merged into Gingko Corp. 12/12/2003
Each share Common 1¢ par exchanged for $3.30 cash and (1) Information Resources Inc. Litigation Contingent Payment Rights Trust Contigent Value Right
(See Information Resources Inc. Litigation Contingent Payment Rights Trust)

INFORMATION RES INC LITIGATION CONTINGENT PMT RTS TR (DE)
Each Contingent Value Right exchanged for $0.7152 cash 6/15/2006

INFORMATION RETRIEVAL SYS CORP (DE)
Charter cancelled and declared inoperative and void for non-payment of taxes 3/1/84

INFORMATION SCIENCE INC (NY)
Assets transferred to InSci Liquidating Trust 12/31/91
(See InSci Liquidating Trust)

INFORMATION SCIENCES INC (OR)
Under plan of merger each share Common no par exchanged for (1) Non-Negotiable Interim Ctf. and $1.60 cash 4/8/76

INFORMATION SOLUTIONS INC (CO)
Each share Common $0.001 par exchanged for (0.25) share Common $0.004 par 03/25/1993
Name changed to Image Software, Inc. 06/27/1994
(See Image Software, Inc.)

INFORMATION STORAGE DEVICES INC (CA)
Issue Information - 2,000,000 shares COM offered at $15 per share on 02/09/1995
Merged into Windbond Acquisition 12/23/98
Each share Common no par exchanged for $7.50 cash

INFORMATION SYS ACQUISITION CORP (DE)
Name changed to HDS Network Systems Inc. 03/02/1995
HDS Network Systems Inc. name changed to Neoware Systems, Inc. 08/01/1997 which name changed to Neoware, Inc. 12/01/2005
(See Neoware, Inc.)

INFORMATION SYS ASSOCS INC (FL)
Common $0.001 par reclassified as Non-Vtg. Class A Common $0.001 par 08/26/2013
Non-Vtg. Class A Common $0.001 par split (3) for (1) issuance of (2) additional shares payable 08/30/2013 to holders of record 08/29/2013 Ex date - 09/03/2013
Each share Non-Vtg. Class A Common $0.001 par exchanged for (0.005) share Common $0.001 par 04/09/2015
Name changed to Duos Technologies Group, Inc. 07/10/2015

INFORMATION SYS CORP (VA)
Automatically dissolved for failure to file reports and pay fees 6/1/73

INFORMATION SYSTEMS, INC. (IL)
Merged into Scam Instrument Corp. (IL) 04/10/1963
Each share Common $1 par exchanged for (1) share Common no par
Scam Instrument Corp. (IL) reincorporated in Delaware 02/17/1970 which name changed to Riley Co. 10/31/1971
(See Riley Co.)

INFORMATION TECHNOLOGY SYS INC (NV)
Recapitalized as IMG Latin America, Inc. 6/8/98
Each share Common $0.001 par exchanged for (0.01) share Common $0.001 par
IMG Latin America, Inc. name changed to International Healthcare Holding Inc. 10/20/98

INFORMATIVE COMPUTER SVC LTD (NY)
Charter cancelled and proclaimed dissolved for failure to pay taxes 12/29/82

INFORMATIX HLDGS INC (DE)
Recapitalized as Autologous Wound Therapy, Inc. 11/08/1999
Each share Common $0.001 par exchanged for (0.5) share Common $0.001 par
Autologous Wound Therapy, Inc. name changed to Cytomedix, Inc. 03/30/2000 which name changed to Nuo Therapeutics, Inc. 11/14/2014

INFORMATRIX 2000 INC (QC)
Acquired by Softkey Software Products Inc. 04/29/1991
Each share Common no par

exchanged for (0.925) share Common no par
SoftKey Software Products Inc. merged into Softkey International Inc. 02/24/1994 which name changed to Learning Co. Inc. 10/24/1996 which merged into Mattel, Inc. 05/13/1999

INFORMAX INC (DE)
Issue Information - 5,000,000 shares COM offered at $16 per share on 07/11/2000
Merged into Invitrogen Corp. 12/9/2002
Each share Common $0.001 par exchanged for $1.36 cash

INFORMEDIA CORP (DE)
Name changed to Strategic Information, Inc. 12/15/88
Strategic Information, Inc. name changed to Strategic Distribution, Inc. 11/9/90
(See Strategic Distribution, Inc.)

INFORMEDICS INC (OR)
Merged into Mediware Information Systems, Inc. 09/24/1998
Each share Common 1¢ par exchanged for (0.1587301) share Common 10¢ par
(See Mediware Information Systems, Inc.)

INFORMEDIX HLDGS INC (NV)
SEC revoked common stock registration 01/29/2014

INFORMISSION GROUP INC (CANADA)
Name changed to Nurun Inc. 04/13/2000
(See Nurun Inc.)

INFORMIX CORP (DE)
Common 1¢ par split (2) for (1) by issuance of (1) additional share 9/15/92
Common 1¢ par split (2) for (1) by issuance of (1) additional share 6/11/93
Common 1¢ par split (2) for (1) by issuance of (1) additional share 6/23/95
Name changed to Ascential Software Corp. 7/3/2001
(See Ascential Software Corp.)

INFORTE CORP (DE)
Merged into Business & Decision Group 07/26/2007
Each share Common $0.001 par exchanged for $4.25 cash

INFORUM COMM INC (DE)
Charter cancelled for failure to pay franchise taxes 3/1/2004

INFORUM INC (TN)
Merged into MEDSTAT Group, Inc. 2/25/93
Each share Common 1¢ par exchanged for (0.9114) share Common 1¢ par
(See MEDSTAT Group, Inc.)

INFOSAFE SYS INC (DE)
Recapitalized as Internet Commerce Corp. 09/25/1998
Each share Class A Common 1¢ par exchanged for (0.2) share Class A Common 1¢ par
Each share Class B Common 1¢ par exchanged for (0.2) share Class B Common 1¢ par
Each share Class E-1 Common 1¢ par exchanged for (0.2) share Class E-1 Common 1¢ par
Each share Class E-2 Common 1¢ par exchanged for (0.2) share Class E-2 Common 1¢ par
Internet Commerce Corp. name changed to EasyLink Services International Corp. 08/20/2007
(See EasyLink Services International Corp.)

INFOSEEK CORP (DE)
Reincorporated 11/18/98
State of incorporation changed from (CA) to (DE) and Common no par changed to $0.001 par 11/18/98
Merged into Disney (Walt) Co. (Holding Co.) 11/17/99
Each share Common $0.001 par exchanged for (1.15) shares Go.Com Common 1¢ par

INFOSERVE INC (MT)
Merged into CD-MAX Inc. 4/15/96
Each share Class A Common $0.003125 par exchanged for (1/3) share Common $0.003125 par
CD-MAX Inc. name changed to IMARK Technologies, Inc. 12/31/97 which recapitalized as Pharm Control Ltd. 11/8/2006

INFOSITE ADVERTISING SYS INC (NY)
Dissolved by proclamation 12/23/92

INFOSMART GROUP INC (CA)
SEC revoked common stock registration 08/20/2014

INFOSOFT INTL INC (DE)
Name changed to Inso Corp. 5/1/95
Inso Corp. name changed to EBT International, Inc. 8/25/2000
(See EBT International, Inc.)

INFOSONICS CORP (MD)
Old Common $0.001 par split (2) for (1) by issuance of (1) additional share payable 06/19/2006 to holders of record 06/09/2006 Ex date - 06/20/2006
Each share old Common $0.001 par exchanged for (0.2) share new Common $0.001 par 10/11/2017
Each share new Common $0.001 par exchanged again for (0.2) share new Common $0.001 par 03/09/2018
Name changed to Cool Holdings, Inc. 06/18/2018

INFOSPACE INC (DE)
Name changed 04/07/2000
Issue Information - 5,000,000 shares COM offered at $15 per share on 12/15/1998
Common $0.0001 par split (2) for (1) by issuance of (1) additional share payable 05/04/1999 to holders of record 04/19/1999
Common $0.0001 par split (2) for (1) by issuance of (1) additional share payable 01/04/2000 to holders of record 12/15/1999
Name changed from Infospace.com, Inc. to InfoSpace, Inc. and (1) additional share issued 04/07/2000
Each share old Common $0.0001 par exchanged for (0.1) share new Common $0.0001 par 09/13/2002
Each share new Common $0.0001 par exchanged again for (1) share new Common $0.0001 par 06/04/2009
Name changed to Blucora, Inc. 06/07/2012

INFOSPI (CA)
Merged into InfoSPI Acquisition Corp. 10/03/2003
Details not available

INFOSPI COM (CA)
Recapitalized as InfoSPI 04/30/2001
Each share Common no par exchanged for (0.25) share Common no par
(See InfoSPI)

INFOSPI COM INC (NV)
Name changed to Innovative Communications Technologies, Inc. 07/12/2000
Innovative Communications Technologies, Inc. recapitalized as Baristas Coffee Co., Inc. 05/07/2010

INFOSPI INC (NV)
Name changed to Onteco Corp. 04/11/2011

Onteco Corp. recapitalized as Inelco Corp. 05/10/2013
(See Inelco Corp.)

INFOSYS TECHNOLOGIES LTD (INDIA)
Sponsored ADR's for Equity Shares split (2) for (1) by issuance of (1) additional ADR payable 02/14/2000 to holders of record 02/11/2000
Sponsored ADR's for Equity Shares split (2) for (1) by issuance of (1) additional ADR payable 07/07/2004 to holders of record 07/02/2004
Basis changed from (1:0.5) to (1:1) 07/07/2004
Sponsored ADR's for Equity Shares split (2) for (1) by issuance of (1) additional ADR payable 07/17/2006 to holders of record 07/14/2006 Ex date - 07/18/2006
Name changed to Infosys Ltd. 06/23/2011

INFOTEC BUSINESS SYS INC (NV)
Old Common $0.001 par split (6) for (1) by issuance of (5) additional shares payable 03/18/2003 to holders of record 03/17/2003 Ex date - 03/19/2003
Each share old Common $0.001 par exchanged for (2.5) shares new Common $0.001 par 10/18/2005
Recapitalized as Wavelit, Inc. 06/13/2007
Each (30) shares new Common $0.001 par exchanged for (1) share Common $0.001 par
Wavelit, Inc. recapitalized as CN Dragon Corp. 01/11/2010

INFOTEC INC (DE)
Recapitalized as Equity Growth Systems Inc. 5/23/95
Each share Common 1¢ par exchanged for (0.1) share Common 1¢ par
Equity Growth Systems Inc. name changed to Amerinet Group.com Inc. 7/19/99 which name changed to Fields Technologies Inc. (DE) 7/3/2001 which reincorporated in Nevada as Park City Group, Inc. 8/8/2002

INFOTEC INDS INC (BC)
Recapitalized as Sellectek Industries Inc. 11/13/1986
Each share Common no par exchanged for (0.28571428) share Common no par
Sellectek Industries Inc. name changed to Global-Pacific Minerals Inc. (BC) 08/29/1989 which reorganized in Wyoming as UNIREX Technologies Inc. 04/23/2001 which recapitalized as UNIREX Corp. 07/19/2001
(See UNIREX Corp.)

INFOTECH MGMT INC (DE)
Chapter 11 Federal Bankruptcy Code converted to Chapter 7 on 1/11/89
Stockholders' equity unlikely

INFOTECH USA INC (DE)
Name changed to IFTH Acquisition Corp. 12/04/2008
IFTH Acquisition Corp. name changed to Steel Vault Corp. 03/18/2009 which merged into PositiveID Corp. 11/10/2009

INFOTECHNOLOGY INC (DE)
Plan of reorganization under Chapter 11 Federal Bankruptcy Code effective 06/21/1996
Each share Common 1¢ par recieved an undetermined amount of AMASYS Corp. Common and Common Stock Purchase Warrants
AMASYS Corp. recapitalized as StemGen, Inc. 02/05/2013

INFOTEL CORP (NJ)
Name changed to Cosmetics International, Inc. and Common 25¢ par changed to 5¢ par 8/9/73
(See Cosmetic International Inc.)

INFOTEX HLDGS INC (DE)
Name changed to Integrated Camera Optics, Corp. 12/19/2005
Integrated Camera Optics, Corp. recapitalized as Global Healthcare & Education Management, Inc. 09/27/2007

INFOTEX HLDGS LTD (NV)
Charter permanently revoked 08/31/1998

INFOTON INC (PA)
Reincorporated under the laws of Delaware as General Terminal Corp. and Common no par changed to 25¢ par 12/31/79
(See General Terminal Corp.)

INFOTOPIA INC (NV)
Each share old Common $0.001 par exchanged for (0.005) share new Common $0.001 par 06/21/2001
Chapter 11 bankruptcy proceedings converted to Chapter 7 on 02/04/2003
No stockholders' equity

INFOTRAX COMMUNICATIONS INC (DE)
Charter cancelled and declared inoperative and void for non-payment of taxes 3/1/95

INFOTRON SYS CORP (PA)
Merged into Gandalf Technologies Inc. 8/2/91
Each share Common 1¢ par exchanged for (0.5) share Common no par
(See Gandalf Technologies Inc.)

INFOTRONICS CORP (TX)
Stock Dividend - 50% 3/20/68
Name changed to Bionic Sciences Corp. 9/19/74
(See Bionic Sciences Corp.)

INFOUSA INC (DE)
Each share Class A Common $0.0025 par exchanged for (1) share Common $0.0025 par 10/21/1999
Each share Class B Common $0.0025 par exchanged for (1) share Common $0.0025 par 10/21/1999
Name changed to infoGroup Inc. 06/04/2008
(See infoGroup Inc.)

INFOUTILITY CORP (ON)
Recapitalized as Lynden Ventures Ltd. (ON) 01/19/2004
Each share Common no par exchanged for (0.25) share Common no par
Lynden Ventures Ltd. (ON) reincorporated in British Columbia 02/02/2006 which name changed to Lynden Energy Corp. 01/17/2008 which merged into Earthstone Energy, Inc. 05/19/2016

INFOVIEW INC (OK)
Charter suspended for failure to pay taxes 02/20/1987

INFOVISTA S A (FRANCE)
Issue Information - 6,000,000 ADR'S offered at $12.80 per ADR on 07/06/2000
ADR agreement terminated 04/05/2007
Each ADR for Ordinary exchanged for $4.91622 cash

INFOWAVE SOFTWARE INC NEW (CANADA)
Each share old Common no par received distribution of (0.1) share Coopers Park Real Estate Corp. Common no par payable 02/01/2005 to holders of record 01/28/2005
Each share old Common no par exchanged for (0.1) share new Common no par 11/22/2006
Dissolved for non-compliance 12/11/2011

FINANCIAL INFORMATION, INC.

INFOWAVE SOFTWARE INC OLD (CANADA)
Name changed 10/04/1999
Reincorporated 06/30/2003
Name changed from Infowave Wireless Messaging Inc. to Infowave Software, Inc. (Old) 10/14/1999
Place of incorporation changed from (BC) to (Canada) 06/30/2003
Reorganized as Infowave Software, Inc. (New) 01/18/2005
Each share Common no par exchanged for (1) share Common no par
(See Infowave Software, Inc. (New))

INFRA ROAST, INC. (DE)
Liquidation completed in 1958
Details not available

INFRABLUE US INC (NV)
Name changed to NextGen Bioscience Inc. 10/29/2007
NextGen Bioscience Inc. recapitalized as Kalahari Greentech Inc. 12/09/2008 which recapitalized as PF Hospitality Group, Inc. 06/11/2015 which name changed to EXOlifestyle, Inc. 09/27/2016 which recapitalized as Sun Pacific Holding Corp. 10/13/2017

INFRACOR INC (VA)
Name changed 08/09/2000
Name changed from InfraCorps Inc. to InfraCor Inc. 08/09/2000
Charter cancelled and proclaimed dissolved for failure to file reports 06/30/2003

INFRARED INDS INC (DE)
Acquired by Rospatch Corp. 10/6/86
Each share Common no par exchanged for (0.393304) share Common $5 par
Rospatch Corp. name changed to Ameriwood Industries International Corp. 12/13/91
(See Ameriwood Industries International Corp.)

INFRARED SYS INTL (NV)
Each share old Common $0.001 par exchanged for (10) shares new Common $0.001 par 06/10/2010
Name changed to Aqualiv Technologies, Inc. 09/19/2011
Aqualiv Technologies, Inc. recapitalized as Verity Corp. 04/04/2013

INFRASONICS INC (CA)
Each share old Common no par exchanged for (0.5) share new Common no par 6/20/91
Merged into Nellcor Puritan Bennett Inc. 6/27/96
Each share Common no par exchanged for (0.12) share Common no par
(See Nellcor Puritan Bennett Inc.)

INFRASOURCE SVCS INC (DE)
Issue Information - 8,600,000 shares COM offered at $13 per share on 05/06/2004
Merged into Quanta Services, Inc. 08/30/2007
Each share Common $0.001 exchanged for (1.223) shares Common $0.00001 par

INFRASTRUCTURE INTL INC (NV)
Charter revoked for failure to file reports and pay taxes 12/01/2001

INFRASTRUCTURE TECHNOLOGIES INC (NV)
Name changed to @ventureworks Inc. 04/03/2000
@ventureworks Inc. name changed to Underground Solutions, Inc. 01/30/2001
(See Underground Solutions, Inc.)

INFRATIONICS INDUSTRIES LTD. (AB)
Struck off register and declared dissolved for failure to file returns 07/30/1977

INFU-TECH INC (DE)
Filed a petition under Chapter 7 Federal Bankruptcy Code 8/21/2001
Stockholders' equity unlikely

INFYNIA COM CORP (CO)
SEC revoked common stock registration 04/01/2013

ING ASIA PAC HIGH DIVID EQUITY INCOME FD (DE)
Issue Information - 11,000,000 shares COM offered at $25 per share on 03/27/2007
Name changed to Voya Asia Pacific High Dividend Equity Income Fund 05/01/2014

ING CDA INC (CANADA)
Name changed to Intact Financial Corp. 05/19/2009

ING CAP FDG TR I (DE)
Issue Information - 20,000,000 GTD TR PFD SECS 7.70% offered at $25 per share on 06/18/1999
7.70% Guaranteed Trust Preferred Securities called for redemption at $25 on 6/30/2004

ING CAP FDG TR II (DE)
Issue Information - 10,000,000 9.20% GTD TR PFD SECS offered at $25 per share on 06/26/2000
9.20% Guaranteed Trust Preferred Securities called for redemption at $25 on 6/30/2005

ING CLARION GLOBAL REAL ESTATE INCOME FD (DE)
Auction Rate Preferred Ser. C called for redemption at $25,000 on 02/18/2009
Auction Rate Preferred Ser. T called for redemption at $25,000 on 02/18/2009
Auction Rate Preferred Ser. W called for redemption at $25,000 on 02/19/2009
Auction Rate Preferred Ser. TH called for redemption at $25,000 on 02/20/2009
Auction Rate Preferred Ser. F called for redemption at $25,000 on 02/23/2009
Auction Rate Preferred Ser. D called for redemption at $25,000 on 02/26/2009
Auction Rate Preferred Ser. A called for redemption at $25,000 on 03/04/2009
Auction Rate Preferred Ser. B called for redemption at $25,000 on 03/12/2009
Name changed to CBRE Clarion Global Real Estate Income Fund 07/11/2011

ING CLARION REAL ESTATE INCOME FD (DE)
Auction Rate Preferred Ser. M called for redemption at $25,000 on 02/17/2009
Auction Rate Preferred Ser. W called for redemption at $25,000 on 03/05/2009
Merged into ING Clarion Global Real Estate Income Fund 10/01/2009
Each share Common $0.001 par exchanged for (0.825226) share Common $0.001 par
ING Clarion Global Real Estate Income Fund name changed to CBRE Clarion Global Real Estate Income Fund 07/11/2011

ING DIVERSIFIED FLOATING RATE SR LN FD (ON)
Name changed to Voya Diversified Floating Rate Senior Loan Fund 08/25/2015
Voya Diversified Floating Rate Senior Loan Fund name changed to Redwood Floating Rate Bond Fund 12/20/2017 which name changed to Purpose Floating Rate Income Fund 06/18/2018

ING EMERGING MKTS HIGH DIVID EQUITY FD (DE)
Issue Information - 19,250,000 shares COM offered at $20 per share on 04/26/2011
Name changed to Voya Emerging Markets High Dividend Equity Fund 05/01/2014

ING FLOATING RATE SR LN FD (ON)
Name changed to Voya Floating Rate Senior Loan Fund 08/25/2015
Voya Floating Rate Senior Loan Fund name changed to Redwood Floating Rate Income Fund 12/20/2017 which name changed to Purpose Floating Rate Income Fund 06/18/2018

ING GLOBAL ADVANTAGE & PREM OPPORTUNITY FD (DE)
Name changed to Voya Global Advantage & Premium Opportunity Fund 05/01/2014

ING GLOBAL EQUITY DIVID & PREM OPPORTUNITY FD (DE)
Name changed to Voya Global Equity Dividend & Premium Opportunity Fund 05/01/2014

ING GROEP N V (NETHERLANDS)
8.50% Perpetual Hybrid Capital Securities called for redemption at $25 on 12/15/2013
(Additional Information in Active)

ING HIGH INCOME FLOATING RATE FD (ON)
Name changed to Voya High Income Floating Rate Fund 08/25/2015
Voya High Income Floating Rate Fund merged into Voya Floating Rate Senior Loan Fund 07/21/2017 which name changed to Redwood Floating Rate Income Fund 12/20/2017 which name changed to Purpose Floating Rate Income Fund 06/18/2018

ING INFRASTRUCTURE INDUSTRIALS & MATLS FD (DE)
Issue Information - 18,500,000 shares COM offered at $20 per share on 01/26/2010
Name changed to Voya Infrastructure, Industrials & Materials Fund 05/01/2014

ING INTL HIGH DIVID EQUITY INCOME FD (DE)
Issue Information - 8,125,000 shares COM offered at $20 per share on 09/25/2007
Name changed to Voya International High Dividend Equity Income Fund 05/01/2014

ING LARGE CO VALUE FD INC (MD)
Reorganized as ING Equity Trust 07/03/2002
Details not available

ING PRIME RATE TR (MA)
Auction Rate Preferred Ser. F 1¢ par called for redemption at $25,000 on 12/19/2011
Auction Rate Preferred Ser. M 1¢ par called for redemption at $25,000 on 12/20/2011
Auction Rate Preferred Ser. T 1¢ par called for redemption at $25,000 on 12/21/2011
Auction Rate Preferred Ser. W 1¢ par called for redemption at $25,000 on 12/22/2011
Auction Rate Preferred Ser. TH 1¢ par called for redemption at $25,000 on 12/23/2011
Name changed to Voya Prime Rate Trust 05/01/2014

ING RISK MANAGED NAT RES FD (DE)
Issue Information - 20,750,000 shares COM offered at $20 per share on 10/24/2006
Name changed to Voya Natural Resources Equity Income Fund 05/01/2014

ING U S INC (DE)
Issue Information - 65,192,307 shares COM offered at $19.50 per share on 05/01/2013
Name changed to Voya Financial, Inc. 04/07/2014

INGENEX CORP (NV)
Charter revoked for failure to file reports and pay fees 06/30/2011

INGENICO (FRANCE)
Name changed to Ingenico Group 06/15/2015

INGENIKA MINES LTD. (BC)
Liquidated 05/19/1976
No stockholders' equity

INGENIUM CAP CORP (NV)
Old Common $0.001 par split (4) for (1) by issuance of (3) additional shares payable 02/06/2006 to holders of record 02/06/2006
Name changed to Nitro Petroleum, Inc. 03/01/2006
Nitro Petroleum, Inc. merged into Core Resource Management, Inc. 03/26/2015

INGENUUS CORP (DE)
Filed plan of liquidation under Chapter 7 Federal Bankruptcy Code 10/29/2003
Stockholders' equity unlikely

INGERSOLL MACH & TOOL LTD (CANADA)
Each share Class A no par or Class B no par exchanged for (4) shares Common no par 10/24/1969
4% Preferred $100 par called for redemption 00/00/1971
98% acquired by Ivaco Industries Ltd. through exchange offer which expired 04/05/1971
Public interest eliminated

INGERSOLL RAND CO (NJ)
Common no par split (3) for (1) by issuance of (2) additional shares 00/00/1954
Common no par changed to $2 par and (1) additional share issued 07/08/1964
6% Preferred $100 par called for redemption 05/31/1973
Each share Exchangeable Dutch Auction Rate Transferable Securities Preference Ser. T-1 exchanged for (1) share Dutch Auction Rate Transferable Securities Preference Ser. D-1 07/01/1987
Each share Exchangeable Dutch Auction Rate Transferable Securities Preference Ser. T-2 exchanged for (1) share Dutch Auction Rate Transferable Securities Preference Ser. D-2 07/01/1987
Common $2 par split (5) for (2) by issuance of (1.5) additional shares 07/10/1987
$2.35 Conv. Preference no par called for redemption 09/14/1987
Dutch Auction Rate Transferable Securities Preference Ser. D-1 called for redemption 03/14/1990
Dutch Auction Rate Transferable Securities Preference Ser. D-2 called for redemption 04/04/1990
Common $2 par split (2) for (1) by issuance of (1) additional share 06/01/1992
Common $2 par split (3) for (2) by issuance of (0.5) additional share payable 09/02/1997 to holders of record 08/19/1997 Ex date - 09/03/1997
Stock Dividend - 100% 06/08/1948
Reorganized under the laws of Bermuda as Ingersoll-Rand Co. Ltd. and Common $2 par reclassified as Class A Common $1 par 12/31/2001
Ingersoll-Rand Co. Ltd. (Bermuda) reincorporated in Ireland as Ingersoll-Rand PLC 07/01/2009

INGERSOLL-RAND CO LTD (BERMUDA)
Class A Common $1 par split (2) for (1) by issuance of (1) additional share payable 09/01/2005 to holders of record 08/16/2005 Ex date - 09/02/2005
Reincorporated under the laws of Ireland as Ingersoll-Rand PLC and Class A Common $1 par reclassified as Ordinary $1 par 07/01/2009

INGERSOLL-RAND CO / INGERSOLL-RAND FING I (DE)
Each Income Preferred Redeemable Increased Dividend Equity Security received (0.5181) share Ingersoll-Rand Co. Ltd. Class A Common $1 par 5/16/2001
Each Growth Preferred Redeemable Increased Dividend Equity Security received (0.5181) share Ingersoll-Rand Co. Ltd. Class A Common $1 par 5/16/2001

INGLEBY COMMUNICATIONS CORP (NV)
Merged into Caribiner International, Inc. 08/09/1993
Details not available

INGLEWOOD GASOLINE CO (CA)
Each share Common no par exchanged for (5) shares Common 20¢ par 00/00/1937
Each share Common 20¢ par exchanged for (0.2) share Common $1 par 00/00/1941
Common $1 par changed to 50¢ par 00/00/1943
Name changed to Pacific American Industries, Inc. 02/20/1968
Pacific American Industries, Inc. name changed to Dr Pepper Bottling Co. of Southern California 06/03/1976 which merged into Dr Pepper Co. 02/23/1977
(See Dr Pepper Co.)

INGLIS LTD (ON)
Name changed 06/04/1973
Capital Stock $6 par changed to no par 00/00/1948
Name changed from Inglis (John) Co., Ltd. to Inglis Ltd. 06/04/1973
Capital Stock no par split (4) for (1) by issuance of (3) additional shares 05/24/1984
Merged into Whirlpool Corp. 02/12/1990
Each share Capital Stock no par exchanged for $33 cash

INGOT RES LTD (BC)
Merged into Candol Developments Ltd. (New) 05/22/1985
Each share Common no par exchanged for (0.7677616) share Common no par
Candol Developments Ltd. (New) recapitalized as Terrastar Development Corp. 03/30/1993
(See Terrastar Development Corp.)

INGRAM & BELL, LTD. (ON)
Acquired by International Bronze Powders, Inc. 00/00/1963
Each share Common no par exchanged for $13.50 cash

INGRAM MICRO INC (DE)
Acquired by Tianjin Tianhai Investment Co., Ltd. 12/05/2016
Each share Class A Common 1¢ par exchanged for $38.90 cash

INGRAM-RICHARDSON, INC. (IN)
Completely liquidated 11/17/65
Each share Common $2 par exchanged for first and final distribution of $11.40 cash

INGRAY YELLOWKNIFE MINES, LTD. (ON)
Charter surrendered 07/28/1958

INGREDIENT TECHNOLOGY CORP (DE)
Reincorporated 06/30/1978
State of incorporation changed from (NY) to (DE) 06/30/1978
Merged into Crompton & Knowles Corp. 06/21/1988
Each share Common $1 par exchanged for $28 cash

INGRES CORP (DE)
Merged into Palette ACQ Corp. 12/14/90
Each share Common $0.001 par exchanged for $9.25 cash

INGRESS MFG INC (IN)
99% acquired by Universal-Rundle Corp. through purchase offer which expired 05/15/1975
Public interest eliminated

INGXABO CORP (NV)
SEC revoked common stock registration 04/05/2016

INHALE THERAPEUTIC SYS INC (DE)
Name changed 7/1/98
Name changed from Inhale Therapeutic Systems (CA) to Inhale Therapeutic Systems, Inc. (DE) and Common no par changed to $0.0001 par 7/1/98
Common $0.0001 par split (2) for (1) by issuance of (1) additional share payable 8/22/2000 to holders of record 8/1/2000
Name changed to Nektar Therapeutics 1/15/2003

INHIBITEX INC (DE)
Issue Information - 5,000,000 shares COM offered at $7 per share on 06/03/2004
Acquired by Bristol-Myers Squibb Co. 02/13/2012
Each share Common $0.001 par exchanged for $26 cash

INHIBITON THERAPEUTICS INC (NV)
Name changed to AlumiFuel Power Corp. 07/06/2009

INI STL CO (KOREA)
Name changed to Hyundai Steel Co. 4/10/2006

INICIA INC (DE)
Name changed to Corporate Universe Inc. 09/21/2010

INITIAL ACQUISITION CORP (DE)
Name changed to Hollis-Eden Pharmaceuticals, Inc. 03/26/1997
Hollis-Eden Pharmaceuticals, Inc. name changed to Harbor BioSciences, Inc. 02/18/2010 which name changed to Harbor Diversified, Inc. 02/28/2012

INITIAL CAP INC (AB)
Recapitalized as Digifonica International Inc. (AB) 05/10/2007
Each share Common no par exchanged for (0.2) share Common no par
Digifonica International Inc. (AB) reincorporated in British Columbia as Dominion Energy Inc. 12/09/2013 which name changed to Dynamic Oil & Gas Exploration Inc. 06/30/2014 which recapitalized as Darien Business Development Corp. 03/14/2017

INITIAL DEVELOPERS LTD (BC)
Delisted from Canadian Dealer Network 05/31/2001

INITIALS PLUS INC (DE)
Company's assets were sold in 1989
No stockholders' equity

INITIATIVE EXPLS INC (ON)
Name changed 02/13/1980
Each share Capital Stock $1 par exchanged for (2) shares Capital Stock 50¢ par 03/21/1969
Under plan of merger name changed from Initiative Explorations Ltd. to Initiative Explorations Inc. 02/13/1980
Each share Capital Stock 50¢ par exchanged for (1) share Common no par
Merged into Canhorn Chemical Corp. 04/26/1995
Each share Common no par exchanged for (0.45) share Common no par
Canhorn Chemical Corp. merged into Nayarit Gold Inc. 05/02/2005 which merged into Capital Gold Corp. 08/02/2010 which merged into Gammon Gold Inc. (QC) 04/08/2011 which reincorporated in Ontario as AuRico Gold Inc. 06/14/2011 which merged into Alamos Gold Inc. (New) 07/06/2015

INITIO INC (DE)
Common 1¢ par split (2) for (1) by issuance of (1) additional share 08/20/1976
Common 1¢ par split (3) for (1) by issuance of (2) additional shares 08/10/1981
Stock Dividends - 15% 08/28/1975; 15% 08/31/1980
Reincorporated under the laws of Nevada 02/01/1994

INJECTO-MATIC SYS INTL INC (DE)
Name changed to Galton Biometrics Inc. 10/26/2004
(See Galton Biometrics Inc.)

INK TECHNOLOGY CORP (CT)
Charter cancelled for failure to pay fees 10/19/1990

INKA PRODUCTIONS CORP (NV)
Name changed to Texas South Energy, Inc. 11/12/2013

INKINE PHARMACEUTICAL INC (NY)
Merged into Salix Pharmaceuticals, Ltd. 10/03/2005
Each share Common $0.0001 par exchanged for (0.1737) share Common $0.0001 par
(See Salix Pharmaceuticals, Ltd.)

INKSURE TECHNOLOGIES INC (DE)
Reincorporated 07/08/2003
State of incorporation changed from (NV) to (DE) 07/08/2003
Name changed to New York Global Innovations Inc. 10/19/2016
New York Global Innovations Inc. recapitalized as Artemis Therapeutics, Inc. 12/20/2016

INKTOMI CORP (DE)
Common $0.001 par split (2) for (1) by issuance of (1) additional share payable 01/27/1999 to holders of record 01/12/1999
Common $0.001 par split (2) for (1) by issuance of (1) additional share payable 12/30/1999 to holders of record 12/14/1999
Merged into Yahoo! Inc. 03/19/2003
Each share Common $0.001 par exchanged for $1.65 cash

INLAND AIR LINES, INC. (WY)
Acquired by Western Air Lines, Inc. 4/10/52
Each share Common exchanged for $15 cash

INLAND AMERN REAL ESTATE TR INC (MD)
Each share Common $0.001 par received distribution of (0.125) share Xenia Hotels & Resorts, Inc. Common 1¢ par payable 02/03/2015 to holders of record 01/20/2015
Name changed to InvenTrust Properties Corp. 06/02/2015

INLAND BANCORP (DE)
Completely liquidated 8/2/71
Each share Common $20 par exchanged for first and final distribution of (0.558) Bank of California, N.A. (San Francisco, CA) Common Capital Stock Purchase Warrant expiring 8/2/76 and $38.1637 cash

INLAND BK (POMONA, CA)
Acquired by Bank of California, N.A. (San Francisco, CA) 07/31/1971
Details not available

INLAND CASINO CORP (UT)
Name changed to Inland Entertainment Corp. 12/11/1997
Inland Entertainment Corp. name changed to Venture Catalyst Inc. 12/10/1999
(See Venture Catalyst Inc.)

INLAND CEMENT CO. LTD. (CANADA)
Merged into Sogemines Ltd. 10/18/1965
Each share Preferred $10 par exchanged for (1.5) shares Common no par
Each share Ordinary $1 par exchanged for (0.15) share Common no par
Sogemines Ltd. name changed to Genstar Ltd. 02/25/1969 which name changed to Genstar Corp. 06/15/1981
(See Genstar Corp.)

INLAND CHEMS CDA LTD (AB)
Name changed to Inland Chemicals Ltd. 06/06/1969
(See Inland Chemicals Ltd.)

INLAND CHEMS LTD (AB)
100% of Common acquired by Canadian Industries Ltd. through purchase offer which expired 00/00/1974
6% Preferred $10 par called for redemption 12/06/1976
Public interest eliminated

INLAND CMNTY BK (RIALTO, CA)
Under plan of reorganization each share Common $1 par automatically became (1) share ICB Financial Common $1 par 10/01/2005
(See ICB Financial)

INLAND CONTAINER CORP (IN)
Class A Common no par and Class B Common no par split (3) for (2) by issuance of (0.5) additional share respectively 2/5/65
Class B Common no par reclassified as Class A Common no par 10/1/71
Class A Common no par reclassified as Common no par 5/10/73
Common no par split (3) for (2) by issuance of (0.5) additional share 7/1/74
Common no par split (2) for (1) by issuance of (1) additional share 6/15/76
Merged into Time Inc. (NY) 11/14/78
Each share Common no par exchanged for (0.425) share $1.575 Conv. Preferred Ser. B $1 par, (0.425) share Common $1 par and $0.0565 cash
Time Inc. (NY) reincorporated in Delaware 12/7/83 which name changed to Time Warner Inc. (Old) 7/25/89 which merged into AOL Time Warner Inc. 1/11/2001 which name changed to Time Warner Inc. (New) 10/16/2003

INLAND COPPER LTD (BC)
Struck off register and declared dissolved for failure to file returns 02/25/1983

INLAND CR CORP (NY)
Charter cancelled and proclaimed dissolved for failure to pay taxes 06/25/2003

INLAND DEVELOPMENT CORP. (DE)
Merged into American Industries, Inc. on a (1) for (4) basis 8/1/62
American Industries, Inc. acquired by Empire Petroleum Co. 11/16/66 which name changed to Empire International, Inc. 7/15/70
(See Empire International, Inc.)

INLAND EMPIRE BK (HERMISTON, OR)
Merged into First Savings Bank of Washington Bancorp, Inc. 8/1/96
Each share Common 1¢ par exchanged for $60.8951 cash

INLAND EMPIRE NATL BK (RIVERSIDE, CA)
Merged into New Inland Empire 7/1/97
Each share Common $5 par exchanged for $8.65 cash

INLAND ENTMT CORP (UT)
Name changed to Venture Catalyst Inc. 12/10/1999
(See Venture Catalyst Inc.)

INLAND FINANCIAL CORP. (WI)
Name changed to Inland Heritage Corp. 4/30/75
Inland Heritage Corp. name changed to Heritage Wisconsin Corp. 4/26/78
(See Heritage Wisconsin Corp.)

INLAND GAS CORP.
Bankrupt in 1935
Details not available

INLAND GOLD & SILVER CORP (WA)
Name changed to Inland Resources Inc. 05/10/1993
(See Inland Resources Inc.)

INLAND GOLD MINES LTD. (BC)
Struck off register and dissolved for failure to file reports and pay fees 05/15/1969

INLAND HERITAGE CORP (WI)
Name changed to Heritage Wisconsin Corp. 4/26/78
(See Heritage Wisconsin Corp.)

INLAND HOMES CORP. (OH)
Under plan of merger name changed to IHC Inc. 8/26/68
IHC Inc. name changed to Portage Industries Corp. 7/23/73 which name changed to Sweitzer Holdings, Inc. 3/18/76
(See Sweitzer Holdings, Inc.)

INLAND INC (MN)
Merged into Computer Graphic in 1984
Details not available

INLAND INVESTORS, INC. (DE)
Capital Stock no par changed to $10 par in 1945
Merged into Broad Street Investing Corp. on a (5.84979) for (1) basis 5/3/62
Broad Street Investing Corp. name changed to Seligman Common Stock Fund, Inc. 5/1/82

INLAND INVS INC (WA)
Charter cancelled and proclaimed dissolved for failure to pay fees 9/30/96

INLAND LIFE INS CO (IL)
Reorganized under the laws of Delaware as Inland National Corp. 7/23/69
Each share Common 50¢ par exchanged for (1) share Common 50¢ par
Inland National Corp. acquired by Zenith United Corp. 6/8/73 which merged into First Continental Life Group, Inc. 10/28/79
(See First Continental Life Group, Inc.)

INLAND MARINE CORP (MN)
Name changed to Inland, Inc. 8/7/70
(See Inland, Inc.)

INLAND METALS PRODUCTS CO. (MI)
Charter declared inoperative and void for failure to file reports in 1923

INLAND MINERAL RES CORP (DE)
Name changed to Parker-Levitt Corp. 4/25/69
Parker-Levitt Corp. name changed to Commercial Property Corp. 6/23/77

which name changed to Shandong Ruitai Chemical Co., Ltd. 11/15/2006 which name changed to China Ruitai International Holdings Co., Ltd. 4/9/2007

INLAND MINING CO. LTD. (BC)
Dissolved 00/00/1950
Details not available

INLAND MINING CORP. LTD. (ON)
Charter cancelled for failure to file reports and pay taxes 00/00/1957

INLAND MONTHLY INCOME FUND II, L.P. (DE)
Company terminated registration of Units of Limited Partnership and is no longer public as of 12/31/2005
Details not available

INLAND MTG INVS FD (DE)
Completely liquidated 12/30/1998
Each Unit of Ltd. Partnership Int. II received first and final distribution of approximately $123.30 cash
Unit of Ltd. Partnership Int. III details not available
Completely liquidated 06/25/1999
Each Unit of Ltd. Partnership Int. received first and final distribution of $57.67 cash

INLAND NAT GAS LTD (BC)
Common $1 par split (2) for (1) by issuance of (1) additional share 11/19/1985
5% Preference Stock $20 par called for redemption 05/01/1989
10% 2nd Preference Stock $25 par called for redemption 05/01/1989
Name changed to BC Gas Inc. (Old) 07/04/1989
BC Gas Inc. (Old) name changed to BC Gas Utility Ltd. 07/01/1993
(See BC Gas Utility Ltd.)

INLAND NATIONAL BANK (WALNUT, CA)
Reorganized as Foothill Independent Bancorp (CA) 11/15/1986
Each share Common $5 par exchanged for (1.1837) shares Common no par
Foothill Independent Bancorp (CA) reincorporated in Delaware 07/18/2000 which merged into First Community Bancorp (CA) 05/10/2006 which reincorporated in Delaware as PacWest Bancorp 05/14/2008

INLAND NATL CORP (DE)
Acquired by Zenith United Corp. 06/08/193
Each share Common 50¢ par exchanged for (0.466667) share Common 80¢ par
Zenith United Corp. merged into First Continental Life Group, Inc. 10/28/1979
(See First Continental Life Group, Inc.)

INLAND NORTHWEST BANCORPORATION INC (WA)
Name changed to Northwest Bancorporation, Inc. 05/21/1999
Northwest Bancorporation, Inc. merged into First Interstate BancSystem, Inc. 08/16/2018

INLAND OIL & URANIUM CORP. (DE)
Recapitalized as Inland Development Corp. 6/1/56
Each share Common 10¢ par exchanged for (0.1) share Common $1 par
Inland Development Corp. merged into American Industries, Inc. 8/1/62 which was acquired by Empire Petroleum Co. 11/16/67 which name changed to Empire International, Inc. 7/15/70
(See Empire International, Inc.)

INLAND OIL CO. (NV)
Name changed to Inland Oil Enterprises, Inc. 5/14/82
(See Inland Oil Enterprises, Inc.)

INLAND OIL ENTERPRISES, INC. (NV)
Charter revoked for failure to file reports and pay fees 10/1/92

INLAND PAC RES INC (NV)
Each share old Common $0.001 par exchanged for (0.05) share new Common $0.001 par 08/05/1994
Recapitalized as Creative Enterprises International Inc. 01/02/2002
Each share new Common $0.001 par exchanged for (0.06123698) share Common $0.001 par
Creative Enterprises International Inc. name changed to Skinny Nutritional Corp. 12/27/2006
(See Skinny Nutritional Corp.)

INLAND PETROLEUM CORP. (FL)
Reorganized under the laws of Delaware as Inland Resources Corp. 3/9/56
Each share Common 1¢ par exchanged for (0.5) share Common 2¢ par
Inland Resources Corp. merged into Universal Major Corp. 10/10/66 which name changed to Universal Major Industries Corp. 12/19/66
(See Universal Major Industries Corp.)

INLAND POWER & LIGHT CORP.
In process of dissolution in 1945
Details not available

INLAND REAL ESTATE CORP (MD)
Each share old Common 1¢ par exchanged for (1) share new Common 1¢ par 12/03/2004
Acquired by DRA Growth & Income Fund VIII, LLC 03/23/2016
Each share new Common 1¢ par exchanged for $10.60 cash
6.95% Preferred Ser. B 1¢ par called for redemption at $25 plus $0.135139 accrued dividends on 05/13/2016
8.125% Preferred Ser. A 1¢ par called for redemption at $25 plus $0.157986 accrued dividends on 05/13/2016

INLAND RECOVERY GROUP LTD (BC)
Recapitalized as Consolidated Inland Recovery Group Ltd. 05/24/1988
Each share Common no par exchanged for (0.14285714) share Common no par
(See Consolidated Inland Recovery Group Ltd.)

INLAND RESOURCES CORP. (DE)
Merged into Universal Major Corp. 10/10/1966
Each share Common 2¢ par exchanged for (0.125) share Common 1¢ par
Universal Major Corp. name changed to Universal Major Industries Corp. 12/19/1966
(See Universal Major Industries Corp.)

INLAND RES INC (WA)
Each share old Common $0.001 par exchanged for (0.1) share new Common $0.001 par 06/03/1996
Each share new Common $0.001 par exchanged again for (0.1) share new Common $0.001 par 12/14/1999
Merged into Inland Resources Inc. (DE) 06/02/2003
Each share new Common $0.001 par exchanged for $1 cash

INLAND RETAIL REAL ESTATE TR (MD)
Merged into Developers Diversified Realty Corp. 02/27/2007
Each share Common 1¢ par exchanged for (0.021569) share Common no par and $12.50 cash

INLAND STEAMSHIP CO.
Dissolved in 1936

INLAND STL CO (DE)
Capital Stock no par split (3) for (1) by issuance of (2) additional shares 05/08/1946
Capital Stock no par split (3) for (1) by issuance of (2) additional shares 05/14/1959
Capital Stock no par reclassified as Common no par 02/17/1970
Under plan of reorganization each share $2.40 Conv. Preferred Ser. A no par, $4.75 Conv. Preferred Ser. B no par and Common no par automatically became (1) share Inland Steel Industries, Inc. $2.40 Conv. Preferred Ser. A no par, $4.75 Conv. Preferred Ser. B no par and Common $1 par respectively 05/01/1986
Inland Steel Industries, Inc. name changed to Ryerson Tull, Inc. (New) 02/26/1999 which name changed to Ryerson, Inc. 01/01/2006
(See Ryerson, Inc.)

INLAND STL INDS INC (DE)
$4.75 Conv. Preferred Ser. B no par called for redemption 12/01/1988
$3.625 Conv. Exchangeable Preferred Ser. C $1 par called for redemption 06/19/1989
$4.625 Conv. Exchangeable Preferred Ser. G $1 par called for redemption 05/31/1994
Under plan of merger name changed to Ryerson Tull, Inc. (New) 02/26/1999
Ryerson Tull, Inc. (New) name changed to Ryerson, Inc. 01/01/2006
(See Ryerson, Inc.)

INLAND SYS INC (OH)
Under plan of merger each share old Common no par exchanged for (4.618) shares new Common no par 02/28/1970
Charter cancelled for failure to file reports and pay fees 12/22/1998

INLAND UNDERGROUND FACILITIES, INC. (KS)
Completely liquidated 7/20/65
Each share Common 50¢ par exchanged for first and final distribution of (0.3308) share Beatrice Foods Co. Common no par 7/21/65
Beatrice Foods Co. name changed to Beatrice Companies, Inc. 6/5/84
(See Beatrice Companies, Inc.)

INLAND UTILITIES INC.
Merged into Southeastern Gas & Water Co. in 1931
Details not available

INLAND VACUUM INDS INC (DE)
Name changed to Ivaco Industries, Inc. 04/09/1987
Ivaco Industries, Inc. name changed to IVAX Corp. (DE) 12/10/1987 which reincorporated in Florida 07/30/1993
(See IVAX Corp.)

INLAND WESTN CORP (UT)
Completely liquidated 09/30/1977
Each share Common 80¢ par exchanged for first and final distribution of $0.0832 cash

INLAND WESTN LN & FIN CORP (AZ)
Acquired by Thompson International Corp. 12/31/1969
Each share Class A Common $1 par or Class B Common $1 par exchanged for (0.125) share Common 80¢ par
Thompson International Corp. name changed to Inland Western Corp. 10/24/1974
(See Inland Western Corp.)

INLAND WIRE & CABLE CO.
Acquired by Anaconda Wire & Cable Co. 00/00/1929
Details not available

INLET DEVICES CORP (AB)
Reorganized under the laws of Ontario as Sangoma.com, Inc. 05/01/2000
Each share Common no par exchanged for (0.5) share Common no par
Sangoma.com, Inc. name changed to Sangoma Technologies Corp. 09/17/2001

INLET MINING CORP. LTD. (ON)
Charter cancelled and company declared dissolved by default 04/15/1965

INLET RES LTD (BC)
Each share old Common no par exchanged for (0.03333333) share new Common no par 01/11/2006
Name changed to Guerrero Ventures Inc. 08/19/2014

INMAC CORP (DE)
Reincorporated 4/29/87
State of incorporation changed from (CA) to (DE) 4/29/87
Merged into Micro Warehouse, Inc. 1/25/96
Each share Common 1¢ par exchanged for (0.276) share Common 1¢ par
(See Micro Warehouse, Inc.)

INMAR CORP (CA)
Name changed to ACA Joe 7/16/85
ACA Joe name changed to ACA Joe, Inc. 11/26/86
(See ACA Joe, Inc.)

INMARK ENTERPRISES INC (DE)
Stock Dividend - 25% payable 06/14/1998 to holders of record 05/14/1998
Name changed to CoActive Marketing Group, Inc. 10/01/1999
CoActive Marketing Group, Inc. name changed to mktg, inc. 09/18/2008
(See mktg, inc.)

INMC MTG HLDGS INC (DE)
Name changed to IndyMac Mortgage Holdings, Inc. 05/20/1998
Indymac Mortgage Holdings, Inc. name changed to IndyMac Bancorp, Inc. 07/03/2000
(See IndyMac Bancorp, Inc.)

INMEDIA PRESENTATIONS INC (BC)
Name changed to PhotoChannel Networks Inc. 07/14/1999
PhotoChannel Networks Inc. name changed to PNI Digital Media Inc. 06/09/2009
(See PNI Digital Media Inc.)

INMEDICA DEV CORP (UT)
Name changed 08/17/1984
Name changed from InMed Development Corp. to InMedica Development Corp. 08/17/1984
Name changed to WindGen Energy Inc. 03/17/2010

INMET MNG CORP (CANADA)
Acquired by First Quantum Minerals Ltd. 04/09/2013
Each share Common no par exchanged for (1.6199) shares Common no par and $36.62 cash

INMOLD INC (IN)
SEC revoked common stock registration 10/12/2007

INMONT COPPER MINES LTD. (ON)
Dissolved 08/09/1972
No stockholders' equity

INMONT CORP (OH)
Acquired by Carrier Corp. 12/27/77
Each share 4-1/2% Preferred $100 par exchanged for (1) share 4-1/2% Preferred $100 par
Each share Common $5 par exchanged for (1) share $1.86 Conv. Preferred $2.50 par
Carrier Corp. acquired by United Technologies Corp. 7/6/79

INMUEBLES CARSO S A B DE C V (MEXICO)
ADR agreement terminated 12/12/2014
Each 144A Sponsored ADR for Ser. B-1 Common exchanged for $3.949614 cash
Each Sponsored ADR for Ser. B-1 Common exchanged for $3.949614 cash

INN HOUSE VIDEO LTD (BC)
Name changed to Sleeping Gold Ltd. 06/08/1988
Sleeping Gold Ltd. recapitalized as Achieva Development Corp. 09/14/1992 which recapitalized as Angus Ventures Corp. 07/09/2008 which name changed to Encanto Potash Corp. 07/15/2009

INN INVT NEWS NETWORK LTD (BC)
Name changed to Interactive Telesis, Inc. (BC) 03/01/1994
Interactive Telesis, Inc. (BC) reincorporated in Delaware 09/23/1996
(See Interactive Telesis, Inc.)

INNCARDIO INC (UT)
Each share old Common $0.001 par exchanged for (0.01) share new Common $0.001 par 07/27/2006
Note: Holders of between (100) and (9,999) shares received (100) shares
Holders of (99) shares or fewer were not affected by the reverse split
Name changed to Long-e International, Inc. 01/11/2007
(See Long-e International, Inc.)

INNER MONGOLIA DEV HLDGS LTD (CAYMAN ISLANDS)
Name changed to Freeman Corp., Ltd. 07/06/2006
Freeman Corp., Ltd. name changed to Freeman Financial Corp. Ltd. 05/14/2012
(See Freeman Financial Corp. Ltd.)

INNER SYS INC (TX)
Plan of reorganization under Chapter 11 Federal Bankruptcy Code effective 04/30/2007
No stockholders' equity

INNER SYS INDS INC (TX)
Each share old Common no par exchanged for (0.5) share new Common no par 12/16/1996
Name changed to Inner Systems, Inc. 08/10/1998
(See Inner Systems, Inc.)

INNERDYNE INC (DE)
Merged into Tyco International Ltd. (Bermuda) 12/06/2000
Each share Common 1¢ par exchanged for (0.1337) share Common 20¢ par
Tyco International Ltd. (Bermuda) reincorporated in Switzerland 03/17/2009 which merged into Johnson Controls International PLC 09/06/2016

INNERGEX PWR INCOME FD (QC)
Merged into Innergex Renewable Energy Inc. 03/29/2010
Each Trust Unit no par exchanged for (1.46) shares Common no par and $0.07946 cash

INNERSPACE CORP (DE)
Recapitalized as SurfNet Media Group, Inc. 06/06/2003
Each share Common $0.001 par exchanged for (0.1) share Common $0.001 par
SurfNet Media Group, Inc. name changed to Modavox, Inc. 09/15/2005 which name changed to Augme Technologies, Inc. 03/23/2010 which name changed to Hipcricket, Inc. 08/26/2013
(See Hipcricket, Inc.)

INNES SHOE CO. (CA)
Acquired by General Shoe Corp. 00/00/1952
Details not available

INNES STR FINL CORP (NC)
Merged into Gaston Federal Bancorp, Inc. 01/02/2002
Each share Common no par exchanged for $18.50 cash

INNICOR SUBSURFACE TECHNOLOGIES INC (AB)
Each share old Common no par exchanged for (0.2) share new Common no par 08/30/2004
Acquired by BJ Services Co. 05/29/2008
Each share Common no par exchanged for $2.50 cash

INNKEEPERS USA TR (MD)
8.625% 144A Conv. Preferred Shares of Bene. Int. Ser. A called for redemption at $25 on 01/20/2004
8.625% Conv. Preferred Shares of Bene. Int. Ser. A called for redemption at $25 on 01/20/2004
Issue Information - 4,690,000 shares COM offered at $10 per share on 09/23/1994
Merged into Grand Prix Holdings LLC 06/29/2007
Each share Common 1¢ par exchanged for $17.75 cash
Plan of reorganization under Chapter 11 Federal Bankruptcy proceedings effective 07/15/2011
Each share 8% Preferred Ser. C 1¢ par exchanged for $0.83 cash
Each share 8% Preferred Ser. C 1¢ par received an initial additional distribution of $0.13 cash payable 06/27/2012 to holders of record 05/13/2011
Each share 8% Preferred Ser. C 1¢ par received a second and final additional distribution of $0.258112 cash payable 12/27/2013 to holders of record 05/13/2011

INNOCENT INC (NV)
Name changed to Panther Energy, Inc. 08/05/2014
Panther Energy, Inc. name changed to Falcon Crest Energy Inc. 09/02/2014 which recapitalized as Cherubim Interests, Inc. 06/16/2015

INNOCOLL AG (GERMANY)
Merged into Innocoll Holdings PLC 03/16/2016
Each Sponsored ADR for Ordinary exchanged for (1) share Ordinary 1¢ par
(See Innocoll Holdings PLC)

INNOCOLL HLDGS PLC (IRELAND)
Acquired by Gurnet Point L.P. 07/24/2017
Each share Ordinary 1¢ par exchanged for (1) Contingent Value Right and $1.75 cash

INNODATA ISOGEN INC (DE)
Name changed 11/14/2003
Each share old Common 1¢ par exchanged for (1/3) share new Common 1¢ par 03/25/1998
New Common 1¢ par split (3) for (1) by issuance of (2) additional shares payable 09/09/1999 to holders of record 08/30/1999
New Common 1¢ par split (2) for (1) by issuance of (1) additional share payable 12/01/2000 to holders of record 11/21/2000 Ex date - 12/04/2000
New Common 1¢ par split (2) for (1) by issuance of (1) additional share payable 03/23/2001 to holders of record 03/13/2001 Ex date - 03/26/2001
Name changed from Innodata Corp. to Innodata Isogen, Inc. 11/14/2003
Name changed to Innodata Inc. 06/05/2002

INNOFONE COM INC (NV)
Each share old Common no par exchanged for (0.00571428) share new Common no par 12/26/2002
Each share new Common no par exchanged for (0.05) share Common $0.001 06/18/2003
SEC revoked common stock registration 01/17/2013

INNOGY HLDGS PLC (UNITED KINGDOM)
Acquired by RWE AG 8/22/2002
Each Sponsored ADR for Ordinary exchanged for $41.86417196 cash

INNOLOG HLDGS CORP (NV)
Ceased operations 02/26/2014
Stockholders' equity unlikely

INNOLUX CORP (TAIWAN)
GDR agreement terminated 05/10/2013
Each Sponsored 144A GDR for Ordinary exchanged for $0.658132 cash
Each Sponsored Reg. S GDR for Ordinary exchanged for $0.658132 cash

INNOLUX DISPLAY CORP (TAIWAN)
Stock Dividends - In Sponsored 144A GDR's for Ordinary to holders of Sponsored 144A GDR's for Ordinary 10% payable 10/10/2008 to holders of record 08/14/2008; 3% payable 10/02/2009 to holders of record 08/14/2009 Ex date - 08/12/2009
In Sponsored Reg. S GDR's for Ordinary to holders of Sponsored Reg. S GDR's for Ordinary 10% payable 10/10/2008 to holders of record 08/14/2008; 3% payable 10/02/2009 to holders of record 08/14/2009
Name changed to Chimei Innolux Corp. 05/10/2010
Chimei Innolux Corp. name changed to Innolux Corp. 01/02/2013
(See Innolux Corp.)

INNOMAT SOLUTIONS CORP (ON)
Recapitalized as Carber Capital Corp. 11/26/1999
Each share Common no par exchanged for (0.025) share Common no par
Carber Capital Corp. recapitalized as Ba Ba Capital Co. 08/17/2010 which recapitalized as Imex Systems Inc. 05/13/2016

INNOPAC INC (CANADA)
Recapitalized as International Innopac Inc. (Canada) 05/27/1991
Each share Common no par exchanged for (0.2) share Common no par
International Innopac Inc. (Canada) reincorporated in British Columbia 05/29/1992 which name changed to Great Pacific Enterprises Inc. 06/01/1994
(See Great Pacific Enterprises Inc.)

INNOPAC INDL CORP (DE)
Name changed to Fortec Pharma, Inc. 3/1/2006

INNOPET BRANDS CORP (DE)
Issue Information - 2,250,000 UNITS consisting of (1) share COM and (1) WT offered at $4 per Unit on 12/05/1996
Charter cancelled and declared inoperative and void for non-payment of taxes 03/01/2000

INNOSERV TECHNOLOGIES INC (CA)
Merged into General Electric Co. 9/15/98
Each share Common 1¢ par exchanged for $3.9699 cash
Note: Each share Common 1¢ par received an additional escrow payment of $0.1775 cash 11/10/98

INNOSUISSE CORP (NV)
Each share old Common $0.001 par

exchanged for (1.02) shares new
Common $0.001 par 05/15/2006
Note: No holder will receive fewer
than (200) post-split shares
Each share new Common $0.001 par
exchanged again for (7) shares new
Common $0.001 par 06/11/2007
Name changed to Noxel Corp.
01/13/2012

INNOTECH AVIATION LTEE (CANADA)
Merged into I.M.P. Aerospace Ltd.
04/05/1989
Each share Common no par
exchanged for $3.10 cash

INNOTECH INC (DE)
Merged into Johnson & Johnson
3/21/97
Each share Common $0.001 par
exchanged for $13.75 cash

INNOTECH MULTIMEDIA CORP (ON)
Recapitalized as Astaware
Technologies Inc. 03/03/1999
Each share Common no par
exchanged for (0.5) share Common
no par

INNOTEK CORP (AR)
Recapitalized as ThermoEnergy Corp.
12/12/96
Each share Common $0.001 par
exchanged for (0.25) share Ser. B
Common $0.001 par

INNOTEK CORP (NY)
Charter cancelled and proclaimed
dissolved for failure to pay taxes
06/24/1981

INNOTEK INC (DE)
Name changed to Dermarx Corp.
12/15/1994
Dermarx Corp. recapitalized as
GoPublicNow.com, Inc. 04/07/2000
which name changed to GPN
Network Inc. 11/08/2000 which
name changed to IR BioSciences
Holdings, Inc. 08/28/2003

INNOTELCO INC (WY)
Each (150) shares old Common no
par exchanged for (1) share new
Common no par 08/28/2007
Recapitalized as Green America Land
Holdings, Inc. 04/24/2008
Each share Common no par
exchanged for (0.01) share Common
no par
Green America Land Holdings, Inc.
name changed to Green Card
Capital Corp. 03/10/2009 which
name changed to CUBA Beverage
Co. 09/27/2010

INNOTRAC CORP (GA)
Acquired by Blue Eagle Holdings, L.P.
01/06/2014
Each share Common 10¢ par
exchanged for $8.20 cash

INNOTRON DIAGNOSTICS (CA)
Charter suspended for failure to file
reports and pay fees 10/01/1987

INNOVA, INC. (CA)
Charter suspended for failure to file
reports and pay taxes 03/03/1975

INNOVA CORP (WA)
Issue Information - 2,750,000 shares
COM offered at $13 per share on
08/08/1997
Merged into Digital Microwave Corp.
10/08/1998
Each share Common no par
exchanged for (1.05) shares
Common no par
Digital Microwave Corp.
name changed to DMC Stratex Networks,
Inc. 08/15/2000 which name
changed to Stratex Networks, Inc.
09/10/2002 which merged into
Harris Stratex Networks,
Inc. 01/26/2007 which name changed to
Aviat Networks, Inc. 01/27/2010

INNOVA EXPL LTD (AB)
Acquired by Crescent Point Energy
Trust 11/05/2007
Each share Common no par
exchanged for $7.55 cash

INNOVA GAMING GROUP INC (CANADA)
Acquired by Pollard Banknote Ltd.
09/19/2017
Each share Common no par
exchanged for $2.50 cash

INNOVA HLDGS INC (DE)
Recapitalized as Innova Robotics &
Automation, Inc. 11/20/2006
Each share Common $0.001 par
exchanged for (0.1) share Common
$0.001 par
Innova Robotics & Automation, Inc.
name changed to CoroWare, Inc.
05/12/2008

INNOVA LIFESCIENCES CORP (ON)
Reincorporated 04/28/1998
Name changed 08/03/2000
Place of incorporation changed from
(BC) to (ON) 04/28/1998
Name changed from Innova
Technologies Corporation to Innova
LifeSciences Corp. 08/03/2000
Merged into Sybron Dental
Specialties, Inc. 10/25/2004
Each share Common no par
exchanged for $1.4106 cash

INNOVA PURE WTR INC (DE)
Reincorporated 07/092007
State of incorporation changed from
(FL) to (DE) 07/09/2007
SEC revoked common stock
registration 02/06/2014

INNOVA ROBOTICS & AUTOMATION INC (DE)
Name changed to CoroWare, Inc.
05/12/2008

INNOVACOM INC (NV)
Chapter 7 Federal Bankruptcy
proceedings closed 11/26/2003
No stockholders' equity

INNOVADENT TECHNOLOGIES LTD (ON)
Liquidation completed 06/01/2000
No stockholders' equity

INNOVASIVE DEVICES INC (MA)
Merged into Johnson & Johnson
02/11/2000
Each share Common $0.0001 par
exchanged for (0.0948) share
Common $1 par

INNOVATE BLDG SYS INC (FL)
Name changed to Xterra Building
Systems, Inc. 09/30/2014
Xterra Building Systems, Inc. name
changed to North America Frac
Sand, Inc. 08/14/2015

INNOVATE ONCOLOGY INC (NV)
Name changed to Avantogen
Oncology, Inc. 07/03/2006
(See Avantogen Oncology, Inc.)

INNOVATION CHEMS INC (UT)
Proclaimed dissolved for failure to
pay taxes 09/30/1986

INNOVATION HLDGS (NV)
Each share old Common 1¢ par
exchanged for (0.002) share new
Common 1¢ par 04/23/2004
Each (6,000) shares new Common 1¢
par exchanged for (1) share
Common $0.001 par 10/27/2004
Each share old Common $0.001 par
exchanged for (0.001) share new
Common $0.001 par 12/01/2004
Name changed to Marketing
Concepts International 10/20/2006

INNOVATION TECHNOLOGIES INC (DE)
Charter cancelled and declared
inoperative and void for
non-payment of taxes 03/01/1991

INNOVATIONS, INC. (KS)
Charter forfeited for failure to file
annual reports 08/17/1981

INNOVATIONS INTL INC (NV)
Recapitalized as Interferon
Pharmaceutical Corp. 02/13/1982
Each share Common $0.0001 par
exchanged for (0.001) share
Common 1¢ par
Interferon Pharmaceutical Corp. name
changed to Chantal Pharmaceutical
Corp. (NV) 10/21/1982 which
reincorporated in Delaware
01/16/1985
(See Chantal Pharmaceutical Corp. (DE))

INNOVATIV MEDIA GROUP INC (WA)
Each share old Common
$0.00000001 par exchanged for
(0.002) share new Common
$0.00000001 par 04/20/2016
Name changed to Demand Brands,
Inc. 10/24/2018

INNOVATIVE BEVERAGE GROUP HLDGS INC (NV)
Reorganized under the laws of
Delaware as Quantum Computing
Inc. 07/03/2018
Each share Common $0.001 par
exchanged for (0.005) share
Common $0.001 par

INNOVATIVE BEVERAGE GROUP INC (NV)
Charter permanently revoked
12/31/2009

INNOVATIVE CAP INC (AB)
Name changed to Vertex Properties
Inc. 07/29/1998
(See Vertex Properties Inc.)

INNOVATIVE CLINICAL SOLUTIONS LTD (DE)
Each share old Common 1¢ par
exchanged for (0.03225806) share
new Common 1¢ par 09/21/2000
Completely liquidated
Each share new Common 1¢ par
received initial distribution of $0.21
cash payable 06/30/2008 to holders
of record 06/23/2008 Ex date -
07/01/2008
Each share new Common 1¢ par
received second and final
distribution of $0.039251 cash
payable 12/16/2010 to holders of
record 12/09/2010

INNOVATIVE COATINGS CORP (NV)
Name changed to Capital Fund
Investment Inc. 12/29/2000
(See Capital Fund Investment Inc.)

INNOVATIVE COMMUNICATIONS INC (NV)
Stock Dividends - 10% 10/10/1973;
10% 08/27/1974
Charter revoked for failure to file
reports and pay fees 12/01/1996

INNOVATIVE COMMUNICATIONS TECHNOLOGIES INC (NV)
Recapitalized as Baristas Coffee Co.,
Inc. 05/07/2010
Each share Common $0.001 par
exchanged for (0.05) share Common
$0.001 par

INNOVATIVE COS INC (FL)
Stock Dividend - 10% payable
03/17/2003 to holders of record
03/01/2003 Ex date - 02/26/2003
Name changed to GeoPharma, Inc.
05/18/2004
(See GeoPharma, Inc.)

INNOVATIVE ENVIRONMENTAL SVCS LTD (AB)
Delisted from Alberta Stock Exchange
08/04/1995

INNOVATIVE GAMING CORP AMER (MN)
Each share old Common 1¢ par
exchanged for (0.1) share new
Common 1¢ par 09/09/2002

Chapter 7 bankruptcy proceedings
terminated 03/23/2010
Stockholders' equity unlikely

INNOVATIVE HEALTH SCIENCES INC (DE)
Reincorporated 02/24/2011
Each share old Common $0.001 par
exchanged for (0.001) share new
Common $0.001 par 11/25/2009
State of incorporation changed from
(NV) to (DE) 02/24/2011
Name changed to Innovative Holdings
Alliance, Inc. 05/27/2011

INNOVATIVE HEALTH SYS INC (DE)
Name changed back to Windsor
Capital Corp. 07/17/1995
Windsor Capital Corp. recapitalized
as Energy Control Technology Inc.
02/12/2001 which name changed to
5Fifty5.com, Inc. 09/26/2005 which
recapitalized as Swap-A-Debt, Inc.
02/26/2008 which name changed to
WikiLoan Inc. 06/26/2009 which
name changed to Wiki Group, Inc.
03/26/2012 which recapitalized as
Source Financial, Inc. 03/21/2013
which name changed to Alltemp, Inc.
04/27/2017

INNOVATIVE HLDGS & TECHNOLOGIES INC (CO)
Administratively dissolved 06/30/2005

INNOVATIVE MATLS INC (DE)
Charter forfeited for failure to maintain
a registered agent 02/18/2005

INNOVATIVE MED SVCS (CA)
Stock Dividend - 2% payable
11/20/2000 to holders of record
11/06/2000 Ex date - 11/02/2000
Name changed to PURE Bioscience
(CA) 10/09/2003
PURE Bioscience (CA) reincorporated
in Delaware as PURE Bioscience,
Inc. 03/24/2011

INNOVATIVE MED TECHNOLOGY INC (NV)
Each share Common $0.00001 par
exchanged for (0.002) share
Common $0.005 par 04/02/1984
Name changed to Monolite Industries
Inc. 09/03/1990
Monolite Industries Inc. recapitalized
as Country World Casinos, Inc.
08/09/1993
(See Country World Casinos, Inc.)

INNOVATIVE PROD OPPORTUNITIES INC (DE)
Each share old Common $0.0001 par
exchanged for (0.001) share new
Common $0.0001 par 06/16/2014
Recapitalized as Two Hands Corp.
09/01/2016
Each share new Common $0.0001
par exchanged for (0.0005) share
Common $0.0001 par

INNOVATIVE PPTY DEV CORP (UT)
Name changed to
ChinaMallUSA.com, Inc. 06/01/1999
(See ChinaMallUSA.com, Inc.)

INNOVATIVE SHIPPING SYS INC (FL)
Each share old Common $0.003 par
exchanged for (0.0625) share new
Common $0.003 par 10/09/1992
Recapitalized as Velocity Aerospace,
Inc. 11/04/2005
Each share new Common $0.003 par
exchanged for (0.01) share Common
no par
Velocity Aerospace, Inc. name
changed to Critical Power Solutions
International, Inc. (FL) 08/08/2007
which reincorporated in Delaware as
Critical Solutions, Inc. 03/03/2008

INNOVATIVE SOFTWARE INC (MO)
Common 1¢ par split (3) for (2) by
issuance of (0.5) additional share
6/1/87
Acquired by Informix Corp. 2/8/88
Each share Common 1¢ par
exchanged for (0.75) share Common
1¢ par

Informix Corp. name changed to Ascential Software Corp. 7/3/2001
(See Ascential Software Corp.)

INNOVATIVE SOFTWARE TECHNOLOGIES INC (CA)
Each share old Common no par exchanged for (1/3) share new Common no par 02/23/2001
Each share new Common no par exchanged again for (3) shares new Common no par 08/10/2001
Reincorporated under the laws of Delaware 11/28/2007

INNOVATIVE TECH SYS INC (IL)
Each share old Common $0.0001 par exchanged for (0.05393743) share new Common $0.0185 par 7/22/94
New Common $0.0185 par split (3) for (1) by issuance of (2) additional shares 9/15/95
Merged into Peregrine Systems, Inc. 7/30/98
Each share new Common $0.0185 par exchanged for (0.2341) share Common $0.001 par
(See Peregrine Systems, Inc.)

INNOVATIVE TECHNOLOGY INC (LA)
Charter revoked 11/19/1990

INNOVATIVE TRACKING SOLUTIONS CORP (DE)
Name changed to Thehealthchannel.com, Inc. 07/28/1999
(See Thehealthchannel.com, Inc.)

INNOVATIVE VALVE TECHNOLOGIES INC (DE)
Issue Information - 3,350,000 shares COM offered at $13 per share on 10/22/1997
Merged into Flowserve Corp. 1/13/2000
Each share Common $0.001 par exchanged for $1.62 cash

INNOVATIVE VIDEO ARCADE INC (NV)
Each share Common $0.00001 par exchanged for (0.001) share Common 1¢ par 04/02/1984
Name changed to Greater Bancshares, Inc. 05/01/1989

INNOVATIVE WASTE TECHNOLOGIES INC (BC)
Recapitalized as International Tire & Manufacturing Corp. 06/08/1995
Each share Class B no par exchanged for (0.1) share Class B no par
International Tire & Manufacturing Corp. recapitalized as Intirmac Industrial Corp. 12/05/1997 which name changed to Sniper Enterprises Inc. 12/07/1998 which name changed to TransAmerican Energy Inc. 08/16/2005 which recapitalized as American Biofuels Inc. 09/12/2018

INNOVATIVE WTR & SWR SYS INC (AB)
Reincorporated under the laws of Canada as Clearford Industries Inc. 07/20/2005
Clearford Industries Inc. name changed to Clearford Water Systems Inc. 06/27/2014

INNOVATIVE WEAPONRY INC (NV)
Name changed to 21st Century Technologies Inc. 11/14/1995
(See 21st Century Technologies Inc.)

INNOVATIVE WIRELINE SOLUTIONS INC (AB)
Creditors announced intention to enforce security interests and all directors have resigned as of 10/27/2011
Stockholders' equity unlikely

INNOVEDA INC (DE)
Merged into Mentor Graphics Corp. 06/05/2002

Each share Common 1¢ par exchanged for $3.95 cash

INNOVENTE INC (QC)
Deemed bankrupt 12/18/2014
Stockholders' equity unlikely

INNOVENTURES INTL INC (AB)
Recapitalized as Hodgins Auctioneers Inc. 08/13/2004
Each share Common no par exchanged for (0.5) share Common no par
(See Hodgins Auctioneers Inc.)

INNOVET INC (FL)
Proclaimed dissolved for failure to file reports and pay fees 09/19/2003

INNOVEX INC (MN)
Common 4¢ par split (2) for (1) by issuance of (1) additional share 08/02/1985
Common 4¢ par split (3) for (2) by issuance of (0.5) additional share 03/21/1986
Common 4¢ par split (3) for (2) by issuance of (0.5) additional share 05/31/1995
Common 4¢ par split (2) for (1) by issuance of (1) additional share payable 12/23/1996 to holders of record 12/16/1996
SEC revoked common stock registration 10/01/2013

INNOVIR LABORATORIES INC (DE)
Charter cancelled and declared inoperative and void for non-payment of taxes 12/2/2002

INNOVIS TECHNOLOGIES CORP (WY)
Reincorporated 10/15/93
Place of incorporation changed from (BC) to (WY) 10/15/93
Delisted from Vancouver Stock Exchange 3/3/97

INNOVISION INTL CORP (FL)
Each share old Common $0.001 par exchanged for (5) shares new Common $0.001 par 07/26/2000
New Common $0.001 par changed to no par 04/19/2002
Each share old Common no par exchanged for (0.02) share new Common no par 10/27/2006
Name changed to Tubearoo, Inc. 03/12/2007
Tubearoo, Inc. recapitalized as Emerging World Pharma, Inc. 11/24/2009

INNOVISIONIX INC (NV)
Name changed to JZZ Technologies, Inc. 4/20/2007

INNOVIUM CAP CORP (BC)
Name changed to Innovium Media Properties Corp. 09/24/2007

INNOVIVE PHARMACEUTICALS INC (DE)
Merged into CytRx Corp. 09/19/2008
Each share Common $0.001 par exchanged for (0.1762) share Common $0.001 par

INNOVO GROUP INC (DE)
Each share old Common 1¢ par exchanged for (0.1) share new Common 1¢ par 06/19/1995
Each share new Common 1¢ par exchanged for (0.1) share Common 10¢ par 09/11/1998
Name changed to Joe's Jeans Inc. 10/15/2007
Joe's Jeans Inc. recapitalized as Differential Brands Group Inc. 01/29/2016

INNOVUS CORP (DE)
Each share old Common no par exchanged for (0.5) share new Common no par 3/1/95
Recapitalized as Esynch Corp. 11/9/98
Each share new Common no par exchanged for (0.1) share Common no par

Esynch Corp. recapitalized as Mergence Corp. 2/13/2004

INNSTAR CORP (UT)
Recapitalized as Guinness Telli-Phone Corp. 09/13/1993
Each share Common no par exchanged for (0.1) share Common no par
(See Guinness Telli-Phone Corp.)

INNUITY INC (WA)
Reincorporated 11/21/2008
State of incorporation changed from (UT) to (WA) 11/21/2008
SEC revoked common stock registration 07/31/2013

INNVEST REAL ESTATE INVT TR / INNVEST OPERATIONS TRUST (ON)
Each Stapled Unit (consisting of (1) InnVest Operations Trust Unit and (1) InnVest Real Estate Investment Trust Unit automatically became (1) InnVest Real Estate Investment Trust, Trust Unit 07/03/2012
Note: Outstanding Units were consolidated to maintain the same number of Units after separation as were outstanding prior to the separation
(See InnVest Real Estate Investment Trust)

INNVEST REAL ESTATE INVT TR (ON)
Name changed to InnVest Real Estate Investment Trust / InnVest Operations Trust and Trust Units no par reclassified as Stapled Units 01/04/2011
InnVest Real Estate Investment Trust / InnVest Operations Trust Stapled Units separated 07/03/2012
Acquired by Bluesky Hotels & Resorts Inc. 08/18/2016
Each Trust Unit par exchanged for $7.25 cash
Note: Unexchanged certificates will be cancelled and become without value 08/18/2022

INOCAN TECHNOLOGIES LTD (BC)
Recapitalized as Arling Resources Ltd. 06/21/1993
Each share Common no par exchanged for (0.33333333) share Common no par
Arling Resources Ltd. name changed to I.D. Internet Direct Ltd. 12/07/1995 which merged into Look Communications Inc. 10/31/1999

INOLEX CORP (DE)
Acquired by American Can Co. 8/28/79
Each share Common 50¢ par exchanged for $2.50 cash

INORE GOLD MINES, LTD. (ON)
Merged into Goldquest Exploration Inc. 08/09/1982
Each share Capital Stock $1 par exchanged for (0.10101010) share Common no par
Goldquest Exploration Inc. merged into Goldcorp Inc. (New) 03/31/1994

INOTEK PHARMACEUTICALS CORP (DE)
Recapitalized as Rocket Pharmaceuticals, Inc. 01/05/2018
Each share Common 1¢ par exchanged for (0.25) share Common 1¢ par

INOTEK TECHNOLOGIES CORP (DE)
Merged into Davis Instruments, LLC 7/11/2001
Each share Common 1¢ par exchanged for $0.65 cash

INOUYE TECHNOLOGIES INC (CANADA)
Dissolved 10/04/2005
Details not available

INOVA OPTICS INC (CANADA)
Bankrupt 01/04/1989

No stockholders' equity

INOVA RES LTD (AUSTRALIA)
Acquired by Shanxi Donghui Coal Coking & Chemicals Group Co., Ltd. 11/27/2013
Each share Ordinary exchanged for $0.22 cash

INOVA TECHNOLOGY INC (NV)
Each share old Common $0.001 par exchanged for (0.0025) share new Common $0.001 par 11/12/2008
New Common $0.001 par split (20) for (1) by issuance of (19) additional shares payable 11/05/2010 to holders of record 10/30/2010
Ex date - 11/08/2010
Each share new Common $0.001 par exchanged again for (0.01) share new Common $0.001 par 06/17/2013
SEC revoked common stock registration 03/20/2015

INOVENT CAP INC (BC)
Name changed to Inomin Mines Inc. 02/02/2017

INOVEX INDS INC (PA)
Recapitalized as Berger Holdings, Ltd. 7/30/90
Each share Common 1¢ par exchanged for (1/6) share Common 1¢ par
(See Berger Holdings, Ltd.)

INOVIO BIOMEDICAL CORP (DE)
Name changed to Inovio Pharmaceuticals, Inc. 05/14/2010

INOVION CORP (UT)
Proclaimed dissolved for failure to file reports and pay fees 3/1/92

INOVISION SOLUTIONS INC (BC)
Name changed to Sierra Geothermal Power Corp. 05/16/2006
Sierra Geothermal Power Corp. merged into Ram Power, Corp. 09/02/2010 which recapitalized as Polaris Infrastructure Inc. 05/19/2015

INOVISION TECHNOLOGIES INC (BC)
Recapitalized as Inovision Solutions Inc. 05/15/2001
Each share Common no par exchanged for (0.125) share Common no par
Inovision Solutions Inc. name changed to Sierra Geothermal Power Corp. 05/16/2006 which merged into Ram Power, Corp. 09/02/2010 which recapitalized as Polaris Infrastructure Inc. 05/19/2015

INPAK SYSTEMS, INC. (NY)
Completely liquidated 12/28/64
Each share Common 1¢ par exchanged for first and final distribution of (0.02) share I.L.I. Corp. Common no par and $3.86 cash
(See I.L.I. Corp.)

INPAR S A (BRAZIL)
Name changed to Viver Incorporadora e Construtora S.A. 07/25/2011
(See Viver Incorporadora e Construtora S.A.)

INPATIENT CLINICAL SOLUTIONS INC (NV)
Name changed to Integrated Inpatient Solutions, Inc. (NV) 05/31/2012
Integrated Inpatient Solutions, Inc. (NV) reincorporated in Marshall Islands as Boston Carriers, Inc. 04/04/2016

INPEX HLDGS INC (JAPAN)
Name changed to Inpex Corp. 06/04/2009

INPHONIC INC (DE)
Plan of reorganization under Chapter 11 Federal Bankruptcy proceedings effective 03/30/2009

No stockholders' equity

INPHYNET MED MGMT INC (DE)
Issue Information - 2,100,000 shares COM offered at $12 per share on 08/19/1994
Merged into MedPartners, Inc. (New) 6/26/97
Each share Common 1¢ par exchanged for (1.18) shares Common 1¢ par
MedPartners, Inc. (New) name changed to Caremark Rx, Inc. 9/13/99 which merged into CVS/Caremark Corp. 3/22/2007 which name changed to CVS Caremark Corp. 5/10/2007

INPLAY TECHNOLOGIES INC (NV)
Completely liquidated
Each share Common $0.001 par received first and final distribution of $0.013 cash payable 02/05/2010 to holders of record 01/22/2010
Note: Certificates were not required to be surrendered and are without value

INPRIMIS INC (FL)
Name changed to Ener1, Inc. 10/28/2002
(See Ener1, Inc.)

INPRISE CORP (DE)
Name changed to Borland Software Corp. 01/22/2001
(See Borland Software Corp.)

INPROJET CORP (DE)
Common $1 par reclassified as Class A Common $1 par 12/23/1981
Merged into Falcon Financial Corp. 01/30/1985
Each share Class A Common $1 par exchanged for $0.30 cash

INPUT BUSINESS MACHS INC (DE)
Merged into BancTec, Inc. 6/20/83
Each share Common 1¢ par exchanged for (0.2458678085) share Common 1¢ par
(See BancTec, Inc.)

INPUT INC (DE)
Charter cancelled and declared inoperative and void for non-payment of taxes 3/1/75

INPUT/OUTPUT INC (DE)
Issue Information - 2,000,000 shares COM offered at $22 per share on 05/19/1994
Common 1¢ par split (2) for (1) by issuance of (1) additional share 05/04/1994
Common 1¢ par split (2) for (1) by issuance of (1) additional share payable 01/09/1996 to holders of record 12/26/1995 Ex date - 01/10/1996
Name changed to ION Geophysical Corp. 09/21/2007

INPUT SOFTWARE INC (DE)
Name changed to ActionPoint, Inc. 04/24/2000
ActionPoint, Inc. name changed to Captiva Software Corp. 08/01/2002
(See Captiva Software Corp.)

INQBATE CORP (DE)
SEC revoked common stock registration 06/24/2013

INQB8 CORP (NV)
Name changed to Aventura Resorts, Inc. 11/25/2005
Aventura Resorts, Inc. recapitalized as Borneo Resource Investments Ltd. 08/05/2011

INRAD INC (NJ)
Name changed to Photonic Products Group, Inc. 10/22/2014
Photonic Products Group, Inc. name changed to Inrad Optics, Inc. 04/09/2012

INRANGE TECHNOLOGIES CORP (DE)
Acquired by Computer Network Technology Corp. 05/05/2003
Each share Class B Common 1¢ par exchanged for $2.31 cash

INREEX INC (NV)
Name changed to Northern Potash Co. 07/29/2008

INREGOLD PROSPECTORS LTD.
Dissolved 00/00/1942
Details not available

INSCI CORP NEW (DE)
Each share Common 1¢ par exchanged for (0.1) share Common 10¢ par 1/2/2004
Name changed to ClearStory Systems, Inc. 11/1/2004

INSCI LIQUIDATING TRUST (NY)
Liquidation completed
Each Share of Bene. Int. received initial distribution of $0.30 cash 4/10/92
Each Share of Bene. Int. received second and final distribution of $7.03 cash 12/21/92

INSCI STATEMENT COM INC (DE)
Name changed 11/9/99
Name changed from INSCI Corp. (Old) to Insci-statement.com Inc. 11/9/99
Name changed to INSCI Corp. (New) 12/5/2001
INSCI Corp. (New) name changed to ClearStory Systems, Inc. 11/1/2004

INSCO MINES LTD. (QC)
Recapitalized as New Insco Mines Ltd. (QUE) 00/00/1953
Each Capital Stock $1 par exchanged for (0.5) share Common $1 par
New Insco Mines Ltd. (QUE) reorganized in British Columbia as Nuinsco Resources Ltd. 10/15/1979 which reincorporated in Ontario 07/26/1989

INSCOR INC (NV)
Recapitalized as Oicintra, Inc. 01/14/2016
Each share Common $0.0001 par exchanged for (0.0001) share Common $0.0001 par

INSCRUTOR INC (DE)
Name changed to Metha Energy Solutions Inc. 10/12/2009
Metha Energy Solutions Inc. name changed to China Network Media Inc. 12/13/2012

INSECTA RESH CORP 1986 INC (CANADA)
Struck off register and declared dissolved for failure to file returns 11/03/1995

INSEQ CORP (DE)
Name changed to GS Energy Corp. 07/19/2006
GS Energy Corp. recapitalized as EcoSystem Corp. 02/12/2008 which recapitalized as Adarna Energy Corp. 07/07/2011
(See Adarna Energy Corp.)

INSHAPE INTL INC (NV)
Name changed to Pierce International Discovery Inc. (New) 01/31/2000
Pierce International Discovery, Inc. (New) name changed to Emergisoft Holding, Inc. 05/14/2001
(See Emergisoft Holding, Inc.)

INSIDE HLDGS INC (YT)
Name changed to SHEP Technologies Inc. 10/07/2002
(See SHEP Technologies Inc.)

INSIDERSTREET COM INC (NV)
Reorganized under the laws of Delaware as Neometrix Technology Group Inc. 04/14/2003
Each share Common $0.001 par exchanged for (1/7) share Common $0.001 par
(See Neometrix Technology Group Inc.)

INSIGHT COMMUNICATIONS INC (DE)
Merged into Carlyle Group 12/16/2005
Each share Class A Common 1¢ par exchanged for $11.75 cash

INSIGHT ENERGY CORP (NV)
Recapitalized as Sun Sports & Entertainment, Inc. 3/7/2007
Each (32) shares Common $0.0001 par exchanged for (1) share Common $0.0001 par

INSIGHT ENTERTAINMENT CORP (DE)
SEC revoked common stock registration 11/23/2009

INSIGHT ENVIRONMENTAL CORP (CO)
Reorganized under the laws of Maryland as American Equity Trust Inc. 07/17/1995
Each (22.5) shares Common no par exchanged for (1) share Common no par
(See American Equity Trust Inc.)

INSIGHT HEALTH SVCS CORP (DE)
Merged into InSight Health Services Acquisition Corp. 10/17/2001
Each share Common $0.001 par exchanged for $18 cash

INSIGHT HEALTH SVCS HLDGS CORP (DE)
Plan of reorganization under Chapter 11 Federal Bankruptcy proceedings effective 03/23/2011
No stockholders' equity

INSIGHT MANAGMENT CORP (FL)
Common $0.001 par changed to $0.00014 par and (6) additional shares issued payable 11/09/2009 to holders of record 11/06/2009 Ex date - 11/10/2009
Each share old Common $0.00014 par exchanged for (0.001) share new Common $0.00014 par 02/23/2011
Each share new Common $0.00014 par exchanged again for (0.002) share new Common $0.00014 par 09/17/2012
Recapitalized as Striper Energy, Inc. 04/20/2016
Each share new Common $0.00014 par exchanged for (0.03333333) share Common $0.0001 par

INSIGHT MED GROUP INC (DE)
SEC revoked common stock registration 03/08/2011

INSIGHTFUL CORP (DE)
Merged into TIBCO Software Inc. 09/03/2008
Each share Common 1¢ par exchanged for $1.87 cash

INSIGHTFULMIND LEARNING INC (BC)
Name changed to Coronus Solar Inc. 01/15/2010

INSIGHTS SVC CORP (FL)
Administratively dissolved 09/26/2008

INSIGNIA / ESG HLDGS INC (DE)
Name changed to Insignia Financial Group, Inc. (New) 10/29/98
(See Insignia Financial Group, Inc. (New))

INSIGNIA ENERGY LTD (AB)
Acquired by Brookfield Capital Partners Ltd. 07/19/2013
Each share Common no par exchanged for $1.35 cash
Note: Unexchanged certificates were cancelled and became without value 07/19/2016

INSIGNIA FINANCIAL GROUP INC NEW (DE)
Merged into CBRE Holdings, Inc. 7/23/2003

Each share Common 1¢ par exchanged for $11.156 cash

INSIGNIA FINL GROUP INC OLD (DE)
Each share old Class A Common 1¢ par exchanged for (1/3) share new Class A Common 1¢ par 8/1/93
New Class A Common 1¢ par split (2) for (1) by issuance of (1) additional share payable 1/29/96 to holders of record 1/15/96 Ex date - 1/30/96
Each share Class A Common 1¢ par received distribution of (0.6667) share Insignia/ESG Holdings, Inc. Common 1¢ par payable 9/21/98 to holders of record 9/15/98 Ex date - 9/22/98
Merged into Apartment Investment & Management Co. 9/24/98
Each share new Class A Common 1¢ par exchanged for (0.238) share Class E Conv. Preferred 1¢ par

INSIGNIA PPTYS TR (MD)
Merged into Apartment Investment & Management Co. 2/26/99
Each share Common 1¢ par exchanged for (0.3601) share Class A Common 1¢ par

INSIGNIA SOLUTIONS PLC (ENGLAND & WALES)
Sponsored ADR's for Ordinary 20p par changed to 1p par 09/30/2005
Merged into America's Suppliers, Inc. 12/14/2009
Each Sponsored ADR for Ordinary 1p par exchanged for (0.1) share Common $0.001 par

INSILCO CORP NEW (CT)
Merged 12/12/88
Each share 7% Preferred $25 par exchanged for (1) share 8% Conv. Preferred $25 par 9/4/69
8% Conv. Preferred $25 par called for redemption 11/6/81
Conv. 2nd Preferred Ser. A no par called for redemption 6/30/83
Insilco Corp. (Old) merged into INR Partners 12/12/88
Each share Common $1 par exchanged for $31.65 cash
Plan of Reorganization under Chapter 11 Bankruptcy Code effective 4/1/93
Each share Insilco Corp. (New) Common received an undetermined amount Common $0.001 par
Merged into Insilco Holding Co. 8/14/98
Each share Common $0.001 par exchanged for (0.03378) share Common $0.001 par and $43.48 cash
(See Insilco Holding Co.)

INSILCO HLDG CO (DE)
Plan of reorganization under Chapter 11 Federal Bankruptcy Code effective 10/6/2004
No stockholders' equity

INSILICON CORP (DE)
Issue Information - 3,500,000 shares COM offered at $12 per share on 03/22/2000
Merged into Synopsys, Inc. 9/20/2002
Each share Common $0.001 par exchanged for $4.05 cash

INSITE VISION INC (DE)
Acquired by Sun Pharmaceutical Industries Ltd. 11/02/215
Each share Common 1¢ par exchanged for $0.35 cash

INSITUFORM EAST INC (DE)
Common 4¢ par split (2) for (1) by issuance of (1) additional share 04/21/1983
Common 4¢ par split (3) for (2) by issuance of (0.5) additional share 10/30/1985
Stock Dividend - 10% 06/27/1986
Name changed to INEI Corp. 09/05/2003
(See INEI Corp.)

INSITUFORM GROUP LTD (ENGLAND)
Ordinary Stock 1p par split (2) for (1) by issuance of (1) additional share 08/29/1986
Merged into Insituform of North America, Inc. 12/09/1992
Each share Ordinary Stock 1p par exchanged for (0.555) share Class A Common 1¢ par
Insituform of North America, Inc. name changed to Insituform Technologies, Inc. 12/09/1992 which name changed to Aegion Corp. 10/26/2011

INSITUFORM GULF SOUTH INC (TX)
Name changed to Naylor Industries Inc. (TX) 03/01/1991
Naylor Industries Inc. (TX) reincorporated in Delaware 06/16/1992
(See Naylor Industries Inc.)

INSITUFORM MID AMER INC (DE)
Class A Common 1¢ par split (4) for (3) by issuance of (1/3) share 01/11/1993
Merged into Insituform Technologies, Inc. 10/26/1995
Each share Class A Common 1¢ par exchanged for (1.15) shares Class A Common 1¢ par
Insituform Technologies, Inc. name changed to Aegion Corp. 10/26/2011

INSITUFORM NORTH AMER INC (DE)
Name changed to Insituform Technologies, Inc. 12/09/1992
Insituform Technologies, Inc. name changed to Aegion Corp. 10/26/2011

INSITUFORM SOUTHEAST CORP (DE)
Name changed to Enviroq Corp. 11/01/1990
Enviroq Corp. merged into Insituform Mid-America, Inc. 04/18/1995 which merged into Insituform Technologies, Inc. 10/26/1995

INSITUFORM TECHNOLOGIES INC (DE)
Name changed to Aegion Corp. 10/26/2011

INSLEY MANUFACTURING CO.
Reorganized as Insley Manufacturing Corp. 00/00/1936
Details not available

INSLEY MFG CORP (IN)
Common no par changed to $10 par 00/00/1950
Common $10 par split (3) for (2) by issuance of (0.5) additional share 03/03/1965
Stock Dividends - 200% 12/27/1946; 100% 12/30/1947; 25% 08/15/1955
Merged into Desa Industries, Inc. 08/31/1971
Each share Common $10 par exchanged for $12 cash

INSO CORP (DE)
Secondary Offering - 1,200,000 shares COM offered at $49.75 per share on 10/31/1996
Common 1¢ par split (2) for (1) by issuance of (1) additional share 9/1/95
Name changed to EBT International, Inc. 8/25/2000
(See EBT International, Inc.)

INSPAN INVTS LTD (AB)
Recapitalized as Slade Energy Inc. 06/12/1998
Each share Common no par exchanged for (0.25) share Common no par
Slade Energy Inc. name changed to Westpoint Energy Inc. 04/10/2000
(See Westpoint Energy Inc.)

INSPEECH INC (DE)
Common 1¢ par split (2) for (1) by issuance of (1) additional share 06/22/1987
Name changed to NovaCare, Inc. 10/19/1989
NovaCare, Inc. name changed to NAHC, Inc. 03/28/2000 which merged into J.L. Halsey Corp. 06/18/2002 which name changed to Lyris, Inc. 11/15/2007
(See Lyris, Inc.)

INSPIRATION CONS COPPER CO (ME)
Common $20 par changed to $10 par and (1) additional share issued 5/10/63
Common $10 par changed to $1 par 4/28/69
Under plan of merger each share Common $1 par exchanged for (1) share $1.80 Class A Preferred no par 1/1/79
$1.80 Preferred Class A no par called for redemption 4/1/92

INSPIRATION LTD (QC)
Common $5 par changed to no par 09/16/1964
Placed in bankruptcy 04/13/1970
Details not available

INSPIRATION MINING & DEVELOPMENT CO., LTD. (QC)
Recapitalized as Inspiration Ltd. 08/31/1962
Each share Capital Stock $1 par exchanged for (0.2) share Common $5 par
(See Inspiration Ltd.)

INSPIRATION MNG CORP (BC)
Reincorporated under the laws of Ontario 08/18/2008

INSPIRATION PRODS GROUP INC (NV)
Name changed to MB-Tech, Inc. 05/18/2003
(See MB-Tech, Inc.)

INSPIRATION RES CORP (MD)
Name changed to Terra Industries Inc. 05/06/1992
Terra Industries Inc. merged into CF Industries Holdings, Inc. 04/15/2010

INSPIRE INS SOLUTIONS INC (TX)
Issue Information - 2,300,000 shares COM offered at $31.50 per share on 05/27/1998
Common 1¢ par split (3) for (2) by issuance of (0.5) additional share payable 8/17/98 to holders of record 7/31/98
Plan of reorganization under Chapter 11 Federal Bankruptcy Code effective 12/2/2002
No stockholders' equity

INSPIRE PHARMACEUTICALS INC (DE)
Issue Information - 5,500,000 shares COM offered at $12 per share on 08/02/2000
Acquired by Merck & Co., Inc. (New) 05/17/2011
Each share Common $0.001 par exchanged for $5 cash

INSPRIT INC (KOREA)
ADR agreement terminated 08/13/2014
No ADR's remain outstanding

INSTA COOL INC NORTH AMER (DE)
Name changed to ThermoGenesis Corp. 01/12/1995
ThermoGenesis Corp. name changed to Cesca Therapeutics Inc. 02/20/2014

INSTA FAX COMMUNICATIONS N Y INC (NY)
Acquired by Great Southwestern Industries, Inc. 9/7/72
Each share Common 10¢ par exchanged for (0.5) share Common 1¢ par
Great Southwestern Industries, Inc. name changed to New American Video, Inc. 2/26/81 which recapitalized as Tropicana, Inc. 6/18/83

INSTA RENT INC (ON)
Acquired by easyhome Ltd. 11/07/2008
Each share Common no par exchanged for $0.50 cash

INSTACARE CORP (NV)
Each share old Common $0.001 par exchanged for (0.0125) share new Common $0.001 par 02/03/2006
Stock Dividend - 8.334% payable 06/16/2006 to holders of record 06/09/2006
Recapitalized as Decision Diagnostics Corp. 12/01/2011
Each (14) shares new Common $0.001 par exchanged for (1) share Common $0.001 par

INSTACOM INC (TX)
Merged into Comdata Network, Inc. 10/28/83
Each share Common 10¢ par exchanged for (0.701) share Common 2¢ par
(See Comdata Network, Inc.)

INSTAFF INTL INC (TX)
SEC revoked common stock registration 02/11/2013

INSTANET INC (NV)
Name changed to VitaCube Systems Holdings, Inc. 09/08/2003
VitaCube Systems Holdings, Inc. name changed to XELR8 Holdings, Inc. 03/19/2007 which name changed to Bazi International, Inc. 10/01/2010 which recapitalized as True Drinks Holdings, Inc. 01/22/2013

INSTANT COMPUTER SYS LTD (DE)
Charter cancelled and declared inoperative and void for non-payment of taxes 4/15/72

INSTANT HOT WTR INC (NV)
Recapitalized as Western Medical Industries, Inc. 08/29/1972
Each share Common 1¢ par exchanged for (1/30) share Common 2¢ par
Western Medical Industries, Inc. name changed to Ameracol Technology, Inc. 11/04/1980 which name changed to Chiropractic 21 International, Inc. 05/31/1983 which name changed to visionGATEWAY, Inc. 03/10/2004
(See visionGATEWAY, Inc.)

INSTANT IDENTIFICATION SYSTEMS CORP. (DE)
Name changed to Faraday National Corp. 11/01/1978
(See Faraday National Corp.)

INSTANT MED TESTS INC (CO)
Charter dissolved 6/3/96

INSTANT PUBLISHER INC (ON)
Name changed to Diversinet Corp. 02/05/1997
(See Diversinet Corp.)

INSTANT TRANSACTIONS CORP AMER (NY)
Completely liquidated 1/18/90
Each share Common 1¢ par received first and final distribution of $1.56 cash
Note: Certificates were not required to be surrendered and are now valueless

INSTANT VIDEO TECHNOLOGIES INC (DE)
Each share old Common $0.00001 par exchanged for (0.07142857) share new Common $0.00001 par 12/21/1992
Name changed to Burst.com, Inc. 01/27/2000
Burst.com, Inc. name changed to Democrasoft, Inc. 04/27/2010 which name changed to Democrasoft Holdings, Inc. 04/22/2013

INSTAPAY SYS INC (UT)
SEC revoked common stock registration 10/17/2007

INSTAR ENERGY CORP (BC)
Struck off register and declared dissolved for failure to file returns 08/22/1994

INSTASAN PHARMACEUTICALS INC (NY)
Charter cancelled and proclaimed dissolved for failure to pay taxes 12/23/1992

INSTENT INC (DE)
Merged into Medtronic Inc. (MN) 06/28/1996
Each share Common 1¢ par exchanged for (0.3833) share Common 10¢ par
Medtronic Inc. (MN) reincorporated in Ireland as Medtronic PLC 01/27/2015

INSTEP MOBILE COMMUNICATIONS INC (BC)
Name changed to eDispatch.com Wireless Data Inc. (BC) 11/20/1998
eDispatch.com Wireless Data Inc. (BC) reincorporated in Canada as AirIQ Inc. 07/31/2002

INSTILL REFINERS, INC. (DE)
No longer in existence having become inoperative and void for non-payment of taxes 4/1/35

INSTINET CORP (DE)
Common 25¢ par split (2) for (1) by issuance of (1) additional share 05/09/1986
Merged into Reuters Holdings PLC 05/13/1987
Each share Common 25¢ par exchanged for (0.1269) ADR for Ordinary B 10p par
Reuters Holdings PLC reorganized as Reuters Group PLC 02/18/1998 which merged into Thomson Reuters PLC 04/17/2008 which exchanged for Thomson Reuters Corp. 09/10/2009

INSTINET GROUP INC (DE)
Issue Information - 32,000,000 shares COM offered at $14.50 per share on 05/17/2001
Merged into Nasdaq Stock Market, Inc. 12/8/2005
Each share Common 1¢ par exchanged for approximately $5.0881 cash

INSTITUTE BROADCAST ARTS INC (WI)
Name changed to IBA, Inc. 01/13/1982
(See IBA, Inc.)

INSTITUTE COMPUTER TECHNOLOGY INC (DE)
Name changed to American List Corp. 12/19/1972
American List Corp. merged into Snyder Communications Inc. 07/11/1997 which merged into Havas Advertising S.A. 09/26/2000 which name changed to Havas S.A. 05/24/2002
(See Havas S.A.)

INSTITUTE COSMETIC SURGERY INC (NV)
Name changed to Petrex Corp. (New) 11/06/2000
Petrex Corp. (New) recapitalized as Force 10 Trading, Inc. 12/30/2001 which recapitalized as F10 Oil & Gas Properties, Inc. 12/03/2002 which name changed to GFY Foods, Inc. 01/12/2004 which recapitalized as Upturn, Inc. 03/20/2009 which recapitalized as Cityside Tickets Inc. 12/10/2009 which name changed to Causeway Entertainment Co. 10/11/2010 which recapitalized as United Bullion Exchange Inc. 05/10/2011

INSTITUTE FOR LAB MED INC (FL)
Each share old Common $0.001 par exchanged for (0.25) share new Common $0.001 par 10/28/1991
Name changed to Specialty Retail Group, Inc. 06/30/1993
Specialty Retail Group, Inc. name changed to TBM Holdings, Inc. 06/15/1999
(See TBM Holdings, Inc.)

INSTITUTE OF CLINICAL PHARMACOLOGY (IRELAND)
Stock Dividend - 200% 02/08/1989
Placed in receivership 00/00/1990
No ADR holders' equity

INSTITUTIONAL EQUITY CORP (DE)
Reincorporated 12/29/1970
State of incorporation changed from (TX) to (DE) 12/29/1970
Completely liquidated 09/14/1984
Each share Common 10¢ par exchanged for first and final distribution of $2.91 cash

INSTITUTIONAL EQUITY HLDGS INC (NV)
Recapitalized as Shing-Mei International, Inc. 04/03/2008
Each share Common 1¢ par exchanged for (0.1) share Common 1¢ par
Shing-Mei International, Inc. name changed to Triad Pro Innovators, Inc. 01/25/2012

INSTITUTIONAL FIDUCIARY TR (MA)
Reincorporated under the laws of Delaware 08/01/2007

INSTITUTIONAL FINL MKTS INC (MD)
Reorganized as Cohen & Co. Inc. (New) 09/05/2017
Each share Common $0.001 par exchanged for (0.1) share Common 1¢ par

INSTITUTIONAL HOLDING CORP. (IL)
Liquidation completed
Each share Common no par exchanged for initial distribution of $1.52 cash 06/15/1970
Each share Common no par received second and final distribution of $0.029733 cash 04/28/1975

INSTITUTIONAL INCOME FUND, INC. (MD)
Name changed to Channing Income Fund, Inc. 04/01/1964
Channing Income Fund, Inc. merged into American General Shares, Inc. 09/02/1975 which merged into American General Enterprise Fund, Inc. 08/31/1979 which name changed to American Capital Enterprise Fund, Inc. (MD) 09/09/1983 which reincorporated in Delaware as Van Kampen American Capital Enterprise Fund 08/03/1995 which name changed to Van Kampen Enterprise Fund 08/31/1998

INSTITUTIONAL INS CO AMER (IL)
Merged into Institutional Holding Corp. 11/06/1969
Each share Common $1 par exchanged for (1) share Common no par
(See Institutional Holding Corp.)

INSTITUTIONAL INVS CORP (DE)
Reorganized 5/27/83
Reorganized from Institutional Investors Trust (MA) to under the laws of Delaware as Institutional Investors Corp. and Shares of Bene. Int. no par reclassified as Common 1¢ par 5/27/83
Under plan of merger name changed to Unicorp American Corp. (New) 2/15/84
Unicorp American Corp. (New) recapitalized as Lincorp Holdings Inc. 9/15/92
(See Lincorp Holdings Inc.)

INSTITUTIONAL INVESTORS FIXED INCOME FUND (NY)
Name changed to Institutional Investors Mutual Funds Convertible Securities Fund 8/1/85

INSTITUTIONAL INVS SYS INC (NY)
Merged into T.N.C. International Publishers Inc. 08/01/1974
Each share Common 1¢ par exchanged for $3 cash

INSTITUTIONAL MORTGAGE INSURANCE CO. (GA)
Merged into Continental Mortgage Insurance, Inc. 1/1/66
Each share Common $2.50 par exchanged for (2/3) share Common $2.50 par
(See Continental Mortgage Insurance, Inc.)

INSTITUTIONAL NETWORKS CORP (DE)
Each share Common 10¢ par exchanged for (0.1) share Common $1 par 06/21/1982
Common $1 par changed to 25¢ par and (3) additional shares issued 06/22/1983
Name changed to Instinet Corp. 06/07/1985
Instinet Corp. merged into Reuters Holdings PLC 05/13/1987 which reorganized as Reuters Group PLC 02/18/1998 which merged into Thomson Reuters PLC 04/17/2008 which was exchanged for Thomson Reuters Corp. 09/10/2009

INSTITUTIONAL SECS COLO INC (CO)
Charter suspended for failure to file annual reports 12/06/1977

INSTITUTIONAL SECURITIES, LTD. (DE)
Name changed to Institutional Shares, Ltd. 03/20/1946
Institutional Shares, Ltd. name changed to Channing Shares, Inc. (DE) 04/01/1964 which reincorporated in Maryland 10/09/1973 which merged into American General Shares, Inc. 09/02/1975 which merged into American General Enterprise Fund, Inc. 08/31/1979 which name changed to American Capital Enterprise Fund, Inc. (MD) 09/09/1983 which reincorporated in Delaware as Van Kampen American Capital Enterprise Fund 08/03/1995 which name changed to Van Kampen Enterprise Fund 08/31/1998

INSTITUTIONAL SHARES, LTD. (DE)
Each old Bank Fund Share 1¢ par exchanged for (0.1) new Bank Fund Share 1¢ par 05/06/1955
Each old Insurance Fund Share 1¢ par exchanged for (0.1) new Insurance Fund Share 1¢ par 05/06/1955
Growth Fund Shares 1¢ par split (2) for (1) by issuance of (1) additional share 05/27/1955
Foundation Fund Shares 1¢ par split (2) for (1) by issuance of (1) additional share 05/27/1955
Each new Bank Fund Share 1¢ par exchanged for (1.201406) Foundation Fund Shares 1¢ par 03/16/1960
Each new Insurance Fund Share 1¢ par exchanged for (1.151764) Foundation Fund Shares 1¢ par 03/16/1960
Name changed to Channing Shares, Inc. (DE) and Foundation Fund Shares reclassified as Balanced Fund Shares 04/01/1964
Channing Shares, Inc. (DE) reincorporated in Maryland 10/09/1973 which merged into American General Shares, Inc. 09/02/1975 which merged into American General Enterprise Fund, Inc. 08/31/1979 which name changed to American Capital Enterprise Fund, Inc. (MD) 09/09/1983 which reincorporated in Delaware as Van Kampen American Capital Enterprise Fund 08/03/1995 which name changed to Van Kampen Enterprise Fund 08/31/1998

INSTITUTIONAL STRATEGIES CORP (DE)
Charter cancelled and declared inoperative and void for non-payment of taxes 3/1/97

INSTORAGE REAL ESTATE INVT TR (ON)
Each old Trust Unit no par exchanged for (0.125) new Trust Unit no par 02/20/2008
Acquired by Canada TKG-StorageMart Partners II, LP 03/19/2009
Each Trust Unit no par exchanged for $4 cash

INSTRACORP (DE)
Recapitalized as Worldwide Web Networx Corp. 05/18/1998
Each share Common no par exchanged for (0.2) share Common no par
(See Worldwide Web Networx Corp.)

INSTRON CORP (MA)
Common $1 par split (5) for (4) by issuance of (0.25) additional share 11/24/1967
Common $1 par split (2) for (1) by issuance of (1) additional share 06/01/1983
Common $1 par split (3) for (2) by issuance of (0.5) additional share 06/05/1985
Common $1 par split (2) for (1) by issuance of (1) additional share 06/04/1986
Stock Dividends - 10% 01/21/1966; 10% 01/20/1967
Preferred Stock Purchase Rights declared for Common stockholders of record 11/14/1988 were redeemed at $0.02 per right 01/03/1992 for holders of record 12/13/1991
Merged into ISN Acquisition Corp. 10/01/1999
Each share Common $1 par exchanged for $22 cash

INSTRON ENGINEERING CORP. (MA)
Name changed to Instron Corp. 6/12/64
(See Instron Corp.)

INSTRUCTIONAL COMPUTER SVCS INC (UT)
Recapitalized as Pacific Basin Resources, Ltd. 06/12/1986
Each share Common $0.0001 par exchanged for (0.01) share Common $0.0001 par

INSTRUCTIONAL MEDIA AMER INC (NY)
Name changed to Prema Facemaster Systems, Inc. 04/30/1971
(See Prema Facemaster Systems, Inc.)

INSTRUCTIVE DEVICES INC (DE)
Merged into Avtek Corp. 01/31/1972
Each share Common 5¢ par exchanged for (0.4) share Common 4¢ par
(See Avtek Corp.)

INSTRUMENT DEV CORP (DE)
Charter cancelled and declared inoperative and void for non-payment of taxes 3/1/84

INSTRUMENT SYS CORP (DE)
Reincorporated 04/15/1971
State of incorporation changed from (NY) to (DE) 04/15/1971
Each share old Common 25¢ par exchanged for (0.1) share new Common 25¢ par 08/10/1981
Each share $12.50 Exchangeable Preferred 25¢ par exchanged for $100 principal amount of 12-1/2% Subordinated Debentures due 11/15/1997 effective 11/15/1988
Stock Dividends - In Common to holders of 2nd Preferred Ser. I - 22% 06/30/1976; 25% 06/30/1977; 25% 06/30/1978; 22% 06/30/1979; 25% 06/30/1980; 25% 06/30/1981; 15% 06/30/1982; 12% 06/29/1984; 14% 06/28/1985
Name changed to Griffon Corp. 03/03/1995

INSTRUMENT TECHNOLOGY CORP (DE)
Name changed to Aerosonic Corp. (DE) 09/21/1970
(See Aerosonic Corp.)

INSTRUMENTARIUM CORP (FINLAND)
ADR's for Ordinary FIM 20 par changed to FIM 10 par and (1) additional ADR issued 04/29/1994
ADR's for Class B FIM 10 par split (2) for (1) by issuance of (0.1) additional share 04/03/2002
ADR basis changed from (1:2) to (1:1) 04/03/2002
Stock Dividends - 50% 12/18/1984; 20% 02/11/1988
Acquired by General Electric Co. 10/09/2003
Each ADR for Class B Ordinary FIM 10 par exchanged for $36 cash

INSTRUMENTATION LAB INC (MA)
Common $1 par split (5) for (4) by issuance of (0.25) additional share 08/08/1978
Merged into Allied Corp. 04/29/1983
Each share Common $1 par exchanged for (0.95) share Common $1 par
Allied Corp. merged into Allied-Signal Inc. 09/19/1985 which name changed to AlliedSignal Inc. 04/26/1993 which name changed to Honeywell International Inc. 12/01/1999

INSTRUMENTATION LAB S P A (ITALY)
ADR agreement terminated 4/29/2006
Each Sponsored ADR for Ordinary exchanged for $0.98 cash

INSU INNOVATIONS GROUP INC (CANADA)
Name changed to MTY Food Group Inc. 07/08/2003

INSUL-8-CORP. (CA)
Each share Common $1 par exchanged for (5) shares Common 20¢ par 05/01/1958
Completely liquidated 11/04/1966
Each share Common 20¢ par exchanged for first and final distribution of (0.142857) share Rucker Co. Common no par
Rucker Co. merged into N L Industries, Inc. 01/21/1977

INSUL-CUP CORP. OF AMERICA (NY)
Bankrupt in 1963; no stockholders' equity

INSULAR, INC. (UT)
Name changed to Gentner Electronics Co. 03/26/1985
Gentner Electronics Co. name changed to Gentner Communications Corp. 07/01/1991 which name changed to ClearOne Communications Inc. 01/02/2002

INSULAR EXPLS LTD (BC)
Name changed to Masuparia Gold Corp. 09/01/1999
Masuparia Gold Corp. name changed to MAS Gold Corp. 04/09/2018

INSULAR LMBR CO (NY)
Liquidation completed
Each share Capital Stock $10 par

received initial distribution of $24 cash 07/23/1973
Each share Capital Stock $10 par received second distribution of $7 cash 02/08/1974
Each share Capital Stock $10 par received third distribution of $6 cash 09/06/1974
Each share Capital Stock $10 par received fourth distribution of $5 cash 08/07/1975
Each share Capital Stock $10 par received fifth and final distribution of $2.53 cash 02/11/1976
Note: Certificates were not required to be surrendered and are without value

INSULATED SHIPPING CONTAINERS INC (CA)
Each share old Common no par exchanged for (0.1) share new Common no par 3/24/93
Merged into Svenska Cellulosa Aktiebolaget SCA 9/17/2001
Each share new Common no par exchanged for $3.73 cash

INSULBLOCK SYS INC (ON)
Struck off register and dissolved dissolved for failure to file returns 09/03/1994

INSULL UTILITY INVESTMENTS, INC.
Bankrupt 00/00/1932
Details not available

INSULPRO INDS INC (CANADA)
Merged into Builder Products of Canada Inc. 12/22/1998
Each share Common no par exchanged for $1.20 cash

INSURANCE & BK STK FD INC (MD)
Name changed to ICM Financial Fund, Inc. 02/24/1970
ICM Financial Fund, Inc. acquired by Pilgrim Fund, Inc. 12/21/1971 which merged into Pilgrim Magnacap Fund, Inc. 06/20/1985

INSURANCE & SECS INC (CA)
Name changed to ISI Corp. 04/17/1969
ISI Corp. recapitalized as California Windsor Co. 05/24/1974 which merged into Hutton (E.F.) Group Inc. 02/21/1978
(See Hutton (E.F.) Group Inc.)

INSURANCE AUTO AUCTIONS INC (IL)
Reincorporated 8/20/97
State of incorporation changed from (CA) to (IL) 8/20/97
Merged into Axle Holdings Inc. 5/25/2005
Each share Common $0.001 par exchanged for $28.25 cash

INSURANCE CITY LIFE CO (CT)
Capital Stock $10 par changed to $1 par and (9) additional shares issued 02/26/1963
Dissolved 04/22/1975
No stockholders' equity

INSURANCE CO. OF OREGON (OR)
Merged into Transpacific Life Insurance Co. 12/31/1965
Each share Common $2.50 par exchanged for (6) shares Common 30¢ par
Transpacific Life Insurance Co. merged into American Guaranty Life Insurance Co. (OR) 10/04/1967 which reorganized as American Guaranty Corp. (OR) 07/01/1969 which name changed to American Guaranty Financial Corp. 12/04/1970 which name changed to Encore Group Inc. 07/18/1990
(See Encore Group Inc.)

INSURANCE CO. OF TEXAS (TX)
Name changed to ICT Insurance Co. in 1954
(See ICT Insurance Co.)

INSURANCE CO. OF THE SOUTH (FL)
Class A Common $10 par & Class B Common $10 par changed to $5 par 06/14/1957
Each share Class A Common $5 par exchanged for (3.5) shares Common $5 par 07/12/1957
Each share Class B Common $5 par exchanged for (1) share Common $5 par 07/12/1957
Each share Common $5 par exchanged for (5) shares Common $1 par 03/25/1959
6% Preferred $100 par called for redemption 00/00/1966
Merged into Carolina Casualty Insurance Co. (FL) 03/31/1966
Each share Common $1 par exchanged for (0.539) share Common $1 par
Carolina Casualty Insurance Co. (FL) merged into Berkley (W. R.) Corp. 01/30/1985

INSURANCE CO NORTH AMER (PA)
Each share Capital Stock $10 par exchanged for (2) shares Capital Stock $5 par 00/00/1951
Stock Dividends - 20% 12/31/1949; 20% 12/31/1953; 20% 05/18/1956; 100% 06/15/1960
Acquired by INA Corp. 05/29/1968
Each share Capital Stock $5 par exchanged for (2) shares Common $1 par
INA Corp. merged into Cigna Corp. 04/01/1982

INSURANCE CO ST PA (PA)
Each share Capital Stock $100 par exchanged for (10) shares Capital Stock $10 par in 1936
Stock Dividend - 20% 10/4/55
Acquired by American Home Assurance Co. 7/26/68
Each share Capital Stock $10 par exchanged for (4) shares Common $2.50 par
(See American Home Assurance Co.)

INSURANCE CORP. OF AMERICA (IN)
Common $1 par changed to 50¢ par and (1) additional share issued 7/16/56
Taken over by Indiana Department of Insurance 9/17/62 which forced liquidation
No stockholders' equity

INSURANCE EXCHANGE BUILDING, INC. (CA)
Liquidated in 1941
Details not available

INSURANCE EXCHANGE BUILDING (MA)
Reorganized as Boston Insurance Exchange Building, Inc. on a share for share basis in 1939
(See Boston Insurance Exchange Building, Inc.)

INSURANCE EXCHANGE BUILDING CORP. (IL)
Each share Common $100 par exchanged for (7.5) shares Common $10 par 00/00/1949
Name changed to I.E.B. Corp. 12/20/1967
(See I.E.B. Corp.)

INSURANCE INDS INC (DE)
Charter cancelled and declared inoperative and void for non-payment of taxes 3/1/76

INS INSURANCE NETWORK SYS INC (BC)
Recapitalized as World Marketing Corp. 03/09/1992
Each share Common no par exchanged for (0.2) share Common no par
(See World Marketing Corp.)

INSURANCE INVT CORP (ID)
Name changed to First Idaho Corp. 5/14/77
(See First Idaho Corp.)

INSURANCE INVESTORS, INC. (IA)
Name changed to Guardsman Insurance Investors Inc. 3/20/63
(See Guardsman Insurance Investors, Inc.)

INSURANCE INVS & HLDG CO (IL)
Merged into Citizens, Inc. 3/12/96
Each share Class A Common $1 par exchanged for (0.125) share Class A Common $1 par

INSURANCE INVS FD INC (DE)
Name changed to First Sierra Fund 06/30/1969
First Sierra Fund merged into Founders Special Fund, Inc. 07/11/1973 which reorganized as Founders Funds, Inc. 08/31/1987 which name changed to Dreyfus Founders Funds, Inc. 12/31/1999 which name changed to Dreyfus Discovery Fund 12/01/2008

INSURANCE INVESTORS TRUST CO. (KY)
Into receivership in September 1967
Holders of Common no par had to file Proof of Claim no later than 8/30/71
For each $1 of allowed claim holders received $0.127 cash 1/25/73

INSURANCE MGMT SOLUTIONS GROUP INC (FL)
Issue Information - 3,350,000 shares COM offered at $11 per share on 02/10/1999
Merged into Fiserv, Inc. 9/24/2003
Each share Common 1¢ par exchanged for $3.30 cash

INSURANCE SECURITIES CO., INC. (LA)
Bankrupt in 1936
No stockholders' equity

INSURANCE SECURITIES INC. (CA)
Capital Stock no par split (3) for (1) by issuance of (2) additional shares 7/20/62
Capital Stock no par split (2) for (1) by issuance of (1) additional share 6/12/64
Name changed to Insurance & Securities Inc. 11/22/67
Insurance & Securities Inc. name changed to ISI Corp. 4/17/69 which recapitalized as California Windsor Co. 5/24/74 which merged into Hutton (E.F.) Group Inc. 2/21/78
(See Hutton (E.F.) Group Inc.)

INSURANSHARES & GENERAL MANAGEMENT CO.
Liquidation completed in 1937
Details not available

INSURANSHARES CERTIFICATES INC. (MD)
Capital Stock no par changed to $1 par 00/00/1933
Liquidation completed
Each share Capital Stock $1 par exchanged for initial distribution of (0.035) share Aetna Casualty & Surety Co. Capital Stock $3.50 par, (0.055) share American Re-Insurance Co. Capital Stock $5 par, (0.017) share Federal Insurance Co. Capital Stock $4 par, (0.336) share Hartford Fire Insurance Co. Capital Stock $5 par, (0.145) share Insurance Co. of North America Capital Stock $5 par, (0.121) share Northwestern National Insurance Co. Capital Stock $5 par and (0.077) share St. Paul Fire & Marine Insurance Co. Capital Stock $6.25 par 12/31/1962
Each share Capital Stock $1 par received second distribution of $0.902563 cash 11/15/1963
Each share Capital Stock $1 par received third distribution of $0.380477 cash 01/29/1965
Each share Capital Stock $1 par received fourth and final distribution of $0.1320948 cash 06/23/1966

INSURANSHARES CORP. OF DELAWARE
Liquidation completed in 1950
Details not available

INSURANSHARES CORP. OF NEW YORK
Reorganized as General Shares, Inc. in 1931
Details not available

INSURANSHARES MANAGEMENT CO.
Name changed to Insuranshares & General Management Co. in 1930
(See Insuranshares & General Management Co.)

INSURCOM FINL CORP (AB)
Name changed to Omega World Inc. and Class A no par reclassified as Common no par 09/17/2007

INSURE COM INC (DE)
Name changed to Life Quotes, Inc. 10/28/2009
(See Life Quotes, Inc.)

INSURED ACCOUNTS FUND, INC. (MA)
Each share old Common $1 par exchanged for (5) shares new Common $1 par 9/1/64
Completely liquidated
Each share new Common $1 par exchanged for first and final distribution of $1,000 cash 4/1/66

INSURED INCOME PPTYS LTD PARTNERSHIP (DE)
Merged into Hardee's Lease Partners L.P. 6/1/94
Each Unit of Ltd. Partnership Int. 1981 Ser. exchanged for (24.021108) shares Common 1¢ par
Each Unit of Ltd. Partnership Int. 1982 Ser. exchanged for (21.628380) shares Common 1¢ par
Each Unit of Ltd. Partnership Int. 1983 Ser. exchanged for (19.183160) shares Common 1¢ par
Each Unit of Ltd. Partnership Int. 1984 Ser. exchanged for (19.807427) shares Common 1¢ par
Each Unit of Ltd. Partnership Int. 1985 Ser. exchanged for (21.997695) shares Common 1¢ par
Each Unit of Ltd. Partnership Int. 1986 Ser. exchanged for (45.420046) shares Common 1¢ par
Each Unit of Ltd. Partnership Int. 1988 Ser. exchanged for (41.804263) shares Common 1¢ par

INSURED MUN INCOME FD (MD)
Auction Rate Preferred Shares Ser. E $0.001 par called for redemption at $50,000 on 10/15/2009
Auction Rate Preferred Shares Ser. F $0.001 par called for redemption at $50,000 on 10/16/2009
Name changed to Special Opportunities Fund, Inc. 12/22/2009

INSURED PENSION INVS LTD PARTNERSHIP (DE)
Merged into Franchise Finance Corp. of America (DE) 6/1/94
Each Unit of Ltd. Partnership Int. 1983 Ser. exchanged for (8.130990) shares Common 1¢ par
Each Unit of Ltd. Partnership Int. 1984 Ser. exchanged for (17.657685) shares Common 1¢ par
Each Unit of Ltd. Partnership Int. 1985 Ser. exchanged for (20.469201) shares Common 1¢ par
Franchise Finance Corp. of America (DE) reincorporated in Maryland 12/31/2000
(See Franchise Corp. of America)

FINANCIAL INFORMATION, INC.   INS-INT

INSURORS INVESTING INC (AR)
Charter revoked for failure to pay taxes 02/16/1973

INSWEB CORP (DE)
Each share old Common $0.001 par exchanged for (0.16666666) share new Common $0.001 par 12/20/2001
Name changed to Internet Patents Corp. 12/21/2011
Internet Patents Corp. name changed to Prism Technologies Group, Inc. 09/23/2015

INSYNERGY PRODS INC (NV)
Name changed to Starco Brands, Inc. 09/14/2017

INSYNQ INC (DE)
Reorganized under the laws of Nevada 12/24/2002
Each share Common $0.001 exchanged for (0.01) share Common $0.001 par
(See InsynQ, Inc. (NV))

INSYNQ INC (NV)
Each share old Common $0.001 par exchanged for (0.02) share new Common $0.001 par 08/02/2004
Each share new Common $0.001 par exchanged again for (0.02) share new Common $0.001 par 11/18/2008
SEC revoked common stock registration 05/18/2011

INSYTE CORP. (DE)
Name changed to Insyte Energy Corp. 1/28/83
Insyte Energy Corp. merged into Shannon Group Inc. (TX) 7/27/84

INSYTE ENERGY CORP (DE)
Merged into Shannon Group Inc. (TX) 7/16/84
Each share Common 1¢ par exchanged for (3) shares Common 1¢ par

INT MEDIA GROUP INC (DE)
Name changed to Jupitermedia Corp. 09/01/2002
Jupitermedia Corp. name changed to WebMediaBrands, Inc. 02/24/2009 which name changed to Mediabistro Inc. 06/13/2013 which name changed to Mecklermedia Corp. (New) 08/25/2014
(See Mecklermedia Corp. (New))

INTAC INTL (NV)
Merged into HSW International, Inc. 10/02/2007
Each share Common $0.001 par exchanged for (1) share Common $0.001 par
HSW International, Inc. name changed to Remark Media, Inc. 01/03/2012 which name changed to Remark Holdings, Inc. 04/11/2017

INTACTA TECHNOLOGIES INC (NV)
SEC revoked common stock registration 10/19/2015

INTAKE COMMUNICATIONS INC (FL)
Common $0.0001 par split (13) for (1) by issuance of (12) additional shares payable 01/25/2011 to holders of record 01/24/2011 Ex date - 01/26/2011
Name changed to Game Face Gaming, Inc. 01/28/2011
Game Face Gaming, Inc. name changed to Face Up Entertainment Group, Inc. 04/27/2012

INTASYS CORP (ON)
Each share old Common no par exchanged for (0.1) share new Common no par 07/13/2001
Name changed to Mamma.com Inc. 01/12/2004
Mamma.com Inc. name changed to Copernic Inc. 06/21/2007 which merged into Comamtech Inc. (ON) 11/04/2010 which reincorporated in Delaware as DecisionPoint Systems, Inc. (New) 06/22/2011

INTEC LTD (AUSTRALIA)
Each old Sponsored ADR for Ordinary exchanged for (0.1) new Sponsored ADR for Ordinary 08/16/2010
Name changed to SciDev Ltd. 03/23/2017
(See SciDev Ltd.)

INTECH INC (CA)
Acquired by a private investor group 03/12/1992
Each share Common no par exchanged for $0.875 cash

INTECH INC (MN)
Each share Common 10¢ par exchanged for (0.5) share Common 20¢ par 04/30/1973
Became private through purchase offer which expired 03/31/1978

INTECHNOLOGIES INC (DE)
SEC revoked common stock registration 02/15/2007

INTECOM INC (TX)
Common no par split (2) for (1) by issuance of (1) additional share 9/21/83
Merged into Wang Laboratories, Inc. (MA) 9/3/86
Each share Common no par exchanged for (0.3783) share Class B Common 50¢ par
Wang Laboratories, Inc. (MA) reorganized in (DE) 12/16/93
(See Wang Laboratories, Inc. (DE))

INTEG INC (MN)
Merged into Inverness Medical Technology Inc. 1/23/2001
Each share Common 1¢ par exchanged for (0.173856) Common $0.001 par
Inverness Medical Technology Inc. merged into Johnson & Johnson 11/21/2001

INTEGCOM CORP (DE)
Name changed to Diversified Security Solutions Inc. 07/13/2001
Diversified Security Solutions Inc. name changed to Henry Bros. Electronics, Inc. 08/08/2005
(See Henry Bros. Electronics, Inc.)

INTEGON CORP (DE)
Ctfs. dated prior to 2/27/81
Reincorporated 5/10/79
Common $2.50 par changed to $1 par and (1.5) additional share issued 9/26/69
State of incorporation changed from (NC) to (DE) 5/10/79
Merged into Ashland Oil, Inc. 2/27/81
Each share Common $1 par exchanged for (1) share $3.96 Conv. Preferred 1981 Ser. no par
Ashland Oil, Inc. name changed to Ashland Inc. (Old) 1/27/95
(See Ashland Inc. (Old))

INTEGON CORP (DE)
Ctfs. dated after 2/13/92
Stock Dividend - 10% 12/15/92
Issue Information - 1,250,000 shares PFD CONV $3.875 offered at $50 per share on 10/12/1994
Merged into General Motors Acceptance Corp. 10/17/97
Each share Common 1¢ par exchanged for $26 cash
$3.875 Conv. Preferred 1¢ par called for redemption at $52.33 plus $0.61354 accrued dividend on 11/11/97
Public interest eliminated

INTEGON CORP NEW (DE)
Ctfs. dated after 6/24/87
Merged into Southmark Life Group Inc. 8/1/90
Each share Common $1 par exchanged for $6 cash

INTEGON GROWTH FD (NC)
Merged into Bullock Fund, Ltd. 01/06/1977
Each share Common $1 par exchanged for (0.6287) share Capital Stock $1 par
Bullock Fund, Ltd. name changed to Bullock Growth Shares, Inc. 04/08/1985 which merged into Chemical Fund, Inc. 03/13/1987 which name changed to Alliance Fund, Inc. 04/01/1987 which name changed to Alliance Mid-Capital Growth Fund Inc. 02/01/2002 which name changed to AllianceBernstein Mid-Capital Growth Fund, Inc. 03/31/2003

INTEGRA-A HOTEL & RESTAURANT CO (DE)
Plan of reorganization under Chapter 11 Federal Bankruptcy proceedings confirmed 02/11/1994
Stockholders' equity unlikely

INTEGRA BK CORP (IN)
Filed a petition under Chapter 7 Federal Bankruptcy Code 07/30/2011
Stockholders' equity unlikely

INTEGRA CAP TR I (IN)
8.25% Trust Preferred Securities no par called for redemption at $25 on 7/26/2003

INTEGRA COMPUTER CORP (DE)
Each share old Common $0.001 par exchanged for (0.05) share new Common $0.001 par 6/26/2002
Name changed to Task Management Inc. 7/2/2002
Task Management Inc. name changed to Integra Distribution, Inc. 5/27/2004 which recapitalized as Powerlock International Corp. 8/25/2005

INTEGRA DISTR INC (DE)
Recapitalized as Powerlock International Corp. 8/25/2005
Each (12) shares Common $0.001 par exchanged for (1) share Common $0.001 par

INTEGRA FINL CORP (PA)
$2.31 Conv. Preferred Ser. A called for redemption 04/01/1993
Merged into National City Corp. 05/03/1996
Each share Common $1 par exchanged for (2) shares Common $1 par
National City Corp. acquired by PNC Financial Services Group, Inc. 12/31/2008

INTEGRA GOLD CORP (BC)
Merged into Eldorado Gold Corp. (New) 07/17/2017
Each share Common no par exchanged for (0.18188) share Common no par and $0.30313 cash
Note: Unexchanged certificates will be cancelled and become without value 07/17/2023

INTEGRA INC (DE)
Plan of reorganization under Chapter 11 Federal Bankruptcy Code effective 08/00/2004
No stockholders' equity

INTEGRA LIFESCIENCES CORP (DE)
Each share old Common 1¢ par exchanged for (0.5) share new Common 1¢ par 5/26/98
Name changed to Integra LifeSciences Holdings Corp. 5/17/99

INTEGRA SYS INC (BC)
Struck off register and declared dissolved for failure to file returns 10/29/1993

INTEGRACARE INC (FL)
Merged into Integrated Health Services, Inc. 8/25/95
Each share Common $0.001 par exchanged for (0.2167) share Common $0.001 par
(See Integrated Health Services, Inc.)

INTEGRAL FDG LTD (CAYMAN ISLANDS)
144A Preferred called for redemption 01/17/2017

INTEGRAL SYS INC (MD)
Common 1¢ par split (3) for (1) by issuance of (2) additional shares payable 07/15/1997 to holders of record 07/01/1997
Common 1¢ par split (2) for (1) by issuance of (1) additional share payable 06/25/1998 to holders of record 06/09/1998
Common 1¢ par split (2) for (1) by issuance of (1) additional share payable 09/05/2008 to holders of record 08/25/2008 Ex date - 09/08/2008
Merged into Kratos Defense & Security Solutions, Inc. 07/27/2011
Each share Common 1¢ par exchanged for (0.588) share Common $0.001 par and $5 cash

INTEGRAMED AMER INC (DE)
Each share old Common 1¢ par exchanged for (0.25) share new Common 1¢ par 11/17/1998
$0.80 Conv. Preferred Ser. A $1 par called for redemption at $10.30 on 10/15/2002
New Common 1¢ par split (5) for (4) by issuance of (0.25) additional share payable 05/04/2007 to holders of record 04/13/2007 Ex date - 05/07/2007
Stock Dividends - 30% payable 06/22/2005 to holders of record 06/08/2005 Ex date - 06/23/2005; 25% payable 06/21/2006 to holders of record 06/07/2006 Ex date - 06/22/2006
Acquired by SCP-325 Holding Corp. 09/20/2012
Each share new Common 1¢ par exchanged for $14.05 cash

INTEGRAND CORP. (NY)
Charter revoked for failure to file reports and pay fees 12/15/66

INTEGRATED ALARM SVCS GROUP INC (DE)
Issue Information - 22,000,000 shares COM offered at $9.25 per share on 07/23/2003
Merged into Protection One, Inc. 04/02/2007
Each share Common $0.001 par exchanged for (0.29) share new Common 1¢ par
(See Protection One, Inc.)

INTEGRATED ART SVCS INC (NV)
Name changed to Worldwide Collectibles, Inc. 02/24/1993
Worldwide Collectibles, Inc. recapitalized as World Wide Net Inc. 07/30/1999 which name changed to Unlimited Coatings Corp. 05/14/2001 which name changed to International American Technologies, Inc. 03/22/2005 which name changed to Hammonds Industries, Inc. 05/14/2007 which recapitalized as Delta Seaboard International, Inc. 06/10/2010 which recapitalized as American International Holdings Corp. 08/13/2012

INTEGRATED AUTOMATIC SYS CORP (DE)
Charter cancelled and declared inoperative and void for non-payment of taxes 4/15/73

INTEGRATED BARTER INTL INC (DE)
Each share Common $0.000166666 par exchanged for (0.1) share Common 1¢ par 12/09/1983
Each share Common 1¢ par exchanged for (0.25) share Common 4¢ par 08/01/1984

Plan of reorganization under Chapter 11 Federal Bankruptcy proceedings confirmed 11/05/1990
No stockholders' equity

INTEGRATED BIO ENERGY RES INC (NV)
Name changed to Onslow Holdings, Inc. 01/30/2014

INTEGRATED BRAND SOLUTIONS INC (NV)
Common $0.001 par split (20) for (1) by issuance of (19) additional shares payable 03/18/2005 to holders of record 03/17/2005 Ex date - 03/21/2005
Common $0.001 par split (3) for (2) by issuance of (0.5) additional share payable 12/22/2005 to holders of record 12/20/2005 Ex date - 12/23/2005
Name changed to Upstream Biosciences Inc. 02/10/2006
Upstream Biosciences Inc. name changed to RealSource Residential, Inc. 08/06/2013

INTEGRATED BRANDS INC (NJ)
Merged into Yogen Fruz World Wide Inc. 03/18/1998
Each share Class A Common 1¢ par exchanged for either (0.557266) share Class B Multiple no par or (0.585129) share Class A Subordinate no par
Note: Option to receive Class B Multiple Stock expired 03/11/1998
Yogen Fruz World-Wide Inc. name changed to CoolBrands International Inc. (NS) 10/06/2000 which reincorporated in Canada 03/27/2006 which reorganized in Delaware as Swisher Hygiene Inc. 11/04/2010

INTEGRATED BUSINESS CORP (FL)
Proclaimed dissolved for failure to file reports and pay fees 8/25/93

INTEGRATED CAMERA OPTICS CORP (DE)
Recapitalized as Global Healthcare & Education Management, Inc. 09/27/2007
Each (44) shares Common 1¢ par exchanged for (1) share Common 1¢ par

INTEGRATED CARBONICS CORP (NV)
Name changed to Urbana.CA, Inc. 08/11/1999
Urbana.CA, Inc. recapitalized as Pitts & Spitts, Inc. 07/17/2002 which name changed to PSPP Holdings, Inc. 06/17/2004 which recapitalized as Mod Hospitality, Inc. 09/22/2008 which recapitalized as Stakool, Inc. 12/16/2009 which name changed to Fresh Promise Foods, Inc. 11/12/2013

INTEGRATED CARD TECHNOLOGIES INC (BC)
Recapitalized as Rizona Ventures Ltd. 07/29/1997
Each share Common no par exchanged for (0.2) share Common no par
Rizona Ventures Ltd. name changed to Admiral Bay Resources, Inc. (BC) 08/31/1998 which reincorporated in Ontario 03/10/2004 which reincorporated back in British Columbia 03/10/2006

INTEGRATED CIRCUIT SYS INC (PA)
Old Common no par split (3) for (2) by issuance of (0.5) additional share 12/31/92
Merged into ICS Merger Corp. 5/11/99
Each share old Common no par exchanged for $21.25 cash
Issue Information - 12,500,000 shares COM offered at $13 per share on 05/22/2000
Merged into Integrated Device Technology, Inc. 9/16/2005
Each share new Common 1¢ par exchanged for (1.3) shares Common $0.001 par and $7.25 cash

INTEGRATED CIRCUITS INC (WA)
Common no par split (2) for (1) by issuance of (1) additional share 3/8/83
Stock Dividend - 10% 3/31/87
Name changed to Interpoint Corp. 2/28/89
Interpoint Corp. merged into Crane Co. 10/17/96

INTEGRATED COMMUNICATION NETWORK INC (DE)
Charter cancelled and declared inoperative and void for non-payment of taxes 03/01/1997

INTEGRATED COMMUNICATION NETWORKS INC (NV)
SEC revoked common stock registration 08/21/2006

INTEGRATED COMMUNICATIONS ACCESS NETWORK INC (NV)
Name changed to Southern Development Inc. (New) 03/05/1996
Southern Development Inc. (New) name changed to EssxSport Corp. 09/10/1998 which name changed to Giant Jr. Investments, Corp. 05/28/2004 which name changed to Financial Media Group, Inc. 09/14/2005 which name changed to Clicker Inc. 07/08/2009
(See Clicker Inc.)

INTEGRATED COMMUNICATIONS INDS INC (BC)
Delisted from Toronto Venture Stock Exchange 06/26/2002

INTEGRATED COMPUTER GRAPHICS INC (GA)
Administratively dissolved 11/29/92

INTEGRATED CONTAINER SVC INC (PA)
Reincorporated under the laws of Delaware as Integrated Container Service Industries Corp. and Common no par changed to $1 par 10/25/68
Integrated Container Service Industries Corp. name changed to Interway Corp. 5/10/71
(See Interway Corp.)

INTEGRATED CONTAINER SVC INDS CORP (DE)
Name changed to Interway Corp. 5/10/71
(See Interway Corp.)

INTEGRATED CTL SYS INC (MA)
Out of business 3/4/74
No stockholders' equity

INTEGRATED DEFENSE TECHNOLOGIES INC (DE)
Issue Information - 7,000,000 shares COM offered at $22 per share on 02/26/2002
Merged into DRS Technologies, Inc. 11/04/2003
Each share Common 1¢ par exchanged for (0.2027) share Common 1¢ par and $12.25 cash
(See DRS Technologies, Inc.)

INTEGRATED DEVICE TECHNOLOGY INC (CA)
Reincorporated under the laws of Delaware and Common no par changed to $0.001 par 9/24/87

INTEGRATED DIRECT INC (DE)
Reorganized under the laws of Nevada as Wolfstone Corp. 02/23/1999
Each share Common $0.001 par exchanged for (0.05) share Common $0.001 par
Wolfstone Corp. recapitalized as FreeGolfStats.com 09/12/2002 which recapitalized as Mobile Nation, Inc. 08/19/2003 which name changed to AuraSource, Inc. 09/09/2008

INTEGRATED ELEC SYS CORP (NV)
Name changed to KollagenX Corp. 07/30/2014

INTEGRATED ELECTRICAL SVCS INC (DE)
Each share old Common 1¢ par exchanged for (0.05850416) share new Common 1¢ par 05/12/2006
Note: Unexchanged certificates were cancelled and became without value 05/12/2008
Name changed to IES Holdings, Inc. 05/25/2016

INTEGRATED ELECTRS CORP (NY)
In process of liquidation
Each share Common 1¢ par received initial distribution of (1) share Color Q Inc. Common no par and $4 cash 07/27/1983
Note: Details on subsequent distributions, if any, are not available

INTEGRATED ENERGY INC (DE)
Merged into MCO Resources, Inc. 7/2/84
Each share Common 1¢ par exchanged for (0.12) share Common 1¢ par
(See MCO Resources, Inc.)

INTEGRATED ENERGY SOLUTIONS INC (NV)
Name changed to Patten Energy Solutions Group, Inc. 05/03/2016

INTEGRATED ENTERPRISES INC (DE)
Recapitalized as SeaLife Corp. (DE) 12/20/2002
Each share Common $0.001 par exchanged for (0.06666666) share Common $0.001 par
SeaLife Corp. (DE) reincorporated in Nevada 10/06/2016

INTEGRATED ENVIRO CAP INC (AB)
Name changed to Canadian Stevia Corp. 12/13/2002
(See Canadian Stevia Corp.)

INTEGRATED ENVIRONMENTAL TECHNOLOGIES LTD (DE)
Reincorporated under the laws of Nevada 01/11/2008

INTEGRATED FINL SYS LTD (DE)
Voluntarily dissolved 10/2/80
Details not available

INTEGRATED FOOD RES INC (NV)
Charter revoked for failure to file reports and pay fees 10/31/2001

INTEGRATED GENERICS INC (NV)
Reincorporated under the laws of Delaware as Biopharmaceutics, Inc. 05/25/1988
Biopharmaceutics, Inc. name changed to Feminique Corp. 06/28/1999 which recapitalized as Receivable Acquisition & Management Corp. 05/11/2004 which name changed to PwrCor, Inc. 03/29/2017

INTEGRATED GENETICS INC (DE)
Merged into Genzyme Corp. (DE) 08/14/1989
Each share Common 1¢ par exchanged for (0.29) share Common 1¢ par
Genzyme Corp. (DE) reincorporated in Massachusetts 12/30/1991
(See Genzyme Corp.)

INTEGRATED GROWTH FD INC (NY)
Out of business 7/7/78
No stockholders' equity

INTEGRATED HEALTH SVCS INC (DE)
Plan of reorganization under Chapter 11 Federal Bankruptcy Code effective 09/09/2003
No stockholders' equity

INTEGRATED HEALTH TECHNOLOGIES INC (DE)
Name changed to Integrated BioPharma, Inc. 4/15/2003

INTEGRATED HEALTHCARE FACS LTD PARTNERSHIP (DE)
Ceased good standing for non-payment of taxes 06/01/1997

INTEGRATED HEALTHCARE HLDGS INC (NV)
Each share old Common $0.001 par exchanged for (0.00000007) share new Common $0.001 par 05/21/2014
Note: In effect holders received $0.203256 per share and public interest was eliminated

INTEGRATED HEALTHCARE INC (WA)
Name changed to Triangle Multi-Media Ltd., Inc. 09/14/1999
Triangle Multi-Media Ltd., Inc. recapitalized as Cinemax Pictures & Production Company International, Inc. 10/05/2007 which name changed to Circa Pictures & Production Company International, Inc. 04/03/2008

INTEGRATED HEALTHCARE SYS INC (DE)
Reincorporated under the laws of Virgina as H.Quotient, Inc. 06/14/1999
(See H.Quotient, Inc.)

INTEGRATED HOMES INC (CO)
Each share Common $0.001 par received distribution of (1) share Integrated Ltd. Restricted Common payable 03/16/2007 to holders of record 02/28/2007
SEC revoked common stock registration 03/27/2007

INTEGRATED INCOME PLUS FD INC (MD)
Name changed to SunAmerica Income Plus Fund, Inc. 02/13/1990
(See SunAmerica Income Plus Fund, Inc.)

INTEGRATED INFORMATION INTL GROUP CO LTD (NV)
Name changed to Intervest Group, Ltd. 04/21/2001
(See Intervest Group, Ltd.)

INTEGRATED INFORMATION SYS INC (DE)
Each share old Common $0.001 par exchanged for (0.2) share new Common $0.001 par 12/30/2002
Chapter 7 bankruptcy proceedings terminated 05/07/2018
Stockholders' equity unlikely

INTEGRATED INPATIENT SOLUTIONS INC (NV)
Reincorporated under the laws of Marshall Islands as Boston Carriers, Inc. 04/04/2016

INTEGRATED LABS INC (DE)
Name changed to Multi-Platform Integrations Inc. 05/30/2002
(See Multi-Platform Integrations Inc.)

INTEGRATED LIVING CMNTYS INC (DE)
Merged into SLC Acquisition Corp. 7/9/97
Each share Common 1¢ par exchanged for $11.50 cash

INTEGRATED LOGIC SYS INC (CO)
Acquired by Simtek Corp. (CO) 5/9/2000
Details not available

INTEGRATED MGMT INFORMATION INC (CO)
Name changed to Where Food Comes From, Inc. 12/03/2012

INTEGRATED MARKETING MGMT INC (UT)
Proclaimed dissolved for failure to file annual report 9/1/88

INTEGRATED MARKETING PROFESSIONALS INC (NV)
Name changed to Casino Airlink Inc. 11/11/96
Casino Airlink Inc. recapitalized as Cotton & Western Mining, Inc. 2/14/2006

INTEGRATED MASONRY SYS INTL (UT)
Charter expired 01/27/2014

INTEGRATED MEASUREMENT SYS INC (OR)
Merged into Credence Systems Corp. 08/01/2001
Each share Common 1¢ par exchanged for (0.9) share Common $0.001 par
Credence Systems Corp. merged into LTX-Credence Corp. 08/29/2008 which name changed to Xcerra Corp. 05/22/2014 which merged into Cohu, Inc. 10/01/2018

INTEGRATED MED RES INC (KS)
Chapter 11 bankruptcy proceedings converted to Chapter 7 on 12/01/1998
Stockholders' equity unlikely

INTEGRATED MED SVCS LTD (DE)
Charter cancelled and declared inoperative and void for non-payment of taxes 3/1/74

INTEGRATED MEDIA COMMUNICATIONS INC (BC)
Recapitalized as IMC Ventures, Inc. (BC) 09/29/1998
Each share Common no par exchanged for (0.1) share Common no par
IMC Ventures, Inc. (BC) reincorporated in Yukon Territory as Triumph Gold Corp. 03/29/2004 which reincorporated in British Columbia 08/26/2004 which recapitalized as Kenai Resources Ltd. 05/01/2007 which merged into Serabi Gold PLC 07/22/2013

INTEGRATED MEDIA HLDGS INC (DE)
Reorganized under the laws of Nevada as Arrayit Corp. 03/19/2009
Each (30) shares Common $0.001 par exchanged for (1) share Common $0.001 par

INTEGRATED MEDICAL VENTURE PARTNERS 2, L.P. (DE)
Name changed to WestMed Venture Partners L.P. and Units of Ltd. Partnership reclassified as Unit of Ltd. Partnership Int. 2 on 07/10/1990
(See WestMed Venture Partners L.P.)

INTEGRATED MICRO PRODS PLC (UNITED KINGDOM)
Liquidation completed
Each Sponsored ADR for Ordinary 10p par received initial distribution of $16.11 cash payable 5/3/96 to holders of record 4/25/95
Each Sponsored ADR for Ordinary 10p par received second distribution of $4.44 cash payable 6/17/96 to holders of record 6/14/96
Each Sponsored ADR for Ordinary 10p par received third and final distribution of approximately $0.375 cash 1/17/2007

INTEGRATED MICROCIRCUITS INC (MN)
Merged into BMC Industries, Inc. 5/13/83
Each share Common 1¢ par exchanged for $0.25 cash

INTEGRATED NETWORK SVCS INC (BC)
Acquired by Call-Net Enterprises Inc. 12/05/1994
Each share Common no par exchanged for (0.9664) share Non-Vtg. Class B Common no par

INTEGRATED OIL NT CORP (ON)
Preferred Shares no par called for redemption at $10 on 04/09/2003
Capital Shares no par called for redemption at $10 on 04/09/2003
Public interest eliminated

INTEGRATED ORTHOPAEDICS INC (NV)
Recapitalized as PowerBrief, Inc. 02/27/2001
Each share Common $0.001 par exchanged for (0.2) share Common $0.001 par
(See PowerBrief, Inc.)

INTEGRATED PACKAGING ASSEMBLY CORP (DE)
Name changed to OSE USA, INC. 7/5/2001
(See OSE USA, Inc.)

INTEGRATED PAV CONCEPTS INC (BC)
Acquired by 0757138 B.C. Ltd. 08/23/2006
Each share Common no par exchanged for $1.30 cash

INTEGRATED PERFORMANCE SYS INC (NY)
Reorganized under the laws of Delaware as Global Innovation Corp. 11/17/2006
Each share Common 1¢ par exchanged for (0.04) share Common 1¢ par

INTEGRATED PHARMACEUTICALS INC (ID)
Administratively dissolved 11/06/2008

INTEGRATED PKG SOLUTIONS INC (NV)
Common $0.001 par changed to $0.0001 par 03/20/2012
Name changed to Integrated Cannabis Solutions, Inc. 04/21/2014

INTEGRATED PROCESS EQUIP CORP (DE)
Merged into SPEEDFAM-IPEC, Inc. 04/06/1999
Each share Common 1¢ par exchanged for (0.71) share Common 1¢ par
SPEEDFAM-IPEC, Inc. merged into Novellus Systems, Inc. 12/06/2002 which merged into Lam Research Corp. 06/04/2012

INTEGRATED PRODTN SVCS LTD (AB)
Acquired by SCF-IV, L.P. 07/03/2002
Each share Common no par exchanged for $3.05 cash

INTEGRATED RES AMERN INSD MTG INVS SER 85 (CA)
Name changed to American Insured Mortgage Investors L.P., Series 85 9/26/91
(See American Insured Mortgage Investors L.P., Series 85)

INTEGRATED RES INC (DE)
Common 10¢ par split (3) for (2) by issuance of (0.5) additional share 10/08/1971
Common 10¢ par split (3) for (2) by issuance of (0.5) additional share 04/15/1983
$3.07 Conv. Preferred $1 par called for redemption 02/28/1983
$3.03 Conv. Preferred $1 par called for redemption 03/21/1986
$3 Preferred $1 par called for redemption 05/28/1986
Plan of reorganization under Chapter 11 Federal Bankruptcy Code effective 11/03/1994
No stockholders' equity

INTEGRATED RES LTD (AB)
Struck off register for failure to file annual returns 10/01/1993

INTEGRATED RES TECHNOLOGIES INC (DE)
Recapitalized as Comprehensive Environmental Systems Inc. 02/06/1995
Each share Common 1¢ par exchanged for (0.1) share Common $0.0001 par
Comprehensive Environmental Systems Inc. name changed to Windswept Environmental Group, Inc. 03/25/1997
(See Windswept Environmental Group, Inc.)

INTEGRATED SEC SYS INC (DE)
Reincorporated 12/17/1991
State of incorporation changed from (TX) to (DE) 12/17/1991
Each share old Common 1¢ par exchanged for (0.01) share new Common 1¢ par 02/17/2011
Name changed to iSatori, Inc. 08/01/2012
iSatori, Inc. merged into FitLife Brands, Inc. 10/01/2015

INTEGRATED SEC TECHNOLOGIES INC (NV)
Name changed to Oramed Pharmaceuticals, Inc. (NV) 04/10/2006
Oramed Pharmaceuticals, Inc. (NV) reincorporated in Delaware 03/11/2011

INTEGRATED SENSOR SOLUTIONS INC (DE)
Merged into Texas Instruments Inc. 08/16/1999
Each share Common $0.001 par exchanged for $8.05 cash

INTEGRATED SVCS GROUP INC (UT)
Charter expired 05/06/2004

INTEGRATED SILICON SOLUTION INC (DE)
Acquired by Uphill Investment Co. 12/07/2015
Each share Common $0.0001 par exchanged for $23 cash

INTEGRATED SILICON SYS INC (NC)
Merged into Avant! Corp. 11/27/1995
Each share Common 1¢ par exchanged for (0.75) share Common 1¢ par
Avant! Corp. merged into Synopsys, Inc. 06/06/2002

INTEGRATED SOFTWARE DEV INC (NV)
Each share old Common no par exchanged for (5) shares new Common no par 02/10/2004
Each share new Common no par exchanged for (0.001) share old Common $0.001 par 04/18/2005
Each share old Common $0.001 par exchanged for (0.001) share new Common $0.001 par 08/22/2006
Each (600) shares new Common $0.001 par exchanged again for (1) share new Common $0.001 par 02/25/2008
Name changed to BSK & Tech, Inc. 05/29/2008

INTEGRATED SOFTWARE SYS CORP (CA)
Merged into Computer Associates International, Inc. 04/15/1987
Each share Common no par exchanged for $12.37 cash

INTEGRATED SPATIAL INFORMATION SOLUTIONS INC (CO)
Name changed to PlanGraphics, Inc. (CO) 04/30/2002
PlanGraphics, Inc. (CO) reorganized in Florida as Integrated Freight Corp. 09/07/2010

INTEGRATED SURGICAL SYS INC (DE)
Each share old Common 1¢ par exchanged for (0.1) share new Common 1¢ par 07/26/2007
Name changed to theMaven, Inc. 12/27/2016

INTEGRATED SYS CONSULTING GROUP INC (PA)
Merged into First Consulting Group, Inc. 12/18/1998
Each share Common $0.005 par exchanged for (0.77) share Common $0.001 par
(See First Consulting Group, Inc.)

INTEGRATED SYS INC (CA)
Common no par split (2) for (1) by issuance of (1) additional share payable 04/04/1996 to holders of record 03/18/1996
Merged into Wind River Systems, Inc. 02/15/2000
Each share Common no par exchanged for (0.92) share Common $0.001 par
(See Wind River Systems, Inc.)

INTEGRATED TECHNOLOGY GROUP (NV)
Recapitalized as Knight Energy Corp. (NV) 06/13/2006
Each share Common $0.001 par exchanged for (0.5) share Common $0.0001 par
Knight Energy Corp. (NV) reincorporated in Maryland 04/30/2007
(See Knight Energy Corp.)

INTEGRATED TECHNOLOGY USA INC (DE)
Name changed to Empire Resources, Inc. 09/15/1999
(See Empire Resources, Inc.)

INTEGRATED TELECOM EXPRESS INC (DE)
Issue Information - 5,600,000 shares COM offered at $18 per share on 08/17/2000
Plan of reorganization under Chapter 11 Federal Bankruptcy Code effective 05/02/2003
Each share Common $0.001 par exchanged for $1.75 cash
Each share Common $0.001 par received an additional distribution of $0.01 cash payable 06/05/2012 to holders of record 05/02/2003

INTEGRATED TELECOM INC (TX)
Name changed to Payless Telecom Solutions, Inc. 12/01/2005
Payless Telecom Solutions, Inc. name changed to WOW Holdings, Inc. 04/14/2008
(See WOW Holdings, Inc.)

INTEGRATED TRANSN NETWORK GROUP INC (DE)
SEC revoked common stock registration 08/01/2011

INTEGRATED TRAVEL SYS INC (TX)
Merged into American Express Travel Related Services 09/24/1992
Each share Common no par exchanged for $0.40 cash

INTEGRATED WASTE SVCS INC (NY)
Dissolved by proclamation 12/27/2000

INTEGRATED WOOD PRODS LTD (BC)
99% acquired by Balco Industries Ltd. through purchase offer which expired 10/30/1977
Public interest eliminated

INTEGRATED WTR TECHNOLOGIES INC (DE)
Each share old Common 1¢ par exchanged for (0.1) share new Common 1¢ par 9/5/97
Name changed to Integrated Water Resources Inc. 3/6/2000

INTEGRITY BANCSHARES INC (GA)
Common no par split (3) for (2) by issuance of (0.5) additional share payable 01/15/2004 to holders of record 12/01/2003
Common no par split (3) for (2) by issuance of (0.5) additional share payable 01/24/2005 to holders of

record 01/10/2005 Ex date - 01/25/2005
Common no par split (2) for (1) by issuance of (1) additional share payable 12/12/2005 to holders of record 11/28/2005 Ex date - 12/13/2005
Chapter 7 bankruptcy proceedings terminated 07/07/2014
No stockholders' equity

INTEGRITY ENTMT CORP (DE)
Common 1¢ par split (2) for (1) by issuance of (1) additional share 11/8/74
Name changed to Wherehouse Entertainment, Inc. 9/7/83
(See Wherehouse Entertainment, Inc.)

INTEGRITY FINL CORP (NC)
Stock Dividends - 10% payable 11/15/2003 to holders of record 10/31/2003 Ex date - 10/29/2003; 10% payable 08/22/2005 to holders of record 08/08/2005 Ex date - 08/04/2005
Merged into FNB United Corp. 04/28/2006
Each share Common $1 par exchanged for (0.8743) share Common $2.50 par and $5.20 cash
FNB United Corp. name changed to CommunityOne Bancorp 07/01/2013 which merged into Capital Bank Financial Corp. 10/26/2016

INTEGRITY FINL GROUP INC (NJ)
Charter revoked for failure to file reports and pay fees 12/31/93

INTEGRITY HLDGS LTD (NV)
Reorganized under the laws of Delaware as Integrity Software Inc. 03/23/2000
Each share Common $0.0025 par exchanged for (0.4) share Common $0.0025 par
(See Integrity Software Inc.)

INTEGRITY MEDIA INC (DE)
Name changed 6/4/2002
Name changed from Integrity Inc. to Integrity Media, Inc. 6/4/2002
Merged into Kona Acquisition Corp. 7/9/2004
Each share Class A Common 1¢ par exchanged for $6.50 cash

INTEGRITY MESSENGER CORP (DE)
Recapitalized as Organa Technologies Group, Inc. 04/27/2006
Each share Common $0.001 par exchanged for (0.01) share Common $0.001 par
(See Organa Technologies Group, Inc.)

INTEGRITY MUSIC INC (DE)
Issue Information - 1,800,000 shares CL A offered at $9 per share on 07/01/1994
Name changed to Integrity Inc. 9/6/95
Integrity Inc. name changed to Integrity Media, Inc. 6/4/2002
(See Integrity Media, Inc.)

INTEGRITY MUT FDS INC (ND)
Name changed to Capital Financial Holdings, Inc. 09/10/2009

INTEGRITY NATL LIFE INS CO (PA)
98.78% acquired by Lincoln Income Life Insurance Co. through purchase offer which expired 03/31/1969
Public interest eliminated

INTEGRITY SOFTWARE INC (DE)
Acquired by Integrity Software Ltd. 12/31/2002
Each share Common $0.0025 par exchanged for $0.65 cash

INTEGRITY TRUST SHARES
Trust terminated 00/00/1942
Details not available

INTEGRYS ENERGY GROUP INC (WI)
Merged into WEC Energy Group, Inc. 06/30/2015
Each share Common $1 par exchanged for (1.128) shares Common 1¢ par and $18.58 cash

INTEK GLOBAL CORP (DE)
Reincorporated 11/28/88
Name changed 2/18/98
State of incorporation changed from (MA) to (DE) 11/28/88
Name changed from Intek Diversified Corp. to Intek Global Corp. 2/18/98
Merged into Security Services PLC 8/25/99
Each share Common 1¢ par exchanged for $3.0125 cash

INTEL CORP (CA)
Capital Stock no par split (3) for (2) by issuance of (0.5) additional share 05/16/1973
Capital Stock no par split (3) for (2) by issuance of (0.5) additional share 05/15/1974
Capital Stock no par split (5) for (4) by issuance of (0.25) additional share 09/08/1978
Capital Stock no par split (3) for (2) by issuance of (0.5) additional share 05/00/1979
Capital Stock no par split (2) for (1) by issuance of (1) additional share 09/08/1980
Capital Stock no par split (2) for (1) by issuance of (1) additional share 06/30/1983
Capital Stock no par split (3) for (2) by issuance of (0.5) additional share 10/28/1987
Stock Dividend - 50% 04/26/1976
Reincorporated under the laws of Delaware and Common no par changed to $0.001 par 05/03/1989
Common Stock Purchase Rights declared for Common stockholders of record 01/30/1989 were redeemed at $0.005 per right 09/01/1994 for holders of record 08/01/1994
(Additional Information in Active)

INTELBAHN INC (NV)
Each share old Common $0.001 par exchanged for (2) shares new Common $0.001 par 06/19/2008
Name changed to Uniontown Energy Inc. 12/31/2010

INTELCOM GROUP INC (BC)
Reorganized as ICG Communications, Inc. 08/02/1996
Each share Common no par exchanged for (1) share Common no par
(See ICG Communications, Inc.)

INTELCOM INDS INC (DE)
Common 50¢ par changed to 10¢ par 01/01/1974
Name changed to IRT Corp. 12/11/1974
(See IRT Corp.)

INTELECOM CORP (DE)
Chapter 11 bankruptcy proceedings converted to Chapter 7 on 11/18/1985
Stockholders' equity unlikely

INTELECOM INC (NV)
Name changed to My Social Income, Inc. (NV) 11/27/2009
My Social Income, Inc. (NV) reincorporated in Wyoming 07/30/2014 which name changed to PDX Partners, Inc. 06/02/2017

INTELECT COMMUNICATIONS INC (DE)
Name changed to TeraForce Technology Corp. 1/31/2001
(See TeraForce Technology Corp.)

INTELECT COMMUNICATIONS SYSTEMS LTD. (BERMUDA)
Reincorporated under the laws of Delaware as Intelect Communications Inc. 12/05/1997
Intelect Communications Inc. name changed to TeraForce Technology Corp. 01/31/2001
(See TeraForce Technology Corp.)

INTELECTIVE COMMUNICATIONS INC (DE)
Name changed to Beacon Redevelopment Industrial Corp. 07/09/2008

INTELECTRON CORP (NY)
Charter cancelled and proclaimed dissolved for failure to pay taxes 6/24/81

INTELEFILM CORP (MN)
Plan of reorganization under Chapter 11 Federal Bankruptcy Code effective
Each share Common 2¢ par received initial distribution of $0.32 cash payable 08/31/2004 to holders of record 04/30/2003 Ex date - 09/01/2004
Each share Common 2¢ par received second and final distribution of $0.0914 cash payable 07/08/2016 to holders of record 04/30/2003

INTELEPLEX CORP (NJ)
Each (26) shares old Common 1¢ par exchanged for (1) share new Common 1¢ par 4/13/88
Charter revoked for failure to file annual reports 6/1/2005

INTELICOM INTL CORP (DE)
Name changed to IntraTel Group, Ltd. 04/01/1997
(See IntraTel Group, Ltd.)

INTELIDATA TECHNOLOGIES CORP (DE)
Merged into Corillian Corp. 10/6/2005
Each share Common $0.001 par exchanged for (0.0957) Common no par and $0.0837 cash
(See Corillian Corp.)

INTELILABS COM INC (DE)
Common $0.0001 par split (8) for (1) by issuance of (7) additional shares payable 04/21/2000 to holders of record 04/11/2000 Ex date - 04/24/2000
Recapitalized as Micro Capital Corp. 07/02/2004
Each share Common $0.0001 par exchanged for (0.1) share Common $0.0001 par
(See Micro Capital Corp.)

INTELIMAX MEDIA INC (BC)
Common USD$0.00001 par changed to no par 12/12/2012
Recapitalized as DraftTeam Fantasy Sports Inc. 01/31/2014
Each share Common no par exchanged for (0.2) share Common no par
DraftTeam Fantasy Sports Inc. merged into DraftTeam Daily Fantasy Sports Corp. 03/13/2015 which name changed to Fantasy Aces Daily Fantasy Sports Corp. 10/06/2015

INTELIQUENT INC (DE)
Acquired by Onvoy, LLC 02/10/2017
Each share Common $0.001 par exchanged for $23 cash

INTELISPAN INC (WA)
Merged into McLeodUSA Inc. 05/31/2001
Each share Common $0.0001 par exchanged for (0.03055) share Common 1¢ par
(See McLeodUSA Inc.)

INTELISYS AVIATION SYS AMER INC (DE)
Each share old Common $0.001 par exchanged for (0.1) share new Common $0.001 par 12/12/2007
Recapitalized as China Yida Holding, Co. (DE) 02/28/2018
Each share Common $0.001 par exchanged for (0.1) share Common $0.001 par
China Yida Holding, Co. (DE) reorganized in Nevada 11/19/2012
(See China Yida Holding, Co.)

INTELLECTUAL TECHNOLOGY INC (DE)
Acquired by ITI Holdings, Inc. 11/15/2012
Each share Common $0.00001 par exchanged for $3.02147174 cash
Each share Common $0.00001 par received an additional distribution of $0.5002714 cash from escrow 05/30/2014

INTELLICALL INC (DE)
Name changed to Wireless WebConnect!, Inc. 04/02/2001
(See Wireless WebConnect!, Inc.)

INTELLICARD INTL INC (CO)
Charter suspended for failure to file annual reports 1/1/93

INTELLICELL BIOSCIENCES INC (NV)
SEC revoked common stock registration 10/04/2017

INTELLICELL CORP (DE)
Each share Common 1¢ par received distribution of (0.5) Common Stock Purchase Warrant expiring 12/10/2000 payable 12/29/1997 to holders of record 12/10/1997
Name changed to Focus Affiliates, Inc. 09/29/1999
Focus Affiliates, Inc. recapitalized as Auric Mining Co. 11/12/2009 which recapitalized as Enterra Corp. (Old) 12/18/2013 which name changed to VinCompass Corp. 04/27/2015 which name changed to Enterra Corp. (New) 11/13/2015

INTELLICHECK MOBILISA INC (DE)
Name changed 03/18/2008
Name changed 10/28/2009
Name changed from Intelli-Check, Inc. to Intelli-Check-Mobilisa, Inc. 03/18/2008
Name changed from Intelli-Check-Mobilisa, Inc. to Intellicheck Mobilisa, Inc. 10/28/2009
Each share old Common $0.001 par exchanged for (0.125) share new Common $0.001 par 08/13/2014
Name changed to Intellicheck, Inc. 05/17/2017

INTELLICHIP HLDGS CORP (UT)
Recapitalized as CompuLoan Originations, Inc. 09/05/1995
Each share Common $0.001 par exchanged for (0.01) share Common $0.001 par
(See CompuLoan Originations, Inc.)

INTELLICORP INC (DE)
Reincorporated 1/12/87
Name changed and reincorporated from IntelliCorp (CA) to IntelliCorp, Inc. (DE) 1/12/87
Plan of reorganization under Chapter 11 Federal Bankruptcy Code effective 2/14/2003
No stockholders' equity

INTELLIDATA INC (CO)
Name changed to Orion Network Solutions Inc. 4/5/88
(See Orion Network Solutions, Inc.)

INTELLIGENETICS, INC. (CA)
Name changed to IntelliCorp (CA) 6/30/84
IntelliCorp (CA) reincorporated in Delaware as IntelliCorp, Inc. 1/12/87
(See IntelliCorp, Inc.)

INTELLIGENT BUSINESS COMMUNICATIONS CORP (DE)
Each share Common $0.0001 par exchanged for (0.25) share Common $0.0004 par
Charter forfeited for failure to maintain a registered agent 10/29/91

INTELLIGENT COMMUNICATION ENTERPRISE CORP (PA)
Each share old Common $0.0001 par

INT-INT

INTELLIGENT COMMUNICATIONS NETWORKS (CA) (continued from previous column)
exchanged for (3) shares new Common $0.0001 par 02/08/2010
Each share new Common $0.0001 par exchanged again for (7) shares new Common $0.0001 par 12/30/2010
Name changed to One Horizon Group, Inc. (PA) 01/31/2013
One Horizon Group, Inc. (PA) reorganized in Delaware 08/29/2013

INTELLIGENT COMMUNICATIONS NETWORKS (CA)
Common no par split (2) for (1) by issuance of (1) additional share 4/28/83
Name changed to Incomnet, Inc. 7/30/86
(See Incomnet, Inc.)

INTELLIGENT CONTENT ENTERPRISES INC (ON)
Recapitalized as Novicius Corp. 05/29/2017
Each share Common no par exchanged for (0.1) share Common no par

INTELLIGENT CTLS INC (ME)
Merged into Franklin Electric Co., Inc. 7/16/2002
Each share Common no par exchanged for $3.95 cash

INTELLIGENT DECISION SYS INC (DE)
Charter cancelled and declared inoperative and void for non-payment of taxes 03/01/2000

INTELLIGENT ELECTRS INC (PA)
Common 1¢ par split (2) for (1) by issuance of (1) additional share 7/13/90
Common 1¢ par split (2) for (1) by issuance of (1) additional share 2/13/92
Acquired by Xerox Corp. 5/20/98
Each share Common 1¢ par exchanged for $7.60 cash

INTELLIGENT ENERGY HLDGS PLC (UNITED KINGDOM)
Name changed to Lb-shell PLC 12/14/2017
(See Lb-shell PLC)

INTELLIGENT FINL CORP (CO)
Name changed to Cell Robotics International Inc. 05/19/1995
(See Cell Robotics International Inc.)

INTELLIGENT LIFE CORP (FL)
Issue Information - 3,500,000 shares COM offered at $13 per share on 05/13/1999
Name changed to ilife.com, Inc. 12/16/1999
ilife.com, Inc. name changed to Bankrate, Inc. 09/18/2000
(See Bankrate, Inc.)

INTELLIGENT LIVING CORP (NV)
Each share old Common $0.001 par exchanged for (0.002) share new Common $0.001 par 09/29/2008
Each share new Common $0.001 par exchanged again for (0.00666666) share new Common $0.001 par 01/18/2012
Recapitalized as Occidental Development Group Inc. 08/19/2013
Each share new Common $0.001 par exchanged for (0.1) share Common $0.001 par

INTELLIGENT LIVING INC (NV)
Recapitalized as Intelligent Living America Inc. 11/24/2014
Each share Common $0.001 par exchanged for (0.02) share Common $0.001 par

INTELLIGENT MED IMAGING INC (DE)
Plan of reorganization under Chapter 11 Federal Bankruptcy proceedings effective 10/06/2000
No stockholders' equity

INTELLIGENT MTR CARS GROUP INC (DE)
Old Common $0.001 par split (7) for (1) by issuance of (6) additional shares payable 01/24/2005 to holders of record 01/20/2005
Each share new Common $0.001 par exchanged for (0.0002) share new Common $0.001 par 03/15/2007
Name changed to Selective Brands Holdings Inc. 05/16/2007
Selective Brands Holdings Inc. recapitalized as East Morgan Holdings Inc. 02/28/2008

INTELLIGENT POLYMERS LTD (BERMUDA)
Acquired by Biovail Corp. 09/29/2000
Each share Common 1¢ par exchanged for USD$39.06 cash

INTELLIGENT SEC NETWORKS INC (DE)
Name changed to Gambino Apparel Group, Inc. 04/10/2006
Gambino Apparel Group, Inc. recapitalized as Patient Portal Technologies, Inc. 09/01/2006

INTELLIGENT SPORTS INC (CA)
Each share old Common no par exchanged for (0.01) share new Common no par 06/14/2007
Name changed to LIGATT Security International, Inc. 04/22/2009

INTELLIGENT SURGICAL LASERS INC (CA)
Each share old Common no par exchanged for (0.4) share new Common no par 11/08/1993
Name changed to Escalon Medical Corp. (CA) 03/12/1996
Escalon Medical Corp. (CA) reincorporated in Delaware 11/17/1999 which reincorporated in Pennsylvania 11/07/2001

INTELLIGENT SYS CORPORATION (GA)
Stock Dividend - 100% 3/4/83
Completely liquidated 12/31/86
Each share Common 5¢ par exchanged for first and final distribution of (1) Intelligent Systems Master, L.P. Depositary Receipt
Intelligent Systems Master, L.P. reorganized as Intelligent Systems Corp. (New) 11/29/91

INTELLIGENT SYS MASTER L P (DE)
Reorganized under the laws of Georgia as Intelligent Systems Corp. (New) 11/29/91
Each Depositary Receipt exchanged for (1) share Common 1¢ par

INTELLIGENT WEB TECHNOLOGIES INC (ON)
Delisted from Toronto Venture Stock Exchange 06/30/2003

INTELLIGENTIAS INC (NV)
All officers and directors resigned as of 09/15/2008
Stockholders' equity unlikely

INTELLIGROUP INC (NJ)
Each share Common 1¢ par received distribution of (1) share SeraNova, Inc. Common 1¢ par payable 07/05/2000 to holders of record 05/12/2000
Merged into NTT Data Corp. 07/21/2010
Each share Common 1¢ par exchanged for $4.65 cash

INTELLIHOME INC (TX)
Reincorporated under the laws of Nevada as Atlas Oil & Gas, Inc. 10/14/2008

INTELLIPHARMACEUTICS LTD (DE)
Merged into IntelliPharmaCeutics International Inc. 10/22/2009
Each share Common $0.001 par exchanged for (0.55278812) share Common no par

INTELLIQUEST INFORMATION GROUP INC (DE)
Merged into WPP Group 12/22/99
Each share Common $0.001 par exchanged for $12.70 cash

INTELLIQUIS INTL INC (NV)
Common $0.001 par split (3) for (1) by issuance of (2) additional shares payable 5/7/99 to holders of record 4/23/99
Recapitalized as NRP Stone, Inc. 4/3/2007
Each share Common $0.001 par exchanged for (0.01) share Common $0.001 par

INTELLIREADY INC (CO)
Reorganized under the laws of Nevada as Unitech Water & Renewable Energy, Inc. 02/29/2008
Each share Common no par exchanged for (0.03367547) share Common $0.001 par
(See Unitech Water & Renewable Energy, Inc.)

INTELLISYNC CORP (DE)
Merged into Nokia Corp. 2/10/2006
Each share Common $0.001 par exchanged for $5.25 cash

INTELLISYS AUTOMOTIVE SYS INC (DE)
Recapitalized as RTAI Systems, Inc. 01/09/1998
Each share Class A Common no par exchanged for (1/6) share Class A Common no par
RTAI Systems, Inc. recapitalized as Production Assistant Technologies, Inc. 01/19/1999
(See Production Assistant Technologies, Inc.)

INTELLISYS GROUP INC (DE)
Chapter 11 Federal Bankruptcy Proceedings converted to Chapter 7 on 1/10/2001
Stockholders' equity unlikely

INTELLISYS SYS INC (DE)
Recapitalized as ISI Technology Corp. 7/18/97
Each share Common exchanged for (0.01) share Common
(See ISI Technology Corp.)

INTELLIWORXX INC (FL)
SEC revoked common stock registration 02/20/2007

INTELLON CORP (DE)
Issue Information - 7,500,000 shares COM offered at $6 per share on 12/13/2007
Merged into Atheros Communications, Inc. 12/15/2009
Each share Common $0.0001 par exchanged for $7.30 cash

INTELOGIC TRACE INC NEW (NY)
Chapter 11 bankruptcy proceedings converted to Chapter 7 on 12/22/95
No stockholders' equity

INTELOGIC TRACE INC OLD (NY)
Stock Dividend - 10% 6/24/86
$1.50 Exchangeable Preferred 1¢ par called for redemption 11/1/86
Reorganized as Intelogic Trace, Inc. (New) 12/8/94
Each share Common 1¢ par exchanged for (0.25) share Common 1¢ par
(See Intelogic Trace, Inc. (New))

INTELPRO MEDIA GROUP INC (AB)
Reorganized under the laws of Ontario as JITE Technologies Inc. 06/20/2006
Each share Common no par exchanged for (0.5) share Common no par
(See JITE Technologies Inc.)

INTELSAT S A (LUXEMBOURG)
Each share 5.75% Mandatory Conv. Jr. Non-Vtg. Preferred 1¢ par automatically became (2.7778) shares Common 1¢ par 05/02/2016

(Additional Information in Active)

INTENSITY CO INC (AB)
Name changed to LX Ventures Inc. 12/07/2012
LX Ventures Inc. name changed to Mobio Technologies Inc. 07/07/2014

INTENSITY RES LTD (AB)
Acquired by Renata Resources Inc. 04/25/1997
For Canadian shareholders:
Each share Common no par exchanged for (0.038948) share Common no par and $2.253262 cash
Note: U.S. shareholders will receive $2.253262 cash plus additional cash in lieu of shares
Renata Resources Inc. merged into Rio Alto Exploration Ltd. 06/21/2000 which merged into Canadian Natural Resources Ltd. 07/01/2002
Gold Oil & Gas Ltd. merged 09/17/1990

INTENSIVA HEALTHCARE CORP (DE)
Issue Information - 2,500,000 shares Common offered at $6 per share on 10/10/1996
Merged into Select Medical Corp. 12/18/98
Each share Common $0.001 par exchanged for $9.625 cash

INTEPAC INC (AB)
Recapitalized 01/18/1999
Recapitalized from Intepac Corp. to Intepac Inc. 01/18/1999
Each share old Common no par exchanged for (0.1) share new Common no par
Completely liquidated 10/00/2003
Each share Common no par received first and final distribution of approximately $0.02 cash
Note: Certificates were not required to be surrendered and are without value

INTEQUEST CORP (AB)
Merged into 1364289 Alberta Ltd. 02/01/2008
Each share Common no par exchanged for $1.70 cash

INTER ACT COMMUNICATIONS INC (UT)
Involuntarily dissolved 07/17/2003

INTER AMERICAN INDUSTRIES, INC. (DE)
No longer in existence having become inoperative and void for non-payment of taxes 4/1/60

INTER AMERN INDS INC (DE)
Name changed to Kendee's International Foods, Inc. 11/20/85
(See Kendee's International Foods, Inc.)

INTER-AMERICAN LIFE INSURANCE CO. (AZ)
Placed in receivership 02/23/1971
No stockholders' equity

INTER AMERN PETE CORP (CO)
Merged into Kenai Corp. 5/2/78
Each share Common 10¢ par exchanged for $24.50 cash

INTER-AMERICAN PHARMACAL CORP. (NY)
Charter revoked for failure to file reports and pay fees 12/16/29

INTER ASIA EQUITIES INC (BC)
Delisted from Toronto Stock Venture Exchange 06/20/2003

INTER ATLANTIC FINL INC (DE)
Issue Information - 7,500,000 UNITS consisting of (1) share COM and (1) WT offered at $8 per Unit on 10/02/2007
Completely liquidated
Each Unit received first and final distribution of $7.95746 cash

INT-INT   **FINANCIAL INFORMATION, INC.**

payable 10/19/2009 to holders of record 10/19/2009
Each share Common $0.0001 par received first and final distribution of $7.95746 cash payable 10/19/2009 to holders of record 10/19/2009
Note: Certificates were not required to be surrendered and are without value

INTER CABLE COMMUNICATIONS INC (BC)
Delisted from Toronto Stock Exchange 07/26/1991

INTER CANADA HOLDINGS LTD. (QC)
Dissolved 10/4/67

INTER-CANADIAN CORP. (DE)
Name changed to Great Northern Investments, Inc. 8/1/58
(See Great Northern Investments, Inc.)

INTER CHEM INC. (UT)
Proclaimed dissolved for failure to pay taxes 9/30/79

INTER-CITIC MINERALS INC (BC)
Name changed 10/04/1999
Name changed 12/19/2003
Name changed from Inter-Citic Envirotec Inc. to Inter-Citic Mineral Technologies Inc. 10/04/1999
Name changed from Inter-Citic Mineral Technologies Inc. to Inter-Citic Minerals Inc. 12/19/2003
Acquired by Western Mining Group Co., Ltd. 11/22/2012
Each share new Common no par exchanged for $2.05 cash

INTER-CITY BAKING CO. LTD. (CANADA)
Each share Capital Stock $100 par exchanged for (5) shares Capital Stock no par 00/00/1949
Acquired by Lake of the Woods Milling Co. Ltd. 06/08/1956
Each share Capital Stock no par exchanged for $20 cash

INTER CITY BK (BENTON HARBOR, MI)
Stock Dividends - 20% 4/11/66; 10% 4/1/74; 10% 4/1/75; 10% 4/1/76; 10% 4/15/77; 10% 4/1/78; 10% 4/1/79; 10% 4/1/80; 10% 5/1/86
Merged into Shoreline Financial Corp. 12/24/87
Each share Common $10 par exchanged for (1.334305) shares Common $1 par
Shoreline Financial Corp. merged into Chemical Financial Corp. 1/9/2001

INTER CITY GAS CORP (MB)
6.5% 2nd Preference Ser. A $20 par called for redemption 03/15/1990
7.5% 2nd Preference Ser. B $20 par called for redemption 03/15/1990
Reorganized as Inter-City Products Corp. 04/18/1990
Each share $2.125 Conv. 3rd Preference 1985 Ser. no par exchanged for (0.4155) share Ordinary Stock no par, (0.4155) Class C Conv. Preference Purchase Warrant and $34.90 cash
Each share Common no par exchanged for (0.25) share Ordinary Stock no par, (0.25) Class C Conv. Preference Purchase Warrant and $21 cash
Inter-City Products Corp. reincorporated in (Canada) 06/05/1992 which name changed to International Comfort Products Corp. (Canada) 07/09/1997
(See International Comfort Products Corp. (Canada))

INTER CITY GAS LTD (MB)
Common no par split (2) for (1) by issuance of (1) additional share 07/24/1970
Common no par split (2) for (1) by issuance of (1) additional share 07/16/1971
6.25% 2nd Preference Ser. A $20 par reclassified as 6.5% 2nd Preference Ser. A $20 par 05/01/1970
Common no par split (2) for (1) by issuance of (1) additional share 07/27/1973
Merged into Inter-City Gas Corp. (MB) 04/14/1980
Each share 6.5% 2nd Preference Ser. A $20 par exchanged for (1) share 6.5% 2nd Preference Ser. A $20 par
Each share 7.5% 2nd Preference Ser. B $20 par exchanged for (1) share 7.5% 2nd Preference Ser. B $20 par
Each share Common no par exchanged for (1) share Common no par
Inter-City Gas Corp. (MB) reorganized as Inter-City Products Corp. (MB) 04/18/1990 which reincorporated in (Canada) 06/05/1992 which name changed to International Comfort Products Corp. (Canada) 07/09/1997
(See International Comfort Products Corp. (Canada))

INTER CITY MFG LTD (MB)
100% of Class A Common no par and Class B Common no par held by Inter-City Gas Ltd. (MB) as of 09/15/1980
Public interest eliminated

INTER CITY NATL BK (BRADENTON, FL)
Merged into First National Bank of Florida (Tampa, FL) 1/2/81
Each share Common $10 par exchanged for (4.72) shares Capital Stock $5 par

INTER-CITY PRODS CORP (CANADA)
Reincorporated 06/05/1992
Each share 8% Class C Preference no par exchanged for (5.5) shares Ordinary Stock no par 07/19/1994
Place of incorporation changed from (MB) to (Canada) 06/05/1992
Name changed to International Comfort Products Corp. 07/09/1997
(See International Comfort Products Corp.)

INTER COMM DATA CORP (DE)
Merged into HRD, Inc. 4/10/77
Each share Common 10¢ par exchanged for $0.15 cash

INTER COMMUNITY BANCORP (NJ)
Acquired by CoreStates Financial Corp 12/17/1993
Each share Common no par exchanged for (0.701) share Common $1 par
CoreStates Financial Corp merged into First Union Corp. 04/28/1998 which name changed to Wachovia Corp. (Ctfs. dated after 09/01/2001) 09/01/2001 which merged into Wells Fargo & Co. (New) 12/31/2008

INTER-COMMUNITY BANK (SPRINGFIELD, NJ)
Reorganized as Inter Community Bancorp 06/27/1985
Each share Capital Stock $5 par exchanged for (1) share Common no par
Inter Community Bancorp acquired by CoreStates Financial Corp 12/17/1993 which merged into First Union Corp. 04/28/1998 which name changed to Wachovia Corp. (Ctfs. dated after 09/01/2001) 09/01/2001 which merged into Wells Fargo & Co. (New) 12/31/2008

INTER-COMMUNITY STATE BANK (SPRINGFIELD, NJ)
Name changed to Inter-Community Bank (Springfield, NJ) and Capital Stock $10 par changed to $5 par 02/07/1974
Inter-Community Bank (Springfield, NJ) reorganized as Inter Community Bancorp 06/27/1985 which was acquired by CoreStates Financial Corp 12/17/1993 which merged into First Union Corp. 04/28/1998 which name changed to Wachovia Corp. (Ctfs. dated after 09/01/2001) 09/01/2001 which merged into Wells Fargo & Co. (New) 12/31/2008

INTER-CON / PC INC (MN)
Each share old Common no par exchanged for (0.01) share new Common no par 04/17/2006
SEC revoked common stock registration 10/27/2008

INTER-CONTINENTAL CORP. (TX)
Charter forfeited for failure to pay taxes 02/26/1973

INTER CONTL ENERGY CORP (BC)
Recapitalized as Tajee Resources Ltd. 08/10/1984
Each share Common no par exchanged for (0.33333333) share Common no par
(See Tajee Resources Ltd.)

INTER CONTL PHOTOCOPY CORP (IL)
Name changed to ICP Inc. (IL) 8/4/69
ICP Inc. (IL) reincorporated in Delaware as Oce-Industries Inc. 4/26/73
(See Oce-Industries Inc.)

INTER CONTL SVCS CORP (MO)
Stock Dividend - 100% 12/31/1980
Reincorporated under the laws of Nevada as Orbital Enterprises and Common no par changed to $0.001 par 08/22/2006
(See Orbital Enterprises)

INTER-CONTL COMPUTING INC (DE)
Completely liquidated 7/31/80
Each share Common 10¢ par exchanged for first and final distribution of $5.07 cash

INTER-CONTL MGMT CO (DE)
Common 10¢ par changed to 1¢ par 6/10/83
Charter cancelled and declared inoperative and void for non-payment of taxes 3/1/93

INTER-COUNTY TELEPHONE & TELEGRAPH CO. (FL)
Common no par changed to $12.50 par and (0.25) additional share issued 2/6/57
Common $12.50 par changed to $4.16-2/3 par and (2) additional shares issued 6/1/60
Common $4.16-2/3 par changed to $2.08-1/3 par and (1) additional share issued 2/1/65
4.65% Preferred Ser. C $25 par called for redemption 6/1/67
5% Preferred Ser. B $25 par called for redemption 6/1/67
Merged into United Utilities, Inc. 9/28/67
Each share 5% Preferred Ser. A $25 par exchanged for (1) share Conv. 1st Preferred no par
Each share Common $2.08-1/3 par exchanged for (1) share Conv. 1st Preferred no par
United Utilities, Inc. name changed to United Telecommunications, Inc. 6/2/72 which name changed to Sprint Corp. 2/26/92 which name changed to Sprint Nextel Corp. 8/12/2005

INTER CNTY TITLE GTY & MTG CO (NY)
Each share Capital Stock $50 par exchanged for (20) shares Capital Stock $2.50 par 4/21/59
Capital Stock $2.50 par changed to $7 par 5/10/63
Stock Dividend - 10% 2/10/62
Acquired by USLIFE Holding Corp. 10/17/69
Each share Capital Stock $7 par exchanged for (0.4) share $4.50 Conv. Preferred Ser. A no par
USLIFE Holding Corp. name changed to USLIFE Corp. 5/22/70 which merged into American General Corp. 6/17/97 which merged into American International Group, Inc. 8/29/2001

INTER ENERGY CORP (AB)
Name changed to Entech Investments Inc. 07/16/2004
Entech Investments Inc. merged into CAPVEST Income Corp. 01/01/2005
(See CAPVEST Income Corp.)

INTER-FACE INTERNATIONAL, INC. (UT)
Name changed to Whitepine Resources, Inc. 12/23/1983
(See Whitepine Resources, Inc.)

INTER FED SVGS BK (CHATTANOOGA, TN)
Merged into First Chattanooga Financial Corp. 4/1/92
Each share Common $1 par exchanged for either (0.700483) share Common $1 par or $11.20 cash

INTER GLOBAL INC USA (DE)
Charter cancelled and declared inoperative and void for non-payment of taxes 3/1/83

INTER GLOBE RES LTD (BC)
Delisted from Vancouver Stock Exchange 3/6/95

INTER IS MORTGAGEE CORP (NY)
Name changed to Continental Management, Inc. 6/1/73
(See Continental Management, Inc.)

INTER IS RESORTS LTD (HI)
Capital Stock $3 par changed to no par 9/26/67
Capital Stock no par split (3) for (2) by issuance of (0.5) additional share 1/31/69
Stock Dividends - 10% 12/19/58; 10% 12/31/59
Assets transferred to Inter-Island Resorts, Ltd. Limited Partnership and Capital Stock no par reclassified as Units of Bene. Int. no par in 1986
(See Inter-Island Resorts, Ltd. Limited Partnership)

INTER-ISLAND RESORTS, LTD. LIMITED PARTNERSHIP (HI)
Liquidation completed
Each Unit of Bene. Int. received cumulative distributions from 1986 - 1989 totaling $16.42 cash per Unit
Note: Certificates were not required to be surrendered and are without value

INTER-ISLAND STEAM NAVIGATION CO. LTD.
Liquidated in 1950

INTER-LEDUC OIL CO., LTD. (ON)
Acquired by Inter-Rock Oil Co. of Canada Ltd. 01/03/1962
Each share Capital Stock $1 par exchanged for (2.5) shares Capital Stock $1 par
Inter-Rock Oil Co. of Canada Ltd. name changed to Inter-Rock Gold Inc. 08/18/1992 which name changed to Inter-Rock Minerals Inc. (ON) 09/22/1998 which reincorporated in Barbados 09/15/2000

INTER-LINK COMMUNICATIONS GROUP INC (NV)
Name changed to EnterTech Media Group, Inc. 04/22/1999
(See EnterTech Media Group, Inc.)

INTER-LINK COMMUNICATIONS INC (AB)
Recapitalized as International Inter-Link Inc. 08/03/1993
Each share Common no par exchanged for (0.2) share Common no par
International Inter-Link Inc. name

changed to Parton Capital Inc. 11/10/1997

INTER-MED INTL INC (DE)
Name changed to Cyclopss Medical Systems Inc. 07/31/1990
Cyclopss Medical Systems Inc. name changed to Cyclopss Corp. 02/02/1995
(See Cyclopss Corp.)

INTER-MED TECHNOLOGIES INC. (BC)
Recapitalized as Botex Industries Corp. 08/07/1998
Each share Common no par exchanged for (0.33333333) share Common no par
Botex Industries Corp. name changed to Radical Elastomers Inc. 08/02/2001

INTER-MOUNTAIN OIL CO. (MT)
Charter expired by time limitation 03/22/1957

INTER-MOUNTAIN TELEPHONE CO. (VA)
Each share 6% Preferred $100 par exchanged for (0.1) shares 6% Preferred $10 par 00/00/1940
Each share Common $100 par exchanged for (0.1) shares Common $10 par 00/00/1940
Merged into United Utilities, Inc. 05/23/1966
Each share Common $10 par exchanged for (1.25) shares Common $2.50 par
United Utilities, Inc. name changed to United Telecommunications, Inc. 06/02/1972 which name changed to Sprint Corp. (KS) 02/26/1992 which name changed to Sprint Nextel Corp. 08/12/2005 which merged into Sprint Corp. (DE) 07/10/2013

INTER MOUNTAIN WATER & POWER CO.
Property sold to Bondholders Committee 00/00/1931
Details not available

INTER MTN DEV INC (BC)
Delisted from Vancouver Stock Exchange 07/07/1989

INTER N CORP (NV)
Reorganized as Safe ID Corp. 09/20/1999
Each share Common $0.001 par exchanged for (3) shares Common no par
Safe ID Corp. name changed to EYI Industries Inc. 12/31/2003
(See EYI Industries Inc.)

INTER NATL BK (MIAMI, FL)
Merged into Royal Trust Co. (Montreal, QC) 09/02/1972
Each share Common $10 par exchanged for (1.93) shares Capital Stock $2 par
Royal Trust Co. (Montreal, QC) merged into Royal Trustco Ltd. 04/03/1979 which name changed to Gentra Inc. 06/25/1993 which name changed to BPO Properties Ltd. 04/19/2001
(See BPO Properties Ltd.)

INTER-NATIONAL SECURITIES CO. (ME)
Charter suspended for failure to file annual reports 00/00/1915

INTER-OCEAN CASUALTY CO.
Name changed to Inter-Ocean Insurance Co. in 1946
Inter-Ocean Insurance Co. reorganized under the laws of Ohio as Inter-Ocean Corp. 12/31/68 which merged into Cincinnati Financial Corp. (DE) 2/23/73 which reincorporated in Ohio 4/9/92

INTER OCEAN CORP (OH)
Common $10 par changed to no par and (9) additional shares issued 10/3/69
Common no par split (2) for (1) by issuance of (1) additional share 8/17/72
Merged into Cincinnati Financial Corp. (DE) 2/23/73
Each share Common no par exchanged for (0.6) share Common $2 par
Cincinnati Financial Corp. (DE) reincorporated in Ohio 4/9/92

INTER OCEAN INS CO (IN)
Each share old Capital Stock $10 par exchanged for (5) shares new Capital Stock $10 par in 1949
Stock Dividend - 100% 2/1/64
Reorganized under the laws of Ohio as Inter-Ocean Corp. 12/31/68
Each share new Capital Stock $10 par exchanged for (1) share Common $10 par
Inter-Ocean Corp. merged into Cincinnati Financial Corp. (DE) 2/23/73 which reincorporated in Ohio 4/9/92

INTER-OCEAN REINSURANCE CO. (IA)
Acquired by American Re-Insurance Co. 12/31/63
Each share Capital Stock $10 par exchanged for (2.2) shares Capital Stock $5 par
(See American Re-Insurance Co.)

INTER-OCEAN SECURITIES CORP. (IA)
Class A and B Common no par changed to $5 par and (1) additional share of each class issued 5/24/55
Completely liquidated 5/2/62
Each share Preferred $25 par exchanged for (0.5) share American Re-Insurance Co. Capital Stock $5 par
Each share Class A or B Common $5 par exchanged for (3.275984) shares American Re-Insurance Co. Capital Stock $5 par
(See American Re-Insurance Co.)

INTER-OCEANIC RES LTD (BC)
Name changed 02/01/1985
Name changed from Inter-Oceanic Oil & Gas Corp. to Inter-Oceanic Resources Ltd. 02/01/1985
Recapitalized as Odin Industries Ltd. 02/11/1987
Each share Common no par exchanged for (0.33333333) share Common no par
(See Odin Industries Ltd.)

INTER PAC RESOURCE CORP (BC)
Merged into QPX Minerals Inc. 03/31/1990
Each share Common no par exchanged for (0.5) share Common no par and (0.3) Common Stock Purchase Warrant expiring 03/31/1993
QPX Minerals Inc. merged into Rea Gold Corp. 08/06/1991
(See Rea Gold Corp.)

INTER PIPELINE FD (AB)
Reorganized as Inter Pipeline Ltd. 09/05/2013
Each Class A Ltd. Partnership Unit exchanged for (1) share Common no par

INTER POLYMER INDS INC (CA)
Charter cancelled for failure to file reports and pay taxes 7/1/85

INTER PROVINCIAL COML DISC LTD (ON)
Name changed to Inter-Provincial Diversified Holdings Ltd. 03/31/1969
(See Inter-Provincial Diversified Holdings Ltd.)

INTER PROVINCIAL DIVERSIFIED HLDGS LTD (ON)
5% Non-Cum. Conv. Preferred no par called for redemption 04/12/1971
Common no par called for redemption at $6.47 on 11/29/1999

INTER RAO UES JSC (RUSSIA)
Basis changed from (1:10,000) to (1:100) 12/29/2014
Name changed to Inter RAO UES PJSC 09/29/2015

INTER REGL FINL GROUP INC (DE)
Common $0.125 par split (3) for (2) by issuance of (0.5) additional share 12/20/95
Stock Dividends - 25% 5/21/81; 20% 4/30/82
Name changed to Interra Financial Inc. 2/4/97
Interra Financial Inc. name changed to Dain Rauscher Corp. 1/2/98
(See Dain Rauscher Corp.)

INTER ROCK MINERALS INC (ON)
Name changed 08/18/1992
Name changed 09/22/1998
Capital Stock $1 par changed to no par 09/08/1972
Name changed from Inter-Rock Oil Co. of Canada Ltd. to Inter-Rock Gold Inc. 08/18/1992
Name changed from Inter-Rock Gold Inc. to Inter-Rock Minerals Inc. (ON) 09/22/1998
Reincorporated under the laws of Barbados 09/15/2000

INTER-STATE ACCEPTANCE CORP. (FL)
Name changed to Growth Equities Corp. 10/02/1961
(See Growth Equities Corp.)

INTER STATE MINERAL PRODUCERS LTD. (ON)
Charter cancelled for failure to file reports and pay taxes in 1969

INTER-STATE ROYALTY CORP., LTD. (CANADA)
Name changed to Lochaber Oil Corp. Ltd. 03/09/1955
(See Lochaber Oil Corp. Ltd.)

INTER STOP TRAVEL CENTERS, INC. (ID)
Charter forfeited for failure to file reports 12/01/1995

INTER TAIN NET INC (ON)
Name changed to CryptoLogic Inc. 06/18/1996
(See CryptoLogic Inc.)

INTER-TECH DRILLING SOLUTIONS LTD (AB)
Merged into Precision Drilling Corp. 06/17/1998
Each share Common no par exchanged for $2.10 cash

INTER TECH RES LTD (BC)
Name changed 06/24/1971
Name changed from Inter-Tech Development & Resources Ltd. to Inter-Tech Resources Ltd. 06/24/1971
Struck off register and declared dissolved for failure to file returns 08/30/1982

INTER TEL DEL INC (DE)
Reincorporated 06/28/2006
Secondary Offering - 3,070,000 shares COM offered at $21 per share on 11/24/1997
Common no par split (2) for (1) by issuance of (1) additional share payable 10/21/1997 to holders of record 10/07/1997
Stock Dividend - 100% 08/14/1981
Name changed and state of incorporation changed from Inter-tel, Inc. (AZ) to Inter-Tel (Delaware), Inc. (DE) and Common no par changed to $0.001 par 06/28/2006
Merged into Mitel Networks Corp. 08/16/2007
Each share Common $0.001 par exchanged for $25.60 cash

INTER UTD FOODS CORP (ON)
Name changed to Mueller Medical International Inc. 06/15/1988
Mueller Medical International Inc.

recapitalized as Vasogen Inc. 04/21/1994 which merged into IntelliPharmaCeutics International Inc. 10/22/2009

INTER VENTURE (NV)
Recapitalized as Digital Power Holding Co. 06/09/1989
Each share Common $0.001 par exchanged for (0.1) share Common $0.001 par
Digital Power Holding Co. name changed to I-Storm, Inc. 07/20/1998
(See I-Storm, Inc.)

INTER WEST ENERGY CORP (BC)
Merged into New Cache Petroleums Ltd. 09/12/1997
Each share Common no par exchanged for (0.08) share Common no par
New Cache Petroleums Ltd. merged into Abraxas Petroleum Corp. 01/12/1999

INTER WORLD TV FILMS, INC. (DE)
Charter cancelled and declared inoperative and void for non-payment of taxes 10/01/1961

INTERA INFORMATION TECHNOLOGIES CORP (CANADA)
Name changed to IITC Holdings Ltd. 11/08/1995
(See IITC Holdings Ltd.)

INTERACT COMM CORP (DE)
Merged into Sage Group plc 5/7/2001
Each share Common $0.001 par exchanged for $12 cash

INTERACT PORTFOLIO SER (MA)
Trust terminated 08/24/1989
Details not available

INTERACTION MEDIA CORP (DE)
Charter forfeited for failure to maintain a registered agent 10/16/1998

INTERACTION RES LTD. (AB)
Name changed 12/22/1982
Reincorporated 04/28/1994
Under plan of merger name changed from Intermet Resources Ltd. to Interaction Resources Ltd. 12/22/1982
Each share Common no par exchanged for (0.66666666) share Common no par
Place of incorporation changed from (BC) to (AB) 04/28/1994
Recapitalized as Ketch Energy Ltd. 06/16/2000
Each share Common no par exchanged for (0.2) share Common no par
Ketch Energy Ltd. merged into Acclaim Energy Trust 10/01/2002
(See Acclaim Energy Trust)

INTERACTION SYS INC (MA)
Each share Class A Common $0.00125 par exchanged for (0.1) share Common $0.0125 par 4/2/86
Involuntarily dissolved 12/31/90

INTERACTIVE BRAND DEV INC (DE)
Company terminated registration of common stock and is no longer public as of 04/11/2008

INTERACTIVE BROADCASTING NETWORK GROUP INC (UT)
Name changed to Baymark Technologies Inc. 08/30/2002
Baymark Technologies Inc. name changed to Implantable Vision, Inc. 01/03/2006 which name changed to Arcland Energy Corp. 08/25/2008
(See Arcland Energy Corp.)

INTERACTIVE BUSINESS DEV INC NEW (NV)
Name changed to American BioDiesel Fuels Corp. 2/2/2007
American BioDiesel Fuels Corp. name changed to Planet Resource Recovery, Inc. 3/9/2007

INTERACTIVE BUSINESS DEV INC OLD (NV)
Name changed to Baby Bee Bright Corp. (Old) 7/27/2005
Baby Bee Bright Corp. (Old) name changed to Lab Holdings, Inc. 5/2/2006 which name changed to Mountain Top Properties, Inc. 12/13/2006

INTERACTIVE BUYERS NETWORK INTL LTD (NV)
Name changed to Vsource, Inc. (NV) 12/03/1999
Vsource, Inc. (NV) reincorporated in Delaware 11/08/2000 which name changed to Tri-Isthmus Group, Inc. 12/30/2005 which name changed to First Physicians Capital Group, Inc. 01/08/2010

INTERACTIVE COMMUNICATIONS CORP (BC)
Recapitalized as ICM Ventures Inc. 12/13/1993
Each share Common no par exchanged for (0.25) share Common no par
ICM Ventures Inc. name changed to RMS Medical Systems Inc. 04/30/1996 which recapitalized as Pacific Genesis Technologies Inc. (BC) 12/21/1999 which reincorporated in Alberta as Ware Solutions Corp. 10/01/2001
(See Ware Solutions Corp.)

INTERACTIVE DATA CORP (DE)
Acquired by Hg Investors L.L.C. 07/29/2010
Each share Common 1¢ par exchanged for $33.86 cash

INTERACTIVE DATA VISION INC (OR)
Recapitalized as Banyan Corp. 02/14/1996
Each share Common no par exchanged for (0.5) share Common no par
(See Banyan Corp.)

INTERACTIVE DIGITAL MULTI MEDIA INC (FL)
Recapitalized as Go Healthy, Inc. 04/11/2008
Each share Common no par exchanged for (1/3) share Common no par
Go Healthy, Inc. name changed to Global Payout, Inc. 12/28/2010

INTERACTIVE DIGITAL SYS CORP (ON)
Recapitalized as CRM Capital Inc. 05/23/1996
Each share Common no par exchanged for (0.1) share Common no par
CRM Capital Inc. recapitalized as Active Control Technology Inc. 04/01/1997
(See Active Control Technology Inc.)

INTERACTIVE ENTERPRISES INC (BC)
Name changed to Interactive Exploration Inc. 02/16/2004
Interactive Exploration Inc. name changed to Anglo-Canadian Uranium Corp. 08/22/2005 which name changed to Anglo-Canadian Mining Corp. 08/29/2011 which name changed to Canada One Mining Corp. 08/30/2017

INTERACTIVE ENTMT LTD (BERMUDA)
Name changed to Creator Capital Ltd. 10/16/2000

INTERACTIVE EXPL INC (BC)
Name changed to Anglo-Canadian Uranium Corp. 08/22/2005
Anglo-Canadian Uranium Corp. name changed to Anglo-Canadian Mining Corp. 08/29/2011 which name changed to Canada One Mining Corp. 08/30/2017

INTERACTIVE FLIGHT TECHNOLOGIES INC (DE)
Issue Information - 2,800,000 UNITS consisting of (1) share CL A, (1) WT CL A, and (1) WT CL B offered at $5 per Unit on 03/07/1995
Each share old Class A Common 1¢ par exchanged for (1/3) share new Class A Common 1¢ par 11/02/1998
Name changed to Global Technologies Ltd. 10/01/1999

INTERACTIVE GAMES INC (NV)
Name changed to China Nuvo Solar Energy, Inc. 08/13/2007
China Nuvo Solar Energy, Inc. name changed to SurgLine International, Inc. 01/27/2012

INTERACTIVE GAMING & COMMUNICATIONS CORP NEW (DE)
Recapitalized as Great American Financial Corp. 4/1/2003
Each share Common $0.001 par exchanged for (0.2) share Common $0.001 par

INTERACTIVE GAMING & COMMUNICATIONS CORP OLD (DE)
Name changed to GlobeSpan Technology Partners, Inc. 2/2/2000
GlobeSpan Technology Partners, Inc. name changed to Interactive Gaming & Communications Corp. (New) 9/27/2000 which recapitalized as Great American Financial Corp. 4/1/2003

INTERACTIVE GIFT EXPRESS INC (UT)
Name changed to E-Data Corp. (UT) 11/08/1995
E-Data Corp. (UT) reincorporated in Delaware 05/23/2002

INTERACTIVE GOLF MARKETING INC (CO)
Name changed to WowStores.Com, Inc. 02/22/1999
WowStores.Com, Inc. name changed to USR Holdings Co. 02/02/2001 which name changed to Technol Fuel Conditioners Inc. (CO) 01/31/2002 which reorganized in Florida as Allied Energy Group, Inc. 08/18/2006 which name changed to Allied Energy, Inc. 04/22/2010

INTERACTIVE GROUP INC (CA)
Merged into DataWorks Corp. (CA) 09/29/1997
Each share Common $0.001 par exchanged for (0.8054) share Common no par
DataWorks Corp. (CA) reincorporated in Delaware 10/30/1998 which merged into Platinum Software Corp. 12/31/1998 which name changed to Epicor Software Corp. 05/04/1999
(See Epicor Software Corp.)

INTERACTIVE GROUP INC (DE)
Recapitalized as Arrowhead Research Corp. 01/15/2004
Each share Common $0.001 par exchanged for (0.01538461) share Common $0.001 par
Arrowhead Research Corp. name changed to Arrowhead Pharmaceuticals, Inc. 04/07/2016

INTERACTIVE INC (DE)
Reincorporated 02/13/2001
State of incorporation changed from (SD) to (DE) 02/13/2001
Name changed to Interactive Group Inc. 02/16/2001
Interactive Group Inc. recapitalized as Arrowhead Research Corp. 01/15/2004 which name changed to Arrowhead Pharmaceuticals, Inc. 04/07/2016

INTERACTIVE INFORMATION SOLUTIONS INC (NY)
Each share old Common $0.001 par exchanged for (0.5) share new Common $0.001 par 12/5/96
Name changed to Microphonics, Inc. 2/5/97

INTERACTIVE INTELLIGENCE GROUP INC (IN)
Acquired by Genesys Telecommunications Laboratories, Inc. 12/01/2016
Each share Common 1¢ par exchanged for $60.50 cash

INTERACTIVE INTELLIGENCE INC (IN)
Name changed to Interactive Intelligence Intelligence Group, Inc. 07/01/2011
(See Interactive Intelligence Group, Inc.)

INTERACTIVE INV INTL PLC (ENGLAND & WALES)
Issue Information - 55,000,000 ADR'S offered at $24.06 per ADR on 02/16/2000
ADR agreement terminated 11/16/2001
Each Sponsored ADR for Ordinary 1p par exchanged for $4.6023 cash

INTERACTIVE LTG SHOWROOMS INC (NV)
Each share old Common $0.001 par exchanged for (0.02) share new Common $0.001 par 10/14/2002
Name changed to Am-Tex Oil & Gas Inc. 07/08/2004
Am-Tex Oil & Gas Inc. name changed to Critical Point Resources, Inc. 04/21/2008 which reorganized as Renewable Energy Solution Systems, Inc. 02/24/2012

INTERACTIVE MAGIC INC (NC)
Issue Information - 2,600,000 shares COM offered at $8 per share on 07/21/1998
Each share Class A Common 10¢ par exchanged for (0.5) share Common 10¢ par 7/1/98
Name changed to Ientertainment Network Inc. 12/30/99

INTERACTIVE MARKETING TECHNOLOGY INC (NV)
Each share Common $0.001 par received distribution of (1) share All Star Marketing Inc. Restricted Common payable 12/21/2004 to holders of record 12/20/2004
Recapitalized as China Artists Agency, Inc. 12/21/2004
Each share Common $0.001 par exchanged for (0.59171597) share Common $0.001 par
China Artists Agency, Inc. name changed to China Entertainment Group, Inc. 08/22/2005 which name changed to Safe & Secure TV Channel, Inc. 08/12/2010 which name changed to Cosmos Group Holdings Inc. 03/31/2016

INTERACTIVE MED TECHNOLOGIES LTD (DE)
Merged into Kaire Holdings Inc. (DE) 02/19/1998
Each share Common $0.001 par exchanged for (0.01333333) share Common $0.001 par
Kaire Holdings Inc. (DE) reorganized in Nevada as International Packaging & Logistics Group, Inc. 05/21/2008 which name changed to YBCC, Inc. 12/22/2016

INTERACTIVE MEDIA TECHNOLOGIES INC (AZ)
Reincorporated under the laws of Delaware and Common $0.001 par changed to 1¢ par 11/30/90
Plan of reorganization under Chapter 11 Federal Bankruptcy Code effective 5/18/94
Holdings of each share old Common 1¢ par received (0.1) share new Common 1¢ par and (0.05) Common Stock Purchase Warrant, Class A expiring 12/31/95
Note: Certificates were not required to be surrendered and are without value
(Additional Information in Active)

INTERACTIVE MOTORSPORTS INC (NV)
Name changed to Black Sea Oil, Inc. (Old) 12/11/2000
(See Black Sea Oil, Inc. (Old))

INTERACTIVE MULTI MEDIA AUCTION CORP (BRITISH VIRGIN ISLANDS)
Each share Common $0.001 par exchanged for (4) shares Common $0.00025 par 02/03/2015
Name changed to Stop Sleep Go Inc. 03/27/2017

INTERACTIVE MULTIMEDIA NETWORK INC (DE)
Recapitalized as RECOV Energy Corp. 03/29/2005
Each share Common $0.001 par exchanged for (0.05) share Common $0.001 par
RECOV Energy Corp. name changed to General Metals Corp. 01/26/2006 which recapitalized as Cibolan Gold Corp. 05/30/2014

INTERACTIVE MULTIMEDIA PUBLISHERS INC (DE)
Charter cancelled and declared inoperative and void for non-payment of taxes 3/1/98

INTERACTIVE MUSIC INC (NV)
Common $0.00001 par split (4) for (1) by issuance of (3) additional shares payable 10/01/1999 to holders of record 09/27/1999
Name changed to Zebramart.com Inc. 01/04/2000
Zebramart.com Inc. name changed to Cottage Investments, Inc. 11/15/2000 which recapitalized as Paving Stone Corp. 12/19/2001
(See Paving Stone Corp.)

INTERACTIVE NETWORK INC (CA)
Merged into Two Way TV (US), Inc. 05/01/2002
Each share Common no par exchanged for (1) share Common $0.001 par
(See Two Way TV (US), Inc.)

INTERACTIVE OBJECTS INC (UT)
Name changed to Fullplay Media Systems, Inc. 1/7/2002
(See Fullplay Media Systems, Inc.)

INTERACTIVE PICTURES CORP (TN)
Issue Information - 3,850,000 shares COM offered at $18 per share on 08/05/1999
Merged into Bamboo.com, Inc. 01/20/2000
Each share Common $0.001 par exchanged for (1.369) shares Common $0.001 par
Bamboo.com, Inc. name changed to Internet Pictures Corp. 01/21/2000 which name changed to IPIX Corp. 03/24/2004
(See IPIX Corp.)

INTERACTIVE PRINCIPLES LTD (DE)
Name changed to Interactive Medical Technologies, Ltd. 02/28/1990
Interactive Medical Technologies, Ltd. recapitalized as Kaire Holdings Inc. (DE) 02/19/1998 which reorganized in Nevada as International Packaging & Logistics Group, Inc. 05/21/2008 which name changed to YBCC, Inc. 12/22/2016

INTERACTIVE PROCESSING INC (NV)
Recapitalized as WorldTradeShow.Com, Inc. 03/01/1999
Each share Common $0.001 par exchanged for (0.01) share Common $0.001 par

WorldTradeShow.Com, Inc. name changed to Business.vn, Inc. 06/25/2007 which recapitalized as Omni Global Technologies, Inc. 11/18/2016 which name changed to Blockchain Industries, Inc. 01/10/2018

INTERACTIVE RADIATION INC (NJ)
Name changed to InRad, Inc. 06/22/1988
InRad, Inc. name changed to Photonic Products Group, Inc. 10/22/2003 which name changed to Inrad Optics, Inc. 04/09/2012

INTERACTIVE SOLUTIONS CORP (NV)
Reorganized under the laws of Wyoming as MyMedicalCD, Ltd. 11/24/2004
Each share Common $0.0001 par exchanged for (0.00125) share Common $0.0001 par
MyMedicalCD, Ltd. recapitalized as United Treatment Centers, Inc. 01/30/2009 which name changed to PotNetwork Holdings, Inc. (WY) 07/24/2015 which reincorporated in Colorado 03/03/2017

INTERACTIVE SYS CORP (CO)
Charter suspended for failure to file annual reports 09/30/1987

INTERACTIVE SYS WORLDWIDE INC. (DE)
SEC revoked common stock registration 11/14/2013

INTERACTIVE TECHNOLOGIES CO (UT)
Name changed to NovaPet Products, Inc. 3/9/98

INTERACTIVE TECHNOLOGIES COM LTD (DE)
Each share Common $0.001 par received distribution of (0.23529411) share International Merchantcard Services Inc. Common payable 01/01/2002 to holders of record 09/01/2001
Reorganized under the laws of Florida as International Coastal Biofuels, Inc. 04/09/2008
Each share Common $0.001 par exchanged for (0.005) share Common no par
International Coastal Biofuels, Inc. recapitalized as IMD Companies Inc. 10/12/2010

INTERACTIVE TECHNOLOGIES CORP (WY)
Name changed to Airtech International Group, Inc. 10/6/98
(See Airtech International Group, Inc.)

INTERACTIVE TECHNOLOGIES INC (MN)
Merged into Network Security Corp. (DE) 6/5/89
Each share Common no par exchanged for $17.375 cash

INTERACTIVE TEL NETWORK INC (DE)
Each share old Common $0.0001 par exchanged for (0.25) share new Common $0.0001 par 11/27/1995
Recapitalized as T House & Co. Ltd. 12/30/1998
Each share new Common $0.0001 par exchanged for (0.01) share Common $0.0001 par
T House & Co. Ltd. name changed to Team Labs Systems Group Inc. 08/28/2000 which name changed to SciLabs Holdings, Inc. 07/17/2001
(See SciLabs Holdings, Inc.)

INTERACTIVE TELESIS INC (DE)
Reincorporated 09/23/1996
Place of incorporation changed from (BC) to (DE) and Common no par changed to $0.001 par 09/23/1996
Each share old Common $0.001 par exchanged for (1/7) share new Common $0.001 par 10/08/1996

Plan of reorganization under Chapter 11 Federal Bankruptcy Code effective 11/15/2003
No stockholders' equity

INTERACTIVE TERMS INC (NV)
Each share old Common $0.0002 par exchanged for (1/60) share new Common $0.0002 par 12/23/1997
Name changed to Elk City Mining, Inc. 04/28/1998
Elk City Mining, Inc. name changed to Chill Tech Industries Inc. 10/05/1998
(See Chill Tech Industries Inc.)

INTERACTIVE THERAPEUTICS INC (CO)
SEC revoked common stock registration 10/03/2011

INTERACTIVE VIDEOSYSTEMS INC (BC)
Name changed 7/19/94
Name changed from Interactive Video Systems Inc. to Interactive VideoSystems Inc. 07/19/1994
Name changed to NCC Mining Corp. 08/16/1995
NCC Mining Corp. recapitalized as BMA Mining Corp. 07/11/1997 which recapitalized as Dasher Energy Corp. 05/26/1999 which name changed to Dasher Resources Corp. 10/03/2002 which recapitalized as Dasher Exploration Ltd. 04/16/2003 which name changed to New World Resource Corp. 06/27/2005

INTERACTIVECORP (DE)
Name changed to IAC/InterActiveCorp 7/14/2004

INTERALLIED CORP (DE)
Dissolved 12/29/66
Details not available

INTERALLIED GROUP INC (NV)
Reincorporated under the laws of Delaware as Pilot Therapeutics Holdings, Inc. 12/06/2001
(See Pilot Therapeutics Holdings, Inc.)

INTERALLIED INVESTING CORP. (DE)
Name changed to Interallied Corp. 12/15/1961
(See Interallied Corp.)

INTERALLIED RES CORP (NY)
Recapitalized as Tri Tec Plastics Corp. 2/24/84
Each share Common 1¢ par exchanged for (1/3) share Common 1¢ par
Tri Tec Plastics Corp. merged into Secom General Corp. 12/17/91
(See Secom General Corp.)

INTERALLIED RESTAURANT GROUP INC (NV)
Each share old Common 1¢ par exchanged for (0.5) share new Common 1¢ par 09/30/1998
Name changed to InterAllied Group, Inc. (NV) 02/08/1999
InterAllied Group, Inc. (NV) reincorporated in Delaware as Pilot Therapeutics Holdings, Inc. 12/06/2001
(See Pilot Therapeutics Holdings, Inc.)

INTERAMERICAN ACQUISITION GROUP INC (DE)
Merged into CNC Development Ltd. 09/09/2009
Each share Common $0.0001 par exchanged for (0.8857955) share Class A Preferred and (0.1850734) share Common $0.0001 par
(See CNC Development Ltd.)

INTERAMERICAN GAMING INC (NV)
SEC revoked common stock registration 02/21/2017

INTERAMERICAN INDS LTD (AB)
Struck from Alberta Registrar of Companies and proclaimed dissolved 12/15/1969

INTERAMERICAN NATIONAL BANK AT SUNNY ISLES (MIAMI BEACH, FL)
Name changed to Jefferson National Bank at Sunny Isles (North Miami Beach, FL) 07/00/1968
(See Jefferson National Bank at Sunny Isles (North Miami Beach, FL))

INTERAMERICAN RES INC (FL)
Each share old Common $0.0005 par exchanged for (0.02) share new Common $0.0005 par 03/27/2003
Name changed to Allixon Corp. 06/04/2004
Allixon Corp. recapitalized as Simcoe Mining Resources Corp. 01/16/2008

INTERAMERICAN TRUST CO. (SC)
Charter dissolved for failure to pay taxes 2/15/65

INTERAMERICAS COMMUNICATIONS CORP (TX)
Name changed to Firstcom Corp. 10/22/98
Firstcom Corp. merged into AT&T Latin America Corp. 8/29/2000
(See AT&T Latin America Corp.)

INTERAND CORP (DE)
Name changed to InventBay.com, Inc. 06/14/2007
InventBay.com, Inc. recapitalized as SMA Alliance, Inc. 05/20/2011

INTERAXX DIGITAL TOOLS INC (FL)
Reincorporated 07/23/2004
State of incorporation changed from (DE) to (FL) 07/23/2004
Name changed to MEDirect Latino Inc. 02/18/2005
(See MEDirect Latino Inc.)

INTERAXX PPTYS INC (DE)
Name changed to Infoterra Corp. 10/20/2005

INTERAXX TECHNOLOGIES INC (DE)
Plan of reorganization under Chapter 11 Federal Bankruptcy Code effective 2/28/2003
Each share Common $0.25 par exchanged for (1) Conv. Preferred Ser. A Unit consisting of (0.125) share Interaxx Digital Tools, Inc. Ser. A Preferred, (0.25) share Interaxx Properties, Inc. Ser. A Preferred, (0.125) share Jefferson Capital Interests, Inc. Ser. A Preferred, (0.5) share Stassi Interaxx, Inc. Ser. A Preferred and (1) Common Stock Purchase Warrant Ser. A, B and C for each company
Note: Certificates were required to be surrendered by 3/7/2002 in order to receive distribution
(See each company's listing)

INTERBANC FINANCIAL GROUP, INC. (FL)
Merged out of existence 07/01/1991
Details not available

INTERBANC INVESTORS, INC.
Dissolved in 1949

INTERBET INC (NV)
Name changed to Virtual Gaming Enterprises, Inc. 05/15/1998
Virtual Gaming Enterprises, Inc. name changed to Asgard Holdings, Inc. 08/25/2004 which recapitalized as Principal Capital Group, Inc. (Old) 02/26/2008
(See Principal Capital Group, Inc. (Old))

INTERBEV PACKAGING CORP (BC)
Merged into Jolt Beverage Co., Ltd. 12/14/1987
Details not available

INTERBOLSA S A (COLOMBIA)
ADR agreement terminated 02/22/2013
Each Sponsored ADR for Ordinary exchanged for (10) shares Ordinary
Note: Company ordered into liquidation 01/04/2013

INTERBOROUGH CONSOLIDATED CORP. (NY)
Charter cancelled and proclaimed dissolved for failure to pay taxes and file reports 12/15/32

INTERBOROUGH RAPID TRANSIT CO.
Acquired by the City of New York 6/12/40
Each share Common exchanged for $2.85 principal amount of 3% New York City Corporate Stock due 6/1/80

INTERBUSINESS CORP (PA)
Merged into DBST Corp. 11/19/98
Each share new Common no par exchanged for $0.625 cash

INTERCALLNET INC (FL)
Assets assigned for the benefit of creditors 11/26/2002
Stockholders' equity unlikely

INTERCAN LEASING INC (CANADA)
Declared bankrupt 11/09/1994
Stockholders' equity undetermined

INTERCAP ECOMMERCE INC (AB)
Name changed 09/01/2000
Name changed from INTERCAP Enterprises Group Inc. to INTERCAP eCommerce Inc. 09/01/2000
Recapitalized as BioNeutra Global Corp. 10/29/2014
Each share Common no par exchanged for (0.1) share Common no par

INTERCAP RES MGMT CO (BC)
Recapitalized as Pine Resources Corp. (BC) 04/07/1999
Each share Common no par exchanged for (0.28571428) share Common no par
Pine Resources Corp. (BC) reincorporated in Canada as Trimble Resources Corp. 01/17/2002
(See Trimble Resources Corp.)

INTERCAPITAL CALIF INSD MUN INCOME TR (MA)
Name changed to Morgan Stanley Dean Witter 12/21/1998
Morgan Stanley Dean Witter name changed to Morgan Stanley Trusts 12/20/2001
(See Morgan Stanley Trusts)

INTERCAPITAL CALIF QUALITY MUN SECS (MA)
Name changed to Morgan Stanley Dean Witter 12/21/1998
Morgan Stanley Dean Witter name changed to Morgan Stanley Trusts 12/20/2001
(See Morgan Stanley Trusts)

INTERCAPITAL DIVID GROWTH SECS INC (MD)
Name changed to Witter (Dean) Dividend Growth Securities Inc. 3/21/83

INTERCAPITAL HIGH YIELD SECS INC (MD)
Name changed to Witter (Dean) High Yield Securities Inc. 03/21/1983
Witter (Dean) High Yield Securities Inc. name changed to Morgan Stanley Dean Witter High Yield Securities Inc. 06/22/1998 which name changed to Morgan Stanley High Yield Securities Inc. 06/18/2001 which merged into Aim Investment Securities Funds (Invesco Investment Securities Funds) (DE) 06/01/2010

INTERCAPITAL INCOME SECS INC (MD)
Name changed to Morgan Stanley Dean Witter 12/21/1998
Morgan Stanley Dean Witter name changed to Morgan Stanley Trusts 12/20/2001
(See Morgan Stanley Trusts)

INTERCAPITAL IND VALUED SECS INC (MD)
Name changed to Dean Witter Industry-Valued Securities Inc. 3/21/83
Dean Witter Industry-Valued Securities Inc. name changed to Dean Witter American Value Fund 4/30/87 which name changed to Morgan Stanley Dean Witter American Value Fund in May 1997 which name changed to Morgan Stanley Dean Witter American Opportunities Fund 3/12/99 which name changed to Morgan Stanley American Opportunities Fund 6/18/2001

INTERCAPITAL INSD CALIF MUN SECS (MA)
Name changed to Morgan Stanley Dean Witter 12/21/1998
Morgan Stanley Dean Witter name changed to Morgan Stanley Trusts 12/20/2001
(See Morgan Stanley Trusts)

INTERCAPITAL INSD MUN BD TR (MA)
Name changed to Morgan Stanley Dean Witter 12/21/1998
Morgan Stanley Dean Witter name changed to Morgan Stanley Trusts 12/20/2001
(See Morgan Stanley Trusts)

INTERCAPITAL INSD MUN INCOME TR (MA)
Name changed to Morgan Stanley Dean Witter 12/21/1998
Morgan Stanley Dean Witter name changed to Morgan Stanley Trusts 12/20/2001
(See Morgan Stanley Trusts)

INTERCAPITAL INSD MUN SECURITIES (MA)
Name changed to Morgan Stanley Dean Witter 12/21/1998
Morgan Stanley Dean Witter name changed to Morgan Stanley Trusts 12/20/2001
(See Morgan Stanley Trusts)

INTERCAPITAL INSD MUN TR (MA)
Name changed to Morgan Stanley Dean Witter 12/21/1998
Morgan Stanley Dean Witter name changed to Morgan Stanley Trusts 12/20/2001
(See Morgan Stanley Trusts)

INTERCAPITAL LIQUID ASSET FD INC (MD)
Name changed to Dean Witter/Sears Liquid Asset Fund Inc. 3/21/83
Dean Witter/Sears Liquid Asset Fund Inc. name changed to Dean Witter Liquid Asset Fund Inc. 2/19/93

INTERCAPITAL N Y QUALITY MUN SECS (MA)
Name changed to Morgan Stanley Dean Witter 12/21/1998
Morgan Stanley Dean Witter name changed to Morgan Stanley Trusts 12/20/2001
(See Morgan Stanley Trusts)

INTERCAPITAL NAT RES DEV SECS INC (MD)
Name changed to Witter (Dean) Natural Resource Development Securities Inc. 3/21/83

INTERCAPITAL QUALITY MUN INCOME TR (MA)
Name changed to Morgan Stanley Dean Witter 12/21/1998
Morgan Stanley Dean Witter name changed to Morgan Stanley Trusts 12/20/2001
(See Morgan Stanley Trusts)

INTERCAPITAL QUALITY MUN INVT TR (MA)
Name changed to Morgan Stanley Dean Witter 12/21/1998
Morgan Stanley Dean Witter name changed to Morgan Stanley Trusts 12/20/2001
(See Morgan Stanley Trusts)

INTERCAPITAL QUALITY MUN SECS (MA)
Name changed to Morgan Stanley Dean Witter 12/21/1998
Morgan Stanley Dean Witter name changed to Morgan Stanley Trusts 12/20/2001
(See Morgan Stanley Trusts)

INTERCAPITAL TAX EXEMPT SECS INC (MD)
Name changed to Witter (Dean) Tax-Exempt Securities Inc. 3/21/83

INTERCAPITAL TAX FREE DAILY INCOME FD INC (MD)
Name changed to Witter (Dean)/Sears Tax Free Daily Income Fund Inc. 3/21/83

INTERCARDIA INC (DE)
Name changed to Incara Pharmaceuticals Corp. (Old) 7/16/99
Incara Pharmaceuticals Corp. (Old) name changed to Incara Pharmaceuticals Corp. (New) 11/21/2003 which recapitalized as Aeolus Pharmaceuticals, Inc. 7/16/2004

INTERCARE COM DX INC (CA)
Name changed 9/18/2002
Name changed from InterCare.com Inc. to InterCare.com-DX Inc. 9/18/2002
Name changed to InterCare DX, Inc. 4/22/2003

INTERCARE INC (DE)
Charter cancelled and declared inoperative and void for non-payment of taxes 3/1/89
No stockholders' equity

INTERCARGO CORP (DE)
Common $1 par split (2) for (1) by issuance of (1) additional share 12/11/1991
Merged into XL Capital Ltd. 05/07/1999
Each share Common $1 par exchanged for $12 cash

INTERCEDENT VENTURES LTD (CANADA)
Merged into ARISE Technologies Corp. 07/30/2003
Each share Common no par exchanged for (0.2051282) share Common no par and (0.1025641) Common Stock Purchase Warrant expiring 06/26/2005
(See ARISE Technologies Corp.)

INTERCEL INC (DE)
Name changed to Powertel Inc. 7/1/97
Powertel Inc. merged into Deutsche Telekom AG 5/31/2001

INTERCELL AG (AUSTRIA)
Merged into Vivalis S.A. 06/27/2013
Each Sponsored ADR for Ordinary exchanged for $2.311548 cash

INTERCELL CORP (CO)
Each (150) shares old Common no par exchanged for (1) share new Common no par 12/24/1992
Reorganized under the laws of Nevada as Intercell International Corp. 05/31/2001
Each share new Common no par exchanged for (0.05) share Common no par
Intercell International Corp. name changed to NewMarket China, Inc. 02/07/2007 which name changed to China Crescent Enterprises, Inc. 07/03/2008

INTERCELL INDS INC (CA)
Charter suspended for failure to file reports and pay fees 05/01/1979

INTERCELL INTL CORP (NV)
Name changed to NewMarket China, Inc. 02/07/2007
NewMarket China, Inc. name changed to China Crescent Enterprises, Inc. 07/03/2008

INTERCEPT, INC. (UT)
Name changed to Unitex, Inc. in May, 1989

INTERCEPT INC (GA)
Name changed 2/25/2002
Name changed from InterCept Group, Inc. to InterCept, Inc. 2/25/2002
Merged into Fidelity National Financial, Inc. 11/8/2004
Each share Common no par exchanged for $18.90 cash

INTERCHANGE CORP (DE)
Issue Information - 2,750,000 shares COM offered at $8 per share on 10/18/2004
Name changed to Local.com Corp. 11/02/2006
Local.com Corp. name changed to Local Corp. 09/17/2012

INTERCHANGE FINL SVCS CORP (NJ)
Common no par split (3) for (2) by issuance of (0.5) additional share payable 04/17/1997 to holders of record 03/20/1997 Ex date - 04/18/1997
Common no par split (3) for (2) by issuance of (0.5) additional share payable 04/17/1998 to holders of record 03/20/1998 Ex date - 04/20/1998
Common no par split (3) for (2) by issuance of (0.5) additional share payable 07/12/2002 to holders of record 06/17/2002
Common no par split (3) for (2) by issuance of (0.5) additional share payable 02/18/2005 to holders of record 02/02/2005 Ex date - 02/22/2005
Stock Dividend - 5% payable 04/19/1996 to holders of record 03/20/1996
Merged into TD Banknorth Inc. 01/02/2007
Each share Common no par exchanged for $23 cash

INTERCHANGE MED INC (FL)
Each share old Common $0.00001 par exchanged for (0.01) share new Common $0.00001 par 10/13/2006
Merged into Maxwell Rand, Inc. 12/10/2007
Each share Common $0.00001 par exchanged for (1) share Common $0.001 par

INTERCHANGE ST BK (SADDLE BROOK, NJ)
Common $2.50 par split (2) for (1) by issuance of (1) additional share 04/22/1985
Reorganized as Interchange Financial Services Corp. 11/28/1986
Each share Common $2.50 par exchanged for (1) share Common no par
(See Interchange Financial Services Corp.)

INTERCHEMICAL CORP (OH)
Each share 6% Preferred $100 par exchanged for (1) share 4-1/2% Preferred $100 par and $5 cash in 1944
Each share Common no par exchanged for (2) shares Common $5 par in 1948
Common $5 par split (5) for (2) by issuance of (1.5) additional shares 4/1/59
Common $5 par split (3) for (2) by issuance of (0.5) additional share 2/15/65
Common $5 par split (1.75) for (1) by issuance of (0.75) additional share 2/28/69
Stock Dividend - 15% 2/1/56
Name changed to Inmont Corp. 4/15/69
Inmont Corp. merged into Carrier Corp. 12/27/77 which was acquired by United Technologies Corp. 7/6/79

INTERCIM CORP (MN)
Merged into Effective Management Systems, Inc. 2/17/95
Each share Common 1¢ par exchanged for (0.0175093) share Common 1¢ par
(See Effective Management Systems, Inc.)

INTERCITIC ENVIROTEC INC (BC)
Name changed to Inter-Citic Mineral Technologies Inc. 10/4/99
Inter-Citic Mineral Technologies Inc. name changed to Inter-Citic Minerals Inc. 12/19/2003

INTERCLICK INC (DE)
Each share old Common $0.001 par exchanged for (0.5) share new Common $0.001 par 10/27/2009
Acquired by Yahoo! Inc. 12/14/2011
Each share new Common $0.001 par exchanged for $9 cash

INTERCO INC NEW (DE)
Name changed to Furniture Brands International, Inc. 03/01/1996
(See Furniture Brands International, Inc.)

INTERCO INC OLD (DE)
Common no par split (2) for (1) by issuance of (1) additional share 04/15/1968
$4.75 Conv. 1st Preferred Ser. A $100 par converted into Common no par 00/00/1973
5.25% Conv. 1st Preferred Ser. B no par called for redemption 04/01/1975
$5.25 Conv. 2nd Preferred Ser. C no par converted into Common no par 03/30/1977
Common no par split (2) for (1) by issuance of (1) additional share 07/22/1986
Plan of reorganization under Chapter 11 Federal Bankruptcy proceedings effective 08/03/1992
No stockholders' equity

INTERCOAST COMPANIES, INC. (CA)
Name changed to Intercoast Life Insurance Co. and Common $10 par changed to $4 par 11/2/64
Intercoast Life Insurance Co. name changed to I.C. Liquidating Corp. 10/20/69 which merged into Pacific Standard Life Co. (AZ) 12/23/70 which reincorporated in Delaware 5/13/74 which merged into Southmark Corp. 8/30/83

INTERCOAST LIFE INS CO (CA)
Name changed to I.C. Liquidating Corp. 10/20/1969
I.C. Liquidating Corp. merged into Pacific Standard Life Co. (AZ) 12/23/1970 which reincorporated in Delaware 05/13/1974 which merged into Southmark Corp. 08/30/1983

INTERCOAST PETROLEUM CORP. (MD)
Common 50¢ par changed to 10¢ par in 1940
Merged into Chesapeake Industries, Inc. 2/14/55
Each share Common 10¢ par exchanged for (4/7) share Common $1 par
Chesapeake Industries, Inc. name changed to America Corp. (OH) 8/10/59 which recapitalized as America Corp. (DE) 12/31/63 which name changed to Pathe Industries, Inc. (DE) 11/20/64
(See Pathe Industries, Inc. (DE))

INTERCOAST RES CORP (BC)
Adjudicated bankrupt 02/17/1981

Stockholders' equity unlikely

INTERCOAST TRADING CORP. (NV)
Acquired by Transamerica Corp.
00/00/1931
Details not available

INTERCOASTAL CAPITAL CORP. (NY)
Charter cancelled and proclaimed dissolved for failure to pay taxes 12/23/1986

INTERCOLE AUTOMATION, INC. (CA)
Stock Dividend - 10% 1/8/80
Name changed to Intercole Inc. 12/8/80
(See Intercole Inc.)

INTERCOLE AUTOMATION, INC. (OH)
Merged into Intercole Automation, Inc. (Calif.) 9/22/72
Each share Common no par exchanged for (0.5) share Common $5 par
Intercole Automation, Inc. (Calif.) name changed to Intercole Inc. 12/8/80
(See Intercole Inc.)

INTERCOLE INC (CA)
Stock Dividends - 10% 1/15/81; 10% 1/20/82; 10% 1/20/83; 10% 1/20/84; 10% 1/8/85
Merged into Northern Group Inc. 4/17/85
Each share Common $1 par exchanged for $9.09 cash

INTERCOLONIAL COAL CO. LTD. (NS)
Liquidation completed 04/18/1955
Details not available

INTERCOLONIAL SALES CO. LTD.
Name changed to Intercolonial Coal Co. Ltd. 00/00/1927
(See Intercolonial Coal Co.)

INTERCOM SYS INC (DE)
SEC revoked common stock registration 11/07/2011

INTERCOM TECHNOLOGIES CORP (NY)
Each share old Common $0.0001 par exchanged for (0.0002941) share new Common $0.0001 par 10/03/1997
Name changed to Radio World Corp. 04/21/1999
(See Radio World Corp.)

INTERCOMMERCE CORP (NV)
Recapitalized as CipherPass Corp. 06/06/2005
Each share Common $0.001 par exchanged for (0.25) share Common $0.001 par
CipherPass Corp. recapitalized as Javalon Technology Group, Inc. (NV) 09/06/2007 which reincorporated in British Virgin Islands as WorldVest Equity, Inc. 11/13/2008

INTERCON DEVELOPMENT CORP. (DE)
Each share Common $1 par exchanged for (0.2) share Common 10¢ par 6/7/61
Acquired by United Improvement & Investing Corp. on a (1) for (30.4) basis 5/24/63
United Improvement & Investing Corp. name changed to U.I.P. Corp. 5/7/68 which merged into Eastmet Corp. 12/20/79
(See Eastmet Corp.)

INTERCON PETE INC (BC)
Struck off register and declared dissolved for failure to file returns 04/10/1992

INTERCONTINENT PETROLEUM CORP.
Out of business 00/00/1933
Details not available

INTERCONTINENTAL APPAREL INC (DE)
Completely liquidated 9/11/79
Each share Common 10¢ par exchanged for first and final distribution of $2.75 cash

INTERCONTINENTAL BK (MIAMI, FL)
Merged into NationsBank Corp. 12/13/95
Each share Common $2 par exchanged for (0.4153) share Common $2 par
NationsBank Corp. reincorporated in Delaware as BankAmerica Corp. (Old) 9/25/98 which merged into BankAmerica Corp. (New) 9/30/98 which name changed to Bank of America Corp. 4/28/99

INTERCONTINENTAL DATA CTL LTD (CANADA)
Placed in receivership 00/00/1987
Details not available

INTERCONTINENTAL DIAMOND CORP (MA)
Name changed to Intek Diversified Corp. (MA) 7/19/83
Intek Diversified Corp. (MA) reincorporated in (DE) 11/28/88 which name changed to Intek Global Corp. 2/18/98
(See Intek Global Corp.)

INTERCONTINENTAL DIVERSIFIED CORP (PANAMA)
Each share Common 50¢ par exchanged for (0.25) share Common $2 par 08/27/1975
Under plan of recapitalization each share Common $2 par automatically became (1) share Class A Common $2 par or Class B Common $2 par 01/27/1981
Class B Common $2 par called for redemption 03/06/1981
Each share Class A Common $2 par exchanged for (0.00002) share Class A Common $100,000 par 07/14/1981
Note: In effect holders received $30 cash per share and public interest was eliminated

INTERCONTINENTAL DYNAMICS CORP (NY)
Merged into Sun Chemical Corp. 3/31/86
Each share Common 10¢ par exchanged for $7.86 cash

INTERCONTINENTAL ELECTRS CORP (NY)
Name changed to IEC Electronics Corp. 2/1/73
(See IEC Electronics Corp.)

INTERCONTINENTAL ENERGY CORP (DE)
Stock Dividend - 20% 9/14/79
Under plan of merger each share Common 40¢ par received (1.21) shares of Greenwood Holdings, Inc. Common 1¢ par 12/17/87
Note: Certificates were not required to be surrendered and are without value
Greenwood Holdings, Inc. name changed to Packaging Research Corp. 2/3/93

INTERCONTINENTAL ENTERPRISES INC (CO)
Administratively dissolved 05/01/1997

INTERCONTINENTAL EQUITIES INC (NV)
Charter permanently revoked 04/30/2003

INTERCONTINENTAL FINL CORP (NJ)
Name changed to Intercontinental Life Corp. (NJ) 07/08/1977
Intercontinental Life Corp. (NJ) reincorporated in Texas 06/19/1997 which merged into Financial Industries Corp. 05/18/2001

(See Financial Industries Corp.)

INTERCONTINENTAL HOLDINGS LTD.
Liquidated in March 1955

INTERCONTINENTAL HOTELS GROUP PLC OLD (UNITED KINGDOM)
Each old Sponsored ADR for Ordinary exchanged for (0.892857) new Sponsored ADR for Ordinary and $1.3893 cash 12/13/2004
Each new Sponsored ADR for Ordinary exchanged for (0.733333) InterContinental Hotels Group PLC (New) Sponsored ADR for Ordinary and $2.85846 cash 06/27/2005

INTERCONTINENTAL INDUSTRIES, INC. (HI)
Merged into Kaneta Family Corp., Inc. 9/30/88
Each share Capital Stock no par exchanged for $2.25 cash

INTERCONTINENTAL INDUSTRIES CORP. (DE)
Charter cancelled and declared inoperative and void for non-payment of taxes 3/1/76

INTERCONTINENTAL INDS INC (NV)
Reincorporated 02/16/1968
State of incorporation changed from (MA) to (NV) 02/16/1968
Completely liquidated 00/00/1982
For holdings of (99) shares or fewer each share Common $1 par exchanged for first and final distribution of $1 cash
For holdings of (100) shares or more each share Common $1 par exchanged for first and final distribution of (0.5) share Commercial Technology, Inc. Common 1¢ par
Commercial Technology, Inc. liquidated for Electric & Gas Technology, Inc. 10/00/1989
(See Electric & Gas Technology, Inc.)

INTERCONTINENTAL INVESTMENT CORP.
Inactive in 1938

INTERCONTINENTAL LIFE CO (NJ)
Recapitalized as Intercontinental Financial Corp. 07/16/1973
Each share Common 20¢ par exchanged for (0.2) share Common $1 par
Intercontinental Financial Corp. name changed to Intercontinental Life Corp. (NJ) 07/08/1977 which reincorporated in Texas 06/19/1997 which merged into Financial Industries Corp. 05/18/2001
(See Financial Industries Corp.)

INTERCONTINENTAL LIFE CORP (TX)
Reincorporated 06/19/1997
Common $1 par changed to 66-2/3¢ par and (0.5) additional share issued 03/01/1983
Common 66-2/3¢ par changed to 22¢ par and (2) additional shares issued 02/21/1990
State of incorporation changed from (NJ) to (TX) 06/17/1997
Common 22¢ par split (2) for (1) by issuance of (1) additional share payable 03/17/1999 to holders of record 03/08/1999
Merged into Financial Industries Corp. 05/18/2001
Each share Common 22¢ par exchanged for (1.1) shares Common 20¢ par
(See Financial Industries Corp.)

INTERCONTINENTAL LIFE INS CO (NJ)
Acquired by Intercontinental Life Co. 06/24/1970
Each share Common 20¢ par exchanged for (1) share Common 20¢ par

Intercontinental Life Co. recapitalized as Intercontinental Financial Corp. 07/16/1973 which name changed to Intercontinental Life Corp. (NJ) 07/08/1977 which reincorporated in Texas 06/19/1997 which merged into Financial Industries Corp. 05/18/2001
(See Financial Industries Corp.)

INTERCONTINENTAL MENS APPAREL INC (DE)
Name changed to Intercontinental Apparel, Inc. 11/20/72
(See Intercontinental Apparel, Inc.)

INTERCONTINENTAL MINERALS & PETE INC (NV)
Recapitalized as # 1 Cousin Organization, Inc. 8/30/85
Each share Common $0.0001 par exchanged for (0.1) share Common $0.0001 par
1 Cousin Organization name changed to J & J Research Inc. 2/11/86

INTERCONTINENTAL MINERALS & PETE INC FLA (UT)
Reorganized under the laws of Florida as American Fuel & Power Corp. 2/16/83
Each share Common 1¢ par exchanged for (1) share Common 1¢ par
(See American Fuel & Power Corp.)

INTERCONTINENTAL MNG & ABRASIVES INC (RI)
Charter forfeited for non-payment of taxes 12/31/1975

INTERCONTINENTAL MNG CORP (BC)
Reincorporated under the laws of Alberta as Maple Leaf Reforestation Inc. 03/03/2005
Maple Leaf Reforestation Inc. name changed to Maple Leaf Green World Inc. 10/05/2012

INTERCONTINENTAL MOTELS, LTD. (DE)
Reorganized 5/19/67
No stockholders' equity

INTERCONTINENTAL RES GROUP INC (DE)
Charter cancelled and declared inoperative and void for non-payment of taxes 3/1/93

INTERCONTINENTAL RES INC (NV)
Each share old Common $0.001 par exchanged for (0.002) share new Common $0.001 par 09/19/2007
Name changed to China Valves Technology, Inc. 01/09/2008

INTERCONTINENTAL RUBBER CO. (DE)
Merged into Texas Instruments, Inc. and each share Capital Stock no par exchanged for (1) share Common $1 par in 1953

INTERCONTINENTAL RUBBER CO. (NJ)
Dissolved in 1926

INTERCONTINENTAL SECURITIES, LTD. (NY)
Name changed to Golconda Investors Ltd. (NY) 03/12/1975
Goldconda Investors Ltd. (NY) reorganized in Maryland as Bull & Bear Gold Investors Ltd. 10/26/1987 which name changed to Midas Investments Ltd. 06/30/1999 which merged into Midas Fund, Inc. (MD) 11/16/2001 which reorganized in Delaware as Midas Series Trust 10/12/2012

INTERCONTINENTAL STRATEGIC MINERALS INC (UT)
Reorganized under the laws of Nevada as Computer Automation Systems, Inc. 2/13/98
Each share Common $0.005 par

exchanged for (0.05) share Common $0.001 par
Computer Automation Systems, Inc. recapitalized as Kahuna Network Security, Inc. 1/20/2004 which name changed to American Security Resources Corp. 8/24/2004

INTERCONTINENTAL SYS INC (CA)
Merged into Itel Corp. (Old) 4/1/70
Each share Common $1 par exchanged for (0.2) share Common $1 par
Itel Corp. (Old) reorganized as Itel Corp. (New) 9/19/83 which name changed to Anixter International Inc. 9/1/95

INTERCONTINENTAL TILE INC (DE)
Charter cancelled and declared inoperative and void for non-payment of taxes 03/01/1995

INTERCONTINENTAL TRAILSEA CORP (DE)
Reincorporated 07/18/1969
State of incorporation changed from (NY) to (DE) 07/18/1969
Common 1¢ par split (3) for (2) by issuance of (0.5) additional share 08/12/1969
Company believed went private 00/00/1999
Details not available

INTERCONTINENTAL VENTURES LTD (BC)
Delisted from Vancouver Stock Exchange 03/01/1989

INTERCONTINENTALEXCHANGE GROUP INC (DE)
Name changed to Intercontinental Exchange, Inc. 06/02/2014

INTERCONTINENTALEXCHANGE INC (DE)
Under plan of merger name changed to IntercontinentalExchange Group, Inc. 11/13/2013
IntercontinentalExchange Group, Inc. name changed to Intercontinental Exchange, Inc. 06/02/2014

INTERCONTINENTS POWER CO.
Reorganized as South American Utilities Corp. 00/00/1936
Details not available

INTERCORE ENERGY INC (DE)
Common $0.0001 par split (9) for (1) by issuance of (8) additional shares payable 05/16/2012 to holders of record 05/16/2012
Recapitalized as InterCore, Inc. 12/31/2013
Each share Common $0.0001 par exchanged for (0.01) share Common $0.0001 par

INTERCORP EXCELLE INC (ON)
Company went private 3/7/2002
Each share Common no par exchanged for $1.15 cash

INTERCOUNTY BANCSHARES INC (OH)
Common no par split (2) for (1) by issuance of (1) additional share payable 10/26/98 to holders of record 10/11/1998
Name changed to NB&T Financial Group, Inc. 05/10/2001
NB&T Financial Group, Inc. merged into Peoples Bancorp Inc. 03/06/2015

INTERCOUNTY PREM ADVANCING CORP (NY)
Name changed to IPA Enterprises Corp. 11/15/1971
IPA Enterprises Corp. name changed to Delhi Chemicals, Inc. 09/10/1975 which name changed to Delhi Consolidated Industries, Inc. 04/21/1981 which name changed to Maritime Transport & Technology Inc. 03/08/1989 which name changed to Bank Store 07/24/1998

which name changed to Banker's Store Inc. 09/18/2001
(See Banker's Store Inc.)

INTERCRAFT INDS CORP (DE)
Merged into IPC Corp. 05/21/1985
Each share Common $2 par exchanged for $29.50 cash

INTERDATA INC (NJ)
Merged into Perkin-Elmer Corp. 07/31/1974
Each share Common 1¢ par exchanged for (0.8) share Common $1 par
Perkin-Elmer Corp. name changed to PE Corp. 05/05/1999 which name changed to Applera Corp. 11/30/2000
(See Applera Corp.)

INTERDENT INC (DE)
Each share old Common $0.001 par exchanged for (0.16666666) share new Common $0.001 par 08/07/2001
Plan of reorganization under Chapter 11 Federal Bankruptcy Code effective 10/09/2003
No stockholders' equity

INTERDIGITAL COMMUNICATIONS CORP (PA)
$2.50 Conv. Preferred 10¢ par called for redemption at $25 on 07/19/2004
Name changed to InterDigital, Inc. 07/02/2007

INTERDOM CORP (NV)
Reorganized as Raystream Inc. 08/22/2011
Each share Common $0.001 par exchanged for (37) shares Common $0.001 par

INTERDYNE CO (CA)
Reorganized under Chapter 11 Federal Bankruptcy Code 05/29/1990
Each share Common 25¢ par exchanged for (0.19334) share Common no par
(Additional Information in Active)

INTERENERGY CORP (KS)
Merged into K N Energy, Inc. 12/19/97
Each share Common no par exchanged for (0.1545) share Common $5 par
K N Energy, Inc. name changed to Kinder Morgan, Inc. (KS) 10/7/99
(See Kinder Morgan, Inc. (KS))

INTEREP NATL RADIO SALES INC (NY)
Chapter 7 bankruptcy proceedings terminated 01/18/2017
Stockholders' equity unlikely

INTEREX MINERALS LTD (AB)
Recapitalized 10/07/1988
Recapitalized from Interex Development Corp. to Interex Minerals Ltd. 10/07/1988
Each share Common no par exchanged for (0.2) share Common no par
Delisted from Toronto Venture Stock Exchange 06/30/2005

INTEREX PRODUCTION CO., INC. (TX)
Charter forfeited for failure to pay taxes 2/14/95

INTERFACE E COM INC (NV)
Common $0.001 par split (9) for (1) by issuance of (8) additional shares payable 07/19/2000 to holders of record 07/18/2000
Name changed to ViaPay Ltd. 09/06/2000
(See ViaPay Ltd.)

INTERFACE FLOORING SYSTEMS, INC. (GA)
Name changed to Interface, Inc. 7/29/87

INTERFACE MECHANISMS INC (WA)
Name changed to Intermec Corp. 7/13/82
(See Intermec Corp.)

INTERFACE SYS INC (DE)
Common 10¢ par split (5) for (4) by issuance of (0.25) additional share 06/16/1986
Stock Dividends - 15% 05/31/1985; 10% 06/16/1987
Merged into Tumbleweed Commmunications Corp. 09/01/2000
Each share Common 10¢ par exchanged for (0.264) share Common $0.001 par
(See Tumbleweed Communications Corp.)

INTERFASHION, INC. (NY)
Reincorporated under the laws of Delaware 7/21/71
Interfashion, Inc. (Del.) charter cancelled 4/15/73

INTERFASHION INC (CO)
Recapitalized as Ceramic Technology Inc. 8/31/92
Each share Common $0.001 par exchanged for (0.25) share Common $0.001 par
(See Ceramic Technology Inc.)

INTERFASHION INC (DE)
Charter cancelled and declared inoperative and void for non-payment of taxes 4/15/73

INTERFERENCE CTL TECHNOLOGIES INC (DE)
Charter cancelled and declared inoperative and void for non-payment of taxes 03/01/1995

INTERFERON PHARMACEUTICAL CORP (NV)
Name changed to Chantal Pharmaceutical Corp. (NV) 10/21/1982
Chantal Pharmaceutical Corp. (NV) reincorporated in Delaware 01/16/1985
(See Chantal Pharmaceutical Corp. (DE))

INTERFERON SCIENCES INC (DE)
Each share old Common 1¢ par exchanged for (0.25) share new Common 1¢ par 03/21/1997
Each share new Common 1¢ par exchanged again for (0.2) share new Common 1¢ par 01/07/1999
Name changed to Stem Cell Innovations, Inc. 02/16/2006
(See Stem Cell Innovations, Inc.)

INTERFILM INC (DE)
Each share old Common 1¢ par exchanged for (0.1) share new Common 1¢ par 7/19/96
Reorganized as Palatin Technologies Inc. 7/19/96
Each share new Common 1¢ par exchanged for (0.1) share Common 1¢ par

INTERFINANCIAL CORP. (MN)
Merged into El Dorado International, Inc. 02/28/1973
Each share Common 10¢ par exchanged for (0.5) share Common 10¢ par
El Dorado International, Inc. name changed to Westamerica Corp. (MN) 06/30/1987 which reincorporated in California 06/28/1988

INTERFINANCIAL HLDGS CORP (NV)
Old Common $0.001 par split (8) for (1) by issuance of (7) additional shares payable 03/17/2005 to holders of record 03/17/2005
Ex date - 03/18/2005
Each share old Common $0.001 par exchanged for (0.04) share new Common $0.001 par 10/17/2005
Charter revoked for failure to file reports and pay fees 03/31/2008

INTERFINANCIAL INC (GA)
Merged into Fortis Amev N.V. 06/30/1980
Each share Common $1 par exchanged for $55 cash

INTERFIRST BANKCORP INC (MI)
Common 1¢ par split (3) for (1) by issuance of (2) additional shares 3/6/92
Common 1¢ par split (6) for (5) by issuance of (0.2) additional share 8/28/92
Common 1¢ par split (2) for (1) by issuance of (1) additional share 2/17/93
Stock Dividend - 10% 3/15/91
Acquired by Standard Federal Bank (Troy, MI) 12/18/93
Each share Common 1¢ par exchanged for $14.26 cash

INTERFIRST CORP (DE)
Merged into First RepublicBank Corp. 06/06/1987
Each share Common $5 par exchanged for (0.02) share Adjustable Rate Preferred Ser. C no par, (0.08) share Common $5 par and (0.1) share Conv. Class A Common $1 par
(See First RepublicBank Corp.)

INTERFOODS AMER (NV)
Merged into Interfoods Acquisition Corp. 5/27/2002
Each share Common $0.001 par exchanged for $1.45 principal amount of 10% Unsecured Debentures due 5/24/2005

INTERFOODS CONS INC (NV)
Common $0.001 par split (3) for (1) by issuance of (2) additional shares payable 07/16/1999 to holders of record 07/14/1999
Name changed to Sitestar Corp. 07/28/1999
Sitestar Corp. recapitalized as Enterprise Diversified, Inc. 07/23/2018

INTERFUND CORP (DE)
Charter cancelled and declared inoperative and void for non-payment of taxes 6/24/92

INTERFUND RES LTD (DE)
Name changed to Interactive Technologies.com, Ltd. (DE) 03/01/1999
Interactive Technologies.com, Ltd. (DE) reorganized in Florida as International Coastal Biofuels, Inc. 04/09/2008 which recapitalized as IMD Companies Inc. 10/12/2010

INTERGEM INC (NV)
Each (4.75) shares old Common 1¢ par exchanged for (1) share new Common 1¢ par 5/29/85
Stock Dividend - 30% 1/30/86
Name changed to Excel InterFinancial Corp. 10/26/87
(See Excel InterFinancial Corp.)

INTERGENERAL INDS INC (DE)
Out of business with no assets
Chapter XI bankruptcy petition filed 6/10/70 was dismissed 11/9/71

INTERGOLD CORP (NV)
Each share old Common $0.001 par exchanged for (0.00333333) share new Common $0.001 par 08/08/2003
Name changed to Lexington Resources, Inc. 11/20/2003
(See Lexington Resources, Inc.)

INTERGOLD LTD (AB)
Acquired by Jostens, Inc. 04/26/2010
Each share Class A Common no par exchanged for $0.16 cash

INTERGOLD RES INC (BC)
Name changed to Internetwork Realty Corp. and Capital Stock no par reclassified as Common no par 04/17/1979

Internetwork Realty Corp. recapitalized as Skalbania Enterprises Ltd. 10/15/1980 which name changed to Selco International Properties Inc. 03/03/1988
(See Selco International Properties Inc.)

INTERGRAPH CORP (AL)
Common 10¢ par split (2) for (1) by issuance of (1) additional share 2/18/83
Common 10¢ par split (2) for (1) by issuance of (1) additional share 6/14/85
Merged into Cobalt Holding Co. 11/29/2006
Each share Common 10¢ par exchanged for $44 cash

INTERGROUP HEALTHCARE CORP (DE)
Merged into Foundation Health Corp. 11/1/94
Each share Common $0.001 par exchanged for (1.9316) shares Common 1¢ par
Foundation Health Corp. merged into Foundation Health Systems, Inc. 4/1/97 which name changed to Health Net, Inc. 11/6/2000

INTERGULF RES CORP (BC)
Acquired by Result Energy Inc. 12/11/2003
Each share Common no par exchanged for (0.4372) share Common no par
Result Energy Inc. merged into PetroBakken Energy Ltd. (Old) 04/01/2010 which reorganized as PetroBakken Energy Ltd. (New) 01/07/2013 which name changed to Lightstream Resources Ltd. 05/28/2013

INTERHOME ENERGY INC (CANADA)
Name changed to Interprovincial Pipe Line Inc. 05/01/1991
Interprovincial Pipe Line Inc. reorganized as Interprovincial Pipe Line Inc. 12/18/1992 which name changed to IPL Energy Inc. 05/10/1994 which name changed to Enbridge Inc. 10/07/1998

INTERIM CAP CORP (BC)
Recapitalized as ERA Carbon Offsets Ltd. 07/28/2008
Each share Common no par exchanged for (0.4) share Common no par
ERA Carbon Offsets Ltd. name changed to Offsetters Climate Solutions Inc. 03/04/2013 which name changed to NatureBank Asset Management Inc. 10/20/2015

INTERIM SVCS INC (DE)
Common 1¢ par split (2) for (1) by issuance of (1) additional share payable 09/05/1997 to holders of record 08/18/1997 Ex date - 09/08/1997
Name changed to Spherion Corp. 07/07/2000
Spherion Corp. name changed to SFN Group, Inc. 03/01/2010
(See SFN Group, Inc.)

INTERIM SYS CORP (DE)
Merged into Block (H & R), Inc. 1/22/91
Each share Common 1¢ par exchanged for $1.66 cash

INTERIOR AIRWAYS, INC. (AK)
Name changed to Alaska International Air, Inc. 9/21/72
Alaska International Air, Inc. name changed to Alaska International Industries, Inc. 5/14/74
(See Alaska International Industries, Inc.)

INTERIOR BREWERIES LTD (BC)
Class B no par reclassified as Common no par 07/15/1968
Common no par split (2) for (1) by issuance of (1) additional share 12/10/1968
Name changed to Columbia Brewing Co. Ltd. 03/24/1972
(See Columbia Brewing Co. Ltd.)

INTERIORS INC (DE)
Each share 10% Conv. Preferred Ser. A 1¢ par received distribution of (0.5) share Class A Common $0.001 par payable 01/06/1998 to holders of record 12/26/1997
Each share 10% Conv. Preferred Ser. A 1¢ par received distribution of (0.16666666) share Class A Common $0.001 par payable 12/31/1998 to holders of record 12/21/1998
Each share 10% Conv. Preferred Ser. A 1¢ par received distribution of (0.15) share Class A Common $0.001 par payable 06/25/1999 to holders of record 06/10/1999
Each share 10% Conv. Preferred Ser. A 1¢ par received distribution of (0.23) share Class A Common $0.001 par payable 12/22/1999 to holders of record 12/10/1999
Charter cancelled and declared inoperative and void for non-payment of taxes 03/01/2002

INTERJET NET CORP (DE)
Name changed to IJNT.net, Inc. 10/01/1998
IJNT.net, Inc. name changed to Universal Broadband Networks Inc. 07/25/2000
(See Universal Broadband Networks, Inc.)

INTERLAKE, INC. (DE)
Common $1 par split (3) for (2) by issuance of (0.5) additional share 10/10/1975
Under plan of reorganization each share Common $1 par automatically became (1) share Interlake Corp. Common $1 par 05/29/1986
(See Interlake Corp.)

INTERLAKE CORP (DE)
Common $1 par split (2) for (1) by issuance of (1) additional share 11/24/1986
Merged into GKN North America Inc. 02/10/1999
Each share Conv. Exchangeable Preferred Ser. A $1 par exchanged for $1,980.87 cash
Each share Common $1 par exchanged for $7.25 cash

INTERLAKE DEV CORP (BC)
Merged into International Interlake Industries Inc. 12/31/1986
Each share Common no par exchanged for (0.2) share Common no par
(See International Interlake Industries Inc.)

INTERLAKE IRON CORP. (NY)
Common no par changed to $1 par 04/25/1957
Under plan of merger name changed to Interlake Steel Corp. (NY) 12/22/1964
Interlake Steel Corp. (NY) reincorporated in Delaware as Interlake, Inc. 05/15/1970 which reorganized as Interlake Corp. 05/29/1986
(See Interlake Corp.)

INTERLAKE STEAMSHIP CO. (DE)
Reincorporated in 1931
State of incorporation changed from (OH) to (DE) in 1931
Merged into Pickands Mather & Co. 8/31/66
Each share Common no par exchanged for (1) share $1.15 Conv. Preferred Ser. A $25 par and (0.9) share Common 50¢ par
Pickands Mather & Co. merged into Diamond Shamrock Corp. 1/3/69 which name changed to Maxus Energy Corp. 4/30/87
(See Maxus Energy Corp.)

INTERLAKE STL CORP (NY)
6.50% Preferred $100 par called for redemption 10/1/65
Reincorporated under the laws of Delaware as Interlake, Inc. 5/15/70
Interlake, Inc. reorganized as Interlake Corp. 5/29/86
(See Interlake Corp.)

INTERLAND INC (GA)
Merged into Interland, Inc. (MN) 08/06/2001
Each share Common no par exchanged for (0.861) share Common 1¢ par
Interland, Inc. (MN) name changed to Web.com, Inc. 03/20/2006 which merged into Website Pros, Inc. 10/01/2007 which name changed to Web.com Group, Inc. 10/27/2008
(See Web.com Group, Inc.)

INTERLAND INC (MN)
Each share old Common 1¢ par exchanged for (0.1) share new Common 1¢ par 08/01/2003
Name changed to Web.com, Inc. 03/20/2006
Web.com, Inc. merged into Website Pros, Inc. 10/01/2007 which name changed to Web.com Group, Inc. 10/27/2008
(See Web.com Group, Inc.)

INTERLEAF INC (MA)
Each share old Common 1¢ par exchanged for (1/3) share new Common 1¢ par 12/31/98
Merged into BroadVision Inc. 4/14/2000
Each share new Common 1¢ par exchanged for (1.0395) shares Common $0.0001 par

INTERLEARN HLDGS LTD (BC)
Delisted from Vancouver Stock Exchange 03/04/1992

INTERLEE INC (DE)
Merged into Intercole Inc. 2/1/83
Each share Conv. Special Preferred $100 par exchanged for $0.27 cash
Each share Common no par exchanged for $0.50 cash

INTERLEUKIN 2 INC (CO)
Name changed to Cel-Sci Corp. 3/7/88

INTERLEUKIN GENETICS INC (DE)
Reincorporated 07/12/2000
State of incorporation changed from (TX) to (DE) and Common no par changed to $0.001 par 07/12/2000
Plan of Complete Liquidation and Dissolution approved 08/14/2017
No stockholders' equity

INTERLIANT INC (DE)
Plan of reorganization under Chapter 11 Federal Bankruptcy Code effective 09/30/2004
No stockholders' equity

INTERLINE BRANDS INC (DE)
Acquired by Isabelle Holding Co., LLC 09/07/2012
Each share Common 1¢ par exchanged for $25.50 cash

INTERLINE RES CORP (UT)
Each share old Common $0.005 par exchanged for (0.0002) share new Common $0.005 par 05/21/2014
Name changed to Automated-X, Inc. 12/03/2014
Automated-X, Inc. name changed to Saddle Ranch Media, Inc. 10/07/2015

INTERLINK COMPUTER SCIENCES INC (DE)
Merged into Sterling Software, Inc. 04/27/1999
Each share Common $0.001 par exchanged for $7 cash

INTERLINK CORP (CA)
Charter cancelled for failure to file reports and pay taxes 5/1/85

INTERLINK ELECTRS INC (DE)
Reincorporated 08/24/1996
State of incorporation changed from (CA) to (DE) and Common no par changed to $0.00001 par 08/24/1996
Common $0.00001 par split (3) for (2) by issuance of (0.5) additional share payable 04/07/2000 to holders of record 03/20/2000
Each share old Common $0.00001 par exchanged for (0.05) share new Common $0.00001 par 01/13/2012
Reincorporated under the laws of Nevada and new Common $0.00001 par changed to $0.001 par 07/03/2012

INTERLINK SYS INC (BC)
Recapitalized as iQuest Networks Inc. (BC) 08/14/2000
Each share Common no par exchanged for (0.5) share Common no par
iQuest Networks Inc. (BC) reorganized in Wyoming as Quest Ventures Inc. 10/28/2003 which recapitalized as Dorato Resources Inc. (WY) 04/24/2006 which reincorporated in British Columbia 08/21/2006 which recapitalized as Xiana Mining Inc. 10/23/2013

INTERLINK US NETWORK LTD (CA)
SEC revoked common stock registration 01/30/2013

INTERLINQ SOFTWARE CORP (WA)
Merged into Harland Financial Solutions, Inc. 10/15/2002
Each share Common 10¢ par exchanged for $6.25 cash

INTERLOCK CONSOLIDATED ENTERPRISES INC (ON)
Delisted from Canadian Dealer Network 12/31/1997

INTERLOCK SVCS INC (NV)
Name changed to 2Dobiz.com, Inc. 02/07/2000
2Dobiz.com, Inc. name changed to New York International Commerce Group, Inc. 01/09/2002
(See New York International Commerce Group, Inc.)

INTERLOGIX INC (DE)
Merged into General Electric Co. 02/21/2002
Each share Common 1¢ par exchanged for (0.5174) share Common 16¢ par and $19.43 cash

INTERLOTT TECHNOLOGIES INC (DE)
Common 1¢ par split (2) for (1) by issuance of (1) additional share payable 12/20/2000 to holders of record 11/30/2000 Ex date - 12/21/2000
Merged into GTECH Holdings Corp. 09/18/2003
Each share Common 1¢ par exchanged for (0.17248) share Common 1¢ par and $1.80 cash
(See GTECH Holdings Corp.)

INTERLUDE CAP CORP (BC)
Name changed to OneMove Technologies Inc. 10/24/2006
(See OneMove Technologies Inc.)

INTERMAC CORP (NY)
Charter cancelled and proclaimed dissolved for failure to pay taxes 12/20/77

INTERMAGNETICS GEN CORP (DE)
Reincorporated 11/29/2004
Common 10¢ par split (5) for (4) by issuance of (0.25) additional share 9/8/94
Common 10¢ par split (3) for (2) by issuance of (0.5) additional share

payable 8/17/2004 to holders of record 7/23/2004
Stock Dividends - 2% payable 8/22/96 to holders of record 8/1/96 Ex date - 7/30/96; 2% payable 9/16/97 to holders of record 8/26/97 Ex date - 8/22/97; 2% payable 9/17/98 to holders of record 8/27/98; 3% payable 8/25/2000 to holders of record 8/4/2000; 2% payable 8/31/2001 to holders of record 8/14/2001
State of incorporation changed from (NY) to (DE) 11/29/2004
Common 10¢ par split (3) for (2) by issuance of (0.5) additional share payable 2/21/2006 to holders of record 2/6/2006 Ex date - 2/22/2006
Merged into Philips Holding USA Inc. 11/9/2006
Each share Common 10¢ par exchanged for $27.50 cash

INTERMAP TECHNOLOGIES LTD (AB)
Recapitalized as Intermap Technologies Corp. 5/25/99
Each share Class A Common no par exchanged for (0.08) share Class A Common no par

INTERMAR SOLUTIONS INC (NV)
Nane changed to SOOoo Good International, Ltd. 07/18/2005
(See SOOoo Good International, Ltd.)

INTERMARK CORP (NY)
Reincorporated under the laws of Delaware as MarkitStar, Inc. 12/10/1986
MarkitStar, Inc. name changed to HMG Worldwide Corp. 10/04/1993
(See HMG Worldwide Corp.)

INTERMARK GAMING INTL INC (DE)
Reincorporated 09/30/1987
Common 1¢ par split (3) for (2) by issuance of (0.5) additional share 10/22/1986
State of incorporation changed from (AZ) to (DE) 09/30/1987
Name changed to Auto Swap USA, Inc. 10/25/1991
Auto Swap USA, Inc. name changed to Water Chef Inc. 08/02/1993 which name changed to PureSafe Water Systems, Inc. 06/16/2009

INTERMARK INC (DE)
Reincorporated 9/13/83
Each share Common $1 par exchanged for (0.3) share Common $3 par 2/2/73
Common $3 par split (3) for (2) by issuance of (0.5) additional share 11/16/79
Common $3 par split (4) for (3) by issuance of (1/3) additional share 9/26/80
Stock Dividends - 10% 6/15/79; 10% 3/24/80; 10% 3/24/81
State of incorporation changed from (CA) to (DE) 9/13/83
Common $1 par split (3) for (2) by issuance of (0.5) additional share 9/15/83
Common $1 par split (5) for (4) by issuance of (0.25) additional share 3/28/86
Stock Dividends - Common 10% 9/23/85; 10% 3/31/89; in Participating Preferred to holders of Common 33-1/3% 8/1/86; Participating Preferred 10% 3/31/89
Reorganized as Triton Group Ltd. (New) 6/25/93
Each share Participating Preferred $1 par exchanged for (0.01128201) share Common $0.0001 par and (0.01768286) Common Stock Purchase Warrant expiring 6/25/98
Each share new Common $1 par exchanged for (0.01128201) share Common $0.0001 par and (0.01768286) Common Stock Purchase Warrant expiring 6/25/98
Triton Group Ltd. (New) name changed to Alarmguard Holdings, Inc. 4/16/97
(See Alarmguard Holdings, Inc.)

INTERMARK INVESTING, INC. (CA)
Name changed to Intermark, Inc. (CA) 10/4/71
Intermark, Inc. (CA) reincorporated in Delaware 9/13/83 which reorganized as Triton Group Ltd. (New) 6/25/93 which name changed to Alarmguard Holdings, Inc. 4/16/97
(See Alarmguard Holdings, Inc.)

INTERMARKET VENTURES INC (UT)
Charter expired 07/11/2001

INTERMEC CORP (WA)
Common 60¢ par split (2) for (1) by issuance of (1) additional share 03/08/1983
Merged into LI Acquisition Corp. 09/09/1991
Each share Common 60¢ par exchanged for $24 cash

INTERMEC INC (DE)
Acquired by Honeywell International Inc. 09/17/2013
Each share Common 1¢ par exchanged for $10 cash

INTERMED INC (AR)
Merged into Beverly Enterprises Arkansas, Inc. 10/20/78
Each share Common 10¢ par exchanged for $11 cash

INTERMED INTERNATIONAL, INC. (AR)
Common $1 par changed to 10¢ par 12/9/71
Name changed to Intermed, Inc. 4/1/74
(See Intermed, Inc.)

INTERMED TECHNOLOGIES INC (BC)
Recapitalized as Botex Industries Corp. 08/07/1998
Each share Common no par exchanged for (1/3) share Common no par
Botex Industries Corp. name changed to Radical Elastomers Inc. 08/02/2001
(See Radical Elastomers Inc.)

INTERMEDCO INC (DE)
Merged into Tilling (Thomas) Ltd. 3/29/77
Each share Common $1 par exchanged for $7.50 cash

INTERMEDIA CAP CORP (AB)
Recapitalized as Savanna Energy Services Corp. 08/21/2003
Each share Common no par exchanged for (0.02222222) share Common no par
Savanna Energy Services Corp. merged into Total Energy Services Inc. 06/23/2017

INTERMEDIA COMMUNICATIONS INC (DE)
Name changed 05/31/1996
Name changed from Intermedia Communications of Florida, Inc. to Intermedia Communications Inc. 05/31/1996
Common 1¢ par split (2) for (1) by issuance of (1) additional share payable 06/15/1998 to holders of record 06/01/1998
Each 7% Conv. Jr. Depositary Preferred Ser. D received distribution of (0.02011581) share Common 1¢ par payable 10/15/1999 to holders of record 10/01/1999
Each 7% Conv. Jr. Depositary Preferred Ser. E received distribution of (0.02011581) share Common 1¢ par payable 10/15/1999 to holders of record 10/01/1999
Each 7% Conv. Jr. Depositary Preferred Ser. F received distribution of (0.02011581) share Common 1¢ par payable 10/15/1999 to holders of record 10/01/1999
Merged into WorldCom, Inc. (New) 07/01/2001
Each share 7% Conv. Jr. Depositary Preferred Ser. D exchanged for (1) share 7% Conv. Jr. Depositary Preferred Ser. D
Each share 7% 144A Conv. Depositary Preferred Ser. E exchanged for (1) share 7% 144A Conv. Depositary Preferred Ser. E
Each 7% Conv. Jr. Depositary Preferred Ser. E exchanged for (1) share 7% Conv. Jr. Depositary Preferred Ser. E
Each 7% Jr. Conv. Depositary Preferred Ser. F exchanged for (1) share 7% Conv. Jr. Depositary Preferred Ser. F
Each share Common 1¢ par exchanged for (1) share Common 1¢ par and (0.04) share MCI Group Common 1¢ par
(See WorldCom, Inc. (New))
Stock Dividends - in 13.5% Exchangeable Preferred Ser. B to holders of 13.5% Exchangeable Preferred Ser. B 3.375% payable 09/30/1999 to holders of record 09/15/1999; 3.375% payable 12/31/1999 to holders of record 12/15/1999; 3.375% payable 03/31/2001 to holders of record 03/15/2001; 3.375% payable 06/30/2001 to holders of record 06/15/2001 Ex date - 06/13/2001; 3.375% payable 12/31/2001 to holders of record 12/15/2001 Ex date - 12/12/2001; 3.375% payable 03/29/2002 to holders of record 03/15/2002 Ex date - 04/04/2002
Plan of reorganization under Chapter 11 Federal Bankruptcy Code effective 04/20/2004
Each 13.5% Exchangeable Preferred Ser. B share $1 par received distribution of $49.34990885 cash
Note: Distributions of less than $100 will not be made, unless requested in writing

INTERMEDIA MARKETING SOLUTIONS INC (NV)
Company terminated common stock registration and is no longer public as of 03/27/2003

INTERMEDIA NET INC (DE)
Each share old Common $0.0001 par exchanged for (0.02) share new Common $0.0001 par 2/12/99
Name changed to Fortune Media, Inc. 5/21/99
Fortune Media, Inc. name changed to Cyberedge Enterprises, Inc. 11/10/2000 which name changed to Wayne's Famous Phillies Inc. 3/10/2003

INTERMEDIA SYS CORP (MA)
Proclaimed dissolved for failure to file reports and pay fees 10/19/1983

INTERMEDIATE MUNI FD INC (MD)
Name changed to Western Asset Intermediate Muni Fund, Inc. 10/09/2006

INTERMEDIATE NURSING CTRS INC (PA)
Name changed to Commonwealth Industries, Inc. 4/16/69
Commonwealth Industries, Inc. name changed to Leader Healthcare Organization, Inc. 5/30/80
(See Leader Healthcare Organization, Inc.)

INTERMEDIATES, INC. (DE)
Common $1 par changed to 1¢ par 8/20/62
Charter cancelled and declared inoperative and void for non-payment of taxes 4/15/69

INTERMEDICS INC (TX)
Common 10¢ par split (3) for (2) by issuance of (0.5) additional share 11/15/78
Common 10¢ par split (3) for (2) by issuance of (0.5) additional share 8/28/80
Common 10¢ par split (3) for (2) by issuance of (0.5) additional share 11/6/87
Merged into Sulzer Bros. Inc. 9/16/88
Each share Common 10¢ par exchanged for $43 cash

INTERMET CORP (GA)
Common 10¢ par split (3) for (2) by issuance of (0.5) additional share 11/26/86
Plan of reorganization under Chapter 11 Federal Bankruptcy Code effective 11/9/2005
No stockholders' equity

INTERMETCO LTD (ON)
Common no par split (2) for (1) by issuance of (1) additional share 09/22/1989
Acquired by Philip Services Corp. 09/03/1997
Each share Common no par exchanged for (0.7976) share Common no par
(See Philip Services Corp.)

INTERMETRICS INC (DE)
Reincorporated 7/1/90
State of incorporation changed from (MA) to (DE) 7/1/90
Merged into Appollo Holding Corp. 8/31/95
Each share Common 1¢ par exchanged for $6.80 cash

INTERMIX MEDIA INC (DE)
Merged into News Corp. 9/30/2005
Each share Common $0.001 par exchanged for $12 cash

INTERMODULEX NDH CORP (DE)
Name changed to ITX Corp. 01/10/1977
(See ITX Corp.)

INTERMONT INC (CANADA)
Each share Common no par received distribution of (0.07692307) share Dachamine Inc. Common no par, (0.07692307) share Dachatech Inc. Common no par and (0.07692307) share Montcalm Resources Inc. Common no par payable 08/30/1996 to holders of record 08/15/1996
Recapitalized as Pebercan Inc. 08/19/1996
Each share Common no par exchanged for (0.1) share Common no par
(See Pebercan Inc.)

INTERMOST CORP (WY)
Reincorporated 02/25/2003
State of incorporation changed from (UT) to (WY) 02/25/2003
Name changed to Uni Core Holdings Corp. 01/29/2010

INTERMOUNTAIN BANKSHARES INC (WV)
Merged into United Bankshares, Inc. 7/1/86
Each share Common $1 par exchanged for (2.2) shares Common $2.50 par

INTERMOUNTAIN CO (MT)
Merged into Hoerner Waldorf Corp. 3/30/73
Each share Common no par exchanged for (0.340136) share Common 50¢ par
Hoerner Waldorf Corp. merged into Champion International Corp. 2/24/77 which merged into International Paper Co. 6/20/2000

INTERMOUNTAIN CMNTY BANCORP (ID)
Common $2.50 par changed to no par and (1) additional share issued payable 12/29/2003 to holders of record 12/18/2003 Ex date - 12/30/2003

Old Common no par split (3) for (2) by issuance of (0.5) additional share payable 03/15/2005 to holders of record 03/10/2005 Ex date - 03/16/2005
Each share old Common no par exchanged for (0.1) share new Common no par 10/10/2012
Stock Dividends - 10% payable 02/09/2001 to holders of record 01/19/2001 Ex date - 01/22/2001; 10% payable 03/06/2002 to holders of record 02/16/2002 Ex date - 02/13/2002; 10% payable 08/15/2003 to holders of record 07/30/2003 Ex date - 07/29/2003; 10% payable 05/31/2006 to holders of record 05/15/2006 Ex date - 05/11/2006; 10% payable 05/31/2007 to holders of record 05/15/2007 Ex date - 05/11/2007
Merged into Columbia Banking System, Inc. 11/01/2014
Each share new Common no par exchanged for (0.6426) share Common no par and $2.293 cash

INTERMOUNTAIN ENERGY CORP (UT)
Involuntarily dissolved 11/01/1992

INTERMOUNTAIN ENERGY INC (CO)
Merged into Bristol Oil & Gas Corp. 07/31/1985
Each share Common 1¢ par exchanged for (0.01) share Common 1¢ par
(See Bristol Oil & Gas Corp.)

INTERMOUNTAIN EXPL CO (UT)
Recapitalized as Future Petroleum Corp. (UT) 2/25/94
Each share Common 10¢ par exchanged for (1/6) share Common 10¢ par
Future Petroleum Corp. (UT) reincorporated in Texas as Bargo Energy Co. 4/29/99 which merged into Mission Resources Corp. 5/16/2001
(See Mission Resources Corp.)

INTERMOUNTAIN GAS CO (ID)
Under plan of merger each share Common $1 par automatically became (1) share Intermountain Gas Industries, Inc. Common $1 par 07/01/1978
$3 Preferred Stock $50 par called for redemption 11/00/1989
Public interest eliminated

INTERMOUNTAIN GAS INDS INC (ID)
Merged into IMG Holdings, Inc. 11/30/84
Each share Common $1 par exchanged for $33.50 cash

INTERMOUNTAIN INDS INC (UT)
Recapitalized as Dynapac, Inc. 9/22/71
Each share Common $1 par exchanged for (0.5) share Common no par
(See Dyanpac, Inc.)

INTERMOUNTAIN LABS INC (UT)
Common no par split (3) for (2) by issuance of (0.5) additional share 8/22/83
Stock Dividend - 100% 8/21/81
Merged into Animed, Inc. 6/7/85
Each share Common no par exchanged for (0.4706) share Common 1¢ par
(See Animed, Inc.)

INTERMOUNTAIN LD DEV CORP (ID)
Name changed to National American Enterprises Inc. 5/18/73
Each share Common 1¢ par exchanged for (1) share Common 1¢ par
(See National American Enterprises Inc.)

INTERMOUNTAIN MORTGAGE CO. (WA)
Under plan of merger name changed to Securities Intermountain, Inc. 12/19/56
(See Securities Intermountain, Inc.)

INTERMOUNTAIN PETE CO (UT)
Common 10¢ par changed to 2¢ par 4/25/69
Proclaimed dissolved for failure to pay taxes 4/1/89

INTERMOUNTAIN PETROLEUM, INC. (UT)
Name changed to Sage Oil Co., Inc. 5/29/59
(See Sage Oil Co., Inc.)

INTERMOUNTAIN REFNG INC (NM)
Reorganized under the laws of Nevada as A.R.E. Wind Corp. 10/23/2008
Each share Common no par exchanged for (0.12987012) share Common $0.001 par
A.R.E. Wind Corp. name changed to Cascade Wind Corp. 12/17/2008 which name changed to XZERES Wind Corp. 05/17/2010 which name changed to XZERES Corp. 05/17/2011
(See XZERES Corp.)

INTERMOUNTAIN RES INC (NV)
Company became insolvent 00/00/2003
No stockholders' equity

INTERMOUNTAIN URANIUM CORP. (UT)
Merged into International Oil & Metals Corp. on a (1) for (200) basis 3/29/56
International Oil & Metals Corp. was liquidated by exchange for Perfect Photo, Inc. 3/24/65 which was acquired by United Whelan Corp. 6/30/66 which name changed to Perfect Film & Chemical Corp. 5/31/67 which name changed to Cadence Industries Corp. 10/22/70

INTERMOUNTAIN VENTURES INC (MN)
Each share old Common $0.001 par exchanged for (0.02) share new Common $0.001 par 06/23/2010
Name changed to Voice One Corp. 01/11/2011

INTERMUNE INC (DE)
Acquired by Roche Holdings, Inc. 09/29/2014
Each share Common $0.001 par exchanged for $74 cash

INTERMUNE LIFE SCIENCES INC (CANADA)
Reincorporated 11/30/1993
Place of incorporation changed from (ON) to (Canada) 11/30/1993
Dissolved for non-compliance 07/12/2004

INTERMUNE PHARMACEUTICALS INC (DE)
Name changed to InterMune, Inc. 04/27/2001
(See InterMune, Inc.)

INTERNACIONAL DE CERAMICA S A DE C V (MEXICO)
ADR agreement terminated 11/1/2004
Each Sponsored ADR for Class B exchanged for $10.34949 cash
Each Sponsored ADR for Ltd. Vtg. Units exchanged for $10.54388 cash

INTERNAL FIXATION SYS (FL)
Common 5¢ par changed to $0.001 par 04/24/2012
Chapter 7 bankruptcy proceedings terminated 01/12/2017
No stockholders' equity

INTERNAL HYDRO INTL INC (FL)
Reincorporated 02/04/2004
State of incorporation changed from (NV) to (FL) 02/04/2004
Common $0.001 par split (5) for (1) by issuance of (4) additional shares payable 09/10/2004 to holders of record 09/03/2004 Ex date - 09/13/2004
Name changed to Renewable Energy Resources, Inc. 02/20/2007
Renewable Energy Resources, Inc. name changed to New Green Technologies, Inc. 07/03/2008 which recapitalized as Spur Ranch, Inc. 08/25/2010 which name changed to Rounder, Inc. 01/24/2012 which name changed to Fortitude Group, Inc. 01/08/2013

INTERNAP NETWORK SVCS CORP (DE)
Reincorporated 09/17/2001
Common $0.001 par split (2) for (1) by issuance of (1) additional share payable 01/07/2000 to holders of record 12/27/1999
State of incorporation changed from (WA) to (DE) 09/17/2001
Each share old Common $0.001 par exchanged for (0.1) share new Common $0.001 par 07/11/2006
Name changed to Internap Corp. 12/04/2014

INTERNATIONAL & COMMON MARKET FUND, INC. (MD)
Name changed to All American Fund, Inc. and Capital Stock $1 par changed to 25¢ par 08/11/1965
All American Fund, Inc. merged into American Birthright Trust 11/01/1976 which name changed to ABT Growth & Income Trust 12/01/1984
(See ABT Growth & Income Trust)

INTERNATIONAL 800 TELECOM CORP (DE)
Common 10¢ par split (2) for (1) by issuance of (1) additional share 06/11/1990
Name changed to Residual Corp. and Common 10¢ par changed to $0.0001 par 02/11/1994
Residual Corp. recapitalized as Residual.com Inc. 08/30/1999
(See Residual.com Inc.)

INTERNATIONAL ABSORBENTS INC (BC)
Each share old Common no par exchanged for (0.25) share new Common no par 04/09/2001
Merged into IAX Canada Acquisition Co. Inc. 05/27/2010
Each share new Common no par exchanged for USD$4.75 cash
Note: Unexchanged certificates were cancelled and became without value 05/27/2013

INTERNATIONAL ACCORD INC (ON)
Delisted from Alberta Stock Exchange 08/27/1997

INTERNATIONAL ACCOUNTANTS SOC INC (IL)
Each share Class A Common no par exchanged for (1) share 6% Part. Preferred $15 par 5/3/65
6% Part. Preferred $15 par called for redemption 2/1/68
Public interest eliminated

INTERNATIONAL ACUVISION SYS INC (DE)
Reincorporated 09/15/1993
Place of incorporation changed from (BC) to (DE) and Common no par changed to $0.001 par 09/15/1993
Recapitalized as AcuBid.Com, Inc. 03/18/1999
Each share Common no par exchanged for (0.5) share Common no par
AcuBid.Com, Inc. name changed to Asia Web Holdings, Inc. 06/01/2000 which name changed to Case Financial, Inc. 05/22/2002
(See Case Financial, Inc.)

INTERNATIONAL AEROPRODUCTS INC (DE)
Name changed to International Transport Industries, Inc. 11/01/1971
(See International Transport Industries, Inc.)

INTERNATIONAL AEROSPACE ENTERPRISES INC (NV)
SEC revoked common stock registration 01/17/2013

INTERNATIONAL AFRICAN AMERICAN CORP. (DE)
Common $1 par changed to 10¢ par and (9) additional shares issued 09/15/1961
Liquidation completed
Each share Common 10¢ par exchanged for initial distribution of (0.5) share Liberian Iron Ore Ltd. Capital Stock no par 04/20/1962
Each share Common 10¢ par received second and final distribution of (0.05) share Liberian Iron Ore Ltd. Capital Stock no par and $0.10 cash 04/05/1963
Liberian Iron Ore Ltd. name changed to LionOre Mining International Ltd. 07/26/1996
(See LionOre Mining International Ltd.)

INTERNATIONAL AGRICULTURAL CORP. (NY)
Name changed to International Minerals & Chemical Corp. 00/00/1941
International Minerals & Chemical Corp. name changed to Imcera Group Inc. 06/14/1990 which name changed to Mallinckrodt Group Inc. 03/15/1994 which name changed to Mallinckrodt Inc. 10/16/1996 which merged into Tyco International Ltd. (Bermuda) 10/17/2000 which reincorporated in Switzerland 03/17/2009 which merged into Johnson Controls International PLC 09/06/2016

INTERNATIONAL AIRBORNE SYS CORP (BC)
Recapitalized as Gateway Waste Systems Inc. 06/10/1994
Each share Common no par exchanged for (0.25) share Common no par
Gateway Waste Systems Inc. name changed to Gateway Technologies Corp. 12/04/1995 which recapitalized as Trevali Resources Corp. 07/06/2006 which name changed to Trevali Mining Corp. 04/07/2011

INTERNATIONAL AIRCRAFT CORP.
Sold to International Aircraft Co. in 1929
Details not available

INTERNATIONAL AIRCRAFT INVS (CA)
Merged into Jetscape Aviation Group, Inc. 12/24/2002
Each share Common 1¢ par exchanged for $1.45 cash

INTERNATIONAL AIRL INC (CO)
Each share Common 10¢ par exchanged for (0.02) share Common 50¢ par 10/11/71
Declared defunct and inoperative for failure to pay taxes and file annual reports 10/19/74
Note: Although it was reported company changed its name to Communications Cybernetics Corp. in 1972, and stock was trading under that name for years, the name change was never filed with the Colorado Secretary of State

INTERNATIONAL AIRL SUPPORT GROUP INC (DE)
Each (27) shares old Common $0.0001 par exchanged for (1) share new Common $0.0001 par 10/3/96
Company terminated registration of Common stock and is no longer public as of 4/15/2003

INTERNATIONAL AIRPORT HOTEL SYSTEM, INC. LIQUIDATING TRUST (FL)
Liquidation completed
Each share Common $1 par exchanged for initial distribution of $0.74 cash 2/26/81
Each share Common $1 par received second distribution of $0.40 cash 1/5/83
Each share Common $1 par received third and final distribution of $0.1695 cash 12/30/83

INTERNATIONAL AKASH VENTURES INC (BC)
Name changed to Healthscreen Solutions Inc. 01/18/2001
(See Healthscreen Solutions Inc.)

INTERNATIONAL ALBANY RES LTD (BC)
Reincorporated under the laws of Bahamas as Brazilian Goldfields Ltd. 03/21/1997
Brazilian Goldfields Ltd. recapitalized as Brazilian International Goldfields Ltd. 11/27/1998 which recapitalized as Aguila American Resources Ltd. (Bahamas) 03/08/2002 which reincorporated in British Columbia 01/14/2008 which name changed to Aguila American Gold Ltd. 05/26/2011

INTERNATIONAL ALL-NORTH RES LTD (BC)
Recapitalized as Kaieteur Resource Corp. 04/14/1999
Each (14) shares Common no par exchanged for (1) share Common no par
Kaieteur Resource Corp. name changed to Samba Gold Inc. 03/22/2005 which recapitalized as Caerus Resource Corp. 02/26/2009 which name changed to Angel Gold Corp. 10/04/2012

INTERNATIONAL ALLIANCE RES INC (QC)
Name changed to Groupe Covitec Inc. 08/27/1993
(See Groupe Covitec Inc.)

INTERNATIONAL ALLIANCE RES INC (YT)
Name changed to Bluenose Gold Corp. 07/25/2012

INTERNATIONAL ALLIANCE SVCS INC (DE)
Name changed to Century Business Services Inc. 12/23/97
Century Business Services name changed to CBIZ, Inc. 8/1/2005

INTERNATIONAL ALLY GROUP INC (DE)
Recapitalized as Green Shores Inc. 07/27/2009
Each share Common $0.001 par exchanged for (0.5) share Common $0.001 par
Green Shores Inc. Name changed to Pacific Shore Holdings, Inc. 10/12/2010

INTERNATIONAL ALUM CORP (CA)
Common $1 par split (3) for (2) by issuance of (0.5) additional share 5/19/72
Common $1 par split (2) for (1) by issuance of (1) additional share 7/10/78
Stock Dividend - 50% 8/15/75
Merged into Genstar Capital, LLC 3/30/2007
Each share Common $1 par exchanged for $53 cash

INTERNATIONAL ALUM LTD (DE)
Assets sold for benefit of creditors under Chapter X bankruptcy petition filed 4/11/69
No stockholders' equity

INTERNATIONAL AMCO CORP (ON)
Reorganized under the laws of England & Wales as Amco Corp. PLC 11/10/1989
Each share Conv. Class A Common no par exchanged for (1) share Ordinary 10p par
Each share Conv. Class B Common no par automatically became (1) share Conv. Class B Common no par
Amco Corp. PLC name changed to Billington Holdings Plc 03/31/2009

INTERNATIONAL AMERA INDS CORP (BC)
Recapitalized as IMA Resource Corp. 02/21/1996
Each share Common no par exchanged for (0.33333333) share Common no par
IMA Resource Corp. recapitalized as IMA Exploration Inc. 07/07/1998 which recapitalized as Kobex Minerals Inc. 09/30/2009 which name changed to Kobex Capital Corp. 08/29/2014 which name changed to Itasca Capital Ltd. 06/23/2016

INTERNATIONAL AMERN HOMES INC (DE)
Each share old Common 1¢ par exchanged for (0.1) share new Common 1¢ par 5/31/95
Each share new Common 1¢ par exchanged again for (1/3) share new Common 1¢ par 12/1/98
Each share new Common 1¢ par exchanged again for (0.002) share new Common 1¢ par 11/16/99
Note: In effect holders received $5.40 cash per share and public interest was eliminated

INTERNATIONAL AMERN INDS (CA)
Common no par split (3) for (1) by issuance of (2) additional shares 01/05/1971
Filed a petition under Chapter XI Bankruptcy Act 04/30/1973
Stockholders' equity unlikely

INTERNATIONAL AMERICAN MINERALS LTD. (NB)
Charter forfeited for failure to file reports and pay fees 03/02/1966

INTERNATIONAL AMERN TECHNOLOGIES INC (NV)
Name changed to Hammonds Industries, Inc. 05/14/2007
Hammonds Industries, Inc. recapitalized as Delta Seaboard International, Inc. 06/10/2010 which recapitalized as American International Holdings Corp. 08/13/2012

INTERNATIONAL ANNAX VENTURES INC (BC)
Merged into Herald Resources Ltd. 10/26/2002
Each share Common no par exchanged for (1) share Ordinary
(See Herald Resources Ltd.)

INTERNATIONAL ANTAM RES LTD (YUKON)
Name changed to Goldsource Mines Inc. (Yukon) 1/23/2004
Goldsource Mines Inc. (Yukon) reincorporated in British Columbia 8/3/2005

INTERNATIONAL APPAREL MARKETING INC (NV)
Name changed to Statewide Corp. 10/19/1990
(See Statewide Corp.)

INTERNATIONAL APPLIED SCIENCES LAB INC (NY)
Charter cancelled and proclaimed dissolved for failure to pay taxes 12/16/74

INTERNATIONAL AQUA FOODS LTD (BC)
Merged into Stolt Sea Farm Inc. 08/17/1999
Each share Common no par exchanged for $1.70 cash

INTERNATIONAL ARIMEX RES INC (BC)
Name changed to WestCan Uranium Corp. 09/10/2007

INTERNATIONAL ARLO RES LTD (YT)
Delisted from Canadian Dealer Network 03/22/2001

INTERNATIONAL ARPT HOTEL SYS INC (FL)
Under plan of liquidation each share Common $1 par stamped to indicate initial distribution of $4 cash 1/5/80
Assets transferred to International Airport Hotel System, Inc. Liquidating Trust 10/6/80
(See International Airport Hotel System, Inc. Liquidating Trust!)

INTERNATIONAL ART SVCS INC (NV)
Name changed to Integrated Art Services Inc. 03/24/1992
Integrated Art Services Inc. name changed to Worldwide Collectibles, Inc. 02/24/1993 which recapitalized as World Wide Net Inc. 07/30/1999 which name changed to Unlimited Coatings Corp. 05/14/2001 which name changed to International American Technologies, Inc. 03/22/2005 which name changed to Hammonds Industries, Inc. 05/14/2007 which recapitalized as Delta Seaboard International, Inc. 06/10/2010 which recapitalized as American International Holdings Corp. 08/13/2012

INTERNATIONAL ARTIFACTS INC (NV)
Name changed to Hawaiian Palisade Homes, Inc. 03/25/2002
Hawaiian Palisade Homes, Inc. name changed to AAA Manufacturing, Inc. 09/27/2004 which recapitalized as Gulf West Property, Inc. (NV) 03/10/2005 which reincorporated in Colorado as Titan Global Entertainment, Inc. 11/10/2005 which recapitalized as Sunset Island Group, Inc. 05/30/2008

INTERNATIONAL ARTWARE CORP (OH)
Name changed to Inarco Corp. 01/15/1968 which name changed back to International Artware Corp. 04/29/1982
Merged into I.A.C. Corp. 05/18/1984
Each share Common no par exchanged for $1 cash

INTERNATIONAL ASBESTOS LTD (QC)
Charter cancelled 05/00/1974

INTERNATIONAL ASSEMBLIX CORP (IL)
Common $10 par changed to no par 12/2/68
Filed Chapter XI bankruptcy proceedings 4/19/76 and the proceedings were closed 9/2/75
No stockholders' equity

INTERNATIONAL ASSETS HLDG CORP (DE)
Issue Information - 800,000 UNITS consisting of (1) share COM and (1) WT offered at $5.50 per Unit on 02/11/1994
Stock Dividends - 10% payable 01/20/1998 to holders of record 12/26/1997; 10% payable 03/26/1999 to holders of record 03/05/1999; 10% payable 03/24/2000 to holders of record 03/10/2000
Name changed to INTL FCStone Inc. 03/02/2011

INTERNATIONAL ATLANTIS RES LTD (AB)
Name changed to Atlantis International Ltd. 11/03/1986
Atlantis International Ltd. name changed to Atlantis Resources Ltd. 07/19/1988
(See Atlantis Resources Ltd.)

INTERNATIONAL ATLAS DEV & EXPL LTD (QC)
Charter annulled for failure to file annual reports 02/09/1980

INTERNATIONAL AVALON AIRCRAFT INC (BC)
Struck off register and declared dissolved for failure to file returns 01/10/1992

INTERNATIONAL AVIATION CORP. (DE)
Acquired by Seaboard & Western Airlines, Inc. 11/1/60
(See Seaboard & Western Airlines, Inc.)

INTERNATIONAL AVINO MINES LTD (BC)
Name changed to Avino Silver & Gold Mines Ltd. 08/29/1997

INTERNATIONAL AVIONICS INC. (UT)
Name changed to Tytan Resources, Inc. 4/25/83
Tytan Resources, Inc. name changed to Sterling Continental Corp. 3/10/88
(See Sterling Continental Corp.)

INTERNATIONAL AZORA MINERALS INC (WY)
Reincorporated 00/00/1990
Place of incorporation changed from (BC) to (WY) 00/00/1990
Name changed to Power Battery Holdings Corp. (WY) 03/05/1991
Power Battery Holdings Corp. (WY) reincorporated in Washington 12/14/1992 which recapitalized as Consolidated Power Battery Corp. 07/09/1998
(See Consolidated Power Battery Corp.)

INTERNATIONAL BALER CORP OLD (DE)
Merged into Waste Technology Corp. 06/27/1997
Each share Common 10¢ par exchanged for (4.1) shares new Common 1¢ par
Waste Technology Corp. name changed to International Baler Corp. (New) 03/16/2009

INTERNATIONAL BALFOUR RES LTD (BC)
Name changed to Quartet Energy Resources Ltd. (BC) 08/28/1980
Quartet Energy Resources Ltd. (BC) reincorporated in Ontario 07/09/1981 which name changed to Oiltex International Ltd. 04/26/1984 which merged into International Oiltex Ltd. 10/01/1989 which merged into Aztec Resources Ltd. 09/02/1994 which recapitalized as Pursuit Resources Inc. (New) 02/13/1997 which merged into EnerMark Income Fund 04/11/2000 which merged into Enerplus Resources Fund 06/22/2001 which reorganized as Enerplus Corp. 01/03/2011

INTERNATIONAL BALLATER RES INC (BC)
Merged into First Quantum Minerals Ltd. (Yukon) 12/12/1997
Each share Common no par exchanged for (2.75) shares Common no par
First Quantum Minerals Ltd. (Yukon) reincorporated in Canada 08/11/2003 which reincorporated in British Columbia 06/03/2005

INTERNATIONAL BANCSHARES CORP. (DE)
Common $1 par split (5) for (4) by issuance of (0.25) additional share 6/20/93
Stock Dividends - 15% 7/28/80; 15% 6/20/90; 15% 6/20/91; 20% 6/25/92
Reincorporated under the laws of Texas 5/18/95

INTERNATIONAL BK (HOUSTON, TX)
Common Capital Stock $10 par changed to $5 par and (1) additional share issued 07/06/1965
Common Capital Stock $5 par changed to $1.25 par and (3) additional shares issued 01/15/1970
Name changed to Greater Houston Bank (Houston, TX) 12/18/1972
(See Greater Houston Bank (Houston, TX))

INTERNATIONAL BK (WASHINGTON, DC)
Common $10 par changed to $5 par 00/00/1945
Common $5 par changed to $1 par and (4) additional shares issued 06/15/1959
Stock Dividend - 12.5% 04/28/1969
Merged into USLICO Corp. 12/31/1985
Each share Class A Common $1 par exchanged for (0.637) share Common $1 par
Each share Common $1 par exchanged for (0.637) share Common $1 par
USLICO Corp. merged into NWNL Companies, Inc. 01/17/1995 which name changed to ReliaStar Financial Corp. 02/13/1995
(See ReliaStar Financial Corp.)

INTERNATIONAL BK CALIF (LOS ANGELES, CA)
Stock Dividends - 5% payable 5/25/2000 to holders of record 3/31/2000; 5% payable 6/14/2001 to holders of record 4/30/2001 Ex date - 6/6/2001
Merged into First Banks, Inc. 9/30/2005
Each share Common $10 par exchanged for $46.28 cash

INTERNATIONAL BK COMM (LAREDO, TX)
Under plan of reorganization each share Capital Stock $5 par automatically became (1) share International Bancshares Corp. (TX) Common $1 par 07/28/1980
International Bancshares Corp. (TX) reincorporated in Delaware 05/18/1995

INTERNATIONAL BANK OF WASHINGTON, D.C. (AZ)
See - International Bank (Washington, DC)

INTERNATIONAL BANKCARD SVCS CORP (DE)
Recapitalized as Integrated Resource Technologies Inc. 07/24/1992
Each share Common 1¢ par exchanged for (0.1) share Common 1¢ par
Integrated Resource Technologies Inc. recapitalized as Comprehensive Environmental Systems Inc. 02/06/1995 which name changed to Windswept Environmental Group, Inc. 03/25/1997
(See Windswept Environmental Group, Inc.)

INTERNATIONAL BANKNOTE INC (NY)
Merged into United States Banknote Corp. (NY) 7/25/90
Each share Common $1 par exchanged for (0.25) share Preferred 1¢ par and (0.5) share Common 1¢ par
United States Banknote Corp. (NY) reincorporated in (DE) 9/21/93 which name changed to American Banknote Corp. 7/3/95

INTERNATIONAL BARON RES LTD (BC)
Recapitalized as Azco Mining Inc. (WY) 02/20/1992
Each share Common no par exchanged for (0.16666666) share Common no par
(See Azco Mining Inc. (WY))

INTERNATIONAL BARRIER CORP (DE)
Charter cancelled and declared inoperative and void for non-payment of taxes 6/17/92

INTERNATIONAL BARRIER TECHNOLOGY INC (BC)
Acquired by Louisiana-Pacific Corp. 10/13/2017
Each share Common no par exchanged for USD$0.41 cash
Note: Unexchanged certificates will be cancelled and become without value 10/13/2022

INTERNATIONAL BARTER CORP (NV)
Common $0.001 par split (2) for (1) by issuance of (1) additional share payable 7/27/98 to holders of record 7/24/98
Name changed to Ubarter.com Inc. 4/21/99
Ubarter.com Inc. merged into Network Commerce Inc. 6/1/2000
(See Network Commerce Inc.)

INTERNATIONAL BARYTEX RES LTD (BC)
Merged into Kobex Minerals Inc. 09/30/2009
Each share Common no par exchanged for (0.09208333) share Common no par
Kobex Minerals Inc. name changed to Kobex Capital Corp. 08/29/2014 which name changed to Itasca Capital Ltd. 06/23/2016

INTERNATIONAL BASE METALS LTD. (MB)
Charter cancelled for failure to file annual reports 00/00/1969

INTERNATIONAL BASIC ECONOMY CORP (NY)
Merged into Booker McConnell Ltd. 6/30/80
Each share Common $1 par exchanged for $8.40 cash

INTERNATIONAL BASIC RES INC (ID)
Recapitalized as International Resort Developers Inc. (ID) 5/19/97
Each (30) shares Common 10¢ par exchanged (1) share Common 10¢ par
International Resort Developers Inc. (ID) reincorporated in Tennessee as Ameristar International Holdings Corp. 1/22/98
(See Ameristar International Holdings Corp.)

INTERNATIONAL BASLEN ENTERPRISES LTD (ON)
Cease trade order effective 07/31/1991
Stockholders' equity unlikely

INTERNATIONAL BD & EQUITY LTD (ON)
Class A $5 par changed to no par and (2) additional shares issued 7/25/69
Stock Dividend - holders of Common received 200% in Class A 7/25/69
Merged into Life Investors International Ltd. 7/14/73
Each share Class A no par exchanged for (1) share Class A $1 par and (0.2) share Common no par
Each share Common no par exchanged for (0.5) share Common no par
(See Life Investors International Ltd.)

INTERNATIONAL BD & EQUITY TR
Units of Bene. Int. Latin America Ser. 1 called for redemption 5/15/97

INTERNATIONAL BEAUTY CORP. (FL)
Name changed to Cement International Corp. 3/15/66
Cement International Corp. name changed to Comp-Tronics, Inc. 9/9/69 which name changed to Silvatex, Inc. 1/7/80 which name changed to Grandma's Inc. 7/30/82
(See Grandma's Inc.)

INTERNATIONAL BELLEVUE VENTURES LTD (BC)
Dissolved 02/00/1989
Details not available

INTERNATIONAL BERYLLIUM CORP. (CO)
Merged into Sterling Beryllium & Oil Co. 02/04/1958
Each share Common exchanged for (0.01666666) share Common 10¢ par
Sterling Beryllium & Oil Co. merged into Elgin Gas & Oil Co. 06/12/1959
(See Elgin Gas & Oil Co.)

INTERNATIONAL BERYLLIUM CORP. LTD. (BC)
Charter cancelled 00/00/1969

INTERNATIONAL BERYLLIUM CORP (BC)
Name changed to IBC Advanced Alloys Corp. 03/06/2009

INTERNATIONAL BEVERAGE CORP (BC)
Recapitalized as Clearly Canadian Beverage Corp. 05/14/1990
Each share Common no par exchanged for (0.28571428) share Common no par
(See Clearly Canadian Beverage Corp.)

INTERNATIONAL BEVERAGE CORP (CO)
Recapitalized as Global Entertainment Holdings/Equities, Inc. 08/27/1998
Each share Common $0.001 par exchanged for (1/7) share Common $0.001 par
(See Global Entertainment Holdings/Equities, Inc.)

INTERNATIONAL BIBIS TIN MINES LTD (ON)
Recapitalized as Laurasia Resources Ltd. 11/29/1973
Each share Capital Stock $1 par exchanged for (0.25) share Capital Stock no par
(See Laurasia Resources Ltd.)

INTERNATIONAL BIGSKY RES CORP (YT)
Dissolved 12/03/2004

INTERNATIONAL BIO RECOVERY CORP (BC)
Name changed to TerraBioGen Technologies Inc. 01/21/2011

INTERNATIONAL BIO WASTE SYS INC (BC)
Recapitalized as Bioflow Environmental Technologies Inc. 04/22/1994
Each share Common no par exchanged for (0.2) share Common no par
Bioflow Environmental Technologies Inc. recapitalized as Strategic Merchant Bancorp Inc. 05/15/1997 which name changed to Strategic Nevada Resources Corp. 08/03/2006 which name changed to SNS Silver Corp. 02/26/2007 which name changed to SNS Precious Metals Inc. 05/17/2010 which recapitalized as Gold Finder Explorations Ltd. 10/08/2010 which recapitalized as Venzee Technologies Inc. 01/05/2018

INTERNATIONAL BIOANALOGICS SYS INC (CANADA)
Reincorporated 09/29/2006
Place of incorporation changed from (OR) to Canada 09/29/2006
Recapitalized as reWORKS Environmental Corp. 05/11/2007
Each (2.9543557) shares Common no par exchanged for (1) share Common no par reWORKS Environmental Corp. name changed to Forterra Environmental Corp. 02/22/2008

INTERNATIONAL BIOCHEMICAL INDS INC (GA)
SEC revoked common stock registration 06/09/2006

INTERNATIONAL BIOFUEL & BIOCHEMICAL CORP (PA)
SEC revoked common stock registration 09/29/2005

INTERNATIONAL BIOREMEDIATION SVCS INC (BC)
Recapitalized as IBIS Ventures Inc. 02/24/2000
Each share Common no par exchanged for (0.1) share Common no par
IBIS Ventures Inc. name changed to Tranzcom Security Networks Inc. 12/12/2001 which name changed to Tranzcom China Security Networks Inc. 06/25/2004 which recapitalized as Pacific Link Mining Corp. 09/12/2007

INTERNATIONAL BIOTECHNOLOGIES INC (DE)
Merged into Eastman Kodak Co. 09/04/1987
Each share Common $2 par exchanged for $6.30 cash

INTERNATIONAL BIOTECHNOLOGY CORP (ON)
Recapitalized as Veris Biotechnology Corp. 03/22/2001
Each share Common no par exchanged for (0.5) share Common no par
Veris Biotechnology Corp. recapitalized as Capital Diagnostic Corp. 05/05/2004

INTERNATIONAL BLDG CONCEPTS LTD (MN)
SEC revoked common stock registration 08/30/2017

INTERNATIONAL BLDG TECHNOLOGIES GROUP, INC. (NV)
SEC revoked common stock registration 09/12/2014

INTERNATIONAL BLDRS LTD INC (FL)
Common $0.001 par split (2) for (1) by issuance of (1) additional share payable 09/26/2005 to holders of record 08/30/2005 Ex date - 09/27/2005
Charter revoked 09/22/2000

INTERNATIONAL BLUE GOLD CORP (BC)
Recapitalized as Buddha Resources Inc. 01/16/1998
Each share Common no par exchanged for (0.5) share Common no par
(See Buddha Resources Inc.)

INTERNATIONAL BLUE SUN RESOURCE CORP (BC)
Name changed to Dalton Enterprises Ltd. (BC) 05/26/1994
Dalton Enterprises Ltd. (BC) reincorporated in Wyoming 01/17/1995 which reincorporated in Delaware as Dalton Specialties, Ltd. 03/01/1996
(See Dalton Specialties, Ltd.)

INTERNATIONAL BOOK CORP (DE)
Reincorporated 7/24/68
Common 10¢ par changed to 2¢ par

and (4) additional shares issued 8/25/66
State of incorporation changed from (FL) to (DE) 7/24/68
Name changed to IBC Industries, Inc. (DE) 8/3/71
(See IBC Industries, Inc.)

INTERNATIONAL BOOK DISTRIBUTORS, INC. (FL)
Stock Dividends - 10% 4/29/64; 25% 5/26/65
Name changed to International Book Corp. (FL) 4/26/66
International Book Corp. (FL) reincorporated in Delaware 7/24/68 which name changed to IBC Industries, Inc. (DE) 8/3/71
(See IBC Industries, Inc. (DE))

INTERNATIONAL BORNITE MINES LTD (BC)
Struck off register and declared dissolved for failure to file retuns 12/00/1976

INTERNATIONAL BRACE RES INC (BC)
Recapitalized as Prescott Resources Inc. (BC) 04/04/1997
Each share Common no par exchanged for (0.2) share Common no par
Prescott Resources Inc. (BC) reincorporated in Yukon as Asia Sapphires Ltd. 06/29/1998
(See Asia Sapphires Ltd.)

INTERNATIONAL BRAID CO.
Name changed to Charles Corp. in 1947 which completed liquidation in 1950

INTERNATIONAL BRANDS INC (NV)
Common 1¢ par split (2) for (1) by issuance of (1) additional share payable 10/31/1998 to holders of record 10/31/1998
SEC revoked common stock registration 01/19/2005

INTERNATIONAL BRAVO RES CORP (BC)
Recapitalized as Bravo Venture Group Inc. 03/15/2002
Each share Common no par exchanged for (0.14285714) share Common no par
Bravo Venture Group Inc. name changed to Bravo Gold Corp. 02/22/2010 which recapitalized as Homestake Resource Corp. 04/16/2012 which merged into Auryn Resources Inc. 09/07/2016

INTERNATIONAL BRENMAC DEV CORP (BC)
Recapitalized as Oberg Industries Ltd. 01/14/1986
Each share Capital Stock no par exchanged for (0.33333333) share Common no par
Oberg Industries Ltd. recapitalized as Consolidated Oberg Industries Ltd. 08/21/1990 which name changed to Hytec Flow Systems Inc. 01/16/1997
(See Hytec Flow Systems Inc.)

INTERNATIONAL BREWERIES, INC. (MI)
Reincorporated under the laws of Delaware as Iroquois Industries, Inc. 5/8/67
Iroquois Industries, Inc. name changed to Iroquois Brands, Ltd. 6/1/73
(See Iroquois Brands, Ltd.)

INTERNATIONAL BREWING & MFG INC (NV)
Each share old Common 2-1/2¢ par exchanged for (0.04) share new Common 2-1/2¢ par 08/13/1990
Each share new Common 2-1/2¢ par exchanged again for (1/3) share new Common 2-1/2 par 08/13/1993
Each share new Common 2-1/2¢ par exchanged again for (0.0005) share new Common 2-1/2¢ par 12/01/1997

Note: No holder will receive fewer than (100) post split shares
Name changed to Juina Mining Corp. 12/16/1997
Juina Mining Corp. name changed to AC Energy, Inc. (NV) 02/23/2007
(See AC Energy, Inc. (NV))

INTERNATIONAL BRICAN RES LTD (BC)
Name changed to C & E Furniture Industries Inc. 02/06/1992
(See C & E Furniture Industries Inc.)

INTERNATIONAL BROADCAST SYS LTD (DE)
Merged into Vidmark, Inc. 12/30/91
Each share Class A Common 10¢ par exchanged for $0.51 cash

INTERNATIONAL BROADCASTING CENTRE LTD (AB)
Recapitalized as Ensel Corp. 10/13/1992
Each share Common no par exchanged for (0.29411764) share Common no par
Ensel Corp. name changed to Surge Resources Inc. 05/04/2005 which name changed to Eaglewood Energy, Inc. 11/05/2007
(See Eaglewood Energy Inc.)

INTERNATIONAL BROADCASTING CORP (DE)
Each share Common 1¢ par exchanged for (10) shares Common $0.001 par 03/04/1983
Each share old Common $0.001 par exchanged for (0.04) share new Common $0.001 par 03/31/1987
Plan of reorganization under Chapter 11 Federal Bankruptcy proceedings confirmed 05/26/1993
Pending the amount of unsecured creditors' claims allowed, holders may receive a cash payment

INTERNATIONAL BROADCASTING CORP (NV)
Each share old Common $0.0001 par exchanged for (0.04) share new Common $0.0001 par 07/06/2007
Name changed to Copper King Mining Corp. 12/19/2007

INTERNATIONAL BROADLANDS RES LTD (BC)
Recapitalized as Broadlands Resources Ltd. (New) 03/15/1999
Each share Common no par exchanged for (0.25) share Common no par
Broadlands Resources Ltd. (New) recapitalized as Pinnacle Mines Ltd. (Ctfs. dated after 07/16/2003) 07/16/2003 which name changed to Jayden Resources Inc. (BC) 06/29/2010 which reincorporated in Cayman Islands 10/03/2012

INTERNATIONAL BRONZE POWDERS LTD (CANADA)
98% of 6% Preference acquired by Foreign Power Securities Corp. Ltd. through purchase offer which expired 11/22/1971
99% of Common acquired by Warnock Hersey International through purchase offer which expired 11/22/71
Public interest eliminated

INTERNATIONAL BROOKS PETE LTD (BC)
Recapitalized as Flying A Petroleum Ltd. 08/14/2003
Each share Common no par exchanged for (0.1) share Common no par

INTERNATIONAL BURGERS NOW LTD (BC)
Dissolved 01/19/1990
Details not available

INTERNATIONAL BUSINESS MACHS CORP (NY)
7.50% Depositary Preferred A called for redemption at $25 on 7/3/2001

(Additional Information in Active)
INTERNATIONAL BUSINESS SCHS INC (ON)
Each share old Common no par exchanged for (0.2) share new Common no par 10/17/1995
Reincorporated under the laws of Canada as Educor International Inc. 08/09/1999
Eudcor International Inc. name changed to LogicalOptions International Inc. 07/20/2000
(See LogicalOptions International Inc.)

INTERNATIONAL BUTEC INDS CORP (BC)
Recapitalized as WebSmart.com Communications, Inc. 10/17/2000
Each share Common no par exchanged for (0.2) share Common no par
WebSmart.com Communications, Inc. name changed to Gold Reach Resources Ltd. 10/13/2004 which name changed to Surge Copper Corp. 02/21/2018

INTERNATIONAL BUTTON HOLE SEWING MACHINE CO.
Merged into Reece Corp. in 1948
Each share Common $10 par exchanged for (0.2) share 5% Preferred $100 par and (1) share Common $1 par
(See Reece Corp.)

INTERNATIONAL BUYERS CLUB CORP (NY)
Name changed to Medical People Holdings, Inc. 06/19/1989
(See Medical People Holdings, Inc.)

INTERNATIONAL BY PRODS LTD (ON)
Charter cancelled and proclaimed dissolved for failure to pay taxes and file returns 8/10/87

INTERNATIONAL CABLECASTING TECHNOLOGIES INC (DE)
Reorganized 09/28/1990
Reorganized from under the laws of (BC) to (DE) 09/28/1990
Each share Common no par exchanged for (1) share Common 1¢ par
Name changed to DMX, Inc. 04/27/1995
DMX, Inc. merged into TCI Music, Inc. 07/11/1997 which name changed to Liberty Digital Inc. 09/10/1999 which merged into Liberty Media Corp. (New) 03/14/2002 which reorganized as Liberty Media Corp. (Incorporated 02/28/2006) 05/10/2006 which name changed to Liberty Interactive Corp. 09/26/2011 which name changed to Qurate Retail, Inc. 04/10/2018

INTERNATIONAL CABLETEL INC (DE)
Common 1¢ par split (4) for (3) by issuance of (1/3) additional share 8/11/95
Name changed to NTL Inc. 3/27/97
NTL Inc. reorganized as NTL Europe, Inc. 1/10/2003
(See NTL Europe, Inc.)

INTERNATIONAL CABLEVISION CORP (DE)
Merged into Columbia Cable Systems, Inc. 6/10/69
Each share Class A Common 10¢ par exchanged for (1.0667) shares Common 5¢ par
Columbia Cable Systems, Inc. name changed to UA-Columbia Cablevision, Inc. 12/29/72
(See UA-Columbia Cablevision, Inc.)

INTERNATIONAL CALNEVA GOLD CORP (BC)
Recapitalized as Tenacity Resources Corp. 09/30/1999
Each share Common no par

exchanged for (1/7) share Common no par
(See Tenacity Resources Corp.)

INTERNATIONAL CAMERO RES LTD (BC)
Name changed to International Pharmadyne Ltd. 03/05/1985
(See International Pharmadyne Ltd.)

INTERNATIONAL CANALASKA RES LTD (BC)
Recapitalized as CanAlaska Ventures Ltd. 12/03/1999
Each share Common no par exchanged for (0.2) share Common no par
CanAlaska Ventures Ltd. name changed to CanAlaska Uranium Ltd. 10/11/2006

INTERNATIONAL CANINE GENETICS INC (DE)
Acquired by Synbiotics Corp. 10/30/1996
Each share Common $0.00006 par exchanged for (0.251) share Common no par
(See Synbiotics Corp.)

INTERNATIONAL CANSTAT PETE CORP (BC)
Recapitalized as Blackwater Gold Corp. 09/16/1993
Each share Common no par exchanged for (0.4) share Common no par
Blackwater Gold Corp. recapitalized as Bonaventure Enterprises Inc. 03/20/2002 which recapitalized as Iconic Minerals Ltd. 03/03/2011

INTERNATIONAL CAP & TECHNOLOGY CORP (MD)
Charter cancelled for failure to file annual reports 10/10/90

INTERNATIONAL CAP DEV CORP (DE)
Charter cancelled and declared inoperative and void for non-payment of taxes 3/1/75

INTERNATIONAL CAP EQUIP LTD (BERMUDA)
Each share Common 5¢ par exchanged for (0.05) share Common $1 par 06/15/1992
Struck off register 00/00/1993

INTERNATIONAL CAPRI RES LTD (BC)
Name changed to Apiva.com Web Corp. 07/19/2000
Apiva.com Web Corp. name changed to Apiva Ventures Ltd. 12/18/2001 which recapitalized as Mark One Global Industries, Inc. 08/13/2008
(See Mark One Global Industries, Inc.)

INTERNATIONAL CAPTAIN INDS CORP (ON)
Recapitalized as Rocklite International Inc. 09/25/1992
Each share Common no par exchanged for (0.33333333) share Common no par
(See Rocklite International Inc.)

INTERNATIONAL CARBON CORP.
Name changed to Darco Corp. 00/00/1935
Darco Corp. acquired by Atlas Powder Co. 00/00/1950 which recapitalized as Atlas Chemical Industries, Inc. 05/31/1961
(See Atlas Chemical Industries, Inc.)

INTERNATIONAL CARDERO RES INC (BC)
Struck from the register and dissolved 02/23/1990

INTERNATIONAL CARGOCARE INC (BC)
Recapitalized as CVAC Industries Inc. 12/14/1993
Each share Common no par exchanged for (0.2) share Common no par

CVAC Industries Inc. recapitalized as Saddlerock Resources Inc. 11/27/1995 which name changed to MDX Medical Inc. 07/07/2000 which name changed to Urodynamix Technologies Ltd. 06/21/2006 which recapitalized as Venturi Ventures Inc. 08/29/2011
(See Venturi Ventures Inc.)

INTERNATIONAL CARRIERS LTD.
Name changed to Carriers & General Corp. 00/00/1935
Carriers & General Corp. merged into Dividend Shares, Inc. 09/15/1981 which name changed to Bullock Dividend Shares, Inc. 01/01/1985 which name changed to Alliance Dividend Shares, Inc. 03/13/1987 which name changed to Alliance Growth & Income Fund, Inc. 10/17/1989 which name changed to AllianceBernstein Growth & Income Fund, Inc. 03/31/2003

INTERNATIONAL CASH PORTFOLIOS (MA)
Eurocash Portfolio Shares of Bene. Int. 1¢ par reclassified as Global Cash Portfolio Shares of Bene. Int. 1¢ par 09/01/1987
Name changed to International Currency Portfolios and Global Cash Portfolio
Shares of Bene. Int. 1¢ par reclassified as Global Currency Portfolio Shares of Bene. Int. 1¢ par 06/01/1991
International Currency Portfolios name changed to Huntington Funds 10/23/1992 which name changed to Franklin/Templeton Global Trust (MA) 11/16/1993 which reincorporated in Delaware 08/01/2007

INTERNATIONAL CASINO CRUISES INC (NV)
Name changed to Mountain Energy Inc. 5/26/98
(See Mountain Energy Inc.)

INTERNATIONAL CATALYST VENTURES INC (YUKON)
Reincorporated 09/08/2000
Place of incorporation changed from (BC) to (Yukon) 09/08/2000
Recapitalized as Aberdeen International Inc. (Yukon) 11/23/2001
Each share Common no par exchanged for (0.33333333) Common no par
Aberdeen International Inc. (Yukon) reincorporated in Ontario 07/04/2006

INTERNATIONAL CAVITATION TECHNOLOGIES INC (CO)
SEC revoked common stock registration 10/03/2011

INTERNATIONAL CDIS SOFTWARE INC (BC)
Name changed to A.T.H. Fund Inc. 07/24/1990
(See A.T.H. Fund Inc.)

INTERNATIONAL CELLUCOTTON PRODUCTS CO. (DE)
Common no par exchanged (2) for (1) in 1936
Each share Common no par exchanged for (2) shares Common $2 par in 1946
Common $2 par changed to $1 par and (1) additional share issued in 1951
Merged into Kimberly-Clark Corp. share for share 9/30/55

INTERNATIONAL CELLULAR ACCESSORIES
Common $0.001 par split (3) for (1) by issuance of (2) additional shares payable 03/08/2010 to holders of record 03/04/2010 Ex date - 03/09/2010

Name changed to Image Metrics, Inc. 03/15/2010

INTERNATIONAL CEMENT CORP.
Name changed to Lone Star Cement Corp. (ME) in 1936
Lone Star Cement Corp. (ME) reincorporated under the laws of Delaware 5/29/69 which name changed to Lone Star Industries, Inc. 5/20/71
(See Lone Star Industries, Inc.)

INTERNATIONAL CERAMIC MNG LTD (ON)
Charter cancelled for failure to pay taxes and file returns 09/26/1973

INTERNATIONAL CETEC INVTS INC (BC)
Preferred no par called for redemption 08/28/1997
Merged into 0731537 B.C. Ltd. 10/31/2005
Each share Common no par exchanged for $1.65 cash

INTERNATIONAL CHALICE RES INC (BC)
Recapitalized as Golden Chalice Resources Inc. 08/15/2003
Each share Common no par exchanged for (0.25) share Common no par
Golden Chalice Resources Inc. recapitalized as Rogue Resources Inc. (Old) 10/15/2010 which name changed to Rogue Iron Ore Corp. 01/23/2012 which reorganized as Rogue Resources Inc. (New) 12/24/2013

INTERNATIONAL CHARGOLD RES LTD (BC)
Recapitalized as Odessa Gold Corp. 05/23/2002
Each share Common no par exchanged for (0.33333333) share Common no par
Odessa Gold Corp. recapitalized as Emerson Exploration Corp. 04/20/2005

INTERNATIONAL CHEM & NUCLEAR CORP (CA)
Each share old Common $1 par exchanged for (0.25) share Common $5 par 11/30/1964
Each share Common $5 par exchanged for (2.5) shares new Common $1 par 01/15/1968
New Common $1 par split (2) for (1) by issuance of (1) additional share 12/16/1968
New Common $1 par split (2) for (1) by issuance of (1) additional share 06/24/1971
Name changed to ICN Pharmaceuticals, Inc. (CA) 04/13/1973
ICN Pharmaceuticals, Inc. (CA) reincorporated in Delaware 10/03/1986 which merged into ICN Pharmaceuticals, Inc. (New) 11/10/1994 which name changed to Valeant Pharmaceuticals International 11/12/2003 which merged into Valeant Pharmaceuticals International, Inc. (Canada) 09/28/2010 which reincorporated in British Columbia 08/09/2013

INTERNATIONAL CHEM DEV CORP (NV)
Recapitalized as Columbia Autocar, Inc. 4/15/80
Each share Capital Stock $1 par exchanged for (0.5) share Capital Stock $0.00025 par
Columbia Autocar, Inc. name changed to American Peat Co. 4/22/82 which name changed to American National Hydrocarbon, Inc. 11/15/82
(See American National Hydrocarbon, Inc.)

INTERNATIONAL CHEMALLOY CORP (ON)
Recapitalized as Denbridge Capital Corp. (ON) 01/20/1986
Each share Capital Stock no par exchanged for (0.01) share Common no par
Denbridge Capital Corp. (ON) reincorporated in Canada 02/24/1994 which recapitalized as Atlantis Systems Corp. 06/11/2001
(See Atlantis Systems Corp.)

INTERNATIONAL CHEROKEE DEVS LTD (BC)
Recapitalized as GLS Global Listing Service Ltd. 11/30/1989
Each share Common no par exchanged for (0.2) share Common no par
GLS Global Listing Service Ltd. name changed to GLS Global Assets Ltd. 08/27/1992 which name changed to Mobile Lottery Solutions Inc. 02/20/2006 which name changed to NuMedia Games Inc. 09/27/2007 which recapitalized as Brandgamz Marketing Inc. 06/04/2008

INTERNATIONAL CHESS ENTERPRISES INC (BC)
Recapitalized as Grandmaster Technologies Inc. 06/22/1994
Each share Common no par exchanged for (0.2) share Common no par
Grandmaster Technologies Inc. recapitalized as EM Net Corp. (BC) 08/31/1998 which reincorporated in Canada as T & E Theatre.com Inc. 11/25/1999 which recapitalized as Manele Bay Ventures Inc. 02/28/2002 which name changed to MBA Gold Corp. 07/15/2003 which name changed to MBA Resources Corp. 10/14/2005 which name changed to Thunderbird Energy Corp. 07/27/2006 which recapitalized as Gordon Creek Energy Inc. 10/24/2013

INTERNATIONAL CHILD CARE CORP (DE)
Common $0.001 par split (2) for (1) by issuance of (1) additional share payable 3/14/2003 to holders of record 3/3/2003 Ex date - 3/17/2003
Recapitalized as World Wide Child Care Corp. 5/21/2007
Each (3.5) shares Common $0.001 par exchanged for (1) share Common $0.001 par

INTERNATIONAL CHOICE VENTURES INC (BC)
Reorganized under the laws of Alberta as Rhodes Resources Corp. 11/20/2002
Each share Common no par exchanged for (0.5) share Common no par
Rhodes Resources Corp. merged into Terra Energy Corp. 1/30/2004

INTERNATIONAL CHS RES CORP (ON)
Recapitalized as CHS Resources Inc. 12/10/2010
Each share Common no par exchanged for (0.5) share Common no par

INTERNATIONAL CIGAR MACHINERY CO. (NJ)
Each share Common $100 par exchanged for (3) shares old Common no par in 1927
Each share old Common no par exchanged for (2) shares new Common no par in 1930
Merged into American Machine & Foundry Co. on a (1.5) for (1) basis 4/19/62
American Machine & Foundry Co. name changed to AMF Inc. 4/30/70
(See AMF Inc.)

INTERNATIONAL CINEMA, INC.
Liquidated in 1938

INTERNATIONAL CINEVISION PRODTNS INC (DE)
Charter cancelled and declared inoperative and void for non-payment of taxes 6/26/85

INTERNATIONAL CITRUS CORP (NY)
Recapitalized as Princeton Commercial Holdings, Inc. 03/03/2004
Each share Common 10¢ par exchanged for (0.1) share Common $0.001 par
Princeton Commercial Holdings, Inc. name changed to EuroWind Energy, Inc. 04/28/2004 which name changed to First Petroleum & Pipeline Inc. 03/31/2005 which recapitalized as Luke Entertainment, Inc. 11/15/2007 which name changed to Greene Concepts, Inc. 01/14/2011

INTERNATIONAL CITY BK & TR CO (NEW ORLEANS, LA)
Under plan of reorganization each share Common $5 par exchanged for (1) share ICB Corp. Common $5 par 12/7/70
(See ICB Corp.)

INTERNATIONAL CLASSIC MOTORCARS INC (NY)
Name changed to ICI Holding Co., Inc. 7/3/87
(See ICI Holding Co., Inc.)

INTERNATIONAL CLINICAL LABORATORIES, INC. OLD (TN)
Merged into International Clinical Laboratories, Inc. (New) 8/31/77
Each share Common $1 par exchanged for (3) shares Common 33-1/3¢ par
(See International Clinical Laboratories, Inc. (New))

INTERNATIONAL CLINICAL LABS INC NEW (TN)
Common 33-1/3¢ par split (3) for (2) by issuance of (0.5) additional share 05/29/1981
Common 33-1/3¢ par split (3) for (2) by issuance of (0.5) additional share 01/07/1983
Merged into SmithKline Beckman Corp. 06/13/1988
Each share Common 33-1/3¢ par exchanged for $37 cash

INTERNATIONAL CMOS TECHNOLOGY INC (CA)
Plan of reorganization under Chapter 11 Federal Bankruptcy proceedings confirmed 09/23/1993
No stockholders' equity

INTERNATIONAL COAL & COKE CO., LTD.
Acquired by Coleman Collieries Ltd. 00/00/1952
Each (1,000) shares Capital Stock $1 par exchanged for (260) shares new Common $1 par, $330 cash and $1,170 in bonds
(See Coleman Collieries Ltd.)

INTERNATIONAL COAL GROUP INC NEW (DE)
Acquired by Arch Coal, Inc. 06/15/2011
Each share Common 1¢ par exchanged for $14.60 cash

INTERNATIONAL COAL GROUP INC OLD (DE)
Name changed to ICG Inc. 08/04/2005
ICG Inc. name changed to International Coal Group, Inc. (New) 11/21/2005
(See International Coal Group, Inc. (New))

INTERNATIONAL COAST MINERALS CORP (BC)
Struck off register and declared

dissolved for failure to file returns 09/02/1994

INTERNATIONAL COASTAL BIOFUELS INC (FL)
Recapitalized as IMD Companies Inc. 10/12/2010
Each share Common no par exchanged for (0.0002) share Common no par

INTERNATIONAL COATING CORP (NM)
Recapitalized as Techrich Corp. 05/30/1984
Each share Common 1¢ par exchanged for (0.25) share Common 4¢ par
(See Techrich Corp.)

INTERNATIONAL COBALT & SILVER MINING CO. LTD. (ON)
Acquired by International Copper & Cobalt Mines Ltd. on a share for share basis 04/01/1958
(See International Copper & Cobalt Mines Ltd.)

INTERNATIONAL COGENERATION CORP (DE)
Name changed to ICC Technologies, Inc. 07/15/1989
ICC Technologies, Inc. name changed to Rare Medium Group, Inc. 03/16/1999 which name changed to SkyTerra Communications, Inc. 09/26/2003
(See SkyTerra Communications, Inc.)

INTERNATIONAL COLIN ENERGY CORP (AB)
Merged into Morgan Hydrocarbons Inc. 07/01/1996
Each share Common no par exchanged for (1.975) shares Common no par
Morgan Hydrocarbons Inc. acquired by Stampeder Exploration Ltd. 10/15/1996 which was acquired by Gulf Canada Resources Ltd. 09/10/1997
(See Gulf Canada Resources Ltd.)

INTERNATIONAL COMBUSTION, INC.
Name changed to Combustion Engineering Co., Inc. 00/00/1933
Combustion Engineering Co., Inc. merged into Combustion Engineering-Superheater, Inc. 12/31/1948 which name changed to Combustion Engineering, Inc. 04/15/1953
(See Combustion Engineering, Inc.)

INTERNATIONAL COMBUSTION ENGINEERING CORP. (DE)
Reorganized as International Combustion Inc. 04/03/1933
Holders received only rights which expired 06/08/1933 to purchase shares in new company
(See International Combustion Inc.)

INTERNATIONAL COMFORT PRODS CORP (CANADA)
Merged into United Technologies Corp. 08/13/1999
Each share Ordinary no par exchanged for $11.75 cash

INTERNATIONAL COML ENTERPRISES INC (CO)
Name changed to Ecotech Ecology Management Corp. 3/2/88

INTERNATIONAL COML ENTERPRISES INC (NV)
Recapitalized as Demil International, Inc. 08/24/1998
Each share Common $0.001 par exchanged for (0.0625) share Common $0.001 par
(See Demil International, Inc.)

INTERNATIONAL COML TELEVISION INC (NV)
Name changed to ICTV Brands Inc. 08/21/2014

INTERNATIONAL COMMODITY RES CORP (NV)
Name changed to Ovutron Corp. 4/7/77
Ovutron Corp. name changed to Colt Energy Corp. 12/4/86
(See Colt Energy Corp.)

INTERNATIONAL COMMUNICATIONS & TECHNOLOGIES CORP (DE)
Recapitalized as GBS Com-Tech Corp. 05/15/1997
Each share Common $0.0001 par exchanged for (0.02) share Common $0.0001 par
(See GBS Com-Tech Corp.)

INTERNATIONAL COMPONENTS CORP (NJ)
Merged into New Intco Inc. 9/21/79
Each share Common 1¢ par exchanged for $0.75 cash

INTERNATIONAL COMPUMEDICS CORP (DE)
Charter cancelled and declared inoperative and void for non-payment of taxes 03/01/1977

INTERNATIONAL COMPUTER APPLICATIONS INC (CO)
Charter suspended for failure to file annual reports 09/30/1986

INTERNATIONAL COMPUTER CORP (DE)
Name changed to Verco Energy Corp. 8/12/75
(See Verco Energy Corp.)

INTERNATIONAL COMPUTER SCIENCES INC (NJ)
Under plan of merger each share Common 1¢ par exchanged for $0.80 cash 06/19/1981

INTERNATIONAL COMPUTERS & TABULATORS LTD (ENGLAND)
Reorganized as International Computers (Holdings) Ltd. 08/06/1968
Each ADR for Ordinary Reg £1 par exchanged for (1) ADR for Ordinary Reg. £1 par
International Computers (Holdings) Ltd. name changed to ICL PLC 02/14/1977 which was acquired by STC PLC 05/16/1986
(See STC PLC)

INTERNATIONAL COMPUTERS HLDGS LTD (ENGLAND)
Name changed to ICL PLC 02/14/1977
ICL PLC acquired by STC PLC 05/16/1986
(See STC PLC)

INTERNATIONAL COMPUTEX INC (GA)
Merged into IHS Itemquest II Inc. 03/25/1999
Each share Common $0.001 par exchanged for $9.50 cash

INTERNATIONAL COMPUTING SERVICE, INC. (FL)
Name changed to XIOX International, Inc. 3/20/69
(See XIOX International, Inc.)

INTERNATIONAL COMSTOCK EXPL LTD (BC)
Recapitalized as Secureview Systems Inc. 09/27/2001
Each share Common no par exchanged for (0.2) share Common no par
Secureview Systems Inc. name changed to Global Immune Technologies Inc. (BC) 05/03/2005 which reincorporated in Wyoming 05/12/2006

INTERNATIONAL CONQUEST EXPL LTD (BC)
Recapitalized as Conquest Ventures Inc. 02/07/2000
Each share Common no par exchanged for (0.33333333) share Common no par
Conquest Ventures Inc. recapitalized as Bellhaven Ventures Inc. 11/26/2003 which name changed to Bellhaven Copper & Gold Inc. 10/06/2006 which merged into GoldMining Inc. 05/30/2017

INTERNATIONAL CONS RLTY INC (DE)
Name changed to San Ti International Corp. 8/14/97

INTERNATIONAL CONSORT INDS INC (BC)
Name changed to Cryopak Industries Inc. 11/12/1993
(See Cryopak Industries Inc.)

INTERNATIONAL CONSORTIUM CORP (NV)
SEC revoked common stock registration 05/31/2011

INTERNATIONAL CONSTR PRODS INC (FL)
Recapitalized as Construction Products International, Inc. 03/30/1999
Each share Common $0.001 par exchanged for (0.00666666) share Common $0.001 par
Construction Products International, Inc. recapitalized as Sports Pouch Beverage Co., Inc. 10/06/2004

INTERNATIONAL CONSTR SYS INC (DE)
Name changed to X-Zel Inc. and Common 10¢ par reclassified as Class A Common 1¢ par 5/10/85
(See X-Zel Inc.)

INTERNATIONAL CONSUMER BRANDS INC (DE)
Charter cancelled and declared inoperative and void for non-payment of taxes 3/1/92

INTERNATIONAL CONSV EQUIP INC (NV)
Name changed to Partners Financial Group, Inc. (Old) 7/29/91
Partners Financial Group, Inc. (Old) name changed to California Food & Vending, Inc. 3/30/92 which name changed to Partners Financial Group, Inc. (New) 8/21/92
(See Partners Financial Group, Inc. (New))

INTERNATIONAL CONTAINER SYS INC (DE)
Common 1¢ par split (3) for (2) by issuance of (0.5) additional share 6/24/86
Merged into Polymer International Corp. 7/20/94
Each share Common 1¢ par exchanged for $3.625 cash

INTERNATIONAL CONTOUR TECHNOLOGY INC (BC)
Name changed to TSI TelSys Corp. (BC) 10/27/1995
TSI TelSys Corp. (BC) reincorporated in New Brunswick 04/01/1996 which reincorporated in Delaware 10/20/2003
(See TSI TelSys Corp.)

INTERNATIONAL CONTROLLED INVTS INC (BC)
Reorganized under the laws of Yukon as New Age Ventures Inc. 08/23/1991
Each share Common no par exchanged for (0.2) share Common no par
New Age Ventures Inc. recapitalized as Great Panther Inc. 01/01/1998 which recapitalized as Great Panther Resources Ltd. (YT) 10/02/2003 which reincorporated in British Columbia 07/14/2004 which name changed to Great Panther Silver Ltd. 01/12/2010

INTERNATIONAL CONVERTER CORP (CO)
Name changed to V.I.P. Global Capital Inc. 11/03/1992
(See V.I.P. Global Capital Inc.)

INTERNATIONAL COPPER & COBALT MINES LTD. (ON)
Charter revoked for failure to file reports and pay fees 11/03/1966

INTERNATIONAL COPPER LTD (BC)
Struck off register and declared dissolved for failure to file returns 09/03/1974

INTERNATIONAL COROMANDEL RES LTD (BC)
Name changed to Sonora Gold Corp. 08/17/2004
Sonora Gold Corp. recapitalized as MetalQuest Minerals Inc. 10/17/2007 which recapitalized as Canada Gold Corp. 09/01/2009 which name changed to STEM 7 Capital Inc. 07/12/2013 which name changed to South Star Mining Corp. 12/22/2017

INTERNATIONAL CORONA CORP (ON)
Under plan of reorganization each share Class A Subordinate no par exchanged for (0.7) share Common no par, (0.3) share Dundee Bancorp Inc. Class A Subordinate no par and (0.25) Dundee Bancorp Inc. Class A Subordinate Stock Purchase Warrant expiring 09/30/1992 on 10/29/1991
Under plan of reorganization each share Conv. Class B Common no par exchanged for (0.7) share Common no par, (0.3) share Dundee Bancorp Inc. Class B Common no par and (0.25) Dundee Bancorp Inc. Class A Subordinate Stock Purchase Warrant expiring 09/30/1992 on 10/29/1991
(See Dundee Bancorp Inc.)
Each share Adjustable Rate 1st Preference Ser. B no par exchanged for either (1) share Adjustable Rate 1st Preference Ser. C no par or (4.562118) shares Common no par 04/30/1992
Merged into Homestake Mining Co. 08/17/1992
Each share Adjustable Rate 1st Preference Ser. A no par exchanged for (0.54) share Common $1 par and $0.50 cash
Each share Adjustable Rate 1st Preference Ser. C no par exchanged for (1.08) shares Common $1 par
Each share Common no par exchanged for (0.35) share Common $1 par
(See Homestake Mining Co.)

INTERNATIONAL CORONA RES LTD (CANADA)
Reincorporated 08/01/1985
Common no par split (2) for (1) by issuance of (1) additional share 10/21/1983
Place of incorporation changed from (BC) to (Canada) 08/01/1985
Common no par split (5) for (1) by issuance of (4) additional shares 02/24/1988
Merged into Corona Corp. 07/01/1988
Each share Common no par exchanged for (1) share Class A Subordinate no par and (1/6) Class A Subordinate Stock Purchase Warrant expiring 06/30/1990
Corona Corp. recapitalized as International Corona Corp. 06/11/1991
(See International Corona Corp.)

INTERNATIONAL CORRESPONDENCE SCHOOLS WORLD LTD. INC. (PA)
Acquired by International Textbook Co. share for share 12/31/64

International Textbook Co. name changed to Intext, Inc. 4/28/72
(See Intext, Inc.)

INTERNATIONAL COSMETICS & CHEMICALS, INC. (NV)
Name changed to International Minerals Corp. 7/1/65
International Minerals Corp. name changed to Dynatron, Inc. 10/7/68
(See Dynatron, Inc.)

INTERNATIONAL COSMETICS MARKETING CO (FL)
SEC revoked common stock registration 03/23/2010

INTERNATIONAL COURIERS CORP (DE)
Merged into Gelco Corp. 12/30/1977
Each share Common $1 par exchanged for $18 cash

INTERNATIONAL CREOSOTING & CONSTRUCTION CO. (TX)
Merged into Kerr-McGee Corp. 9/1/74
Each share Capital Stock $100 par exchanged for $175 cash

INTERNATIONAL CROESUS VENTURES CORP (BC)
Name changed to Zinco Mining Corp. 01/29/2007

INTERNATIONAL CROWN CORP. (DE)
Acquired by United States Crown Corp. 3/31/66
Each share Common 10¢ par exchanged for (0.25) share Common 10¢ par
(See United States Crown Corp.)

INTERNATIONAL CRUISESHIPCENTERS CORP (BC)
Recapitalized as Riley Resources Ltd. 06/24/1991
Each share Common no par exchanged for (0.125) share Common no par
Riley Resources Ltd. recapitalized as International Riley Resources Ltd. 01/23/1998 which recapitalized as Wind River Resources Ltd. 11/22/2001 which recapitalized as Teslin River Resources Corp. 01/03/2008 which recapitalized as Siyata Mobile Inc. 07/29/2015

INTERNATIONAL CRYOGENIC SYS CORP (NV)
Name changed to Powercold Corp. 04/02/1997
(See Powercold Corp.)

INTERNATIONAL CTLS CORP (FL)
Common 10¢ par split (5) for (4) by issuance of (0.25) additional share 3/16/81
Merged into ICC Acquisition Corp. 7/31/87
Each share Common 10¢ par exchanged for $44 cash

INTERNATIONAL CURATOR RES LTD (BC)
Recapitalized as Canadian Gold Hunter Corp. (BC) 12/30/2003
Each share Common no par exchanged for (0.2) share Common no par
Canadian Gold Hunter Corp. (BC) reincorporated in Canada 07/29/2004 which name changed to NGEx Resources Inc. 09/22/2009

INTERNATIONAL CURRENCY PORTFOLIOS (MA)
Name changed to Huntington Funds 10/23/1992
Huntington Funds name changed to Franklin/Templeton Global Trust (MA) 11/16/1993 which reincorporated in Delaware 08/01/2007

INTERNATIONAL CUSTOM PACK INC (NV)
Name changed to Global Seafood Technologies Inc. 12/15/98

INTERNATIONAL DAIRY QUEEN INC (DE)
Each share Common $1 par exchanged for (3) shares Class A Common 1¢ par and (2) shares Conv. Class B Common 1¢ par 2/11/86
Class A Common 1¢ par split (3) for (1) by issuance of (2) additional shares 4/16/91
Conv. Class B Common 1¢ par split (3) for (1) by issuance of (2) additional shares 4/16/91
Merged into Berkshire Hathaway Inc. 1/7/98
Each share Class A Common 1¢ par exchanged for either (0.00056607) share Class A Common $5 par, (0.01698236) share Class B Common $0.1667 par, or $27 cash
Each share Class B Common 1¢ par exchanged for either (0.00056607) share Class A Common $5 par, (0.01698236) share Class B Common $0.1667 par, or $27 cash
Note: Option to make a definitive election expired 1/2/98

INTERNATIONAL DALECO TECHNOLOGIES CORP (CA)
Recapitalized as International Daleco Corp. 06/21/1990
Each share Common no par exchanged for (0.33333333) share Common no par

INTERNATIONAL DAMASCUS RES LTD (BC)
Recapitalized as Ravenhead Recovery Corp. 07/13/1998
Each share Common no par exchanged for (0.33333333) share Common no par
(See Ravenhead Recovery Corp.)

INTERNATIONAL DANCE COLLECTION INC (FL)
Recapitalized as International Wellness Association, Inc. 06/23/1998
Each share Common $0.001 par exchanged for (0.2) share Common $0.001 par
(See International Wellness Association, Inc.)

INTERNATIONAL DASA CORP (MI)
Name changed to Johnson International Corp. 06/18/1984
Each share Common 1¢ par exchanged for (1) share Common 1¢ par
(See Johnson International Corp.)

INTERNATIONAL DATA SVC CORP (BC)
Struck off register and declared dissolved for failure to file returns 01/15/1993

INTERNATIONAL DATA SYSTEMS, INC. (TX)
Completely liquidated 5/28/65
Each share Common 12-1/2¢ par exchanged for (0.1) share Western Equities, Inc. Common 10¢ par 6/29/65
Western Equities, Inc. name changed to Westec Corp. 5/20/66 which name changed to Tech-Sym Corp. 5/25/70
(See Tech-Sym Corp.)

INTERNATIONAL DATACASTING CORP (CANADA)
Merged into Novra Technologies Inc. 06/21/2016
Each share Common no par exchanged for (0.1) share Common no par, (0.2) Common Stock Purchase Warrant expiring 00/00/2017 and $0.01 cash

INTERNATIONAL DATASHARE CORP (AB)
Each share old Common no par exchanged for (0.1) share new Common no par 07/03/2002

Merged into Divestco Inc. 09/24/2003
Each share new Common no par exchanged for (0.501225) share Common no par

INTERNATIONAL DATATRONICS, INC. (CA)
Under plan of partial liquidation each share Common $1 par exchanged for (0.2) share new Common $1 par and $3 cash 12/15/1964
Completely liquidated 06/17/1966
Each share new Common $1 par exchanged for first and final distribution of (1) share Udico Electric Co. Common no par (Holders of (9) or less shares received full distribution 06/17/1966; holders of (10) or more shares actually receive 90% of Udico shares 6/17/66 and final 10% of Udico shares 03/26/1968)
Udico Electric Co. name changed to Udico Corp. 08/17/1966 which name changed to UDO Pacific Corp. 02/16/1972 which reorganized as Winkler/Scheid Corp. 08/30/1972 which name changed to Winkler Scheid Vineyards Inc. 07/29/1974 which name changed to Winkler Scheid Inc. 05/19/1977 which name changed to HS Group Inc. 05/28/1980 which assets were transferred to HG Group Inc. Liquidating Trust 08/23/1985
(See HG Group Inc. Liquidating Trust)

INTERNATIONAL DEBT EXCHANGE ASSOCS INC (TX)
Recapiatlized as China Media Group Corp. 10/06/2005
Each share Common no par exchanged for (0.02222222) share Common no par
China Media Group Corp. name changed to Median Group Inc. 05/25/2016

INTERNATIONAL DELTA RES LTD (CANADA)
Recapitalized as Delpet Resources Ltd. 11/13/1992
Each share Common no par exchanged for (0.33333333) share Common no par
Delpet Resources Ltd. name changed to HTI Ventures Corp. (Canada) 06/06/2000 which reincorporated in British Columbia as Leagold Mining Corp. 08/31/2016

INTERNATIONAL DERRICK & EQUIPMENT CO.
Merged into International-Stacey Corp. in 1931
Details not available

INTERNATIONAL DESIGN GROUP INC (DE)
Each share Common $0.001 par exchanged for (0.02) share old Common 5¢ par 02/11/1991
Each share old Common 5¢ par exchanged for (0.00008) share new Common 5¢ par 07/10/1997
Note: Holders of (12,499) or fewer pre-split shares received $0.38 cash per share
Each share new Common 5¢ par exchanged again for (0.33333333) share new Common 5¢ par 02/24/1998
Note: In effect holders received $4,750 cash per share and public interest was eliminated

INTERNATIONAL DESTRON TECHNOLOGIES INC (CANADA)
Recapitalized as Destron/IDI Inc. (Canada) 06/03/1988
Each share Common no par exchanged for (0.2) share Common no par
Destron/IDI Inc. (Canada) reincorporated in Delaware 10/01/1993 which name changed to Destron Fearing Corp. 08/03/1994

which merged into Applied Digital Solutions, Inc. 09/08/2000 which name changed to Digital Angel Corp. (New) 06/20/2008

INTERNATIONAL DETROLA CORP. (IN)
Name changed to Newport Steel Corp. 03/04/1949
Newport Steel Corp. name changed to Newcorp, Inc. (IN) 09/18/1956
(See Newcorp, Inc. (IN))

INTERNATIONAL DEV CORP (NV)
Recapitalized as Global Wataire, Inc. 04/17/2006
Each share Common $0.001 par exchanged for (0.001) share Common $0.001 par
Global Wataire, Inc. name changed to Global Earth Energy, Inc. 03/10/2008
(See Global Earth Energy, Inc.)

INTERNATIONAL DIAMOND CORP (DE)
Recapitalized as Diginet Systems Corp. 10/1/98
Each share Common $0.000001 par exchanged for (0.01) share Common $0.000001 par

INTERNATIONAL DIODE CORP (NJ)
Each share 6% Preferred $8 par exchanged for $1 cash 2/19/81
Each share Common 10¢ par exchanged for $0.10 cash 2/19/81

INTERNATIONAL DIOXCIDE INC (NY)
Merged into Anthium Chemicals Inc. 3/31/88
Each share Common 10¢ par exchanged for $0.75 cash

INTERNATIONAL DISP CORP (DE)
Charter cancelled and declared inoperative and void for non-payment of taxes 4/15/72

INTERNATIONAL DISPLAY CORP (BC)
Struck off register and declared dissolved for failure to file returns 12/27/91

INTERNATIONAL DISPLAYWORKS INC (DE)
Merged into Flextronics International Ltd. 11/30/2006
Each share Common no par exchanged for (0.5653) share Ordinary S$0.01 par
Flextronics International Ltd. name changed to Flex Ltd. 09/28/2016

INTERNATIONAL DISTILLERS & VINTNERS LTD (ENGLAND)
Ordinary 1s par changed to 5s par plus a 100% stock dividend paid 11/02/1962
ADR's for Ordinary 5s par changed to 25p par per currency change 02/15/1971
Stock Dividends - ADR's for Ordinary - 100% 12/28/1962; 100% 02/10/1969
Stock Dividend - Ordinary - 100% 01/24/1969
Merged into Watney Mann Ltd. 06/03/1972
Each share Ordinary 25p par or ADR for Ordinary 25p par exchanged for (0.666666) share Ordinary 25p par plus 10p cash

INTERNATIONAL DIVERSIFIED DEVELOPERS LTD. (BAHAMAS)
Struck off register 05/31/1971

INTERNATIONAL DIVERSIFIED INDS INC (DE)
Charter forfeited for failure to maintain a registered agent 09/03/1999

INTERNATIONAL DOMESTICATED FURS LTD (BC)
Struck off register and declared dissolved for failure to file returns 05/11/1990

INTERNATIONAL DORADO RES LTD (BC)
Recapitalized as Calco Resources Inc. 12/14/1990
Each share Common no par exchanged for (0.25) share Common no par
Calco Resources Inc. recapitalized as Berkshire International Mining Ltd. 02/19/1997 which recapitalized as Tyner Resources Ltd. 01/24/2002

INTERNATIONAL DRILLING & ENERGY CORP. (DE)
Charter cancelled and declared inoperative and void for non-payment of taxes 3/1/90

INTERNATIONAL DUNLAP MINERALS CORP (YT)
Plan of arrangement effective 08/13/1999
Each share Common no par exchanged for (0.825) share Iriana Resources Corp. new Common no par
Iriana Resources Corp. merged into Polaris Geothermal Inc. 06/21/2004
(See Polaris Geothermal Inc.)

INTERNATIONAL DUNRAINE LTD (CANADA)
Class A Common no par reclassified as Common no par 04/25/1995
Class B Common no par reclassified as Common no par 04/25/1995
Name changed to World Point Terminals Inc. 07/18/1996
(See World Point Terminals Inc.)

INTERNATIONAL DUSTY MAC ENTERPRISES LTD (BC)
Name changed to Dusty Mac Oil & Gas Ltd. 05/10/1994
Dusty Mac Oil & Gas Ltd. name changed to Transglobe Energy Corp. (BC) 04/02/1996 which reincorporated in Alberta 06/09/2004

INTERNATIONAL DYNAMIC PICTURES (NV)
Recapitalized as ID Four Ltd. 11/24/1997
Each share Common 1¢ par exchanged for (0.005) share Common $0.001 par
ID Four Ltd. name changed to Swung, Inc. 08/06/2002 which recapitalized as American Capital Holdings 11/15/2002 which name changed to Symphony Investments, Inc. 05/09/2003 which name changed to International Pharmacy Outlets Inc. 09/29/2003 which name changed to Bionic Products, Inc. 12/11/2006 which recapitalized as Texas Oil & Minerals Inc. 02/01/2012

INTERNATIONAL DYNASTY RESOURCES INC. (BC)
Name changed to Commander Resources Ltd. 10/23/1985
Commander Resources Ltd. name changed to Commander Technologies Corp. 05/15/1992 which recapitalized as SCS Solars Computing Systems Inc. 09/12/1995

INTERNATIONAL DYNERGY INC (DE)
Reincorporated 4/16/84
State of incorporation changed from (UT) to (DE) 4/16/84
Each share old Common $0.001 par exchanged for (0.25) share new Common $0.001 par 8/26/85
Name changed to Unisil Inc. 11/6/91
(See Unisil Inc.)

INTERNATIONAL EAGLE TOOL INC (ON)
Recapitalized as Lignex Inc. 09/22/1995
Each share Common no par exchanged for (0.11111111) share Common no par
Lignex Inc. name changed to International Biotechnology Corp. 08/09/2000 which recapitalized as Veris Biotechnology Corp. 03/22/2001 which recapitalized as Capital Diagnostic Corp. 05/05/2004

INTERNATIONAL ECONOMIC CONSULTANTS INC (NV)
Name changed to ECCO Capital Corp. 08/00/1995
ECCO Capital Corp. recapitalized as Viper Powersports Inc. 03/11/2005
(See Viper Powersports Inc.)

INTERNATIONAL ED & TRAINING INC (DE)
Charter cancelled and declared inoperative and void for non-payment of taxes 3/1/77

INTERNATIONAL EDUCATIONAL PUBLISHING CO.
Merged into International Correspondence Schools World Ltd. Inc. in 1951
Each share Preferred no par exchanged for (1) share new Common $2.50 par
Each (25) shares Common no par exchanged for (1) share new Common $2.50 par
International Correspondence Schools World Ltd. Inc. was acquired by International Textbook Co. 12/31/64 which name changed to Intext, Inc. 4/28/72
(See Intext, Inc.)

INTERNATIONAL ELECTRONIC RESEARCH CORP. (CA)
Name changed to 135 West Magnolia Boulevard Corp. 4/26/63
135 West Magnolia Boulevard Corp. completed liquidation for Dynamics Corp. of America (NY) 4/6/66 which merged into CTS Corp. 10/16/97

INTERNATIONAL ELECTRS CORP (NY)
Class A Common 10¢ par reclassified as Common 10¢ par 01/13/1970
Stock Dividends - 25% 08/24/1972; 25% 09/28/1973
Chapter XI bankruptcy proceedings dismissed 07/31/1979
Attorney opined no stockholders' equity

INTERNATIONAL ELECTRS INC (MA)
Each share old Common 1¢ par exchanged for (1/7) share new Common 1¢ par 10/16/1987
Each share new Common 1¢ par exchanged for (1/3) share new Common 1¢ par 05/27/1993
Merged into Linear LLC 08/06/2007
Each share new Common 1¢ par exchanged for $6.65 cash

INTERNATIONAL ELEVATING CO. (NJ)
Capital Stock $50 par changed to $40 par and $10 in cash distributed in 1933
Capital Stock $40 par changed to $20 par in 1940
Under plan of partial liquidation Common $20 par exchanged (0.1) for (1) plus a distribution of $15 in cash 11/28/58
Liquidation completed 8/29/62

INTERNATIONAL EN-R-TECH INC (BC)
Recapitalized as National Telcom Solutions Inc. 10/16/2000
Each share Common no par exchanged for (0.1) share Common no par
(See National Telcom Solutions Inc.)

INTERNATIONAL ENERGY CO. (DE)
Name changed to International Energy Co. of America in 1980
International Energy Co. of America name changed to AMX International, Inc. 5/8/87
(See AMX International, Inc.)

INTERNATIONAL ENERGY CO AMER (DE)
Name changed to AMX International, Inc. 5/8/87
(See AMX International, Inc.)

INTERNATIONAL ENERGY DEV CORP (DE)
Name changed to Penn Octane Corp. 02/03/1995
(See Penn Octane Corp.)

INTERNATIONAL ENERGY INC (FL)
Name changed 11/06/2009
Each share old Common $0.0001 par exchanged for (0.001) share new Common $0.0001 par 05/22/2007
Name changed from International Energy Group, Inc. to International Energy Ltd., Inc. 11/06/2009
Name changed to Standard Oil Company USA, Inc. 05/13/2010
Standard Oil Company USA, Inc. name changed to Gold Mining USA Inc. 05/24/2012 which name changed to Vita Mobile Systems, Inc. 01/31/2018

INTERNATIONAL ENERGY INC (NV)
Common $0.001 par split (4) for (1) by issuance of (3) additional shares payable 06/20/2005 to holders of record 06/20/2005
Recapitalized as NDB Energy, Inc. 06/29/2011
Each share Common $0.001 par exchanged for (0.2) share Common $0.001 par
NDB Energy, Inc. name changed to Armada Oil, Inc. 05/15/2012

INTERNATIONAL ENEXCO LTD (BC)
Merged into Denison Mines Corp. 06/10/2014
Each share Common no par exchanged for (0.26) share Common no par, (1) share 0999279 B.C. Ltd. Common no par and (1) 0999279 B.C. Ltd. Common Stock Purchase Warrant expiring 12/10/2014

INTERNATIONAL ENVIRONMENTAL CORP (AZ)
Recapitalized as International Fibercom, Inc. 06/06/1994
Each share Common no par exchanged for (0.1) share Common no par
(See International Fibercom, Inc.)

INTERNATIONAL ENVIRONMENTAL MGMT INC (NV)
Name changed to IEMI 11/28/2001
(See IEMI)

INTERNATIONAL EPITEK INC (CANADA)
Name changed to CompAS Electronics Inc. 07/29/1993
CompAS Electronics Inc. acquired by AIM Safety Co., Inc. 12/08/1997 which name changed to AimGlobal Technologies Co., Inc. 01/29/1999
(See AimGlobal Technologies Co., Inc.)

INTERNATIONAL EQUITIES CORP. (DE)
Merged into Standard Equities Corp. in May 1941
Each share Class A exchanged for (3) shares Common $1 par
Each share Class B exchanged for (2.25) shares Common $1 par
Standard Equities Corp. name changed to Sheraton Corp. in 1943 which name changed to United States Realty-Sheraton Corp. 5/17/46 which name changed to Sheraton Corp. of America 8/19/46 which was acquired by International Telephone & Telegraph Corp. (DE) 2/29/68 which name changed to ITT Corp. 12/31/83 which reorganized in Indiana as ITT Industries, Inc. 12/19/95 which name changed to ITT Corp. 7/1/2006

INTERNATIONAL EQUITY FDG CORP (DE)
Name changed to American Land Equity, Inc. 10/5/72
Each share Common 10¢ par exchanged for (1) share Common 10¢ par
(See American Land Equity, Inc.)

INTERNATIONAL EQUITY LTD (BERMUDA)
Name changed to Industrial & Environmental Services Ltd. 2/19/92
Industrial Environmental Services Ltd. name changed to Trask Corp. 1/10/94 which name changed to Med Net International 1/8/96
(See Med Net International Ltd.)

INTERNATIONAL EQUITY RES INC (UT)
Name changed to International Protection Technologies, Inc. 7/27/98
International Protection Technologies, Inc. name changed to HyperSecur Corp. 3/4/99

INTERNATIONAL EROS HLDGS LTD (BC)
Name changed to Global Cable Systems, Inc. 04/12/1996
Global Cable Systems, Inc. recapitalized as Consolidated Global Cable Systems, Inc. 12/19/2000 which name changed to Chelsea Minerals Corp. 01/20/2010 which merged into Sennen Resources Ltd. 05/13/2011 which name changed to Sennen Potash Corp. 04/15/2013

INTERNATIONAL EUROMIN CORP (CANADA)
Merged into Eurogas Corp. 06/30/1995
Each share Common no par exchanged for (0.5) share Common no par
Eurogas Corp. name changed to Dundee Energy Ltd. 06/22/2011

INTERNATIONAL EUROPRIME CAPITAL CORP. (BC)
Dissolved and struck from registry 03/06/1998

INTERNATIONAL EXOTIC MTRS CORP (BC)
Reincorporated under the laws of Wyoming as North American Advanced Materials Corp. 10/05/1993
(See North American Advanced Materials Corp.)

INTERNATIONAL EXPLORATION CORP. (DE)
Charter cancelled and declared inoperative and void for non-payment of taxes 04/01/1961

INTERNATIONAL FACTORS, INC. (TX)
Charter revoked for failure to file reports and pay fees 8/4/60

INTERNATIONAL FAIRHAVEN RES LTD (BC)
Delisted from NEX 06/27/2004

INTERNATIONAL FAMILY ENTMT INC (DE)
Merged into Fox Kid Worldwide, Inc. 9/4/97
Each share Class B Common 1¢ par exchanged for $35 cash

INTERNATIONAL FAST FOOD CORP (FL)
Each share 6% Conv. Preferred Ser. A received distribution of (4.4776) shares Common 1¢ par payable 12/15/1999 to holders of record 11/30/1999
Each share old Common 1¢ par exchanged for (0.01) share new Common 1¢ par 10/03/2000
Administratively dissolved for failure to file annual report 09/19/2003

INTERNATIONAL FDG CORP (FL)
Proclaimed dissolved for failure to file reports and pay fees 11/14/1986

INTERNATIONAL FDG CORP AMER (CA)
Charter suspended for failure to file reports or pay taxes 05/01/1975

INTERNATIONAL FERRO METALS LTD (AUSTRALIA)
ADR agreement terminated 03/09/2017
No ADR's remain outstanding

INTERNATIONAL FIBERCOM INC (AZ)
Issue Information - 1,200,000 shares COM offered at $5.40 per share on 08/12/1994
Chapter 11 bankruptcy proceedings converted to Chapter 7 on 08/25/2003
Stockholders' equity unlikely

INTERNATIONAL FIDELITY INSURANCE CO. (TX)
Merged into Educator's Security Insurance Co. 1/1/66
Each share Common no par exchanged for (1) share Common $1 par
Educator's Security Insurance Co. merged into Superior Equity Corp. 2/28/72
(See Superior Equity Corp.)

INTERNATIONAL FIGHT LEAGUE INC (DE)
Recapitalized as IFLI Acquisition Corp. 07/08/2010
Each share Common 1¢ par exchanged for (0.0025) share Common 1¢ par
IFLI Acquisition Corp. name changed to SimplePons, Inc. 12/27/2011 which recapitalized as Eco-Shift Power Corp. 11/26/2013

INTERNATIONAL FILM PRODTNS INC (TX)
Charter forfeited for failure to pay taxes 12/2/85

INTERNATIONAL FINANCE CORP. (MN)
Name changed to Oakridge Holdings Inc. 06/30/1965
(See Oakridge Holdings Inc.)

INTERNATIONAL FINANCE CORP. (VA)
Merged into Financial Credit Corp. (VA) 00/00/1941
Details not available

INTERNATIONAL FINL INCOME & GROWTH TR (ON)
Trust terminated 12/15/2009
Details not available

INTERNATIONAL FINE FOODS INC (DE)
Each (150) shares Common $0.00005 par exchanged for (1) share Common 1¢ par 3/1/86
Name changed to Fresh Maid, Inc. 2/16/89
(See Fresh Maid, Inc.)

INTERNATIONAL FIRE PREVENTION INC (NV)
Each share old Common $0.001 par exchanged for (0.04620431) share new Common $0.001 par 07/29/1997
Name changed to Trident Media Group Inc. 12/30/1997
(See Trident Media Group Inc.)

INTERNATIONAL FITNESS UNLIMITED CENTRES INC (ON)
Delisted from Alberta Stock Exchange 02/02/1989

INTERNATIONAL FLIGHT CATERERS INC (DE)
Completely liquidated 9/12/69
Each share Common 1¢ par exchanged for first and final distribution of (1) share Lehigh Precision Mfg. Co., Inc. Common 1¢ par
Lehigh Precision Mfg. Co., Inc. name changed to Five Star Coal Co., Inc. 10/28/76 which name changed to Onyx Hydrocarbon Recovery Corp. 5/25/82 which name changed to Magna Diversified Inc. 3/22/84 which name changed to Energizer 500 Inc. 6/8/84 which name changed to Opportunity 21 on 6/16/85
(See Opportunity 21)

INTERNATIONAL FLYER RES LTD (BC)
Name changed to Spectair Industries Inc. 07/30/1987
Spectair Industries Inc. recapitalized as International Spectair Resources Inc. 12/01/1989 which name changed to Camden Oil Corp. 11/05/1991 which name changed to Maxwell Resources Inc. 12/02/1992 which name changed to Maxwell Energy Corp. (BC) 05/12/1993 which reincorporated in Alberta 09/12/1996 which recapitalized as Maxwell Oil & Gas Ltd. 11/18/1996
(See Maxwell Oil & Gas Ltd.)

INTERNATIONAL FOAM SOLUTIONS INC (FL)
Name changed to Hard to Treat Diseases Inc. 6/25/2003

INTERNATIONAL FOCUS RES INC (BC)
Recapitalized as Continental Copper Corp. 12/28/1995
Each share Common no par exchanged for (0.2) share Common no par
Continental Copper Corp. name changed to Continental Energy Corp. 10/23/1997

INTERNATIONAL FOOD & BEVERAGE INC (DE)
Each share Common $0.001 par exchanged for (0.1) share Common 1¢ par 08/03/1990
Name changed to Internet Business's International, Inc. (DE) 02/17/1999
Internet Business's International, Inc. (DE) reincorporated in Nevada 07/15/1999 which name changed to Alpha Wireless Broadband, Inc. 09/17/2004 which recapitalized as Seamless Wi-Fi, Inc. 06/03/2005 which name changed to Seamless Corp. (NV) 08/21/2008 which reincorporated in Florida as GDT TEK, Inc. 11/25/2009
(See GDT TEK, Inc.)

INTERNATIONAL FOOD & DRUG CORP. (IN)
Acquired by Liberty Corp. (CO) 6/30/69
Each share Common 50¢ par exchanged for (0.2) share Capital Stock 10¢ par
Liberty Corp. (CO) name changed to Kryotech International, Inc. 9/17/70
(See Kryotech International, Inc.)

INTERNATIONAL FOOD & WINE CONSULTANTS INC (DE)
Name changed to g8wave Holdings Inc. 08/30/2007
g8wave Holdings Inc. name changed to China Gateway Corp. 07/03/2008

INTERNATIONAL FOOD BK INC (DE)
Recapitalized as Great China Capital Ltd. 9/8/95
Each share Common $0.001 par exchanged for (0.2) share Common $0.001 par

INTERNATIONAL FOOD PRODS GROUP INC (NV)
Each share old Common $0.001 par exchanged for (3) shares new Common $0.001 par 05/10/2005
Name changed to Newport Digital Technologies, Inc. 06/11/2009

INTERNATIONAL FOODSERVICE CORP (DE)
Merged into Acton Corp. 09/29/1980
Each share Common 1¢ par exchanged for (0.058394) share Common 6-2/3¢ par
Acton Corp. name changed to Sunstates Corp. (New) 01/03/1994
(See Sunstates Corp. (New))

INTERNATIONAL FOODSERVICE SYSTEMS, INC. (DE)
Name changed to International Foodservice Corp. 05/06/1974
International Foodservice Corp. merged into Acton Corp. 09/29/1980 which name changed to Sunstates Corp. (New) 01/03/1994
(See Sunstates Corp. (New))

INTERNATIONAL FOREST INDS INC (FL)
Recapitalized as American Financial Holdings, Inc. 02/16/1979
Each share Common 2¢ par exchanged for (0.1) share Common 1¢ par
(See American Financial Holdings, Inc.)

INTERNATIONAL FOREST PRODS LTD (BC)
7% Conv. Preference Ser. 1 no par called for redemption 12/07/1989
Class B Common no par reclassified as Class A Subordinate no par 08/23/2013
Name changed to Interfor Corp. and Class A Subordinate no par reclassified as Common no par 05/12/2014

INTERNATIONAL FORESTECH SYS LTD (BC)
Cease trade order effective 08/21/1991
Stockholders' equity unlikely

INTERNATIONAL FORMING MACHINE, INC. (DE)
Charter cancelled and declared inoperative and void for non-payment of taxes 1/16/61

INTERNATIONAL FRAMING & ARTS LTD (DE)
Recapitalized as J.A. Industries Inc. 11/2/92
Each share Common $0.0005 par exchanged for (0.2) share Common $0.0005 par
J.A. Industries Inc. recapitalized as Electronic Manufacturing Services Group Inc. 7/30/96

INTERNATIONAL FRANCHISE SYS INC (DE)
Merged into IFS Acquisition Corp. 10/8/98
Each share Common 1¢ par exchanged for $3.60 cash

INTERNATIONAL FRECOM COMMUNICATIONS INC (BC)
Delisted from Vancouver Stock Exchange 03/05/1993

INTERNATIONAL FREEGOLD MINERAL DEV INC (BC)
Recapitalized as Freegold Ventures Ltd. 09/04/2002
Each share Common no par exchanged for (0.25) share Common no par

INTERNATIONAL FRONTIERS INDS INC (UT)
Name changed to US-Worldlink Com, Inc. 5/21/99

INTERNATIONAL FST INDS INC (NV)
Each share old Common $0.001 par exchanged for (0.1) share new Common $0.001 par 05/05/1997
Name changed to Flour City International, Inc. 05/16/1997
(See Flour City International, Inc.)

INTERNATIONAL FUEL TECHNOLOGY INC (NV)
Each share old Common 1¢ par exchanged for (0.1) share new Common 1¢ par 07/22/1999
Name changed to Fuel Performance Solutions, Inc. 04/02/2014

INTERNATIONAL FUNERAL SVCS INC (IA)
Common $1 par changed to 50¢ par and (1) additional share issued 09/15/1969
Name changed to IFS Industries Inc. 08/16/1977
IFS Industries Inc. merged into Service Corp. International 12/10/1981 which name changed to IFS Holdings, Inc. 03/16/1999

INTERNATIONAL FURNITURE GALLERIES INC (FL)
Adjudicated bankrupt 03/14/1975
Stockholders' equity unlikely

INTERNATIONAL GAME TECHNOLOGY (NV)
Common 1¢ par changed to $0.005 par and (1) additional share issued 07/13/1990
Common $0.005 par split (2) for (1) by issuance of (1) additional share 08/22/1991
Common $0.005 par changed to $0.00125 par and (1) additional share issued 03/24/1992
Common $0.00125 changed to $0.000625 par and (1) additional share issued 03/17/1993
Common $0.000625 par changed to $0.00015625 par and (3) additional shares issued payable 07/02/2003 to holders of record 06/18/2003
Ex date - 07/03/2003
Merged into International Game Technology PLC 04/07/2015
Each share Common $0.00015625 par exchanged for (0.1819) share Ordinary USD $0.10 par and $14.3396 cash

INTERNATIONAL GAMING GROUP INC (NV)
Old Common 2¢ par split (3) for (1) by issuance of (2) additional shares payable 07/07/1999 to holders of record 06/10/1999
Each share old Common 2¢ par exchanged for (0.01) share new Common 2¢ par 02/04/2002
Name changed to American Standard Energy Inc. 04/16/2002
American Standard Energy Inc. name changed to Sports Wheels, Inc. 04/17/2003 which recapitalized as Automotive Specialty Concepts, Inc. 02/01/2005 which name changed to Drake Gold Resources, Inc. 02/13/2006 which name changed to Universal Apparel & Textile Co. 04/27/2015

INTERNATIONAL GAMING MGMT INC (DE)
Common $0.001 par split (2) for (1) by issuance of (1) additional share 07/28/1988
Charter cancelled and declared inoperative and void for non-payment of taxes 03/01/1996

INTERNATIONAL GEM EXCHANGE INC (DE)
Charter cancelled and declared inoperative and void for non-payment of taxes 3/1/74

INTERNATIONAL GEMINI TECHNOLOGY INC (BC)
Name changed to Widescope Resources Inc. 07/12/2006
Widescope Resources Inc. recapitalized as North American Nickel Inc. 07/07/2010

INTERNATIONAL GEN INDS INC (DE)
Merged into International Bank (Washington, DC) 12/31/79
Each share Common no par exchanged for (3.9) shares Class A Common $1 par

International Bank (Washington, DC) merged into USLICO Corp. 12/31/85 which merged into NWNL Companies, Inc. 1/17/95 which name changed to ReliaStar Financial Corp. 2/13/95
(See ReliaStar Financial Corp.)

INTERNATIONAL GENETIC ENGR INC (CA)
Acquired by Xoma Corp. (Old) (DE) 11/13/1989
Each share Common no par exchanged for (0.278) share Common $0.0005 par
Xoma Corp. (Old) (DE) reincorporated in Bermuda as Xoma Ltd. 12/31/1998 which reincorporated in Delaware as XOMA Corp. (New) 12/31/2011

INTERNATIONAL GEOGRAPHICS LTD (BC)
Acquired by Geographics, Inc. (WY) 07/29/1991
Each share Common no par exchanged for (1.2) shares Common no par
Geographics, Inc. (WY) reincorporated in Delaware 10/18/2000
(See Geographics, Inc.)

INTERNATIONAL GEOPHYSICAL EXPL INC (PANAMA)
Reorganized under the laws of Massachusetts as I.G.E., Inc. 03/03/1972
Each share Common 10¢ par exchanged for (1) share Common 1¢ par
I.G.E., Inc. recapitalized as Life Partners Holdings Inc. (MA) 02/09/2000 which reincorporated in Texas 02/19/2003
(See Life Partners Holdings Inc.)

INTERNATIONAL GERMANIC CO., LTD.
Acquired by Goldman Sachs Trading Corp. 00/00/1930
Details not available

INTERNATIONAL GIANT MNG CORP (BC)
Merged into International Phasor Telecom Ltd. 09/10/1982
Each share Common no par exchanged for (1) share Common no par
(See International Phasor Telecom Ltd.)

INTERNATIONAL GLASS CORP. (CA)
Name changed to Monogram Precision Industries, Inc. 11/01/1957
Monogram Precision Industries, Inc. name changed to Monogram Industries, Inc. (CA) 12/03/1962 which reincorporated in Delaware 11/28/1969 which merged into Nortek, Inc. (RI) 08/26/1983 which reincorporated in Delaware 04/23/1987 which reorganized as Nortek Holdings, Inc. 11/20/2002
(See Nortek Holdings, Inc.)

INTERNATIONAL GLASS FIBRES CORP. (MD)
Charter forfeited for failure to file reports and pay taxes 10/27/54

INTERNATIONAL GLENDALE RES INC (BC)
Name changed to Odessa Petroleum Corp. 03/10/1997
Odessa Petroleum Corp. recapitalized as Aquarius Ventures Inc. (BC) 05/12/1999 which reincorporated in Canada as Citotech Systems Inc. 10/30/2000 which recapitalized as SmartCool Systems Inc. 07/21/2004

INTERNATIONAL GLOW COSMETICS INC (NV)
Recapitalized as International Indigo Industries Inc. 12/16/1996
Each share Common $0.002 par exchanged for (0.01) share Common $0.002 par
International Indigo Industries Inc. name changed to Cavalcade of Sports Network, Inc. 01/07/1999 which name changed to Thin Express Inc. 09/12/2001 which recapitalized as CyberKey Corp. 02/18/2003 which name changed to CyberKey Solutions, Inc. 04/24/2006
(See CyberKey Solutions, Inc.)

INTERNATIONAL GOLD CORP (NV)
Name changed to Lode-Star Mining Inc. 05/28/2015

INTERNATIONAL GOLD MINING & MILLING CO. (CO)
Charter suspended for failure to file annual reports 09/03/1913

INTERNATIONAL GOLD MINING LTD (AUSTRALIA)
Recapitalized as Central Iron Ore Ltd. 01/19/2010
Each share Ordinary exchanged for (0.1) share Ordinary

INTERNATIONAL GOLD RES CORP (ON)
Acquired by Ashanti Goldfields Ltd. 06/17/1996
Each share Common no par exchanged for (0.202) Global Depositary Receipt no par
Ashanti Goldfields Ltd. merged into AngloGold Ashanti Ltd. 04/26/2004

INTERNATIONAL GRAPHICS CORP (MN)
Merged into Moore Business Forms, Inc. 4/30/77
Each share Common 10¢ par exchanged for $13.75 cash

INTERNATIONAL GRAVIS COMPUTER TECHNOLOGY INC (BC)
Merged into Advanced Gravis Computer Technology Ltd. 04/30/1987
Each share Common no par exchanged for (0.33333333) share Common no par
(See Advanced Gravis Computer Technology Ltd.)

INTERNATIONAL GREEN ICE INC (YT)
Reincorporated 03/03/2000
Place of incorporation changed from (BC) to (Yukon) 03/03/2000
Reincorporated under the laws of British Columbia as IGC Resources Inc. 07/21/2004

INTERNATIONAL GRENFELL ACQUISITIONS INC (CANADA)
Name changed to Worldwide Ginseng Corp. 07/21/1995
(See Worldwide Ginseng Corp.)

INTERNATIONAL GROUP HLDGS INC (NV)
Acquired by Energy Producers, Inc. 01/30/2004
Each share Common no par exchanged for (1) share Common $0.001 par
Energy Producers, Inc. name changed to EGPI Firecreek, Inc. 01/30/2004

INTERNATIONAL GROUP INC (DE)
Name changed to Champions Sports Inc. 02/21/1986
Champions Sports Inc. name changed to Champions Biotechnology, Inc. 02/02/2007 which name changed to Champions Oncology, Inc. 04/20/2011

INTERNATIONAL GRYPHON RES INC NEW (AB)
Recapitalized as Wirbac Resources Inc. 12/05/2000
Each share Common no par exchanged for (0.2) share Common no par
Wirbac Resources Inc. recapitalized as Virtus Energy Ltd. 09/12/2001 which merged into Titan Exploration Ltd. 06/23/2005 which was acquired by Penn West Energy Trust 01/11/2008 which reorganized as Penn West Petroleum Ltd. (New) 01/03/2011 which name changed to Obsidian Energy Ltd. 06/29/2017

INTERNATIONAL GRYPHON RES INC OLD (AB)
Merged into International Gryphon Resources Inc. (New) 04/27/1995
Each share Common no par exchanged for (1) share Common no par
International Gryphon Resources Inc. (New) recapitalized as Wirbac Resources Inc. 12/05/2000 which recapitalized as Virtus Energy Ltd. 09/12/2001 which merged into Titan Exploration Ltd. 06/23/2005 which was acquired by Penn Penn West Energy Trust 01/11/2008 which reorganized as Penn West Petroleum Ltd. (New) 01/03/2011 which name changed to Obsidian Energy Ltd. 06/29/2017

INTERNATIONAL H R S INDS INC (BC)
Name changed to Glenex Industries Inc. 05/25/1987
Glenex Industries Inc. merged into Quest Investment Corp. 07/04/2002 which merged into Quest Capital Corp. (BC) 06/30/2003 which reincorporated in Canada 05/27/2008 which name changed to Sprott Resource Lending Corp. 09/10/2010 which merged into Sprott Inc. 07/24/2013

INTERNATIONAL HALLIWELL MINES LTD (QC)
Ceased operations prior to 10/26/1976
No stockholders' equity

INTERNATIONAL HARD SUITS INC (BC)
Recapitalized as Hard Suits Inc. 11/29/1993
Each share Common no par exchanged for (0.33333333) share Common no par
(See Hard Suits Inc.)

INTERNATIONAL HARDWARE INC (DE)
Charter cancelled and declared inoperative and void for non-payment of taxes 03/01/1992

INTERNATIONAL HARVESTER CO. (NJ)
Each share Common $100 par exchanged for (4) shares Common no par 00/00/1928
Common no par changed to $20 par and (1) additional share issued 04/09/1965
Stock Dividend - 200% 06/05/1948
Reorganized under the laws of Delaware 03/17/1966
Each share 7% Preferred $100 par exchanged for $175 principal amount of 4.80% 25-year Subord. Debentures due 03/01/1991
International Harvester Co. (DE) name changed to Navistar International Corp. (Old) 02/21/1986

INTERNATIONAL HARVESTER CO (DE)
Common $20 par changed to no par 2/18/82
$3 Conv. Preferred Ser. A no par called for redemption 1/20/86
Name changed to Navistar International Corp. 2/21/86

INTERNATIONAL HEALTH & BEAUTY INC (BC)
Delisted from Toronto Venture Stock Exchange 08/03/2001

INTERNATIONAL HEALTH & SPORTS INC (DE)
Recapitalized as Medical Health Industries, Inc. 12/28/71
Each share Common 1¢ par exchanged for (0.1) share Common 10¢ par
(See Medical Health Industries, Inc.)

INTERNATIONAL HEALTH ALLIANCE CORP (NV)
Recapitalized as ETI International Inc. 3/10/98
Each share Common $0.001 par exchanged for (0.625) share Common $0.001 par

INTERNATIONAL HEALTH PARTNERS INC (AB)
Each share old Common no par exchanged for (0.2) share new Common no par 03/07/2006
Each share new Common no par exchanged again for (0.1) share new Common no par 11/11/2008
Name changed to Patient Home Monitoring Corp. (AB) 06/08/2010
Patient Home Monitoring Corp. (AB) reincorporated in British Columbia 12/30/2013
(See Patient Home Monitoring Corp.)

INTERNATIONAL HEALTH RESORTS INC (UT)
Each share old Common 1¢ par exchanged for (0.1) share new Common 1¢ par 11/3/84
Each share new Common 1¢ par exchanged for (0.05) share Common $0.001 par 4/15/92
Reorganized under the laws of Utah as Sanguine Corp. 8/23/93
Each share Common $0.001 par exchanged for (1.5) shares Common $0.001 par

INTERNATIONAL HEALTH SCIENCES INC (DE)
Name changed to Gilman Services, Inc. 06/28/1973
(See Gilman Services, Inc.)

INTERNATIONAL HEATER CO. (NY)
Each share Common $100 par exchanged for (4) shares Common $25 par in 1941
Acquired by Weil-McLain Co. Inc. (Ind.) 5/18/65
Each share Common $25 par exchanged for $42.55 cash

INTERNATIONAL HELIUM LTD (ON)
Recapitalized as Mineral Resources International Ltd. 12/22/1970
Each share Capital Stock no par exchanged for (0.1) share Capital Stock no par
Mineral Resources International Ltd. merged into Conwest Exploration Co. Ltd. (ON) 06/01/1990 which merged into Conwest Exploration Co. Ltd. (New) (AB) 09/01/1993 which merged into Alberta Energy Co. Ltd. 01/31/1996 which merged into EnCana Corp. 01/03/2003

INTERNATIONAL HELIX BIOTECHNOLOGIES INC (BC)
Merged into Helix BioPharma Corp. 08/15/1995
Each share Common no par exchanged for (1) share Common no par

INTERNATIONAL HERITAGE FD (MA)
Under plan of reorganization each Government Portfolio Share of Bene. Int. 1¢ par exchanged for (0.943766) Keystone America Government Securities Fund Share of Bene. Int. no par 4/19/89
Under plan of reorganization each High Yield Portfolio Share of Bene. Int. 1¢ par exchanged for (0.909123) Keystone America High Yield Bond Fund Share of Bene. Int. no par 4/19/89
(See each company's listing)

INTERNATIONAL HI-TECH INDS INC (BC)
Common no par split (2) for (1) by issuance of (1) additional share 02/04/1994
Reincorporated under the laws of Canada 05/31/1996

INTERNATIONAL HI-TECH RESEARCH CORP. (UT)
Involuntarily dissolved 02/01/1993

INTERNATIONAL HOLDING CORP. OF GARWOOD
Reorganized as Aeolian Corp. in 1945
No stockholders' equity

INTERNATIONAL HLDG CAP CORP (HI)
Stock Dividend - 10% 5/1/85
Merged into CB Bancshares, Inc. 4/8/94
Each share Common $1 par exchanged for (0.589) share Common $1 par and $15.53 cash
CB Bancshares, Inc. merged into Central Pacific Financial Corp. 9/15/2004

INTERNATIONAL HOME FOODS INC (DE)
Merged into ConAgra, Inc. 08/24/2000
Each share Common 1¢ par exchanged for (0.54692) share Common 5¢ par and $11 cash
ConAgra, Inc. name changed to ConAgra Foods, Inc. 09/28/2000 which name changed to Conagra Brands, Inc. 11/10/2016

INTERNATIONAL HOMESTEAD RES INC (BC)
Name changed to Novawest Resources Inc. 09/11/1996
Novawest Resources Inc. name changed to Apella Resources Inc. 04/02/2008 which name changed to PacificOre Mining Corp. 05/28/2012 which name changed to Vanadiumcorp Resource Inc. 11/22/2013

INTERNATIONAL HOMESTOCK RES LTD (BC)
Reincorporated under the laws of Canada as Coscient Group Inc. 02/14/1989
Coscient Group Inc. name changed to Motion International Inc. 01/25/2000
(See Motion International Inc.)

INTERNATIONAL HORIZONS INC (CO)
Proclaimed dissolved for failure to file reports 9/1/98

INTERNATIONAL HOSP SUPPLY CORP (CA)
Charter suspended for failure to file reports and pay taxes 10/01/1975

INTERNATIONAL HOSPITALITY INC NEW (ON)
Cease trade order effective 02/24/1999
Stockholders' equity unlikely

INTERNATIONAL HOSPITALITY INC OLD (ON)
Reorganized as International Hospitality Inc. (New) 12/05/1996
Each share Common no par exchanged for (0.004) share Common no par
(See International Hospitality Inc. (New))

INTERNATIONAL HOUSE PANCAKES INC (CA)
Name changed to International Industries, Inc. (CA) 02/20/1963
International Industries, Inc. (CA) reincorporated in Delaware 03/07/1969 which merged into IHOP Corp. 09/17/1976
(See IHOP Corp.)

INTERNATIONAL HOUSING CORP. (MN)
Name changed to IHC Liquidating Co. 12/13/1965
(See IHC Liquidating Co.)

INTERNATIONAL HYDRO-ELECTRIC SYSTEM (MA)
Preferred no par changed to $50 par 00/00/1933
Class A no par changed to $25 par 00/00/1933
Under divestment plan each share $3.50 Preferred $50 par exchanged for (5.5) shares Gatineau Power Co. Common no par and $2.50 cash 12/02/1953
(See Gatineau Power Co.)
Name changed to Abacus Fund (MA) and Class A $25 par changed to Common $1 par 06/24/1957
Abacus Fund (MA) reincorporated in Delaware as Abacus Fund, Inc. 03/31/1964 which merged into Paine, Webber, Jackson & Curtis Inc. 04/03/1972 which reorganized as Paine Webber Inc. 02/01/1974 which name changed to Paine Webber Group Inc. 05/21/1984 which merged into UBS AG 11/03/2000
(See UBS AG)

INTERNATIONAL HYDROCARBONS CORP (AB)
Merged into Tudor Corp. Ltd. 01/01/2007
Each share Class A Common no par exchanged for (0.25) share Common no par
(See Tudor Corp. Ltd.)

INTERNATIONAL HYDRODYNAMICS LTD (BC)
Placed in receivership 10/10/1978
No stockholders' equity

INTERNATIONAL HYDROLINES INC (NY)
Charter cancelled and proclaimed dissolved for failure to pay taxes 12/15/75

INTERNATIONAL HYDRON CORP (DE)
Acquired by SmithKline Beckman Corp. 11/12/1987
Each share Common 25¢ par exchanged for $10.45 cash

INTERNATIONAL IMAGING INC (DE)
Each share old Common $0.0001 par exchanged for (0.2) share new Common $0.0001 par 08/25/1997
Name changed to NexTech Enterprises International, Inc. 01/13/1998
(See NexTech Enterprises International, Inc.)

INTERNATIONAL IMAGING MATLS INC (DE)
Merged into PAXAR Corp. 10/28/97
Each share Common 1¢ par exchanged for (1.5) shares Common 10¢ par
PAXAR Corp. name changed to Paxar Corp. 5/1/98

INTERNATIONAL IMAGING SYS INC (DE)
Each share old Common $0.001 par exchanged for (0.03333333) share new Common $0.001 par 06/15/2007
Name changed to China Bio Energy Holding Group Co., Ltd. 12/13/2007
China Bio Energy Holding Group Co., Ltd. name changed to China Integrated Energy, Inc. 09/18/2009
(See China Integrated Energy, Inc.)

INTERNATIONAL IMAGING TECHNOLOGIES INC (DE)
Charter cancelled and declared inoperative and void for non-payment of taxes 3/1/91

INTERNATIONAL IMPALA RES LTD (BC)
Recapitalized as Tapestry Ventures Ltd. 11/13/1992
Each share Common no par exchanged for (0.2) share Common no par
Tapestry Ventures Ltd. recapitalized as Tapestry Resource Corp. 12/23/2004 which name changed to Gran Colombia Gold Corp. 08/24/2010

INTERNATIONAL INCOME PPTY INC (DE)
Common no par changed to 1¢ par 11/00/1979
Completely liquidated 06/29/1990
Each share Common 1¢ par exchanged for first and final distribution of $19.32 cash

INTERNATIONAL INDIGO INDS INC (NV)
Each share old Common $0.002 par exchanged for (0.01) share new Common $0.002 par 08/20/1998
Name changed to Cavalcade of Sports Network, Inc. 01/07/1999
Calvacade of Sports Network, Inc. name changed to Thin Express Inc. 09/12/2001 which recapitalized as CyberKey Corp. 02/18/2003 which name changed to CyberKey Solutions, Inc. 04/24/2006
(See CyberKey Solutions, Inc.)

INTERNATIONAL INDUSTRIES, INC. (MI)
Name changed to Argus, Inc. 00/00/1944
Argus, Inc. name changed to Argus Cameras, Inc. 00/00/1950 which was acquired by Sylvania Electric Products, Inc. 01/02/1957 which merged into General Telephone & Electronics Corp. 03/05/1959 which name changed to GTE Corp. 07/01/1982 which merged into Verizon Communications Inc. 06/30/2000

INTERNATIONAL INDUSTRIES & DEVELOPMENTS, INC. (DE)
No longer in existence having become inoperative and void for non-payment of taxes 4/1/57

INTERNATIONAL INDS INC (DE)
Ctfs. dated after 01/21/1998
Name changed to International Internet Inc. 02/25/1999
International Internet Inc. name changed to Evolve One, Inc. 11/30/2000 which name changed to China Direct, Inc. (DE) 09/19/2006 which reincorporated in Florida 06/21/2007 which name changed to China Direct Industries, Inc. 05/29/2009 which name changed to CD International Enterprises, Inc. 02/29/2012

INTERNATIONAL INDS INC (DE)
Reincorporated 03/07/1969
Common no par split (5) for (3) by issuance of (2/3) additional share 09/20/1967
Common no par split (2) for (1) by issuance of (1) additional share 08/09/1968
State of incorporation changed from (CA) to (DE) and Common no par changed to $1 par 03/07/1969
Merged into IHOP Corp. 09/17/1976
Each share $1.70 Conv. Preference Ser. A $1 par exchanged for (1) share Common $1 par
Each share Common $1 par exchanged for (2/3) share Common $1 par
(See IHOP Corp.)

INTERNATIONAL INFOPET SYS LTD (ON)
Recapitalized as New International Infopet Systems Ltd. 02/26/1997
Each share Common no par exchanged for (0.4) share Common no par
New International Infopet Systems Ltd. name changed to SponsorsOne Inc. 01/13/2014

INTERNATIONAL INFORMATION NETWORK INC (NY)
Reincorporated under the laws of Nevada as Megaphone International, Inc. 6/5/86
Megaphone International, Inc. (NV) reincorporated in (DE) 1/15/87 which was acquired by Votrax, Inc. 1/19/89
(See Votrax, Inc.)

INTERNATIONAL INNOPAC INC (BC)
Reincorporated 05/29/1992
Place of incorporation changed from (Canada) to (BC) 05/29/1992
Name changed to Great Pacific Enterprises Inc. 06/01/1994
(See Great Pacific Enterprises Inc.)

INTERNATIONAL INST APPLIED TECHNOLOGY INC (DC)
Merged into Industrial Training Corp. 06/10/1985
Each share Common 1¢ par exchanged for (0.02) share Common 10¢ par
Industrial Training Corp. name changed to ITC Learning Corp. 05/09/1997
(See ITC Learning Corp.)

INTERNATIONAL INST FOR MED SCIENCES (DE)
Name changed to Techtron, Inc. 07/30/1986
(See Techtron, Inc.)

INTERNATIONAL INTEGRATION INC (DE)
Merged into Razorfish, Inc. 11/02/1999
Each share Common 1¢ par exchanged for (0.875) share Class A Common 1¢ par
(See Razorfish, Inc.)

INTERNATIONAL INTER-LINK INC (AB)
Name changed to Parton Capital Inc. 11/25/1997

INTERNATIONAL INTERCHANGE CORP (NV)
Reorganized 10/2/97
Reorganized from under the laws of (UT) to (NV) 10/2/97
Each share Common $0.001 par exchanged for (0.005) share Common $0.001 par
Common $0.001 par split (2) for (1) by issuance of (1) additional share payable 11/20/97 to holders of record 11/20/97
Name changed to Cardxx Inc. 9/15/98

INTERNATIONAL INTERLAKE INDS INC (BC)
Merged into Newport Petroleum Corp. 04/14/1993
Each share Common no par exchanged for $0.77 cash

INTERNATIONAL INTERNET INC (DE)
Name changed to Evolve One, Inc. 11/30/2000
Evolve One, Inc. name changed to China Direct, Inc. (DE) 09/19/2006 which reincorporated in Florida 06/21/2007 which name changed to China Direct Industries, Inc. 05/29/2009 which name changed to CD International Enterprises, Inc. 02/29/2012

INTERNATIONAL INVESTING CORP.
Liquidated 00/00/1934
Details not available

INTERNATIONAL INVESTING CORP. NEW
Liquidated in 1946
Details not available

INTERNATIONAL INVESTMENT CORP.
Name changed to International

Investing Corp. (New) which
liquidated in 1946

INTERNATIONAL INVT GROUP LTD (DE)
Each share old Common $0.0001 par exchanged for (0.05) share new Common $0.0001 par 2/18/91
Each share new Common $0.0001 par exchanged again for (0.1) share new Common $0.0001 par 6/24/93
Name changed to Intermedia Net Inc. 6/1/96
Intermedia Net Inc. name changed to Fortune Media, Inc. 5/21/99 which name changed to Cyberedge Enterprises, Inc. 11/10/2000 which name changed to Wayne's Famous Phillies Inc. 3/10/2003

INTERNATIONAL INVT INC (PR)
Completely liquidated 02/01/1972
Each share Common $10 par exchanged for first and final distribution of (1.2) shares Robino-Ladd Co. Common $1 par
Robino-Ladd Co. name changed to Inprojet Corp. 08/11/1978
(See Inproject Corp.)

INTERNATIONAL INVESTORS FUND SYSTEM, INC.
Liquidated in 1940

INTERNATIONAL INVS INC (DE)
Capital Stock $1 par split (3) for (1) by issuance of (2) additional shares 09/28/1973
Capital Stock $1 par split (3) for (1) by issuance of (2) additional shares 04/16/1980
Under plan of reorganization each share Common $1 par automatically became (1) share Van Eck Funds International Investors Gold Fund Class A 04/30/1991

INTERNATIONAL INVS LIFE INS INC (TX)
Merged into American Investors Life Insurance Co., Inc. 11/30/77
Each share Common $1 par exchanged for (0.72) share Common $1 par or $2.50 cash
Note: Option to receive cash expired 2/10/87
American Investors Life Insurance Co., Inc. reorganized as AmVestors Financial Corp. 8/27/86 which merged into AmerUs Life Holdings Inc. 12/19/97

INTERNATIONAL INVTS & TRADING INC (DE)
Name changed to Northstar Multimedia Communications, Inc. 9/26/94

INTERNATIONAL IONARC INC (BC)
Ordinary no par reclassified as Common no par 08/31/1981
Struck off register and declared dissolved for failure to file returns 06/04/1993

INTERNATIONAL IRON & METAL CO., LTD. (ON)
Reorganized as Intermetco Ltd. 11/01/1968
Details not available

INTERNATIONAL IRON CARBIDE CORP (CO)
Administratively dissolved 01/04/1996

INTERNATIONAL IRON OF COSTA RICA, INC. (DE)
No longer in existence having become inoperative and void for non-payment of taxes 4/1/64

INTERNATIONAL JAGUAR EQUITIES INC (BC)
Recapitalized as Jaguar International Equities Inc. 02/07/2000
Each share Common no par exchanged for (0.2) share Common no par
Jaguar International Equities Inc.

name changed to Advectus Life Sciences Inc. 03/18/2002

INTERNATIONAL JAMES INDS INC (BC)
Name changed to CDIS Software Inc. 07/08/1988
CDIS Software Inc. recapitalized as International CDIS Software Inc. 03/06/1989 which name changed to A.T.H. Fund Inc. 07/24/1990
(See A.T.H. Fund Inc.)

INTERNATIONAL JAZZMAN VENTURES CORP (BC)
Merged into Oro Belle Resources Inc. 12/14/1995
Each share Common no par exchanged for (1) share Common no par
Oro Belle Resources Inc. merged into Viceroy Resource Corp. 06/30/1998 which merged into Quest Capital Corp. (BC) 06/30/2003 which reincorporated in Canada 05/27/2008 which name changed to Sprott Resource Lending Corp. 09/10/2010 which merged into Sprott Inc. 07/24/2013

INTERNATIONAL JENSEN INC (DE)
Merged into Recoton Corp. 8/28/96
Each share Common 1¢ par exchanged for $11 cash

INTERNATIONAL K C JAKES BBQ & GRILL INC (DE)
Name changed to Cassco Capital Corp. (New) 07/18/1994
Cassco Capital Corp. (New) recapitalized as Diversified Technology Group Inc. 06/23/2000 which name changed to Diversified Technologies Group Inc. 11/14/2000 which name changed to X-Change Corp. 07/30/2001 which name changed to Endocan Corp. 11/06/2013

INTERNATIONAL KAABA GOLD CORP (BC)
Delisted from Vancouver Stock Exchange 11/15/1995

INTERNATIONAL KENERGY RES CORP (SK)
Merged into Interquest Resources Corp. 06/11/1985
Each share Common no par exchanged for (1) share Common no par
Interquest Resources Corp. name changed to Interquest Technologies Inc. 10/23/1992 which recapitalized as Interquest Inc. 09/30/1995
(See Interquest Inc.)

INTERNATIONAL KENGATE VENTURES INC (BC)
Name changed to Latin American Gold Inc. (BC) 03/31/1994
Latin American Gold Inc. (BC) reincorporated in Bermuda as Latin America Gold Ltd 04/27/1995
(See Latin America Gold Ltd.)

INTERNATIONAL KENVILLE GOLD MINES LTD (ON)
Capital Stock $1 par changed to no par 09/25/1972
Charter cancelled for failure to pay taxes and file returns 03/05/1980

INTERNATIONAL KEYSTONE ENTMT INC (BC)
Reincorporated 11/14/1994
Reincorporated 06/15/2005
Place of incorporation changed from (BC) to (Canada) 11/14/1994
Each share old Common no par exchanged for (0.2) share new Common no par 11/09/1998
Place of incorporation changed from (Canada) to (BC) 06/15/2005
Merged into Keystone Pictures Inc. 05/25/2006
Each share new Common no par exchanged for (1) Participation Right to receive, on a pro rata basis, 75%

of the revenue generated from film sales and licensing until 12/31/2008

INTERNATIONAL KING JACK RES LTD (BC)
Recapitalized as Petromin Resources Ltd. 04/18/1996
Each share Common no par exchanged for (0.2) share Common no par

INTERNATIONAL KINGS TABLE INC (OR)
Common no par split (2) for (1) by issuance of (1) additional share 5/2/77
Common no par split (5) for (3) by issuance of (2/3) additional share 8/12/83
Stock Dividend - 10% 9/28/84
Merged into IK Acquisition Corp. 6/14/88
Each share Common no par exchanged for $20.25 cash

INTERNATIONAL KIRBY ENERGY CORP (BC)
Reincorporated under the laws of Bermuda as Kingsway International Holdings Ltd. and Common no par changed to USD$0.01 par 02/23/1996
Kingsway International Holdings Ltd. name changed to Sunwah International Ltd. 01/19/2011

INTERNATIONAL KIRKLAND MINERALS INC (BC)
Each share old Common no par exchanged for (0.2) share new Common no par 05/26/2008
Recapitalized as Legion Resources Corp. 02/22/2010
Each share new Common no par exchanged for (0.14285714) share Common no par
Legion Resources Corp. merged into Samaranta Mining Corp. 05/20/2011 which recapitalized as Icon Exploration Inc. 10/28/2013

INTERNATIONAL KRL RES CORP (BC)
Recapitalized as Acme Resources Inc. 12/07/2009
Each share Common no par exchanged for (0.06666666) share Common no par
Acme Resources Inc. name changed to Affinity Metals Corp. 03/01/2017

INTERNATIONAL LACO RES INC (BC)
Merged into Aurex Resources Inc. 07/11/1985
Each share Capital Stock no par exchanged for (0.4) share Common no par
Aurex Resources Inc. merged into Galveston Resources Ltd. 07/29/1986 which merged into Corona Corp. 07/01/1988 which recapitalized as International Corona Corp. 06/11/1991
(See International Corona Corp.)

INTERNATIONAL LAND & EXPLORATION CORP. (UT)
Name changed to Alhambra Atlanta Gold Mines & Properties, Inc. (UT) 11/10/1977
Alhambra Atlanta Gold Mines & Properties, Inc. (UT) reincorporated in Delaware 01/03/1978 which name changed to Alhambra Mines, Inc. 02/13/1981 which recapitalized as American Eagle Resources, Inc. (DE) 08/31/1989 which reincorporated in British Columbia 02/06/2008 which merged into Lion One Metals Ltd. 01/31/2011

INTERNATIONAL LANDMARK ENVIRONMENTAL INC (BC)
Recapitalized as Shabute Ventures Inc. 01/15/2003
Each share Common no par

exchanged for (0.14285714) share Common no par
Shabute Ventures Inc. name changed to Northern Sun Exploration Co. Inc. 08/19/2004 which recapitalized as Reparo Energy Partners Corp. 11/08/2013

INTERNATIONAL LARDER MINERALS INC (ON)
Merged into Explorers Alliance Corp. 10/13/2000
Each share Common no par exchanged for (0.0491) share Common no par and (0.5) Common Stock Purchase Warrant expiring 05/14/2001
(See Explorers Alliance Corp.)

INTERNATIONAL LASER TECH INC (BC)
Dissolved 12/23/1988
Details not available

INTERNATIONAL LD & DEV CORP (NV)
Name changed to International Chemical Development Corp. 10/25/1968
International Chemical Development Corp. recapitalized as Columbia Autocar, Inc. 04/15/1980 which name changed to American Peat Co. 04/22/1982 which name changed to American National Hydrocarbon, Inc. 11/15/1982
(See American National Hydrocarbon, Inc.)

INTERNATIONAL LD LTD (BC)
Through purchase offer 100% acquired by Hastings West Investment Co. as of 10/00/1978
Public interest eliminated

INTERNATIONAL LEAD & COPPER CO. (ID)
Charter forfeited for failure to file reports 11/30/56

INTERNATIONAL LEASE FIN CORP (CA)
Common 10¢ par split (2) for (1) by issuance of (1) additional share 12/15/1983
Common 10¢ par split (3) for (2) by issuance of (0.5) additional share 07/25/1985
Common 10¢ par split (3) for (2) by issuance of (0.5) additional share 02/13/1987
$1.875 Conv. Preferred Ser. A no par called for redemption 04/03/1987
Dutch Auction Rate Transferable Securities Preferred Ser. A no par called for redemption 08/31/1990
Merged into American International Group, Inc. 08/31/1990
Each share Common 10¢ par exchanged for $32.50 cash
Market Auction Preferred Ser. G called for redemption at $100,000 on 11/27/2001
Market Auction Preferred Ser. D called for redemption at $100,000 on 12/10/2001
Market Auction Preferred Ser. F called for redemption at $100,000 on 12/17/2001
Market Auction Preferred Ser. H called for redemption at $100,000 on 12/31/2001
Market Auction Preferred Ser. E called for redemption at $100,000 on 04/01/2002

INTERNATIONAL LEISURE & CASINO (UT)
Involuntarily dissolved 06/01/1987

INTERNATIONAL LEISURE CORP (NV)
Merged into Hilton Hotels Corp. 03/01/1972
Each share Common $1 par exchanged for (0.35) share Common $2.50 par
(See Hilton Hotels Corp.)

INTERNATIONAL LEISURE ENTERPRISES INC (AZ)
Name changed to ILX Inc. 06/28/1993
ILX Inc. recapitalized as ILX Resorts Inc. 01/13/1998
(See ILX Resorts Inc.)

INTERNATIONAL LEISURE HOSTS LTD (WY)
Certificates dated prior to 05/24/1971
Merged into Brentwood Industries, Inc. 05/24/1971
Each share Common 1¢ par exchanged for (0.8) share Common 10¢ par
(See Brentwood Industries, Inc.)

INTERNATIONAL LEISURE HOSTS LTD NEW (WY)
Certificates dated after 09/12/1973
Liquidation completed
Each share Common 1¢ par received initial distribution of $3 cash payable 05/24/2013 to holders of record 05/17/2013 Ex date - 05/28/2013
Each share Common 1¢ par received second distribution of $2 cash payable 08/20/2014 to holders of record 08/01/2014
Each share Common 1¢ par received third and final distribution of $2.81 cash payable 03/17/2015 to holders of record 02/20/2015 Ex date - 03/18/2015

INTERNATIONAL LEISURE TIME & DEVELOPMENT CORP. (NV)
Recapitalized as G & F T Mfg. Corp. 8/25/75
Each share Common $1 par exchanged for (0.2) share Common $5 par
G & F T Mfg. Corp. name changed to G & FT Oil & Gas Corp. 4/30/80 which name changed to Yankee Energy Group 1/13/81
(See Yankee Energy Group)

INTERNATIONAL LIFE EXTN CORP (NY)
Name changed to Medi-Data International, Inc. 7/8/85

INTERNATIONAL LIFE HLDG CORP (NY)
Stock Dividends - 10% 6/10/74; 10% 6/10/75
Liquidation completed
Each share Common 50¢ par exchanged for initial distribution of $4.30 cash 4/18/80
Each share Common 50¢ par received second and final distribution of $0.3332 cash 12/23/80

INTERNATIONAL LIFE INSURANCE CO. OF THE AMERICAS (PR)
Completely liquidated 12/31/74
Each share Common $1 par exchanged for first and final distribution of $8.10 cash

INTERNATIONAL LIFE INS CO (KY)
Merged into Union Bankers Insurance Co. 6/30/78
Each share Common $1 par exchanged for (1/6) share Common $1 par
(See Union Bankers Insurance Co.)

INTERNATIONAL LIFE INS CO (TX)
Merged into International Life Insurance Co. (KY) 10/10/66
Each share Common no par exchanged for (0.2) share Common $1 par
International Life Insurance Co. (KY) merged into Union Bankers Insurance Co. 6/30/78
(See Union Bankers Insurance Co.)

INTERNATIONAL LIFE INS CO BUFFALO (NY)
Stock Dividend - 10% 5/25/67
Acquired by American General Life Insurance Co. of New York 5/15/80
Each share Capital Stock $2 par exchanged for $20.20 cash

INTERNATIONAL LT AIRCRAFT CORP (BC)
Name changed to Pacific Vista Industries Inc. (BC) 10/16/1992
Pacific Vista Industries Inc. (BC) reincorporated in Yukon 05/27/1993
(See Pacific Vista Industries Inc.)

INTERNATIONAL LIMA RES CORP (BC)
Name changed to Crosshair Exploration & Mining Corp. 03/01/2004
Crosshair Exploration & Mining Corp. name changed to Crosshair Energy Corp. 11/02/2011 which recapitalized as Jet Metal Corp. (BC) 09/23/2013 which reorganized in Canada as Canada Jetlines Ltd. 03/07/2017

INTERNATIONAL LITHIUM MNG LTD (ON)
Name changed to Petroinc Resources Ltd. 04/22/1981
Petroinc Resources Ltd. merged into Barrick Resources Corp. 05/02/1983 which recapitalized as American Barrick Resources Corp. 12/06/1985 which name changed to Barrick Gold Corp. 01/18/1995

INTERNATIONAL LMBR CORP (DE)
Charter cancelled and declared inoperative and void for non-payment of taxes 4/15/72

INTERNATIONAL LMM VENTURES CORP (BC)
Common no par split (5) for (1) by issuance of (4) additional shares payable 01/08/2010 to holders of record 01/06/2010
Name changed to US Oil Sands Inc. (BC) 04/20/2011
US Oil Sands Inc. (BC) reincorporated in Alberta 05/09/2011

INTERNATIONAL LOTTERY & TOTALIZATOR SYS INC (CA)
Each share old Common no par exchanged for (0.33333333) share new Common no par 06/12/1998
Reorganized under the laws of Delaware 01/05/2015
Each (9,245,317) shares new Common no par exchanged for (1) share Common 1¢ par
Note: Holders of (9,245,316) shares or fewer received $1.33 cash per share
Company is now private

INTERNATIONAL LOTTERY INC (DE)
Issue Information - 1,050,000 shares COM offered at $11.50 per share on 04/14/1994
Name changed to Interlott Technologies Inc. 5/8/97
Interlott Technologies Inc. merged into GTECH Holdings Corp. 9/18/2003
(See GTECH Holdings Corp.)

INTERNATIONAL LOUMIC RES LTD (BC)
Name changed to Loumic Exploration Inc. (BC) 02/27/2003
Loumic Exploration Inc. (BC) reorganized as Vast Exploration Inc. (ON) 11/01/2004 which name changed to ARHT Media Inc. 10/17/2014

INTERNATIONAL MACHINE TOOL CORP.
Name changed to International Detrola Corp. in 1943 which name was changed to Newport Steel Corp. 3/4/49
Newport Steel Corp. name changed to Newcorp, Inc. 9/18/56
Newcorp, Inc. liquidation completed 8/31/59

INTERNATIONAL-MADISON BANK & TRUST CO. (NEW YORK, NY)
Dissolved 11/23/43
No stockholders' equity

INTERNATIONAL MAGGIE MINES LTD (BC)
Reincorporated under the laws of Canada as Hall Train Entertainment Inc. 04/24/1995
Hall Train Entertainment Inc. merged into GoldTrain Resources Inc. 04/27/2009 which recapitalized as Idaho Champion Gold Mines Canada Inc. 09/27/2018

INTERNATIONAL MAGNETICS CORP (BC)
Name changed to United Southern Minerals Corp. 11/01/1988
(See United Southern Minerals Corp.)

INTERNATIONAL MAHOGANY CORP (BC)
Class A no par reclassified as Common no par 02/13/1997
Class B Subordinated no par reclassified as Common no par 02/13/1997
Recapitalized as Reliant Ventures Ltd. 06/06/2000
Each share Common no par exchanged for (0.1) share Common no par
Reliant Ventures Ltd. name changed to Esperanza Silver Corp. 05/14/2003 which name changed to Esperanza Resources Corp. 07/19/2010
(See Esperanza Resources Corp.)

INTERNATIONAL MAKAOO LTD (CANADA)
Recapitalized as Non-Par Developments Ltd. (Canada) 12/17/1991
Each share Capital Stock no par exchanged for (0.5) share Common no par
Non-Par Developments Ltd. (Canada) reincorporated in British Columbia as Similkameen Hydro-Power Ltd. 08/17/1992 which recapitalized as Norte Resources Ltd. (BC) 07/25/1996 which reorganized in Yukon as Banks Ventures Ltd. 04/06/1998 which name changed to Banks Energy Inc. 07/26/2004 which merged into Arapahoe Energy Corp. (New) 10/20/2005 which name changed to Canadian Phoenix Resources Corp. 01/07/2008 which recapitalized as Knol Resources Corp. 03/11/2013

INTERNATIONAL MGMT & RESH CORP (PA)
SEC revoked common stock registration 11/07/2011

INTERNATIONAL MANAGEMENT CORP. (NC)
Charter cancelled 2/15/66

INTERNATIONAL MFG & MARKETING CORP (DE)
Name changed to Ultracircuits, Inc. 06/25/1981
(See Ultracircuits, Inc.)

INTERNATIONAL MANUFACTURING CO. (WA)
Charter stricken from record for failure to pay taxes 07/01/1918

INTERNATIONAL MFG SVCS INC (DE)
Issue Information - 5,000,000 shares COM offered at $11.50 per share on 10/22/1997
Merged into Celestica Inc. 12/30/98
Each share Common $0.001 par exchanged for either (0.4) share Common $0.001 par or $7 cash
Note: Option to receive cash expired 12/29/98

INTERNATIONAL MAPLE LEAF RESOURCE CORP. (BC)
Recapitalized as Maple Resource Corp. 08/29/1989
Each share Common no par exchanged for (0.4) share Common no par

Maple Resource Corp. recapitalized as Birchwood Ventures Ltd. 08/17/1992 which recapitalized as Oromin Explorations Ltd. (Old) 09/30/1997 which merged into Oromin Explorations Ltd. (New) 02/25/2002 which merged into Teranga Gold Corp. 10/08/2013

INTERNATIONAL MAPLE LEAF SPRINGS LTD (BC)
Delisted from Vancouver Stock Exchange 03/01/1999

INTERNATIONAL MARCH RES LTD (BC)
Name changed to Mode Products Inc. 04/22/1986
(See Mode Products Inc.)

INTERNATIONAL MARINE, INC. (FL)
Declared dissolved for non-payment of taxes 8/28/64

INTERNATIONAL MARINER RES LTD (BC)
Struck off register and declared dissolved for failure to file returns 03/10/1978

INTERNATIONAL MARKATECH CORP (BC)
Recapitalized as Markatech Industries Corp. 11/03/1995
Each share Common no par exchanged for (0.33333333) share Common no par
Markatech Industries Corp. recapitalized as Ameratech Systems Corp. 02/12/2001
(See Ameratech Systems Corp.)

INTERNATIONAL MARKETING DYNAMICS INC (UT)
Each share old Common $0.001 par exchanged for (0.025) share new Common $0.001 par 3/15/96
Name changed to Two Dog Net, Inc. 12/30/98
(See Two Dog Net, Inc.)

INTERNATIONAL MART CORP (NV)
Recapitalized as Sycamore Development Group, Inc. 11/20/2006
Each share Common $0.001 par exchanged for (0.01) share Common $0.0001 par
Sycamore Development Group, Inc. name changed to ReBuilder Medical Technologies, Inc. 03/20/2007 which name changed to Lion Gold Brazil, Inc. 08/23/2012 which recapitalized as Cannabiz Mobile, Inc. 06/24/2014

INTERNATIONAL MATCH CORP.
Assets acquired by International Match Realization Co. Ltd. in 1936
No stockholders' equity

INTERNATIONAL MATCH REALIZATION CO. LTD.
Dissolved in 1949

INTERNATIONAL MATLS CORP (MA)
Common 1¢ par changed to $0.0025 par and (3) additional shares issued 08/25/1978
Plan of reorganization under Chapter 11 Federal Bankruptcy proceedings confirmed 05/07/1980
No stockholders' equity

INTERNATIONAL MEASUREMENT & CTL CO (ID)
Each share old Common 1¢ par exchanged for (0.2) share new Common 1¢ par 8/18/88
Reorganized as Laser Technology, Inc. (ID) 5/11/89
Each share Common 1¢ par exchanged for (4) shares Common 1¢ par
Laser Technology, Inc. (ID) reincorporated in Delaware 5/30/97
(See Laser Technology, Inc. (DE))

INTERNATIONAL MED IMAGING SPECIALISTS INC (WY)
Reincorporated 08/11/1986
Place of incorporation changed from

(BC) to (WY) 08/11/1986 Charter revoked 11/13/1987

INTERNATIONAL MED SCIENCE INC (DE)
Recapitalized as International Investment Group, Ltd. 7/26/88
Each share Common 1¢ par exchanged for (1) share Common $0.0001 par
International Investment Group, Ltd. name changed to Intermedia Net Inc. 6/1/96 which name changed to Fortune Media, Inc. 5/21/99 which name changed to Cyberedge Enterprises, Inc. 11/10/2000 which name changed to Wayne's Famous Phillies Inc. 3/10/2003

INTERNATIONAL MED STAFFING INC (DE)
Name changed to PureSpectrum, Inc. 10/29/2009

INTERNATIONAL MED SYS INC (NJ)
Name changed to Medical Technology Products, Inc. 12/29/86

INTERNATIONAL MED TECHNOLOGY CORP (NV)
Name changed to North American Bingo, Inc. 9/13/84
(See North American Bingo, Inc.)

INTERNATIONAL MED VENTURES LTD (NV)
Name changed to Amquest International Ltd. 1/29/96
(See Amquest International Ltd.)

INTERNATIONAL MEDIA CORP (FL)
Proclaimed dissolved for failure to file annual reports and pay taxes 10/9/92

INTERNATIONAL MEDIA HLDGS INC (FL)
Administratively dissolved 09/27/2013

INTERNATIONAL MEGA DYNE INDL CORP (BC)
Name changed to ESC Envirotech Systems Corp. 07/12/1991
ESC Envirotech Systems Corp. recapitalized as SWI Steelworks Inc. 03/29/1999
(See SWI Steelworks Inc.)

INTERNATIONAL MEGALINE RES LTD (BC)
Name changed to Dyonix Greentree Technologies Inc. 07/08/1986
(See Dyonix Greentree Technologies Inc.)

INTERNATIONAL MEMBERSHIP MARKETING INC (BC)
Recapitalized as Internova Resources Ltd. 07/30/1991
Each share Common no par exchanged for (0.33333333) share Common no par
Internova Resources Ltd. recapitalized as Parisco Foods Ltd. 01/22/1996
(See Parisco Foods Ltd.)

INTERNATIONAL MENU SOLUTIONS CORP (NV)
Name changed to Dunwynn Resources, Inc. 11/05/2004
Dunwynn Resources, Inc. recapitalized as Dunwynn Exploration, Inc. 06/24/2005
(See Dunwynn Exploration, Inc.)

INTERNATIONAL MERCANTILE CORP (MO)
Each share old Common $1 par exchanged for (0.03225806) share new Common 1¢ par 07/31/1997
Each share new Common 1¢ par exchanged for (0.14285714) share new Common 1¢ par 08/08/2000
Each share new Common 1¢ par exchanged again for (0.09090909) share new Common 1¢ par 07/12/2001
Each share new Common 1¢ par exchanged again for (0.125) share Common $0.001 par 02/21/2002
Reincorporated under the laws of Nevada as T & G2 03/01/2002
T & G2 name changed to Softnet Technology Corp. 08/04/2004

INTERNATIONAL MERCANTILE MARINE CO.
Merged into United States Lines Co. (NJ) on a (2) for (1) basis in 1943
United States Lines Co. (NJ) merged into Kidde (Walter) & Co., Inc. (DE) 1/10/69 which name changed to Kidde, Inc. 4/18/80 which merged into Hanson Trust p.l.c. 12/31/87 which name changed to Hanson PLC (Old) 1/29/88 which reorganized as Hanson PLC (New) 10/15/2003

INTERNATIONAL MERCHANT ADVISORS INC (NV)
Each share old Common $0.001 par exchanged for (0.002) share new Common $0.001 par 04/29/2011
Name changed to DHS Holding Co. 07/15/2011

INTERNATIONAL MERIDIAN RES LTD (BC)
Merged into Meridor Resources Ltd. 04/01/1985
Each share Capital Stock no par exchanged for (0.3381) share Common no par
Meridor Resources Ltd. merged into Hughes Lang Corp. 08/01/1989 which merged into CanGold Resources Inc. (BC) 01/31/1994 which reorganized in Ontario as Amalgamated CanGold Inc. 07/31/1995 which merged into Central Asia Goldfields Corp. 01/08/1996
(See Central Asia Goldfields Corp.)

INTERNATIONAL MESSAGE CTRS INC (BC)
Name changed to Interlearn Holdings Ltd. 11/13/1990
(See Interlearn Holdings Ltd.)

INTERNATIONAL META SYS INC (DE)
SEC revoked common stock registration 10/03/2011

INTERNATIONAL METAL & PETROLEUM CORP. (QC)
Charter annulled for failure to file reports or pay fees 04/13/1974

INTERNATIONAL METAL INDUSTRIES LTD. (CANADA)
Name changed to Wood (John) Industries Ltd. 05/15/1957
Wood (John) Industries Ltd. acquired by Wood (John) Co. 12/03/1962 which was acquired by Anthes Imperial Ltd. 03/00/1964
(See Anthes Imperial Ltd.)

INTERNATIONAL METALS & PETE CORP (DE)
Name changed 1/17/72
Name changed from International Metals Corp. to International Metals & Petroleum Corp. 1/17/72
Charter cancelled and declared inoperative and void for non-payment of taxes 1/17/72

INTERNATIONAL METALS ACQUISITION CORP (DE)
Name changed to Niagara Corp. 5/17/96
(See Niagara Corp.)

INTERNATIONAL METALS STREAMING CORP (NV)
Common $0.0001 par split (5) for (2) by issuance of (1.5) additional shares payable 10/04/2013 to holders of record 10/03/2013 Ex date - 10/07/2013
Common $0.0001 par split (2.17079) for (1) by issuance of (1.17079) additional shares payable 02/15/2017 to holders of record 02/15/2017 Ex date - 02/16/2017

Name changed to Environmental Packaging Technologies Holdings, Inc. 02/28/2017

INTERNATIONAL MICHAM RES INC (BC)
Reorganized under the laws of Ontario as Link Mineral Ventures Ltd. 05/29/1996
Each share Common no par exchanged for (0.1) share Common no par
(See Link Mineral Ventures Ltd.)

INTERNATIONAL MICROCOMPUTER SOFTWARE INC (CA)
Each share old Common no par exchanged for (0.01) share new Common no par 02/23/1991
New Common no par split (3) for (2) by issuance of (0.5) additional share 11/03/1995
New Common no par split (3) for (2) by issuance of (0.5) additional share payable 01/24/1997 to holders of record 12/26/1996
Name changed to Broadcaster, Inc. (CA) 06/12/2006
Broadcaster, Inc. (CA) reincorporated in Delaware 05/21/2007
(See Broadcaster, Inc.)

INTERNATIONAL MICROELECTRONICS PRODS INC (DE)
Name changed to IMP, Inc. 08/12/1993
(See IMP, Inc.)

INTERNATIONAL MINERALS & CHEM CORP (NY)
Each share 7% Prior Preference $100 par exchanged for (1) share 4% Preferred $100 par and (3.5) shares Common $5 par 00/00/1942
Each share Common no par exchanged for (0.25) share Common $5 par 00/00/1942
Common $5 par split (2) for (1) by issuance of (1) additional share 11/25/1964
Common $5 par split (3) for (2) by issuance of (0.5) additional share 10/25/1966
Common $5 par split (4) for (3) by issuance of (1/3) additional share 12/09/1974
Conv. Preferred Ser. B $100 par called for redemption 06/27/1975
Conv. Preferred Ser. C $100 par called for redemption 06/27/1975
Common $5 par split (3) for (2) by issuance of (0.5) additional share 04/25/1980
$3.75 Conv. Exchangeable Preferred Ser. A $1 par called for redemption 07/31/1989
$3.25 Conv. Exchangeable Preferred Ser. B $1 par called for redemption 04/16/1990
Stock Dividend - 100% 12/29/1950
Name changed to Imcera Group Inc. 06/14/1990
Imcera Group Inc. name changed to Mallinckrodt Group Inc. 03/15/1994 which name changed to Mallinckrodt Inc. 10/16/1996 which merged into Tyco International Ltd. (Bermuda) 10/17/2000 which reincorporated in Switzerland 03/17/2009 which merged into Johnson Controls International PLC 09/06/2016

INTERNATIONAL MINERALS CORP (NV)
Name changed to Dynatron, Inc. 10/7/68
(See Dynatron, Inc.)

INTERNATIONAL MINERALS CORP (YT)
Merged into Hochschild Mining PLC 12/27/2013
Each share Common no par exchanged for (1) share Chaparral Gold Corp. Common no par and USD$2.38 cash

Note: Unexchanged certificates will be cancelled and become without value 12/27/2019
(See Chaparral Gold Corp.)

INTERNATIONAL MINERALS MNG GROUP INC (NV)
Each share old Common $0.001 par exchanged for (0.00183486) share new Common $0.001 par 08/31/2007
Each share new Common $0.001 par exchanged again for (0.001) share new Common $0.001 par 12/19/2007
Name changed to Advanced Content Services, Inc. 02/05/2008
Advanced Content Services, Inc. recapitalized as New Wave Holdings, Inc. 12/08/2014 which name changed to PAO Group, Inc. 06/29/2017

INTERNATIONAL MINES DEVELOPMENT CO. (DE)
Charter cancelled and declared inoperative and void for non-payment of taxes 3/22/22

INTERNATIONAL MINING & DEVELOPMENT CORP. (LIBERIA)
Completely liquidated 04/21/1969
Each share Common 1¢ par exchanged for first and final distribution of (0.25) share Precious Metals Ltd. Capital Stock 1¢ par and (0.1) share International Diversified Developers Ltd. Capital Stock 1¢ par plus (0.1) Diversified Land Ltd. Warrant expiring 08/13/1979
(See each company's listing)

INTERNATIONAL MNG & EXPL CORP (DE)
Recapitalized as SPY Depot International Inc. 03/08/2002
Each share Common $0.001 par exchanged for (0.1) share Common $0.001 par
SPY Depot International Inc. name changed to Fortune Graphite Inc. (DE) 01/07/2003 which reorganized in British Columbia 05/01/2010

INTERNATIONAL MINING & MILLING CO. (NV)
Charter revoked for failure to file reports and pay fees 3/4/46

INTERNATIONAL MINING CORP. (DE)
Certificates dated prior to 09/01/1956
Merged into Sunset International Petroleum Corp. 09/01/1956
Each share Common exchanged for (1) share Common $1 par
Sunset International Petroleum Corp. merged into Sunasco Inc. 04/30/1966 which name changed to Scientific Resources Corp. 10/11/1968
(See Scientific Resources Corp.)

INTERNATIONAL MNG CORP (DE)
Ctfs. dated after 6/5/58
Common $5 par changed to $1.66-2/3 par and (2) additional shares issued 2/8/63
Stock Dividend - 12% 10/7/63
Merged into Pacific Holding Corp. 1/27/78
Each share Common $1.66-2/3 par exchanged for $25 principal amount of 9% Subord. Debentures due 1/1/97 and $1 cash

INTERNATIONAL MNG CORP N L (AUSTRALIA)
Struck off register 01/07/1997
No ADR holders' equity

INTERNATIONAL MIRTONE INC (ON)
Name changed to Mirtronics Inc. 03/09/1990
Mirtronics Inc. merged into Genterra Inc. 12/31/2003 which merged into Genterra Capital Inc. (New) 05/10/2010 which merged into Gencan Capital Inc. 10/30/2015

INTERNATIONAL MITEK COMPUTER INC (BC)
Delisted from Vancouver Stock Exchange 05/14/1992

INTERNATIONAL MLG CO (NY)
Merged 9/3/63
Merged from International Milling Co. into International Milling Co., Inc. 9/3/63
Each share 4% 1st Preferred Ser. A $100 par exchanged for (1) share 4% 1st Preferred Ser. A $100 par
Each share 4-1/4% 1st Preferred Ser. C $100 par exchanged for (1) share 4-1/4% 1st Preferred Ser. C $100 par
Each share 4-1/2% 1st Preferred Ser. D $100 par exchanged for (1) share 4-1/2% 1st Preferred Ser. D $100 par
Each share 5-1/4% 1st Preferred Ser. E $100 par exchanged for (1) share 5-1/4% 1st Preferred Ser. E $100 par
Each share Common $1 par exchanged for (4) shares Common $1 par
Reincorporated under the laws of Delaware as International Multifoods Corp. 1/20/70
International Multifoods Corp. merged into Smucker (J.M.) Co. 6/18/2004

INTERNATIONAL MOBILE MACHS CORP (PA)
Preferred Class A 5¢ par called for redemption 06/10/1987
Preferred Class B 5¢ par called for redemption 06/10/1987
Conv. Preferred 1st Ser. 10¢ par called for redemption 07/17/1987
Name changed to InterDigital Communications Corp. 10/15/1992
InterDigital Communications Corp. name changed to InterDigital, Inc. 07/02/2007

INTERNATIONAL MOBILE TEL SYS (CA)
Name changed to LPL Services, Inc. 10/28/1971
LPL Services, Inc. name changed to Transworld Services, Inc. 09/12/1975 which merged into Raycomm Transworld Industries, Inc. 06/04/1986
(See Raycomm Transworld Industries, Inc.)

INTERNATIONAL MOGUL MINES LTD (ON)
Merged into Conwest Exploration Co. Ltd. (Old) (ON) 08/27/1982
Each share 6% Conv. 1st Preference Ser. A $20 par exchanged for (1) share 6% Conv. 1st Preference Ser. A $20 par
Each share Common no par exchanged for (2) shares Class B no par
Conwest Exploration Co. Ltd. (ON) merged into Conwest Exploration Co. Ltd. (New) (AB) 09/01/1993 which merged into Alberta Energy Co. Ltd. 01/31/1996 which merged into EnCana Corp. 01/03/2003

INTERNATIONAL MOLYBDENUM MINES LTD. (ON)
Merged into Pax International Mines Ltd. 01/31/1962
Each share Capital Stock $1 par exchanged for (0.25) share Capital Stock $1 par
Pax International Mines Ltd. recapitalized as Geo-Pax Mines Ltd. 09/00/1968
(See Geo-Pax Mines Ltd.)

INTERNATIONAL MONETARY CORP (CO)
Name changed to Mega Corp. (CO) 11/10/76
Mega Corp. (CO) reincorporated in Delaware 5/5/78
(See Mega Corp. (DE))

INTERNATIONAL MONETARY FDG CORP (NY)
Recapitalized as Hawaiian Sugar Technologies, Inc. 01/20/1983
Each share Common 1¢ par exchanged for (0.25) share Common 1¢ par
Hawaiian Sugar Technologies, Inc. recapitalized as Entertainment Inns of America, Inc. 10/21/1983 which name changed to Tiger Marketing, Inc. 11/08/1984 which recapitalized as U.S. Health Services, Inc. 04/08/1986 which name changed to Diamond Trade Center, Inc. 10/30/1990
(See Diamond Trade Center, Inc.)

INTERNATIONAL MOTOR HOTEL CORP. (AK)
Name changed to Alaska Hotel Properties, Inc. 11/18/68
Alaska Hotel Properties, Inc. name changed to Alaska Diversified Resources, Inc. 9/10/80 which name changed to Microfast Software Corp. 7/1/83

INTERNATIONAL MOVIE GROUP INC (DE)
Reincorporated 12/31/90
Place of incorporation changed from (BC) to (Canada) 12/31/1990
International Movie Group Inc. (Canada) reincorporated in Delaware 05/16/1991
Each share Common no par exchanged for (0.25) share old Common 1¢ par 01/27/1995
Plan of reorganization under Chapter 11 Federal Bankruptcy Code effective 10/03/1997
Each (47) shares old Common 1¢ par exchanged for (1) share new Common 1¢ par
Each share new Common 1¢ par exchanged again for (0.0001) share new Common 1¢ par 06/29/1998
Note: Holdings of (9,999) shares or fewer received $0.93 cash per share
Merged into Lions Gate Entertainment Corp. 06/30/1998
Each share new Common 1¢ par exchanged for (3,750) shares Common no par

INTERNATIONAL MULTIFOODS CORP (DE)
Common $1 par split (2) for (1) by issuance of (1) additional share 09/03/1976
Common $1 par changed to 10¢ par 06/18/1982
Common 10¢ par split (3) for (2) by issuance of (0.5) additional share 07/24/1986
Common Stock Purchase Rights declared for Common stockholders of record 10/10/1986 were redeemed at $0.05 per right 11/09/1990 for holders of record 10/19/1990
Common 10¢ par split (3) for (2) by issuance of (0.5) additional share 07/25/1991
4% 1st Preferred Ser. A $100 par called for redemption 09/01/1995
1st Preferred Ser. C $100 par called for redemption 09/01/1995
5.50% 1st Preferred Ser. D $100 par called for redemption 09/01/1995
5.25% 1st Preferred Ser. E $100 par called for redemption 09/01/1995
Merged into Smucker (J.M.) Co. 06/18/2004
Each share Common 10¢ par exchanged for (0.4103) share Common no par and $5 cash

INTERNATIONAL MUREX TECHNOLOGIES CORP (BC)
Acquired by Abbott Laboratories 04/30/1998
Each share Common no par exchanged for USD$13 cash

INTERNATIONAL MUSTO EXPLS LTD (CANADA)
Reincorporated 06/30/1994
Common no par split (3) for (1) by issuance of (2) additional shares 05/27/1992
Place of incorporation changed from (BC) to (Canada) 06/30/1994
Acquired by RN Galaxy Inc. 06/19/1995
Each share Common no par exchanged for $14.99 cash

INTERNATIONAL NETWORK SVCS (DE)
Reincorporated 12/28/98
State of incorporation changed from (CA) to (DE) and Common no par changed to $0.001 par 12/28/98
Common $0.001 par split (3) for (2) by issuance of (0.5) additional share payable 4/5/99 to holders of record 3/15/99
Merged into Lucent Technologies Inc. 10/18/99
Each share Common $0.001 par exchanged for (0.8473) share Common no par
Lucent Technologies Inc. merged into Alcatel-Lucent S.A. 11/30/2006

INTERNATIONAL NICKEL CO CDA LTD (CANADA)
7% Preferred called for redemption 02/01/1957
Common no par split (2) for (1) by issuance of (1) additional share 05/31/1960
Common no par split (5) for (2) by issuance of (1.5) additional shares 08/16/1968
Common no par reclassified as Conv. Class A Common no par 09/09/1974
Name changed to Inco Ltd. 04/21/1976
(See Inco Ltd.)

INTERNATIONAL NICKEL CO OF N.J.
Merged into International Nickel Co. of Canada Ltd. 00/00/1928
Details not available

INTERNATIONAL NICKEL VENTURES CORP (ON)
Name changed to INV Metals Inc. 06/16/2010

INTERNATIONAL NORFOLK INDS LTD (BC)
Merged into Ventures Resources Corp. 11/20/1996
Each share Common no par exchanged for (0.608608) share Common no par
Ventures Resources Corp. merged into BrazMin Corp. 04/06/2005 which name changed to Talon Metals Corp. 07/09/2007

INTERNATIONAL NORSEMONT VENTURES LTD (BC)
Recapitalized as Consolidated Norsemont Ventures Ltd. 09/29/1999
Each share Common no par exchanged for (0.2) share Common no par
Consolidated Norsemont Ventures Ltd. name changed to Norsemont Mining Inc. 01/27/2005 which was acquired by HudBay Minerals Inc. 07/05/2011

INTERNATIONAL NORTH AMERN RES INC (BC)
Recapitalized as Sonoma Resource Corp. (BC) 01/05/1990
Each share Common no par exchanged for (0.2) share Common no par
Sonoma Resource Corp. (BC) reincorporated in Wyoming as Biometric Security Corp. 10/09/1998 which recapitalized as Safeguard Biometric Corp. (WY) 12/29/1999 which reincorporated in British Columbia 11/30/2001 which name changed to Devon Ventures Corp. 02/11/2002 which name changed to Pender Financial Group Corp. 06/23/2004
(See Pender Financial Group Corp.)

INTERNATIONAL NORTHAIR MINES LTD (BC)
Name changed to Northair Silver Corp. 11/20/2014
Northair Silver Corp. merged into Kootenay Silver Inc. 04/21/2016

INTERNATIONAL NORTHLAND RES INC (BAHAMAS)
Reincorporated 09/10/1997
Place of incorporation changed from (AB) to (Bahamas) 09/10/1997
Merged into Combined Logistics International Ltd. 11/03/1997
Each share Common no par exchanged for (0.1) share Common no par
(See Combined Logistics International Ltd.)

INTERNATIONAL NORVALIE MINES LTD (ON)
Capital Stock $1 par changed to no par 01/28/1971
Charter cancelled for failure to pay taxes and file returns 05/31/1982

INTERNATIONAL NUCLEAR CORP (DE)
Name changed to Inexco Oil Co. 04/06/1970
Inexco Oil Co. merged into Louisiana Land & Exploration Co. 07/22/1986 which merged into Burlington Resources Inc. 10/22/1997 which merged into ConocoPhillips 03/31/2006

INTERNATIONAL NURSING SVCS INC (CO)
Each share old Common $0.001 par exchanged for (0.2) share new Common $0.001 par 08/11/1994
Each share 12% Conv. Preferred no par exchanged for (2.5) shares Common $0.001 par 01/16/1996
Name changed to Medix Resources, Inc. (CO) 02/18/1998
Medix Resources, Inc. (CO) reincorporated in Delaware as Ramp Corp. 12/19/2003
(See Ramp Corp.)

INTERNATIONAL NUTRITION & GENETICS CORP (DE)
Charter forfeited for failure to maintain a registered agent 11/30/1990

INTERNATIONAL NUTRITION TECHNOLOGIES INC (BC)
Struck off register and declared dissolved for failure to file returns 08/14/1992

INTERNATIONAL NUTRONICS INC (DE)
Charter cancelled and declared inoperative and void for non-payment of taxes 3/1/88

INTERNATIONAL OBASKA MINES LTD (CANADA)
Dissolved 12/16/1980

INTERNATIONAL OCEAN TELEGRAPH CO. (NY)
Liquidation completed 12/13/57

INTERNATIONAL OIL & GAS CORP. (DE)
Incorporated 4/15/19
Charter cancelled and declared inoperative and void for non-payment of taxes 4/1/28

INTERNATIONAL OIL & GAS CORP. (DE)
Incorporated 5/28/54
Liquidation completed
Each share Capital Stock $1 par stamped to indicate initial distribution of $10.25 cash 5/27/66
Each share Stamped Capital Stock $1 par exchanged for second and final distribution of $0.645 cash 1/9/67

INTERNATIONAL OIL & GAS HLDGS CORP (NV)
Old Common $0.0001 par split (5) for (1) by issuance of (4) additional shares payable 10/09/2006 to holders of record 10/06/2006
Each share old Common $0.0001 par exchanged for (0.0001) share new Common $0.0001 par 05/14/2008
Name changed to Inscor, Inc. 05/26/2011
Inscor, Inc. recapitalized as Oicintra, Inc. 01/14/2016

INTERNATIONAL OIL & METALS CORP. (DE)
Common $1 par changed to 10¢ par 10/29/1956
Each share Common 10¢ par exchanged for (0.03333333) share Common 25¢ par 06/09/1964
Completely liquidated 03/24/1965
Each share Common 25¢ par exchanged for (0.149797) share Perfect Photo, Inc. Common no par
Perfect Photo, Inc. was acquired by United Whelan Corp. 06/30/1966 which name changed to Perfect Film & Chemical Corp. 05/31/1967 which name changed to Cadence Industries Corp. 10/22/1970
(See Cadence Industries Corp.)

INTERNATIONAL OIL & REFINING CORP. (DE)
Charter cancelled and declared inoperative and void for non-payment of taxes 3/21/23

INTERNATIONAL OIL TOOLS, INC. (NV)
Dissolved 11/12/1997
Details not available

INTERNATIONAL OILTEX LTD (AB)
Merged into Aztec Resources Ltd. 09/02/1994
Each share Common no par exchanged for (0.20833333) share Common no par
Aztec Resources Ltd. recapitalized as Pursuit Resources Inc. (New) 02/13/1997 which merged into EnerMark Income Fund 04/11/2000 which merged into Enerplus Resources Fund 06/22/2001 which reorganized as Enerplus Corp. 01/03/2011

INTERNATIONAL ONWARD LEARNING SYS INC (BC)
Recapitalized as Catalyst Ventures Corp. 04/02/1996
Each share Common no par exchanged for (0.25) share Common no par
Catalyst Ventures Corp. recapitalized as International Catalyst Ventures Inc. (BC) 02/23/2000 which reincorporated in Yukon 09/08/2000 which recapitalized as Aberdeen International Inc. (Yukon) 11/23/2001 which reincorporated in Ontario 07/04/2006

INTERNATIONAL OPPORTUNITY LIFE INSURANCE CO. (CO)
Merged into United American Life Insurance Co. 12/29/1961
Each share Common $1 par exchanged for (0.125) shares Common $1 par
United American Life Insurance Co. (CO) merged into World Service Life Insurance Co. (CO) 07/31/1978 which merged into Western Preferred Corp. 02/21/1979
(See Western Preferred Corp.)

INTERNATIONAL ORE RES CORP (BC)
Recapitalized as Dalphine Enterprises Ltd. 03/16/1993
Each share Common no par exchanged for (0.5) share Common no par
Dalphine Enterprises Ltd. name changed to Inflazyme Pharmaceuticals Ltd. 12/10/1993 which recapitalized as Eacom Timber Corp. 08/26/2008
(See Eacom Timber Corp.)

INTERNATIONAL OSTRICH CORP (DE)
Charter cancelled and declared inoperative and void for non-payment of taxes 03/01/1999

INTERNATIONAL OXYGEN CO.
Acquired by Union Carbide & Carbon Corp. 00/00/1930
Details not available

INTERNATIONAL PAC CYPRESS MINERALS LTD (BC)
Struck off register and declared dissolved for failure to file retuns 01/22/1993

INTERNATIONAL PAC INVTS INC (UT)
Name changed to Berkeley Imaging Technologies, Inc. 2/2/90
Berkeley Imaging Technologies, Inc. recapitalized as U.S. Motor & Safety Inc. 2/2/92

INTERNATIONAL PACKAGING & LOGISTICS GROUP INC (NV)
Name changed to YBCC, Inc. 12/22/2016

INTERNATIONAL PACKERS LTD. (DE)
Common $15 par changed to $1 par 4/25/58
Name changed to IPL Inc. 5/3/68
IPL Inc. acquired by Deltec International Ltd. 3/11/69

INTERNATIONAL PACKINGS CORP (MA)
Name changed 3/26/58
Name changed from International Packings, Inc. to International Packings Corp. 3/26/58
Common no par split (2) for (1) by issuance of (1) additional share 8/26/66
Merged out of existence 8/31/84
Details not available

INTERNATIONAL PAGURIAN LTD (ON)
Name changed to Canadian Express Ltd. (Old) 05/12/1988
Canadian Express Ltd. (Old) recapitalized as Consolidated Canadian Express Ltd. 12/24/1990 which name changed to Canadian Express Ltd. (New) 05/18/2001 which recapitalized as BNN Investments Ltd. 11/02/2001 which name changed to BAM Investments Corp. 07/05/2006 which name changed to Partners Value Fund Inc. 06/10/2013 which name changed to Partners Value Investments Inc. 05/25/2015 which reorganized as Partners Value Investments L.P. 07/04/2016

INTERNATIONAL PAINTS CDA LTD (CANADA)
Each share 7.5% Preferred $30 par exchanged for (1.5) shares 5% Preferred $20 par 00/00/1936
Each share old Class B no par exchanged for new Class B no par 00/00/1936
5% Preferred $20 par reclassified as 6% Preferred $20 par 00/00/1947
Each share Class A no par or new Class B no par exchanged for (1) share Common no par 12/15/1966
6% Preferred $20 par reclassified as $1.20 Part. Preference no par 06/01/1979
Acquired by International Paints Holdings (Canada) Inc. 12/27/1985
Each share $1.20 Participating Preference no par exchanged for $180 cash
Each share Common no par exchanged for $180 cash

INTERNATIONAL PANORAMA RESOURCE CORP (BC)
Recapitalized as Kakanda Development Corp. 09/27/2002
Each share Common no par exchanged for (0.06666666) share Common no par
(See Kakanda Development Corp.)

INTERNATIONAL PAPER & POWER CO.
Recapitalized as International Paper Co. on a share for share basis in 1941

INTERNATIONAL PAPER CAP TR III (DE)
7.875% Capital Securities called for redemption at $25 on 1/14/2004

INTERNATIONAL PAPER CO (NY)
5% Preferred $100 par called for redemption 10/15/1946
$8.75 Ser. A Preferred no par called for redemption 01/01/1988
Dutch Auction Rate Transferable Preferred Ser. A $1 par called for redemption 09/06/1989
Dutch Auction Rate Transferable Preferred Ser. B $1 par called for redemption 09/12/1989
Dutch Auction Rate Transferable Preferred Ser. C $1 par called for redemption 09/26/1989
Dutch Auction Rate Transferable Preferred Ser. D $1 par called for redemption 10/03/1989
(Additional Information in Active)

INTERNATIONAL PARTS CORP. (DE)
Name changed to Midas-International Corp. 09/14/1962
Midas-International Corp. merged into Illinois Central Industries, Inc. 01/25/1972 which name changed to IC Industries, Inc. 05/21/1975 which name changed to Whitman Corp. (Old) 12/01/1988 which name changed to Whitman Corp. (New) 11/30/2000 which name changed to PepsiAmericas, Inc. (DE) 01/24/2001 which merged into PepsiCo, Inc. 02/26/2010

INTERNATIONAL PASTEL FOOD CORP (BC)
Acquired by Comac Food Group Inc. 05/29/1991
Each share Common no par exchanged for (1) share Class B no par, (0.5) Class A Purchase Warrant expiring 07/29/1991 and (0.5) Class B Purchase Warrant expiring 11/29/1991
Comac Food Group Inc. name changed to Canada's Pizza Delivery Corp. 01/22/2004
(See Canada's Pizza Delivery Corp.)

INTERNATIONAL PATENTS & DEV CORP (DE)
Name changed to Ecological Assistance Corp. 2/22/71
(See Ecological Assistance Corp.)

INTERNATIONAL PATHFINDER INC (ON)
Acquired by a private co. 09/22/1988
Each share Common no par exchanged for $3.75 cash

INTERNATIONAL PATHFINDER RES LTD (BC)
Name changed to Pathfinder Financial Corp. 09/06/1983
Pathfinder Financial Corp. name changed to Pathfinder Industries Ltd. 11/17/1986 which recapitalized as International Pathfinder Inc. 05/19/1987
(See International Pathfinder Inc.)

INTERNATIONAL PBX VENTURES LTD (BC)
Recapitalized as Chilean Metals Inc. 02/28/2014
Each share Common no par exchanged for (0.1) share Common no par

INTERNATIONAL PCBX SYS INC (BC)
Name changed to Extreme Technologies Inc. 11/01/1994
Extreme Technologies Inc. name changed to Portacom Wireless, Inc. (BC) 12/05/1995 which reincorporated in Delaware 12/23/1996
(See Portacom Wireless, Inc. (DE))

INTERNATIONAL PEDCO ENERGY CORP (BC)
Merged into Lateral Vector Resources Inc. 02/29/1996
Each share Common no par exchanged for (0.994) share Common no par
(See Lateral Vector Resources Inc.)

INTERNATIONAL PERFUME CO., INC.
Name changed to Bourjois, Inc. 00/00/1930
(See Bourjois, Inc.)

INTERNATIONAL PETE CORP (BC)
Acquired by Sands Petroleum AB 01/15/1998
Each share Common no par exchanged for (0.86956521) Sponsored GDR for B Shares

INTERNATIONAL PETE LTD (BC)
Merged into Consolidated International Petroleum Corp. 06/01/1985
Each share Common no par exchanged for (0.3278688) share Common no par
Consolidated International Petroleum Corp. name changed to International Petroleum Corp. 06/30/1986 which was acquired by Sands Petroleum AB 01/15/1998

INTERNATIONAL PETRODATA INC (DE)
Each share Common 1¢ par exchanged for (0.005) share Class A Common $2 par 04/18/1986
Each share Class A Common $2 par exchanged for (0.002) share Class B Common $1,000 par 03/31/1989
Voluntarily dissolved 09/11/2008
Details not available

INTERNATIONAL PETROLEUM CO., LTD. (CANADA)
Each share Preferred $5 par exchanged for (2) shares Conv. Preferred $2.50 par 00/00/1929
Each share old Common no par exchanged for (2) shares new Common no par 00/00/1929
Each share new Common no par received distribution of $0.361 cash 12/31/1974
Voluntarily dissolved 10/21/1976
Details not available

INTERNATIONAL PETROLEUM CORP. (WA)
Automatically dissolved for non-payment of annual license fees 7/1/57

INTERNATIONAL PETROLEUM HOLDING CORP. (UT)
Name changed to Federal Gold & Silver, Inc. 07/01/1968
(See Federal Gold & Silver, Inc.)

INTERNATIONAL PETROLEUM PROCESS INC. (DE)
Charter cancelled and declared inoperative and void for non-payment of taxes 4/1/52

INTERNATIONAL PETROREAL OIL CORP (AB)
Reincorporated 06/28/2007
Place of incorporation changed from (BC) to (ALTA) 06/28/2007
Each share Common no par exchanged for (0.1) share Common no par
Name changed to PetroReal Energy Inc. 09/15/2008

INTERNATIONAL PHARMACEUTICAL PRODS INC (MN)
Plan of reorganization under Chapter 11 Federal Bankruptcy proceedings confirmed 08/26/1991
No stockholders' equity

INTERNATIONAL PHARMACY OUTLETS INC (NV)
Name changed to Bionic Products, Inc. 12/11/2006
Bionic Products, Inc. recapitalized as Texas Oil & Minerals Inc. 02/01/2012

INTERNATIONAL PHARMADYNE LTD (BC)
Delisted from Vancouver Stock Exchange 03/05/1993

INTERNATIONAL PHASOR TELECOM LTD (BC)
Common no par split (4) for (1) by issuance of (3) additional shares 11/23/1982
Struck off register and declared dissolved for failure to file returns 07/10/1990

INTERNATIONAL PHOENIX CAPITAL CORP. (ON)
Name changed to Fairway Automotive Industries Ltd. 9/25/86
Fairway Automotive Industries Ltd. recapitalized as Fairway Industries Ltd. 2/26/88 which recapitalized as Pharmaglobe Inc. (ONT) 3/14/94 which reincorporated in Delaware 3/1/2001 which name changed to Pharmaglobe America Group, Inc. 5/12/2004

INTERNATIONAL PHOENIX ENERGY CORP (BC)
Merged into Aegis Resources Ltd. 08/01/1990
Each share Common no par exchanged for (0.125) share Common no par
Aegis Resources Ltd. recapitalized as New Aegis Resources Ltd. 03/17/1993 which was acquired by Norcan Resources Ltd. 08/19/1994 which recapitalized as Odyssey Exploration Inc. 06/07/2000 which recapitalized as Consolidated Odyssey Exploration Inc. 12/08/2000 which reorganized as Odyssey Petroleum Corp. 08/25/2005 which recapitalized as Petrichor Energy Inc. 03/03/2011

INTERNATIONAL PHOTOCOPY CORP. (IL)
Involuntarily dissolved 11/12/65

INTERNATIONAL PHOTON CORP. (DE)
Acquired by Photon, Inc. 1/25/68
Each share Capital Stock $1 par exchanged for (0.7) share Common $1 par
(See Photon, Inc.)

INTERNATIONAL PICTURE SHOW CO (GA)
Administratively dissolved 7/23/95

INTERNATIONAL PIPE & CERAMICS CORP. (DE)
Name changed to Interpace Corp. 4/25/68
Interpace Corp. merged into Clevepak Corp. 8/15/83
(See Clevepak Corp.)

INTERNATIONAL PIPE LTD (HONG KONG)
Name changed to K. Wah Construction Materials Ltd. 05/00/1997
K. Wah Construction Materials Ltd. name changed to Galaxy Entertainment Group Ltd. 11/09/2005
(See Galaxy Entertainment Group Ltd.)

INTERNATIONAL PIT BOSS GAMING INC (NV)
Each share old Common $0.001 par exchanged for (0.001) share new Common $0.001 par 09/26/2005
New Common $0.001 par split (10) for (1) by issuance of (9) additional shares payable 03/24/2006 to holders of record 03/20/2006 Ex date - 03/27/2006
Name changed to Logo Industries Corp. 03/23/2006
Logo Industries Corp. reorganized as Malwin Ventures, Inc. 01/22/2009

INTERNATIONAL PIZZA CORP (FL)
Name changed to QPQ Corp. 10/24/1995
QPQ Corp. name changed to Regenesis Holding Inc. 11/04/1997 which name changed to Fuelnation Inc. 10/19/2000
(See Fuelnation Inc.)

INTERNATIONAL PIZZA CORP (UT)
Name changed to Prime Collateral, Inc. 05/22/1990
(See Prime Collateral, Inc.)

INTERNATIONAL PIZZA GROUP INC (FL)
Reincorporated under the laws of Delaware as Technology Horizons Corp. 06/01/1998
Technology Horizons Corp. name changed to CDKnet.com, Inc. 12/16/1998 which name changed to Arkados Group, Inc. 09/06/2006 which name changed to Solbright Group, Inc. 11/07/2017

INTERNATIONAL PK WEST FINL CORP (BC)
Struck off register and declared dissolved for failure to file returns 11/28/86

INTERNATIONAL PLASTICS INC (KS)
Each share Common $1 par exchanged for (0.25) share Common no par 5/1/72
Stock Dividend - 100% 3/31/77
Chapter 11 bankruptcy proceedings converted to Chapter 7 4/27/81
No stockholders' equity

INTERNATIONAL PLATINUM CORP (ON)
Recapitalized as International Precious Metals Corp. (ON) 10/23/1995
Each share Common no par exchanged for (0.1) share Common no par
International Precious Metals Corp. (ON) reorganized in Wyoming as Innotelco, Inc. 04/05/2005 which recapitalized as Green America Land Holdings, Inc. 04/24/2008 which name changed to Green Card Capital Corp. 03/10/2009 which name changed to CUBA Beverage Co. 09/27/2010

INTERNATIONAL PLC AUTOPARK INC (BC)
Delisted from Vancouver Stock Exchange 04/20/1992

INTERNATIONAL POLARIS ENERGY CORP (BC)
Acquired by O'Shanter Development Co. Ltd. 11/13/90
Each share Common no par exchanged for $0.20 principal amount of Secured Promissory Notes due 10/31/92 and $0.20 cash

INTERNATIONAL PORTLAND CEMENT CO.
Name changed to Spokane Portland Cement Co. in 1933
Dissolution of Spokane Portland Cement Co. was approved 1/6/56

INTERNATIONAL POST LTD (DE)
Name changed 2/10/94
Name changed from International Post Group Inc. to International Post Ltd. 2/10/94
Name changed to Video Services Corp. 8/27/97
Video Services Corp. merged into AT&T Corp. 12/21/2000 which merged into AT&T Inc. 11/18/2005

INTERNATIONAL POSTAL SYSTEMS, INC. (NV)
Charter revoked for failure to file reports and pay fees 03/03/1975

INTERNATIONAL POTENTIAL EXPLS INC (BC)
Name changed to Banyan Industries International Inc. 04/12/1991
Banyan Industries International Inc. name changed to Incentive Design Group Ltd. 11/19/1991 which recapitalized as Envoy Communications Group Inc. 01/22/1996 which name changed to Envoy Capital Group, Inc. 04/05/2007 which merged into Merus Labs International Inc. (New) 12/22/2011
(See Merus Labs International Inc. (New))

INTERNATIONAL POTTER DISTILLING CORP (CANADA)
Each share old Common no par exchanged for (0.25) share new Common no par 09/30/1991
Name changed to Cascadia Brands Inc. 03/30/1995
(See Cascadia Brands Inc.)

INTERNATIONAL POULTRY INC (DE)
Recapitalized as Carley Enterprises, Inc. 08/15/2005
Each share Common $0.001 par exchanged for (0.01) share Common $0.001 par
(See Carley Enterprises, Inc.)

INTERNATIONAL POWER & PAPER CO OF NEWFOUNDLAND LTD.
Name changed to Bowater's Newfoundland Pulp & Paper Mills, Ltd. in 1938
Bowater's Newfoundland Pulp & Paper Mills, Ltd. name changed to Bowaters Newfoundland Ltd. 9/19/66

INTERNATIONAL POWER CO. LTD. (CANADA)
99.78% held by Canadian International Power Co. Ltd. as of 12/31/1974
Public interest eliminated

INTERNATIONAL PWR MACHS CORP (DE)
Merged into Exide Electronics Group, Inc. 2/8/95
Each share Common 10¢ par exchanged for (0.2105) share Common 1¢ par
(See Exide Electronics Group, Inc.)

INTERNATIONAL PWR PLC (UNITED KINGDOM)
Each Sponsored ADR for Ordinary no par received distribution of (1) Innogy Holdings PLC Sponsored ADR for Ordinary payable 10/02/2000 to holders of record 09/29/2000 Ex date - 10/03/2000
ADR agreement terminated 07/25/2012
Each Sponsored ADR for Ordinary no par exchanged for $65.05752 cash

INTERNATIONAL POWER SECURITIES CORP.
Reorganized 00/00/1951
Preferred holders received $17.50 in cash and a receipt for any possible future cash payments
No Common stockholders' equity

INTERNATIONAL POWERHOUSE ENERGY CORP (BC)
Name changed to Sea Breeze Power Corp. 7/30/2003

INTERNATIONAL POWERTECH SYS INC (BC)
Class A Common no par split (2) for (1) by issuance of (1) additional share 10/27/1987
Recapitalized as Powertech Industries Inc. 01/20/1992
Each share Class A Common no par exchanged for (0.2) share Class A Common no par
Powertech Industries Inc. name changed to Powertech Uranium Corp. 06/05/2006 which recapitalized as Azarga Uranium Corp. 10/31/2014

INTERNATIONAL PPTYS GROUP LTD (AB)
Each share Common no par exchanged for (1) share Redeemable Preferred no par and (1) share Class A no par 10/22/2001
Each share Pre-Redemption Preferred exchanged for approximately (0.31) share Post-Redemption Preferred and $0.50 cash 11/29/2001
Each share Ser. 1 Post-Redemption Preferred exchanged for approximately (0.5125) share Ser. 2 Post-Redemption Preferred and $0.39975 cash 04/11/2002
Each share Post-Redemption Preferred Ser. 2 exchanged for approximately (0.4818) share old Preferred and $0.424924 cash 08/14/2003
Old Preferred reclassified as new Preferred 04/03/2006
New Preferred called for redemption at $0.40 on 03/13/2007
Recapitalized as Acorn Income Corp. 03/24/2009
Each share Class A no par exchanged for (0.02) share Class A no par
(See Acorn Income Corp.)

INTERNATIONAL PRAXIS RESOURCE CORP (BC)
Struck off register and declared dissolved for failure to file returns 5/3/96

INTERNATIONAL PRECIOUS METALS CORP (ON)
Reorganized under the laws of Wyoming as Innotelco, Inc. 04/05/2005
Each share Common no par exchanged for (0.1) share Common no par
Innotelco, Inc. recapitalized as Green America Land Holdings, Inc. 04/24/2008 which name changed to Green Card Capital Corp. 03/10/2009 which name changed to CUBA Beverage Co. 09/27/2010

INTERNATIONAL PRIME TECHNOLOGIES INC (BC)
Cease trade order effective 01/25/2000

INTERNATIONAL PRINTING INK CORP.
Name changed to Interchemical Corp. in 1937
Interchemical Corp. name changed to Inmont Corp. 4/15/69 which merged into Carrier Corp. 12/27/77 which was acquired by United Technologies Corp. 7/6/79

INTERNATIONAL PRISM EXPL LTD (BC)
Recapitalized as Prism Resources Inc. 3/15/95
Each share Common no par exchanged for (1/3) share Common no par

INTERNATIONAL PRODS INC (UT)
Involuntarily dissolved 05/01/1987

INTERNATIONAL PRODUCTIONS, INC. (CA)
Charter revoked for failure to file reports and pay fees 11/14/67

INTERNATIONAL PRODUCTS CO.
Acquired by International Products Corp. 00/00/1926
Details not available

INTERNATIONAL PRODUCTS CORP. (DE)
Common no par changed to $10 par in 1943
Common $10 par changed to $5 par in 1952
Stock Dividends - 10% 1/14/54; 10% 2/14/57
Name changed to Packers Liquidating Corp. 7/25/66
Packers Liquidating Corp. acquired by Ogden Corp. 7/27/66 which name changed to Covanta Energy Corp. 3/14/2001
(See Covanta Energy Corp.)

INTERNATIONAL PROFESSIONAL COLLEGE INC (FL)
Completely liquidated 9/24/71
Each share Common 1¢ par exchanged for (1) share World Acceptance Corp. (DE) Common 1¢ par
(See World Acceptance Corp. (DE))

INTERNATIONAL PROPERTIES, INC. (MN)
Name changed to Knutson Companies, Inc. 4/24/63
(See Knutson Companies, Inc.)

INTERNATIONAL PROPERTIES, INC. (NM)
Charter forfeited for failure to file returns and pay taxes 10/19/79

INTERNATIONAL PROPERTIES CORP. (UT)
Each share old Common 10¢ par exchanged for (0.1) share new Common 10¢ par 8/21/76
Reorganized under the laws of Delaware as Plasteel International, Inc. 4/12/88
Each share Common 10¢ par exchanged for (0.5) share Common $0.001 par
Plasteel International, Inc. (Del.) name changed to Trans-World Pharmaceuticals, Inc. 3/9/89

INTERNATIONAL PPTY EXCHANGE INC (NV)
Company believed out of business 05/23/1986
Details not available

INTERNATIONAL PROPRIETARIES, INC. (DE)
No longer in existence having become inoperative and void for non-payment of taxes 4/1/64

INTERNATIONAL PROTEINS CORP (NY)
Common $1 par changed to 50¢ par and (1) additional share issued 8/1/66
Common 50¢ par changed to 16-2/3¢ par and (2) additional shares issued 7/1/69
Name changed to GR Foods, Inc. 6/1/90
GR Foods, Inc. name changed to Ground Round Restaurants, Inc. 6/18/91
(See Ground Round Restaurants, Inc.)

INTERNATIONAL PROTN TECHNOLOGIES INC (UT)
Name changed to HyperSecur Corp. 3/4/99

INTERNATIONAL PUBG LTD (ENGLAND)
Acquired by Reed International PLC 08/21/1970
Each ADR for Ordinary exchanged for 22s6d principal amount of 10% Unsecured Loan Stock and (0.3125) ADR's for Ordinary
Reed Intenational PLC name changed to Reed Elsevier PLC 04/22/2002
which reorganized as RELX PLC 07/01/2015

INTERNATIONAL PUBLIC SERVICE CORP.
Dissolved in 1926

INTERNATIONAL PULP CO.
Name changed to International Talc Co., Inc. and Common no par changed to $5 par in 1944

INTERNATIONAL PURSUIT CORP (ON)
Recapitalized as Apollo Gold Corp. (ON) 06/24/2002
Each share Common no par exchanged for (0.02295157) share Common no par
Apollo Gold Corp. (ON) reincorporated in Yukon 05/28/2003 which recapitalized as Brigus Gold Corp. (YT) 06/25/2010 which reincorporated in Canada 06/09/2011
(See Brigus Gold Corp.)

INTERNATIONAL PYRAMID MINES INC (BC)
Merged into American Pyramid Resources Inc. 07/24/1979
Each share Common no par exchanged for (0.2) share Common no par
(See American Pyramid Resources Inc.)

INTERNATIONAL R S V RESOURCE CORP (BC)
Recapitalized as Harambee Mining Corp. 05/05/1997
Each share Common no par exchanged for (0.1) share Common no par
Harambee Mining Corp. recapitalized as Neuer Kapital Corp. 01/03/2002 which name changed to Crescent Resources Corp. 08/03/2005 which recapitalized as Coventry Resources Inc. 01/09/2013
(See Coventry Resources Inc.)

INTERNATIONAL RADIO CORP. (MI)
Name changed to International Industries, Inc. (MI) in 1939
International Industries, Inc. (MI) name changed to Argus, Inc. (MI) in 1944 which name changed to Argus Cameras, Inc. in 1950 which was acquired by Sylvania Electric Products, Inc. 1/2/57 which merged into General Telephone & Electronics Corp. 3/5/59 which name changed to GTE Corp. 7/1/82 which merged into Verizon Communications Inc. 6/30/2000

INTERNATIONAL RAILROADS' WEIGHING CORP. (IN)
Name changed to Railweight, Inc. 3/21/66
Railweight, Inc. merged into Mangood Corp. (Del.) 11/26/79 which name changed to Howe Richardson Inc. 12/31/87
(See Howe Richardson Inc.)

INTERNATIONAL RAILWAY CO.
Reorganized as Niagara Frontier Transit System, Inc. in 1950
No stockholders' equity

INTERNATIONAL RANWICK LTD. (ON)
Name changed to International Molybdenum Mines Ltd. 08/00/1959
International Molybdenum Mines Ltd. merged into Pax International Mines Ltd. 01/31/1962 which recapitalized as Geo-Pax Mines Ltd. 09/00/1968
(See Geo-Pax Mines Ltd.)

INTERNATIONAL RD DYNAMICS INC (CANADA)
Reincorporated 08/28/1997
Place of incorporation changed from (SK) to (Canada) 08/28/1997
Acquired by Wi-LAN Inc. 06/05/2017
Each share Common no par exchanged for $4.25 cash
Note: Unexchanged certificates will be cancelled and become without value 06/05/2020

INTERNATIONAL RE-INSURANCE CORP. (DE)
Reincorporated 5/18/31
State of incorporation changed from (CA) to (DE) 5/18/31
No longer in existence having become inoperative and void for non-payment of taxes 4/1/35

INTERNATIONAL RLTY GROUP INC (DE)
Name changed to Qualton Inc. 10/17/2000
(See Qualton Inc.)

INTERNATIONAL REC & SPORTS INC (CO)
Declared defunct and inoperative for failure to pay taxes and file reports 10/21/72

INTERNATIONAL REC CORP (DE)
Ctfs. dated after 05/06/1970
Merged into Open Road Industries, Inc. 04/24/1974
Each share Common 10¢ par exchanged for $3.75 cash

INTERNATIONAL RECORD CARRIER INC (NY)
Dissolved by proclamation 9/29/93

INTERNATIONAL RECOVERY CORP (FL)
Common 1¢ par split (3) for (2) by issuance of (0.5) additional share 6/27/95
Name changed to World Fuel Services Corp. 8/21/95

INTERNATIONAL RECREATION CORP. (DE)
Ctfs. dated prior to 1/1/67
Charter cancelled and declared inoperative and void for non-payment of taxes 4/1/66
Note: Although some certificates were issued in late 1966, the above cancellation date is correct

INTERNATIONAL RECTIFIER CORP (DE)
Reincorporated 12/03/1979
Stock Dividend - 100% 06/01/1960
State of incorporation changed from (CA) to (DE) 12/03/1979
Common $1 par split (2) for (1) by issuance of (1) additional share 10/28/1983
Common $1 par split (3) for (2) by issuance of (0.5) additional share 12/14/1984
Common $1 par split (2) for (1) by issuance of (1) additional share 12/22/1995
Acquired by Infineon Technologies AG 01/13/2015
Each share Common $1 par exchanged for $40 cash

INTERNATIONAL REEF RES LTD (AB)
Merged into UTS Energy Corp. 06/30/1998
Each share Common no par exchanged for (0.57142857) share Common no par
UTS Energy Corp. merged into SilverBirch Energy Corp. 10/01/2010 which merged into SilverWillow Energy Corp. 04/04/2012
(See SilverWillow Energy Corp.)

INTERNATIONAL REFINERIES, INC. (WI)
Assets sold to Continental Oil Co. (DE) on a (1) for (12.98420255) basis 4/28/59
Continental Oil Co. (DE) name changed to Conoco Inc. 7/2/79 which was acquired by Du Pont (E.I.) De Nemours & Co. 9/30/81

INTERNATIONAL REMOTE IMAGING SYS INC (DE)
Reincorporated 00/00/1987
State of incorporation changed from (CA) to (DE) and Common no par changed to 1¢ 00/00/1987
Each share 7% Conv. Preferred Ser. 1 no par exchanged for (6.5775) shares Common 1¢ par 07/15/1987
Each share old Common 1¢ par exchanged for (0.2) share new Common no par 07/09/1993
Name changed to IRIS International, Inc. 12/18/2003
(See IRIS International, Inc.)

INTERNATIONAL REP AIRCRAFT MFG CORP (BC)
Name changed to Urban Juice & Soda Co. Ltd. (BC) 05/27/1993
Urban Juice & Soda Co. Ltd. (BC) reincorporated in Wyoming 12/31/1999 which reincorporated in Washington as Jones Soda Co. 08/03/2000

INTERNATIONAL RESH & DEV CORP (DE)
Common $1 par split (2) for (1) by issuance of (1) additional share 08/23/1977
Common $1 par changed to 50¢ par and (1) additional share issued 05/24/1978
Common 50¢ par split (2) for (1) by issuance of (1) additional share 09/12/1988
Company filed a petition under Chapter 11 Federal Bankruptcy Code 09/26/1995
Stockholders' equity unlikely

INTERNATIONAL RESH DEV INC (UT)
Name changed to QB Manufacturing & Marketing, Inc. 11/01/1982
QB Manufacturing & Marketing, Inc. name changed to QB International, Inc. 03/07/1983 which recapitalized as Quantec International Corp. 10/24/1983
(See Quantec International Corp.)

INTERNATIONAL RESH LAB INC (NJ)
Name changed to Diagnostic Health Services, Inc. (NJ) 11/8/91
Diagnostic Health Services, Inc. (NJ) reincorporated in Delaware 11/23/92
(See Diagnostic Health Services, Inc. (DE))

INTERNATIONAL RESISTANCE CO. (DE)
Name changed to IRC, Inc. 12/16/65
IRC, Inc. merged into TRW Inc. 2/19/68 which merged into Northrop Grumman Corp. 12/11/2002

INTERNATIONAL RESORT DEVELOPERS INC (ID)
Reincorporated under the laws of Tennessee as Ameristar International Holdings Corp. 1/22/98
(See Ameristar International Holdings Corp.)

INTERNATIONAL RESORTS & ENTMT GROUP INC (FL)
Recapitalized as Raven Moon International, Inc. 12/30/1998
Each (15) shares Common $0.001 par exchanged for (1) share Common $0.001 par
Raven Moon International, Inc. recapitalized as Raven Moon Entertainment, Inc. 09/01/2001 which recapitalized as Made in America Entertainment, Inc. 08/29/2008

INTERNATIONAL RESOURCE MGMT INC (FL)
Name changed to North American Exploration Corp. 6/17/97

INTERNATIONAL RESOURCES FUND, INC. (DE)
Acquired by Investment Co. of America 6/28/65
Each share Capital Stock 1¢ par exchanged for (0.40086) share Common $1 par

INTERNATIONAL RETAIL SYS INC (WY)
Reincorporated 09/11/1992
Place of incorporation changed from (BC) to (WY) 09/11/1992
Name changed to Canmax, Inc. (WY) 11/30/1994
Canmax, Inc. (WY) reincorporated in Delaware as ARDIS Telecom & Technologies, Inc. 02/01/1999 which name changed to Dial-Thru International Corp. 01/20/2000 which name changed to Rapid Link, Inc. 11/28/2005 which name changed to Spot Mobile International Ltd. 06/10/2010
(See Spot Mobile International Ltd.)

INTERNATIONAL REX VENTURES INC (BC)
Recapitalized as Prosperex Minerals Corp. 09/17/1990
Each share Common no par exchanged for (0.5) share Common no par
Prosperex Minerals Corp. name changed to NAV Master Technologies Inc. 08/06/1991 which recapitalized as Starpoint Systems Inc. 02/23/1994 which name changed to Starpoint Goldfields Inc. 05/27/1996
(See Starpoint Goldfields Inc.)

INTERNATIONAL RHODES RES LTD (BC)
Recapitalized as Consolidated Rhodes Resources Ltd. 02/16/1989
Each share Capital Stock no par exchanged for (0.2) share Common no par
Consolidated Rhodes Resources Ltd. recapitalized as Fairhaven Resources Ltd. 03/04/1992 which recapitalized as International Fairhaven Resources Ltd. 05/29/2002
(See International Fairhaven Resources Ltd.)

INTERNATIONAL RICE BRAN INDS LTD (BC)
Recapitalized as Blue Star Investment Ltd. 03/13/1990
Each share Common no par exchanged for (0.33333333) share Common no par
(See Blue Star Investment Ltd.)

INTERNATIONAL RICHEY PAC CABLEVISION LTD (BC)
Name changed to Richey Communications Ltd. 02/13/1995
(See Richey Communications Ltd.)

INTERNATIONAL RILEY RES LTD (BC)
Recapitalized as Wind River Resources Ltd. 11/22/2001
Each share Common no par exchanged for (0.2) share Common no par
Wind River Resources Ltd. recapitalized as Teslin River Resources Corp. 01/03/2008 which recapitalized as Siyata Mobile Inc. 07/29/2015

INTERNATIONAL ROCHESTER ENERGY CORP (BC)
Reorganized under the laws of Alberta as Rochester Energy Corp. 07/29/2004
Each share Common no par exchanged for (0.11111111) share Common no par
Rochester Energy Corp. merged into Southern Pacific Resource Corp. 03/04/2009

INTERNATIONAL RORAIMA GOLD CORP (BC)
Delisted from Canadian Venture Exchange 12/28/2001

INTERNATIONAL ROYALON MINERALS INC (BC)
Recapitalized as International Markatech Corp. 07/20/1987
Each share Common no par exchanged for (0.33333333) share Common no par
International Markatech Corp. recapitalized as Markatech Industries Corp. 11/03/1995 which recapitalized as Ameratech Systems Corp. 02/12/2001
(See Ameratech Systems Corp.)

INTERNATIONAL RTY & OIL CO (NV)
Common 5¢ par changed to $0.0166 par and (2) additional shares issued 06/09/1981
Recapitalized as Signature Motorcars Inc. 08/02/1996
Each share Common $0.0166 par exchanged for (0.04761904) share Common $0.0167 par
Signature Motorcars Inc. recapitalized as Local Telecom Systems Inc. 04/18/2002 which recapitalized as MBI Financial Inc. 06/06/2006
(See MBI Financial Inc.)

INTERNATIONAL RTY & OIL CO NEW (NV)
Recapitalized as Hondo Minerals, Inc. 06/29/2007
Each share Common $0.001 par exchanged for (0.05) share Common $0.001 par

INTERNATIONAL RTY CORP (CANADA)
Merged into Royal Gold, Inc. 02/22/2010
Each share Common no par exchanged for (0.10203093) share Common 1¢ par and $1.86542552 cash
Note: Canadian residents had the option to receive RG Exchangeco Inc. Exchangeable Shares in lieu of Common

INTERNATIONAL RUSTLESS IRON CORP.
Reorganized as Rustless Iron & Steel Corp. in 1933
Details not available

INTERNATIONAL RYS CENT AMER (NJ)
Common $10 par changed to no par 00/00/1928
Charter declared void for non-payment of taxes 05/13/1981

INTERNATIONAL SAFETY INC. (NV)
Charter revoked for failure to file annual reports 12/1/93

INTERNATIONAL SAFETY-JECT INDS INC (BC)
Recapitalized as Specialty Medical Products Inc. 09/30/1993
Each share Common no par exchanged for (0.25) share Common no par
Specialty Medical Products Inc. recapitalized as Fedora Industries Inc. 10/20/1997 which name changed to Airbomb.com Marketing Ltd. (BC) 02/21/2000 which reincorporated in Delaware as airbomb.com, Inc. 05/09/2000 which name changed to RT Petroleum Inc. 05/18/2005
(See RT Petroleum Inc.)

INTERNATIONAL SAFETY RAZOR CORP.
Recapitalized as O'Mahony (Jerry), Inc. in 1951
Each share Class A no par exchanged for (10) shares new Common 10¢ par
Each share Class B no par exchanged for (1) share new Common 10¢ par
O'Mahony (Jerry), Inc. became bankrupt in 1958

INTERNATIONAL SAFFLOWER CORP. (CO)
Bankrupt in May 1963
No stockholders' equity

INTERNATIONAL SALES DEVELOPMENT ASSOCIATION, INC. (OK)
Name changed to Aardvark, Inc. 4/7/70
(See Aardvark, Inc.)

INTERNATIONAL SALES INFORMATION SYS INC (BC)
Name changed to Versatile Mobile Systems (Canada) Inc. (BC) 09/18/2000
Versatile Mobile Systems (Canada) Inc. (BC) reincorporated in Yukon 02/23/2004 which reincorporated in British Columbia as Versatile Systems Inc. 11/16/2005

INTERNATIONAL SALT CO (NJ)
Each share Common $100 par exchanged for (3) shares Common no par 00/00/1930
Common no par split (2) for (1) by issuance of (1) additional share 05/03/1951
Common no par changed to $1 par and (1) additional share issued 11/03/1967
Common $1 par changed to 50¢ par and (1) additional share issued 01/06/1969
Merged into Akzona Inc. 09/30/1970
Each share Common 50¢ par exchanged for (1.3) shares Common $1.25 par
(See Akzona Inc.)

INTERNATIONAL SANTANA RES INC (BC)
Name changed to Image West Entertainment Corp. 12/19/1986

INTERNATIONAL SARGON RES LTD (BC)
Name changed to Canoil Exploration Corp. 07/28/1999
Canoil Exploration Corp. name changed to AMS Homecare Inc. 03/15/2002
(See AMS Homecare Inc.)

INTERNATIONAL SASHA CORP (AB)
Name changed to PanWestern Energy Inc. 06/28/2004
PanWestern Energy Inc. name changed to Valeura Energy Inc. 07/06/2010

INTERNATIONAL SAVANNAH VENTURES LTD (BC)
Name changed to Softcare EC.com, Inc. 06/10/1999
Sofcare EC.com, Inc. name changed to Softcare EC Inc. 10/05/2001 which recapitalized as Open EC Technologies, Inc. 06/23/2003
(See Open EC Technologies, Inc.)

INTERNATIONAL SVGS & LN ASSN LTD (HI)
Reorganized as International Holding Capital Corp. 4/1/85
Each share Common $1 par exchanged for (1) share Common $1 par
International Holding Capital Corp. merged into CB Bancshares, Inc. 4/8/94 which merged into Central Pacific Financial Corp. 9/15/2004

INTERNATIONAL SCANATRON SYS CORP (NY)
Name changed to Victor Graphic Systems, Inc. 1/3/72
(See Victor Graphic Systems, Inc.)

INTERNATIONAL SCANNING DEVICES INC (DE)
Charter cancelled and declared inoperative and void for non-payment of taxes 3/1/75

INTERNATIONAL SEAWAY TRADING CORP (OH)
Common $1 par split (5) for (4) by issuance of (0.25) additional share 1/31/68
Name changed to Resource Recovery Technologies, Inc. 5/26/88
Resource Recovery Technologies, Inc. name changed to Resource Recycling Technologies, Inc. (OH) 11/17/88 which reincorporated in Delaware 6/29/89
(See Resource Recycling Technologies, Inc. (DE))

INTERNATIONAL SECOND HOME CORP (DE)
Adjudicated bankrupt 03/26/1974
Stockholders' equity unlikely

INTERNATIONAL SECS EXCHANGE HLDGS INC (DE)
Name changed 09/01/2006
Issue Information - 10,049,308 shares CL A offered at $18 per share on 03/08/2005
Name changed from International Securities Exchange, Inc. to International Securities Exchange Holdings, Inc. 09/01/2006
Merged into Eurex Frankfurt AG 12/20/2007
Each share Class A Common 1¢ par exchanged for $67.50 cash

INTERNATIONAL SECURITIES CORP. OF AMERICA (MD)
Class A Common no par changed to $1 par 3/27/33
Merged into American General Corp. 11/23/35
Each share 6% Series B and/or 6-1/2% Series C Preferred $100 par exchanged for (1.2) shares $2 Series Preferred $1 par
Each share Class A Common $1 par exchanged for (0.1) share Common 10¢ par
Each share Class B Common exchanged for (0.05) share Common 10¢ par
American General Corp. merged into Equity Corp. 10/17/50 which name changed to Wheelabrator-Frye Inc. 11/4/71 which merged into Signal Companies, Inc. 2/1/83 which merged into Allied-Signal Inc. 9/19/85 which name changed to AlliedSignal Inc. 4/26/93 which name changed to Honeywell International Inc. 12/1/99

INTERNATIONAL SECURITIES TRUST OF AMERICA (MA)
Acquired by International Securities Corp. of America 06/00/1927
Details not available

INTERNATIONAL SECURITY MANAGEMENT CO.
Merged into Wisconsin Investment Co. in 1930
Details not available

INTERNATIONAL SEMI TECH MICROELECTRONICS INC (ON)
Each share Capital Stock no par exchanged for (0.5) share Class A Subordinate no par and (0.5) share Class B Multiple no par 01/27/1992
Name changed to Semi-Tech Corp. 09/14/1994
(See Semi-Tech Corp.)

INTERNATIONAL SEMICONDUCTOR CORP (NV)
Each share old Common $0.001 par exchanged for (0.1) share new Common $0.001 par 03/11/1999
Name changed to Sanitary Environmental Monitoring Labs, Inc. 04/12/2000
Sanitary Environmental Monitoring Labs, Inc. recapitalized as Vietnam United Steel Corp. 08/28/2008 which

INT-INT FINANCIAL INFORMATION, INC.

recapitalized as Vietnam Mining Corp. 07/12/2010 which name changed to Vanguard Mining Corp. 06/03/2014 which name changed to Myson Group, Inc. 06/08/2015

INTERNATIONAL SENIORS HSG CORP (AB)
Name changed to Redux Energy Corp. 09/12/1990
Redux Energy Corp. name changed to Thermal Control Technologies Corp. 10/01/1997
(See Thermal Control Technologies Corp.)

INTERNATIONAL SENSOR TECHNOLOGIES INC (NV)
Recapitalized as BioPulse International, Inc. 3/17/99
Each share Common $0.001 par exchanged for (0.0025) share Common $0.001 par
BioPulse International Inc. recapitalized as Only You, Inc. 1/17/2006

INTERNATIONAL SHARE CORP.
Acquired by Continental Shares, Inc. in 1930
Details not available

INTERNATIONAL SHASTA RES LTD (BC)
Recapitalized as Consolidated Shasta Resources Inc. 05/20/1994
Each share Common $2.50 par exchanged for (0.1) share Common no par
Consolidated Shasta Resources Inc. name changed to Lima Gold Corp. 11/24/1994 which recapitalized as International Lima Resources Corp. 09/20/1999 which name changed to Crosshair Exploration & Mining Corp. 03/01/2004 which name changed to Crosshair Energy Corp. 11/02/2011 which recapitalized as Jet Metal Corp. (BC) 09/23/2013 which reorganized in Canada as Canada Jetlines Ltd. 03/07/2017

INTERNATIONAL SHELTERS INC (TX)
Out of business and declared financially insolvent 1/2/73

INTERNATIONAL SHIPBUILDING CORP. (FL)
Advised bankrupt 00/00/1959
Charter cancelled and company declared dissolved for non-payment of taxes 04/29/1960

INTERNATIONAL SHIPHOLDING CORP (DE)
Each share Common $1 par exchanged for (0.5) share Common no par 10/31/1983
Common no par split (3) for (1) by issuance of (2) additional shares 06/02/1986
Common no par changed to $1 par 10/15/1987
Common $1 par split (5) for (4) by issuance of (0.25) additional share 06/07/1988
Common $1 par split (5) for (4) by issuance of (0.25) additional share 11/17/1995
Plan of reorganization under Chapter 11 Federal Bankruptcy proceedings effective 07/03/2017
No stockholders' equity

INTERNATIONAL SHIPHOLDING CORP (DE)
6% Conv. Exchangeable Preferred called for redemption at $51 plus $0.26 accrued dividends on 02/01/2008
(Additional Information in Active)

INTL SHIPPING ENTERPRISES INC (DE)
Reincorporated under the laws of Marshall Islands as Navios Maritime Holdings Inc. 8/26/2005

INTERNATIONAL SHOE CO. (DE)
Common no par exchanged (4) for (1) 00/00/1927
Name changed to Interco Inc. (Old) 03/02/1966
(See Interco Inc. (Old))

INTERNATIONAL SHOE MFG CORP (DC)
Name changed to GeckoSystems, Inc. (DC) 11/09/2006
GeckoSystems, Inc. (DC) reincorporated in Wyoming as ImagiTrend, Inc. 08/08/2007 which name changed to Castle Technologies, Inc. 04/28/2008 which recapitalized as Hawaiian Hospitality Group, Inc. 08/14/2009

INTERNATIONAL SIGMA SEC INC (BC)
Dissolved 04/28/1989
No stockholders' equity

INTERNATIONAL SIGNAL CO. (AZ)
Charter revoked for failure to file reports and pay fees 9/20/27

INTERNATIONAL SILVER CO. (NJ)
Reorganized under the laws of Connecticut in 1946
Each share 7% Preferred $100 par exchanged for (4) shares 7% Preferred $25 par
Each share Common $50 par exchanged for (4) shares Common $25 par
International Silver Co. (CT) name changed to Insilco Corp. 4/10/69
(See Insilco Corp.)

INTERNATIONAL SILVER CO (CT)
Common $25 par changed to $8.33333333 par and (2) additional shares issued 05/31/1961
Common $8.33333333 par changed to $1 par 04/11/1963
Common $1 par split (3) for (2) by issuance of (1) additional share 11/30/1964
Common $1 par split (5) for (4) by issuance of (0.25) additional share 11/30/1965
Common $1 par split (2) for (1) by issuance of (1) additional share 12/01/1967
Name changed to Insilco Corp. 04/10/1969
(See Insilco Corp.)

INTERNATIONAL SILVER MNG CORP (UT)
Recapitalized as Solar Dynamics Inc. 04/23/1977
Each share Capital Stock 1¢ par exchanged for (0.05) share Capital Stock 1¢ par
Solar Dynamics Inc. name changed to Goldynamics 03/27/1978 which name changed to Nugget Gold Mines, Inc. 10/25/1979
(See Nugget Gold Mines, Inc.)

INTERNATIONAL SILVER RIDGE RES INC (BC)
Each share old Common no par exchanged for (0.33333333) share new Common no par 10/06/2008
Name changed to PNG Gold Corp. 06/13/2011
PNG Gold Corp. name changed to Gen III Oil Corp. 05/16/2017

INTERNATIONAL SINABARB INDS LTD (BC)
Recapitalized as Primero Industries Ltd. 10/15/1990
Each share Common no par exchanged for (0.33333333) share Common no par
Primero Industries Ltd. recapitalized as PMI Ventures Ltd. 03/27/2001 which name changed to PMI Gold Corp. 05/23/2006 which merged into Asanko Gold Inc. 02/10/2014

INTERNATIONAL SKYLINE GOLD CORP (BC)
Merged into International Skyline Gold Corp. (Yukon) 12/18/1996
Each share Common no par exchanged for (1) share Common no par and (1) share Iriana Resources Corp. Common no par
(See each company's listing)

INTERNATIONAL SKYLINE GOLD CORP (YT)
Merged into Skyline Gold Corp. 04/04/2000
Each share Common no par exchanged for (1) share Common no par and (0.125) share Copper Mountain Mines Ltd. Common no par
(See each company's listing)

INTERNATIONAL SLOCAN DEV LTD (BC)
Recapitalized as Slocan Holdings Ltd. 08/15/1995
Each share Common no par exchanged for (0.28571428) share Common no par
Slocan Holdings Ltd. recapitalized as Galaxy Energy Corp. 10/26/1999 which recapitalized as Galaxy Sports Inc. 08/10/2001
(See Galaxy Sports Inc.)

INTERNATIONAL SMART SOURCING INC NEW (DE)
Common $0.001 par split (5) for (1) by issuance of (4) additional shares payable 12/10/2004 to holders of record 12/01/2004 Ex date - 12/13/2004
Name changed to Network 1 Financial Group, Inc. 08/12/2009

INTERNATIONAL SMART SOURCING INC OLD (DE)
Issue Information - 1,250,000 shares COM offered at $4.50 per share on 04/23/1999
Name changed to ChinaB2Bsourcing.com, Inc. 06/15/2000
ChinaB2Bsourcing, Inc. name changed to International Smart Sourcing, Inc. (New) 08/15/2001 which name changed to Network 1 Financial Group, Inc. 08/12/2009

INTERNATIONAL SOFTWARE TECHNOLOGIES CORP (DE)
Recapitalized as TL Industries Inc. 7/21/97
Each share Common $0.001 par exchanged for (0.125) share Common $0.001 par
TL Industries Inc. recapitalized as OT Computer Training Corp. 7/22/98 which recapitalized as COA Development Corp. 7/28/2000 which recapitalized as International Child Care Corp. 12/17/2001 which recapitalized as World Wide Child Care Corp. 5/21/2007

INTERNATIONAL SOVEREIGN ENERGY CORP (AB)
Reorganized under the laws of Canada as Wi2Wi Corp. 02/05/2013
Each share Common no par exchanged for (1) share Preferred no par and (1) share Common no par

INTERNATIONAL SPACE CORP (DE)
Charter cancelled and declared inoperative and void for non-payment of taxes 03/01/1990

INTERNATIONAL SPACE MODULES LTD (BC)
Struck off register and declared dissolved for failure to file returns 08/09/1976

INTERNATIONAL SPECIALTY PRODS INC NEW (DE)
Merged into International Specialty Products Holdings Inc. 2/28/2003

Each share Common 1¢ par exchanged for $10.30 cash

INTERNATIONAL SPECIALTY PRODS INC OLD (DE)
Under plan of reorganization each share Common 1¢ par automatically became (1) share International Specialty Products Inc. (New) Common 1¢ par 7/15/98
(See International Specialty Products Inc. (New))

INTERNATIONAL SPECTAIR RES INC (BC)
Name changed to Camden Oil Corp. 11/05/1991
Camden Oil Corp. name changed to Maxwell Resources Inc. 12/02/1992 which name changed Maxwell Energy Corp. (BC) 05/12/193 which reincorporated in Alberta 09/12/1996 which recapitalized as Maxwell Oil & Gas Ltd. 11/18/1996
(See Maxwell Oil & Gas Ltd.)

INTERNATIONAL SPEEDWAY CORP (FL)
Each (15) shares Common 1¢ par reclassified as (1) share Class B Common 11/4/96
(Additional Information in Active)

INTERNATIONAL SPEEDWAYS, INC. (NC)
Charter suspended for failure to pay taxes 3/1/73

INTERNATIONAL SPIRIT & BEVERAGE GROUP INC (NV)
Recapitalized as International Spirits & Beverage Group, Inc. 09/12/2017
Each share Common $0.00001 par exchanged for (0.00392156) share Common $0.00001 par

INTERNATIONAL SPORTS & MEDIA GROUP INC (NV)
Each share old Common $0.001 par received distribution of (0.01) share Pan American Relations, Inc. Common $0.001 par payable 06/15/2005 to holders of record 06/06/2005 Ex date - 06/02/2005
Each share old Common $0.001 par exchanged for (0.01) share new Common $0.001 par 12/01/2005
Name changed to US Farms, Inc. 07/17/2006

INTERNATIONAL SPORTS AGY INC (NY)
Merged into International Health & Sports, Inc. 3/5/70
Each share Common 1¢ par exchanged for (1) share Common 1¢ par
International Health & Sports, Inc. recapitalized as Medical Health Industries, Inc. 12/28/71
(See Medical Health Industries, Inc.)

INTERNATIONAL SPORTS WAGERING INC (DE)
Name changed to Interactive Systems Worldwide Inc. 03/01/2001
(See Interactive Systems Worldwide Inc.)

INTERNATIONAL SPORTSFEST INC (DE)
Each share old Common $0.00001 par exchanged for (0.005) share new Common $0.002 par 11/09/1992
Name changed to Pride, Inc. 02/01/1994
Pride, Inc. recapitalized as Mason Hill Holdings Inc. 10/01/1999 which name changed to Attitude Drinks Inc. 06/18/2008

INTERNATIONAL-STACEY CORP.
Acquired by Dresser Industries, Inc. (PA) 00/00/1944
Each share Preferred exchanged for (3.6842) shares Common $1 par
Each share Common exchanged for (0.198) share Common no par
(See Dresser Industries, Inc. (PA))

INTERNATIONAL STAR RES LTD (BC)
Delisted from Vancouver Stock Exchange 03/01/1999

INTERNATIONAL STARTECK INDS LTD (BC)
Delisted from NEX 08/07/2008

INTERNATIONAL STD RES LTD (BC)
Recapitalized as First Standard Mining Ltd. 03/15/1988
Each share Capital Stock no par exchanged for (0.2) share Common no par
First Standard Mining Ltd. name changed to First Standard Ventures Ltd. 07/16/1993 which recapitalized as LRG Restaurant Group, Inc. 09/05/1995
(See LRG Restaurant Group, Inc.)

INTERNATIONAL STDS GROUP LTD (DE)
Each share old Common $0.00001 par exchanged for (0.1) share new Common $0.00001 par 04/27/1992
Recapitalized as Total World Telecommunications, Inc. 10/16/1996
Each (15) shares new Common $0.00001 par exchanged for (1) share Common $0.00001 par
Total World Telecommunications, Inc. name changed to Whitehall Enterprises Inc. 02/10/1999
(See Whitehall Enterprises Inc.)

INTERNATIONAL STEEL CO. (IN)
Proclaimed dissolved 5/11/92

INTERNATIONAL STEEL TUBE CO. (DE)
Charter cancelled and declared inoperative and void for non-payment of taxes 3/18/25

INTERNATIONAL STERLING HLDGS INC (BC)
Dissolved 00/00/1994
No stockholders' equity

INTERNATIONAL STL GROUP INC (DE)
Issue Information - 16,500,000 shares COM offered at $28 per share on 12/11/2003
Merged into Mittal Steel Co. N.V. 04/15/2005
Each share Common 1¢ par exchanged for either (1.21740) shares Class A Common 1¢ par or (0.58489548) shares Class A Common 1¢ par and $21.8316 cash
Note: Option to receive stock and cash expired 04/20/2005
Mittal Steel Co. N.V. name changed to ArcelorMittal (Netherlands) 01/30/2007 which reincorporated in Luxembourg 09/03/2007 which merged into ArcelorMittal S.A. 11/13/2007

INTERNATIONAL STRETCH PRODS INC (DE)
Common $1 par split (4) for (3) by issuance of (1/3) additional share 12/10/63
Charter cancelled and declared inoperative and void for non-payment of taxes 3/1/87

INTERNATIONAL SUBMARINE SAFARIS CDA LTD (BC)
Delisted from Vancouver Stock Exchange 01/31/1990

INTERNATIONAL SUNEVA RES LTD (BC)
Recapitalized as Nevsun Resources Ltd. 12/19/1991
Each share Common no par exchanged for (0.25) share Common no par

INTERNATIONAL SUNSTATE VENTURES LTD (BC)
Recapitalized as Thelon Ventures Ltd. 05/23/2002
Each share Common no par exchanged for (0.33333333) share Common no par
Thelon Ventures Ltd. recapitalized as Thelon Capital Ltd. 02/04/2010 which name changed to THC BioMed Intl Ltd. 04/29/2015 which name changed to Global Li-Ion Graphite Corp. 07/14/2017

INTERNATIONAL SUPERCELL LTD (NV)
Name changed to Bargaincity.com, Inc. 03/25/1999
(See Bargaincity.com, Inc.)

INTERNATIONAL SUPERPOWER CORP. (MD)
Common no par changed to $1 par 00/00/1932
Merged into Bullock Fund, Ltd. 11/10/1932
Each share Common $1 par exchanged for (1.1) shares Capital Stock $1 par
Bullock Fund, Ltd. name changed to Bullock Growth Shares, Inc. 04/08/1985 which merged into Chemical Fund, Inc. 03/13/1987 which name changed to Alliance Fund, Inc. 04/01/1987 which name changed to Alliance Mid-Capital Growth Fund Inc. 02/01/2002 which name changed to AllianceBernstein Mid-Capital Growth Fund, Inc. 03/31/2003

INTERNATIONAL SURF RESORTS INC (NV)
Name changed to Biozone Pharmaceuticals, Inc. 03/08/2011
Biozone Pharmaceuticals, Inc. (NV) reincorporated in Delaware as Cocrystal Pharma, Inc. 04/15/2014

INTERNATIONAL SURGICAL & PHARMACEUTICAL CORP (NV)
Charter revoked for failure to file reports and pay fees 5/1/90

INTERNATIONAL SUSTAINABILITY GROUP INC (NV)
Each share old Common $0.001 par exchanged for (0.0005) share new Common $0.001 par 07/06/2016
Name changed to Fuquan Capital Management, Inc. 12/08/2017

INTERNATIONAL SYMBIOTICS, INC. (DE)
Charter cancelled and declared inoperative and void for non-payment of taxes 3/1/74

INTERNATIONAL SYNERGY HLDG CO LTD (NV)
Name changed to Along Mobile Technologies, Inc. 12/27/2005
(See Along Mobile Technologies, Inc.)

INTERNATIONAL SYSTCOMS LTD (CANADA)
Recapitalized as Memotec Data Inc. 04/15/1983
Each share Common no par exchanged for (0.1) share Class A Common no par
Memotec Data Inc. name changed to Teleglobe Inc. 08/12/1991 which was acquired by BCE Inc. 11/01/2000

INTERNATIONAL SYS & CTLS CORP (DE)
Each share $1.50 Conv. Preferred Ser. N no par exchanged for (1) share $1.50 Conv. Preferred Ser. 2 no par 06/27/1972
$1.50 Preferred Ser. A no par called for redemption 02/26/1973
Each share $1.50 Part. Preferred no par exchanged for (1) share $1.50 Conv. Preferred Ser. 2 no par 06/27/1972
Each share $1.50 Conv. Preferred Ser. 1 no par exchanged for (1) share $1.50 Conv. Preferred Ser. AA no par 01/05/1978
Each share $1.50 Conv. Preferred Ser. 2 no par exchanged for (1) share $1.50 Conv. Preferred Ser. AA no par 01/05/1978
Each share $1.50 Conv. Preferred Ser. 2A no par exchanged for (1) share $1.50 Conv. Preferred Ser. AA no par 01/05/1978
Each share $1.50 Conv. Preferred Ser. 2C no par exchanged for (1) share $1.50 Conv. Preferred Ser. AA no par 01/05/1978
Each share $1.50 Conv. Preferred Ser. 2D no par exchanged for (1) share $1.50 Conv. Preferred Ser. AA no par 01/05/1978
Each share $1.50 Conv. Preferred Ser. 2E no par exchanged for (1) share $1.50 Conv. Preferred Ser. AA no par 01/05/1978
Each share $1.50 Conv. Preferred Ser. 2F no par exchanged for (1) share $1.50 Conv. Preferred Ser. AA no par 01/05/1978
Each share $1.50 Conv. Preferred Ser. 2G no par exchanged for (1) share $1.50 Conv. Preferred Ser. AA no par 01/05/1978
Each share $1.50 Conv. Preferred Ser. 2H no par exchanged for (1) share $1.50 Conv. Preferred Ser. AA no par 01/05/1978
Each share $1.50 Conv. Preferred Ser. 2I no par exchanged for (1) share $1.50 Conv. Preferred Ser. AA no par 01/05/1978
Each share $1.50 Conv. Preferred Ser. 2J no par exchanged for (1) share $1.50 Conv. Preferred Ser. AA no par 01/05/1978
Each share $1.50 Conv. Preferred Ser. 2K no par exchanged for (1) share $1.50 Conv. Preferred Ser. AA no par 01/05/1978
Each share $1.50 Conv. Preferred Ser. 2L no par exchanged for (1) share $1.50 Conv. Preferred Ser. AA no par 01/05/1978
Each share $1.50 Conv. Preferred Ser. 2M no par exchanged for (1) share $1.50 Conv. Preferred Ser. AA no par 01/05/1978
Each share $1.50 Conv. Preferred Ser. R no par exchanged for (1) share $1.50 Conv. Preferred Ser. AA no par 01/05/1978
5.50% Preferred $100 par called for redemption at $105 on 06/30/2005 (Additional Information in Active)

INTERNATIONAL SYS & TECHNOLOGY INC (FL)
Each share old Common $0.001 par exchanged for (1/3) share new Common $0.001 par 12/15/1993
Proclaimed dissolved for failure to file reports and pay fees 08/23/1996

INTERNATIONAL SYS ASSOC LTD (NY)
Name changed to Mail Mart Industries, Inc. 1/2/73
(See Mail Mart Industries, Inc.)

INTERNATIONAL SYS CORP (NV)
Charter revoked for failure to file reports and pay fees 3/1/83

INTERNATIONAL TAKO INDS INC (AB)
Reincorporated 11/26/2002
Place of incorporation changed from (BC) to (AB) 11/26/2002
Name changed to Ironhorse Oil & Gas Inc. 05/14/2004
Ironhorse Oil & Gas Inc. recapitalized as Pond Technologies Holdings Inc. 02/06/2018

INTERNATIONAL TAPE CARTRIDGE CORP (DE)
Reincorporated 07/03/1968
State of incorporation changed from (NY) to (DE) 07/03/1968
Adjudicated bankrupt 04/21/1970
Stockholders' equity unlikely

INTERNATIONAL TASTY FRIES INC (NV)
Recapitalized as Filtered Souls Entertainment Inc. 11/25/98
Each share Common $0.001 par exchanged for (0.05) share Common $0.001 par
Filtered Souls Entertainment Inc. name changed to Skyline Entertainment, Inc. 3/31/99 which name changed to Quotemedia.Com Inc. 8/19/99 which name changed to Quotemedia, Inc. 3/11/2003

INTERNATIONAL TAURUS RES INC (BC)
Old Common no par split (4) for (1) by issuance of (3) additional shares payable 01/02/1996 to holders of record 12/27/1995
Each share old Common no par exchanged for (0.5) share new Common no par 10/23/1996
Merged into American Bonanza Gold Corp. 03/31/2005
Each share new Common no par exchanged for (0.2) share Common no par
American Bonanza Gold Corp. merged into Kerr Mines Inc. 07/07/2014

INTERNATIONAL TECHNICAL DEV CORP (UT)
Proclaimed dissolved for failure to pay taxes 11/9/74

INTERNATIONAL TECHNICAL INSTRS INC (CO)
Name changed to October Oil Co. (Old) 10/9/79
October Oil Co. (Old) merged into October Oil Co. (New) 10/18/82
(See October Oil Co. (New))

INTERNATIONAL TECHNOLOGIES CORP (CANADA)
Delisted from Toronto Venture Stock Exchange 07/13/2009

INTERNATIONAL TECHNOLOGIES INC (AB)
Recapitalized as Canadian Crude Separators Inc. 05/31/1993
Each share Common no par exchanged for (0.25) share Common no par
Canadian Crude Separators Inc. recapitalized as CCS Income Trust 05/24/2002
(See CCS Income Trust)

INTERNATIONAL TECHNOLOGIES INC (CO)
Administratively dissolved 08/23/1996

INTERNATIONAL TECHNOLOGY CORP (DE)
Common $1 par split (3) for (2) by issuance of (0.5) additional share 05/10/1985
Common $1 par split (2) for (1) by issuance of (1) additional share 09/05/1986
Each share old Common 1¢ par exchanged for (0.25) share new Common 1¢ par 11/20/1996
Name changed to IT Group, Inc. 12/24/1998
(See IT Group, Inc.)

INTERNATIONAL TECHNOLOGY SYS INC (NV)
Name changed to Immunotech Laboratories, Inc. 02/04/2009

INTERNATIONAL TEL & TELEG CORP (DE)
Reincorporated 04/31/1968
Each share Capital Stock $100 par exchanged for (3) shares Capital Stock no par 00/00/1929
Capital Stock no par split (2) for (1) by issuance of (1) additional share 03/05/1959
Capital Stock no par reclassified as Common no par 05/20/1965
Common no par changed to $1 par

and (1) additional share issued 03/07/1968
State of incorporation changed from (MD) to (DE), 4% Conv. Preferred $100 par reclassified as $4 Conv. Preferred no par, 4% Conv. Preferred Ser. B through F $100 par reclassified as $4 Conv. Preferred Ser. B through F no par respectively and Conv. Preference $10 par exchanged for (1.172) shares $4 Conv. Preferred Ser. H no par and $0.425 cash 01/31/1968
$5.25 Preferred no par called for redemption 12/15/1972
$5.25 Preferred Ser. B no par called for redemption 12/15/1972
$5.50 Preferred Ser. L no par called for redemption 12/15/1972
$6 Preferred Ser. M no par called for redemption 12/15/1972
$4 Conv. Preferred no par called for redemption 01/08/1973
$4 Conv. Preferred Ser. B no par called for redemption 01/08/1973
$4 Conv. Preferred Ser. C no par called for redemption 01/08/1973
$4 Conv. Preferred Ser. D no par called for redemption 01/08/1973
$4 Conv. Preferred Ser. E no par called for redemption 09/14/1977
$4 Conv. Preferred Ser. F no par called for redemption 09/14/1977
Name changed to ITT Corp. (DE) 12/31/1983
(See ITT Corp. (DE))

INTERNATIONAL TELDATA CORP (NV)
Name changed 6/12/84
Name changed from International Teldata II Corp. to International Teldata II Corp. 6/12/84
Each share old Common 1¢ par exchanged for (1/3) share new Common 1¢ par 8/4/86
Charter revoked for failure to file reports and pay fees 3/1/96

INTERNATIONAL TELECHARGE INC (DE)
Merged into LDC Acquisition Inc. 3/31/93
Each share Common 1¢ par exchanged for $0.30 cash

INTERNATIONAL TELECOM SVCS INC (DE)
Name changed to Bullet Sports International, Inc. 03/31/1995
(See Bullet Sports International, Inc.)

INTERNATIONAL TELECOMMUNICATION DATA SYS INC (DE)
Merged into Amdocs Ltd. 11/30/1999
Each share Common 1¢ par exchanged for (0.3717) share Common 1¢ par

INTERNATIONAL TELECOMMUNICATIONS INC (NV)
Each share old Common $0.001 par exchanged for (0.005) share new Common $0.001 par 08/29/2005
Name changed to International Technology Systems, Inc. 11/20/2006
International Technology Systems, Inc. name changed to Immunotech Laboratories, Inc. 02/04/2009

INTERNATIONAL TELECOMPUTER NETWORK CORP (DE)
Charter cancelled and declared inoperative and void for non-payment of taxes 4/15/72

INTERNATIONAL TELEGRAPH CO. OF MAINE (ME)
Dissolved 4/1/59

INTERNATIONAL TELEPOOL CORP (BC)
Name changed to U.S. Pay-Tel, Inc. (BC) 08/11/1986
U.S. Pay-Tel, Inc. (BC) reincorporated in Delaware as U.S. Long Distance Corp. 09/29/1987 which name changed to USLD Communications Corp. 08/19/1997 which merged into LCI International Inc. 12/22/1997 which merged into Qwest Communications International Inc. 06/05/1998 which merged into CenturyLink, Inc. 04/01/2011

INTERNATIONAL TELEPRESENCE CDA CORP (CANADA)
Name changed to Isee3D Inc. 04/30/1999

INTERNATIONAL TELESIS INDS CORP (BC)
Name changed to Madonna Educational Group of Canada Ltd. 02/06/1989
(See Madonna Educational Group of Canada Ltd.)

INTERNATIONAL TELEVISION CORP. (DE)
Incorporated 9/24/29
No longer in existence having become inoperative and void for non-payment of taxes 4/1/34

INTERNATIONAL TELEVISION CORP. (DE)
Incorporated 12/20/47
No longer in existence having become inoperative and void for non-payment of taxes 4/1/57

INTERNATIONAL TELO-SERVICE CORP. (DE)
No longer in existence having become inoperative and void for non-payment of taxes 4/1/58

INTERNATIONAL TESSA CAP CORP (BC)
Name changed to Apex Resorts Corp. 10/05/1993
Apex Resorts Corp. recapitalized as A.M.R. Corporate Group Ltd. 11/12/1996 which recapitalized as Consolidated A.M.R. Corporate Ltd. 12/03/1998 which recapitalized as Consolidated A.M.R. Development Corp. 10/17/2000 which recapitalized as West Hawk Development Corp. 01/09/2002

INTERNATIONAL TESTING SVCS INC (DE)
Recapitalized as Eternal Image, Inc. 02/15/2006
Each share Common 1¢ par exchanged for (0.01) share Common $0.001 par
(See Eternal Image, Inc.)

INTERNATIONAL TEX INDS INC (NV)
Common 20¢ par changed to $0.001 par 09/21/1983
Each share old Common $0.001 par exchanged for (0.0005) share new Common $0.001 par 05/21/1998
Note: No holder will receive fewer than (25) shares
Name changed to Kentex Energy Inc. 06/10/1998
Kentex Energy Inc. recapitalized as Home Financing Centers, Inc. 01/13/2000 which recapitalized as WorldWide Indoor Karting, Inc. 07/23/2003 which name changed to Vault Financial Services Inc. 10/08/2003 which name changed to Prime Restaurants, Inc. 04/18/2007 which name changed to BIH Corp. 03/19/2008
(See BIH Corp.)

INTERNATIONAL TEXCAN TECHNOLOGY CORP (BC)
Delisted from Vancouver Stock Exchange 03/07/1990

INTERNATIONAL TEXORO RES LTD (BC)
Recapitalized as Great Western Gold Corp. 07/24/1991
Each share Common no par exchanged for (0.5) share Common no par
Great Western Gold Corp. name changed to Great Western Minerals Group Ltd. (BC) 08/14/2002 which reincorporated in Canada 12/12/2007
(See Great Western Minerals Group Ltd.)

INTERNATIONAL TEXTBOOK CO (PA)
Each share Capital Stock $100 par exchanged for (2) shares Capital Stock no par in 1931
Capital Stock no par split (6) for (1) by issuance of (5) additional shares 1/2/65
Name changed to Intext, Inc. 4/28/72
(See Intext, Inc.)

INTERNATIONAL TEXTILE GROUP INC (DE)
Acquired by Project Ivory Intermediate Holding II Corp. 10/24/2016
Each share Common 1¢ par exchanged for $0.55 cash

INTERNATIONAL THOMSON ORGANISATION LTD (ON)
Common no par split (2) for (1) by issuance of (1) additional share 06/15/1984
Name changed to Thomson Corp. 06/05/1989
Thomson Corp. name changed to Thomson Reuters Corp. 04/17/2008

INTERNATIONAL THOROUGHBRED BREEDERS INC (DE)
Each share Conv. Preferred Ser. A $5 par exchanged for (0.05) share Conv. Preferred Ser. A $100 par 03/12/1992
Each share Common 10¢ par exchanged for (0.05) share Common $2 par 03/12/1992
Chapter 7 bankruptcy proceedings dismissed 03/07/2011
No stockholders' equity

INTERNATIONAL THUNDERBIRD GAMING CORP (YT)
Reincorporated 02/05/1999
Place of incorporation changed from (BC) to (Yukon) 02/05/1999
Name changed to Thunderbird Resorts, Inc. (Yukon) 10/05/2005
Thunderbird Resorts, Inc. (Yukon) reorganized in British Virgin Islands 11/20/2007

INTERNATIONAL THUNDERWOOD EXPLS LTD (CANADA)
Reincorporated 04/27/1987
Place of incorporation changed from (BC) to (Canada) 04/27/1987
Reorganized under the laws of Ontario as Thunderwood Resources Inc.-Les Ressources Thunderwood Inc. 06/01/1989
Each share Common no par exchanged for (0.02) share Common no par
Thunderwood Resources Inc.-Les Ressources Thunderwood Inc. merged into Thundermin Resources Inc. 11/01/1998 which merged into Rambler Metals & Mining PLC 01/12/2016

INTERNATIONAL TICKER TAPE RES LTD (BC)
Name changed to Econogreen Environmental Systems Ltd. 09/03/1993
Econogreen Environmental Systems Ltd. name changed to Voisey Bay Resources Ltd. 06/28/1995 which merged into Twin Gold Corp. 04/04/1997 which name changed to Twin Mining Corp. 03/15/2000 which recapitalized as Atlanta Gold Inc. 03/28/2007

INTERNATIONAL TICKET SCALE CORP. (DE)
Dissolved 12/18/57

INTERNATIONAL TIKA RES LTD (AB)
Reincorporated 09/24/1984
Place of incorporation changed from (BC) to (AB) 09/24/1984
Charter cancelled 09/02/1999

INTERNATIONAL TILLEX ENTERPRISES LTD (BC)
Each share old Common no par exchanged for (3) shares new Common no par 03/10/1986
Struck off register and declared dissolved for failure to file returns 07/05/1991

INTERNATIONAL TIME CORP. (DE)
(Issued only as part of a unit consisting of (1) share International Time Corp. Common $0.001 par, (1) share TMX Ltd. Capital Stock BD12¢ par and (1) share Timex Corp. Common no par)
Common no par changed to 1¢ par 4/17/57
Common 1¢ par changed to $0.001 par 4/28/60
Merged into TCN Corp. 3/15/82
Each Unit exchanged for $65 cash

INTERNATIONAL TIMESHARING CORP (MN)
Merged into United Telecommunications, Inc. 12/31/1975
Each share Common 20¢ par exchanged for (0.153885) share Common $2.50 par
United Telecommunications, Inc. name changed to Sprint Corp. (KS) 02/26/1992 which name changed to Sprint Nextel Corp. 08/12/2005 which merged into Sprint Corp. (DE) 07/10/2013

INTERNATIONAL TIRE & MFG CORP (BC)
Recapitalized as Intirmac Industrial Corp. 12/05/1997
Each share Class B Common no par exchanged for (0.25) share Common no par
Intirmac Industrial Corp. name changed to Sniper Enterprises Inc. 12/07/1998 which name changed to TransAmerican Energy Inc. 08/16/2005 which recapitalized as American Biofuels Inc. 09/12/2018

INTERNATIONAL TME RES INC (BC)
Merged into Chelsea Oil & Gas Ltd. 10/07/2013
Each share Common no par exchanged for (0.5431) share Common no par

INTERNATIONAL TOPAZ BUSINESS DEV CORP (BC)
Name changed to Leopardus Resources Ltd. 08/09/1996
Leopardus Resources Ltd. merged into Zarara Oil & Gas Ltd. (Channel Islands) 02/12/1999 which reorganized in Wyoming as Zara Trading, Inc. 03/05/2007
(See Zara Trading, Inc.)

INTERNATIONAL TOTAL SVCS INC (OH)
Plan of reorganization under Chapter 11 Federal Bankruptcy proceedings confirmed 02/28/2003
Stockholders' equity unlikely

INTERNATIONAL TOTALIZATOR SYS INC (CA)
Common no par split (2) for (1) by issuance of (1) additional share 03/21/1986
Name changed to International Lottery & Totalizator Systems, Inc. 07/13/1994
(See International Lottery & Totalizator Systems, Inc.)

INTERNATIONAL TOURIST ATTRACTIONS (MN)
Name changed to First American Home Corp. and Common 5¢ par changed to 1¢ par 8/9/71

First American Home Corp. name changed to L-S-K Inns Corp. of America 5/10/77

INTERNATIONAL TOURIST ENTMT CORP (U.S. VIRGIN ISLANDS)
Plan of reorganization under Chapter 11 Federal Bankruptcy Code effective 05/06/1997
Each share old Common $0.001 par exchanged for (0.1) share new Common $0.001 par
Reincorporated under the laws of Nevada as ITEC Attractions Inc. 09/20/1999
(See ITEC Attractions Inc.)

INTERNATIONAL TOURNIGAN CORP (BC)
Recapitalized as Tournigan Ventures Corp. (BC) 03/26/2001
Each share Common no par exchanged for (0.1) share Common no par
Tournigan Ventures Corp. (BC) reincorporated in Yukon as Tournigan Gold Corp. 12/30/2002 which reincorporated back under the laws of British Columbia 03/27/2008 which name changed to Tournigan Energy Ltd. 05/06/2008 which recapitalized as European Uranium Resources Ltd. 03/01/2012 which recapitalized as Azarga Metals Corp. 05/31/2016

INTERNATIONAL TOWER HILL MINES LTD OLD (BC)
Plan of Arrangement effective 08/26/2010
Each share Common no par exchanged for (1) share International Tower Hill Mines Ltd. (New) Common no par and (0.5) share Corvus Gold Inc. Common no par
(See each company's listing)

INTERNATIONAL TRADE CTR INC (UT)
Recapitalized as PAB Oil & Mining, Inc. 10/31/80
Each share Common 5¢ par exchanged for (3) shares Common 5¢ par

INTERNATIONAL TRADING & MFG CORP (NV)
Name changed to Genius Products Inc. (NV) 10/12/99
Genius Products Inc. (NV) reincorporated in Delaware 3/2/2005

INTERNATIONAL TRAINING & ED CORP (UT)
Name changed to Digimedia USA Inc. 02/12/1996
Digimedia USA Inc. name changed to Algorhythm Technologies Corp. 07/24/1997 which name changed to Quikbiz Internet Group, Inc. 07/07/1998
(See Quikbiz Internet Group, Inc.)

INTERNATIONAL TRAINING RINKS CORP (AB)
Recapitalized as National Training Rinks Corp. 12/02/1999
Each share Common no par exchanged for (0.1) share Common no par
(See National Training Rinks Corp.)

INTERNATIONAL TRANS ASIA TRADING CORP (BC)
Recapitalized as ITC International Trading Corp. 07/20/1989
Each share Common no par exchanged for (0.2) share Common no par
(See ITC International Trading Corp.)

INTERNATIONAL TRANS INDS INC (DE)
Merged into New ITII, Inc. 03/29/1974
Each share Common $1 par exchanged for $6 cash

INTERNATIONAL TRANSTECH CORP (TN)
Name changed to Automotive Franchise Corp. 2/26/86
(See Automotive Franchise Corp.)

INTERNATIONAL TRANSTECH INC (BC)
Recapitalized as North American Vanadium Inc. 09/02/2005
Each share Common no par exchanged for (0.2) share Common no par
North American Vanadium Inc. name changed to Veraz Petroleum Ltd. (BC) 06/26/2007 which reincorporated in Alberta 01/24/2008 which name changed to AlkaLi3 Resources Inc. 08/16/2016

INTERNATIONAL TRAVEL CDS INC (CO)
Common no par split (4.5) for (1) by issuance of (3.5) additional shares payable 05/01/2002 to holders of record 04/30/2002 Ex date - 05/02/2002
Recapitalized as Stellar Technologies, Inc. (CO) 03/12/2004
Each share Common no par exchanged for (0.25) share Common $0.001 par
Stellar Technologies, Inc. (CO) reincorporated in Delaware as GeM Solutions, Inc. 10/24/2016
(See GeM Solutions, Inc.)

INTERNATIONAL TRIMARK RES LTD (YT)
Recapitalized as Trimark Oil & Gas Ltd. 06/17/1997
Each share Common no par exchanged for (0.5) share Common no par
Trimark Oil & Gas Ltd. recapitalized as Trimark Energy Ltd. 03/21/2002 which name changed to Halo Resources Ltd. (YT) 02/23/2004 which reincorporated in British Columbia 11/16/2004 which merged into Sendero Mining Corp. 07/09/2013

INTERNATIONAL TROJAN DEV CORP (BC)
Recapitalized as Trojan Ventures Inc. 06/20/1991
Each share Common no par exchanged for (0.5) share Common no par
Trojan Ventures Inc. reorganized in Cayman Islands as Alcanta International Education Ltd. 03/26/1999 which name changed to Access International Education Ltd. 01/17/2001

INTERNATIONAL TROJAN EXPLORATIONS INC. (BC)
Merged into Centurion Exploration Inc. (New) 12/28/1982
Each share Common no par exchanged for (0.66666666) share Common no par
Centurion Exploration Inc. (New) merged into Beaver Resources Inc. (New) 06/13/1983
(See Beaver Resources Inc. (New))

INTERNATIONAL TR & FINL SYS INC (FL)
Reincorporated under the laws of Nevada as Marmion Industries Corp. 7/14/2004

INTERNATIONAL TUNGSTEN & MINERALS CORP (NV)
Reincorporated 10/1/82
State of incorporation changed from (UT) to (NV) 10/1/82
Each share Common 10¢ par exchanged for (0.1) share Common 10¢ par
Charter revoked for failure to file reports and pay fees 4/1/85

INTERNATIONAL TURBINE TECHNOLOGIES INC (BC)
Struck off register and declared dissolved for failure to file returns 08/17/1990

INTERNATIONAL TURBOMIST INC (BC)
Struck off register and declared dissolved for failure to file returns 6/10/94

INTERNATIONAL TWO THOUSAND INC (OK)
Charter suspended for failure to pay taxes 02/19/1985

INTERNATIONAL ULTRASONICS, INC. (NJ)
Adjudicated bankrupt 7/23/64
No stockholders' equity

INTERNATIONAL UN RES INC (BC)
Reorganized as Tropical Submarine Safaris Ltd. 01/08/1987
Each share Common no par exchanged for (1) share Common no par
Tropical Submarine Safaris Ltd. recapitalized as International Submarine Safaris (Canada) Ltd. 08/02/1989
(See International Submarine Safaris (Canada) Ltd.)

INTERNATIONAL-UNITED CORP. (WA)
Adjudicated bankrupt 09/13/1971
No stockholders' equity

INTERNATIONAL UNP HLDGS LTD (CANADA)
Reincorporated 08/04/1993
Class A Subordinate no par reclassified as Common no par 06/28/1991
Class B Multiple no par reclassified as Common no par 06/28/1991
Place of incorporation changed from (BC) to (Canada) 08/04/1993
Merged into CHP Investors N.V. 11/01/1999
Each share Common no par exchanged for USD$0.17 cash

INTERNATIONAL URANIUM CORP (ON)
Under plan of merger name changed to Denison Mines Corp. 12/6/2006

INTERNATIONAL URANIUM MINING CO., LTD.
Recapitalized as Acadia Uranium Mines Ltd. 00/00/1949
Each share Capital Stock $1 par exchanged for (0.25) share Capital Stock $1 par
(See Acadia Uranium Mines Ltd.)

INTERNATIONAL UTIL STRUCTURES INC (AB)
Assets sold for the benefit of creditors 04/01/2005
No stockholders' equity

INTERNATIONAL UTILS CORP (MD)
Each share $7 Preferred no par exchanged for (1) share $7 Prior Preferred no par 00/00/1931
Class B no par changed to $1 par 00/00/1932
Recapitalized 00/00/1944
Each share $3.50 Prior Preferred no par exchanged for (1) share $3.50 Preferred $50 par
Each share $1.75 Preferred no par exchanged for (1.9) shares Common $15 par
Each share Class A no par exchanged for (1.4) shares Common $15 par
Each share Class B $1 par exchanged for (0.01) share Common $15 par
Each share Common $15 par exchanged for (3) shares Common $5 par 00/00/1946
Common $5 par split (2) for (1) by issuance of (1) additional share 08/30/1957
Common $5 par changed to $2.50 par and (1) additional share issued 06/05/1963
$2 Conv. Preferred $25 par called for redemption 06/01/1965
$2 Conv. Preferred no par called for redemption 06/26/1970
$4.50 Conv. Preferred no par called for redemption 01/01/1972
$1.32 Conv. Preferred called for redemption 05/12/1972
$6 Preferred Ser. A no par called for redemption 06/15/1972
$6 Preferred Ser. B no par called for redemption 08/11/1972
Common $2.50 par changed to $1.25 par and (1) additional share issued 10/20/1972
Name changed to IU International Corp. 04/27/1973
(See IU International Corp.)

INTERNATIONAL VENDING TECHNOLOGY CORP (BC)
Recapitalized as Universal Movie Butler Inc. 11/12/1985
Each share Common no par exchanged for (0.25) share Common no par
Universal Movie Butler Inc. name changed to Pacific Vending Technology Ltd. 04/15/1986 which name changed to Nelson Vending Technology Ltd. (BC) 07/10/1987 which reincorporated in Canada 07/23/1987 which was acquired by Cinram Ltd. 07/31/1993 which name changed to Cinram International Inc. 06/12/1997 which reorganized as Cinram International Income Fund 05/08/2006

INTERNATIONAL VENTURE ASSOC INC (DE)
Charter cancelled and declared inoperative and void for non-payment of taxes 3/1/86

INTERNATIONAL VENTURE FDG INC (CO)
Name changed to Action Products, Inc. 6/22/87
(See Action Products, Inc.)

INTERNATIONAL VENTURES GROUP INC (DE)
Charter cancelled and declared inoperative and void for non-payment of taxes 3/1/95

INTERNATIONAL VERIFACT INC (CANADA)
Reincorporated 10/01/1984
Place of incorporation changed from (BC) to (Canada) 10/01/1984
5% Conv. Preferred Ser. A no par called for redemption 06/30/1994
Each share old Common no par exchanged for (0.1) share new Common no par 12/30/1994
Merged into IVI Checkmate Corp. 06/25/1998
Each share Common no par exchanged for either (1) share Common 1¢ par or (1) IVI Checkmate Ltd. Exchangeable Share
Note: Non-electors received Exchangeable Shares
(See each company's listing)

INTERNATIONAL VERONEX RES LTD (BC)
Name changed to Veronex Technologies Inc. 12/04/1997
(See Veronex Technologies Inc.)

INTERNATIONAL VESTOR RES LTD (AB)
Under plan of merger name changed to EuroZinc Mining Corp. 04/21/1999
EuroZinc Mining Corp. merged into Lundin Mining Corp. 11/01/2006

INTERNATIONAL VIDEO CORP (DE)
Name changed to Cezar Industries Ltd. 06/01/1983
(See Cezar Industries Ltd.)

INTERNATIONAL VIDEO TAPE RECORDING & PRODUCTION CO., INC. (CA)
Name changed to International Productions, Inc. 4/7/64
International Productions, Inc. charter revoked 11/14/67

INTERNATIONAL VIKING RES INC (BC)
Recapitalized as Saxony Explorations Ltd. (BC) 11/13/1992
Each share Common no par exchanged for (0.25) share Common no par
Saxony Explorations Ltd. (BC) reorganized in Yukon as Century Mining Corp. 09/24/2003 which reincorporated in Canada 07/22/2004 which merged into White Tiger Gold Ltd. 10/20/2011 which name changed to Mangazeya Mining Ltd. 09/23/2013

INTERNATIONAL VINEYARD INC (DE)
Name changed to Waxess Holdings, Inc. 02/11/2011
Waxess Holdings, Inc. name changed to AirTouch Communications, Inc. 08/18/2011

INTERNATIONAL VISUAL SYS LTD (BC)
Liquidated 00/00/1976
Stockholders' equity unlikely

INTERNATIONAL VITAMIN CORP. (DE)
Ctfs. dated prior to 10/22/1941
Acquired by American Home Products Corp. on a (0.125) for (1) basis 10/22/1941
American Home Products Corp. name changed to Wyeth 03/11/2002 which was acquired by Pfizer Inc. 10/15/2009

INTERNATIONAL VITAMIN CORP (DE)
Ctfs. dated after 02/16/1994
Name changed to IVC Industries, Inc. 03/19/1996
(See IVC Industries Inc.)

INTERNATIONAL WALLCOVERINGS LTD (CANADA)
Filed an assignment in bankruptcy 09/30/1999
No stockholders' equity

INTERNATIONAL WASTEWATER SYS INC (BC)
Recapitalized as Sharc International Systems Inc. 09/11/2017
Each share Common no par exchanged for (0.28571428) share Common no par

INTERNATIONAL WATER-GUARD INDS INC (BC)
Name changed to IWG Technologies Inc. 05/16/2011
(See IWG Technologies Inc.)

INTERNATIONAL WAYSIDE GOLD MINES LTD (BC)
Each share old Common no par exchanged for (0.1) share new Common no par 08/18/2005
Each share new Common no par exchanged again for (0.1) share new Common no par 01/16/2009
Name changed to Barkerville Gold Mines Ltd. 01/21/2010

INTERNATIONAL WELLINGTON RES LTD (BC)
Recapitalized as Consolidated Wellington Resources Ltd. 12/12/1983
Each share Capital Stock no par exchanged for (0.2) share Common no par
Consolidated Wellington Resources Ltd. name changed to First Hospitality (Canada) Corp. 09/24/1987 which recapitalized as Southern Pacific Development Corp. 11/05/1991 which recapitalized as Southern Pacific Resource Corp. (BC) 03/03/2006 which reincorporated in Alberta 11/17/2006

INTERNATIONAL WELLNESS ASSN INC (FL)
Administratively dissolved 09/24/1999

INTERNATIONAL WERNER TECHNOLOGIES INC (BC)
Struck off register and declared dissolved for failure to file returns 08/05/1994

INTERNATIONAL WESTN PETE INC (NV)
Name changed to Norris Industries, Inc. 02/26/2018

INTERNATIONAL WESTWARD DEV CORP (BC)
Recapitalized as J.R. Energy Ltd. 04/23/1986
Each share Common no par exchanged for (0.2) share Common no par
(See J.R. Energy Ltd.)

INTERNATIONAL WEX TECHNOLOGIES INC (CANADA)
Name changed to WEX Pharmaceuticals Inc. 10/22/2004
(See WEX Pharmaceuticals Inc.)

INTERNATIONAL WILDCAT RES LTD (BC)
Recapitalized as Wildcat Trading Corp. 10/02/1991
Each share Common no par exchanged for (0.33333333) share Common no par
Wildcat Trading Corp. name changed to Pacific Wildcat Resources Corp. 04/21/1994

INTERNATIONAL WILDROSE RES LTD (BC)
Merged into Colossus Resource Equities Inc. 12/08/1987
Each share Common no par exchanged for (1) share Common no par
Colossus Resource Equities Inc. merged into Prime Resources Corp. (BC) 02/01/1989 which recapitalized as Prime Resources Group Inc. 01/26/1990 which merged into HomeStake Mining Co. 12/03/1998 which merged into Barrick Gold Corp. 12/14/2001

INTERNATIONAL WIRE GROUP INC (DE)
Name changed to International Wire Group Holdings, Inc. 06/01/2011

INTERNATIONAL WIRELESS INC (MD)
Each (30) shares old Common $0.001 par exchanged for (1) share new Common $0.001 par 11/21/2003
Name changed to Heartland, Inc. 6/22/2004

INTERNATIONAL X-CHEQUER RES INC (QC)
Reorganized under the laws of British Columbia as Passport Metals Inc. 10/18/2007
Each share Common no par exchanged for (3) shares Common no par
Passport Metals Inc. name changed to Passport Potash Inc. 11/10/2009

INTERNATIONAL YACHTING ADVENTURES INC (DE)
Name changed to ResortShips International, Inc. 04/11/2006
ResortShips International, Inc. recapitalized as American Design Inc. (DE) 03/26/2007 which reincorporated in Nevada as Ventana Biotech Inc. 11/20/2008
(See Ventana Biotech Inc.)

INTERNATIONAL YOGURT CO (OR)
Name changed to YoCream International, Inc. 04/07/1999
(See YoCream International, Inc.)

INTERNATIONAL ZIMTU TECHNOLOGIES INC (BC)
Reincorporated under the laws of Canada as Petrol One Corp. 09/26/2006

INTERNATIONALE NEDERLANDEN GROEP N V (NETHERLANDS)
Name changed to ING Groep N.V. 12/01/1995

INTERNATURAL WATERS & BEVERAGES CORP (DE)
Recapitalized as JC Data Solutions, Inc. 7/11/2005
Each share Common $0.001 par exchanged for (0.01) share Common $0.001 par

INTERNET ACQUISITION GROUP INC (CA)
Recapitalized as China Renyuan International, Inc. 08/21/2008
Each share Common $0.001 par exchanged for (0.00429184) share Common $0.001 par

INTERNET ADVISORY CORP (UT)
Each share old Common $0.001 par exchanged for (0.02) share new Common $0.001 par 1/2/2002
New Common $0.001 par split (4) for (1) by issuance of (3) additional shares payable 2/13/2002 to holders of record 1/24/2002 Ex date - 2/14/2002
Recapitalized as Scores Holding Co., Inc. 7/24/2002
Each share new Common $0.001 par exchanged for (0.02) share Common $0.001 par

INTERNET AMER INC (TX)
Liquidation completed
Each share Common 1¢ par received initial distribution of $0.68 cash payable 06/26/2015 to holders of record 06/23/2015 Ex date - 06/29/2015
Each share Common 1¢ par received second and final distribution of $0.04 cash payable 10/30/2015 to holders of record 10/27/2015 Ex date - 11/02/2015

INTERNET ARCHITECTURE HOLDRS TR (DE)
Trust terminated
Each Depositary Receipt received first and final distribution of $60.711846 cash payable 01/08/2013 to holders of record 12/24/2012

INTERNET BRANDS INC (DE)
Issue Information - 6,000,000 shares CL A COM offered at $8 per share on 11/16/2007
Acquired by Micro Holding Corp. (DE) 12/17/2010
Each share Class A Common $0.001 par exchanged for $13.35 cash

INTERNET BROADCAST NETWORKS INC (DE)
Name changed to Mediacom Entertainment Inc. 08/10/2001
(See Mediacom Entertainment Inc.)

INTERNET BUSINESSS INTL INC (NV)
Reincorporated 07/15/1999
State of incorporation changed from (DE) to (NV) 07/15/1999
Each share old Common 1¢ par exchanged for (0.1) share new Common 1¢ par 05/24/2002
Name changed to Alpha Wireless Broadband, Inc. 09/17/2004
Alpha Wireless Broadband, Inc. recapitalized as Seamless Wi-Fi, Inc. 06/03/2005 which name changed to Seamless Corp. (NV) 08/21/2008 which reincorporated in Florida as GDT TEK, Inc. 11/25/2009
(See GDT TEK, Inc.)

INTERNET CABLE CORP (NV)
Common $0.001 par split (3) for (2) by issuance of (0.5) additional share payable 12/31/1997 to holders of record 12/19/1997
SEC revoked common stock registration 08/30/2011

INTERNET CAP GROUP INC (DE)
Old Common $0.001 par split (2) for (1) by issuance of (1) additional share payable 12/27/1999 to holders of record 12/06/1999
Each share old Common $0.001 par exchanged for (0.05) share new Common $0.001 par 05/07/2004
Name changed to ICG Group, Inc. 06/21/2011
ICG Group, Inc. name changed to Actua Corp. 09/03/2014

INTERNET CARD SEC INC (QC)
Issue Information - 3,000,000 shares COM offered at $0.10 per share on 10/18/1996
Delisted from Alberta Stock Exchange 10/21/1998

INTERNET COM CORP (DE)
Name changed to INT Media Group, Inc. 05/29/2001
INT Media Group, Inc. name changed to Jupitermedia Corp. 09/01/2002 which name changed to WebMediaBrands, Inc. 02/24/2009 which name changed to Mediabistro Inc. 06/13/2013 which name changed to Mecklermedia Corp. (New) 08/25/2014
(See Mecklermedia Corp. (New))

INTERNET COMM & COMMUNICATIONS INC (DE)
Chapter 11 bankruptcy proceedings converted to Chapter 7 on 12/28/2001
Stockholders' equity unlikely

INTERNET COMM CORP (DE)
Class E-1 Common 1¢ par called for redemption 06/11/1999
Class E-2 Common 1¢ par called for redemption 06/11/1999
Name changed EasyLink Services International Corp. 08/20/2007
(See EasyLink Services International Corp.)

INTERNET COMMUNICATIONS CORP (CO)
Each share old Common no par exchanged for (0.005) share new Common no par 8/16/91
Each share new Common no par exchanged again for (0.57142857) share new Common no par 10/29/91
Merged into Internet Commerce & Communications, Inc. 11/29/2000
Each share new Common no par exchanged for (0.55) share Common $0.001 par and (1) Common Stock Purchase Warrant expiring 11/29/2002
(See Internet Commerce & Communications, Inc.)

INTERNET CULINARY CORP (NV)
Name changed to Capitol Silver Mines Inc. (New) 03/01/2005
Capitol Silver Mines Inc. (New) name changed to Capitol Toys, Inc. 08/17/2005
(See Capitol Toys, Inc.)

INTERNET EXTRA CORP
Merged into Mediaplex, Inc. 11/24/1999
Each share Ser. B Preferred exchanged for (1) share Common $0.0001 par
Each share Ser. C Preferred exchanged for (1) share Common $0.0001 par
Each share Common exchanged for (1) share Common $0.0001 par

Mediaplex, Inc. merged into ValueClick, Inc. 10/22/2001 which name changed to Conversant, Inc. 02/05/2014 which merged into Alliance Data Systems Corp. 12/11/2014

INTERNET FINL SVCS INC (DE)
Name changed to A.B. Watley Group Inc. 09/01/1999
(See A.B. Watley Group Inc.)

INTERNET GAMING TECHNOLOGIES INC (DE)
Name changed to Virtual Gaming Technologies, Inc. 02/22/1997
Virtual Gaming Technologies, Inc. name changed to VirtGame.com Corp. 09/28/1999 which name changed to VirtGame Corp. 02/25/2002 which merged into Mikohn Gaming Corp. 10/07/2005 which name changed to Progressive Gaming International Corp. 04/03/2006
(See Progressive Gaming International Corp.)

INTERNET GOLF ASSN (NV)
Common $0.001 par split (2) for (1) by issuance of (1) additional share payable 9/24/99 to holders of record 9/13/99
Each share old Common $0.001 par exchanged for (0.01) share new Common $0.001 par 11/19/2001
Name changed to American Oriental Bioengineering Inc. 1/3/2002

INTERNET GROWTH FD INC (MD)
Name changed to Foxby Corp. 7/14/2003

INTERNET HLDGS LTD (UT)
Each share old Common no par exchanged for (0.125) share new Common no par 4/24/97
Each share new Common no par exchanged for (0.5) share Common 1¢ par 6/24/97
Name changed to HTTP Technology, Inc. (UT) 11/28/2000
HTTP Technology, Inc. (UT) reincorporated in Delaware 12/19/2000 which name changed to Medicsight, Inc. 10/28/2001 which name changed to MGT Capital Investments, Inc. 1/24/2007

INTERNET HOLDRS TR (DE)
Trust terminated 01/10/2013
Each share Internet HOLDRS Trust received $98.001177 cash

INTERNET IDENTITY PRESENCE CO (ON)
Name changed to Geophysical Prospecting, Inc. 12/06/2005
Geophysical Prospecting, Inc. name changed to Revolution Technologies Inc. 03/18/2008

INTERNET INFINITY INC (DE)
Common $0.001 par split (2) for (1) by issuance of (1) additional share payable 03/17/1999 to holders of record 02/25/1999
Each share Common $0.001 par received distribution of (0.048) share Electronic Media Central Corp. Common 2¢ par payable 08/21/2002 to holders of record 08/05/2002
Ex date - 08/01/2002
Reincorporated under the laws of Nevada 12/17/2004

INTERNET INFRASTRUCTURE HOLDRS TR (DE)
Trust terminated
Each Depositary Receipt received first and final distribution of $3.824555 cash payable 01/10/2013 to holders of record 12/24/2012

INTERNET LAW LIBR INC (DE)
Each share Common 2¢ par received distribution of (1) share Planet Resources Inc. (New) Common $0.001 par payable 03/26/2001 to holders of record 04/14/1999

Name changed to ITIS Inc. (DE) 10/24/2001
ITIS Inc. (DE) reorganized in Nevada as ITIS Holdings Inc. 09/18/2002
(See ITIS Holdings Inc.)

INTERNET LIQUIDATORS INTL CORP (ON)
Name changed to Bid.Com International, Inc. 07/17/1998
Bid.Com International, Inc. recapitalized as ADB Systems International Inc. 10/18/2001 which name changed to ADB Systems International Ltd. 11/01/2002 which name changed to Northcore Technologies Inc. 07/18/2006

INTERNET MARKETING INC (NV)
SEC revoked common stock registration 08/16/2011

INTERNET MEDIA CORP (NV)
Name changed to USURF America Inc. 07/09/1999
USURF America Inc. name changed to Cardinal Communications, Inc. 06/24/2005
(See Cardinal Communications, Inc.)

INTERNET MEDIA SVCS INC (DE)
Recapitalized as U-Vend Inc. 05/16/2014
Each share Common $0.001 par exchanged for (0.005) share Common $0.001 par
U-Vend Inc. name changed to BoxScore Brands, Inc. 03/01/2018

INTERNET MEDIA TECHNOLOGIES INC (NV)
Each share old Common $0.001 par exchanged for (0.1) share new Common $0.001 par 04/09/2008
Name changed to Star Entertainment Group, Inc. 01/19/2010

INTERNET MULTI-MEDIA CORP (NV)
Recapitalized as AmEurotech Corp. (NV) 12/18/2000
Each (30) shares Common $0.001 par exchanged for (1) share Common $0.001 par
AmEurotech Corp. (NV) reincorporated in Florida 04/18/2007 which recapitalized as Scott Contracting Holdings, Inc. 07/11/2007 which name changed to Liverpool Group, Inc. 04/29/2008

INTERNET PATENTS CORP (DE)
Name changed to Prism Technologies Group, Inc. 09/23/2015

INTERNET PICTURES CORP (DE)
Each share old Common $0.001 par exchanged for (0.1) share new Common $0.001 par 08/23/2001
Name changed to IPIX Corp. 03/24/2004
(See IPIX Corp.)

INTERNET SECURITY SYS INC (DE)
Merged into International Business Machines Corp. 10/20/2006
Each share Common $0.001 par exchanged for $28 cash

INTERNET SHOPPING CATALOG INC (ON)
Cease trade order effective 08/26/2002

INTERNET SOLUTIONS FOR BUSINESS INC (NV)
Recapitalized as GlobalOne Real Estate, Inc. 05/16/2005
Each share Common $0.001 par exchanged for (0.002) share Common $0.001 par
GlobalOne Real Estate, Inc. name changed to Glow Holdings, Inc. 10/07/2011

INTERNET SONG OF THE YR INC (DE)
Each share old Common 1¢ par exchanged for (0.01) share new Common 1¢ par 03/25/2008
Name changed to National Maintenance Group, Inc. 06/11/2008

INTERNET SPORTS NETWORK INC (FL)
Each share old Common $0.001 par exchanged for (0.1666666) share new Common $0.001 par 06/28/2000
Each share new Common $0.001 par exchanged again for (0.02) share new Common $0.001 par 02/15/2002
Name changed to Reibanc USA, Inc. 03/26/2003
Reibanc USA, Inc. name changed to Flair Petroleum Corp. 06/30/2006

INTERNET STK MKT RES INC (DE)
Name changed 09/01/1998
Name changed from Internet Stock Exchange Corp. to Internet Stock Market Resources, Inc. 09/01/1998
Each share old Common $0.001 par exchanged for (1/9) share new Common $0.001 par 06/30/1999
Name changed to VentureNet, Inc. 06/26/2000
VentureNet, Inc. name changed to VentureNet Capital Group, Inc. (DE) 11/06/2001 which reincorporated in Nevada 03/14/2003

INTERNET VENTURE GROUP INC (FL)
Reincorporated under the laws of Delaware as IVG Corp. 02/28/2001
IVG Corp. recapitalized as Group Management Corp. (DE) 12/17/2001 which reincorporated in Georgia as Silver Screen Studios, Inc. 09/05/2003 which name changed to Global 1 Investment Holdings Corp. 11/13/2006
(See Global 1 Investment Holdings Corp.)

INTERNET VIP INC (DE)
Recapitalized as Newtech Brake Corp. 07/01/2002
Each share Common $0.0001 par exchanged for (0.05) share Common $0.0001 par
(See Newtech Brake Corp.)

INTERNETFINANCIALCORP COM INC (NV)
Recapitalized as APO Health Inc. 06/01/2001
Each share Common $0.001 par exchanged for (1/6) share Common $0.0002 par
APO Health Inc. name changed to Paivis, Corp. 05/19/2006
(See Paivis, Corp.)

INTERNETMERCADO COM INC (DE)
Name changed to New Century Companies, Inc. 06/07/2001
New Century Companies, Inc. name changed to U.S. Aerospace, Inc. 04/27/2010

INTERNETSTUDIOS COM INC (NV)
Each share old Common $0.0001 par exchanged for (0.33333333) share new Common $0.0001 par 09/23/1999
Each share new Common $0.0001 par exchanged again for (0.05) share new Common $0.0001 par 12/06/2001
SEC revoked common stock registration 06/04/2007

INTERNETWORK RLTY CORP (BC)
Recapitalized as Skalbania Enterprises Ltd. 10/15/1980
Each share Common no par exchanged for (0.5) share Common no par
Skalbania Enterprises Ltd. name changed to Selco International Properties Inc. 03/03/1988
(See Selco International Properties Inc.)

INTERNEURON PHARMACEUTICALS INC (DE)
Name changed to Indevus Pharmaceuticals, Inc. 04/02/2002

(See Indevus Pharmaceuticals, Inc.)

INTERNORTH INC (DE)
Common $10 par split (2) for (1) by issuance of (1) additional share 04/25/1980
5.5% Preferred $100 par called for redemption 10/01/1981
5.8% Preferred $100 par called for redemption 10/01/1985
Name changed to Enron Corp. (DE) 05/12/1986
Enron Corp. (DE) reincorporated in Oregon 07/01/1997
(See Enron Corp.)

INTERNOVA RES LTD (BC)
Recapitalized as Parisco Foods Ltd. 01/22/1996
Each share Common no par exchanged for (0.2) share Common no par
(See Parisco Foods Ltd.)

INTERNOW AFFILIATES INC (DE)
Name changed to Electronics Communications Corp. 03/00/1994
Electronics Communications Corp. name changed to Northeast Digital Networks Inc. 06/16/1998
(See Northeast Digital Networks Inc.)

INTEROCEAN HLDGS INC (NJ)
Charter declared void for non-payment of taxes 06/26/1990

INTEROCEANIC INDUSTRIES, INC. (IA)
Name changed to First Interoceanic Corp. 5/18/64
First Interoceanic Corp. acquired by Archer-Daniels-Midland Co. in November 1969

INTEROIL CORP (YT)
Reincorporated 08/24/2007
Place of incorporation changed from (NB) to (YT) 08/24/2007
Merged into Exxon Mobil Corp. 02/22/2017
Each share Common no par exchanged for (0.5459) share Common no par
Note: A Contingent Resource Payment has been paid into escrow for possible future distribution

INTERPACE CORP (DE)
Common $1 par split (3) for (2) by issuance of (0.5) additional share 12/2/77
5% Conv. Preferred $100 par called for redemption 7/29/83
Merged into Clevepak Corp. 8/15/83
Each share Common $1 par exchanged for (1) share $1.84 Conv. Preferred Ser. B no par and (1) share $2.23 Preferred Ser. A no par
(See Clevepak Corp.)

INTERPAK HLDGS INC (DE)
Merged into INH Holdings, Inc. 12/31/91
Each share Common 1¢ par exchanged for $1.25 principal amount of 12% Subord. Debentures due 12/31/96 and $0.25 cash

INTERPHARM HLDGS INC (DE)
Each share 10% Conv. Preferred Ser. A 1¢ par automatically became (2) shares Common 1¢ par 07/18/2006
Completely liquidated 06/23/2008
Each share Conv. Preferred Ser. C 1¢ par exchanged for first and final distribution of $1 cash
Common stockholders' equity unlikely

INTERPHARM LABS LTD (ISRAEL)
Acquired by Serono S.A. 02/10/1997
Each share Ordinary NIS 1 par exchanged for $25 cash

INTERPHASE CORP (TX)
Common no par changed to 10¢ par 05/02/2000
Plan of reorganization under Chapter 7 bankruptcy proceedings effective 07/09/2018

Each share Common 10¢ par received $0.109375 cash

INTERPHOTO CORP (DE)
Class A Common $1 par reclassified as Common $1 par 9/15/67
Stock Dividend - 10% 11/2/64
Charter cancelled and declared inoperative and void for non-payment of taxes 3/1/89

INTERPIPE NIZHNEDNEPROVSKY TUBE ROLLING PLT JSC (UKRAINE)
ADR agreement terminated 03/14/2016
Each Sponsored ADR for Ordinary exchanged for (6) shares Ordinary
Note: Unexchanged ADR's will be sold and the proceeds, if any, held for claim after 03/17/2017

INTERPLASTIC CORP (MN)
Each share Common 10¢ par exchanged for (0.2) share Common 50¢ par 09/14/1971
Common 50¢ par changed to 33-1/3¢ par and (0.5) additional share issued 12/15/1972
Common 33-1/3¢ par split (2) for (1) by issuance of (1) additional share 05/31/1978
Merged into Phillips Petroleum Co. 01/16/1980
Each share Common 33-1/3¢ par exchanged for $18 cash

INTERPLEX INTL INC (NV)
Recapitalized as Sportsmans Resorts International, Inc. 10/01/1985
Each (30) shares Common $0.001 par exchanged for (1) share Common $0.001 par
Sportsmans Resorts International, Inc. name changed to Business Resources, Inc. 06/04/1986
(See Business Resources, Inc.)

INTERPLEX MINING & INDUSTRIAL LTD. (BC)
Name changed to Interplex Spa Industries Ltd. 09/15/1971
Each share Capital Stock no par exchanged for (1) share Capital Stock no par
(See Interplex Spa Industries Ltd.)

INTERPLEX SPA INDUSTRIES LTD. (BC)
Each share old Capital Stock no par exchanged for (0.000005) share new Capital Stock no par 12/31/1977
Note: In effect holders received $0.028 cash per share and public interest was eliminated

INTERPOINT CORP (WA)
Common no par split (2) for (1) by issuance of (1) additional share payable 06/27/1996 to holders of record 06/13/1996
Each share Common no par received distribution of (1) share of Advanced Digital Information Corp. Common no par payable 10/18/1996 to holders of record 10/16/1996
Merged into Crane Co. 10/17/1996
Each share Common no par exchanged for (0.091183) share Common $1 par

INTERPOOL INC (DE)
5.75% Conv. Preferred no par called for redemption 03/10/1997
Common $0.001 par split (3) for (2) by issuance of (0.5) additional share payable 03/27/1997 to holders of record 03/21/1997 Ex date - 03/31/1997
Merged into Chariot Acquisition Holding LLC 07/19/2007
Each share Common $0.001 par exchanged for $27.10 cash

INTERPOOL INTL LTD (ON)
Completely liquidated 12/08/1971
Each share Common no par exchanged for first and final distribution of (1) share Interpool Ltd. Capital Stock B$0.02 par
(See Interpool Ltd.)

INTERPOOL LTD (BAHAMAS)
Capital Stock B$0.02 par changed to B$0.01 par and (1) additional share issued 07/05/1972
Each share Capital Stock B$0.01 par exchanged for (0.0005) share Capital Stock B$20 par 04/30/1979
Note: In effect holders received $40 cash per share and public interest eliminated

INTERPORE INTL (CA)
Merged into Biomet, Inc. 6/18/2004
Each share new Common no par exchanged for $14.50 cash

INTERPRO MANANGEMENT CORP (NV)
Common $0.001 par split (35) for (1) by issuance of (34) additional shares payable 03/04/2011 to holders of record 03/04/2011 Ex date - 03/07/2011
Name changed to Stevia Corp. 03/09/2011

INTERPROVINCIAL ALLIED ENTERPRISES LTD. (ON)
Name changed to Comac Communications Ltd. 07/12/1972
(See Comac Communications Ltd.)

INTERPROVINCIAL BRICK CO., LTD. (CANADA)
Charter surrendered 3/3/61

INTERPROVINCIAL BUILDING CREDITS, LTD. (CANADA)
Name changed to Traders Homeplan Ltd. 01/02/1969
(See Traders Homeplan Ltd.)

INTERPROVINCIAL DREDGING & MNG LTD (ON)
Recapitalized as Interprovincial Allied Enterprises Ltd. 09/28/1970
Each share Capital Stock no par exchanged for (0.04) share Common no par
Interprovincial Allied Enterprises Ltd. name changed to Comac Communications Ltd. 07/12/1972
(See Comac Communications Ltd.)

INTERPROVINCIAL PIPE LINE INC (CANADA)
Under plan of reorganization each share Common no par automatically became (1) share Interprovincial Pipe Line System Inc. Common no par 12/18/92
Interprovincial Pipe Line System Inc. name changed to IPL Energy Inc. 5/10/94 which name changed to Enbridge Inc. 10/7/98

INTERPROVINCIAL PIPE LINE LTD (CANADA)
Name changed 08/03/1973
Each share Capital Stock $50 par exchanged for (10) shares Capital Stock $5 par 00/00/1952
Capital Stock $5 par changed to $1 par and (4) additional shares issued 06/02/1967
Name changed from Interprovincial Pipe Line Co. to Interprovincial Pipe Line Ltd. 08/03/1973
Capital Stock $1 par reclassified as Conv. Class A Common $1 par 04/26/1976
Conv. Class A Common $1 par reclassified as Common $1 par 05/07/1979
Conv. Class B Common $1 par reclassified as Common $1 par 05/07/1979
Common $1 par changed to no par 04/09/1980
Name changed to Interhome Energy Inc. 05/09/1988
Interhome Energy Inc. name changed to Interprovincial Pipe Line Inc. 05/01/1991 which reorganized as Interprovincial Pipe Line System Inc. 12/18/1992 which name changed to IPL Energy Inc. 05/10/1994 which name changed to Enbridge Inc. 10/07/1998

INTERPROVINCIAL PIPE LINE SYS INC (CANADA)
Name changed to IPL Energy Inc. 05/10/1994
IPL Energy Inc. name changed to Enbridge Inc. 10/07/1998

INTERPROVINCIAL PROPERTIES CORP.
Liquidated 00/00/1949
Details not available

INTERPROVINCIAL SATELLITE SVCS LTD (CANADA)
Name changed to Wireless Matrix Corp. 05/10/2000
(See Wireless Matrix Corp.)

INTERPROVINCIAL SILVER MINES LTD (BC)
Name changed 01/00/1968
Name changed from Interprovincial Metals Ltd. to Interprovincial Silver Mines Ltd. 01/00/1968
Recapitalized as Turismo Industries Ltd. 10/20/1971
Each share Capital Stock 50¢ par exchanged for (0.2) share Capital Stock no par
Turismo Industries Ltd. recapitalized as General Energy Corp. (BC) 07/31/1978
(See General Energy Corp.)

INTERPROVINCIAL STEEL CORP. LTD. (SK)
Merged into Interprovincial Steel & Pipe Corp. Ltd. on a (1.55) for (1) basis 08/31/1960
Interprovincial Steel & Pipe Corp. Ltd. name changed to IPSCO Inc. 04/06/1984
(See IPSCO Inc.)

INTERPROVINCIAL STL & PIPE LTD (CANADA)
Reincorporated 01/28/1977
Capital Stock no par reclassified as Common no par 11/00/1965
$1.20 Conv. Preference no par called for redemption 12/15/1972
Place of incorporation changed from (SK) to (Canada) 01/28/1977
Name changed to IPSCO Inc. 04/06/1984
(See IPSCO Inc.)

INTERPROVINCIAL UTILITIES, LTD. (CANADA)
Completely liquidated 09/30/1957
Each share Common no par received first and final distribution of $19.35 cash
Note: Certificates were not required to be surrendered and as without value

INTERPUBLIC GROUP COS INC (DE)
Issue Information - 6,500,000 shares PFD CONV SER A 5.375% offered at $50 per share on 12/16/2003
Each share 5.375% Conv. Preferred Ser. A no par converted into (3.7037) shares Common 10¢ par 12/15/2006
Each share 5.25% 144A Conv. Perpetual Preferred Ser. B no par converted into (77.8966) shares Common 10¢ par 10/17/2013
Each share 5.25% Conv. Perpetual Preferred Ser. B no par converted into (77.8966) shares Common 10¢ par 10/17/2013
(Additional Information in Active)

INTERPUBLISHING CDA LTD (QC)
Merged into Pagurian Corp. Ltd. 11/14/1979
Each share Capital Stock no par exchanged for (1.4) shares Class A Special no par
Pagurian Corp. Ltd. name changed to Edper Group Ltd. (Old) 05/10/1995 which merged into Edper Group Ltd. (New) 01/01/1997 which name changed to EdperBrascan Corp. 08/01/1997 which name changed to Brascan Corp. 04/28/2000 which name changed to Brookfield Asset Management, Inc. 11/10/2005

INTERPUMP GROUP S P A (ITALY)
ADR agreement terminated 06/06/2007
No ADR's remain outstanding
(Additional Information in Active)

INTERQUEST INC (ON)
Name changed 10/23/1992
Recapitalized 09/30/1995
Name changed from Interquest Resources Corp. to Interquest Technologies Inc. 10/23/1992
Recapitalized from Interquest Technologies Inc. to Interquest Inc. 09/30/1995
Each share Common no par exchanged for (0.25) share Common no par and (0.05) Common Stock Purchase Warrant expiring 12/31/1997
Placed in receivership 12/13/2007
Stockholders' equity unlikely

INTERRA EXPL INC (BC)
Name changed to Simba Gold Corp. 03/11/2011

INTERRA FINL INC (DE)
Name changed to Dain Rauscher Corp. 1/2/98
(See Dain Rauscher Corp.)

INTERREGIONAL DISTR GRID COS HLDG JSC (RUSSIA)
Sponsored 144A GDR's for Preference split (2) for (1) by issuance of (1) additional GDR payable 07/27/2011 to holders of record 07/26/2011
Sponsored Reg. S GDR's for Preference split (2) for (1) by issuance of (1) additional GDR payable 07/27/2011 to holders of record 07/26/2011
Sponsored 144A GDR's for Ordinary split (2) for (1) by issuance of (1) additional GDR payable 07/27/2011 to holders of record 07/26/2011
Sponsored Reg. S GDR's for Ordinary split (2) for (1) by issuance of (1) additional GDR payable 07/27/2011 to holders of record 07/26/2011
Basis changed from (1:400) to (1:200) 07/27/2011
Name changed to JSC Russian Grids 05/07/2013
JSC Russian Grids name changed to JSC Rosseti 08/22/2014 which name changed to PJSC Rosseti 09/15/2015

INTERRENT INTL PPTYS INC (ON)
Reorganized as InterRent Real Estate Investment Trust 12/07/2006
Each share Common no par exchanged for (0.1) Trust Unit

INTERRENT PPTYS LTD (ON)
Recapitalized as InterRent International Properties Inc. 03/05/2001
Each share Common no par exchanged for (0.25) share Common no par
InterRent International Properties Inc. reorganized as InterRent Real Estate Investment Trust 12/07/2006

INTERRUPTION TELEVISION INC (NV)
Each share old Common $0.001 par exchanged for (0.08695652) share new Common $0.001 par 09/03/2002
Name changed to Bongiovi Entertainment, Inc. 09/17/2002
Bongiovi Entertainment, Inc. name changed to NewGen Technologies, Inc. 08/11/2005
(See NewGen Technologies, Inc.)

INTERSALES LTD (DC)
Out of business in September 1970
No stockholders' equity

INTERSCAN, INC. (MN)
Assets sold for benefit of creditors in 03/00/1972
No stockholders' equity

INTERSCIENCE COMPUTER CORP (CA)
Name changed to CaminoSoft Corp. (CA) 06/14/2000
CaminoSoft Corp. (CA) reincorporated in Delaware as CMSF Corp. 10/12/2010 which recapitalized as Plures Technologies, Inc. 09/27/2011
(See Plures Technologies, Inc.)

INTERSCIENCE SYS INC (NV)
Reincorporated 3/31/81
State of incorporation changed from (CA) to (NV) and Common no par changed to 10¢ par 3/31/81
Charter revoked for failure to file reports and pay fees 11/1/98

INTERSEARCH GROUP INC (DE)
Each share Common $0.0001 par exchanged for (0.125) share Common $0.0008 par 07/22/1991
Charter cancelled and declared inoperative and void for non-payment of taxes 03/01/1993

INTERSEARCH GROUP INC (FL)
Each share old Common $0.001 par exchanged for (0.025) share new Common $0.001 par 10/19/2005
Name changed to Banks.com, Inc. 11/28/2007
Banks.com, Inc. merged into Remark Media, Inc. 07/06/2012 which name changed to Remark Holdings, Inc. 04/11/2017

INTERSECURITY HLDGS CORP (NV)
Recapitalized as Founders Bay Holdings 04/25/2017
Each share Common $0.001 par exchanged for (0.0005) share Common $0.001 par

INTERSERVICE CORP (OH)
Merged out of existence 06/26/1985
Details not available

INTERSHOP COMMUNICATIONS A G (GERMANY)
Issue Information - 3,350,000 ADR'S offered at $32.09 per ADR on 09/28/2000
Each old Sponsored ADR for Ordinary exchanged for (0.1) new Sponsored ADR for Ordinary 02/28/2002
ADR basis changed from (1:0.5) to (1:5) 02/28/2002
ADR agreement terminated 02/17/2004
Each new Sponsored ADR for Ordinary exchanged for $4.3356744 cash

INTERSIL CORP (DE)
Name changed 05/29/2001
Name changed from Intersil Holdings Corp. to Intersil Corp. 05/29/2001
Acquired by Renesas Electronics Corp. 02/24/2017
Each share Class A Common 1¢ par exchanged for $22.50 cash

INTERSIL INC NEW (DE)
Merged into General Electric Co. 2/3/81
Each share Common 10¢ par exchanged for $35 cash

INTERSIL INC OLD (DE)
Merged into Intersil, Inc. (New) 11/9/76
Each share Common 1¢ par exchanged for (0.95) share Common 10¢ par
(See Intersil, Inc. (New))

INTERSOFT TECHNOLOGIES INC (AB)
Delisted from Alberta Stock Exchange 12/10/1991

INTERSOLV INC (DE)
Merged into Micro Focus Group PLC 09/15/1998
Each share Common 1¢ par exchanged for (0.55) Sponsored ADR for Ordinary 10p par
Micro Focus Group PLC name changed to Merant PLC 02/16/1999 which was acquired by Serena Software, Inc. 06/30/2004
(See Serena Software, Inc.)

INTERSPACE ENTERPRISES INC (CO)
Declared defunct and inoperative for failure to pay taxes and file annual reports 05/01/2004

INTERSPEC CORP. (MA)
Name changed to Continental American Industries Corp. 02/00/1980
(See Continental American Industries Corp.)

INTERSPEC INC (PA)
Merged into Advanced Technology Laboratories, Inc. (DE) 5/16/94
Each share Common $0.001 par exchanged for (0.413) share Common 1¢ par
Advanced Technology Laboratories, Inc. (DE) reincorporated in (WA) 5/11/95 which name changed to ATL Ultrasound, Inc. 7/1/97
(See ALT Ultrasound, Inc.)

INTERSPEED INC (DE)
Issue Information - 3,500,000 shares COM offered at $12 per share on 09/24/1999
Terminated registration of securities 2/12/2001
Company is now defunct

INTERSTAR GROUP INC (CANADA)
Name changed 11/12/2003
Name changed from Interstar Mining Group Inc. to Interstar Group Inc. 11/12/2005
Name changed to Theralase Technologies Inc. 11/02/2004

INTERSTAT VENTURES INC (BC)
Recapitalized as Consolidated Interstat Ventures Inc. 04/23/1996
Each share Common no par exchanged for (0.33333333) share Common no par
Consolidated Interstat Ventures Inc. name changed to Diamcor Mining Inc. 11/23/1999

INTERSTATE ADJUSTEZE CORP. (CA)
Name changed to State Industries 9/10/59
State Industries name changed to State Recreation, Inc. 1/14/76 which name changed to State Products Inc. 5/26/92

INTERSTATE AIRCRAFT & ENGINEERING CORP. (CA)
Name changed to Interstate Engineering Corp. 00/00/1946
Interstate Engineering Corp. merged into Automatic Sprinkler Corp. of America (OH) 11/29/1967 which name changed to A-T-O Inc. 10/29/1969 which name changed to Figgie International Inc. (OH) 06/01/1981 which reorganized in Delaware as Figgie International Holdings Inc. 07/18/1983 which name changed to Figgie International Inc. 12/31/1986 which name changed to Scott Technologies, Inc. 05/20/1998 which merged into Tyco International Ltd. (Bermuda) 05/03/2001 which reincorporated in Switzerland 03/17/2009 which merged into Johnson Controls International PLC 09/06/2016

INTERSTATE AMIESITE CO. (DE)
Reorganized as Interstate Amiesite Corp. in 1953
Each share Preferred $50 par exchanged for (10) shares Capital Stock $5 par
Each (50) shares Common no par exchanged for (1) share Capital Stock $5 par
Interstate Amiesite Corp. merged into IA Holdings Corp. 3/24/83
(See IA Holdings Corp.)

INTERSTATE AMIESITE CORP (DE)
Merged into IA Holdings Corp. 3/24/83
Each share Capital Stock $5 par exchanged for (1) share Common $5 par
(See IA Holdings Corp.)

INTERSTATE BAKERIES CORP (DE)
Ctfs. dated prior to 07/25/1969
Plan of merger effective 00/00/1937
Each share Preferred no par exchanged for (1.4) shares $5 Preferred no par and (1) share Common $1 par
Each share Common no par exchanged for (1) share Common $1 par
Each share $5 Preferred no par exchanged for (1-1/3) shares $4.80 Preferred no par 00/00/1947
Common $1 par split (2) for (1) by issuance of (1) additional share 08/18/1967
Stock Dividends - 100% 04/25/1951; 25% 05/03/1954; 25% 01/27/1956
Name changed to Interstate Brands Corp. 07/25/1969
(See Interstate Brands Corp.)

INTERSTATE BAKERIES CORP (DE)
Ctfs. dated after 07/00/1991
Common 1¢ par split (2) for (1) by issuance of (1) additional share payable 11/03/1997 to holders of record 10/15/1997 Ex date - 11/04/1997
Plan of reorganization under Chapter 11 Federal Bankruptcy Code effective 02/03/2009
No stockholders' equity

INTERSTATE BAKERIES CORP NEW (DE)
Ctfs. dated after 11/30/1981
Common 10¢ par split (3) for (2) by issuance of (0.5) additional share 12/01/1986
Under plan of merger each share Common 10¢ par exchanged for (1.62) shares $3.50 Exchangeable Preferred no par 04/29/1988
Name changed to Interstate Brands Corp. 06/02/1990
(See Interstate Brands Corp.)

INTERSTATE BD CO (GA)
Liquidation completed
Each share 7% 1st Preferred Ser. AA $100 par exchanged for first and final distribution of $110 cash 10/1/81
Each share Class A Part. Preferred 1¢ par exchanged for first and final distribution of $2 cash 10/1/81
Each share Class B Common 1¢ par exchanged for initial distribution of $15 cash 1/25/82
Each share Class B Common 1¢ par received second distribution of $7 cash 7/8/82
Each share Class B Common 1¢ par received third distribution of $3 cash 1/17/83
Each share Class B Common 1¢ par received fourth and final distribution of $0.878 cash 8/14/86

INTERSTATE BOWLING CORP. (DE)
Adjudicated bankrupt 10/10/65
No stockholders' equity

INTERSTATE BRANDS CORP (DE)
Merged into DPF Inc. 02/27/1979
Each share Common $1 par exchanged for (1.3) shares Common 10¢ par and $1.71 cash
$3.50 Exchangeable Preferred no par called for redemption 08/23/1991
Plan of reorganization under Chapter 11 Federal Bankruptcy Code effective 02/03/2009
No $4.80 Preferred stockholders' equity

INTERSTATE BRDG CO (OH)
7% Prior Preferred $100 par called for redemption 00/00/1953
7% Preferred $100 par called for redemption 06/01/1991
1st Preferred no par called for redemption 06/03/1991
Voluntarily dissolved 10/31/1991
Details not available

INTERSTATE CAP GROWTH FD INC (GA)
Merged into Ron Thomas, Inc. 1/10/2000
Details not available

INTERSTATE CATTLE LN & OIL CO (MO)
Name changed to Interstate Holdings Inc. 04/22/1982
(See Interstate Holdings Inc.)

INTERSTATE CELLULAR TELECOMMUNICATIONS INC (DE)
Chapter 11 Federal Bankruptcy Code converted to Chapter 7 on 1/10/90
Stockholders' equity unlikely

INTERSTATE CIRCUITS INC (NY)
Each share old Common $0.001 par exchanged for (0.05) share new Common $0.001 par 10/15/82
Name changed to Nyle International Corp. 12/5/84

INTERSTATE CO. (DE)
Common no par changed to old Common $5 par 00/00/1933
Recapitalized 00/00/1938
Each share 7% Preferred $100 par exchanged for (5/6) share 5% Prior Preferred $100 par and (20) shares Common $1 par
Each share old Common $5 par exchanged for (0.5) share Common $1 par
Common $1 par changed to new Common $5 par 00/00/1953
New Common $5 par changed to $2.50 par and (1) additional share issued 12/05/1958
Name changed to Interstate Hosts, Inc. 07/27/1959
Interstate Hosts, Inc. name changed to Host Internatonal, Inc. 04/19/1968
(See Host International, Inc.)

INTERSTATE COMPUTER SVCS INC (NY)
Plan of reorganization under Chapter 11 Federal Bankruptcy proceedings confirmed 09/10/1984
No stockholders' equity

INTERSTATE COMPUTING INC (LA)
Charter revoked for failure to file annual reports 05/13/1982

INTERSTATE CORP (TN)
Merged into Gulf Life Holding Co. 1/30/76
Each share Common Capital Stock $1 par exchanged for (0.833333) share Common $1 par
Gulf Life Holding Co. name changed to Gulf United Corp. 5/16/77
(See Gulf United Corp.)

INTERSTATE CREDIT CORP. (GA)
Plan of Reorganization under Chapter 11 Federal Bankruptcy proceedings confirmed 04/27/1988
No stockholders' equity

INTERSTATE CREDIT CORP. (NY)
Charter cancelled and proclaimed dissolved for failure to pay taxes and file reports 12/15/72

INTERSTATE DEPT STORES INC (DE)
Common no par changed to $1 par in 1953

Common $1 par split (3) for (1) by issuance of (2) additional shares 6/23/61
Common $1 par split (2) for (1) by issuance of (1) additional share 12/29/64
Common $1 par split (5) for (4) by issuance of (0.25) additional share 2/14/68
Name changed to Interstate Stores, Inc. 6/1/70
Interstate Stores, Inc. reorganized as Toys R Us, Inc. 4/6/78
(See Toys R Us, Inc.)

INTERSTATE ELECTRIC CORP.
Acquired by Inland Power & Light Corp. in 1926
Details not available

INTERSTATE ENERGY CORP (BC)
Merged into Aegis Resources Ltd. 08/01/1990
Each share Common no par exchanged for (0.07142857) share Common no par
Aegis Resources Ltd. recapitalized as New Aegis Resources Ltd. 03/17/1993 which was acquired by Norcan Resources Ltd. 08/19/1994 which recapitalized as Odyssey Exploration Inc. 06/07/2000 which recapitalized as Consolidated Odyssey Exploration Inc. 12/08/2000 which reorganized as Odyssey Petroleum Corp. 08/25/2005 which recapitalized as Petrichor Energy Inc. 03/03/2011

INTERSTATE ENERGY CORP (WI)
Name changed to Alliant Energy Corp. 5/19/99

INTERSTATE ENGINEERING CORP. (CA)
Common $5 par changed to $1 par 00/00/1948
Stock Dividends - 20% 07/01/1954; 100% 05/31/1959; 25% 07/19/1961
Merged into Automatic Sprinkler Corp. of America (OH) 11/29/1967
Each share Common $1 par exchanged for (0.15) share Conv. Preference 2nd Ser. $1 par and (0.56) share Common 10¢ par
Automatic Sprinkler Corp. of America (OH) name changed to A-T-O Inc. 10/29/1969 which name changed to Figgie International Inc. (OH) 06/01/1981 which reorganized in Delaware as Figgie International Holdings Inc. 07/18/1983 which name changed to Figgie International Inc. 12/31/1986 which name changed to Scott Technologies, Inc. 05/20/1998 which merged into Tyco International Ltd. (Bermuda) 05/03/2001 which reincorporated in Switzerland 03/17/2009 which merged into Johnson Controls International PLC 09/06/2016

INTERSTATE EQUITIES CORP.
Merged into Equity Corp. (New) 00/00/1935
Details not available

INTERSTATE FIN CORP (IN)
Name changed to Credithrift Financial Corp. 02/01/1967
Credithrift Financial Corp. name changed to American General Finance Corp. 03/20/1989
(See American General Finance Corp.)

INTERSTATE FINANCE CORP. (IA)
Merged into State Loan & Finance Corp. 4/19/67
Each share 5-1/2% Non-Cum. Preferred $100 par exchanged for (4) shares 6% Preferred $25 par
Each share 5-1/2% Cum. Preferred $100 par exchanged for (4) shares 6% Preferred $25 par
Each share Common $5 par or Class B Common $5 par exchanged for (1.6175) shares Class A Common $1 par
State Loan & Finance Corp. name changed to American Finance System Inc. 5/1/68 which merged into Security Pacific Corp. 12/15/78 which merged into BankAmerica Corp. (Old) 4/22/92 which merged into BankAmerica Corp. (New) 9/30/98 which name changed to Bank of America Corp. 4/28/99

INTERSTATE FINL CORP (NY)
Class A Common $5 par reclassified as Common $1 par 06/25/1956
6% Preferred $10 par called for redemption 04/01/1963
Merged into Thrift Interstate Corp. 04/15/1965
Each share $1 Preference $10 par exchanged for (1) share $1 Conv. Preferred $15 par
Each share 75¢ Ser. Part. Preference $10 par exchanged for (0.9) share $1 Conv. Preferred $15 par
Each share 85¢ Preference $10 par exchanged for (1) share 85¢ Preferred $12.50 par
Each share Common $1 par exchanged for (1.5) shares Common $1 par
Thrift Interstate Corp. name changed to Signal Finance Corp. 01/11/1967 which name changed to Signet Corp. 01/09/1969 which merged into Philadelphia National Corp. 06/29/1973 which merged into CoreStates Financial Corp 05/02/1983 which merged into First Union Corp. 04/28/1998 which name changed to Wachovia Corp. (Ctfs. dated after 09/01/2001) 09/01/2001 which merged into Wells Fargo & Co. (New) 12/31/2008

INTERSTATE FINL CORP (OH)
Merged into Society Corp. 5/1/84
Each share Common $5 par exchanged for $31 cash

INTERSTATE FIRE & CAS CO (IL)
Common $10 par changed to $5 par and (1) additional share issued 7/15/59
Reorganized under the laws of Nevada as Interstate National Corp. 1/1/69
Each share Common $5 par exchanged for (2) shares Common $1 par
Interstate National Corp. merged into National Student Marketing Corp. 10/31/69 which reincorporated under the laws of Delaware 4/1/70
(See National Student Marketing Corp. (DE))

INTERSTATE FORGING INDS INC (WI)
Merged into Citation Corp. 10/29/96
Each share Common $1 par exchanged for $32.4917 cash
Note: An initial additional payment of $1.4932 cash per share was made 4/9/97
A second additional payment of $0.19838809 cash per share was made 9/23/97

INTERSTATE FUEL & LIGHT CO.
Dissolved in 1934

INTERSTATE GEN L P (DE)
Each old Unit of Ltd. Partnership exchanged for (0.2) new Unit of Ltd. Partnership 08/31/1998
Each new Unit of Ltd. Partnership received distribution of (0.5) share American Community Properties Trust Common 1¢ par payable 10/5/98 to holders of record 09/01/1998 Ex date - 09/14/1998
Completely liquidated
Holders of (999) or fewer new Units of Ltd. Partnership received first and final distribution of $3 cash payable 12/22/2006 to holders of record 12/04/2006
Holders of (1,000) or more new Units of Ltd. Partnership received initial distribution of (0.01) new Unit of Ltd. Partnership and $2 cash payable 12/22/2006 to holders of record 12/04/2006
Note: New Units were cancelled and holders received a pro-rata distribution of Caribe Waste Technologies, Inc. and Interstate Waste Technologies, Inc. Common stock 12/31/2006

INTERSTATE GOLD & GAS INC (UT)
Reorganized under the laws of Nevada as Cardiovascular Laboratories, Inc. 4/7/98
Each share Common $0.001 par exchanged for (0.002) share Common $0.001 par
Cardiovascular Laboratories, Inc. name changed to Clixhealth.Com Inc. 3/26/99 which name changed to Clix Group Inc. (NV) 8/23/2000 which reorganized in Colorado as RCC Holdings Corp. 4/9/2003

INTERSTATE HLDGS INC
Capital Stock $1 par changed to $10 par 05/28/1982
Stock Dividend - 200% 06/14/1982
Voluntarily dissolved 07/09/1999
Details not available

INTERSTATE HOME EQUIPMENT CO.
Liquidation completed in 1946

INTERSTATE HOSIERY MILLS, INC. (DE)
Name changed to I.H.L. Corp. in 1953 which was liquidated 10/1/59

INTERSTATE HOSTS, INC. (DE)
5% Prior Preferred $100 par called for redemption 8/18/66
Stock Dividends - 33-1/3% 6/30/61; 25% 9/9/63; 33-1/3% 3/10/66; 33-1/3% 7/17/67
Name changed to Host International, Inc. 4/19/68
(See Host International, Inc.)

INTERSTATE HOTELS & RESORTS INC (DE)
Merged into Hotel Acquisition Co., LLC 03/17/2010
Each share Common 1¢ par exchanged for $2.25 cash

INTERSTATE HOTELS CO (PA)
Merged into Patriot American Hospitality, Inc. (DE) 6/2/98
Each share Common 1¢ par exchanged for either (1.341) Paired Certificates 1¢ par or $37.50 cash
Note: Non-electing holders received cash
Patriot American Hospitality, Inc. (DE) merged into Wyndham International, Inc. 6/29/99
(See Wyndham International, Inc.)

INTERSTATE HOTELS CORP (MD)
Merged into Interstate Hotels & Resorts, Inc. 07/31/2002
Each share Class A Common no par exchanged for (0.92) share Common 1¢ par
(See Interstate Hotels & Resorts, Inc.)

INTERSTATE HSG CORP (DE)
Chapter X bankruptcy proceedings Plan of Arrangement confirmed 4/26/74
Common Stock declared worthless

INTERSTATE INVESTMENT CORP. (MI)
Liquidated in 1954

INTERSTATE IRON & STEEL CO.
Acquired by Central Alloy Steel Corp. in 1929
Details not available

INTERSTATE/JOHNSON LANE INC (DE)
Merged into Wachovia Corp. (New) (Ctfs. dated between 05/20/1991 and 09/01/2001) 04/01/1999
Each share Common 20¢ par exchanged for (0.388) share Common $5 par
Wachovia Corp. (New) (Ctfs. dated between 05/20/1991 and 09/01/2001) merged into Wachovia Corp. (Ctfs. dated after 09/01/2001) 09/01/2001 which merged into Wells Fargo & Co. (New) 12/31/2008

INTERSTATE LIFE & ACC INS CO (TN)
Each share Common $4.50 par exchanged for (6.75) shares Common $1 par to effect a (4.5) for (1) split and a 50% stock dividend 7/9/58
Stock Dividends - 33-1/3% 11/12/40; 25% 12/17/43; 100% 10/1/48; 50% 12/22/52; 33-1/3% 2/16/54; 33-1/3% 5/12/61; 25% 11/14/63
Reorganized as Interstate Corp. 5/17/69
Each share Common $1 par exchanged for (1) share Common Capital Stock $1 par
Interstate Corp. merged into Gulf Life Holding Co. 1/30/76 which name changed to Gulf United Corp. 5/16/77
(See Gulf United Corp.)

INTERSTATE LIFE INSURANCE CO. (TX)
Common $10 par changed to no par and (2) additional shares issued 12/30/55
Merged into National Bankers Life Insurance Co. 4/13/65
Each share Common no par exchanged for (1/3) share Common $1 par

INTERSTATE LOAN CORP. (NY)
Name changed to Interstate Financial Corp. 00/00/1947
Interstate Financial Corp. merged into Thrift Interstate Corp. 04/15/1965 which name changed to Signal Finance Corp. 01/11/1967 which name changed to Signet Corp. 01/09/1969 which merged into Philadelphia National Corp. 06/29/1973 which merged into CoreStates Financial Corp 05/02/1983 which merged into First Union Corp. 04/28/1998 which name changed to Wachovia Corp. (Ctfs. dated after 09/01/2001) 09/01/2001 which merged into Wells Fargo & Co. (New) 12/31/2008

INTERSTATE MOTOR FREIGHT SYSTEM (MI)
Certificates dated prior to 09/09/1968
Stock Dividend - 100% 12/01/1958
Merged into Fuqua Industries, Inc. (DE) 09/09/1968
Each share Common $1 par automatically became (1) share new Conv. Preferred of Interstate (represented by Common Ctf.) which was immediately convertible into $20 principal amount of 7% Debentures due 07/01/1988, (0.66666666) share Common $1 par and (0.4) 00/00/1973 Stock Purchase Warrant
Unconverted Preferred shares were called for redemption 10/25/1968 on above same basis as if converted
Fuqua Industries, Inc. (DE) name changed to Actava Group Inc. 07/21/1993 which name changed to Metromedia International Group, Inc. 11/01/1995
(See Metromedia International Group, Inc.)

INTERSTATE MTR FGHT SYS (MI)
Ctfs. dated after 10/31/80
Chapter 11 bankruptcy proceedings converted to Chapter 7 on 12/28/84
Stockholders' equity unlikely

INTERSTATE NATL CORP (NV)
Merged into National Student Marketing Corp. (DC) 10/31/69

Each share Common $1 par exchanged for (12/3) share Common 2-1/2¢ par
National Student Marketing Corp. (DC) reincorporated in Delaware 4/1/70
(See National Student Marketing Corp. (DE))

INTERSTATE NATL DEALER SVCS INC (DE)
Merged into CHL Holdings Corp. 1/16/2003
Each share Common 1¢ par exchanged for $6 cash

INTERSTATE NATURAL GAS CO., INC. (DE)
Acquired by Olin Industries, Inc. at $45 per share in 1953

INTERSTATE OIL & DEVELOPMENT CO. (NV)
Merged into Apex Minerals Corp. 4/14/61
Each share Capital Stock 10¢ par exchanged for (0.1) share Capital Stock $1 par
Apex Minerals Corp. recapitalized as Limotran Corp. 8/1/72

INTERSTATE OIL CORP.
Properties sold to Exeter Oil Co., Ltd. (DE) in 1938
Details not available

INTERSTATE OIL LTD (AUSTRALIA)
Each share old Ordinary Reg. AUD $0.50 par exchanged for (0.25) share new Ordinary Reg. AUD $0.50 par 02/04/1972
Each share old ADR for Ordinary AUD $0.50 par exchanged for (0.25) share new Ordinary Reg. AUD $0.50 par 02/04/1972
Name changed to IOL Petroleum Ltd. 05/01/1974
(See IOL Petroleum Ltd.)

INTERSTATE PETROLEUM CO.
Merged into White Eagle Oil Co. in 1952
Each share Class A Preference $1 par exchanged for (1) share Common 10¢ par
Each share Class B Common 50¢ par exchanged for (1) share Common 10¢ par
White Eagle Oil Co. name changed to Helmerich & Payne, Inc. 8/1/59

INTERSTATE PETROLEUM CORP. (TN)
Charter revoked for non-payment of taxes 1/10/62

INTERSTATE PWR & LT CO (IA)
4.30% Preferred Class A $50 par called for redemption at $51 on 09/16/2002
4.36% Preferred Class A $50 par called for redemption at $52.30 on 09/16/2002
4.68% Preferred Class A $50 par called for redemption at $51.62 on 09/16/2002
4.80% Preferred Class A $50 par called for redemption at $50.25 on 09/16/2002
6.10% Preferred Class A $50 par called for redemption at $51 on 09/16/2002
6.40% Preferred Class A $50 par called for redemption at $53.20 on 09/16/2002
7.76% Preferred Class A $50 par called for redemption at $52.03 on 09/16/2002
7.10% Preferred Ser. C 1¢ par called for redemption at $25 plus $0.221875 accrued dividends on 04/29/2011
8.375% Preferred Ser. B 1¢ par called for redemption at $25 plus $0.0407 accrued dividends on 03/22/2013
(Additional Information in Active)

INTERSTATE PWR CO (DE)
Each share $7 Preferred no par exchanged for (10) units Preferred Escrow Certificates 00/00/1948
Each share $6 Preferred no par exchanged for (9) units Preferred Escrow Certificates 00/00/1948
Each unit Preferred Escrow Certificates exchanged for (0.12) share Common $3.50 par 00/00/1951
9.84% Preferred $50 par called for redemption 09/03/1986
10.64% Preferred $50 par called for redemption 10/01/1986
$2.28 Preference $1 par called for redemption 06/30/1993
8% Preferred $50 par called for redemption 06/30/1993
9% Preferred $50 par called for redemption 06/30/1993
Merged into Interstate Energy Corp. 04/21/1998
Each share Common $3.50 par exchanged for (1.11) shares Common no par
Interstate Energy Corp. name changed to Alliant Energy Corp. 05/19/1999
Merged into Interstate Power & Light Co. 01/01/2002
Each share 4.36% Preferred $50 par exchanged for (1) share 4.36% Preferred Class A $50 par
Each share 4.68% Preferred $50 par exchanged for (1) share 4.68% Preferred Class A $50 par
Each share 6.40% Preferred $50 par exchanged for (1) share 6.40% Preferred Class A $50 par
Each share 7.76% Preferred $50 par exchanged for (1) share 7.76% Preferred Class A $50 par
(See Interstate Power & Light Co.)

INTERSTATE PUBLIC SERVICE CO. (AR)
Acquired in reorganization by Sun Utility Co. in 1940
No stockholders' equity

INTERSTATE PUBLIC SERVICE CO. (IN)
Name changed to Public Service Co. of Indiana in 1931
Public Service Co. of Indiana merged into Public Service Co. of Indiana, Inc. 9/6/41
(See Public Service Co. of Indiana, Inc.)

INTERSTATE RES INC (UT)
Proclaimed dissolved for failure to pay taxes 12/31/1975

INTERSTATE SECS CO (DE)
Incorporated 5/7/24
5-1/2% Prior Preferred Ser. C $100 par called for redemption 7/15/67
5-1/4% Prior Preferred Ser. A $100 par called for redemption 9/15/69
5-1/2% Conv. Preferred $20 par called for redemption 5/15/70
5% Preferred $20 par called for redemption 1/1/76
Completely liquidated 3/31/82
Each share Common $5 par exchanged for first and final distribution of $2.80 cash

INTERSTATE SECS INC (DE)
Incorporated 04/01/1985
Name changed to Interstate/Johnson Lane, Inc. 10/17/1988
Interstate/Johnson Lane, Inc. merged into Wachovia Corp. (New) (Ctfs. dated between 05/20/1991 and 09/01/2001) 04/01/1999 which merged into Wachovia Corp. (Ctfs. dated after 09/01/2001) 09/01/2001 which merged into Wells Fargo & Co. (New) 12/31/2008

INTERSTATE SECURITIES CO. (MO)
Each share Common $100 par exchanged for (5) shares Common $20 par in 1947
Each share Common $20 par exchanged for (4) shares Common $5 par 4/27/55
Stock Dividends - 33.9286% 10/8/48; 66-2/3% 12/20/50; 11-1/9% 1/28/55; 10% 12/4/57
Merged into Interstate Securities Co. (Del.) 4/25/66
Each share 5-1/2% Jr. Preference $20 par exchanged for (1) share 5-1/2% Conv. Preferred $20 par
Each share Common $5 par exchanged for (1) share Common $5 par
(See Interstate Securities Co. (Del.))

INTERSTATE STORES INC (DE)
Reorganized as Toys "R" Us, Inc. 04/06/1978
Each (1.5) shares Common $1 par exchanged for (1) share Common 10¢ par
Note: Unexchanged certificates were cancelled and became without value 06/16/1985
(See Toys "R" Us, Inc.)

INTERSTATE STREET RAILWAY CO.
Out of business 00/00/1934
Details not available

INTERSTATE TECHNOLOGIES INC (DE)
Charter cancelled and declared inoperative and void for non-payment of taxes 3/1/92

INTERSTATE TELEPHONE & TELEGRAPH CO.
Merged into United Telephone Co., Inc. 00/00/1940
Details not available

INTERSTATE TELEPHONE CO. (ID)
Name changed to General Telephone Co. of the Northwest in 1952
(See listing for General Telephone Co. of the Northwest)

INTERSTATE TERMINAL WAREHOUSES, INC.
Acquired by National Terminals Corp. 00/00/1929
Details not available

INTERSTATE UNIFORM SVCS CORP (MA)
Name changed to Unifirst Corp. 1/16/84

INTERSTATE UTD CORP (IL)
Merged into Hanson Industries Inc. 6/19/78
Each share Common $1 par exchanged for $10 cash

INTERSTATE URANIUM, INC. (UT)
Merged into Federal Uranium Corp. (NV) on a (1) for (160) basis 04/28/1955
Federal Uranium Corp. (NV) merged into Federal Resources Corp. 05/02/1960
(See Federal Resources Corp.)

INTERSTATE VENDING CO. (IL)
Name changed to Interstate United Corp. 3/4/64
(See Interstate United Corp.)

INTERSTATE ZINC & LEAD CO.
Reorganized as Oklahoma-Interstate Mining Co. on a (1) for (7) basis in 1937
Oklahoma-Interstate Mining Co. charter cancelled 3/1/78

INTERSTRAT RES INC (BC)
Struck from register 06/12/1992

INTERSYSTEMS INC (DE)
Name changed to EquiFin, Inc. 11/15/2001

INTERSYSTEMS INC (MS)
Common $2 par split (2) for (1) by issuance of (1) additional share 6/15/72
Name changed back to School Pictures, Inc. 6/30/75
(See School Pictures, Inc.)

INTERTAIN GROUP LTD OLD (ON)
Plan of arrangement effective 01/25/2017
Each share Common no par exchanged for either (1) share Jackpotjoy PLC Ordinary or (1) Intertain Group Ltd. (New) Exchangeable Share
Note: Option for eligible Canadian residents to elect to receive Exchangeable Shares expired 01/20/2017
Unexchanged certificates will be cancelled and become without value 01/25/2023

INTERTAN INC (DE)
Common $1 par split (3) for (2) by issuance of (0.5) additional share payable 01/13/2000 to holders of record 12/16/1999 Ex date - 01/14/2000
Merged into Circuit City Stores, Inc. 05/19/2004
Each share Common $1 par exchanged for $14 cash

INTERTEC DATA SYS CORP (MD)
Name changed to Wells American Corp. 9/17/85
(See Wells American Corp.)

INTERTEC NATL INC (DE)
Charter cancelled and declared inoperative and void for non-payment of taxes 3/1/75

INTERTECH CORP (DE)
Common $0.001 par split (15) for (1) by issuance of (14) additional shares payable 3/4/2002 to holders of record 3/4/2002 Ex date - 3/5/2002
Name changed to Kirshner International Inc. 4/12/2002
Kirshner International Inc. name changed to Veracity Management Global, Inc. 10/25/2006

INTERTECH GROUP INC (DE)
Charter cancelled and declared inoperative and void for non-payment of taxes 03/01/1981

INTERTECH MINERALS CORP (BC)
Recapitalized as Mantle Minerals Inc. 04/25/2002
Each share Common no par exchanged for (0.125) share Common no par
Mantle Minerals Inc. recapitalized as Mantle Resources Inc. 08/09/2005 which name changed to Canada Zinc Metals Corp. 09/26/2008 which name changed to ZincX Resources Corp. 05/07/2018

INTERTECH RESEARCH SERVICES, INC. (AL)
Reorganized under the laws of Delaware 5/29/69
Each share Common $1 par exchanged for (2) shares Common $1 par
Intertech Research Services, Inc. (DE) name changed to Intertek Financial Corp. 6/23/72
(See Intertek Financial Corp.)

INTERTECH RESEARCH SERVICES, INC. (DE)
Name changed to Intertek Financial Corp. 06/23/1972
(See Intertek Financial Corp.)

INTERTECHNOLOGY SOLAR CORP (VA)
Charter cancelled and proclaimed dissolved for failure to file reports 09/01/1986

INTERTEK FINL CORP (DE)
Pursuant to Chapter X bankruptcy proceedings stock declared worthless 9/23/77

INTERTEL COMMUNICATIONS INC (BC)
Each share old Common no par

exchanged for (0.2) share new Common no par 01/14/1993
Name changed to Intelcom Group Inc. 09/01/1993
Intelcom Group Inc. reorganized as ICG Communications, Inc. 08/02/1996
(See ICG Communications, Inc.)

INTERTHERM INC (MO)
Common $1 par split (3) for (2) by issuance of (0.5) additional share 08/18/1983
Stock Dividend - 25% 05/01/1979
Merged into Nortek, Inc. 06/10/1985
Each share Common $1 par exchanged for $14.75 cash

INTERTRANS CORP (TX)
Common no par split (3) for (2) by issuance of (0.5) additional share 3/19/87
Common no par split (2) for (1) by issuance of (1) additional share 7/2/93
Acquired by Fritz Companies Inc. 5/31/95
Each share Common no par exchanged for (0.365) share Common 1¢ par
Fritz Companies Inc. merged into United Parcel Service Inc. 5/25/2001

INTERTRUST TECHNOLOGIES CORP (DE)
Issue Information - 6,500,000 shares COM offered at $18 per share on 10/26/1999
Common $0.001 par split (2) for (1) by issuance of (1) additional share payable 2/24/2000 to holders of record 2/10/2000
Merged into Fidelio Acquisition Co., LLC 1/8/2003
Each share Common $0.001 par exchanged for $4.25 cash

INTERTYPE CORP. (NY)
Common no par changed to $5 par and (1) additional share issued 3/15/56
Merged into Harris-Intertype Corp. 6/27/57
Each share Common $5 par exchanged for (0.833333) share Common $1 par
Harris-Intertype Corp. name changed to Harris Corp. 5/15/74

INTERUNION FINL CORP (DE)
Each share old Common $0.001 par exchanged for (0.1) share new Common $0.001 par 10/20/1994
Each share new Common $0.001 par exchanged again for (0.05) share new Common par 05/17/1996
Each share new Common $0.001 par exchanged for (0.1) share new Common $0.001 par 12/07/2000
Each share new Common $0.001 par received distribution of (0.3131) share Kyto BioPharma Inc. Common $0.0001 par payable 08/30/2002 to holders of record 08/23/2002 Ex date - 08/21/2002
Recapitalized as BMB Munai, Inc. (DE) 12/12/2003
Each share Common $0.001 par exchanged for (0.1) share Common no par
BMB Munai, Inc. (DE) reincorporated in Nevada 01/13/2005 which recapitalized as Freedom Holding Corp. 09/05/2017

INTERVAL LEISURE GROUP INC (DE)
Name changed to ILG, Inc. 10/17/2016
ILG, Inc. merged into Marriott Vacations Worldwide Corp. 09/04/2018

INTERVENTIONAL INNOVATIONS CORP
Merged into Medtronic, Inc. 01/26/2000

Each share 5% Conv. Preferred Ser. A exchanged for $6.428158 cash

INTERVEST BANCSHARES CORP (DE)
Class A Common $1 par reclassified as Common $1 par 06/12/2012
Merged into Bank of the Ozarks, Inc. 02/10/2015
Each share Common $1 par exchanged for (0.3014) share Common 1¢ par
Bank of the Ozarks, Inc. reorganized as Bank of the Ozarks (Little Rock, AR) 06/27/2017 which name changed to Bank OZK (Little Rock, AR) 07/16/2018

INTERVEST GROUP LTD (NV)
Charter permanently revoked 06/29/2007

INTERVEST MTG ASSOCS L P (DE)
Partnership terminated 11/01/1999
Details not available

INTERVIA INC (NV)
Name changed to Blue Sky Petroleum Inc. 07/31/2012
Blue Sky Petroleum Inc. name changed to Asian Development Frontier Inc. 07/09/2015 which name changed to Unifunds Ltd. 03/23/2018

INTERVIDEO INC (DE)
Issue Information - 2,800,000 shares COM offered at $14 per share on 07/16/2003
Merged into Corel Corp. (New) 12/12/2006
Each share Common $0.001 par exchanged for $13 cash

INTERVISUAL BOOKS INC (CA)
Reincorporated under the laws of Delaware 2/3/2003

INTERVOICE INC NEW (TX)
Name changed 08/20/1999
Name changed 08/30/2002
Common no par split (2) for (1) by issuance of (1) additional share 10/16/1992
Common no par split (2) for (1) by issuance of (1) additional share 08/16/1993
Common no par split (2) for (1) by issuance of (1) additional share payable 01/11/1999 to holders of record 12/28/1998
Under plan of merger name changed from InterVoice, Inc. (Old) to InterVoice-Brite, Inc. 08/20/1999
Name changed from InterVoice-Brite, Inc. to InterVoice, Inc. (New) 08/30/2002
Acquired by Convergys Corp. 09/04/2008
Each share Common no par exchanged for $8.25 cash

INTERVU INC (DE)
Merged into Akamai Technologies, Inc. 4/20/2000
Each share Common $0.001 par exchanged for (0.5957) share Common 1¢ par

INTERWAVE COMMUNICATIONS INTL LTD (BERMUDA)
Acquired by Alvarion Ltd. 02/09/2005
Each share Common $0.001 par exchanged for $4.18 cash

INTERWAY CORP (DE)
Common $1 par split (3) for (2) by issuance of (0.5) additional share 02/15/1978
Merged into Transamerica Corp. 07/30/1979
Each share Common $1 par exchanged for $42 cash

INTERWEST BANCORP INC (WA)
Common 20¢ par split (3) for (2) by issuance of (0.5) additional share payable 08/17/1998 to holders of record 08/03/1998

Name changed to Pacific Northwest Bancorp 09/01/2000
Pacific Northwest Bancorp merged into Wells Fargo & Co. (New) 11/03/2003

INTERWEST BANK OF ARIZONA (TUCSON, AZ)
Name changed to Arizona Bank (Tucson, AZ) 07/20/1992
Arizona Bank (Tucson, AZ) merged into Compass Bancshares, Inc. 12/15/1998 which merged into Banco Bilbao Vizcaya Argentaria, S.A. 09/07/2007

INTERWEST COMMUNICATIONS CORP (DE)
Each (6) shares old Common $0.0001 par exchanged for (1) share new Common $0.0001 par 5/31/90
Merged into Internet Communications Corp. 9/19/96
Each share new Common $0.0001 par exchanged again for (1) share new Common no par
Internet Communications Corp. merged into Internet Commerce & Communications, Inc. 11/29/2000
(See Internet Commerce & Communications, Inc.)

INTERWEST CORP (NY)
Charter cancelled and proclaimed dissolved for failure to pay taxes 03/25/1992

INTERWEST CORP (UT)
Each share old Common no par exchanged for (0.1) share new Common no par 10/17/1972
Each share new Common no par exchanged again for (0.02) share new Common no par 08/02/1979
Note: In effect holders received $1.17 cash per share and public interest was eliminated

INTERWEST FOOD CORP (UT)
Merged into Interwest General Corp. 6/15/72
Each share Capital Stock 5¢ par exchanged for (0.1) share Common 1¢ par
(See Interwest General Corp.)

INTERWEST GEN CORP (DE)
Charter cancelled and declared inoperative and void for non-payment of taxes 03/01/1974

INTERWEST HOME MED INC (UT)
Each share old Common no par exchanged for (0.25) share new Common no par 12/4/95
Merged into Praxair, Inc. 5/22/2001
Each share new Common no par exchanged for $8.92 cash

INTERWEST MED CORP (OK)
Each (5,000) shares old Common $0.001 par exchanged for (1) share new Common $0.001 par 2/25/2005
Note: In effect holders received $0.10 cash per share and public interest was eliminated

INTERWEST OPPORTUNITIES INC (CO)
Proclaimed dissolved for failure to file reports and pay fees 1/1/96

INTERWEST SVGS BK (OAK HARBOR, WA)
Stock Dividend - 15% 05/06/1993
Recapitalized as Interwest Bancorp, Inc. 07/28/1995
Each share Common $2 par exchanged for (1) share Common 20¢ par
Interwest Bancorp, Inc. name changed to Pacific Northwest Bancorp 09/01/2000 which merged into Wells Fargo & Co. (New) 11/03/2003

INTERWORLD CORP (DE)
Issue Information - 3,000,000 shares COM offered at $15 per share on 08/11/1999

Each share old Common 1¢ par exchanged for (0.02) share new Common 1¢ par 05/21/2001
Chapter 7 bankruptcy proceedings closed 02/07/2008
No stockholders' equity

INTERWOVEN INC (DE)
Old Common $0.001 par split (2) for (1) by issuance of (1) additional share payable 07/13/2000 to holders of record 06/22/2000
Old Common $0.001 par split (2) for (1) by issuance of (1) additional share payable 12/29/2000 to holders of record 12/13/2000 Ex date - 01/02/2001
Each share old Common $0.001 par exchanged for (0.25) share new Common $0.001 par 11/18/2003
Merged into Autonomy Corp. PLC 03/17/2009
Each share Common $0.001 par exchanged for $16.20 cash

INTEVAC INC (CA)
Reincorporated under the laws of Delaware 07/19/2007

INTEX MNG LTD (ON)
Merged into High American Gold Inc. (ON) 06/23/1997
Each share Common no par exchanged for (0.33333333) share Common no par
High American Gold Inc. (ON) reorganized in Alberta as Antioquia Gold Inc. 07/29/2008 which reincorporated in British Columbia 03/24/2016

INTEX OIL CO. (CA)
Merged into Tesoro Petroleum Corp. (CA) 02/01/1968
Each share Common $0.33333333 par exchanged for (1) share Common $0.33333333 par
Tesoro Petroleum Corp. (CA) reincorporated in Delaware as Tesoro Petroleum Corp. 03/03/1969 which name changed to Tesoro Corp. 11/08/2004 which name changed to Andeavor 08/01/2017 which merged into Marathon Petroleum Corp. 10/01/2018

INTEX SOFTWARE SYS INTL LTD (NY)
Dissolved by proclamation 3/24/93

INTEXT INC (PA)
Merged into National Education Corp. 01/31/1980
Each share Capital Stock no par exchanged for $14 cash

INTIER AUTOMOTIVE INC (ON)
Merged into Magna International Inc. 04/03/2005
Each share Class A Subordinate no par exchanged for (0.41) share Class A Subordinate no par

INTIMATE BRANDS INC (DE)
Class A Common 1¢ par split (2) for (1) by issuance of (1) additional share payable 05/30/2000 to holders of record 05/12/2000
Stock Dividend - 5% payable 07/16/1999 to holders of record 07/02/1999
Acquired by Limited, Inc. 03/21/2002
Each share Class A Common 1¢ par exchanged for (1.1) shares Common 50¢ par
Limited, Inc. name changed to Limited Brands, Inc. 05/20/2002 which name changed to L Brands, Inc. 03/28/2013

INTIME RETAIL GROUP CO LTD (CAYMAN ISLANDS)
Name changed 07/19/2013
Name changed from Intime Department Store (Group) Co. Ltd. to Intime Retail (Group) Co. Ltd. 07/19/2013
ADR agreement terminated 06/01/2017

Each ADR for Ordinary exchanged for $25.631538 cash

INTIME SYS INTL INC (DE)
Merged into Aris Corp. 06/30/1998
Each share Class A Common 1¢ par exchanged for (0.3046624) share Common no par
Aris Corp. merged into Ciber, Inc. 0/19/2001 which name changed to CMTSU Liquidation, Inc. 12/22/2017

INTIRMAC INDL CORP (BC)
Name changed to Sniper Enterprises Inc. 12/07/1998
Sniper Enterprises Inc. name changed to TransAmerican Energy Inc. 08/16/2005 which recapitalized as American Biofuels Inc. 09/12/2018

INTIVA BIOPHARMA INC (DE)
Name changed to Nexien BioPharma, Inc. 10/19/2018

INTRA-ASIA ENTMT CORP (NV)
Recapitalized as China TransInfo Technology Corp. 08/23/2007
Each (7.5) shares Common $0.001 par exchanged for (1) share Common $0.001 par
(See China Transinfo Technology Corp.)

INTRABIOTICS PHARMACEUTICALS INC (DE)
Each share old Common $0.001 par exchanged for (0.08333333) share new Common $0.001 par 04/11/2003
Name changed to Ardea Biosciences, Inc. 01/22/2007
(See Ardea Biosciences, Inc.)

INTRAC INC (NV)
Each share old Common $0.001 par exchanged for (0.1) share new Common $0.001 par 12/03/2001
Each share new Common $0.001 par exchanged again for (0.0001052) share new Common $0.001 par 07/03/2002
Reincorporated under the laws of Delaware as Javelin Pharmaceuticals, Inc. 09/07/2005
(See Javelin Pharmaceuticals, Inc.)

INTRACO SYS INC (NV)
Recapitalized as Investco, Inc. 01/28/2002
Each share Common no par exchanged for (0.01) share Common no par
(See Investco, Inc.)

INTRACOASTAL SYS ENGR CORP (BC)
Delisted from Toronto Venture Stock Exchange 06/20/2003

INTRACORP RES CORP (AB)
Name changed to Proteus Environmental Inc. 3/8/96

INTRADO INC (DE)
Merged into West Corp. 04/04/2006
Each share Common $0.001 par exchanged for $26 cash

INTRALASE CORP (DE)
Issue Information - 6,636,314 shares COM offered at $13 per share on 10/06/2004
Merged into Advanced Medical Optics, Inc. 4/2/2007
Each share Common no par exchanged for $25 cash

INTRALINKS HLDGS INC (DE)
Acquired by Synchronoss Technologies, Inc. 01/19/2017
Each share Common $0.001 par exchanged for $13 cash

INTRAMED LABS INC (CA)
Acquired by Baxter International Inc. 11/11/94
Each share Common no par exchanged for (0.10256) share Common $1 par

INTRAMERICAN CORP (PA)
Name changed 07/31/1990
Name changed from Intramerican Oil & Minerals, Inc. to Intramerican Corp. 07/31/1990
Name changed to Hunter Resources Inc. 11/10/1992
Hunter Resources Inc. was liquidated by Magnum Petroleum, Inc. 11/01/1996 which name changed to Magnum Hunter Resources, Inc. 03/18/1997 which merged into Cimarex Energy Co. 06/07/2005

INTRAMERICAN LIFE CORP (NY)
Merged into Colonial Penn Group, Inc. 7/1/68
Each share Class A Common $1 par exchanged for (0.4) share Common 10¢ par and (0.4) Common Stock Purchase Warrant
(See Colonial Penn Group, Inc.)

INTRANET COMPUTING CORP. (DE)
Name changed to Intranet Corp. 12/18/73
Intranet Corp. acquired by Interscience Systems, Inc. (Calif.) 12/28/77 which reincorporated in Nevada 3/31/81

INTRANET CORP (DE)
Reorganized 3/31/72
Name changed 12/18/73
Reorganized from (CO) to under the laws of (DE) 3/31/72
Each share Common 10¢ par exchanged for (0.021) share Common 4¢ par
Name changed from Intranet Computing Corp. to Intranet Corp. 12/18/73
Acquired by Interscience Systems, Inc. (CA) 12/28/77
Each share Common 4¢ par exchanged for (0.25) share Common no par
Interscience Systems, Inc. (CA) reincorporated in Nevada 3/31/81
(See Interscience Systems, Inc.)

INTRANET SOLUTIONS INC (MN)
Each share old Common 1¢ par exchanged for (0.25) share new Common 1¢ par 10/31/96
Name changed to Stellent, Inc. 8/29/2001
(See Stellent, Inc.)

INTRAOP MED CORP (NV)
Old Common $0.001 par split (20) for (1) by issuance of (19) additional shares payable 01/22/2004 to holders of record 01/22/2004 Ex date - 01/22/2004
Each share old Common $0.001 par exchanged for (0.02) share new Common $0.001 par 11/10/2009
Plan of reorganization under Chapter 11 Federal Bankruptcy proceedings effective 02/05/2014
No stockholders' equity

INTRASTATE ASSOCIATES, INC. (NY)
Name changed to I.A. Liquidating Corp. 3/31/70
(See I.A. Liquidating Corp.)

INTRATEL GROUP LTD (DE)
Charter cancelled and declared inoperative and void for non-payment of taxes 03/01/1999

INTRAV INC (MO)
Merged into Kuoni Reisen Holding AG 9/16/99
Each share Common 1¢ par exchanged for $21.32 cash

INTRAVELNET COM INC (ON)
Recapitalized as Forum National Investments Ltd. 7/5/2002
Each share Common no par exchanged for (0.1) share Common no par

INTRAVISION INC (NY)
Charter cancelled and proclaimed dissolved for failure to pay taxes 12/24/91

INTRAWARE INC (DE)
Issue Information - 4,000,000 shares COM offered at $16 per share on 02/25/1999
Each share old Common $0.0001 par exchanged for (0.1) share new Common $0.0001 par 09/27/2005
Merged into Acresso Software Inc. 01/07/2009
Each share Ser. A Preferred $0.0001 par exchanged for $4 cash
Each share Ser. B Preferred $0.0001 par exchanged for $6,000 cash
Each share Ser. B-1 Preferred $0.0001 par exchanged for $6,000 cash
Each share new Common $0.0001 par exchanged for $4 cash

INTRAWEST CORP (CANADA)
Name changed 03/10/1993
Reincorporated 01/14/2002
Name changed from Intrawest Development Corp. to Intrawest Corp. 03/10/1993
Old Common no par reclassified as new Common no par 03/14/1997
Each share new Common no par received distribution of (1) share old Non-Resort Preferred no par payable 03/14/1997 to holders of record 03/14/1997
Each share old Non-Resort Preferred no par exchanged for (1) share 2000 New Non-Resort Preferred no par 10/01/2000
Place of incorporation changed from (BC) to (Canada) 01/14/2002
Merged into Fortress Investment Group LLC 10/26/2006
Each share new Common no par exchanged for $35 cash

INTRAWEST FINL CORP (CO)
Merged into United Banks of Colorado, Inc. 04/30/1987
Each share Common $10 par exchanged for (0.724) share Common $2.50 par
United Banks of Colorado, Inc. merged into Norwest Corp. 04/19/1991 which name changed to Wells Fargo & Co. (New) 11/02/1998

INTRAWEST RESORTS HLDGS INC (DE)
Acquired by Hawk Holding Co., LLC 07/31/2017
Each share Common 1¢ par exchanged for $23.75 cash

INTRAZONE INC (DE)
Each share old Common $0.001 par exchanged for (0.2) share new Common $0.001 par 04/24/1997
Reorganized under the laws of Nevada as PMI Construction Group, Inc. 03/29/1999
Each share new Common $0.001 par exchanged for (0.5) share Common $0.001 par
PMI Construction Group, Inc. recapitalized as Kung Fu Dragon Group Ltd. 06/11/2015

INTRENET INC (IN)
Company ceased operations 1/18/2001
No stockholders' equity

INTREPID GLOBAL IMAGING 3D INC (DE)
Name changed to Spine Pain Management, Inc. 11/27/2009
Spine Pain Management, Inc. name changed to Spine Injury Solutions, Inc. 10/08/2015

INTREPID HLDGS INC (NV)
Recapitalized as My Healthy Access, Inc. 03/12/2008
Each share Common $0.001 par exchanged for (0.1) share Common $0.001 par

INTREPID INC (NV)
Name changed to California ASIC Technical Services Inc. 09/30/1993
California ASIC Technical Services Inc. merged into JMAR Technologies, Inc. 05/01/1998
(See JMAR Technologies, Inc.)

INTREPID MINERALS CORP (CANADA)
Plan of arrangement effective 07/05/2006
Each share Common no par held by Canadian residents exchanged for (1) Intrepid NuStar Exchange Corp. Exchangeable Share
Each share Common no par held by non-Canadian residents exchanged for (1) Intrepid Mines Ltd. Ordinary Share
(See each company's listing)

INTREPID NUSTAR EXCHANGE CORP (CANADA)
Each Exchangeable Share no par exchanged for (1) share Intrepid Mines Ltd. Ordinary 04/30/2009

INTREPID TECHNOLOGY & RES INC (ID)
Each share old Common $0.005 par exchanged for (0.01) share new Common $0.005 par 03/31/2008
Company ceased operations 02/07/2009
Stockholders' equity unlikely

INTREX FINL SVCS INC (DE)
Under plan of reorganization each share Common 10¢ par automatically became (1) share Lawrence Savings Bank (New) (Lawrence, MA) Common 10¢ par 10/25/1991
Lawrence Savings Bank (New) (Lawrence, MA) reorganized as LSB Corp. 07/01/2001
(See LSB Corp.)

INTREX INC (NV)
Name changed 05/19/1999
Each share old Common no par exchanged for (0.04) share new Common no par 02/16/1999
Name and state of incorporation changed from Intrex Inc. (WA) to Intrex.com, Inc. (NV) and Common no par changed to $0.001 par 05/19/1999
Name changed to Financial Commerce Network, Inc. 09/28/1999
Financial Commerce Network, Inc. name changed to Regions Oil & Gas Inc. 01/23/2007 which recapitalized as American Green Group, Inc. 02/27/2008
(See American Green Group, Inc.)

INTRINSIC CAP INC (BC)
Completely liquidated
Each share Common no par received first and final distribution of (0.25) Stealth Ventures Ltd. (BC) Unit consisting of (1) share Common no par and (0.5) Common Stock Purchase Warrant expiring 02/09/2005 payable 04/06/2004 to holders of record 01/30/2004
Stealth Ventures Ltd. (BC) reorganized in Alberta as Stealth Ventures Inc. 08/23/2012

INTRINSYC SOFTWARE INTL INC (CANADA)
Reincorporated 05/01/2003
Name and place of incorporation changed from Intrinsyc Software Inc. (BC) to Intrinsyc Software International, Inc. (Canada) 05/01/2003
Recapitalized as Intrinsyc Technologies Corp. 06/20/2014
Each share Common no par exchanged for (0.125) share Common no par

INTROBUZZ (NV)
Name changed to Cynk Technology Corp. 07/23/2013

INTROGEN THERAPEUTICS INC (DE)
Plan of reorganization under Chapter 11 Federal Bankruptcy proceedings effective 05/17/2010
Stockholders' equity unlikely

INTROL CORP (MN)
Common 10¢ par changed to 5¢ par 11/8/71
Each share Common 5¢ par exchanged for (0.1) share Common 50¢ par 11/17/76
Under plan of merger each share Common 50¢ par exchanged for $3.20 cash 4/20/79

INTRON LTD (DE)
Recapitalized as IMA Medikose Group, Inc. 8/10/90
Each share Common $0.001 par exchanged for (1/3) share Common $0.001 par

INTRON USA COM (NV)
Each share Common $0.001 par exchanged for (0.28571428) share new Common $0.001 par 03/18/2002
Name changed to Mondopolitan Inc. 04/02/2002
Mondopolitan Inc. recapitalized as CGT Resources, Inc. 03/31/2006 which name changed to HealthSonix, Inc. 05/08/2006
(See HealthSonix, Inc.)

INTRUM JUSTITIA AB (SWEDEN)
Name changed to Intrum AB 05/10/2018

INTRUSION COM INC (DE)
Name changed to Intrusion Inc. 11/1/2001

INTRUST CAP TR (DE)
8.24% Trust Preferred Securities called for redemption at $25 on 3/21/2003
Public interest eliminated

INTRUST FINL CORP (KS)
Each share old Common $5 par exchanged for (0.001) share new Common $5 par 5/8/2003
Note: In effect holders received $152 cash per share and public interest was eliminated

INTRYST INC (ID)
Name changed to PTC Group Inc. 12/22/1997
PTC Group Inc. name changed to Ocean Power Corp. 07/12/1999
(See Ocean Power Corp.)

INTUITIVO CAP CORP (ON)
Recapitalized as Argonaut Gold Ltd. 12/31/2009
Each share Common no par exchanged for (0.03333333) share Common no par
Argonaut Gold Ltd. name changed to Argonaut Gold Inc. 10/22/2010

INVADAY MINING & EXPLORATIONS, LTD. (ON)
Charter cancelled 11/05/1962

INVADER EXPL INC (AB)
Merged into Innova Exploration Ltd. 04/16/2004
Each share Common no par exchanged for (0.86) share Common no par
(See Innova Exploration Ltd.)

INVADER OIL CORP. (DE)
Charter cancelled and declared inoperative and void for non-payment of taxes 4/1/30

INVADER RES LTD (BC)
Name changed to Chapel Resources Inc. 02/04/1985
Chapel Resources Inc. recapitalized as Broadway Beverages Ltd. 09/03/1987
(See Broadway Beverages Ltd.)

INVENDA CORP (DE)
Company terminated common stock registration and is no longer public as of 01/08/2009

INVENIO RES CORP (BC)
Name changed to Greatbanks Resources Ltd. 02/12/2015

INVENSENSE INC (DE)
Acquired by TDK Corp. 05/18/2017
Each share Common $0.001 par exchanged for $13 cash

INVENSYS PLC (UNITED KINGDOM)
Each old Sponsored ADR for Ordinary 25p par exchanged for (0.2) new Sponsored ADR for Ordinary 25p par 08/07/2006
ADR basis changed from (1:2) to (1:1) 08/07/2006
Each new Sponsored ADR for Ordinary 25p par exchanged again for (0.8) new Sponsored ADR for Ordinary 25p par 06/12/2013
ADR agreement terminated 03/10/2014
Each new Sponsored ADR for Ordinary 25p par exchanged for $8.3186 cash

INVENT INC (DE)
Merged into Triton Oil & Gas Corp. 8/14/78
Each (4.5) shares Common 5¢ par exchanged for (1) share Common Capital Stock $1 par
Triton Oil & Gas Corp. name changed to Triton Energy Corp. (TX) 12/1/81 which reincorporated in Delaware 5/12/95

INVENTBAY COM INC (DE)
Recapitalized as SMA Alliance, Inc. 05/20/2011
Each share Common $0.001 par exchanged for (0.01) share Common $0.001 par

INVENTION DESIGN ENGR ASSOC INC (DE)
Common 1¢ par split (3) for (2) by issuance of (0.5) additional share 09/14/1984
Name changed to Structural Instrumentation, Inc. 08/02/1993
Structural Instrumentation, Inc. name changed to SI Technologies Inc. 02/12/1996
(See SI Technologies Inc.)

INVENTIV HEALTH INC (DE)
Merged into Papillon Holdings, Inc. 08/03/2010
Each share Common $0.001 par exchanged for $26.05 cash

INVENTORY MARKETING SVCS INC (NV)
Name changed to Sleepsource International Ltd. 5/10/96
(See Sleepsource International Ltd.)

INVENTOY COM INC (DE)
Common $0.001 par split (4) for (1) by issuance of (3) additional shares payable 03/06/2002 to holders of record 02/25/2002 Ex date - 03/07/2002
Name changed to Assure Energy Inc. (DE) 05/01/2002
Assure Energy Inc. (DE) reincorporated in Nevada 09/11/2003 which reincorporated in Alberta 02/10/2004 which was acquired by GEOCAN Energy Inc. 09/08/2005 which merged into Arsenal Energy Inc. (New) 10/08/2008 which merged into Prairie Provident Resources Inc. 09/16/2016

INVENTRONICS LTD (MB)
Reincorporated under the laws of Alberta 10/24/2000

INVENTTECH INC (NV)
Common $0.0001 par split (30) for (1) by issuance of (29) additional shares payable 05/06/2013 to holders of record 05/06/2013
Ex date - 05/07/2013
Name changed to Ener-Core, Inc. (NV) 05/16/2013
Ener-Core, Inc. (NV) reincorporated in Delaware 09/03/2015

INVENTURE CAP CORP (MA)
Acquired by Steadman American Industry Fund, Inc. 9/9/75
Each share Capital Stock $1 par exchanged for (3.9324) shares Common $1 par
Steadman American Industry Fund, Inc. name changed to Ameritor Industry Fund 9/23/98
(See Ameritor Industry Fund)

INVENTURE FOODS INC (DE)
Acquired by Utz Quality Foods, LLC 12/15/2017
Each share Common 1¢ par exchanged for $4 cash

INVENTURE GROUP INC (DE)
Name changed to Inventure Foods, Inc. 05/20/2010
(See Inventure Foods, Inc.)

INVERCOAL INC (CO)
Recapitalized as Core International Ltd. 04/02/2007
Each share Common $0.001 par exchanged for (0.04) share Common $0.001 par
Core International Ltd. recapitalized as Therma-Med, Inc. 12/31/2008

INVERESK RESH GROUP INC (DE)
Issue Information - 12,000,000 shares COM offered at $13 per share on 06/27/2002
Merged into Charles River Laboratories International, Inc. 10/20/2004
Each share Common 1¢ par exchanged for (0.48) share Common 1¢ par and $15.15 cash

INVERMAY RES INC (BC)
Struck off register and declared dissolved for failure to file returns 1/25/91

INVERMERE RES LTD (CANADA)
Name changed to Canalands Resources Corp. 03/07/1983
(See Canalands Resources Corp.)

INVERNESS MED INNOVATIONS INC (DE)
Name changed to Alere Inc. 07/14/2010
(See Alere Inc.)

INVERNESS MED TECHNOLOGY INC (DE)
Each share Common $0.001 par received distribution of (0.2) share Inverness Medical Innovations, Inc. Common $0.001 par payable 11/21/2001 to holders of record 11/21/2001
Merged into Johnson & Johnson 11/21/2001
Each share Common $0.001 par exchanged for (0.5935) share Common $1 par

INVERNESS PETE LTD (CANADA)
7% Conv. Class A Preferred Ser. 3 no par called for redemption 07/30/1993
Merged into Rigel Energy Corp. 03/13/1996
Each share 8.75% Conv. Class B Preferred Ser. 1 no par exchanged for (0.625) share 8.75% Conv. Class B Preferred Ser. 1 no par
Each share Common no par exchanged for (0.625) share Common no par
Rigel Energy Corp. merged into Talisman Energy Inc. 10/05/1999
(See Talisman Energy Inc.)

INVERPOWER CTLS LTD (ON)
Assets sold for the benefit of creditors 07/17/2001
Stockholders' equity unlikely

INVERSIONES AGUAS METROPOLITANAS (CHILE)
ADR agreement terminated 08/07/2015
Each 144A Sponsored ADR for Ordinary exchanged for $34.666245 cash
Each Reg. S Sponsored ADR for Ordinary exchanged for $34.666245 cash

INVERTED PARADIGMS CORP (DE)
Recapitalized as Transfer Technology International Corp. 12/07/2007
Each share Common $0.001 par exchanged for (0.01) share Common $0.001 par
Transfer Technology International Corp. name changed to Enviro-Serv, Inc. 04/23/2013

INVESCO ADVANTAGE GLOBAL HEALTH SCIENCES FD (MD)
Reorganized as INVESCO Counselor Series Funds, Inc. 10/01/2003
Details not available

INVESCO CALIF MUN INCOME TR (MA)
Name changed 01/23/2012
Name changed from Invesco California Insured Municipal Income Trust to Invesco California Municipal Income Trust 01/23/2012
Auction Preferred Ser. 1 1¢ par called for redemption at $50,000 on 06/18/2012
Auction Preferred Ser. 2 1¢ par called for redemption at $50,000 on 06/18/2012
Auction Preferred Ser. 3 1¢ par called for redemption at $50,000 on 06/18/2012
Auction Preferred Ser. 4 1¢ par called for redemption at $50,000 on 06/18/2012
Merged into Invesco Van Kampen California Value Municipal Income Trust 08/27/2012
Each Common Share of Bene. Int. 1¢ par exchanged for (1.16703458) Common Shares of Bene. Int. 1¢ par
Invesco Van Kampen California Value Municipal Income Trust name changed to Invesco California Value Municipal Income Trust 12/03/2012

INVESCO CALIF MUN SECS (MA)
Name changed 01/23/2012
Name changed from Invesco Insured California Municipal Securities to Invesco California Municipal Securities 01/23/2012
Merged into Invesco Van Kampen California Value Municipal Income Trust 08/27/2012
Each Common Share of Bene. Int. 1¢ par exchanged for (1.15599706) Common Shares of Bene. Int. 1¢ par

INVESCO CALIF QUALITY MUN SECS (MA)
Auction Rate Preferred Ser. 1 1¢ par called for redemption at $50,000 on 06/19/2012
Auction Rate Preferred Ser. 3 1¢ par called for redemption at $50,000 on 06/19/2012
Auction Rate Preferred Ser. 1 1¢ par called for redemption at $50,000 on 06/21/2012
Merged into Invesco Van Kampen California Value Municipal Income Trust 08/27/2012
Each Common Share of Bene. Int. 1¢ par exchanged for (1.08388521) Common Shares of Bene. Int. 1¢ par
Invesco Van Kampen California Value Municipal Income Trust name changed to Invesco California Value Municipal Income Trust 12/03/2012

INVESCO CAP APPRECIATION FDS INC (MD)
Reorganized as INVESCO Stock Funds Inc. 06/01/999
Details not available

INVESCO DYNAMICS FD INC (MD)
Name changed to INVESCO Capital Appreciation Funds, Inc. and Common 1¢ par reclassified as Dynamics Fund 1¢ par 07/03/1997
(See INVESCO Capital Appreciation Funds, Inc.)

INVESCO EMERGING OPPORTUNITY FDS INC (MD)
Name changed 12/02/1994
Name changed from INVESCO Emerging Growth Fund, Inc. to INVESCO Emerging Opportunity Funds, Inc. 12/02/1994
Reorganized as INVESCO Stock Funds, Inc. 07/15/1999
Details not available

INVESCO GLOBAL HEALTH SCIENCES FUND (MA)
Reincorporated under the laws of Maryland as INVESCO Advantage Global Health Sciences Fund and Common 1¢ par reclassified as Class A Common 1¢ par 05/15/2001
(See INVESCO Advantage Global Health Sciences Fund)

INVESCO GROWTH FD INC (MD)
Reorganized as Invesco Stock Funds Inc. 07/16/1999
Details not available

INVESCO HIGH YIELD INVTS FD INC (MD)
Merged into Invesco Van Kampen High Income Trust II 08/27/2012
Each share Common 1¢ par exchanged for (0.37313433) share Common 1¢ par
Invesco Van Kampen High Income Trust II name changed to Invesco High Income Trust II 12/03/2012

INVESCO INC (NS)
Each Exchangeable Share no par exchanged for (0.5) share Invesco Ltd. Common U.S. $0.10 par 12/04/2007

INVESCO INCOME FDS INC (MD)
Reorganized as INVESCO Bond Funds, Inc. 11/24/2003
Details not available

INVESCO INDL INCOME FD INC (MD)
Merged into INVESCO Combination Stock & Bond Funds, Inc. 05/28/1999
Details not available

INVESCO INSTL SER TR (MA)
Name changed to Financial Series Trust and Income Fund no par and International Fund no par reclassified as U.S. Government Money Fund no par and International Growth Fund no par respectively 12/28/1990
Financial Series Trust name changed to INVESCO Value Trust 07/01/1993
(See INVESCO Value Trust)

INVESCO INTL CORP (TX)
Reincorporated under the laws of Nevada 04/01/1971

INVESCO INTL FDS INC (MD)
Growth Fund Class A completely liquidated 12/19/2002
Details not available
Growth Fund Class B completely liquidated 12/19/2002
Details not available
Reorganized as AIM International Funds, Inc. II 11/25/2003
Details not available

INVESCO MONEY MKT FDS INC (MD)
Reorganized as AIM Money Market Funds, Inc. 10/01/2003
Details not available

INVESCO MUN INCOME OPPORTUNITIES TR (MA)
Reincorporated under the laws of Delaware 08/27/2012

INVESCO MUN PREM INCOME TR (MA)
Auction Preferred Ser. A 1¢ par called for redemption at $25,000 on 06/13/2012
Auction Preferred Ser. B 1¢ par called for redemption at $25,000 on 06/13/2012
Auction Preferred Ser. C 1¢ par called for redemption at $25,000 on 06/13/2012
Auction Preferred Ser. D 1¢ par called for redemption at $25,000 on 06/13/2012
Auction Preferred Ser. E 1¢ par called for redemption at $25,000 on 06/13/2012
Merged into Invesco Van Kampen Municipal Opportunity Trust 10/15/2012
Each share Common 1¢ par exchanged for (0.6353022) share Common Share of Bene. Int. no par
Invesco Van Kampen Municipal Opportunity Trust name changed to Invesco Municipal Opportunity Trust 12/03/2012

INVESCO MUN INCOME OPPORTUNITIES TR II (MA)
Merged into Invesco Municipal Income Opportunities Trust 08/27/2012
Each share Common 1¢ par exchanged for (1.09433962) shares Common 1¢ par

INVESCO MUN INCOME OPPORTUNITIES TR III (MA)
Merged into Invesco Municipal Income Opportunities Trust 08/27/2012
Each share Common 1¢ par exchanged for (1.18733154) shares Common 1¢ par

INVESCO NY QUALITY MUN SECS (MA)
Auction Preferred Ser. 1 1¢ par called for redemption at $50,000 on 06/12/2012
Auction Preferred Ser. 2 1¢ par called for redemption at $50,000 on 06/15/2012
Merged into Invesco Van Kampen Trust for Investment Grade New York Municipals 08/27/2012
Each share Common 1¢ par exchanged for (1.03140704) shares Common 1¢ par
Invesco Van Kampen Trust for Investment Grade New York Municipals name changed to Invesco Trust for Investment Grade New York Municipals 12/03/2012

INVESCO PLC NEW (ENGLAND & WALES)
Reorganized under the laws of Bermuda as Invesco Ltd. 12/04/2007
Each Sponsored ADR for Ordinary U.S.$0.10 par exchanged for (1) share Common U.S.$0.10 par

INVESCO PLC OLD (ENGLAND & WALES)
Issue Information - 6,000,000 SPONSORED ADR's offered at $33.64 per ADR on 09/24/1995
Name changed to AMVESCO PLC 03/10/1997
AMVESCO PLC name changed to AMVESCAP PLC 05/08/1997 which name changed to INVESCO PLC (New) (England & Wales) 05/23/2007 which reorganized in Bermuda as Invesco Ltd. 12/04/2007

INVESCO QUALITY MUN INCOME TR (MA)
Auction Rate Preferred Ser. 1 1¢ par called for redemption at $50,000 on 06/20/2012
Auction Rate Preferred Ser. 2 1¢ par called for redemption at $50,000 on 06/21/2012
Auction Rate Preferred Ser. 3 1¢ par called for redemption at $50,000 on 06/21/2012
Auction Rate Preferred Ser. 4 1¢ par called for redemption at $50,000 on 06/21/2012
Auction Rate Preferred Ser. 5 1¢ par called for redemption at $50,000 on 06/22/2012
Reincorporated under the laws of Delaware and Common 1¢ par changed to no par 10/15/2012

INVESCO QUALITY MUN INVT TR (MA)
Auction Rate Preferred Ser. A 1¢ par called for redemption at $50,000 on 06/20/2012
Auction Rate Preferred Ser. B 1¢ par called for redemption at $50,000 on 06/22/2012
Merged into Invesco Quality Municipal Income Trust 10/15/2012
Each share Common 1¢ par exchanged for (1.04424157) shares Common no par

INVESCO QUALITY MUN SECS (MA)
Auction Rate Preferred Ser. 1 1¢ par called for redemption at $50,000 on 06/19/2012
Auction Rate Preferred Ser. 4 1¢ par called for redemption at $50,000 on 06/19/2012
Auction Rate Preferred Ser. 5 1¢ par called for redemption at $50,000 on 06/19/2012
Auction Rate Preferred Ser. 2 1¢ par called for redemption at $50,000 on 06/20/2012
Auction Rate Preferred Ser. 3 1¢ par called for redemption at $50,000 on 06/21/2012
Merged into Invesco Quality Municipal Income Trust 10/15/2012
Each share Common 1¢ par exchanged for (1.10744382) shares Common no par

INVESCO SECTOR FDS INC (MD)
Reorganized as AIM Sector Funds, Inc. 11/25/2003
Details not available

INVESCO STRATEGIC PORTFOLIOS INC (MD)
Name changed to INVESCO Sector Funds, Inc. 10/29/1998
(See INVESCO Sector Funds, Inc.)

INVESCO TAX-FREE INCOME FDS INC (MD)
Reorganized as INVESCO Bond Funds, Inc. 05/20/1999
Details not available

INVESCO TREASRS SER TR (MA)
Reincorporated under the laws of Maryland as INVESCO Treasurer's Series Funds, Inc. and Money Market Reserve Fund $1 par and Tax-Exempt Reserve Fund $1 par reclassified as Treasurer's Money Market Reserve Fund $1 par and Treasurer's Tax-Exempt Reserve Fund $1 par respectively 05/28/1999
INVESCO Treasurer's Series Funds, Inc. name changed to AIM Treasurer's Series Funds, Inc. (MD) 10/01/2003 which reincorporated in Delaware as AIM Treasurer's Series Trust 11/25/2003

INVESCO TREASURERS SER FDS INC (MD)
Name changed to AIM Treasurer's Series Funds, Inc. (MD) 10/01/2003
AIM Treasurer's Series Funds, Inc. (MD) reincorporated in Delaware as AIM Treasurer's Series Trust 11/25/2003

INVESCO VALUE MUN BD TR (MA)
Name changed 01/23/2012
Name changed from Invesco Insured Municipal Bond Trust to Invesco Value Municipal Bond Trust 01/23/2012
Auction Preferred 1¢ par called for redemption at $50,000 on 06/14/2012
Merged into Invesco Value Municipal Income Trust 10/15/2012
Each share Common 1¢ par exchanged for (0.94667466) share Common no par

INVESCO VALUE MUN INCOME TR (MA)
Name changed 01/23/2012
Name changed from Invesco Insured Municipal Income Trust to Invesco Value Municipal Income Trust 01/23/2012
Auction Preferred Ser. 1 1¢ par for redemption at $50,000 on 06/11/2012
Auction Preferred Ser. 2 1¢ par for redemption at $50,000 on 06/11/2012
Auction Preferred Ser. 3 1¢ par for redemption at $50,000 on 06/11/2012
Auction Preferred Ser. 4 1¢ par for redemption at $50,000 on 06/11/2012
Auction Preferred Ser. 5 1¢ par for redemption at $50,000 on 06/11/2012
Reincorporated under the laws of Delaware and Common 1¢ par changed to no par 10/15/2012

INVESCO VALUE MUN SECS (MA)
Name changed 01/23/2012
Name changed from Invesco Insured Municipal Securities to Invesco Value Municipal Securities 01/23/2012
Merged into Invesco Value Municipal Income Trust 10/15/2012
Each share Common 1¢ par exchanged for (0.91611744) share Common no par

INVESCO VALUE MUN TR (MA)
Name changed 01/23/2012
Name changed from Invesco Insured Municipal Trust to Invesco Value Municipal Trust 01/23/2012
Auction Preferred Ser. TU 1¢ par called for redemption at $50,000 on 06/13/2012
Auction Preferred Ser. TH 1¢ par called for redemption at $50,000 on 06/15/2012
Merged into Invesco Value Municipal Income Trust 10/15/2012
Each share Common 1¢ par exchanged for (0.94727382) share Common no par

INVESCO VALUE TR (MA)
Merged into INVESCO Stock Funds 05/20/1999
Details not available

INVESCO VAN KAMPEN ADVANTAGE MUN INCOME TR II (DE)
Reincorporated 08/27/2012
Auction Preferred Ser. H 1¢ par called for redemption at $25,000 on 05/22/2012
Auction Preferred Ser. J 1¢ par called for redemption at $25,000 on 05/22/2012
Auction Preferred Ser. F 1¢ par called for redemption at $25,000 on 05/23/2012
Auction Preferred Ser. A 1¢ par called for redemption at $25,000 on 05/24/2012
Auction Preferred Ser. C 1¢ par called for redemption at $25,000 on 05/24/2012
Auction Preferred Ser. D 1¢ par called for redemption at $25,000 on 05/24/2012

Auction Preferred Ser. B 1¢ par called for redemption at $25,000 on 05/25/2012
Auction Preferred Ser. E 1¢ par called for redemption at $25,000 on 05/25/2012
Auction Preferred Ser. G 1¢ par called for redemption at $25,000 on 05/25/2012
Auction Preferred Ser. I 1¢ par called for redemption at $25,000 on 06/04/2012
State of incorporation changed from (MA) to (DE) 08/27/2012
Name changed to Invesco Advantage Municipal Income Trust II 12/03/2012

INVESCO VAN KAMPEN BD FD (DE)
Name changed to Invesco Bond Fund 12/03/2012

INVESCO VAN KAMPEN CALIF VALUE MUN INCOME TR (DE)
Reincorporated 08/27/2012
Auction Preferred Ser. A 1¢ par called for redemption at $25,000 on 05/22/2012
Auction Preferred Ser. C 1¢ par called for redemption at $25,000 on 05/22/2012
Auction Preferred Ser. B 1¢ par called for redemption at $25,000 on 05/25/2012
Auction Preferred Ser. D 1¢ par called for redemption at $25,000 on 06/11/2012
State of incorporation changed from (MA) to (DE) 08/27/2012
Name changed to Invesco California Value Municipal Income Trust 12/03/2012

INVESCO VAN KAMPEN DYNAMIC CR OPPORTUNITIES FD (DE)
Name changed to Invesco Dynamic Credit Opportunities Fund 12/03/2012

INVESCO VAN KAMPEN HIGH INCOME TR II (DE)
Reincorporated 08/27/2012
State of incorporation changed from (MA) to (DE) 08/27/2012
Name changed to Invesco High Income Trust II 12/03/2012

INVESCO VAN KAMPEN MASS VALUE MUN INCOME TR (MA)
Auction Preferred 1¢ par called for redemption at $25,000 on 05/24/2012
Merged into Invesco Van Kampen Municipal Trust 10/15/2012
Each share Common 1¢ par exchanged for (0.94101509) share Common no par
Invesco Van Kampen Municipal Trust name changed to Invesco Municipal Trust 12/03/2012

INVESCO VAN KAMPEN MUN OPPORTUNITY TR (DE)
Reincorporated 10/15/2012
Auction Preferred Ser. B 1¢ par called for redemption at $25,000 on 05/16/2012
Auction Preferred Ser. D 1¢ par called for redemption at $25,000 on 05/16/2012
Auction Preferred Ser. A 1¢ par called for redemption at $25,000 on 05/21/2012
Auction Preferred Ser. E 1¢ par called for redemption at $25,000 on 05/24/2012
Auction Preferred Ser. C 1¢ par called for redemption at $25,000 on 05/30/2012
Auction Preferred Ser. F 1¢ par called for redemption at $25,000 on 05/30/2012
State of incorporation changed from (MA) to (DE) and Common 1¢ par changed to no par 10/15/2012
Name changed to Invesco Municipal Opportunity Trust 12/03/2012

INVESCO VAN KAMPEN MUN TR (DE)
Reincorporated 10/15/2012
Auction Preferred Ser. A 1¢ par called for redemption at $25,000 on 05/24/2012
Auction Preferred Ser. E 1¢ par called for redemption at $25,000 on 05/25/2012
Auction Preferred Ser. C 1¢ par called for redemption at $25,000 on 05/29/2012
Auction Preferred Ser. D 1¢ par called for redemption at $25,000 on 05/30/2012
Auction Preferred Ser. B 1¢ par called for redemption at $25,000 on 06/04/2012
State of incorporation changed from (MA) to (DE) and Common 1¢ par changed to no par 10/15/2012
Name changed to Invesco Municipal Trust 12/03/2012

INVESCO VAN KAMPEN OHIO QUALITY MUN TR (MA)
Auction Rate Preferred Ser. B 1¢ par called for redemption at $25,000 on 05/24/2012
Auction Rate Preferred Ser. A 1¢ par called for redemption at $25,000 on 06/13/2012
Merged into Invesco Van Kampen Municipal Trust 10/15/2012
Each share Common 1¢ par exchanged for (1.10631001) shares Common no par
Invesco Van Kampen Municipal Trust name changed to Invesco Municipal Trust 12/03/2012

INVESCO VAN KAMPEN PA VALUE MUN INCOME TR (PA)
Auction Preferred Ser. D 1¢ par called for redemption at $25,000 on 05/18/2012
Auction Preferred Ser. A 1¢ par called for redemption at $25,000 on 05/22/2012
Auction Preferred Ser. C 1¢ par called for redemption at $25,000 on 05/29/2012
Auction Preferred Ser. B 1¢ par called for redemption at $25,000 on 06/16/2012
State of incorporation changed from (PA) to (DE) 08/27/2012
Name changed to Invesco Pennsylvania Value Municipal Income Trust 12/03/2012

INVESCO VAN KAMPEN SELECT SECTOR MUN TR (MA)
Remarketed Preferred Ser. A 1¢ par called for redemption at $25,000 on 05/18/2012
Remarketed Preferred Ser. C 1¢ par called for redemption at $25,000 on 05/23/2012
Remarketed Preferred Ser. D 1¢ par called for redemption at $25,000 on 05/24/2012
Remarketed Preferred Ser. B 1¢ par called for redemption at $25,000 on 06/12/2012
Merged into Invesco Van Kampen Municipal Opportunity Trust 10/15/2012
Each Common Share of Bene. Int. 1¢ par exchanged for (0.87774725) Common Share of Bene. Int. no par
Invesco Van Kampen Municipal Opportunity Trust name changed to Invesco Municipal Opportunity Trust 12/03/2012

INVESCO VAN KAMPEN SR INCOME TR (MA)
Reincorporated 08/27/2012
State of incorporation changed from (MA) to (DE) 08/27/2012
Auction Rate Preferred Ser. F 1¢ par called for redemption at $25,000 on 11/13/2012
Auction Rate Preferred Ser. M 1¢ par called for redemption at $25,000 on 11/13/2012
Auction Rate Preferred Ser. T 1¢ par called for redemption at $25,000 on 11/14/2012
Auction Rate Preferred Ser. W 1¢ par called for redemption at $25,000 on 11/15/2012
Auction Rate Preferred Ser. TH 1¢ par called for redemption at $25,000 on 11/16/2012
Name changed to Invesco Senior Income Trust 12/03/2012

INVESCO VAN KAMPEN SR LN FD (MA)
Name changed to Invesco Senior Loan Fund 09/24/2012

INVESCO VAN KAMPEN TR INVT GRADE MUNS (DE)
Reincorporated 08/27/2012
Auction Rate Preferred Ser. C 1¢ par called for redemption at $25,000 on 05/15/2012
Auction Rate Preferred Ser. H 1¢ par called for redemption at $25,000 on 05/15/2012
Auction Rate Preferred Ser. G 1¢ par called for redemption at $25,000 on 05/17/2012
Auction Rate Preferred Ser. D 1¢ par called for redemption at $25,000 on 05/21/2012
Auction Rate Preferred Ser. A 1¢ par called for redemption at $25,000 on 05/31/2012
Auction Rate Preferred Ser. E 1¢ par called for redemption at $25,000 on 05/31/2012
Auction Rate Preferred Ser. I 1¢ par called for redemption at $25,000 on 06/05/2012
Auction Rate Preferred Ser. B 1¢ par called for redemption at $25,000 on 06/07/2012
Auction Rate Preferred Ser. F 1¢ par called for redemption at $25,000 on 06/07/2012
State of incorporation changed from (MA) to (DE) 08/27/2012
Name changed to Invesco Trust for Investment Grade Municipals 12/03/2012

INVESCO VAN KAMPEN TR INVT GRADE NEW JERSEY MUNS (MA)
Auction Preferred 1¢ par called for redemption at $25,000 on 05/31/2012
Merged into Invesco Van Kampen Municipal Trust 10/15/2012
Each share Common 1¢ par exchanged for (1.1776406) shares Common no par
Invesco Van Kampen Municipal Trust name changed to Invesco Municipal Trust 12/03/2012

INVESCO VAN KAMPEN TR INVT GRADE NEW YORK MUNS (DE)
Reincorporated 08/27/2012
Auction Rate Preferred Ser. C 1¢ par called for redemption at $25,000 on 05/22/2012
Auction Rate Preferred Ser. A 1¢ par called for redemption at $25,000 on 05/29/2012
Auction Rate Preferred Ser. B 1¢ par called for redemption at $25,000 on 06/01/2012
State of incorporation changed from (MA) to (DE) 08/27/2012
Name changed to Invesco Trust for Investment Grade New York Municipals 12/03/2012

INVESCO VAN KAMPEN TR VALUE MUNS (MA)
Name changed 01/23/2012
Name changed from Invesco Van Kampen Trust for Insured Municipals to Invesco Van Kampen Trust for Value Municipals 01/23/2012
Auction Rate Preferred Ser. B 1¢ par called for redemption at $25,000 on 06/05/2012
Auction Rate Preferred Ser. A 1¢ par called for redemption at $25,000 on 06/06/2012
(Additional Information in Active)

INVESPRINT CORP (ON)
Merged into Metro Label Group Inc. 05/25/2005
Each share Common no par exchanged for $1.20 cash

INVEST A SEARCH INC (CO)
Charter suspended for failure to file annual reports 12/21/1987

INVEST CO (FL)
Class A Common 10¢ par reclassified as Common 10¢ par 1/28/77
Merged into Monumental Corp. 11/15/82
Each (17) shares Common 10¢ par exchanged for (1) share Common $3.50 par
(See Monumental Corp.)

INVESTAMERICA INC (NV)
SEC revoked common stock registration 10/03/2011

INVESTAR INC (MN)
Recapitalized as Sienna Technologies Inc. 2/28/91
Each share Common 1¢ par exchanged for (0.1) share Common 1¢ par

INVESTCO CORP (NV)
Charter permanently revoked 08/31/2007

INVESTCO INC (NV)
SEC revoked common stock registration 11/24/2003

INVESTCOM LLC (LEBANON)
Acquired by MTN International (Mauritius) Ltd. 9/12/2006
Each Regulation S GDR for Ordinary exchanged for $19.20 cash

INVESTEC BK LTD (SOUTH AFRICA)
ADR agreement terminated 10/25/2002
Each Sponsored ADR for Ordinary Rand-60 par exchanged for $12.57057 cash

INVESTED DOLLARS FUND, INC. (MN)
Name changed to Viking Investors Fund, Inc. 12/12/1967
Viking Investors Fund, Inc. merged into Industries Trend Fund Inc. 09/29/1975 which merged into Pilot Fund, Inc. 05/01/1981 which name changed to Transamerica Technology Fund 06/23/1989 which name changed to Transamerica Capital Appreciation Fund 04/19/1991 which merged into Hancock (John) Capital Growth Fund 12/22/1994
(See Hancock (John) Capital Growth Fund)

INVESTEK CORP (DE)
Charter cancelled and declared inoperative and void for non-payment of taxes 03/01/1999

INVESTESTATE (UT)
Each share Common 5¢ par exchanged for (0.1) share Common 50¢ par 09/30/1982
Name changed to Incorp, Inc. and Common 50¢ par changed to 1¢ par 09/30/1987
Incorp, Inc. name changed to Customer Sports, Inc. 01/15/1997
(See Customer Sports, Inc.)

INVESTEX INC (FL)
Filed petition under Chapter 11 Federal Bankruptcy Code 11/20/89
No stockholders' equity

INVESTING CORP. OF AMERICA
Liquidated in 1929

INVESTING PROFESSIONAL INC (DE)
Name changed to Sherinda International, Inc. 5/13/76

Sherinda International, Inc. name changed to North American Energy, Inc. 4/9/81 which reorganized as ORA Electronics, Inc. 12/20/96

INVESTISSEMENTS COMMERCIAUX ET INDUSTRIALS INC. (QC)
Completely liquidated 08/01/1967
Each share Common $5 par exchanged for first and final distribution of $2.41 cash

INVESTITECH LTD (CO)
Name changed to IPM, Inc. 04/19/1988
(See IPM, Inc.)

INVESTMENT & CONSULTING INTL INC NEW (NV)
Recapitalized as KleenAir Systems, Inc. 04/11/1995
Each share Common 1¢ par exchanged for (0.1) share Common 1¢ par
Kleenair Systems, Inc. recapitalized as Migami, Inc. 03/02/2006

INVESTMENT & CONSULTING INTL INC OLD (NV)
Name changed to Currentsea 07/02/1991
Currentsea name changed back to Investment & Consulting International, Inc. (New) 06/02/1993 which recapitalized as KleenAir Systems, Inc. 04/11/1995 which recapitalized as Migami, Inc. 03/02/2006

INVESTMENT AGENTS INC (NV)
Common $0.001 par split (20.18644) for (1) by issuance of (19.18644) additional shares payable 12/11/2002 to holders of record 12/09/2002 Ex date - 12/12/2002
Name changed to City Network, Inc. 03/21/2003
(See City Network, Inc.)

INVESTMENT ANNUITY INC (PA)
Common no par split (3) for (1) by issuance of (2) additional shares 12/22/69
Liquidation completed
Each share Common no par received initial distribution of $1 cash 3/31/78
Each share Common no par received second distribution of $0.50 cash 7/24/78
Each share Common no par received third distribution of $0.12 cash 4/20/79
Each share Common no par received fourth and final distribution of $0.04252 cash 11/21/80
Certificates were not required to be surrendered and are now valueless

INVESTMENT BOOK PUBLISHERS INC (NV)
Recapitalized as Accord Advanced Technologies Inc. 11/06/1997
Each share Common $0.0001 par exchanged for (0.1) share Common $0.0001 par
Accord Advanced Technologies Inc. recapitalized as Central Utilities Production Corp. 07/30/2001
(See Central Utilities Production Corp.)

INVESTMENT CAP ASSOC LTD (NV)
Charter revoked for failure to file reports and pay fees 12/1/89

INVESTMENT CO AMER (MI)
Recapitalized under the laws of Delaware 08/28/1933
Each share 7% Preferred A $100 par exchanged for (1) share Common $10 par
Each share Common no par exchanged for an Option Warrant to purchase (1) share Common $10 par
Each old Option Warrant exchanged for (1) new Option Warrant

INVESTMENT CORP. OF AMERICA (IN)
Adjudicated bankrupt 07/24/1975
Stockholders' equity unlikely

INVESTMENT CORP. OF AMERICA (UT)
Name changed to Consolidated American Corp. 12/13/73
Consolidated American Corp. merged into Dynamic American Corp. 12/21/82
(See Dynamic American Corp.)

INVESTMENT CORP AMER INC (MN)
Common 50¢ par changed to 10¢ par 04/06/1970
Common 10¢ par split (3) for (2) by issuance of (0.5) additional share 11/10/1970
Name changed to River Forest Bancorp 05/18/1982
River Forest Bancorp name changed to River Forest Bancorp, Inc. 04/29/1988 which name changed to Corus Bankshares, Inc. 06/10/1996
(See Corus Bankshares, Inc.)

INVESTMENT CORP FLA (FL)
Merged into Rebus, Inc. 2/5/81
Each share Common 2¢ par exchanged for $4.50 cash
Each share Common 2¢ par received escrow fund distribution of an additional $0.5734 cash 2/5/82

INVESTMENT CORP PHILADELPHIA (DE)
Proclaimed dissolved 2/17/83

INVESTMENT FNDTN LTD (QC)
6% Conv. Preferred $50 par called for redemption 04/15/1965
Common no par reclassified as Conv. Class A Common no par 03/25/1975
Reincorporated under the laws of Canada as IFL Investment Foundation (Canada) Ltd.-La. Fondation de Placements IFL (Canada) Ltee. 10/11/1978
Note: By Court judgement new certificates distributed 12/29/1978
Old certificates are without value and are requested to be surrendered for cancellation
(See IFL Investment Foundation (Canada) Ltd.- La Fondation de Placements IFL (Canada) Ltee.)

INVESTMENT GRADE MUN INCOME FD (MD)
Auction Preferred Ser. C called for redemption at $50,000 on 04/20/2010
Completely liquidated 05/10/2010
Each share Common $0.001 par exchanged for first and final distribution of $14.63 cash

INVESTMENT GRADE TR (ON)
Trust terminated
Each Depositary Receipt received first and final distribution of $9.78 cash payable 01/03/2013 to holders of record 12/31/2012

INVESTMENT GROWTH RES INC (NV)
Recapitalized as Phoenician Olive Oil Inc. 2/12/96
Each share Common $0.001 par exchanged for (0.02) share Common $0.001 par
(See Phoenician Olive Oil Inc.)

INVESTMENT GUARANTY CORP. (MN)
Statutorily dissolved 10/14/88

INVESTMENT INDICATORS FD (CA)
Charter suspended for failure to file reports and pay fees 12/06/1984

INVESTMENT LD INC (CO)
Completely liquidated 6/20/84
Each share Common 1¢ par exchanged for first and final distribution of $6.09 cash

INVESTMENT LIFE & TR CO MULLINS S C (SC)
Stock Dividends - 25% 11/10/72; 25% 6/30/74
Merged into First Republic Financial Corp. 3/16/87
Each share Common $1 par exchanged for $5 cash

INVESTMENT LIFE INS CO AMER (OH)
Merged into Fireman's Fund Insurance Co. 9/4/80
Each share Class A Common $1 par exchanged for $0.20 cash
Each share Class B Common $1 par exchanged for $2 cash

INVESTMENT MANAGEMENT CORP. (NV)
Common $1 par changed to 20¢ par and (4) additional shares issued 8/10/71
Recapitalized as Investment Development Corp. 1/20/81
Each share Common 20¢ par exchanged for (15) shares Common $0.001 par

INVESTMENT MTG CO FLA (FL)
Proclaimed dissolved for failure to file reports and pay fees 11/14/1986

INVESTMENT PORTFOLIOS (MA)
Reincorporated 11/20/1987
Reincorporated from Investment Portfolios Inc. (MD) to under the laws of Massachusetts as Investment Portfolios and each share Equity Portfolio Common no par, Government Plus Portfolio Common no par, High Yield Portfolio Common no par, Intermediate U.S. Government Portfolio Common no par, Money Market Portfolio Common no par, Option Income Portfolio Common no par and Total Return Portfolio Common no par reclassified as Equity Portfolio Shares of Bene. Int. no par, Government Plus Portfolio Shares of Bene. Int. no par, High Yield Portfolio Shares of Bene. Int. no par, Intermediate U.S. Government Portfolio Shares of Bene. Int. no par, Money Market Portfolio Shares of Bene. Int. no par, Option Income Portfolio Shares of Bene. Int. no par and Total Return Portfolio Shares of Bene. Int. no par respectively 11/20/1987
Intermediate U.S. Government Portfolio Shares of Ben. Int. no par reclassified as Short Intermediate Government Portfolio Shares of Bene. Int. no par 01/31/1989
Option Income Portfolio Shares of Bene. Int. no par reclassified as Diversified Income Portfolio Shares of Bene. Int. no par 02/01/1989
Government Plus Portfolio Shares of Bene. Int. no par reclassified as Government Portfolio Shares of Bene. Int. no par 12/01/1989
Name changed to Kemper Investment Portfolios 02/01/1991
Kemper Investment Portfolios name changed to Kemper Portfolios 05/27/1994
(See Kemper Portfolios)

INVESTMENT PPTYS ASSOC (NY)
Completely liquidated
Each Limited Partnership Int. received first and final distribution of $0.7858 cash payable 12/15/2003 to holders of record 12/10/2003 Ex date - 12/16/2003

INVESTMENT PPTY BLDRS INC (DE)
Each share Common 10¢ par exchanged for (0.2) share Common 50¢ par 2/7/71
Name changed to Centree Corp. 10/5/72
Centree Corp. name changed to Air Florida System, Inc. 12/26/73 which name changed to Jet Florida System, Inc. 8/15/85
(See Jet Florida System, Inc.)

INVESTMENT QUALITY INT INC (TX)
Reorganized as Criterion Bond Fund 02/20/1985
Details not available

INVESTMENT REALTY CORP. OF PHILADELPHIA (PA)
Charter revoked for failure to file reports and pay fees 2/16/45

INVESTMENT RESOURCES & PROPERTIES CORP.
Name changed to Kent Industries, Inc. 8/16/62
(See Kent Industries, Inc.)

INVESTMENT RES & TECHNOLOGY INC (CA)
Name changed to Spear Financial Services, Inc. 06/06/1986
Spear Financial Services, Inc. name changed to JMC Group Inc. 06/21/1993 which name changed to Fechtor, Detwiler, Mitchell & Co. Inc. 08/30/1999 which recapitalized as Detwiler, Mitchell & Co. 03/27/2001 which name changed to Detwiler Fenton Group, Inc. 10/20/2008

INVESTMENT SAVINGS & LOAN ASSOCIATION (CA)
Common $20 par changed to $10 par and (1) additional share in December, 1980
Declared insolvent and taken over by FDIC 8/24/90
Stockholders' equity undetermined

INVESTMENT SHARES CORP.
Trust terminated 00/00/1931
Details not available

INVESTMENT TECHNOLOGIES INC (NJ)
Charter declared void for non-payment of taxes 1/31/94

INVESTMENT TECHNOLOGY GROUP INC OLD (DE)
Issue Information - 3,250,000 shares COM offered at $13 per share on 05/04/1994
Merged into Investment Technology Group Inc. (New) 4/27/99
Each share Common 1¢ par exchanged for (1.5955) shares Common 1¢ par

INVESTMENT TRUST & ASSURANCE CORP. (AZ)
Merged into Coastal States Life Insurance Co. 12/30/65
Each share Class A or B Common 50¢ par exchanged for (0.12357) share Common $1 par
Class A Preferred $1 par redeemed at $5.20 per share
Coastal States Life Insurance Co. reorganized as Coastal States Corp. 10/5/72
(See Coastal States Corp.)

INVESTMENT TRUST ASSOCIATES
Acquired by United Founders Corp. (MD) 00/00/1931
Details not available

INVESTMENT TR BOSTON FDS (MA)
Stock Dividend - 100% 08/06/1955
Name changed to TNE Funds Trust 04/01/1992
TNE Funds Trust name changed to New England Funds Trust II 04/18/1994 which name changed to Nvest Funds Trust II 02/01/2000 which name changed to CDC Nvest Funds Trust II 05/01/2001
(See CDC Nvest Funds Trust II)

INVESTMENT TR BOSTON MASS TAX FREE INCOME FD (MA)
Reorganized as Investment Trust of Boston Funds 01/03/1989
Details not available

INVESTMENT TRUST FUND A
Merged into Investors Fund C, Inc. at net asset value 00/00/1938
Investors Fund C, Inc. name changed to Investors Management Fund, Inc. 00/00/1946 which merged into Fundamental Investors, Inc. (DE) 00/00/1954 which reincorporated in Maryland 02/01/1990 which reorganized in Delaware as Fundamental Investors 09/01/2010

INVESTMENT TRUST FUND B
Merged into Investors Fund C, Inc. on a net asset basis 01/30/1946
Investors Fund C, Inc. name changed to Investors Management Fund, Inc. 04/00/1946 which merged into Fundamental Investors, Inc. (DE) 00/00/1954 which reincorporated in Maryland 02/01/1990 which reorganized in Delaware as Fundamental Investors 09/01/2010

INVESTMENT TRUST SHARES-SERIES B
Liquidated in 1936

INVESTNET INC (NV)
Recapitalized as China Kangtai Cactus Bio-Tech, Inc. 08/25/2005
Each (70) shares Common $0.001 par exchanged for (1) share Common $0.001 par

INVESTOOLS INC (DE)
Name changed to thinkorswim Group Inc. 06/06/2008
thinkorswim Group Inc. merged into TD AMERITRADE Holding Corp. 06/11/2009

INVESTOR GTY CORP N V (NETHERLANDS)
Adjudicated bankrupt 11/4/75
No stockholders' equity

INVESTORLINKS COM INC (ON)
Recapitalized as API Electronics Group Inc. (ON) 09/10/2001
Each share Common no par exchanged for 0.33333333) share Common no par
API Electronics Group Inc. (ON) reorganized in Delaware as API Electronics Group Corp. 09/15/2004 which merged into API Nanotronics Corp. 11/07/2006 which name changed to API Technologies Corp. 10/27/2009
(See API Technologies Corp.)

INVESTORS ASSOCIATION
Dissolved in 1934

INVESTORS BANCORP INC OLD (DE)
Reorganized as Investors Bancorp, Inc. (New) 05/07/2014
Each share Common 1¢ par exchanged for (2.55) shares Common 1¢ par

INVESTORS BK CORP MINNETONKA MINN (DE)
Common 1¢ par split (4) for (3) by issuance of (1/3) additional share 12/31/1993
Merged into Firstar Corp. (Old) 04/28/1995
Each share Perpetual Preferred Ser. 1991 1¢ par exchanged for $27.50 cash
Each share Common 1¢ par exchanged for (0.8676) shares Common $1.25 par
Firstar Corp. (Old) merged into Firstar Corp. (New) 11/20/1998 which merged into U.S. Bancorp (DE) 02/27/2001

INVESTORS BOND & SHARE CORP.
Liquidated in 1939

INVESTORS BOND CERTIFICATES SERIES A
Trust terminated 00/00/1935
Details not available

INVESTORS BOOK CLUB INC (NY)
Name changed to IBC Industries, Inc. (NY) and Common 4¢ par changed to 1¢ par 12/9/71
(See IBC Industries, Inc. (NY))

INVESTORS CAP EXCHANGE FD INC (MA)
Merged into Constitution Fund, Inc. 2/15/72
Each share Common $1 par exchanged for (2.5473) shares Common $1 par
Constitution Fund, Inc. merged into Keystone Custodian Funds 10/31/80
(See Keystone Custodian Funds)

INVESTORS CAP HLDGS LTD (DE)
Reincorporated 08/29/2007
State of incorporation changed from (MA) to (DE) 08/29/2007
Merged into RCS Capital Corp. 07/11/2014
Each share Common 1¢ par exchanged for for (0.3334) share Class A Common $0.001 par
(See RCS Capital Corp.)

INVESTORS CASH RESV FD INC (PA)
Fund terminated 11/16/1994
Details not available

INVESTORS CLUB OF THE UNITED STATES, INC. (NV)
Name changed to Noble Financial Group Inc. 06/23/1992
Noble Financial Group Inc. name changed to Newman Energy Technologies Inc. 04/21/1998 which name changed to World Star Asia, Inc. 06/15/1998 which name changed to Comgen Corp. 11/16/1998 which name changed to Planet 411.com Corp. (NV) 02/11/1999 which reincorporated in Delaware as Planet411.com Inc. 10/07/1999 which name changed to Ivany Mining, Inc. 07/27/2007 which name changed to Ivany Nguyen, Inc. 02/16/2010 which name changed to Myriad Interactive Media, Inc. 07/25/2011

INVESTORS COMMERCIAL CORP. (IL)
Name changed to ICC Enterprises, Inc. 12/21/67
(See listing for ICC Enterprises, Inc.)

INVESTORS CONS INS CO (NH)
Acquired by Central United Insurance Co. 11/15/99
Each share Common exchanged for $9.36 cash

INVESTORS CORP. OF RHODE ISLAND
Liquidated in 1940

INVESTORS CORP SOUTH CAROLINA (SC)
Completely liquidated in 2006
Each share Common no par exchanged for approximately $0.38 cash

INVESTORS COUNSEL INC (NY)
6% Preferred $100 par called for redemption 4/15/64
Name changed to Bull & Bear Group, Inc. (NY) 9/26/78
Bull & Bear Group, Inc. (NY) reorganized in Delaware 12/3/85 which name changed to Winmill & Co., Inc. 6/30/99

INVESTORS DATA TECHNOLOGY INC (NY)
Dissolved by proclamation 12/24/91

INVESTORS DIVERSIFIED SVCS INC (DE)
Reincorporated 12/31/1974
Each share Preferred exchanged for (20) shares Class A Common $5 par 00/00/1936
Each share Common $100 par exchanged for (20) shares Common $5 par 00/00/1936
Each share Class A Common $5 par exchanged for (5) shares Class A Common $1 par 00/00/1954
Each share Common $5 par exchanged for (5) shares Common $1 par 00/00/1954
Class A Common $1 par changed to $2 par and (4) additional shares issued 05/18/1964
Common $1 par reclassified as Class B Common 50¢ par and (19) additional shares issued 05/18/1964
State of incorporation changed from (MN) to (DE) 12/31/1974
Merged into Alleghany Corp. (MD) 05/10/1979
Each share Class A Common $2 par exchanged for (1) share Preferred Ser. A $1 par and (0.5) share Common $1 par
Each (4) shares Class B Common 50¢ par exchanged for (1) share Preferred Ser. A $1 par and (0.5) share Common $1 par
(See Alleghany Corp. (MD))

INVESTORS EQUITY, INC. (IA)
Charter cancelled for failure to file reports and pay fees 11/22/76

INVESTORS EQUITY CO., INC.
Acquired by Tri-Continental Corp. in 1932
Details not available

INVESTORS EQUITY CORP. (OK)
Merged into Norin Corp. (Del.) 11/3/72
Each share Common 10¢ par exchanged for (0.016) share Common $1 par
Norin Corp. (Del.) reorganized in Florida 5/31/79
(See Norin Corp. (Fla.))

INVESTORS EQUITY CORP. LTD.
Liquidated in 1939

INVESTORS EQUITY INC (UT)
Recapitalized as Americas Mining Corp. 12/11/1991
Each share Capital Stock $0.005 par exchanged for (0.2) share Common no par
Americas Mining Corp. name changed to Carmina Technologies, Inc. 12/01/2000 which recapitalized as Advanced Integrated Management Services, Inc. 06/29/2004 which reorganized as AIMSI Technologies, Inc. 11/17/2004
(See AIMSI Technologies, Inc.)

INVESTORS EQUITY LIFE INSURANCE CO. (AR)
Merged into National Investors Life Insurance Co. (AR) 06/01/1968
Each share Common 10¢ par exchanged for (0.058823) share $1 par
National Investors Life Insurance Co. (AR) merged into Norin Corp. (DE) 10/31/1972 which reorganized in Florida 05/31/1979
(See Norin Corp. (FL))

INVESTORS EQUITY LIFE INSURANCE CO. OF HAWAII, LTD. (HI)
Completely liquidated 12/29/1994
No stockholders' equity

INVESTORS EQUITY LIFE INSURANCE CO. OF LOUISIANA (LA)
Completely liquidated 7/10/68
Each share Common $1 par exchanged for first and final distribution of $2.15 cash

INVESTORS EQUITY OF IOWA, INC. (IA)
Name changed to Investors Equity, Inc. 01/25/1972
(See Investors Equity, Inc.)

INVESTORS EQUITY OF THE WEST, INC. (HI)
Merged into Norin Corp. (Del.) 11/2/72
Each share Common $1 par exchanged for (0.09) share Common $1 par
Norin Corp. (Del.) reorganized in Florida 5/31/79
(See Norin Corp. (Fla.))

INVESTORS FD SER (MA)
Name changed to Kemper Variable Series 04/03/1999
Kemper Variable Series name changed to Scudder Variable Series II 05/01/2001 which name changed to DWS Variable Series II 01/30/2006

INVESTORS FDG CORP NEW YORK (NY)
Each (12) shares Class A Common 35¢ par exchanged for (1) share Class A Common $5 par 3/24/58
Each (12) shares Class B Common 35¢ par exchanged for (1) share Class B Common $5 par 3/24/58
Class A Common $5 par and Class B Common $5 par reclassified as Common $5 par 2/11/59
Common $5 par reclassified as Class A $5 par 6/27/61
6% Preferred $5 par reclassified as Preferred Ser. A $5 par 5/8/67
Plan of reorganization under Chapter X Bankruptcy Act confirmed 4/10/81
No stockholders' equity

INVESTORS FED SVGS (KS)
Merged into Commercial Federal Bank, A Federal Savings Bank (Omaha, NE) 5/1/97
Each share Common 10¢ par exchanged for $23 cash

INVESTORS FID CORP (DE)
Each share Common 25¢ par exchanged for (0.1) share Common $2.50 par 5/26/70
Merged into Midwestern Fidelity Corp. 10/1/73
Each share Common $2.50 par exchanged for (0.181818) share Common $1.66-2/3 par
Note: The above ratio was issued to holders of (27-1/2) shares or more Holders of fewer than (27-1/2) shares received cash
(See Midwestern Fidelity Corp.)

INVESTORS FID LIFE ASSURN CORP (OH)
Merged into Investors Fidelity Marketing Programs, Inc. 06/09/1987
Each share Class A Common $1 par exchanged for $3.75 cash

INVESTORS FIDELITY CORP. (AL)
Reincorporated under the laws of Delaware 9/27/67
Investors Fidelity Corp. (Del.) merged into Midwestern Fidelity Corp. 10/1/73
(See Midwestern Fidelity Corp.)

INVESTORS FINL CORP (VA)
Assets placed in receivership by Resolution Trust Corp. 12/13/91
No stockholders' equity

INVESTORS FINL SVCS CORP (DE)
Class A Common 1¢ par reclassified as Common 1¢ par 11/14/1997
Common 1¢ par split (2) for (1) by issuance of (1) additional share payable 03/17/1999 to holders of record 03/01/1999
Common 1¢ par split (2) for (1) by issuance of (1) additional share payable 06/15/2000 to holders of record 05/31/2000
Common 1¢ par split (2) for (1) by issuance of (1) additional share payable 06/14/2002 to holders of record 05/24/2002 Ex date - 06/17/2002
Common 1¢ par split (2) for (1) by issuance of (1) additional share payable 06/14/2003 to holders of record 05/24/2003
Merged into State Street Corp. 07/02/2007

Each share Common 1¢ par exchanged for (0.906) share Common $1 par

INVESTORS FIRST FD INC (MD)
Merged into Cornerstone Strategic Value Fund, Inc. 6/28/2004
Each share Common 1¢ par exchanged for (1.6094) shares Common 1¢ par

INVESTORS FORUM INC (DE)
Charter cancelled and declared inoperative and void for non-payment of taxes 3/1/76

INVESTORS FOUNDATION LIFE INSURANCE CO. (OK)
Merged into Investors Preferred Life Insurance Co. (AR) 7/1/64
Each share Common 12¢ par exchanged for (0.25) share Common 12¢ par
(See Investors Preferred Life Insurance Co. (AR))

INVESTORS FUND C, INC.
Name changed to Investors Management Fund, Inc. 00/00/1946
Investors Management Fund, Inc. merged into Fundamental Investors, Inc. (DE) 00/00/1954 which reincorporated in Maryland 02/01/1990 which reorganized in Delaware as Fundamental Investors 09/01/2010

INVESTORS GEN RLTY CORP (NY)
Dissolved by proclamation 06/25/1980

INVESTORS GNMA MTG BACKED SECS TR INC (MD)
Under plan of reorganization each share Common $1 par automatically became (1) share INVG Mortgage Securities Corp. Common 1¢ par 5/12/86
(See INVG Mortgage Securities Corp.)

INVESTORS GROUP INC (CANADA)
Common no par split (2) for (1) by issuance of (1) additional share 01/15/1992
Common no par split (2) for (1) by issuance of (1) additional share 12/22/1993
Common no par split (2) for (1) by issuance of (1) additional share payable 07/13/1998 to holders of record 07/13/1998 Ex date - 07/09/1998
Name changed to IGM Financial Inc. 04/30/2004

INVESTORS GROUP LTD (MB)
Common 5¢ par reclassified as Conv. Common 5¢ par 11/17/1975
Class A Common 5¢ par reclassified as Conv. Class A Common 5¢ par 11/17/1975
Conv. Common 5¢ par reclassified as Common 5¢ par 08/08/1979
Conv. Class A Common 5¢ par reclassified as Class A Common 5¢ par 08/08/1979
Conv. Class B Common 5¢ par reclassified as Common 5¢ par 08/08/1979
Conv. Class C Common 5¢ par reclassified as Class A Common 5¢ par 08/08/1979
Class A Common 5¢ par reclassified as Class A Non-Vtg. 5¢ par 04/30/1984
Name changed to 280 Broadway Holding Corp. 08/28/1986
280 Broadway Holding Corp. merged into Power Financial Corp.-Corporation Financiere Power 12/04/1986

INVESTORS GROWTH INDS INC (DE)
Merged into MEI Corp. 7/13/72
Each share Common $1 par exchanged for (1.61) shares Common 10¢ par
(See MEI Corp.)

INVESTORS GTY LIFE INS CO (CA)
Acquired by Farmers Group, Inc. 8/15/77
Each share Capital Stock $2 par exchanged for (1) share Common $1 par
(See Farmers Group, Inc.)

INVESTORS HERITAGE CAP CORP (KY)
Acquired by Aquarian Investors Heritage Holdings, LLC 03/02/2018
Each share Common $1 par exchanged for $44.75 cash

INVESTORS HERITAGE LIFE INS CO (KY)
Common Capital Stock $1 par changed to $1.12 par 05/08/1969
Common Capital Stock $1.12 par changed to $1 par 05/12/1977
Merged into Kentucky Investors Inc. 12/31/1999
Each share Common $1 par exchanged for (1.24) shares Common $1 par
Kentucky Investors Inc. name changed to Investors Heritage Capital Corp. 06/01/2009

INVESTORS HERITAGE LIFE INS CO OHIO (OH)
Merged into Investors Heritage Life Insurance Co. 6/30/77
Each (4.5) shares Class A Common 50¢ par exchanged for (1) share Common Capital Stock $1 par

INVESTORS HERITAGE LIFE INS CO SOUTH (SC)
Merged into Investors Heritage Life Insurance Co. 11/30/81
Each share Common 30¢ par exchanged for $5 cash

INVESTORS INCOME FD INC (DE)
Ctfs. dated prior to 5/25/76
Acquired by Monthly Income Shares, Inc. 5/25/76
Each share Common $1 par exchanged for (0.3745) share Capital Stock $1 par
Monthly Income Shares, Inc. name changed to Bullock Monthly Income Shares, Inc. 1/14/85 which reorganized as Alliance Bond Fund (MA) 3/13/87 which reorganized in Maryland as Alliance Bond Fund, Inc. 12/7/87 which name changed to AllianceBernstein Bond Fund, Inc. 3/31/2003

INVESTORS INCOME FD INC (DE)
Certificates dated after 05/25/1976
Name changed to Capstone Government Income Fund, Inc. (DE) 01/08/1991
Capstone Government Income Fund, Inc. (DE) reincorporated in Maryland as Capstone Fixed Income Series Inc. 05/11/1992
(See Capstone Fixed Income Series Inc.)

INVESTORS INS CO AMER (NJ)
Name changed to Investors Insurance Holding Corp. 12/30/77
(See Investors Insurance Holding Corp.)

INVESTORS INS CORP (OR)
Common $1 par changed to 25¢ par and split (4) for (1) plus a 20% stock dividend paid effected by exchange of (1) share Common $1 par for (4.8) shares Common 25¢ par 5/6/64
Common 25¢ par changed to $1 par 4/17/85
Stock Dividends - 30% 5/1/63; 20% 5/10/65
Acquired by IIC Inc. 4/1/86
Each share Common $1 par exchanged for $4.00056 cash

INVESTORS INS GROUP INC (FL)
Each share Common 50¢ par received distribution of (0.5) share Gray Peaks, Inc. Common 1¢ par payable 09/06/2007 to holders of record 08/31/2007 Ex date - 09/21/2007
SEC revoked common stock registration 02/03/2010

INVESTORS INS HLDG CORP (NJ)
Merged into IIG Acquisition 10/31/96
Each share Common $1 par exchanged for $12.44 cash

INVESTORS LAND CORP. (GA)
Liquidation completed
Each share Common $5 par exchanged for initial distribution of $4 cash 9/8/67
Each share Common $5 par received second and final distribution of $6.09 cash 3/10/69

INVESTORS LIFE INSURANCE CO. (OK)
Under plan of merger Capital Stock 10¢ par reclassified as Common 5¢ par 11/14/72
Name changed to Investors Life Investment Co. 12/15/75
(See Investors Life Investment Co.)

INVESTORS LIFE INVESTMENT CO. (OK)
Voluntarily dissolved in September 1979
Details not available

INVESTORS LN CORP (MD)
Merged into First Pennsylvania Corp. 06/05/1970
Each share 6% Preferred $50 par exchanged for (1) share 6% Preferred Ser. A no par
Each share Common $1 par exchanged for (2.20777) shares Common $1 par or at option of holder (1.47184) shares Common $1 par plus a Ctf. of Contingent Interest
First Pennsylvania Corp. merged into CoreStates Financial Corp 03/05/1990 which merged into First Union Corp. 04/28/1998 which name changed to Wachovia Corp. (Ctfs. dated after 09/01/2001) 09/01/2001 which merged into Wells Fargo & Co. (New) 12/31/2008

INVESTORS MANAGEMENT FUND, INC. (DE)
Merged into Fundamental Investors, Inc. (DE) on a net asset basis 00/00/1954
Fundamental Investors, Inc. (DE) reincorporated in Maryland 02/01/1990 which reorganized in Delaware as Fundamental Investors 09/01/2010

INVESTORS MORTGAGE & GUARANTY CO.
Name changed to Investors Mortgage Co. in 1938
(See Investors Mortgage Co.)

INVESTORS MTG CO (CT)
Filed a petition under Chapter 7 Federal Bankruptcy Code 11/15/93
Stockholders' equity unlikely

INVESTORS NATL LIFE INS CO (SC)
Merged into South Carolina Insurance Co. 12/31/72
Each share Capital Stock $1 par exchanged for (0.25) share Common $1 par
South Carolina Insurance Co. reorganized as Seibels Bruce Group, Inc. 10/31/78

INVESTORS OF WASHINGTON, INC.
Liquidation completed in 1936

INVESTORS OPTION FUND INC. (DE)
Name changed to Investors Income Fund Inc. 11/9/66
Investors Income Fund Inc. acquired by Monthly Income Shares, Inc. 5/25/76 which name changed to Bullock Monthly Income Shares, Inc. 1/14/85 which reorganized as Alliance Bond Fund Monthly Income Portfolio 3/13/87

INVESTORS OVERSEAS SVCS MGMT LTD (ON)
Each share Capital Stock 20¢ par exchanged for (3) shares Capital Stock no par 4/21/69
Name changed to Transglobal Financial Services Ltd. 9/13/71
(See Transglobal Financial Services Ltd.)

INVESTORS PFD LIFE INS CO (AR)
Common no par split (4) for (1) by issuance of (3) additional shares 5/20/60
Each share Common no par exchanged for (0.2) share Common 12¢ par 4/25/63
Stock Dividend - 20% 1/1/65
Merged into Protective Life Insurance Co. 11/21/79
Each share Common 12¢ par exchanged for $1 cash

INVESTORS PLANNING CORP. OF AMERICA (DE)
Liquidation completed
Each share Capital Stock 10¢ par received initial distribution of (0.142857) share Equity Funding Corp. of America Common 30¢ par 4/25/69
Each share Capital Stock 10¢ par exchanged for second distribution of $2 cash 7/24/69
Name changed to CIP, Inc. 12/22/69
(See CIP, Inc.)

INVESTORS PREF FD FOR INCOME INC (WA)
Reorganized as Victory Fund 04/29/1994
Details not available

INVESTORS PREFERRED LIFE INSURANCE CO. (CO)
Each share old Common 40¢ par exchanged for (6) shares new Common 40¢ par 08/17/1962
New Common 40¢ par changed to 60¢ par 06/10/1963
Name changed to Western Preferred Life Insurance Co. and Common 60¢ par changed to 20¢ par 11/30/1967
Western Preferred Life Insurance Co. merged into Western Preferred Corp. 08/23/1973
(See Western Preferred Corp.)

INVESTORS REAL ESTATE TR
8.25% Preferred Shares of Bene. Int. Ser. A no par called for redemption at $25 plus $0.36 accrued dividends on 12/02/2016
7.95% Preferred Shares of Bene. Int. Ser. B no par called for redemption at $25 plus $0.16563 accrued dividends on 10/30/2017
(Additional Information in Active)

INVESTORS RLTY TR (TN)
Under plan of merger each Share of Bene. Int. $1 par automatically became (1) share IRT Property Co. Common $1 par 06/20/1979
IRT Property Co. merged into Equity One, Inc. 02/13/2003 which merged into Regency Centers Corp. 03/01/2017

INVESTORS RTY INC (DE)
Each share Common $25 par exchanged for (10) shares Common $1 par in 1936
Each share Common $10 par exchanged for (4) shares Common $1 par in 1936
Each share old Common $1 par exchanged for (0.4) share new Common $1 par in 1936
Completely liquidated 10/2/73
Each share Common $1 par exchanged for first and final distribution of (0.294291) share Sabine Royalty Corp. Common no par
Sabine Royalty Corp. reincorporated in Louisiana as Sabine Corp. 1/3/77

(See Sabine Corp.)

INVESTORS SAVINGS & LOAN ASSOCIATION (VA)
Name changed to Investors Savings Bank (Richmond, VA) 07/11/1986
Investors Savings Bank (Richmond, VA) reorganized as Investors Financial Corp. 11/03/1988
(See Investors Financial Corp.)

INVESTORS SVGS BK (RICHMOND, VA)
8-1/2% Conv. Preferred Ser. B $10 par called for redemption 4/24/87
95¢ Conv. Preferred Ser. A $10 par called for redemption 5/8/87
Under plan of reorganization each share Common $1.25 par automatically became (1) share Common $1.25 par of Investors Financial Corp. 11/3/88
(See Investors Financial Corp.)

INVESTORS SVGS BK S C INC (DE)
Merged into First Financial Holdings Inc. (DE) 11/07/1997
Each share Common 1¢ par exchanged for (1.36) shares Common 1¢ par
First Financial Holdings, Inc. (DE) merged into First Financial Holdings, Inc. (SC) 07/30/2013 which name changed to South State Corp. 06/30/2014

INVESTORS SVGS CORP MINNETONKA MINN (DE)
Name changed to Investors Bank Corp. 05/12/1993
Investors Bank Corp. merged into Firstar Corp. (Old) 04/28/1995 which merged into Firstar Corp. (New) 11/20/1998 which merged into U.S. Bancorp (DE) 02/27/2001

INVESTORS SEC LIFE INS CO (IL)
Merged into United Founders Life Insurance Co. 12/27/67
Each share Common 17-1/2¢ par exchanged for (0.47) share Common $1 par
(See United Founders Life Insurance Co.)

INVESTORS SECURITY CORP. (IL)
Completely liquidated 4/30/73
Each share Class A 25¢ par exchanged for first and final distribution of (0.149925) share United Founders Life Insurance Co. Common $1 par
Class B no par did not participate and is now worthless
(See United Founders Life Insurance Co.)

INVESTORS SECURITY CORP. (TN)
Charter revoked for failure to file reports and pay fees 1/24/67

INVESTORS SULPHUR & OIL CO., LTD. (LA)
Voluntarily dissolved 2/13/18
Details not available

INVESTORS SYNDICATE, INC.
Name changed to Investors Diversified Services, Inc. (MN) 00/00/1949
Investors Diversified Services, Inc. (MN) reincorporated in Delaware 12/31/1974 which merged into Alleghany Corp. (MD) 05/10/1979
(See Alleghany Corp. (MD))

INVESTORS SYNDICATE OF CANADA LTD. (MB)
Recapitalized as Investors Group 09/01/1964
Each share Common or Class A Common 25¢ par exchanged for (5) shares Common or Class A Common 5¢ par respectively
Investors Group name changed to 280 Broadway Holding Corp. 08/28/1986 which merged into Power Financial Corp.- Corporation Financiere Power 12/04/1986

INVESTORS TELEPHONE CO. (DE)
Common no par changed to $10 par and (5) additional shares issued in 1950
Stock Dividend - 10% 9/26/52
Merged into United Utilities, Inc. in 1953
Each share Common $10 par exchanged for (1.875) shares new Common $10 par
United Utilities, Inc. name changed to United Telecommunications, Inc. 6/2/72 which name changed to Sprint Corp. 2/26/92 which name changed to Sprint Nextel Corp. 8/12/2005

INVESTORS TR & DEV CORP (AZ)
Charter revoked for failure to file reports and pay fees 9/5/74

INVESTORS TRUST CO. (RI)
Merged into Second Investors Co. 5/1/62
Each share Preferred $25 par exchanged for $50 cash
Each share Common $25 par exchanged for (10) shares Common $2.50 par
Second Investors Co. name changed to Providence Investors Co. 3/19/64 which was acquired by Massachusetts Financial Total Return Trust 12/16/91 which name changed to MFS Total Return Fund 8/3/92

INVESTORS TR INC (IN)
Common 6¢ par changed to 3¢ par and (1) additional share issued 03/17/1975
Voluntarily dissolved 03/13/1996
Details not available

INVESTORS TRUSTEE FOUNDATION OF U.S. INC. SERIES A
Trust terminated 00/00/1932
Details not available

INVESTORS UNITED LIFE INSURANCE CO. (AZ)
Placed in receivership 02/23/1973
No stockholders' equity

INVESTORSBANCORP INC (WI)
Company went private 9/19/2003
Each share Common 1¢ par exchanged for $14.20 cash

INVESTSOURCE COMMUNICATIONS INC (NV)
Name changed to United Resource Holdings Group, Inc. 2/5/2007

INVESTUS REAL ESTATE INC (CANADA)
Merged into Societe de Developpement Alpha 07/05/2011
Each share Common no par exchanged for $0.20 cash

INVEX RES LTD (BC)
Merged into Imperial Metals Corp. (Old) 12/01/1981
Each share Common no par exchanged for (1) share Common no par
Imperial Metals Corp. (Old) reorganized as Imperial Metals Corp. (New) 04/30/2002

INVEX VIRGINIA MINES LTD. (ON)
Charter cancelled for failure to file reports and pay taxes in 1969

INVG MTG SECS CORP (MD)
Merged into Meyrin Sub Corp. 12/11/97
Each share Common 1¢ par exchanged for $13 cash

INVICTA CORP (DE)
Name changed to Executive Hospitality Corp. 05/02/2005
Executive Hospitality Corp. recapitalized as Forest Resources Management Corp. 08/09/2006
(See Forest Resources Management Corp.)

INVICTA ENERGY CORP (AB)
Merged into Whitecap Resources Inc. 05/03/2013
Each share Common no par exchanged for (0.05891) share new Common no par

INVICTA EXPLS LTD (ON)
Completely liquidated 12/31/1975
Each share Common no par received first and final distribution of $1.19 cash

INVICTA GROUP INC (NV)
Each share old Common $0.001 par exchanged for (0.01) share new Common $0.001 par 11/16/2006
Each share new Common $0.001 par exchanged for (0.002) share Common $0.0001 par 09/07/2007
Recapitalized as Alliance Creative Group, Inc. 11/15/2010
Each share Common $0.0001 par exchanged for (0.0005) share Common $0.0001 par

INVICTA OIL & GAS LTD (BC)
Name changed to LNG Energy Ltd. 03/28/2008
LNG Energy Ltd. recapitalized as Esrey Energy Ltd. 11/18/2013 which name changed to Esrey Resources Ltd. 10/16/2017

INVICTUS MINES & OILS LTD (AB)
Recapitalized as Invictus Petro Minerals Ltd. 05/05/1976
Each share Common no par exchanged for (0.5) share Common no par
Invictus Petro Minerals Ltd. merged into Seagull Resources Ltd. 01/03/1978
(See Seagull Resources Ltd.)

INVICTUS OILS & MINERALS LTD (QC)
Merged into Invictus Mines & Oils Ltd. 11/20/1975
Each share Common no par exchanged for (1) share Common no par
Invictus Mines & Oils Ltd. recapitalized as Invictus Petro Minerals Ltd. 05/05/1976 which merged into Seagull Resources Ltd. 01/03/1978
(See Seagull Resources Ltd.)

INVICTUS PETRO MINERALS LTD (AB)
Merged into Seagull Resources Ltd. 01/03/1978
Each share Common no par exchanged for (0.1) share Common no par
(See Seagull Resources Ltd.)

INVINCIBLE METAL FURNITURE CO (WI)
Assets sold for the benefit of creditors 05/13/2008
No stockholders' equity

INVINCIBLE VACUUM CLEANER MANUFACTURING CO. (DE)
Name changed to Invincible Vacuum Corp. 12/13/1965
(See Invincible Vacuum Corp.)

INVINCIBLE VACUUM CORP (DE)
Company believed out of business 11/22/1971
Details not available

INVIRO MED INC (CANADA)
Directors determined the company is no longer a going concern 10/29/2010
No stockholders' equity

INVISA INC (NV)
Each share old Common $0.001 par exchanged for (0.2) share new Common $0.001 par 02/01/2011
Name changed to Uniroyal Global Engineered Products, Inc. 07/16/2015

INVISION CAP INC (NV)
Each share old Common $0.001 par exchanged for (5) shares new Common $0.001 par 03/27/2006
Name changed to Exploration Drilling International, Inc. 10/16/2006
(See Exploration Drilling International, Inc.)

INVISION TECHNOLOGIES INC (DE)
Common $0.001 par split (2) for (1) by issuance of (1) additional share payable 02/07/1997 to holders of record 01/17/1997
Merged into General Electric Co. 12/04/2004
Each share Common $0.001 par exchanged for $50 cash

INVISION TECHNOLOGY INC (NV)
Name changed to Shepherd Surveillance Solutions, Inc. 05/14/1996
(See Shepherd Surveillance Solutions, Inc.)

INVITEL HLDGS A/S (DENMARK)
Acquired by Hungarian Telecom (Netherlands) Cooperatief U.A. 07/05/2010
Each Sponsored ADR for Ordinary exchanged for $4.50 cash

INVITROGEN CORP (DE)
Common 1¢ par split (2) for (1) by issuance of (1) additional share payable 05/27/2008 to holders of record 05/16/2008 Ex date - 05/28/2008
Under plan of merger name changed to Life Technologies Corp. 11/21/2008
(See Life Technologies Corp.)

INVITRON CORP (DE)
Completely liquidated 09/19/1991
Each share Common 2¢ par received first and final distribution of $0.40 cash
Note: Certificates were not required to be exchanged and are without value

INVIVO CORP (DE)
Secondary Offering - 1,000,000 shares COM offered at $14.75 per share on 03/09/1999
Common 1¢ par split (3) for (2) by issuance of (0.5) additional share payable 9/26/2003 to holders of record 9/12/2003 Ex date - 9/29/2003
Merged into Intermagnetics General Corp. (NY) 1/27/2004
Each share Common 1¢ par exchanged for $22 cash

INVNSYS HLDG CORP (FL)
Common $0.001 par split (2) for (1) by issuance of (1) additional share payable 11/06/1998 to holders of record 10/27/1998
Name changed to iBIZ Technology Corp. 01/22/1999
(See iBIZ Technology Corp.)

INVU INC (CO)
Each share Ser. A Conv. Preferred no par converted into (2) shares Common no par 08/31/1998
Merged into Invu PLC 12/07/2007
Each share Common no par exchanged for $0.532 cash

INVUITY INC (DE)
Acquired by Stryker Corp. 10/23/2018
Each share Common $0.001 par exchanged for $7.40 cash

INVVISION CAP INC (NV)
Name changed to RG America, Inc. 08/30/2004
RG America, Inc. (NV) reorganized in Colorado as Sprout Tiny Homes, Inc. 04/21/2015

INWEST RES LTD (CANADA)
Dissolved for non-compliance 05/02/2002

INWORLDS COM INC (NV)
Name changed to Avaterra.Com, Inc. 6/22/99
Avaterra.Com, Inc. recapitalized as

FINANCIAL INFORMATION, INC.

INX-IOR

Xtreme Motorsports of California, Inc. 2/17/2006 which name changed to Extreme Motorsports of California, Inc. 5/21/2007

INX INC (DE)
Acquired by Presidio, Inc. 12/30/2011
Each share Common 1¢ par exchanged for $8.75 cash

INX INSEARCH GROUP COS LTD (BC)
Recapitalized as Nova Marketing Ltd. 5/2/88
Each share Common no par exchanged for (0.5) share Common no par
Nova Marketing Ltd. recapitalized as National Nova Marketing Inc. 7/24/92
(See National Nova Marketing Inc.)

INYO-MONO NATIONAL BANK (BISHOP, CA)
Merged into Security Pacific Corp. 03/30/1980
Each share Common $10 par exchanged for $76.50 cash

INYX INC (NV)
Reincorporated under the laws of Delaware 08/30/2006

INZECO HLDGS INC (AB)
Reincorporated under the laws of Ontario as Rtica Corp. 04/09/2001

INZCON CORP (NV)
Each share old Common $0.001 par exchanged for (0.01) share new Common $0.001 par 09/12/2012
SEC revoked common stock registration 01/16/2014

IOGOLD SYS CDA INC (ON)
Reincorporated 03/29/1999
Place of incorporation changed from (NS) to (ON) 03/29/1999
Recapitalized as Candor Ventures Corp. 07/27/2001
Each share Common no par exchanged for (0.2) share Common no par
Candor Ventures Corp. merged into Canstar Resources Inc. 04/07/2005

IOL PETE LTD (AUSTRALIA)
Each old ADR for Ordinary AUD $0.50 par exchanged for (0.5) new ADR for Ordinary AUD $0.50 par 05/13/1975
Acquired by Conzinc Riotinto of Australia Ltd. 07/30/1976
Details not available

IOMAI CORP (DE)
Issue Information - 5,000,000 shares COM offered at $7 per share on 02/01/2006
Merged into Intercell AG 08/05/2008
Each share Common 1¢ par exchanged for $6.60 cash

IOMED INC (UT)
Issue Information - 1,700,000 shares COM offered at $7.50 per share on 08/23/1998
Merged into ReAble Therapeutics, Inc. 08/10/2007
Each share Common no par exchanged for $2.75 cash

IOMEGA CORP (DE)
Common 3-1/3¢ par split (5) for (4) by issuance of (0.25) additional share 11/23/1994
Each share Conv. Adjustable Dividend Preferred Ser. A 1¢ par exchanged for (0.3969764) share old Common 3-1/3¢ par 06/16/1995
Common 3-1/3¢ par split (3) for (1) by issuance of (2) additional shares payable 01/31/1996 to holders of record 01/15/1996
Common 3-1/3¢ par split (2) for (1) by issuance of (1) additional share payable 05/20/1996 to holders of record 05/06/1996
Common 3-1/3¢ par split (2) for (1) by issuance of (1) additional share payable 12/22/1997 to holders of record 12/01/1997 Ex date - 12/23/1997
Each share old Common 3-1/3¢ par exchanged for (0.2) share new Common 3-1/3¢ par 09/28/2001
Merged into EMC Corp. 06/09/2008
Each share Common 3-1/3¢ par exchanged for $3.85 cash

ION HOLDING, INC. (UT)
Name changed to Laser Holding, Inc. 05/13/1986
Laser Holding, Inc. name changed to Ion Laser Technology, Inc. (New) 08/22/1988 which name changed to BriteSmile, Inc. 08/24/1998 which name changed to BSML, Inc. 11/01/2006
(See BSML, Inc.)

ION LABORATORIES INC
Merged into Skyle, Inc. 12/2/98
Each share Common exchanged for $0.20 cash

ION LASER TECHNOLOGY, INC. OLD (UT)
Merged into Laser Holding, Inc. 8/28/87
Each share Common $0.001 par exchanged for (1) share Common $0.001 par
Laser Holding, Inc. name changed to Ion Laser Technology, Inc. (New) 8/22/88 which name changed to Britesmile, Inc. 8/24/98 which name changed to BSML, Inc. 11/1/2006

ION LASER TECHNOLOGY INC NEW (UT)
Each share old Common $0.001 par exchanged for (0.1) share new Common $0.001 par 10/01/1990
Name changed to BriteSmile, Inc. 08/24/1998
BriteSmile, Inc. name changed to BSML, Inc. 11/01/2006
(See BSML, Inc.)

ION LTD (AUSTRALIA)
ADR agreement terminated 5/1/2007
No ADR holders' equity

ION MEDIA NETWORKS INC (DE)
Through exchange offer 99.6% of 9.75% 144A Conv. Preferred reacquired as of 08/03/2007
Through exchange offer 99.6% of 9.75% Accredited Investors Preferred reacquired as of 08/03/2007
Through exchange offer 90.6% of 13.25% Jr. Exchangeable Preferred reacquired as of 08/03/2007
Note: Remaining outstanding shares cancelled under Chapter 11 reorganization effective 12/18/2009
Each (10,036,763) shares old Class A Common $0.001 par exchanged for (1) share new Class A Common $0.001 par 02/19/2008
Note: In effect holders received $1.46 cash per share and public interest was eliminated
Plan of reorganization under Chapter 11 Federal Bankruptcy Code effective 12/18/2009
No Preferred stockholders' equity

ION NETWORKS INC (DE)
Name changed to HealthWarehouse.com, Inc. 08/05/2009

ION TECHNOLOGIES INC (NV)
Merged into Noise Cancellation Technologies Inc. (FL) 04/04/1985
Each share Common 1¢ par exchanged for (0.1) share Common 1¢ par
Noise Cancellation Technologies Inc. (FL) reincorporated in Delaware 01/00/1987 which name changed to NCT Group, Inc. 10/21/1998
(See NCT Group, Inc.)

ION TECHNOLOGY INC (NV)
Common $0.0005 par changed to $0.001 par and (1) additional share issued payable 10/10/2001 to holders of record 10/08/2001 Ex date - 10/11/2001
Chapter 7 bankruptcy proceedings terminated 11/18/2003
Stockholders' equity unlikely

IONA APPLIANCES INC (ON)
Name changed to Fantom Technologies Inc. 05/01/1997
(See Fantom Technologies Inc.)

IONA ENERGY INC (AB)
Insolvency proceedures commenced on company subsidiaries 01/06/2016
All directors and officers have resigned with no expectation of stockholder equity

IONA INDS INC (BC)
Recapitalized as Aigner Holdings Ltd. 02/20/1987
Each share Common no par exchanged for (0.125) share Common no par
(See Aigner Holdings Ltd.)

IONA SILVER MINES LTD. (BC)
Name changed to Iona Industries Inc. 2/25/82
Iona Industries Inc. recapitalized as Aigner Holdings Ltd. 2/20/87
(See Aigner Holdings Ltd.)

IONA TECHNOLOGIES PLC (IRELAND)
Acquired by Progress Software Corp. 09/12/2008
Each Sponsored ADR for Ordinary exchanged for $4 cash

IONARC SMELTERS LTD (BC)
Recapitalized as International Ionarc Inc. 01/30/1978
Each share Ordinary 50¢ par exchanged for (0.14285714) share Ordinary no par
(See International Ionarc Inc.)

IONATRON INC (DE)
Each share Conv. Preferred Ser. A $0.001 par received distribution of (0.0631) share Common $0.001 par payable 08/01/2006 to holders of record 07/15/2006 Ex date - 07/12/2006
Each share Conv. Preferred Ser. A $0.001 par received distribution of (0.099054) share Common $0.001 par payable 11/01/2006 to holders of record 10/15/2006 Ex date - 10/11/2006
Each share Conv. Preferred Ser. A $0.001 par received distribution of (0.0860958) share Common $0.001 par payable 02/01/2007 to holders of record 01/15/2007 Ex date - 01/10/2007
Each share Conv. Preferred Ser. A $0.001 par received distribution of (0.116632) share Common $0.001 par payable 08/01/2007 to holders of record 07/15/2007 Ex date - 07/11/2007
Each share Conv. Preferred Ser. A $0.001 par received distribution of (0.117378) share Common $0.001 par payable 11/01/2007 to holders of record 10/15/2007 Ex date - 10/11/2007
Stock Dividend - in Common to holders of Preferred 1.625% payable 05/01/2006 to holders of record 04/16/2006 Ex date - 04/20/2006
Name changed to Applied Energetics, Inc. 02/20/2008

IONE INC (DE)
Charter cancelled and declared inoperative and void for non-payment of taxes 5/25/94

IONE MINING CO. (ID)
Name changed to Southwestern Financial Corp. (ID) 08/02/1972
Each share Common 10¢ par exchanged for (1) share Common 10¢ par
Southwestern Financial Corp. (ID) name changed to Univest Technologies, Inc. 10/11/1985 which name changed to Outpatient Treatment Centers, Inc. 12/22/1986
(See Outpatient Treatment Centers, Inc.)

IONIA COUNTY NATIONAL BANK (IONIA, MI)
Reorganized as ICNB Financial Corp. 02/27/1987
Each share Common $20 par exchanged for (3) shares Common $1 par
ICNB Financial Corp. merged into Firstbank Corp. 07/01/2007 which merged into Mercantile Bank Corp. 06/01/2014

IONIC CTLS INC (MN)
Name changed to Western Media Group Corp. (MN) 11/17/1988
Western Media Group Corp. (MN) reorganized in Delaware as MedLink International, Inc. 11/22/2005

IONIC ENERGY INC (AB)
Merged into Shiningbank Energy Income Fund 04/17/2001
Each share Common no par exchanged for (0.306) Trust Unit no par or (0.167685) Trust Unit no par and $2.30524 cash
Note: Option to receive Units and cash expired 06/11/2001
Shiningbank Energy Income Fund merged into PrimeWest Energy Trust 07/13/2007
(See PrimeWest Energy Trust)

IONIC FUEL TECHNOLOGY INC (DE)
Charter cancelled and declared inoperative and void for non-payment of taxes 03/01/2002

IONIC VENTURES INC (AB)
Merged into Ionic Energy Inc. 01/01/1999
Each share Common no par exchanged for (1) share Common no par
Ionic Energy Inc. merged into Shiningbank Energy Income Fund 04/17/2001 which merged into PrimeWest Energy Trust 07/13/2007
(See PrimeWest Energy Trust)

IONICA GROUP PLC (ENGLAND & WALES)
Issue Information - 40,000,000 ADR'S offered at $19.57 per ADR on 07/18/1997
ADR agreement terminated 7/15/99
Each Sponsored ADR for Ordinary 10p par exchanged for $0.7063 cash

IONICRON INC (DE)
Charter cancelled and declared inoperative and void for non-payment of taxes 03/01/1986

IONICS INC (MA)
Merged into General Electric Co. 2/22/2005
Each share Common $1 par exchanged for $44 cash

IONOSPHERE INC (NV)
Recapitalized as Axonyx Inc. (NV) 12/31/1998
Each share Common no par exchanged for (0.5) share Common $0.001 par
Axonyx Inc. (NV) reorganized in Delaware as TorreyPines Therapeutics, Inc. 10/04/2006 which recapitalized as Raptor Pharmaceutical Corp. 09/29/2009
(See Raptor Pharmaceutical Corp.)

IORI ENTERPRISES INC (BC)
Name changed 05/14/1986
Name changed from IORI. International Oil Royalties Inc. to IORI. Enterprises Inc. 05/14/1986
Name changed to Golden Band Resources Inc. (BC) 03/26/1987
Golden Band Resources Inc. (BC)

reincorporated in Saskatchewan 07/04/2006
(See Golden Band Resources Inc.)

IOS CANADIAN VENTURE FUND LTD. (CANADA)
Name changed to Regent Venture Fund Ltd. 04/19/1971
Regent Venture Fund Ltd. name changed to Eaton Venture Fund Ltd. 07/04/1974 which name changed to Eaton/Bay Venture Fund Ltd. 04/12/1978
(See Eaton/Bay Venture Fund Ltd.)

IOS INTERNATIONAL FUND LTD. (ON)
Name changed to Commonwealth International Venture Fund Ltd. 05/04/1971
Commonwealth International Venture Fund Ltd. name changed to Eaton International Fund Ltd. 04/15/1974 which name changed to Eaton Bay International Fund Ltd. (ONT) 04/12/1978 which reincorporated in Canada 04/16/1980 which name changed back to Eaton International Fund 04/16/1986 which name changed to Viking International Fund Ltd. 04/16/1987 which name changed to Laurentian International Fund Ltd. 05/31/1993 which name changed to Strategic Value International Fund Ltd. 06/05/1997 which name changed to StrategicNova World Large Cap Fund Ltd. 09/26/2000
(See StrategicNova World Large Cap Fund Ltd.)

IOS VENTURE FUND LTD. (CANADA)
Name changed to IOS Canadian Venture Fund Ltd. 04/14/1970
IOS Canadian Venture Fund Ltd. name changed to Regent Venture Fund Ltd. 04/19/1971 which name changed to Eaton Venture Fund Ltd. 07/04/1974 which name changed to Eaton/Bay Venture Fund Ltd. 04/12/1978
(See Eaton/Bay Venture Fund Ltd.)

IOTA EXPLS LTD (BC)
Name changed to Mekong International Development Corp. 02/10/1992
Mekong International Developement Corp. recapitalized as Everest Mines & Minerals Ltd. 12/29/1995 which recapitalized as First Narrows Resources Corp. 04/04/2000

IOTA INDS INC (DE)
Adjudicated bankrupt 7/10/78
No stockholders' equity

IOWA AMERN CAP CORP (DE)
Adjustable Rate Preferred $1 par called for redemption 11/15/90
Public interest eliminated

IOWA AMERN WTR CO (DE)
5% Preferred $100 par called for redemption at $105 on 06/30/2002
5.5% Preferred $100 par called for redemption at $100.50 on 06/30/2002

IOWA BANCORP INC (DE)
Merged into First Midwest Financial, Inc. 12/29/95
Each share Common 10¢ par exchanged for $20.39 cash

IOWA BEEF PACKERS INC (DE)
Reincorporated 8/1/69
Common $3 par changed to $1.50 par and (1) additional share issued 9/3/63
6% Preferred $100 par called for redemption 2/28/66
Stock Dividend - 100% 10/1/65
State of incorporation changed from (IA) to (DE) 8/1/69
Name changed to Iowa Beef Processors, Inc. 5/1/70
Iowa Beef Processors, Inc. merged into Occidental Petroleum Corp.

(CA) 8/12/81 which reincorporated in Delaware 5/21/86

IOWA BEEF PROCESSORS INC (DE)
Common $1.50 par split (3) for (2) by issuance of (0.5) additional share 12/20/76
Common $1.50 par split (2) for (1) by issuance of (1) additional share 5/4/79
Stock Dividend - 10% 5/20/74
Merged into Occidental Petroleum Corp. (CA) 8/12/81
Each share Common $1.50 par exchanged for (0.385) share $14.625 Preferred $1 par and (1.328) shares Common 20¢ par
Occidental Petroleum Corp. (CA) reincorporated in Delaware 5/21/86

IOWA BUSINESS INVT CORP (IA)
Merged into Superior Equity Corp. 9/7/71
Each share Common $1 par exchanged for (0.6) share Common no par
(See Superior Equity Corp.)

IOWA CONTINENTAL TELEPHONE CO. (DE)
Name changed to General Telephone Co. of Iowa 11/30/56
(See listing for General Telephone Co. of Iowa)

IOWA CORD TIRE CO. (IA)
Charter revoked for failure to file reports and pay fees 4/21/30

IOWA ELEC LT & PWR CO (IA)
Common $100 par changed to no par in 1932
Each share Common $5 par exchanged for (1.5) shares Common $5 par in 1950
7% Preferred Ser. A $100 par called for redemption 7/1/50
6-1/2% Preferred Ser. B $100 par called for redemption 7/1/50
6% Preferred Ser. C $100 par called for redemption 7/1/50
Common $5 par changed to $2.50 par and (1) additional share issued 5/31/63
Under plan of reorganization each share Common $2.50 par automatically became (1) share IE Industries Inc. Common no par 7/1/86
(See IE Industries Inc.)
7.44% Preference $100 par called for redemption 10/1/86
7.96% Preference $100 par called for redemption 10/1/86
8.65% Preference $100 par called for redemption 10/1/86
8.92% Preference $100 par called for redemption 10/1/86
9.50% Preference $100 par called for redemption 10/1/86
8.55% Preference $100 par called for redemption 10/1/92
Name changed to IES Utilities Inc. 12/31/93
IES Utilities Inc. name changed to Interstate Power & Light Co. 1/1/2002
(See Interstate Power & Light Co.)

IOWA ELECTRIC CO. (IA)
Merged into Iowa Electric Light & Power Co. 4/8/53
Each share 6-1/2% Preferred $100 par exchanged for (8.4) shares Common $5 par
Each share 7% Preferred $100 par exchanged for (8.8) shares Common $5 par
Each share Common $100 par exchanged for (4) shares Common $5 par
Iowa Electric Light & Power Co. name changed to IES Industries Inc. 7/1/91 which merged into Interstate Energy Corp. 4/21/98 which name changed to Alliant Energy Corp. 5/19/99

IOWA ILL GAS & ELEC CO (IL)
Common no par changed to $1 par 07/29/1955
Common $1 par split (2) for (1) by issuance of (1) additional share 04/17/1964
$14 Preference no par called for redemption 03/29/1985
$2.31 Preference no par called for redemption 12/29/1986
$10.75 Preference no par called for redemption 12/29/1986
Common $1 par split (2) for (1) by issuance of (1) additional share 06/01/1990
$4.22 Preferred $100 par called for redemption 12/15/1994
$4.36 Preferred $100 par called for redemption 12/15/1994
$7.50 Preferred $100 par called for redemption 12/15/1994
Merged into MidAmerican Energy Co. 07/01/1995
Each share $5.25 Preferred no par exchanged for (1) share $5.25 Preferred no par
Each share 7.80% Preference no par exchanged for (1) share 7.80% Preference no par
Each share Common $1 par exchanged for (1.47) shares Common no par

IOWA-KANSAS DEVELOPMENT CO. (IA)
Voluntarily dissolved 10/20/27
Details not available

IOWA LIGHT, HEAT & POWER CO.
Merged into Iowa Public Service Co. 00/00/1927
Details not available

IOWA LIQUID ASSETS FD INC (IA)
Name changed to IMG Liquid Assets Fund, Inc. in October 1987

IOWA MICHIGAN CORP. (DE)
Merged into Consolidated Foundries & Mfg. Corp. 3/30/55
Each share Preferred A $5 par exchanged for $5.0625 cash

IOWA NATL BANKSHARES CORP (IA)
Common $50 par changed to $25 par and (1) additional share issued 6/17/85
Common $25 par changed to $12.50 par and (1) additional share issued 5/22/87
Common $12.50 par split (5) for (4) by issuance of (0.25) additional share 5/12/89
Common $12.50 par split (2) for (1) by issuance of (1) additional share 8/16/93
Name changed to Homeland Bankshares Corp. 12/31/94
Homeland Bankshares Corp. merged into Magna Group, Inc. 3/1/97 which merged into Union Planters Corp. 7/1/98 which merged into Regions Financial Corp. (New) 7/1/2004

IOWA PWR INC (IA)
Name changed 01/01/1990
Common $10 par split (3) for (2) by issuance of (0.5) additional share 04/27/1964
Under plan of reorganization each share Common $10 par automatically became (1) share Iowa Resources Inc. Common no par 11/01/1979
(See Iowa Resources Inc.)
9.75% Preferred $100 par called for redemption 00/00/1985
10.20% Preferred $100 par called for redemption 05/01/1986
7.84% Preferred $100 par called for redemption 08/29/1986
8.50% Preferred $100 par called for redemption 08/29/1986
Name changed from Iowa Power & Light Co. to Iowa Power Inc. 01/01/1990

Merged into Midwest Power Systems Inc. 07/22/1992
Each share 3.30% Preferred $100 par exchanged for (1) share 3.30% Preferred no par
Each share 4.35% Preferred $100 par exchanged for (1) share 4.35% Preferred no par
Each share 4.40% Preferred $100 par exchanged for (1) share 4.40% Preferred no par
Each share 4.80% Preferred $100 par exchanged for (1) share 4.80% Preferred no par
Midwest Power Systems Inc. merged into MidAmerican Energy Co. 07/01/1995
(See MidAmerican Energy Co.)

IOWA PUB SVC CO (IA)
Common $5 par split (2) for (1) by issuance of (1) additional share 00/00/1954
Under plan of reorganization each share Common $5 par automatically became (1) share Midwest Energy Co. Common $5 par 05/01/1984
(See Midwest Energy Co.)
10.88% Preferred $100 par called for redemption 06/01/1986
Merged into Midwest Power Systems Inc. 07/22/1992
Each share 3.75% Preferred $100 par exchanged for (1) share 3.75% Preferred no par
Each share 3.90% Preferred $100 par exchanged for (1) share 3.90% Preferred no par
Each share 4.20% Preferred $100 par exchanged for (1) share 4.20% Preferred no par
Each share 7.64% Preferred $100 par exchanged for (1) share 7.64% Preferred no par
Each share 8.08% Preferred $100 par exchanged for (1) share 8.08% Preferred no par
Each share $8.32 Class A Preferred no par exchanged for (1) share $8.32 Class A Preferred no par
Each share $8.52 Class A Preferred no par exchanged for (1) share $8.52 Class A Preferred no par
Midwest Power Systems Inc. merged into MidAmerican Energy Co. 07/01/1995
(See MidAmerican Energy Co.)

IOWA PUBLIC SERVICE CO. (DE)
Merged into Sioux City Gas & Electric Co. share for share whose name was then changed to Iowa Public Service Co. (IA) 00/00/1949
(See Iowa Public Service Co. (IA))

IOWA RAILWAY & LIGHT CORP. (IA)
Name changed to Iowa Electric Light & Power Co. 5/31/32
Iowa Electric Light & Power Co. reorganized as IE Industries Inc. 7/1/86

IOWA REGL TRAN CORP (IA)
Completely liquidated 8/14/74
Each share Common $1 par exchanged for first and final distribution of $0.10 cash

IOWA RES INC (IA)
Common no par split (2) for (1) by issuance of (1) additional share 06/27/1986
Merged into Midwest Resources Inc. 11/07/1990
Each share Common no par exchanged for (1.235) shares Common no par
Midwest Resources Inc. merged into MidAmerican Energy Co. 07/01/1995
(See MidAmerican Energy Co.)

IOWA SOUTHN INC (IA)
Each share Common $5 par received distribution of (1) additional share 6/12/86
Merged into IES Industries Inc. 7/1/91
Each share Common $5 par

exchanged for (1.6) shares Common no par
IES Industries Inc. merged into Interstate Energy Corp. 4/21/98 which name changed to Alliant Energy Corp. 5/19/99

IOWA SOUTHN UTILS CO (IA)
Reincorporated 6/1/86
Each share 7% Preferred $100 par exchanged for (4.2) shares Common $15 par and a Div. Arrears Ctf. for $32.12 in 1938
Each share 6-1/2% Preferred $100 par exchanged for (3.9) shares Common $15 par and a Div. Arrears Ctf. for $29.83 in 1938
Each share 6% Preferred $100 par exchanged for (3.6) shares Common $15 par in 1938
5-1/2% Preferred $30 par called for redemption 11/24/51
$1.76 Preferred $30 par called for redemption 7/3/63
Common $15 par changed to $10 par and (1) additional share issued 7/24/63
10% Preferred $30 par called for redemption 3/1/83
4-3/4% Preferred $30 par called for redemption in December, 1983
State of incorporation changed from (DE) to (IA) 6/1/86
Under plan of reorganization each share Common $10 par automatically became (1) share Iowa Southern Inc. Common $5 par 6/1/86
(See Iowa Southern Inc.)
8-1/2% Preferred $30 par called for redemption 9/1/92
8-3/4% Preferred $30 par called for redemption 9/1/92
Public interest eliminated

IOWA STL MILL INC (IA)
Name changed to Steel Melting Corp. 12/31/74
(See Steel Melting Corp.)

IOWA SURETY CO. (IA)
Name changed to Midwestern Casualty & Surety Co. 12/31/69
Midwestern Casualty & Surety Co. name changed to Midwestern Life Insurance Co. 11/30/83

IOWA TAX FREE LIQUID ASSETS FUND, INC. (IA)
Name changed to IMG Tax Exempt Liquid Assets Fund, Inc. in October, 1987

IOWA TELECOMMUNICATION SVCS INC (IA)
Issue Information - 21,977,895 shares COM offered at $19 per share on 11/17/2004
Merged into Windstream Corp. 06/01/2010
Each share Common 1¢ par exchanged for (0.804) share Common $0.0001 par and $7.90 cash
Windstream Corp. name changed to Windstream Holdings, Inc. 09/03/2013

IOWORLDMEDIA INC (FL)
Reorganized under the laws of Nevada as Radioio, Inc. 12/11/2013
Each share Common $0.001 par exchanged for (0.01) share Common $0.001 par

IP APPLICATIONS CORP (BC)
Each share old Common no par exchanged for (0.2) share new Common no par 01/10/2005
Name changed to Monexa Technologies Corp. 10/28/2009
Monexa Technologies Corp. name changed to Santa Rosa Resources Corp. 04/03/2012

IP FACTORY INC (DE)
Name changed to Dune Energy, Inc. 05/07/2003
(See Dune Energy, Inc.)

IP GATE INC (NV)
Recapitalized as Action Stocks Inc. 01/31/2003
Each share Common $0.001 par exchanged for (0.2) share Common $0.001 par
Action Stocks Inc. recapitalized as Specialized Home Medical Services, Inc. 07/03/2003 which name changed to IGSM Group, Inc. 11/23/2007 which recapitalized as Continental Rail Corp. 08/09/2013 which recapitalized as MediXall Group, Inc. 11/22/2016

IP MATRIX CORP (NV)
Name changed to Airprotek International, Inc. (NV) 03/14/2005
Each share Common $0.001 par exchanged for (1) share Common $0.001 par
Airprotek International, Inc. (NV) reorganized in Wyoming as Rafarma Pharmaceuticals, Inc. 11/20/2012

IP TECHNOLOGY SERVICES, INC. (DE)
Name changed to C2C CrowdFunding, Inc. 11/13/2012

IP TIMBERLANDS LTD (TX)
Merged into International Paper Co. 03/25/1998
Each Class A Depositary Unit no par exchanged for $13.6325 cash

IPA ENTERPRISES CORP (NY)
Name changed to Delhi Chemicals, Inc. 09/10/1975
Delhi Chemicals, Inc. name changed to Delhi Consolidated Industries, Inc. 04/02/1981 which name changed to Maritime Transport & Technology Inc. 03/08/1989 which name changed to Bank Store 07/24/1998 which name changed to Banker's Store Inc. 09/18/2001
(See Banker's Store Inc.)

IPALCO ENTERPRISES INC (IN)
Common no par split (2) for (1) by issuance of (1) additional share 11/12/86
Common no par split (3) for (2) by issuance of (0.5) additional share payable 3/18/96 to holders of record 3/7/96 Ex date - 3/19/96
Common no par split (2) for (1) by issuance of (1) additional share payable 3/18/99 to holders of record 3/5/99 Ex date - 3/19/99
Merged into AES Corp. 3/27/2001
Each share Common no par exchanged for (0.463) share Common 1¢ par

IPARTY CORP (DE)
Merged into Party City Holdings Inc. 05/09/2013
Each share Common $0.001 par exchanged for $0.45 cash

IPAYMENT INC (DE)
Merged into iPayment Holdings, Inc. 05/10/2006
Each share Common 1¢ par exchanged for $43.50 cash

IPC COMMUNICATIONS INC (DE)
Name changed 5/21/99
Issue Information - 3,250,000 shares COM offered at $15 per share on 09/26/1994
Under plan of merger each share old Common 1¢ par exchanged for either (1) share new Common 1¢ par or $21 cash 5/1/98
Note: Non-electing holders received cash
New Common 1¢ par split (2) for (1) by issuance of (1) additional share payable 6/24/98 to holders of record 6/10/98
Name changed from IPC Information Systems Inc. to IPC Communications Inc. 5/21/99
Merged into Global Crossing Ltd. 6/15/2000
Each share Common 1¢ par exchanged for (5.417) shares Common 1¢ par
(See Global Crossing Ltd.)

IPC COMMUNICATIONS INC (NY)
Acquired by Continental Telecom Inc. 1/7/86
Each share Class A Common 1¢ par exchanged for (0.4925) share Common $1 par
Continental Telecom Inc. name changed to Contel Corp. 5/1/86 which merged into GTE Corp. 3/14/91 which merged into Verizon Communications Inc. 6/30/2000

IPC FINL NETWORK INC (ON)
Merged into Investors Group Inc. 05/10/2004
Each share Common no par exchanged for $1.975 cash

IPC HEALTHCARE INC (DE)
Name changed 01/06/2015
Name changed from IPC The Hospitalist Co., Inc. to IPC Healthcare, Inc. 01/06/2015
Acquired by Team Health Holdings, Inc. 11/23/2015
Each share Common $0.001 par exchanged for $80.25 cash

IPC HLDGS LTD (BERMUDA)
Each share Conv. Preferred Ser. A 10¢ par exchanged for (1.0144) shares Common 1¢ par 11/17/2008
Merged into Validus Holdings, Ltd. 09/04/2009
Each share Common 1¢ par exchanged for (0.9727) share Common $0.175 par and $7.50 cash

IPC INTL PROSPECTOR CORP (BC)
Recapitalized as Kingston Resources Ltd. 05/17/1991
Each share Common no par exchanged for (0.4) share Common no par
Kingston Resources Ltd. recapitalized as Butler Developments Corp. 06/29/2001 which recapitalized as Butler Resource Corp. 02/12/2009 which name changed to Quantum Rare Earth Developments Corp. 03/04/2010 which name changed to NioCorp Developments Ltd. 03/04/2013

IPC US REAL ESTATE INVT TR (ON)
Name changed 06/14/2004
Name changed from IPC US Income Commercial Real Estate Investment Trust to IPC US Real Estate Investment Trust 06/14/2004
Merged into Behringer Harvard REIT I, Inc. 12/12/2007
Each CDN$ Trust Unit exchanged for USD$9.7737 cash

IPCO CORP (NY)
Name changed to Sterling Optical Corp. 11/09/1990
(See Sterling Optical Corp.)

IPCO HOSPITAL SUPPLY CORP. (NY)
Common $1 par split (2) for (1) by issuance of (1) additional share 2/20/68
Name changed to IPCO Corp. 11/16/79
IPCO Corp. name changed to Sterling Optical Corp. 11/9/90
(See Sterling Optical Corp.)

IPCOR, LTD. (UT)
Name changed to Luxury Seaside Resorts Inc. (UT) 12/20/1991
Luxury Seaside Resorts Inc. (UT) reincorporated in Nevada as RE/COMM Corp. 03/22/1992 which name changed to Metro Wireless Interactive Corp. 12/27/1993 which name changed to Red Rock International Corp. (NV) 04/01/1996 which reorganized in Kentucky as Page International Inc. 11/05/1997 which reincorporated in Nevada 12/31/1997 which name changed to China TianRen Organic Food, Inc. 06/14/2007

IPCS INC (DE)
Merged into Sprint Nextel Corp. 12/04/2009
Each share Common 1¢ par exchanged for $24 cash

IPEC HLDGS INC (NV)
Each share old Common $0.001 par exchanged for (1) share new Common $0.001 par to reflect a (1) for (1,000,000) reverse split followed by a (1,000,000) for (1) forward split 08/07/2006
Note: In effect holders received $2.90 cash per share and public interest was eliminated

IPEC LTD (AB)
Acquired by Flint Energy Services Ltd. 11/27/2001
Each share Common no par exchanged for (0.0297) share Common no par and $2.67 cash
(See Flint Energy Services Ltd.)

IPERCEPTIONS INC (CANADA)
Acquired by XPND Fund L.P. 03/16/2012
Each share Common no par exchanged for $0.08 cash
Note: Unexchanged certificates were cancelled and became without value 03/16/2018

IPERFORM STRATEGIC PARTNERS HEDGE FUND (ON)
Name changed to Blumont Strategic Partners Hedge Fund 03/24/2003
Blumont Strategic Partners Hedge Fund merged into BluMont Canadian Opportunities Fund 12/31/2006 which merged into BluMont Core Hedge Fund 08/07/2009

IPERFORMANCE FD INC (AB)
Reincorporated under the laws of Ontario as BluMont Capital Inc. 06/30/2003
BluMont Capital Inc. acquired by Integrated Asset Management Corp. 03/02/2007

IPERNICA LTD (AUSTRALIA)
Name changed to Nearmap Ltd. 03/05/2013
(See Nearmap Ltd.)

IPET HLDGS INC (DE)
Liquidation completed
Each share Common $0.00125 par received initial distribution of $0.09 cash payable 9/28/2001 to holders of record 1/18/2001 Ex date - 10/1/2001
Each share Common $0.00125 par received second distribution of $0.075 cash payable 9/27/2002 to holders of record 1/18/2001
Each share Common $0.00125 par received third and final distribution of $0.00747 cash payable 6/23/2004 to holders of record 1/18/2001
Note: Certificates were not required to be surrendered and are without value

IPHONE2 INC (WA)
Each share old Common $0.001 par exchanged for (0.33333333) shares new Common $0.001 par 04/25/2006
SEC revoked common stock registration 10/24/2007

IPI INC (MN)
Liquidation completed
Each share Common 1¢ par received initial distribution of $2.50 cash 1/31/2002
Each share Common 1¢ par received second and final distribution of $3.28 cash payable 12/17/2002 to holders of record 1/31/2001 Ex date - 12/18/2002
Note: Certificates were not required to be surrendered and are now valueless

IPICO INC (CANADA)
Proposal under Bankruptcy and Insolvency Act effective 03/24/2011
No stockholders' equity

IPIX CORP (DE)
Assets sold for the benefit of creditors 03/29/2007
No stockholders' equity

IPL ENERGY INC (CANADA)
Name changed to Enbridge Inc. 10/07/1998

IPL INC (DE)
Completely liquidated 03/11/1969
Each share Common $1 par exchanged for first and final distribution of (1) share Deltec International Ltd. Common $7.50 par
(See Deltec International Ltd.)

IPL INC (QC)
Multiple Shares no par split (2) for (1) by issuance of (1) additional share payable 03/13/2003 to holders of record 03/10/2003
Merged into 9225-8193 Quebec Inc. 10/15/2010
Each Multiple Share no par exchanged for $6.50 cash

IPL SYS INC (MA)
Name changed to Andataco, Inc. 04/21/1998
Andataco, Inc. merged into nStor Technologies, Inc. 11/02/1999
(See nStor Technologies, Inc.)

IPM INC (CO)
Each share old Common no par exchanged for (0.5) share new Common no par 12/19/88
Filed a petition under Chapter 11 Federal Bankruptcy Code in 1993
No stockholders' equity

IPM TECHNOLOGY INC (NY)
Each share Common 10¢ par exchanged for (0.4) share Common 25¢ par 12/19/72
Common 25¢ par split (3) for (2) by issuance of (0.5) additional share 7/31/80
Common 25¢ par split (2) for (1) by issuance of (1) additional share 2/16/81
Stock Dividends - 10% 5/16/83; 10% 7/9/84
Name changed to Mercury Air Group, Inc. (NY) 12/21/89
Mercury Air Group, Inc. (NY) reincorporated in Delaware 3/1/2001
(See Mercury Air Group, Inc.)

IPMC EUROPE CORP (FL)
Name changed to Wholefood Farmacy Corp. 11/10/2004
Wholefood Farmacy Corp. name changed to Wham Inc. 02/21/2012 which recapitalized as Berith Holdings Corp. 06/12/2017 which name changed to Syntrol Corp. 11/29/2017

IPMC HLDGS CORP (FL)
Each share old Common $0.001 par exchanged for (2/3) share new Common $0.001 par 10/03/2005
Reincorporated under the laws of Nevada as Coil Tubing Technology, Inc. 12/22/2005

IPORUSSIA INC (DE)
Each share old Common $0.0001 par exchanged for (0.03435607) share new Common $0.0001 par 12/19/2007
Note: Holders of between (100) and (2,910) shares received (100) shares only
Holders of (99) or fewer were not affected by the reverse split
Name changed to Bonds.com Group, Inc. 01/08/2008
(See Bonds.com Group, Inc.)

IPRINT TECHNOLOGIES INC (DE)
Name changed 05/25/2001
Issue Information - 4,500,000 shares COM offered at $10 per share on 03/07/2000
Name changed from iPrint.com, Inc. to iPrint Technologies, Inc. 05/25/2001
Assets assigned for the benefit of creditors 10/22/2002
No stockholders' equity

IPS COMPUTER MARKETING CORP (DE)
Name changed to Information Processing Systems, Inc. 01/01/1984
(See Information Processing Systems, Inc.)

IPS HEALTH CARE INC (DE)
Name changed to Diagnostic Imaging Services Inc. 10/5/94
(See Diagnostic Imaging Services Inc.)

IPSCO INC (SK)
Common no par split (2) for (1) by issuance of (1) additional share 07/06/1984
Common no par split (3) for (2) by issuance of (0.5) additional share payable 03/09/1998 to holders of record 02/27/1998 Ex date - 03/10/1998
5.5% 1st Preferred Ser. 1 no par called for redemption at $25 plus $0.34375 accrued dividend on 05/14/2004
Merged into SSAB Svenskt Stal AB 07/18/2007
Each share Common no par exchanged for USD$160 cash

IPSWICH BANCSHARES INC (MA)
Merged into Banknorth Group, Inc. (ME) 07/26/2002
Each share Common 10¢ par exchanged for either (0.835) share Common 1¢ par or $20.50 cash
Note: Option to receive stock expired 08/20/2002
Banknorth Group, Inc. (ME) merged into TD Banknorth Inc. 03/01/2005
(See TD Banknorth Inc.)

IPSWICH MILLS
In process of liquidation in 1929

IPSWICH SVGS BK (IPSWICH, MA)
Common 10¢ par split (2) for (1) by issuance of (1) additional share payable 08/27/1997 to holders of record 07/28/1997
Under plan of reorganization each share Common 10¢ par automatically became (1) share Ipswich Bancshares Inc. Common 10¢ par 07/01/1999
Ipswich Bancshares Inc. merged into Banknorth Group, Inc. (ME) 07/26/2002 which merged into TD Banknorth Inc. 03/01/2005
(See TD Banknorth Inc.)

IPSWICH STREET CDO LTD (CAYMAN ISLANDS)
Preference Shares called for redemption at $25,000 on 11/16/2012

IPTEL DIRECT INC (NV)
Name changed to Universal Energy Holdings, Inc. 04/24/2007
(See Universal Energy Holdings, Inc.)

IPTEL GLOBAL INC (NV)
Common $0.001 par split (30) for (1) by issuance of (29) additional shares payable 8/23/2004 to holders of record 8/21/2004
Name changed to Orion Petroleum Corp. 9/21/2004
Orion Petroleum Corp. name changed to Aquarian Gold Corp. 3/14/2005

IPTIMIZE INC (DE)
Reincorporated 10/10/2007
Reorganized from (MN) to under the laws of Delaware 10/10/2007
Each share Common $0.001 par exchanged for (0.33333333) share Common $0.001 par Chapter 7 bankruptcy proceedings terminated 03/23/2011
No stockholders' equity

IPVC COM INC (NV)
Name changed to IPVoice.com, Inc. 6/9/99
IPVoice.com, Inc. name changed to IPVoice Communications, Inc. (New) 10/30/2001 which name changed to NewMarket Technology Inc. 7/16/2004

IPVOICE COMMUNICATIONS INC NEW (NV)
Name changed 01/30/2001
Name changed from IPVoice.com, Inc. to IPVoice Communications, Inc. 01/30/2001
Each shares old Common $0.001 par exchanged for (0.03333333) share new Common $0.001 par 10/29/2002
Name changed to NewMarket Technology, Inc. 07/16/2004

IPVOICE COMMUNICATIONS INC OLD (DE)
Reincorporated under the laws of Nevada as IPVC.Com, Inc. 04/19/1999
IPVC.Com, Inc. name changed to IPVoice.Com, Inc. 06/09/1999 which name changed to IPVoice Communications, Inc. (New) 01/30/2001 which name changed to NewMarket Technology, Inc. 07/16/2004

IQ HLDGS INC (CO)
Reorganized under the laws of Texas as Scenario Systems International, Inc. 08/01/2007
Each share Common no par exchanged for (0.05) share Common $0.00001 par
Scenario Systems International, Inc. (TX) reorganized in Wyoming as Insight ID, Inc. 09/18/2013

IQ MICRO INC (CO)
Name changed 10/23/2006
Name changed from IQ Medical Corp. to IQ Micro Inc. 10/23/2006
SEC revoked common stock registration 01/16/2014

IQ PWR AG (SWITZERLAND)
Company terminated Registered Share registration and no longer trades in North America as of 12/28/2006

IQ PWR TECHNOLOGY INC (CANADA)
Each share old Common no par exchanged for (0.4) share new Common no par 04/10/2000
Reorganized under the laws of Switzerland as iQ Power AG 11/15/2004
Each share new Common no par exchanged for (1) Registered Share
(See iQ Power AG)

IQ SOFTWARE CORP (GA)
Merged into Information Advantage, Inc. 9/24/98
Each share Common $0.00033 par exchanged for (1.96) shares Common 1¢ par
Information Advantage, Inc. merged into Sterling Software, Inc. 8/31/99 which merged into Computer Associates International, Inc. 4/6/2000 which name changed to CA, Inc. 2/1/2006

IQI INC (DE)
Merged into Aegis Communication Group Inc. 7/9/98
Each share Common 1¢ par exchanged for (9.7513) shares Common 1¢ par

IQORDER COM INC
Merged into InfoSpace, Inc. 07/03/2000
Each share Common exchanged for (0.03314666) share Common $0.0001 par
InfoSpace, Inc. name changed to Blucora, Inc. 06/07/2012

IQROM COMMUNICATIONS INC (NV)
Charter revoked for failure to file reports and pay fees 11/01/2002

IQUE INTELLECTUAL PPTYS INC (NV)
Each share old Common $0.001 par exchanged for (0.04255319) share new Common $0.001 par 11/12/2004
Name changed to Safeguard Security Holdings, Inc. 01/05/2005
(See Safeguard Security Holdings, Inc.)

IQUEST NETWORKS INC (BC)
Reorganized under the laws of Wyoming as Quest Ventures Inc. 10/28/2003
Each share Common no par exchanged for (0.25) share Common no par
Quest Ventures Inc. recapitalized as Dorato Resources Inc. (WY) 04/24/2006 which reincorporated in British Columbia 08/21/2006 which recapitalized as Xiana Mining Inc. 10/23/2013

IQUNIVERSE INC (MN)
SEC revoked common stock registration 10/04/2011

IR OPER CORP (DE)
Name changed to Digi Link Technologies, Inc. 02/12/2001
(See Digi Link Technologies, Inc.)

IRA FOOD BROKERS CORP (FL)
Name changed to American International Food Corp. 05/29/1997
American International Food Corp. recapitalized as Travoo, Inc. 06/25/2009 which recapitalized as Yingtui Holdings Ltd. 04/05/2013

IRBY BROTHERS MACHINE & IRON WORKS, INC. (MS)
Name changed to Irby Steel Co. 03/28/1964
Irby Steel Co. acquired by Teledyne, Inc. 04/04/1968 which merged into Allegheny Teledyne, Inc. 08/15/1996 which name changed to Allegheny Technologies Inc. 11/29/1999

IRBY STEEL CO. (MS)
Acquired by Teledyne, Inc. 04/04/1968
Each share Common $1 par exchanged for (0.257449) share Common $1 par
Teledyne, Inc. merged into Allegheny Teledyne, Inc. 08/15/1996 which name changed to Allegheny Technologies Inc. 11/29/1999

IRC, INC. (DE)
Merged into TRW Inc. 2/19/68
Each share Common 10¢ par exchanged for (0.25) share $4.40 Conv. Preference II Ser. 1 no par and (0.333333) share Common $2.50 par
TRW Inc. merged into Northrop Grumman Corp. 12/11/2002

IRCC INC (NY)
Dissolved by proclamation 6/23/93

IRE SER I INC (FL)
Merged into I.R.E Financial Corp. in August 1980
Each share Conv. Preferred Ser. A 50¢ par exchanged for (1) share Common 1¢ par
Each share Common 1¢ par exchanged for (1) share Common 1¢ par
I.R.E. Financial Corp. name changed to BankAtlantic Financial Corp. 1/4/88 which name changed to BFC Financial Corp. 3/27/92

IRE SER II INC (FL)
Merged into I.R.E. Financial Corp. in August 1980
Each share Conv. Preferred Ser. A $1 par exchanged for (1) share Common 1¢ par
Each share Common 1¢ par exchanged for (1) share Common 1¢ par
I.R.E. Financial Corp. name changed to BankAtlantic Financial Corp. 1/4/88 which name changed to BFC Financial Corp. 3/27/92

IRE SER III INC (FL)
Merged into I.R.E. Financial Corp. in August 1980
Each share 10% Preferred Ser. A $1 par exchanged for (1) share Common 1¢ par
Each share Common $1 par exchanged for (1) share Common 1¢ par
I.R.E. Financial Corp. name changed to BankAtlantic Financial Corp. 1/4/88 which name changed to BFC Financial Corp. 3/27/92

IRECO CHEMS (UT)
100% acquired by Gulf Resources & Chemical Corp. through purchase offer which expired 07/29/1975
Public interest eliminated

IRELAND BK GOVERNOR & CO (IRELAND)
Old Sponsored ADR's for Ordinary split (2) for (1) by issuance of (1) additional ADR payable 07/19/1999 to holders of record 07/16/1999 Ex date - 07/20/1999
Each old Sponsored ADR for Ordinary exchanged for (0.1) new Sponsored ADR for Ordinary 10/17/2011
Basis changed from (1:4) to (1:40) 10/17/2011
ADR agreement terminated 04/22/2015
Each new Sponsored ADR for Ordinary exchanged for $11.83548 cash
ADR agreement terminated 08/04/2017
Each ADR for Ordinary exchanged for $13.3934174 cash

IRELANDS RESTAURANTS INC (TN)
Name changed to Southern Hospitality Corp. 2/1/80
(See Southern Hospitality Corp.)

IREX CORP (PA)
Each share Common $1 par received distribution of (0.02) share Specialty Products & Insulation Co. Common 1¢ par payable 01/29/1999 to holders of record 12/28/1998
Merged into North Lime Holdings Corp. 10/20/2006
Each share $2.80 Preferred $1 par exchanged for $30 cash
Each share Common $1 par exchanged for $66 cash

IREX IRON MINES LTD. (ON)
Merged into Choiceland Iron Mines Ltd. 02/26/1962
Each share Capital Stock $1 par exchanged for (0.5) share Common no par
Choiceland Iron Mines Ltd. recapitalized as Atlantic Goldfields Inc. 08/05/1987 which recapitalized as Dexus Inc. 06/22/1990 which was acquired by Trimin Enterprises Inc. (BC) 06/30/1993 which reorganized as Trimin Enterprises Inc. (Canada) 07/27/1998
(See Trimin Enterprises Inc.)

IRG TECHNOLOGIES INC (NV)
Chapter 11 bankruptcy proceedings converted to Chapter 7 on 10/25/1995
Stockholders' equity unlikely

IRI CORP (DE)
Charter cancelled and declared inoperative and void for non-payment of taxes 03/01/2009

IRI INTL CORP (DE)
Issue Information - 12,000,000 shares COM offered at $18 per share on 11/13/1997
Merged into National-Oilwell, Inc. 06/28/2000
Each share Common 1¢ par exchanged for (0.3385) share Common 1¢ par
National-Oilwell, Inc. name changed to National Oilwell Varco, Inc. 03/11/2005

IRIANA RES CORP (YT)
Each share old Common no par exchanged for (0.2) share new Common no par 03/21/1997
Each share new Common no par exchanged again for (0.1) share new Common no par 06/11/2001
Merged into Polaris Geothermal Inc. 06/21/2004
Each share new Common no par exchanged for (0.025) share Class B Common no par
Note: Unexchanged certificates received $1 cash per share 01/28/2005
(See Polaris Geothermal Inc.)

IRIDIUM COMMUNICATIONS INC (DE)
Each share 7% Conv. Preferred Ser. A $0.0001 par automatically became (10.6022) shares Common $0.001 par 03/20/2018
(Additional Information in Active)

IRIDIUM WORLD COMMUNICATIONS LTD (BERMUDA)
Chapter 11 bankrupcy proceedings dismissed 10/28/2009
No stockholders' equity

IRIDIUM WORLD COMMUNICATIONS LTD (BERMUDA)
Issue Information - 12,000,000 shares CL A COM offered at $20 per share on 06/09/1997
Chapter 11 bankruptcy proceedings dismissed 10/28/2009
No stockholders' equity

IRIS COMMUNICATIONS INC (CA)
Name changed to Western Energy Resources, Inc. 2/7/85
Western Energy Resources Inc. recapitalized as Omnipower Inc. 8/23/95
(See Omnipower Inc.)

IRIS INTL INC (DE)
Acquired by Danaher Corp. 10/31/2012
Each share Common 1¢ par exchanged for $19.50 cash

IRIS RES INC (BC)
Name changed to Madison Holdings Ltd. 12/05/1986
Madison Holdings Ltd. recapitalized as Consolidated Madison Holdings Ltd. 04/10/1991 which merged into Ourominas Minerals Inc. 06/27/1996 which recapitalized as Thistle Mining Inc. 04/27/1999
(See Thistle Mining Inc.)

IRISH COPPER MINES LTD (ON)
Capital Stock $1 par changed to no par 08/09/1971
Name changed to Irish International Energy Resources Ltd. 07/11/1978
Irish International Energy Resources Ltd. recapitalized as Irish Energy Oil & Minerals Inc. 03/24/1980 which name changed to Lumax Oil & Gas Inc. 02/27/1981 which recapitalized as First Munich Capital Ltd. 04/28/1989
(See First Munich Capital Ltd.)

IRISH ENERGY OIL & MINERALS INC (ON)
Recapitalized 03/24/1980
Recapitalized from Irish International Energy Resources Ltd. to Irish Energy Oil & Minerals Inc. 03/24/1980
Each share Capital Stock no par exchanged for (0.1) share Capital Stock no par
Name changed to Lumax Oil & Gas Inc. 02/27/1981
Lumax Oil & Gas Inc. recapitalized as First Munich Capital Ltd. 04/28/1989
(See First Munich Capital Ltd.)

IRISH INVT FD INC (MD)
Name changed to New Ireland Fund, Inc. 6/21/2001

IRISH LIFE & PERM PLC (IRELAND)
Name changed 05/26/2010
Name changed from Irish Life & Permanent PLC to Irish Life & Permanent Group Holdings PLC 05/26/2010
Recapitalized as Permanent TSB Group Holdings PLC 10/26/2012
Each ADR for Ordinary exchanged for (0.01) ADR for Ordinary

IRISH MAG INC (FL)
Common 1¢ par split (4.44444444) for (1) by issuance of (3.44444444) additional shares payable 10/02/2006 to holders of record 09/01/2006 Ex date - 10/03/2006
Name changed to China Public Security Technology, Inc. (FL) 02/12/2007
China Public Security Technology, Inc. (FL) reincorporated in Nevada as China Information Security Technology, Inc. 04/07/2008 which name changed to China Information Technology, Inc. 08/26/2010 which reorganized in British Virgin Islands 11/01/2012 which name changed to Taoping Inc. 06/04/2018

IRKUT CORP (RUSSIA)
ADR agreement terminated 06/11/2018
Each Sponsored ADR for Ordinary exchanged for (30) shares Ordinary
Note: Unexchanged ADR's will be sold and the proceeds, if any, held for claim after 12/11/2018

IRKUTSKENERGO AO (RUSSIA)
Each Sponsored ADR for Ordinary received distribution of $2.853431 cash payable 11/03/2009 to holders of record 10/20/2009 Ex date - 10/16/2009
Name changed to Irkutskenergo JSC 04/15/2016

IROC ENERGY SVCS CORP (CANADA)
Merged into Western Energy Services Corp. 04/22/2013
Each share Common no par exchanged for (0.2438) share Common no par and $1.24 cash

IROC SYS CORP (AB)
Merged into IROC Systems Corp. (Canada) 02/28/2003
Each share Common no par exchanged for (1) share Common no par
IROC Systems Corp. (Canada) name changed to IROC Energy Services Corp. 05/22/2007 which marged into Western Energy Services Corp. 04/22/2013

IROC SYS CORP (CANADA)
Name changed to IROC Energy Services Corp. 05/22/2007
IROC Energy Services Corp. merged into Western Energy Services Corp. 04/22/2013

IRON & GLASS BANCORP INC (PA)
Common no par split (2) for (1) by issuance of (1) additional share payable 12/11/1998 to holders of record 12/04/1998
Merged into F.N.B. Corp. 08/19/2008
Each share Common no par exchanged for (5) shares Common 1¢ par

IRON & GLASS BK (PITTSBURGH, PA)
Reorganized as Iron & Glass Bancorp, Inc. 10/01/1987
Each share Capital Stock $100 par exchanged for (50) shares Common no par
Iron & Glass Bancorp, Inc. merged into F.N.B. Corp. 08/19/2008

IRON & GLASS DLR SVGS BK (PITTSBURGH, PA)
Stock Dividends - 100% 07/05/1955; 50% 10/29/1958
Name changed to Iron & Glass Bank (Pittsburgh, PA) 07/24/1969
Iron & Glass Bank (Pittsburgh, PA) reorganized as Iron & Glass Bancorp, Inc. 10/01/1987 which merged into F.N.B. Corp. 08/19/2008

IRON BAY MINES LTD. (ON)
Recapitalized as Calmor Iron Bay Mines Ltd. 12/14/1966
Each share Capital Stock $1 par exchanged for (1) share Capital Stock no par and (1) Trust Share of Iron Bay Trust
(See Calmor Iron Bay Mines Ltd.)

IRON CARBIDE AUSTRALIA LTD (AUSTRALIA)
Name changed to ION Ltd. 2/12/2001
(See ION Ltd.)

IRON CITY MINES LTD (ON)
Name changed to Petrolantic Resources Inc. 10/09/1980
Each share Common no par exchanged for (1) share Common no par
Petrolantic Resources Inc. name changed to Petrolantic Ltd. 10/05/1987 which name changed to Cirque Energy Ltd. 04/01/1994 which recapitalized as Cirque Energy Corp. 05/11/1998 which merged into Tikal Resources Corp. 05/31/1999 which was acquired by BelAir Energy Corp. 12/14/2001 which merged into Purcell Energy Ltd. (New) 09/04/2003
(See Purcell Energy Ltd. (New))

IRON CITY-OHIO RIVER CORP. (MD)
Completely liquidated 06/30/1962
Each share Iron City Series received first and final distribution of $22.60 cash
Each share Ohio River Series received first and final distribution of $19.00 cash

IRON CITY SAND & GRAVEL CO.
Reorganized as Iron City-Ohio River Corp. 00/00/1935
Details not available

IRON CLIFF MINES LTD (ON)
Merged into Gerrard Realty Inc. 01/28/1976
Each share Capital Stock $1 par exchanged for (0.02) share Common no par

IRON CREEK CAP CORP (BC)
Each share old Common no par exchanged for (0.14285714) share new Common no par 04/14/2014
Name changed to Revelo Resources Corp. 12/17/2014

IRON EAGLE GROUP INC (DE)
Each share old Common $0.00001 par exchanged for (0.025) share new Common $0.00001 par 07/13/2010
Each share new Common $0.00001 par exchanged again for (0.125) share new Common $0.00001 par 08/16/2011
SEC revoked common stock registration 05/13/2015

IRON FIREMAN MANUFACTURING CO. (OR)
Common no par changed to $1 par 12/3/58
Merged into Electronic Specialty Co. on a share for share basis 5/31/62

Electronic Specialty Co. merged into International Controls Corp. 8/1/69
(See International Controls Corp.)

IRON HEAD MNG CORP (NV)
Name changed to Connect Corp. 04/16/2009
Connect Corp. name changed to IFCI International Corp. 01/26/2012

IRON HLDGS CORP (NV)
Recapitalized as Monarch Investment Properties, Inc. 07/31/1998
Each share Common $0.001 par exchanged for (0.1) share Common $0.001 par
(See Monarch Investment Properties Inc.)

IRON HORSE PETE CORP (OH)
Charter forfeited for failure to maintain a registered agent 04/17/1986

IRON HORSE RES CORP (BC)
Struck off register and declared dissolved for failure to file returns 06/05/1992

IRON KING CONSOLIDATED MINING CO.
Merged into Eureka Lilly Consolidated Mining Co. 00/00/1937
Each share exchanged for (0.377701) share Common 10¢ par
Eureka Lilly Consolidated Mining Co. merged into Eureka Lilly Standard Consolidated Mining Co. 11/25/1974 which merged into South Standard Mining Co. 07/29/1983 which merged into Chief Consolidated Mining Co. 07/01/1996
(See Chief Consolidated Mining Co.)

IRON KING MINES INC (BC)
Recapitalized as Corriente Resources Inc. 04/23/1992
Each share Common no par exchanged for (0.33333333) share Common no par
(See Corriente Resources Inc.)

IRON LADY RES INC (BC)
Recapitalized as Takepoint Ventures Ltd. (BC) 08/03/1994
Each share Common no par exchanged for (0.2921176) share Common no par
Takepoint Ventures Ltd. (BC) reorganized in Yukon as Consolidated Takepoint Ventures Ltd. 06/25/2002 which name changed to Lake Shore Gold Corp. (YT) 12/18/2002 which reincorporated in British Columbia 06/30/2004 which reincorporated in Canada 07/18/2008 which merged into Tahoe Resources Inc. 04/07/2016

IRON LAKE MINERALS INC (AB)
Reorganized under the laws of Canada as Alturas Minerals Corp. 04/10/2006
Each share Common no par exchanged for (0.33333333) share Common no par

IRON LINK LTD (NV)
Name changed to Wave Uranium Holding 07/19/2007
Wave Uranium Holding name changed to FBC Holding, Inc. 10/26/2009

IRON MANN CORP. (NV)
Charter cancelled for failure to file reports and pay fees 03/01/1965

IRON MASK GOLD MINING CO. (CO)
Charter expired by time limitation 3/18/21

IRON MASK MNG CO (ID)
Name changed to Intrepid Technology & Resources, Inc. 04/12/2002
(See Intrepid Technology & Resources, Inc.)

IRON MNG GROUP INC (FL)
Chapter 11 bankruptcy proceedings converted to Chapter 7 on 11/18/2011
Stockholders' equity unlikely

IRON MTN INC (DE)
Ctfs. dated prior to 07/12/1979
Recapitalized as American Specialty Foods, Inc. 07/12/1979
Each share Common 50¢ par exchanged for (0.02) share Common 1¢ par
(See American Specialty Foods, Inc.)

IRON MTN INC (DE)
Ctfs. dated after 02/06/1996
Common 1¢ par split (3) for (2) by issuance of (0.5) additional share payable 07/31/1998 to holders of record 07/17/1998
Merged into Iron Mountain Inc. (PA) 02/01/2000
Each share Common 1¢ par exchanged for (1) share Common 1¢ par
Iron Mountain Inc. (PA) reincorporated back in Delaware 05/27/2005

IRON MTN INC OLD (DE)
Reincorporated 05/27/2005
Common 1¢ par split (3) for (2) by issuance of (0.5) additional share payable 12/31/2001 to holders of record 12/17/2001 Ex date - 01/02/2002
Common 1¢ par split (3) for (2) by issuance of (0.5) additional share payable 06/30/2004 to holders of record 06/15/2004 Ex date - 07/01/2004
State of incorporation changed from (PA) to (DE) 05/27/2005
Common 1¢ par split (3) for (2) by issuance of (0.5) additional share payable 12/29/2006 to holders of record 12/18/2006 Ex date - 01/03/2007
Reorganized as Iron Mountain Inc. (New) 01/21/2015
Each share Common 1¢ par exchanged for (1) share Common 1¢ par

IRON PRODUCTS CORP.
In process of dissolution in 1936

IRON RIV RES LTD (BC)
Recapitalized as South Duval Gold Corp. 07/09/1996
Each share Common no par exchanged for (0.2) share Common no par

IRON SILVER MINING CO.
In process of liquidation in 1937

IRON SOUTH MNG CORP (BC)
Each share old Common no par exchanged for (0.33333333) share new Common no par 12/22/2014
Name changed to Argentina Lithium & Energy Corp. 09/21/2016

IRON SPRINGS CAP CORP (AB)
Reincorporated under the laws of Canada as Kaboose Inc. 11/28/2005
Kaboose Inc. (Canada) reincorporated in Ontario as KAB Distribution Inc. 06/09/2009
(See KAB Distribution Inc.)

IRON STAR DEV INC (UT)
Name changed to Xinyinhai Technology, Ltd. 10/10/2006

IRON TANK RES CORP (BC)
Name changed to Spriza Media Inc. 03/01/2016
Spriza Media Inc. name changed to Fanlogic Interactive Inc. 03/29/2017

IRON WORKS DEVELOPMENT CORP (MN)
Proclaimed dissolved for failure to file annual reports 1995

IRONBARK ZINC LTD (AUSTRALIA)
Name changed 01/19/2010
Each old Sponsored ADR for Ordinary exchanged for (0.1) new Sponsored ADR for Ordinary 08/14/2008
Basis changed from (1:1) to (1:10) 08/14/2008
Name changed from Ironbark Gold Ltd. to Ironbark Zinc Ltd. 01/19/2010
ADR agreement terminated 08/07/2017
Each new Sponsored ADR for Ordinary exchanged for $0.530171 cash

IRONBOUND BANKCORP (NJ)
Reorganized 7/1/97
Reorganized from Ironbound Bank (Newark, NJ) to Ironbound Bankcorp 7/1/97
Merged into Richmond County Financial Corp. 3/5/99
Each share Common $5 par exchanged for (1.463) shares Common 1¢ par
Richmond County Financial Corp. merged into New York Community Bancorp, Inc. 7/31/2001

IRONCLAD ENCRYPTION CORP (NV)
Reincorporated under the laws of Delaware 10/16/2017

IRONCLAD PERFORMANCE WEAR CORP (NV)
Name changed to ICPW Liquidation Corp. 11/20/2017

IRONCLAD SYS INC (AB)
Name changed to Bikestar Inc. 07/24/1998
Bikestar Inc. recapitalized as Adventurx.Com, Inc. 08/23/1999 which name changed to Nettron.Com, Inc. 09/28/1999 which recapitalized as Valcent Products Inc. 05/03/2005 which name changed to Alterrus Systems Inc. 06/12/2012

IRONHORSE OIL & GAS INC (AB)
Recapitalized as Pond Technologies Holdings Inc. 02/06/2018
Each share Common no par exchanged for (0.14492753) share Common no par

IRONRITE, INC. (MI)
Name changed to Dielectric Products Engineering Co., Inc. 08/23/1961
Dielectric Products Engineering Co., Inc. merged into Sola Basic Industries, Inc. 07/15/1968 which merged into General Signal Corp. 09/30/1977 which merged into SPX Corp. 10/06/1998

IRONRITE IRONER CO.
Name changed to Ironrite, Inc. in 1949
Ironrite, Inc. name changed to Dielectric Products Engineering Co., Inc. 8/23/61 which merged into Sola Basic Industries, Inc. 7/15/68 which merged into General Signal Corp. 9/30/77 which merged into SPX Corp. 10/6/98

IRONWOOD PETE LTD (AB)
Merged into Big Horn Resources Ltd. 11/13/1998
Each share Common no par exchanged for $0.76 cash

IRONWOOD RES INC (AB)
Name changed to Wise Card Holdings Inc. 01/15/1990
Wise Card Holdings Inc. recapitalized as Wise Card Consolidated Inc. 12/31/1990
(See Wise Card Consolidated Inc.)

IRONX MINERACAO S A (BRAZIL)
ADR agreement terminated 12/01/2008
Each Sponsored ADR for Ordinary exchanged for $11.24578 cash

IROQUOIS BANCORP INC (NY)
Common $1 par split (2) for (1) by issuance of (1) additional share 08/31/1995
Floating Rate Preferred Ser. A $1 par called for redemption at $100 on 04/01/1998
Floating Rate Preferred Ser. B $1 par called for redemption at $100 on 10/01/1998
Merged into First Niagara Financial Group, Inc. (Old) 11/06/2000
Each share Common $1 par exchanged for $33.25 cash

IROQUOIS BRANDS LTD (DE)
Each share $1 Conv. Preferred no par exchanged for (2) shares Common $1 par 10/30/1978
Charter cancelled and declared inoperative and void for non-payment of taxes 06/24/1992

IROQUOIS CORP. (MI)
Charter revoked for failure to file reports and pay fees 00/00/1965

IROQUOIS CORP. (MN)
Name changed to EmCom, Inc. 02/06/1973
(See EmCom, Inc.)

IROQUOIS GLASS LTD. (CANADA)
Merged into Sogemines Ltd. 10/18/1965
Each share 6% Part. Preferred $10 par exchanged for (0.75) share Common no par
Sogemines Ltd. name changed to Genstar Ltd. 02/25/1969 which name changed to Genstar Corp. 06/15/1981
(See Genstar Corp.)

IROQUOIS INDS INC (DE)
Name changed to Iroquois Brands, Ltd. 06/01/1973
(See Iroquois Brands, Ltd.)

IROQUOIS KIRKLAND MINES CORP. LTD. (ON)
Charter cancelled for failure to file reports and pay taxes 00/00/1956

IROQUOIS MINES LTD. (BC)
Reorganized as Hertz Industries, Ltd. 08/06/1970
Each share Common $1 par exchanged for (1) share Common $1 par
(See Hertz Industries, Ltd.)

IROQUOIS SHARE CORP.
Acquired by Atlas Utilities Corp. 00/00/1931
Details not available

IRT CORP (DE)
Each share old Common 10¢ par exchanged for (0.05) share new Common 10¢ par 02/16/1978
New Common 10¢ par split (2) for (1) by issuance of (1) additional share 09/06/1985
Chapter 11 bankruptcy proceedings dismissed 12/11/1996
Stockholders' equity unlikely

IRT HLDG CORP (DE)
Name changed to Asthma Disease Management, Inc. 12/03/1998
(See Asthma Disease Management, Inc.)

IRT INDS INC (FL)
Each share old Common $0.0001 par exchanged for (0.02777777) share new Common $0.0001 par 03/25/1994
Each share new Common $0.0001 par exchanged again for (0.1) share new Common $0.0001 par 09/24/1997
Name changed to Xpedian, Inc. 01/26/2000
Xpedian, Inc. name changed to Gala Hospitality Corp. 11/06/2001 which name changed to Gala Holding Corp. 09/04/2002 which recapitalized as Global TransNet Corp. 10/14/2003 which recapitalized as Legacy Brands Holding, Inc. (FL) 11/19/2009 which reincorporated in British Virgin Islands as Revelation MIS, Inc. 10/22/2010 which reincorporated in Florida as Jolen, Inc. 04/08/2015

which name changed to WOWI, Inc. 06/23/2016

IRT PPTY CO (GA)
Common $1 par split (5) for (4) by issuance of (0.25) additional share 08/01/1984
Common $1 par split (5) for (4) by issuance of (0.25) additional share 09/01/1985
Common $1 par split (5) for (4) by issuance of (0.25) additional share 09/01/1986
Common $1 par split (5) for (4) by issuance of (0.25) additional share 06/02/1989
Merged into Equity One, Inc. 02/13/2003
Each share Common $1 par exchanged for (0.9) share Common 1¢ par
Equity One, Inc. merged into Regency Centers Corp. 03/01/2017

IRT RLTY SVCS INC (GA)
Name changed to CP Overseas, Inc. 04/12/1988
CP Overseas, Inc. recapitalized as United Fashions Inc. (GA) 09/28/1990 which reorganized in Delaware as UniHolding Corp. 08/30/1993 which name changed to ULH Corp. 11/21/2000
(See ULH Corp.)

IRV INC (CO)
Name changed to Scarab Systems, Inc. 03/24/2003
Scarab Systems, Inc. name changed to Torrent Energy Corp. 07/30/2004 which recapitalized as 1pm Industries, Inc. 04/06/2015

IRVAN FERROMAGNETICS CORP. (CA)
Reported insolvent 00/00/1962
Charter suspended for non-payment of taxes 12/03/1962

IRVCO RES LTD (BC)
Name changed 06/14/1979
Name changed from Irvco Resources Corp. to Irvco Resources Ltd. 06/14/1979
Struck from the register and dissolved for failure to file returns 11/01/1995

IRVIN INDS INC (NY)
Under plan of merger Common 50¢ par holdings of (50) shares or more exchanged for (1) share 66¢ Preferred Ser. A $1 par per share and holdings of (49) shares or fewer exchanged for $5 cash per share 04/28/1980

IRVINE APT CMNTYS INC (MD)
Reincorporated 5/2/96
State of incorporation changed from (DE) to (MD) 5/2/96
Merged into TIC Acquisition LLC 6/7/99
Each share Common $1 par exchanged for $34 cash

IRVINE NATIONAL BANK (IRVINE, CA)
Merged into Heritage Bank (Anaheim, CA) 12/31/79
Each share Capital Stock $5 par exchanged for (1) share Common no par
Heritage Bank (Anaheim, CA) reorganized as Heritage Bancorp 12/28/81
(See Heritage Bancorp)

IRVINE PAC CORP (CO)
Reincorporated under the laws of Delaware as iMedia International, Inc. 11/26/2003

IRVINE SVGS & LN ASSN (CA)
Merged into Valley Federal Savings & Loan Association 8/1/81
Each share Guarantee Stock $10 par exchanged for $55.52 cash

IRVINE SENSORS CORP (DE)
Reincorporated 05/23/1988
State of incorporation changed from (CA) to (DE) and Common no par changed to 1¢ par 05/23/1988
Each share old Common 1¢ par exchanged for (0.05) share new Common 1¢ par 09/26/2001
Each share new Common 1¢ par exchanged again for (0.1) share new Common 1¢ par 08/27/2008
Name changed to ISC8 Inc. 02/27/2012
(See ISC8 Inc.)

IRVING AIR CHUTE INC (NY)
Common no par changed to $1 par 00/00/1933
Common $1 par changed to 50¢ par and (1) additional share issued 11/08/1963
Stock Dividend - 10% 12/30/1966
Name changed to Irvin Industries Inc. 01/19/1968
(See Irvin Industries Inc.)

IRVING BK & TR CO (IRVING, TX)
Merged into Texas Commerce Bancshares, Inc. 12/11/1973
Each share Capital Stock $5 par exchanged for (0.823528) share Common $4 par
Texas Commerce Bancshares, Inc. acquired by Chemical New York Corp. 05/01/1987 which name changed to Chase Manhattan Corp. (New) 03/31/1996 which name changed to J.P. Morgan Chase & Co. 12/31/2000 which name changed to JPMorgan Chase & Co. 07/20/2004

IRVING BK CORP (NY)
Common $10 par split (2) for (1) by issuance of (1) additional share 06/29/1984
$4 Conv. Preferred $1 par called for redemption 11/30/1988
Merged into Bank of New York Co., Inc. 12/30/1988
Each share Adjustable Rate Preferred $1 par exchanged for (1) share Adjustable Rate Preferred no par
Each share Common $10 par exchanged for (1.675) shares Common $7.50, par (1) Common Stock Purchase Warrant expiring 11/29/1998 and $15 cash
Bank of New York Co., Inc. merged into Bank of New York Mellon Corp. 07/01/2007

IRVING FUND FOR INVESTMENT IN UNITED STATES GOVERNMENT SECURITIES, INC. (DE)
Name changed to Atlantic Fund For Investment In United States Government Securities, Inc. 11/14/1960
Atlantic Fund for Investment in United States Government Securities, Inc. liquidated for Fund for U.S. Government Securities, Inc. 01/13/1972 which name changed to Federated Fund for U.S. Government Securities, Inc. 03/31/1996 which reorganized as Federated Income Securities Trust 10/07/2002

IRVING INVESTORS FUND C, INC.
Name changed to Investors Fund C, Inc. 00/00/1934
Investors Fund C, Inc. name changed to Investors Management Fund, Inc. 00/00/1946 which merged into Fundamental Investors, Inc. (DE) 00/00/1954 which reincorporated in Maryland 02/01/1990 which reorganized in Delaware as Fundamental Investors 09/01/2010

IRVING-PITT MANUFACTURING CO.
Acquired by Wilson-Jones Co. 00/00/1929
Details not available

IRVING (JOHN) SHOE CORP. (DE)
Stock Dividend - 100% 1/15/46
Merged into National Shoes, Inc. 4/9/65
Each share Preferred $25 par exchanged for (4) shares Common $1 par
Each share Common $1 par exchanged for (0.625) share Common $1 par
(See National Shoes, Inc.)

IRVING TRUST CO. (NEW YORK, NY)
Each share Capital Stock $100 par exchanged for (10) shares Capital Stock $10 par 04/17/1929
Acquired by Charter New York Corp. 07/01/1966
Each share Capital Stock $10 par exchanged for (1) share Common $10 par
Charter New York Corp. name changed to Irving Bank Corp. 10/17/1979 which merged into Bank of New York Co., Inc. 12/30/1988 which merged into Bank of New York Mellon Corp. 07/01/2007

IRVINGTON INDS INC (NY)
Charter cancelled and proclaimed dissolved for failure to pay taxes 6/24/81

IRVINGTON MINING CO. LTD. (ON)
Adjudicated bankrupt 12/12/1966
Stockholders' equity unlikely

IRVINGTON PL INC (NY)
Name changed to Irvington Industries Inc. 3/6/70
(See Irvington Industries Inc.)

IRWIN BK & TR CO (IRWIN, PA)
Under plan of reorganization each share Common $1.25 par automatically became (1) share IBT Bancorp, Inc. Common $1.25 par 08/06/1986
IBT Bancorp, Inc. merged into S&T Bancorp, Inc. 06/09/2008

IRWIN ENERGY INC (DE)
Each share old Common $0.0003 par exchanged for (0.01) share new Common $0.0003 par 3/24/2006
Recapitalized as Irwin Resources Inc. 11/20/2006
Each share new Common $0.0003 par exchanged for (0.004) share Common $0.0003 par

IRWIN FINL CORP (IN)
Common $5 par split (3) for (2) by issuance of (0.5) additional share 12/30/1991
Common $5 par split (2) for (1) by issuance of (1) additional share 09/02/1992
Common $5 par split (2) for (1) by issuance of (1) additional share 09/02/1993
Common $5 par split (2) for (1) by issuance of (1) additional share payable 12/30/1996 to holders of record 12/23/1996
Common $5 par split (2) for (1) by issuance of (1) additional share payable 05/27/1998 to holders of record 05/15/1998
Filed a petition under Chapter 7 Federal Bankruptcy Code 09/18/2009
Stockholders' equity unlikely

IRWIN GAS COAL CORP.
Liquidation completed in 1952

IRWIN RICHARD D INC (DE)
Reincorporated 04/18/1967
Common no par split (3) for (2) by issuance of (0.5) additional share 05/24/1965
Common no par split (2) for (1) by issuance of (1) additional share 03/27/1967
State of incorporation changed from (IL) to (DE) 04/18/1967
Common no par changed to 50¢ par 07/18/1969

Merged into Dow Jones & Co., Inc. 09/30/1975
Each share Common 50¢ par exchanged for (1.03) shares Common $1 par
(See Dow Jones & Co., Inc.)

IRWIN MAGNETIC SYS INC (DE)
Merged into Cipher Data Products, Inc. 4/12/89
Each share Common $0.001 par exchanged for $13 cash

IRWIN NATURALS / 4HEALTH INC (UT)
Name changed to Omni Nutraceuticals, Inc. 08/23/1999
(See Omni Nutraceuticals, Inc.)

IRWIN TOY LTD (ON)
Common no par split (2) for (1) by issuance of (1) additional share 07/21/1972
Common no par reclassified as Conv. Class A Common no par 07/09/1973
Conv. Class A Common no par reclassified as Common no par 09/24/1979
Conv. Class B Common no par reclassified as Common no par 09/24/1979
Common no par reclassified as Conv. Ordinary no par 07/07/1982
Each share Conv. Ordinary no par received distribution of (1) share Non-Vtg. Ordinary no par 07/14/1982
Acquired by Livgroup Investments Ltd. 04/30/2001
Each share Conv. Ordinary no par exchanged for $6.25 cash
Each share Non-Vtg. Ordinary no par exchanged for $6.25 cash

IRWIN UN BK & TR CO (COLUMBUS, IN)
Each share Capital Stock $100 par exchanged for (5) shares Capital Stock $25 par to effect a (4) for (1) split and a 25% stock dividend 01/10/1957
Capital Stock $25 par changed to $10 par and (1.5) additional shares issued 01/24/1964
Stock Dividends - 100% 10/17/1953; 10% 01/31/1959; 10% 03/05/1965; 10% 03/03/1967; 25% 02/23/1970; 10% 03/10/1971
Reorganized as Irwin Union Corp. 01/01/1973
Each share Capital Stock $10 par exchanged for (1) share Common $10 par
Irwin Union Corp. name changed to Irwin Financial Corp. 09/04/1990
(See Irwin Financial Corp.)

IRWIN UN CORP (IN)
Common $10 par changed to $5 par 02/01/1974
Common $5 par split (3) for (2) by issuance of (0.5) additional share 09/08/1989
Stock Dividend - 10% 03/01/1974
Name changed to Irwin Financial Corp. 09/04/1990
(See Irwin Financial Corp.)

IS HIMALAYAN FD N V (NETHERLANDS)
ADR agreement terminated 04/22/2010
No ADR's remain outstanding

ISAACS I C & CO INC (DE)
Issue Information - 3,800,000 shares COM offered at $10 per share on 12/17/1997
Recapitalized as Passport Brands, Inc. 01/26/2011
Each share Common $0.0001 par exchanged for (0.02) share Common $0.0001 par

ISABELLA MINES, INC. (CO)
Charter revoked for failure to file reports and pay fees 9/20/57

ISA-ISH FINANCIAL INFORMATION, INC.

ISABELLA MINING & DEVELOPMENT CO. LTD. (AB)
Charter revoked for failure to file reports and pay fees 12/15/61

ISABELLA URANIUM MINES, INC. (CO)
Charter revoked for failure to file reports and pay fees 9/20/57

ISACSOFT INC (CANADA)
Each shares Class A no par exchanged for (0.06666666) share Common no par 10/13/2006
Merged into 4468783 Canada Inc. 07/10/2008
Each share Common no par exchanged for $0.33 cash

ISAGEN S A (COLOMBIA)
ADR agreement terminated 07/07/2016
Each Sponsored ADR for Ordinary exchanged for $12.844374 cash

ISALY INC (DE)
Stock Dividends - 10% 7/21/81; 10% 2/7/84
Name changed to AmBrit Inc. 8/30/85
Ambrit Inc. merged into Empire of Carolina, Inc. 12/29/89
(See Empire of Carolina, Inc.)

ISATORI INC (DE)
Merged into FitLife Brands, Inc. 10/01/2015
Each share Common 1¢ par exchanged for (0.1732) share Common 1¢ par

ISB FINL CORP (IA)
Common $1 par split (2) for (1) by issuance of (1) additional share payable 10/28/1997 to holders of record 10/14/1997
Common $1 par split (2) for (1) by issuance of (1) additional share payable 09/17/2002 to holders of record 09/03/2002 Ex date - 09/18/2002
Common $1 par split (3) for (2) by issuance of (0.5) additional share payable 12/22/2005 to holders of record 12/20/2005 Ex date - 12/23/2005
Common $1 par split (3) for (1) by issuance of (2) additional shares payable 08/18/2006 to holders of record 08/08/2006 Ex date - 08/21/2006
Under plan of merger name changed to MidWestOne Financial Group, Inc. (New) 03/14/2008

ISB FINL CORP (LA)
Name changed to Iberiabank Corp. 5/15/2000

ISB FINL CORP (MI)
Acquired by Detroitbank Corp. 8/1/80
Each share Common $1 par exchanged for $43 cash

ISC FINL CORP (DE)
Chapter 11 bankruptcy proceedings converted to Chapter 7 on 6/9/88
Stockholders' equity unlikely

ISC INDUSTRIES INC. (DE)
5-1/2% Preferred $20 par conversion privilege expired 3/31/70
Name changed to ISC Financial Corp. 9/26/74
(See ISC Financial Corp.)

ISC SYS CORP (WA)
Common no par split (4) for (1) by issuance of (3) additional shares 06/17/1981
Acquired by Olivetti USA, Inc. 05/05/1989
Each share Common no par exchanged for $12.25 cash

ISC8 INC (DE)
Plan of reorganization under Chapter 11 bankruptcy proceedings effective 09/14/2015
No stockholders' equity

ISCO INC (NE)
Stock Dividends - 20% 7/15/88; 15% 9/20/91; 15% 12/9/93
Merged into Teledyne Technologies, Inc. 6/18/2004
Each share Common 10¢ par exchanged for $16 cash

ISCO INTL INC (DE)
Plan of reorganization under Chapter 11 Federal Bankruptcy Code effective 12/23/2009
No stockholders' equity

ISCOPE INC (AB)
Delisted from NEX 12/16/2011

ISCOR LTD (SOUTH AFRICA)
Each Sponsored ADR for Ordinary received distribution of (1) Kumba Resources Ltd. Sponsored ADR for Ordinary payable 12/06/2001 to holders of record 11/23/2001 Ex date - 11/26/2001
Name changed to Ispat Iscor Ltd. 08/27/2004
Ispat Iscor Ltd. name changed to Mittal Steel South Africa Ltd. 03/22/2005 which name changed to ArcelorMittal South Africa 11/02/2007

ISDERA NORTH AMER INC (NV)
Reincorporated 05/29/2008
State of incorporation changed from (NY) to (NV) 05/29/2008
SEC revoked common stock registration 09/14/2015

ISE BLU EQUITY CORP (NV)
Charter revoked for failure to file reports and pay fees 03/01/2010

ISE LTD (CAYMAN ISLANDS)
Filed a petition under Chapter 11 Federal Bankruptcy Code 11/15/2010
Stockholders' equity unlikely

ISEC CDA LTD (CANADA)
Dissolved 12/16/1980

ISECURETRAC CORP (DE)
Each share old Common $0.001 par exchanged for (0.1) share new Common $0.001 par 09/19/2005
Name changed to Technology Monitoring Solutions, Inc. 04/09/2014
(See Technology Monitoring Solutions, Inc.)

ISEEMEDIA INC (CANADA)
Merged into Synchronica PLC 01/06/2011
Each share Common no par exchanged for (0.2687) share Ordinary 1p par

ISEMPLOYMENT COM INC (WY)
Name changed to Idoleyez Corp. 09/10/2003
(See Idoleyez Corp.)

ISG CAP CORP (CANADA)
Reorganized as Firm Capital Property Trust 11/30/2012
Each share Common no par exchanged for (0.03359086) Unit

ISG INTL SOFTWARE GROUP LTD (ISRAEL)
Name changed to Attunity Ltd. 10/27/2000

ISG TECHNOLOGIES INC (ON)
Each share old Common no par exchanged for (0.66) share new Common no par 01/22/1992
Name changed to Cedara Software Corp. 01/04/2000
Cedara Software Corp. merged into Merge Technologies Inc. 06/01/2005 which name changed to Merge Healthcare Inc. (WI) 02/22/2008 which reincorporated in Delaware 12/05/2008
(See Merge Healthcare Inc.)

ISHARES (ON)
Name changed 04/24/2006
Name changed from iUnits Fund to iShares Fund 04/24/2006
TSX Capped Materials Index Fund split (2) for (1) by issuance of (1) additional share payable 08/11/2008 to holders of record 08/08/2008 Ex date - 08/06/2008
CDN DEX Real Return Bond Index Fund name changed to iShares DEX Real Return Bond Index Fund 04/20/2010
CDN Dow Jones Canada Select Dividend Index Fund name changed to iShares Dow Jones Canada Select Dividend Index Fund 04/20/2010
CDN S&P/TSX Income Trust Index Fund name changed to iShares S&P/TSX Income Trust Index Fund 04/20/2010
CDN S&P/TSX Capped Materials Index Fund name changed to iShares S&P/TSX Capped Materials Index Fund 04/20/2010
(See each company's listing)

ISHARES ADVANTAGED CONV BD INDEX FD (ON)
Name changed to iShares Convertible Bond Index ETF 11/26/2013

ISHARES ADVANTAGED SHORT DURATION HIGH INCOME ETF CAD HEDGED (ON)
Name changed 10/18/2013
Name changed 11/04/2014
Name changed from iShares Advantaged Short Duration High Income Fund to iShares Advantaged Short Duration High Income ETF 10/18/2013
Trust terminated 12/10/2013
Each Advisor Unit received USD$19.85873 cash
Each Common Unit received USD$19.61708 cash
Name changed from iShares Advantaged Short Duration High Income ETF to iShares Advantaged Short Duration High Income ETF (CAD-Hedged) 11/04/2014
Name changed to iShares Short Duration High Income ETF (CAD-Hedged) 02/29/2016

ISHARES ADVANTAGED U S HIGH YIELD INDEX ETF CAD HEDGED (ON)
Name changed 11/26/2013
Name changed from iShares Advantaged U.S. High Yield Bond Index Fund (CAD-Hedged) to iShares Advantaged U.S. High Yield Bond Index ETF (CAD-Hedged) 11/26/2013
Name changed to iShares U.S. High Yield Fixed Income Index ETF (CAD-Hedged) 01/14/2015

ISHARES ALTERNATIVES COMPLETION PORT BLDR FD (ON)
Trust terminated 09/27/2017
Each Unit received $28.17802 cash

ISHARES BALANCED GROWTH COREPORTFOLIO FD (ON)
Name changed to iShares Balanced Growth CorePortfolio ETF 06/04/2014

ISHARES BALANCED INCOME COREPORTFOLIO FD (ON)
Name changed to iShares Balanced Income CorePortfolio ETF 06/04/2014

ISHARES BRIC INDEX ETF (ON)
Name changed 06/04/2014
Name changed from iShares BRIC Index Fund to iShares BRIC Index ETF 06/04/2014
Trust terminated 09/27/2017
Each Advisor Class Unit received $26.18438 cash
Each Common Unit received $26.20297 cash

ISHARES BROAD COMMODITY INDEX ETF CAD HEDGED (AB)
Name changed 10/18/2013
Name changed from iShares Broad Commodity Index Fund (CAD-Hedged) to iShares Broad Commodity Index ETF (CAD-Hedged) 10/18/2013
Trust terminated 09/04/2015
Each Advisor Class Unit received $18.55899 cash
Each Common Unit received $19.3502 cash

ISHARES BROAD EMERGING MKTS FD (ON)
Name changed to iShares Emerging Markets Fundamental Index ETF 05/28/2013

ISHARES CDN DEX ALL CORP INDEX FD (ON)
Name changed to iShares DEX All Corporate Bond Index Fund 04/20/2010
iShares DEX All Corporate Bond Index Fund name changed to iShares Canadian Corporate Bond Index ETF 03/27/2014

ISHARES CDN DEX ALL GOVT BD INDEX FD (ON)
Name changed to iShares DEX All Government Bond Index Fund 04/20/2010
iShares DEX All Government Bond Index Fund name changed to iShares Canadian Government Bond Index ETF 03/27/2014

ISHARES CDN DEX LONG TERM BD INDEX FD (ON)
Name changed to iShares DEX Long Term Bond Index Fund 04/20/2010
iShares DEX Long Term Bond Index Fund name changed to iShares Canadian Long Term Bond Index ETF 03/27/2014 which name changed to iShares Core Canadian Long Term Bond Index ETF 07/21/2014

ISHARES CDN DEX REAL RETURN BOND INDEX FUND (ON)
Name changed to iShares DEX Real Return Bond Index Fund 04/20/2010
iShares DEX Real Return Bond Index Fund name changed to iShares Canadian Real Return Bond Index ETF 03/27/2014

ISHARES CDN DEX SHORT TERM BOND INDEX FD (ON)
Name changed to iShares DEX Short Term Bond Index Fund 04/20/2010
iShares DEX Short Term Bond Index Fund name changed to iShares Canadian Short Term Bond Index ETF 03/27/2014 which name changed to iShares Core Canadian Short Term Bond Index ETF 06/15/2017

ISHARES CDN DEX UNIVERSE BD INDEX FD (ON)
Name changed to iShares DEX Universe Bond Index Fund 04/20/2010
iShares DEX Universe Bond Index Fund name changed to iShares Canadian Universe Bond Index ETF 03/27/2014 which name changed to iShares Core Canadian Universe Bond Index ETF 06/15/2017

ISHARES CDN DOW JONES CANADA SELECT DIVIDEND INDEX FUND (ON)
Name changed to iShares Dow Jones Canada Select Dividend Index Fund 04/20/2010
iShares Dow Jones Canada Select Dividend Index Fund name changed to iShares Canadian Select Dividend Index ETF 03/27/2014

ISHARES CDN DOW JONES CDA SELECT GROWTH INDEX FD (ON)
Name changed to iShares Dow Jones Canada Select Growth Index Fund 04/20/2010
iShares Dow Jones Canada Select Growth Index Fund name changed to iShares Canadian Growth Index ETF 03/27/2014

ISHARES CDN DOW JONES CDA SELECT VALUE INDEX FD (ON)
Name changed to iShares Dow Jones Canada Select Value Index Fund 04/20/2010
iShares Dow Jones Canada Select Value Index Fund name changed to iShares Canadian Value Index ETF 03/27/2014

ISHARES CDN FINL MONTHLY INCOME FD (ON)
Name changed to iShares Canadian Financial Monthly Income ETF 10/18/2013

ISHARES CDN FUNDAMENTAL INDEX FD (CANADA)
Name changed to iShares Canadian Fundamental Index ETF 06/04/2014

ISHARES CDN JANTZI SOCIAL INDEX FD (ON)
Name changed to iShares Jantzi Social Index Fund 04/20/2010
iShares Jantzi Social Index Fund name changed to iShares Jantzi Social Index ETF 03/27/2014

ISHARES CDN LONG TERM BD INDEX ETF (ON)
Name changed 03/27/2014
Name changed from iShares DEX Long Term Bond Index Fund to iShares Canadian Long Term Bond Index ETF 03/27/2014
Name changed to iShares Core Canadian Long Term Bond Index ETF 07/21/2014

ISHARES CDN MSCI EMERGING MKTS INDEX FD (ON)
Name changed to iShares MSCI Emerging Markets Index Fund 04/20/2010
iShares MSCI Emerging Markets Index Fund name changed to iShares MSCI Emerging Markets Index ETF 03/27/2014

ISHARES CDN MSCI WORLD INDEX FD (ON)
Name changed to iShares MSCI World Index Fund 04/20/2010
iShares MSCI World Index Fund name changed to iShares MSCI World Index ETF 03/27/2014

ISHARES CDN S&P / TSX CAPPED MATERIALS INDEX FUND (ON)
Name changed to iShares S&P/TSX Capped Materials Index Fund 03/27/2014
iShares S&P/TSX Capped Materials Index Fund name changed to iShares S&P/TSX Capped Materials Index ETF 03/27/2014

ISHARES CDN S&P / TSX INCOME TRUST INCOME FUND (ON)
Name changed to iShares Diversified Monthly Income Fund 04/20/2010
iShares Diversified Monthly Income Fund name changed to iShares Diversified Monthly Income ETF 03/27/2014

ISHARES CDN S&P/TSX 60 INDEX FD (ON)
Name changed 04/25/2006
Name changed from iUnits S&P/TSX 60 Index Fund to iShares CDN S&P/TSX 60 Index Fund 04/25/2006
Units split (4) for (1) by issuance of (3) additional Units payable 08/11/2008 to holders of record 08/08/2008 Ex date - 08/06/2008
Name changed to iShares S&P/TSX 60 Index Fund 04/20/2010
iShares S&P/TSX 60 Index Fund name changed to iShares S&P/TSX 60 Index ETF 03/27/2014

ISHARES CDN S&P/TSX CAPPED COMPOSITE INDEX FD (ON)
Name changed 04/25/2006
Name changed from iUnits Composite CDN Eq Capped Index Fund to iShares CDN S&P/TSX Capped Composite Index Fund 04/25/2006
Units split (4) for (1) by issuance of (3) additional Units payable 08/11/2008 to holders of record 08/08/2008 Ex date - 08/06/2008
Name changed to iShares S&P/TSX Capped Composite Index Fund 04/20/2010
iShares S&P/TSX Capped Composite Index Fund name changed to iShares S&P/TSX Capped Composite Index ETF 03/27/2014 which name changed to iShares Core S&P/TSX Capped Composite Index ETF 07/21/2014

ISHARES CDN S&P/TSX CAPPED ENERGY INDEX FD (ON)
Units split (4) for (1) by issuance of (3) additional Units payable 08/11/2008 to holders of record 08/08/2008 Ex date - 08/06/2008
Name changed to iShares S&P/TSX Capped Energy Index Fund 04/20/2010
iShares S&P/TSX Capped Energy Index Fund name changed to iShares S&P/TSX Capped Energy Index ETF 03/27/2014

ISHARES CDN S&P/TSX CAPPED FINANCIALS INDEX FD (ON)
Units split (2) for (1) by issuance of (1) additional Unit payable 08/11/2008 to holders of record 08/08/2008 Ex date - 08/06/2008
Name changed to iShares S&P/TSX Capped Financials Index Fund 04/20/2010
iShares S&P/TSX Capped Financials Index Fund name changed to iShares S&P/TSX Capped Financials Index ETF 03/27/2014

ISHARES CDN S&P/TSX COMPLETION INDEX FD (ON)
Name changed 04/25/2006
Name changed from iShares CDN S&P/TSX Midcap Index Fund to iShares CDN S&P/TSX Completion Index Fund 04/25/2006
Units split (4) for (1) by issuance of (3) additional Units payable 08/11/2008 to holders of record 08/08/2008 Ex date - 08/06/2008
Name changed to iShares S&P/TSX Completion Index Fund 04/20/2010
iShares S&P/TSX Completion Index Fund name changed to iShares S&P/TSX Completion Index ETF 03/27/2014

ISHARES CDN S&P/TSX GLOBAL GOLD INDEX FD (ON)
Name changed 04/25/2006
Name changed from iShares CDN S&P/TSX Capped Gold Index Fund to iShares CDN S&P/TSX Global Gold Index Fund 04/25/2006
Units split (4) for (1) by issuance of (3) additional Units payable 08/11/2008 to holders of record 08/08/2008 Ex date - 08/06/2008
Name changed to iShares S&P/TSX Global Gold Index Fund 04/20/2010
iShares S&P/TSX Global Gold Index Fund name changed to iShares S&P/TSX Global Gold Index ETF 03/27/2014

ISHARES CDN S&P/TSX SMALLCAP INDEX FD (ON)
Name changed to iShares S&P/TSX SmallCap Index Fund 04/20/2010
iShares S&P/TSX SmallCap Index Fund name changed to iShares S&P/TSX SmallCap Index ETF 03/27/2014

ISHARES CANADIAN SHORT TERM BOND INDEX ETF (ON)
Name changed 03/27/2014
Name changed from iShares DEX Short Term Bond Index Fund to iShares Canadian Short Term Bond Index ETF 03/27/2014
Name changed to iShares Core Canadian Short Term Bond Index ETF 06/15/2017

ISHARES CDN SHORT TERM CORPORATE & MAPLE BD INDEX ETF (ON)
Name changed 03/27/2014
Name changed from iShares DEX Short Term Corporate Bond UPM Index Fund to iShares Canadian Short Term Corporate + Maple Bond Index ETF 03/27/2014
Name changed to iShares Core Canadian Short Term Corporate + Maple Bond Index ETF 07/21/2014

ISHARES CANADIAN UNIVERSE BD INDEX ETF (ON)
Name changed 03/27/2014
Name changed from iShares DEX Universe Bond Index Fund to iShares Canadian Universe Bond Index ETF 03/27/2014
Name changed to iShares Core Canadian Universe Bond Index ETF 06/15/2017

ISHARES CDN RUSSELL 2000 INDEX CDN DLR HEDGED INDEX FD (ON)
Name changed to iShares Russell 2000 Index Fund (CAD-Hedged) 04/20/2010
iShares Russell 2000 Index Fund (CAD-Hedged) name changed to iShares U.S. Small Cap Index ETF (CAD-Hedged) 03/27/2014

ISHARES CHINA ALL CAP INDEX ETF (ON)
Name changed 06/04/2014
Name changed from iShares China All-Cap Index Fund to iShares China All-Cap Index ETF 06/04/2014
Trust terminated 09/04/2015
Each Advisor Class Unit received $23.49701 cash
Each Common Unit received $23.98042 cash

ISHARES CHINA INDEX FD (ON)
Name changed to iShares China Index ETF 03/27/2014

ISHARES CNX NIFTY INDIA INDEX ETF (ON)
Name changed 04/15/2013
Name changed from iShares S&P CNX Nifty India Index Fund to iShares CNX Nifty India Index ETF 04/15/2013
Name changed to iShares India Index ETF 03/27/2014

ISHARES COMEX GOLD TR (NY)
iShares split (10) for (1) by issuance of (9) additional shares payable 06/23/2010 to holders of record 06/21/2010 Ex date - 06/24/2010
Name changed to iShares Gold Trust 09/15/2010

ISHARES COMMODITY OPTIMIZED TR (DE)
Name changed 07/01/2014
Name changed from iShares Dow Jones-UBS Roll Select Commodity Index Trust to iShares Commodity Optimized Trust 07/01/2014
Trust terminated 10/15/2018
Each Share of Bene. Int. received $36.491002 cash

ISHARES CONSERVATIVE CORE PORT BLDR FD (ON)
Trust terminated 09/27/2017
Each Unit received $23.35529 cash

ISHARES CORE HIGH QUALITY CDN BD INDEX ETF (ON)
Name changed 11/20/2013
Name changed 07/21/2014
Name changed from iShares Advantaged Canadian Bond Index Fund to iShares High Quality Canadian Bond Index ETF 11/20/2013
Name changed from iShares High Quality Canadian Bond Index ETF to iShares Core High Quality Canadian Bond Index ETF 07/21/2014
Name changed to iShares High Quality Canadian Bond Index ETF 06/15/2017

ISHARES CORE S&P/TSX COMPOSITE HIGH DIVID INDEX ETF (ON)
Name changed 03/27/2014
Name changed 07/21/2014
Name changed from iShares S&P/TSX Equity Income Index Fund to iShares S&P/TSX Equity Income Index ETF 03/27/2014
Name changed from iShares S&P/TSX Equity Income Index ETF to iShares Core S&P/TSX Composite High Dividend Index ETF 07/21/2014
Name changed to iShares S&P/TSX Composite High Dividend Index ETF 06/15/2017

ISHARES CORE SHORT TERM HIGH QUALITY CDN BD INDEX ETF (ON)
Name changed to iShares Short Term High Quality Canadian Bond Index ETF 06/15/2017

ISHARES DEX ALL CORPORATE BD INDEX FD (ON)
Name changed to iShares Canadian Corporate Bond Index ETF 03/27/2014

ISHARES DEX ALL GOVT BD INDEX FD (ON)
Name changed to iShares Canadian Government Bond Index ETF 03/27/2014

ISHARES DEX FLOATING RATE NT INDEX FD (ON)
Name changed to iShares Floating Rate Index ETF 03/27/2014

ISHARES DEX HYBRID BD INDEX FD (ON)
Name changed to iShares Canadian HYBrid Corporate Bond Index ETF 03/27/2014

ISHARES DEX REAL RETURN BD INDEX FD (ON)
Name changed to iShares Canadian Real Return Bond Index ETF 03/27/2014

ISHARES DIVERSIFIED ALTERNATIVES TR (DE)
Trust terminated 06/04/2013
Each Share of Bene. Int. no par received $53.346807 cash

ISHARES DIVERSIFIED MONTHLY INCOME FD (ON)
Name changed 09/03/2010
Name changed from iShares S&P/TSX Income Trust Index Fund to iShares Diversified Monthly Income Fund 09/03/2010
Name changed to iShares Diversified Monthly Income ETF 03/27/2014

ISHARES DOW JONES CDA SELECT DIVID INDEX FD (ON)
Name changed to iShares Canadian Select Dividend Index ETF 03/27/2014

ISHARES DOW JONES CDA SELECT GROWTH INDEX FD (ON)
Name changed to iShares Canadian Growth Index ETF 03/27/2014

ISHARES DOW JONES CDA SELECT VALUE INDEX FD (ON)
Name changed to iShares Canadian Value Index ETF 03/27/2014

ISHARES EQUAL WEIGHT BANC & LIFECO FD (ON)
Name changed to iShares Equal Weight Banc & Lifeco ETF 10/18/2013

ISHARES FACTORSELECT MSCI CDA INDEX ETF (ON)
Name changed to iShares Edge MSCI Multifactor Canada Index ETF 03/31/2016

ISHARES FACTORSELECT MSCI EAFE INDEX ETF (ON)
Name changed to iShares Edge MSCI Multifactor EAFE Index ETF 03/31/2016

ISHARES FACTORSELECT MSCI USA INDEX ETF (ON)
Name changed to iShares Edge MSCI Multifactor USA Index ETF 03/31/2016

ISHARES FACTORSELECT MSCI USA INDEX ETF CAD HEDGED (ON)
Name changed to iShares Edge MSCI Multifactor USA Index ETF (CAD-Hedged) 03/31/2016

ISHARES FACTORSELECTTM MSCI EAFE INDEX ETF CAD HEDGED (ON)
Name changed to iShares Edge MSCI Multifactor EAFE Index ETF (CAD-Hedged) 03/31/2016

ISHARES GLOBAL AGRICULTURE INDEX FD (ON)
Name changed to iShares Global Agriculture Index ETF 06/04/2014

ISHARES GLOBAL COMPLETION PORT BLDR FD (ON)
Trust terminated 09/27/2017
Each Unit received $30.42603 cash

ISHARES GLOBAL INFRASTRUCTURE INDEX FD (ON)
Name changed to iShares Global Infrastructure Index ETF 06/04/2014

ISHARES GLOBAL MONTHLY DIVID INDEX ETF (ON)
Name changed 11/20/2013
Name changed from iShares Global Monthly Advantaged Dividend Index Fund to iShares Global Monthly Dividend Index ETF 11/20/2013
Name changed to iShares Global Monthly Dividend Index ETF (CAD-Hedged) 06/04/2014

ISHARES GLOBAL REAL ESTATE INDEX FD (ON)
Name changed to iShares Global Real Estate Index ETF 06/04/2014

ISHARES GOLD BULLION FD (ON)
Name changed to iShares Gold Bullion ETF 10/30/2013

ISHARES GROWTH CORE PORT BLDR FD (ON)
Trust terminated 09/27/2017
Each Unit received $28.02788 cash

ISHARES GSCI COMMODITY-INDEXED TR (DE)
Name changed to iShares S&P GSCI Commodity-Indexed Trust 05/09/2007

ISHARES INC (MD)
MSCI Emerging Markets Consumer Discretionary Sector Index Fund reclassified as MSCI Emerging Markets Consumer Discretionary ETF 07/01/2013
MSCI Emerging Markets EMEA Index Fund reclassified as MSCI Emerging Markets EMEA ETF 07/01/2013
MSCI Emerging Markets Eastern Europe Index Fund reclassified as MSCI Emerging Markets Eastern Europe ETF 07/01/2013
MSCI Emerging Markets Energy Sector Capped Index Fund reclassified as MSCI Emerging Markets Energy Capped ETF 07/01/2013
MSCI Emerging Markets Growth Index Fund reclassified as MSCI Emerging Markets Growth ETF 07/01/2013
MSCI Emerging Markets Value Index Fund reclassified as MSCI Emerging Markets Value ETF 07/01/2013
Each share MSCI United Kingdom ETF automatically became (1) share iShares Trust MSCI United Kingdom ETF 09/29/2014
Trust terminated 08/28/2015
Each share MSCI Emerging Markets Consumer Discretionary ETF received $45.650287 cash
Each share MSCI Emerging Markets Eastern Europe ETF received $16.172547 cash
Each share MSCI Emerging Markets EMEA ETF received $37.982466 cash
Each share MSCI Emerging Markets Energy Capped ETF received $24.255819 cash
Each share MSCI Emerging Markets Growth ETF received $46.279167 cash
Each share MSCI Emerging Markets Value ETF received $36.129247 cash
Currency Hedged MSCI ACWI Minimum Volatility ETF reclassified as Edge MSCI Min Vol Global Currency Hedged ETF 05/12/2016
Trust terminated 08/22/2018
Each share Edge MSCI Min Vol EM Currency Hedged ETF received $26.88893 cash
(Additional Information in Active)

ISHARES INTL FUNDAMENTAL INDEX FD (ON)
Name changed to iShares International Fundamental Index ETF 06/04/2014

ISHARES JANTZI SOCIAL INDEX FD (ON)
Name changed to iShares Jantzi Social Index ETF 03/27/2014

ISHARES JAPAN FUNDAMENTAL INDEX FD CAD HEDGED (ON)
Name changed to iShares Japan Fundamental Index ETF (CAD-Hedged) 06/04/2014

ISHARES JPMORGAN USD EMERGING MKTS BD INDEX FD (ON)
Name changed to iShares J.P. Morgan USD Emerging Markets Bond Index ETF (CAD-Hedged) 03/27/2014

ISHARES LATIN AMER INDEX ETF (ON)
Name changed 03/27/2014
Name changed from iShares S&P Latin America 40 Index Fund to iShares Latin America Index ETF 03/27/2014
Trust terminated 09/04/2015
Each Unit received $13.844 cash

ISHARES MANAGED FUTURES INDEX ETF (ON)
Name changed 10/18/2013
Name changed from iShares Managed Futures Index Fund to iShares Managed Futures Index ETF 10/18/2013
Trust terminated 12/05/2013
Each Advisor Unit received $20.50871 cash
Each Common Unit received $20.83083 cash

ISHARES MSCI ALL CTRY WORLD MINIMUM VOLATILITY INDEX ETF (ON)
Name changed 03/27/2014
Name changed from iShares MSCI All Country World Minimum Volatility Index Fund to iShares MSCI All Country World Minimum Volatility Index ETF 03/27/2014
Name changed to iShares Edge MSCI Min Vol Global Index ETF 03/31/2016

ISHARES MSCI BRAZIL INDEX ETF (ON)
Name changed 03/27/2014
Name changed from iShares MSCI Brazil Index Fund to iShares MSCI Brazil Index ETF 03/27/2014
Trust terminated 09/27/2017
Each Unit received $14.67228 cash

ISHARES MSCI CDA MINIMUM VOLATILITY INDEX FET (ON)
Name changed 03/27/2014
Name changed from iShares MSCI Canada Minimum Volatility Index Fund to iShares MSCI Canada Minimum Volatility Index ETF 03/27/2014
Name changed to iShares Edge MSCI Min Vol Canada Index ETF 03/31/2016

ISHARES MSCI EAFE IMI INDEX ETF (ON)
Name changed to iShares Core MSCI EAFE IMI Index ETF 07/21/2014

ISHARES MSCI EAFE INDEX FD (ON)
Name changed 04/20/2010
Name changed from iShares CDN MSCI EAFE 100% Hedged to CAD Dollars Index Fund to iShares MSCI EAFE Index Fund (CAD-Hedged) 04/20/2010
Name changed to iShares MSCI EAFE Index ETF (CAD-Hedged) 03/27/2014

ISHARES MSCI EAFE MINIMUM VOLATILITY INDEX ETF (ON)
Name changed 03/27/2014
Name changed from iShares MSCI EAFE Minimum Volatility Index Fund to iShares MSCI EAFE Minimum Volatility Index ETF 03/27/2014
Name changed to iShares Edge MSCI Min Vol EAFE Index ETF 03/31/2016

ISHARES MSCI EMERGING MKTS IMI INDEX ETF (ON)
Name changed to iShares Core MSCI Emerging Markets IMI Index ETF 07/21/2014

ISHARES MSCI EMERGING MKTS INDEX FD (ON)
Name changed to iShares MSCI Emerging Markets Index ETF 03/27/2014

ISHARES MSCI EMERGING MKTS MINIMUM VOLATILITY INDEX ETF (ON)
Name changed 03/27/2014
Name changed from iShares MSCI Emerging Markets Minimum Volatility Index Fund to iShares MSCI Emerging Markets Minimum Volatility Index ETF 03/27/2014
Name changed to iShares Edge MSCI Min Vol Emerging Markets Index ETF 03/31/2016

ISHARES MSCI USA MINIMUM VOLATILITY INDEX ETF (ON)
Name changed 03/27/2014
Name changed from iShares MSCI USA Minimum Volatility Index Fund to iShares MSCI USA Minimum Volatility Index ETF 03/27/2014
Name changed to iShares Edge MSCI Min Vol USA Index ETF 03/31/2016

ISHARES MSCI WORLD INDEX FD (ON)
Name changed to iShares MSCI World Index ETF 03/27/2014

ISHARES NASDAQ 100 INDEX FD CAD HEDGED (ON)
Name changed to iShares NASDAQ 100 Index ETF (CAD-Hedged) 03/27/2014

ISHARES NAT GAS COMMODITY INDEX FD (AB)
Merged into iShares Broad Commodity Index Fund (CAD-Hedged) 11/30/2012
Each Common Unit received (0.567484) Common Unit iShares Broad Commodity Index Fund (CAD-Hedged) name changed to iShares Broad Commodity Index ETF (CAD-Hedged) 10/18/2013
(See iShares Broad Commodity Index ETF (CAD-Hedged))

ISHARES OIL SANDS INDEX ETF (ON)
Name changed 06/04/2014
Name changed from iShares Oil Sands Index Fund to iShares Oil Sands Index ETF 06/04/2014
Trust terminated 09/04/2015
Each Advisor Class Unit received $6.94812 cash
Each Common Unit received $7.02111 cash

ISHARES 1-5 YR LADDERED CORP BD INDEX FD (ON)
Name changed to iShares 1-5 Year Laddered Corporate Bond Index ETF 06/04/2014

ISHARES 1-5 YR LADDERED GOVT BD INDEX FD (ON)
Name changed to iShares 1-5 Year Laddered Government Bond Index ETF 06/04/2014

ISHARES 1-10 YR LADDERED CORPORATE BD INDEX FD (ON)
Name changed to iShares 1-10 Year Laddered Corporate Bond Index ETF 06/04/2014

ISHARES 1-10 YR LADDERED GOVT BD INDEX FD (ON)
Name changed to iShares 1-10 Year Laddered Goverment Bond Index ETF 06/04/2014

ISHARES PREM MONEY MKT FD (ON)
Name changed to iShares Premium Money Market ETF 10/18/2013

ISHARES RUSSELL 2000 INDEX FD (ON)
Name changed to iShares U.S. Small Cap Index ETF (CAD-Hedged) 03/27/2014

ISHARES S&P 500 INDEX ETF (ON)
Name changed to iShares Core S&P 500 Index ETF 07/21/2014

ISHARES S&P / TSX CAPPED FINANCIALS INDEX FD (ON)
Name changed to iShares S&P/TSX Capped Financials Index ETF 03/27/2014

ISHARES S&P / TSX CAPPED INFORMATION TECHNOLOGY INDEX FD (ON)
Name changed 04/20/2010
Name changed from iShares CDN S&P/TSX Capped Information Technology Index Fund to iShares S&P/TSX Capped Information Technology Index Fund 04/20/2010
Name changed to iShares S&P/TSX Capped Information Technology Index ETF 03/27/2014

ISHARES S&P / TSX CAPPED MATLS INDEX FD (ON)
Name changed to iShares S&P/TSX Capped Materials Index ETF 03/27/2014

ISHARES S&P / TSX CAPPED REIT INDEX FD (ON)
Name changed 04/20/2010
Name changed from iShares CDN S&P/TSX Capped REIT Index Fund to iShares S&P/TSX Capped REIT Index Fund 04/20/2010

Name changed to iShares S&P/TSX Capped REIT Index ETF 03/27/2014

ISHARES S&P / TSX CAPPED UTILS INDEX FD (ON)
Name changed to iShares S&P/TSX Capped Utilities Index ETF 03/27/2014

ISHARES S&P / TSX GLOBAL GOLD INDEX FD (ON)
Name changed to iShares S&P/TSX Global Gold Index ETF 03/27/2014

ISHARES S&P / TSX GLOBAL MNG INDEX ETF (ON)
Name changed 06/04/2014
Name changed from iShares S&P/TSX Global Mining Index Fund to to iShares S&P/TSX Global Mining Index ETF 06/04/2014
Trust terminated 09/04/2015
Each Advisor Class Unit received $9.94296 cash
Each Common Unit received $9.96843 cash

ISHARES S&P / TSX NORTH AMERN PFD STK INDEX FD CAD-HEDGED (ON)
Name changed to iShares S&P/TSX North American Preferred Stock Index ETF (CAD-Hedged) 03/27/2014

ISHARES S&P GLOBAL CONSUMER DISCRETIONARY INDEX FD CAD HEDGED (ON)
Name changed to iShares S&P Global Consumer Discretionary Index ETF (CAD-Hedged) 03/27/2014

ISHARES S&P GLOBAL HEALTHCARE INDEX FD CAD HEDGED (ON)
Name changed to iShares S&P Global Healthcare Index ETF (CAD-Hedged) 03/27/2014

ISHARES S&P GLOBAL INDUSTRIALS INDEX FD CAD HEDGED (ON)
Name changed to iShares S&P Global Industrials Index ETF (CAD-Hedged) 03/27/2014

ISHARES S&P GLOBAL WTR INDEX FD (ON)
Name changed to iShares Global Water Index ETF 06/04/2014

ISHARES S&P/TSX 60 INDEX FD (ON)
Name changed to iShares S&P/TSX 60 Index ETF 03/27/2014

ISHARES S&P/TSX CDN DIVID ARISTOCRATS INDEX FD (ON)
Name changed to iShares S&P/TSX Canadian Dividend Aristocrats Index ETF 06/04/2014

ISHARES S&P/TSX CDN PFD SH INDEX FD (ON)
Name changed to iShares S&P/TSX Canadian Preferred Share Index ETF 06/04/2014

ISHARES S&P/TSX CAPPED COMPOSITE INDEX ETF (ON)
Name changed 03/27/2014
Name changed from iShares S&P/TSX Capped Composite Index Fund to iShares S&P/TSX Capped Composite Index ETF 03/27/2014
Name changed to iShares Core S&P/TSX Capped Composite Index ETF 07/21/2014

ISHARES S&P/TSX CAPPED CONSUMER STAPLES INDEX FD (ON)
Name changed to iShares S&P/TSX Capped Consumer Staples Index ETF 03/27/2014

ISHARES S&P/TSX CAPPED ENERGY INDEX FD (ON)
Name changed to iShares S&P/TSX Capped Energy Index ETF 03/27/2014

ISHARES S&P/TSX COMPLETION INDEX FD (ON)
Name changed to iShares S&P/TSX Completion Index ETF 03/27/2014

ISHARES S&P/TSX GLOBAL BASE METALS INDEX FD (ON)
Name changed to iShares S&P/TSX Global Base Metals Index ETF 03/27/2014

ISHARES S&P/TSX SMALLCAP INDEX FD (ON)
Name changed to iShares S&P/TSX SmallCap Index ETF 03/27/2014

ISHARES S&P/TSX VENTURE INDEX ETF (ON)
Name changed 03/27/2014
Name changed from iShares S&P/TSX Venture Index Fund to iShares S&P/TSX Venture Index ETF 03/27/2014
Trust terminated 09/04/2015
Each Unit received $6.63186 cash

ISHARES S&P US DIVID GROWERS INDEX FD CAD HEDGED (ON)
Name changed to iShares US Dividend Growers Index ETF (CAD-Hedged) 06/04/2014

ISHARES S&P 500 INDEX ETF CAD HEDGED (ON)
Name changed 04/20/2010
Name changed 03/27/2014
Name changed from iShares CDN S&P 500 Hedged to Canadian Dollars Index Fund to iShares S&P 500 Index Fund (CAD-Hedged) 04/20/2010
Name changed from iShares S&P 500 Index Fund (CAD-Hedged) to iShares S&P 500 Index ETF (CAD-Hedged) 03/27/2014
Name changed to iShares Core S&P 500 Index ETF (CAD-Hedged) 07/21/2014

ISHARES SILVER BULLION FD (ON)
Name changed to iShares Silver Bullion ETF 10/30/2013

ISHARES TR (DE)
Trust terminated 12/12/2002
Each share Dow Jones U.S. Chemicals Index Fund received net asset value
Each share Dow Jones U.S. Internet Index Fund received net asset value
Each share S&P/TSE 60 Index Fund received net asset value
FTSE NAREIT Industrial/Office Index Fund reclassified as FTSE NAREIT Industrial/Office Capped Index Fund 03/02/2009
FTSE EPRA/NAREIT Developed Asia Index Fund reclassified as Asia Developed Real Estate ETF 03/23/2009
Trust terminated 08/15/2012
Each share 2012 S&P AMT-Free Municipal Series ETF received $50.62 cash
FTSE China HK Listed Index Fund B - Ca Rated Corporate Bond Fund reclassified as B - Ca Rated Corporate Bond ETF 07/01/2013
Baa - Ba Rated Corporate Bond Fund reclassified as Baa - Ba Rated Corporate Bond ETF 07/01/2013
FTSE China HK Listed Index Fund reclassified as FTSE China ETF 07/01/2013
FTSE EPRA/NAREIT North America Index Fund reclassified as North America Real Estate ETF 07/01/2013
FTSE NAREIT Industrial/Office Capped Index Fund reclassified as Industrial/Office Real Estate Capped ETF 07/01/2013
FTSE NAREIT Retail Capped Index Fund reclassified as Retail Real Estate Capped ETF 07/01/2013
Financials Sector Bond Fund reclassified as Financials Bond ETF 07/01/2013
Global Inflation Linked Bond Fund reclassified as Global Inflation-Linked Bond ETF 07/01/2013
Industrials Sector Bond Fund reclassified as Industrials Bond ETF 07/01/2013
International Inflation Linked Bond Fund reclassified as International Inflation-Linked Bond ETF 07/01/2013
iShares 2018 S&P AMT-Free Muni Ser. reclassified as iShares 2018 AMT-Free Muni Term ETF 07/01/2013
MSCI ACWI ex U.S. Consumer Discretionary Sector Index Fund reclassified as MSCI ACWI ex U.S. Consumer Discretionary ETF 07/01/2013
MSCI ACWI ex U.S. Consumer Staples Sector Index Fund reclassified as MSCI ACWI ex U.S. Consumer Discretionary ETF 07/01/2013
MSCI ACWI ex U.S. Energy Sector Index Fund reclassified as MSCI ACWI ex U.S. Energy ETF 07/01/2013
MSCI ACWI ex U.S. Financials Index Fund reclassified as MSCI ACWI ex U.S. Financials ETF 07/01/2013
MSCI ACWI ex U.S. Health Care Sector Fund reclassified as MSCI ACWI ex U.S. Healthcare ETF 07/01/2013
MSCI ACWI ex U.S. Industrials Sector Index Fund reclassified as MSCI ACWI ex U.S. Industrials ETF 07/01/2013
MSCI ACWI ex U.S. Information Technology Sector Index Fund reclassified as MSCI ACWI ex U.S. Information Technology ETF 07/01/2013
MSCI ACWI ex U.S. Materials Sector Index Fund reclassified as MSCI ACWI ex U.S. Materials ETF 07/01/2013
MSCI ACWI ex U.S. Telecommunication Services Sector Index Fund reclassified as MSCI ACWI ex U.S. Telecommunication Services ETF 07/01/2013
MSCI ACWI ex U.S. Utilities Sector Index Fund reclassified as MSCI ACWI ex U.S. Utilities ETF 07/01/2013
MSCI All Country Asia ex Japan Small-Cap Index Fund reclassified as MSCI All Country Asia ex Japan Small-Cap ETF 07/01/2013
MSCI All Country Asia Information Technology Index Fund reclassified as MSCI All Country Asia Information Technology ETF 07/01/2013
MSCI Australia Small-Cap Index Fund reclassified as MSCI Australia Small-Cap ETF 07/01/2013
MSCI Canada Small-Cap Index Fund reclassified as MSCI Canada Small-Cap ETF 07/01/2013
MSCI Emerging Markets Financials Sector Index Fund reclassified as MSCI Emerging Markets Financials ETF 07/01/2013
MSCI Emerging Markets Latin America Index Fund reclassified as MSCI Emerging Markets Latin America Index ETF 07/01/2013
MSCI Emerging Markets Materials Sector Index Fund reclassified as MSCI Emerging Markets Materials ETF 07/01/2013
MSCI Far East Financials Sector Index Fund reclassified as MSCI Far East Financials ETF 07/01/2013
MSCI Hong Kong Small-Cap Index Fund reclassified as MSCI Hong Kong Small-Cap ETF 07/01/2013
MSCI Singapore Small-Cap Index Fund reclassified as MSCI Singapore Small-Cap ETF 07/01/2013
NYSE Composite Index Fund reclassified as NYSE Composite ETF 07/01/2013
NYSE 100 Index Fund reclassified as NYSE 100 ETF 07/01/2013
S&P Global Nuclear Energy Index Fund reclassified as Global Nuclear Energy ETF 07/01/2013
S&P Target Date Retirement Income Index Fund reclassified as Target Date Retirement Income Index ETF 07/01/2013
S&P Target Date 2010 Index Fund reclassified as Target Date 2010 ETF 07/01/2013
S&P Target Date 2015 Index Fund reclassified as Target Date 2015 ETF 07/01/2013
S&P Target Date 2020 Index Fund reclassified as Target Date 2020 ETF 07/01/2013
S&P Target Date 2025 Index Fund reclassified as Target Date 2025 ETF 07/01/2013
S&P Target Date 2030 Index Fund reclassified as Target Date 2030 ETF 07/01/2013
S&P Target Date 2035 Index Fund reclassified as Target Date 2035 ETF 07/01/2013
S&P Target Date 2040 Index Fund reclassified as Target Date 2040 ETF 07/01/2013
S&P Target Date 2045 Index Fund reclassified as Target Date 2045 ETF 07/01/2013
S&P Target Date 2050 Index Fund reclassified as Target Date 2050 ETF 07/01/2013
Utilities Sector Bond Fund reclassified as Utilities Bond ETF 07/01/2013
Trust terminated 08/15/2013
Each share 2013 S&P AMT-Free Municipal Series ETF received $50.49988 cash
Trust terminated 03/26/2014
Each share MSCI ACWI ex U.S. Industrials ETF received $66.498423 cash
Trust terminated 04/01/2014
Each share MSCI ACWI ex U.S. Consumer Discretionary ETF received $82.360795 cash
Each share MSCI ACWI ex U.S. Consumer Staples ETF received $76.473002 cash
Each share MSCI ACWI ex U.S. Energy ETF received $53.115579 cash
Each share MSCI ACWI ex U.S. Financials ETF received $25.262657 cash
Each share MSCI ACWI ex U.S. Healthcare ETF received $84.733015 cash
Each share MSCI ACWI ex U.S. Information Technology ETF received $66.259945 cash
Each share MSCI ACWI ex U.S. Materials ETF received $48.74831 cash
Each share MSCI ACWI ex U.S. Telecommunication Services ETF received $60.900111 cash
Each share MSCI ACWI ex U.S. Utilities ETF received $45.884773 cash
iSharesBond Dec 2016 Corporate Term ETF reclassified as iShares iBonds Dec 2016 Corporate ETF 07/07/2014
iShares 2016 AMT-Free Muni Term ETF reclassified as iShares iBonds Sep 2016 AMT-Free Muni Bond ETF 07/31/2014
iShares 2015 AMT-Free Muni Term ETF reclassified as iShares iBonds Sep 2015 AMT-Free Muni Bond ETF 07/31/2014
iShares 2018 AMT-Free Muni Term

ETF reclassified as iShares iBonds Sep 2018 AMT-Free Muni Bond ETF 07/31/2014
Trust terminated 08/15/2014
Each share 2014 AMT-Free Municipal Term ETF received $51.175611 cash
Trust terminated 10/21/2014
Each share Global Nuclear Energy ETF received $36.124617 cash
Each share Industrial/Office Real Estate Capped ETF received $31.854402 cash
Each share MSCI Emerging Markets Financials ETF received $24.998031 cash
Each share MSCI Emerging Markets Materials ETF received $14.838592 cash
Each share MSCI Far East Financials ETF received $28.17109 cash
Each share NYSE Composite ETF received $94.312512 cash
Each share NYSE 100 ETF received $86.433849 cash
Each share Retail Real Estate Capped ETF received $39.317509 cash
Each share Target Date 2010 ETF received $35.689524 cash
Each share Target Date 2015 ETF received $37.844007 cash
Each share Target Date 2020 ETF received $39.422192 cash
Each share Target Date 2025 ETF received $40.640619 cash
Each share Target Date 2030 ETF received $41.69748 cash
Each share Target Date 2035 ETF received $42.295133 cash
Each share Target Date 2040 ETF received $43.03308 cash
Each share Target Date 2045 ETF received $33.576288 cash
Each share Target Date 2050 ETF received $33.87869 cash
Each share Target Date Retirement Income ETF received $33.447254 cash
Trust terminated 08/28/2015
Each share Asia Developed Real Estate ETF received $28.870322 cash
Each share Financials Bond ETF received $52.481533 cash
Each share FTSE China ETF received $47.220372 cash
Each share Industrials Bond ETF received $49.170117 cash
Each share MSCI All Country Asia ex Japan Small-Cap ETF received $49.783163 cash
Each share MSCI All Country Asia Information Technology ETF received $30.261123 cash
Each share MSCI Australia Small-Cap ETF received $14.806951 cash
Each share MSCI Canada Small-Cap ETF received $16.19228 cash
Each share MSCI Hong Kong Small-Cap ETF received $22.948042 cash
Each share MSCI Singapore Small-Cap ETF received $20.813924 cash
Each share North America Real Estate ETF received $55.579081 cash
Each share Utilities Bond ETF received $50.718193 cash
iShares iBonds Sep 2016 AMT-Free Muni Bond ETF split (2) for (1) by issuance of (1) additional share payable 05/20/2015 to holders of record 05/18/2015 Ex date - 05/21/2015
iShares iBonds Dec 2016 Corporate ETF split (4) for (1) by issuance of (3) additional shares payable 05/20/2015 to holders of record 05/18/2015 Ex date - 05/21/2015
Trust terminated 09/08/2015
Each share iShares iBonds Sep 2015 AMT-Free Muni Bond ETF received $52.573012 cash
Currency Hedged Global ex USD High Yield Bond ETF reclassified as Currency Hedged International High Yield Bond ETF 10/30/2015
iShares iBonds Sep 2016 AMT-Free Muni Bond ETF reclassified as iShares iBonds Sep 2016 Term Muni Bond ETF 03/01/2016
iShares iBonds Dec 2016 Corporate ETF reclassified as iShares iBonds Dec 2016 Term Corporate ETF 03/01/2016
iShares iBonds Sep 2018 AMT-Free Muni Bond ETF reclassified as iShares iBonds Sep 2018 Term Muni Bond ETF 03/01/2016
Trust terminated 04/05/2016
Each share iShares iBonds Mar 2016 Corporate ETF received $100.820287 cash
Each share iShares iBonds Mar 2016 Corporate ex-Financials ETF received $99.503752 cash
Currency Hedged MSCI ACWI Minimum Volatility ETF reclassified as Edge MSCI Min Vol Global Currency Hedged ETF 05/12/2016
Currency Hedged MSCI EAFE Minimum Volatility ETF reclassified as Edge MSCI Min Vol EM Currency Hedged ETF 05/12/2016
Currency Hedged MSCI Europe Minimum Volatility ETF reclassified as Edge MSCI Min Vol Europe Currency Hedged 05/12/2016
Trust terminated 08/24/2016
Each share B - Ca Rated Corporate Bond ETF received $46.700928 cash
Each share Baa - Ba Rated Corporate Bond ETF received $53.245165 cash
Each share Global Inflation-Linked Bond ETF received $51.123824 cash
Each share International Inflation-Linked Bond ETF received $44.7432 cash
Each share MSCI Emerging Markets Latin America Index ETF received $32.952938 cash
Trust terminated 09/08/2016
Each share iShares iBonds Sep 2016 Term Muni Bond ETF received $26.458058 cash
Trust terminated 12/15/2016
Each share iShares iBonds Dec 2016 Term Corporate ETF received $25.034152 cash
Trust terminated 09/08/2017
Each share iShares iBonds Sep 2017 Term Muni Bond ETF received $27.22 cash
Trust terminated 12/21/2017
Each share iShares iBonds Dec 2017 Term Corporate ETF received $24.843315 cash
Trust terminated 03/21/2018
Each share iShares iBonds Mar 2018 Term Corporate ex-Financials ETF received $24.637358 cash
Trust terminated 04/02/2018
Each share iBonds Mar 2018 Term Corporate ETF received $25.600217 cash
Trust terminated 08/22/2018
Each share Currency Hedged International High Yield Bond ETF received $28.165661 cash
Each share Currency Hedged MSCI ACWI ETF received $30.104827 cash
Each share Currency Hedged MSCI Europe Europe Small-Cap ETF received $30.004893 cash
Each share Edge MSCI Min Vol EAFE Currency Hedged ETF received $27.740942 cash
Each share Edge MSCI Min Vol Europe Currency Hedged ETF received $25.179126 cash
Each share Edge MSCI Min Vol Global Currency Hedged ETF received $30.185427 cash
Each share Edge MSCI Multifactor Financials ETF received $34.56581 cash
Each share Edge MSCI Multifactor Consumer Discretionary ETF received $34.379894 cash
Each share Edge MSCI Multifactor Consumer Staples ETF received $25.340161 cash
Each share Edge MSCI Multifactor Energy ETF received $28.267985 cash
Each share Edge MSCI Multifactor Healthcare ETF received $35.04589 cash
Each share Edge MSCI Multifactor Industrials ETF received $31.674214 cash
Each share Edge MSCI Multifactor Materials ETF received $31.977551 cash
Each share Edge MSCI Multifactor Technology ETF received $42.80651 cash
Each share Edge MSCI Multifactor Utilities ETF received $27.07543 cash
Each share iShares iBonds Sep 2018 Term Muni Bond ETF received $25.449678 cash
(Additional Information in Active)

ISHARES U S ETF TR (DE)
Trust terminated 08/30/2016
Each share Enhanced International Large-Cap ETF received $22.625969 cash
Each share Enhanced International Small-Cap ETF received $24.643013 cash
Each share Enhanced U.S. Large-Cap ETF received $34.5927 cash
Each share Enhanced U.S. Small-Cap ETF received $33.435198 cash
(Additional Information in Active)

ISHARES U S HIGH DIVID EQUITY INDEX FD CAD HEDGED (ON)
Name changed to iShares U.S. High Dividend Equity Index ETF (CAD-Hedged) 03/27/2014

ISHARES U S HIGH YIELD BD INDEX FD CAD HEDGED (ON)
Name changed to iShares U.S. High Yield Bond Index ETF (CAD-Hedged) 03/27/2014

ISHARES U S IG CORPORATE BD INDEX FD (ON)
Name changed to iShares U.S. IG Corporate Bond Index ETF (CAD-Hedged) 03/27/2014

ISHARES US FUNDAMENTAL INDEX FD (ON)
Name changed to iShares US Fundamental Index ETF 06/04/2014

ISHOPPER COM INC (NV)
Name changed to Ensurge, Inc. 10/16/2000

ISHTAR SENIORS COMMUNITIES INC (CANADA)
Name changed 12/01/1998
Reincorporated 12/07/1998
Name changed from Ishtar Investments, Inc. to Ishtar Seniors Communities Inc. 12/01/1998
Place of incorporation changed from (AB) to (Canada) 12/07/1998
Name changed to Amica Mature Lifestyles Inc. 08/31/2000
(See Amica Mature Lifestyles Inc.)

ISI CORP (CA)
Recapitalized as California Windsor Co. 05/24/1974
Each share Capital Stock no par exchanged for (0.1) share Capital Stock no par
California Windsor Co. merged into Hutton (E.F.) Group, Inc. 02/21/1978
(See Hutton (E.F.) Group Inc.)

ISI GROWTH FD INC (CA)
Dissolved 08/19/1991
Details not available

ISI SYS INC (DE)
Merged into Memotec Data Inc. 11/30/1989
Each share Common 1¢ par exchanged for $20 cash

ISI TECHNOLOGY CORP (DE)
Charter cancelled and declared void for failure to pay franchise taxes 3/1/2000

ISI VENTURES INC (AB)
Name changed to Ayotte Music Inc. (AB) 04/02/1998
Ayotte Music Inc. (AB) reincorporated in Canada 05/16/2000 which recapitalized as Verb Exchange Inc. 11/12/2002 which recapitalized as Seymour Ventures Corp. 07/05/2010 which name changed to Rare Earth Industries Ltd. 07/13/2011 which recapitalized as Ackroo Inc. 10/10/2012

ISILON SYS INC (DE)
Issue Information - 8,350,000 shares COM offered at $13 per share on 12/14/2006
Acquired by EMC Corp. 12/21/2010
Each share Common $0.00001 par exchanged for $33.85 cash

ISIS COMMUNICATIONS LTD (AUSTRALIA)
Name changed to AAV Ltd. 03/03/2003
AAV Ltd. name changed to Staging Connections Group Ltd. 01/10/2007
(See Staging Connections Group Ltd.)

ISIS LAB CORP (BC)
Name changed to IMPERUS Technologies Corp. 09/19/2014
IMPERUS Technologies Corp. name changed to Tangelo Games Corp. 06/28/2016
(See Tangelo Games Corp.)

ISIS PHARMACEUTICALS (DE)
Name changed to Ionis Pharmaceuticals, Inc. 12/22/2015

ISKUT GOLD CORP (BC)
Name changed to A&B Geoscience Corp. (BC) 05/02/1994
A&B Geoscience Corp. (BC) reincorporated in British West Indies 04/11/1995 which name changed to Arawak Energy Corp. (British West Indies) 06/18/2003 which reincorporated in Channel Islands as Arawak Energy Ltd. 06/03/2008
(See Arawak Energy Ltd.)

ISKUT RIVER MINES, LTD. (ON)
Charter cancelled and company declared dissolved for default in filing returns 04/15/1965

ISKUT SILVER MINES LTD (BC)
Recapitalized as Commonwealth Minerals Ltd. 04/10/1978
Each share Common no par exchanged for (0.25) share Common no par
Commonwealth Minerals Ltd. merged into Meridor Resources Ltd. 04/01/1985 which merged into Hughes Lang Corp. 08/01/1989 which merged into CanGold Resources Inc. (BC) 01/31/1994 which reorganized in Ontario as Amalgamated CanGold Inc. 07/31/1995 which merged into Central Asia Goldfields Corp. 01/08/1996
(See Central Asia Goldfields Corp.)

ISL INDS LTD (BC)
Struck off register and declared dissolved for failure to file returns 05/15/1987

ISLAMORADA BANK (ISLAMORADA, FL)
Name and location changed to TIB

Bank of the Keys (Key Largo, FL) and Common $10 par changed to $2.50 par 03/14/1987
TIB Bank Of The Keys (Key Largo, FL) reorganized as TIB Financial Corp. 08/31/1996 which merged into Capital Bank Financial Corp. 09/21/2012 which merged into First Horizon National Corp. 11/30/2017

ISLAND ARC EXPL CORP (BC)
Recapitalized as Solace Resources Corp. 05/17/2011
Each share Common no par exchanged for (0.2) share Common no par
Solace Resources Corp. name changed to First Graphite Corp. 03/27/2012 which recapitalized as Desert Star Resources Ltd. (Old) 01/21/2013 merged into Desert Star Resources Ltd. (New) 04/15/2015 which name changed to Kutcho Copper Corp. 12/21/2017

ISLAND ARC EXPL INC (BC)
Recapitalized as Island Arc Mining Corp. 04/30/2003
Each share Common no par exchanged for (0.25) share Common no par
Island Arc Mining Corp. recapitalized as Island Arc Exploration Corp. 05/11/2004 which recapitalized as Solace Resources Corp. 05/17/2011 which name changed to First Graphite Corp. 03/27/2012 which recapitalized as Desert Star Resources Ltd. (Old) 01/21/2013 which merged into Desert Star Resources Ltd. (New) 04/15/2015 which name changed to Kutcho Copper Corp. 12/21/2017

ISLAND ARC MNG CORP (BC)
Recapitalized as Island Arc Exploration Corp. 05/11/2004
Each share Common no par exchanged for (0.5) share Common no par
Island Arc Exploration Corp. recapitalized as Solace Resources Corp. 05/17/2011 which name changed to First Graphite Corp. 03/27/2012 which recapitalized as Desert Star Resources Ltd. (Old) 01/21/2013 merged into Desert Star Resources Ltd. (New) 04/15/2015 which name changed to Kutcho Copper Corp. 12/21/2017

ISLAND ARC RES CORP (BC)
Recapitalized as Island Arc Exploration Inc. 11/12/2001
Each share Common no par exchanged for (0.5) share Common no par
Island Arc Exploration Inc. recapitalized as Island Arc Mining Corp. 04/30/2003 which recapitalized as Island Arc Exploration Corp. 05/11/2004 which recapitalized as Solace Resources Corp. 05/17/2011 which name changed to First Graphite Corp. 03/27/2012 which recapitalized as Desert Star Resources Ltd. (Old) 01/21/2013 merged into Desert Star Resources Ltd. (New) 04/15/2015 which name changed to Kutcho Copper Corp. 12/21/2017

ISLAND BANCORP INC (MA)
Merged into Independent Bank Corp. 05/12/2017
Each share Common 1¢ par exchanged for $500 cash

ISLAND BREEZE INTL INC (DE)
SEC revoked common stock registration 05/14/2015

ISLAND CANYON MINES INC (BC)
Name changed to Access Technologies Inc. 06/26/1987
(See Access Technologies Inc.)

ISLAND COPPER MINES LTD. (BC)
Name changed to Arlington Silver Mines Ltd. 08/08/1964
Arlington Silver Mines Ltd. recapitalized as Western Arlington Resources Ltd. 10/07/1981 which recapitalized as Lightning Creek Mines Ltd. 12/19/1986
(See Lightning Creek Mines Ltd.)

ISLAND CREEK COAL CO. (DE)
Merged into Occidental Petroleum Corp. (CA) 1/29/68
Each share Common 50¢ par exchanged for (0.65) share $4 Conv. Preferred $1 par
(See Occidental Petroleum Corp. (CA))

ISLAND CREEK COAL CO. (ME)
Each share Common $1 par exchanged for (2) shares Common 50¢ par in 1948
Merged into Island Creek Coal Co. (DE) 12/31/64
Each share 6% Preferred $1 par exchanged for (4) shares Common 50¢ par or $140 cash at option of holder
Common 50¢ par exchanged share for share Island Creek Coal Co. (DE) merged into Occidental Petroleum Corp. (CA) 1/29/68
(See Occidental Petroleum Corp. (CA)

ISLAND CRITICAL CARE CORP (DE)
Recapitalized as Kodiak Energy, Inc. 01/18/2016
Each share Common $0.001 par exchanged for (0.01) share Common $0.001 par

ISLAND DATA PROCESSING SYS INC (NY)
Recapitalized as Wellington Communications International, Ltd. 11/14/1973
Each share Common 1¢ par exchanged for (0.33333333) share Common 1¢ par
(See Wellington Communications International, Ltd.)

ISLAND GEM ENTERPRISES LTD. N.V. (NETHERLANDS ANTILLES)
Stock Dividend - 10% 12/00/1974
Name changed to SunResorts Ltd. N.V. 05/00/1985
(See SunResorts Ltd. N.V.)

ISLAND MNG & EXPLS LTD (BC)
Common no par split (2) for (1) by issuance of (1) additional share 04/23/1982
Delisted from Vancouver Stock Exchange 05/28/1991

ISLAND MTN GOLD MINES LTD (BC)
Recapitalized as Lions Gate Energy Inc. 02/01/2006
Each share Common no par exchanged for (0.25) share Common no par
Lions Gate Energy Inc. recapitalized as Starr Peak Exploration Ltd. 07/27/2015

ISLAND MOUNTAIN MINES CO. LTD. (BC)
Liquidation completed 08/05/1957
Details not available

ISLAND NATL BK & TR CO (PALM BEACH, FL)
Merged into 1st United Bancorp 04/01/1997
Each share Common $5 par exchanged for (2.2185) shares Common no par
1st United Bancorp merged into Wachovia Corp. (New) (Ctfs. dated between 05/20/1991 and 09/01/2001) 11/11/1997 which merged into Wachovia Corp. (Ctfs. dated after 09/01/2001) 09/01/2001 which merged into Wells Fargo & Co. (New) 12/31/2008

ISLAND NATL BK PALM BEACH FLA (PALM BEACH, FL)
Name changed to Island National Bank & Trust Co. (Palm Beach, FL) 06/15/1993
Island National Bank & Trust Co. (Palm Beach, FL) merged into 1st United Bancorp 04/01/1997 which merged into Wachovia Corp. (New) (Ctfs. dated between 05/20/1991 and 09/01/2001) 11/11/1997 which merged into Wachovia Corp. (Ctfs. dated after 09/01/2001) 09/01/2001 which merged into Wells Fargo & Co. (New) 12/31/2008

ISLAND OIL & TRANSPORT CORP. (VA)
Charter revoked for failure to file reports and pay taxes 00/00/1928

ISLAND PAC INC (DE)
Name changed to Retail Pro, Inc. 01/29/2008
(See Retail Pro, Inc.)

ISLAND PINEAPPLE CO. LTD.
Dissolved 00/00/1937
Details not available

ISLAND PPTYS INC (OR)
Liquidation completed
Each share Common $0.125 par received initial distribution of $6.75 cash 10/14/1977
Each share Common $0.125 par exchanged for second distribution of $10.55 cash 04/05/1978
Each share Common $0.125 par received third and final distribution of $0.09 cash 01/22/1980

ISLAND RADIO INC (NV)
Name changed to China Herb Group Holdings Corp. 07/17/2012

ISLAND RES INC (NY)
Each share old Common 1¢ par exchanged for (0.002) share new Common 1¢ par 4/1/2000
Merged into Future Educational Systems, Inc. 11/20/2009
Each share new Common 1¢ par exchanged for (1) share Common 1¢ par
(See Future Educational Systems, Inc.)

ISLAND ST BK (PATCHOGUE, NY)
Common $5 par changed to $10 par 03/07/1973
Merged into United Bank Corp. of New York 09/01/1981
Each share Common $10 par exchanged for (2.5) shares Common $5 par
United Bank Corp. of New York name changed to Nortstar Bancorp Inc. 01/04/1982 which merged into Fleet/Norstar Financial Group, Inc. 01/01/1988 which name changed to Fleet Financial Group, Inc. (New) 04/15/1992 which name changed to Fleet Boston Corp. 10/01/1999 which name changed to FleetBoston Financial Corp. 04/18/2000 which merged into Bank of America Corp. 04/01/2004

ISLAND TECHNOLOGIES CORP (BC)
Name changed to Hiburd Properties Inc. 02/11/1987
(See Hiburd Properties Inc.)

ISLAND TELECOM INC (PEI)
Name changed 05/07/1998
Each share Common $100 par exchanged for (10) shares Common $10 par 00/00/1952
Common $10 par changed to $5 par and (1) additional share issued 12/15/1971
Common $5 par changed to $2.50 par and (1) additional share issued 04/16/1987
4.5% Preferred $10 par called for redemption 03/00/1997
4.75% Preferred $10 par called for redemption 03/00/1997
5.5% Preferred $20 par called for redemption 03/00/1997
7.25% Preferred $20 par called for redemption 03/00/1997
9.25% Preferred $20 par called for redemption 03/00/1997
9.25% Preferred 1977 Ser. $20 par called for redemption 03/00/1997
Name changed from Island Telephone Co., Ltd. to Island Telecom Inc. 05/07/1998
Common $2.50 par split (2) for (1) by issuance of (1) additional share payable 05/28/1998 to holders of record 05/22/1998
Merged into Aliant Inc. (Canada) 06/01/1999
Each share Common $2.50 par exchanged for (1) share Common no par
Aliant Inc. (Canada) reorganized in Ontario as Bell Aliant Regional Communications Income Fund 07/10/2006 which reorganized in Canada as Bell Aliant Inc. 01/04/2011 which merged into BCE Inc. 10/31/2014

ISLAND TUG & BARGE LTD (BC)
5% 1st Preference $10 par called for redemption 11/29/1968
Public interest eliminated

ISLANDERS BANK (FRIDAY HARBOR, WA)
Under plan of reorganization each share Common $1 par automatically became (1) share San Juan Bank Holding Co. Common $1 par 08/10/1998
San Juan Bank Holding Co. name changed to San Juan Financial Holding Co. 05/08/2002 which was acquired by Banner Corp. 05/01/2007

ISLE CAPRI CASINOS INC (DE)
Acquired by Eldorado Resorts, Inc. 05/01/2017
Each share Common 1¢ par exchanged for $23 cash

ISLE DIEU MATTAGAMI MINES LTD. (ON)
Acquired by Noranda Inc. 07/16/1987
Each share Capital Stock $1 par exchanged for $9 cash

ISLE OF PINES MINING CO. LTD. (ON)
Recapitalized as Caribbean Gold Mines, Ltd. 00/00/1953
Each share Capital Stock exchanged for (0.14285714) share Capital Stock no par
(See Caribbean Gold Mines, Ltd.)

ISLE RES INC (WI)
Administratively dissolved 12/04/1992

ISLE ROYALE COPPER CO. (MI)
Liquidation completed 00/00/1952
Details not available

ISLE ROYALE COPPER CO. (NJ)
Reorganized under the laws of Michigan 00/00/1937
Details not available

ISLEINVEST LTD (BERMUDA)
Delisted from Alberta Stock Exchange 05/22/1998

ISLESHAVEN CAP CORP (BC)
Name changed to Nortel Communications Inc. 06/17/1991
Nortel Communications Inc. recapitalized as American Nortel Communications Inc. (BC) 05/11/1992 which reincorporated in Wyoming 02/09/1993 which reincorporated in Nevada 08/03/2007

ISLEUTH COM INC (FL)
Name changed to BigHub.com, Inc. 04/29/1999
(See BigHub.com, Inc.)

ISM HLDG CORP (IN)
Reincorporated under the laws of Nevada as Xytos, Inc. 07/16/2004

ISM INFORMATION SYS MGMT CORP (SASK)
Class A Common no par reclassified as Common no par 07/22/1993
Acquired by 607029 Saskatchewan Ltd. 02/03/1995
Each share Common no par exchanged for $14.25 cash

ISMO TECH SOLUTIONS INC (NV)
Name changed to Q BioMed Inc. 07/30/2015

ISO BLOCK PRODS USA INC (CO)
Recapitalized as Cryocon Inc. 09/21/2000
Each share Common no par exchanged for (0.25) share Common no par
(See Cryocon Inc.)

ISO INDS CORP (DE)
Charter cancelled and declared inoperative and void for non-payment of taxes 03/01/1976

ISO MINES LTD (ON)
Capital Stock $1 par changed to no par 07/29/1974
Merged into Teck Corp. 09/28/1979
Each share Capital Stock no par exchanged for (0.2) share Class B Common no par or $16.66 cash
Note: Option to receive cash expired 10/28/1979
Teck Corp. name changed to Teck Cominco Ltd. 09/12/2001 which name changed to Teck Resources Ltd. 04/27/2009

ISO URANIUM MINES LTD. (ON)
Name changed to ISO Mines Ltd. 08/28/1959
ISO Mines Ltd. merged into Teck Corp. 09/28/1979 which name changed to Teck Cominco Ltd. 09/12/2001 which name changed to Teck Resources Ltd. 04/27/2009

ISO VENTURES INC (BC)
Recapitalized as Steadfast Ventures Inc. 06/29/1993
Each share Common no par exchanged for (0.2) share Common no par
(See Steadfast Ventures Inc.)

ISOCOR (CA)
Merged into Critical Path, Inc. 01/19/2000
Each share Common no par exchanged for (0.4707) share Common $0.001 par
(See Critical Path, Inc.)

ISOETEC COMMUNICATIONS INC (VA)
Merged into Executone Information Systems, Inc. (VA) 07/08/1988
Each share Common 1¢ par exchanged for (2.5) shares Common 1¢ par
Executone Information Systems, Inc. (VA) reincorporated in Delaware 06/00/1989 which name changed to eLOT, Inc. (VA) 01/04/2000 which reorganized in Delaware 12/31/2002
(See eLOT, Inc. (DE))

ISOFT INTL INC (NV)
Name changed to Pulse Network, Inc. 04/12/2013

ISOFTSTONE HLDGS LTD (CAYMAN ISLANDS)
Acquired by New iSoftStone Holdings Ltd. 08/29/2014
Each Sponsored ADS for Ordinary exchanged for $5.65 cash

ISOLAGEN INC (DE)
Plan of reorganization under Chapter 11 Federal Bankruptcy proceedings effective 09/03/2009
No stockholders' equity

ISOLVER COM INC (CO)
SEC revoked common stock registration 02/06/2007

ISOLYSER INC (GA)
Issue Information - 3,900,000 shares COM offered at $18 per share on 10/20/1994
Common $0.001 par split (2) for (1) by issuance of (1) additional share 10/02/1995
Name changed to Microtek Medical Holdings, Inc. 07/01/2002
(See Microtek Medical Holdings, Inc.)

ISOMEDIX INC (DE)
Merged into STERIS Corp. 09/17/1997
Each share Common 1¢ par exchanged for $20.50 cash

ISOMER CAP CORP (ON)
Name changed to Gray Wolf Capital Corp. and Class A Common no par reclassified as Class A Preference no par 12/14/2004

ISOMETRY INC (CO)
Name changed to U.S. Mint, Inc. and Common no par changed to $0.0001 par 11/3/89
(See U.S. Mint, Inc.)

ISONEA LTD (AUSTRALIA)
Each old Sponsored ADR for Ordinary exchanged for (0.05) new Sponsored ADR for Ordinary 08/17/2012
Sponsored ADR's for Ordinary split (25) for (1) by issuance of (24) additional ADR's payable 10/11/2013 to holders of record 10/10/2013
Ex date - 10/15/2013
Basis changed from (1:500) to (1:20) 10/15/2013
Name changed to Respiri Ltd. 12/31/2015
(See Respiri Ltd.)

ISOTECHNIKA INC (AB)
Merged into Isotechnika Pharma Inc. 06/23/2009
Each share Common no par exchanged for (1) share Common no par
Isotechnika Pharma Inc. recapitalized as Aurinia Pharmaceuticals Inc. 10/23/2013

ISOTECHNIKA PHARMA INC (AB)
Recapitalized as Aurinia Pharmaceuticals Inc. 10/23/2013
Each share Common no par exchanged for (0.02) share Common no par

ISOTIS INC (DE)
Merged into Integra LifeSciences Holdings Corp. 10/29/2007
Each share Common $0.0001 par exchanged for $7.25 cash

ISOTIS S A (SWITZERLAND)
Acquired by IsoTis, Inc. 07/30/2007
Each share Ordinary CHF 1 par exchanged for (0.1) share Common $0.0001 par
(See IsoTis, Inc.)

ISOTOPE PRODUCTS LTD. (ON)
Name changed to Canadian Curtiss-Wright Ltd. 00/00/1957
Canadian Curtiss-Wright Ltd. recapitalized as Curtiss-Wright of Canada Inc. 06/03/1985
(See Curtiss-Wright of Canada Inc.)

ISOTOPE SOLUTIONS GROUP INC (NY)
Dissolved by proclamation 12/29/2004

ISPAT INTL N V (NETHERLANDS)
Issue Information - 25,000,000 CL A - NY REGISTRY SHS offered at $27 per share on 08/06/1997
Name changed to Mittal Steel Co. N.V. 12/17/2004
Mittal Steel Co. N.V. name changed to ArcelorMittal (Netherlands) 01/30/2007 which reincorporated in Luxembourg 09/03/2007 which merged into ArcelorMittal S.A. 11/13/2007

ISPAT ISCOR LTD (SOUTH AFRICA)
Name changed to Mittal Steel South Africa Ltd. 03/22/2005
Mittal Steel South Africa Ltd. name changed to ArcelorMittal South Africa 11/02/2007

ISRAEL AMERN DIVERSIFIED FD INC (DE)
Charter cancelled and declared inoperative and void for non-payment of taxes 3/1/75

ISRAEL-AMERICAN OIL CORP. (DE)
Common 10¢ par reclassified as Class A Common 10¢ par 4/3/59
Class A Common 10¢ par reclassified as Common 10¢ par 12/3/59
Recapitalized as Isram Corp. 4/17/64
Each (15) shares Common 10¢ par exchanged for (1) share Common $1.50 par
Isram Corp. name changed to ITI Corp. (DE) 1/6/69
ITI Corp. (DE) merged into ITI Corp. (OH) 1/28/77

ISRAEL BK AGRICULTURE LTD (ISRAEL)
Privatized 09/04/2005
93.74% of 7.50% Preferred Ser. C NIS 0.042 par owned by Israeli Government with the remainder to be purchased at 90% of nominal value to be determined at time of surrender

ISRAEL CHEMICALS LTD (ISRAEL)
ADR agreement terminated 10/27/2014
Each ADR for Common exchanged for $7.128328 cash

ISRAEL CONTL OIL LTD (ON)
Capital Stock $1 par changed to no par 04/20/1971
Name changed to Wimberley Resources Ltd. 09/01/1980
(See Wimberley Resources Ltd.)

ISRAEL CORP. OF AMERICA
Merged into Palestine Economic Corp. 1949
(See Palestine Economic Corp.)

ISRAEL CORP LTD (ISRAEL)
ADR agreement terminated 08/06/2018
No ADR's remain outstanding

ISRAEL DEV CORP (NY)
Common $25 par changed to $12.50 par and (2) for (1) split effected 7/30/65
Holders were issued stickers stating each $25 par share now represents (2) $12.50 par shares
Common $12.50 par changed to $5 par 11/20/72
Merged into Ampal-American Israel Corp. 10/5/79
Each share Common $5 par exchanged for (3.3) shares 6-1/2% Conv. Preferred $5 par

ISRAEL DISC BK LTD (ISRAEL)
Each share 7.5% Preference IS10 par exchanged for (10) shares Class A Ordinary IS1 par 5/11/82
(Additional Information in Active)

ISRAEL ENTERPRISES, INC. (DE)
Liquidation completed in 1958
Each share Common $100 par exchanged for an ADR for (55) shares American Israeli Paper Mills Ltd. Ordinary I£1 par; (6) Founders Shares I£1 par and (2.5) Ordinary Shares I£10 par of Mehadrin Ltd.; (1) share Palestine Economic Corp. Common $25 par, and I£3.60 in cash

ISRAEL FUND, INC. (MD)
Merged into Israel American Diversified Fund, Inc. 5/1/67
Each share Common $1 par exchanged for (1.106) shares Common 20¢ par
(See Israel American Diversified Fund, Inc.)

ISRAEL GROWTH PARTNERS ACQUISITION CORP (DE)
Ser. B Units separated 02/19/2009
Completely liquidated 02/19/2009
Each share Class B Common $0.0001 par exchanged for first and final distribution of $5.40403571 cash
Ser. A Units separated 04/11/2013
Merged into Macau Resources Group Ltd. 04/26/2013
Each share Common $0.0001 par exchanged for (0.05) share Ordinary no par
(See Macau Resources Group Ltd.)

ISRAEL HOTELS INTL INC (DE)
Merged into Tel-Aviv Hotels International, Inc. 1/4/77
Each share Common 10¢ par exchanged for $2.50 cash

ISRAEL INDUSTRIAL & MINERAL DEVELOPMENT CORP. (NY)
Each share Common $100 par exchanged for (4) shares Common $25 par 9/14/55
Name changed to Israel Development Corp. 5/17/56
Israel Development Corp. merged into Ampal-American Israel Corp. 10/5/79

ISRAEL INTL CORP (DC)
Common 5¢ par changed to 4¢ par and (0.25) additional share issued in 1973
Charter revoked for failure to file reports 9/9/74

ISRAEL INVS CORP (DE)
Common $1 par split (6) for (1) by issuance of (5) additional shares 2/10/78
Name changed to IIC Industries Inc. 7/18/90
(See IIC Industries Inc.)

ISRAEL LD DEV LTD (ISRAEL)
ADR agreement terminated 7/30/2003
Each Sponsored ADR for Ordinary NIS1 par exchanged for $7.484 cash

ISRAEL-MEDITERRANEAN PETROLEUM INC. (PANAMA)
Merged into Magellan Petroleum Corp. (Panama) on a (0.2) for (1) basis 07/02/1959
Magellan Petroleum Corp. (Panama) reincorporated in Delaware 10/23/1967
(See Magellan Petroleum Corp. (DE))

ISRAEL NEGEV PETE CORP (DE)
Name changed to Penn-Tech Corp. 8/30/68
(See Penn-Tech Corp.)

ISRAEL SEMICONDUCTOR CORP (NV)
Name changed to International Semiconductor Corp. 07/05/1994
International Semiconductor Corp. name changed to Sanitary Environmental Monitoring Labs, Inc. 04/12/2000 which recapitalized as Vietnam United Steel Corp. 08/28/2008 which recapitalized as Vietnam Mining Corp. 07/12/2010 which name changed to Vanguard Mining Corp. 06/03/2014 which name changed to Myson Group, Inc. 06/08/2015

ISRAEL TECH ACQUISITION CORP (DE)
Issue Information - 2,000,000 Units consisting of (1) share COM and (2) WTS offered at $6 per Unit on 04/11/1994
Name changed to Kellstrom Industries Inc. 6/26/95
(See Kellstrom Industries Inc.)

ISRAEL TECHNOLOGY ACQUISITION CORP (DE)
Name changed to IXI Mobile, Inc. 06/06/2007
(See IXI Mobile, Inc.)

ISRAM CORP. (DE)
Name changed to ITI Corp. (DE) 1/6/69
ITI Corp. (DE) merged into ITI Corp. (OH) 1/28/77

ISRAS ISRAEL RASSCO INVT LTD (ISRAEL)
Stock Dividends - 50% 10/28/80; 250% 11/8/81; 300% 11/16/81
Name changed to Isras Investment Co. Ltd. 12/31/87

ISS GROUP INC (DE)
Issue Information - 3,000,000 shares COM offered at $22 per share on 03/23/1998
Common $0.001 par split (2) for (1) by issuance of (1) additional share payable 5/19/99 to holders of record 5/5/99
Name changed to Internet Security Systems Inc. 7/20/2000
(See Internet Security Systems Inc.)

ISS INTL SVC SYS A/S (DENMARK)
ADR agreement terminated 3/1/98
Each Sponsored ADR for Class B Shares Kr.20 par exchanged for (0.5) Class B share Kr.20 par

ISS INTL SVC SYS INC (DE)
Acquired by ISS International Service System A/S 10/30/1990
Each share Common 10¢ par exchanged for $12 cash

ISSAQUAH BANCSHARES INC (WA)
Merged into Cascade Financial Corp. 06/04/2004
Each share Common $1 par exchanged for (4.272) shares Common 1¢ par
(See Cascade Financial Corp.)

ISSAQUAH BK (ISSAQUAH, WA)
Stock Dividend - 10% payable 03/26/1996 to holders of record 01/26/1996
Under plan of reorganization each share Common $1 par automatically became (1) share Issaquah Bancshares Inc. Common $1 par 05/19/1997
Issaquah Bancshares Inc. merged into Cascade Financial Corp. 06/04/2004
(See Cascade Financial Corp.)

ISSC INDL SOLID ST CTLS INC (DE)
Acquired by Honeywell Inc. 11/30/1984
Each share Common $1 par exchanged for $10 cash

ISSG INC (DE)
Name changed to Rubicon Financial Inc. (DE) 09/15/2006
Rubicon Financial Inc. (DE) reincorporated in Nevada 08/29/2011

ISTA PHARMACEUTICALS INC (DE)
Each share old Common $0.001 par exchanged for (0.1) share new Common $0.001 par 11/14/2002
Acquired by Bausch & Lomb Inc. 06/06/2012
Each share new Common $0.001 par exchanged for $9.10 cash

ISTAR FINL INC (MD)
9.2% Preferred Ser. C $0.001 par called for redemption at $25 plus $0.45 accrued dividend on 2/23/2004
9.375% Preferred Ser. B $0.001 par called for redemption at $25 plus $0.46 accrued dividend on 2/23/2004
Name changed to iStar Inc. 08/19/2015

ISTAR INC (MD)
7.8% Preferred Ser. F $0.001 par called for redemption at $25 plus $0.189583 accrued dividends on 10/20/2017
7.875% Preferred Ser. E $0.001 par called for redemption at $25 plus $0.191406 accrued dividends on 10/20/2017
(Additional Information in Active)

ISTAR INTERNET INC (CANADA)
Each (8,500,000) shares old Common no par exchanged for (1) share new Common no par 06/04/1998
Note: In effect holders received $0.510953 cash per share and public interest was eliminated

ISTEC INDS & TECHNOLOGIES LTD (ISRAEL)
Each share Ordinary ILS 1 par exchanged for (0.1) share Ordinary ILS 10 par 11/03/1995
Company terminated registration of Ordinary stock and is no longer public as of 09/17/2003

ISTEL FD INC (DE)
Common $1 par split (2) for (1) by issuance of (1) additional share 5/11/66
Common $1 par split (2) for (1) by issuance of (1) additional share 4/30/82
Name changed to Lepercq-Istel Trust 4/9/86
Lepercq-Istel Trust acquired by Tocqueville Trust 7/9/2002

ISTHMUS STEAMSHIP & SALVAGE CO., INC. (DE)
Out of business 12/00/1960
No stockholders' equity

ISTITUTO BANCARIO SAN PAOLO DI TORINO-INSTITUTO MOBILIARE ITALIANO S.P.A (ITALY)
Name changed to Sanpaolo IMI S.p.A. 10/20/1999
Sanpaolo IMI S.p.A. merged into Intesa Sanpaolo S.p.A. 01/01/2007

ISTITUTO MOBILIARE ITALIANO S P A (ITALY)
Merged into Istituto Bancario San Paolo di Torino-Istituto Mobiliare Italiano S.p.A. 11/1/98
Each Sponsored ADR for Ordinary exchanged for (1.5675) Sponsored ADR's for Ordinary
Istituto Bancario San Paolo di Torino-Istituto Mobiliare Italiano S.p.A. name changed to Sanpaolo IMI S.p.A. 10/20/99 which merged into Intesa Sanpaolo S.p.A. 1/1/2007

ISTITUTO NAZIONALE DELLE ASSICURAZIONI S P A (ITALY)
Each Sponsored ADR for Ordinary 1,000 Lire par received distribution of (10) Unione Immobiliare S.p.A. Ordinary shares payable 10/31/1998 to holders of record 10/30/1998 Ex date - 11/03/1998
Note: Holders who did not elect to receive Ordinary shares prior to 11/09/1998 received $4.8778 cash proceeds of sale
ADR agreement terminated 04/25/2000
Each Sponsored ADR for Ordinary 1,000 Lire par exchanged for $25.4526 cash

ISTORAGE INC (DE)
Name changed to Gamers Ghost, Inc. 10/4/2005
Gamers Ghost, Inc. name changed to Apparel Manufacturing Associates, Inc. 2/7/2006

ISTORAGE NETWORKS INC (DE)
Name changed to Landbank Group, Inc. 02/09/2006
Landbank Group, Inc. name changed to Trist Holdings, Inc. 01/11/2008 which name changed to AtheroNova, Inc. 05/25/2010

ISTRON TECHNOLOGIES INC (CO)
Each share old Common $0.001 par exchanged for (0.05) share new Common $0.001 par 04/20/2007
Name changed to Nanometer Storage Corp. 04/21/2008
Nanometer Storage Corp. Name changed to Success Holding Group Corp. USA 01/09/2013

ISX RES INC (BC)
Reincorporated under the laws of Canada as Potash One Inc. 12/06/2007
(See Potash One Inc.)

ISYS MED INC (DE)
Name changed to FutureWorld Energy, Inc. 04/06/2009
FutureWorld Energy, Inc. name changed to FutureWorld Corp. 07/17/2014

IT BK GROUP COS INC (NV)
Charter permanently revoked 04/01/1997

IT GROUP INC (DE)
Plan of reorganization under Chapter 11 Federal Bankruptcy Code effective 04/30/2004
No stockholders' equity

IT HLDG S P A (ITALY)
ADR agreement terminated 03/12/2009
No ADR's remain outstanding

IT STAFFING LTD (ON)
Name changed to Thinkpath.com Inc. 02/24/2000
Thinkpath.com Inc. name changed to Thinkpath Inc. 06/06/2001
(See Thinkpath Inc.)

IT&E INTL GROUP (DE)
Reincorporated 03/02/2006
State of incorporation changed from (NV) to (DE) 03/02/2006
Name changed to Averion International Corp. 09/22/2006
(See Averion International Corp.)

ITA HLDGS INC (DE)
Liquidation completed
Each share Common $0.001 par received initial distribution of $0.0075 cash payable 10/27/2006 to holders of record 9/29/2006 Ex date - 10/30/2006
Each share Common $0.001 par received second and final distribution of $0.0041 cash payable 12/28/2006 to holders of record 9/29/2006 Ex date - 1/12/2007
Note: Certificates were not required to be surrendered and are without value

ITALCEMENTI FABRICHE RIUNITE SPA (ITALY)
Stock Dividends - 400% 09/24/1990; 4% payable 06/28/2000 to holders of record 05/22/2000
ADR agreement terminated 11/03/2016
Each ADR for Ordinary exchanged for $11.613333 cash

ITALIAN-AMERICAN FIRE & MARINE INSURANCE CO.
Liquidated 00/00/1931
Details not available

ITALIAN OVEN INC (PA)
Each share old Common 1¢ par exchanged for (100) shares new Common 1¢ par 05/22/2009
Name changed to Accredited Business Consolidators Corp. 01/07/2010

ITALIAN SUPERPOWER CORP. (DE)
Recapitalized as Wasatch Corp. 12/04/1952
$7 and $6 Preferred no par exchanged share for share
Each share Class A or B Common no par exchanged for (0.05) share Common no par
Wasatch Corp. merged into Atlas Corp. 05/31/1956
(See Atlas Corp.)

ITALMOBILIARE S P A (ITALY)
ADR agreement terminated 07/20/2017
No ADR's remain outstanding

ITALO-AMERICAN PETROLEUM CORP. (DE)
Name changed to Italo Petroleum Corp. of America 00/00/1928
Italo Petroleum Corp. of America name changed to Westates Petroleum Co. 00/00/1940
(See Westates Petroleum Co.)

ITALO PETROLEUM CORP. OF AMERICA (DE)
Name changed to Westates Petroleum Co. 00/00/1940
(See Westates Petroleum Co.)

ITALY FD INC (MD)
Completely liquidated 02/13/2003
Each share Common 1¢ par received first and final distribution of $6.6497 cash
Note: Certificates were not required to be surrendered and are without value

ITAU UNIBANCO BANCO MULTIPLO SA (BRAZIL)
Name changed to Itau Unibanco Holding S.A. 08/31/2009

ITC DELTACOM INC (DE)
Common 1¢ par split (2) for (1) by issuance of (1) additional share payable 09/04/1998 to holders of record 08/18/1998
Plan of reorganization under Chapter 11 Federal Bankruptcy Code effective 10/29/2002
Each share old Common 1¢ par exchanged for (0.00570033) share new Common 1¢ par
Note: Unexchanged certificates were cancelled and became without value 10/29/2003
Each share new Common 1¢ par exchanged again for (0.33333333) share new Common 1¢ par 09/13/2005
Acquired by EarthLink, Inc. 12/08/2010
Each share new Common 1¢ par exchanged for $3 cash

ITC HLDGS CORP (MI)
Common no par split (3) for (1) by issuance of (2) additional shares payable 02/28/2014 to holders of record 02/18/2014 Ex date - 03/03/2014
Merged into Fortis Inc. 10/14/2016
Each share Common no par exchanged for (0.752) share Common no par and $22.57 cash

ITC INTEGRATED SYS INC (NY)
Dissolved by proclamation 06/26/2002

ITC INTL TRADING CORP (BC)
Struck off register and declared dissolved for failure to file returns 07/15/1994

ITC LEARNING CORP (MD)
Chapter 11 bankruptcy proceedings converted to Chapter 7 on 12/13/2004
Stockholders' equity unlikely

ITC PPTYS GROUP LTD (BERMUDA)
ADR agreement terminated 01/24/2018
No ADR's remain outstanding

ITCO INVT FD LTD (ON)
Merged into Industrial Dividend Fund Ltd. 12/31/1977
Details not available

ITEC ATTRACTIONS INC (NV)
Each (381,426) shares old Common $0.001 exchanged for (1) share new Common $0.001 par 04/04/2006
Note: In effect holders received $0.27 cash per share and public interest was eliminated

ITEC ENVIRONMENTAL GROUP INC (DE)
Each share old Common 1¢ par exchanged for (0.0060606) share new Common 1¢ par 12/20/2004
Name changed to Eco2 Plastics, Inc. 03/26/2007
(See Eco2 Plastics, Inc.)

ITEC-MINERAL INC (QC)
Recapitalized as Electromed Inc. 09/25/2000
Each share Common no par exchanged for (0.13430563) share Common no par
Electromed Inc. recapitalized as Evolved Digital Systems Inc. 10/10/2003

ITECH CAP CORP (YT)
Name changed to Sirit Inc. 05/05/2003
(See Sirit Inc.)

ITEK CORP (DE)
Reincorporated 02/10/1960
Common $1 par split (5) for (1) by issuance of (4) additional shares 01/30/1959
State of incorporation changed from (MA) to (DE) 02/10/1960
Merged into Litton Industries, Inc. 03/04/1983
Each share Common no par exchanged for $48 cash

ITEKNIK HLDG CORP (NV)
Reincorporated under the laws of Wyoming 11/30/2010

ITEL CORP NEW (DE)
$4 Conv. Exchangeable Class B Preferred Ser. B $1 par called for redemption 8/19/87
$8.64 Preferred Class B Ser. A $1 par called for redemption 7/1/88
$3.375 Conv. Exchangeable Class B Preferred Ser. C $1 par called for redemption 8/30/93
Name changed to Anixter International Inc. 9/1/95

ITEL CORP OLD (DE)
Reorganized under Chapter 11 Federal Bankruptcy Code as Itel Corp. (New) 9/19/83
Each share $1.44 Preferred $1 par exchanged for (0.387) share Common $1 par
Each share Common $1 par exchanged for (0.087) share Common $1 par
Itel Corp. (New) name changed to Anixter International Inc. 9/1/95

ITELCO CORP (DE)
Recapitalized as International Design Group, Inc. 03/31/1987
Each share Common $0.001 par exchanged for (0.5) share Common 5¢ par
(See International Design Group, Inc.)

ITEMUS INC (BC)
Filed Notice of Intention under Bankruptcy and Insolvency Act 07/31/2001
No stockholders' equity

ITEQ INC (DE)
Merged into HNT Inc. 07/02/2001
Each share Common $0.001 par exchanged for $0.03 cash

ITERATED SYS INC (GA)
Name changed to Mediabin Inc. 02/09/2001
(See Mediabin Inc.)

ITERATION ENERGY LTD (AB)
Merged into Chinook Energy Inc. (Old) 07/05/2010
Each share Common no par exchanged for (0.5631) share Common no par
Note: Unexchanged certificates were cancelled and became without value 06/29/2015
(See Chinook Energy Inc. (Old))

ITERIS HLDGS INC (DE)
Name changed to Iteris, Inc., Class A Common 10¢ par and Class B Common 10¢ par reclassified as Common 10¢ par 10/22/2004

ITEX BARTER SYS INC (NV)
Recapitalized as Itex Corp. 4/5/91
Each share Common $0.001 par exchanged for (0.1) share Common 1¢ par

ITHACA BANCORP INC (NY)
Acquired by First Empire State Corp. 12/1/94
Each share Common 1¢ par exchanged for $19 cash

ITHACA ENERGY INC (AB)
Acquired by Delek Group Ltd. (New) 06/07/2017
Each share Common no par exchanged for $1.95 cash

ITHACA GROWTH FUND, INC. (NY)
Completely liquidated 08/27/1973
Each share Capital Stock $1 par received first and final distribution of $3.4052294 cash

ITHACA INDS INC NEW (DE)
Recapitalized as American Uranium Mining Inc. 07/05/2007
Each share Common 1¢ par exchanged for (0.02222222) share Common 1¢ par
American Uranium Mining Inc. name changed to F3 Technologies, Inc. 09/29/2008 which name changed to Here to Serve Holding Corp. 11/05/2013

ITHAKA ACQUISITION CORP (DE)
Name changed to Alsius Corp. 06/25/2007
(See Alsius Corp.)

I3 MOBILE INC (DE)
Issue Information - 5,100,000 shares COM offered at $16 per share on 04/06/2000
Merged ino ACE*COMM Corp. 12/08/2003
Each share Common 1¢ par exchanged for (0.18755089) share Common 1¢ par
*(See ACE*COMM Corp.)*

ITI CORP (DE)
Common $1.50 par changed to 10¢ par 01/21/1972
Merged into ITI Corp. (OH) 01/28/1977
Each share Common 10¢ par exchanged for (1) share Common 10¢ par
Note: Holders of (24) or fewer shares received $1 cash per share

ITI ED CORP (CANADA)
Dissolved 09/19/2005
No stockholders' equity

ITI TECHNOLOGIES INC (DE)
Merged into Interlogix, Inc. 5/3/2000
Each share Common 1¢ par exchanged for (1) share Common 1¢ par
Interlogix, Inc. merged into General Electric Co. 2/21/2002

ITI WORLD INVT GROUP INC (AB)
Name changed to First Choice Products Inc. 01/30/2009

ITIS HLDGS INC (NV)
SEC revoked common stock registration 08/16/2011

ITIS INC (DE)
Reorganized under the laws of Nevada as ITIS Holdings Inc. 09/18/2002
Each share Common $0.001 par exchanged for (0.1) share Common $0.001 par
(See ITIS Holdings Inc.)

ITL CAP CORP (BC)
Recapitalized as MPH Ventures Corp. 12/19/2005
Each share Common no par exchanged for (0.2) share Common no par
MPH Ventures Corp. name changed to Cuba Ventures Corp. 03/21/2016 which name changed to CUV Ventures Corp. 03/01/2018

ITLA CAP CORP (DE)
Name changed to Imperial Capital Bancorp, Inc. 08/03/2007
(See Imperial Capital Bancorp, Inc.)

ITLINKZ GROUP INC (DE)
Recapitalized as China YCT International Group, Inc. 11/26/2007
Each share Common $0.001 par exchanged for (0.03571428) share Common $0.001 par
China YCT International Group, Inc. name changed to Spring Pharmaceutical Group, Inc. 08/31/2018

ITM CORP (ON)
Recapitalized as IMC Integrated Marketing Communications Inc. 08/06/1987
Each share Common no par exchanged for (0.13333333) share Common no par
(See IMC Integrated Marketing Communications Inc.)

ITN TECHNOLOGIES INC (AB)
Name changed to Softwex Technologies Inc. 04/02/1998

ITO YOKADO LTD (JAPAN)
Each old ADR for Common 50 Yen par exchanged for (0.5) new ADR for Common 50 Yen par 7/7/77
Stock Dividends - 10% 6/14/78; 10% 6/11/79; 10% 6/5/80; 10% 6/5/81; 10% 6/7/82; 10% 5/18/83; 10% 5/18/84; 10% 5/15/85; 10% 5/16/86; 10% 5/2/89
ADR agreement terminated 5/30/2003
Each new ADR for Common 50 Yen par exchanged for $30.94975 cash
ADR agreement terminated 9/12/2005
Each 2003 ADR for Common exchanged for $30.94975 cash

ITOCO MNG CORP (NV)
Each share old Common $0.001 par exchanged for (0.03333333) share new Common $0.001 par 02/07/2018
Name changed to Itoco Inc. 05/08/2018

ITOGON SUYOC MINES INC (PHILIPPINES)
Common 10 Centavos par reclassified as Class A, 1 Centavo par or Class B, 1 Centavo par and a 25% stock dividend paid 10/7/75
Note: Philippine nationals may hold Class A and Class B shares; Non-Philippine Nationals may hold Class B shares only
Name changed to ISM Communications Corp. and Class A 1 Centavo par and Class B 1 Centavo par reclassified as Common P0.01 par 6/7/2002

ITOH C & CO LTD (JAPAN)
Name changed to Itochu Corp. 10/1/92

ITOS INC (NV)
Recapitalized as Satellite Phone Source Inc. (NV) 08/10/2004
Each share Common $0.001 par exchanged for (0.1) share Common $0.001 par
Satellite Phone Source Inc. (NV) reincorporated in Delaware as Vision Works Media Group, Inc. 04/06/2005 which name changed to Perihelion Global, Inc. (DE) 10/25/2006 which reincorporated in Nevada 04/01/2008 which recapitalized as Nymet Holdings Inc. 04/21/2009

ITP ENERGY CORP (NV)
Name changed to Tristar Acquisition Group 02/26/2018

ITP THERMAL PACKAGING INC (BC)
Recapitalized as Stratford Ventures Ltd. 08/08/1996
Each share Common no par exchanged for (0.11111111) share Common no par
Stratford Ventures Ltd. name changed to MRC Metall Resources Corp. (BC) 08/29/1997 which reincorporated in Canada as Mount Dakota Energy Corp. 08/24/1988 which reincorporated in British Columbia 08/07/2015

ITRACKR TECHNOLOGIES INC (FL)
Name changed to Delivery Technology Solutions, Inc. 03/16/2010

ITRON CORP (CA)
Reorganized as Newport Laboratories, Inc. 9/1/71
Each share Common $1 par exchanged for (1/3) share Common 1¢ par
Newport Laboratories, Inc. name changed to Newport Electronics Inc. 6/27/79
(See Newport Electronics Inc.)

ITS NETWORKS INC (FL)
Each share old Common $0.001 par exchanged for (0.5) share new Common $0.001 par 12/29/2003
Name changed to Teleconnect, Inc. 2/28/2005

ITSA LTD (CAYMAN ISLANDS)
Company terminated registration of Ordinary stock and is no longer public as of 09/26/2005

ITT CDA LTD (CANADA)
9% Retractable 1st Preferred Ser. 1 no par called for redemption 01/31/1990
7.2% Retractable 1st Preferred Ser. 2 no par called for redemption 01/31/1991
Public interest eliminated

ITT CONSUMER SVCS CORP (DE)
2nd Preferred Ser. B $1 par converted into Conv. Preferred Ser. A $1 par in 1971
Conv. Preferred Ser. A $1 par called for redemption 12/20/85
Public interest eliminated

ITT CORP (DE)
$4 Conv. Preferred Ser. H no par called for redemption 06/08/1987
$4 Conv. Preferred Ser. J no par called for redemption 06/08/1987
$4.50 Conv. Preferred Ser. I no par called for redemption 06/08/1987
$4 Conv. Preferred Ser. K no par called for redemption 06/18/1992
$5 Conv. Preferred Ser. O no par called for redemption 06/18/1992
$2.25 Conv. Preferred Ser. N no par called for redemption 06/18/1995
Reorganized under the laws of Indiana as ITT Industries, Inc. 12/19/1995
Each share Common $1 par exchanged for (1) share ITT Hartford Group Inc. Common no par, (1) share ITT Corp. (NV) Common no par and (1) share ITT Industries, Inc. Common $1 par
(See each company's listing)

ITT CORP (IN)
Name changed 07/01/2006
Old Common $1 par split (2) for (1) by issuance of (1) additional share payable 02/21/2006 to holders of record 02/07/2006 Ex date - 02/22/2006
Name changed from ITT Industries, Inc. to ITT Corp. 07/01/2006
Each share old Common $1 par received distribution of (1) share Exelis Inc. Common 1¢ par and (1) share Xylem Inc. Common 1¢ par payable 10/31/2011 to holders of record 10/17/2011
Each share old Common $1 par

FINANCIAL INFORMATION, INC.   ITT-IVE

exchanged for (0.5) share new Common $1 par 10/31/2011
Name changed to ITT Inc. 05/17/2016

ITT CORP (NV)
Merged into Starwood Hotels & Resorts 02/24/1998
Each share Common no par exchanged for (1.543) Paired Certificates
Starwood Hotels & Resorts reorganized as Starwood Hotels & Resorts Worldwide, Inc. 01/06/1999

ITT HARTFORD GROUP INC (DE)
Name changed to Hartford Financial Services Group, Inc. 05/02/1997

ITT LIFE INSURANCE CO. (NY)
Acquired by ITT Hamilton Life Insurance Co. 12/08/1969
Each share Capital Stock $2 par exchanged for $12 cash

ITTIERRE HLDG S P A (ITALY)
Name changed to IT Holding S.p.A. 04/28/2002
(See IT Holding S.p.A.)

ITUNA CAP CORP (BC)
Reincorporated under the laws of Alberta as Tarku Resources Ltd. 08/28/2014

ITURF INC (DE)
Issue Information - 4,200,000 shares CL A offered at $22 per share on 04/09/1999
Under plan of merger name changed to dELiA*s Corp. 11/20/2000
(See dELiA*s Corp.)

ITUS CORP (DE)
Each share old Common 1¢ par exchanged for (0.04) share new Common 1¢ par 06/26/2015
Name changed to Anixa Biosciences, Inc. 10/01/2018

ITV GAMES INC (AB)
Delisted from Toronto Venture Stock Exchange 06/05/2002

I2 TECHNOLOGIES INC (DE)
Old Common $0.00025 par split (2) for (1) by issuance of (1) additional share payable 06/02/1998 to holders of record 05/26/1998
Old Common $0.00025 par split (2) for (1) by issuance of (1) additional share payable 02/17/2000 to holders of record 02/03/2000
Old Common $0.00025 par split (2) for (1) by issuance of (1) additional share payable 12/05/2000 to holders of record 11/28/2000 Ex date - 12/06/2000
Each share old Common $0.00025 par exchanged for (0.04) share new Common $0.00025 par 02/17/2005
Merged into JDA Software Group, Inc. 01/28/2010
Each share new Common $0.00025 par exchanged for (0.2562) share Common 1¢ par and $12.70 cash
(See JDA Software Group, Inc.)

I2 TELECOM INTL INC (WA)
Recapitalized as Geos Communications, Inc. 10/01/2009
Each share Common no par exchanged for (0.1) share Common no par
(See Geos Communications, Inc.)

I2CORP COM (NV)
SEC revoked preferred and common stock registrations 07/27/2011

ITX CORP (DE)
Charter cancelled and declared inoperative and void for non-payment of taxes 06/24/1992

ITXC CORP (DE)
Merged into Teleglobe International Holdings Ltd. 6/1/2004
Each share Common $0.0001 par exchanged for (0.25) share Common U.S. $0.01 par

(See Teleglobe International Holdings Ltd.)

IU INTL CORP (MD)
Common $1.25 par changed to $1.20 par 12/07/1979
$1.25 Conv. Preferred no par called for redemption 09/30/1983
Special Conv. Stock Ser. A no par called for redemption 09/30/1983
$1.36 Conv. Preferred no par called for redemption 09/30/1983
Common $1.20 par changed to $1.15 par 11/21/1983
Acquired by a group of investors 05/06/1988
Each share Common $1.15 par exchanged for $22.25 cash
$5 Preferred no par called for redemption 05/10/1988
Public interest eliminated

IUB CAP TR (DE)
8.75% Trust Preferred Securities called for redemption at $10 on 4/1/2003

IVAC CORP (DE)
Each share old Common 10¢ par exchanged for (0.2) share new Common 10¢ par 11/21/1973
Merged into Lilly (Eli) & Co. 11/30/1997
Each share new Common 10¢ par exchanged for (0.95) share Common 62-1/2¢ par

IVACO INC (CANADA)
Name changed 12/31/1978
Name changed 08/18/1980
Common no par split (2) for (1) by issuance of (1) additional share 07/20/1973
Common no par reclassified as Conv. Class A Common no par 01/28/1975
Name changed from Ivaco Industries Ltd. to Ivaco Ltd. 12/31/1978
6% Conv. Preferred Ser. A $50 par called for redemption 07/06/1979
Conv. Class A Common no par reclassified as Common no par 07/06/1979
Conv. Class B Common no par reclassified as Common no par 07/06/1979
6% Conv. Preferred Ser. B $50 par called for redemption 05/21/1980
Name changed from Ivaco Ltd. to Ivaco Inc. 08/18/1980
8.85% Preferred Ser. C $50 par reclassified as $4.425 Preferred Ser. C no par 09/29/1982
Common no par reclassified as Conv. Class B no par 06/18/1982
Adjustable Rate Exchangeable 2nd Preferred Ser. 4 no par called for redemption at $32 plus $0.57 accrued dividend consisting of $0.261 cash and $0.309 of Ser. 5 2nd Preferred on 07/02/2002
Stock Dividends - in Class A Subordinate to holders of Class A Subordinate 12% 08/19/1982; in Conv. Class B to holders of Conv. Class B 10% 08/19/1982
Assets sold for the benefit of creditors 08/19/2004
Shares deemed worthless 03/13/2009

IVACO INDS INC (DE)
Name changed to Ivax Corp. (DE) 12/10/1987
IVAX Corp. (DE) reincorporated in Florida 07/30/1993
(See IVAX Corp.)

IVANA CAP CORP (CANADA)
Recapitalized as First Ivana Technologies Ltd. 09/29/1992
Each share Class A Common no par exchanged for (0.2) share Class A Common no par
First Ivana Technologies Ltd. recapitalized as Vitamed Biopharmaceuticals Ltd. 04/06/1993 which name changed to Receptagen Ltd. (Canada) 07/12/1993 which

reorganized in Florida as Spantel Communications Inc. 10/16/2001 which recapitalized as Systems America, Inc. 05/27/2010
(See Systems America, Inc.)

IVANA VENTURES INC (BC)
Reincorporated 11/02/2005
Place of incorporation changed from (AB) to (BC) 11/02/2005
Name changed to Ely Gold & Minerals Inc. 07/08/2008
Ely Gold & Minerals Inc. name changed to Ely Gold Royalties Inc. 11/22/2017

IVANCIE WINES INC (CO)
Declared defunct and inoperative for failure to pay taxes and file annual reports 1/31/77

IVANHOE AUSTRALIA LTD (AUSTRALIA)
Name changed to Inova Resources Ltd. 07/08/2013
(See Inova Resources Ltd.)

IVANHOE ENERGY INC (YT)
Each share old Common no par exchanged for (0.33333333) share new Common no par 04/26/2013
Each share new Common no par exchanged again for (0.14285714) share new Common no par 08/18/2014
Discharged from receivership 12/12/2016
No stockholders' equity

IVANHOE FOODS, INC. (NY)
Charter revoked for failure to file reports and pay fees 12/15/55

IVANHOE MINES LTD (CANADA)
Name changed to Turquoise Hill Resources Ltd. 08/08/2012

IVANPLATS LTD (BC)
Name changed to Ivanhoe Mines Ltd. 09/09/2013

IVANY MNG INC (DE)
Name changed to Ivany Nguyen, Inc. 02/16/2010
Ivany Nguyen, Inc. name changed to Myriad Interactive Media, Inc. 07/25/2011

IVANY NGUYEN INC (DE)
Name changed to Myriad Interactive Media, Inc. 07/25/2011

IVASHUK MFG CORP (FL)
Name changed to Control Laser Corp. (FL) 11/26/1969
Control Laser Corp. (FL) reincorporated in Delaware as Control Laser International Corp. 01/01/1987 which merged into Quantronix Corp. 11/22/1988 which was acquired by Excel Technology, Inc. 10/01/1992
(See Excel Technology, Inc.)

IVAX CORP (FL)
Reincorporated 7/30/93
Common 10¢ par split (3) for (2) by issuance of (0.5) additional share 3/25/91
Common 10¢ par split (3) for (2) by issuance of (0.5) additional share 11/15/91
State of incorporation changed from (DE) to (FL) 7/30/93
Common 10¢ par split (3) for (2) by issuance of (0.5) additional share payable 2/22/2000 to holders of record 2/1/2000
Common 10¢ par split (5) for (4) by issuance of (0.25) additional share payable 5/18/2001 to holders of record 5/1/2001 Ex date - 5/21/2001
Common 10¢ par split (5) for (4) by issuance of (0.25) additional share payable 8/24/2004 to holders of record 8/10/2004
Merged into Teva Pharmaceutical Industries Ltd. 1/26/2006
Each share Common 10¢ par exchanged for $26 cash

IVAX DIAGNOSTICS INC (DE)
Name changed to ERBA Diagnostics, Inc. 06/18/2012

IVB FINL CORP (PA)
Acquired by Fidelcor, Inc. 3/31/86
Each share Common $5 par exchanged for $47 cash

IVC INDS INC (DE)
Each share old Common 1¢ par exchanged for (0.125) share new Common 1¢ par 07/12/1999
Merged into Inverness Medical Innovations, Inc. 03/19/2002
Each share new Common 1¢ par exchanged for $2.50 cash

IVCI CORP (DE)
Voluntarily dissolved 4/13/92
Details not available

IVECON CORP (DE)
Common $0.0001 par split (50) for (1) by issuance of (49) additional shares payable 05/06/2009 to holders of record 05/01/2009 Ex date - 05/07/2009
Name changed to Proper Power & Energy Inc. 05/07/2009
(See Proper Power & Energy Inc.)

IVEDA CORP (NV)
Name changed to Iveda Solutions, Inc. 04/25/2011

IVEN S A (BRAZIL)
GDR agreement terminated 10/28/2005
Each Reg. S Sponsored GDR for Preference exchanged for (100) Preference shares
Each Reg. S Sponsored GDR for Common exchanged for (100) Common shares
Note: Unexchanged GDR's will be sold and proceeds, if any, held for claim after 10/27/2006

IVERNIA INC (NB)
Reincorporated 07/23/2008
Place of incorporation changed from (NB) to (Canada) 07/23/2008 07/23/2008
Recapitalized as LeadFX Inc. 11/18/2015
Each share Common no par exchanged for (0.01333333) share Common no par

IVERNIA WEST INC (NB)
Recapitalized as Ivernia Inc. (NB) 07/08/2004
Each share Common no par exchanged for (0.2) share Common no par
Ivernia Inc. (NB) reincorporated in Canada 07/23/2008

IVERS-LEE CO. (DE)
Stock Dividend - 100% 3/15/48
Completely liquidated 11/8/67
Each share Common 25¢ par exchanged for first and final distribution of (1.45) shares Becton, Dickinson & Co. Common $1 par

IVERSON TECHNOLOGY CORP (DE)
Common 1¢ par split (3) for (2) by issuance of (0.5) additional share 03/09/1987
Name changed to D'Brit Corp. 12/05/1995
(See D'Brit Corp.)

IVEST FD INC (MA)
Reincorporated 04/01/1973
Common $1 par split (2) for (1) by issuance of (1) additional share 12/31/1965
Common $1 par split (3) for (2) by issuance of (0.5) additional share 04/14/1972
State of incorporation changed from (MD) to (MA) 04/01/1973
Name changed to Vanguard World Fund, Inc. (MA) and Common $1 par reclassified as U.S. Growth Portfolio $1 par 10/10/1985
Vanguard World Fund, Inc. (MA)

reorganized in Delaware as Vanguard World Fund 06/30/1998

IVEX PACKAGING CORP (DE)
Each share Common 1¢ par received distribution of (0.2) share Packaging Dynamics Corp. Common 1¢ par payable 07/01/2002 to holders of record 06/28/2002
Merged into Alcoa, Inc. 07/01/2002
Each share Common 1¢ par exchanged for $21.50 cash

IVEY CORP (MN)
Acquired by Academic Systems & Management Corp. 10/11/68
Each share Common 1¢ par exchanged for (1) share Common 10¢ par
(See Academic Systems & Management Corp.)

IVEY J B & CO (NC)
Common $5 par changed to $2.50 par and (1) additional share issued 6/9/72
5% Preferred $100 par called for redemption 1/2/73
Merged into Field (Marshall) & Co. (DE) 10/21/80
Each share Common $2.50 par exchanged for (1) share $1.50 Conv. Preferred Ser. C $1 par
(See Field (Marshall) & Co. (DE))

IVEY MED SYS LTD (CANADA)
Proclaimed dissolved for failure to file reports 12/16/1980

IVEY PPTYS INC (NC)
Stock Dividends - 50% 4/1/85; 50% 4/1/87
Merged into BAC, Inc. 11/6/95
Each share Common 1¢ par exchanged for $32.45 cash

IVF AMER INC (DE)
Name changed to IntegraMed America, Inc. 06/11/1996
(See IntegraMed America, Inc.)

IVG CORP (AB)
Recapitalized as IVG Enterprises Ltd. 07/24/2002
Each share Common no par exchanged for (0.25) share Common no par
(See IVG Enterprises Ltd.)

IVG CORP (DE)
Recapitalized as Group Management Corp. (DE) 12/17/2001
Each share Common $0.0001 par exchanged for (0.05) share Common $0.0001 par
Group Management Corp. (DE) reincorporated in Georgia as Silver Screen Studios, Inc. 09/05/2003 which name changed to Global 1 Investment Holdings Corp. 11/13/2006
(See Global 1 Investment Holdings Corp.)

IVG ENTERPRISES LTD (AB)
Delisted from Toronto Venture Stock Exchange 02/08/2008

IVI CHECKMATE CORP (DE)
Merged into Ingenico S.A. 08/08/2001
Each share Common 1¢ par exchanged for $3.30 cash

IVI CHECKMATE LTD (CANADA)
Merged into Ingenico S.A. 08/08/2001
Each Exchangeable Share exchanged for USD$3.30 cash

IVI COMMUNICATIONS INC (NV)
Each share old Common $0.001 par exchanged for (0.0025) share new Common $0.001 par 09/04/2008
SEC revoked common stock registration 05/22/2014

IVI PUBG INC (MN)
Name changed to OnHealth Network Co. 06/16/1998
OnHealth Network Co. merged into WebMD Corp. 09/12/2000 which name changed to Emdeon Corp.

10/17/2005 which name changed to HLTH Corp. 05/21/2007 which merged into WebMD Health Corp. 10/23/2009
(See WebMD Health Corp.)

IVIDEONOW INC (DE)
Reorganized under the laws of Florida as 99 Cent Stuff, Inc. 9/15/2003
Each share Common $0.001 exchanged for (0.00833333) share Common $0.001 par
(See 99 Cent Stuff, Inc.)

IVIE ELECTRS INC (UT)
Acquired by Cetec Corp. (CA) 06/12/1984
Each share Common 5¢ par exchanged for $0.03 cash

IVILLAGE INC (DE)
Issue Information - 3,650,000 shares COM offered at $24 per share on 03/18/1999
Merged into General Electric Co. 5/15/2006
Each share Common 1¢ par exchanged for $8.50 cash

IVISION GROUP LTD (NV)
Recapitalized as Tire International Environmental Solutions Inc. 02/12/2007
Each share Common $0.001 par exchanged for (0.01) share Common $0.001 par

IVOICE INC (DE)
Name changed 8/18/2001
Name changed from iVoice.Com to iVoice, Inc. and Common 1¢ par changed to $0.0001 par 8/18/2001
Reincorporated under the laws of New Jersey and Common $0.0001 par changed to no par 5/5/2003

IVOICE TECHNOLOGY INC (NJ)
Name changed to B Green Innovations, Inc. 12/31/2009
B Green Innovations, Inc. name changed to 024 Pharma, Inc. 11/10/2016

IVOICEIDEAS INC (NV)
Name changed to ZhongKe Holdings Co. 04/12/2018
ZhongKe Holdings Co. recapitalized as Worry Free Holdings Co. 10/04/2018

IVORY CAP CORP (CO)
Each share old Common no par exchanged for (0.002) share new Common no par 10/11/1999
Reorganized under the laws of Delaware as Chelsea Therapeutics International, Ltd. 07/29/2005
Each share new Common no par exchanged for (0.11111111) share Common $0.0001 par
(See Chelsea Therapeutics International, Ltd.)

IVORY ENERGY INC (AB)
Reincorporated 06/22/2007
Place of incorporation changed from (BC) to (AB) 06/22/2007
Merged into Emergo Energy Inc. 03/31/2009
Each share Common no par exchanged for $0.03782 cash

IVORY OILS & MINERALS INC (BC)
Recapitalized as Ivory Energy Inc. (BC) 06/27/2006
Each share Common no par exchanged for (0.5) share Common no par
Ivory Energy Inc. (BC) reincorporated in Alberta 06/22/2007
(See Ivory Energy Inc.)

IVOW INC (DE)
Each share old Common 1¢ par exchanged for (0.1) share new Common 1¢ par 10/11/2005
Name changed to Sound Health Solutions, Inc. 10/29/2007

IVP TECHNOLOGY CORP (NV)
Each share old Common $0.001 par

exchanged for (0.005) share new Common $0.001 par 03/15/1996
Each share new Common $0.001 par exchanged again for (0.08333333) share new Common $0.001 par 01/31/1997
Recapitalized as ActiveCore Technologies, Inc. 03/01/2005
Each share Common $0.001 par exchanged for (0.1) share Common $0.001 par
(See ActiveCore Technologies, Inc.)

IVRNET INC OLD (AB)
Each share old Common no par exchanged for (0.2) share new Common no par 8/15/2002
Merged into IVRnet Inc. (New) 7/31/2003
Each share new Common no par exchanged for (0.42354934) share Common no par

IVS INTELLIGENT VEH SYS INC (BC)
Delisted from Toronto Venture Stock Exchange 06/16/2004

IVT SOFTWARE INC (NV)
Name changed to HWI Global, Inc. 05/27/2011
(See HWI Global, Inc.)

IVY CAP CORP (AB)
Name changed to AdvantEdge International Inc. 08/27/1996

IVY CORP (DE)
Merged into Koppers Co., Inc. 1/24/79
Each share Common 10¢ par exchanged for (0.6) share Common $1.25 par
(See Koppers Co., Inc.)

IVY GROWTH FD (MA)
Reincorporated 04/01/1984
Common $1 par changed to 40¢ par and (1.5) additional shares issued 04/18/1969
Name changed from Ivy Fund, Inc. to Ivy Growth Fund, state of incorporation changed from (DE) to (MA) and Common 40¢ par reclassified as Shares of Bene. Int. no par 04/01/1984
Reorganized as Waddell & Reed Advisors Funds Inc. Accumulative Fund Class A $0.001 par 06/10/2003
Details not available

IVY GROWTH WITH INCOME FD (MA)
Merged into Ivy Funds 06/27/2000
Details not available

IVY INSTITUTIONAL INVESTORS FUND (MA)
Name changed to Ivy Growth With Income Fund 04/30/1990
(See Ivy Growth With Income Fund)

IVY INTL FD (MA)
Merged into Ivy Fund 08/12/1993
Details not available

IVY MICROCOMPUTER CORP (MA)
Proclaimed dissolved for failure to file reports and pay fees 11/14/94

IVY MONEY MKT FD (MA)
Merged into Ivy Fund 01/01/1996
Details not available

IVYNET CORP (ON)
Recapitalized as Saratoga Capital Corp. 08/25/2000
Each share Common no par exchanged for (0.1) share Common no par
(See Saratoga Capital Corp.)

IWAVE COM INC (CANADA)
Recapitalized as iWave Information Systems Inc. 06/28/2002
Each share Common no par exchanged for (1/3) share Common no par
iWave Information Systems Inc. name changed to First Factor Developments Inc. 07/22/2005 which name changed to Millrock Resources Inc. (Canada)

08/14/2007 which reincorporated in British Columbia 07/24/2008

IWAVE INFORMATION SYS INC (CANADA)
Name changed to First Factor Developments Inc. 07/22/2005
First Factor Developments Inc. name changed to Millrock Resources Inc. (Canada) 08/14/2007 which reincorporated in British Columbia 07/24/2008

IWC COMMUNICATIONS LTD (ON)
Recapitalized as Radio IWC Ltd. 04/07/1978
Each share Common no par exchanged for (0.1) share Common no par
(See Radio IWC Ltd.)

IWC INDUSTRIES LTD. (ON)
Name changed to IWC Communications Ltd. 12/05/1972
IWC Communications Ltd. recapitalized as Radio IWC Ltd. 04/07/1978
(See Radio IWC Ltd.)

IWC RES CORP (IN)
Merged into NIPSCO Industries, Inc. 3/25/97
Each share Common no par exchanged for (0.8162) share Common no par

IWEB CORP (NV)
Reorganized as National Health Scan Inc. 05/09/2002
Each share Common $0.001 par exchanged for (3) shares Common $0.001 par
National Health Scan Inc. name changed to Gaensel Energy Group, Inc. 02/24/2015

IWEB GROUP INC (CANADA)
Acquired by Novacap Technologies III, L.P. 06/16/2011
Each share Common no par exchanged for $1.50 cash
Note: Unexchanged certificates were cancelled and became without value 06/16/2017

IWERKS ENTMT INC (DE)
Each share old Common $0.001 par exchanged for (0.28571428) share new Common $0.001 par 01/18/2000
Merged into SimEx Inc. 01/10/2002
Each share new Common $0.001 par exchanged for $0.63 cash

IWG TECHNOLOGIES INC (BC)
Acquired by 1096777 B.C. Ltd. 01/25/2017
Each share Common no par exchanged for $0.43 cash
Note: Unexchanged certificates will be cancelled and become without value 01/25/2023

IWI HOLDING LTD (BRITISH VIRGIN ISLANDS)
Issue Information - 1,500,000 shares COM offered at $8.50 per share on 12/16/1994
Each share old Common no par exchanged for (0.02) share new Common no par 09/21/2009
Reincorporated under the laws of Wyoming as Unilava Corp. 11/10/2009

IWIN COM INC
Merged into Uproar Inc. 10/20/2000
Each share Preferred Ser. B exchanged for (0.8341) share Common 1¢ par
Uproar Inc. merged into Flipside, Inc. 3/21/2000

IWL COMMUNICATIONS INC (TX)
Issue Information - 1,450,000 shares COM offered at $6 per share on 06/12/1997
Under plan of reorganization each share Common 1¢ par automatically became (1) share Caprock

Communications Corp. Common 1¢ par 08/26/1998
Caprock Communications Corp. merged into McLeodUSA Inc. 12/08/2000
(See McLeodUSA Inc.)

IWO HLDGS INC (DE)
Merged into Sprint Nextel Corp. 10/20/2005
Each share new Common 1¢ par exchanged for $42.50 cash

IWORLD PROJS & SYS INC (NV)
Chapter 7 bankruptcy proceedings terminated 03/31/2009
No stockholders' equity

IWT TESORO CORP (NV)
Reincorporated under the laws of Oklahoma as Tesoro Distributors, Inc. 06/17/2009
Tesoro Distributors, Inc. name changed to Tesoro Enterprises, Inc. 03/11/2010

IX CAP INC (BC)
Name changed to P.Z. Resort Systems, Inc. 07/28/2000
P.Z. Resort Systems, Inc. name changed to RSI International Systems, Inc. 01/26/2005

IX SYS INC (NY)
Recapitalized as Guwo Holdings, Inc. 02/02/2007
Each share Common $0.001 par exchanged for (0.01) share Common $0.001 par
Guwo Holdings, Inc. name changed to QED Connect, Inc. 07/23/2007

IXATA GROUP INC (DE)
Name changed to RFP Express Inc. 7/25/2001

IXC COMMUNICATIONS INC (DE)
Each share 7.250% Jr. Conv. Preferred no par received distribution of (0.018125) additional share payable 09/30/1997 to holders of record 09/15/1997
Merged into Cincinnati Bell Inc. (Old) 11/09/1999
Each 6.75% Depositary Preferred exchanged for (1) 6.75% Depositary Preferred
Each share 7.25% Jr. Conv. Preferred no par exchanged for (1) share 7.25% Jr. Conv. Preferred no par
Each share Common 1¢ par exchanged for (2.0976) shares Common 1¢ par
Stock Dividend - in 12.50% Exchangeable Jr. Preferred Ser. B to holders of 12.50% Exchangeable Jr. Preferred Ser. B 3.125% payable 11/15/1999 to holders of record 11/01/1999
Name changed to Broadwing Inc. 11/15/1999
Broadwing Inc. merged into Cincinnati Bell Inc. (New) 05/16/2003

IXI MOBILE INC (DE)
SEC revoked common stock registration 06/17/2013

IXIA (CA)
Acquired by Keysight Technologies, Inc. 04/18/2017
Each share Common no par exchanged for $19.65 cash

IXIS ADVISOR CASH MGMT TR (MA)
Name changed to Natixis Cash Management Trust 06/20/2007
(See Natixis Cash Management Trust)

IXL ENTERPRISES INC (DE)
Issue Information - 6,000,000 shares COM offered at $12 per share on 06/02/1999
Merged into Scient, Inc. 11/8/2001
Each share Common 1¢ par exchanged for (1) share Common $0.0001 par
(See Scient, Inc.)

IXL URANIUM CORP. (NV)
Name changed to Industrial Dynamics, Inc. 10/11/1969
(See Industrial Dynamics, Inc.)

IXNET INC (DE)
Merged into Global Crossing Ltd. 6/15/2000
Each share Common 1¢ par exchanged for (1.184) shares Common 1¢ par
(See Global Crossing Ltd.)

IXORA COMMUNICATION SYS INC (BC)
Struck off register and declared dissolved for failure to file returns 10/4/91

IXOS SOFTWARE A G (GERMANY)
Acquired by OpenText Corp. 04/02/2004
Each Sponsored ADR for Ordinary no par exchanged for $11.0955 cash

IXTAL INTL TECHNOLOGIES CORP (BC)
Recapitalized as Job Industries Ltd. 8/28/92
Each share Common no par exchanged for (1/3) share Common no par

IXYS CORP (DE)
Common 1¢ par split (2) for (1) by issuance of (1) additional share payable 08/10/2000 to holders of record 07/20/2000 Ex date - 08/11/2000
Acquired by Littelfuse, Inc. 01/17/2018
Each share Common 1¢ par exchanged for $23 cash

IZEA HLDGS INC (NV)
Name changed to IZEA Inc. 02/22/2012
IZEA Inc. name changed to IZEA Worldwide, Inc. 08/23/2018

IZEA INC (NV)
Each share old Common $0.0001 par exchanged for (0.025) share new Common $0.0001 par 08/01/2012
Each share new Common $0.0001 par exchanged again for (0.05) share new
Name changed to IZEA Worldwide, Inc. 08/23/2018

IZONE INTL LTD (BC)
Delisted from Toronto Venture Stock Exchange 03/03/1997

J

J. & O. LIQUIDATING CO. (DE)
Liquidation completed
Each share Common $1 par exchanged for initial distribution of (0.393624) share Beatrice Foods Co. Common no par and (1) Ctf. of Interest 3/31/69
Each Ctf. of Interest exchanged for second and final distribution of (0.0000286) share Beatrice Foods Co. Common no par 4/10/72
Beatrice Foods Co. name changed to Beatrice Companies, Inc. 6/5/84
(See Beatrice Companies, Inc.)

J. HERBERT ORR ENTERPRISES, INC. (AL)
See - Orr (J. Herbert) Enterprises, Inc.

J & C INTL INVT GROUP LTD (NV)
Name changed to YAP International, Inc. 7/16/2004
YAP International, Inc. name changed to Nomad International, Inc. 5/13/2005 which recapitalized as iPackets International, Inc. 11/22/2005

J & L CAP VENTURE CORP (AB)
Name changed to Cancoil Integrated Services Inc. 02/18/1999
Cancoil Integrated Services Inc. name changed to Technicoil Corp. 07/26/2002 which merged into Essential Energy Services Ltd. 05/31/2011

J & L SPECIALTY STL INC (PA)
Merged into Usinor 12/17/98
Each share Common 1¢ par exchanged for $6.375 cash

J A B INTL INC (NV)
Common $0.001 split (3) for (1) by issuance of (2) shares payable 02/01/2001 to holders of record 01/25/2001 Ex date - 02/02/2001
SEC revoked common stock registration 09/16/2004

J A INDS INC (DE)
Recapitalized as Electronic Manufacturing Services Group Inc. 7/30/96
Each share Common $0.0005 par exchanged for (0.25) share Common $0.0005 par

J A M INC (NY)
Charter cancelled and proclaimed dissolved for failure to pay taxes 12/29/1999

J.A.P. REALTY & INVESTMENT, INC. (UT)
Name changed to Micro-Jet General Corp. 03/24/1986
Micro-Jet General Corp. recapitalized as E.P. Enterprises, Inc. 01/12/1987 which name changed to F/X Bio-Med, Inc. 03/05/1987

J ALEXANDERS CORP (TN)
Acquired by Fidelity National Financial, Inc. (New) 10/29/2012
Each share Common 5¢ par exchanged for $14.50 cash

J B & T CO (CO)
Declared defunct and inoperative for failure to pay taxes and file annual reports 10/23/72

J B CAP (NV)
Name changed to Computer Plus, Inc. 8/21/90
Computer Plus, Inc. name changed to Education Access Inc. 5/23/97

J B FINL SVCS INC (FL)
Reorganized as Ableauctions.com, Inc. 07/20/1999
Each share Common $0.001 par exchanged for (5) shares Common $0.001 par
Ableauctions.com, Inc. recapitalized as SinoCoking Coal & Coke Chemical Industries, Inc. 02/05/2010 which name changed to Hongli Clean Energy Technologies Corp. 07/28/2015

J-BIRD MUSIC GROUP LTD (PA)
Each share old Common $0.001 par exchanged for (0.025) share new Common $0.001 par 06/01/2001
Name changed to International Biofuel & Biochemical Corp. 12/09/2002
(See International Biofuel & Biochemical Corp.)

J C CAP CORP (DE)
Name changed to Intersearch Group, Inc. 05/21/1991
(See Intersearch Group, Inc.)

J C INTL PETE LTD (AB)
Placed in receivership 06/27/1988
No stockholders' equity

J C S ELEC CO (CA)
Class A Common $10 par changed to Capital Stock no par 5/1/60
Company bankrupt and its charter was suspended for non-payment of franchise taxes 8/1/62

J C SUPPLY INC (UT)
Name changed to Strawberry Valley Estates of the Ozarks 6/23/78
Strawberry Valley Estates of the Ozarks name changed to Continental Industries, Inc. 2/2/82

J CREW GROUP INC (DE)
Issue Information - 18,000,000 shares COM offered at $20 per share on 06/27/2006
Acquired by Chinos Holdings, Inc. 03/07/2011
Each share Common 1¢ par exchanged for $43.50 cash
Note: An additional distribution of approximately $0.2655 cash per share was paid from escrow 01/19/2012

J D HUTT CORP (NV)
Name changed to Code Green Apparel Corp. 09/09/2015

J D S INVTS LTD (ON)
Charter cancelled and proclaimed dissolved for failure to pay taxes and file returns 10/30/1995

J.E. PLASTICS MANUFACTURING CORP. (NY)
Name changed to Logistics Industries Corp. (NY) 9/1/67
Logistics Industries Corp. (NY) reincorporated in Pennsylvania 8/17/70 which merged into Lydall, Inc. (CT) 6/15/77 which reincorporated in Delaware 9/30/87

J ESPOS INC (NY)
Name changed to Globex, Inc. 06/29/2004
Globex, Inc. name changed to UMining Resources Inc. 05/23/2007 which recapitalized as Stargaze Entertainment Group Inc. 03/12/2015

J F CHINA REGION FD INC (MD)
Name changed to JPMorgan China Region Fund, Inc. 12/13/2013

J G WENTWORTH CO (DE)
Plan of reorganization under Chapter 11 Federal Bankruptcy proceedings effective 01/25/2018
No stockholders' equity

J.I.C. MINING & MILLING CO. (NE)
Voluntarily dissolved 11/30/09
Details not available

J JILL GROUP INC (DE)
Common 1¢ par split (3) for (2) by issuance of (0.5) additional share payable 6/28/2002 to holders of record 6/14/2002 Ex date - 7/1/2002
Merged into Talbots, Inc. 5/3/2006
Each share Common 1¢ par exchanged for $24.05 cash

J-K INDUSTRIES, INC. (MI)
Reorganized under the laws of Delaware 12/11/1963
Each share Common no par exchanged for (0.2) share Common $1 par
J-K Industries, Inc. (DE) name changed to Agrow Industries, Inc. 09/16/1977
(See Agrow Industries, Inc.)

J K INDS INC (DE)
Name changed to Agrow Industries, Inc. 9/16/77
(See Agrow Industries, Inc.)

J K M INDS INC (NY)
Dissolved by proclamation 12/20/1977

J-KAN INC (AR)
Reorganized under the laws of Nevada as TrinityCare Senior Living, Inc. 03/17/2009
Each share Common 1¢ par exchanged for (0.03333333) share Common $0.001 par
TrinityCare Senior Living, Inc. name changed to SeaBridge Freight Corp. 10/06/2010 which name changed to University General Health System, Inc. 03/29/2011
(See University General Health System, Inc.)

J L HALSEY CORP (DE)
Name changed to Lyris, Inc. 11/15/2007

(See Lyris, Inc.)

J.M. CONSOLIDATED GOLD MINES LTD.
Recapitalized as Jaculet Mines Ltd. on a (1) for (3) basis in 1949
(See Jaculet Mines Ltd.)

J M RES INC (CO)
Each share Common no par exchanged for (0.1) share Common 10¢ par 4/28/82
Administratively dissolved 2/1/99

J NET ENTERPRISES INC (NV)
Reincorporated under the laws of Delaware as Epoch Holding Corp. 12/09/2004
(See Epoch Holding Corp.)

J P INDS INC (MI)
Common 10¢ par split (2) for (1) by issuance of (1) additional share 06/13/1986
Preferred Stock Purchase Rights declared for Common stockholders of record 04/13/1989 were redeemed at $0.01 per right 08/30/1990 for holders of record 08/20/1990
Merged into T&N PLC 08/30/1990
Each share Common 10¢ par exchanged for $17.30 cash

J P M INDS INC (IL)
Common no par split (3) for (1) by issuance of (2) additional shares 5/8/86
Common no par split (3) for (1) by issuance of (2) additional shares 3/10/87
Involuntarily dissolved 5/1/89

J P MORGAN CHASE CAP IX (DE)
7.5% Capital Securities Ser. I called for redemption at $25 plus $0.177083 accrued dividends on 12/4/2006

J-PACIFIC GOLD INC (BC)
Recapitalized as Sona Resources Corp. 01/27/2010
Each share Common no par exchanged for (0.2) share Common no par
Sona Resources Corp. merged into Skeena Resources Ltd. 09/16/2016

J Q RES INC (ON)
Name changed to International Pursuit Corp. 09/21/1987
International Pursuit Corp. recapitalized as Apollo Gold Corp. (ON) 06/24/2002 which reincorporated in Yukon 05/28/2003 which recapitalized as Brigus Gold Corp. (YT) 06/25/2010 which reincorporated in Canada 06/09/2011
(See Brigus Gold Corp.)

J.R.B. PLASTICS (UT)
Name changed to Q-West Resources, Inc. (Utah) 5/19/82
Q-West Resources, Inc. (Utah) reorganized in Delaware as American Consolidated Holding Corp. 6/30/88

J R CONSULTING INC (NV)
Each share Common $0.0001 par exchanged for (0.0025) share Common 4¢ par 12/20/1988
Recapitalized as Providential Securities Inc. 01/14/2000
Each share Common 4¢ par exchanged for (0.5) share Common 4¢ par
Providential Securities Inc. name changed to Providential Holdings Inc. 02/09/2000 which name changed to PHI Group, Inc. 05/15/2009

J R ENERGY LTD (BC)
Struck off register and declared dissolved for failure to file returns 10/26/1990

J R GOLD MINES INC (FL)
Name changed to Sarah Acquisition Corp. (FL) 01/16/1996
Sarah Acquisition Corp. (FL) reorganized in Nevada as Karts International Inc. 02/23/1996 which name changed to 4D Seismic, Inc. 04/11/2006
(See 4D Seismic, Inc.)

J RISH GROUP INC (LA)
Charter revoked 11/15/2012

J ROBIN SCOTT CREATIVE CONSULTANTS INC (FL)
Proclaimed dissolved for failure to file reports and pay fees 10/9/92

J S INDS INC (DE)
Name changed to American Kitchen Foods, Inc. 01/07/1974
American Kitchen Foods, Inc. name changed to AKF Foods, Inc. 04/05/1979
(See AKF Foods, Inc.)

J TRON INC (UT)
Reincorporated under the laws of Delaware as E.K. Design Corp. 8/11/86
(See E.K. Design Corp.)

J TS RESTAURANTS INC (NV)
Name changed to National Integrated Food Service Corp. 12/10/1998
(See National Integrated Food Service Corp.)

J U M CAP INC (ON)
Recapitalized as West 49 Inc. 12/01/2004
Each share Common no par exchanged for (0.1) share Common no par
(See West 49 Inc.)

J V M MICROWAVE CO (IL)
Acquired by Fidelitone Microwave, Inc. on a (0.1) for (1) basis 3/29/61
Fidelitone Microwave, Inc. name changed to Fidelitone, Inc. 10/17/63
(See Fidelitone, Inc.)

J W GANT FINL INC (DE)
Recapitalized as JJFN Holdings, Inc. 11/27/95
Each share Common 1¢ par exchanged for (0.02) share Common $0.001 par
Preferred affected by name change only
JJFN Holdings, Inc. merged into Priority Financial Inc. 5/15/96

J&E BEAUTY SUPPLY INC (DE)
Recapitalized as International Imaging Inc. 07/27/1994
Each (12) shares Common $0.0001 par exchanged for (1) share Common $0.0001 par
International Imaging Inc. name changed to NexTech Enterprises International, Inc. 01/13/1998
(See NexTech Enterprises International, Inc.)

J P MORGAN CHASE CAP X (DE)
7% Trust Preferred Securities called for redemption at $25 on 05/08/2013

J P MORGAN CHASE CAP XI (DE)
5.875% Capital Securities Ser. K called for redemption at $25 on 05/08/2013

J P MORGAN CHASE CAP XII (DE)
6.25% Capital Securities Ser. L called for redemption at $25 plus $0.390625 accrued dividends on 05/08/2013

JA ENERGY (NV)
Each share old Common $0.001 par received distribution of (1) share Peak Energy Holdings Restricted Common payable 12/11/2014 to holders of record 11/17/2014
Each share old Common $0.001 par exchanged for (0.005) share new Common $0.001 par 02/09/2016
Reincorporated under the laws of Delaware as UBI BlockChain Internet Ltd. 12/08/2016

JA MAR TEMPS INC (DE)
Each share Common $0.0001 par exchanged for (0.025) share new Common $0.0001 par 07/20/1988
Charter forfeited for failure to maintain a registered agent 09/23/1991

JA SOLAR HLDGS CO LTD (CAYMAN ISLANDS)
Old Sponsored ADR's for Ordinary split (3) for (1) by issuance of (2) additional ADR's payable 02/07/2008 to holders of record 02/06/2008 Ex date - 02/08/2008
Basis changed from (1:3) to (1:1) 02/07/2008
Each old Sponsored ADR for Ordinary exchanged for (0.2) new Sponsored ADR for Ordinary 12/10/2012
Basis changed from (1:1) to (1:5) 12/10/2012
Acquired by JASO Acquisition Ltd. 07/16/2018
Each new Sponsored ADR for Ordinary exchanged for $7.50 cash

JABA EXPL INC (AB)
Recapitalized as Dundarave Resources Inc. 12/20/2004
Each share Common no par exchanged for (0.16666666) share Common no par
Dundarave Resources Inc. recapitalized as Nano One Materials Corp. 03/13/2015

JABA INC (AB)
Recapitalized as Consolidated Jaba Inc. 04/07/2000
Each share Common no par exchanged for (0.1) share Common no par
Consolidated Jaba Inc. name changed to Jaba Exploration Inc. 12/11/2003 which recapitalized as Dundarave Resources Inc. 12/20/2004 which recapitalized as Nano One Materials Corp. 03/13/2015

JABIL CIRCUIT INC (DE)
Common $0.001 par split (2) for (1) by issuance of (1) additional share payable 07/22/1997 to holders of record 07/08/1997
Common $0.001 par split (2) for (1) by issuance of (1) additional share payable 02/17/1999 to holders of record 02/05/1999 Ex date - 02/18/1999
Common $0.001 par split (2) for (1) by issuance of (1) additional share payable 03/30/2000 to holders of record 03/23/2000
Name changed to Jabil Inc. 06/05/2017

JACARANDA GOLD MINES, LTD. (ON)
Charter cancelled for failure to file reports and pay taxes 10/07/1957

JACK & HEINTZ, INC. (DE)
4% Preferred $50 par called for redemption 6/30/56
Merged into Siegler Corp. 2/3/61
Each share Common $1 par exchanged for (0.55) share Common no par
Siegler Corp. name changed to Lear Siegler, Inc. 6/5/62
(See Lear Siegler, Inc.)

JACK & HEINTZ PRECISION INDS INC (DE)
Common $5 par changed to $1 par in December 1950
Name changed to Jack & Heintz, Inc. in 1951
Jack & Heintz, Inc. merged into Siegler Corp. 2/3/61 which name changed to Lear Siegler, Inc. 6/5/62
(See Lear Siegler, Inc.)

JACK AMMANN PHOTOGRAMMETRIC ENGINEERS, INC. (TX)
See - Ammann (Jack) Photogrammetric Engineers, Inc.

JACK CARL 312 FUTURES INC (DE)
Reincorporated 5/3/94
State of incorporation changed from (IL) to (DE) 5/3/94
Each share Common $0.001 par exchanged for (0.25) share Common $0.004 par 11/7/94
Name changed to IFX Corp. 6/2/97
(See IFX Corp.)

JACK ECKERD CORP. (FL)
See - Eckerd (Jack) Corp.

JACK-IN-THE-BOX, INC. (DE)
Name changed to Foodmaker, Inc. 6/2/67
(See Foodmaker, Inc.)

JACK LAKE MINES LTD. (ON)
Recapitalized as New Jack Lake Uranium Mines Ltd. 10/11/1955
Each share Capital Stock $1 par exchanged for (0.25) share Capital Stock $1 par
New Jack Lake Uranium Mines Ltd. name changed to Equity Explorations Ltd. 10/10/1962 which recapitalized as Eagle Gold Mines Ltd. 02/08/1967 which merged into Agnico-Eagle Mines Ltd. 06/01/1972 which name changed to Agnico Eagle Mines Ltd. 04/30/2013

JACK THE GRIPPER INC (AB)
Recapitalized as Standard Mining Inc. 09/07/1995
Each share Common no par exchanged for (0.125) share Common no par
Standard Mining Inc. merged into Quest International Resources Corp. 04/03/1999 which recapitalized as Standard Mining Corp. 06/16/1999 which merged into Doublestar Resources Ltd. (YT) 11/01/2001 which reincorporated in British Columbia 10/10/2002 which merged into Selkirk Metals Corp. 07/23/2007
(See Selkirk Metals Corp.)

JACK WAITE CONSOLIDATED MINING CO.
See - Waite (Jack) Consolidated Mining Co.

JACK WAITE MINING CO., LTD.
See - Waite (Jack) Mining Co., Ltd.

JACK WAITE MNG CO (AZ)
Capital Stock $1 par changed to 20¢ par 1/9/58
Charter revoked for failure to file reports or pay fees 8/10/84

JACK WINTER, INC. (WI)
See - Winter (Jack), Inc.

JACKAL INDS INC (NV)
Name changed to First Capital Resources.com Inc. 04/09/1999
First Capital Resources.com Inc. recapitalized as Hampton Berkshire Insurance & Financial Co. 03/25/2003 which recapitalized as Innovate Oncology, Inc. 10/05/2004 which name changed to Avantogen Oncology, Inc. 07/03/2006
(See Avantogen Oncology, Inc.)

JACKES-EVANS MANUFACTURING CO. (MO)
Merged into Cenco Instruments Corp. 10/2/67
Each share Common $1 par exchanged for (0.7709) share Common $1 par
Cenco Instruments Corp. name changed to Cenco Inc. 10/6/72
(See Cenco Inc.)

JACKFISH EXPLS LTD (BC)
Name changed to Watcor Purification Systems Inc. 09/05/1986
(See Watcor Purification Systems Inc.)

JACKIE MINES, LTD. (ON)
Charter cancelled for failure to file reports and pay taxes 00/00/1957

JACKMAY LEAD MINES, LTD. (ON)
Charter cancelled for failure to file reports and pay taxes 05/11/1957

JACKNIFE GOLD MINES LTD. (ON)
Recapitalized as Jacobus Mining Corp. 07/29/1955
Each share Capital Stock no par exchanged for (0.25) share Capital Stock no par
(See Jacobus Mining Corp. Ltd.)

JACKOMATIC CORP.
Out of existence 00/00/1940
Details not available

JACKPINE MNG INC (BC)
Name changed to USV Telemanagement, Inc. 07/12/1996
USV Telemanagement, Inc. reorganized as E*Comnetrix Inc. 06/19/2000 which name changed to Moving Bytes Inc. 07/29/2002 which recapitalized as China International Enterprises Inc. (Canada) 03/23/2006 which reincorporated in Delaware as China Software Technology Group Co., Ltd. 11/16/2006 which recapitalized as American Wenshen Steel Group, Inc. 10/12/2007
(See American Wenshen Steel Group, Inc.)

JACKPOT COPPER MINES LTD (BC)
Recapitalized as Con-Am Resources Ltd. 01/22/1976
Each share Capital Stock 50¢ par exchanged for (0.2) share Capital Stock no par
(See Con-Am Resources Ltd.)

JACKPOT ENTERPRISES INC (NV)
Stock Dividends - 10% 07/11/1983; 10% 07/30/1993
Name changed to J Net Enterprises, Inc. (NV) 12/06/2000
J Net Enterprises, Inc. (NV) reincorporated in Delaware as Epoch Holding Corp. 12/09/2004
(See Epoch Holding Corp.)

JACKPOT OIL CO (CO)
Recapitalized as Canyon State Mining Corp. 3/1/69
Each share Common 5¢ par exchanged for (0.05) share Common $1 par
(See Canyon State Mining Corp.)

JACKPOT URANIUM MINES LTD. (ON)
Name changed to Big Jackpot Mines Ltd. 12/16/1954
(See Big Jackpot Mines Ltd.)

JACKS FOOD SYS INC (DE)
Merged into Florida Capital Corp. 1/30/75
Each share Common 10¢ par exchanged for $5 principal amount of 12% Subord. Debentures due 11/1/89

JACKSON & CURTIS INVESTMENT ASSOCIATES
Acquired by Atlas Utilities Corp. in 1931
Details not available

JACKSON & CURTIS SECURITIES CORP.
Name changed to Fairfield Securities Corp. in 1937
(See Fairfield Securities Corp.)

JACKSON (ANDREW) SAVINGS BANK (TALLAHASSEE, FL)
Name changed to Sun Bank/Tallahassee, N.A. (Tallahassee, FL) 02/17/1994
Sun Bank/Tallahassee, N.A. (Tallahassee, FL) merged into SunTrust Bank, Tallahassee, N.A. (Tallahassee, FL) 07/00/1985
(See SunTrust Bank, Tallahassee, N.A. (Tallahassee, FL))

JACKSON (ANDREW) STATE SAVINGS & LOAN ASSOCIATION (FL)
Name changed to Jackson (Andrew) Savings Bank (Tallahassee, FL) 07/24/1989
Jackson (Andrew) Savings Bank (Tallahassee, FL) name changed to Sun Bank/Tallahassee (Tallahassee, FL) 02/17/1994 which merged into SunTrust Bank, Tallahassee, N.A. (Tallahassee, FL) 07/00/1985
(See SunTrust Bank, Tallahassee, N.A. (Tallahassee, FL))

JACKSON ATLANTIC INC (GA)
Name changed to Munford, Inc. 5/11/71
(See Munford, Inc.)

JACKSON BASIN MINING CO. LTD. (BC)
Recapitalized as Jackson Mines Ltd. 01/19/1956
Each share Capital Stock no par exchanged for (0.33333333) share Capital Stock $2 par
Jackson Mines Ltd. merged into Trojan Consolidated Mines Ltd. 12/09/1956 which recapitalized as B.X. Development Ltd. 11/01/1972 which merged into Brent Petroleum Industries Ltd. 10/07/1981 which recapitalized as B.P.I. Resources Ltd. 05/20/1983 which name changed to Brent Resources Group Ltd. 03/22/1985
(See Brent Resources Group Ltd.)

JACKSON BROS INDS INC (NV)
Reincorporated 05/20/1989
State of incorporation changed from (UT) to (NV) 05/20/1989
Recapitalized as Dynacq International Inc. (NV) 03/08/1993
Each share Common $0.001 par exchanged for (0.125) share Common $0.001 par
Dynacq International Inc. (NV) reincorporated in Delaware as Dynacq Healthcare, Inc. 11/14/2003 which reincorporated in Nevada 03/20/2007

JACKSON CITY BANK & TRUST CO. (JACKSON, MI)
Stock Dividends - 33.33333333% 12/19/1941; 20% 11/13/1944; 33.33333333% 12/17/1947; 25% 10/07/1950
Name changed to City Bank & Trust Co. (Jackson, MI) 03/01/1955
City Bank & Trust Co. (Jackson, MI) name changed to City Bank & Trust Co., (N.A.) (Jackson, MI) 08/04/1964 which reorganized as CB Financial Corp. 08/06/1981 which merged into Citizens Banking Corp. 07/01/1997 which name changed to Citizens Republic Bancorp, Inc. 04/26/2007 which merged into FirstMerit Corp. 04/12/2013 which merged into Huntington Bancshares Inc. 08/16/2016

JACKSON CNTY BK (SEYMOUR, IN)
Reorganized as Bancorp of Southern Indiana 04/04/1983
Each share Capital Stock $10 par exchanged for (1) share Common no par

JACKSON CNTY FED BK (MEDFORD, OR)
Name changed 5/11/90
Name changed from Jackson County Federal Savings & Loan Association (Medford, OR) to Jackson County Federal Bank, FSB (Medford, OR) 5/11/90
Adjustable Rate Preferred Ser. A no par split (2) for (1) by issuance of (1) additional share 1/15/93
Common $1 par split (2) for (1) by issuance of (1) additional share 1/15/93
Merged into KeyCorp (NY) 1/3/94
Each share Adjustable Rate Preferred Ser. A no par exchanged for (0.426) share Common $5 par
Each share Common $1 par exchanged for (0.426) share Common $5 par
KeyCorp (NY) merged into KeyCorp (New) (OH) 3/1/94

JACKSON CNTY ST BK (KANSAS CITY, MO)
99% acquired by Central Mortgage Bancshares, Inc. through exchange offer which expired 09/13/1974
Public interest eliminated

JACKSON COURT CORP. (IL)
Liquidated in 1944

JACKSON DEVS CORP (WY)
Administratively dissolved 05/31/2006

JACKSON DROP FORGE CO. (MI)
Common $10 par changed to no par and (1) additional share issued 06/11/1970
Out of business 00/00/1990
Stockholders' equity unlikely

JACKSON HEWITT INC (VA)
Common 2¢ par split (2) for (1) by issuance of (1) additional share payable 12/03/1997 to holders of record 11/19/1997
Merged into HJ Acquisition Corp. 01/07/1998
Each share Common 2¢ par exchanged for $68 cash

JACKSON HEWITT TAX SVC INC (DE)
Plan of reorganization under Chapter 11 Federal Bankruptcy proceedings effective 08/16/2011
No stockholders' equity

JACKSON HOLE HLDGS CORP (BC)
Delisted from Vancouver Stock Exchange 3/3/97

JACKSON IRON & STL CO (OH)
Each share Common $100 par exchanged for (2) shares Common $50 par 00/00/1948
Merged into Banner Industries, Inc. (MO) 09/30/1969
Details not available

JACKSON LAKE TRAILER PK INC (WY)
Name changed to International Leisure Hosts, Ltd. 09/13/1973
(See International Leisure Hosts, Ltd.)

JACKSON LUMBER CO.
Dissolved in 1951

JACKSON MILLS EMERY CO. (NY)
Charter cancelled and proclaimed dissolved for failure to file reports and pay taxes 12/15/70

JACKSON MINES LTD. (BC)
Merged into Trojan Consolidated Mines Ltd. 12/09/1956
Each share Capital Stock $2 par exchanged for (0.25) share Common $1 par
Trojan Consolidated Mines Ltd. recapitalized as B.X. Development Ltd. 11/01/1972 which merged into Brent Petroleum Industries Ltd. 10/07/1981 which recapitalized as B.P.I. Resources Ltd. 05/20/1983 which name changed to Brent Resources Group Ltd. 03/22/1985
(See Brent Resources Group Ltd.)

JACKSON MOTOR SHAFT CO.
Acquired by Muskegon Motor Specialties Co. in 1930
Details not available

JACKSON NATL BK (JACKSON, TN)
Reorganized as Volunteer Bancshares, Inc. 05/07/1982
Each share Common $5 par exchanged for (1) share Common $1 par
Volunteer Bancshares, Inc. acquired by Bancorp of Mississippi 08/31/1992 which name changed to BancorpSouth, Inc. 10/06/1992 which reorganized as BancorpSouth Bank (Tupelo, MS) 11/01/2017

JACKSON NATL LIFE INS CO (MI)
Class A Common $1 par reclassified as Common $1 par 9/29/64
Common $1 par changed to $1.15 par 6/26/74
Common $1.15 par split (2) for (1) by issuance of (1) additional share 3/16/82
Common $1.15 par split (3) for (2) by issuance of (0.5) additional share 3/7/86
Stock Dividends - 15% 3/16/81; 50% 3/16/83
Acquired by Prudential Corp. 11/25/86
Each share Common $1.15 par exchanged for $51 cash

JACKSON PARK HOSPITAL CO. (IL)
Under plan of merger each share Common $1 par exchanged for (5) shares Common 20¢ par 3/31/62
Completely liquidated 5/8/67
Each share Preferred $100 par exchanged for first and final distribution of $105 cash
Each share Common 20¢ par exchanged for first and final distribution of $130 cash

JACKSON PARK REALTY CO., INC. (VA)
Liquidation completed
Each share Common $25 par exchanged for initial distribution of $40 cash 12/15/80
Each share Common $25 par received second distribution of $50 cash 2/17/81
Each share Common $25 par received third and final distribution of $26 cash 10/15/81

JACKSON RES LTD (BC)
Name changed to Loadmaster Systems, Inc. 05/17/1985
(See Loadmaster Systems, Inc.)

JACKSON RIVS CO (FL)
Each share Common $0.001 par exchanged for (0.001) share old Common $0.00001 par 11/22/2004
Each share old Common $0.00001 par exchanged for (0.0005) share new Common $0.00001 par 2/1/2005
Each share new Common $0.00001 par exchanged again for (0.0005) share new Common $0.00001 par 5/9/2005
Each share new Common $0.00001 par exchanged again for (4) shares new Common $0.00001 par 5/27/2005
Name changed to Interact Holdings Group, Inc. 1/8/2007

JACKSON STATE BANK (HOLLYWOOD, FL)
Name changed to American Bank of Hollywood (Hollywood, FL) 07/01/1974
American Bank of Hollywood (Hollywood, FL) reorganized as Ameribank Bancshares, Inc. 08/31/1983 which merged into Wachovia Corp. (New) (Ctfs. dated between 05/20/1991 and 09/01/2001) 04/01/1998 which merged into Wachovia Corp. (Ctfs. dated after 09/01/2001) 09/01/2001 which merged into Wells Fargo & Co. (New) 12/31/2008

JACKSON STORAGE & VAN CO (IL)
Converted to a limited partnership in 1986
Details not available

JACKSON TECH INC (DE)
Each share old Common $0.001 par exchanged for (0.1) share new Common $0.001 par 03/20/1997
Name changed to Electronic Kourseware International Inc. 08/28/1997

(See Electronic Kourseware International Inc.)

JACKSON VENTURES INC (NV)
Name changed to i-Level Media Group Inc. 02/23/2007
i-Level Media Group Inc. name changed to Telupay International Inc. 10/22/2013

JACKSON'S MINIT MARKETS, INC. (FL)
Stock Dividend - 10% 7/15/66
Merged into Jackson-Atlantic, Inc. 11/15/68
Each share Common $1 par exchanged for (1) share Common $1 par
Jackson-Atlantic, Inc. name changed to Munford, Inc. 5/11/71
(See Munford, Inc.)

JACKSONVILLE BANCORP INC (FL)
Each share old Common 1¢ par exchanged for (0.05) share new Common 1¢ par 10/24/2013
Merged into Ameris Bancorp 03/11/2016
Each share new Common 1¢ par exchanged for (0.5861) share Common $1 par

JACKSONVILLE BANCORP INC (MD)
Acquired by CNB Bank Shares, Inc. 06/05/2018
Each share Common 1¢ par exchanged for $33.70 cash

JACKSONVILLE BANCORP INC (TX)
Merged into Franklin Bank Corp. 12/30/2003
Each share Common 1¢ par exchanged for $37.50 cash

JACKSONVILLE BANCORP INC (USA)
Reorganized under the laws of Maryland 07/15/2010
Each share Common 1¢ par exchanged for (1.0016) shares Common 1¢ par
(See Jacksonville Bancorp, Inc. (MD))

JACKSONVILLE COACH CO. (FL)
Acquired by City Coach Lines, Inc. 00/00/1952
Details not available

JACKSONVILLE GAS CO.
Reorganized as Jacksonville Gas Corp. in 1943
No stockholders' equity

JACKSONVILLE GAS CORP. (FL)
Each share Common $5 par exchanged for (5) shares Common $1 par and 100% stock dividend paid 7/11/56
Merged into Florida Gas Co. on a (2/3) for (1) basis 5/31/62
Florida Gas Co. merged into Continental Group, Inc. 8/28/79

JACKSONVILLE SVGS & LN ASSN (TX)
Reorganized as Jacksonville Bancorp, Inc. 3/29/96
Each share Common 1¢ par exchanged for (1.41785) shares Common 1¢ par
(See Jacksonville Bancorp, Inc.)

JACKSONVILLE SVGS BK (JACKSONVILLE, IL)
Common $1 par split (3) for (2) by issuance of (0.5) additional share payable 01/08/1998 to holders of record 12/24/1997
Under plan of reorganization each share Common $1 par automatically became (1) share Jacksonville Bancorp, Inc. (USA) Common 1¢ par 05/03/2002
Jacksonville Bancorp, Inc. (USA) reorganized in Maryland 07/15/2010
(See Jacksonville Bancorp, Inc. (MD))

JACKSONVILLE TRACTION CO.
Property sold in 1933
No stockholders' equity

JACLYN INC (DE)
Old Common $1 par split (4) for (3) by issuance of (0.33333333) additional share 06/29/1987
Each share old Common $1 par exchanged for (1) share new Common $1 par to reflect a (1) for (250) reverse split followed by a (250) for (1) forward split 05/20/2008
Note: Holders of (249) or fewer pre-split shares received $10.21 cash per share
Acquired by Jaclyn Holdings Parent LLC 02/23/2017
Each share new Common $1 par exchanged for $7.85 cash

JACMAR EXPLS LTD (ON)
Charter cancelled and declared dissolved for failure to file returns and pay fees 11/09/1976

JACOB GOLD CORP (BC)
Recapitalized as Sargon Resources Ltd. 05/31/1990
Each share Common no par exchanged for (0.2) share Common no par
Sargon Resources Ltd. recapitalized as International Sargon Resources Ltd. 07/10/1996 which name changed to Canoil Exploration Corp. 07/28/1999 which name changed to AMS Homecare Inc. 03/15/2002
(See AMS Homecare Inc.)

JACOBS AIRCRAFT ENGINE CO.
Acquired by Republic Industries, Inc. in 1945
Each share Commen exchanged for (1/3) share Common
(See Republic Industries, Inc.)

JACOBS BANK (SCOTTSBORO, AL)
Merged into Regions Financial Corp. (Old) 8/31/98
Each share Common exchanged for (13.5) shares Common $0.625 par
Regions Financial Corp. (Old) merged into Regions Financial Corp. (New) 7/1/2004

JACOBS DISTRIBUTING CO. (TX)
Liquidation completed
Each share 5-1/2% Preferred $10 par exchanged for first and final distribution of $22.65 cash 12/12/73
Each share 6-1/2% Preferred $10 par exchanged for first and final distribution of $24.95 cash 12/12/73
Each share Common $10 par exchanged for initial distribution of $20 cash 12/12/73
Each share Common $10 par received second and final distribution of $15.03 cash 3/18/74

JACOBS ENGR CO (CA)
Under plan of reorganization each share Common no par automatically became (1) share Jacobs Engineering Group Inc. (CA) Common no par 9/26/74
Jacobs Engineering Group Inc. (CA) reincorporated in Delaware 3/4/87

JACOBS ENGR GROUP INC (CA)
Common no par split (3) for (2) by issuance of (0.5) additional share 03/04/1977
Common no par split (3) for (2) by issuance of (0.5) additional share 03/16/1979
Stock Dividend - 10% 03/15/1979
Reincorporated under the laws of Delaware and Common no par changed to $1 par 03/04/1987

JACOBS F L CO (MI)
Reorganized 06/29/1966
Each share 5% Preferred $50 par exchanged for $50 principal amount of 6% Debentures due 08/01/1980 and $19.375 cash
Name changed to Grand Rapids Metalcraft, Inc. 11/28/1977
Grand Rapids Metalcraft, Inc. name changed to GRM Industries, Inc. 11/08/1979 which merged into Redlaw Industries Inc. 12/07/1983
(See Redlaw Industries Inc.)

JACOBS JAY INC (WA)
Each (15) shares old Common 1¢ par exchanged for (1) share new Common 1¢ par 04/03/1998
Recapitalized as Imusic Worldwide Ltd. 03/05/2007
Each share new Common 1¢ par exchanged for (0.001) share Common 1¢ par

JACOBSEN MFG CO (WI)
Each share Common no par exchanged for (4) shares Common $1 par in 1951
Common $1 par split (3) for (2) by issuance of (0.5) additional share 8/31/67
Common $1 par split (3) for (2) by issuance of (0.5) additional share 5/15/68
6% Preferred $1 par called for redemption 8/1/69
Merged into Allegheny Ludlum Steel Corp. 8/1/69
Each share Common $1 par exchanged for (0.5) share $3 Conv. Preferred $1 par
Allegheny Ludlum Steel Corp. name changed to Allegheny Ludlum Industries, Inc. 4/24/70 which name changed to Allegheny International Inc. 4/29/81
(See Allegheny International Inc.)

JACOBSON RESONANCE ENTERPRISES INC (NV)
Plan of reorganization under Chapter 11 Federal Bankruptcy Code effective 12/8/2006
No stockholders' equity

JACOBSON STORES INC (MI)
Common $1 par split (5) for (2) by issuance of (1.5) additional share 11/4/71
6% Conv. Preferred 1965 Ser. $100 par called for redemption 9/15/77
6% Conv. Preferred 1969 Ser. $100 par called for redemption 12/15/83
Common $1 par split (2) for (1) by issuance of (1) additional share 1/21/84
Common $1 par split (3) for (2) by issuance of (0.5) additional share 3/24/86
Common $1 par split (3) for (2) by issuance of (0.5) additional share 3/30/87
Plan of reorganization under Chapter 11 Federal Bankruptcy Code effective 3/21/2004
No stockholders' equity

JACOBUS MNG LTD (ON)
Capital Stock no par changed to 35¢ par 10/01/1957
Charter cancelled and declared dissolved for failure to file returns and pay fees 03/16/1976

JACOLA MINES LTD (ON)
Charter cancelled and declared dissolved for failure to file returns and pay fees 03/16/1976

JACOMAT MINES LTD. (ON)
Charter revoked for failure to file reports and pay fees 01/10/1968

JACOR COMMUNICATIONS INC (DE)
Reincorporated 07/23/1996
Recapitalized 01/11/1993
Each share 15% Preferred Class A $1 par exchanged for (0.2026505) share Class A Common no par and (0.7707796) Class A Common Stock Purchase Warrant expiring 01/14/2000
Each share Common no par exchanged for (0.0423618) share Class A Common no par and (0.1611234) Class A Common Stock Purchase Warrant expiring 01/14/2000
Each share Class B Common no par exchanged for (1) share Class A Common no par 04/23/1993
Class A Common no par reclassified as Common no par 04/23/1993
State of incorporation changed from (OH) to (DE) 07/23/1996
Merged into Clear Channel Communications, Inc. 05/04/1999
Each share Common no par exchanged for (1.1573151) shares Common 10¢ par
(See Clear Channel Communications, Inc.)

JACQUELINE GOLD CORP (BC)
Recapitalized as Stellar Gold Corp. 05/12/1995
Each share Common no par exchanged for (0.14285714) share Common no par
Stellar Gold Corp. name changed to Stellar Metals Inc. 09/23/1996 which recapitalized as Geostar Metals Inc. 10/07/1999 which name changed to Skana Capital Corp. (BC) 11/27/2006 which reincorporated in Alberta as MENA Hydrocarbons Inc. 06/22/2011

JACQUES-MILLER INCOME FD L P (DE)
Company terminated registration of Units of Limited Partnership Interests and is no longer public as of 03/30/2014
Details not available

JACQUINS CHARLES ET CIE INC (PA)
Completely liquidated 04/15/1981
Each share Common 50¢ par exchanged for first and final distribution of $27.20 cash

JACULET MINES LTD. (ON)
Recapitalized as New Jaculet Mines Ltd. 09/06/1955
Each share Capital Stock $1 par exchanged for (1) share Capital Stock 75¢ par and (0.16666666) share Copper Cliff Consolidated Mining Corp. Capital Stock $1 par

JACUZZI BRANDS INC (DE)
Merged into Jupiter Acquisition, LLC 2/7/2007
Each share Common 1¢ par exchanged for $12.50 cash

JADE ENTMT GROUP INC (NY)
Acquired by Dominix, Inc. 12/5/2003
Details not available

JADE FINL CORP (PA)
Merged into PSB Bancorp Inc. 7/2/2001
Each share Common 1¢ par exchanged for $13.55 cash

JADE INTL INDL GROUP LTD (BC)
Cease trade order effective 08/13/1996

JADE MTN CORP (NV)
Each share old Common $0.0001 par exchanged for (0.000005) share new Common $0.0001 par 07/16/2007
New Common $0.0001 par split (100) for (1) by issuance of (99) additional shares payable 09/14/2007 to holders of record 09/04/2007
Ex date - 09/17/2007
Name changed to RINO International Corp. 05/13/2008

JADE OIL & GAS CO (CA)
Common 50¢ par changed to 10¢ par 3/14/72
Name changed to Seaboard Oil & Gas Co. (CA) 11/30/72
Seaboard Oil & Gas Co. (CA) merged into McFarland Energy, Inc. 2/27/76
(See McFarland Energy, Inc.)

JADE OIL CO. (CA)
Capital Stock $1 par changed to 10¢ par in 1935
Each share Capital Stock 10¢ par

JAD-JAL

exchanged for (0.2) share Capital Stock 50¢ par in 1958
Name changed to Jade Oil & Gas Co. 5/18/62
Jade Oil & Gas Co. name changed to Seaboard Oil & Gas Co. (CA) 11/30/72 which merged into McFarland Energy, Inc. 2/27/76
(See McFarland Energy, Inc.)

JADE PANTHER CORPORATION OF AMERICA (NY)
Charter cancelled and proclaimed dissolved for failure to pay taxes 08/27/2004

JADE PETE CORP (TX)
Charter forfeited for failure to pay taxes 2/21/83

JADELA OIL CORP (AB)
Recapitalized as Tenth Avenue Petroleum Corp. 05/19/2015
Each share Common no par exchanged for (0.2) share Common no par

JADRAN REALTY CORP. (NY)
Proclaimed dissolved for failure to file reports and pay fees 12/15/36

JAEGER CDA INC (DE)
Name changed to Jaeger Industries, Inc. 3/1/86
(See Jaeger Industries, Inc.)

JAEGER ENERGY CORP (OH)
Common no par split (2) for (1) by issuance of (1) additional share 09/01/1981
Reincorporated under the laws of Delaware as U.S. Resources, Inc. 09/10/1984
(See U.S. Resources, Inc.)

JAEGER INDUSTRIES, INC. (DE)
Charter cancelled and declared inoperative and void for non-payment of taxes 3/1/91

JAEGER MACHINE CO. (OH)
Common no par changed to $5 par and (1) additional share issued 10/05/1956
Common $5 par changed to $1 par 10/14/1977
Stock Dividend - 100% 02/17/1947
Name changed to Jaeger Energy Corp. (OH) and Common $1 par changed to no par 09/01/1981
Jaeger Energy Corp. (OH) reincorporated Delaware as U S Resources Inc. 09/10/1984
(See U S Resources Inc. (DE))

JAFFEE FD INC (DE)
Name changed to Cambridge Fund, Inc. 2/5/71
Cambridge Fund, Inc. name changed to Assets Investors Fund, Inc. 5/3/76
(See Assets Investors Fund, Inc.)

JAFTA INTL INC (BC)
Recapitalized as Dornoch International Inc. 10/05/1987
Each share Common no par exchanged for (0.6) share Common no par
Dornoch International Inc. name changed to DNI Holdings Inc. 04/28/1988
(See DNI Holdings Inc.)

JAFTEK VENTURES INC (AB)
Struck off register and declared dissolved for failure to file returns 04/01/1991

JAG MEDIA HLDGS INC (NV)
Each share Class A Common $0.00001 par received distribution of (0.01) share Class B Common Ser. 2 payable 04/16/2003 to holders of record 04/14/2003 Ex date - 04/10/2003
Each share Class A Common $0.00001 par exchanged for (1) share Common $0.00001 par 06/04/2004
Each share Class B Common Ser. 1 $0.00001 par exchanged for (1) share Common $0.00001 par 06/04/2004
Name changed to CardioGenics Holdings Inc. 10/27/2009

JAGER H DEVS INC (AB)
Name changed to Westbridge Land Development Corp. 10/15/1999
(See Westbridge Land Development Corp.)

JAGER METAL CORP (BC)
Name changed to Jagercor Energy Corp. 01/27/2014

JAGER RES INC (BC)
Recapitalized as Sora Capital Corp. 02/20/2014
Each share Common no par exchanged for (0.1) share Common no par
Sora Capital Corp. name changed to ProSmart Enterprises Inc. 07/12/2017

JAGGED PEAK INC (NV)
Each share Common $0.001 par received distribution of (0.1) share AcroBoo, Inc. Common $0.001 par payable 05/12/2011 to holders of record 05/10/2011 Ex date - 05/13/2011
Acquired by Singapore Post Ltd. 03/04/2016
Each share Common $0.001 par exchanged for $1 cash

JAGNOTES COM INC (NV)
Recapitalized as JAG Media Holdings, Inc. 04/08/2002
Each (1.1) shares Common $0.001 par exchanged for (1) share Class A Common $0.001 par and (0.1) share Conv. Class B Common Ser. 1 $0.001 par
JAG Media Holdings, Inc. name changed to CardioGenics Holdings Inc. 10/27/2009

JAGOR RES LTD (CANADA)
Acquired by Normandie Resource Corp. 09/12/1985
Each share Common no par exchanged for (1.6) shares Common no par
(See Normandie Resource Corp.)

JAGUAR ACQUISITION CORP (DE)
Reincorporated under the laws of British Virgin Islands as China Cablecom Holdings, Ltd. and Common $0.0001 par reclassified as Ordinary $0.0005 par 04/23/2008

JAGUAR ANIMAL HEALTH INC (DE)
Name changed to Jaguar Health, Inc. 08/16/2017

JAGUAR CAP INC (NV)
Name changed to JCI, Inc. 6/20/90

JAGUAR CARS LTD (ENGLAND)
ADR's for Class A Ordinary 5s par split (2) for (1) by issuance of (1) additional share 04/03/1964
Acquired by British Motor Corp. Ltd. 12/01/1966
Each ADR for Class A Ordinary 5s par exchanged for (2) shares Ordinary 5s par and 10s 3d principal amount of 8% Unsecured Loan Stock due 00/00/1986-00/00/1991
British Motor Corp. Ltd. name changed to British Motor Holdings Ltd. 12/19/1966 which name changed to British Leyland Motor Corp. Ltd. 05/14/1968
(See British Leyland Motor Corp. Ltd.)

JAGUAR CORP (DE)
Name changed to Siberian Natural Gas Corp. 6/7/99

JAGUAR EQUITIES INC (BC)
Recapitalized as International Jaguar Equities Inc. 06/11/1993
Each share Common no par exchanged for (0.2) share Common no par
International Jaguar Equities Inc. recapitalized as Jaguar International Equities Inc. 02/07/2000 which name changed to Advectus Life Sciences Inc. 03/18/2002

JAGUAR FINL INC (QC)
Reincorporated under the laws of Ontario as Jaguar Financial Corp. 07/08/2008

JAGUAR GAMING CORP (NV)
Stock Dividend - 4% payable 12/15/1998 to holders of record 11/18/1998
Recapitalized as Ideal Financial Solutions, Inc. 09/07/2004
Each share Common $0.001 par exchanged for (0.06648936) share Common $0.001 par
(See Ideal Financial Solutions, Inc.)

JAGUAR GROUP LTD (MN)
Name changed to Tech Squared Inc. 5/9/95
Tech Squared Inc. assets transferred to Tech Squared Liquidating Trust 12/17/99
(See Tech Squared Liquidating Trust)

JAGUAR INTL EQUITIES INC (BC)
Name changed to Advectus Life Sciences Inc. 03/18/2002

JAGUAR INVTS INC (NV)
Name changed to Power2Ship, Inc. 05/13/2003
Power2Ship, Inc. name changed to Fittipaldi Logistics, Inc. 10/23/2006 which name changed to NuState Energy Holdings, Inc. (NV) 01/08/2008 which reincorporated in Florida 10/28/2015 which recapitalized as Visium Technologies, Inc. 04/25/2018

JAGUAR MNG ENTERPRISES INC (MN)
Recapitalized as Green Street Capital Corp. 07/16/2010
Each share Common no par exchanged for (0.25) share Common no par

JAGUAR NICKEL INC (QC)
Name changed to Jaguar Financial Inc. (QC) 08/01/2007
Jaguar Financial Inc. (QC) reincorporated in Ontario as Jaguar Financial Corp. 07/08/2008

JAGUAR P L C (ENGLAND)
Each old ADR for Ordinary 25p par exchanged for (1) new ADR for Ordinary 25p par 11/12/1985
Merged into Ford Motor Co. 03/27/1990
Each new ADR for Ordinary 25p par exchanged for $13.72 cash
Each new ADR for Ordinary 25p par received an additional payment of $0.0977 cash 05/14/1990

JAGUAR PETE CORP (AB)
Merged into Probe Exploration Inc. 05/09/1997
Each share Common no par exchanged for (0.34) share Common no par and $0.60 cash
(See Probe Exploration Inc.)

JAGUAR RESORTS INC (MN)
Recapitalized as Iptimize, Inc. (MN) 12/08/2005
Each share Common $0.001 par exchanged for (0.02) share Common $0.001 par
Iptimize, Inc. (MN) reorganized in Delaware 10/10/2007
(See Iptimize, Inc.)

JAGUAR RES CORP (BC)
Name changed to Brazauro Resources Corp. 09/08/2004
(See Brazauro Resources Corp.)

JAHALA LAKE MINES LTD (ON)
Charter cancelled and declared dissolved for failure to file returns and pay fees 11/09/1976

JAHALA LAKE URANIUM MINES LTD. (ON)
Name changed to Jahala Lake Mines Ltd. 11/14/1956
(See Jahala Lake Mines Ltd.)

JAHN & OLLIER ENGRAVING CO. (DE)
Name changed to J. & O. Liquidating Co. (DE) 3/4/69
(See J. & O. Liquidating Co. (DE))

JAHNCKE SVC INC (LA)
Name changed to Consolidated Materials Inc. 6/4/76
(See Consolidated Materials Inc.)

JAKARTA DEV CORP (BC)
Name changed to P.P.M. Development Corp. 07/10/1998
P.P.M. Development Corp. recapitalized as Consolidated P.P.M. Development Corp. 04/27/1999 which name changed to Consolidated Global Diamond Corp. 04/23/2004 which name changed to Gem International Resources Inc. 10/30/2009

JAKARTA GROWTH FD INC (MD)
Reorganized as Indonesia Fund, Inc. 06/12/2001
Each share Common 10¢ par exchanged for (0.7289) share Common $0.001 par
Indonesia Fund, Inc. name changed to Aberdeen Indonesia Fund, Inc. 03/26/2010 which reorganized as Aberdeen Emerging Markets Equity Income Fund, Inc. 04/30/2018

JAKES TRUCKING INTL INC (NV)
Each share old Common $0.001 par exchanged for (10) shares new Common $0.001 par 09/28/2007
Name changed to IndieMV Media Group, Inc. 02/19/2008

JAKO INC (DE)
Each share old Common 1¢ par exchanged for (0.2) share new Common 1¢ par 2/24/92
Charter cancelled and declared inoperative and void for non-payment of taxes 5/25/94

JALAPA RAILROAD & POWER CO. (NJ)
Common $100 par changed to $1 par in 1949
Dissolved 6/20/56

JALNA MINERALS LTD (BC)
Recapitalized as Papuan Precious Metals Corp. 10/01/2010
Each share Common no par exchanged for (0.25) share Common no par
Papuan Precious Metals Corp. name changed to Ironside Resources Inc. 04/21/2015

JALNA MNG CORP (BC)
Recapitalized as Kolyma Goldfields Ltd. 07/27/1998
Each share Common no par exchanged for (0.5) share Common no par
Kolyma Goldfields Ltd. name changed to BidCrawler.com Online Inc. 03/01/2000 which recapitalized as TradeRadius Online Inc. 08/21/2001 which recapitalized as Jalna Resources Ltd. (New) 04/10/2003 which reorganized as Jalna Minerals Ltd. 06/01/2006 which recapitalized as Papuan Precious Metals Corp. 10/01/2010 which name changed to Ironside Resources Inc. 04/21/2015

JALNA RES LTD NEW (BC)
Reorganized as Jalna Minerals Ltd. 06/01/2006
Each share Common no par exchanged for (2) shares Common no par
Jalna Minerals Ltd. recapitalized as Papuan Precious Metals Corp. 10/01/2010 which name changed to Ironside Resources Inc. 04/21/2015

JALNA RES LTD OLD (BC)
Recapitalized as Consolidated Jalna Resources Ltd. 02/17/1988
Each share Common no par exchanged for (0.2) share Common no par
Consolidated Jalna Resources Ltd. recapitalized as Jalna Mining Corp. 04/16/1993 which recapitalized as Kolyma Goldfields Ltd. 07/27/1998 which name changed to BidCrawler.com Online Inc. 03/01/2000 which recapitalized as TradeRadius Online Inc. 08/21/2001 which recapitalized as Jalna Resources Ltd. (New) 04/10/2003 which reorganized as Jalna Minerals Ltd. 06/01/2006 which recapitalized as Papuan Precious Metals Corp. 10/01/2010 which name changed to Ironside Resources Inc. 04/21/2015

JAMA PRODTNS INC (NY)
Charter cancelled and proclaimed dissolved for failure to pay taxes and file reports 12/15/75

JAMAICA BROILERS GROUP LTD (JAMAICA)
Stock Dividends - 30% payable 03/27/1997 to holders of record 11/07/1996; 40% payable 02/04/1998 to holders of record 11/10/1997; 14.28% payable 09/03/2002 to holders of record 08/22/2002; 33.33333333% payable 10/18/2002 to holders of record 10/08/2002 Ex date - 10/04/2002; 20% payable 03/28/2003 to holders of record 03/18/2003 Ex date - 03/14/2003; 16.66666666% payable 09/18/2003 to holders of record 09/10/2003 Ex date - 09/08/2003
ADR agreement terminated 01/22/2014
Each Sponsored ADR for Ordinary exchanged for $1.916624 cash

JAMAICA HLDG INC (UT)
Recapitalized 08/08/1994
Recapitalized from Jamaica Marble Inc. to Jamaica Holding Co. Inc. 08/08/1994
Each share Common $0.001 par exchanged for (0.1) share Common $0.001 par
Recapitalized as Klein Engineered Competition Components Inc. (UT) 05/21/1996
Each share Common $0.001 par exchanged for (0.06666666) share Common $0.001 par
Klein Engineered Competition Components Inc. (UT) reorganized in Delaware as Automotive Performance Group, Inc. 04/15/1998

JAMAICA PUB SVC LTD (CANADA)
Each share Common no par exchanged for (3) shares Common no par 00/00/1940
Each share Common no par exchanged for (3) shares Common no par 10/20/1958
Common no par split (2) for (1) by issuance of (1) additional share 01/24/1962
Liquidation completed
Each share Common no par received initial distribution of (20) shares Jamaica Public Service Co. Ltd. Ordinary 5s par and $3.50 cash 12/22/1967
Each share Common no par received second distribution of $0.30 cash 12/02/1968
Each share Common no par exchanged for third and final distribution of $0.33 cash 11/03/1969

JAMAICA TEL LTD (JAMAICA)
Stock Dividend - ADR's for Ordinary - 100% 9/10/73
Merged into Telecommunications of Jamaica Ltd. 8/10/90

Each ADR for Ordinary J$0.50 par exchanged for $0.837 cash
(Additional Information in Active)

JAMAICA WTR & UTILS INC (NY)
Common no par changed to 10¢ par and (2) additional shares issued 05/02/1969
$15 Preferred Ser. B $100 par reclassified as $1.50 Preferred Ser. B $10 par and (9) additional shares issued 06/18/1971
Name changed to Welsbach Corp. (NY) 11/01/1974
Welsbach Corp. (NY) name changed to Jamaica Water Properties, Inc. 10/21/1976 which name changed to JWP Inc. (NY) 05/12/1986 which reincorporated in Delaware 08/04/1987
(See JWP Inc.)

JAMAICA WTR PPTYS INC (NY)
4-1/2% Conv. Class A Preferred $100 par called for redemption 11/2/83
Common 10¢ par split (2) for (1) by issuance of (1) additional share 5/23/86
Name changed to JWP Inc. (NY) 5/12/86
JWP Inc. (NY) reincorporated in Delaware 8/4/87
(See JWP Inc.)

JAMAICA WTR SUPPLY CO (NY)
$5 Preferred Ser. B no par called for redemption 3/31/63
Common no par split (3) for (1) by issuance of (2) additional shares in December 1963
Completely liquidated
Each share Common no par received first and final distribution of $14 cash payable 10/29/2004 to holders of record 10/22/2004 Ex date - 11/1/2004
Note: Certificates were not required to be surrendered and are without value

JAMAICAN MNG LTD (ON)
Charter cancelled and declared dissolved for failure to file returns and pay fees 11/09/1976

JAMBA INC (DE)
Each share old Common $0.001 par exchanged for (0.2) share new Common $0.001 par 06/03/2013
Acquired by Focus Brands Inc. 09/13/2018
Each share new Common $0.001 par exchanged for $13 cash

JAMCO LTD (CO)
Chapter 11 bankruptcy proceedings converted to Chapter 7 on 4/19/92
No stockholders' equity

JAMDAT MOBILE INC (DE)
Merged into Electronic Arts Inc. 02/14/2006
Each share Common $0.0001 par exchanged for $27 cash

JAMELAND MINES LTD (ON)
Recapitalized as Cotton Valley Resources Inc. (ON) 09/10/1981
Each share Capital Stock $1 par exchanged for (0.4) share Capital Stock $1 par
Cotton Valley Resources Inc. (ON) reincorporated in British Columbia 11/17/1982 which recapitalized as Conscot Resources Ltd. 12/17/1984 which recapitalized as Masters Holdings Inc. 05/08/1992 which name changed to Envirotreat Systems Inc. 01/15/1993 which recapitalized as Treat Systems Inc. 09/02/1999 which name changed to Mega Silver Inc. (BC) 12/18/2007 which reincorporated in Ontario as Mega Precious Metals Inc. 09/14/2009 which merged into Yamana Gold Inc. 06/24/2015

JAMES B. BEAM DISTILLING CO. (IL)
See - Beam (James B.) Distilling Co.

JAMES BARCLAY ALAN INC (NV)
Recapitalized as Titan Consolidated, Inc. 05/28/2003
Each share Common $0.0001 par exchanged for (0.8) share Common $0.0001 par
Titan Consolidated, Inc. name changed to Titan Oil and Gas, Inc. (Ctfs. dated prior to 12/04/2008) 02/21/2005 which name changed to Green Star Energies, Inc. 12/04/2008 which recapitalized as Rock Ridge Resources, Inc. 12/08/2011

JAMES BAY MNG CORP (QC)
Charter annulled for failure to file reports or pay fees 10/20/73

JAMES DISTILLERY, INC.
Name changed to Goldsborough (F.V.) Distilling Corp. 00/00/1950
(See Goldsborough (F.V.) Distilling Corp.)

JAMES FITZGERALD LABORATORIES, INC. (MD)
See - Fitzgerald (James W.) Laboratories, Inc.

JAMES FRED S & CO INC (DE)
Common 50¢ par split (5) for (4) by issuance of (0.25) additional share 01/17/1977
Common 50¢ par split (4) for (3) by issuance of (1/3) additional share 08/31/1978
Stock Dividend - 100% 02/15/1971
Merged into Transamerica Corp. 12/24/1982
Each share Common 50¢ par exchanged for $33.50 cash

JAMES HANLEY CO. (RI)
See - Hanley (James) Co.

JAMES HARDIE INDS LTD (AUSTRALIA)
Each Unsponsored ADR for Ordinary AUD $1 par exchanged for (1) Sponsored ADR for Ordinary AUD $1 par 02/19/1991
Stock Dividends - 12.5% 08/04/1988; 12.5% 03/05/1990
Reorganized under the laws of the Netherlands as James Hardie Industries N.V. 10/22/2001
Each Sponsored ADR for Ordinary AUD $1 par exchanged for (0.4) Sponsored ADR for Units
James Hardie Industries N.V. name changed to James Hardie Industries S.E. (Netherlands) 02/19/2010 which reincorporated in Ireland 06/17/2010

JAMES HARDIE INDS N V (IRELAND)
Name changed 02/19/2010
Reincorporated 06/17/2010
Name changed from James Hardie Industries N.V. to James Hardie Industries S.E. 02/19/2010
Place of incorporation changed from (Netherlands) to (Ireland) 06/17/2010
Name changed to James Hardie Industries PLC 10/15/2012

JAMES INDS INC (BC)
Recapitalized as International James Industries Inc. 04/28/1987
Each share Common no par exchanged for (0.5) share Common no par
International James Industries Inc. name changed to CDIS Software Inc. 07/08/1988 which recapitalized as International CDIS Software Inc. 03/06/1989 which name changed to A.T.H. Fund Inc. 07/24/1990
(See A.T.H. Fund Inc.)

JAMES KILBURG CORP. (CA)
See - Kilburg (James) Corp.

JAMES KIRKLAND MINES, LTD. (ON)
Charter cancelled by the Province of Ontario for default 00/00/1961

JAMES LEES & SONS CO. (PA)
See - Lees (James) & Sons Co.

JAMES MADISON LTD (DE)
Common $10 par changed to $5 par and (1) additional share issued 05/03/1982
Common $5 par split (3) for (2) by issuance of (0.5) additional share 09/30/1985
Common $5 par split (2) for (1) by issuance of (1) additional share 07/01/1986
Common $5 par changed to $1 par 07/23/1986
Charter dissolved 11/24/1992

JAMES MANUFACTURING CO. (WI)
Each share Common $25 par exchanged for (5) shares Common $5 par in 1946
Name changed to Atkinson Finance Corp. 12/30/58
Atkinson Finance Corp. name changed to Atkinson Corp. (WI) 4/20/62 which reincorporated in Delaware 10/6/71 which merged into JMN Corp. 1/1/73
(See JMN Corp.)

JAMES-MCBRIDE APARTMENTS, INC.
In process of liquidation in 1943
Details not available

JAMES MONROE BANCORP INC (VA)
Common $1 par split (3) for (2) by issuance of (0.5) additional share payable 07/25/2002 to holders of record 07/11/2002 Ex date - 07/26/2002
Common $1 par split (5) for (4) by issuance of (0.25) additional share payable 05/16/2003 to holders of record 04/25/2003 Ex date - 05/19/2003
Common $1 par split (3) for (2) by issuance of (0.5) additional share payable 06/01/2004 to holders of record 05/14/2004 Ex date - 06/02/2004
Common $1 par split (5) for (4) by issuance of (0.25) additional share payable 12/28/2005 to holders of record 11/28/2005 Ex date - 12/29/2005
Merged into Mercantile Bankshares Corp. 07/17/2006
Each share Common $1 par exchanged for (0.6033) share Common $2 par
Mercantile Bankshares Corp. merged into PNC Financial Services Group, Inc. 03/02/2007

JAMES MORRISON BRASS MANUFACTURING CO. LTD. (CANADA)
See - Morrison (James) Brass Manufacturing Co. Ltd.

JAMES PETE CORP (DE)
Liquidation completed
Each share Preferred no par received eighty-seventh and final distribution of $5.55 cash 12/16/1974
Note: Above payment brought to a total of $122.90 cash paid through periodic distributions since 00/00/1945
Note: Preferred certificates were not required to be surrendered and are without value
No Common stockholders' equity

JAMES R. KEARNEY CORP. (DE)
See - Kearney (James R.) Corp. (Del.)

JAMES R. KEARNEY CORP. (MO)
See - Kearney (James R.) Corp (Mo.)

JAMES RIV BANKSHARES INC (VA)
Common $5 par split (3) for (2) by issuance of (0.5) additional share

payable 11/7/97 to holders of record 10/10/97
Merged into First Virginia Banks, Inc. 7/2/2001
Each share Common $5 par exchanged for (0.51) share Common $1 par
First Virginia Banks, Inc. merged into BB&T Corp. 7/1/2003

JAMES RIV COAL CO (VA)
New Common 1¢ par split (2) for (1) by issuance of (1) additional share payable 11/05/2004 to holders of record 10/22/2004 Ex date - 11/08/2004
Plan of reorganization under Chapter 11 Federal Bankruptcy proceedings effective 03/22/2016
No stockholders' equity

JAMES RIV CORP (VA)
$5.40 Conv. Preferred Ser. G $10 par called for redemption 12/23/1982
Preferred Ser. H $10 par called for redemption 05/05/1986
Common 10¢ par split (3) for (2) by issuance of (0.5) additional share 06/29/1981
Common 10¢ par split (3) for (2) by issuance of (0.5) additional share 06/30/1983
Common 10¢ par split (3) for (2) by issuance of (0.5) additional share 07/02/1986
Issue Information - 15,000,000 DEPOSITARY SH DIVIDEND ENHANCED CONV SER P 9% offered at $17.25 per share on 06/22/1994
Stock Dividends - 50% 08/03/1978; 50% 06/04/1979
Name changed to Fort James Corp. 08/13/1997
9% Dividend Enhanced Conv. Preferred Ser. P $10 par called for redemption 09/02/1997
Depositary Preferred Ser. P called for redemption 09/02/1997
Depositary Preferred Ser. O called for redemption 10/01/1997
Fort James Corp. merged into Georgia-Pacific Corp. 11/27/2000
(See Georgia-Pacific Corp.)

JAMES RIV GROUP INC (DE)
Merged into D.E. Shaw Group 12/11/2007
Each share Common 1¢ par exchanged for $34.50 cash

JAMES RIVER BRIDGE CORP.
Reorganized in 1938
No stockholders' equity

JAMES RIVER BRIDGE SYSTEM
Liquidation completed in 1953
Details not available

JAMES T. BARNES OF WASHINGTON, D.C., INC. (DC)
See - Barnes (James T.) of Washington, D.C., Inc.

JAMES TALCOTT, INC. (NY)
See - Talcott (James), Inc.

JAMES UTD INDS LTD (CANADA)
Placed in liquidation 07/21/1970
Assets subsequently sold for the benefit of creditors
No stockholders' equity

JAMES UTD STL LTD (CANADA)
Name changed to James United Industries, Ltd. and Common no par changed to $1 par 09/25/1969
(See James United Industries, Ltd.)

JAMESBURY CORP (MA)
Common no par changed to $1 par 5/11/60
6% Preferred $100 par called for redemption 8/30/67
Stock Dividends - 100% 5/11/60; 50% 6/16/75; 50% 4/23/76; 50% 6/1/77; 25% 6/1/79
Merged into Combustion Engineering, Inc. 7/12/84

Each share Common $1 par exchanged for $29.25 cash

JAMESON INNS INC (GA)
$1.70 Conv. Preferred Ser. S called for redemption at $20 on 8/25/2004
9.25% Preferred Ser. A called for redemption at $25 on 8/25/2004
Merged into Argila, LLC 7/27/2006
Each share Common 10¢ par exchanged for $2.97 cash

JAMESON STANFORD RES CORP (NV)
Common $0.001 par split (7) for (1) by issuance of (6) additional shares payable 05/23/2012 to holders of record 05/23/2012
Name changed to Star Mountain Resources, Inc. 12/15/2014

JAMESTOWN EXPLS INC (ON)
Recapitalized as Jamestown Resources Inc. 10/15/1981
Each share Capital Stock no par exchanged for (0.25) share Common no par
(See Jamestown Resources Inc.)

JAMESTOWN RES INC (ON)
Cease trade order effective 6/9/83
Stockholders' equity unlikely

JAMESTOWN TEL CORP (NY)
Each share Common $100 par exchanged for (3) shares Common no par 00/00/1951
Merged into Mid-Continent Telephone Corp. 07/31/1968
Each share 5% 1st Preferred $100 par exchanged for (4) shares 5-1/2% Preferred Ser. F $25 par
Each share Common no par exchanged for (8.15) shares Common no par
Note: Unexchanged certificates were cancelled and became without value 07/31/1972
Mid-Continent Telephone Corp. name changed to Alltel Corp. (OH) 10/25/1983 which reincorporated in Delaware 05/15/1990
(See Alltel Corp.)

JAMESWAY CORP NEW (NY)
Plan of reorganization under Chapter 11 Federal Bankruptcy proceedings confirmed 06/06/1997
No stockholders' equity

JAMESWAY CORP OLD (NY)
Common $10 par changed to $1 par and (9) additional shares issued 6/21/66
Common $1 par split (5) for (4) by issuance of (0.25) additional share 8/1/68
Common $1 par split (3) for (2) by issuance of (0.5) additional share 2/16/71
Common $1 par split (3) for (2) by issuance of (0.5) additional share 7/26/77
Common $1 par split (2) for (1) by issuance of (1) additional share 7/14/83
Common $1 par split (2) for (1) by issuance of (1) additional share 5/22/87
Stock Dividend - 10% 4/20/79
Plan of reorganization under Chapter 11 Federal Bankruptcy Code effective 1/27/95
Each share Common $1 par exchanged for (0.05178749) Jamesway Corp. (New) Common Stock Purchase Warrant expiring 1/27/2010
(See Jamesway Corp. (New))

JAMEX RES LTD (CANADA)
Name changed 01/15/1981
Name changed from Jamex Explorations Ltd. to Jamex Resources Ltd. 01/15/1981
Merged into Claddagh Gold Ltd. 08/09/1989
Each share Capital Stock no par exchanged for (1) share Common no par
Claddagh Gold Ltd. recapitalized as Resorts Unlimited Management Inc. 09/01/2000
(See Resorts Unlimited Management Inc.)

JAMIE FRONTIER RES INC (CANADA)
Dissolved 05/06/2004

JAMIESON (C.E.) & CO.
Acquired by Heyden Chemical Corp. (DE) in 1945
Details not available

JAMIESON INDUSTRIES, INC. (CA)
Completely liquidated 3/5/65
Each (137.528) shares Capital Stock 50¢ par received first and final distribution of (1) share Genisco Technology Corp. (CA) Common $1 par
Genisco Technology Corp. (CA) reincorporated in Delaware 4/9/84
(See Genisco Technology Corp.)

JAMOB LTD (CANADA)
Liquidation completed
Each share Capital Stock no par received initial distribution of 50¢ cash 11/10/1965
Each share Capital Stock no par received second and final distribution of $1.82 cash 09/01/1969
Note: Certificates were not required to be surrendered and are without value

JAN BELL MARKETING INC (DE)
Common $0.0001 par split (3) for (2) by issuance of (0.5) additional share 07/24/1989
Stock Dividend - 50% 10/17/1988
Name changed to Mayor's Jewelers, Inc. 07/17/2000
Mayor's Jewelers, Inc. merged into Birks & Mayors Inc. 11/14/2005 which name changed to Birks Group Inc. 10/01/2013

JAN RES LTD (BC)
Recapitalized as Lode Resource Corp. 10/27/83
Each share Common no par exchanged for (0.2) share Common no par
Lode Resource Corp. recapitalized as Lodex Resource Corp. 6/6/90 which recapitalized as LRX Capital Corp. (BC) which reincorporated in Canada as North American Tungsten Corp. Ltd. 5/1/96

JANAF, INC. (DE)
Common 1¢ par changed to 20¢ par 4/26/55
No longer in existence having become inoperative and void for non-payment of taxes 10/1/61

JANDON MINES LTD (ON)
Charter cancelled for failure to pay taxes and file returns 11/14/1973

JANE BUTEL CORP (FL)
Each share old Common $0.001 par exchanged for (0.01) share new Common $0.001 par 7/25/2005
Name changed to Bootie Beer Corp. 11/7/2005
Bootie Beer Corp. name changed to TMT Capital Corp. 6/8/2007

JANE COLBY INC (NY)
Completely liquidated 2/1/68
Each share Common $1 par exchanged for first and final distribution of (0.2) share U.S. Industries, Inc. Special Conv. Preference Ser. A $2.50 par and (1) Ctf. of Participation no par
(See U.S. Industries, Inc.)

JANEL WORLD TRADE LTD (NV)
Recapitalized as Janel Corp. 04/21/2015
Each share Common $0.001 par exchanged for (0.02) share Common $0.001 par

JANEROS CORP (NV)
Charter revoked for failure to file reports and pay fees 2/1/2002

JANET RED LAKE MINES, LTD. (ON)
Charter cancelled 00/00/1953
No stockholders' equity

JANET'S APPAREL SHOPS, INC. (DE)
No longer in existence having become inoperative and void for non-payment of taxes 4/1/62

JANEX INTL INC (CO)
Proclaimed dissolved for failure to file reports and pay fees 2/1/2002

JANI INTL INC (AB)
Recapitalized as Altech Resource Services Ltd. 10/11/1989
Each share Common no par exchanged for (0.1) share Common no par
(See Altech Resource Services Ltd.)

JANINA RES LTD (BC)
Name changed to International Beryllium Corp. 11/28/2007
International Beryllium Corp. name changed to IBC Advanced Alloys Corp. 03/06/2009

JANIS MARTIN E & CO INC (DE)
Merged into MEJ Holdings, Inc. 4/11/85
Each share Common 5¢ par exchanged for $2.67 cash

JANJOY ENTERPRISES, INC. (NJ)
Name changed to Petro Penn, Inc. 8/2/82
Petro Penn, Inc. name changed to Teksat Corp., Inc. 2/21/85

JANKCO HLDG CORP (FL)
Administratively dissolved 08/26/1994

JANNA SYS INC (ON)
Merged into Siebel Systems, Inc. 11/15/2000
Each share Common no par held by non-Canadian residents exchanged for (0.497) share Common no par
Each share Common no par held by Canadian residents exchanged for (0.497) share Siebel Janna Arrangement, Inc. Common no par
(See Siebel Systems, Inc.)

JANNOCK LTD (ON)
Reorganized 07/05/1977
Reorganized from Jannock Corp. Ltd. to Jannock Ltd. 07/05/1977
Each share Preference 1st Ser. $100 par exchanged for (6) shares 8% 2nd Preference $15 par
Each (10) shares $1.20 Class A no par exchanged for (11) shares 8% 2nd Preference $15 par
Each share 6% Conv. Class B $20 par exchanged for (1) share 8% 2nd Preference $15 par and (1) 1977 Class A Purchase Warrant
Each Conv. Special Share no par exchanged for (1) share Class B no par
Each share Class D no par exchanged for (1) share Class A no par
Class A no par reclassified as Common no par 01/03/1979
Class B no par reclassified as Common no par 01/03/1979
Common no par split (2) for (1) by issuance of (1) additional share 09/13/1979
Common no par split (2) for (1) by issuance of (1) additional share 05/22/1987
8% 2nd Preference no par called for redemption at $17 on 03/10/2000
Plan of arrangement effective 03/10/2000
Each share Common no par exchanged for $2.50 principal amount of Vicwest Corp. 12.50%

Promissory Notes due 2007, (1) share Jannock Properties Ltd. Common no par, and $16 cash
Note: Notes will only be issued in denominations of $250 principal amount and whole multiples thereof. Fractional Notes will be sold and the proceeds distributed on a pro rata basis
(See Jannock Properties Ltd.)

JANNOCK PPTYS LTD (ON)
Common no par reclassified as Units 05/13/2002
Note: Each Unit originally consisted of (175) Class A Special Shares and (1) share Class B Common Final number of Class A shares were reduced to (65) through redemptions
Completely liquidated
Each Unit received first and final distribution of $0.056 cash payable 01/28/2011 to holders of record 01/14/2011

JANSEN ELECTRONICS MANUFACTURING, INC. (MN)
Name changed to Novatron, Inc. 09/09/1969
Novatron, Inc. name changed to Assisted Care Corp. 07/19/1995 which name changed to Quality One Wireless, Inc. 08/27/2002
(See Quality One Wireless, Inc.)

JANSKO INC (FL)
SEC revoked common stock registration 03/05/2009

JANTAR RES CORP (BC)
Name changed to ITP Thermal Packaging Inc. 06/05/1991
ITP Thermal Packaging Inc. recapitalized as Stratford Ventures Ltd. 08/08/1996 which name changed to MRC Metal Resources Corp. (BC) 08/29/1997 which reincorporated in Canada as Mount Dakota Energy Corp. 08/24/1998 which reincorporated in British Columbia 08/07/2015

JANTAR RES LTD (BC)
Common no par split (5) for (1) by issuance of (4) additional shares payable 01/02/2007 to holders of record 01/02/2007 Ex date - 12/28/2006
Name changed to Ultra Lithium Inc. 09/04/2009

JANTRI RES INC (BC)
Name changed to Merit Mining Corp. 12/20/2004
Merit Mining Corp. name changed to Huakan International Mining Inc. 12/23/2010
(See Huakan International Mining Inc.)

JANTZEN INC (NV)
5% Preferred Ser. A $100 par called for redemption 4/15/64
Common $1 par changed to 66-2/3¢ par and (0.5) additional share issued 11/1/68
Stock Dividends - 10% 11/1/56; 15% 11/15/73
Merged into Blue Bell, Inc. 2/28/80
Each share Common 66-2/3¢ par exchanged for $30 cash

JANTZEN KNITTING MILLS, INC. (NV)
Stock Dividends - 10% 2/1/49; 20% 11/1/49; 20% 11/1/50; 10% 11/1/51; 10% 11/1/52; 10% 11/1/53
Name changed to Jantzen, Inc. in January 1954
(See Jantzen, Inc.)

JANTZEN KNITTING MILLS (OR)
Common no par exchanged (2) for (1) in 1930
Common no par changed to $1 par in August 1941
Reincorporated under laws of Nevada as Jantzen Knitting Mills, Inc. 1/20/47
Jantzen Knitting Mills, Inc. name changed to Jantzen, Inc. in January 1954
(See Jantzen, Inc.)

JANTZEN KNITTING MILLS OF CANADA LTD.
Recapitalized in 1947
Each share Preference $100 par exchanged for (22) shares Common no par
Each (50) shares Common no par exchanged for (1) share new Common no par
Name changed to Jantzen of Canada Ltd. in 1952
(See Jantzen of Canada Ltd.)

JANTZEN OF CANADA LTD. (CANADA)
Through several purchase offers all but (6) shares acquired by Jantzen Inc. as of 09/16/1974
Public interest eliminated

JANUARY MNG CO (MT)
Involuntarily dissolved 12/2/87

JANUS AMERN GROUP INC (DE)
Name changed to Janus Hotels & Resorts Inc. 6/1/99
(See Janus Hotels & Resorts Inc.)

JANUS CAP GROUP INC (DE)
Merged into Janus Henderson Group PLC 05/30/2017
Each share Common 1¢ par exchanged for (0.4719) share Ordinary $1.50 par

JANUS DETROIT STR TR (DE)
Janus SG Global Quality Income ETF $0.001 par reclassified as Janus Henderson SG Global Quality Income ETF $0.001 par 06/05/2017
Trust terminated 09/27/2017
Each share The Health and Fitness ETF $0.001 par received $26.15 cash
Trust terminated 03/27/2018
Each share Janus Velocity Tail Risk Hedged Large Cap ETF $0.001 par received $29.488948 cash
Each share Janus Velocity Volatility Hedged Large Cap ETF $0.001 par received $33.464518 cash
Trust terminated 05/25/2018
Each share Janus Henderson SG Global Quality Income ETF $0.001 par received $27.600236 cash
(Additional Information in Active)

JANUS EXPLS LTD (ON)
Charter cancelled for failure to pay taxes and file returns 03/13/1979

JANUS HOTELS & RESORTS INC (DE)
Each share old Common 1¢ par exchanged for (1) share new Common 1¢ par to reflect a (1) for (100) reverse split followed by a (1) for (100) forward split 4/2/2001
Note: Holders of (99) or fewer pre-split shares received $1.496 cash per share
Merged into Janus Acquisition, Inc. 1/29/2004
Each share new Common 1¢ par exchanged for $0.65 cash

JANUS INDS INC (DE)
Name changed to Janus American Group, Inc. 9/29/97
Janus American Group, Inc. name changed to Janus Hotels & Resorts Inc. 6/1/99
(See Janus Hotels & Resorts Inc.)

JANUS INTL INC (NV)
Recapitalized as Diamond Worldwide, Inc. 08/19/2002
Each share Common $0.001 par exchanged for (0.25) share Common $0.001 par
Diamond Worldwide, Inc. name changed to FutureVest, Inc. 12/07/2004 which name changed to Barotex Technology Corp. 01/09/2008

(See Barotex Technology Corp.)

JANUS RES INC (NV)
Name changed to RenovaCare, Inc. 01/09/2014

JANUS TWENTY FD INC (MD)
Name changed 5/22/89
Name changed from Janus Value Fund, Inc. to Janus Twenty Fund, Inc. 5/22/89
Under plan of reorganization each share Common 1¢ par automatically became (1) share Janus Investment Fund Twenty Fund 1¢ par 8/7/92

JANUS VENTURE FD INC (MD)
Under plan of reorganization each share Common 1¢ par automatically became (1) share Janus Investment Fund Venture Fund 1¢ par 8/7/92

JAPAN AIR LINES LTD (JAPAN)
Each old ADR for Common JPY 500 par exchanged for (5) new ADR's for Common JPY 500 par 06/28/1982
New ADR for Common JPY 500 par changed to JPY 50 par and (9) additional ADR's issued 09/07/1990
Recapitalized as Japan Airlines System Corp. 11/20/2002
Each new ADR for Common JPY 50 par exchanged for (0.4) ADR for Common JPY 50 par
Unexchanged ADR's may receive cash upon surrrender after 05/20/2003
Note: Due to ADR's being unsponsored exchange rate may vary dependent upon depositary agent
Japan Airlines System Corp. name changed to Japan Airlines Corp. 06/26/2004
(See Japan Airlines Corp.)

JAPAN AIRLS CORP (JAPAN)
Name changed 06/26/2004
Name changed from Japan Airlines Systems Corp. to Japan Airlines Corp. 06/26/2004
ADR agreement terminated 01/11/2011
No ADR holders' equity

JAPAN EQUITY FD INC (MD)
Name changed to Aberdeen Japan Equity Fund, Inc. 05/01/2014

JAPAN FUND OF CANADA LTD. (CANADA)
Name changed to CSM Japan Fund Ltd. 5/18/71
CSM Japan Fund Ltd. name changed to AGF Japan Fund Ltd. 5/25/73

JAPAN FUTURE INFORMATION TECHNOLOGY & SYS CO LTD (JAPAN)
Merged into CSK Corp. 08/01/2004
Each Sponsored ADR for Common exchanged for (0.28) Sponsored ADR for Ordinary 50 Yen par
CSK Corp. name changed to CSK Holdings Corp. 10/03/2005
(See CSK Holdings Corp.)

JAPAN OTC EQUITY FD INC (MD)
Name changed to Japan Smaller Capitalization Fund, Inc. 2/27/2002

JAPAN TELECOM HLDGS CO LTD (JAPAN)
Name changed 8/5/2002
ADR's for Common split (2) for (1) by issuance of (1) additional ADR payable 6/6/2000 to holders of record 6/5/2000 Ex date - 6/7/2000
ADR's for Common split (5) for (1) by issuance of (4) additional ADR's payable 7/17/2001 to holders of record 7/10/2001 Ex date - 7/9/2001
Name changed from Japan Telecom Co., Ltd. to Japan Telecom Holdings Co., Ltd. 8/5/2002
Name changed to Vodafone Holdings K.K. 1/6/2004
(See Vodafone Holdings K.K.)

JARDEN CORP (DE)
Common 1¢ par split (2) for (1) by issuance of (1) additional share payable 06/03/2002 to holders of record 05/20/2002 Ex date - 06/04/2002
Common 1¢ par split (3) for (2) by issuance of (0.5) additional share payable 11/26/2003 to holders of record 11/12/2003 Ex date - 11/28/2003
Common 1¢ par split (3) for (2) by issuance of (0.5) additional share payable 07/11/2005 to holders of record 06/20/2005 Ex date - 07/12/2005
Common 1¢ par split (3) for (2) by issuance of (0.5) additional share payable 03/18/2013 to holders of record 02/25/2013 Ex date - 03/19/2013
Common 1¢ par split (3) for (2) by issuance of (0.5) additional share payable 11/24/2014 to holders of record 11/03/2014 Ex date - 11/25/2014
Merged into Newell Brands Inc. 04/18/2016
Each share Common 1¢ par exchanged for (0.862) share Common $1 par and $21 cash

JARDIN FINL GROUP INC (AB)
Delisted from Alberta Stock Exchange 10/04/1996

JARDINCAP INC (AB)
Reorganized under the laws of Ontario as Tawsho Mining Inc. 07/28/2008
Each share Common no par exchanged for (0.33333333) share Common no par
Tawsho Mining Inc. merged into Genesis Metals Corp. 03/02/2016

JARDINE CYCLE & CARRIAGE LTD (SINGAPORE)
ADR agreement terminated 7/14/2004
Each Sponsored ADR for Ordinary exchanged for $14.41109 cash

JARDINE FLEMING CHINA REGION FD INC (MD)
Name changed to JF China Region Fund, Inc. 10/15/2003
JF China Region Fund, Inc. name changed to JPMorgan China Region Fund, Inc. 12/13/2013

JARDINE FLEMING INDIA FD INC (MD)
Name changed to Saffron Fund, Inc. 6/20/2003
(See Saffron Fund, Inc.)

JARDINE MATHESON HLDGS LTD (BERMUDA)
Reorganized 06/27/1984
Reorganized from Jardine Matheson & Co., Ltd. (Hong Kong) to Jardine Matheson Holdings Ltd. (Bermuda) 06/27/1984
Each ADR for Ordinary HKD $6 par exchanged for (1) Unsponsored ADR for Ordinary HKD $2 par
Each Unsponsored ADR for Ordinary HKD $2 par exchanged for (1) Sponsored ADR for Ordinary USD $0.25 par 06/24/1991
Stock Dividend - 40% 06/30/1987
ADR agreement terminated 05/28/2004
Each Sponsored ADR for Ordinary USD $0.25 par exchanged for $17.59586 cash

JARDINE MINING CO. (MT)
Adjudicated bankrupt 1/2/58
No stockholders' equity

JARDINE STRATEGIC HLDGS LTD (BERMUDA)
ADR agreement terminated 05/28/2004
Each Sponsored ADR for Ordinary exchanged for $20.37126 cash

FINANCIAL INFORMATION, INC.   JAR-JAV

JARDUN MINES LTD. (ON)
Charter cancelled 06/08/1964

JARECKI CORP (MI)
Reincorporated under the laws of Delaware 5/1/68

JAREX SOLUTIONS CORP (NV)
Name changed to ME Renewable Power Corp. 06/21/2016

JARL ENERGY INC (ON)
Name changed to ALBA Petroleum Corp. 10/26/1989
ALBA Petroleum Corp. merged into Alberta Oil & Gas Ltd. 12/31/1990 which recapitalized as Alberta Oil & Gas Petroleum Corp. 11/19/1997 which recapitalized as Edge Energy Inc. 04/14/1998 which merged into Ventus Energy Ltd. 08/11/2000 which name changed to Navigo Energy Inc. 05/24/2002
(See Navigo Energy Inc.)

JARMACK MINING CO. LTD. (ON)
Dissolved 03/30/1959
Details not available

JARMAN SHOE CO.
Name changed to General Shoe Corp. in 1933
General Shoe Corp. name changed to Genesco Inc. 3/2/59

JARMEL FABRICS INC (NY)
Assets assigned for benefit of creditors 4/14/78
No stockholders' equity

JARRELL-ASH CO. (MA)
Class A Common $2.50 par and Class B Common $2.50 par changed to $1.25 par respectively and (1) additional share issued 8/18/59
Class A Common $1.25 par and Class B Common $1.25 par changed to $1 par respectively and (2) additional shares issued 9/1/61
Completely liquidated 4/5/68
Each share Class A Common $1 par or Class B Common $1 par or VTC for Class B Common $1 par exchanged for first and final distribution of (0.5) share Fisher Scientific Co. Common $2.50 par
Fisher Scientific Co. merged into Allied Corp. 10/27/81 which merged into Allied- Signal Inc. 9/19/85 which name changed to AlliedSignal Inc. 4/26/93 which name changed to Honeywell International Inc. 12/1/99

JARRETT / FAVRE DRIVING ADVENTURE INC (FL)
Name changed to Dale Jarrett Racing Adventure, Inc. 11/21/2002
Dale Jarrett Racing Adventure, Inc. name changed to 24/7 Kid Doc, Inc. 02/18/2016

JARVIS (W.B.) CO.
Merged into Doehler-Jarvis Corp. 12/30/1944
Each share Capital Stock $1 par exchanged for (1) share Common $5 par
Doehler-Jarvis Corp. acquired by National Lead Co. 00/00/1953 which name changed to N L Industries, Inc. 04/16/1971

JARVIS ENTMT GROUP INC (NV)
Each share Common $0.0001 par received distribution of (1) share Jarvis Group Inc. Common $0.0001 par payable 5/5/2002 to holders of record 4/23/2002
Name changed to Westlin Corp. 11/17/2003

JARVIS GROUP INC (NV)
Name changed to Cash 4 Homes 247 05/21/2003
Cash 4 Homes 247 name changed to Vegas Equity International Corp. 02/01/2006
(See Vegas Equity International Corp.)

JARVIS RES LTD (BC)
Recapitalized as Consolidated Stone Industries Inc. 06/11/1999
Each share Common no par exchanged for (0.1) share Common no par
(See Consolidated Stone Industries Inc.)

JAS. H. OLIPHANT & CO., INC.
See - Oliphant (Jas. H.) & Co., Inc.

JASCAN RES INC (ON)
Acquired by Breakwater Resources Ltd. 11/09/2000
Each share Common no par exchanged for either (0.55) share Common no par, $1.15 cash, or (0.33) share Common no par and $0.46 cash
Note: Option to receive stock or cash only expired 11/03/2000
(See Breakwater Resources Ltd.)

JASMINE INTL PUB CO LTD (THAILAND)
ADR agreement terminated 04/23/2018
Each Sponsored ADR for Ordinary exchanged for (10) shares Ordinary
Note: Unexchanged ADR's will be sold and the proceeds, if any, held for claim after 04/26/2019

JASMINE INVTS CORP (UT)
Name changed to Audioventures Corp. 05/17/1989
(See Audioventures Corp.)

JASMINE LTD (DE)
Charter cancelled and declared inoperative and void for non-payment of taxes 3/1/96

JASMINE MNG LTD (CANADA)
Name changed to Rencan Resource Investments Ltd. 03/29/1974
Rencan Resource Investments Ltd. recapitalized as Norminco Developments Ltd. 06/09/1977 which recapitalized as Sumburgh Developments Ltd. 10/17/1983 which recapitalized as Access Banking Network Inc. 09/24/1984 which recapitalized as Access ATM Network Inc. 05/24/1985 which merged into Ancom ATM International Inc. 01/18/1988
(See Ancom ATM International Inc.)

JASMINES GARDEN (NV)
Name changed to China Digital Communication Group 09/24/2004
China Digital Communication Group name changed to New Energy Systems Group 11/18/2009

JASON EMPIRE INC (DE)
Common $1 par split (3) for (2) by issuance of (0.5) additional share 7/15/72
Merged into Noslrac, Inc. 12/31/78
Each share Common $1 par exchanged for $9 cash

JASON GOLD CORP (BC)
Name changed 7/18/83
Name changed from Jason Explorers Ltd. to Jason Gold Corp. 7/18/83
Struck off register and declared dissolved for failure to file returns 8/21/92

JASON INC (WI)
Reincorporated 01/01/1994
Common 10¢ par split (3) for (2) by issuance of (0.5) additional share 05/16/1990
Common 10¢ par split (5) for (4) by issuance of (0.25) additional share 05/15/1991
Common 10¢ par split (3) for (2) by issuance of (0.5) additional share 05/20/1992
Common 10¢ par split (5) for (4) by issuance of (0.25) additional share 05/19/1993
Stock Dividend - 10% 05/12/19989
State of incorporation changed from (DE) to (WI) 01/01/1994
Merged into Calender Holdings, Inc. 08/04/2000
Each share Common 10¢ par exchanged for $11.25 cash

JASON MINES LTD.
Recapitalized as New Jason Mines Ltd. 00/00/1948
Each share Capital Stock exchanged for (0.33333333) share Capital Stock
(See New Jason Mines Ltd.)

JASON MNG LTD (AUSTRALIA)
Name changed to Imperial Mining N.L. 12/04/1996
Imperial Mining N.L. name changed to Imperial One International Ltd. 05/22/2000 which name changed to Imperial One Ltd. 05/30/2000 which name changed to Empire Energy Group Ltd. 07/12/2011

JASPER EXPLORATIONS INC (NV)
Name changed to JPX Global, Inc. 01/31/2013

JASPER OIL CORP. (QC)
Acquired by Okalta Oils, Ltd. 08/17/1955
Each share Common no par exchanged for (1) share Common 90¢ par
Okalta Oils Ltd. recapitalized as Oakwood Petroleums Ltd. 06/10/1970 which was acquired by Sceptre Resources Ltd. 03/14/1989 which merged into Canadian Natural Resources Ltd. 08/15/1996

JASPER PORCUPINE MINES LTD. (ON)
Out of business 06/00/1965
No stockholders' equity

JASPER VENTURES INC (NV)
Common $0.001 par split (7) for (1) by issuance of (6) additional shares payable 10/28/2009 to holders of record 10/05/2009 Ex date - 10/29/2009
Reincorporated under the laws of Delaware as DesignLine Corp. and Common $0.001 par changed to $0.0001 par 11/09/2009
(See DesignLine Corp.)

JASTRZEBSKA SPOLKA WEGLOWA S A (POLAND)
ADR agreement terminated 08/06/2018
No ADR's remain outstanding

JATI TECHNOLOGIES INC (DE)
Recapitalized as Merco Sud Agro-Financial Equities Corp. 03/25/2009
Each (15) shares Common $0.0001 par exchanged for (1) share Common $0.0001 par

JAVA CAP INC (CANADA)
Reincorporated 04/04/2011
Place of incorporation changed from (AB) (Canada) 04/04/2011
Name changed to Peak Positioning Technologies Inc. 07/13/2011

JAVA CENTRALE INC (CA)
Common no par split (5) for (4) by issuance of (0.25) additional share 07/15/1994
Each share old Common no par exchanged for (0.1) share new Common no par 12/19/1997
Reorganized under the laws of Delaware as Paradise Holdings Inc. 05/12/1998
Each share new Common no par exchanged for (1) share Common no par
(See Paradise Holdings Inc.)

JAVA DETOUR INC (DE)
Each share old Common $0.001 par exchanged for (0.125) share new Common $0.001 par 01/03/2007
Chapter 7 bankruptcy proceedings terminated 01/03/2013
Stockholders' equity unlikely

JAVA EXPRESS INC (NV)
Each share old Common $0.001 par exchanged for (1/3) share new Common $0.001 par 11/27/2012
Name changed to Sundance Strategies Inc. 04/17/2013

JAVA GROUP INC (DE)
Name changed to Consolidated General Corp. 04/05/2005
Consolidated General Corp. recapitalized as GoldCorp Holdings, Co. 08/17/2007 which name changed to Goldland Holdings, Co. 10/20/2010 which name changed to Bravo Multinational Inc. 04/07/2016

JAVA INC (NV)
Recapitalized as Wasatch International Corp. 11/06/1995
Each share Common $0.001 par exchanged for (0.005) share Common $0.001 par
Wasatch International Corp. name changed to E-Pawn.com Inc. 02/29/2000 which name changed to UbuyHoldings Inc. 06/01/2001
(See UbuyHoldings Inc.)

JAVA JOES INTL CORP (QC)
Struck off register 05/07/2004

JAVAJUICE NET (NV)
Name changed to MT Ultimate Healthcare Corp. 09/02/2003
MT Ultimate Healthcare Corp. recapitalized as Monarch Staffing, Inc. 03/31/2006
(See Monarch Staffing, Inc.)

JAVAKINGCOFFEE INC (NV)
Common $0.001 par split (10) for (1) by issuance of (9) additional shares payable 08/01/2005 to holders of record 07/29/2005 Ex date - 08/02/2005
Name changed to Zingo, Inc. 09/07/2005
Zingo, Inc. name changed to Superlattice Power, Inc. 05/12/2008 which recapitalized as Sky Power Solutions Corp. 04/25/2011 which recapitalized as Clean Enviro Tech Corp. 01/18/2013 which recapitalized as Cyber Apps World Inc. 04/30/2015

JAVALON TECHNOLOGY GROUP INC (NV)
Reincorporated under the laws of British Virgin Islands as WorldVest Equity, Inc. 11/13/2008

JAVALUTION COFFEE CO (FL)
Reorganized under the laws of Delaware as AL International, Inc. 08/05/2011
Each share Common no par exchanged for (0.5) share Common $0.001 par
AL International, Inc. name changed to Youngevity International, Inc. 07/23/2013

JAVELIN CAP CORP (AB)
Reincorporated 09/20/2004
Place of incorporation changed from (BC) to (AB) 09/20/2004
Recapitalized as Javelin Energy Inc. 03/30/2006
Each share Common no par exchanged for (0.25) share Common no par
(See Javelin Energy Inc.)

JAVELIN ENERGY INC (AB)
Assets sold for the benefit of creditors 05/26/2010
No stockholders' equity

JAVELIN ENTERPRISES LTD. (BC)
Name changed to Canterra Development Corp. Ltd. 06/01/1971
(See Canterra Development Corp. Ltd.)

JAVELIN EXCHANGE-TRADED TR (DE)
Completely liquidated
Each share JETS Dow Jones Islamic

Market International Index Fund no par received first and final distribution of $49.1026354 cash payable 10/29/2010 to holders of record 10/22/2010
Completely liquidated 10/11/2011
Each share JETS Contrarian Opporunities Index Fund no par received first and final distribution of approximately $35.83 cash

JAVELIN INTL LTD (CANADA)
Recapitalized as Nalcap Holdings Inc. 10/06/1987
Each share Capital Stock no par exchanged for (0.2) share Common no par
Nalcap Holdings Inc. recapitalized as Arbatax International Inc. (Canada) 03/28/1996 which reincorporated in Yukon 08/06/1996 which name changed to MFC Bancorp Ltd. (YT) 03/03/1997 which reincorporated in British Columbia 11/03/2004 which name changed to KHD Humboldt Wedag International Ltd. 11/01/2005 which reorganized as Terra Nova Royalty Corp. 03/30/2010 which name changed to MFC Industrial Ltd. 09/30/2011 which name changed to MFC Bancorp Ltd. (BC) 02/16/2016
(See MFC Bancorp Ltd. (BC))

JAVELIN MINES LTD. (BC)
Name changed to Javelin Enterprises Ltd. 01/08/1971
Javelin Enterprises Ltd. name changed to Canterra Development Corp. Ltd. 06/01/1971
(See Canterra Development Corp. Ltd.)

JAVELIN MTG INVT CORP (MD)
Acquired by ARMOUR Residential REIT, Inc. 04/06/2016
Each share Common $0.001 par exchanged for $7.18 cash

JAVELIN PHARMACEUTICALS INC (DE)
Merged into Hospira, Inc. 07/02/2010
Each share Common $0.001 par exchanged for $2.20 cash

JAVELIN SYS INC (DE)
Name changed to Aspeon Inc. 01/31/2000
Aspeon Inc. name changed to ASPI, Inc. 09/24/2009 which name changed to JV Group, Inc. 05/25/2012

JAVELINA RES LTD (BC)
Name changed to Midpoint Holdings Ltd. 05/01/2013

JAVELLE CAP CORP (BC)
Each share old Common no par exchanged for (0.2) share new Common no par 10/07/2016
Recapitalized as Kenadyr Mining (Holdings) Corp. 03/28/2017
Each share Common no par exchanged for (0.5) share Common no par

JAVO BEVERAGE INC (DE)
Plan of reorganization under Chapter 11 Federal Bankruptcy proceedings effective 05/13/2011
No stockholders' equity

JAWZ INC (DE)
Reincorporated 07/07/2000
Name changed 10/02/2000
State of incorporation changed from (NV) to (DE) 07/07/2000
Name changed from Jaws Technologies, Inc. to Jawz Inc. 10/02/2000
Each share old Common $0.001 par exchanged for (0.1) share new Common $0.001 par 03/30/2001
Recapitalized as Ponderosa Lumber, Inc. (DE) 07/27/2006
Each share new Common $0.001 par exchanged for (0.01) share Common $0.001 par

Ponderosa Lumber, Inc. (DE) reincorporated in Nevada as National Automation Services, Inc. 10/11/2007 which name changed to National Energy Services, Inc. 07/15/2015

JAX INTL INC (DE)
Stock Dividends - 1.25% payable 7/15/97 to holders of record 6/30/97; 1.25% payable 10/31/97 to holders of record 9/30/97; 1.25% payable 5/11/98 to holders of record 3/31/98
Charter cancelled and declared inoperative and void for non-payment of taxes 3/1/99

JAXON MINERALS INC (BC)
Each share old Common no par exchanged for (0.1) share new Common no par 08/27/2013
Reorganized as Jaxon Mining Inc. 08/30/2017
Each share new Common no par exchanged for (1.25) shares Common no par

JAY BOY MUSIC CORP (NY)
Charter cancelled and proclaimed dissolved for failure to file reports and pay taxes 12/15/71

JAYARK CORP (NY)
Common $1 par changed to 30¢ par 9/14/71
Each share old Common 30¢ par exchanged for (0.1) share new Common 30¢ par 1/7/2000
Merged into J Acquisition Corp. 12/10/2003
Each share new Common 30¢ par exchanged for $0.40 cash

JAYARK FILMS CORP. (NY)
Name changed to Jayark Corp. 11/13/67
(See Jayark Corp.)

JAYCO INC (DE)
Name changed to Jako Inc. 6/26/91
(See Jako Inc.)

JAYDEN RES INC (BC)
Reincorporated under the laws of Cayman Islands and Common no par reclassified as Ordinary no par 10/03/2012

JAYE EXPLS LTD (ON)
Charter cancelled and declared dissolved for failure to file returns and pay fees 03/16/1976

JAYHAWK ACCEP CORP (TX)
Reincorporated under the laws of Delaware as Bruin Group, Inc. 03/02/2007
Bruin Group, Inc. recapitalized as Fusion Road, Inc. 07/30/2007 which name changed to VZillion, Inc. (DE) 09/10/2007 which reincorporated in Nevada 08/25/2008

JAYHAWK ENERGY INC (CO)
Reincorporated under the laws of Nevada 10/08/2015

JAYHAWK LIFE INS INC (KS)
Merged into I.C.H. Corp. (MO) 1/1/72
Each share Common $1 par exchanged for (2) shares Common $1 par
I.C.H. Corp. (MO) reincorporated in Delaware 8/15/77 which name changed to Southwestern Life Corp. (New) 6/15/94 which name changed to I.C.H. Corp. (New) 10/10/95
(See I.C.H. Corp. (New))

JAYLAC MINES LTD. (ON)
Charter cancelled and company declared dissolved for default in filing returns 05/13/1965

JAYMAX PRECISION PRODUCTS, INC. (NY)
Merged into D.W. Radio Corp. 12/30/67
Each share Common 10¢ par exchanged for $5 cash

JAYMEE INDS INC (NY)
Adjudicated bankrupt 1/18/77

JAYS INDS INC (DE)
Company believed out of business 00/00/2003
Details not available

JAYTEX OIL & GAS CO (OK)
Common 10¢ par split (2) for (1) by issuance of (1) additional share 10/15/80
Charter cancelled for failure to pay taxes 5/5/87

JAZZ AIR INCOME FD (ON)
Reorganized under the laws of Canada as Chorus Aviation Inc. 01/04/2011
Each Unit no par exchanged for (1) share Class B no par
Note: Non-Canadian residents received Class A Variable Shares
Unexchanged certificates were cancelled and became without value 01/04/2017

JAZZ GOLF EQUIP INC (CANADA)
Class B Common no par reclassified as Class A Common no par 02/25/2003
Assets sold for the benefit of creditors and name changed to 2980304 Canada Inc. 11/23/2006
(See 2980304 Canada Inc.)

JAZZ PHARMACEUTICALS INC (DE)
Issue Information - 6,000,000 shares COM offered at $18 per share on 05/31/2007
Reincorporated under the laws of Ireland as Jazz Pharmaceuticals PLC and Common $0.0001 par reclassified as Ordinary $0.0001 par 01/18/2012

JAZZ TECHNOLOGIES INC (DE)
Merged into Tower Semiconductor Ltd. 09/17/2008
Each share Common $0.0001 par exchanged for (1.8) shares Ordinary NIS 1 par

JAZZMAN RES INC (BC)
Recapitalized as International Jazzman Ventures Corp. 11/16/1995
Each share Common no par exchanged for (0.25) share Common no par
International Jazzman Ventures Corp. recapitalized as Oro Belle Resources Inc. 12/14/1995 which merged into Viceroy Resource Corp. 06/30/1998 which merged into Quest Capital Corp. (BC) 06/30/2003 which reincorporated in Canada 05/27/2008 which name changed to Sprott Resource Lending Corp. 09/10/2010 which merged into Sprott Inc. 07/24/2013

JAZZTEL P L C (ENGLAND & WALES)
Issue Information - 10,125,000 ADR'S offered at $17.447 per ADR on 12/08/1999
ADR agreement terminated 7/1/2002
Each Sponsored ADR for Ordinary exchanged for $0.35901 cash

JB CLOTHING CORP (NV)
Name changed to Entest BioMedical, Inc. 07/30/2009
Entest BioMedical, Inc. name changed to Entest Group, Inc. 02/14/2018

JB OXFORD HLDGS INC (DE)
Each share old Common 1¢ par exchanged for (0.1) share new Common 1¢ par 10/15/2002
Each share new Common 1¢ par exchanged again for (0.1) share new Common 1¢ par 12/30/2005
Note: Holders of (99) or fewer pre-split shares received $2.96 cash
New Common 1¢ par split (10) for (1) by issuance of (9) additional shares payable 02/17/2006 to holders of

record 02/15/2006 Ex date - 02/21/2006
Name changed to Cambridge Capital Holdings, Inc. 04/18/2006
(See Cambridge Capital Holdings, Inc.)

JB S RESTAURANTS INC (DE)
Name changed 02/01/1981
Reincorporated 03/05/1985
Name changed from JB's Big Boy Family Restaurants, Inc. to JB's Restaurants, Inc. 02/01/1981
State of incorporation changed from (CA) to (DE) 03/05/1985
Common no par changed to 10¢ par and (0.5) additional share issued 04/08/1985
Name changed to Summit Family Restaurants, Inc. 04/04/1995
Summit Family Restaurants, Inc. merged CKE Restaurants, Inc. 07/15/1996
(See CKE Restaurants, Inc.)

JBI CAP TR I (DE)
9.25% Guaranteed Preferred Securities called for redemption at $25 on 2/3/2003

JBI INC (NV)
Name changed to Plastic2Oil, Inc. 08/06/2014

JBS SOFTWARE TECHNOLOGIES PLC (UNITED KINGDOM)
Name changed to SurfControl plc 08/09/2000
(See SurfControl plc)

JBW VENTURES INC (DE)
Recapitalized as Lifeline Homecare Services, Inc. 11/30/88
Each share Common $0.001 par exchanged for (0.5) share Common $0.0001 par
(See Lifeline Homecare Services, Inc.)

JBZ CAP INC (CANADA)
Each share old Common no par exchanged for (0.33333333) share new Common no par 08/18/2010
Name changed to Strata Minerals Inc. (Canada) 11/08/2011
Strata Minerals Inc. (Canada) reorganized in Ontario 03/21/2017 which name changed to Revival Gold Inc. 07/10/2017

JC GEAR COM (NV)
Charter revoked for failure to file reports and pay fees 02/01/2007

JCC HLDG CO (DE)
Plan of reorganization under Chapter 11 Federal Bankruptcy Code effective 3/30/2001
No stockholders' equity
Merged into Harrah's Operating Co., Inc. 12/12/2002
Each share new Common 1¢ par exchanged for $10.54 cash

JCI LTD (SOUTH AFRICA)
Stock Dividends - 0.7651% payable 5/2/96 to holders of record 3/8/96; 1.1589% payable 11/22/96 to holders of record 9/27/96; 0.6416% payable 5/30/97 to holders of record 4/4/97; 2.55102% payable 11/20/97 to holders of record 9/26/97
ADR agreement terminated in 1998
Each ADR for Ordinary exchanged for $3.43516 cash

JCI TECHNOLOGIES INC (AB)
Recapitalized as JCITech.com Inc. 01/18/2000
Each share Common no par exchanged for (0.125) share Common no par
(See JCITech.com Inc.)

JCITECH COM INC (AB)
Cease trade order effective 02/01/2002

JCP&L CAP L P (DE)
Monthly Income Preferred Securities Ser. A called for redemption at $25

on 6/30/2003

JCT LTD (INDIA)
GDR agreement terminated 03/08/2018
Each 144A GDR for Ordinary exchanged for $0.233949 cash

JD AMERN WORKWEAR INC (DE)
Name changed to American Commerce Solutions Inc. 01/13/2001

JD GROUP LTD (SOUTH AFRICA)
ADR agreement terminated 07/22/2015
Each Sponsored ADR for Ordinary exchanged for $2.66457 cash

JDA SOFTWARE GROUP INC (DE)
Secondary Offering - 2,150,000 shares COM offered at $28 per share on 11/21/1996
Common 1¢ par split (3) for (2) by issuance of (0.5) additional share payable 07/17/1998 to holders of record 06/26/1998 Ex date - 07/20/1998
Acquired by RC Crown Parent, LLC 12/24/2012
Each share Common 1¢ par exchanged for $45 cash

JDL GOLD CORP (BC)
Under plan of merger name changed to Trek Mining Inc. 03/31/2017
Trek Mining Inc. name changed to Equinox Gold Corp. 12/22/2017

JDLPHOTOS COM INC (CO)
Common $0.0001 par split (21) for (1) by issuance of (20) additional shares payable 1/27/2003 to holders of record 1/24/2003 Ex date - 1/28/2003
Name changed to Valde Connections, Inc. 2/10/2003
Valde Connections, Inc. name changed to Signature Leisure, Inc. 8/18/2003

JDMC GLOBAL CORP (CO)
Name changed back to Joe Dandy Mining Co. 8/15/97

JDN RLTY CORP (MD)
Common 1¢ par split (3) for (2) by issuance of (0.5) additional share payable 06/30/1998 to holders of record 06/19/1998 Ex date - 07/01/1998
Merged into Developers Diversified Realty Corp. 03/13/2003
Each share 9.38% Ser. A Preferred 1¢ par exchanged for (1) share 9.375% Preferred no par
Each share Common 1¢ par exchanged for (0.518) share Common no par
Developers Diversified Realty Corp. name changed to DDR Corp. 09/15/2011

JDS CAP LTD (ON)
$2.21875 Retractable 1st Preferred Ser. A no par called for redemption 09/16/1988
Public interest eliminated

JDS FITEL INC (CANADA)
Common no par split (3) for (1) by issuance of (2) additional shares payable 04/15/1998 to holders of record 04/09/1998 Ex date - 04/07/1998
Merged into JDS Uniphase Corp. 07/06/1999
Each share Common no par exchanged for either (0.50855) share Common $0.001 par or (0.50855) JDS Uniphase Canada Ltd. Non-Vtg. Exchangeable share no par
JDS Uniphase Corp. name changed to Viavi Solutions Inc. 08/04/2015

JDS UNIPHASE CDA LTD (CANADA)
Old Non-Vtg. Exchangeable Shares no par split (2) for (1) by issuance of (1) additional share payable 12/29/1999 to holders of record 12/22/1999
Old Non-Vtg. Exchangeable Shares no par split (2) for (1) by issuance of (1) additional share payable 03/10/2000 to holders of record 03/02/2000
Each old Non-Vtg. Exchangeable Share no par exchanged for (0.125) new Non-Vtg. Exchangeable Share no par 10/17/2006
Each new Non-Vtg. Exchangeable Share no par exchanged for (1) share JDS Uniphase Corp. Common $0.001 par 03/31/2014
JDS Uniphase Corp. name changed to Viavi Solutions Inc. 08/04/2015

JDS UNIPHASE CORP (DE)
Old Common $0.001 par split (2) for (1) by issuance of (1) additional share payable 08/03/1999 to holders of record 07/23/1999
Old Common $0.001 par split (2) for (1) by issuance of (1) additional share payable 12/29/1999 to holders of record 12/22/1999
Old Common $0.001 par split (2) for (1) by issuance of (1) additional share payable 03/10/2000 to holders of record 03/02/2000
Each share old Common $0.001 par exchanged for (0.125) share new Common $0.001 par 10/17/2006
Each share new Common $0.001 par received distribution of (0.2) share Lumentum Holdings Inc. Common $0.001 par payable 08/03/2015 to holders of record 07/27/2015 Ex date - 08/04/2015
Name changed to Viavi Solutions Inc. 08/04/2015

JDV CAP CORP (BC)
Recapitalized as Margaret Lake Diamonds Inc. 03/27/2014
Each share Common no par exchanged for (0.5) share Common no par

JEAN COUTU GROUP PJC INC (QC)
Class A Subordinate no par split (2) for (1) by issuance of (1) additional share 03/13/1992
Class A Subordinate no par split (2) for (1) by issuance of (1) additional share payable 10/03/2000 to holders of record 09/29/2000 Ex date - 09/27/2000
Class A Subordinate no par split (2) for (1) by issuance of (1) additional share payable 09/30/2002 to holders of record 09/25/2002
Acquired by Metro Inc. 05/14/2018
Each share Class A Subordinate no par exchanged for $24.50 cash
Note: Unexchanged certificates will be cancelled and become without value 05/14/2024

JEAN LAKE LITHIUM MINES LTD (ON)
Charter cancelled for failure to pay taxes and file returns 6/29/81

JEAN PHILIPPE FRAGRANCES INC (DE)
Each share old Common $0.001 par exchanged for (0.4) share new Common $0.001 par 8/3/90
New Common $0.001 par split (3) for (2) by issuance of (0.5) additional share 12/9/92
Name changed to Inter Parfums, Inc. 7/14/99

JEAN PIERRE COSMETIQUES INC (CANADA)
Dissolved 10/04/1993

JEANETTE MINERALS LTD. (ON)
Charter revoked for failure to file reports and pay fees 10/10/61

JEANNETTE CORP (PA)
Common $1 par split (5) for (4) by ance of (0.25) additional share 8/30/76
Common $1 par split (5) for (4) by ance of (0.25) additional share 3/27/78
Under plan of merger each share Common $1 par exchanged for $20 cash 12/19/78
100% of 7% Preferred $100 par reacquired in 1981
Public interest eliminated

JEANNETTE GLASS CO. (PA)
Recapitalized in 1936
Each share old Preferred $100 par exchanged for (1) share new Preferred $100 par
Each share old Common $1 par exchanged for (3) shares Common no par
Each share Common no par exchanged for (3) shares new Common $1 par in 1946
Each share new Common $1 par split (2) for (1) by issuance of (1) additional share 6/17/69
Name changed to Jeannette Corp. 5/14/71
(See Jeannette Corp.)

JEANTEX GROUP INC (FL)
Name changed to Catalyst Resource Group, Inc. 05/24/2010
(See Catalyst Resource Group, Inc.)

JEBCO INC (GA)
Each share Class A Common 10¢ par exchanged for (1) share Preferred $1 par and (0.5) share Common 10¢ par 6/6/67
Each share Class B Common 10¢ par exchanged for (1) share Common 10¢ par 6/6/67
Common 10¢ par split (2) for (1) by issuance of (1) additional share 3/30/70
Each share Common 10¢ par exchanged for (0.02) share Common $5 par 4/10/74
5% Preferred $1 par called for redemption 1/31/79
Merged into Gregco, Inc. 3/1/79
Each share Common $5 par exchanged for $134.02 cash

JECO2 LASERS INC (NJ)
Name changed to Robotic Lasers, Inc. 02/17/1988
Robotic Lasers, Inc. recapitalized as Genisys Reservation Systems Inc. 07/29/1996 which name changed to Netcruise.com, Inc. 10/20/1999
(See Netcruise.com, Inc.)

JED OIL INC (AB)
Plan of arrangement effective 11/20/2009
No stockholders' equity

JEDA PETE LTD (BC)
Merged into Roseland Resources Ltd. 02/29/2000
Each share Common no par exchanged for (0.5) share Common no par
Roseland Resources Ltd. merged into Rival Energy Ltd. 06/16/2003 which merged into Zargon Energy Trust 01/23/2008 which reorganized as Zargon Oil & Gas Ltd. (New) 01/07/2011

JEDBURGH RES LTD (CANADA)
Recapitalized as OTI Technologies Inc. 01/20/1987
Each share Common no par exchanged for (1/6) share Common no par
(See OTI Technologies Inc.)

JEDDER GOLD MINES LTD.
Out of business in 1947
No stockholders' equity

JEDEDIAH RES CORP (NV)
Name changed to Alterola Biotech Inc. 08/26/2010

JEDI MIND INC (NV)
Name changed to Mind Technologies, Inc. 05/09/2011
(See Mind Technologies, Inc.)

JEDI RESOURCES LTD. (BC)
Name changed to O'Hara Resources Ltd. (BC) 05/22/1985
O'Hara Resources Ltd. (BC) reorganized in Nevada 10/25/1990 which recapitalized as Vision Energy Group, Inc. 03/10/2005 which name changed to Advanced Mineral Technologies, Inc. 04/30/2007
(See Advanced Mineral Technologies, Inc.)

JEEP GOLD MINE LTD. (MB)
Name changed to Transtide Industries Ltd. in May 1969
(See Transtide Industries Ltd.)

JEFFBANKS INC (PA)
9.5% Preferred $1 par called for redemption 10/06/1995
9.50% Conv. Preferred Ser. D $1 par called for redemption 10/06/1995
11% Conv. Preferred Ser. C $1 par called for redemption 10/06/1995
12% Conv. Preferred Ser. B $1 par called for redemption 10/06/1995
8% Conv. Preferred Ser. E $1 par called for redemption 10/31/1995
Common $1 par split (5) for (3) by issuance of (0.66666666) additional share payable 08/20/1998 to holders of record 07/31/1998
Stock Dividends - 5% payable 03/15/1996 to holders of record 02/22/1996; 5% payable 05/13/1997 to holders of record 04/22/1997
Merged into Hudson United Bancorp 11/30/1999
Each share Common $1 par exchanged for (0.9785) share Common no par
Hudson United Bancorp merged into TD Banknorth Inc. 01/31/2006
(See TD Banknorth Inc.)

JEFFERIES GROUP INC NEW (DE)
Common $0.0001 par split (2) for (1) by issuance of (1) additional share payable 08/15/2003 to holders of record 07/31/2003 Ex date - 08/18/2003
Common $0.0001 par split (2) for (1) by issuance of (1) additional share payable 05/15/2006 to holders of record 04/28/2006 Ex date - 05/16/2006
Merged into Leucadia National Corp. 03/01/2013
Each share Common $0.0001 par exchanged for (0.81) share Common $1 par
Leucadia National Corp. name changed to Jefferies Financial Group Inc. 05/24/2018

JEFFERIES GROUP INC OLD (DE)
Common 1¢ par split (2) for (1) by issuance of (1) additional share payable 03/29/1996 to holders of record 03/15/1996 Ex date - 04/01/1996
Common 1¢ par split (2) for (1) by issuance of (1) additional share payable 12/15/1997 to holders of record 11/28/1997 Ex date - 12/16/1997
Each share Common 1¢ par received distribution of (1) share Jefferies Group, Inc. (New) Common $0.0001 par payable 04/27/1999 to holders of record 04/20/1999 Ex date - 04/28/1999
Under plan of merger name changed to Investment Technology Group Inc. (New) 04/27/1999

JEFFERSON & CLEARFIELD COAL & IRON CO.
Merged into Rochester & Pittsburgh Coal Co. in 1928
Details not available

JEFFERSON (THOMAS) INSURANCE CO. (KY)
Stock Dividends - 14% 5/1/62; 10% 9/3/63; 20% 7/1/70
Each share old Common $1 par

exchanged for (0.001666) share new Common $1 par 11/25/72
Note: In effect holders received $6.84 cash per share and public interest was eliminated

JEFFERSON APARTMENT HOTEL, INC. (IN)
Completely liquidated 07/15/1966
Each share Common no par exchanged for first and final distribution of $75.7922 cash

JEFFERSON BANCORP INC (FL)
Common $1 par split (3) for (2) by issuance of (0.5) additional share 11/07/1986
Merged into Colonial BancGroup, Inc. 01/03/1997
Each share Common $1 par exchanged for (0.49090909) share Common $2.50 par
(See Colonial BancGroup, Inc.)

JEFFERSON BANCORP INC (LA)
Merged into ISB Financial Corp. 10/18/96
Each share Common no par exchanged for $23 cash

JEFFERSON BANCSHARES, INC. (LA)
Common $2.50 par changed to $1.25 par and (1) additional share issued 7/2/84
Assets transferred to Jefferson Bancshares Inc. Common Shareholders Liquidating Trust and Common $1.25 par reclassified as Shares of Bene. Int. 8/8/88
(See Jefferson Bancshares Inc. Common Liquidating Trust)

JEFFERSON BANCSHARES INC. COMMON SHAREHOLDERS LIQUIDATING TRUST (LA)
In process of liquidation
Details not available

JEFFERSON BANCSHARES INC (TN)
Merged into HomeTrust Bancshares, Inc. 05/31/2014
Each share Common 1¢ par exchanged for (0.2661) share Common 1¢ par and $4 cash

JEFFERSON BANK & TRUST CO. (METAIRIE, LA)
Under plan of reorganization each share Common $2.50 par automatically became (1) share Jefferson Bancshares, Inc. Common $2.50 par 9/5/80
Jefferson Bancshares, Inc. assets transferred to Jefferson Bancshares Inc. Common Shareholders Liquidating Trust 8/8/88
(See Jefferson Bancshares Inc. Common Shareholders Liquidating Trust)

JEFFERSON BK & TR CO (ST LOUIS, MO)
Stock Dividend - 50% 06/17/1960
Location changed to Eureka, MO 02/01/1989

JEFFERSON BK (HAVERFORD, PA)
Common $3.50 par changed to $1.75 par and (1) additional share issued 1/30/87
Merged into State Bancshares, Inc. 12/3/93
Each share Common $1.75 par exchanged for (0.5) share Common $1 par
State Bancshares, Inc. name changed to JeffBanks, Inc. 5/22/95 which merged into Hudson United Bancorp 11/30/99 which merged into TD Banknorth Inc. 1/31/2006
(See TD Banknorth Inc.)

JEFFERSON BK FLA (OLDSMAR, FL)
Reorganized as Jefferson Bankshares, Inc. 02/27/2014
Each share Common $5 par exchanged for (1) share Common 1¢ par

JEFFERSON BANKSHARES INC (VA)
Common $2.50 par split (3) for (2) by issuance of (0.5) additional share 04/30/1986
Common $2.50 par split (4) for (3) by issuance of (0.33333333) additional share 01/24/1989
Common $2.50 par split (2) for (1) by issuance of (1) additional share 04/30/1993
Merged into Wachovia Corp. (New) (Ctfs. dated between 05/20/1991 and 09/01/2001) 10/31/1997
Each share Common $2.50 par exchanged for (0.625) share Common $5 par
Wachovia Corp. (New) (Ctfs. dated between 05/20/1991 and 09/01/2001) merged into Wachovia Corp. (Ctfs. dated after 09/01/2001) 09/01/2001 which merged into Wells Fargo & Co. (New) 12/31/2008

JEFFERSON BREWING CO.
Dissolved in 1939
Details not available

JEFFERSON CAP CORP (CO)
Name changed to Ohio & Southwestern Energy Co. (CO) 5/9/90
Ohio & Southwestern Energy Co. (CO) reincorporated in Delaware as Strategic Internet Investments, Inc. 10/8/2001

JEFFERSON CAP INC NEW (NV)
Name changed to Future Systems Inc. 1/2/91 which name changed back to Jefferson Capital, Inc. 2/24/92
Name changed to Spirit Gaming Group Inc. 1/23/96

JEFFERSON CAP INTS INC (MD)
Name changed to Trans Global Logistics Inc. 05/02/2005
(See Trans Global Logistics Inc.)

JEFFERSON CONSTRUCTION CO. (MA)
Name changed to Intercontinental Industries, Inc. (MA) 05/19/1967
Intercontinental Industries, Inc. (MA) reincorporated in Nevada 02/16/1968
(See Intercontinental Industries, Inc. (NV))

JEFFERSON CORP. LIQUIDATING TRUST (IN)
Liquidation completed
Each Trust Unit no par received initial distribution of $2.70 cash 12/1/86
Each Trust Unit no par received second distribution of $0.08 cash 12/18/87
Each Trust Unit no par exchanged for third and final distribution of $0.05 cash 11/27/89

JEFFERSON CORP (IN)
Stock Dividends - 10% 10/1/84; 10% 10/1/85
Each share Capital Stock no par received initial distribution of $25 cash 1/20/86
Each share Capital Stock no par received second distribution of $4.81 principal amount of Somerset Group, Inc. 10% Subord. Debentures due 4/1/96 and (2) shares Somerset Group, Inc. Common no par 4/25/86
Assets transferred to Jefferson Corp. Liquidating Trust and Capital Stock no par reclassified as Trust Unit no par 11/15/86
(See Jefferson Corp. Liquidating Trust)

JEFFERSON COUNSEL CORP. (DE)
Dissolved in 1962
Class B Common has no value
Charter subsequently revoked 4/1/65

JEFFERSON CUSTODIAN FUND, INC. (DE)
Stock Dividend - 100% 7/7/53
Acquired by Broad Street Investing Corp. on a (1) for (4.71938) basis 10/10/58
Broad Street Investing Corp. name changed to Seligman Common Stock Fund, Inc. 5/1/82

JEFFERSON ELECTRIC CO. (DE)
Reincorporated 2/10/60
Each share Capital Stock no par exchanged for (2.5) shares Capital Stock $5 par 9/26/52
Reincorporated from under the laws of (IL) to (DE) on a (1.25) for (1) basis 2/10/60
Completely liquidated 2/23/67
Each share Common $5 par exchanged for first and final distribution of (0.15676) share Litton Industries, Inc. Conv. Participating Ser. $2.50 par
(See Litton Industries, Inc.)

JEFFERSON FED SVGS & LN ASSN (USA)
Reorganized as Jefferson Bancshares, Inc. (TN) 07/01/2003
Each share Common $1 par exchanged for (4.2661) shares Common 1¢ par
Jefferson Bancshares, Inc. (TN) merged into HomeTrust Bancshares, Inc. 05/31/2014

JEFFERSON FED SVGS BK (GRETNA, LA)
Reorganized as Jefferson Bancorp, Inc. (LA) 8/18/94
Each share Common 1¢ par exchanged for (2.6528) shares Common no par
Jefferson Bancorp, Inc. (LA) merged into ISB Financial Corp. 10/18/96

JEFFERSON FIRE INSURANCE CO.
Dissolved in 1931
Details not available

JEFFERSON HOTEL CO.
Liquidated in 1951
Details not available

JEFFERSON LAKE ASBESTOS CORP (NV)
Name changed to Pacific Asbestos Corp. 5/27/64
(See Pacific Asbestos Corp.)

JEFFERSON LAKE OIL CO., INC. (LA)
Name changed to Jefferson Lake Sulphur Co., Inc. (LA) in February, 1940
Jefferson Lake Sulphur Co., Inc. (LA) reincorporated in New Jersey as Jefferson Lake Sulphur Co. 12/31/49 which merged into Occidental Petroleum Corp. (CA) 3/2/64 which reincorporated in Delaware 5/21/86

JEFFERSON LAKE PETROCHEMICALS CDA LTD (CANADA)
Merged into Canadian Occidental Petroleum Ltd. 07/12/1971
Each share Common $1 par exchanged for (1) share Common $1 par
Canadian Occidental Petroleum Ltd. name changed to Nexen Inc. 11/02/2000
(See Nexen Inc.)

JEFFERSON LAKE SULPHUR CO., INC. (LA)
Each share Common 25¢ par exchanged for (0.25) share Common $1 par in May, 1945
Reincorporated under laws of New Jersey as Jefferson Lake Sulphur Co. 12/31/49
Jefferson Lake Sulphur Co. merged into Occidental Petroleum Corp. (CA) 3/2/64 which reincorporated in Delaware 5/21/86

JEFFERSON LAKE SULPHUR CO. (NJ)
Common $1 par split (2) for (1) by issuance of (1) additional share 1/18/52
Preferred $10 par called for redemption 3/2/64
Merged into Occidental Petroleum Corp. (CA) 3/2/64
Each share Common $1 par exchanged for (0.676) share Capital Stock 20¢ par
Occidental Petroleum Corp. (CA) reincorporated in Delaware 5/21/86

JEFFERSON NATL BK (MIAMI BEACH, FL)
Common $20 par changed to $10 par and (1) additional share issued 12/03/1968
Through voluntary exchange offer Jefferson Bancorp, Inc. held 100% excluding directors qualifying shares, as of 01/07/1971
Public interest eliminated

JEFFERSON NATL BK (PASSAIC, NJ)
Merged into HUBCO, Inc. 04/05/1995
Each share Common $6 par exchanged for (2.865) shares Common no par
HUBCO, Inc. name changed to Hudson United Bancorp 11/30/1999 which merged into TD Banknorth Inc. 01/31/2006
(See TD Banknorth Inc.)

JEFFERSON NATL BK (WATERTOWN, NY)
Common $1 par split (3) for (2) by issuance of (0.5) additional share 09/02/1986
Common $1 par split (5) for (4) by issuance of (0.25) additional share 09/01/1987
Bank closed and FDIC appointed receiver 02/26/1993
Stockholders' equity undetermined

JEFFERSON NATL BK SUNNY ISLES FLA (NORTH MIAMI BEACH, FL)
99.6% excluding directors qualifying shares acquired by Jefferson Bancorp, Inc. through voluntary exchange offer which expired 04/05/1971
Public interest eliminated

JEFFERSON NATL CORP (DE)
Charter cancelled and declared inoperative and void for non-payment of taxes 03/01/1982

JEFFERSON NATL LIFE INS CO (IN)
Stock Dividends - 33-1/3% 8/3/42; 25% 3/15/44; 33-1/3% 3/15/54; 20% 4/30/58; 20% 6/1/60; 50% 6/15/65; 10% 3/4/70; 100% 10/8/84
Acquired by Lomas & Nettleton Financial Corp. 12/30/85
Each share Common $1 par exchanged for $32.50 cash

JEFFERSON PARK (SD)
Proclaimed dissolved 4/2/90

JEFFERSON PILOT CORP (NC)
Common $2.50 par changed to $1.25 par and (1) additional share issued 6/22/73
Common $1.25 par split (3) for (2) by issuance of (0.5) additional share 6/28/84
Common $1.25 par split (3) for (2) by issuance of (0.5) additional share 6/26/86
Common $1.25 par split (3) for (2) by issuance of (0.5) additional share 4/14/92
Common $1.25 par split (3) for (2) by issuance of (0.5) additional share 12/22/95
Common $1.25 par split (3) for (2) by issuance of (0.5) additional share payable 4/13/98 to holders of record 3/20/98 Ex date - 4/14/98
Common $1.25 par split (3) for (2) by issuance of (0.5) additional share payable 4/9/2001 to holders of record 3/19/2001 Ex date - 4/10/2001

Stock Dividend - 25% 3/14/69
Merged into Lincoln National Corp. 4/3/2006
Each share Common $1.25 par exchanged for $55.96 cash

JEFFERSON SAVINGS & LOAN ASSOCIATION (CA)
Liquidated
Each share Guarantee Stock exchanged for initial distribution of $19 cash 12/23/69
A Second and Final Distribution of approximately 35¢ per share was anticipated to be paid in May 1970 but we have not been able to confirm this

JEFFERSON SVGS & LN ASSN F A (VA)
Each share Common $1 par exchanged for (0.33333333) share Common $3 par 03/18/1993
Merged into Crestar Financial Corp. 01/20/1995
Each share Common $3 par exchanged for (0.449) share Common $5 par
Crestar Financial Corp. merged into SunTrust Banks, Inc. 12/31/1998

JEFFERSON SVGS BANCORP INC (DE)
Common 1¢ par split (2) for (1) by issuance of (1) additional share payable 12/17/97 to holders of record 12/3/97
Merged into Union Planters Corp. 2/12/2001
Each share Common 1¢ par exchanged for (0.433) share Common $5 par
Union Planters Corp. merged into Regions Financial Corp. (New) 7/1/2004

JEFFERSON SMURFIT CORP NEW (DE)
Merged into Smurfit-Stone Container Corp. (Old) 11/18/1998
Each share Common 1¢ par exchanged for (1) share Common 1¢ par
Smurfit-Stone Container Corp. (Old) reorganized as Smurfit-Stone Container Corp. (New) 06/30/2010 which merged into Rock-Tenn Co. 05/27/2011 which merged into WestRock Co. 07/01/2015

JEFFERSON SMURFIT CORP OLD (DE)
Common $1 par split (2) for (1) by issuance of (1) additional share 12/01/1986
Common $1 par split (2) for (1) by issuance of (1) additional share 08/30/1988
Merged into SIBV/MS Acquisition Corp. 12/14/1989
Each share Common $1 par exchanged for $43 cash

JEFFERSON SMURFIT GROUP PLC (IRELAND)
Acquired by Madison Dearborn Partners, L.L.C. 11/4/2002
Each Sponsored ADR for Ordinary 0.25p par exchanged for $21.50 cash

JEFFERSON STD LIFE INS CO (NC)
Each share Capital Stock $100 par exchanged for (10) shares Capital Stock $10 par in 1938
Capital Stock $10 par changed to $5 par and (1) additional share issued 3/15/60
Capital Stock $5 par changed to $2.50 par and (1) additional share issued 3/17/64
Stock Dividends - 100% 12/41; 150% 1/1/46; 50% 12/8/50; 33-1/3% 2/15/54; 25% 3/1/57
Under plan of reorganization each share Capital Stock $2.50 par automatically became (1) share Jefferson-Pilot Corp. Capital Stock $2.50 par 6/26/68
(See Jefferson-Pilot Corp.)

JEFFERSON STORES INC (DE)
Capital Stock $1 par split (3) for (2) issuance of (0.5) additional share 7/5/68
Merged into Marcor Inc. 4/30/73
Each share Capital Stock $1 par exchanged for (0.421) share Common $1 par
Marcor Inc. merged into Mobil Corp. 7/1/76 which merged into Exxon Mobil Corp. 11/30/99

JEFFERSON THOMAS LIFE INS CO AMER (IL)
Merged into Bankers Union Life Insurance Co. 12/31/79
Each share Common $2 par exchanged for (0.1) share Common $5 par
Bankers Union Life Insurance Co. merged into I.C.H. Corp. 10/14/82 which name changed to Southwestern Life Corp. (New) 6/15/94 which name changed to I.C.H. Corp. (New) 10/10/95
(See I.C.H. Corp. (New))

JEFFERSON TRACTION CO.
Property sold in 1927
No stockholders' equity

JEFFERSON TRAVIS CORP.
Name changed to Musicraft Recording Corp. in 1946
(See Musicraft Recording Corp.)

JEFFERSON VY GOLD MINES INC (UT)
Delisted from Alberta Stock Exchange 07/06/1990

JEFFERSON-WILLIAMS ENERGY CORP (TX)
Charter forfeited for failure to maintain a registered agent 9/29/92

JEFFREY MARTIN INC (NJ)
Acquired by Dep Corp. 2/19/87
Each share Common 10¢ par exchanged for $7.30 cash

JEGEROIL CORP (DE)
Recapitalized as Compression Technologies, Inc. 04/29/1991
Each share Common $0.005 par exchanged for (0.05) share Common $0.005 par
Compression Technologies, Inc. recapitalized as Oriental Focus International Ltd. 10/10/1994
(See Oriental Focus International Ltd.)

JEI AIRLS INC (DE)
Charter cancelled and declared inoperative and void for non-payment of taxes 3/1/85

JELEX MINES LTD (ON)
Capital Stock $1 par changed to no par 01/26/1972
Recapitalized as Key Lake Explorations Ltd. 06/21/1978
Each share Common no par exchanged for (0.2) share Common no par
(See Key Lake Explorations Ltd.)

JELLICOE CONSOLIDATED GOLD MINES LTD. (ON)
Acquired by Jellicoe Mines (1939) Ltd. 00/00/1939
Each share Capital Stock $1 par exchanged for (0.33333333) share Capital Stock $1 par
Jellicoe Mines (1939) Ltd. recapitalized as Jelex Mines Ltd. 10/01/1963 which recapitalized as Key Lake Explorations Ltd. 06/21/1978
(See Key Lake Explorations Ltd.)

JELLICOE GOLD MINING CO. LTD.
Merged into Jellicoe Consolidated Gold Mines Ltd. 00/00/1936
Each share Capital Stock $1 par exchanged for (0.66666666) share Capital Stock $1 par
Jellicoe Consolidated Gold Mines Ltd. was acquired by Jellicoe Mines (1939) Ltd. 00/00/1939 which was recapitalized as Jelex Mines Ltd. 10/01/1963 which recapitalized as Key Lake Explorations Ltd. 06/21/1978
(See Key Lake Explorations Ltd.)

JELLICOE MINES (1939) LTD. (ON)
Recapitalized as Jelex Mines Ltd. 10/01/1963
Each share Capital Stock $1 par exchanged for (0.2) share Capital Stock $1 par
Jelex Mines Ltd. recapitalized as Key Lake Explorations Ltd. 06/21/1978
(See Key Lake Explorations Ltd.)

JEM EXPLORATION CORP. LTD. (ON)
Each share Capital Stock $1 par exchanged for (20) shares Capital Stock no par 12/09/1955 Charter dissolved 09/21/1959

JEM GROUP PRODTNS INC (BC)
Recapitalized as Harvard Capital Corp. 08/09/1990
Each share Common no par exchanged for (0.5) share Common no par
Harvard Capital Corp. recapitalized as Harvard International Technologies Ltd. 02/16/1993
(See Harvard International Technologies Ltd.)

JEM RECORDS INC (NJ)
Charter revoked for failure to file reports and pay fees 2/8/95

JEMI FIBRE CORP (BC)
Merged into CanWel Building Materials Group Ltd. 05/16/2016
Each share Common no par exchanged for (0.03212335) share new Common no par
Note: Unexchanged certificates will be cancelled and become without value 05/16/2022

JEN TEK ENTERPRISES & EXPLS INC (ON)
Delisted from Alberta Stock Exchange 08/02/1988

JENANET COM INC (DE)
Reorganized under the laws of Nevada as as Dynamic Media Holdings, Inc. 08/20/2007
Each (167) shares Common $0.0001 par exchanged for (1) share Common $0.0001 par
Dynamic Media Holdings, Inc. name changed to Evermedia Group, Inc. 03/25/2009

JENEX CORP (AB)
Reincorporated under the laws of British Columbia as Therma Bright Inc. 02/08/2018

JENEX EXPLORATION LTD. (AB)
Charter cancelled for failure to file returns in 1970

JENEX GOLD CORP (WA)
Recapitalized as Sun Tzu Corp. 01/15/2009
Each share Common $0.001 par exchanged for (0.005) share Common $0.001 par
(See Sun Tzu Corp.)

JENKINS BROS (NJ)
Non-Vtg. Common $25 par reclassified as Class B Common $10 par 05/06/1977
Stock Dividend - 20% 06/14/1977
Merged into AJY Inc. 06/27/1984
Each share Class B Common $10 par exchanged for $61 cash

JENKINS BROS LTD (CANADA)
Common $25 par changed to $5 par and (4) additional shares issued 05/13/1966
Name changed to Jenkins Canada Inc. and Common $5 par changed to no par 04/17/1979
(See Jenkins Canada Inc.)

JENKINS CDA INC (CANADA)
Declared insolvent 07/28/2003
No stockholders' equity

JENKINS TELEVISION CORP. (DE)
No longer in existence having become inoperative and void for non-payment of taxes 4/1/34

JENKON INTL INC (DE)
Name changed to Multimedia K.I.D., Inc. 06/01/2000
Multimedia K.I.D., Inc. recapitalized as SYCO, Inc. (DE) 12/28/2006 which reincorporated in Colorado as Marine Exploration, Inc. 05/11/2007 which recapitalized as In Ovations Holdings Inc. 10/15/2013

JENN AIR CORP (IN)
Merged into Carrier Corp. 1/15/79
Each share Common no par exchanged for (1.35) shares Common $2.50 par
Carrier Corp. acquired by United Technologies Corp. 7/6/79

JENNA LANE INC (NV)
Reincorporated 12/08/2006
Issue Information - 600,000 UNITS consisting of (2) shares COM and (1) CL A WT offered at $10.125 per Unit on 03/19/1997
Stock Dividend - 10% payable 03/13/1998 to holders of record 03/06/1998
State of incorporation changed from (DE) to (NV) 12/08/2006
Name changed to Propalms USA, Inc. 03/16/2007
Propalms USA, Inc. name changed to Propalms, Inc. 06/21/2007 which name changed to ProTek Capital Inc. 10/27/2010

JENNCOR ACQUISITIONS INC (DE)
Recapitalized as Scantek Medical Inc. 10/09/1991
Each share Common $0.0001 par exchanged for (0.7) share Common $0.0001 par
(See Scantek Medical Inc.)

JENNER INDS INC (NY)
Dissolved by proclamation 12/24/1991

JENNICA INC (CO)
Name changed to Noble Management, Inc. (CO) 4/19/91
Noble Management, Inc. (CO) reorganized in Nevada 5/31/91
(See Noble Management, Inc.)

JENNIFER CONVS INC (DE)
Plan of reorganization under Chapter 11 Federal Bankruptcy proceedings effective 02/22/2011
No stockholders' equity
(Additional Information in Active)

JENNIFER PETES LTD (AB)
Each share Common no par exchanged for (0.5) share Class A Subordinate no par and (0.5) share Class B Common no par 11/15/1983
Delisted from Alberta Stock Exchange 03/29/1989

JENNINGS (ERWIN M.) CO., INC.
Liquidated in 1933
Details not available

JENNISON US EMERGING GROWTH FD INC (MD)
Name changed to Jennison Mid-Cap Growth Fund, Inc. 03/19/2007

JENNISON VALUE FD (MA)
Name changed to JennisonDryden Portfolios 10/09/2007

JENOA INC (CA)
Under plan of partial liquidation each share Common no par received $2.95 cash 3/14/78
Recapitalized as EIP Microwave, Inc. (CA) 9/30/79
Each share Common no par

exchanged for (1) share Common no par and (1) share Cushman Electronics, Inc. Common no par distributed
(See Cushman Electronics, Inc.)
EIP Microwave, Inc. (CA) reincorporated in Delaware 4/29/87
(See EIP Microwave, Inc.)

JENOSYS ENTERPRISES INC (BC)
Recapitalized as Fintry Enterprises Inc. 12/10/2004
Each share Common no par exchanged for (0.1) share Common no par
Fintry Enterprises Inc. recapitalized as Mesa Uranium Corp. 12/23/2005 which name changed to Mesa Exploration Corp. 03/30/2011

JENSEN CORP (FL)
Name changed 9/15/72
Name changed from Jensen Machinery, Inc. to Jensen Corp. 9/15/72
Each share Common 10¢ par exchanged for (0.004444) share Common $22.50 par 4/18/81
In effect holders received $5 cash per share and public interest eliminated

JENSEN-CURTIS (CA)
Name changed back to Jensen Industries 9/17/76
(See Jensen Industries)

JENSEN G LTD (UT)
Name changed to North American Minerals Corp. 3/23/84
North American Minerals Corp. name changed to Tari Group, Inc. 3/18/86 which name changed to Microshare Corp. 11/12/86

JENSEN INDS (CA)
Common $1 par changed to $0.66666666 par and (0.5) additional share issued 09/15/1972
Stock Dividends - 20% 11/23/1976; 20% 04/21/1977; 20% 05/12/1978; 20% 04/20/1979
Name changed to Jensen-Curtis 12/21/1973 which name changed back to Jensen Industries 09/17/1976
Merged into Nortek, Inc. 03/19/1985
Each share Common $0.66666666 par exchanged for $15.36 cash

JENSEN MACHINERY CO., INC. (NY)
Charter cancelled and proclaimed dissolved for failure to pay taxes and file reports 8/30/50

JENSEN MANUFACTURING CO.
Acquired by Muter Co. (IL) in 1948
Details not available

JENSEN YELLOWKNIFE GOLD MINES, LTD. (ON)
Charter cancelled for failure to file reports and pay taxes 00/00/1953

JENSON INTL INC (NV)
SEC revoked common stock registration 10/15/2008

JENTECH VENTURES CORP (BC)
Common no par split (3) for (1) by issuance of (2) additional shares 05/07/1990
Recapitalized as Impact Travel Technology Inc. 04/26/1993
Each share Common no par exchanged for (0.1) share Common no par
Impact Travel Technology Inc. recapitalized as MCF Enterprises, Inc. 03/12/1999 which name changed to Online Consortium Corp. 02/09/2001 which name changed to Equicap Financial Corp. 07/10/2003 which name changed to Zecotek Medical Systems, Inc. 02/10/2005 which name changed to Zecotek Photonics Inc. 11/26/2007

JEPH YELLOWKNIFE GOLD MINES, LTD. (ON)
Liquidated 08/01/1959

Details not available

JEPSON CORP (DE)
Merged into J Acquisition Corp. 9/25/89
Each share Common 1¢ par exchanged for $12 cash

JER ENVIROTECH INTL CORP (YT)
Reincorporated 02/13/2006
Place of incorporation changed from (YT) to (BC) 02/13/2006
Default judgment obtained against the company 11/20/2009
All officers and directors subsequently resigned 12/22/2009
Stockholders' equity unlikely

JEREMIAH CORP (CO)
Under plan of merger Common 1¢ par changed to no par 3/22/78
Merged into October Oil Co. (New) 10/18/82
Each share Common no par exchanged for (0.125) share Common $0.001 par
(See October Oil Co. (New))

JEREMYS MICROBATCH ICE CREAMS INC (DE)
Company terminated registration of securities 9/30/2003
Details not available

JEREZ ENERGY INTL INC (AB)
Name changed 07/25/1996
Name changed from Jerez Investment Corp. to Jerez Energy International Inc. 07/25/1996
Cease trade order effective 06/20/2003
Stockholders' equity unlikely

JERGENS ANDREW CO (OH)
Common $100 par changed to no par 00/00/1939
Each share Preferred $10 par exchanged for (8) shares Common no par 03/23/1965
Common no par split (2) for (1) by issuance of (1) additional share 04/08/1969
Stock Dividend - 50% 04/30/1968
Merged into American Brands, Inc. (NJ) 05/04/1971
Each share Common no par exchanged for $23.50 cash

JERICAP INC (NY)
Reorganized under the laws of Delaware as Graff Pay-Per-View, Inc. 05/14/1992
Each share Common $0.001 par exchanged for (0.1) share Common 1¢ par
Graff Pay-Per-View, Inc. name changed to Spice Entertainment Inc. 12/02/1996
(See Spice Entertainment Inc.)

JERICHO ENERGY CO INC (FL)
SEC revoked common stock registration 09/09/2008

JERICHO MINES LTD (BC)
Recapitalized as New Jericho Development Corp. Ltd. 04/12/1973
Each share Capital Stock $1 par exchanged for (0.2) share Capital Stock $1 par
New Jericho Development Corp. Ltd. recapitalized as Mt. Calvery Resources Ltd. 03/01/1982 which recapitalized as Triumph Resources Ltd. 08/22/1989 which recapitalized as Jericho Resources Ltd. 10/02/1992 which name changed to Regia Resources Ltd. 04/18/1995 which reincorporated in Canada 07/07/1995
(See Regia Resources Ltd.)

JERICHO RES LTD (BC)
Name changed to Regia Resources Ltd. (BC) 04/18/1995
Regia Resources Ltd. (BC) reincorporated in Canada 07/07/1995
(See Regia Resources Ltd.)

JERO INC (DE)
Charter cancelled and declared inoperative and void for non-payment of taxes 3/1/88

JEROCO GOLD MINES, LTD. (ON)
Charter cancelled for failure to file reports and pay taxes 00/00/1952

JEROME EXPLS LTD (ON)
Name changed to Dore Exploration Inc. 05/27/1983
Dore Exploration Inc. merged into Dore-Norbaska Resources Inc. 12/23/1987 which merged into Griffin Corp. 02/23/1998
(See Griffin Corp.)

JEROME GOLD MINES CORP (CANADA)
Merged into Pacific Metals Inc. 05/07/1991
Each share Common no par exchanged for (0.15) share Common no par
Pacific Metals Inc. recapitalized as Crescendo Capital Corp. 06/29/1995 which name changed to Tragoes Inc. 07/24/1996
Tragoes Inc. name changed to Rightsmarket.com Inc. 07/30/1999 which name changed to RightsMarket Inc. 06/07/2000 which reorganized as RightsMarket Ltd. 12/31/2003

JEROME GOLD MINES LTD. (ON)
Charter surrendered and company dissolved 06/30/1969
No stockholders' equity

JEROME GROUP INC (DE)
Reincorporated 12/31/82
Stock Dividend - 25% 8/14/81
State of incorporation changed from (NY) to (DE) 12/31/82
Each share old Common 1¢ par exchanged for (0.0001) share new Common 1¢ par 9/27/96
Note: In effect holders received $0.30 cash per share and public interest was eliminated

JEROME UNDERGROUND TRANSMISSION EQUIP INC (NY)
Name changed to Jerome Group, Inc. (NY) 5/31/81
Jerome Group, Inc. (NY) reincorporated in (DE) 12/31/82
(See Jerome Group, Inc.)

JERRICO INC (KY)
Common no par split (3) for (2) by issuance of (0.5) additional share 7/17/72
Common no par split (5) for (4) by issuance of (0.25) additional share 9/23/74
Common no par split (2) for (1) by issuance of (1) additional share 1/5/76
Common no par split (5) for (4) by issuance of (0.25) additional share 9/17/79
Common no par split (3) for (2) by issuance of (0.5) additional share 9/5/80
Common no par split (3) for (2) by issuance of (0.5) additional share 2/27/81
Common no par split (5) for (4) by issuance of (0.25) additional share 3/3/83
Common no par split (4) for (3) by ance of (1/3) additional share 3/3/86
Stock Dividends - 10% 12/7/70; 10% 12/7/71
Merged into Long John Silver's Holdings, Inc. 5/18/90
Each share Common no par exchanged for $24.25 cash

JERROLD CORP. (DE)
Merged into General Instrument Corp. (Incorporated 06/12/1967) 12/21/1967
Each share Common 10¢ par exchanged for (0.7) share Common $1 par

(See General Instrument Corp. (Incorporated 06/12/1967))

JERROLD ELECTRONICS CORP. (DE)
Name changed to Jerrold Corp. 06/30/1962
Jerrold Corp. merged into General Instrument Corp. (Incorporated 06/12/1967) 12/21/1967
(See General Instrument Corp. (Incorporated 06/12/1967))

JERRY JOHNSON GOLD MNG CO (WY)
Recapitalized as Great American Financial, Inc. 11/2/72
Each share Capital Stock 10¢ par exchanged for (1) share Common 1¢ par
(See Great American Financial, Inc.)

JERRY O'MAHONY, INC. (NJ)
See - O'Mahony (Jerry), Inc.

JERRYS FAMOUS DELI INC (CA)
Each share old Common no par exchanged for (0.33333333) share new Common no par 02/09/2000
Acquired by Acquisitionco Inc. 01/30/2014
Each share new Common no par exchanged for $2.50 cash

JERRYS INC (NV)
Reincorporated 03/16/2004
Each share Common 1¢ par exchanged for (0.25) share Common 4¢ par 09/21/1972
Stock Dividend - 10% 04/30/1984
State of incorporation changed from (FL) to (NV) 03/16/2004
Each share Common 4¢ par received distribution of (1) share Aqua Foods Restricted Common 4¢ par payable 05/18/2004 to holders of record 02/02/2004
Recapitalized as Diamond Ranch Foods, Ltd. 05/10/2004
Each share Common 4¢ par exchanged for (0.02) share Common $0.0001 par
Diamond Ranch Foods, Ltd. name changed to Plandai Biotechnology, Inc. 01/05/2012

JERSEY BK FOR SVGS (MONTVALE, NJ)
Merged into Interchange Financial Services Corp. 6/1/98
Each share Conv. Preferred $5 par exchanged for (1.5) shares Common no par
Each share Common $5 par exchanged for (1.5) shares Common no par
(See Interchange Financial Services Corp.)

JERSEY CENT PWR & LT CO (NJ)
5-1/2% Preferred $100 par called for redemption 7/1/46
6% Preferred $100 par called for redemption 7/1/46
7% Preferred $100 par called for redemption 7/1/46
4% Preferred $100 par changed to no par 10/7/77
7.88% Preferred Ser. E $100 par changed to no par 10/7/77
8% Preferred $100 par changed to no par 10/7/77
8.12% Preferred $100 par changed to no par 10/7/77
9.36% Preferred $100 par changed to no par 10/7/77
13.50% Preferred Ser. F $100 par changed to no par 10/7/77
11% Preferred Ser. G $100 par changed to no par 10/7/77
11% Preferred Ser. G no par called for redemption 6/11/86
13.50% Preferred Ser. F no par called for redemption 6/11/86
9.36% Preferred no par called for redemption 7/1/87
8.75% Preferred Ser. H no par called for redemption 12/16/92

8% Preferred no par called for
redemption 9/17/93
8.12% Preferred no par called for
redemption 9/17/93
8.48% Preferred Ser. I no par called
for redemption at $100 on 5/1/98
7.88% Preferred Ser. E no par called
for redemption at $103.65 on
12/27/99
7.52% Preferred Ser. K no par called
for redemption at $102.51 on
8/1/2002
8.65% Preferred Ser. J no par called
for redemption at $100.87 on
8/1/2002
4% Preferred no par called for
redemption at $106.50 on 9/15/2006

JERSEY CEREAL CO.
Acquired by General Foods Corp. in
1943
Details not available

JERSEY CONS MINES LTD (ON)
Capital Stock $1 par changed to no
par 01/12/1968
Name changed to Holofile Technology
Inc. (ON) 07/27/1976
Holofile Technology Inc. (ON)
reincorporated in Canada
10/08/1976
(See Holofile Technology Inc.)

JERSEY FARM BAKING CO. (DE)
Name changed to Farm Crest
Bakeries, Inc. 3/8/65
Farm Crest Bakeries, Inc. merged into
Ward Foods, Inc. 12/25/65
(See Ward Foods, Inc.)

**JERSEY FARM BAKING CO. OF
CHICAGO (DE)**
Acquired by Jersey Farm Baking Co.
on a (4) for (1) basis in 1956
Jersey Farm Baking Co. name was
changed to Farm Crest Bakeries,
Inc. 3/8/65 which merged into Ward
Foods, Inc. 12/25/65
(See Ward Foods, Inc.)

JERSEY GOLDFIELDS CORP (BC)
Name changed to Jersey Petroleum
Inc. 03/04/1998
Jersey Petroleum Inc. recapitalized as
International Choice Ventures Inc.
(BC) 08/17/2000 which
reincorporated in Alberta as Rhodes
Resources Corp. 11/20/2002 which
merged into Terra Energy Corp.
01/30/2004

**JERSEY INSURANCE CO. OF NEW
YORK (NY)**
Each share Capital Stock $20 par
exchanged for (2) shares Capital
Stock $10 par in 1952
Stock Dividend - 50% 6/10/55
Acquired by Continental Insurance
Co. 9/1/70
Each share Capital Stock $10 par
exchanged for $56 cash

JERSEY INVESTMENT CORP. (NJ)
Merged into Atlantis International
Corp. 02/06/1962
Each share 6% Preferred $10 par
exchanged for (4) shares Common
25¢ par
Each share Common 1¢ par
exchanged for (0.4) share Common
25¢ par
(See Atlantis International Corp.)

**JERSEY MORTGAGE & TITLE
GUARANTY CO.**
Reorganized as Jersey Mortgage Co.
in 1937
Each share Common exchanged for
(0.05) share Common no par
(See Jersey Mortgage Co.)

JERSEY MTG CO (NJ)
Common no par changed to $15 par
and (19) additional shares issued
9/13/68
Merged into Commonwealth Savings
Association 4/3/84
Each share Common $15 par
exchanged for $278.93 cash

Note: Each share Common $15 par
received escrow payment of $15.51
cash 3/8/85

JERSEY PATENTS INC (NJ)
Name changed to Solar Energy
Systems, Inc. 04/27/1978
(See Solar Energy Systems, Inc.)

JERSEY PETE INC (BC)
Recapitalized as International Choice
Ventures Inc. 08/17/2000
Each share Common no par
exchanged for (0.14285714) share
Common no par
International Choice Ventures Inc.
(BC) reincorporated in Alberta as
Rhodes Resources Corp.
11/20/2002 which merged into Terra
Energy Corp. 01/30/2004

**JERSEY SHORE BK
(LONG BRANCH, NJ)**
Common $10 par changed to $5 par
and (1) additional share issued
04/01/1979
Stock Dividends - 10% 06/02/1980;
10% 03/02/1981; 12% 03/01/1982
Merged into National State Bank
(Elizabeth, NJ) 09/24/1982
Each share Common $5 par
exchanged for $21 cash

JERSEY YUKON MINES LTD. (ON)
Recapitalized as Jersey Consolidated
Mines Ltd. 05/11/1964
Each share Capital Stock $1 par
exchanged for (0.2) share Capital
Stock $1 par
Jersey Consolidated Mines Ltd. name
changed to Holofile Technology Inc.
(ON) 07/27/1976 which
reincorporated in Canada
10/08/1976
(See Holofile Technology Inc.)

JERUSALEM EXHIBIT CO. (MO)
Involuntarily dissolved 04/30/1906

JERVIS CORP (MI)
Common $1 par split (4) for (3) by
issuance of (0.33333333) additional
share 01/18/1968
Name changed to Harman
International Industries, Inc.
01/25/1974
Harman International Industries, Inc.
merged into Beatrice Foods Co.
08/01/1977 which name changed to
Beatrice Companies, Inc.
06/05/1984
(See Beatrice Companies, Inc.)

JESKO URANIUM MINES LTD. (ON)
Charter cancelled for failure to pay
taxes and file returns 11/18/1970

JESPERSEN KAY SYS LTD (ON)
Each share old Capital Stock no par
exchanged for (2) shares new
Capital Stock no par 06/30/1969
Completely liquidated 07/19/1972
Each share new Capital Stock no par
exchanged for first and final
distribution of (0.0269) share
National Kinney Corp. Common $1
par
National Kinney Corp. name changed
to Andal Corp. 11/07/1983
(See Andal Corp.)

JESS-MAC GOLD MINES LTD. (ON)
Charter cancelled for failure to pay
taxes and file returns 08/09/1972

JESSCO INC (DE)
Stock Dividend - 10% 10/31/1974
Merged into Rospatch Corp. (DE)
09/20/1978
Each share Common $0.0005 par
exchanged for (0.4) share Common
$5 par
Rospatch Corp. (DE) reincorporated
in Michigan 06/03/1985 which name
changed to Ameriwood Industries
International Corp. 12/13/1991
*(See Ameriwood Industries
International Corp.)*

**JESSEL-ROBERTS PRODUCTIONS
CORP. (DE)**
Dissolved 6/23/58

JESSIAN CAP CORP (AB)
Name changed to Savaria Corp.
03/01/2002

JESSOP MINES LTD. (ON)
Charter cancelled for failure to file
reports and pay taxes 00/00/1968

JESSOP STL CO (PA)
Class A Common $1 par reclassified
as Common $1 par 00/00/1946
Each share 5% Preferred $25 par
exchanged for (2) shares new
Common $1 par and (1) Common
Stock Purchase Warrant 00/00/1950
Each share old Common $1 par
exchanged for (0.1) share new
Common $1 par and (1) Common
Stock Purchase Warrant 00/00/1950
Stock Dividend - 100% 06/01/1944
Merged into Athlone Industries, Inc.
05/08/1969
Each share new Common $1 par
exchanged for $35 principal amount
of Conv. Debentures due 05/15/1984
and (0.33333333) share Common
10¢ par
Athlone Industries, Inc. merged into
Allegheny Ludlum Corp. 11/10/1993
which merged into Allegheny
Teledyne Inc. 08/15/1996 which
name changed to Allegheny
Technologies Inc. 11/29/1999

JESSUP & MOORE PAPER CO. (MA)
Reorganized under the laws of
Maryland in 1934
*(See Jessup & Moore Paper Co.
(MD))*

JESSUP & MOORE PAPER CO. (MD)
Dissolved in 1949

JESUP & LAMONT INC (FL)
Plan of reorganization under Chapter
11 Federal Bankruptcy proceedings
effective 12/21/2011
No stockholders' equity

JESUP GROUP INC (DE)
Each share old Common 1¢ par
exchanged for (0.2) share new
Common 1¢ par 3/1/89
Charter cancelled and declared
inoperative and void for
non-payment of taxes 3/1/93

JET-AERO CORP. (FL)
Name changed to Jet Avion Corp.
10/01/1963
Jet Avion Corp. merged into Heinicke
Instruments Co. 10/16/1974 which
name changed to HEICO Corp.
(Old) 03/18/1986 which reorganized
as HEICO Corp. (New) 04/28/1993

JET AIR FGHT (CA)
Charter suspended for failure to file
reports and pay fees 12/03/1979

JET AMER AIRLS INC (CA)
Merged into Alaska Air Group, Inc.
12/30/86
Each share Common $1 par
exchanged for $4.50 cash

JET AVION CORP (FL)
Each share old Common 10¢ par
exchanged for (1) share new
Common 10¢ par 06/08/1965
(Holders of old Common Stock who
did not file proofs of claim on or
before 04/19/1965 were forever
barred from participating in the Plan
of Exchange)
Merged into Heinicke Instruments Co.
10/16/1974
Each share new Common 10¢ par
exchanged for (0.5) share Common
16-2/3¢ par
Heinicke Instruments Co. name
changed to HEICO Corp. (Old)
03/18/1986 which reorganized as
HEICO Corp. (New) 04/28/1993

JET BRD CORP (DE)
Under plan of merger name changed
to Aeroceanic Corp. 05/15/1970
Aeroceanic Corp. merged into Evans
Industries, Inc. 05/07/1975
(See Evans Industries, Inc.)

JET CAP CORP (DE)
Common 10¢ par reclassified as
Class A Common 1¢ par 08/31/1987
Class A Common 1¢ par split (11) for
(1) by issuance of (10) additional
shares 09/17/1987
Merged into S.M.A. Holdings Corp.
09/13/1990
Each share Class A Common 1¢ par
exchanged for $4.5295 cash
Note: An additional distribution of
$0.0545 cash per share was made
01/03/1994

JET DRILL CDA INC (QC)
Voluntarily dissolved 08/05/2003
Details not available

JET ENERGY CORP (BC)
Merged into Cabre Exploration Ltd.
11/24/1999
Each share Common no par
exchanged for (0.1) share Common
no par and $0.01 cash
Cabre Exploration Ltd. acquired by
EnerMark Income Fund 01/10/2001
which merged into Enerplus
Resources Fund 06/22/2001 which
reorganized as Enerplus Corp.
01/03/2011

JET FLA SYS INC (DE)
Plan of reorganization under Chapter
11 Federal Bankruptcy proceedings
confirmed 08/07/1986
Stockholders' equity unlikely

JET GOLD CORP (BC)
Each share old Common no par
exchanged for (0.2) share new
Common no par 11/04/2010
Each share new Common no par
exchanged again for (0.1) share new
Common no par 01/10/2014
Each share new Common no par
exchanged again for (0.33333333)
share new Common no par
10/09/2014
Recapitalized as Deep-South
Resources Inc. 11/16/2016
Each share new Common no par
exchanged for (0.5) share Common
no par

JET HELICOPTER CORP. (DE)
Charter cancelled and declared
inoperative and void for
non-payment of taxes 04/15/1972

JET INDS INC (TX)
Charter forfeited for failure to pay
taxes 01/20/1987

JET INDS LTD (BC)
Name changed to Jet Energies
International Ltd. 5/4/81

JET LINE PRODUCTS, INC. (NC)
Completely liquidated 03/03/1969
Each share Common $1 par
exchanged for first and final
distribution of (0.166666) share
Thomas Industries Inc. Common $1
par
(See Thomas Industries Inc.)

JET METAL CORP (BC)
Reorganized under the laws of
Canada as Canada Jetlines Ltd.
03/07/2017
Each share Common no par
exchanged for (0.66666666) share
Common no par

JET NEKO INC (DE)
Common $0.001 par split (100) for (1)
by issuance of (99) additional
shares payable 09/20/2011 to
holders of record 09/20/2011
SEC revoked common stock
registration 05/27/2015

JET OILS, LTD. (CANADA)
Merged into Pathfinder Petroleums Ltd. 00/00/1954
Each (4.71) shares Capital Stock no par exchanged for (1) share Capital Stock 50¢ par
Pathfinder Petroleums Ltd. merged into Medallion Petroleums Ltd. 09/11/1956 which merged into Canadian Industrial Gas & Oil Ltd. 03/08/1965 which merged into Norcen Energy Resources Ltd. (AB) 10/28/1975 which reincorporated in Canada 04/15/1977 which merged into Union Pacific Resources Group Inc. 04/17/1998 which merged into Anadarko Petroleum Corp. 07/14/2000

JET SET INTERNATIONAL, LTD. (NV)
Name changed to Coelco Ltd. (NV) 09/27/1982
Coelco Ltd. (NV) reincorporated in Delaware 06/15/1984
(See Coelco Ltd. (DE))

JET SET LIFE USA INC (DE)
Charter cancelled and declared inoperative and void for non-payment of taxes 03/01/2000

JET STAR RES LTD (BC)
Name changed 07/13/1984
Name changed to Radian Petroleum Corp. 06/16/1982 which name changed back to Jet Star Resources Ltd. 07/13/1984
Struck off register and declared dissolved for failure to file returns 04/15/1988

JET TRAVEL SVCS INC (DE)
Charter cancelled and declared inoperative and void for non-payment of taxes 03/01/1975

JET-VAC COOLERS, INC. (NY)
Dissolved in January 1967

JET VACATIONS INC (FL)
Name changed to Precom Technology, Inc. 4/21/98
Precom Technology, Inc. name changed to International Trust & Financial Systems, Inc. (FL) 10/15/2002 which reincorporated in Nevada as Marmion Industries Corp. 7/14/2004

JET X CORP (CO)
Under plan of merger each share Common no par automatically became (1) share Jeremiah Corp. Common no par 03/22/1978
Jeremiah Corp. merged into October Oil Co. (New) 10/18/1982
(See October Oil Co. (New))

JETA PWR INC (NY)
Charter cancelled and proclaimed dissolved for failure to pay taxes and file reports 12/15/1973

JETBORNE INTL INC (DE)
Each share Common 1¢ par exchanged for (0.1) share Common 10¢ par 09/30/1997
Charter cancelled and declared inoperative and void for non-payment of taxes 03/01/2003

JETCO INC (DE)
Under plan of merger name changed to InTechnologies, Inc. 01/25/2000
(See InTechnologies, Inc.)

JETCO INC (TX)
Name changed 09/25/1972
Stock Dividend - 100% 05/03/1971
Name changed from Jetco Electronic Industries, Inc. to Jetco, Inc. 09/25/1972
Charter forfeited for failure to pay taxes 03/19/1979

JETERO CORP (DE)
99.5% acquired by Beeler-Sanders, Inc. through purchase offer which expired 06/14/1982
Public interest eliminated

JETEX RES LTD (BC)
Name changed to California Silver Ltd. 09/09/1980
California Silver Ltd. name changed to California Gold Mines Ltd. 05/27/1986 which merged into Centurion Gold Ltd. 06/06/1988 which merged into Siskon Gold Corp. 08/23/1991
(See Siskon Gold Corp.)

JETFAX INC (DE)
Name changed to EFax.Com, Inc. 02/08/1999
EFax.Com, Inc. name changed to eFax.com 12/23/1999 which merged into J2 Global Communications, Inc. 11/29/2000 which name changed to j2 Global, Inc. 12/05/2011

JETFORM CORP (CANADA)
Common no par split (3) for (2) by issuance of (0.5) additional share 12/15/1993
Name changed to Accelio Corp. 09/12/2001
Accelio Corp. merged into Adobe Systems Inc. 04/15/2002 which name changed to Adobe Inc. 10/09/2018

JETLANDS CORP (DE)
Name changed to Westbury Resources, Inc. 10/03/1973
(See Westbury Resources Inc.)

JETLINE STORES INC (DE)
Name changed to NRX Technologies Inc. and Class A 10¢ par reclassified as Common 1¢ par 01/04/1980
(See NRX Technologies Inc.)

JETORO INC (MN)
Name changed to Modern Merchandising, Inc. 09/03/1971
Modern Merchandising, Inc. merged into Best Products Co., Inc. 09/16/1982
(See Best Products Co., Inc.)

JETPADS INC (NV)
Common $0.001 par split (5) for (1) by issuance of (4) additional shares payable 05/07/2012 to holders of record 05/07/2012 Ex date - 05/08/2012
SEC revoked common stock registration 01/21/2014

JETRONIC INDS INC (PA)
6-1/2% Conv. Senior Preferred $2 par called for redemption 10/31/1968
Each share old Common 10¢ par exchanged for (0.05) share new Common 10¢ par 09/29/2008
Stock Dividends - 10% 08/01/1983; 10% 07/02/1984; 10% 07/17/1985; 10% 09/15/1986
Name changed to New Bastion Development Inc. 02/09/2009
(See New Bastion Development Inc.)

JETT INVT CORP (AB)
Name changed to Jettstar Resource Services Inc. 04/30/1998
Jettstar Resource Services Inc. acquired by Petro Well Energy Services Inc. 06/14/1999 which recapitalized as Cenalta Energy Services Inc. 11/29/1999 which was acquired by Precision Drilling Corp. 10/18/2000
(See Precision Drilling Corp.)

JETTA RES LTD (BC)
Common no par split (3) for (1) by issuance of (2) additional shares 05/11/1984
Recapitalized as Security Environmental Systems, Inc. (BC) 11/05/1986
Each share Common no par exchanged for (0.5) share Common no par
Security Environmental Systems, Inc. (BC) reincorporated in Delaware 04/19/1988
(See Security Environmental Systems, Inc.)

JETTER BREWING CO., INC.
Bankrupt 00/00/1934
Stockholders' equity unlikely

JETTRA RES LTD (BC)
Name changed to Great Canadian Gaming Corp. 03/12/1997

JETTSTAR RESOURCE SVCS INC (AB)
Acquired by Petro Well Energy Services Inc. 06/14/1999
Each (2.4) shares Common no par exchanged for (1) share Common no par
Petro Well Energy Services Inc. recapitalized as Cenalta Energy Services Inc. 11/29/1999 which was acquired by Precision Drilling Corp. 10/18/2000
(See Precision Drilling Corp.)

JEUNESSE COSMETICS, INC. (TX)
Name changed to Fairlane Industries, Inc. 02/26/1971
Fairlane Industries, Inc. name changed to Reliability Inc. 05/01/1980

JEVIC TRANSN INC (NJ)
Merged into Yellow Corp. 07/12/1999
Each share Class A Common no par exchanged for $14 cash
Each share Common no par exchanged for $14 cash

JEWEL BOX STORES CORP. (DE)
Name changed to Carlyle & Co. Jewelers 06/30/1980
(See Carlyle & Co. Jewelers)

JEWEL COS INC (NY)
Common $1 par split (3) for (2) by issuance of (0.5) additional share 07/31/1974
3.75% Preferred $100 par called for redemption 11/01/1983
Merged into American Stores Co. (New) 11/16/1984
Each share $2.31 Conv. Preferred Ser. A $1 par exchanged for (0.6399) share $4.375 Conv. Exchangeable Preferred Ser. A $1 par, (0.1854) share $6.80 Exchangeable Preferred Ser. B $1 par and (0.308) share Common $1 par
Each share Common $1 par exchanged for (0.8976) share Conv. Exchangeable Preferred Ser. A $1 par, (0.26) share $6.80 Exchangeable Preferred Ser. B $1 par and (0.432) share Common $1 par
American Stores Co. (New) merged into Albertson's Inc. 06/23/1999 which merged into Supervalu Inc. 06/02/2006

JEWEL RES INC (BC)
Recapitalized as Wkay Resources Inc. 06/01/1988
Each share Common no par exchanged for (0.4) share Common no par
Wkay Resources Inc. name changed to Magnatron International Corp. 10/18/1990 which recapitalized as QI Technologies Inc. 03/17/1994 which name changed to QI Systems Inc. (BC) 05/25/2001 which reincorporated in Delaware 07/01/2006

JEWEL TEA CO., INC. (NY)
Each share Common no par exchanged for (2) shares Common $1 par in 1953
Common $1 par split (2) for (1) by issuance of (1) additional share 2/27/59
Common $1 par split (3) for (2) by issuance of (0.5) additional share 7/29/65
Under plan of merger name changed to Jewel Companies, Inc. 6/15/66
Jewel Companies, Inc. merged into American Stores Co. (New) 11/16/84 which merged into Albertson's, Inc. 6/23/99 which merged into Supervalu Inc. 6/2/2006

JEWEL URANIUM CO. (UT)
Charter suspended for failure to pay taxes 09/28/1973

JEWELCOR INC (PA)
Common 5¢ par split (3) for (2) by issuance of (0.5) additional share 4/14/72
Common 5¢ par split (3) for (2) by issuance of (0.5) additional share 10/7/86
Stock Dividend - 20% 1/25/71
Merged into S.H. Holdings.Inc. 9/13/88
Each share Common 5¢ par exchanged for $19 cash

JEWELERS EXCHANGE BLDG., INC. (CA)
Liquidated in 1960

JEWELL J D INC (GA)
Petition for reorganization under Chapter X bankruptcy proceedings filed 10/20/1972 Trustee on 04/22/1975 opined stock is without value

JEWELL OIL & GAS CORP. (DE)
No longer in existence having become inoperative and void for non-payment of taxes 4/1/56

JEWELMASTERS INC (DE)
Charter cancelled and declared inoperative and void for non-payment of taxes 3/1/97

JEWELS BY SHALET INC (NY)
Each share old Common 1¢ par exchanged for (0.25) share new Common 1¢ par 4/15/83
Charter cancelled and proclaimed dissolved for failure to pay taxes 3/24/93

JEWELTECH INTL INC (DE)
Charter cancelled and declared inoperative and void for non-payment of taxes 4/15/73

JEWETT CITY TEXTILE NOVELTY CO., INC. (CT)
Charter cancelled for failure to pay fees 6/29/43

JEWETT CITY TR CO (CT)
Merged into Jewett City Savings Bank (Jewett, CT) 9/16/96
Each share Common $10 par exchanged for $575.50 cash

JFAX COM INC (DE)
Issue Information - 8,500,000 shares COM offered at $9.50 per share on 07/23/1999
Name changed to j2 Global Communications, Inc. 11/29/2000 j2 Global Communications, Inc. name changed to j2 Global, Inc. 12/05/2011

JFE HLDGS INC (JAPAN)
ADR agreement terminated 05/27/2009
No ADR's were outstanding

J5 ACQUISITION CORP (ON)
Recapitalized as Trimel Pharmaceuticals Corp. 07/11/2011
Each share Common no par exchanged for (0.03750093) share Common no par
Trimel Pharmaceuticals Corp. name changed to Acerus Pharmaceuticals Corp. 09/11/2015

JFK INC. (UT)
Name changed to Guidon Co. Inc. 12/1/80

JG CAP CORP (ON)
Reorganized under the laws of Canada as VersaPay Corp. 01/20/2010
Each share Common no par exchanged for (0.13333333) share Common no par

JG INDS INC (IL)
Each share old Common no par exchanged for (1/3) share new Common no par 12/27/1996
Liquidation completed
Each share new Common no par received initial distribution of $1 cash payable 10/27/2001 to holders of record 08/11/2000
Each share new Common no par received second distribution of $0.35 cash payable 11/30/2001 to holders of record 08/11/2000
Each share new Common no par received third and final distribution of $0.074 cash payable 01/30/2003 to holders of record 08/11/2000
Ex date - 02/04/2003
Note: Certificates were not required to be surrendered and are without value

JG SUMMIT HLDGS INC (PHILIPPINES)
Stock Dividend - 10% payable 10/22/2001 to holders of record 08/23/2001 Ex date - 08/21/2001
ADR agreement terminated 08/09/2004
Each 144A Sponsored GDR for Class B exchanged for (100) 144A Class B Shares
Note: Unexchanged GDR's will be sold and proceeds held for claim after 02/09/2005
(Additional Information in Active)

JG WEALTH INC (BC)
Common no par split (2) for (1) by issuance of (1) additional share payable 12/20/2017 to holders of record 12/13/2017 Ex date - 12/12/2017
Name changed to Pushfor Investments Inc. 10/16/2018

JG WEALTH MGMT CORP (BC)
Name changed to JG Wealth Inc. 11/24/2017
JG Wealth Inc. name changed to Pushfor Investments Inc. 10/16/2018

JGWPT HLDGS INC (DE)
Name changed to J.G. Wentworth Co. 09/30/2014
(See J.G. Wentworth Co.)

JH DESIGNS INC (NV)
Common $0.001 par split (20) for (1) by issuance of (19) additional shares payable 09/24/2012 to holders of record 09/24/2012
Name changed to Cardinal Resources, Inc. 03/03/2014

JHIRMACK ENTERPRISES INC (CA)
Stock Dividends - 10% 08/18/1978; 10% 08/17/1979; 10% 08/17/1981
Merged into Esmark, Inc. (Inc. 03/14/1969) 05/03/1982
Each share Common no par exchanged for $10.50 cash

JHM MTG SECS L P (DE)
Name changed to Harbourton Financial Services L.P. 4/13/95
(See Harbourton Financial Services L.P.)

JIANGBO PHARMACEUTICALS INC (FL)
SEC revoked common stock registration 07/03/2013

JIAYUAN COM INTL LTD (CAYMAN ISLANDS)
Acquired by LoveWorld Inc. 05/16/2016
Each Sponsored ADR for Ordinary exchanged for $7.56 cash

JIFFY FOOD STORES, INC. (VA)
Common $5 par changed to $2.50 par and (1) additional share issued 10/31/72
Name changed to Hop-In-Food Stores, Inc. 1/11/73
(See Hop-In-Food Stores, Inc.)

JIFFY FOODS CORP (PA)
Chapter 11 bankruptcy proceedings converted to Chapter 7 on 4/22/86
Stockholders' equity unlikely

JIFFY INDS INC (FL)
Each share old Common 1¢ par exchanged for (0.2) share new Common 1¢ par 8/10/82
New Common 1¢ par split (2) for (1) by issuance of (1) additional share 11/15/83
Name changed to Advanced Energy Corp. 5/21/85
(See Advanced Energy Corp.)

JIFFY JOHNS, INC. (FL)
Name changed to Jiffy Industries, Inc. 2/3/82
Jiffy Industries, Inc. name changed to Advanced Energy Corp. 5/21/85
(See Advanced Energy Corp.)

JIFFY LUBE INSD INCOME PARTNERS L P (DE)
Certificate of Cancellation filed 12/29/1995
Details not available

JIFFY LUBE INTL INC (NV)
Common 5¢ par changed to $0.025 par and (1) additional share issued 3/20/87
Each share Common $0.025 par exchanged for (0.1) share Common 25¢ par 9/10/90
Merged into Pennzoil Co. 10/17/91
Each share Common 25¢ par exchanged for $6 cash

JIFFY PUNCH CO., INC. (UT)
Charter expired 07/01/1983

JIFFY STEAK CO. (PA)
Common $1.25 par changed to 62-1/2¢ par and (1) additional share issued 10/23/64
Common 62-1/2¢ par changed to 31-1/4¢ par and (1) additional share issued 2/15/66
Name changed to Jiffy Foods Corp. 1/31/68
(See Jiffy Foods Corp.)

JILBEY EXPL LTD (CANADA)
Name changed 03/16/1990
Reincorporated 09/09/1993
Name changed from Jilbey Industries Ltd. to Jilbey Exploration Ltd. (BC) 03/16/1990
Place of incorporation changed from (BC) to Canada 09/09/1993
Recapitalized as Jilbey Enterprises Ltd./ Les Enterprises Jilbey Ltee. 03/31/1999
Each share Common no par exchanged for (0.2) share Common no par
Jilbey Enterprises Ltd./Les Enterprises Jilbey Ltee. name changed to Jilbey Gold Exploration Ltd. 04/08/2003 which merged into High River Gold Mines Ltd. (Canada) 09/01/2005 which reincorporated in Yukon 02/02/2011
(See High River Gold Mines Ltd.)

JILBEY GOLD EXPL LTD (CANADA)
Name changed 04/08/2003
Name changed from Jilbey Enterprises Ltd./Les Enterprises Ltee. to Jilbey Gold Exploration Ltd. 04/08/2003
Merged into High River Gold Mines Ltd. (Canada) 09/01/2005
Each share Common no par exchanged for (0.75) share Common no par
High River Gold Mines Ltd. (Canada) reincorporated in Yukon 02/02/2011
(See High River Gold Mines Ltd.)

JILBIE MNG LTD (ON)
Charter cancelled for failure to pay taxes and file returns 03/16/1976

JILIN CHEM INDL LTD (CHINA)
ADR agreement terminated 04/03/2006
Each Sponsored ADR for Class H RMB1 par exchanged for $36.01303 cash

JILL KELLY PRODUCTIONS HLDG INC (NV)
Name changed to eWorldCompanies, Inc. 03/13/2007

JILLIANS ENTMT CORP (FL)
Merged into Jillians Entertainment Acquisition Corp. 7/21/97
Each share Common $0.001 par exchanged for $0.50 par

JILLY BEAR & CO INC (DE)
Reorganized under the laws of Texas as Nutec Transmission Ltd. 06/30/1991
Each share Common $0.0001 par exchanged for (0.01) share Common $0.0001 par
Nutec Transmission Ltd. (TX) reorganized in Delaware as Aster Development Enterprises Ltd. 06/01/1992 which name changed to P A N Environmental Services Inc. 04/00/1993 which name changed to PAN Environmental Corp. 02/22/1994 which name changed to Pan International Gaming Inc. 12/30/1998 which name changed to SearchHound.com, Inc. 06/07/2000 which recapitalized as Coach Industries Group, Inc. 08/25/2003
(See Coach Industries Group, Inc.)

JIM HJELMS PRIVATE COLLECTION LTD (DE)
Each share Common $0.0001 par exchanged for (1/3) share Common $0.0002 par 1/10/95
Name changed to JLM Couture, Inc. 7/30/97

JIM ROSS FILM PRODUCTIONS, INC. (TX)
See - Ross (Jim) Film Productions, Inc.

JIM WALTER CORP. (FL)
See - Walter (Jim) Corp.

JIM WALTER INVESTORS (FL)
See - Walter (Jim) Investors

JIMBERLANA MINERALS N L (AUSTRALIA)
ADR agreement terminated 03/11/2003
No ADR holders' equity

JIMBOS JUMBOS INC (DE)
Merged into Chock Full O'Nuts Corp. 07/08/1993
Each share Common $0.001 par exchanged for $6.93 cash

JIMMY VUS TAKE OUT INC (CO)
Voluntarily dissolved 09/12/2005
Details not available

JIN EN INTL GROUP HLDG CO (NV)
Name changed to Nascent Biotech Inc. 09/25/2014

JIN JIE CORP (NV)
Reorganized as Blue Sphere Corp. 02/18/2010
Each share Common $0.001 par exchanged for (35) shares Common $0.001 par

JINGELLIC MINERALS N L (AUSTRALIA)
ADR agreement terminated 03/12/2002
No ADR holders' equity
Note: Name change to Plantcorp Ltd. not applicable to ADR's which were deemed without value 10/19/2007

JINGWEI INTL LTD (NV)
Each share old Common $0.001 par exchanged for (1) share new Common $0.001 par to reflect a (1) for (20,000) reverse split followed by a (20,000) for (1) forward split 03/30/2012
Note: Holders of (19,999) or fewer pre-split shares will receive $2.20 cash per share
Recapitalized as iSocialy, Inc. 01/25/2017
Each share new Common $0.001 par exchanged for (0.001) share Common $0.001 par

JINHAO MTR CO (NV)
SEC revoked common stock registration 03/26/2014

JINHUA CAP CORP (AB)
Each share old Common no par exchanged for (0.16666666) share new Common no par 12/11/2012
Reincorporated under the laws of British Columbia 01/12/2018

JINHUI HLDGS LTD (HONG KONG)
ADR agreement terminated 01/14/2016
No ADR's remain outstanding

JINHUI SHIPPING & TRANSN LTD (HONG KONG)
ADR agreement terminated 07/31/2015
Each Sponsored ADR for Common exchanged for (20) shares Common
Note: Unexchanged ADR's will be sold and the proceeds, if any, held for claim after 08/04/2016

JINMIMI NETWORK INC (NV)
Common $0.0001 par split (10.5) for (1) by issuance of (9.5) additional shares payable 10/05/2011 to holders of record 09/26/2011
Ex date - 10/06/2011
Name changed to One2One Living Corp. 06/04/2012

JINPAN INTERNATIONAL LTD (BRITISH VIRGIN ISLANDS)
Common $0.018 par changed to $0.009 par and (1) additional share issued payable 02/06/2004 to holders of record 01/30/2004
Common $0.009 par changed to $0.0045 par and (1) additional share issued payable 02/15/2010 to holders of record 02/05/2010
Ex date - 02/16/2010
Acquired by FNOF E&M Investment Ltd. 04/18/2016
Each share Common $0.0045 par exchanged for $6 cash

JINSHAN GOLD MINES INC (BC)
Name changed to China Gold International Resources Corp. Ltd. 07/19/2010

JINZANGHUANG TIBET PHARMACEUTICALS INC (DE)
SEC revoked common stock registration 08/26/2016

JITE TECHNOLOGIES INC (ON)
Each share old Common no par exchanged for (0.2) share new Common no par 09/15/2008
Acquired by McVicar Industries Inc. 06/04/2012
Each share new Common no par exchanged for $0.60 cash

JITEC INC (CANADA)
Each share Common no par received distribution of (0.5) share Strateco Resources Inc. Common no par payable 09/21/2000 to holders of record 05/09/2000
Name changed to Advantage Link Inc. 06/19/2001
(See Advantage Link Inc.)

JIU FENG INVT HONG KONG LTD (NV)
Name changed to Jubilant Flame International, Ltd. 05/22/2015

JIVE SOFTWARE INC (DE)
Acquired by Wave Systems Corp. 06/12/2017
Each share Common $0.0001 par exchanged for $5.25 cash

JJ&R VENTURES INC (NV)
Name changed to Blue Calypso, Inc. (NV) 08/05/2011
Blue Calypso, Inc. (NV)

JJF-JOB
FINANCIAL INFORMATION, INC.

reincorporated in Delaware
10/17/2011

JJFN HLDGS INC (DE)
Merged into Priority Financial Inc.
5/15/96
Each (1) share Preferred $2.50 par
exchanged for (1) share Preferred
$2.50 par
Each (1) share Common 1¢ par
exchanged for (1) share Common
1¢ par

JJFN SVCS INC (DE)
Name changed to Strategic Capital
Resources, Inc. (DE) 10/16/98
Strategic Capital Resources, Inc. (DE)
reincorporated in Florida 8/14/2003
*(See Strategic Capital Resources,
Inc. (FL))*

JJR CAP VENTURES INC (ON)
Name changed to Tonbridge Power
Inc. 08/02/2005
(See Tonbridge Power Inc.)

JJR IV ACQUISITION INC (BC)
Reorganized under the laws of
Canada as BIOX Corp. 03/03/2010
Each share Common no par
exchanged for (0.04166666) share
Common no par
(See BIOX Corp.)

JJR VI ACQUISITION CORP (ON)
Reorganized under the laws of
Cayman Islands as Atlas Financial
Holdings, Inc. 01/06/2011
Each share Common no par
exchanged for (0.1) share Ordinary
USD $0.001 par

JJR II ACQUISITION INC (ON)
Name changed to Sino Vanadium Inc.
09/15/2009
(See Sino Vanadium Inc.)

JK ACQUISITION CORP (DE)
Issue Information - 11,500,000 UNITS
consisting of (1) share COM and (2)
WTS offered at $6 per Unit on
04/11/2006
Each old Unit exchanged for
(0.33333333) new Unit and $6.14
cash 06/17/2008
Each share old Common $0.001 par
exchanged for (0.33333333) share
new Common $0.001 par and $6.14
cash
Recapitalized as Golden Gate
Homes, Inc. 03/09/2010
Each new Unit exchanged for
(0.02857143) Unit
Each share new Common $0.001 par
exchanged for (0.02857143) share
Common $0.001 par
Golden Gate Homes, Inc. name
changed to Golden Gate Partners,
Inc. 01/08/2014

JK CORP. (IN)
Liquidation completed
Each share Preferred $25 par
exchanged for first and final
distribution of $25.375 cash
04/05/1966
Each share Common no par
exchanged for initial distribution of
$12.80 cash 04/05/1966
Each share Common no par received
second distribution of $0.5064 cash
03/20/1967
Each share Common no par received
third distribution of $0.02520 cash
01/30/1968
Each share Common no par received
fourth and final distribution of
$0.6780 cash 06/19/1972

JK CORP LTD (INDIA)
Recapitalized as JK Lakshmi Cement
Ltd. 02/11/2008
Each 144A GDR for Ordinary
exchanged for (0.9) 144A
Sponsored GDR for Ordinary
(See JK Lakshmi Cement Ltd.)

JK LAKSHMI CEM LTD (INDIA)
Sponsored 144A GDR's for Ordinary
split (2) for (1) by issuance of (1)
additional ADR payable 01/06/2010
to holders of record 12/28/2009
Ex date - 01/07/2010
GDR agreement terminated
09/15/2014
Each Sponsored 144A GDR for
Ordinary exchanged for $3.463807
cash

JKC GROUP INC (NY)
Name changed to Magic Lantern
Group Inc. 11/08/2002
(See Magic Lantern Group Inc.)

JKN INC (CO)
Name changed to Golf Links Ltd.
12/29/1998
Golf Links Ltd. recapitalized as
American Communication Services
Inc. (CO) 09/23/1993 which
reincorporated in Delaware
09/29/1994 which name changed to
e.spire Communications Inc.
04/15/1998
(See e.spire Communications Inc.)

**JKX OIL & GAS PLC
(UNITED KINGDOM)**
ADR agreement terminated
04/19/2016
Each ADR for Ordinary exchanged for
$6.1091 cash

JLG INDS INC (PA)
Common 20¢ par split (2) for (1) by
issuance of (1) additional share
04/04/1980
Common 20¢ par split (2) for (1) by
issuance of (1) additional share
04/01/1995
Common 20¢ par split (2) for (1) by
issuance of (1) additional share
10/03/1995
Common 20¢ par split (3) for (1) by
issuance of (2) additional shares
payable 07/01/1996 to holders of
record 06/14/1996
Common 20¢ par split (2) for (1) by
issuance of (1) additional share
payable 03/27/2006 to holders of
record 03/13/2006 Ex date -
03/28/2006
Merged into Oshkosh Truck Corp.
12/06/2006
Each share Common 20¢ par
exchanged for $28 cash

JLK DIRECT DIST INC (PA)
Acquired by Kennametal Inc.
11/21/2000
Each share Class A Common 1¢ par
exchanged for $8.75 cash

JLL MIAMI ENTERPRISES INC (NV)
Name changed to BMX Holdings Inc.
01/25/2002
BMX Holdings Inc. recapitalized as
Direct Music Group Inc. 02/07/2003
which name changed to Cell
Bio-Systems, Inc. 04/14/2004 which
name changed to Tulip BioMed, Inc.
(NV) 06/02/2006 which reorganized
in Florida as Bitcoin Services, Inc.
03/21/2016

JLL VENTURES CORP (FL)
Reincorporated under the laws of
Delaware as CNF Technologies Inc.
06/23/1999
(See CNF Technologies Inc.)

JLM INDS INC (DE)
Merged into JLMI Holding Corp.
03/30/2004
Each share Common 1¢ par
exchanged for $1.40 cash

JM CAP CORP (ON)
Name changed to Stans Energy Corp.
12/12/2008

JM GLOBAL HLDG CO (DE)
Units separated 02/07/2018
Name changed to TMSR Holding Co.
Ltd. (DE) 02/07/2018
TMSR Holding Co. Ltd. (DE)
reincorporated in Nevada
06/21/2018

JMAR TECHNOLOGIES INC (DE)
Name changed 05/27/1998
Name changed from JMAR Industries,
Inc. to JMAR Technologies, Inc.
05/27/1998
Assets sold for the benefit of creditors
05/04/2009
Stockholders' equity unlikely

JMB RLTY TR (IL)
Shares of Bene. Int. no par split (2)
for (1) by issuance of (1) additional
share 05/15/1984
Liquidation completed
Each Share of Bene. Int. no par
received initial distribution of $4.60
cash 12/30/1988
Each Share of Bene. Int. no par
received second distribution of $2.75
cash 05/02/1989
Each Share of Bene. Int. no par
received third distribution of $0.35
cash 08/01/1989
Each Share of Bene. Int. no par
received fourth distribution of $0.35
cash 10/31/1989
Each Share of Bene. Int. no par
received fifth distribution of $0.35
cash 01/31/1990
Each Share of Bene. Int. no par
received sixth distribution of $1.10
cash 05/01/1990
Each Share of Bene. Int. no par
received seventh distribution of
$0.35 cash 07/31/1990
Each Share of Bene. Int. no par
received eighth distribution of $2.85
cash 11/05/1990
Each Share of Bene. Int. no par
received ninth distribution of $0.70
cash 04/05/1991
Each Share of Bene. Int. no par
received tenth distribution of $3
cash 09/05/1991
Each Share of Bene. Int. no par
received eleventh distribution of $3
cash 12/31/1992
Each Share of Bene. Int. no par
received twelfth and final distribution
of $0.10 cash 05/28/1993

JMC GROUP INC (CA)
Name changed to Fechtor, Detwiler,
Mitchell & Co. Inc. 08/30/1999
Fechtor, Detwiler, Mitchell & Co. Inc.
recapitalized as Detwiler, Mitchell &
Co. 03/27/2001 which name
changed to Detwiler Fenton Group,
Inc. 10/20/2008

JMG EXPL INC (NV)
Recapitalized as MediaShift, Inc.
03/12/2013
Each share Common $0.001 par
exchanged for (0.5) share Common
$0.001 par
(See MediaShift, Inc.)

JMI TELECOM CORP (DE)
Each share old Common $0.0005 par
exchanged for (0.02) share new
Common $0.0005 par 12/09/2008
Name changed to UA Multimedia Inc.
06/05/2012

JML RES LTD (ON)
Recapitalized as Aquila Resources
Inc. 05/02/2006
Each share Common no par
exchanged for (0.33333333) share
Common no par

JMP GROUP INC (DE)
Under plan of reorganization each
share Common $0.001 par
automatically became (1) JMP
Group LLC Common Share
01/02/2015

JMXI LIQUIDATING TR (DE)
Assets transferred 05/01/2003
Assets transferred from JMXI, Inc. to
JMXI Liquidating Trust and Common
1¢ par reclassified as Shares of
Bene. Int. 05/01/2003
Each Share of Bene. Int. received
initial distribution of $0.10 cash
payable 05/15/2003 to holders of
record 05/01/2003
Each Share of Bene. Int. received
second and final distribution of
approximately $0.0064 cash payable
03/09/2011 to holders of record
05/01/2003
Note: Certificates were not required to
be surrendered and are without
value

JNB DEVS CO LTD (YT)
Name changed to Cooper Minerals
Inc. (YT) 07/14/2004
Cooper Minerals Inc. (YT)
reincorporated in British Columbia
as United Coal Holdings Ltd.
05/28/2012

JNI CORP (DE)
Merged into Applied Micro Circuits
Corp. 10/28/2003
Each share Common $0.001 par
exchanged for $7 cash

JNR RES INC (BC)
Merged into Denison Mines Corp.
02/06/2013
Each share Common no par
exchanged for (0.073) share
Common no par
Note: Unexchanged certificates will
be cancelled and become without
value 02/06/2019

JNS MARKETING INC (CO)
Each share old Common no par
exchanged for (0.01) share new
Common no par 03/03/1999
Common no par split (14) for (1) by
issuance of (13) additional shares
payable 12/15/1999 to holders of
record 11/15/1999
Reincorporated under the laws of
Nevada as Latinocare Management
Corp. and Common no par changed
to $0.001 par 02/28/2002
Latinocare Management Corp. name
changed to Roaming Messenger,
Inc. 05/02/2003 which name
changed to Warp 9, Inc. 11/02/2006
which name changed to
CloudCommerce, Inc. 09/30/2015

JO-AMI GOLD MINES LTD. (ON)
Charter revoked for failure to file
reports and pay fees 09/22/1966

JO-ANN STORES INC (OH)
Each share Class A Common no par
exchanged for (1.15) shares
Common no par 11/05/2003
Each share Class B Common no par
exchanged for (1) share Common
no par 11/05/2003
Acquired by Needle Holdings Inc.
03/18/2011
Each share Common no par
exchanged for $61 cash

JO-LEE CORP (NV)
Name changed to Global Timber
Corp. 11/20/1995
(See Global Timber Corp.)

JOACHIM BANCORP INC (MO)
Merged into First State Community
Bank (De Soto, MO) 06/12/1998
Each share Common 1¢ par
exchanged for $17.25 cash

JOANNES GOLD MINES LTD. (ON)
Charter cancelled and company
declared dissolved for default in
filing returns 03/18/1965

JOANNES GOLDFIELDS LTD.
Name changed to Titanium
Development Corp. 00/00/1952
(See Titanium Development Corp.)

JOAQUIN DEVELOPMENT CO. (CA)
Dissolved 02/11/1969
No stockholders' equity

JOB STORES INC (FL)
Involuntarily dissolved 10/13/1989

JOBSINSITE INC (DE)
Reincorporated 06/17/2009
State of incorporation changed from

(NY) to (DE) 06/17/2009
Name changed to Soleil Capital L.P. and Common $0.001 par reclassified as Common Units 12/31/2013
Soleil Capital L.P. name changed to VPR Brands, L.P. 09/21/2015

JOBURKE GOLD MINES LTD (ON)
Recapitalized as New Joburke Explorations Ltd. 08/21/1973
Each share Capital Stock $1 par exchanged for (0.071422) share Capital Stock no par
New Joburke Explorations Ltd. name changed to Cenex Ltd. 08/16/1977
(See Cenex Ltd.)

JOCIE CORP (UT)
Name changed to Starchild Corp. (UT) 10/16/1989
Starchild Corp. (UT) reorganized in Texas as Ferex Corp. 07/29/1994
(See Ferex Corp.)

JOCKEY CLUB INC (FL)
Each share old Common $0.001 par exchanged for (0.05) share new Common $0.001 par 08/30/1995
SEC revoked common stock registration 03/05/2009

JOCKEY CLUB LTD (ON)
5.50% Conv. 1st Preference $10 par called for redemption 12/17/1971
5.60% 2nd Preference 1963 Ser. $10 par called for redemption 12/17/1971
6% Conv. 1st Preference $10 par called for redemption 12/17/1971
Completely liquidated 12/29/1971
Each share Common no par exchanged for first and final distribution of $6 principal amount of Ontario Jockey Club 10% Secured Debentures due 01/01/1992

JOCOM INC (UT)
Involuntarily dissolved 06/01/1987

JODEE EXPLS LTD (ON)
Charter cancelled for failure to pay taxes and file returns 08/00/1972

JODMAR INDUSTRIES, INC. (NY)
Name changed to Electrogen Industries, Inc. 12/08/1967
Electrogen Industries, Inc. merged into American Lima Corp. 11/08/1968 which reorganized as Brooklyn Poly Industries, Inc. 11/10/1969
(See Brooklyn Poly Industries, Inc.)

JODY TOOTIQUE (CA)
Each share old Common $1 par exchanged for (0.05) share new Common $1 par 8/12/75
Merged into Hartfield-Zodys, Inc. 1/16/78
Each share new Common $1 par exchanged for $620.29 cash
Each share new Common $1 par received additional distribution of $72.68 cash 12/20/78; $102.05 cash 12/19/79 and $62.30 cash 12/17/80

JOE FRANKLIN PRODUCTIONS, INC. (NV)
See - Franklin Joe Prodtns Inc

JOE INDIAN MOUNTAIN METAL MINES LTD. (ON)
Name changed to Indian Mountain Metal Mines Ltd. 00/00/1953
Indian Mountain Metal Mines Ltd. merged into Initiative Explorations Inc. 02/13/1980 which merged into Canhorn Chemical Corp. 04/26/1995 which merged into Nayarit Gold Inc. 05/02/2005 which merged into Capital Gold Corp. 08/02/2010 which merged into Gammon Gold Inc. (QC) 04/08/2011 which reincorporated in Ontario as AuRico Gold Inc. 06/14/2011 which merged into Alamos Gold Inc. (New) 07/06/2015

JOEDOT HOLDINGS, INC. (DE)
Voluntarily dissolved 06/07/1995
Details not available

JOES JEANS INC (DE)
Recapitalized as Differential Brands Group Inc. 01/29/2016
Each share Common 10¢ par exchanged for (0.03333333) share Common 10¢ par

JOEY NEW YORK INC OLD (NV)
Common $0.001 par split (20) for (1) by issuance of (19) additional shares payable 09/13/2013 to holders of record 09/13/2013
Reorganized as Joey New York, Inc. (New) 08/01/2016
Each share Common $0.001 par exchanged for (0.005) share Common $0.001 par

JOFFRE RES LTD (AB)
Assets sold for benefit of creditors 00/00/1984
No stockholders' equity

JOFRAN CONFECTIONERS INTERNATIONAL INC. (UT)
Name changed to Cliff Graphics International Inc. 1/15/87
Cliff Graphics International Inc. name changed to Global Golf Holdings, Inc. 5/8/95 which recapitalized as Dino Minichiello Fashions Inc. 11/20/97 which name chagned to Resort World Enterprises, Inc. 6/15/98 which name changed to Remedent USA, Inc. 10/22/98 which recapitalized as Remedent, Inc. 6/6/2005

JOGRAN MINES LTD (ON)
Charter cancelled and declared dissolved for failure to file returns and pay fees 03/16/1976

JOHANNESBURG CONS INVT LTD (SOUTH AFRICA)
ADR's for Ordinary Rand-2 par changed to Rand-0.10 par and (19) additional ADR's issued 12/15/1989
Name changed to Johnnies Industrial Ltd. 05/15/1995
Johnnies Industrial Ltd. name changed to Johnnic Holdings Ltd. 05/08/2000
(See Johnnic Holdings Ltd.)

JOHANSEN BROS SHOE INC (MO)
Each share Preferred $100 par exchanged for (40) shares Common $1 par 00/00/1939
Each share Common no par exchanged for (1) share Common $1 par 00/00/1939
Charter forfeited for failure to file reports 06/13/1994

JOHN ALDEN FINL CORP (DE)
Issue Information - 6,000,000 shares COM offered at $28.25 per share on 11/02/1993
Merged into Fortis Inc. 8/31/98
Each share Common 1¢ par exchanged for $22.50 cash

JOHN FULHAM & SONS, INC. (MA)
See - Fulham (John) & Sons, Inc.

JOHN MARSHALL BK (RESTON, VA)
Common $5 par split (5) for (4) by issuance of (0.25) additional share payable 07/22/2013 to holders of record 07/01/2013 Ex date - 07/23/2013
Common $5 par split (6) for (5) by issuance of (0.2) additional share payable 07/01/2015 to holders of record 06/01/2015 Ex date - 05/28/2015
Under plan of reorganization each share Common $5 par automatically became (1) share John Marshall Bancorp, Inc. Common 1¢ par 03/02/2017

JOHN NUVEEN CO (DE)
Class A Common 1¢ par split (3) for (2) by issuance of (0.5) additional share payable 09/27/2001 to holders of record 09/20/2001 Ex date - 09/28/2001
Class A Common 1¢ par split (2) for (1) by issuance of (1) additional share payable 06/24/2002 to holders of record 06/03/2002 Ex date - 06/25/2002
Name changed to Nuveen Investments, Inc. 01/31/2003
(See Nuveen Investments, Inc.)

JOHN PHILLIP TUBA CORP (FL)
Proclaimed dissolved for failure to file reports and pay fees 10/9/92

JOHNNIC COMMUNICATIONS (SOUTH AFRICA)
Name changed to Avusa Ltd. 12/27/2007
Avusa Ltd. name changed to Element One Ltd. 06/04/2008
(See Element One Ltd.)

JOHNNIC HLDGS LTD (SOUTH AFRICA)
Each Sponsored ADR for Ordinary Rand-0.10 par received distribution of (3.16473) MTN Group Ltd. Sponsored ADR's for Ordinary payable 06/25/2003 to holders of record 06/20/2003 Ex date - 06/26/2003
Stock Dividend - 2.1497% payable 08/23/2001 to holders of record 07/06/2001 Ex date - 07/03/2001
Acquired by Hosken Consolidated Investments Ltd. 09/25/2008
Each Sponsored ADR for Ordinary Rand-0.10 par exchanged for $2.05669 cash

JOHNNIES INDL LTD (SOUTH AFRICA)
Stock Dividends - 0.3438% payable 05/17/1996 to holders of record 03/22/1996; 1.4189% payable 11/12/1996 to holders of record 09/13/1996; 1.37939% payable 11/18/1997 to holders of record 09/19/1997; 3.0323% payable 11/09/1998 to holders of record 09/18/1998; 1.99846% payable 09/07/1999 to holders of record 07/16/1999
Name changed to Johnnic Holdings Ltd. 05/08/2000
(See Johnnic Holdings Ltd.)

JOHNNY REB INC (GA)
Liquidated and dissolved in 1970
Details not available

JOHNNY UNITAS QUARTERBACK CLUBS, INC. (DE)
See - Unitas (Johnny) Quarterback Clubs, Inc.

JOHNS BARGAIN STORES CORP (NY)
6% Preferred called for redemption 4/30/62
Name changed to Stratton Group, Ltd. 8/18/70
(See Stratton Group, Ltd.)

JOHNS MANVILLE CORP (NY)
Common no par changed to $5 par and (1) additional share issued 3/23/56
Common $5 par changed to $2.50 par and (1) additional share issued 3/31/69
Reincorporated under the laws of Delaware as Manville Corp. 10/30/81
Manville Corp. name changed to Schuller Corp. 3/29/96 which name changed to Johns-Manville Corp. (New) 5/5/97
(See Johns-Manville Corp. (New))

JOHNS-MANVILLE CORP NEW (DE)
Merged into Berkshire Hathaway Inc. 2/28/2001
Each share Common $2.50 par exchanged for $13 cash

JOHNS-MANVILLE (H.W.) INC.
Succeeded by Johns-Manville Corp. (NY) in 1926
(See Johns-Manville Corp. (NY))

JOHNSON (TOM)-NIPIGON MINES LTD.
Succeeded by Tombill Gold Mines Ltd. in 1935
(See Tombill Gold Mines Ltd.)

JOHNSON AUTOMATICS, INC.
In process of dissolution in 1952

JOHNSON BEER CO (DE)
Charter cancelled and declared inoperative and void for non-payment of taxes 3/1/2001

JOHNSON CARPER FURNITURE CO (VA)
Each share Common $100 par exchanged for (15) shares Common $10 par 11/19/1941
Each share Common $10 par exchanged for (3) shares Common $5 par 01/13/1948
Stock Dividend - 100% 12/27/1963
6% Preferred $100 par called for redemption 12/10/1969
Completely liquidated 01/21/1970
Each share Common $5 par exchanged for first and final distribution of (1) share Singer Co. $1.50 Class A Conv. Preferred no par
(See Singer Co.)

JOHNSON (J.N.) CO., INC. (MN)
Statutorily dissolved 8/1/97

JOHNSON CTLS INC (WI)
$2 Part. Conv. Preferred Ser. A $1 par called for redemption 03/31/1977
Common $2.50 par split (2) for (1) by issuance of (1) additional share 09/28/1977
Common $2.50 par changed to $1 par 04/26/1978
$2 Conv. Preferred Ser. B $1 par called for redemption 11/07/1983
Common $1 par changed to 50¢ par 01/26/1984
Common 50¢ par changed to $0.16666666 01/21/1986
Common $0.16666666 par split (2) for (1) by issuance of (1) additional share 01/02/1987
Common $0.16666666 par split (2) for (1) by issuance of (1) additional share payable 03/31/1997 to holders of record 03/07/1997 Ex date - 04/01/1997
Recapitalized 09/30/1987
Each share $4.25 Conv. Exchangeable Preferred Ser. C $1 par exchanged for $50 principal amount of 8.50% Conv. Subord. Debentures due 09/30/2015
Note: Option to receive $1 cash per share in lieu of Debentures expired 09/14/1987
Common $0.16666666 par changed to $0.04166666 par and (1) additional share issued payable 01/02/2004 to holders of record 12/12/2003 Ex date - 01/05/2004
Common $0.04166666 par changed to $0.01388888 par and (2) additional shares issued payable 10/02/2007 to holders of record 09/14/2007 Ex date - 10/03/2007
Each Corporate Unit exchanged for (4.8579) shares Common $0.01388888 par 03/30/2012
Common $0.01388888 par changed to $1 par 01/23/2013
Merged into Johnson Controls International PLC 09/06/2016
Each share Common $1 par exchanged for (0.8357) share Ordinary USD $0.01 par and $5.7293 cash

JOHNSON DEVELOPMENT CORP. (NV)
Charter revoked for failure to file reports and pay fees 3/7/55

JOHNSON E F CO (MN)
Common $1 par changed to 50¢ par and (1) additional share issued 11/14/75
Merged into Western Union Corp. (Old) 11/30/82
Each share Common 50¢ par exchanged for (1) share Common $2.50 par
Western Union Corp. (Old) merged into Western Union Corp. (New) 12/31/87 which name changed to New Valley Corp. (NY) 4/22/91 which reorganized in Delaware 7/29/96 which was acquired by Vector Group Ltd. 12/13/2005

JOHNSON ELEC HLDGS LTD (BERMUDA)
Sponsored ADR's for Ordinary split (4) for (1) by issuance of (3) additional ADR's payable 09/08/2000 to holders of record 08/14/2000 Ex date - 08/14/2000
ADR agreement terminated 08/30/2013
Each Sponsored ADR for Ordinary exchanged for $8.576655 cash
(Additional Information in Active)

JOHNSON ELECTRS INC (FL)
Common $1 par changed to 50¢ par and (1) additional share issued 2/5/81
Common 50¢ par changed to 25¢ par and (1) additional share issued 10/12/82
Name changed to Audio Communications Network, Inc. 6/11/91
(See Audio Communications Network, Inc.)

JOHNSON FARE BOX CO.
Acquired by Bowser, Inc. 00/00/1945
Details not available

JOHNSON HILLS INC (WI)
Each share Common $1 par exchanged for (0.003333) share Common $300 par 11/13/1975
Stock Dividends - 10% 06/30/1965; 10% 06/30/1966
Administratively dissolved 06/22/1991

JOHNSON INDUSTRIES, INC. (DE)
No longer in existence having become inoperative and void for non-payment of taxes 4/1/57

JOHNSON INTL CORP (MI)
Chapter 11 Federal Bankruptcy proceedings converted to Chapter 7 on 02/24/1989
Stockholders' equity unlikely

JOHNSON IRON WORKS, DRY DOCK & SHIPBUILDING CO., INC.
Acquired by Todd-Johnson Dry Docks, Inc. 00/00/1935
Details not available

JOHNSON METAL PRODUCTS CO.
Merged into Detroit Steel Products Co. in 1948
Details not available

JOHNSON MOTOR CO.
Merged into Outboard Marine & Manufacturing Co. in 1936
Details not available

JOHNSON NICKEL MINING CO. (MN)
Charter expired by time limitation 9/22/54

JOHNSON OIL REFINING CO. (DE)
Reincorporated 00/00/1931
State of incorporation changed from (IL) to (DE) 00/00/1931
Merged into Gaseteria, Inc. 03/08/1956
Each share Common no par exchanged for (0.666666) share Capital Stock $7 par
Gaseteria, Inc. acquired by Standard Oil Co. (NJ) 03/31/1958 which name changed to Exxon Corp. 11/01/1972 which name changed to Exxon Mobil Corp. 11/30/1999

JOHNSON PRODS INC (DE)
Common $1 par and Class B Common $1 par changed to 50¢ par and (1) additional share issued respectively 1/12/73
Class B Common 50¢ par reclassified as Common 50¢ par 12/8/76
Under plan of recapitalization each share old Common 50¢ par exchanged for (0.3) share new Common 50¢ par 12/13/90
New Common 50¢ par split (2) for (1) by issuance of (1) additional share 4/20/93
Merged into IVAX Corp. 8/31/93
Each share new Common 50¢ par exchanged for (1) share Common 10¢ par
(See IVAX Corp.)

JOHNSON RANCH ROYALTY CO., INC. (TX)
Common $1 par changed to 25¢ par in 1940
Merged into Magna Oil Corp. 1/30/57
Each share Common 25¢ par exchanged for (1) share Common 50¢ par
Magna Oil Corp. merged into Triton Oil & Gas Corp. 4/28/72 which name changed to Triton Energy Corp. (TX) 12/1/81 which reincorporated in Delaware 5/12/95

JOHNSON SVC CO (WI)
Each share Common $100 par exchanged for (25) shares Common no par 00/00/1929
Each share Common no par exchanged for (4) shares Common $5 par 04/05/1995
Common $5 par split (2) for (1) by issuance of (1) additional share 04/26/1961
Common $5 par changed to $2.50 par and (1) additional share issued 06/05/1969
Name changed to Johnson Controls, Inc. 12/02/1974
Johnson Controls, Inc. merged into Johnson Controls International PLC 09/06/2016

JOHNSON STEPHENS & SHINKLE SHOE CO (MO)
Common no par exchanged (2) for (1) in 1946
Out of business in 1971
No stockholders' equity

JOHNSON WORLDWIDE ASSOC INC (WI)
Name changed to Johnson Outdoors Inc. 03/01/2000

JOHNSON'S ASBESTOS CO. (QC)
Charter cancelled for failure to file reports and pay fees in 1969

JOHNSON'S CO. LTD. (QC)
Charter cancelled for failure to file reports and pay fees in 1969

JOHNSONS WARREN INC (MN)
Reorganized under the laws of Delaware as Commonwealth Equities, Inc. 02/25/1971
Each share Common 10¢ par exchanged for (1) share Common 10¢ par
Commonwealth Equities, Inc. (DE) reorganized as Sun Vacation Properties, Corp. (NV) 04/07/2003
(See Sun Vacation Properties, Corp.)

JOHNSTON & FRYE SECS LTD (BC)
Delisted from Vancouver Stock Exchange 1/10/90

JOHNSTON ACQUISITION CORP (DE)
Acquired by JAQ Corp. 02/24/2009
Details not available

JOHNSTON CAPITAL APPRECIATION FUND (MA)
Name changed to Boston Co. Capital Appreciation Fund 5/1/81

JOHNSTON CONTAINER CORP. (IN)
Name changed to Johnston Industries Corp. 10/4/65
Johnston Industries Corp. acquired by Stanray Corp. 5/31/68 which merged into IC Industries, Inc. 4/26/77

JOHNSTON FOIL MANUFACTURING CO. (NJ)
Merged into Standard Packaging Corp. 6/30/58
Each share Capital Stock $50 par exchanged for (37.5642) shares Common $1 par
Standard Packaging Corp. acquired by Saxon Industries, Inc. (NY) 10/22/70 which reincorporated in Delaware 10/3/75 which reorganized as Paper Corp. of America 4/1/85
(See Paper Corp. of America)

JOHNSTON INDUSTRIES CORP. (IN)
Acquired by Stanray Corp. 05/31/1968
Details not available

JOHNSTON INDS INC (DE)
Reincorporated 12/31/87
State of incorporation changed from (NY) to (DE) 12/31/87
Common 10¢ par split (3) for (2) by issuance of (0.5) additional share 5/30/89
Common 10¢ par split (3) for (2) by issuance of (0.5) additional share 3/6/92
Common 10¢ par split (3) for (2) by issuance of (0.5) additional share 1/24/94
Merged into CGW Southeast Partners IV, L.P. 5/10/2000
Each share Common 10¢ par exchanged for $3 cash

JOHNSTON MUT FD INC (NY)
Stock Dividend - 100% 4/11/55
Capital Stock $1 par split (2) for (1) by issuance of (1) additional share 5/26/60
Reincorporated under the laws of Massachusetts as Johnston Capital Appreciation Fund and Capital Stock $1 par reclassified as Shares of Bene. Int. no par 8/1/79
Johnston Capital Appreciation Fund name changed to Boston Co. Capital Appreciation Fund 5/1/81

JOHNSTON OIL & GAS CO. (DE)
Name changed to Texas National Petroleum Co. 9/1/55
Texas National Petroleum Co. liquidation completed 3/21/72

JOHNSTON TERMS & STORAGE LTD (BC)
Common no par split (3) for (1) by issuance of (2) additional shares 7/25/66
6% Preferred $10 par called for redemption 3/15/71
Acquired by Wescan Transport Ltd. 8/12/71
Each share Common no par exchanged for $12.50 cash
5% 2nd Preferred $10 par acquired by Wescan Transport Ltd. in April 1973
Public interest eliminated

JOHNSTON TESTERS, INC. (DE)
Liquidation completed 1/31/56

JOHNSTON TIN FOIL METAL CO.
Name changed to Johnston Foil Manufacturing Co. in 1949
Johnston Foil Manufacturing Co. merged into Standard Packaging Corp. 6/30/58 which was acquired by Saxon Industries, Inc. (NY) 10/22/70 which reincorporated in Delaware 10/3/75 which reorganized as Paper Corp. of America 4/1/85
(See Paper Corp. of America)

JOHNSTONE TIRE & RUBBER CO. (AZ)
Reorganized under the laws of Delaware as La Porte Rubber Co. in 1928
(See La Porte Rubber Co.)

JOHNSTOWN, GLOVERSVILLE & KINGSBORO HORSE RAILWAY CO.
Acquired by Fonda, Johnstown & Gloversville Railroad Co. 06/01/1944
Each share Common exchanged for $32 amount of 4% 1st Mortgage Series A Bonds, $18 amount of 4-1/2% 2nd Mortgage Income Bonds and (2) shares Common no par
(See Fonda, Johnstown & Gloversville Railroad Co.)

JOHNSTOWN AMER INDS INC (DE)
Name changed to Transportation Technologies Industries, Inc. 6/11/99

JOHNSTOWN AMERN COS (MA)
Shares of Bene. Int. $1 par reclassified as Common $1 par 1/4/85
Name changed to Consolidated Companies 11/28/88
(See Consolidated Companies)

JOHNSTOWN BK & TR CO (JOHNSTOWN, PA)
Stock Dividends - 50% 06/01/1951; 33-1/3% 06/11/1959; 25% 02/11/1966; 33-1/3% 08/15/1968; 25% 08/15/1970; 25% 08/15/1973; 20% 08/16/1976; 10% 08/15/1979; 10% 08/15/1981
Reorganized as BT Financial Corp. 07/01/1983
Each share Capital Stock $10 par exchanged for (2) shares Common $5 par
BT Financial Corp. name changed to Promistar Financial Corp. 11/15/2000 which merged into F.N.B. Corp. (FL) 01/18/2002
00/00/1966, 00/00/1970 & 00/00/1983 Our

JOHNSTOWN CONS INCOME PARTNERS (CA)
Company terminated registration of Units of Limited Partnership Interests 2 and is no longer public as of 08/12/1997
Details not available
Company terminated registration of Units of Limited Partnership Interests and is no longer public as of 11/07/2006
Details not available

JOHNSTOWN CONS RLTY TR (CA)
Name changed to Transcontinental Realty Investors (CA) 7/5/89
Transcontinental Realty Investors (CA) reorganized in Delaware as Transcontinental Realty Investors, Inc. 8/17/90 which reincorporated in Nevada 3/24/92

JOHNSTOWN SVGS BK (JOHNSTOWN, PA)
Name changed 03/09/1993
Name changed from Johnstown Savings Bank, F.S.B. (Johnstown, PA) to Johnstown Savings Bank (Johnstown, PA) 03/09/1993
Merged into USBANCORP, Inc. 07/11/1994
Each share Common $1 par exchanged for (0.4925) share Common $2.50 par and $10.13 cash
USBANCORP, Inc. name changed to AmeriServ Financial, Inc. 05/07/2001

JOHNSTOWN TELEPHONE CO.
Acquired by Associated Telephone Utilities Co. in 1930
Details not available

JOHNSVILLE PACKING CORP (MN)
Completely liquidated 03/23/1972
Each share Common 10¢ par exchanged for first and final distribution of (1) share Black Steer of America, Inc. Common 5¢ par
Black Steer of America, Inc. liquidated for Water Wonderland Corp.

05/00/1972 which name changed to Progressive National Industries, Inc. 08/17/1972
(See Progressive National Industries, Inc.)

JOIE DE VIVRE RESORTS INC (DE)
Recapitalized as Mainstream Semiconductor Corp. 5/10/95
Each share Common 1¢ par exchanged for (0.5) share Common 1¢ par
Mainstream Semiconductor Corp. name changed to Ocotillo Enterprises Inc. 4/18/96
(See Ocotillo Enterprises Inc.)

JOINT INVESTORS, INC.
Dissolved in 1932

JOINT STK CO COMSTAR-UTD TELESYSTEMS (RUSSIA)
Merged into Mobile Telesystems OJSC 04/01/2011
Each Sponsored 144A GDR for Ordinary exchanged for $6.8233 cash
Each Sponsored Reg. S GDR for Ordinary exchanged for $6.8233 cash

JOINT STK CO OPEN INVTS (RUSSIA)
Name changed to Open Investments PJSC 09/04/2015
Open Investments PJSC name changed to Ingrad PJSC 02/08/2018

JOINT STK CO ROSSETI (RUSSIA)
Name changed 08/22/2014
Name changed from JSC Russian Grids to JSC Rosseti 08/22/2014
Name changed to PJSC Rosseti 09/15/2015

JOINTLAND DEV INC (FL)
Name changed to Gold Royalty Corp. 01/14/2011
Gold Royalty Corp. recapitalized as Ally Pharma US, Inc. 12/17/2012 which recapitalized as TPT Global Tech, Inc. 12/02/2014

JOJOBA HORIZONS INC (AZ)
Charter revoked for failure to file annual reports and pay fees 1/10/87

JOLEN INC (FL)
Name changed to WOWI, Inc. 06/23/2016

JOLENE INC (UT)
Charter expired 07/11/2001

JOLIET & CHICAGO RAILROAD CO.
Dissolved in 1950

JOLIET HEATING CORP. (IL)
In process of liquidation in 1954

JOLIET QUE MINES LTD (ON)
Capital Stock $1 par changed to no par 08/09/1972
Recapitalized as J-Q Resources Inc. 09/08/1978
Each share Capital Stock no par exchanged for (0.2) share Capital Stock no par
J-Q Resources Inc. name changed to International Pursuit Corp. 09/21/1987 which recapitalized as Apollo Gold Corp. (ON) 06/24/2002 which reincorporated in Yukon 05/28/2003 which recapitalized as Brigus Gold Corp. (YT) 06/25/2010 which reincorporated in Canada 06/09/2011
(See Brigus Gold Corp.)

JOLIN BOURLAMAQUE MINES LTD. (QC)
Merged into Brominco Inc. 06/01/1976
Each share Common $1 par exchanged for (0.0002) share Capital Stock no par
Brominco Inc. merged into Aur Resources Inc. 05/16/1985 which was acquired by Teck Cominco Ltd. 09/28/2007 which name changed to Teck Resources Ltd. 04/27/2009

JOLLEY MARKETING INC (NV)
Name changed to Creative Medical Technology Holdings, Inc. 05/26/2016

JOLLEY VENDING INC (NV)
Reorganized as Wareforce One Inc. 7/14/98
Each share Common $0.001 par exchanged for (1.85) shares Common $0.001 par
Wareforce One Inc. name changed to Wareforce.Com Inc. 1/26/99
(See Wareforce.Com Inc.)

JOLLOCO EXPLORATIONS LTD. (ON)
Charter cancelled for failure to pay taxes and file returns 03/16/1976

JOLLY JACK URANIUM CO. (UT)
Name changed to International Properties Corp. (UT) 9/20/71
Each share Common 10¢ par exchanged for (1) share Common 10¢ par
International Properties Corp. (UT) reorganized in Delaware as Plasteel International, Inc. 4/12/88 which name changed to Trans-World Pharmaceuticals, Inc. 3/9/89

JOLLY JUMPER PRODS AMER LTD (ON)
Name changed to Sun Valley Ranch Inc. 09/25/1987
Sun Valley Ranch Inc. name changed to Tri-Lateral Free Trade Inc. 03/25/1991 which recapitalized as Tri-Lateral Investments Corp. 06/19/1995 which recapitalized as Tri-Lateral Venture Corp. 11/11/1998 which name changed to Pan American Gold Corp. 05/06/2004 which recapitalized as Newcastle Resources Ltd. (ON) 11/28/2008 which reincorporated in British Columbia as RepliCel Life Sciences Inc. 07/01/2011

JOLT BEVERAGE LTD (BC)
Name changed to International Beverage Corp. 05/13/1988
International Beverage Corp. recapitalized as Clearly Canadian Beverage Corp. 05/14/1990
(See Clearly Canadian Beverage Corp.)

JOLYN ELECTRS MFG CORP (NY)
Name changed to Sovereign Enterprises, Inc. (NY) 06/10/1969
Sovereign Enterprises, Inc. (NY) reincorporated in Delaware as Varlen Corp. 01/30/1970
(See Varlen Corp.)

JOMAC GOLD SYNDICATE LTD.
Liquidated 00/00/1938
Details not available

JOMAC MINES LTD. (ON)
Merged into Jorsco Explorations Ltd. 03/08/1961
Each share Common exchanged for (1) share Common
(See Jorsco Explorations Ltd.)

JOMAR CAP CORP (AB)
Recapitalized as Online Energy Inc. 03/01/2011
Each share Common no par exchanged for (0.16666666) share Common no par
(See Online Energy Inc.)

JOMAR SPECIALTIES INC (FL)
Reorganized as Great East Bottles & Drinks (China) Holdings, Inc. 05/02/2008
Each share Common 1¢ par exchanged for (5) shares Common 1¢ par
Great East Bottles & Drinks (China) Holdings, Inc. name changed to Great China Mania Holdings, Inc. 05/12/2011 which name changed to GME Innotainment, Inc. 07/07/2015

JON DARING GROUP INC (NV)
Name changed to Can-Asia Minerals Inc. 5/4/2006

JONAL CORP (MT)
Common $1 par changed to 10¢ par 6/30/71
Recapitalized as General Ener-Tech, Inc. 4/6/73
Each share Common 10¢ par exchanged for (0.1) share Common $1 par
(See General Ener-Tech, Inc.)

JONAS & NAUMBURG CORP. (NY)
Each share $3 Preferred no par exchanged for (6.5) shares Common $2.50 par in 1935
Each share Common no par exchanged for (0.2) share Common $2.50 par in 1935
Merged into Hat Corp. of America 10/1/61
Each share Common $2.50 par exchanged for (0.4) share Common $1 par
Hat Corp. of America name changed to HCA Industries, Inc. 4/30/70 which name changed to HCA-Martin, Inc. 5/11/73 which name changed to Martin Processing, Inc. 5/16/75
(See Martin Processing, Inc.)

JONATHAN LOGAN INC (DE)
Common 50¢ par split (5) for (4) by issuance of (0.25) additional share 1/29/71
Common 50¢ par split (3) for (2) by issuance of (0.5) additional share 8/26/83
Merged into United Merchants & Manufacturers, Inc. 10/18/84
Each share Common 50¢ par exchanged for $28 principal amount of 15% 20-yr. Subordinated Debentures due 10/15/2004

JONES & FREDERICK, INC. (FL)
Common 10¢ par split (2) for (1) by issuance of (1) additional share 06/20/1961
Merged into Continental Fund, Inc. 02/21/1963
Each share Common 10¢ par exchanged for (0.1) share Common 10¢ par
Continental Fund, Inc. name changed to Manufacturers & Investors Corp. 08/19/1963 which name changed to Landban of Florida Corp. 07/21/1970 which name changed to Transamerica Business Corp. 01/26/1977
(See Transamerica Business Corp.)

JONES & LAMSON MACHINE CO. (VT)
Each share Capital Stock $100 par exchanged for (7) shares Capital Stock $20 par to effect a (5) for (1) split and 40% stock dividend 00/00/1940
Capital Stock $20 par split (2) for (1) by issuance of (1) additional share 01/23/1957
Name changed to Ascutney Fund, Inc. (VT) 02/03/1964
Ascutney Fund, Inc. (VT) reincorporated in Massachusetts 07/10/1964 which was acquired by Loomis-Sayles Mutual Fund, Inc. 06/12/1967 which name changed to CGM Trust 03/01/1991

JONES & LAUGHLIN INDS INC NEW (DE)
Common $1 par split (5) for (2) by issuance of (1.5) additional shares 7/28/69
Merged into Ling-Temco-Vought, Inc. 12/23/69
Each share Common $1 par exchanged for (0.25) share Common 50¢ par
Ling-Temco-Vought, Inc. name changed to LTV Corp. (Old) 5/5/72 which reorganized as LTV Corp. (New) 6/28/93
(See LTV Corp. (New))

JONES & LAUGHLIN STL CORP (PA)
Each share 7% Preferred $100 par exchanged for (0.5) share 5% Preferred Ser. A $100 par, (0.5) share 5% Preferred Ser. B $100 par and (1.25) shares Common no par in 1941
Each share Common $100 par exchanged for (1) share Common no par in 1941
Each share Common no par exchanged for (2) shares Common $10 par in 1951
Common $10 par split (2) for (1) by issuance of (1) additional share 3/12/69
Merged into LTV Corp. 11/23/74
Each share Common $10 par exchanged for $29 cash
Merged into LTV Corp. 6/21/81
Each share 5% Preferred Ser. A $100 par exchanged for $65 cash

JONES & VINING INC (DE)
Common 10¢ par split (2) for (1) by issuance of (1) additional share 5/20/76
Common 10¢ par split (5) for (4) by issuance of (0.25) additional share 1/20/82
Common 10¢ par split (5) for (4) by issuance of (0.25) additional share 5/31/83
Common 10¢ par split (5) for (4) by issuance of (0.25) additional share 5/30/84
Common 10¢ par split (5) for (4) by issuance of (0.25) additional share 5/26/86
Merged into J&V NewCo, Inc. 7/14/87
Each share Common 10¢ par exchanged for $4.90 cash

JONES APOTHECARY INC (TX)
Charter forfeited for failure to pay taxes 1/18/88

JONES APPAREL GROUP INC (PA)
Common 1¢ par split (2) for (1) by issuance of (1) additional share payable 10/02/1996 to holders of record 09/12/1996 Ex date - 10/03/1996
Common 1¢ par split (2) for (1) by issuance of (1) additional share payable 06/25/1998 to holders of record 06/04/1998 Ex date - 06/26/1998
Name changed to Jones Group Inc. 10/18/2010
(See Jones Group Inc.)

JONES BROS. CO. OF CANADA LTD.
Reorganized as Jones Industries Ltd. 10/01/1946
No stockholders' equity

JONES BROTHERS OF CANADA LTD. (CANADA)
Reorganized as Jones Bros. Co. of Canada Ltd. 00/00/1937
Each share Preference exchanged for (5) shares Common no par
Each share Common no par exchanged for (0.2) share Common no par
(See Jones Bros. Co. of Canada Ltd.)

JONES BROTHERS TEA CO., INC.
Name changed to Grand Union Co. in 1928
(See Grand Union Co.)

JONES DAVID LTD (AUSTRALIA)
Stock Dividend - 25% 12/28/1988
ADR agreement terminated 01/01/1996
Each ADR for Ordinary AUD $0.50 par exchanged for $0.006 cash
Each Unsponsored ADR for Ordinary exchanged for (1) Sponsored ADR for Ordinary 04/20/2012
ADR agreement terminated 08/14/2014

Each Sponsored ADR for Ordinary exchanged for $3.675222 cash

JONES DRY GOODS CO. (MO)
Charter forfeited for failure to file reports 12/02/1913

JONES GROUP INC (PA)
Acquired by Jasper Parent LLC 04/08/2014
Each share Common 1¢ par exchanged for $15 cash

JONES HOSPLEX SYS INC (DE)
Reincorporated 6/12/85
State of incorporation changed from (NY) to (DE) 6/12/85
Name changed to Hosplex Systems, Inc. 10/1/85
(See Hosplex Systems, Inc.)

JONES INDUSTRIES, LTD. (CANADA)
Liquidated 12/21/1955
No stockholders' equity

JONES INTERCABLE INC (CO)
Merged into Comcast Corp. (Old) 3/2/2000
Each share Common 1¢ par exchanged for (1.4) shares Class A Special Common $1 par
Each share Class A Common 1¢ par exchanged for (1.4) shares Class A Special Common $1 par
Comcast Corp. (Old) merged into Comcast Corp. (New) 11/18/2002

JONES INTERCABLE INVS LP (CO)
Completely liquidated 9/15/97
Each Class A Unit 1¢ par exchanged for first and final distribution of $16.15 cash

JONES (LEWIS) MANAGEMENT CO. (PA)
Name changed to Pennsylvania Utilities Investment Corp. in July 1954
(See listing for Pennsylvania Utilities Investment Corp.)

JONES MED INDS INC (DE)
Common 4¢ par split (2) for (1) by issuance of (1) additional share 03/15/1991
Common 4¢ par split (3) for (2) by issuance of (0.5) additional share payable 03/01/1996 to holders of record 02/23/1996
Common 4¢ par split (3) for (2) by issuance of (0.5) additional share payable 06/10/1996 to holders of record 06/03/1996
Stock Dividend - 10% 07/07/1989
Name changed to Jones Pharma Inc. 05/20/1998
Jones Pharma Inc. merged into King Pharmaceuticals, Inc. 08/31/2000
(See King Pharmaceuticals, Inc.)

JONES MOTOR CO., INC. (PA)
Common $2 par changed to $1 par 02/14/1968
Alleghany Corp. acquired all outstanding shares through purchase offer as of 03/11/1971
Public interest eliminated

JONES NAUGHTON ENTMT INC (CO)
Reincorporated under the laws of Delaware as Go Online Networks Corp. 09/23/1999
(See Go Online Networks Corp.)

JONES (A.R.) OIL & OPERATING CO.
Liquidated in 1938

JONES OPTICAL CO (CO)
Name changed to Cambridge Holdings, Ltd. 08/19/1988
(See Cambridge Holdings, Ltd.)

JONES PHARMA INC (DE)
Common 4¢ par split (3) for (2) by issuance of (0.5) additional share payable 08/06/1999 to holders of record 07/26/1999
Common 4¢ par split (3) for (2) by issuance of (0.5) additional share payable 03/01/2000 to holders of record 02/15/2000
Merged into King Pharmaceuticals, Inc. 08/31/2000
Each share Common 4¢ par exchanged for (1.125) shares Common no par
(See King Pharmaceuticals, Inc.)

JONES PLUMBING SYS INC (MN)
Statutorily dissolved 12/31/99

JONES PROGRAMMING PARTNERS LTD (CO)
Liquidation completed
Each Unit of Ltd. Partnership Int. 1-A received initial distribution of $9.81 cash payable 08/00/2002 to holders of record 08/00/2002
Each Unit of Ltd. Partnership Int. 2-A received initial distribution of $9.35 cash payable 08/00/2002 to holders of record 08/00/2002
Each Unit of Ltd. Partnership Int. 1-A received second and final distribution of approximately $6.33 cash payable 12/16/2002 to holders of record 12/16/2002
Each Unit of Ltd. Partnership Int. 2-A received second and final distribution of approximately $6.33 cash payable 12/16/2002 to holders of record 12/16/2002
Note: Certificates were not required to be surrendered and are without value

JONES R B CORP (DE)
Common $1 par split (2) for (1) by issuance of (1) additional share 7/15/71
Merged into Alexander & Alexander Services Inc. 1/31/79
Each share Common $1 par exchanged for (1.1601) share Common $1 par
(See Alexander & Alexander Services Inc.)

JONES SPACELINK INCOME / GROWTH FD LTD (CO)
Completely liquidated 12/31/2000
Details not available

JONES SPACELINK LTD NEW (CO)
Name changed to Spacelink, Ltd. 3/30/82 which name changed back to Jones Spacelink, Ltd. 11/26/85
Plan of reorganization and liquidation effective 12/20/94
Each share Class A Common 1¢ par exchanged for (0.9696) share Common 1¢ par and (0.03571) share Class A Common 1¢ par of Jones Intercable, Inc.
Jones Intercable, Inc. merged into Comcast Corp. (Old) 3/2/2000 which merged into Comcast Corp. (New) 11/18/2002

JONES (CHESTER L.) STORES CORP.
Acquired by Sanger Brothers, Inc. in 1938
No stockholders' equity

JONHOP INC (OR)
Name changed to 20/10 Products, Inc. 12/20/79
(See 20/10 Products, Inc.)

JONI BLAIR CALIF INC (CA)
Stock Dividend - 25% 10/12/1978
Acquired by private investors 02/01/1984
Each share Common $1 par exchanged for $5.15 cash

JONKER BUSINESS MACHINES, INC. (DE)
Class A Common no par and Class B Common no par split (10) for (1) respectively by issuance of (9) additional shares 9/30/60
Name changed to Jonker Corp. and Class A Common no par and Class B Common no par changed to 10¢ par 12/17/65
(See Jonker Corp.)

JONKER CORP (DE)
Adjudicated bankrupt 12/2/69
Apparently no stockholders' equity

JONLAB INVESTMENTS LTD. (ON)
99% acquired by Brascan Ltd. through purchase offer which expired 07/19/1977
Public interest eliminated

JONPOL EXPLS LTD (ON)
Merged into Eastern Platinum Ltd. 04/26/2005
Each share Common no par exchanged for (0.25) share Common no par

JONSMITH MINES LTD (ON)
Reorganized under the laws of Alberta as New Jonsmith Exploration Ltd. 08/17/1976
Each share Capital Stock no par exchanged for (0.005) share Capital Stock no par
New Jonsmith Exploration Ltd. name changed to Chal-Bert Drilling (Western) Ltd. 04/27/1977
(See Chal-Bert Drilling (Western) Ltd.)

JONTEX, INC. (NV)
Charter revoked for failure to file reports and pay fees 3/3/58

JOPEC RES LTD (BC)
Recapitalized as Fortuna Ventures Inc. 02/03/1999
Each share Common no par exchanged for (0.14285714) share Common no par
Fortuna Ventures Inc. name changed to Fortuna Silver Mines Inc. 06/29/2005

JOPLIN & PITTSBURGH RAILWAY CO.
Property sold in 1929
No stockholders' equity

JORDAN AMERN HLDGS INC (FL)
Name changed to Gundaker/Jordan American Holdings, Inc. 09/15/2003
(See Gundaker/Jordan American Holdings, Inc.)

JORDAN ENERGY CORP. (UT)
Involuntarily dissolved for failure to file annual reports 6/1/88

JORDAN KANE FLOOR COVERINGS INC (FL)
Each share old Common no par exchanged for (0.01) share new Common no par 01/20/2006
Administratively dissolved 09/14/2007

JORDAN KUWAIT BK (JORDAN)
ADR agreement terminaed 06/20/2017
No ADR's remain outstanding

JORDAN PETE LTD (CANADA)
Class A no par reclassified as Common no par 06/15/1994
Merged into Reserve Royalty Corp. 12/19/1997
Each share Common no par exchanged for $9.80 cash

JORDAN PETE LTD NEW (CANADA)
Conv. Class B no par retraction privilege expired 03/01/1988
Each share Conv. Class B no par exchanged for (0.33333333) share Class A no par 04/29/1988
Class C no par called for redemption 05/31/1988
Merged into New Jordan Petroleum Ltd. 06/01/1990
Each share Class A no par exchanged for (0.2) share Class A Common no par and (0.2) share Class B Common no par
New Jordan Petroleum Ltd. name changed back to Jordan Petroleum Ltd. 05/07/1992
(See Jordan Petroleum Ltd.)

JORDAN PETE LTD OLD (AB)
Reincorporated 06/26/1987
Place of incorporation changed from (AB) to (Canada) 06/26/1987
Merged into Jordan Petroleum Ltd. (New) 12/01/1987
Each share Common no par exchanged for (1) share Class A no par
Jordan Petroleum Ltd. (New) merged into New Jordan Petroleum Ltd. 06/01/1990 which name changed back to Jordan Petroleum Ltd. 05/07/1992
(See Jordan Petroleum Ltd.)

JORDAN TELECOMMUNICATION PRODS INC (DE)
Acquired by Emerson Electric Co. 01/18/2000
Each share 144A Common exchanged for $284.58 cash
13.25% Exchangeable Sr. Preferred Ser. B called for redemption at $1,132.50 on 01/31/2000
Public interest eliminated
Each share 144A Common received an initial distribution of $4.363862 cash from escrow 08/17/2000
Each share 144A Common received a second distribution of $1.8229952 cash from escrow 07/13/2001
Each share 144A Common received a third distribution of $1.8229952 cash from escrow 09/21/2001
Each share 144A Common received a fourth distribution of $1.8229952 cash from escrow 09/11/2002
Each share 144A Common received a fifth distribution of $1.8229952 cash from escrow 03/10/2003
Each share 144A Common received a sixth distribution of $1.8229952 cash from escrow 09/12/2003
Each share 144A Common received a seventh distribution of $1.8229952 cash from escrow 03/08/2004
Each share 144A Common received an eighth distribution of $1.8229952 cash from escrow 09/21/2004
Each share 144A Common received a ninth distribution of $1.8229952 cash from escrow 04/27/2005
Each share 144A Common received a tenth distribution of $1.8229952 cash from escrow 11/02/2005
Each share 144A Common received an eleventh distribution of $0.7781152 cash from escrow 05/30/2006
Each share 144A Common received a twelfth distribution of $0.7781152 cash from escrow 12/06/2006
Each share 144A Common received a thirteenth distribution of $4.7792676 cash from escrow 01/30/2007
Each share 144A Common received a fourteenth and final distribution of $75.1335804 cash from escrow 12/14/2007

JORDAN WESTIN BLDG. LIQUIDATION TRUST
Liquidated in 1945

JORDESCO RES LTD (BC)
Struck off register and declared dissolved for failure to file returns 08/09/1976

JORDEX RES INC (YT)
Reincorporated 07/27/1998
Place of incorporation changed from (BC) to (YT) 07/27/1998
Name changed to iTech Capital Corp. 03/10/2000
iTech Capital Corp. name changed to Sirit Inc. 05/05/2003
(See Sirit Inc.)

JORDYN TAYLOR PPTYS INC (NV)
Name changed to Rent Finders USA, Inc. 4/26/2006
Rent Finders USA, Inc. recapitalized as Church & Crawford, Inc. 3/30/2007

JORE CORP (MT)
Assets sold for the benefit of creditors 4/24/2002
No stockholders' equity

JOREMI ENTERPRISES INC (NY)
Under plan of merger each share Common 10¢ par exchanged for $1.25 cash 2/24/83

JOREX LTD (ON)
Recapitalized as Canadian Jorex Ltd. (ON) 08/01/1984
Each share Common no par exchanged for (0.1) share Common no par
Canadian Jorex Ltd. (ON) reincorporated in Canada 10/30/1984
(See Canadian Jorex Ltd.)

JORGENSEN EARLE M CO (CA)
Stock Dividend - 10% 11/29/1974
Reincorporated under the laws of Delaware 06/30/1975
(See Jorgensen (Earle M.) Co. (DE))

JORGENSEN EARLE M CO (DE)
Common $1 par split (2) for (1) by issuance of (1) additional share 01/07/1977
Common $1 par split (2) for (1) by issuance of (1) additional share 08/28/1981
Merged into EMJ Acquisition, Inc. 05/03/1990
Each share Common $1 par exchanged for $41.50 cash

JORGENSEN EARLE M CO NEW (DE)
Merged into Reliance Steel & Aluminum Co. (CA) 04/03/2006
Each share Common $0.001 par exchanged for (0.0892) share Common no par and $6.50 cash
Reliance Steel & Aluminum Co. (CA) reincorporated in Delaware 06/01/2015

JORN'S GREETING CARD CO., INC. (NY)
Name changed to Metropolitan Greetings Inc. 12/30/63
(See Metropolitan Greetings Inc.)

JORSCO EXPLORATIONS LTD. (ON)
Dissolved 04/29/1970
Opinion of former transfer agent is that shares are without value

JOS. VAILLANCOURT INC. (QC)
See - Villancourt (Jos.) Inc.

JOS A BANK CLOTHIERS INC (DE)
Common 1¢ par split (5) for (4) by issuance of (0.25) additional share payable 08/18/2004 to holders of record 07/30/2004
Common 1¢ par split (3) for (2) by issuance of (0.5) additional share payable 08/18/2010 to holders of record 07/30/2010 Ex date - 08/19/2010
Stock Dividends - 50% payable 02/18/2004 to holders of record 01/30/2004 Ex date - 01/19/2004; 25% payable 02/15/2006 to holders of record 01/27/2006 Ex date - 02/16/2006
Acquired by Men's Wearhouse, Inc. 06/18/2014
Each share Common 1¢ par exchanged for $65 cash

JOSEPH & FEISS CO. (OH)
Recapitalized 00/00/1932
Each share Class A no par exchanged for (1/3) share Common no par
Each share Class B no par exchanged for (1/15) share Common no par
Recapitalized 00/00/1937
Each share Common no par exchanged for (3) shares Common $5 par
Recapitalized 00/00/1951
Each share Common $5 par exchanged for (2) shares Common $2.50 par
Stock Dividends - 40% 09/10/1946; 25% 01/31/1966

Acquired by Phillips-Van Heusen Corp. (NY) 11/28/1966
Each share Common $2.50 par exchanged for (0.927272) share Common $1 par
Phillips-Van Heusen Corp. (NY) reincorporated in Delaware 06/10/1976 which name changed to PVH Corp. 07/14/2011

JOSEPH KREUTZER CORP.
See - Kreutzer (Joseph) Corp.

JOSEPH RANDO INTERNATIONAL (UT)
See - Rando (Joseph) International

JOSEPHSON (MARVIN) ASSOCIATES, INC. (DE)
Common 10¢ par changed to 5¢ par and (1) additional share issued 5/15/75
Stock Dividend - 25% 12/1/78
Name changed to Josephson International Inc. 11/5/81
(See Josephson International Inc.)

JOSEPHSON (MARVIN) ASSOCIATES, INC. (NY)
Reincorporated under the laws of Delaware 4/17/75
Josephson (Marvin) Associates, Inc. (DE) name changed to Josephson International Inc. 11/5/81
(See Josephson International Inc.)

JOSEPHSON INTL INC (DE)
Common 5¢ par split (2) for (1) by issuance of (1) additional share 11/30/81
Merged into LingPei Inc. 6/21/88
Each share Common 5¢ par exchanged for $14.52 cash

JOSHUA DOORE INC (DE)
Adjudicated bankrupt 06/04/1975
Stockholders' equity unlikely

JOSHUA TREE CONSTR INC (NV)
Name changed 07/07/2000
Name changed from Joshua Tree Finishers Inc. to Joshua Tree Construction, Inc. 07/07/2000
Each share old Common $0.001 par exchanged for (0.1) share new Common $0.001 par 12/24/2001
Each share new Common $0.001 par exchanged again for (0.02) share new Common $0.001 par 06/03/2002
Each share new Common $0.001 par exchanged again for (0.00333333) share new Common $0.001 par 12/16/2002
SEC revoked common stock registration 10/29/2008

JOSKE BROTHERS CO.
Acquired by Hahn Department Stores, Inc. in 1929
Details not available

JOSLYN CORP (IL)
Name changed 04/25/1985
Each share 6% Preferred $100 par exchanged for (1) share 4-1/2% Preferred $100 par 12/01/1946
Each share Common $5 par exchanged for (4) shares Common $1.25 par 00/00/1949
4-1/2% Preferred $100 par called for redemption 12/01/1955
Common $1.25 par split (4) for (1) by issuance of (3) additional shares 10/15/1964
Name changed from Joslyn Mfg. & Supply Co. to Joslyn Corp. 04/25/1985
Common $1.25 par split (3) for (2) by issuance of (0.5) additional share 12/17/1992
Stock Dividends - 50% 09/30/1981; 50% 09/16/1982
Acquired by Danaher Corp. 10/31/1995
Each share Common $1.25 par exchanged for $34 cash

JOSS ENERGY LTD (AB)
Class A Common no par reclassified as Common no par 09/20/1985
Merged into StarTech Energy Inc. 07/06/1994
Each share Common no par exchanged for (0.33333333) share Common no par
Startech Energy Inc. merged into Impact Energy Inc. (Canada) 01/31/2001 which merged into Thunder Energy Inc. 04/30/2004
(See Thunder Energy Inc.)

JOSSEY BASS INC (CA)
Merged into Maxwell Communication Inc. 2/23/89
Each share Capital Stock $1 par exchanged for $179.282 cash

JOSTEN GROWTH FD INC (MN)
Name changed to St. Paul Special Fund, Inc. 03/17/1977
St. Paul Special Fund, Inc. name changed to AMEV Special Fund, Inc. 05/01/1985 which name changed to Special Portfolios, Inc. 08/31/1989 which merged into Fortis Growth Fund, Inc. 03/01/1996
(See Fortis Growth Fund, Inc.)

JOSTENS INC (MN)
Class A and B Common $1 par changed to 33-1/3¢ par and (2) additional shares issued respectively 08/10/1961
Class B Common 33-1/3¢ par reclassified as Class A Common 33-1/3¢ par 07/01/1964
Class A Common 33-1/3¢ par reclassified as Common 33-1/3¢ par 10/14/1964
Common 33-1/3¢ par split (3) for (2) by issuance of (0.5) additional share 10/08/1976
Common 33-1/3¢ par split (3) for (2) by issuance of (0.5) additional share 05/31/1978
Common 33-1/3¢ par split (5) for (4) by issuance of (0.25) additional share 05/30/1980
Common 33-1/3¢ par split (5) for (4) by issuance of (0.25) additional share 05/29/1981
Common 33-1/3¢ par split (3) for (2) by issuance of (0.5) additional share 11/28/1984
Common 33-1/3¢ par split (2) for (1) by issuance of (1) additional share 11/28/1986
Stock Dividend - 10% 10/10/1975
Merged into Investcorp 05/10/2000
Each share Common 33-1/3¢ par exchanged for $25.25 cash
Note: Option to retain shares expired 05/04/2000
Common 33-1/3¢ par reclassified as Class A Common 33-1/3¢ par 05/10/2000
Acquired by DLJ Merchant Banking Partners, III, L.P. 07/29/2003
Each share Class A Common 33-1/3¢ par exchanged for approximately $48 cash

JOT IT SOFTWARE CORP (BC)
Name changed to Sideware Systems Inc. (BC) 02/18/1998
Sideware Systems Inc. (BC) reincorporated in Yukon 01/02/2002 which reincorporated in Delaware as Knowledgemax, Inc. 05/21/2002
(See Knowledgemax, Inc.)

JOTAN INC (FL)
Reincorporated 05/14/1996
State of incorporation changed from (ID) to (FL) 05/14/1996
SEC revoked common stock registration 04/30/2012

JOUBI MNG LTD (QC)
Charter annulled for failure to file reports or pay fees 02/12/1977

JOUET INC (NY)
Name changed to Flavos International, Inc. 8/5/69

(See Flavos International, Inc.)

JOULE INC (DE)
Common 1¢ par split (3) for (2) by issuance of (0.5) additional share 4/30/87
Merged into JAC Acquisition Co., Inc. 8/13/2004
Each share Common 1¢ par exchanged for $1.70 cash

JOURDAN RES INC (ON)
Reincorporated under the laws of Canada 12/14/94

JOURNAL COMMUNICATIONS INC (WI)
Each share Class A Common 1¢ par received distribution of (0.195) share Journal Media Group, Inc. Common 1¢ par payable 04/01/2015 to holders of record 03/25/2015
Merged into Scripps (E.W.) Co. 04/01/2015
Each share Class A Common 1¢ par exchanged for (0.5176) share Class A Common 1¢ par

JOURNAL MEDIA GROUP INC (WI)
Acquired by Gannett Co., Inc. (New) 04/08/2016
Each share Common 1¢ par exchanged for $12 cash

JOURNAL RADIOLOGY INC (NV)
Common $0.001 par split (30) for (1) by issuance of (29) additional shares payable 09/11/2012 to holders of record 09/11/2012
Recapitalized as Star Century Pandaho Corp. 04/16/2015
Each share Common $0.001 par exchanged for (0.0002) share Common $0.001 par
Star Century Pandaho Corp. recapitalized as International Leaders Capital Corp. 10/04/2017

JOURNAL REGISTER CO (DE)
Issue Information - 9,375,000 shares COM offered at $14 per share on 05/07/1997
Plan of reorganization under Chapter 11 Federal Bankruptcy proceedings effective 08/07/2009
No stockholders' equity

JOURNEY INTERNATIONAL, INC. (UT)
Reincorporated under the laws of Nevada as Chase American Corp. 3/21/88
(See Chase American Corp.)

JOURNEY RES CORP (BC)
Recapitalized as Musgrove Minerals Corp. 12/17/2010
Each share Common no par exchanged for (0.125) share Common no par
Musgrove Minerals Corp. recapitalized as RewardStream Solutions Inc. 08/04/2016

JOURNEY UNLIMITED OMNI BRAND CORP (BC)
Each share old Common no par exchanged for (0.1) share new Common no par 02/09/2004
Name changed to Journey Resources Corp. 11/29/2005
Journey Resources Corp. recapitalized as Musgrove Minerals Corp. 12/17/2010 which recapitalized as RewardStream Solutions Inc. 08/04/2016

JOURNEYS END CORP (ON)
Name changed 02/28/1989
Name changed from Journey's End Motel Corp. to Journey's End Corp. 02/28/1989
Name changed to UniHost Corp. 12/01/1997
(See UniHost Corp.)

JOUTEL RES LTD (QC)
Name changed 01/08/1980
Capital Stock $1 par changed to 80¢ par 09/11/1975

JOV-JRL — FINANCIAL INFORMATION, INC.

Capital Stock 80¢ par changed to 55¢ par 07/21/1976
Name changed from Joutel Copper Mines Ltd. to Joutel Resources Ltd.-Les Ressources Jout Ltee. and Capital Stock 55¢ par changed to no par 01/08/1980
Common no par reclassified as Subordinated no par 05/30/1985
Merged into Thundermin Resources Inc. 11/01/1998
Each share Subordinated no par exchanged for (0.16666666) share Common no par
Thundermin Resources Inc. merged into Rambler Metals & Mining PLC 01/12/2016

JOVE CORP (MI)
SEC revoked common stock registration 04/25/2012

JOVE MED CARE INC (FL)
Reorganized 08/24/1984
Reorganized from Jove, Inc. (UT) to under the laws of Florida as Jove Med-Care Inc. 08/24/1984
Each share Common 1¢ par exchanged for (0.125) share Common 1¢ par
Stock Dividends - 20% 06/23/1986; 10% 03/10/1988
Proclaimed dissolved for failure to file reports and pay fees 11/09/1990

JOVIAN CAP CORP (CANADA)
Each share old Common no par exchanged for (0.05) share new Common no par 04/29/2009
Acquired by Industrial Alliance Insurance & Financial Services Inc. 10/03/2013
Each share new Common no par exchanged for $10.23 cash

JOWSEY DENTON GOLD MINES, LTD. (ON)
Merged into Eden Roc Mineral Corp. 08/06/1981
Each share Capital Stock $1 par exchanged for (0.1) share Capital Stock no par
(See Eden Roc Mineral Corp.)

JOWSEY R J MNG LTD (ON)
Name changed to Open End Mines Ltd. and Capital Stock $1 par changed to no par 8/4/71
Open End Mines Ltd. liquidated for New York Oils Ltd. (BC) 4/28/72 which reincorporated in Alberta 7/19/82 which was acquired by Sceptre Resources Ltd. 3/14/89 which merged into Canadian Natural Resources Ltd. 8/15/96

JOY GLOBAL INC (DE)
Common $1 par split (3) for (2) by issuance of (0.5) additional share payable 01/21/2005 to holders of record 01/06/2005 Ex date - 01/24/2005
Common $1 par split (3) for (2) by issuance of (0.5) additional share payable 12/12/2005 to holders of record 11/28/2005 Ex date - 12/13/2005
Acquired by Komatsu Ltd. 04/05/2017
Each share Common $1 par exchanged for $28.30 cash

JOY INDS LTD (BC)
Struck off register and declared dissolved for failure to file returns 11/10/1988

JOY MFG CO (PA)
Common $1 par split (2) for (1) by issuance of (1) additional share 02/18/1966
Common $1 par split (2) for (1) by issuance of (1) additional share 11/11/1975
Common $1 par split (3) for (2) by issuance of (0.5) additional share 05/11/1981
Stock Dividend - 100% 12/20/1955
Merged into Joy Technologies Inc. 06/24/1987
Each share Common $1 par exchanged for (1.75) shares $3.25 Exchangeable Preferred $20 par
(See Joy Technologies Inc.)

JOY MNG LTD (BC)
Name changed to Joy Industries Ltd. and Capital Stock 50¢ par changed to no par 06/28/1973
(See Joy Industries Ltd.)

JOY TECHNOLOGIES INC (DE)
$3.25 Exchangeable Preferred $20 par changed to 1¢ par 07/11/1988
$3.25 Exchangeable Preferred 1¢ par called for redemption 12/23/1991
Merged into Harnischfeger Industries, Inc. 11/29/1994
Each share Class A Common 1¢ par exchanged for (0.5652) share Common $1 par
(See Harnischfeger Industries, Inc.)

JOYCE, INC. (CA)
Each share Common no par exchanged for (254) shares Common $1 par 00/00/1947
Acquired by United States Shoe Corp. 04/30/1955
Each share Common $1 par exchanged for (0.08333333) share Common $2 par
(See United States Shoe Corp.)

JOYCE LESLIE INC (NY)
Acquired by Taxi Apparel Corp. 10/2/81
Each share Common 10¢ par exchanged for $4.15 cash

JOYCE PERSONNEL SYS INC (NY)
Ceased operations in January 1975
No stockholders' equity

JOYSTAR INC (CA)
Name changed to Travelstar, Inc. 06/27/2007
(See Travelstar, Inc.)

JOYTOTO USA INC (NV)
Recapitalized as Pollex, Inc. 10/24/2008
Each share Common $0.001 par exchanged for (0.03333333) share Common $0.001 par
Pollex, Inc. name changed to eMARINE Global Inc. 09/12/2017

JP ENERGY PARTNERS LP (DE)
Merged into American Midstream Partners, L.P. 03/08/2017
Each Common Unit exchanged for (0.5775) Common Unit

JP FOODSERVICE INC (DE)
Name changed to U.S. Foodservice 02/27/1998
U.S. Foodservice merged into Koninklijke Ahold N.V. 04/12/2000 which name changed to Koninklijke Ahold Delhaize N.V. 07/25/2016

JP RLTY INC (MD)
Merged into General Growth Properties, Inc. 07/10/2002
Each share Common $0.0001 par exchanged for $26.10 cash

JP 2000 CORP (CO)
Merged into TTG Holdings Inc. 12/23/92
Each share Common $0.001 par exchanged for $0.0323 cash

JPAK GROUP INC (NV)
Acquired by Guo Xin Ltd. 02/09/2018
Each share Common $0.001 par exchanged for $0.20 cash

JPAL INC (NV)
Common $0.001 par split (5) for (1) by issuance of (4) additional shares payable 07/02/2001 to holders of record 07/02/2001 Ex date - 07/03/2001
Name changed to Essential Reality, Inc. (NV) 06/20/2002
Essential Reality, Inc. (NV) reorganized in Delaware as Alliance Distributors Holding Inc. 11/22/2004 which name changed to Alliance Media Holdings Inc. 06/26/2015

JPC CAP PARTNERS INC (DE)
Recapitalized as DIAS Holding, Inc. 08/22/2008
Each share Common $0.001 par exchanged for (0.5) share Common $0.001 par
(See DIAS Holding, Inc.)

JPC CORP (OH)
Recapitalized as Food Products Corp. (OH) 4/28/75
Each share Common no par exchanged for (0.5) share Common no par
Food Products Corp. (OH) reincorporated in South Carolina as Piemonte Foods, Inc. 10/17/86
(See Piemonte Foods, Inc.)

JPE INC (MI)
Voluntarily dissolved 06/17/2003
Stockholders' equity unlikely

JPL ENTERPRISES INC (CO)
Completely liquidated 2/19/82
Each share Common $5 par received first and final distribution of $29.06 cash 2/19/82
Note: Certificates were not required to be surrendered and are without value

JPM CO (PA)
Plan of reorganization under Chapter 11 Federal Bankruptcy Code effective 05/05/2003
No stockholders' equity

JPMORGAN CHASE & CO (DE)
Name changed 07/20/2004
Variable Rate Preferred Ser. E called for redemption at $1,000 on 03/01/2001
Variable Rate Preferred Ser. F called for redemption at $1,000 on 03/08/2001
Variable Rate Preferred Ser. B called for redemption at $1,000 on 03/29/2001
Variable Rate Preferred Ser. C called for redemption at $1,000 on 04/05/2001
Variable Rate Preferred Ser. D called for redemption at $1,000 on 04/12/2001
10.84% Preferred $1 par called for redemption at $25 on 06/30/2001
Name changed from J.P. Morgan Chase & Co. to JPMorgan Chase & Co. 07/20/2004
Adjustable Rate Preferred Ser. A called for redemption at $100 on 12/31/2004
Adjustable Rate Preferred Ser. L $1 par called for redemption at $100 on 12/31/2004
Adjustable Rate Preferred Ser. N $1 par called for redemption at $25 on 12/31/2004
Fixed/Adjustable Rate Preferred $1 par called for redemption at $50 on 05/06/2005
6.625% Depositary Preferred Ser. H called for redemption at $50 on 03/31/2006
5.49% Depositary Preferred Ser. G called for redemption at $50 on 08/20/2010
5.72% Depositary Preferred Ser. F called for redemption at $50 on 08/20/2010
6.15% Depositary Preferred Ser. E called for redemption at $50 on 08/20/2010
8.625% Depositary Preferred Ser. J called called for redemption at $25 on 09/01/2013
5.5% Depositary Preferred Ser. O called for redemption at $25 on 12/01/2017
(Additional Information in Active)

JPMORGAN CHASE CAP XIV (DE)
6.20% Capital Securities Ser. N called for redemption at $25 on 05/08/2013

JPMORGAN CHASE CAP XVI (DE)
6.35% Capital Securities Ser. P called for redemption at $25 on 05/08/2013

JPMORGAN CHASE CAP XIX (DE)
6.625% Capital Securities Ser. S called for redemption at $25 on 05/08/2013

JPMORGAN CHASE CAP XXIV (DE)
6.875% Capital Securities Ser. X called for redemption at $25 on 05/08/2013

JPMORGAN CHASE CAP XXIX (DE)
6.7% Capital Securities Ser. CC called for redemption at $25 on 04/02/2015

JPMORGAN CHASE CAP XXVI (DE)
Fixed-to-Floating Rate Capital Securities Ser. Z called for redemption at $25 on 07/12/2012

JPMORGAN CHASE CAP XXVIII (DE)
Fixed-to-Floating Rate Capital Securities Ser. BB called for redemption at $25 plus $0.45 accured dividends on 07/12/2012

JPS INDS INC (DE)
Name changed 06/24/1999
Plan of reorganization under Chapter 11 Federal Bankruptcy proceedings confirmed 04/02/1991
Each share Exchangeable Adjustable Rate Sr. Preferred 1¢ par exchanged for (1) share Sr. Preferred Ser. A 1¢ par
Plan of reorganization under Chapter 11 Federal Bankruptcy proceedings confirmed 11/17/1997
Each share Adjustable Rate Sr. Preferred Ser. A 1¢ par received an undetermined amount of Warrants expiring 10/10/2000
No Class A Common stockholders' equity
Name changed from JPS Textile Group Inc. to JPS Industries, Inc. 06/24/1999
Acquired by Handy & Harman Ltd. 07/02/2015
Each share Common 1¢ par exchanged for $11 cash

JPS PACKAGING CO (DE)
Merged into Pechiney Plastic Packaging, Inc. 12/1/2000
Each share Common $0.001 par exchanged for $7.86 cash

JPY HLDGS LTD (ON)
Reincorporated under the laws of Canada 11/09/2007

JRE INC (NY)
Common $0.001 par split (2) for (1) by issuance of (1) additional share payable 08/22/2003 to holders of record 08/21/2003 Ex date - 08/25/2003
Name changed to Cyper Media, Inc. 10/13/2003
(See Cyper Media, Inc.)

JRECK SUBS GROUP INC (CO)
Name changed to Ultimate Franchise Systems Inc. (CO) 5/16/2000
Ultimate Franchise Systems Inc. (CO) reincorporated in Nevada 4/25/2002

JRL ENTERPRISES INC (NV)
Name changed to Futurnet Internet Services Inc. 08/28/2000
Futurnet Internet Services Inc. recapitalized as September Group Inc. 04/27/2001 which recapitalized as ProSportsBook.Net Inc. 04/10/2002 which recapitalized as Ibises International Inc. 03/27/2003 which recapitalized as Biomag Corp. 03/28/2006 which name changed to Biomagnetics Diagnostics Corp. 12/18/2006

JRL RES CORP (FL)
Reincorporated under the laws of Nevada as First Ecom.com, Inc. 03/15/1999
First Ecom.com, Inc. name changed

to Brek Energy Corp. 01/31/2002 which merged into Gasco Energy, Inc. 12/14/2007
(See Gasco Energy, Inc.)

JRM HLDGS INC (DE)
Name changed to Harmony Group Ltd. 03/22/1991
(See Harmony Group Ltd.)

JRS FOODS INC (CO)
Reincorporated in Delaware as Southwest Food Products Inc. 02/04/1991

JRTL CAP CORP (BC)
Name changed to Tosca Mining Corp. 12/03/2009
Tosca Mining Corp. recapitalized as Tosca Resources Corp. 10/09/2014 which name changed to Hatch Interactive Technologies Corp. 09/08/2015 which name changed to Fandom Sports Media Corp. 08/03/2016

JRWA INC (NV)
Recapitalized as Secure Solutions Holdings Inc. 04/19/2005
Each share Common $0.001 par exchanged for (0.001) share Common $0.001 par
(See Secure Solutions Holdings Inc.)

JS GROUP CORP (JAPAN)
Name changed to Lixil Group Corp. 07/06/2012

JSB FINL INC (DE)
Merged into North Fork Bancorporation, Inc. 2/29/2000
Each share Common 1¢ par exchanged for (3) shares Common 1¢ par
North Fork Bancorporation, Inc. merged into Capital One Financial Corp. 12/1/2006

JSB INKOMBANK (RUSSIA)
Sponsored ADR's for Ordinary 10,000 Rubles par split (3) for (1) by issuance of (2) additional ADR's payable 9/8/97 to holders of record 9/5/97
ADR agreement terminated 12/1/2005
No ADR holders' equity

JSC CHERNOGORNEFT (RUSSIA)
ADR agreement terminated 10/7/2003
Each Sponsored ADR for Ordinary 100 Rubles par exchanged for $0.47 cash

JSC LENENERGO (RUSSIA)
Name changed to Lenenergo PCSC 11/23/2015

JSC MMC NORILSK NICKEL (RUSSIA)
Each Sponsored ADR for Ordinary received distribution of (1) OJSC Polyus Gold Sponsored ADR payable 07/12/2006 to holders of record 12/30/2005 Ex date - 01/10/2006 Sponsored ADR for Ordinary split (10) for (1) by issuance of (9) additional ADR's payable 02/19/2008 to holders of record 02/18/2008 Ex date - 02/20/2008
Basis changed from (1:1) to (1:0.1) 02/19/2008
Name changed to MMC Norilsk Nickel PJSC 09/18/2015

JSC RUSHYDRO (RUSSIA)
Name changed to PJSC RusHydro 09/11/2015

JSC SURGUTNEFTEGAZ (RUSSIA)
Sponsored ADR's for Ordinary split (4) for (1) by issuance of (3) additional ADR's payable 09/22/1997 to holders of record 09/19/1997
Name changed to Surgutneftegaz AO 09/09/1999
Surgutneftegaz AO name changed to Surgutneftegas PJSC 07/23/2018

JSDC INC (DE)
Common 1¢ par split (7) for (1) by issuance of (6) additional shares payable 4/19/2002 to holders of record 4/5/2002 Ex date - 4/22/2002
Recapitalized as Housing Solutions Hawaii Inc. 11/25/2002
Each share Common 1¢ par exchanged for (0.01) share Common 1¢ par
Housing Solutions Hawaii Inc. name changed to Home Solutions Health, Inc. 5/14/2004

JSFC SISTEMA (RUSSIA)
Basis changed from (1:0.02) to (1:20) on 11/15/2007
Name changed to Sistema PJSFC 09/09/2016

JSL INC (DE)
Reorganized under the laws of Nevada as Infodynamx Corp. 04/21/1994
Each share Common $0.0001 par exchanged for (0.005) share Common $0.0001 par
Infodynamx Corp. name changed to Worldwide Golf Resources, Inc. 09/30/1994
(See Worldwide Golf Resources, Inc.)

JSN INDS INC (DE)
Name changed to Johnston Acquisition Corp. 03/14/2006
(See Johnston Acquisition Corp.)

JSS RES INC (BC)
Name changed to WSI Interactive Corp. 07/26/1999
WSI Interactive Corp. recapitalized as iaNett International Systems Ltd. 05/07/2001 which name changed to Data Fortress Systems Group Ltd. 09/03/2002
(See Data Fortress Systems Group Ltd.)

JSW ISPAT STL LTD (INDIA)
GDR agreement terminated 01/23/2012
Each 144A GDR for Ordinary exchanged for $2.5203 cash
Each Reg. S GDR for Ordinary exchanged for $2.5203 cash

JTH HLDG INC (DE)
Name changed to Liberty Tax, Inc. 07/15/2014

JTS CORP (NV)
Charter forfeited for failure to maintain a registered agent 11/26/98

JTS INTL INC (CO)
Recapitalized as Fuji Construction Company International, Inc. 02/08/2008
Each share Common $0.001 par exchanged for (0.02) share Common $0.001 par
Fuji Construction Company International, Inc. name changed to Hokutou Holdings International, Inc. (CO) 11/06/2008 which reincorporated in Nevada 05/23/2014 which name changed to Platinum Pari-Mutuel Holdings, Inc. 12/09/2014 which name changed to Point to Point Methodics, Inc. 04/27/2017

J2 COMMUNICATIONS (CA)
Each share old Common no par exchanged for (0.33333333) share new Common no par 10/22/1998
Reincorporated under the laws of Delaware as National Lampoon Inc. and new Common no par changed to $0.0001 par 11/05/2002
(See National Lampoon Inc. (DE))

J2 GLOBAL COMMUNICATIONS INC (DE)
Each share old Common 1¢ par exchanged for (0.25) share new Common 1¢ par 02/08/2001
New Common 1¢ par split (2) for (1) by issuance of (1) additional share payable 08/29/2003 to holders of record 08/18/2003 Ex date - 09/02/2003
New Common 1¢ par split (2) for (1) by issuance of (1) additional share payable 05/25/2006 to holders of record 05/15/2006 Ex date - 05/26/2006
Name changed to j2 Global, Inc. 12/05/2011

JUANITA COAL & COKE CO. (CO)
Liquidation completed
Each share Capital Stock $1 par exchanged for initial distribution of $0.15 cash 3/11/76
Each share Capital Stock $1 par received second distribution of $0.76 cash 11/5/76
Each share Capital Stock $1 par received third distribution of $0.40 cash 4/4/77
Each share Capital Stock $1 par received fourth distribution of $0.22 cash 11/3/77
Each share Capital Stock $1 par received fifth distribution of $0.41 cash 4/13/78
Each share Capital Stock $1 par received sixth distribution of $0.68 cash 7/7/78
Each share Capital Stock $1 par received seventh distribution of $0.35 cash 2/21/79
Each share Capital Stock $1 par received eighth distribution of $0.12 cash 4/1/81
Each share Capital Stock $1 par received ninth and final distribution of $0.05305712 cash 12/28/81

JUBILANT CREEK MINES LTD. (ON)
Merged into Jubilant Eagle Holdings & Explorations Ltd. 04/01/1968
Each share Common $1 par exchanged for (0.33333333) share Capital Stock no par
(See Jubilant Eagle Holdings & Explorations Ltd.)

JUBILANT EAGLE HLDGS & EXPLS LTD (ON)
Charter cancelled for failure to pay taxes and file returns 02/26/1980

JUBILANT LIFE SCIENCES LTD (INDIA)
Name changed 10/01/2010
Name changed from Jubilant Organosys Ltd. to Jubilant Life Sciences Ltd. 10/01/2010
GDR agreement terminated 08/14/2017
No GDR's remain outstanding

JUBILEE EXPLS INC (BC)
Struck off register and declared dissolved for failure to file returns 06/06/1986

JUBILEE GOLD INC (ON)
Merged into Jubilee Gold Exploration Ltd. 01/25/2013
Each share Common no par exchanged for (0.212) share Common no par

JUBILEE INDS INC (DE)
Merged into Viewlex, Inc. 03/26/1971
Each share Common $0.075 par exchanged for $2 cash

JUBILEE INVT CORP (UT)
Recapitalized as July Telecommunications Corp. 8/13/84
Each share Common $0.001 par exchanged for (0.025) share Common $0.001 par

JUBILEE IRON CORP (QC)
Reincorporated under the laws of Canada as Dominion Jubilee Corp. Ltd. 07/28/1969
(See Dominion Jubilee Corp. Ltd.)

JUBILEE RES INC (AB)
Acquired by CanScot Resources Ltd. 05/06/2003
Each share Common no par exchanged for $0.11 cash

JUBILEE4 GOLD INC (DE)
Recapitalized as Helix TCS, Inc. 11/03/2015
Each share Common $0.001 par exchanged for (0.25) share Common $0.001 par

JUDEA DEV CORP (NY)
Charter cancelled and proclaimed dissolved for failure to pay taxes and file reports 12/15/1975

JUDEA LIFE INSURANCE CO.
Name changed to Eastern Life Insurance Co. of New York 00/00/1931
Eastern Life Insurance Co. of New York merged into USLIFE Corp. 09/30/1971 which merged into American General Corp. 06/17/1997 which merged into American International Group, Inc. 08/29/2001

JUDELLA URANIUM MINES LTD. (SK)
Charter revoked for failure to file reports and pay fees 10/24/1958

JUDGE GROUP INC (PA)
Name changed 02/14/2000
Issue Information - 3,650,000 shares COM offered at $7.50 per share on 02/14/1997
Name changed from Judge Group, Inc. to JUDGE.com Inc. 02/14/2000 which name changed back to Judge Group, Inc. 02/15/2001
Merged into Judge Group Acquisition Corp. 06/18/2003
Each share Common 1¢ par exchanged for $1.05 cash

JUDGE IMAGING SYS INC (DE)
Merged into Judge Group, Inc. 02/20/1997
Each share Common 1¢ par exchanged for (0.33) share Common 1¢ par
Judge Group, Inc. name changed to JUDGE.com Inc. 02/14/2000 which name changed back to Judge Group, Inc. 01/15/2001
(See Judge Group, Inc.)

JUDICATE INC (DE)
Each share old Common $0.0001 par exchanged for (0.06666666) share new Common $0.0001 par 12/22/1993
Name changed to Questron Technology Inc. 04/02/1996
(See Questron Technology Inc.)

JUDITH GOLD CORP. (MT)
Merged into Crown Resources Corp. 9/26/91
Each share Capital 10¢ par exchanged for (0.04) share Common 1¢ par
Crown Resources Corp. acquired by Kinross Gold Corp. 8/31/2006

JUDSON BROOKS CO (OH)
Acquired by Browne & Co. 7/22/85
Each share Common $1 par exchanged for $556.80 cash

JUDYS INC (DE)
Common 50¢ par split (2) for (1) by issuance of (1) additional share 5/27/86
Stock Dividend - 50% 5/11/79
Merged into Laws International Holdings Ltd. 10/2/89
Each share Common 50¢ par exchanged for $6.7132 cash

JUGGERNAUT ENERGY CORP. (UT)
Name changed to National Power Corp. (UT) 12/08/1981
National Power Corp. (UT) reincorporated in Michigan as World Wide Motion Pictures Corp. 03/19/1984 which name changed to Buckeye Ventures, Inc. (MI) 04/27/2006 which reincorporated in Nevada 10/29/2007 which name changed to Energy King, Inc. 02/26/2008 which name changed to Godfather Media, Inc. 10/18/2011

which name changed to Embark Holdings, Inc. 08/20/2012 which name changed to Muscle Warfare International, Inc. 06/28/2013 which name changed to Cannabusiness Group, Inc. 02/18/2014

JUGOS DEL VALLE S A B DE C V (MEXICO)
Name changed 04/30/2007
Name changed from Jugos Del Valle S.A. de C.V. to Jugos Del Valle S.A.B. de C.V. 04/30/2007
Acquired by Coca-Cola Co. 11/08/2007
Details not available

JUHL WIND INC (DE)
Each share old Common $0.0001 par exchanged for (1) share new Common $0.0001 par 01/13/2012
Name changed to Juhl Energy, Inc. 01/02/2013

JUICE INTL INC (UT)
Name changed to All Western Enterprises, Inc. (UT) 05/12/1987
All Western Enterprises, Inc. (UT) reorganized in Nevada as Fibertrek, Inc. 03/07/2007 which name changed to Capital Group, Inc. 08/01/2007

JUINA MNG CORP (NV)
Each share old Common 2-1/2¢ par exchanged for (1.01) shares new Common 2-1/2¢ par 09/18/1998
New Common 2-1/2¢ par changed to $0.001 par 01/29/2003
Each (350) shares old Common $0.001 par exchanged for (1) share new Common $0.001 par 09/26/2006
Name changed to AC Energy, Inc. (NV) 02/23/2007
(See AC Energy, Inc. (NV))

JULES ORTEIG, LTD. (MD)
See - Orteig (Jules), Ltd.

JULIA PRODS LTD (MT)
Involuntarily dissolved for failure to file annual reports 2/28/85

JULIA RESOURCES CO. (MT)
Name changed to Julia Products, Ltd. 4/29/77
(See Julia Products, Ltd.)

JULIA RES CORP (BC)
Merged into Spokane Resources Ltd. 10/31/1991
Each share Common no par exchanged for (0.25) share Common no par
Spokane Resources Ltd. recapitalized as SKN Resources Ltd. 07/26/2001 which name changed to Silvercorp Metals Inc. 05/02/2005

JULIAN & KONENGE CO (OH)
Merged into Amadac Industries, Inc. 01/30/1970
Each share Common no par exchanged for (6.5) shares Common 10¢ par
Note: Certificates surrendered after 01/30/1972 will receive cash
Unexchanged certificates were cancelled and became without value 01/30/1976
Amadac Industries, Inc. name changed to Miller Shoe Industries, Inc. 01/28/1984 which recapitalized as Apparel America Inc. 01/11/1989
(See Apparel America Inc.)

JULIAN OIL & ROYALTY CO. (AZ)
Common no par changed to $4 par in 1953
Liquidation completed 4/17/62

JULIAN PETROLEUM CORP. (DE)
Acquired by California Eastern Oil Co. 00/00/1927
No stockholders' equity

JULIE RESH LABS INC (NY)
Stock Dividend - 10% 04/06/1964
Charter cancelled and proclaimed dissolved for failure to pay taxes 01/28/2002

JULIUS BAER GLOBAL EQUITY FD INC (MD)
Under plan of reorganization each share Class A and Class B $0.001 par automatically became (1) share Artio Global Investment Funds Global Equity Fund Inc. Class A or Class I $0.001 par respectively 10/13/2008
(See Artio Global Investment Funds)

JULIUS BAER HLDG LTD (SWITZERLAND)
Name changed to GAM Holding Ltd. 10/14/2009

JULIUS BAER INVT FDS (MA)
Global Income Fund Class A and Class I $0.001 par reclassified as Total Return Bond Fund Class A or Class I $0.001 par respectively 06/25/2003
Name changed to Artio Global Investment Funds 10/13/2008
(See Artio Global Investment Funds)

JULIUS GARFINCKEL & CO., INC. (VA)
See - Garfinckel (Julius) & Co., Inc.

JULIUS KAYSER & CO. (NY)
See - Kayser (Julius) & Co.

JULIUS MEINL INTL AG (AUSTRIA)
ADR agreement terminated 12/9/2005
Each Sponsored ADR for Ordinary exchanged for (0.5) Ordinary Share
Note: Unexchanged ADR's will be sold and proceeds, if any, held for claim after 12/9/2006

JULY PROJ I CORP (FL)
Name changed to Pro Roads Systems, Inc. (FL) 03/29/2000
Pro Roads Systems, Inc. (FL) reincorporated in Nevada as International Pit Boss Gaming, Inc. 01/13/2003 which name changed to Logo Industries Corp. 03/23/2006 which reorganized as Malwin Ventures, Inc. 01/22/2009

JULY PROJ III CORP (FL)
Each share old Common $0.001 par exchanged for (0.5) share new Common $0.001 par 08/22/2000
Name changed to Globalgroup Investment Holdings, Inc. (FL) 10/26/2000
Globalgroup Investment Holdings, Inc. (FL) reincorporated in Nevada 04/20/2012 which name changed to Embarr Downs, Inc. 09/09/2013

JULY PROJ IV CORP (FL)
Name changed to Digital Concepts International Inc. 05/22/2000
(See Digital Concepts International Inc.)

JULY RESOURCES CORP (ON)
Merged into ONE Signature Financial Corp. 01/14/2004
Each share Common no par exchanged for (0.1) share Common no par

JULYN SPORTSWEAR INC (NY)
Adjudicated bankrupt 06/19/1978
Stockholders' equity unlikely

JUMA MNG & EXPL LTD (ON)
Charter cancelled and declared dissolved for failure to file returns and pay fees 03/16/1976

JUMA TECHNOLOGY INC (FL)
Name changed to Silverton Mining Corp. Ltd. 07/05/2006
Silverton Mining Corp. Ltd. recapitalized as Fleet Management Solutions Inc. 02/13/2009

JUMBO DEV CORP (AB)
Name changed to Jumbo Petroleum Corp. 06/23/2006

JUMBO ENTMT INC (ON)
Name changed to J.U.M. Capital Inc. 07/09/2004
J.U.M. Capital Inc. recapitalized as West 49 Inc. 12/01/2004
(See West 49 Inc.)

JUMBO LEDGE MINING CO. (SD)
Charter expired by time limitations 4/2/27

JUMBOSPORTS INC (FL)
Plan of reorganization under Chapter 11 Federal Bankruptcy Code effective 08/17/2000
No stockholders' equity

JUMP N JAX INC (UT)
Each (12) shares old Common $0.001 par exchanged for (1) share new Common $0.001 par 10/11/2005
Note: No holder will receive fewer than (100) shares
New Common $0.001 par split (4) for (1) by issuance of (3) additional shares payable 10/03/2009 to holders of record 10/02/2009
Ex date - 09/29/2009
Reincorporated under the laws of Nevada as CuraTech Industries, Inc. 10/04/2006
(See CuraTech Industries, Inc.)

JUMPIN' JAX CORP (NV)
SEC revoked common stock registration 03/05/2009

JUMPING JACK MERGER MINES INC. (NV)
Name changed to Gulf Petroleum Co. 10/8/58
Gulf Petroleum Co. name changed to Wesco General Corp. 2/19/69 which name changed to International Leisure Time & Development Corp. 12/20/71 which recapitalized as G & F T Mfg. Corp. 8/25/75 which name changed to G & FT Oil & Gas Corp. 4/30/80 which name changed to Yankee Energy Group 1/13/81
(See Yankee Energy Group)

JUMPING JACKS SHOES INC (NV)
Reincorporated under the laws of Arkansas as Osage Footwear, Inc. 2/19/91
(See Osage Footwear, Inc.)

JUMPING POUND PETROLEUMS LTD. (AB)
Assets sold to United Oils Ltd. 04/30/1962
Each share Common exchanged for (0.14285714) share Common
(See United Oils Ltd.)

JUMPKICKS INC (DE)
Name changed to Amarantus BioSciences, Inc. 06/08/2011
Amarantus BioSciences, Inc. name changed to Amarantus BioScience, Inc. 12/28/2012 which name changed to Amarantus BioScience Holdings, Inc. 04/18/2013

JUMPMUSIC COM INC (NV)
Recapitalized as PureSpectrum, Inc. (NV) 06/12/2006
Each share Common $0.001 par exchanged for (0.001) share Common $0.001 par
PureSpectrum, Inc. (NV) merged into PureSpectrum, Inc. (DE) 11/04/2009

JUMPTEC INDUSTRIELLE COMPUTERTECHNIK AG (GERMANY)
Merged into Kontron AG 08/14/2002
Details not available

JUMPTV INC (CANADA)
Name changed to NeuLion, Inc. (Canada) 07/16/2009
NeuLion, Inc. (Canada) reincorporated in Delaware 12/01/2010

JUNCTION BIT & TOOL CO (CO)
Name changed to JB & T Co. (CO) 1/2/69
(See JB & T Co.(CO))

JUNCTION EXPLS LTD (ON)
Charter cancelled for failure to file reports and pay taxes 6/1/84

JUNDT GROWTH FD INC (MN)
Completely liquidated
Each share Common 1¢ par received first and final distribution of $7.12 cash payable 11/30/2006 to holders of record 11/30/2006
Note: Certificates were not required to be surrendered and are without value

JUNE RES INC (BC)
Name changed to JNR Resources Inc. 07/25/1995
JNR Resources Inc. merged into Denison Mines Corp. 02/06/2013

JUNESS INDS INC (NY)
Adjudicated bankrupt 04/06/1971
Stockholders' equity unlikely

JUNEX INC (QC)
Recapitalized as Cuda Oil & Gas Inc. 08/22/2018
Each share Common no par exchanged for (0.1) share Common no par

JUNEX RES LTD (BC)
Recapitalized as C.T. Exploranda Ltd. 04/26/1976
Each share Common no par exchanged for (0.25) share Common no par
C.T. Exploranda Ltd. name changed to Izone International Ltd. 04/28/1986
(See Izone International Ltd.)

JUNGLE STR INC (UT)
Each share old Common $0.001 par exchanged for (0.01) share new Common $0.001 par 01/03/1996
Each share new Common $0.001 par exchanged for (0.25) share Common $0.001 par 03/24/1997
Name changed to Orca Technologies Inc. 12/31/1997
(See Orca Technologies Inc.)

JUNIOR FROOD MINES, LTD. (ON)
Recapitalized as Frood Deep Nickel Mines Ltd. 01/16/1967
Each share Capital Stock $1 par exchanged for (5) shares Capital Stock no par
Frood Deep Nickel Mines Ltd. merged into Hoffman Exploration & Minerals Ltd. 06/29/1981 which merged into Consolidated Thompson-Lundmark Gold Mines Ltd. 01/16/1986 which name changed to Consolidated Thompson Iron Mines Ltd. 08/24/2006
(See Consolidated Thompson Iron Mines Ltd.)

JUNIPER CONTENT CORP (DE)
Company terminated common stock registration and is no longer public as of 04/20/2009

JUNIPER GROUP INC (NY)
Name changed 02/12/1997
Name changed from Juniper Features Ltd. to Juniper Group, Inc. 02/12/1997
Reincorporated under the laws of Nevada 02/04/1998

JUNIPER MINES LTD (BC)
Recapitalized as Tally Resources Inc. 08/09/1978
Each share Capital Stock no par exchanged for (0.5) share Capital Stock no par
Talley Resources Inc. recapitalized as Sequoia Resources Ltd. 08/02/1984 which name changed to American Technology & Information, Inc. 08/07/1985
(See American Technology & Information, Inc.)

JUNIPER OIL & GAS CO. (DE)
Liquidation completed
Each share Common 50¢ par

exchanged for initial distribution of $2.75 cash 12/1/67
Each share Common 50¢ par received second and final distribution of $0.07 cash 11/1/68

JUNIPER OIL & MINING CO. (NV)
Merged into Juniper Oil & Gas Co. 5/31/63
Each share Common exchanged for (1) share Common
(See Juniper Oil & Gas Co.)

JUNIPER PARTNERS ACQUISITION CORP (DE)
Name changed to Juniper Content Corp. 1/22/2007
(See Juniper Content Corp.)

JUNIPER PETE CORP (DE)
Merged into Damson Oil Corp. (DE) 2/10/83
Each share Common 10¢ par exchanged for $10 cash
(See Damson Oil Corp. (DE))

JUNIPER PHARMACEUTICALS INC (DE)
Acquired by Catalent, Inc. 08/14/2018
Each share Common 1¢ par exchanged for $11.50 cash

JUNKIEDOG COM INC (NV)
Name changed to Grand Havana, Inc. 07/24/2017

JUNO ACQUISITIONS INC (NV)
Name changed to AremisSoft Corp. (NV) 01/08/1998
AremisSoft Corp. (NV) reorganized in Delaware 03/05/1999 which reorganized as SoftBrands, Inc. 08/02/2002
(See SoftBrands, Inc.)

JUNO CAP CORP (AB)
Recapitalized as North Peace Energy Corp. 02/21/2007
Each share Common no par exchanged for (0.2) share Common no par
North Peace Energy Corp. merged into Southern Pacific Resource Corp. 11/23/2010

JUNO LTG INC (DE)
Common 1¢ par split (2) for (1) by issuance of (1) additional share 5/20/85
Common 1¢ par split (2) for (1) by issuance of (1) additional share 6/8/87
Common 1¢ par split (2) for (1) by issuance of (1) additional share 6/8/92
Merged into Juno Lighting Inc. (New) 8/4/99
Each share old Common 1¢ par exchanged for either (0.5871237) share Common 1¢ par or $23.53219065 cash
Merged into Schneider Electric S.A. 8/24/2005
Each share new Common 1¢ par exchanged for $44 cash

JUNO ONLINE SVCS INC (DE)
Merged into United Online, Inc. 09/25/2001
Each share Common 1¢ par exchanged for (0.357) share Common $0.001 par
(See United Online, Inc.)

JUNO THERAPEUTICS INC (DE)
Acquired by Celgene Corp. 03/06/2018
Each share Common $0.0001 par exchanged for $87 cash

JUNUM INC (DE)
Each share old Common 10¢ par exchanged for (0.1) share new Common 10¢ par 10/04/2002
Recapitalized as WinWin Gaming Inc. 12/31/2002
Each share new Common 10¢ par exchanged for (0.05) share Common 10¢ par
(See WinWin Gaming Inc.)

JUPITER COMMUNICATIONS INC (DE)
Issue Information - 3,125,000 shares COM offered at $21 per share on 10/08/1999
Merged into Jupiter Media Metrix, Inc. 9/20/2000
Each share Common $0.001 par exchanged for (0.946) share Common $0.001 par
Jupiter Media Metrix, Inc. name changed to JMXI, Inc. 4/1/2003
(See JMXI, Inc.)

JUPITER CORP (DE)
Each share Common 15¢ par exchanged for (0.2) share Common 75¢ par 3/1/62
Each share $1.50 Conv. Preferred no par exchanged for (1) share Preferred no par 12/23/68
Merged into Jupiter Industries, Inc. 11/12/71
Each share Preferred no par exchanged for (1) share Preferred no par
Each share Common 75¢ par exchanged for (1) share Common 75¢ par
(See Jupiter Industries, Inc.)

JUPITER DEV LTD (AB)
Struck off register for failure to file annual returns 10/01/1992

JUPITER ENTERPRISES INC (NV)
Old Common $0.001 par split (3) for (1) by issuance of (2) additional shares payable 12/14/2001 to holders of record 12/10/2001 Ex date - 12/17/2001
Each share old Common $0.001 par exchanged for (0.05) share new Common $0.001 par 10/21/2002
SEC revoked common stock registration 06/19/2013

JUPITER EXPLS LTD (BC)
Name changed to Hypaz Technology Corp. 6/29/93
Hypaz Technology Corp. name changed to Calibre Technologies Corp. 9/12/94
(See Calibre Technologies Corp.)

JUPITER GLOBAL HLDGS CORP (NV)
Merged into Paivis, Corp. 05/19/2006
Each share Common $0.00001 par exchanged for (0.46232085) share Common $0.0002 par
(See Paivis, Corp.)

JUPITER GROUP LTD (NV)
Name changed to Scientific Imaging Corp. 4/12/89
Scientific Imaging Corp. name changed to Liberty Communications Inc. 6/18/90 which recapitalized as Big Boy Pacific Inc. 8/14/92

JUPITER INDS INC (TN)
Preferred no par called for redemption 10/15/82
Acquired by a group of investors 10/4/85
Each share Common 75¢ par exchanged for $37 cash

JUPITER INTL RES INC (AB)
Name changed 03/18/1997
Name changed from Jupiter Petroleum Inc. to Jupiter International Resources Inc. 03/18/1997
Name changed to Jupiter Power International Inc. 08/03/1999
Jupiter Power International Inc. name changed to Maxim Power Corp. 12/28/2000

JUPITER MEDIA METRIX INC (DE)
Name changed to JMXI, Inc. 4/1/2003
(See JMXI, Inc.)

JUPITER NATL INC (DE)
Name changed 8/25/92
Name changed from Jupiter Industries, Inc. to Jupiter National, Inc. 8/25/92

Common 40¢ par split (2) for (1) by issuance of (1) additional share 12/15/94
Merged into Johnston Industries Inc. 3/28/96
Each share Common 40¢ par exchanged for $33.97 cash

JUPITER OILS LTD. (AB)
Reorganized under the laws of Delaware as Jupiter Corp. 12/04/1961
Jupiter Corp. merged into Jupiter Industries, Inc. 11/12/1971
(See Jupiter Industries, Inc.)

JUPITER PWR INTL INC (AB)
Name changed to Maxim Power Corp. 12/28/2000

JUPITER RES EXPLS LTD (ON)
Name changed to Video Premiere International Corp. 07/18/1985
Video Premiere International Corp. recapitalized as S.T.I. Industries Inc. 06/12/1990
(See S.T.I. Industries Inc.)

JUPITER RES INC (NV)
Name changed to Rineon Group, Inc. 05/26/2009

JUPITER TELECOMMUNICATION CO LTD (JAPAN)
ADR's for Common split (20) for (3) by issuance of (5.66666666) additional ADR's payable 08/24/2012 to holders of record 08/21/2012 Ex date - 08/27/2012
ADR basis changed from (15:1) to (1:0.01) 08/27/2012
ADR agreement terminated 11/12/2013
Each ADR for Ordinary exchanged for approximately $12.4666759 cash

JUPITER-TEQUESTA NATIONAL BANK (JUPITER, FL)
Name changed to Lighthouse National Bank (Jupiter, FL) 07/01/1981
(See Lighthouse National Bank (Jupiter, FL))

JUPITERMEDIA CORP (DE)
Name changed to WebMediaBrands, Inc. 02/24/2009
WebMediaBrands, Inc. name changed to Mediabistro Inc. 06/13/2013 which name changed to Mecklermedia Corp. (New) 08/25/2014
(See Mecklermedia Corp. (New))

JUPITOR MINES LTD. (BC)
Name changed to Jupitor Resources Ltd. 10/29/1981
Jupitor Resources Ltd. recapitalized as Pacific Western Capital Corp. 03/07/1990 which recapitalized as Telcoplus Enterprises Inc. 10/02/1996 which name changed to Yamiri Gold & Energy Inc. 12/05/2005 which name changed to Cannon Point Resources Ltd. 04/27/2010 which merged into Northern Dynasty Minerals Ltd. 10/29/2015

JUPITOR RES LTD (BC)
Recapitalized as Pacific Western Capital Corp. 03/07/1990
Each share Common no par exchanged for (0.2) share Common no par
Pacific Western Capital Corp. recapitalized as Telcoplus Enterprises Inc. 10/02/1996 which name changed to Yamiri Gold & Energy Inc. 12/05/2005 which name changed to Cannon Point Resources Ltd. 04/27/2010 which merged into Northern Dynasty Minerals Ltd. 10/29/2015

JURAK CORP WORLD WIDE INC (MN)
Old Common no par split (2) for (1) by issuance of (1) additional share payable 10/22/2003 to holders of record 10/14/2003 Ex date - 10/23/2003
Each share old Common no par exchanged for (1/6) share new Common no par 05/23/2006
Name changed to PhytoLabs, Inc. 03/13/2007
PhytoLabs, Inc. recapitalized as LifeQuest World Corp. 08/20/2007

JURASSIC MINERALS, INC. (OK)
Charter cancelled for non-payment of taxes 4/8/58

JURE HLDGS INC (FL)
Name changed to OpenLimit, Inc. 11/14/2003
OpenLimit, Inc. recapitalized as SunVesta, Inc. 08/27/2007

JURGENSENS (CA)
Merged into Yucaipa Capital Corp. 12/30/86
Each share 6% Vtg. Ser. Preferred $25 par exchanged for $25 cash
Each share 6% Conv. Preferred $25 par exchanged for $25 cash
Each share Common $1 par exchanged for $7.73 cash

JURIS TRAVEL (NV)
Name changed to Bed & Biscuit Inns of America Inc. 03/17/2003
Bed & Biscuit Inns of America Inc. name changed to Dogs International 03/24/2003 which name changed to AFV Solutions, Inc. 02/11/2005 which recapitalized as Pure Transit Technologies, Inc. 06/18/2008

JURITEL SYS INC (ON)
Name changed to Huntington Rhodes Inc. 09/23/1993
(See Huntington Rhodes Inc.)

JUSCO LTD (JAPAN)
Name changed to Aeon Co., Ltd. 8/21/2001

JUST ENERGY EXCHANGE CORP (CANADA)
Under plan of reorganization each Exchangeable Share Ser. 1 no par automatically became (1) share Just Energy Group Inc. Common no par 01/04/2011

JUST ENERGY INCOME FD (ON)
Under plan of reorganization each Unit no par automatically became (1) share Just Energy Group Inc. (Canada) Common no par 01/04/2011

JUST FOR FEET INC (AL)
Common $0.0001 par split (3) for (2) by issuance of (0.5) additional share 11/30/1994
Common $0.0001 par split (3) for (2) by issuance of (0.5) additional share 07/10/1995
Common $0.0001 par split (3) for (2) by issuance of (0.5) additional share payable 10/15/1996 to holders of record 09/27/1996
Chapter 11 bankruptcy proceedings converted to Chapter 7 on 03/21/2000
Stockholders' equity unlikely

JUST LIKE HOME INC (FL)
SEC revoked common stock registration 03/05/2009

JUST-RITE MEAT SPECIALTY CORP. (NY)
Charter cancelled and proclaimed dissolved for failure to pay taxes 12/15/69

JUST TOYS INC (DE)
Each share old Common 1¢ par exchanged for (0.5) share new Common 1¢ par 09/04/1998
Recapitalized as Pachinko Inc. 03/24/2006
Each share new Common 1¢ par exchanged for (0.001) share Common 1¢ par
(See Pachinko Inc.)

JUSTEN RES LTD (BC)
Merged into New Penn Energy Corp. (BC) (New) 11/22/1982
Each share Common no par exchanged for (0.19723865) share Common no par
New Penn Energy Corp. (BC) reincorporated in Canada 01/29/1982 which merged into International Interlake Industries Inc. 12/31/1986
(See International Interlake Industries Inc.)

JUSTHEIM PETE CO (NV)
Name changed to C.E.C. Industries Corp. 12/31/1986
C.E.C. Industries Corp. name changed to Advantage Capital Development Corp. 09/01/2004
(See Advantage Capital Development Corp.)

JUSTICE ELECTR MONITORING SYS INC (ON)
Recapitalized as Jemtec Inc. 04/28/1994
Each share Common no par exchanged for (0.1) share Common no par

JUSTICE INVT CORP (FL)
Name changed to American Community Development Group, Inc. 9/30/86
(See American Community Development Corp.)

JUSTICE MNG CORP (BC)
Name changed to Presidential Forest Products Corp. 06/09/1988
(See Presidential Forest Products Corp.)

JUSTICE MTG INVS (MA)
Name changed to Metroplex Realty Trust 12/15/77
Metroplex Realty Trust merged into Vista Mortgage & Realty Inc. 10/31/80
(See Vista Mortgage Realty Inc.)

JUSTIN INDS INC (TX)
Merged into Berkshire Hathaway Inc. 8/1/2000
Each share Common $2.50 par exchanged for $22 cash

JUSTINIAN EXPLORATIONS LTD (AB)
Recapitalized as Connacher Oil & Gas Ltd. (AB) 03/23/2001
Each share Common no par exchanged for (0.1) share Common no par
Connacher Oil & Gas Ltd. (AB) reincorporated in Canada 03/30/2015

JUSTISS MEARS OIL INC (LA)
Name changed to Justiss Oil Co., Inc. 12/1/80

JUSTRITE CORP.
Name changed to Justrite Manufacturing Co. and Common no par changed to $1 par in 1936
Justrite Manufacturing Co. name changed to Packer (C.S.) Associates, Inc. 6/20/65 which completed liquidation 6/29/67
(See listing for Packer (C.S.) Associates Inc.)

JUSTRITE MANUFACTURING CO. (IL)
Name changed to Packer (C.S.) Associates, Inc. 6/29/65
(See Packer (C.S.) Associates, Inc.)

JUSTWEBIT COM INC (NV)
Each share old Common $0.001 par exchanged for (2) shares new Common $0.001 par 5/26/2000
Name changed to Synthetic Turf Corp. of America 11/12/2002
Synthetic Turf Corp. of America recapitalized as City Capital Corp. 12/15/2004

JUTLAND ENTERPRISES INC NEW (DE)
Name changed to Professional Wrestling Alliance Corp. 11/30/99
Professional Wrestling Alliance Corp. recapitalized as TRSG Corp. 11/16/2000 which recapitalized as Worldwide Holdings Corp. 5/21/2003

JUTLAND ENTERPRISES INC OLD (DE)
Name changed to Treats Enterprises Inc. 9/28/89
Treats Enterprises Inc. recapitalized as Jutland Entperises, Inc. (New) 11/23/92
(See Jutland Enterprises, Inc. (New))

JUVENILE SHOE CORP. OF AMERICA (MO)
Common $1 par changed to $50 par 1/17/52
Each share Common $50 par exchanged for (25) shares Common $2 par 1/20/81
Company went out of business in 1990
Details not available

JVWEB INC (DE)
Each share old Common no par exchanged for (1/7) share new Common no par 02/05/2001
Name changed to IQ Biometrix, Inc. 11/12/2002
IQ Biometrix, Inc. name changed to Wherify Wireless, Inc. 08/05/2005
(See Wherify Wireless, Inc.)

JWC ACQUISITION CORP (DE)
Issue Information - 12,500,000 UNITS consisting of (1) share COM and (1) WT offered at $10 per Unit on 11/17/2010
Units separated 08/22/2012
Name changed to Tile Shop Holdings, Inc. 08/22/2012

JWGENESIS FINL CORP (FL)
Common $0.001 par split (3) for (2) by issuance of (0.5) additional share payable 03/24/2000 to holders of record 03/03/2000
Merged into First Union Corp. 01/01/2001
Each share Common $0.001 par exchanged for $12 cash

JWP INC (DE)
Reincorporated 08/04/1987
Common 10¢ par split (2) for (1) by issuance of (1) additional share 05/23/1986
State of incorporation changed from (NY) to (DE) 08/04/1987
Common 10¢ par split (3) for (2) by issuance of (0.5) additional share 06/09/1989
Common 10¢ par split (3) for (2) by issuance of (0.5) additional share 07/13/1990
Plan of reorganization under Chapter 11 Federal Bankruptcy Code effective 12/15/1994
Each share 4.50% Preferred Ser. A $10 par exchanged for (0.00478468) EMCOR Group, Inc. Common Stock Purchase Warrant Ser. Z expiring 12/15/1996
Note: Holdings of (208) shares or fewer did not participate and are without value
Each share $1.50 Preferred Ser. B $10 par exchanged for (0.00478468) EMCOR Group, Inc. Common Stock Purchase Warrant Ser. Z expiring 12/15/1996
Note: Holdings of (208) shares or fewer did not participate and are without value
Each share Common 10¢ par exchanged for (0.00478468) EMCOR Group, Inc. Common Stock Purchase Warrant Ser. Z expiring 12/15/1996
Note: Holdings of (208) shares or fewer did not participate and are without value

JWT GROUP INC (DE)
Common 10¢ par split (3) for (2) by issuance of (0.5) additional share 11/30/84
Stock Distribution - (0.5) share Common 10¢ par for each share held 6/13/80
Merged into WPP Group plc 7/20/87
Each share Common 10¢ par exchanged for $55.50 cash

JX HLDGS INC (JAPAN)
Name changed to JXTG Holdings, Inc. 04/03/2017

JYRA RESH INC (DE)
Assets sold for the benefit of creditors 8/2/2002
No stockholders' equity

JYW CAP CORP (BC)
Name changed to China Coal Corp. 06/11/2010

K

K. & S. TIRE & RUBBER GOODS, LTD.
Acquired by Seiberling Rubber Co. of Canada, Ltd., a wholly owned subsidiary of Seiberling Rubber Co. 00/00/1933
Details not available

K & F INDS HLDGS INC (DE)
Issue Information - 18,000,000 shares COM offered at $17.50 per share on 08/08/2005
Merged into Meggitt PLC 06/22/2007
Each share Common 1¢ par exchanged for $27 cash

K & G MENS CTR INC (GA)
Common 1¢ par split (3) for (2) by issuance of (0.5) additional share payable 04/25/1997 to holders of record 04/07/1997
Merged into Men's Wearhouse, Inc. 06/02/1999
Each share Common 1¢ par exchanged for (0.43) share Common 1¢ par
Men's Wearhouse, Inc. name changed to Tailored Brands, Inc. 02/01/2016

K & M ELECTRS CO (MD)
Adjudicated bankrupt 10/01/1971
Stockholders' equity unlikely

K & M ELECTRS INC (MN)
Name changed to Todd Communications, Inc. 6/15/70
(See Todd Communications, Inc.)

K-5 DEVELOPMENT CO. (UT)
Name changed to K-5 Energy Corp. 07/02/1980

K.A. LIQUIDATING CO. (PA)
Liquidation completed
Each share Common $1 par received initial distribution of (1) share Brown & Grist, Inc. (Va.) Common $1 par and $3.80 cash 2/6/67
Each share Common $1 par exchanged for second and final distribution of $0.17 cash 9/19/72
Brown & Grist, Inc. (Va.) reincorporated under the laws of Delaware 9/29/69 which merged into Consulting Technology, Inc. 2/21/73

K A ELECTRS CORP (NY)
Proclaimed dissolved for failure to file reports and pay taxes 12/15/75

K.B. MINING CO. LTD. (ON)
Liquidation completed
Each share Capital Stock $1 par exchanged for initial distribution of $0.08 cash 12/15/1971
Each share Capital Stock $1 par received second and final distribution of $0.087 cash 11/28/1972

K B ELECTRS INC (NY)
Acquired by K.B. Electronics Acquisition Corp. 1/21/92
Each share Common 1¢ par exchanged for $4.87 cash

K B INDS INC (TX)
Reincorporated under the laws of Nevada as Brake-O Industries, Inc. and Common no par changed to 10¢ par 7/12/76
(See Brake-O Industries, Inc.)

K B MARKETING SYS INC (OH)
Common $2.25 par changed to 10¢ par 5/15/72
Stock Dividend - 10% 5/27/72
Name changed to Kobacker Stores, Inc. 5/5/76
(See Kobacker Stores, Inc.)

K-BRITE SYS INC (ID)
Recapitalized as Service Associates, Inc. 12/1/72
Each share Capital Stock 1¢ par exchanged for (2) shares Capital Stock 1¢ par
(See Service Associates, Inc.)

K-BRO LINEN INCOME FD (AB)
Under plan of reorganization each Unit no par automatically became (1) share K-Bro Linen Inc. Common no par 01/06/2011

K-C COLA CORP. (NJ)
Charter revoked for non-payment of taxes 1/25/66

K C INDS CORP (NY)
In process of liquidation
Each share Common 1¢ par exchanged for initial distribution of (2) shares American Medical Alert Corp. Common 1¢ par and (0.001316) share Unimed Inc. Common 25¢ par 9/17/91
Note: Amount or number of additional distributions, if any, are not available
(See each company's listing)

K CAP INC (DE)
Name changed to Surety Capital Corp. (DE) 04/01/1987
Surety Capital Corp. (DE) reincorporated in Texas 06/12/2014
(See Surety Capital Corp.)

K CARE NUTRITIONAL PRODS INC (NV)
Reorganized as China Wind Energy Inc. 12/17/2007
Each share Common $0.0001 par exchanged for (5) shares Common $0.0001 par
(See China Wind Energy Inc.)

K D I CORP (DE)
Each share Common 75¢ par exchanged for (1/3) share Common $2.25 par 11/13/56
Each share Common $2.25 par exchanged for (2) shares Common 85¢ par in 1958
Common 85¢ par changed to 35¢ par 5/8/61
Merged into KD Holdings Corp. 12/22/88
Each share Common 35¢ par exchanged for $19 cash

K.E. ASSETS CORP. (NY)
Dissolved 08/11/1964
Details not available

K-FED BANCORP (USA)
Under plan of reorganization each share Common 1¢ par automatically became (0.7194) share Kaiser Federal Financial Group, Inc. (MD) Common 1¢ par 11/19/2010
Kaiser Federal Financial Group, Inc. (MD) name changed to Simplicity Bancorp Inc. 11/13/2012 which merged into HomeStreet, Inc. 03/02/2015

K-H CORP (DE)
Merged into Varity Corp. (Canada) 12/1/89
Each share $3.68 Exchangeable

Preferred Ser. A 1¢ par exchanged for $2.85 principal amount of Kelsey-Hayes Co. 13.25% Guaranteed Sr. Subordinated Notes due 11/15/94 and (2) shares Varity Corp. Common no par
Each share Class B Common 1¢ par exchanged for (0.7) share Common no par
Varity Corp. (Canada) reorganized in Delaware 8/1/91 which merged into LucasVarity PLC 9/6/96
(See LucasVarity PLC)

K H F TECHNOLOGIES (NV)
Common $0.001 par changed to $0.0001 par 05/05/2000
Name changed to Lighten Up Enterprises International Inc. (NV) 06/03/2002
Lighten Up Enterprises International Inc. (NV) reincorporated in Delaware as Bionovo, Inc. 06/29/2005
(See Bionovo, Inc.)

K.H.T. CORP. (ME)
Adjudicated bankrupt 6/20/75

K KITZ INC (DE)
Name changed to Bacterin International Holdings, Inc. 07/01/2010
Bacterin International Holdings, Inc. name changed to Xtant Medical Holdings, Inc. 08/05/2015

K MART CORP (MI)
Each Depositary Preferred Ser. A exchanged for (2) shares Common $1 par 9/15/94
Common $1 par split (3) for (2) by issuance of (0.5) additional share 6/5/87
Common $1 par split (2) for (1) by issuance of (1) additional share 6/5/92
Plan of reorganization under Chapter 11 Federal Bankruptcy Code effective 5/6/2003
Holders of Common Stock may receive 2.5% of Kmart Creditor Trust non-transferable interests which will represent proceeds received by the Trust from various claims
Note: Unexchanged certificates were cancelled and became without value 5/6/2005

K MED CTRS INC (TX)
Name changed to Cabre Corp. 05/18/1992
Cabre Corp. name changed to Antenna Products, Inc. 01/30/1998 which name changed to Phazar Corp. 03/12/2001
(See Phazar Corp.)

K N ENERGY INC (KS)
Common $5 par split (3) for (2) by issuance of (0.5) additional share 10/4/93
$8.50 Class A Preferred no par called for redemption 12/31/94
$8.30 Class B Preferred no par called for redemption in 1996
Common $5 par split (3) for (2) by issuance of (0.5) additional share payable 12/31/98 to holders of record 12/15/98 Ex date - 1/4/99
$5 Preferred called for redemption at $105 on 5/14/99
Under plan of merger name changed to Kinder Morgan, Inc. (KS) 10/7/99
(See Kinder Morgan, Inc. (KS))

K-9 CONCEPTS INC (NV)
Common $0.001 par split (3) for (1) by issuance of (2) additional shares payable 01/03/2008 to holders of record 01/03/2008
Name changed to Aussie Soles Group Inc. 03/24/2008
Aussie Soles Group Inc. recapitalized as Global Housing Group 07/29/2010 which name changed to Global Enterprises Group, Inc. 03/12/2014 which name changed to Predictive Technology Group, Inc. 07/16/2015

K-O-T OIL CORP. (OK)
Acquired by Texo Oil Corp. share for share 8/11/55
Texo Oil Corp. acquired by Discovery Oil, Ltd. 12/18/81

K P A COMPUTER TECHNIQUES INC (DE)
Name changed to KPA Nuclear, Inc. 6/17/69

K P A NUCLEAR INC (DE)
No longer in existence having become inoperative and void for non-payment of taxes 04/15/1972

K R M EXPL INC (CO)
Merged into K.R.M. Petroleum Corp. 08/31/1973
Each share Common 1¢ par exchanged for (1) share Common 1¢ par
K.R.M. Petroleum Corp. name changed to PrimeEnergy Corp. 05/17/1990

K R M PETE CORP (DE)
Each share Common 1¢ par exchanged for (0.1) share Common 10¢ par 06/14/1974
Name changed to PrimeEnergy Corp. 05/17/1990

K RANDOLPH INTL INC (UT)
Name changed to Premier Brands Inc. (UT) 4/11/95
Premier Brands Inc. (UT) reincorporated under laws of Delaware as CathayOne, Inc. 8/28/2000
(See CathayOne, Inc.)

K RES INC (DE)
Name changed to Alliance Health, Inc. 07/18/1989

K S I CORP (DE)
Merged into Multimedia Education, Inc. 10/24/69
Each share Common 1¢ par exchanged for (1) share Common 1¢ par
(See Multimedia Education, Inc.)

K S M PRODUCTS, INC. (NJ)
Acquired by Omark Industries, Inc. 07/01/1966
Each share Common $1 par exchanged for (1.17) shares Common no par
(See Omark Industries, Inc.)

K S MEDIA (NV)
SEC revoked common stock registration 10/01/2013

K-SEA TRANSN PARTNERS L P (DE)
Issue Information - 3,625,000 shares COM UNITS offered at $23.50 per share on 01/01/2004
Merged into Kirby Corp. 07/01/2011
Each Common Unit exchanged for $8.15 cash

K-SWISS INC (DE)
Class A Common 1¢ par split (2) for (1) by issuance of (1) additional share payable 03/26/1999 to holders of record 03/15/1999
Class A Common 1¢ par split (2) for (1) by issuance of (1) additional share payable 06/21/2002 to holders of record 06/07/2002 Ex date - 06/24/2002
Class A Common 1¢ par split (2) for (1) by issuance of (1) additional share payable 12/26/2003 to holders of record 12/22/2003 Ex date - 12/29/2003
Acquired by E-Land World Ltd. 04/30/2013
Each share Class A Common 1¢ par exchanged for $4.75 cash

K T OIL CORP (KS)
In process of liquidation 00/00/1983
Details not available

K-TECH INC (NV)
Recapitalized as Ice Age Entertainment, Inc. 05/12/1995
Each share Common $0.001 par exchanged for (0.16666666) share Common $0.001 par
Ice Age Entertainment, Inc. recapitalized as Janus International, Inc. 06/19/1998 which recapitalized as Diamond Worldwide, Inc. 08/19/2002 which name changed to FutureVest, Inc. 12/07/2004 which name changed to Barotex Technology Corp. 01/09/2008
(See Barotex Technology Corp.)

K TEL INTL INC (MN)
Stock Dividend - 33.33333333% 12/22/1972
Reorganized under Chapter 11 Federal Bankruptcy Code 01/20/1986
Each share Common 10¢ par exchanged for (0.0509) share old Common 1¢ par
Old Common 1¢ par split (2) for (1) by issuance of (1) additional share payable 05/08/1998 to holders of record 05/01/1998
Each share old Common 1¢ par exchanged for (1) share new Common 1¢ par to reflect a (1) for (5,000) reverse split followed by a (5,000) for (1) forward split 07/19/2007
Note: Holders of (4,999) or fewer shares received $0.095 cash per share
Acquired by K-5 Leisure Products, Inc. 06/30/2010
Each share new Common 1¢ par exchanged for $0.10 cash

K-III COMMUNICATIONS CORP (DE)
Each share $10 Exchangeable Preferred Ser. C exchanged for (1) share $10 Exchangeable Preferred Ser. D 08/21/1996
11.50% Sr. Exchangeable Preferred 1¢ par called for redemption at $26.45 on 11/03/1997
Name changed to Primedia Inc. 11/18/1997
(See Primedia Inc.)

K TRON INTL INC (NJ)
Acquired by Hillenbrand, Inc. 04/01/2010
Each share Common 1¢ par exchanged for $150 cash

K-TRONIK INTL CORP (NV)
Name changed to Racino Royale, Inc. 07/06/2006
Racino Royale, Inc. name changed to InterAmerican Gaming, Inc. 10/20/2008
(See InterAmerican Gaming, Inc.)

K V PHARMACEUTICAL CO (DE)
Common $1 par changed to 50¢ par and (1) additional share issued 06/16/1981
Common 50¢ par changed to 25¢ par and (1) additional share issued 03/25/1983
Common 25¢ par changed to 17¢ par and (0.5) additional share issued 07/28/1986
Common 17¢ par reclassified as Class B Common 1¢ par 06/09/1987
Each share Conv. Class B Common 1¢ par received distribution of (1) share Class A 1¢ par 12/27/1991
Conv. Class A Common 1¢ par split (3) for (2) by issuance of (0.5) additional share payable 04/17/1998 to holders of record 04/03/1998 Ex date - 04/20/1998
Conv. Class B Common 1¢ par split (3) for (2) by issuance of (0.5) additional share payable 04/17/1998 to holders of record 04/03/1998 Ex date - 04/20/1998
Class A Common 1¢ par split (3) for (2) by issuance of (0.5) additional share payable 09/07/2000 to holders of record 08/28/2000 Ex date - 09/08/2000
Conv. Class B Common 1¢ par split (3) for (2) by issuance of (0.5) additional share payable 09/07/2000 to holders of record 08/28/2000 Ex date - 09/08/2000
Class A Common 1¢ par split (3) for (2) by issuance of (0.5) additional share payable 09/29/2003 to holders of record 09/18/2003 Ex date - 09/30/2003
Conv. Class B Common 1¢ par split (3) for (2) by issuance of (0.5) additional share payable 09/29/2003 to holders of record 09/18/2003 Ex date - 09/30/2003
Plan of reorganization under Chapter 11 Federal Bankruptcy proceedings effective 09/16/2013
No stockholders' equity

K W BATTERY CO (IL)
Common no par changed to $5 par in 1952
Common $5 par changed to $1 par in 1957
Stock Dividends - 100% 9/25/52; 100% 4/25/66
Acquired by Westinghouse Electric Corp. 5/6/68
Each share Common $1 par exchanged for (0.2698) share Common $6.25 par
Westinghouse Electric Corp. name changed to CBS Corp. 12/1/97 which merged into Viacom Inc. (Old) 5/4/2000
(See Viacom Inc. (Old))

K W RES LTD (BC)
Recapitalized as Tako Resources Ltd. 02/14/1992
Each share Common 50¢ par exchanged for (0.25) share Common no par
Tako Resources Ltd. recapitalized as Consolidated Tako Resources Ltd. 03/27/1998 which recapitalized as International Tako Industries Ltd. (BC) 01/18/2000 which reincorporated in Alberta 11/26/2002 which name changed to Ironhorse Oil & Gas Inc. 05/14/2004 which recapitalized as Pond Technologies Holdings Inc. 02/06/2018

K WAH CONSTR MATLS LTD (HONG KONG)
Name changed to Galaxy Entertainment Group Ltd. 11/09/2005
(See Galaxy Entertainment Group Ltd.)

K WAH INTL HLDGS LTD (HONG KONG)
Each Sponsored ADR for Ordinary received distribution of $0.52575 cash payable 07/26/2006 to holders of record 10/13/2005
ADR agreement terminated 04/30/2015
Each Sponsored ADR for Ordinary exchanged for $4.505271 cash

K-ZONE FAULT MINES LTD. (ON)
Charter cancelled 00/00/1953

KT RES 1981 LTD (ON)
Recapitalized 9/28/81
K.T. Resources Ltd. recapitalized as K.T. Resources (1981) Ltd. 9/28/81
Each (3) shares Common $1 par exchanged for (1) share Common $1 par
Charter cancelled 10/29/94

KA-MI-TIN CONCENTRATING CORP. (DE)
Dissolved 1/29/66
No stockholders' equity

KA U SUGAR INC (HI)
Business closed 3/27/96
Details not available

KAABA RES INC (BC)
Recapitalized as International Kaaba Gold Corp. 04/17/1990
Each share Common no par exchanged for (0.16666666) share Common no par
(See International Kaaba Gold Corp.)

KAB DISTR INC (ON)
In process of liquidation
Each share Common no par received initial distribution of $0.65 cash payable 09/22/2009 to holders of record 09/17/2009
Note: Details on subsequent distributions, if any, are not available

KABIN KOACH CO.
Dissolved in 1939

KABOOSE INC (CANADA)
Reincorporated under the laws of Ontario as KAB Distribution Inc. 06/09/2009
(See KAB Distribution Inc.)

KABOUR MINES LTD. (ON)
Charter cancelled for failure to file reports and pay fees 08/06/1957

KACEE EXPL INC (AB)
Name changed to Questar Exploration Inc. 04/09/1996
(See Questar Exploration Inc.)

KACHINA GOLD CORP (NV)
Recapitalized as Osage Energy Corp. (NV) 05/15/2006
Each (750) shares Common $0.0001 par exchanged for (1) share Common $0.0001 par
Osage Energy Corp. (NV) reincorporated in Delaware as Osage Exploration & Development, Inc. 07/17/2007

KACHINA URANIUM CORP. (NV)
Name changed to XI Productions, Inc. 09/13/1968
XI Productions, Inc. acquired by Universal Coverage Corp. 04/02/1969 which recapitalized as Unico American Corp. 08/01/1973

KACHING KACHING INC (DE)
Name changed to KS International Holdings Corp. 12/02/2013

KADREY ENERGY CORP (BC)
Recapitalized as Baroque Resources Ltd. 08/15/1984
Each share Common no par exchanged for (0.33333333) share Common no par
Baroque Resources Ltd. recapitalized as Greenfields Industries Inc. 02/09/1990 which recapitalized as Oracle Minerals Inc. 12/06/1993 which recapitalized as Prophet Minerals Corp. 05/02/1997 which name changed to Meridex Network Corp. 12/21/1999 which recapitalized as Meridex Software Corp. 02/13/2003 which name changed to Cannabis Technologies Inc. 05/21/2014 which name changed to InMed Pharmaceuticals Inc. 10/21/2014

KADYWOOD CAP CORP (BC)
Name changed to Gold Wheaton Gold Corp. 07/16/2008
(See Gold Wheaton Gold Corp.)

KAFUS INDS LTD (BC)
Name changed 09/22/1997
Name changed 06/23/1999
Name changed from Kafus Capital Corp. to Kafus Environmental Industries Ltd. 09/22/1997
Name changed from Kafus Environmental Industries Ltd. to Kafus Industries Ltd. 06/23/1999
Filed an assignment under the Bankruptcy and Insolvency Act 08/22/2000
No stockholders' equity

KAGOLD GARAGE CORP. (NY)
Dissolved by proclamation 9/30/81

KAHALA CORP (DE)
Reincorporated 12/31/2012
Each share old Common $0.001 par exchanged for (0.01) share new Common $0.001 par 09/14/2005
State of incorporation changed from (FL) to (DE) 12/31/2012
Acquired by MTY Food Group Inc. 07/26/2016
Each share new Common $0.001 par exchanged for $159.82186387 cash

KAHIKI FOODS INC (OH)
Common no par split (3) for (1) by issuance of (2) additional shares payable 12/12/2000 to holders of record 12/01/2000 Ex date - 12/13/2000
Common no par split (2) for (1) by issuance of (1) additional share payable 05/12/2003 to holders of record 05/01/2003 Ex date - 05/13/2003
Merged into GTG Foods, Inc. 06/25/2007
Each share Common no par exchanged for $2.163 cash

KAHLER CORP (DE)
Reincorporated 01/27/1987
Each share Common $100 par exchanged for (8) shares Common $25 par to effect a (4) for (1) split and 100% stock dividend 00/00/1941
Common $25 par changed to $5 par 04/08/1968
Common $5 par split (2) for (1) by issuance of (1) additional share 09/12/1968
Common $5 par changed to $2.50 par 04/14/1969
Common $2.50 par split (3) for (1) by issuance of (2) additional shares 06/02/1986
Stock Dividend - 20% 01/31/1968
State of incorporation changed from (MN) to (DE) and Common $2.50 par changed to 10¢ par 01/27/1987
Common 10¢ par split (2) for (1) by issuance of (1) additional share 06/01/1993
Reincorporated under the laws of Minnesota as Kahler Realty Corp. 10/11/1994
(See Kahler Realty Corp.)

KAHLER RLTY CORP (MN)
Merged into Tiger Real Estate Fund, L.P. 08/13/1996
Each share Common 10¢ par exchanged for $17 cash

KAHN INDS INC (DE)
Majority shares acquired through purchase offer 08/29/1980
Public interest eliminated

KAHN'S (E.) SONS CO. (OH)
Each share Class A Part. Preferred $40 par exchanged for (2.5) shares Common no par and $6.78 cash in 1936
Stock Dividends - 25% 5/1/56; 25% 2/1/57
Completely liquidated 12/13/68
Each share Common no par exchanged for first and final distribution of $48 cash

KAHR BEARING CORP (DE)
Completely liquidated 12/31/1973
No stockholders' equity

KAHUKU PLANTATION CO (HI)
Common Capital Stock $20 par changed to $10 par 00/00/1937
Merged into Alexander & Baldwin, Inc. (Old) 06/30/1972
Each share Common Capital Stock $10 par exchanged for (0.5) share Common no par
Alexander & Baldwin, Inc. (Old) name changed to Alexander & Baldwin Holdings, Inc. 06/06/2012 which name changed to Matson, Inc. 06/29/2012

KAHUNA NETWORK SEC INC (NV)
Name changed to American Security Resources Corp. 8/24/2004

KAHZAM INC (DE)
Common $0.0001 par split (3) for (1) by issuance of (2) additional shares payable 07/07/2009 to holders of record 06/12/2009 Ex date - 07/08/2009
Name changed to Madison Ave. Media, Inc. 06/17/2010

KAIBO FOODS CO LTD (DE)
Reincorporated 09/06/2017
State of incorporation changed from (NV) to (DE) 09/06/2017
Recapitalized as C-Cube Genetics, Inc. 07/30/2018
Each share Common $0.001 par exchanged for (0.01) share Common $0.001 par

KAIETEUR RESOURCE CORP (BC)
Name changed to Samba Gold Inc. 03/21/2005
Samba Gold Inc. recapitalized as Caerus Resource Corp. 02/26/2009 which name changed to Angel Gold Corp. 10/04/2012

KAIRE HLDGS INC (DE)
Each share old Common $0.001 par exchanged for (0.005) share new Common $0.001 par 09/02/2003
Reorganized under the laws of Nevada as International Packaging & Logistics Group, Inc. 05/21/2008
Each share new Common $0.001 par exchanged for (0.005) share Common $0.001 par
International Packaging & Logistics Group, Inc. name changed to YBCC, Inc. 12/22/2016

KAIROS CAP CORP (AB)
Name changed to Lithium Chile Inc. 12/20/2017

KAIROS CORP (DE)
Each share old Common 1¢ par exchanged for (0.5) share new Common 1¢ par 07/31/1972
Charter cancelled and declared inoperative and void for non-payment of taxes 03/01/1975

KAIROS HLDGS INC (NV)
Name changed to VitalTrust Business Development Corp. 02/27/2007
VitalTrust Business Development Corp. name changed to Renew Energy Resources, Inc. 05/27/2008
(See Renew Energy Resources Inc.)

KAISER ALUM & CHEM CORP (DE)
Capital Stock $1 par reclassified as Common $1 par in 1951
5% Preferred $50 par called for redemption in 1955
Common $1 par changed to 33-1/3¢ par and (2) additional shares issued 6/3/65
Common 33-1/3¢ par split (2) for (1) by issuance of (1) additional share 11/29/78
4-3/4% Preferred $50 par called for redemption 9/30/81
Stock Dividends - 20% 8/31/50; 10% 8/31/51
Under plan of reorganization each share Common 33-1/3¢ par automatically became (1) share KaiserTech Ltd. Common 33-1/3¢ par 5/1/87
Ser. A Preference called for redemption at $50 on 3/1/2001
Ser. B Preference called for redemption at $50 on 3/1/2001
Plan of reorganization under Chapter 11 Federal Bankruptcy Code effective 7/6/2006
No stockholders' equity

KAISER ALUM CORP (DE)
$6.50 Depositary Preferred Ser. A 5¢ par called for redemption 09/19/1995

$6.50 Preferred Ser. A 5¢ par called for redemption 09/19/1995
8.255% Preferred Increased Dividend Equity Security 5¢ par called for redemption 08/29/1997
Plan of reorganization under Chapter 11 Federal Bankruptcy Code effective 07/06/2006
No old Common stockholders' equity (Additional Information in Active)

KAISER CEM CORP (DE)
Reincorporated 5/4/82
State of incorporation changed from (CA) to (DE) 5/4/82
5% Conv. Preference $50 par called for redemption 4/10/81
$1.375 Conv. Preference no par called for redemption 3/2/87
Merged into HK-9, Inc. 3/3/87
Each share Common $1 par exchanged for $27.50 cash

KAISER CEMENT & GYPSUM CORP. (CA)
Name changed to Kaiser Cement Corp. (Calif.) 5/1/79
Kaiser Cement Corp. (Calif.) reincorporated in Delaware 5/4/82
(See Kaiser Cement Corp. (Del.))

KAISER CORP (MN)
Name changed to Pilot Industries Corp. and Common 10¢ par changed to 5¢ par 7/12/77

KAISER DEVELOPMENT CORP. LTD. (SK)
Struck off register for failure to file annual returns 10/24/1958

KAISER DIVERSIFIED ENTERPRISES INC (DE)
Charter cancelled and declared inoperative and void for non-payment of taxes 3/1/79

KAISER ELECTRONICS, INC. (NJ)
Merged into Utronics, Inc. on a (1/3) for (1) basis 2/6/63
Utronics, Inc. charter cancelled 12/20/77

KAISER FED FINL GROUP INC (MD)
Name changed to Simplicity Bancorp Inc. 11/13/2012
Simplicity Bancorp Inc. merged into HomeStreet, Inc. 03/02/2015

KAISER-FRAZER CORP. (NV)
Name changed to Kaiser Motors Corp. in 1953
Kaiser Motors Corp. recapitalized as Kaiser Industries Corp. 3/16/56
(See Kaiser Industries Corp.)

KAISER GROUP HLDGS INC (DE)
Preferred 1¢ par called for redemption at $55 plus $0.179315 accrued dividends on 11/17/2005
(Additional Information in Active)

KAISER GROUP INTL INC (DE)
Reorganized as Kaiser Group Holdings, Inc. 12/18/2000
Each share Common 1¢ par exchanged for (0.01041666) share Common 1¢ par

KAISER INDS CORP (NV)
6-1/2% Conv. Preferred $50 par called for redemption 9/30/76
Liquidation completed
Each share Common $4 par received initial distribution of (0.2549255) share Kaiser Aluminum & Chemical Corp. Common 33-1/3¢ par, (0.0784243) share Kaiser Cement & Gypsum Corp. Common $1 par, (0.1366646) share Kaiser Steel Corp. Common 66-2/3¢ par and $1 cash 6/3/77
(See each company's listing)
Each share Common $4 par received second distribution of $1 cash 10/3/77
Each share Common $4 par received third distribution of $3 cash 3/9/78
Each share Common $4 par received

fourth distribution of $0.75 cash 6/29/79
Each share Common $4 par received fifth distribution of $1.90 cash 3/28/80
Assets transferred to liquidating agent and certificates requested to be surrendered 4/11/80
Each share Common $4 par received sixth distribution of $0.03 cash 1/30/81
Each share Common $4 par received seventh distribution of $0.04 cash 8/7/81
Each share Common $4 par received eighth distribution of $0.04 cash 7/30/82
Each share Common $4 par received ninth distribution of $0.04 cash 1/31/83
Each share Common $4 par received tenth distribution of $0.04 cash 8/2/83
Each share Common $4 par received eleventh distribution of $0.16 cash 2/16/84
Each share Common $4 par received twelfth distribution of $0.04 cash 7/31/84
Each share Common $4 par received thirteenth distribution of $0.04 cash 2/1/85
Each share Common $4 par received fourteenth distribution of $0.04 cash 8/1/85
Each share Common $4 par received fifteenth and final distribution of $0.62 cash 11/29/85

KAISER MINES OF CANADA LTD. (ON)
Acquired by Mission Financial Corp. Ltd. 05/09/1968
Each share Capital Stock $1 par exchanged for (0.022) share Common no par
Mission Financial Corp. Ltd. merged into H.R.S. Industries, Inc. 05/21/1982 which merged into International H.R.S. Industries Inc. 05/15/1984 which name changed to Glenex Industries Inc. 05/25/1987 which merged into Quest Investment Corp. 07/04/2002 which merged into Quest Capital Corp. (BC) 06/30/2003 which reincorporated in Canada 05/27/2008 which name changed to Sprott Resource Lending Corp. 09/10/2010 which merged into Sprott Inc. 07/24/2013

KAISER MOTORS CORP. (NV)
Recapitalized as Kaiser Industries Corp. 3/16/56
Each share Common $1 par exchanged for (0.25) share Common $4 par
(See Kaiser Industries Corp.)

KAISER PETROLEUM LTD. (AB)
Acquired by Kaiser Resources Ltd. 04/18/1979
Each share Common 45¢ par exchanged for $33.50 cash

KAISER PRODUCE INC (DE)
Name changed to Kaiser Diversified Enterprises, Inc. 12/6/68
(See Kaiser Diversified Enterprises, Inc.)

KAISER RESH INC (UT)
Reincorporated under the laws of Delaware as Pacific Syndication, Inc. 12/02/1994
Pacific Syndication, Inc. recapitalized as Pacific Alliance Corp. 06/08/1997
(See Pacific Alliance Corp.)

KAISER RES INC (DE)
Name changed to Kaiser Ventures Inc. 6/20/95
Kaiser Ventures Inc. merged into Kaiser Ventures LLC 11/30/2001

KAISER RES LTD (BC)
Name changed to B.C. Coal Ltd. and Common $1 par reclassified as Special Shares $1 par 01/16/1981
B.C. Coal Ltd. name changed to Westar Mining Ltd. 06/00/1983
(See Westar Mining Ltd.)

KAISER STL RES INC (DE)
Reincorporated 01/27/1984
Merged 03/31/1984
Name changed 11/17/1988
5-3/4% Conv. Preferred $100 par called for redemption 08/29/1967
Common $1 par changed to 66-2/3¢ par and (0.5) additional share issued 04/12/1968
State of incorporation changed from (NV) to (DE) 01/27/1984
$1.46 Preferred no par called for redemption 03/31/1984
Merged from Kaiser Steel Corp. to Kaiser Steel (Delaware), Inc. 03/31/1984
Each share Common 66-2/3¢ par exchanged for (1) share $1.04 Preferred Ser. A $1 par, (1) share $2.25 Preferred Ser. B $1 par and $22 cash
Plan of reorganization under Chapter 11 Federal Bankruptcy proceedings confirmed 09/23/1988
No Preferred stockholders' equity
Name changed from Kaiser Steel (Delaware), Inc. to Kaiser Steel Resources Inc. 11/17/1988
Each share Common 1¢ par exchanged for (1/3) share Common 3¢ par 10/02/1990
Name changed to Kaiser Resources Inc. 06/15/1993
Kaiser Resources Inc. name changed to Kaiser Ventures Inc. 06/20/1995 which merged into Kaiser Ventures LLC 11/30/2001

KAISER VENTURES INC (DE)
Merged into Kaiser Ventures LLC 11/30/2001
Each share Common 3¢ par exchanged for (1) Class A Unit and $10 cash

KAISERTECH LTD (DE)
Merged into Maxxam Group Inc. 10/28/88
Each share Common 33-1/3¢ par exchanged for $19.375 cash

KAITONE HLDGS LTD (BC)
Recapitalized as Consolidated Kaitone Holdings Ltd. 09/03/1991
Each share Common no par exchanged for (0.33333333) share Common no par
Consolidated Kaitone Holdings Ltd. recapitalized as Largo Resources Ltd. (BC) 05/08/2003 which reincorporated in Ontario 06/10/2004

KAIYUE INTL INC (AB)
Reorganized under the laws of British Columbia as Benchmark Botanics Inc. 11/03/2017
Each share Common no par exchanged for (0.47227732) share Common no par

KAIZEN CAP CORP (AB)
Reincorporated under the laws of British Columbia as Tudor Gold Corp. 05/12/2016

KAIZEN TECHNOLOGIES INC (AB)
Name changed to Underbalanced Drilling Systems Ltd. 11/14/1996
Underbalanced Drilling Systems Ltd. merged into Precision Drilling Corp. 07/30/1999
(See Precision Drilling Corp.)

KAJIMA CONSTRUCTION CO., LTD. (JAPAN)
Name changed to Kajima Corp. 10/14/69

KAKANDA DEV CORP (BC)
Plan of arrangement effective 01/19/2007
Each share Common no par exchanged for (1) share KDC Energy Ltd. Common no par and (1) share Kakanda Resources Corp. Common no par
(See each company's listing)

KAKANDA RES CORP (BC)
Name changed to Otish Energy Inc. 03/28/2008
Otish Energy Inc. name changed to Arrowhead Gold Corp. 08/11/2011 which recapitalized as Kontrol Energy Corp. 08/09/2016

KAL/GRAPHIC INC. (LA)
Charter revoked for failure to file annual reports 11/19/90

KAL-O-MINE INDS INC (UT)
Recapitalized as Amereco, Inc. 06/28/1995
Each share Common $0.001 par exchanged for (0.02) share Common $0.001 par
(See Amereco, Inc.)

KAL RES LTD (BC)
Recapitalized as National Irron Resources Ltd. 11/15/1976
Each share Capital Stock no par exchanged for (0.5) share Capital Stock no par
(See National Irron Resources Ltd.)

KALA CANADA LTD (AB)
Name changed 03/27/1989
Name changed from Kala Feedlots Ltd. to Kala Canada Ltd. 03/27/1989
Assets sold for the benefit of creditors in 05/00/1995
No stockholders' equity

KALA EXPL LTD (AB)
Recapitalized as Kala Feedlots Ltd. 01/06/1987
Each share Class A Common no par exchanged for (0.2) share Class A Common no par
Kala Feedlots Ltd. name changed to Kala Canada Ltd. 03/27/1989
(See Kala Canada Ltd.)

KALADAR MINES LTD. (ON)
Name changed 04/20/1965
Name changed from Kaladar Iron Mines to Kaladar Mines Ltd. 04/20/1965
Charter cancelled 01/03/1983

KALAHARI GREENTECH INC (NV)
Common $0.001 par split (2) for (1) by issuance of (1) additional share payable 12/01/2010 to holders of record 10/18/2010 Ex date - 12/02/2010
Recapitalized as PF Hospitality Group, Inc. 06/11/2015
Each share Common $0.001 par exchanged for (0.0005) share Common $0.0001 par
PF Hospitality Group, Inc. name changed to EXOlifestyle, Inc. 09/27/2016 which recapitalized as Sun Pacific Holding Corp. 10/13/2017

KALAHARI RES INC (BC)
Recapitalized as Integra Gold Corp. 12/22/2010
Each share Common no par exchanged for (0.1) share Common no par
Integra Gold Corp. merged into Eldorado Gold Corp. (New) 07/17/2017

KALAMAX MINING CO. (NV)
Dissolved in 1953

KALAMAZOO ALLEGAN & GRAND RAPIDS RR CO (MI)
Merged into Penn Central Corp. 8/12/82
Each share Capital Stock $100 par exchanged for (10.604) shares Common $1 par
Note: a) distribution is certain only for certificates surrendered between 5/1/85 and 12/31/86 c) no Distribution will be made for certificates surrendered after 12/31/86
Penn Central Corp. name changed to American Premier Underwriters, Inc. 3/25/94 which merged into American Premier Group, Inc. 4/3/95 which name changed to American Financial Group, Inc. 6/9/95 which merged into American Financial Group, Inc. (Holding Co.) 12/2/97

KALAMAZOO FURNACE & APPLIANCE MANUFACTURING CO. (MI)
Name changed to Dowagiac-Kal Co. 4/3/62
(See Dowagiac-Kal Co.)

KALAMAZOO LOOSE LEAF BINDER CO.
Acquired by Remington Rand, Inc. in 1927
(See Remington Rand, Inc.)

KALAMAZOO PAPER CO (MI)
Merged into Georgia-Pacific Corp. 10/20/67
Each share Common $10 par exchanged for (2) shares $1.40 Conv. Preferred no par and (0.7) share Common 80¢ par
(See Georgia-Pacific Corp.)

KALAMAZOO STOVE & FURNACE CO. (MI)
Liquidation completed 6/28/60

KALAMAZOO STOVE CO.
Name changed to Kalamazoo Stove & Furnace Co. in 1937
(See Kalamazoo Stove & Furnace Co.)

KALAMAZOO VEGETABLE PARCHMENT CO. (MI)
Stock Dividends - 25% 9/30/50; 10% 12/18/53; 10% 10/10/57
Merged into KVP Sutherland Paper Co. on a (1.2) for (1) basis 1/4/60
KVP Sutherland Paper Co. merged into Brown Co. (DE) 5/12/66 which merged into James River Corp. of Virginia 10/28/80 which name changed to Fort James Corp. 8/13/97 which merged into Georgia-Pacific Corp. 11/27/2000
(See Georgia-Pacific Corp.)

KALAN GOLD CORP (CO)
Name changed to Digital Broadband Networks, Inc. (CO) 08/20/2001
Digital Broadband Networks, Inc. (CO) reincorporated in Delaware 06/06/2002 which name changed to Secured Digital Applications, Inc. 02/03/2004
(See Secured Digital Applications, Inc.)

KALBARA MNG N L (AUSTRALIA)
Recapitalized as Dioro Exploration N.L. 05/18/1992
Each ADR for Ordinary A$0.25 par exchanged for (0.1) ADR for Ordinary A$0.25 par
(See Dioro Exploration N.L.)

KALBROOK MINING CO., LTD. (ON)
Liquidation completed 06/30/1961
Details not available

KALCO VY MINES LTD (BC)
Recapitalized as Consolidated Kalco Valley Mines Ltd. 09/04/1975
Each share Capital Stock 50¢ par exchanged for (0.2) share Capital Stock no par
Consolidated Kalco Valley Mines Ltd. recapitalized as Brace Resources Ltd. 11/27/1979 which recapitalized as International Brace Resources Inc. 05/11/1988 which recapitalized as Prescott Resources Inc. (BC) 04/04/1997 which reincorporated in Yukon as Asia Sapphires Ltd. 06/29/1998
(See Asia Sapphires Ltd.)

KAL-KAN

KALDENBAUGH MTG & INVT INC (AZ)
Company liquidated in 1985
Details not available

KALE HOMES, INC. (NC)
Name changed to Provident House, Inc. 8/15/63
(See Provident House, Inc.)

KALEEDA RESOURCE INDS INC (AB)
Recapitalized as Kaleeda Enterprises Inc. 06/30/1992
Each share Common no par exchanged for (0.25) share Common no par

KALEIDOSCOPE MEDIA GROUP INC (DE)
Charter cancelled and declared inoperative and void for non-payment of taxes 3/1/2000

KALEX CORP (DE)
Common 1¢ par changed to $0.00001 par 11/30/2010
SEC revoked common stock registration 02/21/2017

KALGOLD MINES, LTD. (ON)
Charter cancelled by Province of Ontario for default 11/21/55

KALI VENTURE CORP (BC)
Struck off register and declared dissolved for failure to file returns 07/24/1992

KALIBAK GOLD MINES LTD. (ON)
Charter revoked for failure to file reports and pay fees 11/09/1967

KALIBER RES LTD (BC)
Name changed to Metro Energy Ltd. 10/04/1989
(See Metro Energy Ltd.)

KALIMANTAN GOLD CORP LTD (BERMUDA)
Reincorporated 12/19/1997
Place of incorporation changed from (ON) to (Bermuda) as Kalimantan Gold Corp. Ltd. and Common no par changed to USD$0.01 par 12/19/1997
Name changed to Asiamet Resources Ltd. 07/27/2015
(See Asiamet Resources Ltd.)

KALIS INC (MN)
Statutorily dissolved 7/29/96

KALLESTAD LABS INC (MN)
Stock Dividend - 200% 2/28/73
Merged into Montedison International Holding Co. 7/14/82
Each share Common 5¢ par exchanged for $25 cash

KALLIMA INTL INC (NV)
Reincorporated 03/23/1988
State of incorporation changed from (UT) to (NV) 03/23/1988
Each share old Common $0.001 par exchanged for (0.01) share new Common $0.001 par 11/13/1993
Reorganized as Peppermint Park Productions Inc. 08/15/1994
Each share new Common $0.001 par exchanged for (2) shares Common $0.001 par
Peppermint Park Productions Inc. recapitalized as Axxess Inc. 02/14/1997 which name changed to Financialweb.Com, Inc. 01/01/1999
(See Financialweb.Com, Inc.)

KALLIO IRON MINES LTD (ON)
Merged into Kalrock Developments Ltd. 10/23/1978
Each share Capital Stock no par exchanged for (0.2) share Capital Stock no par
Kalrock Developments Ltd. merged into Kalrock Resources Ltd. 08/08/1990 which merged into Cercal Minerals Corp. 07/09/1993
(See Cercal Minerals Corp.)

KALLISTO ENERGY CORP (AB)
Name changed to Toro Oil & Gas Ltd. 11/25/2014
(See Toro Oil & Gas Ltd.)

KALNORTH GOLD MINES LTD (AUSTRALIA)
ADR agreement terminated 09/25/2017
Each Sponsored ADR for Ordinary exchanged for $0.075218 cash

KALOBIOS PHARMACEUTICALS INC (DE)
Each share old Common $0.001 par exchanged for (0.125) share new Common $0.001 par 07/14/2015
Name changed to Humanigen, Inc. 08/07/2017

KALOS RES INC (IA)
Name changed to Parallel Development Group, Inc. 09/18/1989
(See Parallel Development Group, Inc.)

KALROCK DEVS LTD (ON)
Merged into Kalrock Resources Ltd. 08/08/1990
Each share Capital Stock no par exchanged for (1) share Common no par
Kalrock Resources Ltd. merged into Cercal Minerals Corp. 07/09/1993
(See Cercal Minerals Corp.)

KALROCK RES LTD (ON)
Merged into Cercal Minerals Corp. 07/09/1993
Each share Common no par exchanged for (1) share Common no par
(See Cercal Minerals Corp.)

KALTMAN (D.) & CO., INC. (NJ)
Name changed to Kalvex, Inc. (NJ) 3/1/68
Kalvex, Inc. (NJ) reincorporated in Delaware 4/2/70 which merged into Allied Artists Industries, Inc. 1/20/76
(See Allied Artists Industries, Inc.)

KALVAR CORP (DE)
Reincorporated 11/12/81
Common 2¢ par split (4) for (1) by issuance of (3) additional shares 12/17/69
State of incorporation changed from (LA) to (DE) 11/12/81
Acquired by MTech Corp. 10/15/87
Each share Common 2¢ par exchanged for $2.70 cash

KALVEX INC (DE)
Reincorporated 4/2/70
State of incorporation changed from (NJ) to (DE) 4/2/70
Merged into Allied Artists Industries, Inc. 1/20/76
Each share Common 50¢ par exchanged for (1) share Common 10¢ par
(See Allied Artists Industries, Inc.)

KAM & RONSON MEDIA GROUP INC (AB)
Each share old Common no par exchanged for (0.2) share new Common no par 03/12/2010
Each share new Common no par exchanged again for (0.0000005) share new Common no par 02/27/2014
Note: In effect holders received $0.02 cash per share and public interest was eliminated
Note: Unexchanged certificates were cancelled and became without value 02/26/2016

KAM CAP CORP (ON)
Name changed to Titan Medical Inc. 07/30/2008

KAM CREED MINES LTD (BC)
Common 50¢ par changed to no par 06/10/1985
Delisted from Toronto Stock Exchange 10/23/1991

KAM KOTIA MINES LTD (ON)
Common $1 par changed to no par 06/25/1975
Merged into Goldcorp Investments Ltd. 05/29/1989
Each share Common no par exchanged for $3 cash

KAM-KOTIA PORCUPINE MINES LTD. (ON)
Acquired by Violamac Mines Ltd. 01/31/1966
Details not available

KAM SCIENTIFIC INC (BC)
Recapitalized as Global Teleworks Corp. 01/15/1993
Each share Common no par exchanged for (0.5) share Common no par

KAMAD SILVER LTD (BC)
Recapitalized as Agate Bay Resources Ltd. 01/19/1993
Each share Common no par exchanged for (0.2) share Common no par
Agate Bay Resources Ltd. recapitalized as Geodex Minerals Ltd. (BC) 04/14/1998 which reincorporated in Ontario as Intercontinental Gold & Metals Ltd. 11/06/2017

KAMALTA EXPL LTD (AB)
Bankrupt 09/09/1970
No stockholders' equity

KAMAN AIRCRAFT CORP. (CT)
Class A & B Common no par changed to $1 par in 1954
Name changed to Kaman Corp. 4/3/67

KAMAN CORP (CT)
$1 Conv. Stock $1 par called for redemption 10/30/78
6.50% Depositary Preferred Ser. 2 $1 par called for redemption at $51.95 on 2/9/98
(Additional Information in Active)

KAMBERN DIVERSIFIED LTD (ON)
Acquired by Berncam International Industries Ltd. 11/23/1970
Each share Common no par exchanged for (1) share Common no par
(See Berncam International Industries Ltd.)

KAMCON MINES LTD (CANADA)
Merged into Nerco Mineral Co. 05/31/1990
Each share Common no par exchanged for $0.25 cash

KAMENSTEIN M INC (NY)
Acquired by CHSMK Corp. 1/10/92
Each share Common 1¢ par exchanged for $10.55 cash

KAMINAK GOLD CORP (BC)
Each share Common no par exchanged for (1) share Class A Common no par and (0.5) Kivalliq Energy Corp. Unit consisting of (0.8) share Common no par and (0.5) Common Stock Purchase Warrant expiring 08/04/2008 on 07/04/2008
Merged into Goldcorp Inc. (New) 07/21/2016
Each share Class A Common no par exchanged for (0.10896) share Common no par
Note: Unexchanged certificates will be cancelled and become without value 07/21/2022

KAMIS COPPER MINES LTD. (ON)
Name changed to Kamis Uranium Mines Ltd. 06/22/1955
Kamis Uranium Mines Ltd. merged into Ver-Million Gold Placer Mining Ltd. 09/27/1960
(See Ver-Million Gold Placer Mining Ltd.)

KAMIS URANIUM MINES LTD. (ON)
Merged into Ver-Million Gold Placer Mining Ltd. 09/27/1960
Each share Common exchanged for (1) share Common
(See Ver-Million Gold Placer Mining Ltd.)

KAMLAC GOLD MINES LTD. (ON)
Under plan of dissolution each (3.5) shares Capital Stock $1 par exchanged for (1) share Kamcon Mines Ltd. Common no par 12/6/60
(See Kamcon Mines Ltd.)

KAMLO GOLD MINES LTD (ON)
Recapitalized as NRT Research Technologies Inc. 10/29/1985
Each share Common no par exchanged for (0.25) share Common no par
NRT Research Technologies Inc. name changed to NRT Industries Inc. 01/20/1988 which recapitalized as Cuda Consolidated Inc. 03/04/1991 which name changed to FoodQuest International Corp. 11/30/1994 which recapitalized as Dealcheck.Com Inc. 01/21/1999 which recapitalized as Bontan Corp. Inc. (ON) 04/17/2003 which reincorporated in British Virgin Islands as Portage Biotech Inc. 08/23/2013

KAMLODE RES INC (BC)
Recapitalized as Symes Resources Ltd. 06/08/1988
Each share Common no par exchanged for (0.4) share Common no par
(See Symes Resources Ltd.)

KAMLOOPS CABLENET LTD (BC)
Merged into CableNet Ltd. 02/01/1988
Details not available

KAMLOOPS COPPER CO. LTD. (BC)
Recapitalized as Kamloops Copper Consolidated Ltd. 07/06/1964
Each share Common no par exchanged for (0.14285714) share Common no par
Kamloops Copper Consolidated Ltd. merged into Davenport Oil & Mining Ltd. 02/29/1972 which name changed to Davenport Industries Ltd. 11/01/1973 which recapitalized as DVO Industries Ltd. 08/19/1991
(See DVO Industries Ltd.)

KAMLOOPS COPPER CONS LTD (BC)
Merged into Davenport Oil & Mining Ltd. 02/29/1972
Each share Common no par exchanged for (0.16666666) share Capital Stock 50¢ par
Davenport Oil & Mining Ltd. name changed to Davenport Industries Ltd. 11/01/1973 which recapitalized as DVO Industries Ltd. 08/19/1991
(See DVO Industries Ltd.)

KAMP A WHILE INDUSTRIES, INC. (IA)
Administratively dissolved for failure to file annual reports 9/14/90

KAMPGROUNDS AMER (MT)
Stock Dividends - 50% 3/20/70; 25% 4/13/79
Merged into KOA Holdings Inc. 5/29/81
Each share Common 12-1/2¢ par exchanged for $15.75 cash

KAN TX ENERGY CO (UT)
Reorganized under the laws of Delaware as Ranger/USA Inc. 05/02/1994
Each share Common $0.001 par exchanged for (0.1) share Common $0.001 par
Ranger/USA Inc. name changed to First Capital International Inc. 08/31/1998
(See First Capital International Inc.)

KANA SOFTWARE INC (DE)
Name changed 06/29/2001
Issue Information - 3,300,000 shares

COM offered at $15 per share on 09/21/1999
Common $0.001 par split (2) for (1) by issuance of (1) additional share payable 02/22/2000 to holders of record 01/28/2000
Name changed from Kana Communications, Inc. to Kana Software, Inc. 06/29/2001
Each share old Common $0.001 par exchanged for (0.1) share new Common $0.001 par 12/13/2001
Name changed to SWK Holdings Corp. 02/04/2010

KANAB URANIUM CORP. (UT)
Merged into Oil Securities & Uranium Corp. 00/00/1955
Each share Common exchanged for (0.02857143) share Common
Oil Securities & Uranium Corp. name changed to Oil Securities & Gas Corp. 07/01/1956 which name changed to Oil Securities & Metals Corp. 02/06/1968 which name changed to Oil Securities, Inc. (UT) 12/10/1969 which reincorporated in Nevada 05/27/1982 which recapitalized as Digital Technologies Media Group Inc. 07/26/1996 which reorganized as Central Capital Ventures Corp. 05/08/2000
(See Central Capital Ventures Corp.)

KANAKARIS WIRELESS (NV)
Name changed 6/2/2000
Name changed from Kanakaris Communications, Inc. to Kanakaris Wireless 6/2/2000
Each share old Common $0.001 par exchanged for (0.05) share new Common $0.001 par 12/7/2001
Recapitalized as Wi-Fi TV, Inc. 4/20/2004
Each share new Common $0.001 par exchanged for (0.02) share Common $0.001 par

KANATA GENESIS LTD (ON)
Recapitalized 10/13/1989
Recapitalized from Kanata Genesis Fund to Kanata Genesis Ltd. 10/13/1989
Each share Common no par exchanged for (0.06896551) share Common no par
Name changed to SFP International Ltd. 10/17/1990
SFP International Ltd. reorganized in Switzerland as Societe Financiere Privee S.A. 01/20/1993 which name changed to Societe Bancaire Privee SA 03/02/2003

KANATA HOTELS INC. (ON)
Recapitalized as Kanata Hotels International Inc. 05/04/1987
Each share Class A Non-Vtg. no par exchanged for (0.5) share Common no par
Each share Conv. Class C no par exchanged for (0.5) share Common no par
Kanata Hotels International Inc. merged into Armbro Enterprises Inc. 02/01/1990 which name changed to Aecon Group Inc. 06/18/2001

KANATA HOTELS INTL INC (ON)
Merged into Armbro Enterprises Inc. 02/01/1990
Each share Common no par exchanged for (0.1222) share Common no par
Armbro Enterprises Inc. name changed to Aecon Group Inc. 06/18/2001

KANAWHA BKG & TR CO (CHARLESTON, WV)
Name changed 7/1/71
Each share Capital Stock $100 par exchanged for (10) shares Capital Stock $20 par to effect a (5) for (1) split and a 100% stock dividend 7/1/62
Capital Stock $20 par changed to $10 par and (1) additional share issued 4/1/68
Name changed from Kanawha Banking & Trust Co. to Kanawha Banking & Trust Co., N.A. 7/1/71
Capital Stock $10 par changed to $5 par and (1) additional share issued 3/21/72
Reorganized as Intermountain Bankshares Inc. 7/1/83
Each share Capital Stock $5 par exchanged for (1) share Common $1 par
Intermountain Bankshares Inc. merged into United Bankshares, Inc. 7/1/86

KANAWHA BLOCK CO. (WV)
Called for redemption 2/1/64
Public interest eliminated

KANAWHA VALLEY BANK (CHARLESTON, WV)
Capital Stock $100 par changed to $10 par and (9) additional shares issued 04/01/1965
Stock Dividends - 20% 12/15/1948; 100% 03/01/1966; 50% 03/20/1970; 50% 03/31/1972
Name changed to Kanawha Valley Bank, N.A. (Charleston, WV) 02/10/1975
Kanawha Valley Bank, N.A. (Charleston, WV) reorganized as One Valley Bancorp of West Virginia, Inc. 09/04/1981 which merged into BB&T Corp. 07/06/2000

KANAWHA VALLEY BK N A (CHARLESTON, WV)
Stock Dividend - 25% 01/20/1977
Reorganized as One Valley Bancorp of West Virginia, Inc. 09/04/1981
Each share Capital Stock $10 par exchanged for (1) share Common $10 par
One Valley Bancorp of West Virginia, Inc. name changed to One Valley Bancorp, Inc. 04/30/1996 which merged into BB&T Corp. 07/06/2000

KANBAY INTL INC (DE)
Acquired by Cap Gemini S.A. 2/9/2007
Each share Common $0.001 par exchanged for $29 cash

KANCANA VENTURES LTD (CANADA)
Recapitalized as Walron Minerals Corp. 12/21/1994
Each share Common no par exchanged for (0.25) share Common no par
(See Walron Minerals Corp.)

KANCO TECH CO (FL)
Name changed to Hotsy Corp. 2/27/76
(See Hotsy Corp.)

KANDAHAR RES LTD (BC)
Recapitalized as First Allied Resources Corp. 07/16/1985
Each share Capital Stock no par exchanged for (0.14285714) share Common no par
(See First Allied Resources Corp.)

KANDI TECHNOLOGIES CORP (DE)
Name changed to Kandi Technologies Group, Inc. 12/31/2012

KANDY PAK INC (MA)
Proclaimed dissolved for failure to file reports and pay fees 7/7/80

KANE ANTHONY INC (DE)
Common 10¢ par split (2) for (1) by issuance of (1) additional share 06/05/1970
Name changed to Maid-Rite Ventures, Inc. 04/12/1985
Maid-Rite Ventures, Inc. name changed to Grandee Corp. 09/23/1985 which name changed to Cassco Capital Corp. (Old) 09/01/1987 which name changed to International K.C. Jakes BBQ & Grill, Inc. 07/20/1992 which name changed back to Cassco Capital Corp. (New) 07/18/1994 which recapitalized as Diversified Technology Inc. 06/23/2000 which name changed to Diversified Technologies Group, Inc. 11/14/2000 which name changed to X-Change Corp. 07/30/2001 which name changed to Endocan Corp. 11/06/2013

KANE CARBURETOR CORP. OF DELAWARE (DE)
No longer in existence having become inoperative and void for non-payment of taxes 4/1/56

KANE CREEK URANIUM CORP. (UT)
Involuntarily dissolved 7/21/58
No stockholders' equity

KANE FURNITURE CORP (FL)
Each share Common 10¢ par exchanged for (0.00004) share Common 1¢ par 4/14/89
Public interest eliminated

KANE INVT CORP (AB)
Voluntarily delisted from Toronto Venture Stock Exchange 06/02/2005
Company is privately held

KANE-MILLER CORP. (NY)
Reincorporated under the laws of Delaware 9/24/64
(See Kane-Miller Corp. (DE))

KANE MILLER CORP (DE)
Common $1 par split (5) for (4) by issuance of (0.25) additional share 7/18/75
Common $1 par split (3) for (2) by issuance of (0.5) additional share 6/22/76
Merged into Kane-Miller Acquisition Corp. 2/28/84
Each share Common $1 par exchanged for $21 cash

KANE STORES OF NEW ENGLAND, INC. (DE)
Dissolved 6/22/56
Details not available

KANEB ENERGY PARTNERS LTD (TX)
Liquidation completed
Each Depositary Receipt received initial distribution of $2.59 cash 10/31/88
Each Depositary Receipt received second and final distribution of $0.67 cash 12/28/88
Note: Certificates were not required to be surrendered and are without value

KANEB PIPE LINE PARTNERS L P (DE)
Each Preference Unit of Ltd. Partnership Int. no par converted into (1) Senior Preference Unit no par 8/17/98
Merged into Valero L.P. 7/1/2005
Each Senior Preference Unit no par exchanged for (1.0231) Common Units no par
Valero L.P. name changed to NuStar Energy L.P. 4/1/2007

KANEB SVCS INC (DE)
Name changed 04/30/1971
6.5% Preferred $100 par called for redemption 03/31/1971
Name changed from Kaneb Pipe Line Co. to Kaneb Services, Inc. 04/30/1971
Common no par split (2) for (1) by issuance of (1) additional share 05/24/1974
Common no par split (2) for (1) by issuance of (1) additional share 05/13/1977
Each share old Adjustable Rate Preferred Class A no par exchanged for (10) shares new Adjustable Rate Preferred Class A no par 09/21/1990
New Adjustable Rate Preferred Class A no par called for redemption at $10.67 on 03/30/2001
Each share Common no par received distribution of (0.33333333) share Kaneb Services LLC Common no par payable 06/29/2001 to holders of record 06/20/2001 Ex date - 07/02/2001
Name changed to Xanser Corp. 08/07/2001
Xanser Corp. name changed to Furmanite Corp. 05/17/2007 which merged into Team, Inc. 02/29/2016

KANEB SVCS LLC (DE)
Merged into Valero L.P. 7/1/2005
Each share Common no par exchanged for $43.31 cash

KANEBO LTD (JAPAN)
ADR agreement terminated 11/5/2004
Each ADR for Common 50 Yen par exchanged for $3.951 cash

KANEH BOSM BIOTECHNOLOGY INC (BC)
Each share old Common no par exchanged for (0.5) share new Common no par 05/17/2017
Name changed to ICC International Cannabis Corp. (New) 09/20/2018

KANGAROO MEDIA INC (CANADA)
Name changed 11/15/2004
Name changed from Kangaroo Capital Inc. to Kangaroo Media Inc. 11/15/2004
Each share old Common no par exchanged for (0.25) share new Common no par 04/18/2006
Acquired by Game Day Entertainment, LLC 12/23/2009
Each share new Common no par exchanged for $0.42 cash
Note: Unexchanged certificates were cancelled and became without value 12/23/2015

KANGELD RES LTD (BC)
Merged into Appian Resources Ltd. 09/06/1989
Each share Common no par exchanged for (0.2131) share Common no par
Appian Resources Ltd. recapitalized as Sultan Minerals Inc. 05/04/1992 which recapitalized as Apex Resources Inc. 07/18/2016

KANIKSU VENTURES INC (ID)
Name changed Intryst Inc. 04/02/1997
Intryst Inc. name changed to PTC Group Inc. 12/22/1997 which changed to Ocean Power Corp. 07/12/1999
(See Ocean Power Corp.)

KANKAKEE BANCORP INC (DE)
Name changed to Centrue Financial Corp. (New) 10/09/2003
Centrue Financial Corp. (New) merged into Midland States Bancorp, Inc. 06/09/2017

KANKAKEE WTR CO (IL)
Reincorporated 07/14/1967
Each share 7% Preferred $100 par exchanged for (1.25) shares 5-1/2% Preferred $100 par 00/00/1940
State of incorporation changed from (ME) to (IL) 07/14/1967
Name changed to Consumers Illinois Water Co. 07/07/1988

KANN ELLERT ELECTRS INC (MD)
Voluntarily dissolved 06/14/1996
Details not available

KANOSAK CAP VENTURE CORP (CANADA)
Name changed to Algold Resources Ltd. 06/28/2013

KANOTEX REFINING CO.
Liquidated in 1953
Details not available

KANSAI MNG CORP (BC)
Reincorporated under the laws of Yukon 07/09/2002 which reincorporated back into British Columbia 01/31/2008

KANSAS & GULF CO. (DE)
Charter cancelled and declared inoperative and void for non-payment of taxes 4/1/30

KANSAS BANKERS SURETY CO (KS)
Common $50 par changed to $12.50 par and (3) additional shares issued 6/1/76
Common $12.50 par changed to $6.25 par and (2) additional shares issued 7/5/85
Common $6.25 par changed to $3.125 par and (1) additional share issued 8/15/92
Common $3.125 par split (2) for (1) by issuance of (1) additional share 12/12/94
Stock Dividends - 100% 6/12/80; 100% 8/17/88; 100% 12/7/90
Merged into Westco Financial Insurance Co. 7/17/96
Each share Common $3.125 par exchanged for $24.7642 cash

KANSAS BEEF INDS INC (DE)
Merged into MBPXL Corp. 9/3/74
Each share Common $1 par exchanged for (0.47619) share Common $1 par
(See MBPXL Corp.)

KANSAS CITY, CLINTON & SPRINGFIELD RAILWAY CO.
Merged into St. Louis, San Francisco Railway Co. (Old) in 1928
Details not available

KANSAS CITY, FORT SCOTT & MEMPHIS RAILWAY CO.
Merged into St. Louis, San Francisco Railway Co. (Old) in 1928
Details not available

KANSAS CITY, LAWRENCE & TOPEKA ELECTRIC RAILROAD CO.
Succeeded by Kansas City, Merriam & Shawnee Railroad 00/00/1928
Details not available

KANSAS CITY, LEAVENWORTH & WESTERN RAILWAY CO.
Succeeded by Kansas City, Leavenworth & Western Transportation Co. in 1932
Details not available

KANSAS CITY, LEAVENWORTH & WESTERN TRANSPORTATION CO.
Reorganized as Kansas City & Leavenworth Transportation Co. in 1938
Details not available

KANSAS CITY, MERRIAM & SHAWNEE RAILROAD
Operations discontinued 00/00/1934
Stockholders' equity unlikely

KANSAS CITY, ST. LOUIS & CHICAGO RAILROAD CO.
Reorganized 00/00/1947
Each share 6% Preferred (on which unpaid dividends for period prior to 01/01/1942 amounted to $7 per share) exchanged for $107 in new First Mortgage Bonds and $32.50 cash
Each share 6% Preferred (on which unpaid dividends for period prior to 01/01/1942 amounted to $16 per share) exchanged for $116 in new First Mortgage Bonds and $32.50 cash
Each share Common exchanged for $100 in new First Mortgage Bonds and $37.92 cash

KANSAS CITY & LEAVENWORTH TRANSPORTATION CO.
In process of liquidation in 1952
Details not available

KANSAS CITY BOLT & NUT CO.
Succeeded by Sheffield Steel Corp. in 1926
Details not available

KANSAS CITY CLAY COUNTY & ST. JOSEPH RAILWAY CO.
Ceased operations in 1933
No stockholders' equity

KANSAS CITY FIRE & MARINE INSURANCE CO. (MO)
Acquired by Glens Falls Insurance Co. through voluntary exchange offer in 1961
Public interest eliminated

KANSAS CITY PWR & LT CO (MO)
Common no par split (2) for (1) by issuance of (1) additional share 01/28/1963
Common no par split (3) for (2) by issuance of (0.5) additional share 11/16/1983
$10.70 Preferred no par called for redemption 08/29/1986
$17.05 Preferred no par called for redemption 03/05/1987
$12.75 Preference no par called for redemption 03/06/1987
$12.875 Preferred no par called for redemption 03/06/1987
$13.75 Preferred no par called for redemption 09/01/1987
$2.20 Preferred no par called for redemption 12/02/1991
$2.33 Preferred no par called for redemption 12/02/1991
7.72% Preferred $100 par called for redemption 02/28/1992
Common no par split (2) for (1) by issuance of (1) additional share 05/29/1992
4% Preferred $100 par called for redemption at $102.25 on 06/01/2001
Under plan of reorganization each share $3.80% Preferred $100 par, 4.20% Preferred $100 par, 4.35% Preferred $100 par, 4.50% Preferred $100 par, and Common no par automatically became (1) share Great Plains Energy Inc. 3.80% Preferred $100 par, 4.20% Preferred $100 par, 4.35% Preferred $100 par, 4.50% Preferred $100 par, and Common no par respectively 10/01/2001
Great Plains Energy Inc. merged into Evergy, Inc. 06/05/2018

KANSAS CITY POWER SECURITIES CORP.
Dissolved in 1931
Details not available

KANSAS CITY PUBLIC SERVICE CO. (MO)
Reorganized 1/6/37
Each share 7% Preferred A no par exchanged for (1) share new Common no par
Each share old Common no par exchanged for (0.1) share new Common no par
New Common no par changed to Common $5 par 12/1/44
Common $5 par changed to $1 par 7/10/51
Name changed to Kansas City Transit Inc. (MO) 6/17/60
Kansas City Transit Inc. (MO) reincorporated in Nevada as Sovereign-Western Corp. 7/1/61 which merged into Westgate-California Corp. Corp. 2/26/62
(See Westgate-California Corp.)

KANSAS CITY SOUTHN (DE)
Name changed 05/02/2002
Common 1¢ par split (3) for (1) by issuance of (2) additional shares 10/02/1978
Common 1¢ par split (2) for (1) by issuance of (1) additional share 10/05/1981
Common Stock Purchase Rights declared for Common stockholders of record 05/27/1986 were redeemed at $0.0125 per right 09/20/1994 for holders of record 08/26/1994
Common 1¢ par split (2) for (1) by issuance of (1) additional share 03/16/1992
Common 1¢ par split (2) for (1) by issuance of (1) additional share 03/17/1993
Common 1¢ par split (3) for (1) by issuance of (2) additional shares payable 09/16/1997 to holders of record 08/25/1997 Ex date - 09/17/1997
Each share old Common 1¢ par received distribution of (2) shares Stilwell Financial, Inc. Common 1¢ par payable 07/12/2000 to holders of record 06/28/2000
Each share old Common 1¢ par exchanged for (0.5) share new Common 1¢ par 07/12/2000
Name changed from Kansas City Southern Industries, Inc. to Kansas City Southern 05/02/2002
Each share 5.125% Conv. Perpetual Preferred Ser. D $1 par exchanged for (33.3333) shares Common 1¢ par 03/10/2011
(Additional Information in Active)

KANSAS CITY SOUTHN RY CO (MO)
Common $100 par changed to no par in 1939
4% Preferred $100 par changed to $50 par and (1) additional share issued in 1953
Common no par split (2) for (1) by issuance of (1) additional share in 1953
Each (7,000) shares 4% Preferred $50 par exchanged for (1) share 4% Preferred $350,000 par 3/10/82
Each (2,000) shares Common no par exchanged for (1) share Common no par 3/10/82
Note: In effect holders received $30 cash per share of Preferred, $210 cash per share of Common and public interest was eliminated

KANSAS CITY STK YDS CO ME (ME)
5% Preferred $100 par called for redemption 12/1/76
Liquidation completed
Each share Common $100 par exchanged for initial distribution of $45 cash plus a Non-Negotiable Receipt 12/15/76
Each share Common $100 par received second distribution of $10 cash 6/24/77
Each share Common $100 par received third distribution of $12 cash 5/15/78
Each share Common $100 par received fourth distribution of $8 cash 5/25/79
Each share Common $100 par received fifth distribution of $4 cash 2/11/80
Each share Common $100 par received sixth distribution of $6 cash 4/23/80
Each share Common $100 par received seventh distribution of $10 cash 12/15/80
Each share Common $100 par received eighth distribution of $8 cash 2/12/82
Note: an additional and final distribution of $128 cash per share was made 4/22/83

KANSAS CITY TRANSIT INC. (MO)
Reincorporated under the laws of Nevada as Sovereign-Western Corp. 7/1/61
Sovereign-Western Corp. merged into Westgate-California Corp. 2/26/62
(See Westgate-California Corp.)

KANSAS CRUDE OIL & GAS CO. (SD)
Charter expired by time limitation 2/24/21

KANSAS ELECTRIC POWER CO.
Merged into Kansas Power & Light Co. and Preferred exchanged share for share 00/00/1949
Kansas Power & Light Co. name changed to Western Resources, Inc. 05/08/1992 which name changed to Westar Energy, Inc. 06/19/2002 which merged into Evergy, Inc. 06/05/2018

KANSAS GAS & ELEC CO. (KS)
Reincorporated 06/01/1973
4.6% Preferred $100 par called for redemption 04/01/1963
Common no par split (2) for (1) by issuance of (1) additional share 06/07/1955
Common no par split (2) for (1) by issuance of (1) additional share 06/08/1962
State of incorporation changed from (WV) to (KS) 06/01/1973
$2.42 Preferred $100 par called for redemption 11/03/1986
7.44% Preferred $100 par called for redemption 11/03/1986
$8.66 Preferred $100 par called for redemption 11/03/1986
$15.50 Preferred $100 par called for redemption 11/03/1986
Merged into Kansas Power & Light Co. 03/31/1992
Each share 4.28% Serial Preferred $100 par exchanged for $101 cash
Each share 4.32% Serial Preferred $100 par exchanged for $101.64 cash
Each share 4.5% Preferred $100 par exchanged for $110 cash
Each share Common no par exchanged for (1.347) shares Common $5 par
Kansas Power & Light Co. name changed to Western Resources, Inc. 05/08/1992 which name changed to Westar Energy, Inc. 06/19/2002 which merged into Evergy, Inc. 06/05/2018

KANSAS NEB NAT GAS INC (KS)
$6 Preferred called for redemption 9/17/43
Common $5 par split (2) for (1) by issuance of (1) additional share 7/15/60
Common $5 par split (3) for (2) by issuance of (0.5) additional share 11/1/71
$5.65 Preferred no par called for redemption 10/1/77
Stock Dividends - 10% 7/1/41; 16-2/3% 5/21/45; 16-2/3% 10/31/47; 10% 1/31/49; 10% 12/20/61; 10% 12/30/66; 10% 7/10/69; 10% 7/25/80; 10% 7/19/82
Name changed to K N Energy, Inc. 4/1/83
K N Energy, Inc. name changed to Kinder Morgan, Inc. (KS) 10/7/99
(See Kinder Morgan, Inc. (KS))

KANSAS OIL CO., INC. (DE)
No longer in existence having become inoperative and void for non-payment of taxes 10/1/56

KANSAS OKLA & GULF RY CO (OK)
6% Ser. A. Preferred $100 par, 6% Non-Cum Ser. B Preferred $100 par and 6% Non-Cum Ser. C Preferred $100 par called for redemption 3/1/65

KANSAS PIPE LINE & GAS CO.
Each share Common $100 par exchanged for (20) shares Common $5 par in 1936
Name changed to Kansas-Nebraska Natural Gas Co., Inc. in 1941
Kansas-Nebraska Natural Gas Co., Inc. name changed to K N Energy, Inc. 4/1/83 which name changed to Kinder Morgan, Inc. (KS) 10/7/99
(See Kinder Morgan, Inc. (KS))

KAN-KAR

KANSAS PWR & LT CO (KS)
Common $8.75 par changed for $5 par and (1) additional share issued 06/01/1965
$2.23 Preferred no par called for redemption 04/01/1987
$2.32 Preferred no par called for redemption 04/01/1987
Common $5 par split (2) for (1) by issuance of (1) additional share 05/21/1987
Name changed to Western Resources, Inc. 05/08/1992
Western Resources, Inc. name changed to Westar Energy, Inc. 06/19/2002 which merged into Evergy, Inc. 06/05/2018

KANSAS POWER CO.
Merged into Western Light & Telephone Co., Inc. in 1945
Each share 7% Preferred exchanged for (4) shares Preferred and $1 cash
Each share 6% Preferred exchanged for (4) shares Preferred
(See Western Light & Telephone Co., Inc.)

KANSAS SEC LIFE INS INC (KS)
Merged into Central United Corp. 3/31/75
Each share Common $1 par exchanged for (2.84) shares Common $1 par
(See Central United Corp.)

KANSAS SOYA PRODS INC (KS)
Liquidation completed
Each share $5 Preferred $95 par exchanged for $142.50 cash in November 1970
Each share Common 25¢ par exchanged for initial distribution of $1 cash in November 1970
Each share Common 25¢ par received second distribution of $1 cash in March 1971
Each share Common 25¢ par received third distribution of $1.50 cash in July 1971
Each share Common 25¢ par received fourth and final distribution of $0.45 cash in September 1971

KANSAS ST BK (WICHITA, KS)
Name changed to Kansas State Bank & Trust Co. (Wichita, KS) 7/3/67

KANSAS ST NETWORK INC (KS)
Common no par changed to 50¢ par 10/30/69
Acquired by Standard Communications Inc. 3/2/81
Each share Common 50¢ par exchanged for $33.50 cash

KANSAS ST TEL CO (DE)
Merged into Continental Telecom Inc. 10/28/82
Each share Common no par exchanged for (5) shares Common $1 par
Continental Telecom Inc. name changed to Contel Corp. 5/1/86 which merged into GTE Corp. 3/14/91 which merged into Verizon Communications Inc. 6/30/2000

KAO CORP (JAPAN)
Each Unsponsored ADR for Common exchanged for (1) Sponsored ADR for Common 03/15/2004
Sponsored ADR's for Common split (10) for (1) by issuance of (9) additional ADR's payable 12/15/2009 to holders of record 12/08/2009 Ex date - 12/16/2009
Basis changed from (1:10) to (1:1) 12/16/2009
Stock Dividends - 10% 06/02/1987; 10% 06/15/1992
ADR agreement terminated 04/30/2018
Each Sponsored ADR for Common exchanged for either (1) share Common or (5) Unsponsored ADR's for Common
Note: Unexchanged ADR's will be sold and the proceeds, if any, held for claim after 10/29/2018
(Additional Information in Active)

KAO SOAP LTD (JAPAN)
Stock Dividends - 10% 12/26/74; 10% 6/23/77; 10% 12/14/77
Name changed to Kao Corp. 10/1/85

KAOLIN CDA INC (ON)
Delisted from Canadian Dealers Network 01/03/1995

KAP RES LTD (YT)
Reincorporated 01/15/1991
Common no par split (2) for (1) by issuance of (1) additional share 09/20/1989
Place of incorporation changed from (BC) to (YT) 01/15/1991
Struck off register 05/17/2005

KAPALUA ACQUISITIONS INC (CO)
Name changed to Startech Environmental Corp. 01/01/1996
(See Startech Environmental Corp.)

KAPALUA GOLD MINES LTD (AB)
Recapitalized as Prize Energy Inc. 11/16/1993
Each share Common no par exchanged for (0.2) share Common no par
Prize Energy Inc. recapitalized as Canadian Superior Energy Inc. 08/28/2000 which recapitalized as Sonde Resources Corp. 06/08/2010
(See Sonde Resources Corp.)

KAPAPALA RANCH, INC. (HI)
Merged into Hawaiian Ranch Co., Inc. on a (0.7) for (1) basis 7/30/62
Hawaiian Ranch Co., Inc. merged into Brewer (C.) & Co., Ltd. 6/16/64 which merged into IU International Corp. 8/14/78
(See IU International Corp.)

KAPHEARST RESOURCE CORP (BC)
Recapitalized as Tri-Alpha Investments Ltd. 06/15/1990
Each share Common no par exchanged for (0.33333333) share Common no par
Tri-Alpha Investments Ltd. name changed to Tri-Gold Resources Corp. 12/20/2004 which recapitalized as Quadro Resources Ltd. 05/04/2009

KAPKICHI NICKEL MINES LTD. (ON)
Merged into Hoffman Exploration & Minerals Ltd. 06/29/1981
Each share Capital Stock no par exchanged for (0.23722653) share Common no par
Hoffman Exploration & Minerals Ltd. merged into Consoldated Thompson-Lundmark Gold Mines Ltd. 01/16/1986 which name changed to Consolidated Thompson Iron Mines Ltd. 08/24/2006
(See Consolidated Thompson Iron Mines Ltd.)

KAPLAN INDS INC (FL)
Each share Common 1¢ par exchanged for (0.25) share Common 4¢ par 05/19/1987
Name changed to Grand Lux, Inc. 11/06/2003
Grand Lux, Inc. recapitalized as World Hockey Association Corp. 09/23/2005

KAPOK CORP (DE)
Name changed to Hampton Healthcare Inc. 11/3/87
Hampton Healthcare Inc. reorganized as Hampton Resources Corp. 12/31/91 which merged into Bellwether Exploration Corp. 3/1/95

KAPOK TREE INNS CORP. (DE)
Stock Dividends - 50% 5/14/71; 50% 3/3/72
Under plan of merger name changed to Kapok Corp. 9/23/83
Kapok Corp. name changed to Hampton Healthcare Inc. 11/3/87 which reorganized as Hampton Resources Corp. 12/31/91 which merged into Bellwether Exploration Co. 3/1/95 which name changed to Mission Resources Corp. 5/16/2001
(See Mission Resources Corp.)

KAPPA ENERGY CORP (AB)
Name changed to Vanguard Oil Corp. 01/17/2000
Vanguard Oil Corp. acquired by Bitech Petroleum Corp. 05/24/2001
(See Bitech Petroleum Corp.)

KAPPA EXPLS LTD (ON)
Name changed to Kappa Investments Ltd. 07/12/1977

KAPPA FROCKS INC (NY)
Dissolved by proclamation 6/23/93

KAPPA INDS INC (OH)
Name changed to Natmar, Inc. 12/31/1979
Natmar, Inc. name changed to Antex Corp. 04/01/1985 which name changed back to Natmar, Inc. 07/05/1985
(See Natmar, Inc.)

KAPPA NETWORKS INC (NJ)
Reincorporated under the laws of Pennsylvania as Polyphase Corp. 6/28/91
Polyphase Corp. (PA) reincorporated in Nevada 6/29/94 which name changed to Overhill Corp. 3/22/2001 which name changed to TreeCon Resources, Inc. 10/28/2002

KAPPA RESOURCE CORP (BC)
Name changed to Offshore Systems International Ltd. 04/23/1990
Offshore Systems International Ltd. name changed to OSI Geospatial Inc. 06/05/2006
(See OSI Geospatial Inc.)

KAPPA RES LTD (AB)
Merged into Aber Resources Ltd. (Old) 08/07/1984
Each share Common no par exchanged for (0.66666666) share Common no par
Aber Resources Ltd. (Old) merged into Aber Resources Ltd. (New) 04/19/1994 which name changed to Aber Diamond Corp. 08/18/2000 which name changed to Harry Winston Diamond Corp. 11/19/2007 which name changed to Dominion Diamond Corp. 03/27/2013
(See Dominion Diamond Corp.)

KAPPA SYS INC (DE)
Reincorporated 6/1/79
Each share old Common no par exchanged for (0.2) share new Common no par 7/18/73
State of incorporation changed from (PA) to (DE) 6/1/79
Each share new Common no par exchanged for (0.5) share Common 1¢ par
Merged into Micronet Services, Inc. 11/24/81
Each share Common 1¢ par exchanged for $3.50 cash

KAPS TRANS LTD (AB)
Common no par split (3) for (1) by issuance of (2) additional shares 11/21/1969
Name changed to Strathcona Resource Industries Ltd. 04/29/1981
Strathcona Resource Industries Ltd. recapitalized as Clarepine Industries Inc. 05/24/1988
(See Clarepine Industries Inc.)

KAPSON SR QUARTERS CORP (DE)
Merged into Prometheus Senior Quarters, LLC 4/7/98
Each share Conv. Exchangeable Accrued Investor Preferred exchanged for $27.93 cash
Each share Conv. Exchangeable Preferred 144A exchanged for $27.93 cash
Each share Common 1¢ par exchanged for $14.50 cash

KAR PRODS INC (DE)
Common $1 par split (3) for (2) by issuance of (0.5) additional share 8/15/75
Merged into Sun Distributors Inc. 5/13/77
Each share Common $1 par exchanged for $18 cash

KAR VENTURES INC (NV)
Name changed to Clarion House, Inc. (NV) 02/27/1991
Clarion House, Inc. (NV) reincorporated in Delaware as Clarion Technologies Inc. 10/02/1998
(See Clarion Technologies, Inc.)

KARA COMMODITY FUND, INC. (DE)
Dissolved 12/23/58

KARA INTL INC (NV)
Each share old Common $0.001 par exchanged for (0.004) share new Common $0.001 par 1/4/95
Each share new Common $0.001 par exchanged again for (0.2) share new Common $0.001 par 4/9/97
Name changed to International Heritage Inc. 3/3/98

KARAT PLATINUM INC (NV)
Charter cancelled 08/01/2011

KARAT PRODUCTIONS INC (NV)
Name changed to Ghiglieri Corp. 06/05/1997
Ghiglieri Corp. name changed to GRG, Inc. 03/03/1998 which recapitalized as HumWare Media Corp. 01/11/2005 which recapitalized as EFT Biotech Holdings, Inc. 11/20/2007 which name changed to EFT Holdings, Inc. 05/27/2011

KARCHER CARL ENTERPRISES INC (CA)
Common no par split (5) for (4) by issuance of (0.25) additional share 02/15/1983
Common no par split (3) for (2) by issuance of (0.5) additional share 08/07/1987
Common no par split (2) for (1) by issuance of (1) additional share 07/14/1989
Reincorporated under the laws of Delaware as CKE Restaurants, Inc. and Common no par changed to 1¢ par 06/21/1994
(See CKE Restaurants, Inc.)

KARDAR CDN OILS LTD (ON)
Charter cancelled and declared dissolved for failure to file returns and pay fees 11/09/1976

KAREL CAP CORP (AB)
Merged into Preo Software Inc. (New) 08/03/2010
Each share Common no par exchanged for (0.33333333) share Common no par
(See Preo Software Inc. (New))

KARI RES EXPLS LTD (ON)
Reorganized as San Paulo Explorations Ltd. 08/09/1983
Each share Common no par exchanged for (0.33333333) share Common no par
San Paulo Explorations Ltd. reorganized as AdvanteXCEL.com Communications Corp. 01/04/1999
(See AdvanteXCEL.com Communications Corp.)

KARIANA RES INC (BC)
Each share old Common no par exchanged for (0.25) share new Common no par 01/27/2014
Name changed to Lifestyle Delivery Systems Inc. 05/06/2015

KARIBA ENTERPRISES LTD (BC)
Recapitalized as Poney Explorations Ltd. 02/14/1977

KAR-KAT   **FINANCIAL INFORMATION, INC.**

Each share Capital Stock 50¢ par exchanged for (1/3) share Capital Stock no par
Poney Explorations Ltd. recapitalized as Steed Ventures Corp. 11/14/1985
(See Steed Ventures Corp.)

KARIBA MINES LTD. (BC)
Name changed to Kariba Enterprises Ltd. 08/19/1974
Each share Capital Stock 50¢ par exchanged for (1) share Capital Stock 50¢ par
Kariba Enterprises Ltd. recapitalized as Poney Explorations Ltd. 02/14/1977 which recapitalized as Steed Ventures Corp. 11/14/1985
(See Steed Ventures Corp.)

KARIN LAKE EXPLS LTD (BC)
Delisted from Vancouver Stock Exchange 11/06/1987

KARISMA CAP CORP (AB)
Recapitalized as EMM Energy Inc. 06/16/2003
Each share Common no par exchanged for (0.5) share Common no par
EMM Energy Inc. merged into SkyWest Energy Corp. 06/22/2010 which recapitalized as Marquee Energy Ltd. (Old) 12/09/2011 which merged into Marquee Energy Ltd. (New) 12/08/2016

KARMA CAP CORP (BC)
Reorganized under the laws of Ontario as Biosign Technologies Inc. 07/10/2006
Each share Common no par exchanged for (0.05) share Common no par
(See Biosign Technologies Inc.)

KARMA MEDIA INC (NV)
Recapitalized as Pit BOSS Entertainment, Inc. 07/18/2005
Each share Common $0.001 par exchanged for (0.1) share Common $0.001 par
Pit BOSS Entertainment, Inc. name changed to US Energy Holdings, Inc. 03/08/2006 which name changed to Lonestar Group Holdings, Co. 01/10/2007 which recapitalized as Guardian Angel Group, Inc. 12/14/2007 which recapitalized as Ree International, Inc. 06/29/2011

KARMA VENTURES INC (BC)
Name changed to Donner Resources Ltd. 12/21/1982
(See Donner Resources Ltd.)

KARNET CAP CORP (NV)
Name changed to Jin Wan Hong International Holdings Ltd. 12/27/2016

KAROO EXPL CORP (BC)
Recapitalized as Bruin Point Helium Corp. 12/11/2017
Each share Common no par exchanged for (0.07407407) share Common no par
Bruin Point Helium Corp. name changed to American Helium Inc. 05/11/2018

KARPUS GOLD MINES LTD. (ON)
Charter surrendered 05/28/1957

KARRINGTON HEALTH INC (OH)
Issue Information - 3,000,000 shares COM offered at $13 per share on 07/18/1996
Merged into Sunrise Assisted Living, Inc. 05/14/1999
Each share Common no par exchanged for (0.3333) share Common 1¢ par
Sunrise Assisted Living, Inc. name changed to Sunrise Senior Living, Inc. 05/30/2003
(See Sunrise Senior Living, Inc.)

KARRINGTON HLDG CORP (NV)
Each share old Common $0.001 par exchanged for (3) shares new Common $0.001 par 12/13/2005
Name changed to World Wide Energy Corp. 03/23/2006
World Wide Energy Corp. recapitalized as Czech Republic Resource Corp. 10/30/2007 which name changed to Global Senior Enterprises Inc. 04/26/2013 which recapitalized as World Financial Holding Group 05/01/2018

KARRISON COMPAGNIE INC (NV)
Recapitalized as American Fidelity Financial Services, Inc. 4/12/2004
Each share Common $0.001 par exchanged for (0.4) share Common $0.001 par
American Fidelity Financial Services, Inc. name changed to Trinity Capital Partners, Inc. 11/10/2006

KARSTADT (RUDOLPH) INC. (GERMANY)
Name changed to Karstadt AG 7/9/63
(See Karstadt AG)

KARSTADT A G (GERMANY)
American Shares DM4-4/9 par changed to DM5-5/9 par to reflect a 25% undistributed stock dividend 06/29/1965
American Shares DM5-5/9 par changed to DM5-25/27 par to reflect a 6-2/3% undistributed stock dividend 06/23/1966
Depositary agreement terminated 02/28/1993
Each American Share DM5-5/9 par exchanged for $40.936 cash

KARTING INTL INC (NV)
SEC revoked common stock registration 09/15/2008

KARTS INTL INC (NV)
Each share old Common $0.001 par exchanged for (0.16666666) share new Common $0.001 par 03/24/1997
Each share new Common $0.001 par exchanged again for (0.002) share new Common $0.001 par 03/06/2006
Note: Holders of (9,999) shares or fewer will receive (20) shares
Name changed to 4D Seismic, Inc. 04/11/2016
(See 4D Seismic, Inc.)

KARVER INTL INC (NY)
Dissolved by proclamation 07/28/2010

KASBA EXPLORATIONS LTD. (ON)
Charter surrendered and company declared dissolved 12/07/1964

KASCO FINL CORP (MI)
Merged into Huntington Bancshares Inc. 11/28/86
Each share Common $10 par exchanged for (4.2775) shares Common no par and $248.5227 cash

KASH N KARRY FOOD STORES INC NEW (DE)
Common 1¢ par split (3) for (2) by issuance of (0.5) additional share 07/17/1995
Merged into Food Lion, Inc. 12/18/1996
Each share Common 1¢ par exchanged for $26 cash

KASH N KARRY FOOD STORES INC OLD (DE)
Each share old Common no par exchanged for (0.025) share new Common no par 11/13/90
Plan of reorganization under Chapter 11 of the Federal Bankruptcy Code effective 12/29/94
No stockholders' equity

KASHIYAMA & CO LTD (JAPAN)
Each old ADR for Common 50 Yen par exchanged for (2) new ADR's for Common 50 Yen par 06/28/1982
Stock Dividend - 8% 04/30/1987
Name changed to Onward Kashiyama Co. Ltd. 09/02/1988
Onward Kashiyama Co. Ltd. name changed to Onward Holdings Co., Inc. 09/06/2007

KASHMIR OIL INC (UT)
Charter suspended for failure to pay taxes 09/15/1970

KASKADA RES LTD (BC)
Merged into Canadian Futurity Oils Ltd. 11/01/1985
Each share Common no par exchanged for (0.15384615) share Class A no par
Canadian Futurity Oils Ltd. recapitalized as Baca Resources Ltd. 08/04/1989 which name changed to CORDEX Petroleums Ltd. 07/11/1994
(See CORDEX Petroleums Ltd.)

KASLER CORP (CA)
Common no par split (3) for (2) by issuance of (0.5) additional share 5/31/91
Stock Dividends - 10% 2/15/83; 10% 2/15/84; 10% 2/15/85
Merged into Kasler Holding Co. 7/12/93
Each share Common no par exchanged for (1) share Common 1¢ par
Kasler Holding Co. name changed Washington Construction Group, Inc. 4/8/96 which name changed to Morrison Knudsen Corp. (New) 9/11/96

KASLER HLDG CO (DE)
Name changed to Washington Construction Group, Inc. 4/8/96
Washington Construction Group, Inc. name changed to Morrison Knudsen Corp. (New) 9/11/96 which changed to Washington Group International, Inc. 9/15/2000
(See Washington Group International, Inc.)

KASLO BASE METALS LTD. (BC)
Struck off register and declared dissolved for failure to file returns 03/12/1964
No stockholders' equity

KASLO MINES CORP. (ID)
Name changed to Victor Industries, Inc. and Class A Capital 7¢ par and Class B Capital 3¢ par reclassified as Common 5¢ par respectively 09/08/1980
Victor Industries, Inc. (ID) reorganized in Nevada as Ethos Environmental, Inc. 11/16/2006 which name changed to Regeneca, Inc. 06/14/2011
(See Regeneca, Inc.)

KASPER A S L LTD (DE)
Plan of reorganization under Chapter 11 Federal Bankruptcy Code effective 12/01/2003
Each share Common 1¢ par exchanged for initial distribution of $4.04 cash 12/01/2003
Each share Common 1¢ par received second distribution of $2.30 cash 01/29/2004
Each share Common 1¢ par received third distribution of $7.20 cash 04/27/2004
Each share Common 1¢ par received fourth distribution of $1.05 cash 06/03/2004
Each share Common 1¢ par received fifth distribution of $0.18 cash 12/16/2004
Each share Common 1¢ par received sixth distribution of $0.28 cash 08/02/2005
Each share Common 1¢ par received seventh distribution of approximately $0.1241 cash payable 06/23/2006 to holders of record 12/01/2003
Each share Common 1¢ par received eighth and final distribution of approximately $0.6225 cash payable 10/24/2008 to holders of record 12/01/2003
Note: Unexchanged certificates were cancelled and became without value 01/31/2006

KASSAN RES INC (BC)
Recapitalized as Consolidated Kassan Resources Inc. 01/15/1993
Each share Common no par exchanged for (0.45454545) share Common no par
Consolidated Kassan Resources Inc. name changed to East Africa Gold Corp. 01/16/1995
(See East Africa Gold Corp.)

KAST TELECOM INC (CANADA)
Reincorporated under the laws of Luxembourg as Kast Telecom Europe S.A. 04/25/2001

KASTEN CHASE APPLIED RESH LTD (AB)
Reincorporated 07/24/2007
Place of incorporation changed from (ON) to (AB) 07/24/2007
Recapitalized as Kasten Energy Inc. 03/02/2010
Each share Common no par exchanged for (0.001) share Common no par

KAT GOLD HLDGS CORP (NV)
Recapitalized as RemSleep Holdings, Inc. 03/26/2015
Each share Common $0.001 par exchanged for (0.0005) share Common $0.001 par

KAT RACING (NV)
Name changed to Prairie West Oil & Gas Ltd. 02/06/2013
Prairie West Oil & Gas Ltd. recapitalized as Pacific Oil Co. 09/16/2013 which name changed to Financial Gravity Companies, Inc. 01/30/2017

KATANA RES LTD (AB)
Struck off register and declared dissolved for failure to file returns 05/01/1992

KATANGA MNG LTD (BERMUDA)
Reincorporated under the laws of Yukon 09/26/2011

KATE GREENAWAY INDS INC (DE)
Common no par changed to 10¢ par 9/22/76
Liquidated under Chapter 7 bankruptcy proceedings 6/24/82
Each share Common 10¢ par received initial distribution of $1.0442 cash 12/24/86
Each share Common 10¢ par received second and final distribution of $0.10585 cash 8/30/88
Note: Certificates were not required to be surrendered and are now valueless

KATE SPADE & CO (DE)
Acquired by Coach, Inc. 07/11/2017
Each share Common $1 par exchanged for $18.50 cash

KATERI MINING CO. LTD. (ON)
Charter cancelled and company declared dissolved for default in filing returns 01/20/1971

KATHOL PETE INC (KS)
Merged into Indian Wells Oil Co. 12/30/76
Each share Common $1 par exchanged for $3 cash

KATHY J INC (NY)
Name changed to BI State Industries Corp. 4/12/74
(See BI State Industries Corp.)

KATIE GOLD CORP (NV)
Common $0.001 par split (20) for (1) by issuance of (19) additional shares payable 03/21/2006 to

holders of record 03/17/2006
Ex date - 03/22/2006
Name changed to Morningstar Industrial Holdings Corp. 04/06/2006
Morningstar Industrial Holdings Corp. name changed to New World Entertainment Corp. 05/01/2006 which name changed to Aultra Gold, Inc. 01/19/2007 which name changed to Shamika 2 Gold, Inc. 02/02/2011
(See Shamika 2 Gold, Inc.)

KATLOR ENVIRONMENTAL TECH INC (BC)
Name changed 07/06/1993
Name changed from Katlor Explorations Ltd. to Katlor Environmental Tech. Inc. 07/06/1993
Recapitalized as Barbican Financial Corp. 06/20/1995
Each share Common no par exchanged for (0.11111111) share Common no par
(See Barbican Financial Corp.)

KATRAK VEHICLE CO. (OR)
Capital Stock $1 par reclassified as Common $1 par 3/23/68
Name changed to Planet Junior Corp. 1/4/73
Planet Junior Corp. name changed to Riverside Metal Products Co. (OR) 7/7/75 which reorganized in Michigan 2/25/77
(See Riverside Metal Products Co. (MI))

KATY INDS INC (DE)
$1.46 Class B Conv. Preferred no par called for redemption 12/21/90
(Additional Information in Active)

KATZ DIGITAL TECHNOLOGIES INC (DE)
Merged into Photobition Group PLC 12/2/98
Each share Common $0.001 par exchanged for $8.78 cash

KATZ DRUG CO (DE)
Stock Dividend - 10% 12/22/67
Voting Trust Agreement terminated 10/9/70
Merged into Skaggs Companies, Inc. 12/31/70
Each share Common $1 par exchanged for (1.25) shares Common $1 par
Skaggs Companies, Inc. name changed to American Stores Co. (New) 7/26/79 which merged into Albertson's, Inc. 6/23/99 which merged into Supervalu Inc. 6/2/2006

KATZ MEDIA GROUP INC (DE)
Merged into Morris Acquisition Corp. 10/28/97
Each share Common 1¢ par exchanged for $11 cash

KATZENBACH & WARREN, INC. (NY)
Merged into Simmons Co. 11/30/68
Each share Common $1 par exchanged for (0.226757) share Common no par
(See Simmons Co.)

KAUAI ENGINEERING WORKS, LTD. (HI)
Name changed to Nawiliwili Canning Co., Ltd. (HI) in 1950
(See Nawiliwili Canning Co., Ltd. (HI))

KAUFEL GROUP LTD (CANADA)
Merged into Thomas & Betts Canada Inc. 11/13/1998
Each share Class A Common no par exchanged for $8 cash
Each share Class B Subordinate no par exchanged for $8 cash

KAUFHOF HLDG AG (GERMANY)
Merged into Metro AG 8/12/96
Each Sponsored ADR for Ordinary no par exchanged for $35.64 cash

KAUFMAN & BROAD BUILDING CO. (MD)
Common $1 par split (3) for (2) by issuance of (0.5) additional share 5/18/67
Common $1 par split (3) for (2) by issuance of (0.5) additional share 2/14/68
Name changed to Kaufman & Broad, Inc. 4/23/68
Kaufman & Broad, Inc. name changed to Broad, Inc. 3/8/89 which name changed to SunAmerica Inc. 2/1/93 which merged into American International Group, Inc. 1/1/99

KAUFMAN & BROAD HOME CORP (DE)
Each share Special Common $1 par exchanged for (0.95) share Common $1 par 11/30/1994
Each $1.52 Depositary Preferred exchanged for (1) share Common $1 par 04/01/1996
Each share $1.52 Mandatory Conversion Preferred Premium Dividend Ser. B $1 par exchanged for (5) shares Common $1 par 04/01/1996
Name changed to KB Home 01/17/2001

KAUFMAN & BROAD INC (MD)
Common $1 par split (2) for (1) by issuance of (1) additional share 1/10/69
Common $1 par split (3) for (2) by issuance of (0.5) additional share 2/13/70
Common $1 par split (2) for (1) by issuance of (1) additional share 8/18/71
Common $1 par split (3) for (2) by issuance of (0.5) additional share 5/12/86
$8.75 Conv. Exchangeable Preferred Ser. B no par called for redemption 3/25/87
Common $1 par split (3) for (2) by issuance of (0.5) additional share 8/28/87
Name changed to Broad, Inc. 3/8/89
Broad Inc. name changed to SunAmerica Inc. 2/1/93

KAUFMAN H W FINL GROUP INC (MI)
Common no par split (3) for (2) by issuance of (0.5) additional share 09/10/1990
Stock Dividends - 10% 05/05/1994; 10% 05/17/1995
Merged into AJK Acquisition Corp. 01/04/1996
Each share Common no par exchanged for $8.20 cash

KAUFMANN DEPARTMENT STORES, INC.
Merged into May Department Stores Co. and each share Common exchanged for (0.2) share $3.40 Preferred and (0.45) share Common in 1946
May Department Stores Co. merged into Federated Department Stores, Inc. 8/30/2005 which name changed to Macy's, Inc. 6/1/2007

KAUFMANN DEPARTMENT STORES SECURITIES CORP.
Acquired by Kaufmann Department Stores, Inc. in 1938
Each share Common exchanged for (0.3069438) share Preferred and (3.069438) shares Common
Kaufmann Department Stores, Inc. merged into May Department Stores Co. in 1946 which merged into Federated Department Stores, Inc. 8/30/2005 which name changed to Macy's, Inc. 6/1/2007

KAUFMANN FD INC (MD)
Reincorporated 02/09/1993
State of incorporation changed from (NY) to (MD) and Common 10¢ par changed to 1¢ par 02/09/1993
Under plan of reorganization each share Common 1¢ par automatically became (1) share Federated Equity Funds Kaufmann Fund Class K 04/20/2001

KAVALMEDIA SVCS LTD (BC)
Name changed to EmerGeo Solutions Worldwide Inc. 08/05/2008
(See EmerGeo Solutions Worldwide Inc.)

KAVANAGH-SMITH & CO. (NC)
Name changed to Key Co. (NC) 2/28/68
(See Key Co. (NC))

KAVANAU CORP. (DE)
Reorganized under the laws of Massachusetts as Kavanau Real Estate Trust 12/31/1966
Each share Common $1 par exchanged for (1) Share of Bene. Int. $1 par
Kavanau Real Estate Trust acquired by BRT Realty Trust (MA) 02/07/1984 which reorganized as BRT Apartments Corp. (MD) 03/18/2017

KAVANAU REAL ESTATE TR (MA)
Acquired by BRT Realty Trust (MA) 02/07/1984
Each Share of Bene. Int. $1 par exchanged for (0.1691) Share of Bene. Int. $1 par
BRT Realty Trust (MA) reorganized as BRT Apartments Corp. (MD) 03/18/2017

KAW-CROW PATRICIA GOLD MINES LTD. (ON)
Charter revoked for failure to file reports and pay fees 03/18/1965

KAWASAKI STL CORP (JAPAN)
Each Unsponsored ADR for Common 50 Yen par exchanged for (1) Sponsored ADR for Common 50 Yen par 1/6/92
ADR agreement terminated 9/16/2002
Each Sponsored ADR for Common 50 Yen par exchanged for $11.813 cash

KAWEAH NATL BK (VISALIA, CA)
Stock Dividends - 5% payable 10/29/99 to holders of record 9/24/99; 5% payable 10/31/2000 to holders of record 9/29/2000 Ex date - 10/11/2000; 5% payable 10/31/2001 to holders of record 9/28/2001 Ex date - 10/2/2001; 5% payable 10/31/2002 to holders of record 9/27/2002 Ex date - 9/30/2002
Merged into CVB Financial Corp. 9/19/2003
Each share Common $5 par exchanged for $29.80 cash

KAWECKI BERYLCO INDS INC (PA)
Merged into Cabot Corp. 5/31/78
Each share Common $1 par exchanged for $29 cash

KAWECKI CHEM CO (PA)
Stock Dividend - 100% 6/30/61
Merged into Kawecki Berylco Industries, Inc. 10/15/68
Each share Capital Stock 25¢ par exchanged for (1) share Common $1 par
(See Kawecki Berylco Industries, Inc.)

KAWNEER CO. (DE)
Reincorporated 02/14/1955
State of incorporation changed from (MI) to (DE) 02/14/1955
Common $5 par split (3) for (1) by issuance of (2) additional shares 06/30/1955
Merged into American Metal Climax, Inc. 08/31/1962
Each share Common $5 par exchanged for (0.33333333) share 4.25% Conv. Preferred $100 par
(See American Metal Climax, Inc.)

KAY (MARY) COSMETICS, INC. (TX)
See - Mary Kay Cosmetics Inc

KAY CORP (DE)
Common $1 par split (5) for (4) by issuance of (0.25) additional share 03/21/1986
Stock Dividends - 10% 03/14/1980; 15% 03/16/1981
Name changed to Balfour Maclaine Corp. 05/26/1988
Balfour Maclaine Corp. recapitalized as Anti Aging Medical Group Corp. 01/23/2006 which name changed to Innolife Pharma, Inc. 05/02/2007

KAY FOODS CORP (MD)
Assets sold for benefit of creditors 6/24/71
No stockholders' equity

KAY HAYS MINES, LTD. (ON)
Charter cancelled for failure to file reports and pay taxes 00/00/1948

KAY JEWELERS INC (DE)
Common $1 par split (5) for (4) by issuance of (0.25) additional share 03/21/1986
Common $1 par split (5) for (4) by issuance of (0.25) additional share 03/20/1987
Common $1 par split (5) for (4) by issuance of (0.25) additional share 03/21/1988
Common $1 par split (5) for (4) by issuance of (0.25) additional share 03/21/1989
Acquired by Ratners Group plc 10/26/1990
Each share Common $1 par exchanged for (1) ADR for Conv. Preferred 1p par
Ratners Group plc name changed to Signet Group PLC (United Kingdom) 09/10/1993 which reorganized in Bermuda as Signet Jewelers Ltd. 09/11/2008

KAY JEWELRY STORES INC (DE)
Capital Stock $1 par split (2) for (1) by issuance of (1) additional share 11/1/66
Name changed to Kay Corp. and Capital Stock $1 par reclassified as Common $1 par 7/28/72
Kay Corp. name changed to Balfour Maclaine Corp. 5/26/88 which recapitalized as Anti Aging Medical Group Corp. 1/23/2006 which name changed to Innolife Pharma, Inc. 5/2/2007

KAY LAB (CA)
Completely liquidated 6/6/57
Each share Class A Common $1 par received first and final distribution of (1) share Cohu Electronics, Inc. Class A Common $1 par
Note: Certificates were not required to be surrendered and are without value
(See Cohu Electronics, Inc.)

KAY LABS INC (CA)
Merged into American Hospital Supply Corp. 8/5/82
Each share Common 10¢ par exchanged for (0.0616597) share Common no par
American Hospital Supply Corp. merged into Baxter Travenol Laboratories, Inc. 11/25/85 which name changed to Baxter International Inc. 5/18/88

KAY LAKE MINES LTD. (MB)
Name changed to Scope Resources Ltd. 2/15/68
Scope Resources Ltd. recapitalized as New Scope Resources Ltd. 3/1/78 which reincorporated in Canada as Newscope Resources Ltd. 9/13/84 which recapitalized as Canadian Newscope Resources Ltd. 12/13/90 which name changed back to Newscope Resources Ltd. 7/11/94

KAY MARY INC (TX)
Name changed to Kay (Mary) Cosmetics, Inc. 4/23/69
(See Kay (Mary) Cosmetics, Inc.)

KAY MERCHANDISING INTL LTD (DE)
Name changed to Betterway Telecom Ltd. 8/11/2004
Betterway Telecom Ltd. recapitalized as KDW Telecom, Inc. 12/31/2004 which recapitalized as KSW Industries, Inc. 9/12/2005

KAY WINDSOR INC (DE)
Class A Common $1 par reclassified as Common $1 par 1/23/69
Merged into V.F. Corp. 5/14/71
Each share Common $1 par exchanged for (0.85) share Common no par

KAYAK SOFTWARE CORP (DE)
Merged into priceline.com, Inc. 05/21/2013
Each share Class A Common $0.001 par exchanged for $40 cash

KAYBEE STORES, INC.
Acquired by Dejay Stores, Inc. in 1932
Details not available

KAYDON CORP (DE)
Common 10¢ par split (2) for (1) by issuance of (1) additional share 05/15/1992
Common 10¢ par split (2) for (1) by issuance of (1) additional share payable 10/21/1997 to holders of record 10/07/1997 Ex date - 10/22/1997
Acquired by Atlas Management, Inc. 10/16/2013
Each share Common 10¢ par exchanged for $35.50 cash

KAYE GROUP INC (DE)
Merged into Hub International Ltd. (ONT) 6/28/2001
Each share Common 1¢ par exchanged for $14 cash

KAYE-HALBERT CORP. (CA)
Charter suspended for failure to pay franchise taxes 11/03/1958

KAYE KOTTS ASSOCS INC (DE)
Chapter 7 bankruptcy proceedings closed 05/02/2003
No stockholders' equity

KAYEL MACHINE & TOOL CORP. (MI)
Charter voided for non-payment of franchise fees 5/15/56

KAYENTA KREATIONS INC (NV)
Reorganized as Geospatial Holdings, Inc. 04/28/2008
Each share Common $0.001 par exchanged for (2.8) shares Common $0.001 par
Geospatial Holdings, Inc. name changed to Geospatial Corp. 08/18/2015

KAYEX CORP (NY)
Common 10¢ par split (3) for (2) by issuance of (0.5) additional share 1/14/80
Acquired by General Signal Corp. 8/19/80
Each share Common 10¢ par exchanged for (0.8) share Common $1 par
General Signal Corp. merged into SPX Corp. 10/6/98

KAYJON MINERALS LTD. (ON)
Name changed to Spartex Oil & Gas Ltd. 07/01/1970
Spartex Oil & Gas Ltd. merged into Newore Developments Ltd. 03/19/1973
(See Newore Developments Ltd.)

KAYMAC GOLD MINES LTD. (ON)
Charter cancelled for failure to pay taxes and file returns 06/21/1972

KAYMARQ CONS CORP (DE)
Dissolved 9/30/71
No stockholders' equity

KAYMO MINERALS LTD. (ON)
Charter cancelled and declared dissolved for failure to file returns and pay fees 04/09/1975

KAYNAR TECHNOLOGIES INC (DE)
Merged into Fairchild Corp. 04/20/1999
Each share Common 1¢ par exchanged for $28.75 cash

KAYNE ANDERSON ENERGY DEV CO (MD)
Merged into Kayne Anderson MLP/Midstream Investment Co. 08/06/2018
Each share Common $0.001 par exchanged for (0.96082101) share Common $0.001 par

KAYNE ANDERSON ENERGY TOTAL RETURN FD INC (MD)
Auction Rate Preferred Ser. C called for redemption at $25,000 on 09/02/2008
Auction Rate Preferred Ser. A called for redemption at $25,000 on 09/03/2008
Auction Rate Preferred Ser. B called for redemption at $25,000 on 09/04/2008
Merged into Kayne Anderson Midstream/Energy Fund, Inc. 08/06/2018
Each share Common $0.001 par exchanged for (0.72863966) share Common $0.001 par

KAYNE ANDERSON MLP INVT CO (MD)
Auction Rate Preferred Ser. D $0.001 par called for redemption at $25,000 on 05/28/2010
4.95% Mandatory Redeemable Preferred Ser. D $0.001 par called for redemption at $25.125 plus $0.144375 accrued dividends on 05/13/2013
4.6% Mandatory Redeemable Preferred Ser. G $0.001 par called for redemption at $25 plus $0.0.0063889 accrued dividends on 10/03/2016
Name changed to Kayne Anderson MLP/Midstream Investment Co. 07/31/2018

KAYOT INC (MN)
Name changed to Harris-Kayot, Inc. and Common 33-1/3¢ par changed to 10¢ par 5/6/83
(See Harris-Kayot, Inc.)

KAYPRO CORP (CA)
Charter cancelled for failure to file reports and pay taxes 8/2/93

KAYRAND MINING & DEVELOPMENT CO. LTD. (ON)
Recapitalized as Chib-Kayrand Copper Mines Ltd. 02/28/1955
Each share Capital Stock no par exchanged for (0.2) share Capital Stock $1 par
Chib-Kayrand Copper Mines Ltd. merged into Cinequity Corp. (New) 11/24/1981
(See Cinequity Corp. (New))

KAYSAM CORP AMER (NJ)
Common $1 par split (4) for (1) by issuance of (3) additional shares 12/4/68
Stock Dividend - 100% 3/28/68
Merged into Kaysam Newco, Inc. 9/29/82
Each share Common $1 par exchanged for $8.50 cash

KAYSER HOSIERY MOTOR-MEND CORP.
Name changed to General Hosiery Motor-Mend Corp. in 1932
(See General Hosiery Motor-Mend Corp.)

KAYSER ROTH CORP (NY)
Name changed 08/01/1958
Common no par changed to $5 par 00/00/1932
Stock Dividend - 100% 01/31/1946
Name changed from Kayser (Julius) & Co. to Kayser-Roth Corp. 08/01/1958
Common $5 par changed to $1 par and (2) additional shares issued 01/11/1960
Merged into Gulf & Western Industries, Inc. (DE) 10/21/1975
Each share Common $1 par exchanged for (0.4) share $2.50 Conv. Preferred Ser. D $2.50 par
(See Gulf + Western Inc.)

KAYTY INC (ON)
Recapitalized 09/10/1987
Reincorporated 09/22/1987
Recapitalized from Kayty Exploration Ltd. to Kayty Inc. 09/10/1987
Each share Common no par exchanged for (0.1) share Common no par
Place of incorporation changed from (ALTA) to (ONT) 09/22/1987
Each share old Common no par exchanged for (1) share new Common no par 12/17/1991
Reorganized as WLD Inc. 12/07/1994
Each share new Common no par exchanged for (1/3) share Common no par
WLD Inc. name changed to Astris Energi Inc. 07/12/1995 which name changed to Carthew Bay Technologies Inc. 08/22/2007

KAZA COPPER LTD (BC)
Dissolved 02/25/1983
Details not available

KAZAKHGOLD GROUP LTD (JERSEY)
Name changed to Polyus Gold International Ltd. 08/03/2011
(See Polyus Gold International Ltd.)

KAZAKHMYS PLC (UNITED KINGDOM)
Name changed to Kaz Minerals PLC 11/28/2014

KAZAKHSTAN MINERALS CORP (YT)
Name changed to European Minerals Corp. (YT) 08/14/2001
European Minerals Corp. (YT) reincorporated in British Virgin Islands 04/08/2005 which name changed to Orsu Metals Corp. 07/14/2008

KAZAKHSTAN GOLDFIELDS CORP (ON)
Delisted from Canadian Dealer Network 10/13/2000

KAZAN CITY TELEPHONE NETWORK (RUSSIA)
Sponsored ADR's for Ordinary 10,000 Rubles par split (28) for (1) by issuance of (27) additional ADR's payable 2/4/2003 to holders of record 12/4/2002 Ex date - 2/5/2003
Merged into Tattelecom 8/9/2006
Each Sponsored ADR for Ordinary 10,000 Rubles par exchanged for $0.02987 cash

KAZANORGSINTEZ PJSC (RUSSIA)
Name changed 01/28/2016
Name changed from Kazanorgsintez A.O. to Kazanorgsintez PJSC 01/28/2016
ADR agreement terminated 11/29/2017
Each Sponsored ADR for Ordinary exchanged for (6) shares Ordinary
Note: Unexchanged ADR's will be sold and the proceeds, if any, held for claim after 12/03/2018

KAZARI INTL INC (NV)
Name changed to e-Auction Global Trading, Inc. 05/04/1999
e-Auction Global Trading, Inc. name changed to Aucxis Corp. 06/12/2001
(See Aucxis Corp.)

KAZAX MINERALS INC (BC)
Acquired by 1069411 B.C. Ltd. 12/15/2016
Each share Common no par exchanged for $0.01 cash
Note: Unexchanged certificates will be cancelled and become without value 12/15/2022

KAZKOMMERTSBANK JSC (KAZAKHSTAN)
Each old Sponsored Reg. S GDR for Ordinary exchanged for (1) new Sponsored Reg. S GDR for Ordinary 12/19/2006
Sponsored Reg. S GDR's for Preferred split (15) for (1) by issuance of (14) additional GDR's payable 07/12/2010 to holders of record 07/09/2010 Ex date - 07/13/2010
Basis changed from (1:30) to (1:2) 07/12/2010
Stock Dividends - 3.08% payable 09/10/2001 to holders of record 08/17/2001; 1,400% payable 09/26/2006 to holders of record 09/22/2006
GDR agreement terminated 09/20/2017
Each Sponsored Reg. S GDR for Preferred exchanged for (0.979981) GDR for Common
Note: Unexchanged GDR's will be sold and the proceeds, if any, held for claim after 09/24/2018

KAZMIR KLIFFS INC (UT)
Recapitalized as Lanstar Semiconductor Inc. 12/01/1995
Each share Common $0.001 par exchanged for (0.5) share Common $0.001 par
(See Lanstar Semiconductor Inc.)

KB COMMUNICATIONS INC (NV)
Each share old Common $0.001 par exchanged for (1/6) share new Common $0.001 par 1/31/90
Charter revoked for failure to file annual reports and pay taxes 1/1/92

KB HOME (DE)
Each Growth Preferred Redeemable Increased Dividend Equity Security exchanged for (0.315) share Common $1 par 08/16/2001
Each Income Preferred Redeemable Increased Dividend Equity Security exchanged for (0.315) share Common $1 par 08/16/2001
(Additional Information in Active)

KB MARKETING INC (CO)
Each share old Common no par exchanged for (0.2) share new Common no par 12/15/86
Charter suspended for failure to maintain a resident agent 1/18/88

KBF POLLUTION MGMT INC (NY)
Reorganized under the laws of Delaware as Veridium Corp. 10/20/2003
Each share Common $0.00001 par exchanged for (0.05) share Common $0.001 par
Veridium Corp. name changed to GS CleanTech Corp. 07/19/2006 which name changed to GreenShift Corp. 02/13/2008

KBH INDS INC (DE)
Charter cancelled and declared inoperative and void for non-payment of taxes 04/15/1972

KBK CAP CORP (DE)
Issue Information - 1,330,000 shares COM offered at $10.50 per share on 06/08/1994
Recapitalized as United States Growth Funds Corp. 04/27/2005
Each share Common 1¢ par exchanged for (0.0002) share Common 1¢ par

KBK CAP TR I (DE)
Company terminated securities registration and is no longer public as of 10/30/2002

KBL HEALTHCARE ACQUISITION CORP (DE)
Name changed to Concord Health Group, Inc. 08/16/1994
(See Concord Health Group, Inc.)

KBL HEALTHCARE ACQUISITION CORP II (DE)
Name changed to Summer Infant, Inc. 03/07/2007

KBL HEALTHCARE ACQUISITION CORP III (DE)
Issue Information - 15,000,000 UNITS consisting of (1) share COM and (1) WT offered at $8 per Unit on 07/19/2007
Completely liquidated 07/27/2009
Each Unit exchanged for first and final distribution of $7.84662104 cash
Each share Common $0.0001 par exchanged for first and final distribution of $7.84662104 cash

KBSH LEADERS TR (ON)
Liquidation completed
Each Unit received initial distribution of $13.92 cash payable 12/05/2005 to holders of record 11/30/2005
Each Unit received second and final distribution of $0.2882 cash payable 12/12/2005 to holders of record 11/30/2005

KBW INC (DE)
Issue Information - 6,800,000 shares COM offered at $21 per share on 11/08/2006
Merged into Stifel Financial Corp. 02/15/2013
Each share Common 1¢ par exchanged for (0.2143) share Common 15¢ par and $10 cash

KCA INTL PLC (UNITED KINGDOM)
Name changed to Bristol Oil & Minerals PLC 12/05/1983
Bristol Oil & Minerals PLC name changed to BOM Holdings PLC 11/06/1986
(See BOM Holdings PLC)

KCC CAP CORP (BC)
Recapitalized as New Era Minerals Inc. 06/02/2014
Each share Common no par exchanged for (0.11890606) share Common no par

KCC CORP (KOREA)
GDR agreement terminated 01/17/2017
Each 144A GDR for Common exchanged for $76.309944 cash

KCD HLDGS INC (NV)
Name changed to Sequester Holdings Inc. 04/01/1997
Sequester Holdings Inc. recapitalized as China Biolife Enterprises Inc. 06/19/2006 which recapitalized as Asia Pacific Energy Inc. 12/07/2007

KCG HLDGS INC (DE)
Acquired by Virtu Financial, Inc. 07/20/2017
Each share Class A Common 1¢ par exchanged for $20 cash

KCM INDS INC (MA)
Adjudicated bankrupt 5/16/79
No stockholders' equity

KCO CAP INC (BC)
Name changed to 3TL Technologies Corp. 11/10/2014
3TL Technologies Corp. name changed to Datable Technologies Corp. 05/18/2018

KCP INCOME FD (ON)
Acquired by Caxton-Iseman Capital, Inc. 05/24/2007
Each Unit of Undivided Int. received $10 cash

KCP RES INC (ON)
Delisted from Alberta Stock Exchange 01/16/1991

KCPL FING I (DE)
8.3% Trust Originated Preferred Securities called for redemption at $25 on 7/21/2004

KCR TECHNOLOGY, INC. TRUST (DE)
In process of liquidation Unitholders' equity to be determined

KCR TECHNOLOGY INC (DE)
Each share Common $0.001 par exchanged for (0.2) share Common $0.005 par 08/30/1985
Plan of reorganization under Chapter 11 Federal Bankruptcy Code effective 04/11/1991
Each share Common $0.005 par exchanged for (1) KCR Technology, Inc. Trust Unit of Bene. Int.
Note: Holders who did not surrender certificates prior to 10/11/1991 are deemed to have unconditionally and irrevocably waived and forfeited all claims to the above consideration
(See KCR Technology, Inc. Trust)

KCS ENERGY INC (DE)
Name changed 02/20/1992
Under plan of recapitalization each share old Common 1¢ par exchanged for (0.5) share new Common 1¢ par 11/03/1989
New Common 1¢ par split (3) for (2) by issuance of (0.5) additional share 01/15/1992
Name changed from KCS Group, Inc. to KCS Energy Inc. 02/20/1992
New Common 1¢ par split (2) for (1) by issuance of (1) additional share 01/15/1993
New Common 1¢ par split (2) for (1) by issuance of (1) additional share 08/31/1993
New Common 1¢ par split (2) for (1) by issuance of (1) additional share payable 06/27/1997 to holders of record 06/03/1997 Ex date - 06/30/1997
Merged into Petrohawk Energy Corp. (DE) 07/12/2006
Each share new Common 1¢ par exchanged for (1.65) shares Common $0.001 par and $9 cash
(See Petrohawk Energy Corp. (DE))

KCS INDS INC (WI)
Completely liquidated 01/31/1975
Each share Common $1 par had the option to receive installment payments totalling $15 cash per share for up to $2,250 per holder or shares in a new investment holding company

KDC ENERGY LTD (AB)
Recapitalized as Clearview Resources Ltd. 01/07/2011
Each (33,000) shares Common no par exchanged for (1) share Common no par

KDT INDS INC (DE)
Merged into Ames Department Stores, Inc. 4/12/84
Each share Common $1 par exchanged for (0.004878) share Common 50¢ par
Escrow account established under Chapter 11 bankruptcy proceedings
Each share Common $1 par received initial distribution of $0.1226 cash 10/15/84
Each share Common $1 par received second and final distribution of $0.1039 cash 4/15/86
Note: Certificates not surrendered for exchange became valueless 4/9/85

KDW ENTERPRISES (NV)
Recapitalized as Boucher-Oehmke Holdings, Inc. 4/11/90
Each share Common $0.001 par exchanged for (0.04) share Common $0.001 par
(See Boucher-Oehmke Holdings, Inc.)

KDW TELECOM INC (DE)
Recapitalized as KSW Industries, Inc. 9/12/2005
Each share Common exchanged for (0.001) share Common

KEANE INC (MA)
Name changed 7/1/80
Name changed from Keane Associates, Inc. to Keane, Inc. 7/1/80
Common 10¢ par split (3) for (2) by issuance of (0.5) additional share 2/14/90
Common 10¢ par split (3) for (2) by issuance of (0.5) additional share 8/18/93
Common 10¢ par split (3) for (2) by issuance of (0.5) additional share 9/7/94
Common 10¢ par split (2) for (1) by issuance of (1) additional share payable 11/29/96 to holders of record 11/14/96 Ex date - 12/2/96
Common 10¢ par split (2) for (1) by issuance of (1) additional share payable 8/29/97 to holders of record 8/14/97 Ex date - 9/2/97
Stock Dividends - In Class B Common to holders of Common 50% 7/21/86; In Common to holders of Class B Common 100% 5/8/89; Common 100% 5/8/89
Class B Common 10¢ par reclassified as Common 10¢ par 2/1/2004
Acquired by Caritor, Inc. 6/4/2007
Each share Common 10¢ par exchanged for $14.30 cash

KEANSBURG MIDDLETOWN NATL BK (MIDDLETOWN, NJ)
Stock Dividend - 50% 07/01/1971
Merged into United Counties Trust Co. (Elizabeth, NJ) 04/03/1972
Each share Common $10 par exchanged for (2.6) shares Common $5 par
United Counties Trust Co. (Elizabeth, NJ) reorganized as United Counties Bancorporation 10/01/1983 which merged into Meridian Bancorp, Inc. 02/23/1996 which merged into CoreStates Financial Corp 04/09/1996 which merged into First Union Corp. 04/28/1998 which name changed to Wachovia Corp. (Ctfs. dated after 09/01/2001) 09/01/2001 which merged into Wells Fargo & Co. (New) 12/31/2008

KEARNEY & TRECKER CORP (WI)
Each share Common $10 par exchanged for (3-1/3) shares Common $3 par in 1941
Common $3 par changed to $2 par and (0.5) additional share issued 1/11/66
Common $2 par split (2) for (1) by issuance of (1) additional share 2/23/68
Stock Dividends - 100% 1/15/53; 50% 9/15/66
Merged into Cross & Trecker Corp. 2/9/79
Each share Common $2 par exchanged for (1) share Common $1 par
Cross & Trecker Corp. merged into Giddings & Lewis, Inc. (New) 10/31/91
(See Giddings & Lewis, Inc. (New))

KEARNEY (JAMES R.) CORP. (DE)
$0.60 Preferred no par called for redemption 1/1/62
Public interest eliminated

KEARNEY JAMES R CORP (MO)
Common no par exchanged (5) for (1) in 1937
Common no par changed to $5 par in 1952
Merged into Kearney (James R.) Corp. (DE) 6/9/59
Each share Common $5 par exchanged for (3) shares $0.60 Preferred no par

(See Kearney (James R.) Corp. (DE))

KEARNEY NATL INC (DE)
Common 50¢ par split (3) for (2) by issuance of (0.5) additional share 4/25/68
Common 50¢ par split (3) for (2) by issuance of (0.5) additional share 6/1/83
Acquired by Dyson-Kissner-Moran Corp. 10/11/88
Each share Common 50¢ par exchanged for $19.35 cash

KEARNS CONSOLIDATED COPPER MINES CO. (WY)
Charter revoked for failure to file reports and pay fees 7/19/27

KEARNY FINL CORP (USA)
Reorganized under the laws of Maryland 05/19/2015
Each share Common 10¢ par exchanged for (1.3804) shares Common 1¢ par

KEARSARGE TELE CO (NH)
5.50% Class B Preferred $50 par called for redemption 12/1/96
(Additional Information in Active)

KEATING CAP INC (MD)
Name changed to BDCA Venture, Inc. 07/02/2014
BDCA Venture, Inc. name changed to Crossroads Capital, Inc. 12/03/2015

KEATON RES LTD (BC)
Name changed to GFM Resources Ltd. (BC) 11/07/1997
GFM Resources Ltd. (BC) reincorporated in Yukon 07/25/2000

KEBA OIL & GAS CO (CO)
Merged into Whiting Petroleum Corp. 12/16/83
Each share Common $0.001 par exchanged for (0.2) share Common 1¢ par
Whiting Petroleum Corp. acquired by IES Industries Inc. 2/18/92 which merged into Interstate Energy Inc. 4/21/98 which name changed to Alliant Energy Corp. 5/19/99

KEC ENVIRONMENTAL CORP (AB)
Struck off register for failure to file annual returns 12/01/1999

KECK OIL CO. (CA)
Acquired by First Leisure Corp. 4/6/72
Each share Common $1 par exchanged for (0.142857) share Common 10¢ par
(See First Leisure Corp.)

KECO INC (UT)
Proclaimed dissolved for failure to pay taxes 1/5/97

KEDEM PHARMACEUTICALS INC (NV)
SEC revoked common stock registration 09/30/2014

KEE EXPL INC (WY)
Each share Common $0.001 par exchanged for (0.2) share Common $0.005 par 05/04/1983
Merged into Wichita River Oil Corp. (VA) (New) 11/04/1987
Each share Common $0.005 par exchanged for (0.013158) share Common no par
Wichita River Oil Corp. (VA) (New) reincorporated in Delaware 03/30/1990
(See Wichita River Oil Corp. (DE))

KEE ZIPPER CORP. (NY)
Proclaimed dissolved for non compliance with New York corporation laws 12/15/60

KEEBEE CORP (DE)
Each share Common $0.001 par exchanged for (0.05) share Common $0.002 par 06/29/1990
Each share Common $0.002 par exchanged for (0.005) share Common $0.001 par 12/11/1995

Recapitalized as Van Harbour International Inc. 04/12/1996
Each share Common $0.001 par exchanged for (0.033333333) share Common $0.001 par
Van Harbour International Inc. name changed to Jackson Tech Inc. 10/14/1996 which name changed to Electronic Kourseware International Inc. 08/28/1997
(See Electronic Kourseware International Inc.)

KEEBEE OIL & GAS CO., INC. (DE)
Name changed to Keebee Corp. 07/25/1983
Keebee Corp. name changed to Van Harbour International Inc. 04/12/1996 which name changed to Jackson Tech Inc. 10/14/1996 which name changed to Electronic Kourseware International Inc. 08/28/1997
(See Electronic Kourseware International Inc.)

KEEBLER CO (DE)
Common no par split (2) for (1) by issuance of (1) additional share 5/3/71
Merged into United Biscuits (Holdings) Ltd. 4/24/74
Each share Common no par exchanged for $30 cash

KEEBLER FOODS CO (DE)
Issue Information - 11,640,575 shares COM offered at $24 per share on 01/29/1998
Merged into Kellogg Co. 03/26/2001
Each share Common 1¢ par exchanged for $42 cash

KEEFER REALTY CORP.
Liquidated in 1947

KEEFER RES INC (BC)
Struck off register and declared dissolved for failure to file returns 11/06/1992

KEEGAN MGMT CO (DE)
Name changed to KMC Enterprises, Inc. 6/14/91
KMC Enterprises, Inc. acquired by Worth Corp. (NV) 7/29/92 which reincorporated in Delaware 7/31/92 which name changed to Krauses Furniture Inc. 12/8/94
(See Krauses Furniture Inc.)

KEEGAN RES INC (BC)
Name changed to Asanko Gold Inc. 03/01/2013

KEEHN-O MANUFACTURING CO. (NV)
Charter revoked for failure to file reports and pay franchise fees 3/2/59

KEEK INC (AB)
Each share old Common no par exchanged for (0.03333333) share new Common no par 01/15/2015
Name changed to Peeks Social Ltd. 03/03/2017

KEELEY-FRONTIER MINES LTD. (ON)
Recapitalized as Canadian Keeley Mines Ltd. 01/23/1964
Each share Capital Stock no par exchanged for (0.5) share Capital Stock no par
Canadian Keeley Mines Ltd. recapitalized as Keeley-Frontier Resources Ltd. 07/22/1981 which merged into Jamie Frontier Resources Inc. 02/15/1984
(See Jamie Frontier Resources Inc.)

KEELEY FRONTIER RES LTD (CANADA)
Merged into Jamie Frontier Resources Inc. 02/15/1984
Each share Common no par exchanged for (0.4) share Common no par
(See Jamie Frontier Resources Inc.)

KEELEY SILVER MINES LTD.
Merged into Anglo-Huronian Ltd. 00/00/1933
Each share Capital Stock exchanged for (0.2) share Capital Stock
Anglo-Huronian Ltd. merged into Kerr Addison Mines Ltd. 11/18/1963 which merged into Noranda Inc. 04/11/1996 which name changed to Falconbridge Ltd. (New) 2005 on 07/01/2005
(See Falconbridge Ltd. (New) 2005)

KEELINE OIL & URANIUM CORP. (CO)
Declared defunct and inoperative for non-payment of franchise taxes 10/11/61

KEEN INDS LTD (AB)
Reincorporated 03/13/1984
Place of incorporation changed from (BC) to (AB) 03/13/1984
Name changed to Delta North Transportation Ltd. 11/14/1986
(See Delta North Transportation Ltd.)

KEENE & WOOLFE OIL CO.
Dissolved in 1929

KEENE CORP (NY)
Reincorporated 12/31/79
Stock Dividend - 300% 1/29/68
State of incorporation changed from (DE) to (NY) 12/31/79
Reorganized as Bairnco Corp. (NY) 4/30/81
Each share Common 10¢ par exchanged for (2) shares Common 5¢ par
Bairnco Corp. (NY) reincorporated in Delaware 5/1/91
(See Bairnco Corp.)

KEENE CORP NEW (DE)
Reorganized under Chapter 11 Federal Bankruptcy Code as Reinhold Industries, Inc. 7/31/96
Each share Common $0.0001 par received (0.091195) share Class A Common 1¢ par
Note: Certificates were not required to be exchanged and are without value
(See Reinhold Industries, Inc.)

KEENE NATL BK (KEENE, NH)
Merged into Indian Head Banks, Inc. in February 1974
Each share Common $50 par exchanged for (2) shares Common $5 par
Indian Head Banks, Inc. acquired by Fleet/Norstar Financial Group, Inc. 12/21/88 which name changed to Fleet Financial Group, Inc. (New) 4/15/92 which name changed to Fleet Boston Corp. 10/1/99 which name changed to FleetBoston Financial Corp. 4/18/2000 which merged into Bank of America Corp. 4/1/2004

KEENE PACKAGING ASSOCIATES (NJ)
Reincorporated under the laws of Delaware as Keene Corp. (Old) 4/15/67
Keene Corp. (DE) (Old) reincorporated in New York 12/31/79 which reorganized as Bairnco Corp. (NY) 4/30/81 which reincorporated in Delaware 5/1/91
(See Bairnco Corp.)

KEENER COPPER CO. (WY)
Charter forfeited for failure to pay taxes 7/19/27

KEENER TECHNOLOGIES INC (CANADA)
Recapitalized as Mindflight Corp. 08/09/1993
Each share Common no par exchanged for (0.25) share Common no par
Mindflight Corp. name changed to RDM Corp. 06/19/1998
(See RDM Corp.)

KEEPER RES INC (AB)
Acquired by Vietnam Resource Investments (Holdings) Ltd. 05/28/2008
Each share Common no par exchanged for $1.50 cash

KEEPRITE INC (CANADA)
Merged into Inter-City Gas Corp. 01/19/1987
Each share Common no par exchanged for $18 cash

KEEPRITE PRODUCTS LTD. (ON)
Class A no par split (3) for (1) by issuance of (2) additional shares 05/20/1969
Each share Class A no par exchanged for (1.25) shares Class B Part. no par 09/05/1972
Reincorporated under the laws of Canada as Keeprite Inc. and Class B Part. no par reclassified as Common no par, Class C Part. no par reclassified as Common no par 08/16/1979
(See Keeprite Inc.)

KEESHIN FREIGHT LINES, INC.
Bankrupt in 1946

KEEVER CO (OH)
Acquired by Staley (A.E.) Manufacturing Co. 07/19/1968
Each share Common $5 par exchanged for $9.60 cash
5% Non-Cum. Preferred $50 par called for redemption 09/30/1968
5% Preferred $100 par called for redemption 09/30/1968
Public interest eliminated

KEEVER STARCH CO. (OH)
Each share Common $100 par exchanged for (4) shares Common $25 par in 1951
Each share Common $25 par exchanged for (2) shares Common $12.50 par in 1954
Name changed to National Industrial Products Co. 10/1/56
(See National Industrial Products Co.)

KEEWATIN WINDPOWER CORP (NV)
Common $0.001 par split (3) for (1) by issuance of (2) additional shares payable 09/25/2006 to holders of record 09/25/2006
Name changed to Sky Harvest Windpower Corp. 09/16/2009
Sky Harvest Windpower Corp. name changed to Sky Harvest Energy Corp. 08/13/2013

KEEWIS REALTY CO., INC. (NY)
Merged into Great Bear Spring Co. 8/1/72
Each share Capital Stock $85 par exchanged for (18.6) shares Capital Stock no par
(See Great Bear Spring Co.)

KEG RESTAURANTS LTD (BC)
Each share old Common no par exchanged for (1) share Non-Vtg. Class A no par and (0.33333333) share new Common no par 04/27/1982
Merged into Whitbread & Co. PLC 10/01/1987
Each share Non-Vtg. Class A no par exchanged for $2 cash
Each share new Common no par exchanged for $2 cash

KEIKA EXPRESS LTD (JAPAN)
ADR agreement terminated 04/30/2009
No ADR's remain outstanding

KEITH-ALBEE-ORPHEUM CORP.
Dissolved in 1944

KEITH CLARK INC (PR)
Common 50¢ par split (3) for (2) by issuance of (0.5) additional share 12/31/75
Merged into Cullman Ventures, Inc. 5/9/78
Each share Common 50¢ par exchanged for $13 principal amount of 6% 30-day Notes or $13.065 cash
Note: Option to receive Notes expired 6/8/78

KEITH (GEO. E.) CO. (MA)
Each share 7% 1st Preferred $100 par exchanged for (1) share $5 Prior Preferred $100 par, (1) share $2 Junior Prior Preferred $10 par and $4 in cash in 1943
Each (2) shares Common no par exchanged for (1) share new Common no par in 1943
Merged into Keith (Geo. E.) Co. (DE) 7/2/62
Each share $5 Prior Preferred $100 par exchanged for (11) shares Common $1 par
Each share $2 Junior Prior Preferred $10 par exchanged for (0.5) share Common $1 par
Each share Common no par exchanged for (0.5) share Common $1 par
(See Keith (Geo. E.) Co. (DE))

KEITH COPPER LTD (BC)
Recapitalized as Tanker Oil & Gas Ltd. 03/12/1982
Each share Common no par exchanged for (0.25) share Common no par
Tanker Oil & Gas Ltd. recapitalized as Tyson Financial Corp. 05/23/1990 which recapitalized as Midd Financial Corp. 06/01/1992
(See Midd Financial Corp.)

KEITH COS INC (CA)
Merged into Stantec Inc. 9/15/2005
Each share Common no par exchanged for (0.4053) share Common no par and $11 cash

KEITH GEORGE E CO (DE)
Stock Dividend - 50% 3/15/68
Merged into Official Industries, Inc. 8/16/79
Each share Common $1 par exchanged for either $3.75 principal amount of 10% Subordinated Notes due 1987 and (1) share Common 10¢ par plus $1 cash or (0.5) share 6% Conv. Preferred Ser. D $10 par and (1) share Common 10¢ par or $4.90 cash

KEITH GROUP COS INC (DE)
Name changed 03/24/1988
Name changed from Keith (Hugh) Enterprises, Ltd. to Keith Group of Companies, Inc. 03/24/1988
Each share Common 1¢ par exchanged for (0.5) share Common 2¢ par 06/17/1988
Stock Dividend - 10% 11/01/1990
SEC revoked common stock registration 10/20/2008

KEITH (HUGH) MOBILE ENTERPRISES, LTD. (DE)
Name changed to Keith (Hugh) Enterprises, Ltd. 06/01/1987
Keith (Hugh) Enterprises, Ltd. name changed to Keith Group of Companies, Inc. 03/24/1988
(See Keith Group of Companies, Inc.)

KEITH PAPER CO. (MA)
Common $50 par changed to $10 par 00/00/1938
Liquidated 10/07/1956
Details not available

KEITH RES LTD (BC)
Recapitalized as Avalon Ventures Ltd. 09/30/1994
Each share Common no par exchanged for (0.2) share Common no par
Avalon Ventures Ltd. name changed to Avalon Rare Metals Inc. (BC) 02/18/2009 which reincorporated in Canada 02/09/2011 which name changed to Avalon Advanced Materials Inc. 03/03/2016

KEITHGOLD MINES, LTD. (ON)
Charter cancelled and declared dissolved for failure to pay taxes and file returns 12/07/1977

KEITHLEY INSTRS INC (OH)
Conv. Class B Common no par split (3) for (1) by issuance of (2) additional shares 04/29/1985
Common no par split (3) for (1) by issuance of (2) additional shares 04/29/1985
Conv. Class B Common no par split (3) for (2) by issuance of (0.5) additional share 10/09/1987
Common no par split (3) for (2) by issuance of (0.5) additional share 10/09/1987
Common no par split (2) for (1) by issuance of (1) additional share 12/11/1995
Conv. Class B Common no par split (2) for (1) issuance of (1) additional share payable 06/01/2000 to holders of record 05/18/2000
Common no par split (2) for (1) by issuance of (1) additional share payable 06/01/2000 to holders of record 05/18/2000
Acquired by Danaher Corp. 12/08/2010
Each share Conv. Class B Common no par exchanged for $21.60 cash
Each share Common no par exchanged for $21.60 cash

KEKAHA SUGAR LTD (HI)
Each share Common $20 par exchanged for (1.666666) shares Common no par 00/00/1937
Merged into Amfac, Inc. 01/10/1969
Each share Common no par exchanged for (1) share $2.50 Conv. Preferred no par
(See Amfac, Inc.)

KEKELAC GOLD MINES LTD. (ON)
Charter cancelled for failure to file reports and pay taxes 00/00/1957

KEL GLEN MINES LTD (BC)
Struck and dissolved from register 12/18/1978

KELAN RES INC (BC)
Recapitalized as Auromar Development Corp. 05/29/1992
Each share Common no par exchanged for (0.28571428) share Common no par
Auromar Development Corp. merged into Casmyn Corp. (CO) 07/30/1996 which reorganized in Nevada as Aries Ventures Inc. 04/11/2000 which reincorporated in Delaware as Cardium Therapeutics, Inc. 01/23/2006 which name changed to Taxus Cardium Pharmaceuticals Group, Inc. 10/07/2014

KELBEE RARE METALS CORP. LTD. (ON)
Charter revoked for failure to file reports and pay fees 12/27/1964

KELCORD INTL INC (NV)
Charter revoked for failure to file reports and pay fees 07/01/1999

KELD OR RES INC (BC)
Recapitalized as Consolidated Keld'or Resources Inc. 09/06/1990
Each share Common no par exchanged for (1/3) share Common no par
Consolidated Keld'or Resources Inc. recapitalized as CKD Ventures Ltd. 03/18/1994 which recapitalized as Alchemy Ventures Ltd. (BC) 05/14/1999 which reincorporated in Canada as i-minerals inc. 01/22/2004 which name changed to I-Minerals Inc. 12/15/2011

KELDON OIL CO (ND)
Common no par split (3) for (2) by issuance of (0.5) additional share 07/21/1980
Merged into Pittencrieff America 12/30/1994
Each share Common no par exchanged for $0.22 cash

KELITE CORP. (CA)
Acquired by Richardson Co. 05/27/1966
Each share Common $1 par exchanged for (0.1472) share 4% Conv. Preferred Ser. A no par

KELKENO COPPER CORP. LTD. (SK)
Charter revoked 09/23/1960
No stockholders' equity

KELKIRK MINES LTD. (ON)
Charter cancelled and company declared dissolved for default in filing returns 01/20/1971

KELLAND MINING CORP. LTD.
Name changed to Leys (Wm.) Mining Corp. Ltd. 00/00/1949
(See Leys (Wm.) Mining Corp. Ltd.)

KELLCAM EXPL LTD (BC)
Struck off register and declared dissolved for failure to file returns 09/09/1974

KELLEHER CONSOLIDATED SHOE CO. (MA)
Charter revoked for failure to file reports and pay fees 03/31/1931

KELLER CORP. (DE)
Bankrupt 07/27/1962
No stockholders' equity

KELLER DORIAN COLORFILM CORP (DE)
Voluntarily dissolved 05/12/1967
Details not available

KELLER H INC (DE)
Charter cancelled and declared inoperative and void for non-payment of 03/01/1987

KELLER INDS INC (FL)
Common 50¢ par split (2) for (1) by issuance of (1) additional share 11/15/1971
Stock Dividend - 20% 10/01/1965
Merged into Keller Holdings, Inc. 10/28/1983
Each share Common 50¢ par exchanged for $24.25 cash

KELLER INDS LTD (ISLE OF MAN)
Each share old Ordinary Stock $0.005 par exchanged for (0.1) share new Ordinary Stock $0.005 par 12/17/1992
Name changed to Tri Kal International Ltd. 08/00/1993
(See Tri Kal International Ltd.)

KELLER MFG INC (IN)
Old Common 1¢ par split (3) for (2) by issuance of (0.5) additional share payable 02/06/1998 to holders of record 02/06/1998
Each share old Common 1¢ par exchanged for (0.002) share new Common 1¢ par 03/29/2004
Note: In effect holders will received $4 cash per share and public interest was eliminated

KELLER TOOL CO. (MI)
Merged into Gardner-Denver Co. 01/31/1955
Each share Common exchanged for (0.625) share Common no par
Gardner-Denver Co. merged into Cooper Industries, Inc. 04/30/1979 which reincorporated in Bermuda as Cooper Industries, Ltd. 05/22/2002 which reincorporated in Ireland as Cooper Industries PLC 09/08/2009 which merged into Eaton Corp. PLC 11/30/2012

KELLERING VICTOR INC (NY)
Each share Common 1¢ par received distribution of (2) shares Pennate Corp. Common 1¢ par 07/21/1984
Each share Common 1¢ par received distribution of (0.9) share Sentry Armoured Courier Corp. Common 1¢ par 07/21/1984
Name changed to Myriad Group Inc. 10/10/1985
Myriad Group Inc. merged into Micron Products Inc. 01/28/1988 which merged into Arrhythmia Research Technology, Inc. 11/25/1992

KELLETT AIRCRAFT CORP (DE)
Name changed to Kellett Corp. 04/21/1969
(See Kellett Corp.)

KELLETT AUTOGIRO CORP.
Name changed to Kellett Aircraft Corp. 00/00/1943
Kellett Aircraft Corp. name changed to Kellett Corp. 04/21/1969
(See Kellett Corp.)

KELLETT CORP (DE)
Common $1 par changed to 10¢ par 12/16/1974
Charter forfeited for failure to maintain a registered agent 10/13/1989

KELLEY ISLAND CO. (OH)
Liquidation completed 12/28/1955
Details not available

KELLEY ISLAND LIME & TRANSPORT CO. (OH)
Each share Common $100 par exchanged for (4) shares Common no par 00/00/1927
Common no par changed to $1 par 00/00/1950
Merged into Kelley Island Co. 00/00/1954
Each share Common $1 par exchanged for (1) share Common $1 par and $22 cash
(See Kelley Island Co.)

KELLEY OIL & GAS CORP (DE)
Recapitalized as Contour Energy Co. 7/30/99
Each share Common 1¢ par exchanged for (0.1) share Common 1¢ par
Preferred not affected except for change of name
(See Contour Energy Co.)

KELLEY OIL & GAS PARTNERS LTD (TX)
Merged into Kelley Oil & Gas Corp. 02/07/1995
Each Unit of Limited Partnership exchanged for either (0.609) share Common 1¢ par and (0.254) share $2.625 Conv. Exchangeable Preferred 1¢ par or (1.2188) shares Common 1¢ par
Note: Option to elect to receive both Preferred and Common expired 04/14/1995
Kelley Oil & Gas Corp. recapitalized as Contour Energy Co. 07/30/1999
(See Contour Energy Co.)

KELLEY OIL CORP (DE)
Merged into Kelley Oil & Gas Corp. 02/07/1995
Each share $2.625 Conv. Exchangeable Preferred 1¢ par exchanged for (1) share $2.625 Conv. Exchangeable Preferred 1¢ par
Each share Common 1¢ par exchanged for (1) share Common 1¢ par
Kelley Oil & Gas Corp. recapitalized as Contour Energy Co. 07/30/1999
(See Contour Energy Co.)

KELLIN CORP. (IL)
Proclaimed dissolved for failure to pay taxes and file reports 11/12/1964

KELLING NUT CO (IL)
Name changed to 2800 Belmont Corp. 08/04/1967
6% Preferred $20 par called for redemption 08/31/1967
2800 Belmont Corp. completed liquidation for Corn Products Co. (DE) 11/22/1968 which name changed to CPC International Inc. 04/23/1969 which name changed to BestFoods 01/01/1998
(See BestFoods)

KELLOGG AMERN INC (NY)
Common 10¢ par split (2) for (1) by issuance of (1) additional share 06/01/1966
Merged into International Compressed Air Corp. 09/30/1971
Each share Common 10¢ par exchanged for $15 cash

KELLOGG (CHARLES C.) & SONS CO. (NY)
Common $100 par changed to no par 00/00/1932
Each share 7% Preferred $100 par exchanged for (1) share 6% Preferred $100 par and (0.5) share Common no par 00/00/1936
Name changed to Kellogg Lumber, Inc. 03/10/1958
(See Kellogg Lumber, Inc.)

KELLOGG (SPENCER) & SONS, INC. (NY)
Each share Capital Stock $100 par exchanged for (5) shares Capital Stock no par 00/00/1928
Each share Capital Stock no par exchanged for (2) shares Capital Stock $1 par 07/11/1947
Stock Dividend - 20% 12/28/1943
Merged into Textron Inc. (RI) 07/28/1961
Each share Capital Stock $1 par exchanged for (6/7) share Common 50¢ par
Textron Inc. (RI) reincorporated in Delaware 01/02/1968

KELLOGG CTZNS NATL BK (GREEN BAY, WI)
Each share Capital Stock $100 par exchanged for (5) shares Capital Stock $20 par 01/09/1964
Stock Dividend - 100% 01/15/1959
Acquired by Associated Bank Services, Inc. 06/01/1970
Each share Capital Stock $20 par exchanged for (4) shares Common $1 par
Associated Bank Services, Inc. name changed to Associated Banc-Corp. 06/15/1977

KELLOGG LUMBER, INC. (NY)
Charter cancelled and proclaimed dissolved for failure to pay taxes and file reports 09/28/1967

KELLOGG SWITCHBOARD & SUPPLY CO.
Acquired by International Telephone & Telegraph Corp. (MD) in 1952
Each share Common no par exchanged for (1.44) shares Capital Stock no par
International Telephone & Telegraph Corp. (MD) reincorporated in Delaware 1/31/68 which name changed to ITT Corp. 12/31/83 which reorganized in Indiana as ITT Industries Inc. 12/19/95 which name changed to ITT Corp. 7/1/2006

KELLOGG UNITED MINES CO. (WA)
Charter stricken from record for failure to pay taxes 7/1/25

KELLSTROM INDS INC (DE)
Secondary Offering - 2,750,000 shares COM offered at $26 per share on 06/11/1998
Plan of reorganization under Chapter 11 Federal Bankruptcy Code effective 9/5/2003
No stockholders' equity

KELLWOOD CO (DE)
Common no par split (2) for (1) by issuance of (1) additional share 03/11/1969
Common no par split (2) for (1) by issuance of (1) additional share 12/17/1985

Common no par changed to 1¢ par 08/00/1986
Common 1¢ par split (3) for (2) by issuance of (0.5) additional share 12/16/1986
Common 1¢ par split (3) for (2) by issuance of (0.5) additional share 03/18/1994
Merged into Cardinal Integrated, LLC 02/20/2008
Each share Common 1¢ par exchanged for $21 cash

KELLY & CLARK MINING & EXPLORATION CO. (NV)
Charter revoked for failure to file reports and pay fees 03/02/1959

KELLY & COHEN INC (PA)
Completely liquidated 04/09/1965
Each share Common 1¢ par exchanged for first and final distribution of $7.50 cash

KELLY DESMOND MNG LTD (ON)
Recapitalized as Premium Letney Canada Inc. 04/20/1994
Each share Common no par exchanged for (0.1) share Common no par
(See Premium Letney Canada Inc.)

KELLY DOUGLAS & CO LTD (BC)
4.5% Preference $100 par called for redemption 03/21/1958
Merged into Loblaw Companies Ltd. 06/18/1989
Each share Class A no par exchanged for $80 cash
Each share Class B no par exchanged for $80 cash

KELLY FIELD BANCSHARES CORP (DE)
Merged into Benson Investment Co. 11/04/1985
Each share Common $1 par exchanged for $25 cash

KELLY FIELD NATL BK (SAN ANTONIO, TX)
Common $10 par changed to $2 par and (4) additional shares issued 10/15/1969
Stock Dividend - 10% 03/15/1971
Reorganized as Kelly Field Bancshares Corp. 05/12/1978
Each share Common $2 par exchanged for (1) share Common $1 par
(See Kelly Field Bancshares Corp.)

KELLY GIRL SERVICE, INC. (DE)
Common $1 par split (3) for (2) by issuance of (0.5) additional share 03/03/1965
Common $1 par split (3) for (2) by issuance of (0.5) additional share 03/04/1966
Name changed to Kelly Services, Inc. 04/05/1966

KELLY GOLD & SILVER MINES, INC. (DE)
No longer in existence having become inoperative and void for non-payment of taxes 04/01/1937

KELLY JOHNSTON ENTERPRISES INC (KS)
Common $1 par split (3) for (2) by issuance of (0.5) additional share 02/25/1983
Stock Dividend - 50% 10/12/1982
Plan of reorganization under Chapter 11 bankruptcy proceedings confirmed 06/17/1986
No stockholders' equity

KELLY JORDAN ENTERPRISES INC (DE)
Charter cancelled and declared inoperative and void for non-payment of taxes 03/01/1976

KELLY-K MINES LTD. (ON)
Merged into Summit Explorations & Holdings Ltd. 09/19/1969
Each share Capital Stock $1 par exchanged for (0.06) share Capital Stock no par
Summit Explorations & Holdings Ltd. name changed to Summit Diversified Ltd. 03/03/1972 which merged into Sumtra Diversified Inc. 08/30/1978

KELLY KERR ENERGY CORP (BC)
Recapitalized as Sirius Resource Corp. 10/19/1988
Each share Common no par exchanged for (0.25) share Common no par
(See Sirius Resource Corp.)

KELLY-KIRKLAND MINES LTD. (ON)
Charter cancelled 00/00/1968

KELLY LAKE NICKEL MINES LTD (MB)
Name changed to Albany Oil & Gas Ltd. (MB) 03/22/1971
Each share Capital Stock no par exchanged for (1) share Capital Stock no par
Albany Oil & Gas Ltd. (MB) reincorporated in Alberta 11/10/1980 which name changed to Albany Corp. 05/17/1988 which merged into LifeSpace Environmental Walls Inc. 08/17/1993 which merged into SMED International Inc. 07/01/1996
(See SMED International Inc.)

KELLY PETE INC (BC)
Merged into New Frontier Petroleum Corp. 01/18/1982
Each share Common no par exchanged for (0.27) share Common no par
New Frontier Petroleum Corp. recapitalized as PetroMac Energy Inc. 08/30/1985
(See PetroMac Energy Inc.)

KELLY RUSSELL STUDIOS INC (MN)
Merged into Global One Distribution & Merchandising Inc. 08/28/1996
Each share Common 1¢ par exchanged for (0.5) share Common 1¢ par
Global One Distribution & Merchandising Inc. recapitalized as Brite-Strike Tactical Illumination Products, Inc. 07/30/2008

KELLY-SPRINGFIELD TIRE CO.
Acquired by Goodyear Tire & Rubber Co. 00/00/1935
Details not available

KELLY VALVE CO. (MI)
Charter declared inoperative and void for failure to file reports 08/31/1930

KELLYS COFFEE GROUP INC (NV)
Reincorporated 10/10/2000
State of incorporation changed from (CO) to (NV) 10/10/2000
Each share Common $0.001 par received distribution of (3) shares Wichita Development Corp. Common $0.001 par payable 01/29/2001 to holders of record 01/01/2001
Name changed to Nexia Holdings, Inc. (NV) 03/21/2002
Nexia Holdings, Inc. (NV) reincorporated in Utah as Sack Lunch Productions, Inc. 04/20/2015

KELMAC MINES LTD.
Merged into Baldwin Consolidated Mines Ltd. 00/00/1946
Each share Capital Stock $1 par exchanged for (0.14285714) share Capital Stock $1 par
Baldwin Consolidated Mines Ltd. recapitalized as Canadian Baldwin Holdings Ltd. 07/11/1989 which recapitalized as Canadian Baldwin Resources Ltd. 07/25/2005 which name changed to Aura Gold Inc. (ON) 03/22/2006 which reincorporated in Canada 04/20/2006 which name changed to Aura Minerals Inc. (Canada) Inc.
08/16/2007 which reorganized in British Virgin Islands 01/05/2017

KELMAC OILS LTD. (AB)
Completely liquidated 00/00/1963
Liquidator advised company has been wound up and all holders have received distribution

KELMAN TECHNOLOGIES INC (CANADA)
Each share old Common no par exchanged for (0.0125) share new Common no par 08/18/2009
Acquired by Seyco Operations Ltd. 05/13/2010
Each share new Common no par exchanged for $2 cash
Note: Unexchanged certificates were cancelled and became without value 05/13/2016

KELMOUNT EXPLS LTD (BC)
Name changed to Almahurst Energy Corp. 04/26/1982
Almahurst Energy Corp. name changed to Canadian Entech Research Corp. 01/17/1984 which recapitalized as Canadian Entech Resources Inc. 03/31/1995 which name changed to H2O Entertainment Corp. 07/15/1996 which recapitalized as Consolidated H2O Entertainment Corp. 07/14/2005 which name changed to Tri-River Ventures, Inc. 07/30/2007

KELORE MINES LTD. (ON)
Recapitalized as New Kelore Mines Ltd. 00/00/1953
Each share Capital Stock no par exchanged for (0.2) share Capital Stock no par
New Kelore Mines Ltd. merged into Orvana Minerals Corp. 02/24/1992

KELROWE GOLD MINES LTD. (ON)
Recapitalized as Kelwren Gold Mines Ltd. 00/00/1946
Each share Capital Stock no par exchanged (0.41666666) share Capital Stock no par
Kelwren Gold Mines Ltd. recapitalized as Kelore Mines Ltd. 00/00/1948 which recapitalized as New Kelore Mines Ltd. 00/00/1953 which merged into Orvana Minerals Corp. 02/24/1992

KELSEY HAYES CDA LTD (ON)
Capital Stock no par split (3) for (1) by issuance of (2) additional shares 07/21/1981
Capital Stock no par split (2) for (1) by issuance of (1) additional share 02/06/1986
Merged into Varity Corp. 01/28/1991
Each share Capital Stock no par exchanged for $20 cash

KELSEY HAYES CO (DE)
Common $1 par split (2) for (1) by issuance of (1) additional share 09/06/1966
Merged into Fruehauf Corp. (MI) 10/31/1973
Each share Common $1 par exchanged for (1.25) shares Common $1 par
Fruehauf Corp. (MI) merged into Fruehauf Corp. (DE) 12/23/1986 which name changed to K-H Corp. 08/04/1989 which merged into Varity Corp. (Canada) 12/01/1989 which reorganized in Delaware 08/01/1991 which merged into LucasVarity PLC 09/06/1996
(See LucasVarity PLC)

KELSEY-HAYES WHEEL CO. (DE)
Class B $1 par changed to Common $1 par 00/00/1953
Stock Dividend - 100% 07/01/1953
Name changed to Kelsey-Hayes Co. 12/20/1956
Kelsey-Hayes Co. merged into Fruehauf Corp. (MI) 10/31/1973 which merged into Fruehauf Corp. (DE) 12/23/1986 which name changed to K-H Corp. 08/04/1989 which merged into Varity Corp. (Canada) 12/01/1989 which reorganized in Delaware 08/01/1991 which merged into LucasVarity PLC 09/06/1996
(See LucasVarity PLC)

KELSEY-HAYES WHEEL CORP.
Reorganized as Kelsey-Hayes Wheel Co. 00/00/1933
Details not available

KELSEY LAKE DEVELOPMENT CO. LTD. (ON)
Merged into Choiceland Iron Mines Ltd. 02/26/1962
Each share Common no par exchanged for (1) share Common no par
Choiceland Iron Mines Ltd. recapitalized as Atlantic Goldfields Inc. 08/05/1987 which recapitalized as Dexus Inc. 06/22/1990 which was acquired by Trimin Enterprises Inc. (BC) 06/30/1993 which reorganized as Trimin Enterprises Inc. (Canada) 07/27/1998
(See Trimin Enterprises Inc.)

KELSEY MOTOR CO. (DE)
No longer in existence having become inoperative and void for non-payment of taxes 03/17/1926

KELSEY WHEEL CO.
Merged into Kelsey-Hayes Wheel Corp. 00/00/1927
Details not available

KELSEY WHEEL CO., LTD. (ON)
Name changed to Kelsey-Hayes Canada Ltd. 01/31/1967
(See Kelsey-Hayes Canada Ltd.)

KELSEYS INTL INC (ON)
Reincorporated 02/10/1994
Place of incorporation changed from (AB) to (ON) 02/10/1994
Merged into Cara Operations Ltd. 07/05/1999
Each share Common no par exchanged for $3 cash

KELSO ENERGY INC (AB)
Recapitalized as COSTA Energy Inc. 04/28/2006
Each share Common no par exchanged for (0.125) share Common no par
COSTA Energy Inc. recapitalized as Artek Exploration Ltd. 01/20/2010 which merged into Kelt Exploration Ltd. 04/21/2015

KELSO EXPLS LTD (BC)
Charter cancelled 00/00/1980

KELSO RES LTD (BC)
Name changed to Kelso Technologies Inc. 07/21/1994

KELSON RED LAKE GOLD MINES, LTD. (ON)
Charter surrendered in 1943

KELSPAR URANIUM DEVELOPERS LTD. (AB)
Struck off the register of companies and deemed dissolved by the Province of Alberta 06/15/1962

KELTEC INC (IN)
Completely liquidated 12/31/1973
Each share Common $10 par exchanged for first and final distribution of $1.58 cash

KELTEC INDUSTRIES, INC. (VA)
Acquired by Aiken Industries, Inc. 08/15/1967
Each share Capital Stock 40¢ par exchanged for (2/3) share Common $1 par
(See Aiken Industries, Inc.)

KELTEY ENERGY LTD (AB)
Recapitalized as Kappa Energy Corp. 10/18/1996
Each share Class A Common no par exchanged for (0.13755158) share Common no par

FINANCIAL INFORMATION, INC. KEL-KEM

Kappa Energy Corp. name changed to Vanguard Oil Corp. 01/17/2000 which was acquired by Bitech Petroleum Corp. 05/24/2001
(See Bitech Petroleum Corp.)

KELTIC INC (NS)
Name changed to CrossOff Inc. and Class A Subordinate no par reclassified as (5) shares Common no par 08/08/2000
CrossOff Inc. name changed to Nexient Learning Inc. 06/22/2006
(See Nexient Learning Inc.)

KELTIC MNG LTD (ON)
Charter cancelled and declared dissolved for failure to file returns and pay fees 05/09/1977

KELTNER ELECTRONICS, INC. (CO)
Declared defunct and inoperative for failure to file reports and pay franchise taxes 10/19/1965

KELTRON CORP (MA)
Each share old Common 1¢ par exchanged for (0.00008) share new Common 1¢ par 10/14/2015
Note: In effect holders received $0.385 cash per share and public interest was eliminated

KELVER MINES LTD (BC)
Recapitalized as New Kelver Resources Ltd. 05/22/1974
Each share Common no par exchanged for (0.5) share Common no par
New Kelver Resources Ltd. recapitalized as Access Resources Ltd. 03/31/1982
(See Access Resources Ltd.)

KELVIN CREEK EXPLORATIONS LTD. (BC)
Charter cancelled for failure to file returns 00/00/1969

KELVIN ENERGY LTD (AB)
Reported bankrupt 01/00/1993
No stockholders' equity

KELVINATOR CDA LTD (CANADA)
Each share old Common no par exchanged for (4) shares new Common no par 00/00/1950
Name changed to WCI Canada Ltd. 10/03/1972
(See WCI Canada Ltd.)

KELVINATOR CORP.
Merged into Nash-Kelvinator Corp. on a (1.375) for (1) basis 00/00/1936
Nash-Kelvinator Corp. merged into American Motors Corp. 00/00/1954 which merged into Chrysler Corp. 08/05/1987 which merged into DaimlerChrysler AG 11/12/1998 which name changed to Daimler AG 10/19/2007

KELWREN GOLD MINES LTD.
Recapitalized as Kelore Mines Ltd. 00/00/1948
Each share Capital Stock no par exchanged for (0.5) share Capital Stock no par
Kelore Mines Ltd. recapitalized as New Kelore Mines Ltd. 00/00/1953 which merged into Orvana Minerals Corp. 02/24/1992

KELWYNN INC (UT)
Reincorporated under the laws of Delaware and Common no par changed to $1 par 12/16/1983

KEM-ICAL CORP.
In process of liquidation 00/00/1944
Details not available

KEMANO RES LTD (AB)
Recapitalized 04/13/1993
Recapitalized from Kemano Gold Corp. to Kemano Resources Ltd. 04/13/1993
Each share Class A Common no par exchanged for (0.2) share Class A Common no par

Merged into Purcell Energy Ltd. (Old) 11/19/1993
Each share Class A Common no par exchanged for (0.9) share Common no par
Purcell Energy Ltd. (Old) recapitalized as Purcell Energy Ltd. (New) 03/07/1997
(See Purcell Energy Ltd. (New))

KEMGAS HLDGS LTD (BC)
Reorganized 06/15/1988
Reorganized from Kemgas International Ltd. (UT) to Kemgas Holdings Ltd. (BC) 06/15/1988
Each share Common 1¢ par exchanged for (0.5) share Common 1¢ par
Name changed to Envirochem Inc. 11/10/1993

KEMGAS INTL LTD (BERMUDA)
Reincorporated 06/23/1995
Place of incorporation changed from (BC) to Bermuda 06/23/1995
Name changed to Kemgas Ltd. 05/28/1996
Kemgas Ltd. name changed to CalciTech Ltd. 07/25/2000

KEMGAS LTD (BERMUDA)
Name changed to CalciTech Ltd. 07/25/2000

KEMGAS SYDNEY INC (BC)
Name changed to Kemgas International Ltd. (BC) 02/15/1995
Kemgas International Ltd. (BC) reincorporated in Bermuda 06/23/1995 which name changed to Kemgas Ltd. 05/28/1996 which name changed to CalciTech. Ltd. 07/25/2000

KEMIRA OY (FINLAND)
Name changed to Kemira Oyj 11/02/1999

KEMLINE INDUSTRIES, INC. (DE)
No longer in existence having become inoperative and void for non-payment of taxes 4/1/65

KEMP INDS INC (DE)
Charter cancelled and declared inoperative and void for non-payment of taxes 03/01/2000

KEMP URANIUM MINES LTD. (QC)
Ceased operations and charter lapsed 01/01/1957

KEMPER / CYRMOT REAL ESTATE INVT L P (DE)
Plan of liquidation effective 7/1/95
Each Unit of Limited Partnership Int. A exchanged for $88 cash minus expenses

KEMPER CORP OLD (DE)
Common $5 par split (3) for (2) by issuance of (0.5) additional share 01/31/1979
Common $5 par split (4) for (3) by issuance of (1/3) additional share 01/31/1980
Common $5 par split (3) for (1) by issuance of (2) additional shares 06/20/1986
Merged into Zurich Insurance Co. 01/04/1996
Each share $2 Conv. Preferred Ser. A no par exchanged for (1) share Preferred
Each share Common $5 par exchanged for $49.80 cash

KEMPER DOUBLE PLAY TRUST (MO)
Name changed to Kemper Bond Enhanced Securities Trust 01/07/1987
(See Kemper Bond Enhanced Securities Trust)

KEMPER GLOBAL/INTL SER INC (MD)
Name changed to Scudder International Research Fund Inc. 05/25/2001

(See Scudder International Research Fund Inc.)

KEMPER GROWTH FD (MA)
Reincorporated 01/31/1986
Reincorporated from Kemper Growth Fund, Inc. (MD) to under the laws of Massachusetts as Kemper Growth Fund and Common 50¢ par reclassified as Shares. of Bene. Int. 50¢ par 01/31/1986
Name changed to Scudder Growth Fund 06/25/2001
Scudder Growth Fund name changed to Scudder Growth Trust 01/15/2003
(See Scudder Growth Trust)

KEMPER HIGH INCOME TR (MA)
Name changed to Scudder High Income Trust 01/01/2001
Scudder High Income Trust name changed to DWS High Income Trust 02/06/2006 which name changed to Deutsche High Income Trust 08/11/2014
(See Deutsche High Income Trust)

KEMPER HIGH YIELD FD (MA)
Reincorporated 01/31/1986
Reincorporated from Kemper High Yield Fund, Inc. (MD) to under the laws of Massachusetts as Kemper High Yield Fund and Common $0.001 par reclassified as Shares of Bene. Int. $0.001 par 01/31/1986
Name changed to Scudder High Yield Series 05/25/2001
Scudder High Yield Series name changed to Scudder High Income Series 04/01/2003 which name changed to DWS High Income Series 12/19/2005

KEMPER INCOME & CAP PRESERVATION FD (MD)
Reorganized 01/31/1986
Under plan of reorganization each share Kemper Income & Capital Preservation Fund, Inc. Common 50¢ par automatically became (1) share Kemper Income & Capital Preservation Fund Share of Bene. Int. no par 01/31/1986
Merged into Scudder Portfolio Trust 06/25/2001
Details not available

KEMPER INTER GOVT TR (MA)
Name changed to Scudder Intermediate Government Trust 01/01/2001
Scudder Intermediate Government Trust name changed to Scudder Intermediate Government & Agency Trust 04/01/2004
(See Scudder Intermediate Government & Agency Trust)

KEMPER INTL FD INC (MD)
Reincorporated under the laws of Massachusetts as Kemper International Fund and Common $0.001 par reclassified as Shares of Bene. Int. $0.001 par 01/31/1986

KEMPER INVS FD (MA)
Name changed to Investors Fund Series 05/06/1997
Investors Fund Series name changed to Kemper Variable Series 04/30/1999 which name changed to Scudder Variable Series II 05/01/2001 which name changed to DWS Variable Series II 01/30/2006

KEMPER MONEY MKT FD (MA)
Reincorporated 11/29/1985
Reincorporated from Kemper Money Market Fund, Inc. (MD) to under the laws of Massachusetts as Kemper Money Market Fund and Common $0.001 par reclassified as Shares of Bene. Int. no par 11/29/1985
Name changed to Scudder Money Funds 04/17/1997
Scudder Money Funds name changed to DWS Money Funds 12/19/2005

KEMPER MULTI-MARKET INCOME TR (MA)
Name changed to Scudder Multi-Market Income Trust 01/01/2001
Scudder Multi-Market Income Trust name changed to DWS Multi-Market Income Trust 02/06/2006 which name changed to Deutsche Multi-Market Income Trust 08/11/2014

KEMPER MUN BD FD INC (MD)
Reincorporated under the laws of Massachusetts as Kemper Municipal Bond Fund and Common $0.001 par reclassified as Shares of Bene. Int. $0.001 par 01/31/1986

KEMPER MUN INCOME TR (MA)
Name changed to Scudder Municipal Income Trust 01/01/2001
Scudder Municipal Income Trust name changed to DWS Municipal Income Trust (Old) 02/06/2006 which name changed to Deutsche Municipal Income Trust 08/11/2014 which name changed to DWS Municipal Income Trust (New) 07/02/2018

KEMPER MUNICIPAL BOND FUND, LTD. (NE)
Reorganized under the laws of Maryland as Kemper Municipal Bond Fund, Inc. and Shares of Ltd. Partnership Int. reclassified as Common $0.001 par 1/1/77
Kemper Municipal Bond Fund, Inc. (Md.) reincorporated in Massachusetts as Kemper Municipal Bond Fund 1/31/86

KEMPER NEW EUROPE FD INC (MD)
Name changed to Scudder New Europe Fund, Inc. (New) 05/25/2001
Scudder New Europe Fund, Inc. (New) merged into Scudder International Fund, Inc. 03/14/2005 which name changed to DWS International Fund, Inc. 02/06/2006

KEMPER OPT INCOME FD (MA)
Name changed to Kemper Diversified Income Fund 02/01/1989

KEMPER OPTION INCOME FUND, INC. (MD)
Reincorporated under the laws of Massachusetts as Kemper Option Income Fund and Common $0.001 par reclassified as Shares of Bene. Int. $0.001 par 1/31/86
Kemper Option Income Fund name changed to Kemper Diversified Income Fund 2/1/89

KEMPER PORTFOLIOS (MA)
Name changed 05/27/1994
Name changed from Kemper Investment Portfolios to Kemper Portfolios and Government Portfolio no par, Money Market Portfolio no par and Short Intermediate Government Portfolio no par reclassified as U.S Mortgage Fund Class B no par, Cash Reserves Fund Class B no par and Short Intermediate Government Fund Class B no par respectively 05/27/1994
Diversified Income Portfolio, Growth Portfolio, High Yield Portfolio and Total Return Portfolio merged into Kemper Total Return Fund 05/27/1994
Details not available
Short Intermediate Government Fund Class B merged into Kemper Adjustable Rate U.S. Government Fund 12/16/1998
Details not available
Name changed to Scudder Portfolios 07/02/2001
(See Scudder Portfolios)

KEMPER STRATEGIC INCOME TR (MA)
Name changed 01/20/1999
Name changed from Kemper Strategic Income Fund to Kemper Strategic Income Trust 01/20/1999
Name changed to Scudder Strategic Income Trust 01/01/2001
Scudder Strategic Income Trust name changed to DWS Strategic Income Trust 02/06/2006 which name changed to Deutsche Strategic Income Trust 08/11/2014

KEMPER STRATEGIC MUN INCOME TR (MA)
Name changed to Scudder Strategic Municipal Income Trust 01/01/2001
Scudder Strategic Municipal Income Trust name changed to DWS Strategic Municipal Income Trust (Old) 02/06/2006 which name changed to Deutsche Strategic Municipal Income Trust 08/11/2014 which name changed to DWS Strategic Municipal Income Trust (New) 07/02/2018

KEMPER SUMMIT FD (MA)
Reincorporated 01/31/1986
Name, place of incorporation changed from Kemper Summit Fund, Inc. (MD) to Kemper Summit Fund (MA) and Common 50¢ par reclassified as (5) Shares of Bene. Int. 50¢ par 01/31/1986
Reorganized as Kemper Small Capitalization Equity Fund 02/01/1992
Details not available

KEMPER TECHNOLOGY FD (MA)
Name changed to Scudder Technology Fund 06/25/2001
Scudder Technology Fund name changed to DWS Technology Fund 02/06/2006

KEMPER TOTAL RETURN FD (MA)
Reincorporated 01/31/1986
Reincorporated from Kemper Total Return Fund, Inc. (MD) to under the laws of Massachusetts as Kemper Total Return Fund and Common $1 par reclassified as Shares of Bene. Int. $1 par 01/31/1986
Shares of Bene. Int. $1 par split (2) for (1) by issuance of (1) additional share 01/29/1988
Name changed to Scudder Total Return Fund 06/08/2001
Scudder Total Return Fund name changed to DWS Balanced Fund 02/06/2006

KEMPER U S GOVT SECS FD (MA)
Reorganized 01/31/1986
Reorganized from Kemper U.S. Government Securities Fund, Inc. (MD) to under the laws of Massachusetts as Kemper U.S. Government Securities Fund and Common $0.001 par reclassified as Shares of Bene. Int. $0.001 par 01/31/1986
Name changed to Scudder U.S. Government Securities Fund 05/25/2001
Scudder U.S. Government Securities Fund name changed to DWS U.S Government Securities Fund 02/06/2006 which name changed to DWS Strategic Government Securities Fund 03/25/2008

KEMPER VAR SER (MA)
Name changed to Scudder Variable Series II 05/01/2001
Scudder Variable Series II name changed to DWS Variable Series II 01/30/2006

KEMPERCO INC (DE)
Name changed to Kemper Corp. (Old) 01/15/1974
(See Kemper Corp. (Old))

KEMPTON CAP PARTNERS INC (ON)
Name changed to Gensel Biotechnologies Ltd. 12/08/1997
Gensel Biotechnologies Ltd. recapitalized as Greenfield Commercial Credit (Canada) Inc. 01/01/2003 which name changed to Greenfield Financial Group Inc. 08/17/2005 which name changed to Wheels Group Inc. 01/18/2012 which merged into Radiant Logistics, Inc. 04/08/2015

KEMSLEY MILLBOURN & CO. LTD.
Acquired by Commercial Credit Co. in 1928
Details not available

KEMWALL FINANCIAL CORP. (TN)
Name changed to Allied Mortgage & Development Co., Inc. 6/10/63
Allied Mortgage & Development Co., Inc. name changed to Alodex Corp. 4/18/69
(See Alodex Corp.)

KEN BAY GOLD MINES LTD. (ON)
Name changed to K.B. Mining Co. Ltd. 00/00/1955
(See K.B. Mining Co. Ltd.)

KEN-MOORE MINES, LTD. (BC)
Struck off the register and dissolved by the Province of British Columbia 12/28/1950

KEN-RAD TUBE & LAMP CORP. (DE)
Under plan of liquidation
Each share Class A Common no par stamped to indicate initial distribution of (0.2) share Westinghouse Electric Corp. Common $12.50 par and $22.50 cash to holders of record 10/15/1945
Cash liquidation completed 12/23/1946

KEN VENTURI GOLF INC (NV)
Recapitalized as Transcontinental Waste Industries Inc. 12/05/1997
Each share Common 1¢ par exchanged for (0.01) share Common 1¢ par
Transcontinental Waste Industries Inc. name changed to Para Mas Internet Inc. 08/27/1999
(See Para Mas Internet Inc.)

KENAI CORP (DE)
Common 1¢ par split (3) for (2) by issuance of (0.5) additional share 9/29/80
Plan of reorganization under Chapter 11 Federal Bankruptcy Code effective 7/10/89
No stockholders' equity

KENAI DRILLING LTD. (DE)
Name changed to Kenai Corp. 06/28/1978
(See Kenai Corp.)

KENAI RES LTD (BC)
Merged into Serabi Gold PLC 07/22/2013
Each share Common no par exchanged for (0.85) share Ordinary 5p par
Note: Unexchanged certificates will be cancelled and become without value 07/22/2019

KENAN TRANS CO (NC)
Common no par split (2) for (1) by issuance of (1) additional share 2/1/80
Common no par split (2) for (1) by issuance of (1) additional share 7/20/81
Common no par split (2) for (1) by issuance of (1) additional share 1/16/84
Merged into Advantage Management Holdings Corp. 5/1/2001
Each share Common no par exchanged for $35 cash

KENAR ENTERPRISES INC (DE)
Assets sold for the benefit of creditors 9/3/99
Stockholders' equity unlikely

KENAR RES LTD (BC)
Name changed to Western Commonwealth Developments Inc. 01/22/1990
(See Western Commonwealth Developments Inc.)

KENARE PETROLEUMS CORP. LTD. (AB)
Recapitalized as Maverick Mines & Oils Ltd. 03/19/1964
Each share Capital Stock no par exchanged for (0.2) share Capital Stock no par
Maverick Mines & Oils Ltd. recapitalized as Peregrine Petroleum Ltd. 05/15/1972 which recapitalized as Peregrine Oil & Gas Ltd. 09/15/1994 which merged into Surge Petroleum Inc. 07/07/2000 which merged into Innova Exploration Ltd. 04/16/2004
(See Innova Exploration Ltd.)

KENCOPE ENERGY COS (TX)
Name changed to New London Inc. 03/02/1989
(See New London Inc.)

KENCORP INC (DE)
Name changed to Interface Systems, Inc. and Common 5¢ par changed to 10¢ par 07/10/1969
Interface Systems, Inc. merged into Tumbleweed Communications Corp. 09/01/2000
(See Tumbleweed Communications Corp.)

KENCOUR GOLD MINES, LTD. (ON)
Charter cancelled by Province of Ontario for default 01/04/1960

KENDA PERSHING MINES LTD. (QC)
Charter voluntarily surrendered 11/15/1968
No stockholders' equity

KENDAL MNG & EXPL LTD (BC)
Recapitalized as Velvet Exploration Co., Ltd. (BC) 05/10/1978
Each share Capital Stock 50¢ par exchanged for (0.2) share Capital Stock no par
Velvet Exploration Co. Ltd. (BC) reincorporated in Alberta as Velvet Exploration Ltd. 05/26/1998
(See Velvet Exploration Ltd. (AB))

KENDALE STATE BANK (KENDALE, FL)
Name changed to Capital Bank of Kendale (Kendale, FL) 5/1/75
Capital Bank of Kendale (Kendale, FL) merged into Capital Bank (North Bay Village, FL) 12/30/77 which was acquired by Capital Bancorp in September 1982 which merged into Union Planters Corp. 12/31/97 which merged into Regions Financial Corp. (New) 7/1/2004

KENDALL CO (MA)
Common no par changed to $16 par and (0.25) additional share issued 00/00/1953
Common $16 par changed to $8 par and (1) additional share issued 08/19/1960
Common $8 par split (3) for (2) by issuance of (0.5) additional share 05/14/1965
Common $8 par changed to $4 par and (1) additional share issued 08/14/1969
Stock Dividend - 100% 11/16/1948
Merged into Colgate-Palmolive Co. 08/16/1972
Each share $3 Conv. 2nd Preferred Ser. A no par exchanged for (1) share $3 Conv. 2nd Preferred no par
Each share Common $4 par exchanged for (1) share Common $1 par
$4.50 Preferred Ser. A no par called for redemption 08/18/1972
Public interest eliminated

KENDALL INDS INC (CA)
Adjudicated bankrupt 04/00/1968
No stockholders' equity

KENDALL INTL INC (DE)
Merged into Tyco International Ltd. (MA) 10/19/1994
Each share Common 1¢ par exchanged for (1.29485) shares Common 50¢ par
Tyco International Ltd. (MA) merged into Tyco International Ltd. (Bermuda) 07/02/1997 which reincorporated in Switzerland 03/17/2009 which merged into Johnson Controls International PLC 09/06/2016

KENDALL MGMT CORP (UT)
Reincorporated under the laws of Nevada as Medical Resources Management Inc. 08/20/1996
Medical Resources Management Inc. merged into Emergent Group Inc. 07/06/2001
(See Emergent Group Inc.)

KENDALL MNG INTL INC (NV)
Name changed 11/10/1982
Name changed from Kendall Medical International Inc. to Kendall Mining International Inc. 11/10/1982
Charter revoked for failure to file reports and pay fees 03/01/2004

KENDALL PRODUCTS CORP. (DE)
Charter cancelled and declared inoperative and void for non-payment of taxes 00/00/1926

KENDALL REFINING CO. (PA)
Capital Stock $10 par changed to $5 par and (1) additional share issued 02/20/1966
Merged into Witco Chemical Co., Inc. 03/18/1966
Each share Capital Stock $5 par exchanged for (0.5) share $2.65 Conv. Preferred $1 par
Witco Chemical Co., Inc. name changed to Witco Chemical Corp. 04/25/1968 which name changed to Witco Corp. 10/01/1985 which merged into CK Witco Corp. 09/01/1999 which name changed to Crompton Corp. 04/27/2000 which name changed to Chemtura Corp. 07/01/2005
(See Chemtura Corp.)

KENDALL SQUARE RESH CORP (DE)
Reorganized under the laws of Nevada as National Hyberbaric Rehab Center, Inc. 08/25/2005
Each share Common 1¢ par exchanged for (0.002) share Common 1¢ par
National Hyperbaric Rehab Center, Inc. recapitalized as SanCuro Corp. 02/07/2008 which name changed to Kendall Square Research Corp. 09/08/2009

KENDALLVILLE BANK & TRUST CO. (KENDALLVILLE, IN)
Acquired by SummCorp 9/2/86
Each share Capital Stock $11.25 par exchanged for (4.8) shares Common no par
SummCorp merged into NBD Bancorp, Inc. 7/1/92 which name changed to First Chicago NBD Corp. 12/1/95 which merged into Bank One Corp. 10/2/98 which merged into J.P. Morgan Chase & Co. 12/31/2000 which name changed to JPMorgan Chase & Co. 7/20/2004

KENDEES INTL FOODS INC (DE)
Charter forfeited for failure to maintain a registered agent 01/23/1988

KENDER ENERGY INC (NV)
Common $0.001 par split (5) for (1) by issuance of (4) additional shares payable 07/31/2009 to holders of record 07/24/2009 Ex date - 08/03/2009

Recapitalized as Bettwork Industries Inc. 07/02/2014
Each share Common $0.001 par exchanged for (0.002) share Common $0.0001 par

KENDLE INTL INC (OH)
Issue Information - 3,600,000 shares COM offered at $14 per share on 08/22/1997
Secondary Offering - 2,100,000 shares COM offered at $23.50 per share on 06/24/1998
Acquired by INC Research, L.L.C. 07/08/2011
Each share Common no par exchanged for $15.25 cash

KENDON COPPER MINES LTD (ON)
Charter cancelled for failure to pay taxes and file reports 03/16/1976

KENDON ELECTRONICS CO., INC. (NY)
Charter cancelled and proclaimed dissolved for failure to pay taxes 12/15/1967

KENDRA GOLD RES LTD (BC)
Name changed to Koda Resources Ltd. (BC) 05/13/1994
Koda Resources Ltd. (BC) reorganized in Ontario as African Gold Group, Inc. 03/18/2004

KENDREX SYS INC (NV)
Recapitalized as HLHK World Group, Inc. 11/18/1996
Each share Common $0.001 par exchanged for (0.2) share new Common $0.001 par
HLHK World Group, Inc. name changed to TrimFast Group, Inc. 09/04/1998 which recapitalized as eDollars Inc. 11/21/2006 which recapitalized as Forex Inc. 06/18/2007 which name changed to Petrogulf Inc. 03/26/2008 which name changed to Novagant Corp. 01/02/2014

KENECHO GOLD MINES, LTD. (ON)
Charter cancelled 03/19/1963
No stockholders' equity

KENERGY RES CORP (SK)
Recapitalized as International Kenergy Resource Corp. 11/08/1984
Each share Common no par exchanged for (0.25) share Common no par
International Kenergy Resource Corp. merged into Interquest Resources Corp. 06/11/1985 which name changed to Interquest Technologies Inc. 10/23/1992 which recapitalized as Interquest Inc. 09/30/1995
(See Interquest Inc.)

KENERGY SCIENTIFIC INC (NJ)
Each share old Class A Common no par exchanged for (0.00125) share new Class A Common no par 06/02/2011
Reincorporated under the laws of Wyoming and new Class A Common no par changed to 1¢ par 09/28/2017

KENETECH CORP (DE)
Each share 8.25% Depositary Preferred exchanged for (1) share Common $0.0001 par 5/14/98
Merged into ValueAct Capital Partners, L.P. 12/29/2000
Each share Common $0.0001 par exchanged for $1.04 cash

KENEXA CORP (PA)
Issue Information - 5,000,000 shares COM offered at $12 per share on 06/24/2005
Acquired by International Business Machines Corp. 12/03/2012
Each share Common 1¢ par exchanged for $46 cash

KENFIL INC (DE)
Merged into AmeriQuest Technologies, Inc. 9/13/94
Each share Common 1¢ par exchanged for (0.34) share Common 1¢ par
(See AmeriQuest Technologies, Inc.).

KENFLO CORP (FL)
Acquired by Collins Foods International, Inc. (CA) 05/24/1971
Each share Common 10¢ par exchanged for (0.32724) share Common 10¢ par
Under escrow agreement additional shares distributed 05/13/1974
Collins Foods International, Inc. (CA) reincorporated in Delaware 10/31/1980 which merged into PepsiCo, Inc. 03/18/1991

KENGATE RES LTD (BC)
Recapitalized as International Kengate Ventures Inc. 03/02/1990
Each share Common no par exchanged for (0.33333333) share Common no par
International Kengate Ventures Inc. name changed to Latin American Gold Inc. (BC) 03/31/1994 which reincorporated in Bermuda as Latin American Gold Ltd. 04/27/1995
(See Latin American Gold Ltd.)

KENICS CORP. (MA)
Acquired by Chemineer Inc. 9/16/77
Each share Common $1 par exchanged for $35.924 cash

KENIEBA GOLDFIELDS LTD (BC)
Each share old Common no par exchanged for (0.33333333) share new Common no par 06/02/2014
Name changed to EA Education Group Inc. (BC) 02/20/2015
EA Education Group Inc. (BC) reincorporated in Canada 08/17/2015

KENILIND OIL & GAS CO., INC. (DE)
Merged into Baruch Kenilind Oil Corp. 10/9/56
Each share Common 10¢ par exchanged for (1) share Capital Stock 10¢ par
Baruch Kenilind Oil Corp. merged into Baruch-Foster Corp. 1/11/60
(See Baruch-Foster Corp.)

KENILWORTH CORP. (DE)
Acquired by Texas Industries, Inc. 04/30/1955
Each share Common 50¢ par exchanged for (0.29442) share Common $1 par
Texas Industries, Inc. merged into Martin Marietta Materials, Inc. 07/01/2014

KENILWORTH EXPLORATIONS LTD. (ON)
Charter cancelled 01/00/1960
No stockholders' equity

KENILWORTH RLTY TR (MA)
Assets transferred 08/04/1981
In process of liquidation
Each share of Bene. Int. $1 par received initial distribution of $6 cash 12/03/1980
Each share of Bene. Int. $1 par received second distribution of $25 cash 05/21/1981
Each Share of Bene. Int. $1 par received third distribution of $3 cash 08/03/1981
Assets transferred to Kenilworth Realty Liquidating Trust 08/04/1981
Each Share of Bene. Int. $1 par received fourth distribution of $2 cash 01/06/1982
Each Share of Bene. Int. $1 par received fifth distribution of $3 cash 06/21/1983
Each Share of Bene. Int. $1 par received sixth distribution of $2 cash 01/24/1984
Each Share of Bene. Int. $1 par received seventh distribution of $2 cash 03/21/1984
Each Share of Bene. Int. $1 par received eighth distribution of $1 cash 07/25/1984
Each Share of Bene. Int. $1 par received ninth distribution of $0.50 cash 03/15/1985
Each Share of Bene. Int. $1 par received tenth distribution of $0.30 cash 08/08/1985
Note: Details on subsequent distributions, if any, are not available

KENILWORTH RESH & DEV CORP (NY)
Name changed to Kenilworth Systems Corp. 12/14/1979

KENILWORTH ST BK (KENILWORTH, NJ)
Stock Dividend - 10% 11/16/1973
Merged into United Counties Trust Co. (Elizabeth, NJ) 03/01/1983
Each share Common $10 par exchanged for (3.5) shares Common $5 par
United Counties Trust Co. (Elizabeth, NJ) reorganized as United Counties Bancorporation 10/01/1983 which merged into Meridian Bancorp, Inc. 02/23/1996 which merged into CoreStates Financial Corp 04/09/1996 which merged into First Union Corp. 04/28/1998 which name changed to Wachovia Corp. (Ctfs. dated after 09/01/2001) 09/01/2001 which merged into Wells Fargo & Co. (New) 12/31/2008

KENLAWN BUILDING CORP. (IL)
Dissolved 00/00/1954
Details not available

KENLEW MINES LTD. (ON)
Charter cancelled 01/01/1969

KENMAR OIL CO. (DE)
Charter cancelled for non-payment of taxes 1/27/23

KENMAYO YUKON MINES LTD. (ON)
Recapitalized as Mercedes Exploration Co. Ltd. 03/21/1956
Each share Capital Stock exchanged for (0.28571428) share Capital Stock
(See Mercedes Exploration Co. Ltd.)

KENMORE FOREIGN CORP. (NY)
Dissolved by proclamation 6/23/93

KENN HLDGS & MNG LTD (ON)
Charter cancelled for default in filing returns and paying fees 11/24/1973

KENNA CAP CORP (SK)
Name changed to Kenna Resources Corp. (SK) 06/19/2012
Kenna Resources Corp. (SK) reincorporated in British Columbia 09/04/2014 which recapitalized as LOOPShare Ltd. 07/08/2016

KENNA RES CORP (BC)
Reincorporated 09/04/2014
Place of incorporation changed from (SK) to (BC) 09/04/2014
Each share old Common no par exchanged for (0.1) share new Common no par 09/15/2014
Recapitalized as LOOPShare Ltd. 07/08/2016
Each share new Common no par exchanged for (0.68047337) share Common no par

KENNADY DIAMONDS INC (ON)
Merged into Mountain Province Diamonds Inc. 04/17/2018
Each share Common no par exchanged for (0.975) share Common no par
Note: Unexchanged certificates will be cancelled and become without value 04/17/2024

KENNARD (J.) & SONS, INC.
Dissolved 00/00/1934
Details not available

KENNARD (J.) & SONS CARPET CO.
Name changed to Kennard (J.) & Sons, Inc. 00/00/1929
(See Kennard (J.) & Sons, Inc.)

KENNEBEC CONS MNG CO (UT)
Name changed to Health Industries, Inc. 10/17/1969
(See Health Industries, Inc.)

KENNECOM INC (ON)
Recapitalized as Deltona Industries Inc. 01/25/1995
Each share Common no par exchanged for (0.05) share Common no par
(See Deltona Industries Inc.)

KENNECOTT COPPER CORP. (NY)
Capital Stock no par changed to $5 par and (2) additional share issued 06/20/1966
Name changed to Kennecott Corp. and Capital Stock $5 par reclassified as Common $5 par 05/07/1980
(See Kennecott Corp.)

KENNECOTT CORP (NY)
Acquired by Standard Oil Co. (OH) 06/04/1981
Each share Common $5 par exchanged for $62 cash

KENNEDY & COHEN INC (FL)
Ceased operations and adjudicated bankrupt 03/11/1976
Stockholders' equity unlikely

KENNEDY (D.S.) & CO. (MA)
Merged into Electronic Specialty Co. 03/31/1961
Each share Common $1 par exchanged for (0.8) share Common 50¢ par
Electronic Specialty Co. merged into International Controls Corp. 08/01/1969
(See International Controls Corp.)

KENNEDY BANK & TRUST CO. (BETHESDA, MD)
Merged into Citizens Bank & Trust Co. of Maryland (Riverdale, MD) 12/17/82
Each share Capital Stock $10 par exchanged for $43 cash

KENNEDY CONCEPTS INC (NY)
Name changed 04/16/1973
Name changed from Kennedy Computer Institute, Inc. to Kennedy Concepts, Inc. 04/16/1973
Stock Dividends - 10% 06/25/1976; 10% 12/24/1976
Name changed to Belmont Group, Inc. 02/08/1984
(See Belmont Group, Inc.)

KENNEDY MINERALS LTD. (ON)
Charter cancelled 01/01/1969

KENNEDY MINING CO., INC. (NV)
Charter revoked for failure to file reports and pay fees 3/3/52

KENNEDY NATL LIFE INS CO AMER (IN)
Merged into International Financial Services 2/6/97
Each share Common $1 par exchanged for $4.35 cash

KENNEDY RIV GOLD INC (BC)
Cease trade order effective 01/30/1991
Stockholders' equity unlikely

KENNEDY-WILSON INC (DE)
Each share old Common 1¢ par exchanged for (0.1) share new Common 1¢ par 11/21/1995
New Common 1¢ par split (3) for (1) by issuance of (2) additional share payable 04/10/1998 to holders of record 03/30/1998
New Common 1¢ par split (3) for (2) by issuance of (0.5) additional share payable 12/15/1998 to holders of record 12/04/1998
Stock Dividend - 20% payable 11/17/1997 to holders of record 10/27/1997
Merged into Kennedy-Wilson Holdings, Inc. 11/13/2009

Each share new Common 1¢ par exchanged for (3.8031) shares Common $0.0001 par

KENNEDYS INC (MA)
$1.25 Preferred no par called for redemption 03/15/1975
Public interest eliminated

KENNER PARKER TOYS INC (DE)
Common no par changed to $1 par 04/21/1987
Merged into Tonka Corp. 12/08/1987
Each share Common $1 par exchanged for $51 cash

KENNER PRODUCTS CO. (DE)
Name changed to Rennek Co. 12/20/1967
(See Rennek Co.)

KENNESAW LIFE & ACC INS CO (GA)
Old Common $1 par changed to 50¢ par 03/08/1961
Under plan of merger each share Common 50¢ par exchanged for (0.2) share Common $1.25 par 12/28/1962
Common $1.25 par changed to new Common $1 par 05/27/1966
Each share new Common $1 par exchanged for (0.25) share Common $1.50 par 06/05/1968
Merged into Lykes-Youngstown Financial Corp. 11/14/1969
Each share Common $1.50 par exchanged for (1) share Common $1.50 par
Lykes-Youngstown Financial Corp. name changed to LifeSurance Corp. 05/10/1971 which merged into Regan Holding Corp. 10/31/1991
(See Regan Holding Corp.)

KENNESAW PLASTIC CO (DE)
Name changed to Kenplasco, Inc. 2/2/71
(See Kenplasco, Inc.)

KENNETH DION OF SCOTTSDALE, INC. (UT)
See - Dion (Kenneth) of Scottsdale, Inc.

KENNETH RES INC (DE)
Name changed to National Reference Publishing, Inc. 4/8/86
National Reference Publishing, Inc. name changed to NRP Inc. 7/13/88 which name changed to Aegis Communications Group, Inc. 7/9/98
(See Aegis Communications Group, Inc.)

KENNINGTON CORP (NY)
Completely liquidated 01/31/1973
Each share Common 1¢ par exchanged for first and final distribution of (0.02) share Woodford Corp. Common 1¢ par
(See Woodford Corp.)

KENNINGTON INC (CA)
Stock Dividends - 10% 12/10/1975; 50% 05/10/1976; 50% 06/26/1979; 50% 07/07/1980
Merged into C & T Acquisition Corp. 03/20/1987
Each share Common 10¢ par exchanged for $8.50 cash

KENNSINGTON CAP & EQUITY CORP (FL)
Common $0.001 par split (2) for (1) by issuance of (1) additional share payable 11/08/1999 to holders of record 10/25/1999
Name changed to Geotec Thermal Generators, Inc. 11/05/1999
Geotec Thermal Generators, Inc. name changed to Geotec, Inc. 06/04/2007
(See Geotec, Inc.)

KENO HILL MINING CO. LTD.
Recapitalized as United Keno Hill Mines Ltd. on a (0.5) for (1) basis in 1948
(See United Keno Hill Mines Ltd.)

KENO INDS INC (ON)
Recapitalized as Dayak Goldfields Corp. 06/03/1996
Each share Common no par exchanged for (0.33333333) share Common no par
Dayak Goldfields Corp. merged into International Pursuit Corp. 05/22/1997 which recapitalized as Apollo Gold Corp. (ON) 06/24/2002 which reincorporated in Yukon 05/28/2003 which recapitalized as Brigus Gold Corp. (YT) 06/25/2010 which reincorporated in Canada 06/09/2011
(See Brigus Gold Corp.)

KENO OILS LTD. (AB)
Name changed to Monterey Petroleum Corp. Ltd. 09/01/1961
Monterey Petroleum Corp. Ltd. recapitalized as Monterey Petroleum Corp. (1971) Ltd. 11/15/1971
(See Monterey Petroleum Corp. (1971) Ltd.)

KENOGAMISIS GOLD MINES LTD (ON)
Name changed to Anglo Keno Developments Ltd. 00/00/1973
Anglo Keno Developments Ltd. name changed to Lumsden Building Corp., Inc. (Old) 01/10/1978 which merged into Lumsden Building Corp., Inc. (New) 08/15/1978
(See Lumsden Building Corp., Inc. (New))

KENORATOMIC MINES LTD. (ON)
Dissolved 12/27/1960
No stockholders' equity

KENPAT MINES LTD. (ON)
Completely liquidated 11/21/1967
Each share Capital Stock $1 par received first and final distribution of $0.010875266 cash

KENPLASCO INC (DE)
Dissolved 12/31/1977
No stockholders' equity

KENRELL RES INC (BC)
Recapitalized as New Kenrell Resources Inc. (BC) 05/22/1984
Each share Common no par exchanged for (0.2) share Common no par
New Kenrell Resources Inc. (BC) reincorporated in Alberta as International Broadcasting Centre Ltd. 08/31/1987 which recapitalized as Ensel Corp. 10/13/1992 which name changed to Surge Resources Inc. 05/04/2005 which name changed to Eaglewood Energy, Inc. 11/05/2007
(See Eaglewood Energy Inc.)

KENRICH CORP (DE)
Each share Class A Common 20¢ par exchanged for (0.1) share Common 1¢ par 04/18/1983
Note: To holdings of (300) shares or fewer option to receive $0.25 cash expired 6/2/83
Merged into WS Acquisition Inc. 12/05/1988
Each share Common 1¢ par exchanged for $1.50 cash

KENRICH-ESKAY MNG CORP (BC)
Name changed to Eskay Mining Corp. (BC) 11/03/2009
Eskay Mining Corp. (BC) reincorporated in Ontario 11/02/2010

KENRICH MNG CORP NEW (BC)
Recapitalized as Kenrich-Eskay Mining Corp. 11/19/2001
Each share Common no par exchanged for (1/3) share Common no par
Kenrich-Eskay Mining Corp. name changed to Eskay Mining Corp. (BC) 11/03/2009 which reincorporated in Ontario 11/02/2010

KENRICH MNG CORP OLD (BC)
Merged into Kenrich Mining Corp. (New) 08/15/1994
Each share Common no par exchanged for (1) share Common no par
Kenrich Mining Corp. (New) recapitalized as Kenrich-Eskay Mining Corp. 11/19/2001 which name changed to Eskay Mining Corp. (BC) 11/03/2009 which reincorporated in Ontario 11/02/2010

KENRICH PETROCHEMICALS INC (DE)
Name changed to Kenrich Corp. 8/3/62
(See Kenrich Corp.)

KENRIDGE INVT CORP (ON)
Reorganized under the laws of Yukon Territory as Exploro Minerals Corp. Ltd. 03/06/1997
Each share Common no par exchanged for (0.33333333) share Common no par
(See Exploro Minerals Corp. Ltd.)

KENRIDGE MINERAL CORP (BC)
Recapitalized as Pacific Kenridge Ventures Inc. 03/20/1987
Each share Common no par exchanged for (0.5) share Common no par
(See Pacific Kenridge Ventures Inc.)

KENRIDGE RED LAKE MINES, LTD. (ON)
Charter cancelled for failure to file reports and pay fees 02/00/1958

KENSBROOK DEV CORP (AB)
Delisted from Alberta Stock Exchange 06/01/1995

KENSEY NASH CORP (DE)
Acquired by Koninklijke DSM N.V. 06/22/2012
Each share Common $0.001 par exchanged for $38.50 cash

KENSINGTON CT VENTURES INC (BC)
Recapitalized as Para Resources Inc. 03/10/2014
Each share Common no par exchanged for (0.2) share Common no par

KENSINGTON ENERGY CORP (NV)
Each share old Common $0.001 par exchanged for (0.05) share new Common $0.001 par 12/13/2010
Name changed to Emerald Organic Products Inc. 08/28/2012

KENSINGTON ENERGY LTD (AB)
Acquired by Viking Energy Royalty Trust 03/09/2005
Each share Class A Common no par exchanged for $0.52 cash

KENSINGTON HYGEIA ICE CO.
Out of business 00/00/1948
Details not available

KENSINGTON INTL HLDG CORP (MN)
Name changed to Voice & Wireless Corp. 08/16/2000
Voice & Wireless Corp. recapitalized as MIXED Entertainment Inc. 08/25/2004 which name changed to Conscious Co. 08/30/2006 which name changed to American Environmental Energy, Inc. 05/06/2008

KENSINGTON INTL INC (NV)
Each share old Common 1¢ par exchanged for (0.1) share new Common 1¢ par 03/01/1996
Each share new Common 1¢ par exchanged again for (2) shares new Common 1¢ par 03/31/1997
Charter revoked for failure to file reports and pay fees 12/01/2000

KENSINGTON LEASING LTD (NV)
Name changed to Wikifamilies, Inc. 12/20/2011

Wikifamilies, Inc. name changed to Gepco, Ltd. 10/08/2013

KENSINGTON RES LTD (YUKON)
Merged into Shore Gold Inc. 10/28/2005
Each share Common no par exchanged for (0.64) share Common no par
Shore Gold Inc. name changed to Star Diamond Corp. 02/12/2018

KENSINGTON STEEL CO.
Acquired by Poor & Co. 00/00/1945
Details not available

KENSULL GOLD MINES LTD. (ON)
Charter cancelled and company declared dissolved for default in filing returns 07/29/1965

KENT AUTOMATIC PARKING GARAGE, INC.
Bankrupt 00/00/1931
Details not available

KENT DRY CLEANERS INC (NY)
Name changed to Kent Industries Inc. 2/18/69
(See Kent Industries Inc.)

KENT ELECTRIC LIGHT & POWER CO.
Merged into Connecticut Light & Power Co. 00/00/1929
Details not available

KENT ELECTRS CORP (TX)
Common no par split (3) for (2) by issuance of (0.5) additional share 3/1/95
Common no par split (2) for (1) by issuance of (1) additional share payable 3/1/96 to holders of record 2/15/96 Ex date - 3/4/96
Merged into Avnet, Inc. 6/8/2001
Each share Common no par exchanged for (0.87) share Common $1 par

KENT ENERGY CORP (BC)
Recapitalized as Kerf Petroleums Corp. 10/29/1982
Each share Common no par exchanged for (0.25) share Common no par
Kerf Petroleums Corp. name changed to Kaskada Resources Ltd. 09/30/1985 which merged into Canadian Futurity Oils Ltd. 11/01/1985 which recapitalized as Baca Resources Ltd. 08/04/1989 which name changed to CORDEX Petroleums Ltd. 07/11/1994
(See CORDEX Petroleums Ltd.)

KENT EXPL INC (BC)
Reincorporated 05/03/2010
Place of incorporation changed from (Canada) to (BC) 05/03/2010
Each share old Common no par received distribution of (0.25) share Archean Star Resources Inc. Common no par payable 01/28/2011 to holders of record 01/28/2011 Ex date - 01/26/2011
Each share old Common no par exchanged for (0.1) share new Common no par 10/15/2012
Name changed to Bayhorse Silver Inc. 12/16/2013

KENT FINL SVCS INC (NV)
Reincorporated 12/15/2006
Each share old Common 10¢ par exchanged for (1/6) share new Common 10¢ par 09/26/1991
New Common 10¢ par split (2) for (1) by issuance of (1) additional share payable 11/09/1998 to holders of record 10/26/1998
New Common 10¢ par split (2) for (1) by issuance of (1) additional share payable 05/03/2004 to holders of record 04/30/2004 Ex date - 05/04/2004
State of incorporation changed from (DE) to (NV) 12/15/2006
Each share new Common 10¢ par exchanged again for (0.00000112)

share new Common 10¢ par 03/04/2013
Note: In effect holders received $1.75 cash per share and public interest was eliminated

KENT FINNELL INDUSTRIES, INC. (IN)
Name changed to Keltec, Inc. 03/04/1963
(See Keltec, Inc.)

KENT GARAGE INVESTING CORP.
Declared bankrupt 00/00/1931
Details not available

KENT HLDGS LTD (NV)
Charter revoked for failure to file reports and pay fees 08/01/1992

KENT INDUSTRIES, INC. (UT)
Charter suspended for failure to pay taxes 03/31/1964

KENT INDS INC (NY)
Charter cancelled and proclaimed dissolved for failure to pay taxes 9/30/81

KENT INTL HLDGS INC (NV)
Each (950,000) shares old Common $0.002 par exchanged for (1) share new Common $0.002 par 12/09/2011
Note: In effect holders received $2.50 cash per share and public interest was eliminated

KENT MINES LTD. (ON)
Charter cancelled and company declared dissolved for default 03/28/1960

KENT MOORE CORP (DE)
Reincorporated 7/31/70
State of incorporation changed from (MI) to (DE) 7/31/70
Common $1 par split (7) for (5) by issuance of (0.4) additional share 7/15/71
Common $1 par split (3) for (2) by issuance of (0.5) additional share 9/27/76
Common $1 par split (3) for (2) by issuance of (0.5) additional share 10/2/78
Merged into Sealed Power Corp. (DE) 2/1/82
Each share Common $1 par exchanged for (1.22) shares Common $10 par
Sealed Power Corp. (DE) name changed to SPX Corp. 4/27/88

KENT-MOORE ORGANIZATION, INC. (MI)
Common $1 par split (5) for (4) by issuance of (0.25) additional share 7/30/63
Name changed to Kent-Moore Corp. (MI) 6/17/65
Kent-Moore Corp. (MI) reincorporated in Delaware 7/31/70 which merged into Sealed Power Corp. (DE) 2/1/82 which name changed to SPX Corp. 4/27/88

KENT ORGANIZATION INC (CA)
Charter suspended for failure to file reports and pay fees 02/01/1973

KENT PETROLEUM CORP. (CA)
Name changed to Kent Organizations, Inc. 09/21/1960
(See Kent Organizations, Inc.)

KENT TOYS INC (UT)
Each share old Common $0.001 par exchanged for (0.005) share new Common $0.001 par 09/19/1995
Stock Dividend - 100% 06/06/1986
Reorganized under the laws of Delaware as L.A. Group Inc. 03/20/1996
Each (300) shares Common $0.001 par exchanged for (1) share Common $0.001 par
L.A. Group Inc. name changed to ONTV, Inc. 04/03/2000 which name changed to True Product ID, Inc. 05/22/2006

KENT TRUST & SAVINGS CO. (CHATHAM, ONT)
Merged into Metropolitan Trust Co. (Toronto, ON) 06/30/1969
Each share Common $10 par exchanged for (0.5) share Common $10 par
Metropolitan Trust Co. (Toronto, ON) merged into Victoria Grey Metro Trust Co. (Stratford, ON) 10/31/1979 which name changed to Victoria & Grey Trust Co. (Stratford, ON) 04/07/1980 which merged into National Victoria & Grey Trust Co. (Toronto, ON) 08/31/1984 which name changed to National Trust Co. (Toronto, ON) 10/28/1985
(See National Trust Co. (Toronto, ON))

KENT WASHINGTON INC (MD)
Stock Dividend - 10% 06/30/1968
Merged into Presidential Realty Corp. (Old) 11/12/1971
Each share Common $1 par exchanged for (1/3) share Class B Common 10¢ par
Presidential Realty Corp. (Old) reorganized as Presidential Realty Corp. (New) 07/06/1983

KENTANA DEV INC (CA)
Each share old Common no par exchanged for (0.005) share new Common no par 12/10/91
Reorganized as Silicon Disk Corp. 03/01/1992
Each share new Common no par exchanged for (4) shares Common no par
Silicon Disk Corp. recapitalized as Canadian Piper Air Corp. 06/23/1992

KENTEK INFORMATION SYS INC (DE)
Merged into KE Acquisition Corp. 10/28/99
Each share Common 1¢ par exchanged for $8.29 cash

KENTEX ENERGY INC (NV)
Each share old Common $0.001 par exchanged for (0.0005) share new Common $0.001 par 07/16/1998
Recapitalized as Home Financing Centers, Inc. 01/13/2000
Each share new Common $0.001 par exchanged for (0.02) share Common $0.001 par
Note: No holder will receive fewer than (1) share
Home Financing Centers, Inc. recapitalized as WorldWide Indoor Karting, Inc. 07/23/2003 which name changed to Vault Financial Services Inc. 10/08/2003 which name changed to Prime Restaurants, Inc. 04/18/2007 which name changed to BIH Corp. 03/19/2008
(See BIH Corp.)

KENTEX PETE INC (NV)
Each share old Common $0.001 par exchanged for (0.004) share new Common $0.001 par 10/05/1999
Note: No holder of (100) or more pre-split shares received fewer than (100) shares
Holders of (99) or fewer pre-split shares were not affected
Name changed to Northern Oil & Gas, Inc. (NV) 04/03/2007
Northern Oil & Gas, Inc. (NV) reincorporated in Minnesota 06/30/2010 which reincorporated in Delaware 05/09/2018

KENTING AVIATION LTD (CANADA)
Capital Stock 50¢ par reclassified as Common 50¢ par 09/08/1967
Name changed to Kenting Ltd. 04/22/1968
Kenting Ltd. merged into Trimac Ltd. 10/03/1977
(See Kenting Ltd.)

KENTING ENERGY SVCS INC (AB)
Merged into Precision Drilling Corp. 05/28/1997
Each share Common no par exchanged for (0.1752) share Common no par
(See Precision Drilling Corp.)

KENTING LTD (CANADA)
Merged into Trimac Ltd. 10/03/1977
Each share Common 50¢ par exchanged for (1) Conv. Class A Common Stock Purchase Warrant expiring 05/17/1982 and $21.25 cash

KENTON CORP (DE)
Common 50¢ par split (3) for (2) by issuance of (0.5) additional share 7/31/69
Each share Common 50¢ par exchanged for (0.1) share Common 1¢ par 8/29/75
Each share $4 Class A Conv. Preferred exchanged for (1.17648) shares Common 1¢ par 9/19/75
Merged into Rapid-American Corp. 1/31/81
Each share Conv. Preferred 1¢ par exchanged for $22.50 cash
Each share 6% Preferred $100 par exchanged for $22.50 cash
Each share Common 1¢ par exchanged for $22.50 cash
Each share Conv. Preferred 1¢ par, 6% Preferred $100 par and Common 1¢ par received additional distribution of $0.22 cash respectively in August 1981

KENTON NAT RES CORP (CANADA)
Recapitalized as Pacalta Resources Ltd. 10/01/1990
Each share Common no par exchanged for (0.2) share Common no par
Pacalta Resources Ltd. merged into Alberta Energy Co. Ltd. 05/28/1999 which merged into EnCana Corp. 01/03/2003

KENTON TELEPHONE CO. (OH)
Merged into Mid-Continent Telephone Corp. 06/30/1961
Each share Capital Stock no par exchanged for (15) shares Common no par
Mid-Continent Telephone Corp. name changed to Alltel Corp. (OH) 10/25/1983 which reincorporated in Delaware 05/15/1990
(See Alltel Corp.)

KENTRON INTL INC (TX)
Merged into Planning Research Corp. 03/08/1985
Each share Common 10¢ par exchanged for $4.25 cash

KENTUCKY-AMERICAN WATER CO (KY)
5% Preferred Ser. D $100 par called for redemption at $100 plus $0.069444 accrued dividends on 07/06/2012
5.50% Preferred Ser. C $100 par called for redemption at $100.50 plus $0.076388 accrued dividends on 07/06/2012
5.75% Ser. B $100 par called for redemption at $101 plus $0.079861 accrued dividends on 07/06/2012
Public interest eliminated

KENTUCKY BANCORPORATION INC (KY)
Merged into Star Banc Corp. 07/01/1991
Each share Common no par exchanged for $19.85247 cash

KENTUCKY BANCSHARES INC (KY)
Incorporated 05/12/1993
Merged into Peoples Bancorp Inc. 05/09/2003
Each share Common $1 par exchanged for either (30.33333333) shares Common $1 par and $1,813 cash, (102.5) shares Common $1 par or $2,575 cash
Note: Option to receive stock or cash only expired 06/05/2003

KENTUCKY BARLEY LAKES AREA DEVELOPMENT CO. (KY)
Charter revoked for failure to file annual reports 3/27/78

KENTUCKY BOONE COAL CO. (DE)
Liquidated 00/00/1954
Details not available

KENTUCKY BREWING CO.
Acquired by Frankenmuth Brewing Co. 00/00/1939
Details not available

KENTUCKY CARDINAL COAL CORP (VA)
Charter cancelled and proclaimed dissolved for failure to file reports 06/01/1966

KENTUCKY CASH CREDIT CORP.
Merged into Franklin Plan Corp. 00/00/1932
Details not available

KENTUCKY CENT LIFE INS CO (KY)
Each share Common $1 par exchanged for (0.01) share Common $100 par 09/06/1972
Each share Common $100 par received distribution of (200) shares Non-Vtg. Class A Common $1 par 04/20/1987
Stock Dividend - In Non-Vtg. Class A Common to holders of Non-Vtg. Class A Common 200% 04/20/1987
Charter revoked for failure to file annual reports 11/01/2007

KENTUCKY CENTRAL LIFE & ACCIDENT INSURANCE CO. (KY)
Stock Dividends - 25% 12/08/1944; 20% 12/06/1946; 25% 12/03/1948; 33-1/3% 12/01/1950
Name changed to Kentucky Central Life Insurance Co. 03/08/1963
(See Kentucky Central Life Insurance Co.)

KENTUCKY CONSOLIDATED STONE CO.
Reorganized as Kentucky Stone Co. 00/00/1936
No stockholders' equity

KENTUCKY ELEC STL INC (DE)
Chapter 11 bankruptcy petition dismissed 11/21/2003
No stockholders' equity

KENTUCKY ELECTRIC DEVELOPMENT CO., INC.
Acquired by Kentucky Utilities Co. 00/00/1940
Details not available

KENTUCKY ELECTRIC POWER CO.
Liquidation completed 00/00/1951
No Common stockholders' equity

KENTUCKY ENERGY INC (UT)
Each share old Common $0.0001 par exchanged for (0.04) share new Common $0.0001 par 02/02/2011
SEC revoked common stock registration 10/27/2014

KENTUCKY ENTERPRISE BANCORP INC (OH)
Merged into Fifth Third Bancorp 3/15/96
Each share Common 1¢ par exchanged for (0.5735) share Common no par

KENTUCKY FAMILY RESTAURANTS, INC. (KY)
Liquidation completed
Each share Common no par exchanged for initial distribution of $4 cash 02/16/1968
Each share Common no par received second and final distribution of $1 cash 07/01/1968

KENTUCKY FAMILY SEC INS CO (KY)
Under plan of merger name changed to American Family Security Insurance Co. 09/13/1976
American Family Security Insurance Co. merged into Kentucky Central Life Insurance Co. 01/01/1983
(See Kentucky Central Life Insurance Co.)

KENTUCKY FIN INC (KY)
Stock Dividend - 19% 07/11/1966
Merged into Kentucky Central Life Insurance Co. 07/31/1973
Each share Common $1 par exchanged for $12 cash
6% Preferred $10 par called for redemption 09/00/1992
$1.40 Preferred $20 par called for redemption 09/00/1992
Public interest eliminated

KENTUCKY FIRST BANCORP INC (KY)
Merged into Kentucky Bancshares, Inc. 11/7/2003
Each share Common 1¢ par exchanged for $23.25 cash

KENTUCKY FRIED CHICKEN CORP (DE)
Merged into Heublein, Inc. 07/08/1971
Each share Common $1 par exchanged for (0.53) share Common no par
Heublein, Inc. merged into Reynolds (R.J.) Industries, Inc. 10/13/1982 which name changed to RJR Nabisco, Inc. 04/25/1986 which merged into RJR Holdings Group, Inc. 04/28/1989
(See RJR Holdings Group, Inc.)

KENTUCKY FRIED CHICKEN CORP (KY)
Common no par split (5) for (4) by issuance of (0.25) additional share 01/14/1967
Common no par split (3) for (1) by issuance of (2) additional shares 12/29/1967
Common no par split (2) for (1) by issuance of (1) additional share 11/01/1968
Acquired by Kentucky Fried Chicken Corp. (DE) 07/31/1970
Each share Common no par exchanged for (1) share Common $1 par
Kentucky Fried Chicken Corp. (DE) merged into Heublein, Inc. 07/08/1971 which merged into Reynolds (R.J.) Industries, Inc. 10/13/1982 which name changed to RJR Nabisco, Inc. 04/25/1986 which merged into RJR Holdings Group, Inc. 04/28/1989
(See RJR Holdings Group, Inc.)

KENTUCKY FUEL GAS CORP.
Plan of reorganization under Chapter X Bankruptcy Act effective 06/06/1960
No stockholders' equity

KENTUCKY HORSE CTR INC (DE)
Name changed to Racing Corp. of America Inc. 03/29/1990
(See Racing Corp. of America Inc.)

KENTUCKY HOTEL, INC.
In process of liquidation 00/00/1949
Details not available

KENTUCKY INDUSTRIES TRUST CO. (KY)
Name changed to National Industries, Inc. (KY) and Class A Common no par reclassified as Common $1 par 05/14/1963
National Industries, Inc. (KY) merged into Fuqua Industries, Inc. 01/03/1978 which name changed to Actava Group Inc. 07/21/1993 which name changed to Metromedia International Group, Inc. 11/01/1995
(See Metromedia International Group, Inc.)

KENTUCKY INS CO (KY)
Merged into KIC Investment Insurance Co. 12/19/1980
Each share Common $1 par exchanged for $3.91 cash

KENTUCKY INVS INC (KY)
Name changed to Investors Heritage Capital Corp. 06/01/2009

KENTUCKY JOCKEY CLUB INC (KY)
Reorganized 12/09/1963
Common $1 par holders lost equity; received only rights, which expired 10/19/1964 to purchase new Common no par
Voluntarily dissolved 12/29/1987
Details not available

KENTUCKY MED INS CO (KY)
Class A Common $2.80 par split (3) for (2) by issuance of (0.5) additional share 09/14/1989
Class A Common $2.80 par split (4) for (3) by issuance of (1/3) additional share 05/24/1990
Stock Dividends - 10% 05/23/1991; 10% 09/06/1991
Merged into Michigan Physicians Mutual Liability Co. 01/01/1996
Each share Class A Common $2.80 par exchanged for $12.37 cash

KENTUCKY NATL BK (ELIZABETHTOWN, KY)
Under plan of reorganization each share Common 1¢ par automatically became (1) share Kentucky National Bancorp Inc. (IN) Common 1¢ par 05/18/1999

KENTUCKY OHIO GAS CO (DE)
Common $1 par changed to no par 01/30/1958
93% owned by Spectrum Resources Inc. as of 00/00/1985
Public interest eliminated

KENTUCKY OIL & DISTRIBUTING CORP. (DE)
Charter cancelled for non-payment of taxes 4/1/53

KENTUCKY OIL & GAS CORP. (DE)
Dissolved 12/30/55

KENTUCKY OIL & GAS INC (BC)
Name changed to Integrated Card Technologies Inc. 06/06/1994
Integrated Card Technologies Inc. recapitalized as Rizona Ventures Ltd. 07/29/1997 which name changed to Admiral Bay Resources, Inc. (BC) 08/31/1998 which reincorporated in Ontario 03/10/2004 which reincorporated back in British Columbia 03/10/2006

KENTUCKY POWER CO., INC.
Dissolved in 1935

KENTUCKY PRODUCERS & REFINERS CORP. (ME)
Charter revoked for failure to file reports and pay fees in 1920

KENTUCKY PPTY TR (KY)
Name changed to RealAmerica Co. (KY) 2/25/82
RealAmerica Co. (KY) reorganized in Delaware 12/15/82 which name changed to RA Global Services, Inc. 3/6/2007

KENTUCKY REFRIGERATING CO. (DE)
Charter cancelled and declared inoperative and void for non-payment of taxes 4/1/33

KENTUCKY RIVER COAL CORP (VA)
Each share Common $100 par exchanged for (4) shares Common $25 par 00/00/1953
Under plan of merger each share Common $25 par exchanged for (1) Kentucky River Properties LLC Subscription Right expiring 12/30/2002 and $4,000 cash 07/31/2002

KENTUCKY ROCK ASPHALT CO. (DE)
Reorganized in 1936
Each (2) shares Common no par exchanged for (1) share new Common no par
Each share Preferred $100 par exchanged for (1) share Class A Common $25 par and (2) shares Common no par
Recapitalized in 1945
Common no par changed to $1 par
Liquidation approved 6/14/57
Class A Common liquidated 7/1/57

KENTUCKY SECURITIES CO.
Liquidation completed in 1945

KENTUCKY SECURITIES CORP.
Reorganized as Kentucky Securities Co. in 1936 which was completely liquidated in 1945

KENTUCKY SOUTHN BANCORP INC (KY)
Name changed to Trans Financial Bancorp, Inc. 09/24/1985
Trans Financial Bancorp, Inc. name changed to Trans Financial, Inc. 04/24/1995 which merged into Star Banc Corp. 08/31/1998 which merged into Firstar Corp. (New) 11/20/1998 which merged into U.S. Bancorp (DE) 02/27/2001

KENTUCKY STATE LIFE INSURANCE CO
Merged into American Life & Accident Insurance Co. in 1930
Details not available

KENTUCKY STATE TELEPHONE CORP.
Bankrupt in 1931

KENTUCKY TELEPHONE CORP. (DE)
Name changed to General Telephone Co. of Kentucky in 1952
General Telephone Co. of Kentucky merged into General Telephone Co. of the South 12/31/85 which name changed to GTE South Inc. 1/1/88

KENTUCKY USA ENERGY INC (DE)
Common $0.0001 par split (12) for (1) by issuance of (11) additional shares payable 11/19/2007 to holders of record 11/13/2007 Ex date - 11/20/2007
SEC revoked common stock registration 06/12/2013

KENTUCKY-UTAH MINING CO. (UT)
Merged into Federal Uranium Corp. (NV) on a (0.1) for (1) basis 04/28/1955
Federal Uranium Corp. (NV) merged into Federal Resources Corp. 05/02/1960
(See Federal Resources Corp.)

KENTUCKY UTILS CO (KY)
6% Jr. Preferred $100 par called for redemption 11/20/47
7% Preferred $50 par called for redemption 11/20/47
Common no par split (2) for (1) by issuance of (1) additional share 4/12/63
7.84% Preferred $100 par changed to no par 4/26/77
4-3/4% Preferred $100 par changed to no par 4/27/77
10.60% Preferred $100 par changed to no par 4/26/77
10.60% Preferred no par called for redemption 3/1/86
Common $10 par changed to no par and (1) additional share issued 5/19/87
13.36% Preferred no par called for redemption 9/2/87
Under plan of reorganization each share Common no par automatically became (1) share KU Energy Corp. Common no par 12/1/91
7.84% Preferred no par called for redemption 2/1/94
4.75% Preferred no par called for redemption at $101 plus $0.699305 accrued dividends on 10/24/2005
6.53% Preferred called for redemption at $102.939 plus $0.961361 accrued dividends on 10/24/2005

KENTUCKY VALLEY DISTILLING CO.
Acquired by Oldetyme Distillers Corp. in 1937
Details not available

KENTY GOLD MINES LTD.
Dissolved 00/00/1936
Details not available

KENTY RES LTD (ON)
Recapitalized as Browning Communications Inc. 02/09/1987
Each share Common no par exchanged for (0.33333333) share Common no par
(See Browning Communications Inc.)

KENVER RES INC (BC)
Struck off register and declared dissolved for failure to file returns 10/04/1985

KENVILLE GOLD MINES, LTD. (ON)
Recapitalized as International Kenville Gold Mines Ltd. 07/24/1964
Each share Capital Stock $1 par exchanged for (0.25) share Capital Stock $1 par
(See International Kenville Gold Mines Ltd.)

KENVILLE GOLD MINES LTD. (BC)
Charter cancelled in March 1975

KENWAY CORP (DE)
Charter cancelled and declared inoperative and void for non-payment of taxes 04/15/1972

KENWELL OILS & MINES LTD. (ON)
Acquired by Sapphire Petroleums Ltd. 00/00/1954
Each share Common no par exchanged for (1) share Common no par
Sapphire Petroleums Ltd. recapitalized as Cabol Enterprises, Ltd. 01/19/1962
(See Cabol Enterprises, Ltd.)

KENWICK INDS INC (FL)
Name changed 07/30/1998
Name changed from Kenwick Inc. to Kenwick Industries, Inc. 07/30/1998
Recapitalized as Southern California Beverage Corp. 09/03/2003
Each (150) shares Common $0.001 par exchanged for (1) share Common $0.001 par
Southern California Beverage Corp. name changed to Tropical Beverage, Inc. 09/12/2003 which recapitalized as ViviCells International, Inc. 05/09/2008

KENWIN SHOPS INC (NY)
Common $1 par changed to 1¢ par 10/00/1995
Stock Dividend - 50% 05/15/1968
Chapter 11 bankruptcy proceedings dismissed 11/03/2004
Stockholders' equity unlikely

KENWOOD BANCORP INC (DE)
Acquired by Peoples Community Bancorp, Inc. 04/26/2002
Each share Common 1¢ par exchanged for $25.22 cash

KENWOOD CAP CORP (FL)
Reorganized under the laws of Delaware as Envirotech Systems, Inc. 08/16/1989
Each share Common $0.0001 par exchanged for (0.05) share Common 2¢ par
(See Envirotech Systems, Inc.)

KENWOOD PRODUCTS, INC. (KY)
Charter revoked for failure to file annual reports 4/11/78

KENWOOD SVGS & LN ASSN (CINCINNATI, OH)
Under plan of reorganization each share Common 10¢ par automatically became (1) share Kenwood Bancorp Inc. (DE) Common 1¢ par 5/13/96
(See Kenwood Bancorp Inc. (DE))

KENWOOD STORAGE & WAREHOUSE CORP. (NY)
Charter revoked for failure to file reports and pay fees 12/15/34

KEOKUK BANCSHARES INC (DE)
Merged into Heartland Financial USA Inc. 06/30/1994
Each share Common 1¢ par exchanged for (2.0689) shares Common $1 par

KEORA MINES LTD. (ON)
Charter cancelled and company declared dissolved for default in filing returns 06/24/1965

KEPPEL LD LTD (SINGAPORE)
ADR agreement terminated 07/02/2015
Each ADR for Ordinary exchanged for $31.303988 cash

KEPPEL SHIPYARD LTD (SINGAPORE)
Stock Dividend - 25% 6/15/82
Name changed to Keppel Corp. Ltd. 5/8/86

KEPTEL INC (NJ)
Merged into Antec Corp. 11/17/1994
Each share Common no par exchanged for either (0.7) share Common 1¢ par or $18 cash
Note: Option to elect to receive cash expired 11/22/1994
Antec Corp. name changed to ARRIS Group, Inc. (Old) 08/03/2001 which reorganized as ARRIS Group, Inc. (New) 04/16/2013 which merged into ARRIS International PLC 01/05/2016

KERAVISION INC (DE)
Chapter 7 bankruptcy proceedings closed 05/21/2007
No stockholders' equity

KERECO ENERGY LTD (AB)
Name changed to Cadence Energy Inc. 05/14/2008
(See Cadence Energy Inc.)

KEREMEOS MINES LTD. (BC)
Charter cancelled for failure to file returns in 1969

KERF PETES CORP (BC)
Name changed to Kaskada Resources Ltd. 09/30/1985
Kaskada Resources Ltd. merged into Canadian Futurity Oils Ltd. 11/01/1985 which recapitalized as Baca Resources Ltd. 08/04/1989 which name changed to CORDEX Petroleums Ltd. 07/11/1994
(See CORDEX Petroleums Ltd.)

KERITE CO (CT)
Stock Dividends - 20% 7/15/48; 20% 7/20/51; 66-2/3% 10/1/55
Merged into Hubbell (Harvey), Inc. 5/6/69
Each share Capital Stock $10 par exchanged for (2) shares $1.75 Conv. Preferred Ser. A no par
(See Hubbell (Harvey), Inc.)

KERKHOFF INDS INC (CANADA)
Company dissolved 00/00/1993
Details not available

KERLYN OIL CO. (DE)
Name changed to Kerr-McGee Oil Industries, Inc. and each share Common $1 par exchanged for (2) shares Common $1 par 2/23/46
Kerr-McGee Oil Industries, Inc. name changed to Kerr-McGee Corp. 11/1/65

KERMAN ST BK (KERMAN, CA)
Stock Dividend - 2% payable 4/16/99 to holders of record 3/27/99
Merged into Westamerica Bancorporation 6/21/2002
Each share Common no par exchanged for (0.2487) share Common no par

KERMODE CAP LTD (BC)
Name changed to NSGold Corp. 06/30/2010

KERMODE EXPL LTD (ON)
Name changed to Rencore Resources Ltd. 06/01/2010
Rencore Resources Ltd. merged into Bold Ventures Inc. 02/13/2012

KERMODE RES LTD (AB)
Reincorporated under the laws of British Columbia 03/23/1999

KERN (GEORGE), INC.
Merged into Gobel (Adolf), Inc. in 1929
Details not available

KERN COUNTY LAND CO. (CA)
Each share Capital Stock $100 par exchanged for (20) shares Capital Stock $5 par in 1939
Capital Stock $5 par changed to $2.50 par and (1) additional share issued in 1951
Acquired by Tenneco Inc. 8/30/67
Each share Capital Stock $2.50 par exchanged for (1) share $5.50 Conv. Preference no par
(See Tenneco Inc.)

KERN FIDELITY CO.
Liquidated in 1945

KERN FINANCIAL CORP. (DE)
Liquidated 2/13/70

KERN FRONT OIL & GAS CORP. (DE)
No longer in existence having become inoperative and void for non-payment of taxes 4/1/57

KERN MUTUAL TELEPHONE CO. (CA)
5.36% Preferred Ser. A $25 par called for redemption 9/21/64
Acquired by Continental Independent Telephone Corp. 12/31/64
Each share Common $10 par exchanged for (5) shares Common $1 par
Continental Independent Telephone Corp. name changed to Continental Telephone Corp. 5/11/65 which name changed to Continental Telecom Inc. 5/6/82 which name changed to Contel Corp. 5/1/86 which merged into GTE Corp. 3/14/91 which merged into Verizon Communications Inc. 6/30/2000

KERN OIL CO. LTD. (ENGLAND)
Stock Dividend - 20% 01/24/1957
Acquired by Rio Tinto Co. Ltd. on a (0.32) for (1) basis 00/00/1958
Rio Tinto Co. Ltd. merged into Rio-Tinto Zinc Corp. Ltd. 07/09/1962 which name changed to RTZ Corp. PLC 08/26/1987 which name changed to Rio Tinto PLC 06/02/1997

KERN RIVER MINING CO. (CA)
Charter suspended for failure to file reports and pay fees 01/04/1950

KERNOW RES & DEVS LTD (BC)
Merged into Galena International Resources Ltd. 02/26/2010
Each share Common no par exchanged for (0.33333333) share Common no par
Galena International Resources Ltd. name changed to Aurelius Minerals Inc. 01/09/2017

KERONIX INC (CA)
Name changed to Investment Resources & Technology, Inc. 12/15/1983
Investment Resources & Technology, Inc. name changed to Spear Financial Services, Inc. 06/06/1986 which name changed to JMC Group Inc. 06/21/1993 which name changed to Fechtor, Detwiler, Mitchell & Co. Inc. 08/30/1999 which recapitalized as Detwiler, Mitchell & Co. 03/27/2001 which name changed to Detwiler Fenton Group, Inc. 10/20/2008

KERR ADDISON GOLD MINES, LTD. (ON)
Merged into Kerr Addison Mines Ltd. 11/18/1963
Each share Capital Stock no par exchanged for (1) share Capital Stock no par
Kerr Addison Mines Ltd. merged into Noranda Inc. 04/11/1996 which name changed to Falconbridge Ltd. (New) 2005 on 07/01/2005
(See Falconbridge Ltd. (New) 2005)

KERR ADDISON MINES LTD (ON)
Capital Stock no par reclassified as Conv. Class A no par 09/18/1974
Conv. Class A no par reclassified as Common no par 05/07/1979
Conv. Class B no par reclassified as Common no par 05/07/1979
Merged into Noranda Inc. 04/11/1996
Each share Common no par exchanged for (1) share Common no par
Noranda Inc. name changed to Falconbridge Ltd. (New) 2005 on 07/01/2005
(See Falconbridge Ltd. (New) 2005)

KERR GROUP INC (DE)
Name changed 4/28/92
Name changed from Kerr Glass Manufacturing Corp. to Kerr Group Inc. 4/28/92
Merged into Fremont Partners 12/31/97
Each share $1.70 Conv. Class B Preferred Ser. D 50¢ par exchanged for $12.50 cash
Each share Common 50¢ par exchanged for $5.40 cash

KERR INCOME FUND, INC. (DE)
Name changed to Convertible Securities Fund, Inc. 03/14/1963
Convertible Securities Fund, Inc. name changed to Harbor Fund, Inc. (DE) 04/30/1969 which reincorporated in Maryland 12/31/1978 which name changed to American General Harbor Fund, Inc. 12/10/1980 which name changed to American Capital Harbor Fund, Inc. (MD) 09/12/1983 which reincorporated in Delaware as Van Kampen American Capital Harbor Fund 08/19/1995 which name changed to Van Kampen Harbor Fund 07/14/1998

KERR LAKE MINES LTD. (ON)
Capital Stock $4 par changed to $1 par 00/00/1935
Capital Stock $1 par changed to 40¢ par 07/02/1957
Name changed to United Principal Properties Ltd. and Capital Stock 40¢ par changed to no par 05/20/1958
United Principal Properties Ltd. recapitalized as Canadian Interurban Properties Ltd. 08/28/1963 which merged into Campeau Corp. 10/09/1973
(See Campeau Corp.)

KERR MANUFACTURING CO. (MI)
Each share Common $10 par exchanged for (10) shares Common $1 par plus a 33-1/3% stock dividend paid in 1948
Acquired by Ritter Co., Inc. 5/1/64
Each (6-2/3) shares 6% Participating Class A $3 par exchanged for (1) share Common $2.50 par
Each (7.53) shares Common $1 par exchanged for (1) share Common $2.50 par
Ritter Co., Inc. name changed to Ritter Corp. 4/27/65 which merged into Ritter Pfaudler Corp. 11/1/65 which merged into Sybron Corp. 10/7/68
(See Sybron Corp.)

KERR MCGEE CORP (DE)
Common $1 par split (3) for (1) by issuance of (2) additional shares 08/13/1971
$4.50 Conv. Preferred Ser. A no par called for redemption 11/27/1973
Common $1 par split (2) for (1) by issuance of (1) additional share 11/20/1981
Each share Common $1 par received distribution of (0.20164) share Tronox Inc. Common 1¢ par payable 03/30/2006 to holders of record 03/20/2006 Ex date - 03/31/2006
Common $1 par split (2) for (1) by issuance of (1) additional share payable 06/14/2006 to holders of record 06/02/2006 Ex date - 06/15/2006
Merged into Anadarko Petroleum Corp. 08/10/2006
Each share Common $1 par exchanged for $70.50 cash

KERR MCGEE OIL INDS (DE)
Common $1 par split (4) for (3) by issuance of (1/3) additional share 4/1/55
Common $1 par split (2) for (1) by issuance of (1) additional share 5/26/61
Stock Dividend - 10% 6/2/52
4-1/2% Prior Conv. Preferred $25 par called for redemption 6/15/61
Name changed to Kerr-McGee Corp. 11/1/65

KERRISDALE MNG CORP (NV)
Name changed to China Jo-Jo Drugstores, Inc. 09/24/2009

KERRISDALE RES LTD (BC)
Struck off register and declared dissolved for failure to file returns 06/05/1992

KERRY MNG LTD (BC)
Common 50¢ par changed to no par 11/14/1984
Merged into Berkley Resources Inc. (New) 08/18/1986
Each share Common no par exchanged for (0.33333333) share Capital Stock no par
Berkley Resources Inc. (New) recapitalized as Berkley Renewables Inc. 04/16/2012

KERZNER INTL LTD (BAHAMAS)
Acquired by K-Two Holdco Ltd. 09/01/2006
Each share Ordinary $0.001 par exchanged for $81 cash

KESA ELECTRICALS PLC (UNITED KINGDOM)
ADR agreement terminated 09/01/2016
No ADR's remain outstanding

KESANG CORP BERHAD (MALAYSIA)
ADR agreement terminated 12/21/2006
Details not available

KESSEF TECHNOLOGIES INC (DE)
Name changed to Maxoil Inc. 11/29/1988
Maxoil Inc. recapitalized as LCA-Vision Inc. 08/15/1995
(See LCA-Vision Inc.)

KESSLER GRAPHICS CORP (NY)
Dissolved by proclamation 3/24/93

KESSLER MANUFACTURING CO.
Acquired by Cannon Mills Co. 00/00/1928
Details not available

KESSLER OIL & GAS CO.
Dissolution approved in 1941

KESTRAL CORP. (MA)
Common no par changed to $5 par in 1953
Merged into Coleco Industries, Inc. 12/31/65
Each share Common $5 par exchanged for (2.5) shares Common $1 par
(See Coleco Industries, Inc.)

KESTREL ENERGY INC (CO)
Each share old Common no par exchanged for (0.01) share new Common no par 8/23/2005
Note: Holders of (99) or fewer pre-split shares received $1.42 cash per share
Acquired by Samson Oil & Gas 7/14/2006
Each share new Common no par exchanged for $142 cash

KESTREL EQUITY CORP (AZ)
Name changed to Stereo Vision Entertainment, Inc. 2/7/2000

KESTREL RES LTD (BC)
Merged into Ella Resources Inc. 06/01/1993
Each share Common no par exchanged for (0.35) share Common no par
Ella Resources Inc. name changed to Kinetic Energy Inc. 01/25/2001 which recapitalized as Torque Energy Inc. 02/19/2003
(See Torque Energy Inc.)

KETAY INSTRUMENT CORP. (IL)
Name changed to Norden-Ketay Corp. 2/11/55
Norden-Ketay Corp. merged into United Aircraft Corp. 7/1/58 which name changed to United Technologies Corp. 4/30/75

KETAY MANUFACTURING CORP. (IL)
Name changed to Ketay Instrument Corp. 9/10/54
Ketay Instrument Corp. name changed to Norden-Ketay Corp. 2/11/55 which merged into United Aircraft Corp. 7/1/58 which name changed to United Technologies Corp. 4/30/75

KETCH ENERGY LTD (BC)
Acquired by Acclaim Energy Trust 10/01/2002
Each share Common no par exchanged for (1.15) Trust Units and (0.33333333) share Ketch Resources Ltd. Common no par
(See each company's listing)

KETCH RES LTD (AB)
Under plan of merger each share Common no par exchanged for (0.4) share Bear Ridge Resources Ltd. Common no par, (0.4) share Kereco Energy Ltd. Common no par, and (0.1) Ketch Resources Trust, Trust Unit 01/18/2005
(See each company's listing)

KETCH RES TR (AB)
Merged into Advantage Energy Income Fund 06/23/2006
Each Trust Unit no par exchanged for (0.565) Trust Unit no par
Advantage Energy Income Fund reorganized as Advantage Oil & Gas Ltd. 07/09/2009

KETCHUM & CO INC (NY)
Merged into OCP International, Inc. 06/28/1991
Each share Common $1 par exchanged for $2.425 cash

KETCHUM CAP CORP (AB)
Recapitalized as Ammonite Energy Ltd. 01/22/2009
Each share Common no par exchanged for (0.2) share Common no par

Ammonite Energy Ltd. merged into Novus Energy Inc. 12/11/2009
(See Novus Energy Inc.)

KETEMA INC (DE)
Merged into KTM Acquisition Corp. 12/13/94
Each share Common $1 par exchanged for $15 cash

KETNER GLOBAL INVTS INC (NV)
Name changed to Kelyniam Global, Inc. 12/05/2007

KETONA RED LAKE MINES LTD.
Name changed to Marcourt Nickel Mines Ltd. in 1948
(See Marcourt Nickel Mines Ltd.)

KETRIA INC (FL)
Reincorporated 06/25/1969
State of incorporation changed from (CA) to (FL) 06/25/1969
Name changed to United Resources, Inc. and Common no par changed to 1¢ par 12/08/1969
(See United Resources, Inc.)

KETTELLE JOHN D CORP (PA)
Name changed to Kappa Systems, Inc. (PA) 12/06/1971
Kappa Systems, Inc. (PA) reorganized in Delaware 06/01/1979
(See Kappa Systems, Inc. (DE))

KETTERING INDS INC (DE)
Merged into Newco Acquisition Corp. 04/06/1984
Each share Common 10¢ par exchanged for $6.50 cash

KETTLE RIV GROUP INC (NV)
Common $0.001 par split (3) for (1) by issuance of (2) additional shares payable 10/4/2001 to holders of record 10/3/2001 Ex date - 10/5/2001
Name changed to Koala International Wireless, Inc. 12/6/2001
Koala International Wireless Inc. name changed to KIWI Network Solutions, Inc. 1/14/2004 which name changed to Trimax Corp. 2/15/2005

KETTLE RIV RES LTD (BC)
Merged into New Nadina Explorations Ltd. 11/06/2015
Each share Common no par exchanged for (1) share Common no par
Note: Unexchanged certificates will be cancelled and become without value 11/06/2021

KETTLEMAN HILLS ROYALTY SYNDICATE NO. 1
Trust terminated 05/03/1955
Details not available

KEUFFEL & ESSER CO (CA)
Acquired by Azon Corp. 05/18/1987
Details not available

KEUFFEL & ESSER CO (NJ)
Common $1 par split (5) for (4) by issuance of (0.25) additional share 11/10/1980
Acquired by Kratos, Inc. 03/24/1982
Each share Common $1 par exchanged for $3 cash

KEUHNE MANUFACTURING CO. (IL)
Adjudicated bankrupt 12/7/66
No stockholders' equity

KEURIG GREEN MTN INC (DE)
Acquired by Acorn Holdings B.V. 03/03/2016
Each share Common 10¢ par exchanged for $92 cash

KEVCO INC (TX)
Plan of reorganization under Chapter 11 Federal Bankruptcy Code effective 12/05/2002
No stockholders' equity

KEVCORP SVCS INC (NV)
Common $0.001 par split (10) for (1) by issuance of (9) additional shares payable 03/07/2005 to holders of record 03/07/2005

Recapitalized as Center For Wound Healing, Inc. 02/15/2006
Each share Common $0.001 par exchanged for (0.1) share Common $0.001 par
(See Center For Wound Healing, Inc.)

KEVEX CORP (DE)
Stock Dividend - 100% 11/20/1980
Acquired by VG Instruments PLC 04/29/1988
Each share Common 1¢ par exchanged for $13 cash

KEVIN-FLATHEAD OIL CO. (MT)
Dissolved 1/6/30

KEVIN SPORTS TOYS INTL INC (AB)
Recapitalized as Gobi Oil & Gas Ltd. 12/31/1993
Each share Common no par exchanged for (0.1) share Common no par
Gobi Oil & Gas Ltd. merged into Dominion Explorers Inc. (New) 12/31/1994 which merged into Neutrino Resources Inc. 02/28/1997
(See Neutrino Resources Inc.)

KEVLIN CORP (MA)
Name changed 10/2/91
Common 10¢ par split (2) for (1) by issuance of (1) additional share 7/6/82
Common 10¢ par split (3) for (2) by issuance of (0.5) additional share 12/30/82
Name changed from Kelvin Microwave Corp. to Kelvin Corp. 10/2/91
Merged into Chelton Communications Systems, Inc. 3/7/96
Each share Common 10¢ par exchanged for $4.54 cash

KEVLIN MANUFACTURING CO. (MA)
Common 20¢ par changed to 10¢ par 2/24/74
Name changed to Kevlin Microwave Corp. 6/3/81
Kevlin Microwave Corp. name changed to Kevlin Corp. 10/2/91

KEVTRON ELECTRS CORP (NY)
Dissolved by proclamation 3/24/93

KEWAGAMA GOLD MINES QUE LTD (QC)
Name changed to KWG Resources Inc. 10/09/1991

KEWANEE INDS INC (DE)
Name changed 07/01/1975
Each share Common $100 par exchanged for (10) shares Common $10 par 00/00/1950
Each share Common $10 par exchanged for (1) share Class A Common $10 par and (2) shares Class B Common $10 par 04/01/1960
Each share Class A Common $10 par exchanged for (1) share Conv. Common $10 par 05/10/1966
Each share Class B Common $10 par exchanged for (1) share Ordinary Common $10 par 05/10/1966
Conv. Common $10 par and Ordinary Common $10 par changed to $5 par and (1) additional share issued respectively 12/11/1972
$2 Conv. Preferred Ser. A no par called for redemption 03/01/1973
Stock Dividend - 21% in Class B Common to Common holders of record 04/01/1960 paid 05/16/1960
Name changed from Kewanee Oil Co. to Kewanee Industries, Inc. 07/01/1975
Merged into Gulf Oil Corp. 09/19/1977
Each share Conv. Common $5 par exchanged for $47.50 cash
Each share Ordinary Common $5 par exchanged for $47.50 cash

KEWAUNEE GREEN BAY & WESTN RR CO (WI)
Merged into Green Bay & Western Railroad Co. 1/1/69

Each share Preferred $100 exchanged for for $200 cash
Each share Common $100 par exchanged for $200 cash

KEWAUNEE SCIENTIFIC EQUIPMENT CORP. (DE)
Common $2.50 par split (3) for (2) by issuance of (0.5) additional share 1/4/84
Common $2.50 par split (3) for (2) by issuance of (0.5) additional share 1/4/85
Name changed to Kewaunee Scientific Corp. 8/27/86

KEWAUNEE SCIENTIFIC EQUIPMENT CORP. (MI)
Reincorporated under the laws of Delaware 9/1/70
Kewaunee Scientific Equipment Corp. (Del.) name changed to Kewaunee Scientific Corp. 8/27/86

KEWEENAW COPPER CO.
Liquidated in 1945

KEWL CORP (CANADA)
Each share old Common no par exchanged for (0.05) share new Common no par 08/13/2004
Each share new Common no par exchanged again for (0.000002) share new Common no par 02/07/2005
Note: In effect holders received $0.01 cash per share and public interest was eliminated

KEWL INTL INC (NV)
Recapitalized as Meg Athletic Corp. 11/15/2004
Each share Common 1¢ par exchanged for (0.01) share Common 1¢ par
Meg Athletic Corp. recapitalized as Pure H2O Inc. 05/10/2006 which recapitalized as Newron Sport 10/03/2008

KEY ANACON MINES LTD (ON)
Merged into Hunter Brook Holdings Ltd. 01/01/1999
Each share Common no par exchanged for $1.65 cash

KEY BANCSHARES W VA INC (WV)
Merged into Key Centurion Bancshares, Inc. 11/30/1985
Each share Common $3 par exchanged for (1) share Common $3 par
Key Centurion Bancshares, Inc. merged into Banc One Corp. 05/03/1993 which merged into Bank One Corp. 10/02/1998 which merged into J.P. Morgan Chase & Co. 12/31/2000 which name changed to JPMorgan Chase & Co. 07/20/2004

KEY BANK OF FLORIDA (TAMPA, FL)
Under plan of reorganization each share Common $5 par automatically became (1) share Key Bancshares, Inc. Common $5 par in January, 1985

KEY BANK OF TAMPA (TAMPA, FL)
Common $10 par changed to $5 par 6/28/76
Name changed to Key Bank of Florida (Tampa, Fla.) 4/20/83
Key Bank of Florida (Tampa, Fla.) reorganized as Key Bancshares, Inc. in January, 1985

KEY BKS INC (NY)
Common $5 par split (3) for (2) by issuance of (0.5) additional share 05/10/1984
Name changed to KeyCorp (NY) 08/28/1985
KeyCorp (NY) merged into KeyCorp (New) (OH) 03/01/1994

KEY BISCAYNE ENTERPRISES INC (DE)
Liquidation completed

Each share Common 10¢ par exchanged for initial distribution of $0.24 cash 06/17/1991
Each share Common 10¢ par received second and final distribution of $0.062 cash 06/08/1992

KEY BOILER EQUIPMENT CO., INC.
Name changed to Key Co. (Mo.) in 1935
Key Co. (Mo.) acquired by ACF Industries, Inc. 8/9/55
(See ACF Industries, Inc.)

KEY CAP GROUP INC (BC)
Name changed to AccelRate Power Systems Inc. 10/24/2003
AccelRate Power Systems Inc. name changed to Goldstrike Resources Ltd. 06/21/2011

KEY CENTURION BANCSHARES INC (WV)
Common $3 par split (3) for (2) by issuance of (0.5) additional share 12/31/85
Common $3 par split (2) for (1) by issuance of (1) additional share 7/29/88
Stock Dividends - 10% 12/31/86; 10% 12/18/87; 10% 12/21/88
Merged into Banc One Corp. 5/3/93
Each share Common $3 par exchanged for (0.434783) share Common no par
Banc One Corp. merged into Bank One Corp. 10/2/98 which merged into J.P. Morgan Chase & Co. 12/31/2000 which name changed to JPMorgan Chase & Co. 7/20/2004

KEY CO. (MO)
Acquired by ACF Industries, Inc. on a (1) for (4) basis 8/9/55
(See ACF Industries, Inc.)

KEY CO (NC)
Common $1 par split (2) for (1) by issuance of (1) additional share 6/3/83
Common $1 par reclassified as Class B Common $1 par 9/17/85
Each share Class B Common $1 par received distribution of (1) share Class A Common $1 par 9/23/85
Stock Dividend - 10% 9/30/68
Completely liquidated and dissolved 11/26/91
No stockholders' equity

KEY COLOR LABORATORIES INC. (NY)
Name changed to T.K.C.L., Inc. 01/27/1977
T.K.C.L., Inc. recapitalized as Outdoor Sportman's Travel, Ltd. 09/06/1977 which name changed to Anglo American Properties, Inc. 03/31/1978
(See Anglo American Properties, Inc.)

KEY COLOR STUDIOS, INC. (NY)
Name changed to Key Color Laboratories Inc. 09/29/1967
Key Color Laboratories Inc. name changed to T.K.C.L., Inc. 01/27/1977 which recapitalized as Outdoor Sportman's Travel, Ltd. 09/06/1977 which name changed to Anglo American Properties, Inc. 03/31/1978
(See Anglo American Properties, Inc.)

KEY CORP. PHARMACEUTICALS (FL)
Reorganized as Key Pharmaceuticals, Inc. 12/20/1961
Each share Class A or B Common $1 par exchanged for (2) shares Common no par
Key Pharmaceuticals, Inc. merged into Schering-Plough Corp. 06/26/1986 which merged into Merck & Co., Inc. (New) 11/03/2009

KEY DEVELOPMENT CORP. (MN)
Name changed to Minnesota Equity Corp. and Common $1 par changed to 10¢ par 9/27/66
Minnesota Equity Corp. liquidated for Minnesota Equities Corp. 12/27/68 which name changed to Interfinancial Corp. 9/30/69 which merged into El Dorado International, Inc. 2/28/73 which name changed to Westamerica Inc. (Minn.) 6/30/87 which reincorporated in California 6/28/88

KEY ENERGY ENTERPRISES INC (FL)
Stock Dividend - 10% 6/16/80
Chapter 11 bankruptcy proceedings converted to Chapter 7 on 11/3/89
Stockholders' equity unlikely

KEY ENERGY SVCS INC (MD)
Name changed 12/09/1998
Name changed from Key Energy Group, Inc. to Key Energy Services Inc. 12/09/1998
Plan of reorganization under Chapter 11 Federal Bankruptcy proceedings effective 12/15/2016
Each share Common 10¢ par received (0.005105) share Key Energy Services, Inc. (DE) Common 1¢ par, (0.005751) Common Stock Purchase Warrant expiring 12/15/2020 and (0.005751) Common Stock Purchase Warrant expiring 12/15/2021
Note: No distribution was made to holders entitled to fewer than (1) share

KEY FLA BANCORP INC (FL)
Merged into Regions Financial Corp. (Old) 3/19/98
Each share Common 1¢ par exchanged for (0.3666) share Common $0.625 par
Regions Financial Corp. (Old) merged into Regions Financial Corp. (New) 7/1/2004

KEY GOLD CORP (NV)
Common $0.001 par split (8) for (1) by issuance of (7) additional shares payable 05/17/2004 to holders of record 05/10/2004 Ex date - 05/18/2004
Name changed to Strategic Resources, Ltd. 12/26/2006
(See Strategic Resources, Ltd.)

KEY GOLD HLDG INC (QC)
Recapitalized as Pangolin Diamonds Corp. 03/20/2013
Each share Common no par exchanged for (0.5) share Common no par

KEY HOSPITALITY ACQUISITION CORP (DE)
Issue Information - 6,000,000 UNITS consisting of (1) share COM and (1) WT offered at $8 per Unit on 10/20/2005
Completely liquidated
Each share Common $0.001 par received first and final distribution of approximately $7.6876 cash payable 12/12/2007 to holders of record 12/11/2007
Note: Certificates were not required to be surrendered and are without value

KEY IMAGE SYS INC (CA)
Reorganized under Chapter 11 Federal Bankruptcy Code as Electrotek Industries, Inc. 8/28/90
Each share Class A Common no par exchanged for (0.25) share Common no par

KEY INDS LTD (BC)
Recapitalized as New Key Industries Ltd. 09/27/1976
Each share Common no par exchanged for (0.25) share Common no par
New Key Industries Ltd. merged into Ambassador Industries Ltd. (Old) 06/01/1978
(See Ambassador Industries Ltd. (Old))

KEY INTL FILMS DISTRS INC (CO)
Name changed to Image Entertainment Inc. 06/30/1983
Image Entertainment Inc. reincorporated in California 06/19/1990 which reincorporated in Delaware 09/09/2005 which merged into RLJ Entertainment, Inc. 10/03/2012

KEY INTL MFG INC (NY)
Completely liquidated 4/9/86
Each share 5-1/2% Prior Preferred $100 par exchanged for first and final distribution of $100 cash
Each share Common 1¢ par exchanged for first and final distribution of $5.20 cash

KEY LAKE EXPLS LTD (ON)
Delisted from Canadian Dealer Network 1/3/95

KEY LARGO RES LTD (BC)
Recapitalized as World Organics Inc. 03/16/1993
Each share Common no par exchanged for (0.5) share Common no par

KEY LEARNING SYS INC (DE)
Charter cancelled and declared inoperative and void for non-payment of taxes 3/1/76

KEY LIFE INSURANCE CO. OF IOWA (IA)
Name changed to Circle Key Life Insurance Co. 7/14/65
Circle Key Life Insurance Co. name changed to Central United Life Insurance Co. 4/30/71 which merged into Central United Corp. 3/31/75
(See Central United Corp.)

KEY LIFE INS CO (IL)
Merged into Central-National Financial Corp. 12/20/1971
Each share Capital Stock $1 par exchanged for (0.444444) share Common $1 par
(See Central-National Financial Corp.)

KEY LINK ASSETS CORP (DE)
Common $0.0001 par split (4) for (1) by issuance of (3) additional shares payable 05/16/2016 to holders of record 05/16/2016 Ex date - 05/17/2016
Name changed to Foothills Exploration, Inc. 08/05/2016

KEY OIL & GAS (1955) LTD. (BC)
Name changed to Consolidated Key Oils, Ltd. 10/15/1968
Consolidated Key Oils, Ltd. name changed to Commonwealth Drilling (BC) Ltd. 02/09/1970
(See Commonwealth Drilling (BC) Ltd.)

KEY OIL & GAS CO. LTD. (AB)
Struck off register and declared dissolved for failure to file reports and pay fees 12/15/61

KEY PHARMACEUTICALS INC (FL)
Each share Common no par exchanged for (1/3) share Common $1 par 11/04/1966
Common $1 par changed to 50¢ par and (1) additional share issued 11/10/1978
Common 50¢ par changed to 25¢ par and (1) additional share issued 06/11/1979
Common 25¢ par changed to $0.16666 par and (0.5) additional share issued 10/03/1980
Common $0.1666 par changed to $0.1111 par and (0.5) additional share issued 06/25/1981
Common $0.1111 par changed to $0.074 par and (0.5) additional share issued 09/07/1982
Common $0.074 par changed to $0.0493 par and (0.5) additional share issued 11/03/1983
Merged into Schering-Plough Corp. 06/26/1986
Each share Common $0.0493 par exchanged for (0.265625) share Common $1 par and (1) right to purchase (1) share Common $1 par
Schering-Plough Corp. merged into Merck & Co., Inc. (New) 11/03/2009

KEY PRODTN INC (DE)
Merged into Cimarex Energy Co. 9/30/2002
Each share Common 25¢ par exchanged for (1) share Common 1¢ par

KEY PUNCH COMPUTER TEMPS INC (NY)
Company became private 00/00/1988
Details not available

KEY SAVINGS & LOAN ASSOCIATION (CO)
Out of business 02/28/1987
No stockholders' equity

KEY ST BK (OWOSSO, MI)
Common $10 par changed to $5 par and (1) additional share issued 06/20/1986
Stock Dividends - 10% 04/15/1987; 10% 04/12/1991
Acquired by Chemical Financial Corp. 10/21/1993
Each share Common $5 par exchanged for (1.017) shares Common $10 par

KEY SYSTEM TRANSIT CO.
Reorganized as Railway Equipment & Realty Co., Ltd. in 1930 which completed liquidation 11/4/63

KEY TECHNOLOGY INC (OR)
Conv. Preferred Ser. B 1¢ par called for redemption at $10 on 7/12/2005
Acquired by Duravant LLC 03/20/2018
Each share Common no par exchanged for $26.75 cash

KEY WASTE MGMT INC (UT)
Recapitalized as Ammonia Hold, Inc. 07/12/1994
Each share Common $0.001 par exchanged for (0.05) share Common $0.001 par
Ammonia Hold, Inc. name changed to TS&B Holdings, Inc. 10/11/2001 which recapitalized as CALI Holdings Inc. 04/08/2005 which name changed to Sovereign Exploration Associates International, Inc. 10/27/2005

KEY WEST ELECTRIC CO.
Liquidated in 1943

KEY WEST ST BK (KEY WEST, FL)
Name changed to First State Bank of the Florida Keys (Key West, FL) 06/30/1978

KEY-WESTERN INVESTMENT CORP. (TX)
Charter forfeited for failure to file reports and pay fees 3/16/67

KEYBOYCON MINES LTD. (ON)
Recapitalized as Con-Key Mines Ltd. 08/16/1956
Each share Capital Stock no par exchanged for (0.25) share Capital Stock no par
Con-Key Mines Ltd. merged into Can-Con Enterprises & Explorations Ltd. 11/30/1970 which name changed to Aubet Resources Inc. 09/08/1981 which recapitalized as Aubet Explorations Ltd. 09/30/1998 which name changed to Visa Gold Explorations Inc. 08/25/1999
(See Visa Gold Explorations Inc.)

KEYCLUB NET INC (FL)
Recapitalized as Global Wide Web, Inc. 3/16/2001
Each share Common $0.001 par

exchanged for (0.1) share Common $0.001 par
Global Wide Web, Inc. name changed to TIE Technologies, Inc. 4/5/2002

KEYCON INDS INC (NV)
Merged into LLC Corp. 09/17/1985
Each share Common 1¢ par exchanged for (11.5) shares Common $1 par
LLC Corp. name changed to Valhi, Inc. 03/10/1987

KEYCORP (NY)
Common $5 par split (3) for (2) by issuance of (0.5) additional share 01/31/1986
Common $5 par split (3) for (2) by issuance of (0.5) additional share issued 04/14/1992
Common $5 par split (2) for (1) by issuance of (1) additional share 03/22/1993
Adjustable Rate Preferred Ser. A $5 par called for redemption 08/02/1993
Merged into KeyCorp (New) (OH) 03/01/1994
Each Depositary Preferred Ser. B exchanged for (1) 10% Depositary Preferred Class A
Each share Preferred Ser. B $5 par exchanged for (1) share 10% Preferred Class A $5 par
Each share Common $5 par exchanged for (1.205) shares Common $1 par

KEYCORP CAP V (DE)
5.875% Trust Preferred Securities called for redemption at $25 on 09/01/2011

KEYCORP CAP VI (DE)
Issue Information - 3,000,000 shares TR PFD SECS 6.125% offered at $25 per share on 12/02/2003
6.125% Trust Preferred Securities called for redemption at $25 on 09/01/2011

KEYCORP CAP VIII (DE)
7% Trust Preferred Securities called for redemption at $25 on 09/01/2011

KEYCORP CAP IX (DE)
6.750% Enhanced Trust Preferred Securities called for redemption at $25 on 12/15/2011

KEYCORP CAP X (DE)
8% Enhanced Trust Preferred Securities called for redemption at $25 on 07/12/2012

KEYCORP INDS LTD (BC)
Recapitalized as Belkin Inc. 10/01/1985
Each share Common no par exchanged for (4) shares Common no par
(See Belkin Inc.)

KEYCORP NEW (OH)
10% Class A Depositary Preferred called for redemption at $25 on 06/25/1996
Fixed-to-Floating Rate Non-Cum. Perpetual Preferred Ser. C $1 par called for redemption at $25 on 02/15/2017
Each share 7.75% Non-Cum. Conv. Perpetual Preferred Ser. A $1 par automatically became (7.0922) shares Common $1 par 03/20/2017
(Additional Information in Active)

KEYDATA CORP (DE)
Each share Common 1¢ par exchanged for (0.277) share Common 25¢ par 07/30/1982
Ceased operations 04/00/1988
No stockholders' equity

KEYERA FACS INCOME FD (AB)
Each Trust Unit no par received distribution of (0.00988576) additional Unit and $0.225 cash payable 12/15/2009 to holders of record 11/23/2009 Ex date - 11/19/2009
Under plan of reorganization each Trust Unit no par automatically became (1) share Keyera Corp. Common no par 01/17/2011

KEYES FIBRE CO (ME)
Common no par changed to $1 par 00/00/1950
Common $1 par split (2) for (1) by issuance of (1) additional share 12/28/1959
4.8% 1st Preferred $25 par called for redemption 11/01/1963
Stock Dividends - 100% 04/15/1955; 50% 05/12/1976
Merged into Arcata Corp. 11/30/1978
Each share Common $1 par exchanged for (1) share $2.16 Conv. Preferred Ser. A $5 par
Arcata Corp. name changed to Atacra Liquidating Corp. 06/04/1982
(See Atacra Liquidating Corp.)

KEYES FLA PPTYS LTD-85 (FL)
Name changed to KFP 85-Ltd. 12/21/1992
(See KFP 85-Ltd.)

KEYES OFFSHORE LTD PARTNERSHIP (DE)
Under plan of reorganization each Depositary Receipt exchanged for (9.5) shares Marine Holding Co. Common 10¢ par 03/13/1990
Marine Holding Co. name changed to Marine Drilling Companies, Inc. 06/27/1991 which merged into Pride International, Inc. (DE) 09/13/2001 which merged into Ensco PLC 06/01/2011

KEYLOCK RES INC (AB)
Name changed to Eurasia Gold Corp. (AB) 05/15/1997
Eurasia Gold Corp. (AB) reincorporated in Yukon 06/17/1999 which reorganized in Canada as Eurasia Gold Inc. 05/25/2006 which reincorporated in British Columbia 04/05/2007
(See Eurasia Gold Inc. (BC))

KEYMARK RES INC (BC)
Name changed to Alabama Graphite Corp. 08/31/2012
Alabama Graphite Corp. merged into Westwater Resources, Inc. 04/23/2018

KEYMASTER CORP (AR)
Merged into Solomon, Inc. 3/8/73
Each share 6% Class A Conv. Preferred $5 par exchanged for (0.25) share Common 10¢ par
Each share 8% Non-Cum. Preferred $5 par exchanged for (2.25) shares Common 10¢ par
Each share Common $1 par exchanged for (0.25) share Common 10¢ par
(See Solomon, Inc.)

KEYMET MINES LTD. (ON)
Acquired by Anacon Lead Mines Ltd. 00/00/1955
Each share Common exchanged for (0.25) share Common
Anacon Lead Mines Ltd. recapitalized as Key Anacon Mines Ltd. 02/14/1964
(See Key Anacon Mines Ltd.)

KEYMOR GOLD MINES, LTD. (ON)
Charter cancelled and company declared dissolved for default in filing returns 03/18/1965

KEYNOTE RECORDINGS, INC. (DE)
No longer in existence having become inoperative and void for non-payment of taxes 4/1/54

KEYNOTE RES INC (BC)
Struck off register and declared dissolved for failure to file returns 04/23/1993

KEYNOTE SYS INC (CA)
State of incorporation changed from (CA) to (DE) 03/00/2000
Acquired by Thoma Bravo, LLC 08/22/2013
Each share Common $0.001 par exchanged for $20 cash

KEYON COMMUNICATIONS HLDGS INC (DE)
Each share old Common $0.001 par exchanged for (0.5) share new Common $0.001 par 11/02/2007
Company terminated common stock registration 12/23/2011

KEYREIT (ON)
Acquired by Plazacorp Retail Properties Ltd. (NB) 06/28/2013
Each Trust Unit exchanged for (1.0396) shares Common no par and $3.26 cash
Plazacorp Retail Properties Ltd. (NB) reorganized in Ontario as Plaza Retail REIT 01/08/2014

KEYSER RES INC (NV)
Name changed to Lone Star Gold, Inc. 06/20/2011

KEYSOURCE FINL INC (NC)
Merged into BNC Bancorp 09/14/2012
Each share Common $1 par exchanged for (1) share Common no par
BNC Bancorp merged into Pinnacle Financial Partners, Inc. 06/16/2017

KEYSPAN CORP (NV)
7.95% Preferred Ser. AA $25 par called for redemption at $25 on 06/01/2000
Merged into National Grid PLC 08/24/2007
Each share Common $0.33333333 par exchanged for $42 cash

KEYSPAN ENERGY (NY)
Name changed to KeySpan Corp. 05/20/1999
(See KeySpan Corp.)

KEYSPAN ENERGY CORP (NY)
Merged into MarketSpan Corp. 05/29/1998
Each share Common $0.33-1/3 par exchanged for (1) share Common $0.33-1/3 par
MarketSpan Corp. name changed to KeySpan Energy 09/10/1998 which name changed to KeySpan Corp. 05/20/1999
(See KeySpan Corp.)

KEYSPAN FACS INCOME FUND (AB)
Name changed to Keyera Facilities Income Fund 02/10/2005
Keyera Facilities Income Fund reorganized as Keyera Corp. 01/17/2011

KEYSTONE AIRCRAFT CORP.
Merged into Curtiss-Wright Corp. in 1929
Details not available

KEYSTONE ALLOYS CO. (PA)
Name changed to K.A. Liquidating Co. 12/31/66
(See K.A. Liquidating Co.)

KEYSTONE AMER CAP PRESERVATION & INCOME FD (MA)
Merged into Keystone America Capital Preservation & Income Fund II (MA) 1/3/95
Each Share of Bene. Int. no par exchanged for (1) Class B Share of Bene. Int. no par
Keystone America Capital Preservation & Income Fund II (MA) reincorporated in Delaware as Evergreen Capital Preservation & Income Fund 10/31/97

KEYSTONE AMER CAP PRESERVATION & INCOME FD-II (MA)
Shares of Bene. Int. no par reclassified as Class B Shares of Bene. Int. no par 2/1/93
Reincorporated under the laws of Delaware as Evergreen Capital Preservation & Income Fund 10/31/97

KEYSTONE AMER FD GROWTH STKS (MA)
Merged into Keystone America Omega Fund, Inc. (MA) 8/28/92
Each Share of Bene. Int. no par exchanged for (0.810653) share Common $1 par
Keystone America Omega Fund, Inc. (MA) reincorporated in Delaware as Evergreen Omega Fund 10/31/97

KEYSTONE AMER FDS (MA)
Name changed 3/1/96
Shares of Bene. Int. no par reclassified as Class A Shares of Bene. Int. no par 2/1/93
Name changed from Keystone America Government Securities Fund to Keystone America Funds 3/1/96
Merged into Evergreen Funds 7/31/97
Each share Government Securities Class A exchanged for (1.018497) shares U.S. Government Portfolio Class A
Each share Government Securities Class B exchanged for (1.018363) shares U.S. Government Portfolio Class B
Each share Government Securities Class C exchanged for (1.019528) shares U.S. Government Portfolio Class C
Merged into Evergreen Small Co. Growth Fund 1/28/98
Each share Small Co. Growth Fund II exchanged for (1.361175) shares Class A
Each share Small Co. Growth Fund II exchanged for (1.338161) shares Class B
Each share Small Co. Growth Fund II exchanged for (1.338842) shares Class C
(See each company's listing)

KEYSTONE AMER FUND FOR TOTAL RETURN (MA)
Name changed 9/15/94
Shares of Bene. Int. no par reclassified as Class A Shares of Bene. Int. no par 2/1/93
Name changed from Keystone America Equity Income Fund to Keystone America Fund For Total Return 9/15/94
Reincorporated under the laws of Delaware as Evergreen Fund For Total Return 10/31/97
Evergreen Fund For Total Return name changed to Evergreen Equity Income Fund 4/6/99

KEYSTONE AMER GLOBAL OPPORTUNITIES FD (MA)
Global Opportunities Portfolio reclassified as Class A Global Opportunities Portfolio 2/1/93
Reincorporated under the laws of Delaware as Evergreen Global Opportunities Fund 10/31/97

KEYSTONE AMER HARTWELL EMERGING GROWTH FD INC (MA)
Merged into Evergreen Trust 08/01/1997
Each share Class A no par exchanged for (1.088213) Agressive Growth Fund Class A shares
Each share Class B no par exchanged for (1.045411) Agressive Growth Fund Class B shares
Each share Class C no par exchanged for (1.055627) Agressive Growth Fund Class C shares
(See Evergreen Trust)

KEYSTONE AMER HARTWELL GROWTH FD INC (MA)
Merged into Keystone America

Omega Fund, Inc. (MA) 4/1/96
Each share Class A no par exchanged for (0.957195) Class A no par
Each share Class B no par exchanged for (0.955660) share Class B no par
Each share Class C no par exchanged for (0.947018) share Class C no par
Keystone America Omega Fund, Inc. (MA) reincorporated in Delaware as Evergreen Omega Fund, Inc. 10/31/97

KEYSTONE AMER HIGH YIELD BD FD (MA)
Name changed to Keystone America Strategic Income Fund (MA) 2/1/93
Keystone America Strategic Income Fund (MA) reincorporated in Delaware as Evergreen Strategic Income Fund 10/31/97

KEYSTONE AMER INTER TERM BD FD (MA)
Reincorporated under the laws of Delaware as Evergreen Intermediate Term Bond Fund 10/31/1997
(See Evergreen Intermediate Term Bond Fund)

KEYSTONE AMER INVT GRADE BD FD (MA)
Name changed to Keystone America Intermediate Term Bond Fund (MA) 2/1/93
Keystone America Intermediate Term Bond Fund (MA) reincorporated in Delaware as Evergreen Intermediate Term Bond Fund 10/31/97

KEYSTONE AMER MONEY MKT FD (MA)
Merged into Keystone Liquid Trust 7/29/92
Each Share of Bene. Int. no par exchanged for (1) Share of Bene. Int. 10¢ par
Keystone Liquid Trust merged into Evergreen Money Market Trust 7/31/97

KEYSTONE AMER OMEGA FD INC (MA)
Common $1 par reclassified as Class A Common $1 par 2/1/93
Reincorporated under the laws of Delaware as Evergreen Omega Fund 10/31/97

KEYSTONE AMER ST TAX FREE FD (MA)
Florida Tax Free Fund reclassified as Class A Florida Tax Free Fund 2/1/93
Pennsylvania Tax Free Fund reclassified as Class A Pennsylvania Tax Free Fund 2/1/93
Texas Tax Free Fund reclassified as Class A Texas Tax Free Fund 2/1/93
Merged into Keystone Tax Free Fund 4/30/96
Each share Texas Tax Free Fund Class A, B, and C no par exchanged for (1.070238) Share of Bene. Int. no par
Reincorporated under the laws of Delaware as Evergreen Florida Tax Free Fund and Florida Tax Free Fund Class A, B, and C automatically became a like number of respective Series 10/31/97
Reincorporated under the laws of Delaware as Evergreen Massachusetts Tax Free Fund and Massachusetts Tax Free Fund Class A, B, and C automatically became a like number of respective Series 10/31/97
Reincorporated under the laws of Delaware as Evergreen Pennsylvania Tax Free Fund and Pennsylvania Tax Free Fund Class A, B, and C automatically became a like number of respective Series 10/31/97

Reincorporated under the laws of Delaware as Evergreen New York Tax Free Fund and New York Tax Free Fund Class A, B and C automatically became a like number of respective Series 10/31/97
Keystone Tax Free Fund merged into Evergreen Tax Free Trust 1/23/98 which name changed to Evergreen Municipal Bond Fund 1/4/99

KEYSTONE AMER ST TAX FREE FD SER II (MA)
Reincorporated under the laws of Delaware as Evergreen California Tax Free Fund and California Insured Tax Free Fund Class A, B, and C automatically became a like number of respective Series 10/31/97
Reincorporated under the laws of Delaware as Evergreen Missouri Tax Free Fund and Missouri Tax Free Fund Class A, B, and C automatically became a like number of respective Series 10/31/97

KEYSTONE AMER STRATEGIC INCOME FD (MA)
Reincorporated under the laws of Delaware as Evergreen Strategic Income Fund 10/31/97

KEYSTONE AMER TAX FREE INCOME FD (MA)
Shares of Bene. Int. no par reclassified as Class A Shares of Bene. Int. no par 2/1/93
Reincorporated under the laws of Delaware as Evergreen Tax Free Income Fund 10/31/97

KEYSTONE AMER TAX FREE MONEY MKT FD (MA)
Fund dissolved 7/16/92
Each Share of Bene. Int. no par exchanged for net asset value

KEYSTONE AMER WORLD BD FD (MA)
Name changed 12/29/89
Name changed from Keystone America Global Income Fund to Keystone America World Bond Fund 12/29/89
Merged into Keystone Strategic Income Fund (MA) 7/1/97
Each Share of Bene. Int. no par exchanged for (1.244823) shares Class A no par
Each share Class B no par exchanged for (1.241767) shares Class B no par
Each share Class C no par exchanged for (1.238490) shares Class C no par
Keystone Strategic Income Fund (MA) reincorporated in Delaware as Evergreen Strategic Income Fund 10/31/97

KEYSTONE APOLLO FD INC (MA)
Stock Dividend - 100% 5/15/72
Merged into Polaris Fund Inc. 12/16/77
Each share Common 10¢ par exchanged for (1.212) shares Common $1 par
Polaris Fund Inc. name changed to Keystone International Fund Inc. 9/21/79

KEYSTONE AUSTRALIA FDS INC (MA)
Income Fund no par reclassified as Class A Income Fund no par 02/01/1993
Short Term Income Fund no par reclassified as Class A Short Term Income Fund no par 02/01/1993
Each share Class A Short Term Income Fund no par exchanged for (0.904715) share Class A Income Fund no par 09/24/1993
Merged into Keystone America World Bond Fund 12/30/1994
Each share Class A Income Fund no par exchanged for (1.55354) Shares of Bene. Int. no par
Keystone America World Bond Fund merged into Keystone America Strategic Income Fund (MA) 07/01/1997 which reincorporated in Delaware as Evergreen Strategic Income Fund 10/31/1997

KEYSTONE AUTOMOTIVE INDS INC (CA)
Merged into LKQ Corp. 10/12/2007
Each share Common no par exchanged for $48 cash

KEYSTONE BK (LOWER BURRELL CITY, PA)
Merged into First Seneca Bank & Trust Co. (Oil City, PA) 08/15/1980
Each share Common $13.50 par exchanged for $30 principal amount of 9% Subordinated Capital Notes due 08/15/1997, (2/3) share Capital Stock $5 par and $4 cash
First Seneca Bank & Trust Co. (Oil City, PA) reorganized as First Seneca Corp. 06/01/1982 which merged into Pennbancorp 12/31/1983 which merged into Integra Financial Corp. 01/26/1989 which merged into National City Corp. 05/03/1996 which was acquired by PNC Financial Services Group, Inc. 12/31/2008

KEYSTONE BERYLLIUM CORP. (CO)
Became defunct in 1960
No stockholders' equity

KEYSTONE BUSINESS CONTROLS INC. (NY)
Name changed to Romanoff Industries, Inc. 11/9/70
Romanoff Industries, Inc. name changed to Cannon Industries, Inc. 11/1/71 which name changed to Pud Industries, Inc. 5/9/77
(See Pud Industries, Inc.)

KEYSTONE BUSINESS FORMS LTD (BC)
Name changed to Keycorp Industries Ltd. 04/02/1976
Keycorp Industries Ltd. recapitalized as Belkin Inc. 10/01/1985
(See Belkin Inc.)

KEYSTONE CAMERA PRODS CORP (DE)
Chapter 11 bankruptcy proceedings converted to Chapter 7 on 4/16/91
No stockholders' equity

KEYSTONE COAL & COKE CO.
Liquidation completed in 1948

KEYSTONE CONS INDS INC (DE)
Common $1 par split (3) for (2) by issuance of (0.5) additional share 06/08/1990
Plan of reorganization under Chapter 11 Federal Bankruptcy Code effective 08/31/2005
No stockholders' equity
Acquired by Contran Corp. 07/22/2013
Each share Common 1¢ par exchanged for $9 cash

KEYSTONE CONSOLIDATED MINES, INC. (DE)
No longer in existence having become inoperative and void for non-payment of taxes 4/1/32

KEYSTONE CORP. (DE)
Completely liquidated for cash 1/3/64

KEYSTONE CTRS INC (PA)
Acquired by Rite Aid Corp. 10/29/76
Each share Common 1¢ par exchanged for $3.75 cash
Note: An additional distribution of $0.637784 cash per share was made 11/29/79

KEYSTONE CUSTODIAN FDS (PA)
Low-Priced Bond Fund Ser. B-3 merged into High-Return Bond Fund Ser. B-4 08/01/1966
Each share Ser. B-3 $1 par

exchanged for (1.661) shares Ser. B-4 $1 par
Each share Income Common Stock Fund Ser. S-2 $1 par exchanged for (0.5285) share High-Grade Common Stock Fund Ser. S-1 $1 par 06/27/1977
Ser. B-1 $1 par reclassified as Quality Bond Fund Class B 05/01/1995
Ser. B-2 $1 par reclassified as Diversified Bond Fund Class B 05/01/1995
Ser. B-4 $1 par reclassified as High Income Bond Fund B-4 05/01/1995
Ser. K-1 $1 par reclassified as Balanced Fund Class B 05/01/1995
Ser. K-2 $1 par reclassified as Strategic Growth Fund K-2 05/01/1995
Ser. S-1 $1 par reclassified as Growth & Income Fund S-1 05/01/1995
Ser. S-3 $1 par reclassified as Mid-Cap Growth Fund S-3 05/01/1995
Ser. S-4 $1 par reclassified as Small Co. Growth Fund Class B 05/01/1995
Stock Dividends - K-2 & S-1 200% S-2 & S-3 100% 1/2/54; K-1 100% 05/01/1956; S-4 200% 09/01/1961; K-2 200% 10/02/61; 100% 10/15/1966
Each share Mid-Cap Growth Fund S-3 exchanged for (0.923582) share Evergreen Equity Trust Strategic Growth Fund Class 07/22/1997
Each share Growth & Income Fund S-1 exchanged for (1) share Evergreen Equity Trust Blue Chip Fund A 01/09/1998
Each share Balanced Fund Class B exchanged for (1) Evergreen Equity Trust Balanced Fund Class B 01/28/1998
Each share Diversified Bond Fund Class B exchanged for (1) share Evergreen Fixed Income Trust Diversified Bond Fund Class B 01/28/1998
Each share High Income Bond Fund B-4 exchanged for (0.966562) Evergreen Fixed Income Trust High Yield Bond Fund B 1/28/98
Each share Quality Bond Fund Class B exchanged for (1) share Evergreen Fixed Income Trust Diversified Bond Fund Class B 01/28/1998
Each share Small Co. Growth Fund Class B exchanged for (1) share Evergreen Equity Trust Small Co. Growth Fund Class B 01/28/1998
Each share Strategic Growth Fund K-2 exchanged for (1) share Evergreen Equity Trust Strategic Growth Fund Class A 01/28/1998
(See each company's listing)

KEYSTONE CUSTODIAN FDS INC (DE)
Class A Common no par split (3) for (1) by issuance of (2) additional shares 10/15/1959
Acquired by Travelers Corp. 01/26/1979
Each share Class A Common no par exchanged for (0.497) share Common $2.50 par
Travelers Corp. merged into Travelers Inc. 12/31/1993 which name changed to Travelers Group Inc. 04/26/1995 which name changed to Citigroup Inc. 10/08/1998

KEYSTONE DISC STORES INC (PA)
Merged into Philadelphia Pharmaceuticals & Cosmetics, Inc. 12/29/67
Each share Common $1 par exchanged for (0.125) share $2 Conv. Preferred Ser. A $1 par
Philadelphia Pharmaceuticals & Cosmetics, Inc. name changed to PP & C Companies, Inc. 4/17/69 which merged into Keystone

Centers, Inc. 4/18/75 which was acquired by Rite Aid Corp. 10/29/76

KEYSTONE DRILLER CO. (PA)
Name changed to Stardrill-Keystone Co. in 1952
(See Stardrill-Keystone Co.)

KEYSTONE ELECTRONICS CO., INC. (DE)
Name changed to Odell, Inc. 11/30/1964
Odell, Inc. merged into Papercraft Corp. 03/26/1971
(See Papercraft Corp.)

KEYSTONE ENERGY SVCS INC (MN)
SEC revoked common stock registration 8/21/2006
Stockholders' equity unlikely

KEYSTONE ENTMT GROUP INC (BC)
Name changed 02/27/1992
Name changed from Keystone Explorations Ltd. to Keystone Entertainment Group, Inc. 02/27/1992
Recapitalized as International Keystone Entertainment Inc. (BC) 04/20/1994
Each share Common no par exchanged for (0.25) share Common no par
International Keystone Entertainment Inc. (BC) reincorporated in Canada 11/14/1994 which reincorporated in British Columbia 06/15/2005
(See International Keystone Entertainment Inc.)

KEYSTONE FD AMERS (MA)
Reincorporated under the laws of Delaware as Evergreen Latin America Fund 10/31/97

KEYSTONE FINL INC (PA)
Common $2 par split (3) for (2) by issuance of (0.5) additional share 01/22/1986
Common $2 par split (5) for (4) by issuance of (0.25) additional share 08/31/1990
Common $2 par split (3) for (2) by issuance of (0.5) additional share payable 08/23/1996 to holders of record 08/06/1996
Merged into M&T Bank Corp. 10/06/2000
Each share Common $2 par exchanged for either (0.05) share Common 50¢ par, $21.50 cash, or a combination thereof
Note: Option to receive stock or stock and cash only expired 09/20/2000

KEYSTONE FOODS CORP (DE)
Common 10¢ par split (3) for (2) by issuance of (0.5) additional share 8/10/78
Stock Dividends - 10% 7/27/79; 10% 8/11/80; 10% 8/10/81
Acquired by Northern Foods plc 5/6/82
Each share Common 10¢ par exchanged for $22 cash

KEYSTONE FUND OF CANADA, LTD. (CANADA)
Name changed to Keystone International Fund, Ltd. (Canada) 7/1/61
Keystone International Fund, Ltd. (Canada) reincorporated under the laws of Massachusetts as Keystone International Fund, Inc. 11/1/63 which name changed to Polaris Fund Inc. 7/23/68 which name changed back to Keystone International Fund 9/21/79 which name changed to Evergreen International Trust in January 1998

KEYSTONE HERITAGE GROUP INC (PA)
Common $5 par split (5) for (4) by issuance of (0.25) additional share 11/10/94
Common $5 par split (4) for (3) by issuance of (1/3) additional share payable 2/9/96 to holders of record 1/31/96 Ex date - 2/12/96
Stock Dividends - 10% 2/10/85; 10% 5/10/88; 10% 5/10/89; 10% 5/10/90; 10% 11/8/91
Merged into Fulton Financial Corp. 3/27/98
Each share Common $5 par exchanged for (1.83) shares Common $5 par

KEYSTONE INDS INC (DE)
Class A 50¢ par reclassified as Common 50¢ par 11/01/1973
Name changed to Le Chantecler, Inc. 10/21/1977
(See Le Chantecler, Inc.)

KEYSTONE INTL FD INC (MA)
Name changed 11/1/63
Reincorporated from Keystone International Fund, Ltd. (Canada) to Keystone International Fund Inc. (MA) 11/1/63
Name changed to Polaris Fund, Inc. 7/23/68 which name changed back to Keystone International Fund Inc. 9/21/79
Name changed to Evergreen International Trust and Common $1 par reclassified as International Growth Fund A in January 1998

KEYSTONE INTL INC (TX)
Class A Common $2.50 par reclassified as Common $2.50 par 11/15/1970
Common $2.50 par changed to $1 par 04/20/1971
Stock Dividends - 55% 06/14/1971; 55% 06/30/1972; 50% 02/28/1974; 50% 02/27/1976; 50% 05/31/1977; 25% 05/31/1978; 25% 05/31/1979; 25% 05/30/1980; 25% 05/29/1981; 25% 05/28/1982; 25% 05/30/1985; 25% 05/25/1989
Merged into Tyco International Ltd. (Bermuda) 08/29/1997
Each share Common $1 par exchanged for (0.48726) share Common 50¢ par
Tyco International Ltd. (Bermuda) reincorporated in Switzerland 03/17/2009 which merged into Johnson Controls International PLC 09/06/2016

KEYSTONE INVT MGMT GROUP INC (NV)
Name changed to KIMG Management Group, Inc. 03/18/1999
KIMG Management Group, Inc. recapitalized as Fortune Real Estate Development Corp. 09/09/2004 which recapitalized as Andros Isle Development Corp. 04/18/2005
(See Andros Isle Development Corp.)

KEYSTONE LAUNDRIES, INC. (DE)
Each share Preferred $25 par exchanged for (2-1/2) shares Preferred $10 par in 1938
Common no par changed to $5 par in 1938
Voluntarily dissolved 9/15/76
Details not available

KEYSTONE LIQUID TR (MA)
Shares of Bene. Int. 10¢ par reclassified as Class A Shares of Bene. Int. no par 2/1/93
Merged into Evergreen Money Market Trust 7/31/97
Each Class A Share of Bene. Int. no par exchanged for (1) share Class A no par
Each Class B Share of Bene. Int. no par exchanged for (1) share Class B no par
Each Class C Share of Bene. Int. no par exchanged for (1) share Class C no par

KEYSTONE MANUFACTURING CO. (MI)
Completely liquidated 12/23/60
Each share Common $1 par exchanged for first and final distribution of $10.50 cash

KEYSTONE MED CORP (DE)
Each share Common 1¢ par exchanged for (0.1) share new Common 1¢ par 12/11/1992
Name changed to Proactive Technologies, Inc. 01/13/1995
Proactive Technologies, Inc. name changed to Flightserv.com 06/21/1999 which name changed to eResource Capital Group, Inc. 10/06/2000 which name changed to RCG Companies Inc. 11/14/2003 which name changed to OneTravel Holdings, Inc. 06/08/2005
(See OneTravel Holdings, Inc.)

KEYSTONE MICRO SCAN INC (DE)
Reincorporated 07/02/1971
State of incorporation changed from (NY) to (DE) and Common 2-1/2¢ par changed to 10¢ par 07/02/1971
Adjudicated bankrupt 11/26/1973
Stockholders' equity unlikely

KEYSTONE MINES LTD (NV)
Common $0.00001 par split (20) for (1) by issuance of (19) additional shares payable 01/22/2003 to holders of record 01/20/2003 Ex date - 01/23/2003
Name changed to C-Chip Technologies Corp. 02/28/2003
C-Chip Technologies Corp. name changed to Manaris Corp. 08/09/2005 which name changed to Avensys Corp. 12/12/2007 which name changed to Manaris (2010) Corp. 08/23/2010

KEYSTONE MNG CO (WY)
Completely liquidated 9/24/69
Each share Capital Stock $1 par exchanged for (0.1) share United Park City Mines Co. Capital Stock $1 par
(See United Park City Mines Co.)

KEYSTONE MORTGAGE INVESTMENT CO. (DE)
Name changed to Keystone Corp. in 1949 which was liquidated 1/3/64

KEYSTONE NATL BK (PUNXSUTAWNEY, PA)
Each share Common $25 par exchanged for (10) shares Common $2.50 par 12/20/1972
Acquired by Union National Corp. 01/01/1983
Each share Common $2.50 par exchanged for $36.50 cash

KEYSTONE NORTH AMER INC (ON)
Each share old Common no par automatically became (0.16666666) share new Common no par 06/30/2008
Each old Income Participating Security automatically became (0.16666666) new Income Participating Security 07/02/2008
Notes: Each new IPS consists of (1) share Common and $25.716 principal amount of 14.5% Subordinated Notes of Keystone North America Inc.
Income Participating Securities separated 04/26/2010
Acquired by Service Corporation International 04/29/2010
Each share new Common no par received $8.07 cash
Each share new Common represented by Income Participating Securities received $8.07 cash

KEYSTONE OIL PRODUCTS CORP. (DE)
No longer in existence having become inoperative and void for non-payment of taxes 4/1/32

KEYSTONE OTC FD INC (MA)
Merged into Polaris Fund Inc. 12/16/1977
Each share Common no par exchanged for (3.431) shares Common $1 par
Polaris Fund Inc. name changed to Keystone International Fund Inc. 09/21/1979

KEYSTONE PIPE & SUPPLY CO (PA)
Recapitalized 00/00/1937
Each share 7% Preferred $100 par exchanged for (1) share 5% Preferred $100 par and (4) shares Common no par
Each share Common $100 par exchanged for (4) shares Common no par
5% Preferred $100 par called for redemption 11/30/1956
Acquired by Marmon Group, Inc. (DE) 12/31/1970
Details not made public and interested party must contact Marmon Group, Inc. directly

KEYSTONE PORTLAND CEM CO (PA)
$7 Preferred $75 par called for redemption 11/3/50
Each share Common no par exchanged for (4) shares Common $3 par in 1954
Merged into Giant Portland & Masonry Cement Co. 1/11/85
Each share Common $3 par exchanged for (0.55) share $25 Conv. Preferred $1 par and $13.50 cash
Note: Option to receive either (1) share $25 Conv. Preferred $1 par or a variable amount of $25 Conv. Preferred $1 par and cash expired 2/21/85
Giant Portland & Masonry Cement Co. reorganized as Giant Group Ltd. 6/7/85
(See Giant Group Ltd.)

KEYSTONE POWER CORP.
Merged into West Penn Power Co. 00/00/1927
Details not available

KEYSTONE PRECIOUS METALS HLDGS INC (DE)
Name changed to Evergreen International Trust and Common $1 par reclassified as Precious Metals Fund A in January 1998

KEYSTONE PPTY TR (MD)
Merged into ProLogis Six Rivers Ltd. Partnership L.P. 8/4/2004
Each share Common $0.001 par exchanged for $23.80 cash
Issue Information - 2,400,000 shares PFD SER D 9.125% offered at $25 per share on 02/12/2003
9.125% Preferred Ser. D called for redemption at $25 plus $0.209 accrued dividends on 9/3/2004
7.375% Preferred Ser. E $0.001 par called for redemption at $$25 plus $0.169 accrued dividends on 9/3/2004
Public interest eliminated

KEYSTONE RAILWAY EQUIPMENT CO. (DE)
Name changed to Keystone Industries, Inc. 12/31/68
Keystone Industries, Inc. name changed to Le Chantecler, Inc. 10/21/77
(See Le Chantecler, Inc.)

KEYSTONE RAILWAY EQUIPMENT CO. (IL)
Reorganized under the laws of Delaware 10/24/66
Each share Class A $1 par exchanged for (2) shares Class A 50¢ par
Keystone Railway Equipment Co. (Del.) name changed to Keystone Industries, Inc. 12/31/68 which name changed to Le Chantecler, Inc. 10/21/77
(See Le Chantecler, Inc.)

KEYSTONE SILVER MINES INC (ID)
Each share old Common 5¢ par exchanged for (0.01428571) share new Common 5¢ par 08/03/1999
Name changed to Scope Industries, Inc. 12/01/2000
Scope Industries, Inc. name changed to American Motorcycle Corp. 12/23/2002
(See American Motorcycle Corp.)

KEYSTONE SOLUTIONS INC (DE)
Merged into Novume Solutions, Inc. 08/28/2017
Each share Preferred Ser. A $0.0001 par exchanged for (1) share Preferred Ser. A $0.0001 par
Each share Common $0.0001 par exchanged for (1.9399449) shares Common $0.0001 par

KEYSTONE STL & WIRE CO (DE)
Reincorporated 06/30/1955
Each share Common $100 par exchanged for (6) shares old Common no par 00/00/1928
Each share old Common no par exchanged for (4) shares new Common no par 00/00/1936
Stock Dividend - 200% 10/14/1948
State of incorporation changed from (IL) to (DE) and new Common no par changed to $1 par 06/30/1955
Name changed to Keystone Consolidated Industries Inc. 10/07/1968
(See Keystone Consolidated Industries Inc.)

KEYSTONE TAX EXEMPT TR (MA)
Merged into Keystone Tax Free Fund (MA) 2/29/96
Each Share of Bene. Int. no par exchanged for (1.390347) shares Class A no par
Keystone Tax Free Fund (MA) reincorporated in Delaware as Evergreen Municipal Trust 10/31/97

KEYSTONE TAX FREE FD (MA)
Reincorporated under the laws of Delaware as Evergreen Municipal Trust and Class A, B, and C no par automatically became shares of Tax Free Fund Class A, B, and C respectively 10/31/97

KEYSTONE TELEPHONE CO. OF NEW JERSEY
Name changed to Telephone Securities, Inc. 00/00/1929
(See Telephone Securities, Inc.)

KEYSTONE TELEPHONE CO. OF PHILADELPHIA
Liquidated in 1944

KEYSTONE VALVE CORP (TX)
Name changed to Keystone International, Inc. 05/06/1970
Keystone International, Inc. merged into Tyco International Ltd. (Bermuda) 08/29/1997 which reincorporated in Switzerland 03/17/2009 which merged into Johnson Controls International PLC 09/06/2016

KEYSTONE WATCH CASE CORP.
Merged into Riverside Metal Co. on a (3) for (1) basis in 1942
Riverside Metal Co. was acquired by Porter (H.K.) Co., Inc. (Pa.) for cash in 1954

KEYSTONE WATER WORKS & ELECTRIC CORP.
Reorganized as Northeastern Public Service Co. and Northeastern Utilities Co. in 1931
(See each company's listing)

KEY3MEDIA GROUP INC (CA)
Plan of reorganization under Chapter 11 Federal Bankruptcy Code effective 6/19/2003
No stockholders' equity

KEYUAN PETROCHEMICALS INC (NV)
Acquired by XinKe Petrochemicals Inc. 05/15/2017
Each share Common $0.001 par exchanged for $0.104 cash

KEYWEST ENERGY CORP (CANADA)
Acquired by Viking Energy Royalty Trust 02/26/2003
Each share Common no par exchanged for (0.5214) Trust Unit no par and (0.1) share Luke Energy Ltd. Common no par
(See each company's listing)

KEYWEST RESOURCES LTD. (BC)
Incorporated 09/18/1972
Name changed to K.W. Resources Ltd. 04/12/1984
K.W. Resources Ltd. recapitalized as Tako Resources Ltd. 02/14/1992 which recapitalized as Consolidated Tako Resources Ltd. 03/27/1998 which recapitalized as International Tako Industries Inc. (BC) 01/18/2000 which reincorporated in Alberta 11/26/2002 which name changed to Ironhorse Oil & Gas Inc. 05/14/2004 which recapitalized as Pond Technologies Holdings Inc. 02/06/2018

KEYWEST RES LTD (BC)
Incorporated 01/25/1988
Cease trade order effective 08/17/2001

KEYWORLD INVTS PLC (UNITED KINGDOM)
ADR agreement terminated 09/16/2008
No ADR's remain outstanding

KFORCE COM INC (FL)
Name changed to Kforce Inc. 6/20/2001

K45 CAP CORP (CANADA)
Name changed to VisionSky Corporation (Canada) 12/08/2004
VisionSky Corporation (Canada) reincorporated in Alberta as VisionSky Corp. 02/16/2006 which reorganized as Dixie Energy Trust 03/01/2013

KFP 85-LTD. (FL)
Partnership revoked for failure to file annual report 09/28/2001

KFX INC (DE)
Name changed to Evergreen Energy Inc. 11/09/2006
(See Evergreen Energy Inc.)

KGA INDS INC (DE)
Merged into Todlau, Inc. 12/30/77
Each share Common 1¢ par exchanged for $0.05 cash

KGHM POLSKA MIEDZ S A (POLAND)
GDR agreement terminated 12/22/2009
No GDR's remain outstanding

KGI SECS CO LTD (TAIWAN)
Stock Dividend - 1.98% payable 10/14/2011 to holders of record 08/29/2011
GDR agreement terminated 03/19/2013
Each Sponsored 144A GDR for Common exchanged for $9.852369 cash
Each Sponsored Reg. S GDR for Common exchanged for $9.852369 cash

KGIC INC (CANADA)
Placed in receivership 01/25/2017
Stockholders' equity unlikely

KHALKOS EXPL INC (CANADA)
Name changed to Pershimex Resources Corp. 02/15/2018

KHANTYMANSIYSKOKRTELECOM OPEN JT STK CO (RUSSIA)
ADR agreement terminated 12/19/2002
Each Sponsored ADR for Ordinary 1 Ruble par exchanged for $2.13574 cash

KHARTSYZSK PIPE PLT (UKRAINE)
GDR agreement terminated 05/14/2018
Each Reg. S GDR for Ordinary exchanged for (50) shares Ordinary
Note: Unexchanged GDR's will be sold and the proceeds, if any, held for claim after 11/13/2018

KHAYYAM MINERALS LTD (BC)
Under plan of dissolution each share Common no par received approximately (0.6397) share Kincora Copper Ltd. Common no par and (0.6397) Common Stock Purchase Warrant expiring 05/22/2016 payable 05/23/2014 to holders of record 05/20/2014

KHC LIQUIDATING CO. (IL)
Liquidation completed
Each share Common $10 par exchanged for initial distribution of $57 cash 3/4/66
Each share Common $10 par received second and final distribution of $8.4161 cash 11/18/66

KHD HUMBOLDT WEDAG INTL LTD (BC)
Each share Common no par received distribution of (1) share Mass Financial Corp. Class A Common no par payable 02/14/2006 to holders of record 01/31/2006
Common no par split (2) for (1) by issuance of (1) additional share payable 09/07/2007 to holders of record 08/23/2007 Ex date - 09/10/2007
Reorganized as Terra Nova Royalty Corp. 03/30/2010
Each share Common no par exchanged for (1) share Common no par and (0.286) share KHD Humboldt Wedag International AG Ordinary
Terra Nova Royalty Corp. name changed to MFC Industrial Ltd. 09/30/2011 which name changed to MFC Bancorp Ltd. (BC) 02/16/2016
(See MFC Bancorp Ltd. (BC))

KHMELNITSKOBLENERGO (UKRAINE)
ADR agreement terminated 09/05/2017
No ADR's remain outstanding

KHOT INFRASTRUCTURE HLDGS LTD (BRITISH VIRGIN ISLANDS)
Name changed to Blockchain Holdings Ltd. 10/12/2018

KIA MTRS CORP (KOREA)
Each old Sponsored 144A GDR for Ordinary exchanged for (0.1) new Sponsored 144A ADR for Ordinary 03/05/1999
Stock Dividend - 1.50% payable 04/24/1996 to holders of record 12/29/1995
GDR agreement terminated 08/31/2012
Each new 144A Sponsored GDR for Ordinary exchanged for $48.89303 cash

KIABAB INTERNATIONAL, INC. (UT)
Recapitalized as Telegift International, Inc. 11/17/70
Each share Capital Stock 2¢ par exchanged for (0.05) share Capital Stock no par
Telegift International, Inc. name changed to Turbotron Corp. 8/11/72

KIABAB URANIUM CORP. (UT)
Name changed to Kiabab International, Inc. 10/20/70

Kiabab International, Inc. recapitalized as Telegift International, Inc. 11/17/70 which name changed to Turbotron Corp. 8/11/72

KIAWANDA PRODUCTS, INC. (NV)
Charter revoked for failure to file reports and pay fees 1965

KICK ENERGY CORP (AB)
Merged into Highpine Oil & Gas Ltd. 08/01/2006
Each share Common no par exchanged for (0.32) share Common no par
Highpine Oil & Gas Ltd. merged into Daylight Resources Trust 10/08/2009 which reorganized as Daylight Energy Ltd. 05/12/2010
(See Daylight Energy Ltd.)

KICKING HORSE ENERGY INC (AB)
Acquired by ORLEN Upstream Canada Ltd. 12/02/2015
Each share Common no par exchanged for $4.75 cash
Note: Unexchanged certificates will be cancelled and become without value 12/02/2018

KICKING HORSE RES INC (AB)
Merged into Kicking Horse Resources Ltd. 08/13/1999
Each share Common no par exchanged for (0.3678913) share Common no par
Kicking Horse Resources Ltd. name changed to Launch Resources Inc. 10/02/2003
(See Launch Resources Inc.)

KICKING HORSE RES LTD (AB)
Name changed to Launch Resources Inc. 10/02/2003
(See Launch Resources Inc.)

KID BRANDS INC (NJ)
Chapter 11 Federal bankruptcy proceedings dismissed 01/05/2018
No stockholders' equity

KID KRITTER USA INC (DE)
Name changed to Primebuy International Inc. 02/22/2002
Primebuy International Inc. name changed to Russian Resources Group Inc. 05/08/2003 which name changed to Petro Resources Corp. 06/20/2005 which name changed to Magnum Hunter Resources Corp. 07/14/2009
(See Magnum Hunter Resources Corp.)

KID ROM INC (DE)
Each share old Common $0.0001 par exchanged for (0.05) share new Common $0.0001 par 12/09/1996
Each share new Common $0.0001 par exchanged again for (0.001) share new Common $0.0001 par 12/22/1997
Name changed to Millennium Direct Inc. 12/01/1999
Millennium Direct Inc. recapitalized as Viyon Corp. 05/17/2004 which name changed to First Guardian Financial Corp. 07/22/2005 which name changed to New Capital Funding Corp. 05/07/2007 which recapitalized as Ulysses Holding Corp. 10/29/2007 which name changed to Ulysses Diversified Holdings Corp. 05/08/2008 which name changed to JNS Holdings Corp. 02/16/2012

KIDD COPPER MINES LTD (ON)
Charter cancelled for failure to pay taxes and file returns 02/14/1978

KIDD RES LTD (BC)
Merged into Monte Carlo Resources Ltd. 12/31/1987
Each share Common no par exchanged for (0.2) share Common no par
Monte Carlo Resources Ltd. name changed to Provini (C.R.) Financial

Services Corp. 05/17/1989 which recapitalized as DataWave Vending Inc. 01/24/1994 which name changed to DataWave Systems Inc. (BC) 01/15/1997 which reincorporated in Yukon 09/19/2000 which reincorporated in Delaware 02/23/2005
(See DataWave Systems Inc.)

KIDDE (WALTER) & CO., INC. (DE)
Reincorporated 07/02/1968
Each share Common no par exchanged for (5) shares Common $10 par 00/00/1939
Each share Common $10 par exchanged for (2) shares Common $5 par 00/00/1942
Common $5 par changed to $2.50 par and (1) additional share issued 00/00/1954
Stock Dividend - 100% 04/25/1944
$2.20 Conv. Preference Ser. A $1 par called for redemption 11/15/1979
Name changed to Kidde, Inc. 04/18/1980
(See Kidde, Inc.)

KIDDE INC (DE)
Common $2.50 par split (2) for (1) by issuance of (1) additional share 12/30/1981
Common $2.50 par changed to $1.25 par 05/00/1982
$1.64 Conv. Preference Ser. D $1 par called for redemption 12/28/1987
$4 Conv. Preference Ser. B $1 par called for redemption 12/28/1987
$4 Conv. Preference Ser. C $1 par called for redemption 12/28/1987
Merged into Hanson Trust p.l.c. 12/31/1987
Each share Common $1.25 par exchanged for (1) ADR Purchase Warrant expiring 09/30/1994 and $60.10 cash

KIDDE PLC (UNITED KINGDOM)
ADR agreement terminated 7/18/2005
Each Sponsored ADR for Ordinary exchanged for $28.9512 cash

KIDDER, PEABODY ACCEPTANCE CORP.
Merged into Consolidated Investment Trust in 1933
(See Consolidated Investment Trust)

KIDDER, PEABODY CALIFORNIA TAX EXEMPT MONEY FUND (MA)
Name changed to PaineWebber/Kidder, Peabody California Tax Exempt Money Market Fund 02/17/1995
(See PaineWebber/Kidder, Peabody California Tax Exempt Money Market Fund)

KIDDER, PEABODY CASH RESERVE FUND, INC. (MD)
Merged into Paine Webber RMA Money Fund, Inc. 02/20/1996
Details not available

KIDDER, PEABODY GOVERNMENT MONEY FUND, INC. (MD)
Reorganized as PaineWebber RMA U.S. Government Portfolio 11/10/1995
Details not available

KIDDER, PEABODY PREMIUM ACCOUNT FUND (MA)
Ceased operations 02/20/1996
Details not available

KIDDER PARTICIPATIONS, INC. 1, 2 & 3
Merged into Consolidated Investment Trust in 1933
Details not available

KIDDER PEABODY EQUITY INCOME FD INC (MD)
Merged into PaineWebber Growth & Income Fund 01/30/1996
Details not available

KIDDER PEABODY EXCHANGE GROUP MONEY FD (MA)
Fund terminated 00/00/1990
Details not available

KIDDER PEABODY GOVT INCOME FD INC (MD)
Merged into PaineWebber U.S. Government Income Fund 01/30/1996
Details not available

KIDDER PEABODY MARKETGUARD APPRECIATION FD (MA)
Fund terminated 03/31/1993
Details not available

KIDDER PEABODY SPL GROWTH FD INC (MD)
Charter forfeited 10/03/1994

KIDDER PEABODY TAX EXEMPT MONEY FD INC (MD)
Merged into PaineWebber RMA Tax-Free Fund, Inc. 11/20/1995
Details not available

KIDDIE ACADEMY INTL INC (DE)
Plan of reorganization under Chapter 11 Federal Bankruptcy Code effective 4/1/99
No stockholders' equity

KIDDIE CARE CORP (DE)
Name changed to Concordia Corp. 10/06/1972

KIDDIE PRODS INC (MA)
Common 10¢ par split (2) for (1) by issuance of (1) additional share 6/14/91
Common 10¢ par split (3) for (1) by issuance of (2) additional shares 12/15/92
Name changed to First Years Inc. 5/18/95
(See First Years Inc.)

KIDDO TECHNOLOGIES INC (CANADA)
Dissolved for non-compliance 01/06/2004

KIDEO PRODUCTIONS INC (DE)
Reincorporated 07/31/1995
State of incorporation changed from (NY) to (DE) 07/31/1995
Issue Information - 1,400,000 shares COM offered at $5 per share on 06/04/1996
Charter cancelled and declared inoperative and void for non-payment of taxes 03/01/2001

KIDIHAWK MINES, LTD. (ON)
Charter cancelled 03/29/1955
No stockholders' equity

KIDS BOOK WRITER INC (NV)
Recapitalized as Eternity Healthcare Inc. 11/15/2010
Each share Common $0.001 par exchanged for (0.1) share Common $0.001 par

KIDS COMPUTER COLLEGE INC (DE)
Charter forfeited for failure to maintain a registered agent 10/25/88

KIDS GERM DEFENSE CORP (FL)
Name changed to Topaz Resources, Inc. 04/16/2010

KIDS MART INC (FL)
Chapter 11 bankruptcy proceedings terminated 8/22/1997
No stockholders' equity

KIDS ONLY MKT INC (NV)
Name changed to Stevia Agritech Corp. 05/07/2012
Stevia Agritech Corp. name changed to Rightscorp, Inc. 07/17/2013

KIDS STUFF EUROPE INC (NV)
Name changed to Don Primo, Inc. 10/17/2005
Don Primo, Inc. reorganized as Bedford Energy, Inc. 4/26/2006

KIDS STUFF INC (DE)
Company believed out of business 05/00/2002
Details not available

KIDSATIONAL INC (NV)
Name changed to Stratton Holdings Inc. 02/09/2009
Stratton Holdings Inc. recapitalized as Profitable Developments, Inc. 12/24/2012

KIDSFUTURES INC (CANADA)
Name changed to Futura Loyalty Group Inc. 05/24/2007
(See Futura Loyalty Group Inc.)

KIDSTON GOLD MINES LTD (AUSTRALIA)
Each Sponsored ADR for Ordinary exchanged for (0.5) Sponsored ADR for Ordinary 02/19/2003
ADR basis changed from (1:2.5) to (1.0.5) 02/19/2003
ADR agreement terminated 03/02/2003
Each Sponsored ADR for Ordinary exchanged for $0.0714 cash

KIDSTOYSPLUS COM INC (NV)
Recapitalized as Stealth MediaLabs, Inc. (NV) 09/30/2002
Each share Common $0.001 par exchanged for (0.004) share Common $0.001 par
Stealth MediaLabs, Inc. (NV) reincorporated in Oklahoma as Crosswind Renewable Energy Corp. 09/24/2010

KIDWELL-GRAVER CORP. (DE)
Charter cancelled and declared inoperative and void for non-payment of taxes in 1935

KIEHL INDUSTRIES, INC. (DE)
Merged into AVP Holding Corp. 11/23/77
Each share Common 1¢ par exchanged for $0.12 cash

KIENA GOLD MINES LTD (ON)
Common no par split (2) for (1) by issuance of (1) additional share 05/01/1987
Merged into Placer Dome Inc. 06/17/1988
Each share Common no par exchanged for (0.92) share Common no par
Placer Dome Inc. merged into Barrick Gold Corp. 03/08/2006

KIERLAND CAP CORP (AB)
Merged into GASFRAC Energy Services Inc. 08/12/2010
Each share Common no par exchanged for (0.02083333) share Common no par
(See GASFRAC Energy Services Inc.)

KIERLAND RES LTD (AB)
Recapitalized as PetroSands Resources (Canada) Inc. 11/30/2010
Each share Common no par exchanged for (0.1) share Common no par
PetroSands Resources (Canada) Inc. name changed to CanRock Energy Corp. 01/03/2012 which merged into Alston Energy Inc. 07/24/2012
(See Alston Energy Inc.)

KIEWIT PETER SONS INC (DE)
Class D Common $0.0625 par split (5) for (1) by issuance of (4) additional shares payable 12/31/1997 to holders of record 12/26/1997
Name changed to Level 3 Communications, Inc. and Class D Common $0.0625 par reclassified as Common 1¢ par 01/19/1998
Level 3 Communications, Inc. merged into CenturyLink, Inc. 11/01/2017

KIK POLYMERS INC (BC)
Name changed to Edgewater Wireless Systems Inc. 02/01/2012

KIK TECHNOLOGY INTL INC (CA)
SEC revoked common stock registration 06/08/2011

KIK TIRE TECHNOLOGIES INC (BC)
Recapitalized as Kik Polymers Inc. 06/20/2006
Each share Common no par exchanged for (0.1) share Common no par
Kik Polymers Inc. name changed to Edgewater Wireless Systems Inc. 02/01/2012

KILAUEA SUGAR CO. LTD. (HI)
All but (2) shares acquired by C. Brewer & Co. Ltd. as of 05/09/1973
Public interest eliminated

KILAUEA SUGAR PLANTATION CO. (CA)
Reincorporated under laws of Hawaii as Kilauea Sugar Co. Ltd. in 1956

KILBANON CORP. (MA)
Name changed to Synergistics, Inc. 10/10/67
(See Synergistics, Inc.)

KILBARRY RED LAKE GOLD MINES, LTD. (ON)
Charter cancelled 10/17/1955

KILBURG (JAMES) CORP. (CA)
Name changed to Dialaphone 3/3/60 which name changed to Perini Electronic Corp. 6/21/62 which name changed to Dasa Corp. (CA) 9/29/64
Dasa Corp. (CA) merged into Dasa Corp. (MA) 4/1/66
(See Dasa Corp. (MA))

KILBURN MILL (MA)
Proclaimed dissolved for failure to file reports and pay taxes 7/7/80

KILDUN MINING CORP. (DE)
Dissolved in 1944

KILE TECHNOLOGY CORP (DE)
Charter cancelled and declared inoperative and void for non-payment of taxes 6/26/90

KILEMBE COPPER COBALT LTD (CANADA)
Name changed to Renabie Mines Ltd. (Canada) 06/29/1979
Renabie Mines Ltd. (Canada) name changed to Sungate Resources Ltd. 12/24/1980 which merged into Barrick Resources Corp. 10/14/1983 which recapitalized as American Barrick Resources Corp. 12/06/1985 which name changed to Barrick Gold Corp. 01/18/1995

KILEMBE RES LTD (BC)
Recapitalized as Liquid Gold Resources Inc. 07/10/1991
Each share Common no par exchanged for (0.25) share Common no par
Liquid Gold Resources Inc. name changed to West African Ventures Exchange Corp. 05/07/1999 which recapitalized as Wave Exploration Corp. 09/17/2002 which recapitalized as Roxgold Inc. 01/16/2007

KILEY BREWING CO., INC.
Merged into Fox De Luxe Brewing Co. of Indiana, Inc. 00/00/1942
Details not available

KILGEN (GEORGE) & CO., INC.
Dissolution and liquidation approved in 1939

KILGORE COMMUNITY HOTEL MOTEL CO. (TX)
Voluntarily dissolved 3/30/64
Details not available

KILGORE MINERALS LTD (CANADA)
Merged into Bayswater Uranium Corp. (New) 07/24/2007
Each share Common no par exchanged for (1.25) shares Common no par

Bayswater Uranium Corp. (New) recapitalized as Green Thumb Industries Inc. 06/13/2018

KILIMANJARO CAP LTD (BELIZE)
Ordinary EUR 1 par changed to EUR 0.01 and (99) additional shares issued payable 03/03/2014 to holders of record 02/21/2014
Ex date - 03/03/2014
Name changed to N1 Technologies Inc. 02/11/2015

KILKENNEY RES LTD (BC)
Name changed to Ghana Goldfields Ltd. 09/18/1995
Ghana Goldfields Ltd. recapitalized as Icon Industries Ltd. 11/18/1999 which name changed to ICN Resources Ltd. 11/16/2009 which merged into Corazon Gold Corp. 10/17/2012 name changed to NanoSphere Health Sciences Inc. 12/05/2017

KILLALA LAKE MINES, LTD. (ON)
Charter cancelled and company declared dissolved for failure to file reports and pay fees 08/24/1964

KILLAM PPTYS INC (CANADA)
Each share old Common no par exchanged for (0.25) share new Common no par 05/24/2007
Reorganized as Killam Apartment REIT 01/07/2016
Each share new Common no par exchanged for (1) Trust Unit

KILLBEAR ACQUISITION CORP (ON)
Voluntarily dissolved
Each share Common no par received first and final distribution of approximately (0.1363995) share Yangaroo Inc. Common no par payable 08/28/2014 to holders of record 07/15/2014

KILLDEER MINERALS INC (BC)
Each share old Common no par exchanged for (0.1) share new Common no par 01/19/2015
Name changed to Glacier Lake Resources Inc. 03/01/2017

KILLEARN PPTYS INC (FL)
Merged into Killearn, Inc. 8/9/99
Each share Common 10¢ par exchanged for $5.50 cash

KILLEBREW INC (UT)
Name changed to Mac Energy, Inc. 12/22/1980

KILLER WAVES HAWAII INC (NV)
Name changed to Acro Biomedical Co. Ltd. 02/27/2017

KILLICK CAP CORP (BC)
Name changed to Sila Industrial Group Ltd. 08/06/2009
Sila Industrial Group Ltd. name changed to West Cirque Resources Ltd. 07/08/2011 which merged into Kaizen Discovery Inc. 07/08/2014

KILLICK GOLD LTD (BC)
Struck off register and declared dissolved for failure to file returns 07/03/1992

KILLUCAN RES LTD (AB)
Merged into Skill Resources Ltd. 08/17/1983
Each share Class A Common no par exchanged for (0.7143) share Common no par
Skill Resources Ltd. recapitalized as Unicorp Resources Ltd. 06/27/1984 which merged into Asamera Inc. 05/01/1986 which was acquired by Gulf Canada Resources Ltd. 08/04/1988
(See Gulf Canada Resources Ltd.)

KILMER INDS INC (DE)
Charter cancelled and declared inoperative and void for non-payment of taxes 3/1/77

KILO GOLD MINES LTD (AB)
Recapitalized as Newmex Minerals Inc. 05/05/1998
Each share Common no par exchanged for (0.2) share Common no par
Newmex Minerals Inc. name changed to Pearl Exploration & Production Ltd. 02/28/2006 which name changed to BlackPearl Resources Inc. 05/14/2009

KILROY RLTY CORP (MD)
7.5% Preferred Ser. F 1¢ par called for redemption at $25 on 04/16/2012
7.8% Preferred Ser. E 1¢ par called for redemption at $25 on 04/16/2012
6.875% Preferred Ser. G 1¢ par called for redemption at $25 plus $0.21 accrued dividends on 03/30/2017
6.375% Preferred Ser. H 1¢ par called for redemption at $25 on 08/15/2017
(Additional Information in Active)

KIM MANGANESE CO. (WV)
Bankrupt in 1957

KIMACLO MINES LTD. (BC)
Struck off register and declared dissolved for failure to file returns 04/03/1969

KIMASCA PORCUPINE GOLD MINES, LTD. (ON)
Charter cancelled 12/16/1954
No stockholders' equity

KIMBALL BUILDING TRUST
Trust terminated in 1948
No stockholders' equity

KIMBALL-KROUGH PUMP CO.
Acquired by Victor Equipment Co. 00/00/1931
Details not available

KIMBALL PORCUPINE GOLD MINES, LTD. (ON)
Charter cancelled by Province of Ontario for default 11/18/1958

KIMBARK HOTEL
Trust terminated in 1951
Details not available

KIMBARK OIL & GAS CO (CO)
Under plan of reorganization name changed to Hallador Petroleum Co. and Common 10¢ par changed to 1¢ par 12/14/1989
Hallador Petroleum Co. name changed to Hallador Energy Co. 03/17/2010

KIMBELL DECAR CORP (CO)
Each share old Common no par exchanged for (0.04166666) share new Common no par 04/19/1999
Name changed to TangibleData, Inc. 04/20/2000
TangibleData, Inc. name changed to TDI Holding Corp. 10/25/2002 which recapitalized as Fashion House Holdings, Inc. 08/30/2005
(See Fashion House Holdings, Inc.)

KIMBER CORP (DE)
Each share Common $0.002 par exchanged for (0.05) share Common $0.04 par 02/25/1978
Charter cancelled and declared inoperative and void for non-payment of taxes 03/01/1985

KIMBER RES INC (BC)
Acquired by Invecture Group, S.A. de C.V. 01/13/2014
Each share Common no par exchanged for $0.15 cash
Note: Unexchanged certificates will be cancelled and become without value 01/13/2020

KIMBER-X RES CORP (DE)
Name changed to Radium Resources Corp. 12/21/2007

KIMBERLEY COPPER MINES LTD. (BC)
Recapitalized as Nor-West Kim Resources Ltd. 03/08/1971
Each share Capital Stock no par exchanged for (0.33333333) share Capital Stock no par
(See Nor-West Kim Resources Ltd.)

KIMBERLEY YELLOWKNIFE GOLD MINES, LTD. (ON)
Charter cancelled 06/04/1953
No stockholders' equity

KIMBERLITE MNG LTD (ON)
Charter cancelled for failure to pay taxes and file returns 03/16/1976

KIMBERLY CLARK CORP (DE)
6% Preferred $100 par called for redemption 01/02/1945
4% 2nd Preferred $100 par called for redemption 10/02/1950
4.5% Preferred $100 par called for redemption 12/17/1951
(Additional Information in Active)

KIMBERLY CLARK DE MEXICO S A (MEXICO)
Name changed to Kimberly-Clark de Mexico, S.A.B. de C.V. 11/17/2006

KIMBERLY COPPER MINES LTD. (ON)
Charter cancelled and company declared dissolved for default in filing returns 3/18/65

KIMBERLY CORP. (CA)
Common no par changed to $1 par in 1950
Stock Dividends - 100% 10/2/50; 33-1/3% 10/31/52
Name changed to Eversharp Pen Co. 4/28/64
(See Eversharp Pen Co.)

KIMBERLY GOLD INC (NV)
Reincorporated 3/5/74
State of incorporation changed from (NY) to (NV) 3/5/74
Name changed to Goodtime Gourmet Inc. 1/12/79
Goodtime Gourmet Inc. name changed to Kimberly Oil & Gas, Inc. 8/24/79 which name changed to Resorts International, Ltd. 3/13/85
(See Resorts International, Ltd.)

KIMBERLY MINES INC (NV)
Each (12) shares old Common $0.001 par exchanged for (1) new Common $0.001 par 03/25/1996
Recapitalized as Mine-A-Max Corp. 08/18/1997
Each share new Common $0.001 par exchanged for (0.05) share Common $0.001 par
Mine-A-Max Corp. name changed to Peabody's Coffee, Inc. 03/15/1999
(See Peabody's Coffee, Inc.)

KIMBERLY OIL & GAS INC (NV)
Name changed to Resorts International, Ltd. 3/13/85
(See Resorts International, Ltd.)

KIMBLE GLASS CO.
Acquired by Owens-Illinois Glass Co. 00/00/1946
Details not available

KIMBROUGH INVT CO (MS)
Merged into KIC, Inc. 01/28/1982
Each share Common no par exchanged for $1.35 cash

KIMCO ENERGY CORP (DE)
Charter cancelled and declared inoperative and void for non-payment of taxes 3/1/92

KIMCO RLTY CORP (MD)
Reincorporated 08/04/1994
State of incorporation changed from (DE) to (MD) 08/04/1994
7.5% Depositary Preferred Class D called for redemption at (0.93168) share Common 1¢ par on 01/03/2002
8.5% Depositary Preferred called for redemption at $25 on 06/02/2003
7.75% Depositary Preferred Class A called for redemption at $25 plus $0.129167 accrued dividends on 06/09/2003
8.375% Depositary Preferred Class C called for redemption at $25 plus $0.31407 accrued dividends on 06/09/2003
6.65% Depositary Preferred Class F called for redemption at $25 plus $0.1385 accrued dividends on 08/15/2012
7.75% Depositary Preferred Class G called for redemption at $25 plus $0.457465 accrued dividends on 10/10/2012
6.9% Depositary Preferred Class H called for redemption at $25 plus $0.191667 accrued dividends on 11/25/2015

KIMG MGMT GROUP INC (NV)
Recapitalized as Fortune Real Estate Development Corp. 09/09/2004
Each share Common $0.00005 par exchanged for (0.005) share Common $0.00005 par
Fortune Real Estate Development Corp. recapitalized as Andros Isle Development Corp. 04/18/2005
(See Andros Isle Development Corp.)

KIMMINS CORP NEW (FL)
Reincorporated 10/14/1999
State of incorporation changed from (DE) to (FL) 10/14/1999
Each share old Common $0.001 par exchanged for (0.01) share new Common $0.001 par 03/14/2003
Note: Holders of (99) or fewer pre-split shares received $1 cash per share
Each share new Common $0.001 par exchanged again for (0.02) share new Common $0.001 par 05/22/2009
Each share new Common $0.001 par exchanged again for (0.04) share new Common $0.001 par 07/13/2012
Note: In effect holders received $5,000 cash per share and public interest was eliminated

KIMMINS CORP OLD (DE)
Name changed 09/11/1986
Name changed from Kimmins Industrial Service Corp. to Kimmins Corp. (Old) 09/11/1986
Common 1¢ par split (3) for (2) by issuance of (0.5) additional share 04/24/1987
Merged into Kimmins Environmental Service Corp. 10/31/1988
Each share Common 1¢ par exchanged for (2) shares Common $0.001 par
Kimmins Environmental Service Corp. recapitalized as Kimmins Corp. (New) (DE) 01/11/1996 which reincorporated in Florida 10/14/1999
(See Kimmins Corp. (New))

KIMMINS ENVIRONMENTAL SVC CORP (DE)
Common $0.001 par split (3) for (2) by issuance of (0.5) additional share 02/19/1990
Recapitalized as Kimmins Corp. (New) (DE) 01/11/1996
Each share Common $0.001 par exchanged for (0.33333333) share Common $0.001 par
Kimmins Corp. (New) (DE) reincorporated in Florida 10/14/1999
(See Kimmins Corp. (New))

KIMMINS RESIDENTIAL FUND, L.P. (DE)
Filed Certificate of Cancellation 12/31/1995
Details not available

KIMPEX INTL INC (QC)
Assets sold for the benefit of creditors 06/15/1999
No stockholders' equity

KIN ARK OIL CO (DE)
Name changed to Kin-Ark Corp. 05/01/1969
Kin-Ark Corp. name changed to Kinark Corp. 06/14/1978 which name changed to North American Galvanizing & Coatings, Inc. 07/01/2003
(See North American Galvanizing & Coatings, Inc.)

KIN'EL URANIUM CORP. (NV)
Name changed to Alpha Enterprises, Inc. 4/2/70
Alpha Enterprises, Inc. charter revoked 3/7/77

KINAI TECHNOLOGIES INC (BC)
Name changed 11/29/1985
Name changed from Kinai Resources Corp. to Kinai Technologies Inc. 11/29/1985
Struck off register and declared dissolved for failure to file returns 06/12/1992

KINAM GOLD INC (DE)
Reincorporated under the laws of Nevada 5/29/2001

KINARK CORP (DE)
Name changed 06/14/1978
Name changed from Kin-Ark Corp. to Kinark Corp. 06/14/1978
Common Stock Purchase Rights declared for Common stockholders of record 01/02/1990 were redeemed at $0.01 per right 11/01/1990 for holders of record 10/15/1990
Name changed to North American Galvanizing & Coatings, Inc. 07/01/2003
(See North American Galvanizing & Coatings, Inc.)

KINASCO EXPLORATION & MINING LTD. (ON)
Charter revoked for failure to file reports and pay fees 03/30/1967

KINAUTICS INTL INC (DE)
Recapitalized as Independent Companies of America, Inc. 1/11/72
Each share Common 20¢ par exchanged for (0.5) share Common 1¢ par
Independent Companies of America, Inc. name changed to I.I.B. Ltd. 10/19/77 which recapitalized as Sparkling Water of Austria, Inc. 12/22/80 which recapitalized as Dairy Whey Foods Corp. 7/27/83 which name changed to Novar International Corp. 6/8/84
(See Novar International Corp.)

KINBAURI GOLD CORP (CANADA)
Acquired by Orvana Minerals Corp. 09/25/2009
Each share Common no par exchanged for $0.75 cash

KINCAID FURNITURE INC (DE)
Merged into La-Z-Boy Chair Co. 05/20/1988
Each share Common $1.33-1/2 par exchanged for $15.50 cash

KINCAID INDUSTRIES, INC. (PA)
Recapitalized as Drinks By The Case Inc. 10/11/85
Each share Common 10¢ par exchanged for (1) share Common 10¢ par
Drinks By The Case Inc. name changed to Acustar Corp. 12/1/86

KINCAID INDS INC (PA)
Name changed to Drinks By The Case Inc. 10/11/1985
Drinks By The Case Inc. name changed to Acustar Corp. 12/01/1986
(See Acustar Corp.)

KINCHO GLOBAL ENTERPRISES INC (NV)
Recapitalized as Millennium Gold Corp. 03/26/2003
Each share Common $0.001 par exchanged for (0.005) share Common $0.001 par
Millennium Gold Corp. name changed to Prairie Oil & Gas Inc. 04/01/2005 which recapitalized as Prairie Energy Inc. 07/10/2007
(See Prairie Energy Inc.)

KINDER CARE INC (DE)
Name changed 02/12/1987
Common 50¢ par split (2) for (1) by issuance of (1) additional share 06/30/1978
Common 50¢ par split (4) for (3) by issuance of (1/3) additional share 05/31/1983
Common 50¢ par split (3) for (2) by issuance of (0.5) additional share 09/05/1984
Common 50¢ par split (4) for (3) by issuance of (1/3) additional share 05/22/1986
Stock Dividends - 100% 10/26/1977; 25% 12/30/1980; 25% 11/15/1982
Name changed from Kinder-Care Learning Centers, Inc. to Kinder-Care, Inc. 02/12/1987
Name changed to Enstar Group, Inc. (DE) 11/06/1989
(See Enstar Group, Inc. (DE))

KINDER HLDG CORP (DE)
Recapitalized as Intiva BioPharma Inc. 11/29/2017
Each share Common $0.0001 par exchanged for (0.16666666) share Common $0.0001 par
Intiva BioPharma Inc. name changed to Nexien BioPharma Inc. 10/19/2018

KINDER MORGAN ENERGY PARTNERS L P (DE)
Units of Ltd. Partnership Int. split (2) for (1) by issuance of (1) additional Unit payable 10/01/1997 to holders of record 09/15/1997 Ex date - 10/02/1997
Units of Ltd. Partnership Int. split (2) for (1) by issuance of (1) additional Unit payable 08/31/2001 to holders of record 08/17/2001 Ex date - 09/04/2001
Merged into Kinder Morgan, Inc. 11/26/2014
Each Unit of Ltd. Partnership Int. exchanged for (2.1931) shares Common 1¢ par and $10.77 cash

KINDER MORGAN INC (KS)
Merged into Knight Holdco LLC 05/30/2007
Each share Common $5 par exchanged for $107.50 cash

KINDER MORGAN INC OLD (DE)
Merged into Kinder Morgan, Inc. (KS) 10/07/1999
Each share Common no par exchanged for (3,917.957) shares Common $5 par
(See Kinder Morgan, Inc. (KS))

KINDER MORGAN MGMT LLC (DE)
Shares split (2) for (1) by issuance of (1) additional share payable 08/31/2001 to holders of record 08/17/2001 Ex date - 09/04/2001
Each Share received distribution of (0.0009853) share Kinder Morgan, Inc. Common $5 par payable 07/29/2002 to holders of record 07/23/2002 Ex date - 07/24/2002
Stock Dividend - 0.5625% payable 08/13/2004 to holders of record 07/30/2004
Merged into Kinder Morgan, Inc. 11/26/2014
Each Share exchanged for (2.4849) shares Common 1¢ par

KINDER TRAVEL INC (NV)
Name changed to Genova Biotherapeutics Inc. and Common $0.001 par changed to $0.00001 par 07/13/2009
(See Genova Biotherapeutics Inc.)

KINDERCARE LEARNING CTRS INC (DE)
Name changed 06/02/1994
Name changed from Kinder-Care Learning Centers, Inc. to KinderCare Learning Centers, Inc. 06/02/1994
Under plan of merger each share old Common 1¢ par exchanged for $19 cash 02/13/1997
New Common 1¢ par split (2) for (1) by issuance of (1) additional share payable 08/19/2002 to holders of record 08/09/2002 Ex date - 08/20/2002
Merged into Knowledge Learning Corp. 01/14/2005
Each share new Common 1¢ par exchanged for $24.757169 cash
Each share new Common 1¢ par received an initial distribution of $0.99 cash from escrow 02/08/2006

KINDERWORKS CORP (NH)
Administratively dissolved 09/01/2005

KINDRED HEALTHCARE INC (DE)
Common 25¢ par split (2) for (1) by issuance of (1) additional share payable 05/27/2004 to holders of record 05/10/2004
Each share Common 25¢ par received distribution of (0.3660241) share PharMerica Corp. Common 1¢ par payable 07/31/2007 to holders of record 07/20/2007 Ex date - 08/01/2007
Each 7.5% Tangible Equity Unit automatically became (50.6329) shares Common 25¢ par 12/01/2017
Acquired by Kentucky Homecare Holdings, Inc. 07/02/2018
Each share Common 25¢ par exchanged for $9 cash

KINEMOTIVE CORP (DE)
Reorganized 09/30/1986
Common $1 par changed to 1¢ par 09/13/1973
Reorganized from (NY) to under the laws of (DE) 09/30/1986
Each share Common 1¢ par exchanged for (0.5) share Common 2¢ par
Each (5,050) shares Common 2¢ par exchanged for (1) share Common $101 par 05/04/2007
Note: In effect holders received $0.39 cash per share and public interest was eliminated

KINEMOTIVE ENERGY CORP (NY)
Recapitalized as K.C. Industries Corp. 12/2/83
Each share Common 1¢ par exchanged for (6) shares Common 1¢ par
(See K.C. Industries Corp.)

KINERET ACQUISITION CORP (DE)
Name changed to Hain Food Group, Inc. 12/06/1994
Hain Food Group, Inc. name changed to Hain Celestial Group, Inc. 05/30/2000

KINESYS PHARMACEUTICAL INC (AB)
Name changed to Green River Petroleum Inc. 08/20/1997
Green River Petroleum Inc. recapitalized as Green River Holdings Inc. 07/06/1999 which recapitalized as Netco Energy Inc. 10/03/2000 which name changed to Netco Silver Inc. (AB) 07/14/2011 which reincorporated in British Columbia as Brisio Innovations Inc. 02/12/2014

KINESYS PHARMACEUTICALS INC (NV)
Recapitalized as Database Solutions Ltd. 03/31/2003
Each share Common $0.00001 par exchanged for (0.001) share Common $0.00001 par
Database Solutions Ltd. recapitalized as Blue Data Group, Inc. 10/17/2007 which name changed to Expert Group, Inc. 11/07/2007 which name changed to American Premium Water Corp. 12/19/2013

KINETIC CONCEPTS INC (TX)
Merged into Fremont/RCBA 01/05/1998
Each share old Common $0.001 par exchanged for $19.25 cash
Issue Information - 20,700,000 shares COM offered at $30 per share on 02/23/2004
Acquired by Chiron Holdings, Inc. 11/04/2011
Each share new Common $0.001 par exchanged for $68.50 cash

KINETIC DESIGN SYS LTD (CO)
Chapter 11 Federal Bankruptcy Code converted to Chapter 7 00/00/1987
No stockholders' equity

KINETIC ENERGY INC (BC)
Recapitalized as Torque Energy Inc. 02/19/2003
Each share Common no par exchanged for (0.125) share Common no par
(See Torque Energy Inc.)

KINETIC MINERALS INC (UT)
Involuntarily dissolved for failure to file annual reports 04/01/1990

KINETIC MULTIMEDIA INC (NY)
Charter cancelled and proclaimed dissolved for failure to pay taxes 12/27/2000

KINETIC RES CORP (NV)
Common $0.001 par split (17.85715) for (1) by issuance of (16.85715) additional shares payable 02/10/2012 to holders of record 02/10/2012 Ex date - 02/13/2012
Name changed to Crown Alliance Capital Ltd. 02/23/2012
(See Crown Alliance Capital Ltd.)

KINETIC SCIENCE CORP (DE)
Charter cancelled and declared inoperative and void for non-payment of taxes 03/01/1974

KINETIC VENTURES LTD (DE)
Recapitalized as Suite101.com, Inc. 12/04/1998
Each share old Common $0.001 par exchanged for (0.16666666) share Common $0.001 par
Suite101.com, Inc. name changed to GeoGlobal Resources Inc. 02/02/2004

KINETICS CORP. (CA)
Acquired by Teledyne, Inc. 06/02/1966
Each share Common no par exchanged for (1/7) share Common $1 par
Teledyne, Inc. merged into Allegheny Teledyne, Inc. 08/15/1996 which name changed to Allegheny Technologies Inc. 11/29/1999

KINETIKS COM INC (DE)
Name changed to eLinear, Inc. 07/27/2000
(See eLinear, Inc.)

KING BALL INTL TECHNOLOGY CORP (FL)
Recapitalized as Kid Castle Educational Corp. 8/22/2002
Each share Common no par exchanged for (0.02) share Common no par

KING BROS. INDUSTRIES, INC. (CA)
Name changed to Macrodyne, Inc. 3/5/68
Macrodyne, Inc. merged into Macrodyne- Chatillon Corp. 4/1/69 which merged into Macrodyne Industries, Inc. 1/1/74
(See Macrodyne Industries, Inc.)

KING BROS. PRODUCTIONS, INC. OLD (CA)
Name changed to King Bros. Industries, Inc. 10/29/65
King Bros. Industries, Inc. name changed to Macrodyne, Inc. 3/5/68 which merged into Macrodyne-Chatillon Corp. 4/1/69 which merged into Macrodyne Industries, Inc. 1/1/74
(See Macrodyne Industries, Inc.)

KING BROS PRODTNS INC NEW (CA)
Ctfs. dated after 4/25/68
Name changed to King International Corp. "The Sensate Co." 10/17/69
King International Corp. "The Sensate Co." name changed to King International Corp. 10/25/73
(See King International Corp.)

KING CAP CORP (AB)
Name changed to King Energy Inc. 07/26/2001
(See King Energy Inc.)

KING CAP HLDGS INC (FL)
Name changed to BTX Holdings, Inc. 01/17/2006
BTX Holdings, Inc. recapitalized as Rebornne (USA) Inc. 03/22/2010

KING CITY FED SVGS BK (MT VERNON, IL)
Merged into CNB Bancshares Inc. 2/1/95
Each share Common $1 par exchanged for (1.1517) shares Common no par
CNB Bancshares Inc. merged into Fifth Third Bancorp 10/29/99

KING COLA BOTTLING CORP. (NJ)
Charter revoked for non-payment of taxes 2/3/65

KING-COLA CORP. (NJ)
Declared bankrupt 10/9/62
No stockholders' equity

KING COPPER MINING CORP. (QC)
Merged into International Metal & Petroleum Corp. 11/04/1957
Each share Capital Stock exchanged for (0.25) share Capital Stock
(See International Metal & Petroleum Corp.)

KING DAVID MINING CO. (UT)
Merged into Tintic Lead Co. on a (0.5) for (1) basis 12/22/1964
Tintic Lead Co. name changed to Tintic Minerals Resources, Inc. 06/27/1969 which merged into Horn Silver Mines, Inc. 07/20/1983
(See Horn Silver Mines, Inc.)

KING DIGITAL ENTMT PLC (IRELAND)
Acquired by Activision Blizzard, Inc. 02/23/2016
Each share Ordinary $0.00008 par exchanged for $18 cash

KING EDWARD HOTEL CORP. (NY)
Liquidation completed 01/20/1955
Details not available

KING EDWARD HOTEL (TORONTO) LTD.
Acquired by Cardy Corp. Ltd. 00/00/1947
Each share Capital Stock exchanged for (0.2) share Class A $20 par, $4.825 principal amount in Debentures and $2.81 cash
Cardy Corp. Ltd. name changed to Sheraton Ltd. 00/00/1950
(See Sheraton Ltd.)

KING ENERGY INC (AB)
Acquired by Vanquish Oil & Gas Corp. 04/07/2006
Each share Common no par exchanged for $1.25 cash

KING ERRINGTON RES LTD (BC)
Name changed to Daimler Resources Inc. 12/21/1987
(See Daimler Resources Inc.)

KING GEORGE DEV CORP (BC)
Reincorporated under the laws of Canada as Allied Hotel Properties Inc. 10/21/1999
Allied Hotel Properties Inc. (Canada) reincorporated in British Columbia 06/22/2009

KING INTL CORP (CA)
Name changed 10/25/73
Name changed from King International Corp. "The Sensate Co." to King International Corp. 10/25/73
Acquired by King Merger Corp. 4/18/89
Each share Common $1 par exchanged for $13.50 cash

KING IS MINES LTD (ON)
Charter cancelled for failure to pay taxes and file returns 03/16/1976

KING ISLAND CO. (CO)
Recapitalized as Allied Executive Industries, Inc. 6/20/68
Each share Common 50¢ par exchanged for (1) share Capital Stock $0.001 par
Allied Executive Industries, Inc. name changed to Pacific Resource Group, Inc. 4/15/80

KING ISLAND COSMETIC CO. (CO)
Name changed to King Island Co. 4/6/63
King Island Co. recapitalized as Allied Executive Industries, Inc. 6/20/68 which name changed to Pacific Resource Group, Inc. 4/15/80

KING JACK RES LTD (BC)
Recapitalized as International King Jack Resources Ltd. 07/24/1990
Each share Common no par exchanged for (0.2) share Common no par
International King Jack Resources Ltd. recapitalized as Petromin Resources Ltd. 04/18/1996

KING JAMES CORPORATIONS (NJ)
Completely liquidated 02/20/1985
Each share Capital Stock 20¢ par exchanged for first and final distribution of $18 cash

KING JAMES EXTENDED CARE, INC. (NJ)
Name changed to King James Corp. in May 1979
(See King James Corp.)

KING JUICES INC (PA)
Name changed to Jayrik Industries, Inc. 05/08/1974

KING KIRKLAND GOLD MINES LTD (ON)
Charter cancelled 12/20/1982
No stockholders' equity

KING KULLEN GROCERY INC (NY)
Class A $1 par reclassified as Common $1 par 2/13/79
Merged into King Kullen Transaction Corp. 12/12/2005
Each share Common $1 par exchanged for $315 cash

KING LOUIE BOWLING CORP. (DE)
Merged into King Louie International, Inc. 9/1/64
Each share Common 25¢ par exchanged for (1/6) share Common $1 par
(See King Louie International, Inc.)

KING LOUIE INTL INC (KS)
Acquired by King Louie Enterprises, Inc. 03/30/1981
Each share Common $1 par exchanged for $38.90 cash

KING MEDIA HLDGS INC (NV)
Recapitalized as Extreme Fitness, Inc. 10/09/2007
Each share Common $0.001 par exchanged for (0.03333333) share Common $0.001 par
(See Extreme Fitness, Inc.)

KING MIDAS MINES LTD. (BC)
Struck off register and declared dissolved for failure to file returns 12/16/1966

KING MIDAS URANIUM CORP. (UT)
Merged into Oil Securities & Uranium Corp. 00/00/1955
Each share Common exchanged for (0.02857143) share Common
Oil Securities & Uranium Corp. name changed to Oil Securities & Gas Corp. 07/01/1956 which name changed to Oil Securities & Metals Corp. 02/06/1968 which name changed to Oil Securities, Inc. (UT) 12/10/1969 which reincorporated in Nevada 05/27/1982 which recapitalized as Digital Technologies Media Group Inc. 07/26/1996 which reorganized as Central Capital Venture Corp. 05/08/2000
(See Central Capital Venture Corp.)

KING MINES, INC. (OH)
Charter revoked for failure to file reports and pay fees 8/31/62

KING MINING CO.
Merged into Day Mines Inc. 00/00/1947
Details not available

KING OF THE ROAD ENTERPRISES, INC. (TN)
Adjudicated bankrupt 6/23/75

KING OF VIDEO INC (NV)
Common 1¢ par split (5) for (1) by issuance of (4) additional shares 11/20/1974
Charter revoked for failure to file reports and pay fees 11/01/1990

KING OIL, INC. (DE)
Recapitalized as Lane Wood, Inc. 08/10/1964
Each share Common exchanged for (10) shares Common
(See Lane Wood, Inc.)

KING OIL CO. (DE)
Completely liquidated 12/18/1941
Details not available

KING OIL CO (UT)
Name changed to Alta Loma Oil Co. 5/6/77
(See Alta Loma Oil Co.)

KING OPTICAL CORP (NV)
Charter revoked for failure to file reports and pay fees 02/01/1983

KING PAC INTL HLDGS LTD (BERMUDA)
Placed in receivership 06/03/2002
ADR holders' equity unlikely

KING PHARMACEUTICALS INC (TN)
Common no par split (3) for (2) by issuance of (0.5) additional share payable 11/11/1999 to holders of record 10/28/1999
Common no par split (3) for (2) by issuance of (0.5) additional share payable 06/21/2000 to holders of record 06/12/2000 Ex date - 06/22/2000
Common no par split (4) for (3) by issuance of (0.33333333) additional share payable 07/19/2001 to holders of record 07/03/2001 Ex date - 07/20/2001
Acquired by Pfizer Inc. 02/28/2011
Each share Common no par exchanged for $14.25 cash

KING PHARR CANNING OPERATIONS, INC. (AL)
Company dissolved 01/05/1979
Details not available

KING PHILIP MILLS
Acquired by Berkshire Fine Spinning Associates, Inc. 00/00/1930
Details not available

KING PWR INTL GROUP LTD (NV)
Merged into KP (Thailand) Co. Ltd. 10/29/2003

Each share Common $0.001 par exchanged for $3.27 cash
Each share Common $0.001 par received an additional distribution of approximately $0.50 cash in March 2004

KING PRODS INC (ON)
Reorganized under the laws of British Columbia as Moto Goldmines Ltd. 05/24/2005
Each share Common no par exchanged for (0.01194172) share Commmon no par and (0.00597086) share Common Stock Purchase Warrant expiring 05/31/2006
Moto Goldmines Ltd. merged into Randgold Resources Ltd. 10/15/2009

KING RADIO CORP (KS)
Common 30¢ par split (3) for (2) by issuance of (0.5) additional share 01/22/1979
Stock Dividend - 33.33333333% 02/17/1969
Acquired by Allied Corp. 01/31/1985
Each share Common 30¢ par exchanged for $40.50 cash

KING RES CO (ME)
Reorganized 03/31/1967
Reorganized from (NV) to under the laws of Maine 03/31/1967
Each share Common $1 par exchanged for (2) shares Common $1 par
Common $1 par split (3) for (1) by issuance of (2) additional shares 02/19/1968
Common $1 par split (3) for (1) by issuance of (2) additional shares 07/28/1969
Petition filed under Chapter X Federal Bankruptcy Act 08/16/1971
No stockholders' equity

KING ROYALTY CO.
Merged into King Oil Co. (DE) on a (13) for (1) basis in 1936
(See King Oil Co. (DE))

KING-SEELEY CORP. (MI)
Under plan of merger name changed to King-Seeley Thermos Co. and (1) additional share Common $1 par issued 12/9/60
King-Seeley Thermos Co. merged into Household Finance Corp. 9/30/68 which reorganized as Household International, Inc. 6/26/81 which merged into HSBC Holdings PLC 3/28/2003

KING-SEELEY THERMOS CO. (MI)
Common $1 par split (2) for (1) by issuance of (1) additional share 12/14/64
Merged into Household Finance Corp. 9/30/68
Each share Common $1 par exchanged for (1) share $2.375 Conv. Preferred no par
Household Finance Corp. reorganized as Household International, Inc. 6/26/81
(See Household International, Inc.)

KING SILVER CORP (UT)
Name changed to Altex Oil Corp. (UT) 05/17/1972
Altex Oil Corp. (UT) reorganized in Delaware as Altex Industries Inc. 10/30/1985

KING SOLOMON MINES LTD. (AB)
Recapitalized as King Solomon Resources Ltd. 03/10/1967
Each share Common no par exchanged for (0.1) share Common no par
King Solomon Resources Ltd. merged into Acroll Oil & Gas Ltd. 06/29/1967 which recapitalized as Acroll Petroleums Ltd. 12/30/1977 which merged into Trans-Canada Resources Ltd. (New) 11/01/1982 which recapitalized as Consolidated Trans-Canada Resources Ltd.

09/22/1988 which merged into Ranchmen's Resources Ltd. 09/30/1989 which merged into Crestar Energy Inc. 10/11/1995 which was acquired by Gulf Canada Resources Ltd. 11/13/2000
(See Gulf Canada Resources Ltd.)

KING SOLOMON MINING CO., INC. (NV)
Charter revoked for failure to file reports and pay fees 3/3/58

KING SOLOMON RESOURCES LTD. (AB)
Merged into Acroll Oil & Gas Ltd. 06/29/1967
Each share Common no par exchanged for (1) share Common no par
Acroll Petroleums Ltd. merged into Trans-Canada Resources Ltd. (New) 11/01/1982 which recapitalized as Consolidated Trans-Canada Resources Ltd. 09/22/1988 which merged into Ranchmen's Resources Ltd. 09/30/1989 which merged into Crestar Energy Inc. 10/11/1995 which was acquired by Gulf Canada Resources Ltd. 11/13/2000
(See Gulf Canada Resources Ltd.)

KING SOLOMON RES LTD (BC)
Delisted from Vancouver Stock Exchange 04/03/1987

KING W R INDL LTD (AB)
Name changed to Tropic Trading Co., Ltd. 08/12/1994
(See Tropic Trading Co., Ltd.)

KING WORLD PRODTNS INC (DE)
Common 1¢ par split (2) for (1) by issuance of (1) additional share 7/15/85
Common 1¢ par split (3) for (1) by issuance of (2) additional shares 9/10/86
Common 1¢ par split (3) for (2) by issuance of (0.5) additional share 7/23/90
Common 1¢ par split (2) for (1) by issuance of (1) additional share payable 2/17/98 to holders of record 2/3/98 Ex date - 2/18/98
Merged into CBS Corp. 11/15/99
Each share Common 1¢ par exchanged for (0.81) share Common $1 par
CBS Corp. merged into Viacom Inc. (Old) 5/4/2000
(See Viacom Inc. (Old))

KING'S OFFICE SUPPLIES & EQUIPMENT, INC. (CA)
Name changed to King's Office Products Centers, Inc. 12/31/88

KINGAN & CO., INC. (NJ)
Merged into Hygrade Food Products Corp. 9/29/53
Each share 4% Preferred $100 par exchanged for (1) share 4% Preferred A $100 par
Each share Common $10 par exchanged for (0.2) share Common $5 par
(See Hygrade Food Products Corp.)

KINGBIRD PRODUCTS, INC. (CA)
Dissolved 5/28/64
No stockholders' equity

KINGBIRD RES INC (CANADA)
Reincorporated 08/29/1988
Place of incorporation changed from (AB) to (Canada) 08/29/1988
Recapitalized as Gold Bar Resources Inc. 09/29/1988
Each share Common no par exchanged for (0.2) share Common no par
(See Gold Bar Resources Inc.)

KINGBOARD CHEM HLDGS LTD (CAYMAN ISLANDS)
Name changed to Kingboard Holdings Ltd. 07/31/2018

KINGBRIDGE CAP CORP (ON)
Name changed 10/08/1987
Name changed from Kingbridge Mines Ltd. to Kingbridge Capital Corp. 10/08/1987
Name changed to Blue Mountain Beverages Inc. 12/06/1993
(See Blue Mountain Beverages Inc.)

KINGDOM KONCRETE INC (NV)
Name changed to Latitude 360, Inc. 06/17/2014

KINGDOM OIL CO. (DE)
Merged into Ambassador Oil Corp. on a (2) for (1) basis 12/31/55
(See Ambassador Oil Corp.)

KINGDOM RES LTD (BC)
Recapitalized as KRL Resources Corp. 09/27/1989
Each share Common no par exchanged for (0.33333333) share Common no par
KRL Resources Corp. recapitalized as International KRL Resources Corp. 03/06/2002 which recapitalized as Acme Resources Inc. 12/07/2009 which name changed to Affinity Metals Corp. 03/01/2017

KINGDOM VENTURES INC (NV)
Each share Common $0.002 par received distribution of (2) shares Restricted Class B Common $0.002 par payable 05/09/2003 to holders of record 02/05/2003
Recapitalized as Denim Apparel Group, Inc. 10/24/2005
Each share Common $0.002 par exchanged for (0.001) share Common $0.001 par
Denim Apparel Group, Inc. recapitalized as Bolivar Mining Corp. 10/15/2007

KINGDON MINING CO. LTD. (ON)
Completely liquidated 06/06/1966
Each share Capital Stock $1 par exchanged for first and final distribution of $0.099915 cash

KINGFISHER PLC (UNITED KINGDOM)
Sponsored ADR's for Ordinary 25p par split (2) for (1) by issuance of (1) additional ADR payable 7/9/98 to holders of record 7/2/98
Plan of demerger effective 8/28/2001
Each Sponsored ADR for Ordinary 25p par exchanged for (0.9090909) Sponsored ADR for Ordinary 15-5/7p and $0.9692 cash
(Additional Information in Active)

KINGFISHER VENTURES INC (YT)
Acquired by eMedia Networks International Corp. 02/25/2002
Each share Common no par exchanged for (0.9090909) Unit consisting of (1) share Common no par and (1) Common Stock Purchase Warrant expiring 02/22/2003
(See eMedia Networks International Corp.)

KINGHORN PETE CORP (BC)
Recapitalized 04/30/1991
Recapitalized from Kinghorn Energy Corp. to Kinghorn Petroleum Corp. 04/30/1991
Each share Common no par exchanged for (0.25) share Common no par
Recapitalized as Triple 8 Energy Corp. (BC) 11/17/1992
Each share Common no par exchanged for (0.25) share Common no par
Triple 8 Energy Corp. (BC) reincorporated in Alberta 02/24/1994 which name changed to Oilexco Inc. 03/01/1994 which recapitalized as ScotOil Petroleum Ltd. (AB) 06/09/2011 which reincorporated in British Columbia as 0915988 B.C. Ltd. 07/27/2011
(See 0915988 B.C. Ltd.)

KINGLAKE RES INC (NV)
Common $0.00001 par split (3) for (1) by issuance of (2) additional shares payable 12/10/2007 to holders of record 11/28/2007 Ex date - 12/11/2007
Name changed to K's Media 03/26/2008
(See K's Media)

KINGLY ENTERPRISES INC (ON)
Each share old Common no par exchanged for (0.0005) share new Common no par 08/05/2008
Note: In effect holders received $0.05 cash per share and public interest was eliminated

KINGMAN CAP CORP (AB)
Recapitalized as Enterra Communications Inc. 07/12/1999
Each share Common no par exchanged for (0.5) share Common no par

KINGS BAY GOLD CORP (CANADA)
Each share old Class A Common no par exchanged for (0.1) share new Class A Common no par 07/06/2016
Name changed to King's Bay Resources Corp. 08/14/2017

KINGS CNTY DEV CO (CA)
In process of liquidation
Each share Capital Stock $1 par received initial distribution of $10 cash 4/17/82
Each share Capital Stock $1 par received second distribution of $8 cash 1/7/83
Each share Capital Stock $1 par received third distribution of $2.15 cash 3/24/83
Details not available

KINGS CNTY LAFAYETTE TR CO (BROOKLYN, NY)
Name changed to Kings Lafayette Bank (Brooklyn, NY) 03/17/1970
Kings Lafayette Bank (Brooklyn, NY) merged into Kings Lafayette Corp. 05/03/1974 which merged into Republic New York Corp. 07/01/1974
(See Republic New York Corp.)

KINGS CNTY LTG CO (NY)
Recapitalized 00/00/1948
Each share 7% Preferred $100 par exchanged for (1) share 4% Preferred $50 par, (11) shares Common no par and $9 cash
Each share 6% Preferred $100 par exchanged for (1) share 4% Preferred $50 par, (9.2285 plus) shares Common no par and $8 cash
Each share 5% Preferred $100 par exchanged for (1) share 4% Preferred $50 par, (8) shares Common no par and $1 cash
Each share Common no par exchanged for (66/100) share new Common no par
Merged into Brooklyn Union Gas Co. on a (21) for (44) basis 01/15/1957
Brooklyn Union Gas Co. reorganized as KeySpan Energy Corp. 9/30/1997 which merged into MarketSpan Corp. 05/29/1998 which name changed to KeySpan Energy 09/10/1998 which name changed to KeySpan Corp. 05/20/1999
(See KeySpan Corp.)

KINGS COUNTY POSTAL REORGANIZATION CORP.
Liquidated in 1949

KINGS COUNTY REAL ESTATE CORP. (NY)
Charter cancelled and proclaimed dissolved for failure to pay taxes 12/16/35

KINGS COUNTY TRUST CO. (BROOKLYN, NY)
Each share Capital Stock $100 par exchanged for (10) shares Capital Stock $40 par to effect a (2.5) for (1) split plus 300% stock dividend 00/00/1954
Capital Stock $40 par changed to $20 par and (1) additional share issued plus a 10% stock dividend paid 02/01/1956
Capital Stock $20 par changed to $10 par and (1) additional share issued 02/01/1961
Capital Stock $10 par changed to $15 par 12/15/1963
Stock Dividends - 10% 02/01/1957; 10% 02/02/1959
Merged into Kings County Lafayette Trust Co. (Brooklyn, NY) 11/30/1965
Each share Capital Stock $15 par exchanged for (1.526478) shares Capital Stock $12.50 par
Kings County Lafayette Trust Co. (Brooklyn, NY) name changed to Kings Lafayette Bank (Brooklyn, NY) 03/17/1970 which merged into Kings Lafayette Corp. 05/03/1974 which merged into Republic New York Corp. 07/01/1974
(See Republic New York Corp.)

KINGS DEPT STORES INC (DE)
Common $1 par split (5) for (4) by issuance of (0.25) additional share 1/14/65
Common $1 par split (5) for (4) by issuance of (0.25) additional share 6/21/67
Common $1 par split (2) for (1) by issuance of (1) additional share 3/30/68
Common $1 par split (2) for (1) by issuance of (1) additional share 3/22/71
Stock Dividend - 10% 5/27/66
Name changed to KDT Industries, Inc. 6/5/81
(See KDT Industries, Inc.)

KINGS LAFAYETTE BANK (BROOKLYN, NY)
Merged into Kings Lafayette Corp. 05/03/1974
Each share Capital Stock $12.50 par exchanged for (1) share Common $1 par
Kings Lafayette Corp. merged into Republic New York Corp. 07/01/1974
(See Republic New York Corp.)

KINGS LAFAYETTE CORP (NY)
Merged into Republic New York Corp. 07/01/1974
Each share Common $1 par exchanged for (1.1) shares Common $5 par
(See Republic New York Corp.)

KINGS MINERALS NL (AUSTRALIA)
Name changed to Cerro Resources NL 12/10/2010
(See Cerro Resources NL)

KINGS RD ENTMT INC (DE)
Each share old Common 1¢ par exchanged for (1/3) share new Common 1¢ par 04/17/1998
SEC revoked common stock registration 03/13/2012

KINGS RIVER BANCORP (CA)
Merged into VIB Corp. 1/7/2000
Each share Common no par exchanged for $72.22 cash

KINGS RIVER MINERAL CO (NV)
Recapitalized as Commonwealth Western Corp. 08/26/1976
Each share Common $0.005 par exchanged for (0.01) share Common $0.005 par
(See Commonwealth Western Corp.)

KINGS RIVER STATE BANK (REEDLEY, CA)
Under plan of reorganization each share Common no par automatically became (1) share Kings River Bancorp Common no par 12/31/82
(See Kings River Bancorp)

KINGSBRIDGE HLDGS LTD (DE)
Name changed to Masco Sports, Inc. 7/13/87
(See Masco Sports, Inc.)

KINGSBURG COTTON OIL CO. (CA)
Liquidation completed 6/15/61

KINGSBURY BREWERIES CO. (WI)
Merged into Heileman (G.) Brewing Co. Inc. on a (5/62) for (1) basis 12/31/62
(See Heileman (G.) Brewing Co., Inc. (Wisc.))

KINGSCROSS CMMTYS INC (ON)
Ceased operations 12/21/2000
Stockholders' equity unlikely

KINGSFIELD ENVIRONMENTAL CORP (AB)
Name changed 10/13/1995
Name changed from Kingsfield Capital Corp Corp. to Kingsfield Environmental Corp. 10/13/1995
Recapitalized as KEC Environmental Corp. 06/25/1997
Each share Common no par exchanged for (0.2) share Common no par
(See KEC Environmental Corp.)

KINGSFORD CO (IL)
Each share Common $1.25 par exchanged for (0.2) share Common $6.25 par 02/15/1965
6% Conv. Preferred $80 par called for redemption 03/15/1966
Common $6.25 par split (5) for (4) by issuance of (0.25) additional share 05/31/1968
Each share Common $6.25 par exchanged for (3) shares Common $2 par 06/11/1969
Merged into Clorox Co. (CA) 03/12/1973
Each share Common $2 par exchanged for (0.444444) share Common $1 par
Clorox Co. (CA) reincorporated in Delaware 10/22/1986

KINGSFORD INDS INC (IN)
Merged into Kingsford Acquisition Corp. 05/31/1991
Each share Common Capital Stock no par exchanged for $0.10 cash

KINGSLAKE ENERGY INC (NV)
Common $0.001 par split (5) for (1) by issuance of (4) additional shares payable 06/22/2007 to holders of record 06/15/2007 Ex date - 06/25/2007
Charter revoked 07/31/2010

KINGSLEY COACH INC (DE)
Each share old Common $0.00001 par exchanged for (0.5) share new Common $0.00001 par 11/22/1999
SEC revoked common stock registration 09/21/2011

KINGSMAN RES INC (BC)
Each share old Common no par exchanged for (0.11111111) share new Common no par 07/31/2012
Recapitalized as Contagious Gaming Inc. 09/23/2014
Each share Common no par exchanged for (0.5) share Common no par

KINGSMERE CAPITAL INC. (AB)
Cease trade order effective 10/10/2003
Stockholders' equity unlikely

KINGSMILL CAP VENTURES INC (ON)
Merged into Innovative Composites International Inc. 10/20/2009
Each share Common no par exchanged for (0.5165) share Common no par

KINGSMILL CAP VENTURES II INC (ON)
Merged into Innovative Composites International Inc. 10/20/2009
Each share Common no par exchanged for (1) share Common no par

KINGSPORT PRESS INC (DE)
Each share Common no par exchanged for (10) shares Common $2.50 par 00/00/1946
Under plan of merger Common $2.50 par changed to $1.25 par and (1) additional share issued 11/01/1960
Stock Dividend - 20% 07/01/1955
Acquired by Arcata National Corp. 07/24/1969
Each share Common $1.25 par exchanged for (0.25) share $2 Conv. Preferred Ser. C $5 par and (0.4) share Common 25¢ par
Arcata National Corp. name changed to Arcata Corp. 11/30/1978 which name changed to Atacra Liquidating Corp. 06/04/1982
(See Atacra Liquidating Corp.)

KINGSTIP COMMUNICATIONS INC (DE)
Merged into Mid-Texas Broadcasting Inc. 09/04/1979
Each share Common $1 par exchanged for $18.35 cash

KINGSTIP INC (DE)
Merged into Justin Industries Inc. 1/31/77
Each share Common $1 par exchanged for (0.38) share Common $2.50 par
(See Justin Industries, Inc.)

KINGSTON CMNTY HOTEL (NY)
Voluntarily dissolved 6/24/76
Details not available

KINGSTON CONSOLIDATED R.R. CO.
Dissolved in 1949

KINGSTON GOLD & COPPER MINING CO. LTD.
Liquidated in 1937

KINGSTON HYDRAULICS, INC. (DE)
Acquired by Avien, Inc. 01/10/1961
Each share Common $1 par exchanged for (0.143678) share Class A 10¢ par
(See Avien, Inc.)

KINGSTON MINES LTD (NV)
Common $0.0001 par split (7) for (1) by issuance of (6) additional shares payable 06/03/2008 to holders of record 06/02/2008 Ex date - 06/04/2008
Name changed to Laureate Resources & Steel Industries Inc. 06/04/2008
(See Laureate Resources & Steel Industries Inc.)

KINGSTON NATL BK (KINGSTON, PA)
Name changed to State Bank of Eastern Pennsylvania (Kingston, PA) 4/8/70
State Bank of Eastern Pennsylvania (Kingston, PA) merged into First Valley Corp. 5/1/72 which acquired by United Jersey Banks 1/29/88 which name changed to UJB Financial Corp. 6/30/89 which name changed to Summit Bancorp 3/1/96 which merged into FleetBoston Financial Corp. 3/1/2001 which merged into Bank of America Corp. 4/1/2004

KINGSTON PRODUCTS CORP. (IN)
Each share Common no par exchanged for (7) shares Common $1 par in 1935
Merged into Scott & Fetzer Co. 4/30/68
Each share Common $1 par exchanged for (1/3) share Common no par
(See Scott & Fetzer Co.)

KINGSTON RES LTD (BC)
Recapitalized as Butler Developments Corp. 06/29/2001
Each share Common no par exchanged for (1/6) share Common no par
Butler Developments Corp. recapitalized as Butler Resource Corp. 02/12/2009 which name changed to Quantum Rare Earth Developments Corp. 03/04/2010 which name changed to NioCorp Developments Ltd. 03/04/2013

KINGSTON SECURITIES CORP. (PA)
Merged into Eastern Pennsylvania Corp. 10/25/1973
Each share Common no par exchanged for (1) share Capital Stock $10 par

KINGSTON TR CO (KINGSTON, NY)
Capital Stock $100 par changed to $20 par and (9) additional shares issued 09/20/1957
Stock Dividend - 163% 03/01/1970
Acquired by First Commercial Banks, Inc. 06/30/1972
Each share Capital Stock $20 par exchanged for (5.25) shares Common $5 par
First Commercial Banks, Inc. name changed to Key Banks Inc. 04/23/1979 which name changed to KeyCorp (NY) 08/28/1985 which merged into KeyCorp (New) (OH) 03/01/1994

KINGSVALE RES LTD (BC)
Recapitalized as Niche Peripherals, Inc. 11/26/1993
Each share Common no par exchanged for (0.36363636) share Common no par
Niche Peripherals, Inc. recapitalized as Consolidated Niche Peripherals Inc. 10/31/1994
(See Consolidated Niche Peripherals Inc.)

KINGSVILLE ST BANCSHARES INC (TX)
Shares reacquired 12/8/99
Each share Common exchanged for $115 cash

KINGSWAY ARMS RETIREMENT RESIDENCES INC (ON)
Reincorporated under the laws of British Columbia as Mainstreet Health Investments Inc. 04/12/2016
Mainstreet Health Investments Inc. name changed to Invesque Inc. 01/08/2018

KINGSWAY ENTERPRISES INC (DE)
Name changed to Geriaco International Inc. 03/23/1986
Geriaco International Inc. recapitalized as American Business Financial Services, Inc. 02/12/1993
(See American Business Financial Services, Inc.)

KINGSWAY INTL HLDGS LTD (BERMUDA)
Each share Common USD $0.01 par exchanged for (0.25) share Common USD $0.04 par 05/09/2002
Name changed to Sunwah International Ltd. 01/19/2011

KINGSWAY LINKED RETURN CAP TR (ON)
LROC Preferred Units called for redemption at $25 on 06/30/2015

KINGSWAY LMBR LTD (ON)
Charter cancelled 06/25/1979

KINGSWOOD RES INC (CANADA)
Recapitalized 8/21/85
Recapitalized 7/20/92
Recapitalized from Kingswood Explorations 1985 Ltd. to Kingswood Explorations Ltd. 8/21/85
Each share Capital Stock no par exchanged for (0.5) share Common no par
Recapitalized from Kingswood Explorations Ltd. to Kingswood Resources Inc. 7/20/92
Each share Common no par exchanged for (0.2) share Common no par
Recapitalized as Southern Africa Minerals Corp. 5/5/94
Each share Common no par exchanged for (0.4) share Common no par
Southern Africa Minerals Corp. name changed to Tango Mineral Resources Inc. 7/2/2002 which recapitalized as RNC Gold Inc. 12/4/2003 which merged into Yamana Gold Inc. 2/28/2006

KINGTHOMASON GROUP INC (NV)
Each share old Common $0.001 par exchanged for (0.2) share new Common $0.001 par 08/08/2008
Name changed to Hardwired Interactive, Inc. 11/03/2008
Hardwired Interactive, Inc. recapitalized as iGlue, Inc. 01/27/2012 which recapitalized as AC Partners Inc. 02/05/2018

KINGTONE WIRELESSINFO SOLUTION HLDG LTD (BRITISH VIRGIN ISLANDS)
Each Sponsored ADR for Ordinary exchanged for (0.1) Sponsored ADR for Ordinary 11/06/2012
Name changed to Luokung Technology Corp. 09/13/2018
(See Luokung Technology Corp.)

KINGTRON INTL CORP (CANADA)
Struck off register and declared dissolved for failure to file returns 10/19/1999

KINGWOOD CORP. (OK)
Acquired by National Industries, Inc. (KY) 01/07/1966
Each share Common $1 par exchanged for (1) share Common $1 par
National Industries, Inc. (KY) merged into Fuqua Industries, Inc. 01/03/1978 which name changed to Actava Group Inc. 07/21/1993 which name changed to Metromedia International Group, Inc. 11/01/1995
(See Metromedia International Group, Inc.)

KINGWOOD OIL CO. (OK)
Name changed to Kingwood Corp. 07/23/1965
Kingwood Corp. acquired by National Industries, Inc. (KY) 01/07/1966 which merged into Fuqua Industries, Inc. 01/03/1978 which name changed to Actava Group Inc. 07/21/1993 which name changed to Metromedia International Group, Inc. 11/01/1995
(See Metromedia International Group, Inc.)

KINIKA GOLD MINES LTD. (ON)
Charter cancelled for noncompliance with the Ontario Companies Act 03/07/1959

KINLAW ENERGY PARTNERS CORP (TX)
Name changed to Environmental Plus, Inc. 07/11/1996
Environmental Plus, Inc. recapitalized as TTI Industries Inc. 04/27/1998
(See TTI Industries Inc.)

KINLOCH-BLOOMINGTON TELEPHONE CO.
Dissolved in 1931

KINLOCH RES INC (AB)
Reincorporated 06/29/2001
Place of incorporation changed from (ON) to (AB) 06/29/2001
Recapitalized as Stylus Energy Inc. 03/01/2005
Each share Common no par exchanged for (0.33333333) share Common no par
(See Stylus Energy Inc.)

KINNARD COS INC (KS)
Reincorporated 9/11/80
State of incorporation changed from (MN) to (KS) 9/11/80
Common 10¢ par split (2) for (1) by issuance of (1) additional share 10/20/80
Merged into Kelly-Johnston Enterprises, Inc. 12/28/81
Each share Common 10¢ par exchanged for (0.125) share Common $1 par
Note: Holders also received (1) Common Stock Purchase Warrant expiring 2/28/83 for each (50) shares of Common 10¢ par
(See Kelly-Johnston Enterprises, Inc.)

KINNARD INVTS INC (MN)
Common 2¢ par split (6) for (5) by issuance of (0.2) additional share 1/30/87
Common 2¢ par split (6) for (5) by issuance of (0.2) additional share 6/17/91
Stock Dividends - 20% 2/10/84; 20% 6/29/88
Merged into Stockwalk.com Group, Inc. 9/11/2000
Each share Common 2¢ par exchanged for (0.7676) share Common no par and $6 cash
Stockwalk.com Group, Inc. name changed to Stockwalk Group, Inc. 1/1/2001
(See Stockwalk Group, Inc.)

KINNEAR STORES CO.
Merged into National Bellas Hess Co. Inc. in 1929
Details not available

KINNER AIRPLANE & MOTOR CORP., LTD.
Bankrupt in 1938

KINNER MOTORS, INC. (CA)
Name changed to Gladden Products Corp. in 1945 which name changed to Buckner Industries, Inc. 3/9/62 which completely liquidated 9/7/67

KINNEY COASTAL OIL CO. (ME)
Liquidation completed 6/21/61

KINNEY (G.R.) CO., INC. (NY)
Preferred $100 par changed to no par 00/00/1932
Recapitalized 00/00/1937
Each share $8 Preferred no par exchanged for (1.33333333) shares $5 Prior Preferred no par and (1) share Common $1 par
Common no par changed to $1 par
Merged into Brown Shoe Co., Inc. (Old) 05/01/1956
Each share Common $1 par exchanged for (0.66666666) share Common $15 par
Brown Shoe Co., Inc. (Old) name changed to Brown Group, Inc. 01/14/1972 which name changed to Brown Shoe Co., Inc. (New) 05/28/1999 which name changed to Caleres, Inc. 05/29/2015

KINNEY MANUFACTURING CO. (MA)
Merged into New York Air Brake Co. in 1954
Each share $6 Preferred no par exchanged for (4.25) shares Common $5 par
Each share Common no par exchanged for for (3) shares Common $5 par
New York Air Brake Co. merged into General Signal Corp. 9/20/67 which merged into SPX Corp. 10/6/98

KINNEY NATL SVC INC (NY)
Name changed 08/12/1966
Under plan of merger name changed from Kinney Service Corp. to Kinney National Service, Inc. 08/12/1966
Common $1 par split (2) for (1) by issuance of (1) additional share 02/14/1969
Name changed to Kinney Services, Inc. (NY) 02/17/1971

Kinney Services, Inc. (NY) reincorporated in Delaware as Warner Communications Inc. 02/11/1972 which merged into Time Warner Inc. (Old) 01/10/1990 which merged into Time Warner Inc. 01/11/2001 which name changed to Time Warner Inc. (New) 10/16/2003 which merged into AT&T Inc. 06/15/2018

KINNEY SERVICE CORP. (NY)
Under plan of merger name changed to Kinney National Service, Inc. 08/12/1966
Kinney National Service, Inc. name changed to Kinney Services, Inc. (NY) 02/17/1971 which reincorporated in Delaware as Warner Communications Inc. 02/11/1972 which merged into Time Warner Inc. 01/10/1990

KINNEY SVCS INC (NY)
Conv. Preferred 1966 Ser. A $1 par called for redemption 09/29/1971
Reincorporated under the laws of Delaware as Warner Communications Inc. 02/11/1972
Warner Communications Inc. merged into Time Warner Inc. (Old) 01/10/1990 which merged into AOL Time Warner Inc. 01/11/2001 which name changed to Time Warner Inc. (New) 10/16/2003 which merged into AT&T Inc. 06/15/2018

KINNEY SYS INC (DE)
Merged into Cromwell Group Inc. 10/16/1986
Each share $1.375 Conv. Exchangeable Preferred 1¢ par exchanged for $12 cash
Each share Common 1¢ par exchanged for $10.50 cash

KINOJEVIS MINING CO. LTD.
Recapitalized as Bowes Gold Mines Ltd. on a (6) for (1) basis in 1936

KINOJEVIS RIVER MINES, LTD. (ON)
Charter cancelled 5/13/57
No stockholders' equity

KINROSS MINES LTD (SOUTH AFRICA)
Under plan of merger name changed to Evander Gold Mines Ltd. 11/18/96
Evander Gold Mines Ltd. merged into Harmony Gold Mining Co. Ltd. 8/28/98

KINSEL DRUG CO. (MI)
Merged into Cunningham Drug Stores, Inc. on a (0.05) for (1) basis 11/24/58
(See Cunningham Drug Stores, Inc.)

KINSHIP SYS INC (UT)
Name changed to Caribbean Clubs International Inc. 11/18/2002
Caribbean Clubs International Inc. name changed to CCI Group, Inc. 08/29/2003
(See CCI Group, Inc.)

KINSMAN MANUFACTURING CO., INC. (NH)
Liquidation completed 7/1/63

KINSTAR RES LTD (CANADA)
Merged into Summit Resources Ltd. 11/10/88
Each (33) shares Common no par exchanged for (1) share Common no par
(See Summit Resources Ltd.)

KINTAIL ENERGY INC (AB)
Merged into Canadian Hunter Exploration Ltd. 12/23/99
Each share Common no par exchanged for $3.10 cash

KINTANA RES LTD (BC)
Delisted from Vancouver Stock Exchange 05/04/1993

KINTERA INC (DE)
Acquired by Blackbaud, Inc. 07/09/2008

Each share Common $0.001 par exchanged for $1.12 cash

KINTI MNG LTD (DE)
Name changed to Swift International, Inc. 05/27/2011

KINVARA VENTURES INC (AB)
Recapitalized as Ivana Ventures Inc. (AB) 05/20/2005
Each share Common no par exchanged for (0.2) share Common no par
Ivana Ventures Inc. (AB) reincorporated in British Columbia 11/02/2005 which name changed to Ely Gold & Minerals Inc. 07/08/2008 which name changed to Ely Gold Royalties Inc. 11/22/2017

KINZUA LUMBER CO. (WV)
Dissolved in 1954

KIO OIL & DEVELOPMENT CO. (DE)
Under plan of merger name changed to Christiana Oil Corp. 03/26/1956
Christiana Oil Corp. name changed to Christiana Companies, Inc. (DE) 12/01/1970 which reincorporated in Wisconsin 10/31/1992 which merged into Weatherford International Inc. (New) (DE) 02/08/1999 which reincorporated in Bermuda as Weatherford International Ltd. 06/26/2002 which reincorporated in Switzerland 02/25/2009 which reincorporated in Ireland as Weatherford International PLC 06/18/2014

KIOR INC (DE)
Plan of reorganization under Chapter 11 Federal Bankruptcy proceedings effective 06/30/2015
No stockholders' equity

KIPP & ZONEN INC (SK)
Assets sold for the benefit of creditors in May 2004
No stockholders' equity

KIPPER CORP. (UT)
Name changed to Energy Research Corp. 06/04/1973
Each share Common 1¢ par exchanged for (1) share Common 1¢ par
Energy Research Corp. name changed to Billings Energy Research Corp. 05/06/1974 which name changed to Billings Energy Corp. 06/10/1976 which name changed to Billings Corp. 08/04/1981 which name changed to Hydrogen Energy Corp. 08/21/1985

KIPPER TASHOTA GOLD MINING CO. LTD.
Name changed to Lincoln Gold Mines Ltd. in 1928
(See Lincoln Gold Mines Ltd.)

KIPWATER MINES LTD (ON)
Charter cancelled for failure to file reports and pay taxes 04/23/1969

KIR-VIT MINES, LTD. (ON)
Charter cancelled 12/3/62
Stock valueless

KIRANA KIRKLAND GOLD MINES LTD. (ON)
Charter cancelled in November 1954
Stock is valueless

KIRBY COGESHALL STEINAU INC (WI)
Name changed to KCS Industries Inc. 06/14/1968
(See KCS Industries Inc.)

KIRBY ENERGY INC (BC)
Recapitalized as International Kirby Energy Corp. (BC) 08/03/1995
Each share Common no par exchanged for (1/3) share Common no par
International Kirby Energy Corp. (BC) reincorporated in Bermuda as Kingsway International Holdings Ltd. 02/23/1996 which name changed to

Sunwah International Ltd. 01/19/2011

KIRBY EXPLORATION CO. (NV)
Common $1 par changed to 10¢ par and (9) additional shares issued 05/11/1981
Under plan of reorganization each share Common 10¢ par automatically became (1) share Kirby Exploration Co., Inc. Common 10¢ par 08/01/1984
Kirby Exploration Co., Inc. name changed to Kirby Corp. 05/01/1990

KIRBY EXPL INC (NV)
Name changed to Kirby Corp. 5/1/90

KIRBY INDS INC (NV)
Assets transferred 10/15/1976
Stock Dividend - 100% 01/03/1968
Liquidation completed
Each share Common $1 par received initial distribution of $22 cash 01/16/1976
Each share Common $1 par received second distribution of $4 cash 07/08/1976
Each share Common $1 par received third distribution of (1) share Caribbean Finance Co., Inc. Common $1 par and (1) share Kirby Exploration Co. Common $1 par 09/30/1976
Each share Common $1 par exchanged for fourth distribution of $1.25 cash 12/28/1976
Assets transferred to Kirby Industries, Inc. Liquidating Trust and Common $1 par reclassified as Share of Bene. Int. 10/15/1976
Each Share of Bene. Int. received initial distribution of $2.962 cash 05/13/1977
Each Share of Bene. Int. received second distribution of $1.10 cash 12/15/1977
Each Share of Bene. Int. received third distribution of $2.29 cash 12/18/1979
Each Share of Bene. Int. received fourth distribution of $0.634053 cash 08/08/1980
Each Share of Bene. Int. received fifth distribution of $1 cash 12/15/1980
Each Share of Bene. Int. received sixth distribution of $0.08 cash 12/17/1981
Each Share of Bene. Int. received seventh and final distribution of $0.0213 cash 12/22/1983

KIRBY LMBR CORP (DE)
Each share old Common no par exchanged for (10) shares new Common no par 12/23/1946
New Common no par changed to Common $1 par 12/18/1956
Merged into Santa Fe Industries, Inc. 08/31/1974
Each share Common $1 par exchanged for $150 cash

KIRBY LUMBER CO. (TX)
Reorganized as Kirby Lumber Corp. 7/13/36
Stockholders received short-term rights only

KIRBY OIL & GAS CO. (DE)
Merged into Kirby Vensyn Petroleum Co. on a (1.75) for (1) basis 2/15/57
Kirby Vensyn Petroleum Co. name changed to Kirby Petroleum Co. (Nev.) 1/3/58 which name changed to Kirby Industries, Inc. 11/13/67
(See Kirby Industries, Inc.)

KIRBY PETROLEUM CO. (DE)
Capital Stock no par changed to $1 par in 1934
Capital Stock $1 par redesignated as Common $1 par in 1951
Liquidated 4/29/55
Each share Common $1 par exchanged for $2 cash plus (1) Ctf. of Bene. Int. in each of Kirby

Petroleum Trusts Numbers One and Two

KIRBY PETROLEUM CO. (NV)
Each share Common 20¢ par exchanged for (0.2) share Common $1 par 1/20/61
Name changed to Kirby Industries, Inc. 11/13/67
(See Kirby Industries, Inc.)

KIRBY VENSYN PETROLEUM CO. (NV)
Name changed to Kirby Petroleum Co. (NV) 1/3/58
Kirby Petroleum Co. (NV) name changed to Kirby Industries, Inc. 11/13/67
(See Kirby Industries, Inc.)

KIRIN BREWERY LTD (JAPAN)
Each Unsponsored ADR for Common 50 Yen exchanged for (10) Sponsored ADR's for Common 50 Yen 09/03/2002
Name changed to Kirin Holdings Co., Ltd. 07/02/2007

KIRIN INTL HLDG INC (NV)
Name changed to Yangtze River Development Ltd. 01/22/2016
Yangtze River Development Ltd. name changed to Yangtze River Port & Logistics Ltd. 02/14/2018

KIRK ASBESTOS MINES LTD.
Name changed to Donegal Petroleums Ltd. 00/00/1952
Donegal Petroleums Ltd. acquired by D'Arcy Oil & Gas Ltd. 00/00/1953 which name changed to Lariat Exploration & Development Ltd. 00/00/1953 which was acquired by Dominion Asbestos Mines Ltd. 00/00/1954 which name changed to Daine Mining Corp. Ltd. 09/11/1956 which recapitalized as Cable Mines & Oils Ltd. 08/15/1957 which merged into St. Fabien Copper Mines Ltd. 07/27/1967 which name changed to St. Fabien Explorations Inc. 02/11/1981 which recapitalized as Fabien Explorations Inc. 07/18/1983
(See Fabien Explorations Inc.)

KIRK C F LABS INC (NJ)
Charter declared void for non-payment of taxes 9/9/82

KIRK CORP (MD)
Name changed to 25th Street Corp. 1/10/80
(See 25th Street Corp.)

KIRK-HUDSON MINES LTD. (ON)
Recapitalized as Northgate Exploration Ltd. (ON) 12/05/1958
Each (4.5) shares Capital Stock $1 par exchanged for (1) share Capital Stock $1 par
Northgate Exploration Ltd. (ON) reincorporated in British Columbia 07/01/2001 which name changed to Northgate Minerals Corp. 05/20/2004 which merged into AuRico Gold Inc. 10/26/2011

KIRK INDS INC (PA)
Each share Common $10 par exchanged for (10) shares Common $1 par 04/00/1955
Liquidation completed
Each share Common $1 par received initial distribution of (0.2) North European Oil Royalty Trust Ctf. of Bene. Int. no par 08/16/1982
Each share Common $1 par exchanged for second distribution of (0.1) North European Oil Royalty Trust Ctf. of Bene. Int. no par, (0.1) Jamaica Water Properties, Inc. Common Stock Purchase Warrant expiring 12/31/1994 and $0.50 cash 04/15/1983
Note: Holdings not entitled to (100) or more Warrants received $10 cash per Warrant

(See North European Oil Royalty Trust)
Each share Common $1 par received third and final distribution of $1.20 cash 07/28/1983

KIRK URANIUM CORP. (DE)
Dissolved in 1954

KIRKCALDY CAP CORP (AB)
Reorganized under the laws of Jersey as Royal Road Minerals Ltd. 04/20/2015
Each share Common no par exchanged for (0.5) share Ordinary no par

KIRKEBY CORP. (DE)
Merged into Natus Corp. on a (33.903) for (1) basis 5/26/61
Natus Corp. name changed to Kirkeby-Natus Corp. 6/30/61 which name changed to United Ventures, Inc. 6/24/66 which merged into Federated Development Co. 7/31/70
(See Federated Development Co.)

KIRKEBY HOTELS, INC. (PA)
Name changed to Kirkeby Corp. in 1957
Kirkeby Corp. merged into Natus Corp. 5/26/61 which name changed to Kirkeby-Natus Corp. 6/30/61 which name changed to United Ventures, Inc. 6/24/66 which merged into Federated Development Co. 7/31/70
(See Federated Development Co.)

KIRKEBY-NATUS CORP. (MD)
Name changed to United Ventures, Inc. 06/24/1966
United Ventures, Inc. merged into Federated Development Co. 07/31/1970
(See Federated Development Co.)

KIRKHAM ENGINEERING & MANUFACTURING CORP.
Name changed to Liberty Aircraft Products Corp. in 1940
Liberty Aircraft Products Corp. name changed to Liberty Products Corp. (NY) in 1947 which merged into Penn-Texas Corp. 12/12/55 which name changed to Fairbanks Whitney Corp. 5/29/59 which recapitalized as Colt Industries Inc. (PA) 5/15/64 which reincorporated in Delaware 10/17/68 then reincorporated in Pennsylvania 5/6/76
(See Colt Industries Inc. (PA))

KIRKKING MINES LTD.
Succeeded by King Kirkland Gold Mines Ltd. share for share in 1938

KIRKLAND BASIN GOLD MINES LTD. (ON)
Charter cancelled for failure to pay taxes and file returns 3/15/72

KIRKLAND CONSOLIDATED GOLD MINES, LTD. (ON)
Name changed to Kirkland Consolidated Mines Ltd. in 1934
(See Kirkland Consolidated Mines Ltd.)

KIRKLAND CONSOLIDATED MINES LTD. (ON)
Charter cancelled in February 1949

KIRKLAND DIORITE GOLD MINES LTD. (ON)
Acquired by Gordon-Lebel Mines Ltd. 00/00/1957
Each share Common exchanged for (0.1) share Common $1 par
Gordon-Lebel Mines Ltd. merged into Hoffman Exploration & Minerals Ltd. 06/29/1981 which merged into Consolidated Thompson-Lundmark Gold Mines Ltd. 01/16/1986 which name changed to Consolidated Thompson Iron Mines Ltd. 08/24/2006
(See Consolidated Thompson Iron Mines Ltd.)

KIRKLAND GATEWAY GOLD MINES, LTD. (ON)
Recapitalized as Upper Kirkland Mines Ltd. 6/3/65
Each share Capital Stock $1 par exchanged for (0.2) share Capital Stock $1 par
(See Upper Kirkland Mines Ltd.)

KIRKLAND GOLD RAND LTD.
Acquired by Hudson Rand Gold Mines Ltd. in 1947
Each share Common exchanged for (1/3) share Common
Hudson Rand Gold Mines Ltd. name changed to Hudson Rand Mines Ltd. 6/13/56 which recapitalized as Canorama Explorations Ltd. 12/2/57 which recapitalized as Consolidated Canorama Explorations Ltd. 10/8/63
(See Consolidated Canorama Explorations Ltd.)

KIRKLAND GOLDEN GATE MINES LTD. (ON)
Recapitalized as Gateford Mines Ltd. (ONT) 00/00/1950
Each share Common no par exchanged for (0.1) share Common no par
Gateford Mines Ltd. (ONT) reincorporated in Canada as Gateford Resources Inc. 07/03/1986 which merged into Landmark Corp. (New) 01/31/1992 which recapitalized as Landmark Global Financial Corp. 07/05/1996

KIRKLAND-HUDSON BAY GOLD MINES LTD. (ON)
Name changed to Kirk-Hudson Mines Ltd. 05/10/1956
Kirk-Hudson Mines Ltd. recapitalized as Northgate Exploration Ltd. (ON) 12/05/1958 which reincorporated in British Columbia 07/01/2001 which name changed to Northgate Minerals Corp. 05/20/2004 which merged into AuRico Gold Inc. 10/26/2011

KIRKLAND HUNTON MINES LTD.
Merged into Amalgamated Kirkland Mines Ltd. 00/00/1939
Each share Common exchanged for (0.083) share Common
Amalgamated Kirkland Mines Ltd. merged into Mayfield Explorations & Developments Ltd. 06/21/1971 which merged into Microsolve Computer Capital Inc. 02/11/1998 which name changed to Homebank Technologies Inc. 12/20/2000 which name changed to Selient Inc. 06/15/2005
(See Selient Inc.)

KIRKLAND LAKE GOLD INC (CANADA)
Merged into Kirkland Lake Gold Ltd. 12/06/2016
Each share Common no par exchanged for approximately (1.0000175) shares Common no par

KIRKLAND LAKE GOLD MINING CO. LTD. (ON)
Recapitalized as Kirkland Minerals Corp. Ltd. 05/03/1956
Each share Capital Stock $1 par exchanged for (0.181818) share Capital Stock $1 par
Kirkland Minerals Corp. Ltd. acquired by Groundstar Resources Ltd. (BC) 08/31/1973 which reincorporated in Alberta 10/28/2005

KIRKLAND LARDER MINES LTD. (ON)
Charter revoked for failure to file reports and pay fees 12/23/1965

KIRKLAND MINERALS LTD (ON)
Capital Stock $1 par changed to no par 07/13/1971
Acquired by Groundstar Resources Ltd. (BC) 08/31/1973
Each share Capital Stock no par

exchanged for (0.1) share Capital Stock no par
Groundstar Resources Ltd. (BC) reincorporated in Alberta 10/28/2005

KIRKLAND PREMIER MINES LTD.
Acquired by Kirkland Gold Rand Ltd. in 1937
Each share Common exchanged for (1/3) share Common
Kirkland Gold Rand Ltd. was acquired by Hudson Rand Gold Mines Ltd. in 1947 which name changed to Hudson Rand Mines Ltd. 6/13/56 which recapitalized as Canorama Explorations Ltd. 12/2/57 which recapitalized as Consolidated Canorama Explorations Ltd. 10/8/63
(See Consolidated Canorama Explorations Ltd.)

KIRKLAND RAND LTD.
Succeeded by Kirkland Premier Mines Ltd. on an (8) for (15) basis 00/00/1927
Kirkland Premier Mines Ltd. acquired by Kirkland Gold Rand Ltd. 00/00/1937 which was acquired by Hudson Rand Gold Mines Ltd. 00/00/1947 which name changed to Hudson Rand Mines Ltd. 06/13/1956 which recapitalized as Canorama Explorations Ltd. 12/02/1957 which recapitalized as Consolidated Canorama Explorations Ltd. 10/08/1963
(See Consolidated Canorama Explorations Ltd.)

KIRKLAND TOWNSITE GOLD MINES LTD (ON)
Name changed to K.T. Mining Ltd. 03/29/1971
K.T. Mining Ltd. name changed to K.T. Resources Ltd. 09/29/1980 which recapitalized as K.T. Resources (1981) Ltd. 09/28/1981
(See K.T. Resources (1981) Ltd.)

KIRKLEES CAP INC (AB)
Name changed to IPerformance Fund Inc. (AB) 01/12/2001
IPerformance Fund Inc. (AB) reincorporated in Ontario as BluMont Capital Inc. 06/30/2003 which was acquired by Integrated Asset Management Corp. 03/02/2007

KIRKROYALE GOLD MINES, LTD. (ON)
Dissolved 00/00/1959
Details not available

KIRKSTONE VENTURES LTD (BC)
Name changed to Balaton Power Inc. 07/24/2000
(See Balaton Power Inc.)

KIRKSVILLE BANCSHARES INC (DE)
Merged into Roosevelt Financial Group, Inc. 12/29/1995
Each share Common 1¢ par exchanged for (2.4437) shares Common 1¢ par
Roosevelt Financial Group, Inc. merged into Mercantile Bancorporation, Inc. 07/01/1997 which merged into Firstar Corp. (New) 09/20/1999 which merged into U.S. Bancorp (DE) 02/27/2001

KIRKTWIN GOLD MINES LTD. (ON)
Name changed to Athabaska Goldfields & Uranium Ltd. 08/12/1949
(See Athabaska Goldfields & Uranium Ltd.)

KIRKWIN GOLD MINES, LTD. (ON)
Charter cancelled by the Provincial Secretary of Ontario 02/02/1952

KIRLIN HLDG CORP (DE)
Old Common $0.0001 par split (2) for (1) by issuance of (1) additional share payable 12/22/1997 to holders of record 12/08/1997
Old Common $0.0001 par split (2) for (1) by issuance of (1) additional

share payable 07/30/1999 to holders of record 07/14/1999
Old Common $0.0001 par split (2) for (1) by issuance of (1) additional share payable 03/01/2000 to holders of record 02/15/2000
Each share old Common $0.0001 par exchanged for (0.125) share new Common $0.0001 par 01/06/2003
Name changed to Zen Holdings Corp. 08/12/2008
Zen Holdings Corp. name changed to Millennium Healthcare Inc. 07/26/2011

KIRMAQUE GOLD MINES, LTD. (ON)
Charter cancelled 04/23/1953
No stockholders' equity

KIRRIEMUIR OIL & GAS LTD (AB)
Name changed to WWB Oil & Gas Ltd. 12/06/1994
WWB Oil & Gas Ltd. recapitalized as Cigar Oil & Gas Ltd. 10/22/1997 which merged into Pivotal Energy Ltd. 01/10/2003 which merged into Fairborne Energy Ltd. (Old) 07/08/2003
(See Fairborne Energy Ltd. (Old))

KIRRIN RES INC (AB)
Ceased operations 02/27/2013
Stockholders' equity unlikely

KIRSCH CO (MI)
Each share $1.80 Preferred no par exchanged for (1) share Preferred no par and (1) share Class A Common no par 00/00/1937
Each share Common no par exchanged for (1) share Class B Common no par
Class B Common no par reclassified as Common $5 par 00/00/1947
Common $5 par split (3) for (2) by issuance of (0.5) additional share 11/19/1971
Stock Dividends - 200% 12/06/1950; 25% 01/02/1953; 25% 12/12/1955; 10% 07/01/1960; 100% 01/20/1964
Merged into Cooper Industries, Inc. 04/01/1981
Each share Common $5 par exchanged for $35.51 cash

KIRSCH MANUFACTURING CO.
Reorganized as Kirsch Co. 00/00/1928
Details not available

KIRSCHNER MED CORP (DE)
Merged into Biomet, Inc. 11/04/1994
Each share Common 10¢ par exchanged for $10.75 cash
Note: Option to receive (0.916) share Common no par in lieu of cash expired 12/05/1994
(See Biomet, Inc.)

KIRSHNER ENTMT & TECHNOLOGIES INC (FL)
Each share old Common $0.001 par exchanged for (0.1) share new Common $0.001 par 03/24/2005
Name changed to Linkwell Corp. 08/17/2005
(See Linkwell Corp.)

KIRSHNER ENTMT CORP (NY)
Liquidation completed
Each share Common $1 par received initial distribution of $2 cash 09/19/1977
Each share Common $1 par received second distribution of $0.50 cash 10/28/1977
Each share Common $1 par received third distribution of $0.30 cash 03/27/1978
Each share Common $1 par received fourth and final distribution of $0.30 cash 05/19/1978
Note: Certificates were not required to be surrendered and are without value

KIRSHNER INTL INC (DE)
Name changed to Veracity

Management Global, Inc. 10/25/2006

KIRYAN GOLD MINES, LTD. (ON)
Charter cancelled 10/14/1952
No stockholders' equity

KISH INDUSTRIES, INC. (MI)
Acquired by Grow Chemical Corp. 10/30/1964
Each share 6% Conv. Class A or Common $1 par exchanged for (0.01) share Common 10¢ par
Note: Unexchanged certificates were cancelled and became without value 10/30/1969
Grow Chemical Corp. name changed to Grow Group, Inc. 04/20/1979
(See Grow Group, Inc.)

KISHACOQUILLAS VALLEY NATL BK (BELLEVILLE, PA)
Under plan of reorganization each share Common $2.50 par automatically became (1) share Kish Bancorp, Inc. Common $2.50 par 12/31/1986

KISKA METALS CORP (YT)
Merged into AuRico Metals Inc. 03/14/2017
Each share Common no par exchanged for (0.06666666) share Common no par and $0.016 cash
Note: Unexchanged certificates will be cancelled and become without value 03/14/2023
(See AuRico Metals Inc.)

KISKOBA MINING CO. LTD. (MB)
Charter cancelled 02/26/1966
No stockholders' equity

KISLAK NATL BK (NORTH MIAMI, FL)
Merged into Banco Popular North America (New York, NY) 01/04/2005
Details not available

KISMET ENERGY CORP (NV)
Recapitalized as Global Bancorp Inc. 03/26/2002
Each share Common $0.001 par exchanged for (0.005) share Common $0.001 par
Global Bancorp Inc. name changed to Voxbox World Telecom, Inc. 07/06/2005 which name changed to Internet Media Technologies, Inc. 11/21/2007

KISMET URANIUM & OIL CORP. (NV)
Charter revoked for failure to file reports and pay fees 03/03/1958

KISMET VENTURES INC (BC)
Name changed to Mighty Beaut Minerals Inc. (BC) 12/15/1998
Mighty Beaut Minerals, Inc. (BC) reincorporated in Yukon 08/30/2000 which recapitalized as MBMI Resources Inc. (YT) 12/20/2002 which reincorporated in British Columbia 11/15/2005 which reorganized in Ontario 06/22/2012

KISPIOX INC (AZ)
Recapitalized as Sue Wong International, Inc. (AZ) 04/28/1989
Each (15) shares Common $0.0015 par exchanged for (1) share Common $0.0015 par
Sue Wong International, Inc. (AZ) reorganized in Colorado as Amalgamated Explorations, Inc. 08/03/1995
(See Amalgamated Explorations, Inc.)

KISSACOQUILLAS VALLEY R.R. CO.
Operations discontinued 00/00/1940
Stockholders' equity unlikely

KISSELL CO (OH)
Each share Class B Common no par exchanged for (1) share Class A Common no par 03/16/1967
Merged into Pittsburgh National Corp. 02/25/1970
Each share Class A Common no par exchanged for $15 cash

KIT FARMS INC (IN)
Name changed to Total Entertainment Inc. 02/18/1998
Total Entertainment Inc. name changed to Total Luxury Group, Inc. (IN) 06/08/2004 which reincorporated in Nevada as Total Apparel Group, Inc. 08/27/2008

KIT KARSON CORP (WA)
Name changed to Ness Energy International Inc. (WA) 07/06/1999
Ness Energy International Inc. (WA) reincorporated in Texas 03/05/2008
(See Ness Energy International Inc.)

KIT MFG CO (CA)
Charter suspended for failure to file reports and pay fees 07/20/2006

KIT RES LTD (ON)
Ctfs. dated prior to 03/06/2000
Reincorporated 03/03/2000
Place of incorporation changed from (Canada) to (ON) 03/03/2000
Merged into Wheaton River Minerals Ltd. 03/06/2000
Each share Common no par exchanged for (0.408) share Common no par
Wheaton River Minerals Ltd. merged into Goldcorp Inc. 04/15/2005
Ctfs. dated after 03/06/2000
Place of incorporation changed from (ON) to (BC) 12/29/2006
Name changed to Bayou Bend Petroleum Ltd. 02/09/2007
Bayou Bend Petroleum Ltd. name changed to ShaMaran Petroleum Corp. 10/21/2009

KITALTA OIL, LTD. (ON)
Charter cancelled and dissolved 12/12/1955
No stockholders' equity

KITARA HOLDCO CORP (DE)
Name changed to Propel Media, Inc. 02/09/2015

KITARA MEDIA CORP (DE)
Reorganized as Kitara Holdco Corp. 01/28/2015
Each share Common $0.0001 par exchanged for (1) share Common $0.0001 par
Kitara Holdco Corp. name changed to Propel Media, Inc. 02/09/2015

KITCHEN BAZAAR INC (DE)
Liquidated under Chapter 11 Federal Bankruptcy Code 01/00/1996
Stockholders' equity unlikely

KITCHEN CRAFT FOODS CORP (NY)
Charter cancelled and proclaimed dissolved for failure to pay taxes 06/27/1979

KITCHENER MNG N L (AUSTRALIA)
Acquired by Haoma Mining 09/16/1996
Each ADR for Ordinary A$0.25 par exchanged for $0.379 cash

KITCHER RES INC (NV)
Each share old Common $0.001 par exchanged for (0.025) share new Common $0.001 par 06/13/2011
Recapitalized as Amogear Inc. 03/01/2012
Each share new Common $0.001 par exchanged for (0.002) share Common $0.001 par

KITE PHARMA INC (DE)
Acquired by Gilead Sciences, Inc. 10/03/2017
Each share Common $0.001 par exchanged for $180 cash

KITE RLTY GROUP TR (MD)
8.25% Perpetual Preferred Ser. A 1¢ par called for redemption at $25 plus $0.0287 accrued dividends on 12/07/2015
(Additional Information in Active)

KITOV PHARMACEUTICALS HLDGS LTD. (ISRAEL)
Name changed to Kitov Pharma Ltd. 01/31/2018

KITRINOR METALS INC (ON)
Each share old Common no par exchanged for (0.1) share new Common no par 12/05/2016
Recapitalized as Scythian Biosciences Corp. 08/08/2017
Each share new Common no par exchanged for (0.05) share Common no par
Note: Holders of (19) or fewer pre-split shares were cancelled

KITSAP BK (PORT ORCHARD, WA)
Under plan of reorganization each share Common $10 par automatically became (1) share Olympic Bancorp Inc. Common $10 par 11/01/1997

KITTANNING TELEPHONE CO. (PA)
Acquired by Mid-Continent Telephone Corp. 01/01/1964
Each share 4% Preferred A, B or C $25 par exchanged for (1) share 5% Preferred $25 par
Each share Common $25 par exchanged for (3-1/8) shares Common no par
Mid-Continent Telephone Corp. name changed to Alltel Corp. (OH) 10/25/1983 which reincorporated in Delaware 05/15/1990
(See Alltel Corp.)

KITTITAS VY BANCORP (WA)
Merged into Interwest Bancorp, Inc. 08/31/1998
Each share Common $10 par exchanged for either (1.714) shares Common 20¢ par, $72 cash, or a combination thereof
Interwest Bancorp, Inc. name changed to Pacific Northwest Bancorp 09/01/2000 which merged into Wells Fargo & Co. (New) 11/03/2003

KITTY HAWK INC (DE)
Plan of reorganization under Chapter 11 Federal Bankruptcy Code effective 09/30/2002
No old Common stockholders' equity
Plan of reorganization under Chapter 11 Federal Bankruptcy Code effective 07/09/2008
No new Common stockholders' equity

KITTYHAWK TV CORP (OH)
Adjudicated bankrupt 07/16/1971
Stockholders' equity unlikely

KIVA CORP (NV)
Charter revoked for failure to file annual reports 11/01/1989

KIVALLIQ ENERGY CORP (BC)
Recapitalized as ValOre Metals Corp. 06/28/2018
Each share Common no par exchanged for (0.1) share Common no par

KIWA BIO-TECH PRODS GROUP CORP (UT)
Reincorporated under the laws of Delaware 07/22/2004

KIWI HLDGS INC (DE)
Name changed to Chariot International Holdings Inc. 04/30/1999
(See Chariot International Holdings Inc.)

KIWI NETWORK SOLUTIONS INC (NV)
Each share old Common $0.001 par exchanged for (0.01) share new Common $0.001 par 11/5/2004
Name changed to Trimax Corp. 2/15/2005

KIWI III LTD (CO)
Recapitalized as Petro Union Inc. 9/18/92
Each share Common $0.0001 par

exchanged for (0.0008) share Common $0.125 par
Petro Union Inc. name changed to Horizontal Ventures, Inc. 7/13/98 which name changed to GREKA Energy Corp. 3/24/99
(See GREKA Energy Corp.)

KKR & CO GUERNSEY LP (UNITED KINGDOM)
Reorganized under the laws of Delaware as KKR & Co. L.P. 07/14/2010
Each Common Unit exchanged for (1) Common Unit KKR & Co. L.P. reorganized as KKR & Co. Inc. 07/02/2018

KKR & CO L P (DE)
Under plan of reorganization each 6.5% Preferred Unit, 6.75% Preferred Unit and Common Unit automatically became (1) share KKR & Co. Inc. 6.5% Preferred Ser. B, 6.75% Preferred Ser. A or Class A Common 1¢ par 07/02/2018

KKR FINL CORP (MD)
Merged into KKR Financial Holdings LLC 05/04/2007
Each share Common 1¢ par exchanged for (1) share Common no par
KKR Financial Holdings LLC merged into KKR & Co. L.P. 04/30/2014 which reorganized as KKR & Co. Inc. 07/02/2018

KKR FINL HLDGS LLC (DE)
Merged into KKR & Co. L.P. 04/30/2014
Each share Common no par exchanged for (0.51) Common Unit 7.375% Ser. A LLC Preferred no par called for redemption at $25 on 01/16/2018
KKR & Co. L.P. reorganized as KKR & Co. Inc. 07/02/2018

KKS VENTURE MGMT INC (NV)
Recapitalized as Codima, Inc. 06/09/2008
Each share Common $0.001 par exchanged for (0.00333333) share Common $0.001 par
(See Codima, Inc.)

KL ENERGY CORP (NV)
Common $0.001 par split (3) for (1) by issuance of (2) additional shares payable 09/08/2008 to holders of record 09/08/2008
Company terminated common stock registration and is no longer public as of 11/17/2011

KLA INSTRS CORP (DE)
Common $0.001 par split (2) for (1) by issuance of (1) additional share 1/7/83
Common $0.001 par split (2) for (1) by issuance of (1) additional share 12/8/83
Common $0.001 par split (3) for (2) by issuance of (0.5) additional share 12/14/84
Common $0.001 par split (2) for (1) by issuance of (1) additional share 9/29/95
Under plan of merger name changed to KLA-Tencor Corp. 4/30/97

KLAD ENTERPRISES LTD (AB)
Merged into Diamond Hawk Mining Corp. (ALTA) 2/9/2005
Each share Common no par exchanged for (1) share Common no par
Diamond Hawk Mining Corp. (ALTA) reincorporated in British Columbia 7/4/2005

KLAMATH FIRST BANCORP INC (OR)
Merged into Sterling Financial Corp. 01/02/2004
Each share Common 1¢ par exchanged for (0.77) share Common $1 par
Sterling Financial Corp. merged into Umpqua Holdings Corp. 04/18/2014

KLARER CO. (KY)
Name changed to Klarer of Kentucky, Inc. 3/1/63
(See Klarer of Kentucky, Inc.)

KLARER KY INC (KY)
Preferred $100 par called for redemption 05/15/1964
Acquired by Armour & Co. 12/29/1972
Each share Common $5 par exchanged for $44 cash

KLASSEN ENTERPRISES, INC. (CA)
Completely liquidated 9/27/67
Each share Capital Stock $1 par received first and final distribution of $0.0212195 cash
Certificates were not retired and are now without value

KLEANZA MINES LTD. (BC)
Recapitalized as Kendal Mining & Exploration Co. Ltd. 8/17/72
Each share Capital Stock 50¢ par exchanged for (0.2) share Capital Stock 50¢ par
Kendal Mining & Exploration Co. Ltd. recapitalized as Velvet Exploration Co., Ltd. (BC) 5/10/78 which reincorporated in Alberta as Velvet Exploration Ltd. 5/27/98
(See Velvet Exploration Ltd. (ALTA))

KLEARFOLD INC (PA)
Merged into KFI Heritage Acquisition 6/7/96
Each share Common 1¢ par exchanged for $3.4793 cash

KLEBER LABS INC (DE)
Common 2¢ par changed to 1¢ par 03/11/1969
Name changed to Three Dimensional Circuits, Inc. 05/15/1969
(See Three Dimensional Circuits, Inc.)

KLEENA KLEENE GOLD MINES LTD (CANADA)
Merged into Maiden Creek Mining Co., Inc. 09/01/1994
Each share Common no par exchanged for (1) share Common no par
(See Maiden Creek Mining Co., Inc.)

KLEENAIR SYS INC (NV)
Each share old Common $0.001 par exchanged for (0.06666666) share new Common $0.001 par 06/10/1997
New Common $0.001 par split (2) for (1) by issuance of (1) additional share payable 03/20/2000 to holders of record 03/15/2000
Recapitalized as Migami, Inc. 03/02/2006
Each share new Common $0.001 par exchanged for (0.2) share Common $0.001 par

KLEER PAK CORP (DE)
Each share old Common 10¢ par exchanged for (1/3) share new Common 10¢ par 08/12/1974
Merged into KPC Acquisitions, Inc. 09/28/1982
Each share new Common 10¢ par exchanged for $2 cash

KLEER VU INDS INC (DE)
Reincorporated 07/15/1983
Common 10¢ par split (2) for (1) by issuance of (1) additional share 03/15/1983
State of incorporation changed from (NY) to (DE) 07/15/1983
Common 10¢ par split (3) for (2) by issuance of (0.5) additional share 09/15/1983
Common 10¢ par split (5) for (4) by issuance of (0.25) additional share 05/15/1987
Each share old Common 10¢ par exchanged for (0.1) share new Common 10¢ par 09/28/1990
Stock Dividends - 10% 06/30/1982; 25% 12/10/1982 ;10% 12/31/1984; 10% 01/10/1985; 10% 04/13/1992; 10% 01/15/1993; 20% 10/15/1993
Recapitalized as Calypso Wireless Inc. 11/08/2002
Each share new Common 10¢ par exchanged for (0.05) share Common 10¢ par
(See Calypso Wireless Inc.)

KLEGG ELECTRONICS INC (NV)
Each share old Common $0.001 par exchanged for (6) shares new Common new Common $0.001 par 09/16/2005
Each share new Common $0.001 par exchanged again for (0.1) share new Common $0.001 par 05/08/2007
Company reported out of business 00/00/2012

KLEIN (D. EMIL) CO., INC. (NY)
Name changed to Demlein Corp. 1/25/55
Demlein Corp. name changed to Industrial Enterprises, Inc. (NY) 10/25/55 which name changed to Novo Industrial Corp. 4/28/60 which name changed to Novo Corp. 5/5/69
(See Novo Corp.)

KLEIN (S.) DEPARTMENT STORES, INC. (NY)
Merged into McCrory Corp. 11/13/1967
Each share Common $1 par exchanged for $10 principal amount of 5% Jr. S.F. Subord. Debentures due 07/15/1981, (1) 1981 Ser. Stock Purchase Warrant and $0.50 cash or $8 principal amount of 6-1/2% Conv. Subord. Debentures due 02/15/1992, (0.6) 1981 Ser. Stock Purchase Warrant and $0.50 cash
Option to elect to receive 6-1/2% Conv. Debentures expired 12/13/1967

KLEIN ENGINEERED COMPETITION COMPONENTS INC (UT)
Reorganized under the laws of Delaware as Automotive Performance Group, Inc. 4/15/98
Each share Common $0.001 par exchanged for (0.05) share Common $0.001 par

KLEINERT I B RUBR INC (NY)
Common no par changed to $10 par in 1933
Common $10 par changed to $5 par and (1) additional share issued 1/12/56
Common $5 par changed to $2.50 par and (1) additional share issued 1/3/62
Name changed to Kleinert's Inc. (NY) 6/18/69
Kleinert's, Inc. (NY) reincorporated in Pennsylvania 7/31/70
(See Kleinert's Inc. (PA))

KLEINERTS INC (PA)
Reincorporated 7/31/70
State of incorporation changed from (NY) to (PA) 7/31/70
Common $2.50 par split (5) for (2) by issuance of (1.5) additional shares 3/26/92
Chapter 11 bankruptcy proceedings converted to Chapter 7 on 8/14/2003
No stockholders' equity

KLEINWORT BENSON AUSTRALIAN INCOME FD INC (MD)
Name changed to Dresdner RCM Global Strategic Income Fund, Inc. 11/09/1999
Dresdner RCM Global Strategic Income Fund, Inc. merged into RCM Strategic Global Government Fund, Inc. 01/18/2002 which name changed to PIMCO Strategic Global Government Fund, Inc. 03/19/2002 which name changed to PIMCO Strategic Income Fund, Inc. 03/03/2014

KLEINWORT BENSON INVT STRATEGIES (MA)
Merged into Centerland Fund 07/11/1993
Details not available

KLEVER MARKETING INC (DE)
Name changed to DarkPulse, Inc. 09/04/2018

KLG SYSTEL LTD (INDIA)
GDR agreement terminated 06/11/2015
Each Reg. S GDR for Ordinary exchanged for (1) share Ordinary
Note: Unexchanged GDR's will be sold and the proceeds, if any, held for claim after 06/15/2015

KLH COMPUTERS INC (TX)
Chapter 11 bankruptcy proceedings converted to liquidating Chapter 11 proceedings 9/2/92
Stockholders' equity unlikely

KLH ENGR GRP INC (DE)
Name changed to Ameriresource Technologies, Inc. 07/16/1996

KLICKITAT VY BANK (GOLDENDALE, WA)
Merged into Columbia Bancorp (OR) 06/13/1996
Each share Common 1¢ par exchanged for (8.5) shares Common no par
(See Columbia Bancorp (OR))

KLIKLOK CORP (DE)
Merged into International General Industries, Inc. 12/31/1975
Each share Common $1 par exchanged for $11 cash

KLINAIR ENVIRONMENTAL TECHNOLOGIES LTD (CAYMAN ISLANDS)
Recapitalized as GSI Securitization Ltd. (Cayman Islands) 07/11/2003
Each Ordinary share 1¢ par exchanged for (0.5) Ordinary share 2¢ par
GSI Securitization Ltd. (Cayman Islands) reincorporated in Nevada as GSI Securitization Inc. 10/18/2007
(See GSI Securitization Inc.)

KLINTAR OILS LTD. (AB)
Assets sold to Humber Oils Ltd. on a (2) for (1) basis in 1958
Humber Oils Ltd. completely liquidated for cash in 1958

KLION (H.L.), INC. (NY)
Liquidation completed
Each share Common 25¢ par exchanged for initial distribution of (0.02587) share Korvette (E.J.), Inc. Common $1 par and $0.18885 cash 08/23/1965
Each share Common 25¢ par received second and final distribution of $0.086 cash 12/27/1965
Korvette (E.J.), Inc. merged into Spartan Industries, Inc. (NY) 09/25/1966 which merged into Arlen Realty & Development Corp. 02/26/1971 which name changed to Arlen Corp. 10/16/1985
(See Arlen Corp.)

KLION (H.L.), INC. (PA)
Under plan of merger reincorporated under the laws of New York 10/31/1963
Klion (H.L.), Inc. (NY) acquired by Korvette (E.J.), Inc. 08/23/1965 which merged into Spartans Industries, Inc. (NY) 09/25/1966 which merged into Arlen Realty & Development Corp. 02/26/1971 which name changed to Arlen Corp. 10/16/1985
(See Arlen Corp.)

KLIPFEL-WASHBURN-BERKLEY CO. (OH)
Charter cancelled for failure to pay taxes 2/15/26

KLLM TRANS SVCS INC (DE)
Common $1 par split (4) for (3) by issuance of (1/3) additional share 5/15/92
Merged into High Road Acquisition Corp. 7/21/2000
Each share Common $1 par exchanged for $8.05 cash

KLM ROYAL DUTCH AIRLS (NETHERLANDS)
New York Registry Shares 100 ANG par changed to 20 ANG par and (4) additional Shares issued 10/24/1984
Each old New York Registry Share 20 ANG par exchanged for (0.75) new New York Registry Share 20 ANG par 10/11/1999
96.33% acquired by Air France as of 05/21/2004
Public interest eliminated

KLOECKNER WERKE AKTIENGESELLSCHAFT (GERMANY)
ADR agreement terminated 11/20/2000
No ADR holder's equity

KLONDEX INC (NY)
Name changed to World Institutes of Technology, Inc. and Class A 1¢ par reclassified as Common 1¢ par 02/21/1969
World Institutes of Technology, Inc. recapitalized as Investors General Realty Corp. 03/30/1973
(See Investors General Realty Corp.)

KLONDEX MINES LTD (BC)
Merged into Hecla Mining Co. 07/25/2018
Each share Common no par exchanged for (0.4136) share Common 25¢ par, (0.125) share Havilah Mining Corp. Common no par and USD$0.8411 cash
Note: Unexchanged certificates will be cancelled and become without value 07/25/2021

KLONDIKE CAP CORP (AB)
Recapitalized as Pacific Iron Ore Corp. 07/21/2008
Each share Common no par exchanged for (0.66666666) share Common no par

KLONDIKE EXPLS LTD (BC)
Recapitalized as Kenver Resources Inc. 07/03/1979
Each share Common 50¢ par exchanged for (0.33333333) share Common no par
(See Kenver Resources Inc.)

KLONDIKE LODE GOLD MINES CORP (BC)
Struck off register and declared dissolved for failure to file returns 08/12/1974

KLONDIKE STAR MINERAL CORP (DE)
Merged into Klondike Star Mineral Corp. 12/20/2016
Each share Common $0.001 par exchanged for either (0.025) share Common no par or $0.0035 cash
Note: Stock option available only to accredited investors or non-U.S. citizens living outside the U.S.

KLONDYKE-CRIPPLE CREEK & GALENA MINING CO. (KS)
Charter cancelled for failure to file annual reports 00/00/1911

KLONDYKE KENO MINES LTD. (ON)
Recapitalized as Jaye Explorations Ltd. 02/00/1955
Each share Capital Stock exchanged for (0.25) share Capital Stock
(See Jaye Explorations Ltd.)

KLOOF GOLD MNG LTD (SOUTH AFRICA)
Each ADR for Ordinary Reg. Rand-1 par exchanged for (4) ADR's for Ordinary Reg. Rand-0.25 par 09/09/1985
Each Unsponsored ADR for Ordinary Reg. Rand-0.25 par exchanged for (1) Sponsored ADR for Ordinary Reg. Rand-0.25 par 12/27/1994
Merged into Gold Fields Ltd. (Old) 02/02/1998
Each Sponsored ADR for Ordinary Rand-0.25 par exchanged for (0.4746) Sponsored ADR for Ordinary 1¢ par
Gold Fields Ltd. (Old) merged into Gold Fields Ltd. (New) 05/10/1999

KLOSS VIDEO CORP (MA)
Out of business 04/00/1988
Details not available

KLR ENERGY ACQUISITION CORP (DE)
Name changed to Rosehill Resources Inc. 04/28/2017

KLX INC (DE)
Each share Common 1¢ par received distribution of (0.4) share KLX Energy Services Holdings, Inc. Common 1¢ par payable 09/14/2018 to holders of record 09/03/2018 Ex date - 09/17/2018
Acquired by Boeing Co. 10/09/2018
Each share Common 1¢ par exchanged for $63 cash

KMA HLDG INC (WY)
Administratively dissolved 04/12/2013

KMART FING I (DE)
Plan of reorganization under Chapter 11 Federal Bankruptcy Code effective 5/6/2003
Each 7.75% Conv. Trust Preferred Security exchanged for approximately $0.03 cash
Note: Unexchanged certificates were cancelled and became without value 05/06/2005

KMART HLDG CORPORATION (DE)
Under plan of merger name changed to Sears Holdings Corp. 03/24/2005

KMC ENTERPRISES INC (DE)
Acquired by Worth Corp. (NV) 7/29/92
Each share Common $0.001 par exchanged for (1.1) shares Common 2¢ par
Worth Corp. (NV) reincorporated in Delaware 7/31/92 which name changed to Krauses Furniture Inc. 12/8/94
(See Krauses Furniture Inc.)

KMC MTG INVS (KY)
Name changed to Kentucky Property Trust 11/30/77
Kentucky Property Trust name changed to RealAmerica Co. (KY) 2/25/82 which reorganized in Delaware 12/15/82 which name changed to RA Global Services, Inc. 3/6/2007

KMG AMERICA CORP (VA)
Acquired by Humana Inc. 11/30/2007
Each share Common 1¢ par exchanged for $6.20 cash

KMG B INC (TX)
Name changed to KMG Chemicals, Inc. 12/11/97

KMI CONTL INC (NY)
Acquired by Kiewit Investment Corp. 01/13/1986
Each share $4.25 Preferred no par exchanged for $55.50 cash
Each share $4.50 Preference Ser. C $1 par exchanged for $45 cash

KMS INDS INC (DE)
Each share Common 1¢ par exchanged for (0.125) share Common 8¢ par 06/10/1987
SEC revoked common stock registration 10/20/2008

KMS PWR INCOME FD (AB)
Acquired by Algonquin Power Income Fund 06/10/2002
Each Trust Unit no par exchanged for (0.7428) Trust Unit no par
Algonquin Power Income Fund merged into Algonquin Power & Utilities Corp. 10/27/2009

KMT GLOBAL HLDGS INC (NV)
Recapitalized as StarPower ON Systems, Inc. 03/23/2017
Each share Common $0.001 par exchanged for (0.02) share Common $0.001 par

KMW SYS CORP (DE)
Common 10¢ par split (3) for (2) by issuance of (0.5) additional share 9/21/86
Merged into Andrew Corp. 1/12/90
Each share Common 10¢ par exchanged for $5.25 cash

KNAPE & VOGT MFG CO (DE)
Reincorporated 2/26/85
Common $2 par split (2) for (1) by issuance of (1) additional share 3/3/72
State of incorporation changed from (MI) to (DE) 2/26/85
Common $2 par split (3) for (1) by issuance of (2) additional shares 12/30/86
Note: Option to receive (1) share Common and (1) share Conv. Class B Common or (2) shares Conv. Class B Common expired 12/15/86
Stock Dividends - 10% 9/7/90; 10% 9/6/91; 10% 9/11/92; 10% 9/9/94; 10% payable 5/19/2000 to holders of record 5/5/2000 Ex date - 5/3/2000
Merged into Wind Point Partners VI, L.P. 7/28/2006
Each share Common $2 par exchanged for $19 cash
Each share Class B Common $2 par exchanged for $19 cash

KNAPIC ELECTRO-PHYSICS, INC. (MN)
Adjudicated bankrupt 4/23/64
No stockholders' equity

KNAPP & TUBBS, INC. (DE)
Completely liquidated
Each share Common 50¢ par exchanged for first and final distribution of $3 cash 5/2/66

KNAPP MONARCH CO (DE)
Reincorporated 00/00/1946
State of incorporation changed from (MO) to (DE) 00/00/1946
Liquidation completed
Each share Common $1 par exchanged for initial distribution of (0.2227) share Hoover Co. (DE) Common $2.50 par 07/18/1969
Each share Common $1 par received second distribution of $0.035 cash 07/15/1970
Each share Common $1 par received third distribution of (0.031284) share Hoover Co. (DE) Common $2.50 par 03/24/1971
Each share Common $1 par received fourth and final distribution of $0.01041 cash 11/05/1971
(See Hoover Co. (DE))

KNAPP OIL & GAS, INC. (UT)
Name changed to American Resources, Ltd. (UT) and Common $1 par changed to no par 10/24/61
American Resources, Ltd. (UT) reincorporated in Delaware as Resources International, Ltd. 12/21/82
(See Resources International, Ltd.)

KNAPP SECURITIES CORP. (DE)
Dissolved 5/22/61

KNAPP URANIUM DEVELOPMENT CO. (UT)
Recapitalized as Knapp Oil & Gas, Inc. 4/25/60
Each share Common 1¢ par exchanged for (0.01) share Common $1 par
Knapp Oil & Gas, Inc. name changed to American Resources, Ltd. 10/24/61
(See American Resources, Ltd.)

KNBT BANCORP INC (PA)
Merged into National Penn Bancshares, Inc. 02/01/2008
Each share Common 1¢ par exchanged for (1.03) shares Common no par
National Penn Bancshares, Inc. merged into BB&T Corp. 04/01/2016

KNE GRAPHICS INC (MA)
Reincorporated under the laws of Delaware as Hera Resources, Inc. 08/02/1982

KNEE HILL ENERGY CDA LTD (CANADA)
Acquired by 158154 Canada Inc. 03/03/1989
Each share Common no par exchanged for $0.47 cash

KNEE LAKE GOLD MINES LTD.
Acquired by Amalgamated Knee Lake Mines Ltd. on a (1) for (5) basis in 1947
Amalgamated Knee Lake Mines Ltd. charter cancelled 3/31/76

KNEWTRINO INC (NV)
Name changed to Vanguard Minerals Corp. 10/04/2007
Vanguard Minerals Corp. name changed to Zoned Properties, Inc. 10/25/2013

KNEXA SOLUTIONS INC (BC)
Name changed 02/18/2003
Name changed from Knexa.com Enterprises Inc. to Knexa Solutions Inc. 02/18/2003
Name changed to ClearFrame Solutions Inc. 02/13/2004
ClearFrame Solutions Inc. recapitalized as ClearFrame Solutions Corp. 05/02/2005 which name changed to Clear Gold Resources Inc. 02/25/2013

KNICKERBOCKER ANTHRACITE COAL CO. (PA)
Out of existence 09/03/1880
Details not available

KNICKERBOCKER BIOLOGICALS, INC. (NY)
Acquired by Pfizer (Chas.) & Co., Inc. (Del.) on a (0.12308) for (1) basis 11/15/62
Pfizer (Chas.) & Co., Inc. (Del.) name changed to Pfizer Inc. 4/27/70

KNICKERBOCKER BUILDING CORP.
Liquidated in 1951

KNICKERBOCKER CAP CORP (NV)
Reincorporated 02/25/2004
Each share old Common $0.001 par exchanged for (0.0001) share new Common $0.001 par 03/21/2000
State of incorporation changed from (CO) to (NV) 02/25/2004
New Common $0.001 par split (10) for (1) by issuance of (9) additional shares payable 08/16/2005 to holders of record 08/16/2005
Charter revoked for failure to file reports and pay fees 02/28/2007

KNICKERBOCKER HOTEL CO. (IL)
Name changed to KHC Liquidating Co. 2/19/66 which completed liquidation 11/18/66

KNICKERBOCKER INSURANCE CO. OF NEW YORK
Merged into American Equitable Assurance Co. of New York on a (1) for (2) basis in 1944
American Equitable Assurance Co. of New York merged into Reliance Insurance Co. 6/30/65
(See Reliance Insurance Co.)

KNICKERBOCKER INS CO (NY)
Liquidated by Court Order 11/18/1971
No stockholders' equity

KNICKERBOCKER L L INC (CA)
Each share old Common no par exchanged for (5) shares new Common no par 08/30/1995
Reorganized under Chapter 11 Federal Bankruptcy Code 09/06/2002
Each share new Common no par exchanged for (0.0225647) share RG Global Lifestyles, Inc. Common no par
Note: Unexchanged certificates were cancelled and became without value 12/17/2004
RG Global Lifestyles, Inc. name changed to Sustainable Environmental Technologies Corp. 08/24/2010
(See Sustainable Environmental Technologies Corp.)

KNICKERBOCKER SECURITIES CORP. (NY)
Dissolved 6/12/58

KNICKERBOCKER TOY INC (NY)
Common 10¢ par changed to 5¢ par and (1) additional share issued 02/06/1973
Common 5¢ par split (2) for (1) by issuance of (1) additional share 02/11/1977
Stock Dividend - 50% 08/20/1976
Merged into Warner Communications Inc. 06/30/1977
Each share Common 5¢ par exchanged for $10 principal amount 9.125% Subord. Sinking Fund Debentures, due 11/15/1996 and $9 cash

KNICKERBOCKER VILLAGE INC (NY)
Each (4,000) shares old Common $2.15 par exchanged for (1) share new Common $2.15 par 7/10/2001
Note: In effect holders will receive $6.28 cash per share and public interest was eliminated

KNIE RES INC (BC)
Recapitalized as Alta Explorations Inc. 07/17/1987
Each share Common no par exchanged for (0.25) share Common no par
Alta Explorations Inc. recapitalized as Akash Ventures Inc. 03/15/1994 which recapitalized as International Akash Ventures Inc. 12/08/1999 which name changed to Healthscreen Solutions Inc. 01/18/2001
(See Healthscreen Solutions Inc.)

KNIGHT & MILLER OIL CORP (CO)
Name changed to Domestic Energy Co., Inc. 10/23/1973
Domestic Energy Co., Inc. merged into Dietrich Exploration Co., Inc. (CO) 03/04/1976 which reorganized in Delaware as Dietrich Resources Corp. 05/15/1981 which name changed to DRX, Inc. 04/29/1987
(See DRX, Inc.)

KNIGHT AIRLS INC (FL)
Name changed to Southern Airlines, Inc. 5/1/80
Southern Airlines, Inc. proclaimed dissolved 11/1/85

KNIGHT CAP GROUP INC (DE)
Merged into KCG Holdings, Inc. 07/01/2013
Each share Common 1¢ par exchanged for for (0.33333333) share Class A Common 1¢ par
(See KCG Holdings, Inc.)

KNIGHT (B.B. & R.) CORP.
Reorganized as Fruit of the Loom, Inc. (DE) 00/00/1938
Each share Preferred exchanged for (1) share Preferred and (1) share Common
Each share Class A exchanged for (0.5) share Preferred and (0.5) share Common
Each share Class B and/or C exchanged for (1) share Common
(See Fruit of the Loom, Inc. (DE))

KNIGHT ENERGY CORP (MD)
Reincorporated 04/30/2007
State of incorporation changed from (NV) to (MD) 04/30/2007
Chapter 11 bankruptcy proceedings converted to Chapter 7 on 04/08/2010
Stockholders' equity unlikely

KNIGHT FULLER INC (DE)
Name changed to CenterStaging Corp. 02/07/2006
(See CenterStaging Corp.)

KNIGHT INDS INC (OK)
Common 50¢ par split (3) for (2) by issuance of (0.5) additional share 12/3/75
Merged into Ingersoll-Rand Co. (NJ) 4/2/80
Each share Common 50¢ par exchanged for $13.50 cash

KNIGHT INVT LTD (NV)
Name changed to Northeast Mortgage Corp. 02/25/2002
(See Northeast Mortgage Corp.)

KNIGHT KNOX DEV CORP (NV)
Name changed to Reactive Medical Inc. 02/10/2017
Reactive Medical Inc. name changed to Artelo Biosciences, Inc. 05/02/2017

KNIGHT METALS LTD (BC)
Name changed to Africa Hydrocarbons Inc. (BC) 02/02/2012
Africa Hydrocarbons Inc. (BC) reincorporated in Alberta 04/25/2013 which name changed to Blockchaink2 Corp. 05/30/2018

KNIGHT MNG CORP (AB)
Name changed to Choice Software Systems Ltd. 10/03/1991
Choice Software Systems Ltd. recapitalized as Timbuktu Gold Corp. 12/29/1995 which name changed to Marchmont Gold Corp. 06/11/1997 which recapitalized as Adulis Minerals Corp. 05/18/2000 which recapitalized as Adulis Resources Inc. 05/01/2001 which name changed to Solana Resources Ltd. 10/18/2005 which merged into Gran Tierra Energy Inc. (NV) 11/17/2008 which reincorporated in Delaware 10/31/2016

KNIGHT NEWSPAPERS INC (OH)
Common 16-2/3¢ par changed to 8-1/3¢ par and (1) additional share issued 4/25/72
Under plan of merger name changed to Knight-Ridder Newspapers, Inc. (OH) 11/30/74
Knight-Ridder Newspapers, Inc. (OH) reincorporated in Florida 8/31/76 which name changed to Knight-Ridder, Inc. 4/30/86 which merged into McClatchy Co. 6/27/2006

KNIGHT PETE CORP (BC)
Name changed to Knight Resources Ltd. 03/07/2003
Knight Resources Ltd. recapitalized as Knight Metals Ltd. 05/25/2011 which name changed to Africa Hydrocarbons Inc. (BC) 02/02/2012 which reincorporated in Alberta 04/25/2013 which name changed to Blockchaink2 Corp. 05/30/2018

KNIGHT RES LTD (BC)
Recapitalized as Knight Metals Ltd. 05/25/2011
Each share Common no par exchanged for (0.05263157) share Common no par
Knight Metals Ltd. name changed to Africa Hydrocarbons Inc. (BC) 02/02/2012 which reincorporated in Alberta 04/25/2013 which name changed to Blockchaink2 Corp. 05/30/2018

KNIGHT RIDDER INC (FL)
Reincorporated 08/31/1976
Name changed 04/30/1986
$3.60 Preferred $10 par called for redemption 06/10/1976
State of incorporation changed from (OH) to (FL) 08/31/1976
Common 8-1/3¢ par changed to 4-1/6¢ par and (1) additional share issued 09/08/1978
Conv. Preference Ser. 1 no par called for redemption 01/02/1980
Common 4-1/6¢ par changed to 2-1/12¢ par and (1) additional share issued 11/28/1983
Name changed from Knight-Ridder Newspapers, Inc. to Knight-Ridder, Inc. 04/30/1986
Common 2-1/12¢ par split (2) for (1) by issuance of (1) additional share payable 07/31/1996 to holders of record 07/10/1996
Merged into McClatchy Co. 06/27/2006
Each share Common 2-1/12¢ par exchanged for (0.5118) share Class A Common 1¢ par and $40 cash

KNIGHT RTY CORP (CO)
Under plan of merger each share Common 1¢ par automatically became (1) share Sheffield Exploration Co., Inc. (CO) Common 1¢ par 1/1/85
Sheffield Exploration Co., Inc. (CO) reorganized in Delaware 3/6/91 which merged into Transmontaigne Oil Co. 6/4/96 which name changed to Transmontaigne Inc. 8/26/98
(See Transmontaigne Inc.)

KNIGHT TRADING GROUP INC (DE)
Name changed to Knight Capital Group, Inc. 05/11/2005
Knight Capital Group, Inc. merged into KCG Holdings, Inc. 07/01/2013
(See KCG Holdings, Inc.)

KNIGHT TRANSN INC (AZ)
Common 1¢ par split (3) for (2) by issuance of (0.5) additional share payable 05/18/1998 to holders of record 05/01/1998
Common 1¢ par split (3) for (2) by issuance of (0.5) additional share payable 06/01/2001 to holders of record 05/18/2001 Ex date - 06/04/2001
Common 1¢ par split (3) for (2) by issuance of (0.5) additional share payable 12/28/2001 to holders of record 12/07/2001 Ex date - 12/31/2001
Common 1¢ par split (3) for (2) by issuance of (0.5) additional share payable 07/20/2004 to holders of record 07/12/2004 Ex date - 07/21/2004
Common 1¢ par split (3) for (2) by issuance of (0.5) additional share payable 12/23/2005 to holders of record 11/30/2005 Ex date - 12/27/2005
Merged into Knight-Swift Transportation Holdings Inc. 09/11/2017
Each share Common 1¢ par exchanged for (1) share Class A Common 1¢ par

KNIGHT/TRIMARK GROUP INC (DE)
Class A Common 1¢ par split (2) for (1) by issuance of (1) additional share payable 05/14/1999 to holders of record 04/30/1999
Name changed to Knight Trading Group, Inc. 05/14/2000
Knight Trading Group, Inc. name changed to Knight Capital Group, Inc. 05/11/2005 which merged into KCG Holdings, Inc. 07/01/2013
(See KCG Holdings, Inc.)

KNIGHTHAWK AIRLS INC (CANADA)
Reincorporated 9/29/98
Place of incorporation changed from (BC) to (Canada) 9/29/98
Name changed to KnightHawk Inc. 4/15/99

KNIGHTS DEVELOPING & TRADING CO., INC. (NY)
Proclaimed dissolved for failure to file reports and pay fees 12/15/36

KNIGHTS LIFE INSURANCE CO. OF AMERICA (DE)
Stock Dividends - 33-1/3% 2/21/42; 25% 3/26/44; 50% 4/30/47; 33-1/3% 3/30/49; 50% 12/1/50; 66-2/3% 4/15/53; 20% 5/1/56; 25% 12/1/58
Acquired by American General Insurance Co. on a (2) for (1) basis 8/1/60
American General Insurance Co. reorganized as American General Corp. 7/1/80 which merged into American International Group, Inc. 8/29/2001

KNIGHTSBRIDGE CORP (NV)
Each share old Common $0.001 par exchanged for (0.25) share new Common $0.001 par 7/24/98
Under plan of merger name changed to Western Oil & Tire Distributors, Inc. 8/11/98
Western Oil & Tire Distributors, Inc. name changed to Saratoga International Holdings Corp. 3/24/99 which name changed to Fortune Credit & Insurance Services, Inc. 9/27/2001

KNIGHTSBRIDGE FINE WINES INC (NV)
Name changed to 360 Global Wine Co. 02/15/2005
(See 360 Global Wine Co.)

KNIGHTSBRIDGE SHIPPING LTD (BERMUDA)
Name changed 10/07/2014
Name changed from Knightsbridge Tankers Ltd. to Knightsbridge Shipping Ltd. 10/07/2014
Under the plan of merger name changed to Golden Ocean Group Ltd. (New) 04/01/2015

KNIGHTSWOOD FINL CORP (BC)
Common no par split (3) for (1) by issuance of (2) additional shares payable 04/18/2017 to holders of record 04/12/2017 Ex date - 04/10/2017
Name changed to Cannabis Wheaton Income Corp. 05/08/2017
Cannabis Wheaton Income Corp. name changed to Auxly Cannabis Group Inc. 06/08/2018

KNOBBY LAKE MINES LTD (CANADA)
Recapitalized as Consolidated Knobby Lake Mines Ltd. 7/6/84
Each share Common no par exchanged for (0.2) share Common no par
Consolidated Knobby Lake Mines Ltd. recapitalized as Kancana Ventures Ltd. 9/23/88 which recapitalized as Walron Minerals Corp. 12/21/94
(See Walron Minerals Corp.)

KNOBHILL GOLD MINES, LTD. (ON)
Charter cancelled 11/5/62

KNOBIAS INC (DE)
Each share old Common 1¢ par exchanged for (0.01) share new Common 1¢ par 12/03/2007
Assets assigned to senior secured creditor 07/30/2009
Stockholders' equity unlikely

KNOCKOUT HLDGS INC (DE)
SEC revoked common stock registration 09/09/2011

KNOGO CORP (NY)
Common 1¢ par split (2) for (1) by issuance of (1) additional share 09/20/1980
Merged into Sensormatic Electronics Corp. 12/29/1994
Each share Common 1¢ par exchanged for (0.5513) share Common 1¢ par
Sensormatic Electronics Corp. merged into Tyco International Ltd. 11/13/2001

KNOGO CORP (ON)
Name changed to Plumbing Mart Corp. 07/03/1974
Plumbing Mart Corp. recapitalized as PMC Corp. 03/01/1988 which name changed to Floorco Ltd. 07/06/1994
(See Floorco Ltd.)

KNOGO NORTH AMER INC (DE)
Merged into Sentry Technology Corp. 02/12/1997
Each share Common 1¢ par exchanged for (0.83180835) share 5% Class A Preferred $0.001 par and (0.83180835) share Common $0.001 par

KNOLL INC (DE)
Issue Information - 8,000,000 shares COM offered at $17 per share on 05/09/1997
Merged into Warburg, Pincus Ventures, L.P. 11/4/99
Each share Common 1¢ par exchanged for $28 cash
(Additional Information in Active)

KNOLL INTL INC (DE)
Merged into General Felt Industries, Inc. 01/22/1987
Each share Class A Common 10¢ par exchanged for $12 cash

KNOLOGY INC (DE)
Issue Information - 6,000,000 shares COM offered at $9 per share on 12/18/2003
Acquired by WideOpenWest Finance L.L.C. 07/17/2012
Each share Common 1¢ par exchanged for $19.75 cash

KNOMEX RES INC (ON)
Recapitalized as Afitex Financial Services Inc. 11/10/1998
Each share Common no par exchanged for (0.1) share Common no par
(See Afitex Financial Services Inc.)

KNOT INC (DE)
Issue Information - 3,500,000 shares COM offered at $10 per share on 12/01/1999
Name changed to XO Group Inc. 06/28/2011

KNOTT CORP.
Recapitalized as Knott Hotels Corp. in 1950
Each share Common $1 par exchanged for (2) shares Common $5 par
(See Knott Hotels Corp.)

KNOTT HOTELS CORP (DE)
Common $5 par split (2) for (1) by issuance of (1) additional share 10/22/1969
Merged into Trust Houses Forte Ltd. 03/03/1977
Each share Common $5 par exchanged for $5.73 cash

KNOVA SOFTWARE INC (DE)
Merged into Consona Corp. 3/13/2007
Each share Common 1¢ par exchanged for $5 cash

KNOWAY VENTURES INC (DE)
Recapitalized as Olympus Mountain Gold Ltd. 8/5/2004
Each share Common $0.0001 par exchanged for (0.005) share Common $0.0001 par

KNOWLEDGE COMMUNICATION FD INC (OH)
Under plan of merger name changed to Cardinal Fund Inc. 05/30/1975
(See Cardinal Fund Inc.)

KNOWLEDGE DATA SYS INC (DE)
Merged into AIS Acquisition Corp. 02/08/1991
Each share Common 1¢ par exchanged for $0.9428 cash

KNOWLEDGE FOUNDATIONS INC (DE)
Name changed to BSI2000 Inc. 4/4/2003

KNOWLEDGE HOUSE PUBG LTD (NS)
Name changed to Knowledge House Inc. 1/3/2000

KNOWLEDGE MACH INTL INC (NV)
Common $0.001 par split (10) for (1) by issuance of (9) additional shares payable 11/10/2014 to holders of record 11/10/2014
Recapitalized as Dthera Sciences 11/02/2016
Each share Common $0.001 par exchanged for (0.19571865) share Common $0.001 par

KNOWLEDGE MECHANICS GROUP INC (DE)
Charter cancelled and declared inoperative and void for non-payment of taxes 03/01/2003

KNOWLEDGE NETWORKS ACQUISITIONS INC (NV)
Recapitalized as Wattage Monitor, Inc. 02/19/1999
Each (36) shares Common $0.001 par exchanged for (1) share Common 1¢ par
(See Wattage Monitor, Inc.)

KNOWLEDGE NETWORKS INC (NV)
Each share old Common $0.001 par exchanged for (1.333) shares new Common $0.001 par 11/06/2000
Each share new Common $0.001 par exchanged again for (0.1) share new Common $0.001 par 07/05/2001
Each share new Common $0.001 par exchanged again for (0.1) share new Common $0.001 par 02/15/2002
Each share new Common $0.001 par exchanged again for (0.33333333) share new Common 09/18/2002
Note: Holders of (100) to (300) shares will receive (100) shares only
Holders of (99) shares or fewer were not affected by the reverse split
Recapitalized as KNW Networks, Inc. 10/23/2002
Each share new Common $0.001 par exchanged for (0.2) share Common $0.001 par
Note: Holders of between (100) to (500) shares will receive (100) shares only
Holders of (100) or fewer pre-split shares were not afffected by reverse split
KNW Networks, Inc. name changed to Austin Chalk Oil & Gas, Ltd. 06/10/2004 which recapitalized as Mercantile Resources, Ltd. 07/08/2010 which recapitalized as Sharewell Capital Group, Inc. 03/25/2011 which name changed to Artemis Energy Holdings Inc. 04/11/2013 which name changed to Findit, Inc. 02/20/2015

KNOWLEDGE PLUS MULTIMEDIA PUBG LTD (AB)
Issue Information - 1,250,000 shares COM offered at $0.60 per share on 12/08/1993
Delisted from Alberta Stock Exchange 07/23/1998

KNOWLEDGE TRANSFER SYS INC (NV)
Each share old Common $0.001 par exchanged for (0.002) share new Common $0.001 par 07/16/2004
Name changed to Global General Technologies Inc. 07/08/2005
Global General Technologies, Inc. recapitalized as Turbine Aviation, Inc. 12/19/2014

KNOWLEDGEMAX INC (DE)
Ceased operations and assets sold for the benefit of creditors 2/20/2003
No stockholders' equity

KNOWLEDGEWARE INC (GA)
Merged into Sterling Software, Inc. 11/30/1994
Each share Common no par exchanged for (0.1322) share Common 10¢ par
Note: Additional shares are being held in escrow to cover certain claims pursuant to the terms of the merger
Sterling Software, Inc. merged into Computer Associates International, Inc. 04/07/2000 which name changed to CA, Inc. 02/01/2006

KNOWLTON CAP INC NEW (CANADA)
Recapitalized as LGC Capital Ltd. 07/19/2016
Each share Common no par exchanged for (0.78249998) share Common no par

KNOWLTON CAP INC OLD (CANADA)
Name changed to Buzz Telecommunications Services Inc. 01/26/2007
Buzz Telecommunications Services Inc. name changed to Knowlton Capital Inc. (New) 01/21/2014 which recapitalized as LGC Capital Ltd. 07/19/2016

KNOX-ARIZONA COPPER MINING CORP. (AZ)
Name changed to Knox-Arizona Corp. and Common $1 par changed to no par 5/20/69

KNOX CORP. (DE)
Merged into National Homes Corp. 8/10/59
Each (1.538) shares Class A Common $1 par exchanged for (1) share Class A Common 50¢ par
Each (1.538) shares Class B Common $1 par exchanged for (1) share Class A Common 50¢ par
National Homes Corp. name changed to National Enterprises, Inc. 6/3/86 which name changed to Empire Gold Inc. 9/30/97
(See Empire Gold Inc.)

KNOX FURNITURE MANUFACTURING CO.
Property sold 00/00/1931
Details not available

KNOX GLASS, INC. (PA)
Common $25 par changed to $6.25 par and (3) additional shares issued 9/22/58
Merged into Hunt Foods & Industries, Inc. 9/30/65
Each share Common $6.25 par exchanged for (0.2) share 5% Preferred Ser. A $100 par
(See Hunt Foods & Industries, Inc.)

KNOX GLASS BOTTLE CO. (PA)
Name changed to Knox Glass, Inc. 5/19/55
Knox Glass, Inc. merged into Hunt Foods & Industries, Inc. 9/30/65
(See Hunt Foods & Industries, Inc.)

KNOX HAT CO., INC. (NY)
Name changed to Byrndun Corp. in 1932
Byrndun Corp. merged into Hat Corp. of America 5/2/60 which name changed to HCA Industries, Inc. 4/30/70 which name changed to HCA-Martin, Inc. 5/11/73 which name changed to Martin Processing, Inc. 5/16/75
(See Martin Processing, Inc.)

KNOX LMBR CO (MN)
Stock Dividend - 50% 03/22/1978
Merged into Southwest Forest Industries, Inc. 12/24/1980
Each share Common 25¢ par exchanged for $11.86 cash

KNOX NURSERY INC (FL)
Each share old Common $0.001 par exchanged for (0.001) share new Common $0.001 par 08/08/2012
Note: Holders entitled to (149) or fewer post-split shares received $0.021 cash per share
Common $0.001 par changed to $0.0001 par 02/14/2013
Common $0.0001 par split (7) for (1) by issuance of (6) additional shares payable 12/06/2013 to holders of record 11/21/2013 Ex date - 12/09/2013
Reincorporated under the laws of Oklahoma as Upper Street Marketing, Inc. 02/18/2014

KNOX WESTN CAP INC (CANADA)
Delisted from Alberta Stock Exchange 12/10/1991

KNOXFORT CORP (NJ)
Charter declared void for non-payment of taxes 04/12/1973

KNOXVILLE GAS CO.
Properties sold to City of Knoxville 00/00/1945
Details not available

KNOXVILLE GRAY EAGLE MARBLE CO.
Out of business 00/00/1935
Details not available

KNOXVILLE LAND & IMPROVEMENT CO.
Liquidated in 1950

KNUDSEN CORP (CA)
Stock Dividends - 100% 06/15/1971; 10% 06/15/1976; 10% 12/14/1978
Merged into Builders Investment Group 06/01/1983
Each share Common $1 par exchanged for $27.50 cash

KNUDSEN CREAMERY CO.
Name changed to Knudsen Creamery Co. of California in 1935
Knudsen Creamery Co. of California name changed to Knudsen Corp. 7/16/68
(See Knudsen Corp.)

KNUDSEN CREAMERY CO. OF CALIFORNIA (CA)
Each share Class A no par exchanged for (2.5) shares Preferred no par and (1) share Common no par in 1939
Each share Class B no par exchanged for (5) shares Common no par in 1939
Common no par changed to $1 par in 1945
$0.60 Preferred no par called for redemption 11/25/58
Voting Trust Agreement terminated 3/25/65
Each VTC for Common $1 par exchanged for (1) share Common $1 par
Stock Dividends - 300% 12/2/46; 10% 2/10/59
Name changed to Knudsen Corp. 7/16/68
(See Knudsen Corp.)

KNUDSEN LABORATORIES, INC.
Acquired by Knudsen Creamery Co. 00/00/1929
Details not available

KNUSAGA CORP (NV)
Reincorporated 05/19/2002
State of incorporation changed from (DE) to (NV) and Common 1¢ par changed to $0.001 par 05/19/2002

Each (36) shares old Common $0.001 par exchanged for (1) share new Common $0.001 par 08/01/2005
Note: In effect holders received $0.25 cash per share and public interest was eliminated

KNUTSON COS INC (MN)
Each share Common 50¢ par exchanged for (0.1) share Common $5 par 04/27/1967
Each share old Common $5 par exchanged for (1) share Preferred $5 par 06/30/1978
Note: Option to convert Preferred $5 par into new Common $5 par expired 08/18/1978
Preferred $5 par called for redemption 10/06/1980
Each (300) shares new Common $5 par exchanged for (1) share Common $5 par 10/28/1980
Note: In effect holders received $30 cash per share and public interest was eliminated

KNUTSON MTG CORP (DE)
Acquired by Temple Inland Mortgage Corp. 5/31/97
Details not available

KNW NETWORKS INC (NV)
Each share old Common $0.001 par exchanged for (0.06666666) share new Common $0.001 par 02/27/2004
Each share new Common $0.001 par exchanged again for (3) new shares Common $0.001 par 05/13/2004
Name changed to Austin Chalk Oil & Gas, Ltd. 06/10/2004
Austin Chalk Oil & Gas, Ltd. recapitalized as Mercantile Resources, Ltd. 07/08/2010 which recapitalized as Sharewell Capital Group, Inc. 03/25/2011 which name changed to Artemis Energy Holdings Inc. 04/11/2013 which name changed to Findit, Inc. 02/20/2015

KNY-SCHEERER CORP.
Merged into Vadsco Sales Corp. 00/00/1929
Details not available

KOAL-KRUDES, INC. (WA)
Charter revoked for failure to file reports and pay fees 7/1/63

KOALA BEVERAGES LTD (BC)
Name changed to Tribridge Enterprises Corp. 7/21/97
Tribridge Enterprises Corp. recapitalized as Vision Gate Ventures Ltd. 3/16/99 which name changed to Northern Lion Gold Corp. 7/10/2003

KOALA CAP CORP (NV)
Name changed to Sterling Worldwide Corp. 01/07/1997
Sterling Worldwide Corp. name changed to Sun Quest Holdings Inc. 12/23/1999 which name changed to Sunrise Consulting Group, Inc. 12/04/2007

KOALA CONE INC (NJ)
Charter revoked for failure to file reports and pay fees 6/6/95

KOALA CORP (CO)
Issue Information - 700,000 shares COM offered at $6 per share on 10/12/1993
Common 10¢ par split (2) for (1) by issuance of (1) additional share payable 10/28/1999 to holders of record 10/18/1999
Plan of reorganization under Chapter 11 Federal Bankruptcy Code effective 09/04/2007
No stockholders' equity

KOALA INTL WIRELESS INC (NV)
Name changed to KIWI Network Solutions, Inc. 1/14/2004
KIWI Network Solutions, Inc. name changed to Trimax Corp. 2/15/2005

KOALA KREME INC (CANADA)
Recapitalized as Sur American Gold Corp. (Canada) 06/15/1995
Each share Common no par exchanged for (0.16666666) share Common no par
Sur American Gold Corp. (Canada) reincorporated in British Columbia as Cadan Resources Corp. 08/28/2007 which name changed to Rizal Resources Corp. 10/07/2016

KOALA RES LTD (BC)
Recapitalized as Dragon Gem Corp. 3/30/93
Each share Common no par exchanged for (0.2) share Common no par
Dragon Gem Corp. recapitalized as Consolidated Alliance Resource Corp. 4/15/98 which name changed to Dyna Haul Corp. 7/9/99
(See Dyna Haul Corp.)

KOALA TECHNOLOGIES CORP (DE)
Recapitalized as Rotonics Manufacturing Inc. 12/17/92
Each share Common no par exchanged for (1/3) share Common no par
(See Rotonics Manufacturing Inc.)

KOBACKER SHOE CO (PA)
Reincorporated under the laws of Ohio as K B Marketing Systems, Inc. 03/20/1969
K B Marketing Systems, Inc. name changed to Kobacker Stores, Inc. 05/05/1976
(See Kobacker Stores, Inc.)

KOBACKER STORES, INC. (OH)
Incorporated 1/25/25
Each share Common no par exchanged for (6) shares Common $1 par and (0.5) share Preferred $20 par in 1945
Common $1 par changed to $7.50 par in 1951
Name changed to Kostin Corp. 1/31/61

KOBACKER STORES INC (OH)
Incorporated 2/21/69
$0.82 Conv. Preferred Ser. A no par called for redemption 06/24/1977
Stock Dividend - 200% 03/01/1979
Merged into Kobacker Co. 03/03/1984
Each share Common 10¢ par exchanged for $19 cash

KOBE, INC.
Acquired by Dresser Industries, Inc. (PA) 00/00/1945
Each share Class A Preferred exchanged for (0.4) share Common
Each share Class B Preferred exchanged for (0.02) share Common
Each share Common exchanged for (0.19841269) share new Common
Dresser Industries, Inc. (PA) reincorporated in Delaware 08/01/1956
(See Dresser Industries, Inc. (DE) (Plain) (Old))

KOBE STL LTD (JAPAN)
Basis changed from (1:5) to (1:0.5) 10/03/2016
ADR agreement terminated 04/26/2018
Each Sponsored ADR for Common exchanged for $5.202433 cash

KOBER CORP (CO)
Each share old Common $0.001 par exchanged for (0.1) share new Common $0.001 par 8/29/84
Each share new Common $0.001 par exchanged for (0.1) share Common 1¢ par 6/1/92
Administratively dissolved 1/2/2000

KOBEX CAP CORP (BC)
Name changed to Itasca Capital Ltd. 06/23/2016

KOBEX MINERALS INC (BC)
Name changed to Kobex Capital Corp. 08/29/2014

Kobex Capital Corp. name changed to Itasca Capital Ltd. 06/23/2016

KOBEX RES LTD (BC)
Merged into Kobex Minerals Inc. 09/30/2009
Each share Common no par exchanged for (0.54625) share Common no par
Kobex Minerals Inc. name changed to Kobex Capital Corp. 08/29/2014 which name changed to Itasca Capital Ltd. 06/23/2016

KOBOLD RES LTD (BC)
Recapitalized as Canton Ventures Ltd. 02/01/1990
Each share Common no par exchanged for (0.5) share Common no par
Canton Ventures Ltd. name changed to Seacorp Capital Corp. 03/01/1993 which recapitalized as Seacorp Communications Inc. 04/07/1995
(See Seacorp Communications Inc.)

KOCH PIPELINES CDA LP (AB)
Name changed to Inter Pipeline Fund 11/15/2002
Inter Pipeline Fund reorganized as Inter Pipeline Ltd. 09/05/2013

KODA RES LTD (BC)
Reorganized under the laws of Ontario as African Gold Group, Inc. 03/18/2004
Each share Common no par exchanged for (0.28571428) share Common no par

KODEL ELECTRIC & MANUFACTURING CO.
Out of existence 00/00/1931
Details not available

KODEL RADIO CORP.
Name changed to Kodel Electric & Manufacturing Co. 00/00/1928
(See Kodel Electric & Manufacturing Co.)

KODIAK ENERGY SVCS LTD (AB)
Placed in receivership 08/10/2005
Stockholders' equity unlikely

KODIAK EXPLORATION CO., INC. (AK)
Out of business 00/00/1964
Details not available

KODIAK EXPL LTD (BC)
Name changed to Prodigy Gold Inc. 01/04/2011
Prodigy Gold Inc. merged into Argonaut Gold Inc. 12/11/2012

KODIAK GAMING INC (DE)
Name changed to Straight Up Brands, Inc. 8/7/2006

KODIAK GRAPHICS CO (NV)
Name changed to SportsPrize Entertainment Inc. 5/24/99
(See SportsPrize Entertainment Inc.)

KODIAK INC (MN)
Class A Common 10¢ par reclassified as Common 10¢ par 10/01/1962
Each share Common 10¢ par exchanged for (0.2) share Common 50¢ par 02/25/1964
Recapitalized as Kodicor, Inc. 05/10/1972
Each share Common 50¢ par exchanged for (0.1) share Common $5 par
(See Kodicor, Inc.)

KODIAK INTL INC (NV)
Name changed to Amerilithium Corp. 03/09/2010
Amerilithium Corp. name changed to Integrated Energy Solutions, Inc. 09/26/2014 which name changed to Patten Energy Solutions Group, Inc. 05/03/2016

KODIAK MINERALS LTD (MB)
Charter cancelled and declared dissolved for failure to file returns 03/09/1972

KODIAK OIL & GAS CORP (YT)
Merged into Whiting Petroleum Corp. 12/08/2014
Each share Common no par exchanged for (0.177) share Common $0.001 par
Note: Unexchanged certificates will be cancelled and become without value 12/08/2020

KODIAK PETE CORP (DE)
Each share Common $0.0001 par exchanged for (0.004) share Common $0.025 par or $0.0025 cash 12/23/1983
Note: Option to receive cash expired 01/11/1984
Name changed to American Pipeline & Exploration Co. 12/09/1984
(See American Pipeline & Exploration Co.)

KODIAK PETROLEUMS LTD. (AB)
Recapitalized 01/08/1965
Each share Non-Cum. Preference Ser. A $10 exchanged for (1) share Common no par
Each share Non-Cum. Conv. 1st Preference Ser. B $10 par exchanged for (2) shares Common no par
Completely liquidated 10/02/1969
Each share Common no par exchanged for first and final distribution of (0.800004) share Manhattan Continental Development Corp. Common 10¢ par
(See Manhattan Continental Development Corp.)

KODIAK RES INC (NV)
Name changed to Group Capital Corp. 02/25/1987

KODIAK VENTURES INC (NV)
Each share old Common $0.001 par exchanged for (1.4) shares new Common $0.001 par 2/18/2000
Name changed to Sonika Inc. 8/25/2000
Sonika Inc. name changed to Cavio International Inc. 3/4/2002 which name changed to Allied Energy Inc. 9/18/2003 which name changed to FloodSmart, Inc. 9/29/2005 which name changed to Axis Energy Corp. 8/1/2006

KODICOR INC (MN)
Each share old Common $5 par exchanged for (0.00005) share new Common $5 par 12/17/1979
Note: In effect holders received $7.50 cash per share and public interest was eliminated

KOEHLER MANAGEMENT CORP. (OH)
Out of business in 09/00/1975
No stockholders' equity

KOEHRING CO (WI)
Reorganized 00/00/1936
Each share Preferred $100 par exchanged for (3.25) shares new Common no par
Each share old Common no par exchanged for (0.1) share new Common no par
Each share new Common no par exchanged for (4) shares Common $5 par 00/00/1945
Each share Common $5 par exchanged for (3) shares Common $2 par 12/03/1956
5% Conv. Preferred Ser. A $50 par called for redemption 03/31/1965
5-1/2% Preferred Ser. C $50 par called for redemption 03/31/1965
$1.68 Conv. Preferred Ser. E no par called for redemption 02/02/1968
$2.75 Conv. Preferred Ser. D no par called for redemption 08/02/1968
Stock Dividend - 10% 01/21/1952
Merged into AMCA International Corp. 10/31/1980
Each share $2.75 Conv. Preferred

Ser. H no par exchanged for $50 cash
Each share $2.50 Conv. Preferred Ser. I no par exchanged for $50 cash
Each share Common $2 par exchanged for $37 cash

KOELLER AIR PRODS INC (NJ)
Charter declared void for non-payment of taxes 1/14/82

KOENIG INC (TX)
Name changed to Rawson-Koenig, Inc. 9/18/87
(See Rawson-Koenig, Inc.)

KOERING CYANIDING PROCESS CO. (AZ)
Charter revoked for failure to file reports and pay fees 7/17/28

KOFAX IMAGE PRODS INC (DE)
Issue Information - 2,000,000 shares COM offered at $11 per share on 10/10/1997
Merged into Imaging Components Corp. 10/18/99
Each share Common $0.001 par exchanged for $12.75 cash

KOFAX LTD (BERMUDA)
Acquired by Lexmark International Inc. 05/21/2015
Each share Common $0.001 par exchanged for $11 cash

KOFFEE KORNER INC (DE)
Common $0.0001 par split (4.4) for (1) by issuance of (3.4) additional shares payable 02/14/2014 to holders of record 01/09/2014
Name changed to Cardax, Inc. 02/21/2014

KOFFLER STORES LTD (CANADA)
Reincorporated 02/09/1978
Common no par split (4) for (1) by issuance of (3) additional shares 05/30/1969
Common no par split (2) for (1) by issuance of (1) additional share 06/29/1973
Common no par reclassified as Class A Conv. Common no par 06/27/1975
Place of incorporation changed from (ONT) to (Canada) 02/09/1978
7% 1st Preference Ser. A $10 par called for redemption 09/15/1978
Acquired by Imasco Ltd.-Imasco Ltee. 06/21/1978
Each share Class A Conv. Common no par exchanged for (1) share Conv. Preference Ser. A no par and $55 cash
Each share Class B Conv. Common no par exchanged for (1) share Conv. Preference Ser. A no par and $55 cash
(See Imasco Ltd. - Imasco Ltee.)

KOGEL INC (DE)
Name changed to Chemstat Corp. 11/07/1968
(See Chemstat Corp.)

KOGER CO (FL)
Merged into Koger Properties, Inc. 08/05/1988
Each share Common 10¢ par exchanged for (1.015) shares Common 10¢ par
(See Koger Properties, Inc.)

KOGER EQUITY INC (FL)
Name changed to CRT Properties, Inc. 07/01/2004
(See CRT Properties, Inc.)

KOGER PPTYS INC (FL)
Reincorporated 9/11/81
Stock Dividends - 50% 3/2/71; 100% 6/6/72
State of incorporation changed from (DE) to (FL) 9/11/81
Plan of reorganization under Chapter 11 Federal Bankruptcy Code effective 12/21/93
Each share Common 10¢ par exchanged for (0.02) Koger Equity Inc. Common Stock Purchase Warrant expiring 6/30/99

KOGETO INC (NV)
SEC revoked common stock registration 12/19/2016

KOHALA PINEAPPLE CO. LTD.
Operations discontinued 00/00/1934
Stockholders' equity unlikely

KOHLBERG CAP CORP (DE)
Issue Information - 14,462,000 shares COM offered at $15 per share on 12/11/2006
Name changed to KCAP Financial, Inc. 06/28/2012

KOHLER CO (WI)
Each share old Common no par exchanged for (0.05) share new Common no par 12/19/78
Public interest eliminated

KOHLS CORP (DE)
Reincorporated under the laws of Wisconsin 06/04/1993

KOHNSTAMM H & CO INC (NY)
Common $6 par changed to $2 par and (2) additional shares issued 10/3/75
Merged into Universal Foods Corp. 9/7/88
Each share Common $2 par exchanged for (0.315) share Common 10¢ par
Note: Approximately 50% of the above ratio will be held in escrow for future distribution
Universal Foods Corp. name changed to Sensient Technologies Corp. 11/6/2000

KOKANEE EXPLS LTD (BC)
Acquired by Consolidated Ramrod Gold Corp. 09/17/1992
Each share Common no par exchanged for (1) share Common no par
Consolidated Ramrod Gold Corp. recapitalized as Quest International Resources Corp. 04/09/1996 which recapitalized as Standard Mining Corp. 06/16/1999 which merged into Doublestar Resources Ltd. (YT) 11/01/2001 which reincorporated in British Columbia 10/10/2002 which merged into Selkirk Metals Corp. 07/23/2007
(See Selkirk Metals Corp.)

KOKANEE MINERALS INC (BC)
Name changed to Declan Resources Inc. 04/05/2012
Declan Resources Inc. name changed to Declan Cobalt Inc. 08/30/2018

KOKANEE RES LTD (BC)
Name changed to Integra Systems Inc. 03/03/1987
(See Integra Systems Inc.)

KOKEN COMPANIES, INC. (MO)
Liquidation completed
Each share Common $1 par exchanged for initial distribution of $15 cash 12/1/71
Each share Common $1 par received second distribution of $2 cash 1/24/72
Each share Common $1 par received third distribution of $2 cash 11/16/72
Each share Common $1 par received fourth distribution of $1 cash 5/1/73
Each share Common $1 par received fifth and final distribution of $0.89 cash 8/30/74

KOKICARE INC (DE)
Recapitalized as AIT Therapeutics, Inc. 01/10/2017
Each share Common $0.0001 par exchanged for (0.01) share Common $0.0001 par

KOKKO CREEK MINING CORP. LTD. (QC)
Acquired by Quebec Chibougamau Goldfields 04/07/1955
Each share Capital Stock exchanged for (0.14285714) share Capital Stock $1 par
Quebec Chibougamau Goldfields Ltd. merged into Allied Mining Corp. 09/22/1969 which merged into United Asbestos Inc. 06/29/1973 which merged into Campbell Resources Inc. (New) 06/08/1983
(See Campbell Resources Inc. (New))

KOKO LTD (NV)
Recapitalized as Cardinal Energy Group, Inc. 11/02/2012
Each share Common $0.00001 par exchanged for (0.4) share Common $0.00001 par

KOKO PETE INC (NV)
Common no par split (2) for (1) by issuance of (1) additional share payable 11/02/2004 to holders of record 11/01/2004 Ex date - 11/03/2004
Charter permanently revoked 04/30/2009

KOKOMO ENTERPRISES INC (BC)
Recapitalized as High 5 Ventures Inc. 08/29/2012
Each share Common no par exchanged for (0.06666666) share Common no par
High 5 Ventures Inc. recapitalized as 37 Capital Inc. 07/07/2014

KOKOMO GAS & FUEL CO (IN)
Acquired by NIPSCO Industries, Inc. 02/10/1992
Details not available

KOKOMO NATIONAL LIFE INSURANCE CO. (IN)
Common $1 par changed to no par 08/17/1970
Stock Dividend - 10% 01/31/1971
Placed in liquidation 11/02/1981
No stockholders' equity

KOKOS GROUP INC (NV)
Name changed to China WuYi Mountain, Ltd. 05/25/2018

KOLA MNG CORP (BC)
Each share old Common no par exchanged for (0.1) share new Common no par 01/06/2012
Each share new Common no par exchanged again for (0.5) share new Common no par 10/15/2013
Name changed to Mitchell Resources Ltd. 05/27/2015
Mitchell Resources Ltd. name changed to Hannan Metals Ltd. 01/10/2017

KOLD-HOLD MANUFACTURING CO.
Name changed to Tranter Manufacturing, Inc. in 1953
Tranter Manufacturing, Inc. name changed to Tranter, Inc. 1/28/74
(See Tranter, Inc.)

KOLDECK INC (NV)
Name changed to Global House Holdings Ltd. 04/03/2018

KOLFF MED INC (UT)
Name changed to Symbion, Inc. 6/25/84
(See Symbion, Inc.)

KOLL MGMT SVCS INC (DE)
Merged into KMS Acquisition Corp. 11/23/94
Each share Common 1¢ par exchanged for $16 cash

KOLL REAL ESTATE GROUP INC (DE)
Plan of reorganization under Chapter 11 Federal Bankruptcy proceedings effective 09/02/1997
Each share Conv. Preferred Ser. A 1¢ par exchanged for (0.0175) share new Common 5¢ par
Each share old Common 5¢ par exchanged for (0.01) share new Common 5¢ par
Note: Unexchanged certificates were cancelled and became without value 09/02/1998
Name changed to California Coastal Communities Inc. 05/29/1998
(See California Coastal Communities Inc.)

KOLL REAL ESTATE SVCS (DE)
Merged into CB Commercial Real Estate Services Group Inc. 8/28/97
Each share Common 1¢ par exchanged for (0.776) share Common 1¢ par and an undetermined amount of warrants
CB Commercial Real Estate Services Group Inc. name changed to CB Richard Ellis Services Inc. 5/19/98
(See CB Richard Ellis Services Inc.)

KOLLMORGEN CORP (NY)
Merged into Danaher Corp. 06/20/2000
Each share Common $2.50 par exchanged for $23 cash

KOLOA SUGAR CO.
Merged into Grove Farm Co., Ltd. in 1948 which name was changed to Grove Farm Co., Inc. 4/23/62

KOLORFUSION INTL INC (CO)
Plan of reorganization under Chapter 11 Federal Bankruptcy proceedings effective 10/04/2011
No stockholders' equity

KOLORWOOD LTD. (ON)
Charter declared cancelled for non-compliance with the Ontario Companies Act 3/7/59

KOLPAK INDS INC (TN)
Merged into Dalton Enterprises, Inc. 12/27/1983
Each share Common no par exchanged for $1 cash

KOLSTER-BRANDES LTD.
Liquidated in 1938

KOLSTER RADIO CORP.
Liquidated in 1931

KOLVOX COMMUNICATIONS INC (AB)
Merged into Wildcard Technologies, Inc. 7/2/96
Each share Common no par exchanged for (0.125) share Common no par

KOLYMA GOLDFIELDS LTD (BC)
Name changed to BidCrawler.com Online Inc. 03/01/2000
BidCrawler.com Online Inc. recapitalized as TradeRadius Online Inc. 08/21/2001 which recapitalized as Jalna Resources Ltd. (New) 04/10/2003 which reorganized as Jalna Minerals Ltd. 06/01/2006 which recapitalized as Papuan Precious Metals Corp. 10/01/2010 name changed to Ironside Resources Inc. 04/21/2015

KOLYNOS CO.
Acquired by American Home Products Corp. 06/00/1928
Details not available

KOMAG INC (DE)
Old Common 1¢ par split (2) for (1) by issuance of (1) additional share payable 01/10/1996 to holders of record 12/21/1995
Plan of reorganization under Chapter 11 Federal Bankruptcy Code effective 06/30/2002
No old Common stockholders' equity
Acquired by Western Digital Corp. 09/05/2007
Each share new Common 1¢ par exchanged for $32.25 cash

KOMATSU MANUFACTURING CO. LTD. (KABUSHIKA KAISHA KOMATSU SEISAKUSHO) (JAPAN)
Name changed to Komatsu Ltd. 11/1/69

KOMBAT COPPER INC (CANADA)
Each share old Common no par exchanged for (0.1) share new Common no par 12/06/2016

Name changed to Trigon Metals Inc. 12/28/2016

KOMERCNI BANKA A S (CZECH REPUBLIC)
Each Reg. S 1999 GDR for Ordinary exchanged for (1) GDR for Ordinary 05/08/2000
GDR's for Ordinary split (5) for (1) by issuance of (4) additional GDR's payable 05/18/2016 to holders of record 05/16/2016 Ex date - 05/19/2016
GDR agreement terminated 06/03/2016
Each GDR for Ordinary exchanged for (0.33333333) share Ordinary
Note: Unexchanged GDR's will be sold and the proceeds, if any, held for claim after 06/08/2017

KOMET MFRS INC (QC)
Name changed to Komet Resources Inc. 12/19/2013

KOMO EXPLS LTD (BC)
Recapitalized as Canzona Minerals Inc. 07/05/1976
Each share Common 50¢ par exchanged for (0.1) share Common no par
Canzona Minerals Inc. merged into American Energy Corp. 08/03/1982 which recapitalized as Nickling Resources Inc. 06/05/1984 which recapitalized as Florin Resources Inc. 05/09/1989 which merged into Crimsonstar Mining Corp. 06/19/1991 which recapitalized as Mountain View Ventures Inc. 05/21/1993 which recapitalized as Blackrun Ventures Inc. 04/08/1997 which recapitalized as Blackrun Minerals Inc. 06/10/1999 which name changed to Diversified Industries Ltd. 03/29/2000
(See Diversified Industries Ltd.)

KOMODO INC (NV)
Common $0.001 par split (4) for (1) by issuance of (3) additional shares payable 05/08/2002 to holders of record 05/01/2002 Ex date - 05/09/2002
SEC revoked common stock registration 10/01/2013

KOMPASS TRAVEL LTD (CO)
Recapitalized as Imagexpress, Inc. 08/19/2003
Each share Common $0.001 par exchanged for (0.001) share Common $0.001 par
Imagexpress, Inc. name changed to Imagexpres Corp. 10/01/2003

KONA HAI CORP (AZ)
Name changed to World Video Arts 11/15/72
(See World Video Arts)

KONA INDL CAP CORP (AB)
Name changed to Mobilift Inc. 07/03/1996
(See Mobilift Inc.)

KONAMI CORP (JAPAN)
Name changed to Konami Holdings Corp. 10/01/2015

KONDFIL KHMELNITSKY CONFECTIONARY J S C (UKRAINE)
GDR agreement terminated 03/14/2014
No GDR's remain outstanding

KONEXUS TECHNOLOGIES LTD (ON)
Ceased operations 09/11/2002
Stockholders' equity unlikely

KONGA INTERNATIONAL, INC. (DE)
In receivership in 1948

KONGZHONG CORP (CAYMAN ISLANDS)
Acquired by Linkedsee Ltd. 04/13/2017
Each Sponsored ADR for Ordinary exchanged for $7.50 cash

KONICA CAP CORP 1 (DE)
Market Auction Preferred Ser. C called for redemption at $1,000,000 on 2/23/99
Market Auction Preferred Ser. D called for redemption at $1,000,000 on 3/2/99
Market Auction Preferred Ser. A called for redemption at $1,000,000 on 3/16/99
Market Auction Preferred Ser. B called for redemption at $1,000,000 on 3/23/99

KONICA CORP (JAPAN)
Merged into Konica Minolta Holdings, Inc. 8/5/2003
Each share Common exchanged for (1) share Common ADR agreement terminated 9/12/2003
Each ADR for Ordinary 10 Yen par exchanged for $133.7154 cash

KONICA MINOLTA HLDGS INC (JAPAN)
ADR's for Common split (5) for (1) by issuance of (4) additional ADR's payable 12/07/2010 to holders of record 11/30/2010 Ex date - 12/08/2010
ADR basis changed from (1:10) to (1:2) 12/08/2010
Name changed to Konica Minolta Inc. 04/01/2013

KONIG HOUSE FOODS INC (CO)
Adjudicated bankrupt 06/13/1978
Stockholders' equity unlikely

KONIGSBERG CORP (NV)
Each share old Common $0.001 par exchanged for (4) shares new Common $0.001 par 04/25/2006
Name changed to GoldMountain Exploration Corp. 05/29/2007
(See GoldMountain Exploration Corp.)

KONINKLIJKE AHOLD NV (NETHERLANDS)
Each old Sponsored ADR for Ordinary exchanged for (2) new Sponsored ADR's for Ordinary 11/00/1993
New Sponsored ADR's for Ordinary split (3) for (1) by issuance of (2) additional ADR's payable 07/29/1997 to holders of record 07/18/1997 Ex date - 07/30/1997
Each new Sponsored ADR for Ordinary exchanged again for (0.8) new Sponsored ADR for Ordinary and $2.56984 cash 08/22/2007
Each new Sponsored ADR for Ordinary exchanged again for (0.92307692) new Sponsored ADR for Ordinary 04/03/2014
Each new Sponsored ADR for Ordinary exchanged again for (0.94117647) new Sponsored ADR for Ordinary 07/20/2016
Stock Dividend - 100% 01/09/1991
Name changed to Koninklijke Ahold Delhaize N.V. 07/25/2016

KONINKLIJKE BIJENKORF BEHEER KBB N V (NETHERLANDS)
ADR agreement terminated 11/04/1999
Each ADR for Ordinary 10 Gldrs. par exchanged for $46.513 cash

KONINKLIJKE BOLS WESSANEN N V (NETHERLANDS)
Name changed to Koninklijke Wessanen N.V. (New) 01/20/1999
(See Koninklijke Wessanen N.V. (New))

KONINKLIJKE HOOGOVENS N V (NETHERLANDS)
Each Unsponsored ADR for Ordinary exchanged for (2) Sponsored ADR's for Ordinary 02/14/1997
ADR agreement terminated 11/26/1999
Each Sponsored ADR for Ordinary exchanged for $29.0658 cash

KONINKLIJKE PHILIPS ELECTRS N V (NETHERLANDS)
Each N Y Registry Share 10 Gldrs. par exchanged for (0.92) N Y Registry Share EUR 0.25 par 05/28/1999
N Y Registry Shares EUR 0.25 par changed to EUR 1 par and (3) additional shares issued payable 04/17/2000 to holders of record 04/14/2000
Each N Y Registry Shares EUR 1 par exchanged for (0.97) N Y Registry Share 2000 EUR 0.20 par 08/01/2000
Stock Dividends - 2.763851% payable 04/28/2010 to holders of record 03/31/2010 Ex date - 03/29/2010; 5.343593% payable 05/31/2012 to holders record 05/04/2012 Ex date - 05/02/2012
Name changed to Koninklijke Philips N.V. 05/15/2013

KONINKLIJKE VENDEX KBB N V (NETHERLANDS)
ADR agreement terminated 10/26/2004
No ADR holders' equity

KONINKLIJKE WESSANEN N V (OLD) (NETHERLANDS)
Each Unsponsored ADR for Ordinary Bearer exchanged for (1) Sponsored ADR for Ordinary Bearer 07/01/1988
Reorganized as Koninklijke Bols Wessanen N.V. 04/07/1993
Each Sponsored ADR for Ordinary exchanged for (2.5) Sponsored ADR's for Ordinary
Koninklijke Bols Wessanen N.V. name changed to Koninklijke Wessanen N.V. (New) 01/20/1999
(See Koninklijke Wessanen N.V. (New))

KONINKLIJKE WESSANEN N V NEW (NETHERLANDS)
Sponsored ADR's for Bearer shares NLG 2 par changed to EUR 1 par 08/22/2001
Each old Sponsored ADR for Bearer shares EUR 1 par exchanged for (0.9) new Sponsored ADR for Bearer shares EUR 1 par 01/15/2002
ADR agreement terminated 11/08/2010
Each new Sponsored ADR for Bearer shares EUR 1 par exchanged for $4.349336 cash

KONINKLIJKE ZOUT-KETJEN N.V. (NETHERLANDS)
Merged into Koninklijke Zout-Organon N.V. 12/04/1967
Each ADR for Ordinary Bearer 10 Gldrs. par exchanged for (1) ADR for Ordinary Bearer 10 Gldrs. par Koninklijke Zout-Organon N.V. acquired by AKZO N.V. 01/29/1970 which name changed to AKZO Nobel N.V. 02/25/1994

KONINKLIJKE ZOUT ORGANON N V (NETHERLANDS)
Acquired by AKZO N.V. 01/29/1970
Each ADR for Ordinary Bearer 10 Gldrs. par exchanged for (0.833333) Bearer Share 50 Gldrs. par
AKZO N.V. name changed to AKZO Nobel N.V. 02/25/1994

KONINKLIJKE ZWANENBERG-ORGANON N.V. (NETHERLANDS)
Merged into Koninklijke Zout-Organon N.V. 12/04/1967
Each ADR for Ordinary Bearer 10 Gldrs. par exchanged for (1.25) ADR's for Ordinary Bearer 10 Gldrs. par
Koninklijke Zout-Organon N.V. acquired by AKZO N.V. 01/29/1970 which name changed to AKZO Nobel N.V. 02/25/1994

KONOVER PPTY TR INC (MD)
Merged into Kimco Realty Corp. 11/22/2002
Each share Common no par exchanged for $2.10 cash

KONTIKI LEAD & ZINC MINES LTD (ON)
Recapitalized as Olympic Victor Corp. 09/11/1985
Each share Capital Stock $1 par exchanged for (1/3) share Common no par
Olympic Victor Corp. recapitalized as Olympic Victor Enterprises Inc. 09/19/1986 which name changed to TCS Energy Systems Ltd. 11/17/1992 which name changed to Advanced Pultrusion Technologies Inc. 06/29/1993
(See Advanced Pultrusion Technologies Inc.)

KONTRON MOBILE COMPUTING INC (MN)
Merged into Kontron AG 10/01/2004
Each share Common $0.001 par exchanged for $0.55 cash

KOO KOO ROO ENTERPRISES INC (DE)
Name changed to Prandium, Inc. 04/01/1999
(See Prandium, Inc.)

KOO KOO ROO INC (DE)
Merged into Koo Koo Roo Enterprises, Inc. 10/30/1998
Each share Common 1¢ par exchanged for (1) share Common 1¢ par
Koo Koo Roo Enterprises, Inc. name changed to Prandium, Inc. 04/01/1999
(See Prandium, Inc.)

KOOKABURRA RES LTD (BC)
Name changed 01/21/1993
Reincorporated 07/16/2004
Name changed from Kookaburra Gold Corp. to Kookaburra Resources Ltd. 01/21/1993
Place of incorporation changed from (BC) to (YT) 06/18/2001
Each share old Common no par exchanged for (0.06666666) share new Common no par 10/02/2003
Place of incorporation changed from (YT) back to (BC) 07/16/2004
Recapitalized as Consolidated Kookaburra Resources Ltd. 03/08/2006
Each share Common no par exchanged for (0.5) share Common no par
Consolidated Kookaburra Resources Ltd. name changed to Salazar Resources Ltd. 03/09/2007

KOOKMIN BK NEW (KOREA)
Stock Dividend - 6% payable 04/19/2002 to holders of record 12/28/2001
Merged into KB Financial Group Inc. 09/29/2008
Each Sponsored ADR for Common exchanged for (1) Sponsored ADR for Common

KOOKMIN BK OLD (KOREA)
Stock Dividend - 2.47% payable 03/24/1998 holders of record 01/05/1998
Merged into Kookmin Bank (New) 11/01/2001
Each 144A GDR for Common exchanged for (0.59229565) Sponsored ADR for Common
Each Reg. S GDR for Common exchanged for (0.59229565) Sponsored ADR for Common
Kookmin Bank (New) merged into KB Financial Group Inc. 09/29/2008

KOOL-AID BOTTLING CO. INC. OF CALIFORNIA (WI)
Charter forfeited for failure to file reports 1/1/53

KOOL-AID BOTTLING CO. OF OHIO (OH)
Charter revoked for non payment of franchise taxes 10/15/48

KOOLY KUPP INC (PA)
Adjudicated bankrupt 05/25/1977
Stockholders' equity unlikely

KOOR INDS LTD (ISRAEL)
ADR agreement terminated 06/20/2007
Each Sponsored ADR for Ordinary NIS 0.001 par exchanged for $16.15253 cash

KOOTENAI CORP (DE)
Reorganized as BizAuctions, Inc. 08/17/2006
Each share Common $0.001 par exchanged for (2) shares Common $0.001 par
BizAuctions, Inc. name changed to CannaGrow Holdings, Inc. 11/05/2014

KOOTENAI DIKE MINES, INC. (ID)
Charter revoked for failure to renew annual corporation license taxes 11/30/54

KOOTENAY BASE METALS (CONSOLIDATED) LTD. (BC)
Name changed to Great Alaska Services Ltd. 11/25/1969
Great Alaska Services Ltd. recapitalized as Great Alaska Services Consolidated Ltd. 07/10/1972 which name changed to Vanstates Resources Ltd. 01/09/1980 which recapitalized as Southport Resources Inc. 07/16/1990 which recapitalized as Olds Industries Inc. 06/03/1992
(See Olds Industries Inc.)

KOOTENAY BASE METALS LTD. (BC)
Recapitalized as Kootenay Base Metals (Consolidated) Ltd. 05/18/1962
Each share Capital Stock 50¢ par exchanged for (0.2) share Capital Stock no par
Kootenay Base Metals (Consolidated) Ltd. name changed to Great Alaska Services Ltd. 11/25/1969 which recapitalized as Great Alaska Services Consolidated Ltd. 07/10/1972 which name changed to Vanstates Resources Ltd. 01/09/1980 which recapitalized as Southport Resources Inc. 07/16/1990 which recapitalized as Olds Industries Inc. 06/03/1992
(See Olds Industries Inc.)

KOOTENAY COPPER MINES, INC. (MT)
Recapitalized as Kootenay Resources Inc. 1/11/82
Each share Common 1¢ par exchanged for (0.5) share Common $0.001 par
Kootenay Resources Inc. name changed to Ameriquest Inc. 3/24/82 which name changed to Hair Analysis, Inc. 6/11/82 which recapitalized as OTC Stock Journal, Inc. 3/16/83
(See OTC Stock Journal, Inc.)

KOOTENAY ENERGY INC (AB)
Acquired by Golden Oil Corp. 09/22/2008
Each share Common no par exchanged for $0.66 cash

KOOTENAY GOLD INC (BC)
Reincorporated 11/09/2006
Place of incorporation changed from (AB) to (BC) 11/09/2006
Name changed to Kootenay Silver Inc. 02/21/2012

KOOTENAY GRANITE PRODUCTS LTD. (AB)
Struck off register and declared dissolved for failure to file returns 10/15/63

KOOTENAY KING MINING CO., LTD. (BC)
Struck off the register and dissolved by the Province of British Columbia 10/10/46

KOOTENAY KING RES INC (BC)
Recapitalized as Intercap Resource Management Corp. 6/13/95
Each share Common no par exchanged for (0.2) share Common no par
Intercap Resource Management Corp. recapitalized as Pine Resources Corp. (BC) 4/7/99 which reincorporated in Canada as Trimble Resources Corp. 1/17/2002
(See Trimble Resources Corp.)

KOOTENAY RESOURCES INC. (MT)
Name changed to Ameriquest Inc. 3/24/82
Ameriquest Inc. name changed to Hair Analysis, Inc. 6/11/82 which recapitalized as OTC Stock Journal, Inc. 3/16/83
(See OTC Stock Journal, Inc.)

KOPAN DEVS LTD (BC)
Recapitalized as Jordesco Resources Ltd. 08/14/1972
Each share Capital Stock no par exchanged for (0.2) share Capital Stock no par
(See Jordesco Resources Ltd.)

KOPEL LTD (ISRAEL)
ADR agreement terminated 04/20/2009
No ADR's remain outstanding

KOPJAGGERS INC (FL)
Name changed to National Waste Management Holdings, Inc. 10/31/2014

KOPP SCIENTIFIC, INC. (NY)
Each share Common 25¢ par exchanged for (2.5) shares Common 10¢ par in 1953
Merged into Camdale Corp. share for share 8/31/56
(See Camdale Corp.)

KOPPERS CO.
Merged into Koppers Co., Inc. 00/00/1944
Details not available

KOPPERS GAS & COKE CO.
Name changed to Koppers Co. in 1936 which merged into Koppers Co., Inc. in 1944
(See Koppers Co., Inc.)

KOPPERS INC (DE)
4-3/4% Preferred $100 par called for redemption 08/31/1946
Common $10 par changed to $5 par and (1) additional share issued 04/26/1966
Common $5 par changed to $2.50 par and (1) additional share issued 10/20/1975
Common $2.50 par changed to $1.25 par and (1) additional share issued 10/29/1976
$10 Conv. Preference no par called for redemption 07/31/1986
4% Preferred $100 par called for redemption 08/31/1988
Merged into BNS Inc. 11/14/1988
Each share Common $1.25 par exchanged for $61 cash

KOPPERS UNITED CO.
Merged into Koppers Co., Inc. in 1944
Each share $4 Preferred exchanged for (5.2) shares Common $10 par
Each share Common exchanged for (0.19) share Common $10 par
(See Koppers Co., Inc.)

KOPPITZ-MELCHERS, INC.
Acquired by Goebel Brewing Co. in 1947
Details not available

KOPR RES CORP (DE)
Each share old Common $0.001 par exchanged for (0.17391304) share new Common $0.001 par 04/05/2011
New Common $0.001 par split (51.7449549) for (1) by issuance of (50.7449549) additional shares payable 07/27/2011 to holders of record 07/25/2011 Ex date - 07/28/2011
Name changed to Bullfrog Gold Corp. 08/11/2011

KORACH (S.) CO.
Liquidation completed in 1936

KORACORP INDS INC (DE)
Reincorporated 07/03/1970
State of incorporation changed from (CA) to (DE) 07/03/1970
Common $1 par split (3) for (2) by issuance of (0.5) additional share 06/26/1978
Merged into Levi Strauss & Co. (DE) 09/10/1979
Each share Common $1 par exchanged for $18.68 cash

KORAKUEN STAD LTD (JAPAN)
Name changed to Tokyo Dome Corp. 09/01/1990
(See Tokyo Dome Corp.)

KORAM BK (KOREA)
Name changed to Citibank Korea Inc. 11/1/2004

KORBY GOLD MINES, LTD. (ON)
Charter cancelled for failure to file reports and pay taxes in 1955

KORDOL EXPLORATIONS LTD. (ON)
Merged into Junction Explorations Ltd. 12/12/78
Each share Capital Stock $1 par exchanged for (0.2) share Common no par
(See Junction Explorations Ltd.)

KORE HLDGS INC (NV)
Chapter 7 bankruptcy proceedings terminated 01/09/2013
No stockholders' equity

KORE RES INC (NV)
Each share old Common $0.001 par exchanged for (10) shares new Common $0.001 par 12/24/2013
Name changed to UNEEQO, Inc. 05/27/2016

KOREA EQUITY FD INC (MD)
Stock Dividend - 33.27904% payable 01/18/2012 to holders of record 11/30/2011 Ex date - 11/28/2011
Completely liquidated
Each share Common 10¢ par received first and final distribution of $7.0491 cash payable 08/07/2017 to holders of record 07/17/2017

KOREA MOBILE TELECOMMUNICATIONS CORP (KOREA)
Name changed to SK Telecom Co., Ltd. 3/24/97

KOREA TELECOM CORP (KOREA)
Issue Information - 90,191,012 Sponsored ADR's offered at $27.56 per ADR on 05/26/1999
Name changed to KT Corp. 3/22/2002

KOREA THRUNET CO LTD (KOREA)
Issue Information - 10,100,000 shares COM offered at $18 per share on 11/16/1999
Each share old Common W2,500 par exchanged for (1/3) share new Common W2,500 par 01/21/2003
Each share new Common W2,500 par exchanged again for (0.025) share new Common W2,500 par 06/15/2004
Each share new Common W2,500 par exchanged again for (0.5) share new Common W2,500 par 10/17/2005
Merged into Hanarotelecom Inc. 01/01/2006
Each share new Common W2,500 par exchanged for (0.3570308)
Sponsored ADR for Common W5,000 par
(See Hanarotelecom Inc.)

KOREA TOB & GINSENG CORP (KOREA)
Name changed to KT&G Corp. 1/23/2003

KOREAN INVT FD INC (MD)
Completely liquidated 6/6/2003
Each share Common $0.001 par, Class A $0.001 par, Class B $0.001 par, and Class C $0.001 par received net asset value

KOREASTATION CORP (NV)
Name changed to E4World Corp. 01/01/2001
E4World Corp. name changed to Xcelplus Global Holdings, Inc. 08/18/2006 which name changed to Clean Energy Pathways, Inc. 02/04/2011

KORET INC (DE)
Merged into Kellwood Co. 04/30/1999
Each share Class A Common 1¢ par exchanged for (0.6025391) share Common 1¢ par
Each share Class C Common 1¢ par exchanged for (0.6025391) share Common 1¢ par
(See Kellwood Co.)

KORET OF CALIFORNIA, INC. (CA)
Name changed to Koracorp Industries Inc. (Calif.) 2/13/68
Koracorp Industries Inc. (Calif.) reincorporated under the laws of Delaware 7/3/70 which merged into Levi Strauss & Co. (Del.) 9/10/79
(See Levi Strauss & Co. (Del.))

KORFUND INC (DE)
Merged into Korfund-Lowell, Inc. 08/15/1978
Each share Common 10¢ par exchanged for $0.83 cash

KORICH MINING CO. LTD. (ON)
Recapitalized as TPB&T Ltd. 02/09/1990
Each share Capital Stock $1 par exchanged for (0.2) share Capital Stock $1 par
(See TPB&T Ltd.)

KORN FERRY INTL (CA)
Stock Dividend - 25% 4/25/77
Reincorporated under the laws of Delaware and Common no par changed to 1¢ par 9/13/99

KORNHANDLER (LOU), INC. (CA)
Name changed to California Girl Manufacturing, Inc. 6/15/64
(See California Girl Manufacturing, Inc.)

KORVETTE (E.J.), INC. (NY)
Common $1 par split (3) for (1) by issuance of (2) additional shares 12/15/1961
Under plan of merger name changed to Spartans Industries, Inc. (NY) 09/25/1966
Spartans Industries, Inc. (NY) merged into Arlen Realty & Development Corp. 02/26/1971 which name changed to Arlen Corp. 10/16/1985
(See Arlen Corp.)

KOS PHARMACEUTICALS INC (FL)
Issue Information - 4,150,000 shares COM offered at $15 per share on 03/07/1997
Acquired by Abbott Laboratories 12/15/2006
Each share Common 1¢ par exchanged for $78 cash

KOSA RES LTD (BC)
Struck off register and declared dissolved for failure to file returns 07/24/1992

KOSAN BIOSCIENCES INC (DE)
Issue Information - 5,000,000 shares COM offered at $14 per share on 10/05/2000
Merged into Bristol-Myers Squibb Co. 06/26/2008

Each share Common $0.001 par exchanged for $5.50 cash

KOSHER KITCHENS INC (NY)
Reorganized under the laws of Nevada as Power Conservation Corp. 6/16/78
Each share Common 1¢ par exchanged for (0.2) share Common 2¢ par
Power Conservation Corp. name changed to Power Capital Corp. 10/29/82 which recapitalized as Huayang International Holdings, Inc. 1/18/96 which recapitalized as China Energy & Carbon Black Holdings, Inc. 10/25/2004 which recapitalized as CO2 Tech Ltd. 1/9/2007

KOSS ELECTRONICS, INC. (NY)
Reincorporated under the laws of Delaware as Koss Corp. 10/12/71

KOSTER-DANA CORP. (NY)
Each share 7% Preferred $100 par exchanged for (1) share 7-1/2% Preferred $100 par 9/3/65
Name changed to Liquidonics Industries, Inc. 9/24/65
Liquidonics Industries, Inc. name changed to Greer Hydraulics, Inc. 12/27/79
(See Greer Hydraulics, Inc.)

KOTAK MAHINDRA BK LTD (INDIA)
Sponsored 144A GDR's for Equity Shares split (2) for (1) issuance of (1) additional GDR payable 09/22/2010 to holders of record 09/14/2010 Ex date - 09/23/2010
Sponsored Reg. S GDR's for Equity Shares split (2) for (1) issuance of (1) additional GDR payable 09/22/2010 to holders of record 09/14/2010
GDR agreement terminated 09/04/2015
Each Sponsored 144A GDR for Equity Shares exchanged for $5.335842 cash
Each Sponsored Reg. S GDR for Equity Shares exchanged for $5.335842 cash

KOTKIN LAWRENCE ASSOC INC (NY)
Merged into Philips, Appel & Walden, Inc. 01/26/1973
Each share Common 1¢ par exchanged for (0.3923) share Class A Voting Common 10¢ par
Philips, Appel & Walden, Inc. reorganized as P.A.W. Management Corp. 10/27/1977

KOTROZO MUTUAL FUND GROUP, INC. (AZ)
Ceased operations 10/07/1993
Details not available

KOVAL RES LTD (AB)
Recapitalized as Ironwood Petroleum Ltd. 01/17/1994
Each share Common no par exchanged for (1/6) share Common no par
(See Ironwood Petroleum Ltd.)

KOVR BROADCASTING CO. (CA)
Acquired by McClatchy Newspapers 00/00/1964
Details not available

KOWABUNGA INC (NV)
Name changed to Inuvo, Inc. 07/30/2009

KOWKASH GOLD CORP (BC)
Struck off register and declared dissolved for failure to file returns 03/26/1993

KOWKASH HOLDINGS, LTD.
Acquired by Tashota Goldfields, Ltd. 00/00/1936
Details not available

KOWTOW INC (NV)
Reorganized as Affordable Homes of America, Inc. 3/31/99
Each share Common $0.001 par exchanged for (2) shares Common $0.001 par
Affordable Homes of America, Inc. name changed to World Homes Inc. 10/16/2000 which name changed to Composite Industries of America, Inc. 8/23/2001 which recapitalized as Composite Holdings, Inc. 5/8/2002 which name changed to Gold Rock Holdings, Inc. 1/7/2005

KPC INVTS (UT)
Name changed to Medizone Canada Ltd. 01/09/1989
Medizone Canada Ltd. name changed to One World Online.com Inc. 06/29/1999
(See One World Online.com Inc.)

KPI INTL INC (QC)
Struck off register for failure to file reports or pay fees 05/02/2003

KPMG CONSULTING INC (DE)
Issue Information - 112,482,000 shares COM offered at $18 per share on 02/17/2001
Name changed to BearingPoint, Inc. 10/02/2002
(See BearingPoint, Inc.)

KPNQWEST B V (NETHERLANDS)
Name changed to KPNQWEST N.V. 6/2/99
(Additional Information in Active)

KPS VENTURES LTD (BC)
Name changed to Energentia Resources Inc. 03/05/2007
Energentia Resources Inc. merged into Mega Uranium Ltd. 05/06/2008

KRAFT CHEESE CO.
Name changed to Kraft-Phenix Cheese Co. Kraft-Phenix Cheese Co. reorganized as Kraft-Phenix Cheese Corp. in 1928
(See Kraft-Phenix Cheese Corp.)

KRAFT FOODS GROUP INC (VA)
Merged into Kraft Heinz Co. 07/02/2015
Each share Common no par exchanged for (1) share Common 1¢ par and $16.50 cash

KRAFT FOODS INC (VA)
Issue Information - 280,000,000 shares CL A offered at $31 per share on 06/12/2001
Each share Class A Common no par received distribution of (1/3) share Kraft Foods Group, Inc. Common no par payable 10/01/2012 to holders of record 09/19/2012 Ex date - 10/02/2012
Name changed to Mondelez International, Inc. 10/02/2012

KRAFT INC NEW (DE)
Merged into Morris (Philip) Companies Inc. 12/7/88
Each share Common $1 par exchanged for $106 cash

KRAFT INC OLD (DE)
Under plan of reorganization each share Common $2.50 par automatically became (1) share Dart & Kraft, Inc. Common $2.50 par 9/25/80
Dart & Kraft, Inc. name changed to Kraft, Inc. (New) 11/21/86
(See Kraft, Inc. (New))

KRAFT-PHENIX CHEESE CO.
Reorganized as Kraft-Phenix Cheese Corp. 00/00/1928
Details not available

KRAFT-PHENIX CHEESE CORP.
Acquired by National Dairy Products Corp. 00/00/1930
Details not available

KRAFTCO CORP. (DE)
Name changed to Kraft, Inc. (Old) 10/27/76
Kraft, Inc. (Old) reorganized as Dart & Kraft, Inc. 9/25/80 which name changed to Kraft, Inc. (New) 11/21/86
(See Kraft, Inc. (New))

KRAIN COPPER LTD. (BC)
Merged into Comet-Krain Mining Corp. Ltd. 3/28/66
Each share Capital Stock exchanged for (0.5) share Capital Stock no par
Comet-Krain Mining Corp. Ltd. name changed to Comet Industries Ltd. 4/26/71

KRAKEN SONAR INC (CANADA)
Name changed to Kraken Robotics Inc. 09/22/2017

KRAMB MANUFACTURING CORP. (NV)
Charter revoked for failure to file reports and pay fees 3/7/55

KRAMER & LEE INTL (NV)
Each (33) shares old Common $0.001 par exchanged for (1) share new Common $0.001 par 6/15/92
Name changed to Water U.S.A., Inc. 7/31/92
(See Water U.S.A., Inc.)

KRAMER-AMERICAN CORP. (CA)
Charter suspended for non-payment of taxes 03/01/1965

KRAMER CAP CORP (BC)
Reincorporated 08/16/2016
Place of incorporation changed from (AB) to (BC) 08/16/2016
Reorganized under the laws of Canada as 48North Cannabis Corp. 06/05/2018
Each share Common no par exchanged for (0.5) share Common no par

KRAMONT RLTY TR (MD)
9.5% Preferred Ser. D 1¢ par called for redemption at $25 plus $0.066 accrued dividends on 01/30/2004
Merged into Centro Watts America III, L.P. 04/18/2005
Each share 8.25% Preferred Ser. E 1¢ par exchanged for $25 cash
Each share 9.75% Conv. Preferred Share of Bene. Int. Ser. B-1 1¢ par exchanged for $25 cash
Each share Common 1¢ par exchanged for $23.50 cash

KRANCOR OIL & GAS LTD (BC)
Recapitalized as Sanilogical Industries Ltd. 04/19/1976
Each share Capital Stock no par exchanged for (0.5) share Capital Stock no par
Sanilogical Industries Ltd. recapitalized as Encom Environmental & Communications Systems Ltd. 07/05/1988 which recapitalized as ST Systems Corp. 11/14/1994 which recapitalized as Sky Ridge Resources Ltd. 12/24/2007 which recapitalized as Japan Gold Corp. 09/19/2016

KRANEM CORP (CO)
Common no par split (5) for (1) by issuance of (4) additional shares payable 07/28/2011 to holders of record 07/25/2011 Ex date - 07/29/2011
Company terminated common stock registration and is no longer public as of 06/27/2014

KRANTI RES INC (NV)
Each share old Common $0.001 par exchanged for (10) shares new Common $0.001 par 06/09/2009
Reorganized as Horiyoshi Worldwide Inc. 07/19/2010
Each share new Common $0.001 par exchanged for (2.1622) shares Common $0.001 par
Horiyoshi Worldwide Inc. name changed to HW Holdings, Inc. 03/02/2015

KRANTOR CORP (DE)
Each (12) shares old Common $0.001 par exchanged for (1) share new Common $0.001 par 09/25/1992
Each share new Common $0.001 par exchanged again for (0.04) share new Common $0.001 par 05/02/1997
Name changed to Synergy Brands Inc. 06/29/1998
(See Synergy Brands Inc.)

KRANZCO RLTY TR (MD)
Each Conv. Preferred Share of Bene. Int. B-2 1¢ par exchanged for (1) Conv. Preferred Share of Bene. Int. B-1 1¢ par 02/28/2000
Merged into Kramont Realty Trust 06/16/2000
Each share 9.50% Preferred Ser. D 1¢ par exchanged for (1) share 9.50% Preferred Ser. D 1¢ par
Each share Conv. Preferred Share of Bene. Int. Ser. B-1 1¢ par exchanged for (1) share Conv. Preferred Share of Bene. Int. Ser. B-1 1¢ par
Each share Common Bene. Int. 1¢ par exchanged for (1) share Common 1¢ par
(See Kramont Realty Trust)

KRASNOW INDUSTRIES, INC. (NY)
Merged into American Safety Equipment Corp. 6/30/66
Each share Common 10¢ par exchanged for (0.84) share Common 25¢ par
(See American Safety Equipment Corp.)

KRATON PERFORMANCE POLYMERS INC (DE)
Name changed to Kraton Corp. 09/14/2016

KRATOS INC (CA)
Name changed 08/08/1977
Each share old Common no par exchanged for (0.2) share new Common no par 08/10/1973
Name changed from Kratos to Kratos, Inc. 08/08/1977
Common no par split (2) for (1) by issuance of (1) additional share 03/09/1979
Stock Dividends - 10% 04/29/1977; 50% 03/04/1980
Name changed to Keuffel & Esser Co. (CA) and Common no par changed to $1 par 03/27/1986
(See Keuffel & Esser Co. (CA))

KRATTER CORP. (DE)
$1.20 Preferred $1 par called for redemption 09/14/1961
Class A Common $1 par and Class B Common $1 par reclassified as Common $1 par 01/30/1963
Stock Dividend - 10% 05/02/1960
Name changed to Countrywide Realty, Inc. 05/11/1965
Countrywide Realty, Inc. acquired by Realty Equities Corp. of New York 11/01/1967
(See Realty Equities Corp. of New York)

KRAUS AUTOMATIC MACHINES CORP. (DE)
Recapitalized as KDI Corp. 5/7/56
Each share Common 15¢ par exchanged for (0.2) share Common 75¢ par
(See KDI Corp.)

KRAUSES FURNITURE INC (DE)
Each share old Common 2¢ par exchanged for (1/3) share new Common 2¢ par 8/2/95
Chapter 11 Federal Bankruptcy proceedings converted to Chapter 7 on 4/4/2002
No stockholders' equity

KREDYT BK PBI S A (POLAND)
GDR agreement terminated 4/30/2003
Each GDR for Ordinary exchanged for $12.5576 cash

KREE TECH INTL CORP (CANADA)
Dissolved for non-compliance 10/14/2009

KREISLER MFG CORP (DE)
Stock Dividend - 15% 03/15/1984
Common 50¢ par changed to $0.125 par and (3) additional shares issued payable 12/02/1997 to holders of record 11/25/1997
Acquired by United Flexible Technologies, Inc. 07/21/2016
Each share Common $0.125 par exchanged for $18 cash

KRELITZ INDS INC (MN)
Common $1 par split (2) for (1) by issuance of (1) additional share 12/17/82
Common $1 par split (5) for (4) by issuance of (0.25) additional share 6/20/83
Common $1 par split (2) for (1) by issuance of (1) additional share 6/28/85
Common $1 par split (3) for (2) by issuance of (0.5) additional share 11/15/91
Stock Dividend - 25% 12/18/87
Acquired by D & K Healthcare Resources Inc. in 1995
Details not available

KRESGE DEPARTMENT STORES, INC.
Liquidation completed in 1948

KRESGE S S CO (MI)
Each share Common $100 par exchanged for (10) shares Common $10 par in 1926
Common $10 par changed to $5 par and (1) additional share issued 6/30/66
Common $5 par changed to $1.66-2/3 par and (2) additional shares issued 6/28/68
Common $1.66-2/3 par changed to $1 par and (2) additional shares issued 7/26/72
Name changed to K mart Corp. 5/17/77
(See K mart Corp.)

KRESS S H & CO (NY)
Each share Common $100 par exchanged for (8) shares old Common no par 00/00/1927
Each share old Common no par exchanged for (2) shares new Common no par 00/00/1936
6% Special Preferred called for redemption 12/14/1944
New Common no par changed to $10 par 05/22/1958
Merged into Genesco Inc. 03/27/1970
Each share Common $10 par exchanged for (0.322684) share $6 Conv. Preference Ser. C no par

KREUGER & TOLL CO.
Bankrupt in 1932
Liquidating dividend of $0.0235 paid in 1939

KREUTZER (JOSEPH) CORP.
Bankrupt in 1930

KRG MGMT INC (ON)
Merged into 1379114 Ontario Inc. 07/05/2000
Each share Common no par exchanged for $1.32 cash

KRG TELEVISION LTD (AB)
Recapitalized as IntelPro Media Group Inc. (AB) 03/07/2003
Each share Common no par exchanged for (0.5) share Common no par
IntelPro Media Group Inc. (AB) reorganized in Ontario as JITE Technologies Inc. 06/20/2006
(See JITE Technologies Inc.)

KRIA RES LTD (ON)
Merged into Trevali Mining Corp. 04/07/2011
Each share Common no par exchanged for (0.2) share Common no par

KRICKET CORP. (UT)
Name changed to International Health Resorts, Inc. (UT) 12/5/77
International Health Resorts, Inc. (UT) reorganized in Nevada as Sanguine Corp. 8/23/93

KRIEGER DATA INTL CORP (BC)
Name changed to Promark Software Inc. 11/17/1987
Promark Software Inc. name changed to clipclop.com Enterprises Inc. 08/30/1999 which recapitalized as Worldwide Technologies Inc. 09/10/2001
(See Worldwide Technologies Inc.)

KRIFTER HLDGS INC (NV)
Each share old Common $0.001 par exchanged for (25) shares new Common $0.001 par 08/29/2005
SEC revoked common stock registration 09/04/2009

KRIGOLD RES LTD (BC)
Struck off register and declared dissolved for failure to file returns 9/24/93

KRISCH AMERN INNS INC (VA)
Converted from Chapter 11 to Chapter 7 bankruptcy code 8/9/94
No stockholders' equity

KRISPY KREME DOUGHNUTS INC (NC)
Common no par split (2) for (1) by issuance of (1) additional share payable 03/19/2001 to holders of record 03/05/2001 Ex date - 03/20/2001
Common no par split (2) for (1) by issuance of (1) additional share payable 06/14/2001 to holders of record 05/29/2001 Ex date - 06/15/2001
Acquired by JAB Holdings B.V. 07/27/2016
Each share Common no par exchanged for $21 cash

KRISTIANSEN CYCLE ENGINES LTD (CANADA)
Dissolved in 1986
Details not available

KRISTINA CAP CORP (AB)
Reorganized under the laws of British Virgin Islands as Black Marlin Energy Holdings Ltd. 03/22/2010
Each share Common no par exchanged for (0.5) share Common no par
(See Black Marlin Energy Holdings Ltd.)

KRISTINA COPPER MINES LTD. (ON)
Recapitalized as Coppercrest Mines Ltd. 02/20/1956
Each share Capital Stock $1 par exchanged for (0.2) share Capital Stock $1 par
Coppercrest Mines Ltd. name changed to Peerless Canadian Explorations Ltd. 00/00/1957
(See Peerless Canadian Explorations Ltd.)

KRL RES CORP (BC)
Recapitalized as International KRL Resources Corp. 03/06/2002
Each share Common no par exchanged for (0.2) share Common no par
International KRL Resources Corp. recapitalized as Acme Resources Inc. 12/07/2009 which name changed to Affinity Metals Corp. 03/01/2017

KROEHLER MFG CO (DE)
Reincorporated 05/31/1969
Common no par changed to $5 par 00/00/1948
Stock Dividends - 100% 12/28/1954; 20% 05/06/1966
State of incorporation changed from (IL) to (DE) and Common $5 par changed to $1 par 05/31/1969
4-1/2% Preferred Ser. A $100 par called for redemption 05/02/1977
Name changed to Rymer Co. 11/30/1983
Rymer Co. name changed to Rymer Foods Inc. 04/11/1989
(See Rymer Foods Inc.)

KROES ENERGY INC (AB)
Name changed to Vecta Energy Corp. 06/23/2009

KROGER CO (OH)
4.30% Conv. Preferred Ser. A $50 par called for redemption 12/02/1968
6% 1st Preferred $100 par called for redemption 00/00/1969
Auction Preferred Ser. B $100 par called for redemption 01/03/1989
Auction Preferred Ser. C $100 par called for redempion 01/17/1989
Auction Preferred Ser. A $100 par called for redemption 01/31/1989
Auction Preferred Ser. D $100 par called for redemption 02/07/1989
(Additional Information in Active)

KROGER GROCERY & BAKING CO. (OH)
Name changed to Kroger Co. 3/11/46

KROHN INDS INC (NY)
Merged into Krohn Enterprises Inc. 6/30/94
Each share Common 1¢ par exchanged for $0.425 cash

KROLL INC (DE)
Reincorporated 07/02/2002
State of incorporation changed from (OH) to (DE) 07/02/2002
Acquired by Marsh & McLennan Companies, Inc. 07/08/2004
Each share Common 1¢ par exchanged for $37 cash

KROLL O GARA CO (OH)
Name changed to Kroll Inc. (OH) 08/23/2001
Kroll Inc. (OH) reincorporated in in Delaware 07/02/2002
(See Kroll Inc.)

KROMA, INC. (OH)
Completely liquidated 6/14/67
Each share Common $1 par exchanged for first and final distribution of $0.27 cash

KROMEX CORP. (OH)
Completely liquidated
Each share Capital Stock $1 par exchanged for initial distribution of $9 cash 9/30/64
Each share Capital Stock $1 par received second and final distribution of $0.107 cash 12/15/65

KROMONA CONSOLIDATED MINES, INC. (WA)
Charter cancelled and proclaimed dissolved for failure to pay fees 12/30/83

KROMONA MINES CORP. (WA)
Assets acquired by Victory Mines Corp. and company liquidated 9/19/57
(See listing for Victory Mines Corp.)

KRON CHOCOLATIER INC (NV)
Recapitalized 12/3/87
Details not available
Charter revoked for failure to file reports and pay fees 11/1/95

KRONOFUSION TECHNOLOGIES INC (YT)
Recapitalized as Consolidated Kronofusion Technologies Inc. 08/13/2003
Each share Common no par exchanged for (0.25) share Common no par
Consolidated Kronofusion Technologies Inc. recapitalized as JER Envirotech International Corp. (YT) 09/22/2004 which reincorporated in British Columbia 02/13/2006
(See JER Envirotech International Corp.)

KRONOS ADVANCED TECHNOLOGIES INC (NV)
Company terminated common stock registration and is no longer public as of 02/13/2009

KRONOS INC (MA)
Common 1¢ par split (3) for (2) by issuance of (0.5) additional share payable 1/29/96 to holders of record 1/15/96
Common 1¢ par split (3) for (2) by issuance of (0.5) additional share payable 3/9/99 to holders of record 2/23/99
Common 1¢ par split (3) for (2) by issuance of (0.5) additional share payable 11/15/2001 to holders of record 11/5/2001 Ex date - 11/16/2001
Common 1¢ par split (3) for (2) by issuance of (0.5) additional share payable 10/31/2003 to holders of record 10/20/2003 Ex date - 11/3/2003
Merged into Hellman & Friedman LLC 6/11/2007
Each share Common 1¢ par exchanged for $55 cash

KROPP FORGE CO. (IL)
Each share Common $1 par exchanged for (3) shares Common 33-1/3¢ par in 1946
Merged into Anadite, Inc. (CA) 9/13/67
Each share Common 33-1/3¢ par exchanged for (0.088237) share 3-1/2% Conv. Preferred $50 par and (0.088237) share Common no par
Anadite, Inc. (CA) reincorporated in Nevada 12/21/78
(See Anadite, Inc. (NV))

KROSSBOW HLDG CORP (NV)
Reorganized as Scio Diamond Technology Corp. 08/05/2011
Each share Common $0.001 par exchanged for (2) shares Common $0.001 par

KROY INC (MN)
Capital Stock 50¢ par split (2) for (1) by issuance of (1) additional share 8/28/81
Acquired by a group of investors 12/23/86
Each share Capital Stock 50¢ par exchanged for $11.50 cash

KROY INDUSTRIES INC. (MN)
Capital Stock 50¢ par split (2) for (1) by issuance of (1) additional share 8/17/79
Capital Stock 50¢ par split (2) for (1) by issuance of (1) additional share 8/22/80
Stock Dividend - 50% 3/16/79
Name changed to Kroy Inc. 7/23/81
(See Kroy Inc.)

KROY OILS LTD. (AB)
Common no par changed to 20¢ par 00/00/1952
Name changed to Pamoil Ltd. 10/09/1959
Pamoil Ltd. merged into Canadian Industrial Gas & Oil Ltd. 03/08/1965 which merged into Norcen Energy Resources Ltd. (AB) 10/28/1975 which reincorporated in Canada 04/15/1977 which merged into Union Pacific Resources Group Inc. 04/17/1998 which merged into Andarko Petroleum Corp. 07/14/2000

KRUEGER (H.R.) & CO.
Acquired by Commercial Credit Co. in 1943
Details not available

KRUEGER (G.) BREWING CO. (DE)
Name changed to GKB Co., Inc. 5/1/61
(See GKB Co., Inc.)

KRUEGER W A CO (WI)
Common $5 par changed to $2.50 par and (1) additional share issued 05/27/1977
$1.44 2nd Conv. Preferred Ser. A $1 par called for redemption 03/15/1978
Common $2.50 par changed to $1.25 par and (1) additional share issued 10/13/1978
Common $1.25 par changed to $0.625 par and (1) additional share issued 05/23/1983
Common $0.625 par changed to $0.3125 par and (1) additional share issued 05/29/1984
Common $0.3125 par changed to 20¢ par and (1) additional share issued 06/16/1987
Each share Common 20¢ par exchanged for (0.0000002) share Common 1¢ par 06/27/1989
Note: In effect holders received $10.49 cash per share and public interest was eliminated

KRUG (FRED) BREWING CO.
Sold to Falstaff Brewing Corp. (MD) in 1935
Details not available

KRUG INTL CORP (OH)
Stock Dividend - 10% 12/23/1994
Name changed to SunLink Health Systems, Inc. 08/20/2001

KRUGER CAP CORP (BC)
Name changed 09/03/1993
Name changed from Kruger Explorations Ltd. to Kruger Capital Corp. 09/03/1993
Name changed to Nextraction Energy Corp. 11/05/2008

KRUGER COPPER & SILVER MINING CO. (SD)
Charter expired by time limitation 00/00/1923

KRUGER MTN RES INC (NV)
Charter revoked for failure to file reports and pay fees 2/1/89

KRUPP CASH PLUS LTD PARTNERSHIP (MA)
Filed a Certificate of Cancellation 12/30/1998
Details not available

KRUPP CASH PLUS II LTD PARTNERSHIP (MA)
Filed a Certificate of Cancellation 12/30/1998
Details not available

KRUPP CASH PLUS III LTD PARTNERSHIP (MA)
Merged into Berkshire Realty Co., Inc. 06/28/1991
Each Depositary Receipt exchanged for (1.01) shares Common 1¢ par
(See Berkshire Realty Co., Inc.)

KRUPP CASH PLUS IV LTD PARTNERSHIP (MA)
Merged into Berkshire Realty Co., Inc. 06/28/1991
Each Unit of Depositary Receipts exchanged for (1.07) shares Common 1¢ par
(See Berkshire Realty Co., Inc.)

KRUPP GOVT INCOME TR (MA)
Trust terminated 11/30/2004
Details not available

KRUPP GOVT INCOME TR II (MA)
Trust terminated 11/01/2005
Details not available

KRUPP INSD MTG LTD PARTNERSHIP (MA)
Completely liquidated 12/30/2003
Each Depositary Receipt received first and final distribution of approximately $0.29 cash

KRUPP INSD PLUS LTD PARTNERSHIP (MA)
Completely liquidated 09/08/2004
Each Depositary Receipt received first and final distribution of approximately $0.247 cash

KRUPP INSD PLUS-II LTD PARTNERSHIP (MA)
Completely liquidated 07/29/2003
Each Depositary Receipt received first and final distribution of approximately $0.21 cash

KRUPP INSD PLUS-III LTD PARTNERSHIP (MA)
Completely liquidated 09/29/2004
Each Depositary Receipt received first and final distribution of approximately $0.20 cash

KRUPP MANUFACTURING CO. (PA)
Completely liquidated 05/31/1972
No stockholders' equity

KRUPP YIELD PLUS LTD PARTNERSHIP (MA)
Filed a Certificate of Cancellation 04/30/1996
Details not available

KRUTEX ENERGY CORP (UT)
Each share old Common $0.001 par exchanged for (0.1) share new Common $0.001 par 8/13/86
Merged into Foreland Corp. 6/28/91
Each share new Common $0.001 par exchanged for (0.1123595) share Common $0.001 par
(See Foreland Corp.)

KRUTH ASSOCS INC (DE)
Completely liquidated 11/19/1991
Each share Common 10¢ par received an undetermined amount of cash
Note: Certificates were not required to be surrendered and are without value

KRYLON, INC. (PA)
Acquired by Borden Co. 01/18/1966
Each share Common no par exchanged for (0.378) share Capital Stock $3.75 par
Borden Co. name changed to Borden, Inc. 04/17/1968 which merged into RJR Nabisco Holdings Corp. 03/14/1995 which name changed to Nabisco Group Holdings Corp. 06/15/1999
(See Nabisco Group Holdings Corp.)

KRYOTECH INTERNATIONAL, INC. (CO)
Each share Capital Stock 10¢ par exchanged for (0.1) share Capital Stock 1¢ par 5/14/71
Declared defunct and inoperative for failure to pay taxes and file annual reports 10/15/73

KRYPTAR CORP.
Bankrupt in 1948

KRYPTIC ENTMT INC (NV)
Name changed to Farm Lands of Guinea, Inc. 04/01/2011
Farm Lands of Guinea, Inc. name changed to Farm Lands of Africa, Inc. 03/28/2012

KRYPTON DISTR CORP (FL)
Recapitalized as Sobik's International Franchising, Inc. 02/02/2001
Each share Common $0.001 par exchanged for (0.025) share Common $0.001 par
Sobik's International Franchising, Inc. name changed to Quality Restaurant Ventures, Inc. 01/12/2004 which name changed to Airborne Security & Protective Services, Inc. (Ctfs. dated after 05/25/2010) 05/25/2010

KRYSTAL CO (TN)
Merged into Port Royal Holdings Inc. 9/26/97
Each share Common no par exchanged for $14.50 cash

KRYSTAL DIGITAL CORP (DE)
Recapitalized as Sunningdale, Inc. 04/16/2004
Each share Common $0.0001 par exchanged for (0.2) share Common $0.0001 par
Sunningdale, Inc. name changed to AdAl Group, Inc. 11/05/2004
(See AdAl Group, Inc.)

KRYSTINEL CORP (NY)
Merged into MMG Acquisition Corp. 02/14/1989
Each share Class A 1¢ par exchanged for $8.50 cash

KRYVYI RIH CEM OJSC (UKRAINE)
GDR agreement terminated 04/21/2017
No GDR's remain outstanding

KS E-MEDIA HLDGS INC (DE)
Name changed to Genex Pharmaceutical, Inc. 06/24/2004

KSAT SATELLITE NETWORKS INC (YT)
Reincorporated 04/14/1998
Place of incorporation changed from (BC) to (YT) 04/14/1998
Voluntarily dissolved 05/13/2004
No stockholders' equity

KSB BANCORP INC (ME)
Common 1¢ par split (3) for (1) by issuance of (2) additional shares payable 07/10/1997 to holders of record 06/30/1997
Stock Dividend - 10% payable 08/12/1996 to holders of record 07/29/1996
Merged into Camden National Corp. 12/20/1999
Each share Common 1¢ par exchanged for (1.136) shares Common 1¢ par

K7 CAP CORP (CA)
Name changed to Cosmetic Group U.S.A., Inc. 06/07/1993
Cosmetic Group U.S.A., Inc. name changed to Zegarelli Group International Inc. 10/01/1997 which recapitalized as 2050 Motors, Inc. 05/05/2014

KSF CHEM PROCESSES LTD (ON)
Name changed to KCP Resources Inc. 01/21/1982
(See KCP Resources Inc.)

KSIGN INTL INC (NV)
Each share old Common $0.001 par exchanged for (0.0005) share new Common $0.001 par 04/16/2007
Name changed to Columbus Geographic Systems (GIS) Ltd. 09/06/2007
(See Columbus Geographic Systems (GIS) Ltd.)

KSIX MEDIA HLDGS INC (NV)
Name changed to Surge Holdings, Inc. 01/16/2018

KSTV HLDG CO (NV)
Name changed to Bahamas Development Corp. 07/15/2016

KSW INC (DE)
Stock Dividend - 5% payable 06/11/2007 to holders of record 05/24/2007 Ex date - 05/22/2007
Acquired by Kool Acquisition Corp. 10/11/2012
Each share Common 1¢ par exchanged for $5 cash

KT CAP CORP (AB)
Ceased operations 01/17/2005
Stockholders' equity unlikely

KT HIGH-TECH MARKETING INC (DE)
Name changed to KULR Technology Group, Inc. 08/30/2018

KT MNG LTD (ON)
Name changed to K.T. Resources Ltd. 09/29/1980
K.T. Resources Ltd. recapitalized as K.T. Resources (1981) Ltd. 09/28/1981
(See K.T. Resources (1981) Ltd.)

KTI INC (NY)
Each share old Common 1¢ par exchanged for (1/3) share new Common 1¢ par 3/24/95
Stock Dividend - 5% payable 3/28/97 to holders of record 3/14/97
Merged into Casella Waste Systems, Inc. 12/15/99
Each share new Common 1¢ par exchanged for (0.51) share Class A Common 1¢ par

KTL BAMBOO INTL CORP (NV)
Common $0.001 par split (1.801801) for (1) by issuance of (0.801801) additional share payable 06/02/2016 to holders of record 05/31/2016 Ex date - 06/09/2016
Name changed to Miramar Labs, Inc. 06/16/2016
(See Miramar Labs, Inc.)

K2 DESIGN INC (DE)
Name changed to K2 Digital, Inc. 11/16/2000
K2 Digital, Inc. recapitalized as Accelerated Building Concepts Corp. 09/10/2007 which recapitalized as WhereverTV Broadcasting Corp. 09/12/2012

K2 DIGITAL INC (DE)
Recapitalized as Accelerated Building Concepts Corp. 09/10/2007
Each share Common 1¢ par exchanged for (0.1) share Common 1¢ par
Accelerated Building Concepts Corp. recapitalized as WhereverTV Broadcasting Corp. 09/12/2012

K2 ENERGY CORP (AB)
Recapitalized as Resilient Resources Ltd. 05/24/2005
Each share Common no par exchanged for (0.03333333) share Common no par
Resilient Resources Ltd. merged into Guardian Exploration Inc. 04/21/2006

K2 INC (DE)
Merged into Jarden Corp. 08/08/2007
Eash share Common $1 par exchanged for (0.1118) share Common 1¢ par and $10.85 cash

K 2 RES INC (BC)
Name changed to Jazz Resources Inc. 05/29/1996

KU ENERGY CORP (KY)
Merged into LG&E Energy Corp. 05/04/1998
Each share Common no par exchanged for (1.67) shares Common no par
(See LG&E Energy Corp.)

KUALA HEALTHCARE INC (DE)
Filed a petition under Chapter 7 Federal Bankruptcy Code 8/21/2001
Stockholders' equity unlikely

KUALA LUMPUR KEPONG BERHAD (MALAYSIA)
Each Unsponsored ADR for Ordinary exchanged for (1) Sponsored ADR for Ordinary 05/03/1999
Stock Dividends - 50% payable 06/06/1996 to holders of record 03/19/1996; 50% payable 03/30/2007 to holders of record 03/01/2007 Ex date - 02/27/2007
ADR agreement terminated 08/04/2014
Each Sponsored ADR for Ordinary exchanged for (10) shares Ordinary
Note: Unexchanged ADR's were sold and the proceeds, if any, held for claim after 02/02/2015

KUALTA RES LTD (AB)
Recapitalized as Capco Resources Ltd. 10/6/93
Each share Common no par

KUA-KUZ

KUAN CORP (HI)
exchanged for (1/3) share Common no par
Each share Common no par exchanged for (0.002) share Common no par 3/1/83
Note: In effect holders received $0.03 cash per share and public interest was eliminated

KUBANELECTROSVYAZ OPEN JT STK CO (RUSSIA)
Name changed to Southern Telecommunications Co. 11/29/2001
(See Southern Telecommunications Co.)

KUBLA KHAN INC (UT)
Name changed to China Finance, Inc. 8/9/2004

KUBOTA LTD (JAPAN)
Stock Dividend - 10% 07/09/1976
Name changed to Kubota Corp. 04/01/1990

KUHLMAN CO (NV)
Ceased operations 04/13/2007
Stockholders' equity unlikely

KUHLMAN CORP (DE)
Reincorporated 06/09/1993
Common $2 par changed to $1 par and (1) additional share issued 05/05/1967
Common $1 par split (3) for (2) by issuance of (0.5) additional share 06/05/1984
Common $1 par split (3) for (2) by issuance of (0.5) additional share 06/05/1985
Stock Dividend - 100% 05/13/1968
State of incorporation changed from (MI) to (DE) 06/09/1993
Merged into Borg-Warner Automotive, Inc. 03/01/1999
Each share Common $1 par exchanged for (0.85545) share Common 1¢ par
Borg-Warner Automotive, Inc. name changed to BorgWarner Inc. 02/04/2000

KUHLMAN ELECTRIC CO. (MI)
5-1/2% Preferred Ser. A $10 par called for redemption 12/22/1965
Name changed to Kuhlman Corp. (MI) 05/01/1967
Kuhlman Corp. (MI) reincorporated in Delaware 06/09/1993 which merged into Borg-Warner Automotive, Inc. 03/01/1999 which name changed to BorgWarner Inc. 02/04/2000

KUHNER PACKING CO. (IN)
Name changed to Marhoefer Packing Co., Inc. in 1952
Marhoefer Packing Co., Inc. adjudicated bankrupt 6/2/78

KUHNS BIG K STORES CORP (TN)
Stock Dividend - 50% 05/19/1976
Acquired by Wal-Mart Stores, Inc. 08/11/1981
Each share Common $1 par exchanged for (0.11) share 8% Conv. Preferred Ser. A 10¢ par
(See Wal-Mart Stores, Inc.)

KUL WATCH INC (DE)
Reorganized as Fit After Fifty Inc. 7/18/2005
Each share Common $0.0001 par exchanged for (1,000) shares Common $0.0001 par

KULCZYK OIL VENTURES INC (AB)
Recapitalized as Serinus Energy Inc. (AB) 06/27/2013
Each share Common no par exchanged for (0.1) share Common no par
Serinus Energy Inc. (AB) reincorporated in Jersey as Serinus Energy PLC 05/15/2018
(See Serinus Energy PLC)

KULEHED, INC. (MA)
Charter revoked for failure to file reports and pay fees 3/31/31

KULICKE & SOFFA MANUFACTURING CO. (PA)
Name changed to Kulicke & Soffa Industries, Inc. 1/18/66

KULKA ELECTRONICS CORP. (NY)
6-1/2% Preferred $10 par called for redemption 11/23/61
Name changed to Kulka Smith Electronics Corp. 4/27/62
Kulka Smith Electronics Corp. merged into Consolidated Electronics Industries Corp. 9/14/64 which name changed to North American Philips Corp. 2/14/69
(See North American Philips Corp.)

KULKA SMITH ELECTRONICS CORP. (NY)
Class A 10¢ par reclassified as Common 10¢ par 6/13/62
Merged into Consolidated Electronics Industries Corp. on a (1) for (5.2) basis 9/14/64
Consolidated Electronics Industries Corp. name changed to North American Philips Corp. 2/14/69
(See North American Philips Corp.)

KUM RES LTD (BC)
Name changed to Futurtek Communications Inc. 08/16/1983
(See Futurtek Communications Inc.)

KUMA RES LTD (AB)
Name changed to Algonquin Petroleum Corp. 03/18/1997
Algonquin Petroleum Corp. recapitalized as Algonquin Oil & Gas Ltd. 04/10/2000 which recapitalized as PetroShale Inc. 03/19/2012

KUMAGAI GUMI (HONG KONG) LTD (HONG KONG)
Name changed to Hong Kong Construction (Holdings) Ltd. 02/12/1999
(See Hong Kong Construction (Holdings) Ltd.)

KUMAGAI GUMI LTD (JAPAN)
Stock Dividend - 10% 12/10/85
ADR agreement terminated 9/26/2003
Each Sponsored ADR for Common 5 Yen par exchanged for $1.978 cash

KUMBA RES LTD (SOUTH AFRICA)
Each Sponsored ADR for Ordinary received distribution of (1) Kumba Iron Ore Ltd. Sponsored ADR for Ordinary payable 11/27/2006 to holders of record 11/24/2006 Ex date - 11/28/2006
Name changed to Exxaro Resources Ltd. 12/4/2006

KUMGANG KOREA CHEMICAL CO LTD (KOREA)
Name changed to KCC Corp. 03/14/2005
(See KCC Corp.)

KUMIX RES CORP (BC)
Struck off register and declared dissolved for failure to file returns 12/15/1989

KUN RUN BIOTECHNOLOGY INC (NV)
Acquired by Hua Kun, Inc. 03/26/2018
Each share Common $0.001 par exchanged for $0.20 cash

KUNDAN INVT CORP (NY)
Name changed to Silent Partner Body Armor, Inc. 01/26/1989
(See Silent Partner Body Armor, Inc.)

KUNER EMPSON CO (CO)
6% Preferred $10 par called for redemption 3/1/71
Merged into Stokely-Van Camp, Inc. 5/21/71
Each share Common $5 par exchanged for $5.25 cash

KUONI REISEN HLDG AG (SWITZERLAND)
ADR agreement terminated 12/02/2016
Each ADR for Common issued by Bank of New York exchanged for $7.316116 cash
Each ADR for Common issued by Deutsche Bank exchanged for $7.282613 cash

KUPPER PARKER COMMUNICATIONS INC (NY)
Recapitalized as Principal Solar, Inc. (NY) 05/25/2011
Each share Common 1¢ par exchanged for (0.025) share Common 1¢ par
Principal Solar, Inc. (NY) reincorporated in Delaware 10/24/2012

KURCHATOV RESH HLDGS LTD (DE)
Name changed to Advanced Technology Industries, Inc. 2/18/2000
Advanced Technology Industries, Inc. name changed to Brilliant Technologies Corp. 5/1/2006

KURITA WTR INDS LTD (JAPAN)
ADR agreement terminated 03/07/2014
No ADR's were issued

KURMAN ELECTRIC CO., INC. (NY)
Name changed to K.E. Assets Corp. 08/29/1957
(See K.E. Assets Corp.)

KURRANT FOOD ENTERPRISES INC (CO)
Each share Common $0.001 par received distribution of (0.1) share Kurrant Mobile Catering, Inc. Common $0.001 par payable 02/05/2008 to holders of record 01/10/2008 Ex date - 01/31/2008
Name changed to Zhidali Radio & Television Network, Inc. 05/06/2011
(See Zhidali Radio & Television Network, Inc.)

KURRANT MOBILE CATERING INC (CO)
SEC revoked common stock registration 01/23/2013

KURTZ CHATTERTON COPPER MINING CO. (WY)
Charter forfeited for non-payment of taxes 7/19/27

KURZ KASCH INC (OH)
Preferred $100 par called for redemption 12/13/1975
Each share Common $1 par exchanged for (0.001) share Common no par 03/20/1981
Note: In effect holders received $7 cash per share and public interest was eliminated

KURZWEIL APPLIED INTELLIGENCE INC (DE)
Merged into Lernout & Hauspie Speech Products N.V. 6/27/97
Each share Common 1¢ par exchanged for (0.047549) share Common no par and $4.20 cash
(See Lernout & Hauspie Speech Products N.V.)

KURZWEIL MUSIC SYS INC (DE)
Filed a petition under Chapter 11 Federal Bankruptcy Code 4/20/90
Stockholders' equity unlikely

KUSAN INC (KY)
Common $1 par split (3) for (2) by issuance of (0.5) additional share 3/30/68
Completely liquidated 2/27/70
Each share Common $1 par exchanged for first and final distribution of (0.93) share Bethlehem Steel Corp. (DE) Common $8 par
(See Bethlehem Steel Corp.)

KUSBASS ENERGO STK CO OF OPEN TYPE (RUSSIA)
GDR agreement terminated 10/16/2014
Each Sponsored Reg. S GDR for Ordinary exchanged for $0.340605 cash
Each Sponsored 144A GDR for Ordinary exchanged for $0.340605 cash

KUSH BOTTLES INC (NV)
Name changed to KushCo Holdings, Inc. 09/04/2018

KUSHEQUA RAILROAD CO.
Dissolved in 1932

KUSHI MACROBIOTICS CORP (DE)
Name changed to American Phoenix Group, Inc. (DE) 09/26/1996
American Phoenix Group, Inc. (DE) name changed to TAL Wireless Networks, Inc. 05/22/1997
(See TAL Wireless Networks, Inc.)

KUSHI NAT FOODS CORP (DE)
Recapitalized as HanKersen International Corp. 12/09/2005
Each share Common $0.0001 par exchanged for (0.16666666) share Common $0.0001 par
HanKersen International Corp. name changed to Asia Cork, Inc. 07/28/2008
(See Asia Cork, Inc.)

KUSHI RES INC (NV)
Common $0.0001 par split (2.6) for (1) by issuance of (1.6) additional shares payable 03/23/2010 to holders of record 12/15/2009 Ex date - 03/24/2010
Name changed to TheraBiogen, Inc. 03/29/2010
(See TheraBiogen, Inc.)

KUSHNER-LOCKE CO (CA)
Each share old Common no par exchanged for (1/6) share new Common no par 09/05/1997
Plan of reorganization under Chapter 11 Federal Bankruptcy proceedings effective 02/01/2010
No stockholders' equity

KU6 MEDIA CO LTD (CAYMAN ISLANDS)
ADR agreement terminated 07/12/2016
Each Sponsored ADR for Ordinary exchanged for $1.03 cash

KUSTOM ELECTRS INC (DE)
Charter cancelled and declared inoperative and void for non-payment of taxes 3/1/93

KUT KWICK CORP (GA)
Name changed to Treshco Enterprises, Inc. 04/18/1978

KUT-KWICK TOOL CORP. (DE)
Reorganized under the laws of Georgia as Kut-Kwick Corp. 5/1/54
Each share 6% Preferred $5 par exchanged for (100) shares Class B Common 1¢ par and $3 principal amount of 6% Debentures
Each share Common 1¢ par exchanged for (1) share Class A Common 1¢ par
Kut-Kwick Corp. name changed to Treshco Enterprises, Inc. 4/18/78

KUTZ CANON OIL & GAS CO. (CO)
Merged into King Oil, Inc. 05/25/1961
Each share Common exchanged for (10) shares Common
King Oil, Inc. recapitalized as Lane Wood, Inc. 08/10/1964
(See Lane Wood, Inc.)

KUZBASSENERGO JSC (RUSSIA)
Sponsored ADR's for Ordinary split (2) for (1) by issuance of (1) additional ADR payable 04/21/2008 to holders of record 04/18/2008 Ex date - 04/22/2008
ADR basis changed from (1:10) to (1:500) 04/21/2008
ADR agreement terminated 10/16/2014
Each Sponsored ADR for Ordinary exchanged for $0.340605 cash

KVAERNER A S (NORWAY)
Each old Sponsored ADR for Free Class A NOK 12.50 par exchanged for (0.25) new Sponsored ADR for Class A NOK 12.50 par 10/30/1995
Each old Sponsored ADR for Class B NOK 12.50 par exchanged for (0.25) new Sponsored ADR for Class B NOK par 10/30/1995
Each new Sponsored ADR for Class A NOK 12.50 par exchanged for (0.25) Sponsored ADR for Ordinary Share 2000 on 10/16/2000
Each new Sponsored ADR for Class B NOK 12.50 par exchanged for (0.25) Sponsored ADR for Ordinary Share 2000 on 10/16/2000
Name changed to Aker Kvaerner A.S.A. 12/19/2003
Aker Kvaerner A.S.A. name changed to Kvaerner A.S.A. (New) 04/14/2004
(See Kvaerner A.S.A. (New))

KVAERNER A S A NEW (NORWAY)
ADR agreement terminated 04/14/2004
Each Sponsored ADR for Ordinary NOK 12.50 par exchanged for $0.2194 cash
(Additional Information in Active)

KVP SUTHERLAND PAPER CO. (DE)
Merged into Brown Co. (DE) 05/12/1966
Each share Common $5 par exchanged for (1) share $1.50 Conv. Preferred Ser. A $1 par
(See Brown Co. (DE))

KWANTRA NATL INC (MN)
Completely liquidated 08/31/1978
Each share Common 1¢ par exchanged for first and final distribution of $0.258 cash

KWEST INVT INTL LTD (NV)
Name changed to Fuhuiyuan International Holdings Ltd. 08/07/2013 Fuhuiyuan International Holdings Ltd. recapitalized as Wellness Matrix Group, Inc. 09/10/2018

KWIK PRODS INTL CORP (BC)
Common no par split (2) for (1) by issuance of (1) additional share 03/20/1986
Recapitalized as Trend Vision Technologies, Inc. 05/20/1992
Each share Common no par exchanged for (0.5) share Common no par
(See Trend Vision Technologies, Inc.)

KWIKSTAR COMMUNICATIONS LTD (AB)
Recapitalized as Digital Courier International Corp. 05/02/1996
Each share Common no par exchanged for (1/3) share Common no par
(See Digital Courier International Corp.)

KWIKWEB COM INC (NV)
SEC revoked common stock registration 09/15/2008

KYBER RES LTD (BC)
Recapitalized as Magin Energy Inc. (Old) 02/29/1996
Each share Common no par exchanged for (0.33333333) share Common no par
Magin Energy Inc. (Old) reorganized as Magin Energy Inc. (New) 09/26/1996 which was acquired by NCE Petrofund 07/03/2001 which name changed to Petrofund Energy Trust 11/01/2003 which merged into Penn West Energy Trust 07/04/2006 which reorganized as Penn West Petroleum Ltd. (New) 01/03/2011 which name changed to Obsidian Energy Ltd. 06/29/2017

KYLE DEV CORP (DE)
Name changed to Ferrara Food Inc. 5/11/92
(See Ferrara Food Inc.)

KYLE GOLD MINES LTD. (ON)
Charter revoked for failure to file reports and pay fees 12/23/65

KYLE RES INC (BC)
Recapitalized as Consolidated Kyle Resources Inc. 05/29/1990
Each share Common no par exchanged for (0.2) share Common no par
Consolidated Kyle Resources Inc. recapitalized as Zappa Resources Ltd. 07/27/1992 which recapitalized as AKA Ventures Inc. 07/02/2008 which name changed to Phoenix Copper Corp. 09/07/2012 which recapitalized as Phoenix Metals Corp. 12/04/2013 which name changed to Envirotek Remediation Inc. 04/27/2018

KYLE TECHNOLOGY CORP (CA)
Acquired by KTC Acquisition Corp. 04/06/1990
Each share Common no par exchanged for $1.12 cash

KYNB BANCSHARES INC (KY)
Acquired by Banc One Corp. 00/00/1985
Details not available

KYOCERA MGMT LTD (NV)
Common $0.001 par split (2.273) for (1) by issuance of (1.273) additional shares payable 9/4/98 to holders of record 8/27/98
Name changed to Cathayonline Inc. 4/8/99

KYOMEDIX CORP (NV)
Name changed back to First Deltavision, Inc. 11/18/2002
First Deltavision, Inc. name changed to Integrated Healthcare Holdings, Inc. 03/04/2004
(See Integrated Healthcare Holdings, Inc.)

KYOTO CERAMIC LTD (JAPAN)
Stock Dividends - 25% 07/29/1977; 20% 07/09/1979; 20% 07/14/1980; 10% 07/21/1982
Name changed to Kyocera Corp. 10/01/1982

KYOWA BK LTD (JAPAN)
Name changed to Kyowa Saitama Bank, Ltd. 04/01/1991
Kyowa Saitama Bank, Ltd. name changed to Asahi Bank Ltd. 09/21/1992
(See Asahi Bank Ltd.)

KYOWA SAITAMA BK LTD (JAPAN)
Name changed to Asahi Bank Ltd. 09/21/1992
(See Asahi Bank Ltd.)

KYPHON INC (DE)
Issue Information - 6,000,000 shares COM offered at $15 per share on 05/16/2002
Merged into Medtronic, Inc. 11/02/2007
Each share Common $0.001 par exchanged for $71 cash

KYRGOIL HOLDING CORP (BRITISH VIRGIN ISLANDS)
Reincorporated 01/04/2001
Reincorporated from Kyrgoil Corp. (ON) to Kyrgoil Holding Corp. (British Virgin Islands) 01/04/2001
Recapitalized as Serica Energy Corp. (British Virgin Islands) 01/30/2004
Each share Common no par exchanged for (0.1) share Common no par
Serica Energy Corp. (British Virgin Islands) reincorporated in United Kingdom as Serica Energy PLC 09/07/2005
(See Serica Energy PLC)

KYSOR HEATER CO. (MI)
Stock Dividend - 10% 3/20/62
Name changed to Kysor Industrial Corp. (MI) 10/8/62
Kysor Industrial Corp. (MI) reincorporated under the laws of Delaware 5/14/70 which incorporated again in Michigan 5/31/85
(See Kysor Industrial Corp. (MI))

KYSOR INDL CORP (MI)
Reincorporated 5/14/70
Reincorporated 5/31/85
Common $1 par split (2) for (1) by issuance of (1) additional share 10/27/78
Common $1 par split (2) for (1) by issuance of (1) additional share 5/24/66
State of incorporation changed from (MI) to (DE) 5/14/70
State of incorporation changed from (DE) back to (MI) 5/31/85
Common $1 par split (2) for (1) by issuance of (1) additional share 9/14/87
Stock Dividends - 10% 7/25/63; 10% 3/20/64
Merged into Scotsman Industries, Inc. 3/12/97
Each share Voting Conv. Preferred Ser. A $1 par exchanged for $43 cash
Each share Common $1 par exchanged for $43 cash

KYTHERA BIOPHARMACEUTICALS INC (DE)
Acquired by Allergan PLC 10/01/2015
Each share Common $0.00001 par exchanged for $75 cash

KYTO BIOPHARMA INC (FL)
Each share old Common $0.0001 par exchanged for (0.1) share new Common $0.0001 par 11/04/2015
Name changed to Kyto Technology & Life Science, Inc. 06/05/2018

KYZEN CORP (UT)
Reincorporated under the laws of Tennessee 5/12/99

L

L & B FINL INC (TX)
Merged into Jefferson Savings Bancorp, Inc. 2/28/97
Each share Common 1¢ par exchanged for (0.3328) share Common 1¢ par and $9.2778 cash
Jefferson Savings Bancorp, Inc. merged into Union Planters Corp. (New) 2/12/2001 which merged into Regions Financial Corp. (New) 7/1/2004

L & C LTD. (HI)
5% Preferred $20 par called for redemption 9/30/65
Merged into Dillingham Corp. 3/5/68
Each share Common $5 par exchanged for (0.5) share $2 Conv. Preferred March 1968 Ser. no par and (0.5) share Common no par
(See Dillingham Corp.)

L & D PPTY OPERATIONS CDA LTD (BC)
Name changed to Uni-Way Pacific Holdings Inc. 04/06/1992
Uni-Way Pacific Holdings Inc. recapitalized as New Uni-Way Holdings Ltd. 09/16/1993 which name changed to Full Riches Investments Ltd. 02/26/1998 which was acquired by Medoro Resources Ltd. 03/02/2004 which merged into Gran Colombia Gold Corp. 06/14/2011

L & H CAPITAL SERVICES CORP. (OR)
Voluntarily dissolved 6/18/85
Details not available

L & H COMPUTER CORP (DE)
Out of business 06/01/1972
No stockholders' equity

L & L SCRAP IRON CORP. (NV)
Charter revoked for failure to file reports and pay fees 3/6/61

L & N HSG CORP (MD)
Name changed to LNH Reit, Inc. 5/5/92
LNH Reit, Inc. merged into Eastgroup Properties 5/14/96 which reorganized as Eastgroup Properties, Inc. 6/5/97

L & N MINING CO. (NV)
Charter revoked for failure to file reports and pay fees 3/3/69

L & S ELECTRS INC (NY)
Voluntarily dissolved 3/14/95
Details not available

L A C INDS LTD (NY)
Charter cancelled and proclaimed dissolved for failure to pay taxes 03/25/1981

L.A.D. CORP. (DE)
Merged into Marmon Group, Inc. (Del.) 6/30/69
Each share Common $1 par exchanged for $12.13 cash

L A ENTMT INC (DE)
Name changed to Gerant Industries, Inc. 12/28/92
Gerant Industries, Inc. reorganized as Xplorer, S.A. 12/16/96 which name changed to Netholdings.com Inc. 12/8/99 which name changed to Global Avcess Corp. 5/9/2001

L A GEAR INC (CA)
Common no par split (2) for (1) by issuance of (1) additional share 08/02/1988
Common no par split (2) for (1) by issuance of (1) additional share 09/25/1989
Second amended plan of reorganization under Chapter 11 Federal Bankruptcy Code effective 10/21/1998
No stockholders' equity

L A GROUP INC (DE)
Name changed to ONTV, Inc. 04/03/2000
ONTV, Inc. name changed to True Product ID, Inc. 05/22/2006

L A T SPORTSWEAR INC (GA)
Issue Information - 1,200,000 shares COM offered at $10 per share on 01/25/1994
Name changed to Full Line Distributors, Inc. 3/2/2000
(See Full Line Distributors, Inc.)

L AIGLON APPAREL INC (PA)
Assets assigned for benefit of creditors 10/22/1975
No stockholders' equity

L AIR HLDG INC (NV)
Recapitalized as Hansheng Industrial Equipment Manufacturing (USA) Inc. 10/3/2006
Each share Common $0.001 par exchanged for (0.01) share Common $0.001 par

L AUTREC INC (DE)
Recapitalized as IRT Holding Corp. 03/11/1992
Each share Common $0.001 par exchanged for (0.25) share Common $0.001 par
IRT Holding Corp. name changed to Asthma Disease Management, Inc. 12/03/1998
(See Asthma Disease Management, Inc.)

L C M EQUITY INC (NV)
Name changed to Regma Bio Technologies Ltd. 2/1/2002
Regma Bio Technologies Ltd. name changed to Phage Genomics, Inc. 11/26/2003 which name changed to

Searchlight Minerals Corp. 6/24/2005

L D V ELECTRO SCIENCE INDS INC (NY)
Proclaimed dissolved 9/25/96

L E H VENTURES LTD (BC)
Name changed to Discovery PGM Exploration Ltd. 09/16/2005
Discovery PGM Exploration Ltd. acquired by Marathon PGM Corp. 06/13/2008
(See Marathon PGM Corp.)

L.F.I. CORP. (DE)
Name changed to Gerli & Co., Inc. 08/01/1960
(See Gerli & Co., Inc.)

L F INDS INC (DE)
Name changed to Flair Communications Inc. 7/14/89
Flair Communications Inc. name changed to Tier Environmental Services Inc. 10/6/94 which name changed to Gulfstar Industries, Inc. 1/4/96 which recapitalized as Media Vision Productions Inc. 1/5/99 which name changed to eCONTENT, Inc. 10/1/99 which name changed to Earthworks Entertainment, Inc. 1/15/2004

L G INDS INC (NY)
Name changed to Sunbelt Airlines, Inc. 7/9/79
Sunbelt Airlines, Inc. recapitalized as Florida Publishers, Inc. 10/15/80
(See Florida Publishers, Inc.)

L G R RES LTD (BC)
Recapitalized as Stream Oil & Gas Ltd. 04/09/2008
Each share Common no par exchanged for (0.25) share Common no par
(See Stream Oil & Gas Ltd.)

L H M CORP (DE)
Name changed to International Sportsfest, Inc. 06/27/1990
International Sportsfest, Inc. name changed to Pride, Inc. 02/01/1994 which recapitalized as Mason Hill Holdings Inc. 10/01/1999 which name changed to Attitude Drinks Inc. 06/18/2008

L.I. CHROMATEL, INC. (NY)
Liquidation completed
Each share Class A 10¢ par received initial distribution of (0.1) share Giannini Scientific Corp. Common 10¢ par 10/11/1962
Each share Class A 10¢ par received second distribution of (0.1) share Giannini Scientific Corp. Common 10¢ par 03/15/1963
Each share Class A 10¢ par exchanged for third and final distribution of (0.5) share Giannini Scientific Corp. Common 10¢ par 06/01/1964
Giannini Scientific Corp. name changed to Geotel, Inc. 05/16/1968
(See Geotel, Inc.)

L I F E INC (NV)
Charter revoked for failure to file reports and pay fees 03/01/1976

L I F T SYS INC (AB)
Name changed to Laniuk Industries Inc. 06/25/1999
Laniuk Industries Inc. reorganized as TerraVest Income Fund 07/08/2004 which reorganized as TerraVest Capital Inc. 11/05/2012 which name changed to TerraVest Industries Inc. (New) 02/28/2018

L I INC (CO)
Recapitalized as Imaging Management Associates, Inc. 06/25/1990
Each share Common no par exchanged for (0.25) share Common no par
Imaging Management Associates, Inc.

recapitalized as Gulf Energy Corp. 07/23/2007 which name changed to Indie Ranch Media Inc. 11/19/2007

L INTL COMPUTERS INC (DE)
Charter cancelled and declared inoperative and void for non-payment of taxes 03/01/2007

L J B VENTURES INC (NV)
Name changed to American Quality Products, Inc. 07/26/1987

L.J.N. TOYS, LTD. (NY)
Name changed to LJN Toys, Ltd. 7/22/84
(See LJN Toys, Ltd.)

L J SIMONE INC (DE)
Name changed to Simone Group, Inc. 09/22/1992
(See Simone Group, Inc.)

L K RES LTD (AB)
Each share Common no par exchanged for (0.5) share Class B Common no par 02/12/1981
Name changed to XL Food Systems Ltd. and Class A Special Stock no par and Class B Common no par reclassified as Common no par 04/21/1986
XL Foods Systems Ltd. name changed to XL Foods Ltd. 06/15/1989 which name changed to Sevenway Capital Corp. 03/09/1999 which merged into Glacier Ventures International Corp. (Canada) (New) 04/28/2000 which name changed to Glacier Media Inc. 07/01/2008

L L BROWN INTL INC (NV)
Recapitalized as Terra Block International, Inc. 3/3/2003
Each share Common $0.001 par exchanged for (0.5) share Common $0.001 par
Terra Block International, Inc. name changed to EarthBlock Technologies, Inc. 4/1/2005

L.M. LIQUIDATING CO. (DE)
In process of liquidation
Each share Common 50¢ par exchanged for initial distribution of (0.296667) share Gulton Industries, Inc. Common $1 par 9/15/70
Details on subsequent distributions, if any, are not available

L-O-F GLASS FIBERS CO. (OH)
Assets sold to Johns-Manville Corp. (NY) 12/31/58
Each share Common $5 par exchanged for (0.4) share Common $5 par
Johns-Manville Corp. (NY) reincorporated in Delaware as Manville Corp. 10/30/81 which name changed to Schuller Corp. 3/29/96 which name changed to Johns-Manville Corp. (New) 5/5/97
(See Johns-Manville Corp. (New))

L-1 IDENTITY SOLUTIONS INC (DE)
Acquired by Safran S.A. 07/25/2011
Each share Common $0.001 par exchanged for $12 cash

L.P.C. LIQUIDATING CO. (PA)
Liquidation completed
Each share Common no par or Class B Common no par exchanged for initial distribution of $9 cash 7/20/72
Each share Common no par or Class B Common no par received second and final distribution of $0.50 cash 5/31/73

L P INDS LTD (BC)
Recapitalized as May-Ralph Resources Ltd. 7/25/79
Each share Capital Stock no par exchanged for (0.2) share Capital Stock no par
(See May-Ralph Resources Ltd.)

L P R CYBERTEK INC (CO)
Name changed to Thermoelastic Technologies, Inc. 12/10/1999
Thermoelastic Technologies, Inc.

name changed to Wannigan Capital Corp. 06/30/2003
(See Wannigan Capital Corp.)

L Q CORP INC (DE)
Each share Common $0.001 par automatically became (0.14) share Common $0.001 par to reflect a (1) for (250) reverse split followed by a (35) for (1) forward split 06/08/2004
Merged into Sielox, Inc. 07/31/2007
Each share Common $0.001 par exchanged for (3.68) shares Common $0.001 par

L.R. CORP. (DE)
Merged into Westinghouse Air Brake Co. in April 1954
Each share Common $2.50 par exchanged for (0.36) share Common $10 par
Westinghouse Air Brake Co. merged into American Standard Inc. 6/7/68
(See American Standard Inc.)

L.R. STEEL COMPANY, INC. (DE)
Company went bankrupt 00/00/1923
Common stock declared worthless 00/00/1926

L R C INTL PLC (ENGLAND)
ADR's for Ordinary Reg. 2s par changed to 10p par per currency change 02/15/1971
Stock Dividend - 10% 10/18/1983
Name changed to London International Group PLC 11/15/1985
(See London International Group PLC)

L-R HEAT TREATING CO. (NJ)
Name changed to L-R Metal Treating Corp. 11/02/1959
L-R Metal Treating Corp. name changed to Thermo National Industries, Inc. 10/09/1967
(See Thermo National Industries, Inc.)

L-R METAL TREATING CORP. (NJ)
Name changed to Thermo National Industries, Inc. 10/09/1967
(See Thermo National Industries, Inc.)

L REX INTL INC (VIRGIN ISLANDS)
Each (410) shares old Common $0.0001 par exchanged for (1) share new Common $0.0001 par 06/05/1992
SEC revoked common stock registration 04/08/2009

L S B BANCSHARES INC S C (SC)
Name changed 5/1/86
Common $5 par changed to $2.50 par and (1) additional share issued 1/31/86
Name changed from L.S.B. Bancshares, Inc. to L.S.B. Bancshares, Inc. of South Carolina 5/1/86
Stock Dividend - 10% 12/15/89
Merged into BB&T Financial Corp. 6/30/94
Each share Common $2.50 par exchanged for (1.2593) shares Common $2.50 par
BB&T Financial Corp. merged into Southern National Corp. 2/28/97 which name changed to BB&T Corp. 5/19/97

L S CAP INC (DE)
Name changed to Nacoma Consolidated Industries, Inc. 12/11/1990
(See Nacoma Consolidated Industries, Inc.)

L S K INNS CORP AMER (MN)
Statutorily dissolved 09/26/1991

L.T. GROWTH, INC. (UT)
Recapitalized as Sweany Gold Corp. 02/17/1986
Each share Common $0.001 par exchanged for (12) shares Common $0.001 par

L-3 COMMUNICATIONS HLDGS INC (DE)
Common 1¢ par split (2) for (1) by

issuance of (1) additional share payable 05/20/2002 to holders of record 05/06/2002 Ex date - 05/21/2002
Each share Common 1¢ par received distribution of (0.16666666) share Engility Holdings, Inc. (Old) Common 1¢ par payable 07/17/2012 to holders of record 07/16/2012 Ex date - 07/18/2012
Name changed to L3 Technologies, Inc. 01/03/2017

L.V. INTST DEVELOPING INC (NV)
Recapitalized as Today.Com, Inc. 02/01/1998
Each (2.75) shares Common $0.001 par exchanged for (1) share Common $0.001 par
Today.com, Inc. recapitalized as Online Sales Strategies, Inc. 09/27/2007

L W RES LTD (AB)
Issue Information - 2,000,000 shares COM offered at $0.10 per share on 12/22/1997
Name changed to Bancorp Financial Group Inc. 6/12/2000
(See Bancorp Financial Group Inc.)

L&L ACQUISITION CORP (DE)
Issue Information - 4,000,000 UNITS consisting of (1) share COM and (1) WT offered at $10 per Unit on 11/23/2010
Completely liquidated
Each Unit received first and final distribution of $10.10 cash payable 05/31/2012 to holders of record 05/29/2012
Each share Common $0.0001 par received first and final distribution of $10.10 cash payable 05/31/2012 to holders of record 05/29/2012
Note: Holders will also be entitled to distribution from any Trust Account income tax refund received

LA BARGE INC (DE)
Acquired by Ducommun Inc. 06/28/2011
Each share Common 1¢ par exchanged for $19.25 cash

LA BUENA ESPERANZA MINES CO. (NM)
Charter forfeited for failure to file reports and pay taxes 5/7/34

LA BURBUJA CAFE INC (NV)
Name changed to WaferGen Bio-systems, Inc. 02/09/2007
(See WaferGen Bio-systems, Inc.)

LA CASA MEXICANA, INC. (CO)
Name changed to Casa Grande Mining Co. 4/13/83
Casa Grande Mining Co. name changed to Datafusion Corp. 7/11/84

LA CEMENTO NACIONAL C A (ECUADOR)
144A GDR's for Ordinary split (15) for (1) by issuance of (14) additional GDR's payable 05/06/2003 to holders of record 12/30/2002 Ex date - 12/26/2002
Name changed to Holcim Ecuador S.A. 04/21/2005
(See Holcim Ecuador S.A.)

LA CHIB MINES LTD (ON)
Recapitalized as Lachib Development Corp. 12/23/1987
Each share Common $1 par exchanged for (0.1) share Common no par
Lachib Development Corp. name changed to Syntech Diamond Films Inc. 06/26/1991 which merged into Structured Biologicals Inc. 07/27/1993 which recapitalized as Ben-Abraham Technologies Inc. 12/06/1996 which name changed to BioSante Pharmaceuticals, Inc. (WY) 12/17/1999 which reincorporated in Delaware 06/26/2001 which recapitalized as

ANI Pharmaceuticals, Inc.
07/18/2013

LA CHOY FOOD PRODUCTS, INC.
Acquired by Beatrice Creamery Co.
00/00/1943
Details not available

LA CIEBA MINERALS CORP (BC)
Reincorporated under the laws of
Canada as Lowell Petroleum Inc.
09/26/1995
Lowell Petroleum Inc. recapitalized as
Hedong Energy, Inc. 08/17/1998
which recapitalized as Benchmark
Energy Corp. 02/09/2004 which
name changed to Bolivar Energy
Corp. (Canada) 10/29/2010 which
reorganized in Alberta as Anatolia
Energy Corp. 12/13/2011 which
merged into Cub Energy Inc.
07/01/2013

LA CO INC (DE)
Charter cancelled and declared
inoperative and void for
non-payment of taxes 4/15/73

LA COMPAGNIE FONCIERE DU MANITOBA (1967) LTEE. (MB)
Merged into CIIT Inc. 10/01/1983
Each share Common no par
exchanged for (8.5) shares Common
no par
(See CIIT Inc.)

LA COMPAGNIE FONCIERE DU MANITOBA LTEE. (MB)
Merged into La Compagnie Fonciere
du Manitoba (1967) Ltee.
12/28/1967
Each share Common $75 par
exchanged for (1) share Common
no par
La Compagnie Fonciere du Manitoba
(1967) Ltee. merged into CIIT Inc.
10/01/1983
(See CIIT Inc.)

LA CORPORATION DES PRODUITS LATIERS LAURENTIDE (QC)
Bankrupt in 1955

LA CORTEZ ENTERPRISES INC (NV)
Name changed to La Cortez Energy,
Inc. 02/21/2008

LA COSTA CORP (NV)
Name changed to Alto Casino Corp.
05/20/1989
(See Alto Casino Corp.)

LA CREMERIE DE WEEDON LTEE. (QC)
Charter annulled for failure to file
annual reports 9/2/78

LA CROSSE COOLER CO. (WI)
Name changed to La Crosse Cooler
Holding Corp. 1/4/78

LA CROSSE DREDGING CO (DE)
Preferred $100 par called for
redemption 08/01/1976
Public interest eliminated

LA CROSSE PLOW CO.
Acquired by Allis-Chalmers
Manufacturing Co. in 1929
Details not available

LA CROSSE RUBR MLS CO (WI)
Acquired by LaCrosse Products, Inc.
5/1/82
Each share Common $5 par
exchanged for $10.08 cash

LA CROSSE TEL CORP (WI)
Each share Common $50 par
exchanged for (5) shares Common
$10 par 00/00/1941
Common $10 par split (11) for (10) by
issuance of (0.1) additional share
10/01/1958
99.78% held by Century Telephone
Enterprises, Inc. as of 05/17/1979
Public interest eliminated

LA CUMBRE SVGS BK (SANTA BARBARA, CA)
Merged into First Banks Inc. 9/1/95

Each share Common $10 par
exchanged for $8.75 cash

LA DELITE LTD (NY)
Stock Dividend - In Common to
holders of Conv. Preferred Ser. A
25% 07/21/1986
Chapter 11 Federal Bankruptcy Code
converted to Chapter 7 on
03/17/1989
Stockholders' equity unlikely

LA FONDERIE DE L'ISLET LTEE. (QC)
Adjudicated bankrupt 4/5/67
No stockholders' equity

LA FORTUNA MINING & MILLING CO. (TX)
Charter forfeited for failure to pay
taxes 5/19/50

LA FRANCE GOLD MINES, LTD. (ON)
Charter cancelled in May 1958

LA FRANCE INDUSTRIES, INC. (DE)
Name changed to L.F.I. Corp.
10/15/1959
L.F.I. Corp. name changed to Gerli &
Co., Inc. 08/01/1960
(See Gerli & Co., Inc.)

LA FRANCE INDUSTRIES (PA)
Each share Common $1 par received
distribution of (1.5) shares La
France Industries, Inc. (DE)
Common $1 par 01/21/1952
Merged into La France Industries, Inc.
(DE) 02/00/1952
Each share Common $1 par
exchanged for (1) share Common
$1 par
La France Industries, Inc. (DE) name
changed to L.F.I. Corp. 10/15/1959
which name changed to Gerli & Co.,
Inc. 08/01/1960
(See Gerli & Co., Inc.)

LA FRANCE-REPUBLIC CORP.
Out of existence 00/00/1939
Details not available

LA FRANCE TEXTILE INDUSTRIES (PA)
Name changed to La France
Industries (PA) 00/00/1929
La France Industries (PA) merged into
La France Industries, Inc. (DE)
02/00/1952 which name changed to
L.F.I. Corp. 10/15/1959 which name
changed to Gerli & Co., Inc.
08/01/1960
(See Gerli & Co., Inc.)

LA GRANGE ST BK (LA GRANGE, IL)
Common $25 par changed to $12.50
par and (1) additional share issued
01/17/1977
Stock Dividends - 50% 01/14/1969;
33-1/3% 01/08/1973; 25%
01/13/1975; 25% 02/12/1979
Under plan of reorganization each
share Common $12.50 par
automatically became (1) share First
Burlington Corp. Common $12.50
par 03/31/1982
(See First Burlington Corp.)

LA GRANGE ST BK (LA GRANGE, TX)
Merged into Premier Bancshares Inc.
6/21/96
Each share Common $10 par
exchanged for $75 cash

LA GUARDIA EAST SIRE PLAN HOTEL, INC. (NY)
Company declared insolvent in 1964
No stockholders' equity

LA GUARDIA HOTEL SIRE PLAN INC. (NY)
Company declared insolvent in 1964
No stockholders' equity

LA INVT ASSOCS INC (NV)
Name changed to World Associates
Inc. 9/28/2000

LA JOLLA BANCORP (CA)
Merged into Security Pacific Corp.
8/23/90
Each share Capital Stock no par
exchanged for (0.392157) share
Common $10 par
Security Pacific Corp. merged into
BankAmerica Corp. (Old) 4/22/92
which merged into BankAmerica
Corp. (New) 9/30/98 which name
changed to Bank of America Corp.
4/28/99

LA JOLLA BANK & TRUST CO. (LA JOLLA, CA)
Capital Stock $10 par changed to $5
par 5/14/75
Capital Stock $5 par changed to $2
par 1/2/79
Capital Stock $2 par changed to no
par and (0.6644) additional share
issued 7/16/81
Reorganized as La Jolla Bancorp
7/31/82
Each share Capital Stock no par
exchanged for (1) share Capital
Stock no par
La Jolla Bancorp merged into Security
Pacific Corp. 8/23/90 which merged
into BankAmerica Corp. (Old)
4/22/92 which merged into
BankAmerica Corp. (New) 9/30/98
which name changed to Bank of
America Corp. 4/28/99

LA JOLLA CAP INC (UT)
Involuntarily dissolved 05/01/1994

LA JOLLA DIAGNOSTICS INC (CA)
Name changed to NatureWell, Inc.
(CA) 01/04/2001
NatureWell, Inc. (CA) reincorporated
in Delaware 10/25/2001 which
recapitalized as Brazil Interactive
Media, Inc. 05/30/2013 which name
changed to American Cannabis Co.,
Inc. 10/10/2014

LA JOLLA FRESH SQUEEZED COFFEE CO INC (WA)
Name changed 06/21/1999
Name changed from La Jolla Coffee
Co. Inc. to La Jolla Fresh Squeezed
Coffee Co. Inc. 06/21/1999
Reincorporated under the laws of
Delaware as Javo Beverage Co.,
Inc. 08/21/2002
(See Javo Beverage Co., Inc.)

LA JOLLA PHARMACEUTICAL CO (DE)
Issue Information - 2,600,000 UNITS
consisting of (1) share COM and (1)
WT offered at $5 per Unit on
06/03/1994
Each share old Common 1¢ par
exchanged for (0.2) share new
Common 1¢ par 12/22/2005
Each share new Common 1¢ par
exchanged for (0.01) share old
Common $0.0001 par 04/15/2011
Each share old Common $0.0001 par
exchanged for (0.01) share new
Common $0.0001 par 02/17/2012
Reincorporated under the laws of
California 06/07/2012

LA LASINE INTERNATIONAL, INC.
Bankrupt in 1933

LA LUZ MINES LTD (ON)
Merged into Barrick Resources Corp.
7/26/85
Each share Capital Stock no par
exchanged for (0.5) share Common
no par
Barrick Resources Corp. recapitalized
as American Barrick Resources
Corp. 12/6/85 which name changed
to Barrick Gold Corp. 1/18/95

LA MAN CORP (NV)
Each share old Common $0.001 par
exchanged for (0.33333333) share
new Common $0.001 par
10/28/1992
Stock Dividend - 5% payable
08/07/1996 to holders of record
07/26/1996; 5% payable 12/01/1997
to holders of record 11/14/1997
Name changed to Display
Technologies Inc. 11/02/1998
(See Display Technologies Inc.)

LA MANCHA RES INC (BC)
Acquired by Weather Investments II
SARL 11/12/2012
Each share Common no par
exchanged for $3.50 cash

LA MAR TECHNOLOGY INC (DE)
Charter cancelled and declared
inoperative and void for
non-payment of taxes 3/1/74

LA MAUR INC (MN)
Common 10¢ par changed to
$0.06666666 par and (0.5)
additional share issued 05/07/1964
Common $0.06666666 par changed
to $0.03333333 par and (1)
additional share issued 05/06/1968
Common $0.03333333 par split (5) for
(4) by issuance of (0.25) additional
share 06/16/1982
Stock Dividend - 20% 06/17/1981
Name changed to Lamaur, Inc.
04/26/1983
(See Lamaur, Inc.)

LA MED TECH INC (UT)
Name changed to Entertainment
Concepts International 00/00/1987
Entertainment Concepts International
name changed to Lord & Lazarus,
Inc. 00/00/1988 which name
changed to Utility Communications
International, Inc. 00/00/1996 which
reorganized as Intermost Corp. (UT)
11/10/1998 which reincorporated in
Wyoming 02/25/2003 which name
changed to Uni Core Holdings Corp.
01/29/2010

LA MIRADA SAVINGS & LOAN ASSOCIATION (CA)
Acquired by United Financial Corp. of
California 7/15/69
Each share Guarantee Stock $10 par
exchanged for (2/3) share Capital
Stock $1 par
(See United Financial Corp. of California)

LA PALME PORCUPINE MINES LTD.
Succeeded by Pamour Porcupine
Mines Ltd. 00/00/1934
Each share Capital Stock exchanged
for (0.11627906) share Capital Stock
no par
Pamour Porcupine Mines Ltd. name
changed to Pamour Inc. 07/11/1986
which merged into Royal Oak Mines
Inc. 07/23/1991 which recapitalized
as Royal Oak Ventures Inc.
02/14/2000
(See Royal Oak Ventures Inc.)

LA PETITE ACADEMY INC (DE)
Common 10¢ par split (2) for (1) by
issuance of (1) additional share
9/12/84
Common 10¢ par split (4) for (3) by
issuance of (1/3) additional share
3/19/85
Common 10¢ par split (4) for (3) by
issuance of (1/3) additional share
9/12/86
Stock Dividend - 25% 1/31/86
Shares reacquired 7/23/93
Each share Common 10¢ par
exchanged for $10 cash

LA PLACE BANCSHARES INC (LA)
Merged into Union Planters Corp.
12/31/98
Each share Common $1 par
exchanged for (2.97) shares
Common $5 par
Union Planters Corp. merged into
Regions Financial Corp. (New)
7/1/2004

LA PLANT CHOATE MANUFACTURING CO., INC. (DE)
Merged into Allis-Chalmers
Manufacturing Co. 00/00/1952

Each share Common $5 par exchanged for (0.2) share Common no par
Allis-Chalmers Manufacturing Co. name changed to Allis-Chalmers Corp. 05/28/1971 which name changed to Allis-Chalmers Energy, Inc. 01/01/2005
(See Allis-Chalmers Energy, Inc.)

LA PLATA GOLD CORP (BC)
Name changed to Alphamin Resources Corp. (BC) 10/27/2008
Alphamin Resources Corp. (BC) reincorporated in Mauritius 09/30/2014

LA PLATE OIL & MINING, INC. (UT)
Name changed to Gold Coast Resources (UT) 10/1/82
Gold Coast Resources (UT) reincorporated in Nevada 12/23/96 which recapitalized as Global Datatel Inc. 12/2/98 which name changed to Cana Petroleum Corp. 8/30/2006 which name changed to XCana Petroleum Corp. 5/22/2007

LA POINTE INDS INC (CT)
Name changed 01/01/1957
Name changed from La Pointe Electronics, Inc. to La Pointe Industries, Inc. 01/01/1957
Each (75) shares old Common $1 par exchanged for (1) share new Common $1 par 02/07/1990
Name changed to Titan International Inc. (CT) 03/29/1996
Titan International Inc. (CT) reorganized in Utah as Enrol Corp. 07/18/1997 which name changed to E-Power International Inc. 01/22/2001 which recapitalized as Integrated Services Group Inc. 01/29/2003
(See Integrated Services Group Inc.)

LA POINTE-PLASCOMOLD CORP. (CT)
Each share Common $5 par exchanged for (3) shares Common $1 par 00/00/1949
Name changed to La Pointe Electronics, Inc. 00/00/1953
La Pointe Electronics, Inc. name changed to La Pointe Industries, Inc. 01/01/1957 which name changed to Titan International Inc. (CT) 03/29/1996 which reorganized in Utah as Enrol Corp. 07/18/1997 which name changed to E-Power International Inc. 01/22/2001 which recapitalized as Integrated Services Group Inc. 01/29/2003
(See Integrated Services Group Inc.)

LA PORTE CORP. (IL)
Involuntarily dissolved in the Superior Court of Cook County, IL 12/13/1954
Stockholders' equity unlikely

LA PORTE RUBBER CO. (DE)
Charter cancelled for failure to pay taxes in 1932

LA PORTE STATE BANK (LA PORTE, TX)
Acquired by First City Bancorporation of Texas, Inc. (TX) 09/26/1972
Each share Common $10 par exchanged for (1.375) shares Common $10 par
(See First City Bancorporation of Texas, Inc. (TX))

LA QUINTA CORP (DE)
Note: Issued and transferred only in Non-Separable Units of (1) share La Quinta Corp. Common 10¢ par and (1) share La Quinta Properties, Inc. Class B Common 10¢ par
Acquired by Blackstone Group 1/25/2006
Each Paired Certificate 10¢ par exchanged for $11.25 cash

LA QUINTA HLDGS INC (DE)
Each share Common 1¢ par exchanged for (0.5) share Common 2¢ par 05/30/2018
Each share Common 2¢ par received distribution of (1) share CorePoint Lodging Inc. Common 1¢ par payable 05/30/2018 to holders of record 05/30/2018
Acquired by Wyndham Worldwide Corp. 05/30/2018
Each share Common 2¢ par exchanged for $16.80 cash

LA QUINTA INNS INC (TX)
Reincorporated 10/12/1978
Name changed 05/27/1993
State of incorporation changed from (DE) to (TX) 10/12/1978
Common 10¢ par split (3) for (1) by issuance of (2) additional shares 11/17/1978
Common 10¢ par split (5) for (4) by issuance of (0.25) additional share 03/30/1981
Common 10¢ par split (4) for (3) by issuance of (1/3) additional share 02/08/1982
Stock Dividends - 10% 02/18/1977; 10% 02/20/1978; 10% 02/09/1979; 10% 02/08/1980
Common Stock Purchase Rights declared for Common stockholders of record 10/09/1990 were redeemed at $0.02 per right 09/20/1991 for holders of record 09/05/1991
Name changed from La Quinta Motor Inns, Inc. to La Quinta Inns, Inc. 05/27/1993
Common 10¢ par split (3) for (2) by issuance of (0.5) additional share 10/01/1993
Common 10¢ par split (3) for (2) by issuance of (0.5) additional share 03/15/1994
Common 10¢ par split (3) for (2) by issuance of (0.5) additional share 10/25/1994
Common 10¢ par split (3) for (2) by issuance of (0.5) additional share payable 07/15/1996 to holders of record 06/24/1996
Merged into Meditrust Corp. 07/17/1998
Each share Common 10¢ par exchanged for (0.738) Paired Certificate
Meditrust Corp. name changed to La Quinta Properties, Inc. 06/20/2001 which reorganized as La Quinta Corp. 01/02/2002
(See La Quinta Corp.)

LA QUINTA MTR INNS LTD PARTNERSHIP (DE)
Merged into LQI Acquisition Corp. 1/25/94
Each Depositary Unit exchanged for $13 cash

LA QUINTA PPTYS INC (DE)
Note: Issued and transferred only in Non-Separable Units of (1) share La Quinta Corp. Common 10¢ par and (1) share La Quinta Properties, Inc. Common 10¢ par
Reorganized as La Quinta Corp. 1/2/2002
Each Paired Certificate 10¢ par exchanged for (1) Paired Certificate 10¢ par
9% Depositary Preferred Ser. A called for redemption at $25 plus $0.275 accrued dividends on 2/12/2006
(See La Quinta Corp.)

LA QUINTA RES CORP (BC)
Each share old Common no par exchanged for (0.1) share new Common no par 05/28/2013
Recapitalized as Black Mammoth Metals Corp. 02/19/2016
Each share new Common no par exchanged for (0.25) share Common no par

LA REINA CORP (FL)
Merged into Dominion Development Corp. 01/01/1971
Each share Common 1¢ par exchanged for (0.033333) share Common 1¢ par
Dominion Development Corp. name changed to First Continental Oil & Gas Co. Inc. 05/10/1971 which merged into Continental Resources, International 07/31/1972
(See Continental Resources, International)

LA REINE MOLYBDENUM MINES, LTD.
Charter cancelled for failure to file reports in 1968

LA RINASCENTE S P A (ITALY)
ADR agreement terminated 02/07/2012
Each ADR for Ordinary exchanged for $20.255337 cash

LA ROCK MNG CORP (BC)
Recapitalized as Avola Industries Inc. 7/19/2001
Each share Common no par exchanged for (0.1) share Common no par
Avola Industries Inc. recapitalized as Auramex Resource Corp. 1/16/2003

LA RONCIERE GOLD MINES LTD. (ON)
Charter revoked for failure to file reports and pay fees 11/9/64

LA RONGE GOLD CORP (BC)
Name changed to Select Sands Corp. 11/14/2014

LA RONGE RES INC (AB)
Name changed to IAE Hong Kong Equities Inc. 01/04/1991
(See IAE Hong Kong Equities Inc.)

LA RONGE URANIUM MINES LTD. (ON)
Charter cancelled 12/9/70
Stock is valueless

LA ROSE ROUYN MINES, LTD.
Each share Capital Stock $1 par exchanged for (1) share Mastermet Cobalt Mines Ltd. Capital Stock $1 par and (1) share Capital Stock of New La Rose Mining & Smelting Ltd. Capital Stock $1 par in 1952
(See each company's listing)

LA SAL URANIUM CORP. (UT)
Merged into Resource Ventures Corp. 6/11/56
Each share Common 5¢ par exchanged for (0.04) share Common $1 par
Resource Ventures Corp. merged into Petroleum Resources Corp. 6/30/65 which name changed to PRC Corp. 11/9/70 which name changed to CorTerra Corp. 11/28/72 which assets were transferred to CorTerra Corp. Liquidating Corp. 10/8/80
(See CorTerra Corp. Liquidating Corp.)

LA SALLE CASUALTY CO. (IL)
Merged into La Salle National Insurance Co. 12/16/66
Each share Common $1 par exchanged for (0.62) share Common $1 par

LA SALLE COPPER CO.
Acquired by Calumet & Hecla Consolidated Copper Co. in 1936
Details not available

LA SALLE DEITCH INC (IN)
Stock Dividend - 100% 11/6/69
Merged into Magnavox Co. 2/18/71
Each share Common no par exchanged for (0.333333) share Common $1 par
(See Magnavox Co.)

LA SALLE INDUSTRIAL FINANCE CORP.
Merged into Wacker Corp. in 1944
Each share Class A exchanged for (0.6) share Class B Preferred and $7 in cash
Each share Common exchanged for (0.01) share Class B Preferred and $1.65 in cash
Wacker Corp. name changed to G.F.C. Corp. 9/29/49 which filed for dissolution 5/5/61

LA SALLE MADISON HOTEL CO (IL)
Completely liquidated 02/14/1972
Each share Common no par exchanged for first and final distribution of $50 cash

LA SALLE NATL BK (CHICAGO, IL)
Capital Stock $50 par changed to $25 par and (1) additional share issued 00/00/1951
Capital Stock $25 par changed to $10 par and (1.5) additional shares issued 01/30/1962
Capital Stock $10 par reclassified as Common $10 par 08/14/1967
5.75% Preferred $60 par called for redemption 11/08/1968
Stock Dividends - 20% 03/02/1959; 11-1/9% 03/09/1961; 10% 10/27/1964; 10% 01/24/1967
Through exchange offer 99% acquired by Algemene Bank Nederland N.V. as of 08/14/1979
Public interest eliminated

LA SALLE NATL INS CO (IL)
Declared insolvent and ordered into liquidation by Court 12/28/1971
No stockholders' equity

LA SALLE-PERU INDUSTRIAL CORP. (IL)
Involuntarily dissolved 9/5/67

LA SALLE STR CAP CORP (DE)
Reincorporated 09/29/1967
Partial liquidating distribution paid and each share Common $1 par received (0.25) share Wagner Industries, Inc. Common 50¢ par 06/30/1967
State of incorporation changed from (IL) to (DE) 09/29/1967
Common $1 par changed to 33-1/3¢ par and (2) additional shares issued 01/21/1969
Under plan of merger each share Common 33-1/3¢ par automatically became (1) share Atlanta/La Salle Corp. Common $1 par 11/01/1971
(See Atlanta/La Salle Corp.)

LA SALLE STR FDG CORP (CO)
Name changed to J.P. 2000 Corp. 3/1/90
(See J.P. 2000 Corp.)

LA SALLE STREET BUILDINGS, INC. (IL)
Liquidation completed
Each VTC for Capital Stock 1¢ par received initial distribution of $3.50 cash 10/7/55
Each VTC for Capital Stock 1¢ par exchanged for second and final distribution of $0.397 cash 5/1/56

LA SALLE TOWERS CORP. (IL)
Liquidation completed
Each share Common no par exchanged for initial distribution of $120 cash 3/25/66
Each share Common no par received second and final distribution of $9.50 cash 7/22/66

LA SALLE TOWERS LIQUIDATION TRUST
Trust terminated and property transferred to La Salle Towers Corp. in 1947
(See La Salle Towers Corp.)

LA SALLE WINES & CHAMPAGNE INC (MI)
Completely liquidated 01/08/1974
Each share Common $2 par exchanged for first and final distribution of $3.10 cash

LA SALLE YELLOWKNIFE GOLD MINES LTD. (ON)
Succeeded by Ormsby Mines Ltd. 00/00/1954
Each share Common exchanged for (0.1) share Common $1 par
Ormsby Mines Ltd. merged into Discovery Mines Ltd. (ON) 04/14/1964 which reincorporated in Canada 01/15/1982 which merged into Discovery West Corp. 03/01/1987
(See Discovery West Corp.)

LA SENZA CORP (CANADA)
Acquired by Limited Brands, Inc. 1/17/2007
Each share Subordinate no par exchanged for $48.25 cash

LA SOCIETE GENERALE DE FINANCEMENT DU QUEBEC (QC)
See - General Investment Corp. of Quebec

LA SOLUCION INC (DE)
Common $0.0001 par split (4.20168) for (1) by issuance of (3.20168) additional shares payable 12/20/2007 to holders of record 12/20/2007 Ex date - 12/21/2007
Name changed to ESYS Holdings, Inc. 01/14/2008
ESYS Holdings, Inc. name changed to PERF Go-Green Holdings, Inc. 05/09/2008

LA TEKO RES LTD (BC)
Merged into Kinross Gold Corp. 02/26/1999
Each share Common no par exchanged for (0.44444444) share Common no par

LA TOUR OIL CO. (DE)
Charter cancelled and for failure to pay taxes in 1931

LA TUQUE TELEPHONE CO.-LA CIE DE TELEPHONE DE LA TUQUE (QC)
Acquired by Bell Telephone Co. of Canada-La Compagnie de Telephone Bell du Canada 06/00/1967
Details not available

LA VERENDRYE MGMT CORP (QC)
Common no par split (3) for (1) by issuance of (2) additional shares 10/12/72
Common no par split (2) for (1) by issuance of (1) additional share 6/1/79
6% Preferred $8 par called for redemption 7/31/79
Common no par reclassified as Class A Common no par 1/8/81
Merged into Milihuit Inc. 3/21/91
Each share Class A Common no par exchanged for $1.60 cash
Each share Class B Common no par exchanged for $1.60 cash

LA Z BOY CHAIR CO (MI)
Capital Stock $1 par split (4) for (1) by issuance of (3) additional shares 9/14/87
Name changed to La-Z-Boy Inc. 8/30/96

LAACO INC (CA)
Reorganized as LAACO, Ltd. 12/30/1986
Each share Common $10 par exchanged for (1) Unit of Ltd. Partnership

LAAN-TEX OIL CORP. (DE)
Assets sold to New Idria Mining & Chemical Co. 7/20/56
Each share Common $1 par exchanged for (0.25) share Common 50¢ par
New Idria Mining & Chemical Co. name changed to New Idria, Inc. 11/5/75 which merged into Buckhorn Inc. (Del.) 12/22/81
(See Buckhorn Inc. (Del.))

LAAND CORP (NV)
Note: Although it was reported that this company changed its name to Geolectric Corp. in 1971, and stock certificates were issued under such name, the change in name was subsequently rescinded in that same year and the company is still known as Laand Corp.
Name changed to Digital Energy Corp. 12/2/81
(See Digital Energy Corp.)

LAB HLDGS INC (MO)
Common $1 par split (3) for (2) by issuance of (0.5) additional share payable 8/11/99 to holders of record 8/9/99
Under plan of merger name changed to LabOne, Inc. (New) and Common $1 par changed to 1¢ par 8/10/99
(See LabOne, Inc. (New))

LAB HLDGS INC (NV)
Name changed to Mountain Top Properties, Inc. 12/13/2006

LAB INTL INC (CANADA)
Name changed to Akela Pharma Inc. 07/13/2007
(See Akela Pharma Inc.)

LAB RESH INC (CANADA)
Assets sold for the benefit of creditors 04/27/2011
Stockholders' equity unlikely

LAB-VOLT SYS INC (NJ)
Acquired by Festo Didactic 06/20/2014
Each share Common $1 par exchanged for $21.33824945 cash

LABATT BREWERIES OF BRITISH COLUMBIA LTD. (CANADA)
Merged into Labatt Brewing Co. Ltd. 00/00/1979
Details not available

LABATT JOHN LTD (CANADA)
Common no par split (3) for (1) by issuance of (2) additional shares 10/12/1961
Common no par split (2) for (1) by issuance of (1) additional share 10/23/1967
Common no par reclassified as Conv. Class A Common no par 10/26/1973
Conv. Preferred Ser. A $18 par called for redemption 02/16/1980
Conv. Class A Common no par reclassified as Common no par 09/30/1983
Conv. Class B Common no par reclassified as Common no par 09/30/1983
Common no par split (2) for (1) by issuance of (1) additional share 10/04/1983
Common no par split (2) for (1) by issuance of (1) additional share 07/15/1986
Merged into Interbrew S.A./N.V. 07/27/1995
Each share Common no par exchanged for $28.50 cash

LABCO PHARMACEUTICALS CORP (NV)
Each share old Common $0.001 par exchanged for (0.01) share new Common $0.001 par 04/15/1998
Each share new Common $0.001 par exchanged for (0.1) share new Common $0.001 par 10/10/1999
Recapitalized as Checkpoint Genetics Pharmaceuticals Inc. 08/15/2000
Each share new Common $0.001 par exchanged for (0.05) share Common $0.001 par
Checkpoint Genetics Pharmaceuticals Inc. recapitalized as InterNatural Pharmaceuticals, Inc. 07/13/2001

LABE FED BK FOR SVGS (CHICAGO, IL)
Name changed 4/27/94
Name changed from Labe Federal Savings & Loan Association to Labe Federal Bank for Savings (Chicago, IL) 4/27/94
Under plan of reorganization each share Common $1 par automatically became (1) share LDF, Inc. Common $1 par 11/6/97
(See LDF, Inc.)

LABEL DEPOT CORP (AB)
Name changed to LDC Ventures Inc. 09/20/2001
LDC Ventures Inc. recapitalized as Mint Technology Corp. 01/22/2004 which recapitalized as Mint Corp. 08/12/2013

LABELLE AIR TRANSN CO (MN)
Became insolvent and went out of business 1/31/75

LABINE-MCCARTHY URANIUM MINES LTD. (ON)
Charter revoked for failure to file reports and pay fees 11/30/64

LABMAHON PORCUPINE GOLD MINES LTD.
Name changed to McBine Porcupine Gold Mines Ltd. 00/00/1937
(See McBine Porcupine Gold Mines Ltd.)

LABMIN RES LTD (NL)
Merged into Hollinger Inc. 09/17/1985
Each share Common no par exchanged for (3.5) shares Common no par
(See Hollinger Inc.)

LABONE INC NEW (MO)
Acquired by Quest Diagnostics Inc. 11/1/2005
Each share Common 1¢ par exchanged for $43.90 cash

LABONE INC OLD (DE)
Merged into LabOne, Inc. (New) 8/10/99
Each share Common 1¢ par exchanged for (1) share Common 1¢ par
(See LabOne, Inc. (New))

LABOPHARM INC (QC)
Acquired by Paladin Labs Inc. 10/07/2011
Each share Common no par exchanged for $0.2857 cash
Note: Unexchanged certificates were cancelled and became without value 10/07/2017

LABOR LYCEUM LOAN ASS'N, INC. (CT)
Charter expired by time limitation 9/10/60

LABOR READY INC (WA)
Each share old Common no par exchanged for (0.1) share new Common no par 01/15/1993
New Common no par split (3) for (2) by issuance of (0.5) additional share 11/28/1995
New Common no par split (3) for (2) by issuance of (0.5) additional share payable 08/09/1996 to holders of record 07/31/1996
New Common no par split (3) for (2) by issuance of (0.5) additional share payable 10/31/1997 to holders of record 10/24/1997
New Common no par split (3) for (2) by issuance of (0.5) additional share payable 06/09/1998 to holders of record 05/29/1998
New Common no par split (3) for (2) by issuance of (0.5) additional share payable 07/12/1999 to holders of record 06/24/1999 Ex date - 07/13/1999
Name changed to TrueBlue, Inc. 12/18/2007

LABORATORIO CHILE S A (CHILE)
Issue Information - 1,825,000 SPONSORED ADR offered at $14.50 per ADR on 06/28/1994
99.9% acquired by IVAX Corp. at $25 per ADR through purchase offer which expired 09/13/2001
ADR agreement terminated 04/27/2007
Each Sponsored ADR for Ordinary no par exchanged for (20) Ordinary shares no par
Note: Unexchanged ADR's will be sold and proceeds, if any, held for claim after 04/26/2008

LABORATORY CORP AMER HLDGS INC (DE)
Stock Dividends - in 8.50% Pay-In-Kind Conv. Preferred Ser. B to holders of 8.50% Pay-In-Kind Conv. Preferred Ser. B 0.02125% payable 9/30/98 to holders of record 9/21/98; 0.02125% payable 9/30/99 to holders of record 9/17/99; 0.02125% payable 12/31/99 to holders of record 12/17/99
8.50% Conv. Exchangeable Preferred Ser. A 1¢ par called for redemption at $52.83 on 7/7/2000
8.50% Pay-in Kind Conv. Preferred Ser. B 1¢ par called for redemption at $52.83 on 7/7/2000
(Additional Information in Active)

LABORATORY DATA CTL INC (DE)
Merged into Milton Roy Co. 02/23/1972
Each share Common 1¢ par exchanged for (0.199531) share Common $1 par
(See Milton Roy Co.)

LABORATORY ELECTRS INC (DE)
Common $1 par split (2) for (1) by issuance of (1) additional share 00/00/1954
Name changed to LFE Corp. 11/03/1969
(See LFE Corp.)

LABORATORY OF ELECTRONIC ENGINEERING, INC. (MD)
Out of business in July 1962
No stockholders' equity

LABORATORY PROCEDURES INC. (CA)
Completely liquidated 6/16/67
Each share Common 1¢ par exchanged for first and final distribution of (0.052173) share Upjohn Co. (DE) Common $1 par
Upjohn Co. (DE) merged into Pharmacia & Upjohn, Inc. 11/2/95 which merged into Pharmacia Corp. 3/31/2000 which merged into Pfizer Inc. 4/16/2003

LABORATORY PRODUCTS CO.
Name changed to S.M.A. Corp. 00/00/1930
S.M.A. Corp. merged into American Home Products Corp. 07/23/1938 which name changed to Wyeth 03/11/2002 which was acquired by Pfizer Inc. 10/15/2009

LABORATORY SPECIALISTS AMER INC (OK)
Merged into Kroll O'Gara Co. 12/11/1998
Each share Common $0.001 par exchanged for (0.2102) share Common 1¢ par
Kroll O'Gara Co. name changed to Kroll Inc. (OH) 08/23/2001 which reincorporated in Delaware 07/02/2002
(See Kroll Inc.)

LABRADOR ACCEP CORP (QC)
Name changed 10/15/65
$1.40 Conv. Preferred $25 par called for redemption 4/14/65
Name changed from Labrador Acceptance Corp. to Labrador Acceptance Corp. - La Societe De Financemment Labrador Inc. and $1.50 Preferred reclassified as 1st Preferred Ser. A $25 par and Class A $5 par and Class B $1 par changed to no par 10/15/65
Adjudicated bankrupt 1/22/69

LABRADOR INTL MNG LTD (BC)
Recapitalized as Royal International Venture Corp. 3/18/99
Each share Common no par exchanged for (0.2) share Common no par
Royal International Venture Corp. recapitalized as RCOM Venture Corp. 7/28/2000 which name changed to Wellstar Energy Corp. 7/21/2005

LABRADOR IRON ORE ROYALTY INCOME FD (ON)
Reorganized under the laws of Canada as Labrador Iron Ore Royalty Corp. 07/05/2010
Each Trust Unit no par exchanged for (1) Stapled Unit
Note: Unexchanged certificates were cancelled and became without value 07/05/2016

LABRADOR MNG & EXPL LTD (NL)
Under plan of reorganization each share Capital Stock $1 par automatically became (1) share Labmin Resources Ltd. Common no par 07/06/1983
Labmin Resources Ltd. merged into Hollinger Inc. 09/17/1985
(See Hollinger Inc.)

LABRADOR UNGAVA EXPLORATIONS LTD. (QC)
Name changed to Little Tex Mining Corp. 8/28/64
Little Tex Mining Corp. charter cancelled 9/9/72

LABRANCHE & CO INC (DE)
Merged into Cowen Group, Inc. (New) 06/28/2011
Each share Common 1¢ par exchanged for (0.998) share Class A Common 1¢ par
Cowen Group, Inc. (New) name changed to Cowen Inc. 05/23/2017

LABSTYLE INNOVATIONS CORP (DE)
Each share old Common $0.0001 par exchanged for (0.2) share new Common $0.0001 par 10/06/2014
Each share new Common $0.0001 par exchanged again for (0.05555555) share new Common $0.0001 par 03/04/2016
Name changed to DarioHealth Corp. 07/28/2016

LABTEC INC (MA)
Each share old Common 1¢ par exchanged for (0.5) share new Common 1¢ par 12/1/99
Merged into Logitech International S.A. 3/23/2001
Each share new Common 1¢ par exchanged for (0.2644) Sponsored ADR for Ordinary Srf 20 par and $11 cash

LABTEST EQUIP CO (CA)
Merged into Systron-Donner Corp. 08/05/1971
Each share Common 10¢ par exchanged for (0.166666) share Capital Stock no par
(See Systron-Donner Corp.)

LABURNUM VENTURES INC (NV)
Name changed to AGR Tools, Inc. 09/29/2009

LABYRINTH RESOURCE CORP (BC)
Name changed to El Callao Mining Corp. 12/20/93
El Callao Mining Corp. merged into Crystallex International Corp. 8/19/2004

LAC CHEMICALS, INC.
Acquired by American-Marietta Co. 00/00/1947
Details not available

LAC D'OR MINES LTD.
Name changed to Yukore Mines Ltd. in 1951
Yukore Mines Ltd. merged into Continental Consolidated Mines & Oils Co. Ltd. 10/4/57
(See Consolidated Mines & Oils Co. Ltd.)

LAC DE RENZY NICKEL LTD. (ON)
Merged into Delahey Consolidated Nickel Mines Ltd. 04/10/1957
Each (3.4) shares Capital Stock no par exchanged for (1) share Common no par
Delahey Consolidated Nickel Mines Ltd. merged into Hoffman Exploration & Minerals Ltd. 06/29/1981 which merged into Consolidated Thompson-Lundmark Gold Mines Ltd. 01/16/1986 which name changed to Consolidated Thompson Iron Mines Ltd. 08/24/2006
(See Consolidated Thompson Iron Mines Ltd.)

LAC MINERALS LTD NEW (ON)
Common no par split (3) for (1) by issuance of (2) additional shares 09/18/1987
Acquired by American Barrick Resources Corp. 10/17/1994
Each share Common no par exchanged for (0.487) share Common no par
American Barrick Resources Corp. name changed to Barrick Gold Corp. 01/18/1995

LAC MINERALS LTD OLD (ON)
Merged into LAC Minerals Ltd. (New) 07/29/1985
Each share Common no par exchanged for (1) share Common no par
LAC Minerals Ltd. (New) acquired by American Barrick Resources Corp. 10/17/1994 which name changed to Barrick Gold Corp. 01/18/1995

LACAL OIL CORP. (UT)
Proclaimed dissolved for failure to pay taxes 11/9/74

LACANA MNG CORP (ON)
Deposit Receipts not exchanged for Common no par 10/23/87
Note: Unexchanged Receipts were sold and proceeds distributed after 4/11/88
Merged into Corona Corp. 7/1/88
Each share Common no par exchanged for (1.32) shares Class A Subordinate no par
Corona Corp. recapitalized as International Corona Corp. 6/11/91
(See International Corona Corp.)

LACANEX MNG LTD (ON)
Merged into Lacana Mining Corp. 09/29/1975
Each share Common no par exchanged for (0.3) share Common no par
Lacana Mining Corp. merged into Corona Corp. 07/01/1988 which recapitalized as International Corona Corp. 06/11/1991
(See International Corona Corp.)

LACHANCE MINES LTD. (QC)
Voluntarily dissolved 5/20/72
Details not available

LACHIB DEV CORP (ON)
Name changed to Syntech Diamond Films Inc. 06/26/1991
Syntech Diamond Films Inc. merged into Structured Biologicals Inc. 07/27/1993 which recapitalized as Ben-Abraham Technologies Inc. 12/06/1996 which name changed to BioSante Pharmaceuticals, Inc. (WY) 12/17/1999 which reincorporated in Delaware 06/26/2001 which recapitalized as ANI Pharmaceuticals, Inc. 07/18/2013

LACKAWANNA & MONTROSE RAILROAD
Absorbed by Delaware, Lackawanna & Western Railroad Co. in 1927
Delaware, Lackawanna & Western Railroad Co. merged into Erie-Lackawanna Railroad Co. 10/17/60 which merged into Dereco, Inc. 4/1/68
(See Dereco, Inc.)

LACKAWANNA & WYOMING VALLEY RAILROAD (PA)
Reorganized as Lackawanna & Wyoming Valley Railway Co. (Del.) 2/23/60
Stockholders' had no equity

LACKAWANNA OIL CORP. (OK)
Charter revoked for failure to file reports and pay fees 12/15/30

LACKAWANNA RAILROAD CO. OF N.J.
Merged into Delaware, Lackawanna & Western Railroad Co. in 1945
Capital Stock received 75% in 4% Series A Bonds and 25% in Series B Bonds

LACKAWANNA SECURITIES CO.
Dissolved in 1932

LACLEDE GAS & ELECTRIC CO.
Liquidated in 1929

LACLEDE GAS CO (MO)
4.32% Conv. Preferred Ser. A $25 par called for redemption 04/15/1966
Common $4 par changed to $2 par and (1) additional share issued 03/07/1984
Common $2 par changed to $1 par and (1) additional share issued 03/07/1994
Stock Dividend - 10% 06/05/1963
Reorganized as Laclede Group, Inc. 10/01/2001
Each share Common $1 par exchanged for (1) share Common $1 par
4.56% Preferred Ser. C $25 par called for redemption at $25 on 03/31/2009
5% Preferred Ser. B $25 par called for redemption at $25 on 03/31/2009
Laclede Group, Inc. name changed to Spire Inc. 04/29/2016

LACLEDE GAS LIGHT CO.
Name changed to Laclede Gas Co. 00/00/1950
Laclede Gas Co. reorganized as Laclede Group, Inc. 10/01/2001 which name changed to Spire Inc. 04/29/2016

LACLEDE GROUP INC (MO)
Name changed to Spire Inc. 04/29/2016

LACLEDE PACKING CO.
Acquired by Mickelberry's Food Products Co. 00/00/1945
Details not available

LACLEDE POWER & LIGHT CO.
Properties sold in 1945

LACLEDE STL CO (DE)
Reincorporated 3/31/69
Each share Common $100 par exchanged for (5) shares Common $20 par in 1929
State of incorporation changed from (MO) to (DE) 3/31/69
Old Common $20 par split (4) for (1) by issuance of (3) additional shares 8/23/74
Old Common $20 par changed to $13.33 par and (0.5) additional share issued 10/21/88
Stock Dividend - 100% 9/29/72
Plan of reorganization under Chapter 11 Federal Bankruptcy Code effective 12/29/2000
No stockholders' equity for old Common
Plan of reorganization under Chapter 11 Federal Bankruptcy Code effective 5/31/2005
No stockholders' equity for new Common

LACO MINES LTD. (ON)
Acquired by Oklend Gold Mines Ltd. in 1960
Each share Capital Stock $1 par exchanged for (1/6) share Capital Stock no par
Oklend Gold Mines Ltd. charter revoked 11/16/67

LACO RES INC (BC)
Recapitalized as International Laco Resources Inc. 9/1/82
Each share Capital Stock no par exchanged for (0.2) share Capital Stock no par
International Laco Resources Inc. merged into Aurex Resources Inc. 7/11/85 which merged into Galveston Resources Ltd. 7/29/86 which merged into Corona Corp. 7/1/88 which recapitalized as International Corona Corp. 6/11/91
(See International Corona Corp.)

LACOCK JOLLY OIL CO. (PA)
Liquidation completed
Each share Capital Stock $25 par exchanged for initial distribution of $30 cash 3/15/75
Each share Capital Stock $25 par received second distribution of $30 cash 1/16/76
Each share Capital Stock $25 par received third and final distribution of $0.86 cash 12/29/76

LACOMA GOLD MINE LTD.
Assets acquired by New Barber-Larder Mines Ltd. on a (1) for (20) basis in 1943

LACONIA WATER CO. (NH)
Liquidation completed 12/23/59

LACOP CORP (PA)
Name changed to Life of Pennsylvania Financial Corp. 04/26/1972
(See Life of Pennsylvania Financial Corp.)

LACORNE LITHIUM MINES LTD. (ON)
Charter surrendered 2/17/58

LACOTAH OIL & GAS CO. (DE)
Charter cancelled and declared inoperative and void for non-payment of taxes 3/16/21

LACROIX INC (QC)
Acquired by Russel (Hugh) Ltd. 04/01/1976
Each share Common no par exchanged for $8.50 cash

LACROSSE FOOTWEAR INC (WI)
Acquired by ABC-Mart, Inc. 08/16/2012
Each share Common 1¢ par exchanged for $20 cash

LACY SALES INST INC (MA)
Recapitalized as American International Health Services, Inc. 06/30/1980
Each share Common 5¢ par received (0.05) share Common 1¢ par
Note: Certificates were not required to be surrendered and are without value
American International Health Services, Inc. recapitalized as PHC, Inc. 11/24/1992 which merged into Acadia Healthcare Co., Inc. 11/01/2011

LADA DEV LTD (BC)
Struck off register 02/04/1983

LADBROKE GROUP PLC (ENGLAND & WALES)
Each Unsponsored ADR for Ordinary exchanged for (1) Sponsored ADR for Ordinary 05/22/1998
Stock Dividends - 100% 07/02/1981; 100% 07/31/1989

Name changed to Hilton Group PLC 05/14/1999
Hilton Group PLC recapitalized as Ladbrokes PLC 04/17/2006 which name changed to Ladbrokes Coral Group PLC 11/03/2016
(See Ladbrokes Coral Group PLC)

LADBROKES CORAL GROUP PLC (ENGLAND & WALES)
Name changed 11/03/2016
Name changed from Ladbrokes PLC to Ladbrokes Coral Group PLC 11/03/2016
ADR agreement terminated 04/23/2018
Each Sponsored ADR for Ordinary exchanged for $2.196885 cash

LADCO CORP (NV)
Adjudicated bankrupt 00/00/1969
No stockholders' equity

LADD ENTERPRISES INC (NV)
Reincorporated 09/15/1972
Name changed 08/10/1973
Name changed from Ladd Mountain Mining Co. of Nevada to Ladd Mountain Mining Co. and state of incorporation changed from (SD) to (NV) 09/15/1972
Name changed from Ladd Mountain Mining Co. to Ladd Enterprises, Inc. 08/10/1973
Company believed out of business 00/00/1989
Details not available

LADD FURNITURE INC (NC)
Common 10¢ par split (4) for (3) by issuance of (1/3) additional share 1/10/86
Common 10¢ par split (2) for (1) by issuance of (1) additional share 9/26/86
Each share Common 10¢ par exchanged for (1/3) share Common 30¢ par 5/16/95
Merged into La-Z-Boy Inc. 1/29/2000
Each share Common 30¢ par exchanged for (1.18) shares Common $1 par

LADD PETE CORP (DE)
Merged into Utah International Inc. 11/30/1973
Each share Common 10¢ par exchanged for (0.25) share Common $2 par
Utah International Inc. merged into General Electric Co. 12/20/1976

LADDIE GOLD MINES LTD (ON)
Merged into Goldquest Exploration Inc. 08/09/1982
Each share Capital Stock $1 par exchanged for (0.06570302) share Common no par
Goldquest Exploration Inc. merged into Goldcorp Inc. (New) 03/31/1994

LADERA VENTURES CORP (BC)
Recapitalized as MedMen Enterprises Inc. 05/29/2018
Each share Common no par exchanged for (0.10796454) share Class B Subordinate no par

LADISH INC (WI)
Each share old Common no par exchanged for (0.16666666) share new Common 1¢ par 12/12/1997
Merged into Allegheny Technologies Inc. 05/10/2011
Each share new Common 1¢ par exchanged for (0.4556) share Common 10¢ par and $24 cash

LADORIC MINES LTD. (DE)
No longer in existence having become inoperative and void for non-payment of taxes 4/1/58

LADUBORO ENTERPRISES LTD (QC)
Name changed 05/12/1965
Name changed 07/04/1985
Name changed from Laduboro Oil Ltd. to Laduboro Oil Ltd.-Les Petroles Laduboro Ltee. 05/12/1965

Capital Stock $1 par changed to no par 12/28/1984
Name changed from Laduboro Oil Ltd.-Les Petroles Laduboro Ltee. to Laduboro Enterprises Ltd.-Les Entreprises Laduboro Ltee. 07/04/1985
Recapitalized as Laduboro Ltd. 06/02/1987
Each share Capital Stock no par exchanged for (0.2) share Class A Common no par
Laduboro Ltd. reorganized as Monterey Capital Inc. 11/30/1989 which merged into Nymox Pharmaceutical Corp. (Canada) 12/18/1995 which reincorporated in Bahamas 11/20/2015

LADUBORO LTD (QC)
Reorganized as Monterey Capital Inc. 11/30/1989
Each share Class A Common no par exchanged for (1) share Class A Common no par
Monterey Capital Inc. merged into Nymox Pharmaceutical Corp. (Canada) 12/18/1995 which reincorporated in Bahamas 11/20/2015

LADULAMA GOLD MINES LTD. (ON)
Recapitalized as Nudulama Mines Ltd. on a (1) for (2) basis 00/00/1953
Nudulama Mines Ltd. recapitalized as Anglo Dominion Gold Exploration Ltd. 03/06/1979 which merged into QSR Ltd. 09/07/1993 which name changed to Coniagas Resources Ltd. 06/25/1999 which name changed to Lithium One Inc. 07/23/2009
(See Lithium One Inc.)

LADY BALTIMORE FOODS INC (KS)
Class A Common $1 par changed to 50¢ par and (1) additional share issued 11/17/1992
Plan of reorganization under Chapter 11 Federal Bankruptcy proceedings confirmed 10/12/2006
No stockholders' equity

LADY GOLDIE BRACELET INC (NY)
Name changed to Trans National Marketing Industries Inc. 08/07/1972
(See Trans National Marketing Industries Inc.)

LADY JANE RES INC (UT)
Merged into First Midwest Financial Corp. 12/10/1982
Each (99) shares Common $0.001 par exchanged for (1) share Common $0.005 par
(See First Midwest Financial Corp.)

LADY LUCK GAMING CORP (DE)
Each share old Common $0.001 par exchanged for (0.16666666) share new Common $0.001 par 06/04/1998
Merged into Isle of Capri Casinos, Inc. 03/02/2000
Each share new Common $0.006 par exchanged for $12 cash

LADY ROBYN RES INC (BC)
Name changed to Sino Business Machines Inc. 11/23/87
(See Sino Business Machines Inc.)

LADY ROUYN MINES, LTD. (ON)
Charter cancelled for failure to file reports and pay taxes 6/1/59

LADYSMITH EXPLORATIONS LTD. (ON)
Charter cancelled and company declared dissolved for default in filing returns 12/30/70

LAFARGE CDA INC (CANADA)
Acquired by Lafarge S.A. 08/02/2006
Each share Exchangeable Preference no par exchanged for USD$85.26 cash

LAFARGE CDA LTD (BC)
Acquired by Canada Cement Lafarge Ltd. - Ciments Canada Lafarge Ltee. 08/03/1970
Each share 6% Conv. Preferred $10 par exchanged for (0.4) share Common no par
Each share Common $10 par exchanged for (0.4) share Common no par
Canada Cement Lafarge Ltd. - Ciments Canada Lafarge Ltee. name changed to Lafarge Canada Inc. 01/12/1988
(See Lafarge Canada Inc.)

LAFARGE CEM NORTH AMER LTD (BC)
Name changed to Lafarge Canada Ltd. and Class A $10 par reclassified as 6% Conv. Preferred $10 par 06/30/1969
(See Lafarge Canada Ltd.)

LAFARGE CEM QUE LTD (CANADA)
Merged into Canada Cement Lafarge Ltd. - Ciments Canada Lafarge Ltee. 05/31/1979
Each share Capital Stock no par exchanged for (2) shares Common no par
Canada Cement Lafarge Ltd. - Ciments Canada Lafarge Ltee. name changed to Lafarge Canada Inc. 01/12/1988
(See Lafarge Canada Inc.)

LAFARGE NORTH AMER INC (MD)
Name changed 09/01/2001
$2.44 Conv. Preferred $1 par called for redemption 09/18/1987
Name changed from Lafarge Corp. to Lafarge North America Inc. 09/01/2001
Acquired by Lafarge S.A. 05/16/2006
Each share Common $1 par exchanged for $85.50 cash

LAFARGE S A (FRANCE)
Name changed 05/02/1997
Name changed from Lafarge Coppee to Lafarge S.A. 05/02/1997
Each old Sponsored ADR for Ordinary exchanged for (0.25) new Sponsored ADR for Ordinary 07/23/2001
Basis changed from (1:3) to (1:4) 07/23/2001
ADR agreement terminated 08/15/2003
Each 144A Sponsored ADR for Common exchanged for approximately $89.54 cash
ADR agreement terminated 11/19/2015
Each new Sponsored ADR for Ordinary exchanged for $16.363 cash

LAFAYETTE ACADEMY INC (DE)
Merged into Lafayette United Corp. 07/01/1972
Each share Common 1¢ par exchanged for (2) shares Common 8¢ par

LAFAYETTE AMERN BK & TR CO (HAMDEN, CT)
Reorganized 02/23/1994
Under plan of reorganization each share Lafayette American Bancorp, Inc. Common $1 par automatically became (1) share Lafayette American Bank & Trust Co. (Hamden, CT) Common no par 02/23/1994
Each share old Common no par exchanged for (0.5) share new Common no par 06/01/1994
Merged into HUBCO, Inc. 07/01/1996
Each share new Common no par exchanged for (0.588) share Common no par
HUBCO, Inc. name changed to Hudson United Bancorp 04/21/1999 which merged into TD Banknorth Inc. 01/31/2006

(See TD Banknorth Inc.)

LAFAYETTE ASBESTOS CO. LTD. (QC)
Recapitalized as New Lafayette Asbestos Co. Ltd. on a (0.25) for (1) basis 7/11/55
New Lafayette Asbestos Co. Ltd. name was changed to North American Asbestos Co. Ltd. 3/2/57 which name changed to Bishop Resources International Exploration Inc. 9/30/93 which recapitalized as Caldera Resources Inc. 11/30/95

LAFAYETTE BANCORP INC (CT)
Merged into Constitution Bancorp of New England, Inc. 05/31/1988
Each share Common 10¢ par exchanged for (2.05) shares Common $1 par
Constitution Bancorp of New England, Inc. name changed to Lafayette American Bancorp, Inc. 05/21/1991 which reorganized as Lafayette American Bank & Trust Co. (Hamden, CT) 02/23/1994 which merged into HUBCO Inc. 07/01/1996 which name changed to Hudson United Bancorp 04/21/1999 which merged into TD Banknorth Inc. 01/31/2006
(See TD Banknorth Inc.)

LAFAYETTE BANCORPORATION (IN)
Common $5 par split (3) for (2) by issuance of (0.5) additional share payable 11/1/99 to holders of record 9/30/99
Stock Dividends - 10% payable 11/1/97 to holders of record 9/30/97; 10% payable 11/2/98 to holders of record 9/30/98; 10% payable 11/1/2000 to holders of record 10/2/2000 Ex date - 9/28/2000
Merged into First Merchants Corp. 4/2/2002
Each share Common $5 par exchanged for (1.11) shares Common no par

LAFAYETTE BANK & TRUST CO. (FAYETTEVILLE, NC)
Merged into Southern National Bank of North Carolina (Lumberton, N.C.) 4/1/77
Each share Common $3 par exchanged for $6.70 cash

LAFAYETTE BK & TR CO (BRIDGEPORT, CT)
Capital Stock $10 par changed to $5 par and (1) additional share issued 2/1/66
Capital Stock $5 par changed to $2.50 par and (1) additional share issued 10/19/77
Reorganized as Lafayette Bancorp, Inc. 9/24/84
Each share Capital Stock $2.50 par exchanged for (2) shares Common 10¢ par
Lafayette Bancorp, Inc. merged into Constitution Bancorp of New England, Inc. 5/31/88 which name changed to Lafayette American Bancorp, Inc. 5/21/91 which reorganized as Lafayette American Bank & Trust Co. (Hamden, CT) 2/23/94 which merged into HUBCO, Inc. 7/1/96 which name changed to Hudson United Bancorp 4/21/99 which merged into TD Banknorth Inc. 1/31/2006
(See TD Banknorth Inc.)

LAFAYETTE CMNTY BANCORP (IN)
Merged into Horizon Bancorp 09/01/2017
Each share Common no par exchanged for (0.5878) share Common no par and $1.73 cash
Note: Holders of (99) or fewer shares received $17.25 cash
Horizon Bancorp name changed to Horizon Bancorp, Inc. 05/08/2018

LAFAYETTE ENTERPRISES LTD (CO)
Name changed to Colorado Select Products Inc. 01/10/1991

LAFAYETTE FIRE INSURANCE CO.
Name changed to Lafayette Insurance Co. and each share Capital Stock $25 par exchanged for (2) shares new Capital Stock $25 par in 1951

Lafayette Insurance Co. merged into ICB Corp. 7/31/73

(See ICB Corp.)

LAFAYETTE INDS INC (DE)
SEC revoked common stock registration 03/06/2017

LAFAYETTE INS CO (LA)
Capital Stock $25 par changed to $15 par 02/28/1966

Stock Dividend - 100% 03/19/1959

Merged into ICB Corp. 07/31/1973

Each share Capital Stock $15 par exchanged for (5.5357) shares Common $4 par

Note: The above ratio includes (1.25) for (1) split of ICB Corp. Common issued 08/06/1973

(See ICB Corp.)

LAFAYETTE LONG LAC GOLD MINES, LTD. (ON)
Charter revoked for failure to file reports and pay fees 12/7/67

LAFAYETTE NATIONAL BANK (BROOKLYN, NY)
Each share Common $100 par exchanged for (5) shares Common $20 par 00/00/1945

Common $20 par changed to $10 par and (1) additional share issued 04/23/1962

Stock Dividend - 50% 12/31/1941

Merged into Kings County Lafayette Trust Co. (Brooklyn, NY) 11/30/1965

Each share Common $10 par exchanged for (1.291743) shares Capital Stock $12.50 par

Kings County Lafayette Trust Co. (Brooklyn, NY) name changed to Kings Lafayette Bank (Brooklyn, NY) 03/17/1970 which merged into Kings Lafayette Corp. 05/03/1974 which merged into Republic New York Corp. 07/01/1974

(See Republic New York Corp.)

LAFAYETTE NATL BK (LITTLETON, NH)
Merged into Indian Head Banks, Inc. 6/12/81

Each share Common Capital Stock $10 par exchanged for (0.5) share 12% Conv. Preferred Ser. I $100 par

Indian Head Banks, Inc. acquired by Fleet/Norstar Financial Group, Inc. 12/21/88 which name changed to Fleet Financial Group, Inc. (New) 4/15/92 which name changed to Fleet Boston Corp. 10/1/99 which name changed to FleetBoston Financial Corp. 4/18/2000 which merged into Bank of America Corp. 4/1/2004

LAFAYETTE NATL BK IND (LAFAYETTE, IN)
Stock Dividends - 150% 8/19/44; 50% 7/25/56; 42.857% 10/20/58

Under plan of reorganization each share Capital Stock $20 par automatically became (1) share Lafayette National Corp. Common no par 8/19/74

(See Lafayette National Corp.)

LAFAYETTE NATL CORP (IN)
Merged into Indiana National Corp. 11/1/85

Each share Common no par exchanged for $149 cash

LAFAYETTE NOBLE HOMES INC. (OR)
Involuntarily dissolved 7/30/74
No stockholders' equity

LAFAYETTE RADIO ELECTRS CORP (NY)
Common $1 par split (2) for (1) by issuance of (1) additional share 04/30/1969

Merged into Wards Co., Inc. 06/24/1981

Each (100) shares Common $1 par exchanged for (1.3999) shares Ser. D Preferred $20 par and (5.5) shares Common $1 par

Wards Co., Inc. name changed to Circuit City Stores, Inc. 06/21/1984

(See Circuit City Stores, Inc.)

LAFLAMME BARRAUTE MINES, LTD. (ON)
Charter cancelled for failure to file reports and pay taxes in 1956

LAFORZA AUTOMOBILES INC (NV)
Common $0.001 par split (2) for (1) by issuance of (1) additional share payable 05/01/1999 to holders of record 04/12/1999

Name changed to U.S. Sustainable Energy Corp. 11/01/2006

U.S. Sustainable Energy Corp. recapitalized as Zeons Corp. 02/26/2010

LAGARDERE GROUPE S C A (FRANCE)
ADR agreement terminated 03/05/2007

Each Sponsored ADR for Ordinary exchanged for $77.00509 cash

LAGASCO CORP (ON)
Reincorporated under the laws of British Columbia as El Condor Minerals Inc. 08/04/2010

El Condor Minerals Inc. recapitalized as Worldwide Resources Corp. 06/08/2015

LAGAVA MINERALS LTD. (ON)
Name changed to Fox Lake Mines Ltd. 9/8/61

(See Fox Lake Mines Ltd.)

LAGO DOURADO MINERALS LTD (CANADA)
Each share old Common no par exchanged for (0.1) share new Common no par 04/02/2016

Name changed to Sandy Lake Gold Inc. 07/21/2016

LAGO OIL & TRANSPORT CORP.
Merged into Pan American Petroleum & Transport Co. in 1930
Details not available

LAGO PETROLEUM CORP.
Assets acquired by Creole Petroleum Corp. and liquidated 00/00/1943
Details not available

LAGO RES LTD (ON)
Recapitalized as RUX Resources Inc. 01/16/1997

Each share Common no par exchanged for (0.2) share Common no par

RUX Resources Inc. name changed to Galaxy Online Inc. 12/08/1999

(See Galaxy Online Inc.)

LAGONDA NATL BK (SPRINGFIELD, OH)
Each share Common $20 par exchanged for (2) shares Common $12.50 par 00/00/1945

Stock Dividend - 100% 06/01/1967

Name changed to Huntington Lagonda National Bank (Springfield, OH) 03/31/1975

Huntington Lagonda National Bank (Springfield, OH) merged into Huntington Bancshares Inc. 12/31/1979

LAGOON GROUP CORP (NV)
Name changed to TRHF Co. Ltd., Inc. 07/09/2015

LAGUERRE GOLD MINES LTD.
Recapitalized as New Laguerre Mines Ltd. on a (0.5) for (1) basis 00/00/1950

New Laguerre Mines Ltd. recapitalized as Can-Erin Mines Ltd. 00/00/1956 which recapitalized as Argosy Mining Corp. Ltd. 11/16/1964

(See Argosy Mining Corp.)

LAGUNA BANK, N.A. (LAGUNA BEACH, CA)
Merged into Orange Bank (Orange, CA) 8/7/92
Details not available

LAGUNA BLENDS INC (BC)
Each share old Common no par exchanged for (0.4) share new Common no par 01/06/2016

Name changed to Isodiol International Inc. 06/09/2017

LAGUNA CAP CORP (CO)
Name changed to Las Vegas Discount Golf & Tennis, Inc. 12/27/1988

Las Vegas Discount Golf & Tennis, Inc. name changed to Sports Entertainment Enterprises, Inc. (CO) 06/04/1999 which reincorporated in Delaware as CKX, Inc. 03/25/2005

(See CKX, Inc.)

LAGUNA CO. (PA)
Liquidated in 1951

LAGUNA FINL CORP (CA)
Merged into Swanton (Norman F.) Associates, Inc. 1/30/76

Each share Common 1¢ par exchanged for (0.22) share Common 10¢ par

Swanton (Norman F.) Associates, Inc. name changed to Swanton Corp. 8/9/76

(See Swanton Corp.)

LAGUNA GOLD MINES LTD.
Liquidated in 1939

LAGUNA HILLS UTIL CO (CA)
Each share old Common no par exchanged for (0.1) share new Common no par 05/09/1979

Assets transferred to Laguna Hills Utility Co. Liquidating Trust and certificates required to be surrendered 10/14/1983

(See Laguna Hills Utility Co. Liquidating Trust)

LAGUNA HILLS UTILITY CO. LIQUIDATING TRUST (CA)
In process of liquidation
Each Trust share received the following distributions: Initial $0.50 cash 03/27/1984
Second $0.60 cash 06/15/1984
Third $0.75 cash 09/21/1984
Fourth $0.75 cash 12/14/1984
Fifth $0.75 cash 03/15/1985
Sixth $0.75 cash 06/17/1985
Seventh $0.75 cash 09/13/1985
Eighth $0.75 cash 12/13/1985
Ninth $0.75 cash 03/14/1986
Tenth $2.35 cash 06/13/1986
Eleventh $0.775 cash 09/15/1986
Twelfth $0.775 cash 12/15/1986
Thirteenth $0.78 cash 03/16/1987
Fourteenth $0.78 cash 06/15/1987
Fifteenth $0.78 cash 09/14/1987
Sixteenth $0.78 cash 12/14/1987
Seventeenth $0.78 cash 03/14/1988
Eighteenth $0.78 cash 06/14/1988
Nineteenth $0.78 cash 09/14/1988
Twentieth $0.78 cash 12/13/1988
Twenty-first $0.78 cash 03/13/1989
Twenty-second $0.78 cash 06/13/1989
Twenty-third $0.78 cash 09/13/1989
Twenty-forth $0.78 cash 12/13/1989
Twenty-fifth $0.78 cash 03/13/1990
Twenty-sixth $0.78 cash 06/13/1990
Twenty-seventh $0.78 cash 09/13/1990
Twenty-eight $0.78 cash 12/13/1990
Twenty-ninth $0.78 cash 03/13/1991
Thirtieth $0.78 cash 06/13/1991
Thirty-first $0.78 cash 09/13/1991
Thirty-second $0.78 cash 12/13/1991
Thirty-third $0.78 cash 03/13/1992
Thirty-fourth $0.78 cash 06/15/1992
Thirty-fifth $0.78 cash 09/14/1992
Thirty-sixth $0.78 cash 12/14/1992
Thirty-seventh $0.78 cash 03/15/1993
Thirty-eight $0.78 cash 06/14/1993
Thirty-ninth $0.78 cash 09/13/1993
Fortieth $0.79 cash 12/13/1993
Forty-first $0.79 cash 03/14/1994
Forty-second $0.79 cash 06/14/1994
Forty-third $0.79 cash 09/13/1994
Forty-fourth $0.79 cash 12/13/1994
Forty-fifth $0.79 cash 03/14/1995
Forty-sixth $0.79 cash 06/13/1995
Forty-seventh $0.78 cash 09/12/1995
Forty-eighth $0.79 cash 12/12/1995
Forty-ninth $0.79 cash 03/13/1996
Fiftieth $0.79 cash 06/13/1996
$0.79 cash 06/12/2002
$0.79 cash 09/12/2002
$0.79 cash 12/12/2002
$0.79 cash 03/12/2003
$0.79 cash 06/11/2003
$0.78 cash 09/11/2003
$0.79 cash 12/11/2003
$0.79 cash 06/14/2004
$0.79 cash 09/13/2004
$0.79 cash 12/13/2004
$0.79 cash 03/14/2005
$0.79 cash 06/14/2005
$0.79 cash 09/12/2005
$0.79 cash 12/15/2005
$0.79 cash 03/14/2006
$0.79 cash 09/14/2006
$0.79 cash 12/12/2006
$0.79 cash 03/13/2007
$0.79 cash 06/12/2007
$0.79 cash 03/12/2008
$0.78 cash 09/11/2008
$0.79 cash 12/12/2008
$0.79 cash 03/12/2009
$0.79 cash 06/15/2009
$0.79 cash 09/16/2009
$0.79 cash 12/13/2009
$0.79 cash 03/15/2010
$0.78 cash 06/14/2010
$0.79 cash 09/14/2010
$0.79 cash 12/15/2010
$0.79 cash 03/15/2011
$0.79 cash 06/15/2011
$0.79 cash 09/14/2011
$0.79 cash 12/14/2011

Note: Number and amount of distributions made between 1999-2001 or after 12/14/2011 are not available

LAGUNA NIGUEL CORP (CA)
Class B no par reclassified as Common no par 06/24/1966

Each share old Common no par exchanged for (0.0002) share new Common no par 05/14/1971

Note: In effect holders received $5.625 cash per share and public interest was eliminated

LAGUNA RES LTD (BC)
Recapitalized as Laco Resources Inc. 1/30/78

Each share Capital Stock no par exchanged for (0.2) share Capital Stock no par

Laco Resources Inc. recapitalized as International Laco Resources Inc. 9/1/82 which merged into Aurex Resources Inc. 7/11/85 which merged into Galveston Resources Ltd. 7/29/86 which merged into Corona Corp. 7/1/88 which recapitalized as International Corona Corp. 6/11/91

(See International Corona Corp.)

LAGUNA RES NL (AUSTRALIA)
Each old Sponsored ADR for Ordinary exchanged for (0.04) new Sponsored ADR for Ordinary 06/21/2011

ADR basis changed from (1:40) to (1:8) 06/21/2011

Acquired by Kingsgate Consolidated Ltd. 02/01/2012

Each new Sponsored ADR for Ordinary exchanged for $30.844603 cash

LAHAINA ACQUISITIONS INC (CO)
Name changed to UCAP Inc.
07/19/2002
(See UCAP Inc.)

LAHONTON OIL & GAS CO. (NV)
Charter forfeited for non-payment of taxes 2/28/24

LAI WORLDWIDE INC (FL)
Merged into TMP Worldwide Inc. 08/26/1999
Each share Common 1¢ par exchanged for (0.1321) share Common $0.001 par
TMP Worldwide Inc. name changed to Monster Worldwide, Inc. 05/01/2003
(See Monster Worldwide, Inc.)

LAID BACK ENTERPRISES INC (OK)
Name changed to Gift Liquidators Inc. 12/20/2002
Gift Liquidators Inc. (OK) reincorporated in Maryland as Excellency Investment Realty Trust, Inc. 09/20/2006
(See Excellency Investment Realty Trust, Inc.)

LAIDLAW ENVIRONMENTAL SVCS INC (DE)
Name changed to Safety-Kleen Corp. (New) 7/1/98
(See Safety-Kleen Corp. (New))

LAIDLAW GLOBAL CORP (DE)
Common $0.00001 par split (3) for (2) by issuance of (0.5) additional share payable 10/14/1999 to holders of record 09/23/1999
Each share old Common $0.00001 par exchanged for (0.01) share new Common $0.00001 par 05/22/2006
Name changed to Allegro Group, Inc. 06/27/2006
Allegro Group, Inc. name changed to Brandt Inc. 03/13/2008

LAIDLAW INC (CANADA)
Conv. 1st Preference Ser. F no par called for redemption 10/17/1988
Each share Non-Vtg. Class B Common no par exchanged for (1) share Common no par 07/31/1997
Class A Common no par reclassified as Common no par 07/31/1997
Each share Common no par received distribution of (0.15) additional share payable 08/05/1997 to holders of record 07/31/1997
Plan of reorganization under Chapter 11 Federal Bankruptcy Code effective 06/23/2003
No stockholders' equity

LAIDLAW INDS INC (DE)
Common $1 par changed to 50¢ par and (1) additional share issued 1/31/83
Common 50¢ par changed to 25¢ par and (1) additional share issued 6/24/83
Conv. Preferred Ser. A $1 par called for redemption 8/30/85
Merged into Laidlaw Transportation Ltd. 12/31/87
Each share Common 25¢ par exchanged for $22 cash

LAIDLAW INTL INC (DE)
Merged into FirstGroup PLC 10/01/2007
Each share Common 1¢ par exchanged for $35.25 cash

LAIDLAW MOTORWAYS LTD. (ON)
Common no par split (3) for (1) by issuance of (2) additional shares 5/15/72
Name changed to Laidlaw Transportation Ltd. (Ont.) 11/1/73
Laidlaw Transportation Ltd. (Ont.) reincorporated in Canada 3/15/79 which name changed to Laidlaw Inc. 1/2/90
(See Laidlaw Inc.)

LAIDLAW TRANSN LTD (CANADA)
Reincorporated 3/15/79
Common no par reclassified as Conv. Class A Common no par 2/17/75
5% Conv. 1st Preference Ser. B $10 par called for redemption 8/30/78
7% Conv. 1st Preference Ser. A $10 par called for redemption 3/13/79
Conv. Class A Common no par split (2) for (1) by issuance of (1) additional share 3/12/79
Conv. Class B Common no par split (2) for (1) by issuance of (1) additional share 3/15/79
Place of incorporation changed from (ONT) to (Canada) 3/15/79
Conv. Class A Common no par reclassified as Class A Common no par and (1) share Non-Vtg. Class B Common no par distributed 9/10/79
Each share Conv. Class B Common no par exchanged for (1) share Class A Common no par and (1) share Non-Vtg. Class B Common no par 9/10/79
Class A Common no par split (2) for (1) by issuance of (1) additional share 7/11/83
Non-Vtg. Class B Common $1 par split (2) for (1) by issuance of (1) additional share 7/11/83
Class A Common no par split (2) for (1) by issuance of (1) additional share 1/29/85
Non-Vtg. Class B Common $1 par split (2) for (1) by issuance of (1) additional share 1/29/85
9-3/4% 1st Preference Ser. C $10 par called for redemption 3/1/85
Class A Common no par split (3) for (2) by issuance of (0.5) additional share 9/17/86
Non-Vtg. Class B Common no par split (3) for (2) by issuance of (0.5) additional share 9/17/86
80¢ 1st Preference Ser. E no par called for redemption 3/4/87
Class A Common no par split (3) for (2) by issuance of (0.5) additional share 5/25/87
Non-Vtg. Class B Common no par split (3) for (2) by issuance of (0.5) additional share 5/25/87
Name changed to Laidlaw Inc. 1/2/90

LAINA INVESTMENT CORP. (UT)
Recapitalized as Zaplink International, Inc. 2/27/87
Each (4.667) shares Common $0.001 par exchanged for (1) share Common $0.001 par
(See Zaplink International, Inc.)

LAIR DOR CORP (ON)
Name changed to Tagalder Inc. 7/26/96
Tagalder Inc. name changed to Tagalder (2000) Inc. 9/1/2000

LAIRD GROUP INC (CANADA)
6% Preferred $100 par called for redemption 03/05/1984
Merged into Printera Corp. 11/22/1996
Each (18) shares Common no par exchanged for (1) share Common no par
Each (18) shares Conv. Class A no par exchanged for (1) share Common no par
(See Printera Corp.)

LAIRD PLC (ENGLAND & WALES)
ADR agreement terminated 06/14/2018
No ADR's remain outstanding

LAITERIES PAPINEAU INC. (QC)
Charter cancelled for failure to file reports 08/03/1974

LAKE AIRCRAFT CORP. (DE)
Merged into Consolidated Aeronautics, Inc. 4/5/62
Each share Class A Common 10¢ par exchanged for (0.5) share Class A Common 50¢ par

(See Consolidated Aeronautics, Inc.)

LAKE ARIEL BANCORP INC (PA)
Each share Common $5 par exchanged for (4) shares Common $1.25 par 4/2/87
Common $1.25 par changed to 42¢ par and (2) additional shares issued 8/16/93
Common 42¢ par split (2) for (1) by issuance of (1) additional share payable 11/10/97 to holders of record 10/31/97
Stock Dividends - 5% payable 10/1/96 to holders of record 9/20/96; 5% payable 10/1/97 to holders of record 9/19/97
Merged into NBT Bancorp Inc. 2/17/2000
Each share Common 42¢ par exchanged for (0.9961) share Common 1¢ par

LAKE ARROWHEAD DEVELOPMENT CO. (CA)
Liquidation completed
Each share Common no par received initial distribution of (0.36) share Boise Cascade Corp. Common $2.50 par 1/20/68
Each share Common no par exchanged for second and final distribution of (0.04) share Boise Cascade Corp. Common $2.50 par 10/16/68

LAKE BEAVERHOUSE MINES LTD (ON)
Capital Stock $1 par changed to no par 05/28/1971
Charter cancelled for failure to pay taxes and file returns 02/20/1980

LAKE CAPITAL CORP. (ON)
Name changed to Valavaara Environmental Technologies Ltd. 7/14/93
Valavaara Environmental Technologies Ltd. recapitalized as Kenridge Investment Corp. (ONT) 4/12/96 which reorganized in Yukon Territory as Exploro Minerals Corp. Ltd. 3/6/97
(See Exploro Minerals Corp.)

LAKE CENT AIRLS INC (DE)
Merged into Allegheny Airlines, Inc. 7/1/68
Each share Conv. Preferred $20 par exchanged for (1.17) shares Common $1 par
Each share Common $1 par exchanged for (0.44) share Common $1 par
Allegheny Airlines, Inc. name changed to U S Air, Inc. 10/29/79 which reorganized as USAir Group, Inc. 2/1/83 which name changed to US Airways Group, Inc. 2/21/97
(See US Airways Group, Inc.)

LAKE CENTRAL MINES LTD. (BC)
Charter cancelled for failure to file returns in 1969

LAKE CHANDALAR GOLD MINES, LTD. (ON)
Charter cancelled for failure to file reports and pay taxes in March 1961

LAKE CHARLES NAVAL STORES INC (LA)
Each share old Common no par exchanged for (0.25) share new Common no par 10/01/2010
Note: In effect holders received $1,287.50 cash per share and public interest was eliminated

LAKE CINCH MINES LTD. (ON)
Merged into Dickenson Mines Ltd. (Old) on a (1) for (4.5) basis 10/14/60
Dickenson Mines Ltd. (Old) merged into Dickenson Mines Ltd. (New) 10/31/80 which merged into Goldcorp Inc. (New) 3/31/94

LAKE CITY GAMING CORP (BC)
Acquired by Gateway Casinos Inc. 8/13/2002
Each share Common no par exchanged for $3.25 cash

LAKE CITY MINES INC (CO)
Involuntarily dissolved for failure to file annual reports 01/01/1989

LAKE CMNTY BK (LAKEPORT, CA)
Merged into Western Sierra Bancorp 05/03/1999
Each share Common no par exchanged for (0.6905) share Common no par
Western Sierra Bancorp merged into Umpqua Holdings Corp. 06/05/2006

LAKE COPPER CO.
Liquidated in 1930

LAKE COUNTY NATIONAL BANK (PAINESVILLE, OH)
Common $10 par changed to $5 par and (1) additional share issued 2/26/69
Stock Dividends - 10.75% 2/2/61; 20% 12/6/63; 20% 12/21/65; 15% 2/19/68; 10% 3/15/73; 15% 5/12/78
Name changed to Lake National Bank (Painesville, OH) 12/1/79
Lake National Bank (Painesville, OH) merged into Banc One Corp. (DE) 9/1/81 which reincorporated in Ohio 5/1/89 which merged into Bank One Corp. 10/2/98 which merged into J.P. Morgan Chase & Co. 12/31/2000 which name changed to JPMorgan Chase & Co. 7/20/2004

LAKE DUFAULT MINES LTD (QC)
Merged into Falconbridge Copper Ltd. 12/16/1971
Each share Capital Stock $1 par exchanged for (1.5) shares Capital Stock no par
Falconbridge Copper Ltd. name changed to Corporation Falconbridge Copper 07/09/1980 which name changed to Minnova Inc. 05/26/1987 which merged into Metall Mining Corp. 05/05/1993 which name changed to Inmet Mining Corp. 05/04/1995 which was acquired by First Quantum Minerals Ltd. 04/09/2013

LAKE ERIE BOLT & NUT CO.
Merged into Lamson & Sessions Co. 00/00/1929
Details not available

LAKE ERIE GAS LTD. (ON)
Merged into Erieshore Industries Inc. 05/10/1971
Each share Common $1 par exchanged for (0.133333) share Common no par
Erieshore Industries Inc. merged into Portfield Industries Inc. 10/22/1980 which recapitalized as Canmine Resources Corp. 05/01/1991
(See Canmine Resources Corp.)

LAKE ERIE POWER & LIGHT CO.
Dissolved in 1938

LAKE EXPANSE GOLD MINES LTD. (ON)
Recapitalized as Lakex Mines Ltd. 8/15/72
Each share Capital Stock $1 par exchanged for (1.5) shares Capital Stock no par
(See Lakex Mines Ltd.)

LAKE FOREST ATLANTIC BANK (JACKSONVILLE, FL)
100% acquired by Atlantic Bancorporation through exchange offer which expired 10/01/1973
Public interest eliminated

LAKE FOREST BANCORP INC (IL)
Merged into Wintrust Financial Corp. 9/1/96
Each share Common $20 par exchanged for (9.6734) shares Common no par

LAKE FORTUNE GOLD MINES, LTD.
Reorganized as New Fortune Mines Ltd. on a (1) for (4) basis in 1952
New Fortune Mines Ltd. recapitalized as United New Fortune Mines Ltd. 7/11/58
(See United New Fortune Mines Ltd.)

LAKE GENEVA MINING CO. LTD. (ON)
Succeeded by Geneva Lake Mines Co. Ltd. share for share 00/00/1949
Geneva Lake Mines Co. Ltd. recapitalized as Genex Mines Ltd. 04/12/1956 which recapitalized as Irvington Mining Co. 10/17/1966
(See Irvington Mining Co.)

LAKE HORWOOD GOLD MINES, LTD. (ON)
Charter cancelled for failure to file reports and pay taxes in April 1958

LAKE HURON URANIUM MINES LTD. (ON)
Charter surrendered 8/1/58

LAKE KAGINU MINES LTD. (ON)
Merged into Crowpat Minerals Ltd. on a (0.5) for (1) basis in 1955
Crowpat Minerals Ltd. recapitalized as Crowbank Mines Ltd. 7/29/68 which recapitalized as Patmore Developments Ltd. 2/14/74 which name changed to Patmore Group Ltd. 11/1/76 which merged into Uranco Inc. 10/23/80

LAKE KINGSTON MINES LTD (ON)
Charter cancelled for failure to pay taxes and file returns 03/05/1975

LAKE KOZAK MINES LTD (ON)
Charter cancelled and declared dissolved for failure to file returns and pay fees 04/09/1975

LAKE LANE LIQUIDATION TRUST
Trust liquidated in 1951

LAKE LAUZON MINES LTD. (ON)
Charter revoked for failure to file reports and pay fees 4/1/65

LAKE LINGMAN GOLD MINING CO., LTD. (ON)
Recapitalized as Lakelyn Mines Ltd. on a (0.2857142) for (1) basis 11/30/1964
Lakelyn Mines Ltd. recapitalized as Lakelyn Mines Inc. 11/16/1978 which name changed to Twin Gold Mines Ltd. 11/09/1979
(See Twin Gold Mines Ltd.)

LAKE MARON GOLD MINES LTD.
Acquired by Maralgo Mines Ltd. (ON) 00/00/1937
Each share Common no par exchanged for (0.25) share Common no par
Maralgo Mines Ltd. (ON) reincorporated in British Columbia 06/06/1984 which recapitalized as Rich Coast Sulphur Ltd. 03/13/1986 which recapitalized as Consolidated Rich Coast Sulphur Ltd. 06/19/1991 which merged into Rich Coast Resources Ltd. (BC) 01/25/1993 which reincorporated in Delaware as Rich Coast Inc. 09/16/1996 which reincorporated in Nevada 07/14/1998 which recapitalized as Media Pal Holdings, Corp. 03/16/2010

LAKE MCIVOR MINES LTD (ON)
Charter cancelled for failure to pay taxes and file returns 08/02/1972

LAKE MEAD MEMORIAL PARKS CORP. (NV)
Name changed to General American Corp. 06/24/1965
(See General American Corp.)

LAKE NATL BK (PAINESVILLE, OH)
Merged into Banc One Corp. (DE) 09/01/1981
Each share Common $5 par exchanged for (1.5) shares Common no par
Banc One Corp. (DE) reincorporated in Ohio 05/01/1989 which merged into Bank One Corp. 10/02/1998 which merged into J.P. Morgan Chase & Co. 12/31/2000 which name changed to JPMorgan Chase & Co. 07/20/2004

LAKE NORDIC URANIUM MINES LTD. (ON)
Merged into Northspan Uranium Mines Ltd. 7/5/56
Each share Common $1 par exchanged for (0.75) share Capital Stock $1 par
Northspan Uranium Mines Ltd. merged into Rio Algom Mines Ltd. 6/30/60 which name changed to Rio Algom Ltd. 4/30/75
(See Rio Algom Ltd.)

LAKE OF THE WOODS MILLING CO. LTD. (CANADA)
Each share Common $100 par exchanged for (3) shares Common no par 00/00/1928
Acquired by Ogilvie Flour Mills Co., Ltd. 00/00/1955
Each share 7% Preferred $100 par exchanged for $130 cash 00/00/1960
Each share Common no par exchanged for (1) share Common no par and $10 cash
Ogilvie Flour Mills Co. Ltd. name changed to Ogilvie Mills Ltd./Les Minoteries Ogilvie Ltee. 09/15/1975
(See Ogilvie Mills Ltd./Les Minoteries Ogilvie Ltee.)

LAKE ONT CEM LTD (CANADA)
5% Preferred $10 par called for redemption 03/31/1965
Common $1 par changed to no par 04/17/1980
Merged into Societe des Ciments Francais 12/08/1986
Each share Common no par exchanged for $36.25 cash

LAKE ONTARIO PORTLAND CEMENT CO. LTD. (CANADA)
Name changed to Lake Ontario Cement Ltd. 02/01/1965
(See Lake Ontario Cement Ltd.)

LAKE OSU MINES LTD (ON)
Charter cancelled for failure to file reports and pay fees 11/8/77

LAKE OTTER URANIUM MINES LTD (QC)
Declared dissolved for failure to file reports and pay fees 11/27/76

LAKE PLACID RES LTD (AB)
Merged into Electra Energy Corp. 2/22/95
Each share Common no par exchanged for (0.1) share Common no par

LAKE PONASK GOLD CORP (ON)
Recapitalized as Leadley Gunning & Culp International Corp. 11/25/91
Each share Common no par exchanged for (0.125) share Common no par
(See Leadley Gunning & Culp International Corp.)

LAKE RENZY MINES LTD. (QC)
Recapitalized as Renzy Mines Ltd. 6/28/65
Each share Capital Stock $1 par exchanged for (0.25) share Common $1 par

LAKE-RIDGE MINES LTD. (ON)
Charter revoked for failure to file reports and pay fees 8/25/66

LAKE ROWAN (1945) MINES LTD. (ON)
Recapitalized as Rowan Consolidated Mines Ltd. 01/29/1951
Each share Capital Stock $1 par exchanged for (0.25) share Capital Stock $1 par
Rowan Consolidated Mines Ltd. recapitalized as Rowan Gold Mines Ltd. 04/01/1974 which merged into Goldquest Exploration Inc. 08/09/1982 which merged into Goldcorp Inc. (New) 03/31/1994

LAKE ROWAN GOLD MINES LTD. (ON)
Recapitalized as Lake Rowan (1945) Mines Ltd. 00/00/1945
Each share Capital Stock $1 par exchanged for (1/3) share Capital Stock $1 par
Lake Rowan (1945) Mines Ltd. recapitalized as Rowan Consolidated Mines Ltd. 01/29/1951 which recapitalized as Rowan Gold Mines Ltd. 04/01/1974 which merged into Goldquest Exploration Inc. 08/09/1982 which merged into Goldcorp Inc. (New) 03/31/1994

LAKE SHORE BANCORP INC (DE)
Common $10 par split (5) for (4) by issuance of (0.25) additional share 01/21/1983
Common $10 par split (3) for (2) by issuance of (0.5) additional share 12/27/1985
Common $10 par split (4) for (3) by issuance of (1/3) additional share 12/19/1986
Common $10 par split (5) for (4) by issuance of (0.25) additional share 12/18/1989
Common $10 par split (5) for (4) by issuance of (0.25) additional share 02/08/1993
Stock Dividends - 10% 12/28/1983; 10% 12/28/1984
Merged into First Chicago Corp. 07/08/1994
Each share Common $10 par exchanged for (0.617) share Common $5 par

LAKE SHORE ELECTRIC RWY. CO.
Properties sold at foreclosure in 1938
No stockholders' equity

LAKE SHORE ENGINEERING CO. (MI)
Name changed to Lake Shore, Inc. 5/23/55
(See Lake Shore, Inc.)

LAKE SHORE FINL CORP (DE)
Stock Dividend - 10% 06/07/1976
Merged into Detroitbank Corp. 12/01/1977
Each share Common $5 par exchanged for $23 principal amount of 9% 15-yr. Conv. Subord. Debentures due 11/30/1992 and $0.21 cash
Note: Holders entitled to receive less than $990 principal amount of Debentures received cash only

LAKE SHORE GOLD CORP (CANADA)
Reincorporated 06/30/2004
Reincorporated 07/18/2008
Place of incorporation changed from (YT) to (BC) 06/30/2004
Place of incorporation changed from (BC) to Canada 07/18/2008
Merged into Tahoe Resources Inc. 04/07/2016
Each share Common no par exchanged for (0.1467) share Common no par
Note: Unexchanged certificates will be cancelled and become without value 04/07/2022

LAKE SHORE HOMES, INC. (NC)
Name changed to North American Funding, Inc. 12/22/1969
(See North American Funding, Inc.)

LAKE SHORE HOTEL INC (OH)
Liquidation completed
Each share Common no par exchanged for initial distribution of $300 cash 07/01/1964
Each share Common no par received second distribution of $25 cash 02/08/1965
Each share Common no par received third and final distribution of $6 cash 03/02/1965

LAKE SHORE INC (MI)
Common no par split (4) for (1) by issuance of (3) additional shares 7/24/70
Merged into Oldenburg Group, Inc. 3/28/88
Each share Common no par exchanged for $23 cash

LAKE SHORE MINES LTD (ON)
Merged into LAC Minerals Ltd. (New) 07/29/1985
Each share Capital Stock $1 par exchanged for (2.871) shares Common no par
LAC Minerals Ltd. (New) acquired by American Barrick Resources Corp. 10/17/1994 which name changed to Barrick Gold Corp. 01/18/1995

LAKE SHORE NATL BK (CHICAGO, IL)
Capital Stock $50 par changed to $10 par and (4) additional shares issued plus a 25% stock dividend paid 07/13/1960
Stock Dividends - 25% 12/21/1943; 50% 12/26/1945; 33-1/3% 12/15/1949; 25% 11/20/1952; 20% 11/17/1954; 33-1/3% 12/05/1956; 20% 07/18/1962; 33-1/3% 12/14/1966; 25% 12/18/1968; 11.1316% 03/27/1972; 20% 07/18/1973; 25% 01/08/1976; 33-1/3% 05/08/1978
Under plan of reorganization each share Capital Stock $10 par automatically became (1) share Lake Shore Bancorp., Inc. Common $10 par 04/01/1982
Lake Shore Bancorp., Inc. merged into First Chicago Corp. 07/08/1994

LAKE ST BK (LUTZ, FL)
Merged into SouthTrust Corp. 06/28/1996
Each share Common $8 par exchanged for (0.84) share Common $2.50 par
SouthTrust Corp. merged into Wachovia Corp. (Ctfs. dated after 09/01/2001) 11/01/2004 which merged into Wells Fargo & Co. (New) 12/31/2008

LAKE SUNAPEE BK GROUP (DE)
Merged into Bar Harbor Bankshares 01/13/2017
Each share Common 1¢ par exchanged for (0.497) share Common $2 par

LAKE SUNAPEE SVGS BK FSB (NEWPORT, NH)
Common $1 par split (2) for (1) by issuance of (1) additional share 06/19/1987
Reorganized under the laws of Delaware as New Hampshire Thrift Bancshares, Inc. 07/05/1989
Each share Common $1 par exchanged for (1) share Common 1¢ par
New Hampshire Thrift Bancshares, Inc. name changed to Lake Sunapee Bank Group 06/01/2015 which merged into Bar Harbor Bankshares 01/13/2017

LAKE SUPERIOR & ISHPEMING R R CO (MI)
Each share Common $100 par exchanged for (5) shares Common $20 par in 1941
Merged into a private company 3/23/2001
Each share Common $20 par exchanged for approximately $700 cash

FINANCIAL INFORMATION, INC. LAK-LAK

LAKE SUPERIOR DIST PWR CO (WI)
Common $100 par changed to $75 par in 1936
Each share Common $75 par exchanged for (3.75) shares Common $20 par in 1945
5% 2nd Preferred $20 par called for redemption 12/1/52
Common $20 par changed to $10 par and (1) additional share issued 4/30/55
Stock Dividend - 100% 6/9/72
Acquired by Northern States Power Co. 2/20/84
Each share Common $10 par exchanged for (0.48) share Common $5 par
5% Preferred $100 par called for redemption 12/29/86
Northern States Power Co. name changed to Xcel Energy Inc. 8/18/2000

LAKE SUPERIOR INVESTMENT CO.
Liquidated in 1946

LAKE SUPERIOR IRON LTD. (QC)
Recapitalized as St. Lawrence Columbium & Metals Corp. on a (0.04) for (1) basis 9/28/60
(See St. Lawrence Columbium & Metals Corp.)

LAKE SUPERIOR MINING CORP. LTD. (ON)
Charter revoked for failure to file reports and pay fees 2/25/65

LAKE TAHOE RAILWAY & TRANSPORTATION CO.
Property sold in 1933

LAKE TORPEDO BOAT CO.
Liquidated in 1930

LAKE VENTURES LTD (BC)
Struck off register and declared dissolved for failure to file returns 3/2/90

LAKE VIEW TR & SVGS BK (CHICAGO, IL)
Capital Stock $100 par changed to $20 par and (4) additional shares issued 02/11/1960
Stock Dividends - 100% 08/24/1954; 50% 01/10/1956; 66-2/3% 08/21/1958; 100% 01/24/1967; 50% 01/31/1968
99.9% held by National Lead Co. as of 01/00/1969
Public interest eliminated

LAKE WASA MINING CORP. (QC)
Recapitalized as Wasamac Mines Ltd. 10/07/1960
Each share Capital Stock $1 par exchanged for (0.33333333) share Capital Stock $1 par
Wasamac Mines Ltd. acquired by Wright-Hargreaves Mines, Ltd. 01/03/1969 which merged into LAC Minerals Ltd. (New) 07/29/1985 which was acquired by American Barrick Resources Corp. 10/17/1994 which name changed to Barrick Gold Corp. 01/18/1995

LAKE WIFI INC (NV)
Charter revoked for failure to file reports and pay fees 09/30/2009

LAKEFIELD MARKETING CORP (ON)
Name changed 01/23/2004
Name changed from Lakefield Minerals Ltd. to Lakefield Marketing Corp. 01/23/2004
Delisted from CNQ 10/17/2008

LAKEFIELD PORCUPINE GOLD MINES LTD.
Each (8) shares Capital Stock no par exchanged for (3) shares Goldhawk Porcupine Mines Ltd. and (2) shares Cocallen Porcupine Gold Mines Ltd. in 1947
(See each company's listing)

LAKEFIELD RESEARCH LTD. (CANADA)
Assets sold and each share Capital Stock no par exchanged for (0.3) share Quebec Lithium Corp. Capital Stock $1 par, (0.1) share Lakefield Research of Canada Ltd. Capital Stock no par and 95¢ cash 12/15/58
(See each company's listing)

LAKEFIELD VENTURES INC (NV)
Each share old Common $0.001 par exchanged for (11.14) shares new Common $0.001 par 02/02/2005
Reorganized as Urex Energy Corp. 07/03/2006
Each share new Common $0.001 par exchanged for (2) shares Common $0.001 par
Urex Energy Corp. recapitalized as Mustang Geothermal Corp. 07/22/2010 which recapitalized as Dakota Territory Resource Corp. 09/26/2012

LAKEFRONT REALTY CORP. (IL)
Each share Common $10 par exchanged for (2) shares Common $5 par 9/25/57
Liquidation completed
Each share Common $5 par exchanged for (1) Receipt and initial distribution of $10.40 cash 5/1/78
Each share Common $5 par received second distribution of $1.6165 cash 4/12/79
Each share Common $5 par received third distribution of $25.04 cash 6/3/81
Each share Common $5 par received fourth and final distribution of $0.79667 cash 7/14/82
Note: Receipts were not required to be surrendered and are now valueless

LAKEHEAD MINES LTD (ON)
Capital Stock $1 par changed to no par 07/21/1971
Merged into Parlake Resources Ltd. 06/18/1979
Each share Capital Stock no par exchanged for (0.125) share Common no par
Parlake Resources Ltd. name changed to Concord Capital Corp. 07/23/1991
(See Concord Capital Corp.)

LAKEHEAD PIPE LINE PARTNERS L P (DE)
Name changed to Enbridge Energy Partners, L.P. 09/05/2001

LAKELAND BASE METALS LTD (BC)
Merged into BrenMac Mines Ltd. 4/26/68
Each share Common 50¢ par exchanged for (1) share Capital Stock no par
BrenMac Mines Ltd. recapitalized as International BrenMac Development Corp. 11/28/75 which recapitalized as Oberg Industries Ltd. 1/14/86 which recapitalized as Consolidated Oberg Industries Ltd. 8/21/90 which name changed to Hytec Flow Systems Inc. 1/16/97
(See Hytec Flow Systems Inc.)

LAKELAND CAP TR (DE)
9% Trust Preferred called for redemption at $10 on 10/1/2003

LAKELAND DEV CORP (TN)
Administratively dissolved 08/18/1995

LAKELAND FIRST FINL GROUP INC (NJ)
Stock Dividend - 10% 10/14/94
Merged into Valley National Bancorp 6/30/95
Each share Common 10¢ par exchanged for (1.286) shares Common no par

LAKELAND FIRST MORTGAGE CORP. (FL)
Name changed to Anchor Investment Corporation of Fla. 07/01/1975
(See Anchor Investment Corporation of Fla.)

LAKELAND HARVESTING CORP. (FL)
Merged into Dominion Development Corp. 1/1/71
Each share Common 1¢ par exchanged for (2) shares Common 1¢ par
Dominion Development Corp. name changed to First Continental Oil & Gas Co. Inc. 5/10/71 which merged into Continental Resources, International 7/31/72

LAKELAND NAT GAS LTD (ON)
Capital Stock $1 par reclassified as Common $1 par 05/09/1963
Merged into Northern & Central Gas Corp. Ltd. 01/01/1968
Each share 5.4% Preference Ser. A $20 par exchanged for (1) share $2.70 1st Preference 2nd Series $50 par
Each share Common $1 par exchanged for (0.666666) share Common no par
(See Northern & Central Gas Corp. Ltd.)

LAKELAND RES INC (BC)
Recapitalized as ALX Uranium Corp. 09/25/2015
Each share Common no par exchanged for (0.33333333) share Common no par

LAKELAND RTY & PETE CORP (BC)
Cease trade order effective 07/19/2000
Stockholders' equity unlikely

LAKELAND SAVINGS & LOAN ASSOCIATION (NJ)
Stock Dividend - 10% 8/24/87
Name changed to Lakeland Savings Bank, S.L.A. (Succasunna, NJ) 10/27/87
Lakeland Savings Bank, S.L.A. (Succasunna, NJ) reorganized as Lakeland First Financial Group, Inc. 5/1/89 which merged into Valley National Bancorp 6/30/95

LAKELAND SVGS BK S L A (SUCCASUNNA, NJ)
Common $1 par split (3) for (2) by issuance of (0.5) additional share 4/13/88
Stock Dividend - 10% 3/31/89
Under plan of reorganization each share Common $1 par automatically became (1) share Lakeland First Financial Group, Inc. Common 10¢ par 5/1/89
Lakeland First Financial Group, Inc. merged into Valley National Bancorp 6/30/95

LAKELAND ST BK (NEWFOUNDLAND, NJ)
Under plan of reorganization each share Common $2.50 par automatically became (1) share Lakeland Bancorp, Inc. Common $2.50 par 05/19/1988

LAKELYN MINES INC. (ON)
Name changed to Twin Gold Mines Ltd. 11/09/1979
(See Twin Gold Mines Ltd.)

LAKELYN MINES LTD (ON)
Capital Stock $1 par changed to no par 00/00/1974
Recapitalized as Lakelyn Mines Inc. 11/16/1978
Each share Capital Stock no par exchanged for (0.2) share Capital Stock no par
Lakelyn Mines Inc. name changed to Twin Gold Mines Ltd. 11/09/1979
(See Twin Gold Mines Ltd.)

LAKEPORT BREWING INCOME FD (ON)
Acquired by Labatt Brewing Co., Ltd. 3/29/2007
Each Unit no par received $28 cash

LAKER RES LTD (BC)
Name changed to Videogram International Corp. 06/11/1990
Videogram International Corp. recapitalized as Interactive Video Systems Inc. 10/08/1992 which name changed to Interactive VideoSystems Inc. 07/19/1994 which name changed to NCC Mining Corp. 08/16/1995 which recapitalized as BMA Mining Corp. 07/11/1997 which recapitalized as Dasher Energy Corp. 05/26/1999 which name changed to Dasher Resources Corp. 10/03/2002 which recapitalized as Dasher Exploration Ltd. 04/16/2003 which name changed to New World Resource Corp. 06/27/2005

LAKERIDGE HOTEL CO. (IL)
Liquidation completed 11/3/58

LAKES ENTMT INC (MN)
Name changed 06/05/2002
Name changed from Lakes Gaming, Inc. to Lakes Entertainment, Inc. 06/05/2002
Old Common 1¢ par split (2) for (1) by issuance of (1) additional share payable 05/03/2004 to holders of record 04/26/2004 Ex date - 05/04/2004
Each share old Common 1¢ par exchanged for (0.5) share new Common 1¢ par 09/10/2014
Name changed to Golden Entertainment, Inc. 08/04/2015

LAKESHORE COMMERCIAL FINANCE CORP. (WI)
99.8% acquired by Lakeshore Financial Corp. through exchange offer which expired 07/26/1972
Public interest eliminated

LAKESHORE FINL CORP (WI)
Merged into Lakeshore Commercial Finance Corp. (New) 09/27/2006
Details not available

LAKESHORE MINERALS INC (ON)
Recapitalized as Leggo Holdings Inc. 07/18/1990
Each share Common no par exchanged for (0.25) share Common no par
Leggo Holdings Inc. name changed to Transarctic Petroleum Corp. 09/29/1997 which name changed to ivyNET Corp. 03/26/1999 which recapitalized as Saratoga Capital Corp. 08/25/2000
(See Saratoga Capital Corp.)

LAKESIDE BANCSHARES INC (LA)
Merged into First Commerce Corp. 8/3/95
Each share Common $2.50 par exchanged for (1.96844) shares Common $5 par
First Commerce Corp. merged into Banc One Corp. 6/12/98 which merged into Bank One Corp. 10/2/98 which merged into J.P. Morgan Chase & Co. 12/31/2000 which name changed to JPMorgan Chase & Co. 7/20/2004

LAKESIDE INDS INC (DE)
Name changed to Leisure Dynamics, Inc. 9/2/69
(See Leisure Dynamics, Inc.)

LAKESIDE KIRKLAND GOLD MINES, LTD. (ON)
Charter cancelled for failure to file reports and pay taxes in 1956

LAKESIDE LABORATORIES, INC. (WI)
Merged into Colgate-Palmolive Co. on an (1.2424) for (1) basis 2/1/60

LAKESIDE MINERALS INC (ON)
Each share old Common no par exchanged for (0.25) share new Common no par 06/16/2014
Each share new Common no par exchanged again for (0.33333333)

share new Common no par 11/09/2016
Name changed to Lineage Grow Co. Ltd. 07/25/2017

LAKESIDE MONARCH MINING CO. (UT)
Each (4) shares Capital Stock 10¢ par exchanged for (1) share Capital Stock 40¢ par 12/20/55
Merged into Micro Copper Corp. (DE) 7/13/57
Each share Capital Stock 40¢ par exchanged for (1) share Common 4¢ par
Micro Copper Corp. (DE) reincorporated in Nevada 5/8/85

LAKESIDE NATL BK (LAKE CHARLES, LA)
Capital Stock $10 par changed to $2.50 par and (3) additional shares issued 5/15/78
Reorganized as Lakeside Bancshares, Inc. 4/15/83
Each share Capital Stock $2.50 par exchanged for $6 principal amount of 15% Debentures due 4/15/95 and (1) share Common $2.50 par
Lakeside Bancshares, Inc. merged into First Commerce Corp. 8/3/95

LAKESIDE OIL & GAS LTD. (ON)
Merged into Erieshore Industries Inc. 05/10/1971
Each share Common $1 par exchanged for (0.4) share Common no par
Erieshore Industries Inc. merged into Portfield Industries Inc. 10/22/1980 which recapitalized as Canmine Resources Corp. 05/01/1991
(See Canmine Resources Corp.)

LAKESIDE STL INC (ON)
Acquired by JMC Steel Group, Inc. 03/30/2012
Each share Common no par exchanged for $0.2983 cash

LAKETOWN LEASING CORP. (NV)
Name changed to Admor Memory Corp. 10/21/1996
Admor Memory Corp. recapitalized as Atlas Resources, Inc. 12/24/2003 which recapitalized as Globaltech Holdings, Inc. 08/01/2007

LAKEVIEW FINL CORP (NJ)
Common $2 par split (2) for (1) by issuance of (1) additional share payable 10/15/1997 to holders of record 10/01/1997
Stock Dividends - 10% 02/06/1995; 10% payable 01/30/1996 to holders of record 01/16/1996; 10% payable 11/13/1996 to holders of record 10/30/1996
Merged into Dime Bancorp, Inc. (New) 05/21/1999
Each share Common $2 par exchanged for (0.9) share Common 1¢ par
Dime Bancorp, Inc. (New) merged into Washington Mutual, Inc. 01/04/2002
(See Washington Mutual, Inc.)

LAKEVIEW HOTEL REAL ESTATE INVT TR (MB)
Under plan of reorganization each Class A Trust Unit automatically became (1) share Lakeview Hotel Investment Corp. (Canada) Common no par 01/02/2013

LAKEVIEW SVGS BK (PATERSON, NJ)
Under plan of reorganization each share Common $2 par automatically became (1) share Lakeview Financial Corp. Common $2 par 08/26/1994
Lakeview Financial Corp. merged into Dime Bancorp, Inc. (New) 05/21/1999 which merged into Washington Mutual, Inc. 01/04/2002
(See Washington Mutual, Inc.)

LAKEWAY CHEMS INC (MI)
Common $1 par changed to $5 par and (1) additional share issued 06/01/1965
Stock Dividends - 10% 03/01/1968; 10% 05/12/1971; 25% 11/29/1974; 15% 11/28/1975
Merged into Bofors America, Inc. 10/21/1977
Each share Common $5 par exchanged for $29.42 cash

LAKEWOOD BK & TR CO (DALLAS, TX)
Common $5 par changed to $3 par and (2/3) additional share issued 11/03/1977
Common $3 par split (3) for (2) by issuance of (0.5) additional share 08/18/1979
Stock Dividends - 50% 10/02/1974; 14.58% 04/15/1977; 10% 04/13/1979; 10% 05/11/1981
Merged into Allied Bancshares, Inc. (TX) 03/31/1982
Each share Common $3 par exchanged for (0.825) share Common $1 par
Allied Bancshares, Inc. (TX) reincorporated in Delaware 04/22/1987 which merged into First Interstate Bancorp 01/29/1988 which merged into Wells Fargo & Co. (Old) 04/01/1996 which merged into Wells Fargo & Co. (New) 11/02/1998

LAKEWOOD BOWL, INC. (CA)
Charter revoked for failure to file reports and pay fees 12/1/69

LAKEWOOD ENERGY INC (CANADA)
Each Royalty Unit exchanged for (1.033) shares Common no par 8/10/93
Plan of arrangement effective 8/4/94
Each share Common no par exchanged for (0.686) share Serenpet Inc. Common no par 8/4/94
(See Serenpet Inc.)

LAKEWOOD ENGINEERING CO.
Merged into Jaeger Machine Co. 00/00/1928
Details not available

LAKEWOOD FST PRODS LTD (BC)
Struck off register and declared dissolved for failure to file returns 09/04/1992

LAKEWOOD MNG LTD (BC)
Recapitalized as Golden Secret Ventures Ltd. 11/18/2013
Each share Common no par exchanged for (0.06666666) share Common no par

LAKEWOOD STORAGE, INC. (OH)
Liquidation completed
Each share Common $100 par received initial distribution of $100 cash 6/25/71
Each share Common $100 par received second distribution of $400 cash 8/12/71
Each share Common $100 par received third and final distribution of $311.41 cash 9/24/71
Certificates were not required to be surrendered and are now valueless

LAKEWOOD TRUST CO. (LAKEWOOD, NJ)
Name changed to Trust Co. of Ocean County (Lakewood, NJ) 01/00/1963
Trust Co. of Ocean County (Lakewood, NJ) merged into First National State Bancorporation 11/10/1972 which name changed to First Fidelity Bancorporation (Old) 05/01/1985 which merged into First Fidelity Bancorporation (New) 02/29/1988 which merged into First Union Corp. 01/01/1996 which name changed to Wachovia Corp. (Ctfs. dated after 09/01/2001) 09/01/2001

which merged into Wells Fargo & Co. (New) 12/31/2008

LAKEX MINES LTD (ON)
Charter cancelled for failure to file reports and pay taxes 6/2/86

LAKEY FDRY CORP (MI)
Adjudicated bankrupt 10/11/1972
Stockholders' equity unlikely

LAKEY FOUNDRY & MACHINE CO.
Name changed to Lakey Foundry Corp. in 1952
(See Lakey Foundry Corp.)

LAKOTA ENERGY INC (CO)
Name changed to Lakota Technolgies, Inc. 08/04/1999
Lakota Technologies, Inc. name changed to 2-Infinity.com, Inc. 04/12/2000 which name changed to 2-Infinity, Inc. 08/25/2000
(See 2-Infinity, Inc.)

LAKOTA RES INC (ON)
Common no par split (2) for (1) by issuance of (1) additional share payable 12/16/2002 to holders of record 12/13/2002
Recapitalized as Tembo Gold Corp. 09/26/2011
Each (18) shares Common no par exchanged for (1) share Common no par

LAKOTA TECHNOLOGIES INC (CO)
Name changed to 2-Infinity.com, Inc. 04/12/2000
2-Infinity.com, Inc. name changed to 2-Infinity, Inc. 08/25/2000
(See 2-Infinity, Inc.)

LAKSHMI ENTERPRISES INC (DE)
SEC revoked common stock registration 04/08/2009

LAL VENTURES CORP (FL)
Name changed to Cyberoad.com Corp. (FL) 05/03/1999
Cyberoad.com Corp. (FL) reincorporated in Delaware as Strata Capital Corp. 01/11/2008 which name changed to Metrospaces, Inc. 02/13/2013

LALANCE & GROSJEAN MANUFACTURING CO. (NY)
Liquidated 6/30/55

LALO VENTURES LTD (BC)
Reincorporated 07/29/2005
Place of incorporation changed from (YT) to (BC) 07/29/2005
Name changed to Sunrise Minerals Inc. 12/20/2005
Sunrise Minerals Inc. recapitalized as Cronus Resources Ltd. (BC) 03/10/2008 which reincorporated in Ontario 06/25/2009 which merged into Continental Gold Ltd. (New) (Bermuda) 03/30/2010 which reorganized in Ontario as Continental Gold Inc. 06/12/2015

LAM INDS INC (DE)
Name changed to Easton Pharmaceuticals Inc. 03/17/2010

LAM LIANG CORP (NV)
Name changed to Blacksands Petroleum, Inc. 06/21/2006
(See Blacksands Petroleum, Inc.)

LAM PHARMACEUTICAL CORP (DE)
Recapitalized as LAM Industries Inc. 04/30/2009
Each (3,000) shares Common $0.0001 par exchanged for (1) share Common $0.0001 par
LAM Industries Inc. name changed to Easton Pharmaceuticals Inc. 03/17/2010

LAM RESH CORP (CA)
Reincorporated under the laws of Delaware and Common no par changed to $0.001 par in March 1990

LAMA EXPLORATION & MINING CO. LTD. (ON)
Charter cancelled in 1963

LAMA TONY INC (TX)
Common $1 par split (2) for (1) by issuance of (1) additional share 6/30/72
Merged into Justin Industries, Inc. 10/15/90
Each share Common $1 par exchanged for $9 cash

LAMALIE ASSOCS INC (FL)
Under plan of reorganization each share Common 1¢ par automatically became (1) share LAI Worldwide Inc. Common 1¢ par 12/31/1998
LAI Worldwide Inc. merged into TMP Worldwide Inc. 08/26/1999 which name changed to Monster Worldwide, Inc. 05/01/2003
(See Monster Worldwide, Inc.)

LAMAQUE GOLD MINES, LTD. (CANADA)
Merged into Teck Corp. Ltd. on a (0.8) for (1) basis 09/11/1963
Teck Corp. Ltd. name changed to Teck Corp. 11/21/1978 which name changed to Teck Cominco Ltd. 09/12/2001 which name changed to Teck Resources Ltd. 04/27/2009

LAMAR ADVERTISING CO OLD (DE)
Class A Common $0.001 par split (3) for (2) by issuance of (0.5) additional share payable 02/27/1998 to holders of record 02/13/1998
Class B Common $0.001 par split (3) for (2) by issuance of (0.5) additional share payable 02/27/1998 to holders of record 02/13/1998
Merged into Lamar Advertising Co. (New) 11/19/2014
Each share Class A Common $0.001 par exchanged for (1) share Class A Common $0.001 par
Each share Class B Common $0.001 par exchanged for (1) share Class B Common $0.001 par

LAMAR AUTO PTS INC (DE)
Charter cancelled and declared inoperative and void for non-payment of taxes 03/01/1987

LAMAR CAP CORP (MI)
Merged into Hancock Holding Co. 07/01/2001
Each share Common 50¢ par exchanged for $11 cash

LAMAR LIFE CORP (MS)
Stock Dividends - 116% 06/15/1973; 15% 05/01/1974
Name changed to Capitol Street Corp. 12/15/1988
(See Capitol Street Corp.)

LAMAR LIFE INS CO (MS)
Each share Common $10 par exchanged for (5) shares Common $2 par 08/12/1960
Stock Dividends - 233-1/3% 07/25/1950; 50% 01/15/1962; 10% 04/15/1963; 10% 04/15/1964; 10% 02/15/1965; 10% 04/15/1966; 10% 02/03/1967
Reorganized as Lamar Life Corp. 10/04/1972
Each share Common $2 par exchanged for (1) share Common $1 par
Lamar Life Corp. name changed to Capitol Street Corp. 12/15/1988
(See Capitol Street Corp.)

LAMAR LUMBER CO., INC.
Acquired by Mengel Co. 00/00/1935
Details not available

LAMARTINE MINES, INC. (CO)
Charter revoked for failure to file reports and pay fees 10/15/64

LAMAUR CORP (DE)
Filed a petition under Chapter 7 Federal Bankruptcy Code 06/19/2002
No stockholders' equity

LAMAUR INC (MN)
Common $0.03333333 par split (2) for

(1) by issuance of (1) additional
  share 05/17/1983
Common $0.03333333 par split (4) for
  (3) by issuance of (0.33333333)
  additional share 03/20/1985
Merged into Dow Chemical Co.
  01/05/1988
Each share Common $0.03333333
  par exchanged for $28.50 cash

LAMB COMMUNICATIONS, INC. (DE)
Common no par changed to 50¢ par
  11/30/70
Merged into Lamb Enterprises, Inc.
  3/31/78
Each share Common 50¢ par
  exchanged for $2.60 cash

LAMB FD INC (MD)
Completely liquidated 03/27/1973
Each share Common $1 par received
  first and final distribution of $8.86
  cash
Note: Certificates were not required to
  be surrendered and are without
  value

LAMB INDUSTRIES, INC. (DE)
Common $3 par changed to no par
  7/6/65
Name changed to Lamb
  Communications, Inc. 8/28/67
(See Lamb Communications, Inc.)

LAMB WESTON INC (OR)
Merged into Amfac, Inc. 08/25/1971
Each share Common no par
  exchanged for (0.9) share Common
  no par
(See Amfac, Inc.)

LAMBDA MERCANTILE CORP (ON)
Recapitalized 02/20/1979
Recapitalized from Lambda
  Mercantile Corp. Ltd. to Lambda
  Mercantile Corp. 02/20/1979
Each share Class A Preference no
  par exchanged for (2) shares Class
  A Preference no par
Each share Common no par
  exchanged for (2) shares Common
  no par
Common no par split (5) for (2) by
  issuance of (1.5) additional share
  10/24/1983
Class A Preference no par split (2) for
  (1) by issuance of (1) additional
  share 11/16/1984
Common no par split (2) for (1) by
  issuance of (1) additional share
  11/16/1984
Reorganized as Consolidated
  Mercantile Corp. 09/30/1987
Each share Class A Preference no
  par exchanged for (0.5) share
  Preference Ser. 1 no par
Each share Common no par
  exchanged for (0.5) share Common
  no par
Consolidated Mercantile Corp.
  recapitalized as Consolidated
  Mercantile Inc. 11/23/1998 which
  merged into Genterra Capital Inc.
  (New) 05/10/2010 which merged
  into Gencan Capital Inc. 10/30/2015

LAMBENT SOLUTIONS CORP (NV)
Name changed to USA InvestCo
  Holdings, Inc. 11/07/2012

LAMBERT ALFRED INC (QC)
Each share Common $5 par
  exchanged for (5) shares Common
  $1 par 00/00/1944
Each share Common $1 par
  exchanged for (0.5) share Class A
  $1 par and (0.5) share Class B $1
  par 00/00/1951
5% Conv. Preferred. 1956 Ser. $20
  par called for redemption
  06/28/1963
6-1/2% Preferred 1959 Ser. $20 par
  called for redemption 06/28/1963
Through purchase offer F.I.C. Fund
  Inc. acquired 100% of Class A $1
  par as of 08/28/1974
Public interest eliminated

LAMBERT CO. (DE)
Deferred Stock no par exchanged for
  Common no par in 1928
Merged into Warner-Lambert
  Pharmaceutical Co. 3/31/55
Each share Common no par
  exchanged for (1) share Common
  $1 par
Warner-Lambert Pharmaceutical Co.
  name changed to Warner-Lambert
  Co. 11/13/70 which merged into
  Pfizer Inc. 6/19/2000

LAMBERT COMMUNICATIONS INC (DE)
Plan of reorganization under Chapter
  11 Federal Bankruptcy proceedings
  confirmed 01/31/1996
No stockholders' equity

LAMBERT TIRE & RUBBER CO. (AZ)
Charter expired by time limitation
  9/18/38

LAMBERTVILLE NATL BK (LAMBERTVILLE, NJ)
Merged into First Trenton National
  Bank (Trenton, NJ) 12/01/1969
Each share Capital Stock $20 par
  exchanged for (2.5) shares Common
  $5 par
First Trenton National Bank (Trenton,
  NJ) name changed to New Jersey
  National Bank (Trenton, NJ)
  05/11/1970 which reorganized as
  NJN Bancorporation 07/01/1971
  which name changed to New Jersey
  National Corp. 03/21/1972 which
  was acquired by CoreStates
  Financial Corp 10/30/1986 which
  merged into First Union Corp.
  04/28/1998 which name changed to
  Wachovia Corp. (Ctfs. dated after
  09/01/2001) 09/01/2001 which
  merged into Wells Fargo & Co.
  (New) 12/31/2008

LAMBRECHT KELLY CO (MI)
Liquidation completed
Each share Common $1 par received
  initial distribution of $0.50 cash
  04/04/1968
Each share Common $1 par received
  second distribution of $0.50 cash
  10/25/1968
Each share Common $1 par received
  third distribution of $0.50 cash
  01/14/1969
Each share Common $1 par received
  fourth distribution of $1 cash
  01/05/1970
Each share Common $1 par
  exchanged for fifth and final
  distribution of $0.90 cash
  03/31/1970

LAMBTON LN & INVT CO (ON)
Each share Common $10 par
  exchanged for (5) shares Common
  $2 par 08/16/1963
Over 99.6% acquired by Victoria &
  Grey Trust Co. (Toronto, ON)
  10/31/1973
Public interest eliminated

LAMCOR INC (MN)
Merged into Packaging Acquisition
  Co. 1/6/97
Each share Common no par
  exchanged for $4 cash
Note: An additional $0.12 cash per
  share is being held in escrow for
  possible future distribution

LAMELEE IRON ORE INC (CANADA)
Each share old Common no par
  exchanged for (0.05) share new
  Common no par 08/02/2016
Reincorporated under the laws of
  Ontario as Aura Health Inc.
  08/16/2018

LAMINAIRE CORP (DE)
Recapitalized as Agent 155 Media
  Group, Inc. 11/19/2004
Each share Common $0.001 par
  exchanged for (0.005) share
  Common $0.001 par
Agent 155 Media Group, Inc.
  recapitalized as Cavico Corp.
  05/12/2006
(See Cavico Corp.)

LAMINAR CORP (MN)
Creditors took possession of
  equipment and operations ceased
  12/10/1970
Stockholders' equity unlikely

LAMINATING TECHNOLOGIES INC (DE)
Name changed to LTI Holdings, Inc.
  06/25/1999
LTI Holdings, Inc. recapitalized as
  SPEEDCOM Wireless Corp.
  09/27/2000 which name changed to
  SP Holding Corp. 07/05/2005 which
  name changed to Organic To Go
  Food Corp. 05/21/2007
(See Organic To Go Food Corp.)

LAMINCO RES INC (BC)
Reorganized under the laws of Yukon
  as Zaruma Resources Inc.
  11/01/2000
Each share Common no par
  exchanged for (0.1) share Common
  no par
Zaruma Resources Inc. recapitalized
  as Red Tiger Mining Inc. 11/08/2011

LAMONTAGNE LTD (QC)
Each share Class A $1 par
  exchanged for (4) shares Class A no
  par 12/11/1967
Acquired by Couvrette & Provost
  Ltee. 11/05/1969
Each share Class A no par
  exchanged for (0.714285) share
  Common no par
Each share Class B $1 par
  exchanged for (0.714285) share
  Common no par
Couvrette & Provost Ltee. name
  changed to Provigo Inc. (Old)
  09/14/1970 which name changed to
  Univa Inc. 05/22/1992 which name
  changed to Provigo Inc. (New)
  05/25/1994 which was acquired by
  Loblaw Companies Ltd. 12/10/1998

LAMONTS APPAREL INC (DE)
Recapitalized 11/2/92
Recapitalized from Lamonts Corp. to
  Lamonts Apparel, Inc. 11/2/92
Each share old Common 1¢ par
  exchanged for (1/30) share new
  Common 1¢ par
Each share Preferred Ser. A 1¢ par
  exchanged for (2) shares new
  Common 1¢ par 3/21/94
Each share new Common 1¢ par
  exchanged again for (0.01117315)
  share new Common 1¢ par and
  (0.00558655) Common Stock
  Purchase Warrants, Class B expiring
  1/31/2008 on 1/31/98
Plan of reorganization under Chapter
  11 Federal Bankruptcy Code
  effective 11/16/2000
No stockholders' equity

LAMORINDA FINANCIAL CORP. (CA)
Merged into Mission-Valley Bancorp
  12/16/88
Each share Common no par
  exchanged for (0.3577) share
  Common no par
Mission-Valley Bancorp merged into
  California Bancshares Inc. 7/1/91

LAMOUR (DOROTHY), INC. (DE)
No longer in existence having
  become inoperative and void for
  non-payment of taxes 4/1/63

LAMP FASHION INC (DE)
Adjudicated bankrupt 4/13/80
Stockholders' equity unlikely

LAMPERT AGENCY, INC. (NY)
Name changed to Lampert
  Communications, Inc. 2/13/74
(See Lampert Communications, Inc.)

LAMPERT COMMUNICATIONS INC (NY)
Completely liquidated 11/17/1978
Each share Common 10¢ par
  exchanged for first and final
  distribution of $0.46 cash

LAMPLIGHTER ENERGY LTD (AB)
Each share old Common no par
  exchanged for (0.16666666) share
  new Common no par 05/30/2003
Merged into Blackdog Resources Ltd.
  01/12/2006
Each share new Common no par
  exchanged for (1) share Common
  no par
Blackdog Resources Ltd. name
  changed to StonePoint Energy Inc.
  11/06/2014
(See StonePoint Energy Inc.)

LAMSON & SESSIONS CO (OH)
Each share Common $25 par
  exchanged for (1.725) shares
  Common no par 00/00/1929
Each share 7% Preferred $100 par
  exchanged for (3) shares $2.50
  Preferred no par and (1) share
  Common $10 par 00/00/1941
Each share Common no par
  exchanged for (1) share Common
  $10 par 00/00/1941
$2.50 Preferred no par called for
  redemption 11/18/1954
$4.75 Conv. Class A Preferred $50
  par called for redemption
  08/01/1967
Common $10 par changed to $5 par
  and (1) additional share issued
  08/24/1967
Common $5 par split (3) for (2) by
  issuance of (0.5) additional share
  12/07/1978
Common $5 par split (3) for (2) by
  issuance of (0.5) additional share
  09/10/1979
Common $5 par changed to no par
  06/28/1984
Stock Dividends - 10% 08/03/1948;
  20% 12/29/1950; 10% 12/06/1951;
  10% 06/10/1974; 15% 02/28/1975
Merged into Thomas & Betts Corp.
  11/05/2007
Each share Common no par
  exchanged for $27.30 cash

LAMSON BUILDING CO. (OH)
Liquidated in 1953

LAMSON CORP. (NY)
6% Prior Preferred called for
  redemption 06/30/1965
Merged into Diebold, Inc. 07/16/1965
Each share Common $5 par
  exchanged for (1) share Common
  $2.50 par
Diebold, Inc. name changed to
  Diebold Nixdorf Inc. 12/12/2016

LAMSON CORP. OF DELAWARE (DE)
6% Preferred $50 par reclassified as
  6% Prior Preferred $50 par
  05/01/1948
Reincorporated under the laws of
  New York as Lamson Corp.
  03/26/1962
Lamson Corp. merged into Diebold,
  Inc. 07/16/1965 which name
  changed to Diebold Nixdorf Inc.
  12/12/2016

LAMSTON M H INC (NY)
Each share Class A no par or Class B
  no par exchanged for (1) share
  Common $1 par in 1945
$6 Preferred no par called for
  redemption 1/24/57
Common $1 par split (6) for (5) by
  issuance of (0.2) additional share
  6/1/62
Common $1 par split (6) for (5) by
  issuance of (0.2) additional share
  6/1/65
Common $1 par split (2) for (1) by
  issuance of (1) additional share
  6/16/80
Stock Dividends - 100% 12/31/45;
  100% 11/20/47; 10% 2/1/51; 20%
  3/1/57; 20% 4/1/59
Merged into Stonlam Holdings, Inc.
  7/11/83

Each share Common $1 par exchanged for $40 cash

LAMTEX INDUSTRIES, INC. (NY)
Name changed to Pomel, Inc. 07/01/1963
(See Pomel, Inc.)

LAMTRON INDS INC (FL)
Recapitalized 2/20/69
Class A Common 10¢ par split (3) for (1) by issuance of (2) additional shares
Class B Common 10¢ par reclassified as Class A Common 10¢ par and (2) additional shares issued
Adjudicated bankrupt 12/23/71
Stockholders' equity not determined

LAN AIRLINES S A (CHILE)
Name changed 09/08/2004
Name changed from Lan Chile S.A. to Lan Airlines S.A. 09/08/2004
Sponsored ADR's for Ordinary split (5) for (1) by issuance of (4) additional ADR's payable 08/15/2007 to holders of record 08/14/2007 Ex date - 08/16/2007
Name changed to LATAM Airlines Group S.A. 10/11/2012

LAN MGMT INC (DE)
Name changed to Transworld Temporaries, Inc. 05/24/1989
(See Transworld Temporaries, Inc.)

LAN SYS INC (MN)
Statutorily dissolved 12/31/93

LANA GOLD CORP (BC)
Recapitalized as Global Technologies Inc. 03/07/1995
Each share Common no par exchanged for (0.33333333) share Common no par
Global Technologies Inc. recapitalized as Consolidated Global Technologies Inc. 12/05/2001 which name changed to Garnet Point Resources Corp. 12/17/2003 which name changed to Hastings Resources Corp. 02/21/2008 which recapitalized as Trigen Resources Inc. 09/22/2010 which recapitalized as BlissCo Cannabis Corp. 03/02/2018

LANACORT CORP. (NY)
Liquidation completed
Each share Common $1 par exchanged for initial distribution of $2.05 cash 5/22/72
Each share Common $1 par received second distribution of $0.13 cash 2/23/73
Each share Common $1 par received third and final distribution of $0.05 cash 5/23/75

LANAI INDUSTRIES INC. (DE)
Charter cancelled and declared inoperative and void for non-payment of taxes 4/15/71

LANAI LECTRONICS INC (DE)
Name changed to Lanai Industries Inc. 10/14/1969
(See Lanai Industries Inc.)

LANARK SILVER MINES LTD. (ON)
Charter revoked for failure to file reports and pay fees 11/10/66

LANARK URANIUM MINES LTD. (ON)
Charter cancelled for failure to file reports and pay taxes in 1956

LANATIN CORP.
Out of existence 00/00/1940
Details not available

LANCASHIRE STEEL CORP. LTD. (ENGLAND)
Nationalized by the United Kingdom 08/08/1967
Each ADR for Ordinary £1 par exchanged for £1 6s 6.0462d principal amount of 6-1/2% Treasury Stock due 01/28/1971

LANCASTER, MECHANICSBURG & NEW HOLLAND RAILWAY CO.
Merged into Conestoga Transportation Co. 00/00/1932
Details not available

LANCASTER, PETERSBURG & MANHEIM RAILWAY CO.
Merged into Conestoga Transportation Co. 00/00/1932
Details not available

LANCASTER, WILLOW STREEET, LAMPETER & STRASBURG RAILWAY CO.
Merged into Conestoga Transportation Co. 00/00/1932
Details not available

LANCASTER & EASTERN STREET RAILWAY CO.
Merged into Conestoga Transportation Co. 00/00/1932
Details not available

LANCASTER & QUARRYVILLE STREET RAILWAY CO.
Merged into Conestoga Transportation Co. 00/00/1932
Details not available

LANCASTER & ROCKY SPRINGS RAILWAY CO.
Merged into Conestoga Transportation Co. 00/00/1932
Details not available

LANCASTER CAP CORP (BC)
Name changed to NxGold Ltd. 11/18/2016

LANCASTER COLONY CORP (DE)
$1 Conv. Preferred Ser. A no par called redemption 10/12/69
Common $4 par split (6) for (5) by issuance of (0.2) additional share 6/30/71
Common $4 par split (3) for (2) by issuance of (0.5) additional share 3/30/72
Common $4 par split (3) for (2) by issuance of (0.5) additional share 2/17/78
Common $4 par changed to $1 par 11/20/78
Common $1 par split (3) for (2) by issuance of (0.5) additional share 1/4/83
Common $1 par split (5) for (4) by issuance of (0.25) additional share 7/28/86
Stock Dividend - 10% 1/25/88
Reincorporated under the laws of Ohio 1/2/92

LANCASTER CORP. (PA)
Class A Common $1 par and Class B Common $1 par reclassified as Common $1 par 1/30/63
Recapitalized as Safeguard Industries, Inc. 4/5/66
Each share Common $1 par exchanged for (3) shares Common 10¢ par
Safeguard Industries, Inc. name changed to Safeguard Scientifics, Inc. 5/15/81

LANCASTER CNTY FMRS NATL BK (LANCASTER, PA)
Merged into National Central Bank (Lancaster, PA) 12/07/1970
Each share Common $10 par exchanged for (1.4) shares Common $10 par
National Central Bank (Lancaster, PA) reorganized as National Central Financial Corp. 12/31/1972 which merged into CoreStates Financial Corp 05/02/1983 which merged into First Union Corp. 04/28/1998 which name changed to Wachovia Corp. (Ctfs. dated after 09/01/2001) 09/01/2001 which merged into Wells Fargo & Co. (New) 12/31/2008

LANCASTER COUNTY NATIONAL BANK (LANCASTER, PA)
Each share Common $50 par exchanged for (5) shares Common $10 par 00/00/1954
Merged into Lancaster County Farmers National Bank (Lancaster, PA) 12/11/1963
Each share Common $10 par exchanged for (1.25) shares Common $10 par
Lancaster County Farmers National Bank (Lancaster, PA) merged into National Central Bank (Lancaster, PA) 12/07/1970 which reorganized as National Central Financial Corp. 12/31/1972 which merged into CoreStates Financial Corp 05/02/1983 which merged into First Union Corp. 04/28/1998 which name changed to Wachovia Corp. (Ctfs. dated after 09/01/2001) 09/01/2001 which merged into Wells Fargo & Co. (New) 12/31/2008

LANCASTER IRON WORKS, INC.
Name changed to Posey Iron Works, Inc. in 1948
(See Posey Iron Works, Inc.)

LANCASTER MILLS
Liquidation completed in 1932

LANCASTER NATL BK (LANCASTER, NH)
Common $60 par changed to $30 par and (1) additional share issued 02/24/1970
Common $30 par changed to $5 par and (4) additional shares issued 03/27/1989
Common $5 par split (5) for (1) by issuance of (4) additional shares payable 09/27/2002 to holders of record 08/02/2002 Ex date - 10/01/2002
Merged into Passumpsic Savings Bank (Lancaster, NH) 07/14/2008
Each share Common $5 par exchanged for $57 cash

LANCASTER RESOURCE CORP (BC)
Name changed to Synex International Inc. 07/08/1985

LANCASTER SIERRA CAP CORP
Name changed to EFT Canada Inc. 05/12/2006
(See EFT Canada Inc.)

LANCE CREEK RYTS CO (WY)
Charter revoked for failure to file annual reports 4/3/96

LANCE INC (NC)
Common $2.50 par changed to $1.25 par and (1) additional share issued 05/16/1972
Common $1.25 par changed to $0.83333333 par and (0.5) additional share issued 05/16/1978
Common $0.83333333 par split (4) for (3) by issuance of (0.33333333) additional share 04/10/1985
Common $0.83333333 par split (2) for (1) by issuance of (1) additional share 08/28/1987
Stock Dividend - 50% 03/31/1982
Name changed to Snyder's-Lance, Inc. 12/13/2010
(See Snyder's-Lance, Inc.)

LANCE SYS INC (UT)
Each share old Common $0.001 par exchanged for (0.00285714) share new Common $0.001 par 06/30/2003
Name changed to Conspiracy Entertainment Holdings, Inc. 08/01/2003
(See Conspiracy Entertainment Holdings, Inc.)

LANCER CDA LTD (BC)
100% acquired through purchase offer which expired 08/18/1977
Public interest eliminated

LANCER CORP (FL)
Proclaimed dissolved for failure to file reports and pay fees 12/5/79

LANCER CORP (TX)
Common 1¢ par split (3) for (2) by issuance of (0.5) additional share 7/11/95
Common 1¢ par split (3) for (2) by issuance of (0.5) additional share payable 7/9/96 to holders of record 6/25/96
Common 1¢ par split (3) for (2) by issuance of (0.5) additional share payable 7/8/97 to holders of record 6/24/97 Ex date - 7/9/97
Merged into Hoshizaki America, Inc. 2/2/2006
Each share Common 1¢ par exchanged for $22 cash

LANCER GRAPHIC INDS INC (DE)
Each share old Common 10¢ par exchanged for (0.1) share new Common 10¢ par 10/15/73
Name changed to LGI Corp. 3/1/76
(See LGI Corp.)

LANCER HOMES INC (TX)
Name changed to Lanchart Industries, Inc. 01/23/1973
(See Lanchart Industries, Inc.)

LANCER INDUSTRIES INC. (FL)
Common 10¢ par split (2) for (1) by issuance of (1) additional share 8/15/59
Name changed to Strato Industries Inc. 9/11/62
(See Strato Industries Inc.)

LANCER INDS INC (DE)
Merged into a wholly owned subsidiary 9/21/94
Each share Class A Preferred $0.0025 par exchanged for $0.95 cash
Each share Class B Preferred $0.0025 par exchanged for $0.95 cash
Each share new Class A Common $0.0025 par exchanged for $0.95 cash
Each share new Class B Common $0.0025 par exchanged for $0.95 cash

LANCER PACIFIC, INC. (CA)
Name changed to Lancer Orthodontics, Inc. 1/23/87

LANCER RES INC (BC)
Recapitalized as V-Tech Diagnostics (Canada) Inc. 01/29/1991
Each share Common no par exchanged for (0.2) share Common no par
(See V-Tech Diagnostics (Canada) Inc.)

LANCHART INDS INC (TX)
Merged into LDB Corp. 05/04/1979
Each share Common 10¢ par exchanged for $6 cash

LANCIA MOTORS OF AMERICA, INC.
Bankrupt in 1929

LANCIT MEDIA ENTMT LTD (NY)
Name changed from Lancit Media Productions, Ltd. to Lancit Media Entertainment Ltd. 12/18/96
Merged into RCN Corp. 6/15/98
Each share Common $0.001 par exchanged for (0.05) share Common $1 par

LAND & GENERAL FINANCE CORP. (FL)
Merged into Coral Ridge Properties, Inc. 08/24/1959
Details not available

LAND & HSES PUB CO LTD (THAILAND)
ADR agreement terminated 05/21/2018
No ADR's remain outstanding

LAND & LEISURE INC (FL)
Proclaimed dissolved for failure to file reports and pay fees 10/04/2002

LAND & SEA RES INC (NV)
Charter revoked for failure to file reports and pay fees 12/01/1989

LAND CONSULTANTS AMER INC (DE)
Completely liquidated 04/12/1972
Each share Common 1¢ par exchanged for first and final distribution of (0.4) share NHA, Inc. Common $1 par
(See NHA, Inc.)

LAND CORP. OF AMERICA, INC. (MN)
Name changed to Future Homes, Inc. 1/19/78

LAND DYNAMICS (CA)
Completely liquidated 04/18/2007
Each share Common $1 par exchanged for first and final distribution of $3.40 cash

LAND EQUITIES INC (NV)
Name changed to Intercontinental Equities, Inc. 11/21/1972
(See Intercontinental Equities, Inc.)

LAND INVS AMER INC (OK)
Reorganized as U.S. Development Corp. 01/20/2005
Each share Common $0.001 par exchanged for (10) shares Common $0.001 par
U.S. Development Corp. recapitalized as Gulf Ethanol Corp. 07/31/2006 which recapitalized as Gulf Alternative Energy Corp. 03/24/2009

LAND O FABRICS INC (GA)
Adjudicated bankrupt 03/29/1976
No stockholders' equity

LAND OF LINCOLN LIFE INSURANCE CO. (IL)
Each share Common 35¢ par exchanged for (4) shares Common $0.0875 par 7/26/63
Acquired by Wabash Life Insurance Co. 8/29/65
Each share Common $0.0875 par exchanged for (0.1869159) share Common $1 par
Wabash Life Insurance Co. name changed to Wabash International Corp. 12/28/67
(See Wabash International Corp.)

LAND OF LINCOLN SVGS & LN ASSN (IL)
Merged into Household Bank, f.s.b. (Newport Beach, CA) 06/16/1989
Each share Common $1 exchanged for $21 cash

LAND RESOURCES LTD. (UT)
Reincorporated under the laws of Nevada as CSD, Inc. 1/16/79
CSD, Inc. name changed to Capital Energy & Operating Co. 5/6/81
(See Capital Energy & Operating Co.)

LAND SECS GROUP PLC (ENGLAND & WALES)
ADR agreement terminated 09/01/2016
Each Sponsored ADR for Ordinary exchanged for $14.6672 cash
(Additional Information in Active)

LAND TITLE GTY & TR CO (OH)
100% acquired by Chicago Title & Trust Co. through exchange offer which expired 06/02/1969
Public interest eliminated

LAND TITLE INSURANCE CO. (CA)
Stock Dividends - 20% 11/20/1957; 20% 02/20/1959; 20% 08/20/1959
Merged into Security Title Insurance Co. 11/17/1959
Each share Capital Stock $2.50 par exchanged for (0.6) share Capital Stock $1 par
Security Title Insurance Co. name changed to Financial Corp. of America 04/30/1962 which merged into General America Corp. 07/31/1964 which name changed to Safeco Corp. 04/30/1968
(See Safeco Corp.)

LAND TITLE INS CO (MO)
8% Preferred $100 par called for redemption 00/00/1946
Merged into First American Corp. 06/30/2009
Details not available

LANDA INDUSTRIES, INC.
Bankrupt in 1930

LANDA INDS INC (DE)
Recapitalized as Surveyor Companies, Inc. 11/12/1971
Each share Common 10¢ par exchanged for (0.2) share Common $0.001 par
Surveyor Companies, Inc. name changed to Forum Companies, Inc. 09/23/1974
(See Forum Companies, Inc.)

LANDA MGMT SYS CORP (CA)
Reincorporated under the laws of Delaware as Landacorp Inc. 12/3/99
(See Landacorp Inc.)

LANDA OIL CO OLD (DE)
Name changed to Landa Industries, Inc. 04/07/1967
Landa Industries, Inc. recapitalized as Surveyor Companies, Inc. 11/12/1971 which name changed to Forum Companies, Inc. 09/23/1974
(See Forum Companies, Inc.)

LANDACORP INC (DE)
Merged into SHPS Holdings, Inc. 4/27/2004
Each share Common $0.001 par exchanged for $3.09 cash

LANDAIR CORP (TN)
Common 1¢ par split (3) for (2) by issuance of (0.5) additional share payable 9/9/2002 to holders of record 8/30/2002 Ex date - 9/10/2002
Merged into Landair Acquisition Corp. 2/28/2003
Each share Common 1¢ par exchanged for $13 cash

LANDAIR SVCS INC (TN)
Name changed to Forward Air Corp. 8/27/98

LANDALL CORP (DE)
Name changed to Shongum Corp. 06/26/1984
Shongum Corp. name changed to American Water Resources, Inc. 07/19/1989
(See American Water Resources, Inc.)

LANDAMERICA FINL GROUP INC (VA)
Plan of reorganization under Chapter 11 Federal Bankruptcy proceedings effective 12/07/2009
No stockholders' equity

LANDAUER INC (DE)
Common no par split (2) for (1) by issuance of (1) additional share 01/17/1992
Common no par changed to 10¢ par 02/03/1993
Acquired by Fortive Corp. 10/19/2017
Each share Common 10¢ par exchanged for $67.25 cash

LANDBAN FLA CORP (FL)
Name changed to Transamerica Business Corp. 01/26/1977
(See Transamerica Business Corp.)

LANDBANK GROUP INC (DE)
Each share old Common $0.00001 par exchanged for (0.1) share new Common $0.0001 par 06/30/2006
Name changed to Trist Holdings, Inc. 01/11/2008
Trist Holdings, Inc. name changed to AtheroNova Inc. 05/25/2010

LANDCARE USA INC (DE)
Issue Information - 5,000,000 shares COM offered at $8 per share on 06/04/1998
Merged into ServiceMaster Co. 03/18/1999
Each share Common no par exchanged for (0.55) share Common 1¢ par
(See ServiceMaster Co.)

LANDCO INC (DE)
Name changed to Milbrook Financial Corp. 01/17/1984
(See Milbrook Financial Corp.)

LANDDRILL INTL INC (BC)
Declared bankrupt 05/30/2013
Stockholders' equity unlikely

LANDEC CORP (CA)
Reincorporated under the laws of Delaware 11/06/2008

LANDEN CAP CORP (BC)
Name changed to Sama Resources Inc. (BC) 06/22/2010
Sama Resources Inc. (BC) reincorporated in Canada 05/21/2013

LANDEN CORP. (CT)
Proclaimed dissolved 11/28/73

LANDER ENERGY CO (CO)
Reincorporated 7/8/86
State of incorporation changed from (WY) to (CO) 7/8/86
Recapitalized as Voice It Worldwide Inc. 12/29/94
Each (4.98) shares Common 10¢ par exchanged for (1) share Common 10¢ par
(See Voice It Worldwide Inc.)

LANDER ENERGY CORP (ON)
Reincorporated under the laws of British Columbia as Prosper Gold Corp. 04/27/2012

LANDERS, FRARY & CLARK (CT)
Common $25 par changed to no par 4/27/60
Merged into Williams (J.B.) Co., Inc., for cash 5/28/65

LANDIS ENERGY CORP (AB)
Acquired by AltaGas Income Trust 03/23/2010
Each share Common no par exchanged for $0.80 cash

LANDIS MACHINE CO. (PA)
Acquired by Teledyne, Inc. 02/24/1968
Each share Common $2 par exchanged for (0.5) share $6 Conv. Preferred $1 par and (0.4) share $3.50 Conv. Preferred $1 par
(See Teledyne, Inc.)

LANDIS MNG CORP (AB)
Name changed to Landis Energy Corp. 07/26/2006
(See Landis Energy Corp.)

LANDIS TOOL CO. (PA)
Common no par split (2) for (1) by issuance of (1) additional share 04/20/1966
Completely liquidated 01/16/1968
Each share Common no par exchanged for first and final distribution of (1) share Litton Industries, Inc. $2 Conv. Preferred Ser. B $5 par
(See Litton Industries, Inc.)

LANDMARK AMERN CORP (GA)
Administratively dissolved 7/17/94

LANDMARK BANCORP LA HABRA CALIF (CA)
Merged into California State Bank (Covina, CA) 4/12/96
Each share Common no par exchanged for (0.796) share Common no par and $8.22 cash
California State Bank (Covina, CA) merged into First Security Corp. 5/30/98 which merged into Wells Fargo & Co. (New) 10/26/2000

LANDMARK BANCSHARES CORP (MO)
Common $5 par changed to no par and (0.5) additional share issued 05/29/1981
Common no par split (3) for (2) by issuance of (0.5) additional share 12/01/1983
Conv. Preferred Ser. II 10¢ par called for redemption 12/06/1984
Variable Rate Conv. Preferred Ser. I 10¢ par called for redemption 04/17/1990
Merged into Magna Group, Inc. 12/20/1991
Each share 7.5% Preferred $20 par exchanged for (1) share 7.5% Class B Preferred $20 par
Each share Common no par exchanged for (0.81) share Common $2 par and $0.50 cash
Magna Group, Inc. merged into Union Planters Corp. 07/01/1998 which merged into Regions Financial Corp. (New) 07/01/2004

LANDMARK BANCSHARES INC (KS)
Under plan of merger each share Common 10¢ par automatically became (1) share Landmark Bancorp, Inc. (DE) Common 10¢ par 10/09/2001

LANDMARK BANK (HARTFORD, CT)
Reorganized as Landmark Financial Corp. (Conn.) 9/22/86
Each share Common $3.33 par exchanged for (1) share Common $3 par
Landmark Financial Corp. (Conn.) merged into Landmark/Community Bancorp. Inc. 7/29/88

LANDMARK BANK (LA HABRA, CA)
Under plan of reorganization each share Common $6.25 par automatically became (1) share Landmark Bancorp Common no par 2/26/83
Landmark Bancorp merged into California State Bank (Covina, CA) 4/12/96 which merged into First Security Corp. 5/30/98 which merged into Wells Fargo & Co. (New) 10/26/2000

LANDMARK BK FOR SVGS (WHITMAN, MA)
Common 10¢ par split (3) for (2) by issuance of (0.5) additional share 05/18/1987
Placed in receivership with FDIC 06/12/1992
No stockholders' equity

LANDMARK BANK OF CLEARWATER, N.A. (CLEARWATER, FL)
Bank closed 01/03/1977
No stockholders' equity

LANDMARK BKG CORP FLA (FL)
Stock Dividends - 10% 1/2/81; 10% 1/3/83
Merged into Citizens & Southern Georgia Corp. 8/30/85
Each share Common $1 par exchanged for (0.92) share Common $2.50 par
Citizens & Southern Georgia Corp. name changed to Citizens & Southern Corp. 5/20/86 which merged into C&S/Sovran Corp. 9/1/90 which merged into NationsBank Corp. 12/31/91 which reincorporated in Delaware as BankAmerica Corp. (Old) 9/25/98 which merged into BankAmerica Corp. (New) 9/30/98 which name changed to Bank of America Corp. 4/28/99

LANDMARK CAP CORP (AB)
Issue Information - 2,500,000 shares COM offered at $0.20 per share on 01/08/2002
Name changed to Landmark Oil & Gas Corp. 12/10/2003
(See Landmark Oil & Gas Corp.)

LANDMARK CAP GROWTH FD (MA)
Reorganized as Landmark Funds II 04/26/1990
Details not available

LANDMARK CENTRAL BANK & TRUST CO. (WELLSTON, MO)
100% acquired by Landmark Bancshares through exchange offer which expired 12/09/1976
Public interest eliminated

LANDMARK/CMNTY BANCORP INC (DE)
Declared insolvent and taken over by FDIC 03/28/1991
Stockholders' equity unlikely

LANDMARK CMNTY BK (PITTSTON, PA)
Under plan of reorganization each share Common $1 par automatically became (1) share Landmark Bancorp, Inc. Common $1 par 10/30/2008

LANDMARK CORP. OF INDIANA (IN)
Charter revoked for failure to file reports 9/15/66

LANDMARK CORP NEW (ON)
Recapitalized as Landmark Global Financial Corp. 7/5/96
Each share Common no par exchanged for (0.1) share Common no par

LANDMARK CORP OLD (ON)
Merged into Landmark Corp. (New) 1/31/92
Each share Subordinate no par exchanged for (0.84615384) share Common no par
Landmark Corp. (New) recapitalized as Landmark Global Financial Corp. 7/5/96

LANDMARK ENERGY ENTERPRISE INC (NV)
Common $0.001 par split (8) for (1) by issuance of (7) additional shares payable 04/19/2010 to holders of record 04/19/2010
SEC revoked common stock registration 05/21/2015

LANDMARK ENVIRONMENTAL INC (BC)
Recapitalized as International Landmark Environmental Inc. 06/12/1997
Each share Common no par exchanged for (0.1) share Common no par
International Landmark Environmental Inc. recapitalized as Shabute Ventures Inc. 01/15/2003 which name changed to Northern Sun Exploration Co. Inc. 08/19/2004 which recapitalized as Reparo Energy Partners Corp. 11/08/2013

LANDMARK FDS TAX FREE RESVS (MA)
Name changed to CitiFunds Tax Free Reserves 1/2/97
CitiFunds Tax Free Reserves name changed to Citi Tax Free Reserves 12/28/2000

LANDMARK FINL CORP (CT)
Common $3 par split (3) for (2) by issuance of (0.5) additional share 10/15/86
Stock Dividends - 20% 6/26/87; 10% 7/29/80
Merged into Landmark/Community Bancorp, Inc. 7/29/88
Each share Exchangeable Auction Preferred $1 par exchanged for an undetermined amount of Auction Rate Notes expiring 8/2/99
Each share Common $3 par exchanged for (1) share Common 1¢ par

LANDMARK FINL CORP (DE)
Merged into TrustCo Bank Corp NY 7/28/2000

Each share Common 10¢ par exchanged for $21 cash

LANDMARK FIRST NATIONAL BANK (FORT LAUDERDALE, FL)
Thru voluntary exchange offer in 1971 Consolidated Bankshares of Florida, Inc. acquired 92.06% excluding directors' qualifying shares, as of 3/31/71

LANDMARK GRAPHICS CORP (DE)
Merged into Halliburton Co. 10/4/96
Each share Common 5¢ par exchanged for (0.574) share Common $2.50 par

LANDMARK INTL INC (NV)
Name changed to LMKI Inc. 07/20/1999
LMKI Inc. name changed to Myrient Inc. 02/08/2001
(See Myrient Inc.)

LANDMARK LAND CO., INC. (NY)
Reincorporated under the laws of Delaware 6/26/84

LANDMARK MINERALS INC (BC)
Merged into Ucore Uranium Inc. 08/17/2007
Each share Common no par exchanged for (0.68) share Common no par
Ucore Uranium Inc. name changed to Ucore Rare Metals Inc. 06/29/2010

LANDMARK MINES LTD. (ON)
Charter cancelled for failure to pay taxes and file returns 11/01/1972

LANDMARK NATL BANK (SOLANA BEACH, CA)
Acquired by 1st Pacific Bancorp 07/01/2007
Each share Common $5 par exchanged for either (0.778125) share Common no par or $9.40426188 cash and (0.19035863) share Common no par
Note: Option to receive stock and cash expired 08/17/2007
(See 1st Pacific Bancorp)

LANDMARK NORTHWEST PLAZA BANK (ST. ANN, MO)
Merged into Landmark Bank (Clayton, MO) 3/1/85
Details not available

LANDMARK OIL & GAS CORP (AB)
Plan of reorganization under Bankruptcy and Insolvency Act effective 06/27/2008
No stockholders' equity

LANDMARK OIL & GAS LTD (CO)
Charter suspended for failure to file annual reports 9/30/83

LANDMARK PUBLISHERS CORP. (UT)
Charter suspended for failure to pay taxes 9/30/78

LANDMARK RES LTD (BC)
Name changed to Landmark Environmental Inc. 10/10/1995
Landmark Environmental Inc. name changed to International Landmark Environmental Inc. 06/12/1997 which recapitalized as Shabute Ventures Inc. 01/15/2003 which name changed to Northern Sun Exploration Co. Inc. 08/19/2004 which recapitalized as Reparo Energy Partners Corp. 11/08/2013

LANDMARK SVGS ASSN PITTSBURGH (PA)
Stock Purchase Rights redeemed at $0.01 per right 06/30/1992 for holders of record 06/29/1992
Merged into Integra Financial Corp. 06/30/1992
Each share Common $1 par exchanged for (0.317) share Common $1 par
Integra Financial Corp. merged into National City Corp. 05/03/1996 which was acquired by PNC

Financial Services Group, Inc. 12/31/2008

LANDMARK SYS CORP (VA)
Issue Information - 3,200,000 shares COM offered at $7 per share on 11/17/1997
Merged into Allen Systems Group, Inc. 2/19/2002
Each share Common 1¢ par exchanged for $4.75 cash

LANDMARK TECHNOLOGY CORP (GA)
Recapitalized as Landmark American Corp. 8/10/87
Each share Common 1¢ par exchanged for (0.4) share Common 1¢ par
(See Landmark American Corp.)

LANDMARK TOWNES INC (OR)
Placed in receivership 11/30/72
Assets not sufficient to pay taxes
No stockholders' equity

LANDMARK UNION TRUST BANK OF ST. PETERSBURG, N.A. (ST. PETERSBURG, FL)
99.59% held by holding company 00/00/1979
Public interest eliminated

LANDON RADIATOR CO., INC.
Dissolved in 1930

LANDON RES LTD (BC)
Name changed to Adikann Goldfields Ltd. 03/24/1995
Adikann Goldfields Ltd. recapitalized as Harben Industries Ltd. 05/03/1999 which name changed to Merit Industries Inc. 07/19/2000 which recapitalized as Ialta Industries Ltd. 07/02/2002
(See Ialta Industries Ltd.)

LANDORAMA INC (UT)
Recapitalized as Mitec Corp. 03/01/1986
Each share Common $0.001 par exchanged for (0.1) share Common $0.001 par
Mitec Corp. name changed to Baldwin Aircraft International Inc. 10/30/1986
(See Baldwin Aircraft International Inc.)

LANDORE RES INC (AB)
Merged into Landore Resources Ltd. (Channel Islands) 4/5/2005
Each share Common no par exchanged for (1) share Common no par

LANDOVER ENERGY INC (AB)
Merged into Viking Energy Royalty Trust 7/9/2002
Each share Common no par exchanged for $0.625 cash

LANDOVER HOLDING CORP.
Dissolved in 1928

LANDOVER OILS & MINES LTD. (ON)
Recapitalized as Belcher Mining Corp. Ltd. in 1954
Each share Capital Stock $1 par exchanged for (0.2) share Capital Stock $1 par
Belcher Mining Corp. merged into Little Long Lac Mines Ltd. (Old) 1/8/71 which name changed to Little Long Lac Gold Mines Ltd. (New) 7/3/75 which merged into LAC Minerals Ltd. (New) 7/29/85 which was acquired by American Barrick Resources Corp. 10/17/94 which name changed to Barrick Gold Corp. 1/18/95

LANDRYS RESTAURANTS INC (DE)
Name changed 06/05/2001
Common 1¢ par split (2) for (1) by issuance of (1) additional share 06/23/1995
Each share Class A Conv. Preferred 1¢ par exchanged for (1) share Common 1¢ par 12/31/1998
Name changed from Landry's Seafood Restaurants, Inc. to

Landry's Restaurants, Inc. 06/05/2001
Acquired by Fertitta Group, Inc. 10/06/2010
Each share Common 1¢ par exchanged for $24.50 cash

LANDS END INC OLD (DE)
Common 1¢ par split (2) for (1) by issuance of (1) additional share 09/01/1987
Common 1¢ par split (2) for (1) by issuance of (1) additional share 06/15/1994
Merged into Sears, Roebuck & Co. 06/17/2002
Each share Common 1¢ par exchanged for $62 cash

LANDSING INSTL PPTYS TR V (CA)
Merged into Landsing Pacific Fund (DE) 12/12/1988
Each Share of Bene. Int. no par exchanged for (0.25) share Common $0.001 par
Landsing Pacific Fund (DE) reincorporated in Maryland as Landsing Pacific Fund, Inc. 09/30/1993 which assets were transferred to Landsing Pacific Fund Liquidating Trust 12/29/1995
(See Landsing Pacific Fund Liquidating Trust)

LANDSING INSTL PPTYS TR VI (CA)
Merged into Landsing Pacific Fund (DE) 12/12/1988
Each Share of Bene. Int. no par exchanged for (0.5) share Common $0.001 par
Landsing Pacific Fund (DE) reincorporated in Maryland as Landsing Pacific Fund, Inc. 01/30/1993 which assets were transferred to Landsing Pacific Fund Liquidating Trust 12/29/1995
(See Landsing Pacific Fund Liquidating Trust)

LANDSING INSTL PPTYS TR VII (CA)
Merged into Landsing Pacific Fund (DE) 12/12/1988
Each Share of Bene. Int. no par exchanged for (0.5) share Common $0.001 par
Landsing Pacific Fund (DE) reincorporated in Maryland as Landsing Pacific Fund, Inc. 09/30/1993 which assets were transferred to Landsing Pacific Fund Liquidating Trust 12/29/1995
(See Landsing Pacific Fund Liquidating Trust)

LANDSING PAC FD LIQUIDATING TR (MD)
Reincorporated 09/30/1993
State of incorporation changed from (DE) to (MD) 09/30/1993
Assets transferred from Landsing Pacific Fund Inc. to Landsing Pacific Fund Liquidating Trust 12/29/1995
Each share Common $0.001 par received initial distribution of $4.54 cash
Note: Details on subsequent distribution(s), if any, are not available

LANDSTAR DEV GROUP INC (NV)
Recapitalized as Solar Integrated Roofing Corp. 11/12/2015
Each share Common $0.00001 par exchanged for (0.03333333) share Common $0.00001 par

LANDSVERK CORP (CA)
Common no par changed to 10¢ par 11/05/1970
Charter suspended for failure to file reports and pay taxes 08/01/1973

LANDSVERK ELECTROMETER CO (CA)
Name changed to Landsverk Corp. 8/12/69
(See Landsverk Corp.)

LANDVEST DEV CORP (MN)
Each (2,500) shares old Common 5¢ par exchanged for (1) share new Common 5¢ par 4/30/2001
Note: In effect holders received $0.05 cash per share and public interest was eliminated

LANE BRYANT INC (DE)
Common no par changed to $1 par 00/00/1953
Common $1 par changed to no par and (0.5) additional share issued 06/16/1961
Common no par split (3) for (2) by issuance of (0.5) additional share 06/16/1965
Common no par split (2) for (1) by issuance of (1) additional share 07/01/1970
Stock Dividends - 100% 08/18/1945; 100% 09/02/1946; 10% 05/11/1959; 10% 06/08/1964
Merged into Limited Stores, Inc. 05/28/1982
Each share Common no par exchanged for $29 cash

LANE COTTON MILLS (LA)
Capital Stock no par changed to $10 par 00/00/1946
Acquired by Lowenstein (M.) & Sons, Inc. 00/00/1955
Details not available

LANE FINANCE, INC. (IN)
98.78% owned by Indian Finance Corp. as of 07/12/1968
Public interest eliminated

LANE FINL INC (DE)
Merged into ABN/LaSalle North America, Inc. 06/14/1988
Each share Common $1 par exchanged for $28.1496504 cash

LANE INC (VA)
Common $20 par reclassified as Class A Common $20 par 4/1/60
Each share Class A Common $20 par or Class B Common $20 par exchanged for (8) shares Common $5 par 8/15/66
Common $5 par split (3) for (2) by issuance of (0.5) additional share 1/28/83
Common $5 par split (3) for (2) by issuance of (0.5) additional share 1/27/84
Common $5 par split (3) for (2) by issuance of (0.5) additional share 1/31/86
5% Preferred $20 par called for redemption 3/6/87
Merged into Interco Inc. (Old) 4/14/87
Each share Common $5 par exchanged for (1.5) shares Common no par
(See Interco Inc. (Old))

LANE INDS INC (TX)
Merged into Tecor, Inc. 4/30/71
Each share Common $1 par exchanged for (0.92) share Common 25¢ par
(See Tecor, Inc.)

LANE TELECOMMUNICATIONS INC (TX)
Name changed to LTI Technologies, Inc. 8/23/89

LANE TRAVIS POLLARD INC (MO)
Name changed to Synergistic Communications Group Inc. 7/17/72
(See Synergistic Communications Group Inc.)

LANE-WELLS CO. (DE)
Common no par changed to $10 par 01/00/1938
Common $10 par changed to $1 par 07/00/1938
Stock Dividend - 100% 05/02/1951
Merged into Dresser Industries, Inc. (PA) 03/29/1955
Each share Common $1 par exchanged for (0.8) share Common 50¢ par

Dresser Industries, Inc. (PA) reincorporated under the laws of Delaware 08/01/1956
(See Dresser Industries, Inc. (DE) (Old))

LANE WOOD INC (DE)
Common no par changed to $1 par 07/28/1976
Each share Common $1 par exchanged for (0.05) share old Common no par 11/01/1986
Each share old Common no par exchanged for (0.05) share new Common no par 09/09/1988
Charter cancelled and declared inoperative and void for non-payment of taxes 03/01/2002

LANECO INC (PA)
Merged into Wetterau Inc. 02/15/1983
Each share Common $1 par exchanged for (1.44) shares Common $1 par
(See Wetterau Inc.)

LANETT BLEACHERY & DYE WORKS (AL)
Merged into West Point Manufacturing Co. (GA) in 1955
Each share Common $10 par exchanged for (2) shares Capital Stock $5 par
West Point Manufacturing Co. (GA) name changed to West Point-Pepperell Inc. 3/29/65
(See West Point-Pepperell, Inc.)

LANG & CO (WA)
Completely liquidated 03/10/1981
Each share Common $1 par exchanged for first and final distribution of (2.21959) shares Safeco Income Fund, Inc. (WA) Common 10¢ par
Safeco Income Fund, Inc. (WA) reincorporated in Delaware 09/30/1993
(See Safeco Income Fund, Inc.)

LANG BAY RES LTD (BC)
Recapitalized as Hibright Minerals Inc. 11/06/1995
Each share Common no par exchanged for (0.2) share Common no par
Hibright Minerals Inc. name changed to Frontier Pacific Mining Corp. 10/25/1996 which was acquired by Eldorado Gold Corp. (New) 07/15/2008

LANG BODY CO.
Acquired by Iron Fireman Manufacturing Co. 00/00/1938
Details not available

LANG CO., INC. (UT)
Merged into Union Tank Car Co. (N.J.) on a (1) for (3) basis 7/1/58
Union Tank Car Co. (N.J.) reincorporated under the laws of Delaware 4/30/68 which reorganized as Trans Union Corp. 6/1/69
(See Trans Union Corp.)

LANG CONSTRUCTION EQUIPMENT CO. (NV)
Merged into L.I.F.E. Inc. 01/26/1972
Each share Common 10¢ par exchanged for (1) share Common 1¢ par
(See L.I.F.E. Inc.)

LANGDON GROUP INC (NY)
Charter cancelled and proclaimed dissolved for failure to pay taxes 6/24/81

LANGE CO (IA)
Merged into Garcia Corp. 09/05/1972
Each share Common 10¢ par or Class B Common 10¢ par exchanged for (0.125) share Common $1 par
Garcia Corp. name changed to TGC Inc. 12/31/1980 which recapitalized as Equion Corp. 01/31/1985
(See Equion Corp.)

LANGENDORF BAKING CO.
Name changed to Langendorf United Bakeries, Inc. in 1928
Lagendorf United Bakeries, Inc. acquired by American Bakeries Co. (Del.) 5/22/64
(See American Bakeries Co. (Del.))

LANGENDORF UNITED BAKERIES, INC. (DE)
Each share Class A no par exchanged for (7/50) share 6% Preferred $50 par and (1) share new Class A no par in 1938
Each share Class B no par exchanged for (1) share new Class B no par in 1938
Each share Class A no par exchanged for (1) share $1.80 Preferred $25 par and (0.4) share Common $1 par in 1948
Each share Class B no par exchanged for (2) shares Common $1 par in 1948
Stock Dividend - 100% 12/31/56
Merged into American Bakeries Co. (Del.) 5/22/64
Each share $1.80 Preferred $25 par exchanged for (1) share $1.80 Prior Preferred $25 par
Each share Common $1 par exchanged for (0.23) share 5% Convertible Preferred $100 par
(See American Bakeries Co. (Del.))

LANGER INC (DE)
Name changed 07/31/2001
Name changed from Langer Biomechanics Group, Inc. to Langer, Inc. (NY) 07/31/2001
State of incorporation changed from (NY) to (DE) 06/28/2002
Name changed to PC Group, Inc. 07/24/2009
(See PC Group, Inc.)

LANGHAM CORP.
Dissolved in 1938

LANGHAM CREEK NATL BK (HOUSTON, TX)
Under plan of reorganization each share Common no par automatically became (1) share LCNB Bancorporation, Inc. Common no par 7/2/98
(See LCNB Bancorporation, Inc.)

LANGIS SILVER & COBALT MNG CO (ON)
Common $1 par changed to no par 07/08/1975
Name changed to Aranka Gold Inc. 07/27/2005
Aranka Gold Inc. merged into Guyana Goldfields Inc. 01/28/2009

LANGLEY BAY URANIUM MINES LTD. (ON)
Charter revoked for failure to file reports and pay fees 11/30/64

LANGLEY CORP (CA)
Reincorporated under the laws of Delaware as Langly Corp. 4/12/83
(See Langly Corp.)

LANGLY CORP (DE)
Under plan of merger each share Common $1 par exchanged for (1) share Fleet Aerospace Inc. 10% Conv. Preferred 1¢ par, (1) share Common 1¢ par and $0.50 cash 2/2/89
(See Fleet Aerospace Inc.)

LANGMUIR LONGLAC GOLD MINES LTD.
Acquired by Maralgo Mines Ltd. (ON) 00/00/1937
Each share Common no par exchanged for (0.2) share Common no par
Maralgo Mines Ltd. (ON) reincorporated in British Columbia 06/06/1984 which recapitalized as Rich Coast Sulphur Ltd. 03/13/1986 which recapitalized as Consolidated Rich Coast Sulphur Ltd. 06/19/1991

which merged into Rich Coast Resources Ltd. (BC) 01/25/1993 which reincorporated in Delaware as Rich Coast Inc. 09/16/1996 which reincorporated in Nevada 07/14/1998 which recapitalized as Media Pal Holdings, Corp. 03/16/2010

LANGTEC CAP CORP (BC)
Name changed VisionQuest Enterprise Group Inc. 08/25/1997
VisionQuest Enterprise Group Inc. name changed to VisionQuest Energy Group Inc. 11/03/2006

LANGUAGE ACCESS NETWORK INC (NV)
Each share old Common $0.001 par exchanged for (0.005) share new Common $0.001 par 08/21/2008
Name changed to IB3 Networks, Inc. 10/10/2008
(See IB3 Networks, Inc)

LANGUAGE ARTS CORP (NV)
Name changed to FLASR Inc. 09/22/2014

LANGUAGE ENTERPRISES CORP (NV)
Each share old Common $0.001 par exchanged for (25) shares new Common $0.001 par 01/09/2008
Name changed to Doral Energy Corp. 04/30/2008
Doral Energy Corp. name changed to Cross Border Resources, Inc. 01/06/2011

LANGUAGE 2 LANGUAGE UNVL HLDGS INC (NV)
Charter revoked for failure to file reports and pay fees 02/01/2010

LANGUAGEWARE NET (COMPANY) LTD (ISRAEL)
Filed an application for liquidation on the grounds of insolvency 02/27/2001
Stockholders' equity unlikely

LANIER BK & TR (CUMMING, GA)
Merged into Premier Bancshares Inc. (New) 6/9/98
Each share Common no par exchanged for (1.98) shares Common $5 par
Premier Bancshares Inc. (New) merged into BB&T Corp. 1/13/2000

LANIER BANKSHARES INC (GA)
Merged into Century South Banks, Inc. 2/15/2000
Each share Common $1 par exchanged for (1.44186) shares Common $1 par
Century South Banks, Inc. merged into BB&T Corp. 6/7/2001

LANIER BUSINESS PRODS INC (GA)
Common $1 par split (3) for (2) by issuance of (0.5) additional share 12/1/79
Common $1 par split (2) for (1) by issuance of (1) additional share 9/1/81
Merged into Harris Corp. 10/28/83
Each share Common $1 par exchanged for (0.525) share Common $1 par

LANIER WORLDWIDE INC (DE)
Merged into Ricoh Co. Ltd. 01/26/2001
Each share Common 1¢ par exchanged for $3 cash

LANIUK INDS INC (AB)
Reorganized as TerraVest Income Fund 07/08/2004
Each share Common no par exchanged for (0.16666666) Trust Unit
TerraVest Income Fund reorganized as TerraVest Capital Inc. 11/05/2012 which name changed to TerraVest Industries Inc. (New) 02/28/2018

LANNET DATA COMMUNICATIONS LTD (ISRAEL)
Merged into Madge Networks N.V. 11/28/1995
Each share Ordinary NIS0.1 par exchanged for (0.734) Common 1 Gldr. par
(See Madge Networks N.V.)

LANNETT INC (PA)
Each share Capital Stock no par received distribution of (1) share Vesco Corp. no par 09/21/1968
Stock Dividend - 10% 09/16/1983
Reincorporated under the laws of Delaware and Capital Stock no par changed to Common $0.001 par 02/20/1991

LANOLIN PLUS, INC. (DE)
Stock Dividend - 400% 6/16/55
Merged into Bishop (Hazel) Inc. 1/23/62
Each share Common 1¢ par exchanged for (1) share Common 10¢ par
Bishop (Hazel) Inc. name changed to Bishop Industries Inc. (N.Y.) 5/19/67

LANOPTICS LTD (ISRAEL)
Name changed to EZchip Semiconductor Ltd. 08/01/2008
(See EZchip Semiconductor Ltd.)

LANPAR TECHNOLOGIES INC (CANADA)
Placed in receivership 3/15/89
No stockholders' equity

LANSCO PETE INC (BC)
Recapitalized as Lansco Resources Ltd. 03/03/1983
Each share Common no par exchanged for (1) share Common no par
Lansco Resources Ltd. recapitalized as Bomax Resource Corp. 11/22/1993
(See Bomax Resource Corp.)

LANSCO RES LTD (BC)
Recapitalized as Bomax Resource Corp. 11/22/1993
Each share Common no par exchanged for (0.1) share Common no par
(See Bomax Resource Corp.)

LANSDALE MICROELECTRONICS INC (DE)
Name changed to L.M. Liquidating Co. 9/15/70
(See L.M. Liquidating Co.)

LANSDALE SILK HOSIERY MILLS, INC.
Acquired by Interstate Hosiery Mills, Inc. 00/00/1928
Details not available

LANSDOWNE EXPLS LTD (ON)
Charter cancelled for failure to pay taxes and file returns 2/20/80

LANSDOWNE MINERALS LTD (BC)
Name changed to Conquistador Mines Ltd. (Old) 04/13/1995
Conquistador Mines Ltd. (Old) merged into Conquistador Mines Ltd. (New) 02/02/1998 which recapitalized as Western Platinum Holdings Ltd. 12/14/2001 which recapitalized as Orsa Ventures Corp. (YT) 07/23/2002 which reincorporated in British Columbia 12/31/2007
(See Orsa Ventures Corp.)

LANSDOWNE OIL & MINERALS LTD (BC)
Recapitalized as Lansdowne Minerals Ltd. 11/03/1987
Each share Common no par exchanged for (1) share Common no par
Lansdowne Minerals Ltd. name changed to Conquistador Mines Ltd. (Old) 04/13/1995 which merged into Conquistador Mines Ltd. (New) 02/02/1998 which recapitalized as Western Platinum Holdings Ltd. 12/14/2001 which recapitalized as Orsa Ventures Corp. (YT) 07/23/2002 which reincorporated in British Columbia 12/31/2007
(See Orsa Ventures Corp.)

LANSDOWNE SEC INC (NV)
Charter revoked 07/31/2012

LANSING CO. (MI)
Common $10 par changed to $5 par in 1955
Common $5 par changed to $1 par 9/13/56
Charter voided for failure to file reports and pay fees 5/15/73

LANSING DEVELOPMENT CORP. (MI)
Each share Common no par exchanged for (0.2) share Common $1 par 11/9/61
Charter voided for failure to file report and pay fees 5/15/63

LANSING ENTERPRISES INC (BC)
Recapitalized as White Hawk Ventures Inc. 1/19/93
Each share Common no par exchanged for (0.5) share Common no par
White Hawk Ventures Inc. recapitalized as E-Energy Ventures Inc. 1/9/2001

LANSING STAMPING CO. (MI)
Name changed to Deep Drawing Corp. 9/29/65
Deep Drawing Corp. name changed to Metal Flo Corp. 5/28/68 which merged into AO Industries, Inc. 9/1/71 which name changed to Aegis Corp. 6/1/74
(See Aegis Corp.)

LANSTAR SEMICONDUCTOR INC (UT)
Each share Common $0.001 par received distribution of (1) share Celex Technology Inc. Common $0.001 par payable 09/01/1999 to holders of record 08/31/1999
Charter expired 11/30/2000

LANSTON INDUSTRIES, INC. (VA)
Stock Dividend - 100% 8/17/59
Merged into United States Banknote Corp. on a (1/3) for (1) basis 3/3/65
Each share Common $5 par exchanged for (0.333333) share Common $1 par
(See United States Banknote Corp.)

LANSTON MONOTYPE MACHINE CO. (VA)
Common $100 par changed to $25 par in 1943
Each share Common $25 par exchanged for (5) shares Common $5 par in 1945
Name changed to Lanston Industries, Inc. 8/11/56
Lanston Industries, Inc. merged into United States Banknote Corp. 3/3/65
(See United States Banknote Corp.)

LANSVIEW RES CORP (BC)
Name changed to Neumed Systems Corp. 10/16/85
Neumed Systems Corp. recapitalized as Reneaux Capital Inc. 3/19/88 which name changed to Naturally Niagara, Inc. 6/29/93 which recapitalized as Northern Gaming Inc. 1/22/96 which recapitalized as Icon Laser Eye Centers Inc. 9/1/99

LANTE CORP (DE)
Issue Information - 4,000,000 shares COM offered at $20 per share on 02/10/2000
Merged into SBI & Co. 9/5/2002
Each share Common 1¢ par exchanged for $1.10 cash

LANTERN GAS & OIL LTD (BC)
Merged into Stand-Skat Resources Ltd. 10/16/1978
Each share Capital Stock no par exchanged for (0.17728) share Capital Stock no par
Stand-Skat Resources Ltd. merged into Ramrod Energy Corp. 03/01/1983 which recapitalized as Consolidated Ramrod Gold Corp. 08/27/1986 which name changed to Quest International Resources Corp. 04/09/1996 which recapitalized as Standard Mining Corp. 06/16/1999 which merged into Doublestar Resources Ltd. (YT) 11/01/2001 which reincorporated in British Columbia 10/10/2002 which merged into Selkirk Metals Corp. 07/23/2007
(See Selkirk Metals Corp.)

LANTIS LASER INC (NV)
Each share old Common $0.001 par exchanged for (0.5) share new Common $0.001 par 06/16/2006
Name changed to Raptor Resources Holdings Inc. 03/28/2012

LANVIN CHARLES RITZ INC (DE)
Class B Common $1 par reclassified as Common $1 par 12/15/68
Stock Dividend - 30% 2/8/68
Merged into Squibb Corp. 4/30/71
Each share $0.80 Preferred no par exchanged for (0.7326) share Common $1 par
Each share Common $1 par exchanged for (0.5635) share Common $1 par
Squibb Corp. merged into Bristol-Myers Squibb Co. 10/4/89

LANVIN-PARFUMS, INC. (DE)
Merged into Lanvin-Charles of the Ritz, Inc. 1/21/64
Each share Common $1 par exchanged for (0.3) share $0.80 Preferred no par and (0.7) share Common $1 par
Lanvin-Charles of the Ritz, Inc. merged into Squibb Corp. 4/30/71 which merged into Bristol-Myers Squibb Co. 10/4/89

LANVISION SYS INC (DE)
Name changed to Streamline Health Solutions, Inc. 7/5/2006

LANWERX ENTMT INC (NV)
Name changed to GameState Entertainment, Inc. 9/24/2003
GameState Entertainment, Inc. name changed to Quest Oil Corp. 9/16/2004

LANXIDE CORP (DE)
Recapitalized as VoIPCom USA, Inc. 05/05/2005
Each share new Common 1¢ par exchanged for (0.01) share Common 1¢ par
VoIPCom USA, Inc. name changed to Maplex Alliance Ltd. 01/26/2011

LANZET LIZA LINGERIE LTD (BC)
Name changed to First Venture Developments Ltd. 03/30/1995
First Venture Developments Ltd. recapitalized as Knightswood Financial Corp. 12/08/1998 which name changed to Cannabis Wheaton Income Corp. 05/08/2017 which name changed to Auxly Cannabis Group Inc. 06/08/2018

LAPA CADILLAC GOLD MINES LTD. (ON)
Recapitalized as Zulapa Mining Corp. Ltd. on a (1) for (4) basis 04/01/1955
(See Zulapa Mining Corp.)

LAPALARTIC GOLD MINES, LTD. (ON)
Charter cancelled for failure to file reports and pay taxes in 1953

LAPASKA MINES, LTD. (ON)
Recapitalized as Can-Met Explorations Ltd. on a (1) for (3) basis in 1955
Can-Met Explorations Ltd. merged into Denison Mines Ltd. 4/7/60 which recapitalized as Denison Energy Inc. (ONT) 5/30/2002 which reorganized in Alberta 3/8/2004 which name changed to Calfrac Well Services Ltd. 3/29/2004

LAPEER COUNTY BANK & TRUST CO. (LAPEER, MI)
Stock Dividend - 10% 3/9/79
Reorganized as County Bank Corp. 12/31/88
Each share Capital Stock $5 par exchanged for (1) share Common $5 par

LAPEXCO GOLD MINES LTD. (ON)
Name changed to Regal Mining & Development Ltd. 10/9/58
Regal Mining & Development Ltd. merged into Resource Exploration & Development Co. Ltd. 6/11/68
(See Resource Exploration & Development Co. Ltd.)

LAPIS TECHNOLOGIES INC (DE)
Recapitalized as Micronet Enertec Technologies, Inc. 03/18/2013
Each share Common $0.001 par exchanged for (0.5) share Common $0.001 par
Micronet Enertec Technologies, Inc. name changed to MICT, Inc. 07/16/2018

LAPLANTE RED LAKE GOLD MINES LTD.
Name changed to New Mic Mac Mines Ltd. 00/00/1947
New Mic Mac Mines Ltd. name changed to United Mic Mac Mines Ltd. 00/00/1949 which merged into Indian Lake Mines Ltd 00/00/1956 which merged into Hydra Explorations Ltd. 11/16/1959 which name changed to Hydra Capital Corp. 12/30/1992 which name changed to Waterford Capital Management Inc. 11/12/1996 which merged into CPI Plastics Group Ltd. 09/21/1998
(See CPI Plastics Group Ltd.)

LAPOLLA INDS INC (DE)
Acquired by Icynene U.S. Holding Corp. 11/30/2017
Each share Common 1¢ par exchanged for $1.03 cash

LAPORTE BANCORP INC (MD)
Merged into Horizon Bancorp 07/18/2016
Each share Common 1¢ par exchanged for (0.629) share Common no par
Horizon Bancorp name changed to Horizon Bancorp, Inc. 05/08/2018

LAPORTE BANCORP INC (USA)
Reorganized under the laws of Maryland 10/05/2012
Each share Common 1¢ par exchanged for (1.319) shares Common 1¢ par
LaPorte Bancorp, Inc. (MD) merged into Horizon Bancorp 07/18/2016 which name changed to Horizon Bancorp, Inc. 05/08/2018

LAR-KIRK GOLD MINES, LTD. (ON)
Charter cancelled for failure to file reports and pay taxes in 1955

LARACA INTL INC (NV)
Name changed to Loraca International Inc. 06/30/1999
(See Loraca International Inc.)

LARAGO ELECTRONIC MANUFACTURERS, INC. (FL)
Capital Stock $1 par changed to 50¢ par and (1) additional share issued 6/23/69
Each share Capital Stock 50¢ par exchanged for (0.25) share Capital Stock 1¢ par 10/23/71
Proclaimed dissolved for failure to file reports and pay fees 12/8/80

LARAMIDE RES LTD (BC)
Reincorporated under the laws of Canada 06/27/1996

LARANDONA MINES LTD (ON)
Charter cancelled for failure to file reports and pay fees 4/9/75

LARBEL GOLD MINES LTD.
Merged into Aurlando Consolidated Mining Corp., Ltd. 00/00/1947
Each share Capital Stock $1 par exchanged for (0.2) share Capital Stock $1 par
(See Aurlando Consolidated Mining Corp. Ltd.)

LARCAN-TTC INC (DE)
Merged into Larcan, Inc. 3/10/98
Each share Common 4¢ par exchanged for $0.0625 cash

LARCH RES LTD (BC)
Recapitalized as Manticore Petroleum Corp. 01/28/1987
Each share Common no par exchanged for (1) share Common no par
Manticore Petroleum Corp. recapitalized as Dexx Energy Corp. 05/31/1988
(See Dexx Energy Corp.)

LARCHFIELD CORP (RI)
Under plan of merger each share Common $1 par exchanged for (0.1) share Common $2 par 4/30/55
Charter forfeited for non-payment of taxes 12/31/77

LARCHMONT MINES LTD (ON)
Charter cancelled for failure to pay taxes and file returns in 1973
No stockholders' equity

LARDEAU CONSOLIDATED MINES LTD.
Dissolved in 1948

LARDEGO GOLD MINES, LTD. (ON)
Charter cancelled 3/20/60
No stockholders' equity

LARDER RES INC (ON)
Merged into International Larder Minerals Inc. 05/01/1986
Each share Capital Stock no par exchanged for (0.5) share Common no par
International Larder Minerals Inc. merged into Explorers Alliance Corp. 10/13/2000
(See Explorers Alliance Corp.)

LARDER U ISLAND MINES LTD. (ON)
Recapitalized as New Larder U Island Mines Ltd. on a (1) for (3) basis in 1952
New Larder U Island Mines Ltd. was acquired by Anacon Lead Mines Ltd. in January 1955 which was recapitalized as Key Anacon Mines Ltd. 2/14/64
(See Key Anacon Mines Ltd.)

LARDON GOLD MINES, LTD. (ON)
Charter cancelled for failure to file reports and pay taxes 2/1/60

LAREDO INVT CORP (NV)
Recapitalized as GFR Pharmaceuticals Inc. 8/9/2004
Each (30) shares Common $0.001 par exchanged for (1) share Common $0.001 par

LAREDO LIMESTONE LTD (BC)
Acquired by Kamad Silver Co. Ltd. 08/31/1972
Each share Capital Stock $1 par exchanged for (0.2) share Common no par
Kamad Silver Co. Ltd. recapitalized as Agate Bay Resources Ltd. 01/19/1993 which recapitalized as Geodex Minerals Ltd. (BC) 04/14/1998 which reincorporated in Ontario as Intercontinental Gold & Metals Ltd. 11/06/2017

LAREDO MINES LTD. (BC)
Name changed to Largo Mines Ltd. 7/7/67
Largo Mines Ltd. recapitalized as Advanced Growth Systems Inc. 6/12/86
(See Advanced Growth Systems Inc.)

LAREDO MNG INC (DE)
Name changed to Laredo Oil, Inc. 11/05/2009

LAREDO NATL BK (LAREDO, TX)
Under plan of reorganization each share Capital Stock $100 par automatically became (1) share Laredo National Bancshares, Inc. Common no par 12/31/80

LAREDO PETE HLDGS INC (DE)
Issue Information - 17,500,000 shares COM offered at $17 per share on 12/14/2011
Name changed to Laredo Petroleum, Inc. 01/02/2014

LAREDO PETES LTD (BC)
Recapitalized as Pedco Energy Ltd. 10/23/86
Each share Capital Stock no par exchanged for (1/3) share Common no par
Pedco Energy Ltd. merged into International Pedco Energy Corp. 11/26/93 which merged into Lateral Vector Resources Inc. 2/29/96
(See Lateral Vector Resources Inc.)

LARGE SCALE BIOLOGY CORP (DE)
Issue Information - 5,000,000 shares COM offered at $17 per share on 08/09/2000
Each share old Common $0.001 par exchanged for (0.2) share new Common $0.001 par 12/12/2005
Plan of reorganization under Chapter 11 Federal Bankruptcy Code effective 10/23/2006
No stockholders' equity

LARGO GROUP LTD (DE)
Charter cancelled and declared inoperative and void for non-payment of taxes 3/1/76

LARGO MINES LTD (BC)
Recapitalized as Advanced Growth Systems Inc. 6/12/86
Each share Capital Stock 50¢ par exchanged for (0.25) share Common no par
(See Advanced Growth Systems Inc.)

LARGO OILS & MINES LTD. (ON)
Name changed to Wardean Drilling Co. Ltd. and Common $1 par changed to no par 1/8/68
(See Wardean Drilling Co. Ltd.)

LARGO RES LTD (BC)
Reincorporated under the laws of Ontario 06/10/2004

LARGO VISTA GROUP LTD (NV)
SEC revoked common stock registration 02/22/2013

LARGOLD MINING CO., LTD. (ON)
Charter surrendered 10/28/57

LARI CORP (FL)
Name changed to Neptune Society Inc. 4/18/99
(See Neptune Society Inc.)

LARIAT ENERGY LTD (BC)
Reincorporated 04/01/2006
Place of incorporation changed from (YT) (BC) 04/01/2006
Each share old Common no par exchanged for (0.5) share new Common no par 08/27/2015
Name changed to Global Daily Fantasy Sports Inc. 07/11/2016

LARIAT EXPLORATION & DEVELOPMENT LTD. (ON)
Acquired by Dominion Asbestos Mines Ltd. on a (0.1) for (1) basis 00/00/1954
Dominion Asbestos Mines Ltd. name changed to Daine Mining Corp. Ltd. 09/11/1956 which recapitalized as Cable Mines & Oils Ltd. 08/15/1957 which merged into St. Fabien Copper Mines Ltd. 07/27/1967 which name changed to St. Fabien Explorations Inc. 02/11/1981 which recapitalized as Fabien Explorations Inc. 07/18/1983
(See Fabien Explorations Inc.)

LARIAT OIL & GAS LTD (AB)
Merged into Jordan Petroleum Ltd. (New) 12/01/1987
Each share Common no par exchanged for (1) share Class A no par, (1) share Conv. Retractable Class B no par and (0.25) share Conv. Class C no par
Jordan Petroleum Ltd. (New) merged into New Jordan Petroleum Ltd. 06/01/1990 which name changed back to Jordan Petroleum Ltd. 05/07/1992
(See Jordan Petroleum Ltd.)

LARIAT PPTY CORP (YT)
Name changed to Lariat Resources Ltd. 06/02/2003
Lariat Resources Ltd. recapitalized as Lariat Energy Ltd. (YT) 09/23/2004 which reincorporated in British Columbia 04/01/2006 which name changed to Global Daily Fantasy Sports Inc. 07/11/2016

LARIAT RES LTD (YT)
Recapitalized as Lariat Energy Ltd. (YT) 09/23/2004
Each share Common no par exchanged for (0.5) share Common no par
Lariat Energy Ltd. (YT) reincorporated in British Columbia 04/01/2006 which name changed to Global Daily Fantasy Sports Inc. 07/11/2016

LARIBEE WIRE INC (DE)
Name changed to LW Industries 5/7/83
(See LW Industries)

LARIZZA INDS INC (OH)
Merged into Collins & Aikman Corp. 1/3/96
Each share Common no par exchanged for $6.50 cash

LARK & CO. (NM)
Name changed to Geoexplorations, Inc. 9/15/58
Geoexplorations, Inc. recapitalized as Harold's Coin-O-Matic, Inc. 9/1/61 which name was changed to Harold's Coin-O-Matics, Inc. 11/27/61 which name changed to Geo Explorations, Inc. 9/25/62
(See Geo Explorations, Inc.)

LARK TECHNOLOGIES INC (DE)
Each share old Common $0.001 par exchanged for (1) share new Common $0.001 par to reflect a (1) for (100) reverse split followed by a (100) for (1) forward split 08/28/2003
Note: Holders of (99) or fewer pre-split shares received $4.31 cash per share
Merged into Genaissance Pharmaceuticals, Inc. 04/01/2004
Each share new Common $0.001 par exchanged for (1.81) shares Common $0.001 par
Genaissance Pharmaceuticals, Inc. merged into Clinical Data, Inc. (New) 10/07/2005
(See Clinical Data, Inc. (New))

LARKFIELD CAP CORP (ON)
Recapitalized as Rentcash Inc. 02/01/2002
Each share Common no par exchanged for (1/3) share Common no par
Rentcash Inc. name changed to Cash Store Financial Services Inc. 04/07/2008

LARKIN BANK (ELGIN, IL)
Merged into Financial National Bancshares, Co. 7/31/84
Each share Capital Stock $1 par exchanged for (0.5) share Common $2.50 par
Financial National Bancshares, Co. name changed to FNW Bancorp, Inc. 12/9/86 which merged into NBD Bancorp, Inc. 10/1/91 which name changed to First Chicago NBD Corp. 12/1/95 which merged into Bank One Corp. 10/2/98 which merged into J.P. Morgan Chase & Co. 12/31/2000 which name changed to JPMorgan Chase & Co. 7/20/2004

LARKIN LECTRO PRODUCTS CORP. (AR)
Name changed to Central Transformer Corp. in 1952
Central Transformer Corp. merged into Colt Industries Inc. (Del.) 11/4/68 which reincorporated in Pennsylvania 5/6/76
(See Colt Industries Inc. (Pa.))

LARKINS-WARR TRUST (OK)
Liquidation completed 9/19/56

LARMONT MINES LTD. (ON)
Charter revoked for failure to file reports and pay fees 1/26/67

LAROCHE MCCAFFREY & MCCALL INC (NY)
Name changed to McCaffrey & McCall, Inc. 12/16/71
(See McCaffrey & McCall, Inc.)

LAROMA MIDLOTHIAN MINES LTD (ON)
Charter cancelled for failure to file reports and pay fees 11/08/1977

LARONEX COPPER MINES LTD. (MB)
Name changed to Northern Copper Ltd. 10/30/1967
(See Northern Copper Ltd.)

LARONEX MINING & EXPLORATION CO. LTD. (MB)
Thru share for share voluntary exchange offer substantially all Capital Stock no par was acquired by Northern Copper Ltd. in 1969

LARONGE MNG LTD (BC)
Recapitalized as La Teko Resources Ltd. 08/11/1977
Each share Common no par exchanged for (0.33333333) share Common no par
La Teko Resources Ltd. merged into Kinross Gold Corp. 02/26/1999

LARR CAP CORP (ON)
Recapitalized as Pembridge Inc. 11/3/94
Each share Common no par exchanged for (0.025) share Common no par
(See Pembridge Inc.)

LARR OPTICS & ELECTRONICS CO. (CO)
Name changed to Cash Industries, Inc. 03/20/1972
(See Cash Industries, Inc.)

LARROWE MILLING CO.
Acquired by General Mills, Inc. 00/00/1929
Details not available

LARRYS ICE CREAM INC (DE)
Name changed to Abco Ice Cream, Inc. 10/22/1990
(See Abco Ice Cream, Inc.)

LARSCOM INC (DE)
Each share old Class A Common 1¢ par exchanged for (0.14285714) share new Common 1¢ par 06/05/2003
Merged into Verilink Corp. 07/29/2004
Each share new Common 1¢ par exchanged for (1.166) shares Common 1¢ par
Verilink Corp. name changed to LMK Global Resources, Inc. 08/29/2012 which name changed to Alas Aviation Corp. 07/23/2013 which name changed to Energie Holdings, Inc. 02/13/2014 which name

changed to ExeLED Holdings Inc. 12/30/2015

LARSEN CO (WI)
Common $6-2/3 par changed to $1 par 10/01/1976
Common $1 par split (3) for (2) by issuance of (0.5) additional share 06/25/1982
Common $1 par changed to 40¢ par and (2) additional shares issued 06/27/1983
Common 40¢ par split (2) for (1) by issuance of (1) additional share 06/21/1985
Stock Dividend - 100% 06/30/1977
Acquired by Dean Foods Co. (Old) 04/28/1986
Each share Common 40¢ par exchanged for (0.62) share Common $1 par
Dean Foods Co. (Old) merged into Dean Foods Co. (New) 12/21/2001

LARSEN INDUSTRIES, INC. (DE)
Name changed to United Technical Industries, Inc. 03/22/1961
United Technical Industries, Inc. liquidated for Stickelber & Sons, Inc. 12/02/1964 which merged into Marion Corp. 02/01/1965
(See Marion Corp.)

LARSON DAVIS INC (NV)
Recapitalized as Sensar Corp. 05/03/1999
Each share Common $0.001 par exchanged for (0.2) share Common $0.001 par
Sensar Corp. name changed to VitalStream Holdings, Inc. 07/26/2002 which merged into Internap Network Services Corp. 02/20/2007 which name changed to Internap Corp. 12/04/2014

LARSON INDS INC (MN)
Common 10¢ par changed to 1¢ par 11/28/77
Merged into Federal Financial Corp. 11/30/79
Each share Common 1¢ par exchanged for $0.05 cash

LARTIC MINES LTD. (ON)
Charter cancelled for failure to file reports and pay taxes in 1959

LARUM MINES LTD (ON)
Merged into Glenarum Mining Explorations Ltd. 5/10/76
Each share Capital Stock $1 par exchanged for (0.25) share Capital Stock no par
(See Glenarum Mining Explorations Ltd.)

LARUS & BROTHER INC (VA)
Each share Common $100 par exchanged for (20) shares Common $5 par 6/29/60
8% Preferred $100 par called for redemption 7/1/61
Name changed to Larus Investing Co., Inc. 7/1/68
(See Larus Investing Co., Inc.)

LARUS INVESTING CO., INC. (VA)
Liquidation completed
Each share Class B Common $100 par exchanged for first and final distribution of $100 cash 12/16/68
Each share Common $5 par received initial distribution of $30 cash 12/16/68
Each share Common $5 par received second distribution of $35 cash 1/15/69
Each share Common $5 par received third distribution of $1.50 cash 6/3/69
Each share Common $5 par exchanged for fourth and final distribution of $2.10 cash 10/18/72

LARUTAN FUEL CO.
Name changed to Larutan Gas Corp. in 1927 which dissolved in 1935

LARUTAN GAS CORP.
Dissolved in 1935

LARUTAN PETROLEUM CORP. LTD. (ON)
Merged into Cessland Corp. Ltd. 3/15/62
Each share Capital Stock $1 par exchanged for (0.13) share Capital Stock no par
(See Cessland Corp. Ltd.)

LARWIN MTG INVS (CA)
Name changed to LMI Investors 1/3/75
LMI Investors name changed to Growth Realty Investors 5/31/78 which reorganized as Growth Realty Companies 2/9/79 which name changed to British Land of America (Calif.) which reincorporated in Delaware as British Land of America Inc. 12/15/86 which merged into Medical Management of America, Inc. 9/23/88
(See Medical Management of America, Inc.)

LARWIN RLTY & MTG TR (CA)
Name changed to United Realty Trust 5/19/75
United Realty Trust reorganized in Delaware as United Realty Investors, Inc. 7/11/80 which merged into Butterfield Equities Corp. 10/27/83
(See Butterfield Equities Corp.)

LAS AMERICAS BROADBAND INC (CO)
Plan of reorganization under Chapter 11 Federal Bankruptcy Code effective 11/11/2006
No stockholders' equity

LAS MADERAS MNG & PETE LTD (BC)
Struck off register and dissolved for failure to file returns 8/30/76

LAS PALMAS MOBILE ESTATES (NV)
Common $0.001 par split (15) for (1) by issuance of (14) additional shares payable 11/15/2007 to holders of record 11/14/2007
Ex date - 11/16/2007
Name changed to Energy Composites Corp. 10/15/2008
Energy Composites Corp. name changed to Trailblazer Resources, Inc. 10/27/2011

LAS ROCAS MNG CORP (DE)
Name changed to Kentucky USA Energy, Inc. 11/07/2007

LAS TUNAS WATER CO. (CA)
Completely liquidated for cash 8/20/63

LAS VEGAS AIRLS INC (DE)
Recapitalized as LASV Enterprises, Inc. 05/18/2000
Each share Common $0.001 par exchanged for (0.16666666) share Common $0.001 par
(See LASV Enterprises, Inc.)

LAS VEGAS BUSINESS BK (LAS VEGAS, NV)
Common $1 par split (5) for (4) by issuance of (0.25) additional share payable 04/30/1998 to holders of record 04/16/1998
Under plan of reorganization each share Common $1 par automatically became (1) share Business Bank Corp. Common $1 par 02/01/1999
(See Business Bank Corp.)

LAS VEGAS CINEMA INC (NV)
Reincorporated under the laws of Delaware as Kimber Corp. 01/01/1974
(See Kimber Corp.)

LAS VEGAS DISC GOLF & TENNIS INC (CO)
Each share old Common no par exchanged for (0.01) share new Common no par 07/17/1989
Name changed to Sports Entertainment Enterprises, Inc. (CO) 06/04/1999
Sports Entertainment Enterprises, Inc. (CO) reincorporated in Delaware as CKX, Inc. 03/25/2005
(See CKX, Inc.)

LAS VEGAS ENTMT NETWORK INC (DE)
Each share old Common $0.001 par exchanged for (0.05) share new Common $0.001 par 10/30/1998
SEC revoked common stock registration 10/09/2002

LAS VEGAS FROM HOME COM ENTMT INC (BC)
Each share old Common no par exchanged for (0.125) share new Common no par 04/05/2013
Name changed to Jackpot Digital Inc. 06/18/2015

LAS VEGAS HACIENDA INC (CA)
Merged into LVH, Inc. 9/4/75
Each share Common $1 par exchanged for $1.125 cash

LAS VEGAS INTL INC (NV)
Name changed to Rising Star International Inc. 2/14/97

LAS VEGAS JOCKEY CLUB (NV)
Bankrupt in 1954
Details not available

LAS VEGAS MAJOR LEAGUE SPORTS INC (NV)
Issue Information - 640,000 UNITS consisting of (2) shares COM and (1) WT offered at $8 per share on 04/07/1994
Each share old Common $0.001 par exchanged for (0.02) share new Common $0.001 par 03/23/1998
Name changed to Pacific Medical Group Inc. 05/00/1998
Pacific Medical Group Inc. recapitalized as Tandem Energy Holdings Inc. 03/07/2005
(See Tandem Energy Holdings Inc.)

LAS VEGAS MGMT SYS INC (NV)
Name changed to WSS Resources, Inc. 12/27/2005
WSS Resources, Inc. recapitalized as Trendsetter Industries Inc. 03/06/2006
(See Trendsetter Industries Inc.)

LAS VEGAS PROPERTIES TRUST (NV)
Dissolved 2/7/66

LAS VEGAS RESORTS CORP (NV)
Each share old Common $0.001 par exchanged for (0.00066666) share new Common $0.001 par 10/26/2005
Name changed to Winner Medical Group, Inc. 03/06/2006
(See Winner Medical Group, Inc.)

LAS VEGAS RY EXPRESS (DE)
Each share old Common $0.0001 par exchanged for (0.05) share new Common $0.0001 par 12/02/2013
Each share new Common $0.0001 par exchanged again for (0.0001) share new Common $0.0001 par 08/14/2015
Reorganized under the laws of Nevada as United Rail, Inc. 10/12/2018
Each share new Common $0.0001 par exchanged for (0.001) share Common $0.0001 par

LAS VEGAS SANDS CORP (NV)
10% Perpetual Preferred Ser. A $0.001 par called for redemption at $110 on 11/15/2011
(Additional Information in Active)

LAS VEGAS THOROUGHBRED RACING ASSOCIATION (NV)
Reorganized as Las Vegas Jockey Club 02/02/1953
Each share 6% Preferred $5 par exchanged for either $3 principal amount of 6% 10-yr. Trust Notes or (1.5) shares Class B Common no par
Note: Option to receive stock expired 08/01/1953
No Common stockholders' equity
(See Las Vegas Jockey Club)

LAS WESTN ENTMT INC (AB)
Name changed to mBase.com Inc. 10/26/99
mBase.com Inc. name changed to mBase Commerce Inc. 7/5/2002 which recapitalized as Bri-Chem Corp. 1/11/2007

LASALLE BRANDS CORP (NV)
Charter revoked for failure to file reports and pay taxes 08/31/2009

LASALLE CAP CORP (DE)
Name changed to SilentRadio, Inc. 7/24/91
SilentRadio, Inc. name changed to Cybernetic Services, Inc. 4/24/96
(See Cybernetic Services, Inc.)

LASALLE CAP CORP (FL)
Name changed to Seertech Corp. 3/28/2006
(See Seertech Corp.)

LASALLE EXTENSION UNIVERSITY (IL)
Common $10 par changed to $5 par 00/00/1933
Each share old 7% Preferred exchanged for (8) shares Common $5 par and $2 cash 00/00/1937
Through voluntary purchase offer Crowell Collier & MacMillan, Inc. acquired 92% as of 11/30/1961
Balance was subsequently acquired by 12/31/1970

LASALLE FD INC (MD)
Merged into Acorn Fund, Inc. (DE) 3/15/77
Each share Common 1¢ par exchanged for (0.5922952) share Capital Stock $1 par
Acorn Fund, Inc. (DE) reincorporated in Maryland 1/1/81 which reorganized in Massachusetts as Acorn Investment Trust 7/1/92

LASALLE HOTEL PPTYS (MD)
10.25% Preferred Shares of Bene. Int. Ser. A 1¢ par called for redemption at $25 on 03/06/2007
8.375% Preferred Shares of Bene. Int. Ser. B 1¢ par called for redemption at $25 plus $0.348954 accrued dividends on 03/14/2011
7.5% Preferred Shares of Bene. Int. Ser. D 1¢ par called for redemption at $25 on 05/21/2012
8% Preferred Shares of Bene. Int. Ser. E 1¢ par called for redemption at $25 on 05/21/2012
7.25% Preferred Shares of Bene. Int. Ser. G 1¢ par called for redemption at $25 plus $0.468229 accrued dividends on 07/03/2014
7.5% Preferred Shares of Bene. Int. Ser. H 1¢ par called for redemption at $25 plus $0.088541 accrued dividends on 05/04/2017
(Additional Information in Active)

LASALLE NATL CORP (DE)
Remarketed Preferred Ser. G called for redemption at $100,000 on 06/12/1997
Remarketed Preferred Ser. H called for redemption at $100,000 on 06/19/1997
Remarketed Preferred Ser. E called for redemption at $100,000 on 07/03/1997
Remarketed Preferred Ser. F called for redemption at $100,000 on 07/17/1997
Fixed/Adjustable Rate Preferred Ser. C called for redemption at $50 on 01/21/2000
Remarketed Preferred Ser. G called for redemption at $100,000 on 08/29/2000

Remarketed Preferred Ser. A called for redemption at $100,000 on 09/06/2000
Remarketed Preferred Ser. B called for redemption at $100,000 on 09/12/2000
Remarketed Preferred Ser. C called for redemption at $100,000 on 09/19/2000
Remarketed Preferred Ser. D called for redemption at $100,000 on 09/26/2000
Remarketed Preferred Ser. E called for redemption at $100,000 on 10/03/2000
Remarketed Preferred Ser. F called for redemption at $100,000 on 10/10/2000
Market Auction Preferred Ser. A called for redemption at $100,000 on 10/10/2000

LASALLE PARTNERS INC (MD)
Name changed to Jones Lang LaSalle Inc. 03/10/1999

LASALLE RE HLDGS LTD (BERMUDA)
Merged into Trenwick Group Ltd. 09/27/2000
Each share Common $1 par exchanged for (1) share Common 10¢ par
(See Trenwick Group Ltd.)
Completely liquidated
Each share Preferred Ser. A $1 par received initial distribution of $10.50 cash payable 07/28/2008 to holders of record 07/17/2008
Each share Preferred Ser. A $1 par received second and final distribution of $0.10 cash payable 02/15/2013 to holders of record 02/12/2013

LASCO, INC. (MS)
Merged out of existence 11/24/1986
Details not available

LASCO INDS (CA)
Merged into Philips Industries Inc. 12/3/69
Each share Common no par exchanged for (0.461) share Common par
(See Philips Industries Inc.)

LASER ALIGNMENT INC (DE)
Acquired by Leica Geosystems Finance plc 1/8/2001
Each share Common 10¢ par exchanged for $5.83 cash
Note: Holders received additional payments
Details not available

LASER ARMS CORP. (DE)
Charter forfeited for failure to maintain a registered agent 10/3/86

LASER BLADE TECHNOLOGIES INC (AB)
Name changed to Laser Blade Systems Inc. 3/31/97

LASER CAPITAL CORP. (UT)
Reincorporated under the laws of Delaware as Tededata International, Inc. (Del.) 7/14/86
Teledata International, Inc. (Del.) reincorporated in Utah as US Fax, Inc. 6/15/87

LASER CORP (UT)
Each share old Common 1¢ par exchanged for (0.2) share new Common 1¢ par 06/29/1992
New Common 1¢ par split (5) for (4) by issuance of (0.25) additional share payable 02/18/1998 to holders of record 01/30/1998
Recapitalized as Broadcast International, Inc. (New) 01/23/2004
Each share new Common 1¢ par exchanged for (0.1) share Common 1¢ par
Broadcast International, Inc. (New) merged into Wireless Ronin Technologies, Inc. 08/01/2014 which name changed to Creative Realities, Inc. 09/17/2014

LASER CRAFT INDS INC (NY)
Name changed to Laser Master International, Inc. 4/8/85

LASER ENDO TECHNIC CORP (DE)
Recapitalized as Laser Medical Technology Inc. 03/02/1992
Each share Common $0.001 par exchanged for (0.5) share Common $0.001 par
Laser Medical Technology Inc. name changed to Biolase Technology Inc. 05/24/1994 which name changed to Biolase,

LASER ENERGY INC (NY)
Dissolved by proclamation 3/31/82

LASER EXPRESSIONS INC (ON)
Recapitalized as Speer Darrow Management Inc. 11/25/1992
Each share Common no par exchanged for (0.25) share Common no par
Speer Darrow Management Inc. name changed to Rex Diamond Mining Corp. (ON) 09/14/1995 which reincorporated in Yukon 07/13/2000 which reorganized in Ontario as Rex Opportunity Corp. 11/09/2011

LASER FRIENDLY INC (ON)
Each share old Common no par exchanged for (0.4) share new Common no par 02/01/1994
Name changed to Gaming Lottery Corp. (ON) 08/01/1995
Gaming Lottery Corp. (ON) reorganized in British Virgin Islands as Gaming Lottery Corp. Ltd. 01/17/1997 which name changed to GLC Ltd. 09/30/1998 which name changed to Galaxiworld.com Ltd. 08/30/1999
(See Galaxiworld.com Ltd.)

LASER HLDG INC (UT)
Name changed to Ion Laser Technology, Inc. (New) 08/22/1988
Ion Laser Technology, Inc. (New) name changed to BriteSmile, Inc. 08/24/1998 which name changed to BSML, Inc. 11/01/2006
(See BSML, Inc.)

LASER INDS LTD (ISRAEL)
Ordinary IS 0.10 chg changed to ILS 0.0001 par per currency change 01/01/1986
Merged into ESC Medical Systems Ltd. 02/22/1998
Each share Ordinary ILS 0.0001 par exchanged for (0.75) share Ordinary ILS 0.10 par
ESC Medical Systems Ltd. name changed to Lumenis Ltd. 09/24/2001
(See Lumenis Ltd.)

LASER LINK CORP (DE)
Merged into Chromalloy American Corp. (DE) 12/29/1977
Each share Common 10¢ par exchanged for (0.1) share Common $1 par
Chromalloy American Corp. (DE) merged into Sun Chemical Corp. 12/23/1986 which name changed to Sequa Corp. 05/08/1987
(See Sequa Corp.)

LASER MAGIC INTL INC (CANADA)
Dissolved 05/02/2002

LASER MEASUREMENTS INC (ID)
Name changed to Affordable Housing Constructors, Inc. 11/01/1993

LASER MED TECHNOLOGY INC (DE)
Each share old Common $0.001 par exchanged for (0.25) share new Common $0.001 par 02/15/1994
Name changed to Biolase Technology Inc. 05/24/1994
Biolase Technology Inc. name changed to Biolase, Inc. 05/29/2012

LASER MTG MGMT INC (DE)
Reincorporated 08/01/2001
Issue Information - 15,000,000 shares COM offered at $15 per share on 11/26/1997
State of incorporation changed from (MD) to (DE) 08/01/2001
Liquidation completed
Each share Common $0.001 par received initial distribution of $3 cash payable 12/28/2001 to holders of record 12/17/2001 Ex date - 12/31/2001
Each share Common $0.001 par received second distribution of $0.50 cash payable 04/08/2003 to holders of record 03/31/2003 Ex date - 04/09/2003
Each share Common $0.001 par received third and final distribution of $0.8623029 cash payable 07/20/2004 to holders of record 07/05/2004 Ex date - 7/21/2004
Note: Certificates were not required to be surrendered and are without value

LASER OPTICS INC (CT)
Acquired by Photonic Products Group, Inc. 11/26/2003
Details not available

LASER-PAC MEDIA CORP (DE)
Merged into Eastman Kodak Co. 10/31/2003
Each share Common $0.0001 par exchanged for $4.22 cash

LASER PHOTONICS INC (DE)
Each share old Common 1¢ par exchanged for (0.03910374) share new Common 1¢ par 02/01/1996
Name changed to PhotoMedex, Inc. (DE) 08/22/2000
PhotoMedex, Inc. (DE) reincorporated in Nevada 12/29/2010 which name changed to FC Global Realty Inc. 11/01/2017

LASER PWR CORP (DE)
Issue Information - 1,650,000 shares COM offered at $5.50 per share on 06/19/1997
Merged into II-VI Inc. 10/12/2000
Each share Common $0.001 par exchanged for (0.104) share Common no par and $3.08 cash

LASER PRECISION CORP (NV)
Common 10¢ par split (2) for (1) by issuance of (1) additional share 02/15/1983
Stock Dividend - 10% 12/01/1987
Merged into Helios Acquisition Corp. 12/19/1994
Each share Common 10¢ par exchanged for $8 cash

LASER PUBG INC (BC)
Delisted from Vancouver Stock Exchange 07/07/1989

LASER QUEST CORP (ON)
Recapitalized as Versent Corp. 02/26/1998
Each share Common no par exchanged for (0.2) share Common no par
(See Versent Corp.)

LASER RECORDING SYS INC (NJ)
Recapitalized as Weida Communications, Inc. 06/16/2004
Each share Common no par exchanged for (0.25) share Common no par
(See Weida Communications, Inc.)

LASER REJUVENATION CLINICS INC (AB)
Merged into 1024386 Alberta Ltd. 10/24/2003
Each share Common no par exchanged for $0.22 cash

LASER REJUVENATION CLINICS LTD (AB)
Issue Information - 2,000,000 shares CL A offered at $0.60 per share on 12/08/1997
Recapitalized as Laser Rejuvenation Clinics Inc. 2/17/2003
Each share Class A Common no par exchanged for (0.1) share Class A Common no par
(See Laser Rejuvenation Clinics Inc.)

LASER SCAN INTL INC (DE)
Merged into Imtec Group plc 6/15/88
Each share Common $0.0001 par exchanged for $0.25 cash

LASER SCIENCES INC (NY)
Charter cancelled and proclaimed dissolved for failure to pay taxes 12/20/77

LASER STORM INC (CO)
Reorganized under the laws of Delaware as Devonshire Consolidated, Inc. 09/25/2008
Each (30) shares Common $0.001 par exchanged for (1) share Common $0.001 par

LASER SYS & ELECTRS INC (TN)
Merged into Keuffel & Esser Co. (NJ) 06/30/1979
Each share Common 50¢ par exchanged for $0.85 cash

LASER SYS CORP (DE)
Each share old Common $1 par exchanged for (0.1) share new Common $1 par 6/6/73
Recapitalized as International Cinevision Productions, Inc. 12/31/83
Each share new Common $1 par exchanged for (2) shares Common 1¢ par
(See International Cinevision Productions, Inc.)

LASER TECH INC (NY)
Charter cancelled and proclaimed dissolved for failure to pay taxes 3/25/81

LASER TECHNOLOGY INC (DE)
Reincorporated 5/30/97
Each share old Common 1¢ par exchanged for (0.25) share new Common 1¢ par 12/23/92
State of incorporation changed from (ID) to (DE) 5/30/97
Merged into LTI Acquisition Corp. 12/31/2003
Each share new Common 1¢ par exchanged for $2.06 cash

LASER VIDEO NETWORK INC (DE)
Name changed to UC Television Network Corp. 7/30/96
UC Television Network recapitalized as College Television Network, Inc. 11/12/97
College Television Network, Inc. name changed to CTN Media Group Inc. 11/18/99

LASER VISION CTRS INC (DE)
Common 1¢ par split (2) for (1) by issuance of (1) additional share payable 8/9/99 to holders of record 7/2/99
Merged into TLC Vision Corp. 5/16/2002
Each share Common 1¢ par exchanged for (0.98) share Common no par

LASERCAD REPROGRAPHICS LTD (NY)
Chapter 11 Federal Bankruptcy Code converted to Chapter 7 on 9/10/87
Stockholders' equity unlikely

LASERCARD CORP (DE)
Acquired by Assa Abloy AB 01/28/2011
Each share Common 1¢ par exchanged for $6.25 cash

LASERGATE SYS INC (FL)
Each (120) shares Common $0.0001 par exchanged for (1) share Common 1¢ par 7/31/89
Each share old Common 1¢ par exchanged exchanged for (1/3) share new Common 1¢ par 11/29/91

Each (12) shares new Common 1¢ par exchanged for (1) share Common 3¢ par 6/16/94
Merged into Tickets.com, Inc. 12/21/99
Each share Common 3¢ par exchanged for $0.10 cash

LASERLOCK TECHNOLOGIES INC (NV)
Recapitalized as VerifyMe, Inc. 07/23/2015
Each share Common $0.001 par exchanged for (0.0117647) share Common $0.001 par

LASERLOGIC INC (WA)
Charter cancelled and proclaimed dissolved for failure to pay fees 2/9/88

LASERMASTER TECHNOLOGIES INC (MN)
Name changed to Virtualfund.com, Inc. 4/1/98
Virtualfund.com, Inc. recapitalized as ASFG, Inc. 8/11/2004

LASERMAX CORP (CO)
Name changed to RXSYS International, Inc. 11/28/1990

LASERMED CORP (CA)
Charter suspended for failure to file reports and pay fees 02/02/1987

LASERMEDIA COMMUNICATIONS CORP (ON)
Name changed to ActFit.com Inc. 08/05/1999
ActFit.com Inc. name changed to Telum International Corp. 12/05/2001
(See Telum International Corp.)

LASERMEDICS INC (TX)
Name changed to Henley Healthcare, Inc. 06/17/1997
(See Henley Healthcare, Inc.)

LASERMETRICS INC (NJ)
Assets sold for the benefit of creditors 10/00/1991
No stockholders' equity

LASERS FOR MEDICINE INC (DE)
Merged into Newcomb Inc. 12/14/1987
Each share Common 1¢ par exchanged for $1 cash

LASERSCOPE, INC. (NV)
Acquired by Trimedyne, Inc. pursuant to terms of an option 07/15/1982
Details not available

LASERSCOPE (CA)
Merged into American Medical Systems Holdings, Inc. 07/25/2006
Each share Common no par exchanged for $31 cash

LASERSIGHT INC (DE)
Old Common $0.001 par split (2) for (1) by issuance of (1) additional share 12/04/1992
Reorganized under Chapter 11 Federal Bankruptcy Code 06/30/2004
Each share old Common 1¢ par exchanged for (0.01929458) share Common 1¢ par
SEC revoked common stock registration 04/27/2010

LASERTEC INTL INC (FL)
Reorganized under the laws of Nevada as Chaichem Holdings Inc. 02/18/2005
Each share Common $0.0001 par exchanged for (0.01) share Common $0.0001 par
Chaichem Holdings Inc. name changed to Excelsior Biotechnology, Inc. 05/16/2005 which name changed to Targetviewz, Inc. 03/03/2006 which recapitalized as Greenway Energy 11/15/2007 which name changed to Greenway Technology 09/19/2008

LASERTECHNICS INC (DE)
Recapitalized as AXCESS Inc. 4/2/98
Each share Common 1¢ par exchanged for (0.05) share Common 1¢ par
AXCESS Inc. name changed to Axcess International, Inc. 4/15/2003

LASERTEK NUCLEAR LABS INC (ON)
Name changed to Hydrol-Tek International Inc. 07/14/2008

LASH INC (NV)
Name changed to Artisan Consumer Goods, Inc. 05/09/2018

LASHBURN PETROLEUMS LTD.
Acquired by Scarlet Oils Ltd. on a (1) for (3) basis in 1952
Scarlet Oils Ltd. was acquired by Oil Selections Ltd. in 1953 which was acquired by Quonto Petroleums Ltd. in 1957 which name was changed to Quonto Explorations Ltd. 7/27/62
(See Quonto Explorations Ltd.)

LASIDON GOLD MINES, LTD. (ON)
Charter cancelled for failure to file reports and pay taxes in January 1958

LASIK AMER INC (NV)
Name changed to Critical Care, Inc. 10/27/2004
Critical Care, Inc. name changed to Cost Containment Technologies, Inc. 03/21/2007 which recapitalized as American Diversified Holdings Corp. 10/16/2007

LASIK VISION CORP (BC)
Acquired by Icon Laser Eye Centers, Inc. 3/13/2001
Each share Common no par exchanged for (0.5) share Common no par

LASIR GOLD INDS INC (BC)
Name changed 02/13/1989
Name changed from Lasir Gold Inc. to Lasir Gold Industries Inc. 02/13/1989
Recapitalized as First Fortune Investments Inc. 11/22/1995
Each share Common no par exchanged for (0.1) share Common no par
First Fortune Investments Inc. name changed to Hansa Resources Ltd. 09/18/2007

LASMO CDA INC (AB)
Name changed to Elan Energy Inc. 10/29/92
Elan Energy Inc. merged into Ranger Oil Ltd. (Canada) 10/9/97
Ranger Oil Ltd. (Canada) merged into Canadian Natural Resources Ltd. 7/28/2000

LASMO PLC (ENGLAND)
Sponsored ADR's for Preference Ser. A 25p par called for redemption at $25 on 02/16/2000
Acquired by Eni S.p.A. 04/17/2001
Each Sponsored ADR for Ordinary 25p par exchanged for (8.5636) Sponsored ADR's for Ordinary

LASON INC (DE)
Plan of reorganization under Chapter 11 Federal Bankruptcy Code effective 07/01/2002
No old Common stockholders' equity
Merged into Charter Larson, Inc. 08/12/2004
Each share new Common 1¢ par exchanged for $0.125 cash

LASORDA FOODS HLDG CORP (CO)
Acquired by Modami Services Inc. 00/00/1993
Details not available

LASSIE RED LAKE GOLD MINES LTD (ON)
Merged into Placer Dome Ltd. 10/15/1998
Each share Common $1 par exchanged for $1.50 cash

LASSITER CORP. (NC)
Merged into Riegel Paper Corp. (Del.) on a (0.975) for (1) basis 10/24/60
(See Riegel Paper Corp. (Del.))

LASSITER KUMA OILS LTD (AB)
Recapitalized as Baloil Lassiter Petroleum Ltd. 05/21/1986
Each share Capital Stock no par exchanged for (0.1) share Common no par
Baloil Lassiter Petroleum Ltd. name changed to Baloil Resources Ltd. 03/21/1989 which merged into Kuma Resources Ltd. 08/27/1993 which name changed to Algonquin Resources Petroleum Corp. 03/18/1997 which recapitalized as Algonquin Oil & Gas Ltd. 04/10/2000 which recapitalized as PetroShale Inc. 03/19/2012

LASSITER PETE LTD (AB)
Merged into Lassiter Kuma Oils Ltd. 10/14/1971
Each share Capital Stock no par exchanged for (0.25) share Capital Stock no par
Lassiter Kuma Oils Ltd. recapitalized as Baloil Lassiter Petroleum Ltd. 05/21/1986 which name changed to Baloil Resources Ltd. 03/21/1989 which merged into Kuma Resources Ltd. 08/27/1993 which name changed to Algonquin Resources Petroleum Corp. 03/18/1997 which recapitalized as Algonquin Oil & Gas Ltd. 04/10/2000 which recapitalized as PetroShale Inc. 03/19/2012

LAST CO CLOTHING INC (NV)
Common $0.001 par split (20) for (1) by issuance of (19) additional shares payable 12/4/2000 to holders of record 12/1/2000 Ex date - 12/4/2000
Name changed to Premier Axiom ASP, Inc. 3/27/2001
Premier Axiom ASP, Inc. name changed to Core Solutions Inc. 7/15/2002 which recapitalized as Sunshine Ventures Inc. 5/12/2003 which name changed to Christine's Precious Petals Inc. 7/14/2003 which name changed to Global Business Markets, Inc. 9/5/2003 which name changed to GREM USA 3/3/2005

LAST CO CLOTHING INC OLD (NV)
Name changed to MIVI Biomedical Technologies Inc. and (1) additional share issued 7/31/2000
MIVI Biomedical Technologies Inc. name changed to Last Company Clothing, Inc. (New) 12/4/2000 which name changed to Premeir Axiom ASP, Inc. 3/27/2001

LAST MILE LOGISTICS GROUP INC (FL)
Administratively dissolved 09/18/2013

LASTARMCO INC (LA)
Each share Common $10 par exchanged for (0.01) share Common $1,000 par 12/28/1977
Merged into Louisiana State Rice Milling Co., Inc. (DE) 03/06/1986
Each share Common $1,000 par exchanged for (1,000) shares Common 1¢ par
(See Louisiana State Rice Milling Co., Inc.)

LASTHOPE LAKE GOLD MINES LTD. (MB)
Charter cancelled and declared dissolved for failure to file returns in September, 1977

LASTMINUTE COM PLC (ENGLAND & WALES)
Issue Information - 33,000,000 SPONSORED ADR'S offered at $30.02 per ADR on 03/14/2000
ADR agreement terminated 8/18/2004
Each Sponsored ADR for Ordinary 1p par exchanged for $9.7752 cash

LASV ENTERPRISES INC (DE)
Each share old Common $0.001 par exchanged for (0.2) share new Common $0.001 par 01/24/2001
SEC revoked common stock registration 04/02/2004

LATAH BANCORPORATION INC (WA)
Stock Dividends - 5% payable 02/15/2000 to holders of record 02/01/2000; 5% payable 03/01/2001 to holders of record 02/01/2001 Ex date - 01/30/2001; 5% payable 02/20/2002 to holders of record 01/16/2002 Ex date - 01/31/2002
Merged into AmericanWest Bancorporation 08/01/2002
Each share Common no par exchanged for (0.5192) share Common no par and $21.22 cash
(See AmericanWest Bancorporation)

LATASA S A (BRAZIL)
Name changed 04/19/2001
Name changed from Latas de Aluminio S.A. to Latasa S.A. 04/19/2001
GDR agreement terminated 06/12/2003
Each 144A GDR for Ordinary exchanged for $13.60037 cash
Each Reg. S GDR for Ordinary exchanged for $13.60037 cash

LATEEGRA GOLD CORP (BC)
Each share old Common no par exchanged for (0.1) share new Common no par 04/14/2009
Merged into Excellon Resources Inc. (BC) 08/05/2011
Each share new Common no par exchanged for (0.54) share Common no par
Note: Unexchanged certificates were cancelled and became without value 08/05/2017
Excellon Resources Inc. (BC) reincorporated in Ontario 06/05/2012

LATEEGRA RES CORP (BC)
Recapitalized as Lateegra Gold Corp. 01/12/2006
Each share Common no par exchanged for (0.1) share Common no par
Lateegra Gold Corp. merged into Excellon Resources Inc. (BC) 08/05/2011 which reincorporated in Ontario 06/05/2012

LATELCO INTL INC (WY)
Reincorporated 12/01/2000
Place of incorporation changed from (BC) to (WY) 12/01/2000
Administratively dissolved 06/11/2002

LATERAL CAP CORP (AB)
Name changed to Jaguar Resources Inc. 07/21/2014

LATERAL GOLD CORP (BC)
Each share old Common no par exchanged for (0.1) share new Common no par 01/14/2015
Recapitalized as Trakopolis IoT Corp. 10/26/2016
Each share new Common no par exchanged for (0.25) share Common no par

LATERAL VECTOR RES INC (SK)
Issue Information - 5,700,000 UNITS consisting of (1) share COM and (1) WT offered at $1 per Unit on 04/20/1994
Acquired by CanArgo Energy Corp. 06/28/2001
Each share Common no par exchanged for $0.11 cash

LATEX RES INC (DE)
Merged into Alliance Resources plc (United Kingdom) 4/30/97
Each share Common 1¢ par exchanged for (0.85981) share new Ordinary Stock 10p par
Alliance Resources plc merged into AROC Inc. 12/8/99

(See AROC Inc.)

LATHAM PROCESS CORP (DE)
Recapitalized as London & Pacific Healthcare, Inc. 11/06/2006
Each share Common 10¢ par exchanged for (0.1) share Common 10¢ par
London & Pacific Healthcare, Inc. name changed to London Pacific & Partners, Inc. 10/08/2009 which recapitalized as Valentine Mark Corp. 03/20/2015

LATHAM SQUARE CO. (CA)
Liquidation completed
Each share Capital Stock no par received initial distribution of $50 cash in 1945
Each share Capital Stock no par received second distribution of $140 cash in 1950
Each share Capital Stock no par exchanged for third and final distribution of $11.15 cash 12/7/54

LATHERIZER CORP. (DE)
No longer in existence having become inoperative and void for non-payment of taxes 4/1/34

LATHWELL RES LTD (BC)
Recapitalized as Optima Energy Corp. (BC) 2/5/88
Each share Common no par exchanged for (0.2) share Common no par
Optima Energy Corp. (BC) recapitalized as Optima Petroleum Corp. (BC) 7/9/92 which reincorporated in Delaware as Petroquest Energy Inc. 9/1/98

LATIGO CAP CORP (AB)
Merged into Cumberland Oil & Gas Ltd. 02/26/2010
Each share Common no par exchanged for (0.3879) share Common no par
Note: Unexchanged certificates were cancelled and became without value 02/26/2015
Cumberland Oil & Gas Ltd. merged into Kallisto Energy Corp. 10/15/2012 which name changed to Toro Oil & Gas Ltd. 11/25/2014
(See Toro Oil & Gas Ltd.)

LATIGO RES INC (BC)
Name changed to LGO Net.Com Inc. (BC) 7/5/99
LGO Net.Com Inc. (BC) reincorporated in Alberta as Prolific Technology Inc. 1/26/2001 which recapitalized as Klad Enterprises Ltd. 3/18/2002 which merged into Diamond Hawk Mining Corp. (ALTA) 2/9/2005 which reincorporated in British Columbia 7/4/2005

LATIN AMER DLR INCOME FD INC (MD)
Name changed to Scudder Global High Income Fund, Inc. 11/14/1997
Scudder Global High Income Fund, Inc. name changed to DWS Global High Income Fund, Inc. 02/06/2006 which name changed to Deutsche Global High Income Fund, Inc. 08/11/2014
(See Deutsche Global High Income Fund, Inc.)

LATIN AMER EQUITY FD INC NEW (MD)
Name changed to Aberdeen Latin America Equity Fund, Inc. (New) 03/26/2010
Aberdeen Latin America Equity Fund, Inc. reorganized as Aberdeen Emerging Markets Equity Income Fund, Inc. 04/30/2018

LATIN AMER EQUITY FD INC OLD (MD)
Merged into Latin America Equity Fund, Inc. (New) 11/10/2000
Common $0.001 par exchanged for Common $0.001 par on a net asset basis
Latin America Equity Fund, Inc. (New) name changed to Aberdeen Latin America Equity Fund, Inc. 03/26/2010

LATIN AMER INVT FD INC (MD)
Under plan of merger name changed to Latin America Equity Fund, Inc. (New) 11/10/2000
Latin America Equity Fund, Inc. (New) name changed to Aberdeen Latin America Equity Fund, Inc. 03/26/2010

LATIN AMER SMALLER COS FD INC (MD)
Name changed 2/15/98
Name changed from Latin America Growth Fund, Inc. to Latin America Smaller Companies Fund, Inc. 2/15/98
Liquidation completed
Each share Common $0.001 par exchanged for initial distribution of $5.92 cash 2/18/99
Each share Common $0.001 par received second and final distribution of $0.015 cash 8/24/99

LATIN AMER VENTURES INC (NV)
Common $0.001 par split (2.4) for (1) by issuance of (1.4) additional shares payable 08/06/2009 to holders of record 08/03/2009
Ex date - 08/07/2009
Name changed to Chile Mining Technologies Inc. 07/23/2010

LATIN AMERICAN AIRWAYS, INC. (DE)
Out of business 00/00/1949
Details not available

LATIN AMERN CASINOS INC (DE)
Name changed to NuWay Energy, Inc. 8/15/2001
NuWay Energy, Inc. name changed to NuWay Medical, Inc. 10/29/2002 which recapitalized as BioLargo, Inc. 3/21/2007

LATIN AMERN GOLD LTD (BERMUDA)
Reincorporated 04/27/1995
Name and place of incorporation changed from Latin American Gold Inc. (BC) to Latin American Gold Ltd. (Bermuda) and Common no par changed to 1¢ par 04/27/1995
Cease trade order effective 01/21/1998
Stockholders' equity unlikely

LATIN AMERN MINES LTD (ON)
Common 50¢ par changed to 20¢ par 02/29/1960
Charter cancelled for failure to file reports and pay taxes 08/02/1972

LATIN AMERN TELECOMMUNICATIONS CORP (BC)
Name changed to Latelco International, Inc. (BC) 10/17/1997
Latelco International, Inc. (BC) reincorporated in Wyoming 12/01/2000
(See Latelco International, Inc.)

LATIN AMERN TELECOMMUNICATIONS VENTURE CO - LATVCO (NV)
Charter permanently revoked 01/30/2009

LATIN HEAT ENTMT INC (NV)
Recapitalized as ProOne Holdings, Inc. 03/27/2008
Each share Common $0.001 par exchanged for (0.0076923) share Common $0.001 par

LATIN RES LTD (AUSTRALIA)
ADR agreement terminated 08/22/2017
Each Sponsored ADR for Ordinary exchanged for $0.067824 cash

LATIN TELEVISION INC NEW (NV)
Recapitalized as Pure Play Music, Ltd. 07/10/2008
Each share Common $0.001 par exchanged for (0.001) share Common $0.001 par
(See Pure Play Music, Ltd.)

LATIN TELEVISION INC OLD (NV)
Name changed to The League Publishing Inc. 09/07/2007
The League Publishing Inc. name changed to Good Life China Corp. 04/08/2008

LATIN VENTURE PARTNERS INC (FL)
Name changed to C3D Inc. 3/31/99
C3D Inc. name changed to Constellation 3D, Inc. (FL) 12/28/99 which reincorporated in Delaware 2/8/2001
(See Constellation 3D, Inc. (DE))

LATINGOLD INC (ON)
Name changed to Travelbyus.Com Ltd. 6/11/99
(See Travelbyus.Com Ltd.)

LATINOCARE MGMT CORP (NV)
Name changed to Roaming Messenger, Inc. 05/02/2003
Roaming Messenger, Inc. name changed to Warp 9, Inc. 11/02/2006 which name changed to CloudCommerce, Inc. 09/30/2015

LATITUDE COMMUNICATIONS INC (DE)
Issue Information - 3,000,000 shares COM offered at $12 per share on 05/06/1999
Merged into Cisco Systems, Inc. 1/12/2004
Each share Common $0.001 par exchanged for $3.95 cash

LATITUDE INDS INC (FL)
Each share old Common $0.0001 par exchanged for (7) shares new Common $0.0001 par 11/03/2006
Each share new Common $0.0001 par exchanged again for (0.1) share new Common $0.0001 par 05/04/2007
Each share new Common $0.0001 par exchanged for (0.001) share Common $0.00001 par 11/03/2008
Recapitalized as Water Technologies International, Inc. 06/20/2011
Each share Common $0.00001 par exchanged for (0.05) share Common $0.00001 par

LATITUDE MINERALS CORP (BC)
Recapitalized as Coal Creek Energy Inc. 05/21/2002
Each share Common no par exchanged for (0.1) share Common no par
Coal Creek Energy Inc. name changed to Corex Gold Corp. 11/18/2003 which merged into Minera Alamos Inc. 04/18/2018

LATITUDE NETWORK INC (NV)
Name changed to Orbis Development, Inc. (Ctfs. dated prior to 06/18/1998) 06/08/1998
Orbis Development, Inc. (Ctfs. dated prior to 06/18/1998) name changed to Struthers Inc. 06/18/1998 which name changed to Global Marine Ltd. 08/02/2004
(See Global Marine Ltd.)

LATOKA INC (TX)
Each share Common $0.0005 par exchanged for (0.04) share Common $0.0125 par 6/22/89
Merged into Lomak Petroleum, Inc. 7/23/91
Each (2.65) shares Common $0.0125 par exchanged for (1) share Common 1¢ par
Lomak Petroleum, Inc. name changed to Range Resources Corp. 8/25/98

LATOMIC RED LAKE GOLD MINES LTD. (ON)
Acquired by Loisan Red Lake Gold Mines Ltd. 00/00/1954
Each share Common no par exchanged for (0.33333333) share Common no par
Loisan Red Lake Gold Mines Ltd. name changed to Grandview Energy Resources Inc. 11/09/1979 which recapitalized as Consolidated Grandview Inc. 09/22/1983 which name changed to Grandview Gold Inc. 07/06/2004 which recapitalized as PUDO Inc. 07/13/2015

LATOURAINE-BICKFORDS FOODS INC (DE)
Name changed to Bickford Corp. 5/2/78
(See Bickford Corp.)

LATOURAINE COFFEE CO., INC. (MA)
Class B $1 par split (10) for (1) by issuance of (9) additional shares 11/30/66
Merged into LaTouraine Foods, Inc. 5/31/70
LaTouraine Foods, Inc. merged into LaTouraine-Bickford's Foods, Inc. 11/30/70 which name changed to Bickford Corp. 5/2/78
(See Bickford Corp.)

LATOURAINE FOODS INC (DE)
Merged into LaTouraine-Bickford's Foods, Inc. 11/30/1970
Each share Common 5¢ par exchanged for (1/3) share Common 10¢ par
LaTouraine-Bickford's Foods, Inc. name changed to Bickford Corp. 05/02/1978
(See Bickford Corp.)

LATROBE CONNELLSVILLE COAL & COKE CO.
Ceased operations 00/00/1929
Details not available

LATROBE STL CO (PA)
Name changed 00/00/1952
Name changed from Latrobe Electric Steel Co. to Latrobe Steel Co. 00/00/1952
Common $10 par changed to $5 par and (1) additional share issued plus a 25% stock dividend paid 08/22/1955
Common $5 par changed to $2.50 par and (1) additional share issued 02/05/1960
Merged into Timken Co. 04/25/1975
Each share Common $2.50 par exchanged for (0.48) share Common no par

LATSHAW ENTERPRISES INC (DE)
Each share Common $2 par exchanged for (0.02) share Class A Common $100 par 12/18/1996
Class A Common $100 par split (20) for (1) by issuance of (19) additional shares payable 05/16/1997 to holders of record 05/05/1997
Acquired by Latco Inc. 05/30/2002
Each share Class A Common $100 par exchanged for $55 cash

LATTICE CAP CORP (BC)
Acquired by Verb Exchange Inc. 06/24/2003
Each share Common no par exchanged for (0.36) share Common no par
Verb Exchange Inc. recapitalized as Seymour Ventures Corp. 07/05/2010 which name changed to Rare Earth Industries Ltd. 07/13/2011 which recapitalized as Ackroo Inc. 10/10/2012

LATTICE GROUP PLC (ENGLAND)
Merged into National Grid Transco plc 10/21/2002
Each share Ordinary exchanged for (0.375) share Ordinary

LATVIJAS UNIBANKA A/S (LATVIA)
Stock Dividend - 14.29107% payable 09/11/1998 to holders of record 09/09/1998
Merged into SEB (Stockholm) 08/24/2007
Each Sponsored 144A GDR for Ordinary exchanged for $4.376 cash
Each Sponsored Reg. S GDR for Ordinary exchanged for $4.376 cash

LAU BLOWER CO (OH)
Stock Dividend - 100% 03/30/1955
Merged into Philips Industries Inc. 09/30/1969
Each share Common $1 par exchanged for (1) Conv. Special Preferred no par
(See Philips Industries Inc.)

LAUD RES INC (NV)
Name changed to MASS Petroleum Inc. 07/11/2008
MASS Petroleum Inc. name changed to Cannamed Corp. 04/07/2014 which name changed to Chuma Holdings, Inc. 08/29/2014

LAUDA AIR LUFTFAHRT AG (AUSTRIA)
Acquired by Austrian Airlines AG 11/00/2001
Details not available

LAUDER ESTEE AUTOMATIC COM EXCHANGE SEC TR II (NY)
Each share 6.25% Trust Automatic Common Exchange Securities exchanged for $73.154 plus $1.3516 accrued dividends on 5/23/2002

LAUFER BRDG ENTERPRISES INC (NV)
Name changed to Creative Edge Nutrition, Inc. 05/02/2012

LAUFER CO (CA)
Common 10¢ par split (3) for (2) by issuance of (0.5) additional share 8/9/71
Stock Dividend - 50% 2/15/78
Each share Common 10¢ par exchanged for (0.0002) share Common $500 par 10/9/79
Note: In effect holders received $10 cash per share and public interest eliminated

LAUGHLIN ALLOY STEEL CO., INC. (NV)
Charter revoked for failure to file reports and pay fees 3/7/60

LAUNCH MEDIA INC (DE)
Merged into Yahoo! Inc. 08/14/2001
Each share Common $0.001 par exchanged for $0.92 cash
Yahoo! Inc. name changed to Altaba Inc. 06/19/2017

LAUNCH RES INC (AB)
Placed in receivership 02/10/2005
Stockholders' equity unlikely

LAUNDRIMATION INC (DE)
Name changed to Venturevest Corp. 12/30/1969
(See Venturevest Corp.)

LAUNDRY & CLEANER SUPPLIES CORP. (NY)
Liquidation completed 2/15/61

LAURA ASHLEY HLDGS PLC (UNITED KINGDOM)
ADR agreement terminated 4/14/2005
Each ADR for Ordinary 5p par exchanged for $1.12596 cash

LAURA INDS & RES LTD (BC)
Recapitalized as Lorcan Resources Ltd. 9/20/78
Each share Capital Stock no par exchanged for (0.2) share Capital Stock no par
(See Lorcan Resources Ltd.)

LAURA LEE MINING & LEASING CO. (CO)
Charter suspended for failure to file annual reports 10/19/1918

LAURA MINES LTD. (BC)
Name changed to Laura Industries & Resources Ltd. and Capital Stock 50¢ par changed to no par 12/4/73
Laura Industries & Resources Ltd. recapitalized as Lorcan Resources Ltd. 9/20/78
(See Lorcan Resources Ltd.)

LAURA SECORD CANDY SHOPS LTD. (CANADA)
See - Secord (Laura) Candy Shops Ltd.

LAURAAN CORP (NV)
Recapitalized as Special Projects Group, Ltd. 2/17/2006
Each share Common $0.001 par exchanged for (0.001) share Common $0.001 par

LAURAL RES INC (NV)
Common $0.001 par split (20) for (1) by issuance of (19) additional shares payable 03/10/2008 to holders of record 02/14/2008
Ex date - 03/11/2008
Name changed to Abtech Holdings, Inc. 06/16/2010

LAURASIA RES LTD (ON)
Merged into StarTech Energy Inc. 2/9/98
Each share Common no par exchanged for (0.0362) share Common no par and $0.24 cash
StarTech Energy Inc. merged into Impact Energy Inc. (Canada) 1/31/2001 which merged into Thunder Energy Inc. 4/30/2004
(See Thunder Energy Inc.)

LAURE EXPLORATION CO., INC. (DE)
No longer in existence having become inoperative and void for non-payment of taxes 4/1/65

LAUREATE ED INC (MD)
Merged into Wengen Alberta L.P. 08/17/2007
Each share Common 1¢ par exchanged for $62 cash

LAUREATE RES & STL INDS INC (NV)
SEC revoked common stock registration 09/12/2013

LAUREL BANCORP INC (MD)
Common 1¢ par split (2) for (1) by issuance of (1) additional share 7/15/93
Merged into FCNB Corp. 1/26/96
Each share Common 1¢ par exchanged for (0.7656) share Common $1 par
FCNB Corp. merged into BB&T Corp. 1/8/2001

LAUREL BANCSHARES INC (MO)
Merged into Ameribanc, Inc. 06/30/1982
Each share Common $1 par exchanged for (1.057) shares Common $5 par
(See Ameribanc, Inc.)

LAUREL CAP GROUP INC (PA)
Common 1¢ par split (5) for (4) by issuance of (0.25) additional share 11/15/94
Common 1¢ par split (3) for (2) by issuance of (0.5) additional share 9/15/95
Common 1¢ par split (3) for (2) by issuance of (0.5) additional share payable 1/16/98 to holders of record 1/2/98
Merged into First Commonwealth Financial Corp. 8/28/2006
Each share Common 1¢ par exchanged for (2.229) shares Common $1 par

LAUREL ENTMT INC (DE)
Acquired by Spelling Entertainment, Inc. 3/1/89
Each share Common $0.001 par exchanged for (0.282188) share Class A Common 1¢ par and $1.70 cash
Spelling Entertainment, Inc. merged into Charter Co. 7/30/92

LAUREL EXPLS LTD (BC)
Recapitalized as Linden Explorations Inc. 2/22/91
Each share Common no par exchanged for (0.25) share Common no par
Linden Explorations Inc. name changed to Australian Oilfields Property Ltd. (BC) 5/23/96 which reincorporated in Alberta as Equatorial Energy Inc. 9/15/97 which name changed to Resolute Energy Inc. 11/14/2002
(See Resolute Energy Inc.)

LAUREL FDS INC (MD)
Government Money Market II Portfolio $0.001 par reclassified as Institutional Government Money Market Fund Class I $0.001 par 03/01/1994
Prime Money Market II Portfolio $0.001 par reclassified as Institutional Prime Money Market Fund Class I $0.001 par 03/01/1994
Short-Term Bond Portfolio $0.001 par reclassified as Institutional Short-Term Bond Fund Class I $0.001 par 03/01/1994
Name changed to Dreyfus/Laurel Funds, Inc. and Tactical Asset Allocation Portfolio $0.001 par reclassified as Tactical Asset Allocation Fund Class R $0.001 par 10/14/1994

LAUREL MILLS, INC. (DE)
Charter cancelled and declared inoperative and void for non-payment of taxes 04/01/1963

LAUREL SVGS ASSN (PA)
Common $1 par split (5) for (4) by issuance of (0.25) additional share 8/14/92
Common $1 par split (5) for (4) by issuance of (0.25) additional share 9/17/93
Under plan of reorganization each share Common $1 par automatically became (1) share Laurel Capital Group Inc. Common 1¢ par 12/3/93
Laurel Capital Group Inc. merged into First Commonwealth Financial Corp. 8/28/2006

LAUREL WAY PRODTNS (NV)
Name changed to LWAY Productions 10/1/87
LWAY Productions name changed to Marquee Entertainment, Inc. 5/4/93 which recapitalized as Progresssive Telecommunications Corp. 8/4/99

LAUREL WEST PUBG INC (CANADA)
Reincorporated 01/22/1990
Place of incorporation changed from (AB) to (Canada) 01/22/1990
Name changed to Elite Real Estate Canada Inc. 03/22/1990
Elite Real Estate Canada Inc. recapitalized as Far Eastern Energy Corp. 03/21/1995
(See Far Eastern Energy Corp.)

LAUREN INC (FL)
Proclaimed dissolved for failure to file reports and pay fees 08/13/1993

LAURENCE ASSOCS CONSULTING INC (NV)
Reincorporated under the laws of Delaware as Beacon Energy Holdings, Inc. and (2/3) additional share issued 07/11/2008
Beacon Energy Holdings, Inc. recapitalized as EQM Technologies & Energy, Inc. 02/10/2011

LAURENCE LEE GOLD MINES LTD. (ON)
Charter cancelled for failure to file reports and pay taxes 10/27/58

LAURENT VENTURE CAPITAL CORP (CANADA)
Name changed to Carbon2Green Corp. 10/07/2009
Carbon2Green Corp. recapitalized as TomaGold Corp. 01/04/2012

LAURENTIAN AMERICAN EQUITY FUND LTD. (CANADA)
Name changed to Strategic Value American Equity Fund Ltd. 06/05/1997
Strategic Value American Equity Fund Ltd. name changed to StrategicNova U.S. Large Cap Growth Fund Ltd. 09/26/2000
(See StrategicNova U.S. Large Cap Growth Fund Ltd.)

LAURENTIAN BK CDA (MONTREAL, QC)
Class A Preferred Ser. 3 no par called for redemption 09/30/1988
$2.625 Retractable Class A Preferred Ser. 1 no par called for redemption 02/02/1990
Class A Preferred Ser. 6 no par called for redemption at $25 plus $0.546875 accrued dividends on 11/26/2001
Class A Preferred Ser. 7 no par called for redemption at $25.50 on 06/16/2004
Class A Preferred Ser. 8 no par called for redemption at $25.50 on 06/16/2004
Class A Preferred Ser. 9 no par called for redemption at $25 plus $0.375 accrued dividends on 03/15/2013
Class A Preferred Ser. 10 no par called for redemption at $25 on 06/16/2014
Class A Preferred Ser. 11 no par called for redemption at $25 on 12/15/2017
(Additional Information in Active)

LAURENTIAN CANADIAN EQUITY FUND LTD. (CANADA)
Name changed to Strategic Value Canadian Equity Fund Ltd. 06/05/1997
Strategic Value Canadian Equity Fund Ltd. name changed to StrategicNova Canadian Large Cap Value Fund Ltd. 09/26/2000
(See StrategicNova Canadian Large Cap Value Fund Ltd.)

LAURENTIAN CAP CORP (DE)
Reincorporated 7/24/87
State of incorporation changed from (FL) to (DE) 7/24/87
Each share old Common 5¢ par exchanged for (0.5) share new Common 5¢ par 1/1/91
$6 Conv. Preferred Ser. A 1¢ par called for redemption 11/13/95
Merged into American Annuity Group, Inc. 11/13/95
Each share Common 5¢ par exchanged for $14.125 cash

LAURENTIAN COMMONWEALTH FUND LTD. (CANADA)
Name changed to Strategic Value Commonwealth Fund Ltd. 06/05/1997
Strategic Value Commonwealth Fund Ltd. name changed to StrategicNova Commonwealth Fund Ltd. 09/26/2000
(See StrategicNova Commonwealth Fund Ltd.)

LAURENTIAN DIVIDEND FUND LTD. (CANADA)
Name changed to Strategic Value Dividend Fund Ltd. 06/05/1997
Strategic Value Dividend Fund Ltd. name changed to StrategicNova Canadian Dividend Fund Ltd. 09/26/2000
(See StrategicNova Canadian Dividend Fund Ltd.)

LAURENTIAN GOLDFIELDS LTD (BC)
Each share old Common no par exchanged for (0.1) share new Common no par 11/23/2012
Name changed to Pure Gold Mining Inc. 06/27/2014

LAURENTIAN GROUP CORP (QC)
Merged into Desjardins-Laurentian Financial Corp. 2/16/94
Each share Class B Subordinate no par exchanged for (0.0996) share Class A Preferred no par, (0.1794) share Class A Subordinate no par and $6.22 cash
$1.875 Conv. Retractable Class III Preferred Ser. 1 no par called for redemption at $25 plus $0.3955548 accrued dividends on 3/18/94
Desjardins-Laurentian Financial Corp. name changed to Desjardins Financial Corp. 3/31/2003
(See Desjardins Financial Corp.)

LAURENTIAN INTERNATIONAL FUND LTD. (CANADA)
Name changed to Strategic Value International Fund Ltd. 06/05/1997
Strategic Value International Fund Ltd. name changed to StrategicNova World Large Cap Fund Ltd. 09/26/2000
(See StrategicNova World Large Cap Fund Ltd.)

LAURENTIAN LIFE INS CO INC (QC)
$2.22 Class A Preferred $25 par called for redemption 9/30/90
Public interest eliminated

LAURENTIAN MUTUAL INSURANCE (QC)
Name changed to Laurentian Life Insurance Co. Inc. 1/16/89
(See Laurentian Life Insurance Co. Inc.)

LAURENTIDE CO.
Merged into Consolidated Paper Corp. Ltd. 00/00/1932
Details not available

LAURENTIDE FIN CORP CALIF (DE)
5% Preference $20 par called for redemption 04/17/1967
5% 1st Preferred $20 par called for redemption 04/17/1967
6% Jr. Preferred Ser. 1966 $16 par called for redemption 04/17/1967
Merged into Eliminator, Inc. 06/01/1967
Each share Common $5 par exchanged for $90 cash

LAURENTIDE FINANCIAL CORP. LTD.-LE FINANCIER LAURENTIDE LTEE. (CANADA)
Preferred no par called for redemption 10/29/82
Public interest eliminated

LAURENTIDE FINL LTD (BC)
Class A Common no par reclassified as Common no par 04/10/1963
Class B Common no par reclassified as Common no par 04/10/1963
Reorganized under the laws of Canada as Laurentide Financial Corp. Ltd.-Le Financier Laurentide Ltee. 02/12/1979
Each (2.75) shares Common no par exchanged for (2) shares Preferred no par
$1.25 Preferred $20 par called for redemption 06/30/1979
$1.40 Preferred $25 par called for redemption 06/30/1979
$2 2nd Preferred $38 par called for redemption 06/30/1979
5.25% Preferred $20 par called for redemption 06/30/1979
6.25% Preferred $20 par called for redemption 06/30/1979
Public interest eliminated

LAURENTIDE POWER CO.
Acquired by Shawinigan Water & Power Co. in 1928

Details not available

LAURIAT CORP (DE)
Adjudicated bankrupt 05/27/1976
Stockholders' equity unlikely

LAURIC INDS INC (NY)
Dissolved by proclamation 12/15/75

LAURIER INTL INC (DE)
Each share old Common $0.0001 par exchanged for (1/3) share new Common $0.0001 par 05/09/2008
Name changed to Arno Therapeutics, Inc. 07/17/2008

LAURIER RES INC (BC)
Name changed to Zarcan International Resources Inc. 11/08/1999
Zarcan International Resources Inc. name changed to Bighorn Petroleum Ltd. 01/30/2006 which recapitalized as Sunset Pacific Petroleum Ltd. 05/07/2009

LAURIER RES LTD (QC)
Acquired by Humboldt Energy Corp. 00/00/1982
Each share Common $1 par exchanged for (0.6) share Subordinate no par
Humboldt Energy Corp. recapitalized as HEC Investments Ltd. 08/04/1989 which name changed to Humboldt Capital Corp. 08/29/1994
(See Humboldt Capital Corp.)

LAURION GOLD INC (ON)
Name changed to Laurion Mineral Exploration Inc. 11/03/2006

LAUSON CO.
Acquired by Hart-Carter Co. 00/00/1941
Details not available

LAUTARO NITRATE CO., LTD.
Merged into Anglo-Lautaro Nitrate Corp. in 1951
Each share Class A Ordinary £1 par exchanged for (1) share Class A $2.40 par
Each share Class B Ordinary 5d par exchanged for (1) share Class B 5¢ par
Anglo-Lautaro Nitrate Corp. reorganized as Anglo-Lautaro Nitrate Co. Ltd. 7/8/68 which name changed to Anglo Co. Ltd. 5/10/72 which name changed to Anglo Energy Ltd. 12/17/80 which reorganized in Delaware as Anglo Energy, Inc. 7/14/86 which name changed to Nabors Industries, Inc. (DE) 3/7/89 which reincorprated in Bermuda as Nabors Industries Ltd. 6/24/2002

LAUTARO NITRATE CORP.
Dissolved. Final liquidating dividend of Compania de Salitre de Chile stock distributed 00/00/1931 which was acquired by Compania Salitrera de Tarapaca Y Antofagasta 00/00/1934

LAVA CAP CORP (ON)
Recapitalized as Samoth Capital Corp. 02/17/1988
Each share Common no par exchanged for (0.2) share Common no par
Samoth Capital Corp. name changed to Sterling Financial Corp. 06/14/2000 which name changed to Sterling Centrecorp Inc. 06/08/2001
(See Sterling Centrecorp Inc.)

LAVA CAP GOLD MINING CORP. (DE)
Acquired by New Goldvue Mines Ltd. 00/00/1953
Each share Common $1 par exchanged for (0.25) share Capital Stock $1 par
New Goldvue Mines Ltd. recapitalized as Lava Cap Resources Ltd. 04/06/1979 which name changed to Lava Capital Corp. 11/14/1985 which recapitalized as Samoth Capital Corp. 02/17/1988 which name changed to Sterling Financial Corp. 06/14/2000 which name changed to Sterling Centrecorp Inc. 06/08/2001
(See Sterling Centrecorp Inc.)

LAVA CAP RESOURCES LTD. (ON)
Capital Stock no par reclassified as Common no par 07/03/1980
Name changed to Lava Capital Corp. 11/14/1985
Lava Capital Corp. recapitalized as Samoth Capital Corp. 02/17/1988 which name changed to Sterling Financial Corp. 06/14/2000 which name changed to Sterling Centrecorp Inc. 06/08/2001
(See Sterling Centrecorp Inc.)

LAVAL RES LTD (AB)
Merged into International Oiltex Ltd. 10/01/1989
Each share Common no par exchanged for (1) share Common no par
International Oiltex Ltd. merged into Aztec Resources Ltd. 09/02/1994 which recapitalized as Pursuit Resources Inc. (New) 02/13/1997 which merged into EnerMark Income Fund 04/11/2000 which merged into Enerplus Resources Fund 06/22/2001 which reorganized as Enerplus Corp. 01/03/2011

LAVALIE MINES LTD. (ON)
Recapitalized as Norvalie Mines Ltd. on a (1) for (4) basis 11/25/55
Norvalie Mines Ltd. recapitalized as International Norvalie Mines Ltd. 12/20/65

LAVALIN INDS INC (QC)
Discharged from bankruptcy 05/05/1997
No stockholders' equity

LAVANDIN MINING CO. (QC)
Acquired by Malartic Hygrade Gold Mines Ltd. 10/2/61
Each share Capital Stock $1 par exchanged for (1) share Capital Stock $1 par
Malartic Hygrade Gold Mines Ltd. recapitalized under the laws of Quebec as Malartic Hygrade Gold Mines (Quebec) Ltd. 8/15/68 which reincorporated under the laws of Ontario as Malartic Hygrade Gold Mines (Canada) Ltd. 3/1/75 which name changed to Republic Goldfields Inc. 6/10/91

LAVANT IRON MINES LTD. (ON)
Name changed to Lavant Mines Ltd. 07/10/1959
(See Lavant Mines Ltd.)

LAVANT MINES LTD. (ON)
Charter revoked for failure to file reports and pay fees 7/8/65

LAVCO INC (AB)
Issue Information - 1,500,000 shares COM offered at $0.20 per share on 05/16/1997
Name changed to Entercor Entertainment Corp. 11/10/99
Entercor Entertainment Corp. recapitalized as Entercor Resource Corp. 2/25/2005

LAVENDER URANIUM CORP. (UT)
Completely liquidated 03/19/1956
Each share Capital Stock 5¢ par received (0.16666) share Wycotah Oil & Uranium, Inc. Common 1¢ par
Note: Certificates were not required to be surrendered and are without value

LAVERTON GOLD N L (WESTERN AUSTRALIA)
Delisted from Australian Stock Exchange 10/06/1998
Stockholders' equity unlikely

LAVERTY INDL DEV LTD (ON)
Merged into GHP Exploration Corp. (BC) 02/18/1997
Each share Common no par exchanged for (0.0666) share Common no par
GHP Exploration Corp. (BC) reincorporated in Yukon 04/30/1997 which merged into TransAtlantic Petroleum Corp. (AB) 12/02/1998 which reincorporated in Bermuda as TransAtlantic Petroleum Ltd. 10/01/2009

LAVERTY RED LAKE MINES, LTD. (ON)
Charter surrendered in May 1958

LAVICHA GOLD MINES, LTD. (ON)
Charter cancelled for failure to file reports and pay taxes in 1952

LAVOIE LABORATORIES, INC. (NJ)
Adjudicated bankrupt 10/28/66

LAVORIS CO. (DE)
Each share Common no par exchanged for (5) shares Common $4 par 9/26/56
Acquired by Vick Chemical Co. on a (4/7) for (1) basis 10/1/58
Vick Chemical Co. name changed to Richardson-Merrell Inc. 10/21/60 which merged into Dow Chemical Co. 3/10/81

LAW CENTER OF AMERICA MANAGEMENT CORP. (NV)
Name changed to American Excel, Ltd. 6/12/82

LAW ENFORCEMENT ASSOCS CORP (NV)
Chapter 7 bankruptcy proceedings terminated 10/05/2017
No stockholders' equity

LAW RESH SVC INC (NY)
Charter cancelled and proclaimed dissolved for failure to pay taxes 09/30/1981

LAWBECK CORP.
Merged into Consolidated Dearborn Corp. in 1940
Each share Preferred exchanged for $100 in Debentures and (2.5) shares Common
(See Consolidated Dearborn Corp.)

LAWHON JOHN F FURNITURE CO (DE)
Name changed to Sloane (W & J) Corp. 7/17/85
(See Sloane (W & J) Corp.)

LAWLEY (GEO.) & SON CORP.
Dissolution approved in 1946

LAWLOR INDS INC (IL)
Adjudicated bankrupt 10/7/76
No stockholders' equity

LAWN A MAT CHEM & EQUIP CORP (NY)
Dissolved by proclamation 3/24/93

LAWN ELECTRONICS CO., INC. (NY)
Assets liquidated for benefit of creditors in 1963
No stockholders' equity

LAWN SAVINGS & LOAN ASSOCIATION (IL)
Receivership terminated 6/24/75
Each Permanent Reserve share exchanged for $1 cash

LAWNAMERICA INC (DE)
Chapter 11 bankruptcy proceedings converted to Chapter 7 on 3/2/92
Stockholders' equity unlikely

LAWNDALE NATIONAL BANK (CHICAGO, IL)
Stock Dividend - 100% 10/29/63
Name changed to Lawndale Trust & Savings Bank (Chicago, IL) 11/25/70
(See Lawndale Trust & Savings Bank (Chicago, IL))

LAWNDALE TR & SVGS BK (CHICAGO, IL)
Acquired by Bank of Chicago/Garfield Ridge (Chicago, IL) 11/30/92
Details not available

LAWNLITE CO (FL)
Name changed to Reiter (Victor) Corp. 10/15/81
(See Reiter (Victor) Corp.)

LAWRENCE (A.C.) LEATHER CO. (ME)
Acquired by Swift & Co. in 1952
Each share Capital Stock $10 par received $18 cash

LAWRENCE CONSERVATIVE PAYOUT RATIO TR (ON)
Merged into Lawrence Payout Ratio Trust (New) 12/30/2005
Each Trust Unit no par exchanged for (1.0149904) Trust Units no par
Lawrence Payout Ratio Trust (New) name changed to Lawrence Income & Growth Fund 08/27/2007 which name changed to Navina Income & Growth Fund 01/04/2010

LAWRENCE ELECTRIC CO. (MA)
Merged into Merrimack-Essex Electric Co. on a (1.25) for (1) basis 7/30/57 which Common was acquired by New England Electric System 6/30/59
(See New England Electric System)

LAWRENCE FINL HLDGS INC (MD)
Merged into Oak Hill Financial, Inc. 04/02/2005
Each share Common 1¢ par exchanged for approximately (0.17685504) share Common no par and $17.575 cash
Oak Hill Financial, Inc. merged into WesBanco, Inc. 11/30/2007

LAWRENCE GAS & ELECTRIC CO. (MA)
Each share Capital Stock $25 par exchanged for (1) share Lawrence Gas Co. Capital Stock $10 par and (1.5) shares Lawrence Electric Co. Capital Stock $10 par in 1953
(See each company's listing)

LAWRENCE GAS CO. (MA)
Acquired by Bay State Gas Co. (Old) 11/29/73
Each share Capital Stock $10 par exchanged for $39.89 cash

LAWRENCE HOLDING CORP. (CA)
Name changed to Lawrence Investment Corp. 00/00/1946
(See Lawrence Investment Corp.)

LAWRENCE INCOME & GROWTH FUND (ON)
Name changed to Navina Income & Growth Fund 01/04/2010

LAWRENCE INS GROUP INC (DE)
Common 1¢ par split (3) for (2) by issuance of (0.5) additional share 07/26/1988
Assets placed in receivership 10/22/1997
No stockholders' equity

LAWRENCE INVESTING INC (NY)
Each share 7% Preferred exchanged for (1) share Part. Preferred $100 par 00/00/1940
Each share Common no par exchanged for (1) share old Common $1 par 00/00/1940
Each share Part. Preferred $100 par exchanged for (1) share $5 Preferred $100 par 00/00/1948
Each share old Common $1 par exchanged for (1) new Common $1 par 00/00/1948
5% Preferred $100 par called for redemption 03/01/1959
Charter cancelled and proclaimed dissolved for failure to pay taxes 06/14/2004

LAWRENCE INVT CORP (CA)
3% Preferred Ser. A $10 par called for redemption 12/01/1967
8% Preferred $10 par called for redemption 12/01/1967
In process of liquidation
Each share Common $1 par received initial distribution of $7 cash 12/22/1969
Note: Details on additional distributions are not available

LAWRENCE MANOR APARTMENTS LIQUIDATION TRUST
Trust terminated and liquidated in 1951
Details not available

LAWRENCE MANUFACTURING CO.
Liquidated in 1939

LAWRENCE MNG CORP (BC)
Struck off register and declared dissolved for failure to file returns 02/04/1994

LAWRENCE PAYOUT RATIO TR II (ON)
Merged into Lawrence Payout Ratio Trust (New) 12/30/2005
Each Trust Unit no par exchanged for (1) Trust Unit no par
Lawrence Payout Ratio Trust (New) name changed to Lawrence Income & Growth Fund 08/27/2007 which name changed to Navina Income & Growth Fund 01/04/2010

LAWRENCE PAYOUT RATIO TR NEW (ON)
Name changed to Lawrence Income & Growth Fund and Units reclassified as Class X Units 08/27/2007
Lawrence Income & Growth Fund name changed to Navina Income & Growth Fund 01/04/2010

LAWRENCE PAYOUT RATIO TR OLD (ON)
Merged into Lawrence Payout Ratio Trust (New) 12/30/2005
Each Trust Unit no par exchanged for (1.19326995) Trust Units no par
Lawrence Payout Ratio Trust (New) name changed to Lawrence Income & Growth Fund 08/27/2007 which name changed to Navina Income & Growth Fund 01/04/2010

LAWRENCE PORTLAND CEMENT CO.
Merged into Dragon Cement Co., Inc. 11/30/1951
Each share Common exchanged for (1) share Common $10 par
Dragon Cement Co., Inc. acquired by American-Marietta Co. 10/01/1956 which merged into Martin Marietta Corp. (Old) 10/10/1961 which merged into Martin Marietta Corp. (New) 04/02/1993 which merged into Lockheed Martin Corp. 03/15/1995

LAWRENCE RES INC (DE)
Name changed to Consolidated Mines International, Inc. 9/6/85
(See Consolidated Mines International, Inc.)

LAWRENCE SVGS & TR CO (NEW CASTLE, PA)
Capital Stock $100 par changed to $10 par and (9) additional shares issued plus a 100% stock dividend paid 03/31/1959
Merged into First Seneca Bank & Trust Co. (Oil City, PA) 09/29/1972
Each share Capital Stock $10 par exchanged for (1.3) shares Capital Stock $5 par
First Seneca Bank & Trust Co. (Oil City, PA) reorganized as First Seneca Corp. 06/01/1982 which merged into Pennbancorp 12/31/1983 which merged into Integra Financial Corp. 01/26/1989 which merged into National City Corp. 05/03/1996 which was acquired by PNC Financial Services Group, Inc. 12/31/2008

LAWRENCE SVGS BK NEW (LAWRENCE, MA)
Under plan of reorganization each share Common 10¢ par automatically became (1) share LSB Corp. Common 10¢ par 07/01/2001
(See LSB Corp.)

LAWRENCE SVGS BK OLD (LAWRENCE, MA)
Under plan of reorganization each share Common 10¢ par automatically became (1) share Intrex Financial Services, Inc. (DE) 01/07/1988
Intrex Financial Services, Inc. (DE) reorganized as Lawrence Savings Bank (New) (Lawrence, MA) 10/25/1991 which reorganized as LSB Corp. 07/01/2001
(See LSB Corp.)

LAWRENCE SERVES IND INC (NY)
Acquired by ECCO Service Group Inc. 07/10/1978
Each share Common 10¢ par exchanged for $1.50 cash

LAWRENCE SYS INC (CA)
Merged into INA Corp. 9/25/72
Each share Common no par exchanged for $338 cash
Note: Additional funds held in escrow may have been distributed

LAWRENCE WAREHOUSE CORP. (CA)
Name changed to Lawrence Holding Corp. 00/00/1942
Lawrence Holding Corp. name changed to Lawrence Investment Corp. 00/00/1946
(See Lawrence Investment Corp.)

LAWRENCE WHSE CO (CA)
6% Preferred $25 par called for redemption 1/31/41
Name changed to Lawrence Systems, Inc. 6/30/71
Lawrence Systems, Inc. merged into INA Corp. 9/25/72 which merged into Cigna Corp. 4/1/82

LAWRENCE WINTHROP BUILDING (IL)
See - Winthrop (Lawrence) Building

LAWRYS FOODS INC (CA)
Common $2 par split (5) for (4) by issuance of (0.25) additional share 4/25/72
Stock Dividends - 25% 1/24/69; 25% 3/28/69
Merged into Lipton (Thomas J.) Inc. 7/6/79
Each share Common $2 par exchanged for $43.75 cash

LAWSON & JONES LTD (CANADA)
Class A no par reclassified as Conv. Class A no par 9/11/74
Class B no par reclassified as Conv. Class B no par 9/11/74
Conv. Class A no par reclassified as Class A no par 5/28/79
Conv. Class B no par reclassified as Class B no par 5/28/79
Conv. Class C no par reclassified as Class A no par 5/28/79
Conv. Class D no par reclassified as Class B no par 5/28/79
Class A no par reclassified as Class A Preference no par 5/30/84
Class B no par reclassified as Class B Common no par 5/30/84
Acquired by Lawson Mardon Group Ltd. 11/20/85
Each share Class A Preference no par exchanged for $18 cash
Each share Class B Common no par exchanged for $200 cash

LAWSON MARDON GROUP LTD (ON)
Acquired by A-L Acquisition Inc. 1/14/94
Each share Class A Subordinate Vtg. no par exchanged for $14 cash

LAWSON PRODS INC (IL)
Common no par split (3) for (2) by issuance of (0.5) additional share 08/31/1971
Common no par split (2) for (1) by issuance of (1) additional share 04/14/1972
Common no par split (3) for (2) by issuance of (0.5) additional share 03/06/1973
Common no par split (3) for (2) by issuance of (0.5) additional share 06/25/1981
Reincorporated under the laws of Delaware 05/28/1982

LAWSON SOFTWARE INC NEW (DE)
Acquired by GGC Software Holdings, Inc. 07/06/2011
Each share Common 1¢ par exchanged for $11.25 cash

LAWSON SOFTWARE INC OLD (DE)
Issue Information - 14,000,000 shares COM offered at $14 per share on 12/06/2001
Under plan of merger each share Common 1¢ par automatically became (1) share Lawson Software, Inc. (New) Common 1¢ par 04/25/2006
(See Lawson Software, Inc. (New))

LAWTER INTL INC (DE)
Name changed 4/29/81
Capital Stock $1 par split (5) for (4) by issuance of (0.25) additional share 5/10/63
Capital Stock $1 par split (5) for (4) by issuance of (0.25) additional share 5/12/64
Capital Stock $1 par split (4) for (3) by issuance of (1/3) additional share 3/30/65
Capital Stock $1 par split (4) for (3) by issuance of (1/3) additional share 3/31/66
Capital Stock $1 par split (5) for (4) by issuance of (0.25) additional share 3/31/67
Capital Stock $1 par split (5) for (4) by issuance of (0.25) additional share 3/26/68
Capital Stock $1 par reclassified as Common $1 par 7/3/68
Common $1 par split (5) for (4) by issuance of (0.25) additional share 3/31/69
Common $1 par split (5) for (4) by issuance of (0.25) additional share 3/20/70
Common $1 par split (5) for (4) by issuance of (0.25) additional share 3/15/71
Common $1 par split (5) for (4) by issuance of (0.25) additional share 3/15/72
Common $1 par split (5) for (4) by issuance of (0.25) additional share 3/15/73
Common $1 par split (5) for (4) by issuance of (0.25) additional share 3/15/74
Common $1 par split (5) for (4) by issuance of (0.25) additional share 3/17/75
Common $1 par split (5) for (4) by issuance of (0.25) additional share 3/15/76
Name changed from Lawter Chemicals, Inc. to Lawter International, Inc. 4/29/81
Common $1 par split (3) for (2) by issuance of (0.5) additional share 5/25/84
Common $1 par split (4) for (3) by issuance of (1/3) additional share 3/14/88
Common $1 par split (4) for (3) by issuance of (1/3) additional share 12/18/90
Common $1 par split (4) for (3) by

issuance of (1/3) additional share 12/6/91
Merged into Eastman Chemical Co. 6/9/99
Each share Common $1 par exchanged for $12.25 cash

LAWTON MILLS CORP.
Acquired by General Cotton Corp. 00/00/1936
Details not available

LAWTON OIL CORP. (DE)
Acquired by Colorado Oil & Gas Corp. 6/12/56
Each (25.14245) shares Common $3 par exchanged for (1) share Common no par
Colorado Oil & Gas Corp. liquidated 7/1/64
(See Colorado Oil & Gas Corp.)

LAWTON SPINNING CO.
Liquidation approved in 1935

LAWTON YORK CORP (DE)
Name changed to AuctionAnything.Com, Inc. 03/03/1999
AuctionAnything.Com, Inc. name changed to Disease Sciences Inc. 07/16/2001 which name changed to IceWEB, Inc. 05/30/2002 which recapitalized as UnifiedOnline, Inc. 01/05/2015

LAWYERS-CLINTON TITLE INSURANCE CO. OF NEW JERSEY (NJ)
Completely liquidated for cash 11/1/65

LAWYERS FINL CORP (CA)
Charter suspended for failure to file reports and pay fees 01/02/1986

LAWYERS MORTGAGE & TITLE CO. (NY)
Each share Common 65¢ par exchanged for (0.1) share Common $6.50 par 05/29/1959
Under plan of merger name changed to Guaranteed Title Co. and Common $6.50 par changed to $4 par 08/02/1961
(See Guaranteed Title Co.)

LAWYERS MORTGAGE CO. (NY)
Reorganized as Lawyers Mortgage Corp. in December 1939
Stockholders received only rights to subscribe to VTC's Rights expired 3/18/40

LAWYERS MORTGAGE CORP. (NY)
Capital Stock Voting Trust terminated 6/1/49
Name changed to Lawyers Mortgage & Title Co. in January 1950
Lawyers Mortgage & Title Co. name changed to Guaranteed Title Co. 8/2/61
(See Guaranteed Title Co.)

LAWYERS TITLE & GUARANTY CO. (NY)
Liquidated in 1936

LAWYERS TITLE CORP (VA)
Common no par split (3) for (2) by issuance of (0.5) additional share 05/06/1993
Name changed to LandAmerica Financial Group, Inc. 02/27/1998
(See LandAmerica Financial Group, Inc.)

LAWYERS TITLE GUARANTY CO. OF NEW JERSEY
Assets purchased by Clinton Title & Mortgage Guaranty Co. 00/00/1949
Details not available

LAWYERS TITLE INS CO (VA)
Each share Class A Common $100 par or Class B Common $100 par exchanged for (5) shares Common $20 par 00/00/1941
Each share Common $20 par exchanged for (2) shares Common $10 par 00/00/1949

Each share Common $10 par exchanged for (2) shares Capital Stock $5 par 00/00/1951
Stock Dividends - 20% 12/17/1941; 57-1/7% 12/15/1947; 50% 11/01/1949; 16-2/3% 02/19/1954; 14-2/7% 09/20/1955; 25% 12/20/1956
Merged into Continental Group, Inc. 11/19/1980
Each share Capital Stock $5 par exchanged for (2.583) shares Common $1 par
(See Continental Group, Inc.)

LAWYERS TITLE OF ARIZONA (AZ)
98% held by Lawyers Title Insurance Corp. as of 00/00/1976
Public interest eliminated

LAWYERS TRUST DEED CORP. (CA)
Name changed to Lawyers Financial Corp. 07/03/1962
(See Lawyers Financial Corp.)

LAWYERS WESTCHESTER MORTGAGE & TITLE CO.
Liquidation ordered by Court in 1935
Details not available

LAY (H.W.) & CO., INC. (TN)
Each share Common $1 par exchanged for (2) shares Common 50¢ par 7/10/56
Class A Common 50¢ par changed to no par and (0.25) additional share issued 1/13/61
Merged into Frito-Lay, Inc. 9/22/61
Each (1.65) shares Common 50¢ par exchanged for (1) share Common $2.50 par
Frito-Lay, Inc. merged into PepsiCo, Inc. (DE) 6/10/65 which reincorporated in North Carolina 12/4/86

LAYCOR VENTURES CORP (NV)
Common $0.001 par split (3) for (1) by issuance of (2) additional shares payable 02/08/2008 to holders of record 02/07/2008 Ex date - 02/11/2008
Name changed to Blackwater Midstream Corp. 03/24/2008
(See Blackwater Midstream Corp.)

LAYFIELD RES INC (BC)
Recapitalized as Playfair Mining Ltd. 10/30/2000
Each share Common no par exchanged for (0.2) share Common no par

LAYMEN LIFE INS CO (IN)
Stock Dividends - 10% 10/31/1965; 10% 04/28/1967; 10% 04/30/1968; 10% 03/14/1969
Reorganized as Associated Companies, Inc. 07/31/1969
Each share Common $1 par exchanged for (1) share Common no par
Associated Companies, Inc. merged into Acap Corp. 07/05/1989 which merged into UTG, Inc. 11/14/2011

LAYNE & BOWLER PUMP CO (CA)
Stock Dividend - 200% 11/20/61
Merged into General Signal Corp. 12/31/74
Each share Capital Stock $1 par exchanged for $12.56 cash
General Signal Corp. merged into SPX Corp. 10/6/98

LAYNE CHRISTENSEN CO (DE)
Name changed 03/28/1996
Name changed from Layne Inc. to Layne Christensen Co. 03/28/1996
Merged into Granite Construction Inc. 06/14/2018
Each share Common 1¢ par exchanged for (0.27) share Common 1¢ par

LAYTON PK FINL GROUP INC (WI)
Acquired by North Shore Interim Corp. 10/28/2016
Each share Common exchanged for $87 cash

LAZ FINL CORP (CO)
Name changed to American Teletronics 05/16/1994
American Teletronics, Inc. recapitalized as Shine Holdings, Inc. 03/13/2006
(See Shine Holdings, Inc.)

LAZARD FRERES INSTL FD INC (MD)
Name changed to Scudder Institutional Fund, Inc. and Bond Index Portfolio Shares of Bene. Int. $0.001 par, Cash Portfolio Shares of Bene. Int. $0.001 par, Government Portfolio Shares of Bene. Int. $0.001 par, Intermediate Cash Portfolio Shares of Bene. Int. $0.001 par, Municipal Income Portfolio Shares of Bene. Int. $0.001 par, Prime Portfolio Shares of Bene. Int. $0.001 par, Tax-Free Portfolio Shares of Bene. Int. $0.001 par and Treasury Portfolio Shares of Bene. Int. $0.001 par reclassified as Institutional Bond Index Portfolio Shares of Bene. Int. $0.001 par, Institutional Cash Portfolio Shares of Bene. Int. $0.001 par, Institutional Government Portfolio Shares of Bene. Int. $0.001 par, Institutional Intermediate Cash Portfolio Shares of Bene. Int. $0.001 par, Institutional Prime Portfolio Shares of Bene. Int. $0.001 par and Institutional Federal Portfolio Shares of Bene. Int. $0.001 par respectively 05/01/1989
(See Scudder Institutional Fund, Inc.)

LAZARD FRERES INSTL TAX EXEMPT FD INC (MD)
Merged into Lazard Freres Institutional Fund, Inc. 05/01/1987
Each Municipal Bond Portfolio Share of Bene. Int. $0.001 par exchanged for (1) Bond Index Portfolio Share of Bene. Int. $0.001 par
Each Tax-Free Portfolio Share of Bene. Int. $0.001 par exchanged for (1) Tax- Tax-Free Portfolio Share of Bene. Int. $0.001 par
Lazard Freres Institutional Fund, Inc. name changed to Scudder Institutional Fund, Inc. 05/01/1989

LAZARD GLOBAL CONV BD FD (ON)
Name changed to Aston Hill Global Convertible Bond Fund 06/14/2011

LAZARD LTD (BERMUDA)
Each 6.625% Equity Unit received (0.83333333) share Class A Common 1¢ par 05/15/2008
(Additional Information in Active)

LAZARD SPL EQUITY FD INC (MD)
Reorganized as Lazard Funds Inc. 08/19/1991
Details not available

LAZARE KLEIN CO.
Acquired by Hale Brothers Stores, Inc. 00/00/1931
Details not available

LAZARUS (F & R) & CO.
Acquired by Federated Department Stores, Inc. in 1949
Each share Common no par exchanged for (2.5) shares Common $5 par
Federated Department Stores, Inc. name changed to Macy's, Inc. 6/1/2007

LAZARUS HLDGS INC (OR)
Involuntarily dissolved for failure to file reports and pay fees 12/20/89

LAZARUS INDS INC (UT)
Recapitalized as American Dairy, Inc. 05/07/2003
Each share Common $0.001 par exchanged for (0.05263157) share Common $0.001 par
American Dairy, Inc. name changed to Feihe International, Inc. 11/08/2010
(See Feihe International, Inc.)

LAZER MAZE INDS INC (BC)
Struck off register and declared dissolved for failure to file returns 9/29/95

LAZER-TRON CORP (CA)
Issue Information - 1,100,000 shares COM offered at $8 per share on 05/26/1994
Merged into Acclaim Entertainment, Inc. 8/31/95
Each share Common no par exchanged for (0.314) share Common 2¢ par
(See Acclaim Entertainment, Inc.)

LAZURUS DISTRG CORP (BC)
Name changed 10/21/1988
Name changed from Lazurus Resources Ltd. to Lazurus Distributing Corp. 10/21/1988
Recapitalized as Discovery Distributing Corp. 04/23/1990
Each share Common no par exchanged for (1/3) share Common no par
Discovery Distributing Corp. name changed to Discovery Technologies Corp. 07/29/1993
(See Discovery Technologies Corp.)

LB CTR INC (GA)
Name changed to Berman Center, Inc. 09/16/2005
(See Berman Center, Inc.)

LB-SHELL PLC (UNITED KINGDOM)
ADR agreement terminated 05/28/2018
Each Sponsored ADR for Ordinary exchanged for $0.012046 cash

LBE CO (NE)
Name changed to Commerce Group Lincoln East Inc. 05/22/1978 which name changed back to LBE Co. 05/23/1980
Merged into Lincoln East Bancshares Inc. 01/05/1982
Each share Common $2 par exchanged for $4.50 cash

LBI MANUFACTURING, INC. (NY)
Charter cancelled and proclaimed dissolved for failure to pay taxes 06/26/1996

LBKL CAP OPPORTUNITY FD INC (MD)
Name changed to Lehman Opportunity Fund, Inc. 01/01/1985

LBL SKYSYSTEMS CORP (CANADA)
Dissolved 12/14/2005

LBM-US INC (DE)
Name changed to GK Intelligent Systems, Inc. 08/19/1994
GK Intelligent Systems, Inc. recapitalized as M Power Entertainment, Inc. 05/18/2005 which recapitalized as eDoorways Corp., Inc. 09/04/2007 which name changed to eDoorways International Corp. (DE) 09/02/2010 which reincorporated in Nevada 05/06/2013 which recapitalized as Escue Energy, Inc. 06/23/2015

LBP INC (DE)
Liquidation completed
Each share Common 1¢ par received initial distribution of $5.10 cash payable 10/25/2001 to holders of record 10/15/2001 Ex date - 10/26/2001
Each share Common 1¢ par received second and final distribution of $0.8475 cash payable 10/15/2002 to holders of record 10/15/2001
Note: Certificates were not required to be surrendered and are valueless

LBT BANCSHARES INC (DE)
Name changed to Midwest BankCentre, Inc. 01/03/2000

LBT CORP (LA)
Assets sold 02/17/1989
No stockholders' equity

LBU INC (NV)
Each share old Class A Common $0.001 par exchanged for (0.05) share new Class A Common $0.001 par 08/16/1995
Each share new Class A Common $0.001 par received distribution of (0.01) share New Century Media Corp. Common $0.001 par payable 11/10/1995 to holders of record 09/29/1995
Charter permanently revoked 11/01/1999

LBY HLDG CORP (NY)
Charter cancelled and proclaimed dissolved for failure to pay taxes 09/02/1988

LC LUXURIES LTD (NV)
Name changed to General Cannabis, Inc. 11/19/2010
General Cannabis, Inc. name changed to SearchCore, Inc. 01/06/2012 which name changed to Wisdom Homes of America, Inc. 03/05/2015

LCA CORP (DE)
Common $1 par changed to 50¢ par and (1) additional share issued 4/8/72
Merged into Kidde (Walter) & Co., Inc. (DE) 3/4/76
Each share Common 50¢ par exchanged for (0.2) share $4 Conv. Preference Ser. C $1 par
Kidde (Walter) & Co., Inc. (DE) name changed to Kidde, Inc. 4/18/80
(See Kidde, Inc.)

LCA-VISION INC (DE)
Each share old Common $0.0001 par exchanged for (0.25) share new Common $0.001 par 06/05/1996
Each share new Common $0.001 par exchanged again for (0.25) share new Common $0.001 par 11/12/2002
New Common $0.001 par split (3) for (2) by issuance of (0.5) additional share payable 12/15/2004 to holders of record 12/06/2004 Ex date - 12/16/2004
Acquired by PhotoMedex, Inc. 05/12/2014
Each share new Common $0.001 par exchanged for $5.37 cash

LCB BANCORP INC (OH)
Common $5 par changed to no par and (2) additional shares issued 03/27/1987
Name changed to CoBancorp Inc. 05/01/1992
CoBancorp Inc. merged into FirstMerit Corp. 05/22/1998 which merged into Huntington Bancshares Inc. 08/16/2016

LCC INTL INC (DE)
Each share old Class A Common 1¢ par exchanged for (0.0000001) share new Class A Common 1¢ par 01/20/2010
Note: In effect holders received $0.000056 cash per share and public interest was eliminated

LCI INDS INC (DE)
Company believed out of business 04/25/1985
Details not available

LCI INTL INC (DE)
Common 1¢ par split (2) for (1) by issuance of (1) additional share 07/06/1994
Common 1¢ par split (2) for (1) by issuance of (1) additional share 09/29/1995
5% Conv. Preferred 1¢ par called for redemption 09/03/1996
Merged into Qwest Communications International Inc. 06/05/1998
Each share Common 1¢ par exchanged for (1.1661) shares Common 1¢ par
Qwest Communications International Inc. merged into CenturyLink, Inc. 04/01/2011

LCM INTERNET GROWTH FD INC (MD)
Name changed to Internet Growth Fund, Inc. 7/14/2002
Internet Growth Fund, Inc. name changed to Foxby Corp. 7/14/2003

LCNB BANCORPORATION, INC. (TX)
Merged into SouthTrust Corp. 3/12/99
Each share Common no par exchanged for $11.6093488 cash

LCS BANCORP INC (DE)
Merged into Jacksonville Savings Bank (Jacksonville, IL) 01/02/1997
Each share Common 1¢ par exchanged for $17.75 cash

LCS GROUP INC (DE)
Name changed to Conversion Services International, Inc. 02/03/2004
(See Conversion Services International, Inc.)

LCS INDS INC (DE)
Common 1¢ par split (4) for (3) by issuance of (1/3) additional share 3/10/78
Each share old Common 1¢ par exchanged for (2) shares new Common 1¢ par 6/2/83
Stock Dividend - 10% 1/31/95
Merged into CustomerONE Holding Corp. 1/27/99
Each share new Common 1¢ par exchanged for $17.50 cash

LDB CORP (FL)
Recapitalized 2/5/88
Name changed from LDB Corp. to LDBrinkman Corp. 1/25/83
Recapitalized back from LDBrinkman Corp. to LDB Corp. 2/5/88
Each share Common $1 par exchanged for (0.2) share Common $5 par
Merged into LDB Merger Corp. 1/30/95
Each share Common $5 par exchanged for $7.50 cash

LDC VENTURES INC (AB)
Recapitalized as Mint Technology Corp. 01/22/2004
Each share Common no par exchanged for (0.10435727) share Common no par
Mint Technology Corp. recapitalized as Mint Corp. 08/12/2013

LDDS COMMUNICATIONS INC (DE)
Class A Common 1¢ par split (3) for (2) by issuance of (0.5) additional share 07/17/1990
Class A Common 1¢ par split (3) for (2) by issuance of (0.5) additional share 06/25/1991
Class A Common 1¢ par split (3) for (2) by issuance of (0.5) additional share 01/14/1993
Merged into Resurgens Communications Group, Inc. 09/15/1993
Each share Class A Common 1¢ par exchanged for (0.9599) share new Common 1¢ par
Resurgens Communications Group, Inc. name changed to LDDS Communications, Inc. (GA) 09/15/1993 which name changed to Worldcom, Inc. 05/26/1995 which name changed to MCI WorldCom, Inc. 09/14/1998 which name changed to WorldCom Inc. (New) 05/01/2000
(See WorldCom Inc. (New))

LDDS COMMUNICATIONS INC (GA)
Common 1¢ par split (2) for (1) by issuance of (1) additional share 01/06/1994
Name changed to WorldCom, Inc. 05/26/1995
WorldCom, Inc. name changed to MCI WorldCom, Inc. 09/14/1998 which name changed to WorldCom Inc. (New) 05/01/2000
(See WorldCom Inc. (New))

LDF INC (DE)
Merged into Western States Opportunity LLC 4/26/2006
Each share Common $1 par exchanged for $125 cash

LDG INC (NV)
Name changed to Modigene, Inc. 03/12/2007
Modigene, Inc. name changed to PROLOR Biotech, Inc. 06/12/2009 which merged into OPKO Health, Inc. 08/29/2013

LDI CORP (DE)
Acquired by NationsBank Corp. 4/29/96
Each share Common 1¢ par exchanged for $4.10 cash

LDR HLDG CORP (DE)
Acquired by Zimmer Biomet Holdings, Inc. 07/13/2016
Each share Common $0.001 par exchanged for $37 cash

LDS DENTAL SUPPLIES INC (NY)
Name changed to Krohn Industries, Inc. 1/3/74
(See Krohn Industries, Inc.)

LDS SYS INC (DE)
Merged into International Remote Imaging Systems Inc. 05/03/1995
Each share Common 1¢ par exchanged for (2.5765) shares new Common no par
International Remote Imaging Systems, Inc. name changed to IRIS International, Inc. 12/18/2003
(See IRIS International, Inc.)

LE BATEAU INC (NY)
Dissolved by proclamation 03/31/1982

LE BLOND-SCHACHT TRUCK CO.
Name changed to Ahrens-Fox Fire Engine Co. in 1939 which dissolved in 1940

LE BON TABLE BRAND FOODS CORP (CA)
Each share old Common no par exchanged for (0.00571428) share new Common no par 12/20/2007
SEC revoked common stock registration 07/08/2010

LE CARBONE LORRAINE SA (FRANCE)
Name changed to Mersen 08/09/2010

LE CHANTECLER, INC. (DE)
Liquidation completed
Each share Common 50¢ par exchanged for initial distribution of $10 cash 10/21/77
Each share Common 50¢ par received second distribution of $2 cash 1/4/78
Each share Common 50¢ par received third and final distribution of $0.715 cash 12/31/85

LE GAGA HLDGS LTD (CAYMAN ISLANDS)
Acquired by Harvest Parent Ltd. 12/02/2014
Each Sponsored ADR for Ordinary exchanged for $4.01 cash

LE GOURMET CO INC (NV)
Common $0.001 par split (5) for (1) by issuance of (4) additional shares payable 03/03/2003 to holders of record 02/28/2003 Ex date - 03/04/2003
Name changed to Estelle Reyna, Inc. 03/24/2003
Estelle Reyna, Inc. name changed to Karma Media, Inc. 09/24/2003 which recapitalized as Pit BOSS Entertainment, Inc. 07/18/2005 which name changed to US Energy Holdings, Inc. 03/08/2006 which name changed to Lonestar Group Holdings, Co. 01/10/2007 which recapitalized as Guardian Angel Group, Inc. 12/14/2007 which recapitalized as Ree International, Inc. 06/29/2011

LE GRAN CORP (CA)
Stock Dividends - 25% 04/09/1971; 25% 04/17/1972
Merged into Lucky Stores, Inc. (CA) 04/22/1974
Each share Common $1 par exchanged for (0.8) share Common $1.25 par
Lucky Stores, Inc. (CA) reincorporated in Delaware 12/22/1986
(See Lucky Stores, Inc. (DE))

LE MAIRE MACH TOOL CO (MI)
Charter declared inoperative and void for failure to file reports 05/15/1987

LE MAIRE TOOL & MANUFACTURING CO. (MI)
Name changed to Le Maire Machine Tool Co. 12/02/1957
(See Le Maire Machine Tool Co.)

LE MANS EXPLORATIONS LTD. (ON)
Charter cancelled for failure to pay taxes and file returns 11/28/1973

LE MONDE CORSET CO. (MI)
Charter declared inoperative and void for failure to file reports 5/15/72

LE MOYNE EXPLORATIONS LTD. (ON)
Charter surrendered 10/7/68
No stockholders' equity

LE MOYNE UNGAVA MINES LTD. (QC)
Dissolved 6/1/68
No stockholders' equity

LE MUR CO.
Merged into Nestle-LeMur Co. 00/00/1928
Details not available

LE O ENTERPRISES INC (CO)
Each (45) shares Common no par exchanged for (1) share Common $0.001 par 07/11/1986
Name changed to Tellis Gold Mining Co., Inc. 12/05/1986
Tellis Gold Mining Co., Inc. recapitalized as Bannockburn Resources Inc. (CO) 03/21/2002 which reorganized in British Columbia as Bannockburn Resources Ltd. 04/02/2004 which name changed to Lucara Diamond Corp. 08/14/2007

LE PEEP RESTAURANTS INC (DE)
Each share old Common 1¢ par exchanged for (0.001) share new Common 1¢ par 12/31/92
Each share new Common 1¢ par exchanged again for (0.0002) share new Common 1¢ par 5/29/98
Note: In effect holders received $0.24 cash per share and public interest was eliminated

LE PRINT EXPRESS INTL INC (ON)
Each share old Common no par exchanged for (0.33333333) share new Common no par 12/29/1995
Each share new Common no par received distribution of (1.3515) shares BrandEra.com Inc. Common no par payable 02/21/2000 to holders of record 02/07/2000
SEC revoked common stock registration 03/25/2009

LE ROI CO. (WI)
Each share Common $10 par exchanged for (4) shares Common $2.50 par in 1946
Reincorporated under the laws of Delaware as L.R. Corp. in January 1954
L.R. Corp. merged into Westinghouse Air Brake Co. in April 1954 which merged into American Standard Inc. 6/7/68
(See American Standard Inc.)

LE ROY MINES LTD.
Acquired by Roybell Mines Ltd. on an (18) for (100) basis in 1943

LE TOURNEAU ASBESTOS CORP. (DE)
Charter cancelled for non-payment of taxes 4/1/63

LE-WOOD HOMES, INC. (VA)
Charter revoked 6/1/66

LEA FABRICS, INC. (DE)
Recapitalized in 1936
Each share Preference no par exchanged for (1.2) shares Capital Stock $5 par
Each share Common no par exchanged for (0.043956) share Capital Stock $5 par
Stock Dividend - 100% 11/7/47
No longer in existence having become inoperative and void for non-payment of taxes 4/1/59

LEA MFG CO (CT)
Common $5 par changed to $2.50 par and (1) additional share issued 5/1/68
Name changed to CKC Liquidating Co. 9/27/83
(See CKC Liquidating Co.)

LEA RONAL INC (NY)
Common $1 par split (3) for (2) by issuance of (0.5) additional share 10/31/68
Common $1 par split (3) for (2) by issuance of (0.5) additional share 5/31/72
Stock Dividend - 10% 6/3/74
Name changed to LeaRonal, Inc. 7/27/78
(See LeaRonal, Inc.)

LEACH CORP. (DE)
Ctfs. dated prior to 2/28/69
Under plan of merger each share Common 20¢ par exchanged for (0.1) share Common $2 par 1/3/66
Completely liquidated 2/28/69
Each share Common $2 par exchanged for first and final distribution of (35.6) shares Subscription Television, Inc. Common 1¢ par

LEAD KING MINES, INC. (NV)
Charter revoked for failure to pay fees and file reports 3/5/62

LEAD-URA MINES, LTD.
Name changed to Rare Earth Mining Corp. of Canada Ltd. in 1951 which was acquired by Rare Earth Mining Co. Ltd. 3/5/56 which merged into Amalgamated Earth Mines Ltd. 5/27/57
(See Amalgamated Earth Mines Ltd.)

LEADER CAP CORP (ON)
Each share old Common no par exchanged for (1) share new Common no par to reflect a (1) for (50) reverse split followed by a (50) for (1) forward split 10/22/2007
Note: Holders of (49) or fewer pre-split shares received $0.245 cash per share
Each share new Common no par exchanged again for (0.000002) share new Common no par 02/25/2009
Note: In effect holders received $0.51 cash per share and public interest was eliminated

LEADER DEV CORP (OH)
Name changed to Clinton Gas Systems Inc. 12/31/87
(See Clinton Gas Systems Inc.)

LEADER-DURST CORP. (DE)
Completely liquidated 12/11/64
Each share Class A Common 50¢ par exchanged for first and final distribution (1/3) Prudential Real Estate Trust Ctf. of Bene. Int. $1 par
Prudential Real Estate Trust name changed to Prudent Resources Trust 5/1/68 which name changed to Prudent Real Estate Trust 5/26/71
(See Prudent Real Estate Trust)

LEADER ENERGY SVCS LTD (AB)
Each share old Common no par exchanged for (0.33333333) share new Common no par 08/11/2009
Deemed bankrupt 08/20/2015
Stockholders' equity unlikely

LEADER ENTERPRISES, INC. (DE)
Merged into Science & Government Publications, Inc. 11/14/61
Each share 6% Preferred $5 par exchanged for (1) share Common 10¢ par
Each share Common 10¢ par exchanged for (0.1) share Common 10¢ par
Science & Government Publications, Inc. acquired by ABC Industries, Inc. 4/7/72
(See ABC Industries, Inc.)

LEADER FILLING STATIONS CORP. (MA)
Reorganized in 1943
Each share 8% Preferred $50 par exchanged for (1) share 5% Preferred $15 par
Class A and B had no equity
Dissolved 7/14/58

LEADER FINL CORP (TN)
Merged into Union Planters Corp. 10/1/96
Each share Common $1 par exchanged for (1.525) shares Common $5 par
Union Planters Corp. merged into Regions Financial Corp. (New) 7/1/2004

LEADER HEALTHCARE ORGANIZATION INC (PA)
Common no par split (3) for (1) by issuance of (2) additional shares 1/16/81
Merged into Cenco Inc. 9/1/81
Each share Common no par exchanged for $20 cash

LEADER INDS INC (QC)
Assets sold for the benefit of creditors 06/00/2002
No stockholders' equity

LEADER INTL INDS INC (DE)
Common $2 par changed to $1.33-1/3 par and (0.5) additional share issued 07/21/1972
Adjudicated bankrupt 02/24/1975
Stockholders' equity unlikely

LEADER MFG INC (QC)
Recapitalized as Leader Industries Inc. 05/28/1992
Each share Common no par exchanged for (0.1) share Common no par
(See Leader Industries Inc.)

LEADER MNG CORP (AB)
Recapitalized as Leader Mining International Inc. 7/29/94
Each share Common no par exchanged for (0.2) share Common no par

LEADER NATL CORP (OH)
Class A Common $1 par and Class B Common $1 par reclassified as Common no par and (1) additional share issued 5/3/72
Common no par split (1.5) for (1) by issuance of (0.5) additional share 1/31/79
Through purchase offer over 96% acquired by Leader Financial Corp. as of 5/31/79
Public interest eliminated

LEADER OIL & GAS LTD (AB)
Name changed to Canadian Leader Energy Inc. 7/18/94
Canadian Leader Energy Inc. merged into Centurion Energy International Inc. 5/20/97
(See Centurion Energy International Inc.)

LEADER RES INC (BC)
Recapitalized as United Leader Resources Inc. 11/29/84
Each share Common no par exchanged for (0.2) share Common no par
United Leader Resources Inc. name changed to Vertica Systems Corp. 4/13/87 which recapitalized as Siscoe Callahan Mining Corp. 8/3/88
(See Siscoe Callahan Mining Corp.)

LEADERS EQUITY CORP (BC)
Struck off register and declared dissolved for failure to file returns 07/20/1990

LEADERS OF INDUSTRY SHARES
Trusts Series B and C terminated and liquidated 00/00/1933
Details not available

LEADERSHIP FD INC (CANADA)
Name changed to NSP Pharma Corp. 05/02/2005
(See NSP Pharma Corp.)

LEADERSHIP HSG INC (DE)
Preferred Ser. A 50¢ par called for redemption 12/21/73
Merged into Cerro Corp. 12/28/73
Each share Common 10¢ par exchanged for $5.50 cash
(See Cerro Corp.)

LEADERSHIP PPTYS INC (OK)
Charter suspended for failure to pay taxes 03/27/1989

LEADING - EDGE EARTH PRODS INC (OR)
Name changed to LEEP, Inc. 01/03/2005

LEADING BRANDS INC (BC)
Each share old Common no par exchanged for (0.2) share new Common no par 02/02/2010
Name changed to Liquid Media Group Ltd. 08/13/2018

LEADING EDGE INDS INC (FL)
Proclaimed dissolved for failure to file reports and pay fees 10/13/89

LEADING EDGE PACKAGING INC (DE)
Issue Information - 1,250,000 shares COM offered at $6 per share on 12/02/1996
Chapter 11 bankruptcy proceedings converted to Chapter 7 on 11/20/2000
No stockholders' equity

LEADINGSIDE INC (DE)
SEC revoked common stock registration 03/12/2009

LEADIS TECHNOLOGY INC (DE)
Liquidation completed
Each share Common $0.001 par received initial distribution of $0.95 cash payable 12/14/2009 to holders of record 10/27/2009
Each share Common $0.001 par received second distribution of $0.23 cash payable 12/31/2012 to holders of record 12/21/2012 Ex date - 01/02/2013
Each share Common $0.001 par received third and final distribution of $0.003 cash payable 12/28/2017 to holders of record 12/26/2017 Ex date - 12/29/2017

LEADLEY GUNNING & CULP INTL CORP (ON)
Charter cancelled for failure to pay taxes and file returns 10/15/94

LEADPOINT CONS MINES CO (WA)
Reincorporated under the laws of Nevada as Point Acquisition Corp. and Common 5¢ par changed to $0.001 par 09/01/2006
Point Acquisition Corp. name changed to China Minerals Technologies, Inc. 06/13/2007 which name changed to China GengSheng Minerals, Inc. 07/30/2007

LEADVILLE CORP (CO)
SEC revoked common stock registration 02/15/2006

LEADVILLE LAND & WATER CO. (ME)
Liquidation completed
Each share Capital Stock $1 par exchanged for initial distribution of $0.40 cash 12/10/69
Each share Capital Stock $1 par received second and final distribution of $1.39 cash 12/24/70

LEADVILLE LEAD & URANIUM CORP. (CO)
Name changed to Leadville Lead Corp. 11/04/1957
Leadville Lead Corp. name changed to Leadville Corp. 10/07/1970
(See Leadville Corp.)

LEADVILLE LEAD CORP (CO)
Name changed to Leadville Lead & Uranium Corp. 00/00/1954 which name changed back to Leadville Lead Corp. 11/04/1957
Name changed to Leadville Corp. 10/07/1970
(See Leadville Corp.)

LEADVILLE MNG & MLG CORP (NV)
Each share Common $0.0001 par exchanged for (0.1) share Common $0.001 par 04/11/1997
Name changed to Capital Gold Corp. (NV) 03/07/2003
Capital Gold Corp. (NV) reincorporated in Delaware 11/21/2005 which merged into Gammon Gold Inc. (QC) 04/08/2011 which reincorporated in Ontario as AuRico Gold Inc. 06/14/2011 which merged into Alamos Gold Inc. (New) 07/06/2015

LEADVILLE WTR CO (CO)
Liquidation completed
Each share Common $100 par exchanged for initial distribution of $130 cash 5/18/65
Each share Common $100 par received second distribution of (4) shares Leadville Land & Water Co. Capital Stock $1 par and $4 cash 12/1/65
Each share Common $100 par received third and final distribution of $13.30 cash 4/2/69
(See Leadville Land & Water Co.)

LEAGUE NOW HLDGS CORP (FL)
Each share old Common $0.001 par exchanged for (0.16666666) share new Common $0.001 par 07/23/2009
New Common $0.001 par split (2) for (1) by issuance of (1) additional share payable 01/29/2010 to holders of record 01/19/2010 Ex date - 02/01/2010
Each share new Common $0.001 par exchanged again for (0.33333333) share new Common $0.001 par 06/01/2010
New Common $0.001 par split (16) for (1) by issuance of (15) additional shares payable 10/25/2010 to holders of record 10/22/2010 Ex date - 10/26/2010
Name changed to NYBD Holding, Inc. 06/20/2013
NYBD Holding, Inc. name changed to Pleasant Kids, Inc. 10/29/2014 which name changed to Next Group Holdings, Inc. 12/30/2015 which recapitalized as Cuentas Inc. 08/13/2018

LEAH INDS INC (CO)
Each share Common 1¢ par received distribution of (0.5) share Fire Environmental Inc. Common no par 01/26/1999 to holders of record 12/17/1998

LEAHI INVT TR (MA)
Proclaimed dissolved for failure to file reports and pay fees 02/01/2002
Trust terminated in 2000
Details not available

LEAK-X ENVIRONMENTAL CORP (DE)
Name changed 05/22/1992
Reincorporated 02/02/1996
Name changed from Leak-X Corp. to Leak-X Environmental Corp. 05/22/1992
State of incorporation changed from (NY) to (DE) 02/02/1996
Each (13) shares old Common no par exchanged for (1) share new Common no par 01/31/1997
SEC revoked common stock registration 03/25/2009
Stockholders' equity unlikely

LEAMAC PETROLEUMS LTD. (CANADA)
Recapitalized as Embassy Petroleums Ltd. 8/8/61
Each share Capital Stock no par exchanged for (0.05) share Capital Stock 25¢ par
Embassy Petroleums Ltd. merged into Cavalier Energy Inc. (ONT) 3/1/74 which reincorporated in Alberta as Cavalier Energy Ltd. 2/7/78
(See Cavalier Energy Ltd.)

LEAMINGTON HOTEL
Reorganized as Leamington, Inc. in 1933
Stockholders did not participate.

LEAP GROUP INC (DE)
Name changed to Leapnet, Inc. 4/22/99
(See Leapnet, Inc.)

LEAP WIRELESS INTL INC (DE)
Plan of reorganization under Chapter 11 Federal Bankruptcy Code effective 08/16/2004
No old Common stockholders' equity
Merged into AT&T Inc. 03/13/2014
Each share new Common $0.0001 par exchanged for (1) Contingent Value Right and $15 cash

LEAPFROG ENTERPRISES INC (DE)
Acquired by VTech Holdings Ltd. 04/05/2016
Each share Class A Common $0.0001 par exchanged for $1 cash
Each share Class B Common $0.0001 par exchanged for $1 cash

LEAPFROG SMART PRODS INC (CO)
Recapitalized as Red Alert Group, Inc. 7/15/2003
Each share Common no par exchanged for (1.875) shares Common no par

LEAPNET INC (DE)
Each share old Common 1¢ par exchanged for (0.2) share new Common 1¢ par 6/6/2001
Merged into SPRI, Ltd. 2/8/2002
Each share new Common 1¢ par exchanged for $1.85 cash

LEAR, INC. (IL)
Each share old Common 50¢ par exchanged for (0.05) share 5% Preferred $5 par and (1) share new Common 50¢ par 6/20/52
5% Preferred $5 par called for redemption 6/17/55
Merged into Lear Siegler, Inc. 6/5/62
Each share new Common 50¢ par exchanged for (5/7) share Common no par

LEAR CORP (DE)
Plan of reorganization under Chapter 11 Federal Bankruptcy proceedings effective 11/09/2009
No old Common stockholders' equity
Each share Conv. Participating Ser. A Preferred 1¢ par automatically became (1) share new Common 1¢ par 11/10/2010
(Additional Information in Active)

LEAR JET INDS INC (DE)
Name changed 10/17/66
Name changed from Lear Jet Corp. to Lear Jet Industries, Inc. 10/17/66
Name changed to Gates Learjet Corp. 1/12/70
(See Gates Learjet Corp.)

LEAR OIL & GAS CORP (BC)
Recapitalized as Priority Ventures Ltd. 12/23/87
Each share Common no par exchanged for (0.033) share Common no par

LEAR PETE CORP (DE)
Reincorporated 5/18/84
Common 10¢ par split (5) for (4) by issuance of (0.25) additional share 9/30/77
Common 10¢ par split (5) for (4) by issuance of (0.25) additional share 5/24/78
Common 10¢ par split (5) for (4) by issuance of (0.25) additional share 3/7/79
Common 10¢ par split (4) for (3) by issuance of (1/3) additional share 5/31/79
Common 10¢ par split (3) for (2) by issuance of (0.5) additional share 2/20/80
Stock Dividends - 10% 6/16/75; 10% 7/20/76; 10% 5/16/77
State of incorporation changed from (TX) to (DE) 5/18/84
Merged into BP America Inc. 6/22/88
Each share $2.875 Conv. Exchangeable Preferred $1 par exchanged for $8.50 cash
Each share Common 10¢ par exchanged for $2.65 cash

LEAR PETE PARTNERS L P (DE)
Completely liquidated 12/30/88
Each Depositary Unit exchanged for first and final distribution of $1.18 cash

LEAR SEATING CORP (DE)
Issue Information - 9,375,000 shares COM offered at $15.50 per share on 04/06/1994
Name changed to Lear Corp. 05/09/1996
(See Lear Corp.)

LEAR SIEGLER INC (DE)
$5.75 Conv. Preferred Ser. A no par called for redemption 3/1/66
Each share $4.50 Conv. Preferred no par exchanged for (2) shares $2.25 Conv. Preferred no par 11/19/68
Common no par split (2) for (1) by issuance of (1) additional share 12/16/68
$4.50 Preferred Ser. D no par called for redemption 6/11/79
$5 Preferred Ser. E no par called for redemption 6/11/79
Merged into L Acquisition Corp. 2/11/87
Each share $2.25 Conv. Preferred no par exchanged for $230 cash
Each share Common $1 par exchanged for $92 cash

LEARMONTH & BURCHETT MGMT SYS PLC (ENGLAND)
Acquired by PLATINUM Technology, Inc. 05/12/1998
Each Sponsored ADR for Ordinary exchanged for (0.2094) share Common $0.001 par
PLATINUM Technology, Inc. name changed to Platinum Technology International Inc. 01/04/1999 which merged into Computer Associates International, Inc. 06/29/1999 which name changed to CA, Inc. 02/01/2006

LEARNCO INTL INC (AB)
Delisted from Toronto Venture Stock Exchange 06/20/2005

LEARNCOM INC (NV)
SEC revoked common stock registration 12/01/2004

LEARNERS WORLD INC (NY)
Common no par changed to $0.0001 par 02/25/1999
Each (30) shares old Common $0.0001 par exchanged for (1) share new Common $0.0001 par 03/01/1999
Each share new Common $0.0001 par exchanged for (0.005) share Common $0.0001 par 09/10/2001
Reincorporated under the laws of Florida as Liquidix, Inc. 09/27/2001
Liquidix, Inc. recapitalized as Anscott Industries Inc. 04/09/2003
(See Anscott Industries Inc.)

LEARNING, INC. (DE)
Charter cancelled and declared inoperative and void for non-payment of taxes 04/15/1969

LEARNING AIDS GROUP INC (NY)
Merged into Chein Industries, Inc. 10/1/73
Each share Common 1¢ par exchanged for $0.75 cash

LEARNING ANNEX INC (NY)
Name changed to TLA, Inc. 9/19/97
(See TLA, Inc.)

LEARNING CARE GROUP INC (MI)
Merged into A.B.C. Learning Centres Ltd. 01/10/2006
Each share Common no par exchanged for $7.50 cash

LEARNING CO (CA)
Merged into Softkey International, Inc. 12/27/95
Each share Common no par exchanged for $67.50 cash

LEARNING CO INC (DE)
Merged into Mattel, Inc. 05/13/1999
Each share Common 1¢ par exchanged for (1.2) shares Common $1 par

LEARNING LIBRARY INC (ON)
Recapitalized as Street Resources Inc. 01/05/2005
Each (2.75) shares Common no par exchanged for (1) share Common no par
Street Resources Inc. name changed to EXMIN Resources Inc. 07/19/2005 which merged into Dia Bras Exploration Inc. 10/01/2009 which name changed to Sierra Metals Inc. 12/07/2012

LEARNING MATLS PUBG CORP (NY)
Dissolved by proclamation 12/15/73

LEARNING PRIORITY INC (NV)
SEC revoked common stock registration 10/15/2008

LEARNING QUEST TECHNOLOGIES INC (NV)
Each share old Common $0.001 par exchanged for (0.5) share new Common $0.001 par 12/19/2007
Note: No holder will receive fewer than (100) post-split shares
Stock Dividend - 5% payable 01/22/2008 to holders of record 01/18/2008 Ex date - 01/16/2008
Name changed to China Infrastructure Investment Corp. 04/23/2008

LEARNING RESOURCE CENTER, INC. (OR)
Name changed to Therapeutic Medco, Inc. 7/7/86
(See Therapeutic Medco, Inc.)

LEARNING TECHNOLOGY INC (DE)
Charter cancelled and declared inoperative and void for non-payment of taxes 03/01/2005

LEARNINGSTAR CORP (DE)
Name changed to Excelligence Learning Corp. 5/3/2002
(See Excelligence Learning Corp.)

LEARNSOFT CORP (BC)
Reincorporated 01/06/2004
Place of incorporation changed from (ON) to (BC) 01/06/2004
Recapitalized as Reva Resources Corp. 12/13/2007
Each share Common no par exchanged for (0.33333333) share Common no par
Reva Resources Corp. recapitalized as Grosvenor Resource Corp. 08/10/2016

LEARN2 COM INC (DE)
Merged into Learn2 Corp. 09/26/2001
Each share Common 1¢ par exchanged for (0.4747) share Common $0.001 par
Learn2 Corp. name changed to LTWC Corp. 09/06/2002
(See LTWC Corp.)

LEARN2 CORP (DE)
Name changed to LTWC Corp. 09/06/2002
(See LTWC Corp.)

LEARONAL INC (NY)
Common $1 par split (4) for (3) by issuance of (1/3) additional share 3/3/80
Common $1 par split (2) for (1) by issuance of (1) additional share 3/5/81
Common $1 par split (5) for (4) by issuance of (0.25) additional share 3/1/83
Common $1 par split (5) for (4) by issuance of (0.25) additional share 6/17/86
Common $1 par split (5) for (4) by issuance of (0.25) additional share 11/17/87
Common $1 par split (3) for (2) by issuance of (0.5) additional share payable 8/19/97 to holders of record 7/29/97 Ex date - 8/20/97
Stock Dividend - 25% 3/1/79
Merged into Rohm & Haas Co. 1/26/99
Each share Common $1 par exchanged for $34 cash

LEASCO CORP (DE)
Ctfs. dated prior to 12/14/73
Name changed to Reliance Group, Inc. 12/14/73
(See Reliance Group, Inc.)

LEASCO CORP NEW (DE)
Ctfs. dated after 5/14/79
Merged into Reliance Financial Group, Inc. 1/8/82
Each share Common 10¢ par exchanged for $52.50 principal amount 17% (18% for the first year) 15-yr. Sr. Debentures due 12/15/96 and $13 cash

LEASCO DATA PROCESSING EQUIP CORP (DE)
Common 25¢ par split (5) for (2) by issuance of (1.5) additional shares 03/10/1969
Stock Dividend - 100% 05/27/1968
Name changed to Leasco Corp. 02/24/1971
Leasco Corp. name changed to Reliance Group, Inc. 12/14/1973
(See Reliance Group, Inc.)

LEASE 64 LTD.
Merged into Triad Oil Co. Ltd. 10/17/51
Each share Capital Stock no par exchanged for (2.5) shares Capital Stock no par
Triad Oil Co. Ltd. name changed to BP Oil & Gas Ltd. 7/2/70 which merged into BP Canada Ltd. (Ont.) 10/18/72 which name changed to BP Canada Ltd.-BP Canada Ltee. 4/27/73 which reincorporated in Canada as BP Canada Inc. 7/6/79
(See BP Canada Inc.)

LEASE PLAN INTERNATIONAL CORP. (DE)
Common $1 par split (2) for (1) by issuance of (1) additional share 2/10/64
Acquired by PepsiCo, Inc. (DE) 1/5/66
Each share Common $1 par exchanged for (0.454545) share Capital Stock 33-1/3¢ par
PepsiCo, Inc. (DE) reincorporated in North Carolina 12/4/86

LEASE PUR CORP (DE)
Charter cancelled and declared inoperative and void for non-payment of taxes 6/27/89

LEASE RITE INC (ON)
Recapitalized as Kermode Exploration Ltd. 06/06/2006
Each share Common no par exchanged for (0.1) share Common no par
Kermode Exploration Ltd. name changed to Rencore Resources Ltd. 06/01/2010 which merged into Bold Ventures Inc. 02/13/2012

LEASEMORE EQUIP INC (NY)
Common 1¢ par split (2) for (1) by issuance of (1) additional share 9/17/71
Charter cancelled and proclaimed dissolved for failure to pay taxes 6/24/81

LEASEPAC CORP (DE)
Charter cancelled and declared inoperative and void for non-payment of taxes 3/1/81

LEASEQUIP CORP (CA)
Name changed to Franklin Financial Corp. 10/31/73
(See Franklin Financial Corp.)

LEASESMART INC (CA)
Charter suspended for failure to file reports and pay fees 01/02/2009

LEASEWAY TRANSN CORP NEW (DE)
Merged into Penske Truck Leasing Co., L.P. 4/25/95
Each share Common 1¢ par exchanged for $20 cash

LEASEWAY TRANSN CORP OLD (DE)
Common $1 par split (3) for (2) by issuance of (0.5) additional share 2/1/72
Common $1 par split (3) for (2) by issuance of (0.5) additional share 1/12/79
Stock Dividend - 100% 5/25/64
Acquired by a group of investors 6/25/87
Each share Common $1 par exchanged for $51 cash

LEASING CONSULTANTS INC (NY)
Stock Dividend - 10% 10/1/69
Name changed to Action Staffing Inc. and Common 5¢ par changed to $0.001 par 6/28/87
(See Action Staffing Inc.)

LEASING CR CORP NEW (DE)
Merged 1/1/84
Class A 10¢ par reclassified as Common 10¢ par 6/2/69
Leasing Credit Corp. (Old) merged into Leasing Credit Corp. (New) 1/1/84
Each share Common 10¢ par exchanged for (1.04) shares Common 10¢ par
Charter cancelled and declared inoperative and void for non-payment of taxes 3/1/87

LEASING EDGE CORP (DE)
Name changed to LEC Technologies, Inc. 03/20/1997
LEC Technologies, Inc. name changed to Golf Entertainment, Inc. (DE) 02/18/1999 which reincorporated in Nevada as Contemporary Solutions, Inc. 05/02/2005
(See Contemporary Solutions, Inc.)

LEASING INTL INC (GA)
Merged into Gelco Corp. 6/14/79
Each share Common 25¢ par exchanged for $3.08 cash

LEASING SOLUTIONS INC (CA)
Name changed to Le Bon Table Brand Foods Corp. 11/13/2007
(See Le Bon Table Brand Foods Corp.)

LEASING TECHNOLOGY INC (UT)
Each share old Common $0.001 par exchanged for (0.1) share new Common $0.001 par 12/02/1991
Recapitalized as American Resources & Development Co. 02/27/1997
Each share new Common $0.001 par exchanged for (0.05) share Common $0.001 par
(See American Resources & Development Co.)

LEATH & CO (DE)
Each share Preferred no par exchanged for (1) share $2.50 Preferred no par and (2) shares new Common no par in 1936
Each share old Common no par exchanged for (1) share new Common no par in 1936
$2.50 Preferred no par called for redemption 10/1/58
Common no par split (3) for (1) by issuance of (2) additional shares 10/1/68
Common no par split (2) for (1) by issuance of (1) additional share 3/1/72
Acquired by Gamble-Skogmo Inc. 2/28/78
Each share Common no par exchanged for $19 cash

LEATHER FACTORY INC (CO)
State of incorporation changed from (CO) to (DE) 6/17/94
Name changed to Tandy Leather Factory, Inc. 5/25/2005

LEATHERHIDE INDUSTRIES, INC. (DE)
Adjudicated bankrupt 8/30/58
No stockholders' equity

LEAVENWORTH, TOPEKA & WESTERN RAILROAD
Out of business 00/00/1932
Details not available

LEAVENWORTH & TOPEKA R.R. CO.
Acquired by Leavenworth, Topeka & Western Railroad in 1931 which went out of business in 1932

LEAVITT LUSITANIA SALVAGE CO., INC. (DE)
Charter cancelled and declared inoperative and void for non-payment of taxes 3/17/26

LEAWOOD NATL BK (KANSAS CITY, MO)
100% acquired by First National Charter Corp. through exchange offer as of 09/30/1969
Public interest eliminated

LEBANESE CO FOR DEV & RECON OF BEIRUT CENT DIST S A L (LEBANON)
Stock Dividends - In 144A to holders of 144A 3.33333% payable 12/01/2011 to holders of record 09/19/2011 Ex date - 09/15/2011; 2% payable 11/19/2012 to holders of record 08/14/2012 Ex date - 08/10/2012; 2% payable 11/03/2015 to holders of record 07/31/2015 Ex date - 07/30/2015; 1.25% payable 10/20/2016 to holders of record 07/18/2016 Ex date - 07/15/2016
In Reg. S to holders of Reg. S 3.33333% 12/01/2011 to holders of record 09/19/2011 Ex date - 09/15/2011; 2% payable 11/19/2012 to holders of record 08/14/2012 Ex date - 08/10/2012; 2% payable 11/03/2015 to holders of record 07/31/2015 Ex date - 07/30/2015; 1.25% payable 10/20/2016 to holders of record 07/18/2016 Ex date - 07/15/2016
GDR agreement terminated 08/25/2017
Each 144A GDR for Ordinary exchanged for $5.955696 cash
Each Reg. S GDR for Ordinary exchanged for $5.955696 cash

LEBANON CTZNS NATL BK (LEBANON, OH)
Reorganized as LCNB Corp. 5/18/99
Each share Common $60 par exchanged for (10) shares Common no par

LEBANON CNTY TR CO (LEBANON, PA)
Each share Capital Stock $25 par exchanged for (5) shares Capital Stock $10 par to effect a (2.5) for (1) split and a 100% stock dividend 12/30/1967
Stock Dividends - 10% 02/10/1976; 10% 02/28/1977
Merged into National Central Financial Corp. 12/03/1979
Each share Capital Stock $10 par exchanged for (5.0875) shares Common $5 par
National Central Financial Corp. merged into CoreStates Financial Corp 05/02/1983 which merged into First Union Corp. 04/28/1998 which name changed to Wachovia Corp. (Ctfs. dated after 09/01/2001) 09/01/2001 which merged into Wells Fargo & Co. (New) 12/31/2008

LEBANON IRON CO.
Acquired by Wrought Iron Co. of America in 1928
Details not available

LEBANON STEEL & IRON CO.
Liquidation completed in 1948

LEBANON VALLEY NATL BK (LEBANON, PA)
Stock Dividends - 10% 3/6/61; 10% 1/15/62; 10% 1/31/64; 10% 1/28/65; 10% 1/28/66; 10% 2/20/70; 10% 9/28/73; 10% 4/11/77; 10% 7/17/81; 10% 10/15/82
Under plan of reorganization each share Capital Stock $10 par automatically became (2) shares Keystone Heritage Group, Inc. Common $5 par 6/24/83
Keystone Heritage Group, Inc. merged into Fulton Financial Corp. 3/27/98

LEBEL ORO MINES LTD.
Each share Capital Stock $1 par exchanged for (1/3) share Capital Stock $1 par 9/12/35
Recapitalized as Consolidated Lebel Oro Mines Ltd. in 1949
Each share Capital Stock $1 par exchanged for (1/3) share Capital Stock $1 par
Consolidated Lebel Oro Mines Ltd. recapitalized as Copper-Man Mines Ltd. in 1952 which merged into Hartland Mines Ltd. 7/25/74
(See Hartland Mines Ltd.)

LEBERTA REDWATER OIL CO., LTD. (ON)
Charter cancelled and declared dissolved for failure to file reports and pay fees 12/12/60

LEBLANC PETE INC (NV)
Reincorporated 12/1/2001
State of incorporation changed from (AZ) to (NV) 12/1/2001
Name changed to Petrosun Drilling, Inc. 8/31/2005
Petrosun Drilling, Inc. name changed to PetroSun, Inc. 9/29/2006

LEBOEUF FOUNTAIN PEN CO., INC. (MA)
Dissolved 1/1/35
No stockholders' equity

LEBOLDUS CAP INC (AB)
Name changed to Viper Gold Ltd. 10/26/2010
Viper Gold Ltd. name changed to QuikFlo Health Inc. 11/30/2015 which recapitalized as Friday Night Inc. (AB) 06/16/2017 which reincorporated in British Columbia as 1933 Industries Inc. 10/01/2018

LEBON GOLD MINES LTD (BC)
Reincorporated 12/19/2007
Place of incorporation changed from (ON) to (BC) 12/19/2007
Merged into American Consolidated Minerals Corp. 01/30/2009
Each share Common no par exchanged for (1.2) shares Common no par
American Consolidated Minerals Corp. merged into Starcore International Mines Ltd. 12/03/2014

LEC TECHNOLOGIES INC (DE)
Each share old Common 1¢ par exchanged for (0.25) share new Common 1¢ par 09/16/1998
Name changed to Golf Entertainment, Inc. (DE) 02/18/1999
Golf Entertainment, Inc. (DE) reincorporated in Nevada as Contemporary Solutions, Inc. 05/02/2005
(See Contemporary Solutions, Inc.)

LECG CORP (DE)
Issue Information - 7,500,000 shares COM offered at $17 per share on 11/19/2003
Assets sold for the benefit of creditors 03/31/2011
Stockholders' equity unlikely

LECG INC (CA)
Issue Information - 4,500,000 shares COM offered at $9 per share on 12/18/1997
Merged into Metzler Group, Inc. 08/19/1998
Each share Common $0.001 par exchanged for (0.6) share Common $0.001 par
Metzler Group, Inc. name changed to Navigant Consulting, Inc. 07/16/1999

LECHAMP CAP CORP (AB)
Reorganized under the laws of Ontario as HydraLogic Systems Inc. 01/16/2004
Each share Common no par exchanged for (0.25) share Common no par, (0.125) Common Stock Purchase Warrant, Class A expiring 6/30/2005 and (0.125) Common Stock Purchase Warrant, Class B expiring 12/31/2005

LECHE OIL CO., INC. (TX)
Charter revoked for failure to file reports and pay fees 6/12/63

LECHTERS INC (NJ)
Common no par split (2) for (1) by issuance of (1) additional share 04/24/1992
Assets sold for the benefit of creditors 10/12/2001
No stockholders' equity

LECROY CORP (DE)
Acquired by Teledyne Technologies Inc. 08/03/2012
Each share Common 1¢ par exchanged for $14.30 cash

LECSTAR CORP (TX)
SEC revoked preferred and common stock registration 03/12/2009

LECTEC CORP (MN)
Name changed to AxoGen, Inc. 10/13/2011

LECTRO COMPUTER LEASING CORP (NY)
Name changed to Lectro Management Inc. 9/2/70
(See Lectro Management Inc.)

LECTRO MGMT INC (NY)
Assets assigned for benefit of creditors 8/26/75
No stockholders' equity

LECTUS DEVS LTD (BC)
Recapitalized as Swannell Minerals Corp. 05/15/1991
Each share Common no par exchanged for (0.2) share Common no par
Swannell Minerals Corp. recapitalized as Globenet Resources Inc. 04/01/1997 which name changed to Terra Nova Gold Corp. 01/28/2003 which name changed to Terra Nova Minerals Inc. (BC) 02/19/2008 which reincorporated in Canada 02/05/2009 which reincorporated in Alberta as Terra Nova Energy Ltd. 08/21/2012 which reincorporated in British Columbia 10/31/2016 which recapitalized as Claren Energy Corp. 11/14/2016

LECUNO OIL CORP. (DE)
Merged into Texas Gas Producing Co. 04/19/1963
Each share Capital Stock 10¢ par exchanged for (0.08) share Common 25¢ par
Texas Gas Producing Co. acquired by Landa Oil Co. (Old) 10/15/1965 which name changed to Landa Industries, Inc. 04/07/1967 which recapitalized as Surveyor Companies, Inc. 11/12/1971 which name changed to Forum Companies, Inc. 09/23/1974
(See Forum Companies, Inc.)

LED PWR GROUP INC (NV)
Each share old Common $0.001 par exchanged for (0.01) share new Common $0.001 par 08/10/2009
Recapitalized as Nyxio Technologies Corp. 06/14/2011
Each share new Common $0.001 par exchanged for (0.6060606) share Common $0.001 par

LEDERIC GROUP INC (QC)
Recapitalized 12/1/72
Recapitalized from Lederic Mines Ltd. to Lederic Group Inc. 12/1/72
Each share Capital Stock $1 par exchanged for (0.2) share Capital Stock no par
Charter annulled for failure to file annual reports 10/25/80

LEDERLE LABORATORIES, INC.
Merged into American Cyanamid Co. 00/00/1946
Details not available

LEDGER CAP CORP (WI)
Merged into Anchor BanCorp Wisconsin Inc. 11/9/2001
Each share Common $1 par exchanged for either (1.1) shares Common 10¢ par or $17.325 cash
Note: Option to receive cash expired 12/31/2001

LEDGETT, INC. (UT)
Recapitalized as Tunex International, Inc. 09/16/1983
Each share Common $0.001 par exchanged for (0.125) share Common 10¢ par
Tunex International, Inc. recapitalized as Aone Dental International Group, Inc. 03/15/2011
(See Aone Dental International Group, Inc.)

LEDUC CALMAR OIL LTD (AB)
Recapitalized as Liberty Resources Ltd. 7/27/70
Each share Capital Stock no par exchanged for (0.05) share Capital Stock no par
Liberty Resources Ltd. name changed to Turbo Resources Ltd. 10/21/71 which recapitalized as Canadian Turbo Inc. 11/8/90
(See Canadian Turbo Inc.)

LEDUC CONSOLIDATED OILS LTD. (AB)
Merged into Mill City Petroleums Ltd. and each share Capital Stock no par exchanged for (1) share new Common no par in 1953

LEDUC LEASEHOLDS LTD. (AB)
Ceased operations 04/00/1960
Details not available

LEDUC-WEST OIL CO. LTD.
Merged into Trans Empire Oils Ltd. in 1950
Each share Capital Stock no par exchanged for (1/3) share Capital Stock no par
Trans Empire Oils Ltd. name changed to West Canadian Oil & Gas Ltd. 3/10/58 which merged into Canadian Delhi Oil Ltd. 1/1/62 which recapitalized as CanDel Oil Ltd. 1/10/72
(See CanDel Oil Ltd.)

LEDYARD NATL BK (HANOVER, NH)
Under plan of reorganization each share Common $1 par automatically became (1) share Ledyard Financial Group, Inc. Common $1 par 10/16/2007

LEE BROADCASTING CORP. (IA)
Merged into Lee Enterprises, Inc. 6/30/67
Each share Capital Stock no par exchanged for (1.07349) shares Capital Stock no par

LEE BROS., INC. (CA)
Name changed to Lee Bros., Value World Inc. 3/1/65

LEE (MARY) CANDIES, INC. (MI)
Common no par changed to $1 par in 1945
Adjudicated bankrupt 6/1/59
No stockholders' equity

LEE (MARY) CANDY SHOPS, INC.
Reorganized as Lee (Mary) Candies, Inc. 00/00/1932
Details not available

LEE-CARLSON OILS LTD. (AB)
Merged into Campo United Petroleums Ltd. on a (1) for (7) basis 00/00/1952
(See Campo United Petroleums Ltd.)

LEE COMMUNICATIONS INC. (NY)
Proclaimed dissolved for failure to file reports and pay taxes 12/15/66

LEE DATA CORP (MN)
Name changed to Apertus Technologies Inc. 7/19/90
Apertus Technologies Inc. name changed to Carleton Corp. 8/1/98
(See Carleton Corp.)

LEE ELECTRONICS, INC. (DE)
Adjudicated bankrupt 7/7/64
No stockholders' equity
Charter subsequently revoked 4/1/65

LEE EXPLORATION LTD. (NV)
Name changed to Kismet Energy Corp. 05/21/1998
Kismet Energy Corp. recapitalized as Global Bancorp Inc. 03/26/2002 which name changed to Voxbox World Telecom, Inc. 07/06/2005 which name changed to Internet Media Technologies, Inc. 11/21/2007 which name changed to Star Entertainment Group, Inc. 01/19/2010

LEE FILTER CORP (NJ)
Merged into Filter Dynamics International, Inc. 2/6/69
Each share Capital Stock $1 par exchanged for (1) share Common $1 par
Filter Dynamics International, Inc. name changed to FDI, Inc. 10/15/74 which recapitalized as Interlee, Inc. 12/18/81
(See Interlee, Inc.)

LEE GOLD MINES LTD. (ON)
Recapitalized as Greenlee Mines Ltd. 00/00/1936
Each share Capital Stock exchanged for (0.2) share Capital Stock
Greenlee Mines Ltd. acquired by New Athona Mines Ltd. 00/00/1954 which recapitalized as Lakota Resources Inc. 11/21/1994 which recapitalized as Tembo Gold Corp. 09/26/2011

LEE H D INC CO (KS)
Capital Stock no par split (4) for (1) by issuance of (3) additional shares 11/19/59
Capital Stock no par reclassified as Common no par 10/14/68
Common no par split (2) for (1) by issuance of (1) additional share 12/3/68
Completely liquidated 8/7/69
Each share Common no par exchanged for first and final distribution of (0.8) share V.F. Corp. Common no par

LEE JEFFREYS INC (NY)
Adjudicated bankrupt 3/11/75
Stockholders' equity unlikely

LEE (H.D.) MERCANTILE CO.
Name changed to Lee (H.D.) Co., Inc. in 1943
Lee (H.D.) Co., Inc. acquired by V.F. Corp. 8/7/69

LEE MTR PRODS INC (OH)
Name changed to Florida Automotive Marketing Corp. 11/02/1976
(See Florida Automotive Marketing Corp.)

LEE NATL BANC CORP (DE)
Merged into City Savings Bank of Pittsfield (Pittsfield, MA) 12/5/97
Each share Common 1¢ par exchanged for $39.40 cash

LEE NATL CORP (NY)
Capital Stock $5 par reclassified as Common $5 par 2/24/66
Common $5 par changed to $2.50 par and (1) additional share issued 3/15/67
Stock Dividend - 13.3% 6/4/69
Merged into Surrey Associates Corp. 8/3/78
Each share Common $2.50 par exchanged for $3.68 cash

LEE NATL LIFE INS CO (LA)
Merged into Wilder Corp. of Louisiana 12/31/80
Each share Common 50¢ par exchanged for $8 cash

LEE OIL & NATURAL GAS CO. (MD)
Each share Common 25¢ par exchanged for (2) shares Class A Common 12-1/2¢ par 5/1/53 Charter annulled 10/31/62

LEE PAPER CO. (MI)
Merged into Simpson Lee Paper Co. 9/14/59
Each share Common $10 par exchanged for (2) shares Common $10 par
(See Simpson Lee Paper Co.)

LEE PHARMACEUTICALS (CA)
Common 10¢ par split (3) for (1) by issuance of (2) additional shares 01/15/1972
Common 10¢ par split (2) for (1) by issuance of (1) additional share 01/11/1973
Common 10¢ par split (2) for (1) by issuance of (1) additional share 10/24/1986
Company terminated common stock registration 09/28/2005

LEE RUBBER & TIRE CORP. (NY)
Capital Stock no par changed to $5 par in 1932
Capital Stock $5 par split (3) for (1) by issuance of (2) additional shares 3/15/55
Name changed to Lee National Corp. 2/26/64
(See Lee National Corp.)

LEE SPRING CO., INC. (NY)
Name changed to Leetronics, Inc. 2/7/56
(See Leetronics, Inc.)

LEE TEL CO (VA)
Acquired by Central Telephone & Utilities Corp. 12/01/1971
Each share Common $10 par exchanged for (2) shares Common $2.50 par
Central Telephone & Utilities Corp. name changed to Centel Corp. 04/30/1982 which was acquired by Sprint Corp. (KS) 03/09/1993 which name changed to Sprint Nextel Corp. 08/12/2005 which merged into Sprint Corp. (DE) 07/10/2013

LEE WAY MTR FGHT INC (DE)
Common $1 par split (5) for (4) by issuance of (0.25) additional share 10/04/1968
Common $1 par split (3) for (2) by issuance of (0.5) additional share 05/19/1969
Class B Common $1 par reclassified as Common $1 par 05/05/1971
Common $1 par split (3) for (2) by issuance of (0.5) additional share 10/16/1972
Merged into PepsiCo, Inc. (DE) 08/18/1976
Each share Common $1 par exchanged for (0.241546) share Capital Stock 16-2/3¢ par
PepsiCo, Inc. (DE) reincorporated in North Carolina 12/04/1986

LEE WILSON ENGR INC (OH)
Completely liquidated in May, 1994
Each share Common no par exchanged for first and final distribution of approximately $0.22 cash

LEECE NEVILLE CO (OH)
Common $1 par changed to 50¢ par and (1) additional share issued 5/15/62
Common 50¢ par split (3) for (2) by issuance of (0.5) additional share 12/21/66
Merged into Victoreen Leece Neville, Inc. 2/1/69
Each share Common 50¢ par exchanged for (0.25) share $3 Conv. Preferred Ser. A no par and (0.75) share Common $1 par
Victoreen Leece Neville, Inc. name changed to VLN Corp. 4/29/70 which merged into Sheller-Globe Corp. 9/30/74
(See Sheller-Globe Corp.)

LEECO DIAGNOSTICS INC (MI)
Merged into Endogen, Inc. 03/19/1993
Each share Common 1¢ par exchanged for (0.45) share Common 1¢ par
(See Endogen, Inc.)

LEECOBY MINES LTD.
Dissolved in 1948
Details not available

LEED NT CORP (CANADA)
Capital Shares called for redemption at $54.41255 on 9/7/2001
Equity Dividend Shares called for redemption at $29.80991 on 9/7/2001

LEEDS & NORTHRUP CO (PA)
Common $1 par changed to 50¢ par and (1) additional share issued 8/1/56
Common 50¢ par changed to 25¢ par and (1) additional share issued 2/1/66

5% Preferred Ser. B $25 par called for redemption 5/1/64
5% Preferred Ser. A $25 par called for redemption 3/15/66
Common 25¢ par split (3) for (2) by issuance of (0.5) additional share 7/31/77
Stock Dividend - 10% 1/31/77
Merged into General Signal Corp. 9/29/78
Each share Common 25¢ par exchanged for (1.375) shares Common $1 par
General Signal Corp. merged into SPX Corp. 10/6/98

LEEDS CAP CORP (DE)
Name changed to Tech-Holdings, Inc. 7/9/90
Tech-Holdings, Inc. recapitalized as Prostar Holdings Inc. 5/26/94
(See Prostar Holdings Inc.)

LEEDS FED BANKSHARES INC (USA)
Merged into Leeds Federal Savings Bankshares 1/24/2003
Each share Common $1 par exchanged for $32 cash

LEEDS FED SVGS BK (BALTIMORE, MD)
Common $1 par split (3) for (2) by issuance of (0.5) additional share payable 11/19/97 to holders of record 11/5/97
Under plan of reorganization each share Common $1 par automatically became (1) share Leeds Federal Bankshares, Inc.
Common $1 par 1/21/98
(See Leeds Federal Bankshares, Inc.)

LEEDS HOMES INC (TN)
Reorganized 9/1/64
No stockholders' equity

LEEDS METALS LTD (QC)
Charter cancelled for failure to file reports and pay fees 10/12/74

LEEDS SHOES INC (FL)
Proclaimed dissolved for failure to file reports and pay fees 11/14/86

LEEDS TRAVELWEAR, INC. (DE)
Class A Common $1 par reclassified as Common $1 par 11/4/64
Merged into Rapid-American Corp. (OH) 11/15/67
Each share Common $1 par exchanged for (0.4666) share $2.25 Conv. Preferred $2 par
Rapid-American Corp. (OH) merged into Rapid-American Corp. (DE) 11/6/72
(See Rapid-American Corp. (DE))

LEEL ELECTRICALS LTD (INDIA)
GDR agreement terminated 03/08/2018
Each Reg. S GDR for Ordinary exchanged for (2) shares Ordinary

LEEMAC MINES LTD (BC)
Recapitalized as LMC Resources Ltd. 5/10/76
Each share Common no par exchanged for (0.2) share Common no par
LMC Resources Ltd. merged into Seadrift Resources Ltd. 11/14/78 which recapitalized as Pacific Seadrift Resources Ltd. (BC) 8/13/80 which reincorporated in Alberta 6/3/82 which recapitalized as Seadrift International Exploration Ltd. 6/1/85 which merged into Deak International Resources Corp. 12/30/88 which name changed to Deak Resources Corp. 3/27/89 which name changed to AJ Perron Gold Corp. 10/7/94
(See AJ Perron Gold Corp.)

LEEMAC RED LAKE MINES LTD. (ON)
Charter cancelled for failure to pay taxes and file returns 4/6/78

LEEMICK INDS INC (DE)
Charter cancelled and declared inoperative and void for non-payment of taxes 4/15/73

LEENLIFE PHARMA INTL INC (BC)
Name changed to LeanLife Health Inc. 01/15/2018

LEES (JAMES) & SONS CO. (PA)
Each share Common $100 par exchanged for (33-1/3) shares Common $3 par 00/00/1946
Stock Dividend - 12-1/2% 07/02/1959
Assets sold to Burlington Industries, Inc. (Old) on a (2-1/3) for (1) basis 03/25/1960
(See Burlington Industries, Inc. (Old))

LEES INNS AMER INC (IN)
Merged into LIA Acquisition Corp. 6/7/94
Each share Common no par exchanged for $1.50 cash

LEESBURG LD & MNG INC (NV)
Reincorporated 12/23/98
Each share old Common no par exchanged for (0.025) share new Common no par 6/10/85
State of incorporation changed from (CO) to (NV) 12/23/98
Recapitalized as Intelliquis International, Inc. 2/6/99
Each (30) shares new Common no par exchanged for (1) share Common $0.001 par
Intelliquis International, Inc. recapitalized as NRP Stone, Inc. 4/3/2007

LEESONA CORP (MA)
Common $5 par split (2) for (1) by issuance of (1) additional share 11/30/64
Merged into Brown (John) & Co. Ltd. 4/25/80
Each share Common $5 par exchanged for $40 cash

LEESPORT FINL CORP (PA)
Stock Dividends - 5% payable 04/15/2003 to holders of record 04/01/2003 Ex date - 03/28/2003; 5% payable 01/14/2005 to holders of record 01/03/2005 Ex date - 12/30/2004; 5% payable 06/15/2006 to holders of record 06/01/2006 Ex date - 05/30/2006; 5% payable 06/15/2007 to holders of record 06/01/2007 Ex date - 05/30/2007
Name changed to VIST Financial Corp. 03/03/2008
VIST Financial Corp. merged into Tompkins Financial Corp. 08/01/2012

LEESVILLE, SLAGLE & EASTERN RAILWAY CO.
Road abandoned in 1931
Details not available

LEETA GOLD CORP (BC)
Name changed to HIVE Blockchain Technologies Inc. 09/18/2017

LEETRONICS, INC. (NY)
Acquired by Maxson Electronics Corp. 9/30/68
Each share Common 50¢ par exchanged for $12.50 principal amount of 6% Subord. Debentures due 9/30/78 and (0.25) Common Stock Purchase Warrant

LEEWARD CAP CORP (BC)
Reincorporated under the laws of Alberta 8/20/2002

LEEZAMAX CAP CORP (AB)
Name changed to iFabric Corp. 09/13/2011

LEFCOURT REALTY CORP. (DE)
Common no par changed to $1 par in 1933
Under plan of partial liquidation each share Common $1 par exchanged for (2) shares Common 25¢ par and $16.50 in cash in 1953
Common 25¢ par reclassified as Class A 25¢ par 1/29/58 which was reclassified back to Common 25¢ par 4/16/59
Name changed to World-Wide Realty & Investing Corp. 10/28/64
(See World-Wide Realty & Investing Corp.)

LEFEBURE, INC. (DE)
Acquired by Kidde (Walter) & Co., Inc. (NY) 5/26/66
Each share Common $1 par exchanged for (0.2) share $2.20 Conv. Preference Ser. A $1 par Kidde (Walter) & Co., Inc. (NY) reincorporated in Delaware 7/2/68
(See Kidde (Walter) & Co., Inc. (DE))

LEFIER CORP. (DE)
Charter cancelled and declared inoperative and void for non-payment of taxes 4/1/53

LEFT BEHIND GAMES INC (NV)
Reincorporated 11/29/2010
Common $0.001 par split (3) for (2) by issuance of (0.5) additional share payable 10/13/2009 to holders of record 10/09/2009 Ex date - 10/14/2009
State of incorporation changed from (WA) to (NV) 11/29/2010
SEC revoked common stock registration 02/24/2014

LEFT RT MARKETING TECHNOLOGY INC (DE)
Each share old Common 1¢ par exchanged for (0.001) share new Common 1¢ par 09/21/2005
Name changed to Strategic Gaming Investments, Inc. 04/21/2006
Strategic Gaming Investments, Inc. recapitalized as Amerigo Energy, Inc. 09/11/2008 which name changed to Quest Solution, Inc. 06/10/2014

LEGACY ABILITY PRODS & SVCS INC (BC)
Recapitalized as Canadian Medical Legacy Corp. 4/23/96
Each share Common no par exchanged for (1/6) share Common no par
Canadian Medical Legacy Corp. name changed to Continental Home Healthcare Ltd. 10/16/98

LEGACY BANCORP INC (DE)
Merged into Berkshire Hills Bancorp, Inc. 07/21/2011
Each share Class A Common 1¢ par exchanged for (0.56385) share Common 1¢ par and $1.30 cash
Note: Each share Class A Common 1¢ par received additional distribution of $0.1422 cash 12/28/2011

LEGACY BANK (HARRISBURG, PA)
Name changed 1/1/2003
Under plan of merger name changed from Legacy Bank of Harrisburg (Harrisburg, PA) to Legacy Bank (Harrisburg, PA) 1/1/2003
Merged into F.N.B. Corp. (FL) 5/26/2006
Each share Common $5 par exchanged for (1) share Common 1¢ par

LEGACY BK N A (CAMPBELL, CA)
Merged into United Security Bancshares Inc. 02/16/2007
Each share Common exchanged for (0.583259) share Common 1¢ par

LEGACY BRANDS HLDG INC (FL)
Reincorporated under the laws of British Virgin Islands as Revelation MIS, Inc. and Common $0.0001 par changed to 1¢ par 10/22/2010
Revelation MIS, Inc. (British Virgin Islands) reincorporated in Florida as Jolen, Inc. 04/08/2015 which name changed to WOWI, Inc. 06/23/2016

LEGACY CAP INC (CO)
Name changed to Welcom Capital, Inc. 07/16/1990
Welcom Capital, Inc. recapitalized as Great Earth Vitamin Group Inc. 01/10/1994 which name changed to Kelly's Coffee Group, Inc. (CO) 04/22/1994 which reincorporated in Nevada 10/10/2000 which name changed to Nexia Holdings Inc. (NV) 03/21/2002 which reincorporated in Utah as Sack Lunch Productions, Inc. 04/20/2015

LEGACY COMMUNICATIONS CORP (NV)
Recapitalized as Mint Leasing, Inc. 07/23/2008
Each share Common $0.001 par exchanged for (0.05) share Common $0.001 par

LEGACY EXPLS LTD (ON)
Recapitalized as Trinexus Holdings Ltd. 06/18/1999
Each share Common no par exchanged for (0.5) share Common no par
(See Trinexus Holdings Ltd.)

LEGACY FINE ART INC (NV)
Name changed to Art-Exchange.com Inc. 2/8/2000

LEGACY HLDG INC (DE)
SEC revoked common stock registration 12/10/2012

LEGACY HOTELS REAL ESTATE INVT TR (AB)
Acquired by InnVest Real Estate Investment Trust 09/18/2007
Each share Common no par exchanged for $12.60 cash

LEGACY MNG LTD (NV)
Name changed to Legacy Wine & Spirits International Ltd. 05/27/2008
Legacy Wine & Spirits International Ltd. name changed to Legacy Platinum Group Inc. 03/15/2013 which name changed to Wee-Cig International Corp. 05/20/2014

LEGACY OIL PLUS GAS INC (AB)
Each share old Common no par exchanged for (0.16666666) share new Common no par 12/03/2009
Merged into Crescent Point Energy Corp. 07/06/2015
Each share new Common no par exchanged for (0.095) share Common no par
Note: Unexchanged certificates were cancelled and became without value 07/06/2018

LEGACY PETE LTD (AB)
Delisted from Alberta Stock Exchange 05/02/1994

LEGACY PLATINUM GROUP INC (NV)
Each share old Common $0.0001 par exchanged for (0.11111111) share new Common $0.0001 par 11/15/2013
Name changed to Wee-Cig International Corp. 05/20/2014

LEGACY RESERVES LP (DE)
Merged into Legacy Reserves Inc. 09/21/2018
Each share 8% Fixed-to-Floating Rate Perpetual Preferred Unit Ser. A exchanged for (2.92033118) shares Common 1¢ par
Each share 8% Fixed-to-Floating Rate Perpetual Preferred Unit Ser. B exchanged for (2.90650421) shares Common 1¢ par
Each Unit of Ltd. Partnership exchanged for (1) share Common 1¢ par

LEGACY SOFTWARE INC (DE)
Each share old Common $0.001 par exchanged for (1/3) share new Common $0.001 par 09/08/1998

LEGACY STORAGE SYS INTL INC (CANADA)
Name changed to Talk Visual Corp. (DE) 02/17/1999
Talk Visual Corp. (DE) reincorporated in Nevada 06/24/1999 which name changed to TVC Telecom, Inc. 09/19/2003

LEGACY STORAGE SYS INTL INC (CANADA)
Each share old Common no par exchanged for (0.1) share new Common no par 11/1/96
Name changed to Tecmar Technologies International, Inc. 12/17/96
Tecmar Technologies International, Inc. name changed to Xencet Investments Inc. 3/31/98 which name changed to Games Trader Inc. 11/11/98 which name changed GTR Group Inc. 6/29/99 which name changed to Mad Catz Interactive, Inc. 9/5/2001

LEGACY WEST VENTURES CORP (NV)
Name changed to Columbus Networks Corp. (New) 01/19/2005
(See Columbus Networks Corp. (New))

LEGACY WINE & SPIRITS INTL LTD (NV)
Name changed to Legacy Platinum Group Inc. 03/15/2013
Legacy Platinum Group Inc. name changed to Wee-Cig International Corp. 05/20/2014

LEGAL ACCESS TECHNOLOGIES INC (NV)
Each share old Common $0.001 par exchanged for (0.03333333) share new Common $0.001 par 11/18/2004
Name changed to UnderSea Recovery Corp. 07/21/2010
(See Undersea Recovery Corp.)

LEGAL LIFE PLANS INC (DE)
SEC revoked common stock registration 09/12/2016

LEGAL LIST INVTS INC (DE)
Reincorporated under the laws of Maryland as American General Total Return Fund, Inc. 1/12/79
American General Total Return Fund, Inc. merged into Fund of America, Inc. (NY) 12/31/79 which name changed to American Capital Growth & Income Fund, Inc. (NY) 7/23/90 which reincorporated in Maryland 7/6/93 which reincorporated in Delaware as Van Kampen American Capital Growth & Income Fund 7/31/95 which name changed to Van Kampen Growth & Income Fund 7/14/98

LEGAL RESERVE LIFE INSURANCE CO. OF CALIFORNIA (CA)
Merged into Surety Life Insurance Co. 11/22/65
Each share Capital Stock $10 par exchanged for (11.5) shares Common $1 par
Surety Life Insurance Co. acquired by Surety Financial Corp. 5/2/72 which merged into Witter (Dean) Organization Inc. 12/30/76 which name changed to Witter (Dean) Organization Inc. 1/3/78 which merged into Sears, Roebuck & Co. 12/31/81 which merged into Sears Holdings Corp. 3/24/2005

LEGAL RESH CLEARINGHOUSE INC (CO)
Charter dissolved for failure to file annual reports 1/1/94

LEGAL RESH CTR INC (MN)
Each share old Common 1¢ par exchanged for (0.00125) share new Common 1¢ par 08/19/2015
Note: In effect holders received $0.14 cash per share and public interest was eliminated

LEGAL SOFTWARE SOLUTIONS INC (NV)
Each (18.1313) shares Common $0.001 par exchanged for (1) share Common 1¢ par 6/23/88
Charter revoked for failure to file reports and pay fees 12/1/91

LEGALDOCUMENTSCENTER INC (FL)
Each share old Common 1¢ par exchanged for (0.1) share new Common 1¢ par 01/05/2001
Name changed to Seafood Harvest Group Inc. 09/17/2002
Seafood Harvest Group Inc. name changed to Vision Media Technologies, Inc. 03/17/2004 which recapitalized as ASF Group, Inc. (FL) 08/01/2008 which reincorporated in Georgia as American Seniors Association Holding Group, Inc. 04/28/2010

LEGALOPINION COM (UT)
Recapitalized as Drayton Richdale Corp. 4/14/2004
Each share Common $0.0001 par exchanged for (0.25) share Common $0.0001 par

LEGALPLAY ENTMT INC (FL)
Recapitalized as Synthenol Inc. (FL) 12/18/2006
Each share Common 1¢ par exchanged for (0.02) share Common 1¢ par
Synthenol Inc. (FL) reincorporated in Nevada as SinoCubate, Inc. 11/25/2008 which name changed to Viking Investments Group, Inc. 07/16/2012 which name changed to Viking Energy Group, Inc. 05/08/2017

LEGATO SYS INC (DE)
Common $0.0001 par split (2) for (1) by issuance of (1) additional share payable 07/05/1996 to holders of record 07/05/1996
Common $0.0001 par split (2) for (1) by issuance of (1) additional share payable 04/17/1998 to holders of record 04/03/1998
Common $0.001 par split (2) for (1) by issuance of (1) additional share payable 08/16/1999 to holders of record 08/02/1999
Merged into EMC Corp. 10/21/2003
Each share Common $0.0001 par exchanged for (0.9) share Common $0.0001 par
EMC Corp. merged into Dell Technologies Inc. 09/07/2016

LEGEND CAP CORP (AB)
Merged into Arsenal Energy Inc. (New) 05/29/2003
Each share Common no par exchanged for (0.37913365) share Common no par
Arsenal Energy Inc. (New) merged into Prairie Provident Resources Inc. 09/16/2016

LEGEND CITY, INC. (AZ)
Under plan of merger each share Common automatically became (1) share Saberdyne, Inc. (AZ) Common 25¢ par 8/11/70
Saberdyne, Inc. (AZ) recapitalized as Saberdyne Systems, Inc. 9/20/71
(See Saberdyne Systems, Inc.)

LEGEND FOODS INC (NY)
Each share Common $0.0001 par exchanged for (0.1) share Common $0.001 par 3/9/89
Name changed to American Complex Care, Inc. 6/22/92
(See American Complex Care, Inc.)

LEGEND GOLD CORP (BC)
Reincorporated 06/20/2014
Each share old Common no par exchanged for (0.16666666) share new Common no par 09/10/2013
Place of incorporation changed from (ON) to (BC) 06/20/2014
Each share new Common no par exchanged again for (0.1) share new Common no par 07/17/2017
Plan of arrangement effective 02/01/2018
Each share new Common no par exchanged for (3) shares Altus Strategies PLC Ordinary 1p par
Note: Unexchanged certificates will be cancelled and become without value 02/01/2018

LEGEND GROUP LTD (HONG KONG)
Name changed 04/25/2002
Sponsored ADR's for Ordinary split (4) for (1) by issuance of (3) additional ADR's payable 03/15/2000 to holders of record 03/08/2000
Each Sponsored ADR for Ordinary received distribution of $0.0513936 cash payable 09/10/2001 to holders of record 08/02/2001
Name changed from Legend Holdings Ltd. to Legend Group Ltd. 04/25/2002
Name changed to Lenovo Group Ltd. 04/13/2004

LEGEND INTL HLDGS INC (DE)
Common $0.001 par split (3) for (2) by issuance of (0.5) additional share payable 12/11/2006 to holders of record 11/17/2006 Ex date - 12/12/2006
Common $0.001 par split (3) for (2) by issuance of (0.5) additional share payable 01/10/2007 to holders of record 12/31/2006 Ex date - 01/11/2007
SEC revoked common stock registration 10/06/2017

LEGEND INVT CORP (DE)
Name changed to GiraSolar, Inc. 04/10/2006
(See GiraSolar, Inc.)

LEGEND MNG INC (NV)
Name changed to Stevia First Corp. 10/12/2011
Stevia First Corp. recapitalized as Vitality Biopharma, Inc. 07/20/2016

LEGEND MOBILE INC (DE)
Name changed to Cephas Holding Corp. 01/14/2009
(See Cephas Holding Corp.)

LEGEND PPTYS INC (DE)
Merged into RGI Holdings Inc. 08/31/2000
Each share Common 1¢ par exchanged for $0.50 cash

LEGEND RES INC (NV)
Each share old Common $0.001 par exchanged for (0.05) share new Common $0.001 par 07/18/2001
Name changed to SMS @ctive Technologies Corp. 07/31/2001
SMS @ctive Technologies Corp. recapitalized as Exchange Mobile Telecommunications Corp. 11/17/2006 which recapitalized as Anything Technologies Media, Inc. 09/20/2010

LEGENDARY SUPERSTARS INC (NV)
Name changed to Gatekeeper USA, Inc. 01/09/2008

LEGENDS CO CHICAGO INC (DE)
Charter cancelled and declared inoperative and void for non-payment of taxes 3/1/92

LEGENDS FOOD CORP (NV)
Name changed to Republic of Texas Brands, Inc. 11/07/2011
Republic of Texas Brands, Inc. name changed to Totally Hemp Crazy Inc. 08/05/2014 which name changed to Rocky Mountain High Brands Inc. 10/16/2015

LEGENDS OF THE FAITH INC (NV)
Recapitalized as Kingdom Ventures, Inc. 07/08/2002
Each share Common $0.002 par exchanged for (0.5) share Common $0.002 par
Kingdom Ventures, Inc. recapitalized as Denim Apparel Group, Inc. 10/24/2005 which recapitalized as Bolivar Mining Corp. 10/15/2007

LEGENT CORP (DE)
Merged into Computer Associates International, Inc. 11/06/1995
Each share Common 1¢ par exchanged for $47.95 cash

LEGETTES, INC. (ID)
Charter forfeited for failure to pay franchise taxes 11/30/63

LEGG MASON BW GLOBAL INCOME OPPORTUNITIES FD INC (MD)
Name changed to BrandywineGLOBAL - Global Income Opportunities Fund Inc. 01/02/2018

LEGG MASON BW INVT GRADE FOCUS FD (ON)
Under plan of merger each Trust Unit automatically became (0.38166219) Limited Duration Investment Grade Preferred Securities Fund Class A Unit 03/14/2014
Limited Duration Investment Grade Preferred Securities Fund merged into Purpose US Preferred Share Fund 08/24/2018

LEGG MASON CDA HLDGS LTD (NB)
Exchangeable Shares split (3) for (2) by issuance of (0.5) additional share payable 09/24/2004 to holders of record 09/08/2004 Ex date - 09/03/2004
Each Exchangeable Share exchanged for (1) share Legg Mason, Inc. Common 10¢ par 05/26/2010

LEGG MASON CASH RESV TR (MA)
Completely liquidated 02/28/2006
Each Share of Bene. Int. no par received net asset value

LEGG MASON ETF EQUITY TR (MD)
Name changed to Legg Mason ETF Investment Trust 02/15/2017

LEGG MASON FOCUS TR (MD)
Name changed to Legg Mason Growth Trust, Inc. 5/1/2004

LEGG MASON INC (MD)
Each Corporate Unit automatically became (0.8881) share Common 10¢ par 06/30/2011

LEGG MASON PARTNERS CALIF MUNS FD INC (MD)
Class Y 1¢ par reclassified as Class I 1¢ par 11/20/2006
Name changed to Legg Mason Partners Income Trust and Class A 1¢ par, Class B 1¢ par, Class C 1¢ par, and Class I 1¢ par reclassified as California Municipal Fund Class A, Class B, Class C, or Class I respectively 04/16/2007

LEGG MASON PARTNERS EQUITY FD INC (MD)
Name changed to Legg Mason Partners Equity Trust 04/16/2007

LEGG MASON TOTAL RETURN TR INC (MD)
Merged into Legg Mason Investors Trust, Inc. 06/14/2001
Details not available

LEGGETT & PLATT SPRING BED MANUFACTURING CO.
Name changed to Leggett & Platt, Inc. in 1942

LEGGO HLDGS INC (ON)
Name changed to Transarctic Petroleum Corp. 09/29/1997
Transarctic Petroleum Corp. name changed to ivyNET Corp. 03/26/1999 which recapitalized as Saratoga Capital Corp. 08/25/2000
(See Saratoga Capital Corp.)

LEGGOONS INC (MO)
Common 1¢ par split (14) for (1) by issuance of (13) additional shares 05/28/1993
Name changed to Betting, Inc. (MO) 03/01/1997
Betting, Inc. (MO) reincorporated in Nevada as eConnect 06/04/1999 which name changed to EyeCashNetworks, Inc. 01/24/2003
(See EyeCashNetworks, Inc.)

LEGHORN INC (MN)
Name changed to Purchase Point Media Corp. and (3) additional shares issued 04/25/1997
Purchase Point Media Corp. recapitalized as Power Sports Factory, Inc. 06/10/2008
(See Power Sports Factory, Inc.)

LEGION OILS LTD. (AB)
Merged into Medallion Petroleums Ltd. 2/22/60
Each share Common no par exchanged for (0.04) share Common $1.25 par
Medallion Petroleums Ltd. merged into Canadian Industrial Gas & Oil Ltd. 3/8/65 which merged into Norcen Energy Resources Ltd. (ALTA) 10/28/75 which reincorporated under the laws of Canada 4/15/77 which merged into Union Pacific Resources Group Inc. 4/17/98 which merged into Anadarko Petroleum Corp. 7/14/2000

LEGION RES CORP (BC)
Merged into Samaranta Mining Corp. 05/20/2011
Each share Common no par exchanged for (0.25) share Common no par
Note: Unexchanged certificates were cancelled and became without value 05/20/2018
Samaranta Mining Corp. recapitalized as Icon Exploration Inc. 10/28/2013

LEGION RES LTD (BC)
Reorganized under the laws of Cayman Islands as Earl Resources Ltd. 06/02/1998
Each share Common no par exchanged for (0.5) share Common no par
Earl Resources Ltd. (Cayman Islands) reorganized in British Columbia 03/02/2018

LEGUME INC (DE)
Charter cancelled and declared inoperative and void for non-payment of taxes 6/24/91

LEGUMEX WALKER INC (CANADA)
Name changed to LWP Capital Inc. 12/02/2015

LEHI CORP. (UT)
Charter suspended for failure to pay taxes 09/15/1972

LEHIGH & WILKES-BARRE COAL CO. OF NEW JERSEY
Liquidation completed in 1943
Details not available

LEHIGH & WILKES-BARRE CORP.
Liquidated in 1951
Details not available

LEHIGH BUILDING & DEVELOPMENT CO. (FL)
Dissolved 12/14/64
Details not available

LEHIGH COAL & NAV CO (PA)
Each share Common $50 par exchanged for (3) shares Common no par in 1929
Common no par changed to $10 par in 1944
Under plan of reorganization Common $10 par changed to $1 par 4/30/62
Liquidation completed
Each share Common $1 par exchanged for initial distribution of $0.725 cash 9/15/85
Each share Common $1 par received second and final distribution of $0.1558 cash 12/31/86

LEHIGH GAS PARTNERS L P (DE)
Name changed to CrossAmerica Partners L.P. 10/06/2014

LEHIGH GROUP INC (DE)
Recapitalized as First Medical Group, Inc. 11/13/1997
Each (30) shares Common $0.001 par exchanged for (1) share Common $0.001 par
(See First Medical Group, Inc.)

LEHIGH INDS & INVESTING CORP (DE)
Charter dissolved 4/9/65

LEHIGH PORTLAND CEM CO (PA)
Recapitalized in 1936
Each share 7% Preferred $100 par exchanged for (1) share 4% Preferred $100 par, (0.5) share Common $25 par and $12.50 cash
Common $50 par changed to $25 par
Common $25 par changed to $15 par and (1) additional share issued 4/27/56
Stock Dividend - 100% 5/4/51
Merged into Heidelberg Cement of Pennsylvania, Inc. 12/14/77
Each share Common $15 par exchanged for $25 cash

LEHIGH POWER SECURITIES CORP.
Liquidated in 1939

LEHIGH PRECISION MFG INC (DE)
Name changed to Five Star Coal Co., Inc. 10/28/76
Five Star Coal Co., Inc. name changed to Onyx Hydrocarbon Recovery Corp. 5/25/82 which name changed to Magna Diversified 3/22/84 which name changed to Energizer 500 Inc. 6/8/84 which name changed to Opportunity 21 on 6/16/85
(See Opportunity 21)

LEHIGH PRESS INC (PA)
Common no par split (5) for (4) by issuance of (0.25) additional share 10/31/68
Common no par split (2) for (1) by issuance of (1) additional share 3/15/85
Stock Dividends - 10% 1/31/64; 10% 10/29/66
Merged into LP Acquisition Corp. 3/6/87
Each share Common no par exchanged for $45 cash

LEHIGH VALLEY COAL CORP. (DE)
Common no par changed to $1 par 03/30/1946
Name changed to Lehigh Valley Industries, Inc. 03/21/1958
Lehigh Valley Industries, Inc. name changed to LVI Group Inc. 06/04/1986 which name changed to Lehigh Group Inc. 01/27/1995 which recapitalized as First Medical Group, Inc. 11/13/1997
(See First Medical Group, Inc.)

LEHIGH VALLEY COAL SALES CO. (DE)
Name changed to Lehval Industries, Inc. 3/30/59
Lehval Industries, Inc. merged into Lehigh Valley Industries, Inc. 6/3/60 which name changed to LVI Group Inc. 6/4/86 which name changed to Lehigh Group Inc. 1/27/95

LEHIGH VALLEY COAL SALES CO. (NJ)
Each share Common $50 par exchanged for (1) share Common $25 par and $25 in cash distributed in 1932
Each share Common $25 par exchanged for (1) share Common $22.50 par and $2.50 in cash distributed in 1938
Each share Common $22.50 par exchanged for (1) share Common $20 par and $1 in cash distributed in 1939
Reincorporated under the laws of Delaware in August 1942
Lehigh Valley Coal Sales Co. (DE) name changed to Lehval Industries, Inc. 3/30/59 which merged into Lehigh Valley Industries, Inc. 6/3/60 which name changed to LVI Group Inc. 6/4/86 which name changed to Lehigh Group Inc. 1/27/95 which recapitalized as First Medical Group, Inc. 11/13/97

LEHIGH VALLEY ELECTRS INC (PA)
Merged into Tech Serv, Inc. 9/12/72
Each share Common 10¢ par exchanged for (0.444444) share Common 10¢ par
(See Tech Serv, Inc.)

LEHIGH VALLEY INDS INC (DE)
Each share $3 1st Preferred no par exchanged for (1) share $1.50 Preferred Ser. A no par and (12) shares Common 50¢ par 06/03/1960
Each share 50¢ 2nd Preferred no par exchanged for (0.25) share $1.50 Preferred Ser. A no par and (3) shares Common 50¢ par 06/03/1960
Each share 6% Preferred $50 par exchanged for (1.25) shares $1.50 Preferred Ser. A no par and (16) shares Common 50¢ par 06/03/1960
Each share Common $1 par exchanged for (1) share Common 50¢ par 06/03/1960
Each share $1.50 Conv. Preferred Ser. A no par exchanged for (16.7640) shares Common 50¢ par 01/02/1986
Name changed to LVI Group Inc. 06/04/1986
LVI Group Inc. name changed to Lehigh Group Inc. 01/27/1995 which recapitalized as First Medical Group, Inc. 11/13/1997
(See First Medical Group, Inc.)

LEHIGH VALLEY OIL CO., INC. (DE)
Liquidated in 1954

LEHIGH VALLEY RR CO (PA)
Common $50 par changed to no par in 1949
Reorganized under Section 77 (d) of the bankruptcy Act 7/16/82
Each share Common no par exchanged for $10 cash

LEHIGH VALLEY TR CO (ALLENTOWN, PA)
Stock Dividend - 100% 9/15/55
Capital Stock $100 par changed to $10 par and (9) additional shares issued plus a 20% stock dividend paid 2/15/61
Merged into Industrial Valley Bank & Trust Co. (Jenkintown, PA) 12/23/68
Each share Capital Stock $10 par exchanged for (3.333333) shares Common $5 par
Industrial Valley Bank & Trust Co. (Jenkintown, PA) reorganized as IVB Financial Corp. 1/1/84
(See IVB Financial Corp.)

LEHIGH WATER CO.
Acquired by City of Easton, Pa. in 1935

LEHMAN BARTEL & CO INC (UT)
Name changed to Integrated Marketing Management, Inc. 09/19/1978
(See Integrated Marketing Management, Inc.)

LEHMAN BROS / FIRST TR INCOME OPPORTUNITY FD (DE)
Issue Information - 11,000,000 SHS BEN INT offered at $15 per share on 07/28/2003
Money Market Preferred called for redemption at $25,000 on 11/13/2008
Name changed to Neuberger Berman High Yield Strategies Fund (DE) 12/19/2008
Neuberger Berman High Yield Strategies Fund (DE) reincorporated in Maryland as Neuberger Berman High Yield Strategies Fund Inc. 08/06/2010

LEHMAN BROS HLDGS INC (DE)
Common 10¢ par split (2) for (1) by issuance of (1) additional share payable 10/20/2000 to holders of record 10/05/2000 Ex date - 10/23/2000
5% Conv. Preferred Ser. B $1 par called for redemption at $39.10 on 12/15/2000
8.3% Quarterly Income Capital Securities Ser. A called for redemption at $25 on 01/04/2002
Fixed/Adjustable Rate Depositary Preferred Ser. E called for redemption at $50 on 05/31/2005
Common 10¢ par split (2) for (1) by issuance of (1) additional share payable 04/28/2006 to holders of record 04/18/2006 Ex date - 05/01/2006
Each Premium Income Exchangeable Security for General Mills received (0.4609) share General Mills, Inc. Common 10¢ par 10/15/2007
Plan of reorganization under Chapter 11 Federal Bankruptcy proceedings effective 03/06/2012
Holders received a beneficial interest in LBHI Plan Trust which will make a distribution only in the event that all Allowed Claims are satisfied
Each Premium Income Exchangeable Security for General Mills received initial distribution of $1.597977 cash payable 04/17/2012 to holders of record 03/06/2012
Each Premium Income Exchangeable Security for General Mills received second distribution of $1.016432 cash payable 10/01/2012 to holders of record 03/06/2012
Each Premium Income Exchangeable Security for General Mills received third distribution of $1.325221 cash payable 04/04/2013 to holders of record 03/06/2012
Each Premium Income Exchangeable Security for General Mills received fourth distribution of $1.529825 cash payable 10/03/2013 to holders of record 03/06/2012
Each Premium Income Exchangeable Security for General Mills received fifth distribution of $1.697841 cash payable 04/03/2014 to holders of record 03/06/2012
Each Premium Income Exchangeable Security for General Mills received sixth distribution of $1.233233 cash payable 10/02/2014 to holders of record 03/06/2012
Each Premium Income Exchangeable Security for General Mills received seventh distribution of $0.848074 cash payable 04/02/2015 to holders of record 03/06/2012
Each Premium Income Exchangeable Security for General Mills received eighth distribution of $0.634204 cash payable 10/01/2015 to holders of record 03/06/2012
Each Premium Income Exchangeable Security for General Mills received ninth distribution of $0.181135 cash payable 03/31/2016 to holders of record 03/06/2012
Each Premium Income Exchangeable Security for General Mills received tenth distribution of $0.265533 cash payable 06/16/2016 to holders of record 03/06/2012
Each Premium Income Exchangeable Security for General Mills received eleventh distribution of $0.449897

cash payable 10/06/2016 to holders of record 03/06/2012
Each Premium Income Exchangeable Security for General Mills received twelfth distribution of $0.347764 cash payable 04/06/2017 to holders of record 03/06/2012
Each Premium Income Exchangeable Security for General Mills received thirteenth distribution of $0.234862 cash payable 10/05/2017 to holders of record 03/06/2012
Each Premium Income Exchangeable Security for General Mills received fourteenth distribution of $0.314207 cash payable 12/07/2017 to holders of record 03/06/2012
Each Premium Income Exchangeable Security for General Mills received fifteenth distribution of $0.19587 cash payable 04/05/2018 to holders of record 03/06/2012
Each Premium Income Exchangeable Security for General Mills received sixteenth distribution of $0.207221 cash payable 10/04/2018 to holders of record 03/06/2012

LEHMAN BROS INC CUSTODIAL RCPTS FOR PFD SHS OF VAR
Money Market Preferred Citigroup Custodial Receipts called for redemption at $100,000 on 06/20/2007

LEHMAN BROS LATIN AMER GROWTH FD INC (MD)
Issue Information - 4,000,000 shares COM offered at $15 per share on 10/28/1994
Name changed to Latin America Growth Fund, Inc. 9/29/95
Latin America Growth Fund, Inc. name changed to Latin America Smaller Companies Fund, Inc. 2/15/98
(See Latin America Smaller Companies Fund, Inc.)

LEHMAN BROS HLDGS CAP TR I (DE)
8% Preferred Securities Ser. I called for redemption at $25 on 3/31/2004

LEHMAN BROS HLDGS CAP TR II (DE)
7.875% Preferred Securities Ser. J called for redemption at $25 on 6/30/2004

LEHMAN BROS HLDGS CAP TR III (DE)
Issue Information - 12,000,000 PFD SECS K 6.375% offered at $25 per share on 03/12/2003
Plan of reorganization under Chapter 11 Federal Bankruptcy proceedings effective 03/06/2012
Holders received a beneficial interest in LBHI Plan Trust which will make a distribution only in the event that all Allowed Claims are satisfied

LEHMAN BROS HLDGS CAP TR IV (DE)
Issue Information - 12,000,000 shares PFD SER L 6.375% offered at $25 per share on 10/09/2003
Plan of reorganization under Chapter 11 Federal Bankruptcy proceedings effective 03/06/2012
Holders received a beneficial interest in LBHI Plan Trust which will make a distribution only in the event that all Allowed Claims are satisfied

LEHMAN BROS HLDGS CAP TR V (DE)
Issue Information - 16,000,000 PFD SECS SER M 6% offered at $25 per share on 04/01/2004
Plan of reorganization under Chapter 11 Federal Bankruptcy proceedings effective 03/06/2012
Holders received a beneficial interest in LBHI Plan Trust which will make a distribution only in the event that all Allowed Claims are satisfied

LEHMAN BROS HLDGS CAP TR VI (DE)
Issue Information - 8,000,000 TR PFD SECS SER N 6.24% offered at $25 per share on 01/05/2005
Plan of reorganization under Chapter 11 Federal Bankruptcy proceedings effective 03/06/2012
Holders received a beneficial interest in LBHI Plan Trust which will make a distribution only in the event that all Allowed Claims are satisfied

LEHMAN CORP (MD)
Reincorporated 04/30/1977
Capital Stock no par changed to $1 par 00/00/1937
Capital Stock $1 par split (2) for (1) by issuance of (1) additional share 00/00/1953
Capital Stock $1 par split (2) for (1) by issuance of (1) additional share 11/08/1956
Capital Stock $1 par split (2) for (1) by issuance of (1) additional share 11/20/1967
State of incorporation changed from (DE) to (MD) 04/30/1977
Name changed to Salomon Brothers Fund Inc. 05/01/1990
Salomon Brothers Fund Inc. name changed to Legg Mason Partners Equity Fund, Inc. 11/20/2006 which name changed to Legg Mason Partners Equity Trust 04/16/2007

LEHN & FINK PRODUCTS CO.
Merged into Lehn & Fink Products Corp. on a share for share basis in 1936
Lehn & Fink Products Corp. acquired by Sterling Drug Inc. 6/28/66
(See Sterling Drug Inc.)

LEHN & FINK PRODUCTS CORP. (DE)
Common $5 par changed to $1 par and (2) additional shares issued 5/10/61
Acquired by Sterling Drug Inc. 6/28/66
Each share Common $1 par exchanged for (1) share $1.50 Conv. Preferred $2.50 par
(See Sterling Drug Inc.)

LEHNDORFF CDN PPTYS (AB)
Units of Ltd. Partnership split (2) for (1) by issuance of (1) additional unit 1/9/84
Completely liquidated 10/1/99
Each Unit of Ltd. Partnership received first and final distribution of $0.22 cash

LEHRENKRAUSS CORP.
Reorganized as Fulton Service Corp. in 1935

LEHVAL INDUSTRIES, INC. (DE)
Merged into Lehigh Valley Industries, Inc. 06/03/1960
Each share Capital Stock $20 par exchanged for (1) share $1.50 Conv. Preferred A no par
Lehigh Valley Industries, Inc. name changed to LVI Group Inc. 06/04/1986 which name changed to Lehigh Group Inc. 01/27/1995 which recapitalized as First Medical Group, Inc. 11/13/1997
(See First Medical Group, Inc.)

LEICA PLC (UNITED KINGDOM)
Acquired by Form-Feed (Netherlands) B.V. 10/11/91
Each ADR for Ordinary 5p par exchanged for $11.86 cash

LEICESTER DIAMOND MINES LTD (BC)
Recapitalized as Target Exploration & Mining Corp. 04/30/2004
Each share Common no par exchanged for (0.1) share Common no par
Target Exploration & Mining Corp. merged into Crosshair Exploration & Mining Corp. 03/31/2009 which name changed to Crosshair Energy Corp. 11/02/2011 which recapitalized as Jet Metal Corp. (BC) 09/23/2013 reorganized in Canada as Canada Jetlines Ltd. 03/07/2017

LEICHARDT EXPL LTD (AUSTRALIA)
Acquired by Victoria Exploration N.L. 07/26/1984
Each ADR for Ordinary A$0.20 par exchanged for (1/3) ADR for Ordinary A$0.20 par
Victoria Exploration N.L. name changed to Victoria Petroleum N.L. 02/09/1989 which name changed to Senex Energy Ltd. 05/07/2012

LEICOM INDS INC (NY)
Charter cancelled and proclaimed dissolved for failure to pay taxes and file reports 12/15/71

LEIDY PROSPECTING CO., INC. (PA)
Merged into Devonian Gas & Oil Co. (PA) in 1953
Each share Common 10¢ par exchanged for (1) share Capital Stock 10¢ par
Devonian Gas & Oil Co. (PA) merged into Devonian Gas & Oil Co. (DE) 12/20/57
(See Devonian Gas & Oil Co. (DE))

LEIGH INSTRS LTD (CANADA)
Common no par split (2) for (1) by issuance of (1) additional share 12/22/69
Common no par reclassified as Conv. Class 2 Common no par 6/16/81
Each share Conv. Class 2 Common no par received distribution of (1) share Class 1 Common no par 6/23/81
Class 1 Common no par reclassified as Common no par 12/22/81
Conv. Class 2 Common no par reclassified as Common no par 12/22/81
Non-Vtg. Conv. 2nd Preference 1982 R&D Ser. no par called for redemption 11/2/87
Acquired by Plessey Co. 5/19/88
Each share $1.75 Conv. 2nd Preference Ser. 2 no par exchanged for $29.25 cash
Each share Common no par exchanged for $7 cash
$2.60 1st Preference Ser. A $50 par called for redemption 6/23/88
Public interest eliminated

LEIGH PRODS INC (DE)
Merged into Harrow Corp. 8/1/79
Each share Common $1 par exchanged for $25 cash

LEIGH RESOURCE CORP (BC)
Recapitalized as Upland Resource Corp. (BC) 11/6/2000
Each share Common no par exchanged for (0.1) share Common no par
Upland Resource Corp. (BC) reorganized in Canada as New Sleeper Gold Corp. 3/25/2004 which name changed to Reunion Gold Corp. 6/6/2006

LEIGHTON HLDG LTD (AUSTRALIA)
Name changed to CIMIC Group Ltd. 07/16/2015

LEINER P NUTRITIONAL PRODS CORP (CA)
Common no par split (3) for (2) by issuance of (0.5) additional share 10/24/89
Merged into PLI Investors Inc. 5/4/92
Each share Common no par exchanged for $15 cash

LEISURE & LEARNING INC (DE)
Merged into Majestic Penn State, Inc. (DE) 06/29/1973
Each share Common 10¢ par exchanged for (0.081311) share Common 10¢ par
Each share Common 10¢ par received additional distribution of $0.018335 cash 05/27/1976
Majestic Penn State, Inc. (DE) reincorporated in Pennsylvania 02/01/1976
(See Majestic Penn State, Inc. (PA))

LEISURE + TECHNOLOGY, INC. (DE)
Name changed to Leisure Technology Inc. (Old) 8/11/87
(See Leisure Technology Inc. (Old))

LEISURE CDA INC (ON)
Name changed to 360 VOX Corp. 10/17/2011
360 VOX Corp. merged into Dundee Corp. 07/03/2014

LEISURE CAP CORP AMER (FL)
Proclaimed dissolved for failure to file reports and pay fees 8/13/93

LEISURE CONCEPTS INC (NY)
Common 1¢ par split (2) for (1) by issuance of (0.5) additional share 10/27/1978
Common 1¢ par split (2) for (1) by issuance of (1) additional share 06/30/1986
Name changed to 4 Kids Entertainment Inc. (NY) 11/16/1995
4 Kids Entertainment Inc. (NY) reorganized in Delaware as 4Licensing Corp. 12/21/2012
(See 4Licensing Corp.)

LEISURE CONCEPTS INTL INC (DE)
Name changed to CI4net.com, Inc. 11/30/1999
(See CI4net.co, Inc.)

LEISURE DEVS LTD (BC)
Name changed to Leisure Gold Ltd. and Capital Stock 50¢ par changed to no par 09/19/1974
Leisure Gold Ltd. recapitalized as United Leisure Gold Ltd. 04/14/1975 which recapitalized as Forum Resources Ltd. 04/17/1978 which name changed to Forum Beverages Inc. 02/16/1989
(See Forum Beverages Inc.)

LEISURE DIRECT INC (NV)
Name changed to LD Holdings, Inc. 10/27/2008

LEISURE DYNAMICS INC (DE)
Merged into LD Acquisition Corp. 2/6/86
Each share Common $1 par exchanged for $2.10 cash

LEISURE EXPOSITIONS CORP (DE)
Name changed to Restaurant Concepts, Inc. 12/21/82
(See Restaurant Concepts, Inc.)

LEISURE GOLD LTD (BC)
Recapitalized as United Leisure Gold Ltd. 04/14/1975
Each share Capital Stock no par exchanged for (0.33333333) share Capital Stock no par
United Leisure Gold Ltd. recapitalized as Forum Resources Ltd. 04/17/1978 which name changed to Forum Beverages Inc. 02/16/1989
(See Forum Beverages Inc.)

LEISURE GROUP INC (DE)
Stock Dividend - 100% 7/17/69
Common no par changed to 1¢ par 1/24/80
Each share Common 1¢ par exchanged for (0.05) share Common 20¢ par 5/11/82
Merged into TLG Merger Corp. 6/3/87
Each share Common 20¢ par exchanged for $0.35 cash

LEISURE HLDGS INC (DE)
Name changed to Amsnax, Inc. 08/15/1989
(See Amsnax, Inc.)

LEISURE INNS & RESORTS INC (DE)
Charter cancelled and declared inoperative and void for non-payment of taxes 3/1/74

LEISURE INTERNATIONAL INC. (UT)
Name changed to IMABV Ltd. 9/22/88
(See IMABV Ltd.)

LEISURE LIVING CMNTYS INC (MA)
Proclaimed dissolved for failure to file reports and pay fees 07/07/1980

LEISURE LODGES INC (AR)
Completely liquidated 10/15/1975
Each share Common $1 par exchanged for first and final distribution of $12 cash

LEISURE PLANNING CORP (DE)
Adjudicated bankrupt 09/29/1970
Stockholders' equity unlikely

LEISURE SERVICES, INC. (UT)
Name changed to Tucker Drilling Co., Inc. (UT) 7/16/74
Tucker Drilling Co., Inc. (UT) reincorporated under the laws of Delaware 1/13/75 which merged into Patterson Energy Inc. 7/30/96 which name changed to Patterson-UTI Energy, Inc. 5/9/2001

LEISURE SVCS INC (CO)
Name changed to Havelock Resources International, Inc. 5/7/82
(See Havelock Resources International, Inc.)

LEISURE SHOPPERS INC (LA)
Each share old Common no par exchanged for (0.01) share new Common no par 08/18/2005
Name changed to LOM Logistics, Inc. 12/08/2006
(See LOM Logistics, Inc.)

LEISURE TECHNOLOGY CORP (DE)
Common 10¢ par split (3) for (2) by issuance of (0.5) additional share 12/15/69
Name changed to Leisure + Technology, Inc. 8/23/82
Leisure + Technology, Inc. name changed to Leisure Technology Inc. (Old) 8/11/87
(See Leisure Technology Inc. (Old))

LEISURE TECHNOLOGY INC NEW (DE)
Merged into Realmark Holdings Corp. 06/30/1999
Each (14) shares Common no par exchanged for (1) share new Common no par
Note: Holders entitled (99) of fewer post-merger shares will receive $0.90 cash per share
Realmark Holdings Corp. acquired by Realmark Acquisitions LLC 04/13/2005 which name changed to Realmark Acquisitions II LLC 07/12/2005

LEISURE TECHNOLOGY INC OLD (DE)
Plan of reorganization under Chapter 11 Federal Bankruptcy Code effective 2/15/93
No stockholders' equity

LEISURE TIME CASINOS & RESORTS INC (CO)
Issue Information - 700,000 shares COM offered at $12 per share on 09/15/1999
Chapter 11 bankruptcy proceedings converted to Chapter 7 on 4/11/2002
Stockholders' equity unlikely

LEISURE TIME PRODS INC (IN)
Second Amended Plan of Reorganization under Chapter 11 Federal Bankruptcy Act confirmed 11/23/83
No stockholders' equity

LEISURE TRENDS INC (DE)
Charter cancelled and declared inoperative and void for non-payment of taxes 03/01/1978

LEISURE WORLD SVCS INC (DE)
Each share old Common 1¢ par exchanged for (0.142857) share new Common 1¢ par 12/15/72

Charter cancelled and declared inoperative and void for non-payment of taxes 3/1/74

LEISURECRAFT INDS INC (CO)
Name changed to Super Seer Corp. 4/10/73

LEISURECRAFT PRODS LTD (DE)
Name changed to Webcor Electronics Inc. 6/2/81
(See Webcor Electronics Inc.)

LEISUREPLANET HLDGS LTD (BERMUDA)
Name changed to Silverstar Holdings, Ltd. 12/14/2000
(See Silverstar Holdings, Ltd.)

LEISURETECH SPORTS CORP (BC)
Recapitalized as Concept Industries Inc. 02/22/1994
Each share Common no par exchanged for (1/3) share Common no par
Concept Industries Inc. name changed to Concept Wireless Inc. 06/23/2000 which recapitalized as Candao Enterprises Inc. 02/27/2003
(See Candao Enterprises Inc.)

LEISUREWAYS MARKETING LTD (YT)
Reincorporated 11/10/1997
Each share old Common no par exchanged for (0.33333333) share new Common no par 03/03/1997
Place of incorporation changed from (BC) to (YT) 11/10/1997
Name changed to LML Payment Systems Inc. (YT) 07/15/1998
LML Payment Systems Inc. (YT) reincorporated in British Columbia 09/07/2012
(See LML Payment Systems Inc.)

LEISUREWORLD SR CARE CORP (BC)
Name changed to Sienna Senior Living Inc. 05/01/2015

LEITAK ENTERPRISES LTD (CAYMAN ISLANDS)
Delisted from Toronto Venture Stock Exchange 06/22/2003

LEITCH GOLD MINES LTD (ON)
Name changed to Leitch Mines Ltd. 03/18/1970
Leitch Mines Ltd. liquidated for Teck Corp. Ltd. 04/30/1971 which name changed to Teck Corp. 11/21/1978 which name changed to Teck Cominco Ltd. 09/12/2001 which name changed to Teck Resources Ltd. 04/27/2009

LEITCH MINES LTD (ON)
Completely liquidated 04/30/1971
Each share Common $1 par exchanged for first and final distribution of (1/3) share Teck Corp. Ltd. Class B Common no par
Teck Corp. Ltd. name changed to Teck Corp. 11/21/1978 which name changed to Teck Cominco Ltd. 09/12/2001 which name changed to Teck Resources Ltd. 04/27/2009

LEITCH TECHNOLOGY CORP (ON)
Common no par split (2) for (1) by issuance of (1) additional share payable 09/27/1996 to holders of record 09/26/1996 Ex date - 09/24/1996
Merged into Harris Corp. 10/25/2005
Each share Common no par exchanged for $14 cash
Note: Unexchanged certificates were cancelled and became without value 10/25/2015

LEITRIM GROUP INC (AB)
Name changed to Savers Plus International Inc. 7/24/2006
Savers Plus International Inc. name changed to Intertainment Media Inc. 4/30/2007

LEJAY CORP (UT)
Name changed to Drumm Corp. 9/24/83
Drumm Corp. name changed to Horti-Tech Inc. 1/7/86
(See Horti-Tech Inc.)

LEK TROL INC (TX)
Charter forfeited for non-payment of taxes 9/26/73

LEL, INC. (NY)
Name changed to Standard Resources Corp. (N.Y.) 2/5/65
Standard Resources Corp. (N.Y.) reincorporated under the laws of Delaware 11/28/69 which name changed to Microsemiconductor Corp. 3/22/72 which name changed to Microsemi Corp. 2/10/83

LELAND ELECTRIC CO.
Acquired by American Machine & Foundry Co. in 1952
Each share Common $3 par exchanged for (1.025) shares Common no par
American Machine & Foundry Co. name changed to AMF Inc. 4/30/70
(See AMF Inc.)

LELAND PUBG LTD (ON)
Trustee in bankruptcy appointed 03/16/1964
No stockholders' equity

LELAND-RACINE BUILDING CO. (IL)
Liquidation completed 5/8/57

LEM CORP (TX)
Charter forfeited for failure to pay taxes 03/15/1976

LEMANS RES LTD (BC)
Struck off register and declared dissolved for failure to file returns 2/25/83

LEMAY BK & TR CO (ST LOUIS, MO)
Under plan of reorganization each share Common $20 par automatically became (1) share LBT Bancshares, Inc. Common $20 par 07/14/1999
LBT Bancshares, Inc. name changed to Midwest BankCentre, Inc. 01/03/2000

LEMCKE (R.A.) REALTY CO. (IN)
Name changed to Consolidated Office Building, Inc. 2/12/57

LEMIEUX COPPER EXPLS LTD (QC)
Completely liquidated 07/18/1969
Each share Common $1 par exchanged for first and final distribution of (0.5) share Lemtex Developments Ltd. Common no par
Lemtex Developments Ltd. name changed to B.Y.G. Natural Resources Inc. 07/29/1982
(See B.Y.G. Natural Resources Inc.)

LEMKE B L & CO INC (NJ)
Merged into Lemke Chemicals, Inc. 3/13/71
Each share Common 50¢ par exchanged for $3 cash

LEMMING RES LTD (BC)
Recapitalized as Dimitra Developments Corp. 10/11/1994
Each share Common no par exchanged for (0.25) share Common no par
Dimitra Developments Corp. name changed to Jeda Petroleum Ltd. 08/22/1996 which merged into Roseland Resources Ltd. 02/29/2000 which merged into Rival Energy Ltd. 06/16/2003 which merged into Zargon Energy Trust 01/23/2008 which reorganized as Zargon Oil & Gas Ltd. (New) 01/07/2011

LEMMON PHARMACAL CO (PA)
Stock Dividend - 100% 07/31/1964
Name changed to L.P.C. Liquidating Co. 07/20/1972
(See L.P.C. Liquidating Co.)

LEMOINE CHIBOUGAMAU MINING CORP. (QC)
Dissolved in 1961
No stockholders' equity

LEMONT INC (NY)
Each share old Class A Common $0.0001 par exchanged for (0.00348432) share new Class A Common $0.0001 par 07/11/2017
Name changed to Smoke Cartel, Inc. 08/29/2017

LEMONTONIC INC (ON)
Recapitalized as Pioneering Technology Inc. 04/05/2006
Each share Common no par exchanged for (0.2) share Common no par
Pioneering Technology Inc. recapitalized as Pioneering Technology Corp. 09/18/2008

LEMP BREWING CO.
Name changed to EMS Brewing Co. in 1942
EMS Brewing Co. acquired by Columbia Brewing Co. in 1947 which was acquired by Falstaff Brewing Corp. (DE) in 1948
(See Falstaff Brewing Corp. (DE))

LEMP (WM. J.) BREWING CO.
Bankrupt in 1941

LEMTEX DEVS LTD (ON)
Name changed to B.Y.G. Natural Resources Inc. 07/29/1982
(See B.Y.G. Natural Resources Inc.)

LENA HORNE BEAUTY PRODUCTS, INC. (DE)
See - Horne (Lena) Beauty Products, Inc.

LENAHAN ALUMINUM WINDOW CORP. (FL)
Merged into Pacific Coast Co. (DE) 5/14/63
Each share Common exchanged for (1/3) share Common
(See Pacific Coast Co. (DE))

LENAPE ST BK (WEST DEPTFORD, NJ)
Acquired by Commercial Bancshares, Inc. (NJ) 11/27/85
Each share Capital Stock $10 par exchanged for (1.8375) shares Common $5 par
Commercial Bancshares, Inc. (NJ) merged into United Jersey Banks 12/1/86 which name changed to UJB Financial Corp. 6/30/89 which name changed to Summit Bancorp 3/1/96 which merged into FleetBoston Financial Corp. 3/1/2001 which merged into Bank of America Corp. 4/1/2004

LENAWEE BANCORP INC (MI)
Common $10 par split (2) for (1) by issuance of (1) additional share payable 07/30/1999 to holders of record 07/01/1999
Stock Dividend - 10% 09/30/1994
Name changed to Pavilion Bancorp, Inc. 04/22/2002
Pavilion Bancorp, Inc. merged into First Defiance Financial Corp. 03/17/2008

LENCE LANES, INC. (DE)
No longer in existence having become inoperative and void for non-payment of taxes 4/1/66

LENCO MOBILE INC (DE)
Plan of reorganization under Chapter 11 Federal Bankruptcy proceedings effective 12/29/2015
No stockholders' equity

LENCOURT GOLD MINES, LTD. (QC)
Recapitalized as Canadian Lencourt Mines Ltd. 01/19/1965
Each share Capital Stock $1 par exchanged for (0.25) share Capital Stock $1 par
Canadian Lencourt Mines Ltd.

recapitalized as Lencourt Ltd./Lencourt Ltee. 05/22/1987
(See Lencourt Ltd./Lencourt Ltee.)

LENCOURT LTD (QC)
Cease trade order effective 01/02/1996
Stockholders' equity unlikely

LEND LEASE LTD (AUSTRALIA)
Name changed to Lendlease Corp. Ltd. 12/10/2015

LENDER PROCESSING SVCS INC (DE)
Merged into Fidelity National Financial, Inc. (New) 01/02/2014
Each share Common $0.0001 par exchanged for (0.28742) share Class A Common $0.0001 par and $28.10 cash

LENDINGTREE INC (DE)
Issue Information - 3,650,000 shares COM offered at $12 per share on 02/15/2000
Merged into InterActiveCorp 8/8/2003
Each share Common 1¢ par exchanged for (0.6199) share Common 1¢ par
InterActiveCorp name changed to IAC/InterActiveCorp 7/14/2004

LENENERGO A O (RUSSIA)
ADR agreement terminated 06/08/2005
Each Sponsored ADR for Ordinary exchanged for $168.783647 cash

LENNARD OIL N L (AUSTRALIA)
ADR agreement terminated 01/11/1996
No ADR holders' equity

LENNIE RED LAKE GOLD MINES LTD (BC)
Reincorporated 05/29/1984
Common $1 par changed to no par 07/26/1974
Place of incorporation changed from (ON) to (BC) 05/29/1984
Recapitalized as Sun Valley Id., & Red Lake Resources Ltd. 05/29/1985
Each share Common no par exchanged for (0.2) share Common no par
Sun Valley Id., & Red Lake Resources Ltd. name changed to Red Lake & Sun Valley Resources Ltd. 09/04/1987 which recapitalized as International R.S.V. Resource Corp. 12/27/1989 which recapitalized as Harambee Mining Corp. 05/05/1997 which recapitalized as Neuer Kapital Corp. 01/03/2002 which name changed to Crescent Resources Corp. 08/03/2005 which recapitalized as Coventry Resources Inc. 01/09/2013
(See Coventry Resources Inc.)

LENNOC VENTURES INC (NV)
Name changed to Wireless Age Communications Inc. 10/23/2002
Each share Common no par exchanged for (5) shares Common no par

LENNOX HOTEL CO. (MO)
Under plan of merger name changed to Mayfair-Lennox Hotels, Inc. 3/31/62
(See Mayfair-Lennox Hotels, Inc.)

LENOIR FINANCE CO. (NC)
Acquired by Sterling Discount Corp. 4/1/62
Each share Common $10 par exchanged for (1) share Common $1 par and $8 cash
(See Sterling Discount Corp.)

LENORA EXPLS LTD (ON)
Merged into Greater Lenora Resources Corp. (ON) 01/05/1989
Each share Common no par exchanged for (0.25) share Common no par
Greater Lenora Resources Corp.

(ON) reincorporated in Canada 05/03/2001
(See Greater Lenora Resources Corp.)

LENOX BANCORP INC (OH)
Name changed to Lenox Wealth Management Inc. 11/16/2004

LENOX FD (DE)
Acquired by Bayrock Growth Fund, Inc. 4/24/74
Each share Common $1 par exchanged for (1.01) shares Common 10¢ par
Bayrock Growth Fund, Inc. acquired by Affiliated Fund, Inc. (DE) 9/3/75 which reincorporated in Maryland 11/26/75

LENOX GROUP INC (DE)
Plan of reorganization under Chapter 11 Federal Bankruptcy proceedings effective 12/31/2009
No stockholders' equity

LENOX INC (NJ)
Common $2.50 par split (3) for (2) by issuance of (0.5) additional share 6/16/64
Common $2.50 par split (3) for (2) by issuance of (0.5) additional share 12/27/68
Common $2.50 par changed to $1.25 par and (1) additional share issued 12/30/70
Common $1.25 par changed to $1 par and (1) additional share issued 7/1/83
Merged into Brown-Forman Distillers Corp. 8/1/83
Each share Common $1 par exchanged for $45 cash

LENOX POLYMERS LTD (ON)
Delisted from Canadian Dealer Network 10/3/2000

LENTEC IMAGING INC (UT)
Reorganized under the laws of Nevada as RTO Holdings, Inc. 06/21/2006
Each share Common no par exchanged for (0.001) share Common $0.001 par
Note: Holders of between (100) and (99,999) shares received (100) shares
Holders of (99) or fewer shares were not affected
RTO Holdings, Inc. name changed to Orion Ethanol, Inc. 11/07/2006

LENWOOD MINING & EXPLORATIONS, LTD. (ON)
Charter revoked for failure to file reports and pay fees 7/8/65

LENZING AG (AUSTRIA)
ADR agreement terminated 3/21/2003
Each Sponsored ADR for Ordinary 100 Schillings par exchanged for $42.3641 cash

LEO RES INC (BC)
Incorporated 03/13/2013
Each share old Common no par exchanged for (0.2) share new Common no par 05/21/2014
Each share new Common no par exchanged again for (0.2) share new Common no par 05/04/2017
Name changed to Global Health Clinics Ltd. 08/29/2018

LEO RES INC (BC)
Incorporated 00/00/1980
Name changed to Uni-Globe International Energy Corp. 03/03/1986
(See Uni-Globe International Energy Corp.)

LEON LD & CATTLE CO (TX)
5% Preferred no par called for redemption 10/15/1957
Merged into Dixel Industries Inc. 04/01/1971
Each share Common 10¢ par

exchanged for (1.2) shares Common 10¢ par
Dixel Industries Inc. name changed to Weatherford International Inc. (Old) 02/17/1975 which recapitalized as Weatherford Enterra, Inc. 10/05/1995 which merged into EVI Weatherford, Inc. 05/27/1998 which name changed to Weatherford International Inc. (New) (DE) 09/21/1998 which reincorporated in Bermuda as Weatherford International Ltd. 06/26/2002 which reincorporated in Switzerland 02/25/2009 which reincorporated in Ireland as Weatherford International PLC 06/18/2014

LEONA ENTERPRISES INC (DE)
Charter cancelled and declared inoperative and void for non-payment of taxes 3/1/93

LEONARD, FITZPATRICK MUELLER STORES CO.
Acquired by National Bellas Hess Co., Inc. in 1929
Details not available

LEONARD INVESTMENTS CORP. (IA)
Charter cancelled for failure to file annual reports 11/23/81

LEONARD OIL DEV CO (DE)
Charter cancelled and declared inoperative and void for non-payment of taxes 7/1/49

LEONARD REFINERIES INC (MI)
Each (3) shares Common $1 par exchanged for (1) share Common $3 par in 1939
Merged into Total Petroleum (North America) Ltd. 10/2/70
Each share Common $3 par exchanged for (1) share 70¢ Non-Cum. Conv. Preferred Ser. A $20 par (U.S.)
(See Total Petroleum (North America) Ltd.)

LEONARD SILVER INTL INC (MA)
Reincorporated 4/5/77
State of incorporation changed from (NY) to (MA) 4/5/77
Common 1¢ par split (3) for (2) by issuance of (0.5) additional share 2/1/78
Completely liquidated 9/11/78
Each share Common 1¢ par exchanged for first and final distribution of (1/3) share Preferred Ser. A $1 par and (2/3) share Common no par of Towle Manufacturing Co.
(See Towle Manufacturing Co.)

LEONARDO FINMECCANICA S P A (ITALY)
Name changed to Leonardo S.p.A. 01/06/2017

LEONIDAS FILMS INC (NV)
Recapitalized as Consolidated Pictures Group, Inc. 06/09/2009
Each share Common 1¢ par exchanged for (0.04) share Common 1¢ par
(See Consolidated Pictures Group, Inc.)

LEONIDS INVTS INC (CANADA)
Name changed to iWeb Group Inc. 08/25/2004
(See iWeb Group Inc.)

LEONORA MINING & MILLING CO. (UT)
Each share Common 10¢ par exchanged for (0.1) share Common no par 8/28/63
Merged into Moviematic Industries, Corp. 2/1/66
Each share Common no par exchanged for (1) share Common no par

LEOPARD CAP INC (NV)
Each share old Common $0.001 par

exchanged for (0.1) share new Common $0.001 par 04/24/2003
Note: Holders of (999) or fewer pre-split shares will receive (100) post-split shares
Each share new Common $0.001 par exchanged again for (1.3) shares new Common $0.001 par 12/29/2003
Name changed to China Expert Technology, Inc. 03/29/2004
(See China Expert Technology, Inc.)

LEOPARD HLDGS INC (TX)
Name changed to Passport Restaurants, Inc. (TX) 07/21/2003
Passport Restaurants, Inc. (TX) reincorporated in Delaware as Pacific Restaurant Holdings, Inc. 03/30/2009
(See Pacific Restaurant Holdings, Inc.)

LEOPARDUS RES LTD (BC)
Merged into Zarara Oil & Gas Ltd. (Channel Islands) 02/12/1999
Each share Common no par exchanged for (1) share Common no par
Zarara Oil & Gas Ltd. (Channel Islands) reorganized in Wyoming as Zara Trading, Inc. 03/05/2007
(See Zara Trading, Inc.)

LEORA MINERALS LTD. (BC)
Completely liquidated 10/15/69
Each share Common 50¢ par exchanged for (0.15) share Ulster Petroleums Ltd. Capital Stock no par 10/15/69
Ulstar Petroleums Ltd. merged into Anderson Exploration Ltd. 5/23/2000
(See Anderson Exploration Ltd.)

LEOS INDS INC (DE)
Charter cancelled and declared inoperative and void for non-payment of taxes 03/01/1993

LEP GROUP PLC (ENGLAND & WALES)
ADR agreement terminated 00/00/1992
Details not available

LEPAGE A E CAP PPTYS (ON)
Name changed to Royal LePage Capital Properties 12/16/1985
(See Royal LePage Capital Properties)

LEPANTO CONS MNG CO (PHILIPPINES)
ADR agreement terminated 03/13/2018
No ADR's remain outstanding

LEPAS FLIN FLON MINES LTD. (ON)
Charter cancelled for failure to file reports and pay taxes in 1958

LEPERCQ ISTEL TR (DE)
Acquired by Tocqueville Trust 7/9/2002
Each share Leperq Istel Fund $1 par exchanged for approximately (0.8353286) share Tocqueville Fund Class A 1¢ par

LEPINE LAKE GOLD MINES LTD. (ON)
Acquired by Courville Mines Ltd. 12/31/1964
Each share Capital Stock $1 par exchanged for (0.025) share Capital Stock $1 par
(See Courville Mines Ltd.)

LEQUER MINES & INVESTMENTS LTD. (ON)
Name changed to Mobilex Development Corp. Ltd. and Capital Stock $1 par changed to no par 10/28/70
(See Mobilex Development Corp. Ltd.)

LEQUER MINES LTD. (ON)
Name changed to Lequer Mines & Investments Ltd. 6/19/69
Lequer Mines & Investments Ltd.

name changed to Mobilex Development Corp. Ltd. 10/28/70
(See Mobilex Development Corp. Ltd.)

LERNER MARKETS, INC. (PA)
Liquidated 11/09/1962
Class A Common $1 par surrendered for 16¢ per share
Class B Common $1 par has no value

LERNER STORES CORP (MD)
Each share old Common no par exchanged for (2) shares new Common no par in 1936
Stock Dividend - 200% 11/25/44
New Common no par split (4) for (1) by issuance of (3) additional shares 11/1/65
4-1/2% Preferred $100 par called for redemption 10/6/67
Merged into McCrory Corp. 9/18/73
Each share Common no par exchanged for $50 principal amount of 7-3/4% Subord. S.F. Debentures due 9/15/95 and $8 cash

LERNOULT INVT FD INC (MD)
Auction Market Preferred Ser. A 144A called for redemption at $100,000 on 11/25/98
Auction Market Preferred Ser. B 144A called for redemption at $100,000 on 12/2/98
Auction Market Preferred Ser. C 144A called for redemption at $100,000 on 12/9/98

LERNOUT & HAUSPIE SPEECH PRODS N V (BELGIUM)
Common no par split (2) for (1) by issuance of (1) additional share payable 04/15/1998 to holders of record 04/01/1998
Common no par split (2) for (1) by issuance of (1) additional share payable 04/28/2000 to holders of record 04/19/2000
Plan of reorganization under Chapter 11 Federal Bankruptcy Code effective 04/02/2004
No stockholders' equity

LERO GOLD CORP (BC)
Merged into European Minerals Corp. (British Virgin Islands) 06/19/2008
Each share Common no par exchanged for (1) share Common
Note: Unexchanged certificates were cancelled and became without value 06/19/2014
European Minerals Corp. (British Virgin Islands) name changed to Orsu Metals Corp. 07/14/2008

LEROY MINING CORP. LTD. (QC)
No results obtained and went out of existence 03/00/1962
Stockholders' equity unlikely

LEROY PHARMACIES INC (NY)
Name changed to Accuhealth, Inc. 8/15/90
(See Accuhealth, Inc.)

LEROY PPTYS & DEV CORP (NV)
Name changed 9/28/76
Name changed from Leroy Corp. to Leroy Properties & Development Corp. 9/28/76
Charter revoked for failure to file reports and pay fees 8/1/96

LEROY VENTURES INC (BC)
Name changed to Unbridled Energy Corp. 07/20/2006
Unbridled Energy Corp. merged into Altima Resources Ltd. 02/11/2010

LES ENTREPRISES MICROTEC INC (QC)
Plan of arrangement effective 06/21/2005
Each share Subordinate no par exchanged for (0.2501202) First National AlarmCap Income Fund Class A Trust Unit
(See First National AlarmCap Income Fund)

LES INDS CHARAN INC (CANADA)
Common no par split (2) for (1) by issuance of (1) additional share 12/22/1986
Dissolved 00/00/1993
Stockholders' equity undetermined

LES LAITERIES LECLERC INC (QC)
Acquired by La Societe de Cooperative Agricola de Granby 06/16/1972
Each share Class A no par exchanged for $8.70 principal amount of debenture maturing 00/00/1981 and $3.47 cash

LES MINES D ARGENT ABCOURT INC (QC)
Name changed to Abcourt Mines Inc.-Mines Abcourt Inc. 04/23/1985

LES MINES D OR THOMPSON BOUSQUET LTEE (QC)
Merged into Long Lac Minerals Ltd. 11/02/1981
Each share Capital Stock $1 par exchanged for (1.25) shares Common $1 par
Long Lac Minerals Ltd. merged into Lac Minerals Ltd. (Old) 12/31/1982 which merged into LAC Minerals Ltd. (New) 07/29/1985 which was acquired by American Barrick Resources Corp. 10/17/1994 which name changed to Barrick Gold Corp. 01/18/1995

LES MINES EST MALARTIC LTEE (QC)
Merged into Lac Minerals Ltd. (Old) 12/31/1982
Each share Capital Stock $1 par exchanged for (0.94) share Common no par and $0.01 Promissory Note payable within one year
Lac Minerals Ltd. (Old) merged into LAC Minerals Ltd. (New) 07/29/1985 which was acquired by American Barrick Resources Corp. 10/17/1994 which name changed to Barrick Gold Corp. 01/18/1995

LES RESSOURCES CAMCHIB INC.- CAMCHIB RESOURCES INC. (QC)
See - Camchib Res Inc

LES TERRAINS AURIFERES MALARTIC QUE LTEE (QC)
Merged into Lac Minerals Ltd. (Old) 12/31/1982
Each share Capital Stock $1 par exchanged for (0.84) share Common no par and $0.01 Promissory Note payable within one year
Lac Minerals Ltd. (Old) merged into LAC Minerals Ltd. (New) 07/29/1985 which was acquired by American Barrick Resources Corp. 10/17/1994 which name changed to Barrick Gold Corp. 01/18/1995

LESCARDEN, LTD. (NY)
Name changed to Lescarden Inc. 1/12/83

LESCO INC (OH)
Common no par split (2) for (1) by issuance of (1) additional share 04/15/1986
Common no par split (3) for (2) by issuance of (0.5) additional share 07/30/1993
Common Stock Purchase Rights declared for Common stockholders of record 05/31/2001 were redeemed at $0.01 per right 09/10/2001 for holders of record 08/24/2001
Merged into Deere & Co. 05/07/2007
Each share Common no par exchanged for $14.50 cash

LESLIE BLDG PROD INC (DE)
Name changed to LBP Inc. 6/19/98
(See LBP Inc.)

LESLIE-CALIFORNIA SALT CO.
Merged into Leslie Salt Co. in 1936
Each share old Capital Stock exchanged for (1) share new Capital Stock $10 par
(See Leslie Salt Co.)

LESLIE FAY COS INC OLD (DE)
Plan of reorganization under Chapter 11 Federal Bankruptcy Code effective 6/4/97
No stockholders' equity

LESLIE FAY INC (NY)
Class A $1 par split (3) for (2) by issuance of (0.5) additional share 7/15/65
Class A $1 par reclassified as Common $1 par 9/12/68
Common $1 par split (3) for (2) by issuance of (0.5) additional share 4/21/71
Name changed to Fayless Investors, Inc. 4/30/82
(See Fayless Investors, Inc.)

LESLIE FAY INC NEW (DE)
Common 1¢ par split (2) for (1) by issuance of (1) additional share payable 7/1/98 to holders of record 6/17/98
Acquired by TCR Acquisition 8/25/99
Each share Common 1¢ par exchanged for $7 cash
Note: Cash was paid for 77.8% of total holdings surrendered with the balance of shares retained by holder
Option to receive cash expired 8/17/99
Acquired by Three Cities Research 11/20/2001
Each share Common 1¢ par exchanged for $5 cash

LESLIE GOLD MINES LTD (SOUTH AFRICA)
Merged into Evander Gold Mines Ltd. 11/18/96
Each ADR for Ordinary Rand-1 par exchanged for (0.58825) ADR for Ordinary Rand-1 par
Evander Gold Mines Ltd. merged into Harmony Gold Mining Co. Ltd. 8/28/98

LESLIE OIL & GAS LTD (BC)
Struck off register and declared dissolved for failure to file returns 5/27/88

LESLIE PRODUCTIONS, INC. (SC)
Name changed to Columbia Films, Inc. and Common $1 par changed to 25¢ par 10/01/1958
(See Columbia Films, Inc.)

LESLIE SALT CO (DE)
Capital Stock $10 par split (2) for (1) by issuance of (1) additional share 02/10/1976
Merged into Cargill Inc. 05/31/1978
Each share Capital Stock $10 par exchanged for $40 cash

LESLIES POOLMART INC (CA)
Acquired by Hancock Park Associates II L.P. 6/11/97
Each share Common no par exchanged for $14.50 cash

LESON MICHAEL DESIGNS LTD (DE)
Recapitalized as Diversified Foods Inc. 01/29/1987
Each (27) shares Common $0.001 par exchanged for (1) share Common $0.001 par
(See Diversified Foods Inc.)

LESS MESS STORAGE INC (BC)
Acquired by Less Mess Holdings Inc. 12/14/2015
Each share Common no par exchanged for $1.415 cash
Note: Unexchanged certificates will be cancelled and become without value 12/14/2021

LESSARD BEAUCAGE LEMIEUX INC (CANADA)
Name changed to LBL Skysystems Corp. 08/13/1998
(See LBL Skysystems Corp.)

LESSER (LOUIS) ENTERPRISES, INC. (DE)
Name changed to Western Orbis Co. 11/20/1967
(See Western Orbis Co.)

LESSONWARE LTD (YT)
Delisted from Vancouver Stock Exchange 03/04/1994

LESSTUDS CORP (NY)
Name changed to Trans Southern Holding Corp. 02/11/1970
(See Trans Southern Holding Corp.)

LESTOIL PRODS INC (DE)
Merged into Standard International Corp. 11/19/1964
Each share Common 50¢ par exchanged for (1/3) share Common no par
Class A no par called for redemption 12/15/1964
Standard International Corp. name changed to Standex International Corp. (OH) 07/24/1973 which reincorporated in Delaware 06/30/1975

LETCHWORTH INDPT BANCSHARES CORP (NY)
Common $1 par split (3) for (1) by issuance of (2) additional shares payable 6/8/98 to holders of record 5/8/98
Merged into Tompkins Trustco, Inc. 12/31/99
Each share Common $1 par exchanged for (0.685) share Common 10¢ par
Tompkins Trustco, Inc. name changed to Tompkins Financial Corp. 6/4/2007

LETHBRIDGE BREWERIES, LTD.
Acquired by Associated Breweries of Canada, Ltd. in 1928
Details not available

LETOURNEAU R G INC (CA)
Stock Dividend - 400% 10/15/65
Name changed to Marathon LeTourneau Co. 8/13/71
Marathon LeTourneau Co. merged into Marathon Manufacturing Co. 11/1/71 which merged into Penn Central Corp. 12/18/79 which name changed to American Premier Underwriters, Inc. 3/25/94 which merged into American Premier Group, Inc. 4/3/95 which name changed to American Financial Group, Inc. 6/9/95 which merged into American Financial Group, Inc. (Holding Co) 12/2/97

LETS GOWEX S A (SPAIN)
Stock Dividend - 400% payable 04/10/2013 to holders of record 04/05/2013 Ex date - 04/11/2013
ADR agreement terminated 05/31/2016
ADR holders' equity unlikely

LETS TALK CELLULAR & WIRELESS INC (FL)
Issue Information - 2,337,245 shares COM offered at $12 per share on 11/24/1997
Plan of reorganization under Chapter 11 Federal Bankruptcy Code effective 5/1/2001
No stockholders' equity

LETS TALK RECOVERY INC (DE)
Reorganized under the laws of Nevada as Columbia Energy Corp. 11/26/2010
Each share Common 1¢ par exchanged for (0.01) share Common $0.001 par
Columbia Energy Corp. name changed to Cornwall Resources, Inc. 04/16/2012

LEUCADIA INC. (NY)
Jr. Preferred Ser. A 50¢ par called for redemption 03/26/1982
Public interest eliminated

LEUCADIA NATL CORP (NY)
Common $1 par split (2) for (1) by issuance of (1) additional share 04/06/1983
$5.50 Conv. Preferred Ser. C $1 par called for redemption 04/07/1983
$1.85 Preferred Ser. E $1 par called for redemption 10/01/1984
Common $1 par split (3) for (2) by issuance of (0.5) additional share 02/14/1985
$2 Conv. Exchangeable Preferred Ser. F $1 par called for redmption 04/15/1985
Common $1 par split (2) for (1) by issuance of (1) additional share 01/06/1987
Common $1 par split (2) for (1) by issuance of (1) additional share 01/08/1993
Common $1 par split (2) for (1) by issuance of (1) additional share 11/15/1995
Common $1 par split (3) for (2) by issuance of (0.5) additional share payable 12/31/2004 to holders of record 12/23/2004 Ex date - 01/03/2005
Common $1 par split (2) for (1) by issuance of (1) additional share payable 06/14/2006 to holders of record 05/30/2006 Ex date - 06/15/2006
Each share Common $1 par received distribution of (0.1) share Crimson Wine Group, Ltd. Common 1¢ par payable 02/25/2013 to holders of record 02/11/2013 Ex date - 02/26/2013
Name changed to Jefferies Financial Group Inc. 05/24/2018

LEUKOSITE INC (DE)
Issue Information - 2,500,000 shares COM offered at $6 per share on 08/15/1997
Merged into Millennium Pharmaceuticals, Inc. 12/23/1999
Each share Common 1¢ par exchanged for (0.4296) share Common 1¢ par
(See Millennium Pharmaceuticals, Inc.)

LEV PHARMACEUTICALS INC (DE)
Merged into ViroPharma Inc. 10/21/2008
Each share Common 1¢ par exchanged for (0.042146) share Common $0.002 par, (1) Contingent Value Right and $2.25 cash
Note: Each Contingent Value Right received $0.50 cash 08/17/2012
(See ViroPharma Inc.)

LEV SCIENTIFIC INDS LTD (BC)
Common no par split (3) for (1) by issuance of (2) additional shares 9/18/86
Cease trade order effective 3/16/93
Stockholders' equity unlikely

LEVACK MINES LTD (ON)
Name changed 02/00/1964
Name changed from Levack Nickel Mines Ltd. to Levack Mines Ltd. 02/00/1964
Charter cancelled for failure to pay taxes and file returns 09/05/1979

LEVEL 8 SYS INC (DE)
Reincorporated 06/23/1999
State of incorporation changed from (NY) to (DE) and Common 1¢ par changed to $0.001 par 06/23/1999
Recapitalized as Cicero, Inc. 01/16/2007
Each share Common $0.001 par exchanged for (0.01) share Common $0.001 par

LEVEL JUMP FINL GROUP INC (FL)
SEC revoked common stock registration 02/15/2006

LEVEL ONE COMMUNICATIONS INC (CA)
Common no par split (3) for (2) by issuance of (0.5) additional share 1/20/94
Common no par split (3) for (2) by issuance of (0.5) additional share payable 8/26/97 to holders of record 8/15/97
Common no par split (3) for (2) by issuance of (0.5) additional share payable 3/30/98 to holders of record 3/9/98
Merged into Intel Corp. 8/10/99
Each share Common no par exchanged for (0.86) share Common $0.001 par

LEVEL 3 COMMUNICATIONS INC (DE)
Old Common 1¢ par split (2) for (1) by issuance of (1) additional share payable 08/07/1998 to holders of record 07/30/1998
Each share old Common 1¢ par exchanged for (0.06666666) share new Common 1¢ par 10/20/2011
Merged into CenturyLink, Inc. 11/01/2017
Each share new Common 1¢ par exchanged for (1.4286) shares Common $1 par and $26.50 cash

LEVELLAND ENERGY & RES LTD (BC)
Recapitalized as Endeavour Gold Corp. 8/27/2002
Each share Common no par exchanged for (0.25) share Common no par
Endeavour Gold Corp. name changed to Endeavour Silver Corp. 9/13/2004

LEVEL20 INC (NV)
Name changed to Spriza, Inc. 11/07/2013

LEVENGOOD OIL & GAS INC (CANADA)
Recapitalized as Fortune Resources Corp. 08/08/1995
Each share Common no par exchanged for (1/6) share Common no par
(See Fortune Resources Corp.)

LEVERAGE FD BOSTON INC (MA)
Under plan of reorganization each Capital Share $1 par automatically became (1) share Common $1 par 01/04/1982
Under plan of reorganization each Income Share $1 par automatically became (1) share Common $1 par 01/04/1982
Common $1 par changed to 33-1/3¢ par and (2) additional shares issued 08/06/1982
Merged into Eaton Vance Special Equities Fund, Inc. 06/00/1989
Each share Common 33-1/3¢ par exchanged for (0.32200516) share Common $1 par
Eaton Vance Special Equities Fund, Inc. name changed to Eaton Vance Special Investment Trust 07/21/1992

LEVERAGE FIXED TRUST SHARES
Trust terminated in 1936
Details not available

LEVERAGE FUND OF CANADA LTD. (CANADA)
Name changed to Commonwealth International Leverage Fund Ltd. 7/26/60
Commonwealth International Leverage Fund Ltd. name changed to Eaton Leverage Fund Ltd. 4/15/74 which name changed to Eaton/Bay Leverage Fund Ltd. 4/12/78

LEVERICH REALTY CORP. (NY)
Proclaimed dissolved 12/15/36

LEVESQUE BEAUBIEN & CO (QC)
Merged into National Bank of Canada (Montreal, QC) 10/31/1988
Each share Class A Subordinate no par exchanged for (0.3) share Common no par and $3.075 cash

LEVI DEVS INC (BC)
Recapitalized as R.I.S. Resources International Corp. 6/9/94
Each share Common no par exchanged for (1/6) share Common no par
R.I.S. Resources International Corp. recapitalized as Ultra Holdings Inc. 12/1/99
(See Ultra Holdings Inc.)

LEVI STRAUSS & CO (DE)
Common $1 par split (2) for (1) by issuance of (1) additional share 7/30/76
Common $1 par split (2) for (1) by issuance of (1) additional share 1/2/80
Merged into HHF Corp. 8/30/85
Each share Common $1 par exchanged for $50 cash

LEVIATHAN GAS PIPELINE PARTNERS L P (DE)
Common Unit split (2) for (1) by issuance of (1) additional share payable 1/15/97 to holders of record 12/31/96 Ex date - 1/16/97
Name changed to El Paso Energy Partners, L.P. 11/30/99
El Paso Energy Partners, L.P. name changed to Gulfterra Energy Partners, L.P. 5/15/2003 which merged into Enterprise Products Partners L.P. 9/30/2004

LEVIATHAN INTL LTD (FL)
Proclaimed dissolved for failure to file reports and pay fees 10/ /92

LEVIN COMPUTER CORP. (NJ)
Common no par split (2) for (1) by issuance of (1) additional share 7/16/79
Name changed to Levin International Corp. 10/4/84
(See Levin International Corp.)

LEVIN INTL CORP (NJ)
Charter declared void for non-payment of taxes 6/26/90

LEVIN TOWNSEND COMPUTER CORP (NJ)
Common 50¢ par changed to 25¢ par and (1) additional share issued 2/7/66
Common 25¢ par split (3) for (2) by issuance of (0.5) additional share 7/18/68
Name changed to Rockwood Computer Corp. 8/24/71
Rockwood Computer Corp. reorganized as Rockwood National Corp. 8/8/73
(See Rockwood National Corp.)

LEVIN TOWNSEND SVC CORP (NJ)
Name changed to Tolley International Corp. (NJ) 1/12/71
Tolley International Corp. (NJ) reincorporated in Delaware 3/31/76 which name changed to TIC International Corp. 11/6/81
(See TIC International Corp.)

LEVINE'S, INC. (TX)
Acquired by Zale Corp. 12/29/66
Each share Common $4 par exchanged for (0.28) share 4% Conv. Preferred $25 par and (0.5) share Common $1 par

LEVINGSTON SHIPBUILDING CO. (DE)
Common $6 par changed to $2 par and (2) additional shares issued 11/14/1969
Merged into Ashland Oil, Inc. 09/10/1975
Each share Common $2 par exchanged for (0.9) share Common $1 par
Ashland Oil, Inc. name changed to Ashland Inc. (Old) 01/27/1995
(See Ashland Inc. (Old))

LEVITT & SONS, INC. (NY)
Merged into International Telephone & Telegraph Corp. (DE) 2/1/68
Each share Capital Stock 70¢ par exchanged for (0.285) share Common $1 par
International Telephone & Telegraph Corp. (DE) name changed to ITT Corp. 12/31/83 which reorganized in Indiana as ITT Industries, Inc. 12/19/95 which name changed to ITT Corp. 7/1/2006

LEVITT CORP (FL)
Name changed to Woodbridge Holdings Corp. 05/20/2008
Woodbridge Holdings Corp. merged into BFC Financial Corp. 09/22/2009 which name changed to BBX Capital Corp. (New) 02/03/2017

LEVITT CORP (MD)
Merged into Starrett Housing Corp. 01/19/1989
Each share Common 5¢ par exchanged for (1) share Common $1 par
Starrett Housing Corp. name changed to Starrett Corp. 06/23/1995
(See Starrett Corp.)

LEVITT INDS INC (MA)
Merged into Optel Corp. 06/30/1978
Each share Common 50¢ par exchanged for $10.8788 cash
Note: An additional distribution of $0.5742 cash per share was paid from escrow 07/27/1978

LEVITZ FURNITURE CORP (PA)
Common 10¢ par split (2) for (1) by issuance of (1) additional share 2/14/69
Common 10¢ par split (2) for (1) by issuance of (1) additional share 6/18/71
Common 10¢ par split (3) for (1) by issuance of (2) additional shares 4/21/72
Each share Common 10¢ par exchanged for (0.25) share Common 40¢ par 8/17/77
Common 40¢ par split (2) for (1) by issuance of (1) additional share 8/1/83
Merged into LFC Holding Corp. 6/26/85
Each share Common 40¢ par exchanged for $39 cash

LEVITZ FURNITURE INC (DE)
Plan of reorganization under Chapter 11 Federal Bankruptcy proceedings confirmed 12/14/2000
No stockholders' equity

LEVON RES LTD OLD (BC)
Reorganized as SciVac Therapeutics Inc. 07/14/2015
Each share Common no par exchanged for (1) share Common no par and (0.5) share Levon Resources Ltd. (New) Common no par
(See each company's listing)

LEVTECH MED TECHNOLOGIES LTD (BC)
Struck off register and declared dissolved for failure to file returns 5/28/93

LEVY ACQUISITION CORP (DE)
Name changed to Del Taco Restaurants, Inc. 07/01/2015

LEVY ADLER COHEN LTD (NY)
Name changed to Lac Industries Ltd. 10/19/1972
(See Lac Industries Ltd.)

LEVY BANCORP (CA)
6% Non-Cum. Centennial Participating Preferred $0.125 par split (8) for (1) by issuance of (7) additional shares 08/31/1987
Common $5 par split (8) for (1) by issuance of (7) additional shares 08/31/1987
Merged into First Interstate Bancorp 01/31/1995
Each share 6% Non-Cum. Centennial

Participating Preferred $0.125 par exchanged for $0.125 cash
Each share Common $5 par exchanged for (0.457262) share Common $2 par
Note: Each share 6% Non-Cum. Centennial Participating Preferred $0.125 par received an additional distribution of $0.125 cash 03/23/1995
First Interstate Bancorp merged into Wells Fargo & Co. (Old) 04/01/1996 which merged into Wells Fargo & Co. (New) 11/02/1998

LEVY BROS. & ADLER ROCHESTER, INC. (NY)
Liquidation completed in 1954

LEVY INDS LTD (ON)
7% 1st Preference Class A $20 par called for redemption 5/15/63
5-1/2% Conv. Class B Preference $20 par called for redemption 6/27/69
6% 2nd Preference $12 par reclassified as 6% Class A Preference $12 par 5/5/64
Placed in receivership 4/2/87
Stockholders' equity undetermined

LEW CORP (NV)
Each share old Common $0.001 par exchanged for (0.1) share new Common $0.001 par 03/20/2007
Name changed to Vintage Energy & Exploration, Inc. 10/02/2007
(See Vintage Energy & Exploration, Inc.)

LEWERS & COOKE LTD. (HI)
Common $20 par changed to $10 par and (1) additional share issued 4/20/59
Common $10 par changed to $5 par and (1) additional share issued 9/23/60
Name changed to L & C Ltd. 5/21/65
L & C Ltd. merged into Dillingham Corp. 3/5/68
(See Dillingham Corp.)

LEWES RIV MINES LTD (BC)
Recapitalized as Olympian International Resources Ltd. 10/9/73
Each share Common $1 par exchanged for (1/6) share Common no par
(See Olympian International Resources Ltd.)

LEWIS & KAUFMAN ELECTRONICS CORP. (CA)
Name changed to Cascade Research Corp. 11/5/62
Cascade Research Corp. name changed to Evergreen Western 10/23/63 which merged into S.O. Systems, Inc. (Calif.) 11/27/64 which was acquired by Kalvar Corp. (La.) 4/3/68 which reincorporated in Delaware 11/12/81
(See Kalvar Corp. (Del.))

LEWIS (A.T.) & SON DRY GOODS CO.
Bankrupt in 1933

LEWIS AMERICAN AIRWAYS, INC. (CO)
Placed in receivership 5/10/40
No stockholders' equity

LEWIS BROOK RES LTD (ON)
Merged into ChondroGene Ltd. 6/27/2000
Each share Common no par exchanged for (1) share Common no par
ChondroGene Ltd. name changed to GeneNews Ltd. 10/26/2006

LEWIS BUSINESS FORMS, INC. (FL)
Common $1 par split (3) for (2) by issuance of (0.5) additional share 3/15/68
Common $1 par split (1.333) for (1) by issuance of (0.333) additional share 4/15/74
Common $1 par split (5) for (4) by issuance of (0.25) additional share 4/30/75
Stock Dividend - 25% 3/17/67
Reincorporated under the laws of Delaware as Lewis Business Products, Inc. 3/1/77
Lewis Business Products, Inc. merged into Duplex Products Inc. 1/31/78
(See Duplex Products Inc.)

LEWIS BUSINESS PRODS INC (DE)
Merged into Duplex Products Inc. 1/31/78
Each share Common $1 par exchanged for (0.362) share $1.45 Conv. Preferred Ser. A $1 par or $8.50 cash
Option to receive $8.50 cash expired 2/21/78
(See Duplex Products Inc.)

LEWIS (E.L.) CO., INC. (SC)
Acquired by Mac (W.W.) Co. 12/01/1960
Details not available

LEWIS EDGAR P & SONS INC (MA)
Conv. Preferred $10 par called for redemption 11/01/1946
Common no par exchanged (3) for (1) 00/00/1937
Common no par changed to $1 par 09/28/1956
Company believed out of business 11/17/1971
Details not available

LEWIS ENERGY CORP (CO)
Charter cancelled and proclaimed dissolved for failure to file annual reports 9/30/88

LEWIS (TILLIE) FOODS, INC. (CA)
Merged into Ogden Corp. in September 1967
Each share Common $1 par exchanged for $16 cash

LEWIS GROUP LTD (SOUTH AFRICA)
ADR agreement terminated 05/21/2018
No ADR's remain outstanding

LEWIS JONES MANAGEMENT CO. (PA)
See - Jones (Lewis) Management Co.

LEWIS MORRIS APARTMENTS, INC. (NY)
See - Morris (Lewis) Apartments, Inc.

LEWIS OIL CORP. (DE)
Incorporated 3/28/21
No longer in existence having become inoperative and void for non-payment of taxes 4/1/30

LEWIS OIL CORP. (DE)
Incorporated 9/8/32
No longer in existence having become inoperative and void for non-payment of taxes 4/1/36

LEWIS PALMER G INC (WA)
Common $2.50 par changed to $1.66-2/3 par and (0.5) additional share issued 06/30/1972
Common $1.66-2/3 par changed to $1 par and (1) additional share issued 06/25/1976
Stock Dividend - 25% 05/16/1978
Acquired by Crane Co. 08/18/1988
Each share Common $1 par exchanged for $11 cash

LEWIS PUBLISHING CO. (SD)
Charter expired by time limitation 4/16/23

LEWIS RED LAKE MINES LTD (ON)
Name changed to Arcap Diversified Inc. 06/01/1973
Arcap Diversified Inc. recapitalized as First United Capital Corp. 10/25/1982
(See First United Capital Corp.)

LEWIS REFRIG CO (WA)
Common $2 par changed to 66-2/3¢ par and (2) additional shares issued 07/01/1968
Merged into Refrigeration Holdings Ltd. 03/11/1974
Each share Common 66-2/3¢ par exchanged for $3.50 cash

LEWIS RES INC (NV)
Recapitalized as Israel Semiconductor Corp. 11/30/1993
Each share Common $0.001 par exchanged for (0.16666666) share Common $0.001 par
Israel Semiconductor Corp. name changed to International Semiconductor Corp. 07/05/1994 which name changed to Sanitary Environmental Monitoring Labs, Inc. 04/12/2000 which recapitalized as Vietnam United Steel Corp. 08/28/2008 which recapitalized as Vietnam Mining Corp. 07/12/2010 which name changed to Vanguard Mining Corp. 06/03/2014 which name changed to Myson Group, Inc. 06/08/2015

LEWIS TOTAL MARKETING GROUP INC (NY)
Name changed to Radix Ventures, Inc. 12/2/75
(See Radix Ventures, Inc.)

LEWIS WELDING & ENGR CORP (OH)
Common $1 par changed to no par 12/28/1963
Merged into McDowell-Wellman Engineering Co. 11/30/1971
Each share Common no par exchanged for (1) share Class A Common $5 par
(See McDowell-Wellman Engineering Co.)

LEWIS WHARF CO. (MA)
Liquidation for cash completed 10/15/63

LEWISBURG BRIDGE CO.
Acquired by Pennsylvania Railroad Co. 00/00/1944
Details not available

LEWISBURG TR & SAFE DEP CO (LEWISBURG, PA)
Name changed to Lewisburg Trust Bank (Lewisburg, PA) 12/19/1977
Lewisburg Trust Bank (Lewisburg, PA) merged into Commonwealth Bancshares Corp. 09/21/1984 which was acquired by Meridian Bancorp, Inc. 08/31/1993 which merged into CoreStates Financial Corp 04/09/1996 which merged into First Union Corp. 04/28/1998 which name changed to Wachovia Corp. (Ctfs. dated after 09/01/2001) 09/01/2001 which merged into Wells Fargo & Co. (New) 12/31/2008

LEWISBURG TRUST BANK (LEWISBURG, PA)
Capital Stock $25 par changed to $5 par and (4) additional shares issued 02/00/1978
Merged into Commonwealth Bancshares Corp. 09/21/1984
Each share Capital Stock $5 par exchanged for (13) shares Common $3.50 par
Commonwealth Bancshares Corp. acquired by Meridian Bancorp, Inc. 08/31/1993 which merged into CoreStates Financial Corp 04/09/1996 which merged into First Union Corp. 04/28/1998 which name changed to Wachovia Corp. (Ctfs. dated after 09/01/2001) 09/01/2001 which merged into Wells Fargo & Co. (New) 12/31/2008

LEWISOHN COPPER CORP (DE)
Merged into Leisure Planning Corp. 12/05/1969
Each share Common 10¢ par exchanged for (0.2) share Common 10¢ par
(See Leisure Planning Corp.)

LEWISON ENTERPRISES INC (NV)
Name changed to Omega Development Corp. 01/19/1994
Omega Development Corp. recapitalized as BBJ Environmental Technologies, Inc. 06/01/2000
(See BBJ Environmental Technologies, Inc.)

LEWISTON GAS LIGHT CO. (ME)
Stock Dividend - 50% 10/1/55
Merged into Northern Utilities, Inc. (ME) 8/1/66
Each share Preferred $100 par exchanged for (1) share 5% Preferred $100 par
Each share Common $10 par exchanged for (1.62) shares Common $5 par
Northern Utilities, Inc. (ME) merged into Northern Utilities, Inc. (NH) 6/30/69 which merged into Bay State Gas Co. (New) 5/1/79 which merged into Nipsco Industries, Inc. 2/12/99 which name changed to NiSource Inc. (IN) 4/14/99 which reincorporated in Delaware 11/1/2000

LEWISTON-GORHAM RACEWAYS, INC. (ME)
Name changed to Lewiston Raceways, Inc. 04/11/1969
(See Lewiston Raceways, Inc.)

LEWISTON GREENE & MONMOUTH TEL CO (ME)
Each share 5% Preferred $10 par exchanged for (1) share Common $10 par 02/11/1965
Name changed to Community Service Telephone Co. 02/08/1973
Community Service Telephone Co. reorganized as Community Service Communications, Inc. 10/01/1988
(See Community Service Communications, Inc.)

LEWISTON RACEWAYS INC (ME)
Reported out of business 02/00/1990
Details not available

LEWISTON TR CO (PA)
Merged into Juniata Valley Financial Corp. 7/1/98
Each share Common $1.25 par exchanged for (1) share Common $1 par

LEWMUL GOLD MINES LTD. (ON)
Name changed to Denlake Mining Co. Ltd. 3/10/52
(See Denlake Mining Co. Ltd.)

LEWRON, LTD. (MD)
Merged into Lewron Television, Inc. 02/00/1967
Each share Class A Common $1 par exchanged for (1) share Class A Common $1 par
Each share Class B Common $1 par exchanged for (1) share Class B Common $1 par
(See Lewron Television, Inc.)

LEWRON TELEVISION INC (MD)
Class A Common $1 par and Class B Common $1 par split (3) for (1) respectively by issuance of (2) additional shares 04/15/1968
Class A Common $1 par reclassified as Common $1 par 06/30/1969
Class B Common $1 par reclassified as Common $1 par 06/30/1969
Stock Dividend - Class A & B Common - 10% 04/07/1969
Charter annulled for failure to file annual reports 07/30/1974

LEX CORP (AB)
Name changed to Home Ticket Network Corp. 11/26/96
Home Ticket Network Corp. name changed to Applause Corp. 9/18/2001
(See Applause Corp.)

LEXA INDUSTRIES (DE)
Name changed to Lexa Industries, Inc. 1/17/72

Lexa Industries, Inc. acquired by Oral-Visual Medical, Inc. 8/11/72 which name changed to Florida Sunshine Plants, Inc. 12/23/76 which recapitalized as General Growth Industries, Inc. 7/24/79 which name changed to Silver Reclamation Industries, Inc. 5/1/80 which recapitalized as Inter America Industries, Inc. 1/28/83 which name changed to Kendee's International Foods, Inc. 11/20/85
(See Kendee's International Foods, Inc.)

LEXA INDS INC (DE)
Acquired by Oral-Visual Medical, Inc. 08/11/1972
Each share Common 10¢ par exchanged for (1/3) share Common 1¢ par
Oral-Visual Medical, Inc. name changed to Florida Sunshine Plants, Inc. 12/23/1976 which recapitalized as General Growth Industries, Inc. 07/24/1979 which name changed to Silver Reclamation Industries, Inc. 05/01/1980 which recapitalized as Inter America Industries, Inc. 01/28/1983 which name changed to Kendee's International Foods, Inc. 11/20/1985
(See Kendee's International Foods, Inc.)

LEXA OIL CORP (DE)
Recapitalized as Lexa Industries 09/30/1970
Each share Common 1¢ par exchanged for (0.1) share Common 10¢ par
Lexa Industries name changed to Lexa Industries, Inc. 01/17/1972 which was acquired by Oral-Visual Medical, Inc. 08/11/1972 which name changed to Florida Sunshine Plants, Inc. 12/23/1976 which recapitalized as General Growth Industries, Inc. 07/24/1979 which name changed to Silver Reclamation Industries, Inc. 05/01/1980 which recapitalized as Inter America Industries, Inc. 01/28/1983 which name changed to Kendee's International Foods, Inc. 11/20/1985
(See Kendee's International Foods, Inc.)

LEXACAL INVT CORP (CANADA)
Name changed to New West Energy Services Inc. 10/26/2007

LEXAM EXPLS INC (ON)
Merged into Lexam VG Gold Inc. 01/04/2011
Each share Common no par exchanged for (2.1) shares Common no par
Lexam VG Gold Inc. merged into McEwen Mining Inc. 05/01/2017

LEXAM VG GOLD INC (ON)
Merged into McEwen Mining Inc. 05/01/2017
Each share Common no par exchanged for (0.056) share Common no par
Note: Unexchanged certificates will be cancelled and become without value 05/01/2023

LEXAR MEDIA INC (DE)
Issue Information - 6,500,000 shares COM offered at $8 per share on 08/14/2000
Merged into Micron Technology, Inc. 06/21/2006
Each share Common $0.0001 par exchanged for (0.5925) share Common 10¢ par

LEXARIA CORP (NV)
Each share old Common $0.001 par exchanged for (0.25) share new Common $0.001 par 06/23/2009
Each share new Common $0.001 par exchanged again for (1.1) shares new Common $0.001 par 12/16/2015
Name changed to Lexaria Bioscience Corp. 05/12/2016

LEXCOM INC (NC)
Non-Vtg. Class B Common no par split (2) for (1) by issuance (1) additional share payable 08/14/1998 to holders of record 07/31/1998
Acquired by Windstream Corp. 12/02/2009
Each share Common no par exchanged for $83.955495 cash
Each share Non-Vtg. Class B Common no par exchanged for $79.957614 cash

LEXENT INC (DE)
Issue Information - 6,000,000 shares COM offered at $15 per share on 07/27/2000
Merged into LX Merger Corp. 12/23/2003
Each share Common $0.001 par exchanged for $1.50 cash

LEXFORD INC (OH)
Merged into Lexford Residential Trust 3/18/98
Each share Common no par exchanged for (2) Shares of Bene. Int. no par
Lexford Residential Trust merged into Equity Residential Properties Trust 10/1/99 which name changed to Equity Residential 5/15/2002

LEXFORD RESIDENTIAL TR (MD)
Merged into Equity Residential Properties Trust 10/1/99
Each Share of Bene. Int. no par exchanged for (0.463) Share of Bene. Int. 1¢ par
Equity Residential Properties Trust name changed to Equity Residential 5/15/2002

LEXICO RES INTL CORP (NV)
Each share old Common $0.001 par exchanged for (0.05) share new Common $0.001 par 10/03/2012
Stock Dividend - 2% payable 04/22/1999 to holders of record 03/22/1999 Charter revoked 12/30/2016

LEXICON CORP (DE)
$1.30 Conv. Preferred 10¢ par called for redemption 08/29/1983
Each share Common 5¢ par exchanged for (0.5) share Common 10¢ par 02/10/1986
Each share old Common 10¢ par exchanged for (0.1) share new Common 10¢ par 09/30/1992
Name changed to Florida Gaming Corp. 03/21/1994
(See Florida Gaming Corp.)

LEXICON GENETICS INC (DE)
Issue Information - 10,000,000 shares COM offered at $22 per share on 04/07/2000
Name changed to Lexicon Pharmaceuticals, Inc. 4/27/2007

LEXICON UTD INC (DE)
Name changed to Accres Holding, Inc. 07/29/2011

LEXIDATA CORP (MA)
Merged into Adage, Inc. (MA) 03/21/1986
Each share Common 1¢ par exchanged for (0.3636) share Common 10¢ par
Adage, Inc. (MA) reincorporated in Pennsylvania 05/31/1991 which reincorporated in Nevada as RELM Wireless Corp. 01/30/1998 which name changed to BK Technologies, Inc. 06/05/2018

LEXINDIN GOLD MINES, LTD. (ON)
Recapitalized as Norlex Mines Ltd. 2/25/63
Each share Capital Stock no par exchanged for (0.2) share Capital Stock no par
Norlex Mines Ltd. recapitalized as NLX Resources Inc. 10/7/87
(See NLX Resources Inc.)

LEXINGTON AVE & 42ND ST CORP (NY)
Each share Class C Common 1¢ par exchanged for (1) share Class D Common 1¢ par 09/01/1970
Acquired by Lexington Acquisition Corp. 11/30/1988
Each share Class D Common 1¢ par exchanged for $238.31 cash

LEXINGTON B & L FINL CORP (MO)
Acquired by NASB Financial, Inc. 07/13/2016
Each share Common 1¢ par exchanged for $29.35 cash

LEXINGTON BARRON TECHNOLOGIES INC (CO)
Name changed to AGU Entertainment Corp. (CO) 03/26/2004
AGU Entertainment Corp. (CO) reincorporated in Delaware 10/21/2004 which name changed to Tube Media Corp. 03/07/2006
(See Tube Media Corp.)

LEXINGTON CAP CORP (CO)
Name changed to Club America, Inc. 09/12/1989
Club America, Inc. recapitalized as Plancapital U S A Inc. 01/15/1992 which recapitalized as Continental Capital Corp. 01/31/1995 which recapitalized as RFID Ltd. 06/21/2005 which name changed to OptimizeRx Corp. (CO) 04/30/2008 which reincorporated in Nevada 09/04/2008

LEXINGTON COMMUNICATIONS INC (NC)
Name changed to Lexcom Inc. 05/29/1988
(See Lexcom Inc.)

LEXINGTON CORP PPTYS INC (MD)
Reincorporated 6/27/94
State of incorporation changed from (DE) to (MD) 6/27/94
Name changed to Lexington Corporate Properties Trust 12/31/97
Lexington Corporate Properties Trust name changed to Lexington Realty Trust 12/31/2006

LEXINGTON CORPORATE LEADERS FD INC (DE)
Dissolved 07/08/1971
Each share Capital Stock $1 par exchanged for $8.626 cash

LEXINGTON CORPORATE LEADERS TR FD (NY)
Name changed to Pilgrim Corporate Leaders Trust Fund 08/07/2000
Pilgrim Corporate Leaders Trust Fund name changed to ING Corporate Leaders Trust Fund 03/01/2002

LEXINGTON ENERGY SVCS INC (NV)
Recapitalized as Suburban Minerals Corp. 03/14/2013
Each share Common $0.0001 par exchanged for (0.0002) share Common $0.0001 par

LEXINGTON FDG INC (CO)
Name changed to Eldorado Artesian Springs, Inc. 06/00/1987

LEXINGTON GLOBAL ASSET MANAGERS INC (DE)
Merged into ReliaStar Financial Corp. 07/26/2000
Each share Common exchanged for (0.11) share Common $0.001 par and $4.798 cash
(See ReliaStar Financial Corp.)

LEXINGTON GNMA INCOME FD INC (MD)
Name changed 12/22/80
Name changed from Lexington Income Fund, Inc. to Lexington GNMA Income Fund, Inc. 12/22/80
Capital Stock $1 par changed to 1¢ par 4/5/83
Name changed to Pilgrim GNMA Income Fund, Inc. 7/26/2000
Pilgrim GNMA Income Fund, Inc. name changed to ING GNMA Income Fund, Inc. 3/1/2002

LEXINGTON GROUP INC (NY)
Name changed to Harris & Harris Group, Inc. 08/15/1988
Harris & Harris Group, Inc. name changed to 180 Degree Capital Corp. 03/27/2017

LEXINGTON GROWTH & INCOME FD INC (MD)
Name changed to Pilgrim Growth & Income Fund, Inc. 07/26/2000
Pilgrim Growth & Income Fund, Inc. name changed to ING Large Company Value Fund, Inc. 03/01/2002
(See ING Large Company Value Fund, Inc.)

LEXINGTON HEALTHCARE GROUP INC (DE)
Issue Information - 1,125,000 shares COM offered at $5 per share on 05/14/1997
Chapter 11 bankruptcy proceedings converted to Chapter 7 on 05/19/2004
Stockholders' equity unlikely

LEXINGTON INCOME TR (NY)
Name changed to Magna Income Trust 01/22/1970
Magna Income Trust name changed to Pilgrim High Yield Trust 03/01/1985

LEXINGTON INDS INC (CO)
Charter suspended for failure to file annual reports 09/30/1989

LEXINGTON INSTRS CORP (MA)
Proclaimed dissolved for failure to file reports and pay fees 12/13/90

LEXINGTON INTL FD INC (MD)
Name changed to Pilgrim International Fund, Inc. 7/26/2000
Pilgrim International Fund, Inc. name changed to ING International Fund, Inc. 3/1/2002

LEXINGTON MINES LTD (BC)
Recapitalized as Kent Energy Corp. 12/1/75
Each share Common no par exchanged for (0.2) share Common no par
Kent Energy Corp. recapitalized as Kerf Petroleums Corp. 10/29/82 which name changed to Kaskada Resources Ltd. 9/30/85 which merged into Canadian Futurity Oils Ltd. 11/1/85 which recapitalized as Baca Resources Ltd. 8/4/89 which name changed to Cordex Petroleums Ltd. 7/11/94

LEXINGTON MONEY MKT TR (NJ)
Name changed to ING Lexington Money Market Trust 3/1/2002

LEXINGTON PRECISION CORP (DE)
Plan of reorganization under Chapter 11 Federal Bankruptcy proceedings effective 07/30/2010
No stockholders' equity

LEXINGTON RLTY TR (MD)
Name changed 12/31/2006
Under plan of merger name changed from Lexington Corporate Properties Trust to Lexington Realty Trust 12/31/2006
8.05% Preferred Ser. B $0.0001 par called for redemption at $25 plus $0.335417 accrued dividends on 05/31/2012
7.55% Preferred Ser. D $0.0001 par called for redemption at $25 plus $0.099618 accrued dividends on 04/19/2013
(Additional Information in Active)

LEX-LEY

LEXINGTON RESH & MGMT CORP (NY)
Merged into Piedmont Equities, Inc. 02/24/1969
Each share Class A Common 10¢ par exchanged for $15 cash
Each share Class B Common 10¢ par exchanged for $15 cash

LEXINGTON RESH FD INC (NJ)
Reincorporated under the laws of Maryland as Lexington Growth & Income Fund, Inc. 04/30/1991
Lexington Growth & Income Fund, Inc. name changed to Pilgrim Growth & Income Fund, Inc. 07/26/2000 which name changed to ING Large Company Value Fund, Inc. 03/01/2002
(See ING Large Company Value Fund, Inc.)

LEXINGTON RESH INVESTING CORP (NJ)
Name changed to Lexington Research Fund, Inc. (NJ) 04/28/1969
Lexington Research Fund, Inc. (NJ) reincorporated in Maryland as Lexington Growth & Income Fund, Inc. 04/30/1991 which name changed to Pilgrim Growth & Income Fund, Inc. 07/26/2000 which name changed to ING Large Company Value Fund, Inc. 03/01/2002
(See ING Large Company Value Fund, Inc.)

LEXINGTON RES INC (AB)
Name changed to Nett-Workk Inc. 02/15/1988
(See Nett-Workk Inc.)

LEXINGTON RES INC (NV)
Common $0.001 par split (3) for (1) by issuance of (2) additional shares payable 01/28/2004 to holders of record 01/26/2004 Ex date - 01/29/2004
SEC revoked common stock registration 06/04/2009

LEXINGTON RES LTD (BC)
Recapitalized as Churchill Resources Ltd. 04/27/1992
Each share Common no par exchanged for (0.2) share Common no par
Churchill Resources Ltd. merged into Greystar Resources Ltd. (New) 08/15/1997 which name changed to Eco Oro Minerals Corp. 08/19/2011

LEXINGTON RUSSIA FUND, INC. (MD)
Name changed to Lexington Troika Dialog Russia Fund, Inc. 4/2/96
Lexington Troika Dialog Russia Fund, Inc. name changed to Pilgrim Troika Dialog Russia Fund, Inc. 7/26/2000 which name changed to Pilgrim Russia Fund, Inc. 3/1/2001 which name changed to ING Russia Fund, Inc. 3/1/2002

LEXINGTON SVGS BK (LEXINGTON, MA)
Merged into Affiliated Community Bancorp, Inc. 10/19/95
Each share Common 30¢ par exchanged for (1) share Common 10¢ par
Affiliated Community Bancorp, Inc. merged into UST Corp. 8/7/98
(See UST Corp.)

LEXINGTON SILVER FD INC (MD)
Name changed to Pilgrim Silver Fund, Inc. 08/07/2000
Pilgrim Silver Fund, Inc. merged into Pilgrim Gold Fund, Inc. 02/20/2001 which name changed to Pilgrim Precious Metals Fund, Inc. 03/01/2001 which name changed to ING Precious Metals Fund, Inc. 03/01/2002
(See ING Precious Metals Fund, Inc.)

LEXINGTON ST BK (LEXINGTON, NC)
Under plan of reorganization each share Capital Stock $5 par automatically became (1) share LSB Bancshares, Inc. (NC) Common $5 par 07/01/1983
LSB Bancshares, Inc. (NC) name changed to NewBridge Bancorp 07/31/2007 which merged into Yadkin Financial Corp. 03/01/2016 which merged into F.N.B. Corp. 03/11/2017

LEXINGTON ST BK S C (LEXINGTON, SC)
Capital Stock $10 par changed to $5 par and (1) additional share issued in 1981
Reorganized as L.S.B. Bancshares, Inc. (SC) 10/1/84
Each share Capital Stock $5 par exchanged for (1) share Common $5 par
L.S.B. Bancshares, Inc. (SC) name changed to L.S.B. Bancshares, Inc. of South Carolina 5/1/86 which merged into BB&T Financial Corp. 6/30/94 which merged into Southern National Corp. 2/28/95 which name changed to BB&T Corp. 5/19/97

LEXINGTON STRATEGIC ASSET CORP (DE)
Acquired by Lexington Realty Trust 06/29/2007
Each share Common $0.0001 par exchanged for $10 cash

LEXINGTON STRATEGIC SILVER FD INC (MD)
Name changed to Lexington Silver Fund, Inc. 05/10/1999
Lexington Silver Fund Inc. name changed to Pilgrim Silver Fund, Inc. 08/07/2000 which merged into Pilgrim Gold Fund, Inc. 02/20/2001 which name changed to Pilgrim Precious Metals Fund, Inc. 03/01/2001 which name changed to ING Precious Metals Fund, Inc. 03/01/2002
(See ING Precious Metals Fund, Inc.)

LEXINGTON TAX FREE MONEY FD INC (MD)
Name changed 04/30/1980
Name changed 04/12/1983
Name changed from Lexington Tax Free Income Fund, Inc. to Lexington Tax Free Daily Income Fund, Inc. 04/30/1980
Name changed from Lexington Tax Free Daily Income Fund, Inc. to Lexington Tax Free Money Fund, Inc. 04/12/1983
Completely liquidated 09/08/1997
Each share Common $1 par received $1 cash

LEXINGTON TECHNICAL STRATEGY FD INC (MD)
Voluntarily dissolved 08/02/1993
Details not available

LEXINGTON TEL CO (NC)
Under plan of reorganization each share Common no par or Non-Vtg. Class B Common no par automatically became (1) share Lexington Communications Inc. Common no par or Non-Vtg. Class B Common no par respectively 01/01/1996
Lexington Communications Inc. name changed to Lexcom Inc. 05/29/1998
(See Lexcom Inc.)
Preferred Ser. A no par called for redemption at $100 on 03/29/1999
Public interest eliminated

LEXINGTON TELEPHONE CO. (DE)
Name changed to Kentucky Telephone Corp. 00/00/1950
Kentucky Telephone Corp. name changed to General Telephone Co. of Kentucky 00/00/1952 which merged into General Telephone Co. of the South 12/31/1985 which name changed to GTE South Inc. 01/01/1988

LEXINGTON TROIKA DIALOG RUSSIA FD INC (MD)
Name changed to Pilgrim Troika Dialog Russia Fund, Inc. 7/26/2000
Pilgrim Troika Dialog Russia Fund, Inc. name changed to Pilgrim Russia Fund, Inc. 3/1/2001 which name changed to ING Russia Fund, Inc. 3/1/2002

LEXINGTON TROTS BREEDERS ASSN (KY)
Merged into Red Mile Renaissance 7/6/2000
Each share Common no par exchanged for $44 cash

LEXINGTON TRUST FUND SHARES
Each Trust share 25¢ par exchanged for (0.25) Trust share $1 par 00/00/1950
Name changed to Lexington Income Trust 06/01/1960
Lexington Income Trust name changed to Magna Income Trust 01/22/1970 which name changed to Pilgrim High Yield Trust 03/01/1985

LEXINGTON UNION STATION CO. (KY)
Dissolved 8/18/58

LEXINGTON VENTURE FUNDS (DE)
Name changed to Federated Growth Fund, Inc. 06/06/1960
Federated Growth Fund, Inc. name changed to Pligrowth Fund, Inc. 01/01/1971 which merged into Plitrend Fund, Inc. 07/23/1982 which name changed to U.S. Trend Fund, Inc. (PA) 02/00/1986 which reincorporated in Maryland as Capstone U.S. Trend Fund, Inc. 05/11/1992 which name changed to Capstone Growth Fund, Inc. 08/26/1994 which name changed to Capstone Series Fund, Inc. 01/22/2002

LEXINGTON WATER CO. (KY)
Name changed to Kentucky-American Water Co. 03/30/1973
(See Kentucky-American Water Co.)

LEXITECH INTL DOCUMENTATION NETWORK INC (DE)
Charter cancelled and declared inoperative and void for non-payment of taxes 3/1/91

LEXITRON CORP (DE)
Merged into Raytheon Co. 1/12/78
Each share Common 20¢ par exchanged for $3.90 cash

LEXMARK INTL INC (DE)
Name changed 07/01/2000
Class B Common 1¢ par reclassified as Class A Common 1¢ par 02/00/1998
Name changed from Lexmark International Group, Inc. to Lexmark International Inc. 07/01/2000
Acquired by Ninestar Group Co. Ltd. 11/29/2016
Each share Class A Common 1¢ par exchanged for $40.50 cash

LEXOIL INC (AB)
Acquired by Aquest Explorations Ltd. 11/21/2003
Each share Common no par exchanged for (0.2) share Common no par and (0.1) Common Stock Purchase Warrant expiring 09/22/2008
Aquest Explorations Ltd. recapitalized as Aquest Energy Ltd. 02/04/2004 which recapitalized as Anderson Energy Ltd. 09/01/2005 which name changed to Anderson Energy Inc. 01/27/2015 which name changed to InPlay Oil Corp. 11/10/2016

LEXON INC (OK)
Recapitalized as ProVision Operation Systems, Inc. 8/16/2004
Each (3.7346) shares Common $0.001 par exchanged for (1) share Common $0.001 par

LEXON TECHNOLOGIES INC (DE)
Each share old Common $0.001 par exchanged for (0.1) share new Common $0.001 par 05/29/2002
Each share new Common $0.001 par exchanged again for (0.00158478) share new Common $0.001 par 09/14/2011
Name changed to Social Cube Inc. 03/28/2012

LEXOR HLDGS INC (FL)
Name changed to Jeantex Group, Inc. 07/25/2005
Jeantex Group, Inc. name changed to Catalyst Resource Group, Inc. 05/24/2010
(See Catalyst Resource Group, Inc.)

LEXOR INTL INC (DE)
Each share old Common $0.001 par exchanged for (0.1) share new Common $0.001 par 12/19/2001
Recapitalized as Grayling Wireless USA, Inc. 01/16/2003
Each share Common $0.001 par exchanged for (0.005) share Common $0.001 par

LEX2000 INC (ON)
Merged into Cognos Inc. 2/24/99
Each share Common no par exchanged for $0.6235 cash

LEXXIT LIFE INC (TX)
Name changed to Replen-K Inc. 01/14/1992

LEXXOR ENERGY INC (AB)
Each share Class A Common no par exchanged for (0.2) share Common no par 10/31/2001
Plan of Arrangement effective 09/05/2003
Each share Common no par exchanged for (0.5) share Find Energy Ltd. Common no par and (0.1) Common Stock Purchase Warrant expiring 10/30/2003
Note: Holders of (199) or fewer shares received $1.6872 cash per share
Find Energy Ltd. acquired by Shiningbank Energy Income Fund 09/22/2006 which merged into PrimeWest Energy Trust 07/13/2007
(See PrimeWest Energy Trust)

LEY-FRED CORP.
Dissolved in 1938

LEY FRED T & CO INC (DE)
Capital Stock no par changed to $1 par 00/00/1936
Liquidation completed
Each share Capital Stock $1 par received initial distribution of $1.20 cash 06/00/1979
Each share Capital Stock $1 par exchanged for second and final distribution of $0.59 cash 02/06/1981

LEYGHTON-PAIGE CORP. (MN)
Name changed to Ten-Tex, Inc. 10/10/62
(See Ten-Tex, Inc.)

LEYS (WM.) MINING CORP. LTD. (ON)
Charter cancelled for failure to pay taxes and file returns 2/4/70

LEYSHON RES LTD (AUSTRALIA)
Each Sponsored ADR for Ordinary received distribution of $0.0483 cash payable 05/31/2005 to holders of record 05/24/2005 Ex date - 05/20/2005
Each Sponsored ADR for Ordinary received distribution of $0.45015 cash payable 02/18/2014 to holders of record 02/10/2014 Ex date - 02/06/2014

ADR agreement terminated 08/16/2017
Each Sponsored ADR for Ordinary exchanged for (5) shares Ordinary
Note: Unexchanged ADR's will be sold and the proceeds, if any, held for claim after 08/20/2018

LEZAK ENERGY GROUP INC (NV)
Name changed to Enterprise Oil & Gas Corp. 11/2/82
Enterprise Oil & Gas Corp. name changed to Enterprise Technologies Inc. 7/27/83 which reorganized as Enterprise Entertainment Group, Inc. 10/3/89 which recapitalized as Andromeda Capital Corp. 7/29/94
(See Andromeda Capital Corp.)

LEZAK GROUP INC (NV)
Recapitalized as International Dynamic Pictures 10/22/1993
Each (133) shares Class A Common 1¢ par exchanged for (1) share Class A Common 1¢ par
International Dynamic Pictures recapitalized as ID Four Ltd. 11/24/1997 which name changed to Swung, Inc. 08/06/2002 which recapitalized as American Capital Holdings 11/15/2002 which name changed to Symphony Investments, Inc. 05/09/2003 which name changed to International Pharmacy Outlets Inc. 09/29/2003 which name changed to Bionic Products, Inc. 12/11/2006 which recapitalized as Texas Oil & Minerals Inc. 02/01/2012

LF BANCORP INC (DE)
Merged into BancorpSouth Inc. 03/31/1995
Each share Common 1¢ par exchanged for (1.013) shares Common $2.50 par
BancorpSouth, Inc. reorganized as BancorpSouth Bank (Tupelo, MS) 11/01/2017

LFC FINL CORP (DE)
Merged into Great Western Financial Corp. 12/22/1970
Each share Capital Stock $1 par exchanged for (0.25) share Capital Stock $1 par
Great Western Financial Corp. merged into Washington Mutual Inc. 07/01/1997
(See Washington Mutual, Inc.)

LFC HLDG CORP (DE)
Variable Rate Exchangeable Preferred $1 par called for redemption 8/1/93
Public interest eliminated

LFC INC. (CO)
Each share Common $0.001 par exchanged for (0.00001) share Common $0.001 par 4/16/90
Note: In effect holders received $0.02 cash per share and public interest was eliminated

LFE CORP (DE)
50¢ Conv. Preferred Ser. A no par called for redemption 07/15/1985
Stock Dividends - 10% 07/17/1978; 10% 08/01/1979; 10% 08/01/1980
Merged into Mark IV Industries, Inc. 06/17/1985
Each share Common $1 par exchanged for $19 cash

LFG INTL INC (NV)
Each (300) shares old Common $0.001 par exchanged for (1) share new Common $0.001 par 04/08/2005
Each (15) shares new Common $0.001 par exchanged again for (1) share new Common $0.001 par 01/03/2006
Name changed to Nano-Jet Corp. 11/07/2006
Nano-Jet Corp. name changed to Hitor Group, Inc. 01/09/2008

LFS BANCORP INC (DE)
Acquired by Great Financial Corp. 06/07/1996
Each share Common 1¢ par exchanged for $19.50 cash

LG CHEM INVT LTD (KOREA)
GDR agreement terminated 05/11/2002
Each 144A Sponsored GDR for Ordinary exchanged for $9.7681 cash

LG CHEM LTD NEW (KOREA)
Old Sponsored 144A GDR's for Common split (2) for (1) by issuance of (1) additional GDR payable 12/28/2005 to holders of record 12/22/2005 Ex date - 12/20/2005
Basis changed from (1:1) to (1:0.5) 12/28/2005
Each old Sponsored 144A GDR for Common exchanged for (0.88) new Sponsored 144A GDR for Common 05/20/2009
GDR agreement terminated 11/25/2015
Each new Sponsored 144A GDR for Common exchanged for $119.432751 cash

LG CHEM LTD OLD (KOREA)
Each 144A GDR for Ordinary received distribution of (0.66) LG Chemical Ltd. New 144A Sponsored GDR for Ordinary payable 05/02/2001 to holders of record 04/30/2001
Each 144A GDR for Ordinary received distribution of (0.16) LG Household & Health Care Ltd. 144A Sponsored GDR for Ordinary payable 05/02/2001 to holders of record 04/30/2002
Merged into LG Chemical Investment Ltd. 05/02/2001
Each 144A GDR for Ordinary exchanged for (0.18) 144A Sponsored GDR for Ordinary
(See LG Chemical Investment Ltd.)

LG ELECTRONICS INC (KOREA)
Merged into LG Electronics Inc. (New) 04/01/2002
Each 144A GDR for Non-Vtg. Common exchanged for (0.9) Sponsored GDR for Non-Vtg. Common and $0.943183 cash
Each 144A GDR for Common exchanged for (0.9) Sponsored GDR for Non-Vtg. Common and $0.943183 cash

LG HLDG CORP (CO)
Reincorporated under the laws of Delaware as Mikojo Inc. and Common $0.001 par changed to $0.0001 par 09/11/2009
(See Mikojo Inc.)

LG HOUSEHOLD & HEALTH CARE LTD (KOREA)
ADR agreement terminated 05/01/2006
Each 144A Sponsored GDR for Common exchanged for $99.3584 cash

LG PHILIPS LCD CO LTD (KOREA)
Issue Information - 24,960,000 ADRS offered at US$15 per ADR on 07/15/2004
Name changed to LG Display Co., Ltd. 03/03/2008

LG&E ENERGY CORP (KY)
Merged into Powergen PLC 12/11/2000
Each share Common no par exchanged for $24.85 cash

LGC SKYROTA WIND ENERGY CORP (CANADA)
Ceased operations 11/23/2010
Stockholders' equity unlikely

LGF BANCORP INC (DE)
Merged into First of America Bank Corp. 05/01/1994
Each share Common 1¢ par exchanged for (0.8754) share Common $10 par
First of America Bank Corp. merged into National City Corp. 03/31/1998 which was acquired by PNC Financial Services Group, Inc. 12/31/2008

LGI CORP (DE)
Each (850) shares old Common 10¢ par exchanged for (1) share new Common 10¢ par 05/17/1978
Note: In effect holders received $3 cash per share and public interest was eliminated

LGL GROUP INC (IN)
Reincorporated under the laws of Delaware 08/31/2007

LGM ACQUISITION CORP (NV)
Name changed to Home Dish Satellite Networks, Inc. 01/12/1989
(See Home Dish Satellite Networks, Inc.)

LGM BIOPHARMA INC (NV)
Name changed to Syncronys International, Inc. 12/11/2007
Syncronys International, Inc. name changed to Seeker Tec International, Inc. 04/24/2013

LGO NET COM INC (BC)
Reincorporated under the laws of Alberta as Prolific Technology Inc. 1/26/2001
Prolific Technology Inc. recapitalized as Klad Enterprises Ltd. 3/18/2002 which merged into Diamond Hawk Mining Corp. (ALTA) 2/9/2005 which reincorporated in British Columbia 7/4/2005

LGS GROUP INC (CANADA)
Acquired by International Business Machines Corp. 05/15/2000
Each share Class A Subordinate no par held by Canadian residents exchanged for either (1) Exchangeable share or $19 cash
Each share Class A Subordinate no par held by non-residents exchanged for U.S. dollar equivalent of C$19 cash

LGX OIL PLUS GAS INC (CANADA)
Reincorporated under the laws of Alberta 06/27/2013

LHS GROUP INC (DE)
Issue Information - 4,800,000 shares COM offered at $16 per share on 05/15/1997
Common 1¢ par split (2) for (1) by issuance of (1) additional share payable 5/28/98 to holders of record 4/3/98
Merged into Sema Group PLC 7/28/2000
Each share Common 1¢ par exchanged for either (2.6) Ordinary or (1.3) ADR's for Ordinary
Note: Option to receive Ordinary expires 9/26/2000
Sema Group PLC name changed to Sema PLC 12/18/2000
(See Sema PLC)

LI FALCO MANUFACTURING CO., INC. (NY)
Proclaimed dissolved by the Secretary of State of New York 12/15/61

LI-ION MTRS CORP (NV)
Each share old Common $0.001 par exchanged for (0.2) share new Common $0.001 par 01/26/2012
Stock Dividend - 20% payable 05/28/2010 to holders of record 05/28/2010 Ex date - 05/26/2010
Recapitalized as Terra Inventions Corp. 12/21/2012
Each share new Common $0.001 par exchanged for (0.1) share Common $0.001 par
(See Terra Inventions Corp.)

LI'L GENERAL STORES, INC. (MN)
Each share Common $1 par exchanged for (0.5) share Common $2 par 10/29/1965
Merged into General Host Corp. 07/19/1968
Each share Common $2 par exchanged for (0.9) share Common $1 par
(See General Host Corp.)

LIARD RES LTD (AB)
Name changed to CMX Gold & Silver Corp. 02/11/2011

LIBANON GOLD MNG LTD (SOUTH AFRICA)
Each ADR for Ordinary Reg. Rand-1 par exchanged for (5) ADR's for Ordinary Reg. Rand-0.20 par 11/13/1987
Merged into Kloof Gold Mining Co. Ltd. 09/18/1992
Each ADR for Ordinary Reg. Rand-0.20 par exchanged for (0.09) ADR for Ordinary Reg. Rand-0.25 par
Kloof Gold Mining Co. Ltd. merged into Gold Fields Ltd. (Old) 02/02/1998 which merged into Gold Fields Ltd. (New) 05/10/1999

LIBBEY GLASS MANUFACTURING CO.
Acquired by Owens-Illinois Glass Co. 00/00/1935
Details not available

LIBBEY OWENS FORD CO (OH)
Name changed to Trinova Corp. 08/01/1986
Trinova Corp. name changed to Aeroquip-Vickers, Inc. 04/17/1997
(See Aeroquip-Vickers, Inc.)

LIBBEY-OWENS-FORD GLASS CO. (OH)
Each share Common no par exchanged for (2) shares Common $10 par in 1950
Common $10 par changed to $5 par and (1) additional share issued 5/18/59
Name changed to Libbey-Owens-Ford Co. 8/27/68
Libbey-Owens-Ford Co. name changed to Trinova Corp. 8/1/86 which name changed to Aeroquip-Vickers, Inc. 4/17/97
(See Aeroquip-Vickers, Inc.)

LIBBEY-OWENS GLASS CO.
Name changed to Libbey-Owens-Ford Glass Co. in 1930
Libbey-Owens-Ford Glass Co. name changed to Libbey-Owens-Ford Co. 8/27/68 which name changed to Trinova Corp. 8/1/86 which name changed to Aeroquip-Vickers, Inc. 4/17/97
(See Aeroquip-Vickers, Inc.)

LIBBEY-OWENS SHEET GLASS CO.
Name changed to Libbey-Owens Glass Co. in 1929
Libbey-Owens Glass Co. name changed to Libbey-Owens-Ford Glass Co. in 1930 which name changed to Libbey-Owens-Ford Co. 8/27/68 which name changed to Trinova Corp. 8/1/86 which name changed to Aeroquip-Vickers, Inc. 4/17/97
(See Aeroquip-Vickers, Inc.)

LIBBY & LIBBY COLD STORAGE CO.
Dissolved in 1928

LIBBY (LOUIS L.) FOOD PRODUCTS, INC. (DE)
Name changed to Red L Foods Corp. 9/21/55
Red L Foods Corp. merged into Gortons of Gloucester, Inc. 4/1/63 which name changed to Gorton Corp. (Mass.) 6/14/65 which reincorporated under the laws of Delaware 7/1/66 which merged into General Mills, Inc. 8/16/68

LIBBY GOLD CORP. (MT)
Charter expired by time limitation 5/8/73

LIBBY MCNEILL & LIBBY (ME)
Recapitalized 00/00/1935
Each share 1st Preferred $100 par exchanged for (1) share 6% Preferred $100 par
Each share 2nd Preferred $100 par exchanged for (10) shares Common no par
Common $10 par changed to no par
Recapitalized 00/00/1940
Each share 6% Preferred $100 par exchanged for (12) shares Common $7 par
Common no par changed to $7 par
Common $7 par changed to $1 par 10/28/1970
Merged into Nestle Alimentana S.A. 04/06/1976
Each share Common $1 par exchanged for $8.125 cash

LIBCO CORP (DE)
Each share Common $1 par exchanged for (0.058823) share Common 1¢ par 05/20/1975
Each share Common 1¢ par exchanged for (0.01) share Common 2¢ par 10/03/1979
Recapitalized as RDIS Corp. 12/14/1992
Each share Common 2¢ par exchanged for (0.05) share Common 2¢ par
RDIS Corp. recapitalized as TenthGate International, Inc. 03/14/2007 which recapitalized as TGI Solar Power Group, Inc. 07/25/2008

LIBERAL FINANCE SYSTEMS, INC. (MO)
Adjudicated bankrupt 6/11/69
No stockholders' equity

LIBERAL KING MINING CO.
Liquidated in 1950

LIBERAL PETROLEUMS LTD. (AB)
Capital Stock no par changed to 25¢ par in 1955
Acquired by Canadian Husky Oil Ltd. 2/28/58
Each share Common 25¢ par exchanged for (0.125) share Common $1 par
Canadian Husky Oil Ltd. name changed to Husky Oil Canada Ltd. 5/13/63 which name changed to Husky Oil Ltd. 9/3/68
(See Husky Oil Ltd.)

LIBERATE TECHNOLOGIES (DE)
Old Common 1¢ par split (2) for (1) by issuance of (1) additional share payable 01/14/2000 to holders of record 12/31/1999
Each share old Common 1¢ par exchanged for (1) share new Common 1¢ par to reflect a (1) for (250,000) reverse split followed by a (250,000) for (1) forward split 12/19/2005
Note: In effect holders received $0.20 cash per share and public interest was eliminated

LIBERATOR INC (FL)
Name changed to Luvu Brands, Inc. 11/05/2015

LIBERATOR MED HLDGS INC (NV)
Acquired by Bard (C.R.), Inc. 01/21/2016
Each share Common $0.001 par exchanged for $3.35 cash

LIBERIAN INTL AMERN CORP (DE)
Each VTC for Common 5¢ par exchanged for (1) share Common 5¢ par 05/25/1972
Charter cancelled and declared inoperative and void for non-payment of taxes 03/01/1986

LIBERIAN IRON ORE LTD (CANADA)
Name changed to LionOre Mining International Ltd. 07/26/1996
(See LionOre Mining International Ltd.)

LIBERO MNG CORP (BC)
Name changed to Libero Copper Corp, 11/01/2017

LIBERTAS PFD FDG IV LTD (CHANNEL ISLANDS)
144A Preference Shares in default 08/08/2008
Assets sold for the benefit of A-1 Noteholders Stockholders' equity unlikely
Note: All holders are requested to surrender certificates, regardless of whether or not they are expected to receive any distributions

LIBERTE INVS (MA)
Reincorporated under the laws of Delaware as Liberte Investors Inc. 08/16/1996
Liberte Investors Inc. name changed to First Acceptance Corp. 04/30/2004

LIBERTE INVS INC (DE)
Name changed to First Acceptance Corp. 4/30/2004

LIBERTEL N V (NETHERLANDS)
Name changed to Vodafone Libertel N.V. 12/13/2001
(See Vodafone Libertel N.V.)

LIBERTO INC (NV)
Name changed to 4Cable TV International, Inc. 05/06/2013

LIBERTY ACORN TR (MA)
Name changed to Columbia Acorn Trust 10/13/2003

LIBERTY ACQUISITION HLDGS CORP (DE)
Issue Information - 90,000,000 UNITS consisting of (1) share COM and (0.5) WT offered at $10 per Unit on 12/06/2007
Merged into Promotora de Informaciones, S.A. 11/29/2010
Each Unit exchanged for (0.43125) Sponsored ADR for Class A Ordinary, (0.75) Sponsored ADR for Conv. Non-Vtg. Class B and $0.95 cash
Each share Common $0.0001 par exchanged for (0.375) Sponsored ADR for Class A Ordinary, (0.75) Sponsored ADR for Conv. Non-Vtg. Class B and $0.50 cash

LIBERTY ACQUISITIONS CORP (CO)
Name changed to Caribbean Select, Inc. 1/9/87
(See Caribbean Select, Inc.)

LIBERTY ADVANTAGE TR (MA)
Under plan of reorganization Tax Free Bond Fund or U.S. Government Securities Fund automatically became Liberty Financial Trust Tax Free Bond Fund or U.S. Government Securities Fund respectively 08/03/1992
(See Liberty Financial Trust)

LIBERTY AIRCRAFT PRODUCTS CORP.
Name changed to Liberty Products Corp. (NY) in 1947
Liberty Products Corp. (NY) merged into Penn-Texas Corp. 12/12/55 which name changed to Fairbanks Whitney Corp. 5/29/59 which recapitalized as Colt Industries Inc. (PA) 5/15/64 which reincorporated in Delaware 10/17/68 which reincorporated in Pennsylvania 5/6/76
(See Colt Industries Inc. (PA))

LIBERTY AIRLINES INC (OH)
Ceased operations 12/20/1984
No stockholders' equity

LIBERTY ALLIANCE INC NEW (DE)
Recapitalized as SinoHub, Inc. 07/18/2008
Each share Common $0.001 par exchanged for (0.28571428) share Common $0.001 par

LIBERTY ALLIANCE INC OLD (DE)
Name changed to Vestige, Inc. 08/17/2006
Vestige, Inc. name changed to Liberty Alliance, Inc. (New) 02/28/2007 which recapitalized as SinoHub, Inc. 07/18/2008

LIBERTY AMERN LIFE INS CO (OH)
Common $2 par changed to $1 par 11/24/65
Merged into Coastal States Life Insurance Co. 12/31/69
Each share Common $1 par exchanged for (0.298989) share Common $1 par
Coastal States Life Insurance Co. reorganized as Coastal States Corp. 10/5/72
(See Coastal States Corp.)

LIBERTY BAKING CO. (PA)
Out of business 10/31/1968
Details not available

LIBERTY BAKING CORP. (DE)
Reorganized in 1935
Each share 7% Preferred $100 par exchanged for (1) share $4 Preferred no par and (1) share new Common no par
Each (20) shares Common no par exchanged for (1) share new Common no par
Reorganized 1/4/60
No stockholders' equity

LIBERTY BANCORP INC (OK)
Merged into Banc One Corp. 6/1/97
Each share Common 10¢ par exchanged for (1.175) share Common no par
Banc One Corp. merged into Bank One Corp. 10/2/98 which merged into J.P.Morgan Chase & Co. 12/31/2000 which name changed to JPMorgan Chase & Co. 7/20/2004

LIBERTY BANCORP INC (PA)
Merged into First Eastern Corp. 10/22/1987
Each share Common $25 par exchanged for (56.2) shares Common $10 par
(See First Eastern Corp.)

LIBERTY BANCORP INC (USA)
Merged into NSB Holding Corp. 12/31/2002
Each share Common $1 par exchanged for $26.50 cash

LIBERTY BANCORP INC DEL (DE)
Merged into Alliance Bancorp 2/10/97
Each share Common no par exchanged for (1.054) shares Common 1¢ par
Alliance Bancorp merged into Charter One Financial, Inc. 7/2/2001
(See Charter One Financial, Inc.)

LIBERTY BANCSHARES INC (ALTON, IL)
Reorganized 02/03/1997
Under plan of reorganization each share Liberty Bank (Alton, IL) Common no par automatically became (1) share Liberty BancShares Inc. Common no par 02/03/1997
Merged into United Community Bancorp, 03/10/2018
Details not available

LIBERTY BANCSHARES INC (AR)
Merged into Home BancShares, Inc. 10/24/2013
Each share Common 1¢ par exchanged for (7.4591) share Common 1¢ par and $25.53 cash

LIBERTY BANCSHARES INC (MO)
Merged into Simmons First National Corp. 02/27/2015
Each share Common $1 par exchanged for (1) share Class A Common 1¢ par

LIBERTY BANCSHARES INC (WV)
Merged into United Bankshares, Inc. 10/21/1992
Each share Common $1.25 par exchanged for (1.8) shares Common $2.50 par

LIBERTY BANK & TRUST CO. (BUFFALO, NY)
Name changed to Liberty National Bank & Trust Co. (Buffalo, NY) 4/19/63
Liberty National Bank & Trust Co. (Buffalo, NY) reorganized as United Bank Corp. of New York 12/31/71 which name changed to Norstar Bancorp Inc. 1/4/82 which merged into Fleet/Norstar Financial Group, Inc. 1/1/88 which name changed to Fleet Financial Group, Inc. (New) 4/15/92 which name changed to Fleet Boston Corp. 10/1/99 which name changed to FleetBoston Financial Corp. 4/18/2000 which merged into Bank of America Corp. 4/1/2004

LIBERTY BANK & TRUST CO. (DURHAM, NC)
Acquired by Planters National Bank & Trust Co. (Rocky Mount, NC) 08/31/1979
Each share Capital Stock $10 par exchanged for $22 cash

LIBERTY BK & TR CO (BOSTON, MA)
Common $10 par changed to $4 par in November 1976
Acquired by GBC Bancorp 2/28/2002
Each share Common $4 par exchanged for $81.50 cash

LIBERTY BK (HONOLULU, HI)
Capital Stock $20 par changed to $5 par and (3) additional shares issued 03/30/1962
Merged into BankAmerica Corp. (Old) 07/07/1994
Each share Common $5 par exchanged for (0.58008) share Common $1.5625 par
BankAmerica Corp. (Old) merged into BankAmerica Corp. (New) 09/30/1998 which name changed to Bank of America Corp. 04/28/1999

LIBERTY BANK (SEATTLE, WA)
Declared insolvent and taken over by the FDIC 6/17/88
Stockholders' equity undetermined

LIBERTY BK (SOUTH SAN FRANCISCO, CA)
Reorganized as Liberty Bancorp 7/1/2001
Each share Common no par exchanged for (1) share Common no par

LIBERTY BAY FINL CORP (WA)
Merged into Frontier Financial Corp. 7/20/2000
Each share Common no par exchanged for (10.5) shares Common no par

LIBERTY BELL BK (CHERRY HILL, NJ)
Stock Dividend - 3% payable 06/15/2009 to holders of record 06/01/2009 Ex date - 05/28/2009
Merged into Delmar Bancorp 03/01/2018
Each share Common $5 par exchanged for $1.70 cash

LIBERTY BELL CORP (NJ)
Plan of reorganization effective 03/16/1972
No stockholders' equity

LIBERTY BELL MINES INC (BC)
Recapitalized as Canadian Liberty Developments Corp. 05/23/1990
Each share Common no par exchanged for (0.25) share Common no par
(See Canadian Liberty Developments Corp.)

LIBERTY BELL PK INC (PA)
Liquidated 12/26/86
Details not available

LIBERTY BELL RACING ASSN (PA)
Class A Common $10 par and Class B Common no par changed to $1 par and (4) additional shares issued respectively 12/9/70
Liquidated 12/26/86
Details not available

LIBERTY BIOPHARMA INC (BC)
Each share old Common no par exchanged for (0.06666666) share new Common no par 07/23/2018
Name changed to HooXi Network Inc. 10/11/2018

LIBERTY BOND & SHARE CORP.
Merged into Liberty Share Corp. 00/00/1929
Details not available

LIBERTY CAP ASSET MGMT INC (DE)
Name changed to Las Vegas Railway Express (DE) 03/30/2010
Las Vegas Railway Express (DE) reorganized in Nevada as United Rail, Inc. 10/12/2018

LIBERTY CASH MGMT FD INC (MD)
Charter forfeited 10/03/1995

LIBERTY CENTRE BANCORP INC (PA)
Acquired by GNB Financial Services, Inc. 03/28/2014
Each share Common $1 par exchanged for $2.68 cash

LIBERTY CIRCLE CORP (DE)
Name changed to Equilink Corp. 6/11/76
Equilink Corp. name changed to MacGregor Sporting Goods Inc. 1/3/84 which name changed to M Holdings Corp. 9/14/89
(See M Holdings Corp.)

LIBERTY COMMUNICATIONS INC (NV)
Recapitalized as Big Boy Pacific Inc. 08/14/1992
Each share Common $0.001 par exchanged for (0.33333333) share Common $0.001 par

LIBERTY CONSUMER (GEORGIA)
GDR agreement terminated 11/30/2017
Each 144A Sponsored GDR for Ordinary exchanged for (20) shares Ordinary
Each Reg. S Sponsored GDR for Ordinary exchanged for (20) shares Ordinary
Note: Unexchanged GDR's will be sold and the proceeds, if any, held for claim after 12/04/2017

LIBERTY CORP. (CO)
Name changed to Kryotech International, Inc. 9/17/70
(See Kryotech International, Inc.)

LIBERTY CORP. (OK)
99.9% acquired by Palomar Financial through exchange offer 00/001970
Public interest eliminated

LIBERTY CORP (SC)
40¢ Conv. Preferred $2 par called for redemption 6/30/77
5% Conv. Preferred Ser. 1995-A called for redemption at $35 plus $0.32 accrued dividend on 9/5/2000
Common $2 par changed to $1 par and (1) additional share issued 7/19/79
Common $1 par split (2) for (1) by issuance of (1) additional share 12/2/91
Common $1 par changed to no par 5/14/92
Merged into Raycom Media, Inc. 1/31/2006
Each share Common no par exchanged for $47.35 cash

LIBERTY DAIRY PRODUCTS CORP.
Acquired by Beatrice Creamery Co. 00/00/1930
Details not available

LIBERTY DIGITAL INC (DE)
Merged into Liberty Media Corp. (New) 03/14/2002
Each share Class A Common 1¢ par exchanged for (0.25) share Common 1¢ par
Liberty Media Corp. (New) reorganized as Liberty Media Corp. (Incorporated 02/28/2006) 05/10/2006 which name changed to Liberty Interactive Corp. 09/26/2011 which name changed to Qurate Retail, Inc. 04/10/2018

LIBERTY DIVERSIFIED HLDGS INC (NV)
Each (3,000) shares old Common $0.001 par exchanged for (1) share new Common $0.001 par 08/14/2007
Name changed to Nutripure Beverages, Inc. 01/17/2008

LIBERTY DIVIDE MINING CO. (NV)
Charter forfeited for non-payment of taxes 2/28/24

LIBERTY ENTMT INC (DE)
Under plan of merger name changed to DIRECTV and each share Ser. A Common 1¢ par and Ser. B Common 1¢ par automatically became (1.1113) shares Class A Common 1¢ par 11/20/2009
DIRECTV merged into AT&T Inc. 07/24/2015

LIBERTY EQUITIES CORP (FL)
Name changed to Smithfield Foods, Inc. (FL) 01/12/1971
Smithfield Foods, Inc. (FL) reincorporated in Delaware 06/10/1971 which reincorporated in Virginia 09/02/1997
(See Smithfield Foods, Inc.)

LIBERTY EQUITY INCOME FD INC (MD)
Capital Stock no par reclassified as Class A no par 04/30/1993
Name changed to Federated Equity Income Fund, Inc. 03/31/1996

LIBERTY FABRICS NEW YORK INC (NY)
5% Preferred $10 par called for redemption 12/23/1983
Name changed to LBY Holding Corp. 01/03/1984
(See LBY Holding Corp.)

LIBERTY FEDERAL SAVINGS & LOAN ASSOCIATION (USA)
Chartered 00/00/1901
Name changed to Liberty Federal Savings Bank (Philadelphia, PA) 04/25/1985
Liberty Federal Savings Bank (Philadelphia, PA) reorganized as Liberty Financial Group, Inc. 02/13/1986

LIBERTY FED SVGS & LN ASSN MACON GA (USA)
Chartered 00/00/1926
Common $1 par split (3) for (2) by issuance of (0.5) additional share 12/05/1985
Reorganized as First Liberty Financial Corp. 04/01/1986
Each share Common $1 par exchanged for (1) share Common $1 par
(See Liberty Financial Group, Inc.)

LIBERTY FED SVGS BK (PHILADELPHIA, PA)
Reorganized under the laws of Delaware as Liberty Financial Group, Inc. 02/13/1986
Each share Common $1 par exchanged for (1) share Common $1 par
(See Liberty Financial Group, Inc.)

LIBERTY FINL CORP (IL)
Involuntarily dissolved 12/01/1975

LIBERTY FINL COS INC (MO)
Common 1¢ par split (3) for (2) by issuance of (0.5) additional share payable 12/10/97 to holders of record 11/26/97 Ex date - 12/11/97
Conv. Preferred Ser. A 1¢ par called for redemption at $51.54688 on 8/23/2001
Merged into Liberty Mutual Insurance Co. 12/12/2001
Each share Common 1¢ par exchanged for $33.70 cash

LIBERTY FINL GROUP INC (DE)
Merged into Equimark Corp. 12/30/1987
Each share Common $1 par exchanged for $47.96 cash

LIBERTY FINL TR (MA)
Merged into Colonial Trust III 3/24/95
Contact fund for details

LIBERTY FIRE INSURANCE CO.
In process of dissolution in 1940

LIBERTY GEM SILVER MINES, INC. (ID)
Recapitalized as Watling Industries, Inc. 11/19/1979
Each share Common 10¢ par exchanged for (0.1) share Common 10¢ par
Watling Industries, Inc. name changed to Watronics, Inc. 06/30/1981 which name changed to Measurements Game Technology, Inc. 08/30/1982
(See Measurements Game Technology, Inc.)

LIBERTY GLOBAL INC (DE)
Each share Ser. A Common 1¢ par received distribution of (1) share Ser. C Common 1¢ par payable 09/06/2005 to holders of record 08/26/2005
Each share Ser. B Common 1¢ par received distribution of (1) share Ser. C Common 1¢ par payable 09/06/2005 to holders of record 08/26/2005
Reorganized under the laws of England & Wales as Liberty Global PLC 06/10/2013
Each share Ser. A Common 1¢ par exchanged for (1) share Class A Ordinary 1¢ par
Each share Ser. B Common 1¢ par exchanged for (1) share Class B Ordinary 1¢ par
Each share Ser. C Common 1¢ par exchanged for (1) share Class C Ordinary 1¢ par

LIBERTY GLOBAL PLC (ENGLAND & WALES)
Each share LiLAC Class A, Class B and Class C Ordinary USD $0.01 par received distribution of (1) share Liberty Latin America Ltd. Class A, Class B or Class C Common 1¢ par respectively payable 12/29/2017 to holders of record 12/26/2017 Ex date - 01/02/2018
Note: LiLAC Ordinary Shares were delisted, redesignated as "deferred shares" and transferred to a third-party designee
(Additional Information in Active)

LIBERTY GOLD CORP (BC)
Name changed to Parksice Ventures Inc. 04/02/1992
Parkside Ventures Inc. recapitalized as International Parkside Products Inc. 02/03/1995

LIBERTY GOLD CORP (DE)
Common $0.0001 par split (50) for (1) by issuance of (49) additional shares payable 05/24/2011 to holders of record 05/19/2011
Ex date - 05/25/2011
SEC revoked common stock registration 08/08/2016

LIBERTY GROUP HLDGS INC (DE)
Company reported no assets or ongoing operations as of 00/00/2012

LIBERTY GROUP LTD (SOUTH AFRICA)
Each old Sponsored ADR for Ordinary exchanged for (0.9067361) new Sponsored ADR for Ordinary and $0.077538 cash 02/11/2005
Acquired by Liberty Holdings Ltd. 12/01/2008
Each Sponsored ADR for Ordinary exchanged for $5.73605 cash

LIBERTY GROUP PUBG INC (DE)
Stock Dividends - 3.6875% payable 11/1/99 to holders of record 10/22/99; 3.6875% payable 2/1/2000 to holders of record 1/21/2000; 3.6875% payable 5/1/2000 to holders of record 4/20/2000; 3.6875% payable 8/1/2000 to holders of record 7/21/2000; 3.6875% payable 11/1/2000 to holders of record 10/20/2000; 3.6875% payable 8/1/2001 to holders of record 7/27/2001; 3.6875% payable 11/1/2001 to holders of record 10/19/2001 Ex date - 11/2/2001; 3.6875% payable 2/1/2002 to holders of record 1/18/2002; 3.6875% payable 5/1/2002 to holders of record /19/2002 Ex date - 4/25/2002; 3.6875% payable 8/1/2002 to holders of record 7/19/2002 Ex date - 8/5/2002; 3.6875% payable 11/1/2002 to holders of record 10/21/2002 Ex date - 10/28/2002; 3.6875% payable 2/1/2003 to holders of record 1/17/2003 Ex date - 3/7/2003; 3.6875% payable 5/1/2003 to holders of record 4/25/2003 Ex date - 4/30/2003; 3.6875% payable 8/1/2003 to holders of record 7/18/2003; 3.6875% payable 11/1/2003 to holders of record 10/17/2003 Ex date - 10/30/2003; 3.6875% payable 2/1/2004 to holders of record 1/16/2004; 3.6875% payable 5/1/2004 to holders of record 4/23/2004 Ex date - 5/6/2004; 3.6875% payable 8/1/2004 to holders of record 7/20/2004 Ex date - 7/29/2004; 3.6875% payable 11/1/2004 to holders of record 10/25/2004; 3.6875% payable 2/1/2005 to holders of record 1/26/2005 Ex date - 2/17/2005
14.75% Sr. Exchangeable Preferred $25 par called for redemption at $25 on 3/15/2005

LIBERTY HIGH INCOME BD FD INC (MD)
Name changed to Federated High Income Bond Fund, Inc. 3/31/96

LIBERTY HOMES INC (IN)
Common $1 par split (3) for (2) by issuance of (0.5) additional share 09/20/1971
Each share Common $1 par exchanged for (0.5) share Class A $1 par and (0.5) share Conv. Class B $1 par 04/25/1985
Voluntarily dissolved 05/25/2017
Details not available

LIBERTY INCOME PPTYS LTD PARTNERSHIP (MA)
Filed a Certificate of Cancellation 03/26/1996

Details not available

LIBERTY INSURANCE CO. OF TEXAS (TX)
Name changed to Liberty Universal Insurance Co. 12/14/61
(See Liberty Universal Insurance Co.)

LIBERTY INTERACTIVE CORP (DE)
Incorporated 02/28/2006
Name changed 09/26/2011
Each share Liberty Capital Ser. A Common 1¢ par received distribution of (4) shares Liberty Entertainment Ser. A Common 1¢ par payable 03/03/2008 to holders of record 03/03/2008 Ex date - 03/04/2008
Each share Liberty Capital Ser. B Common 1¢ par received distribution of (4) shares Liberty Entertainment Ser. B Common 1¢ par payable 03/03/2008 to holders of record 03/03/2008 Ex date - 03/04/2008
Each share Liberty Entertainment Ser. A Common 1¢ par exchanged for (0.1) share Liberty Starz Ser. A Common 1¢ par and (0.9) share Liberty Entertainment, Inc. Ser. A Common 1¢ par 11/20/2009
Each share Liberty Entertainment Ser. B Common 1¢ par exchanged for (0.1) share Liberty Starz Ser. B Common 1¢ par and (0.9) share Liberty Entertainment, Inc. Ser. B Common 1¢ par 11/20/2009
Each share Liberty Capital Common Ser. A 1¢ par exchanged for (1) Liberty Media Corp. (Ctfs. dated after 09/26/2011) Liberty Capital Common Ser. A 1¢ par 09/26/2011
Each share Liberty Capital Common Ser. B 1¢ par exchanged for (1) Liberty Media Corp. (Ctfs. dated after 09/26/2011) Liberty Capital Common Ser. B 1¢ par 09/26/2011
Each share Liberty Starz Common Ser. A 1¢ par exchanged for (1) Liberty Media Corp. (Ctfs. dated after 09/26/2011) Liberty Starz Common Ser. A 1¢ par 09/26/2011
Each share Liberty Starz Common Ser. B 1¢ par exchanged for (1) Liberty Media Corp. (Ctfs. dated after 09/26/2011) Liberty Starz Common Ser. A 1¢ par 09/26/2011
Name changed from Liberty Media Corp. to Liberty Interactive Corp. 09/26/2011
Each share Interactive Common Ser. A 1¢ par received distribution of (0.05) share Liberty Ventures old Common Ser. A 1¢ par and (0.01666666) Liberty Ventures Ser. A Right payable 08/09/2012 to holders of record 08/09/2012 Ex date - 08/10/2012
Each share Interactive Common Ser. B 1¢ par received distribution of (0.05) share Liberty Ventures old Common Ser. B 1¢ par and (0.01666666) Liberty Ventures Ser. A and (0.01666666) Liberty Ventures Ser. A Right payable 08/09/2012 to holders of record 08/09/2012 Ex date - 08/10/2012
Liberty Ventures old Common Ser. A 1¢ par split (2) for (1) by issuance of (1) additional share payable 04/11/2014 to holders of record 04/04/2011 Ex date - 04/14/2014
Liberty Ventures old Common Ser. B 1¢ par split (2) for (1) by issuance of (1) additional share payable 04/11/2014 to holders of record 04/04/2011 Ex date - 04/14/2014
Each share Liberty Ventures old Common Ser. A 1¢ par received distribution of (1) share Liberty TripAdvisor Holdings, Inc. Common Ser. A 1¢ par payable 08/27/2014 to holders of record 08/21/2014 Ex date - 08/28/2014
Each share Liberty Ventures old Common Ser. B 1¢ par received distribution of (1) share Liberty TripAdvisor Holdings, Inc. Common Ser. B 1¢ par payable 08/27/2014 to holders of record 08/21/2014 Ex date - 08/28/2014
Each share Liberty Interactive Common Ser. A 1¢ par received distribution of (0.14217) share Liberty Ventures old Common Ser. A 1¢ par payable 10/20/2014 to holders of record 10/13/2014 Ex date - 10/15/2014
Interactive Common Ser. A 1¢ par reclassified as QVC Group Common Ser. A 1¢ par 06/08/2015
Interactive Common Ser. B 1¢ par reclassified as QVC Group Common Ser. B 1¢ par 06/08/2015
Each share Liberty Ventures old Common Ser. A 1¢ par received distribution of (0.1) share CommerceHub, Inc. Common Ser. A 1¢ par payable 07/22/2016 to holders of record 07/08/2016 Ex date - 07/25/2016
Each share Liberty Ventures old Common Ser. A 1¢ par received distribution of (0.2) share CommerceHub, Inc. Common Ser. C 1¢ par payable 07/22/2016 to holders of record 07/08/2016 Ex date - 07/25/2016
Each share Liberty Ventures old Common Ser. B 1¢ par received distribution of (0.1) share CommerceHub, Inc. Common Ser. B 1¢ par payable 07/22/2016 to holders of record 07/08/2016 Ex date - 07/25/2016
Each share Liberty Ventures old Common Ser. B 1¢ par received distribution of (0.2) share CommerceHub, Inc. Common Ser. C 1¢ par payable 07/22/2016 to holders of record 07/08/2016 Ex date - 07/25/2016
Each share Liberty Ventures old Common Ser. A 1¢ par exchanged for (0.6) share new Common Ser. A 1¢ par and (0.4) share Liberty Expedia Holdings, Inc. Common Ser. A 1¢ par 11/07/2018
Each share Liberty Ventures old Common Ser. B 1¢ par exchanged for (0.6) share new Common Ser. B 1¢ par and (0.4) share Liberty Expedia Holdings, Inc. Common Ser. B 1¢ par 11/07/2018
Each share Liberty Ventures new Common Ser. A 1¢ par automatically became (1) share GCI Liberty, Inc. Class A Common no par 03/12/2018
Each share Liberty Ventures new Common Ser. B 1¢ par automatically became (1) share GCI Liberty, Inc. Class B Common no par 03/12/2018
Name changed to Qurate Retail, Inc. 04/10/2018

LIBERTY INTL PLC (UNITED KINGDOM)
Name changed to Capital Shopping Centres Group PLC 05/14/2010
(See Capital Shopping Centres Group PLC)

LIBERTY INVESTMENT CORP. (IL)
Name changed to Liberty Financial Corp. 12/8/69
Liberty Financial Corp. dissolved 12/1/75

LIBERTY INVESTORS, INC. (KS)
Name changed to Ammest Inc. 02/01/1972
Ammest Inc. name changed to Ammest Group, Inc. 06/05/1973 which merged into Academy Insurance Group, Inc. 08/31/1978
(See Academy Insurance Group, Inc.)

LIBERTY INVS LIFE INS CO (OK)
Common Capital Stock 5¢ par changed to 2¢ par 09/25/1975
Placed in receivership 09/02/1983
No stockholders' equity

LIBERTY LEASING INC (DE)
Stock Dividend - 50% 10/30/1968
Name changed to Libco Corp. 07/10/1973
Libco Corp. recapitalized as RDIS Corp. 12/14/1992 which recapitalized as TenthGate International, Inc. 03/14/2007 which recapitalized as TGI Solar Power Group, Inc. 07/25/2008

LIBERTY LIFE & ACCIDENT INSURANCE CO. (MI)
Each share Class A $1 par exchanged for (0.75) share Part. Common $1 par 04/08/1956
Each share Class B $1 par exchanged for (1.5) shares Common $1 par 04/08/1956
Each share Part. Common $1 par or old Common $1 par exchanged for (1) share new Common $1 par 06/15/1958
Merged into Independent Liberty Life Insurance Co. 03/30/1966
Each share Common $1 par exchanged for (0.534) share Common $1 par
(See Independent Liberty Life Insurance Co.)

LIBERTY LIFE ASSN AFRICA LTD (SOUTH AFRICA)
Each old Sponsored ADR for Ordinary Rand-10 par exchanged for (0.5) new Sponsored ADR for Ordinary Rand-10 par 02/22/1999
Name changed to Liberty Group Ltd. 05/29/2000
(See Liberty Group Ltd.)

LIBERTY LIFE INSURANCE CO. (KS)
Acquired by Business Men's Assurance Co. of America 07/00/1941
Details not available

LIBERTY LIFE INSURANCE CO. (SC)
Each share Capital Stock $10 par exchanged for (4-1/6) shares Vtg. Capital Stock $2 par and (4-1/6) shares Non-Vtg. Capital Stock $2 par to effect a (2.5) for (1) split and 66-2/3% stock dividend 10/28/1959
Non-Vtg. Capital Stock $2 par reclassified as Vtg. Capital Stock $2 par 06/28/1963
Stock Dividends - 100% 10/01/1940; 25% 10/31/1942; 50% 10/15/1944; 33-1/3% 10/15/1947; 100% 03/26/1952; 50% 04/15/1957; 20% 10/20/1961; 25% 04/30/1963; 10% 05/10/1965; 21.21212% 04/24/1967
Each share Vtg. Capital Stock $2 par exchanged for (0.0002) share Common $10,000 par 04/23/1971
Public interest eliminated

LIBERTY LIVEWIRE CORP (DE)
Name changed to Ascent Media Group, Inc. 11/20/2002
Ascent Media Group, Inc. merged into Liberty Media Corp. (New) 07/01/2003 which reorganized as Liberty Media Corp. (Incorporated 02/28/2006) 05/10/2006 which name changed to Liberty Interactive Corp. 09/26/2011 which name changed to Qurate Retail, Inc. 04/10/2018

LIBERTY LN CORP (DE)
Class A Common no par changed to $5 par in 1944
Each share Class A Common $5 par exchanged for (1) share Common $1 par in 1954
Each share Class B Common no par exchanged for (13-1/3) shares Common $1 par in 1954
Common $1 par split (1.75) for (1) by issuance of (0.75) additional share 7/10/59
Common $1 par split (5) for (4) by issuance of (0.25) additional share 11/26/63
Name changed to LLC Corp. 3/14/80

LLC Corp. name changed to Valhi, Inc. 3/10/87

LIBERTY MEDIA CORP (DE)
Ctfs. dated after 09/26/2011
Each share Liberty Starz Common Ser. A 1¢ par exchanged for (0.88129) share Liberty Capital Common Ser. A 1¢ par 11/29/2011
Each share Liberty Starz Common Ser. B 1¢ par exchanged for (0.88129) share Liberty Capital Common Ser. B 1¢ par 11/29/2011
Each share Common Ser. A 1¢ par received distribution of (1) share Liberty Media Corp. (Ctfs. dated after 01/11/2013)
Common Ser. A 1¢ par payable 01/11/2013 to holders of record 01/10/2013 Ex date - 01/14/2013
Each share Common Ser. B 1¢ par received distribution of (1) share Liberty Media Corp. (Ctfs. dated after 01/11/2013) Common Ser. B 1¢ par payable 01/11/2013 to holders of record 01/10/2013 Ex date - 01/14/2013
Name changed to Starz 01/14/2013
Starz merged into Lions Gate Entertainment Corp. 12/08/2016

LIBERTY MEDIA CORP NEW (DE)
Each share Common Ser. A 1¢ par received distribution of (0.05) share Liberty Media International, Inc. Common Ser. A 1¢ par payable 06/07/2004 to holders of record 06/01/2004 Ex date - 06/08/2004
Each share Common Ser. B 1¢ par received distribution of (0.05) share Liberty Media International, Inc. Common Ser. B 1¢ par payable 06/07/2004 to holders of record 06/01/2004
Each share Common Ser. A 1¢ par received distribution of (0.1) share Discovery Holding Co. Common Ser. A 1¢ par payable 07/20/2005 to holders of record 07/15/2005 Ex date - 07/21/2005
Each share Common Ser. B 1¢ par received distribution of (0.1) share Discovery Holding Co. Common Ser. B 1¢ par payable 07/20/2005 to holders of record 07/15/2005 Ex date - 07/21/2005
Reorganized as Liberty Media Corp. (Incorporated 02/28/2006) 05/10/2006
Each share Common Ser. A 1¢ par exchanged for (0.25) share Liberty Interactive Common Ser. A 1¢ par and (0.05) share Liberty Capital Ser. A Common 1¢ par
Each share Common Ser. B 1¢ par exchanged for (0.25) share Liberty Interactive Common Ser. B 1¢ par and (0.05) share Liberty Capital Ser. B Common 1¢ par
Liberty Media Corp. (Incorporated 02/28/2006) name changed to Liberty Interactive Corp. 09/26/2011 which name changed to Qurate Retail, Inc. 04/10/2018

LIBERTY MEDIA CORP OLD (DE)
Each share old Class A Common $1 par exchanged for (2) shares 6% Class E Preferred $1 par and (20) shares new Class A Common $1 par 3/12/92
Each share old Class B Common $1 par exchanged for (2) shares 6% Class E Preferred $1 par and (20) shares new Class B Common $1 par 3/12/92
New Class A Common $1 par split (4) for (1) by issuance of (3) additional shares 12/3/92
New Class B Common $1 par split (4) for (1) by issuance of (3) additional shares 12/3/92
New Class A Common $1 par split (2) for (1) by issuance of (1) additional share 3/17/93
New Class B Common $1 par split (2)

for (1) by issuance of (1) additional share 3/17/93
Merged into Tele-Communications, Inc. (New) 8/5/94
Each share 6% Class E Preferred 1¢ par exchanged for (1) share 6% Class B Jr. Preferred 1¢ par
Each share new Class A Common $1 par exchanged for (0.975) share Class A Common $1 par
Each share new Class B Common $1 par exchanged for (0.975) share Class B Common $1 par
Tele-Communications, Inc. (New) merged into AT&T Corp. 3/9/99 which merged into AT&T Inc. 11/18/2005

LIBERTY MEDIA INTL INC (DE)
Merged into Liberty Global, Inc. (DE) 06/15/2005
Each share Common Ser. A 1¢ par exchanged for (1) share Common Ser. A 1¢ par
Each share Common Ser. B 1¢ par exchanged for (1) share Common Ser. B 1¢ par
Liberty Global, Inc. (DE) reorganized in England & Wales as Liberty Global PLC 06/10/2013

LIBERTY MILITARY SALES INC (DE)
Plan of reorganization under Chapter 11 Federal Bankruptcy proceedings confirmed 04/26/1991
No stockholders' equity

LIBERTY MINERAL EXPL INC (ON)
Reincorporated 08/17/2004
Place of incorporation changed from (AB) to (ON) 08/17/2004
Name changed to Liberty Mines Inc. 07/19/2005
Liberty Mines Inc. name changed to Northern Sun Mining Corp. 10/25/2013
(See Northern Sun Mining Corp.)

LIBERTY MINES CORP. (NV)
Charter revoked for failure to file reports and pay fees 3/7/27

LIBERTY MINES INC (ON)
Each share old Common no par exchanged for (0.02) share new Common no par 08/13/2014
Name changed to Northern Sun Mining Corp. 10/25/2013
(See Northern Sun Mining Corp.)

LIBERTY MINES LTD. (BC)
Struck off register and declared dissolved for failure to file returns 7/9/72

LIBERTY MINT LTD (NV)
Reincorporated 10/00/1999
State of incorporation changed from (CO) to (NV) 10/00/1999
Each share old Common no par exchanged for (1/6) share new Common no par 05/12/1999
Each share new Common no par exchanged again for (6) shares new Common no par 08/14/2000
Each share new Common no par exchanged for (0.02) share old Common $0.001 par 02/13/2003
Each share old Common $0.001 par exchanged for (0.05) share new Common $0.001 par 05/04/2004
Note: No holder will receive fewer than (100) shares
Name changed to Akesis Pharmaceuticals, Inc. 01/19/2005
(See Akesis Pharmaceuticals, Inc.)

LIBERTY MTG INS CO (IL)
Acquired by American Financial Corp. 9/24/71
Each share Common $1 par exchanged for (0.093457) share Common no par
(See American Financial Corp.)

LIBERTY MUN SECS FD INC (MD)
Name changed to Federated Municipal Securities Fund, Inc. 3/31/96

LIBERTY MUT TAX EXEMPT INCOME TR (MA)
Trust terminated 06/06/1990
Details not available

LIBERTY NATL BANCORP INC (KY)
Under plan of merger name changed to Liberty United Bancorp, Inc. 12/23/82 which name changed back to Liberty National Bancorp, Inc. 4/17/86
Common no par split (3) for (2) by issuance of (0.5) additional share 5/15/86
Common no par split (4) for (3) by issuance of (1/3) additional share 5/14/87
Common no par split (3) for (2) by issuance of (0.5) additional share 2/17/92
Common no par split (4) for (3) by issuance of (1/3) additional share 5/17/93
Merged into Banc One Corp. 8/15/94
Each share Common no par exchanged for (0.9617) share Common no par
Banc One Corp. merged into Bank One Corp. 10/2/98 which merged into J.P. Morgan Chase & Co. 12/31/2000 which name changed to JPMorgan Chase & Co. 7/20/2004

LIBERTY NATL BANCSHARES INC (GA)
Common $1 par split (2) for (1) by issuance of (1) additional share payable 8/15/2002 to holders of record 7/31/2002 Ex date - 8/16/2002
Merged into United Community Banks, Inc. 12/1/2004
Each share Common $1 par exchanged for (0.20467) share Common $1 par and $16.946 cash

LIBERTY NATL BK & TR CO (BUFFALO, NY)
Stock Dividends - 10% 1/69; 10% 3/1/71
Reorganized as United Bank Corp. of New York 12/31/71
Each share Common $10 par exchanged for (2.25) shares Common $5 par
United Bank Corp. of New York name changed to Norstar Bancorp Inc. 1/4/82 which merged into Fleet/Norstar Financial Group, Inc. 1/1/88 which name changed to Fleet Financial Group, Inc. (New) 4/15/92 which name changed to Fleet Boston Corp. 10/1/99 which name changed to FleetBoston Financial Corp. 4/18/2000 which merged into Bank of America Corp. 4/1/2004

LIBERTY NATL BK & TR CO (LOUISVILLE, KY)
Common $2.50 par changed to $2.75 par in 1943
Each share Common $2.75 par exchanged for (0.2) share Common $13.75 par in January 1944
Common $13.75 par changed to $15 par in December 1944
Common $15 par changed to $16 par in August 1945
Common $16 par changed $17.50 par in December 1945
Common $17.50 par changed to $20 par in 1946
Common $20 par changed to $21 par in 1947
Common $21 par changed to $22.50 par in 1948
Common $22.50 par changed to $25 par in 1949
Common $25 par changed to $12.50 par and (1) additional share issued 11/18/63
Voting Trust Agreement terminated 1/10/77
Each VTC for Common $12.50 par exchanged for (1) share Common $12.50 par
Common $12.50 par changed to $8.333333 par and (0.5) additional share issued 5/1/78
Stock Dividends - 20% 12/28/70; 100% 11/15/72
Merged into Liberty National Bancorp, Inc. 10/1/80
Each share Common $8.333333 par exchanged for (1) share Common $8.333333 par
Liberty National Bancorp, Inc. merged into Liberty United Bancorp, Inc. 12/23/82 which name changed back to Liberty National Bancorp, Inc. 4/17/86 which merged into Banc One Corp. 8/15/94 which merged into Bank One Corp. 10/2/98 which merged into J.P. Morgan Chase & Co. 12/31/2000 which name changed to JPMorgan Chase & Co. 7/20/2004

LIBERTY NATL BK & TR CO (OKLAHOMA CITY, OK)
Each share Capital Stock $100 par exchanged for (5) shares Capital Stock $20 par 00/00/1945
Each share Capital Stock $20 par exchanged for (2) shares Capital Stock $10 par 12/30/1955
Stock Dividends - 33-1/3% 12/01/1949; (1.5) for (7) 12/30/1955; 27.118644% 01/31/1963; 12-1/2% 01/31/1966
Reorganized as Liberty National Corp. 10/01/1969
Each share Capital Stock $10 par exchanged for (1) share Common $10 par
Liberty National Corp. merged into Banks of Mid-America, Inc. (DE) 07/17/1984 which reincorporated in Oklahoma as Liberty Bancorp Inc. 05/26/1992 which merged into Banc One Corp. 06/01/1997 which merged into Bank One Corp. 10/02/1998 which merged into J.P. Morgan Chase & Co. 12/31/2000 which name changed to JPMorgan Chase & Co. 07/20/2004

LIBERTY NATL BK & TR CO (SAVANNAH, GA)
Each share Capital Stock $100 par exchanged for (10) shares Capital Stock $10 par 00/00/1942
Capital Stock $10 par split (1.666) for (1) by issuance of (0.666) additional share 03/28/1974
Stock Dividend - 100% 12/27/1965
Name changed to Trust Co. of Georgia Bank of Savannah, N.A. (Savannah, GA) 08/12/1974
Trust Co. of Georgia Bank of Savannah, N.A. (Savannah, GA) merged into Trust Co. of Georgia 08/17/1978 which merged into SunTrust Banks, Inc. 07/01/1985

LIBERTY NATL BK (BRADENTON, FL)
Merged into Key Florida Bancorp Inc. 7/30/96
Each share Common $5 par exchanged for (1.5) shares Common $5 par
Key Florida Bancorp Inc. merged into Regions Financial Corp. (Old) 3/19/98 which merged into Regions Financial Corp. (New) 7/1/2004

LIBERTY NATL BK (DANBURY, CT)
Merged into Village Bancorp Inc. 11/18/94
Each share Common $5 par exchanged for (0.11494252) share Common $3.33 par
Village Bancorp Inc. merged into Webster Financial Corp. 5/19/99

LIBERTY NATL BK (HILLSDALE, NJ)
Merged into Valley National Bank (Passaic, NJ) 12/31/1981
Each share Common $6 par exchanged for (1) Common Stock Purchase Warrant expiring 02/16/1982 and $24 cash
Note: Above ratio applied to shares surrendered by 02/16/1982 after which holders received $30 cash per share

LIBERTY NATL BK (HUNTINGTON BEACH, CA)
Each share Common $0.83333333 par exchanged for (0.25) share Common $3.33333333 par 08/26/1991
Merged into SDN Bancorp Inc. 04/01/1996
Each share Common $3.33333333 par exchanged for $14.80 cash

LIBERTY NATL BK (PARIS, TX)
Under plan of reorganization each share Common $1 par automatically became (1) share Paris Bancshares, Inc. Common $1 par 11/01/1996

LIBERTY NATL BK (PITTSTON, PA)
Stock Dividend - 10% 10/21/70
Merged into First Valley Corp. 12/31/73
Each share Common $25 par exchanged for (7) shares Common $1 par
First Valley Corp. acquired by United Jersey Banks 1/29/88 which name changed to UJB Financial Corp. 6/30/89 which name changed to Summit Bancorp 3/1/96 which merged into FleetBoston Financial Corp. 3/1/2001 which merged into Bank of America Corp. 4/1/2004

LIBERTY NATL BK (SAN FRANCISCO, CA)
Merged into Chartered Bank of London (San Francisco, CA) 07/01/1974
Each share Common $2 par exchanged for $16.33 cash

LIBERTY NATL BK (ST. PETERSBURG, FL)
Name changed to Flagship Bank of St. Petersburg, N.A. (St. Petersburg, FL) 11/08/1974
(See Flagship Bank of St. Petersburg, N.A. (St. Petersburg, FL))

LIBERTY NATL CORP (DE)
Common $10 par changed to $5 par and (1) additional share issued 04/15/1977
Common $5 par split (4) for (3) by issuance of (1/3) additional share 10/17/1980
Common $5 par split (3) for (2) by issuance of (0.5) additional share 07/17/1981
$2.125 Conv. Preferred $1 par called for redemption 09/19/1981
Stock Dividends - 10% 11/23/1973; 33-1/3% 01/19/1983
Merged into Banks of Mid-America, Inc. (DE) 07/17/1984
Each share Adjustable Rate Preferred Ser. A $1 par exchanged for (1) share Adjustable Rate Preferred Ser. A $1 par
Each share Common $5 par exchanged for (1) share Common $1 par
Banks of Mid-America, Inc. (DE) reincorporated in Oklahoma as Liberty Bancorp Inc. 05/26/1992 which merged into Banc One Corp. 06/01/1997 which merged into Bank One Corp. 10/02/1998 which merged into J.P. Morgan Chase & Co. 12/31/2000 which name changed to JPMorgan Chase & Co. 07/20/2004

LIBERTY NATL INS HLDG CO (DE)
Name changed to Torchmark Corp. 07/01/1982

LIBERTY NATL LIFE INS CO (AL)
Capital Stock $10 par changed to $2 par and (4) additional shares issued plus a 20% stock dividend paid 04/19/1957
Capital Stock $2 par split (2) for (1)

by issuance of (1) additional share 05/21/1969
Capital Stock $2 par split (4) for (3) by issuance of (1/3) additional share 05/18/1973
Stock Dividends - 44% 00/00/1939; 33-1/3% 03/11/1941; 25% 12/17/1942; 100% 03/10/1948; 100% 03/10/1953; 25% 04/17/1959; 33-1/3% 04/03/1961; 25% 03/29/1963; (3) for (17) 05/25/1966
Under plan of reorganization each share Capital Stock $2 par automatically became (1) share Liberty National Insurance Holding Co. (DE) Common $2 par 12/31/1980
Liberty National Insurance Holding Co. (DE) name changed to Torchmark Corp. 07/01/1982

LIBERTY OIL & GAS 1998 LTD (SK)
Acquired by Lexxor Energy Inc. 07/23/2002
Each share Common no par exchanged for (0.05655532) share Common no par and (0.05655332) Common Stock Purchase Warrant expiring 07/23/2004
Lexxor Energy Inc. reorganized as Find Energy Ltd. 09/05/2003 which was acquired by Shiningbank Energy Income Fund 09/22/2006 which merged into PrimeWest Energy Trust 07/13/2007
(See PrimeWest Energy Trust)

LIBERTY OIL & REFINING CO. (CA)
Charter suspended for failure to file reports and pay fees 03/01/1919

LIBERTY OIL & URANIUM CO. (CO)
Each share Common 1¢ par exchanged for (0.1) share Common 10¢ par 12/30/55
Name changed to Liberty Corp. (CO) 5/21/69
Liberty Corp. (CO) name changed to Kryotech International, Inc. 9/17/70
(See Kryotech International, Inc.)

LIBERTY OIL CO.
Dissolved in 1927

LIBERTY OIL CORP. (UT)
Name changed to Coastal Investments Corp. 7/6/81
(See Coastal Investments Corp.)

LIBERTY PETE INC (CANADA)
Name changed to Power Oil & Gas Inc. 06/26/2008
Power Oil & Gas Inc. recapitalized as Power Resource Exploration Inc. 01/03/2012

LIBERTY PETES INC (BC)
Acquired by Corrida Oils Ltd. 05/06/1982
Each share Common no par exchanged for (0.16666666) Common Stock Purchase Warrant, Ser. B expiring 11/20/1982 and (0.25) share Common no par
(See Corrida Oils Ltd.)

LIBERTY PLAN OF AMERICA, INC. (OK)
Charter cancelled for failure to pay taxes 6/13/68

LIBERTY PRESIDENTIAL INVT FDS (CA)
Each share Common no par exchanged for (0.03333333) share Common $0.001 par 02/26/2008
Name changed to American Pacific Rim Commerce Group (CA) 03/28/2008
American Pacific Rim Commerce Group (CA) reincorporated in Florida as American Pacific Rim Commerce Corp. 11/21/2012

LIBERTY PRODUCTS CORP.
Acquired by Beatrice Creamery Co. 00/00/1930
Details not available

LIBERTY PRODUCTS CORP. (NY)
Stock Dividends - 10% 12/28/48; 10% 12/27/50
Merged into Penn-Texas Corp. 12/12/55
Each share Common 50¢ par exchanged for (1/3) share $1.60 Conv. Preferred $40 par and (0.6) share Common $10 par
Penn-Texas Corp. name changed to Fairbanks Whitney Corp. 5/29/59 which recapitalized as Colt Industries Inc. (PA) 5/15/64 which reincorporated in Delaware 10/17/68 which reincorporated in Pennsylvania 5/6/76
(See Colt Industries Inc. (PA))

LIBERTY PPTY TR (MD)
Issue Information - 5,000,000 PFD SHS BEN INT SER A 8.80% offered at $25 per share on 08/05/1997
8.80% Preferred Shares of Bene. Int. Ser. A $0.001 par called for redemption at $25 on 08/28/2002
(Additional Information in Active)

LIBERTY REAL ESTATE BANK & TRUST CO. (PHILADELPHIA, PA)
Stock Dividends - 10% 03/07/1956; 10% 03/04/1959; 10% 03/07/1962
Merged into Fidelity-Philadelphia Trust Co. (Philadelphia, PA) 01/10/1964
Each share Capital Stock $10 par exchanged for (0.7) share Capital Stock $10 par
Fidelity-Philadelphia Trust Co. (Philadelphia, PA) name changed to Fidelity Bank (Philadelphia, PA) 04/03/1967 which reorganized as Fidelity Corp. of Pennsylvania 04/14/1969 which name changed to Fidelcor, Inc. 05/15/1974 which merged into First Fidelity Bancorporation (New) 02/29/1988 which merged into First Union Corp. 01/01/1996 which name changed to Wachovia Corp. (Ctfs. dated after 09/01/2001) 09/01/2001 which merged into Wells Fargo & Co. (New) 12/31/2008

LIBERTY REAL ESTATE TRUST (FL)
Reorganized as Liberty Equities Corp. 08/01/1966
Each Ctf. of Bene. Int. $1 par exchanged for (1) share Common $1 par
Liberty Equities Corp. name changed to Smithfield Foods, Inc. (FL) 01/12/1971 which reincorporated in Delaware 06/10/1971 which reincorporated in Virginia 09/02/1997
(See Smithfield Foods, Inc.)

LIBERTY RECORDS, INC. (CA)
Merged into Avnet Electronics Corp. on a (0.6) for (1) basis 5/29/62 which name was changed to Avnet, Inc. 12/2/64

LIBERTY RES INC (DE)
Name changed to Bristol-Sterling Financial Corp. 10/05/1988
(See Bristol-Sterling Financial Corp.)

LIBERTY RES LTD (AB)
Name changed to Turbo Resources Ltd. 10/12/1971
Turbo Resources Ltd. recapitalized as Canadian Turbo Inc. 11/08/1990
(See Canadian Turbo Inc.)

LIBERTY RES LTD (AUSTRALIA)
Each old Sponsored ADR for Ordinary exchanged for (0.5) new Sponsored ADR for Ordinary 05/29/2015
ADR agreement terminated 11/06/2015
Each new Sponsored ADR for Ordinary exchanged for $0.85156 cash

LIBERTY SATELLITE & TECHNOLOGY INC (DE)
Each share old Class A Common $8 par exchanged for (0.1) share new Class A Common $8 par 04/01/2002
Each share old Class B Common $8 par exchanged for (0.1) share new Class B Common $8 par 04/01/2002
Merged into Liberty Media Corp. (New) 11/12/2003
Each share new Class A Common $8 par exchanged for (0.275) share Class A Common 1¢ par
Each share new Class B Common $8 par exchanged for (0.275) share Class B Common 1¢ par
Liberty Media Corp. (New) reorganized as Liberty Media Corp. (Incorporated 02/28/2006) 05/10/2006 which name changed to Liberty Interactive Corp. 09/26/2011 which name changed to Qurate Retail, Inc. 04/10/2018

LIBERTY SVGS & LN ASSN (CA)
Merged into Equity Funding Corp. of America 04/12/1971
Each share Guarantee Stock $1 par exchanged for (1/3) share Conv. Preferred Ser. B $100 par
Equity Funding Corp. of America reorganized as Orion Capital Corp. 03/31/1976
(See Orion Capital Corp.)

LIBERTY SVGS & LN ASSN (WARRENTON, VA)
Placed in conservatorship by the RTC 7/17/92
No stockholders' equity

LIBERTY SVGS BK (MARIETTA, OH)
Placed in receivership 05/03/1991
No stockholders' equity

LIBERTY SVGS BK (MAYFIELD, KY)
Each share Common $100 par exchanged for (10) shares Common $10 par 09/15/1960
Stock Dividends - 100% 05/01/1972; 100% 12/28/1979
Reorganized as Libsab Bancorp, Inc. 12/05/1983
Each share Common $10 par exchanged for (1) share Common no par
(See Libsab Bancorp, Inc.)

LIBERTY SVGS BK F S B (POTTSVILLE, PA)
Under plan of reorganization each share Common $1 par automatically became (1) share Liberty Centre Bancorp, Inc. Common $1 par 08/13/1999
(See Liberty Centre Bancorp, Inc.)

LIBERTY SVGS BK FSB (LIBERTY, MO)
Name changed 3/1/95
Name changed from Liberty Savings Bank (Liberty, MO) to Liberty Savings Bank, F.S.B. (Liberty, MO) 3/1/95
Reorganized as Liberty Bancorp, Inc. 7/24/2006
Each share Common $1 par exchanged for (3.5004) shares Common 1¢ par

LIBERTY SELF STOR INC (MD)
Name changed to John D. Oil & Gas Co. 6/27/2005

LIBERTY SHARE CORP.
Merged into Western New York Fund, Inc. in 1941 which was completely liquidated in 1946

LIBERTY SHS INC (GA)
Name changed to Heritage Bancorporation, Inc. 06/07/2017

LIBERTY SILVER CORP (NV)
Old Common 1¢ par split (20) for (1) by issuance of (19) additional shares payable 03/15/2010 to holders of record 03/15/2010
Each share old Common 1¢ par exchanged for (0.06666666) share new Common 1¢ par 02/02/2015
Name changed to Bunker Hill Mining Corp. 11/29/2017

LIBERTY ST BK (MOUNT CARMEL, PA)
Merged into Commonwealth Bancshares Corp. 09/18/1987
Each share Capital Stock $50 par exchanged for (180.356) shares Common $3.50 par
Commonwealth Bancshares Corp. acquired by Meridian Bancorp, Inc. 08/31/1993 which merged into CoreStates Financial Corp 04/09/1996 which merged into First Union Corp. 04/28/1998 which name changed to Wachovia Corp. (Ctfs. dated after 09/01/2001) 09/01/2001 which merged into Wells Fargo & Co. (New) 12/31/2008

LIBERTY STAR GOLD CORP (NV)
Reorganized as Liberty Star Uranium & Metals Corp. 04/13/2007
Each share Common $0.001 par exchanged for (1) share Common $0.001 par

LIBERTY STEEL CO.
Acquired by Trumbull Steel Co. 00/00/1927
Details not available

LIBERTY SURETY BOND INSURANCE CO.
Merged into Commonwealth Casualty Co. 07/00/1931
Details not available

LIBERTY TECHNOLOGIES INC (DE)
Recapitalized as DomiKnow, Inc. 02/15/2013
Each share Common $0.001 par exchanged for (0.1) share Common $0.001 par
DomiKnow, Inc. name changed to Gooi Global, Inc. 04/02/2015

LIBERTY TECHNOLOGIES INC (PA)
Merged into Crane Co. 10/14/1998
Each share Common 1¢ par exchanged for $3.50 cash

LIBERTY TERM TR INC - 1999 (MD)
Trust terminated 12/17/99
Each share Common $0.001 par exchanged for $9.15720015 cash

LIBERTY TRUST CO. (CUMBERLAND, MD)
Capital Stock $15 par changed to $20 par 00/00/1945
Capital Stock $20 par changed to $10 par 00/00/1948
Name changed to Liberty Trust Co. of Maryland (Cumberland, MD) 02/01/1966
Liberty Trust Co. of Maryland (Cumberland, MD) reorganized as LTC Bancorp 09/01/1983 which merged into WM Bancorp 10/01/1986 which was acquired by Keystone Financial, Inc. 01/07/1994

LIBERTY TR CO MD (CUMBERLAND, MD)
Stock Dividends - 10% 10/6/70; 20% 5/1/73; 20% 5/3/76; 50% 7/26/78
Reorganized as LTC Bancorp 9/1/83
Each share Common $10 par exchanged for (1) share Common $10 par
LTC Bancorp merged into WM Bancorp 10/1/86 which was acquired by Keystone Financial, Inc. 1/7/94 which merged into M&T Bank Corp. 10/6/2000

LIBERTY UTD BANCORP INC (KY)
Common $8.333333 par split (3) for (2) by issuance of (0.5) additional share 5/17/83
Common $8.333333 par changed to no par 4/17/85
Common no par split (3) for (2) by issuance of (0.5) additional share 5/9/85
Name changed back to Liberty National Bancorp, Inc. 4/17/86
Liberty National Bancorp, Inc. merged into Banc One Corp. 8/15/94 which merged into Bank One Corp.

10/2/98 which merged into J.P. Morgan Chase & Co. 12/31/2000 which name changed to JPMorgan Chase & Co. 7/20/2004

LIBERTY UNVL INS CO (TX)
Placed in permanent receivership and charter cancelled by the Texas Insurance Department 10/20/1970
No stockholders' equity

LIBERTY UTIL FD INC (MD)
Name changed to Federated Utility Fund, Inc. 3/31/96
Federated Utility Fund, Inc. reorganized in Massachusetts as Federated Capital Income Fund, Inc. 12/20/2002

LIBERTY VENTURES LTD (CO)
Name changed to UniComp, Inc. 11/20/1986
(See UniComp, Inc.)

LIBERTY VISION INC (NV)
Name changed to Jiu Feng Investment Hong Kong Ltd. 01/22/2013
Jiu Feng Investment Hong Kong Ltd. name changed to Jubilant Flame International, Ltd. 05/22/2015

LIBRA ALLIANCE CORP (NV)
Name changed to Lightyear Network Solutions, Inc. 04/23/2010

LIBRA ENERGY INC. (BC)
Name changed to Libra Industries Inc. 11/21/1985
(See Libra Industries Inc.)

LIBRA GOLD CORP (ON)
Name changed to Riphean Platinum Corp. 3/30/2001

LIBRA INDS INC (BC)
Delisted from Vancouver Stock Exchange 03/04/1991

LIBRA SYS INC (DE)
Chapter 11 bankruptcy proceedings converted to Chapter 7 on 11/00/1991
No stockholders' equity

LIBRARY BUR INC (NY)
Name changed to LBI Manufacturing, Inc. 07/11/1995
(See LBI Manufacturing, Inc.)

LIBRARY INFORMATION SOFTWARE CORP (ON)
Class A Common no par reclassified as Common no par 05/03/2006
Name changed to Starwood Industries Inc. 05/03/2006
(See Starwood Industries Inc.)

LIBSAB BANCORP, INC. (KY)
Acquired by Peoples First Corp. 10/07/1994
Each share Common no par exchanged for (12.632) shares Common no par

LIBYA MERCURY PETE CORP (DE)
Name changed back to Consolidated Development Corp. (DE) and Common 20¢ par changed to 5¢ par 09/29/1969
(See Consolidated Development Corp. (DE))

LICEFA INTL INC (BC)
Recapitalized as Continuum Arts Inc. 12/24/1996
Each share Common no par exchanged for (0.125) share Common no par
Continuum Arts Inc. recapitalized as Continuum Resources Ltd. 05/13/1999 which was acquired by Fortuna Silver Mines Inc. 03/06/2009

LICON INTL INC (DE)
Each share old Common $0.001 par exchanged for (0.1) share new Common $0.001 par 10/14/94
Name changed to Emerald Capital Holdings Inc. 6/14/95
(See Emerald Captial Holdings Inc.)

LICONT CORP (NV)
Name changed to Maverick Technology Solutions 09/20/2018

LIDA INC (DE)
Name changed to Olas Inc. 9/1/95
Olas Inc. recapitalized as Ediets.com, Inc. 11/17/99

LIDAK PHARMACEUTICALS (CA)
Name changed to Avanir Pharmaceuticals (CA) 11/30/1998
Avanir Pharmaceuticals (CA) reincorporated in Delaware as Avanir Pharmaceuticals, Inc. 03/23/2009
(See Avanir Pharmaceuticals, Inc.)

LIDCO INDS INC (AB)
Struck off register for failure to file annual returns 10/1/94

LIDO CORP. (DE)
Stock Dividend - 10% 7/6/64
Name changed to Bala Industries, Inc. 10/1/65
Bala Industries, Inc. merged into Babbitt (B.T.), Inc. 1/2/68 which name changed to B.T.B. Corp. 12/5/69 which name changed to International Banknote Co., Inc. 1/2/73 which merged into United States Banknote Corp. (NY) 7/25/90 which reincorporated in (DE) 9/21/93 which name changed to American Banknote Corp. 7/3/95

LIDO INTL CORP (NV)
Common $0.001 par split (33.519553) for (1) by issuance of (32.519553) additional shares payable 09/12/2013 to holders of record 09/09/2013 Ex date - 09/13/2013
Name changed to HBP Energy Corp. 12/06/2013

LIDO METAL & HOLDINGS LTD. (ON)
Struck off register and declared dissolved for failure to file returns in 1980

LIDO MINERALS LTD. (ON)
Name changed to Lido Metal & Holdings Ltd. and Capital Stock $1 par changed to no par 12/22/70

LIEBER (RICHARD) BREWING CORP.
Liquidated in 1937

LIEBERMAN ENTERPRISES INC (MN)
Common no par split (3) for (2) by issuance of (0.5) additional share 6/28/85
Reorganized under the laws of Delaware as Live Entertainment Inc. and Common no par changed to 1¢ par 11/23/88
(See Live Entertainment Inc.)

LIEBERT CORP (OH)
Common no par split (3) for (2) by issuance of (0.5) additional share 1/4/82
Common no par split (4) for (3) by issuance of (1/3) additional share 2/25/83
Merged into Emerson Electric Co. 3/10/87
Each share Common no par exchanged for (0.3322) share Common $1 par

LIECO, INC. (NY)
Name changed to Leicom Industries, Inc. 03/12/1968
(See Leicom Industries, Inc.)

LIF-O-GEN, INC. (DE)
Capital Stock 10¢ par changed to 1¢ par 02/28/1973
Voluntarily dissolved 01/12/1983
Details not available

LIFE & ACCIDENT INSURANCE CO. OF ALABAMA (AL)
Merged into Life Insurance Co. of Alabama on a (1) for (3) basis 3/12/58

LIFE & CASUALTY CO. OF CHICAGO
Name changed to Alliance Life Insurance Co. in 1934 which was acquired by Republic National Life Insurance Co. in 1949

LIFE & CASUALTY INSURANCE CO. OF TENNESSEE (TN)
Each share Capital Stock $100 par exchanged for (20) shares Capital Stock $5 par in 1929
Capital Stock $5 par changed to $2 par in 1934
Capital Stock $2 par changed to $3 par in 1937
Stock Dividend - 100% 11/12/43; 25% 11/1/45; 20% 10/6/47; 33-1/3% 12/16/50; 25% 12/15/53; 50% 10/31/56; 20% 3/18/63; 20% 4/14/67
Merged into American General Insurance Co. 1/1/68
Each share Common $3 par exchanged for (0.2) share $1.80 Conv. Preferred $1.50 par and (0.8) share Common $1.50 par
American General Insurance Co. reorganized as American General Corp. 7/1/80 which merged into American International Group, Inc. 8/29/2001

LIFE & HEALTH INS CO ST LOUIS (MO)
Merged into Independent Liberty Life Insurance Co. 10/31/72
Each share Common $1 par exchanged for (0.434782) share Common $1 par
(See Independent Liberty Life Insurance Co.)

LIFE & SAFETY CONCEPTS, INC. (UT)
Proclaimed dissolved for failure to file annual report 11/1/92

LIFE AFFILIATES INC (NY)
Charter revoked for failure to file reports and pay fees 12/16/1968

LIFE AID CORP (DE)
Charter cancelled and declared inoperative and void for non-payment of taxes 3/1/88

LIFE AID PRODUCTS LTD. (ON)
Name changed to Millmore Products Ltd. 11/12/1970
(See Millmore Products Ltd.)

LIFE ASSURN CO CAROLINA (NC)
Merged into National Savings Life Insurance Co. 10/01/1975
Each share Common $1 par exchanged for $2.40 cash

LIFE ASSURN CO PA (PA)
Capital Stock $5 par changed to $4 par and (0.25) additional share issued 12/10/1963
Capital Stock $4 par changed to $3 par and (1/3) additional share issued 05/15/1965
Acquired by Lacop Corp. 01/01/1970
Each share Capital Stock $3 par exchanged for (1) share Common $1 par
Lacop Corp. name changed to Life of Pennsylvania Financial Corp. 04/26/1972
(See Life of Pennsylvania Financial Corp.)

LIFE ASSURN CO WEST (CO)
Each share Common 20¢ par exchanged for (5) shares Common 4¢ par 11/8/61
Common 4¢ par changed to 8¢ par 1/29/71
Merged into Western Preferred Corp. 8/12/75
Each share Common 8¢ par exchanged for (0.077339) share 8% Conv. Preferred Ser. A $5 par
(See Western Preferred Corp.)

LIFE BANCORP INC (VA)
Merged into BB&T Corp. 3/2/98
Each share Common 1¢ par exchanged for (0.58) share Common $5 par

LIFE BOSTON INS CO (MA)
Merged into Laurentian Mutual Insurance Co. 4/15/88
Each share Common $1 par exchanged for $7 cash

LIFE CARE CMNTYS CORP (PA)
Name changed to Inovex Industries, Inc. 11/29/89
Inovex Industries, Inc. recapitalized as Berger Holdings, Ltd. 7/30/90
(See Berger Holdings, Ltd.)

LIFE CHEMISTRY INC (CA)
Charter suspended for failure to file reports and pay fees 07/01/1986

LIFE COMPANIES, INC. (VA)
Liquidation completed
Each share Common $1 par stamped to indicate initial distribution of $10 cash 3/20/61
Each share Stamped Common $1 par stamped to indicate second distribution of $2.77 cash 7/18/61
Each share Stamped Common $1 par stamped to indicate third distribution of (0.99999) share Insurance Securities Inc. Capital Stock no par 1/15/62
Each share Stamped Common $1 par stamped to indicate fourth distribution of (0.04) share Leach Corp. Common 20¢ par 9/24/62
Each share Stamped Common $1 par exchanged for fifth and final distribution $0.5882 cash 7/16/71
(See each company's listing)

LIFE CONCEPTS INC (WY)
Recapitalized as World Vision Holding Inc. 11/26/1997
Each share Common $0.001 par exchanged for (0.001) share Common $0.001 par
(See World Vision Holding Inc.)

LIFE CORP. (OH)
Reorganized as Progressive Industries Corp. 12/11/67
Each share Class A $5 par exchanged for (1) share Common no par
Each share Class B $5 par exchanged for (0.333333) share Common no par

LIFE CORP AMER (OK)
Under plan of merger name changed to Twain (Mark) Life Corp. 08/13/1971
Twain (Mark) Life Corp. recapitalized as Twain (Mark) Life Insurance Corp. 04/15/1976
(See Twain (Mark) Life Insurance Corp.)

LIFE CTRS INC (MN)
Each share old Common 1¢ par exchanged for (0.1) share new Common 1¢ par 4/24/87
New Common 1¢ par split (3) for (2) by issuance of (0.5) additional share 1/16/90
Name changed to Oxboro Medical International, Inc. 4/16/90
Oxboro Medical International, Inc. name changed to Oxboro Medical, Inc. 3/17/2000 which name changed to Sterion, Inc. 1/15/2002 which name changed to STEN Corp. 1/31/2005

LIFE DIAGNOSTICS INC (OH)
Merged into GE Medical 9/15/2000
Each share Common no par exchanged for $3.10 cash

LIFE ENERGY & TECHNOLOGY HLDGS INC (DE)
Name changed to Global Environmental Energy Corp. (DE) 8/30/2004
Global Environmental Energy Corp. (DE) reincorporated in Bahamas 2/25/2005

LIFE EXTN SVCS INC (NV)
Each share old Common $0.001 par

exchanged for (0.2) share new Common $0.001 par 10/28/91
Recapitalized as Anglo Resource & Technology Corp. 2/24/92
Each share new Common $0.001 par exchanged for (0.14285714) share Common $0.001 par

LIFE FD BOSTON (MA)
Name changed to Greateastern Fund of Boston, Inc. 06/07/1974
(See Greateastern Fund of Boston, Inc.)

LIFE FINL CORP (DE)
Each share old Common 1¢ par exchanged for (0.2) share new Common 1¢ par 6/12/2001
Name changed to Pacific Premier Bancorp, Inc. 8/24/2002

LIFE GROUP INC (NY)
Name changed to Global Capital Group, Inc. 04/01/1988

LIFE HOLDING CORP. (NJ)
Capital Stock 50¢ par changed to 12-1/2¢ par and (3) additional shares issued 11/30/65
Completely liquidated 7/17/67
Each share Capital Stock 12-1/2¢ par exchanged for (0.574) share Hale (Nathan) Life Insurance Co. of New York Capital Stock $1.60 par
Hale (Nathan) Life Insurance Co. of New York acquired by Washington National Corp. 6/20/72

LIFE IMAGING CORP (CO)
Chapter 11 bankruptcy proceedings converted to Chapter 7 on 08/26/1984
No stockholders' equity

LIFE IND CORP (IN)
Stock Dividends - 10% 9/30/80; 25% 5/1/81; 20% 11/1/82; 20% 8/29/83; 20% 7/3/84
Administratively dissolved 12/30/91

LIFE INDS INC (NV)
Recapitalized as Quill Industries Inc. 09/19/1997
Each share Common $0.001 par exchanged for (0.01) share Common $0.001 par
Quill Industries Inc. recapitalized as Ostrich Products of America, Inc. 06/01/2005 which name changed to PayPro, Inc. 07/11/2005 which name changed to Panamersa Corp. 02/16/2007 which recapitalized as Eagle Worldwide Inc. 01/12/2012

LIFE INSTRS CORP (CO)
Name changed to Life Imaging Corp. 05/15/1981
(See Life Imaging Corp.)

LIFE INSURANCE CO. OF MISSOURI (MO)
Liquidation completed 6/30/57

LIFE INSURANCE CO. OF SOUTH CAROLINA (SC)
Merged into Empire Life Insurance Co. (S.C.) 9/3/60
Each share Preferred $10 par exchanged for (2.12799) shares Common 25¢ par
Each share Common no par exchanged for (0.42626) share Common 25¢ par
Empire Life Insurance Co. (S.C.) merged into Atlantic American Life Insurance Co. 1/29/65

LIFE INSURANCE CO. OF THE SOUTH (NC)
Merged into Kentucky Central Life & Accident Insurance Co. 07/01/1960
Each share Capital Stock $5 par exchanged for (0.9) share Class A $1 par and (0.1) share Common $1 par
Kentucky Central Life & Accident Insurance Co. name changed to Kentucky Central Life Insurance Co. 03/08/1963

(See Kentucky Central Life Insurance Co.)

LIFE INSURANCE CO. OF VIRGINIA (VA)
Each share Capital Stock $100 par exchanged for (5) shares Capital Stock $20 par in 1928
Capital Stock $20 par changed to $10 par and (1) additional share issued 9/26/58
Capital Stock $10 par changed to $5 par and (1) additional share issued 3/11/64
Stock Dividend - 100% 2/15/50
Merged into Continental Group, Inc. 10/16/81
Each share Capital Stock $5 par exchanged for (4.234) shares Common $1 par
(See Continental Group, Inc.)

LIFE INS CO AMER (AL)
Merged into Pacific American Corp. (NV) 5/9/69
Each share Common $1 par exchanged for (0.6) share Common $1 par
(See Pacific American Corp. (NV))

LIFE INS CO AMER (WA)
Placed in receivership 02/20/1987
No stockholders' equity

LIFE INS CO CONN (CT)
Common $5 par changed to $3.75 par 01/07/1969
Under plan of reorganization each share Common $3.75 par automatically became (2) shares Connsurance Corp. Capital Stock $1 par 10/08/1969
(See Connsurance Corp.)

LIFE INS CO FLA (FL)
Reorganized as Life of Florida Corp. 12/31/1968
Each share Common $1 par exchanged for (1) share Common $1 par
Life of Florida Corp. name changed to Context Industries, Inc. 05/28/1970
(See Context Industries, Inc.)

LIFE INS CO GA (GA)
Capital Stock $10 par changed to $2.50 par and (3) additional shares issued 04/23/1965
Stock Dividends - 25% 04/26/1963; 14-2/7% 05/12/1965; 50% 03/26/1973
Each (6,000) shares Capital Stock $2.50 par exchanged for (1) share Capital Stock $15,000 par 11/15/1979
Note: In effect holders received $60 cash per share and public interest was eliminated

LIFE INS CO KY (KY)
Common $1 par changed to $2 par 03/26/1964
Common $2 par changed to $1 par and (1) additional share issued 11/16/1964
Stock Dividend - 10% 11/04/1968
Acquired by Hamilton International Corp. 12/31/1969
Each share Common $1 par exchanged for (1.5) shares Class C Conv. Common 10¢ par and (1.25) shares Common $1 par
(See Hamilton International Corp.)

LIFE INS CO N H (PA)
Acquired by New Hampshire Insurance Co. 04/07/1976
Each share Capital Stock $5 par exchanged for $17.50 cash

LIFE INS CO NORTHWEST (WA)
Common $10 par changed to $2 par and (4) additional shares issued 03/17/1972
99% acquired by Canadian Pioneer Management Ltd. through purchase offer which expired 08/28/1978
Public interest eliminated

LIFE INSURANCE CORP. OF AMERICA (UT)
Capital Stock $30 par changed to $10 par 11/03/1955
Name changed to Freedom National Life Insurance Co. 05/19/1964
(See Freedom National Life Insurance Co.)

LIFE INSURANCE INVESTMENT CORP. (ME)
Name changed to Life Insurance Securities Corp. 09/25/1957
(See Life Insurance Securities Corp.)

LIFE INS INVS INC (MD)
Stock Dividends - 100% 07/12/1961; 100% 07/17/1964
Acquired by Security Equity Fund, Inc. 11/12/1981
Each share Common $1 par exchanged for (1.5097) shares Common 25¢ par
Security Equity Fund, Inc. name changed to Security Equity Fund 12/11/1981

LIFE INS SECS CORP (ME)
Charter suspended for non-payment of franchise taxes 01/01/1975

LIFE INSURORS, INC. (OK)
Completely liquidated 10/29/71
Each share 8% Preferred $1 par received first and final distribution of (3.333333) shares Western American Life Insurance Co. (N. Mex.) Capital Stock $1 par
Each share Common 50¢ par received first and final distribution of (0.076923) share Western American Life Insurance Co. (N. Mex.) Capital Stock $1 par
Certificates were not surrendered and are now valueless
Western American Life Insurance Co. (N. Mex.) became worthless 5/14/75

LIFE INVESTORS, INC. (DE)
Merged into Life Investors Inc. (IA) 8/21/68
Each share Preferred $25 par exchanged for (1) share 3-1/2% Conv. Preferred $25 par
(See Life Investors Inc. (IA))

LIFE INVS INC (IA)
Common $1 par split (3) for (2) by issuance of (0.5) additional share 09/06/1972
3% Conv. Preferred $25 par called for redemption 12/31/1981
Merged into Aegon U.S. Holding Corp. 02/24/1988
Each share Common $1 par exchanged for $54.45 cash

LIFE INVS INS CO AMER (IA)
Acquired by Life Investors, Inc. (IA) 12/31/1969
Each share Capital Stock $1 par exchanged for (1) share Common $1 par

LIFE INVS INTL LTD (ON)
Charter cancelled for failure to pay taxes and file returns 3/16/76

LIFE INVS LTD (ON)
Merged into Life Investors International Ltd. 7/14/73
Each share Common no par exchanged for (5) shares Class A $1 par and (1) share Common no par
(See Life Investors International Ltd.)

LIFE INVS NEB INC (NE)
Reincorporated under the laws of Delaware as Investors Growth Industries, Inc. 1/31/69
Investors Growth Industries, Inc. merged into MEI Corp. 7/13/72
(See MEI Corp.)

LIFE INVESTORS OF IOWA, INC. (IA)
Name changed to Life Investors, Inc. (IA) 06/30/1968
(See Life Investors, Inc. (IA))

LIFE KY FINL CORP (DE)
Adjudicated bankrupt 06/29/1972

Stockholders' equity unlikely

LIFE MED CORP (AB)
Delisted from Toronto Venture Stock Exchange 06/26/2006

LIFE MED SCIENCES INC (DE)
Name changed to SyntheMed, Inc. 04/28/2005
SyntheMed, Inc. name changed to Pathfinder Cell Therapy, Inc. 09/16/2011

LIFE MED TECHNOLOGIES INC (DE)
Reincorporated 08/29/1994
State of incorporation changed from (CO) to (DE) 08/29/1994
Recapitalized as I-Sim International Inc. 06/04/1999
Each share Common no par exchanged for (0.001) share Common no par
I-Sim International Inc. name changed back to Life Medical Technologies Inc. 01/26/2000 which name changed to iBonZai.com, Inc. 05/12/2000 which name changed to IbonZi.com, Inc. (DE) 01/10/2002 which reorganized in Nevada as China Global Development, Inc. 01/23/2002 which recapitalized as Arizona Ventures, Inc. 11/18/2002 which name changed to Fox River Holdings, Inc. 10/13/2003 which name changed to Zynex Medical Holdings, Inc. 12/23/2003 which name changed to Zynex, Inc. 07/08/2008

LIFE MONT INS CO (MT)
Name changed to American Plan Life Insurance Co. 12/1/83
(See American Plan Life Insurance Co.)

LIFE NUTRITION PRODS INC (DE)
Name changed to ADGS Advisory, Inc. 07/19/2013

LIFE OF AMERICA INSURANCE CORP. OF BOSTON (MA)
Conv. Preferred A no par and Conv. Preferred C no par changed to $1 par 9/15/71
Common no par changed to $1 par 6/30/72
Conv. Preferred C $1 par reclassified as Conv. Preferred A $1 par in 1978
Conv. Preferred A $1 par called for redemption 2/10/84
Stock Dividend - 10% 5/15/73
Name changed to Life of Boston Insurance Co. 11/5/86
(See Life of Boston Insurance Co.)

LIFE OF FLORIDA CORP. (FL)
Name changed to Context Industries, Inc. 5/29/70
(See Context Industries, Inc.)

LIFE PA FINL CORP (PA)
Liquidation completed
Each share Common $1 par exchanged for initial distribution of $2.40 cash 03/31/1978
Each share Common $1 par received second and final distribution of $0.30 cash 09/15/1978

LIFE PARTNERS GROUP INC (DE)
Merged into Conseco, Inc. 8/2/96
Each share Common $0.001 par exchanged for (0.5833) share Common no par
(See Conseco, Inc.)

LIFE PARTNERS HLDGS INC (MA)
Reincorporated 02/19/2003
State of incorporation changed from (MA) to (TX) 02/19/2003
Common 1¢ par split (5) for (4) by issuance of (0.25) additional share payable 09/27/2007 to holders of record 09/14/2007 Ex date - 09/28/2007
Common 1¢ par split (5) for (4) by issuance of (0.25) additional share payable 02/16/2009 to holders of record 02/06/2009 Ex date - 02/17/2009

FINANCIAL INFORMATION, INC.

LIF-LIF

Common 1¢ par split (5) for (4) by issuance of (0.25) additional share payable 12/31/2010 to holders of record 12/21/2010 Ex date - 01/03/2011
Plan of reorganization under Chapter 11 Federal Bankruptcy proceedings effective 12/09/2016
No stockholders' equity

LIFE PETE INC (FL)
Recapitalized as TAG Group, Inc. 09/04/2003
Each (80.32955) shares Common $0.0001 par exchanged for (1) share Common $0.0001 par
(See TAG Group, Inc.)

LIFE PT INC (DE)
Assets assigned for the benefit of creditors 04/28/2005
Stockholders' equity unlikely

LIFE QUOTES INC (DE)
Acquired by LQ Acquisition Inc. 08/13/2010
Each share Common $0.003 par exchanged for $4 cash

LIFE RE CORP / LIFE RE CAP TR II (DE)
Issue Information - 1,800,000 UNITS consisting of a Purchase Contract and a Quarterly Income Preferred Security offered at $66 per Unit on 03/11/1998
Each Quarterly Income Preferred Security received $77.86865 cash 03/15/2001

LIFE RE CORP (DE)
Secondary Offering - 3,850,000 shares COM offered at $66 per share on 03/11/1998
Merged into Swiss Reinsurance Co. 12/01/1998
Each share Common $0.001 par exchanged for $95 cash

LIFE RES INC (OR)
Each share old Common 1¢ par exchanged for (0.04) share new Common 1¢ par 06/30/1995
SEC revoked common stock registration 07/22/2010

LIFE SAVERS, INC.
Acquired by Drug, Inc. in 1929 which in accordance with a plan of segregation issued stock of five new companies in exchange for its own stock in 1933

LIFE SAVERS CORP. (DE)
Capital Stock $5 par split (2) for (1) by issuance of (1) additional share 10/4/55
Stock Dividend - 100% 12/17/45
Merged into Beech-Nut Life Savers, Inc. 8/1/56
Each share Capital Stock $5 par exchanged for (1) share Common $10 par
Beech-Nut Life Savers, Inc. merged into Squibb Beech-Nut, Inc. 1/15/68 which name changed to Squibb Corp. 4/30/71 which merged into Bristol-Myers Squibb Co. 10/4/89

LIFE SAVINGS & LOAN ASSOCIATION (CA)
Name changed to Life Savings Bank (San Bernardino, CA) in 1985
Life Savings Bank (San Bernardino, CA) name changed to Life Savings FSB (San Bernardino, CA) 6/27/91 which reorganized in Delaware as Life Financial Corp. 6/27/97 which name changed to Pacific Premier Bancorp, Inc. 8/24/2002

LIFE SVGS & LN ASSN (FL)
Name changed to Life Savings Bank (Clearwater, FL) 6/30/86
(See Life Savings Bank (Clearwater, FL))

LIFE SAVINGS BANK (SAN BERNARDINO, CA)
Name changed to Life Savings FSB (San Bernardino, CA) 6/27/91
Life Savings FSB (San Bernardino, CA) reorganized in Delaware as Life Financial Corp. 6/27/97 which name changed to Pacific Premier Bancorp, Inc. 8/24/2002

LIFE SVGS BK FED SVGS BK (CLEARWATER, FL)
Placed in conservatorship 10/11/91
Stockholders' equity unlikely

LIFE SVGS BK FED SVGS BK (SAN BERNARDINO, CA)
Common $8 par split (2) for (1) by issuance of (1) additional share payable 3/29/96 to holders of record 2/28/96
Reorganized under the laws of Delaware as Life Financial Corp. 6/27/97
Each share Common $8 par exchanged for (3) shares Common 1¢ par

LIFE SCIENCES INC (DE)
Common 10¢ par split (3) for (2) by issuance of (0.5) additional share 11/14/1983
Stock Dividend - 100% 02/10/1971
Chapter 11 bankruptcy proceedings converted to Chapter 7 on 10/21/2009
No stockholders' equity

LIFE SCIENCES INST INC (AB)
Recapitalized as Quattro Exploration & Production Ltd. 11/23/2011
Each share Common no par exchanged for (0.33333333) share Common no par

LIFE SCIENCES RESH INC (MD)
Acquired by Lion Holdings, Inc. 11/24/2009
Each share Common 1¢ par exchanged for $8.50 cash

LIFE SECS IOWA INC (IA)
Common Capital Stock $1 par reclassified as Class A Common $1 par 03/00/1971
Recapitalized as Financial Security Life Corp. 08/23/1978
Each share Class A Common $1 par exchanged for (0.5) share Common $2 par
Each share Class B Common 1¢ par exchanged for (0.005) share Common $2 par

LIFE SIGNS GROUP INC (UT)
Each share Common $0.001 par exchanged for (0.2) share Common $0.005 par 04/10/1992
Involuntarily dissolved 05/01/1994

LIFE STOCKS OF MINNESOTA, INC. (MN)
Name changed to LSM Corp. 05/13/1969
LSM Corp. merged into American Trustee Inc. 12/21/1981
(See American Trustee Inc.)

LIFE SUPPORT EQUIP CORP (MA)
Adjudicated bankrupt 05/00/1978
No stockholders' equity

LIFE SUPPORT MEDICAL EQUIPMENT CORP. (MA)
Name changed to Life Support Equipment Corp. 03/19/1973
(See Life Support Equipment Corp.)

LIFE SYS CORP (NV)
Each share old Common $0.001 par exchanged for (0.05555555) share new Common $0.001 par 05/10/2005
Charter permanently revoked 02/28/2011

LIFE SYS INTL INC (DE)
Recapitalized as Mesquite Country, Inc. 06/08/1990
Each share Common $0.001 par exchanged for (0.00833333) share Common $0.001 par
Mesquite Country, Inc. name changed to Gimmeabid.com, Inc. 10/14/1999
(See Gimmeabid.com, Inc.)

LIFE TECHNOLOGIES CORP (DE)
Acquired by Thermo Fisher Scientific Inc. 02/03/2014
Each share Common 1¢ par exchanged for $76.1311786 cash

LIFE TECHNOLOGIES INC (DE)
Each share old Common no par exchanged for (1.5) shares new Common 1¢ par 05/21/1986
New Common 1¢ par split (3) for (2) by issuance of (0.5) additional share payable 08/28/1996 to holders of record 08/09/1996
Merged into Invitrogen Corp. 09/14/2000
Each share new Common 1¢ par exchanged for either (1) share Common 1¢ par, (0.72) share Common 1¢ par and $16.80 cash, or $60 cash
Note: Option to receive stock or cash only expired 10/05/2000
Invitrogen Corp. name changed to Life Technologies Corp. 11/21/2008
(See Life Technologies Corp.)

LIFE THERAPEUTICS LTD (AUSTRALIA)
Recapitalized as Arturus Capital Ltd. 08/14/2012
Each Sponsored ADR for Ordinary exchanged for (0.25) Sponsored ADR for Ordinary
(See Arturus Capital Ltd.)

LIFE TIME COS INC (MA)
Each share Common 1¢ par exchanged for (0.0001) share Common $100 par 1/5/81
In effect holders received $0.50 cash per share and public interest was eliminated

LIFE TIME FITNESS INC (MN)
Acquired by Leonard Green & Partners L.P. 06/10/2015
Each share Common 2¢ par exchanged for $72.10 cash

LIFE UNDERWRITERS, INC. (TX)
Charter forfeited for non-payment of franchise taxes 3/7/63

LIFE UNDERWRITERS INC. (GA)
Liquidation completed 11/3/64
Holders of each share Class A Common 50¢ par recieved an initial distribution of (0.2587) share Kennesaw Life & Accident Insurance Co. Common $1.25 par 11/13/63 and the second and final distribution of $0.02571865 in cash 11/3/64
Holders of each share Class B Common 1/100 of 1¢ par received an initial distribution of (0.0487) share Kennesaw Life & Accident Insurance Co. Common $1.25 par 11/13/63 and the second and final distribution of $0.02571865 in cash 11/3/64
Certificates were not required to be surrendered and are now valueless

LIFE UNDERWRITERS INC. (SC)
Merged into Public Savings Insurance Co. 12/31/62
Each share Class A Common exchanged for (1/3) share Common 50¢ par
(See Public Savings Insurance Co.)

LIFE UNDERWRITERS INS CO (LA)
Completely liquidated 11/30/1971
Each share Common 20¢ par exchanged for first and final distribution of (0.08) share Life Investors Inc. Common $1 par
(See Life Investors Inc.)

LIFE USA HLDG INC (MN)
Each share old Common 1¢ par exchanged for (1/3) share new Common 1¢ par 4/9/92
Merged into Allianz Life 10/1/99
Each share new Common 1¢ par exchanged for $20.75 cash

LIFE USA INC (CO)
Recapitalized as Legacy Technology Holdings, Inc. 05/29/2008
Each share Common $0.0001 par exchanged for (0.1) share Common $0.0001 par

LIFEAPPS DIGITAL MEDIA INC (DE)
Recapitalized as LifeApps Brands Inc. 01/07/2016
Each share Common $0.001 par exchanged for (0.06666666) share Common $0.001 par

LIFEBANK CORP (CANADA)
Acquired by Insception Biosciences Inc. 10/01/2012
Each share Common no par exchanged for $0.495 cash

LIFEBANK CRYOGENICS CORP (CANADA)
Reincorporated 11/20/2002
Place of incorporation changed from (BC) to Canada 11/20/2002
Name changed to Lifebank Corp. 01/16/2006
(See Lifebank Corp.)

LIFEBLEND INC (MN)
Name changed to BEC, Inc. 04/26/1988
BEC, Inc. name changed to Gran Prix Enterprises, Inc. 12/02/1988
(See Gran Prix Enterprises, Inc.)

LIFECALL AMER INC (NV)
Reorganized under the laws of Delaware as Response USA, Inc. 4/1/92
Each share Common $0.002 par exchanged for (1/7) share Common $0.002 par
(See Response USA, Inc.)

LIFECALL CDA INC (CANADA)
Name changed to Voxcom, Inc. 8/23/93
(See Voxcom, Inc.)

LIFECELL CORP (DE)
Merged into Kinetic Concepts, Inc. 05/27/2008
Each share Common $0.001 par exchanged for $51 cash

LIFECHOICE INC (UT)
Reorganized under the laws of Delaware as Fix-Corp International, Inc. 10/30/1995
Each share Common $0.001 par exchanged for (0.02) share Common $0.001 par
(See Fix-Corp International, Inc.)

LIFECO SPLIT CORP INC (QC)
Preferred no par called for redemption at $25 on 7/31/2005
Class C Preferred no par split (1.39) for (1) by issuance of (0.39) additional share payable 08/05/2010 to holders of record 08/05/2010 Ex date - 08/03/2010
Class C Preferred no par called for redemption at $36.84 on 07/31/2012
Class A Capital Shares no par called for redemption at $4.4466 on 07/31/2012

LIFECORE BIOMEDICAL INC (MN)
Merged into SBT Holdings Inc. 03/24/2008
Each share Common 1¢ par exchanged for $17 cash

LIFEF/X INC (NV)
Plan of reorganization under Chapter 11 Federal Bankruptcy Code effective 11/26/2002
No stockholders' equity

LIFEGUARD MFG CORP (NY)
Petition filed under Chapter 11 Federal Bankruptcy Code 04/12/1977 was subsequently terminated 03/29/2001
Stockholders' equity undetermined

LIFEKEEPERS INTL INC (FL)
Common $0.001 par split (2) for (1) by issuance of (1) additional share payable 2/29/2000 to holders of record 2/15/2000
Reorganized under the laws of Nevada as East Coast Diversified Corp. 10/23/2003
Each share Common $0.001 par exchanged for (0.04) share Common $0.001 par

LIFELINE BENEFITS GROUP INC (FL)
Name changed to American Benefits Group Inc. 2/14/97
American Benefits Group Inc. name changed to Prom Resources, Inc. 10/19/2006

LIFELINE EMPLOYMENT SERVICE, INC. (UT)
Each (3) shares old Common $0.001 par exchanged for (4) shares new Common $0.001 par 12/29/83
Name changed to Carb-A-Drink International, Inc. 1/12/84
Carb-A-Drink International, Inc. name changed to Fountain Fresh International 4/26/88 which name changed to Bevex, Inc. 8/17/98 which recapitalized as GTG Ventures, Inc. 11/1/2005

LIFELINE HEALTHCARE GROUP LTD (DE)
Reorganized 09/02/1988
Reorganized from under the laws of (CO) to Delaware 09/02/1988
Each share Common $0.0001 par exchanged for (0.001) share Common $0.0001 par 09/02/1988
Each share old Common $0.0001 par exchanged for (2) shares new Common $0.0001 par 05/01/1989
Reorganized under Chapter 11 Federal Bankruptcy Code 06/04/1991
Each share new Common $0.0001 par exchanged for (1.1125) shares Naturade, Inc. old Common $0.001 par, (7) Common Stock Purchase Warrants, Class A expiring 12/04/1991 and (7) Common Stock Purchase Warrants Class B expiring 06/04/1993
Note: Unexchanged certificates were cancelled and became without value 09/02/1991

LIFELINE HOMECARE SVCS INC (DE)
Charter cancelled and declared inoperative and void for non-payment of taxes 3/1/90

LIFELINE SHELTER SYS INC (OH)
Acquired by LSS of Ohio Inc. 2/8/2000
Each share Common exchanged for $0.32 cash

LIFELINE SYS INC (MA)
Common 2¢ par split (3) for (2) by issuance of (0.5) additional share 07/15/1991
Common 2¢ par split (2) for (1) by issuance of (1) additional share payable 12/17/2003 to holders of record 12/03/2003 Ex date - 12/18/2003
Merged into Koninklijke Philips Electronics N.V. 03/22/2006
Each share Common 2¢ par exchanged for $47.75 cash

LIFELINE THERAPEUTICS INC (CO)
Name changed to LifeVantage Corp. (CO) 02/02/2007
LifeVantage Corp. (CO) reincorporated in Delaware 03/09/2018

LIFELOCK INC (DE)
Acquired by Symantec Corp. 02/09/2017
Each share Common $0.001 par exchanged for $24 cash

LIFEMARK CORP (DE)
Common 1¢ par split (4) for (3) by issuance of (1/3) additional share 07/15/1980
Common 1¢ par split (3) for (2) by issuance of (0.5) additional share 06/30/1981
Common 1¢ par split (3) for (2) by issuance of (0.5) additional share 05/31/1983
Merged into American Medical International, Inc. 01/20/1984
Each share Common 1¢ par exchanged for (1.7143) shares Common $1 par
American Medical International, Inc. merged into American Medical Holdings, Inc. 04/12/1990 which merged into National Medical Enterprises, Inc. 02/28/1995 which name changed to Tenet Healthcare Corp. 06/23/1995

LIFEMARK CORP (DE)
Merged into UnitedHealth Group Inc. 2/9/2001
Each share Common 1¢ par exchanged for (0.18672) share Common 1¢ par

LIFEMASTER, INC. (OH)
Charter cancelled for failure to file reports and pay fees 2/20/65

LIFEMINDERS COM INC (DE)
Issue Information - 4,200,000 shares COM offered at $14 per share on 11/18/1999
Name changed to Lifeminders, Inc. 6/14/2000
Lifeminders, Inc. merged into Cross Media Marketing Corp. 10/25/2001
(See Cross Media Marketing Corp.)

LIFEMINDERS INC (DE)
Merged into Cross Media Marketing Corp. 10/25/2001
Each share Common 1¢ par exchanged for (0.2596) share Common $0.001 par
(See Cross Media Marketing Corp.)

LIFEN INC (DE)
Name changed to Crdentia Corp. 05/30/2003
(See Crdentia Corp.)

LIFEONE INC (LA)
Plan of reorganization under Chapter 11 Federal Bankruptcy Code effective 05/16/2003
No stockholders' equity

LIFEPOINT HOSPS INC (DE)
Name changed to LifePoint Health, Inc. 05/12/2015

LIFEQUEST INTL INC (CANADA)
Common no par split (3) for (1) by issuance of (2) additional shares 10/28/1987
Recapitalized as Amswiss Pharmaceuticals Inc. 09/21/1988
Each share Common no par exchanged for (1/7) share Common no par
Amswiss Pharmaceuticals Inc. recapitalized as Amswiss Scientific Inc. 03/05/1990
(See Amswiss Scientific Inc.)

LIFEQUEST MED INC (DE)
Name changed to Dexterity Surgical Inc. 03/18/1999
Dexterity Surgical Inc. name changed to China INSOline Corp. 03/17/2008 which recapitalized as China Bio-Energy Corp. 02/03/2011 which name changed to Wave Sync Corp. 10/05/2015

LIFERATE SYS INC (MN)
SEC revoked common stock registration 06/04/2010

LIFESCIENCES CAP CORP (ON)
Name changed to Bio-Extraction Inc. 05/16/2007
Bio-Extraction Inc. name changed to BioExx Specialty Proteins Ltd. 01/04/2010
(See BioExx Specialty Proteins Ltd.)

LIFESMART NUTRITION TECHNOLOGIES INC (UT)
SEC revoked common stock registration 02/22/2010

LIFESOFT CORP (DE)
Each share old Common 1¢ par exchanged for (0.02) share new Common 1¢ par 4/27/2001
Recapitalized as PetsMarketing, Inc. 6/15/2001
Each share new Common 1¢ par exchanged for (0.02) share Common $0.0001 par
PetsMarketing, Inc. name changed to PS Management Holdings Inc. 5/15/2002
(See PS Management Holdings Inc.)

LIFESOUTH INC (DE)
Merged into MAI Corp. 10/31/96
Details not available

LIFESPACE ENVIRONMENTAL WALLS INC (AB)
Merged into SMED International Inc. 07/01/1996
Each share Common no par exchanged for (0.02918591) share Common no par
(See SMED International Inc.)

LIFESPAN INC (NV)
SEC revoked common stock registration 04/30/2010

LIFESTAR CORP (UT)
Each (35) shares old Common no par exchanged for (1) share new Common no par 11/28/2001
SEC revoked common stock registration 07/22/2010

LIFESTART MULTIMEDIA CORP (AB)
Recapitalized as GLK Strategies Inc. 11/20/2000
Each share Common no par exchanged for (1/3) share Common no par
GLK Strategies Inc. recapitalized as Yankee Hat Industries Corp. (ALTA) 02/18/2003 which reincorporated in British Columbia as Yankee Hat Minerals Ltd. 02/09/2005

LIFESTEM INTL INC (NV)
Recapitalized as International Aerospace Enterprises, Inc. 04/30/2009
Each share Common $0.001 par exchanged for (0.02) share Common $0.001 par
(See International Aerospace Enterprises, Inc.)

LIFESTORE FINL GROUP (NC)
Name changed to LifeStore Financial Group, Inc. 06/01/2018

LIFESTREAM TECHNOLOGIES INC (NV)
Chapter 11 bankruptcy proceedings converted to Chapter 7 on 05/14/2007
No stockholders' equity

LIFESTYLE BEVERAGE CORP (BC)
Name changed to Australian Corporate Holdings Ltd. 10/23/1987

LIFESTYLE COS INC (DE)
Merged into Care Corp. 01/06/1981
Each share Common 10¢ par exchanged for $3.21 cash

LIFESTYLE ENHANCEMENT SYS INC (NV)
Name changed to Australian Agriculture & Property Development Inc. 12/08/2003
Australian Agriculture & Property Development Inc. name changed to WorldSource, Inc. 06/21/2005
(See WorldSource, Inc.)

LIFESTYLE INNOVATIONS INC (NV)
Recapitalized as Vought Defense Systems Corp. 02/16/2010
Each share Common $0.001 par exchanged for (0.00183486) share Common $0.001 par
Vought Defense Systems Corp. name changed to Alas Defense Systems, Inc. 06/29/2010 which name changed to ALAS International Holdings, Inc. 07/11/2011 which name changed to PV Enterprises International, Inc. 08/19/2013 which recapitalized as Drone Services USA, Inc. 04/29/2015

LIFESTYLE RESTAURANTS INC (DE)
Merged into Bombay Palace Restaurants, Inc. 9/14/87
Each (6) shares Common 10¢ par exchanged for (1) share Common 1¢ par
(See Bombay Palace Restaurants, Inc.)

LIFESTYLES N A BEVERAGE CORP (BC)
Recapitalized as Sasha Ventures Ltd. 6/6/96
Each share Common no par exchanged for (0.18867924) share Common no par
Sasha Ventures Ltd. recapitalized as eShippers.com Management Ltd. 10/24/2000 which recapitalized as eShippers Management Ltd. 2/28/2003

LIFESURANCE CORP (DE)
Merged into Regan Holding Corp. 10/31/1991
Each share Common $1.50 par exchanged for (3.3) shares Ser. B Common no par
(See Regan Holding Corp.)

LIFETECH CORP (ON)
Name changed to IATRA Life Sciences Corp. 3/12/2002

LIFETECH INDS CORP (DE)
Charter cancelled and declared inoperative and void for non-payment of taxes 03/01/1986

LIFETECH INDS INC (NV)
Name changed to mCig, Inc. 08/29/2013

LIFETIME CAP GROWTH TR (MA)
Name changed to MFS Lifetime Capital Growth Fund 8/1/92

LIFETIME CMNTYS INC (DE)
Name changed to BEI Holdings Ltd. 05/30/1986
BEI Holdings Ltd. name changed to Amresco, Inc. 05/23/1994
(See Amresco, Inc.)

LIFETIME CORP (DE)
Each share old Common 1¢ par exchanged for (0.16666666) share new Common 1¢ par 07/06/1989
Acquired by Olsten Corp. 07/30/1993
Each share new Common 1¢ par exchanged for (1.27) shares Common 10¢ par
Olsten Corp. merged into Adecco SA 03/15/2000 which name changed to Adecco Group AG 06/03/2016

LIFETIME EMERGING GROWTH TR (MA)
Name changed to MFS Lifetime Emerging Growth Fund 8/1/92

LIFETIME GLOBAL EQUITY TR (MA)
Name changed to MFS Lifetime Worldwide Equity Fund 8/1/92

LIFETIME GOLD & NAT RES TR (MA)
Name changed 4/1/92
Name changed from Lifetime Gold & Precious Metals Trust to Lifetime Gold & Natural Resources Trust Metals Inc. 4/1/92
Name changed to MFS Lifetime Gold & Natural Resources Fund 8/1/92

LIFETIME GOVT INCOME PLUS TR (MA)
Name changed to MFS Lifetime

LIF-LIG   **FINANCIAL INFORMATION, INC.**

Government Income Plus Fund 8/1/92

LIFETIME GOVT SEC TR (MA)
Name changed 4/1/92
Name changed from Lifetime Quality Bond Trust to Lifetime Government Securities Trust 4/1/92
Name changed to MFS Lifetime Government Securities Fund 8/1/92

LIFETIME HIGH INCOME TR (MA)
Name changed to MFS Lifetime High Income Fund 8/1/92

LIFETIME HOAN CORP (DE)
Common 1¢ par split (3) for (2) by issuance of (0.5) additional share 12/3/93
Stock Dividends - 10% 2/21/92; 10% 2/26/93; 10% 1/13/95; 10% 12/15/95; 10% payable 2/26/97 to holders of record 2/18/97
Name changed to Lifetime Brands, Inc. 7/1/2005

LIFETIME INTER INCOME TR (MA)
Name changed to MFS Lifetime Intermediate Income Fund 8/1/92

LIFETIME MANAGED MUN BD TR (MA)
Name changed to MFS Lifetime Municipal Bond Fund 8/1/92

LIFETIME MANAGED SECTORS TR (MA)
Name changed to MFS Lifetime Managed Sectors Fund 8/1/92

LIFETIME MONEY MKT TR (MA)
Name changed to MFS Lifetime Money Market Fund 8/1/92

LIFETIME POOLS EQUIPMENT CORP. (NY)
Merged into Lancer Industries, Inc. on a (1) for (2.5) basis 11/6/61
Lancer Industries, Inc. name changed to Strato Industries Inc. 9/11/62
(See Strato Industries Inc.)

LIFETIME SEALANT PRODS INC (CO)
Recapitalized as Southern Plains Oil Corp. 05/20/2008
Each share Common 1¢ par exchanged for (0.1) share Common 1¢ par

LIFETIME SEC LIFE INS CO (TX)
Merged into Progressive National Corp. 6/8/78
Each share Common $1 par exchanged for (2.75) shares Common no par
Progressive National Corp. merged into I.C.H. Corp. 11/14/79 which name changed to Southwestern Life Corp. (New) 6/15/94 which name changed to I.C.H. Corp. (New) 10/10/95
(See I.C.H. Corp. (New))

LIFETIME TOTAL RETURN TR (MA)
Name changed 04/01/1990
Name changed from Lifetime Dividends Plus Trust to Lifetime Total Return Trust 04/01/1990
Name changed to MFS Lifetime Total Return Fund 08/01/1992

LIFETRENDS BEHAVIORIAL SYS INC (BC)
Company dissolved 7/28/89
Details not available

LIFEVANTAGE CORP (CO)
Each share old Common $0.0001 par exchanged for (0.14285714) share new Common $0.0001 par 10/19/2015
Reincorporated under the laws of Delaware 03/09/2018

LIFEWORKS HLDGS INC (NV)
SEC revoked common stock registration 07/22/2010

LIFSCHULTZ INDS INC (DE)
Each share old Common $0.001 par exchanged for (0.02) share new Common $0.001 par 01/28/1998
Merged into Danaher Corp. 07/03/2001
Each share new Common $0.001 par exchanged for $22.80 cash

LIGAND PHARMACEUTICALS INC (DE)
Each share Class A Common $0.001 par exchanged for (1.33) shares Class B Common $0.001 par which was then reclassified as Common $0.001 par 11/25/94
(Additional Information in Active)

LIGGETT & MYERS INC. (DE)
Name changed to Liggett Group Inc. 4/28/76
(See Liggett Group Inc.)

LIGGETT & MYERS TOB CO (NJ)
Class B Common $25 par reclassified as Common $25 par 00/00/1947
Reincorporated under the laws of Delaware as Liggett & Myers Inc. 05/31/1968
Liggett & Myers Inc. name changed to Liggett Group Inc. 04/28/1976
(See Liggett Group Inc.)

LIGGETT GROUP INC (DE)
Ctfs. dated prior to 08/07/1980
Merged into Grand Metropolitan Ltd. 08/07/1980
Each share 7% Preferred $100 par exchanged for $70 cash
Each share $5.25 Conv. Preference $1 par exchanged for $158.62 cash
Each share Common $1 par exchanged for $69 cash

LIGGETT GROUP INC NEW (DE)
Ctfs. dated after 10/08/1987
Name changed to Brooke Group Ltd. 07/24/1990
Brooke Group Ltd. name changed to Vector Group Ltd. 05/24/2000

LIGHT & POWER SECURITIES CO. (DE)
Liquidated 5/31/71
Details not available

LIGHT DEV INC (CO)
Name changed to Microtec Development, Inc. 09/06/1989
(See Microtec Development, Inc.)

LIGHT ENERGY MGMT INC (NV)
Each share old Common $0.001 par exchanged for (0.2) share new Common $0.001 par 09/15/1999
Name changed to Forlink Software Corp. Inc. 12/15/1999
(See Forlink Software Corp. Inc.)

LIGHT METALS REFINING CORP. (DE)
No longer in existence having become inoperative and void for non-payment of taxes 4/1/57

LIGHT SAVERS U S A INC (NY)
Name changed to Hospitality Worldwide Services, Inc. 09/26/1996
Hospitality Worldwide Services, Inc. name changed to Hotelworks.com, Inc. 12/23/1999
(See Hotelworks.com, Inc.)

LIGHT THE BRD (UT)
Name changed to Hi-Tech Corp. (UT) 2/2/81
Hi-Tech Corp. (UT) reorganized in Delaware as Hi-Tech Ventures, Inc. 6/1/90 which recapitalized as Rubicon Medical Corp. 11/16/2000
(See Rubicon Medical Corp.)

LIGHTBRIDGE INC (DE)
Issue Information - 3,800,000 shares COM offered at $10 per share on 09/27/1996
Name changed to Authorize.Net Holdings, Inc. 04/30/2007
Authorize.Net Holdings, Inc. was acquired by CyberSource Corp. 11/01/2007
(See CyberSource Corp.)

LIGHTCOLLAR INC (NV)
Common $0.001 par split (5) for (1) by issuance of (4) additional shares payable 12/23/2014 to holders of record 12/23/2014
Name changed to EMS Find, Inc. 03/20/2015
EMS Find, Inc. name changed to Integrated Ventures, Inc. 07/27/2017

LIGHTCRAFT-GENERAL (CA)
Acquired by NuTone, Inc. 3/25/66
Each share Common $1 par or Class B Common $1 par exchanged for (0.90667) share $1.28 Conv. Preferred Ser. A $5 par
NuTone, Inc. merged into Scovill Manufacturing Co. 9/15/67 which name changed to Scovill Inc. 7/6/79
(See Scovill Inc.)

LIGHTEN UP ENTERPRISES INTL INC (NV)
Reincorporated under the laws of Delaware as Bionovo, Inc. 06/29/2005
(See Bionovo, Inc.)

LIGHTFOOT ENTERPRISES INC (NV)
Each share old Common $0.001 par exchanged for (0.2) share new Common $0.001 par 08/04/1989
Merged into Jelco Energy, Inc. 06/16/2000
Details not available

LIGHTHOUSE FAST FERRY INC (NJ)
SEC revoked common stock registration 03/27/2007

LIGHTHOUSE FD B INC (DE)
Acquired by Sigma Capital Shares, Inc. 06/25/1976
Each share Common $1 par exchanged for (0.78448) share Common $1 par
Sigma Capital Shares, Inc. name changed to ProvidentMutual Growth Fund, Inc. 03/01/1990
(See ProvidentMutual Growth Fund, Inc.)

LIGHTHOUSE LANDINGS INC (NJ)
Name changed to Lighthouse Fast Ferry, Inc. 9/19/2000
(See Lighthouse Fast Ferry, Inc.)

LIGHTHOUSE NATIONAL BANK (JUPITER, FL)
Acquired by Florida National Banks of Florida, Inc. 12/15/1984
Details not available

LIGHTHOUSE PETE INC (DE)
Each share old Common $0.001 par exchanged for (0.004) share new Common $0.001 par 11/10/2011
Each share new Common $0.001 par exchanged again for (0.002) share new Common $0.001 par 12/18/2013
Name changed to Supurva Healthcare Group, Inc. 06/30/2015

LIGHTHOUSE RES INC (BC)
Recapitalized as Saxon Capital Corp. 06/22/1995
Each share Common no par exchanged for (0.33333333) share Common no par
Saxon Capital Corp. name changed to Saxon Gold Corp. 05/16/1997 which name changed to Avatar Petroleum Inc. 12/18/2000 which merged into Quest Capital Corp. (BC) 06/30/2003 which reincorporated in Canada 05/27/2008 which name changed to Sprott Resource Lending Corp. 09/10/2010 which merged into Sprott Inc. 07/24/2013

LIGHTING CORP. OF AMERICA (PA)
Completely liquidated 6/19/67
Each share Common $1 par exchanged for first and final distribution of (0.1756) share Kidde (Walter) & Co., Inc. (NY) $2.20 Conv. Preference Ser. A $1 par and (0.3618) share Common $2.50 par

Kidde (Walter) & Co., Inc. (NY) reincorporated under the laws of Delaware 7/2/68 which name changed to Kidde, Inc. 4/18/80 which merged into Hanson Trust p.l.c. 12/31/87 which name changed to Hanson PLC (Old) 1/29/88 which reorganized as Hanson PLC (New) 10/15/2003

LIGHTLAKE THERAPEUTICS INC (NV)
Each share old Common $0.001 par exchanged for (0.01) share new Common $0.001 par 12/31/2014
Name changed to Opiant Pharmaceuticals, Inc. (NV) 03/08/2016
Opiant Pharmaceuticals, Inc. (NV) reincorporated in Delaware 10/02/2017

LIGHTMAN GRNT INC (DE)
Name changed to QMIS Finance Securities Corp. 03/01/2013

LIGHTNING BOLT INTL INC (NV)
Each share old Common $0.001 par exchanged for (0.04) share new Common $0.001 par 2/6/91
Name changed to Sportsland Sales Inc. 12/12/91
Sportsland Sales Inc. recapitalized as Medtex Corp. 11/13/94 which recapitalized as Opal Technologies Inc. 7/7/97

LIGHTNING CREEK MINES LTD (BC)
Struck off register and declared dissolved for failure to file returns 7/10/92

LIGHTNING ENERGY LTD (AB)
Plan of Arrangement effective 04/26/2005
Each share Common no par exchanged for (0.25) Sequoia Oil & Gas Trust Trust Unit and (0.25) share White Fire Energy Ltd. Common no par
(See each company's listing)

LIGHTNING JACK FILM TR (AUSTRALIA)
ADR agreement terminated 05/14/1997
Each ADR for Ordinary no par exchanged for (4) Trust Units
Note: Unexchanged ADR's were sold and the proceeds, if any, held for claim after 05/14/1998

LIGHTNING MINERALS INC (BC)
Recapitalized as Vangold Resources Inc. 08/25/1988
Each share Common no par exchanged for (0.25) share Common no par
Vangold Resources Inc. recapitalized as Pacific Vangold Mines Ltd. 03/24/1994 which recapitalized as Paccom Ventures Inc. 04/18/2000 which name changed to Vangold Resources Ltd. 08/29/2003 which name changed to Vangold Mining Corp. 05/10/2017

LIGHTNING ROD SOFTWARE INC (DE)
Each share Common 10¢ par received distribution of (1) share CE Software Inc. Common 10¢ par payable 06/13/2000 to holders of record 04/28/2000
SEC revoked common stock registration 02/22/2010

LIGHTNING URANIUM CO (UT)
Recapitalized as Polyastics Corp. 11/24/70
Each share Capital Stock 1¢ par exchanged for (0.033333) share Common 30¢ par
(See Polyastics Corp.)

LIGHTOLIER INC (NY)
Merged into Bairnco Corp. 11/10/81
Each share Common 5¢ par exchanged for $28 cash

LIGHTPATHS TP TECHNOLOGIES INC (NJ)
Name changed to mPhase Technologies Inc. 05/15/1997

LIGHTSPAN INC (DE)
Each share old Common $0.001 par exchanged for (0.1) share new Common $0.001 par 08/25/2003
Merged into Plato Learning, Inc. 11/17/2003
Each share new Common $0.001 par exchanged for (1.33) shares Common $0.001 par
(See Plato Learning, Inc.)

LIGHTSPAN PARTNERSHIP INC (DE)
Issue Information - 7,500,000 shares COM offered at $12 per share on 02/10/2000
Name changed to Lightspan, Inc. 04/10/2000
Lightspan, Inc. merged into Plato Learning, Inc. 11/17/2003
(See Plato Learning, Inc.)

LIGHTTOUCH VEIN & LASER INC (NV)
Each share old Common $0.001 par exchanged for (0.01) share new Common $0.001 par 07/09/2013
Note: No holder of (100) or more pre-split shares will receive fewer than (100) shares
Name changed to Grow Solutions Holdings, Inc. 07/09/2015

LIGHTVIEW INC (NV)
Reincorporated under the laws of Delaware as Geeks On Call Holdings, Inc. 02/01/2008

LIGHTWAVE CABLEVISION SYS INC (CA)
Filed bankruptcy 00/00/1992
Details not available

LIGNEX INC (ON)
Name changed to International Biotechnology Corp. 8/9/2000
International Biotechnology Corp. recapitalized as Veris Biotechnology Corp. 3/22/2001 which recapitalized as Capital Diagnostic Corp. 5/5/2004

LIGNIN INDS INC (NV)
Name changed to Heritage Media Corp. 06/05/2006
Heritage Media Corp. recapitalized as Oliveda International, Inc. 03/24/2017

LIHIR GOLD LTD (PAPUA NEW GUINEA)
Sponsored ADR's for Ordinary split (2) for (1) by issuance of (1) additional ADR payable 10/03/2006 to holders of record 10/02/2006 Ex date - 10/04/2006
Acquired by Newcrest Mining Ltd. 08/30/2010
Each share Ordinary exchanged for (0.12236652) share Ordinary no par and AUD $0.08329 cash
Each Sponsored ADR for Ordinary no par exchanged for (1.22366519) Sponsored for Ordinary AUD $0.50 par and $0.77834505 cash

LIHUE PLANTATION LTD (HI)
Each share Common $100 par exchanged for (5) shares Common no par 00/00/1937
Merged into Amfac, Inc. 01/09/1969
Each share Common no par exchanged for (1.68) shares Common no par
(See Amfac, Inc.)

LIKE DEVELOPMENT INC. (UT)
Reincorporated under the laws of Michigan as Tubby's Sub Shops, Inc. 5/23/86
Tubby's Sub Shops, Inc. merged into Tubby's Inc. 4/2/90
(See Tubby's Inc.)

LIKLY (HENRY) & CO., INC. (NY)
Acquired by Likly Luggage, Inc. 05/00/1928

Details not available

LIKLY LUGGAGE, INC. (DE)
Charter revoked for failure to file reports and pay fees in 1932

LIL CHAMP FOOD STORES INC (FL)
Common 10¢ par split (3) for (2) by issuance of (0.5) additional share 01/02/1983
Common 10¢ par split (3) for (2) by issuance of (0.5) additional share 01/03/1984
100% acquired by LCFS Acquisition Corp. through purchase offer which expired 02/27/1985
Public interest eliminated

LIL MARC INC (NV)
Each share old Common 1¢ par exchanged for (0.54) share new Common 1¢ par 10/23/2002
Name changed to InkSure Technologies Inc. (NV) 10/28/2002
InkSure Technologies Inc. (NV) reincorporated in Delaware 07/08/2003 which name changed to New York Global Innovations Inc. 10/19/2016 which recapitalized as Artemis Therapeutics, Inc. 12/20/2016

LILAC TIME INC (FL)
Reorganized 04/01/1973
Reorganized from (NY) to under the laws of (FL) 04/01/1973
Each share Common 5¢ par exchanged for (5) shares Common 1¢ par
Name changed to Southern Atlantic Corp. 07/13/1976
(See Southern Atlantic Corp.)

LILAC TIME OF ROCHESTER INC. (NY)
Stock Dividend - 100% 10/21/70
Name changed to Lilac Time, Inc. (NY) 4/25/72
Lilac Time, Inc. (NY) recapitalized in Florida 4/1/73 which name changed to Southern Atlantic Corp. 7/13/76
(See Southern Atlantic Corp.)

LILLI ANN CORP (DE)
Reincorporated 07/02/1979
Stock Dividends - 50% 03/25/1965; 10% 12/22/1969; 10% 06/15/1971; 10% 06/30/1972
State of incorporation changed from (CA) to (DE) 07/02/1979
Merged into Schuman Associates, Inc. 10/04/1982
Each share Common no par exchanged for $16 cash

LILLIAN VERNON CORP (DE)
Common 1¢ par split (3) for (2) by issuance of (0.5) additional share 8/14/90
Merged into LVC Holdings LLC 7/3/2003
Each share Common 1¢ par exchanged for $7.25 cash

LILLY ELI & CO (IN)
Each share old 5% Preferred $100 par exchanged for (1) share new 5% Preferred $100 par 12/20/1955
5% Preferred $100 par called for redemption 06/10/1968
  (Additional Information in Active)

LILLY INDS INC (IN)
Name changed 12/01/1991
Name changed from Lilly Industrial Coating Inc. 12/01/1991 to Lilly Industries, Inc. 12/01/1991
Class A no par split (3) for (2) by issuance of (0.5) additional share 03/10/1993
Class B no par split (3) for (2) by issuance of (0.5) additional share 03/10/1993
Class A no par split (3) for (2) by issuance of (0.5) additional share 06/01/1994
Class B no par split (3) for (2) by issuance of (0.5) additional share 06/01/1994

Merged into Valspar Corp. 12/20/2000
Each share Class A Common no par exchanged for $31.75 cash
Each share Class B Common no par exchanged for $31.75 cash

LILLY VARNISH CO. (IN)
Name changed to Lilly Industrial Coatings, Inc. 5/15/65
Lilly Industrial Coatings, Inc. name changed to Lilly Industries, Inc. 12/1/91

LILM INC (NV)
Name changed to Great Plains Holdings, Inc. 12/04/2013
Great Plains Holdings, Inc. name changed to Jerrick Media Holdings, Inc. 03/04/2016

LILY LYNN INC (MA)
Name changed to Lynnwear Corp. 5/21/76
(See Lynnwear Corp.)

LILY-TULIP CUP CORP. (DE)
Common no par changed to $10 par and (1) additional share issued 5/13/55
Common $10 par changed to $5 par and (1) additional share issued 5/14/59
Stock Dividends - 75% 7/12/50; 50% 2/18/54
Merged into Owens-Illinois, Inc. 11/1/68
Each share Common $5 par exchanged for (0.22) share $4.75 Conv. Preference no par and (0.39) share Common $3.125 par
(See Owens-Illinois, Inc.)

LILY TULIP INC (DE)
Acquired by Fort Howard Paper Co. 06/24/1986
Each share Common no par exchanged for $18.50 cash

LIMA CORD SOLE & HEEL CO. (OH)
Name changed to Gro-Cord Rubber Co. 10/30/45 which was adjudicated bankrupt 10/24/63

LIMA GOLD CORP (BC)
Recapitalized as International Lima Resources Corp. 09/21/1999
Each share Common no par exchanged for (0.33333333) share Common no par
International Lima Resources Corp. name changed to Crosshair Exploration & Mining Corp. 03/01/2004 which name changed to Crosshair Energy Corp. 11/02/2011 which recapitalized as Jet Metal Corp. (BC) 09/23/2013 which reorganized in Canada as Canada Jetlines Ltd. 03/07/2017

LIMA-HAMILTON CORP.
Merged into Baldwin-Lima-Hamilton Corp. and each share Capital Stock $5 par exchanged for (1) share new Capital Stock $13 par in 1950
Baldwin-Lima-Hamilton Corp. was acquired by Armour & Co. (Del.) 7/2/65

LIMA LOCOMOTIVE WORKS, INC.
Merged into Lima-Hamilton Corp. on a (5.375) for (1) basis 00/00/1947
Lima-Hamilton Corp. merged into Baldwin-Lima-Hamilton Corp. 00/00/1950 which was acquired by Armour & Co. (DE) 07/02/1965 which merged into Greyhound Corp. (DE) 12/28/1970 which reincorporated in Delaware 03/18/1992 which name changed to Viad Corp. 08/15/1996

LIMCO PIEDMONT INC (DE)
Issue Information - 4,400,000 shares COM offered at $11 per share on 07/18/2007
Merged into TAT Technologies Ltd. 07/06/2009
Each share Common 1¢ par exchanged for (0.5) share new Ordinary NIS 0.15 par

LIME COLA CO., INC.
Reorganized as Lime Cola Co. of Tennessee on a (1) for (4) basis in 1948
Lime Cola Co. of Tennessee name changed to General Beverages, Inc. in 1952
(See General Beverages, Inc.)

LIME COLA CO. OF TENNESSEE
Name changed to General Beverages, Inc. in 1952
(See General Beverages, Inc.)

LIME COLA DISTRIBUTORS OF AMERICA
Name changed to Lime Cola Co., Inc. in 1946
Lime Cola Co., Inc. reorganized as Lime Cola Co. of Tennessee in 1948 which name changed to General Beverages, Inc. in 1952
(See General Beverages, Inc.)

LIME HILL CAP CORP (CANADA)
Issue Information - 7,553,000 shares COM offered at $0.10 per share on 04/28/2010
Recapitalized as Liquid Nutrition Group Inc. 05/25/2011
Each share Common no par exchanged for (0.125) share Common no par

LIMELIGHT MEDIA GROUP INC (NV)
Recapitalized as Impart Media Group, Inc. 12/22/2005
Each share Common $0.001 par exchanged for (0.05) share Common $0.001 par
(See Impart Media Group, Inc.)

LIMELIGHT PRODUCTIONS LTD (NV)
SEC revoked common stock registration 12/01/2006

LIMESTONE MILLS
Acquired by Lowenstein (M) & Sons Inc. 00/00/1947
Details not available

LIMESTONE PRODS CORP AMER (NJ)
Merged into Penn Virginia Corp. (Old) 08/30/1974
Each share Common no par exchanged for (6) shares Capital Stock $12.50 par
(See Penn Virginia Corp. (Old))

LIMITED BRANDS INC (DE)
Name changed 05/20/2002
Common 50¢ par split (2) for (1) by issuance of (1) additional share 11/22/1982
Common 50¢ par split (2) for (1) by issuance of (1) additional share 06/13/1983
Common 50¢ par split (2) for (1) by issuance of (1) additional share 06/25/1985
Common 50¢ par split (3) for (2) by issuance of (0.5) additional share 06/23/1986
Common 50¢ par split (2) for (1) by issuance of (1) additional share 06/19/1990
Each share Common 50¢ par received distribution of (0.013673) share Abercrombie & Fitch Co. Class A Common 1¢ par payable 06/01/1998 to holders of record 05/29/1998 Ex date - 06/02/1998
Each share Common 50¢ par received distribution of (0.14285714) share Too, Inc. Common no par payable 08/23/1999 to holders of record 08/11/1999 Ex date - 08/24/1999
Common 50¢ par split (2) for (1) by issuance of (1) additional share payable 05/30/2000 to holders of record 05/12/2000
Name changed from Limited, Inc. to Limited Brands, Inc. 05/20/2002
Name changed to L Brands, Inc. 03/28/2013

LIM-LIN

LIMITED DURATION INVT GRADE PFD SECS FD (ON)
Under plan of merger each Class A, Class F, Class U and Class V Unit automatically became (0.881314), (0.963747), (1.301973) or (1.379099) Purpose US Preferred Share Fund ETF Unit, ETF Unit, ETF Non-Currency Hedged Units or ETF Non-Currency Hedged Units respectively 08/24/2018

LIMITED OIL CO.
Merged into Superior Oil Co. (CA) in 1937
Details not available

LIMITED STORES INC (OH)
Common no par split (2) for (1) by issuance of (1) additional share 10/28/1975
Common no par split (3) for (2) by issuance of (0.5) additional share 07/16/1976
Common no par split (2) for (1) by issuance of (1) additional share 07/07/1977
Common no par split (3) for (2) by issuance of (0.5) additional share 06/09/1978
Reincorporated under the laws of Delaware as Limited, Inc. and Common no par changed to 50¢ par 06/04/1982
Limited, Inc. (DE) name changed to Limited Brands, Inc. 05/20/2002 which name changed to L Brands, Inc. 03/28/2013

LIMITED TERM MUN FD INC (MD)
Reorganized as Thornburg Investment Trust 01/29/2004
Details not available

LIMOGES PORCELAINES LTD (BC)
Recapitalized as Boch & Limoges Ltd. 10/20/1988
Each share Common no par exchanged for (0.1) share Common no par
Boch & Limoges Ltd. recapitalized as Vannessa Ventures Ltd. 07/21/1994 which name changed to Infinito Gold Ltd. 05/28/2008

LIMONEIRA CO (CA)
Reincorporated under the laws of Delaware 00/00/1990

LIMPIA ROYALTIES, INC. (DE)
Completely liquidated 10/1/64
Each share Common $1 par received first and final distribution of $8.41 cash
Certificates were not surrendered and are now without value

LIMTECH LITHIUM INDS INC (QC)
Assets sold for the benefit of creditors 3/30/2004
No stockholders' equity

LIMTECH LITHIUM METAL TECHNOLOGIES INC (QC)
Recapitalized as Limtech Lithium Industries Inc. 12/16/2002
Each share Common no par exchanged for (0.1) share Common no par
(See Limtech Lithium Industries Inc.)

LIN BROADCASTING CORP (DE)
Common $2 par split (2) for (1) by issuance of (1) additional share 12/5/80
Common $2 par split (2) for (1) by issuance of (1) additional share 3/4/82
Common $2 par split (2) for (1) by issuance of (1) additional share 6/24/83
Common $2 par changed to 1¢ par 5/29/86
Common 1¢ par split (2) for (1) by issuance of (1) additional share 3/31/87
Merged into AT&T Corp. 10/3/95
Each share Common 1¢ par exchanged for $129.9003 cash

LIN MEDIA LLC (DE)
Merged into Media General, Inc. (New) 12/22/2014
Each share Class A Common 1¢ par exchanged for (1.4714) shares Common no par
Media General, Inc. (New) merged into Nexstar Media Group, Inc. 01/18/2017

LIN TELEVISION CORP (DE)
Merged into Hicks, Muse, Tate & Furst Inc. 3/3/98
Each share Common 1¢ par exchanged for $55.1929 cash

LIN TSO CORP (DE)
Charter cancelled and declared inoperative and void for non-payment of taxes 4/15/72

LIN TV CORP (DE)
Merged into LIN Media LLC 07/31/2013
Each share Class A Common 1¢ par exchanged for (1) share Class A Common 1¢ par
LIN Media LLC merged into Media General, Inc. (New) 12/22/2014 which merged into Nexstar Media Group, Inc. 01/18/2017

LINAIR ENGINEERING, INC. (CA)
Liquidated 01/22/1962
Each share Capital Stock $1 par exchanged for (0.1) share Teledyne, Inc. Capital Stock $1 par
Teledyne, Inc. merged into Allegheny Teledyne, Inc. 08/15/1996 which name changed to Allegheny Technologies Inc. 11/29/1999

LINAMAR MACH LTD (ON)
Common no par split (2) for (1) by issuance of (1) additional share 11/25/86
Name changed to Linamar Corp. 11/2/92

LINC CAP INC (DE)
Issue Information - 2,000,000 shares COM offered at $13 per share on 11/05/1997
Plan of reorganization under Chapter 11 Federal Bankruptcy Code effective 1/27/2002
No stockholders' equity

LINC ENERGY LTD (AUSTRALIA)
Each old Sponsored ADR for Ordinary exchanged for (0.16666666) new Sponsored ADR for Ordinary 03/09/2016
ADR agreement terminated 08/31/2016
ADR holders' equity unlikely

LINCAM PPPTYS LTD (IL)
Liquidation completed
Each Unit of Limited Partnership Int. Ser. 85 received initial distribution of $510 cash in 1996
Each Unit of Limited Partnership Int. Ser. 85 received second distribution of $75 cash in 1997
Each Unit of Limited Partnership Int. Ser. 85 received third and final distribution of $136 cash 7/15/98

LINCARE HLDGS INC (DE)
Common 1¢ par split (2) for (1) by issuance of (1) additional share 11/30/1993
Common 1¢ par split (2) for (1) by issuance of (1) additional share payable 05/29/1998 to holders of record 05/15/1998
Common 1¢ par split (2) for (1) by issuance of (1) additional share payable 06/22/2001 to holders of record 06/07/2001 Ex date - 06/25/2001
Common 1¢ par split (3) for (2) by issuance of (0.5) additional share payable 06/15/2010 to holders of record 06/03/2010 Ex date - 06/16/2010
Acquired by Linde AG 08/13/2012

Each share Common 1¢ par exchanged for $41.50 cash

LINCO CORP. (OH)
Dissolved 11/28/47

LINCO INTERNATIONAL, INC. (MO)
Name changed to International Super Stores, Inc. 10/17/66

LINCOLN-ALLIANCE BANK & TRUST CO. (ROCHESTER, NY)
Merged into Lincoln Rochester Trust Co. (Rochester, N.Y.) 7/6/45
Lincoln Rochester Trust Co. (Rochester, N.Y.) merged into Lincoln First Group Inc. 5/16/67 which name changed to Lincoln First Banks Inc. 5/22/68

LINCOLN AMERN CORP (NY)
Conv. Preference $1 par called for redemption 06/27/1980
Merged into American General Corp. 09/01/1980
Each share Common $1 par exchanged for (0.4) share $3.25 Conv. Jr. Pfd. 1980 Ser. $1.50 par
American General Corp. merged into American International Group, Inc. 08/29/2001

LINCOLN AMERN CORP (TN)
Merged into Lincoln American Corp. (NY) 5/1/72
Each share Common $1 par exchanged for (2/3) share Common $1 par
Lincoln American Corp. (NY) merged into American General Corp. 9/1/80 which merged into American International Group, Inc. 8/29/2001

LINCOLN AMERN LIFE INS CO (TN)
Reorganized as Lincoln American Corp. (TN) 4/1/69
Each share Common Capital Stock $1 par exchanged for (1) share Common $1 par
Lincoln American Corp. (TN) merged into Lincoln American Corp. (NY) 5/1/72 which merged into American General Corp. 9/1/80 which merged into American International Group, Inc. 8/29/2001

LINCOLN ARMS APARTMENTS LIQUIDATION TRUST
Trust terminated and liquidated 00/00/1951
Details not available

LINCOLN BANCORP (CA)
Common no par split (6) for (5) by issuance of (0.2) additional share 02/20/1985
Common no par split (6) for (5) by issuance of (0.2) additional share 05/15/1990
Stock Dividend - 20% 05/19/1989
Name changed to CU Bancorp 08/01/1990
(See CU Bancorp)

LINCOLN BANCORP (IN)
Acquired by First Merchants Corp. 12/31/2008
Each share Common no par exchanged for either (0.7004) share Common no par or (0.41869912) share Common no par and $6.338672 cash
Note: Option to receive stock and cash expired 01/02/2009

LINCOLN BK & TR CO (JEFFERSON BOROUGH, PA)
Name changed to Three Rivers Bank & Trust Co. (Jefferson Borough, PA) 4/1/70
Three Rivers Bank & Trust Co. (Jefferson Borough, PA) merged into USBANCORP, Inc. 6/30/84 which name changed to AmeriServ Financial, Inc. 5/7/2001

LINCOLN BK N C (LINCOLNTON, NC)
Reorganized as Carolina First Bancshares, Inc. 06/00/1989

Each share Common $2.50 par exchanged for (1) share Common $2.50 par
Carolina First Bancshares, Inc. merged into First Charter Corp. 04/04/2000 which merged into Fifth Third Bancorp 06/06/2008

LINCOLN BK SOUTH (LINCOLN, NE)
Common $2 par split (5) for (4) by issuance of (0.25) additional share 1/12/87
Stock Dividends - 33-1/3% 11/20/75; 25% 5/14/76; 15% 5/23/77; 15% 6/14/78; 15% 5/16/79; 10% 1/10/89; 10% 1/10/92
Merged into First Commerce Bancshares, Inc. 10/1/94
Each share Common $2 par exchanged for (0.6174) share Class B $1 par
First Commerce Bancshares, Inc. merged into Wells Fargo & Co. 6/16/2000

LINCOLN BLDG. CO. (DE)
Liquidated in 1955

LINCOLN BUILDING CORP.
Liquidation for cash completed 4/15/52

LINCOLN CAP CORP (ON)
Name changed to Jumbo Entertainment Inc. 07/30/1996
Jumbo Entertainment Inc. name changed to J.U.M. Capital Inc. 07/09/2004 which recapitalized as West 49 Inc. 12/01/2004
(See West 49 Inc.)

LINCOLN CAP INC (UT)
Name changed to Page Impero Holdings, Inc. 03/22/1993
Page Impero Holdings, Inc. name changed to China Continental Inc. (UT) 01/18/1994 which reincorporated in Nevada 01/11/2002
(See China Continental Inc.)

LINCOLN CONS INC (NV)
Acquired by Illinois Central Industries, Inc. 04/11/1972
Each share Common $1 par exchanged for (0.35) share Common no par
Illinois Central Industries, Inc. name changed to IC Industries, Inc. 05/21/1975 which name changed to Whitman Corp. (Old) 12/01/1988 which name changed to Whitman Corp. (New) 11/30/2000 which name changed to PepsiAmericas, Inc. (DE) 01/24/2001 which merged into PepsiCo, Inc. 02/26/2010

LINCOLN DIVIDE MNG CO (NV)
Name changed to Cheroke Minerals & Oil, Inc. 02/25/1980
Cheroke Minerals & Oil, Inc. name changed to HydroMaid International, Inc. 01/20/1999
(See HydroMaid International, Inc.)

LINCOLN DRILLING CO.
Name changed to Lincoln Petroleum Co. in 1931
Lincoln Petroleum Co. acquired by Great Basins Petroleum Co. in 1956
(See Great Basins Petroleum Co.)

LINCOLN ELEC CO (OH)
Common no par split (10) for (1) by issuance of (9) additional shares 06/02/1993
Each share Common no par received distribution of (1) share Non-Vtg. Class A Common no par 06/12/1995
Reorganized as Lincoln Electric Holdings, Inc. 06/02/1998
Each share Non-Vtg. Class A Common no par exchanged for (2) shares Common no par
Each share Common no par exchanged for (2) shares Common no par

LINCOLN ENGINEERING CO. (MO)
Merged into McNeil Machine & Engineering Co. 4/27/56
Each share Common no par exchanged for (1) share 5% Preferred A $40 par
(See McNeil Machine & Engineering Co.)

LINCOLN EQUITIES, INC.
Liquidated in 1939

LINCOLN EQUITIES CORP (CO)
Name changed to Action Dynamics, Inc. 07/03/1989
(See Action Dynamics, Inc.)

LINCOLN FINANCE CO., INC. (KY)
Name changed to Lincoln International Corp. (KY) 01/05/1970
Lincoln International Corp. (KY) reincorporated in Delaware 11/03/2004 which recapitalized as China Display Technologies, Inc. 11/26/2007

LINCOLN FINL BANCORP INC (DE)
Merged into First Southern Bancorp, Inc. 9/5/96
Each share Common 1¢ par exchanged for $22.01 cash

LINCOLN FINL CORP (IN)
Common no par split (2) for (1) by issuance of (1) additional share 05/15/1986
Common no par split (3) for (2) by issuance of (0.5) additional share 10/23/1986
Stock Dividends - 25% 02/03/1975; 10% 05/01/1976; 16-2/3% 02/01/1978
Acquired by Norwest Corp. 02/09/1993
Each share Common no par exchanged for (0.588) share Common $1-2/3 par
Northwest Corp. name changed to Wells Fargo & Co. (New) 11/02/1998

LINCOLN FIRE INSURANCE CO. OF NEW YORK
Name changed to American Fidelity Fire Insurance Co. and Preferred $1 par changed to $5 par in 1944
(See American Fidelity Fire Insurance Co.)

LINCOLN 1ST BKS INC (NY)
Common $10 par changed to $1 par 5/6/83
Merged into Chase Manhattan Corp. (Old) 7/1/84
Each share $1.05 Conv. Preferred $4.50 par exchanged for (0.596387) share Adjustable Rate Preferred Ser. F no par and (0.060801) share Common $12.50 par
Each share Common $1 par exchanged for (1.334198) shares Adjustable Rate Preferred Ser. F no par and (0.136021) share Common $12.50 par
Chase Manhattan Corp. (Old) merged into Chase Manhattan Corp. (New) 3/31/96 which name changed to J.P. Morgan Chase & Co. 12/31/2000 which name changed to JPMorgan Chase & Co. 7/20/2004

LINCOLN 1ST GROUP INC (NY)
Name changed to Lincoln First Banks Inc. 5/22/68
Lincoln First Banks Inc. merged into Chase Manhattan Corp. (Old) 7/1/84 which merged into Chase Manhattan Corp. (New) 3/31/96 which name changed to J.P. Morgan Chase & Co. 12/31/2000 which name changed to JPMorgan Chase & Co. 7/20/2004

LINCOLN FLOORPLANNING CO INC (NV)
Name changed to China Power Technology, Inc. 10/13/2010

LINCOLN FOODSERVICE PRODS INC (IN)
Merged into Welbilt Corp. (DE) 8/17/94
Each share Common no par exchanged for $15.60 cash

LINCOLN GOLD CORP (BC)
Reincorporated 02/18/2009
Place of incorporation changed from (Canada) to (BC) 02/18/2009
Merged into Lincoln Mining Corp. 08/12/2009
Each share Common no par exchanged for (0.31) share Common no par
Note: Unexchanged certificates were cancelled and became without value 08/17/2015

LINCOLN GOLD CORP (NV)
Reincorporated under the laws of Canada and Common $0.001 par changed to no par 04/04/2008
Lincoln Gold Corp. (Canada) reincorporated in British Columbia 02/18/2009 which merged into Lincoln Mining Corp. 08/12/2009

LINCOLN GOLD MINES LTD. (ON)
Charter revoked for failure to file reports and pay fees 4/1/65

LINCOLN HALL CORP. (NY)
Liquidation completed 5/10/61

LINCOLN HERITAGE CORP (TX)
Name changed to Forever Enterprises, Inc. 03/09/2000
(See Forever Enterprises, Inc.)

LINCOLN HIGHWAY TIRE CO. (SD)
Charter expired by time limitation in 1941

LINCOLN INCOME LIFE INS CO (KY)
Stock Dividends - 100% 03/30/1950; 10% 02/25/1955; 10% 03/01/1956; 10% 03/01/1957; 10% 03/01/1958; 10% 02/28/1959; 10% 03/01/1960; 100% 06/17/1960
Merged into Conseco, Inc. 05/08/1986
Each share Common $1 par exchanged for $29 cash

LINCOLN INTL CORP (DE)
Recapitalized as China Display Technologies, Inc. 11/26/2007
Each share Class A Common $0.0001 par exchanged for (0.13333333) share Common $0.001 par

LINCOLN INTL CORP (KY)
Each share old Non-Vtg. Class A Common no par exchanged for (0.0025) share new Non-Vtg. Class A Common no par 04/05/1998
Each share new Non-Vtg. Class A Common no par exchanged again for (1/3) share new Non-Vtg. Class A Common no par 02/18/2003
Reincorporated under the laws of Delaware and Common no par changed to $0.0001 par 11/03/2004
Lincoln International Corp. (DE) recapitalized as China Display Technologies, Inc. 11/26/2007

LINCOLN INTERSTATE HOLDING CO.
Acquired by Niagara Share Corp. of Delaware 00/00/1929
Details not available

LINCOLN INVS (CA)
Merged into Builders Investment Group 03/01/1982
Each Share of Bene. Int. no par exchanged for (0.75) Common Share of Bene. Int. 10¢ par
Builders Investment Group name changed to Winn Enterprises 08/17/1983
(See Winn Enterprises)

LINCOLN LD CO (NE)
Dissolved 08/05/1974
Details not available

LINCOLN LIBERTY LIFE INS CO (NE)
Each share Common $100 par exchanged for (156.7755) shares Common $1 par 07/29/1958
Acquired by Lincoln Financial, Inc. 04/24/1974
Each share Common $1 par exchanged for $14 cash

LINCOLN LIFE & CASUALTY CO. (NE)
Under plan of merger each share Common 50¢ par exchanged for (2/3) share Common $1 par 12/30/65
Stock Dividend - 10% 11/28/77
Merged into Federal Credit Corp. 5/8/89
Each share Common $1 par exchanged for $4.10 cash

LINCOLN LIFE INSURANCE CO. OF GEORGIA (GA)
Acquired by Public Savings Life Insurance Co. 12/31/62
Each share Common $5 par received (1) share Common $1 par
Certificates were not surrendered and are now without value

LINCOLN LOGS LTD (NY)
Each share old Common 1¢ par exchanged for (0.08) share new Common 1¢ par 02/24/1986
Each share new Common 1¢ par exchanged again for (0.002) share new Common 1¢ par 09/14/2005
Note: Holders of (499) or fewer pre-split shares received $0.49 cash per share
Stock Dividend - 10% 06/03/1988
Plan of reorganization under Chapter 11 Federal Bankruptcy proceedings effective 07/20/2009
No stockholders' equity

LINCOLN MANUFACTURING CO.
Merged into General Cotton Corp. 00/00/1930
Details not available

LINCOLN MNG CO (ID)
Completely liquidated 01/18/1972
Each share Common 10¢ par exchanged for first and final distribution of (0.125) share Sunshine Mining Co. (WA) Capital Stock 5¢ par
Sunshine Mining Co. (WA) reincorporated in Delaware 03/12/1980 which name changed to Sunshine Mining & Refining Co. 06/20/1994
(See Sunshine Mining & Refining Co.)

LINCOLN MNG CORP (NV)
Name changed to Liberty Silver Corp. 03/15/2010
Liberty Silver Corp. name changed to Bunker Hill Mining Corp. 11/29/2017

LINCOLN MORTGAGE & TITLE GUARANTY CO.
Assets sold to Bondholders Committee in 1938

LINCOLN MORTGAGE CO. (LOS ANGELES, CA)
Out of business 00/00/1931
Details not available

LINCOLN MORTGAGE CO. (NEWARK, NJ)
Dissolved in 1946

LINCOLN MORTGAGE CO. (NY)
Liquidation completed in 1947

LINCOLN MTG INVS (CA)
Name changed to Lincoln Investors 09/03/1980
Lincoln Investors merged into Builders Investment Group 03/01/1982 which name changed to Winn Enterprises 08/17/1983
(See Winn Enterprises)

LINCOLN MUTUAL INVESTMENT TRUST
Liquidated in 1931

LINCOLN N C RLTY FD INC (MD)
Name changed to North American Trust, Inc. 10/29/1993
(See North American Trust, Inc.)

LINCOLN NATL BALANCED FD (DE)
Name changed to Lincoln National Income Fund Inc. 07/01/1972
Lincoln National Income Fund Inc. merged into Selected American Shares, Inc. 11/17/1976

LINCOLN NATIONAL BANK & TRUST CO. (SYRACUSE, NY)
Each share Capital Stock $20 par exchanged for (2) shares Capital Stock $10 par in 1953
Name changed to Lincoln National Bank & Trust Co. of Central New York (Syracuse, NY) 4/1/49
Lincoln National Bank & Trust Co. of Central New York (Syracuse, NY) merged into Lincoln First Group Inc. 5/16/67 which name changed to Lincoln First Banks Inc. 5/22/68 which merged into Chase Manhattan Corp. (Old) 7/1/84 which merged into Chase Manhattan Corp. (New) 3/31/96 which name changed to J.P. Morgan Chase & Co. 12/31/2000 which name changed to JPMorgan Chase & Co. 7/20/2004

LINCOLN NATIONAL BANK & TRUST CO. OF CENTRAL NEW YORK (SYRACUSE, NY)
Merged into Lincoln First Group Inc. 5/16/67
Each share Capital Stock $10 par received (0.381) share Common $10 par
Each share Capital Stock $10 par subsequently exchanged for (1) share Common $10 par
Lincoln First Group Inc. name changed to Lincoln First Banks Inc. 5/22/68 which merged into Chase Manhattan Corp. (Old) 7/1/84 which merged into Chase Manhattan Corp. (New) 3/31/96 which name changed to J.P. Morgan Chase & Co. 12/31/2000 which name changed to JPMorgan Chase & Co. 7/20/2004

LINCOLN NATL BK & TR CO (FORT WAYNE, IN)
Capital Stock $20 par changed to $10 par and (0.6) additional share issued 07/18/1961
Stock Dividends - 33-1/3% 01/10/1951; 20% 07/16/1957; 25% 02/17/1964; 10% 02/09/1966
Reorganized as Lincoln Tower Corp. 11/01/1969
Each share Capital Stock $10 par exchanged for (1) share Common no par
Lincoln Tower Corp. name changed to Lincoln Financial Corp. 05/01/1974 which was acquired by Norwest Corp. 02/09/1993 which name changed to Wells Fargo & Co. (New) 11/02/1998

LINCOLN NATL BK (BUFFALO, NY)
Merged into Chase Manhattan Corp. (Old) 6/29/73
Each share Common $5 par exchanged for (0.508775) share Common $12.50 par
Chase Manhattan Corp. (Old) merged into Chase Manhattan Corp. (New) 3/31/96 which name changed to J.P. Morgan Chase & Co. 12/31/2000 which name changed to JPMorgan Chase & Co. 7/20/2004

LINCOLN NATL BK (CHICAGO, IL)
Stock Dividend - 100% 02/02/1970
Acquired by Corus Banksharks, Inc. 09/14/1996
Each share Common $25 par exchanged for $500 cash

LINCOLN NATL BK (GAITHERSBURG, MD)
Acquired by First American Bank of

Maryland (Silver Spring, MD) 09/01/1981
Details not available

LINCOLN NATL BK (MIAMI, FL)
Name changed to National Industrial Bank (Miami, FL) 11/4/68
National Industrial Bank (Miami, FL) name changed to Capital Bank of Miami, N.A. (Miami, FL) 12/1/75 which merged into Capital Bank (North Bay Village, FL) 12/30/77 which was acquired by Capital Bancorp in September 1982 which merged into Union Planters Corp. 12/31/97 which merged into Regions Financial Corp. (New) 7/1/2004

LINCOLN NATL BK (PHILADELPHIA, PA)
Reorganized as Lincoln National Co. 06/17/1969
Each share Capital Stock $10 par exchanged for (1) share Common $10 par
(See Lincoln National Co.)

LINCOLN NATL BK (STAMFORD, CT)
Merged into Hartford National Bank & Trust Co. (Hartford, CT) 12/12/69
Each share Common $5 par exchanged for (1/6) share Hartford National Corp. Common $6.25 par
Hartford National Corp. merged into Shawmut National Corp. 2/29/88 which merged into Fleet Financial Group Inc. (New) 11/30/95 which name changed to Fleet Boston Corp. 10/1/99 which name changed to FleetBoston Financial Corp. 4/18/2000 which merged into Bank of America Corp. 4/1/2004

LINCOLN NATL CAP FD (DE)
Merged into Selected Special Shares, Inc. 11/18/1976
Each share Common $1 par exchanged for (0.4492) share Common 25¢ par
Selected Special Shares, Inc. name changed to Selected International Fund, Inc. 05/01/2011

LINCOLN NATL CAP I (DE)
8.750% Guaranteed Quarterly Income Preferred Securities A called for redemption at $25 on 9/13/2001

LINCOLN NATL CAP III (DE)
7.40% Trust Originated Preferred Ser. C called for redemption at $25 on 7/24/2003

LINCOLN NATL CAP IV (DE)
Preferred called for redemption at $25 on 8/15/2003

LINCOLN NATL CAP V (DE)
7.65% Guaranteed Trust Preferred Securities called for redemption at $25 on 11/19/2006

LINCOLN NATL CAP VI (DE)
6.750% Trust Preferred Securities called for redemption at $25 on 12/15/2010

LINCOLN NATL CO (PA)
Acquired by Continental Bank (Norristown, PA) 06/28/1982
Each share Common $10 par exchanged for $45 cash

LINCOLN NATL CORP (IN)
Short Term Auction Rate Preferred Ser. C no par called for redemption 06/21/1990
Short Term Auction Rate Preferred Ser. D no par called for redemption 06/28/1990
Short Term Auction Rate Preferred Ser. B no par called for redemption 07/12/1990
$3 Preferred Ser. A no par called for redemption at $80 plus $0.2225 accrued dividends on 07/02/2013
(Additional Information in Active)

LINCOLN NATL CORP (NJ)
Out of business and liquidated 10/31/1969
Details not available

LINCOLN NATL INCOME FD INC (DE)
Merged into Selected American Shares, Inc. 11/17/76
Each share Common $1 par exchanged for (1.2461) shares Common $1.25 par

LINCOLN NATL LIFE INS CO (IN)
Common $10 par changed to $5 par and (1) additional share issued plus a 25% stock dividend paid 03/23/1961
Common $5 par changed to $2.50 par and (1) additional share issued 04/01/1965
Stock Dividends - 40% 12/16/1943; 42-6/7% 12/16/1946; 100% 11/22/1950; 100% 03/23/1956
Reorganized as Lincoln National Corp. (IN) 06/04/1968
Each share Common $2.50 par exchanged for (1) share Common $2.50 par

LINCOLN OIL & GAS CO. (CO)
Charter dissolved for failure to file annual reports 1/1/29

LINCOLN PETROLEUM CO. (CA)
Acquired by Great Basins Petroleum Co. in 1956
Each share Capital Stock 10¢ par exchanged for (1.25) shares Common $1 par
(See Great Basins Petroleum Co.)

LINCOLN PETROLEUM CORP. LTD.
Acquired by Lincoln Petroleum Co. on a (0.25) for (1) basis in 1936
Lincoln Petroleum Co. was acquired by Great Basins Petroleum Co. in 1956
(See Great Basins Petroleum Co.)

LINCOLN PLAZA CORP. (OK)
Common 50¢ par changed to 10¢ par and (4) additional shares issued 2/20/81
Name changed to Lincoln Plaza Resources, Inc. 6/3/81
(See Lincoln Plaza Resources, Inc.)

LINCOLN PLAZA RES INC (OK)
Liquidation completed
Each share Common 10¢ par exchanged for initial distribution of $1 cash 07/05/1983
Each share Common 10¢ par received second distribution of $0.15 cash 01/12/1984
Each share Common 10¢ par received third distribution of $0.15 cash 03/19/1985
Each share Common 10¢ par received fourth and final distribution of $0.1235 cash 05/06/1987

LINCOLN PRINTING CO. (DE)
Preference $50 par changed to no par in 1936
Each share Common no par exchanged for (0.25) share Common $1 par in 1944
Common $1 par changed to 50¢ par and (2) additional shares issued 11/13/61
No longer in existence having become inoperative and void for non-payment of taxes 4/1/67

LINCOLN RES INC (BC)
Recapitalized as United Lincoln Resources Inc. 06/21/1988
Each share Common no par exchanged for (0.1) share Common no par
United Lincoln Resources Inc. merged into Continental Gold Corp. (New) 03/15/1989
(See Continental Gold Corp. (New))

LINCOLN-ROBEY CORP. (DE)
Completely liquidated 9/22/65
Each share Capital Stock $1 par or Capital Stock Trust Ctfs. $1 par exchanged for first and final distribution of $27.90 cash

LINCOLN ROCHESTER TRUST CO. (ROCHESTER, NY)
Capital Stock $20 par changed to $10 par and (1) additional share issued 2/19/65
Stock Dividends - 10% 2/1/51; 11-1/9% 2/1/54
Merged into Lincoln First Group Inc. 5/16/67
Each share Capital Stock $10 par received (0.25) share Common $10 par
Each share Capital Stock $10 par then subsequently exchanged for (1) share Common $10 par
Lincoln First Group Inc. name changed to Lincoln First Banks Inc. 5/22/68 which merged into Chase Manhattan Corp. (Old) 7/1/84 which merged into Chase Manhattan Corp. (New) 3/31/96 which name changed to J.P. Morgan Chase & Co. 12/31/2000 which name changed to JPMorgan Chase & Co. 7/20/2004

LINCOLN SVGS & LN ASSN (OR)
Reserve Fund Stock $10 par changed to $2 par and (4) additional shares issued 8/1/70
Reserve Fund Stock $2 par changed to no par in October 1977
Company reported as inactive 1/1/87
Stockholders' equity unknown

LINCOLN SVGS & LN ASSN (VA)
Capital Stock $1 par changed to 10¢ par 08/19/1987
Name changed to Seasons Savings Bank (Richmond, VA) 02/18/1988
(See Seasons Savings Bank (Richmond, VA))

LINCOLN SVGS BK (CARNEGIE, PA)
Merged into Integra Bank/Pittsburgh (Pittsburgh, PA) 1/5/95
Each share Common $1 par exchanged for $58 cash

LINCOLN SERVICE CORP. (DE)
Stock Dividends - 300% 10/23/50; 100% 4/20/56; 50% 6/12/57; 20% 7/1/58
Merged into State Loan & Finance Corp. 3/16/59
Each share $1.50 Preferred no par or $1.50 Preferred 2nd Ser. no par exchanged for (1) share 6% Preferred $25 par
Each share Common $1 par exchanged for (1.375) shares Class A Common $1 par
State Loan & Finance Corp. name changed to American Finance System Inc. 5/1/68 which merged into Security Pacific Corp. 12/15/78 which merged into BankAmerica Corp. (Old) 4/22/92 which merged into BankAmerica Corp. (New) 9/30/98 which name changed to Bank of America Corp. 4/28/99

LINCOLN SNACKS CO (DE)
Issue Information - 2,150,000 shares COM offered at $4.50 per share on 06/14/1994
Merged into Brynwood Partners III L.P. 10/15/2001
Each share Common 1¢ par exchanged for $3.50 cash

LINCOLN SQUARE BUILDING CO. (IL)
Liquidation completed 5/22/62

LINCOLN STATE BANK (EAST ORANGE, NJ)
98% acquired by Dreyfus Corp. through purchase offer which expired 12/03/1982
Public interest eliminated

LINCOLN STORES INC (MA)
Each share Common no par exchanged for (2) shares Common $5 par 00/00/1951
Name changed to Hurlkapp, Inc. 08/13/1969
(See Hurlkapp, Inc.)

LINCOLN TEL & TELEG CO (DE)
Each share Class A Common no par exchanged for (2) shares Common $16.66-2/3 par 00/00/1948
Common $16.66-2/3 par changed to $25 par 04/09/1957
Common $25 par changed to $6.25 par and (3) additional shares issued 07/15/1964
5% Conv. Preferred $100 par called for redemption 10/01/1964
Common $6.25 par changed to $3.125 par and (1) additional share issued 05/25/1979
Under plan of reorganization each share Common $3.125 par automatically became (1) share Lincoln Telecommunications Co. Common $3.125 par 02/23/1981
Lincoln Telecommunications Co. name changed to Aliant Communications Inc. 09/03/1996 which merged into Alltel Corp. 07/02/1999
(See Alltel Corp.)
Name changed to Aliant Communications Co. 09/03/1996
(See Aliant Communications Co.)

LINCOLN TELECOMMUNICATIONS CO (NE)
Common $3.125 par changed to $1 par 04/23/1987
Common $1 par split (2) for (1) by issuance of (1) additional share 08/17/1987
Common $1 par changed to 25¢ and (1) additional share issued 11/17/1989
Common 25¢ par split (2) for (1) by issuance of (1) additional share 01/06/1994
Name changed to Aliant Communications Inc. 09/03/1996
Aliant Communications Inc. merged into Alltel Corp. 07/02/1999
(See Alltel Corp.)

LINCOLN TELEPHONE & TELEGRAPH CO. (NE)
Acquired by Lincoln Telephone & Telegraph Co. (DE) 01/01/1937
Details not available

LINCOLN TELEPHONE SECURITIES CO. (DE)
Name changed to Lincoln Telephone & Telegraph Co. (DE) 12/00/1936
Lincoln Telephone & Telegraph Co. reorganized as Lincoln Telecommunications Co. 02/23/1981 which name changed to Aliant Communications Inc. 09/03/1996 which merged into Alltel Corp. 07/02/1999
(See Alltel Corp.)

LINCOLN TOWER CORP (IN)
Stock Dividend - 25% 12/22/1969
Name changed to Lincoln Financial Corp. 05/01/1974
Lincoln Financial Corp. acquired by Norwest Corp. 02/09/1993 which name changed to Wells Fargo & Co. (New) 11/02/1998

LINCOLN TR & SVGS CO (NIAGARA FALLS, ON)
Common $10 par and VTC's for Common $10 par changed to $5 par respectively 12/04/1969
Voting Trust Agreement terminated 01/12/1970
Each VTC for Common $5 par exchanged for (1) share Common $5 par
Merged into Canada Trustco Mortgage Co. 12/31/1976
Each share 8% 1st Preference Ser. A $25 par exchanged for (1) share 1st Preference Ser. B $25 par
Each share Common $5 par exchanged for (2) shares Common $2 par
Canada Trustco Mortgage Co. reorganized as CT Financial Services Inc. 11/25/1987

(See CT Financial Services Inc.)
LINCOLN URANIUM CORP. (NV)
Merged into Atomic Minerals Corp. on a (1) for (20) basis 6/5/56

LINCOLN WASTE MGMT INC (ON)
Name changed to Philip Environmental Inc. 7/10/91
Philip Environmental Inc. name changed to Philip Services Corp. (ONT) 5/22/97 which reorganized in Delaware as Philip Services Corporation 4/7/2000
(See Philip Services Corporation)

LINCOLNBERG CAP CORP (AB)
Name changed to Mancap Global Ventures Inc. 6/30/95
(See Mancap Global Ventures Inc.)

LINCOLNLAND BANCSHARES, INC. (DE)
Merged into AMBANC Corp. 6/1/94
Each share Common $10 par exchanged for (3.3904) shares Common $10 par
AMBANC Corp. merged into Union Planters Corp. 8/31/98 which merged into Regions Financial Corp. (New) 7/1/2004

LINCORP HLDGS INC (DE)
Charter cancelled and declared inoperative and void for non-payment of taxes 3/1/2005

LINCTON ENTERPRISES, INC. (NY)
Charter cancelled and proclaimed dissolved for failure to pay taxes 12/16/74

LINDAL CEDAR HOMES INC (WA)
Common $1 par split (2) for (1) by issuance of (1) additional share 11/29/85
Common $1 par split (5) for (4) by issuance of (0.5) additional share 4/27/92
Stock Dividends - 10% 3/15/85; 10% 2/16/87; 10% 3/15/88; 10% 12/23/88; 10% 5/12/89; 10% 6/18/90; 10% 5/27/91; 10% 5/12/93
93% acquired at $4.55 per share thru purchase offer which expired 1/26/2001

LINDAS DIVERSIFIED HLDGS INC (DE)
Name changed 07/11/1996
Name changed from Linda's Flame Roasted Chicken Inc. to Linda's Diversified Holdings Inc. 07/11/1996
Charter cancelled and declared inoperative and void for non-payment of taxes 03/01/1999

LINDATECH INC (DE)
Assets placed in foreclosure 09/24/1999
Stockholders' equity unlikely

LINDBERG CORP (IL)
Class A $5 par and Class B $5 par reclassified as Common $2.50 par and (1) additional share issued 9/1/67
Common $2.50 par split (2) for (1) by issuance of (1) additional share 3/7/75
Common $2.50 par split (2) for (1) by issuance of (1) additional share 9/1/77
Merged into Bodycote International PLC 1/19/2001
Each share Common $2.50 par exchanged for $18.125 cash

LINDBERG STEEL TREATING CO., INC. (IL)
Name changed to Lindberg Corp. 8/1/67
(See Lindberg Corp.)

LINDE AG (GERMANY)
Unsponsored ADR's for Ordinary reclassified as Sponsored ADR's for Ordinary 01/11/2010
ADR agreement terminated 09/29/2017
Each Sponsored ADR for Ordinary exchanged for $20.390024 cash

LINDELL TR CO (ST. LOUIS, MO)
Capital Stock $20 par changed to $10 par and (1) additional share issued 01/29/1960
Capital Stock $10 par split (4) for (3) by issuance of (1/3) additional share 02/20/1981
Stock Dividends - 25% 02/20/1946; 20% 02/20/1950; 25% 04/10/1951
Acquired by First Illinois Bancorp, Inc. 10/30/1987
Each share Capital Stock $10 par exchanged for $94 cash

LINDEMANN (A.J.) & HOVERSON CO. (WI)
Acquired by Norris-Thermador Corp. in 1953
Norris-Thermador Corp. name changed to Norris Industries, Inc. 7/29/66
(See Norris Industries, Inc.)

LINDEN CORP (DE)
99% acquired by Avemco Corp. through exchange offer which expired 00/00/1971
Public interest eliminated

LINDEN EXPLS INC (BC)
Name changed to Australian Oilfields Property Ltd. (BC) 5/23/96
Australian Oilfields Property Ltd. (BC) reincorporated in Alberta as Equatorial Energy Inc. 9/15/97 which name changed to Resolute Energy Inc. 11/14/2002
(See Resolute Energy Inc.)

LINDEN HOTEL REALTY CORP. (IN)
Liquidation completed 10/3/55

LINDEN LABORATORIES, INC. (PA)
Merged into Resource Management Corp. 12/29/72
Each share Common $1 par exchanged for (0.425527) share Common 10¢ par
(See Resource Management Corp.)

LINDEN LAWRENCE BLDG., INC.
Liquidated in 1945

LINDEX EXPLORATIONS LTD. (BC)
Name changed to Lectus Developments Ltd. 02/28/1986
Lectus Developments Ltd. recapitalized as Swannell Minerals Corp. 05/15/1991 which recapitalized as Globenet Resources Inc. 04/01/1997 which name changed to Terra Nova Gold Corp. 01/28/2003 which name changed to Terra Nova Minerals Inc. (BC) 02/19/2008 which reincorporated in Canada 02/05/2009 which reincorporated in Alberta as Terra Nova Energy Ltd. 08/21/2012 which reincorporated in British Columbia 10/31/2016 which recapitalized as Claren Energy Corp. 11/14/2016

LINDLY & CO (NY)
Common 10¢ par changed to 1¢ par 5/10/88
Dissolved by proclamation 6/26/96

LINDNER CO. (OH)
Name changed to Linco Corp. 11/17/47 which was dissolved on 11/28/47

LINDNER FD FOR INCOME INC (MO)
Name changed to Lindner Dividend Fund, Inc. 1/19/84

LINDSAY (C.W.) & CO. LTD. (QC)
6-1/2% Preferred $100 par called for redemption 3/25/57
Completely liquidated 10/24/67
Each share Common no par exchanged for first and final distribution of $48.90 cash

LINDSAY CHEMICAL CO. (IL)
Recapitalized in 1954
Each share 7% Preferred $10 par exchanged for (5) shares 7% Preferred $2 par
Each share Common no par exchanged for (5) shares Common $1 par
Merged into American Potash & Chemical Corp. 5/1/58
Each share 7% Preferred $2 par exchanged for (0.03) share $5 Special Preferred no par
Each share Common $1 par exchanged for (1) share Common no par
American Potash & Chemical Corp. merged into Kerr-McGee Corp. 12/29/67

LINDSAY EXPLORATINS LTD (ON)
Recapitalized as Sapawe Gold Mines Ltd. in 1963
Each share Common no par exchanged for (0.2) share Common no par
(See Sapawe Gold Mines Ltd.)

LINDSAY LIGHT & CHEMICAL CO.
Name changed to Lindsay Chemical Co. in 1952
Lindsay Chemical Co. merged into American Potash & Chemical Corp. 5/1/58 which merged into Kerr-McGee Corp. 12/29/67

LINDSAY LIGHT CO.
Name changed to Lindsay Light & Chemical Co. in 1935
Lindsay Light & Chemical Co. name changed to Lindsay Chemical Co. in 1952 which merged into American Potash & Chemical Corp. 5/1/58 which merged into Kerr-McGee Corp. 12/29/67

LINDSAY MFG CO (DE)
Common $1 par split (3) for (2) by issuance of (0.5) additional share 05/15/1990
Common $1 par split (3) for (2) by issuance of (0.5) additional share 09/15/1991
Common $1 par split (3) for (2) by issuance of (0.5) additional share payable 02/22/1996 to holders of 02/07/1996
Common $1 par split (3) for (2) by issuance of (0.5) additional share payable 03/10/1997 to holders of record 03/03/1997
Common $1 par split (3) for (2) by issuance of (0.5) additional share payable 06/15/1998 to holders of 06/05/1998 Ex date - 06/16/1998
Name changed to Lindsay Corp. 12/11/2006

LINDSAY URANIUM MINES LTD. (ON)
Name changed to Lindsay Explorations Ltd. in 1955
Lindsay Exploratins Ltd. recapitalized as Sapawe Gold Mines Ltd. in 1963
(See Sapawe Gold Mines Ltd.)

LINDSEY MORDEN GROUP INC (CANADA)
Name changed to Cunningham Lindsey Group Inc. 4/13/2006
(See Cunningham Lindsey Group Inc.)

LINDY HYDROTHERMAL PRODUCTS, INC. (NY)
Name changed to Lindy Products, Inc. 06/29/1966
Lindy Products, Inc. name changed to Fecor Industries Ltd. (NY) 05/28/1969 which reincorporated in Pennsylvania 08/20/1973 which name changed to Farrier Industries, Inc. 02/13/1976
(See Farrier Industries, Inc.)

LINDY PRODS INC (NY)
Name changed to Fecor Industries Ltd. (NY) and Common 10¢ par changed to 1¢ par 05/28/1969
Fecor Industries Ltd. (NY) reincorporated in Pennsylvania 08/20/1973 which name changed to Farrier Industries, Inc. 02/13/1976

(See Farrier Industries, Inc.)

LINDYS FOOD PRODS INC (NY)
Dissolved by proclamation 9/29/93

LINE IS EXPLORATION INC (CANADA)
Name changed to Dia Bras Exploration Inc. 01/31/2000
Dia Bras Exploration Inc. name changed to Sierra Metals Inc. 12/07/2012

LINE MATERIAL CO.
Merged into McGraw Electric Co. in 1949
Each share Capital Stock $5 par exchanged for (2/3) share Common $1 par
McGraw Electric Co. name changed to McGraw-Edison Co. 1/2/57
(See McGraw-Edison Co.)

LINE UP ADVERTISEMENT INC (NV)
Name changed to Tactical Services, Inc. 10/23/2017

LINEA AEREA NACIONAL CHILE S A (CHILE)
Issue Information - 7,150,000 ADR'S offered at $14 per ADR on 11/06/1997
Name changed to Lan Chile S.A. 07/13/1998
Lan Chile S.A. name changed to Lan Airlines S.A. 09/08/2004 which name changed to LATAM Airlines Group S.A. 10/11/2012

LINEAR CORP (CA)
Merged into Nortek, Inc. 02/22/1988
Each share Common 1¢ par exchanged for $12.50 cash 07/19/1983)

LINEAR FILMS INC (DE)
Common $1 par split (3) for (2) by issuance of (0.5) additional share 6/2/86
Merged into LF Acquisition Corp. 7/15/88
Each share Common $1 par exchanged for $12.625 cash

LINEAR GOLD CORP (CANADA)
Reincorporated 11/10/2004
Place of incorporation changed from (AB) to (Canada) 11/10/2004
Each share Common no par received distribution of (1) Linear Metals Corp. Unit consisting of (0.8) share Common no par and (0.1) Common Stock Purchase Warrant expiring 07/27/2006 payable 06/30/2006 to holders of record 06/26/2006 Ex date - 06/22/2006
Merged into Brigus Gold Corp. (YT) 06/25/2010
Each share Common no par exchanged for (1.3686) shares Common no par
Note: Unexchanged certificates were cancelled and became without value 06/25/2016
Brigus Gold Corp. (YT) reincorporated in Canada 06/09/2011
(See Brigus Gold Corp.)

LINEAR INSTRS CORP (CA)
Common no par changed to 1¢ par 1/17/82
Merged into Spectra-Physics, Inc. 12/7/88
Each share Common 1¢ par exchanged for $1.75 cash

LINEAR METALS CORP (CANADA)
Name changed to Stockport Exploration Inc. 05/01/2012
Stockport Exploration Inc. name changed to Sona Nanotech Inc. 10/04/2018

LINEAR RES INC (AB)
Name changed to Linear Gold Corp. (AB) 11/24/2003
Linear Gold Corp. (AB) reincorporated in Canada 11/10/2004 which merged into Brigus Gold Corp. (YT)

06/25/2010 which reincorporated in Canada 06/09/2011
(See Brigus Gold Corp.)

LINEAR TECH INC (ON)
Name changed to Gennum Corp. 12/03/1990
(See Gennum Corp.)

LINEAR TECHNOLOGY CORP (DE)
Reincorporated 01/02/2001
Common no par split (2) for (1) by issuance of (1) additional share 11/24/1992
Common no par split (2) for (1) by issuance of (1) additional share 09/01/1995
Common no par split (2) for (1) by issuance of (1) additional share payable 02/19/1999 to holders of record 01/29/1999
Common no par split (2) for (1) by issuance of (1) additional share payable 03/27/2000 to holders of record 03/06/2000
State of incorporation changed from (CA) to (DE) and Common no par changed to $0.001 par 01/02/2001
Merged into Analog Devices, Inc. 03/10/2017
Each share Common $0.001 par exchanged for (0.2321) share Common $0.16666666 par and $46 cash

LINEN SERVICE CORP. OF TEXAS
Merged into National Linen Service Corp. on a (1) for (3) basis in 1947
National Linen Service Corp. name changed to National Service Industries, Inc. 12/14/64
(See National Service Industries, Inc.)

LINENS N THINGS INC (DE)
Issue Information - 13,000,000 shares COM offered at $15.50 per share on 11/25/1996
Common 1¢ par split (2) for (1) by issuance of (1) additional share payable 5/7/98 to holders of record 4/24/98 Ex date - 5/8/98
Under plan of merger each share Common 1¢ par exchanged for $28 cash 2/14/2006

LING-ALTEC ELECTRONICS, INC. (DE)
6% Preferred $1 par called for redemption 9/30/59
Under plan of merger name changed to Ling-Temco Electronics, Inc. 7/19/60
Ling-Temco Electronics, Inc. name changed to Ling-Temco-Vought, Inc. 8/16/61 which name changed to LTV Corp. (Old) 5/5/72 which reorganized as LTV Corp. (New) 6/28/93
(See LTV Corp. (New))

LING ELECTRIC, INC. (TX)
Stock Dividend - 10% 1/31/56
Name changed to Ling Industries, Inc. 1/23/57
Ling Industries, Inc. merged into Ling Electronics, Inc. (CA) 3/10/58 which reincorporated under the laws of Delaware 11/20/58 which name changed to Ling-Altec Electronics, Inc. 6/1/59 which name changed to Ling-Temco Electronics, Inc. 7/19/60 which name changed to Ling-Temco-Vought, Inc. 8/16/61 which name changed to LTV Corp. (Old) 5/5/72 which reorganized as LTV Corp. (New) 6/28/93
(See LTV Corp. (New))

LING ELECTRONICS, INC. (DE)
Reincorporated 11/20/58
State of incorporation changed from (CA) to (DE) 11/20/58
Name changed to Ling-Altec Electronics, Inc. 6/1/59
Ling-Altec Electronics, Inc. name changed to Ling-Temco-Vought Electronics, Inc. 7/19/60 which name changed to Ling-Temco-Vought, Inc. 8/16/61 which name changed to LTV Corp. (Old) 5/5/72 which reorganized as LTV Corp. (New) 6/28/93
(See LTV Corp. (New))

LING FD INC (TX)
Name changed to Dallas Fund, Inc. 08/13/1973
Dallas Fund, Inc. liquidated for Selected Special Shares, Inc. 01/30/1975 which name changed to Selected International Fund, Inc. 05/01/2011

LING INDUSTRIES, INC. (TX)
Merged into Ling Electronics, Inc. (CA) 3/10/58
Each share Common $1 par exchanged for (0.75) share 6% Preferred $1 par and (0.25) share Common 50¢ par
Ling Electronics, Inc. (CA) reincorporated under the laws of Delaware 11/20/58 which name changed to Ling-Altec Electronics, Inc. 6/1/59 which name changed to Ling-Temco Electronics, Inc. 7/19/60 which name changed to Ling-Temco-Vought, Inc. 8/16/61 which name changed to LTV Corp. (Old) 5/5/72 which reorganized as LTV Corp. (New) 6/28/93
(See LTV Corp. (New))

LING-TEMCO ELECTRONICS, INC. (DE)
Name changed to Ling-Temco-Vought, Inc. 8/16/61
Ling-Temco-Vought, Inc. name changed to LTV Corp. (Old) 5/5/72 which reorganized as LTV Corp. (New) 6/28/93
(See LTV Corp. (New))

LING TEMCO VOUGHT INC (DE)
4-1/2% Conv. Preferred Ser. A $30 par called for redemption 12/30/66
Common 50¢ par split (3) for (2) by issuance of (0.5) additional share 7/31/67
$3 Conv. Preferred Ser. B $1 par called for redemption 4/19/68
Name changed to LTV Corp. (Old) 5/5/72
LTV Corp. (Old) reorganized as LTV Corp. (New) 6/28/93
(See LTV Corp. (New))

LINGAS RES INC (NV)
Name changed to Lingas Ventures, Inc. 06/19/2013
Lingas Ventures, Inc. recapitalized as Cannabis Kinetics Corp. 05/15/2014 which name changed to Monarch America, Inc. 12/26/2014

LINGAS VENTURES INC (NV)
Common $0.001 par split (5.8) for (1) by issuance of (4.8) additional shares payable 06/19/2013 to holders of record 06/19/2013
Recapitalized as Cannabis Kinetics Corp. 05/15/2014
Each share Common $0.001 par exchanged for (0.1) share Common $0.001 par
Cannabis Kinetics Corp. name changed to Monarch America, Inc. 12/26/2014

LINGMAN LAKE GOLD MINES, LTD. (ON)
Recapitalized as Lake Lingman Gold Mining Co., Ltd. on a (0.5) for (1) basis 00/00/1948
Lake Lingman Gold Mining Co., Ltd. recapitalized as Lakelyn Mines Ltd. 11/30/1964 which recapitalized as Lakelyn Mines Inc. 11/16/1978 which name changed to Twin Gold Mines Ltd. 11/09/1979
(See Twin Gold Mines Ltd.)

LINGNORA GOLD MINES LTD. (ON)
Charter revoked for failure to file reports and pay fees 12/27/67

LINGO MEDIA INC (ON)
Recapitalized as Lingo Media Corp. 10/16/2007
Each share Common no par exchanged for (1/7) share Common no par

LINGSIDE COPPER MNG LTD (ON)
Charter cancelled for failure to pay taxes and file returns 05/05/1982

LINGSIDE GOLD MINES LTD. (ON)
Name changed to Lingside Copper Mining Co. Ltd. 05/00/1953
(See Lingside Copper Mining Co. Ltd.)

LINGUISTIX INC (UT)
Recapitalized as Buyers United International Inc. (UT) 10/22/1997
Each share Common no par exchanged for (0.04) share Common no par
Buyers United International Inc. (UT) reincorporated in Delaware as BUI Inc. 04/09/1999 which name changed to Buyersonline.com Inc. 04/20/2000 which name changed to Buyers United Inc. 11/20/2001 which name changed to UCN, Inc. 07/15/2004 which name changed to inContact, Inc. 01/01/2009
(See inContact, Inc.)

LINGXIAN CAP INC (BC)
Name changed to Crownia Holdings Ltd. 09/15/2015

LINIUM TECHNOLOGY INC (FL)
Reincorporated 03/11/1993
Each share old Common $0.0001 par exchanged for (0.02) share new Common $0.0001 par 08/04/1989
Each share new Common $0.0001 par exchanged again for (1/6) share new Common $0.0001 par 08/10/1992
State of incorporation changed from (DE) to (FL) 03/11/1993
Name changed to Value Holdings, Inc. 07/29/1994
Value Holdings, Inc. recapitalized as Galea Life Sciences Inc. 07/24/2007
(See Galea Life Sciences Inc.)

LINK BELT CO. (IL)
Common $50 par changed to no par in 1929
Each share Common no par exchanged for (2) shares Common $5 par in 1951
Common $5 par split (3) for (2) by issuance of (0.5) additional share 4/23/65
Merged into FMC Corp. 6/30/67
Each share Common $5 par exchanged for (1) share $2.25 Conv. Preferred no par

LINK COM INC (NV)
Name changed to eClickMD, Inc. 07/25/2000
eClickMD, Inc. reorganized as SecureCARE Technologies, Inc. 12/15/2003 which name changed to Scrypt, Inc. 03/11/2014

LINK CORP (CO)
Name changed to Banyan Industries, Inc. 04/29/1988

LINK ENERGY LLC (DE)
Assets sold for the benefit of creditors 04/01/2004
No stockholders' equity

LINK ENTERPRISES INC. (DE)
Name changed to Edan Corp. 3/9/71
Edan Corp. name changed to Edan Enterprise, Inc. 3/25/71 which was completely liquidated 5/13/74

LINK MEDIA PUBG LTD (NV)
Each share old Common $0.001 par exchanged for (5) shares new Common $0.001 par 07/14/2003
Name changed to Crown Medical Systems, Inc. 12/16/2003
Crown Medical Systems, Inc. name changed to PaperFree Medical Solutions, Inc. 12/06/2004

LINK MINERAL VENTURES LTD (ON)
Delisted from Canadian Dealer Network 10/13/2000

LINK RES INC (BC)
Recapitalized as Haddington Resources Ltd. (BC) 07/14/1992
Each share Common no par exchanged for (0.2) share Common no par
Haddington Resources Ltd. (BC) reorganized in Yukon as Haddington International Resources Ltd. 05/20/1999 which reincorporated in Australia 06/23/2000 which name changed back to Haddington Resources Ltd. 01/16/2003

LINK RES INC (NV)
Name changed to Bohai Pharmaceuticals Group, Inc. 02/09/2010

LINKED COS INC (ID)
Recapitalized as Worldwide Entertainment Inc. (ID) 09/16/1996
Each share Common $0.0001 par exchanged for (0.05) share Common $0.0001 par
Worldwide Entertainment Inc. (ID) reorganized in Nevada as EJH Entertainment Inc. 11/12/1997 which name changed to Findex.com, Inc. 05/10/1999

LINKED MEDIA GROUP INC (WY)
Common 1¢ par split (31) for (1) by issuance of (30) additional shares payable 04/15/2009 to holders of record 04/14/2009 Ex date - 04/16/2009
Administratively dissolved for failure to pay taxes 02/24/2011

LINKEDIN CORP (DE)
Acquired by Microsoft Corp. 12/08/2016
Each share Class A Common $0.0001 par exchanged for $196 cash

LINKLETTER ROBERT INC (CO)
Administratively dissolved 03/01/1999

LINKON CORP (NV)
Recapitalized as Packetport.com, Inc. 12/08/1999
Each share Common $0.001 par exchanged for (1/3) share Common $0.003 par
Packetport.com, Inc. name changed to Wyndstorm Corp. 05/05/2008
(See Wyndstorm Corp.)

LINKTONE LTD (CAYMAN ISLANDS)
Name changed to MNC Media Investment Ltd. 07/16/2014
(See MNC Media Investment Ltd.)

LINK2 TECHNOLOGIES INC (NV)
Recapitalized as CinTel Corp. 10/31/2003
Each share Common $0.001 par exchanged for (0.4) share Common $0.001 par
CinTel Corp. recapitalized as Chun Can Capital Group 03/16/2017

LINKWELL CORP (FL)
Each share old Common $0.0005 par exchanged for (0.005) share new Common $0.0005 par 11/16/2012
Shares reacquired 10/27/2014
Each share new Common $0.0005 par exchanged for $0.88 cash

LINLAND EQUIP SALES LTD (ON)
Charter cancelled and declared dissolved for failure to file returns and pay fees 11/09/1976

LINMOR INC (AB)
Merged into NUVO Network Management Inc. 05/21/2004
Each share Common no par exchanged for (0.00865501) share Common no par
(See NUVO Network Management Inc.)

LIN-LIO

LINN BENTON BK (ALBANY, OR)
Common no par split (2) for (1) by issuance of (1) additional share payable 4/3/98 to holders of record 1/30/98
Common no par split (5) for (4) by issuance of (0.25) additional share payable 1/12/99 to holders of record 12/31/98
Stock Dividend - 20% payable 2/3/2000 to holders of record 12/31/99
Merged into Umpqua Holdings Corp. 12/28/2001
Each share Common no par exchanged for $12.75 cash

LINN COACH & TRUCK CORP.
Acquired by Great American Industries, Inc, in 1948
Each (6-2/3) shares Common 10¢ par exchanged for (1) share Common 10¢ par
(See Great American Industries, Inc.)

LINN ENERGY INC (DE)
Each share Class A Common $0.001 par received distribution of (1) share Riviera Resources, Inc. Common 1¢ par payable 08/07/2018 to holders of record 08/03/2018 Ex date - 08/08/2018
Name changed to Roan Resources, Inc. 09/25/2018

LINN ENERGY LLC (DE)
Plan of reorganization under Chapter 11 Federal Bankruptcy proceedings effective 02/28/2017
No stockholders' equity

LINNCO LLC (DE)
Plan of reorganization under Chapter 11 Federal Bankruptcy proceedings effective 02/28/2017
No stockholders' equity

LINOGRAPH CO. (ME)
Voluntarily dissolved 11/4/31
Details not available

LINPRO SPECIFIED PPTYS (MD)
Name changed to Brandywine Realty Trust 6/21/93

LINTEX MINERALS LTD (BC)
Recapitalized as New Lintex Minerals Ltd. 12/07/1987
Each share Common no par exchanged for (0.33333333) share Common no par
New Lintex Minerals Ltd. merged into Globaltex Industries Inc. 03/05/1993 which name changed to Pine Valley Mining Corp. 05/14/2003

LINTEX RES INC (UT)
Recapitalized as Spa Faucet, Inc. 02/26/1996
Each share Common $0.001 par exchanged for (0.025) share Common $0.001 par
(See Spa Faucet, Inc.)

LINTRONICS INTL LTD (BC)
Recapitalized as Bi-Petro Resources Inc. 8/9/88
Each share Common no par exchanged for (0.5) share Common no par
(See Bi-Petro Resources Inc.)

LINUXWIZARDRY SYS INC (BC)
Name changed to Linux Gold Corp. 3/19/2003

LION BIOSCIENCE AKTIENGESELLSCHAFT (GERMANY)
ADR agreement terminated 12/22/2004
Each Sponsored ADR for Ordinary exchanged for $1.3757 cash

LION BIOTECHNOLOGIES INC (DE)
Reincorporated 06/01/2017
State of incorporation changed from (NV) to (DE) 06/01/2017
Name changed to Iovance Biotherapeutics, Inc. 06/28/2017

LION BRAND SHIRT & COLLAR CORP.
Merged into Nirenberg (M.) Sons, Inc. 00/00/1931
Details not available

LION BREWERY INC (PA)
Acquired by a group of investors 1/11/99
Each share Common 1¢ par exchanged for $4.70 cash

LION CAP HLDGS INC (DE)
Old Common $0.001 par split (2) for (1) by issuance of (1) additional share payable 08/19/2003 to holders of record 08/12/2003 Ex date - 09/26/2003
Each share old Common $0.001 par exchanged for (0.1) share new Common $0.001 par 01/24/2007
Name changed to DeFi Global, Inc. 06/11/2010
(See DeFi Global, Inc.)

LION COLLARS & SHIRTS, INC.
Reorganized as Lion Collar Holding Corp.
Details not available

LION CONSULTING GROUP INC (DE)
Reorganized as Cantabio Pharmaceuticals Inc. 10/16/2015
Each share Common $0.001 par exchanged for (5) shares Common $0.001 par

LION CONTROLS CORP (MA)
Name changed 6/24/86
Name changed from Lion Precision Corp. to Lion Controls Corp. 6/24/86
Involuntarily dissolved 12/31/90

LION CTRY SAFARI INC (DE)
Name changed to United Leisure Corp. 04/01/1987
(See United Leisure Corp.)

LION ENERGY CORP (BC)
Acquired by Africa Oil Corp. 06/20/2011
Each share Common no par exchanged for (0.2) share Common no par
Note: Unexchanged certificates were cancelled and became without value 06/20/2014

LION ENERGY CORP (DE)
Charter cancelled and declared inoperative and void for non-payment of taxes 06/23/1988

LION GOLD BRAZIL INC (NV)
Recapitalized as Cannabiz Mobile, Inc. 06/24/2014
Each share Common $0.001 par exchanged for (0.125) share Common $0.001 par

LION-GRI INTL INC (CO)
Recapitalized as Promotora Valle Hermoso, Inc. 07/24/2006
Each share Common $0.001 par exchanged for (0.05) share Common $0.001 par
Promotora Valle Hermoso, Inc. name changed to UNR Holdings, Inc. 10/15/2009

LION INC (WA)
Reincorporated 12/15/2000
State of incorporation changed from (MN) to (WA) 12/15/2000
Liquidation completed
Each share Common 1¢ par exchanged for initial distribution of $0.065 cash 08/21/2008
Each share Common 1¢ par received second distribution of $0.026 cash payable 10/20/2008 to holders of record 08/11/2008
Each share Common 1¢ par received third and final distribution of $0.013 cash payable 12/29/2008 to holders of record 08/11/2008

LION INDS CORP BERHAD (SINGAPORE)
ADR agreement terminated 10/31/2016
No ADR's remain outstanding

LION INDS USA INC (NV)
Each share old Common no par exchanged for (0.04) share new Common no par 6/27/2002
Name changed to Sedona Horizons Corp. 7/3/2002
Sedona Horizons Corp. name changed to Cornerstone Entertainment, Inc. 7/21/2003 which name changed to Beverly Hills Film Studios, Inc. 10/28/2003 which name changed to Big Screen Entertainment Group, Inc. 4/1/2005

LION LAND BERHAD (SINGAPORE)
Name changed to Lion Industries Corp. Berhad 04/08/2003
(See Lion Industries Corp. Berhad)

LION MATCH CO., INC. (DE)
Capital Stock no par split (2) for (1) by issuance of (1) additional share 5/31/60
Merged into Lion Match Corp. of America 12/1/65
Each share Capital Stock no par exchanged for (1) share Common no par
(See Lion Corp. of America)

LION MATCH CORP AMER (NJ)
Merged into Newlion Inc. 7/20/84
Each share Common no par exchanged for $0.01 cash

LION MINES LTD (BC)
Struck off register and declared dissolved for failure to file returns 9/20/85

LION NICKEL MINES OF CANADA LTD. (ON)
Merged into Indian Mountain Metal Mines Ltd. 06/24/1971
Each share Capital Stock $1 par exchanged for (0.235294) share Capital Stock $1 par
Indian Mountain Metal Mines Ltd. merged into Initiative Explorations Inc. 02/13/1980 which merged into Canhorn Chemical Corp. 04/26/1995 which merged into Nayarit Gold Inc. 05/02/2005 which merged into Capital Gold Corp. 08/02/2010 which merged into Gammon Gold Inc. (QC) 04/08/2011 which reincorporated in Ontario as AuRico Gold Inc. 06/14/2011 which merged into Alamos Gold Inc. (New) 07/06/2015

LION OIL CO. (DE)
Stock Dividends - 100% 7/18/47; 100% 5/4/49
Merged into Monsanto Chemical Co. 9/30/55
Each share Capital Stock no par exchanged for (1.5) shares Common $2 par 9/30/55
Monsanto Chemical Co. name changed to Monsanto Co. 4/1/64 which name changed to Pharmacia Corp. 3/31/2000 which merged into Pfizer Inc. 4/16/2003

LION OIL REFINING CO.
Name changed to Lion Oil Co. in 1945 which merged into Monsanto Chemical Co. 9/30/55 which name was changed to Monsanto Co. 4/1/64

LION PRESS INC (NY)
Merged into KDI Corp. 11/25/1969
Each share Common 10¢ par exchanged for (0.055) share Common 35¢ par
(See KDI Corp.)

LION RESH CORP (MA)
Name changed to Lion Precision Corp. 1/20/70
Lion Precision Corp. name changed to Lion Controls Corp. 6/24/86
(See Lion Controls Corp.)

LION RES CORP (DE)
Merged into Bull & Bear Group, Inc. 06/03/1986
Each share Common 1¢ par exchanged for (0.05) share Class A Common 1¢ par
Bull & Bear Group, Inc. name changed to Winmill & Co. Inc. 06/30/1999

LIONBRIDGE TECHNOLOGIES INC (DE)
Acquired by LBT Acquisition, Inc. 02/28/2017
Each share Common 1¢ par exchanged for $5.75 cash

LIONEL CORP (NY)
Each share Preferred $10 par exchanged for (1) share Common $10 par 00/00/1937
Each share Class A Common $100 par or Class B Common $100 par exchanged for (10) shares Common $10 par 00/00/1937
Common $10 par changed to $5 par and (1) additional share issued 00/00/1948
Common $5 par changed to $2.50 par and (1) additional share issued 00/00/1951
3.75% Conv. Preferred $20 par called for redemption 02/20/1969
Common $2.50 par changed to 10¢ par 05/01/1975
Plan of reorganization under Chapter 11 Federal Bankruptcy Code effective 12/28/1994
No stockholders' equity

LIONEL D. EDIE CAPITAL FUND, INC. (DE)
See - Edie (Lionel D.) Capital Fund, Inc.

LIONEL D. EDIE READY ASSETS TRUST (MD)
See - Edie (Lionel D.) Ready Assets Trust

LIONHEART CAP CORP (BC)
Merged into 1726 Holdings Ltd. 10/12/1988
Each share Common no par exchanged for $3.28 cash

LIONHEART ENERGY CORP (AB)
Merged into Search Energy Corp. 05/02/1997
Each share Common no par exchanged for (0.81) share Common no par
Search Energy Corp. merged into Advantage Energy Income Fund 05/24/2001 which reorganized as Advantage Oil & Gas Ltd. 07/09/2009

LIONHEART RESOURCES CORP. (BC)
Common no par split (3) for (1) by issuance of (2) additional shares 6/12/86
Name changed to Lionheart Capital Corp. 7/14/87
(See Lionheart Capital Corp.)

LIONORE MNG INTL LTD (CANADA)
Merged into OJSC MMC Norilsk Nickel 08/14/2007
Each share Common no par exchanged for $27.50 cash

LIONS GATE ENERGY INC (BC)
Recapitalized as Starr Peak Exploration Ltd. 07/27/2015
Each share Common no par exchanged for (0.16666666) share Common no par

LIONS GATE INVT LTD (NV)
Common $0.001 par split (4) for (1) by issuance of (3) additional shares payable 11/06/2002 to holders of record 11/06/2002 Ex date - 11/07/2002
Reincorporated under the laws of Delaware as DOBI Medical International, Inc. 01/30/2004
(See DOBI Medical International, Inc.)

LIONS GATE LTG CORP (NV)
Name changed to Umami Sustainable Seafood Inc. 08/20/2010

LIONS GATE METALS INC (BC)
Each share old Common no par exchanged for (0.25) share new Common no par 11/11/2013
Each share new Common no par exchanged again for (0.25) share new Common no par 11/16/2016
Name changed to Block X Capital Corp. 01/25/2018

LIONS PETE INC (DE)
SEC revoked common stock registration 03/30/2012

LIONSGATE MINES LTD. (ON)
Completely liquidated 06/00/1968
Each share Capital Stock $1 par exchanged for first and final distribution of (0.03171) share Mission Financial Corp. Ltd. Common no par
Mission Financial Corp. Ltd. merged into H.R.S. Industries, Inc. 05/21/1982 which merged into International H.R.S. Industries Inc. 05/15/1984 which name changed to Glenex Industries Inc. 05/25/1987 which merged into Quest Investment Corp. 07/04/2002 which merged into Quest Capital Corp. (BC) 06/30/2003 which reincorporated in Canada 05/27/2008 which name changed to Sprott Resource Lending Corp. 09/10/2010 which merged into Sprott Inc. 07/24/2013

LIONSHARE GROUP INC (DE)
Each old share Common $0.0001 par exchanged for (0.1) share new Common $0.0001 par 09/08/1998
Each share new Common $0.0001 par exchanged again for (0.1) share new Common $0.0001 par 08/01/2002
SEC revoked common stock registration 04/27/2010

LIONSHEAD ENTMT CORP (NV)
Name changed to Trans-Global Holdings Inc. 3/17/99
Trans-Global Holdings Inc. name changed to Clear Cut Film Technology Studios, Inc. 4/17/2006 which recapitalized as Trans-Global Capital Management, Inc. 2/13/2007

LIPARI ENERGY INC (BC)
Common no par split (1.070775) for (1) by issuance of (0.070775) additional share payable 03/14/2011 to holders of record 03/14/2011
Acquired by Lipari Private Holdings, Inc. 11/01/2013
Each share Common no par exchanged for $0.48 cash
Note: Unexchanged certificates will be cancelled and become without value 11/01/2019

LIPE (W.C.) INC.
Name changed to Lipe-Rollway Corp. in 1942
Lipe-Rollway Corp. merged into Emerson Electric Co. 9/3/96

LIPE ROLLWAY CORP (NY)
$1 Preferred $10 par called for redemption 03/04/1955
Each share Class A $1 par exchanged for (0.5) share $1 Conv. Preferred $10 par and (1-2/3) shares Common 50¢ par 06/21/1967
Each share Class B 50¢ par exchanged for (2.5) shares Common 50¢ par 06/21/1957
$1 Preferred $10 par conversion privilege expired 09/15/1977
Merged into Emerson Electric Co. 09/03/1996
Each share $1 Preferred $10 par exchanged for (0.23195129) share Common $1 par
Each share Common 50¢ par exchanged for (0.05465603) share Common $1 par
Each share Common 50¢ par received an initial additional distribution of (0.01448114) share Common $1 par 02/01/1997
Each share Common 50¢ par received an second additional distribution of (0.0157047) share Emerson Electric Co. Common $1 par 08/14/1997

LIPID SCIENCES INC (DE)
Reincorporated 06/19/2002
State of incorporation changed from (AZ) to (DE) 06/19/2002
Filed a petition under Chapter 7 Federal Bankruptcy Code 10/03/2008
Stockholders' equity unlikely

LIPIDLABS INC NEW (TX)
Name changed to Telemedicus, Inc. 09/21/2007
Telemedicus, Inc. recapitalized as National Wind Solutions Inc. 10/01/2008 which recapitalized as National Clean Fuels Inc. 03/17/2010 which recapitalized as Quantum International Corp. 01/20/2012

LIPIDLABS INC OLD (TX)
Reorganized as LipidLabs, Inc. (New) 12/15/2006
Each share Common $0.0001 par exchanged for (0.25) share Common $0.0001 par
LipidLabs, Inc. (New) name changed to Telemedicus, Inc. 09/21/2007 which recapitalized as National Wind Solutions Inc. 10/01/2008 which recapitalized as National Clean Fuels Inc. 03/17/2010 which recapitalized as Quantum International Corp. 01/20/2012

LIPIDVIRO TECH INC (NV)
Each share old Common $0.001 par exchanged for (7) shares new Common $0.001 par 04/18/2006
Each share new Common $0.001 par exchanged again for (0.07142857) share new Common $0.001 par 09/05/2008
Name changed to NAC Global Technologies, Inc. 07/18/2014

LIPMAN ELECTRONIC ENGINEERING LTD (ISRAEL)
Merged into VeriFone Holdings, Inc. 11/01/2006
Each share Ordinary ILS 1 par exchanged for (0.9336) share Common 1¢ par
VeriFone Holdings, Inc. name changed to VeriFone Systems, Inc. 05/18/2010
(See VeriFone Systems, Inc.)

LIPONEX INC (ON)
Recapitalized as ImaSight Corp. 06/30/2008
Each share Common no par exchanged for (0.2) share Common no par

LIPOSCIENCE INC (DE)
Acquired by Laboratory Corp. of America Holdings 11/20/2014
Each share Common $0.001 par exchanged for $5.25 cash

LIPOSOME INC (DE)
7.75% Depositary Preferred Ser. A called for redemption 10/14/1996
Merged into Elan Corp., PLC 05/12/2000
Each share Common 1¢ par exchanged for (0.385) share Common 1¢ par and (1) Contingent Value Right
Elan Corp., PLC merged into Perrigo Co. PLC 12/18/2013

LIPOSOME TECHNOLOGY INC (DE)
Stock Dividend - 10% 08/05/1988
Name changed to Sequus Pharmaceuticals, Inc. 06/26/1995
Sequus Pharmaceuticals, Inc. merged into Alza Corp. 03/16/1999 which merged into Johnson & Johnson 06/22/2001

LIPPINCOTT J B CO (PA)
Merged into Harper & Row, Publishers, Inc. 09/20/1978
Each share Common no par exchanged for (0.885) share Common 10¢ par
(See Harper & Row, Publishers, Inc.)

LIPPOBANK (SAN FRANCISCO, CA)
Merged into First Banks America, Inc. 02/29/2000
Each share Common $5 par exchanged for $15.13 cash

LIPSETT (EDWARD) LTD. (BC)
Name changed to E.L. Products Ltd. 01/11/1965
(See E.L. Products Ltd.)

LIPTON (THOMAS J.) INC. (DE)
Recapitalized in 1950
Each share Class A $1 par exchanged for (0.2725) share Common $50 par
Each share Class B no par exchanged for (0.06) share Common $50 par
All but (3) shares held by Unilever as of 6/11/70
Public interest eliminated

LIQUENT INC (DE)
Merged into Information Holdings, Inc. 12/28/2001
Each share Common $0.001 par exchanged for $2.27 cash

LIQUEST INTL MARKETING CORP (BC)
Recapitalized as Massey Mercantile Ltd. 04/09/1992
Each share Common no par exchanged for (0.5) share Common no par
Massey Mercantile Ltd. name changed to Riosun Resources Corp. 01/22/1997
(See Riosun Resources Corp.)

LIQUI BOX CORP (OH)
Common no par split (2) for (1) by issuance of (1) additional share 09/15/1986
Common no par split (3) for (1) by issuance of (2) additional shares 06/15/1992
Merged into DuPont Canada Inc. 05/31/2002
Each share Common no par exchanged for $67 cash

LIQUID AIR CORP. (DE)
Merged into AAL Acquisition Corp. 4/20/88
Each share Common no par exchanged for $37 cash

LIQUID AIR CORP NORTH AMER (DE)
Name changed to Liquid Air Corp. 2/22/80
(See Liquid Air Corp.)

LIQUID AUDIO INC (DE)
Issue Information - 4,200,000 shares COM offered at $15 per share on 07/08/1999
Each share Common $0.001 par received distribution of $2.50 cash payable 01/29/2003 to holders of record 12/10/2002 Ex date - 01/30/2003
Name changed to L Q Corporation, Inc. 01/07/2004
L Q Corporation, Inc. merged into Sielox, Inc. 07/31/2007

LIQUID CAP INCOME TR (MA)
Name changed 04/07/1982
Name changed from Liquid Capital Income, Inc. to Liquid Capital Income Trust and Common 10¢ par reclassified as Shares of Bene. Int. 10¢ par 04/07/1982
Completely liquidated 11/19/1999
Each Share of Bene. Int. 10¢ par received $1 cash
Note: Certificates were not required to be surrendered and are without value

LIQUID CARBONIC CORP. (DE)
Common no par changed to $15 par 4/12/56
Merged into General Dynamics Corp. share for share 9/30/57

LIQUID CARBONIC INDS INC (DE)
Merged into Houston Natural Gas Corp. (TX) 01/31/1969
Each share Common $1 par exchanged for (1) share $2.50 Conv. Preference Ser. A $1 par
(See Houston Natural Gas Corp. (TX))

LIQUID GOLD RES INC (BC)
Name changed to West African Venture Exchange Corp. 5/7/99
West African Venture Exchange Corp. recapitalized as Wave Exploration Corp. 9/17/2002 which recapitalized as Roxgold Inc. 1/16/2007

LIQUID GREEN GOVT TR (IN)
Voluntarily dissolved 02/23/1993
Details not available

LIQUID GREEN TAX FREE TR (IN)
Voluntarily dissolved 02/23/1993
Details not available

LIQUID GREEN TR (IN)
Voluntarily dissolved 02/23/1993
Details not available

LIQUID INVTS CO (MD)
Fund dissolved and assets liquidated
Details not available

LIQUID METAL OIL & GAS CO. (NV)
Charter revoked 3/4/63; stock valueless

LIQUID MOTION INDS (NV)
Reorganized as Pacific Global Communications Group, Inc. 03/25/1996
Each share Common $0.001 par exchanged for (0.04) share Common $0.001 par, (0.04) Common Stock Purchase Warrant Ser. A expiring 08/15/1996 and (0.04) Common Stock Purchase Warrant Ser. B expiring 08/15/1999
Note: No holder will receive fewer than (10) shares
(See Pacific Global Communications Group, Inc.)

LIQUID OPTICS CORP (NY)
Charter cancelled and proclaimed dissolved for failure to pay taxes 12/15/1972

LIQUID TRANSPORTERS INC (KY)
Stock Dividends - 10% 06/01/1977; 10% 12/01/1978
Merged into Trimac Transportation, Inc. 09/30/1980
Each share Common $2.50 par exchanged for $17 cash

LIQUIDATING SHARES, INC.
Liquidated 00/00/1941
Details not available

LIQUIDATION CTL INC (DE)
Name changed to Romlock Inc. 10/27/83
Romlock Inc. recapitalized as Newlock Inc. 10/29/97
(See Newlock Inc.)

LIQUIDATION WORLD INC (AB)
Each share old Common no par exchanged for (0.2) share new Common no par 05/26/1995
New Common no par split (2) for (1) by issuance of (1) additional share payable 04/23/1998 to holders of record 04/16/1998 Ex date - 04/14/1998
Acquired by Big Lots, Inc. 07/18/2011
Each share new Common no par exchanged for $0.06 cash
Note: Unexchanged certificates were cancelled and became without value 07/18/2017

LIQUIDATIONBID COM INC (NV)
Name changed to SoftLead, Inc. 09/12/2003
SoftLead, Inc. recapitalized as Sysorex Global Holdings Corp. 06/03/2011 which name changed to Sysorex Global 01/04/2016 which recapitalized as Inpixon 03/01/2017

LIQUIDGOLF HLDG CORP (DE)
Reincorporated 09/29/2003
State of incorporation changed from (NV) to (DE) 09/29/2003
Name changed to Horizon Holding Corp. 09/02/2004
Horizon Holding Corp. name changed to Inverted Paradigms Corp. 05/12/2006 which recapitalized as Transfer Technology International Corp. 12/07/2007 which name changed to Enviro-Serv, Inc. 04/23/2013

LIQUIDICS INC (NV)
Name changed to Global Web TV, Inc. (Old) 12/13/2001
Global Web TV, Inc. (Old) recapitalized as QOL Holdings, Inc. 12/15/2003 which name changed to Global Web TV, Inc. (New) 10/05/2005 which reorganized as Amore TV, Inc. 01/27/2006 which recapitalized as Rapid Fitness, Inc. 05/11/2007 which name changed to Tri-Star Holdings Inc. 08/27/2008 which recapitalized as Macada Holding, Inc. (NV) 08/20/2009 which reincorporated in Wyoming 02/22/2011 which recapitalized as KMA Holding, Inc. 03/17/2011
(See KMA Holding, Inc.)

LIQUIDIX INC (FL)
Recapitalized as Anscott Industries Inc. 04/09/2003
Each share Common $0.0001 par exchanged for (0.05) share Common $0.0001 par
(See Anscott Industries Inc.)

LIQUIDMETAL TECHNOLOGIES (CA)
Reincorporated under the laws of Delaware as Liquidmetal Technologies, Inc. and Common no par changed to $0.001 par 05/21/2003

LIQUIDOMETER CORP. (DE)
Recapitalized in 1933
Each share Class A no par exchanged for (1) share Common $1 par
Each (5) shares Class B no par exchanged for (1) share Common $1 par
Stock Dividends - 10% 12/10/59; 100% 11/25/60
Merged into Simmonds Products, Inc. 12/3/65
Each share Common $1 par exchanged for $9.50 cash

LIQUIDONICS INDS INC (NY)
7-1/2% Preferred $100 par called for redemption 09/30/1975
Each share Common 1¢ par exchanged for (0.04) share Common 25¢ par 09/30/1976
Name changed to Greer Hydraulics, Inc. 12/27/1979
(See Greer Hydraulics, Inc.)

LIQUIDPURE CORP (DE)
Name changed to Coventure International Inc. 2/14/2002
Coventure International Inc. name changed to China Natural Gas, Inc. 12/19/2005

LIQUITEK ENTERPRISES INC (NV)
SEC revoked common stock registration 10/24/2007

LIQUOR BARN INCOME FUND (AB)
Merged into Liquor Stores Income Fund (AB) 06/08/2007
Each Trust Unit received (0.57) Trust Unit
Liquor Stores Income Fund (AB) reorganized in Canada as Liquor Stores N.A. Ltd. 01/07/2011 which name changed to Alcanna Inc. 05/14/2018

LIQUOR GROUP WHSL INC (CO)
Each share old Common $0.0001 par exchanged for (0.005) share new Common $0.0001 par 04/28/2010
Chapter 7 bankruptcy proceedings terminated 01/20/2017
Stockholders' equity unlikely

LIQUOR STORES INCOME FD (AB)
Reorganized under the laws of Canada as Liquor Stores N.A. Ltd. 01/07/2011
Each Trust Unit exchanged for (1) share share Common no par
Note: Unexchanged certificates were cancelled and became without value 01/07/2016
Liquor Stores N.A. Ltd. name changed to Alcanna Inc. 05/14/2018

LIQUOR STORES N A LTD (CANADA)
Name changed to Alcanna Inc. 05/14/2018

LISA INTL LTD (NY)
Name changed to Interfashion, Inc. (NY) 06/02/1970
Interfashion, Inc. (NY) reincorporated in Delaware 07/21/1971
(See Interfashion, Inc. (DE))

LISBOA LEISURE INC (NV)
Name changed to GroGenesis, Inc. 11/01/2013

LISBON URANIUM CORP. (UT)
Merged into Hidden Splendor Mining Co. (DE) 10/19/1959
Each share Capital Stock 15¢ par exchanged for (0.28) share 6% Preferred $11 par
(See Hidden Splendor Mining Co. (DE))

LISBON VALLEY URANIUM CO. (CO)
Recapitalized as Ocean Data Industries, Inc. 12/20/1968
Each share Common 1¢ par exchanged for (0.05) share Common 1¢ par
Ocean Data Industries, Inc. name changed to Universal Investment Properties, Inc. 10/18/1972
(See Universal Investment Properties, Inc.)

LISBON VALLEY URANIUM CORP. (UT)
Merged into Universal Uranium & Milling Corp. 4/22/55
(See Universal Uranium & Milling Corp.)

LISCO CORP. (IL)
Acquired by Empire Life Insurance Co. (AL) 12/16/1964
Each share Common 25¢ par exchanged for (2/3) share Class A Common $1 par
Empire Life Insurance Co. (AL) name changed to Empire Life Insurance Co. of America (AL) 06/18/1965
(See Empire Life Insurance Co. of America (AL))

LISCO NATL CORP (NY)
Name changed to Summit National Corp. and Common $1 par changed to 10¢ par 05/16/1972

LISK MANUFACTURING CO. LTD.
Merged into Lisk Savory Corp. 00/00/1944
Details not available

LISK SAVORY CORP (NY)
Common $100 par changed to $1 par 06/08/1979
Dissolved 03/20/1987
Details not available

LISSOME TRADE CORP (NV)
Name changed to Tianhe Union Holdings Ltd. 09/22/2015
Tianhe Union Holdings Ltd. recapitalized as National Art Exchange, Inc. 08/24/2017

LIST INDUSTRIES CORP. (DE)
Merged into Glen Alden Corp. (Pa.) share for share 4/21/59
Glen Alden Corp. (Pa.) reincorporated under the laws of Delaware 5/18/67 which merged into Rapid-American Corp. (Del.) 11/6/72
(See Rapid-American Corp. (Del.))

LISTA, INC. (NV)
Recapitalized as Saberdyne, Inc. (NV) 10/1/69
Each share Capital Stock 1¢ par exchanged for (0.03) share Common 1¢ par and $1 and cash per certificate regardless of amount of shares
Saberdyne, Inc. (NV) merged into Saberdyne, Inc. (AZ) 8/11/70 which recapitalized as Saberdyne Systems, Inc. 9/20/71
(See Saberdyne Systems, Inc.)

LISTED SECURITIES CORP.
Operations discontinued 00/00/1938
Details not available

LISTED VENTURES INTL INC (AB)
Recapitalized 5/3/93
Recapitalized from Listed Ventures Inc. to Listed Ventures International Inc. 5/3/93
Each share Common no par exchanged for (1/3) share Common no par
Name changed to Command Performance Network Ltd. 7/5/94
(See Command Performance Network Ltd.)

LISTER ENERGY GROUP (NV)
Recapitalized as American Minerals & Research Corp. 11/8/82
Each share Common $0.001 par exchanged for (0.25) share Common $0.001 par

LISTFAX CORP (NY)
Class A 5¢ par changed to 2¢ par and (1.5) additional shares issued 03/10/1970
Charter cancelled and proclaimed dissolved for failure to pay taxes 09/29/1982

LIT BROTHERS
Merged into City Stores Co. in 1951
Each (7) shares Common no par exchanged for (1) share 4-1/4% Preferred $100 par
(See City Stores Co.)

LITAS INTL INC (DE)
Charter cancelled and declared inoperative and void for non-payment of taxes 3/1/95

LITCHFIELD CAP TR I (DE)
10% Guaranteed Trust Preferred Securities Ser. A called for redemption at $10 on 6/30/2004

LITCHFIELD CNTY NATL BK (NEW MILFORD, CT)
Merged into Colonial Bank & Trust Co. (Waterbury, CT) 12/6/68
Each share Common Capital Stock $5 par exchanged for (1.5) shares Capital Stock $10 par
Colonial Bank & Trust Co. (Waterbury, CT) reorganized as Colonial Bancorp, Inc. (CT) 6/1/70 which merged into Bank of Boston Corp. 6/20/85 which name changed to BankBoston Corp. 4/25/97 which merged into Fleet Boston Corp. 10/1/99 which name changed to FleetBoston Financial Corp. 4/18/2000 which merged into Bank of America Corp. 4/1/2004

LITCHFIELD FINL CORP (MA)
Common 1¢ par split (3) for (2) by issuance of (0.5) additional share 7/16/93
Stock Dividend - 5% payable 8/9/96 to holders of record 7/23/96
Merged into Textron Financial Corp. 11/4/99
Each share Common 1¢ par exchanged for $24.50 cash

LITCO BANCORPORATION N Y INC (NY)
Merged into Banca Commerciale Italiana 07/09/1982
Each share Common $5 par exchanged for $36.25 cash

LITCO CORP. OF NEW YORK (NY)
Common $5 par split (3) for (2) by issuance of (0.5) additional share 02/15/1978
Name changed to Litco Bancorporation of New York, Inc. 05/04/1979
(See Litco Bancorporation of New York, Inc.)

LITE KING CORP (NY)
SEC revoked common stock registration 04/27/2010

LITE OIL CORP (BC)
Recapitalized as Wescal Resources Inc. 2/8/84
Each share Common no par exchanged for (0.2) share Common no par
Wescal Resources Inc. recapitalized as CCC Coded Communications Corp. 11/26/87 which recapitalized as CCI Coded Communications Inc. 10/21/92 which reincorporated in Delaware as Coded Communications Corp. 8/27/93

LITE RES LTD (AB)
Struck off register for failure to file annual returns 12/01/1993

LITE VENT INDS INC (MI)
Charter voided for failure to file reports and pay fees 5/15/70

LITECRAFT INDS LTD (NJ)
Merged into Silvray-Litecraft Corp. on a (1.6) for (1) basis 11/18/63
Silvray-Litecraft Corp. name changed to Bluebird Inc. (N.Y.) 6/30/69 which reincorporated under the laws of Pennsylvania 8/3/70
(See Bluebird Inc. (Pa.))

LITEGLOW INDS INC (UT)
Each share old Common $0.001 par exchanged for (0.01666666) share new Common $0.001 par 12/28/1998
Plan of reorganization under Chapter 11 Federal Bankruptcy Code effective 08/03/2004
No stockholders' equity

LITERA GROUP INC (NV)
Name changed to First Foods Group, Inc. 02/27/2017

LITERARY PLAYPEN INC (DE)
Name changed to American Pallet Leasing, Inc. 12/23/2004
(See American Pallet Leasing, Inc.)

LITEX ENERGY INC (DE)
Recapitalized as International Ostrich Corp. 11/24/1997
Each share Common 1¢ par exchanged for (0.47619047) share Common 1¢ par
(See International Ostrich Corp.)

LITFIBER INC (NV)
Recapitalized as Grifco International, Inc. 11/19/2004
Each share Common no par exchanged for (0.05) share Common $0.0001 par
(See Grifco International, Inc.)

LITFUNDING CORP (NV)
Stock Dividend - 10% payable 11/01/2004 to holders of record 10/28/2004 Ex date - 10/26/2004
Recapitalized as Global Entertainment Holdings, Inc. 12/17/2007
Each share Common $0.001 par

exchanged for (0.1) share Common $0.001 par

LITHANIUM MINES LTD (ON)
Charter cancelled for failure to pay taxes and file returns 11/28/1979

LITHIC RES LTD (CANADA)
Name changed to InZinc Mining Ltd. 02/19/2014

LITHIUM AMERS CORP OLD (ON)
Merged into Western Lithium USA Corp. 09/04/2015
Each share Common no par exchanged for (0.789) share Common no par
Note: Unexchanged certificates will be cancelled and become without value 09/04/2021
Western Lithium USA Corp. name changed to Lithium Americas Corp. (New) 03/30/2016

LITHIUM CORP. OF AMERICA, INC. (MN)
Merged into Gulf Resources & Chemical Corp. 06/19/1967
Each share Common Capital Stock $1 par exchanged for (0.5) share Conv. Preferred Ser. A $1 par
Gulf Resources & Chemical Corp. name changed to Gulf USA Corp. 05/01/1992
(See Gulf USA Corp.)

LITHIUM CORP CDA LTD (MB)
Name changed to Rusty Lake Resources Inc. 01/07/1991
Rusty Lake Resources Inc. reorganized in British Columbia as Seven Seas Petroleum Inc. 06/29/1995 which reincorporated in Yukon 08/12/1996 which reincorporated in Cayman Islands 03/01/2001
(See Seven Seas Petroleum Inc.)

LITHIUM DEVELOPMENTS, INC. (DE)
Name changed to Northern Minerals, Inc. 12/12/1958
(See Northern Minerals, Inc.)

LITHIUM ONE INC (ON)
Acquired by Galaxy Resources Ltd. 07/03/2012
Each share Common no par exchanged for either (1.96) shares Ordinary or (1.96) Galaxy Lithium One Inc. Exchangeable Shares no par

LITHIUM TECHNOLOGY CORP (DE)
Reorganized 02/08/1996
Reorganized from Nevada to under the laws of Delaware 02/08/1996
Each share Common $0.0001 par exchanged for (0.03333333) share Common 1¢ par
Each share old Common 1¢ par exchanged for (0.05) share new Common 1¢ par 07/28/2003
Chapter 7 bankruptcy proceedings terminated 01/03/2018
Stockholders' equity unlikely

LITHIUM X ENERGY CORP (BC)
Acquired by NNEL Holding Corp. 03/13/2018
Each share Common no par exchanged for $2.61 cash
Note: Unexchanged certificates will be cancelled and become without value 03/10/2020

LITHO-WEB, INC. (NC)
Name changed to Automation Business Systems, Inc. 5/1/65
Automation Business Systems, Inc. merged into American Business Products, Inc. (DE) 11/17/68 which reincorporated in Georgia 4/30/86
(See American Business Products, Inc. (GA))

LITHOID INC (NJ)
Merged into LYB Holding Corp. 05/02/1988
Each share Common 10¢ par exchanged for $22.53 cash

LITHOMAT CORP.
Name changed to Photon, Inc. and Common no par changed to $1 par 00/00/1950
(See Photon, Inc.)

LITHONIA LTG INC (GA)
Merged into National Service Industries, Inc. 6/27/69
Each share Common no par exchanged for (0.4901) share Common $1 par
(See National Service Industries, Inc.)

LI3 ENERGY INC (NV)
Common $0.001 par split (15.625) for (1) by issuance of (14.625) additional shares payable 11/23/2009 to holders of record 11/20/2009 Ex date - 11/24/2009
Merged into Bearing Lithium Corp. (Old) 09/28/2017
Each share Common $0.001 par exchanged for (0.02877054) share Common no par
Bearing Lithium Corp. (Old) reorganized as Bearing Lithium Corp. (New) 07/20/2018

LITRONIC INC (DE)
Issue Information - 3,700,000 shares COM offered at $11 per share on 06/09/1999
Name changed to SSP Solutions, Inc. 08/23/2001
SSP Solutions, Inc. merged into Saflink Corp. 08/09/2004 which recapitalized as IdentiPHI, Inc. 02/19/2008
(See IdentiPHI, Inc.)

LITRONIX INC (CA)
Merged into New Sitronix, Inc. 03/01/1979
Each share Common 5¢ par exchanged for $3.625 cash

LITTELFUSE, INC. (IL)
Completely liquidated 5/8/68
Each share Common $2.50 par exchanged for first and final distribution of (0.5) share Tracor, Inc. (Tex.) 75¢ Conv. Preferred $1 par and $0.1875 cash
Tracor, Inc. (Tex.) reincorporated under the laws of Delaware 6/20/73
(See Tracor, Inc. (Del.))

LITTLE & IVES CO., INC. (NY)
Adjudicated bankrupt 2/15/66
No stockholders' equity

LITTLE (J.J.) & IVES CO. (NY)
Name changed to Little & Ives Co. Inc. 07/24/1962
(See Little & Ives Co. Inc.)

LITTLE ABITIBI RIVER RES INC (ON)
Name changed to LARR Capital Corp. 1/15/90
LARR Capital Corp. recapitalized as Pembridge Inc. 11/3/94
(See Pembridge Inc.)

LITTLE ARTHUR D INC (MA)
Common $1 par split (3) for (2) by issuance of (0.5) additional share 8/18/78
Acquired by Memorial Drive Trust 6/14/88
Each share Common $1 par exchanged for $60 cash

LITTLE BK INC (KINSTON, NC)
Common no par split (5) for (4) by issuance of (0.25) additional share payable 12/15/2006 to holders of record 11/30/2006 Ex date - 12/18/2006
Stock Dividends - 5% payable 01/31/2001 to holders of record 01/15/2001; 5% payable 01/31/2002 to holders of record 01/15/2002; 5% payable 11/28/2003 to holders of record 11/14/2003 Ex date - 11/12/2003; 5% payable 11/30/2004 to holders of record 11/15/2004 Ex date - 11/10/2004; 5% payable 11/30/2005 to holders of record 11/15/2005 Ex date - 11/10/2005; 5% payable 12/15/2009 to holders of record 11/30/2009 Ex date - 11/25/2009; 5% payable 11/30/2010 to holders of record 11/15/2010 Ex date - 11/10/2010; 5% payable 11/30/2011 to holders of record 11/15/2011 Ex date - 11/10/2011; 5% payable 12/07/2012 to holders of record 11/26/2012 Ex date - 11/21/2012; 5% payable 11/29/2013 to holders of record 11/15/2013 Ex date - 11/13/2013; 5% payable 11/28/2014 to holders of record 11/14/2014 Ex date - 11/12/2014; 5% payable 11/30/2015 to holders of record 11/13/2015 Ex date - 11/10/2015; 5% payable 11/30/2016 to holders of record 11/15/2016 Ex date - 11/10/2016
Name and location changed to Union Bank (Greenville, NC) 07/10/2017

LITTLE BEAR RES LTD (BC)
Name changed to Response Biomedical Corp. 10/11/1991
(See Response Biomedical Corp.)

LITTLE CREEK INC (UT)
Reincorporated under the laws of Delaware as TMSF Holdings Inc. 11/07/2002
(See TMSF Holdings Inc.)

LITTLE DUDE TRAILER INC (TX)
Name changed to Columbia General Corp. (TX) 10/14/1968
Columbia General Corp. (TX) reincorporated in Delaware 03/07/1969
(See Columbia General Corp. (DE))

LITTLE FALLS AGWAY COOPERATIVE, INC. (NY)
Merged into Agway, Inc. 9/23/72
Each share Preferred $5 par exchanged for $5 cash

LITTLE FALLS BANCORP INC (NJ)
Merged into Hudson United Bancorp 5/21/99
Each share Common 10¢ par exchanged for either (0.6408) share Common no par or $20.64 cash
Note: Option to receive stock expired 5/17/99
Hudson United Bancorp merged into TD Banknorth Inc. 1/31/2006
(See TD Banknorth Inc.)

LITTLE FALLS COOPERATIVE GLF SERVICE, INC. (NY)
Name changed to Little Falls Agway Cooperative, Inc. 12/11/65
(See Little Falls Agway Cooperative, Inc.)

LITTLE FALLS WATER CO.
Acquired by Federal Water Service Corp. 00/00/1926
Details not available

LITTLE FORT BANK & TRUST CO. (WAUKEGAN, IL)
Name changed to American National Bank & Trust Co. (Waukegan, IL) 12/01/1966
(See American National Bank & Trust Co. (Waukegan, IL))

LITTLE GIANT FOOD MART INC (NC)
Administratively dissolved 12/8/93

LITTLE JIM MINING & DEVELOPMENT CORP.
Charter cancelled and proclaimed dissolved for failure to pay taxes 12/16/63

LITTLE JOE MINES (NV)
Name changed to Republic Oil & Mining Co. 06/01/1974
Each share Common 1¢ par exchanged for (1) share Common 1¢ par

LITTLE KANAWHA RAILROAD
Dissolved in 1937

LITTLE LAKE RES LTD (BC)
Name changed to I.C.E.-ICE Factory Inc. 5/4/87
(See I.C.E.-ICE Factory Inc.)

LITTLE LONG LAC GOLD MINES LTD. (THE) (ON)
Merged into Little Long Lac Mines Ltd. (Old) 1/8/71
Each share Capital Stock no par exchanged for (1) share Capital Stock no par
Little Long Lac Mines Ltd. name changed to Little Long Lac Gold Mines Ltd. (New) 7/3/75 which merged into LAC Minerals Ltd. (New) 7/29/85 which was acquired by American Barrick Resources Corp. 10/17/94 which name changed to Barrick Gold Corp. 1/18/95

LITTLE LONG LAC GOLD MINES LTD. OLD (ON)
Under plan of merger each share Capital Stock no par exchanged for (1) share Capital Stock no par 6/15/66
Merged into Little Long Lac Gold Mines Ltd. (The) 4/27/67
Each share Capital Stock no par exchanged for (1) share Capital Stock no par
Little Long Lac Gold Mines Ltd. (The) merged into Little Long Lac Mines Ltd. (Old) 1/8/71 which name changed to Little Long Lac Gold Mines Ltd. (New) 7/3/75 which merged into LAC Minerals Ltd. (New) 7/29/85 which was acquired by American Barrick Resources Corp. 10/17/94 which name changed to Barrick Gold Corp. 1/18/95

LITTLE LONG LAC GOLD MINES LTD NEW (ON)
Merged into LAC Minerals Ltd. (New) 07/29/1985
Each share Capital Stock no par exchanged for (2.377) shares Common no par
LAC Minerals Ltd. (New) acquired by American Barrick Resources Corp. 10/17/1994 which name changed to Barrick Gold Corp. 01/18/1995

LITTLE LONG LAC MINES LTD OLD (ON)
Name changed to Little Long Lac Gold Mines Ltd. (New) 7/3/75
Little Long Lac Gold Mines Ltd. (New) merged into LAC Minerals Ltd. (New) 7/29/85 which was acquired by American Barrick Resources Corp. 10/17/94 which name changed to Barrick Gold Corp. 1/18/95

LITTLE MAY MINING CO. (UT)
Recapitalized as Investment Resources & Properties Corp. 11/28/60
Each share Common 5¢ par exchanged for (0.05) share Common $1 par
Investment Resources & Properties Corp. name changed to Kent Industries, Inc. 8/16/62
(See Kent Industries, Inc.)

LITTLE MIAMI RR CO (OH)
Merged into Penn Central Corp. 10/5/79
Each share Special Betterment Guaranty $50 par exchanged for (0.2431) share Conv. Preference Ser. B $20 par, (0.1096) share Common $1 par, $4.8622 principal amount of 7% General Mortgage Bonds Ser. A due 12/31/87 and $20.4153 cash
Each share Capital Stock $50 par exchanged for (0.9432) share Conv. Preference Ser. B $20 par, (0.4251) share Common $1 par, $18.8633 principal amount of 7% General Mortgage Bonds Ser. A due 12/31/87 and $20.4153 cash
Note: a) Distribution is certain only for

certificates surrendered prior to 5/1/85 b) Distribution may also be made for certficates surrendered between 5/1/85 and 12/31/86 c) No distribution will be made for certificates surrendered after 12/31/86

Penn Central Corp. name changed to American Premier Underwriters, Inc. 3/25/94 which merged into American Premier Group, Inc. 4/3/95 which name changed to American Financial Group, Inc. 6/9/95 which merged into American Financial Group, Inc. (Holding Co.) 12/2/97

LITTLE MTN RES LTD (BC)
Name changed to PetroStar Petroleum Corp. 08/10/2005
PetroStar Petroleum Corp. name changed to Cerus Energy Group Ltd. 09/01/2015

LITTLE PRINCE PRODTNS LTD (NY)
Reorganized under the laws of Colorado as Atlantic Industries Inc. 2/12/97
Each share Common 1¢ par exchanged for (0.005) share Common 1¢ par

LITTLE QUEEN MINES, INC. (ID)
Out of business and charter subsequently revoked 11/30/73
No stockholders' equity

LITTLE RIVER BK & TR CO (MIAMI, FL)
Each share Capital Stock $25 par exchanged for (2.5) shares Capital Stock $10 par 00/00/1952
Stock Dividends - 50% 00/00/1949; 33-1/3% 02/18/1955; 10% 02/19/1957; 20% 02/19/1960; 20% 02/20/1963; 12-1/2% 02/28/1968; 10% 02/27/1970
Name changed to First State Bank (Miami, FL) 04/01/1970
(See First State Bank (Miami, FL))

LITTLE RUFFY TOGS, INC. (NY)
Out of business in November 1964
Common stock is worthless

LITTLE SCHUYLKILL NAVIGATION RAILROAD & COAL CO.
Merged into Reading Co. 4/30/52
Each share Capital Stock $50 par exchanged for (1) share 1st Preferred $50 par
Reading Co. merged into Reading Entertainment Inc. (DE) 10/15/96 which reincorporated in Nevada 12/29/99 which merged into Reading International, Inc. 12/31/2001

LITTLE SHEEP GROUP LTD (CAYMAN ISLANDS)
ADR agreement terminated 02/17/2012
No ADR's remain outstanding

LITTLE SQUAW GOLD MNG CO (AK)
Name changed to Goldrich Mining Co. 07/11/2008

LITTLE STAR URANIUM CO., INC. (WY)
Merged into Anschutz Drilling Co., Inc. on a (1) for (37.85) basis 7/27/56
Anschutz Drilling Co. recapitalized as Webb Resources, Inc. 10/17/61 which merged into Standard Oil Co. (OH) 12/11/79
(See Standard Oil Co. (OH))

LITTLE STORE INC (DE)
Reincorporated 08/05/1970
State of incorporation changed from (FL) to (DE) 08/05/1970
Name changed to Leisure World Services, Inc. 07/22/1971
(See Leisure World Services, Inc.)

LITTLE SWITZ INC (DE)
Merged into Tiffany & Co. (New) 11/20/2002
Each share Common 1¢ par exchanged for $2.40 cash

LITTLE TEX MINING CORP. (QC)
Charter revoked for failure to file reports and pay fees 9/9/72

LITTLE VALLEY OIL CO. (WY)
Recapitalized as California Press Bureau, Inc. 04/01/1971
Each share Common $1 par exchanged for (1) share Common 1¢ par
California Press Bureau, Inc. name changed to Atronic, Inc. 09/02/1981
(See Atronic, Inc.)

LITTLEFIELD ADAMS & CO (NJ)
Common $1 par split (3) for (2) by issuance of (0.5) additional share 07/15/1993
SEC revoked common stock registration 03/01/2010

LITTLETON NATL BK (LITTLETON, NH)
Common Capital Stock $50 par changed to $25 and (1) additional share issued 1/14/69
Common Capital Stock $25 par changed to $10 par and (2) additional shares issued 1/2/71
Name changed to Lafayette National Bank (Littleton, NH) 10/1/75
Each share Common Capital Stock $10 par exchanged for (1) share Common Capital Stock $10 par
Lafayette National Bank (Littleton, NH) merged into Indian Head Banks, Inc. 6/12/81 which was acquired by Fleet/Norstar Financial Group, Inc. 12/21/88 which name changed to Fleet Financial Group, Inc. (New) 4/15/92 which name changed to Fleet Boston Corp. 10/1/99 which name changed to FleetBoston Financial Corp. 4/18/2000 which merged into Bank of America Corp. 4/1/2004

LITTMAN PROJ CORP (FL)
Name changed to National Conglomerated Food Services Inc. 11/17/97

LITTMAN RES INC (FL)
Name changed to NuOncology Labs, Inc. 6/24/98

LITTMAN VENTURES CORP (FL)
Name changed to United Media Group, Inc. 04/16/1997
United Media Group, Inc. name changed to 21st Century Frontier Group, Inc. 08/04/1997 which recapitalized as Goldplate Holdings Enterprises Inc. 02/10/1999 which recapitalized as Eagletech Communications, Inc. 03/17/1999
(See Eagletech Communications, Inc.)

LITTON INDS INC (DE)
Common 10¢ par changed to $1 par and (1) additional share issued 12/18/1959
Common $1 par split (2) for (1) by issuance of (1) additional share 08/15/1962
Common $1 par split (2) for (1) by issuance of (1) additional share 01/14/1966
$2 Preferred Ser. B $5 par conversion privilege expired 09/19/1974
Conv. Preference Part. Ser. 2.50 par called for redemption 01/15/1981
$3 Conv. Preferred Ser. a $5 par called for redemption 01/15/1981
Common $1 par split (2) for (1) by issuance of (1) additional share 05/08/1992
Merged into Northrop Gruman Corp. (Holding Company) 05/30/2001
Each share $2 Preferred Ser. B $5 par exchanged for $35 cash
Each share Common $1 par exchanged for $80 cash

LIUSKI INTL INC (DE)
Each share old Common 1¢ par exchanged for (0.4) share new Common 1¢ par 07/01/1998

Chapter 7 bankruptcy proceedings terminated 04/18/2003
Stockholders' equity unlikely

LIUYANG FIREWORKS LTD (BERMUDA)
Each (6,000,000) shares old Common CAD$0.02 par exchanged for (1) share new Common CAD$0.02 par 10/01/2015
Note: In effect holders received CAD$0.048 cash per share and public interest was eliminated

LIVE ENTMT CDA INC (ON)
Name changed to Livent, Inc. 5/18/95
(See Livent, Inc.)

LIVE ENTMT INC (DE)
Common 1¢ par split (3) for (2) by issuance of (0.5) additional share 5/31/89
Plan of reorganization under Chapter 11 Federal Bankruptcy Code effective 3/23/93
Each share Conv. Preferred Ser. A 1¢ par exchanged for $2.98 principal amount of Variable Rate Senior Secured Subordinated Notes due 1999 and (0.447) share Conv. Preferred Ser. B 1¢ par
Each share old Common 1¢ par exchanged for (0.2) share new Common 1¢ par 12/8/94
Acquired by an investor group 7/9/97
Each share Conv. Preferred Ser. B 1¢ par exchanged for $10 cash
Each share new Common 1¢ par exchanged for $6 cash

LIVE EVENT MEDIA INC (NV)
Name changed to Eventure Interactive, Inc. 03/14/2013

LIVE FIT CORP (NV)
Name changed to Starlight Supply Chain Management Co. 06/16/2016

LIVE NATION INC (DE)
Under plan of merger name changed to Live Nation Entertainment, Inc. 01/27/2010

LIVE OAK STATE BANK (ROCKPORT, TX)
Merged into Allied Bancshares, Inc. (TX) 01/03/1982
Each share Capital Stock $5 par exchanged for (1.02659) shares Common $1 par
Allied Bancshares, Inc. (TX) reincorporated in Delaware 04/22/1987 which merged into First Interstate Bancorp 01/29/1988 which merged into Wells Fargo & Co. (Old) 04/01/1996 which merged into Wells Fargo & Co. (New) 11/02/1998

LIVE STK NATL BK (KANSAS CITY, MO)
Stock Dividend - 20% 2/8/66
Merged into First National Charter Corp. 8/8/72
Each share Common $10 par exchanged for (1) share Common $12.50 par
First National Charter Corp. name changed to CharterCorp 6/25/82 which merged into Boatmen's Bancshares, Inc. 1/28/85 which merged into NationsBank Corp. 1/7/97 which reincorporated in Delaware as BankAmerica Corp. (Old) 9/25/98 which merged into BankAmerica Corp. (New) 9/30/98 which name changed to Bank of America Corp. 4/28/99

LIVE STOCK NATIONAL BANK (CHICAGO, IL)
Acquired by Central National Bank (Chicago, Ill.) 3/26/65
Each share Capital Stock $20 par exchanged for (3.8607) shares Capital Stock $10 par
Central National Bank (Chicago, Ill.) reorganized as Central National Chicago Corp. 9/30/69 which merged into Exchange International

Corp. 8/21/82 which name changed to Exchange Bancorp, Inc. 5/17/88
(See Exchange Bancorp, Inc.)

LIVEDEAL INC (NV)
Each share old Common $0.001 par exchanged for (0.1) share new Common $0.001 par 09/07/2010
New Common $0.001 par split (3) for (1) by issuance of (2) additional shares payable 02/11/2014 to holders of record 02/03/2014
Ex date - 02/12/2014
Stock Dividend - 5.263% payable 08/10/2011 to holders of record 07/29/2011 Ex date - 07/27/2011
Name changed to Live Ventures Inc. 10/09/2015

LIVENT INC (ON)
Plan of reorganization under Chapter 11 Federal Bankruptcy Code effective 12/22/2003
No stockholders' equity

LIVEREEL MEDIA CORP (CANADA)
Name changed to CordovaCann Corp. 08/08/2018

LIVERPOOL INDS INC (NY)
Charter cancelled and proclaimed dissolved for failure to pay taxes 06/27/2001

LIVESTAR ENTMT GROUP INC (NV)
Each share old Common $0.0001 par exchanged for (0.001) share new Common $0.0001 par 09/02/2004
Note: Holders of (100) or fewer pre-split shares were not affected
Each share new Common $0.0001 par exchanged for (0.0005) share Common $0.00001 par 11/09/2004
Name changed to Jupiter Global Holdings Corp. 12/22/2004
Jupiter Global Holdings Corp. merged into Paivis, Corp. 05/19/2006
(See Paivis, Corp.)

LIVESTOCK FINL CORP (CO)
Name changed to LFC Inc. 10/22/1987
(See LFC Inc.)

LIVESTOCK FINL CORP (NY)
Name changed to Lisco National Corp. 09/30/1968
Lisco National Corp. name changed to Summit National Corp. 05/16/1972

LIVEWIRE MOBILE INC (DE)
Each share old Common 1¢ par exchanged for (0.1) share new Common 1¢ par 12/21/2009
Name changed to Live Microsystems, Inc. 08/29/2013

LIVING & LEARNING CTRS INC (MA)
Merged into Kinder-Care Learning Centers, Inc. 10/31/1980
Each share Common 10¢ par exchanged for $5.249 principal amount Promissory Notes due 10/01/1987 and $1.556 cash

LIVING ALUMINUM, INC. (NY)
Name changed to Living Industries, Inc. (NY) 1/5/67
Living Industries, Inc. (NY) reorganized as Living Industries, Inc. (DE) 11/2/77
(See Living Industries, Inc.)

LIVING CARD CO INC (NV)
Name changed to Integrated Technology Group, Inc. 06/20/2000
Integrated Technology Group, Inc. recapitalized as Knight Energy Corp. (NV) 06/13/2006 which reincorporated in Maryland 04/30/2007
(See Knight Energy Corp.)

LIVING CTRS AMER INC (DE)
Merged into Paragon Health Network, Inc. 11/4/97
Each share Common 1¢ par exchanged for (1) share Common 1¢ par or $40.50 cash
Note: Due to over-election 9.46% of

total shares were exchanged for stock and 90.54% for cash
Non-electors received $40.50 cash per share
Paragon Health Network, Inc. name changed to Mariner Post-Acute Network Inc. 7/31/98
(See Mariner Post-Acute Network, Inc.)

LIVING INDS INC (DE)
Reorganized 1/2/77
Common $1 par changed to 1¢ par 8/28/70
Living Industries, Inc. (NY) reorganized as Living Industries, Inc. (DE) 11/2/77
Each share Common 1¢ par exchanged for (0.1) share Common 10¢ par 10/12/79
Common 10¢ par changed to 2¢ par 10/31/80
Charter cancelled and declared inoperative and void for non-payment of taxes 3/1/92

LIVING WELL INC (DE)
Chapter 11 Federal Bankruptcy Code converted to Chapter 7 on 10/5/90
Stockholders' equity unlikely

LIVINGSTON INDS LTD (ON)
Common no par split (3) for (1) by issuance of (2) additional shares 11/5/69
6% 1st Preference Ser. A $50 par called for redemption 11/30/78
Merged into Allpak Holdings Ltd. 12/1/78
Each share Common no par exchanged for $36 cash

LIVINGSTON INTL INCOME FD (ON)
Issue Information - 15,102,600 UNITS offered at $10 per Unit on 01/31/2002
Acquired by CPP Investment Board 01/20/2010
Each Unit received $9.50 cash

LIVINGSTON NATL BK N J (LIVINGSTON, NJ)
Merged into First Jersey National Corp. 11/26/1984
Each share Common $50 par exchanged for (4.34) shares Common $5 par
(See First Jersey National Corp.)

LIVINGSTON OIL CO (DE)
Stock Dividend - 10% 6/30/61
Name changed to LVO Corp. 9/24/69
LVO Corp. merged into Utah International Inc. 10/31/74 which merged into General Electric Corp. 12/20/76
(See General Electric Corp.)

LIVINGSTON OIL CORP. (DE)
No longer in existence having become inoperative and void for non-payment of taxes 4/1/29

LIVINGSTON WOOD MFG LTD (ON)
Name changed to Livingston Industries Ltd. 04/17/1967
(See Livingston Industries Ltd.)

LIVINGSTONE ENERGY CORP (BC)
Under plan of merger name changed to World Tec Industries Inc. 06/30/1987
World Tec Industries Inc. name changed to Solucorp Industries Inc. (BC) 08/19/1994 which reincorporated in Yukon 04/04/1997

LIVINGSTONE MINING CO., INC.
Property sold to Kenville Gold Mines, Ltd. in 1945
(See Kenville Gold Mines, Ltd.)

LIVONIA NATL BK (LIVONIA, MI)
Stock Dividends - 10% 10/29/1955; 10% 10/24/1959; 10% 02/25/1963; 25% 03/31/1969; 10% 03/31/1970; 10% 03/26/1971
98% held by Michigan National Corp. as of 11/03/1972
Public interest eliminated

LIZ CLAIBORNE INC (DE)
Common $1 par split (2) for (1) by issuance of (1) additional share 08/10/1983
Common $1 par split (2) for (1) by issuance of (1) additional share 12/04/1984
Common $1 par split (2) for (1) by issuance of (1) additional share 04/07/1986
Common $1 par split (2) for (1) by issuance of (1) additional share 06/08/1987
Common $1 par split (2) for (1) by issuance of (1) additional share payable 01/16/2002 to holders of record 12/31/2001
Stock Dividend - 50% 11/29/1982
Name changed to Fifth & Pacific Companies, Inc. 05/15/2012
Fifth & Pacific Companies, Inc. name changed to Kate Spade & Co. 02/26/2014
(See Kate Spade & Co.)

LJ INTL INC (BRITISH VIRGIN ISLANDS)
Acquired by Flora Bloom Holdings 07/30/2013
Each share Common 1¢ par exchanged for $2 cash

LJC CORP (UT)
Merged into Immunotechnology Corp. 10/07/1989
Each share Common $0.001 par exchanged for (1.1) shares Common $0.00001 par
Immunotechnology Corp. recapitalized as Petals Decorative Accents, Inc. 09/21/2006
(See Petals Decorative Accents, Inc.)

LJL BIOSYSTEMS INC (DE)
Merged into Molecular Devices Corp. 08/30/2000
Each share Common $0.001 par exchanged for (0.3) share Common $0.001 par
(See Molecular Devices Corp.)

LJM ENERGY CORP (NV)
Name changed to American Energy Development Corp. 07/15/2011

LJN TOYS LTD (NY)
Acquired by MCA Inc. 09/19/1985
Each share Common 10¢ par exchanged for $14.26 cash

LKA INTL INC (DE)
Recapitalized as LKA Gold Inc. 03/15/2013
Each share Common $0.001 par exchanged for (0.5) share Common $0.001 par

LKL FRANCHISES INC (MN)
Name changed to Automated Services, Inc. (MN) 8/10/71
Automated Services, Inc. (MN) name changed to Dameron, Inc. 11/2/71
(See Dameron, Inc.)

LL & E RTY TR (MI)
SEC revoked Unit of Bene. Int. registration 07/27/2015

LL CAP CORP (ON)
Recapitalized as Syncordia Technologies & Healthcare Solutions, Corp. 07/08/2015
Each share Common no par exchanged for (0.05) share Common no par

LLC CORP (DE)
Under plan of merger each share $1.25 Conv. Preference $25 par, 5% Preferred $25 par, 5-1/2% Conv. Preferred $25 par and 5-3/4% Preference 1960 Ser. $25 par exchanged for (8.0782) shares Common $1 par 9/17/85
Under plan of merger name changed to Valhi, Inc. and Common $1 par changed to 1¢ par 3/10/87

LLIFELINE HLDGS INC (NV)
Company reported out of business 00/00/1998
Details not available

LLOYD ELEC & ENGR LTD (INDIA)
Name changed to LEEL Electricals Ltd. 06/16/2017
(See LEEL Electricals Ltd.)

LLOYD S ELECTRS INC (DE)
Merged into Bacardi Corp. 12/30/1983
Each share Common 75¢ par exchanged for $6 cash

LLOYDAL PETROLEUMS LTD. (ON)
Merged into Continental Consolidated Mines & Oils Co. Ltd. on a (0.1) for (1) basis 10/4/57
(See Continental Consolidated Mines & Oils Co. Ltd.)

LLOYDBROOK OIL CO., LTD. (AB)
Struck off register and deemed dissolved for failure to file reports 12/15/70

LLOYDMINSTER DEVELOPMENT CO. LTD. (SK)
Acquired by Kodiak Petroleums Ltd. 02/13/1963
Each share Capital Stock $1 par exchanged for (0.075) share Common no par
Kodiak Petroleums Ltd. was acquired by Manhattan Continental Development Corp. 10/02/1969
(See Manhattan Continental Development Corp.)

LLOYDS ACCEP CORP (NV)
Each share old Common 10¢ par exchanged for (1/3) share new Common 10¢ par 7/25/88
Recapitalized as Latrobe Corp. 7/21/97
Each share new Common 10¢ par exchanged for (0.025) share Common 10¢ par

LLOYDS CASUALTY CO.
Merged into Lloyds Insurance Co. of America in 1932 the liquidation of which company was ordered by the court in 1933

LLOYDS INSURANCE CO. OF AMERICA
Liquidation ordered by court in 1933

LLOYDS PLATE GLASS INSURANCE CO.
Name changed to Lloyds Casualty Co. in 1929 which merged into Lloyds Insurance Co. of America in 1932 the liquidation of which company was ordered by the court in 1933

LLOYDS SHOPPING CTRS INC (NY)
Each share Common 5¢ par exchanged for (1) share Class B Common 5¢ par 01/13/1995
SEC revoked common stock registration 04/30/2012

LLOYDS TSB GROUP PLC (UNITED KINGDOM)
Under plan of merger name changed to Lloyds Banking Group PLC 01/20/2009

LLX LOGISTICA S A (BRAZIL)
Name changed to Prumo Logistica S.A. 12/31/2013
(See Prumo Logistica S.A.)

LMC DATA INC (NY)
Name changed to Distinctive Devices, Inc. (NY) 9/2/76
Distinctive Devices, Inc. (NY) reorganized in Delaware 11/8/2002

LMC RES LTD (BC)
Merged into Seadrift Resources Ltd. 11/14/78
Each share Common no par exchanged for (1/3) share Common no par
Seadrift Resources Ltd. recapitalized as Pacific Seadrift Resources Ltd.

(BC) 8/13/80 which reincorporated in Alberta 6/3/83 which recapitalized as Seadrift International Exploration Ltd. 6/1/85 which merged into Deak International Resources Corp. 12/30/88 which name changed to Deak Resources Corp. 3/27/89 which name changed to AJ Perron Gold Corp. 10/7/94
(See AJ Perron Gold Corp.)

LMF CORP (MO)
Common $1 par changed to 40¢ par and (1.5) additional shares issued 12/15/1971
Stock Dividend - 10% 08/22/1977
Merged into Diamond International Corp. 11/15/1978
Each share Common 40¢ par exchanged for (1) share $1.20 Conv. Preferred Ser. A $1 par
(See Diamond International Corp.)

LMI AEROSPACE INC (MO)
Acquired by Sonaca S.A. 06/27/2017
Each share Common 2¢ par exchanged for $14 cash

LMI INVS (CA)
Name changed to Growth Realty Investors 05/31/1978
Growth Realty Investors reorganized as Growth Realty Companies 02/09/1979 which name changed to British Land of America (CA) 11/17/1983 which reincorporated in Delaware as British Land of America Inc. 12/15/1986 which merged into Medical Management of America, Inc. 09/23/1988
(See Medical Management of America, Inc.)

LMIC INC (DE)
Name changed to Z Holdings Group, Inc. and Common $0.001 par reclassified as Class A Common $0.000006 par 10/15/2012
Z Holdings Group, Inc. name changed to Ariel Clean Energy, Inc. 08/20/2015

LMK ENERGY INC (AB)
Delisted from Alberta Stock Exchange 02/27/1997

LMK GLOBAL RES INC (DE)
Name changed to Alas Aviation Corp. 07/23/2013
Alas Aviation Corp. name changed to Energie Holdings, Inc. 02/13/2014 which name changed to ExeLED Holdings Inc. 12/30/2015

LMKI INC (NV)
Name changed to Myrient Inc. 02/08/2001
(See Myrient Inc.)

LML PMT SYS INC (BC)
Reincorporated 09/07/2012
Place of incorporation changed from (YT) to (BC) 09/07/2012
Acquired by Digital River, Inc. 01/10/2013
Each share Common no par exchanged for USD$3.45 cash

LMP CORPORATE LN FD INC (MD)
Auction Rate Preferred Ser. A called for redemption at $25,000 on 12/24/2015
Auction Rate Preferred Ser. B called for redemption at $25,000 on 12/31/2015
Name changed to Western Asset Corporate Loan Fund Inc. 04/04/2016

LMP REAL ESTATE INCOME FD INC (MD)
Taxable Auction Rate Preferred Ser. M
$0.001 par called for redemption at $25,000 on 08/26/2008
(Additional Information in Active)

LMS MED SYS INC (CANADA)
Name changed to Maclos Capital Inc. 08/20/2012

LMX RES LTD (BC)
Recapitalized as Merrex Resources Inc. 09/09/2004
Each share Common no par exchanged for (0.1) share Common no par
Merrex Resources Inc. name changed to Merrex Gold, Inc. 05/25/2006 which merged into IAMGOLD Corp. 03/01/2017

LNB BANCORP INC (OH)
Common $2.50 par changed to $1.25 par and (1) additional share issued 04/18/1989
Common $1.25 par changed to $1 par and (0.25) additional share issued 04/00/1993
Common $1 par split (5) for (4) by issuance of (0.25) additional share 04/18/1995
Common $1 par split (3) for (2) by issuance of (0.5) additional share payable 03/14/2003 to holders of record 03/10/2003 Ex date - 03/17/2003
Stock Dividends - 2% payable 04/22/1996 to holders of record 04/16/1996; 2% payable 07/01/2000 to holders of record 06/12/2000; 2% payable 07/02/2001 to holders of record 06/18/2001 Ex date - 06/14/2001; 2% payable 07/01/2002 to holders of record 06/17/2002 Ex date - 06/13/2002
5% Perpetual Preferred Ser. B no par called for redemption at $1,000 plus $8.6111 accrued dividends on 01/17/2014
Merged into Northwest Bancshares, Inc. 08/14/2015
Each share Common $1 par exchanged for (1.4588085) shares Common 1¢ par and $0.02805 cash

LNC CORP (PA)
Liquidation completed
Common $1 par changed to no par and each share stamped to indicate initial distribution of $5 cash 08/17/1964
Each share Stamped Common no par received second distribution of $2.50 cash 10/25/1965
Each share Stamped Common no par received third distribution of (1) share Blue Ridge Real Estate Co. Common no par, (1) share Split Rock Lodge, Inc. Common no par and $1 cash 09/23/1966
Each share Stamped Common no par received fourth distribution of $0.80 cash 01/18/1968
Each share Stamped Common no par exchanged for fifth and final distribution of (0.166666) share Lehigh Coal & Navigation Co. Common $1 par 11/11/1969
(See each company's listing)

LNG ENERGY LTD (BC)
Recapitalized as Esrey Energy Ltd. 11/18/2013
Each share Common no par exchanged for (0.001) share Common no par
Note: Holders of (999) or fewer pre-split shares received $0.01 cash per share
Esrey Energy Ltd. name changed to Esrey Resources Ltd. 10/16/2017

LNH REIT INC (MD)
Merged into Eastgroup Properties 05/14/1996
Each share Common 50¢ par exchanged for (0.3671) Share of Bene. Int. $1 par
Eastgroup Properties reorganized as Eastgroup Properties, Inc. 06/05/1997

L90 INC (DE)
Reorganized as MaxWorldwide, Inc. 07/10/2002
Each share Common $0.001 par exchanged for (1) share Common $0.001 par
(See MaxWorldwide, Inc.)

LNR PPTY CORP (DE)
Merged into Riley Property Holdings LLC 2/3/2005
Each share Common 10¢ par exchanged for $63.10 cash
Each share Class B Common exchanged for $63.10 cash

LO BOY INC (UT)
Proclaimed dissolved for failure to file reports 1/1/96

LO JACK CORP (MA)
Name changed 08/16/1990
Name changed from Lo-Jack Corp. to LoJack Corp. 08/16/1990
Acquired by CalAmp Corp. 03/18/2016
Each share Common 1¢ par exchanged for $6.45 cash

LOAD GUARD LOGISTICS INC (NV)
Name changed to Nemus Bioscience, Inc. 11/04/2014

LOAD RES LTD (BC)
Name changed to GIS Global Imaging Solutions Inc. 05/31/2000
GIS Global Imaging Solutions Inc. name changed to Segami Images, Inc. 02/05/2001
(See Segami Images, Inc.)

LOADMASTER SYS INC (BC)
Cease trade order effective 12/8/88
Stockholders' equity unlikely

LOAN AMER FINL CORP (FL)
Stock Dividends - 25% 8/30/85; 10% 5/26/92; 15% 12/17/92
Merged into Barnett Banks, Inc. 10/1/94
Each share Common 10¢ par exchanged for $12.61259 cash

LOBANOR GOLD MINES LTD. (ON)
Charter revoked for failure to file reports and pay fees 12/2/65

LOBELL OIL & GAS LTD (AB)
Recapitalized 12/76
Reincorporated 9/26/77
Name changed from Lobell Mines Ltd. to Lobell Oil & Gas Ltd. and each share Capital Stock no par exchanged for (1/3) share Common no par December, 1976
Place of incorporation changed from (BC) to (ALTA) 9/26/77
Struck off register and declared dissolved for failure to file returns 4/6/80

LOBITOS OILFIELDS LTD. (ENGLAND)
Acquired by Burmah Oil Co., PLC 01/18/1963
Each share Ordinary Reg. 5s par exchanged for (0.8) share Ordinary Reg. £1 par
Each ADR for Ordinary Reg. 5s par exchanged for (0.8) ADR for Ordinary Reg. £1 par
Burmah Oil Co., PLC name changed to Burmah Castrol PLC 07/30/1990
(See Burmah Castrol PLC)

LOBLAW COS LTD (CANADA)
7.3% 2nd Preferred 3rd Ser. no par called for redemption 09/01/1993
$2.40 Preferred $50 par called for redemption 09/30/1998
$3.70 1st Preferred 2nd Ser. no par called for redemption 09/30/1998
2nd Preferred Ser. A no par called for redemption at $25 on 07/31/2015
(Additional Information in Active)

LOBLAW GROCETERIAS, INC.
Name changed to Loblaw, Inc. in 1950
(See Loblaw, Inc.)

LOBLAW GROCETERIAS LTD (ON)
Each share old Common no par exchanged for (2) shares Class A no par and (2) shares Class B no par 00/00/1929
Recapitalized 01/07/1957
Class A no par reclassified as 2nd Preference no par
Class B no par reclassified as new Common no par
Name changed to Loblaws Ltd. 12/14/1973
Loblaws Ltd. merged into Loblaw Companies Ltd. 01/09/1984

LOBLAW INC (NY)
Capital Stock $6 par changed to $1 par and (9) additional shares issued 2/17/60
Merged into Loblaw Interim Inc. 10/4/75
Each share Capital Stock $1 par exchanged for $6 cash

LOBLAWS LTD (ON)
Merged into Loblaw Companies Ltd. 1/9/84
Each share $1.50 1st Preference Ser. A $30 par exchanged for (0.5) share 1st Preferred 2nd Ser. no par
Each share $1.60 1st Preference Ser. B $30 par exchanged for (0.5) share 1st Preferred 2nd Ser. no par

LOBO CAPITAL INC (ON)
Name changed to Q & A Communications Inc. 03/01/1993
Q & A Communications Inc. recapitalized as Q & A Capital Inc. 11/05/1997 which recapitalized as Leader Capital Corp. 08/17/1998
(See Leader Capital Corp.)

LOBO GOLD & RES INC (ON)
Recapitalized as Lobo Capital Inc. 06/11/1992
Each (15) shares Common no par exchanged for (1) share Common no par
Lobo Capital Inc. name changed to Q & A Communications Inc. 03/01/1993 which recapitalized as Q & A Capital Inc. 11/05/1997 which recapitalized as Leader Capital Corp. 08/17/1998
(See Leader Capital Corp.)

LOBO MINES EXPLS LTD (ON)
Merged into Lobo Gold & Resources Inc. 07/06/1983
Each share Common no par exchanged for (0.1) share Common no par
Lobo Gold & Resources Inc. recapitalized as Lobo Capital Inc. 06/11/1992 which name changed to Q & A Communications Inc. 03/01/1993 which recapitalized as Q & A Capital Inc. 11/05/1997 which recapitalized as Leader Capital Corp. 08/17/1998
(See Leader Capital Corp.)

LOBSTER FD INC (CO)
Name changed to International Technologies, Inc. (CO) 10/06/1988
(See International Technologies, Inc. (CO))

LOCAL COM CORP (DE)
Name changed to Local Corp. 09/17/2012

LOCAL FED SVGS & LN ASSN OKLA CITY OKLA (USA)
Acquired by a private company 08/21/1989
Each share Common 1¢ par exchanged for $15 cash

LOCAL FIN CORP (RI)
Common $1 par reclassified as Class B Common 25¢ par 10/20/1959
Class A Non-Cum. Preferred $1 par reclassified as Non-Callable Preferred $1 par 06/21/1960
Class A Common 25¢ par and Class B Common 25¢ par reclassified as Common 25¢ par 11/03/1969
Merged into Fidelity Corp. of Pennsylvania 06/29/1973
Each share Preferred $5 par or Non-Callable Preferred $1 par exchanged for (0.149813) share Common $1 par
Each share Common 25¢ par exchanged for (0.792153) share Common $1 par
Fidelity Corp. of Pennsylvania name changed to Fidelcor, Inc. 05/15/1974 which merged into First Fidelity Bancorporation (New) 02/29/1988 which merged into First Union Corp. 01/01/1996 which name changed to Wachovia Corp. (Ctfs. dated after 09/01/2001) 09/01/2001 which merged into Wells Fargo & Co. (New) 12/31/2008

LOCAL FINL CORP (DE)
Merged into International Bancshares Corp. 6/21/2004
Each share Common 1¢ par exchanged for (0.517) share Common $1 par

LOCAL TELECOM SYS INC (NV)
Recapitalized as MBI Financial Inc. 06/06/2006
Each share Common $0.0167 par exchanged for (0.02) share Common $0.0167 par
(See MBI Financial Inc.)

LOCALSHARES INVT TR (DE)
Trust terminated 02/16/2018
Each share Nashville Area ETF no par received $29.07 cash

LOCAN INC (DE)
SEC revoked common stock registration 02/02/2016

LOCANA MINERAL HLDGS LTD (CANADA)
Name changed to NSI Marketing Ltd. 8/11/71
(See NSI Marketing Ltd.)

LOCATEPLUS HLDGS CORP (DE)
Each share Class A Common 1¢ par exchanged for (0.02) share Common 1¢ par 12/12/2005
Each share Class B Common 1¢ par exchanged for (0.02) share Common 1¢ par 12/12/2005
SEC revoked common stock registration 07/30/2012

LOCATING DEVICES INC (NY)
Name changed to Gallo Pet Supplies, Inc. 3/19/74
(See Gallo Pet Supplies, Inc.)

LOCATOR EXPLS LTD (BC)
Merged into Duration Mines Ltd. 6/30/88
Each share Common no par exchanged for (1.45) shares Common no par
(See Duration Mines Ltd.)

LOCH EXPL INC (TX)
Reorganized under Chapter 11 Federal Bankruptcy Code 12/20/1989
Each share Common 1¢ par exchanged for (0.125) share Common $0.001 par
Each share Common $0.001 par exchanged for (0.02) share Common 1¢ par 02/28/1997
Name changed to Design Automation Systems, Inc. 04/12/1999
Design Automation Systems, Inc. name changed to EpicEdge, Inc. 03/17/2000
(See EpicEdge, Inc.)

LOCH HARRIS INC (NV)
Each share Common $0.001 par exchanged for (0.5) share Common $0.002 par 10/08/1993
Class Action settlement effective 03/11/2003
Each share Common $0.002 par exchanged for (0.02207572) share CDEX-Inc. Class A Common $0.001 par
Note: Unexchanged certificates except for class members who opted

out, were cancelled and became without value 08/15/2003

LOCHABER OIL LTD (CANADA)
Each share Class A $10 par exchanged for (4) shares Common no par 11/05/1956
Each share Class B no par exchanged for (1) share Common no par 11/05/1956
Stock Dividend - 50% 12/27/1956
Acquired by Texas Land & Mortgage Co., Inc. 03/12/1975
Each share Common no par exchanged for (0.17565805) share Common
Note: Texas Land & Mortgage Co., Inc. is privately held

LOCHAVEN FED SVGS LN ASSN (ORLANDO, FL)
Merged into Republic Bancshares, Inc. 11/5/98
Each share Common 1¢ par exchanged for (0.2776) share Common $2 par
Republic Bancshares, Inc. merged into BB&T Corp. 4/14/2004

LOCHGOLD MINES, LTD. (ON)
Charter annulled in 1948

LOCHIEL EXPL LTD (AB)
Common no par reclassified as Class B Common no par 1/9/81
Each share Class B Common no par received distribution of (1) share Class A Common no par 1/23/81
Class A Common no par reclassified as Class A Non-Vtg. Common no par 6/21/84
Placed in receivership 10/16/86
No stockholders' equity

LOCK HAVEN DEVELOPMENT CORP. (PA)
Out of existence affidavit filed 9/29/66
No stockholders' equity

LOCK JOINT PIPE CO. (NJ)
Each share 8% Preferred $100 par exchanged for (2) shares 8% Preferred $50 par in 1949
Each share Common no par exchanged for (40) shares Common $1 par 3/27/58
Common $1 par changed to 33-1/3¢ par and (2) additional shares issued 4/3/59
8% Preferred $50 par called for redemption 7/1/59
Merged into International Pipe & Ceramics Corp. 9/27/62
Each share Common 33-1/3¢ par exchanged for (1) share Common $1 par
International Pipe & Ceramics Corp. name changed to Interpace Corp. 4/25/68 which merged into Clevepak Corp. 8/15/83
(See Clevepak Corp.)

LOCK NUT CORP. OF AMERICA
Bankrupt
Assets sold in 1950
No stockholders' equity

LOCK THREAD CORP (DE)
Each share Common no par exchanged for (10) shares Common 10¢ par in 1951
Each share old Common 10¢ par exchanged for (0.1) share new Common 10¢ par 3/10/83
Stock Dividend - 10% 5/15/79
Under plan of merger name changed to Shelby Universal Corp. (DE) 12/1/83
Shelby Universal Corp. (DE) recapitalized as NA American Technologies, Inc. 4/3/2006 which name changed to JSX Energy, Inc. 8/30/2006

LOCKE MFG INC (CT)
Stock Dividends - 10% 12/01/1964; 30% 09/10/1968
Merged into Stellar Industries, Inc. (DE) 01/06/1970

Each share Common $2.50 par exchanged for (1) share Common 10¢ par
(See Stellar Industries, Inc. (DE))

LOCKE RICH MINERALS LTD (BC)
Delisted from Vancouver Stock Exchange 03/05/1996

LOCKE SCHULER CORP (DE)
Charter cancelled and declared inoperative and void for non-payment of taxes 3/1/76

LOCKE STEEL CHAIN CO. (CT)
Common $5 par changed to $2.50 par and (1) additional share issued 1/29/62
Stock Dividend - 10% 7/20/59
Name changed to Locke Manufacturing Companies, Inc. 12/3/63
Locke Manufacturing Companies, Inc. merged into Stellar Industries, Inc. (DE) 1/6/70
(See Stellar Industries, Inc. (DE))

LOCKERBIE & HOLE INC (AB)
Acquired by Aecon Group Inc. 04/01/2009
Each share Common no par exchanged for approximately (0.581024) share Common no par and $2.64 cash

LOCKHART CORP. (NV)
Merged into Zions Utah Bancorporation (NV) 01/10/1966
Each share Common $1 par exchanged for (1.3) shares Common no par
Zions Utah Bancorporation (NV) reincorporated in Utah 06/08/1971 which name changed to Zions Bancorporation 04/30/1987 which merged into Zions Bancorporation, N.A. (Salt Lake City, UT) 10/01/2018

LOCKHEED AIRCRAFT CORP. (CA)
Capital Stock $1 par split (2) for (1) by issuance of (1) additional share 07/16/1951
Capital Stock $1 par split (2) for (1) by issuance of (1) additional share 02/02/1959
Capital Stock $1 par split (4) for (3) by issuance of (0.33333333) additional share 06/28/1963
Capital Stock $1 par reclassified as Common $1 par 09/29/1976
Stock Dividend - 10% 01/26/1953
Name changed to Lockheed Corp. (CA) 09/30/1977
Lockheed Corp. (CA) reincorporated in Delaware 06/30/1986 which merged into Lockheed Martin Corp. 03/15/1995

LOCKHEED AIRCRAFT CORP. (DE)
Name changed to Southern California Aviation Corp. 00/00/1933
(See Southern California Aviation Corp.)

LOCKHEED CORP (DE)
Reincorporated 06/30/1986
$11.25 Conv. Preferred no par called for redemption 07/02/1982
Common no par split (3) for (1) by issuance of (2) additional shares 09/08/1983
State of incorporation changed from (CA) to (DE) 06/30/1986
Merged into Lockheed Martin Corp. 03/15/1995
Each share Common $1 par exchanged for (1.63) shares Common $1 par

LOCKLIN OIL CO (UT)
Voluntarily dissolved 07/31/2002
Details not available

LOCKPORT LIGHT HEAT & POWER CO.
Acquired by New York State Electric & Gas Corp. 00/00/1929
Details not available

LOCKSLEY CAP PARTNERS INC (AB)
Issue Information - 1,500,000 shares COM offered at $0.20 per share on 02/10/1997
Name changed to IPEC Ltd. 03/11/1998
IPEC Ltd. was acquired by Flint Energy Services Ltd. 11/27/2001
(See Flint Energy Services Ltd.)

LOCKWAVE TECHNOLOGIES INC (NV)
Recapitalized as Edison Renewables, Inc. 05/19/2003
Each share Common $0.001 par exchanged for (0.005) share Common $0.001 par
Edison Renewables, Inc. name changed to NextPhase Wireless, Inc. 01/26/2005 which name changed to MetroConnect Inc. 02/02/2009
(See MetroConnect Inc.)

LOCKWIN OIL & GAS CO. (CA)
Charter suspended for failure to file reports 10/01/1969

LOCKWOOD, GREENE & CO., INC.
Liquidated in 1929
Details not available

LOCKWOOD CO.
Name changed to Lockwood-Dutchess Inc. in 1947
(See Lockwood-Dutchess Inc.)

LOCKWOOD CORP (DE)
Merged into Alaska Interstate Co. (Alaska) 5/21/70
Each share Common $1 par exchanged for (0.71856) share Common $1 par
Alaska Interstate Co. (Alaska) reincorporated in Delaware as Enstar Corp. 6/4/82
(See Enstar Corp. (DE))

LOCKWOOD-DUTCHESS INC. (ME)
Liquidated in 1955
Details not available

LOCKWOOD GRADER CORP. (NE)
Class A Common $2 par and Class B Common $2 par changed to $1 par in 1963
Name changed to Marlow Corp. 5/2/66
(See Marlow Corp.)

LOCKWOOD KESSLER & BARTLETT INC (NY)
Reincorporated under the laws of Delaware as Viatech Inc. and Class A 25¢ par reclassified as Common 25¢ par 7/30/71
Viatech Inc. name changed to Continental Can Co., Inc. 10/21/92 which merged into Suiza Foods Corp. 5/29/98 which name changed to Dean Foods Co. (New) 12/21/2001

LOCKWOOD PETE INC (BC)
Merged into Appian Resources Ltd. 09/06/1989
Each share Common no par exchanged for (0.1586) share Common no par
Appian Resources Ltd. recapitalized as Sultan Minerals Inc. 05/04/1992 which recapitalized as Apex Resources Inc. 07/18/2016

LOCOMOTIVE FIREBOX CO.
Liquidation completed in 1952
Details not available

LOCTITE CORP (CT)
Common $1 par changed to no par and (1) additional share issued 10/25/1972
Common no par split (3) for (2) by issuance of (0.5) additional share 10/15/1973
Common no par split (2) for (1) by issuance of (1) additional share 11/30/1987
Common no par split (2) for (1) by

issuance of (1) additional share 03/19/1991
Stock Dividends - 100% 12/22/1966; 100% 01/15/1969; 150% 01/12/1970
Merged into Henkel KGaA 01/15/1997
Each share Common no par exchanged for $61 cash

LOCUST ARMS OPERATING CORP. (NY)
Liquidation completed in 1957
Details not available

LODDING ENGR CORP (MA)
Common $1 par reclassified as Class A Common $1 par in November 1963
Merged into Thermo Electron Corp. 11/15/71
Each share Class A Common $1 par exchanged for $8 cash

LODE RES CORP (BC)
Recapitalized as Lodex Resource Corp. 06/06/1990
Each share Common no par exchanged for (0.2) share Common no par
Lodex Resource Corp. recapitalized as LRX Capital Corp. (BC) 02/01/1993 which reincorporated in Canada as North American Tungsten Corp. Ltd. 05/01/1996

LODESTAR DRILLING CO. LTD. (AB)
Bankrupt in 1953
Details not available

LODESTAR ENERGY INC (AB)
Merged into Torrington Resources Ltd. 04/06/1998
Each share Class A Common no par exchanged for $1.15 cash
Each share Class B Common no par exchanged for either (0.6) share Common no par or $3 cash
Torrington Resources Ltd. acquired by Magin Energy Inc. (New) 07/18/1998 which was acquired by NCE Petrofund 07/03/2001 which name changed to Petrofund Energy Trust 11/01/2003 which merged into Penn West Energy Trust 07/04/2006 which reorganized as Penn West Petroleum Ltd. (New) 01/03/2011 which name changed to Obsidian Energy Ltd. 06/29/2017

LODESTAR ENERGY INC (BC)
Name changed 02/01/1980
Name changed from Lodestar Mines Ltd. to Lodestar Energy Inc. and Capital Stock $1 par changed to no par 02/01/1980
Recapitalized as Controlled Environment Farming International Ltd. 12/30/1985
Each share Capital Stock no par exchanged for (0.25) share Common no par
Controlled Environment Farming International Ltd. recapitalized as International Controlled Investments Inc. (BC) 10/09/1987 which reincorporated in Yukon as New Age Ventures Inc. 08/23/1991 which recapitalized as Great Panther Inc. 01/01/1998 which recapitalized as Great Panther Resources Ltd. (YT) 10/02/2003 which reincorporated in British Columbia 07/14/2004 which name changed to Great Panther Silver Ltd. 01/12/2010

LODESTAR EXPLS INC (BC)
Recapitalized as Precision International Resources Corp. 10/24/1994
Each share Common no par exchanged for (0.2) share Common no par
Precision International Resources Corp. recapitalized as Range Petroleum Corp. 05/07/1996 which recapitalized as Range Energy Inc. 05/15/2002
(See Range Energy Inc.)

FINANCIAL INFORMATION, INC.

LODESTAR MNG INC (DE)
Common $0.000001 par split (5.05) for (1) by issuance of (4.05) additional shares payable 01/28/2010 to holders of record 01/27/2010 Ex date - 01/29/2010
Name changed to Atlantic Green Power Holding Co. 03/03/2010
Atlantic Green Power Holding Co. recapitalized as Southern USA Resources Inc. 04/23/2012

LODESTAR YELLOWKNIFE GOLD MINES, LTD. (ON)
Charter cancelled for failure to file reports and pay taxes in 1956

LODEX RESOURCE CORP (BC)
Recapitalized as LRX Capital Corp. (BC) 2/1/93
Each share Common no par exchanged for (1/3) share Common no par
LRX Capital Corp. (BC) reincorporated in Canada as North American Tungsten Corp. Ltd. 5/1/96

LODGE & SHIPLEY CO (OH)
Liquidation completed
Each share Common $1 par exchanged for initial distribution of $0.60 cash 3/13/87
Assets transferred to LSP Liquidating Co. 3/20/87
(See LSP Liquidating Co.)

LODGE URANIUM MINES LTD. (ON)
Merged into St. Michael Uranium Mines Ltd. on a (1) for (2) basis in December 1954
St. Michael Uranium Mines Ltd. merged into Cadamet Mines Ltd. 11/17/58 which recapitalized as Terrex Mining Co. Ltd. 9/8/66
(See Terrex Mining Co. Ltd.)

LODGENET INTERACTIVE CORP (DE)
Name changed 01/15/2008
Name changed from LodgeNet Entertainment Corp. to LodgeNet Interactive Corp. 01/15/2008
Plan of reorganization under Chapter 11 Federal Bankruptcy proceedings effective 03/28/2013
No stockholders' equity

LODGIAN CAP TR I (DE)
Plan of reorganization under Chapter 11 Federal Bankruptcy Code effective 11/15/2002
Each Conv. Redeemable Equity Structured Trust Security 144A share received (0.24799988) share Lodgian Inc. new Common 1¢ par, (0.35966048) Common Stock Purchase Warrant, Class A expiring 11/25/2007 and (0.7173189) Common Stock Purchase Warrant, Class B expiring 11/25/2009

LODGIAN INC (DE)
Plan of reorganization under Chapter 11 Federal Bankruptcy Code effective 11/25/2002
Each share old Common 1¢ par exchanged for (0.0072999) share new Common 1¢ par, (0.0088417) Common Stock Purchase Warrant, Class A expiring in 2005 and (0.0273224) Common Stock Purchase Warrant, Class B expiring in 2005
Note: Unexchanged certificates were cancelled and became without value 11/29/2003
Each share new Common 1¢ par exchanged again for (1/3) share new Common 1¢ par 04/29/2004
Preferred called for redemption at $25 on 07/26/2004
Merged into LSREF Lodging Investments LLC 04/19/2010
Each share new Common 1¢ par exchanged for $2.50 cash

LODGISTIX INC (KS)
Merged into Sulcus Computer Corp. 02/25/1991
Each (13.479) shares Common no par exchanged for (1) Unit consisting of (2) shares Common no par and (2) Common Stock Purchase Warrants expiring 01/29/1995
Sulcus Computer Corp. name changed to Sulcus Hospitality Technologies Corp. 08/27/1997 which merged into Eltrax Systems, Inc. 03/25/1999 which name changed to Verso Technologies, Inc. 10/02/2000
(See Verso Technologies, Inc.)

LODI LIQUIDATING CORP. (NY)
Liquidation completed
Each share Common 10¢ par received initial distribution of (0.02) share Kawecki Chemical Co. Capital Stock 25¢ par 7/27/62
Each share Common 10¢ par received second and final distribution of (0.048065) share Kawecki Chemical Co. Capital Stock 25¢ par 6/18/63
Certificates were not retired and are now without value
(See listing for Kawecki Chemical Co.)

LODI METALS INC (BC)
Recapitalized as Valley High Ventures Ltd. 06/26/1996
Each share Common no par exchanged for (0.125) share Common no par
(See Valley High Ventures Ltd.)

LOEB M LTD (ON)
Capital Stock no par split (3) for (1) by issuance of (2) additional shares 6/12/64
Capital Stock no par reclassified as Common no par 7/30/65
5-3/4% Preference $50 par called for redemption 6/15/79
Merged into Provigo Inc. (Old) 6/16/79
Each share Common no par exchanged for (0.5) share Common no par
Provigo Inc. (Old) name changed to Univa Inc. 5/22/92 which name changed to Provigo Inc. (New) 5/25/94 which was acquired by Loblaw Companies Ltd. 12/10/98

LOEHMANNS HLDGS INC (MD)
Merged into Loehmann's Inc. (New) 5/8/96
Each share Class B Common no par exchanged for (0.223446) share Common 1¢ par
$0.056 Preferred Ser. A no par called for redemption 6/14/96
Acquired by Crescent Capital Investments, Inc. 10/13/2004
Each share Common 1¢ par exchanged for $23 cash

LOEHMANNS INC (NY)
Common $1 par split (3) for (2) by issuance of (0.5) additional share 11/30/67
Stock Dividends - 50% 8/6/69; 50% 11/14/77
Merged into AEA Investors Inc. 1/8/81
Each share Common $1 par exchanged for $31.30 cash

LOEHMANNS INC NEW (DE)
Plan of reorganization under Chapter 11 Federal Bankruptcy Code effective 10/10/2000
No stockholders' equity

LOETZER DON INC (NY)
Recapitalized as Quality Packaging Supply Corp. 11/15/90
Each share Common $0.0001 par exchanged for (0.04) share Common $0.001 par
(See Quality Packaging Supply Corp.)

LOEW DRUG CO., INC. (DE)
Bankrupt in 1951
Details not available

LOEW'S BOSTON THEATRES (MA)
Completely liquidated 8/25/66
Each share Common $25 par exchanged for first and final distribution of $20 par

LOEW'S BUFFALO THEATRES INC. (NY)
Name changed to Midland Properties, Inc. 3/6/31
(See Midland Properties, Inc.)

LOEW'S DAYTON THEATRE CO. (OH)
Land Trust Certificates $1000 par called for redemption 4/1/72

LOEW'S INC. NEW (DE)
Name changed to Metro-Goldwyn-Mayer Inc. (Old) 2/5/60
Metro-Goldwyn-Mayer Inc. (Old) name changed to MGM Grand Hotels, Inc. 5/30/80
(See MGM Grand Hotels, Inc.)

LOEW'S INC. OLD (DE)
Common no par split (3) for (1) by issuance of (2) additional shares 5/9/45
Under plan of reorganization each share Common no par exchanged for (0.5) share Loew's Inc. (DE) (New) Common no par and (0.5) share Common $1 par of Loew's Theatres, Inc. 3/12/59
(See each company's listing)

LOEW'S LONDON THEATRES LTD.
Liquidated in 1943
Details not available

LOEW'S OHIO THEATRES
Property sold at foreclosure in 1934
Details not available

LOEWEN GROUP CAP L P (DE)
Reorganized as Alderwoods Group Inc. 1/2/2002
Each 9.45% Monthly Income Preferred Security Ser. A no par exchanged for (0.1656) Common Stock Purchase Warrant expiring 1/2/2007
Note: Unexchanged certificates were cancelled and became without value 1/2/2004

LOEWEN GROUP INC (BC)
7.75% Conv. 1st Preferred Ser. A $10 par called for redemption 5/29/90
Common no par split (2) for (1) by issuance of (1) additional share 7/12/91
Plan of reorganization under Chapter 11 Federal Bankruptcy Code effective 1/2/2002
No stockholders' equity

LOEWEN ONDAATJE MCCUTCHEON INC (ON)
Name changed to Ondaatje Corp. 12/09/1992
Ondaatje Corp. name changed to Global Equity Corp. 06/27/1996 which merged into PICO Holdings Inc. (CA) 12/16/1998 which reincorporated in Delaware 05/31/2017

LOEWS CINEPLEX ENTMT CORP (DE)
Plan of reorganization under Chapter 11 Federal Bankruptcy Code effective 3/21/2002
No stockholders' equity

LOEWS CORP (DE)
Each share Carolina Group Stock 1¢ par exchanged for (1) share Lorillard, Inc. Common 1¢ par 06/10/2008
(See Lorillard, Inc.)
(Additional Information in Active)

LOEWS MARCUS THEATRES LTD (CANADA)
Proclaimed dissolved 12/6/76

LOEWS THEATRES INC (NY)
Common $1 par split (5) for (2) by issuance of (1.5) additional shares 1/30/68
Common $1 par split (3) for (1) by issuance of (2) additional shares 12/19/68
Reincorporated under the laws of Delaware as Loews Corp. 2/1/71

LOFT, INC.
Under plan of merger name changed to Pepsi-Cola Co. in 1941
Pepsi-Cola Co. name changed to PepsiCo, Inc. (DE) 6/10/65 which reincorporated in North Carolina 12/4/86

LOFT CANDY CORP (NY)
Name changed to Briarcliff Candy Corp. 5/5/71
(See Briarcliff Candy Corp.)

LOFTWERKS INC (NV)
Name changed to Sulja Bros. Building Supplies, Ltd. 7/31/2006

LOG ON AMERICA INC (DE)
Issue Information - 2,200,000 shares COM offered at $10 per share on 04/22/1999
Chapter 7 bankruptcy proceedings terminated 07/13/2011
No stockholders' equity

LOG PT TECHNOLOGIES INC (CO)
SEC revoked common stock registration 07/22/2010

LOGAL EDUCATIONAL SOFTWARE & SYS LTD (ISRAEL)
Name changed to SimPlayer.com Ltd 10/28/1999
(See SimPlayer.com Ltd.)

LOGAN COAL CO.
Insolvent in 1940
Details not available

LOGAN GEAR CO. (OH)
Name changed to Bingham Stamping Co. 00/00/1940
Bingham Stamping Co. name changed to Bingham-Herbrand Corp. 00/00/1947 which was acquired by Van Norman Industries Inc. 12/05/1956 which merged into Universal American Corp. (DE) (Ctfs. dtd. prior to 01/12/1968) 01/31/1962 which merged into Gulf & Western Industries, Inc. (DE) 01/12/1968
(See Gulf & Western Industries, Inc. (DE))

LOGAN (JONATHAN), INC. (DE)
See - Jonathan Logan Inc

LOGAN INTL CORP (WA)
Name changed to Trimaine Holdings Inc. 11/8/2001

LOGAN INTL INC (AB)
Acquired by Rubicon Oilfield International Holdings, L.P. 10/26/2016
Each share Common no par exchanged for $1.58886 cash
Note: Unexchanged certificates will be cancelled and become without value 10/26/2019

LOGAN MANOR CO. (IL)
Liquidation completed 9/28/56
Details not available

LOGAN MINES LTD (BC)
Recapitalized as Consolidated Logan Mines Ltd. 7/21/92
Each share Common no par exchanged for (1/3) share Common no par
Consolidated Logan Mines Ltd. recapitalized as Logan Resources Ltd. 1/29/2002

LOGAN PORCUPINE MINES, LTD. (ON)
Adjudicated bankrupt in 1962
No stockholders' equity

LOGAN RES (AB)
Acquired by Rio Alto Exploration Ltd. 11/1/91
Each share Common no par exchanged for (1.45) shares Common no par
Rio Alto Exploration Ltd. merged into Canadian Natural Resources Ltd. 7/1/2002

LOGANS ROADHOUSE INC (TN)
Common 1¢ par split (3) for (2) by issuance of (0.5) additional share payable 06/10/1996 to holders of record 05/20/1996
Merged into CBRL Group Inc. 02/16/1999
Each share Common 1¢ par exchanged for 24¢ cash

LOGETRONICS (DE)
Merged into DBA Systems, Inc. 04/27/1984
Each share Common $0.16666666 par exchanged for (0.5996) share Common 10¢ par
Note: An additional (0.0914) share was placed in escrow
DBA Systems, Inc. merged into Titan Corp. 02/27/1998
(See Titan Corp.)

LOGIBEC GROUPE INFORMATIQUE LTEE (CANADA)
Acquired by OMERS LGI Inc. 08/04/2010
Each share Common no par exchanged for $26 cash

LOGIC CORP. (PA)
Reincorporated under the laws of Delaware and Capital Stock no par changed to 5¢ par 6/17/71
(See Logic Corp. (DE))

LOGIC CORP (DE)
Merged into General Telephone & Electronics Corp. 11/2/73
Each share Capital Stock 5¢ par exchanged for $1.22 cash

LOGIC ELECTRS INC (MA)
Declared dissolved for failure to file reports and pay taxes 12/11/74

LOGIC WKS INC (DE)
Merged into PLATINUM Technology, Inc. 05/28/1998
Each share Common 1¢ par exchanged for (0.5769) share Common 1¢ par
PLATINUM Technology, Inc. name changed to Platinum Technology International Inc. 01/04/1999 which merged into Computer Associates International, Inc. 06/29/1999 which name changed to CA, Inc. 02/01/2006

LOGICA HLDGS INC (NV)
Name changed to Dolphin Digital Media, Inc. (NV) 08/18/2008
Dolphin Digital Media, Inc. (NV) reincorporated in Florida 12/03/2014 which recapitalized as Dolphin Entertainment, Inc. 09/18/2017

LOGICAL COMPUTER SVCS NY LTD (NY)
Recapitalized as Coronado Industries Inc. (NY) 08/31/1996
Each share Common $0.001 par exchanged for (0.2) share Common $0.001 par
Coronado Industries Inc. (NY) reincorporated in Nevada 10/29/1996 which name changed to Continental Fuels, Inc. 03/23/2007
(See Continental Fuels Inc.)

LOGICALOPTIONS INTL INC (CANADA)
Each (2,700,000) shares old Common no par exchanged for (1) share new Common no par 12/31/2002
Note: In effect holders received $0.01

cash per share and public interest was eliminated

LOGICIEL SYS LTD (AB)
Struck off register and declared dissolved for failure to file returns 8/1/93

LOGICOM INC (NV)
Each share old Common $0.001 par exchanged for (0.727273) shares new Common $0.001 par 12/16/2005
Name changed to Skins Inc. 04/18/2006
(See Skins Inc.)

LOGICON INC (CA)
Reincorporated 8/14/78
Each share Common $1 par exchanged for (13) shares Common 10¢ par 4/29/69
State of incorporation changed from (CA) to (DE) 8/14/78
Common 10¢ par split (2) for (1) by issuance of (1) additional share 3/8/82
Common 10¢ par split (3) for (2) by issuance of (0.5) additional share 9/1/83
Common 10¢ par split (2) for (1) by issuance of (1) additional share 12/3/91
Common 10¢ par split (2) for (1) by issuance of (1) additional share 9/13/95
Merged into Northrop Grumman Corp. 8/1/97
Each share Common 10¢ par exchanged for (0.6161) share Common no par
Northrop Grumman Corp. reorganized as Northrop Grumman Corp. (Holding Company) 4/2/2001

LOGICON PRODS LTD (BC)
Struck off register and declared dissolved for failure to file returns 3/26/93

LOGICSYS INC (ON)
Name changed to Wisper Inc. 01/29/2001
Wisper Inc. recapitalized as Eclips Inc. 03/29/2004 which recapitalized as Cadillac Mining Corp. (ON) 07/10/2006 which reincorporated in British Columbia 05/22/2007 which merged into Pilot Gold Inc. 08/29/2014 which name changed to Liberty Gold Corp. 05/12/2017

LOGICVISION INC (DE)
Each share old Common $0.0001 par exchanged for (0.4) share new Common $0.0001 par 03/12/2008
Merged into Mentor Graphics Corp. 08/18/2009
Each share Common $0.0001 par exchanged for (0.2006) share Common no par
(See Mentor Graphics Corp.)

LOGILITY INC (GA)
Issue Information - 2,200,000 shares COM offered at $14.50 per share on 10/07/1997
Acquired by American Software, Inc. 07/06/2009
Each share Common no par exchanged for $7.02 cash

LOGIMETRICS INC (DE)
Class A Common 10¢ par split (5) for (4) by issuance of (0.25) additional share 6/24/86
Liquidation approved 9/20/2002
No stockholders' equity

LOGIO INC (NV)
Merged into Pacific WebWorks, Inc. 01/31/2001
Each share Common $0.001 par exchanged for (0.15151515) share Common $0.001 par
Pacific WebWorks, Inc. name changed to Heyu Biological Technology Corp. 06/28/2018

LOGIPHONE GROUP INC (DE)
New Common 1¢ par split (2) for (1) by issuance of (1) additional share payable 3/21/97 to holders of record 11/29/96
Charter cancelled and declared inoperative and void for non-payment of taxes 3/1/99

LOGIQ ADVANTAGE BD FD (ON)
Trust terminated 12/29/2017
Each Class A Unit received $8.47664 cash
Each Class F Unit received $9.675 cash

LOGIQ ADVANTAGE OIL & GAS INCOME FD (ON)
Name changed to Redwood Energy Income Fund 12/20/2017
(See Redwood Energy Income Fund)

LOGIQ ADVANTAGE VIP INCOME FD (ON)
Name changed to Redwood Advantage Monthly Income Fund 12/20/2017
Redwood Advantage Monthly Income Fund merged into Purpose Multi-Asset Income Fund 05/04/2018

LOGIQ ASSET MGMT INC (AB)
Reorganized under the laws of British Columbia as Flow Capital Corp. 06/11/2018
Each share Common no par exchanged for (0.08333333) share Common no par

LOGIQ VIP INCOME FD (ON)
Name changed to Redwood Monthly Income Fund 12/20/2017
Redwood Monthly Income Fund merged into Purpose Multi-Asset Income Fund 05/04/2018

LOGISOFT CORP (DE)
Name changed to Team Sports Entertainment, Inc. 05/18/2001
Team Sports Entertainment, Inc. name changed to Idea Sports Entertainment Group, Inc. 11/09/2004 which recapitalized as HealthSport, Inc. 05/16/2006
(See HealthSport, Inc.)

LOGISTIC DISTR SYS INTL GROUP INC (NV)
Recapitalized as Vortices, Inc. 12/6/95
Each share Common $0.001 par exchanged for (0.25) share Common $0.001 par
Vortices, Inc. name changed to Simulator Systems, Inc. 4/21/98 which name changed to Casino Pirata.Com Ltd. 5/5/99 which name changed to Advantage Technologies, Inc. 11/30/99 which recapitalized as Expo Holdings Inc. 5/30/2006

LOGISTICS INDS CORP (PA)
Reincorporated 08/17/1970
State of incorporation changed from (NY) to (PA) 08/17/1970
Merged into Lydall, Inc. (CT) 06/15/1977
Each share Conv. Preferred $1 par exchanged for (1) share $1 Preferred $11 par
Each share Common 10¢ par exchanged for (0.42) share Common $3.33-1/3 par or $3.60 cash
Note: Option to receive cash or stock per share Common expired (21) days after the effective date after which holders received cash
Lydall, Inc. (CT) reincorporated in Delaware 09/30/1987

LOGISTICS MGMT RES INC (CO)
Name changed to American Business Corp. 6/28/2004

LOGITECH CORP (DE)
Name changed to Toxic Control Technologies Inc. 8/16/83
(See Toxic Control Technologies Inc.)

LOGITECH INTL S A (SWITZERLAND)
Issue Information - 2,000,000 ADR'S offered at $16 per ADR on 03/27/1997
Sponsored ADR's for Ordinary split (2) for (1) by issuance of (1) additional ADR payable 07/10/2000 to holders of record 07/03/2000
Sponsored ADR's for Ordinary split (2) for (1) by issuance of (1) additional ADR payable 06/30/2005 to holders of record 06/29/2005
Ex date - 07/01/2005
Sponsored ADR's for Ordinary split (2) for (1) by issuance of (1) additional ADR payable 07/14/2006 to holders of record 07/13/2006
Ex date - 07/17/2006
ADR agreement terminated 10/20/2006
Each Sponsored ADR for Ordinary exchanged for $32.98595 cash
(Additional Information in Active)

LOGITEK INC (NY)
Common 1¢ par split (4) for (1) by issuance of (3) additional shares 12/20/85
Common 1¢ par split (2) for (1) by issuance of (1) additional share 10/10/86
Common 1¢ par split (2) for (1) by issuance of (1) additional share 8/6/90
Merged into North Atlantic Instruments, Inc. 8/24/99
Each share Common 1¢ par exchanged for $0.88 cash

LOGIX ENTERPRISES INC (BC)
Recapitalized as Transac Enterprise Corp. 11/27/2002
Each share Common no par exchanged for (0.125) share Common no par
Transac Enterprise Corp. name changed to Evergreen Gaming Corp. 11/1/2006

LOGO INDS CORP (NV)
Common $0.001 par split (10) for (1) by issuance of (9) additional shares payable 02/05/2007 to holders of record 01/31/2007 Ex date - 02/06/2007
Reorganized as Malwin Ventures, Inc. 01/22/2009
Each share Common $0.001 par exchanged for (4) shares Common $0.001 par

LOGO RES LTD (BC)
Delisted from Vancouver Stock Exchange 03/01/1989

LOGOS CORP (DE)
Name changed 7/9/81
Name changed 4/14/83
Name changed from Logos Development Corp. to Logos Computer Systems, Inc. 7/9/81
Name and state of incorporation changed from Logos Computer Systems, Inc. (NY) to Logos Corp. (DE) 4/14/83
Each share old Common 1¢ par exchanged for (0.004) share new Common 1¢ par 4/1/91
Each share new Common 1¢ par exchanged again for (0.1) share new Common 1¢ par 1/25/93
Acquired by a private company in 1993
Details not available

LOGOS INTL INC (NV)
Recapitalized 5/15/92
Recapitalized from Logos Scientific, Inc. to Logos International Inc. 5/12/92
Each share Common $0.001 par exchanged for (0.01) share Common $0.001 par
Each (18) shares old Common $0.001 par exchanged for (1) share new Common $0.001 par 7/8/92

Each share new Common $0.001 par exchanged again for (0.05) share new Common $0.001 par 6/29/94
Name changed to Omap Holdings Inc. 10/25/95
Omap Holdings Inc. recapitalized as China Food & Beverage Co. 4/10/97

LOGSEARCH INC (NV)
Name changed to Guilin Paper, Inc. 06/21/2007
(See Guilin Paper, Inc.)

LOGTUNG RES LTD (BC)
Merged into Regional Resources Ltd. 8/28/82
Each share Capital Stock no par exchanged for (1) share Class A Common no par
Regional Resources Ltd. merged into Imperial Metals Corp. (Old) 11/15/96 which reorganized as Imperial Metals Corp. (New) 4/30/2002

LOHENGRIN INC (NV)
Name changed to Western Capital Financial Corp. 04/22/1988
Western Capital Financial Corp. recapitalized as Global Diamond Resources, Inc. 07/17/1995
(See Global Diamond Resources, Inc.)

LOHS SINFULLY GOOD ICE CREAM & COOKIES INC (CANADA)
Dissolved for non-compliance 08/31/1989

LOIL CORP (CO)
Recapitalized as Medsafe Products International Ltd. 7/7/87
Each share Common $0.001 par exchanged for (0.1) share Common no par
(See Medsafe Products International Ltd.)

LOIS / USA INC (DE)
Chapter 11 bankruptcy proceedings terminated 08/20/2009
No stockholders' equity

LOISAN RED LAKE GOLD MINES LTD (ON)
Name changed to Grandview Energy Resources Inc. and Common $1 par changed to no par 11/09/1979
Grandview Energy Resources Inc. recapitalized as Consolidated Grandview Inc. 09/22/1983 which name changed to Grandview Gold Inc. 07/06/2004 which recapitalized as PUDO Inc. 07/13/2015

LOISLAW COM INC (DE)
Merged into Wolters Kluwer N.V. 02/01/2001
Each share Common $0.001 par exchanged for $4.3545 cash

LOJAS AMERICANAS S A (BRAZIL)
ADR agreement terminated 1/5/2004
Each Sponsored ADR for Preferred exchanged for $13.59 cash

LOJAS ARAPUA S A (BRAZIL)
GDR agreement terminated 03/18/2011
No GDR's remain outstanding

LOKI GOLD CORP (BC)
Merged into Viceroy Resource Corp. 05/30/1996
Each share Common no par exchanged for (0.426) share Common no par
Viceroy Resource Corp. merged into Quest Capital Corp. (BC) 06/30/2003 which reincorporated in Canada 05/27/2008 which name changed to Sprott Resource Lending Corp. 09/10/2010 which merged into Sprott Inc. 07/24/2013

LOKI MINES LTD. (ON)
Charter cancelled for failure to pay taxes and file returns 5/6/80

LOKI RESOURCES INC. (ON)
Reorganized under the laws of Canada as Mill City Gold Inc. 7/14/87
Each share Common no par exchanged for (0.1) share Common no par
Mill City Gold Inc. reorganized as Mill City Gold Mining Corp. 12/14/88 which name changed to Mill City International Inc. 1/8/98 which recapitalized as E3 Energy Inc. 12/23/2002
(See E3 Energy Inc.)

LOLLIPOP DAYCARE LTD (BC)
Struck off register and declared dissolved for failure to file returns 2/25/94

LOM LOGISTICS INC (LA)
SEC revoked common stock registration 03/25/2009

LOM RIV GOLD CORP (BC)
Name changed to Catalina Energy Corp. 10/17/2001
Catalina Energy Corp. recapitalized as Catalina Metals Corp. 02/14/2011 which name changed to True Grit Resources Ltd. 06/28/2012

LOMA CORP. (CO)
Dissolved 11/30/64
No stockholders' equity

LOMA PETE RES LTD (AB)
Recapitalized as Loma Oil & Gas Ltd. 11/21/1997
Each share Common no par exchanged for (0.5) share Common no par

LOMA URANIUM CORP. (CO)
Name changed to Loma Corp. in 1958
(See Loma Corp.)

LOMA VERDE INC (NV)
Each share old Common $0.001 par exchanged for (56) shares new Common $0.001 par 3/21/2007
Name changed to Clean Power Concepts, Inc. 4/2/2007

LOMA VISTA CAP INC (ON)
Reorganized under the laws of Canada as as BitGold Inc. 05/13/2015
Each share Common no par exchanged for (0.06060606) share Common no par
BitGold Inc. name changed to GoldMoney Inc. 07/30/2015

LOMAK PETE INC (DE)
Each share old Common 1¢ par exchanged for (0.06666666) share new Common 1¢ par 11/23/1992
Under plan of merger name changed to Range Resources Corp. 08/25/1998

LOMART INDS INC (DE)
Merged into Hoffinger Holding Corp. 7/27/82
Each share Common 50¢ par exchanged for $7 cash

LOMART PERFECTED DEVICES, INC. (DE)
Common 50¢ par split (3) for (2) by issuance of (0.5) additional share 12/29/67
Name changed to Lomart Industries, Inc. 6/30/75
(See Lomart Industries, Inc.)

LOMAS & NETTLETON MTG INVS (MA)
Shares of Bene. Int. no par split (3) for (2) by issuance of (0.5) additional share 02/19/1985
Name changed to Liberte Investors and Shares of Bene. Int. no par reclassified as Common no par 12/21/1992
Liberte Investors (MA) reincorporated in Delaware as Liberte Investors Inc. 08/16/1996 which name changed to First Acceptance Corp. 04/30/2004

LOMAS FINL CORP NEW (DE)
Plan of reorganization under Chapter 11 Federal Bankruptcy Code effective 3/7/97
No Common stockholders' equity

LOMAS FINL CORP OLD (DE)
Name changed 10/28/88
Common $2 par split (2) for (1) by issuance of (1) additional share 10/31/83
Common $2 par split (3) for (2) by issuance of (0.5) additional share 10/31/86
Name changed from Lomas & Nettleton Financial Corp. to Lomas Financial Corp. (Old) 10/28/88
Reorganized under Chapter 11 Federal Bankruptcy Code 1/31/92
Each share Common $2 par exchanged for (0.00928446) share Lomas Financial Corp. (New) Common $1 par, (0.14884283) Common Stock Purchase Warrant expiring 11/1/2001 and (0.08235013) share Vista Properties, Inc. Class A Common $1 par
(See each company's listing)

LOMAS MTG CORP (MD)
Name changed to Capstead Mortgage Corp. 11/06/1989

LOMAS MTG SECS FD INC (MD)
Name changed to Tyler Cabot Mortgage Securities Fund, Inc. 2/19/91
Tyler Cabot Mortgage Securities Fund, Inc. acquired by Capstead Mortgage Corp. 12/2/92

LOMBARDI MEDIA CORP (ON)
Each (300,000) shares old Common no par exchanged for (1) share new Common no par 09/14/2007
Note: In effect holders received $0.22 cash per share and public interest was eliminated

LOMBARDI MICHAEL PUBG INC (ON)
Name changed to Lombardi Media Corp. 11/19/1996
(See Lombardi Media Corp.)

LOMBARDY HOTEL CORP (NY)
Liquidation completed 3/27/57
Details not available

LOMEGA EXPLORATIONS LTD. (ON)
Charter cancelled in January 1962

LOMEGA GOLD MINES LTD. (ON)
Name changed to Lomega Explorations Ltd. in 1956
(See Lomega Explorations Ltd.)

LOMIKO ENTERPRISES LTD (BC)
Recapitalized as Lomiko Resources Inc. 07/28/2006
Each share Common no par exchanged for (0.2) share Common no par
Lomiko Resources Inc. name changed to Lomiko Metals Inc. 09/29/2008

LOMIKO RESOURCES INC (BC)
Name changed to Lomiko Metals Inc. 09/29/2008

LOMMA INTL INC (PA)
Name changed to Carlton International Corp. 7/28/75

LOMO JSC (RUSSIA)
GDR agreement terminated 04/16/2018
No GDR's remain outstanding

LOMPOC SAVINGS & LOAN ASSOCIATION (CA)
Acquired by Imperial Corp. of America (CA) 3/14/73
Each share Common $10 par exchanged for (6) shares Common $1 par
Imperial Corp. of America (CA) reincorporated in Delaware 9/21/87
(See Imperial Corp. of America (DE))

LONDON & OVERSEAS FREIGHTERS LTD (BERMUDA)
Reorganized 7/30/92
Reorganized from London & Overseas Freighters Plc (England) to London & Overseas Freighters Ltd (Bermuda) 7/30/92
Each ADR for Ordinary 25p exchanged for (1) ADR for Ordinary 25¢ par
Unsponsored ADR's for Ordinary 25¢ par reclassified as Sponsored ADR's for Ordinary 25¢ par 11/15/93
Name changed to Frontline Ltd. 5/11/98
(See Frontline Ltd.)

LONDON & PAC HEALTHCARE INC (DE)
Name changed to London Pacific & Partners, Inc. 10/08/2009
London Pacific & Partners, Inc. recapitalized as Valentine Mark Corp. 03/20/2015

LONDON & SCOTTISH MARINE OIL PLC (ENGLAND)
Recapitalized as Lasmo PLC 10/16/1989
Each Unsponsored ADR for Ordinary 25p par exchanged for (0.25) Sponsored ADR for Ordinary 25p par
Lasmo PLC acquired by Eni S.p.A. 04/17/2001

LONDON CANADIAN INVESTMENT CORP. (QC)
Recapitalized in 1951
Each share 5% Preferred $100 par exchanged for $20 of 3% Notes, (1) share $3 Preferred $25 par, (1) share Class A $5 par and $20 cash
Common no par changed to $1 par
Assets acquired by United Corporations Ltd. 12/23/59
Each share $3 Preferred $25 par exchanged for (2) shares 5% Preferred 1959 Ser. $30 par and (0.5) share Class B no par
Each share Class A $5 par exchanged for (1.5) shares 5% Preferred 1959 Ser. $30 and (0.5) share Class B no par
Each share Common $1 par exchanged for (0.5) share Class B no par and $1.26 cash

LONDON DRY LTD (SC)
Common 20¢ par and Class A Common 20¢ par split (2) for (1) by issuance of additional share respectively 7/1/68
Class A Common 20¢ par reclassified as Common 20¢ par 4/22/71
Common 20¢ par changed to 10¢ par and (1) additional share issued 8/23/71
Involuntarily dissolved for failure to file reports and pay taxes 5/20/88

LONDON ELECTRICITY PLC (UNITED KINGDOM)
ADR agreement terminated 5/2/97
Each Final Instalment ADR for Ordinary 50p par exchanged for $11.43 cash

LONDON FIN & INVT GROUP P L C (ENGLAND)
ADR agreement terminated 06/03/2009
Each ADR for Ordinary 10p par exchanged for $0.21015 cash

LONDON FINL CORP (OH)
Merged into Camco Financial Corp. 08/20/2004
Each share Common no par exchanged for either (1.56342) shares Common $1 par or $26.50 cash
Note: Option to receive cash expired 09/17/2004
(See Camco Financial Corp.)

LONDON GROCERS LTD. (ENGLAND)
Stock Dividends - ADR's for Ordinary Reg. and A Ordinary Reg.; 25% in ADR's for A Ordinary Reg. 08/22/1962; 20% in ADR's for A Ordinary Reg. 08/12/1963
Name changed to Victor Value (Holdings) Ltd. 09/11/1964
Victor Value (Holdings) Ltd. acquired by Tesco Stores (Holdings) Ltd. 11/08/1968 which name changed to Tesco PLC 07/29/1983

LONDON GULL LAKE MINES LTD.
Liquidated in 1936
Details not available

LONDON HOUSE INC (DE)
Acquired by Maxwell Communication Corp. PLC 11/4/88
Each share Common 10¢ par exchanged for $13.25 cash

LONDON INS GROUP INC (ON)
Merged into Great-West Lifeco Inc. 12/18/97
Each share Common no par exchanged for $34 cash
Adjustable Rate Preferred Class 1 Ser. A no par called for redemption 12/22/97
7.25% Preferred Class I Ser. D no par called for redemption at $25 on 12/31/2002
7.20% Preferred Class I Ser. E no par called for redemption at $25 on 12/31/2002
Public interest eliminated

LONDON INTL GROUP PLC (ENGLAND)
Each Unsponsored ADR for Ordinary Reg. 10p par exchanged for (0.2) Sponsored ADR for Ordinary Reg. 10p par 11/26/1986
ADR agreement terminated 11/04/1999
Each Sponsored ADR for Ordinary 10p par exchanged for $12.0425 cash

LONDON LIFE INS CO (CANADA)
Name changed 6/29/66
Name changed from London Life Insurance Co. to London Life Insurance Co.-London Life, Compagnie d'Assurance-Vie 6/29/66
Acquired by Great-West Life Assurance Co. in 1997
Details not available

LONDON LIGHT & POWER CO.
Merged into Ohio Edison Co. 7/5/30
Details not available

LONDON PAC & PARTNERS INC (DE)
Recapitalized as Valentine Mark Corp. 03/20/2015
Each share Common $0.001 par exchanged for (0.001) share Common $0.001 par

LONDON PAC GROUP LTD (CHANNEL ISLANDS)
Sponsored ADR's for Ordinary 5p par split (4) for (1) by issuance of (3) additional ADR's payable 03/24/2000 to holders of record 03/23/2000 Ex date - 03/27/2000
Each old Sponsored ADR for Ordinary 5p par exchanged for (0.1) new Sponsored ADR for Ordinary 5p par 06/24/2002
Name changed to Berkeley Technology Ltd. 06/16/2003
(See Berkeley Technology Ltd.)

LONDON PRIDE SILVER MINES LTD (BC)
Recapitalized as L.P. Industries Ltd. 9/27/73
Each share Capital Stock 50¢ par exchanged for (0.2) share Capital Stock par
L.P. Industries Ltd. recapitalized as May-Ralph Resources Ltd. 7/25/79
(See May-Ralph Resources Ltd.)

LONDON RUBR LTD (ENGLAND)
Name changed to L.R.C. International PLC 05/23/1969
L.R.C. International plc name changed to London International Group PLC 11/15/1985
(See London International Group PLC)

LONDON SILVER CORP (BC)
Delisted from Vancouver Stock Exchange 03/01/1989

LONDON SOFTWARE INDS INC (DE)
Name changed to Corspan, Inc. 12/14/2001
Corspan, Inc. recapitalized as Oncthera Inc. 03/19/2003 which name changed to Evolve Oncology Inc. 11/26/2003 which recapitalized as Reparotech, Inc. 09/26/2007 which name changed to Nextrata Energy Inc. 01/07/2010

LONDON STRAUSS CAP CORP (ON)
Name changed to Viking Gold Corp. 9/5/96
(See Viking Gold Corp.)

LONDON STREET RWY. CO. (CANADA)
Acquired by the City of London, ONT in 1952
Details not available

LONDON TER INC (NY)
Completely liquidated 1/19/78
Each share Class A Common $1 par exchanged for first and final distribution of $55.14 cash
Each share Class B Common $1 par exchanged for first and final distribution of $55.14 cash

LONDON TIN LTD (ENGLAND)
Reorganized 00/00/1937
Each share 7-1/2% Preference 10s par exchanged for (3) shares Ordinary 4s par and 6d cash
Each share Ordinary 10s par exchanged for (2) shares Ordinary 4s par
Ordinary 4s par and ADR's for Ordinary 4s par changed to 20p par per currency change 02/15/1971
ADR basis changed from (1:10) to (1:1) 08/14/1974
Stock Dividend Ordinary - 20% 10/16/1961
Stock Dividend - ADR's - 20% 10/20/1961
Merged into LTMB Corp. 10/12/1976
Each share Ordinary 20p par exchanged for $6.04 cash
Each ADR for Ordinary 2p par exchanged for $2.31 cash

LONDONDERRIE TRAIL INC (AB)
Issue Information - 2,000,000 shares COM offered at $0.15 per share on 02/08/2002
Name changed to Mosaic Mapping Corp. 10/02/2002
Mosaic Mapping Corp. merged into Pulse Data Inc. 05/25/2004 which name changed to Pulse Seismic Inc. 05/28/2009

LONDONTOWN CORP (MD)
Merged into Interco Inc. (Old) 2/25/76
Each share Common 25¢ par exchanged for (0.6) share Common no par
(See Interco Inc. (Old))

LONDONTOWN HLDGS CORP (DE)
Common went private under the name of London Fog Corp. 5/7/92
Details not available

LONDONTOWN MANUFACTURING CO. (MD)
Common $1 par changed to 50¢ par and (1) additional share issued 5/27/64
Common 50¢ par changed to 25¢ par and (1) additional share issued 4/15/66
Name changed to Londontown Corp. 5/17/74

Londontown Corp. merged into Interco Inc. (Old) 2/25/76
(See Interco Inc. (Old))

L1 CAP CORP (AB)
Merged into Breaking Point Developments Inc. 07/22/2010
Each share Common no par exchanged for (1.333) shares Class A Common no par

LONE CREEK MINES LTD (AB)
Struck off register for failure to file annual returns 2/15/77

LONE JACK RES LTD (BC)
Name changed to Performance Minerals of Canada Ltd. 2/14/89
(See Performance Minerals of Canada Ltd.)

LONE MTN FEDT GAS & OIL LTD (BC)
Struck off register and declared dissolved for failure to file returns 6/12/69

LONE MTN MINES INC (NV)
Name changed to Convenientcast, Inc. 09/21/2009
Convenientcast, Inc. name changed to Dewmar International BMC, Inc. 05/17/2012

LONE MTN MNG CORP (DE)
Charter cancelled and declared inoperative and void for non-payment of taxes 03/01/1997

LONE OAK ACQUISITION CORP (CAYMAN ISLANDS)
Issue Information - 4,000,000 UNITS consisting of (1) share ORD and (1) WT offered at $8 per Unit on 03/24/2011
Name changed to Arabella Exploration, Inc. 02/27/2014

LONE OAK INC (DE)
Each (15) shares old Common 1¢ par exchanged for (1) share new Common 1¢ par 3/26/99
Name changed to Politics.com Inc. 7/27/99
Politics.com Inc. recapitalized as English Language Learning & Instruction Systems, Inc. 2/1/2001
(See English Language Learning & Instruction Systems, Inc.)

LONE PINE HLDGS INC (NV)
Name changed to Flux Power Holdings, Inc. 06/11/2012

LONE PINE RES EXPLS LTD (ON)
Recapitalized as M.S.M. Marketing Ltd. 09/15/1983
Each share Common no par exchanged for (0.16666666) share Common no par
M.S.M. Marketing Ltd. recapitalized as Sea Hawk Energy Inc. 06/16/1986 which name changed to Jarl Energy Inc. 08/05/1987 which name changed to ALBA Petroleum Corp. 10/26/1989 which merged into Alberta Oil & Gas Ltd. 12/31/1990 which recapitalized as Alberta Oil & Gas Petroleum Corp. 11/19/1997 which recapitalized as Edge Energy Inc. 04/14/1998 which merged into Ventus Energy Ltd. 08/11/2000 which name changed to Navigo Energy Inc. 05/24/2002
(See Navigo Energy Inc.)

LONE PINE RES INC (DE)
Issue Information - 15,000,000 shares COM offered at $13 per share on 05/25/2011
Plan of arrangement under Companies' Creditors Arrangement Act effective 01/31/2014
No stockholders' equity

LONE ROCK OILS, LTD. (AB)
Liquidated 09/28/1961
For each share Capital Stock no par holders of record 09/28/1961 were entitled to receive (0.2) share Inter-Rock Oil Co. of Canada Ltd.

Capital Stock $1 par 60% of distribution paid 09/28/1961 and 40% held in escrow pending consent of authorities to release same
Note: Certificates were not required to be surrendered and are without value
Inter-Rock Oil Co. of Canada Ltd. name changed to Inter-Rock Gold Inc. 08/18/1992 which name changed to Inter-Rock Minerals Inc. (ON) 09/22/1998 which reincorporated in Barbados 09/15/2000

LONE STAR BREWING CO (TX)
Each share Common $3 par exchanged for (3) shares Common $1 par in 1949
Stock Dividends - 25% 6/1/49; 25% 8/1/54; 10% 11/6/56; 200% 5/7/65
Completely liquidated 1/6/77
Each share Common $1 par exchanged for first and final distribution of (0.2667) share Olympia Brewing Co. Common $10 par
Olympia Brewing Co. merged into Pabst Brewing Co. 3/18/83
(See Pabst Brewing Co.)

LONE STAR CASINO CORP (DE)
Recapitalized as LS Capital Corp. 07/01/1996
Each share Common 10¢ par exchanged for (0.04) share Common 10¢ par
LS Capital Corp. recapitalized as Eurbid.com Inc. 10/03/2000 which name changed to Junum Inc. 12/14/2000 which recapitalized as WinWin Gaming Inc. 12/31/2002
(See WinWin Gaming Inc.)

LONE STAR CEM CORP (DE)
Reincorporated 05/29/1969
Each share Common no par exchanged for (3) shares Common $10 par 00/00/1951
Common $10 par changed to $4 par and (1.5) additional shares issued 01/15/1957
State of incorporation changed from (ME) to (DE) and $4.50 Conv. Preferred no par changed to $1 par and Common $4 par changed to $1 par 05/29/1969
Name changed to Lone Star Industries, Inc. 05/20/1971
(See Lone Star Industries, Inc.)

LONE STAR COAL MINING CO. (DE)
Charter cancelled and declared inoperative and void for non-payment of taxes 1/23/24

LONE STAR FUEL SUPPLY CO.
Name changed to Lone Star Gas Corp. in 1926
(See Lone Star Gas Corp.)

LONE STAR FUND, INC. (DE)
Name changed to Morton (B.C.) Fund, Inc. 12/30/60
Morton (B.C.) Fund, Inc. name changed to Admiralty Fund 1/23/70 which merged into Oppenheimer A.I.M. Fund, Inc. 12/7/76 which name changed to Oppenheimer Global Fund 2/1/87

LONE STAR GAS CO (TX)
4.75% Preferred called for redemption 11/8/56
Common $10 par split (2) for (1) by issuance of (1) additional share 2/20/61
4.75% Conv. Preferred $100 par called for redemption 9/23/64
Name changed to Enserch Corp. 10/10/75
(See Enserch Corp.)

LONE STAR GAS CORP.
Liquidated in 1943
Details not available

LONE STAR INDS INC (DE)
$5.375 Conv. Preferred $1 par called for redemption 2/13/87
Reorganized under Chapter 11 Federal Bankruptcy Code 4/14/94
Each share $4.50 Conv. Preferred $1 par exchanged for (3.26815) shares new Common $1 par and (3.24221) Common Stock Purchase Warrants expiring 12/31/2000
Each share old Common $1 par exchanged for (0.032442) share new Common $1 par and (0.165413) Common Stock Purchase Warrant expiring 12/31/2000
New Common $1 par split (2) for (1) by issuance of (1) additional share payable 12/28/98 to holders of record 12/14/98
Merged into Dycherhoff AG 10/8/99
Each share new Common $1 par exchanged for $50 cash

LONE STAR INTL ENERGY INC (NV)
Charter permanently revoked 12/31/1998

LONE STAR INVESTMENT CO. (DE)
Liquidated 00/00/1948
Details not available

LONE STAR LIFE INS CO (TX)
Common no par changed to $1 par 05/13/1965
Stock Dividend - 25% 09/16/1968
Each share Common $1 par exchanged for (0.001) share Common no par 11/10/1975
Note: In effect holders received $21.34 cash per share and public interest was eliminated

LONE STAR LIQUIDATING TR (TX)
Liquidation completed
Each Trust Certificate received initial distribution of $0.03 cash payable 05/27/1997 to holders of record 05/05/1997 Ex date - 06/03/1997
Each Trust Certificate received second distribution of $0.2469 cash payable 09/10/1997 to holders of record 08/19/1997 Ex date - 09/10/1997
Each Trust Certificate received third distribution of $0.05 cash per share payable 02/27/1998 to holders of record 02/05/1998 Ex date - 03/06/1998
Each Trust Certificate received fourth distribution of $0.0273 cash payable 09/30/1998 to holders of record 09/08/1998 Ex date - 10/01/1998
Each Trust Certificate received fifth distribution of $0.07 cash payable 04/07/2003 to holders of record 03/17/2003 Ex date - 04/09/2003
Each Trust Certificate received sixth distribution of $0.02 cash payable 03/31/2006 to holders of record 03/10/2006 Ex date - 04/03/2006
Each Trust Certificate received seventh and final distribution of $0.0088 cash payable 03/26/2008 to holders of record 03/05/2008
Note: Certificates were not required to be surrendered and are without value

LONE STAR MINING & DEVELOPMENT CORP. (DE)
Charter cancelled and declared inoperative and void for non-payment of taxes 3/1/83

LONE STAR OIL CO. (CO)
Declared defunct and inoperative for failure to pay taxes and file annual reports 10/25/26

LONE STAR PETROLEUM CORP. (BC)
Name changed to Lone Star Resource Corp. 10/26/83
Lone Star Resource Corp. recapitalized as Consolidated Lone Star Resource Corp. 11/24/86
(See Consolidated Lone Star Resource Corp.)

LONE STAR RESOURCE CORP (BC)
Recapitalized as Consolidated Lone Star Resource Corp. 11/24/86
Each share Common no par exchanged for (0.5) share Common no par
(See Consolidated Lone Star Resource Corp.)

LONE STAR STEAKHOUSE SALOON (DE)
Common 1¢ par split (2) for (1) by issuance of (1) additional share 8/7/92
Common 1¢ par split (2) for (1) by issuance of (1) additional share 4/26/93
Merged into Lone Star U.S. Acquisitions LLC 12/13/2006
Each share Common 1¢ par exchanged for $27.35 cash

LONE STAR STEEL CO. (TX)
Incorporated 4/8/42
Common no par changed to $1 par in 1950
Stock Dividends - 10% 5/1/57; 10% 6/2/58; 10% 6/1/59; 10% 6/1/60
Acquired by Philadelphia & Reading Corp. (NY) 4/15/66
Each share Common $1 par exchanged for (0.25) share $5 Class A Preferred $100 par
Philadelphia & Reading Corp. (NY) reincorporated in Delaware 10/27/82
(See Philadelphia & Reading Corp. (DE))

LONE STAR STL CO (TX)
Incorporated 03/16/1966
Reincorporated under the laws of Delaware as Lone Star Technologies, Inc. 05/15/1986
(See Lone Star Technologies, Inc.)

LONE STAR SULPHUR CORP (DE)
Charter cancelled and declared inoperative and void for non-payment of taxes 4/1/57

LONE STAR TECHNOLOGIES INC (DE)
Acquired by United States Steel Corp. (New) 06/14/2007
Each share Common $1 par exchanged for $67.50 cash

LONE STAR URANIUM & DRILLING CO. (UT)
Charter suspended 3/30/62; stock valueless

LONE STAR VENTURES INC (UT)
Recapitalized as Intellichip Holdings Corp. 04/22/1988
Each share Common $0.0001 par exchanged for (0.1) share Common $0.001 par
Intellichip Holdings Corp. recapitalized as CompuLoan Originations, Inc. 09/05/1995
(See CompuLoan Originations, Inc.)

LONE WOLF ENERGY INC (CO)
Name changed to Zenex Telecom 11/20/2001
Zenex Telecom name changed to Zenex International, Inc. (CO) 8/6/2002 which reincorporated in Oklahoma as Aduddell Industries, Inc. 6/19/2006

LONERGAN CORP (IN)
Merged into Guerdon Industries, Inc. 12/31/71
Each share Common no par exchanged for (1/3) share Common no par
Guerdon Industries, Inc. merged into City Investing Co. 9/29/72
(See City Investing Co.)

LONERGAN MANUFACTURING CO. (MI)
Class B Common no par changed to $1 par in 1939
Stock Dividend - 250% 1946
Merged into McGraw Electric Co. in 1955
Each (16.7239) shares Class B Common $1 par exchanged for (2) shares Common $1 par
McGraw Electric Co. name was changed to McGraw Edison Co. 1/2/57
(See McGraw-Edison Co.)

LONESTAR CAP CORP (BC)
Name changed to Acro Energy Technologies Corp. 05/29/2009
(See Acro Energy Technologies Corp.)

LONESTAR GROUP HLDGS CO (NV)
Common $0.001 par split (2) for (1) by issuance of (1) additional share payable 02/14/2007 to holders of record 02/07/2007 Ex date - 02/15/2007
Recapitalized as Guardian Angel Group, Inc. 12/14/2007
Each share Common $0.001 par exchanged for (0.001) share Common $0.001 par
Guardian Angel Group, Inc. recapitalized as Ree International, Inc. 06/29/2011

LONESTAR HOSPITALITY CORP (DE)
Each share Common 2¢ par exchanged for (0.2) share Common 1¢ par 12/11/1995
Common 1¢ par split (3) for (2) by issuance of (0.5) additional share payable 02/02/1996 to holders of record 01/02/1996
Recapitalized as Citadel Computer Systems Inc. 05/01/1996
Each share Common 1¢ par exchanged for (0.5) share Common 1¢ par
Citadel Computer Systems Inc. name changed to Citadel Technology Inc. 02/27/1998 which name changed to CT Holdings, Inc. 11/30/1999 which recapitalized as CT Holdings Enterprises, Inc. 02/28/2007 which recapitalized as Xcorporeal, Inc. 10/15/2007

LONESTAR RES LTD (AUSTRALIA)
ADR agreement terminated 06/20/2014
Details not available

LONESTAR RES LTD (AUSTRALIA)
Each share old Ordinary exchanged for (0.02) share new Ordinary 05/12/2015
Reorganized under the laws of Delaware as Lonestar Resources US Inc. 07/05/2016
Each share new Ordinary exchanged for (0.5) share Class A Common $0.001 par

LONESTAR WEST INC (CANADA)
Acquired by Clean Harbors, Inc. 07/18/2017
Each share Common no par exchanged for $0.72 cash
Note: Unexchanged certificates will be cancelled and become without value 07/18/2023

LONG BAY GOLD MINES, LTD. (ON)
Charter revoked for failure to file reports and pay fees 4/29/65

LONG BEACH CONSOLIDATED OIL CO. (CA)
Charter cancelled for failure to file reports and pay taxes in 1923

LONG BEACH FINL CORP (DE)
Merged into Washington Mutual, Inc. 10/01/1999
Each share Common $0.001 par exchanged for either (0.5389) share Common no par, (0.1902) share Common no par and $10.03 cash, or $15.50 cash
Note: Non-electors received stock only
(See Washington Mutual, Inc.)

LONG-BELL LUMBER CO. (MO)
Each Certificate of Beneficial Interest for Common $50 par exchanged for (10) shares Capital Stock $5 par in 1943
Merged into Internatonal Paper Co. 11/5/56
Each share Capital Stock $5 par exchanged for (0.42642) share Common $7.50 par and (0.02508) Unit of Contingent Interest 11/5/56

LONG-BELL LUMBER CORP. (MD)
Merged into International Paper Co. 11/5/56
Each share Class A Common no par exchanged for (0.65085) share Common $7.50 par and (0.03829) Unit of Contingent Interest
Each share Class B Common no par exchanged for (0.08134) share Common $7.50 par and (0.00478) Unit of Contingent Interest

LONG DISTANCE DIRECT HLDGS INC (NV)
SEC revoked common stock registration 08/05/2004

LONG DISTANCE TEL CO (UT)
Proclaimed dissolved for failure to pay taxes 3/31/86

LONG-E INTL INC (UT)
SEC revoked common stock registration 04/11/2012

LONG HARBOUR CAP CORP (BC)
Name changed to Long Harbour Exploration Corp. 06/09/2011
Long Harbour Exploration Corp. name changed to Lancaster Capital Corp. 10/19/2015 which name changed to NxGold Ltd. 11/18/2016

LONG HARBOUR EXPL CORP (BC)
Each share old Common no par exchanged for (0.1) share new Common no par 10/10/2013
Name changed to Lancaster Capital Corp. 10/19/2015
Lancaster Capital Corp. name changed to NxGold Ltd. 11/18/2016

LONG HUGH W & CO INC (DE)
Name changed to Anchor Corp. 4/2/62
Anchor Corp. merged into Washington National Corp. 8/22/69
(See Washington National Corp.)

LONG IS ARENA INC (NY)
Reorganized 05/06/1965
No stockholders' equity

LONG IS BANCORP INC (DE)
Merged into Astoria Financial Corp. 09/30/1998
Each share Common 1¢ par exchanged for (1.15) shares Common 1¢ par
Astoria Financial Corp. merged into Sterling Bancorp 10/02/2017

LONG IS COML BK (ISLANDIA, NY)
Under plan of reorganization each share Common $3 par automatically became (1) share Long Island Financial Corp. Common $3 par 1/28/99
Long Island Financial Corp. merged into New York Community Bancorp, Inc. 12/30/2005

LONG IS FINL CORP (NY)
Merged into New York Community Bancorp, Inc. 12/30/2005
Each share Common $3 par exchanged for (2.32) shares Common 1¢ par

LONG IS ICED TEA CORP (DE)
Name changed to Long Blockchain Corp. 01/05/2018

LONG IS VIDEO TIME (NV)
Name changed to Espley, Inc. 04/03/1984

LONG ISLAND BK (HICKSVILLE, NY)
Name changed 9/7/76
Capital Stock $10 par changed to $5

par and additional share issued 1/8/57
Name changed from Long Island National Bk (Hicksville, NY) to Long Island Bank (Hicksville, NY) 9/7/76
Acquired by Litco Corp. of New York 11/22/76
Each share Capital Stock $5 par exchanged for (0.5) share Common $5 par and $3.375 cash
Litco Corp. of New York name changed to Litco Bancorporation of New York, Inc. 5/4/79
(See Litco Bancorporation of New York, Inc.)

LONG ISLAND BANKERS, INC. (NY)
Out of business in 1948
Details not available

LONG ISLAND CITY FINL CORP (NY)
Merged into Independence Savings Bank (Brooklyn, NY) 4/7/92
Each share Common 1¢ par exchanged for $29.49 cash

LONG ISLAND FIRE INSURANCE CO.
Merged into New York Fire Insurance Co. in 1931
Details not available

LONG ISLAND LTG CO (NY)
Each share Common no par exchanged for (10) shares Common no par 00/00/1929
Each share 7% Preferred Ser. A $100 par exchanged for (10.4) shares Common no par 00/00/1950
Each share 6% Preferred Ser. B $100 par exchanged for (9.2) shares Common no par 00/00/1950
Each share Common no par exchanged for (0.06) share Common no par 00/00/1950
Common no par changed to $10 par 00/00/1953
5.25% Preferred Ser. A $100 par called for redemption 05/21/1954
5.25% Preferred Ser. C $100 par called for redemption 05/21/1954
4.40% Preferred Ser. G $100 par called for redemption 08/04/1960
Common $10 par changed to $5 par and (1) additional share issued 06/05/1963
13% Preferred Ser. N $100 par called for redemption 12/02/1977
$3.50 Preferred Ser. V $25 par called for redemption 11/06/1989
$3.50 Preferred Ser. X $25 par called for redemption 11/06/1989
$3.52 Preferred Ser. W $25 par called for redemption 11/06/1989
$4.25 Preferred Ser. U $25 par called for redemption 11/06/1989
$3.31 Preferred Ser. T $25 par called for redemption 06/13/1991
$2.65 Preferred Ser. Y $25 par called for redemption 06/28/1992
9.80% Preferred Ser. S $25 par called for redemption 09/03/1992
$2.47 Preferred Ser. O $25 par called for redemption 03/29/1993
$2.43 Preferred Ser. P $25 par called for redemption 03/31/1993
$2.35 Preferred Ser. Z $25 par called for redemption 06/04/1993
8.12% Preferred Ser. J $100 par called for redemption 11/18/1993
8.30% Preferred Ser. K $100 par called for redemption 11/18/1993
$1.95 Preferred Ser. NN $100 par called for redemption at $26.95 plus $0.4225 accrued dividend on 05/19/1998
4.25% Preferred Ser. D $100 par called for redemption at $102 plus $0.5667 accrued dividend on 05/19/1998
4.35% Preferred Ser. E $100 par called for redemption at $102 plus $0.58 accrued dividend on 05/19/1998
4.35% Preferred Ser. F $100 par called for redemption at $102 plus $0.58 accrued dividend on 05/19/1998
5% Preferred Ser. B $100 par called for redemption at $101 plus $0.6667 accrued dividend on 05/19/1998
5.125% Preferred Ser. H $100 par called for redemption at $102 plus $0.6833 accrued dividend on 05/19/1998
5.75% Conv. Preferred Ser. I $100 par called for redemption at $100 on 05/19/1998
6.875% Preferred Ser. UU $25 par called for redemption at $27.4846 on 05/28/1998
7.05% Preferred Ser. QQ $25 par called for redemption at $26.6515 on 05/28/1998
7.66% Preferred Ser. CC $100 par called for redemption at $111.0522 on 05/28/1998
$1.67 Preferred Ser. GG $25 par called for redemption at $25.4489 on 05/28/1998
Merged into MarketSpan Corp. 05/29/1998
Each share 7.95% Preferred Ser. AA $25 par exchanged for (1) share 7.95% Preferred Ser. AA $25 par
Each share Common $5 par exchanged for (0.88) share Common $0.33-1/3 par
MarketSpan Corp. name changed to KeySpan Energy 09/10/1998 which name changed to KeySpan Corp. 05/20/1999
(See KeySpan Corp.)

LONG ISLAND PETROLEUMS LTD. (AB)
Recapitalized as Canadian Long Island Petroleums Ltd. on a (1) for (5.5) basis 01/26/1962
Canadian Long Island Petroleums Ltd. recapitalized as First Calgary Petroleums Ltd. 08/15/1979
(See First Calgary Petroleums Ltd.)

LONG ISLAND PLASTICS CORP (NY)
Name changed to Fibrothane Industries Corp. 5/5/72
Fibrothane Industries Corp. name changed to A O K Enterprises Ltd. 9/20/84 which reorganized as Environmental Protective Industries Inc. 11/30/87
(See Environmental Protective Industries Inc.)

LONG ISLAND TITLE GUARANTEE CO.
Taken over by New York State Insurance Department for liquidation in 1935
Details not available

LONG ISLAND TR CO (GARDEN CITY, NY)
Capital Stock $10 par changed to $5 par and (1) additional share issued 4/23/59
Stock Dividends - 10% 4/22/68; 10% 4/8/70
Reorganized as Litco Corp. of New York 4/6/73
Each share Capital Stock $5 par exchanged for (1) share Common $5 par
Litco Corp. of New York name changed to Litco Bancorporation of New York, Inc. 5/4/79
(See Litco Bancorporation of New York, Inc.)

LONG LAC MINERALS LTD (QC)
Merged into Lac Minerals Ltd. (Old) 12/31/1982
Each share Common $1 par exchanged for (1) share Common no par and $0.01 Promissory Note Payable within one year
Lac Minerals Ltd. (Old) merged into LAC Minerals Ltd. (New) 07/29/1985 which was acquired by American Barrick Resources Corp. 10/17/1994 which name changed to Barrick Gold Corp. 01/18/1995

LONG LAKE ENERGY CORP (DE)
Each share Common $0.001 par received initial distribution of $1 cash 09/28/1992
Each share Common $0.001 par received second distribution of $0.15 cash 12/06/1993
Recapitalized as DGW Financial Ltd. (DE) 10/20/2004
Each share Common $0.001 par exchanged for (0.00125) share Common $0.001 par
DGW Financial Ltd. (DE) reorganized in Nevada as YNOT Education, Inc. (Old) 03/10/2006 which name changed to Physiognomy Interface Technologies, Inc. 05/01/2006 which name changed to Ynot Education, Inc. (New) 01/10/2007 which name changed to King Media Holdings Inc. 10/04/2007 which recapitalized as Extreme Fitness, Inc. 10/09/2007
(See Extreme Fitness, Inc.)

LONG LIFE VALVE CO. (OH)
Charter cancelled for failure to pay taxes 3/1/23

LONG-LOK CORP. (CA)
Stock Dividend - 50% 6/27/66
Name changed to 1425 Liquidating Corp. 8/23/67
1425 Liquidating Corp. acquired by Whittaker Corp. (CA) 8/31/67 which reincorporated in Delaware 6/16/86
(See Whittaker Corp. (DE))

LONG POINT GAS & OIL INC. (ON)
Merged into New Force Crag Mines Ltd. 11/22/74
Each (3) shares Common no par exchanged for (1) share Common no par
(See New Force Crag Mines Ltd.)

LONG POINT GAS & OIL LTD. (ON)
Acquired by Consolidated West Petroleum, Ltd. on a (1) for (17.5) basis 4/7/64
(See Consolidated West Petroleum, Ltd.)

LONG POINT NATL BK (HOUSTON, TX)
Merged into Southwest Bancshares, Inc. 5/18/72
Each share Capital Stock $20 par exchanged for (0.8) share Common $5 par
Southwest Bancshares, Inc. merged into MCorp 10/11/84
(See MCorp)

LONG RANGE RES LTD (AB)
Name changed to Sport Specific International Inc. 11/16/92
(See Sport Specific International Inc.)

LONG RD ENTMT INC (DE)
Each share old Common $0.0001 par exchanged for (3) shares new Common $0.0001 par 07/14/2003
Recapitalized as Alternative Ethanol Technologies, Inc. 02/21/2007
Each share new Common $0.0001 par exchanged for (0.01) share Common $0.0001 par
Alternative Ethanol Technologies, Inc. name changed to Clean Tech Biofuels, Inc. 11/14/2007

LONG RESERVE LIFE RESOURCE FD (ON)
Name changed to Navina Global Resource Fund 06/23/2010
Navina Global Resource Fund name changed to Aston Hill Global Resource Fund (Old)
(See Aston Hill Global Resource Fund (Old))

LONG RUN EXPL LTD (AB)
Acquired by Calgary Sinoenergy Investment Corp. 07/05/2016
Each share Common no par exchanged for $0.52 cash
Note: Unexchanged certificates will be cancelled and become without value 07/04/2019

LONG SHORE DEV CORP (DE)
Each share Common $0.0001 par exchanged for (1/6) share Common $0.0006 par 10/1/86
Charter cancelled and declared inoperative and void for non-payment of taxes 3/1/91

LONG VIEW RES CORP (AB)
Merged into Reece Energy Exploration Corp. (New) 05/15/2007
Each share Common no par exchanged for (0.25) share Common no par
Reece Energy Exploration Corp. (New) merged into Penn West Energy Trust 04/30/2009 which reorganized as Penn West Petroleum Ltd. (New) 01/03/2011 which name changed to Obsidian Energy Ltd. 06/29/2017

LONG WHARF LIQUIDATING CO., INC. (CT)
Liquidation completed
Each share Capital Stock $15 par or VTC's for Capital Stock $15 par exchanged for initial distribution of (0.882) share Kidde (Walter) & Co., Inc. (NY) $2.20 Conv. Preference Ser. A $1 par 4/21/67
Kidde (Walter) & Co., Inc. (NY) reincorporated in Delaware 7/2/68
Each share Capital Stock $15 par or VTC's for Capital Stock $15 par received second and final distribution of (0.0196) share Kidde (Walter) & Co., Inc. (DE) $2.20 Conv. Preference Ser. A $1 par 6/8/70
(See Kidde (Walter) & Co., Inc. (DE))

LONGBOAT CAP CORP (AB)
Issue Information - 2,250,000 shares COM offered at $0.10 per share on 04/07/1997
Recapitalized as YMG Ventures Inc. 5/24/2001
Each (1.5) shares Common no par exchanged for (1) share Common no par
(See YMG Ventures Inc.)

LONGBOAT RES INC (BC)
Struck off register and declared dissolved for failure to file returns 9/27/91

LONGBOW ENERGY CORP NEW (AB)
Recapitalized as LongBow Resources Inc. 04/11/2007
Each share Common no par exchanged for (0.1) share Common no par
(See LongBow Resources Inc.)

LONGBOW ENERGY CORP OLD (AB)
Merged into LongBow Energy Corp. (New) 02/25/2004
Each share Common no par exchanged for (1) share Common no par
LongBow Energy Corp. (New) recapitalized as LongBow Resources Inc. 04/11/2007
(See LongBow Resources Inc.)

LONGBOW MNG CORP (NV)
Each share old Common $0.001 par exchanged for (10) shares new Common $0.001 par 02/24/2004
Name changed to BonusAmerica Worldwide Corp. 06/09/2004
BonusAmerica Worldwide Corp. name changed to Asia Global Holdings Corp. 07/17/2006
(See Asia Global Holdings Corp.)

LONGBOW RES INC (AB)
Acquired by TriAxon Resources Ltd. 06/19/2008
Each share Common no par exchanged for $0.70 cash

LONGCHAMPS CORP (DE)
Merged into Longchamps, Inc. 1/3/69
Each share Common 50¢ par exchanged for (1) share Capital Stock $1 par
Longchamps, Inc. merged into Beefsteak Charlie's, Inc. 12/29/80 which name changed to Lifestyle Restaurants, Inc. 4/29/85 which merged into Bombay Palace Restaurants, Inc. 9/14/87
(See Bombay Palace Restaurants, Inc.)

LONGCHAMPS INC (NY)
Merged into Beefsteak Charlie's, Inc. 12/29/80
Each share Common $1 par exchanged for (0.7) share Common 10¢ par
Beefsteak Charlie's, Inc. name changed to Lifestyle Restaurants, Inc. 4/29/85 which merged into Bombay Palace Restaurants, Inc. 9/14/87
(See Bombay Palace Restaurants, Inc.)

LONGFOR PPTYS CO LTD (CAYMAN ISLANDS)
Name changed to Longfor Group Holdings Ltd. 07/12/2018

LONGFORD CORP (ON)
Recapitalized as Longford Energy Inc. 12/24/2007
Each share Common no par exchanged for (0.1) share Common no par
Longford Energy Inc. recapitalized as UrtheCast Corp. 06/27/2013

LONGFORD ENERGY INC (ON)
Recapitalized as UrtheCast Corp. 06/27/2013
Each share Common no par exchanged for (0.07457288) share Common no par

LONGFORD EQUIP INTL LTD (ON)
Each share old Common no par exchanged for (0.000025) share new Common no par 3/21/90
Note: In effect holders received $0.82 cash per share and public interest was eliminated

LONGHORN DEV INC (DE)
Each share old Common $0.0001 par exchanged for (0.2) share new Common $0.0001 par 08/26/1988
Name changed to Single Chip Systems International, Inc. 08/25/1988
Single Chip Systems International, Inc. recapitalized as Triple Chip Systems, Inc. (DE) 07/16/1996 which reincorporated in Tennessee as Miller Petroleum Inc. 01/13/1997 which name changed to Miller Energy Resources, Inc. 04/12/2011

LONGHORN ENERGY SVCS INC (MN)
Recapitalized as Equisure, Inc. 5/10/96
Each share Common 1¢ par exchanged for (0.05) share Common 1¢ par
(See Equisure, Inc.)

LONGHORN ENTERPRISES INC (UT)
Each share old Common $0.005 par exchanged for (0.2) share new Common $0.005 par 10/27/1986
Name changed to Republic International Corp. 09/25/1987
Republic International Corp. recapitalized as Axiom Security Solutions, Inc. 10/02/1995
(See Axiom Security Solutions, Inc.)

LONGHORN OIL CO. (TX)
Charter forfeited for failure to pay taxes 2/11/30

LONGHORN PORTLAND CEMENT CO. (TX)
Common no par changed to $5 par in 1944
Each share Common $5 par exchanged for (2) shares Common $2.50 par in 1949
Common $2.50 par changed to $1.25 par and (1) additional share issued 3/24/56
Merged into Kaiser Cement & Gypsum Corp. 11/10/65
Each share Common $1.25 par exchanged for (1) share $1.375 Conv. Preference no par
Kaiser Cement & Gypsum Corp. name changed to Kaiser Cement Corp. (CA) 5/1/79 which reincorporated in Delaware 5/4/82
(See Kaiser Cement Corp. (DE))

LONGHORN STEAKS INC (GA)
Name changed to RARE Hospitality International, Inc. 01/13/1997
(See RARE Hospitality International, Inc.)

LONGINES WITTNAUER WATCH INC (NY)
Each share Class C $1 par exchanged for (2) shares Common $1 par in 1946
Common $1 par and VTC's for Common $1 par split (2) for (1) respectively by issuance of (1) additional share 9/6/68
Common $1 par and VTC's for Common $1 par split (2) for (1) respectively by issuance of (1) additional share 9/8/69
Voting Trust Agreement terminated 12/23/70
Each VTC for Common $1 par exchanged for (1) share Common $1 par
Merged into Westinghouse Electric Corp. 12/23/70
Each share Common $1 par exchanged for (0.45129) share Common $6.25 par
Westinghouse Electric Corp. name changed to CBS Corp. 12/1/97 which merged into Viacom Inc. (Old) 5/4/2000
(See Viacom Inc. (Old))

LONGOLD RES INC (BC)
Recapitalized as Cascadia Technologies Ltd. 3/9/93
Each share Common no par exchanged for (0.2941176) share Common no par
(See Cascadia Technologies Ltd.)

LONGREACH OIL & GAS LTD (CHANNEL ISLANDS)
Name changed to PetroMaroc Corp. PLC 07/14/2014

LONGREACH RES LTD (BC)
Struck from the register and dissolved 8/14/92

LONGREN AIRCRAFT CO., INC. (CA)
Merged into Aeronca Manufacturing Corp. 4/10/59
Each share Common $1 par exchanged for (0.02) share 5-1/2% Prior Preferred $20 par and (0.1) share Common $1 par 4/10/59
Aeronca Manufacturing Corp. name changed to Aeronca, Inc. 5/17/66
(See Aeronca, Inc.)

LONGROSE GOLD MINES, LTD. (ON)
Charter cancelled and company dissolved by default 11/9/64

LONGS DRUG STORES CORP (MD)
Reincorporated 05/24/1985
Common $2 par changed to $1 par and (1) additional share issued 06/04/1965
Common $1 par changed to no par and (1) additional share issued 06/12/1968
Common no par split (2) for (1) by issuance of (1) additional share 06/07/1971
Common no par split (2) for (1) by issuance of (1) additional share 05/28/1976
Common no par split (2) for (1) by issuance of (1) additional share 03/26/1985
Name and state of incorporation changed from Longs Drug Stores, Inc. (CA) to Longs Drug Stores Corp. (MD) and Common no par changed to 50¢ par 05/24/1985
Common 50¢ par split (2) for (1) by issuance of (1) additional share payable 01/10/1997 to holders of record 12/03/1996 Ex date - 01/13/1997
Acquired by CVS Caremark Corp. 10/30/2008
Each share Common 50¢ par exchanged for $71.50 cash

LONGTOP FINL TECHNOLOGIES LTD (CAYMAN ISLANDS)
SEC revoked ADR registration 12/14/2011

LONGVIEW BRIDGE CO.
Liquidated 00/00/1950
No Class B stockholders' equity

LONGVIEW CAP PARTNERS INC (BC)
Name changed to Resinco Capital Partners Inc. 11/30/2009

LONGVIEW FIBRE CO (WA)
Reincorporated 4/6/90
Common $7.50 par split (10) for (1) by issuance of (9) additional shares 2/22/80
Stock Dividend - 400% 3/20/53
State of incorporation changed from (DE) to (WA) 4/6/90
Common $7.50 par changed to $1.50 par and (4) additional shares issued 4/20/90
Each share Common $1.50 par received distribution of $2.0778 cash payable 8/7/2006 to holders of record 6/26/2006 Ex date - 6/22/2006
Merged into Brookfield Asset Management Inc. 4/20/2007
Each share Common $1.50 par exchanged for $24.75 cash

LONGVIEW NATL BK (LONGVIEW, TX)
Each share Capital Stock $100 par exchanged for (5) shares Capital Stock $20 par 04/25/1950
Capital Stock $20 par changed to $10 par and (1) additional share issued 01/21/1969
Stock Dividend - 10% 02/02/1970
Acquired by Texas Commerce Bancshares, Inc. 10/25/1976
Each share Capital Stock $10 par exchanged for (0.2963621) share Common $4 par
Texas Commerce Bancshares, Inc. acquired by Chemical New York Corp. 05/01/1987 which name changed to Chemical Banking Corp. 04/29/1988 which name changed to Chase Manhattan Corp. (New) 03/31/1996 which name changed to J.P. Morgan Chase & Co. 12/31/2000 which name changed to JPMorgan Chase & Co. 07/20/2004

LONGVIEW OIL CORP (AB)
Merged into Surge Energy Inc. 06/10/2014
Each share Common no par exchanged for (0.975) share Common no par
Note: Unexchanged certificates were cancelled and became without value 06/10/2017

LONGVIEW PETE CORP (AB)
Recapitalized as Rival Energy Inc. 10/28/2002
Each share Common no par exchanged for (1/6) share Common no par
Rival Energy Inc. name changed to Rival Energy Ltd. 06/16/2003 which merged into Zargon Energy Trust 01/23/2008 which reorganized as Zargon Oil & Gas Ltd. (New) 01/07/2011

LONGVIEW REAL ESTATE INC (DE)
Common $0.0001 par split (110) for (1) by issuance of (109) additional shares payable 08/02/2013 to holders of record 08/02/2013
Name changed to Cannabis-Rx Inc. 02/05/2014
Cannabis-Rx Inc. name changed to Praetorian Property, Inc. (DE) 10/26/2015 which reincorporated in Nevada 12/30/2015

LONGVIEW RES INC (AB)
Name changed to Olympia Energy Inc. 04/20/1990
Olympia Energy Inc. merged into Provident Energy Trust 06/01/2004

LONGVIEW STRATEGIES INC (BC)
Name changed to Longview Capital Partners Inc. 10/25/2006
Longview Capital Partners Inc. name changed to Resinco Capital Partners Inc. 11/30/2009

LONGWOOD BROADCASTING CO (OH)
Charter cancelled for failure to pay taxes 12/30/88

LONGWOOD GROUP LTD (DE)
Recapitalized as DRS Industries Inc. 5/26/92
Each share Common $0.0001 par exchanged for (1/3) share Common $0.0001 par
DRS Industries Inc. name changed to Family Bargain Corp. 1/13/94 which merged into Factory 2-U Stores, Inc. 11/23/98

LONRHO AFRICA PLC (UNITED KINGDOM)
ADR agreement terminated 12/29/2003
Each Sponsored ADR for Ordinary exchanged for $0.2169 cash

LONRHO PLC (ENGLAND & WALES)
ADR agreement terminated 08/23/2013
Each Sponsored ADR for Ordinary exchanged for $15.58535 cash

LONRHO PLC (ENGLAND)
Each Unsponsored ADR for Ordinary 25p par exchanged for (1) old Sponsored ADR for Ordinary 25p par 01/30/1995
Each old Sponsored ADR for Ordinary 25p par exchanged for (0.25) new Sponsored ADR for Ordinary 25p par 04/27/1998
Stock Dividends - 10% 05/01/1974; 10% 04/25/1975; 20% 04/26/1976; 10% 05/23/1986; 10% 05/11/1987; (1) for (6) 05/09/1988; 16.6666% 05/09/1989; 10% 05/14/1990
Note: Common Market regulation required all publicly held British companies to replace LTD with PLC 00/00/1982
Name changed to Lonmin PLC 03/18/1999

LONSDALE CO. NEW (RI)
Acquired by Textron, Inc. (RI) in 1952
Each (30) shares Common $1 par exchanged for (1) share new 4% Preferred Series A $100 par
Textron, Inc. (RI) name changed to Textron American Inc. 2/24/55 which name changed back to Textron, Inc. (RI) 5/16/56

LONSDALE CO. OLD (RI)
Acquired by Textron, Inc. (RI) in 1945
Details not available

LONSDALE PUB VENTURES INC (ON)
Reorganized under the laws of Canada as Cannasat Therapeutics Inc. 03/22/2006
Each share Common no par exchanged for (0.83752093) share Common no par

Cannasat Therapeutics Inc. name changed to Cynapsus Therapeutics Inc. 04/24/2010
(See Cynapsus Therapeutics Inc.)

LONVEST CORP (ON)
Name changed to London Insurance Group Inc 6/18/90
(See London Insurance Group Inc.)

LOOK COMMUNICATIONS INC (BC)
Each share Class A Limited no par exchanged for (0.01) share Common no par 02/11/2002
Each share Common no par exchanged for (0.5) share Multiple no par and (0.5) share Subordinate no par 04/11/2005
Name changed to ONEnergy Inc. 07/12/2013

LOOK ENTMT INC (NV)
Recapitalized as VTEC, Inc. 07/05/2007
Each share Common $0.0001 par exchanged for (0.05) share Common $0.0001 par
VTEC, Inc. name changed to United Consortium, Ltd. (Old) 03/10/2008 which reorganized as United Consortium, Ltd. (New) 05/05/2010

LOOK TELEVISION CORP. (IL)
Involuntarily dissolved by Court order 10/16/74

LOOKOUT MOUNTAIN MNG & MLG CO (ID)
Charter forfeited for failure to file reports 12/1/93

LOOKOUT MOUNTAIN MINING CO. LTD. (CA)
Charter revoked for failure to file reports and pay fees 1/4/52

LOOKSMART GROUP INC OLD (NV)
Reorganized as LookSmart Group, Inc. (New) 03/23/2017
Each share Common $0.001 par exchanged for (0.01) share Common $0.001 par

LOOKSMART LTD (DE)
Each share old Common $0.001 par exchanged for (0.2) share new Common $0.001 par 10/26/2005
Each share new Common $0.001 par exchanged again for (0.33333333) share new Common $0.001 par 11/06/2013
Each share new Common $0.001 par exchanged again for (0.15116279) share new Common $0.001 par 10/28/2015
Merged into Pyxis Tankers Inc. 10/28/2015
Each share new Common $0.001 par exchanged for (1.0667) shares Common $0.001 par

LOOMIS COAL CORP. (DE)
No longer in existence having become inoperative and void April 1, 1964 and proclaimed by the Governor in January 1965 for non-payment of taxes

LOOMIS CORP (NV)
Common 50¢ par changed to 33-1/3¢ par and (0.5) additional share issued 3/1/72
Merged into Mayne Nickless Ltd. 11/30/79
Each share Common 33-1/3¢ par exchanged for $10.50 cash

LOOMIS SAYLES CDN & INTL FD LTD (CANADA)
Acquired by Scudder International Investments Ltd. (Canada) 03/07/1973
Each share Common $1 par exchanged for (1.761481) shares Common 25¢ par
Scudder International Investments Ltd. (Canada) reincorporated in Maryland as Scudder International Fund, Inc. 07/31/1975 which name changed to DWS International Fund, Inc. 02/06/2006

LOOMIS SAYLES CAP DEV FD INC (MA)
Name changed to CGM Capital Development Fund 03/01/1991
CGM Capital Development Fund merged into CGM Trust 06/27/2008

LOOMIS-SAYLES FUND OF CANADA LTD. (CANADA)
Name changed to Loomis-Sayles Canadian & International Fund Ltd. 06/21/1962
Loomis-Sayles Canadian & International Fund Ltd. acquired by Scudder International Investments Ltd. (Canada) 03/07/1973 which reincorporated in Maryland as Scudder International Fund, Inc. 07/31/1975 which name changed to DWS International Fund, Inc. 02/06/2006

LOOMIS SAYLES MUT FD INC (MA)
Capital Stock no par changed to $1 par 00/00/1952
Stock Dividends - 200% 03/00/1950; 200% 03/10/1960
Name changed to CGM Trust 03/01/1991

LOOMIS-SAYLES SECOND FUND, INC.
Merged into Loomis-Sayles Mutual Fund, Inc. in 1952 which name changed to CGM Mutual Fund 3/1/91

LOON ENERGY INC (AB)
Plan of arrangement effective 12/11/2008
Each share Common no par exchanged for (1) share Loon Energy Corp. Common no par and (1) share Kulczyk Oil Ventures Inc. Common no par
(See each company's listing)

LOOP HOTEL CO. (DE)
Completely liquidated 7/17/45
Each Capital Stock Trust Ctf. no par exchanged for first and final distribution of $26.02 cash

LOOPNET INC (DE)
Issue Information - 6,000,000 shares COM offered at $12 per share on 06/06/2006
Merged into CoStar Group, Inc. 04/30/2012
Each share Common $0.001 par exchanged for (0.03702) share Common 1¢ par and $16.50 cash

LOOSE-WILES BISCUIT CO.
Recapitalized as Sunshine Biscuits, Inc. 00/00/1946
Each share Common $25 par exchanged for (2) shares Capital Stock $12.50 par
Sunshine Biscuits, Inc. merged into American Tobacco Co. 05/31/1966 which name changed to American Brands, Inc. (NJ) 07/01/1969 which reincorporated in Delaware 01/01/1986 which name changed to Fortune Brands, Inc. 05/30/1997 which name changed to Beam Inc. 10/04/2011
(See Beam Inc.)

LOPAT INDS INC (DE)
Name changed to Safe-Waste Systems, Inc. 05/31/1990
(See Safe-Waste Systems, Inc.)

LOPEZ HLDGS CORP (PHILIPPINES)
GDR agreement terminated 11/07/2017
Each Sponsored GDR for SPURs exchanged for (20) shares Common
Each 144A GDR for Common exchanged for (20) shares Common
Note: Unexchanged GDR's will be sold and the proceeds, if any, held for claim after 11/13/2017

LOR CAP INC (CANADA)
Recapitalized as Decision Dynamics Technology Ltd. 08/04/2005
Each (3.0435) shares Common no par exchanged for (1) share Common no par
Decision Dynamics Technology Ltd. merged into Acorn Energy, Inc. 05/14/2010

LORACA INTL INC (NV)
Charter permanently revoked 04/01/2002

LORADO URANIUM MINES LTD. (ON)
Merged into International Mogul Mines Ltd. 11/20/68
Each share Common $1 par exchanged for (0.112359) share Capital Stock no par
International Mogul Mines Ltd. merged into Conwest Exploration Co. Ltd. (Old) (ONT) 8/27/82 which merged into Conwest Exploration Co. Ltd. (New) (ALTA) 9/1/93 which merged into Alberta Energy Co. Ltd. 1/31/96 which merged into EnCana Corp. 1/3/2003

LORAIN BANKING CO. (LORAIN, OH)
Under plan of merger name changed to Lorain National Bank (Lorain, OH) 01/01/1961
Lorain National Bank (Lorain, OH) reorganized as LNB Bancorp, Inc. 03/30/1984 which merged into Northwest Bancshares, Inc. 08/14/2015

LORAIN COAL & DOCK CO. (OH)
Each share 7% Preferred $100 par exchanged for (1) share 5% Preferred $50 par and (3.5) shares Common no par in 1944
Liquidation completed
Each share Common no par stamped to indicate initial distribution of $1.50 cash 12/20/63
Each share Stamped Common no par stamped to indicate second distribution of $1.50 cash 5/8/64
Each share Stamped Common no par stamped to indicate third distribution of $7 cash 10/30/64
Each share Stamped Common no par stamped to indicate fourth distribution of $7.50 cash 4/16/65
Each share Stamped Common no par stamped to indicate fifth distribution of $1 cash 1/11/66
Each share Stamped Common no par stamped to indicate sixth distribution of $0.50 cash 7/6/66
Each share Stamped Common no par stamped to indicate seventh distribution of $0.75 cash 9/6/66
Each share Stamped Common no par exchanged for eighth and final distribution of $0.0812 cash 6/18/69

LORAIN COUNTY RADIO CORP. (OH)
Name changed to Lorain Electronics Corp. 4/7/65
Lorain Electronics Corp. acquired by Oakmont Marine Corp. 8/19/76 which name changed to Lorain Telecom Corp. (TX) 11/7/83 which reorganized in Delaware 4/10/85
(See Lorain Telecom Corp.)

LORAIN CNTY SVGS & TR CO (ELYRIA, OH)
Each share Capital Stock $25 par exchanged for (3) shares Capital Stock $12.50 par 02/28/1956
Each share Capital Stock $12.50 par exchanged for (1.5) shares Capital Stock $10 par 10/14/1965
Capital Stock $10 par changed to $5 par and (1) additional share issued 09/15/1978
Stock Dividends - 10% 04/14/1967; 10% 04/15/1968; 10% 09/15/1970; 10% 04/15/1974
Under plan of reorganization each share Capital Stock $5 par automatically became (1) share LCB Bancorp Inc. Common $5 par 09/02/1984
LCB Bancorp Inc. name changed to CoBancorp Inc. 05/01/1992 which merged into FirstMerit Corp. 05/22/1998 which merged into Huntington Bancshares Inc. 08/16/2016

LORAIN COUNTY TELEPHONE CO.
Acquired by Lorain Telephone Co. 00/00/1928
Details not available

LORAIN ELECTRS CORP (OH)
Acquired by Oakmont Marine Corp. 8/19/76
Each share Common no par exchanged for (0.6) share $6 Conv. Preferred Ser. C $100 and (65) shares Common no par
Oakmont Marine Corp. name changed to Lorain Telecom Corp. (TX) 11/7/83 which reorganized in Delaware 4/10/85
(See Lorain Telecom Corp.)

LORAIN NATL BK (LORAIN, OH)
Capital Stock $10 par changed to $5 par and (1) additional share issued 01/27/1971
Capital Stock $5 par changed to $2.50 par and (1) additional share issued 04/06/1982
Stock Dividend - 10% 01/28/1964
Reorganized as LNB Bancorp, Inc. 03/30/1984
Each share Capital Stock $2.50 par exchanged for (1) share Common $1 par
LNB Bancorp, Inc. merged into Northwest Bancshares, Inc. 08/14/2015

LORAIN TEL CO (OH)
Merged into Central Telephone & Utilities Corp. 3/1/78
Each share Preferred $100 par exchanged for $105 cash
Each share Common no par exchanged for (5) shares Common $2.50 par
Central Telephone & Utilities Corp. name changed to Centel Corp. 4/30/82 which was acquired by Sprint Corp. 3/9/93 which name changed to Sprint Nextel Corp. 8/12/2005

LORAIN TELECOM CORP (DE)
Reorganized 04/10/1985
Reorganized from under the laws of (TX) to (DE) 04/10/1985
Each share $6 Conv. Preferred Ser. C $100 par exchanged for (48) shares Common no par
Common no par changed to 1¢ par
Charter cancelled and declared inoperative and void for non-payment of taxes 03/01/1998

LORAINE GOLD MINES LTD (SOUTH AFRICA)
Consolidated into Avgold Ltd. 1/3/97
Each ADR for Ordinary Rand-1 par exchanged for (0.1106443) ADR for Ordinary
(See Avgold Ltd.)

LORAL CORP (NY)
Common 25¢ par split (2) for (1) by issuance of (1) additional share 3/20/80
Common 25¢ par split (2) for (1) by issuance of (1) additional share 9/15/83
Common 25¢ par split (2) for (1) by issuance of (1) additional share 10/7/93
Common 25¢ par split (2) for (1) by issuance of (1) additional share 9/29/95
Each share Common 25¢ par received distribution of (1) share Loral Space & Communications Ltd. Common no par payable 5/6/96 to holders of record 4/22/96

Merged into Lockheed Martin Corp. 4/29/96
Each share Common 25¢ par exchanged for $38 cash

LORAL ELECTRS CORP (NY)
Common $1 par changed to 25¢ par and (2) additional shares issued 11/25/60
Name changed to Loral Corp. 10/30/64
(See Loral Corp.)

LORAL SPACE & COMMUNICATIONS LTD (BERMUDA)
Each share old Common no par exchanged for (0.1) share new Common no par 06/13/2003
Plan of reorganization under Chapter 11 Federal Bankruptcy Code effective 11/21/2005
No stockholders' equity

LORAN CONNECTION CORP (NV)
Name changed to PetroTerra Corp. 01/30/2012
PetroTerra Corp. recapitalized as Transportation & Logistics Systems, Inc. 07/18/2018

LORCAN RES LTD (BC)
Struck off register and declared dissolved for failure to file returns 10/30/92

LORD & BURNHAM CO.
Merged into Burnham Corp. (NY) 00/00/1947
Each share 7% Preferred $100 par exchanged for (1) share 6% Preferred $50 par and (10) shares Common $15 par
Each share Common $65 par exchanged for (1) share new Common $15 par
Burnham Corp. (NY) reincorporated in Delaware 04/29/2002 which name changed to Burnham Holdings, Inc. 01/08/2003

LORD & LAZARUS INC (UT)
Name changed to Utility Communications International, Inc. 00/00/1996
Utility Communications International, Inc. reorganized as Intermost Corp. (UT) 11/10/1998 which reincorporated in Wyoming 02/25/2003 which name changed to Uni Core Holdings Corp. 01/29/2010

LORD & TAYLOR
Merged into Associated Dry Goods Corp. 8/24/51
Each share 1st Preferred $100 par exchanged for (1.3) shares 5.25% 1st Preferred $100 par
Each share 2nd Preferred $100 par exchanged for (1.5) shares 6% 2nd Preferred $100 par
Each share Common $100 par exchanged for (18) shares new Common $1 par
Associated Dry Goods Corp. merged into May Department Stores Co. (NY) 10/4/86 which reincorporated in Delaware 5/24/96 which merged into Federated Department Stores, Inc. 8/30/2005 which name changed to Macy's, Inc. 6/1/2007

LORD ABBETT BD DEB FD INC (DE)
Reincorporated under the laws of Maryland 4/29/76

LORD ABBETT CALIF TAX FREE INCOME FD INC (MD)
Reorganized as Lord Abbett Tax-Free Income Fund, Inc. 07/12/1996
Details not available

LORD ABBETT CASH RESV FD INC (MD)
Name changed to Lord Abbett U.S. Government Securities Money Market Fund Inc. and Common $0.001 par reclassified as Common-A $0.001 par 12/16/93
Lord Abbett U.S. Government Securities Money Market Fund Inc.

name changed to Lord Abbett U.S. Government & Government Sponsored Enterprises Money Market Fund Inc. 10/1/2003

LORD ABBETT DEVELOPING GROWTH FD INC OLD (MD)
Merged into Lord Abbett Developing Growth Fund, Inc. (New) 2/6/79
Each share Capital Stock $1 par exchanged for (1.37562) shares Capital Stock $1 par

LORD ABBETT EQUITY FD (MA)
Under plan of merger each Share of Bene. Int. 1990 Ser. no par automatically became Lord Abbett Large-Cap Growth Fund Class A on a net asset basis 05/31/2000

LORD ABBETT FUNDAMENTAL VALUE FD INC (MD)
Reorganized as Lord Abbett Securities Trust 07/12/1996
Details not available

LORD ABBETT INCOME FD INC (MD)
Reincorporated 07/09/1975
State of incorporation changed from (DE) to (MD) 07/09/1975
Name changed to Lord Abbett U.S. Government Securities Fund, Inc. 09/23/1985
(See Lord Abbett U.S. Government Securities Fund, Inc.)

LORD ABBETT TAX FREE INCOME FD INC (MD)
National Series $0.001 par reclassified as National Tax Free Income Fund $0.001 par 01/20/1999
New York Series $0.001 par reclassified as New York Tax Free Income Fund $0.001 par 01/20/1999
Name changed to Lord Abbett Municipal Income Fund, Inc. 01/28/2005

LORD ABBETT U S GOVT SECS FD INC (MD)
Reorganized under the laws of Delaware as Lord Abbett Investment Trust 07/12/1996
Details not available

LORD ABBETT U S GOVT SECS MONEY MKT FD INC (MD)
Name changed to Lord Abbett U.S. Government & Government Sponsored Enterprises Money Market Fund, Inc. 10/1/2003

LORD ABBETT VALUE APPRECIATION FD INC (MD)
Name changed to Lord Abbett Mid-Cap Value Fund Inc. 2/13/96

LORD ABBOTT INC (CO)
Recapitalized as Platinum Productions Inc. 11/24/92
Each share Common no par exchanged for (1/300) share Common no par

LORD ADAM/LADY EVE PRODUCTS, INC. (NJ)
Charter revoked for failure to file reports and pay fees 1/25/66

LORD BALTIMORE HOTEL CO. (MD)
Liquidation completed
Each share 2nd Preferred $100 par exchanged for first and final distribution of $100 cash plus $1.75 accrued dividends 8/1/60
Each share Common $2 par or VTC for Common $2 par exchanged for initial distribution of $100 cash 8/1/60
Each share Common $2 par or VTC for Common $2 par received second distribution of $25 cash 11/4/60
Each share Common $2 par or VTC for Common $2 par received third distribution of $5 cash 1/12/61
Each share Common $2 par or VTC for Common $2 par received fourth distribution of $240.42 principal amount of Ctfs. of Participation no par 1/16/61

Each share Common $2 par or VTC for Common $2 par received fifth and final distribution of $20.90 cash 4/12/61
Each Ctf. of Participation no par received initial distribution of $4.81 cash in July 1961
Each Ctf. of Participation no par received second distribution of $4.81 cash in July 1962
Each Ctf. of Participation no par received third distribution of $4.81 cash in July 1963
Each Ctf. of Participation no par received fourth distribution of $4.81 cash in July 1964
Each Ctf. of Participation no par received fifth distribution of $25 cash in December 1964
Each Ctf. of Participation no par received sixth distribution of $4.80 cash in July 1965
Each Ctf. of Participation no par received seventh distribution of $2.50 cash in October 1965
Each Ctf. of Participation no par received eighth distribution of $2.51 cash in January 1966
Each Ctf. of Participation no par received ninth distribution of $2.51 cash in April 1966
Each Ctf. of Participation no par received tenth distribution of $2.51 cash in July 1966
Each Ctf. of Participation no par received eleventh distribution of $2.51 cash in October 1966
Each Ctf. of Participation no par received twelfth distribution of $2.51 cash in January 1967
Each Ctf. of Participation no par received thirteenth distribution of $2.51 cash in April 1967
Each Ctf. of Participation no par received fourteenth distribution of $2.51 cash in July 1967
Each Ctf. of Participation no par received fifteenth distribution of $2.51 cash in October 1967
Each Ctf. of Participation no par received sixteenth distribution of $30.30 cash in April 1969
Each Ctf. of Participation no par received seventeenth distribution of $20.03 cash in February 1970
Each Ctf. of Participation no par exchanged for eighteenth and final distribution of $5.02 cash 5/19/70

LORD ELECTRIC CO., INC. (DE)
Charter forfeited for failure to maintain a registered agent 2/25/91

LORD ELGIN HOTEL LTD. (ON)
Charter revoked for failure to file reports and pay fees 11/11/65

LORD HARDWICKE LTD (DE)
Name changed to Hardwicke Companies Inc. 10/26/1970
(See Hardwicke Companies Inc.)

LORD-REBEL INDS (CA)
Stock Dividend - 50% 04/12/1972
Merged into Topps & Trowsers 06/30/1978
Each share Common 10¢ par exchanged for $1.51 cash

LORD RIV GOLD MINES LTD (BC)
Recapitalized as Aquamin Resources Inc. 07/02/1992
Each share Common no par exchanged for (0.25) share Common no par
Aquamin Resources Inc. name changed to Peruvian Gold Ltd. 05/10/1994 which merged into Quest Investment Corp. 07/04/2002 which merged into Quest Capital Corp. (BC) 06/30/2003 which reincorporated in Canada 05/27/2008 which name changed to Sprott Resource Lending Corp. 09/10/2010 which merged into Sprott Inc. 07/24/2013

LORD SIMCOE HOTEL LTD (ON)
Dissolution completed
Each share Class A $1 par received initial distribution of $1.75 cash 11/30/88
Each share Common no par received initial distribution of $1.75 cash 11/30/88
Each share Class A $1 par received second and final distribution of $0.265 cash 6/28/89
Each share Common no par received second and final distribution of $0.265 cash 6/28/89
Note: Certificates were not required to be surrendered and are now valueless

LORD TECH INC (WY)
Administratively dissolved for failure to pay taxes 03/14/2009

LORD WHEATLEY ASSOC INC (DE)
Name changed to Roan Financial Services Inc. 7/17/87
(See Roan Financial Services Inc.)

LOREDI RES LTD (BC)
Recapitalized as Marlin Developments Ltd. 01/15/1987
Each share Common no par exchanged for (0.2) share Common no par
Marlin Developments Ltd. name changed to Matrix Petroleum Inc. 12/13/2001 which was acquired by Berens Energy Ltd. 12/12/2003
(See Berens Energy Ltd.)

LOREN INDS INC (NY)
Each (125,000) shares old Common 1¢ par exchanged for (1) share new Common 1¢ par 12/14/1990
Note: In effect holders received $1.25 cash per share and public interest was eliminated

LORETO RES CORP (NV)
Name changed 07/24/2008
Common $0.0015 par changed to $0.001 par 07/03/2008
Common $0.001 par split (2) for (1) by issuance of (1) additional share payable 07/23/2008 to holders of record 07/18/2008 Ex date - 07/24/2008
Name changed from Loreto Corp. to Loreto Resources Corp. 07/24/2008
Common $0.001 par split (2) for (1) by issuance of (1) additional share payable 01/30/2009 to holders of record 01/26/2009 Ex date - 02/02/2009
Common $0.001 par split (2) for (1) by issuance of (1) additional share payable 01/28/2010 to holders of record 01/25/2010 Ex date - 01/29/2010
Recapitalized as HK International Group Inc. 04/16/2013
Each share Common $0.001 par exchanged for (0.01) share Common $0.001 par
HK International Group Inc. name changed to Hygeialand Biomedical Corp. 07/11/2013 which name changed to Angstron Holdings Corp. 08/19/2013 which name changed to HK Graphene Technology Corp. 07/31/2015

LORETTO MNG CO (DE)
Charter cancelled and declared inoperative and void for non-payment of taxes 3/1/75

LOREX MINERALS INC (BC)
Recapitalized as Alinghi Minerals Inc. 12/01/2003
Each share Common no par exchanged for (0.25) share Common no par
Alinghi Minerals Inc. name changed to Dorex Minerals Inc. 04/05/2006 which name changed to Cipher Resources Inc. 09/18/2017

LOREX TECHNOLOGY INC (ON)
Acquired by FLIR Systems, Inc. 12/20/2012
Each share Common no par exchanged for $1.30 cash

LORI CORP (DE)
Name changed to COMFORCE Corp. 12/01/1995
(See COMFORCE Corp.)

LORI EXPL LTD (BC)
Recapitalized as O'Lori Holdings Ltd. 10/24/78
Each share Capital Stock 50¢ par exchanged for (0.5) share Capital Stock no par
(See O'Lori Holdings Ltd.)

LORIAN CAP CORP (CANADA)
Name changed to Medworxx Solutions Inc. 12/17/2007
(See Medworxx Solutions Inc.)

LORICA RES LTD (BC)
Recapitalized as Lom River Gold Corp. 08/18/1999
Each share Common no par exchanged for (1/3) share Common no par
Lom River Gold Corp. name changed to Catalina Energy Corp. 10/17/2001 which recapitalized as Catalina Metals Corp. 02/14/2011 which name changed to True Grit Resources Ltd. 06/28/2012

LORIE MINES LTD.
Name changed to New Lorie Mines Ltd. in 1945
New Lorie Mines Ltd. recapitalized as Lorie Resources Inc. 3/10/81 which recapitalized as Theme Restaurants Inc. 12/30/86
(See Theme Restaurants Inc.)

LORIE RES INC (ON)
Recapitalized as Theme Restaurants Inc. 12/30/76
Each share Common no par exchanged for (0.5) share Common no par
(See Theme Restaurants Inc.)

LORILLARD CORP (DE)
Merged into Loew's Theatres, Inc. 11/29/1968
Each share Common $5 par exchanged for $62 principal amount of 6-7/8% Subord. Debentures due 12/01/1993 and (1) Common Stock Purchase Warrant expiring 11/29/1980

LORILLARD INC (DE)
Common 1¢ par split (3) for (1) by issuance of (2) additional shares payable 01/15/2013 to holders of record 12/14/2012 Ex date - 01/16/2013
Merged into Reynolds American Inc. 06/12/2015
Each share Common 1¢ par exchanged for (0.2909) share Common $0.0001 par and $50.50 cash
Reynolds American Inc. merged into British American Tobacco PLC 07/25/2017

LORILLARD P CO (NJ)
Common $25 par changed to no par in 1929
Common no par changed to $10 par in 1933
Common $10 par changed to $5 par and (1) additional share issued 5/1/59
Recapitalized under the laws of Delaware as Lorillard Corp. 4/9/68
Each share 7% Preferred $100 par exchanged for $140 principal amount of 6-5/8% Subord. Debentures due 4/1/93
Each share Common $5 par exchanged for (1) share Common $5 par
Lorillard Corp. merged into Loew's Theatres, Inc. 11/29/68

(See listing for Loew's Theatres, Inc.)

LORIMAR (DE)
Name changed 01/27/1985
Name changed from Lorimar (CA) to Lorimar, Inc. (DE) 01/27/1985
Merged into Lorimar-Telepictures Corp. 02/18/1986
Each share Common no par exchanged for (2.2) shares Common 1¢ par
Lorimar-Telepictures Corp. acquired by Warner Communications Inc. 01/11/1989 which merged into Time Warner Inc. (Old) 01/10/1990 which merged into AOL Time Warner Inc. 01/11/2001 which name changed to Time Warner Inc. (New) 10/16/2003 which merged into AT&T Inc. 06/15/2018

LORIMAR FILM PARTNERS L P (DE)
Option to purchase Limited Partnership Interests exercised 6/29/96
No Unitholders' equity

LORIMAR TELEPICTURES CORP (NY)
Acquired by Warner Communications Inc. 01/11/1989
Each share Common 1¢ par exchanged for (0.3675) share Common $1 par
Warner Communications Inc. merged into Time Warner Inc. (Old) 01/10/1990 which merged into AOL Time Warner Inc. 01/11/2001 which name changed to Time Warner Inc. (New) 10/16/2003 which merged into AT&T Inc. 06/15/2018

LORING INDS INC (UT)
Involuntarily dissolved 06/13/1969

LORING WARD INTL LTD (CANADA)
Each share old Common no par exchanged for (0.1) share new Common no par 06/29/2005
Merged into Werba Reinhard, Inc. 01/23/2009
Each share Common no par exchanged for $11.25 cash

LORNE GOLD MINES LTD.
Acquired by Bralorne Mines Ltd. in 1931
Each share Capital Stock exchanged for (0.125) share Capital Stock no par
Bralorne Mines Ltd. name changed to Bralorne Pioneer Mines Ltd. 3/19/59 which name changed to Bralorne Can-Fer Resources Ltd. 12/3/69 which name changed to Bralorne Resources Ltd. 5/29/72 which recapitalized as BRL Enterprises Inc. 11/27/90
(See BRL Enterprises Inc.)

LORNE TRAIL HLDGS LTD (CANADA)
Name changed to Brake Check Canada Inc. 8/13/90
(See Brake Check Canada Inc.)

LORNEX CAP INC (CANADA)
Each share old Common no par exchanged for (0.33333333) share new Common no par 08/29/2011
Reincorporated under the laws of British Columbia as Norsemont Capital Inc. 02/16/2016

LORNEX MNG LTD (ON)
Reincorporated 12/30/88
Capital Stock 50¢ par changed to no par 8/14/70
Capital Stock no par changed to $1 par 9/28/70
Place of incorporation changed from (BC) to (ONT) 12/30/88
Merged into Rio Algom Ltd. 12/30/88
Each share Capital Stock $1 par exchanged for (3) shares 8.5% Non-Vtg. 2nd Preference Ser. C $5 par
(See Rio Algom Ltd.)

LORONIX INFORMATION SYS INC (NV)
Issue Information - 2,400,000 shares COM offered at $6 per share on 08/24/1994
Merged into Comverse Technology, Inc. 07/17/2000
Each share Common $0.001 par exchanged for (0.385) share Common 10¢ par
Comverse Technology, Inc. merged into Verint Systems Inc. 02/05/2013

LORRAINE COURT APARTMENTS, INC.
Liquidated in 1940

LORRY BAY & CO INC (FL)
Recapitalized as Sentech EAS Corp. 09/22/1995
Each share Common $0.0001 par exchanged for (0.0128381) share Common $0.0001 par

LORTOGS INC (DE)
Charter cancelled and declared inoperative and void for non-payment of taxes 3/1/80

LORUS THERAPEUTICS INC (CANADA)
Each share old Common no par exchanged for (0.03333333) share new Common no par 05/31/2010
Name changed to Aptose Biosciences Inc. 09/03/2014

LORUS THERAPEUTICS INC (ON)
Reorganized under the laws of Canada as Lorus Therapeutics Inc. (New) 07/10/2007
Each share Common no par exchanged for (1) share Common no par and (0.08) share 4325231 Canada Inc. Common no par
Note: U.S. holders received CAD$0.00407751 cash in lieu of 4325231 Canada Inc. shares
(See 4325231 Canada Inc.)
Lorus Therapeutics Inc. (New) name changed to Aptose Biosciences Inc. 09/03/2014

LOS ALAMITOS RACE COURSE (CA)
Capital Stock $200 par changed to $20 par and (9) additional shares issued 08/15/1971
Capital Stock $20 par changed to $5 par and (3) additional shares issued 08/14/1972
Completely liquidated 08/08/1984
Each share Capital Stock $5 par exchanged for first and final distribution of $24.25 cash

LOS ANGELES ALBERTA PETROLEUM LTD. (AB)
Charter struck off register and deemed dissolved for failure to file reports 9/15/65

LOS ANGELES ATHLETIC CLUB (CA)
Name changed to LAACO Inc. 05/01/1975
LAACO Inc. reorganized as LAACO, Ltd. 12/30/1986

LOS ANGELES BILTMORE CO.
Dissolved 00/00/1934
Details not available

LOS ANGELES BILTMORE HOTEL CO.
Acquired by Corrigan Hotel Co. 00/00/1951
Details not available

LOS ANGELES CREAMERY CO.
Assets acquired by Golden State Co., Ltd. 00/00/1934
Details not available

LOS ANGELES DRUG CO (CA)
Completely liquidated 09/06/1968
Each share Capital Stock no par exchanged for first and final distribution of (1) share Di Giorgio Corp. 88¢ Conv. Preferred Ser. A no par
(See Di Giorgio Corp.)

LOS ANGELES GAS & ELECTRIC CORP.
Merged into Southern California Gas Co. on a (4) for (1) basis in 1937

LOS ANGELES INDUSTRIES, INC.
Name changed to Blue Diamond Corp. in 1940 which was acquired by Flintkote Co. 5/14/59
(See Flintkote Co.)

LOS ANGELES INVT CO (CA)
Each share Capital Stock $1 par exchanged for (0.1) share Capital Stock $10 par 00/00/1929
Each share Capital Stock $10 par exchanged for (0.1) share Capital Stock $100 par 00/00/1945
Each share Capital Stock $100 par exchanged for (26) shares Capital Stock no par to effect a (20) for (1) split plus a 30% stock dividend 06/21/1965
Merged into First Colony Life Insurance Co. 12/07/1971
Each share Capital Stock no par exchanged for (6) shares Common $1 par
(See First Colony Life Insurance Co.)

LOS ANGELES LIFE INS CO (CA)
Each share Common $17 par exchanged for (3) shares Common $5.67 par 02/05/1970
Declared insolvent 03/30/1973
No stockholders' equity

LOS ANGELES LUMBER PRODUCTS CO. LTD.
Reorganized as Los Angeles Shipbuilding & Drydock Corp. in 1940
No stockholders' equity

LOS ANGELES NATL BK (BUENA PARK, CA)
Acquired by Royal Business Bank (Los Angeles, CA) 05/17/2013
Each share Common $3 par exchanged for $9.7467 cash

LOS ANGELES-NEW MEXICO OIL CO. LTD.
Assets sold and dissolution approved in 1937
Details not available

LOS ANGELES PACIFIC PROPERTIES CORP.
Properties sold Inactive in 1930

LOS ANGELES RAILWAY CORP. (CA)
Name changed to Los Angeles Transit Lines in 1945 which was completely liquidated 2/27/59

LOS ANGELES SECS GROUP (UT)
Name changed to Above Technologies, Inc. 04/20/1990

LOS ANGELES SHIPBUILDING & DRYDOCK CORP. (CA)
Liquidation completed 9/16/63

LOS ANGELES SOAP CO (CA)
Liquidation completed
Each share Common $100 par received initial distribution of $115 cash 1/10/90
Each share Common $100 par received second distribution of $3.30 cash 9/4/90
Each share Common $100 par received third distribution of $115 cash 12/3/90
Each share Common $100 par received fourth distribution of $4.60 cash 1/10/91
Each share Common $100 par received fifth distribution of $1.40 cash 3/15/91
Each share Common $100 par received sixth distribution of $3.80 cash 9/10/91
Each share Common $100 par received seventh distribution of $118.50 cash 1/10/92
Each share Common $100 par received eighth distribution of $1.60 cash 4/3/92

Each share Common $100 par exchanged for ninth and final distribution of $110.85 cash 11/30/92

LOS ANGELES STEAMSHIP CO.
Merged into Matson Navigation Co. 00/00/1930
Details not available

LOS ANGELES SYND TECHNOLOGY INC (NV)
Name changed to Invent Ventures, Inc. 09/19/2012

LOS ANGELES TRANSIT LINES (CA)
Liquidation completed 2/27/59

LOS ANGELES TURF CLUB, INC. (CA)
Recapitalized 2/29/60
Each share Capital Stock $5,000 par exchanged for (50) shares Capital Stock $100 par
Each share Capital Stock $500 par exchanged for (5) shares Capital Stock $100 par
Each share Capital Stock $100 par exchanged for (2) shares Capital Stock $50 par 2/17/64
Name changed to Santa Anita Consolidated, Inc. in November 1964
Santa Anita Consolidated, Inc. reorganized as Santa Anita Realty Enterprises Inc. 12/31/79 which merged with Meditrust Corp. 1/5/97 which name changed to La Quinta Properties, Inc. 6/20/2001 which reorganized as La Quinta Corp. 1/2/2002
(See La Quinta Corp.)

LOS GATOS TELEPHONE CO. (CA)
Name changed to Western California Telephone Co. in 1956
Western California Telephone Co. acquired by General Telephone & Electronics Corp. 5/29/64 which name changed to GTE Corp. 7/1/82 which merged into Verizon Communications Inc. 6/30/2000

LOS GAUCHOS CAP CORP (AB)
Issue Information - 1,000,000 shares COM offered at $0.20 per share on 05/08/1997
Name changed Service Track Enterprises Inc. 9/22/97

LOS PADRES SVGS BK (SOLVANG, CA)
Acquired by Henrington West Financial Group in April 1996
Each share Common exchanged for $17.50 cash

LOS ROBLES BANCORP (CA)
Merged into Pacific Capital Bancorp 06/30/2000
Each share Common $5 par exchanged for $23.1375 cash

LOS ROBLES NATL BK (THOUSAND OAKS, CA)
Under plan of reorganization each share Common $5 par automatically became (1) share Los Robles Bancorp Common $5 par 7/31/95

LOS TRES AMIGOS LTD (CO)
Name changed to Venture Frontiers Corp. 01/30/1984

LOST CANYON URANIUM & OIL CO. (NM)
Out of business 06/13/1961
Details not available

LOST CHORD MINING CO. INC. (WA)
Charter cancelled and declared dissolved for failure to pay fees 7/1/58

LOST CREEK OIL & URANIUM CO. (WY)
Name changed to Western Nuclear Corp. 03/25/1957
Western Nuclear Corp. recapitalized as Western Nuclear, Inc. 12/23/1959 which merged into Phelps Dodge Corp. 05/07/1971 which merged into Freeport-McMoRan Copper & Gold Inc. 03/19/2007 which name changed to Freeport-McMoRan Inc. 07/14/2014

LOST DUTCHMAN URANIUM MINING CORP. (UT)
Merged into Uranium Corp. of America (UT) on a (1) for (2) basis 4/5/55
Uranium Corp. of America (UT) merged into Chemical & Metallurgical Enterprises, Inc. 11/5/56
(See Chemical & Metallurgical Enterprises, Inc.)

LOST LAKE RES LTD (BC)
Name changed to Equivest International Financial Corp. 09/12/1985
Equivest International Financial Corp. name changed to Allegro Property Inc. 03/25/1996 which name changed to Valdor Fiber Optics Inc. 07/05/2000 which recapitalized as Valdor Technology International Inc. 07/21/2008

LOST RIV MNG LTD (ON)
Capital Stock $1 par changed to no par 10/6/71
Assets sold for benefit of creditors in 1984
No stockholders' equity

LOTO INC (NV)
Name changed to Mobile Integrated Systems, Inc. 03/27/2012
Mobile Integrated Systems, Inc. name changed to Epcylon Technologies, Inc. 08/08/2013

LOTON CORP (NV)
Common $0.001 par split (2) for (1) by issuance of (1) additional share payable 09/27/2016 to holders of record 09/22/2016 Ex date - 09/28/2016
Reincorporated under the laws of Delaware as LiveXLive Media, Inc. 08/03/2017

LOTSOFF CORP (DE)
Preferred Ser. A 1¢ par called for redemption at $5 on 12/30/1997
Chapter 7 bankruptcy proceedings terminated 07/16/2007
No stockholders' equity

LOTT HOTELS CO. (IL)
Liquidation completed 11/11/54

LOTTA COAL INC (FL)
Administratively dissolved 09/24/2010

LOTTE SHOPPING CO LTD (KOREA)
GDR agreement terminated 05/30/2017
Each 144A GDR for Common exchanged for $8.536525 cash

LOTTERY ENTERPRISES INC (NV)
Name changed to On-Point Technology Systems, Inc. 08/15/1996
On-Point Technology Systems, Inc. name changed to Global ePoint, Inc. 06/05/2001

LOTTO OIL CO (UT)
Name changed to Personal Puzzle, Inc. 09/22/1988
(See Personal Puzzle, Inc.)

LOTTOMATICA S P A (ITALY)
Stock Dividend - 2% payable 06/06/2011 to holders of record 05/25/2011 Ex date - 05/23/2011
Name changed to GTECH S.p.A. 06/03/2013
GTECH S.p.A. merged into International Game Technology PLC 04/07/2015

LOTTOWORLD INC (FL)
Plan of reorganization under Chapter 11 Federal Bankruptcy Code effective 10/1/99
No stockholders' equity

LOTUS BANCORP INC (MI)
Acquired by Level One Bancorp, Inc. 03/02/2015
Each share Common 1¢ par exchanged for $12 cash

LOTUS COSMETICS INTL LTD (BC)
Recapitalized as Creative Products Inc. 3/27/89
Each share Common no par exchanged for (0.5) share Common no par
(See Creative Products Inc.)

LOTUS DEV CORP (DE)
Common 1¢ par split (3) for (1) by issuance of (2) additional shares 2/23/87
Merged into White Acquisition Corp. 7/10/95
Each share Common 1¢ par exchanged for $64 cash

LOTUS ENTERPRISES INC (NV)
Name changed to Clubcharlie.com, Inc. 03/23/1999
Clubcharlie.com, Inc. name changed to ViaStar Holdings, Inc. 01/22/2001 which name changed to Viastar Media Corp. 01/23/2004 which name changed to Pop3 Media Corp. 01/21/2005
(See Pop3 Media Corp.)

LOTUS PAC INC (DE)
Name changed to Opta Corp. 9/28/2004
(See Opta Corp.)

LOTUS RES LTD (NS)
Name changed to Ashgrove Resources Ltd. 08/02/1990
Ashgrove Resources Ltd. recapitalized as Ashgrove Energy Ltd. 08/19/1993 which name changed to Search Energy Inc. 08/29/1995 which merged into Search Energy Corp. 01/09/1997 which merged into Advantage Energy Income Fund 05/24/2001 which reorganized as Advantage Oil & Gas Ltd. 07/09/2009

LOU KORNHANDLER, INC. (CA)
See - Kornhandler (Lou), Inc.

LOU MEX MINES LTD (BC)
Recapitalized as Continental Minerals Corp. (Incorporated 06/15/1970) 03/08/1977
Each share Common no par exchanged for (0.25) share Common no par
(See Continental Minerals Corp. Corp. (Incorporated 06/15/1970))

LOUANNA GOLD MINES LTD (ON)
Recapitalized as Consolidated Louanna Gold Mines Ltd. 03/07/1973
Each share Common $1 par exchanged for (0.25) share Common no par
(See Consolidated Louanna Gold Mines Ltd.)

LOUBAC TOP ENVIRONMENTAL INC (CANADA)
Reincorporated under the laws of British Columbia as Novus Gold Corp. 03/20/2009
Novus Gold Corp. merged into PanTerra Gold Ltd. 04/19/2012

LOUBEL EXPL INC (QC)
Recapitalized as Lounor Exploration Inc. 4/17/2006
Each share Common no par exchanged for (0.1) share Common no par

LOUDCLOUD INC (DE)
Issue Information - 25,000,000 shares COM offered at $6 per share on 03/08/2001
Name changed to Opsware Inc. 08/16/2002
(See Opsware Inc.)

LOUDEN MACHY CO (IA)
Each share Common $100 par exchanged for (10) shares Common $10 par 00/00/1949
All Common $10 par acquired by Mechanical Handling Systems Inc. following voluntary purchase offer 00/00/1953
5% Preferred $100 par called for redemption 02/00/1966
Public interest eliminated

LOUDER FINL GROUP INC (AB)
Struck off register and declared dissolved for failure to file returns 1/1/91

LOUDEYE CORP (DE)
Name changed 6/4/2002
Issue Information - 4,500,000 shares COM offered at $16 per share on 03/15/2000
Name changed from Loudeye Technologies, Inc. to Loudeye Corp. 6/4/2002
Each share old Common $0.001 par exchanged for (0.1) share new Common $0.001 par 5/23/2006
Merged into Nokia Corp. 10/17/2006
Each share new Common $0.001 par exchanged for $4.50 cash

LOUDON PACKING CO.
Dissolved in 1943

LOUDONG GEN NICE RES CHINA HLDGS LTD (HONG KONG)
Stock Dividend - 20% payable 06/18/2012 to holders of record 06/05/2012 Ex date - 06/01/2012
ADR agreement terminated 02/23/2016
Each Sponsored ADR for Ordinary exchanged for $2.582 cash

LOUGAN INVTS INC (AB)
Recapitalized as Shearhart Corp. 11/20/1990
Each share Common no par exchanged for (0.5) share Common no par
(See Shearhart Corp.)

LOUGHBOROUGH GOLD MINES LTD. (BC)
Dissolved in 1949

LOUIS DREYFUS NAT GAS CORP (OK)
$2.25 Depositary Preferred called for redemption at $26.35 plus $0.5625 accrued dividends 12/31/1997
Merged into Dominion Resources, Inc. (New) 11/01/2001
Each share Common 1¢ par exchanged for (0.3226) share Common no par and $20 cash
Dominion Resources, Inc. (New) name changed to Dominion Energy, Inc. 05/11/2017

LOUIS SHERRY INC (NY)
Name changed 11/01/1965
Name changed from Louis Sherry Preserves, Inc. to Louis Sherry, Inc. 11/01/1965
Merged into Norin Corp. (DE) 12/20/1978
Each share Common 10¢ par exchanged for (0.0441) share Common $1 par
Norin Corp. (DE) reorganized in Florida 05/31/1979
(See Norin Corp. (FL))

LOUIS VUITTON S A (FRANCE)
Merged into LVMH Moet Hennessey Louis Vuitton 10/22/87
Each ADR for Ordinary 10 Frs. par exchanged for (0.625) Sponsored ADR for Ordinary 50 Frs. par
(See LVMH Moet Hennessey Louis Vuitton)

LOUISE APARTMENTS, INC.
Liquidated in 1940

LOUISIANA & NORTH WEST RR CO (LA)
Acquired by Patriot Rail Co. LLC 06/00/2008
Details not available

LOUISIANA & SOUTHN LIFE INS CO (LA)
Each share old Common $1 par exchanged for (0.333333) share new Common $1 par 8/15/75
Merged into Charter Co. 10/3/77
Each share new Common $1 par exchanged for $6 cash

LOUISIANA BANCORP INC NEW (LA)
Acquired by Home Bancorp, Inc. 09/15/2015
Each share Common 1¢ par exchanged for $24.25 cash

LOUISIANA BANCORP INC OLD (LA)
Out of business 12/10/1987
Stockholders' equity unlikely

LOUISIANA BANCSHARES INC (LA)
Name changed to Premier Bancorp, Inc. 4/15/87
Premier Bancorp, Inc. merged into Banc One Corp. 1/2/96 which merged into Bank One Corp. 10/2/98 which merged into J.P. Morgan Chase & Co. 12/31/2000 which name changed to JPMorgan Chase & Co. 7/20/2004

LOUISIANA BK & TR CO (CROWLEY, LA)
Reorganized as Louisiana Bancorp, Inc. (Old) 07/28/1982
Each share Capital Stock $10 par exchanged for (1) share Common $10 par
(See Louisiana Bancorp, Inc. (Old))

LOUISIANA BK & TR CO (SHREVEPORT, LA)
Common $20 par changed to $10 par and (1) additional share issued 06/00/1978
Reorganized as LBT Corp. 04/16/1984
Each share Common $10 par exchanged for (2) shares Common $5 par
(See LBT Corp.)

LOUISIANA CENT OIL & GAS CO (DE)
Each share Common automatically became (1) Net Profit Unit 12/23/1968
In process of liquidation
Details not available

LOUISIANA CENTRAL BANK (FERRIDAY, LA)
Under plan of reorganization each share Common $6 par automatically became (1) share Central Louisiana Capital Corp. Common $6 par 8/15/84

LOUISIANA-DELTA OFFSHORE CORP. (DE)
Mergedd into Zapata Off-Shore Co. 07/06/1966
Each share Common 2¢ par exchanged for (0.2325581) share Capital Stock 50¢ par
Zapata Off-Shore Co. name changed to Zapata Norness Inc. 11/25/1968 which name changed to Zapata Corp. (DE) 02/15/1972 which reincorporated in Nevada 04/30/1999 which reincorporated in Delaware as Harbinger Group Inc. 12/23/2009 which name changed to HRG Group, Inc. 03/11/2015 which recapitalized as Spectrum Brands Holdings, Inc. (New) 07/16/2018

LOUISIANA DIVERSIFIED CORP. (LA)
Charter revoked for failure to file annual reports 5/13/82

LOUISIANA FIRE INSURANCE CO. (LA)
Name changed to Louisiana Companies 4/29/71

LOUISIANA FOOD CO (NV)
Common $0.001 par changed to $0.00001 par 09/21/2012
Recapitalized as MMA Global, Inc. 09/14/2018
Each share Common $0.00001 par exchanged for (0.002) share Common $0.00001 par

LOUISIANA GAS & FUEL CO.
Acquired by United Gas Corp. 00/00/1930
Details not available

LOUISIANA GAS SVC CO (FL)
Under plan of reorganization each share Common $10 par automatically became (1) share Louisiana General Services, Inc. Common $1 par 2/26/71
Louisiana General Services, Inc. merged into Citizens Utilities Co. 12/4/90 which name changed to Citizens Communication Co. 5/18/2000

LOUISIANA GEN SVCS INC (LA)
Common $1 par split (2) for (1) by issuance of (1) additional share 05/15/1972
Common $1 par split (2) for (1) by issuance of (1) additional share 02/29/1980
Common $1 par split (3) for (2) by issuance of (0.5) additional share 06/12/1981
Merged into Citizens Utilities Co. 12/04/1990
Each share Common $1 par exchanged for (0.8) share Ser. B Common 25¢ par
Citizens Utilities Co. name changed to Citizens Communications Co. 05/18/2000 which name changed to Frontier Communications Corp. 07/31/2008

LOUISIANA ICE & ELECTRIC CO., INC. (LA)
Name changed to Central Louisiana Electric Co., Inc. in 1945
(See Central Louisiana Electric Co., Inc.)

LOUISIANA ICE & UTILITIES, INC. (LA)
Reorganized as Louisiana Ice & Electric Co., Inc. 1/1/35
No stockholders' equity

LOUISIANA LD & EXPL CO (MD)
Common no par changed to $1 par 00/00/1934
Common $1 par changed to 30¢ par and (2) additional shares issued 05/21/1956
Common 30¢ par changed to 15¢ par and (1) additional share issued 10/30/1964
Common 15¢ par split (2) for (1) by issuance of (1) additional share 06/15/1971
Merged into Burlington Resources Inc. 10/22/1997
Each share Common 15¢ par exchanged for (1.525) shares Common 1¢ par
Burlington Resources Inc. merged into ConocoPhillips 03/31/2006

LOUISIANA LD OFFSHORE EXPL INC (MD)
Reincorporated 06/03/1976
State of incorporation changed from (DE) to (MD) 06/03/1976
Class B Common $1 par reclassified as Common $1 par 01/01/1979
Merged into Louisiana Land & Exploration Co. 10/31/1984
Each share Common $1 par exchanged for $10 cash

LOUISIANA MNG CORP (BC)
Delisted from Alberta Stock Exchange 05/06/1991

LOUISIANA MOTOR CAR CO., INC. (LA)
Charter revoked for failure to file annual reports 5/13/82

LOUISIANA NATL BK (BATON ROUGE, LA)
Each share Capital Stock $100 par exchanged for (20) shares Capital Stock and a 100% stock dividend paid 10/24/1957
Each share Capital Stock $10 par exchanged for (1.5) shares Capital Stock $5 par to effect a (2) for (1) split and a 25% stock dividend 02/22/1973
Stock Dividends - 100% 12/28/1942; 14-2/7% 01/28/1964; 25% 02/15/1965; 25% 01/20/1967; 10% 01/25/1968; 25% 08/21/1969; 14-2/7% 01/28/1971; 10% 09/15/1978; 10% 05/31/1979; 10% 11/28/1980
Under plan of reorganization each share Capital Stock $5 par automatically became (1) share First Bancshares of Louisiana, Inc. Common $5 par 06/19/1981
First Bancshares of Louisiana, Inc. merged into Louisiana Bancshares, Inc. 01/10/1985 which name changed to Premier Bancorp, Inc. 04/15/1987 which merged into Banc One Corp. 01/02/1996 which merged into Bank One Corp. 10/02/1998 which merged into J.P. Morgan Chase & Co. 07/01/2004 which name changed to JPMorgan Chase & Co. 07/20/2004

LOUISIANA NATL SEC BK (DONALDSONVILLE, LA)
Merged into Whitney Holding Corp. 05/16/1998
Each share Common no par exchanged for (16.9011) shares Common no par
Whitney Holding Corp. merged into Hancock Holding Co. 06/04/2011 which name changed to Hancock Whitney Corp. 05/25/2018

LOUISIANA PAC RES INC (UT)
Proclaimed dissolved for failure to file annual reports 6/1/91

LOUISIANA POSTAL SYSTEMS, INC. (LA)
Charter revoked for failure to file annual reports 5/13/82

LOUISIANA PWR & LT CO (LA)
Reincorporated 2/28/75
6% Preferred no par called for redemption 6/1/53
State of incorporation changed from (FL) to (LA) 2/28/75
19.20% Preferred $25 par called for redemption 8/2/89
11.48% Preferred $100 par called for redemption 12/4/91
15.20% Preferred $25 par called for redemption 11/1/92
9.44% Preferred $100 par called for redemption 11/30/92
9.52% Preferred $100 par called for redemption 11/30/92
14.72% Preferred $25 par called for redemption 5/1/94
13.12% Preferred $25 par called for redemption 10/1/94
10.72% Preferred $25 par called for redemption 7/1/95
Name changed to Entergy Louisiana, Inc. 4/22/96
Entergy Louisiana, Inc. name changed to Entergy Louisiana Holdings, Inc. 2/13/2006

LOUISIANA STATE RICE MILLING CO., INC. (DE)
Voluntarily dissolved 12/17/2007
Details not available

LOUISIANA STATE RICE MILLING CO., INC. (LA)
Common $100 par changed to $10 par 00/00/1939
Stock Dividend - 400% 06/08/1950
Name changed to Lastarmco Inc. 08/23/1966
Lastarmco Inc. merged into Louisiana State Rice Milling Co., Inc. (DE) 03/06/1986
(See Louisiana State Rice Milling Co., Inc. (DE))

LOUISVILLE & NASHVILLE RR CO (KY)
Each share Capital Stock $100 par exchanged for (2) shares Capital Stock $50 par 00/00/1945
Capital Stock $50 par reclassified as Common $50 par 05/15/1970
Merged into Seaboard Coast Line Industries, Inc. (DE) 11/10/1972
Each share $2.10 Conv. Preferred Ser. A $35 par exchanged for (0.816666) share Common $20 par
Each share Common $50 par exchanged for (2.45) shares Common $20 par
Seaboard Coast Line Industries, Inc. (DE) merged into CSX Corp. 11/01/1980

LOUISVILLE BEDDING CO (KY)
Common $10 par changed to no par 11/15/1951
Common no par split (5) for (1) by issuance of (4) additional shares 01/15/1965
Stock Dividends - 10% 11/22/1968; 10% 01/21/1982; 10% payable 08/01/2002 to holders of record 07/26/2002 Ex date - 09/03/2002; 15% payable 02/06/2004 to holders of record 01/30/2004 Ex date - 02/23/2004
Acquired by LBC Capital, Inc. 03/31/2014
Each share Common no par exchanged for $8.16 principal amount of a 7.5% Note due 00/00/2015 and $6.21 cash

LOUISVILLE CEM CO (KY)
Each share Common $100 par exchanged for (5) shares Common $20 par 00/00/1937
Common $20 par changed to $5 par and (3) additional shares issued 02/10/1960
Stock Dividends - 100% 11/27/1951; 100% 11/08/1955
Acquired by Coplay Cement Co. 02/19/1985
Each share Common $5 par exchanged for $72 cash

LOUISVILLE DOWNS, INC. (KY)
Acquired by a private investor in November, 1986
Each share Common $1 par exchanged for approximately $15 cash

LOUISVILLE GAS & ELEC CO (KY)
Common no par split (2) for (1) by issuance of (1) additional share 12/14/56
Common no par split (2) for (1) by issuance of (1) additional share 1/19/62
Under plan of reorganization each share Common no par automatically became (1) share LG&E Energy Corp. Common no par 8/17/90
$8.72 Preferred no par called for redemption 3/16/92
$9.54 Preferred no par called for redemption 3/16/92
$8.90 Preferred no par called for redemption 7/1/93
7.45% Preferred $25 par called for redemption 12/15/95
Auction Preferred Ser. A no par called for redemption at $100 on 4/16/2007
5% Preferred $25 par called for redemption at $28 on 4/16/2007
$5.875 Preferred no par called for redemption at $100 on 4/16/2007

LOUISVILLE GAS & ELECTRIC CO. (DE)
Liquidated in 1948

LOUISVILLE HEATING CO.
Dissolved in 1927

LOUISVILLE INDUSTRIAL FOUNDATION (KY)
Liquidation completed
Each share Capital Stock $100 par

exchanged for initial distribution of $420.80 cash 12/30/86
Each share Capital Stock $100 par received second distribution of $200.04 cash 12/31/87
Each share Capital Stock $100 par received third distribution of $3.17 cash 12/19/88
Each share Capital Stock $100 par received fourth and final distribution of $20.04 cash 12/29/89

LOUISVILLE INVT CO (KY)
5% Preferred $80 par called for redemption 07/01/1953
Liquidation completed
Each share Common $10 par exchanged for initial distribution of $275 cash 10/31/1986
Each share Common $10 par received second distribution of $4 cash 12/01/1986
Each share Common $10 par received third and final distribution of $0.83567 cash 12/01/1987

LOUISVILLE PROPERTY CO. (KY)
Liquidation completed
Each share Capital Stock $100 par exchanged for initial distribution of $55 cash 9/3/63
Each share Capital Stock $100 par received second distribution of $8 cash 3/23/64
Each share Capital Stock $100 par received third and final distribution of $1.89 cash 6/3/66

LOUISVILLE TAXICAB & TRANSFER CO. (KY)
Each share Common $100 par exchanged for (8) shares Common $25 par to effect a (4) for (1) split and a 100% stock dividend 00/00/1950
Acquired by National Industries, Inc. (KY) 12/31/1967
Each share Common $25 par exchanged for (15) shares Common $1 par
National Industries, Inc. (KY) merged into Fuqua Industries, Inc. 01/03/1978 which name changed to Actava Group Inc. 07/21/1993 which name changed to Metromedia International Group, Inc. 11/01/1995
(See Metromedia International Group, Inc.)

LOUISVILLE TITLE CO. (KY)
Acquired by Louisville Title Mortgage Co. 08/12/1932
Details not available

LOUISVILLE TITLE CO (DE)
LOUISVILLE TITLE CO. (DE)
Acquired by Commonwealth Land Title Insurance Co. 10/07/1964
Each share Common no par exchanged for (1.7) shares Common $1.66-2/3 par
Commonwealth Land Title Insurance Co. acquired by Provident National Corp. 10/31/1969 which merged into PNC Financial Corp. 01/19/1983 which name changed to PNC Bank Corp. 02/08/1993 which name changed to PNC Financial Services Group, Inc. 03/15/2000

LOUISVILLE TITLE MORTGAGE CO. (DE)
Name changed to Louisville Title Co. (DE) 02/11/1960
Louisville Title Co. (DE) acquired by Commonwealth Land Title Insurance Co. 10/07/1964 which was acquired by Provident National Corp. 10/31/1969 which merged into PNC Financial Corp 01/19/1983 which name changed to PNC Bank Corp. 02/08/1993 which name changed to PNC Financial Services Group, Inc. 03/15/2000

LOUISVILLE TR CO (LOUISVILLE, KY)
Stock Dividends - 100% 1/24/57; 100% 1/25/62; 100% 3/20/73
Reorganized as United Kentucky, Inc. 12/19/75
Each share Common $10 par exchanged for (1) share Common $10 par
United Kentucky, Inc. merged into Liberty United Bancorp, Inc. 12/23/82 which name changed back to Liberty National Bancorp, Inc. 4/17/86 which merged into Banc One Corp. 8/15/94 which merged into Bank One Corp. 10/2/98 which merged into J.P. Morgan Chase & Co. 12/31/2000 which name changed to JPMorgan Chase & Co. 7/20/2004

LOUMIC EXPL INC (BC)
Common no par split (3) for (1) by issuance of (2) additional shares payable 03/03/2003 to holders of record 03/03/2003
Reorganized under the laws of Ontario as Vast Exploration Inc. 11/01/2004
Each share Common no par exchanged for (0.1) share Common no par
Vast Exploration Inc. name changed to ARHT Media Inc. 10/17/2014

LOUMIC RES LTD (BC)
Recapitalized as International Loumic Resources Ltd. 04/14/1998
Each share Common no par exchanged for (0.1) share Common no par
International Loumic Resources Ltd. name changed to Loumic Exploration Inc. (BC) 03/03/2003 which reorganized as Vast Exploration Inc. (ON) 11/01/2004 which name changed to ARHT Media Inc. 10/17/2014

LOURAY GAS & OIL CORP. (PA)
Out of business 00/00/1954
Details not available

LOUVICOURT GOLD MINES INC (QC)
Name changed 06/16/1981
Name changed from Louvicourt Goldfield Corp. to Louvicourt Gold Mines Inc. 06/16/1981
Delisted from NEX 10/04/2006

LOUVRE GOLD MINES LTD. (QC)
Recapitalized as New Louvre Gold Mines Ltd. 00/00/1945
Each share Capital Stock $1 par exchanged for (0.33333333) share Capital Stock $1 par
New Louvre Gold Mines Ltd. name changed to Fano Mining & Explorations, Inc. 12/30/1955 which recapitalized as Fanex Resources Ltd. 08/26/1971
(See Fanex Resources Ltd.)

LOVE CALENDAR INC (UT)
Reincorporated under the laws of Nevada as Perfect Health Care Corp. 04/07/2003
(See Perfect Health Care Corp.)

LOVE CORP. (TX)
Adjudicated bankrupt 4/29/64
No stockholders' equity

LOVE OIL INC (WY)
Charter revoked for failure to file annual reports 4/5/95

LOVE PETE CO (DE)
Each share Class A $1 par exchanged for (0.01) share Class A $100 par 1/28/82
Each share Class B $1 par exchanged for (0.01) share Class B $100 par 1/28/82
Note: Minority holders received an undetermined amount of cash and public interest was eliminated

LOVE VALLEY, INC. (NC)
Name changed to Love Valley Enterprises, Inc. 4/3/63

LOVELADY IKE INC (TX)
Name changed to Petromark Resources Co. and Common $1 par changed to 1¢ par 06/08/1985
(See Petromark Resources Co.)

LOVEN CHEMICAL OF CALIFORNIA (CA)
Name changed to Alcylite Plastics & Chemical Corp. 1/2/59 which was adjudicated bankrupt in January 1963

LOVENIA CORP. (DE)
Recapitalized as CALCOL, Inc. 12/30/1987
Each share Common no par exchanged for (0.5) share Common $0.001 par

LOVITT NUTRICEUTICAL CORP (BC)
Name changed to Lovitt Resources Inc. 09/10/2008

LOVLE PRODS INC (FL)
Reincorporated under the laws of Delaware as National Priorities Corp. 02/29/1972
(See National Priorities Corp.)

LOW MOOR IRON CO. OF VIRGINIA
Liquidated in 1927

LOW-PRICED SHARES
Trust terminated 00/00/1935
Details not available

LOW VOLATILE COAL CO.
Liquidated in 1943

LOW VOLATILITY CDN EQUITIES INCOME FD (ON)
Name changed to Redwood Low Volatility High Income Fund 12/20/2017
(See Redwood Low Volatility High Income Fund)

LOWCOUNTRY SVGS BK INC (SC)
Merged into Carolina First Corp. 07/18/1997
Each share Common $5 par exchanged for either (0.938) share Common $1 par, (0.469) share Common $1 par and $7.375 cash, or $14.75 cash
Note: Option to receive stock or cash only expired 08/08/1997
Carolina First Corp. name changed to South Financial Group, Inc. 04/24/2000 which merged into Toronto-Dominion Bank (Toronto, ON) 09/30/2010

LOWE (JOE) CORP. (DE)
Completely liquidated 06/25/1965
Each share Class A Common no par or Class B Common no par exchanged for first and final distribution of (2.514919) shares Consolidated Foods Corp. Common $1.33333333 par
Consolidated Foods Corp. name changed to Sara Lee Corp. 04/02/1985 which recapitalized as Hillshire Brands Co. 06/29/2012
(See Hillshire Brands Co.)

LOWE MANUFACTURING CO.
Bankrupt in 1933

LOWELL & FITCHBURG ST. RWY. CO.
Sold at foreclosure 00/00/1929
Stockholders' equity unlikely

LOWELL ADAMS FACTORS CORP. (NY)
Bankrupt in 1953

LOWELL BUILDING CORP.
Liquidated in 1944

LOWELL COPPER LTD (BC)
Recapitalized as JDL Gold Corp. 10/07/2016
Each share Common no par exchanged for (0.15503875) share Common no par

JDL Gold Corp. name changed to Trek Mining Inc. 03/31/2017 which name changed to Equinox Gold Corp. 12/22/2017

LOWELL CORP (NY)
Charter cancelled and proclaimed dissolved for non-payment of taxes 12/15/1969

LOWELL ELECTRIC LIGHT CORP. (MA)
Merged into Merrimack-Essex Electric Co. on a (2.5) for (1) basis 7/30/57 which company was acquired by New England Electric System 6/30/59
(See New England Electric System)

LOWELL GAS CO (MA)
Each share Common $25 par exchanged for (2.5) shares Common $10 par 6/14/62
Merged into Colonial Gas Co. 7/30/81
Each share Common $10 par exchanged for (2) shares Common $5 par
Colonial Gas Co. merged into Eastern Enterprises 8/31/99
(See Eastern Enterprises)

LOWELL INSTN FOR SVGS (LOWELL, MA)
Reorganized under the laws of Delaware as Merrimack Bancorp, Inc. 10/06/1987
(See Merrimack Bancorp, Inc.)

LOWELL LIQUIDATION CORP. (MA)
Liquidation completed 3/25/59

LOWELL NATIONAL BANCORP (IN)
Merged into Indiana National Corp. 11/27/85
Each share Common $5 par exchanged for $62.42 cash

LOWELL PETE INC (CANADA)
Recapitalized as Hedong Energy, Inc. 08/17/1998
Each share Common no par exchanged for (0.1) share Common no par
Hedong Energy, Inc. recapitalized as Benchmark Energy Corp. 02/09/2004 which name changed to Bolivar Energy Corp. (Canada) 10/29/2010 which reorganized in Alberta as Anatolia Energy Corp. 12/13/2011 which merged into Cub Energy Inc. 07/01/2013

LOWELL PORCUPINE GOLD MINES LTD.
Bankrupt in 1949
No stockholders' equity

LOWELL TOY MANUFACTURING CORP. (NY)
Name changed to Lowell Corp. 11/25/64
Lowell Corp. charter cancelled 12/15/69

LOWENSTEIN (M.) & SONS, INC. (NY)
Common $1 par split (2) for (1) by issuance of (1) additional share in 1954
4-1/4% Preferred Ser. A $100 par called for redemption 3/22/56
Stock Dividend - 25% 11/15/50
Name changed to Lowenstein (M.) Corp. 5/17/79
(See Lowenstein (M.) Corp.)

LOWENSTEIN FURNITURE GROUP INC (FL)
Merged into WinsLoew Furniture, Inc. 12/19/94
Each share Common 1¢ par exchanged for (1.05) shares Common 1¢ par
(See WinsLoew Furniture, Inc.)

LOWENSTEIN M CORP (NY)
Common $1 par split (5) for (4) by issuance of (0.25) additional share 6/30/84
Merged into Springs Industries, Inc. 12/23/85

Each share Common $1 par exchanged for $63 cash

LOWER CANADA GOLD MINES, LTD. (ON)
Charter revoked for failure to file reports and pay fees 11/30/64

LOWER FREDERICK TOWNSHIP GAS CO.
Merged into Philadelphia Electric Co. 00/00/1929
Details not available

LOWER ST. LAWRENCE POWER CO. (QC)
Stock Dividend - 150% 06/01/1954
Acquired by the Quebec Hydro-Electric Commission 09/27/1963
Each share Common no par exchanged for $37 cash
Each share 4-1/2% Preferred $20 par exchanged for $20 principal amount of 4-1/2% 10-Year Debentures 12/06/1963
Public interest eliminated

LOWER SALEM COML BK (LOWER SALEM, OH)
Merged into Peoples Bancorp Inc. 02/23/2001
Each share Common exchanged for either (4.6367) shares Common $10 par or $85.72 cash
Note: Option to receive stock expired 03/15/2001

LOWER VY MINES LTD (BC)
Recapitalized as Groton Minerals Ltd. 07/22/1974
Each share Capital Stock no par exchanged for (0.2) share Capital Stock no par
(See Groton Minerals Ltd.)

LOWERY PETROLEUMS LTD.
Liquidated in 1951

LOWES COS INC (NC)
Common Stock Purchase Rights declared for Common stockholders of record 09/09/1998 were redeemed at $0.0005 per right 04/30/2004 for holders of record 04/16/2004
(Additional Information in Active)

LOWNDES BK (CLARKSBURG, WV)
Reorganized as Consolidated Banc Shares, Inc. 10/1/84
Each share Common $5 par exchanged for (1) share Common $5 par
Consolidated Banc Shares, Inc. acquired by CB&T Financial Corp. 9/1/89 which was acquired by Huntington Bancshares Inc. 6/25/93

LOWNEY (WALTER M.) CO., LTD. (CANADA)
Acquired by Standard Brands Ltd. 11/8/68
Each share Common no par exchanged for $68.22 cash

LOWRANCE ELECTRS INC (DE)
Acquired by Simrad Yachting AS 3/14/2006
Each share Common 10¢ par exchanged for $37 cash

LOYAL AMERICAN LIFE INSURANCE CO., INC. (AL)
Common $1 par changed to 50¢ par in 1958
Under plan of merger name changed to Loyal American Life Insurance Co. 6/1/64
(See Loyal American Life Insurance Co.)

LOYAL AMERN LIFE INS CO (AL)
Each share Common 50¢ par exchanged for (1/3) share Common $1 par 12/30/1964
Merged into Imperial Life Assurance Co. of Canada 04/01/1980
Each share Common $1 par exchanged for $25 cash

LOYAL PROT LIFE INS CO (MA)
Each share Capital Stock $100 par exchanged for (2) shares Capital Stock $50 par 00/00/1950
Capital Stock $50 par changed to $20 par and (1.5) additional shares issued plus a 33-1/3% stock dividend paid 05/18/1956
Capital Stock $20 par changed to $10 par and (1) additional share issued plus a 50% stock dividend paid 05/04/1960
Stock Dividends - 66-2/3% 11/15/1946; 50% 12/01/1950; 66-2/3% 06/07/1965
Merged into Massachusetts General Life Insurance Co. 09/08/1978
Each share Capital Stock $10 par exchanged for $19.70 cash

LOYALIST GROUP LTD (CANADA)
Reincorporated 12/11/2013
Place of incorporation changed from (AB) to (Canada) 12/11/2013
Name changed to KGIC Inc. 10/01/2015
(See KGIC Inc.)

LOYALIST INS GROUP LTD (AB)
Name changed to Loyalist Group Ltd. (AB) 06/24/2010
Loyalist Group Ltd. (AB) reincorporated in Canada 12/11/2013 which name changed to KGIC Inc. 10/01/2015
(See KGIC Inc.)

LOYALIST MINES LTD (NB)
Merged into Proto Explorations & Holdings Inc. 5/31/72
Each share Capital Stock $1 par exchanged for (0.083333) share Common no par
Proto Explorations & Holdings Inc. name changed to Baxter Resources Corp. 6/26/81 which merged into Baxter Technologies Corp. 12/31/81 which name changed to Standard-Modern Technologies Corp. 10/8/85
(See Standard-Modern Technologies Corp.)

LOYALIST RES LTD (BC)
Name changed to IBS Technologies Ltd. 1/2/86
(See IBS Technologies Ltd.)

LOYALTY FING CORP (NJ)
Charter declared void for non-payment of taxes 01/17/1968

LOYALTY SAVINGS & LOAN ASSOCIATION (CA)
Acquired by Trans-World Financial Co. 09/12/1969
Each share Guarantee Stock $10 par exchanged for (1.68) shares Common $1 par
Trans-World Financial Co. merged into Golden West Financial Corp. (DE) 10/31/1975
(See Golden West Financial Corp. (DE))

LOYALTYPOINT INC (DE)
Company terminated common stock registration and is no longer public as of 07/21/2005

LOYOLA CAP CORP (MD)
Reincorporated 00/00/1989
State of incorporation changed from (DE) to (MD) 00/00/1989
Common 10¢ par split (2) for (1) by issuance of (1) additional share 09/30/1992
Merged into Crestar Financial Corp. 12/31/1995
Each share Common 10¢ par exchanged for (0.64) share Common no par
Crestar Financial Corp. merged into SunTrust Banks, Inc. 12/31/1998

LP HLDGS INC (NV)
Each share old Common $0.0001 par exchanged for (0.0025) share new Common $0.0001 par 04/23/2007
Name changed to Tanke, Inc. 10/17/2007

LPATH INC (NV)
Reincorporated 07/21/2014
Each share old Class A Common $0.001 par exchanged for (0.14285714) share new Class A Common $0.001 par 10/09/2012
State of incorporation changed from (NV) to (DE) and new Class A Common $0.001 par reclassified as old Common $0.001 par 07/21/2014
Each share old Common $0.001 par exchanged for (0.07142857) share new Common $0.001 par 06/13/2016
Recapitalized as Apollo Endosurgery, Inc. 12/30/2016
Each share new Common $0.001 par exchanged for (0.18181818) share Common $0.001 par

LPBP INC (ON)
Completely liquidated
Each share Class A no par received first and final distribution of $0.0099 cash payable 10/29/2009 to holders of record 10/23/2009

LPI DATA COMMUNICATION SYS INC (DE)
Charter cancelled and declared inoperative and void for non-payment of taxes 5/30/96

LPL INVT GROUP INC (DE)
Name changed to LPL Technologies Inc. 07/03/1989
(See LPL Technologies Inc.)

LPL INVT HLDGS INC (DE)
Issue Information - 15,657,482 shares COM offered at $30 per share on 11/17/2010
Name changed to LPL Financial Holdings Inc. 06/20/2012

LPL SVCS INC (CA)
Name changed to Transworld Services, Inc. 09/12/1975
Transworld Services, Inc. merged into Raycomm Transworld Industries, Inc. 06/04/1986
(See Raycomm Transworld Industries, Inc.)

LPL TECHNOLOGIES INC (DE)
Class A Common 2¢ par split (3) for (2) by issuance of (0.5) additional share 09/08/1989
Merged into LPL Acquisition Corp. 05/09/1990
Each share Class A Common 2¢ par exchanged for $25 cash

LQ MTR INNS INC (DE)
Name changed to La Quinta Motor Inns, Inc. (DE) 10/8/75
La Quinta Motor Inns, Inc. (DE) reincorporated in Texas 10/12/78 which name changed to La Quinta Inns, Inc. 5/27/93 which merged into Meditrust Corp. 7/17/98 which name changed to La Quinta Properties, Inc. 6/20/2001 which reorganized as La Quinta Corp. 1/2/2002
(See La Quinta Corp.)

LRC INC (CO)
Merged into Cutler-Hammer, Inc. 7/2/79
Each share Common 10¢ par exchanged for $4.50 cash

LRC INC (OR)
Name changed to LRC Oregon Inc. 3/25/2005

LRG RESTAURANT GROUP INC (BC)
SEC revoked common stock registration 08/05/2004

LRH INCOME PROPERTIES LTD. (NY)
Partnership terminated in 1991
Details not available

LRL CORP. (NY)
In process of liquidation
Each (2.6) shares Common 10¢ par exchanged for (1) share Loral Electronics Corp. Common 25¢ par 03/20/1963
Note: Holders; had the option to receive a lesser number of shares with the potential of receiving, after five years, additional Common which may become issuable
(See Loral Electronics Corp.)

LRN "2" VIDEO, INC. (UT)
Name changed to Satco Power Corp. 8/5/85

LRNN CORP (NV)
SEC revoked common stock registration 07/22/2010

LRR ENERGY LP (DE)
Merged into Vanguard Natural Resources, LLC 10/05/2015
Each Common Unit exchanged for (0.55) Common Unit
(See Vanguard Natural Resources, LLC)

LRS CAP INC (DE)
Name changed to GL Energy & Exploration Inc. 10/29/2001
GL Energy & Exploration Inc. recapitalized as American Southwest Music Distribution, Inc. 8/24/2006

LRX CAP CORP (BC)
Reincorporated under the laws of Canada as North American Tungsten Corp. Ltd. 5/1/96

LS CAPITAL CORP (DE)
Recapitalized as Eurbid.com Inc. 10/03/2000
Each share Common 10¢ par exchanged for (0.04) share Common 10¢ par
Eurbid.com Inc. name changed to Junum Inc. 12/14/2000 which recapitalized as WinWin Gaming Inc. 12/31/2002
(See WinWin Gaming Inc.)

LS LASER SYS LTD (AB)
Struck off register for failure to file annual returns 07/01/1992

LSB BANCSHARES INC (NC)
Common $5 par split (4) for (3) by issuance of (0.33333333) additional share 04/17/1989
Common $5 par split (5) for (4) by issuance of (0.25) additional share 03/31/1992
Common $5 par split (5) for (4) by issuance of (0.25) additional share 03/31/1994
Common $5 par split (5) for (4) by issuance of (0.25) additional share payable 02/15/1996 to holders of record 02/01/1996
Common $5 par split (5) for (4) by issuance of (0.25) additional share payable 02/16/1998 to holders of record 02/02/1998
Stock Dividends - 10% 07/01/1985; 10% 06/01/1987; 25% 04/16/1990
Under plan of merger name changed to NewBridge Bancorp 07/31/2007
NewBridge Bancorp merged into Yadkin Financial Corp. 03/01/2016 which merged into F.N.B. Corp. 03/11/2017

LSB CORP (MA)
Acquired by People's United Financial, Inc. 11/30/2010
Each share Common 10¢ par exchanged for $21 cash

LSB FINL CORP (IN)
Common 1¢ par split (3) for (2) by issuance of (0.5) additional share payable 06/04/1999 to holders of record 05/14/1999
Stock Dividends - 5% payable 06/30/1997 to holders of record 06/03/1997; 5% payable 06/30/1998 to holders of record 06/08/1998; 5% payable 10/29/2004 to holders of record 10/08/2004 Ex date - 10/06/2004; 5% payable 10/30/2005

to holders of record 10/07/2005
Ex date - 10/05/2005
Merged into Old National Bancorp 10/31/2014
Each share Common 1¢ par exchanged for (2.269) shares Common no par and $10.63 cash

LSB INDS INC (DE)
Reincorporated 06/14/1977
State of incorporation changed from (OK) to (DE) 06/14/1977
$2.20 Conv. Exchangeable Preferred Class C Ser. 1 no par called for redemption 03/23/1993
$3.25 Conv. Exchangeable Class C Ser. 2 Preferred no par called for redemption at $50 plus $26.25 accrued dividends on 08/27/2007
10% Conv. Preferred $100 par called for redemption at $100 on 03/14/2012
(Additional Information in Active)

LSI COMMUNICATIONS INC (NV)
Each share old Common $0.001 par exchanged for (1/30) share new Common $0.001 par 04/08/1998
Recapitalized as Peregrine Inc. 02/01/2002
Each share new Common $0.001 par exchanged for (0.01) share Common $0.001 par
Peregrine Inc. name changed to Nighthawk Systems, Inc. 07/01/2002 which name changed to Video River Networks, Inc. 03/03/2011

LSI CORP (DE)
Reincorporated 06/11/1987
Name changed 04/06/2007
Common no par split (3) for (2) by issuance of (0.5) additional share 03/14/1986
State of incorporation changed from (CA) to (DE) and Common no par changed to 1¢ par 06/11/1987
Common 1¢ par split (2) for (1) by issuance of (1) additional share 06/21/1995
Common 1¢ par split (2) for (1) by issuance of (1) additional share payable 02/16/2000 to holders of record 02/04/2000 Ex date - 02/17/2000
Name changed from LSI Logic Corp. to LSI Corp. 04/06/2007
Acquired by Avago Technologies Wireless (U.S.A.) Manufacturing Inc. 05/06/2014
Each share Common 1¢ par exchanged for $11.15 cash

LSI LOGIC CORP CDA INC (CANADA)
Each share old Common no par exchanged for (0.00000062) share new Common no par 09/14/1995
Note: In effect holders received $4 cash per share and public interest was eliminated

LSI LTG SYS INC (DE)
Common 1¢ par split (3) for (2) by issuance of (0.5) additional share 8/30/85
Common 1¢ par split (3) for (2) by issuance of (0.5) additional share 6/5/89
Reincorporated under the laws of Ohio as LSI Industries Inc. 11/16/89

LSL CORP (TX)
Merged into I.C.H. Corp. 11/14/79
Each (12.75) shares Common $1 par exchanged for (1) share 45¢ Preferred Ser. A no par
I.C.H. Corp. name changed to Southwestern Life Corp. (New) 6/15/94 which name changed to I.C.H. Corp. (New) 10/10/95
(See I.C.H. Corp. (New))

LSM CORP (MN)
Merged into American Trustee Inc. 12/21/1981
Each share Common 10¢ par exchanged for (1/3) share Common $1 par
(See American Trustee Inc.)

LSP LIQUIDATING CO. (OH)
Liquidation completed
Each Unit of Bene. Int. received second distribution of $0.15 cash 4/29/88
Each Unit of Bene. Int. received third and final distribution of $0.115 cash 4/16/90
(See Lodge & Shipley Co. for previous distribution)

LTC BANCORP (MD)
Merged into WM Bancorp 10/1/86
Each share Common $10 par exchanged for (2) shares Common $2.50 par
WM Bancorp acquired by Keystone Financial, Inc. 1/7/94 which merged into M&T Bank Corp. 10/6/2000

LTC HEALTHCARE INC (NV)
Name changed to CLC Healthcare, Inc. 2/27/2002
(See CLC Healthcare, Inc.)

LTC PHARMACEUTICALS CORP (IL)
Declared involuntarily dissolved by Court 11/16/1972
Stockholders' equity unlikely

LTC PPTYS INC (MD)
9.5% Conv. Preferred Ser. A 1¢ par called for redemption at $25 plus $0.1583 accrued dividends on 03/25/2004
9% Preferred Ser. B called for redemption at $25 plus $0.01875 accrued dividends on 03/31/2004
8.5% Conv. Preferred Ser. E 1¢ par called for redemption at $25 plus $0.4191 accrued dividends on 09/09/2010
8% Preferred Ser. F 1¢ par called for redemption at $25 plus $0.1333 accrued dividends on 04/25/2011
(Additional Information in Active)

L3 CORP (DE)
Name changed to Longview Real Estate, Inc. 08/02/2013
Longview Real Estate, Inc. name changed to Cannabis-Rx Inc. 02/05/2014 which name changed to Praetorian Property, Inc. (DE) 10/26/2015 which reincorporated in Nevada 12/30/2015

LTI HLDGS INC (DE)
Recapitalized as SPEEDCOM Wireless Corp. 09/27/2000
Each (4.26) shares Common 1¢ par exchanged for (1) share Common $0.001 par
SPEEDCOM Wireless Corp. name changed to SP Holding Corp. 07/05/2005 which name changed to Organic To Go Food Corp. 05/21/2007
(See Organic To Go Food Corp.)

LTT CAP CORP (CANADA)
Name changed to Arura Pharma Inc. 07/13/2007
(See Arura Pharma Inc.)

LTV AEROSPACE CORP (DE)
Common 50¢ par split (5) for (2) by issuance of (1.5) additional shares 02/25/1966
Reorganized 05/05/1972
Each share $4 Preferred Ser. A $20 par exchanged for $100 cash
Each share Common 50¢ par exchanged for (1.3) shares E-Systems Inc. Common 50¢ par and (1) share Altec Corp. Common 50¢ par plus $1.25 cash
(See each company's listing)

LTV CORP NEW (DE)
Assets sold for the benefit of creditors 12/7/2001
Plan of reorganization under Chapter 11 Federal Bankruptcy Code effective 12/17/2003
No stockholders' equity

LTV CORP OLD (DE)
$5 Preferred Ser. $5 par conversion privilege expired 04/29/1977
$2.60 Conv. Preferred Ser. B $1 par called for redemption 12/26/1980
Part. Conv. Preference Ser. 1, 50¢ par called for redemption 02/23/1984
Special Conv. Class AA 50¢ par called for redemption 10/24/1988
Stock Dividend - Special Cv. Class AA 15.93% 05/27/1975
Reorganized under Chapter 11 Federal Bankruptcy Code as LTV Corp. (New) 06/28/1993
Each share $1.25 Conv. Preferred Ser. D $1 par exchanged for (0.0194) Common Stock Purchase Warrants, Class A expiring 06/28/1998
Each share $3.06 Conv. Preferred Ser. B $1 par exchanged for (0.0207) Common Stock Purchase Warrants, Class A expiring 06/28/1998
Each share $5 Preferred Ser. A $5 par exchanged for (0.1553) Common Stock Purchase Warrants, Class A expiring 06/28/1998
Each share $5.25 Conv. Preferred Ser. C $1 par exchanged for (0.0776) Common Stock Purchase Warrants, Class A expiring 06/28/1998
Each share Common 50¢ par exchanged for (0.0116) Common Stock Purchase Warrants, Class A expiring 06/28/1998
(See LTV Corp. (New))

LTV ELECTROSYSTEMS INC (DE)
Common 50¢ par split (2) for (1) by issuance of (1) additional share 4/8/66
6% Preferred Ser. B $25 par called for redemption 2/1/68
Name changed to E-Systems Inc. 4/27/72
(See E-Systems Inc.)

LTV LING ALTEC INC (DE)
Common 50¢ par split (2) for (1) by issuance of (1) additional share 5/15/67
Name changed to Altec Corp. 4/27/72
(See Altec Corp.)

LTWC CORP (DE)
Plan of reorganization under Chapter 11 Federal Bankruptcy proceedings effective 4/12/2004
No stockholders' equity

L2 MED DEV CO (NV)
Name changed to Enerpulse Technologies, Inc. 10/04/2013

LTX CORP (MA)
Stock Dividend - 100% 03/21/1983
Under plan of merger name changed to LTX-Credence Corp. 08/29/2008
LTX-Credence Corp. name changed to Xcerra Corp. 05/22/2014 which merged into Cohu, Inc. 10/01/2018

LTX-CREDENCE CORP (MA)
Each share old Common 5¢ par exchanged for (0.33333333) share new Common 5¢ par 10/01/2010
Name changed to Xcerra Corp. 05/22/2014
Xcerra Corp. merged into Cohu, Inc. 10/01/2018

LUAARON METALS LTD (BC)
Recapitalized as Lynx Resources Ltd. (BC) 07/10/1981
Each share Common no par exchanged for (0.33333333) share Common no par
Lynx Resources Ltd. (BC) name changed to Avatar Resource Corp. (BC) 01/21/1987 which recapitalized as Blackline Oil Corp. (BC) 12/21/1993 which reincorporated in Alberta as Resourcexplorer Inc. 02/19/2001 which recapitalized as Exchequer Resource Corp. (AB) 07/24/2002 which reincorporated in British Columbia 10/25/2004 which recapitalized as CBD MED Research Corp. 07/18/2014

LUBBOCK ENTERPRISES INC (UT)
Name changed to Asset Holding Co. 09/01/1989
(See Asset Holding Co.)

LUBBOCK NATL BK (LUBBOCK, TX)
Each share Common $100 par exchanged for (12.5) shares Common $10 par to effect a (10) for (1) split and a 25% stock dividend 8/13/58
Stock Dividends - 125% 1/4/51; 20% 4/20/60; 10% 12/15/61; 21.22% 12/31/64; 12.5% 6/20/66; 11.11% 6/1/68; 10% 11/25/69; 10% 1/15/73; 10% 5/1/74; 11.57% 10/75; 10% 9/78
Merged into RepublicBank Corp. 8/2/82
Each share Common $10 par exchanged for (2.4) shares Common $5 par
RepublicBank Corp. merged into First RepublicBank Corp. 6/6/87
(See First RepublicBank Corp.)

LUBECK BREWING CO.
Bankrupt in 1938
Details not available

LUBICON MNG LTD (BC)
Name changed to Lubicon Petroleum & Mining Ltd. in 1972
Libicon Petroleum & Mining Ltd. acquired by Alberta Petroleum & Resources Ltd. 8/25/72
(See Alberta Petroleum & Resources Ltd.)

LUBICON PETROLEUM & MINING LTD. (BC)
Acquired by Alberta Petroleum & Resources Ltd. 08/25/1972
Each share Common no par exchanged for (0.1) share Common 50¢ par
(See Alberta Petroleum & Resources Ltd.)

LUBRICON PETROLEUMS LTD.
Acquired by Scarlet Oils Ltd. on a (1) for (1.5) basis in 1952
Scarlet Oils Ltd. was acquired by Oil Selections Ltd. in 1953 which was acquired by Quonto Petroleums Ltd. in 1957 which name changed to Quonto Explorations Ltd. 7/27/62
(See Quonto Explorations Ltd.)

LUBRIZOL CORP (OH)
Common $1 par changed to no par and (5) additional shares issued 04/03/1964
Common no par split (2) for (1) by issuance of (1) additional share 08/30/1968
Common no par split (2) for (1) by issuance of (1) additional share 09/03/1971
Common no par split (2) for (1) by issuance of (1) additional share 05/29/1981
Common no par split (2) for (1) by issuance of (1) additional share 08/31/1992
Stock Dividend - 50% 05/16/1966
Acquired by Berkshire Hathaway Inc. 09/16/2011
Each share Common no par exchanged for $135 cash

LUBY CORP (DE)
Name changed to Fleet Control Corp. 9/11/74
(See Fleet Control Corp.)

LUBY LEASING SYS INC (DE)
Name changed to Luby Corp. 4/24/70
Luby Corp. name changed to Fleet Control Corp. 9/11/74
(See Fleet Control Corp.)

LUBYS CAFETERIAS INC (DE)
Reincorporated 1/8/99
Common 32¢ par split (3) for (2) by

issuance of (0.5) additional share 8/24/81
Common 32¢ par split (5) for (4) by issuance of (0.25) additional share 2/11/83
Common 32¢ par split (4) for (3) by issuance of (1/3) additional share 8/31/84
Common 32¢ par split (3) for (2) by issuance of (0.5) additional share 8/11/86
Common 32¢ par split (3) for (2) by issuance of (0.5) additional share 8/3/90
State of incorporation changed from (TX) to (DE) 12/31/91
Name changed to Luby's Inc. 1/8/99

LUCA CAP INC (AB)
Name changed to VentriPoint Diagnostics Ltd. 09/26/2007

LUCAS CNTY ST BK (TOLEDO, OH)
Name changed 7/1/63
Name changed from Lucas County Bank (Toledo, OH) to Lucas County State Bank (Toledo, OH) 7/1/63
Stock Dividends - 50% 1/22/62; 10% 9/2/69
Acquired by Huntington Bancshares Inc. in 1970
Details not available

LUCAS ENERGY INC (NV)
Each share old Common $0.001 par exchanged for (0.25) share new Common $0.001 par 02/04/2008
Each share new Common $0.001 par exchanged again for (0.04) share new Common $0.001 par 07/15/2015
Name changed to Camber Energy, Inc. 01/05/2017

LUCAS GOLD RES CORP (ON)
Merged into Altaur Gold Explorations Inc. 12/27/96
Each share Preferred Ser. B no par exchanged for (1/6) share Common no par
Each share Common no par exchanged for (1/6) share Common no par

LUCASVARITY PLC (UNITED KINGDOM)
Merged into TRW Inc. 5/10/99
Each Sponsored ADR for Ordinary 25p exchanged for £28.80 cash

LUCAYAN BEACH HOTEL CO. LTD. (BAHAMAS)
Recapitalized as Lucayan Beach Hotel & Development Ltd. 6/11/65
Each share Ordinary and Deferred 2s 6d par exchanged for (2.5) shares Ordinary and Deferred 5s par respectively 6/11/65

LUCE FURNITURE SHOPS
Sold at foreclosure in 1933
Details not available

LUCENT TECHNOLOGIES CAP TR I (DE)
7.75% 144A Conv. Trust Preferred Securities called for redemption at $1,000 plus $6.03 accrued dividends on 01/13/2014
7.75% Conv. Trust Preferred Securities called for redemption at $1,000 plus $6.03 accrued dividends on 01/13/2014

LUCENT TECHNOLOGIES INC (DE)
Common no par split (2) for (1) by issuance of (1) additional share payable 4/1/98 to holders of record 3/6/98 Ex date - 4/2/98
Common no par split (2) for (1) by issuance of (1) additional share payable 4/1/99 to holders of record 3/5/99 Ex date - 4/5/99
Each share Common no par received distribution of (1) share Avaya Inc. Common 1¢ par payable 9/29/2000 to holders of record 9/20/2000 Ex date - 10/2/2000
Each share Common no par received distribution of (0.01077976) share Agere Systems Inc. Class A Common 1¢ par and (0.264563) share Class B Common 1¢ par payable 5/31/2002 to holders of record 5/3/2002 Ex date - 6/3/2002
Each share 8% Conv. Preferred exchanged for $1,000 principal amount of 144A Conv. Subordinated Debentures due 2017 on 11/24/2003
Merged into Alcatel-Lucent S.A. 11/30/2006
Each share Common no par exchanged for (0.1952) Sponsored ADR for Ordinary

LUCERO RESOURCE CORP (BC)
Recapitalized as C Squared Developments Inc. 07/19/2001
Each share Common no par exchanged for (0.1) share Common no par
C Squared Developments Inc. name changed to Dynasty Gold Corp. 05/14/2003

LUCK ENERGY INC. (UT)
Name changed to Spectrum Resources Inc. (UT) 1/11/85
Each share Common $0.001 par exchanged for (1) share Common $0.001 par
Spectrum Resources Inc. (UT) reincorporated in Delaware 4/18/89
(See Spectrum Resources Inc.)

LUCK'S, INC. (NC)
Stock Dividend - 100% 02/15/1966
Name changed to SLP Associates, Inc. 10/13/1967
SLP Associates, Inc. liquidated for American Home Products Corp. 12/15/1970 which name changed to Wyeth 03/11/2002 which was acquired by Pfizer Inc. 10/15/2009

LUCKRIDGE PHOSPHATE MINES LTD. (ON)
Struck off register and declared dissolved for failure to file returns 11/26/94

LUCKY BOY MINES INC (BC)
Name changed to Dundarave Resources Inc. 11/29/88
Dundarave Resources Inc. recapitalized as SRR Mercantile Inc. 2/4/93
(See SRR Mercantile Inc.)

LUCKY BOY SILVER CORP (NV)
Reincorporated 03/22/2011
Common $0.001 par split (15) for (1) by issuance of (14) additional shares payable 03/31/2010 to holders of record 03/31/2010
State of incorporation changed from (WY) to (NV) 03/22/2011
Name changed to National Graphite Corp. 06/06/2012

LUCKY BREWERIES INC (CA)
Name changed to General Brewing Co. 8/8/72
(See General Brewing Co.)

LUCKY CHANCE MNG INC (AZ)
Reorganized as Turbo Inc. 6/30/92
Each share Common 1¢ par exchanged for (0.0333333) Unit consisting of (1) share Common 1¢ par and (1) Common Stock Purchase Warrant, Class A expiring 11/1/94
Turbo Inc. recapitalized as A Priori AG 12/22/2000

LUCKY CREEK MINING CO. LTD. (ON)
Charter cancelled and declared dissolved for failure to file returns and pay fees in 1972

LUCKY D URANIUM MINING CO. (CO)
Declared defunct and inoperative for failure to pay franchise taxes 10/15/62

LUCKY FIVE MINING CO. (WA)
Recapitalized as TDL, Inc. 9/4/70
Each share Capital Stock 10¢ par exchanged for (0.1) share Capital Stock $1 par

LUCKY FRIDAY SILVER-LEAD MINES CO. (ID)
Acquired by Hecla Mining Co. (Wash.) on a (1.5) for (1) basis 3/31/64
Hecla Mining Co. (Wash.) reincorporated in Delaware 6/6/83

LUCKY GIRL MINES, LTD. (ON)
Dissolved 8/1/58

LUCKY GOLD HILL CO. (NV)
Name changed to Apple Wear Co. 7/25/85
Apple Wear Co. name changed to American Blood Protection Systems, Inc. 4/7/86 which name changed to Energex Corp. 3/23/87

LUCKY JIM LEAD & ZINC CO. LTD. (BC)
Struck off register and declared dissolved for failure to file returns 11/16/44

LUCKY JOE MNG CO (ID)
Merged out of existence 08/04/2008
Details not available

LUCKY KIRKLAND GOLD MINES LTD.
Recapitalized as Baldwin Consolidated Mines Ltd. 00/00/1946
Each share Capital Stock $1 par exchanged for (0.05) share Capital Stock
Baldwin Consolidated Mines Ltd. recapitalized as Canadian Baldwin Holdings Ltd. 07/11/1989 which recapitalized as Canadian Baldwin Resources Ltd. 07/25/2005 which name changed to Aura Gold Inc. (ON) 03/22/2006 which reincorporated in Canada 04/20/2006 which name changed to Aura Minerals Inc. (Canada) Inc. 08/16/2007 which reorganized in British Virgin Islands 01/05/2017

LUCKY LAGER BREWERIES 1954 LTD. (CANADA)
Name changed to Lucky Lager Breweries Ltd. 11/25/1957
Lucky Lager Breweries Ltd. name changed to Labatt Breweries of British Columbia Ltd. 05/24/1967
(See Labatt Breweries of British Columbia Ltd.)

LUCKY LAGER BREWERIES LTD. (CANADA)
5% Preferred $50 par called for redemption 09/01/1965
Name changed to Labatt Breweries of British Columbia Ltd. 05/24/1967
(See Labatt Breweries of British Columbia Ltd.)

LUCKY LAGER BREWING CO. (CA)
Each share Common no par exchanged for (5) shares Common $1 par 03/29/1955
Name changed to General Brewing Corp. (New) 08/02/1963
General Brewing Corp. (New) name changed to Lucky Breweries Inc. 06/17/1969 which name changed to General Brewing Co. 08/08/1972
(See General Brewing Co.)

LUCKY LAKE MINES LTD (NB)
Voluntarily dissolved 9/18/73
Details not available

LUCKY LANES INC (CA)
Reorganized as Bay Area Holdings, Inc. 07/20/1990
Each share Class A $10 par exchanged for (5) shares Conv. Preferred no par and (5) shares Common no par
(See Bay Area Holdings, Inc.)

LUCKY MC URANIUM CORP. (NV)
Common $1 par changed to 10¢ par 2/27/57
Merged into Utah Construction & Mining Co. 2/1/60
Each share Common 10¢ par exchanged for (0.1) share Capital Stock $2 par
Utah Construction & Mining Co. name changed to Utah International Inc. 10/18/71 which merged into General Electric Co. 12/20/76

LUCKY MINING CO. (NV)
Charter revoked for failure to file reports and pay fees 3/3/58

LUCKY 1 ENTERPRISES INC (BC)
Recapitalized as Bronx Ventures Inc. 01/24/2005
Each share Common no par exchanged for (0.02857142) share Common no par
Bronx Ventures Inc. reorganized as ZAB Resources Inc. 03/19/2007 which recapitalized as Kokomo Enterprises Inc. 04/15/2009 which recapitalized as High 5 Ventures Inc. 08/29/2012 which recapitalized as 37 Capital Inc. 07/07/2014

LUCKY 7 EXPL LTD (BC)
Name changed to Brett Resources Inc. 01/31/1995
Brett Resources Inc. acquired by Osisko Mining Corp. 08/13/2010
(See Osisko Mining Corp.)

LUCKY SEVEN GOLD MINES INC (PA)
Merged into American Precious Metals Inc. 03/16/1998
Each share Common exchanged for (1) share Common $0.00001 par
American Precious Metals Inc. name changed to American International Ventures Inc. 02/06/2001

LUCKY STAR MNG CO (WA)
Common 5¢ par changed to no par 07/20/1977
Name changed to Mountain View Investment Corp. (WA) 12/18/1984
Mountain View Investment Corp. (WA) reorganized in Delaware as Maratech Corp. 03/19/1987

LUCKY STAR URANIUM CO. (UT)
Merged into Sun Tide Corp. 11/15/1957
Each share Capital Stock 1¢ par exchanged for (0.05) share Capital Stock 10¢ par
Sun Tide Corp. name changed to Maxa Corp. 04/13/1974
(See Maxa Corp.)

LUCKY STORES INC (DE)
Reincorporated 12/22/86
Common $1.25 par split (2) for (1) by issuance of (1) additional share 9/28/66
Common $1.25 par split (2) for (1) by issuance of (1) additional share 9/29/69
Common $1.25 par split (2) for (1) by issuance of (1) additional share 9/27/71
Each share Common $100 par exchanged for (80) shares Common $1.25 par in 1974
4.2% Preferred Ser. A $50 par conversion privilege expired 9/30/75
State of incorporation changed from (CA) to (DE) and Common $1.25 par changed to 1¢ par 12/22/86
Acquired by Alpha Beta Acquisition Corp. 6/1/88
Each share Common 1¢ par exchanged for $65 cash

LUCKY STRIKE DRILLING CO. (DE)
Merged into Seneca Oil Co. 03/01/1962
Each share Common $1 par exchanged for (1) share Common 50¢ par, (1) share Class A Preferred 50¢ par, (1) share Class B Preferred

50¢ par and (1) share Class C Preferred 50¢ par
(See Seneca Oil Co.)

LUCKY STRIKE EXPLORATIONS INC (NV)
Name changed to Western Graphite Inc. 02/27/2013

LUCKY STRIKE GOLD MINING CO. LTD. (BC)
Struck off register and deemed dissolved by Province of British Columbia 09/30/1948

LUCKY STRIKE RES LTD (BC)
Name changed 06/21/1980
Name changed from Lucky Strike Mines Ltd. to Lucky Strike Resources Ltd. 06/21/1980
Each share old Common no par exchanged for (0.1) share new Common no par 03/09/2010
Recapitalized as Rojo Resources Ltd. 02/18/2015
Each share new Common no par exchanged for (0.125) share Common no par

LUCKY STRIKE SILVER INC (ID)
Merged into Silver Champion, Inc. 10/01/1969
Each share Common 10¢ par exchanged for (0.6) share Common 10¢ par
Silver Champion, Inc. name changed to Champion Gold & Silver, Inc. 05/22/1973 which recapitalized as Western Continental, Inc. 06/17/1993
(See Western Continental, Inc.)

LUCKY THREE MNG CO (WA)
Reincorporated under the laws of Nevada as Pellet American Corp. 06/02/1995
Pellet American Corp. recapitalized as Sunflower Ltd. 10/05/1998 recapitalized as Sunflower (USA) Ltd. 03/01/1999
(See Sunflower (USA) Ltd.)

LUCKYCOM INC (NV)
Name changed to Luckycom Pharmaceuticals Inc. 04/18/2017
Luckycom Pharmaceuticals Inc. name changed to Luckwel Pharmaceuticals Inc. 04/13/2018

LUCKYCOM PHARMACEUTICALS INC (NV)
Name changed to Luckwel Pharmaceuticals Inc. 04/13/2018

LUCKYTEX URANIUM CO. (DE)
Merged into Old Texas Mining & Oil Co. share for share 3/25/56
Old Texas Mining & Oil Co. dissolved 1/15/64

LUCOR INC (FL)
Each share Class A Common 2¢ par exchanged for (0.05) share old Class A Common 40¢ par 05/04/2001
Each share old Class A Common 40¢ par exchanged for (0.005) share new Class A Common 40¢ par 09/16/2010
Note: In effect holders received $400 cash per share and public interest was eliminated

LUCRE VENTURES LTD (BC)
Recapitalized as Strathclair Ventures Ltd. 09/05/2001
Each share Common no par exchanged for (0.15384615) share Common no par
Strathclair Ventures Ltd. name changed to SilverCrest Mines Inc. 05/28/2003 which merged into First Majestic Silver Corp. 10/07/2015

LUCRO CAP LTD (CANADA)
Name changed to Intrepid Minerals Corp. 8/16/96
(See Intrepid Minerals Corp.)

LUCRUM CAP CORP (BC)
Name changed to Sheltered Oak Resources Corp. 12/17/2008
Sheltered Oak Resources Corp. merged into Foundation Resources Inc. 04/10/2013 which recapitalized as Birch Hill Gold Corp. 10/28/2013 which merged into Canoe Mining Ventures Corp. 06/04/2014

LUCYS CAFE INC (NV)
Name changed to InterMetro Communications, Inc. 06/07/2007

LUCYS WTR WORLD INC (NV)
SEC revoked common stock registration 04/22/2016

LUDLOW CORP (MA)
Common no par split (2) for (1) by issuance of (1) additional share 11/25/1964
Common no par split (2) for (1) by issuance of (1) additional share 09/27/1968
Merged into Tyco Laboratories, Inc. 11/16/1981
Each share Common no par exchanged for $27.50 cash

LUDLOW INDS INC (DE)
Merged into International Metals & Machines, Inc. 7/15/76
Each share Preference $10 par exchanged for $100 cash
Each share Common $10 par exchanged for $17.50 cash

LUDLOW MANUFACTURING & SALES CO. (MA)
Stock Dividend - 200% 5/48
Name changed to Ludlow Corp. 3/21/60

LUDLOW MANUFACTURING ASSOCIATES
Reorganized as Ludlow Manufacturing & Sales Co. share for share in 1942
Ludlow Manufacturing & Sales Co. name changed to Ludlow Corp. 3/21/60
(See Ludlow Corp.)

LUDLOW MINING CO. (MT)
Charter expired by time limitation 6/2/60

LUDLOW SAVINGS BANK & TRUST CO. (LUDLOW, VT)
Merged into Vermont National Bank (Brattleboro, VT) 01/13/1967
Each share Common 10¢ par exchanged for (0.027) share Common $10 par
Vermont National Bank (Brattleboro, VT) reorganized as Vermont Financial Services Corp. (VT) 02/28/1983 which reincorporated in Delaware 04/17/1990 which merged into Chittenden Corp. 05/28/1999
(See Chittenden Corp.)

LUDLOW TYPOGRAPH CO (DE)
Reorganized 06/30/1958
Common no par changed to $5 par 00/00/1932
Recapitalized 00/00/1936
Each share 7% Preferred $100 par exchanged for (1) share Preference $10 par and $1 cash
Each share old Common $5 par exchanged for (1) share new Common $5 par
Stock Dividend - 200% 11/15/1950
Reorganized from (IL) to under the laws of Delaware 06/30/1958
Each share Preference $10 par exchanged for (1) share Preference $10 par
Each share Common $5 par exchanged for (1) share Common $10 par
Stock Dividend - 300% 07/07/1958
Name changed to Ludlow Industries, Inc. 03/23/1971
(See Ludlow Industries, Inc.)

LUDLOW VALVE MANUFACTURING CO.
Reorganized under plan of merger and consolidation as Ludlow Valve Manufacturing Co., Inc. 00/00/1939
Each share Preferred $100 par exchanged for (8) shares 5-1/2% Preferred $20 par
Each share General Stock no par exchanged for (1) share new Common $5 par
Ludlow Valve Manufacturing Co., Inc. liquidated for Banner Industries, Inc. (MO) 08/13/1968 which reincorporated in Delaware 11/13/1970 which name changed to Fairchild Corp. 11/15/1990
(See Fairchild Corp.)

LUDLOW VALVE MANUFACTURING CO., INC. (NY)
Completely liquidated 08/13/1968
Each share 5-1/2% Preferred $20 par exchanged for first and final distribution of (0.5) share Banner Industries, Inc. (MO) Common 10¢ par
Each share Common $5 par exchanged for first and final distribution of (1) share Banner Industries, Inc. (MO) Common 10¢ par
Banner Industries, Inc. (MO) reincorporated in Delaware 11/13/1970 which name changed to Fairchild Corp. 11/15/1990
(See Fairchild Corp.)

LUDLUM STEEL CO. (NJ)
Merged into Allegheny Ludlum Steel Corp. on a share for share basis 8/16/38
Allegheny Ludlum Steel Corp. name changed to Allegheny Ludlum Industries, Inc. 4/24/70 which name changed to Allegheny International Inc. 4/29/81
(See Allegheny International Inc.)

LUDMAN CORP. (FL)
Bankrupt in 1959
Stock worthless

LUDVIK CAP INC (DE)
Common $0.0001 par split (2) for (1) by issuance of (1) additional share payable 09/28/2007 to holders of record 09/21/2007 Ex date - 10/01/2007
Name changed to SavWatt USA, Inc. 10/27/2010

LUDWIG ENGINEERING & SCIENCE (CA)
Completely liquidated 9/12/68
Each share Common no par exchanged for first and final distribution of (0.333333) share Zurn Industries, Inc. Common 50¢ par
Zurn Industries, Inc. merged into U.S. Industries, Inc. (Holding Co.) 6/11/98

LUDWIG MNG CO (NV)
Name changed to Lifetech Enterprises Inc. 6/4/97

LUFKIN, HEMPHILL & GULF RWY. CO.
Road abandoned 00/00/1937
Stockholders' equity unlikely

LUFKIN INDS INC (TX)
Common $1 par split (3) for (1) by issuance of (2) additional shares 12/03/1990
Common $1 par split (2) for (1) by issuance of (1) additional share payable 04/19/2005 to holders of record 04/04/2005 Ex date - 04/20/2005
Common $1 par split (2) for (1) by issuance of (1) additional share payable 06/01/2010 to holders of record 05/19/2010 Ex date - 06/02/2010
Acquired by General Electric Co. 07/01/2013
Each share Common $1 par exchanged for $88.50 cash

LUFKIN RULE CO. (MI)
Merged into Cooper Industries, Inc. (OH) 10/31/1967
Each share Common $5 par exchanged for (0.4) share $5 Conv. Preferred Ser. A no par
(See Cooper Industries, Inc.)

LUGANO RES LTD (BC)
Merged into Ethicorp Resources Ltd. 04/15/1986
Each share Common no par exchanged for (0.5) share Common no par
Ethicorp Resources Ltd. name changed to Central Explorers Ltd. 10/26/1987
(See Central Explorers Ltd.)

LUIRI GOLD LTD (BC)
Reincorporated under the laws of Bermuda and Common no par changed to USD $0.01 par 09/13/2012

LUKE ENERGY LTD (CANADA)
Merged into Connacher Oil & Gas Ltd. (AB) 03/16/2006
Each share Common no par exchanged for (0.75) share Common no par and $2.31 cash
Note: Unexchanged certificates were cancelled and became without value 03/16/2012
Connacher Oil & Gas Ltd. (AB) reincorporated in Canada 03/30/2015

LUKE ENTMT INC (NY)
Name changed to Greene Concepts, Inc. 01/14/2011

LUKEN RES LTD (BC)
Merged into IVS Intelligent Vehicle Systems Inc. 10/15/1992
Each share Common no par exchanged for (1) share Common no par
(See IVS Intelligent Vehicle Systems Inc.)

LUKENS INC (DE)
Reincorporated 1/29/87
State of incorporation changed from (PA) to (DE) 1/29/87
Common 1¢ par split (3) for (2) by issuance of (0.5) additional share 9/9/88
Common 1¢ par split (3) for (2) by issuance of (0.5) additional share 9/28/92
Merged into Bethlehem Steel Corp. 5/29/98
Each share Common 1¢ par exchanged for either (1.05) shares Common $1 par and $19.07 cash or $30 cash
Note: Option to receive cash only expired 5/27/98
(See Bethlehem Steel Corp.)

LUKENS MED CORP (DE)
Merged into Medisys PLC 9/28/98
Each share Common 1¢ par exchanged for $4 cash

LUKENS STEEL CO. (PA)
Common $50 par changed to $10 par in 1933
Common $10 par changed to $3.33-1/3 par and (2) additional shares issued 1/11/57
Common $3.33-1/3 par changed to no par and (2) additional shares issued 10/15/65
Common no par split (2) for (1) by issuance of (1) additional share 8/14/78
Name changed to Lukens, Inc. (PA) 4/14/82
Lukens, Inc. (PA) reincorporated in Delaware 1/29/87 which merged into Bethlehem Steel Corp. 5/29/98
(See Bethlehem Steel Corp.)

LUMA NET CORP (NV)
Recapitalized as Riviera International Casinos Inc. 8/22/97
Each share Common $0.001 par

exchanged for (0.1) share Common $0.001 par
Riviera International Casinos Inc. name changed to International Casino Cruises Inc. 11/21/97 which name changed to Mountain Energy Inc. 5/26/98
(See Mountain Energy Inc.)

LUMAC INTL INC (MN)
Name changed to El Dorado International, Inc. 10/31/72
El Dorado International, Inc. name changed to Westamerica Inc. 6/30/87
(See Westamerica Inc.)

LUMAC LEASING, INC. (MN)
Name changed to Lumac International, Inc. 2/18/72
Lumac International, Inc. name changed to El Dorado International, Inc. 10/31/72 which name changed to Westamerica Inc. 6/30/87
(See Westamerica Inc.)

LUMALITE HLDGS INC (NV)
Each share old Common 10¢ par exchanged for (0.005) share new Common 10¢ par 12/18/2003
Note: Holders of between (100) and (19,999) shares will receive (100) post-split shares
Holders of (99) shares or fewer were not affected by the reverse split
Name changed to MEMS USA, Inc. 01/19/2004
MEMS USA, Inc. name changed to Convergence Ethanol, Inc. 12/13/2006
(See Convergence Ethanol, Inc.)

LUMALURE MFG INC (NV)
Recapitalized as Sairam Technologies Ltd. 12/29/89
Each (7) shares Common 1¢ par exchanged for (1) share Common $0.001 par
Sairam Technologies Ltd. name changed to Balanced Environmental Services Technology Inc. 4/5/91 which recapitalized as United States Indemnity & Casualty, Inc. 7/8/93 which name changed to Birch Financial, Inc. 1/20/2000

LUMAX OIL & GAS INC (ON)
Recapitalized as First Munich Capital Ltd. 04/28/1989
Each share Capital Stock no par exchanged for (0.2) share Common no par
(See First Munich Capital Ltd.)

LUMBER LIQUIDATORS INC (DE)
Issue Information - 10,000,000 shares COM offered at $11 per share on 11/08/2007
Name changed to Lumber Liquidators Holdings, Inc. 12/31/2009

LUMBERMANS ACCEP CO (CA)
Each share 7.2% Conv. Preferred Ser. A $100 par exchanged for (9) shares 7.2% Conv. Preferred Ser. A $1 par and (10) shares Common $1 par 12/29/1972
Stock Dividends - 100% 04/10/1970; 100% 10/10/1970; 100% 09/10/1971
Name changed to Equestrian Centers of America, Inc. 01/23/1984
(See Equestrian Centers of America, Inc.)

LUMBERMANS MTG CORP (CA)
Charter cancelled for failure to file reports and pay taxes 1/21/88

LUMBERMEN'S INSURANCE CO.
Merged into Fire Association of Philadelphia on a (1.479) for (1) basis in 1950
Fire Association of Philadelphia name changed to Reliance Insurance Co. 1/1/58
(See Reliance Insurance Co.)

LUMBERMENS LIFE INSURANCE CO. (IN)
Acquired by Indiana Lumbermens Mutual Insurance Co. 4/30/77
Each share Common no par exchanged for $4 cash

LUMBERMENS MTG CORP
6% Non-Voting Preferred called for redemption at $200 on 6/4/98

LUMBY RES CORP (BC)
Name changed to Rock Resources Inc. 10/01/1996
Rock Resources Inc. recapitalized as Adroit Resources Inc. 02/10/2004 which recapitalized as iMetal Resources Inc. 11/09/2015

LUMEN TECHNOLOGIES INC (DE)
Merged into EG&G, Inc. 1/4/99
Each share Common 1¢ par exchanged for $7.75 cash

LUMENIS LTD (ISRAEL)
Each share Ordinary ILS 0.10 par exchanged for (0.11764706) share Ordinary ILS 0.85 par 02/14/2014
Ordinary ILS 0.85 par reclassified as Ordinary B ILS 0.85 par 08/26/2014
Acquired by XIO Fund I L.P. 10/12/2015
Each share Ordinary B ILS 0.85 par exchanged for $14 cash

LUMENON INNOVATIVE LIGHTWAVE TECHNOLOGY INC (DE)
SEC revoked Common stock registration 08/05/2008

LUMENPULSE INC (CANADA)
Acquired by 10191051 Canada Inc. 06/22/2017
Each share Common no par exchanged for $21.25 cash

LUMERA CORP (DE)
Acquired by GigOptix, Inc. 12/09/2008
Each share Common $0.001 par exchanged for (0.125) share Common $0.001 par
GigOptix, Inc. name changed to GigPeak, Inc. 04/06/2016
(See GigPeak, Inc.)

LUMEX CAP CORP (BC)
Merged into Tasman Metals Ltd. 11/03/2009
Each share Common no par exchanged for (1.0806) shares Common no par
Tasman Metals Ltd. merged into Leading Edge Materials Corp. 08/26/2016

LUMEX INC (NY)
Common 10¢ par split (3) for (2) by issuance of (0.5) additional share 05/01/1980
Common 10¢ par split (3) for (2) by issuance of (0.5) additional share 10/01/1981
Common 10¢ par split (2) for (1) by issuance of (1) additional share 05/20/1983
Name changed to CYBEX International, Inc. 08/07/1996
(See CYBEX International, Inc.)

LUMIDOR INDS INC (FL)
Proclaimed dissolved for failure to file reports and pay fees 12/5/78

LUMIERE INTL CORP (FL)
Name changed to Air Temp North America, Inc. 01/30/2007
(See Air Temp North America, Inc.)

LUMINA COPPER CORP NEW (BC)
Acquired by First Quantum Minerals Ltd. 08/21/2014
Each share Common no par exchanged for $10 cash

LUMINA COPPER CORP OLD (BC)
Plan of arrangement effective 05/18/2005
Each share Common no par exchanged for (1) share Regalito Copper Corp. Common no par, (1) share Global Copper Corp. Common no par, (1) share Lumina Resources Corp. Common no par and (1) share Northern Peru Copper Corp. Common no par
(See each company's listing)

LUMINA INVT CORP (BC)
Recapitalized as Latitude Minerals Corp. 12/02/1996
Each share Common no par exchanged for (0.2) share Common no par
Latitude Minerals Corp. recapitalized as Coal Creek Energy Inc. 05/21/2002 which name changed to Corex Gold Corp. 11/18/2003 which merged into Minera Alamos Inc. 04/18/2018

LUMINA RES CORP (BC)
Acquired by Western Copper Corp. 11/30/2006
Each share Common no par exchanged for (1) share Common no par
Western Copper Corp. reorganized as Western Copper & Gold Corp. 10/17/2011

LUMINA RTY CORP (BC)
Merged into Franco-Nevada Corp. 12/01/2011
Each share Common no par exchanged for (0.03487) share Common no par and (0.01917) Common Stock Warrant expiring 06/16/2017
Note: Unexchanged certificates were cancelled and became without value 12/01/2017

LUMINALL PAINTS INC (DE)
Stock Dividend - 10% 8/16/65
Charter dissolved 2/22/96

LUMINANT WORLDWIDE CORP (DE)
Issue Information - 4,060,000 shares COM offered at $18 per share on 09/15/1999
Plan of reorganization under Chapter 11 Federal Bankruptcy Code effective 1/8/2003
No stockholders' equity

LUMINART CORP (WY)
Reincorporated 05/27/2009
State of incorporation changed from (NV) to (WY) 05/27/2009
Administratively dissolved 08/21/2016

LUMINART INC (ON)
Acquired by a private company in 1998
Details not available

LUMINATOR-HARRISON, INC. (IL)
Name changed to Luminator, Inc. 5/8/67
Luminator, Inc. merged into Gulton Industries, Inc. (Del.) 1/2/69
(See Gulton Industries, Inc. (Del.))

LUMINATOR INC (IL)
Merged into Gulton Industries, Inc. (DE) 01/02/1969
Each share Common $1 par exchanged for (1.1) shares Common $1 par
(See Gulton Industries, Inc. (DE))

LUMINENT INC (DE)
Merged into MRV Communications, Inc. 12/28/2001
Each share Common $0.001 par exchanged for (0.43) share Common $0.0017 par
(See MRV Communications, Inc.)

LUMINENT MTG CAP INC (MD)
Issue Information - 13,110,000 shares COM offered at $13 per share on 12/18/2003
Plan of reorganization under Chapter 11 Federal Bankruptcy proceedings effective 07/14/2009
No stockholders' equity

LUMINEX VENTURES INC (BC)
Recapitalized as Lateegra Resources Corp. 06/12/2002
Each share Common no par exchanged for (1/6) share Common no par
Lateegra Resources Corp. recapitalized as Lateegra Gold Corp. 01/12/2006 which merged into Excellon Resources Inc. (BC) 08/05/2011 which reincorporated in Ontario 06/05/2012

LUMINOR MED TECHNOLOGIES INC (CANADA)
Name changed to RISE Life Science Corp. 03/14/2018

LUMISYS INC (DE)
Acquired by Eastman Kodak Co. 12/26/2000
Each share Common $0.001 par exchanged for $4.05 cash

LUMMI DEV INC (DE)
Common $0.0001 par split (46) for (1) by issuance of (45) additional shares payable 11/03/2002 to holders of record 10/29/2002
Ex date - 11/04/2002
Name changed to Signature Horizons Group, Inc. 03/31/2003
Signature Horizons Group, Inc. recapitalized as Summit Dental Clinics, Inc. 07/21/2008 which recapitalized as AyreTrade, Inc. 08/14/2012 which name changed to Rocky Mountain Ayre, Inc. 02/05/2015

LUMONALL INC (NV)
SEC revoked common stock registration 03/21/2014

LUMONICS INC NEW (ON)
Reincorporated under the laws of New Brunswick as GSI Lumonics Inc. 03/22/1999
GSI Lumonics Inc. name changed to GSI Group Inc. (Old) 06/06/2005 which reorganized as GSI Group Inc. (New) 07/23/2010 which name changed to Novanta Inc. 05/12/2016

LUMONICS INC OLD (ON)
Common no par split (2) for (1) by issuance of (1) additional share 01/04/1984
Merged into SHI Acquisition Corp. 06/19/1989
Each share Common no par exchanged for $7.75 cash

LUMOS NETWORKS CORP (DE)
Acquired by MTN Infrastructure TopCo, Inc. 11/17/2017
Each share Common 1¢ par exchanged for $18 cash

LUMS INC (FL)
Class A Common 10¢ par reclassified as Common 10¢ par 7/31/66
Common 10¢ par split (3) for (1) by issuance of (2) additional shares 11/27/67
Common 10¢ par split (3) for (1) by issuance of (2) additional shares 8/1/69
Name changed to Caesars World, Inc. 12/17/71
(See Caesars World, Inc.)

LUMSDEN BLDG INC NEW (ON)
Charter cancelled for failure to file reports and pay taxes 08/27/1990

LUMSDEN BUILDING INC (ON)
Merged into Lumsden Building Corp., Inc. (New) 8/15/78
Details not available

LUN-ECHO GOLD MINES, LTD. (ON)
Recapitalized as Lundor Mines Ltd. 3/10/71
Each share Capital Stock $1 par exchanged for (0.2) share Capital Stock no par
(See Lundor Mines Ltd.)

LUN-MAT MINES LTD. (ON)
Charter cancelled for failure to file reports and pay taxes in 1970

LUNA D'OR MINES, LTD. (ON)
Charter cancelled for failure to file

reports and pay taxes in December 1957

LUNA GOLD CORP (CANADA)
Reincorporated 12/01/2005
Place of incorporation changed from (WY) to (Canada) 12/01/2005
Each share old Common no par exchanged for (0.2) share new Common no par 02/24/2012
Each share new Common no par exchanged again for (0.1) share new Common no par 11/03/2016
Merged into Trek Mining Inc. 03/31/2017
Each share new Common no par exchanged for (1.105) shares Common no par
Note: Unexchanged certificates will be cancelled and become without value 03/31/2023
Trek Mining Inc. name changed to Equinox Gold Corp. 12/22/2017

LUNA INDS INC (DE)
Charter cancelled and declared inoperative and void for non-payment of taxes 3/1/89

LUNA MED TECHNOLOGIES INC (NV)
Name changed to LanWerX Entertainment, Inc. 5/15/2003
LanWerX Entertainment, Inc. name changed to GameState Entertainment, Inc. 9/24/2003 which name changed to Quest Oil Corp. 9/16/2004

LUNA MNG CO (NV)
Merged into Tancor International Inc. 9/22/72
Each share Capital Stock 2-1/2¢ par exchanged for (1) share Common 2-1/2¢ par
(See Tancor International Inc.)

LUNA TECHNOLOGIES INTL INC (DE)
SEC revoked common stock registration 03/16/2012

LUNAR CORP (WI)
Common 1¢ par split (3) for (2) by issuance of (0.5) additional share 12/21/1995
Each share Common 1¢ par received distribution of (0.5) share Bone Care International Inc. Common 1¢ par payable 05/08/1996 to holders of record 04/02/1996
Merged into General Electric Co. 08/08/2000
Each share Common 1¢ par exchanged for (0.322) share Common 16¢ par

LUNAR OIL & GAS INC. (UT)
Name changed to All-American Technology, Inc. 6/11/84

LUNAR RES LTD (BC)
Cease trade order effective 10/26/1988
Stockholders' equity unlikely

LUND AMERN INC (MN)
Stock Dividends - 100% 1/23/73; 20% 4/26/74
Merged into Arctic Enterprises, Inc. 1/23/78
Each share Common 10¢ par exchanged for $3 cash

LUND GOLD LTD (BC)
Recapitalized as Lund Enterprises Corp. 12/19/2013
Each share Common no par exchanged for (0.1) share Common no par

LUND INTL HLDGS INC (DE)
Name changed 10/11/89
Name changed from Lund Enterprises Inc. to Lund International Holdings Inc. 10/11/89
Merged into Aftermarket Holdings, Inc. 3/13/2003
Each share Common 10¢ par exchanged for $2.50 cash

LUND METALCRAFT, INC. (MN)
Stock Dividend - 20% 3/26/70
Name changed to Lund American, Inc. 8/3/71
(See Lund American, Inc.)

LUND VENTURES LTD (BC)
Recapitalized as Lund Gold Ltd. 07/10/2003
Each share Common no par exchanged for (0.5) share Common no par
Lund Gold Ltd. recapitalized as Lund Enterprises Corp. 12/19/2013

LUNDBERG EXPLORATIONS LTD. (ON)
Each share Capital Stock no par exchanged for (10) shares Capital Stock $6 par 10/20/1955
Liquidation commenced 10/28/1960 and all marketable assets sold for benefit of creditors which were still owed $35,000 as of 06/28/1971
Note: Liquidator's opinion is that there will be no stockholders' equity

LUNDELL TECHNOLOGIES INC (WA)
Name changed to Worldtek Corp. 12/17/2003
(See Worldtek Corp.)

LUNDIN EXPLS LTD (BC)
Company wound up in June 1991
Details not available

LUNDIN OIL AB (SWEDEN)
GDR agreement terminated 11/5/2001
Each Sponsored GDR for B Shares exchanged for $0.50107 cash

LUNDOR MINES LTD. (ON)
Completely liquidated 9/18/78
Each share Capital Stock no par exchanged for first and final distribution of $1.6499 cash

LUNDY ELECTRS & SYS INC (NY)
Merged into TransTechnology Corp. (CA) 07/01/1986
Each share Common 10¢ par exchanged for $14.50 cash

LUNDY PACKING CO (NC)
Merged into Premium Standard Farms 08/25/2000
Each share Class A Common no par exchanged for $104.552858 cash

LUNKENHEIMER CO. (DE)
Stock Dividend - 10% 12/28/66
Merged into Condec Corp. (N.Y.) 6/14/68
Each share Common 10¢ par exchanged for (1) share 7% Preferred $25 par and (1) share 10¢ Conv. Preferred $25 par
Condec Corp. (N.Y.) reincorporated in Delaware 3/2/84

LUNKENHEIMER CO. (OH)
6% Preferred $100 par changed to 6-1/2% Preferred $100 par 00/00/1930
Common no par changed to $2.50 par and (1) additional share issued 01/07/1957
Name changed to Elco Investment Co. 02/05/1964
Elco Investment Co. liquidated for Scudder, Stevens & Clark Common Stock Fund, Inc. 12/27/1966 which name changed to Scudder Common Stock Fund, Inc. 03/07/1979 which name changed to Scudder Growth & Income Fund 12/31/1984
(See Scudder Growth & Income Fund)

LUNN INDS INC (NY)
Name changed 5/18/77
Stock Dividend - 20% 4/30/54
Name changed from Lunn Laminates, Inc. to Lunn Industries, Inc. 5/18/77
Merged into Advanced Technical Products Inc. 11/4/97
Each share Common 25¢ par exchanged for (0.1) share Common 1¢ par

(See Advanced Technical Products Inc.)

LUNT & GLENWOOD CORP. (IL)
Liquidated in 1946

LUNWARD GOLD MINES LTD.
Property and assets sold and each share Capital Stock exchanged for (2) shares Capital Stock of Newlund Mines Ltd. and (10) shares Capital Stock of Warlund Mines Ltd. in 1949
(See each company's listing)

LUOKUNG TECHNOLOGY CORP (BRITISH VIRGIN ISLANDS)
ADR agreement terminated 09/19/2018
Each Sponsored ADR for Ordinary exchanged for (1) share Ordinary
Note: Unexchanged ADR's will be sold and the proceeds, if any, held for claim after 01/21/2019

LUPTON REAL ESTATE CO.
Liquidated in 1939

LUPTONS (DAVID) SONS CO.
Bankrupt in 1932

LUPUS CAP PLC (UNITED KINGDOM)
Name changed to Tyman PLC 02/22/2013
(See Tyman PLC)

LURIA L & SON INC (FL)
Proclaimed dissolved for failure to file reports and pay fees 10/16/98

LUSCAR COAL INCOME FD (AB)
Acquired by Sherritt International Corp. (NB) 07/20/2001
Each Trust Unit no par exchanged for either (0.33482) Restricted Share no par and $1.33928 cash or $4 cash
Note: Non-electing and U.S holders received cash only
Sherritt International Corp. (NB) reincorporated in Ontario 08/01/2007

LUSCAR OIL & GAS LTD (AB)
Merged into Encal Energy Ltd. 07/13/1994
Each share Common no par exchanged for (0.37735849) share Common no par
Encal Energy Ltd. merged into Calpine Canada Holdings Ltd. 04/19/2001 which was exchanged for Calpine Corp. 05/27/2002
(See Calpine Corp.)

LUSCOMBE AIRPLANE CORP. (NJ)
Merged into Temco Aircraft Corp. in 1953
Each share Common 50¢ par exchanged for (0.333333) share Common $1 par
Temco Aircraft Corp. merged into Ling- Temco Electronics, Inc. 7/19/60 which name changed to Ling-Temco-Vought, Inc. 8/16/61 which name changed to LTV Corp. (Old) 5/5/72 which reorganized as LTV Corp. (New) 6/28/93
(See LTV Corp. (New))

LUSK CORP (DE)
Each share Common $1 par exchanged for (0.1) share Common 10¢ par 12/7/70
Charter cancelled and declared inoperative and void for non-payment of taxes 3/1/91

LUSK RTY CO (WY)
Name changed to L.R. Co. 06/17/1970

LUSKINS INC (MD)
Plan of reorganization under Chapter 11 Federal Bankruptcy proceedings confirmed 9/16/97
No stockholders' equity

LUSORA HEALTHCARE SYS INC (NV)
Name changed to Western Standard Energy Corp. 09/07/2007
Western Standard Energy Corp.

name changed to Dominovas Energy Corp. 04/24/2014

LUSTRE RES INC (BC)
Name changed 3/30/79
Name changed from Lustre Gold Mines Inc. to Lustre Resources Inc. 3/30/79
Struck off register and declared dissolved for failure to file returns 2/14/86

LUSTROS INC (UT)
SEC revoked common stock registration 03/06/2017

LUTAH URANIUM & OIL, INC. (NV)
Acquired by Shelton-Warren Oil Co. on a (1) for (10.1245) basis 11/15/58
(See Shelton-Warren Oil Co.)

LUTCAM INC (NV)
Name changed to Midwest Uranium Corp. 08/30/2007
Midwest Uranium Corp. name changed to American Patriot Corp. 04/15/2009
(See American Patriot Corp.)

LUTHER MED PRODS INC (CA)
Each share old Common $0.001 par exchanged for (0.1) share new Common $0.001 par 12/1/83
New Common $0.001 par changed to no par 2/22/91
Under plan of reorganization state of incorporation changed from (NV) to (CA) 6/19/91
Each (7) shares Common no par exchanged for (1) share Common no par
Merged into Becton, Dickinson & Co. 1/26/99
Each share Common no par exchanged for $4.70 cash

LUTHERAN BROTHERHOOD FD INC (MD)
Common $1 par reclassified as Class A $1 par 10/31/1997
Merged into Thrivent Mutual Funds 07/16/2004
Details not available

LUTHERAN BROTHERHOOD HIGH YIELD FD INC (MN)
Common 1¢ par reclassified as Class A 1¢ par 10/31/1997
Merged into Thrivent Mutual Funds 07/16/2004
Details not available

LUTHERAN BROTHERHOOD INCOME FD INC (MD)
Common $1 par reclassified as Class A $1 par 10/31/1997
Merged into Thrivent Mutual Funds 07/16/2004
Details not available

LUTHERAN BROTHERHOOD MONEY MKT TR (MA)
Merged into Thrivent Mutual Funds 07/16/2004
Details not available

LUTHERAN BROTHERHOOD MUN BD FD INC (MD)
Common 1¢ par reclassified as Class A 1¢ par 10/31/1997
Merged into Thrivent Mutual Funds 07/16/2004
Details not available

LUTHERAN BROTHERHOOD U S GOVT SECS FD INC (MD)
Merged into Lutheran Brotherhood Income Fund, Inc. 11/18/1983
Each share Capital Stock 10¢ par exchanged for (1.05) shares Capital Stock $1 par
(See Lutheran Brotherhood Income Fund, Inc.)

LUVE SPORTS INC (NV)
SEC revoked common stock registration 08/08/2016

LUVOO INT INC (NV)
Each share old Common $0.001 par

exchanged for (0.01) share new Common $0.001 par 10/23/2006
Charter revoked for failure to file reports and pay taxes 03/02/2009

LUX CLOCK MANUFACTURING CO., INC. (CT)
Each share Capital Stock $100 par exchanged for (10) shares Capital Stock $10 par 00/00/1937
Acquired by Robertshaw-Fulton Controls Co. 07/17/1961
Each share Capital Stock $10 par exchanged for (0.5) share Common $1 par
Robertshaw-Fulton Controls Co. name changed to Robertshaw Controls Co. 04/10/1963
(See Robertshaw Controls Co.)

LUX DIGITAL PICTURES INC (WY)
Recapitalized as StreamTrack, Inc. 03/07/2013
Each share Common $0.001 par exchanged for (0.00083333) share Common $0.001 par
StreamTrack, Inc. recapitalized as Total Sports Media, Inc. 12/06/2016

LUX ENERGY CORP (NV)
Each share old Common $0.001 par exchanged for (3) shares new Common $0.001 par 12/10/2009
Recapitalized as Sunbelt International Corp. 10/03/2011
Each share new Common $0.001 par exchanged for (0.001) share Common $0.001 par
Sunbelt International Corp. recapitalized as Nevcor Business Solutions Inc. 02/06/2014 which name changed to CPSM, Inc. 07/15/2014 which name changed to Astro Aerospace Ltd. 07/24/2018

LUXCEL GROUP INC (DE)
Charter cancelled and declared inoperative and void for non-payment of taxes 03/01/1996

LUXELL TECHNOLOGIES INC (ON)
Issue Information - 4,400,000 shares COM offered at $1.25 per share on 08/12/1996
Acquired by Lux Acquisition Corp. 05/13/2009
Each share Common no par exchanged for $0.10 principal amount of a Promissory Note due 00/00/2012

LUXELLO PPTYS INC (DE)
Recapitalized as Organic Solutions, Inc. (DE) 10/31/1994
Each share Common $0.001 par exchanged for (0.125) share Common $0.001 par
Organic Solutions, Inc. (DE) reincorporated in Nevada 04/28/2000 which recapitalized as iWorld Projects & Systems, Inc. 01/11/2005
(See iWorld Projects & Systems, Inc.)

LUXENE, INC. (DE)
Merged into Howmet Corp. 04/20/1969
Details not available

LUXFER HLDGS PLC (ENGLAND & WALES)
Basis changed from (1:0.5) to (1:1) 06/09/2014
Each Sponsored ADR for Ordinary exchanged for (1) share Ordinary £0.50 par 12/10/2017

LUXMAR RES INC (ON)
Struck off register and declared dissolved for failure to file returns 9/3/94

LUXMATIC TECHNOLOGIES N V (NETHERLANDS)
Recapitalized as Warrior Energy N.V. 11/18/2002
Each share Common no par exchanged for (0.1) share Common Euro 0.15 par
Warrior Energy N.V. name changed to Summus Solutions N.V. 11/16/2012

LUXOR BUILDING CO. (OH)
Completely liquidated for cash 6/25/64
Distribution was made to holders of record and stock certificates are now worthless

LUXOR DEVS INC (AB)
Reincorporated under the laws of Canada as Amorfix Life Sciences Ltd. 09/21/2005
Amorfix Life Sciences Ltd. name changed to ProMIS Neurosciences Inc. 07/14/2015

LUXOR EXPLS LTD (ON)
Name changed 10/26/1981
Name changed from Luxor Red Lake Mines, Ltd. to Luxor Explorations Inc. 10/26/1981
Delisted from Canadian Dealer Network 01/03/1995

LUXOR GROUP N A INC (UT)
Name changed to NorStar Group Inc. 03/04/1992
NorStar Group Inc. recapitalized as Gaming & Entertainment Group, Inc. 01/20/2004
(See Gaming & Entertainment Group, Inc.)

LUXOR INDL CORP (BC)
Placed in receivership 03/20/2017
Stockholders' equity unlikely

LUXOR RESOURCES CORP. (BC)
Name changed to Palmyria Resources Corp. 08/02/1983
Palmyria Resources Corp. reorganized as Med-Tech Systems Inc. 09/24/1986
(See Med-Tech Systems Inc.)

LUXOR RES LTD (BC)
Name changed to Luxor Industrial Corp. 3/30/92

LUXTEC CORP (MA)
Each share old Common $0.001 par exchanged for (0.1) share new Common $0.001 par 4/13/92
Name changed to PrimeSource Healthcare, Inc. 6/27/2001
PrimeSource Healthcare, Inc. name changed to LXU Healthcare, Inc. 12/10/2004
(See LXU Healthcare, Inc.)

LUXURIOUS TRAVEL CORP (FL)
Name changed to US Lighting Group, Inc. 09/07/2016

LUXURY SEASIDE RESORTS, INC. (UT)
Reincorporated under the laws of Nevada as RE/COMM Corp. 03/22/1992
RE/COMM Corp. (NV) name changed to Metro Wireless Interactive Corp. 12/27/1993 which name changed to Red Rock International Corp. (NV) 04/01/1996 which reorganized in Kentucky as Page International Inc. 11/05/1997 which reincorporated in Nevada 12/31/1997 which name changed to China TianRen Organic Food, Inc. 06/14/2007

LUZ DEL SUR S A (PERU)
ADR agreement terminated 12/13/2001
Each 144A Sponsored ADR for Class B exchanged for $15.04533 cash
Each Sponsored ADR for Class B exchanged for $15.04533 cash

LUZERNE COUNTY GAS & ELECTRIC CORP.
Merged into United Gas Improvement Co. in 1952
Each share 4-1/4% Preferred $100 par exchanged for (1) share 4-1/4% Preferred $100 par
(See United Gas Improvement Co.)

LUZERNE NATL BK CORP (PA)
Reorganized 11/10/1987
Reorganized from Luzerne National Bank (Luzerne, PA) to Luzerne National Bank Corp. 11/10/1987
Each share Common Capital $25 par exchanged for (10) shares Common $2.50 par
Common $2.50 par split (2) for (1) by issuance of (1) additional share payable 04/01/1995 to holders of record 04/01/1995
Common $2.50 par split (2) for (1) by issuance of (1) additional share payable 06/30/2000 to holders of record 06/30/2000 Ex date - 07/06/2000
Merged into Penns Woods Bancorp, Inc. 06/01/2013
Each share Common $2.50 par exchanged for (1.4393433) shares Common $8.33 par and $4.542002 cash

LUZON MINERALS LTD (BC)
Recapitalized as Black Isle Resources Corp. 01/14/2010
Each share Common no par exchanged for (0.1) share Common no par

LUZON YELLOWKNIFE GOLD MINES, LTD. (ON)
Charter cancelled for failure to file reports and pay taxes 4/28/54

LVI GROUP INC (DE)
Each share $2.0625 Conv. Exchangeable Preferred no par exchanged for (34) shares Common 50¢ par 03/15/1991
Each (35) shares Common 50¢ par exchanged for (1) share Common $0.001 par 12/27/1991
Name changed to Lehigh Group Inc. 01/27/1995
Lehigh Group Inc. recapitalized as First Medical Group, Inc. 11/13/1997
(See First Medical Group, Inc.)

LVMH MOET HENNESSY LOUIS VUITTON (FRANCE)
Sponsored ADR's for Ordinary 50 Frcs. par split (5) for (1) by issuance of (4) additional ADR's 3/21/94
Sponsored ADR's for Ordinary 50 Frcs. par split (5) for (1) by issuance of (4) additional ADR's payable 7/6/2000 to holders of record 6/30/2000 Ex date - 7/3/2000
Stock Dividend - 10% 10/4/91
ADR agreement terminated 11/25/2002
Each Sponsored ADR for Ordinary 50 Frcs. par exchanged for $10.4059 cash
(Additional Information in Active)

LVO CABLE INC (DE)
Name changed to United Cable Television Corp. 07/29/1974
(See United Cable Television Corp.)

LVO CORP (DE)
Merged into Utah International Inc. 10/31/1974
Each share 30¢ Conv. Preferred no par exchanged for (1) share 30¢ Conv. Preferred no par
Each share Common 10¢ par exchanged for (0.185) share Common $2 par
Utah International Inc. merged into General Electric Co. 12/20/1976

LW CAP POOL INC (CANADA)
Recapitalized as Tweed Marijuana Inc. 04/04/2014
Each share Common no par exchanged for (0.2) share Common no par
Tweed Marijuana Inc. name changed to Canopy Growth Corp. 09/22/2015

LW INDS INC (DE)
Petition under Chapter 11 Federal Bankruptcy Code dismissed 12/22/92
No stockholders' equity

LWAY PRODTNS (NV)
Name changed to Marquee Entertainment, Inc. 5/4/93
Marquee Entertainment, Inc. recapitalized as Progressive Telecommunications Corp. 8/4/99 which name changed to Businessmall.com Inc. 3/24/2000
(See Businessmall.com Inc.)

LX VENTURES INC (AB)
Name changed to Mobio Technologies Inc. 07/07/2014

LXE INC (GA)
Merged into Electromagnetic Sciences Inc. 12/31/1996
Each share Common 1¢ par exchanged for (0.75) share Common 10¢ par
Electromagnetic Sciences Inc. name changed to EMS Technologies Inc. 03/15/1999
(See EMS Technologies Inc.)

LXR BIOTECHNOLOGY INC (DE)
Issue Information - 2,500,000 shares COM offered at $4.50 per share on 05/06/1994
Completely liquidated 12/27/2000
Each share Common $0.0001 par received first and final distribution of $0.018 cash
Note: Certificates were not required to be surrendered and are without value

LXU HEALTHCARE INC (MA)
Each share old Common 1¢ par exchanged for (1) share new Common 1¢ par to reflect a (1) for (1,000) reverse split followed by a (1,000) for (1) forward split 12/14/2005
Note: Holders of (999) or fewer pre-split shares received $0.19 cash per share
Merged into Integra LifeSciences Holdings Corp. 05/07/2007
Each share new Common 1¢ par exchanged for $0.08079 cash
Note: An additional initial distribution of approximately $0.00229 cash per share was paid from escrow 04/28/2008
An additional second distribution of approximately $0.03378 cash per share was paid from escrow 02/18/2009
An additional third distribution of approximately $0.0306 cash per share was paid from escrow 09/02/2010
An additional fourth and final distribution of approximately $0.00426 cash per share was paid from escrow 01/19/2012

LYCEUM COS INC (PA)
Name changed to MVC Industries, Inc. 09/15/1969
(See MVC Industries, Inc.)

LYCOMING MANUFACTURING CO.
Acquired by Aviation Corp. 00/00/1939
Details not available

LYCOR CO. (MO)
Liquidated in 1959

LYCOS INC (DE)
Common 1¢ par split (2) for (1) by issuance of (1) additional share payable 8/25/98 to holders of record 8/14/98
Common 1¢ par split (2) for (1) by issuance of (1) additional share payable 7/26/99 to holders of record 7/16/99
Merged into Terra Networks, S.A. 10/27/2000
Each share Common 1¢ par exchanged for (2.15) Sponsored ADR's for Ordinary
Terra Networks, S.A. merged into Telefonica, S.A. 7/18/2005

LYDALL INC (DE)
Reincorporated 9/30/87
$1.50 Preferred $25 par called for redemption in 1983 80¢ Conv. Preferred Ser. A no par called for redemption 9/15/83
Common $3.33-1/3 par split (3) for (2) by issuance of (0.5) additional share 6/29/84
State of incorporation changed from (CT) to (DE) 9/30/87
$1 Preferred $11 par called for redemption 6/15/89
(Additional Information in Active)

LYDENBURG PLATINUM LTD (SOUTH AFRICA)
ADR agreement terminated 9/11/96
Each ADR for Ordinary Rand-0.125 par exchanged for $14.762 cash

LYKENS VALLEY R.R. & COAL CO. (PA)
Merged into Penndel Co. through payment of $19.50 per share plus accrued dividends of $0.13-1/3 per share 8/31/56

LYKES BROS. STEAMSHIP CO., INC. (LA)
Stock Dividend - 10% 12/20/67
Name changed to Lykes Corp. (LA) 5/1/68
Lykes Corp. (LA) merged into Lykes-Youngstown Corp. 5/28/69 which name changed to Lykes Corp. (DE) 5/11/76 which merged into LTV Corp. (Old) 12/5/78 which reorganized as LTV Corp. (New) 6/28/93
(See LTV Corp. (New))

LYKES CORP (DE)
Merged into LTV Corp. (Old) 12/5/78
Each share $2.50 Conv. Preferred Ser. A $1 par exchanged for (1) share $2.60 Conv. Preferred Ser. B $1 par and $3.25 cash
Each share $4 Conv. Preferred $1 par exchanged for (2) shares $2.60 Conv. Preferred Ser. B $1 par and $5.20 cash
Each share Common $10 par exchanged for (0.15) share Part. Conv. Preference Ser. 1, 50¢ par and (1.1) shares Common 50¢ par
LTV Corp. (Old) reorganized as LTV Corp. (New) 6/28/93
(See LTV Corp. (New))

LYKES CORP (LA)
Common $10 par split (2) for (1) by issuance of (1) additional share 7/8/68
Merged into Lykes-Youngstown Corp. 5/28/69
Each share Common $10 par exchanged for (1) share Common $10 par
Lykes-Youngstown Corp. name changed to Lykes Corp. (DE) 5/11/76 which merged into LTV Corp. (Old) 12/5/78 which reorganized as LTV Corp. (New) 6/28/93
(See LTV Corp. (New))

LYKES-YOUNGSTOWN CORP. (DE)
Name changed to Lykes Corp. (DE) 5/11/76
Lykes Corp. (DE) merged into LTV Corp. (Old) 12/5/78 which reorganized as LTV Corp. (New) 6/28/93
(See LTV Corp. (New))

LYKES YOUNGSTOWN FINL CORP (DE)
Name changed to LifeSurance Corp. 05/10/1971
LifeSurance Corp. merged into Regan Holding Corp. 10/31/1991
(See Regan Holding Corp.)

LYLE STUART, INC. (DE)
See - Stuart (Lyle), Inc.

LYMAN MILLS
Liquidated in 1927

LYNALDA GOLD MINES LTD. (ON)
Former transfer agent advised charter was reported cancelled in April 1963

LYNBAR MNG LTD (ON)
Charter cancelled for failure to pay taxes and file returns 03/16/1976

LYNCH CARRIER SYSTEMS, INC. (DE)
Name changed to Lynch Communication Systems Inc. 3/24/60
(See Lynch Communication Systems Inc.)

LYNCH COMMUNICATIONS SYS INC (DE)
Common $1 par split (2) for (1) by issuance of (1) additional share 6/23/67
Common $1 par split (2) for (1) by issuance of (1) additional share 9/6/68
Common $1 par split (3) for (2) by issuance of (0.5) additional share 7/3/85
Merged into Alcatel Acquisition, Inc. 12/31/86
Each share Common $1 par exchanged for $15.50 cash

LYNCH CORP (IN)
Common no par changed to $5 par 00/00/1933
Each share Common $5 par exchanged for (2.5) shares Common $2 par 00/00/1946
Common $2 par changed to no par 05/31/1973
Each share Common no par received distribution of (1) share East/West Communications, Inc. Common $0.001 par payable 12/05/1997 to holders of record 12/04/1997 Ex date - 12/08/1997
Each share Common no par received distribution of (1) share Lynch Interactive Corp. Common $0.0001 par payable 09/01/1999 to holders of record 08/23/1999
Common no par changed to 1¢ par 05/02/2002
Name changed to LGL Group, Inc. (IN) 06/21/2006
LGL Group, Inc. (IN) reincorporated in Delaware 08/31/2007

LYNCH GLASS MACHINE CO.
Name changed to Lynch Corp. 00/00/1930
Lynch Corp. name changed to LGL Group, Inc. (IN) 06/21/2006 which reincorporated in Delaware 08/31/2007

LYNCH INTERACTIVE CORP (DE)
Common $0.0001 par split (2) for (1) by issuance of (1) additional share payable 9/11/2000 to holders of record 8/28/2000 Ex date - 9/12/2000
Each share Common $0.0001 par received distribution of (1) share Sunshine PCS Corp. Class A Common $0.0001 par payable 2/23/2001 to holders of record 2/22/2001
Each share Common $0.0001 par received distribution of (1) share Morgan Group Holding Co. Common payable 1/24/2002 to holders of record 12/18/2001
Each share Common $0.0001 par exchanged for (0.01) share Common 1¢ par 11/10/2005
Note: Holders of (99) or fewer pre-split shares received $29.9352 cash per share
Name changed to LICT Corp. 6/14/2007

LYNCHBURG & ABINGDON TELEGRAPH CO. (VA)
Out of existence 08/07/1958
Details not available

LYNCHBURG COAL & COKE CO.
In process of liquidation in 1941

LYNCHBURG FOUNDRY CO. (VA)
Stock Dividends - 100% 11/23/1948; 100% 05/15/1956
Merged into Woodward Iron Co. 10/30/1961
Each share Common exchanged for (0.925) share Common $10 par
4.25% Preferred $25 par called for redemption on 12/01/1961
Woodward Iron Co. name changed to Woodward Corp. 04/19/1968 which merged into Mead Corp. 11/30/1968
(See Mead Corp.)

LYNCHBURG GAS CO (VA)
Common $10 par changed to $5 par and (1) additional share issued 5/1/82
Stock Dividends - 20% 12/1/76; 20% 9/1/78; 20% 12/21/79; 10% 3/6/81; 15% 9/1/83
Acquired by Columbia Gas System, Inc. 5/23/88
Each share Common $5 par exchanged for (1.447) shares Common $10 par
Columbia Gas System, Inc. name changed to Columbia Energy Group 1/16/98 which merged into NiSource Inc. 11/1/2000

LYNCHBURG HOTEL CORP (VA)
Liquidated for benefit of creditors only and charter subsequently dissolved 12/24/1969
No stockholders' equity

LYNDEN ENERGY CORP (BC)
Merged into Earthstone Energy, Inc. 05/19/2016
Each share Common no par exchanged for (0.02842) share Common no par
Note: Unexchanged certificates will be cancelled and become without value 05/19/2022

LYNDEN INC (WA)
Merged into Lynden Acquisition, Inc. 12/18/1987
Each share Common $1 par exchanged for $27.50 cash

LYNDEN TRANS INC (WA)
Stock Dividend - 200% 06/22/1981
Under plan of reorganization each share Common $1 par automatically became (1) share Lynden Inc. Common $1 par 07/01/1982
(See Lynden Inc.)

LYNDEN VENTURES LTD (BC)
Reincorporated 02/02/2006
State of incorporation changed from (ON) to (BC) 02/02/2006
Name changed to Lynden Energy Corp. 01/17/2008
Lynden Energy Corp. merged into Earthstone Energy, Inc. 05/19/2016

LYNDEX EXPLS LTD (CANADA)
Delisted from Canadian Dealer Network 10/13/2000

LYNDHURST MNG LTD (QC)
Recapitalized as Globex Mining Enterprises Inc. 06/04/1974
Each share Common $1 par exchanged for (0.1) share Common $1 par

LYNDON PROSPECTING SYNDICATE (ON)
Liquidated 12/17/56

LYNDONBANK (LYNDONVILLE, VT)
Name changed 08/25/2006
Common $1 par split (2) for (1) by issuance of (1) additional share payable 08/25/2003 to holders of record 08/18/2003 Ex date - 09/17/2003
Name changed from Lyndonville Savings Bank & Trust Co. (Lyndonville, VT) to LyndonBank (Lyndonville, VT) 08/25/2006
Merged into Community Bancorp 01/03/2008
Each share Common $1 par exchanged for $25.25 cash

LYNN CARBON BLACK CO. (DE)
No longer in existence having become inoperative and void for non-payment of taxes 4/1/66

LYNN ELECTRIC CO. (MA)
Acquired by New England Electric System on a (2.25) for (1) basis 10/31/61
(See New England Electric System)

LYNN ENGR & MFG INC (AZ)
Common no par split (4) for (1) by issuance of (3) additional shares 07/01/1970
Adjudicated bankrupt 06/30/1972
Stockholders' equity unlikely

LYNN GAS & ELECTRIC CO. (MA)
Each share Capital Stock $25 par exchanged for (2.5) shares Capital Stock $10 par 00/00/1950
Reorganized as Lynn Electric Co. 02/05/1960
Each share Capital Stock $10 par exchanged for (0.7) share Capital Stock $10 par and (0.3) share Lynn Gas Co. Capital Stock $10 par
(See each company's listing)

LYNN GAS CO (MA)
Completely liquidated 12/28/1973
Each share Capital Stock $10 par exchanged for first and final distribution of $55.59 cash

LYNN TECH, INC (AZ)
Name changed to Staggs Enterprises, Inc. 04/29/14970
Staggs Enterprises, Inc. recapitalized as Staggs-Bilt Homes, Inc. 10/20/1971 which name changed to SBH, Inc. 01/30/1973
(See SBH, Inc.)

LYNNGOLD RES INC (ON)
Assets sold for the benefit of creditors 12/12/89
No stockholders' equity

LYNNITA CONSOLIDATED GOLD MINES, LTD. (ON)
Charter cancelled and dissolved 6/6/55
No stockholders' equity

LYNNWEAR CORP (MA)
Involuntarily dissolved 8/31/98

LYNTEX CORP (DE)
Reorganized under Chapter X Federal Bankruptcy Act 07/30/1976
No stockholders' equity

LYNTEX INTL INC (DE)
Charter cancelled and declared inoperative and void for non-payment of taxes 03/01/1986

LYNTEX RES INC (DE)
Each share old Common 1¢ par exchanged for (4) shares new Common 1¢ par 03/29/1985
Name changed to Lyntex International, Inc. 03/29/1985
(See Lyntex International, Inc.)

LYNTON GROUP INC (DE)
Each share Common 1¢ par exchanged for (0.2) share Common 5¢ par 08/26/1991
Each share Common 5¢ par exchanged for (1/6) share old Common 30¢ par 06/02/1994
Each share old Common 30¢ par exchanged for (0.0005) share new Common 30¢ par 04/29/1999
Note: Holders of (1,999) shares or fewer received $1 cash per share
Each share new Common 30¢ par exchanged again for (0.1) share new Common 30¢ par 11/30/1999
Note: In effect holders received $2,000 cash per share and public interest was eliminated

LYNWATIN NICKEL COPPER LTD. (CANADA)
Merged into Resource Exploration & Development Co. Ltd. 06/11/1968
Each share Capital Stock no par

LYN-M &

exchanged for (0.050761) share
Capital Stock no par
(See Resource Exploration & Development Co. Ltd.)

LYNWOOD CAP INC (BC)
Name changed to Tantalex Resources Corp. 10/18/2013

LYNX CDA EXPLS LTD (ON)
Capital Stock 50¢ par changed to no par 08/29/1978
Recapitalized as CS Resources Ltd./Les Ressources CS Ltee. 09/06/1989
Each share Capital Stock no par exchanged for (0.04) share Common no par
(See CS Resources Ltd./Les Ressources CS Ltee.)

LYNX ENERGY INC (UT)
Name changed to Teamway, Inc. 1/9/84
Teamway, Inc. name changed to Health & Fitness Retreats, Inc. 8/1/84 which name changed to Ormc Laboratories, Inc. 1/11/85
(See Ormc Laboratories, Inc.)

LYNX ENERGY SVCS CORP (AB)
Each share Class A Common no par received distribution of (0.5) Serval Growth Fund Trust Unit no par payable 5/28/97 to holders of record 5/27/97
Each share Class B Subordinate no par received distribution of (0.5) Serval Growth Fund Trust Unit no par payable 5/28/97 to holders of record 5/27/97
Merged into Precision Drilling Corp. 5/28/97
Each share Class A Common no par exchanged for (0.19507) share Common no par
Each Class B Subordinate no par exchanged for (0.19507) share Common no par
(See Precision Drilling Corp.)

LYNX EXPL CO (CO)
Each share old Common $0.001 par exchanged for (0.000005) share new Common $0.001 par 7/1/93
Note: In effect holders received $0.022 cash per share and public interest was eliminated

LYNX RES LTD (BC)
Name changed to Avatar Resource Corp. 01/21/1987
Avatar Resource Corp. recapitalized as as Blackline Oil Corp. (BC) 12/21/1993 which reincorporated in Alberta as Resourcexplorer Inc. 02/19/2001 which recapitalized as Exchequer Resource Corp. (AB) 07/24/2002 which reincorporated in British Columbia 10/25/2004 which recapitalized as CBD MED Research Corp. 07/18/2014

LYNX SEC INC (BC)
Struck from the register and dissolved 3/27/92

LYNX THERAPEUTICS INC (DE)
Name changed to Solexa, Inc. 3/4/2005
Solexa, Inc. merged into Illumina, Inc. 1/26/2007

LYNX YELLOWKNIFE GOLD MINES LTD (ON)
Charter cancelled for failure to pay taxes and file returns 03/16/1976

LYON CAP VENTURE CORP (NV)
Name changed to UTEC, Inc. 03/21/2007
UTEC, Inc. name changed to Tiger Oil & Energy, Inc. 09/23/2010

LYON LAKE MINES LTD (BC)
Each share old Common no par exchanged for (0.5) share new Common no par 02/11/1999
Ceased operations 05/09/2001
Stockholders' equity unlikely

LYON LUMBER CO.
Merged into Cascades Plywood Corp. 00/00/1947
Each share Capital Stock $20 par exchanged for (1) share Preferred $67 par and (3) shares Common $1 par
Cascades Plywood Corp. merged into United States Plywood Corp. 02/23/1962 which merged into U.S. Plywood-Champion Papers Inc. 02/28/1967 which name changed to Champion International Corp. 05/12/1972 which merged into International Paper Co. 06/20/2000

LYON METAL PRODS INC (DE)
Reincorporated 04/27/1970
Common $20 par changed to $10 par 00/00/1936
Each share Common $10 par exchanged for (2) shares Common $5 par 00/00/1948
5% Preferred $50 par called for redemption 08/01/1956
Common $5 par changed to $2.50 par and (1) additional share issued 05/12/1961
Stock Dividends - 100% 05/12/1958; 25% 05/20/1966; 40% 05/15/1968
State of incorporation changed from (IL) to (DE) 04/27/1970
Acquired by an employee group 08/29/1985
Each share Common $2.50 par exchanged for $20.55 cash

LYON MTN INC (NV)
Reorganized as Falken Investment, AG 03/17/1998
Each share Common $0.001 par exchanged for (2) shares Common $0.001 par
Falken Investment, AG name changed to Holter Technologies Holding, AG 03/00/1999 which recapitalized as International Consortium Corp. 06/17/2008
(See International Consortium Corp.)

LYON WILLIAM HOMES (DE)
Acquired by WLH Acquisition Corp. 07/27/2006
Each share Common 1¢ par exchanged for $109 cash
(Additional Information in Active)

LYONDELL CHEMICAL CO (DE)
Name changed 08/24/1998
Name changed from Lyondell Petrochemical Co. to Lyondell Chemical Co. 08/24/1998
Merged into Basell AF 12/20/2007
Each share Common $1 par exchanged for $48 cash

LYONS EDUCATIONAL ENTERPRISES INC (DE)
Common 10¢ par split (2) for (1) by issuance of (1) additional share 5/9/83
Name changed to Lyons Holding Co., Inc. 8/17/83
(See Lyons Holding Co., Inc.)

LYONS FINANCE SERVICE, INC. (DE)
Merged into Time Finance Corp. 07/21/1955
Each share 42¢ Preferred $5 par exchanged for (1) share $0.50 Preferred $5 par
Each share 50¢ Preferred $5 par exchanged for (1.2) shares $0.50 Preferred $5 par
Each share 56¢ Class A par exchanged for (1.5) shares $0.50 Preferred $5 par

LYONS HLDG INC (DE)
Charter cancelled and declared inoperative and void for non-payment of taxes 3/1/89

LYONS LIQUORS (NV)
Name changed to Hengyi International Industries Group Inc. 04/16/2013

LYONS-MAGNUS, INC. (DE)
Class B no par changed to $1 par 00/00/1958
Class B $1 par reclassified as Common $1 par 05/10/1963
Stock Dividends - 25% 02/28/1964; 25% 02/23/1965; 75% 03/08/1966
Name changed to 2545-16th Street Corp. 12/07/1966
(See 2545-16th Street Corp.)

LYPHOMED INC (DE)
Common 1¢ par split (3) for (2) by issuance of (0.5) additional share 6/20/84
Common 1¢ par split (3) for (2) by issuance of (0.5) additional share 4/8/85
Common 1¢ par split (3) for (2) by issuance of (0.5) additional share 11/1/85
Common 1¢ par split (3) for (2) by issuance of (0.5) additional share 6/20/86
Merged into Fujisawa Pharmaceutical Co., Ltd. 4/5/90
Each share Common 1¢ par exchanged for $31.87 cash

LYRA RES LTD (BC)
Common no par split (4) for (1) by issuance of (3) additional shares payable 07/25/2007 to holders of record 07/25/2007 Ex date - 07/23/2007
Name changed to Cicada Ventures Ltd. 07/02/2008

LYRIC CO (MD)
Voting Trust Agreement terminated 06/30/1970
Each VTC for Capital Stock $25 par exchanged for (1) share Capital Stock $25 par
Completely liquidated 10/10/1970
Each share Capital Stock $25 par exchanged for first and final distribution of $1.38 cash

LYRIC INTL INC (CO)
Recapitalized 08/13/1998
Recapitalized from Lyric Energy, Inc. to Lyric International, Inc. 08/13/1998
Each (240.597) shares Common 1¢ par exchanged for (1) share Common 1¢ par
SEC revoked common stock registration 04/22/2016

LYRIS INC (DE)
Each share old Common 1¢ par exchanged for (0.06666666) share new Common 1¢ par 03/12/2012
Acquired by Aurea Software, Inc. 06/22/2015
Each share new Common 1¢ par exchanged for $0.89 cash

LYSANDER GOLD CORP (BC)
Recapitalized as Lysander Minerals Corp. 07/22/1999
Each share Common no par exchanged for (0.2) share Common no par
Lysander Minerals Corp. name changed to EastCoal Inc. 01/31/2011

LYSANDER MINERALS CORP (BC)
Each share Common no par received distribution of (0.914) share Lorraine Copper Corp. Common no par payable 04/24/2008 to holders of record 04/16/2008 Ex date - 04/14/2008
Name changed to EastCoal Inc. 01/31/2011

LYSOZYME PRODS INC (CA)
Charter suspended for failure to file reports and pay fees 02/01/1973

LYTLE CORP. (IL)
Reincorporated under the laws of New Mexico 2/19/62
(See Lytle Corp. (NM))

LYTLE CORP. (NM)
Charter cancelled for failure to pay taxes 1/21/65

LYTTON & TOLLEY INC (FL)
Name changed to Wheeler Construction Inc. 7/2/93

LYTTON FINL CORP (DE)
Stock Dividend - 25% 01/31/1964
Name changed to LFC Financial Corp. 12/20/1968
LFC Financial Corp. merged into Great Western Financial Corp. 12/22/1970 which merged into Washington Mutual Inc. 07/01/1997
(See Washington Mutual, Inc.)

LYTTON MINERALS LTD (BC)
Class B no par reclassified as Class A no par 12/21/1964
Each share Class A no par exchanged for (1) share Common no par and $0.65 cash 01/27/1981
Merged into Tahera Corp. 03/01/1999
Each share Common no par exchanged for (1) share Common no par
Tahera Corp. name changed to Tahera Diamond Corp. 06/23/2004
(See Tahera Diamond Corp.)

LYTTONS HENRY C LYTTON & CO (IL)
100% held by Cluett, Peabody & Co., Inc. as of 07/01/1978
Public interest eliminated

LYYNKS INC (NV)
Reincorporated under the laws of Delaware as Vancord Capital Inc. 01/06/2015

M

M. & D. STORE FIXTURES, INC. (CA)
Stock Dividend - 25% 3/12/64
Completely liquidated 10/22/65
Each share Common $1 par exchanged for first and final distribution of (0.430863) share Kidde (Walter) & Co., Inc. (N.Y.) Common $2.50 par
Kidde (Walter) & Co., Inc. (NY) reincorporated in Delaware 7/2/68 which name changed to Kidde, Inc. 4/18/80 which merged into Hanson Trust p.l.c. 12/31/87 which name changed to Hanson PLC (OLd) 1/29/88 which reorganized as Hanson PLC (New) 10/15/2003

M. & T. SECURITIES CORP.
Dissolved in 1937

M. LIQUIDATING CORP. (CO)
Voluntarily dissolved 2/9/79
Details not available

M. R. P. INC. (MI)
Name changed to Michigan Rotary Press, Inc. 9/21/53
(See Michigan Rotary Press, Inc.)

M & A HLDG CORP (NV)
Name changed to Mullan Agritech, Inc. 07/11/2016

M & A WEST INC (CO)
Each share Common no par received distribution of (0.5) share Digital Bridge Inc. Common $0.001 par payable 01/10/2000 to holders of record 09/30/1999
Each share Common no par received distribution of (0.1) share Venturelist.com Inc. Common payable 08/10/2000 to holders of record 07/10/2000
Each share Common no par received distribution of (0.2) share Venturelist.com Inc. Common $0.001 par payable 08/18/2001 to holders of record 11/15/2000
SEC revoked common stock registration 05/01/2006

M & F WORLDWIDE CORP (DE)
Acquired by MacAndrews & Forbes Holdings Inc. 12/21/2011
Each share Common 1¢ par exchanged for $25 cash

M & H LIQUIDATING CORP. (NY)
7% Preferred $100 par called for redemption 06/29/1962
Liquidation completed
Each share Common $100 par stamped to indicate initial distribution of $150 cash 08/08/1962
Each share Stamped Common $100 par stamped to indicate second distribution of $50 cash 01/17/1963
Each share Stamped Common $100 par stamped to indicate third and final distribution of $14.85 cash 12/20/1965
Certificates were not surrendered and are now without value

M & M COMPUTER INDS INC (DE)
Merged into Singer Co. 02/28/1973
Each share Common 30¢ par exchanged for $6 cash

M & M HYDROELECTRIC CORP (UT)
Recapitalized as Fundamental Financial Corp. 03/14/1995
Each share Common no par exchanged for (0.1) share Common $0.025 par
Fundamental Financial Corp. name changed to Ikar Mineral Corp. (UT) 09/22/1997 which reincorporated in Delaware 03/31/1997 which recapitalized as Ethos Capital Inc. 11/02/2000 which name changed to Patriot Energy Corp. 02/04/2002 which name changed to BigBrews Holdings Inc. (DE) 02/18/2003 which reincorporated in Nevada as Patriot Energy Corp. 09/09/2003 which name changed to Healing Hand Network International, Inc. 12/22/2003 which name changed to Patriot Energy Corp. (NV) 10/10/2005
(See Patriot Energy Corp.)

M & M INTL RLTY INC (DE)
Name changed to Sonic Systems Corp. 10/30/1998
Sonic Systems Corp. name changed to Unity Wireless Corp. 07/20/2000
(See Unity Wireless Corp.)

M & M PORCUPINE GOLD MINES LTD (CANADA)
Reincorporated 7/19/77
Reincorporated 6/28/95
Common $1 par changed to no par 8/21/75
Place of incorporation changed from (Ont) to (BC) 7/19/77
Place of incorporation changed from (BC) to (Canada) 6/28/95
Name changed to Diasyn Technologies Ltd. 1/15/88
Diasyn Technologies Ltd. merged into Strucutures Biologicals Inc. 7/27/93 which recapitalized as Ben-Abraham Technologies Inc. 12/6/96 which name changed to BioSante Pharmaceuticals, Inc. (WY) 12/17/99 which reincorporated in Delaware 6/26/2001

M & M PRECISION SYSTEMS, INC. (CO)
Merged into Acme-Cleveland Corp. 11/27/81
Each share Common no par exchanged for $20.09 cash

M & M WOOD WORKING CO. (OR)
Each share Capital Stock $10 par exchanged for (2) shares Capital Stock $5 par and dividend of (1) additional share paid in December 1947
Stock Dividend - 100% 2/47
Assets sold and company liquidated 8/17/56
Details not available

M & R DIETETIC LABORATORIES, INC. (OH)
Common no par split (5) for (1) by issuance of (4) additional shares 4/13/56
Common no par split (3) for (1) by issuance of (2) additional shares 3/31/60
Merged into Abbott Laboratories on a (0.300609) for (1) basis 2/28/64

M & S BANCORP (WI)
Common $5 par changed to $2.50 par and (1) additional share issued 08/01/1972
Common $2.50 par split (3) for (2) by issuance of (0.5) additional share 12/31/1973
Name changed to Bancwis Corp. 07/09/1980
(See Bancwis Corp.)

M & T BANK CORP (NY)
6.875% Depositary Preferred Ser. D called for redemption at $1,000 on 12/15/2016
(Additional Information in Active)

M-A-C PLAN OF HARTFORD, INC.
Dissolution approved in 1935

M A COM INC (MA)
Common $1 par split (3) for (2) by issuance of (0.5) additional share 06/05/1978
Common $1 par split (2) for (1) by issuance of (1) additional share 04/06/1979
Common $1 par split (3) for (2) by issuance of (0.5) additional share 04/07/1980
Common $1 par split (2) for (1) by issuance of (1) additional share 10/21/1980
Common Stock Purchase Rights redeemed at $0.01 per right 06/29/1995 for holders of record 06/29/1995
Merged into AMP Inc. 06/30/1995
Each share Common $1 par exchanged for (0.28) share Common $1 par
AMP Inc. merged into Tyco International Ltd. (Bermuda) 04/01/1999 which reincorporated in Switzerland 03/17/2009 which merged into Johnson Controls International PLC 09/06/2016

M/A-COM TECHNOLOGY SOLUTIONS HLDGS INC (DE)
Name changed to MACOM Technology Solutions Holdings, Inc. 06/03/2016

M.A.G. LIQUIDATING CORP. (TX)
Liquidation completed
Each share Common $1 par exchanged for initial distribution of $16.15 cash 6/30/78
Each share Common $1 par received second distribution of $10 principal amount of 9% Secured Debentures due 8/1/93 of Houston First Financial Group, Inc. 8/13/78
Each share Common $1 par received third and final distribution of $0.50 cash 10/15/78

M A G HLDGS INC (UT)
Proclaimed dissolved for failure to file reports and pay fees 01/01/1991

M A I D PLC (ENGLAND)
Name changed to Dialog Corp. PLC 11/17/1997
Dialog Corp. PLC name changed to Bright Station PLC 05/08/2000 which name changed to Smartlogik Group PLC 07/09/2001
(See Smartlogik Group PLC)

M A R C INC (TX)
Common $1 par split (6) for (5) by issuance of (0.2) additional share 03/31/1972
Common $1 par split (3) for (2) by issuance of (0.5) additional share payable 02/28/1997 to holders of record 02/07/1997
Stock Dividends - 150% 12/15/1984; 50% 12/19/1985
Merged into Omnicom Group Inc. 11/04/1999
Each share Common $1 par exchanged for $20 cash

M&I MARSHALL & ILSLEY INVT II CORP (NV)
8.875% Preferred Ser. C called for redemption at $100,000 on 06/15/2007

M B A HLDGS INC (NV)
Each share old Common $0.001 par exchanged for (0.33333333) share new Common $0.001 par 06/11/1996
Each share new Common $0.001 par exchanged for (10) shares Common no par 04/05/2004
Stock Dividends - 1% payable 11/26/2004 to holders of record 11/26/2004 Ex date - 11/23/2004; 0.5% payable 11/26/2005 to holders of record 11/25/2005 Ex date - 11/22/2005
SEC revoked common stock registration 08/31/2011

M.B.C. NOME CO. (CA)
Charter suspended for failure to pay franchise taxes 07/01/1963

M-B HOLDING CORP.
Dissolved in 1943

M C BEVERAGES LTD (BC)
Delisted from Vancouver Stock Exchange 10/06/1989

M C D HLDGS INC (MD)
Name changed to Chesapeake Investors, Inc. 8/14/80
(See Chesapeake Investors, Inc.)

M-CELL LTD (SOUTH AFRICA)
Name changed to MTN Group Ltd. 10/14/2002

M CORP. (CT)
Merged out of existence 10/31/2007
Details not available

M CORP INC (ON)
Common no par split (2) for (1) by issuance of (1) additional share 06/05/1986
Name changed to Mikes Restaurants Inc. 12/08/1998
(See Mikes Restaurants Inc.)

M D C ASSET INVS INC (MD)
Name changed to Asset Investors Corp. (MD) 01/01/1989
Asset Investors Corp. (MD) reincorporated in Delaware 05/25/1999 which name changed to American Land Lease, Inc. 08/11/2000
(See American Land Lease, Inc.)

M D C CORP (CO)
Common 1¢ par split (4) for (1) by issuance of (3) additional shares 3/15/79
Stock Dividend - 20% 4/29/80552676
Reincorporated under the laws of Delaware as M.D.C. Holdings, Inc. 6/20/85

M D NAT VITAMINS INC (DE)
Charter cancelled and declared inoperative and void for non-payment of taxes 3/1/89

M E C SYS INC (NY)
Charter cancelled and proclaimed dissolved for failure to pay taxes 03/01/1982

M E COMPU SOFTWARE INC (CANADA)
Name changed to Goldrite Mining Corp. 3/31/88
Goldrite Mining Corp. recapitalized as Consolidated Goldrite Mining Corp. (Canada) 7/28/93 which reincorporated in Cayman Islands as Bestar International Group Ltd. 4/30/96
(See Bestar International Group Ltd.)

M E P C CDN PPTYS LTD (ON)
Merged into Pensionfund Properties Ltd. 09/30/1977
Each share 6% Preferred Ser. A $25 par exchanged for $25.50 cash
Each share Common no par exchanged for $13.60 cash

M.F. CORP. (DE)
Dissolved 5/11/56

M.F.F. EQUITIES LTD. (ON)
Liquidation completed
Each share Common no par received initial distribution of $11.50 cash 7/29/68
Each share Common no par received second distribution of $1.2316 cash 5/30/69
Each share Common no par received third and final distribution of $0.0705 cash 8/16/71
Certificates were not surrendered and are now without value

M G F MGMT LTD (CANADA)
Acquired by Gdn. Management Ltd. 03/06/1973
Each share Class A no par exchanged for (0.5) share Common no par
Gdn. Management Ltd. name changed to Guardian Capital Group Ltd. 07/18/1973

M G GOLD CORP (NV)
Name changed to MG Natural Resources Corp. 10/12/98
MG Natural Resources Corp. name changed to Xenolix Technologies Inc. 6/14/2000 which name changed to Pershing Resources Co., Inc. 4/27/2004

M G N MGMT CORP (NY)
Charter cancelled and proclaimed dissolved for failure to pay taxes 06/30/2004

M G NAT RES CORP (NV)
Name changed to Xenolix Technologies Inc. 6/14/2000
Xenolix Technologies Inc. name changed to Pershing Resources Co., Inc. 4/27/2004

M G PRODS INC (CA)
SEC revoked common stock registration 12/01/2009

M-GAB DEV CORP (FL)
Name changed to China Agro Sciences Corp. 05/01/2006
China Agro Sciences Corp. name changed to China HGS Real Estate Inc. 11/24/2009

M H MEYERSON & CO INC (NJ)
Name changed to Crown Financial Group, Inc. 10/16/2003
Crown Financial Group, Inc. name changed to Crown Financial Holdings, Inc. 1/11/2005
(See Crown Financial Holdings, Inc.)

M HOLDINGS CORP. (DE)
Charter cancelled and declared inoperative and void for non-payment of taxes 3/1/90

M I ACQUISITIONS INC (DE)
Units separated 07/27/2018
Name changed to Priority Technology Holdings, Inc. 07/27/2018

M/I HOMES INC (OH)
Name changed 01/12/2004
Common 1¢ par split (2) for (1) by issuance of (1) additional share payable 06/19/2002 to holders of record 06/05/2002 Ex date - 06/20/2002
Name changed from M/I Schottenstein Homes, Inc. to M/I Homes, Inc. 01/12/2004
9.75% Depositary Preferred Ser. A called for redemption at $25 plus

$0.209896 accrued dividends on 10/16/2017
(Additional Information in Active)

M I M HLDGS LTD (AUSTRALIA)
Each Unsponsored ADR for Ordinary A$0.50 par exchanged for (2) Sponsored ADR's for Ordinary A$0.50 par 03/06/1991
Old Sponsored ADR's for Ordinary A$0.50 par reclassified as new ADR's for Ordinary A$0.50 par 03/29/1991
Stock Dividends - 25% 11/01/1979; 25% 10/28/1980; 50% 06/12/1987
ADR agreement terminated 07/11/2003
Each Sponsored ADR for Ordinary A$0.50 par exchanged for $2.2513 cash

M I SCHOTTENSTEIN HOMES INC (DE)
Merged into M/I Homes Acquisition Corp. 06/29/1990
Each share Common 1¢ par exchanged for $7.50 cash

M I T S INC (NM)
Merged into Pertec Computer Corp. 05/20/1977
Each share Common 1¢ par exchanged for (0.7721) share Common 10¢ par
(See Pertec Computer Corp.)

M INC (NV)
Recapitalized as Parallel Technologies Inc. 06/04/1991
Each (60) shares Common $0.0001 par exchanged for (1) share Common $0.006 par
Parallel Technologies Inc. recapitalized as Fushi International, Inc. 01/30/2006 which name changed to Fushi Copperweld, Inc. 01/15/2008

M.J. & M. & M. CONSOLIDATED (CA)
Name changed to M J M & M Oil Co. in 1951
M J M & M Oil Co. merged into Anza Pacific Corp. 6/12/64
(See Anza Pacific Corp.)

M J M & M OIL CO. (CA)
Merged into Anza Pacific Corp. 6/12/64
Each share Capital Stock 10¢ par exchanged for (0.1) share Capital Stock $1 par
(See Anza Pacific Corp.)

M J MAILLIS S A INDL PACKAGING SYS & TECHNOLOGIES (GREECE)
Name changed 09/21/2010
Name changed from M.J. Maillis S.A. to M.J. Maillis S.A. - Industrial Packaging Systems & Technologies 09/21/2010
ADR agreement terminated 12/17/2014
Each Sponsored ADR for Ordinary exchanged for $0.125178 cash

M-K ENERGY INC. (UT)
Name changed to Cache Drilling, Inc. 06/02/1982
Cache Drilling, Inc. name changed to Almur Cosmetics, Inc. 07/26/1988 which recapitalized as Multi-Media Industries Corp. 06/19/1995 which recapitalized as Worldnet Resources Group Inc. 02/14/2000 which recapitalized as Asset Equity Group, Inc. 12/12/2001
(See Asset Equity Group, Inc.)

M.L.J.W. CORP. (DE)
Liquidation completed
Each share Common 50¢ par received initial distribution of $0.75 cash 2/28/84
Each share Common 50¢ par received second and final distribution of $0.63 cash 2/8/85
Note: Certificates were not required to be surrendered and are now valueless

M.M. LEAD CO. (UT)
Name changed to Basic Energy, Inc. 2/22/80

M M CORK ENTERPRISES INC (NV)
Name changed to International Forest Industries, Inc. 10/01/1996
International Forest Industries, Inc. name changed to Flour City International, Inc. 05/16/1997
(See Flour City International, Inc.)

M P C INC (DE)
Common 10¢ par changed to 5¢ par and (1) additional shares issued 1/15/69
Acquired by Swanton Corp. 12/30/83
Each share Common 5¢ par exchanged for $11.90 principal amount of 10-1/2% Conv. Subordinated Debentures due 10/31/93

M P F CONSULTING CORP (NV)
Recapitalized as Amco Resources, Inc. 05/20/1983
Each share Common $0.0001 par exchanged for (0.0625) share Common 1¢ par
Amco Resources, Inc. name changed to Amco Building Corp. 03/31/1988

M P G INVT LTD (CANADA)
$1.30 Preferred 1964 Ser. $25 par reclassified as Class A 1964 Ser. no par 11/21/1979
Class A 1964 Ser. no par reclassified as Preferred 1964 Ser. no par 12/05/1984
Class B Ser. 1985 no par called for redemption 01/31/1991
Common no par split (5) for (3) by issuance of (1/3) additional share 06/30/1993
Preferred Ser. 1964 no par called for redemption 03/29/1996
Common no par split (7) for (4) by issuance of (0.75) additional shares payable 05/22/1996 to holders of record 05/15/1996
Stock Dividends - 100% 10/14/1981; 60% 11/10/1986
Each share Common no par exchanged for $6.22 cash 08/15/1996

M PHARMACEUTICAL INC (AB)
Each share old Common no par exchanged for (0.1) share new Common no par 04/17/2015
Recapitalized as Callitas Health Inc. 09/20/2017
Each share new Common no par exchanged for (0.1) share Common no par

M PWR ENTMT INC (DE)
Recapitalized as eDoorways Corp., Inc. 09/04/2007
Each share Common $0.001 par exchanged for (0.0005) share Common $0.001 par
eDoorways Corp., Inc. name changed to eDoorways International Corp. (DE) 09/02/2010 reincorporated in Nevada 05/06/2013 which recapitalized as Escue Energy, Inc. 06/23/2015

M R A HLDGS LTD (NB)
5% Part. Preferred $25 par called for redemption 1/30/62
Each share Class A no par or Class B no par exchanged for (1) share Common no par 2/14/74

M.R.B., INC. (MA)
Completely liquidated 4/13/67
Each share Class A Common $1 par or Class B Common $1 par exchanged for first and final distribution of (0.115273) share Genesco Inc. $6 Conv. Preference Ser. B no par

M-REAL CORP (FINLAND)
Name changed to Metsa Board Corp. 07/27/2012
(See Metsa Board Corp.)

M S CARRIERS INC (TN)
Common 1¢ par split (2) for (1) by issuance of (1) additional share 6/11/87
Common 1¢ par split (2) for (1) by issuance of (1) additional share 9/16/92
Merged into Swift Transportation Co., Inc. 7/2/2001
Each share Common 1¢ par exchanged for (1.7) shares Common $0.001 par
(See Swift Transportation Co., Inc.)

M S E CABLE SYS INC (DE)
Each share old Common 1¢ par exchanged for (1/11) share new Common 1¢ par 06/30/1986
Merged into Cable Plus of Michigan Inc. 07/21/1995
Each share new Common 1¢ par exchanged for $0.685 cash

M S M MARKETING LTD (ON)
Recapitalized as Sea Hawk Energy Inc. 06/16/1986
Each share Common no par exchanged for (0.25) share Class A Common no par
Sea Hawk Energy Inc. name changed to Jarl Energy Inc. 08/05/1987 which name changed to ALBA Petroleum Corp. 10/26/1989 which merged into Alberta Oil & Gas Ltd. 12/31/1990 which recapitalized as Alberta Oil & Gas Petroleum Corp. 11/19/1997 which recapitalized as Edge Energy Inc. 04/14/1998 which merged into Ventus Energy Ltd. 08/11/2000 which name changed to Navigo Energy Inc. 05/24/2002
(See Navigo Energy Inc.)

M STR GALLERY INC (FL)
Name changed to Enhance-Your-Reputation.com, Inc. 10/03/2014
Enhance-Your-Reputation.com, Inc. name changed to Force Protection Video Equipment Corp. 03/05/2015

M-SYS FLASH DISK PIONEERS LTD (ISRAEL)
Ordinary ILS 0.001 par split (2) for (1) by issuance of (1) additional share payable 09/21/2000 to holders of record 09/14/2000 Ex date - 09/22/2000
Merged into SanDisk Corp. 11/19/2006
Each share Ordinary ILS 0.001 par exchanged for (0.76368) share Common $0.001 par
SanDisk Corp. merged into Western Digital Corp. 05/12/2016

M T FINL GROUP INC (NV)
Name changed to Photogen Technologies, Inc. 5/16/97
Photogen Technologies, Inc. name changed to IMCOR Pharmaceutical Co. 2/5/2004

M T P R CORP (MI)
Charter dissolved for failure to file annual reports 05/15/1980

M III ACQUISITION CORP (DE)
Units separated 03/28/2018
Name changed to Infrastructure & Energy Alternatives, Inc. 03/28/2018

M 2003 PLC (ENGLAND & WALES)
Assets sold for the benefit of creditors 10/25/2005
No stockholders' equity

M.V. CO., INC. (NV)
Charter revoked for failure to pay fees and file reports 3/3/58

M V I D INTL CORP (NV)
Recapitalized as Micro-Lite Television 3/14/94
Each share Common $0.001 par exchanged for (1/30) share Common $0.001 par
Micro-Lite Television name changed to Superior Wireless Communications, Inc. 11/1/96 which recapitalized as JustWebit.Com, Inc. 8/16/99 which name changed to Synthetic Turf Corp. of America 11/12/2002 which recapitalized as City Capital Corp. 12/15/2004

M.W. SAVAGE FACTORIES, INC. (ME)
Liquidated by Court order 1/24/35
Details not available

M W PETE CORP (UT)
Reorganized as Parkford Petroleum Inc. 10/11/1978
Each share Common $0.001 par exchanged for (6) shares Common $0.000833 par

M-WAVE INC (DE)
Common 1¢ par split (2) for (1) by issuance of (1) additional share payable 11/28/2000 to holders of record 11/13/2000 Ex date - 11/29/2000
Common 1¢ par changed to $0.005 par 00/00/2002
Each share old Common $0.005 par exchanged for (0.25) share new Common $0.005 par 12/18/2006
Name changed to Green St. Energy, Inc. 01/16/2009

M&I CENTRAL BANK & TRUST (MARSHFIELD, WI)
Acquired by M&I Marshall & Ilsley Bank (Milwaukee, WI) 4/1/2001
Details not available

M&I FIRST AMERICAN NATIONAL BANK (WAUSAU, WI)
99% acquired by Marshall & Ilsley Corp. through purchase offer which expired 08/15/1990
Public interest eliminated

M&I MARSHALL & ILSLEY BANK (MILWAUKEE, WI)
99.9% held by Marshall & Ilsley Corp. as of 05/21/1971
Public interest eliminated

M&K INVTS INC (UT)
Recapitalized as Dynamic Information Systems & Exchange Inc. (UT) 11/07/1994
Each share Common $0.001 par exchanged for (0.5) share Common $0.001 par
Dynamic Information Systems & Exchange Inc. (UT) reincorporated in Nevada as Career Worth, Inc. 11/17/2000 which name changed to U.S. Homes & Properties, Inc. 11/22/2002
(See U.S. Homes & Properties, Inc.)

M&M FINANCIAL CORP. (DE)
Acquired by Southern Bankshares Inc. 7/1/88
Each share Common 20¢ par exchanged for $62.50 cash

M&M FINANCIAL CORP (SC)
Merged into Anchor Financial Corp. 08/31/1998
Each share Common $5 par exchanged for (0.87) share Common no par
Anchor Financial Corp. merged into South Financial Group, Inc. 06/07/2000 which merged into Toronto-Dominion Bank (Toronto, ON) 09/30/2010

M&N CAP CORP (NY)
Reincorporated under the laws of Delaware as Analytical Nursing Management Corp. 8/3/94
Analytical Nursing Management Corp. name changed to AMEDISYS, Inc. 8/11/95

M&T CAP TR IV (DE)
8.5% Enhanced Trust Preferred Securities called for redemption at $25 plus $0.425 accrued dividends on 02/27/2014

M&T MTG INVS (TX)
Merged into Commonwealth Financial Group Real Estate Investment Trust 08/31/1983

Each Share of Bene. Int. $1 par exchanged for (1.17) Shares of Bene. Int. $1 par
Commonwealth Financial Group Real Estate Investment Trust name changed to First Continental Real Estate Investment Trust 06/28/1985 which merged into Parkway Co. (TX) 06/14/1994 which reincorporated in Maryland as Parkway Properties, Inc. 08/02/1996

MAANSHAN IRON & STL LTD (CHINA)
ADR agreement terminated 08/05/2013
Each 144A Sponsored ADR for H shares exchanged for (100) H shares
Note: Unexchanged ADR's will be sold and the proceeds, if any, held for claim after 08/05/2014

MAAX INC (QC)
Common no par split (2) for (1) by issuance of (1) additional share payable 4/3/97 to holders of record 4/1/97
Merged into a group of companies 6/4/2004
Each share Common no par exchanged for $22.50 cash

MABAIE INC (QC)
Acquired by MBE Acquisition Inc. 9/14/2001
Each share Common no par exchanged for $0.80 cash

MABEE MINERALS INC (BC)
Struck off register and declared dissolved for failure to file returns 11/23/1984

MABL HOLDINGS LTD. (MB)
Liquidation completed
Each share Common no par received initial distribution of $80 cash payable 07/06/2006 to holders of record 07/04/2006
Each share Common no par received second distribution of $20 cash payable 03/30/2007 to holders of record 03/19/2007
Each share Common no par received third and final distribution of $5 cash payable 09/28/2007 to holders of record 09/06/2007
Note: Certificates were not required to be surrendered and are without value

MABWE MINERALS INC (WY)
Reorganized under the laws of Delaware as Fonon Corp. 07/29/2015
Each share Common $0.001 par exchanged for (0.1) share Common $0.001 par

MAC (W.W.) CO. (DE)
Stock Dividends - 25% 2/15/51; 10% 10/24/60
No longer in existence having become inoperative and void for non-payment of taxes 4/1/67

MAC AM RES CORP (BC)
Merged into Colossus Resource Equities Inc. 12/08/1987
Each share Common no par exchanged for (1) share Common no par
Colossus Resource Equities Inc. merged into Prime Resources Corp. (BC) 02/01/1989 which recapitalized as Prime Resources Group Inc. 01/26/1990 which merged into HomeStake Mining Co. 12/03/1998 which merged into Barrick Gold Corp. 12/14/2001

MAC AVIATION CORP (NY)
Charter cancelled and proclaimed dissolved for failure to pay taxes 12/20/1977

MAC FARLANES CANDIES (CA)
Merged into Riviana Foods Inc. (Old) 10/1/71
Each share Common $1 par exchanged for (0.291117) share Common $3.50 par
Riviana Foods, Inc. (Old) acquired by Colgate-Palmolive Co. 6/14/76

MAC FILMWORKS INC (DE)
Each share old Common $0.0001 par exchanged for (0.03333333) share new Common $0.0001 par 09/11/2008
Name changed to Sahara Media Holdings, Inc. 09/26/2008
Sahara Media Holdings, Inc. name changed to YouBlast Global, Inc. 06/16/2010
(See YouBlast Global, Inc.)

MAC FRUGALS BARGAINS CLOSE OUTS INC (DE)
Merged into Consolidated Stores Corp. (DE) 1/16/98
Each share Common $0.02778 par exchanged for (0.94) share Common 1¢ par
Consolidated Stores Corp. (DE) reincorporated in Ohio as Big Lots, Inc. 5/16/2001

MAC-GRAY CORP (DE)
Acquired by CSC ServiceWorks, Inc. 01/09/2014
Each share Common 1¢ par exchanged for $21.25 cash

MAC MEL FINL CORP INC (AB)
Name changed to Sparta Capital Ltd. 06/04/1996

MAC-RYAN ENTERPRISES, LTD. (ON)
Charter cancelled in February 1939
No stockholders' equity

MACABE CO., INC. (OR)
Company dissolved and assets distributed to shareholders 1/21/59

MACADA HLDG INC (WY)
Reincorporated 02/22/2011
State of incorporation changed from (NV) to (WY) 02/22/2011
Recapitalized as KMA Holding, Inc. 03/17/2011
Each share Common $0.0001 par exchanged for (0.001) share Common $0.0001 par
(See KMA Holding, Inc.)

MACANDREWS & FORBES CO (NJ)
Common no par changed to $10 par 00/00/1932
Common $10 par changed to $3 par and (2) additional shares issued 06/01/1966
Stock Dividend - 10% 01/03/1975
Merged into Cohen-Hatfield Industries, Inc. 04/18/1980
Each share Common $3 par exchanged for $24 cash

MACANDREWS & FORBES GROUP INC (DE)
Merged into MacAndrews & Forbes Holdings Inc. 03/14/1984
Each share Common $1 par exchanged for $56 cash

MACARTHUR COAL LTD (AUSTRALIA)
Acquired by PEAMCoal Property Ltd. 12/22/2011
Each ADR for Ordinary exchanged for $34.335 cash

MACARTHUR DIAMONDS LTD (AUSTRALIA)
Reincorporated 12/02/2002
Place of incorporation changed from (BC) to Australia 12/02/2002
Recapitalized as Macarthur Minerals Ltd. 07/07/2005
Each share Common no par exchanged for (0.1) share Common no par

MACASSA GOLD MINES LTD (ON)
Merged into Willroy Mines Ltd. 01/08/1971
Each share Capital Stock $1 par exchanged for (0.8) share Capital Stock no par
Willroy Mines Ltd. merged into Lac Minerals Ltd. (Old) 12/31/1982 which merged into LAC Minerals Ltd. (New) 07/29/1985 which was acquired by American Barrick Resources Corp. 10/17/1994 which name changed to Barrick Gold Corp. 01/18/1995

MACASSA MINES LTD. (ON)
Merged into Macassa Gold Mines Ltd. 11/1/61
Each share Capital Stock $1 par exchanged for (1) share Capital Stock $1 par
Macassa Gold Mines Ltd. merged into Willroy Mines Ltd. 1/8/71 which merged into Lac Minerals Ltd. (Old) 12/31/82 which merged into LAC Minerals Ltd. (New) 7/29/85 which was acquired by American Barrick Resources Corp. 10/17/94 which name changed to Barrick Gold Corp. 1/18/95

MACAU RESOURCES GROUP LTD (BRITISH VIRGIN ISLANDS)
SEC revoked common stock registration 07/06/2016

MACAW CAP INC (NV)
Recapitalized as Unidyn, Corp. 12/03/1997
Each share Common $0.001 par exchanged for (0.125) share Common $0.001 par

MACAW ONE INC (NV)
Name changed to Westgate Energy, Inc. 6/10/96
Westgate Energy, Inc. name changed to Taco, Inc. 12/16/96 which name changed to Communique Wireless Corp. 4/10/97 which name changed to Communique Corp. 10/10/97 which name changed to Formal Systems America Inc. 12/17/98
(See Formal Systems America Inc.)

MACBART MINES, LTD. (ON)
Charter cancelled 1/1/62
No stockholders' equity

MACBETH-EVANS GLASS CO.
Merged into Corning Glass Works 00/00/1936
Details not available

MACC PRIVATE EQUITIES INC (DE)
Stock Dividends - 10% payable 03/31/1997 to holders of record 03/14/1997; 20% payable 03/31/1998 to holders of record 03/13/1998; 30% payable 03/31/1999 to holders of record 03/15/1999; 20% payable 03/31/2000 to holders of record 03/15/2000; 20% payable 03/30/2001 to holders of record 03/15/2001 Ex date - 03/13/2001
Liquidation completed
Each share Common 1¢ par received initial distribution of $1.46 cash payable 04/16/2012 to holders of record 01/20/2012
Each share Common 1¢ par received second distribution of $0.61 cash payable 05/20/2013 to holders of record 01/20/2012
Each share Common 1¢ par received third distribution of $1.30 cash payable 08/08/2013 to holders of record 01/20/2012
Each share Common 1¢ par received fourth and final distribution of $0.75896 cash payable 12/29/2015 to holders of record 01/20/2012

MACCABI VENTURES INC (BC)
Recapitalized as Lead Ventures Inc. 03/15/2018
Each share Common no par exchanged for (0.1) share Common no par

MACCLARE MINES, LTD. (ON)
Charter cancelled for failure to file reports and pay taxes 8/1/58

MACCO CHEMICAL CO. (OH)
Each share Common no par exchanged for (10) shares Common $1 par 8/14/57
Merged into Glidden Co. 3/1/64
Each share Common $1 par exchanged for (0.3) share $2.125 Conv. Preferred no par
(See Glidden Co.)

MACCO CORP. (DE)
Merged into Great Southwest Corp. (TX) 2/26/69
Each share 6% Class A Preferred $14 par exchanged for (1) share 8.4% Preferred Ser. E $10 par
Great Southwest Corp. (TX) reincorporated in Delaware 12/31/72
(See Great Southwest Corp.)

MACCO CORP. (NV)
Each share Capital Stock $1 par exchanged for (1) share Common $1 par and (1) share Macoil Corp. Capital Stock $1 par 01/07/1948
Stock Dividends - 10% 12/01/1952; 10% 08/31/1959; 100% 01/22/1960
Name changed to Paramount Pacific Inc. 06/01/1967
Paramount Pacific Inc. merged into Zapata Norness Inc. 09/30/1969 which name changed to Zapata Corp. (DE) 02/15/1972 which reincorporated in Nevada 04/30/1999 which reincorporated in Delaware as Harbinger Group Inc. 12/23/2009 which name changed to HRG Group, Inc. 03/11/2015 which recapitalized as Spectrum Brands Holdings, Inc. (New) 07/16/2018

MACCO INTL CORP (NV)
Name changed to Success Holding Group International, Inc. 07/08/2014

MACCO REALTY CO. (DE)
Name changed to Macco Corp. (DE) 10/3/68
Macco Corp. (DE) merged into Great Southwest Corp. (TX) 2/26/69 which reincorporated in Delaware
(See Great Southwest Corp.)

MACCO RLTY CO (CA)
Merged into Macco Realty Co. (DE) 7/25/66
Each share Common $1 par exchanged for (1) share 6% Class A Preferred $14 par
Macco Realty Co. (DE) name changed to Macco Corp. (DE) 10/3/68 which merged into Great Southwest Corp. (TX) 2/26/69 which reincorporated in Delaware 12/31/72
(See Great Southwest Corp.)

MACCS SUSTAINABLE YIELD TR (ON)
Each Unit no par received distribution of (1) Sustainable Yield Trust Warrant expiring 02/15/2007 payable 09/08/2006 to holders of record 09/08/2006 Ex date - 09/06/2006
Each Unit no par received distribution of (1) Sustainable Yield Trust Warrant expiring 12/13/2007 payable 08/27/2007 to holders of record 08/27/2007 Ex date - 08/23/2007
Under plan of merger name changed to Crown Hill Fund 12/31/2008
Crown Hill Fund merged into Citadel Income Fund 12/02/2009

MACDERMID INC (CT)
Common no par split (2) for (1) by issuance of (1) additional share 8/20/69
Common no par split (2) for (1) by issuance of (1) additional share 9/4/84
Common no par split (3) for (1) by issuance of (2) additional shares

payable 11/15/96 to holders of record 11/1/96
Common no par split (3) for (1) by issuance of (2) additional shares payable 2/6/98 to holders of record 1/26/98
Merged into Court Square Capital Partners, L.P. 4/12/2007
Each share Common no par exchanged for $35 cash

MACDONALD DETTWILER & ASSOC LTD NEW (BC)
Reincorporated 05/16/2016
Place of incorporation changed from (Canada) to (BC) 05/16/2016
Name changed to Maxar Technologies Ltd. 10/10/2017

MACDONALD DETTWILER & ASSOC LTD OLD (CANADA)
Plan of arrangement effective 11/17/1995
Each share Common no par exchanged for (0.36067) MacDonald Dettwiler Holdings Inc. Non-Vtg. Exchangeable Share no par
Note: Shares are exchangeable for Orbital Sciences Corp. Common share for share for a five-year period

MACDONALD DETTWILER HLDGS INC (CANADA)
Merged into MacDonald Dettwiler & Associates Ltd. (New) (Canada) 12/22/1999
Each share Common no par exchanged for (1) share Common no par
MacDonald, Dettwiler & Associates Ltd. (New) (Canada) reincorporated in British Columbia 05/16/2016 which name changed to Maxar Technologies Ltd. 10/10/2017

MACDONALD E F CO (DE)
Class A Common and Common $1 par changed to 33-1/3¢ par respectively and (2) additional shares issued 6/12/62
Each share Class A Common 33-1/3¢ par exchanged for (1.85) shares Common 33-1/3¢ par 1/26/68
Merged into Carlson Cos. 10/28/81
Each share Common 33-1/3¢ par exchanged for $10 cash

MACDONALD MINES EXPL LTD (QC)
Name changed 11/18/1988
Name changed from MacDonald Mines Ltd. to MacDonald Mines Exploration Ltd. (QC) 11/18/1988
Each share old Common no par exchanged for (0.1) share new Common no par 09/02/2003
Reincorporated under the laws of Canada 11/01/2011

MACDONALD OIL EXPL LTD (ON)
Delisted from Toronto Stock Venture Exchange 06/05/2002

MACDONALD PROSPECTING & MINING CO. LTD.
Liquidated in 1941
Details not available

MACDOR QUEBEC MINES LTD. (ON)
Completely liquidated 00/00/1963
Each share Capital Stock no par received first and final distribution of (0.5) share Tinex Development & Exploration Ltd. Capital Stock $1 par
Note: Certificates were not required to be surrendered and are without value
Tinex Development & Exploration Ltd. merged into Can-Con Enterprises & Explorations Ltd. 11/30/1970 which name changed to Aubet Resources Inc. 09/08/1981 which recapitalized as Aubet Explorations Ltd. 09/30/1998 which name changed to Visa Gold Explorations Inc. 08/25/1999
(See Visa Gold Explorations Inc.)

MACDOUGALL DEV CORP (BC)
Struck off register and declared dissolved for failure to file returns 1/15/93

MACE GOLD MINES LTD.
Liquidated in 1948
Details not available

MACE INC (UT)
Recapitalized as Action Covers, Inc. 6/12/89
Each share Common $0.001 par exchanged for (0.5) share Common $0.002 par
(See Action Covers, Inc.)

MACE TECHNOLOGY INC (BC)
Struck off register and declared dissolved for failure to file returns 3/13/87

MACFADDEN-BARTELL CORP. (DE)
Name changed to Bartell Media Corp. 6/18/65
(See Bartell Media Corp.)

MACFADDEN PUBLICATIONS, INC. (NY)
Each (6) shares Capital Stock $5 par exchanged for (1) share Preferred no par or each (4) shares Capital Stock $5 par exchanged for (1) share Common no par in 1929
Recapitalized in 1944
Each share $6 Cum. Preferred no par exchanged for (1) share $1.50 Part. Preference $1 par and $50 of 6% Debentures
Each share Common no par exchanged for (1) share Common $1 par
Stock Dividend - 50% 1/15/56
Merged into MacFadden-Bartell Corp. on a (2) for (1) basis 2/9/62
MacFadden-Bartell Corp. name changed to Bartell Media Corp. 6/18/65
(See Bartell Media Corp.)

MACFARLANE CONSOLIDATED MINES, LTD. (ON)
Charter cancelled for failure to file reports and pay taxes 05/08/1952

MACFIE EXPLORATIONS LTD. (ON)
Recapitalized as United Macfie Mines Ltd. on a (1) for (5) basis 5/21/63
United Macfie Mines Ltd. name changed to Macfie Resources Inc. 6/12/80
(See Macfie Resources Inc.)

MACFIE RED LAKE MINES, LTD. (ON)
Name changed to Macfie Explorations Ltd. in 1952
Macfie Explorations Ltd. recapitalized as United Macfie Mines Ltd. 5/21/63 which name changed to Macfie Resources Inc. 6/12/80
(See Macfie Resources Inc.)

MACFIE RES INC (ON)
Delisted from Vancouver Stock Exchange 3/2/88

MACGREGOR BOWLING CTRS INC (TX)
Name changed to MacGregor Leisure Corp. 2/11/70
(See MacGregor Leisure Corp.)

MACGREGOR LEISURE CORP (TX)
In process of liquidation
Each share Common 20¢ par exchanged for initial distribution of $0.75 cash in March 1979
Each share Common 20¢ par received second distribution of $0.85 cash in February 1980
Each share Common 20¢ par received third distribution of $0.75 cash in August 1980
Each share Common 20¢ par received fourth distribution of $0.60 cash in February 1981
Each share Common 20¢ par received fifth distribution of $0.70 cash in August 1981
Note: Details on subsequent distributions, if any, are not available

MACGREGOR SPORTING GOODS INC (DE)
Name changed to M Holdings Corp. 9/14/89
(See M Holdings Corp.)

MACGREGOR SPORTS & FITNESS INC (MN)
Name changed to Intranet Solutions, Inc. 7/31/96
Intranet Solutions, Inc. name changed to Stellent, Inc. 8/29/2001
(See Stellent, Inc.)

MACGUIDE MAGAZINE INC (DE)
Charter cancelled and declared inoperative and void for non-payment of taxes 3/1/91

MACH FIVE MARKETING CORP (NV)
Reorganized under the laws of Washington as Sunrise Petroleum Resources, Inc. 09/05/2006
Each share Common $0.001 par exchanged for (0.001) share Common $0.001 par
(See Sunrise Petroleum Resources, Inc.)

MACH ONE CORP (NV)
Each share old Common $0.001 par exchanged for (0.05) share new Common $0.001 par 04/19/1995
Each share new Common $0.001 par exchanged again for (0.03333333) share new Common $0.001 par 05/01/2002
Each share new Common $0.001 par exchanged again for (0.03333333) share new Common $0.001 par 06/24/2005
Name changed to Capsalus Corp. 10/20/2010
Capsalus Corp. recapitalized as ForU Holdings, Inc. 07/03/2014

MACHEEZMO MOUSE RESTAURANTS INC (OR)
Chapter 7 bankruptcy proceedings terminated 02/04/2005
Stockholders' equity unlikely

MACHINE TECHNOLOGY INC (NJ)
SEC revoked common stock registration 04/07/2008

MACHINE VISION INTL CORP (MI)
Name changed to CompuCom Systems, Inc. (MI) 11/4/87
CompuCom Systems, Inc. (MI) reincorporated in Delaware 6/15/89
(See CompuCom Systems, Inc.)

MACHINETALKER INC (DE)
Each share old Common $0.001 par exchanged for (0.2) share new Common $0.001 par 05/13/2009
Recapitalized as Solar3D, Inc. 10/25/2010
Each share new Common $0.001 par exchanged for (0.2) share Common $0.001 par
Solar3D, Inc. name changed to Sunworks, Inc. 03/01/2016

MACHLETT LABORATORIES, INC. (CT)
Each share Capital Stock no par exchanged for (10) shares Capital Stock $5 par 9/16/55
Merged into Raytheon Co. and each (5.9594) shares Capital Stock $5 par exchanged for (1) share 5-1/2% Preferred $50 par 5/25/59

MACHO RIVER GOLD MINES LTD.
Recapitalized as Aumacho River Mines Ltd. 00/00/1953
Each share Capital Stock $1 par exchanged for (0.33333333) share Capital Stock $1 par
Aumacho River Mines, Ltd. recapitalized as Urban Quebec Mines Ltd. 12/05/1962 which name changed to Urban Resources Ltd. 04/18/1982 which recapitalized as Urbana Corp. 06/06/1985

MACINAR, INC. (DE)
No longer in existence having become inoperative and void for non-payment of taxes 4/1/62

MACINTOSH CORP (UT)
Reorganized under the laws of Nevada as Sixty Eight Thousand, Inc. 10/01/1992
Each share Common $0.001 par exchanged for (0.1) share Common $0.001 par
Sixty Eight Thousand, Inc. name changed to Arrisystems Inc. 01/17/1995
(See Arrisystems Inc.)

MACINTOSH VIDEO NEWS INC (CO)
Recapitalized as Best Collateral Inc. 6/17/92
Each share Common $0.001 par exchanged for (0.01) share Common 10¢ par
(See Best Collateral Inc.)

MACJOE STURGEON GOLD MINES LTD.
Dissolved in 1942

MACK CALI RLTY CORP (MD)
8% Depositary Preferred Ser. C called for redemption at $25 on 10/28/2011
(Additional Information in Active)

MACK LAKE MINING CORP. LTD. (CANADA)
Declared dissolved for failure to file annual reports 5/6/72

MACK-LANG URANIUM CORP. (WY)
Charter revoked for failure to pay corporate taxes 3/28/58

MACK SHIRT CORP (OH)
Name changed to Shapely Inc. 04/29/1981
(See Shapely Inc.)

MACK TRUCKS, INC. (NY)
Each share Common no par exchanged for (2) shares Common $5 par in 1948
Common $5 par split (4) for (3) by issuance of (1/3) additional share 12/10/56
Stock Dividend - 10% 12/23/55
Merged into Signal Oil & Gas Co. 9/1/67
Each share 5-1/4% Preferred $50 par exchanged for (1) share 5-1/4% Sr. Preferred $50 par
Each share Common $5 par exchanged for (1) share $2.20 Conv. Preferred no par
Signal Oil & Gas Co. name changed to Signal Companies, Inc. 5/1/68 which merged into Allied-Signal Inc. 9/19/85 which name changed to AlliedSignal Inc. 4/26/93 which name changed to Honeywell International Inc. 12/1/99

MACK TRUCKS INC (PA)
Merged into ITM Acquisition Corp. 10/5/90
Each share Common $1 par exchanged for $6.25 cash

MACKAY COMPANIES
Name changed to Associated Companies in 1938
Associated Companies reorganized as Postal Telegraph, Inc. in 1940 which was acquired by Western Union Telegraph Co. in 1943
(See Western Union Telegraph Co.)

MACKAY LIFE SCIENCES INC (DE)
SEC revoked common stock registration 05/28/2014

MACKE CO (DE)
Class A Common $1 par split (2) for (1) by issuance of (1) additional share 3/18/66
Class A Common $1 par reclassified as Common $1 par 3/9/70
Acquired by Allegheny Beverage Corp. 1/30/81
Each share Common $1 par exchanged for $14.50 cash

MACKE (G.B.) CORP. (DE)
Name changed to Macke Vending Co. 3/9/61
Macke Vending Co. name changed to Macke Co. 8/23/65
(See Macke Co.)

MACKE VENDING CO. (DE)
Name changed to Macke Co. 8/23/65
(See Macke Co.)

MACKELLAR BAY MINES LTD. (ON)
Name changed to MacKellar Bay Mining & Exploration Co. Ltd. 10/03/1956
(See MacKellar Bay Mining & Exploration Co. Ltd.)

MACKELLAR BAY MINING EXPLORATION CO. LTD. (ON)
Charter cancelled and company declared dissolved for default in filing returns 8/29/60

MACKENO MINES LTD. (ON)
Recapitalized as Galkeno Mines Ltd. on a (1) for (3) basis 1/4/57
Galkeno Mines Ltd. name changed to Canadian Northwest Mines & Oils Ltd. 6/13/58
(See Canadian Northwest Mines & Oils Ltd.)

MACKENZIE AIR SERVICE LTD.
Dissolved 00/00/1949
Details not available

MACKENZIE ENERGY CORP (BC)
Recapitalized as Mac-Am Resources Corp. 3/26/84
Each share Common no par exchanged for (0.2) share Common no par
Mac-Am Resources Corp. merged into Colossus Resources Equities Inc. 12/8/87 which merged into Prime Resources Corp. (BC) 2/1/89 which recapitalized as Prime Resources Group Inc. 1/26/90 which merged into HomeStake Mining Co. 12/3/98 which merged into Barrick Gold Corp. 12/14/2001

MACKENZIE FINL CORP (ON)
Name changed 9/24/87
Common no par split (2) for (1) by issuance of (1) additional share 9/19/83
Common no par split (3) for (1) by issuance of (2) additional shares 1/22/86
Name changed from Mackenzie Financial Corp. to MacKenzie Financial Corp.-Corporation Financiere MacKenzie 9/24/87
Common no par split (3) for (1) by issuance of (2) additional shares 10/1/87
Common no par split (2) for (1) by issuance of (1) additional share payable 11/20/97 to holders of record 11/10/97
Acquired by Investors Group Inc. 5/31/2001
Each share Common no par exchanged for (0.280668) share Common no par
Investors Group Inc. name changed to IGM Financial Inc. 4/30/2004

MACKENZIE HILL MINES LTD. (ON)
Merged into Alchib Developments Ltd. 7/10/69
Each share Capital Stock $1 par exchanged for (0.28) share Capital Stock no par
Alchib Developments Ltd. merged into Kalrock Developments Ltd. 10/23/78 which merged into Kalrock Resources Ltd. 8/8/90 which merged into Cercal Minerals Corp. 7/9/93
(See Cercal Minerals Corp.)

MACKENZIE INCOME TR (ON)
Each Instalment Receipt plus final payment of $10 cash received (1) Preferred A Unit no par
Trust terminated
Each Preferred A Unit no par received a final distribution of $1.5048 cash payable 1/15/2003 to holders of record 12/31/2002

MACKENZIE INVT MGMT INC (DE)
Common no par split (2) for (1) by issuance of (1) additional share payable 9/2/97 to holders of record 8/25/97
Completely liquidated 12/20/2002
Each share Common no par exchanged for first and final distribution of $4.05 cash

MACKEY AIRLINES, INC. (FL)
Merged into Eastern Air Lines, Inc. 1/8/67
Each share Common 33-1/3¢ par exchanged for (0.125) share Common $1 par
Eastern Air Lines, Inc. merged into Texas Air Corp. 11/25/86

MACKEY JOHN ENTERPRISES INC (DE)
Name changed to Venture Corp. of America 8/11/72
(See Venture Corp.)

MACKIE DESIGNS INC (WA)
Name changed to LOUD Technologies, Inc. 9/12/2003

MACKINAC FINL CORP (MI)
Fixed Rate Perpetual Preferred Ser. A no par called for redemption at $1,000 on 12/31/2013
(Additional Information in Active)

MACKINNIE OIL & DRILLING CO.
Liquidated in 1951

MACKINNON STEEL CORP. LTD.
Acquired by MacKinnon Structural Steel Co. Ltd. in 1943
Details not available

MACKINNON STRUCTURAL STL LTD (CANADA)
Name changed to QSP Ltd.-QSP Ltee. 12/31/69
(See QSP Ltd.-QSP Ltee.)

MACKINTOSH-HEMPHILL CO. (DE)
Common no par changed to $10 par in 1936
Each share Common $10 par exchanged for (2) shares Common $5 par in 1946
Acquired by Bliss (E.W.) Co. 4/29/55
Each share Common $5 par exchanged for (0.9) share Common $1 par
Bliss (E.W.) Co. merged into Gulf & Western Industries, Inc. (Del.) 1/11/68

MACKS STORES INC (NC)
Common 50¢ par split (1.5) for (1) by issuance of (0.5) additional share 6/23/72
Merged into N.V. Koninklijke Bijenkorf Beheer KBB 10/9/80
Each share Common 50¢ par exchanged for $14.25 cash

MACKTOWN ST BK (ROCKTON, IL)
Acquired by Centre 1 Bancorp, Inc. 02/28/2001
Each share Common $20 par exchanged for $164.04 cash

MACKWA MINES, LTD. (ON)
Charter cancelled for failure to file reports and pay taxes February 1958

MACLAN EXPL INC (QC)
Name changed to Can-Mac Exploration Ltd. and Common $1 par changed to no par 11/03/1986
(See Can-Mac Exploration Ltd.)

MACLAN EXPLORATION LTD. (QC)
Name changed to MacLan Exploration Inc. 12/02/1980
MacLan Exploration Inc. name changed to Can-Mac Exploration Ltd. 11/03/1986
(See Can-Mac Exploration Ltd.)

MACLAND INC (NV)
Each share old Common $0.001 par exchanged for (1/6) share new Common $0.001 par 04/26/1994
Name changed to Ameripage, Inc. 12/07/1994
(See Ameripage, Inc.)

MACLAREN POWER & PAPER CO. (QC)
Each share Capital Stock no par exchanged for (2) shares Class A $2.50 par and (2) shares Class B $2.50 par 09/30/1960
Class A $2.50 par and Class B $2.50 par reclassified as Conv. Class A $2.50 par and Conv. Class B $2.50 par respectively 06/13/1974
1% Preferred $1 par called for redemption 10/11/1974
Name changed to MacLaren Power & Paper Co./La Compagnie d'Energie & de Papier MacLaren 05/11/1976
(See MacLaren Power & Paper Co./La Compagnie d'Energie & de Papier MacLaren)

MACLAREN PWR & PAPER CO (QC)
Conv. Class A $2.50 par reclassified as Class A no par 02/07/1979
Conv. Class B $2.50 par reclassified as Class B no par 02/07/1979
Conv. Class C $2.50 par reclassified as Class A no par 02/07/1979
Conv. Class D $2.50 par reclassified as Class B no par 02/07/1979
Class A no par split (3) for (1) by issuance of (2) additional shares 02/12/1979
Class B no par split (3) for (1) by issuance of (2) additional shares 02/12/1979
Through voluntary exchange offer 100% acquired by Noranda Mines Ltd. 02/22/1980
Public interest eliminated

MACLEAN HUNTER CABLE TV LTD (ON)
Merged into MacLean-Hunter Ltd./MacLean Hunter Ltee. 9/30/79
Each share Common $1 par exchanged for $14 cash

MACLEAN HUNTER LTD (ON)
Common no par split (4) for (1) by issuance of (3) additional shares 04/15/1968
Common no par reclassified as Class A no par and (1) additional share issued 12/22/1971
Class B no par reclassified as Participating Class B no par 12/22/1971
Class A no par split (2) for (1) by issuance of (1) additional share 05/19/1980
Participating Class B no par split (2) for (1) by issuance of (1) additional share 05/19/1980
Class A no par reclassified as Conv. Class X no par 01/07/1981
Participating Class B no par reclassified as Conv. Class X no par 01/07/1981
Each share Conv. Class X no par received distribution of (1) share Conv. Class Y no par 01/30/1981
Conv. Class X no par split (2) for (1) by issuance of (1) additional share 05/13/1985
Class Y no par split (2) for (1) by issuance of (1) additional share 05/13/1985
Conv. Class X no par split (2) for (1) by issuance of (1) additional share 05/24/1988
Class Y no par split (2) for (1) by issuance of (1) additional share 05/24/1988
Conv. Class X no par reclassified as Common no par 12/18/1989
Class Y no par reclassified as Common no par 12/18/1989
Merged into Rogers Communications Inc. 05/13/1994
Each share new Common no par exchanged for $17 cash

MACLEAN-HUNTER PUBLISHING CO. LTD. (ON)
Name changed to MacLean-Hunter Ltd./MacLean-Hunter Ltee. 4/9/68
(See MacLean-Hunter Ltd./MacLean-Hunter Ltee.)

MACLEOD-COCKSHUTT GOLD MINES LTD. (ON)
Merged into MacLeod Mosher Gold Mines Ltd. 06/15/1967
Each share Capital Stock $1 par exchanged for (1) share Common no par
MacLeod Mosher Gold Mines Ltd. acquired by Lake Shore Mines Ltd. 12/31/1968 which merged into LAC Minerals Ltd. (New) 07/29/1985 which was acquired by American Barrick Resources Corp. 10/17/1994 which name changed to Barrick Gold Corp. 01/18/1995

MACLEOD MOSHER GOLD MINES LTD (ON)
Acquired by Lake Shore Mines, Ltd. 12/31/1968
Each share Common no par exchanged for (0.25) share Capital Stock $1 par
Lake Shore Mines, Ltd. merged into LAC Minerals Ltd. (New) 07/29/1985 which was acquired by American Barrick Resources Corp. 10/17/1994 which name changed to Barrick Gold Corp. 01/18/1995

MACLEOD'S LTD. (MB)
6% Part. 1st Preference Ser. A $20 par called for redemption 06/15/1964
Public interest was eliminated

MACMARR STORES, INC.
Acquired by Safeway Stores, Inc. 00/00/1931
Details not available

MACMILLAN, BLOEDEL & POWELL RIVER LTD. (BC)
Name changed to MacMillan Bloedel Ltd. 5/10/66
MacMillan Bloedel Ltd. merged into Weyerhaeuser Co. 11/3/99

MACMILLAN & BLOEDEL, LTD. (CANADA)
Merged into Macmillan, Bloedel & Powell River Ltd. 1/4/60
Each (3) shares Class A and/or B no par exchanged for (7) shares Ordinary no par
MacMillan, Bloedel & Powell River Ltd. name changed to MacMillan Bloedel Ltd. 5/10/66 which merged into Weyerhaeuser Co. 11/3/99

MACMILLAN BLOEDEL LTD (BC)
Preference $1 par called for redemption 2/28/73
$2 Class B Conv. Preferred Ser. 1 no par called for redemption 1/19/87
$2.08 Class B Conv. Preferred Ser. 2 no par called for redemption 3/20/87
$2.21 Class B Retractable Preferred Ser. 6 no par called for redemption 3/1/88
Adjustable Rate Preferred Class B Ser. 10 no par called for redemption 10/27/99
Floating Rate Preferred Class B Ser. 8 no par called for redemption 10/27/99
Ordinary Stock no par reclassified as Common no par 4/26/77
Common no par split (3) for (1) by issuance of (2) additional shares 4/14/87
Merged into Weyerhaeuser Co. 11/3/99
Each share Common no par exchanged for (0.28) share Common $1.25 par
Note: Canadian residents had the option to elect to receive Weyerhaeuser Co. Ltd. Exchangeable Shares until 10/26/99

MAC-MAC FINANCIAL INFORMATION, INC.

MACMILLAN CO. (NY)
Each share Class A & B $100 par exchanged for (3) shares Common no par and (0.3) share Preferred no par in 1929
Common no par changed to $1 par in 1950
Merged into Crowell-Collier Publishing Co. 12/30/60
Each share Common $1 par exchanged for (1.6) shares Common $1 par
Crowell-Collier Publishing Co. name changed to Crowell Collier & Macmillan, Inc. 5/7/65 which name changed to Macmillan, Inc. 1/1/73
(See Macmillan, Inc.)

MACMILLAN (H.R.) EXPORT CO., LTD. (CANADA)
Name changed to MacMillan & Bloedel, Ltd. 10/00/1951
MacMillan & Bloedel, Ltd. merged into MacMillan, Bloedel & Powell River Ltd. 01/04/1960 which name changed to MacMillan Bloedel Ltd. 05/10/1966 which merged into Weyerhaeuser Co. 11/03/1999

MACMILLAN GOLD CORP (BC)
Name changed 10/14/1988
Name changed from MacMillan Energy Corp. to MacMillan Gold Corp. 10/14/1988
Merged into Duran Ventures Inc. 10/31/2008
Each share Common no par exchanged for (0.5) share Common no par and (0.5) share MacMillan Minerals Inc. Common no par
Note: Unexchanged certificates were cancelled and became without value 10/31/2014
(See each company's listing)

MACMILLAN INC (DE)
$1.20 Conv. Preferred $1 par called for redemption 08/01/1983
Common $1 par split (2) for (1) by issuance of (1) additional share 04/15/1985
$2.50 Conv. Preferred $1 par called for redemption 09/13/1985
Merged into Mills Acquisition Co. 12/12/1988
Each share Common $1 par exchanged for $90.25 cash

MACMILLAN MINERALS INC (CANADA)
Each share old Common no par exchanged for (0.1) share new Common no par 08/04/2015
Recapitalized as Maverix Metals Inc. 07/12/2016
Each share new Common no par exchanged for (0.5) share Common no par

MACMILLAN PETROLEUM CORP. (DE)
Common $25 par changed to $5 par 00/00/1936
Each share Common $5 par exchanged for (10) shares Common 50¢ par 00/00/1953
Name changed to MacMillan Ring-Free Oil Co., Inc. 05/05/1961
(See MacMillan Ring-Free Oil Co., Inc.)

MACMILLAN RING FREE OIL INC (DE)
Capital Stock 50¢ par split (5) for (4) by issuance of (0.25) additional share 11/13/1964
Stock Dividend - In Preferred 10% 01/31/1980
Plan of reorganization under Chapter 11 Federal Bankruptcy proceedings confirmed 05/26/1989
No stockholders' equity

MACNEAL SCHWENDLER CORP (DE)
Reincorporated 09/22/1994
Common 10¢ par split (2) for (1) by issuance of (1) additional share 03/25/1987
Stock Dividend - 50% 03/15/1984
State of incorporation changed from (CA) to (DE) and Common 10¢ par changed to 1¢ par 09/22/1994
Name changed to MSC.Software Corp. 06/24/1999
(See MSC.Software Corp.)

MACNEILL INTL INDS INC (BC)
Name changed 10/30/89
Common no par split (2) for (1) by issuance of (1) additional share 2/2/89
Name changed from MacNeill Industrial Inc. to MacNeill International Industries Inc. 10/30/89
Merged into Spokane Resources Ltd. 10/31/91
Each share Common no par exchanged for (0.25) share Common no par
Spokane Resources Ltd. recapitalized as SKN Resources Ltd. 7/26/2001 which name changed to Silvercorp Metals Inc. 5/2/2005

MACOID INDS INC (MI)
Name changed to Howell Industries, Inc. 11/30/71
(See Howell Industries, Inc.)

MACOIL CORP. (NV)
Dissolved 08/08/1951
Details not available

MACOMB BIOTECHNOLOGY INC (MT)
Involuntarily dissolved 12/1/92

MACOMB FEDERAL SAVINGS BANK (SAINT CLAIR SHORES, MI)
Merged into D&N Financial Corp. 04/10/1996
Each share Common $1 par exchanged for (3.7494) shares Common $1 par
D&N Financial Corp. merged into Republic Bancorp Inc. 05/17/1999 which merged into Citizens Banking Corp. 12/29/2006 which name changed to Citizens Republic Bancorp, Inc. 04/26/2007 which merged into FirstMerit Corp. 04/12/2013 which merged into Huntington Bancshares Inc. 08/16/2016

MACOMBER INC (OH)
Each share Common no par exchanged for (4) shares Common $1 par 5/1/56
Thru voluntary exchange offer of each share Common $1 par for (0.68) share Sharon Steel Corp. Common no par, 100% was acquired by 8/31/62

MACON LINEN SERVICE, INC. (GA)
Proclaimed dissolved for failure to file annual reports 4/6/79

MACON RAILWAY & LIGHT CO.
Merged into Georgia Power Co. 00/00/1928
Details not available

MACOTTA CORP. (MI)
Proclaimed dissolved for failure to file reports 5/15/74

MACPHERSON VITAMIN INC (NY)
Reincorporated under the laws of Nevada as Trojan Energy Corp. 4/20/81
Trojan Energy Corp. name changed to Petro-Med, Inc. 9/10/84
(See Petro-Med, Inc.)

MACQUARIE BK LTD (AUSTRALIA)
Name changed to Macquarie Group Ltd. 11/13/2007

MACQUARIE EMERGING MKTS INFRASTRUCTURE INCOME FD (ON)
Combined Units separated 03/14/2011
Trust terminated 03/31/2017
Each Unit received $0.10 cash

MACQUARIE GLOBAL INFRASTRUCTURE INCOME FD (ON)
Name changed to Redwood Global Infrastructure Income Fund 12/20/2017
Redwood Global Infrastructure Income Fund merged into Purpose Fund Corp. 08/24/2018

MACQUARIE INFRASTRUCTURE CO LLC (DE)
Under plan of reorganization each Membership Int. no par automatically became (1) share Macquarie Infrastructure Corp. Common $0.001 par 05/21/2015

MACQUARIE INFRASTRUCTURE CO TR (DE)
Merged into Macquarie Infrastructure Co. LLC 06/25/2007
Each Share of Bene. Int. 1¢ par exchanged for (1) Membership Int. no par
Macquarie Infrastructure Co. LLC reorganized as Macquarie Infrastructure Corp. 05/21/2015

MACQUARIE NEXGEN GLOBAL INFRASTRUCTURE CORP (ON)
Merged into NexGen Canadian Balanced Growth Tax Managed Fund 05/13/2011
Each share Class A Common no par automatically became Class A Common no par on a net asset basis
Each share Class B Common no par automatically became Class B Common no par on a net asset basis

MACQUARIE PWR & INFRASTRUCTURE CORP (BC)
Name changed to Capstone Infrastructure Corp. 04/21/2011
(See Capstone Infrastructure Corp.)

MACQUARIE PWR & INFRASTRUCTURE INCOME FD (ON)
Under plan of reorganization each Trust Unit automatically became (1) share Macquarie Power & Infrastructure Corp. (BC) Common no par 01/10/2011
Macquarie Power & Infrastructure Corp. name changed to Capstone Infrastructure Corp. 04/21/2011
(See Capstone Infrastructure Corp.)

MACQUARIE PWR INCOME FD (ON)
Name changed to Macquarie Power & Infrastructure Income Fund (ON) 02/24/2006
Macquarie Power & Infrastructure Income Fund (ON) reorganized in British Columbia as Macquarie Power & Infrastructure Corp. 01/10/2011 which name changed to Capstone Infrastructure Corp. 04/21/2011
(See Capstone Infrastructure Corp.)

MACQUEST RES LTD (AB)
Recapitalized as Polo Petroleums Ltd. 09/21/1989
Each share Common no par exchanged for (0.1) share Class A Common no par
Polo Petroleums Ltd. merged into Attock Oil Corp. 02/04/1991 which recapitalized as Attock Energy Corp. 08/02/1995
(See Attock Energy Corp.)

MACRO COMMUNICATIONS INC (NY)
Reincorporated under the laws of Nevada as First Capital Holdings Corp. 4/27/83
(See First Capital Holdings Corp.)

MACRO SYNETIC SYS INC (CA)
Charter cancelled for failure to file reports and pay taxes 10/1/85

MACRO TECHNOLOGY HLDG CORP (UT)
Name changed to Benchmark Enterprises Inc. 5/26/92
Benchmark Enterprises Inc. recapitalized as Coconino SMA Inc. 6/16/95 which name changed to Veltex Corp. 4/1/99

MACROCHEM CORP (DE)
Each share old Common 1¢ par exchanged for (1/7) share new Common 1¢ par 01/03/2006
Each share new Common 1¢ par exchanged again for (1/6) share new Common 1¢ par 02/10/2006
Merged into Access Pharmaceuticals, Inc. 02/25/2009
Each share Common 1¢ par exchanged for (0.054217) share Common 1¢ par

MACROCHEM CORP (MA)
Reincorporated under the laws of Delaware and Common $0.005 par changed to 1¢ par 05/15/1992
MacroChem Corp. (DE) merged into Access Pharmaceuticals, Inc. 02/25/2009 which recapitalized as PlasmaTech Biopharmaceuticals, Inc. 10/24/2014 which name changed to Abeona Therapeutics Inc. 06/22/2015

MACROCURE LTD (ISRAEL)
Merged into Leap Therapeutics, Inc. 01/24/2017
Each share Ordinary ILS 0.01 par exchanged for (0.1815) share Common $0.001 par

MACRODATA CORP (CA)
Acquired by Cutler-Hammer, Inc. 12/15/1977
Each share Common $1 par exchanged for (0.165) share Common $5 par
(See Cutler-Hammer, Inc.)

MACRODYNE CHATILLON CORP (NY)
Merged into Macrodyne Industries, Inc. 1/1/74
Each share Conv. Preferred Ser. A $1 par exchanged for (2) shares Common 10¢ par and (0.5) Common Stock Purchase Warrant expiring 1/1/78
Each share Common 10¢ par automatically became (1) share Common 10¢ par
Note: Conv. Preferred Ser. A $1 par certificates not surrendered by February 28, 1974 received Common Stock Purchase Warrants by mail but it is necessary to surrender certificates in order to receive Common Shares
(See Macrodyne Industries, Inc.)

MACRODYNE INC (CA)
Common $1 par split (3) for (2) by issuance of (0.5) additional share 7/26/68
Merged into Macrodyne-Chatillon Corp. 4/1/69
Each share Common $1 par exchanged for (0.4) share Conv. Preferred Ser. A $1 par and (0.6) share Common 10¢ par
Macrodyne-Chatillon Corp. merged into Macrodyne Industries, Inc. 1/1/74
(See Macrodyne Industries, Inc.)

MACRODYNE INDS INC (DE)
Reorganized 1/4/88
Each share Common 10¢ par exchanged for a Bearer Coupon representing the right to receive a pro rata share of $337,000 cash on 1/4/93
Note: Unexchanged certificates were cancelled and became without value 7/6/88

MACROMEDIA INC (DE)
Common $0.001 par split (2) for (1)

by issuance of (1) additional share 10/13/1995
Merged into Adobe Systems Inc. 12/03/2005
Each share Common $0.001 par exchanged for (1.38) shares Common $0.0001 par
Adobe Systems Inc. name changed to Adobe Inc. 10/09/2018

MACRONIX INTL CO LTD (TAIWAN)
Each old Sponsored ADR for Common TWD $10 par exchanged for (0.5837135) new Sponsored ADR for Common TWD $10 par 05/17/2006
Stock Dividends - 21.1762% payable 09/30/1998 to holders of record 08/04/1998; 10% payable 10/08/1999 to holders of record 08/06/1999; 12.9242% payable 07/14/2000 to holders of record 06/12/2000; 10% payable 08/22/2002 to holders of record 07/03/2002 Ex date - 07/05/2002; 1.7577% payable 10/29/2007 to holders of record 09/18/2007 Ex date - 09/14/2007
ADR agreement terminated 10/29/2007
Each new Sponsored ADR for Common TWD $10 par exchanged for $2.71692 cash
Each 144A Sponsored ADR for Common TWD $10 par exchanged for $2.71692 cash

MACROPORE BIOSURGERY INC (DE)
Name changed to Cytori Therapeutics, Inc. 07/11/2005

MACROSE INDS CORP (NY)
Each share Capital Stock 1¢ par exchanged for (0.25) share Capital Stock 4¢ par 10/01/1970
Stock Dividend - 150% 04/14/1980
Charter cancelled and proclaimed dissolved for failure to pay taxes 09/27/1995

MACROSHARES MAJOR METRO HSG DOWN TR (DE)
Trust terminated 01/06/2010
Each Down MacroShare received $24.95006 cash

MACROSHARES MAJOR METRO HSG UP TR (DE)
Trust terminated 01/06/2010
Each Up MacroShare received $21.86689 cash

MACROSHARES OIL DOWN TRADEABLE TR (NY)
Completely liquidated 06/30/2008
No stockholders' equity

MACROSHARES OIL UP TRADEABLE TR (NY)
Completely liquidated
Each Share $20 par received first and final distribution of $40.000343 cash payable 07/03/2008 to holders of record 06/30/2008

MACROSHARES 100 OIL DOWN TR (NY)
Units split (4) for (1) by issuance of (3) additional Units payable 01/29/2009 to holders of record 01/23/2009 Ex date - 01/30/2009
Trust terminated 07/06/2009
Each Unit received net asset value

MACROSHARES 100 OIL UP TR (NY)
Units split (4) for (1) by issuance of (3) additional Units payable 01/29/2009 to holders of record 01/23/2009 Ex date - 01/30/2009
Trust terminated 07/06/2009
Each Unit received net asset value

MACROSOLVE INC (OK)
Reorganized under the laws of Nevada as Drone Aviation Holding Corp. 05/05/2014
Each share Common 1¢ par exchanged for (0.01977775) share Common $0.0001 par

MACROSONIC INC (NV)
Each share old Common $0.001 par exchanged for (0.001) share new Common $0.001 par 09/12/2005
Note: No holder will receive fewer than (20) shares
Name changed to Sunx Energy, Inc. 11/09/2007
Sunx Energy, Inc. recapitalized as Suntex Enterprises, Inc. 01/23/2017

MACROTRENDS INTL VENTURES INC (BC)
Recapitalized as Global Election Systems Inc. 11/22/1991
Each share Common no par exchanged for (0.125) share Common no par
Global Election Systems Inc. acquired by Diebold, Inc. 01/22/2002 which name changed to Diebold Nixdorf Inc. 12/12/2016

MACROTRENDS VENTURES INC (BC)
Merged into Macrotrends International Ventures Inc. 08/17/1988
Each share Common no par exchanged for (1) share Common no par
Macrotrends International Ventures Inc. recapitalized as Global Election Systems Inc. 11/22/1991 which was acquired by Diebold, Inc. 01/22/2002 which name changed to Diebold Nixdorf Inc. 12/12/2016

MACROVISION CORP (DE)
Common $0.001 par split (2) for (1) by issuance of (1) additional share payable 08/31/1999 to holders of record 08/06/1999
Common $0.001 par split (2) for (1) by issuance of (1) additional share payable 03/17/2000 to holders of record 02/25/2000
Merged into Macrovision Solutions Corp. 05/05/2008
Each share Common $0.001 par exchanged for (1) share Common $0.001 par
Macrovision Solutions Corp. name changed to Rovi Corp. 07/16/2009 which name changed to TiVo Corp. 09/08/2016

MACROVISION SOLUTIONS CORP (DE)
Name changed to Rovi Corp. 07/16/2009
Rovi Corp. name changed to TiVo Corp. 09/08/2016

MACSIM BAR PAPER CO.
Sold to United Biscuit Co. of America in 1947
United Biscuit Co. of America name changed to Keebler Co. 6/8/66 which merged into United Biscuits (Holdings) Ltd. 4/24/74

MACTAVISH INTL INC (NV)
Name changed to On Queue, Inc. (New) 08/10/1992
On Queue, Inc. (New) name changed to Sunlogic, Inc. 07/01/1994 which name changed to Dawson Science Corp. (NV) 03/17/1995 which reorganized in Delaware as Integrated Transportation Network Group Inc. 06/30/1998
(See Integrated Transportation Network Group Inc.)

MACTELL CORP (TX)
Company reported out of business 10/25/1999
Stockholders' equity unlikely

MACTIER PUBLISHING CORP. (DE)
Charter cancelled and declared inoperative and void for non-payment of taxes 4/15/73

MACU MINES LTD. (ON)
Acquired by Cusco Mines Ltd. 00/00/1955
Details not available

MACUSANI YELLOWCAKE INC (ON)
Recapitalized as Plateau Uranium Inc. 05/01/2015
Each share Common no par exchanged for (0.125) share Common no par
Plateau Uranium Inc. name changed to Plateau Energy Metals Inc. 03/16/2018

MACWHYTE CO. (IL)
Common $25 par changed to no par in 1933
Recapitalized under the laws of Wisconsin in 1944
Each share Preferred $100 par exchanged for (1) share 8% Preferred $100 par
Each share Common no par exchanged for (3) shares Common $10 par
(See MacWhyte Co. (Wisc.))

MACWHYTE CO. (WI)
Stock Dividend - 50% 11/12/63
Merged into Amsted Industries Inc. (Del.) 9/30/69
Each share Common $10 par exchanged for $41.50 cash

MACY R H & CO INC (NY)
Common no par changed to $1 par 11/16/60
Common $1 par changed to 50¢ par and (1) additional share issued 12/1/64
Common 50¢ par changed to 25¢ par and (1) additional share issued 12/19/67
4% Preferred Ser. B $100 par called for redemption 12/1/75
Common 25¢ par split (3) for (2) by issuance of (0.5) additional share 4/1/80
Common 25¢ par split (2) for (1) by issuance of (1) additional share 4/1/82
Stock Distribution - (0.1) share 4-1/4% Preferred Ser. A for each share Common 8/1/44
Common 25¢ par split (3) for (2) by issuance of (0.5) additional share 4/1/83
Acquired by a management group 7/15/86
Each share Common 25¢ par exchanged for $68 cash
4-1/4% Preferred Ser. A $100 par called for redemption 8/15/86
Public interest eliminated

MACYRO GROUP INC (CANADA)
Merged into RED Holdings Group, Inc. 07/04/2007
Each share Common no par exchanged for $1.77 cash

MAD JACK HLDGS LTD (AB)
Issue Information - 1,500,000 shares COM offered at $0.20 per share on 07/10/1997
Name changed to Staccato's Inc. 03/24/2000
Staccato's Inc. name changed to Gravity West Mining Corp. 04/14/2005 which recapitalized as Rock Tech Resources Inc. (AB) 03/09/2009 which reincorporated in British Columbia as Rock Tech Lithium Inc. 05/12/2010

MAD JACKS CORP (CO)
Each share Common $0.00001 par exchanged for (0.01) share Common $0.001 par 4/10/89
Name changed to Jacks Inc. 5/14/90

MAD RIVER RES INC (BC)
Name changed to Canadian Educational Courseware Inc. 07/16/1992
Canadian Educational Courseware Inc. name changed to Can West Exploration Inc. 08/28/1997 which recapitalized as Watch Resources Ltd. (BC) 10/13/2000 which reincorporated in Alberta 07/20/2006 which recapitalized as Watch Resources Ltd. (New) 01/17/2007 which merged into Pearl Exploration & Production Ltd. 10/21/2007 which name changed to BlackPearl Resources Inc. 05/14/2009

MADA YELLOWKNIFE GOLD MINES, LTD. (ON)
Charter cancelled for failure to file reports and pay taxes in 1952

MADACY ENTMT INCOME FD (QC)
Acquired by Clarke Inc. 03/25/2009
Each Unit no par received $0.39 cash

MADALENA VENTURES INC (AB)
Reincorporated 08/22/2006
Place of incorporation changed from (BC) to (AB) 08/22/2006
Each share Common no par received distribution of (0.06666666) share Great Bear Resources Ltd. Common no par payable 08/28/2006 to holders of record 08/22/2006
Name changed to Madalena Energy Inc. 08/02/2013

MADAWASKA MINING CO. LTD. (QC)
Name changed to Dominion Industrial Mineral Corp. 12/19/1960
(See Dominion Industrial Mineral Corp.)

MADDEN STEVEN LTD (NY)
Reincorporated under the laws of Delaware 11/18/1998

MADDOCK'S (THOMAS) SONS CO.
Assets acquired by American Radiator & Sanitary Corp. for stock 8/16/29

MADDONA RESOURCE CORP (BC)
Name changed to Maddona Resources Ltd. 1/31/84
Maddona Resources Ltd. name changed to Aricana Resources Inc. 8/30/84
(See Aricana Resources Inc.)

MADDONA RESOURCES LTD. (BC)
Name changed to Aricana Resources Inc. 8/30/84
(See Aricana Resources Inc.)

MADDUX AIR LINES, INC.
Acquired by Transcontinental Air Transport, Inc. in 1929
Details not available

MADE IN AMER ENTMT INC (FL)
SEC revoked common stock registration 09/18/2013

MADE2MANAGE SYS INC (IN)
Merged into Battery Ventures VI, L.P. 08/08/2003
Each share Common no par exchanged for $5.73 cash

MADECO S A (CHILE)
Each old Sponsored ADR for Ordinary no par exchanged for (0.1) new Sponsored ADR for Ordinary no par 05/12/2003
ADR basis changed from (1:10) to (1:100) 05/12/2003
ADR agreement terminated 10/10/2009
Each Sponsored ADR for Ordinary no par exchanged for $5.90213 cash

MADEIRA, HILL & CO.
Bankrupt in 1937

MADEIRA INC (UT)
Proclaimed dissolved for failure to pay taxes 6/1/90

MADELEINE MINES LTD (CANADA)
Name changed to North American Palladium Ltd. (Old) 07/07/1993
North American Palladium Ltd. (Old) reorganized as North American Palladium Ltd. (New) 08/10/2015

MADENTA COMMUNICATIONS INC (AB)
Issue Information - 2,400,000 shares COM offered at $0.25 per share on 07/30/1997
Name changed to Madenta, Inc. 2/24/98

MADERA GARDENS DEVELOPMENT CO. (CA)
Liquidation completed
Each share Common $100 par exchanged for initial distribution of $75 cash
Each share Common $100 par received second distribution of $2.75 cash 8/16/71
Each share Common $100 par received third distribution of $2.75 cash 11/8/71
Each share Common $100 par received fourth distribution of $125 cash 12/16/71
Each share Common $100 par received fifth distribution of $10.855 cash 2/28/72
Each share Common $100 par received sixth distribution of $2.25 cash 5/12/72
Each share Common $100 par received seventh distribution of $2.25 cash 4/12/73
Each share Common $100 par received eighth distribution of $2.25 cash 7/2/74
Each share Common $100 par received ninth distribution of $4.50 cash 3/3/75
Each share Common $100 par received tenth and final distribution of $5.48 cash 1/28/76

MADERA GUARANTEE SAVINGS & LOAN ASSOCIATION (CA)
Acquired by Golden West Financial Corp. (CA) 5/17/74
Each share Guarantee Stock $10 par exchanged for $102 cash

MADERA INTL INC (NV)
Each share old Common 1¢ par exchanged for (0.33333333) share new Common 1¢ par 08/11/1994
SEC revoked common stock registration 10/22/2001

MADERAS Y SINTETICOS SOCIEDAD ANONIMA MASISA (CHILE)
Name changed to Masisa S.A. (Old) 07/28/1998
Masisa S.A. (Old) merged into Masisa S.A. (New) 08/04/2005
(See Masisa S.A. (New))

MADERO INC (NV)
Name changed to GetFugu, Inc. (NV) 03/25/2009
GetFugu, Inc. (NV) reincorporated in Delaware 11/15/2010

MADGE NETWORKS N V (NETHERLANDS)
Name changed 07/17/1995
Name changed from Madge N.V. to Madge Networks N.V. 07/17/1995
Placed in bankruptcy 05/22/2003
Stockholders' equity unlikely

MADHUCON PROJS LTD (INDIA)
GDR agreement terminated 09/07/2017
Each Reg. S Sponsored GDR for Ordinary exchanged for $0.198923 cash

MADIGAN CORP (TX)
Merged into Contran Corp. 1/1/72
Each share Class B Preferred $10 par exchanged for (1) share Class B Preferred $10 par
Each share Preferred $1 par exchanged for (1) share Preferred $1 par
Each share Common $1 par exchanged for (1) share Common $1 par
(See Contran Corp.)

MADIGAN ELECTR CORP (NY)
Adjudicated bankrupt 2/23/71
Trustee's opinion: No stockholders' equity

MADING DRUG STORES CO (MD)
Stock Dividend - 100% 8/25/55
Name changed to Mading-Dugan Drug Co. (MD) 8/30/68
Mading-Dugan Drug Co. (MD) reorganized under the laws of Texas 5/29/69 which name changed to Madigan Corp. 11/4/69 which merged into Contran Corp. 1/1/72
(See Contran Corp.)

MADING DUGAN DRUG CO (TX)
Reincorporated 5/29/69
Common $1 par split (3) for (1) by issuance of (2) additional shares 11/1/68
State of incorporation changed from (MD) to (TX) and each share Common $1 par exchanged for (5) shares Common $1 par 5/29/69
Name changed to Madigan Corp. 11/4/69
Madigan Corp. merged into Contran Corp. 1/1/72
(See Contran Corp.)

MADISON, INC. (NY)
Liquidation completed 11/29/57

MADISON & BURKE CAP (CA)
Charter suspended for failure to file reports and pay taxes 05/03/1976

MADISON AMERICAN GUARANTY INSURANCE CORP. (WI)
Name changed to Wisconsin Insurance Corp. of America 7/16/65
Wisconsin Insurance Corp. of America merged into Wayne National Life Insurance Co. 12/31/66 which merged into Hamilton (Alexander) Life Insurance Co. of America 11/6/67 which merged into Hamilton International Corp. 8/15/69
(See Hamilton International Corp.)

MADISON AVE CAP INC (DE)
Recapitalized as Tree Technology International Inc. 12/9/91
Each share Common $0.0001 par exchanged for (0.2) share Common $0.0005 par
(See Tree Technology International Inc.)

MADISON AVE INC (CO)
Name changed to Guide Energy Inc. 3/31/86
(See Guide Energy Inc.)

MADISON AVE SPORTS NETWORK LTD (ON)
Recapitalized 3/27/92
Recapitalized from Madison Avenue Partners Inc. to Madison Avenue Sports Network Ltd. 3/27/92
Each share Common no par exchanged for (0.2) share Common no par
Name changed to Madison Partners Ltd. 5/17/94
Madison Partners Ltd. recapitalized as Madison Holdings Ltd. 10/18/96 which name changed to Northpoint Corp. 12/19/97

MADISON AVENUE & 58TH STREET CORP. (NY)
Completely liquidated 11/29/57
Each share Common 10¢ par exchanged for first and final distribution of $16.65 cash

MADISON BANCORP INC (MD)
Acquired by Codorus Valley Bancorp, Inc. 01/16/2015
Each share Common 1¢ par exchanged for $22.90 cash

MADISON BANCORP INC (MI)
Common $1 par split (6) for (5) by issuance of (0.2) additional share payable 05/21/1997 to holders of record 03/01/1997
Merged into Peoples State Bank (Hamtramck, MI) 05/15/1998
Each share Common $1 par exchanged for (29.4449) shares Common $1 par
Peoples State Bank (Hamtramck, MI) reorganized as PSB Group, Inc. 05/31/2003
(See PSB Group, Inc.)

MADISON BANCSHARES GROUP LTD (PA)
Stock Dividends - 7.5% payable 02/15/1996 to holders of record 01/31/1996; 7.5% payable 02/20/1997 to holders of record 02/05/1997; 20% payable 11/21/1997 to holders of record 11/07/1997; 20% payable 06/17/1998 to holders of record 06/03/1998; 10% payable 09/16/1999 to holders of record 09/01/1999
Merged into Leesport Financial Corp. 10/01/2004
Each share Common $1 par exchanged for (0.6028) share Common $5 par
Leesport Financial Corp. name changed to VIST Financial Corp. 03/03/2008 which merged into Tompkins Financial Corp. 08/01/2012

MADISON BANCSHARES INC (FL)
Common 1¢ par split (5) for (4) by issuance of (0.25) additional share payable 05/15/2003 to holders of record 05/05/2003 Ex date - 05/16/2003
Stock Dividend - 5% payable 12/23/2002 to holders of record 12/09/2002 Ex date - 12/05/2002
Merged into Whitney Holding Corp. 08/20/2004
Each share Common 1¢ par exchanged for (0.46735) share Common no par and $10.4615 cash
Whitney Holding Corp. merged into Hancock Holding Co. 06/04/2011 which name changed to Hancock Whitney Corp. 05/25/2018

MADISON BK & TR CO (CHICAGO, IL)
Common $10 par changed to $5 par and (1) additional share issued plus a (1) for (13) stock dividend paid 3/20/69
Stock Dividend - 10% 3/23/70
Under plan of reorganization each share Common $5 par automatically became (1) share Madison Financial Corp. (DE) Common $5 par 8/15/74
Madison Financial Corp. (DE) acquired by River Forest Bancorp, Inc. 11/1/90 which name changed to Corus Bankshares, Inc. 6/10/96

MADISON BK & TR CO (MADISON, IN)
Each share Capital Stock $20 par exchanged for (3-1/3) shares Capital Stock $10 par to effect a (2) for (1) split and a 66-2/3% stock dividend 02/03/1971
Reorganized as Ohio Valley Bancorp 07/08/1981
Each share Capital Stock $10 par exchanged for (5) shares Common no par
Ohio Valley Bancorp merged into Merchants National Corp. 08/31/1987 which merged into National City Corp. 05/02/1992 which was acquired by PNC Financial Services Group, Inc. 12/31/2008

MADISON BK & TR CO (MADISON, WI)
Name changed to United Bank & Trust (Madison, WI) 7/10/72
(See United Bank & Trust (Madison, MI))

MADISON BK (PALM HARBOR, FL)
Common $10 par split (5) for (1) by issuance of (4) additional shares payable 12/09/1998 to holders of record 09/30/1998
Stock Dividends - 5% payable 05/15/2000 to holders of record 05/01/2000 Ex date - 04/27/2000; 5% payable 12/20/2000 to holders of record 12/01/2000 Ex date - 12/05/2000; 5% payable 05/15/2001 to holders of record 05/01/2001 Ex date - 05/07/2001
Reorganized as Madison Bancshares, Inc. 08/31/2001
Each share Common $10 par exchanged for (1) share Common 1¢ par
Madison Bancshares, Inc. merged into Whitney Holding Corp. 08/20/2004 which merged into Hancock Holding Co. 06/04/2011 which name changed to Hancock Whitney Corp. 05/25/2018

MADISON BK (RICHMOND, KY)
Under plan of reorganization each share Common $10 par automatically became (1) share Madison Financial Corp. Common $10 par 12/28/1998
Madison Financial Corp. merged into Kentucky Bancshares, Inc. 07/24/2015

MADISON BAY HLDGS INC (UT)
Each share old Common $0.0001 par exchanged for (0.03333333) share new Common $0.0001 par 05/21/2007
Recapitalized as Middle East Oil Corp. 01/08/2010
Each share new Common $0.0001 par exchanged for (0.001) share Common $0.0001 par
(See Middle East Oil Corp.)

MADISON BUS CO (WI)
Out of business 5/1/70
Details not available

MADISON CAP CORP (AB)
Reorganized under the laws of Canada as Radient Technologies Inc. 06/02/2014
Each share Common no par exchanged for (0.1) share Common no par

MADISON CENTRAL PARK BUILDING CORP.
Property sold 00/00/1947
Details not available

MADISON/CLAYMORE COVERED CALL & EQUITY STRATEGY FD (DE)
Name changed 10/31/2007
Issue Information - 17,350,000 shares COM offered at $15 per share on 07/27/2004
Name changed from Madison/Claymore Covered Call Fund to Madison/Claymore Covered Call & Equity Strategy Fund 10/31/2007
Name changed to Madison Covered Call & Equity Strategy Fund 01/02/2013

MADISON CO (DE)
Merged into Independence Holding Co. (Old) 8/9/83
Each share Common $1 par exchanged for (0.5) share Common $1 par
Independence Holding Co. (Old) name changed to Stamford Capital Group, Inc. 11/4/87 which name changed to Independence Holding Co. (New) 9/10/90

MADISON ENERGY CORP (AB)
Reincorporated 08/29/2003
Place of incorporation changed from (BC) to (AB) 08/29/2003
Merged into Clampett Energy Ltd. 04/08/2010
Each share Common no par exchanged for $0.20 cash
Note: Unexchanged certificates were cancelled and became without value 04/08/2016

MADISON ENTERPRISES CORP (BC)
Recapitalized as Madison Minerals Inc. 10/29/2004
Each share Common no par

FINANCIAL INFORMATION, INC.   MAD-MAD

exchanged for (0.2) share Common no par
Madison Minerals Inc. recapitalized as Battle Mountain Gold Inc. 05/14/2014 which merged into Gold Standard Ventures Corp. 06/15/2017

MADISON EQUITIES INC (DE)
Each share old Common $0.00001 par exchanged for (0.02) share new Common $0.00001 par 5/13/91
Name changed to Buckeye Communications Inc. 1/23/92
(See Buckeye Communications Inc.)

MADISON EXPLORATIONS INC (NV)
Recapitalized as Madison Technologies Inc. 03/11/2015
Each share Common $0.001 par exchanged for (0.1) share Common $0.001 par

MADISON FD INC (DE)
$1.20 Conv. Preferred $25 par called for redemption 6/16/69
Name changed to Madison Resources, Inc. 6/13/84
Madison Resources, Inc. merged into Adobe Resources Corp. 10/31/85 which merged into Santa Fe Energy Resources, Inc. 5/19/92 which name changed to Santa Fe Snyder Corp. 5/5/99 which merged into Devon Energy Corp. (New) 8/29/2000

MADISON FDG INC (NV)
Name changed to Medizone International Inc. 3/25/86

MADISON FINL CORP (DE)
Common $5 par reclassified as Class B Common $5 par 05/12/1987
Class B Common $5 par split (3) for (1) by issuance of (2) additional shares 05/28/1987
Acquired by River Forest Bancorp, Inc. 11/01/1990
Each share Class B Common $5 par exchanged for $7.01 cash
Note: An escrow account has been established for possible future payments

MADISON FINL CORP (KY)
Merged into Kentucky Bancshares, Inc. 07/24/2015
Each share Common $10 par exchanged for (1.1927) shares Common no par

MADISON FOODS INC (NE)
Merged into Iowa Beef Processors, Inc. 5/28/76
Each share Common $1 par exchanged for $13 cash

MADISON GAS & ELEC CO (WI)
Preferred Ser. D $25 par called for redemption 8/2/85
Preferred Ser. A $25 par called for redemption 12/29/86
Preferred Ser. B $25 par called for redemption 12/29/86
Preferred Ser. C $25 par called for redemption 12/29/86
Common $16 par changed to $8 par and (1) additional share issued 5/20/60
Common $8 par split (3) for (2) by issuance of (0.5) additional share 1/21/92
Common $8 par changed to $1 par and (0.5) additional share issued payable 2/20/96 to holders of record 2/1/96
Stock Dividend - 100% 2/25/66
Under plan of reorganization each share Common $1 par automatically became (1) share MGE Energy, Inc. Common $1 par 8/12/2002

MADISON GNT RES INC (QC)
Reorganized under the laws of Canada as Banro International Capital Inc. 3/2/95
Each share Common $1 par exchanged for (1/6) share Common $1 par
Banro International Capital Inc. name changed to Banro Resources Corp. (Canada) 5/6/96 which reincorporated in Ontario 10/24/96 which recapitalized as Banro Corp. (ONT) 1/22/2001 which reincorporated in Canada 4/2/2004

MADISON GOLD MINES, LTD. (QC)
Charter surrendered for failure to file reports and pay fees in 1949

MADISON GROUP ASSOC INC (DE)
Each share Common 50¢ par exchanged for (0.2) share Common $0.0001 par 07/15/1993
Each share Common $0.0001 par exchanged for (0.1) share Common $0.001 par 06/21/1996
SEC revoked common stock registration 09/15/1999

MADISON HLDGS LTD (BC)
Recapitalized as Consolidated Madison Holdings Ltd. 04/10/1991
Each share Common no par exchanged for (0.25) share Common no par
Consolidated Madison Holdings Ltd. merged into Ourominas Minerals Inc. 06/27/1996 which recapitalized as Thistle Mining Inc. 04/27/1999
(See Thistle Mining Inc.)

MADISON HLDGS LTD (ON)
Name changed to Northpoint Corp. 12/19/97
(See Northpoint Corp.)

MADISON IMPROVEMENT CORP. (WI)
Completely liquidated 10/22/70
Each share Common $10 par exchanged for first and final distribution of $16 cash

MADISON INDS INC (DE)
Each share Common 10¢ par exchanged for (0.33333333) share Common 30¢ par 05/21/1969
Merged into MDS Merging Corp. 03/03/1983
Each share Common 30¢ par exchanged for $3.25 cash

MADISON-KEDZIE CORP. (DE)
Declared inoperative and void for non-payment of taxes 2/26/53

MADISON MGMT INC (NV)
Name changed to E & M Group, Inc. 02/25/2010

MADISON MINERALS INC (BC)
Recapitalized as Battle Mountain Gold Inc. 05/14/2014
Each share Common no par exchanged for (0.25) share Common no par
Battle Mountain Gold Inc. merged into Gold Standard Ventures Corp. 06/15/2017

MADISON MINES CO. (UT)
Merged into Oil Securities & Uranium Corp. 00/00/1955
Each share Common exchanged for (0.02857143) share Common
Oil Securities & Uranium Corp. name changed to Oil Securities & Gas Corp. 07/01/1956 which name changed to Oil Securities & Metals Corp. 02/06/1968 which name changed to Oil Securities, Inc. (UT) 12/10/1969 which reincorporated Nevada 05/27/1982 which recapitalized as Digital Technologies Media Group Inc. 07/26/1996 which reorganized as Central Capital Venture Corp. 05/08/2000
(See Central Capital Venture Corp.)

MADISON MORTGAGE CORP.
Bankrupt in 1936

MADISON NATL BANCORP INC (NY)
Stock Dividend - 10% payable 06/30/2009 to holders of record 06/18/2009 Ex date - 06/22/2009
Acquired by FNBNY Bancorp, Inc. 04/03/2012
Each share Common 1¢ par exchanged for $9.09 cash

MADISON NATL BK (HAUPPAUGE, NY)
Under plan of reorganization each share Common 1¢ par automatically became (1) share Madison National Bancorp, Inc. Common 1¢ par 06/11/2009
(See Madison National Bancorp, Inc.)

MADISON NATL BK (WASHINGTON, DC)
Stock Dividend - 10% 3/22/71
Reorganized as James Madison Ltd. 5/29/81
Each share Capital Stock $10 par exchanged for (1) share Common $10 par
(See James Madison Ltd.)

MADISON NATL BK OF VIRGINIA (MCLEAN, VA)
Bank failed 05/11/1991
No stockholders' equity

MADISON NATIONAL LIFE INSURANCE CO., INC. (WI)
Name changed to Madison National Life Insurance Co., Inc. of Wisconsin 8/17/64
Madison National Life Insurance Co., Inc. of Wisconsin reorganized as Madison Co. 12/1/75 which merged into Independence Holding Co. (Old) 8/9/83 which name changed to Stamford Capital Group, Inc. 11/4/87 which name changed to Independence Holding Co. (New) 9/10/90

MADISON NATIONAL LIFE INSURANCE CO., INC. OF WISCONSIN (WI)
Under plan of reorganization each share Common $1 par automatically became (1) share Madison Co. Common $1 par 12/1/75
Madison Co. merged into Independence Holding Co. (Old) 8/9/83 which name changed to Stamford Capital Group, Inc. 11/4/87 which name changed to Independence Holding Co. (New) 9/10/90

MADISON OIL & GAS LTD (CANADA)
Recapitalized as Knee Hill Energy Canada Ltd. 2/27/87
Each share Common no par exchanged for (1) share Common no par
(See Knee Hill Energy Canada Ltd.)

MADISON OIL CO (DE)
Merged into Toreador Resources Corp. 12/31/2001
Each share Common no par exchanged for (0.118) share Common 15-5/8¢ par
Toreador Resources Corp. merged into ZaZa Energy Corp. 02/22/2012

MADISON OIL CO INC (BC)
Reincorporated under the laws of Delaware 07/12/2000
Madison Oil Co. Inc. (DE) merged into Toreador Resources Corp. 12/31/2001 which merged into ZaZa Energy Corp. 02/22/2012

MADISON OILS LTD. (CANADA)
Each share old Capital Stock no par exchanged for (0.1) share new Capital Stock no par 8/8/51
Recapitalized as Madison Oil & Gas Ltd. 7/9/84
Each share new Capital Stock no par exchanged for (0.1) share Common no par
Madison Oil & Gas Ltd. recapitalized as Knee Hill Energy Canada Ltd. 2/27/87
(See Knee Hill Energy Canada Ltd.)

MADISON PARK HOTEL CO.
Property sold 00/00/1946
Details not available

MADISON PARTNERS LTD (ON)
Recapitalized as Madison Holdings Ltd. 10/18/96
Each share Common no par exchanged for (0.1) share Common no par
Madison Holdings Ltd. name changed to Northpoint Corp. 12/19/97

MADISON PK PFD FDG INC
144A Auction Rate Preferred Ser. A called for redemption at $100,000 on 6/23/2005
144A Auction Rate Preferred Ser. B called for redemption at $100,000 on 6/23/2005
144A Auction Rate Preferred Ser. C called for redemption at $100,000 on 6/23/2005
144A Auction Rate Preferred Ser. D called for redemption at $100,000 on 6/23/2005
144A Auction Rate Preferred Ser. E called for redemption at $100,000 on 6/23/2005
144A Auction Rate Preferred Ser. F called for redemption at $100,000 on 6/23/2005
144A Auction Rate Preferred Ser. G called for redemption at $100,000 on 6/23/2005

MADISON POWER CO.
Merged into Republic Service Corp. 00/00/1929
Details not available

MADISON RAILWAYS CO.
Reorganized as Madison Bus Co. in 1940
Each (10) shares Preferred exchanged for (1) share Common
No Common stockholders' equity
(See Madison Bus Co.)

MADISON RES INC (DE)
Merged into Adobe Resources Corp. 10/31/85
Each share Common $1 par exchanged for (1) share Common 1¢ par
Adobe Resources Corp. merged into Santa Fe Energy Resources, Inc. 5/19/92 which name changed to Santa Fe Snyder Corp. 5/5/99 which merged into Devon Energy Corp. (New) 8/29/2000

MADISON SQUARE GARDEN CO OLD (DE)
Name changed 05/05/2011
Name changed from Madison Square Garden, Inc. to Madison Square Garden Co. 05/05/2011
Each share Class A Common 1¢ par received distribution of (0.33333333) share Madison Square Garden Co. (New) Class A Common 1¢ par payable 09/30/2015 to holders of record 09/21/2015 Ex date - 10/01/2015
Name changed to MSG Networks Inc. 10/01/2015

MADISON SQUARE GARDEN CORP. (NY)
Stock Dividend - 200% 7/10/46
Merged into Graham-Paige Corp. 4/20/60
Each share Capital Stock no par exchanged for (2.25) shares 60¢ Preferred no par
Graham-Paige Corp. name changed to Madison Square Garden Corp. (Mich.) 4/4/62
(See Madison Square Garden Corp. (Mich.))

MADISON SQUARE GARDEN CORP (MI)
Common $1 par changed to no par 4/7/64
60¢ Conv. Preferred no par called for redemption 5/31/67
Common no par changed to $1 par 10/18/68
Each share old Common $1 par exchanged for (0.2) share new Common $1 par 5/29/73
Merged into Gulf & Western Industries 8/19/77

Each share new Common $1 par exchanged for $10 cash

MADISON ST BK (MADISON TOWNSHIP, NJ)
Acquired by United Jersey Banks 7/1/72
Each share Capital Stock $10 par exchanged for (0.625) share Common $5 par
United Jersey Banks name changed to UJB Financial Corp. 6/30/89 which name changed to Summit Bancorp 3/1/96 which merged into FleetBoston Financial Corp. 3/1/2001 which merged into Bank of America Corp. 4/1/2004

MADISON STRATEGIC SECTOR PREM FD (DE)
Under plan of merger each Common Share of Bene. Int. 1¢ par automatically became (1.493683) Madison Covered Call & Equity Strategy Fund Common Shares of Bene. Int. 1¢ par 10/08/2018

MADISON VENTURES INC (NV)
Each share old Common $0.001 par exchanged for (4) shares new Common $0.001 par 04/11/2016
Recapitalized as Viabuilt Ventures Inc. 10/09/2018
Each share new Common $0.001 par exchanged for (0.04) share Common $0.001 par

MADISON WELLS BUILDING CO. (IL)
Liquidated in 1948

MADJAC DATA INC (NY)
Charter cancelled and proclaimed dissolved for failure to pay taxes and file reports 12/20/77

MADOC MNG LTD (BC)
Recapitalized as Adobe Ventures Inc. 01/28/1999
Each share Common no par exchanged for (0.2) share Common no par
Adobe Ventures Inc. name changed to Coalcorp Mining Inc. 10/27/2005 which name changed to Melior Resources Inc. 09/29/2011

MADONNA EDL GROUP CDA LTD (BC)
Delisted from Vancouver Stock Exchange 07/14/1989

MADONNA MINES LTD. (ON)
Name changed to Outlook Explorations Ltd. 05/15/1959
(See Outlook Explorations Ltd.)

MADRE MNG LTD (AB)
Recapitalized as Cortez Corp. 03/19/1986
Each share Common no par exchanged for (0.2) share Common no par
Cortez Corp. recapitalized as Cortez International Ltd. 06/02/1986
(See Cortez International Ltd.)

MADRONA EXPLS LTD (BC)
Merged into International Mariner Resources Ltd. 2/9/71
Each share Common 50¢ par exchanged for (0.210526) share Common no par and (0.105263) Ser. C Common Stock Purchase Warrant which expired 7/31/72
(See International Mariner Resources Ltd.)

MADRONA RES INC (BC)
Struck off register and declared dissolved for failure to file returns 1/22/93

MADRONA VENTURES INC (NV)
Common $0.001 par split (20) for (1) by issuance of (19) additional shares payable 08/19/2009 to holders of record 08/05/2009
Ex date - 08/20/2009
Name changed to Lightlake Therapeutics Inc. 10/07/2009
Lightlake Therapeutics Inc. name changed to Opiant Pharmaceuticals, Inc. (NV) 03/08/2016 which reincorporated in Delaware 10/02/2017

MADSEN GOLD CORP (ON)
Merged into Claude Resources Inc. 06/25/1998
Each share Common no par exchanged for (0.28571428) share Common no par
Claude Resources Inc. merged into Silver Standard Resources Inc. 06/06/2016 which name changed to SSR Mining Inc. 08/03/2017

MADSEN RED LAKE GOLD MINES LTD (ON)
Name changed to McChip Resources Inc. and Capital Stock $1 par reclassified as Common $1 par 7/3/81

MADWAY MAIN LINE HOMES INC (PA)
Adjudicated bankrupt 1/10/68
No stockholders' equity

MAESA GAMING MGMT INC (DE)
Reincorporated 7/30/96
Place of incorporation changed from (BC) to (DE) 7/30/96
Recapitalized as Mako Capital Inc. 7/15/98
Each share Common no par exchanged for (0.01) share Common no par
Mako Capital Inc. name changed to O Media, Inc. 4/7/99 which name changed to Original Media, Inc. 1/4/2000 which recapitalized as OMDA Oil & Gas Inc. 6/7/2002

MAESA PETROLEUM INC. (BC)
Name changed to Maesa Gaming Management Inc. (BC) 5/4/94
Maesa Gaming Management Inc. (BC) reincorporated in Delaware 7/30/96 which recapitalized as Mako Capital Inc. 7/15/98 which name changed to O Media, Inc. 4/7/99 which name changed to Original Media, Inc. 1/4/2000 which recapitalized as OMDA Oil & Gas Inc. 6/7/2002

MAESTRAL GROUP INC (BC)
Struck off register and declared dissolved for failure to file returns 6/4/93

MAESTRO CAP CORP (AB)
Each share Common no par received distribution of (0.25) Relevium Technologies Inc. Unit consisting of (1) share Common no par and (1) Common Stock Purchase Warrant expiring 08/18/2019 payable 12/21/2016 to holders of record 12/19/2016
Voluntarily dissolved 02/21/2017

MAESTRO VENTURES LTD (BC)
Recapitalized as Invenio Resources Corp. 10/06/2010
Each share Common no par exchanged for (0.33333333) share Common no par
Invenio Resources Corp. name changed to Greatbanks Resources Ltd. 02/12/2015

MAF BANCORP INC (DE)
Common 1¢ par split (3) for (2) by issuance of (0.5) additional share 08/26/1993
Common 1¢ par split (3) for (2) by issuance of (0.5) additional share payable 07/09/1997 to holders of record 06/17/1997
Common 1¢ par split (3) for (2) by issuance of (0.5) additional share payable 07/10/1998 to holders of record 06/18/1998
Stock Dividend - 10% 08/31/1995
Merged into National City Corp. 09/01/2007
Each share Common 1¢ par exchanged for (1.9939) shares Common $4 par
National City Corp. acquired by PNC Financial Services Group, Inc. 12/31/2008

MAFCO CONS GROUP INC (DE)
Merged into Mafco Consolidated Holdings Inc. 07/09/1997
Each share Common 1¢ par exchanged for $33.50 cash
Value Support Rights called for redemption at $0.56 on 01/30/1998

MAFRICOR RESOURCES (QC)
Struck off register and declared dissolved for failure to file reports or pay fees 11/05/1999

MAG COPPER LTD (ON)
Each share old Common no par exchanged for (0.2) share new Common no par 09/08/2015
Each share new Common no par exchanged again for (0.2) share new Common no par 01/31/2017
Recapitalized as Integra Resources Corp. 08/22/2017
Each share new Common no par exchanged for (0.4) share Common no par

MAG ENTERPRISES INC (UT)
Each share Common $0.001 par exchanged for (0.05) share Common $0.0001 par 08/29/1983
Recapitalized as Safari Associates, Inc. 10/08/1993
Each share Common $0.0001 par exchanged for (0.1) share Common $0.0001 par
Safari Associates, Inc. recapitalized as Power-Save Energy Co. 11/28/2006 which name changed to Lustros, Inc. 04/25/2012
(See Lustros, Inc.)

MAG-IRON MINING & MILLING, LTD. (ON)
Charter revoked for failure to file reports and pay fees 4/22/65

MAG-TRONICS CORP. (MN)
Assets sold 1/1/63
No stockholders' equity

MAGAININ PHARMACEUTICALS INC (DE)
Name changed to Genaera Corp. 03/12/2001
Genaera Corp. assets transferred to Genaera Liquidating Trust 07/08/2009
(See Genaera Liquidating Trust)

MAGAR HOME PRODUCTS, INC. (DE)
No longer in existence having become inoperative and void for non-payment of taxes 4/1/56

MAGAZIJN DE BIJENKORF BEHEER N V (NETHERLANDS)
Name changed to Bijenkorf Beheer N.V. 02/01/1966
Bijenkorf Beheer N.V. name changed to Koninklijke Bijenkorf Beheer KBB N.V. 09/03/1971
(See Koninklijke Bijenkorf Beheer N.V. KBB)

MAGAZINE REPEATING RAZOR CO.
Acquired by Eversharp, Inc. on a (1.5) for (1) basis in 1946
(See listing for Eversharp, Inc.)

MAGDALENA MINING & MILLING CO. (CO)
Dissolved 12/31/62

MAGDALENA RED LAKE MINES LTD. (ON)
Merged into Pardee Amalgamated Mines Ltd. on a (1) for (20) basis 12/31/54
Pardee Amalgamated Mines Ltd. liquidated for Rio Algom Mines Ltd. 11/9/61 which name changed to Rio Algom Ltd. 4/30/75
(See Rio Algom Ltd.)

MAGELLAN BIOTECH INC (CANADA)
Name changed to Miraculins Inc. 10/11/2002
Miraculins Inc. recapitalized as Luminor Medical Technologies Inc. 04/14/2016 which name changed to RISE Life Science Corp. 03/14/2018

MAGELLAN CORP (CO)
Name changed to Power-Cell, Inc. and Common 1¢ par changed to $0.00001 par 2/22/88
Power-Cell, Inc. name changed to Park Pharmacy Corp. 10/20/99
(See Park Pharmacy Corp.)

MAGELLAN FD (MA)
Under plan of merger name changed to Fidelity Magellan Fund, Inc. 6/22/81

MAGELLAN HEALTH SVCS INC (DE)
Plan of reorganization under Chapter 11 Federal Bankruptcy Code effective 01/05/2004
Each share Common 25¢ par exchanged for (0.003247) share Common 1¢ par and (0.003247) share Common Stock Purchase Warrant expiring 01/05/2011
Note: Unexchanged certificates were cancelled and became without value 01/05/2005
Name changed to Magellan Health, Inc. 06/13/2014

MAGELLAN INDS INC (NV)
Recapitalized 09/21/2004
Each share old Common $0.0001 par exchanged for (0.25) share new Common $0.0001 par 05/29/2001
Recapitalized from Magellan Filmed Entertainment, Inc. to Magellan Industries, Inc. 09/21/2004
Each share Common $0.0001 par exchanged for (0.0001) share Common $0.0001 par
Charter permanently revoked 02/28/2005

MAGELLAN MIDSTREAM HLDGS L P (DE)
Issue Information - 22,000,000 COM UNITS REPSTG LTD PARTNER INTS offered at $24.50 per share on 02/09/2006
Merged into Magellan Midstream Partners, L.P. 09/25/2009
Each Common Unit exchanged for (0.6325) Common Unit

MAGELLAN MINERALS LTD (BC)
Merged into Anfield Nickel Corp. 05/06/2016
Each share Common no par exchanged for (0.0863) share Common no par
Note: Unexchanged certificates will be cancelled and become without value 05/06/2022
Anfield Nickel Corp. name changed to Anfield Gold Corp. 05/11/2016 which merged into Equinox Gold Corp. 12/22/2017

MAGELLAN PETE AUSTRALIA LTD (AUSTRALIA)
Stock Dividends - 10% 03/04/1988; 10% 11/04/1988; 10% 01/09/1990; 10% 02/12/1991; 5% payable 11/19/1998 to holders of record 10/23/1998
Acquired by Magellan Petroleum Corp. 10/20/2006
Each ADR for Ordinary exchanged for (0.75) share Common 1¢ par and $0.04523 cash
Magellan Petroleum Corp. name changed to Tellurian Inc. 02/10/2017

MAGELLAN PETE CORP (DE)
Reincorporated 10/23/1967
Place of incorporation changed from (Panama) to (DE) 10/23/1967
Voting Trust Agreement terminated 04/01/1969
Each VTC for Common 1¢ par

exchanged for (1) share Common 1¢ par
Each share old Common 1¢ par exchanged for (0.125) share new Common 1¢ par 07/13/2015
Under plan of merger name changed to Tellurian Inc. 02/10/2017

MAGELLAN RES CORP (BC)
Common no par split (2) for (1) by issuance of (1) additional share 04/18/1986
Merged into International Mahogany Corp. 12/10/1990
Each share Common no par exchanged for (0.22) share Class B Subordinate no par
International Mahogany Corp. recapitalized as Reliant Ventures Ltd. 06/06/2000 which name changed to Esperanza Silver Corp. 05/14/2003 which name changed to Esperanza Resources Corp. 07/19/2010
(See Esperanza Resources Corp.)

MAGELLAN RESTAURANT SYS INC (DE)
Name changed to Grill Concepts Inc. (DE) 02/27/1995
Grill Concepts Inc. (DE) reincorporated in Nevada 08/03/2011
(See Grill Concepts Inc.)

MAGELLAN TECHNOLOGY INC (UT)
Each share old Common $0.0001 par exchanged for (1/30) share new Common $0.0001 par 10/17/94
Each share new Common $0.0001 par exchanged again for (0.5) share new Common $0.0001 par 3/8/96
Name changed to Biomeridian Corp. 8/1/2000

MAGENTA CORP (NV)
Recapitalized as China Resources Development, Inc. (NV) 12/16/94
Each share Common $0.001 par exchanged for (0.14992503) share Common $0.001 par
China Resources Development, Inc. (NV) reincorporated in British Virgin Islands as China Natural Resources, Inc. 11/24/2004

MAGENTA DEV CORP (BC)
Struck off register and declared dissolved for failure to file returns 10/14/94

MAGES SPORTING GOODS CO. (IL)
Name changed to Community Discount Centers, Inc. 12/12/1961
Community Discount Centers, Inc. merged into TSC Industries, Inc. 02/19/1968 which was acquired by National Industries, Inc. (KY) 12/06/1969 which merged into Fuqua Industries, Inc. 01/03/1978 which name changed to Actava Group Inc. 07/21/1993 which name changed to Metromedia International Group, Inc. 11/01/1995
(See Metromedia International Group, Inc.)

MAGGIE MINES LTD (BC)
Recapitalized as International Maggie Mines Ltd. 04/18/1985
Each share Capital Stock no par exchanged for (0.5) share Common no par
International Maggie Mines Ltd. name changed to Hall Train Entertainment Inc. 04/24/1995 which merged into GoldTrain Resources Inc. 04/27/2009 which recapitalized as Idaho Champion Gold Mines Canada Inc. 09/27/2018

MAGHEMITE INC (BC)
Delisted from Vancouver Stock Exchange 03/04/1992

MAGIC CHEF, INC. (NJ)
Common no par changed to $1 par 7/27/56
Name changed to Magic Chef-Food Giant Markets, Inc. 8/5/57
Magic Chef-Food Giant Markets, Inc. name changed to Food Giant Markets, Inc. 2/17/58 which merged into Vornado, Inc. (DE) 9/29/67 which reorganized as Vornado Realty Trust (MD) 5/6/93

MAGIC CHEF-FOOD GIANT MARKETS, INC. (NJ)
Name changed to Food Giant Markets, Inc. 2/17/58
Food Giant Markets, Inc. merged into Vornado, Inc. (DE) 9/29/67 which reorganized as Vornado Realty Trust (MD) 5/6/93

MAGIC CHEF INC (DE)
Class B Common $3 par reclassified as Common $3 par 5/17/67
Common $3 par split (3) for (2) by issuance of (0.5) additional share 10/1/69
Common $3 par split (2) for (1) by issuance of (1) additional share 10/6/72
Stock Dividend - Common & Class B Common 33-1/3% 2/11/66
Merged into Maytag Co. 5/30/86
Each share Common $3 par exchanged for (1.671) shares Common $1.25 par
Maytag Co. name changed to Maytag Corp. 4/29/87 which merged into Whirlpool Corp. 3/31/2006

MAGIC CIRCLE ENERGY CORP (OK)
Merged into MCEN Corp. 3/13/92
Each share Common 10¢ par exchanged for $0.24 cash

MAGIC COMMUNICATIONS INC (DE)
Name changed to American Post Tension, Inc. 09/27/2007
American Post Tension, Inc. name changed to Crown City Pictures, Inc. 10/07/2011 which recapitalized as World Poker Fund Holdings, Inc. 01/06/2015

MAGIC FINGERS INC (DE)
Each share old Common $0.0001 par exchanged for (0.025) share new Common $0.0001 par 03/04/1997
Name changed to Magicinc.com 07/23/1999
Magicinc.com name changed to Magic Media Networks, Inc. 04/15/2002 which name changed to Destination Television, Inc. 02/27/2007 which name changed to Movie Studio, Inc. 06/09/2014

MAGIC FOODS INC (ON)
Reorganized under the laws of British Columbia as Lucre Ventures Ltd. 05/15/1998
Each share Common no par exchanged for (0.5) share Common no par
Lucre Ventures Ltd. recapitalized as Strathclair Ventures Ltd. 09/05/2001 which name changed to SilverCrest Mines Inc. 05/28/2003 which merged into First Majestic Silver Corp. 10/07/2015

MAGIC GOLD INC (UT)
Name changed to Cardinal Technologies, Inc. 10/08/1987
(See Cardinal Technologies, Inc.)

MAGIC-KELLER SOAP WORKS, LTD. (LA)
Charter revoked for failure to file annual reports 5/13/82

MAGIC LANTERN GROUP INC (NV)
Name changed to CasinoBuilders.com, Inc. 05/13/1999
CasinoBuilders.com, Inc. name changed to Proxity Digital Networks Inc. 10/31/2001 which name changed to Proxity, Inc. 01/14/2005 which recapitalized as CAVU Resources Inc. 05/06/2009

MAGIC LANTERN GROUP INC (NY)
Voluntarily dissolved 08/14/2006

Details not available

MAGIC MARKER CORP (DE)
Reincorporated 09/00/1975
Common 50¢ par split (3) for (2) by issuance of (0.5) additional share 08/09/1972
State of incorporation changed from (NY) to (DE) 09/00/1975
Reorganized under Chapter 11 Bankruptcy Code 01/09/1981
No stockholders' equity

MAGIC MARKER INDS INC (DE)
Each share Common 1¢ par exchanged for (0.25) share Common 4¢ par 02/01/1984
Chapter 11 bankruptcy proceedings terminated 12/21/1992
Stockholders' equity unlikely

MAGIC MEDIA NETWORKS INC (DE)
Name changed 04/15/2002
Each share old Common $0.0001 par exchanged for (0.1) share new Common $0.0001 par 10/12/2001
Name changed from Magicinc.com to Magic Media Networks, Inc. 04/15/2002
Name changed to Destination Television, Inc. 02/27/2007
Destination Television, Inc. name changed to Movie Studio, Inc. 06/09/2014

MAGIC METALS URANIUM CO., INC. (UT)
Charter suspended for non-payment of taxes 03/29/1957

MAGIC MOUNTAIN, INC. (CO)
Bankrupt in August 1962
No stockholders' equity

MAGIC MOUNTAIN CORP. (VT)
Charter revoked for failure to file annual reports 8/9/90

MAGIC RESTAURANTS INC (DE)
Each share old Common $0.001 par exchanged for (2/3) share new Common $0.001 par 05/23/1991
Name changed to Redheads, Inc. 03/00/1997
(See Redheads, Inc.)

MAGIC TASTE FOOD PRODS INC (DE)
Name changed to Atlas American Corp. 12/12/69
(See Atlas American Corp.)

MAGIC 3 INDS LTD (BC)
Name changed to Rent-A-Wreck Industries Corp. 10/15/1986
Rent-A-Wreck Industries Corp. recapitalized as Practicar Industries Corp. 09/07/1988
(See Practicar Industries Corp.)

MAGIC URANIUM CO., INC. (NV)
Charter revoked for failure to file reports and pay fees 3/3/57

MAGIC VALLEY FROZEN FOODS, INC. (TX)
Merged into Vahlsing, Inc. 10/31/67
Each share Common no par exchanged for (0.17) share Common 10¢ par
(See Vahlsing, Inc.)

MAGIC YRS CHILD CARE & LEARNING CTRS INC (PA)
Merged into Children's Discovery Centers of America, Inc. 4/15/91
Each share Common no par exchanged for (0.4925) share Class A Common 1¢ par
(See Children's Discovery Centers of America, Inc.)

MAGICAL MARKETING INC (WY)
Name changed to ISEmployment.com, Inc. 6/12/2002
ISEmployment.com, Inc. name changed to Idoleyez Corp. 9/10/2003

MAGICIAN INDS HLDGS LTD (HONG KONG)
ADR agreement terminated 09/11/2006
No ADR's remain outstanding

MAGICORP ENTMT INC (ON)
Reincorporated 7/4/2001
Place of incorporation changed from (BC) to (ONT) 7/4/2001
Recapitalized as Lucid Entertainment Inc. 7/5/2004
Each share Common no par exchanged for (0.1) share Common no par

MAGICSILK INC (NY)
Name changed to Vader Group Inc. 04/13/1988
Vader Group Inc. name changed to SoftNet Systems, Inc. (NY) 06/29/1993 which reincorporated in Delaware 04/13/1999 which name changed to American Independence Corp. 11/14/2002
(See American Independence Corp.)

MAGICWORKS ENTMT INC (DE)
Merged into SFX Entertainment, Inc. 09/11/1998
Each share Common $0.001 par exchanged for $4 cash

MAGIN ENERGY INC NEW (AB)
Each share old Common no par exchanged for (0.33333333) share new Common no par 05/05/1998
Acquired by NCE Petrofund 07/03/2001
Each share new Common no par exchanged for (0.2986) new Trust Unit 2001
NCE Petrofund name changed to Petrofund Energy Trust 11/01/2003 which merged into Penn West Energy Trust 07/04/2006 which reorganized as Penn West Petroleum Ltd. (New) 01/03/2011 which name changed to Obsidian Energy Ltd. 06/29/2017

MAGIN ENERGY INC OLD (AB)
Reorganized as Magin Energy Inc. (New) 09/26/1996
Each share Common no par exchanged for (1) share old Common no par
Magin Energy Inc. (New) acquired by NCE Petrofund 07/03/2001 which name changed to Petrofund Energy Trust 11/01/2003 which merged into Penn West Energy Trust 07/04/2006 which reorganized as Penn West Petroleum Ltd. (New) 01/03/2011 which name changed to Obsidian Energy Ltd. 06/29/2017

MAGINDUSTRIES CORP (ON)
Reincorporated under the laws of Canada 01/10/2006

MAGINO GOLD MINES, LTD. (ON)
Assets sold to satisfy Bond Mortgage in 1947
No stockholders' equity
Dissolved by default 10/19/50

MAGISTRAL BIOTECH INC (CANADA)
Recapitalized as Immunotec Inc. 01/24/2007
Each share Common no par exchanged for (0.025) share Common no par
(See Immunotec Inc.)

MAGMA CHIEF COPPER CO. (AZ)
Charter revoked for failure to file reports or pay taxes 4/17/28

MAGMA COPPER CO (ME)
Capital Stock no par changed to $10 par 00/00/1933
Capital Stock $10 par changed to $3-1/3 par and (2) additional shares issued 05/29/1963
Stock Dividend - 10% 12/01/1953
Merged into Newmont Mining Corp. 05/06/1969
Each share Capital Stock $3-1/3 par

MAG-MAG

exchanged for (0.85) share $4.50 Conv. Preferred Ser. A $5 par
(See Newmont Mining Corp.)

MAGMA COPPER CO NEW (DE)
Class B Common 1¢ par reclassified as Common 1¢ par 11/2/92
Merged into Broken Hill Propietary Co., Ltd. 1/18/96
Each share 5.625% Conv. Preferred Ser. D 1¢ par exchanged for $28 cash
Each share 6% Conv. Preferred Ser. E 1¢ par exchanged for $28 cash
Each share Common 1¢ par exchanged for $28 cash

MAGMA DESIGN AUTOMATION INC (DE)
Issue Information - 4,850,010 shares COM offered at $13 per share on 11/19/2001
Acquired by Synopsys, Inc. 02/22/2012
Each share Common $0.0001 exchanged for $7.35 cash

MAGMA ENERGY CORP (BC)
Under plan of merger name changed to Alterra Power Corp. 05/17/2011
Alterra Power Corp. merged into Innergex Renewable Energy Inc. 02/07/2018

MAGMA ENERGY INC (NV)
Each share Common 10¢ par exchanged for (5) shares Common 2¢ par 11/22/1976
Acquired by Magma Power Co. (New) 03/11/1988
Each (1.9) shares Common 2¢ par exchanged for (1) share Common 10¢ par
(See Magma Power Co. (New))

MAGMA KING MANGANESE MINING CO. (AZ)
Charter revoked for failure to file reports and pay fees 9/25/59

MAGMA METALS LTD (AUSTRALIA)
Acquired by Panoramic Resources Ltd. 07/05/2012
Each share Common exchanged for (0.14285714) share Common

MAGMA PWR CO NEW (NV)
Merged into CE Acquisition Co., Inc. 02/24/1995
Each share Common 10¢ par exchanged for $38.4772 cash

MAGMA PWR CO OLD (NV)
6% Conv. Preferred $10 par called for redemption 8/11/64
Merged into Natomas Co. 4/23/82
Each share Common 10¢ par exchanged for $45 cash
(See Natomas Co.)

MAGMA RES (UT)
Each share old Common no par exchanged for (0.05) share new Common no par 4/2/93
Name changed to Cellular Telecommunications & Technologies Inc. 7/15/93
Cellular Telecommunications & Technologies Inc. recapitalized as China Biomedical Group Inc. 4/3/95 which name changed to Internet Holdings Inc. 6/30/96 which name changed to HTTP Technology, Inc. (UT) 11/28/2000 which reincorporated in Delaware 12/19/2000 which name changed to Medicsight, Inc. 10/28/2002 which name changed to MGT Capital Investments, Inc. 1/24/2007

MAGNA AMERICAN CORP. (MS)
Reincorporated 12/31/66
State of incorporation changed from (OH) to (MS) 12/31/66
Voluntarily dissolved 10/17/88
Details not available

MAGNA BANCORP INC (DE)
Common 1¢ par split (2) for (1) by issuance of (1) additional share 6/7/93
Common 1¢ par split (2) for (1) by issuance of (1) additional share 6/6/94
Common 1¢ par split (2) for (1) by issuance of (1) additional share payable 8/15/96 to holders of record 7/29/96
Stock Dividend - 20% 11/26/92
Merged into Union Planters Corp. 11/1/97
Each share Common 1¢ par exchanged for (0.5165) share Common $5 par
Union Planters Corp. merged into Regions Financial Corp. (New) 7/1/2004

MAGNA BK (MEMPHIS, TN)
Reorganized 03/26/2012
Each share Common $1 par held by holders of (2,499) or fewer shares exchanged for (1) share Non-Vtg. Preferred Ser. D $1 par
Each share Non-Vtg. Preferred Ser. D $1 reclassified as (1) share Common $1 par 09/01/2015
Merged into Pinnacle Financial Partners, Inc. 09/01/2015
Each share Common $1 par exchanged for (0.28626558) share Common $1 par and $2.15222583 cash

MAGNA-BOND, INC. (DE)
Reincorporated 03/30/1961
State of incorporation changed from (NJ) to (DE) 03/30/1961
Adjudicated bankrupt 03/22/1962
No stockholders' equity

MAGNA CARTA RES INC (AB)
Recapitalized as Allyn Resources Inc. (AB) 11/05/1992
Each share Common no par exchanged for (0.5) share Common no par
Allyn Resources Inc. (AB) reincorporated in British Columbia 00/00/2004 which recapitalized as Troy Energy Corp. (BC) 01/14/2008 which reincorporated in Alberta 02/24/2011

MAGNA CORP. (CA)
Acquired by Baker International Corp. (CA) 03/31/1977
Each share Common no par exchanged for (0.81300813) share Common $1 par
Baker International Corp. (CA) reincorporated in Delaware 01/27/1983 which merged into Baker Hughes Inc. 04/03/1987 which merged into Baker Hughes, a GE company 07/05/2017

MAGNA CORP (MS)
Common no par split (3) for (1) by issuance of (2) additional shares 7/15/72
Merged into Contractors Material Co., Inc. 4/30/89
Details not available

MAGNA DIVERSIFIED INC (DE)
Name changed to Energizer 500 Inc. 6/8/84
Energizer 500 Inc. name changed to Opportunity 21 on 6/16/85
(See Opportunity 21)

MAGNA ELECTRS LTD (ON)
Name changed to Magna International Inc. 5/2/73

MAGNA ENTMT CORP (DE)
Each share old Class A Subordinate 1¢ par exchanged for (0.05) share new Class A Subordinate 1¢ par 07/22/2008
Plan of reorganization under Chapter 11 Federal Bankruptcy proceedings effective 04/30/2010
No stockholders' equity

MAGNA GROUP INC (DE)
Common $4 par changed to $2 par and (2) additional shares issued 11/10/83
Merged into Union Planters Corp. 7/1/98
Each share 7-1/2% Class B Preferred $20 par exchanged for $20 cash
Each share Common $2 par exchanged for (0.9686) share Common $5 par
Union Planters Corp. merged into Regions Financial Corp. (New) 7/1/2004

MAGNA INCOME TR (NY)
Name changed to Pilgrim High Yield Trust 3/1/85

MAGNA INTL INC (ON)
Each share Common no par exchanged for (3) shares Conv. Class B no par 12/15/1978
6.5% Preference $100 par called for redemption 12/15/1983
Each share Conv. Class B Common no par received distribution of (0.2) share MEC Holdings (Canada) Inc. Common no par payable 03/10/2000 to holders of record 02/25/2000
Each share Conv. Class B Common no par received distribution of (0.5) share MI Developments Inc. Class B no par payable 09/02/2003 to holders of record 08/29/2003
8.875% US$ Preferred Securities Ser. B called for redemption at $25 plus $0.41335 accrued dividends on 09/21/2004
8.65% CDN$ Preferred Securities Ser. A called for redemption at $25 plus $0.54507 accrued dividends on 09/30/2004
Plan of Arrangement effective 09/20/2007
Each share Conv. Class B Common no par exchanged for $114 cash (Additional Information in Active)

MAGNA INVT & DEV CORP (UT)
Reorganized as Magna Investment & Development, Ltd. 12/31/86
Each share Common $1 par exchanged for (1) Ltd. Partnership Int.
Each share Class A $1 par exchanged for (1) Ltd. Partnership Int.

MAGNA OIL CORP (DE)
Merged into Triton Oil & Gas Corp. 4/28/72
Each share Common 50¢ par exchanged for (1) share Common Capital Stock $1 par
Triton Oil & Gas Corp. name changed to Triton Energy Corp. (TX) 12/1/81 which reincorporated in Delaware 5/12/95

MAGNA PICTURES CORP (DE)
Each share Common 5¢ par exchanged for (0.2) share Common 25¢ par 05/27/1965
Name changed to Todd-AO Corp. 02/04/1986
Todd-AO Corp. merged into Liberty Livewire Corp. 06/09/2000 which name changed to Ascent Media Group, Inc. 11/20/2002 which merged into Liberty Media Corp. (New) 07/01/2003 which reorganized as Liberty Media Holding Corp. (Incorporated 02/28/2006) 05/10/2006

MAGNA PIPE LINE CO. LTD. (BC)
Acquired by Cascade Natural Gas Corp. 12/00/1962
Each share Common no par exchanged for $5.25 (U.S.) principal amount of 5-1/4% Debentures due 12/31/1970

MAGNA PWR CORP (AB)
Name changed to Canyon Creek Food Co., Ltd. 2/8/96

MAGNA RES LTD (BC)
Common no par split (2) for (1) by issuance of (1) additional share payable 12/30/2011 to holders of record 12/30/2011 Ex date - 12/28/2011
Name changed to American Potash Corp. 08/19/2014
American Potash Corp. name changed to New Tech Lithium Corp. 01/22/2018

MAGNA TECHNOLOGIES INC (FL)
Proclaimed dissolved for failure to file reports and pay fees 11/14/1986

MAGNA-TEK, INC. (MN)
Name changed to Moulded Products, Inc. 06/21/1966
(See Moulded Products, Inc.)

MAGNA THEATRE CORP. (DE)
Name changed to Magna Pictures Corp. 7/20/60
Magna Pictures Corp. name changed to Todd-AO Corp. 2/4/86 which merged into Liberty Livewire Corp. 6/9/2000 which name changed to Ascent Media Group, Inc. 11/20/2002

MAGNA VENTURES LTD (BC)
Common no par split (3) for (1) by issuance of (2) additional shares 05/17/1985
Recapitalized as Consolidated Magna Ventures Ltd. 08/09/1990
Each share Common no par exchanged for (1/7) share Common no par
Consolidated Magna Ventures Ltd. name changed to Skinny Technologies Inc. 01/10/2002 which recapitalized as Pediment Exploration Ltd. 09/22/2004 which name changed to Pediment Gold Corp. 02/26/2009 which merged into Argonaut Gold Inc. 02/01/2011

MAGNACAP FD INC (MD)
Capital Stock 10¢ par split (2) for (1) by issuance of (1) additional share 08/14/1972
Under plan of merger name changed to Pilgrim Magnacap Fund, Inc. 06/20/1985

MAGNACARD INC (NJ)
Each share old Common no par exchanged for (0.1) share new Common no par 10/31/1983
Recapitalized as Highlander International Corp. 12/15/1988
Each share new Common no par exchanged for (0.05) share Common no par
Highlander International Corp. name changed to Worldwide Collections Fund, Inc. 09/25/1991
(See Worldwide Collections Fund, Inc.)

MAGNADATA INC (DE)
Name changed to MortgageBrokers.com Holdings, Inc. 02/17/2005
MortgageBrokers.com Holdings, Inc. name changed to MoPals.com, Inc. 04/11/2013

MAGNADYN FINL CORP (FL)
Stock Dividend - 100% 10/17/1972
Proclaimed dissolved for failure to file annual reports 11/09/1990

MAGNAGEM INDS INC (NY)
Dissolved by proclamation 9/30/81

MAGNAGRAPH CORP. (CA)
Dissolved in 1953

MAGNASONIC CDA INC (CANADA)
Name changed 09/04/1981
Name changed from Magnasonic Canada Ltd. to Magnasonic Canada Inc. 09/04/1981
Reacquired 03/07/1983
Each share Common no par exchanged for $5.70 cash

MAGNASYNC CORP. (CA)
Name changed to Magnasync/Moviola Corp. 8/1/66
Magnasync/Moviola Corp. merged

into Magnasync Craig Corp. 6/24/69 which name changed to Craig Corp. (DE) 10/30/69 which reincorporated in Nevada 12/29/99 which merged into Reading International, Inc. 12/31/2001

MAGNASYNC CRAIG CORP (DE)
Name changed to Craig Corp. (DE) 10/30/69
Craig Corp. (DE) reincorporated in Nevada 12/29/99 which merged into Reading International, Inc. 12/31/2001

MAGNASYNC MOVIOLA CORP (CA)
Merged into Magnasync Craig Corp. 6/24/69
Each share Common $1 par exchanged for (1) share Common 25¢ par
Magnasync Craig Corp. name changed to Craig Corp. (DE) 10/30/69 which reincorporated in Nevada 12/29/99 which merged into Reading International, Inc. 12/31/2001

MAGNATE VENTURES INC (BC)
Merged into Thor Explorations Ltd. (New) 09/01/2009
Each share Common no par exchanged for (0.42) share Common no par

MAGNATRON INTL CORP (BC)
Recapitalized as QI Technologies Corp. 3/17/94
Each share Common no par exchanged for (0.2) share Common no par
QI Technologies Corp. name changed to QI Systems Inc. (BC) 5/25/2001 which reincorporated under the laws of Delaware 7/1/2006

MAGNAVEST CORP (DE)
Merged into F.C.H.C. Acquiring Corp. 04/30/1984
Each share Common 10¢ par exchanged for $8.345726 cash
Each share Common 10¢ par received an additional initial payment of $4.172863 cash 01/17/1985
Each share Common 10¢ par received second payment of $2.4569 cash 01/10/1986
Each share Common 10¢ par received third and final payment of $2.10960 cash 03/12/1986

MAGNAVISION CORP (DE)
Each share old Common $0.00001 par exchanged for (0.05) share new Common $0.00001 par 5/9/97
Merged into Blue Acquisition Corp. 9/11/2001
Each share new Common $0.00001 par exchanged for $4.01 cash

MAGNAVOX CO. LTD.
Name changed to Magnavox Co. in 1942
(See Magnavox Co.)

MAGNAVOX CO (DE)
4-3/4% Preferred called for redemption 2/5/59
Common $1 par split (2) for (1) by issuance of (1) additional share 11/16/59
Common $1 par split (3) for (1) by issuance of (2) additional shares 8/3/61
Common $1 par split (2) for (1) by issuance of (1) additional share 5/20/66
Stock Dividends - 20% 6/1/46; 20% 10/1/47; 10% 1/15/49
Merged into North American Philips Development Corp. 7/24/75
Each share Common $1 par exchanged for $9 cash

MAGNESITA REFRATARIOS S A (BRAZIL)
Each old Sponsored ADR for Common exchanged for (0.2) new Sponsored ADR for Common to reflect a (1) for (25) reverse split followed by a (5) for (1) forward split 01/15/2016
ADR agreement terminated 03/05/2018
Each new Sponsored ADR for Common exchanged for (2) shares Common

MAGNESIUM ALLOY CORP (ON)
Name changed to MagIndustries Corp. (ONT) 2/4/2005
MagIndustries Corp. (ONT) reincorporated in Canada 1/10/2006

MAGNESIUM TECHNOLOGIES INC (NV)
Recapitalized as Relax Investments Ltd. 09/20/2000
Each share Common $0.001 par exchanged for (0.1) share Common $0.001 par

MAGNET BK FSB (CHARLESTON, WV)
Common 1¢ par split (2) for (1) by issuance of (1) additional share 7/25/85
Assets acquired 2/10/88
No stockholders' equity

MAGNET CONSOLIDATED MINES LTD. (ON)
Recapitalized as Conigo Mines Ltd. 2/22/65
Each share Capital Stock $1 par exchanged for (0.2) share Capital Stock $1 par
Conigo Mines Ltd. acquired by Amos Mines Ltd. 11/19/71 which merged into Jonpol Explorations Ltd. 4/28/80 which merged into Eastern Platinum Ltd. 4/26/2005

MAGNET EXPLORATIONS LTD. (BC)
Merged into Ballinderry Explorations Ltd. 07/28/1969
Each share Capital Stock 50¢ par exchanged for (0.33333333) share Common $1 par
Ballinderry Explorations Ltd. recapitalized as Prairie Pacific Energy Corp. 03/06/1970
(See Prairie Pacific Energy Corp.)

MAGNET GROUP LTD (AUSTRALIA)
Name changed 04/23/1985
Name changed from Magnet Metals Ltd. to Magnet Group Ltd. 04/23/1985
ADR agreement terminated 09/16/1996
Each ADR for Ordinary exchanged for (4) shares Ordinary
Note: Unexchanged ADR's were sold and the proceeds, if any, held for claim after 03/16/1997

MAGNET LAKE GOLD MINES LTD.
Acquired by Magnet Consolidated Mines Ltd. and Numalake Mines Ltd. 00/00/1936
Each share Common exchanged for (0.2) share of each company
(See each company's listing)

MAGNET OIL CO. (CA)
Charter suspended for failure to pay fees 03/01/1941

MAGNETECH CORP (DE)
Common $0.0001 par split (4) for (1) by issuance of (3) additional shares 03/12/1990
Each share Common $0.0001 par exchanged for (0.125) share Common $0.0002 par 10/01/1992
Name changed to Digital Communications Technology Corp. 05/03/1994

MAGNETEK INC (DE)
Each share old Common 1¢ par exchanged for (0.1) share new Common 1¢ par 12/05/2011
Acquired by Columbus McKinnon Corp. 09/02/2015
Each share new Common 1¢ par exchanged for $50 cash

MAGNETIC AMPLIFIERS, INC. (NY)
Acquired by Siegler Corp. 4/6/60
Each (3.5) shares Common 50¢ par exchanged for (1) share Common no par
Siegler Corp. name changed to Lear Siegler Inc. 6/5/62
(See Lear Siegler, Inc.)

MAGNETIC CORE CORP (DE)
Charter cancelled and declared inoperative and void for non-payment of taxes 3/1/80

MAGNETIC CTLS CO (MN)
Each share Common 4¢ par exchanged for (0.2) share Common 20¢ par 03/25/1966
Common 20¢ par split (3) for (2) by issuance of (0.5) additional share 06/23/1982
Common 20¢ par split (3) for (2) by issuance of (0.5) additional share 04/29/1983
Stock Dividend - 50% 05/01/1980
Name changed to ADC Telecommunications, Inc. 04/08/1985
(See ADC Telecommunications, Inc.)

MAGNETIC HEAD CORP (NY)
Dissolved by proclamation 6/23/93

MAGNETIC INFORMATION TECHNOLOGY (CA)
Charter suspended for failure to file reports and pay fees 05/01/1986

MAGNETIC MEDIA CORP (NY)
Voluntarily dissolved 11/28/1997
Details not available

MAGNETIC METALS CO (NJ)
Merged into Magmetco Inc. 09/05/1975
Each share Common $1 par exchanged for $6.50 cash

MAGNETIC TAPE ENGR CORP (CA)
Charter suspended for failure to file reports and pay fees 05/01/1980

MAGNETIC TECHNOLOGIES CORP (DE)
Each share Common 10¢ par exchanged for (0.1) share Common 15¢ par 01/29/1988
Common 15¢ par split (5) for (4) by issuance of (0.25) additional share 02/28/1992
Common 15¢ par split (3) for (2) by issuance of (0.5) additional share 02/15/1994
Merged into SPS Technologies, Inc. 12/02/1997
Each share Common 15¢ par exchanged for $5 cash

MAGNETIC VIDEO CORP (MI)
Each share Common $1 par exchanged for (2) shares Common no par 08/14/1978
Acquired by Twentieth Century-Fox Film Corp. 02/21/1979
Each share Common no par exchanged for $15.75 cash

MAGNETICS INC (PA)
Name changed to Spang Industries Inc. 2/1/70
(See Spang Industries Inc.)

MAGNETICS INTL INC (OH)
Stock Dividends - 10% 12/30/1980; 10% 12/30/1981
Merged into Porter (H.K.) Co., Inc. 09/15/1986
Each share Common no par exchanged for $12 cash

MAGNETICS INTL LTD (QC)
Name changed 11/20/70
Name changed from Magnetics International Ltd. to Magnetics International Ltd.- Magnetique International Ltee. and Capital Stock $5 par changed to no par 11/20/70
Name changed to Mavtech Holdings Inc. 8/31/87
(See Mavtech Holdings Inc.)

MAGNIFOAM TECHNOLOGY INC. (ON)
Merged into Magnifoam Technology International Inc. 12/05/1995
Each share Common no par exchanged for (2.5) shares Common no par
Magnifoam Technology International Inc. name changed to MTI Global Inc. 05/12/2005 which name changed to Zuni Holdings Inc. (New) 07/15/2010 which merged into Pacific Safety Products Inc. 01/04/2011

MAGNIFOAM TECHNOLOGY INTL INC (ON)
1st Preferred Ser. 1 no par called for redemption at $0.01 on 01/10/1999
Name changed to MTI Global Inc. 05/12/2005
MTI Global Inc. name changed to Zuni Holdings Inc. (New) 07/15/2010 which merged into Pacific Safety Products Inc. 01/04/2011

MAGNIN (I.) & CO.
Acquired by Bullock's, Inc. through offer of (1) share for each (3.5) shares in 1944
Bullock's, Inc. merged into Federated Department Stores, Inc. 8/29/64 which name changed to Macy's, Inc. 6/1/2007

MAGNIN JOSEPH INC (CA)
8% Preferred $1 par and Common $1 par changed to no par respectively and (1) additional share issued 01/15/1966
Acquired by Amfac, Inc. 03/26/1969
Each share 8% Preferred no par exchanged for $0.50 cash
Each share Common no par exchanged for $16.67 principal amount of 5% Conv. Subord. Debentures due 03/01/1989 and $33.33 cash

MAGNITUDE INFORMATION SYS INC (DE)
Name changed to Kiwibox.Com, Inc. 03/02/2010

MAGNOLIA CHEM INC (TX)
Name changed to Arrow Magnolia International Inc. 6/6/87
(See Arrow Magnolia International Inc.)

MAGNOLIA EXPLORATIONS CO. LTD. (DE)
Name changed to Northern Resources Ltd. in 1958
(See Northern Resources Ltd.)

MAGNOLIA FOODS INC (OK)
Common 1¢ par changed to $0.005 par 00/00/1997
Name changed to Creative Restaurants Concepts Inc. 06/28/1997
Creative Restaurants Concepts Inc. name changed to Cala Corp. 12/02/1999
(See Cala Corp.)

MAGNOLIA INDS INC (NY)
Completely liquidated 12/17/98
Each share Common 1¢ par received first and final distribution of $2.60 cash
Note: Certificates were not required to be exchanged and are without value

MAGNOLIA LANE INCOME FD (DE)
Name changed to Huntwicke Capital Group Inc. 09/23/2016

MAGNOLIA LEAD & OIL CO.
Name changed to Magnolia Uranium & Oil Co. and Common 10¢ par changed to 5¢ par in 1954
Magnolia Uranium & Oil Co. recapitalized as Intermountain Petroleum, Inc. 4/19/57 which name changed to Sage Oil Co., Inc. 5/29/59
(See Sage Oil Co., Inc.)

MAGNOLIA LEAD CO.
Name changed to Magnolia Lead & Oil Co. in 1950
Magnolia Lead & Oil Co. name changed to Magnolia Uranium & Oil Co. in 1954 which recapitalized as Intermountain Petroleum, Inc. 4/19/57 which name changed to Sage Oil Co., Inc. 5/29/59
(See Sage Oil Co., Inc.)

MAGNOLIA MANOR APARTMENTS LIQUIDATION TRUST
Trust terminated in 1951
Details not available

MAGNOLIA METAL CORP (NE)
Each share Common $1 par exchanged for (0.004) share Common $250 par 09/17/1982
Note: In effect holders received $60 cash per share Common $1 par and public interest was eliminated

MAGNOLIA PARK, INC. (LA)
Under plan of reorganization each share Common 10¢ par exchanged for $0.003 cash 3/8/66

MAGNOLIA SOLAR CORP (NV)
Common $0.001 par split (1.315789) for (1) by issuance of (0.315789) additional share payable 02/12/2010 to holders of record 02/12/2010
Ex date - 02/16/2010
Recapitalized as Ecoark Holdings, Inc. 03/28/2016
Each share Common $0.001 par exchanged for (0.004) share Common $0.001 par

MAGNOLIA TERRACE APTS., INC.
Liquidated in 1941

MAGNOLIA URANIUM & OIL CO. (UT)
Recapitalized as Intermountain Petroleum, Inc. 4/19/57
Each share Common 10¢ par exchanged for (0.1) share Common $1 par
Intermountain Petroleum, Inc. name changed to Sage Oil Co., Inc. 5/29/59
(See Sage Oil Co., Inc.)

MAGNOLIA VENTURES INC (NV)
Name changed to AP Henderson Group and (1.875) additional shares issued 02/10/2003
(See AP Henderson Group)

MAGNOR MINING CORP. LTD. (ON)
Charter cancelled and declared dissolved for failure to file returns and pay fees 10/23/74

MAGNOTTA WINERY CORP (ON)
Merged into Magnotta Family Holdings Ltd. 01/20/2012
Each share Common no par exchanged for $2.90 cash
Note: Unexchanged certificates were cancelled and became without value 01/20/2017

MAGNUM CAP CORP (AB)
Name changed to Magnum Goldcorp Inc. (AB) 11/13/2013
Magnum Goldcorp Inc. (AB) reincorporated in British Columbia 07/25/2014

MAGNUM COMMUNICATIONS CORP (DE)
Name changed to Vacation Ownership Marketing, Inc. 12/12/1980
Vacation Ownership Marketing, Inc. recapitalized as Capital Solutions I, Inc. 05/11/2004 which name changed to Fuda Faucet Works, Inc. 01/03/2008

MAGNUM CONS MNG LTD (BC)
Completely liquidated 03/11/1970
Each share Capital Stock no par exchanged for first and final distribution of (0.392156) share Brameda Resources Ltd. Common no par and $0.01 cash
Brameda Resources Ltd. merged into Teck Corp. 02/08/1979 which name changed to Teck Cominco Ltd. 09/12/2001 which name changed to Teck Resources Ltd. 04/27/2009

MAGNUM D OR RES INC (NV)
Each share old Common $0.001 par exchanged for (0.025) share new Common $0.001 par 04/24/2006
Note: Holders of between (100) to (3,999) shares will receive (100) shares
Holders of (99) shares or fewer were not affected
Each share new Common $0.001 par received distribution of (1) share Sunrise Mining Corp. Common $0.001 par payable 09/20/2007 to holders of record 01/23/2007
Ex date - 11/08/2007
SEC revoked common stock registration 08/03/2011

MAGNUM ENERGY INC (BC)
Reincorporated under the laws of Alberta 02/18/2010

MAGNUM FUND LTD. (NETHERLANDS)
Reincorporated 12/13/1971
Each share Common $10 par exchanged for (2) shares Common $5 par 03/14/1969
Place of incorporation changed from (Canada) to (Netherlands) and Common $5 par changed to $25 par 12/13/1971
Acquired by Copthall (Tilburg) B.V. 08/10/1978
Each share Common $25 par exchanged for $42.552 cash

MAGNUM GOLD MINES, LTD. (ON)
Charter cancelled for failure to file reports and pay taxes in 1929

MAGNUM GOLDCORP INC (AB)
Reincorporated under the laws of British Columbia 07/25/2014

MAGNUM HUNTER RES CORP (DE)
Each share Common 1¢ par received distribution of (0.1) Common Stock Purchase Warrant expiring 04/15/2016 payable 10/15/2013 to holders of record 09/16/2013
Plan of reorganization under Chapter 11 Federal Bankruptcy proceedings effective 05/06/2016
No stockholders' equity
Name changed to Blue Ridge Mountain Resources, Inc. 04/04/2017

MAGNUM HUNTER RES INC (NV)
Name changed 03/18/1997
Each share Common $0.002 par exchanged for (0.5) share Common $0.002 par 06/01/1993
$1.10 Conv. Preferred Ser. C $0.001 par called for redemption 08/16/1996
Name changed from Magnum Petroleum Inc. to Magnum Hunter Resources, Inc. 03/18/1997
Each share Common $0.002 par received distribution of (0.2) Common Stock Purchase Warrant expiring 03/21/2005 payable 03/21/2002 to holders of record 01/10/2002
Each share Common $0.002 par received distribution of (1) TEL Offshore Trust Unit of Bene. Int. payable 05/13/2005 to holders of record 04/18/2005 Ex date - 04/14/2005
Merged into Cimarex Energy Co. 06/07/2005
Each share Common $0.002 par exchanged for (0.415) share Common 1¢ par

MAGNUM MINERALS CORP (BC)
Name changed to Magnum Uranium Corp. 10/03/2005
Magnum Uranium Corp. acquired by Energy Fuels Inc. 07/02/2009

MAGNUM OIL INC (NV)
Name changed to USA Graphite Inc. 04/17/2012
(See USA Graphite Inc.)

MAGNUM RES INC (DE)
Reorganized 02/14/1991
Reorganized from (UT) to under the laws of Delaware 02/14/1991
Each share old Common 1¢ par exchanged for (0.05) share new Common 1¢ par
Each share new Common 1¢ par exchanged again for (0.33333333) share new Common 1¢ par 09/20/1993
SEC revoked common stock registration 09/11/2009

MAGNUM RES LTD (AB)
Delisted from Alberta Stock Exchange 08/08/1994

MAGNUM SPORTS & ENTMT INC (DE)
SEC revoked common stock registration 04/07/2008

MAGNUM URANIUM CORP (BC)
Acquired by Energy Fuels Inc. 07/02/2009
Each share Common no par exchanged for (0.78) share Common no par

MAGNUM VENTURES INC (NV)
Name changed to RadioTower.com, Inc. 05/18/1999
RadioTower.com, Inc. name changed to Pacific Fuel Cell Corp. 08/27/2001
(See Pacific Fuel Cell Corp.)

MAGNUS ENERGY INC (AB)
Acquired by Questerre Energy Corp. 11/02/2007
Each share Class A Common no par exchanged for (0.015316) share Common no par
Each share Class B Common no par exchanged for (0.15316) share Common no par

MAGNUS INTL INC (NY)
Name changed back to Illustrated World Encyclopedia, Inc. 07/05/1978

MAGNUS RES LTD (BC)
Name changed to Enerteck Energy Technologies Corp. 12/3/86
(See Enerteck Energy Technologies Corp.)

MAGNUSON COMPUTER SYS INC (CA)
Plan of reorganization under Chapter 11 bankruptcy proceedings confirmed 10/08/1984
No stockholders' equity

MAGOMA MINES LTD (ON)
Charter cancelled and declared dissolved for failure to file returns and pay fees 03/00/1976

MAGOR CAR CORP (DE)
Each share Common no par exchanged for (4) shares Capital Stock $6 par 00/00/1945
Dissolved 12/31/1966
Details not available

MAGRA COMPUTER TECHNOLOGIES CORP (ON)
Delisted from Canadian Dealer Network 10/10/2000

MAGUIRE INDUSTRIES, INC. (NY)
Name changed to Components Corp. of America 4/3/61
(See Components Corp. of America)

MAGUIRE PPTYS INC (MD)
Issue Information - 9,000,000 shares PFD SER A 7.625% offered at $25 per share on 01/15/2004
Issue Information - 36,510,000 shares COM offered at $19 per share on 06/24/2003
Name changed to MPG Office Trust, Inc. 05/17/2010
(See MPG Office Trust, Inc.)

MAGWELL LONG LAC GOLD MINES, LTD. (ON)
Charter cancelled for failure to pay taxes and file returns 10/28/57

MAGYAR PUBLISHING CO., INC. (NY)
Bankrupt 1962
No stockholders' equity

MAGYAR TELEKOM LTD (HUNGARY)
Name changed 05/06/2005
Name changed from Magyar Tavkozlest Rt to Magyar Telekom Ltd. 05/06/2005
Name changed to Magyar Telekom Telecommunications PLC 03/01/2006

MAHALO ENERGY LTD (AB)
Plan of arrangement under Companies' Creditors Arrangement Act approved 09/16/2010
No stockholders' equity

MAHANAGAR TEL NIGAM LTD (INDIA)
GDR agreement terminated 05/21/2001
Each 144A Sponsored GDR for Ordinary exchanged for (2) 144A Ordinary shares
Note: Agent advised 100% of 144A GDR's were exchanged
GDR agreement terminated 11/29/2001
Each Reg. S Sponsored GDR for Ordinary exchanged for $5.8921 cash
(Additional Information in Active)

MAHARAJA MINERALS LTD (BC)
Recapitalized as Mecca Minerals Ltd. 03/14/1978
Each share Capital Stock no par exchanged for (0.5) share Capital Stock no par
(See Mecca Minerals Ltd.)

MAHARG CO., INC. (NY)
Liquidation completed
Each share Common 10¢ par exchanged for initial distribution of (0.10461) share Revlon, Inc. Common $1 par 4/8/66
Each share Common 10¢ par received second and final distribution of (0.000947) share Revlon, Inc. Common $1 par 5/14/68
(See Revlon, Inc.)

MAHASKA INVT CO (IA)
Common $5 par split (5) for (3) by issuance of (0.66666666) additional share payable 11/10/1997 to holders of record 10/20/1997
Name changed to MidWestOne Financial Group, Inc. (Old) 05/09/2003
MidWestOne Financial Group, Inc. (Old) merged into MidWestOne Financial Group, Inc. (New) 03/14/2008

MAHDIA GOLD CORP (AB)
Reincorporated under the laws of Ontario 03/25/2013

MAHER COLLIERIES CO.
Property sold 00/00/1928
Details not available

MAHER INC (ON)
Assets sold for the benefit of creditors in May 1993
No stockholders' equity

MAHER SHOES LTD. NEW (ON)
Name changed to Maher Inc. 10/23/78
(See Maher Inc.)

MAHER SHOES LTD. OLD (ON)
Merged into Maher Shoes Ontario Ltd. 4/24/65
Each share Common no par exchanged for (1) share 60¢ Class B Preference no par and $31 cash
Maher Shoes Ontario Ltd. name changed to Maher Shoes Ltd. (New)

6/29/66 which name changed to Maher Inc. 10/23/78
(See Maher Inc.)

MAHER SHOES ONTARIO LTD. (ON)
Name changed to Maher Shoes Ltd. (New) 6/29/66
(See Maher Inc.)

MAHINDRA GESCO DEVELOPERS LTD (INDIA)
Name changed to Mahindra Lifespace Developers Ltd. 10/25/2007

MAHLSTEDT (J.A.) LUMBER & COAL CO.
Reorganized as Mahlstedt Materials, Inc. in 1935
(See Mahlstedt Materials, Inc.)

MAHLSTEDT MATERIALS, INC. (NY)
Dissolved by proclamation of the New York Secretary of State 12/15/47

MAHOGANY MINERALS RESOURCES INC. OLD (BC)
Common no par split (2) for (1) by issuance of (1) additional share 11/26/86
Common no par reclassified as Class B Subordinate no par 3/30/87
Merged into Mahogany Mineral Resources Inc. (New) 7/7/87
Each share Class B Subordinate no par exchanged for (1-1/9) share Class B Subordinate no par
Mahogany Minerals Resources Inc. (New) recapitalized as International Mahogany Corp. 9/8/88 which recapitalized as Reliant Ventures Ltd. 6/6/2000 which name changed to Esperanza Silver Corp. 5/14/2003

MAHOGANY MINERALS RES INC NEW (BC)
Recapitalized as International Mahogany Corp. 09/08/1988
Each share Class B Subordinate no par exchanged for (0.5) share Class B Subordinate no par
International Mahogany Corp. recapitalized as Reliant Ventures Ltd. 06/06/2000 which name changed to Esperanza Silver Corp. 05/14/2003 which name changed to Esperanza Resources Corp. 07/19/2010

MAHOGANY MINING CO. LTD. (BC)
Name changed to Mahogany Minerals Resources Inc. (Old) 12/17/1981
Each share Common no par exchanged for (1) share Common no par
Mahogany Minerals Resources Inc. (Old) merged into Mahogany Minerals Resources Inc. (New) 07/07/1987 which recapitalized as International Mahogany Corp. 09/08/1988 which recapitalized as Reliant Ventures Ltd. 06/06/2000 which name changed to Esperanza Silver Corp. 05/14/2003 which name changed to Esperanza Resources Corp. 07/19/2010

MAHON TECHNOLOGY GROUP INC (DE)
Merged into Banbury Corp. 12/13/71
Each share Common $1 par exchanged for $11.50 cash

MAHONEY-RYAN AIRCRAFT CORP.
Acquired by Detroit Aircraft Corp. 00/00/1929
Details not available

MAHONING COAL RR CO (OH)
Preferred $50 par called for redemption 12/31/79
Liquidation completed
Each share Common $50 par received initial distribution of $293.54 cash 2/29/80
Each share Common $50 par received second distribution of $177 cash 3/11/80
Each share Common $50 par received third distribution of $46.84 cash 2/27/81

Each share Common $50 par received fourth distribution of $550 cash 2/27/81
Each share Common $50 par exchanged for fifth and final distribution of $120 cash 1/7/82
Note: a) Distribution is certain only for certificates surrendered prior to 5/1/85 b) Distribution may also be made for certificates surrendered between 5/1/85 and 12/31/86 c) No distribution will be made for certificates surrendered after 12/31/86

MAHONING INVESTMENT CO.
Merged into Rochester & Pittsburgh Coal Co. in 1950
Each share Common exchanged for (0.25) share Common
(See Rochester & Pittsburgh Coal Co.)

MAHONING NATL BANCORP INC (OH)
Common $10 par changed to no par 02/12/1996
Common no par split (2) for (1) by issuance of (1) additional share payable 05/15/1996 to holders of record 04/30/1996
Merged into Sky Financial Group, Inc. 10/01/1999
Each share Common no par exchanged for (1.66) shares Common no par
Sky Financial Group, Inc. merged into Huntington Bancshares Inc. 07/02/2007

MAHONING NATL BK (YOUNGSTOWN, OH)
Each share Common $25 par exchanged for (2) shares Common $12.50 par 00/00/1951
Each share Common $12.50 par exchanged for (1.25) shares Common $10 par 07/21/1957
Common $10 par split (3) for (1) by issuance of (2) additional shares 04/30/1990
Stock Dividends - 10% 01/19/1956; 16-2/3% 10/15/1971; 50% 06/10/1977
Under plan of reorganization each share Common $10 par automatically became (1) share Mahoning National Bancorp, Inc. Common $10 par 04/30/1992
Mahoning National Bancorp, Inc. merged into Sky Financial Group, Inc. 10/01/1999 which merged into Huntington Bancshares Inc. 07/02/2007

MAI CORP (DE)
Charter cancelled and declared inoperative and void for non-payment of taxes 8/1/2000

MAI LIQUIDATING CO. (NJ)
Liquidation completed
Each share Capital Stock $2.50 par exchanged for initial distribution of $7.50 cash 6/13/77
Each share Capital Stock $2.50 par received second distribution of $4.50 cash 9/21/77
Each share Capital Stock $2.50 par received third distribution of $0.70 cash 1/30/81
Each share Capital Stock $2.50 par received fourth and final distribution of $2.925 cash 12/15/81

MAI SYS CORP (DE)
Name changed 11/07/1990
Name changed from MAI Basic Four, Inc. to MAI Systems Corp. 11/07/1990
Plan of reorganization under Chapter 11 Federal Bankruptcy Code effective 01/27/1994
No stockholders' equity for old Common 25¢ par
New Common 1¢ par split (5) for (4)

by issuance of (0.25) additional share 08/10/1995
Each share new Common 1¢ par exchanged for (0.00666666) share new Common 1¢ par 11/23/2005
Note: Holders of (149) or fewer pre-split shares received $0.17 cash per share
Acquired by SoftBrands, Inc. 08/14/2006
Each share new Common 1¢ par exchanged for $32.32 cash
Note: Each share new Common 1¢ par received an additional distribution of $6.29306417 cash from escrow 01/02/2008

MAIC HLDGS INC (DE)
Stock Dividends - 6% payable 2/5/96 to holders of record 1/4/96; 6% payable 2/17/97 to holders of record 1/17/97
Name changed to Medical Assurance, Inc. 6/1/97

MAID RITE INDS INC (UT)
Name changed to Delta Rental Systems Inc. 12/15/87
(See Delta Rental Systems Inc.)

MAID-RITE VENTURES INC (DE)
Name changed to Grandee Corp. and Common 1¢ par changed to $0.00333 par 09/23/1985
Grandee Corp. name changed to Cassco Capital Corp. (Old) 09/01/1987 which name changed back to International K.C. Jakes BBQ & Grill, Inc. 07/20/1992 which name changed to Cassco Capital Corp. 07/18/1994 which recapitalized as Diversified Technology Inc. (DE) 06/23/2000 which reincorporated in Nevada 10/04/2000 which reorganized as Diversified Technologies Group, Inc. 11/14/2000 which name changed to X-Change Corp. 07/30/2001 which name changed to Endocan Corp. 11/06/2013

MAIDEN CAPITAL FINANCING TR (DE)
144A Trust Preferred Securities called for redemption at $1,000 on 01/15/2014
Trust Preferred Securities called for redemption at $1,000 on 01/15/2014

MAIDEN CREEK MINING CO INC (CANADA)
Dissolved for non-compliance 06/10/2004

MAIDEN HLDGS LTD (BERMUDA)
Each share 7.25% Mandatory Conv. Preference Ser. B 1¢ par automatically became (3.6573) shares Common 1¢ par 09/15/2016 (Additional Information in Active)

MAIDEN HLDGS NORTH AMER LTD (DE)
8.25% Non-Cum Preference Ser. A 1¢ par called for redemption at $25 on 06/15/2016

MAIDENFORM BRANDS INC (DE)
Issue Information - 12,794,067 shares COM offered at $17 per share on 07/22/2005
Acquired by HanesBrands Inc. 10/07/2013
Each share Common 1¢ par exchanged for $23.50 cash

MAIDSTONE CAP INC (FL)
Name changed to Check Express, Inc. 12/23/88
(See Check Express, Inc.)

MAII HLDGS INC (TX)
SEC revoked common stock registration 10/21/2008

MAIL BOXES COAST TO COAST INC (DE)
Each (15) shares Common 1¢ par exchanged for (1) share Common $0.0007 par 08/10/1992

Name changed to North American Technologies Group, Inc. 02/01/1993
(See North American Technologies Group, Inc.)

MAIL BOXES ETC (CA)
Common no par split (6) for (5) by issuance of (0.2) additional share 7/15/88
Common no par split (3) for (2) by issuance of (0.5) additional share 10/16/89
Common no par split (4) for (3) by issuance of (1/3) additional share 4/12/91
Common no par split (2) for (1) by issuance of (1) additional share 4/13/92
Stock Dividend - 20% 2/9/87
Merged into U.S. Office Products Co. 11/21/97
Each share Common no par exchanged for (1.349) shares Common $0.001 par
(See U.S. Office Products Co.)

MAIL COM INC (DE)
Issue Information - 6,850,000 shares CL A offered at $7 per share on 06/17/1999
Name changed to EasyLink Services Corp. 04/03/2001
(See EasyLink Services Corp.)

MAIL HOUSE INC (MN)
Under plan of merger each share Common 10¢ par exchanged for $2.50 cash 5/25/83

MAIL MART INDUSTRIES, INC. (NY)
Assets sold for benefit of creditors 3/29/73
No stockholders' equity

MAIL-WELL INC (CO)
Reincorporated 05/30/1997
Common 1¢ par split (3) for (2) by issuance of (0.5) additional share payable 06/06/1997 to holders of record 06/02/1997 Ex date - 06/09/1997
State of incorporation changed from (DE) to (CO) 05/30/1997
Common 1¢ par split (2) for (1) by issuance of (1) additional share payable 06/10/1998 to holders of record 06/01/1998 Ex date - 06/11/1998
Name changed to Cenveo, Inc. 05/17/2004
(See Cenveo, Inc.)

MAILE INTL INC (NV)
Recapitalized as Simex/NK Technologies, Inc. (NV) 04/28/1998
Each share Common $0.001 par exchanged for (0.45248868) share Common $0.001 par
Simex/NK Technologies, Inc. (NV) reincorporated in Delaware as Simex Technologies, Inc. 04/06/1999 which recapitalized as College Tonight, Inc. 03/28/2008 which name changed to CT Holdings, Inc. 09/03/2009

MAILKEY CORP (NV)
Name changed to IElement Corp. 08/25/2005
(See IElement Corp.)

MAILMAN CORP., LTD. (QC)
Reverted to private company by purchase of all but (2) stockholders' shares by offer made in August 1964

MAILTEC INC (NV)
Each share old Common $0.001 par exchanged for (0.25) share new Common $0.001 par 10/30/2007
Name changed to Provision Holding, Inc. 02/14/2008

MAIN BK & TR CO (SAN ANTONIO, TX)
Stock Dividends - 10% 1/2/62; 10% 1/19/63; 10% 1/21/64; 10% 2/10/65; 11.31% 2/7/66; 10% 2/23/67; 10.3% 2/10/68; 12.3% 2/17/69; 10%

2/13/70; 10.61% 3/22/71; 10% 5/11/73
Merged into First International Bancshares, Inc. 8/6/74
Each share Common $5 par exchanged for (0.58) share Common $5 par
First International Bancshares, Inc. name changed to InterFirst Corp. 12/31/81 which merged into First RepublicBank Corp. 6/6/87
(See First RepublicBank Corp.)

MAIN DLR STORES INC (TN)
Merged into Walker Delaware, Inc. 5/1/75
Each share Common $1 par exchanged for $5.77 cash

MAIN LINE BANCSHARES INC (PA)
Merged into Keystone Financial Inc. 08/03/1992
Each share Common $5 par exchanged for (0.92) share Common $2 par
Keystone Financial Inc. merged into M&T Bank Corp. 10/06/2000

MAIN LINE FLEETS INC (PA)
Charter revoked for failure to file reports and pay fees 12/31/2001

MAIN ST TR INC (IL)
Stock Dividends - 5% payable 09/21/2000 to holders of record 09/01/2000 Ex date - 09/05/2000; 5% payable 09/21/2001 to holders of record 09/04/2001
Merged into First Busey Corp. 08/01/2007
Each share Common 1¢ par exchanged for (1.55) shares Common $0.001 par

MAIN STR A C INC (CA)
Name changed 10/24/1997
Name changed from Main Street Athletic Clubs, Inc. to Main Street AC, Inc. 10/24/1997
Recapitalized as Mentor Capital, Inc. (CA) 04/07/2008
Each share Common no par exchanged for (0.001) share Common no par
Mentor Capital, Inc. (CA) reincorporated in Delaware 09/24/2015

MAIN STR BANCORP INC (MI)
Company's sole asset placed in receivership 10/10/2008
Stockholders' equity unlikely

MAIN STR BANCORP INC (PA)
Stock Dividend - 7% payable 12/15/1998 to holders of record 11/30/1998
Merged into Sovereign Bancorp, Inc. 03/08/2002
Each share Common $1 par exchanged for (1.25988) shares Common no par
Sovereign Bancorp, Inc. merged into Banco Santander, S.A. 01/30/2009

MAIN STR BKS INC (GA)
Merged into BB&T Corp. 6/1/2006
Each share Common no par exchanged for (0.6602) share Common $5 par

MAIN STR BKS INC (PA)
Common $1 par split (4) for (1) by issuance of (3) additional shares payable 9/16/98 to holders of record 9/1/98
Merged into First Sterling Banks, Inc. (Old) 5/24/2000
Each share Common $1 par exchanged for (1.01) shares Common no par
First Sterling Banks, Inc. (Old) name changed to First Sterling Banks, Inc. (New) 5/24/2000 which name changed to Main Street Banks, Inc. (GA) 1/2/2001

MAIN STR BANKSHARES INC (NC)
Merged into Yadkin Valley Bank & Trust Co. (Elkin, NC) 08/02/2002

Each share Common $5 par exchanged for (1.176) shares Common $5 par and $5.55 cash
Yadkin Valley Bank & Trust Co. (Elkin, NC) reorganized as Yadkin Valley Financial Corp. 07/01/2006 which recapitalized as Yadkin Financial Corp. 05/28/2013 which recapitalized as Yadkin Financial Corp. 05/28/2013 which merged into F.N.B. Corp. 03/11/2017

MAIN STR CMNTY BANCORP INC (MA)
Merged into Affiliated Community Bancorp, Inc. 10/19/95
Each share Common 1¢ par exchanged for (1) share Common 10¢ par
Affiliated Community Bancorp, Inc. merged into UST Corp. 8/7/98
(See UST Corp.)

MAIN STR RESTAURANT GROUP INC (DE)
Name changed 7/15/2004
Each share old Common $0.001 par exchanged for (0.25) share new Common $0.001 par 7/24/95
Name changed from Main St. & Main Inc. to Main Street Restaurant Group, Inc. 7/15/2004
Acquired by Braid Main Street, Inc. 6/30/2006
Each share Common $0.001 par exchanged for $6.40 cash

MAIN STREET EQUITIES INC. (UT)
Recapitalized as Aledo Oil & Gas Co. 12/11/81
Each share Common 1¢ par exchanged for (0.2) share Common 1¢ par
Aledo Oil & Gas Co. name changed to Spindletop Oil & Gas Co. (UT) 1/24/83 which merged into Spindletop Oil & Gas Co. (TX) 7/13/90

MAINBREAK GOLD MINES LTD. (ON)
Charter revoked for failure to file reports and pay fees 8/25/66

MAINE & MARITIMES CORP (ME)
Acquired by BHE Holdings Inc. 12/21/2010
Each share Common $7 par exchanged for $45 cash

MAINE & NEW BRUNSWICK ELECTRICAL POWER CO., LTD. (NB)
Each share 6% Perpetual Debenture Stock $100 par exchanged for $100 cash 3/26/74
Public interest eliminated

MAINE CENT RR CO (ME)
Merged into United States Filter Corp. 12/10/80
Each share Common $100 par exchanged for $100 cash
(Additional Information in Active)

MAINE FIDELITY FIRE & CASUALTY CO. (ME)
Name changed to Maine Insurance Co. in 1955
Maine Insurance Co. placed in receivership 2/12/71

MAINE FIDELITY LIFE INSURANCE CO. (ME)
Capital Stock $10 par changed to $6 par 9/5/57
Capital Stock $6 par changed to $4 par 4/11/58
Capital Stock $4 par changed to $1.50 par and (1) additional share issued 4/22/59
Capital Stock $1.50 par changed to $1.34 par 5/25/62
Capital Stock $1.34 par changed to $1.24 par 8/31/62
Capital Stock $1.24 par changed to $1.15 par 11/29/63
Acquired by NGM Corp. 3/28/74
Each share Capital Stock $1.15 par exchanged for $10 cash

MAINE GAS COMPANIES
Merged into Portland Gas Light Co. share for share in 1936
Portland Gas Light Co. merged into Northern Utilities, Inc. (ME) 8/11/66 which merged into Northern Utilities, Inc. (NH) 6/30/69 which merged into Bay State Gas Co. (New) 10/30/79 which merged into Nipsco Industries, Inc. 2/12/99 which name changed to NiSource Inc. (IN) 4/14/99 which reincorporated in Delaware 11/1/2000

MAINE INS CO (ME)
Common $3 par changed to $1 par and (1) additional share issued 8/28/59
Common $1 par changed to 60¢ par 7/18/61
Common 60¢ par changed to 50¢ par 3/28/62
Each share Common 50¢ par exchanged for (0.5) share Common $1 par 8/26/66
Declared insolvent and placed in receivership 2/12/71
Receiver opined assets insufficient to pay claims and stock is apparently worthless

MAINE MINING & EXPLORATION CORP. (ME)
Charter suspended for non-payment of franchise taxes 00/00/1956

MAINE NATL BK (PORTLAND, ME)
Stock Dividends - 10% 5/1/74; 10% 6/1/79
Reorganized as Maine National Corp. 2/18/83
Each share Capital Stock $10 par exchanged for (2) shares Common $5 par
Maine National Corp. merged into Bank of New England Corp. 12/18/85
(See Bank of New England Corp.)

MAINE NATL CORP (ME)
Stock Dividends - 20% 3/31/83; 10% 1/19/84
Merged into Bank of New England Corp. 12/18/85
Each share Common $5 par exchanged for (0.997) share Common $5 par
(See Bank of New England Corp.)

MAINE PUB SVC CO (ME)
Common $10 par changed to $7 par and (0.5) additional share issued 05/31/1955
Common $7 par split (2) for (1) by issuance of (1) additional share 03/03/1989
4.75% Preferred $50 par called for redemption 03/31/1990
9-5/8% Preferred $50 par called for redemption 04/02/1990
9-7/8% Preferred $50 par called for redemption 04/02/1990
Stock Dividend - 30% 07/14/1961
Under plan of reorganization each share Common $7 par automatically became (1) share Maine & Maritimes Corp. Common $7 par 06/30/2003
(See Maine & Maritimes Corp.)

MAINE SLATE PRODUCTS CORP. (DE)
No longer in existence having become inoperative and void for non-payment of taxes 4/1/55

MAINE SUGAR INDS INC (ME)
Charter suspended 7/22/92

MAINE YANKEE ATOMIC PWR CO (ME)
7.48% Preferred $100 par called for redemption at $100 on 1/17/2000
Public interest eliminated

MAINFORT MARINE INTL CORP (BC)
Struck off register and declared dissolved for failure to file returns 03/04/1994

MAINFRAME ENTMT INC (CANADA)
Acquired by Rainmaker Income Fund 10/31/2006
Each share Common no par exchanged for $0.24 cash

MAINLAND BK (LINWOOD, NJ)
Stock Dividend - 50% 11/11/74
Merged into National Community Bank of New Jersey (Rutherford, NJ) 12/31/81
Each share Capital Stock $10 par exchanged for $9.70 cash

MAINLAND CAP ASSOC INC (DE)
Name changed to Southeast First Capital Corp. 3/14/89

MAINLAND FINL SVCS INC (DE)
Charter cancelled and declared inoperative and void for non-payment of taxes 3/1/79

MAINLAND RES INC (NV)
Old Common $0.0001 par split (20) for (1) by issuance of (19) additional shares payable 03/10/2008 to holders of record 02/26/2008 Ex date - 03/11/2008
Old Common $0.0001 par split (3) for (2) by issuance of (0.5) additional share payable 05/28/2008 to holders of record 05/16/2008 Ex date - 05/29/2008
Old Common $0.0001 par split (2) for (1) by issuance of (1) additional share payable 07/10/2009 to holders of record 06/16/2009 Ex date - 07/13/2009
Each share old Common $0.0001 par exchanged for (0.1) share new Common $0.0001 par 03/23/2012
Charter revoked 06/30/2014

MAINLINE BANCORP INC (PA)
Merged into S&T Bancorp, Inc. 03/09/2012
Each share Common no par exchanged for (0.04152662) share Common $2.50 par and $61.11 cash

MAINLINE CABLEVISION KAMLOOPS LTD (BC)
Name changed to Kamloops Cablenet Ltd. 5/13/81
(See Kamloops Cabienet Ltd.)

MAINLINE HLDG CORP (UT)
Recapitalized as Tulsa Oil & Gas Co. 6/27/83
Each share Common 1¢ par exchanged for (0.1) share Common $0.001 par

MAINSOURCE FINL GROUP INC (IN)
Common no par split (3) for (2) by issuance of (0.5) additional share payable 04/16/2004 to holders of record 03/31/2004 Ex date - 04/19/2004
Stock Dividends - 5% payable 01/17/2003 to holders of record 12/31/2002 Ex date - 12/27/2002; 5% payable 01/09/2004 to holders of record 12/22/2003 Ex date - 12/18/2003; 5% payable 01/15/2005 to holders of record 12/31/2004 Ex date - 12/29/2004; 5% payable 01/16/2007 to holders of record 12/31/2006 Ex date - 12/27/2006
Merged into First Financial Bancorp 04/02/2018
Each share Common no par exchanged for (1.3875) shares Common no par

MAINSPRING INC (DE)
Issue Information - 4,000,000 shares COM offered at $12 per share on 07/26/2000
Merged into International Business Machines Corp. 6/7/2001
Each share Common 1¢ par exchanged for $4 cash

MAINSTAY DEFINEDTERM MUN OPPORTUNITIES FD (DE)
Name changed to MainStay MacKay DefinedTerm Municipal Opportunities Fund 03/01/2018

MAINSTREAM ENGR INC (CA)
Merged into Raycomm Transworld Industries, Inc. 12/11/89
Each share Common 2¢ par exchanged for (0.6) share Preferred Ser. B $10 par and (0.6) Common Stock Purchase Warrant expiring 9/30/94
(See Raycomm Transworld Industries, Inc.)

MAINSTREAM ENTMT INC (FL)
Name changed to First Power & Light, Inc. 07/22/2013
First Power & Light, Inc. name changed to Volt Solar Systems, Inc. 05/01/2014
(See Volt Solar Systems, Inc.)

MAINSTREAM SEMICONDUCTOR CORP (ID)
Name changed to Ocotillo Enterprises Inc. 4/18/96
(See Octillo Enterprises Inc.)

MAINSTREET BK (FAIRFAX, VA)
Location changed 08/13/2012
Location changed from (Herndon, VA) to (Fairfax, VA) 08/13/2012
Under plan of reorganization each share Common $4 par automatically became (1) share MainStreet Bancshares, Inc. Common $4 par 07/15/2016

MAINSTREET BANKSHARES INC (VA)
Stock Dividend - 10% payable 12/15/2006 to holders of record 11/30/2006 Ex date - 12/04/2006
Merged into American National Bankshares Inc. 12/31/2014
Each share Common no par exchanged for (0.482) share Common $1 par and $3.46 cash

MAINSTREET FINL CORP (USA)
Reported out of business 07/16/2010
Stockholders' equity unlikely

MAINSTREET FINL CORP (VA)
Name changed 6/1/98
Common $5 par split (2) for (1) by issuance of (1) additional share payable 3/15/96 to holders of record 3/4/96
Name changed from MainStreet BankGroup Inc. to MainStreet Financial Corp. 6/1/98
Merged into BB&T Corp. 3/8/99
Each share Common $5 par exchanged for (1.18) shares Common $5 par

MAINSTREET HEALTH INVTS INC (BC)
Each share old Common no par exchanged for (0.004) share new Common no par 06/02/2016
Name changed to Invesque Inc. 01/08/2018

MAIONE COS INC (NJ)
Name changed 9/18/88
Name changed from Maione-Hirschberg Companies, Inc. to Maione Companies, Inc. 9/18/88
Charter revoked for failure to file reports and pay fees 10/11/95

MAIRS & POWER FUND, INC. (MN)
Name changed to Mairs & Power Growth Fund, Inc. 3/19/62

MAIRS & POWER INCOME FD INC (MN)
Name changed to Mairs & Power Balanced Fund, Inc. 5/19/97

MAISLIN INDS LTD (QC)
Declared dissolved for failure to file reports and pay fees 7/28/90

MAISON PORTIER HLDGS LTD (NV)
Each (500) shares old Common $0.001 par exchanged for (1) share new Common $0.001 par 8/25/98
Note: No holder will receive fewer than (100) post-split shares

Name changed to Global Healthcare Communications USA Corp. 9/30/98

MAISONDOR GOLD MINES LTD.
Succeeded by Dencroft Mines Ltd. 00/00/1955
Details not available

MAISONETTE INTL ENTERPRISES LTD (NV)
Each share old Common no par exchanged for (2) shares new Common no par 10/07/2004
Recapitalized as New Asia Inc. 03/21/2008
Each share new Common no par exchanged for (0.002) share Common no par
(See New Asia Inc.)

MAJESCO ENTERTAINMENT CO (DE)
Name changed 04/11/2005
Each share old Common $0.001 par exchanged for (0.14285714) share new Common $0.001 par 12/31/2004
Name changed from Majesco Holdings, Inc. to Majesco Entertainment Co. 04/11/2005
Each share new Common $0.001 par exchanged again for (0.14285714) share new Common $0.001 par 06/13/2014
Each share new Common $0.001 par exchanged again for (0.16666666) share new Common $0.001 par 08/01/2016
Name changed to PolarityTE, Inc. 01/11/2017

MAJESCO INC (DE)
Each share Common 10¢ par exchanged for (0.333333) share Common 30¢ par 4/26/71
Adjudicated bankrupt 6/9/77
Stockholders' equity unlikely

MAJESTIC APARTMENT BUILDING CORP. (IL)
Dissolved in 1955
Details not available

MAJESTIC CAP CORP (CO)
Declared defunct and inoperative for failure to file reports and pay taxes 10/21/72

MAJESTIC CONTRACTORS LTD (ON)
Merged into Banister Pipelines 1/15/93
Each share Common no par exchanged for $6.65 cash

MAJESTIC COS LTD (NV)
Each share old Common $0.001 par received distribution of (0.14285714) share Global Diversified Industries Inc. Common $0.001 par payable 03/18/2002 to holders of record 12/11/2001
Each share old Common $0.001 par exchanged for (0.03333333) share new Common $0.001 par 06/06/2002
SEC revoked common stock registration 04/07/2008

MAJESTIC CREATIONS INC (NY)
Merged into Teledata, Inc. 6/5/70
Each share Common 1¢ par exchanged for (0.5) share Common 10¢ par
Teledata, Inc. name changed to TDA Industries, Inc. 12/2/70
(See TDA Industries, Inc.)

MAJESTIC DEV MGMT CORP (MN)
Recapitalized as Worldwide Leisure Corp. 02/20/1997
Each share Common no par exchanged for (0.5) share Common no par
Worldwide Leisure Corp. name changed to Wellness Universe Corp. 06/04/1999
(See Wellness Universe Corp.)

MAJESTIC DEVELOPMENT CORP. (FL)
Name changed to Afram Inc. 2/24/70
(See Afram Inc.)

MAJESTIC ELECTR STORES INC (ON)
Acquired by Adventure Electronics Inc. 7/11/94
Each share Common no par exchanged for (0.0092) share Common no par and (0.021) Common Stock Purchase Warrant expiring 7/11/96
(See Adventure Electronics Inc.)

MAJESTIC ELECTRO INDS LTD (DE)
Stock Dividend - 25% 8/3/81
Charter cancelled and declared inoperative and void for non-payment of taxes 3/1/83

MAJESTIC EXPLS LTD (BC)
Involuntarily dissolved 9/25/78
Details not available

MAJESTIC FIRE INSURANCE CO.
Merged into American Colony Insurance Co. in 1933
(See American Colony Insurance Co.)

MAJESTIC GOLD MINES, LTD. (ON)
Charter revoked for failure to file reports and pay fees 11/9/50

MAJESTIC HOUSEHOLD UTILITIES CORP.
Acquired by Grigsby-Grunow Co. in 1931 which became bankrupt in 1934

MAJESTIC MINES LTD. (BC)
Recapitalized as Majestic Explorations Ltd. 6/5/69
Each share Capital Stock 50¢ par exchanged for (1) share Capital Stock 50¢ par
Majestic Explorations Ltd. involuntarily dissolved 9/25/78

MAJESTIC MNG CORP (BC)
Name changed to Majestic Resources Corp. 12/17/1981
Majestic Resources Corp. recapitalized as International Majestic Holdings Ltd. 12/02/1985

MAJESTIC OIL & MINING CO. (UT)
Each share Capital Stock 5¢ par exchanged for (0.05) share Capital Stock $1 par 07/18/1962
Recapitalized as American Mining Co. (UT) 05/05/1964
Each share Capital Stock $1 par exchanged for (0.1) share Capital Stock $10 par
American Mining Co. (UT) merged into Toledo Mining Co. 09/16/1968 which name changed to Toledo Technology, Inc. 03/26/1984 which recapitalized as HIPP International Inc. 08/31/1994 which name changed to Assembly & Manufacturing Systems Corp. 04/12/1995 which recapitalized as American Ship Inc. 09/05/1997 which name changed to Petshealth, Inc. 05/20/1998
(See Petshealth, Inc.)

MAJESTIC PENN ST INC (DE)
Reincorporated 06/29/1973
Stock Dividends - 10% 07/31/1967; 10% 07/31/1968; 10% 08/06/1969
State of incorporation changed from (PA) to (DE) and Common no par changed to 10¢ par 06/29/1973
Reincorporated under the laws of Pennsylvania 02/01/1976

MAJESTIC PENN ST INC (PA)
Each share old Common 10¢ par exchanged for (1/6,000) share new Common 10¢ par 05/31/1983
Note: In effect holders received $2.50 cash per share and public interest was eliminated

MAJESTIC RADIO & TELEVISION CORP. (DE)
Bankrupt 00/00/1949

Charter cancelled and declared inoperative and void for non-payment of taxes 04/01/1952

MAJESTIC RES CORP (BC)
Recapitalized as International Majestic Holdings Ltd. 12/2/85
Each share Common no par exchanged for (0.2) share Common no par

MAJESTIC RESOURCES INC. (UT)
Reorganized under the laws of Texas as Alta Energy Corp. 6/3/81
Each share Common 1¢ par exchanged for (0.25) share Common 1¢ par
Alta Energy Corp. (TX) reorganized in Delaware 1/29/93 which merged into Devon Energy Corp. (DE) 5/18/94 which reincorporated in (OK) 6/7/95 which merged into Devon Energy Corp. (New) (DE) 8/17/99

MAJESTIC SILVER-LEAD MINES INC (ID)
Capital Stock 10¢ par changed to 5¢ par 5/19/69
Merged into Sogelec America Corp. 1/10/94
Details not available

MAJESTIC SPECIALTIES, INC. (OH)
Acquired by Genesco Inc. on a (1) for (2.8512) basis 2/24/65

MAJESTIC UTILITIES CORP. (CO)
Stock Dividend - 10% 5/15/62
Proclaimed defunct and inoperative for failure to pay taxes 10/13/66

MAJESTIC WILEY CONTRACTORS LTD (AB)
Reincorporated under the laws of Ontario 12/17/77
Majestic Wiley Contractors Ltd. (Ont.) name changed to Majestic Contractors Ltd. 5/6/83
(See Majestic Contractors Ltd.)

MAJOR AUTOMOTIVE COS INC (NV)
Each share old Common 1¢ par exchanged for (1) share new Common 1¢ par to reflect a (1) for (1,000) reverse split followed by a (1,000) for (1) forward split 03/13/2006
Note: Holders of (999) or fewer pre-split shares received $1.90 cash per share
Each (3,000,000) shares new Common 1¢ par exchanged again for (1) share new Common 1¢ par 02/18/2011
Note: In effect holders received $0.44 cash per share and public interest was eliminated

MAJOR CREATIONS INC (NV)
Common $0.001 par split (36) for (1) by issuance of (35) additional shares payable 10/12/2006 to holders of record 10/12/2006
Name changed to Aegis Industries, Inc. 12/18/2006
Aegis Industries, Inc. name changed to Fortified Holdings Corp. 06/19/2007
(See Fortified Holdings Corp.)

MAJOR D CORP (CA)
Reincorporated 03/27/1970
State of incorporation changed from (UT) to (CA) 03/27/1970
Charter suspended for failure to file reports and pay taxes 02/01/1973

MAJOR ELECTRS CORP (NJ)
Reincorporated 4/15/77
Common 10¢ par split (2) for (1) by issuance of (1) additional share 3/29/72
State of incorporation changed from (NY) to (NJ) 4/15/77
Name changed to Emerson Radio Corp. (NJ) 5/3/77
(See Emerson Radio Corp. (NJ))

MAJOR EXPL INC (CO)
Proclaimed dissolved for failure to file reports and pay fees 1/1/90

MAJOR FIN CORP (DE)
Each share Class A Common $10 par exchanged for (5) shares Common $2 par 07/31/1961
Merged into Centran Bancshares Corp. 07/31/1973
Each share Common $2 par or Class B Common no par exchanged for $6.80 cash
Note: Each share Common $2 par or Class B Common no par received an additional $1.70 cash upon completion of escrow agreement 10/01/1973
6% Preferred $10 par called for redemption 08/30/1973
Public interest eliminated

MAJOR GEN RES LTD (BC)
Plan of arrangement effective 5/3/2002
Each share Common no par exchanged for (1/3) share Commander Resources Ltd. Common no par and (0.095238) share Diamonds North Resources Ltd. (Old) Common no par
(See each company's listing)

MAJOR GROUP INC (FL)
Merged into Stoneridge Resources, Inc. 09/25/1992
Each share Common 20¢ par exchanged for (0.04) share Common 10¢ par
Stoneridge Resources, Inc. recapitalized as Acceptance Insurance Companies Inc. 12/22/1992
(See Acceptance Insurance Companies Inc.)

MAJOR (ALFRED J.) INC.
Dissolved in 1947

MAJOR LEAGUE BOWLING & REC INC (VA)
Each share Common $1 par exchanged for (0.1) share Common $10 par 11/21/1966
Common $10 par changed to $2 par and (2) additional shares issued 12/07/1971
Merged into MLB Corp. 01/02/1980
Each share Common $2 par exchanged for $13.50 cash

MAJOR LEAGUE ENTERPRISES INC (NY)
Name changed 8/17/87
Name changed from Major League Standardbreds, Inc. to Major League Enterprises, Inc. 8/17/87
Reorganized under the laws of Delaware as Arxa International Energy Inc. 10/17/95
Each share Common $0.001 par exchanged for (1) share Common $0.001 par
Arxa International Energy Inc. name changed to King Resources Inc. 12/11/2000

MAJOR MINERALS, INC. (NV)
Charter revoked for failure to file reports and pay fees 6/1/92

MAJOR MINES LTD. (BC)
Struck off register and declared dissolved for failure to file returns 5/15/69

MAJOR MOLYBDENITE MINES, LTD. (ON)
Charter cancelled in May 1956
No stockholders' equity

MAJOR OIL CORP (UT)
Proclaimed dissolved for failure to pay taxes 12/31/1982

MAJOR OIL INVESTMENTS LTD. (AB)
Acquired by Globe Oil Co. (1958) Ltd. 9/10/59
Each (1/40) Unit, Royalty Trust Certificates, Ordinary, Preferred or Net exchanged for Globe Oil Co. (1958) Ltd. Common $5 par on the following basis: No. 1 Well - (5) shares No. 2 Well - (10) shares No. 3 Well - (50) shares No. 4 Well - (5) shares No. 6 Well - (3) shares No. 7 Well - (2) shares No. 8 Well - (1) share No. 9 Well - (10) shares
Globe Oil Co. (1958) Ltd. merged into Trans-Canada Resources Ltd. (New) 11/1/82 which recapitalized as Consolidated Trans-Canada Resources Ltd. 9/22/88 which merged into Ranchmen's Resources Ltd. 9/30/89 which merged into Crestar Energy Inc. 10/11/95 which was acquired by Gulf Canada Resources Ltd. 11/13/2000
(See Gulf Canada Resources Ltd.)

MAJOR OIL LTD. (AB)
Merged into Majortrans Oil & Mines Ltd. on a (1) for (5) basis 1/16/57
Majortrans Oil & Mines Ltd. charter revoked 11/9/67

MAJOR PETE CO (UT)
Name changed to Tyche Petroleum Corp. and Common 20¢ par changed to 1¢ par 03/16/1977

MAJOR POOL EQUIP CORP (NJ)
Common 10¢ par split (6) for (5) by issuance of (0.2) additional share 9/30/67
Stock Dividends - 10% 9/30/63; 10% 9/30/64; 10% 9/30/65; 10% 9/30/66; 20% 9/30/69
Chapter 11 bankruptcy proceedings converted to Chapter 7 on 12/9/82
Stockholders' equity unlikely

MAJOR RLTY CORP (DE)
Merged into PBD Holdings, L.P. 5/19/98
Each share Common 1¢ par exchanged for $1.25 cash

MAJOR RES LTD (BC)
Recapitalized as Anvil Resources Ltd. 11/03/1982
Each share Common no par exchanged for (0.25) share Common no par
Anvil Resources Ltd. recapitalized as Geocore Exploration Inc. 07/24/2003 which recapitalized as Emerick Resources Corp. 12/31/2007 which name changed to Medgold Resources Corp. 12/17/2012

MAJOR TELEPHONE CORP. OF AMERICA (NV)
Charter permanently revoked for failure to file reports and pay fees in April 1990

MAJOR VIDEO CORP (NV)
Merged into Blockbuster Entertainment Corp. 1/17/89
Each share Common $0.025 par exchanged for (0.79051383) share Common 10¢ par
Blockbuster Entertainment Corp. merged into Viacom Inc. (Old) 9/30/94
(See Viacom Inc. (Old))

MAJOREM MINERALS LTD (BC)
Recapitalized as Radcliffe Resources Ltd. 08/27/1986
Each share Capital Stock no par exchanged for (0.2) share Capital Stock no par
Radcliffe Resources Ltd. recapitalized as Madison Energy Corp. (BC) 11/01/1993 which reincorporated in Alberta 08/29/2003
(See Madison Energy Corp.)

MAJORTECK INDS INC (BC)
Struck off register and declared dissolved for failure to file returns 2/15/91

MAJORTRANS OIL & MINES LTD. (ON)
Charter revoked for failure to file reports and pay fees 11/9/67

MAKAHA INC (DE)
Each share old Common $0.001 par exchanged for (0.02) share new Common $0.001 par 07/12/1993
Name changed to TerraCom Inc. 12/24/1993
(See TerraCom Inc.)

MAKALOT CORP.
Liquidated in 1945

MAKAOO DEV LTD (CANADA)
Recapitalized as International Makaoo Ltd. 03/07/1980
Each share Capital Stock no par exchanged for (1/3) share Capital Stock no par
International Makaoo Ltd. recapitalized as Non-Par Developments Ltd. (Canada) 12/17/1991 which reincorporated in British Columbia as Similkameen Hydro-Power Ltd. 08/17/1992 which recapitalized as Norte Resources Ltd. (BC) 7/25/96 which reorganized in Yukon as Banks Ventures Ltd. 04/06/1998 which name changed to Banks Energy Inc. 07/26/2004 which merged into Arapahoe Energy Corp. (New) 10/20/2005 which name changed to Canadian Phoenix Resources Corp. 01/07/2008 which recapitalized as Knol Resources Corp. 03/11/2013

MAKE IT HAPPEN MGMT (NV)
Name changed to E-Channels Corp. and (4) additional shares issued 05/23/2000
E-Channels Corp. recapitalized as ETI Expertise Technology Innovation Corp. 12/18/2001 which name changed to UC Hub Group, Inc. 06/21/2004
(See UC Hub Group, Inc.)

MAKE YOUR MOVE INC (NV)
Each (150) shares old Common $0.001 par exchanged for (1) share new Common $0.001 par 6/14/2004
Note: Holders of between (15,000) and (101) shares will receive (100) post split shares
Holders of (100) or fewer shares are not affected by the reverse split
Name changed to Texhoma Energy, Inc. 9/27/2004

MAKEMUSIC INC (MN)
Name changed 06/09/2006
Each share old Common no par exchanged for (0.1) share new Common no par 01/16/2003
Name changed from MakeMusic! Inc. to MakeMusic, Inc. 06/09/2006
Acquired by LaunchEquity Acquisition Partners, LLC Designated Series Education Partners 05/01/2013
Each share new Common no par exchanged for $4.85 cash

MAKEPEACE CAP CORP (TX)
Reorganized under the laws of Delaware as NetSalon Corp. 10/18/2000
Each share Common $0.001 par exchanged for (0.5) share Common $0.001 par
NetSalon Corp. name changed to Military Communications Technologies, Inc. 4/17/2003 which name changed to Carbon Race Corp. 10/16/2006

MAKER COMMUNICATIONS INC (DE)
Issue Information - 3,350,000 shares COM offered at $13 per share on 05/10/1999
Merged into Conexant Systems, Inc. 03/10/2000
Each share Common 1¢ par exchanged for (0.66) share Common $1 par
(See Conexant Systems, Inc.)

MAKEUP COM LTD (NV)
Each share old Common $0.001 par exchanged for (0.05) share new Common $0.001 par 08/08/2008
Name changed to LC Luxuries Ltd. 04/01/2010
LC Luxuries Ltd. name changed to General Cannabis, Inc. 11/19/2010 which name changed to SearchCore, Inc. 01/06/2012 which name changed to Wisdom Homes of America, Inc. 03/05/2015

MAKH GROUP CORP (NV)
Name changed to WeWin Group Corp. 08/03/2017

MAKHTESHIM-AGAN INDS LTD (ISRAEL)
Acquired by National Chemical Agrochemical Corp. Ltd. 10/18/2011
Each ADR for Ordinary exchanged for $11.099 cash
Note: An additional distribution of $0.394139 cash per ADR was paid 01/19/2012

MAKITA ELEC WKS LTD (JAPAN)
Stock Dividends - 10% 11/04/1976; 10% 05/30/1977; 10% 11/16/1979; 10% 11/19/1980; 10% 05/08/1981; 10% 05/10/1982; 10% 05/04/1984; 10% 05/06/1985; 10% 06/06/1990
Under plan of reorganization each ADR for Common automatically became (1) Makita Corp. Sponsored ADR for Common 04/01/1991

MAKKANOTTI GROUP CORP (NV)
Name changed to CURE Pharmaceutical Holding Corp. 12/19/2016

MAKLAW CORP. (DE)
Liquidation completed
Each share Capital Stock no par received initial distribution of $1 cash 12/29/1964
Each share Capital Stock no par received second distribution of $1.30 cash 01/15/1965
Each share Capital Stock no par received third distribution of 50¢ cash 04/21/1965
Each share Capital Stock no par exchanged for fourth and final distribution of (1) share Adobe Brick & Supply Co. Common $1 par 06/11/1965
(See Adobe Brick & Supply Co.)

MAKLYN VENTURE CAP CORP (AB)
Reorganized under the laws of Ontario as QuStream Corp. 04/07/2005
Each share Common no par exchanged for (0.5) share Common no par
QuStream Corp. name changed to PESA Corp. 04/10/2014

MAKO CAP INC (DE)
Name changed to O Media, Inc. 4/7/99
O Media, Inc. name changed to Original Media, Inc. 1/4/2000 which recapitalized as OMDA Oil & Gas Inc. 6/7/2002

MAKO HYDROCARBONS LTD (AUSTRALIA)
Name changed 05/18/2012
Name changed from Mako Energy Ltd. to Mako Hydrocarbons Ltd. 05/18/2012
ADR agreement terminated 04/16/2013
Each Sponsored ADR for Ordinary exchanged for (20) shares Ordinary
Note: Unexchanged ADR's will be sold and the proceeds, if any, held for claim after 08/15/2013

MAKO MARINE INTL INC (FL)
Issue Information - 1,500,000 Units consisting of (1) share COM and (1) WT offered at $4 per Unit on 08/23/1995
Merged into Trackaq, Inc. 12/29/97
Each share Common 1¢ par exchanged for $1.25 cash

MAKO SURGICAL CORP (DE)
Issue Information - 5,100,000 shares

COM offered at $10 per share on 02/14/2008
Acquired by Stryker Corp. 12/17/2013
Each share Common $0.001 par exchanged for $30 cash

MAKOVER INVT INC (GA)
Merged into Scudder Managed Municipal Bonds 06/22/1979
Each share Common $1 par exchanged for (0.857707) Share of Bene. Int. no par
(See Scudder Managed Municipal Bonds)

MAKRO ATACADISTA S A (BRAZIL)
GDR agreement terminated 02/12/2002
Each 144A GDR for Ordinary exchanged for $6.4076 cash

MAKUS RES INC (BC)
Struck off register and declared dissolved for failure to file returns 6/26/92

MALA NOCHE RES CORP (BC)
Recapitalized as Primero Mining Corp. 08/06/2010
Each share Common no par exchanged for (0.05) share Common no par
Primero Mining Corp. merged into First Majestic Silver Corp. 05/11/2018

MALABAR MINES LTD (BC)
Recapitalized as Majorem Minerals Ltd. 10/04/1982
Each share Capital Stock no par exchanged for (0.25) share Capital Stock no par
Majorem Minerals Ltd. recapitalized as Radcliffe Resources Ltd. 08/27/1986 which recapitalized as Madison Energy Corp. (BC) 11/01/1993 which reincorporated in Alberta 08/29/2003
(See Madison Energy Corp.)

MALABAR MINING CO. LTD. (BC)
Merged into Cosmic Nickel Mines Ltd. 02/23/1970
Each share Capital Stock no par exchanged for (1) share Capital Stock no par
Cosmic Nickel Mines Ltd. recapitalized as New Cosmic Industries Ltd. 05/16/1972 which name changed to Cosmic Industries Ltd. 08/08/1977
(See Cosmic Industries Ltd.)

MALABAR SILVER MINES LTD. (BC)
Name changed to Malabar Mines Ltd. 06/28/1978
Each share Capital Stock no par exchanged for (1) share Capital Stock no par
Malabar Mines Ltd. recapitalized as Majorem Minerals Ltd. 10/04/1982 which recapitalized as Radcliffe Resources Ltd. 08/27/1986 which recapitalized as Madison Energy Corp. (BC) 11/01/1993 which reincorporated in Alberta 08/29/2003
(See Madison Energy Corp.)

MALAGA BK (PALOS VERDES ESTATES, CA)
Common no par split (3) for (2) by issuance of (0.5) additional share payable 09/30/1998 to holders of record 09/15/1998
Common no par split (4) for (3) by issuance of (1/3) additional share payable 07/31/2000 to holders of record 07/21/2000 Ex date - 08/01/2000
Common no par split (5) for (3) by issuance of (1/6) additional share payable 04/30/2002 to holders of record 04/19/2002 Ex date - 05/01/2002
Stock Dividend - 5% payable 06/01/1999 to holders of record 05/10/1999
Reorganized as Malaga Financial Corp 06/05/2003

Each share Common no par exchanged for (1) share Common $0.001 par

MALAGA INC (QC)
Each share Common no par received distribution of (0.11699874) share Dynacor Gold Mines Inc. Common no par payable 11/01/2007 to holders of record 10/26/2007 Ex date - 10/24/2007
Filed a Notice of Intention to Make a Proposal under the Bankruptcy and Insolvency Act 06/06/2013
Stockholders' equity unlikely

MALAHAT ENERGY CORP (NV)
Name changed to PHC Holdings 12/22/2004
PHC Holdings recapitalized as Rudy 45 on 09/26/2005 which name changed to NMI Group, Inc. 07/13/2007

MALAHIDE PETE CORP (ON)
Reorganized under the laws of Yukon as Stratic Energy Corp. 12/12/1997
Each share Common no par exchanged for (0.05) share Common no par
(See Stratic Energy Corp.)

MALAN LIQUIDATING TR
Assets transferred 08/27/2004
Issue Information - 3,530,000 shares COM offered at $17 per share on 06/17/1994
Liquidation completed
Each share Common 1¢ par received initial distribution of $0.51 cash payable 09/30/2003 to holders of record 09/19/2003 Ex date - 09/17/2003
Each share Common 1¢ par received second distribution of $0.30 cash payable 01/26/2004 to holders of record 12/31/2003
Assets transferred from Malan Realty Investors, Inc. (MI) to Malan Liquidating Trust (DE) and Common 1¢ par reclassified as Units of Bene. Int. 08/27/2004
Each Unit of Bene. Int. received third distribution of $1 cash payable 10/29/2004 to holders of record 10/19/2004
Each Unit of Bene. Int. received fourth distribution of $0.50 cash payable 03/02/2005 to holders of record 01/31/2005
Each Unit of Bene. Int. received fifth distribution of $0.50 cash payable 08/03/2005 to holders of record 07/26/2005
Each Unit of Bene. Int. received sixth distribution of $2.25 cash payable 11/14/2005 to holders of record 11/10/2005
Each Unit of Bene. Int. received seventh distribution of $0.20 cash payable 10/09/2006 to holders of record 10/02/2006
Each Unit of Bene. Int. received eighth distribution of $1.25 cash payable 09/25/2007 to holders of record 09/17/2007
Each Unit of Bene. Int. received ninth and final distribution of $0.02 cash payable 01/12/2009 to holders of record 12/31/2008
Note: Certificates were not required to be surrendered and are without value

MALARTIC GOLD FIELDS QUEBEC LTD (QC)
Name changed 10/05/1965
Under plan of merger name changed from Malarctic Gold Fields Ltd. to Malarctic Gold Fields (Quebec) Ltd. and each share Capital Stock $1 par exchanged for (1) share Capital Stock $1 par 10/05/1965
Name changed to Les Terrains Auriferes Malartic (Quebec) Ltee. 09/13/1979
Les Terrains Auriferes Malartic

(Quebec) Ltee. merged into Lac Minerals Ltd. (Old) 12/31/1982 which merged into LAC Minerals Ltd. (New) 07/29/85 which was acquired by American Barrick Resources Corp. 10/17/1994 which name changed to Barrick Gold Corp. 01/18/1995

MALARTIC GOLD MINES LTD.
Reorganized as Canadian Malartic Gold Mines Ltd. on a (1) for (2) basis 00/00/1933
Canadian Malartic Gold Mines Ltd. merged into Canray Resources Ltd. 12/21/1976 which recapitalized as Exall Resources Ltd. 12/09/1983 which merged into Gold Eagle Mines Ltd. 12/27/2006 which was acquired by Goldcorp Inc. 09/25/2008

MALARTIC HYGRADE GOLD MINES (QUEBEC) LTD. (QC)
Reincorporated under the laws of Ontario as Malartic Hygrade Gold Mines (Canada) Ltd. 03/01/1975
Malartic Hygrade Gold Mines (Canada) Ltd. name changed to Republic Goldfields Inc. 06/10/1991
(See Republic Goldfields Inc.)

MALARTIC HYGRADE GOLD MINES CDA LTD (ON)
Name changed to Republic Goldfields Inc. 06/10/1991
(See Republic Goldfields Inc.)

MALARTIC HYGRADE GOLD MINES LTD. (ON)
Reorganized under the laws of Quebec as Malartic Hygrade Gold Mines (Quebec) Ltd. (QC) 08/15/1968
Each share Capital Stock $1 par exchanged for (0.1) share Capital Stock no par
Malartic Hygrade Gold Mines (Quebec) Ltd. (QC) reincorporated in Ontario as Malartic Hygrade Gold Mines (Canada) Ltd. 03/01/1975 which name changed to Republic Goldfields Inc. 06/10/1991
(See Republic Goldfields Inc.)

MALASPINA CAP LTD (AB)
Issue Information - 3,000,000 shares COM offered at $0.10 per share on 03/25/1997
Reorganized under the laws of Yukon as Miranda Mining Corp. 11/21/2001
Each share Common no par exchanged for (0.25) share Common no par
(See Miranda Mining Corp.)

MALAYAN CR LTD (SINGAPORE)
ADR agreement terminated 1/23/98
Each ADR for Ordinary S$1 par exchanged for $0.5082 cash

MALAYSIA ARPTS HLDGS BERHAD (MALAYSIA)
ADR agreement terminated 01/09/2017
No ADR's remain outstanding

MALAYSIA FD INC (MD)
Completely liquidated
Each share Common 1¢ par received first and final distribution of $9.48 cash payable 08/24/2012 to holders of record 08/17/2012

MALAYSIA PRO-GUARDIANS SEC MGMT CORP (NV)
Recapitalized as Shenzhen-ZhongRong Morgan Investment Holding Group Co., Ltd. 06/21/2017
Each share Common $0.001 par exchanged for (0.01428571) share Common $0.001 par

MALBAK LTD (SOUTH AFRICA)
ADR agreement terminated 3/30/98
Each Sponsored ADR for Ordinary no par exchanged for (1) Ordinary share no par
Note: Unclaimed Ordinary shares will

be sold and proceeds held for claim after 3/30/99

MALBAR GOLDFIELDS, LTD. (ON)
Charter revoked for failure to file reports and pay fees 8/24/64

MALBEC GOLD MINES, LTD. (ON)
Charter cancelled for failure to file reports and pay taxes 8/18/58

MALBEX RES INC (ON)
Each share old Common no par exchanged for (0.1) share new Common no par 01/08/2016
Name changed to Coin Hodl Inc. 09/10/2018

MALBOHM MOTORS CO. (OH)
Charter cancelled for failure to pay taxes 3/1/23

MALCOLM RES LTD (BC)
Name changed to Pan Pacific Petroleum Inc. 10/18/1988
(See Pan Pacific Petroleum Inc.)

MALDEN & MELROSE GAS LIGHT CO. (MA)
Under plan of merger each share Capital Stock $25 par exchanged for (1) share Common $25 par of Mystic Valley Gas Co. in 1953
Mystic Valley Gas Co. completely liquidated 12/28/73

MALDEN ELECTRIC CO. (MA)
Under plan of merger each share Capital Stock $25 par exchanged for (1) share Common $25 par of Suburban Electric Co. in 1953

MALDEN TR CO (MALDEN, MA)
Stock Dividends - 10% 02/15/1962; 10% 02/26/1969; 10% 03/15/1972; 50% 03/16/1981
Under plan of reorganization each share Capital Stock $10 par automatically became (1) share Malden Trust Corp. Common $10 par 08/15/1985
(See Malden Trust Corp.)

MALDEN TR CORP (MA)
Common $10 par split (6) for (1) by issuance of (5) additional shares 04/15/1987
Out of business 05/15/1992
No stockholders' equity

MALERS INC (DE)
Each share old Common $0.0001 par exchanged for (0.0005) share new Common $0.0001 par 6/19/2006
Name changed to Dot VN, Inc. 8/7/2006

MALETTE INC (ON)
Acquired by Tembec Inc. (QC) 07/25/1995
Each share Subordinate $1 par exchanged for (1.138) shares Class A Common no par, $16.50 cash or combination thereof
Each share Class A Common $1 par exchanged for (1.138) shares Class A Common no par, $16.50 cash or a combination thereof
Tembec Inc. (QC) reorganized in Canada 02/29/2008 which merged into Rayonier Advanced Materials Inc. 11/21/2017

MALETTE INDS INC (CANADA)
Dissolved for non-compliance 10/17/2008

MALETTE QUE INC (CANADA)
Acquired by Tembec Inc. 02/29/2000
Each share Common no par exchanged for $3.20 cash

MALEX INC (DE)
Common $0.00002 par changed to $0.001 par 11/13/2007
Name changed to China Wind Systems, Inc. 01/03/2008
China Wind Systems, Inc. name changed to Cleantech Solutions International, Inc. (DE) 06/16/2011 which reincorporated in Nevada 08/10/2012 which name changed to

Sharing Economy International Inc. 01/08/2018

MALIBU GRAND PRIX CORP (DE)
Merged into Malibu Acquisition Corp. 04/28/1989
Each share Common 1¢ par exchanged for $0.95 cash

MALIBU MINERALS INC (NV)
Name changed to Flex Fuels Energy, Inc. 07/16/2007
Flex Fuels Energy, Inc. name changed to Bio-AMD, Inc. 05/18/2011

MALKA RES LTD (BC)
Name changed to Electra Title Corp. 01/30/1985
Each share Common no par exchanged for (1) share Common no par
Electra Title Corp. recapitalized as B.I. Ventures Ltd. 02/13/1987
(See B.I Ventures Ltd.)

MALL BANK (WEST PALM BEACH, FL)
Reorganized as TMB Bankshares Inc. 6/13/83
Each share Common $1 par exchanged for (3) shares Common $1 par
(See TMB Bankshares Inc.)

MALLARD COACH INC (DE)
Plan of reorganization under Chapter 11 Federal Bankruptcy proceedings confirmed 09/00/1994
No stockholders' equity

MALLEN RED LAKE GOLD MINES LTD. (ON)
Recapitalized as New Mallen Red Lake Mines Ltd. 03/20/1961
Each share Common exchanged for (0.33333333) share Common
(See New Mallen Red Lake Mines Ltd.)

MALLICH QUEBEC GOLD MINES, LTD. (ON)
Charter cancelled for failure to file reports and pay taxes in 1962

MALLINCKRODT CHEMICAL WORKS (MO)
Class A Common $10 par and Class B Common $10 par changed to $3-1/3 par and (2) additional shares issued respectively 10/15/67
Class A Common $3-1/3 par and Class B Common $3-1/3 par changed to $1-2/3 par and (1) additional share issued respectively 11/15/71
Class A Common $1-2/3 par and Class B Common $1-2/3 par changed to $1 par and (1) additional share issued respectively 5/15/73
Recapitalized as Mallinckrodt, Inc. 4/23/74
Each share Class A Common $1 par automatically became (1) share Common $1 par
Each share Class B Common $1 par exchanged for (1) share Common $1 par
Mallinckrodt, Inc. merged into Avon Products, Inc. 3/9/82

MALLINCKRODT GROUP INC (NY)
Name changed to Mallinckrodt Inc. 10/16/1996
Mallinckrodt Inc. merged into Tyco International Ltd. (Bermuda) 10/17/2000 which reincorporated in Switzerland 03/17/2009 which merged into Johnson Controls International PLC 09/06/2016

MALLINCKRODT INC (MO)
Common $1 par split (3) for (2) by issuance of (0.5) additional share 5/25/81
Merged into Avon Products, Inc. 3/9/82
Each share Common $1 par exchanged for (1.667) shares Capital Stock 50¢ par

MALLINCKRODT INC (NY)
4% Preferred $100 par called for redemption at $110 on 11/30/2000
Merged into Tyco International Ltd. (Bermuda) 10/17/2000
Each share Common $1 par exchanged for (0.9384) share Common 20¢ par
Tyco International Ltd. (Bermuda) reincorporated in Switzerland 03/17/2009 which merged into Johnson Controls International PLC 09/06/2016

MALLINSON (H.R.) & CO., INC.
Bankrupt in 1947

MALLON MINERALS CORP (CO)
Reorganized as Mallon Resources Corp. 12/21/88
Each share Common $0.001 par exchanged for (0.07737286456) share Common 1¢ par
Mallon Resources Corp. merged into Black Hills Corp. 3/10/2003

MALLON RES CORP (CO)
Secondary Offering - 2,300,000 shares COM offered at $9.25 per share on 12/16/1997
Each share old Common 1¢ par exchanged for (0.25) share new Common 1¢ par 9/10/96
Merged into Black Hills Corp. 3/10/2003
Each share new Common 1¢ par exchanged for (0.044) share Common $1 par

MALLORY P R & CO INC (DE)
Common no par split (3) for (2) by issuance of (0.5) additional share 9/15/55
Common no par changed to $1 par 3/29/56
4-1/2% Preferred $50 par called for redemption 2/28/57
5% Conv. Preference Ser. A $50 par called for redemption 3/22/63
Common $1 par split (5) for (4) by issuance of (0.25) additional share 12/31/63
Common $1 par split (2) for (1) by issuance of (1) additional share 6/2/72
Stock Dividends - 20% 11/10/43; 20% 9/15/50; 25% 12/10/52
Merged into Dart Industries, Inc. 1/31/79
Each share Common $1 par exchanged for $51 cash

MALLORY RANDALL CORP (DE)
Each share Common 10¢ par exchanged for (1/6) share Common 60¢ par 5/8/76
Each share Class A 30¢ par exchanged for (1) share Common 60¢ par 3/2/79
Merged into Savoy Industries, Inc. 12/31/81
Each share Common 60¢ par exchanged for (2.75) shares Common 1¢ par
(See Savoy Industries, Inc.)

MALLORY RESTAURANTS INC (NY)
Completely liquidated 12/20/1971
Each share Class A Common 1¢ par exchanged for first and final distribution of (0.303902) share Pillsbury Co. Common no par
(See Pillsbury Co.)

MALLVISION INC (CO)
Recapitalized as Instant Medical Tests Inc. 4/12/87
Each share Common no par exchanged for (0.2) share Common no par
(See Instant Medical Tests Inc.)

MALOFILM COMMUNICATIONS INC (CANADA)
Each share Common no par exchanged for (0.5) share Class A Multiple no par and (0.5) share Class B Subordinate no par 07/05/1995
Name changed to Behaviour Communications Inc. 11/28/1997
Behaviour Communications Inc. name changed to MDP Worldwide Entertainment Inc. 06/05/2000 which name changed to M8 Entertainment Inc. 04/14/2004

MALONE & HYDE INC (TN)
Common $1 par split (5) for (4) by issuance of (0.25) additional share 11/10/67
Common $1 par split (2) for (1) by issuance of (1) additional share 11/15/68
Common $1 par split (3) for (2) by issuance of (0.5) additional share 2/28/72
Common $1 par split (2) for (1) by issuance of (1) additional share 10/15/82
Stock Dividends - 10% 10/20/64; 10% 12/3/74
Acquired by Pittco Acquisition Corp. 8/30/84
Each share Common $1 par exchanged for $35 cash

MALONE LIGHT & POWER CO.
Merged into Niagara Hudson Public Service Corp. which name was changed to Central New York Power Corp. 7/31/37
Each share $6 Preferred exchanged for (10) shares Common no par
Central New York Power Corp. merged into Niagara Mohawk Power Corp. 1/5/50

MALRITE COMMUNICATIONS GROUP INC (DE)
Stock Dividend - In Class A to holders of Common - 50% 06/27/1985
Acquired by MCG Merger Co. 02/21/1989
Each share Class A 1¢ par exchanged for $11.142 cash
Each share Common 1¢ par exchanged for $11.142 cash

MALTACOM P L C (MALTA)
Name changed to GO PLC 02/19/2007
(See GO PLC)

MALTOP, INC.
Succeeded by Toddy Corp. in 1928
(See Toddy Corp.)

MALVERN FED BANCORP INC (USA)
Reorganized under the laws of Pennsylvania as Malvern Bancorp, Inc. 10/12/2012
Each share Common 1¢ par exchanged for (1.0748) shares Common 1¢ par

MALVY TECHNOLOGY INC (DE)
Each share old Common no par exchanged for (0.05) share new Common no par 02/17/1995
Name changed to Metal Recovery Technologies Inc. 06/30/1995
(See Metal Recovery Technologies Inc.)

MAMBULAO CONSOLIDATED MINING (PHILIPPINES)
Dissolved 06/30/1968
Details not available

MAMIT LAKE MINING LTD. (BC)
Merged into New Copper Mountain Mines Ltd. 8/9/74
Each (2.5) shares Capital Stock no par exchanged for (1) share Capital Stock no par

MAMMA COM INC (ON)
Name changed to Copernic Inc. 06/21/2007
Copernic Inc. merged into Comamtech Inc. (ON) 11/04/2010 which reincorporated in Delaware as DecisionPoint Systems, Inc. (New) 06/22/2011

MAMMATECH CORP (FL)
Each share old Common $0.0001 par exchanged for (0.05) share new Common $0.0001 par 12/02/2004
Reorganized as Dynamic Energy Alliance Corp. 12/05/2011
Each share new Common $0.0001 par exchanged for (3) shares Common $0.0001 par
Dynamic Energy Alliance Corp. recapitalized as Elite Data Services, Inc. 12/31/2013 which recapitalized as WOD Retail Solutions Inc. 09/05/2018

MAMMON INDS INC (NY)
Reincorporated under the laws of Delaware as United Marine Industries, Inc. 7/22/69
(See United Marine Industries, Inc.)

MAMMON OIL & GAS, INC. (UT)
Name changed to Volt Research, Inc. (UT) 02/24/1986
Volt Research, Inc. (UT) reincorporated in Delaware as Age Research, Inc. 05/12/1987 which name changed to SalesTactix, Inc. 08/02/2004 which name changed to Strativation, Inc. 10/14/2005 which name changed to CNS Response, Inc. 03/09/2007 which name changed to MYnd Analytics, Inc. 01/12/2016

MAMMOTH CAP CORP (BC)
Incorporated 01/07/2011
Name changed to Mammoth Resources Corp. 12/28/2011

MAMMOTH CAP CORP (BC)
Incorporated 02/27/2007
Completely liquidated
Each share Common no par received first and final distribution of approximately (1.2988) shares Primary Petroleum Corp. Common no par payable 11/16/2009 to holders of record 09/02/2009
Note: Certificates were not required to be surrendered and are without value
Primary Petroleum Corp. name changed to Keek Inc. 03/10/2014 which name changed to Peeks Social Ltd. 03/03/2017

MAMMOTH ENERGY GROUP INC (WY)
Reorganized 08/19/2013
Each share old Common $0.0001 par exchanged for (0.01) share new Common $0.0001 par 07/24/2007
State of incorporation changed from (NV) to (WY) 08/19/2013
Each share new Common $0.0001 par exchanged for (0.0005) share Common $0.0001 par
Recapitalized as Strategic Asset Leasing Inc. 11/12/2014
Each share Common $0.0001 par exchanged for (0.002) share Common $0.0001 par

MAMMOTH ENERGY INC (BC)
Recapitalized as Cierra Pacific Ventures Ltd. 02/25/1998
Each share Common no par exchanged for (0.25) share Common no par
Cierra Pacific Ventures Ltd. recapitalized as Alange Energy Corp. 07/15/2009 which recapitalized as PetroMagdalena Energy Corp. 07/19/2011
(See PetroMagdalena Energy Corp.)

MAMMOTH INDUSTRIES, INC. (MN)
Liquidation completed
Each share Common 10¢ par exchanged for initial distribution of (0.32) share Lear Siegler, Inc. Common $1 par 1/6/66
Each share Common 10¢ par received second and final distribution of (0.305) share Lear Siegler, Inc. Common $1 par 3/23/67
(See Lear Siegler, Inc.)

MAMMOTH LIFE & ACC INS CO (KY)
Capital Stock no par changed to $12.50 par 01/13/1978
Merged into Atlanta Life Insurance Co. 12/30/1985
Each share Capital Stock $12.50 par exchanged for $55 cash

MAMMOTH MART INC (DE)
Reincorporated 6/25/69
Common $1 par split (5) for (4) by issuance of (0.25) additional share 12/15/65
Common $1 par split (5) for (4) by issuance of (0.25) additional share 5/15/68
State of incorporation changed from (ME) to (DE) 6/25/69
Common $1 par split (3) for (2) by issuance of (0.5) additional share 5/5/71
Stock Dividends - 10% 2/1/67; 100% 5/23/69
Merged into King's Department Stores, Inc. 7/30/77
Each share Common $1 par exchanged for $9 cash

MAMMOTH MTN INN CORP (CA)
Adjudicated bankrupt 06/20/1975
Stockholders' equity unlikely

MAMMOTH PETROLEUMS LTD. (ON)
Acquired by Ellesmere Oil & Development Ltd. on a (1) for (10) basis which then merged into New Concord Development Corp. Ltd. in 1952
(See New Concord Development Corp. Ltd.)

MAMMOTH RES INC (UT)
Each share old Common $0.001 par exchanged for (0.1) share new Common $0.001 par 06/27/1990
Recapitalized as Symphony Telecom International Inc. (UT) 03/20/2000
Each share new Common $0.001 par exchanged for (0.2) share Common $0.001 par
Symphony Telecom International Inc. (UT) reincorporated in Delaware as Symphony Telecom Corp. 07/18/2001
(See Symphony Telecom Corp.)

MAMMOTH RES LTD (BC)
Recapitalized as Sicanna Industries Ltd. 12/18/86
Each share Common no par exchanged for (0.25) share Common no par
Sicanna Industries Ltd. name changed to Decorstone Industries Inc. 3/28/88
(See Decorstone Industries Inc.)

MAN AG (GERMANY)
Name changed to Man SE 06/22/2009

MAN-ECHO MINES LTD. (ON)
Merged into Milestone Exploration Ltd. 07/23/1968
Each share Capital Stock $1 par exchanged for (0.075694) share Capital Stock no par
Milestone Exploration Ltd. merged into Jubilee Gold Inc. 01/01/2010 which merged into Jubilee Gold Exploration Ltd. 01/25/2013

MAN GLG EMERGING MKTS INCOME FD (ON)
Name changed to Next Edge GLG Emerging Markets Income Fund 06/19/2014
Next Edge GLG Emerging Markets Income Fund merged into Next Edge Theta Yield Fund 12/30/2014

MAN INDS INDIA LTD (INDIA)
Sponsored Reg. S GDR's for Equity Shares split (2) for (1) by issuance of (1) additional GDR payable 01/15/2008 to holders of record 10/16/2007
GDR agreement terminated 11/30/2012
Each Sponsored Reg. S GDR for Equity Shares exchanged for (1) Equity Share
Note: Unexchanged GDR's will be sold and the proceeds, if any, held for claim after 11/30/2012

MAN O WAR INC (CO)
Recapitalized as Versailles Capital Corp. 11/26/96
Each share Common $0.0001 par exchanged for (0.002) share Common 5¢ par
Versailles Capital Corp. name changed to Amerimmune Pharmaceuticals Inc. 8/6/99
(See Amerimmune Pharmaceuticals Inc.)

MAN SANG HLDGS INC (NV)
Each share old Common $0.001 par exchanged for (0.25) share new Common $0.001 par 10/17/1996
New Common $0.001 par split (5) for (4) by issuance of (0.25) additional share payable 08/05/2005 to holders of record 07/22/2005 Ex date - 08/08/2005
Reorganized under the laws of British Virgin Islands as Man Sang International (B.V.I.) Ltd. 08/25/2009
Each share Common $0.001 par exchanged for (1) share Ordinary $0.001 par
Man Sang International (B.V.I.) Ltd. name changed to China Metro-Rural Holdings Ltd. 03/19/2010
(See China Metro-Rural Holdings Ltd.)

MAN SANG INTL B V I LTD (BRITISH VIRGIN ISLANDS)
Name changed to China Metro-Rural Holdings Ltd. 03/19/2010
(See China Metro-Rural Holdings Ltd.)

MANABI EXPLORATION CO., INC. (DE)
Capital Stock no par exchanged (6) for (1) in 1951
Capital Stock no par changed to Common 10¢ par in 1952
Dissolution approved and each share Common 10¢ par received (1.4) shares of Pan-Israel Oil Co., Inc. Common Voting Trust 1¢ par and (1.4) shares of Israel-Mediterranean Petroleum, Inc. Common Voting Trust 1¢ par 10/31/58

MANAC INC (QC)
Acquired by a group of investors 10/08/2015
Each Subordinate Share exchanged for $10.20 cash
Note: Unexchanged certificates will be cancelled and become without value 10/08/2021

MANAGED CARE SOLUTIONS INC (DE)
Name changed to Lifemark, Corp. 7/12/99
Lifemark, Corp. merged into UnitedHealth Group Inc. 2/9/2001

MANAGED DURATION INVT GRADE MUN FD (DE)
Auction Market Preferred Ser. M7 $0.001 par called for redemption at $25,000 on 08/01/2017
Auction Market Preferred Ser. W28 $0.001 par called for redemption at $25,000 on 08/03/2017
In process of liquidation
Each Common Share of Bene. Int. $0.001 par received initial distribution of $11.3406733 cash payable 09/21/2018 to holders of record 08/03/2018

MANAGED FUNDS, INC. (DE)
Stock Dividends - Paper Shares 100% 03/31/1955; Steel Shares 100% 06/30/1955; Electric Shares 100% 08/19/1955; Petroleum Shares 100% 12/30/1955
General Industries Shares and Special Investment Shares split (2) for (1) by issuance of (1) additional share 02/27/1963
Shares of Electric & Electronics Shares, Metal Shares, Paper Shares, Petroleum Shares and Transport Shares merged into General Industries Shares (after split) on a (1.41548), (1.15752), (1.75372), (1.42870) and (1.69176) for (1) basis respectively 02/27/1963
Name changed to Channing Investment Funds, Inc. and General Industries Shares and Special Investment Shares reclassified as Common Stock Fund and Special Fund respectively 04/01/1964
Channing Investment Funds, Inc. name changed to Channing Securities, Inc. (DE) 04/01/1965 which reincorporated in Maryland 10/09/1973 which merged into American General Shares, Inc. 09/02/1975 which merged into American General Enterprise Fund, Inc. 08/31/1979 which name changed to American Capital Enterprise Fund, Inc. (MD) 09/09/1983 which reincorporated in Delaware as Van Kampen American Capital Enterprise Fund 08/03/1995 which name changed to Van Kampen Enterprise Fund 08/31/1998

MANAGED HEALTH BENEFITS CORP (DE)
Under plan of merger name changed to Avitar Inc. (New) 5/19/95

MANAGED HIGH INCOME PORTFOLIO INC (MD)
Name changed 03/26/1993
Name changed from Managed High Yield Portfolio Inc. to Managed High Income Portfolio Inc. 02/26/1993
Name changed to Western Asset Managed High Income Fund Inc. 10/09/2006
Western Asset Managed High Income Fund Inc. merged into Western Asset High Income Opportunity Fund, Inc. 08/29/2016

MANAGED HIGH YIELD FD (MD)
Merged into Managed High Yield Plus Fund Inc. 06/02/2000
Each share Common $0.001 par exchanged for (0.96853364) share Common $0.001 par
(See Managed High Yield Plus Fund Inc.)

MANAGED HIGH YIELD PLUS FD INC (MD)
Completely liquidated
Each share Common $0.001 par received first and final distribution of $1.8855 cash payable 06/29/2016 to holders of record 06/22/2016

MANAGED MUNS PORTFOLIO II INC (MD)
Reorganized as Managed Municipals Portfolio Inc. 4/29/2002
Each share Common $0.001 par exchanged for (0.98036) share Common $0.001 par
Managed Municipals Portfolio Inc. name changed to Western Asset Managed Municipals Fund Inc. 10/9/2006

MANAGED MUNS PORTFOLIO INC (MD)
Name changed to Western Asset Managed Municipals Fund Inc. 10/9/2006

MANAGEMENT, ENGINEERING & DEVELOPMENT CO.
Acquired by Mead Corp. 00/00/1930
Details not available

MANAGEMENT & DEVELOPMENT CORP. (MD)
Merged into Canada Dry-Frostie Corp. 03/08/1966
Details not available

MANAGEMENT & TECHNOLOGY INC (NY)
Adjudicated bankrupt 02/16/1971
Stockholders' equity unlikely

MANAGEMENT ADVISORY SOFTWARE INC (DE)
Each share Common $0.0001 par exchanged for (0.1) share Common $0.001 par 2/29/88
Charter cancelled and declared inoperative and void for non-payment of taxes 3/1/92

MANAGEMENT ASSISTANCE INC LIQUIDATING TR (NY)
Reorganized 01/09/1986
Common 10¢ par split (2) for (1) by issuance of (1) additional share 12/15/1964
Preferred Ser. B $1 par called for redemption 12/23/1975
Each share Common 10¢ par exchanged for (0.25) share Common 40¢ par 10/28/1976
Preferred Ser. C $1 par called for redemption 09/28/1978
Stock Dividend - 100% 12/15/1965
Liquidation completed
Each share Common 40¢ par received initial distribution of $7.89165 principal amount of MAI Holdings, Inc. 16% Guaranteed Subordinated Debentures due 11/15/1997 on 02/05/1985
Each share Common 40¢ par received distribution of $18 cash 02/22/1985
Each share Common 40¢ par received third distribution of $1 cash 01/03/1986
Assets transferred from Management Assistance Inc. to Management Assistance Inc. Liquidating Trust and Common 40¢ par reclassified as Units of Bene. Int. 01/09/1986
Each Unit of Bene. Int. received fourth distribution of $0.75 cash 09/08/1986
Each Unit of Bene. Int. received fifth distribution of $0.30 cash 12/30/1986
Each Unit of Bene. Int. received sixth distribution of $0.80 cash 08/07/1987
Each Unit of Bene. Int. received seventh distribution of $0.20 cash 12/31/1987
Each Unit of Bene. Int. received eighth distribution of $0.20 cash 09/19/1988
Each Unit of Bene. Int. received ninth distribution of $0.15 cash 01/12/1989
Each Unit of Bene. Int. received tenth distribution of $0.10 cash 12/22/1989
Each Unit of Bene. Int. received eleventh distribution of $0.43 cash 01/09/1992
Each Unit of Bene. Int. received twelfth distribution of $0.25 cash 01/31/1996
Each Unit of Bene. Int. received thirteenth distribution of $0.25 cash 09/30/1996
Each Unit of Bene. Int. received fourteenth and final distribution of $0.126 cash 01/09/1997
Note: Certificates were not required to be surrendered and are without value

MANAGEMENT CO ENTMT GROUP INC (DE)
Reorganized as MCEG Sterling Inc. 03/30/1992
For every approximate (110) shares Common $0.001 par held holders received (1) share Common $0.001 par
Note: Certificates were not required to be surrendered and are without value

MCEG Sterling Inc. merged into Metromedia International Group, Inc. 11/01/1995
(See Metromedia International Group, Inc.)

MANAGEMENT DATA CORP (PA)
Name changed to MDC Corp. (PA) 03/20/1973
MDC Corp. (PA) name changed to Bouton Corp. (PA) 07/14/1982 which reincorporated in Delaware 06/29/1992
(See Bouton Corp.)

MANAGEMENT DATA PROCESSING SYS (NJ)
Charter declared void for non-payment of taxes 1/16/80

MANAGEMENT DYNAMICS INC (NJ)
Charter declared void for non-payment of taxes 09/18/1978

MGMT ENERGY INC (NV)
Name changed to Management Energy, Inc. 07/01/2009
Management Energy, Inc. name changed to MMEX Mining Corp. 03/04/2011 which name changed to MMEX Resources Corp. 06/03/2016

MANAGEMENT ENERGY INC (NV)
Common $0.001 par split (5) for (1) by issuance of (4) additional shares payable 07/01/2009 to holders of record 07/01/2009
Name changed to MMEX Mining Corp. 03/04/2011
MMEX Mining Corp. name changed to MMEX Resources Corp. 06/03/2016

MANAGEMENT GRAPHICS INC (ON)
Company reported out of business 00/00/1999
Details not available

MANAGEMENT INFORMATION SYS INC (NJ)
Completely liquidated 4/30/70
Each share Common 25¢ par exchanged for first and final distribution of (0.18) share Cummins Engine Co., Inc. Common $2.50 par
Cummins Engine Co., Inc. name changed to Cummins Inc. 4/5/2001

MANAGEMENT NETWORK GROUP INC (DE)
Each share Common $0.001 par exchanged for (0.2) share Common $0.005 par 02/08/2010
Name changed to Cartesian, Inc. 06/19/2014
(See Cartesian, Inc.)

MANAGEMENT OF ENVIRONMENTAL SOLUTIONS & TECHNOLOGY CORP (DE)
SEC revoked common stock registration 04/07/2008

MANAGEMENT RECRUITERS INTL INC (DE)
Stock Dividend - 50% 03/31/1970
Merged into Comprehensive Designers, Inc. 02/08/1972
Each share Common 10¢ par exchanged for (0.114) share Common no par
Comprehensive Designers, Inc. name changed to CDI Corp. 10/01/1973
(See CDI Corp.)

MANAGEMENT SCIENCE AMER INC (GA)
Stock Dividend - 100% 12/17/1982
Merged into Dun & Bradstreet Corp. 01/05/1990
Each share Common $0.0025 par exchanged for $18.50 cash

MANAGEMENT SCIENCE INC (WI)
Administratively dissolved 09/03/1993

MANAGEMENT SVCS INC (GA)
Proclaimed dissolved for failure to file annual reports 11/29/1990

MANAGEMENT SVCS INC (NJ)
Recapitalized as Centriforce Technology Corp. 08/15/2008
Each share Common $0.001 par exchanged for (0.1) share Common $0.001 par
Centriforce Technology Corp. recapitalized as ADB International Group, Inc. (NJ) 05/20/2010 which reorganized in Delaware 08/04/2014 which name changed to E- Qure Corp. 10/09/2014

MANAGEMENT SYS INC (OK)
Merged into Vanier Graphics Corp. in April 1974
Each share Common 33-1/3¢ par exchanged for cash

MANAGEMENT TECHNOLOGIES INC (NY)
Common 1¢ par split (2) for (1) by issuance of (1) additional share 01/15/1988
Each share old Common 1¢ par exchanged for (0.14285714) share new Common 1¢ par 05/15/1995
SEC revoked common stock registration 10/31/2006

MANAGEMENT TELEVISION SYS INC (DE)
Charter cancelled and declared inoperative and void for non-payment of taxes 3/1/81

MANAGERS FD INC (MD)
Name changed to GOC Fund, Inc. 06/11/1993
(See GOC Fund, Inc.)

MANAKOA SVCS CORP (NV)
Recapitalized as TeslaVision Corp. 12/15/2008
Each share Common $0.001 par exchanged for (0.2) share Common $0.001 par
(See TeslaVision Corp.)

MANALTA COAL INCOME TR (AB)
Acquired by Luscar Coal Income Fund 10/01/1998
Each Instalment Receipt no par exchanged for (0.4) Trust Unit no par and $4 cash
Luscar Coal Income Fund acquired by Sherritt International Corp. (NB) 07/20/2001 which reincorporated in Ontario 08/01/2007

MANAR CDA INC (AB)
Struck off register and declared dissolved for failure to file returns 1/1/96

MANARIS CORP (NV)
Name changed to Avensys Corp. 12/12/2007
Avensys Corp. name changed to Manaris (2010) Corp. 08/23/2010

MANAS PETE CORP (NV)
Name changed to MNP Petroleum Corp. 01/20/2014

MANATECH INTL LTD (NJ)
Stock Dividend - 10% 05/30/1972
Adjudicated bankrupt 12/30/1977
Stockholders' equity unlikely

MANATEE NATL BK (BRADENTON, FL)
Stock Dividends - 20% 10/27/1959; 33-1/3% 01/23/1963; 50% 04/02/1971
100% acquired by Southeast Banking Corp. through voluntary exchange offer as of 12/29/1972
Public interest eliminated

MANATEE RIVER BANK & TRUST CO. (BRADENTON, FL)
Stock Dividend - 100% 2/15/50
Name changed to Manatee River National Bank (Bradenton, Fla.) 5/13/54
Manatee River National Bank (Bradenton, Fla.) name changed to Manatee National Bank (Bradenton, Fla.) 10/27/59

(See Manatee National Bank (Bradenton, Fla.))

MANATEE RIVER NATIONAL BANK (BRADENTON, FL)
Each share Capital Stock $100 par exchanged for (15) shares Capital Stock $10 par to effect a (10) for (1) split and a 50% stock dividend 11/01/1956
Stock Dividend - 25% 04/17/1958
Name changed to Manatee National Bank (Bradenton, FL) 10/27/1959
(See Manatee National Bank (Bradenton, FL))

MANATI SUGAR CO (NY)
Each share Preferred $100 par exchanged for (3) shares Common $1 par 00/00/1937
Each share Common $100 par exchanged for (0.5) share Common $1 par 00/00/1937
Common $1 par changed to 10¢ par 11/21/1966
Name changed to Manati Industries, Inc. 04/22/1970

MANATRON INC (MI)
Merged into Manatron Intermediate Holdings, Inc. 04/01/2008
Each share Common no par exchanged for $12 cash

MANCAP GLOBAL VENTURES INC (AB)
Merged into Mancap Ventures Inc. 6/10/2002
Each share Common no par exchanged for $0.07 cash

MANCHESTER BK (ST. LOUIS, MO)
Each share Common $100 par exchanged for (5) shares Common $20 par 00/00/1947
Common $20 par changed to $10 par and (1) additional share issued 10/08/1959
Stock Dividend - 10% 04/01/1967
99.8% held by Manchester Financial Services Corp. as of 03/29/1971
Public interest eliminated

MANCHESTER CORP (NH)
VTC's for Common $5 par split (2) for (1) by issuance of (1) additional VTC 02/05/1973
Name changed to First Financial Group of New Hampshire, Inc. 01/01/1974
First Financial Group of New Hampshire, Inc. name changed to BankEast Corp. 04/22/1981
(See BankEast Corp.)

MANCHESTER COTTON MILLS
Merged into Callaway Mills in 1932 which was completely liquidated in 1947

MANCHESTER ELEC CO (MA)
Each share Capital Stock $100 par exchanged for (4) shares Capital Stock $25 par in 1927
Merged into New England Electric System 7/1/83
Each share Capital Stock $25 par exchanged for (2.5) shares Common $1 par
(See New England Electric System)

MANCHESTER EQUIP INC (NY)
Name changed to Manchester Technologies, Inc. 1/29/2001
(See Manchester Technologies, Inc.)

MANCHESTER FINL CORP (MO)
Acquired by Commerce Bancshares, Inc. 11/20/1978
Each share Common $1 par exchanged for (1.2) shares Common $5 par

MANCHESTER FINANCIAL SERVICES CORP. (MO)
Name changed to Manchester Financial Corp. 3/17/72
Manchester Financial Corp. acquired by Commerce Bancshares, Inc. 11/20/78

MANCHESTER GAS CO (NH)
Common $100 par changed to $20 par and (4) additional shares issued plus a 100% stock dividend paid 11/8/63
Each share Common $20 par exchanged for (4) shares Common $5 par 3/29/66
Under plan of merger each share Common $5 par exchanged for (1) share EnergyNorth
Common $1 par 12/31/82
Acquired by EnergyNorth, Inc. 4/30/86
Each share 7% Preferred $100 par exchanged for (5) shares Common $1 par
(See EnergyNorth Inc.)

MANCHESTER INC (NV)
Each share old Common $0.001 par exchanged for (11) shares new Common $0.001 par 09/17/2004
Plan of reorganization under Chapter 11 Federal Bankruptcy Code effective 06/23/2008
No stockholders' equity

MANCHESTER LIFE & CAS MGMT CORP (MO)
Name changed 3/30/65
Name changed from Manchester Insurance Management & Investment Corp. to Manchester Life & Casualty Management Corp. 3/30/65
Administratively dissolved 8/28/2000

MANCHESTER NATL BK (MANCHESTER, NH)
Merged into Bank of New Hampshire, N.A. (Manchester, NH) 11/30/69
Each share Capital Stock $100 par exchanged for (20) shares Common Capital Stock $10 par
Bank of New Hampshire, N.A. (Manchester, NH) reorganized as Bank of New Hampshire Corp. 4/30/80

MANCHESTER RES CORP (BC)
Name changed 3/7/84
Name changed from Manchester Oil Corp. to Manchester Resources Corp. 3/7/84
Recapitalized as Danoil Energy Ltd. 9/1/95
Each share Common no par exchanged for (0.1) share Common no par
Danoil Energy Ltd. merged into Acclaim Energy Trust 4/20/2001
(See Acclaim Energy Trust)

MANCHESTER ST BK CONN (MANCHESTER, CT)
Merged into New England Community Bancorp, Inc. 7/11/96
Each share Common $10 par exchanged for (5.493) shares Class A Common 10¢ par and $35.20 cash

MANCHESTER TECHNOLOGIES INC (NY)
Merged into Electrograph Holdings, Inc. 8/1/2005
Each share Common 1¢ par exchanged for $6.40 cash

MANCHESTER TERM CORP (TX)
Reorganized 00/00/1938
Each share Preferred $100 par exchanged for (4) VTC's for Common $1 par
Each share Common $10 par exchanged for (0.04) VTC for Common $1 par
Voting Trust Agreement terminated 10/01/1957
Each VTC for Common $1 par exchanged for (1) share Common $1 par
Name changed to MTC Liquidating Corp. 09/25/1973
(See MTC Liquidating Corp.)

MANCHESTER TRACTION LIGHT & POWER CO.
Merged into Public Service Co. of New Hampshire 00/00/1926
Details not available

MANCHURIA OIL & GAS CO. (OK)
Charter cancelled for failure to pay taxes 8/8/21

MANCO GOLD MINES, LTD. (CANADA)
Charter cancelled and declared dissolved 1/9/42

MANCOS CORP. (CO)
Acquired by Union Oil Co. of California 11/27/78
Each share Capital Stock 1¢ par exchanged for (0.0039) share Common $8-1/3 par
Union Oil Co. of California reorganized as Unocal Corp. 4/25/83 which merged into Chevron Corp. 8/10/2005

MANDALAY CAP CORP (NV)
Name changed to Save The World Air, Inc. 02/11/1999
Save The World Air, Inc. name changed to QS Energy, Inc. 08/12/2015

MANDALAY DIGITAL GROUP INC (DE)
Each share old Common $0.0001 par exchanged for (0.2) share new Common $0.0001 par 04/15/2013
Name changed to Digital Turbine, Inc. 01/20/2015

MANDALAY GOLD MINES, LTD. (MB)
Charter cancelled for failure to file annual reports in 1955

MANDALAY INC (WA)
Name changed to LaserLogic Inc. 9/16/85
(See LaserLogic Inc.)

MANDALAY MEDIA INC (DE)
Name changed to NeuMedia, Inc. 06/21/2010
NeuMedia, Inc. name changed to Mandalay Digital Group, Inc. 02/28/2012 which name changed to Digital Turbine, Inc. 01/20/2015

MANDALAY RESORT GROUP (NV)
Merged into MGM Mirage 4/25/2005
Each share Common 5¢ par exchanged for $71 cash

MANDALLA RES LTD (BC)
Delisted from Vancouver Stock Exchange 10/31/1994

MANDARIN CAP CORP (BC)
Reorganized as H.I.S.A. Investments Ltd. 12/29/1989
Each share Common no par exchanged for (1) share Common no par
(See H.I.S.A. Investments Ltd.)

MANDARIN INDS LTD (CAYMAN ISLANDS)
Reincorporated 10/08/1997
Place of incorporation changed from (BC) to (Cayman Islands) 10/08/1997
Recapitalized as Leitak Enterprises Ltd. 10/09/1997
Each share Common no par exchanged for (0.25) share Common no par
(See Leitak Enterprises Ltd.)

MANDARIN MINES LTD (ON)
Charter cancelled for failure to file reports and pay taxes 1/7/96

MANDARIN ORIENTAL INTL LTD (BERMUDA)
ADR agreement terminated 5/28/2004
Each Sponsored ADR for Ordinary U.S. $0.05 par exchanged for $9.44522 cash

MANDATORY COM EXCHANGE TR (DE)
Issue Information - 2,000,000 TR

ISSUED MAND EXCHANGE SECS offered at $48.875 per share on 09/12/1997
Each Trust Issued Mandatory Exchange Security exchanged for (1) share FIRSTPLUS Financial Group, Inc. Common 1¢ par 8/15/2000

MANDEL (HENRY) ASSOCIATES, INC. (NY)
Charter cancelled and proclaimed dissolved for non-payment of taxes 12/15/36

MANDEL BROTHERS, INC. (DE)
Stock Dividend - 20% 12/28/45
Merged into Wieboldt Stores, Inc. and each share Capital Stock no par exchanged for (0.02) share 3-1/4% Junior Preferred $100 par and (0.21716) share Common no par 8/18/60
(See Wieboldt Stores, Inc.)

MANDO MACHY CORP (KOREA)
GDR's for Common split (6) for (5) by issuance of (0.2) additional receipt payable 01/27/1998 to holders of record 12/16/1997
GDR agreement terminated 05/07/2003
Details not available

MANDORIN GOLDFIELDS INC (YT)
Reincorporated 06/11/1999
Place of incorporation changed from (BC) to (Yukon) 06/11/1999
Name changed to Sphere Resources Inc. 11/27/2007

MANDRAKE FOOD & ALE (UT)
Each share old Common 1¢ par exchanged for (10) shares new Common 1¢ par 05/23/1978
Recapitalized as International Leisure & Casino Inc. 08/06/1979
Each share new Common 1¢ par exchanged (0.33333333) share Common 1¢ par
(See International Leisure & Casino Inc.)

MANDREL INDUSTRIES, INC. (MI)
Common $1 par changed to no par and (1) additional share issued 1/15/62
Acquired by Ampex Corp. 3/12/64
Each share Common no par exchanged for (0.9) share Common $1 par
Ampex Corp. merged into Signal Companies, Inc. 1/15/81 which merged into Allied- Signal Inc. 9/19/85 which name changed to AlliedSignal Inc. 4/26/93 which name changed to Honeywell International Inc. 12/1/99

MANDUSA RES LTD (BC)
Common no par split (3) for (1) by issuance of (2) additional shares 04/01/1986
Recapitalized as MSA Petroleum Ltd. 08/22/1988
Each share Common no par exchanged for (0.2) share Common no par
MSA Petroleum Ltd. merged into Tygas Resource Corp. 01/04/1989 which merged into Alberta Oil & Gas Ltd. 08/02/1990 which recapitalized as Alberta Oil & Gas Petroleum Corp. 11/19/1997 which recapitalized as Edge Energy Inc. 04/14/1998 which merged into Ventus Energy Ltd. 08/11/2000 which name changed to Navigo Energy Inc. 05/24/2002
(See Navigo Energy Inc.)

MANDY MINES LTD.
Liquidated in 1942

MANEAST URANIUM LTD (CANADA)
Charter cancelled for failure to file reports 02/28/1973

MANEKI MNG INC (NV)
Common $0.001 par split (17) for (1)

by issuance of (16) additional shares payable 09/26/2006 to holders of record 09/22/2006
Ex date - 09/27/2006
Name changed to Red Rock Pictures Holdings, Inc. 11/15/2006
Red Rock Pictures Holdings, Inc. name changed to OSL Holdings Inc. 11/28/2011
(See OSL Holdings Inc.)

MANELE BAY VENTURES INC (CANADA)
Name changed to MBA Gold Corp. 07/15/2003
MBA Gold Corp. name changed to MBA Resources Corp. 10/14/2005 which name changed to Thunderbird Energy Corp. 07/27/2006 which recapitalized as Gordon Creek Energy Inc. 10/24/2013

MANERA CAP CORP (BC)
Name changed to GT Gold Corp. 11/22/2016

MANFREY CAP CORP (BC)
Delisted from Canadian Stock Venture Exchange 01/14/2000

MANGAPETS INC (DE)
Each share old Common $0.001 par exchanged for (0.5) share new Common $0.001 par 09/18/2006
Name changed to Intrepid Global Imaging 3D, Inc. 03/01/2007
Intrepid Global Imaging 3D, Inc. name changed to Spine Pain Management, Inc. 11/27/2009 which name changed to Spine Injury Solutions, Inc. 10/08/2015

MANGEL STORES CORP (DE)
Each share Preferred $100 par exchanged for (1) share $5 Preferred no par and (3) shares Common $1 par in 1936
Each share Common no par exchanged for (1) share Common $1 par in 1936
$5 Preferred no par called for redemption 2/14/45
Common $1 par split (3) for (2) by issuance of (0.5) additional share 12/15/69
Stock Dividend - 100% 5/28/57
Name changed to Russell Burdsall & Ward Corp. 2/23/78
Russell Burdsall & Ward Corp. name changed to RB&W Corp. 4/24/86 which merged into Park-Ohio Industries, Inc. 3/31/95

MANGO RES LTD (BC)
Recapitalized as Consolidated Mango Resources Ltd. (BC) 10/07/1999
Each share Common no par exchanged for (0.2) share Common no par
Consolidated Mango Resources Ltd. (BC) reincorporated in Delaware 03/10/2000 which recapitalized as U.S. Geothermal Inc. 12/22/2003
(See U.S. Geothermal Inc.)

MANGOOD CORP (DE)
Reincorporated 4/22/68
State of incorporation changed from (IL) to (DE) 4/22/68
Common $16-2/3 par changed to no par and (1.5) additional shares issued 5/15/68
Common no par split (2) for (1) by issuance of (1) additional share 2/6/84
Name changed to Howe Richardson Inc. 12/31/87
(See Howe Richardson Inc.)

MANGOSOFT INC (NV)
Each share old Common $0.001 par exchanged for (0.03703703) share new Common $0.001 par 02/28/2003
Name changed to Mango Capital, Inc. 02/17/2011

MANGURIANS INC (FL)
Common 10¢ par split (3) for (2) by

issuance of (0.5) additional share 3/9/70
Acquired by General Portland Cement Co. 12/29/70
Each share Common 10¢ par exchanged for (0.666666) share Common $1 par
General Portland Cement Co. name changed to General Portland Inc. 5/31/72
(See General Portland Inc.)

MANHATTAN BAGEL INC (NJ)
Plan of reorganization under Chapter 11 Federal Bankruptcy Code effective 11/25/98
No stockholders' equity

MANHATTAN BANCORP (CA)
Merged into Plaza Bancorp 06/29/2015
Each share Common no par exchanged for either (1.1996) shares Common 1¢ par or $5.59 cash
Plaza Bancorp merged into Pacific Premier Bancorp, Inc. 11/01/2017

MANHATTAN BOND FUND, INC. (DE)
Merged into Diversified Investment Fund, Inc. on an approximately (0.71492) for (1) basis 10/23/58
Diversified Investment Fund, Inc. name changed to Anchor Income Fund, Inc. 9/2/69 which merged into Income Fund of America, Inc. (Del.) 7/31/78 which reincorporated in Maryland 9/22/83

MANHATTAN BRIDGE THREE-CENT LINE
Purchased by City of New York in 1929

MANHATTAN BUFFALO MINING CO. (SD)
Charter expired by time limitation in 1926

MANHATTAN COIL CORP. (NY)
6% Preferred $25 par changed to $100 par in 1948
Name changed to Holfast Rubber Co. Inc. in 1953 which completed liquidation 10/29/54

MANHATTAN CONS MINES DEV CO (NV)
Recapitalized as Aero-Trails Corp. 09/02/1969
Each share Common 10¢ par exchanged for (0.25) share Common 40¢ par
Aero-Trails Corp. name changed to Techni-Culture, Inc. 01/15/1971

MANHATTAN CONTL DEV CORP (NV)
Charter revoked for failure to file reports and pay fees 03/03/1975

MANHATTAN-DEARBORN CORP.
Merged into Consolidated Dearborn Corp. share for share in 1940
Consolidated Dearborn Corp. completed liquidation 5/11/62

MANHATTAN ELECTRICAL SUPPLY CO., INC.
Succeeded by American Machine & Metals, Inc. in 1930
(See American Machine & Metals, Inc.)

MANHATTAN EXPRESS MINING CO. (AZ)
Charter expired by time limitation 4/4/31

MANHATTAN FINANCIAL CORP. (NY)
Recapitalized in 1937
Each share Class A no par exchanged for (1) share Class A $10 par plus a 25% Stock Dividend
Each share Class B no par exchanged for (1) share Class B $1 par
Liquidation completed 4/17/61

MANHATTAN FUND, INC. (DE)
Incorporated 12/23/37
Name changed to Manhattan Bond Fund, Inc. 3/28/39
Manhattan Bond Fund, Inc. merged into Diversified Investment Fund, Inc. 10/23/58 which name changed to Anchor Income Fund, Inc. 9/2/69 which merged into Income Fund of America, Inc. (Del.) 7/31/78 which reincorporated in Maryland 9/22/83

MANHATTAN FUND, INC. (DE)
Incorporated 12/27/65
Reincorporated under the laws of Maryland 3/21/73

MANHATTAN GOLD MINES CO (NV)
Name changed to Manhattan Continental Development Corp. 02/19/1969
(See Manhattan Continental Development Corp.)

MANHATTAN INDS INC (NY)
Common $5 par changed to $1 par 6/5/79
Merged into Salant Acquisition Corp. 8/12/88
Each share Common $1 par exchanged for $18.50 cash

MANHATTAN LIFE CORP (DE)
Name changed to Manhattan National Corp. 12/31/82
Manhattan National Corp. assets transferred to Manhattan National Corp. Liquidating Trust and Common $2 par reclassified as Units of Bene. Int. no par 12/31/91
(See Manhattan National Corp. Liquidating Trust)

MANHATTAN LIFE INS CO NEW (NY)
Each Guaranty Capital Share $2 par exchanged for (0.00000329) Guaranty Capital Share $835,406 par 01/28/1997
Note: In effect holders received $7.50 cash per share and public interest was eliminated

MANHATTAN LIFE INS CO OLD (NY)
Each share Guarantee Capital Stock $50 par exchanged for (10) shares Guarantee Capital Stock $5 par 12/29/1961
Guarantee Capital Stock $5 par changed to $2 par and (1.5) additional shares issued 01/22/1964
Stock Dividends - 18.1% 03/31/1961; (5) for (26) 03/30/1962; (5) for (31) 04/01/1963; 16-2/3% 04/01/1964; 14-2/7% 04/01/1965; 13-1/3% 12/15/1970
Acquired by Manhattan Life Corp. 04/06/1977
Each share Guarantee Capital Stock $2 par exchanged for $6.30 cash
Manhattan Life Corp. name changed to Manhattan National Corp. 12/31/1982 which assets were transferred to Manhattan National Corp. Liquidating Trust and Common $2 par reclassified as Units of Bene. Int. no par 12/31/1991
(See Manhattan National Corp. Liquidating Trust)

MANHATTAN MERGER CO. (NV)
Charter forfeited for non-payment of taxes 7/1/26

MANHATTAN MINERAL CORP (BC)
Name changed to Safety-Ject Medical Products Ltd. 07/12/1989
Safety-Ject Medical Products Ltd. recapitalized as International Safety-Ject Industries Inc. 09/23/1991 which recapitalized as Specialty Medical Products Inc. 09/30/1993 which recapitalized as Fedora Industries Inc. 10/20/1997 which name changed to Airbomb.com Marketing Ltd. (BC) 02/21/2000 which reincorporated in Delaware as airbomb.com, Inc. 05/09/2000 which name changed to RT Petroleum Inc. 05/18/2005
(See RT Petroleum Inc.)

MANHATTAN MINERALS CORP (BC)
Name changed to Mediterranean Minerals Corp. 02/23/2005
Mediterranean Minerals Corp. recapitalized as Mediterranean Resources Ltd. 12/19/2005 which name changed to Blockchain Power Trust 01/04/2018

MANHATTAN MORTGAGE CO.
Dissolved and assets taken over by New York Realty & Improvement Co. 00/00/1928
Details not available

MANHATTAN NATIONAL CORP. LIQUIDATING TRUST (DE)
Liquidation completed
Each Unit of Bene. Int. no par received initial distribution of $1.05 cash 2/5/93
Each Unit of Bene. Int. no par received second distribution of $1 cash 3/28/94
Each Unit of Bene. Int. no par received third and final distribution of $1.15 cash 11/11/94

MANHATTAN NATL CORP (DE)
Liquidation completed
Each share Common $2 par exchanged for initial distribution of (0.53) share Manhattan Life Insurance Co. (NY) (New) Guarantee Capital Stock $2 par and $3.25 cash 12/31/1991
(See Manhattan Life Insurance Co. (NY) (New))
Assets transferred to Manhattan National Corp. Liquidating Trust 12/31/1991
(See Manhattan National Corp. Liquidating Trust)

MANHATTAN NATL LIFE INS CO (ND)
Each share Common $1 par exchanged for (0.0001) share Common $10,000 par 06/10/1987
Note: In effect holders received $6 cash per share
5% Conv. Preferred $1 par called for redemption 06/15/1987
Public interest eliminated

MANHATTAN OIL CO. OF DELAWARE
Merged into Independent Oil & Gas Co. 00/00/1928
Details not available

MANHATTAN OIL LTD (BC)
Recapitalized as Tulsa Crude Oil Corp. 12/17/81
Each share Common no par exchanged for (0.2) share Common no par
Tulsa Crude Oil Corp. name changed to Perkins Oil Ltd. 3/26/82
(See Perkins Oil Ltd.)

MANHATTAN PHARMACEUTICALS INC (DE)
Each share old Common $0.001 par exchanged for (0.2) share new Common $0.001 par 09/25/2003
Each share Preferred Ser. A $0.001 par exchanged for (9.0909) shares new Common $0.001 par 08/26/2005
Each share new Common $0.001 par exchanged again for (0.02) share new Common $0.001 par 07/14/2011
Recapitalized as TG Therapeutics, Inc. 04/30/2012
Each share new Common $0.001 par exchanged for (0.01777777) share Common $0.001 par

MANHATTAN RAILWAY CO.
Acquired by the City of New York 00/00/1940
Details not available

MANHATTAN RES INC (NV)
Each share Common 5¢ par exchanged for (0.05) share Common 1¢ par 09/28/1983
Each share new Common 1¢ par exchanged for (0.1) share Common $0.001 par 03/31/1993
Charter permanently revoked 12/31/2008

MANHATTAN RES LTD (AB)
Merged into Pivotal Energy Ltd. 01/10/2003
Each share Common no par exchanged for (0.14285714) share Common no par
Pivotal Energy Ltd. merged into Fairborne Energy Ltd. (Old) 07/08/2003
(See Fairborne Energy Ltd. (Old))

MANHATTAN RUBBER MANUFACTURING CO.
Merged into Raybestos-Manhattan, Inc. (NJ) 00/00/1929
Details not available

MANHATTAN SECURITIES CO. (NJ)
Common $5 par changed to 10¢ par 3/4/66
Merged into Haven Industries, Inc. 10/26/67
Each share Common 10¢ par exchanged for (50) shares Common 10¢ par
Haven Industries, Inc. name changed to Federated Communications Corp. 4/29/75
(See Federated Communications Corp.)

MANHATTAN SHIRT CO. (NY)
Common $25 par changed to $5 par in 1945
Common $5 par split (4) for (3) by issuance of (1/3) additional share 5/20/66
Stock Dividend - 100% 7/19/56
Name changed to Manhattan Industries, Inc. 5/21/68
(See Manhattan Industries, Inc.)

MANHATTAN STORAGE & WAREHOUSE CO. (NY)
Each share Capital Stock $100 par exchanged for (4) shares Capital Stock $25 par in 1948
Liquidated under plan of merger 2/14/56

MANHATTAN UNION CORP. (NV)
Merged into Globe Hill Co. in September 1971
Each share Capital Stock 10¢ par exchanged for (1) share Common 10¢ par
Globe Hill Co. name changed to Aadan Corp. 11/1/72
(See Aadan Corp.)

MANHATTAN YELLOWKNIFE MINES, LTD. (ON)
Charter cancelled for failure to file reports and pay taxes in 1961

MANICOUAGAN MINERALS INC (CANADA)
Each share old Common no par exchanged for (0.1) share new Common no par 06/21/2011
Recapitalized as Murchison Minerals Ltd. 06/05/2014
Each share new Common no par exchanged for (0.2) share Common no par

MANIKURU GOLDFIELDS LTD. (ON)
Dissolved in 1950

MANILA ELEC CO (PHILIPPINES)
Stock Dividends - 50% 07/14/1995; 30% payable 11/29/1996 to holders of record 07/23/1996; 30% payable 07/18/1997 to holders of record 05/15/1997; 20% payable 08/30/2000 to holders of record 05/15/2000; 10% payable 10/16/2007 to holders of record 09/07/2007 Ex date - 09/05/2007
ADR agreement terminated 11/26/2007
Each Sponsored ADR for Class B Common P10 par exchanged for $1.1596315 cash
GDR agreement terminated 11/26/2007
Each GDR for 144A Class B Common P10 par exchanged for $5.9981575 cash

MANION (JOE RAINEY) & CO. (TX)
Completely liquidated 11/01/1971
Each share Capital Stock $1 par exchanged for first and final distribution of (0.5) share Pacer Corp. Common 1¢ par
(See Pacer Corp.)

MANISCHEWITZ B CO (OH)
Merged into Mano Acquisition Corp. 01/18/1991
Each share Common no par exchanged for $800 cash

MANITEX CAP INC (ON)
Recapitalized from Manitex Minerals Inc. to Manitex Capital Inc. 06/16/1992
Each share Common no par exchanged for (1/6) share Common no par
Reincorporated under the laws of Canada 03/12/1998

MANITO BK SVCS INC (DE)
Under plan of merger each share Common $10 par exchanged for $120 cash 11/16/2004

MANITOBA & EASTERN MINES LTD. (CANADA)
Recapitalized as Maneast Uranium Corp. Ltd. in 1954
Each share Capital Stock no par exchanged for (0.2) share Capital Stock no par
Maneast Uranium Corp. Ltd. charter cancelled 2/28/73

MANITOBA BASIN CONSOLIDATED MINES LTD. (ON)
Charter cancelled in March 1963

MANITOBA BASIN MINING CO. LTD.
Acquired by Manitoba Basin Consolidated Mines Ltd. on a (1) for (3) basis in 1947
(See Manitoba Basin Consolidated Mines Ltd.)

MANITOBA BRIDGE & IRON WORKS, INC.
Acquired by Dominion Bridge Co. Ltd. 00/00/1930
Details not available

MANITOBA CHROMIUM LTD (CANADA)
Reorganized as Helvetique Gold Exploration Ltd. 11/25/1987
Details not available

MANITOBA FLIN FLON MINES LTD.
Adjudicated bankrupt in 1935

MANITOBA PPTYS INC (CANADA)
9.25% Retractable Preferred Ser. A no par called for redemption 8/31/92
Public interest eliminated

MANITOBA TELECOM SVCS INC (MB)
Name changed 01/07/1997
Name changed from Manitoba Telephone System to Manitoba Telecom Services Inc. 01/07/1997
Each share Non-Vtg. Exchangeable Preference Class B no par exchanged for (1) share Common no par 12/01/2004
Merged into BCE Inc. 03/20/2017
Each share Common no par exchanged for (0.3311) share Common no par and $20.3977 cash
Note: Unexchanged certificates will be cancelled and become without value 03/20/2023

MANITOU ACRES, INC. (AR)
Charter revoked for failure to pay taxes 2/19/74

MANITOU BARVUE MINES LTD (ON)
Capital Stock $1 par changed to no par 07/19/1972
Name changed to Terratech Resources Inc. 08/31/1983
(See Terratech Resources Inc.)

MANITOU CAP CORP (ON)
Issue Information - 1,500,000 shares COM offered at $0.20 per share on 02/03/1998
Acquired by MTF Acquisitionco Ltd. 05/27/2009
Each share Common no par exchanged for $0.23 cash

MANITOU REEF RES INC (BC)
Recapitalized as Consolidated Manitou Resources Inc. 07/15/1988
Each share Common no par exchanged for (1/3) share Common no par
Consolidated Manitou Resources Inc. name changed to A.C.T. Industrial Corp. 07/05/1991 which name changed to Rhona Online.com Inc. 07/06/2000 which recapitalized as Winchester Minerals & Gold Exploration Ltd. 04/16/2004

MANITOWOC FOODSERVICE INC (DE)
Name changed to Welbilt, Inc. 03/06/2017

MANITOWOC INC (WI)
1st Preferred $100 par called for redemption 6/30/60
2nd Preferred $100 par called for redemption 6/30/65
(Additional Information in Active)

MANITOWOC SAVINGS BANK (MANITOWOC, WI)
Each share Capital Stock $100 par exchanged for (10) shares Capital Stock $10 par in 1955
Acquired by Associated Bank Services, Inc. 6/1/70
Each share Capital Stock $10 par exchanged for (1.17) shares Common $1 par

MANITOWOC SHIPBUILDING CO. (WI)
Reorganized as Manitowoc Co., Inc. on a share for share basis in 1952

MANIWAKI MINES LTD.
Liquidated in 1940

MANIWAKI MOLYBDENUM MINES LTD.
Bankrupt in 1940

MANIX MINES LTD (QC)
Recapitalized as Ziebart Corp. 12/05/1972
Each share Common no par exchanged for (0.1) share Common no par
(See Ziebart Corp.)

MANKATO CTZNS TEL CO (MN)
Common Capital Stock no par split (4) for (1) by issuance of (3) additional shares 07/18/1966
Common Capital Stock no par split (2) for (1) by issuance of (1) additional share 11/20/1972
Stock Dividend - 10% 08/15/1967
Under plan of reorganization each share Common Capital Stock no par automatically became (1) share Hickory Tech Corp. Common no par 06/17/1985
Hickory Tech Corp. name changed to Enventis Corp. 05/08/2014 which merged into Consolidated Communications Holdings, Inc. 10/16/2014

MANLEY INDS INC (IA)
Each share Common 20¢ par exchanged for (0.25) share Common 80¢ par 05/31/1975
Merged into K & T Corp. 04/08/1976

Each share Common 80¢ par exchanged for $4 cash

MANN INDICATOR CO. (WV)
Charter revoked for failure to file reports and pay fees 02/23/1917

MANN MFG INC (TX)
Merged into Billy The Kid, Inc. 02/08/1977
Each share Common 50¢ par exchanged for (0.192864) share Conv. Preferred Ser. A $1 par
Billy The Kid, Inc. name changed to BTK Industries, Inc. 03/01/1982
(See BTK Industries, Inc.)

MANN OIL RES INC (CANADA)
Name changed to Consolidated Mann Oil Inc. 10/26/1989
(See Consolidated Mann Oil Inc.)

MANN RESEARCH LABORATORIES, INC. (NY)
Acquired by Becton, Dickinson & Co. on a (0.0866) for (1) basis 5/12/64

MANN STREET CAR INDICATOR & ADVERTISING CO. (WV)
Name changed to Mann Indicator Co. 5/23/10
(See Mann Indicator Co.)

MANNE BUILDING, INC.
Liquidated in 1944

MANNESMANN A G (GERMANY)
Each Unsponsored ADR for Ordinary DM50 par exchanged for (1) Sponsored ADR for Ordinary DM50 par 12/20/1995
Sponsored ADR's for Ordinary DM50 par split (10) for (1) by issuance of (9) additional ADR's payable 06/08/1998 to holders of record 06/04/1998
Name changed to Vodafone AG 11/08/2001
(See Vodafone AG)

MANNING, BOWMAN & CO. (CT)
Succeeded by Manning, Bowman & Co. (Delaware) in 1926 whose assets were sold in 1941

MANNING, BOWMAN & CO. (DE)
Assets sold in 1941

MANNING, MAXWELL & MOORE, INC. (NJ)
Each share Common $100 par exchanged for (8) shares Common no par 00/00/1937
Each share Common no par exchanged for (1.) shares Common $12.50 par 00/00/1946
Stock Dividends - 10% 09/10/1953; 10% 11/09/1956
Name changed to Two Hundred & Fifty East Main Street Corp. 11/25/1964
(See Two Hundred & Fifty East Main Street Corp.)

MANNING & RUDOLPH, INC. (MN)
Name changed to Gordon-Miles Mining Co. 10/13/70
Gordon-Miles Mining Co. name changed to U.S. Coal Corp. 1/21/75
(See U.S. Coal Corp.)

MANNING GAS & OIL CO (OH)
Liquidation completed
Each share Common no par exchanged for initial distribution of $8.50 cash 08/08/1977
Each share Common no par received second and final distribution of $1.1896 cash 04/25/1980

MANNING GREG AUCTIONS INC (DE)
Reincorporated 01/25/2001
State of incorporation changed from (NY) to (DE) 01/25/2001
Name changed to Escala Group, Inc. 09/28/2005
Escala Group, Inc. name changed to Spectrum Group International, Inc. 05/21/2009

MANNING MARTHA CO (DE)
Stock Dividends - 10% 08/23/1976; 10% 09/27/1977
Charter cancelled and declared inoperative and void for non-payment of taxes 03/01/1987

MANNING MAY OIL CO (CO)
Reorganized under the laws of Delaware as The 1411 Holding Co. 09/17/1985
Each (24) shares Common no par exchanged for (1) share Common $0.001 par
(See The 1411 Holding Co.)

MANNIX RES INC (BC)
Each share old Common no par exchanged for (0.1) share new Common no par 07/25/2012
Name changed to International Tungsten Inc. 02/27/2014

MANNVILLE OIL & GAS LTD (AB)
Merged into Gulf Canada Resources Ltd. 8/14/95
Each share Common no par exchanged for $4.50 cash

MANO RIV RES INC (BC)
Reincorporated 07/19/2004
Place of incorporation changed from (YT) to (BC) 07/19/2004
Recapitalized as African Aura Mining Inc. 10/14/2009
Each share Common no par exchanged for (0.125) share Common no par
(See African Aura Mining Inc.)

MANOBEC PROSPECTORS LTD.
Liquidated in 1946

MANOIR INDS LTD (CANADA)
Common no par changed to 40¢ par 05/13/1969
Recapitalized as Canadian Manoir Industries Ltd. 06/08/1971
Each share 6% Preferred $10 par automatically became (1) share 6% Preferred $10 par
Each share Common 40¢ par exchanged for (0.4) share Common $1 par

MANOKA MNG & SMLT LTD (ON)
Recapitalized as Cat Lake Mines Ltd. 10/18/71
Each share Common $1 par exchanged for (0.0625) share Common no par
Cat Lake Mines Ltd. merged into Fundy Chemical International Ltd. 3/16/73
(See Fundy Chemical International Ltd.)

MANOMET MILLS
Liquidated in 1929

MANONTQUEB EXPLORATIONS, LTD. (ON)
Charter cancelled for failure to file reports and pay taxes in 1952

MANOR CARE INC (DE)
Common 10¢ par split (3) for (2) by issuance of (0.5) additional share 01/30/1980
Common 10¢ par split (3) for (2) by issuance of (0.5) additional share 02/27/1981
Common 10¢ par split (5) for (4) by issuance of (0.25) additional share 09/10/1981
Common 10¢ par split (3) for (2) by issuance of (0.5) additional share 02/25/1983
Common 10¢ par split (3) for (2) by issuance of (0.5) additional share 07/18/1983
Common 10¢ par split (3) for (2) by issuance of (0.5) additional share 12/05/1984
Common 10¢ par split (3) for (2) by issuance of (0.5) additional share 09/30/1985
Common 10¢ par split (3) for (2) by issuance of (0.5) additional share 03/27/1992

Each share Common 10¢ par received distribution of (1) share Choice Hotels Holdings, Inc. Common 1¢ par payable 11/01/1996 to holders of record 10/10/1996
Ex date - 11/04/1996
Merged into HCR Manor Care, Inc. 09/25/1998
Each share Common 10¢ par exchanged for (1) share Common 1¢ par
HCR Manor Care, Inc. name changed to Manor Care, Inc. (New) 09/30/1999
(See Manor Care, Inc. (New))

MANOR CARE INC NEW (DE)
Merged into MCHCR-CP Holdings, Inc. 12/21/2007
Each share Common 1¢ par exchanged for $67 cash

MANOR GLOBAL INC (CANADA)
Name changed to Martina Minerals Corp. 12/09/2011

MANOR GOLD MINES, LTD. (ON)
Charter cancelled for failure to file reports and pay taxes 8/6/57

MANOR MINES LTD (BC)
Struck off register and declared dissolved for failure to file returns 01/17/1977

MANOR NATL BK (MANOR, PA)
Reorganized as Manor Bank (Manor, PA) 12/15/2005
Each share Common $100 par exchanged for (4) shares Common $100 par

MANOR NURSING CTRS INC (DE)
Acquired by Capital Cities Nursing Centres, Inc. 8/3/70
Each share Common 5¢ par exchanged for (1) share 5% Non-Cum. Conv. Preferred no par
(See Capital Cities Nursing Centres, Inc.)

MANOR RES INC (CANADA)
Recapitalized as American Manor Corp. 06/29/1994
Each share Common no par exchanged for (0.1) share Common no par
American Manor Corp. recapitalized as American Manor Enterprises Inc. 08/10/2000 which name changed to Overland Realty Ltd. 10/25/2006
(See Overland Realty Ltd.)

MANOTTO MTRS INC (NV)
Charter revoked for failure to file reports and pay fees 03/01/1984

MANOX PETE LTD (BC)
Recapitalized as Petrox Petroleum Corp. 06/15/1977
Each share Capital Stock 50¢ par exchanged for (0.2) share Capital Stock no par
Petrox Petroleum Corp. name changed to Petrox Energy & Minerals Corp. (BC) 12/24/1982 which reincorporated in Canada 08/12/1985 which name changed to HuMedaTech International Inc. 02/04/1997 which recapitalized as Feathertouch E-Comm Inc. 11/10/1999
(See Feathertouch E-Comm Inc.)

MANPOWER INC (DE)
Ctfs. dated prior to 03/01/1976
Common $1 par changed to 66-2/3¢ par and (0.5) additional share issued 11/30/1961
Stock Dividends - 25% 07/01/1964; 25% 07/01/1965; 25% 07/01/1966
Merged into Parker Pen Co. 03/01/1976
Each share Common 66-2/3¢ par exchanged for $15.27 cash

MANPOWER INC (WI)
Name changed to ManpowerGroup 04/18/2011

MANPOWER INC NEW (DE)
Ctfs. dated after 1/31/86
Merged into Blue Arrow PLC 9/15/87
Each share Common $1.50 par exchanged for $82.50 cash

MANPOWER PLC (UNITED KINGDOM)
Reorganized under the laws of Wisconsin as Manpower Inc. 05/13/1991
Each Sponsored ADR for Ordinary 5p par exchanged for (1) share Common 1¢ par
Manpower Inc. name changed to ManpowerGroup 04/18/2011

MANQUEEN CORP. (NY)
Liquidation completed 3/12/58

MANRESA, INC. (NV)
Declared defunct in 1974
No stockholders' equity

MANRIDGE EXPLS LTD (ON)
Merged into Equisure Financial Network Inc. 09/16/1992
Each share Common no par exchanged for (0.04) share Common no par
(See Equisure Financial Network Inc.)

MANSA EXPLORATIONS LTD. (ON)
Charter cancelled for failure to pay taxes and file returns 3/15/72

MANSFIELD INDUSTRIES, INC. (DE)
Name changed to Argus, Inc. (DE) 05/14/1962
Argus, Inc. (DE) name changed to Spiratone International, Inc. 10/14/1988
(See Spiratone International, Inc.)

MANSFIELD INSURANCE CORP. (OH)
Merged into Acceleration Corp. (OH) 12/16/75
Each share Common $2 par exchanged for $2 cash

MANSFIELD INVTS INC (UT)
Name changed to Sea Alive Wellness Inc. 5/13/2005
Each share Common $1 par exchanged for (1) share Common $1 par

MANSFIELD MEDIA CORP (DE)
Name changed to Starlight Energy Corp. 04/27/2011

MANSFIELD MINERALS INC (BC)
Each share Common no par received distribution of (1) share Pachamama Resources Ltd. Common no par payable 11/27/2008 to holders of record 11/20/2008
Name changed to Goldrock Mines Corp. 01/22/2013
Goldrock Mines Corp. merged into Fortuna Silver Mines Inc. 07/28/2016

MANSFIELD SAVINGS TRUST NATIONAL BANK (MANSFIELD, OH)
Merged into First National Bank (Mansfield, OH) 4/1/53
Each share Capital Stock $100 par exchanged for (4) shares Capital Stock $25 par
First National Bank (Mansfield, OH) name changed to First Buckeye Bank, N.A. (Mansfield, OH) 3/12/80 which merged into Toledo Trustcorp, Inc. 12/30/82 which name changed to Trustcorp, Inc. 4/10/86 which was acquired by Society Corp. 1/5/90 which merged into KeyCorp (New) 3/1/94

MANSFIELD SHEET & TIN PLATE CO.
Merged into Empire Steel Corp. (Old) 00/00/1927
Details not available

MANSFIELD TELEPHONE CO. (OH)
5% Preferred $50 par called for redemption 09/30/1965
Acquired by United Utilities, Inc. 01/04/1966
Each share Common no par exchanged for (0.14285714) shares Common $2.50 par
United Utilities, Inc. name changed to United Telecommunications, Inc. 06/02/1972 which name changed to Sprint Corp. (KS) 02/26/1992 which name changed to Sprint Nextel Corp. 08/12/2005 which merged into Sprint Corp. (DE) 07/10/2013

MANSFIELD THEATRE CO. LTD.
Dissolved in 1943

MANSFIELD TIRE & RUBR CO (OH)
Each share Common no par exchanged for (3) shares Common $5 par 00/00/1952
6% Preferred $20 par called for redemption 03/10/1952
Common $5 par changed to $2.50 par and (1) additional share issued 05/28/1959
Common $2.50 par changed to no par 04/30/1979
Plan of liquidation filed under Chapter 11 Federal Bankruptcy Act confirmed 12/30/1985
No stockholders' equity

MANSION INDS INC (CA)
Merged into Netcoast Communications, Inc. 03/18/1996
Each share Common 16-2/3¢ par exchanged for (0.5) share Common 16-2/3¢ par
Netcoast Communications, Inc. recapitalized as SmartData, Inc. 10/26/2004 which name changed to Coastal Technologies Inc. 10/10/2005 which recapitalized as Cyclone Power Technologies, Inc. 07/02/2007

MANSON CREEK RES LTD (AB)
Reincorporated 06/02/1995
Place of incorporation changed from (BC) to (AB) 06/02/1995
Each share old Common no par exchanged (0.2) share new Common no par 04/23/2014
Name changed to Jade Leader Corp. 03/21/2018

MANSUR INDS INC (FL)
Issue Information - 1,000,000 shares COM offered at $7.50 per share on 09/27/1996
Name changed to SystemOne Technologies, Inc. 07/21/2000
(See SystemOne Technologies, Inc.)

MANTAUR PETE CORP (ON)
Name changed 06/25/1997
Name changed from Mantaur Goldfields Corp. to Mantaur Petroleum Corp. 06/25/1997
Merged into Videoflicks.com Inc. 03/24/1999
Each share Common no par exchanged for (0.2) Unit consisting of (1) share Common no par and (0.5) Common Stock Purchase Warrant Ser. A expiring 07/23/1999
(See Videoflicks.com Inc.)

MANTEX S A I C A (VENEZUELA)
Sponsored ADR's for Ordinary VEB 0.10 par split (3) for (2) by issuance of (0.5) additional ADR payable 07/23/1996 to holders of record 07/19/1996
Stock Dividend - 15% 08/26/1994
ADR agreement terminated 08/27/2012
Each Sponsored ADR for Ordinary VEB 0.10 par exchanged for (15) shares Ordinary VEB 0.10 par
Note: Unexchanged ADR's will be sold and the proceeds, if any, held for claim after 08/23/2013

MANTICORE PETE CORP (BC)
Recapitalized as Dexx Energy Corp. 05/31/1988
Each share Common no par exchanged for (0.2) share Common no par
(See Dexx Energy Corp.)

MANTIS MINERAL CORP (ON)
Each share old Common no par exchanged for (0.2) share new Common no par 09/21/2007
Name changed to Gondwana Oil Corp. 02/26/2014
Gondwana Oil Corp. name changed to European Metals Corp. 11/07/2014

MANTLE MINERALS INC (BC)
Recapitalized as Mantle Resources Inc. 08/09/2005
Each share Common no par exchanged for (0.5) share Common no par
Mantle Resources Inc. name changed to Canada Zinc Metals Corp. 09/26/2008 which name changed to ZincX Resources Corp. 05/07/2018

MANTLE RES INC (BC)
Name changed to Canada Zinc Metals Corp. 09/26/2008
Canada Zinc Metals Corp. name changed to ZincX Resources Corp. 05/07/2018

MANTLES MICKEY CTRY COOKIN INC (TX)
Name changed to Invesco International Corp. (TX) and Common no par changed to $1 par 06/30/1970
Invesco International Corp. (TX) reincorporated in Nevada 04/01/1971

MANTRA CAP INC (BC)
Common no par split (4) for (1) by issuance of (3) additional shares payable 12/31/2013 to holders of record 12/27/2013
Name changed to SolidusGold Inc. 09/04/2014

MANTRA MNG INC (BC)
Name changed to TintinaGold Resources Inc. 09/28/2009
TintinaGold Resources Inc. name changed to Tintina Resources Inc. 05/26/2011 which name changed to Sandfire Resources America Inc. 02/02/2018

MANTRA RESOURCES LTD (AUSTRALIA)
Acquired by JSC Atomredmetzoloto 06/07/2011
Each share Ordinary exchanged for $6.87 cash

MANTRA VENTURE GROUP LTD (BC)
Reincorporated 12/15/2008
Place of incorporation changed from (NV) to (BC) 12/15/2008
Name changed to Spectrum Global Solutions, Inc. (BC) 12/15/2017
Spectrum Global Solutions, Inc. (BC) reincorporated in Nevada 02/05/2018

MANUFACTURED HOME CMNTYS INC (MD)
Common 1¢ par split (2) for (1) by issuance of (1) additional share 04/22/1994
Name changed to Equity LifeStyle Properties, Inc. 11/16/2004

MANUFACTURED HOMES INC (NC)
Common 50¢ par split (2) for (1) by issuance of (1) additional share 6/3/85
Stock Dividend - 25% 11/26/84
Chapter 11 Federal Bankruptcy petition converted to Chapter 7 on 9/20/91
Stockholders' equity unlikely

MANUFACTURED RUBBER CO.
In process of dissolution in 1936

MANUFACTURERS & DEALERS FINANCE CORP. (IL)
Common $5 par changed to $40 par in 1950
Liquidation for cash completed 4/30/65

MANUFACTURERS & INVS CORP (FL)
Name changed to Landban of Florida Corp. 07/21/1970
Each share Common 10¢ par exchanged for (1) share Common 10¢ par
Landban of Florida Corp. name changed to Transamerica Business Corp. 01/26/1977
(See Transamerica Business Corp.)

MANUFACTURERS & INVS TECHNOLOGIES INC (UT)
Proclaimed dissolved for failure to file annual reports 8/1/91

MANUFACTURERS & JOBBERS FIN CORP (NC)
Merged into Northwestern Financial Corp. 10/31/1969
Each share 5% Preferred $100 par and 6% Preferred $100 par exchanged for $100 principal amount of a 7% Note
Each share Class A $10 par exchanged for (4) shares Common $5 par
Each share Class B $10 par exchanged for (4) shares Common $5 par
Northwestern Financial Corp. merged into First Union Corp. 12/02/1985 which name changed to Wachovia Corp. (Ctfs. dated after 09/01/2001) 09/01/2001 which merged into Wells Fargo & Co. (New) 12/31/2008

MANUFACTURERS & MERCHANTS MUT INS CO (NH)
Company went private in 1986
Details not available

MANUFACTURERS & TRADERS TR CO (BUFFALO, NY)
Each share Capital Stock $10 par exchanged for (2) shares Capital Stock $5 par 8/8/55
Reorganized as First Empire State Corp. 12/31/69
Each share Capital Stock $5 par exchanged for (1) share Common $5 par
First Empire State Corp. name changed to M&T Bank Corp. 6/1/98

MANUFACTURERS BANCORP INC (MO)
Merged into Ameribanc, Inc. 08/01/1983
Each share Common $1 par exchanged for (3-1/3) shares Common $5 par
(See Ameribanc, Inc.)

MANUFACTURERS BANCSHARES INC (FL)
Merged into Colonial BancGroup, Inc. 10/25/2001
Each share Common no par exchanged for (1.6) shares Common $2.50 par
(See Colonial BancGroup, Inc.)

MANUFACTURERS BK & TR CO (ST LOUIS, MO)
Capital Stock $20 par changed to $10 par and (1) additional share issued 01/19/1965
Stock Dividends - 25% 03/14/1949; 20% 02/04/1955; 11-1/9% 01/26/1962
Merged into Manufacturers Bancorp, Inc. 06/12/1980
Each share Capital Stock $10 par exchanged for (1) share Common $1 par
Manufacturers Bancorp, Inc. merged into Ameribanc, Inc. 08/01/1983
(See Ameribanc, Inc.)

MANUFACTURERS BK (LOS ANGELES, CA)
Capital Stock $7.50 par changed to $3.75 par and (1) additional share issued 09/03/1964
Capital Stock $3.75 par changed to $2.8125 par and (1/3) additional share issued 03/24/1980
Stock Dividends - 10% 03/15/1978; 10% 04/13/1979
Merged into Mitsui Bank, Ltd. 06/30/1981
Each share Capital Stock $2.8125 par exchanged for $45 cash

MANUFACTURERS BK OF FLA (TAMPA, FL)
Under plan of reorganization each share Common no par automatically became (1) share Manufacturers Bancshares, Inc. Common no par 06/23/1999
Manufacturers Bancshares, Inc. merged into Colonial BancGroup, Inc. 10/25/2001
(See Colonial BancGroup, Inc.)

MANUFACTURERS CREDIT CORP. (MD)
Dissolved 12/31/59

MANUFACTURERS EXCHANGE BUILDING, INC.
Dissolved in 1945

MANUFACTURERS FINANCE CO.
Liquidation approved and assets sold in 1939

MANUFACTURERS HANOVER CORP (DE)
Common $15 par changed to $7.50 par and (1) additional share issued 05/14/1971
5-1/2% Preferred Ser. A no par called for redemption 03/01/1979
Common $7.50 par changed to $1 par 04/22/1988
Merged into Chemical Banking Corp. 12/31/1991
Each share Adjustable Rate Preferred no par exchanged for (1) share Adjustable Rate Preferred Ser. E no par
Each share Adjustable Rate Preferred Ser. B no par exchanged for (1) share Adjustable Rate Preferred Ser. F no par
Each share 10.96% Preferred no par exchanged for (1) share 10.96% Preferred no par
Each share Common $1 par exchanged for (1.14) shares Common $1 par
Chemical Banking Corp. name changed to Chase Manhattan Corp. (New) 03/31/1996 which name changed to J.P. Morgan Chase & Co. 12/31/2000 which name changed to JPMorgan Chase & Co. 07/20/2004

MANUFACTURERS HANOVER TR CO (NEW YORK, NY)
Stock Dividend - 12% 05/05/1967
Reorganized under the laws of Delaware as Manufacturers Hanover Corp. 04/28/1969
Each share Capital Stock $15 par exchanged for (1) share Common $15 par
Manufacturers Hanover Corp. merged into Chemical Banking Corp. 12/31/1991 which name changed to Chase Manhattan Corp. (New) 03/31/1996 which name changed to J.P. Morgan Chase & Co. 12/31/2000 which name changed to JPMorgan Chase & Co. 07/20/2004

MANUFACTURERS LIABILITY INSURANCE CO.
Liquidated in 1941

MANUFACTURERS LIFE CAP CORP (CANADA)
Reincorporated 00/00/1984
Reincorporated 00/00/1985
Name changed 05/07/1986
Place of incorporation changed from (ON) to (BC) 00/00/1984
Place of incorporation changed from (BC) to (Canada) 00/00/1985
Name changed from Manufacturers Life Capital Corp. to Manufacturers Life Capital Corp. Inc. 05/07/1986
7.25% 1st Preferred Ser. A no par called for redemption at $25 plus $0.0149 accrued dividends on 01/04/1993
Public interest eliminated

MANUFACTURERS LIFE INSURANCE CO. (CANADA)
Each share Capital Stock $100 par exchanged for (10) shares Capital Stock $10 par in 1953
Completely mutualized over a five-year period ending on 1/7/63
Each share Capital Stock $10 par received total distribution of $275 cash
Note: Certificates were not required to be surrendered and are without value

MANUFACTURERS LIFE INS CO (CANADA)
6.10% Class A Preferred Ser. 6 no par called for redemption at $26 on 12/31/2007

MANUFACTURERS NATL BK (CHICAGO, IL)
Stock Dividends - 100% 06/20/1950; 100% 01/18/1960; 50% 01/20/1964
Reorganized as Manufacturers National Corp. 08/28/1968
Details not available

MANUFACTURERS NATL BK (DETROIT, MI)
Each share Common $50 par exchanged for (3) shares Common $20 par to effect a (2.5) for (1) split plus a 50% stock dividend 00/00/1951
Each share Common $20 par changed to $10 par and (1) additional share issued 07/26/1955
Stock Dividends - 33-1/3% 01/11/1946; 11-1/9% 01/25/1955; 10% 01/20/1961; 10% 03/12/1968; 20% 01/11/1971
Under plan of reorganization each share Common $10 par automatically became (1) share Manufacturers National Corp. Common $10 par 04/24/1973
Manufacturers National Corp. merged into Comerica, Inc. 06/18/1992

MANUFACTURERS NATIONAL BANK (TROY, NY)
Name changed to Marine Midland National Bank (Troy, N.Y.) 12/1/65
Marine Midland National Bank (Troy, N.Y.) name changed to Marine Midland Bank-Eastern, N.A. (Troy, N.Y.) 12/31/71
(See Marine Midland Bank-Eastern, N.A. (Troy, N.Y.))

MANUFACTURERS NATIONAL CORP. (IL)
Acquired by MB Financial, Inc. 11/15/2001
Details not available

MANUFACTURERS NATL CORP (DE)
Common $10 par split (3) for (2) by issuance of (0.5) additional share 07/06/1973
Common $10 par split (2) for (1) by issuance of (1) additional share 10/11/1985
Common $10 par split (2) for (1) by issuance of (1) additional share 08/15/1991
Stock Dividend - 50% 10/31/1978
Merged into Comerica, Inc. 06/18/1992
Each share Common $10 par exchanged for (0.81) share Common $5 par

MANUFACTURERS NATL CORP (IL)
Each share old Common exchanged for (0.00001) share new Common 11/10/1998
Note: In effect holders received approximately $11.66 cash per share and public interest was eliminated

MANUFACTURERS REALTY CO. (DE)
Liquidation completed 11/26/56

MANUFACTURERS SVCS LTD (DE)
Issue Information - 11,000,000 shares COM offered at $16 per share on 06/22/2000
Merged into Celestica Inc. 3/12/2004
Each share Common $0.001 par exchanged for (0.375) share Subordinate no par

MANUFACTURERS SYS INC (MN)
Stock Dividend - 10% 06/30/1976
Acquired by Standex International Corp. 10/31/1977
Each share Common 20¢ par exchanged for $8 cash

MANUFACTURERS TRADING CORP.
Declared insolvent by court in 1949

MANUFACTURERS TRUST CO. (NEW YORK, NY)
Capital Stock $20 par changed to $10 par and (1) additional share issued 01/20/1956
Capital Stock $10 par changed to $20 par 01/30/1959
Merged into Manufacturers Hanover Trust Co. (New York, NY) 09/08/1961
Each share Capital Stock $20 par exchanged for (1-1/3) shares Capital Stock $15 par
Manufacturers Hanover Trust Co. (New York, NY) reorganized in Delaware as Manufacturers Hanover Corp. 04/28/1969 which merged into Chemical Banking Corp. 12/31/1991 which name changed to Chase Manhattan Corp. (New) 03/31/1996 which name changed to J.P. Morgan Chase & Co. 12/31/2000 which name changed to JPMorgan Chase & Co. 07/20/2004

MANUFACTURING DATA SYS INC (DE)
Acquired by Schlumberger Ltd. 01/21/1981
Each share Common 1¢ par exchanged for (0.6375) share Common $1 par

MANUGISTICS GROUP INC (DE)
Issue Information - 2,400,000 shares COM offered at $10 per share on 08/13/1993
Common $0.002 par split (2) for (1) by issuance of (1) additional share payable 07/11/1997 to holders of record 05/23/1997
Common $0.002 par split (2) for (1) by issuance of (1) additional share payable 12/07/2000 to holders of record 11/20/2000 Ex date - 12/08/2000
Merged into JDA Software Group, Inc. 07/05/2006
Each share Common $0.002 par exchanged for $2.50 cash

MANULIFE BROMPTON ADVANTAGED BD FD (ON)
Name changed to Aston Hill Advantage Bond Fund 09/16/2011
Aston Hill Advantage Bond Fund name changed to LOGiQ Advantage Bond Fund 05/12/2017
(See LOGiQ Advantage Bond Fund)

MANULIFE DIVERSIFIED CANADA FUND (ON)
Under plan of merger each share Advisor Ser. and Ser. F automatically became Manulife Canadian Focused Fund Advisor Ser. or Ser. F on a net asset basis 11/04/2011

MANULIFE FINL CORP (CANADA)
Class A Preferred Ser. 4 called for redemption at $25 plus $0.4125 accrued dividends on 06/19/2014
Non-Cum. Rate Reset Preferred Class 1 Ser. 1 called for redemption at $25 on 09/19/2014
Non-Cum. Preferred Class A Ser. 1 called for redemption at $25 on 06/19/2015
(Additional Information in Active)

MANULIFE STRATEGIC INCOME OPPORTUNITIES FD (ON)
Name changed to Manulife Global Tactical Credit Fund and Trust Units reclassified as Advisor Ser. Units 06/28/2013

MANUS INDS INC (BC)
Recapitalized as Consolidated Manus Industries Inc. 11/10/1992
Each share Common no par exchanged for (0.38461538) share Common no par
Consolidated Manus Industries Inc. recapitalized as Westmount Resources Ltd. (New) 02/08/1996 which recapitalized as Mt. Tom Minerals Corp. 05/20/1998 which name changed to Global Net Entertainment Corp. 10/14/1999 which recapitalized as Guildhall Minerals Ltd. 02/21/2006 which name changed to Edge Resources Inc. 07/28/2009
(See Edge Resources Inc.)

MANUWEB SOFTWARE SYS INC (BC)
Recapitalized as VisualVault Corp. 12/21/2011
Each share Common no par exchanged for (0.14285714) share Common no par
VisualVault Corp. recapitalized as Certive Solutions Inc. 10/07/2013

MANVILLE CORP (DE)
Plan of reorganization under Chapter 11 Federal Bankruptcy proceedings confirmed 11/28/1988
Each share $5.40 Preferred $1 par exchanged for (1) share Preference Ser. B $1 par and (2.16091) shares new Common $2.50 par
Each share old Common $2.50 par exchanged for (0.12499) share new Common $2.50 par
Note: Unexchanged certificates were cancelled and became without value 11/30/1993
$2.70 Preferred Ser. B $1 par called for redemption 03/28/1996
Name changed to Schuller Corp. 03/29/1996
Schuller Corp. name changed to Johns-Manville Corp. (New) 05/05/1997
(See Johns-Manville Corp. (New))

MANVILLE JENCKES CO.
Reorganized as Manville Jenckes Corp. in 1933 which was acquired by Textron Inc. (R.I.) in 1945

MANVILLE JENCKES CORP.
Acquired by Textron Inc. (R.I.) through purchase of Common in 1945

MANVILLE MFG CORP (MI)
Charter declared inoperative and void for failure to file reports 07/15/2007

MANVILLE NATL BK (MANVILLE, NJ)
Merged into First National Bank of Central Jersey (Bridgewater Township, NJ) in October 1982
Details not available

MANVILLE OIL & URANIUM CO., INC. (WY)
Charter revoked for failure to pay corporate license taxes 3/15/61

MANWEB PLC (UNITED KINGDOM)
ADR agreement terminated 12/14/95
Each Final Installment Sponsored ADR for Ordinary 50p par exchanged for $151.65 cash

MAP PHARMACEUTICALS INC (DE)
Acquired by Allergan, Inc. 03/01/2013
Each share Common 1¢ par exchanged for $25 cash

MAPAN ENERGY LTD (AB)
Merged into Tourmaline Oil Corp. 08/17/2015
Each share Common no par exchanged for (0.0379) share Common no par
Note: Unexchanged certificates were cancelled and became without value 08/17/2018

MAPCO INC (DE)
$1.12 Conv. Preferred Ser. A no par called for redemption 06/21/1972
Common no par split (2) for (1) by issuance of (1) additional share 09/13/1972
Common no par changed to $1 par 10/30/1972
Common $1 par split (2) for (1) by issuance of (1) additional share 02/01/1974
Common $1 par split (2) for (1) by issuance of (1) additional share 05/12/1989
Common $1 par split (2) for (1) by issuance of (1) additional share payable 09/30/1996 to holders of record 09/16/1996 Ex date - 10/01/1996
Merged into Williams Companies, Inc. 03/28/1998
Each share Common $1 par exchanged for (1.665) shares Common $1 par

MAPES CONSOLIDATED MANUFACTURING CO. (DE)
Merged into Central Fibre Products Co., Inc. in 1954
Each share Capital Stock no par exchanged for (2/3) share Common $2.50 par and and (2/3) share Non-Voting Common $2.50 par
Central Fibre Products Co., Inc. name changed to Central Fibre Products Co. 1/1/55 which merged into Packaging Corp. of America 7/31/59 which was acquired by Tennessee Gas Transmission Co. 6/8/65 which name changed to Tenneco Inc. 4/11/66 which merged into El Paso Natural Gas Co. 12/12/96 which reorganized as El Paso Energy Corp. 8/1/98 which name changed to El Paso Corp. 2/5/2001

MAPICS INC (MA)
Merged into Infor Global Solutions 4/18/2005
Each share Common 1¢ par exchanged for $12.75 cash

MAPIN GOLD MINES LTD. (ON)
Charter cancelled for failure to file reports and pay taxes 9/9/58

MAPINFO CORP (DE)
Reincorporated 11/06/1997
State of incorporation changed from (NY) to (DE) 11/06/1997
Common $0.002 par split (3) for (2) by issuance of (0.5) additional share payable 01/10/2000 to holders of record 12/20/1999
Common $0.002 par split (3) for (2) by issuance of (0.5) additional share payable 09/28/2000 to holders of record 09/08/2000 Ex date - 09/29/2000
Merged into Pitney Bowes Inc. 04/19/2007
Each share Common $0.002 par exchanged for $20.25 cash

MAPIT CORP (CO)
Proclaimed dissolved for failure to file annual reports 1/1/93

MAPLE ENTERPRISES INC (NV)
Name changed to Warner Technologies Inc. 11/29/88
Warner Technologies Inc. name changed to MGPX Ventures Inc. 4/22/98 which name changed to Contango Oil & Gas Co. (NV) 10/7/99 which reorganized in Delaware 12/1/2000

MAPLE LEAF FOODS INC OLD (CANADA)
Merged into Maple Leaf Foods Inc. (New) 04/26/1995
Each share Common no par exchanged for either (2.143) shares Common no par or $15 cash

MAPLE LEAF GARDENS LTD (ON)
Each share old Common no par exchanged for (4) shares Common no par in 1947
New Common no par split (5) for (1) by issuance of (4) additional shares 12/7/65
New Common no par split (5) for (1) by issuance of (4) additional shares 1/12/87
Merged into MGL Ventures 8/6/96
Each share Common no par exchanged for $49.50 cash

MAPLE LEAF GOLD MINING CO., INC. (WA)
Charter revoked for failure to file reports and pay fees 7/1/65

MAPLE LEAF MINES & SECURITIES (1936) LTD.
Liquidated in 1941

MAPLE LEAF MINES LTD.
Liquidated in 1936

MAPLE LEAF MLS LTD (ON)
5-1/2% Class B Preferred $100 par called for redemption 11/29/74
Common no par split (3) for (1) by issuance of (2) additional shares 7/15/77
Merged into Norin Corp. (DE) 2/1/79
Each share Common no par exchanged for $20 cash

MAPLE LEAF MLS ONT INC (ON)
Each share 1st Preferred $100 par exchanged for (7) shares Common no par
Each share Class B no par exchanged for (1) share Common no par 00/00/1934
Each (5) shares Common no par exchanged for (1) share new Common no par 00/00/1937
Merged into Maple Leaf Mills Ltd. 03/31/1961
Each share 5% Preferred $100 par exchanged for 5-1/2% Class B Preferred $100 par
Each share Common no par exchanged for (1.4) shares Common no par
(See Maple Leaf Mills Ltd.)

MAPLE LEAF OIL CO., LTD.
Acquired by New Pacalta Oils Co., Ltd. in 1949
Details not available

MAPLE LEAF PETE LTD (BC)
Recapitalized as International Maple Leaf Resource Corp. 04/23/1986
Each share Common no par exchanged for (0.2) share Common no par
International Maple Leaf Resource Corp. recapitalized as Maple Resource Corp. 08/29/1989 which recapitalized as Birchwood Ventures Ltd. 08/17/1992 which recapitalized as Oromin Explorations Ltd. (Old) 09/30/1997 which merged into Oromin Explorations Ltd. (New) 02/25/2002 which merged into Teranga Gold Corp. 10/08/2013

MAPLE LEAF REFORESTATION INC (AB)
Name changed to Maple Leaf Green World Inc. 10/05/2012

MAPLE LEAF RESOURCE CORP (BC)
Recapitalized as Maple Leaf Royalties Corp. 11/21/2014
Each share Common no par exchanged for (0.25) share Common no par
Maple Leaf Royalties Corp. merged into Eagle Energy Inc. 02/01/2016

MAPLE LEAF ROYALTIES CORP (BC)
Merged into Eagle Energy Inc. 02/01/2016
Each share Common no par exchanged for (0.0947) share Common no par
Note: Unexchanged certificates were cancelled and became without value 02/01/2018

MAPLE LEAF SHORT DURATION 2010 FLOW THRU LTD PARTNERSHIP (BC)
Assets transferred to Maple Leaf Corporate Funds Ltd. 10/21/2011
Each Unit of Ltd. Partnership received (1.337) shares Maple Leaf Resource Class Ser. A

MAPLE LEAF SHORT DURATION 2011 FLOW THRU LTD PARTNERSHIP (BC)
Assets transferred to Maple Leaf Corporate Funds Ltd. 05/08/2012
Each Unit of Ltd. Partnership received (1.2001) shares Maple Leaf Resource Class Ser. A

MAPLE LEAF SHORT DURATION 2011 II FLOW THRU LTD PARTNERSHIP (BC)
Assets transferred to Maple Leaf Corporate Funds Ltd. 05/08/2012
Each National Class Unit of Ltd. Partnership received (1.327) shares Maple Leaf Resource Class Ser. A
Each Quebec Class Unit of Ltd. Partnership received (1.4204) shares Maple Leaf Resource Class Ser. A

MAPLE LEAF SPRINGS WTR CORP (BC)
Merged into International Maple Leaf Springs Ltd. 02/24/1998
Each share Common no par exchanged for (0.2) share Common no par
(See International Maple Leaf Springs Ltd.)

MAPLE MARK INTL INC (AB)
Recapitalized as Linear Resources Inc. 10/15/1999
Each share Common no par exchanged for (0.1) share Common no par
Linear Resources Inc. name changed to Linear Gold Corp. (AB) 11/24/2003 which reincorporated in Canada 11/10/2004 which merged into Brigus Gold Corp. (YT) 06/25/2010 which reincorporated in Canada 06/09/2011
(See Brigus Gold Corp.)

MAPLE MINERALS CORP (ON)
Name changed to Mega Uranium Ltd. 10/19/2005

MAPLE MINERALS INC (ON)
Recapitalized as Maple Minerals Corp. 11/9/2001
Each share Common no par exchanged for (1/3) share Common no par
Maple Minerals Corp. name changed to Mega Uranium Ltd. 10/19/2005

MAPLE MTN EXPLORATIONS INC (NV)
Name changed to Pegasi Energy Resources Corp. 02/06/2008

MAPLE MTN PUMPKINS & AGRICULTURE INC (NV)
Each share old Common $0.001 par exchanged for (2.5) shares new Common $0.001 par 10/21/2008
Name changed to Piccolo Educational Systems, Inc. 05/08/2009

MAPLE PLAIN INC (MN)
Liquidation completed
Each share Common 10¢ par exchanged for initial distribution of $1.60 cash 04/14/1977
Each share Common 10¢ par received second and final distribution of $0.1288 cash 03/24/1978

MAPLE PWR CAP CORP (ON)
Recapitalized as Intrinsic4D Inc. 06/22/2015
Each share Common no par exchanged for (0.25) share Common no par

MAPLE RESOURCE CORP (BC)
Recapitalized as Birchwood Ventures Ltd. 08/17/1992
Each share Common no par exchanged for (0.22727272) shares Common no par
Birchwood Ventures Ltd. recapitalized as Oromin Explorations Ltd. (Old) 09/30/1997 which merged into Oromin Explorations Ltd. (New) 02/25/2002 which merged into Teranga Gold Corp. 10/08/2013

MAPLE TECHNOLOGY LTD (BC)
Recapitalized as Peritronics Medical Inc. (Old) 10/24/1987
Each share Common no par exchanged for (1) share Common no par
Peritronics Medical Inc. (Old) recapitalized as Consolidated Peritronics Medical Inc. 11/06/1989 which recapitalized as Peritronics Medical Inc. (New) 11/15/1996
(See Peritronics Medical Inc. (New))

MAPLE TREE KIDS INC (NV)
Recapitalized as Aerkomm Inc. 01/20/2017
Each share Common $0.001 par exchanged for (0.1) share Common $0.001 par

MAPLE VALLEY EXPLORATIONS LTD. (BC)
Name changed to Maple Technology Ltd. 06/07/1985
Maple Technology Ltd. recapitalized as Peritronics Medical Inc. (Old) 10/24/1987 which recapitalized as Consolidated Peritronics Medical Inc. 11/06/1989 which recapitalized as Peritronics Medical Inc. (New) 11/15/1996
(See Peritronics Medical Inc. (New))

MAPLES PARTNERS INVTS INC (AB)
2nd Preferred Ser. A called for redemption at $0.25 plus $0.1062 accrued dividends on 01/30/2004
Public interest eliminated

MAPLEWOOD BK & TR CO (MAPLEWOOD, MO)
Capital Stock $20 par changed to $40 par 5/17/60
Name changed to Pioneer Bank & Trust Co. (Maplewood, MO) 8/1/70
(See Pioneer Bank & Trust Co. (Maplewood, MO))

MAPLEWOOD BK & TR CO (MAPLEWOOD, NJ)
Each share Capital Stock $100 par exchanged for (5) shares Capital Stock $20 par in 1954
Capital Stock $20 par changed to $5 par and (3) additional shares issued 8/1/67
Stock Dividends - 14-2/7% 12/23/59; 25% 1/15/64; 10% 6/30/70
Merged into Summit Bancorporation 4/1/81
Each share Capital Stock $5 par exchanged for (1.16) shares Ser. A Preferred no par
Summit Bancorporation merged into

Summit Bancorp 3/1/96 which merged into FleetBoston Financial Corp. 3/1/2001 which merged into Bank of America Corp. 4/1/2004

MAPLEX MGMT & HLDGS LTD (CANADA)
Each share Common no par exchanged for (1) share Class A no par and (1) share Class B no par 04/24/1981
Stock Dividend - 50% 02/24/1987
Merged into M.E.R. Financial Corp. 03/11/1987
Each share Class A no par exchanged for $14.26 cash
Each share Class B no par exchanged for $14.26 cash

MAPQUEST COM INC (DE)
Merged into America Online, Inc. 06/29/2000
Each share Common $0.001 par exchanged for (0.31558) share Common 1¢ par
America Online, Inc. merged into AOL Time Warner Inc. 01/11/2001 which name changed to Time Warner Inc. (New) 10/16/2003 which merged into AT&T Inc. 06/15/2018

MAR GOLD RES LTD (BC)
Recapitalized as West-Mar Resources Ltd. 12/24/84
Each share Capital Stock no par exchanged for (0.25) share Common no par
West-Mar Resources Ltd. recapitalized as Mar-West Resources Ltd. 6/2/93 which merged into Glamis Gold Ltd. 10/19/98 which merged into Goldcorp Inc. (New) 11/4/2006

MAR KED MINERAL EXPL INC (NV)
Common $0.001 par split (3) for (2) by issuance of (0.5) additional share payable 07/18/2008 to holders of record 07/13/2008 Ex date - 07/21/2008
Name changed to North American Energy Resources, Inc. 08/15/2008
North American Energy Resources, Inc. name changed to KSIX Media Holdings, Inc. 08/03/2015 which name changed to Surge Holdings, Inc. 01/16/2018

MAR-SEARCH INC. (TN)
Adjudicated bankrupt 1/24/74
No stockholders' equity

MAR-TEX OIL & GAS CO. (NV)
Liquidation completed 4/20/59
Details not available

MAR-TEX OIL CO.
Mar-Tex Realization Corp. formed for purpose of liquidation in 1943 which became an operating company in 1946 which name was changed to Mar-Tex Oil & Gas Co. in 1953 and then completely liquidated 4/20/59

MAR-TEX REALIZATION CORP. (NV)
Common no par changed to 10¢ par in 1944
Name changed to Mar-Tex Oil & Gas Co. in 1953
(See Mar-Tex Oil & Gas Co.)

MAR TIERRA, INC. (LIBERIA)
Completely liquidated 12/00/1984
Each share Common 1¢ par exchanged for $1.90 cash

MAR VENTURES INC (DE)
Name changed to PYR Energy Corp. (DE) 11/12/97
PYR Energy Corp. (DE) reincorporated in Maryland 7/30/2001
(See PYR Energy Corp.)

MAR VISTA COMMERCIAL & SAVINGS BANK (BEVERLY HILLS, CA)
Name changed to Fidelity Bank (Beverly Hills, Calif.) 10/1/56

MAR-WEST RES LTD (BC)
Merged into Glamis Gold Ltd. 10/19/98
Each share Common no par exchanged for (0.5) share Common no par
Glamis Gold Ltd. merged into Goldcorp Inc. (New) 11/4/2006

MARA MINERALS & OILS INC (BC)
Merged into Cymric Resources Ltd. (BC) 09/23/1983
Each share Capital Stock no par exchanged for (0.25) share Common no par
Cymric Resources Ltd. (BC) reincorporated in Canada 04/29/1985 which name changed to Rimoil Corp. 12/06/1988 which merged into Barrington Petroleum Ltd. 09/22/1995 which merged into Petrobank Energy & Resources Ltd. (Old) 07/18/2001 which reorganized as Petrobank Energy & Resources Ltd. (New) 01/07/2013 which recapitalized as Touchstone Exploration Inc. 05/20/2014

MARACAIBO OIL EXPLORATION CORP. (DE)
Capital Stock no par changed to $1 par 00/00/1935
Liquidated 03/06/1964
Each share Capital Stock $1 par exchanged for (1) Tribune Oil Corp. Common Stock Purchase Warrant expiring 06/26/1964, $12 principal amount of Tribune Oil Corp. 5% Sub. Debentures due 00/00/1979 and $1.50 cash

MARACAMBEAU MINES LTD (ON)
Charter cancelled for failure to pay taxes and file returns 10/18/78

MARACOTE INTL RES INC (BC)
Recapitalized as Lund Ventures Ltd. 05/28/2001
Each share Common no par exchanged for (0.2) share Common no par
Lund Ventures Ltd. recapitalized as Lund Gold Ltd. 07/10/2003 which recapitalized as Lund Enterprises Corp. 12/19/2013

MARADEL PRODUCTS, INC. (DE)
Name changed to Del Laboratories, Inc. 04/18/1966
(See Del Laboratories, Inc.)

MARALGO MINES LTD (BC)
Reincorporated 06/06/1984
Each share old Common no par exchanged for (0.16666666) share new Common no par 04/22/1983
Place of incorporation changed from (ON) to (BC) 06/06/1984
Recapitalized as Rich Coast Sulphur Ltd. 03/13/1986
Each share Common no par exchanged for (0.5) share Common no par
Rich Coast Sulphur Ltd. recapitalized as Consolidated Rich Coast Sulphur Ltd. 06/19/1991 which merged into Rich Coast Resources Ltd. (BC) 01/25/1993 which reincorporated in Delaware as Rich Coast Inc. 09/16/1996 which reincorporated in Nevada on 07/14/1998 which recapitalized as Media Pal Holdings, Corp. 03/16/2010

MARAMAR VENTURES INC (AB)
Name changed to IMS Petroleum Inc. 04/04/2001
IMS Petroleum Inc. recapitalized as Pocaterra Energy Inc. 01/14/2005 which was acquired by Buffalo Oil Corp. 01/01/2007 which name changed to Buffalo Resources Corp. 08/03/2007 which merged into Twin Butte Energy Ltd. 10/15/2009

MARANCHA CORP.
Dissolved in 1935

MARAND COURT LIQUIDATION TRUST
Liquidated in 1944

MARANTHA II INC (CO)
Name changed to Equity Financial Group, Inc. 09/07/1988

MARANTZ INC (DE)
Reincorporated 07/17/1986
State of incorporation changed from (CA) to (DE) 07/17/1986
Merged into Dynascan Corp. 02/27/1987
Each share Common $1 par exchanged for $6 cash

MARAPHARM VENTURES INC (BC)
Name changed to Liht Cannabis Corp. 10/25/2018

MARATHON ACQUISITION CORP (DE)
Issue Information - 37,500,000 UNITS consisting of (1) share COM and (1) WT offered at $8 per Unit on 08/24/2006
Reincorporated under the laws of Marshall Islands as Global Ship Lease, Inc. and Common $0.0001 par reclassified as Class A Common 1¢ par 08/14/2008

MARATHON BANCORP (CA)
Common no par split (5) for (4) by issuance of (0.25) additional share 02/24/1986
Common no par split (5) for (4) by issuance of (0.25) additional share 06/30/1987
Merged into First Community Bancorp 08/23/2002
Each share Common no par exchanged for $5.55 cash

MARATHON BAR CORP (DE)
Recapitalized as Lipocine Inc. 07/25/2013
Each share Common $0.0001 par exchanged for (0.01) share Common $0.0001 par

MARATHON BATTERY CO. (WI)
Merged into Gould-National Batteries, Inc. 3/6/68
Each share Capital Stock 10¢ par exchanged for (0.232473) share Common $4 par
Gould-National Batteries, Inc. name changed to Gould Inc. 7/31/69
(See Gould Inc.)

MARATHON CORP. (WI)
Each share Common $12.50 par exchanged for (2) shares Common $6.25 par in 1946
Stock Dividend - 100% 1/25/52
Assets sold to American Can Co. on a (0.8) for (1) basis 12/3/57
American Can Co. name changed to Primerica Corp. (NJ) 4/28/87 which was acquired by Primerica Corp. (DE) 12/15/88 which name changed to Travelers Inc. 12/31/93 which name changed to Travelers Group Inc. 4/16/95 which name changed to Citigroup Inc. 10/8/98

MARATHON ENTERPRISES INC (NJ)
Merged into Charmont, Inc. 02/05/1979
Each share Capital Stock no par exchanged for $6.35 cash

MARATHON FINL CORP (VA)
Under plan of reorganization each share Common $1 par automatically became (1) share Premier Community Bankshares, Inc. Common $1 par 11/20/2000
Premier Community Bankshares, Inc. merged into United Bankshares, Inc. 07/16/2007

MARATHON FOODS INC (BC)
Delisted from Toronto Venture Stock Exchange 06/05/2002

MARATHON GOLD CORP (UT)
Reorganized under the laws of Delaware as American Consolidated Gold Corp. 09/08/1987
Each share Common $0.0016 par exchanged for (0.1) share Common 10¢ par
American Consolidated Gold Corp. name changed to American Consolidated Growth Corp. 05/31/1991
(See American Consolidated Growth Corp.)

MARATHON GROUP CORP (ID)
Reincorporated under the laws of Wyoming and Common $0.001 par changed to $0.000001 par 06/02/2011

MARATHON LETOURNEAU CO. (CA)
Merged into Marathon Manufacturing Co. 11/1/71
Each share Common $1 par exchanged for (0.5) share Common $1 par
Marathon Manufacturing Co. merged into Penn Central Corp. 12/18/79 which name changed to American Premier Underwriters, Inc. 3/25/94 which merged into American Premier Group, Inc. 4/3/95 which name changed to American Financial Group, Inc. 6/9/95 which merged into American Financial Group, Inc. (Holding Co.) 12/2/98

MARATHON MFG CO (DE)
Common $1 par split (3) for (2) by issuance of (0.5) additional share 12/9/77
Common $1 par split (5) for (4) by issuance of (0.25) additional share 5/31/79
Merged into Penn Central Corp. 12/18/79
Each share Common $1 par exchanged for (1) share $5.27 Conv. Special Preference no par
Penn Central Corp. name changed to American Premier Underwriters, Inc. 3/25/94 which merged into American Premier Group, Inc. 4/3/95 which name changed to American Financial Group, Inc. 6/9/95 which merged into American Financial Group, Inc. (Holding Co.) 12/2/97

MARATHON MED EQUIP CORP (CO)
Charter dissolved for failure to file annual reports 01/01/1989

MARATHON MINERALS INC (BC)
Struck off register and declared dissolved for failure to file returns 08/25/1995

MARATHON MINES LTD. (ON)
Merged into Trimar Holdings & Explorations Ltd. 6/22/67
Each share Capital Stock $1 par exchanged for (0.2) share Capital Stock no par
(See Trimar Holdings & Explorations Ltd.)

MARATHON MTR SUPPLIES LTD (ON)
Thru purchase offer 100% of Common no par acquired by Gas Machinery Co. Ltd. 00/00/1968
7% Preference $10 par called for redemption 02/13/1978
Public interest eliminated

MARATHON OFFICE SUPPLY INC (DE)
Common 30¢ par split (100) for (1) by issuance of (99) addtional shares 05/13/1982
Charter forfeited for failure to maintain a registered agent 02/25/1991

MARATHON OIL CANADA LTD (ON)
Exchangeable Shares no par called for redemption at (1) share of USX-Marathon Group Inc. new Common $1 par 8/13/2001

MARATHON OIL CO (OH)
Common no par split (2) for (1) by

issuance of (1) additional share 1/26/68
Common no par split (2) for (1) by issuance of (1) additional share 6/14/79
Merged into United States Steel Corp. 3/11/82
Each share Common no par exchanged for $100 principal amount of USS Holdings Co. 12-1/2% 12-yr. Guaranteed Notes due 3/1/94

MARATHON PAPER MILLS CO.
Recapitalized as Marathon Corp. on a (2) for (1) basis in 1944
Marathon Corp. acquired by American Can Co. 12/3/57 which name changed to Primerica Corp. (NJ) 4/28/87 which was acquired by Primerica Corp. (DE) 12/15/88 which name changed to Travelers Inc. 12/31/93 which name changed to Travelers Group Inc. 4/16/95 which name changed to Citigroup Inc. 10/8/98

MARATHON PGM CORP (CANADA)
Merged into Stillwater Mining Co. 12/02/2010
Each share Common no par exchanged for (0.112) share Common 1¢ par, (0.5) share Marathon Gold Corp. Common no par and $1.775 cash
Note: Unexchanged certificates were cancelled and became without value 12/02/2016
(See each company's listing)

MARATHON SECS CORP (DE)
Liquidation completed
Each share Common $1 par received initial distribution of (0.1154) share Bonanza International, Inc. Common no par; (0.027) share Buttes Gas & Oil Co. Common no par; (0.0314) share Digital Computer Controls, Inc. Common 1¢ par (0.0754) share HCA-Martin, Inc. Common $3 par; (0.0368) share Hydron Pacific, Ltd. Common $0.025 par; (0.0614) share Marlboro Enterprises, Inc. Common 10¢ par; (0.0645) share National Patent Development Corp. Common 1¢ par; (0.1474) share Puritan Fashions Corp. Common $1 par; (0.086) share Sonesta International Hotels Corp. Common 80¢ par; (0.0803) share Starrett Housing Corp. Common $1 par; (0.0485) share Tishman Realty & Construction Co., Inc. Common $1 par and (0.0293) share Vindale Corp. Common no par 12/9/74
(See each company's listing)
Each share Common $1 par received second distribution of $0.50 cash 11/18/75
Each share Common $1 par received third distribution of $0.25 cash 12/23/76
Each share Common $1 par received fourth distribution of $0.30 cash 2/8/78
Each share Common $1 par received fifth distribution of $0.50 cash 8/7/78
Each share Common $1 par received sixth and final distribution of $0.08 cash 12/20/78
Certificates were not required to be surrendered and are now valueless

MARATHON SHOE CO.
Liquidated in 1935

MARATHON TELECOM CORP (BC)
Struck off register and declared dissolved for failure to file returns 3/3/95

MARAYNE APARTMENTS
Property sold 00/00/1948
Details not available

MARBACO RES LTD (AB)
Struck off register and declared dissolved for failure to file returns 3/29/85

MARBANC FINL CORP (IN)
Common no par split (2) for (1) by issuance of (1) additional share payable 07/17/1999 to holders of record 07/15/1999 Ex date - 07/27/1999
Merged into Independent Alliance Banks, Inc. 05/01/2005
Each share Common no par exchanged for (1) share Common
Note: Non-Indiana residents holding (199) or fewer shares received $71.50 cash
Independent Alliance Banks, Inc. merged into First Merchants Corp. 07/14/2017

MARBENOR MALARTIC MINES LTD. (ON)
Recapitalized as Consolidated Marbenor Mines Ltd. 00/00/1955
Each share Capital Stock $1 par exchanged for (0.2) share Capital Stock $1 par
Consolidated Marbenor Mines Ltd. merged into Canhorn Mining Corp. 01/09/1986 which merged into Canhorn Chemical Corp. 04/26/1995 which merged into Nayarit Gold Inc. 05/02/2005 which merged into Capital Gold Corp. 08/02/2010 which merged into Gammon Gold Inc. (QC) 04/08/2011 which reincorporated in Ontario as AuRico Gold Inc. 06/14/2011

MARBLE CANYON URANIUM, INC. (UT)
Recapitalized as Marcan Corp. 3/11/69
Each share Common 1¢ par exchanged for (0.01) share Common 10¢ par
Marcan Corp. name changed to Modulearn, Inc. 10/18/72 which name changed to Micro General Corp. (UT) 1/25/82 which reincorporated in Delaware 7/1/88 which merged into Fidelity National Information Solutions, Inc. 7/10/2002 which merged into Fidelity National Financial, Inc. 9/30/2003 which merged into Fidelity National Information Services, Inc. 11/9/2006

MARBLE FINL CORP (VT)
Merged into Albank Financial Corp. 1/3/96
Each share Common $1 par exchanged for $18 cash

MARBLE HOLDING CO.
Liquidated in 1945

MARBLE MORTGAGE CO. (CA)
Acquired by exchange for Western Bancorporation 11/30/65
(See Western Bancorporation)

MARBLE PRODS CO GA (GA)
Acquired by Walter (Jim) Corp. 7/14/72
Each share Capital Stock $1 par exchanged for (1/3) share Common 16-2/3¢ par
(See Walter (Jim) Corp.)

MARBLEDGE GROUP INC (DE)
Each share old Common $0.001 par exchanged for (1/3) share new Common $0.001 par 10/04/1993
Recapitalized as AR Growth Finance Corp. 03/13/2007
Each share new Common $0.001 par exchanged for (0.02) share Common $0.001 par
(See AR Growth Finance Corp.)

MARBLEX CORP. OF CANADA LTD. (AB)
Name changed to United International Industries Ltd. 5/15/70

MARBOY MINES LTD (ON)
Involuntarily dissolved 10/24/1973

MARBUAN GOLD MINES LTD.
Acquired by Buffalo Ankerite Gold Mines Ltd. on a (1) for (6) basis in 1936
Buffalo Ankerite Gold Mines Ltd. name changed to Buffalo Ankerite Holdings Ltd. 9/27/62 which name changed to Romfield Building Corp. Ltd. 7/21/64 which recapitalized as Dolphin Quest Inc. 9/30/96 which name changed to Naftex Energy Corp. (ONT) 4/10/97 which reincorporated in Yukon 9/16/98
(See Naftex Energy Corp.)

MARBURN STORES INC (NJ)
Merged into Marhold Stores, Inc. 12/28/78
Each share Common 1¢ par exchanged for $0.50 cash

MARCADE GROUP INC (NY)
Reorganized as Aris Industries, Inc. 6/30/93
Each share Common 10¢ par exchanged for (0.1) share Common 1¢ par
(See Aris Industries, Inc.)

MARCAM CORP (MA)
Each share Common 1¢ par received distribution of (0.5) share Marcam Solutions Inc. Common 1¢ par payable 7/29/97 to holders of record 7/23/97
Name changed to MAPICS, Inc. 7/28/97
(See MAPICS, Inc.)

MARCAM SOLUTIONS INC (DE)
Merged into Invensys PLC 07/14/1999
Each share Common 1¢ par exchanged for $7.50 cash

MARCAN CORP (UT)
Name changed to Modulearn, Inc. 10/18/1972
Modulearn, Inc. name changed to Micro Micro General Corp. (UT) 01/25/1982 which reincorporated in Delaware 07/01/1988 which merged into Fidelity Information Solutions, Inc. 07/10/2002 which merged into Fidelity National Financial, Inc. 09/30/2003 which merged into Fidelity National Information Services, Inc. 11/09/2006

MARCANA PETE LTD (AB)
Name changed to Compact Power Holdings Ltd. 11/09/1994
Compact Power Holdings Ltd. name changed to Exceed Capital Holdings Ltd. 09/05/2000 which name changed to Gallic Energy Ltd. 07/16/2007 which merged into Petromanas Energy Inc. 01/04/2013 which recapitalized as PMI Resources Ltd. 06/14/2016 which name changed to PentaNova Energy Corp. 06/05/2017 which recapitalized as CruzSur Energy Corp. 09/04/2018

MARCANA RES LTD (BC)
Reorganized under the laws of Canada as FMG Telecomputer Ltd. 04/04/1983
Each share Capital Stock $1 par exchanged for (0.2) share Common no par
FMG Telecomputer Ltd. name changed to SOK Properties Ltd. 07/04/1989 which name changed to Impact Telemedia International Ltd. 08/03/1990 which name changed to UC'NWIN Systems Ltd. (Canada) 07/17/1992 which reincorporated in Delaware as UC'NWIN Systems Corp. 12/11/1995 which recapitalized as Winner's Edge.com, Inc. 10/29/1999 which name changed to Sealant Solutions Inc. 08/06/2001 which name changed to PowerChannel, Inc. 07/28/2003 which recapitalized as Qualibou Energy Inc. 02/05/2008

MARCH DYNAMICS, INC. (NY)
Adjudicated bankrupt 3/9/65
No stockholders' equity

MARCH INDY INTL INC (NV)
Old Common $0.001 par split (1.77) for (1) by issuance of (0.77) additional share payable 11/19/1999 to holders of record 11/10/1999
Each share old Common $0.001 par exchanged for (0.33333333) share new Common $0.001 par 07/05/2000
Name changed to Bancorp International Group 08/08/2001
Bancorp International Group reorganized as Energy Source, Inc. 06/27/2008
(See Energy Source, Inc.)

MARCH MINERALS LTD. (ON)
Charter revoked for failure to file reports and pay fees 3/11/70

MARCH NETWORKS CORP (CANADA)
Acquired by Shenzhen Infinova Ltd. 04/27/2012
Each share Common no par exchanged for $5 cash

MARCH RES CORP (AB)
Recapitalized as Ranger Energy Ltd. (AB) 08/21/2009
Each share Common no par exchanged for (1/3) share Common no par
Ranger Energy Ltd. (AB) reorganized in Ontario as North Sea Energy Inc. 10/21/2011

MARCH RES INC (AB)
Struck off register and declared dissolved for failure to file returns 08/01/1991

MARCH RES LTD (BC)
Common no par split (2) for (1) by issuance of (1) additional share 04/03/1981
Recapitalized as International March Resources Ltd. 03/12/1985
Each share Common no par exchanged for (1/3) share Common no par
International March Resources Ltd. name changed to Mode Products Inc. 04/22/1986
(See Mode Products Inc.)

MARCHANT CALCULATING MACHINE CO.
Stock Dividend - 25% 12/21/50
Recapitalized as Marchant Calculators, Inc. and Common $5 par split (2) for (1) by issuance of (1) additional share in 1952
Marchant Calculators, Inc. merged into Smith-Corona Marchant, Inc. 6/30/58 which name changed to SCM Corp. 11/30/62
(See SCM Corp.)

MARCHANT CALCULATORS, INC. (CA)
Stock Dividend - 100% 8/15/52
Merged into Smith-Corona Marchant, Inc. 6/30/58
Each share Common $5 par exchanged for (1.25) shares Common $5 par
Smith-Corona Marchant, Inc. name changed to SCM Corp. 11/30/62
(See SCM Corp.)

MARCHANT MNG LTD (QC)
Completely liquidated 01/10/1972
Each share Capital Stock $1 par exchanged for (0.46666666) share Wright-Hargreaves Mines, Ltd. Capital Stock no par and $0.10 cash
Wright-Hargreaves Mines, Ltd. merged into LAC Minerals Ltd. (New) 07/29/1985 which was acquired by American Barrick Resources Corp. 10/17/1994 which name changed to Barrick Gold Corp. 01/18/1995

MARCHANT VALVE CORP. (NV)
Name changed to M.V. Co., Inc. 2/21/56
(See M.V. Co., Inc.)

MARCHAUD MINES LTD. (ON)
Merged into Garrison Creek Consolidated Mines Ltd. on a (1) for (2) basis 12/09/1954
Garrison Creek Consolidated Mines Ltd. merged into QSR Ltd. 09/07/1993 which name changed to Coniagas Resources Ltd. 06/25/1999 which name changed to Lithium One Inc. 07/23/2009
(See Lithium One Inc.)

MARCHE UN INC (QC)
Adjudicated bankrupt 12/07/1977
Stockholders' equity unlikely

MARCHEX INC (DE)
4.75% Conv. Exchangeable Preferred 1¢ par called for redemption at $258.31 plus $1.41 accrued dividends on 10/01/2008
(Additional Information in Active)

MARCHFIRST INC (DE)
Chapter 11 bankruptcy proceedings converted to Chapter 7 on 04/30/2001
Stockholders' equity unlikely

MARCHING MOOSE CAP CORP (BC)
Each share old Common no par exchanged for (0.5) share new Common no par 04/25/2017
Name changed to Avidian Gold Corp. 12/04/2017

MARCHMONT GOLD CORP (AB)
Recapitalized as Adulis Minerals Corp. 05/18/2000
Each share Common no par exchanged for (0.5) share Common no par
Adulis Minerals Corp. recapitalized as Adulis Resources Inc. 05/01/2001 which name changed to Solana Resources Ltd. 10/18/2005 which merged into Gran Tierra Energy Inc. (NV) 11/17/2008 which reincorporated in Delaware 10/31/2016

MARCHWELL CAP CORP (AB)
Recapitalized as Eurasian Minerals Inc. (AB) 12/03/2003
Each share Common no par exchanged for (0.5) share Common no par
Eurasian Minerals Inc. (AB) reincorporated in British Columbia 09/24/2004

MARCHWELL VENTURES LTD (CANADA)
Recapitalized as Sante Vertias Holdings Inc. 04/11/2018
Each share Common no par exchanged for (0.33333333) share Common no par

MARCI INTL IMPORTS INC (GA)
Recapitalized as FAB Global, Inc. 04/02/1999
Each (18) shares Common 1¢ par exchanged for (1) share Common 1¢ par
FAB Global, Inc. name changed to Dupont Direct Financial Holdings, Inc. 03/10/2000

MARCO CMNTY BANCORP INC (FL)
Common 1¢ par split (3) for (2) by issuance of (0.5) additional share payable 12/15/2005 to holders of record 11/15/2005 Ex date - 12/16/2005
Company's principal asset placed in receivership 02/19/2010
Stockholders' equity unlikely

MARCO DENTAL PRODS INC (OR)
Reincorporated 06/25/1975
State of incorporation changed from (MN) to (OR) 06/25/1975
Common 2¢ par changed to no par 07/29/1975
Charter dissolved for failure to pay taxes 08/07/1981

MARCO FOODS INC (CO)
Administratively dissolved 03/01/2004

MARCO MFG CO (DE)
Common $1 par changed to 1¢ par 11/15/1961
Completely liquidated 05/19/1971
Each share Common 1¢ par exchanged for first and final distribution of $0.0575 cash

MARCO POLO INVTS LTD (AB)
Name changed to Cobalt Coal Corp. 10/08/2009
Cobalt Coal Corp. recapitalized as Cobalt Coal Ltd. 07/08/2011

MARCO RES LTD (BC)
Struck off register and declared dissolved for failure to file returns 4/16/93

MARCO VENTURES (NV)
Each share old Common $0.001 par exchanged for (0.01) share new Common $0.001 par 08/05/1992
Name changed to International Cryogenic Systems Corp. 12/28/1992
International Cryogenic Systems Corp. name changed to Powercold Corp. 04/02/1997
(See Powercold Corp.)

MARCO VIDEO SYS INC (PA)
Liquidated and dissolved 03/24/1978
No stockholders' equity

MARCOIN, INC. (VA)
Charter cancelled and proclaimed dissolved for failure to file reports 09/30/2005

MARCOM FINL GROUP (ME)
Name changed to Firstmark Corp. 04/15/1987
(See Firstmark Corp.)

MARCOM INC (NY)
Reincorporated under the laws of Maine as Marcom Financial Group 05/09/1984
Marcom Financial Group name changed to Firstmark Corp. 04/15/1987
(See Firstmark Corp.)

MARCOM TELECOMMUNICATIONS INC (FL)
Name changed to Aril Group, Inc. 12/04/1989
(See Aril Group, Inc.)

MARCON COMMUNICATIONS INC (DE)
Common 10¢ par changed to 5¢ par and (1) additional share issued 08/30/1971
Name changed to Britmar Corp. 07/22/1985
(See Britmar Corp.)

MARCON ELECTRS CORP (NJ)
Adjudicated bankrupt 04/24/1969
No stockholders' equity

MARCON MINES LTD. (ON)
Recapitalized as Conmar Explorations Ltd. 10/12/66
Each share Capital Stock $1 par exchanged for (0.25) share Capital Stock $1 par
Conmar Explorations Ltd. charter cancelled 4/9/75

MARCONI INTERNATIONAL MARINE COMMUNICATION CO. LTD. (ENGLAND)
Stock Distribution - (2) for (3) Ordinary 07/29/1960; ADR 08/12/1960
Name changed to Marconi International Marine Co. Ltd. 09/11/1962
(See Marconi International Marine Co. Ltd.)

MARCONI INTL MARINE LTD (ENGLAND)
Acquired by General Electric Co. Ltd. 08/19/1971
Each share Ordinary Reg. GBP 1 par exchanged for 165p cash
Each ADR for Ordinary GBP 1 par exchanged for $4.07 cash

MARCONI PLC (ENGLAND)
Each Unsponsored ADR for Ordinary 5p par exchanged for (0.5) Sponsored ADR for Ordinary 5p par 09/11/2000
Each Sponsored ADR for Ordinary received distribution of (0.0003524) Marconi Corp plc Sponsored ADR for Ordinary and $0.0077 cash 05/29/2003
Name changed to M (2003) plc 01/16/2004
(See M (2003) plc)

MARCONI PLC NEW (ENGLAND & WALES)
ADR agreement terminated 12/31/2005
Each Sponsored ADR for Ordinary exchanged for $13.69538 cash

MARCONI WIRELESS TELEGRAPH CO. OF CANADA, LTD. (CANADA)
Name changed to Canadian Marconi Co. 6/12/25
Canadian Marconi Co. name changed to BAE Systems Canada Inc. 2/8/2000
(See BAE Systems Canada Inc.)

MARCONI'S WIRELESS TELEGRAPH CO. LTD.
Merged into Cables & Wireless Ltd. in 1929
Details not available

MARCONSULT INC (CA)
Adjudicated bankrupt 11/27/1973
No stockholders' equity

MARCOPOLO S A (BRAZIL)
ADR agreement terminated 6/4/2003
Each Sponsored ADR for Ordinary exchanged for $16.3735 cash

MARCOR DEV INC (NV)
Reincorporated 08/31/1988
State of incorporation changed from (CA) to (NV) 08/31/1988
Name changed to MarCor Resorts, Inc. 07/13/1989
MarCor Resorts, Inc. name changed to Rio Hotel & Casino Inc. 03/02/1992 which merged into Harrah's Entertainment, Inc. 01/01/1999
(See Harrah's Entertainment, Inc.)

MARCOR INC (DE)
Common $1 par split (2) for (1) by issuance of (1) additional share 07/15/1970
Merged into Mobil Corp. 07/01/1976
Each share $2 Conv. Preferred Ser A. $1 par exchanged for (0.32) share Common $7.50 par and $60 principal amount of 8.5% Sinking Fund Debentures due 06/15/2001
Each share Common $1 par exchanged for (0.16) share Common $7.50 par and $30 principal amount of 8.5% Sinking Fund Debentures due 06/15/2001
Mobil Corp. merged into Exxon Mobil Corp. 11/30/1999

MARCOR RESORTS INC (NV)
Each share old Common 1¢ par exchanged for (0.5) share new Common 1¢ par 10/11/1989
Name changed to Rio Hotel & Casino Inc. 03/02/1992
Rio Hotel & Casino Inc. merged into Harrah's Entertainment, Inc. 01/01/1999
(See Harrah's Entertainment, Inc.)

MARCORP INC (DE)
Each share old Common $0.001 par exchanged for (0.125) share new Common $0.001 par 12/15/92
Each share new Common $0.001 par exchanged again for (1/6) share new Common $0.001 par 11/25/94
Charter cancelled and declared void for failure to pay franchise taxes 3/1/96

MARCOURT NICKEL MINES, LTD. (ON)
Charter cancelled 11/11/57

MARCUM NAT GAS SVCS INC (DE)
Each share old Common 1¢ par exchanged for (0.25) share new Common 1¢ par 07/06/1998
Name changed to Metretek Technologies, Inc. 06/08/1999
Metretek Technologies, Inc. name changed to PowerSecure International, Inc. 08/22/2007
(See PowerSecure International, Inc.)

MARCUS CORP (DE)
Stock Dividends - 10% 09/22/1975; 10% 08/11/1976; 10% 09/30/1977; 10% 08/30/1978; 10% 09/15/1979; 10% 09/22/1980; 10% 09/21/1981; 50% 05/01/1987
Reincorporated under the laws of Wisconsin 10/10/1992

MARCUS ENERGY HLDGS INC (ON)
Name changed to Au Martinique Silver Inc. 7/21/2005

MARCUS ENERGY INC (ON)
Recapitalized as Marcus Energy Holdings Inc. 11/27/2000
Each share Common no par exchanged for (0.1) share Common no par
Marcus Energy Holdings Inc. name changed to Au Martinique Silver Inc. 7/21/2005

MARCUS GOLD MINES LTD. (ON)
Acquired by Consolidated Marcus Gold Mines Ltd. in 1956
Details not available

MARCUS HERMAN INC (TX)
Merged into Southwestern Apparel, Inc. 12/10/1981
Each share Common 50¢ par exchanged for $5 cash

MARCUS J ENTERPRISES INC (FL)
Name changed to Global Eco-Logical Services, Inc. 1/21/99
Global Eco-Logical Services, Inc. name changed to Intercontinental Holdings Inc. 3/31/2002

MARCUS TRANSFORMER CO., INC. (NJ)
Adjudicated bankrupt 6/25/65
No stockholders' equity

MARCY SHENANDOAH CORP (DE)
Completely liquidated 01/02/1961
Each share Common 10¢ par received first and final distribution of $0.58 cash

MAREAST EXPL LTD (ON)
Name changed to Cascade Pacific Resources Ltd. 03/01/1984
(See Cascade Pacific Resources Ltd.)

MAREE URANIUM LTD. (ON)
Charter cancelled by the Province of Ontario for default in September 1960

MAREIGHT CORP (DE)
Charter cancelled and declared inoperative and void for non-payment of taxes 04/15/1973

MAREMONT AUTOMOTIVE PRODUCTS, INC. (IL)
Each share old Common $1 par exchanged for (4) shares new Common $1 par 2/16/53
Stock Dividend - 100% 8/11/59
Name changed to Maremont Corp. (Ill.) 5/8/61
Maremont Corp. (Ill.) reincorporated in Delaware 4/30/74
(See Maremont Corp. (Del.))

MAREMONT CORP (DE)
Reincorporated 04/30/1974
Common $1 par split (3) for (2) by issuance of (0.5) additional share 05/31/1972
4.5% Conv. Preferred 1963 Ser. $100 par called for redemption 11/12/1973
State of incorporation changed from (IL) to (DE) 04/30/1974
5.75% Preferred $100 par called for redemption 09/14/1979
6% Preferred 1960 Ser. $100 par called for redemption 09/14/1979
Merged into Swiss Aluminum Ltd. 09/26/1979
Each share Common $1 par exchanged for $42 cash

MARENGO EXPL LTD (AB)
Acquired by True Energy Inc. 2/28/2001
Each share Class A no par exchanged for (1.71) shares Common no par
Each share Class B no par exchanged for (1.69) shares Common no par
(See True Energy Inc.)

MARENGO MNG CDA LTD (CANADA)
Name changed to Marengo Mining Ltd. 01/17/2013
Marengo Mining Ltd. recapitalized as Era Resources Inc. 11/25/2015
(See Era Resources Inc.)

MARENGO MNG LTD (AUSTRALIA)
Reincorporated under the laws of Canada as Marengo Mining Canada Ltd. and Ordinary reclassified as Common no par 01/08/2013
Marengo Mining Canada Ltd. name changed to Marengo Mining Ltd. 01/17/2013 which recapitalized as Era Resources Inc. 11/25/2015
(See Era Resources Inc.)

MARENGO MNG LTD (CANADA)
Recapitalized as Era Resources Inc. 11/25/2015
Each share Common no par exchanged for (0.01) share Common no par
(See Era Resources Inc.)

MAREX INC (FL)
Name changed 05/29/2001
Name changed from Marex.com, Inc. to Marex, Inc. 05/29/2001
Each share old Common 1¢ par received distribution of (1) share Vigilant Applied Technologies Inc. Restricted Share payable 09/05/2002 to holders of record 08/03/2002
Each share old Common 1¢ par exchanged for (0.1) share new Common 1¢ par 08/26/2002
SEC revoked common stock registration 05/14/2007

MARFIN POPULAR BK PUB CO LTD (CYPRUS)
Stock Dividend - 10% payable 07/05/2011 to holders of record 05/31/2011 Ex date - 05/26/2011
Name changed to Cyprus Popular Bank Public Co., Ltd. 04/27/2012
(See Cyprus Popular Bank Public Co., Ltd.)

MARFRANK CORP (NY)
Dissolved by proclamation 12/7/76

MARFRIG ALIMENTOS SA (BRAZIL)
Name changed to Marfrig Global Foods S.A. 01/29/2014

MARG LTD (INDIA)
Name changed 12/17/2007
Name changed from MARG Constructions Ltd. to MARG Ltd. 12/17/2007
GDR agreement terminated 03/20/2015
No GDR's remain outstanding

MARGANETSKY ORE MNG & JT STK CO (UKRAINE)
ADR agreement terminated 08/16/2017
Each Sponsored ADR for Ordinary exchanged for (100) shares Ordinary
Note: Unexchanged ADR's will be sold and the proceeds, if any, held for claim after 08/20/2018

MARGARET RED LAKE MINES (1940) LTD. (ON)
Charter cancelled 3/11/70
Stock is valueless

MARGARET RED LAKE MINES LTD. (ON)
Dissolved and each share Capital Stock exchanged for (0.25) share of McMarmac Red Lake Gold Mines Ltd. Capital Stock $1 par and (0.1) share of Margaret Red Lake Mines (1940) Ltd. Capital Stock $1 par in November, 1940
(See each Company's listing)

MARGARETTEN FINL CORP (DE)
Merged into MFC Acquisition Corp. 7/22/94
Each 8.25% Depositary Preferred Ser. A exchanged for $25 cash
Each share Common 1¢ par exchanged for $25 cash

MARGATE INDS INC (DE)
Name changed 07/12/1991
Name changed from Margate Ventures, Inc. to Margate Industries, Inc. 07/12/1991
Each share Common $0.001 par exchanged for (0.2) share Common $0.005 par 01/21/1994
Each share Common $0.005 par exchanged for (1/3) share Common $0.015 par 11/16/1998
Stock Dividend - 5% payable 11/15/1999 to holders of record 10/15/1999
Company terminated common stock registration and is no longer public as of 05/30/2002

MARGAUX CONTROLS, INC. (CA)
Name changed to Margaux Inc. 11/10/87
(See Margaux Inc.)

MARGAUX INC (CA)
In process of liquidation
Each share Common no par received initial distribution of $0.20 cash per share 6/30/95
Note: Holders received a pro rata share of $840,000 cash in June 1996
Additional distributions and amounts, if any, are unknown

MARGAUX RED CAP INC (CANADA)
Recapitalized as Sigma Lithium Resources Corp. 06/22/2018
Each share Common no par exchanged for (0.1) share Common no par

MARGAY OIL CORP.
Acquired by Standard Oil Co. (Ohio) and liquidated in 1945
Each share Capital Stock exchanged for (0.2) share 3-3/4% Preferred and (0.25) share Common
(See Standard Oil Co. (Ohio))

MARGE ENTERPRISES LTD (BC)
Name changed to Thunderbird Projects Ltd. 09/27/1996
Thunderbird Projects Ltd. recapitalized as Consolidated Thunderbird Projects Ltd. 12/17/1998 which name changed to Jenosys Enterprises, Inc. 08/16/1999 which recapitalized as Fintry Enterprises Inc. 12/10/2004 which recapitalized as Mesa Uranium Corp. 12/23/2005 which name changed to Mesa Exploration Corp. 03/30/2011

MARGO CORP. (TX)
Merged into Appell Petroleum Corp. share for share 9/17/57
Appell Petroleum Corp. charter cancelled 4/15/68

MARGO NURSERY FARMS INC (PR)
Reincorporated 12/31/97
State of incorporation changed from (FL) to (PR) 12/31/97
Under plan of reorganization each share Common $0.001 par automatically became (1) share Margo Caribe, Inc. Common $0.001 par 6/1/98

MARGO'S INC. (TX)
Name changed to Margo's La Mode, Inc. 4/1/66
(See Margo's La Mode, Inc.)

MARGOLIS & CO INC (MN)
Out of business 00/00/1978
No stockholders' equity

MARGOS LAMODE INC (TX)
Stock Dividend - 10% 03/06/1978
Acquired by Alexander's Inc. 07/26/1979
Each share Common $1 par exchanged for $10.30 cash

MARHOEFER PACKING INC (IN)
$6 Preferred $110 par called for redemption 12/31/1959
Each share Common $10 par exchanged for (7) shares Common $1 par 06/29/1965
Adjudicated bankrupt 06/02/1978
Stockholders' equity unlikely

MARIA MINING CORP. LTD. (ON)
Charter cancelled and declared dissolved for failure to file returns and pay fees 3/16/76

MARIAH INTL INC (UT)
Merged into MG Gold Corp. 5/15/97
Each share Common 5¢ par exchanged for (0.1) share Common $0.0001 par
MG Gold Corp. name changed to MG Natural Resources Corp. 10/12/98 which name changed to Xenolix Technologies Inc. 6/14/2000 which name changed to Pershing Resources Co., Inc. 4/27/2004

MARIAH OIL & GAS CORP (DE)
Charter cancelled and declared inoperative and void for non-payment of taxes 6/27/84

MARIAH RES LTD (BC)
Struck off register and declared dissolved for failure to file returns 4/3/92

MARIAN CAP CORP (AB)
Name changed to Advance Multimedia Corp. 07/27/1994
Advance Multimedia Corp. name changed to Discoverware Inc. 04/22/1996
(See Discoverware Inc.)

MARIAN LAKE MINES LTD. (ON)
Charter revoked for failure to file reports and pay fees 2/18/65

MARIAN LAKE URANIUM MINES LTD. (ON)
Name changed to Marian Lake Mines in August 1958
(See Marian Lake Mines Ltd.)

MARIAN MINERALS CORP (BC)
Recapitalized as Lumina Investment Corp. 09/08/1992
Each share Common no par exchanged for (0.33333333) share Common no par
Lumina Investment Corp. recapitalized as Latitude Minerals Ltd. 12/02/1996 which recapitalized as Coal Creek Energy Inc. 05/21/2002 which name changed to Corex Gold Corp. 11/18/2003 which merged into Minera Alamos Inc. 04/18/2018

MARIAN NAVIGATION CO. (PANAMA)
Liquidated 00/00/1951
Details not available

MARIANA RES LTD (GUERNSEY)
Each share old Ordinary £0.0001 par exchanged for (0.1) share new Ordinary £0.0001 par 07/01/2016
Note: Shares previously transferred to UK register 03/12/2013 began trading on TSXV 07/26/2015
Merged into Sandstorm Gold Ltd. 07/06/2017
Each share new Ordinary £0.0001 par exchanged for (0.2573) share Common no par and approximately CDN$0.48 cash

MARIANNA LIME PRODUCTS CO. (FL)
Charter revoked for failure to file reports and pay fees 12/20/39

MARICANA ENTPRISES LTD 1971 (CANADA)
Declared dissolved for failure to file reports 12/15/1980

MARICONA MINERALS LTD. (ON)
Bankrupt in 1958

MARICOPA RANCHES, INC. (AZ)
Liquidated in 1956
No stockholders' equity

MARICULTURE SYS INC (FL)
SEC revoked common stock registration 04/07/2008

MARIE ANTOINETTE, INC. (TX)
Common $2.50 par changed to $1 par 6/26/62
Voluntarily dissolved 4/30/82
Details not available

MARIE PIGALLE INC (NY)
Name changed to Time-Off, Inc. 02/26/1970
(See Time-Off, Inc.)

MARIETTA CONCRETE CORP. (OH)
Merged into American-Marietta Co. 06/01/1959
Each share Common no par exchanged for (0.333333) share Common $2 par
American-Marietta Co. merged into Martin Marietta Corp. (Old) 10/10/1961 which merged into Martin Marietta Corp. (New) 04/02/1993 which merged into Lockheed Martin Corp. 03/15/1995

MARIETTA CORP (NY)
Merged into BFMA Holding Corp. 3/8/96
Each share Common 1¢ par exchanged for $10.25 cash

MARIETTA RES CORP (BC)
Recapitalized as Garrison Enterprises Inc. 12/21/93
Each share Common no par exchanged for (1/3) share Common no par
Garrison Enterprises Inc. recapitalized as GNI Petroleum Inc. 4/2/98 which recapitalized as Logix Enterprises Inc. 10/11/2001 which recapitalized as Transac Enterprise Corp. 11/27/2002 which name changed to Evergreen Gaming Corp. 11/1/2006

MARIEVALE CONSOLIDATED MINES LTD. (SOUTH AFRICA)
ADR's for Ordinary Rand-80¢ par changed to Rand-70¢ par 6/28/74
Name changed to Marievale Ltd. 2/8/88
Marievale Ltd. name changed to Randex Ltd. 7/10/89

MARIEVALE LTD (SOUTH AFRICA)
Name changed to Randex Ltd. 07/10/1989
(See Randex Ltd.)

MARIFARMS INC (DE)
Incorporated 5/23/91
Name changed to Marine Harvest International Inc. 12/16/92
(See Marine Harvest International Inc.)

MARIFARMS INC (DE)
Incorporated 07/20/1967
Each share old Common no par exchanged for (3) shares new Common no par 01/31/1972
New Common no par changed to 10¢ par 05/22/1974
Each share old Common 10¢ par exchanged for (0.04) share new Common 10¢ par 08/24/1978
Each share new Common 10¢ par exchanged for (0.1) share new Common 10¢ par 04/07/1981
Charter forfeited for failure to maintain a registered agent 08/22/1983

MARIFIL MINES LTD (YT)
Reincorporated under the laws of British Columbia 01/17/2014

MARIGOLD OILS LTD. (AB)
Recapitalized as Unisphere Explorers Ltd. on a (1) for (3) basis 5/16/62
Unisphere Explorers Ltd. recapitalized as New Unisphere Resources Ltd. 10/6/69
(See New Unisphere Resources Ltd.)

MARIJUANA INC (CO)
Name changed to Hemp, Inc. 08/30/2012

MARIKA INC (NV)
Common $0.001 par split (2.272727) for (1) by issuance of (1.272727) additional shares payable 12/05/2014 to holders of record 12/02/2014 Ex date - 12/08/2014
Name changed to Pieris Pharmaceuticals, Inc. 12/17/2014

MARILLAC ROUYN MINES, LTD. (ON)
Charter revoked for failure to file reports and pay fees 11/9/64

MARILYN GOLD MINES INC (BC)
Name changed to Titan Resources Ltd. 02/18/1981
Titan Resources Ltd. recapitalized as Golden Titan Resources Ltd. 09/08/1987 which merged into Titan Pacific Resources Ltd. 12/28/1989 which name changed to Titan Logix Corp. (BC) 06/01/2002 which reincorporated in Alberta 03/27/2013

MARILYN RES INC (BC)
Delisted from Vancouver Stock Exchange 03/02/1990

MARIMAC MINES LTD. (ON)
Merged into Alchib Developments Ltd. 7/10/69
Each share Capital Stock no par exchanged for (0.06) share Capital Stock no par
Alchib Developments Ltd. merged into Kalrock Developments Ltd. 10/23/78 which merged into Kalrock Resources Ltd. 8/8/90 which merged into Cercal Minerals Corp. 7/9/93
(See Cercal Minerals Corp.)

MARIMBA CAP CORP (AB)
Name changed to Phoenix Coal Inc. (AB) 06/30/2008
Phoenix Coal Inc. (AB) reincorporated in Ontario 07/11/2008 which recapitalized as Elgin Mining Inc. 05/10/2010 which merged into Mandalay Resources Corp. 09/11/2014

MARIMBA INC (DE)
Issue Information - 4,000,000 shares COM offered at $20 per share on 04/29/1999
Merged into BMC Software, Inc. 7/15/2004
Each share Common $0.0001 par exchanged for $8.25 cash

MARIN CNTY FINL CORP (CA)
Completely liquidated 04/01/1970
Each share Capital Stock $1 par exchanged for first and final distribution of (1.53406) shares Pacific Coast Holdings, Inc. Common $2 par
Pacific Coast Holdings, Inc. name changed to Bell National Corp. (CA) 01/03/1983 which reincorporated in Delaware as Ampersand Medical Corp. 05/26/1999 which name changed to CytoCore, Inc. 08/17/2006 which name changed to Medite Cancer Diagnostics, Inc. 12/11/2014

MARIN FD INC (CO)
Each share old Common no par exchanged for (0.01) share new Common no par 12/31/90
Name changed to Albara Corp. 8/30/91
Albara Corp. recapitalized as Leapfrog Smart Products, Inc. 2/23/2000 which name changed to Red Alert Group, Inc. 7/15/2003

MARIN HLDG CORP (NV)
Each share old Common $0.001 par exchanged for (0.02) share new Common $0.001 par 3/4/98
Charter revoked for failure to file reports and pay fees 5/1/2004

MARIN NATL BANCORP (CA)
Each share old Common $5 par exchanged for (0.0001) share new Common $5 par 12/15/95
Note: In effect holders received $0.08 cash per share and public interest was eliminated

MARINA BK (CHICAGO, IL)
Acquired by NBD Bancorp, Inc. 12/01/1992
Details not available

MARINA BK (MARINA DEL REY, CA)
Merged into First Coastal Bancshares 6/26/97
Each share Common no par exchanged for $13 cash

MARINA BIOTECH INC (DE)
Each share old Common $0.006 par exchanged for (0.1) share new Common $0.006 par 12/23/2011
Each share new Common $0.006 par exchanged again for (0.1) share new Common $0.006 par 08/03/2017
Name changed to Adhera Therapeutics, Inc. 10/09/2018

MARINA CAP INC (UT)
SEC revoked common stock registration 04/07/2008
Stockholders' equity unlikely

MARINA CITY BK (CHICAGO, IL)
Name changed to Marina Bank (Chicago, IL) 09/29/1975
(See Marina Bank (Chicago, IL))

MARINA CORP (IN)
Assets transferred to Marina Limited Partnership and Common $1 par reclassified as Units of Ltd. Partnership 12/31/86
(See Marina Limited Partnership)

MARINA EXPLS LTD (BC)
Recapitalized as Consolidated Marina Explorations Ltd. 06/11/1992
Each share Common no par exchanged for (0.33333333) share Common no par
Consolidated Marina Explorations Ltd. name changed to Watson Bell Communications Inc. 02/25/1994 which recapitalized as Cosworth Ventures Ltd. (BC) 11/22/1995 which reincorporated in Yukon as Cosworth Minerals Ltd. 03/30/1998 which name changed to Palcan Fuel Cells Ltd. 02/13/2002 which name changed to Palcan Power Systems Inc. 08/10/2004

MARINA INDS INC (MA)
Involuntarily dissolved 08/31/1998

MARINA LTD PARTNERSHIP (IN)
Each (300) old Units of Ltd. Partnership exchanged for (1) new Unit of Ltd. Partnership 9/7/2001
Note: In effect holders received $40 cash per Unit and public interest was eliminated

MARINA ST BK (MARINA DEL REY, CA)
Name changed to Marina Bank (Marina Del Rey, CA) 6/30/95
(See Marina Bank (Marina Del Rey, CA))

MARINAS INTL INC (DE)
Charter cancelled and declared inoperative and void for non-payment of taxes 03/01/2006

MARINDUQUE IRON MINES AGENTS, INC. (PHILIPPINES)
Name changed to Marinduque Mining & Industrial Corp. 5/9/63
(See Marinduque Mining & Industrial Corp.)

MARINDUQUE MNG & INDL CORP (PHILIPPINES)
Each share Capital Stock P0.10 par exchanged for (0.006666) share Capital Stock P15 par 11/3/67
Capital Stock P15 par split (5) for (4) by issuance of (0.25) additional share 9/27/68
Capital Stock P15 par split (3) for (2) by issuance of (0.5) additional share 3/20/70
Capital Stock P15 par split (5) for (4) by issuance of (0.25) additional share 2/26/71
Each share Capital Stock P15 par exchanged for (0.25) share Capital Stock P60 par 7/29/71
Capital Stock P60 par split (5) for (4) by issuance of (0.25) additional share 10/20/72
Capital Stock P60 par split (5) for (4) by issuance of (0.25) additional share 3/24/73
Each share Capital Stock P60 par exchanged for (6) shares Class A Capital Stock P60 par or (6) shares Class B Capital Stock P10 par 8/17/73 (See Note)
Note: Only Philippine Nationals may hold Class A Capital Shares; Non-Philippine Nationals can hold Class B Capital Shares only
Class A Capital Stock P10 par and Class B Capital Stock P10 par split (5) for (4) by issuance of (0.25) additional share 12/28/73
Class A Capital Stock P10 par and Class B Capital Stock P10 par split (5) for (4) by issuance of (0.25) additional share 3/29/74
Class A Capital Stock P10 par and Class B Capital Stock P10 par split (5) for (4) by issuance of (0.25) additional share respectively 7/12/75
Assets foreclosed upon by Philippine National Bank 8/31/84
No stockholders' equity

MARINE & ELECTRS MFG INC (MD)
Taken over by Environmental Air Control Inc. 00/00/1972
Details not available

MARINE AIRCRAFT CORP.
Bankrupt in 1954

MARINE AIRWAYS, INC. (AK)
Merged into Alaska Coastal-Ellis Airlines 4/1/62
Each share 5-1/2% Preferred $1 par exchanged for (1) share 5-1/2% Preferred $1 par
Each share Common $1 par exchanged for (2.19184041) shares Common $1 par
Alaska Coastal-Ellis Airlines name changed to Alaska Coastal Airlines, Inc. 5/16/66 which merged into Alaska Airlines, Inc. 4/1/68 which reorganized in Delaware as Alaska Air Group, Inc. 5/23/85

MARINE APARTMENTS BUILDING CORP. (IL)
Liquidation completed 2/26/62

MARINE BANCORP INC (IL)
Name changed to Marine Corp. 7/1/84
Marine Corp. merged into Banc One Corp. 1/1/92 which merged into Bank One Corp. 10/2/98 which merged into J.P. Morgan Chase & Co. 12/31/2000 which name changed to JPMorgan Chase & Co. 7/20/2004

MARINE BANCORP INC (PA)
Merged into PNC Financial Corp. 01/23/1984
Each share $2.20 Conv. Preferred Ser. A no par exchanged for (1) share $1.60 Conv. Preferred Ser. C $1 par and (0.55) share Common $5 par
Each share Common $5 par exchanged for (1) share $1.60 Conv. Preferred Ser. C $1 par and (0.55) share Common $5 par
PNC Financial Corp. name changed to PNC Bank Corp. 02/08/1993 which name changed to PNC Financial Services Group, Inc. 03/15/2000

MARINE BANCORPORATION (WA)
Fully Participating Stock no par reclassified as Common $2.50 par and (9) additional shares issued 2/20/69
Initial Stock no par reclassified as Common $2.50 par and (29) additional shares issued 2/20/69
Name changed to Rainier Bancorporation 11/8/74
Rainier Bancorporation acquired by Security Pacific Corp. 8/31/87 which merged into BankAmerica Corp. (Old) 4/22/92 which merged into BankAmerica Corp. (New) 9/30/98 which name changed to Bank of America Corp. 4/28/99

MARINE BANCSHARES INC (FL)
Merged into Old Florida Bankshares, Inc. 08/22/2003
Each share Common 1¢ par exchanged for (0.62) share Common 1¢ par
Old Florida Bankshares, Inc. merged into Bank of Florida Corp. 04/24/2007
(See Bank of Florida Corp.)

MARINE BK & TR CO (TAMPA, FL)
Each share Capital Stock $100 par exchanged for (6.25) shares Capital Stock $20 par to effect a (5) for (1) split and 25% stock dividend 06/30/1952
Stock Dividends - 14-2/7% 12/31/1953; 20% 12/18/1957; 25% 01/10/1961; 10% 10/01/1964; 10% 01/11/1966
Name changed to Flagship Bank of Tampa (Tampa, FL) 11/08/1974
Flagship Bank of Tampa (Tampa, FL) name changed to Sun Bank of Tampa Bay (Tampa, FL) 01/01/1984

MARINE BK (MEADVILLE, PA)
Under plan of reorganization each share Capital Stock $5 par automatically became (1) share Marine Bancorp, Inc. (PA) Common $5 par 12/21/1981
Marine Bancorp, Inc. (PA) merged into PNC Financial Corp. 01/23/1984 which name changed to PNC Bank Corp. 02/08/1993 which name changed to PNC Financial Services Group, Inc. 03/15/2000

MARINE BIOPRODUCTS INTL CORP (BC)
Reorganized under the laws of Alberta as Phoenix Oilfield Hauling Inc. 06/06/2006

Each share Common no par exchanged for (0.00645161) share Common no par
Phoenix Oilfield Hauling Inc. name changed to Aveda Transportation & Energy Servives Inc. 06/25/2012 which merged into Daseke, Inc. 06/08/2018

MARINE CAPITAL CORP. (WI)
Liquidation completed
Each share Common $1 par received initial distribution of $10 cash 8/10/66
Each share Common $1 par received second distribution consisting of (0.2479) share Dextra Corp. Common 10¢ par; (0.123) share Empire Gas Corp. Common no par; and (0.0833) share Racine Hydraulics & Machinery, Inc. Common $1 par 8/18/66
Each share Common $1 par received third and final distribution of $0.4667 cash 11/23/66
Certificates were not required to be surrendered and are now without value
(See each company's listing)

MARINE CHEMICALS CO., LTD.
Name changed to Marine Magnesium Products Corp. 00/00/1940
Marine Magnesium Products Corp. acquired by Merck & Co., Inc. (Old) 00/00/1951 which merged into Merck & Co., Inc. (New) 11/03/2009

MARINE COLLOIDS INC (DE)
Merged into FMC Corp. 11/30/1977
Each share Common 56¢ par exchanged for $22.10 cash

MARINE CORP. (DE)
Merged into California Eastern Oil Co. in 1926
Details not available

MARINE CORP (IL)
Common $12.50 par changed to $3.125 par and (3) additional shares issued 8/1/84
Common $3.125 par changed to $1.5625 par and (1) additional share issued 3/17/86
Common $1.5625 par changed to $0.78125 par and (1) additional share issued 6/13/86
Merged into Banc One Corp. 1/1/92
Each share Common $0.78125 par exchanged for (0.849) share Common no par
Banc One Corp. merged into Bank One Corp. 10/2/98 which merged into J.P. Morgan Chase & Co. 12/31/2000 which name changed to JPMorgan Chase & Co. 7/20/2004

MARINE CORP (WI)
Common $10 par changed to $5 par 05/07/1984
Common $5 par split (2) for (1) by issuance of (1) additional share 08/01/1984
$2 Conv. Preferred $1 par called for redemption 07/01/1985
$3 Conv. Preferred Ser. A $1 par called for redemption 09/08/1987
$3 Conv. Preferred Ser. B $1 par called for redemption 09/08/1987
$3 Conv. Preferred Ser. C $1 par called for redemption 09/08/1987
Stock Dividends - 50% 01/15/1970; 50% 07/17/1977
Merged into Banc One Corp. (DE) 04/01/1988
Each share Common $5 par exchanged for (2.5652) shares Common no par
Banc One Corp. (DE) reincorporated in Ohio 05/01/1989 which merged into Bank One Corp. 10/02/1998 which merged into J.P. Morgan Chase & Co. 12/31/2000 which name changed into JPMorgan Chase & Co. 07/20/2004

MARINE DRILLING, INC. (DE)
Name changed to Great National Corp. 07/08/1964
Great National Corp. name changed to GNC Energy Corp. 08/05/1981
(See GNC Energy Corp.)

MARINE DRILLING CO (TX)
Under plan of reorganization each share Common 10¢ par automatically became (1) share Marine Holding Co. Common 10¢ par 03/13/1990
Marine Holding Co. name changed to Marine Drilling Companies, Inc. 06/27/1991 which merged into Pride International, Inc. (DE) 09/13/2001 which merged into Ensco PLC 06/01/2011

MARINE DRILLING COS INC (TX)
Each share 14% Exchangeable Preferred $1 par exchanged for (44.322568) shares Common 1¢ par 10/29/1992
Each share Common 10¢ par exchanged for (0.04) share Common 1¢ par 10/29/1992
Merged into Pride International, Inc. (DE) 09/13/2001
Each share Common 1¢ par exchanged for (1) share Common 1¢ par
Pride International, Inc. (DE) merged into Ensco PLC 06/01/2011

MARINE DRIVE MOBILE CORP (NV)
Each share old Common $0.001 par exchanged for (0.01) share new Common $0.001 par 09/11/2013
Name changed to Gamzio Mobile, Inc. 11/15/2013

MARINE ELEVATOR CO. (NY)
Each share Capital Stock $100 par exchanged for (1) share Common $100 par in 1945
Common $100 par changed to Capital Stock $10 par in 1947
Liquidation completed 12/12/57

MARINE EXPL INC (CO)
Each share old Common $0.001 par exchanged for (0.002) share new Common $0.001 par 11/18/2010
Recapitalized as In Ovations Holdings Inc. 10/15/2013
Each share new Common $0.001 par exchanged for (0.001) share Common $0.001 par

MARINE EXPL INC (FL)
Proclaimed dissolved for failure to file reports and pay fees 11/9/90

MARINE FIBER-GLASS & PLASTICS, INC. (WA)
Completely liquidated 4/7/89
Each share Common 10¢ par exchanged for first and final distribution of $1.70 cash

MARINE HARVEST INTL INC (DE)
Merged into Harvest Holdings, Inc. 12/1/94
Each share Common 16-2/3¢ par exchanged for $10.20 cash

MARINE HLDG CO (TX)
Name changed to Marine Drilling Companies, Inc. 06/27/1991
Marine Drilling Companies, Inc. merged into Pride International, Inc. (DE) 09/13/2001 which merged into Ensco PLC 06/01/2011

MARINE INTL CORP (NJ)
Each share Common no par exchanged for (1/7) share Common 1¢ par 2/7/80
Name changed to Southern Reserve Oil Corp. 3/10/80
Southern Reserve Oil Corp. name changed to Southern Reserve, Inc. 12/23/83
(See Southern Reserve, Inc.)

MARINE INVS INC (KS)
Charter forfeited for failure to file annual reports 01/15/1989

MARINE JET TECHNOLOGY CORP (NV)
Recapitalized as Blue Holdings, Inc. 06/07/2005
Each (29) shares Common $0.001 par exchanged for (1) share Common $0.001 par
Note: Holders of between (2,899) and (100) shares received (100) shares only
Holders of (99) shares or fewer were not affected by reverse split

MARINE MAGNESIUM PRODUCTS CORP.
Acquired by Merck & Co., Inc. (Old) 00/00/1951
Each (9.43) shares Capital Stock $1 par exchanged for (1) share new Common 50¢ par
Merck & Co., Inc. (Old) merged into Merck & Co., Inc. (New) 11/03/2009

MARINE MGMT SYS INC (DE)
Company terminated registration of common stock and is no longer public as of 02/09/1999
Details not available

MARINE MIDLAND BANK (NEW YORK, NY)
Merged into Marine Midland Banks, Inc. 1/1/76
Each share Capital Stock $10 par exchanged for $84.76 cash

MARINE MIDLAND BANK-CENTRAL (SYRACUSE, NY)
Merged into Marine Midland Banks, Inc. 1/1/76
Each share Capital Stock $10 par exchanged for $67.44 cash

MARINE MIDLAND BANK-EASTERN, N.A. (TROY, NY)
Merged into Marine Midland Banks, Inc. 1/1/76
Each share Capital Stock $25 par exchanged for $169.12 cash

MARINE MIDLAND BANK OF SOUTHEASTERN NEW YORK, N.A. (POUGHKEEPSIE, NY)
Merged into Marine Midland Banks, Inc. 1/1/76
Each share Common $40 par exchanged for $144.82 cash

MARINE MIDLAND BANK-ROCHESTER (ROCHESTER, NY)
Merged into Marine Midland Banks, Inc. 1/1/76
Each share Capital Stock $30 par exchanged for $158.47 cash

MARINE MIDLAND BANK-SOUTHERN (ELMIRA, NY)
Merged into Marine Midland Banks, Inc. 1/1/76
Each share Capital Stock $75 par exchanged for $191.17 cash

MARINE MIDLAND BANK-WESTERN (BUFFALO, NY)
Capital Stock $30 par changed to $50 par 2/25/71
Merged into Marine Midland Banks, Inc. 1/1/76
Each share Capital Stock $50 par exchanged for $119.40 cash

MARINE MIDLAND BKS INC (DE)
Merged into Hongkong & Shanghai Banking Corp. 12/15/87
Each share Common $5 par exchanged for $83.51 cash
Note: Preferred stocks were unaffected by the merger and remain outstanding as Marine Midlands Banks, Inc.
Money Market Preferred Ser. A $1 par called for redemption 6/22/90
Money Market Preferred Ser. B $1 par called for redemption 6/28/90
Name changed to HSBC Americas, Inc. 12/4/95
(See HSBC Americas, Inc.)

MARINE MIDLAND CORP (DE)
Capital Stock $10 par changed to $5 par in 1934
Capital Stock $5 par reclassified as Common $5 par in 1951
4% Preferred no par called for redemption 1/15/60
Name changed to Marine Midland Banks, Inc. 4/16/68
(See Marine Midland Banks, Inc.)

MARINE MIDLAND GRACE TRUST CO. (NEW YORK, NY)
Name changed to Marine Midland Bank (New York, NY) 10/14/70
(See Marine Midland Bank (New York, NY))

MARINE MIDLAND NATIONAL BANK (TROY, NY)
Name changed to Marine Midland Bank-Eastern, N.A. (Troy, N.Y.) 12/31/70
(See Marine Midland Bank-Eastern, N.A. (Troy, N.Y.))

MARINE MIDLAND TINKER NATIONAL BANK (EAST SETAUKET, NY)
Merged into Marine Midland Banks, Inc. 01/01/1976
Each share Common $5 par exchanged for $30.28 cash

MARINE MIDLAND TRUST CO. (NEW YORK, NY)
Name changed to Marine Midland Grace Trust Co. (New York, NY) 8/18/65
Marine Midland Grace Trust Co. (New York, NY) name changed to Marine Midland Bank (New York, NY) 10/17/70
(See Marine Midland Bank (New York, NY))

MARINE MIDLAND TRUST CO. (ROCHESTER, NY)
Name changed to Marine Midland Bank- Rochester (Rochester, N.Y.) 6/5/70
(See Marine Midland Bank-Rochester (Rochester, N.Y.))

MARINE MIDLAND TRUST CO. OF CENTRAL NEW YORK (SYRACUSE, NY)
Under plan of merger name changed to Marine Midland Bank-Central (Syracuse, NY) 2/1/71
(See Marine Midland Bank-Central (Syracuse, NY))

MARINE MIDLAND TRUST CO. OF ROCKLAND COUNTY (NYACK, NY)
Merged into Marine Midland Bank of Southeastern New York, N.A. (Poughkeepsie, N.Y.) 12/31/69
Each share Capital Stock $8 par exchanged for (0.18) share Common $40 par
(See Marine Midland Bank of Southeastern New York, N.A. (Poughkeepsie, N.Y.))

MARINE MIDLAND TRUST CO. OF SOUTHERN NEW YORK (ELMIRA, NY)
Name changed to Marine Midland Bank- Southern (Elmira, NY) and Capital Stock $25 par changed to $75 par 12/30/70
(See Marine Midland Bank-Southern (Elmira, NY))

MARINE MIDLAND TRUST CO. OF WESTERN NEW YORK (BUFFALO, NY)
Name changed to Marine Midland Bank- Western (Buffalo, NY) 8/1/70
(See Marine Midland Bank-Western (Buffalo, NY))

MARINE MIDLAND TR CO MOHAWK VY (UTICA, NY)
Merged into Marine Midland Bank-Central (Syracuse, NY) 2/1/71
Each share Common $5 par

exchanged for (1) share Marine Midland Banks, Inc. Common $5 par
(See Marine Midland Bank-Central (Syracuse, NY))

MARINE NATIONAL BANK (ERIE, PA)
Each share Capital Stock $66-2/3 par exchanged for (4) shares Capital Stock $20 par 00/00/1945
Under plan of merger each share Capital Stock $20 par exchanged for (2) shares Capital Stock $10 par 10/02/1964
Capital Stock $10 par changed to $5 par and (1) additional share issued 03/05/1974
Stock Dividend - 150% 11/07/1969
Name changed to Marine Bank (Meadville, PA) 12/23/1976
Marine Bank (Meadville, PA) reorganized as Marine Bancorp, Inc. 12/21/1981 which merged into PNC Financial Corp. 01/23/1984 which name changed to PNC Financial Services Group, Inc. 03/15/2000

MARINE NATL BK (JACKSONVILLE, FL)
Acquired by Alliance Capital Partners 01/02/2001
Details not available

MARINE NATL BK (SANTA ANA, CA)
Merged into Shinhan Bank 9/24/96
Each share Common $4 par exchanged for $9.90 cash

MARINE NATL BK (WILDWOOD, NJ)
Merged into Horizon Bancorp 06/04/1980
Each share Capital Stock $10 par exchanged for (4.5) shares Common $4 par
(See Horizon Bancorp)

MARINE NATIONAL EXCHANGE BANK (MILWAUKEE, WI)
Stock Dividend - 100% 1/14/57
Acquired by Banc One Corp. 4/1/88
Each share Capital Stock $20 par exchanged for (2.5652) shares Common no par
Banc One Corp. merged into Bank One Corp. 10/2/98 which merged into J.P. Morgan Chase & Co. 12/31/2000 which name changed to JPMorgan Chase & Co. 7/20/2004

MARINE PROPULSION ENGR INC (MA)
Adjudicated bankrupt 12/04/1975
Stockholders' equity unlikely

MARINE PROTEIN CORP (DE)
Reincorporated 8/5/71
State of incorporation changed from (NY) to (DE) 8/5/71
Each share Common 1¢ par exchanged for (1) share Common 1¢ par
Filed for Chapter 11 bankruptcy proceedings 4/13/79
Stockholders' equity unlikely

MARINE RES INC (NY)
Name changed to MRI Liquidating, Inc. 04/13/1979
(See MRI Liquidating, Inc.)

MARINE SAFETY RAPID TRANSIT CO. (NH)
Proclaimed dissolved in 1925

MARINE SAVINGS & LOAN ASSOCIATION OF FLORIDA (FL)
Acquired by Fortune Savings Bank (Clearwater, Fla.) 3/11/88
Each share Common $3 par exchanged for $16.75 cash

MARINE SHARE CORP.
Acquired by Marine Union Investors Inc. 00/00/1929
Details not available

MARINE SHUTTLE OPERATIONS INC (NV)
SEC revoked common stock registration 03/11/2010

MARINE TRANS CORP (DE)
Merged into Crowley Maritime Corp. 2/8/2001
Each share Common 50¢ par exchanged for $7 cash

MARINE TRANS LINES INC (DE)
Acquired by Intrepid Acquisition Corp. 11/16/1989
Each share Common 10¢ par exchanged for $25.25 cash

MARINE TRUST CO. OF WESTERN NEW YORK (BUFFALO, NY)
Capital Stock $20 par changed to $30 par 4/23/64
Name changed to Marine Midland Trust Co. of Western New York (Buffalo, NY) 9/30/65
Marine Midland Trust Co. of Western New York (Buffalo, NY) name changed to Marine Midland Bank-Western (Buffalo, NY) 8/1/70
(See Marine Midland Bank-Western (Buffalo, NY))

MARINE UNION INVESTORS, INC.
Acquired by Niagara Share Corp. of Maryland 07/00/1930
Details not available

MARINE VIEW ELECTRONICS, INC. (NY)
Adjudicated bankrupt 6/23/65

MARINELAND PAC INC (DE)
Completely liquidated 11/10/1971
Each share Common $1 par exchanged for first and final distribution of (0.173611) share Hollywood Turf Club (CA) Capital Stock $3.33333333 par
Hollywood Turf Club (CA) reincorporated in Delaware as Hollywood Park, Inc. (Old) 01/31/1974 which reorganized as Hollywood Park Realty Enterprises, Inc. 04/13/1982 which reorganized as Hollywood Park, Inc. (New) 01/02/1992 which name changed to Pinnacle Entertainment, Inc. (Old) 02/23/2000 which merged into Gaming & Leisure Properties, Inc. 04/28/2016

MARINEMAX INC (DE)
Reincorporated under the laws of Florida 03/20/2015

MARINER CAP CORP (FL)
Recapitalized as First Commercial Bancorporation 11/14/86
Each share Common $0.001 par exchanged for (0.04) share Common $0.001 par
(See First Commerical Bancorporation)

MARINER CAP TR (MD)
8.3% Preferred Securities called for redemption at $10 on 10/1/2003

MARINER ENERGY INC (DE)
Merged into Apache Corp. 11/10/2010
Each share Common $0.0001 par exchanged for (0.17043) share Common $0.625 par and $7.80 cash

MARINER EXPLS INC (BC)
Recapitalized as Argosy Resources Corp. 02/15/1991
Each (3.5) shares Common no par exchanged for (1) share Common no par
Argosy Resources Corp. name changed to Motion Works Corp. 10/24/1991 which name changed to Motion Works Group Ltd. 08/08/1995
(See Motion Works Group Ltd.)

MARINER HEALTH CARE INC (DE)
Merged into National Senior Care, Inc. 12/10/2004
Each share Common 1¢ par exchanged for $30 cash

MARINER HEALTH CARE INC (NV)
Name changed to Advanced Healthcare Technologies Inc. 08/12/2002
Advanced Healthcare Technologies Inc. recapitalized as Global Resource Corp. 09/14/2004
(See Global Resource Corp.)

MARINER HEALTH GROUP INC (DE)
Merged into Mariner Post-Acute Network, Inc. 7/31/98
Each share Common 1¢ par exchanged for (1) share Common 1¢ par
(See Mariner Post-Acute Network, Inc.)

MARINER MINES LTD (ON)
Merged into International Mariner Resources Ltd. 2/9/71
Each share Capital Stock $1 par exchanged for (0.4) share Common no par and (0.2) Ser. C Common Stock Purchase Warrant which expires 7/31/72
(See International Mariner Resources Ltd.)

MARINER POST-ACUTE NETWORK INC (DE)
Plan of reorganization under Chapter 11 Federal Bankruptcy Code effective 05/13/2002
No stockholders' equity

MARINERS BANCORP (CA)
Merged into Eldorado Bancorp 10/20/95
Each share Common no par exchanged for (1) share Common no par
(See Eldorado Bancorp)

MARINERS CHOICE INTL INC (WY)
Reorganized 09/02/2014
Reorganized from Nevada to under the laws of Wyoming 09/02/2014
Each share Common $0.001 par exchanged for (0.001) share Common $0.0001 par
Name changed to Han Tang Technology, Inc. 09/28/2015

MARINERS FINL CORP (DE)
Merged into Fidelity Federal Savings & Loan Association 11/06/1978
Each share Capital Stock $1 par exchanged for $20.75 principal amount of a savings account

MARINEX MULTIMEDIA CORP (NV)
Name changed to Texas Equipment Corp. 10/2/96
(See Texas Equipment Corp.)

MARINO INVESTMENTS, INC. (UT)
Reincorporated under the laws of Delaware as Rattlesnake Gold, Inc. 4/12/88
Rattlesnake Gold, Inc. recapitalized as Shadow Wood Corp. 9/5/95 which recapitalized as Magicworks Entertainment Inc. 7/24/96 which merged into SFX Entertainment, Inc. 9/11/98 which merged into Clear Channel Communications, Inc. 8/1/2000

MARINUS LABORATORIES, INC. (FL)
Charter cancelled and proclaimed dissolved for non-payment of taxes 6/28/71

MARION BANCORP (IN)
Merged into Banc One Corp. (DE) 10/01/1986
Each share Common no par exchanged for (2.42) shares Common no par
Banc One Corp. (DE) reincorporated in Ohio 05/01/1989 which merged into Bank One Corp. 10/02/1998 which merged into J.P. Morgan Chase & Co. 12/31/2000 which name changed to JPMorgan Chase & Co. 07/20/2004

MARION BK (MARION, OH)
Under plan of reorganization each share Common $10 par automatically became (1) share Ohio State Bancshares, Inc. Common $10 par 05/16/1996

MARION BRICK CORP (OH)
Merged into Medusa Portland Cement Co. 02/29/1972
Each share Common no par exchanged for (0.56) share Common no par
Medusa Portland Cement Co. name changed to Medusa Corp. 03/31/1972
(See Medusa Corp.)

MARION CAP HLDGS INC (IN)
Merged into Mutualfirst Financial, Inc. 12/11/2000
Each share Common no par exchanged for (1.862) shares Common 1¢ par

MARION CORP (NV)
Each share Common no par exchanged for (0.25) share Common $1 par 12/24/1969
Common $1 par split (2) for (1) by issuance of (1) additional share 01/25/1980
Common $1 par split (3) for (2) by issuance of (0.5) additional share 01/30/1981
Stock Dividend - 100% 12/01/1971
Reorganized under Chapter 11 Federal Bankruptcy Code 01/27/1986
For holdings of (99) shares or fewer each share Common $1 par exchanged for $0.05 cash
For holdings of (100) shares or more each share Common $1 par exchanged for (0.1) share Skylink America Inc. (AL) Common 1¢ par or $0.05 cash
Note: Unexchanged certificates were cancelled and became without value 08/06/1987
Skylink America Inc. (AL) reincorporated in Texas 09/28/1989 which name changed to Crown Casino Corp. 11/09/1993 which name changed to Grown Group, Inc. 10/02/1997 which name changed to America's Car-Mart, Inc. 03/28/2002

MARION FABRICS INC (CA)
Believed out of business 00/00/1976
Details not available

MARION LABS INC (DE)
Common $1 par split (2) for (1) by issuance of (1) additional share 09/06/1966
Common $1 par split (3) for (2) by issuance of (0.5) additional share 09/18/1967
Common $1 par split (2) for (1) by issuance of (1) additional share 09/12/1968
Common $1 par split (2) for (1) by issuance of (1) additional share 04/20/1972
Common $1 par split (2) for (1) by issuance of (1) additional share 05/27/1983
Common $1 par split (2) for (1) by issuance of (1) additional share 04/18/1985
Common $1 par split (2) for (1) by issuance of (1) additional share 06/03/1986
Common $1 par split (2) for (1) by issuance of (1) additional share 04/20/1987
Common $1 par changed to 10¢ par 11/12/1987
Under plan of reorganization name changed to Marion Merrell Dow Inc. and each share Common 10¢ par received distribution of (1) Dow Chemical Co. Contingent Value Right 12/01/1989
(See Dow Chemical Co.)
Marion Merrell Dow Inc. merged into Hoechst A.G. 07/18/1995

MARION MFG CO (NC)
Each share Common $100 par exchanged for (5) shares Common $20 par 00/00/1946

Stock Dividend - 166-2/3% 03/06/1950
Completely liquidated 11/07/1986
Details not available

MARION MERRELL DOW INC (DE)
Merged into Hoechst AG 07/18/1995
Each share Common 10¢ par exchanged for $25.75 cash

MARION NATL BK (MARION, IN)
Stock Dividends - 20% 05/29/1957; 25% 02/15/1965; 20% 02/15/1966
Name changed to American Bank & Trust Co. (Marion, IN) 05/26/1978
(See American Bank & Trust Co. (Marion, IN))

MARION NATL CORP (IN)
Administratively dissolved 12/31/87

MARION POWER SHOVEL CO. (OH)
Common no par changed to $10 par in 1947
Liquidation for cash completed in 1957

MARION STEAM SHOVEL CO.
Name changed to Marion Power Shovel Co. in 1946
Marion Power Shovel Co. completed liquidation for cash in 1957

MARION WATER CO. (OH)
Name changed to Ohio-American Water Co. 01/01/1980
(See Ohio-American Water Co.)

MARIONETTE PRODUCTIONS, INC. (DE)
No longer in existence having become inoperative and void for non-payment of taxes 4/1/61

MARIPOSA RES INC (BC)
Recapitalized as Adagio Investments Inc. 7/24/89
Each share Common no par exchanged for (0.25) share Common no par
(See Adagio Investments Inc.)

MARIPOSA RES LTD (NV)
Common $0.001 par split (10) for (1) by issuance of (9) additional shares payable 05/06/2009 to holders of record 05/06/2009
Name changed to Lithium Exploration Group, Inc. 12/07/2010

MARISA CHRISTINA INC (DE)
Acquired by Hampshire Group, Ltd. 05/19/2006
Each share Common 1¢ par exchanged for $0.6015 cash

MARISHELL PRODS LTD (BC)
Recapitalized as Boulevard Capital Ltd. 05/12/1999
Each share Common no par exchanged for (0.125) share Common no par
Boulevard Capital Ltd. name changed to Urban Communications Inc. 06/28/2001
(See Urban Communications Inc.)

MARITEK CORP (DE)
SEC revoked common stock registration 02/15/2006

MARITIME ACCESSORIES LTD (NS)
Assets sold in 1980
Details not available

MARITIME BK & TR CO (ESSEX, CT)
Merged into Webster Financial Corp. 4/21/99
Each share Common $1 par exchanged for (1.091) shares Common 1¢ par

MARITIME BANK OF CALIFORNIA (WILMINGTON, CA)
Taken over by FDIC 8/27/93
Stockholders' equity unlikely

MARITIME-BARYTES, LTD. (ON)
Charter cancelled for failure to file reports and pay taxes 5/2/60

MARITIME CADILLAC GOLD MINES LTD.
Bankrupt in 1939

MARITIME COAL, RAILWAY & POWER CO. LTD. (NS)
Liquidation completed
Each share Preferred $10 par presented for initial distribution of $3.50 cash plus return of certificate 07/27/1962
Each share Preferred $10 par presented for second distribution of $4 cash plus return of certificate 02/20/1963
Each share Preferred $10 par exchanged for third and final distribution of $0.681088 cash 01/00/1965
Common $22 par did not participate and certificates are now valueless

MARITIME CORP (MA)
Liquidation completed
Each share Class A Common no par or Class B Common no par stamped to indicate initial distribution of (1) share LaTouraine Coffee Co., Inc. Class B $1 par and $12.09979916 cash 01/01/1966
(See LaTouraine Coffee Co.)
Each share Stamped Class A Common no par or Stamped Class B Common no par stamped to indicate second distribution of $37.077089 cash 05/23/1966
Each share Stamped Class A Common no par or Stamped Class B Common no par exchanged for third and final distribution of $4.86 cash 11/28/1966

MARITIME ELEC LTD (CANADA)
14-3/4% Retractable Preferred Ser. C no par called for redemption 9/1/88
Common no par split (3) for (1) by issuance of (2) additional shares 8/15/73
Common no par reclassified as Conv. Class A Common no par 10/24/74
Conv. Class A Common no par reclassified as Common no par 11/14/79
Conv. Class B Common no par reclassified as Common no par 11/14/79
Common no par split (3) for (1) by issuance of (2) additional shares 6/12/86
Acquired by Fortis Inc. 8/26/94
Each share Common no par exchanged for either (0.6725) share Common no par and $7.94 cash or $24.25 cash

MARITIME FINANCE, LTD. (NS)
Voluntarily dissolved 2/10/75
Details not available

MARITIME LIFE ASSRN CO (NS)
Capital Stock $100 par changed to $50 par 09/03/1969
Each share Capital Stock $50 par exchanged for (10) shares Capital Stock $5 par 02/19/1970
99% held by Hancock (John) Mutual Life Insurance Co. as of 12/31/1975
Public interest eliminated

MARITIME LIFE ASSRN CO NEW (NS)
Adjustable Dividend 1st Preferred Ser. A $25 par called for redemption at $25 plus $0.028 accrued dividends on 10/15/2004
Each share old 2nd Preferred Ser. 3 exchanged for (0.000001) share new 2nd Preferred Ser. 3 on 11/30/2004
Note: In effect holders received $27.07279 cash per share
Floating Dividends 2nd Preferred Ser. 1 called for redemption at $25 plus $0.38125 accrued dividends on 12/31/2004

MARITIME RESORTS INTL (UT)
Each share old Common $0.001 par exchanged for (0.01) share new Common $0.001 par 10/07/1992
Each share new Common $0.001 par exchanged for (1.5) shares Class A Common $0.001 par 04/19/1993
Name changed to Palace Casinos Inc. 12/13/1993
Palace Casinos Inc. recapitalized as Xcel Management Inc. (UT) 08/09/1999 which reincorporated in Delaware as InsynQ, Inc. 08/04/2000 which reincorporated in Nevada 12/24/2002
(See InsynQ, Inc. (NV))

MARITIME ROCK PRODUCTS LTD. (NB)
Petitioned into Bankruptcy 12/11/61
No stockholders' equity

MARITIME STEEL & FOUNDRIES, LTD. (NS)
Preferred $100 par called for redemption 5/1/69
(Additional Information in Active)

MARITIME TELEG & TEL LTD (NS)
Common $10 par changed to no par and (2) additional shares issued 04/25/1985
9.40% Preferred $10 par called for redemption 03/17/1986
8.60% Preference $10 par called for redemption 03/16/1992
7.10% Preference $10 par called for redemption 01/29/1993
7.65% Preferred $10 par called for redemption 01/29/1993
$1.9625 Retractable Class E Preferred $25 par called for redemption 01/15/1994
Merged into Aliant Inc. (Canada) 06/01/1999
Each share 7% Preference Ser. B $10 par exchanged for (0.605) share Common no par
Each share Common no par exchanged for (1.667) shares Common no par
Aliant Inc. (Canada) reorganized in Ontario as Bell Aliant Regional Communications Income Fund 07/10/2006 which reorganized in Canada as Bell Aliant Inc. 01/04/2011 which merged into BCE Inc. 10/31/2014

MARITIME TRANS & TECHNOLOGY INC (NY)
Each share old Class A Common 1¢ par exchanged for (0.1) share new Class A Common 1¢ par 04/23/1998
Name changed to Bank Store 07/24/1998
Bank Store name changed to Banker's Store Inc. 09/18/2001
(See Banker's Store Inc.)

MARITIMES MINING CORP. LTD. (NB)
Recapitalized as First Maritime Mining Corp. Ltd. on a (1) for (2.5) basis 5/22/64
(See First Maritime Mining Corp. Ltd.)

MARITRANS INC (DE)
Merged into Overseas Shipholding Group, Inc. 11/28/2006
Each share Common 1¢ par exchanged for $37.50 cash

MARITRANS PARTNERS L P (DE)
Reorganized as Maritrans Inc. 04/01/1993
Each Depositary Unit exchanged for (1) share Common 1¢ par
(See Maritrans Inc.)

MARIUPOL HEAVY MACHY PLT AZOV (UKRAINE)
GDR agreement terminated 05/25/2017
Each Reg. S Sponsored GDR for Ordinary exchanged for (1) share Ordinary
Note: Unexchanged GDR's will be sold and the proceeds, if any, held for claim after 11/24/2017

MARJAS RED LAKE GOLD MINES, LTD. (ON)
Charter cancelled for failure to file reports and pay taxes in 1953

MARK-CAN INVT CORP (BC)
Name changed to Yale Resources Ltd. 09/30/2003
Yale Resources Ltd. recapitalized as Alta Vista Ventures Ltd. 05/29/2013 which name changed to Global UAV Technologies Ltd. 05/17/2017

MARK COMPUTER SYS INC (NY)
Plan of arrangement with creditors confirmed 09/15/1971
Details not available

MARK CORRECTIONAL SYS INC (DE)
Under plan of merger name changed to Mark Solutions, Inc. 11/10/1993
Mark Solutions, Inc. name changed to Mark Holdings Inc. 12/26/2001
(See Mark Holdings Inc.)

MARK CTLS CORP NEW (DE)
Merged into Crane Co. 4/27/94
Each share Common 1¢ par exchanged for $19.50 cash

MARK CTLS CORP OLD (DE)
Common $1 par split (3) for (2) by issuance of (0.5) additional share 6/2/75
Common $1 par split (3) for (2) by issuance of (0.5) additional share 3/4/76
Common $1 par split (3) for (2) by issuance of (0.5) additional share 3/3/77
Common $1 par split (3) for (2) by issuance of (0.5) additional share 6/1/81
$1.20 Conv. Preferred Ser. A $1 par called for redemption 9/15/87
Merged into Landis & Gyr, Inc. 10/13/87
Each share Common $1 par exchanged for $27.50 cash

MARK CTRS TR (MD)
Name changed to Acadia Realty Trust 8/12/98

MARK V MINES LTD. (BC)
Name changed to Mark V Petroleums & Mines Ltd. 02/14/1972
Each share Capital Stock 50¢ par exchanged for (1) share Capital Stock 50¢ par
Mark V Petroleums & Mines Ltd. recapitalized as TLC Ventures Corp. 10/05/1994 which name changed to Calibre Mining Corp. 06/18/2007

MARK IV HOMES, INC. (DE)
Common 1¢ par split (3) for (2) by issuance of (0.5) additional share 4/5/72
Name changed to Mark IV Industries, Inc. 7/26/77
(See Mark IV Industries, Inc.)

MARK IV INDS INC (DE)
Common 1¢ par split (3) for (2) by issuance of (0.5) additional share 11/10/1983
Common 1¢ par split (3) for (2) by issuance of (0.5) additional share 01/04/1985
Common 1¢ par split (3) for (2) by issuance of (0.5) additional share 06/06/1986
Common 1¢ par split (3) for (2) by issuance of (0.5) additional share issued 01/30/1987
Common 1¢ par split (3) for (2) by issuance of (0.5) additional share 11/17/1989
Common 1¢ par split (3) for (2) by issuance of (0.5) additional share 04/01/1992
Stock Dividends - 5% payable 04/26/1996 to holders of record 04/12/1996; 5% payable 05/01/1997 to holders of record
Merged into MIV Holdings S.A. 09/14/2000

MARK FOUR RES INC (DE)
Each share Common 1¢ par exchanged for $23 cash

MARK FOUR RES INC (DE)
Recapitalized as Ecology Pure Air International Inc. 6/19/96
Each share Common $0.001 par exchanged for (1/3) share Common $0.001 par
(See Ecology Pure Air International Inc.)

MARK HLDGS INC (DE)
Charter cancelled and declared inoperative and void for non-payment of taxes 03/01/2003

MARK HOPKINS, INC. (CA)
Each share Class A or B no par exchanged for (10) shares Class A or B $1 par in 1947
Name changed to California-Mason Realty Co. 2/5/62
(See California-Mason Realty Co.)

MARK HOPKINS HOTEL CO., LTD.
Reorganized as Mark Hopkins, Inc. in 1937
Mark Hopkins, Inc. name changed to California-Mason Realty Co. 2/5/62
(See California-Mason Realty Co.)

MARK INC. (DE)
Name changed to Digitran Systems, Inc. 10/15/1985
Digitran Systems, Inc. recapitalized as TGFIN Holdings, Inc. 09/30/2002 which recapitalized as Redify Group, Inc. 02/28/2014

MARK ONE GLOBAL INDS INC (BC)
SEC revoked common stock registration 10/14/2015

MARK I INDS INC (DE)
Each share old Common $0.001 par exchanged for (0.02) share new Common $0.001 par 01/21/1999
Each share new Common $0.001 par exchanged again for (0.5) share new Common $0.001 par 01/26/1999
Name changed to Foodvision.com Inc. 06/00/1999
(See Foodvision.com Inc.)

MARK 1 OFFSET INC (DE)
Adjudicated bankrupt 10/16/1975
Stockholders' equity unlikely

MARK PRODS INC (TX)
Common no par split (2) for (1) by issuance of (1) additional share 8/20/75
Common no par split (4) for (1) by issuance of (3) additional shares 6/15/81
Merged into Bralone Resources Ltd. 2/22/85
Each share Common no par exchanged for $5.2751 cash

MARK RES INC (AB)
Each share Conv. Preferred Ser. A no par exchanged for (0.66666666) share Common no par 04/16/1987
Acquired by EnerMark Income Fund 04/09/1996
Each share Common no par exchanged for (1) Trust Unit no par and $2 cash
EnerMark Income Fund merged into Enerplus Resources Fund 06/22/2001 which reorganized as Enerplus Corp. 01/03/2011

MARK VII INC (DE)
Reincorporated 5/22/96
State of incorporation changed from (MO) to (DE) 5/22/96
Common 10¢ par changed to 5¢ par and (1) additional share issued payable 11/21/97 to holders of record 11/14/97
Merged into Ocean Group plc 9/1/99
Each share Common 5¢ par exchanged for $23 cash

MARK (LOUIS) SHOES, INC.
Liquidated in 1930

MARK SOLUTIONS INC (DE)
Each share old Common 1¢ par exchanged for (0.25) share new Common 1¢ par 06/14/1999
Name changed to Mark Holdings Inc. 12/26/2001
(See Mark Holdings Inc.)

MARK SYS INC (CA)
Merged into Intech Inc. 01/13/1982
Each share Common 20¢ par exchanged for (0.04) share Common no par
(See Intech Inc.)

MARK TWAIN BANCSHARES INC (MO)
9-1/4% Conv. Preferred Ser. 1 $25 par called for redemption 01/19/1990
Common $5 par changed to $2.50 par and (1) additional share issued 05/17/1979
Common $2.50 par changed to $1.25 par and (1) additional share issued 05/20/1983
Common $1.25 par split (3) for (2) by issuance of (0.5) additional share 11/05/1987
Common $1.25 par split (3) for (2) by issuance of (0.5) additional share 06/21/1993
Merged into Mercantile Bancorporation, Inc. 04/25/1997
Each share Common $1.25 par exchanged for (0.952) share Common $5 par

MARK TWAIN LIFE CORP (OK)
Recapitalized as Twain (Mark) Life Insurance Corp. 4/15/76
Each share Class A 25¢ par exchanged for (0.25) share Class A $1 par
Each share Class B 25¢ par exchanged for (0.25) share Class B $1 par
(See Twain (Mark) Life Insurance Corp.)

MARK TWAIN LIFE INS CO (MO)
Merged into Twain (Mark) Life Corp. 08/13/1971
Each share Common $1 par exchanged for (2.18) shares Class A Common 25¢ par
Twain (Mark) Life Corp. recapitalized as Twain (Mark) Life Insurance Corp. 04/15/1976
(See Twain (Mark) Life Insurance Corp.)

MARK TWAIN LIFE INS CORP (OK)
Each share Class A Common $1 par exchanged for (0.01) share Class A Common $100 or $7 cash 10/15/84
Note: Option to receive cash expired 1/15/85
Stock Dividends - 25% 4/30/80; 10% 4/30/81; 10% 4/30/82; 10% 4/29/83
Merged into MTL Holding Co. 11/18/85
Each share Class A Common $100 par exchanged for $7 cash

MARK TWAIN MARINE INC (DE)
Stock Dividend - 100% 8/16/76
Charter cancelled and declared inoperative and void for non-payment of taxes 3/1/89

MARK V PETES & MINES LTD (BC)
Recapitalized as TLC Ventures Corp. 10/05/1994
Each share Common 50¢ par exchanged for (1/3) share Common no par
TLC Ventures Corp. name changed to Calibre Mining Corp. 06/18/2007

MARKAN INC (KS)
Each share Common 10¢ par exchanged for (0.090909) share Common $2 par 10/22/68
Charter dissolved for failure to file annual report 12/6/96

MARKATECH INDS CORP (BC)
Recapitalized as Ameratech Systems Corp. 2/12/2001
Each (12) shares Common no par exchanged for (1) share Common no par
(See Ameratech Systems Corp.)

MARKBOROUGH PPTYS INC (CANADA)
Merged into Cambridge Shopping Centres Ltd. 6/9/97
For Canadian residents: Each share Common no par exchanged for $0.148 principal amount of 6% Conv. Subordinate Debentures due 6/30/2007 and $0.216 cash
For Non-Canadian residents: Each share Common no par exchanged for $0.148 principal amount of 6% Conv. Subordinate Debentures due 6/30/2007 and $0.316 cash

MARKBOROUGH PPTYS LTD (ON)
Merged into Hudson's Bay Co. 8/1/81
Each share Common no par exchanged for $30 cash

MARKEL FINL HLDGS LTD (CANADA)
Capital Stock no par reclassified as Subordinate Vtg. no par 07/30/1986
Name changed to Fairfax Financial Holdings Ltd. 05/15/1987

MARKER INTL (UT)
Name changed to MKR Holdings 8/3/2000
(See MKR Holdings)

MARKER LABS INC (MN)
Name changed to California Cami'z, Inc. 6/30/88
California Cami'z, Inc. recapitalized as Cami'z Inc. 2/9/90 which name changed to B.U.M. International Inc. 11/2/94
(See B.U.M. International Inc.)

MARKER RES LTD (AB)
Merged into Varna Gold Inc. 12/14/1987
Each share Common no par exchanged for (0.75) share Common no par
Varna Gold Inc. name changed to New Island Minerals Ltd. 01/18/1993 which name changed to New Island Resources Inc. 04/22/1997

MARKET AMER INC (NC)
Merged into Miracle Marketing Inc. 7/22/2002
Each share Common $0.00001 par exchanged for $8 cash

MARKET BASKET (CA)
Each share Common $1 par exchanged for (2) shares Common 50¢ par in 1946
Stock Dividend - 100% 7/1/55
99.9% held by Kroger Co. as of 12/4/63 and on 5/25/72 advised will purchase minority shares at $35 per share

MARKET BASKET CORP. (NY)
Merged into American Stores Co. (Old) 4/10/56
Each share 2nd Preferred no par exchanged for (2.1) shares Common $1 par
Each share Common no par exchanged for (0.546) share Common $1 par
American Stores Co. (Old) name changed to Acme Markets, Inc. 6/28/62 which name changed back to American Stores Co. (Old) 12/29/73 which merged into American Stores Co. (New) 7/26/79 which merged into Albertson's, Inc. 6/23/99 which merged into Supervalu Inc. 6/2/2006

MARKET BASKET ENTERPRISES INC (NV)
Reorganized as J.T.'s Restaurants Inc. 11/12/1996
Each share Common exchanged for (0.01666666) share Common J.T.'s Restaurants Inc. name changed to National Integrated Food Service Corp. 12/20/98
(See National Integrated Food Service Corp.)

MARKET CENT INC (DE)
Name changed to Scientigo, Inc. 02/17/2006
Scientigo, Inc. recapitalized as Incumaker, Inc. 06/01/2011

MARKET DATA CORP (TX)
Reorganized under the laws of Nevada as Time Financial Services, Inc. 07/01/1997
Each share Common $0.001 par exchanged for (0.05) share Common $0.001 par
Time Financial Services, Inc. recapitalized as Interruption Television, Inc. 07/20/2000 which name changed to Bongiovi Entertainment, Inc. 09/17/2002 which name changed to NewGen Technologies, Inc. 08/11/2005
(See NewGen Technologies, Inc.)

MARKET FACTS INC (DE)
Common $1 par split (3) for (2) by issuance of (0.5) additional share 5/31/72
Common $1 par split (3) for (2) by issuance of (0.5) additional share 8/25/80
Common $1 par split (4) for (3) by issuance of (1/3) additional share 8/24/81
Common $1 par split (2) for (1) by issuance of (1) additional share 10/7/85
Common $1 par split (2) for (1) by issuance of (1) additional share payable 12/13/96 to holders of record 11/22/96
Common $1 par split (2) for (1) by issuance of (1) additional share payable 5/27/97 to holders of record 5/12/97
Merged into Aegis Group plc 6/10/99
Each share Common $1 par exchanged for $31 cash

MARKET FINL CORP (OH)
Merged into People's Community Bancorp Inc. 3/30/2001
Each share Common no par exchanged for either (0.8386) share Common $1 par or $13 cash

MARKET FORMULATION & RESH CORP NEW (TX)
Reorganized as 649.com Inc. 05/27/1999
Each share Common $0.001 par exchanged for (5) shares Common $0.001 par
649.com Inc. name changed to Infinite Holdings Group, Inc. 01/24/2007
(See Infinite Holdings Group, Inc.)

MARKET FORMULATION & RESH CORP OLD (TX)
Name changed to Convenience Concepts Inc. 06/09/1998
Convenience Concepts Inc. name changed to Market Formulation & Research Corp. (New) 11/12/1998 which reorganized as 649.com Inc. 05/27/1999 which name changed to Infinite Holdings Group, Inc. 01/24/2007
(See Infinite Holdings Group, Inc.)

MARKET GROWTH FD INC (MD)
Acquired by Pennsylvania Mutual Fund, Inc. 10/26/1973
Each share Common $1 par exchanged for (0.868) share Capital Stock $1 par
Pennsylvania Mutual Fund, Inc. merged into Royce Fund 06/28/1996

MARKET GUIDE INC (NY)
Each share old Common $0.001 par exchanged for (0.25) share new Common $0.001 par 10/16/95

Merged into Multex.com, Inc. 9/24/99
Each share Common $0.001 par exchanged for (1) share Common 1¢ par
(See Multex.com, Inc.)

MARKET LEAD INTL CORP (DE)
Each share old Common $0.0666 par exchanged for (0.1) share new Common $0.0666 par 08/17/1995
Recapitalized as Primesource Communications Holdings Inc. 06/13/1998
Each (1.333) shares new Common $0.0666 par exchanged for (1) share Common $0.0666 par
Primesource Communications Holdings Inc. name changed to Primeholdings.com Inc. 07/20/1999 which reincorporated in Nevada 02/27/2004 which name changed to Mindpix Corp. 10/16/2007

MARKET LEADER INC (WA)
Merged into Trulia, Inc. 08/20/2013
Each share Common $0.001 par exchanged for (0.1553) share Common $0.00001 par and $6 cash
Trulia, Inc. merged into Zillow Group, Inc. 02/18/2015

MARKET LINE INTL INC (NJ)
Charter declared void for non-payment of taxes 12/31/93

MARKET MONITOR DATA INC (DE)
Adjudicated bankrupt 10/13/1970
No stockholders' equity

MARKET PL PRODS INC (NY)
Charter cancelled and proclaimed dissolved for failure to pay taxes and file reports 12/15/1975

MARKET PLANNING SOLUTIONS INC (DE)
Acquired by KSS Ltd. 05/31/2011
Each share Common 5¢ par exchanged for $201.9688 cash

MARKET PROGRAMS INC (DE)
Charter cancelled and declared inoperative and void for non-payment of taxes 3/1/81

MARKET PUBLICATIONS, INC. (DE)
In liquidation and trustee appointed 1/6/76
No stockholders' equity

MARKET STREET INVESTMENT CORP.
Liquidation completed in 1939

MARKET STREET NATIONAL BUILDING, INC.
Liquidation completed in 1949

MARKET STREET RAILWAY CO. (CA)
In process of liquidation since 1950
Stock Transfer books closed 7/27/53

MARKET TREND INC (NV)
Charter revoked for failure to file reports and pay fees 4/11/2001

MARKET 2000 HOLDRS TR (DE)
Trust terminated
Each Depositary Receipt received first and final distribution of $55.382076 cash payable 01/08/2013 to holders of record 12/24/2012

MARKET VECTORS ETF TR (DE)
Nuclear Energy ETF no par reclassified as Uranium+Nuclear Energy ETF no par 01/05/2011
Indonesia Index ETF no par split (3) for (1) by issuance of (2) additional shares payable 01/31/2011 to holders of record 01/28/2011 Ex date - 02/01/2011
Bank & Brokerage ETF no par split (2) for (1) by issuance of (1) additional share payable 02/13/2012 to holders of record 02/10/2012 Ex date - 02/14/2012
Biotech ETF no par split (3) for (1) by issuance of (2) additional shares payable 02/13/2012 to holders of record 02/10/2012 Ex date - 02/14/2012
Oil Services ETF no par split (3) for (1) by issuance of (2) additional shares payable 02/13/2012 to holders of record 02/10/2012 Ex date - 02/14/2012
Pharmaceutical ETF no par split (2) for (1) by issuance of (1) additional share payable 02/13/2012 to holders of record 02/10/2012 Ex date - 02/14/2012
Retail ETF no par split (3) for (1) by issuance of (2) additional shares payable 02/13/2012 to holders of record 02/10/2012 Ex date - 02/14/2012
Each (15) shares old Solar Energy ETF no par automatically became (1) share new Solar Energy ETF no par 07/02/2012
Morningstar Wide Moat Research ETF no par reclassified as Wide Moat ETF no par 02/01/2013
Each share old Egypt Index ETF no par automatically became (0.25) share new Egypt Index ETF no par 07/01/2013
Each share old Global Alternative Energy ETF no par automatically became (0.33333333) share new Global Alternative Energy ETF no par 07/01/2013
Each share old India Small-Cap Index ETF no par automatically became (0.25) share new India Small-Cap Index ETF no par 07/01/2013
Each share old Junior Gold Miners ETF no par automatically became (0.25) share new Junior Gold Miners ETF no par 07/01/2013
Each share old Rare Earth/Strategic Metals ETF no par automatically became (0.25) share new Rare Earth/Strategic Metals ETF no par 07/01/2013
Each share old Russia Small-Cap ETF no par automatically became (0.33333333) share new Russia Small-Cap ETF no par 07/01/2013
Each share old Uranium+Nuclear Energy ETF no par automatically became (0.33333333) share new Uranium+Nuclear Energy ETF no par 07/01/2013
LatAm Aggregate Bond ETF no par reclassified as Emerging Markets Aggregate Bond ETF no par 12/10/2013
China A Shares ETF no par reclassified as ChinaAMC A-Share ETF no par 01/08/2014
RVE Hard Assets Producers ETF no par reclassified as Natural Resources ETF no par 05/01/2014
Wide Moat ETF no par reclassified as Morningstar Wide Moat ETF no par 09/16/2014
Trust terminated 12/23/2014
Each share Bank & Brokerage ETF no par received $53.83809 cash
Each share Colombia ETF no par received $12.40072 cash
Each share Germany Small-Cap ETF no par received $27.57117 cash
Each share Latin America Small-Cap ETF no par received $13.97573 cash
Each share Renminbi Bond ETF no par received $24.81173 cash
Emerging Markets Local Currency Bond ETF no par reclassified as J.P. Morgan EM Local Currency Bond ETF no par 10/01/2015
Trust terminated 10/28/2015
Each share MSCI Emerging Markets Quality Dividend ETF no par received $39.61686 cash
Each share MSCI Emerging Markets Quality ETF no par received $44.39892 cash
Each share MSCI International Quality Dividend ETF no par received $40.32661 cash
Each share MSCI International Quality ETF no par received $44.68016 cash
Intermediate Municipal Index ETF no par reclassified as AMT-Free Intermediate Municipal Index ETF no par 02/03/2016
Long Municipal Index ETF no par reclassified as AMT-Free Long Municipal Index ETF no par 02/03/2016
Short Municipal Index ETF no par reclassified as AMT-Free Short Municipal Index ETF no par 02/03/2016
ChinaAMC A-Share ETF no par reclassified as ChinaAMC CSI 300 ETF no par 05/01/2016
Name changed to VanEck Vectors ETF Trust 05/02/2016

MARKETCENTRAL NET CORP (TX)
Each share old Common $0.001 par exchanged for (0.0625) share new Common $0.001 par 09/28/2001
Recapitalized as Trezac Corp. 09/16/2002
Each share Common $0.001 par exchanged for (0.01) share Common $0.001 par
Trezac Corp. name changed to Trezac International Corp. 02/26/2003 which recapitalized as Millagro International Corp. 01/20/2004 which name changed to Telatinos Inc. 11/08/2004 which name changed to Netco Investments, Inc. 11/04/2005
(See Netco Investments, Inc.)

MARKETFAX INFOSERVICES LTD (BC)
Struck off register and declared dissolved for failure to file returns 06/30/1994

MARKETIME CORP. (DE)
Assets assigned for benefit of creditors 2/13/76
No stockholders' equity

MARKETING ACQUISITION CORP (NV)
Each (48) shares old Common $0.001 par exchanged for (1) share new Common $0.001 par 05/18/2007
Note: No holder will receive fewer than (100) post-split shares
Name changed to USA Zhimingde International Group Corp. 02/07/2013

MARKETING COMMUNICATIONS INC (NJ)
Common no par split (2) for (1) by issuance of (1) additional share 4/21/72
Name changed to Janjoy Enterprises, Inc. 1/8/74
Janjoy Enterprises, Inc. name changed to Petro Penn, Inc. 8/2/82 which name changed to Teksat Corp., Inc. 2/21/85

MARKETING EDL CORP (FL)
Reincorporated under the laws of Nevada as Marketing Acquisition Corp. 06/13/2006
Marketing Acquisition Corp. name changed to USA Zhimingde International Group Corp. 02/07/2013

MARKETING FACTORS INC (MN)
Merged into Unisource Corp. 03/18/1969
Each share Common $1 par exchanged for for (0.333333) share Common 10¢ par

MARKETING RESEARCH CORP. OF AMERICA (TN)
Name changed to Mar-Search Inc. 11/09/1970
(See Mar-Search Inc.)

MARKETING RES & APPLICATIONS INC (NY)
Reincorporated under the laws of Delaware as Simera Corp. and Common 1¢ par changed to 10¢ par 07/03/1972
(See Simera Corp.)

MARKETING SVCS GROUP INC (NV)
Each share old Common 1¢ par exchanged for (0.16666666) share new Common 1¢ par 10/15/2001
Name changed to MKTG Services, Inc. 03/26/2002
MKTG Services, Inc. name changed to Media Services Group, Inc. 12/26/2003 which name changed to MSGI Security Solutions, Inc. 02/09/2005
(See MSGI Security Solutions, Inc.)

MARKETING SPECIALISTS CORP (DE)
Plan of reorganization under Chapter 11 Federal Bankruptcy Code effective 5/26/2002
No stockholders' equity

MARKETING SYS USA INC (FL)
Each share old Common $0.001 par exchanged for (0.02) share new Common $0.001 par 12/21/2005
Name changed to Icon International Holdings, Inc. 04/11/2006
(See Icon International Holdings, Inc.)

MARKETING-247 INC (NV)
Merged into MidAmerica Oil & Gas, Inc. 12/30/2003
Each share Common $0.001 par exchanged for (0.0076923) share Common $0.001 par

MARKETINGMOBILE TEXT INC (NV)
Name changed to Progressive Green Solutions, Inc. 05/02/2014

MARKETKAST INC (FL)
Name changed to Engage Mobility, Inc. 04/04/2013

MARKETLINK INC (MN)
Name changed to OneLink Communications, Inc. 01/09/1997
OneLink Communications, Inc. recapitalized as OneLink Inc. 12/01/2003 which name changed to Spectre Gaming, Inc. 01/22/2004
(See Spectre Gaming, Inc.)

MARKETMASTER TR (MA)
Name changed to Nations Fund 4/1/92
Nations Fund name changed to Nations Fund Trust 9/22/92

MARKETO INC (DE)
Acquired by Milestone Holdco, LLC 08/16/2016
Each share Common $0.0001 par exchanged for $35.25 cash

MARKETPLACE PUBLICATIONS, INC. (DE)
Under plan of merger each share Class A Common 10¢ par and Class B Common 10¢ par automatically became (1) share Market Publications, Inc. Class A 10¢ par or Class B 10¢ par respectively 11/30/1970
(See Market Publications, Inc.)

MARKETSHARE RECOVERY INC (UT)
Each (12) shares old Common 1¢ par exchanged for (1) share new Common 1¢ par 12/20/2004
Name changed to bioMETRX, Inc. 10/10/2005
(See bioMETRX, Inc.)

MARKETSPAN CORP (NY)
Name changed to KeySpan Energy 09/10/1998
KeySpan Energy name changed to KeySpan Corp. 05/20/1999
(See KeySpan Corp.)

MARKETU INC (NV)
Name changed to Most Home Corp. 03/28/200/2
(See Most Home Corp.)

MARKETVISION DIRECT INC (DE)
Name changed to APIC Petroleum Corp. (DE) 05/24/2011
APIC Petroleum Corp. (DE) reincorporated in Canada 06/08/2012 which merged into Longreach Oil & Gas Ltd. 12/20/2012 which name changed to PetroMaroc Corp. PLC 07/14/2014

MARKETWATCH INC (DE)
Name changed 1/16/2004
Name changed 8/11/2004
Issue Information - 2,750,000 shares COM offered at $17 per share on 01/15/1999
Under plan of merger name changed from Marketwatch.com, Inc. (Old) to Marketwatch.com, Inc. (New) 1/16/2004
Name changed from Marketwatch.com, Inc. (New) to Marketwatch, Inc. 8/11/2004
Merged into Dow Jones & Co., Inc. 1/24/2005
Each share Common no par exchanged for $18 cash

MARKIT LTD (BERMUDA)
Under plan of merger name changed to IHS Markit Ltd. 07/13/2016

MARKITE CORP (NJ)
Merged into GCA Corp. 03/31/1971
Each share Common 25¢ par exchanged for $1.87 cash

MARKITSTAR INC (DE)
Each share old Common 1¢ par exchanged for (0.1) share new Common 1¢ par 02/14/1992
Name changed to HMG Worldwide Corp. 10/04/1993
(See HMG Worldwide Corp.)

MARKLAND AGF PRECIOUS METALS CORP (ON)
Completely liquidated 12/13/2013
Each Equity Share received $5.941135 cash

MARKLAND TECHNOLOGIES INC (FL)
Each share old Common $0.0001 par exchanged for (0.016666666) share new Common $0.0001 par 10/27/2003
Each share new Common $0.0001 par received distribution of (0.0515464) share Technest Holdings, Inc. Common $0.0001 par payable 05/04/2007 to holders of record 04/25/2007 Ex date - 05/07/2007
SEC revoked common stock registration 02/27/2009

MARKLE BANKING & TRUST CO. (HAZLETON, PA)
Merged into Northeastern Pennsylvania National Bank & Trust Co. (Scranton, Pa.) 8/1/58
Each share Capital Stock $50 par exchanged for $205 cash

MARKON MFG INC (CO)
In process of liquidation
Each share Common 25¢ par exchanged for initial distribution of $2.25 cash 06/05/1978
Details on subsequent distributions, if any are not available

MARKS & SPENCER CDA INC (CANADA)
Common no par split (2) for (1) by issuance of (1) additional share 6/27/84
Merged into Marks & Spencer PLC 8/7/86
Each share Common no par exchanged for $24 cash

MARKS & SPENCER PLC (UNITED KINGDOM)
Each Unsponsored ADR for Ordinary 25p par exchanged for (1) Sponsored ADR for Ordinary 25p par 3/31/88
Stock Dividend - 100% 8/17/84

Note: Common Market regulation required all publicly held British companies to replace LTD with PLC in 1982
Recapitalized as Marks & Spencer Group PLC 3/19/2002
Each Sponsored ADR for Ordinary 25p par exchanged for (0.8095238) Sponsored ADR for Ordinary 25p par and $5.9736 cash

MARKS BROS JEWELERS INC (DE)
Secondary Offering - 2,202,000 shares COM exchanged at $22.25 per share on 11/01/1996
Name changed to Whitehall Jewellers, Inc. 1/20/99
(See Whitehall Jewellers, Inc.)

MARKS MARKET CORP (AB)
Issue Information - 3,000,000 shares COM offered at $0.10 per share on 01/07/1997
Name changed to Patchgear.Com Inc. 06/24/1999
(See Patchgear.Com Inc.)

MARKS POLARIZED CORP (NY)
Name changed to Upward Technology Corp. 04/25/1989
(See Upward Technology Corp.)

MARKS TECHNOLOGIES INC (CO)
Name changed to Americorp International Inc. 12/5/83
Americorp International Inc. recapitalized as Double Eagle Resources, Inc. 1/13/89 which name changed to Biomed Science International Corp. 5/14/93

MARKS WK WEARHOUSE LTD (AB)
Acquired by Canadian Tire Corp., Ltd. 2/11/2002
Each share Common no par exchanged for $4.10 cash

MARKSMEN CAP INC (BC)
Name changed to Brixton Metals Corp. 12/07/2010

MARKSMEN RES LTD (AB)
Issue Information - 2,000,000 shares CL A offered at $0.15 per share on 10/03/1997
Each share old Class A Common no par exchanged for (0.2) share new Class A Common no par 06/06/2002
Each share new Class A Common no par received distribution of (1) share Signet Minerals Inc. Common no par payable 10/17/2005 to holders of record 10/11/2005
New Class A Common no par reclassified as Common no par 10/17/2005
Recapitalized as Marksmen Energy Inc. 08/23/2010
Each share Common no par exchanged for (0.1) share Common no par

MARKWAY RES LTD (BC)
Name changed to So-Luminaire Systems Corp. 8/9/84
(See So-Luminaire Systems Corp.)

MARKWEST ENERGY PARTNERS L P (DE)
Common Units split (2) for (1) by issuance of (1) additional Unit payable 02/28/2007 to holders of record 02/22/2007 Ex date - 03/01/2007
Merged into MPLX L.P. 12/04/2015
Each Common Unit exchanged for (1.09) Common Units and $6.20 cash

MARKWEST HYDROCARBON INC (DE)
Stock Dividends - 10% payable 08/11/2003 to holders of record 07/31/2003 Ex date - 07/29/2003; 10% payable 11/19/2004 to holders of record 11/09/2004 Ex date - 11/05/2004; 10% payable 05/23/2006 to holders of record 05/11/2006 Ex date - 05/09/2006

Merged into MarkWest Energy Partners, L.P. 02/22/2008
Each share Common 1¢ par exchanged for approximately (1.8325) Common Units and $2.34 cash
MarkWest Energy Partners, L.P. merged into MPLX L.P. 12/04/2015

MARKWOOD INDUSTRIES INC. (DE)
No longer in existence having become inoperative and void for non-payment of taxes 4/1/59

MARL RES CORP (ON)
Under plan of merger name changed to Pelangio Mines Inc. 05/25/2000
Pelangio Mines Inc. name changed to PDX Resources Inc. 09/03/2008 which merged into Detour Gold Corp. 03/27/2009

MARLA INDS INC (DE)
Charter cancelled and declared inoperative and void for non-payment of taxes 3/1/74

MARLAND ENVIRONMENTAL SYS INC (DE)
Each share Capital Stock 1¢ par exchanged for (0.1) share Capital Stock 10¢ par 1/1/79
Charter cancelled and declared inoperative and void for non-payment of taxes 3/1/94

MARLAND OIL CO. (DE)
Name changed to Continental Oil Co. (DE) 6/26/29
Continental Oil Co. (DE) name changed to Conoco Inc. 7/2/79 which was acquired by Du Pont (E.I.) De Nemours & Co. 9/30/81

MARLAT RES LTD (BC)
Name changed to Renco Resources Ltd. 6/18/96

MARLBORO ENTERPRISES INC (NY)
Charter cancelled and proclaimed dissolved for failure to pay taxes and file reports 09/15/1976

MARLBORO MINES (1968) LTD. (ON)
Merged into Boeing Holdings & Explorations Ltd. 12/13/68
Details not available

MARLBORO MINES LTD. (ON)
Merged into Boeing Holdings & Explorations Ltd. 12/13/1968
Each share Capital Stock $1 par exchanged for (0.5) share Common no par
Note: on 12/10/1968 the company recapitalized as Marlboro Mines (1968) Ltd. on a (0.5) for (1) basis, changing the Capital Stock $1 par to no par
Certificates were not surrendered at time of recapitalization
Marlboro Mines (1968) Ltd. merged into Boeing Holdings & Explorations Ltd. on a share for share basis
Subsequently as a result of the merger each share Marlboro Mines Ltd. Capital Stock $1 par (which actually represents (1/2) share Marlboro Mines (1968) Ltd. Capital Stock no par) is exchanged for (0.5) share Boeing Holdings & Explorations Ltd. Common no par
Boeing Holdings & Explorations Ltd. recapitalized as Consolidated Boeing & Explorations Ltd. 01/06/1972 which name changed to Academy Explorations Ltd. 04/10/1980
(See Academy Explorations Ltd.)

MARLBORO VENTURES INC (NV)
Name changed to Dial-A-Brand Inc. 04/16/1986
Dial-A-Brand Inc. recapitalized as China Container Holdings Ltd. (NV) 05/22/1995 which reincorporated in Delaware as Asiana Dragons, Inc. 12/22/2009 which recapitalized as Annabidiol Corp. 01/08/2018

MARLBOROUGH ELECTRIC CO.
Merged into Worcester Suburban Electric Co. in 1938
(See Worcester Suburban Electric Co.)

MARLBOROUGH PRODTNS LTD (BC)
Delisted from Vancouver Stock Exchange 11/16/1990

MARLBOROUGH SOFTWARE DEV HLDGS INC (DE)
Acquired by Pageflex Acquisitions Inc. 12/09/2013
Each share Common 1¢ par exchanged for $0.091 cash

MARLEAU LEMIRE INC (CANADA)
Each share old Common no par exchanged for (1/3) share new Common no par 06/23/1995
Name changed to Peelbrooke Capital Inc. 06/01/1998
(See Peelbrooke Capital Inc.)

MARLENE INDS CORP (NY)
Common 10¢ par split (3) for (1) by issuance of (2) additional shares 10/25/68
Name changed to MI Fund, Inc. 11/2/79
MI Fund, Inc. merged into Oppenheimer Tax-Free Bond Fund, Inc. 3/30/94 which name changed to Oppenheimer Municipal Bond Fund 11/22/2002 which name changed to Oppenheimer AMT-Free Municipals 10/27/2003

MARLENNAN CORP (DE)
Common no par changed to $1 par 04/22/1970
Name changed to Marsh & McLennan Companies, Inc. 05/21/1975

MARLEX MINING CORP. LTD. (BC)
Name changed to Marlex Enviro-Systems & Resources Ltd. and Common 50¢ par changed to no par 3/31/71

MARLEY CO (DE)
Common $2 par split (2) for (1) by issuance of (1) additional share 10/30/67
Common $2 par split (2) for (1) by issuance of (1) additional share 7/20/77
Stock Dividends - 50% 12/31/62; 10% 10/30/64; 50% 10/29/65; 10% 10/31/66
Preferred Ser. A $30 par called for redemption 6/18/81
Completely liquidated 6/19/81
Each share Common $2 par exchanged for first and final distribution of $38.50 cash

MARLEY COFFEE INC (NV)
Name changed to Jammin Java Corp. 09/17/2009

MARLEY MINES LTD (BC)
Delisted from Vancouver Stock Exchange 03/04/1991

MARLIN CAP FOODS LTD (ON)
Recapitalized as Meranto Technology Ltd. 10/04/1994
Each share Common no par exchanged for (0.1) share Common no par
Meranto Technology Ltd. recapitalized as World Sports Merchandising Inc. 02/01/1998 which name changed to World Sales & Merchandising Inc. 02/22/2000
(See World Sales & Merchandising Inc.)

MARLIN DEVS LTD (BC)
Name changed to Matrix Petroleum Inc. 12/13/2001
Matrix Petroleum Inc. acquired by Berens Energy Ltd. 12/12/2003
(See Berens Energy Ltd.)

MARLIN ENTERPRISES INC (NV)
Name changed to National Telephone

Information Network, Inc. 01/13/1988

MARLIN GOLD MNG LTD OLD (BC)
Each share old Common no par exchanged for (0.1) share new Common no par 07/14/2014
Plan of arrangement effective 12/22/2017
Each share new Common no par exchanged for (1) share Marlin Gold Mining Ltd. (New) Common no par and (0.2) share Sailfish Royalty Corp. Common no par
Note: Unexchanged certificates will be cancelled and become without value 12/22/2023

MARLIN MIDSTREAM PARTNERS LP (DE)
Name changed to Azure Midstream Partners, L.P. 05/20/2015
(See Azure Midstream Partners, L.P.)

MARLIN OIL CO (CO)
Common 1¢ par split (4) for (1) by issuance of (3) additional shares 3/14/80
Stock Dividend - 150% 4/10/81
Merged into Churchill Technology Inc. 9/23/87
Each (3.64479562624) shares Common 1¢ par exchanged for (1) share Common $0.001 par
(See Churchill Technology Inc.)

MARLIN-ROCKWELL CORP. (DE)
Stock Dividend - 300% 10/10/52
Acquired by Thompson Ramo Wooldridge, Inc. 6/16/64
Each share Capital Stock $1 par exchanged for (0.25) share $4.25 Conv. Preference Ser. A no par and (0.25) share Common $5 par
Thompson Ramo Wooldridge, Inc. name changed to TRW Inc. 4/30/65 which merged into Northrop Grumman Corp. 12/11/2002

MARLIN-ROCKWELL CORP. (NY)
Reincorporated under the laws of Delaware in 1935
Marlin-Rockwell Corp. acquired by Thompson Ramo Wooldridge, Inc. 6/16/64 which name changed to TRW Inc. 4/30/65 which merged into Northrop Grumman Corp. 12/11/2002

MARLINE OIL CORP (DE)
Each share Ser. A Common 1¢ par exchanged for (0.4) share Ser. A Common 3¢ par 06/17/1976
Name changed to Marquest Resources Corp. 06/20/1985
(See Marquest Resources Corp.)

MARLON ROUYN GOLD MINES LTD. (ON)
Recapitalized as New Marlon Gold Mines Ltd. on a (1) for (2) basis in 1947
New Marlon Gold Mines Ltd. recapitalized as Marcon Mines Ltd. 3/16/56 which recapitalized as Conmar Explorations Ltd. 10/12/66
(See Conmar Explorations Ltd.)

MARLOW CORP. (NE)
Liquidation completed
Each share Class A Common $1 par or Class B Common $1 par exchanged for initial distribution of $7.50 cash 1/16/67
Each share Class A Common $1 par or Class B Common $1 par received second distribution of $0.20 cash 4/12/67
Each share Class A Common $1 par or Class B Common $1 par received third and final distribution of $0.13 cash 9/23/68

MARLOWE CHEMICAL CO., INC. (DE)
Declared inoperative and void for non- payment of taxes 4/1/63

MARLOWE EQUIPMENT, INC.
Name changed to Exercycle Corp. in 1939
(See Exercycle Corp.)

MARLOWE PRODUCTS, INC.
Name changed to Marlowe Equipment, Inc. in 1937
Marlowe Equipment, Inc. name changed to Exercycle Corp. in 1939
(See Exercycle Corp.)

MARLTON TECHNOLOGIES INC (PA)
Reincorporated 11/20/2001
State of incorporation changed from (NJ) to (PA) 11/20/2001
Each share old Common 10¢ par exchanged for (0.0002) share new Common 10¢ par 12/21/2005
Note: Holders of (4,999) or fewer pre-split shares received $1.25 cash per share
Acquired by Sparks Marketing Group, Inc. 11/30/2006
Each share new Common 10¢ par exchanged for $8,750 cash

MARMAC CORP (DE)
Common 1¢ par split (3) for (1) by issuance of (2) additional shares 3/4/70
Charter cancelled and declared inoperative and void for non-payment of taxes 3/1/78

MARMAC INDS INC (NJ)
Reincorporated under the laws of Delaware as Educor Inc. 06/17/1968
Educor Inc. name changed to Vocational Advancement Services Inc. 05/08/1972
(See Vocational Advancement Services Inc.)

MARMAL NICKEL MINES LTD. (ON)
Struck off register and declared dissolved for failure to file returns 12/20/2000

MARMON GROUP, INC. (DE)
Incorporated 10/22/1963
Ctfs. dated prior to 12/14/1967
99.7% acquired by Marmon Group, Inc. (MI) as of 12/14/1967
Public interest eliminated

MARMON GROUP INC (DE)
Ctfs. dated after 12/31/1970
Reincorporated 12/31/1970
Common $10 par changed to $1 par and (1) additional share issued 12/28/1970
State of incorporation changed from (MI) to (DE) 12/31/1970
Merged into Bess Corp. 10/26/1971
Each share Common $1 par exchanged for $12 cash

MARMON GROUP INC (DE)
Incorporated 11/25/1975
Preferred Ser. A $1 par called for redemption 05/30/1986
Public interest eliminated

MARMON-HERRINGTON CO., INC. (DE)
Acquired by Marmon Group, Inc. (Del.) 9/30/66
Each share Common $1 par exchanged for $30 cash

MARMON-HERRINGTON CO., INC. (IN)
Reincorporated under the laws of Delaware 9/30/65
Marmon-Herrington Co., Inc. (Del.) acquired by Marmon Group, Inc. (Del.) for cash 9/30/66

MARMON MOTOR CAR CO.
Liquidation completed in 1943

MARMORA MINERAL PRODS INC (ON)
Merged into Gitennes Exploration Inc. 5/13/93
Each share Common no par exchanged for (1) share Common no par

MARMOT LEAD & ZINC MINES LTD. (ON)
Charter cancelled in September, 1961

MARNETICS BROADBAND TECHNOLOGIES LTD (ISRAEL)
Company began the process of liquidating and all members of the Board of Directors resigned 12/15/2004
Stockholders' equity unlikely

MAROSA MINES LTD. (ON)
Charter revoked for failure to file reports and pay fees 12/27/67

MARPIC EXPLORATIONS LTD. (ON)
Charter cancelled 3/12/62

MARPOINT GAS & OIL CORP. LTD. (ON)
Assets acquired by Dynamic Petroleum Products Ltd. share for share 7/19/62
Dynamic Petroleum Products Ltd. liquidated for Pan Ocean Oil Corp. 1/1/72
(See Pan Ocean Oil Corp.)

MARQUARDT AIRCRAFT CO. (CA)
Capital Stock $1 par split (2) for (1) by issuance of (1) additional share 07/01/1957
Stock Dividends - 10% 06/30/1954; 100% 03/15/1955
Recapitalized as Marquardt Corp. and (1) additional share issued 06/15/1959
Marquardt Corp. merged into CCI Marquardt Corp. 06/12/1968 which name changed to CCI Corp. 09/26/1969
(See CCI Corp.)

MARQUARDT CORP. (CA)
Capital Stock $1 par reclassified as Common $1 par 08/08/1967
Merged into CCI Marquardt Corp. 06/12/1968
Each share Common $1 par exchanged for (0.1) share $1.25 Conv. Preferred Ser. A $1 par and (0.375) share Common 50¢ par
CCI Marquardt Corp. name changed to CCI Corp. 09/26/1969
(See CCI Corp.)

MARQUEE ENERGY LTD OLD (AB)
Merged into Marquee Energy Ltd. (New) 12/08/2016
Each share Common no par exchanged for (1.67) shares Common no par
Note: Unexchanged certificates will be cancelled and become without value 12/08/2019

MARQUEE ENTMT GROUP (NV)
Name changed to Allstate Industries Corp. (NV) 10/3/88
Allstate Industries Corp. (NV) name changed to Creative Classics International 12/18/89
(See Creative Classics International)

MARQUEE ENTMT INC (NV)
Each share old Common $0.001 par exchanged for (0.025) share new Common $0.001 par 3/22/96
Recapitalized as Progressive Telecommunications Corp. 8/4/99
Each share new Common $0.001 par exchanged for (0.2) share Common $0.001 par
Progressive Telecommunications Corp. name changed to Businessmall.com Inc. 3/24/2000
(See Businessmall.com Inc.)

MARQUEE GROUP INC (DE)
Merged into SFX Entertainment, Inc. 03/16/1999
Each share Common 1¢ par exchanged for (0.0815) share Class A Common 1¢ par
SFX Entertainment, Inc. merged into Clear Channel Communications, Inc. 08/01/2000
(See Clear Channel Communications, Inc.)

MARQUEE PETE LTD (AB)
Merged into SkyWest Energy Corp. 12/09/2011
Each share Common no par exchanged for (1.35) shares Common no par
SkyWest Energy Corp. recapitalized as Marquee Energy Ltd. (Old) 12/09/2011 which merged into Marquee Energy Ltd. (New) 12/08/2016

MARQUEST CDN EQUITY INCOME FD (ON)
Trust terminated 01/02/2018
Each Trust Unit received $5.322501 cash

MARQUEST MED PRODS INC (CO)
Merged into Vital Signs Inc. 7/28/97
Each share Common no par exchanged for $0.797 cash

MARQUEST RES CORP (CO)
Charter cancelled and declared inoperative and void for non-payment of taxes 11/16/90

MARQUETTE CAP CORP (BC)
Name changed to On-Track Learning Systems Ltd. 1/13/2003
On-Track Learning Systems Ltd. recapitalized as Torq Media Corp. 5/18/2004 which recapitalized as Quizam Media Corp. 5/18/2005

MARQUETTE CEMENT MANUFACTURING CO. (DE)
Reincorporated 3/2/73
6% Preferred $100 par changed to $50 par in 1948
Each share Preferred $50 par exchanged for (2.5) shares 6% Preferred $20 par in 1951
Each share Common $25 par exchanged for (2.5) shares Common $10 par in 1951
Each share 6% Preferred $20 par exchanged for (2.5) shares 6% Preferred $8 par 11/7/55
Each share Common $10 par exchanged for (2.5) shares Common $4 par 11/7/55
State of incorporation changed for (IL) to (DE) 3/2/73
Name changed to Marquette Co. 5/30/75
Marquette Co. merged into Gulf & Western Industries, Inc. (DE) 9/16/76 which name changed to Gulf + Western Inc. 5/1/86 which name changed to Paramount Communications Inc. 6/5/89 which merged into Viacom Inc. (Old) 7/7/94
(See Viacom Inc. (Old))

MARQUETTE CO (DE)
Merged into Gulf & Western Industries, Inc. (DE) 9/16/76
Each share 6% Preferred $8 par exchanged for (0.1) share $5.75 S.F. Preferred $2.50 par
Each share Common $4 par exchanged for (0.34) share $2.50 Conv. Preferred Ser. D $2.50 par
Gulf & Western Industries Inc. (DE) name changed to Gulf + Western Inc. 5/1/86 which name changed to Paramount Communications Inc. 6/5/89 which merged into Viacom Inc. (Old) 7/7/94
(See Viacom Inc. (Old))

MARQUETTE CORP (DE)
Merged into Applied Power Industries, Inc. 12/31/70
Each share Common $1 par exchanged for (0.222222) share Conv. Preferred Ser. B $1 par
Applied Power Inc. name changed to Applied Power Industries, Inc. 1/17/73 which name changed to Actuant Corp. 1/12/2001

MARQUETTE ELECTRS INC (WI)
Name changed to Marquette Medical Systems, Inc. 08/15/1996
Marquette Medical Systems, Inc.

merged into General Electric Co. 11/20/1998

MARQUETTE MED SYS INC (WI)
Merged into General Electric Co. 11/20/1998
Each share Common 10¢ par exchanged for (0.508) share Common 16¢ par

MARQUETTE NATL BK (CHICAGO, IL)
Stock Dividend - 42% 01/25/1962
Reorganized as Marquette National Corp. (IL) 03/15/1983
Each share Capital Stock $20 par exchanged for (1) share Common $20 par
Marquette National Corp. (IL) reincorporated in Delaware 06/30/1994

MARQUETTE NATL CORP (IL)
Reincorporated under the laws of Delaware 06/30/1994

MARQUETTE OIL CORP.
Sold to Oklahoma Co. in 1931 which was acquired by Oklahoma Oil Corp. in 1932

MARQUETTE REAL ESTATE FDG CORP
Step Down Preferred 144A called for redemption 6/30/97

MARQUETTE SVGS BK S A (WEST ALLIS, WI)
Merged into North Shore Bank FSB (Milwaukee, WI) 7/31/2000
Each share Common 1¢ par exchanged for $12 cash

MARQUIS DEV LTD (BC)
Merged into Colt Exploration Ltd. (BC) 07/08/1982
Each (1.2837) shares Common no par exchanged for (1) share Common no par
Colt Exploration Ltd. (BC) reorganized in Alberta as Colt Exploration (Western) Ltd. 05/17/1983 which recapitalized as Colt Exploration (1988) Ltd. 06/30/1988 which reorganized as Stampede Oils Inc. 12/29/1988
(See Stampede Oils Inc.)

MARQUIS EXPLORATIONS LTD. (ON)
Merged into New Force Crag Mines Ltd. 11/22/74
Each (2.5) shares Common $1 par exchanged for (1) share Common no par
New Force Crag Mines Ltd. charter cancelled 7/12/82

MARQUIS RES CORP (AB)
Name changed to Panorama Trading Co. Ltd. 10/22/1992
Panorama Trading Co. Ltd. name changed to Perfect Fry Corp. 05/21/1993 which name changed to Woodrose Corp. (AB) 09/01/2010 which reincorporated in British Columbia as Woodrose Ventures Corp. 11/07/2016 which recapitalized as Novoheart Holdings Inc. 10/03/2017

MARQUIS TECH HLDGS INC (PA)
Each share old Common $0.001 par exchanged for (1.05) shares new Common $0.001 par 12/07/2011
Recapitalized as Tritent Int'l Agriculture, Inc. 07/11/2012
Each share new Common $0.001 par exchanged for (0.0005) share Common $0.001 par

MARQUIS VENTURES INC (BC)
Name changed to PowerBand Solutions Inc. 02/09/2018

MARRET INVT GRADE BD FD (ON)
Name changed to First Asset Investment Grade Bond ETF 08/22/2016

MARRIAS NICKEL PROSPECTING SYNDICATE
Acquired by Marcourt Nickel Mines, Ltd. 00/00/1948
Details not available

MARRIOTT CORP (DE)
Common $1 par split (2) for (1) by issuance of (1) additional share 04/08/1968
Common $1 par split (2) for (1) by issuance of (1) additional share 04/24/1972
Common $1 par split (5) for (1) by issuance of (4) additional shares 06/20/1986
Name changed to Host Marriott Corp. (DE) 10/08/1993
Host Marriott Corp. (DE) reorganized in Maryland 12/29/1998

MARRIOTT-HOT SHOPPES, INC. (DE)
Common $1 par split (2) for (1) by issuance of (1) additional share 6/11/65
Name changed to Marriott Corp. 11/21/67
Marriott Corp. name changed to Host Marriott Corp. (DE) 10/8/93 which reorganized in Maryland 12/29/98

MARRIOTT INTL INC OLD (DE)
Each share Common $1 par received distribution of (1) share Marriott International Inc. (New) Common $1 par and (1) share Class A Common $1 par payable 03/30/1998 to holders of record 03/27/1998
Recapitalized as Sodexho Marriott Services, Inc. 03/27/1998
Each share Common $1 par exchanged for (0.25) share Common $1 par
(See Sodexho Marriott Services, Inc.)

MARROW-TECH INC (DE)
Name changed to Advanced Tissue Sciences, Inc. 12/19/91
Advanced Tissue Sciences, Inc. reorganized as ATS Liquidating Trust 3/31/2003

MARRUD, INC. (MA)
Stock Dividend - 100% 4/30/62
Name changed to Interequity Industries, Inc. and Common $2 par changed to $1 par 11/6/68

MARS ACQUISITIONS INC (NV)
SEC revoked common stock registration 03/06/2017

MARS BARGAINLAND INC (MA)
Name changed to Mars Stores, Inc. 07/17/1979
(See Mars Stores, Inc.)

MARS DELORO GOLD MINES, LTD. (ON)
Charter cancelled for failure to file reports and pay taxes September 1962

MARS GRAPHIC SVCS INC (NJ)
Stock Dividends - 10% 9/17/90; 20% 9/12/91
Name changed to Dimark Inc. 4/24/92
Dimark Inc. merged into Harte-Hanks Communications, Inc. 4/30/96 which name changed to Harte-Hanks, Inc. 5/5/98

MARS INDS INC (MN)
Name changed 03/15/1963
Name changed from Mars Industries to Mars Industries Inc. and Common 50¢ par changed to 10¢ par 03/15/1963
Completely liquidated 03/31/1977
No stockholders' equity

MARS NATL BANCORP INC (PA)
Name changed to Mars Bancorp, Inc. 06/29/2017

MARS STORES INC (MA)
Plan of reorganization under Chapter 11 Federal Bankruptcy proceedings confirmed 03/21/1991
No stockholders' equity

MARSA ENERGY INC (AB)
Merged into Condor Petroleum Inc. 03/30/2016
Each share Common no par exchanged for (0.184326) share Common no par
Note: Unexchanged certificates will be cancelled and become without value 03/30/2019

MARSAM PHARMACEUTICALS INC (DE)
Common 1¢ par split (3) for (2) by issuance of (0.5) additional share 7/20/89
Common 1¢ par split (3) for (2) by issuance of (0.5) additional share 5/2/91
Merged into Schein Pharmaceutical, Inc. 9/11/95
Each share Common 1¢ par exchanged for $21 cash

MARSAN CAP CORP (FL)
Proclaimed dissolved for failure to file reports and pay fees 12/14/1982

MARSAN INDUSTRIES, INC. (MN)
Recapitalized as Snow Sports Publications, Inc. 07/22/1971
Each share Common 20¢ par exchanged for (0.5) share Common 10¢ par
(See Snow Sports Publications, Inc.)

MARSAN INDUSTRIES, INC. (NJ)
Adjudicated bankrupt 5/13/64
No stockholders' equity

MARSCO DEVELOPMENT CORP. (CA)
Completely liquidated 4/30/75
Each share Common $1 par exchanged for cash

MARSH & MCLENNAN INC (DE)
Common no par split (2) for (1) by issuance of (1) additional share 5/25/67
Reorganized as Marlennan Corp. 6/3/69
Each share Common no par exchanged for (2) shares Common no par
Marlennan Corp. name changed to Marsh & McLennan Companies, Inc. 5/21/75

MARSH MINES CONSOLIDATED
In process of liquidation in 1947

MARSH STEEL & ALUMINUM CO. (MO)
Under voluntary purchase offer each share Capital Stock $1 par exchanged for $9 cash and a Certificate of Participation 1/10/66
Liquidation completed
Each Certificate of Participation received initial distribution of $1 cash 5/5/66
Each Certificate of Participation received second and final distribution of $0.50646 cash 9/26/66
Certificates of Participation were not surrendered and are now without value

MARSH STEEL CORP. (MO)
Name changed to Marsh Steel & Aluminum Co. 1/23/59
Marsh Steel & Aluminum Co. completed liquidation 9/26/66

MARSH SUPERMARKETS INC (IN)
Name changed 8/5/60
Name changed from Marsh Foodliners, Inc. to Marsh Supermarkets, Inc. 8/5/60
Common no par split (2) for (1) by issuance of (1) additional share 9/4/68
Common no par split (2) for (1) by issuance of (1) additional share 9/5/78
Common no par split (3) for (2) by issuance of (0.5) additional share 9/15/86
Common no par split (3) for (2) by issuance of (0.5) additional share 9/12/88
Common no par reclassified as (0.5) share Class A Common no par and (0.5) share Class B Common no par 5/15/91
Merged into Sun Capital Partners, Inc. 9/28/2006
Each share Class A Common no par exchanged for $11.125 cash
Each share Class B Common no par exchanged for $11.125 cash

MARSH WALL PRODUCTS, INC. (OH)
Each share Capital Stock $100 par exchanged for (100) shares Capital Stock $1 par in 1937
Stock Dividend - 100% 10/25/48
Acquired by Masonite Corp. 8/31/63
Each share Capital Stock $1 par exchanged for $21 cash

MARSHALL & ILSLEY BANK (MILWAUKEE, WI)
Stock Dividends - 33-1/3% 12/29/41; 25% 12/26/47; 20% 9/30/52; 33-1/3% 9/2/54; 25% 12/5/58; 20% 7/30/65; 50% 1/30/70
Preferred $50 par called for redemption 8/1/65
Name changed to M&I Marshall & Ilsley Bank (Milwaukee, Wisc.) 5/1/72
(See M&I Marshall & Ilsley Bank (Milwaukee, Wisc.))

MARSHALL & ILSLEY CORP NEW (WI)
Merged into Bank of Montreal (Montreal, QC) 07/05/2011
Each share Common $1 par exchanged for (0.1257) share Common no par

MARSHALL & ILSLEY CORP OLD (WI)
Name changed 12/30/1971
Common $10 par changed to $2.50 par and (1) additional share issued 05/14/1968
Name changed from Marshall & Ilsley Bank Stock Corp. to Marshall & Ilsley Corp. 12/30/1971
Common $2.50 par changed to $1 par 04/24/1984
$7.50 Conv. Preferred Ser. A no par called for redemption 06/03/1985
Common $1 par split (3) for (1) by issuance of (2) additional shares 05/30/1986
Common $1 par split (3) for (1) by issuance of (2) additional shares 05/28/1993
Common $1 par split (2) for (1) by issuance of (1) additional share payable 06/14/2002 to holders of record 05/31/2002 Ex date - 06/17/2002
Each 6.50% Common SPACES received approximately (0.57672122) share Common $1 par 08/15/2007
Stock Dividend - 100% 05/26/1978
Reorganized as Marshall & Ilsley Corp. (New) 11/01/2007
Each share Common $1 par exchanged for (1) share Common $1 par and (1/3) share Metavante Technologies, Inc. Common 1¢ par
Note: Holders of (2) or fewer pre-reorganization shares received $42.70 cash per share
(See each company's listing)

MARSHALL-BARWICK INC (CANADA)
Class A Subordinated no par reclassified as Common no par 07/22/1999
Class B Multiple no par reclassified as Common no par 07/22/1999
Merged into CEL Marshares Inc. 09/19/2002
Each share Common no par exchanged for $4.40 cash

MARSHALL BOSTON IRON MINES LTD (ON)
Name changed to Marshall Minerals Corp. 10/15/1981
(See Marshall Minerals Corp.)

MARSHALL CREEK COPPER LTD (BC)
Recapitalized as Shalmar Resources Ltd. 03/16/1973
Each share Capital Stock no par exchanged for (0.25) share Capital Stock no par
(See Shalmar Resources Ltd.)

MARSHALL DRUMMOND MCCALL INC (CANADA)
Each share Class A Conv. Common no par exchanged for (1) share Class A Subordinate no par 05/30/1986
Each share Class B Conv. Common no par exchanged for (1) share Conv. Class B Multiple no par 05/30/1986
Name changed to Marshall Steel Ltd. 03/09/1987
Marshall Steel Ltd. name changed to Marshall-Barwick, Inc. 05/29/1996
(See Marshall-Barwick, Inc.)

MARSHALL EDWARDS INC (DE)
Issue Information - 2,080,000 UNITS consisting of (1) share COM and (1) WT offered at $7.50 per Unit on 12/18/2003
Each share old Common $0.00000002 par exchanged for (0.1) share new Common $0.00000002 par 03/31/2010
Name changed to MEI Pharma, Inc. 07/02/2012

MARSHALL ELECTRS CO (NJ)
Reincorporated under the laws of Delaware as GLM Industries, Inc. and Common 10¢ par changed to 1¢ par 12/1/70
(See GLM Industries, Inc.)

MARSHALL ENERGY LTD (BC)
Name changed to Stockmen Resources Corp. 01/21/1991
Stockmen Resources Corp. recapitalized as Panhandle Resources Corp. 10/16/1992 which name changed to Abacan Resource Corp. (Old) 01/27/1993 which merged into Abacan Resource Corp. (New) 02/10/1995
(See Abacan Resource Corp. (New))

MARSHALL FDS INC (WI)
Completely liquidated
Each share BMO Large-Cap Focus Fund Class I $0.0001 par received first and final distribution of $10.89 cash payable 09/28/2012 to holders of record 09/28/2012
Each share BMO Large-Cap Focus Fund Class Y $0.0001 par received first and final distribution of $10.88 cash payable 09/28/2012 to holders of record 09/28/2012
(Additional Information in Active)

MARSHALL FIELD & CO (DE)
Reincorporated 5/15/70
Each share 7% Preferred $100 par exchanged for (1) share 6% Preferred $100 par which was subsequently called and (0.833333) share Common no par in 1937
Common no par split (2) for (1) by issuance of (1) additional share 6/2/61
Common no par split (2) for (1) by issuance of (1) additional share 6/13/69
State of incorporation changed from (IL) to (DE) and Common no par changed to $1 par 5/15/70
$2.40 Preferred Ser. A $1 par called for redemption 10/15/80
Merged into BATUS Inc. 6/11/82
Each share $1.50 Conv. Preferred Ser. C $1 par exchanged for $54 cash

Each share Common $1 par exchanged for $30 cash

MARSHALL FOODS INC (MN)
Name changed to Food Formula One Inc. 02/07/1986
(See Food Formula One Inc.)

MARSHALL HLDGS INTL INC (NV)
Each share old Common $0.001 par exchanged for (0.000025) share new Common $0.001 par 06/10/2008
Charter revoked for failure to file reports and pay fees 05/31/2011

MARSHALL INDS (CA)
Common $1 par split (2) for (1) by issuance of (1) additional share 7/12/83
Common $1 par split (2) for (1) by issuance of (1) additional share 7/7/86
Common $1 par split (2) for (1) by issuance of (1) additional share 2/28/94
Merged into Avnet, Inc. 10/20/99
Each share Common $1 par exchanged for (0.82063) share Common $1 par, $39 cash, or a combination thereof

MARSHALL (JOHN) LIFE INSURANCE CO. OF AMERICA (IN)
Capital Stock 75¢ par changed to 50¢ par 7/14/65
Acquired by United Standard Asset Growth Corp. 6/17/70
Each share Capital Stock 50¢ par exchanged for (0.351) share Common no par
(See United Standard Asset Growth Corp.)

MARSHALL (JOHN) LIFE INSURANCE CO. OF INDIANA (IN)
Capital Stock $1.50 par changed to 75¢ par 5/26/61
Name changed to Marshall (John) Life Insurance Co. of America 2/8/65
Marshall (John) Life Insurance Co. of America acquired by United Standard Asset Growth Corp. 6/17/70
(See United Standard Asset Growth Corp.)

MARSHALL MINERALS CORP (ON)
Each share old Common no par exchanged for (0.4) share new Common no par 01/09/1997
Delisted from Toronto Stock Exchange 08/31/2001

MARSHALL MORTGAGE CORP.
Dissolved in 1945

MARSHALL NATL BK & TR CO (MARSHALL, VA)
Merged into Mercantile Bankshares Corp. 03/31/1998
Each share Common $2 par exchanged for (1.75) shares Common $2 par
Mercantile Bankshares Corp. merged into PNC Financial Services Group, Inc. 03/02/2007

MARSHALL RED LAKE MINES LTD. (ON)
Charter cancelled for failure to file reports and pay taxes in 1956

MARSHALL STL LTD (CANADA)
Name changed to Marshall-Barwick, Inc. 05/29/1996
(See Marshall-Barwick, Inc.)

MARSHALL-WELLS CO. (DE)
Merged into Larchfield Corp. on a (4) for (1) basis 4/30/65
Larchfield Corp. charter forfeited 12/31/77

MARSHALL-WELLS CO. (NJ)
Reincorporated under laws of Delaware 4/30/65
Marshall-Wells Co. (Del.) merged into Larchfield Corp. 4/30/65 which charter forfeited 12/31/77

MARSHALL WELLS OF CANADA LTD. (CANADA)
Merged into Marshall Wells Ltd. 11/15/65
Each share Common no par exchanged for (1) share 6-1/2% 1st Preferred $5 par

MARSHALL'S U.S. AUTO SUPPLY, INC. (MO)
Charter revoked for failure to file annual registration report and anti-trust affidavit 1/1/60

MARSHALLTOWN FINL CORP (DE)
Merged into HMN Financial Inc. 12/5/97
Each share Common 1¢ par exchanged for $17.51 cash

MARSHFIELD CORP. (MA)
Merged into Kilburn Mill on a share for share basis 8/29/61
Kilburn Mill proclaimed dissolved 7/7/80

MARSTON CO. (CA)
Acquired by Broadway-Hale Stores, Inc. (DE) 1/31/61
Each share Common $10 par exchanged for (0.571428) share Common $5 par
Broadway-Hale Stores, Inc. (DE) merged into Broadway-Hale Stores, Inc. (CA) 8/27/70 which name changed to Carter Hawley Hale Stores Inc. (CA) 5/30/74 which reincorporated in Delaware 7/26/84 which name changed to Broadway Stores, Inc. 6/17/94 which merged into Federated Department Stores, Inc. 10/11/95 which name changed to Macy's, Inc. 6/1/2007

MARSULEX INC (CANADA)
Merged into Chemtrade Logistics Income Fund 06/28/2011
Each share Common no par exchanged for either (1) share Investis U.S., Inc. Common no par and $10.50 cash or $13.80 cash
Note: Option to receive stock and cash expired 06/17/2011
Unexchanged certificates were cancelled and became without value 06/28/2017

MART INDS INC (DE)
Stock Dividend - 100% 02/22/1971
Recapitalized as Dandor International Inc. 08/07/1973
Each share Common 1¢ par exchanged for (0.1) share Common 10¢ par
(See Dandor International Inc.)

MART RES INC (AB)
Acquired by San Leon Energy PLC 03/29/2016
Each share Common no par exchanged for $0.25 cash
Note: Unexchanged certificates will be cancelled and become without value 03/28/2021

MARTA DRILLING & DEVELOPMENT CO. LTD. (BC)
Acquired by Peak Oils Ltd. share for share 00/00/1952
Peak Oils Ltd. recapitalized as Consolidated Peak Oils Ltd. 00/00/1953 which was acquired by Western Allenbee Oil & Gas Co. Ltd. 06/20/1960 which name changed to Convoy Capital Corp. 04/28/1989 which recapitalized as Hariston Corp. 09/25/1992 which recapitalized as Midland Holland Inc. (Canada) 02/10/1999 which reincorporated in Yukon 03/11/1999 which name changed to Mercury Partners & Co. Inc. 02/22/2000 which name changed to Black Mountain Capital Corp. 05/02/2005 which recapitalized as Grand Peak Capital Corp. (YT) 11/20/2007 which reincorporated in British Columbia 04/27/2010

MARTECH USA INC (DE)
Chapter 11 bankruptcy proceedings converted to Chapter 7 on 12/22/1994
No stockholders' equity

MARTEK BIOSCIENCES CORP (DE)
Acquired by Koninklijke DSM N.V. 02/28/2011
Each share Common 10¢ par exchanged for $31.50 cash

MARTEK INVS INC (NY)
Name changed to Rochester Fund Municipals, Inc. 03/31/1986

MARTEL MICRO SYS INC (NY)
Charter cancelled and proclaimed dissolved for failure to pay taxes 12/23/1992

MARTEL MILLS, INC.
Reorganized as Martel Mills Corp. in 1932
Details not available

MARTEL MILLS CORP. (DE)
Recapitalized 00/00/1936
Each share Preferred $100 par exchanged for (1) share $3 Preferred $50 par and (1) share Common $1 par
Each share Common $1 par exchanged for (1) share new Common $1 par
Name changed to Valfour Corp. 08/29/1957
(See Valfour Corp.)

MARTEL OIL & GAS LTD (BC)
Recapitalized as Mylan Ventures Ltd. (BC) 11/27/87
Each (2.7) shares Common no par exchanged for (1) share Common no par
Mylan Ventures Ltd. (BC) reincorporated in Wyoming 9/10/96
(See Mylan Ventures Ltd. (WY))

MARTEN TRANS LTD (WI)
Reincorporated under the laws of Delaware 5/13/88

MARTHA STEWART LIVING OMNIMEDIA INC (DE)
Merged into Sequential Brands Group, Inc. (New) 12/07/2015
Each share Class A Common 1¢ par exchanged for (0.6958) share Common 1¢ par

MARTHA, INC. (TN)
See - White (Martha) Inc.

MARTHA WHITE FOODS INC (TN)
Common $1 par split (3) for (2) by issuance of (0.5) additional share 10/16/67
Merged into Beatrice Foods Co. 11/18/75
Each share Common $1 par exchanged for (1.25) shares Common no par
Beatrice Foods Co. name changed to Beatrice Companies, Inc. 6/5/84
(See Beatrice Companies, Inc.)

MARTHA WHITE MILLS, INC. (TN)
See - White (Martha) Mills, Inc.

MARTI (HUGH A.) CO.
Property sold to Bondholders' Committee in 1932

MARTIN BROWER CORP (DE)
Reincorporated 3/31/70
Common $1 par split (3) for (2) by issuance of (0.5) additional share 12/1/69
State of incorporation changed from (IL) to (DE) 3/31/70
Merged into Clorox Co. (OH) 7/25/72
Each share Common $1 par exchanged for (0.675) share Common no par
Clorox Co. (OH) reincorporated in California 3/12/73 which reincorporated in Delaware 10/22/86

MARTIN CO. (MD)
Common $1 par changed to no par

and (1) additional share issued 02/10/1961
Merged into Martin Marietta Corp. (Old) 10/10/1961
Each share Common $1 par exchanged for (1.3) shares Common $1 par
Martin Marietta Corp. (Old) merged into Martin Marietta Corp. (New) 04/02/1993 which merged into Lockheed Martin Corp. 03/15/1995

MARTIN COLOR-FI INC (SC)
Plan of reorganization under Chapter 11 Federal Bankruptcy proceedings confirmed 06/26/2000
No stockholders' equity

MARTIN (GLENN L.) CO. (MD)
Common no par changed to $1 par 00/00/1935
Stock Dividend - 10% 12/15/1954
Name changed to Martin Co. 04/23/1957
Martin Co. merged into Martin Marietta Corp. (Old) 10/10/1961 which merged into Martin Marietta Corp. (New) 04/02/1993 which merged into Lockheed Martin Corp. 03/15/1995

MARTIN E. JANIS & CO., INC. (DE)
See - Janis (Martin E.) & Co., Inc.

MARTIN GAS CO. (WV)
Dissolved 12/23/59

MARTIN HEALTH GROUP INC (AB)
Placed in receivership 07/05/2004
No stockholders' equity

MARTIN-HUNT MINING LTD. (ON)
Charter cancelled for failure to pay taxes and file returns in March, 1972

MARTIN INDS INC (DE)
Ctfs. dated prior to 3/29/77
Charter cancelled and declared inoperative and void for non-payment of taxes 3/1/76

MARTIN INDS INC (DE)
Ctfs. dated after 7/1/95
Plan of reorganization under Chapter 11 Federal Bankruptcy Code effective 8/12/2003
No stockholders' equity

MARTIN LAWRENCE LTD EDITIONS INC (DE)
Reincorporated 06/19/1987
State of incorporation changed from (NV) to (DE) and Common $0.001 par changed to 1¢ par 06/19/1997
Filed a petition under Chapter 11 Federal Bankruptcy Code 12/17/1996
No stockholders' equity

MARTIN MARIETTA ALUM INC (CA)
Merged into Martin Marietta Corp. (Old) 06/27/1974
Each share Common $1 par exchanged for (1.15) shares Common $1 par
Martin Marietta Corp. (Old) merged into Martin Marietta Corp. (New) 04/02/1993 which merged into Lockheed Martin Corp. 03/15/1995

MARTIN MARIETTA CORP NEW (MD)
Common $1 par split (2) for (1) by issuance of (1) additional share 09/30/1993
Merged into Lockheed Martin Corp. 03/15/1995
Each share Common $1 par exchanged for (1) share Common $1 par

MARTIN MARIETTA CORP OLD (MD)
Common $1 par split (3) for (2) by issuance of (0.5) additional share 10/19/1981
Common $1 par split (3) for (2) by issuance of (0.5) additional share 10/17/1983
$4.875 Conv. Exchangeable Preferred no par called for redemption 03/27/1985
Common $1 par split (3) for (2) by issuance of (0.5) additional share 06/28/1985
Under plan of merger each share Common $1 par became (1) share Martin Marietta Corp. (New) 04/29/1993
Martin Marietta Corp. (New) merged into Lockheed Martin Corp. 03/15/1995

MARTIN MCNEELY MINES LTD (ON)
Capital Stock $1 par changed to no par 5/29/74
Recapitalized as Neomar Resources Ltd. 5/10/78
Each share Capital Stock no par exchanged for (1/7) share Common no par
Neomar Resources Ltd. name changed to Tarragon Oil & Gas Ltd. 7/3/87 which merged into Marathon Oil Canada Ltd. 9/11/98
(See Marathon Oil Canada Ltd.)

MARTIN MILLER INTERNET MALLS INC (NV)
Name changed to Golden Age Resources, Inc. 03/18/2009

MARTIN NUTRACEUTICALS INC (NV)
Each share old Common $0.001 par exchanged for (0.005) share new Common $0.001 par 10/03/2005
Each share new Common $0.001 par exchanged again for (0.125) share new Common $0.001 par 01/17/2006
Recapitalized as MNI Nutraceuticals Inc. 05/05/2008
Each share Common $0.001 par exchanged for (0.0005) share Common $0.001 par
MNI Nutraceuticals Inc. recapitalized as Green Hygienics, Inc. 05/20/2011

MARTIN-PARRY CORP. (DE)
Merged into Ward Industries Corp. 3/15/56
Each share Capital Stock no par exchanged for (0.08) share $1.25 Preferred Ser. A $25 par and (1) share Common $1 par
Ward Industries Corp. name changed to Dragor Shipping Corp. 8/14/64 which merged into American Export Industries, Inc. 10/17/67 which name changed to Aeicor, Inc. 3/31/78 which name changed to Doskocil Companies Inc. 9/30/83 which name changed to Foodbrands America Inc. 5/15/95 which merged into IBP, Inc. 5/7/97 which merged into Tyson Foods, Inc. 9/28/2001

MARTIN PROCESSING INC (DE)
Common $3 par changed to $1 par and (2) additional shares issued 06/01/1986
Merged into Courtaulds PLC 08/12/1987
Each share Common $1 par exchanged for $20 cash

MARTIN PYCNOGENOL PRODS INC (AB)
Issue Information - 2,500,000 shares COM offered at $0.10 per share on 12/18/1997
Name changed to Martin Health Group Inc. 02/24/1999
(See Martin Health Group Inc.)

MARTIN YALE BUSINESS MACHS CORP (IL)
Stock Dividends - 10% 03/15/1968; 20% 03/15/1969
Name changed to Yale (Martin) Industries, Inc. 10/14/1969
Yale (Martin) Industries, Inc. merged into Williams Manufacturing Co. (OH) 01/05/1972 which reincorporated in Delaware as Escalade, Inc. 03/23/1973 which reincorporated in Indiana 07/23/1987

MARTIN YALE INDS INC (IL)
Common 10¢ par split (5) for (4) by issuance of (0.25) additional share 03/16/1970
Common 10¢ par split (6) for (5) by issuance of (0.2) additional share 07/01/1971
Merged into Williams Manufacturing Co. (OH) 01/05/1972
Each share Common 10¢ par exchanged for (1) share Common no par
Williams Manufacturing Co. (OH) reincorporated in Delaware as Escalade, Inc. 03/23/1973 which reincorporated in Indiana 07/23/1987

MARTINALL INDUSTRIES, INC. (DE)
Completely liquidated 1/3/67
Each share Common $1.25 par exchanged for first and final distribution of (0.9) share Bates Manufacturing Co., Inc. Capital Stock $5 par
(See Bates Manufacturing Co., Inc.)

MARTINEZ & MURPHEY INC (CA)
Name changed 06/17/1987
Name changed from Martinez & Murphey Vestments Makers, Inc. to Martinez & Murphey, Inc. 06/17/1987
Plan of reorganization under Chapter 11 Federal Bankruptcy proceedings confirmed 09/29/1993
Stockholders' equity unlikely

MARTINIQUE VENTURES CORP (DE)
Name changed to TAO Partners Inc. 4/21/98
TAO Partners Inc. name changed to Inetvisionz.Com Inc. 5/12/99
(See Inetvisionz.Com Inc.)

MARTINKA GOLD MINES LTD. (ON)
Charter cancelled for failure to file reports and pay taxes 7/2/63

MARTLET VENTURE MGMT LTD (AB)
Merged into Knorr Capital Partners AG 9/28/2000
Each share Common no par exchanged for (0.28571428) Ordinary share

MARU URANIUM MINES LTD. (BC)
Struck off register and declared dissolved for failure to file returns 06/27/1977

MARUI LTD (JAPAN)
Each old ADR for Common 50 Yen par exchanged for (5) new ADR's for Common 50 Yen par 06/28/1982
Stock Dividends - 10% 04/20/1973; 15% 04/29/1975; 10% 05/21/1976; 10% 05/20/1977; 10% 04/17/1981; 10% 04/28/1982; 10% 05/16/1983; 10% 04/05/1984; 10% 04/01/1991
Name changed to Marui Group Co., Ltd. 10/01/2007

MARUM RES INC (AB)
Name changed to StrikePoint Gold Inc. (AB) 06/26/2009
StrikePoint Gold Inc. (AB) reincorporated in British Columbia 08/12/2015

MARVA INDS INC (DE)
Name changed to Razor Industries, Inc. 12/17/1984
(See Razor Industries, Inc.)

MARVAC MATERIALS CORP. (NY)
Name changed to Marvac Industries Corp. 2/25/70

MARVAS DEVS LTD (ON)
Reorganized as Pan American Resources Inc. 01/23/1996
Each share Common no par exchanged for (1) share Common no par
Pan American Resources Inc. name changed to ONTZINC Corp. 08/08/2002 which recapitalized as HudBay Minerals Inc. (ONT) 12/24/2004 which reincorporated in Canada 10/25/2005

MARVEL CARBURETOR CO.
Merged into Borg-Warner Corp. (IL) 00/00/1928
Details not available

MARVEL CORP (DE)
Name changed to Leisure Holdings Inc. 04/18/1989
Leisure Holdings Inc. name changed to Amsnax, Inc. 08/15/1989
(See Amsnax, Inc.)

MARVEL ENTERPRISES INC (DE)
Each share 8% Conv. Exchangeable Preferred exchanged for (1.039) shares Common 1¢ par 03/30/2003
Common 1¢ par split (3) for (2) by issuance of (0.5) additional share payable 03/26/2004 to holders of record 03/12/2004 Ex date - 03/29/2004
Stock Dividends - In Preferred to holders of Preferred 2% payable 01/04/1999 to holders of record 12/31/1998; 2% payable 04/01/1999 to holders of record 03/31/1999; 2% payable 07/01/1999 to holders of record 06/30/1999; 2% payable 10/01/1999 to holders of record 09/30/1999; 2% payable 01/03/2000 to holders of record 12/31/1999; 2% payable 04/03/2000 to holders of record 03/31/2000; 2% payable 07/30/2000 to holders of record 06/30/2000; 2% payable 10/02/2000 to holders of record 09/30/2000; 2% payable 01/02/2001 to holders of record 12/29/2000; 2% payable 04/06/2001 to holders of record 03/30/2001; 2% payable 07/13/2001 to holders of record 06/29/2001; 2% payable 10/05/2001 to holders of record 09/28/2001 Ex date - 10/03/2001; 2% payable 01/04/2002 to holders of record 12/28/2001; 2% payable 04/03/2002 to holders of record 03/28/2002 Ex date - 04/04/2002; 2% payable 07/01/2002 to holders of record 06/28/2002 Ex date - 06/26/2002; 2% payable 10/01/2002 to holders of record 09/30/2002 Ex date - 09/26/2002
Name changed to Marvel Entertainment, Inc. 09/16/2005
Marvel Entertainment, Inc. merged into Disney (Walt) Co. 12/31/2009

MARVEL ENTMT GROUP INC (DE)
Common 1¢ par split (2) for (1) by issuance of (1) additional share 03/03/1992
Common 1¢ par split (2) for (1) by issuance of (1) additional share 12/21/1992
Common 1¢ par split (2) for (1) by issuance of (1) additional share 11/01/1993
Plan of reorganization under Chapter 11 Federal Bankruptcy Code effective 10/01/1998
Each share Common 1¢ par received (0.0281653) Marvel Enterprises Inc. Common Stock Purchase Warrant, Class A expiring 10/02/2001, (0.0180576) Common Stock Purchase Warrant, Class B expiring 06/23/1999 and (0.0476993) Common Stock Purchase Warrant, Class C expiring 10/02/2002
Note: Certificates were not required to be surrendered and are without value
Marvel Enterprises Inc. name changed to Marvel Entertainment, Inc. 09/16/2005 which merged into Disney (Walt) Co. 12/31/2009

MARVEL ENTMT INC (DE)
Merged into Disney (Walt) Co. 12/31/2009
Each share Common 1¢ par exchanged for (0.7452) share Common 1¢ par and $30 cash

MARVEL HEMSLEY LTD (QC)
Declared dissolved for failure to file reports or pay fees 03/00/1976

MAR-MAR

MARVEL MINERALS LTD (ON)
Charter cancelled and declared dissolved for failure to file returns and pay fees 03/00/1976

MARVEL OILS LTD (CANADA)
Recapitalized as New Marvel Oils Ltd. 05/05/1969
Each share Common $1 par exchanged for (0.2) share Common no par
(See New Marvel Oils Ltd.)

MARVEL ROUYN MINES LTD. (ON)
Name changed to Marvel Uranium Mines, Ltd. 5/4/53
(See Marvel Uranium Mines, Ltd.)

MARVEL URANIUM MINES, LTD. (ON)
Charter cancelled and company declared dissolved by default 6/29/64

MARVEND, INC. (GA)
Ceased operations in October 1973
Registered Agent opined no stockholders' equity

MARVENS LTD (NB)
100% acquired by Weston (George) Ltd. through purchase offer which expired 00/00/1978
Public interest eliminated

MARVIL PACKAGE CO.
Acquired by Atlas Plywood Corp. 00/00/1946
Details not available

MARVIN ELECTRIC MANUFACTURING CO. (CA)
Acquired by Progress Manufacturing Co., Inc. 04/30/1956
Each share Common exchanged for (0.18382352) share Common $1 par
Progress Manufacturing Co., Inc. name changed to Lighting Corp. of America 05/04/1966 which was acquired by Kidde (Walter) & Co., Inc. (NY) 06/19/1967 which reincorporated in Delaware 07/02/1968 which name changed to Kidde, Inc. 04/18/1980 which merged into Hanson Trust PLC 12/31/1987 which name changed to Hanson PLC (Old) 01/29/1988 which reorganized as Hanson PLC (New) 10/15/2003

MARVINS PL INC (NV)
Name changed to Atlas Therapeutics Corp. 07/14/2010
Atlas Therapeutics Corp. name changed to MYOS Corp. 05/21/2012 which name changed to MYOS RENS Technology Inc. 03/22/2016

MARWAYNE OILS, LTD. (ON)
Merged into Consolidated Dragon Oils Ltd. 12/30/1954
Each share Capital Stock no par exchanged for (0.33333333) share Capital Stock $1 par
Consolidated Dragon Oils Ltd. acquired by Plains Petroleums Ltd. 03/27/1965
(See Plains Petroleum Ltd.)

MARWICH II LTD (CO)
Common no par split (4) for (1) by issuance of (3) additional shares payable 06/14/2006 to holders of record 06/12/2006 Ex date - 06/15/2006
Reincorporated under the laws of Nevada as AE Biofuels, Inc. and Common no par changed to $0.001 par 12/11/2007
AE Biofuels, Inc. name changed to Aemetis, Inc. 11/15/2011

MARWOOD MINING CORP. LTD. (ON)
Charter cancelled and proclaimed dissolved for failure to pay taxes and file returns 10/13/58

MARX TOYS & ENTMT CORP (NV)
Recapitalized as Toyshare, Inc. 07/03/2007
Each share Common $0.001 par exchanged for (0.001) share Common $0.001 par
Toyshare, Inc. name changed to Capital Financial Global, Inc. 05/27/2011

MARY ANN GOLD MINES INC. (CO)
Charter dissolved for failure to file annual reports 1/1/47

MARY CREEK RESOURCE CORP (BC)
Name changed to Pundata Gold Corp. 03/24/1986
Each share Common no par exchanged for (1) share Common no par
(See Pundata Gold Corp.)

MARY ELLEN RES LTD (BC)
Merged into Greater Lenora Resources Corp. 1/5/89
Each share Common no par exchanged for (1/6) share Common no par
(See Greater Lenora Resources Corp.)

MARY KAY, INC. (TX)
See - Kay (Mary), Inc.

MARY KAY COSMETICS INC (TX)
Common 10¢ par split (2) for (1) by issuance of (1) additional share 8/29/80
Common 10¢ par split (2) for (1) by issuance of (1) additional share 7/2/81
Common 10¢ par split (2) for (1) by issuance of (1) additional share 3/31/83
Stock Dividends - 100% 7/12/71; 100% 4/12/73
Merged into Kay (Mary) Holding Corp. 12/4/85
Each share Common 10¢ par exchanged for $8.25 principal amount of Kay (Mary) Corp. Discount Debentures due 11/30/2000 and $11 cash

MARY MOPPETS DAY CARE SCHS INC (DE)
Merged into Children's Discovery Centers of America, Inc. 10/24/85
Each share Common 10¢ par exchanged for $8.50 cash

MARYGOLD MINES, LTD. (ON)
Charter surrendered for failure to file reports and pay taxes in 1951

MARYLAND APARTMENTS, INC. (MA)
Dissolved in 1954

MARYLAND BK & TR CO (LEXINGTON PARK, MD)
96% acquired by Maryland Bancorp, Inc. through exchange offer which expired 03/31/1971
Public interest eliminated

MARYLAND BANKCORP, INC. (MD)
Ctfs. dated prior to 09/29/1994
Stock Dividend - 10% 12/23/1985
Merged into MBTC Corp., Inc. 09/29/1994
Details not available

MARYLAND BANKCORP INC (MD)
Ctfs. dated after 05/17/2001
Stock Dividend - 10% payable 12/12/2001 to holders of record 11/14/2001
Merged into Old Line Bancshares, Inc. 04/01/2011
Each share Common 1¢ par exchanged for (3.4826) shares Common 1¢ par

MARYLAND CABLE HLDGS CORP (MD)
Plan of reorganization under Chapter 11 Federal Bankruptcy Code effective 9/30/94
No stockholders' equity

MARYLAND CAS CO (MD)
Each share Common $25 par exchanged for (2) shares Common $10 par 00/00/1930
Common $10 par changed to $2 par 00/00/1932
Common $2 par changed to $1 par in 00/00/1933
Stock Dividend - 10% 05/22/1964
Each share Common $1 par exchanged for (0.00025) share Common $4,000 par 09/05/1969
Public interest eliminated

MARYLAND CASH CREDIT CORP.
Merged into Franklin Plan Corp. in 1932 which became bankrupt in 1933

MARYLAND CREDIT FINANCE CORP. (DE)
Each share Common no par exchanged for (2) shares Common $15 par in 1952
Merged into Oxford Finance Companies, Inc. 1/1/63
Each share 6% Preferred $100 par exchanged for (4) shares Preferred $19.25 par and (4) Common Stock Purchase Warrants
Each share Common $5 par exchanged for (0.5) share Common $1 par
(See Oxford Finance Companies, Inc.)

MARYLAND CUP CORP (MD)
Common $1 par split (5) for (4) by issuance of (0.25) additional share 12/23/64
Common $1 par split (5) for (4) by issuance of (0.25) additional share 1/15/68
Common $1 par split (3) for (2) by issuance of (0.5) additional share 11/15/78
Common $1 par split (3) for (2) by issuance of (0.5) additional share 2/15/83
Merged into Fort Paper Howard Paper Co. 8/31/83
Each share Common $1 par exchanged for (0.85) share Common $1 par
Fort Howard Paper Co. name changed to Fort Howard Corp. 4/23/87
(See Fort Howard Corp.)

MARYLAND DRYDOCK CO. (MD)
Each share Common no par exchanged for (5) shares Common $1 par in 1941
Each share Common $1 par exchanged for (2) shares Common 50¢ par in 1948
Stock Dividend - 10% 5/26/52
Name changed to Maryland Shipbuilding & Drydock Co. 4/20/55
(See Maryland Shipbuilding & Drydock Co.)

MARYLAND FED BANCORP INC (MD)
Common 1¢ par split (2) for (1) by issuance of (1) additional share payable 11/21/97 to holders of record 11/7/97
Stock Dividend - 10% 9/18/92; 5% payable 12/12/96 to holders of record 12/2/96
Merged into BB&T Corp. 9/30/98
Each share Common 1¢ par exchanged for (1.2078) shares Common $5 par

MARYLAND FED SVGS & LN ASSN HYATTSVILLE (MD)
Reorganized as Maryland Federal Bancorp, Inc. 11/17/1989
Each share Common $1 par exchanged for (1) share Common 1¢ par
Maryland Federal Bancorp, Inc. merged into BB&T Corp. 09/30/1998

MARYLAND FINE & SPECIALTY WIRE CO., INC. (MD)
Name changed to Maryland Specialty Wire, Inc. 7/20/64

Maryland Specialty Wire, Inc. was acquired by Handy & Harman 7/12/67
(See Handy & Harman)

MARYLAND FUND, INC.
Merged into American Business Shares, Inc. on a (1.645052) for (1) basis 00/00/1944
American Business Shares, Inc. name changed to Lord Abbett Income Fund, Inc. (DE) 11/17/1975 which reincorporated in Maryland 07/09/1975 which name changed to Lord Abbett U.S. Government Securities Fund, Inc. 09/23/1985
(See Lord Abbett U.S. Government Securities Fund, Inc.)

MARYLAND FURNITURE CO., INC. (MD)
Incorporated 12/23/31
Charter forfeited for failure to file annual reports 2/15/35

MARYLAND FURNITURE CO., INC. (MD)
Incorporated 10/30/63
Charter annulled for failure to file annual reports 10/7/81

MARYLAND INCOME BOND CO.
Name changed to Homewood Holding Co. in 1946
(See Homewood Holding Co.)

MARYLAND LIFE INSURANCE CO. OF BALTIMORE (MD)
Stock Dividend - 20% 5/1/61
Merged into Philadelphia Life Insurance Co. on a share for share basis 7/12/62
Philadelphia Life Insurance Co. merged into Tenneco Inc. 3/1/78 which merged into El Paso Natural Gas Co. 12/12/96 which reorganized as El Paso Energy Corp. 8/1/98 which name changed to El Paso Corp. 2/5/2001

MARYLAND MORTGAGE & NATIONAL TITLE CO.
Reorganized as Mortbon Corp. of New York in 1935
Mortbon Corp. of New York acquired by Telfair Stockton & Co., Inc. in 1945 which merged into Stockton, Whatley, Davin & Co. in 1952 which was acquired by General American Oil Co. of Texas 5/19/64
(See General American Oil Co. of Texas)

MARYLAND MORTGAGE CO.
Name changed to Maryland Mortgage & National Title Co. in 1928
Maryland Mortgage & National Title Co. reorganized as Mortbon Corp. of New York in 1935 which was acquired by Telfair Stockton & Co., Inc. in 1945 which merged into Stockton, Whatley, Davin & Co. in 1952 which was acquired by General American Oil Co. of Texas 5/19/64
(See General American Oil Co. of Texas)

MARYLAND NATL BK (BALTIMORE, MD)
Stock Dividend - 50% 10/08/1965
Reorganized as Maryland National Corp. 05/01/1969
Each share Capital Stock $10 par exchanged for (2.2) shares Common $5 par
Maryland National Corp. name changed to MNC Financial, Inc. 04/29/1987 which merged into NationsBank Corp. (NC) 10/01/1993 which reincorporated in Delaware as BankAmerica Corp. (Old) 09/25/1998 which merged into BankAmerica Corp. (New) 09/30/1998 which name changed to Bank of America Corp. 04/28/1999

MARYLAND NATL CORP (MD)
Common $5 par changed to $2.50 par

and (1) additional share issued 4/3/74
Common $2.50 par split (2) for (1) by issuance of (1) additional share 3/22/85
Name changed to MNC Financial, Inc. 4/29/87
MNC Financial, Inc. merged into NationsBank Corp. 10/1/93 which reincorporated in Delaware as BankAmerica Corp. (Old) 9/25/98 which merged into BankAmerica Corp. (New) 9/30/98 which name changed to Bank of America Corp. 4/28/99

MARYLAND NATIONAL INSURANCE CO. (MD)
Acquired by Kennesaw Life & Accident Insurance Co. 00/00/1964
Each share Common $4.50 par exchanged for (1.5) shares Common $1.25 par
Kennesaw Life & Accident Insurance Co. merged into Lykes-Youngstown Financial Corp. 11/14/1969 which name changed to LifeSurance Corp. 05/10/1971 which merged into Regan Holding Corp. 10/31/1991
(See Regan Holding Corp.)

MARYLAND OLD LINE CORP (MD)
Each share Preferred $10 par exchanged for (2) shares Common 1¢ par 11/14/1969
Common 1¢ par changed to $1 par 08/21/1970
Merged into Consumers Financial Corp. (PA) 05/31/1983
Each share Common $1 par exchanged for (0.5) share $5 Conv. Preferred Ser. 1 $1 par
Consumers Financial Corp. (PA) reincorporated in Nevada 02/26/2008
(See Consumers Financial Corp.)

MARYLAND PERM BK & TR CO (OWINGS, MD)
Merged into Northwest Bancorp, Inc. 5/19/2006
Each share Common $1 par exchanged for $4.75 cash

MARYLAND PETROLEUMS, LTD. (AB)
Acquired by Globe Oil Co. (1958) Ltd. 11/30/59 Each (1/40) Unit of Class A Preferred or Deferred Royalty Unit exchanged for (5) shares Common no par
Globe Oil Co. (1958) Ltd. merged into Trans-Canada Resources Ltd. (New) 11/1/82 which recapitalized as Consolidated Trans-Canada Resources Ltd. 9/22/88 which merged into Ranchmen's Resources Ltd. 9/30/89

MARYLAND PORCUPINE GOLD MINES, LTD. (ON)
Charter cancelled in February 1957
Stock is valueless

MARYLAND PPTY CAP TR INC (MD)
Under plan of merger name changed to Property Capital Trust Inc. 5/28/99
(See Property Capital Trust Inc.)

MARYLAND RLTY TR (MD)
Reorganized under the laws of Delaware as Maxxus, Inc. and each Share of Bene. Int. $1 par automatically became (1) share Common 1¢ par 11/30/1983
(See Maxxus, Inc. (DE))

MARYLAND SHIPBUILDING & DRYDOCK CO (MD)
4.5% Preferred Ser. A $100 par called for redemption 11/26/1962
Merged into Fruehauf Corp. (MI) 12/31/1973
Each share Common 50¢ par exchanged for $35 cash

MARYLAND SPECIALTY WIRE, INC. (MD)
Completely liquidated 7/12/67
Each share Common $1 par exchanged for first and final distribution of (1.333333) shares Handy & Harman Common $1 par
(See Handy & Harman)

MARYLAND TELECOMMUNICATIONS, INC. (MD)
Completely liquidated 11/22/1967
Each share Common 50¢ par exchanged for first and final distribution of (0.75) share KMS Industries, Inc. Common 1¢ par
(See KMS Industries, Inc.)

MARYLAND THEATRE BUILDING CORP. (IL)
Liquidation completed
Each share Capital Stock no par exchanged for initial distribution of $47 cash 04/01/1965
Each share Capital Stock no par received second and final distribution of $3.65 cash 01/12/1966

MARYLAND TITLE SECURITIES CORP.
Liquidated in 1941

MARYLAND TRUST CO. (BALTIMORE, MD)
Stock Dividends - 25% 2/1/54; 10% 12/5/57
Merged into Baltimore National Bank (Baltimore, MD) 6/24/60
Each share Capital Stock $10 par exchanged for (1.8) shares Capital Stock $10 par
Baltimore National Bank (Baltimore, MD) merged into Maryland National Bank (Baltimore, MD) 11/14/61 which reorganized as Maryland National Corp. 5/1/69 which name changed to MNC Financial, Inc. 4/29/87 which merged into NationsBank Corp. 10/1/93 which reincorporated in Delaware as BankAmerica Corp. (Old) 9/25/98 which merged into BankAmerica Corp. (New) 9/30/98 which name changed to Bank of America Corp. 4/28/99

MAS, INC. (UT)
Name changed to American Energy Partners Inc. (UT) 8/4/82
(See American Energy Partners Inc. (UT))

MAS ACQUISITION VIII INC. (IN)
Name changed to Netstaff, Inc. (IN) 9/15/99
Netstaff, Inc. (IN) reincorporated in Delaware as Financial Systems Group, Inc. 7/15/2002
(See Financial Systems Group, Inc.)

MAS ACQUISITION IX CORP (IN)
Merged into Airtrax Inc. 11/19/99
Each (74.170997) shares Common no par exchanged for (1) share Common no par

MAS ACQUISTION XI CORP (IN)
Recapitalized as Bluepoint Linux Software Corp. 02/25/2000
Each (15) shares Common $0.001 par exchanged for (1) share Common $0.001 par

MAS TECHNOLOGY LTD (NEW ZEALAND)
Issue Information - 2,000,000 SPONSORED ADR's offered at $14 per ADR on 06/19/1997
Merged into Digital Microwave Corp. 03/24/1998
Each Sponsored ADR for Ordinary no par exchanged for (1.2) shares Common 1¢ par
Digital Microwave Corp. name changed to DMC Stratex Networks, Inc. 08/15/2000 which name changed to Stratex Networks, Inc. 09/10/2002 which merged into Harris Stratex Networks, Inc. 01/26/2007 which name changed to Aviat Networks, Inc. 01/27/2010

MAS VENTURES LTD (CO)
Name changed to Continental American Transportation, Inc. 07/29/1994
(See Continental American Transportation, Inc.)

MASBATE CONSOLIDATED MINING CO.
Merged into Atlas Consolidated Mining & Development Corp. and each share Common P0.10 par exchanged for (1) share Capital Stock P0.10 par in 1953

MASCAN CORP (ON)
Under plan of merger each share Common no par exchanged for (1) share 128508 Canada Ltd. Common Stock Purchase Warrant expiring 09/30/1984 and $15 cash 04/09/1984
9% 1st Preferred Ser. A $25 par called for redemption 05/01/1984
10% 2nd Preferred $20 par called for redemption 05/01/1984
Public interest eliminated

MASCO CORP (MI)
Stock Dividends - 100% 12/18/1961; 100% 06/17/1963; 50% 12/11/1967
Reincorporated under the laws of Delaware 08/31/1968

MASCO INDS INC (DE)
Common $1 par split (3) for (1) by issuance of (2) additional shares 8/26/85
Common $1 par split (2) for (1) by issuance of (1) additional share 6/20/86
Common $1 par split (2) for (1) by issuance of (1) additional share 6/29/87
Depository Conv. Exchangeable Preferred $1 par called for redemption 9/28/87
Name changed to Mascotech, Inc. 6/23/93
(See Mascotech Inc.)

MASCO SCREW PRODUCTS CO. (MI)
Name changed to Masco Corp. (Mich.) 6/14/61
Masco Corp. (Mich.) reincorporated under the laws of Delaware 8/31/68

MASCO SPORTS INC (DE)
Each share Common 1¢ par exchanged for (0.002) share Common 1¢ par 2/16/88
Charter cancelled and declared inoperative and void for non-payment of taxes 3/1/96

MASCOT GOLD MINES LTD (BC)
Merged into Corona Corp. 07/01/1988
Each share Common no par exchanged for (1.11) shares Class A Subordinate no par
Corona Corp. recapitalized as International Corona Corp. 06/11/1991
(See International Corona Corp.)

MASCOT MALARTIC MINES LTD. (ON)
Charter cancelled for failure to file reports and pay taxes in 1952

MASCOT MINES, INC. (ID)
Capital Stock 35¢ par changed to 17-1/2¢ par 6/22/56
Name changed to Mascot Silver-Lead Mines, Inc. and Capital Stock 17-1/2¢ par changed to 10¢ par 3/25/65

MASCOT OIL CO. (CA)
Assets acquired by Mt. Diablo Oil Co. on a (0.605) for (1) basis in 1956

MASCOT PPTYS INC (NV)
Name changed to MamaMancini's Holdings, Inc. 03/11/2013

MASCOT VENTURES INC (NV)
Name changed to eMONEco, Inc. 12/23/2019

MASCOTECH INC (DE)
$17.50 Conv. Exchangeable Preferred $1 par called for redemption in September 1987
$1.20 Dividend Enhanced Conv. Preferred $1 par called for redemption at $20 plus $0.29 accrued dividend on 6/27/97
Merged into Saturn Electronics & Engineering Inc. 11/28/2000
Each share Common $1 par exchanged for $16.90 cash
Note: Each share Common $1 par received second and final distribution of $0.05 cash in February 2005

MASCOTT CORP (NJ)
Each share old Common no par exchanged for (0.2) share new Common no par 02/04/1994
Acquired by DINE, LLC 05/22/1995
Each share Common no par exchanged for $1.55 cash

MASER OPTICS, INC. (DE)
Name changed to General Laser Corp. 4/24/68

MASEV COMMUNICATIONS INTL INC (BC)
Delisted from Toronto Venture Stock Exchange 06/16/2004

MASHIACH CAP INC (BC)
Recapitalized as Animatronix Entertainment Corp. 03/26/1993
Each share Common no par exchanged for (0.5) share Common no par
Animatronix Entertainment Corp. name changed to Creative Entertainment Technologies Inc. 07/13/1995
(See Creative Entertainment Technologies Inc.)

MASISA S A NEW (CHILE)
ADR agreement terminated 04/28/2008
Each Sponsored ADR for Common exchanged for $8.55532 cash

MASISA S A OLD (CHILE)
Merged into Masisa S.A. (New) 08/04/2005
Each Sponsored ADR for Common exchanged for (1.536) Sponsored ADR's for Common
(See Masisa S.A. (New))

MASK RES INC (BC)
Name changed to American Nevada Gold Corp. 10/01/2002
American Nevada Gold Corp. recapitalized as Northern Canadian Minerals Inc. 08/06/2004 which name changed to Northern Canadian Uranium Inc. 04/09/2007 which merged into Bayswater Uranium Corp. (New) 12/21/2007 which recapitalized as Green Thumb Industries Inc. 06/13/2018

MASKAL ENERGY INC (AB)
Recapitalized as Maskal Energy Ltd. 08/13/2007
Each share Common no par exchanged for (0.25) share Common no par
(See Maskal Energy Ltd.)

MASKAL ENERGY LTD (AB)
Assets sold for the benefit of creditors 08/13/2010
Stockholders' equity unlikely

MASLAND C H & SONS (PA)
Merged into Burlington Industries, Inc. 09/09/1986
Each share Common $1.66-2/3 par exchanged for $73 cash

MASLAND CORP (DE)
Merged into Lear Corp. 07/01/1996

Each share Common 1¢ par exchanged for $26 cash

MASON (JAMES S.) CO. (DE)
Company became private 00/00/1978
Details not available

MASON BLOCK REALTY CORP.
Property sold 00/00/1947
Details not available

MASON DENTAL INC (MT)
Recapitalized 12/01/1990
Recapitalized from Mason Dental Ceramics, Inc. to Mason Dental Inc. 12/01/1990
Each share Common $0.0015 par exchanged for (0.01) share Common 15¢ par
Merged into Princeton Dental Management Corp. 12/31/1992
Holders received a pro rata distribution in a 10-yr. note

MASON-DIXON BANCSHARES INC (MD)
Common $10 par changed to $1 par and (2) additional shares issued 10/28/94
Merged into BB&T Corp. 7/14/99
Each share Common $1 par exchanged for (1.3) shares Common $5 par

MASON-DIXON CAP TR (DE)
$2.5175 Preferred Securities called for redemption at $25.75525 on 05/02/2012

MASON DIXON CAP TR II (DE)
8.40% Preferred Securities called for redemption at $20 on 04/01/2005

MASON GRAPHITE INC (ON)
Reincorporated under the laws of Canada 03/03/2016

MASON HILL HLDGS INC (DE)
Each share old Common $0.001 par exchanged for (0.02) share new Common $0.001 par 07/31/2006
Name changed to Attitude Drinks Inc. 06/18/2008

MASON (WESLEY) MILLS LTD. (CANADA)
Wound up in 1964
No stockholders' equity

MASON MORTGAGE & INVESTMENT CORP. (DE)
Reorganized 05/22/1967
Each share 6% Preferred $200 par exchanged for $4.25 cash
No equity for holders of Class A Common and Class B Common

MASON OIL INC (UT)
Each share old Common $0.001 par exchanged for (0.05) share new Common $0.001 par 03/18/1996
Name changed to Brandmakers Inc. 11/16/1999

MASON PERSONNEL ASSOC INC (NY)
Dissolved by proclamation 1/11/73

MASON ST BK (MASON, MI)
Reorganized as Capital Directions, Inc. 07/22/1988
Each share Capital Stock $5 par exchanged for (1) share Common $5 par
(See Capital Directions, Inc.)

MASON TIRE & RUBBER CO.
Name changed to Mason Tire & Rubber Corp. in 1929 which liquidated in 1943

MASON TIRE & RUBBER CORP.
Liquidated in 1943

MASONEILAN INTL INC (DE)
Merged into Studebaker-Worthington, Inc. 05/26/1977
Each share Common $1 par exchanged for (0.8416) share Common $1 par
(See Studebaker-Worthington, Inc.)

MASONITE CORP (DE)
Each share Common no par exchanged for (2) shares Common no par in 1936
Common no par split (3) for (2) by issuance of (0.5) additional share 12/21/64
Common no par split (2) for (1) by issuance of (1) additional share 12/22/69
Common no par split (2) for (1) by issuance of (1) additional share 1/9/73
Each share old Common no par exchanged for (1/3) share new Common no par 8/27/82
New Common no par split (2) for (1) by issuance of (1) additional share 1/3/84
Stock Dividends - 100% 12/28/50; 20% 10/18/68
Merged into United States Gypsum Co. 5/3/84
Each share Common no par exchanged for $38 cash

MASONITE INTL CORP (ON)
Acquired by Stile Acquisition Corp. 04/06/2005
Each share Common no par exchanged for $42.25 cash

MASS FINANCIAL CORP (BARBADOS)
Merged into Terra Nova Royalty Corp. 12/30/2010
Each share Class A Common no par exchanged for (1) share Common no par
Terra Nova Royalty Corp. name changed to MFC Industrial Ltd. 09/30/2011 which name changed to MFC Bancorp Ltd. (BC) 02/16/2016
(See MFC Bancorp Ltd. (BC))

MASS MEGAWATTS POWER INC (MA)
Name changed 1/2/2001
Name changed from Mass Megawatts, Inc. to Mass Megawatts Power, Inc. 1/2/2001
Name changed to Mass Megawatts Wind Power Inc. 2/25/2002

MASS MERCHANDISERS INC (AR)
Common 50¢ par split (3) for (2) by issuance of (0.5) additional share 07/12/1976
Stock Dividends - 10% 06/15/1973; 25% 03/16/1977
Merged into Napco Industries, Inc. 01/09/1979
Each share Common 50¢ par exchanged for $14 cash

MASS MERCHANDISERS INC (IN)
Acquired by McKesson Corp. (MD) 10/29/1985
Each share $0.25 Preferred no par exchanged for (0.1) share Common $2 par
Each share Common $1 par exchanged for (0.3262) share Common $2 par
McKesson Corp. (MD) reincorporated in Delaware 07/31/1987
(See McKesson Corp. (Old) (DE))

MASS MICROSYSTEMS INC (CA)
Merged into Ramtek Corp. 4/30/93
Each share Common no par exchanged for (0.39328) share Common 1¢ par

MASS PETE INC (NV)
Each share old Common $0.0001 par exchanged for (0.001) share new Common $0.0001 par 02/17/2012
Name changed to Cannamed Corp. 04/07/2014
Cannamed Corp. name changed to Chuma Holdings, Inc. 08/29/2014

MASSACHUSETTS ACCIDENT CO.
Declared insolvent in 1940

MASSACHUSETTS BAY BANCORP INC (MA)
Merged into New England Merchants Co., Inc. 5/31/80
Each share Common $1 par exchanged for (0.9798) share Common $5 par
New England Merchants Co., Inc. name changed to Bank of New England Corp. 5/1/82
(See Bank of New England Corp.)

MASSACHUSETTS BAY CO (DE)
Charter cancelled and declared inoperative and void for non-payment of taxes 4/15/73

MASSACHUSETTS BONDING & INSURANCE CO. (MA)
Each share Capital Stock $100 par exchanged for (4) shares Capital Stock $25 par 00/00/1929
Capital Stock $25 par changed to $12.50 par 00/00/1934
Each share Capital Stock $12.50 par exchanged for (2.5) shares Capital Stock $5 par 00/00/1947
Merged into Hanover Insurance Co. (NY) 06/30/1961
Each share Capital Stock $5 par exchanged for (1) share Capital Stock $10 par
Hanover Insurance Co. (NY) reincorporated in New Hampshire 01/01/1973 which merged into Allmerica Property & Casualty Companies, Inc. 12/11/1992 which merged into Allmerica Financial Corp. 07/16/1997 which name changed to Hanover Insurance Group, Inc. 12/01/2005

MASSACHUSETTS CAP DEV FD INC (MA)
Stock Dividends - 100% 9/8/78; 100% 3/23/81
Name changed to MFS Capital Development Fund and Common $1 par reclassified as Shares of Bene. Int. $1 par 8/3/92

MASSACHUSETTS CHAIN STORE TERMINALS, INC. (MD)
Liquidation completed 4/24/56

MASSACHUSETTS CITIES REALTY CO. (MA)
Liquidation completed 7/1/61

MASSACHUSETTS CO., INC. (MA)
100% acquired by Travelers Corp. through exchange offer which expired 06/13/1969
Public interest eliminated

MASSACHUSETTS COMPUTER CORP (DE)
Under plan of merger name changed to Concurrent Computer Corp. (New) 09/27/1988
Concurrent Computer Corp. (New) name changed to CCUR Holdings, Inc. 01/11/2018

MASSACHUSETTS CONSOLIDATED MINING CO.
Property sold in 1929

MASSACHUSETTS COTTON MILLS, INC.
Acquired by Pepperell Manufacturing Co. 12/13/1926
Details not available

MASSACHUSETTS ELEC CO (MA)
9.44% Preferred $100 par called for redemption 03/31/1977
7.80% Preferred $100 par called for redemption 11/01/1993
7.84% Preferred $100 par called for redemption 11/01/1993
6.84% Preferred $100 par called for redemption at $25.80 on 10/31/1998
6.99% Preferred called for redemption at $103.50 on 08/01/2003
4.76% Preferred called for redemption at $103.73 on 12/31/2007

MASSACHUSETTS FD (MA)
Merged into Keystone Custodian Funds 11/17/84
Each Trust Ctf. of Bene. Int. $1 par exchanged for (1.47437) shares Keystone Income Fund Ser. K-1 $1 par
(See Keystone Custodian Funds)

MASSACHUSETTS FD FOR TAX EXEMPT INCOME (MA)
Name changed to Keystone Tax Free Fund 1/1/80
Keystone Tax Free Fund reorganized as Evergreen Municipal Trust 10/31/97

MASSACHUSETTS FD INCOME (MA)
Merged into Keystone Custodian Funds 10/24/1980
Each Share of Bene. Int. no par exchanged for (0.714) share Medium-Grade Bond Fund Ser. B-2 $1 par
(See Keystone Custodian Funds)

MASSACHUSETTS FINL BD FD INC (MA)
Reorganized as MFS Fixed Income Trust 08/03/1992
Details not available

MASSACHUSETTS FINL DEV FD INC (MA)
Stock Dividend - 100% 05/12/1980
Name changed to MFS Research Fund 02/01/1992

MASSACHUSETTS FINL EMERGING GROWTH TR (MA)
Name changed to MFS Emerging Growth Fund 8/3/92

MASSACHUSETTS FINL HIGH INCOME TR (MA)
Name changed to MFS Series III Trust - High Income Fund 8/3/92

MASSACHUSETTS FINL TOTAL RETURN TR (MA)
Name changed to MFS Total Return Fund 08/03/1992

MASSACHUSETTS FINCORP INC (DE)
Stock Dividend - 10% payable 5/21/2001 to holders of record 5/7/2001
Merged into Abington Bancorp, Inc. (New) 9/13/2002
Each share Common 1¢ par exchanged for either (1.6175) shares Common 10¢ par or $30 cash
Note: Option to receive stock expired 10/9/2002
(See Abington Bancorp, Inc. (New))

MASSACHUSETTS GAS COMPANIES
Dissolved and properties transferred to Eastern Gas & Fuel Associates in 1936
(See Eastern Gas & Fuel Associates)

MASSACHUSETTS GEN LIFE INS CO (MA)
Acquired by Bankers Union Life Insurance Co. 12/31/1979
Each share Capital Stock $3 par exchanged for $6.75 cash

MASSACHUSETTS HEALTH & ED TAX EXEMPT TR (MA)
Auction Preferred Ser. B 1¢ par called for redemption at $50,000 on 06/20/2012
Auction Preferred Ser. A 1¢ par called for redemption at $50,000 on 06/20/2012
Name changed to BlackRock Massachusetts Tax-Exempt Trust 08/13/2013

MASSACHUSETTS HOSPITAL LIFE INSURANCE CO. (MA)
Common $100 par changed to $20 par in 1949
Common $20 par changed to $200 par in 1963
Common $200 par reclassified as Voting Common $7 par share for share and (29) shares Non-Voting Common $7 par issued 5/9/66
Name changed to Massachusetts Co., Inc. 4/30/67
(See Massachusetts Co., Inc.)

MASSACHUSETTS INCOME DEV FD INC (MA)
Common $1 par split (2) for (1) by issuance of (1) additional share 5/16/83
Name changed to Massachusetts Financial Total Return Trust 1/28/86
Massachusetts Financial Total Return Trust name changed to MFS Total Return Fund 8/3/92

MASSACHUSETTS INDEMNITY INSURANCE CO. (MA)
Each share Capital Stock $10 par exchanged for (20) shares Capital Stock $5 par 8/8/55
Stock Dividend - 50% 12/4/50
Name changed to Massachusetts Indemnity & Life Insurance Co. 7/26/56
Massachusetts Indemnity & Life Insurance Co. acquired by Mayflower, Inc. 12/30/74

MASSACHUSETTS INDTY & LIFE INS CO (MA)
Stock Dividends - 33-1/3% 01/29/1958; 25% 12/09/1963
Acquired by Mayflower, Inc. 12/30/1974
Each share Capital Stock $5 par exchanged for $57 cash

MASSACHUSETTS INVESTORS GROWTH STOCK FUND, INC. (DE)
Capital Stock $1 par changed to 33-1/3¢ par and (2) additional shares issued 10/8/55
Reincorporated under the laws of Massachusetts and Capital Stock 33-1/3¢ par changed to $1 par 2/27/59

MASSACHUSETTS INVESTORS SECOND FUND, INC. (DE)
Name changed to Massachusetts Investors Growth Stock Fund, Inc. (DE) in 1952
Massachusetts Investors Growth Stock Fund, Inc. (DE) reincorporated in Massachusetts 2/27/59

MASSACHUSETTS LIFE FUND (MA)
Trust Ctfs. of Bene. Int. no par split (4) for (1) in 1951
Trust Ctfs. of Bene. Int. no par changed to $1 par in 1952
Trust Ctfs. of Bene. Int. $1 par split (2) for (1) 3/1/57
Trust Ctfs. of Bene. Int. $1 par split (2) for (1) 4/10/64
Name changed to Massachusetts Fund 4/30/67
Massachusetts Fund merged into Keystone Custodian Funds 11/17/84
(See Keystone Custodian Funds)

MASSACHUSETTS LIFE INS CO (MA)
Capital Stock $2 par changed to $1 par and (1) additional share issued 9/15/64
Capital Stock $1 par changed to no par 6/6/69
Stock Dividend - 100% 6/30/64
Name changed to Life of America Insurance Corp. of Boston 9/25/69
Life of America Insurance Corp. of Boston name changed to Life of Boston Insurance Co. 11/5/86
(See Life of Boston Insurance Co.)

MASSACHUSETTS LIGHTING COMPANIES
Liquidated in 1938

MASSACHUSETTS MORTGAGE CO. (MA)
Proclaimed dissolved for failure to file reports and pay taxes 4/10/46

MASSACHUSETTS NORTHEASTN TRANSN CO (MA)
Each share Common $5 par exchanged for (5) shares Common $1 par 00/00/1945
Common $1 par changed to $10 par 08/06/1957
Bankrupt and placed into receivership 05/06/1964

Declared dissolved by Supreme Judicial Court, Suffolk County, MA 09/11/1969
Stockholders' equity unlikely

MASSACHUSETTS POWER & LIGHT ASSOCIATES
Merged into New England Electric System 6/3/47
Each share $2 Preferred no par exchanged for (1.1) shares Common $20 par and $8 in cash
Each share $2 2nd Preferred no par exchanged for (0.03) share Common $20 par
Each share Common no par exchanged for (0.01) share Common $20 par
(See New England Electric System)

MASSACHUSETTS PROTECTIVE ASSOCIATION, INC. (MA)
Capital Stock $25 par changed to $10 par and (1.5) additional shares issued 12/30/52
Capital Stock $10 par changed to $5 par and (1) additional share issued 7/12/57
Stock Dividend - 50% 11/3/55
Name changed to Revere (Paul) Corp. 1/1/67
Revere (Paul) Corp. merged into Avco Corp. 11/28/68
(See Avco Corp.)

MASSACHUSETTS REAL ESTATE INVESTMENT FUND (MA)
Completely liquidated for cash 8/20/62

MASSACHUSETTS UTILITIES ASSOCIATES
Common and Common VTC's no par changed to $1 par in 1935
Merged into New England Electric System 6/3/47
Each share Preferred $50 par exchanged for (1.5) shares Common $20 par and $16.50 in cash
Each share Common or Common VTC $1 par exchanged for (0.15) share Common $20 par
(See New England Electric System)

MASSACHUSETTS UTILITIES INVESTMENT TRUST
Name changed to Massachusetts Utilities Associates in 1928
Massachusetts Utilities Associates merged into New England Electric System 6/3/47
(See New England Electric System)

MASSACHUSETTS VARIABLE ANNUITY INS CO (MA)
Name changed to Patriot General Life Insurance Co. 01/09/1969
(See Patriot General Life Insurance Co.)

MASSAPEQUA VENTURES, INC. (DE)
Name changed to Code-Care, Inc. 08/00/1991
Code-Care, Inc. recapitalized as Netgates Inc. 04/12/1996 which recapitalized as Netgates Holdings, Inc. 06/29/2006 which name changed to Sustainable Energy Development, Inc. 09/05/2006 which recapitalized as United States Oil & Gas Corp. 04/17/2008

MASSASOIT CORP.
Liquidated in 1932

MASSAWIPPI VALLEY RY CO (CANADA)
Company liquidated in June 2001
Details not available

MASSBANK CORP READING MASS (DE)
Common $1 par split (3) for (2) by issuance of (0.5) additional share 09/09/1994
Common $1 par split (4) for (3) by issuance of (1/3) additional share payable 09/15/1997 to holders of record 08/29/1997

Common $1 par split (3) for (2) by issuance of (0.5) additional share payable 04/19/2002 to holders of record 03/29/2002 Ex date - 03/26/2002
Merged into Eastern Bank Corp. 09/02/2008
Each share Common $1 par exchanged for $40 cash

MASSBANK FOR SVGS (READING, MA)
Under plan of reorganization each share Common $1 par automatically became (1) share MASSBANK Corp. Common $1 par 12/02/1986
(See MASSBANK Corp.)

MASSBERYL LITHIUM CO. LTD. (QC)
Merged into Massval Resources Inc. 11/10/1959
Each share Capital Stock $1 par exchanged for (0.25) share Common $1 par
Massval Resources Inc. recapitalized as MSV Resources Inc. 10/10/1986 which merged into Campbell Resources Inc. (New) 06/03/2001
(See Campbell Resources Inc. (New))

MASSENGILL S E CO (TN)
Stock Dividend - 100% 07/17/1969
Merged into Beecham-Massengill Corp. 10/31/1971
Each share Common $1 par exchanged for $27.25 cash

MASSEY ENERGY CO (DE)
Each share Common $0.625 par received distribution of (1) share Fluor Corp. (New) Common 1¢ par payable 12/21/2000 to holders of record 11/30/2000 Ex date - 12/22/2000
Merged into Alpha Natural Resources, Inc. 06/01/2011
Each share Common $0.625 par exchanged for (1.025) share Common 1¢ par and $10 cash
(See Alpha Natural Resources, Inc.)

MASSEY EXPL CORP (DE)
Reincorporated 07/08/2011
State of incorporation changed from (NV) to (DE) 07/08/2011
Name changed to Nevada Gold Corp. 07/27/2012

MASSEY EXPL CORP (NV)
Reincorporated under the laws of Delaware 07/08/2011

MASSEY FERGUSON LTD (CANADA)
4-1/2% Conv. Preferred $100 par called for redemption 8/28/64
5-1/2% Conv. Preferred $100 par called for redemption 8/28/64
Each share $2.50 Preferred Ser. A $25 par exchanged for (7.8042) shares Common no par 5/9/86
Each share $2.50 Preferred Ser. B $25 par exchanged for (7.8042) shares Common no par 5/9/86
Name changed to Varity Corp. (Canada) 6/19/86
Varity Corp. (Canada) reorganized in Delaware 8/1/91 which merged into LucasVarity PLC 9/6/96
(See LucasVarity PLC)

MASSEY-HARRIS CO. LTD. (CANADA)
Each share Common $100 par exchanged for (4) shares Common no par 00/00/1927
Each share 5% Preference $100 par exchanged for (4) shares Preference $20 par and (3) shares Common no par 00/00/1942
Each share Common no par exchanged for (0.5) share new Common no par 00/00/1942
Each share old Common no par exchanged for (5) shares new Common no par 00/00/1951
Name changed to Massey-Harris-Ferguson Ltd. 00/00/1953
Massey-Harris-Ferguson Ltd. name

changed to Massey-Ferguson Ltd. 04/28/1958 which name changed to Varity Corp. (Canada) 06/19/1986 which reorganized in Delaware 08/01/1991 which merged into LucasVarity PLC 09/06/1996
(See LucasVarity PLC)

MASSEY-HARRIS-FERGUSON LTD. (CANADA)
Name changed to Massey-Ferguson Ltd. 04/28/1958
Massey-Ferguson Ltd. name changed to Varity Corp. (Canada) 06/19/1986 which reorganized in Delaware 08/01/1991 which merged into LucasVarity PLC 09/06/1996
(See LucasVarity PLC)

MASSEY MERCANTILE INC (BC)
Name changed to Riosun Resources Corp. 01/22/1997
(See Riosun Resources Corp.)

MASSIF MINERALS CORP (BC)
Recapitalized as World Wide Oil & Gas Inc. 6/25/91
Each share Common no par exchanged for (0.5) share Common no par
(See World Wide Oil & Gas Inc.)

MASSILLON & CLEVELAND R.R. CO.
Purchased by Pittsburgh, Fort Wayne & Chicago Railway Co. in 1928
(See Pittsburgh, Fort Wayne & Chicago Railway Co.)

MASSILLON STL CASTING CO (OH)
Chapter 11 Bankruptcy petition dismissed 04/03/1984
No stockholders' equity

MASSIMO DA MILANO INC (DE)
Recapitalized as Uptrend Corp. 3/22/2004
Each share Common $0.001 par exchanged for (0.002) share Common $0.001 par

MASSIVE DYNAMICS INC (NV)
Common $0.001 par split (20) for (1) by issuance of (19) additional shares payable 09/17/2012 to holders of record 09/14/2012 Ex date - 09/18/2012
SEC revoked common stock registration 07/25/2016

MASSIVE G MEDIA CORP (NV)
Name changed to International Minerals Mining Group, Inc. 06/21/2007
International Minerals Mining Group, Inc. name changed to Advanced Content Services, Inc. 02/05/2008 which recapitalized as New Wave Holdings, Inc. 12/08/2014 which name changed to PAO Group, Inc. 06/29/2017

MASSIVE RES LTD (BC)
Name changed 5/5/87
Common no par split (2) for (1) by issuance of (1) additional share 7/13/84
Name changed from Massive Energy Ltd. to Massive Resources Ltd. 5/5/87
Delisted from Vancouver Stock Exchange 3/4/91

MASSIVE YELLOWKNIFE MINES, LTD. (ON)
Charter cancelled 11/28/60

MASSMUTUAL CORPORATE INVS INC (MA)
Reincorporated 11/29/1985
Name and state of incorporation changed from MassMutual Corporate Investors Inc. (DE) to MassMutual Corporate Investors (MA) 11/29/1985
Common $1 par split (2) for (1) by issuance of (1) additional share payable 01/20/1998 to holders of record 12/31/1997 Ex date - 01/21/1998
Common $1 par split (2) for (1) by

issuance of (1) additional share payable 02/18/2011 to holders of record 02/04/2011 Ex date - 02/22/2011
Name changed to Babson Capital Corporate Investors 12/19/2011
Babson Capital Corporate Investors name changed to Barings Corporate Investors 09/12/2016

MASSMUTUAL INCOME INVS INC (MD)
Reorganized under the laws of Massachusetts as MassMutual Integrity Funds and Capital Stock $1 par reclassified as Investment Grade Bond Fund Share of Bene. Int. no par 04/15/1988

MASSMUTUAL LIQUID ASSETS TR (MA)
Under plan of reorganization each Share of Bene. Int. no par automatically became (1) MassMutual Integrity Funds Money Market Fund Share of Bene. Int. no par 04/15/1988

MASSMUTUAL MTG & RLTY INVS (MA)
Shares of Bene. Int. no par reclassified as Common no par 06/02/1982
Merged into Massachusetts Mutual Life Insurance Co. 06/25/1985
Each share Common no par exchanged for $19.50 cash

MASSMUTUAL PARTN INVS (MA)
Name changed to Babson Capital Participation Investors 12/19/2011
Babson Capital Participation Investors name changed to Barings Participation Investors 09/12/2016

MASSTOR SYS CORP (DE)
Reincorporated 03/09/1988
State of incorporation changed from (CA) to (DE) and Common no par changed to $0.001 par 03/09/1988
Bankruptcy proceedings converted from Chapter 11 to Chapter 7 00/00/1996
No stockholders' equity

MASSVAL RES INC (QC)
Recapitalized as MSV Resources Inc. 10/10/1986
Each share Common $1 par exchanged for (0.33333333) share Class A no par
MSV Resources Inc. merged into Campbell Resources Inc. (New) 06/03/2001
(See Campbell Resources Inc. (New))

MAST KEYSTONE INC (IA)
Each share old Common $0.001 par exchanged for (0.04) share new Common $0.001 par 03/16/1990
SEC revoked common stock registration 02/18/2010

MAST TECHNOLOGY INC (IA)
Certificate of Cancellation filed 11/30/1988
Details not available

MAST THERAPEUTICS INC (DE)
Recapitalized as Savara Inc. 04/28/2017
Each share Common $0.001 par exchanged for (0.01428571) share Common $0.001 par

MASTAN CO., INC. (DE)
Merged into Lee National Corp. 9/2/77
Each share Common $1 par exchanged for $3 cash

MASTEC INC (DE)
Common 10¢ par split (3) for (2) by issuance of (0.5) additional share payable 02/28/1997 to holders of record 02/03/1997 Ex date - 03/03/1997
Reincorporated under the laws of Florida 05/29/1998

MASTECH COMPUTER SYS INC (DE)
Merged into National Information Systems Corp. 11/09/1970
Each share Common 1¢ par exchanged for (0.2857) share Common no par
(See National Information Systems Corp.)

MASTECH CORP (PA)
Common 1¢ par split (2) for (1) by issuance of (1) additional share payable 04/10/1998 to holders of record 03/27/1998
Name changed to iGate Capital Corp. 03/07/2000
iGate Capital Corp. name changed to iGate Corp. 03/25/2002
(See iGate Corp.)

MASTECH HLDGS INC (PA)
Common 1¢ par split (5) for (4) by issuance of (0.25) additional share payable 11/29/2013 to holders of record 11/15/2013 Ex date - 12/02/2013
Name changed to Mastech Digital, Inc. 09/15/2016

MASTER ACQUISITIONS INC (DE)
Merged into Master Products Manufacturing Co., Inc. 12/30/87
Details not available

MASTER ARTISTS CORP. (CA)
Charter revoked for failure to file reports and pay fees 01/03/1966

MASTER CAP CORP (NV)
Name changed to Stresscare Systems, Inc. 04/10/1989

MASTER COMMUNICATIONS CORP (FL)
Common $0.0001 par split (3) for (1) by issuance of (2) additional shares payable 11/24/99 to holders of record 11/22/99
Name changed to i-Incubator.com, Inc. 11/24/99

MASTER COMMUNICATIONS INC (NY)
Charter cancelled and proclaimed dissolved for failure to pay taxes 12/15/1975

MASTER CONSOLIDATED INC. (OH)
Completely liquidated 6/30/67
Each share Common no par exchanged for first and final distribution of (0.2) share Koehring Co. Common $2 par and (0.228) share 5-1/2% Conv. Preferred Ser. H no par
(See Koehring Co.)

MASTER CRAFT CORP (MI)
Name changed to Shaw-Walker Ventures Corp. 08/03/1988
(See Shaw-Walker Ventures Corp.)

MASTER CTL INC (TX)
Merged into Dataflo, Inc. 06/11/1974
Each (150) shares Common par exchanged for (1) share Common 1¢ par
(See Dataflo, Inc.)

MASTER DEVELOPERS INC (IN)
Name changed to Signature Inns, Inc. 01/31/1984
Signature Inns, Inc. merged into Jameson Inns, Inc. 05/10/1999
(See Jameson Inns, Inc.)

MASTER DOWNHOLE CDA INC (AB)
Name changed to Wenzel Downhole Tools Ltd. and Class A Common no par reclassified as Common no par 02/27/1998
(See Wenzel Downhole Tools Ltd.)

MASTER ELECTRIC CO. (OH)
Stock Dividends - 100% 7/15/47; 10% 3/26/51; 10% 12/23/53; 10% 12/21/56
Merged into Reliance Electric & Engineering Co. (OH) 7/30/57
Each share Common exchanged for (0.67637) share Common Reliance Electric & Engineering Co. (OH) reincorporated in Delaware as Reliance Electric Co. 2/28/69
(See Reliance Electric Co.)

MASTER GLAZIERS KARATE INTL INC (DE)
Each share old Common no par exchanged for (0.2) share new Common no par 04/30/1997
Company terminated registration of common stock and is no longer public as of 03/04/2008
Details not available

MASTER GRAPHICS INC (TN)
Plan of reorganization under Chapter 11 Federal Bankruptcy Code effective 3/7/2001
No stockholders' equity

MASTER HOSTS INTL INC (DE)
Merged into International Industries, Inc. (DE) 02/13/1973
Each share Common $1 par exchanged for (1.857) shares Common $1 par
International Industries, Inc. (DE) merged into IHOP Corp. 09/17/1976
(See IHOP Corp.)

MASTER INDS INC (DE)
Each share Common 10¢ par exchanged for (1/3) share Common 30¢ par 4/30/73
Charter cancelled and declared inoperative and void for non-payment of taxes 3/1/81

MASTER METALS MNG LTD (ON)
Charter cancelled and declared dissolved for failure to file returns and pay fees 11/09/1976

MASTER PLAN MINERAL & PETE DEVELOPERS CORP (BERMUDA)
Reincorporated 12/07/1995
Place of incorporation changed from (Canada) to (Bermuda) 12/07/1995
Recapitalized as Isleinvest Ltd. 01/31/1996
Each share Common no par exchanged for (0.2) share Common no par
(See Isleinvest Ltd.)

MASTER PLAYER HOME ENTMT CORP (BC)
Recapitalized as International Player Enterprises Inc. 03/17/1997
Each share Common no par exchanged for (0.25) share Common no par

MASTER PRINTERS BUILDING OPERATING CORP. (NY)
Liquidation completed 5/31/56

MASTER RLTY PPTYS INC (DE)
Name changed 05/14/1999
Each share old Common 1¢ par exchanged for (0.0004) share new Common 1¢ par 04/30/1998
Conv. Preferred Class A 1¢ par split (75) for (1) by issuance of (74) additional shares 06/30/1998
New Common 1¢ par split (75) for (1) by issuance of (74) additional shares 06/30/1998
Name changed from Master Mortgage Investment Fund, Inc. to Master Realty Properties, Inc. 05/14/1999
Company terminated registration of preferred and common stock and is no longer public as of 01/31/2001
Details not available

MASTER RES LTD (NV)
Charter permanently revoked 07/31/2004

MASTER SEC SVCS INC (WA)
Charter expired 07/31/2007

MASTER SILICON CARBIDE INDS INC (NV)
Reincorporated 11/02/2009
State of incorporation changed from (DE) to (NV) 11/02/2009
Charter revoked 08/01/2016

MASTER TIRE & RUBBER CORP.
Name changed to Cooper Tire & Rubber Co. in 1946

MASTER TRANSN COMPUTING CORP (MN)
Company ceased operations due to financial difficulties 04/00/1971
Stockholders' equity unlikely

MASTER VENTURES INC (NV)
Name changed to Magnum Petroleum, Inc. 10/1/90
Magnum Petroleum, Inc. name changed to Magnum Hunter Resources, Inc. 3/18/97 which merged into Cimarex Energy Co. 6/7/2005

MASTERCRAFT ELECTRS CORP (DE)
Charter cancelled and declared inoperative and void for non-payment of taxes 04/15/1971

MASTERCRAFT LITHOGRAPHERS INC (DE)
Completely liquidated 09/28/1990
Each share Common no par exchanged for first and final distribution of $2 cash

MASTERCRAFT MED & INDL CORP (NY)
Merged into Mastercraft Products Corp. 04/01/1990
Each share Common 10¢ par exchanged for (1) share Common 10¢ par

MASTERING INC (DE)
Merged into PLATINUM Technology, Inc. 04/21/1998
Each share Common $0.001 par exchanged for (0.467) share Common $0.001 par
PLATINUM Technology, Inc. name changed to Platinum Technology International Inc. 01/04/1999 which merged into Computer Associates International, Inc. 06/29/1999 which name changed to CA, Inc. 02/01/2006

MASTERMET COBALT MINES LTD (ON)
Name changed to Master Resources & Developments Ltd. 10/15/84

MASTERPIECE GAMES INC (BC)
Recapitalized as Maestro Ventures Ltd. 08/27/2003
Each share Common no par exchanged for (0.2) share Common no par
Maestro Ventures Ltd. recapitalized as Invenio Resources Corp. 10/06/2010 which name changed to Greatbanks Resources Ltd. 02/12/2015

MASTERPIECE QUALITY PRODS INC (BC)
Recapitalized as Aruma Ventures, Inc. 03/21/1997
Each share Common no par exchanged for (0.1) share Common no par
Aruma Ventures, Inc. recapitalized as dot.com Technologies Inc. 09/07/1999 which recapitalized as BCS Collaborative Solutions Inc. 07/12/2002 which recapitalized as BCS Global Networks Inc. 09/02/2003
(See BCS Global Networks Inc.)

MASTERPIECE TECHNOLOGY GROUP INC (UT)
SEC revoked common stock registration 12/04/2009

MASTERS ENERGY CORP (DE)
Merged into Harken Oil & Gas, Inc. 3/18/86
Each (17.45505324) shares Common 1¢ par exchanged for (1) share Common $1 par
Harken Oil & Gas, Inc. name changed to Harken Energy Corp. 1/1/89

which recapitalized as HKN, Inc. 6/6/2007

MASTERS ENERGY INC (AB)
Merged into Zargon Energy Trust 04/29/2009
Each share Common no par exchanged for approximately (0.096) Trust Unit no par and $0.366 cash
Zargon Energy Trust reorganized as Zargon Oil & Gas Ltd. (New) 01/07/2011

MASTERS HLDGS INC (BC)
Name changed to Envirotreat Systems Inc. 01/15/1993
Envirotreat Systems Inc. recapitalized as Treat Systems Inc. 09/02/1999 which name changed to Mega Silver Inc. (BC) 12/18/2007 which reincorporated in Ontario as Mega Precious Metals Inc. 09/14/2009 which merged into Yamana Gold Inc. 06/24/2015

MASTERS INC (NY)
Merged into LMJ Group, Inc. 07/10/1981
Each share Common $1 par exchanged for $10 cash

MASTERS MERCHANDISE MART INC (FL)
Name changed to Congress Video Group, Inc. 10/07/1985
(See Congress Video Group, Inc.)

MASTERS OILS & GAS, LTD. (ON)
Charter cancelled for failure to file reports and pay taxes 7/2/63

MASTERSLINK COMMUNICATIONS INC (NV)
Each share old Common $0.001 par exchanged for (0.01) share new Common no par 08/14/2003
Name changed to IQue Intellectual Properties, Inc. and (9) additional shares issued 12/02/2003
IQue Intellectual Properties, Inc. name changed to Safeguard Security Holdings, Inc. 01/05/2005
(See Safeguard Security Holdings, Inc.)

MASTHEAD RES LTD (AB)
Name changed to C.A. Bancorp Inc. 01/17/2006
C.A. Bancorp Inc. name changed to Crosswinds Holdings Inc. 09/26/2014

MASTIC ASPHALT CORP. (IN)
Name changed to Mastic Corp. 5/1/59
Mastic Corp. merged into Bethlehem Steel Corp. 6/28/74

MASTIC CORP (IN)
Merged into Bethlehem Steel Corp. 6/28/74
Each share Common $1 par exchanged for (0.71556) share Common $8 par
(See Bethlehem Steel Corp.)

MASTORAK LTD (CANADA)
Name changed to Matthew Moody Enterprises Inc. 11/1/82
(See Matthew Moody Enterprises Inc.)

MASTRO INDS INC (NY)
Dissolved by proclamation 6/23/93

MASTT RES INC (BC)
Struck off register and declared dissolved for failure to file returns 9/29/89

MASUPARIA GOLD CORP (BC)
Each share old Common no par exchanged for (0.03333333) share new Common no par 12/16/2005
Each share new Common no par exchanged again for (0.1) share new Common no par 07/17/2009
Name changed to MAS Gold Corp. 04/09/2018

MASURY-YOUNG CO. (MA)
Acquired by Alberto-Culver Co. (Old) 5/20/65

Details not available

MATACHEWAN CDN GOLD LTD (ON)
Merged into Triton Explorations Ltd. 12/15/69
Each share Capital Stock $1 par exchanged for (0.166666) share Capital Stock $1 par
(See Triton Explorations Ltd.)

MATACHEWAN HUB PIONEER MINES, LTD. (ON)
Charter surrendered for failure to file reports and pay taxes in 1949

MATADOR CAP INC (AB)
Name changed to Canadian Public Venture Equities I Inc. (AB) 07/24/2003
Canadian Public Venture Equities I Inc. (AB) reorganized in Ontario as Vanguard Response Systems Inc. 11/24/2003 which name changed to Allen-Vanguard Corp. 03/25/2005
(See Allen-Vanguard Corp.)

MATADOR DEVS LTD (BC)
Recapitalized as Betina Resources Inc. 03/12/1975
Each share Capital Stock no par exchanged for (0.2) share Capital Stock no par
Betina Resources Inc. recapitalized as Nevcal Resources Ltd. 09/06/1983 which recapitalized as Arapahoe Mining Corp. 12/03/1986 which recapitalized as Salus Resource Corp. 5/6/96 which name changed to Brandon Gold Corp. 12/04/1996 which recapitalized as Redmond Ventures Corp. 09/16/1999 which recapitalized as Crown Point Ventures Ltd. (BC) 03/12/2002 which reincorporated in Alberta as Crown Point Energy Inc. 07/31/2012

MATADOR EXPL INC (AB)
Merged into Committee Bay Resources Ltd. 12/01/2005
Each share Common no par exchanged for (0.72) share Common no par and (0.5) share Dahava Resources Ltd. Common no par
(See each company's listing)

MATAGORDA DRILLING & EXPL CO (TX)
Each share old Common 1¢ par exchanged for (0.5) share new Common 1¢ par 03/02/1981
Name changed to Stanley Well Service, Inc. 12/13/1983
Stanley Well Service, Inc. merged into Alliance Well Service, Inc. 09/28/1984 which recapitalized as Alliance Northwest Industries, Inc. 07/30/1993
(See Alliance Northwest Industries, Inc.)

MATAGORDA OIL ROYALTY TRUST
Leases expired and trust terminated 00/00/1948
Details not available

MATAMEC EXPLORATIONS INC (QC)
Merged into Quebec Precious Metals Corp. 07/05/2018
Each share Common no par exchanged for (0.26769731) share Common no par
Note: Unexchanged certificates will be cancelled and become without value 07/05/2024

MATANUSKA VALLEY BK (ANCHORAGE, AK)
Capital Stock $100 par changed to $10 par and (9) additional shares issued in 1963
Changed location from (Palmer, AK) to (Anchorage, AK) 1/7/71
Matanuska Valley Bank (Anchorage, AK) name changed to Alaska Bank of Commerce (Anchorage, AK) 3/3/73 which name changed to First Interstate Bank of Alaska (Anchorage, AK) 10/6/83 which

reorganized as First Interstat Corp. of Alaska 8/1/85
(See First Interstate Corp. of Alaska)

MATANZAS-AMERICAN SUGAR CO.
Acquired by Hershey Chocolate Corp. in 1929
Details not available

MATARROW LEAD MINES LTD. (ON)
Recapitalized as Consolidated Matarrow Mines Ltd. on a (1) for (4) basis 3/9/53
Consolidated Matarrow Mines Ltd. recapitalized as Jeanette Minerals Ltd. 6/16/55
(See Jeanette Minerals Ltd.)

MATAV-CABLE SYS MEDIA LTD (ISRAEL)
ADR agreement terminated 6/30/2006
Each Sponsored ADR for Ordinary NIS1 par exchanged for $13.39585 cash

MATCH CORP. OF AMERICA (DE)
Charter cancelled and declared inoperative and void for non-payment of taxes 3/18/25

MATCHNET PLC (ENGLAND & WALES)
Name changed to Spark Networks PLC (England & Wales) 01/10/2005
Spark Networks PLC (England & Wales) reorganized in Delaware as Spark Networks, Inc. 07/09/2007 which merged into Spark Networks S.E. 11/03/2017

MATCHTRADE INC (DE)
Assets assigned for the benefit of creditors 09/23/2014
Stockholders' equity unlikely

MATCO ENTERPRISES INC (NV)
Recapitalized as PetroQuest Resources, Inc. 11/30/2005
Each share new Common $0.0005 par exchanged for (0.2) share Common $0.005 par

MATCO RAVARY INC (QC)
Name changed 04/03/1992
Name changed from Matco Mart Inc. to Matco Ravary Inc. 04/03/1992
Common no par reclassified as Class B Multiple no par 05/02/1994
Name changed to MCO Capital Inc. 06/13/2005
MCO Capital Inc. recapitalized as IOU Financial Inc. 02/28/2011

MATEC CORP (DE)
Reincorporated 07/01/1987
State of incorporation changed from (NY) to (DE) 07/01/1987
Reorganized under the laws of Maryland 07/02/1998
Each share Common 5¢ par exchanged for (1) share Common 5¢ par to reflect a (1) for (100) reverse split followed by a (100) for (1) forward split
Note: Holders of (99) shares or fewer received $4.03 cash per share
Matec Corp. (MD) name changed to Valpey-Fisher Corp. 06/03/2002
(See Valpey-Fisher Corp.)

MATEC CORP (MD)
Common 5¢ par split (3) for (2) by issuance of (0.5) additional share payable 11/27/2000 to holders of record 11/09/2000 Ex date - 11/28/2000
Name changed to Valpey-Fisher Corp. 06/03/2002
(See Valpey-Fisher Corp.)

MATECH CORP (DE)
SEC revoked common stock registration 03/24/2014

MATERIAL SCIENCE INDS INC (DE)
Name changed to Faratron Corp. 04/18/1972
(See Faratron Corp.)

MATERIAL SCIENCES CORP (DE)
Common 2¢ par split (3) for (2) by

issuance of (0.5) additional share 04/06/1992
Common 2¢ par split (3) for (2) by issuance of (0.5) additional share 07/28/1994
Preferred Stock Purchase Rights declared for Common stockholders of record 07/02/1996 were redeemed at $0.01 per right 05/16/2003 for holders of record 04/28/2003
Acquired by Insight Equity Holdings LLC 03/30/2014
Each share Common 2¢ par exchanged for $12.75 cash

MATERIAL SCIENCES INC (DE)
Class A Common 5¢ par changed to $0.025 par and (1) additional share issued 05/08/1970
Charter cancelled and declared inoperative and void for non-payment of taxes 03/01/1975

MATERIAL SERVICE CORP. (IL)
Merged into General Dynamics Corp. and each share Common $10 par exchanged for (35.884655) shares Conv. Preference no par 12/31/59

MATERIAL TECHNOLOGIES INC (DE)
Each share old Class A Common $0.001 par exchanged for (0.001) share new Class A Common $0.001 par 09/23/2003
Each share new Class A Common $0.001 par exchanged again for (0.00333333) share new Class A Common $0.001 par 11/08/2006
Recapitalized as Matech Corp. 10/03/2008
Each share Class A Common $0.001 par exchanged for (0.001) share Class A Common $0.001 par
(See Matech Corp.)

MATERIAL TECHNOLOGY INC (DE)
Recapitalized as Securfone America Inc. 8/18/97
Each share Common $0.001 par exchanged for (0.1) share Common $0.001 par
Securfone America Inc. name changed to Ixata Group, Inc. 2/4/2000 which name changed to RFP Express Inc. 7/25/2001

MATERIALS PROTN TECHNOLOGIES INC (ON)
Delisted from Toronto Venture Stock Exchange 06/20/2003

MATERIALS RESH CORP (NY)
Common $1 par split (3) for (2) by issuance of (0.5) additional share 3/9/79
Common $1 par split (2) for (1) by issuance of (1) additional share 2/1/80
Common $1 par split (4) for (3) by issuance of (1/3) additional share 3/13/81
Stock Dividend - 25% 3/10/78
Merged into Sony MRC Acquisition Corp. 10/30/89
Each share Common $1 par exchanged for $14 cash

MATERIALS TECHNOLOGY INC (NJ)
Adjudicated bankrupt 12/02/1974
Stockholders' equity unlikely

MATERIALS TECHNOLOGY LTD (AUSTRALIA)
ADR agreement terminated 01/25/1989
ADR holders' equity unlikely

MATES INVT FD INC (DE)
Name changed to Rainbow Fund Inc. 10/1/75
(See Rainbow Fund Inc.)

MATEWAN BANCSHARES INC (DE)
Stock Dividends - 10% 6/15/95; 10% payable 4/15/98 to holders of record 4/1/98
Acquired by BB&T Corp. 8/30/99
Each share 7-1/2% Conv. Preferred

Ser. A $1 par exchanged for (0.8375) share Common $5 par
Each share Common $1 par exchanged for (0.67) share Common $5 par

MATH BOX INC (MD)
Name changed to MBI Business Centers, Inc. 06/27/1985
(See MBI Business Centers, Inc.)

MATHEMATICA INC (NJ)
Common 10¢ par split (3) for (2) by issuance of (0.5) additional share 04/19/1982
Merged into Martin Marietta Corp. (Old) 07/22/1983
Each share Common 10¢ par exchanged for (0.4689) share Common $1 par
Matin Marietta Corp. (Old) merged into Martin Marietta Corp. (New) 04/02/1993 which merged into Lockheed Martin Corp. 03/15/1995

MATHEMATICAL APPLICATIONS GROUP INC (DE)
Name changed to Advanced Technology Group International, Inc. 3/29/74 which name changed back to Mathematical Applications Group, Inc. 8/5/75
Stock Dividend - 50% 11/14/80
Dissolved 9/1/87
Each share Common 5¢ par exchanged for $0.15 cash

MATHERS FD INC (MD)
Stock Dividend - 100% 02/26/1969
Reincorporated under the laws of Delaware as GAMCO Mathers Fund and Common $1 par reclassified as Class AAA $0.001 par 10/01/1999
(See GAMCO Mathers Fund)

MATHES MANUFACTURING CO. (TX)
Name changed to Curtis Mathes Manufacturing Co. 8/28/59
Curtis Mathes Manufacturing Co. merged into Curtis Mathes Corp. 1/19/70

MATHESON CO., INC. (NJ)
Each share Common no par exchanged for (4) shares Common $1 par in 1953
6% Preferred $20 par called for redemption 5/1/59
Merged into Will Ross, Inc. 7/13/67
Each share Class A Ser. 1 no par exchanged for (1.032) shares Common $1.25 par
Each share Common $1 par exchanged for (0.8411) share Common $1.25 par
Will Ross, Inc. merged into Searle (G.D.) & Co. (Del.) 12/31/73
(See Searle (G.D.) & Co. (Del.))

MATHEWS CO (MI)
Charter declared inoperative and void for failure to file annual reports 05/15/1977

MATHEWS CONVEYER CO. (PA)
Each share Common no par exchanged for (10) shares Common $1 par in 1946
Stock Dividends - 10% 12/19/52; 10% 12/18/53; 100% 2/24/56
Merged into Rex Chainbelt Inc. 12/31/64
Each share Common $1 par exchanged for (0.51988) share Capital Stock $10 par
Rex Chainbelt Inc. name changed to Rexnord Inc. 1/26/73
(See Rexnord Inc.)

MATHEWS INDUSTRIES, INC.
Acquired by Mathews Co. 00/00/1930
Details not available

MATHIAS (A.L.) CO. (MD)
Liquidated 2/18/64
Each share Common no par exchanged for (0.25) share Servomation Corp. Common $1 par
(See Servomation Corp.)

MATHIESON ALKALI WORKS, INC.
Name changed to Mathieson Chemical Corp. in 1948
Mathieson Chemical Corp. merged into Olin Mathieson Chemical Corp. in 1954 which name changed to Olin Corp. 9/1/69

MATHIESON CHEMICAL CORP. (VA)
Each share Common no par exchanged for (2) shares Common $5 par in 1950
Each share 7% Preferred $100 par exchanged for (4) shares Common $5 par in 1951
Merged into Olin Mathieson Chemical Corp. share for share in 1954
Olin Mathieson Chemical Corp. name changed to Olin Corp. 9/1/69

MATHIESON HYDROCARBON CHEMICAL CORP.
Merged into Mathieson Chemical Corp. in 1951
Each share Common $1 par exchanged for (0.666666) share Common $5 par
Mathieson Chemical Corp. merged into Olin Mathieson Chemical Corp. in 1954 which name changed to Olin Corp. 9/1/69

MATHSOFT INC (MA)
Reincorporated under the laws of Delaware as Insightful Corp. 06/07/2001
(See Insightful Corp.)

MATHSTAR INC (DE)
Each share old Common 1¢ par exchanged for (0.2) share new Common 1¢ par 05/27/2008
Name changed to Sajan, Inc. 02/26/2010
(See Sajan, Inc.)

MATIADEKA VENTURES INC (ON)
Name changed to Avante Security Corp. 04/04/2008
Avante Security Corp. name changed to Avante Logixx Inc. 10/13/2010

MATICA GRAPHITE INC (BC)
Name changed to Matica Enterprises Inc. 07/04/2014

MATINECOCK BK (LOCUST VALLEY, NY)
Merged into Hempstead Bank (Hempstead, NY) 08/29/1969
Each share Capital Stock $2.50 par exchanged for (1.387347) shares Capital Stock $5 par
Hempstead Bank (Hempstead, NY) merged into United Bank Corp. of New York 09/30/1977 which name changed to Norstar Bancorp Inc. 01/04/1982
(See Norstar Bancorp Inc.)

MATINENDA URANIUM MINES LTD. (ON)
Charter cancelled for failure to file reports and pay taxes 12/7/59

MATLACK SYS INC (DE)
Common $1 par split (3) for (2) by issuance of (0.5) additional share 09/15/1994
Chapter 11 Federal Bankruptcy proceedings converted to Chapter 7 on 10/18/2002
Stockholders' equity unlikely

MATLO OILS LTD. (AB)
Acquired by Sweet Grass Oils Ltd. in 1952
Each (2.5) shares Capital Stock no par exchanged for (1) share Capital Stock 25¢ par
Sweet Grass Oils Ltd. recapitalized as Great Sweet Grass Oils Ltd. 4/22/54 which was recapitalized as Kardar Canadian Oils Ltd. 6/29/62
(See Kardar Canadian Oils Ltd.)

MATLOCK COMMUNICATIONS COS INC (UT)
Recapitalized as Persimmon Corp. (UT) 06/15/1989

Each (15) shares Common $0.001 par exchanged for (1) share Common $0.015 par
Persimmon Corp. (UT) reorganized in Delaware as Amalgamated Entertainment Inc. 01/29/1992 which name changed to MegaMedia Networks, Inc. 11/15/1999
(See MegaMedia Networks, Inc.)

MATNIC RES INC (BC)
Each share old Common no par exchanged for (0.5) share new Common no par 01/15/2014
Name changed to Graphene 3D Lab Inc. 08/11/2014

MATODZI RES LTD (SOUTH AFRICA)
Name changed to White Water Resources Ltd. 03/02/2009
White Water Resources Ltd. name changed to Goliath Gold Mining Ltd. 05/26/2011
(See Goliath Gold Mining Ltd.)

MATONA GOLDS LTD. (ON)
Charter cancelled for failure to file reports and pay taxes 11/27/61

MATRIA HEALTHCARE INC (DE)
Each share old Common 1¢ par exchanged for (0.25) share new Common 1¢ par 12/06/2000
New Common 1¢ par split (3) for (2) by issuance of (0.5) additional share payable 02/04/2005 to holders of record 01/19/2005 Ex date - 02/07/2005
Merged into Inverness Medical Innovations, Inc. 05/09/2008
Each share new Common 1¢ par exchanged for (0.08125) share Conv. Perpetual Preferred Ser. B $0.001 par and $6.50 cash
Inverness Medical Innovations, Inc. name changed to Alere Inc. 07/14/2010
(See Alere Inc.)

MATRIKON INC (AB)
Merged into Honeywell International Inc. 06/28/2010
Each share Common no par exchanged for $4.50 cash
Note: Unexchanged certificates were cancelled and became without value 06/28/2016

MATRITECH INC (DE)
Assets transferred to MZT Holdings, Inc. 12/12/2007
(See MZT Holdings, Inc.)

MATRIX ASSET MGMT INC (CANADA)
Voluntarily dissolved 01/27/2017
No stockholders' equity

MATRIX BANCORP CAP TR I (DE)
10% Guaranteed Trust Preferred Securities called for redemption at $25 on 10/13/2006

MATRIX BANCORP INC (CO)
Name changed 12/09/1998
Name changed from Matrix Capital Corp. to Matrix Bancorp, Inc. 12/09/1998
Name changed to United Western Bancorp, Inc. 09/07/2006
(See United Western Bancorp, Inc.)

MATRIX CONCEPTS INC (CA)
Merged into University Patents, Inc. 09/18/1972
Each share Common 10¢ par exchanged for (0.32) share Common $1 par and (0.16) Common Stock Purchase Warrant expiring 07/31/1979
University Patents, Inc. name changed to Competitive Technologies, Inc. 12/20/1994 which name changed to Calmare Therapeutics Inc. 06/04/2015

MATRIX CORP. (DE)
Certificates dated after 04/19/1988
Acquired by Agfa Gevaert Inc. 11/10/1988

Each share Common $1 par exchanged for $10 cash

MATRIX CORP (DE)
Certificates dated prior to 04/15/1972
Charter cancelled and declared inoperative and void for non-payment of taxes 04/15/1972

MATRIX CORP (NJ)
Common $1 par split (5) for (4) by issuance of (0.25) additional share 04/02/1979
Common $1 par split (4) for (3) by issuance of (0.33333333) additional share 04/25/1980
Common $1 par split (3) for (2) by issuance of (0.5) additional share 04/23/1981
Common $1 par split (5) for (4) by issuance of (0.25) additional share 12/17/1982
Common $1 par split (3) for (2) by issuance (0.5) additional share 09/29/1983
Common $1 par split (5) for (4) by issuance of (0.25) additional share 09/28/1984
Common $1 par split (5) for (4) by issuance of (0.25) additional share 09/20/1985
Reincorporated under the laws of Delaware 04/19/1988
(See Matrix Corp. (DE))

MATRIX ELECTRONICS, INC. (CA)
Business terminated 10/22/63
No stockholders' equity

MATRIX ENERGY INC (BC)
Recapitalized as Promax Energy Inc. (BC) 2/3/99
Each share Common no par exchanged for (0.2) share Common no par
Promax Energy Inc. (BC) reincorporated in Alberta 6/8/200
(See Promax Energy Inc.)

MATRIX ENERGY SVCS CORP (NV)
Common 2¢ par split (3) for (1) by issuance of (2) additional shares payable 06/28/2002 to holders of record 06/17/2002
Common 2¢ par changed to $0.002 par 10/31/2002
Each share Common $0.002 par exchanged for (0.001) share Common $0.001 par 11/23/2007
Note: Holders of between (500) and (500,000) shares received (500) shares
Holders of (499) shares or fewer received no distribution
Name changed to Shi Corp. 04/09/2009

MATRIX INCOME FD (AB)
Merged into MINT Income Fund 05/24/2007
Each Unit no par received (0.68846815) Trust Unit no par

MATRIX INVTS LTD (AB)
Name changed 3/26/86
Name changed from Matrix Exploration Ltd. to Matrix Investments Ltd. 3/26/86
Voluntarily dissolved 3/22/93
Each share Common no par received first and final distribution of $0.034613 cash

MATRIX MEMBRANES INC (CO)
Name changed 06/02/1989
Each share Common 1¢ par exchanged for (0.125) share Common 2¢ par 09/04/1987
Name changed from Matrix Medica, Inc. to Matrix Membranes, Inc. 06/02/1989
Dissolved 01/01/1995
Details not available

MATRIX PETE INC (BC)
Acquired by Berens Energy Ltd. 12/12/2003
Each share Common no par

exchanged for (0.51) share Common no par
(See Berens Energy Ltd.)

MATRIX PHARMACEUTICAL INC (DE)
Merged into Chiron Corp. 3/29/2002
Each share Common 1¢ par exchanged for $2.21 cash

MATRIX RESH & DEV CORP (NH)
Class A Common $1 par and Class B Common $1 par reclassified as Common $1 par 02/09/1965
Each share Common $ par exchanged for (0.1) share Common no par 06/01/1965
Merged into American Electromedics Corp. 12/18/1980
Each share Common no par exchanged for $1.50 cash

MATRIX SCIENCE CORP (DE)
Common 1¢ par split (2) for (1) by issuance of (1) additional share 05/07/1987
Acquired by AMP Inc. (NJ) 08/17/1988
Each share Common 1¢ par exchanged for (0.3417) Endorsed Share of Common no par
AMP Inc. (NJ) reincorporated in Pennsylvania 04/21/1989 which merged into Tyco International Ltd. (Bermuda) 04/01/1999 which reincorporated in Switzerland 03/17/2009 which merged into Johnson Controls International PLC 09/06/2016

MATRIX TELECOMMUNICATIONS LTD (AUSTRALIA)
Each Unsponsored ADR for Ordinary A$0.50 par exchanged for (0.25) Sponsored ADR for Ordinary A$0.20 par 12/06/1993
ADR agreement terminated 09/25/1995
Details not available

MATRIX VENTURES INC (NV)
Name changed to Fsona Systems Corp. 04/19/2007
(See Fsona Systems Corp.)

MATRIXONE INC (DE)
Merged into Dassault Systemes S.A. 05/11/2006
Each share Common 1¢ par exchanged for $7.25 cash

MATRIXX INITIATIVES INC (DE)
Acquired by Wonder Holdings Acquisition Corp. 02/22/2011
Each share Common $0.001 par exchanged for $8.75 cash

MATRIXX RESOURCE HLDGS INC (DE)
Each share old Common $0.001 par exchanged for (0.004) share new Common new Common $0.001 par 11/20/2007
SEC revoked common stock registration 03/06/2013

MATSON INTL CORP (DE)
Charter cancelled and declared inoperative and void for non-payment of taxes 3/1/86

MATSON NAV CO (CA)
Each share Capital Stock $100 par exchanged for (5) shares Capital Stock no par 00/00/1936
Capital Stock no par split (3) for (1) by issuance of (2) additional shares 07/17/1968
Merged into Alexander & Baldwin, Inc. (Old) 03/24/1969
Each share Capital Stock no par exchanged for (1.6) shares Common no par
Alexander & Baldwin, Inc. (Old) name changed to Alexander & Baldwin Holdings, Inc. 06/06/2012 which name changed to Matson, Inc. 06/29/2012

MATSUSHITA ELEC INDL LTD (JAPAN)
Under new plan of deposit agreement each ADR for Dollar-Validated Common 50 Yen par exchanged for (1) ADR for Common 50 Yen par 04/28/1970
After 11/28/1970 old ADR's for Dollar-Validated Common will be exchanged for cash
ADR's for Common 50 Yen par split (10) for (1) by issuance of (9) additional ADR's payable 12/08/2000 to holders of record 12/01/2000
(Note: In 1969 Cusip assigned 576879 20 9 to ADR's for Dollar-Validated Common and has not assigned a new number to ADR's for Common which are different securities and of different value. Suggest caution and use of your own number to differentiate)
Stock Dividends - 20% 01/28/1971; 10% 02/08/1974; 10% 02/09/1979; 10% 02/03/1981; 10% 02/04/1982; 10% 02/01/1985
Name changed to Panasonic Corp. 10/01/2008

MATSUSHITA ELEC WKS LTD (JAPAN)
ADR's for Common JPY 50 par split (11) for (10) by issuance of (0.1) additional ADR 02/05/1992
Stock Dividends - 10% 02/20/1976; 10% 03/07/1977; 10% 03/14/1979; 10% 02/13/1981
Name changed to Panasonic Electric Works Co. Ltd. 10/01/2008
(See Panasonic Electric Works Co. Ltd.)

MATT BERRY INC (BC)
Recapitalized 12/31/1992
Recapitalized from Matt Berry Ltd. to Matt Berry Inc. 12/31/1992
Each share Common no par exchanged for (0.5) share Common no par
Recapitalized as SIRIT Technologies Inc. 12/23/1993
Each share Common no par exchanged for (0.33333333) share Common no par
SIRIT Technologies Inc. was acquired by iTech Capital Corp. 11/01/2002 which name changed to Sirit Inc. 05/05/2003
(See Sirit Inc.)

MATTA-KING MINING CORP. LTD. (ON)
Merged into Bayfor Corp. Inc. in May 1972
Each share Capital Stock no par exchanged for (0.142857) share Capital Stock no par
Bayfor Corp. Inc. charter cancelled 2/20/80

MATTAGAMI EXPLORERS CORP. (QC)
Charter annulled for failure to file annual reports 9/29/79

MATTAGAMI LAKE MINES LTD (QC)
Capital Stock $1 par changed to no par and (1) additional share issued 5/28/74
Capital Stock no par reclassified as Conv. Class A Capital Stock no par 8/11/75
Merged into Noranda Mines Ltd. 3/30/79
Each (2.25) shares Conv. Class A Capital Stock no par exchanged for (1) share Conv. Class A no par
Each (2.25) shares Conv. Class B Capital Stock no par exchanged for (1) share Conv. Class A no par
Noranda Mines Ltd. name changed to Noranda Inc. 5/28/84 which name changed to Falconbridge Ltd. (New) 2005 on 7/1/2005
(See Falconbridge Ltd. (New) 2005)

MATTATUCK BK & TR CO (WATERBURY, CT)
Merged into Hartford National Corp. 1/29/83
Each share Capital Stock $10 par exchanged for (0.31) share Common $6.25 par
Hartford National Corp. merged into Shawmut National Corp. 2/29/88 which merged into Fleet Financial Group Inc. (New) 11/30/95 which name changed to Fleet Boston Corp. 10/1/99 which name changed to FleetBoston Financial Corp. 4/18/2000 which merged into Bank of America Corp. 4/1/2004

MATTAWIN GOLD MINES LTD. (ON)
Charter revoked for failure to file reports and pay fees 6/3/65

MATTEL INC (CA)
Common $1 par split (5) for (2) by issuance of (1.5) additional shares 02/09/1962
Reincorporated under the laws of Delaware 05/31/1968
$25 Conv. Preferred Ser. A $1 par called for redemption 06/17/1985
15.25% Exchangeable Preference Ser. B-1 1¢ par called for redemption 05/12/1986
15.75% Exchangeable Preference Ser. B-2 1¢ par called for redemption 05/12/1986
5% Conv. Preference Ser. C 1¢ par called for redemption 08/27/1987
Each Depositary Preferred Ser. C exchanged for (0.400637) share Common $1 par 07/01/1999
Each share Mandatorily Conv. Preferred Ser. C exchanged for (10.015914) shares Common $1 par 07/01/1999
(Additional Information in Active)

MATTERSIGHT CORP (DE)
Acquired by NICE Ltd. 08/20/2018
Each share 7% Conv. Preferred Ser. B 1¢ par exchanged for $7.80 cash
Each share Common 1¢ par exchanged for $2.70 cash

MATTHEW MOODY ENTERPRISES INC. (CANADA)
Company went private 12/31/85
Details not available

MATTHEWS & WRIGHT GROUP INC (DE)
Name changed to Helmstar Group Inc. 12/02/1991
Helmstar Group Inc. name changed to CareerEngine Network, Inc. 03/28/2000 which name changed to CNE Group, Inc. 06/09/2003 which name changed to Arrow Resources Development, Inc. 12/20/2005

MATTHEWS CORP. (NV)
Charter revoked for non-compliance of Nevada laws 3/2/64

MATTHEWS ROTARY PRESS, INC. (CA)
Adjudicated bankrupt 6/17/64
No stockholders' equity

MATTHEWS STUDIO EQUIP GROUP (CA)
Assets sold for the benefit of creditors 09/19/2001
No stockholders' equity

MATTHIESSEN & HEGELER ZINC CO (IL)
Common $25 par and Common no par changed to $20 par 00/00/1948
Common $20 par changed to $10 par and (1) additional share issued 01/05/1967
Ceased operations 07/25/1978
No stockholders' equity

MATTMAN SPECIALTY VEHS INC (NV)
Name changed to Remote Surveillance Technologies, Inc. 01/11/2007
Remote Surveillance Technologies,
Inc. name changed to Stratera, Inc. 07/15/2008 which recapitalized as Gulf West Investment Properties, Inc. 12/16/2009

MATTMAR MINERALS INC (NV)
Reincorporated under the laws of Delaware 09/19/2008

MATTRESS FIRM HLDG CORP (DE)
Acquired by Steinhoff International Holdings N.V. 09/16/2016
Each share Common 1¢ par exchanged for $64 cash

MATTSON TECHNOLOGY INC (DE)
Reincorporated 09/00/1997
Place of incorporation changed from (CA) to (DE) and Common no par changed to $0.001 par 09/00/1997
Acquired by Beijing E-Town Dragon Semiconductor Industry Investment Center L.P. 05/11/2016
Each share Common $0.001 par exchanged for $3.80 cash

MATURE CONCEPTS INC (DE)
Charter cancelled and declared inoperative and void for non-payment of taxes 03/01/1991

MAUCH CHUNK TR CO (JIM THORPE, PA)
Common $1 par split (3) for (1) by issuance of (2) additional shares payable 5/31/98 to holders of record 5/10/98
Reorganized as Mauch Chunk Trust Financial Corp. 1/1/2002
Each share Common $1 par exchanged for (1) share Common no par

MAUCHLY ASSOCIATES, INC. (PA)
Completely liquidated 10/11/68
Each share Common no par exchanged for first and final distribution of (1.7) shares Scientific Resources Corp. Common 10¢ par
(See Scientific Resources Corp.)

MAUCHLY MGMT SVCS INC (DE)
Charter cancelled and declared inoperative and void for non-payment of taxes 03/01/1976

MAUD MULLER CANDY CO. (OH)
See - Muller (Maud) Candy Co.

MAUDE LAKE EXPL LTD (ON)
Recapitalized as Maudore Minerals Ltd. 11/10/2004
Each share Common no par exchanged for (0.16666666) share Common no par
(See Maudore Minerals Ltd.)

MAUDEGASCON GOLD MINES, LTD. (ON)
Charter cancelled in 1952

MAUDIES FLEA MKT LTD (CO)
Charter cancelled and proclaimed dissolved for failure to file annual reports and pay taxes 01/01/1981

MAUDORE MINERALS LTD (ON)
Assets assigned under the Bankruptcy and Insolvency Act 05/16/2016
No stockholders' equity

MAUI AGRICULTURAL CO. LTD.
Merged into Hawaiian Commercial & Sugar Co. Ltd. on a (3) for (1) basis 00/00/1948
Hawaiian Commercial & Sugar Co. Ltd. merged into Alexander & Baldwin Inc. (Old) 01/01/1962 which name changed to Alexander & Baldwin Holdings, Inc. 06/06/2012 which name changed to Matson, Inc. 06/29/2012

MAUI CAP CORP (CO)
Each share Common $0.0001 par exchanged for (0.005) share Common no par 3/8/95
Reincorporated under the laws of Nevada as Charter Communications International, Inc. 4/15/96
Charter Communications

International, Inc. name changed to Pointe Communications Corp. 9/9/98 which merged into Telscape International Inc. (New) 6/2/2000
(See Telscape International Inc. (New))

MAUI ELECTRIC CO. LTD. (HI)
Merged into Hawaiian Electric Co., Inc. 11/1/68
Each share Common $10 par exchanged for (1) share $1.44 Conv. Preferred Ser. L $20 par

MAUI GEN STORE INC (NY)
Recapitalized as China Digital Animation Development, Inc. 02/05/2009
Each share Common $0.001 par exchanged for (0.04) share Common $0.001 par
(See China Digital Animation Development, Inc.)

MAUI PINEAPPLE CO. LTD. (HI)
Name changed to Maui Land & Pineapple Co., Inc. 9/11/69

MAUL BROS INC (NJ)
Common 25¢ par split (2) for (1) by issuance of (1) additional share 12/1/61
Common 25¢ par split (2) for (1) by issuance of (1) additional share 1/16/69
Stock Dividend - 10% 11/15/76
Merged into Maul Technology Corp. 9/30/77
Each share Common 25¢ par exchanged for (1) share Common no par
(See Maul Technology Corp.)

MAUL MACOTTA CORP (MI)
Stock Dividends - 10% 04/14/1950; 10% 01/31/1952
Name changed to Macotta Corp. 09/28/1966
(See Macotta Corp.)

MAUL TECHNOLOGY CORP (IN)
Merged into L-G-M Corp. 12/18/1981
Each share Common no par exchanged for $9 cash

MAULE INDS INC (FL)
Each share Common $1 par exchanged for (1/3) share Common $3 par 5/8/57
Common $3 par split (3) for (2) by issuance of (0.5) additional share 6/30/74
Stock Dividend - 10% 2/10/67
Adjudicated bankrupt 12/16/77
No stockholders' equity

MAUMEE COLLIERIES CO. (OH)
Acquired by Peabody Coal Co. in 1959
Peabody Coal Co. name changed to PDY Coal Co. 3/29/68 which liquidation completed 3/31/71

MAUNA CORP (DE)
Name changed to White Hall Investments, Inc. 7/10/90
(See White Hall Investments, Inc.)

MAUNA KEA SUGAR INC (HI)
Merged into Brewer (C.) & Co., Ltd. 04/25/1973
Each share Common $10 par exchanged for $13.50 cash

MAUNA LOA MACADAMIA PARTNERS L P (DE)
Name changed to ML Macadamia Orchards L.P. 09/16/1998
ML Macadamia Orchards L.P. name changed to Royal Hawaiian Orchards, L.P. 10/15/2012 which name changed to Hawaiian Macadamia Nut Orchards, L.P. 10/17/2018

MAURY FED SVGS BK (COLUMBIA, TN)
Acquired by Trans Financial Bancorp, Inc. 03/27/1992
Each share Common $1 par exchanged for $18.50 cash

MAUST COAL & COKE CORP (WV)
Liquidation completed
Each share Common $1 par received initial distribution of $2.25 cash 4/5/73
Each share Common $1 par received second and final distribution of $0.54 cash 2/10/78
Certificates were not required to be surrendered and are now valueless

MAVEN MEDIA HLDGS INC (DE)
Name changed to Waste2Energy Holdings, Inc. 07/22/2019
(See Waste2Energy Holdings, Inc.)

MAVENIR SYS INC (DE)
Merged into Mitel Networks Corp. 04/29/2015
Each share Common $0.001 par exchanged for (1.832) shares Common no par

MAVERICK DRILLING & EXPL LTD (AUSTRALIA)
Name changed to Freedom Oil & Gas Ltd. 11/14/2016

MAVERICK MINES & OILS LTD (AB)
Recapitalized as Peregrine Petroleum Ltd. 05/15/1972
Each share Capital Stock no par exchanged for (0.2) share Capital Stock no par
Peregrine Petroleum Ltd. recapitalized as Peregrine Oil & Gas Ltd. 09/15/1994 which merged into Surge Petroleum Corp. 07/07/2000 which merged into Innova Exploration Ltd. 04/16/2004
(See Innova Exploration Ltd.)

MAVERICK MTN RES LTD (BC)
Merged into Pioneer Metals Corp. (Old) 9/26/86
Each (2.4) shares Common no par exchanged for (1) share Common no par
(See Pioneer Metals Corp. (Old))

MAVERICK NATURALITE BEEF CORP (BC)
Name changed to Golden Iskut Resources Inc. 09/06/1988
Golden Iskut Resources Inc. merged into Aegis Resources Ltd. 08/01/1990 which recapitalized as New Aegis Resources Ltd. 03/17/1993 which was acquired by Norcan Resources Ltd. 08/19/1994 which recapitalized as Odyssey Exploration Inc. 06/07/2000 which recapitalized as Consolidated Odyssey Exploration Inc. 12/08/2000 which reorganized as Odyssey Petroleum Corp. 08/25/2005 which recapitalized as Petrichor Energy Inc. 03/03/2011

MAVERICK OIL & GAS INC (NV)
Each share old Common $0.001 par exchanged for (0.02) share new Common $0.001 par 10/24/2008
SEC revoked common stock registration 03/04/20013

MAVERICK RESTAURANT CORP (KS)
Name changed to Amarillo Mesquite Grill, Inc. 5/27/97
(See Amarillo Mesquite Grill, Inc.)

MAVERICK TUBE CDA LTD (AB)
Each Exchangeable Share no par exchanged for (1) share Maverick Tube Corp. Common 1¢ par 9/30/2005
(See Maverick Tube Corp.)

MAVERICK TUBE CORP (DE)
Common 1¢ par split (2) for (1) by issuance of (1) additional share payable 8/21/97 to holders of record 8/12/97
Merged into Tenaris S.A. 10/5/2006
Each share Common 1¢ par exchanged for $65 cash

MAVES COFFEE INC (NY)
Completely liquidated 03/18/1977
Each share Common 1¢ par exchanged for first and final distribution of $0.666 cash

MAVESA S A (VENEZUELA)
Sponsored ADR's for Common split (3) for (2) by issuance of (0.5) additional ADR payable 05/22/1996 to holders of record 05/13/1996
Each 144A Sponsored ADR for Common exchanged for (1) Sponsored ADR for Common 07/07/1997
Stock Dividend - 33% 03/16/1994
ADR agreement terminated 05/29/2001
Each Sponsored ADR for Common exchanged for (60) shares Common

MAVOR SYS CORP (DE)
Name changed to Toltec Corp. 12/22/71
(See Toltec Corp.)

MAVRIX BALANCED INCOME & GROWTH TR (ON)
Merged into Mavrix Canadian Income Trust Fund 10/02/2006
Each Trust Unit no par received (0.903638) Class A Unit
Mavrix Canadian Income Trust Fund name changed to Mavrix Balanced Monthly Pay Fund 06/27/2008

MAVRIX CANADIAN INCOME TRUST FUND (ON)
Name changed to Mavrix Balanced Monthly Pay Fund 06/27/2008

MAVRIX FD MGMT INC (ON)
Merged into GrowthWorks Capital Ltd. 07/06/2009
Each share Common no par exchanged for $0.25 cash

MAVRIX RESOURCE FD 2005-I LTD PARTNERSHIP (ON)
Acquired by Mavrix Multi Series Fund 03/09/2007
Each Unit of Ltd. Partnership exchanged for (1.117688) shares Explorer Series

MAVTECH HLDGS INC (QC)
Merged into Ingram & Bell Acquisition, Inc. 05/26/1990
Each share Common no par exchanged for $0.75 cash

MAWANA SUGARS LTD NEW (INDIA)
GDR agreement terminated 11/14/2014
Each 144A GDR for Ordinary exchanged for $0.0511 cash
Each Reg. S GDR for Ordinary exchanged for $0.0511 cash

MAWANA SUGARS LTD OLD (INDIA)
Merged into Siel Ltd. 01/07/2008
Each Sponsored 144A GDR for Ordinary exchanged for (1.5) Sponsored 144A GDR's for Ordinary
Each Sponsored Reg. S GDR for Ordinary exchanged for (1.5) Sponsored Reg. S GDR's for Ordinary

MAWENZI RES LTD (SOUTH AFRICA)
Stock Dividend - 10.1186% payable 12/21/1998 to holders of record 10/30/1998
Name changed to Zarara Energy Ltd. 10/27/2000
(See Zarara Energy Ltd.)

MAWSON PAC LTD (AUSTRALIA)
Acquired by Elders Resources NZFP Ltd. 05/01/1990
Each ADR for Ordinary AUD $0.20 par exchanged for $0.964 cash

MAWSON RES LTD OLD (BC)
Reorganized as Mawson Resources Ltd. (New) 05/02/2012
Each share Common no par exchanged for (1) share Common no par, (0.33333333) share Darwin Resources Corp. Common no par and approximately (0.2) share European Uranium Resources Ltd. Common no par
(See each company's listing)

MAWSON WEST LTD (AUSTRALIA)
Name changed 12/27/2012
Name changed from Mawson West Ltd. to Mawson West Limited 12/27/2012
Acquired by Galena Private Equity Resources Fund L.P. 12/13/2016
Each share Ordinary exchanged for CAD$0.01 cash

MAX & ERMAS RESTAURANTS INC (DE)
Common 10¢ par split (4) for (3) by issuance of (1/3) additional share 04/21/1989
Common 10¢ par split (5) for (4) by issuance of (0.25) additional share 03/26/1993
Stock Dividend - 10% 04/21/1995
Merged into G&R Acquisition, Inc. 07/10/2008
Each share Common 10¢ par exchanged for $4 cash

MAX CAP GROUP LTD (BERMUDA)
Name changed 05/04/2007
Issue Information - 12,000,000 shares COM offered at $16 per share on 08/13/2001
Name changed from Max Re Capital Ltd. to Max Capital Group Ltd. 05/04/2007
Name changed to Alterra Capital Holdings, Ltd. 05/13/2010
Alterra Capital Holdings, Ltd. merged into Markel Corp. 05/01/2013

MAX CASH MEDIA INC (NV)
Name changed to BOLDFACE Group, Inc. 06/05/2012

MAX COMMUNICATIONS CORP (BC)
Recapitalized as Speyside Ventures Inc. 9/29/95
Each share Common no par exchanged for (0.2) share Common no par
Speyside Ventures Inc. name changed to Trandirect.com Technologies Inc. 7/19/99 which recapitalized as Consolidated Trandirect.com Technologies Inc. 8/14/2000 which name changed to International Samuel Exploration Corp. 6/20/2001

MAX DEV INC (CO)
Each share old Common $0.001 par exchanged for (0.5) share new Common $0.001 par 09/26/2000
Name changed to Image World Media, Inc. 01/29/2002
(See Image World Media, Inc.)

MAX ENTMT HLDGS INC (DE)
Name changed to Cyclon Capital Corp. 12/15/2007

MAX INC (NV)
Charter revoked for failure to file reports and pay fees 12/01/1985

MAX INTERNET COMMUNICATIONS INC (NV)
Recapitalized as China Health Management Corp. 08/04/2006
Each share Common $0.001 par exchanged for (0.01) share Common $0.001 par
(See China Health Management Corp.)

MAX MEDIA GROUP INC (NV)
Each share old Common $0.001 par exchanged for (0.0025) share new Common $0.001 par 10/09/2012
Name changed to Altavoz Entertainment, Inc. 04/20/2016

MAX MINERALS INC (BC)
Delisted from Vancouver Stock Exchange 03/01/1989

MAX MINERALS LTD (CANADA)
Name changed to Standard Exploration Ltd. 10/08/2010

MAX RET INC (DE)
Recapitalized as Telescan, Inc. 11/15/1989
Each share Common $0.0001 par exchanged for (0.01) share Common $0.0001 par
Telescan, Inc. merged into INVESTools Inc. 12/06/2001 which name changed to thinkorswim Group Inc. 06/06/2008 which merged into TD AMERITRADE Holding Corp. 06/11/2009

MAXA CORP (UT)
Proclaimed dissolved for failure to pay taxes 03/31/1983

MAXAD INC (CA)
Name changed to Morehouse Industries, Inc. 1/25/74
Morehouse Industries, Inc. recapitalized as Summa Industries 12/22/93
(See Summa Industries)

MAXAM, INC. (DE)
Adjudicated bankrupt 7/26/66
No stockholders' equity

MAXAM GOLD CORP (WY)
Name changed 01/03/1996
Reincorporated 09/02/1999
Reorganized 10/14/2014
Name changed from Maxam International Corp. to Maxam Gold Corp. 01/03/1996
State of incorporation changed from (UT) to (NV) 09/02/1999
Reorganized from Nevada to under the laws of Wyoming 10/14/2014
Each share Common $0.00001 par exchanged for (0.001) share Common $0.00001 par
Recapitalized as X Rail Enterprises, Inc. (WY) 11/20/2015
Each share Common $0.00001 par exchanged for (0.001) share Common $0.00001 par
X Rail Enterprises, Inc. (WY) reincorporated in Nevada 03/29/2016 which name changed to X Rail Entertainment, Inc. 05/17/2017 which recapitalized as Las Vegas Xpress, Inc. 09/17/2018

MAXAM TECHNOLOGIES INC (DE)
Charter cancelled and declared inoperative and void for non-payment of taxes 3/1/89

MAXAXAM CORP (DE)
Charter cancelled and declared inoperative and void for non-payment of taxes 03/01/1991

MAXCARD SYS INTL INC (BC)
Delisted from Vancouver Stock Exchange 03/06/1995

MAXCO INC (MI)
10% Preferred Ser. 3 called for redemption at $60 on 03/31/2007
10% Preferred Ser. 4 called for redemption at $51.50 on 03/31/2007
10% Preferred Ser. 5 called for redemption at $120 on 03/31/2007
Stock Dividend - 20% 08/01/1978
Liquidation completed
Each share Common $1 par received initial distribution of $0.75 cash payable 02/25/2010 to holders of record 02/16/2010 Ex date - 02/17/2010
Each share Common $1 par received second distribution of $1 cash payable 06/02/2010 to holders of record 05/24/2010 Ex date - 06/03/2010
Each share Common $1 par received third distribution of $0.75 cash payable 03/30/2011 to holders of record 03/23/2011 Ex date - 03/31/2011
Each share Common $1 par received fourth distribution of $0.40 cash payable 06/07/2013 to holders of record 05/31/2013 Ex date - 06/10/2013
Each share Common $1 par received fifth and final distribution of $0.10 cash payable 07/28/2014 to holders of record 07/18/2014 Ex date - 07/29/2014

MAXCOM CORP (DE)
Charter cancelled and declared inoperative and void for non-payment of taxes 3/1/95

MAXCOR FINL GROUP INC (DE)
Merged into BGC Partners, L.P. 5/20/2005
Each share Common $0.001 par exchanged for $14 cash

MAXI GROUP INC (NV)
Each share Common $0.001 par exchanged for (0.1) share new Common $0.001 par 03/09/1999
Reincorporated under the laws of Delaware as Enigma Software Group, Inc. 04/15/2005
Enigma Software Group, Inc. name changed to City Loan, Inc. (DE) 06/05/2008 which reorganized in Nevada 09/17/2008

MAXICARE HEALTH PLANS INC (DE)
Reorganized 12/05/1990
Common no par split (3) for (2) by issuance of (0.5) additional share 07/08/1985
Reorganized from (CA) to (DE) 12/05/1990
Each (173) shares Common no par exchanged for (1) share Common 1¢ par
Note: Unexchanged certificates were cancelled and became without value 12/05/1992
Each share old Common 1¢ par exchanged for (0.2) share new Common 1¢ par 03/28/2001
Company reported officers resigned and all financial resources exhausted 03/30/2007
Stockholders' equity unlikely

MAXILL INC (ON)
Acquired by 2277832 Ontario Inc. 05/01/2011
Each share Common no par exchanged for $0.08 cash
Note: Unexchanged certificates were cancelled and became without value 05/01/2017

MAXIM CRANE WKS HLDGS INC (PA)
Merged into Platinum Equity Capital Partners II, L.P. 07/02/2008
Each share Common exchanged for $42.50 cash

MAXIM DEV LTD (BC)
Struck off register and declared dissolved for failure to file returns 01/11/1991

MAXIM ENERGY GROUP LTD (AB)
Merged into Maxim Power Corp. 12/28/2000
Each share Common no par exchanged for (1.55) shares Common no par

MAXIM FINL MGMT INC (NV)
Name changed to Hammertime Holdings Inc. 06/28/2001
Hammertime Holdings Inc. name changed to VR Systems, Inc. 12/10/2003 which name changed to Hansen Gray & Co., Inc. 03/29/2004 which recapitalized as AMF Capital, Inc. 06/22/2007 which name changed to Pro Motors Group Corp. 10/29/2007 which recapitalized as Hydrogen Hybrid Corp. 11/25/2008 which name changed to Get Real USA Inc. 01/12/2011

MAXIM GROUP INC (DE)
Name changed to Flooring America, Inc. 01/10/2000
(See Flooring America, Inc.)

MAXIM MTG CORP (DE)
Recapitalized as Thomas Equipment, Inc. 10/19/2004
Each share Common $0.001 par exchanged for (0.025) share Common $0.001 par
Thomas Equipment, Inc. name changed to Osiris Corp. 01/29/2008

MAXIM PHARMACEUTICALS INC (DE)
Merged into EpiCept Corp. 01/05/2006
Each share Common $0.001 par exchanged for (0.203969) share Common $0.001 par
EpiCept Corp. recapitalized as Immune Pharmaceuticals Inc. 08/21/2013

MAXIM RES INC (AB)
Each share old Common no par exchanged for (0.25) share new Common no par 07/29/2010
Reincorporated under the laws of Ontario 01/16/2015

MAXIM TEP INC (TX)
Recapitalized as Conquest Petroleum Inc. 08/05/2009
Each share Common $0.00001 par exchanged for (0.1) share Common $0.00001 par
(See Conquest Petroleum Inc.)

MAXIMIZER SOFTWARE INC (CANADA)
Merged into MSI Acquisition Corp. 12/10/2009
Each share Common no par exchanged for $0.12 cash
Note: Unexchanged certificates were cancelled and became without value 12/10/2015

MAXIMUM ACCEPTANCE CORP. LTD. (ON)
Charter cancelled for failure to pay taxes and file returns 09/29/1980

MAXIMUM AWARDS INC (NV)
Each share Common $0.001 par exchanged for (1) share Common $0.015 par 05/18/2007
Name changed to Logica Holdings, Inc. 07/27/2007
Logica Holdings, Inc. name changed to Dolphin Digital Media, Inc. (NV) 08/18/2008 which reincorporated in Florida 12/03/2014 which recapitalized as Dolphin Entertainment, Inc. 09/18/2017

MAXIMUM DYNAMICS INC (CO)
Common no par split (5) for (2) by issuance of (1.5) additional shares payable 11/30/2002 to holders of record 11/29/2002 Ex date - 12/02/2002
SEC revoked common stock registration 02/07/2008

MAXIMUM ENERGY TR (AB)
Name changed to Ultima Energy Trust 11/13/2001
Ultima Energy Trust merged into Petrofund Energy Trust 06/16/2004 which merged into Penn West Energy Trust 07/04/2006 which reorganized as Penn West Petroleum Ltd. (New) 01/03/2011 which name changed to Obsidian Energy Ltd. 06/29/2017

MAXIMUM VENTURES INC (BC)
Recapitalized 05/31/1999
Recapitalized from Maximum Resources Inc. to Maximum Ventures Inc. 05/31/1999
Each share Common no par exchanged for (1/7) share Common no par
Recapitalized as Whistler Gold Exploration Inc. 10/23/2009
Each share Common no par exchanged for (0.2) share Common no par

MAXIMUS EXPL CORP (NV)
Name changed to Next 1 Interactive, Inc. 10/22/2008
Next 1 Interactive, Inc. recapitalized as Monaker Group, Inc. 06/25/2015

MAXIMUS RES INC (BC)
Struck from register and dissolved 5/27/94

MAXIMUS VENTURES LTD (BC)
Merged into Bear Lake Gold Ltd. 09/17/2008
Each share Common no par exchanged for (1) share Common no par
Bear Lake Gold Ltd. merged into Kerr Mines Inc. 05/26/2014

MAXIMUSIC NORTH AMER CORP (BC)
Recapitalized as Trivalence Mining Corp. 03/02/1995
Each share Common no par exchanged for (0.2) share Common no par
Trivalence Mining Corp. name changed to Azure Resources Corp. 03/26/2008 which recapitalized as Panorama Petroleum Inc. 06/13/2014 which recapitalized as Stamper Oil & Gas Corp. 04/06/2017

MAXIN INCOME FD (ON)
Merged into YIELDPLUS Income Fund 09/27/2007
Each Unit received (1.20015552) Trust Units
YIELDPLUS Income Fund merged into MINT Income Fund 03/21/2017

MAXIS INC (DE)
Issue Information - 3,000,000 shares COM offered at $16 per share on 05/24/1995
Merged into Electronic Arts Inc. 07/25/1997
Each share Common $0.0001 par exchanged for (0.3644) share Common 1¢ par

MAXNET INC (DE)
Name changed to MaxPlanet, Corp. 08/06/1999
MaxPlanet, Corp. recapitalized as Youth Enhancement Systems, Inc. 06/21/2006 which name changed to Dynamic Response Group, Inc. 03/30/2007
(See Dynamic Response Group, Inc.)

MAXOIL (DE)
Recapitalized as LCA-Vision Inc. 08/15/1995
Each share Common $0.0001 par exchanged for (0.1) share Common $0.001 par
(See LCA-Vision Inc.)

MAXON COMPUTER SYS INC (ON)
Name changed to Quartex Corp. 10/31/1990
Quartex Corp. name changed to PC Docs Group International Inc. 06/29/1994
(See PC Docs Group International Inc.)

MAXON ENERGY INC (CANADA)
Merged into Neutrino Resources Inc. 11/08/1995
Each share Common no par exchanged for (0.5) share Common no par and (0.5) Common Stock Purchase Warrant expiring 10/05/1997
(See Neutrino Resources Inc.)

MAXON INDS INC (CA)
Plan of reorganization under Chapter 11 Federal Bankruptcy proceedings confirmed 09/12/1990
No stockholders' equity

MAXPHARMA INC (TN)
Charter revoked for non payment of taxes 08/18/1989

MAXPLANET CORP (DE)
Recapitalized as Youth Enhancement Systems, Inc. 06/21/2006
Each share Common $0.00001 par exchanged for (0.01) share Common $0.00001 par
Youth Enhancement Systems, Inc.

MAX-MAX

name changed to Dynamic Response Group, Inc. 03/30/2007
(See Dynamic Response Group, Inc.)

MAXPOINT INTERACTIVE INC (DE)
Each share old Common $0.00005 par exchanged for (0.25) share new Common $0.00005 par 04/26/2016
Acquired by Harland Clarke Holdings Corp. 10/10/2017
Each share new Common $0.00005 par exchanged for $13.86 cash

MAXRAY OPTICAL TECHNOLOGY CO LTD (DE)
SEC revoked common stock registration 04/22/2016

MAXSERV INC (DE)
Reincorporated 05/04/1994
State of incorporation changed from (TX) to (DE) 05/04/1994
Merged into Sears, Roebuck & Co. 03/18/1997
Each share Common 1¢ par exchanged for $7.75 cash

MAXSON (W.L.) CORP. (NY)
Capital Stock 25¢ par changed to $3 par in 1945
Capital Stock $3 par split (2) for (1) by issuance of (1) additional share 4/14/55
Name changed to Maxson Electronics Corp. 1/18/61
Maxson Electronics Corp. merged into Riker-Maxson Corp. 3/31/69 which recapitalized as Unimax Group, Inc. 9/2/75 which name changed to Unimax Corp. 9/11/80
(See Unimax Corp.)

MAXSON ELECTRS CORP (NY)
Capital Stock $3 par split (3) for (2) by issuance of (0.5) additional share 04/01/1968
Merged into Riker-Maxson Corp. 03/31/1969
Each share Capital Stock $3 par exchanged for (1.2) shares Special Conv. Preference Ser. A Class A $1 par and (0.8) shares Common 25¢ par
Riker-Maxson Corp. recapitalized as Unimax Group, Inc. 09/02/1975 which name changed to Unimax Corp. 09/11/1980
(See Unimax Corp.)

MAXSON FOOD SYSTEMS, INC.
Merged into Foremost Dairies, Inc. (NY) 00/00/1949
Each (100) shares 50¢ Preferred $1 par exchanged for (6) shares 4% Preferred $50 par
Each (100) shares Common 25¢ par exchanged for (1.2) shares 4% Preferred $50 par
Foremost Dairies, Inc. (NY) merged into Foremost-McKesson, Inc. 07/19/1957 which name changed to McKesson Corp. (MD) 07/27/1983 which reincorporated in Delaware 07/31/1987
(See McKesson Corp. (Old) (DE))

MAXSON FOODS SYSTEMS, LTD.
Acquired by General Merchandise Co., Ltd. 00/00/1947
Details not available

MAXTOR CORP (DE)
Common no par split (2) for (1) by issuance of (1) additional share 06/12/1986
Acquired by Hyundai Electronics of America 01/11/1996
Each share old Common no par exchanged for $6.70 cash
Secondary Offering - 11,000,000 shares COM NEW offered at $13 per share on 02/09/1999
Merged into Seagate Technology (Cayman Islands) 05/19/2006
Each share new Common 1¢ par exchanged for (0.37) share Common $0.00001 par
Seagate Technology (Cayman Islands) reincorporated in Ireland as Seagate Technology PLC 07/06/2010

MAXUM DEV INC (NV)
Each share old Common $0.001 par exchanged for (0.01) share new Common $0.001 par 12/18/2000
Name changed to Tropical Leisure Resorts, Inc. 09/10/2001
Tropical Leisure Resorts, Inc. recapitalized as eWorldMedia Holdings, Inc. 10/22/2002 which name changed to Liberty Diversified Holdings, Inc. 01/09/2006 which name changed to Nutripure Beverages, Inc. 01/17/2008

MAXUM HEALTH CORP (DE)
Merged into InSight Health Services Corp. 6/26/96
Each share Common 1¢ par exchanged for (0.598) share Common $0.001 par
(See InSight Health Services Corp.)

MAXUS ENERGY CORP (DE)
Each share $2.07 Conv. Preferred $1 par exchanged for (1) share $4 Conv. Preferred $1 par 07/15/1987
Preferred Stock Purchase Rights declared for Common stockholders of record 09/12/1988 were redeemed at $0.10 per right 03/31/1995 for holders of record 03/22/1995
Merged into YPF Sociedad Anonima 06/08/1995
Each share Common $1 par exchanged for $5.50 cash
$4 Conv. Preferred $1 par called for redemption 08/13/1996
$2.50 Preferred $1 par called for redemption at $25 on 05/14/1999
Public interest eliminated

MAXUS TECHNOLOGY CORP (DE)
SEC revoked common stock registration 09/11/2009

MAXWELD CORP. (NY)
Charter cancelled and proclaimed dissolved for failure to pay taxes 12/15/39

MAXWELL COMMUNICATION CORP PLC (UNITED KINGDOM)
ADR agreement terminated 9/25/92
No stockholders' equity

MAXWELL-COX GROUP INC (DE)
Each share Common $0.0001 par exchanged for (0.2) share Common 1¢ par 02/05/1990
Note: Unexchanged certificates became without value 03/31/1990
Name changed to Digicom Corp. 06/18/1993
Digicom Corp. name changed to Emery Ferron Energy Corp. 06/27/1994
(See Emery Ferron Energy Corp.)

MAXWELL HARMAN ENTERPRISES INC (DE)
Name changed to Technology Expositions, Ltd. 04/05/1977
Technology Expositions, Ltd. recapitalized as World-Wide Patents, Ltd. 05/15/1978

MAXWELL INDS INC (NY)
Charter cancelled and proclaimed dissolved for failure to file reports and pay taxes 12/29/1972

MAXWELL LABS INC (CA)
Reincorporated 10/27/86
State of incorporation changed from (CA) to (DE) and Common $1 par changed to 10¢ par 10/27/86
Name changed to Maxwell Technologies, Inc. 8/30/96

MAXWELL, LTD. (ON)
Completely liquidated 06/15/1964
Each share $6 Preference no par exchanged for (10) shares of Maxwell (1964) Ltd. Common no par, $30 principal amount of Butler Metal Products Co. Ltd. 7% Conv. Debentures plus dividend arrears of $10.25 cash
Each share Common no par exchanged for (1) share Maxwell (1964) Ltd. Common no par and $3 principal amount of Butler 7% Conv. Debentures

MAXWELL (1964) LTD. (ON)
97.3% acquired by Mindustrial Corp. Ltd. through purchase offer which expired 01/05/1970
Public interest eliminated

MAXWELL OIL & GAS LTD (AB)
Reincorporated 9/12/96
Recapitalized 11/18/96
Place of incorporation changed from (BC) to (Alta) 9/12/96
Recapitalized from Maxwell Energy Corp. to 11/18/96
Each share Common no par exchanged for (0.2) share Common no par
Acquired by Tethys Energy Inc. 6/29/2000
Each share Common no par exchanged for $0.88 cash

MAXWELL RAND HLDGS INC (MN)
Reorganized under the laws of Florida as Maxwell Rand, Inc. 01/29/2001
Each share Common $0.001 par exchanged for (0.1) share Common $0.001 par

MAXWELL RES INC (BC)
Name changed to Maxwell Energy Corp. (BC) 05/12/1993
Maxwell Energy Corp. (BC) reincorporated in Alberta 09/12/1996 which recapitalized as Maxwell Oil & Gas Ltd. 11/18/1996
(See Maxwell Oil & Gas Ltd.)

MAXWELL SHOE INC (DE)
Class A Common 1¢ par split (3) for (2) by issuance of (0.5) additional share payable 05/17/2002 to holders of record 05/03/2002 Ex date - 05/20/2002
Merged into Jones Apparel Group, Inc. 07/08/2004
Each share Class A Common 1¢ par exchanged for $23.25 cash

MAXWELL-UINTAH INC (UT)
Name changed 06/24/1970
Name changed from Maxwell-Uintah Oil, Inc. to Maxwell-Uintah, Inc. and each share Capital Stock 1¢ par received (0.1) share Common 1¢ par 06/24/1970
Note: Certificates were not required to be surrendered and are without value
Proclaimed dissolved for failure to pay taxes 11/09/1974

MAXWIFI COMMUNICATIONS INC (DE)
Recapitalized as Tivus, Inc. 01/27/2010
Each (300) shares Common $0.001 par exchanged for (1) share Common $0.001 par

MAXWORLDWIDE INC (DE)
Liquidation completed
Each share Common $0.001 par received initial distribution of $0.50 cash payable 03/24/2004 to holders of record 03/15/2004 Ex date - 03/25/2004
Each share Common $0.001 par received second distribution of $0.40 cash payable 05/15/2008 to holders of record 04/15/2008 Ex date - 05/16/2008
Each share Common $0.001 par received third and final distribution of $0.014199 cash payable 06/22/2018 to holders of record 02/01/2018 Ex date - 06/25/2018

MAXX INTL INC (UT)
Common 1¢ par split (2) for (1) by issuance of (1) additional share payable 07/06/2000 to holders of record 06/30/2000 Ex date - 07/07/2000
SEC revoked common stock registration 07/30/2004
Stockholders' equity unlikely

MAXX PETE LTD (AB)
Each share old Common no par exchanged for (0.25) share new Common no par 05/11/1998
Acquired by Provident Energy Trust 05/25/2001
Each share new Common no par exchanged for (0.4523) Trust Unit no par and $1.97445 cash
Provident Energy Trust reorganized as Provident Energy Ltd. (New) 01/03/2011 which merged into Pembina Pipeline Corp. 04/02/2012

MAXXAM GROUP INC (DE)
Reincorporated 01/16/1985
State of incorporation changed from (NY) to (DE) 01/16/1985
Merged into MCO Holdings, Inc. 05/20/1988
Each share Common $8.33333333 par exchanged for (0.25) share Common 50¢ par, $6 principal amount of 0.135% Sr. Subordinated Reset Notes due 00/00/2000 and $6 cash
MCO Holdings, Inc. name changed to MAXXAM Inc. 10/06/1988
(See MAXXAM Inc.)

MAXXAM INC (DE)
Each share Conv. Class A Preferred 50¢ par exchanged for (0.004) share Conv. Class A Preferred $125 par 12/24/2009
Note: Holders of (249) or fewer pre-split shares received $11.75 cash per share
Each share Common 50¢ par exchanged for (0.004) share Common $125 par 12/24/2009
Note: Holders of (249) or fewer pre-split shares received $11 cash per share
Shares reacquired 03/21/2016
Each share Common $125 par exchanged for $850 cash

MAXXCOM INC (ON)
Acquired by MDC Corp. Inc. 07/31/2003
Each share Common no par exchanged for (0.1904761) share Class A Subordinate no par
MDC Corp. Inc. name changed to MDC Partners Inc. (ONT) 01/01/2004 which reincorporated in Canada 06/28/2004

MAXXIM INTL CORP (DE)
Name changed to Global Link Technologies, Inc. (DE) 05/00/1995
Global Link Technologies, Inc. (DE) reorganized in Wyoming as MutuaLoan Corp. 01/12/2009 which name changed to Nexus Enterprise Solutions, Inc. 02/27/2012

MAXXIM MED INC (TX)
Acquired by a management group 11/12/99
Each share Common $0.001 par exchanged for $26 cash

MAXXIMA CORP (FL)
Proclaimed dissolved for failure to file reports and pay fees 11/9/90

MAXXON INC (NV)
Recapitalized as Revolutions Medical Corp. 1/18/2007
Each share Common $0.001 par exchanged for (0.05) share Common $0.001 par

MAXXUS INC (DE)
Acquired by Maxxam Group Inc. (DE) 01/16/1985
Each share Common 1¢ par exchanged for $5.85 cash

MAXXZONE COM INC (NV)
Common $0.001 par split (2) for (1) by issuance of (1) additional share

payable 03/10/2003 to holders of record 03/07/2003
Name changed to ACS Holdings Inc. 06/08/2004
ACS Holdings Inc. recapitalized as Kairos Holdings Inc. 05/27/2005 which name changed to VitalTrust Business Development Corp. 02/27/2007 which name changed to Renew Energy Resources, Inc. 05/27/2008
(See Renew Energy Resources, Inc.)

MAXY GOLD CORP (BC)
Merged into Lara Exploration Ltd. 12/21/2009
Each share Common no par exchanged for (0.125) share Common no par
Note: Unexchanged certificates were cancelled and became without value 12/21/2015

MAXY OIL & GAS INC (BC)
Recapitalized as Maxy Gold Corp. 11/10/2003
Each share Common no par exchanged for (0.25) share Common no par
Maxy Gold Corp. merged into Lara Exploration Ltd. 12/21/2009

MAXYGEN INC (DE)
Each share Common $0.0001 par received distribution of (0.187039) share Codexis, Inc. Common $0.0001 par payable 12/14/2010 to holders of record 12/03/2010 Ex date - 12/15/2010
Liquidation completed
Each share Common $0.0001 par exchanged for initial distribution of $2.50 cash 08/29/2013
Each share Common $0.0001 par received second and final distribution of $0.093 cash payable 06/30/2014 to holders of record 08/29/2013

MAY, MC EWEN, KAISER CO.
Acquired by Burlington Mills Corp. on a (2/3) for (1) basis 7/14/48, which name was changed to Burlington Industries, Inc. 2/3/55
(See Burlington Industries, Inc.)

MAY & SPEH INC (DE)
Merged into Acxiom Corp. 09/17/1998
Each share Common 1¢ par exchanged for (0.8) share Common 10¢ par
Acxiom Corp. reorganized as Acxiom Holdings, Inc. 09/21/2018 which name changed to LiveRamp Holdings, Inc. 10/02/2018

MAY DEPT STORES CO (DE)
Reincorporated 5/24/96
Common $25 par changed to $10 par in 1933
Each share Common $10 par exchanged for (2) shares Common $5 par in 1945
Common $5 par changed to $2.50 par and (1) additional share issued 6/30/64
$1.80 Preferred no par conversion privilege expired 9/30/75
Common $2.50 par changed to $1.66-2/3 par and (0.5) additional share issued 6/30/76
Common $1.66-2/3 par split (3) for (2) by issuance of (0.5) additional share 10/3/84
3-3/4% Preferred $100 par called for redemption 12/21/84
Common $1.66-2/3 par changed to $1 par and (1) additional share issued 7/21/86
Common $1 par changed to 50¢ par and (1) additional share issued 6/14/93
$1.80 Preferred no par called for redemption 4/30/96
$3.40 Preferred no par called for redemption 4/30/96
$3.75 Preferred Ser. 45 no par called for redemption 4/30/96

$3.75 Preferred Ser. 47 no par called for redemption 4/30/96
State of incorporation changed from (NY) to (DE) 5/24/96
Common 50¢ par split (3) for (2) by issuance of (0.5) additional share payable 3/22/99 to holders of record 3/1/99 Ex date - 3/23/99
Stock Dividend - 100% 6/28/51
Merged into Federated Department Stores, Inc. 8/30/2005
Each share Common 50¢ par exchanged for (0.3115) share Common 1¢ par and $17.75

MAY DRUG STORES CORP.
Acquired by Drug, Inc. in 1929 which issued stock of five new companies in exchange for its own stock in accordance with plan of segregation in 1933

MAY ENERGY PARTNERS LTD (TX)
Acquired by Energy Development Partners, Ltd. 3/31/87
Each Unit of Ltd. Partnership exchanged for (0.35) Depositary Units no par
Note: Holdings of (99) Units or fewer exchanged for cash
Energy Development Partners, Ltd. merged into Hallwood Energy Partners, L.P. 5/10/90 which reorganized as Hallwood Energy Corp. 6/8/99
(See Hallwood Energy Corp.)

MAY EXPLORATION VENTURES INC. (DE)
Name changed to May Petroleum Inc. 11/16/72
May Petroleum Inc. name changed to Hall Financial Group, Inc. 8/15/88
(See Hall Financial Group, Inc.)

MAY HOSIERY MILLS, INC.
Each share Common no par exchanged for (2) shares Common $1 par in September 1940
Name changed to May, McEwen, Kaiser Co. in January 1941, which was acquired by Burlington Mills Corp. 7/14/48
Burlington Mills Corp. name changed to Burlington Industries, Inc. 2/3/55
(See Burlington Industries, Inc.)

MAY LEE INDS INC (NY)
Name changed 07/29/1972
Name changed from May Lee Import-Export Corp. to May Lee Industries Inc. 07/29/1972
Chapter XI bankruptcy proceedings dismissed 05/19/1976
Stockholders' equity unlikely

MAY OIL BURNER CORP. (MD)
Name changed to Gerotor May Corp. in 1944
Gerotor May Corp. acquired by Edy Corp. 1/21/72
(See Edy Corp.)

MAY PETE INC (DE)
Common 5¢ par split (3) for (2) by issuance of (0.5) additional share 10/21/80
Name changed to Hall Financial Group, Inc. 8/15/88
(See Hall Financial Group, Inc.)

MAY RALPH RES LTD (BC)
Struck off register and declared dissolved for failure to file returns 7/24/87

MAY SPIERS GOLD MINES LTD.
Liquidated in 1938

MAYA GOLD LTD (AB)
Recapitalized as Centram Exploration Ltd. (AB) 04/19/2002
Each share Common no par exchanged for (0.2) share Common no par
Centram Exploration Ltd. (AB) reincorporated in Canada as Pancontinental Uranium Corp. 09/10/2007 which name changed to Pancontinental Gold Corp.

07/29/2016 which name changed to Pancontinental Resources Corp. 07/13/2018

MAYAN ENERGY INC (BC)
Recapitalized as Leo Resources Inc. 03/01/1985
Each share Common no par exchanged for (0.5) share Common no par
Leo Resources Inc. name changed to Uni-Globe International Energy Corp. 03/03/1986
(See Uni-Globe International Energy Corp.)

MAYBELLINE INC (DE)
Merged into Rainbow Acquisition Corp. 2/13/96
Each share Common 1¢ par exchanged for $44 cash

MAYBRUN MINES LTD (ON)
Recapitalized as Consolidated Maybrun Mines Ltd. 07/10/1978
Each share Capital Stock $1 par exchanged for (0.1) share Capital Stock no par
(See Consolidated Maybrun Mines Ltd.)

MAYCOM INTL INC (WA)
Name changed to Celerex Corp. 7/9/87
(See Celerex Corp.)

MAYDAO CORP (UT)
Voluntarily dissolved 12/29/2011
No stockholders' equity

MAYDAY URANIUM INC (UT)
Recapitalized as Recreation Corp. of America, Inc. 4/10/72
Each share Capital Stock 50¢ par exchanged for (0.02) share Capital Stock 25¢ par
Recreation Corp. of America, Inc. name changed to Engineered Construction Industries, Inc. 5/31/74
(See Engineered Construction Industries, Inc.)

MAYEN MINERALS LTD (BC)
Name changed to Rift Basin Resources Corp. 09/25/2012
Rift Basin Resources Corp. name changed to Asean Energy Corp. 08/25/2014 which name changed to Genovation Capital Corp. 08/20/2015 which name changed to Valens Groworks Corp. 11/24/2016

MAYER GUS STORES INC (DE)
Acquired by Warnaco Inc. 09/30/1969
Each share Class A $1 par exchanged for (0.75) share Common no par
Each share Class B $1 par exchanged for (0.75) share Common no par
(See Warnaco Inc.)

MAYER OIL CO.
Name changed to Mayflower Petroleum Co. in 1936 which was liquidated in 1948

MAYER OSCAR & CO INC (DE)
Reincorporated 2/6/70
Common $10 par split (5) for (4) by issuance of (0.25) additional share 10/29/64
Common $10 par changed to $5 par and (1) additional share issued 2/18/66
Common $5 par split (2) for (1) by issuance of (1) additional share 1/19/70
State of incorporation changed from (IL) to (DE) 2/6/70
Common $5 par split (3) for (2) by issuance of (0.5) additional share 3/10/77
Stock Dividends - 400% 10/29/48; 20% 10/26/55; 25% 10/26/56; 50% 2/1/60
Acquired by General Foods Corp. 5/5/81
Each share Common $5 par exchanged for $29 cash

MAYETOK INC (NV)
Name changed to First American Silver Corp. 06/16/2010
First American Silver Corp. name changed to Century Cobalt Corp. 06/18/2018

MAYFAIR FINANCIAL CORP. (FL)
Merged into Mayfair Trading Corp. (Bahamas) 4/9/93
Details not available

MAYFAIR HOTEL, INC. (MO)
Merged into Mayfair-Lennox Hotels, Inc. on a (10) for (1) basis 3/31/62
(See Mayfair-Lennox Hotels, Inc.)

MAYFAIR HOTEL CO. (MO)
Reorganized as Mayfair Hotel, Inc. in 1943
No stockholders' equity

MAYFAIR INDUSTRIES, INC. (DE)
Ctfs. dated prior to 1/25/67
Bankrupt 1/25/67
Common Stock worthless

MAYFAIR INDS INC (DE)
Incorporated 08/21/1972
Merged into Empire Acquisition Inc. 05/15/1989
Each share Common 1¢ par exchanged for $11.35 cash

MAYFAIR INVESTMENT CO.
Dissolved in 1949

MAYFAIR LENNOX HOTELS INC (MO)
Merged into M-L Restaurant Inc. 01/27/1977
Each share Common $1 par exchanged for $1.73 cash

MAYFAIR MANOR DEVELOPMENT CORP. (OK)
Completely liquidated 02/19/1970
Each share Common 5¢ par exchanged for first and final distribution of (0.014925) share Four Seasons Nursing Centers of America, Inc. Common 25¢ par
(See Four Seasons Nursing Centers of America, Inc.)

MAYFAIR MARKETS (CA)
Stock Dividend - 25% 05/01/1962
6% Preferred $50 par called for redemption 09/01/1964
Merged into Arden Farms Co. (New) 10/31/1964
Each share Common $1 par exchanged for (1) share Common $1 par
Arden Farms Co. (New) name changed to changed to Arden-Mayfair, Inc. 04/24/1965 which reorganized as Arden Group, Inc. 12/19/1978
(See Arden Group, Inc.)

MAYFAIR MEDIA CORP (AB)
Name changed to MF Media Corp. 12/15/98

MAYFAIR MINES LTD (ON)
Merged into Mayfair Resources & Developments Ltd. 04/12/1978
Each share Capital Stock $1 par exchanged for (0.2) share Common no par
(See Mayfair Resources & Developments Ltd.)

MAYFAIR MNG & MINERALS INC (NV)
SEC revoked common stock registration 12/05/2011

MAYFAIR MOLY MINES LTD. (BC)
Struck off register and declared dissolved for failure to file returns 10/21/74

MAYFAIR POTTERIES LTD.
Bankrupt in 1942

MAYFAIR RES & DEVS LTD (ON)
Cease trade order effective 01/28/1982

MAYFAIR SUPER MKTS INC (DE)
Common $1 par reclassified as Class A Common 1¢ par 06/07/1984
Each share Class A Common 1¢ par received distribution of (0.5) share Conv. Class B Common 1¢ par 08/10/1984
Class A Common 1¢ par split (3) for (2) by issuance of (0.5) additional share 08/26/1985
Conv. Class B Common 1¢ par split (3) for (2) by issuance of (0.5) additional share 08/26/1985
Class A Common 1¢ par split (2) for (1) by issuance of (1) additional share 08/26/1986
Conv. Class B Common 1¢ par split (2) for (1) by issuance of (1) additional share 08/26/1986
Class A Common 1¢ par split (2) for (1) by issuance of (1) additional share 08/24/1987
Conv. Class B Common 1¢ par split (2) for (1) by issuance of (1) additional share 08/24/1987
Acquired by Mayfair Acquisition Corp. 11/01/1989
Each share Class A Common 1¢ par exchanged for $24.70 cash
Each share Conv. Class B Common 1¢ par exchanged for $24.70 cash

MAYFIELD ENGR CO (CO)
Name changed to M. Liquidating Corp. 11/14/1977
(See M. Liquidating Corp.)

MAYFIELD EXPLS & DEV LTD (QC)
Merged into Microsolve Computer Capital Inc. 02/11/1998
Each share Common no par exchanged for (0.1) share Common no par
Microsolve Computer Capital Inc. name changed to Homebank Technologies Inc. 12/20/2000 which name changed to Selient Inc. 06/15/2005
(See Selient Inc.)

MAYFLOWER ASSOCIATES, INC.
Dissolved in 1936

MAYFLOWER BANCORP INC (MA)
Acquired by Independent Bank Corp. 11/15/2013
Each share Common $1 par exchanged for $17.50 cash

MAYFLOWER CO (UT)
Each share Common 1¢ par exchanged for (0.1) share Common 25¢ par 06/09/1961
Each share Common 25¢ par exchanged for (0.4) share Common no par 12/16/1966
Merged into WellTech, Inc. 12/31/1973
Each share Common no par exchanged for (0.25) share Common 10¢ par
(See WellTech, Inc.)

MAYFLOWER CO-OPERATIVE BK (MIDDLEBORO, MA)
Common $1 par split (3) for (2) by issuance of (0.5) additional share payable 03/31/1999 to holders of record 03/25/1999
Common $1 par split (3) for (2) by issuance of (0.5) additional share payable 11/28/2003 to holders of record 11/21/2003 Ex date - 12/01/2003
Under plan of reorganization each share Common $1 par automatically became (1) share Mayflower Bancorp, Inc. Common $1 par 02/15/2007
(See Mayflower Bancorp, Inc.)

MAYFLOWER CORP (IN)
Common no par split (3) for (2) by issuance of (0.5) additional share 6/7/85
Stock Dividends - 10% 1/10/77; 10% 12/9/77; 10% 11/10/78; 15% 10/16/81; 10% 12/27/82; 20% 10/15/84
Name changed to Mayflower Group Inc. (Old) 5/1/86
(See Mayflower Group Inc. (Old))

MAYFLOWER DRUG STORES, INC.
Assets sold in 1933
No stockholders' equity

MAYFLOWER FINL CORP (DE)
Acquired by Valley National Bancorp 12/31/1990
Each share Common 1¢ par exchanged for (0.3686) Common Stock Purchase Warrant expiring 12/31/1995 and $15.75 cash

MAYFLOWER GROUP INC NEW (IN)
Merged into MCS Transit Inc. 3/31/95
Each share Common no par exchanged for $10.37 cash

MAYFLOWER GROUP INC OLD (IN)
Merged into MG Holdings, Inc. 12/19/86
Each share Common no par exchanged for $31.50 cash

MAYFLOWER HOTEL CORP. (DE)
Merged into Hilton Hotels Corp. and each share Capital Stock $1 par exchanged for (1) share Common $5 par 00/00/1952
(See Hilton Hotels Corp.)

MAYFLOWER-ILLINOIS, INC. (IL)
Name changed to Mayflower Investors, Inc. (IL) 2/3/65
Mayflower Investors, Inc. (IL) reincorporated under the laws of Delaware 6/18/70 which recapitalized as Seago Group, Inc. 9/2/76
(See Seago Group, Inc.)

MAYFLOWER INSURANCE CO. (OH)
Liquidation completed
Each share Capital Stock no par exchanged for initial distribution of $30 cash 10/25/65
Each share Capital Stock no par received second and final distribution of (1) Ctf. of Equitable Int. and $23.30 cash 1/14/66
Each Ctf. of Equitable Int. received first and final distribution of $0.18249 cash 12/30/71
Certificates of Equitable Int. were not required to be surrendered and are now valueless

MAYFLOWER INVESTMENT TRUST (MA)
In process of dissolution but there is no stockholders' equity Stock declared worthless 02/28/1968

MAYFLOWER INVS INC (DE)
Reincorporated 06/18/1970
State of incorporation changed from (IL) to (DE) and Common 50¢ par changed to 10¢ par 06/18/1970
Recapitalized as Seago Group, Inc. 09/02/1976
Each share Common 10¢ par exchanged for (0.1) share Common 10¢ par
(See Seago Group, Inc.)

MAYFLOWER LIFE INSURANCE CO. OF AMERICA (IL)
Acquired by Pennsylvania Life Co. (Del.) 10/1/69
Each share Common $1 par exchanged for (0.162419) share Common $1 par
Pennsylvania Life Co. (Del.) name changed to Penncorp Financial, Inc. 6/5/79

MAYFLOWER LIFE INSURANCE CO. OF ILLINOIS (IL)
Merged into Mayflower Life Insurance Co. of America 12/30/66
Each share Common $1 par exchanged for (1) share Common $1 par
Mayflower Life Insurance Co. of America acquired by Pennsylvania Life Co. (DE) 10/1/69 which name changed to Penncorp Financial, Inc. 6/5/79

MAYFLOWER LIFE INSURANCE CO. OF WISCONSIN, INC. (WI)
Merged into Mayflower Life Insurance Co. of America 12/30/66
Each share Common exchanged for (0.95) share Common $1 par Mayflower Life Insurance Co. of America acquired by Pennsylvania Life Co. (Del.) 10/1/69 which name changed to Penncorp Financial, Inc. 6/5/79

MAYFLOWER LIFE INS CO MICH (MI)
Name changed to Mid-America Life Assurance Co. 05/18/1969
(See Mid-America Life Assurance Co.)

MAYFLOWER PETROLEUM CO.
Liquidated in 1948

MAYGILL PETROLEUM CO. LTD. (ON)
Recapitalized as West Maygill Gas & Oil Ltd. on a (0.1) for (1) basis in 1954
West Maygill Gas & Oil Ltd. name changed to Ranger Oil (Canada) Ltd. (Ont.) 9/9/58 which reincorporated in Canada as Ranger Oil Ltd. 6/30/80 which merged into Canadian Natural Resources Ltd. 7/28/2000

MAYHEW CAPITAL CORP. (UT)
Recapitalized as Da-Jon Inc. 3/8/77
Each share Common 1¢ par exchanged for (10) shares Common $0.001 par
Da-Jon Inc. recapitalized as Omega Energy, Inc. 3/12/79 which recapitalized as Olivier International Energy, Inc. 1/7/80

MAYLAC GOLD MINES LTD (ON)
Charter cancelled for failure to file reports and pay taxes 6/11/94

MAYMAC PETE CORP (BC)
Name changed 08/19/1985
Name changed from Maymac Explorations Ltd. to Maymac Petroleum Corp. 08/19/1985
Recapitalized as Consolidated Maymac Petroleum Corp. (BC) 05/28/1999
Each share Common no par exchanged for (0.05263157) share Common no par
Consolidated Maymac Petroleum Corp. (BC) reincorporated in Yukon as Northern Star Mining Corp. 01/16/2003 which reincorporated in British Columbia 07/17/2006

MAYNARD-ALLEN STATE BANK (PORTLAND, MI)
Merged into First Michigan Bank Corp. 12/31/90
Each share Common $2 par exchanged for (2.4) shares Common $1 par
First Michigan Bank Corp. merged into Huntington Bancshares Inc. 9/30/97

MAYNARD ENERGY INC (CANADA)
Over 98% acquired by Tintagel Energy Corp. as of 12/20/1985
Public interest eliminated

MAYNARD OIL CO (DE)
Common 50¢ par changed to 10¢ par 5/7/73
Merged into Plantation Petroleum Holdings 7/17/2002
Each share Common 10¢ par exchanged for $17 cash

MAYNE GROUP LTD (AUSTRALIA)
Name changed 01/27/2002
Stock Dividend - 20% 10/31/1988
Name changed from Mayne Nickless Ltd. to Mayne Group Ltd. 01/27/2002
Name changed to Symbion Health, Ltd. 12/01/2005
(See Symbion Health, Ltd.)

MAYNE INTL LTD (DE)
Name changed to Black Dragon Entertainment Inc. 09/22/2000
Black Dragon Entertainment Inc. recapitalized as Vita Biotech Corp. 08/10/2002 which name changed to August Energy Corp. 07/02/2004 which recapitalized as Canyon Gold Corp. 05/02/2011 which name changed to Defense Technologies International Corp. 06/15/2016

MAYO MINES, LTD. (CANADA)
Acquired by Maybrun Mines Ltd. 00/00/1953
Each (3) shares Capital Stock no par exchanged for (1) share Capital Stock $1 par
Maybrun Mines Ltd. recapitalized as Consolidated Maybrun Mines Ltd. 07/10/1978
(See Consolidated Maybrun Mines Ltd.)

MAYO SILVER MINES LTD. (BC)
Struck off register and declared dissolved for failure to file returns in August, 1974

MAYORS JEWELERS INC (DE)
Merged into Birks & Mayors Inc. 11/14/2005
Each share Common $0.0001 par exchanged for (0.08695) share Class A no par
Birks & Mayors Inc. name changed to Birks Group Inc. 10/01/2013

MAYRAND INC. (NC)
6% Preferred $50 par called for redemption 06/30/1963
Name changed to Mayrand Pharmaceuticals, Inc. 03/29/1990
(See Mayrand Pharmaceuticals, Inc.)

MAYRAND PHARMACEUTICALS, INC. (NC)
Acquired by Merz GmbH & Co. 05/01/1995
Details not available

MAYS MANUFACTURING CO. (NC)
Dissolved 6/18/27
No stockholders' equity

MAYTAG CORP (DE)
Name changed 4/29/87
Each share old Common no par exchanged for (0.05625) share $6 1st Preferred no par, (0.2) share $3 Preference no par and (1) share new Common no par in 1928
$3 Preference no par called for redemption 5/1/59
New Common no par split (2) for (1) by issuance of (1) additional share 7/10/59
New Common no par split (2) for (1) by issuance of (1) additional share 1/12/62
New Common no par changed to $2.50 par and (1) additional share issued 1/20/69
Common $2.50 par changed to $1.25 par and (1) additional share issued 1/17/86
Name changed from Maytag Co. to Maytag Corp. 4/29/87
Common $1.25 par split (2) for (1) by issuance of (1) additional share 10/26/87
Merged into Whirlpool Corp. 3/31/2006
Each share Common $1.25 par exchanged for (0.1196) share Common $1 par and $10.50 cash

MAYWOOD PROVISO ST BK (MAYWOOD, IL)
Name changed to Continental Community Bank & Trust Co. (Aurora, IL) 05/16/1997
(See Continental Community Bank & Trust Co. (Aurora, IL))

MCDONOUGH MINING SYNDICATE (1940), LTD. (CANADA)
Charter surrendered 04/10/1964

MCDOUGALL MINES LTD.
Dissolved 00/00/1930
Details not available

MCDOUGALL-SEGUR EXPLORATION CO. OF CANADA LTD. (CANADA)
Acquired by Pathfinder Petroleums Ltd. 00/00/1954
Each share Capital Stock no par exchanged for (0.25) share Capital Stock 50¢ par
Pathfinder Petroleums Ltd. merged into Medallion Petroleums Ltd. 09/11/1956 which merged into Canadian Industrial Gas & Oil Ltd. 03/08/1965 which merged into Norcen Energy Resources Ltd. (AB) 10/28/1975 which reincorporated in Canada 04/15/1977
(See Norcen Energy Resources Ltd.)

MCDOWELL & CO LTD (INDIA)
Name changed to United Spirits Ltd. 11/14/2006

MCDOWELL ENTERPRISES INC (TN)
Common no par split (4) for (3) by issuance of (0.33333333) additional share 05/15/1979
Common no par changed to $1 par 05/06/1980
Stock Dividends - 10% 01/04/1974; 25% 01/04/1978
Name changed to Maxpharma, Inc. 08/20/1987
(See Maxpharma, Inc.)

MCDOWELL NATL BK (SHARON, PA)
Capital Stock $10 par split (4) for (3) by issuance of (0.33333333) additional share 06/22/1981
Stock Dividend - 150% 00/00/1952
Merged into Union National Corp. 09/01/1983
Each share Capital Stock $10 par exchanged for $53.65 cash

MCDOWELL WELLMAN ENGR CO (OH)
Through purchase offer 100% acquired by Helix Technology Corp. 00/00/1978
Public interest eliminated

MCDUFFIE BK & TR (THOMSON, GA)
Under plan of reorganization each share Common $0.001 par automatically became (1) share Georgia-Carolina Bancshares, Inc. Common $0.001 par 06/06/1997
Georgia-Carolina Bancshares, Inc. merged into State Bank Financial Corp. 01/01/2015

MCEG STERLING INC (DE)
Merged into Metromedia International Group, Inc. 11/01/1995
Each share Common $0.001 par exchanged for (0.04627) share Common $1 par
(See Metromedia International Group, Inc.)

MCELWAIN (J.F.) CO.
Merged into Melville Shoe Corp. 00/00/1939
Each share Preferred exchanged for (1.05) shares new Preferred
Each share Common exchanged for (354726/1047260) share Preferred and (1-4762/104726) shares new Common
Melville Shoe Corp. name changed to Melville Corp. (NY) 04/14/1976 which reorganized in Delaware as CVS Corp. 11/20/1996 which name changed to CVS/Caremark Corp. 03/22/2007 which name changed to CVS Caremark Corp. 05/10/2007 which name changed to CVS Health Corp. 09/04/2014

MCENANEY GOLD MINES LTD. (ON)
Charter cancelled and company declared dissolved by default 4/30/62

MCEWEN KNITTING CO.
Merged into May Hosiery Mills, Inc. on a (23.288) for (1) basis in 1940
May Hosiery Mills, Inc. name changed to May, McEwen, Kaiser Co. in January 1941 which was acquired by Burlington Mills Corp. 7/14/48 which name was changed to Burlington Industries, Inc. 2/3/55
(See Burlington Industries, Inc.)

MCEWEN MNG MINERA ANDES ACQUISITION CORP (AB)
Each Exchangeable Share exchanged for (1) share McEwen Mining Inc. Common no par 08/22/2016

MCF CORP (DE)
Each share old Common $0.0001 par exchanged for (1/7) share new Common $0.0001 par 11/16/2006
Name changed to Merriman Curhan Ford Group, Inc. 05/20/2008
Merriman Curhan Ford Group, Inc. recapitalized as Merriman Holdings, Inc. 08/16/2010

MCF ENTERPRISES INC (BC)
Name changed to Online Consortium Corp. 02/09/2001
Online Consortium Corp. name changed to Equicap Financial Corp. 07/10/2003 which name changed to Zecotek Medical Systems, Inc. 02/10/2005 which name changed to Zecotek Photonics Inc. 11/26/2007

MCFADDEN STORES, INC. (CA)
Out of business 00/00/1954
Details not available

MCFARLAND ENERGY INC (CA)
Merged into Monterey Resources, Inc. 7/24/97
Each share Common no par exchanged for $18.55 cash

MCFARLANE, SON & HODGSON LTD. (CANADA)
6-1/2% 1st Preferred $50 par called for redemption 9/18/78
Public interest eliminated

MCFINLEY MINES LTD (ON)
Reorganized 07/20/1984
Each (10) shares Capital Stock $1 par exchanged for (4.25) shares McFinley Red Lake Mines Ltd. Common no par and (5) shares Redaurum Red Lake Mines Ltd. Common no par
(See each company's listing)

MCFINLEY RED LAKE GOLD MINES LTD. (ON)
Recapitalized as McFinley Mines Ltd. 01/31/1975
Each share Capital Stock $1 par exchanged for (0.2) share Capital Stock no par
(See McFinley Mines Ltd.)

MCG CAP CORP (DE)
Merged into PennantPark Floating Rate Capital Ltd. 08/18/2015
Each share Common 1¢ par exchanged for (0.32044) share Common $0.001 par and $0.30595 cash

MCG DIVERSIFIED INC (FL)
Name changed to Electro Energy Inc. 06/09/2004
(See Electro Energy Inc.)

MCGAW INC (DE)
Merged into IVAX Corp. 3/25/94
Each share Common $0.001 par exchanged for (0.523) share Common 10¢ par
(See IVAX Corp.)

MCGEARY SMITH LABORATORIES, INC. (DE)
Name changed to Capital Film Laboratories, Inc. in 1954
(See Capital Film Laboratories, Inc.)

MCGILL MFG INC (IN)
Each share Common no par exchanged for (2) shares Common $50 par 10/09/1953
Each share Common $50 par exchanged for (3) shares Common no par 10/09/1959
Common no par split (5) for (4) by issuance of (0.25) additional share 10/26/1965
Common no par split (2) for (1) by issuance of (1) additional share 10/26/1973
Common no par split (2) for (1) by issuance of (1) additional share 09/29/1978
Stock Dividend - 20% 03/05/1965
Preferred Stock Purchase Rights declared for Common stockholders of record 10/23/1989 were redeemed at $0.01 per right 02/28/1990 for holders of record 02/14/1990
Merged into Emerson Electric Co. 04/04/1990
Each share Common no par exchanged for $93 cash

MCGILL METAL PRODS CO (IL)
Name changed 05/27/1987
Name changed from Mc Gill Metal Products Co. to Mc Gill Metal Products Co. of Marengo 05/27/1987
Voluntarily dissolved 12/24/1990
Details not available

MCGILLIVARY CREEK COAL & COKE CO. LTD. (CANADA)
Acquired by Coleman Collieries Ltd. 00/00/1952
Each (1,000) shares Capital Stock $1 par exchanged for (19.8) shares new Common $1 par, $682 in Bonds and $180 cash
(See Coleman Collieries Ltd.)

MCGINN GOLD MINES LTD. (ON)
Charter revoked for failure to file reports and pay fees 12/2/65

MCGLEN INTERNET GROUP INC (DE)
Recapitalized as Northgate Innovations, Inc. 03/20/2002
Each share Common 3¢ par exchanged for (0.1) share Common 3¢ par
Northgate Innovations, Inc. name changed to Digital Lifestyles Group, Inc. 06/25/2004 which name changed to TN-K Energy Group Inc. 10/29/2009

MCGOWEN GLASS FIBERS CORP (NJ)
Name changed to Wyndmoor Industries, Inc. 03/05/1971

MCGOWEN RES INC (UT)
Each (3.5) shares old Common $0.001 par exchanged for (1) share new Common $0.001 par 3/7/96
Name changed to Trek Resources Inc. (UT) 6/15/2000
Trek Resources Inc. (UT) reincorporated in Delaware 2/7/2001

MCGRATH CORP (WA)
Adjudicated bankrupt 03/23/1972
Stockholders' equity unlikely

MCGRATH ST PAUL CO (MN)
Each share Preferred $5 par exchanged for (2) shares Common 50¢ par 01/31/1969
Common 50¢ par changed to 1¢ par 10/24/1969
Recapitalized as Budget Systems Corp. 02/07/1973
Each share Common 1¢ par exchanged for (0.2) share Common 5¢ par

MCGRAW EDISON CO (DE)
Common $1 par split (2) for (1) by issuance of (1) additional share 05/21/1965
Merged into Cooper Industries, Inc. (OH) 05/30/1985
Each share Common $1 par exchanged for $65 cash

MCGRAW ELECTRIC CO. (DE)
Each share Common $5 par exchanged for (2) shares Common $1 par in 1937
Common $1 par split (2) for (1) by issuance of (1) additional share in 1955
Name changed to McGraw Edison Co. and (1) additional share issued 1/31/57
(See McGraw-Edison Co.)

MCGRAW F H & CO (NJ)
Common 10¢ par changed to $2 par 00/00/1949
Common $2 par changed to 10¢ par 11/30/1964
Adjudicated bankrupt 02/06/1970
Stockholders' equity unlikely

MCGRAW HILL FINL INC (NY)
Name changed 04/28/1995
Name changed 05/02/2013
Common $1 par split (2) for (1) by issuance of (1) additional share 07/17/1967
Class A $1 par called for redemption 03/01/1968
$5.50 Conv. Preferred $10 par called for redemption 04/05/1971
Common $1 par split (2) for (1) by issuance of (1) additional share 06/01/1983
Name changed from McGraw-Hill, Inc. to McGraw-Hill Companies, Inc. 04/28/1995
Common $1 par split (2) for (1) by issuance of (1) additional share payable 04/26/1996 to holders of record 03/28/1996
Common Stock Purchase Rights declared for holders of record 11/06/1989 were redeemed at $0.005 per right 08/27/1998 for holders of record 08/14/1998
Common $1 par split (2) for (1) by issuance of (1) additional share payable 03/08/1999 to holders of record 02/24/1999 Ex date - 03/09/1999
Common $1 par split (2) for (1) by issuance of (1) additional share payable 05/17/2005 to holders of record 05/06/2005 Ex date - 05/18/2005
$1.20 Conv. Preference $10 par called for redemption at $40 on 08/30/2002
Name changed from McGraw-Hill Companies, Inc. to McGraw Hill Financial, Inc. 05/02/2013
Name changed to S&P Global Inc. 04/28/2016

MCGRAW-HILL PUBLISHING CO., LTD. (NY)
Common no par changed to $5 par and (1) additional share issued 00/00/1953
Common $5 par changed to $3 par and (2) additional shares issued 08/08/1956
Common $3 par changed to $1 par and (2) additional shares issued 03/17/1961
Name changed to McGraw-Hill, Inc. 01/02/1964
McGraw-Hill, Inc. name changed to McGraw-Hill Companies, Inc. 04/28/1995 which name changed to McGraw Hill Financial, Inc. 05/02/2013 which name changed to S&P Global Inc. 04/28/2016

MCGRAW HILL RYERSON LTD (ON)
Acquired by McGraw-Hill Global Education Holdings, LLC 06/18/2014
Each share Common no par exchanged for $50 cash
Note: Unexchanged certificates will be cancelled and become without value 06/18/2020

MCGRAW TIRE & RUBBER CO. (OH)
Charter cancelled for failure to pay taxes 2/14/25

MCGREGOR CAP CORP (AB)
Name changed to Canadian Platinum Corp. 11/22/2011

MCGREGOR CAP CORP (CO)
Name changed to Ultima International Corp. 10/14/1988

MCGREGOR CORP (NY)
Merged into Rapid-American Corp. 03/13/1985
Each share Common 1¢ par exchanged for $23 cash

MCGREGOR DONIGER INC (NY)
Class A $1 par split (3) for (2) by issuance of (0.5) additional share 06/04/1969
Class B $1 par split (3) for (2) by issuance of (0.5) additional share 06/04/1969
Merged into Rapid-American Corp. (DE) 05/01/1979
Each share Class A $1 par exchanged for $2 cash
Each share Class B $1 par exchanged for $2 cash

MCGUIRE BONDS (MI)
Dissolved 4/28/55

MCGUIRE CHRIS INC (FL)
Proclaimed dissolved for failure to file reports and pay fees 12/05/1978

MCGUIRE WTR CONDITIONING CORP (MO)
Charter forfeited for failure to file reports 01/01/1970

MCI CAP I (DE)
Plan of reorganization under Chapter 11 Federal Bankruptcy Code effective 4/20/2004
Each 8% Guaranteed Quarterly Income Preferred Security received initial distribution of $10.90 cash
Note: Distributions of less than $100 will not be made, unless requested in writing

MCI COMMUNICATIONS CORP (DE)
$2.64 Conv. Preferred 10¢ par called for redemption 3/14/80
Conv. Preferred Ser. B 10¢ par called for redemption 11/1/80
$1.80 Conv. Sr. Preferred 10¢ par called for redemption 5/8/81
$1.84 Conv. Preferred 10¢ par called for redemption 11/18/81
Common 10¢ par split (2) for (1) by issuance of (1) additional share 8/19/83
Common 10¢ par split (2) for (1) by issuance of (1) additional share 7/9/93
Stock Dividend - 100% 9/10/82
Merged into MCI WorldCom, Inc. 9/14/98
Each share Common 10¢ par exchanged for (1.2439) shares Common 1¢ par
MCI WorldCom, Inc. name changed to WorldCom Inc. (New) 5/1/2000
(See WorldCom Inc. (New))

MCI INC (GA)
Merged into Verizon Communications Inc. 1/6/2006
Each share Common 1¢ par exchanged for (0.5743) share Common 10¢ par and $2.738 cash

MCI LIQUIDATING CO., INC. (KY)
Liquidation completed
Each share Common no par exchanged for initial distribution of $13.75 cash 5/3/79
Each share Common no par received second and final distribution of $0.65 cash 3/3/86

MCI WORLDCOM INC (GA)
Common 1¢ par split (3) for (2) by issuance of (0.5) additional share payable 12/30/99 to holders of record 12/15/99
$2.25 Conv. Exchangeable Preferred Ser. C 1¢ par called for redemption at $50.75 plus $0.55625 accrued dividends on 1/14/2000
Name changed to WorldCom Inc. (New) 5/1/2000
(See WorldCom Inc. (New))

MCI WORLDCOM SYNERGIES MGMT INC
Plan of reorganization under Chapter 11 Federal Bankruptcy Code effective 4/20/2004
No stockholders' equity

MCINTOSH & SEYMOUR CORP.
Acquired by American Locomotive Co. in 1929
Details not available

MCINTOSH BANCSHARES INC (GA)
Common $2.50 par split (5) for (4) by issuance of (0.25) additional share payable 03/01/2001 to holders of record 02/15/2001 Ex date - 03/02/2001
Common $2.50 par split (5) for (4) by issuance of (0.25) additional share payable 06/01/2005 to holders of record 05/15/2005 Ex date - 06/02/2005
Common $2.50 par split (2) for (1) by issuance of (1) additional share payable 06/01/2007 to holders of record 05/15/2007 Ex date - 06/04/2007
Common $2.50 par changed to $1 par 06/07/2010
Stock Dividends - 10% payable 03/01/1999 to holders of record 02/15/1999; 10% payable 03/01/2000 to holders of record 02/15/2000
Principal asset placed in receivership 06/17/2011
Stockholders' equity unlikely

MCINTOSH CORP (DE)
Merged into Norris Industries, Inc. 06/30/1977
Each share Common $1 par exchanged for (0.8) share Common 50¢ par
(See Norris Industries, Inc.)

MCINTOSH (J.R.C.), INC. (NV)
Out of business in November 1963
Common stock is worthless

MCINTOSH LAB INC (DE)
Each share Common $10 par exchanged for (20) shares Common 50¢ par 10/10/1969
Merged into CCL Acquisition Co. 07/13/1990
Each share 6% Preferred $10 par exchanged for $159.78 cash
Each share Common 50¢ par exchanged for $159.78 cash

MCINTYRE MINES LTD (ON)
Name changed 5/31/74
Name changed from McIntyre Porcupine Mines Ltd. to McIntyre Mines Ltd. 5/31/74
Merged into Falconbridge Ltd. 1/24/89
Each share Common no par exchanged for (2.5186) shares Common no par
(See Falconbridge Ltd.)

MCIVOR DRILLING CO. LTD. (AB)
Name changed to Hi-Tower Drilling Co. Ltd. 00/00/1954
Hi-Tower Drilling Co. Ltd. name changed to Bow Valley Industries Ltd. 06/01/1962 which name changed to Bow Valley Energy Inc. 05/07/1993 which was acquired by Talisman Energy Inc. 08/11/1994
(See Talisman Energy Inc.)

MCK COMMUNICATIONS INC (DE)
Merged into Verso Technologies, Inc. 09/26/2003
Each share Common $0.001 par exchanged for (0.8517) share Common 1¢ par
(See Verso Technologies, Inc.)

MCK DISTRIBUTION CO. (WA)
Liquidation completed
Each share Class A $3 par or Class B $3 par exchanged for initial distribution of $10 cash 1/4/65
Each share Class A $3 par or Class B $3 par received second and final distribution of $5.13 cash 10/15/65

MCK MNG CORP (ON)
Name changed to PhosCan Chemical Corp. (ON) 08/01/2006
PhosCan Chemical Corp. (ON) reincorporated in Canada 10/19/2006
(See PhosCan Chemical Corp.)

MCKALE'S CORP. (WA)
Each share Common no par exchanged for (2) shares Class A $3 par and (1) share Class B $3 par 00/00/1949
Name changed to MCK Distribution Co. 11/17/1964
(See MCK Distribution Co.)

MCKALE'S INC. (WA)
Name changed to McKale's Corp. in 1950
McKale's Corp. name was changed to MCK Distribution Co. 11/17/64 which completed liquidation 10/15/65

MCKAY CO (PA)
Merged into Teledyne, Inc. 10/30/1969
Details not available

MCKAY CORMACK HLDGS LTD (BC)
Placed in receivership 04/29/1970
No stockholders' equity

MCKAY MACHINE CO. (OH)
Stock Dividends - 20% 1/20/50; 10% 11/16/53; 25% 2/1/55; 10% 2/3/58; 10% 2/3/61; 10% 2/5/62; 10% 1/31/66
Merged into Wean Industries, Inc. 5/1/67
Each share Common no par exchanged for (2.333333) shares 5-1/4% Conv. Preferred $24 par

MCKEE ARTHUR G & CO (DE)
Each share Class B no par exchanged for (2) shares Common no par in 1952
Common no par split (2) for (1) by issuance of (1) additional share 10/9/59
Common no par split (3) for (2) by issuance of (0.5) additional share 12/17/73
Common no par split (2) for (1) by issuance of (1) additional share 6/14/76
Stock Dividend - 200% 10/24/47
Under plan of reorganization each share Common no par automatically became (1) share McKee Corp. Common no par 9/1/77
(See McKee Corp.)

MCKEE CORP (DE)
Merged into Davy Corp. Ltd. 11/28/1978
Each share Common no par exchanged for $33 cash

MCKEE ROBERT E INC (NV)
Merged into Santa Fe Industries, Inc. 01/16/1973
Each share Common $5 par exchanged for either (A) $16.50 prinicipal amount of 6-1/4% Conv. Subord. Debentures due 08/01/1998 or (B) (0.542) share Common $10 par
Option to receive (B) expired 01/16/1973
Santa Fe Industries, Inc. merged into Santa Fe Southern Pacific Corp. 12/23/1983 which name changed to Santa Fe Pacific Corp. 04/25/1989 which merged into Burlington Northern Santa Fe 09/22/1995
(See Burlington Northern Santa Fe Corp.)

MCKEESPORT NATL BK (MCKEESPORT, PA)
Common $10 par changed to $5 par and (1) additional share issued 4/6/77
Stock Dividends - 10% 8/31/73; 10% 5/31/78
Reorganized as McKeesport National Corp. 6/30/84
Each share Common $5 par exchanged for (1) share Common no par
McKeesport National Corp. merged into USBANCORP, Inc. 12/1/85 which name changed to AmeriServ Financial, Inc. 5/7/2001

MCKEESPORT NATL CORP (PA)
Stock Dividend - 10% 08/15/1984
Merged into USBANCORP, Inc. 12/01/1985
Each share Common no par exchanged for (0.375) share Common $2.50 par
USBANCORP, Inc. name changed to AmeriServ Financial, Inc. 05/07/2001

MCKEESPORT OIL & DRILLING CO. (DE)
Charter cancelled and declared inoperative and void for non-payment of taxes 3/16/27

MCKEESPORT TIN PLATE CO.
Merged into McKeesport Tin Plate Corp. on a (2) for (1) basis in 1937
McKeesport Tin Plate Corp. name changed to National Can Corp. in 1941
(See National Can Corp.)

MCKEESPORT TIN PLATE CORP.
Name changed to National Can Corp. in 1941
(See National Can Corp.)

MCKELVEY G M CO (OH)
Acquired by Higbee Co. 07/03/1969
Each share Common no par exchanged for (1.2) shares Common $1 par
(See Higbee Co.)

MCKENZIE BAY INTL LTD (DE)
Recapitalized as CGE Energy, Inc. 09/14/2015
Each share Common $0.001 par exchanged for (0.04) share Common $0.001 par

MCKENZIE RED LAKE GOLD MINES LTD. (ON)
Merged into Little Long Lac Gold Mines Ltd. (Old) 6/15/66
Each share Capital Stock $1 par exchanged for (0.05) share Capital Stock no par
Little Long Lac Gold Mines Ltd. (Old) merged into Little Long Lac Gold Mines Ltd (The) 4/27/67 which merged into Little Long Lac Mines Ltd. 1/8/71 which name changed to Little Long Lac Gold Mines Ltd. 7/3/75 which merged into LAC Minerals Ltd. (New) 7/29/85 which was acquired by American Barrick Resources Corp. 10/17/94 which name changed to Barrick Gold Corp. 1/18/95

MCKENZIE ST BK (SPRINGFIELD, OR)
Merged into Umpqua Holdings Corp. 12/31/2001
Each share Class A Common exchanged for (1.3) shares Common 83-1/3¢ par

MCKEON CONSTR (CA)
Name changed to McKeon Liquidating Co. 04/16/1981
(See McKeon Liquidating Co.)

MCKEON LIQUIDATING CO. (CA)
Liquidation completed
Each share Common $1 par received initial distribution of $3.58 cash 04/16/1981
Each share Common $1 par

FINANCIAL INFORMATION, INC. MCK-MCL

exchanged for second and final distribution of (1) E & J Properties, Ltd. Unit of Limited Partnership Int. and $4.75 cash 10/26/1981
(See E & J Properties, Ltd.)

MCKESSON & ROBBINS, INC. (MD)
Common no par changed to $5 par 00/00/1932
Each share 7% Preference $50 par exchanged for (1.25) shares $3 Preference no par, (0.5) share Common $5 par and 50¢ cash 00/00/1935
Each share $3 Preference no par exchanged for (2.3) shares Common $18 par 00/00/1941
Each share Common $5 par exchanged for (0.25) share Common $18 par 00/00/1941
Common $18 par changed to $9 par and (1) additional share issued 08/10/1959
Stock Dividend - 10% 07/23/1951
Merged into Foremost-McKesson, Inc. 07/19/1967
Each share Common $9 par exchanged for (1) share $1.80 Conv. Preferred Ser. A $35 par and (0.75) share Common $2 par
Foremost-McKesson, Inc. name changed to McKesson Corp. (MD) 07/27/1983 which reincorporated in Delaware 07/31/1987
(See McKesson Corp. (Old) (DE))

MCKESSON & ROBBINS LTD.
Dissolved in 1941

MCKESSON CORP NEW (DE)
Common 1¢ par split (2) for (1) by issuance of (1) additional share payable 1/2/98 to holders of record 12/1/97 Ex date - 1/5/98
Under plan of merger name changed to McKesson HBOC Inc. 1/12/99
McKesson HBOC Inc. name changed to McKesson Corp. 7/30/2001

MCKESSON CORP OLD (DE)
Reincorporated 07/31/1987
Common $2 par split (2) for (1) by issuance of (1) additional share 10/01/1986
State of incorporation changed from (MD) to (DE) 07/31/1987
$1.80 Conv. Preferred Ser. A $35 par called for redemption 08/29/1994
Merged into ECO Acquisition Corp. 11/30/1994
Each share Common $2 par exchanged for $76 cash

MCKESSON FING TR (DE)
Issue Information - 3,500,000 TR CONV PFD SECS 5% offered at $50 per share on 02/13/1997
5% Trust Conv. Preferred Securities called for redemption at $50.50 plus $0.145833 accrued dividends on 6/22/2005

MCKESSON HBOC INC (DE)
Name changed to McKesson Corp. 07/30/2001

MCKINLEY DARRAGH SAVAGE MINES OF COBALT LTD.
Sold to McKinley Mines Securities Co. Ltd. on a (0.25) for (1) basis in 1928
McKinley Mines Securities Co. was acquired by Argus Interests Ltd. in 1939 which liquidated in 1943

MCKINLEY MINES SECURITIES CO. LTD.
Acquired by Argus Interests Ltd. in 1939 which liquidated in 1943

MCKINNEY GOLD HOLDINGS LTD.
Dissolved in 1948

MCKINNEY GOLD MINES LTD. (BC)
Recapitalized as Continental McKinney Mines Ltd. 3/10/67
Each share Capital Stock no par exchanged for (0.2) share Capital Stock no par
Continental McKinney Mines Ltd. recapitalized as Chandalar Resources Ltd. 6/13/73 which merged into International Park West Financial Corp. 6/20/78
(See International Park West Financial Corp.)

MCKINNEY MFG CO (PA)
Common $10 par changed to old Common $1 par 00/00/1939
Each share old Common $1 par exchanged for (5) shares new Common $1 par 00/00/1947
Stock Dividend - 100% 06/00/1950
Completely liquidated 12/29/1971
Each share 5% Preferred $100 par exchanged for first and final distribution of $100 cash
Each share new Common $1 par exchanged for first and final distribution of $2.65 cash

MCKINNEY RES INC (BC)
Recapitalized as Consolidated McKinney Resources, Inc. 09/03/1986
Each share Common no par exchanged for (0.4) share Common no par
Consolidated McKinney Resources, Inc. recapitalized as AZTEK Technologies Inc. 12/09/1996 which recapitalized as Aztek Resource Development Inc. 11/19/2004
(See Aztek Resource Development Inc.)

MCKINNON INDUSTRIES LTD.
Acquired by General Motors Corp. 00/00/1929
Details not available

MCKITTRICK OIL CO. (CA)
Completely liquidated 07/31/1964
Each (51.73734) shares Capital Stock $1 par exchanged (1) share Shell Oil Co. Common $1 par
(See Shell Oil Co.)

MCKONE TIRE & RUBBER CO.
Property sold 00/00/1928
Details not available

MCL CAP INC (ON)
Recapitalized as Feel Good Cars Corp. 02/02/2006
Each share Common no par exchanged for (0.33333333) share Common no par
Feel Good Cars Corp. name changed to Zenn Motor Co. Inc. which name changed to EEStor Corp. 04/06/2015

MCLACHLEN BANCSHARES CORP. (DC)
Merged into Citizens Bancorp (MD) 10/13/87
Each share Capital Stock $10 par exchanged for (0.95) share Common $10 par
Citizens Bancorp (MD) merged into Crestar Financial Corp. 12/31/96 which merged into SunTrust Banks, Inc. 12/31/98

MCLACHLEN BANKING CORP. (DC)
Each share Capital Stock $50 par exchanged for (2) shares Capital Stock $25 par 1/10/61
Stock Dividend - 12.5% 1/16/64
Name changed to McLachlen National Bank (Washington, DC) 7/5/68
McLachlen National Bank (Washington, DC) reorganized as McLachlen Bancshares Corp. 6/27/87 which merged into Citizens Bancorp (MD) 10/13/87 which merged into Crestar Financial Corp. 12/31/96 which merged into SunTrust Banks, Inc. 12/31/98

MCLACHLEN NATL BK (WASHINGTON, DC)
Capital Stock $25 par changed to $10 par and (1.5) additional shares issued 2/27/70
Under plan of reorganization each share Capital Stock $10 par automatically became (1) share McLachlen Bancshares Corp. Capital Stock $10 par 6/27/87
McLachlen Bancshares Corp. merged into Citizens Bancorp (MD) 10/13/87 which merged into Crestar Financial Corp. 12/31/96 which merged into SunTrust Banks, Inc. 12/31/98

MCLAIN GROCERY CO (OH)
Common $100 par split (4) for (3) by issuance of (1/3) additional share 9/20/57
Common $100 par changed to $10 par 11/1/62
Common $10 par changed to $5 par 9/1/65
Common $5 par changed to no par 6/21/71
Stock Dividends - 100% 2/27/52; 50% 9/1/65; 100% 6/21/71; 10% 10/28/75
Merged into Fleming Companies, Inc. 12/19/81
Each share Common no par exchanged for (1.5513) shares Common $2.50 par
(See Fleming Companies, Inc.)

MCLAREN CONSOLIDATED CONE CORP.
Acquired by National Biscuit Co. 00/00/1931
Details not available

MCLAREN PERFORMANCE TECHNOLOGIES INC (DE)
Name changed 4/20/2000
Name changed from McLaren Automotive Group, Inc. to McLaren Performance Technologies, Inc. 04/20/2000
Merged into Linamar Corp. 09/26/2003
Each share Common $0.00001 par exchanged for $0.8875 cash

MCLEAN BANK (MCLEAN, VA)
Name changed to McLean Bank N.A. (McLean, VA) 01/01/1987
McLean Bank N.A. (McLean, VA) name changed to Madison National Bank of Virginia (McLean, VA) 04/01/1988
(See Madison National Bank of Virginia (McLean, VA))

MCLEAN BANK N.A. (MCLEAN, VA)
Name changed to Madison National Bank of Virginia (McLean, VA) 04/01/1988
(See Madison National Bank of Virginia (McLean, VA))

MCLEAN INDS INC (DE)
Ctfs. dated prior to 05/13/1969
Common 1¢ par changed to Class A Common 1¢ par 06/03/1957
Stock Dividend - 500% 11/16/1955
$3 Preferred $5 par called for redemption 05/13/1969
$4 Preferred $5 par called for redemption 05/13/1969
Merged into Reynolds (R.J.) Tobacco Co. (NJ) 05/13/1969
Each share Class A Common 1¢ par or Class B Common 1¢ par exchanged for (1) share $2.25 Conv. Preferred no par
Reynolds (R.J.) Tobacco Co. (NJ) reincorporated in Delaware as Reynolds (R.J.) Industries, Inc. 06/29/1970 which name changed to RJR Nabisco, Inc. 04/25/1986 which merged into RJR Holdings Group, Inc. 04/28/1989
(See RJR Holdings Group, Inc.)

MCLEAN INDS INC NEW (DE)
Incorporated 00/00/1976
Plan of reorganization under Chapter 11 Federal Bankruptcy proceedings confirmed 05/16/1989
No stockholders' equity

MCLEAN SECURITIES CORP. (DE)
Name changed to McLean Industries, Inc. 07/06/1955
McLean Industries, Inc. merged into Reynolds (R.J.) Tobacco Co. (NJ) 05/13/1969 which reincorporated in Delaware as Reynolds (R.J.) Industries, Inc. 06/29/1970 which name changed to RJR Nabisco, Inc. 04/25/1986 which merged into RJR Holdings Group, Inc. 04/28/1989
(See RJR Holdings Group, Inc.)

MCLEAN TRUCKING CO (NC)
Class A Common $1 par reclassified as Common $1 par 12/31/56
6% Preferred called for redemption 9/1/57
Common $1 par changed to 50¢ par and (1) additional share issued 2/11/72
Common 50¢ par split (2) for (1) by issuance of (1) additional share 8/1/76
Stock Dividend - 25% 8/1/57
Merged into Meridian Express Co. 9/1/82
Each share Common 50¢ par exchanged for $18 cash

MCLELLAN GOLD MINES LTD.
Merged into Dyno Mines Ltd. 00/00/1953
Each share Capital Stock $1 par exchanged for (0.25) share Capital Stock $1 par
Dyno Mines Ltd. recapitalized as Canadian Dyno Mines Ltd. 12/06/1956 which merged into International Mogul Mines Ltd. 11/20/1968 which merged into Conwest Exploration Co. Ltd. (Old) (ON) 08/27/1982 which merged into Conwest Exploration Co. Ltd. (New) (AB) 09/01/1993 which merged into Alberta Energy Co. Ltd. 01/31/1996 which merged into EnCana Corp. 01/03/2003

MCLELLAN LONG LAC GOLD MINES LTD.
Acquired by McLellan Gold Mines Ltd. 00/00/1940
Details not available

MCLELLAN STORES CO. (DE)
Recapitalized 00/00/1935
Each share Class A & B Preferred $100 par exchanged for (1) share 6% Preferred $100 par and (1.5) shares Common $1 par
Common no par changed to $1 par
Merged into McCrory-McLellan Stores Corp. on a (1.25) for (1) basis
McCrory-McLellan Stores Corp. name changed to McCrory Corp. 07/16/1960
(See McCrory Corp.)

MCLEOD COPPER LTD (BC)
Recapitalized as MCP Resources Corp. 08/31/1977
Each share Capital Stock $1 par exchanged for (0.25) share Capital Stock no par
MCP Resources Corp. recapitalized as Petro-American Energy Inc. 07/06/1981
(See Petro-American Energy Inc.)

MCLEODUSA INC (DE)
Name changed 05/29/1997
Secondary Offering - 5,200,000 shares CL A offered at $28 per share on 11/15/1996
Name changed from McLeod Inc. to McLeodUSA Inc. 05/29/1997
Class A Common 1¢ par split (2) for (1) by issuance of (1) additional share payable 07/26/1999 to holders of record 07/12/1999
Class A Common 1¢ par split (3) for (1) by issuance of (2) additional shares payable 04/24/2000 to holders of record 04/04/2000
Plan of reorganization under Chapter 11 Federal Bankruptcy Code effective 04/16/2002
Each share 6.75% Conv. Preferred Ser. A exchanged for approximately (29.32) shares new Class A Common 1¢ par
Each share Conv. Preferred Ser. D

exchanged for approximately (284.38) shares new Class A Common 1¢ par
Each share Conv. Preferred Ser. E exchanged for approximately (284.38) shares new Class A Common 1¢ par
Each share old Class A Common 1¢ par exchanged for (0.05854) share new Class A Common 1¢ par
Note: Unexchanged certificates were cancelled and became without value 04/16/2003
Plan of reorganization under Chapter 11 Federal Bankruptcy Code effective 01/06/2006
No stockholders' equity
Merged into PAETEC Holding Corp. 02/08/2008
Each share Common 1¢ par exchanged for (1.3) shares Common 1¢ par
PAETEC Holding Corp. merged into Windstream Corp. 12/01/2011 which name changed to Windstream Holdings, Inc. 09/03/2013

MCLOONE METAL GRAPHICS INC (WI)
Merged into JSJ Corp. 07/31/1980
Each share Common 10¢ par exchanged for $35 cash

MCLOUGHLIN TEXTILE CORP.
In process of liquidation in 1936

MCLOUTH STL CORP (MI)
Each share Common no par exchanged for (2) shares Common $5 par in 1945
Each share Common $5 par exchanged for (2) shares Common $2.50 par in 1948
5% Preferred $100 par called for redemption 2/19/59
Common $2.50 par split (2) for (1) by issuance of (1) additional share 5/6/60
5-1/4% Preferred called for redemption 3/31/61
Common $2.50 par split (3) for (2) by issuance of (0.5) additional share 9/20/74
Stock Dividends - 100% 9/29/50; 25% 10/1/53; 25% 4/10/56
Reorganized under Chapter 11 Federal Bankruptcy Code as MLX Corp. 12/11/84
Each share Common $2.50 par exchanged for (0.063816) share Common 1¢ par
Note: Unexchanged shares became valueless 12/11/89
MLX Corp. merged into Morton Industrial Group Inc. 1/20/98

MCM CAP GROUP INC (DE)
Issue Information - 2,500,000 shares COM offered at $10 per share on 07/08/1999
Name changed to Encore Capital Group, Inc. 4/2/2002

MCM CAP ONE INC (ON)
Name changed to Enerdynamic Hybrid Technologies Corp. 09/11/2014

MCM CORP (NC)
Each (3,000) shares old Common $1 par exchanged for (1) share new Common $1 par 7/20/2000
Note: In effect holders received $2.31 cash per share and public interest was eliminated

MCM SPLIT SHARE CORP (ON)
Preferred reclassified as Priority Equity Shares 12/12/2007
Completely liquidated
Each Priority Equity Share received first and final distribution of $13.1874 cash payable 03/31/2011 to holders of record 03/31/2011
No equity for Class A Shares

MCMANN INVTS INC (NV)
Name changed to Bulls On The Run Productions, Corp. 06/15/1988

Bulls On The Run Productions, Corp. name changed to China Treasure, Inc. 04/18/1994 which name changed to China Pacific, Inc. 01/25/1996
(See China Pacific, Inc.)

MCMANUS RED LAKE GOLD MINES LTD (ON)
Recapitalized as New McManus Red Lake Gold Mines Ltd. 09/13/1977
Each share Capital Stock $1 par exchanged for (0.1) share Common no par
New McManus Red Lake Gold Mines Ltd. recapitalized as Milestone Resource Corp. 08/26/1987 which reorganized as Horizontal Petroleum Exploration Ltd. 07/26/1990
(See Horizontal Petroleum Exploration Ltd.)

MCMANUS STEEL & IRON CO.
Bankrupt in 1930

MCMARMAC RED LAKE GOLD MINES LTD (ON)
Charter cancelled for failure to pay taxes and file returns 03/14/1978

MCMARTIN INC (CA)
Charter suspended for failure to file reports and pay fees 9/3/91

MCMILLAN GOLD MINES LTD. (ON)
Charter cancelled and declared dissolved for failure to pay taxes and file returns 4/10/79

MCMILLAN RADIATION LABS INC (MA)
Adjudicated bankrupt 11/15/1973
Stockholders' equity unlikely

MCMILLEN CO.
Acquired by Allied Mills, Inc. 00/00/1929
Details not available

MCMILLEN CORP (DE)
Merged into Peninsular Life Insurance Co. (New) 9/30/76
Each share Common $3 par exchanged for (1) share Common $3 par
Peninsular Life Insurance Co. (New) merged into McM Corp. 8/20/79
(See McM Corp.)

MCMORAN EXPLORATION CO. OLD (DE)
Reincorporated 03/31/1978
State of incorporation changed from (UT) to (DE) 03/31/1978
Name changed to McMoRan Oil & Gas Co. (Old) 01/31/1979
McMoRan Oil & Gas Co. (Old) merged into Freeport-McMoRan Inc. 04/07/1981 which merged into IMC Global Inc. 12/22/1997 which merged into Mosaic Co. (Old) 10/22/2004 which merged into Mosaic Co. (New) 05/25/2011

MCMORAN EXPLORATION CO NEW (DE)
Each share 5% Conv. Preferred exchanged for (5.1975) shares Common 1¢ par 06/30/2007
Each share 6.75% Mandatory Conv. Preferred automatically became (6.7204) shares Common 1¢ par 11/15/2010
Merged into Freeport-McMoRan Copper & Gold Inc. 06/03/2013
Each share Common 1¢ par exchanged for (1.15) Gulf Coast Ultra Deep Royalty Trust Royalty Trust Units and $14.75 cash
(Additional Information in Active)

MCMORAN OIL & GAS CO NEW (DE)
Merged into McMoRan Exploration Co. 11/17/1998
Each share Common 1¢ par exchanged for (0.2) share Common 1¢ par
(See McMoRan Exploration Co.)

MCMORAN OIL & GAS CO OLD (DE)
Common no par split (2) for (1) by issuance of (1) additional share 05/19/1980
Merged into Freeport-McMoRan Inc. 04/07/1981
Each share Common $1 par exchanged for (1) share Common $1 par
Freeport-McMoRan Inc. merged into IMC Global Inc. 12/22/1997 which merged into Mosaic Co. (Old) 10/22/2004 which merged into Mosaic Co. (New) 05/25/2011

MCMS INC (DE)
Plan of reorganization under Chapter 11 Federal Bankruptcy Code effective 1/13/2004
No stockholders' equity

MCN ENERGY GROUP INC (MI)
Name changed 4/28/97
Common 1¢ par split (2) for (1) by issuance of (1) additional share 1/23/89
Common 1¢ par split (2) for (1) by issuance of (1) additional share 11/28/94
Name changed from MCN Corp. to MCN Energy Group Inc. 4/28/97
Each share 8.75% Preferred Increased Dividend Equity no par exchanged for (0.255) share Common 1¢ par 4/30/99
Each Income Pride exchanged for (1.7241) shares Common 1¢ par 5/16/2000
Merged into DTE Energy Co. 5/31/2001
Each share Common 1¢ par exchanged for either (0.715) share Common no par or $24 cash
Note: Option to receive stock expired 5/31/2001

MCN FING I (DE)
8.625% Trust Originated Preferred Securities called for redemption at $25 on 02/21/2002

MCN FING II (DE)
8.75% Guaranteed Trust Preferred Securities called for redemption at $25 on 1/15/2004

MCN FING III (DE)
Issue Information - 2,300,000 GTD TR PFD SECS 7.25% offered at $50 per share on 03/19/1997
7.25% Guaranteed Trust Preferred Securities called for redemption at $50 on 05/16/2002

MCN MICH LTD PARTNERSHIP (MI)
9.375% Preferred Ser. A called for redemption at $25 on 2/21/2002

MCN MULTICAST NETWORKS INC (NV)
Each share old Common $0.001 par exchanged for (0.25) share new Common $0.001 par 3/7/2005
Name changed to Downtown America Funding Corp. 9/8/2005
Downtown America Funding Corp. name changed to Savior Energy Corp. 12/22/2006

MCNAB CREEK GOLD CORP (NV)
Name changed to Utah Uranium Corp. 04/27/2007
Utah Uranium Corp. name changed to Universal Potash Corp. 06/16/2008

MCNAUGHTON APPAREL GROUP INC (DE)
Merged into Jones Apparel Group, Inc. 06/19/2001
Each share Common 1¢ par exchanged for (0.282) share Common 1¢ par and $10.50 cash
Jones Apparel Group, Inc. name changed to Jones Group Inc. 10/18/2010
(See Jones Group Inc.)

MCNEIL CORP (OH)
Common no par split (2) for (1) by issuance of (1) additional share 12/16/1968
Merged into Pentair, Inc. 09/02/1986

Each share Common no par exchanged for $39 cash

MCNEIL MACHINE & ENGINEERING CO. (OH)
Common $5 par changed to no par and (1) additional share issued 8/8/59
5% Preferred Ser. A $40 par called for redemption 4/1/61
Stock Dividend - 10% 8/31/54
Name changed to McNeil Corp. 12/28/64
(See McNeil Corp.)

MCNEIL REAL ESTATE FUND LTD (CA)
Merged into a private company 1/31/2000
Each Unit of Limited Partnership Int. Ser. IX exchanged for $429.13 cash
Each Unit of Limited Partnership Int. Ser. X exchanged for $234.37 cash
Each Unit of Limited Partnership Int. Ser. XI exchanged for $221.39 cash
Each Unit of Limited Partnership Int. Ser. XII exchanged for $73.17 cash
Each Unit of Limited Partnership Int. Ser. XV exchanged for $161.75 cash
Each Unit of Limited Partnership Int. Ser. XXI exchanged for $99.46 cash
Each Unit of Limited Partnership Int. Ser. XXII exchanged for $0.27 cash
Each Unit of Limited Partnership Int. Ser. XXIII exchanged for $0.27 cash
Each Unit of Limited Partnership Int. Ser. XXIV exchanged for $357.13 cash
Note: Above amounts include special cash distributions payable 1/31/2000

MCNEIL REAL ESTATE FUND XX L.P. (CA)
Merged into a private company 02/15/2000
Each Unit of Ltd. Partnership Int. received $105 cash
Note: Above amount includes special cash distribution payable 02/15/2000

MCNEIL REAL ESTATE FD XXVII LP (DE)
Merged into a private company 01/20/2000
Each Unit of Ltd. Partnership Int. exchanged for $10.98 cash
Note: Amount includes special cash distribution payable 01/20/2000

MCNELLEN RES INC (BC)
Common no par split (2) for (1) by issuance of (1) additional share 01/27/1987
Merged into Golden Goose Resources Inc. 09/30/1996
Each share Common no par exchanged for (0.04395604) share Common no par
Golden Goose Resources Inc. merged into Kodiak Exploration Ltd. 12/16/2010 which name changed to Prodigy Gold Inc. 01/04/2011 which merged into Argonaut Gold Inc. 12/11/2012

MCNELLEY MINES (1937) LTD. (ON)
Acquired by Barymin Explorations Ltd. 07/15/1966
Each share Capital Stock $1 par exchanged for (2) shares Capital Stock 50¢ par
(See Barymin Explorations Ltd.)

MCNICKEL INC (ON)
Recapitalized as Sahelian Goldfields Inc. 09/09/1996
Each share Common no par exchanged for (0.125) share Common no par
Sahelian Goldfields Inc. recapitalized as Sage Gold Inc. 03/03/2005

MCO CAP INC (QC)
Recapitalized as IOU Financial Inc. 02/28/2011
Each share Class B Common no par exchanged for (0.25) share Class B Common no par

MCO HLDGS INC (DE)
Name changed to MAXXAM Inc. 10/06/1988
(See MAXXAM Inc.)

MCO RES INC (DE)
Acquired by United Meridian Corp. 07/11/1988
Each share Common 1¢ par exchanged for $0.40 cash

MCORP (DE)
Liquidating plan of reorganization under Chapter 11 Federal Bankruptcy proceedings confirmed 10/01/1993
No stockholders' equity

MCP RES CORP (BC)
Reorganized as Petro-American Energy Inc. 07/06/1981
Each share Capital Stock no par exchanged for (1) share Common no par
(See Petro-American Energy Inc.)

MCPHAIL INDS INC (DE)
Name changed 3/9/66
Name changed from McPhail Candy Corp. to McPhail Industries, Inc. 3/9/66
Voluntarily dissolved 6/12/96
Stockholders' equity undetermined

MCPHAR INSTR CORP (ON)
Merged into Androck Inc. 1/31/84
Each share Common no par exchanged for (0.2) share Non-Vtg. Class A no par and (0.1) share Class B no par
Androck Inc. name changed to Autrex Inc. 1/20/86 which merged into Basis 100 Inc. 10/29/99

MCPHERSONS LTD (AUSTRALIA)
Stock Dividend - 100% 07/28/1987
ADR agreement terminated 07/11/1996
Each ADR for Ordinary AUD 50¢ par exchanged for (5) shares Ordinary AUD 50¢ par

MCQUAY INC NEW (MN)
5% Preferred called for redemption 7/1/60
Stock Dividend - 100% 6/30/67
Under plan of merger name changed to McQuay-Perfex Inc. 6/23/71 which name changed back to McQuay Inc. 5/31/83
Merged into Snyder General Corp. 11/2/84
Each share Common $1 par exchanged for $19 cash

MCQUAY NORRIS MFG CO (DE)
Each share Common no par exchanged for (3) shares Common $10 par in 1944
Common $10 par split (5) for (4) by issuance of (0.25) additional share 2/29/60
Stock Dividends - 20% 3/1/55; 10% 2/28/69
Merged into Eaton Yale & Towne Inc. 10/31/69
Each share Common $10 par exchanged for (0.8) share Common 50¢ par
Eaton Yale & Towne Inc. name changed to Eaton Corp. 4/21/71

MCQUAY PERFEX INC (MN)
Stock Dividends - 50% 10/01/1976; 50% 10/02/1978
Name changed to McQuay Inc. 05/31/1983
(See McQuay Inc.)

MCQUILLAN GOLD LTD (BC)
Merged into Nexus Resource Corp. 10/25/1982
Each share Common no par exchanged for (0.25) share Common no par
Nexus Resource Corp. recapitalized as Pacific Gold Corp. (BC) 07/05/1990 which reincorporated in Alberta 05/12/1994 which reincorporated in Ontario 06/27/1995 which name changed to Worldtek (Canada) Ltd. 07/04/1996
(See Worldtek (Canada) Ltd.)

MCR CAP INC (ON)
Recapitalized as Covesco Capital Corp. 10/22/1993
Each share $0.026 1st Preferred Ser. A no par exchanged for (1) share $0.026 1st Preferred Ser. A no par
Each share 2nd Preferred Ser. Y no par exchanged for (1) share 2nd Preferred Ser. Y no par
Each (15) shares Class A Special Stock no par exchanged for (1) share Class A Special Stock no par
Each (15) shares Common no par exchanged for (1) share Common no par
Covesco Capital Corp. merged into Magra Computer Technologies Corp. 08/14/1996
(See Magra Computer Technologies Corp.)

MCR INDL DISTR & SVC CORP (DE)
Name changed 2/25/88
Each share Common $0.0001 par exchanged for (0.01) share Common 1¢ par 11/12/85
Name changed from MCR Associates, Inc. to MCR Industrial Distribution & Service Corp. 2/25/88
Charter cancelled and declared inoperative and void for non-payment of taxes 3/1/91

MCRAE CONS OIL & GAS INC (DE)
Common 1¢ par split (3) for (2) by issuance of (0.5) additional share 8/16/79
Common 1¢ par split (2) for (1) by issuance of (1) additional share 4/21/80
Completely liquidated 12/29/83
Each share Common 1¢ par exchanged for first and final distribution of $3.50 principal amount of Lear Petroleum Corp. 9% Conv. Subordinated Debentures due 12/29/2003, (0.12227) share Lear Petroleum Corp. (TX) Common 10¢ par and $7 cash
Lear Petroleum Corp. (TX) reincorporated in Delaware 5/18/84
(See Lear Petroleum Corp. (DE))

MCRAE INDS INC (NC)
Reincorporated under the laws of Delaware and Common no par reclassified as Conv. Class B $1 par 09/23/1983

MCRAE OIL & GAS CORP. (DE)
Stock Dividend - 10% 12/16/55
Merged into Sunset International Petroleum Corp. on a (0.77981) for (1) basis 7/2/58
Sunset International Petroleum Corp. merged into Sunasco Inc. 4/30/66 which name changed to Scientific Resources Corp. 10/11/68
(See Scientific Resources Corp.)

MCRAE SHOE INC (NC)
Name changed to McRae Industries, Inc. (NC) 07/14/1969
McRae Industries, Inc. (NC) reincorporated in Delaware 09/23/1983

MCS GLOBAL CORP (AB)
Reorganized under the laws of British Columbia as Newstrike Capital Inc. 05/08/2006
Each share Common no par exchanged for (0.33333333) share Common no par
Newstrike Capital Inc. merged into Timmins Gold Corp. 05/28/2015 which recapitalized as Alio Gold Inc. 05/16/2017

MCS TELECOMMUNICATIONS INC (AZ)
Each (300,000) shares old Common no par exchanged for (1) share new Common no par 12/21/90
Note: In effect holders received $0.24 cash per share and public interest was eliminated

MCSEV EXPL LTD (AB)
Name changed to Eco-Dynamics Industries Inc. 07/24/1990
(See Eco-Dynamics Industries Inc.)

MCSI INC (MD)
Chapter 11 bankruptcy petition dismissed 05/22/2008
No stockholders' equity

MCSMOOTHIES INC (CA)
Reorganized as Ameri-Dream Entertainment, Inc. 05/30/2002
Each share Common $0.001 par exchanged for (5) shares Common $0.001 par
Ameri-Dream Entertainment, Inc. name changed to Soleil Film & Television, Inc. 11/07/2003 which reorganized as Soleil Film, Inc. 07/13/2004 which name changed to Imperia Entertainment, Inc. (CA) 08/04/2005 which reincorporated in Nevada 08/28/2006 which recapitalized as Viratech Corp. 10/11/2011

MCT HLDG CORP (NV)
Name changed to Dakota Plains Holdings, Inc. 03/28/2012
(See Dakota Plains Holdings, Inc.)

MC2 LEARNING SYS INC (CANADA)
Name changed to Centrinity Inc. 3/24/2000
(See Centrinity Inc.)

MCVICAR INDS INC (ON)
Acquired by 1909734 Ontario Ltd. 04/30/2014
Each share Common no par exchanged for $0.50 cash
Note: Unexchanged certificates will be cancelled and become without value 04/30/2020

MCVICAR MINERALS LTD (CANADA)
Issue Information - 1,250,000 shares COM offered at $0.40 per share on 05/01/1997
Acquired by Hanfeng Evergreen Inc. 6/5/2003
Each share Common no par exchanged for (0.5054922) share Common no par and (1) Class A Special Share no par

MCVICAR MINING CO. LTD. (BC)
Acquired by Western Surf Inlet Mines Ltd. on (1/7) for (1) basis 04/00/1962
Western Surf Inlet Mines Ltd. acquired by Matachewan Consolidated Mines, Ltd. 04/26/1966

MCVICAR RES INC (ON)
Name changed to McVicar Industries Inc. 09/08/2008

MCVITTIE GOLD MINES LTD.
Bankrupt in 1937

MCVITTIE-GRAHAM MINES, LTD.
Assets acquired by McVittie-Graham Mining Co., Ltd. in 1944
Each (10) shares Capital Stock $1 par received (2) shares Conwest Exploration Co., Ltd. (Old) (ONT) Capital Stock no par and (1) share McVittie - Graham Mining Co., Ltd. Capital Stock $1 par
(See each company's listing)

MCVITTIE GRAHAM MNG LTD (ON)
Merged into Central Patricia Ltd. 6/19/80
Each share Capital Stock $1 par exchanged for (1) share 6% Non-Vtg. Non-Cum. Retractable Preference $8 par
(See Central Patricia Ltd.)

MCVITTIE KIRKLAND GOLD MINES, LTD. (ON)
Charter surrendered for failure to file reports and pay taxes in 1956

MCW ENERGY GROUP LTD (ON)
Recapitalized as Petroteq Energy Inc. 05/05/2017
Each share Common no par exchanged for (0.03333333) share Common no par

MCW ENTERPRISES LTD (BC)
Reincorporated under the laws of Ontario as MCW Energy Group Ltd. 12/20/2012
MCW Energy Group Ltd. recapitalized as Petroteq Energy Inc. 05/05/2017

MCWATTERS GOLD MINES LTD (CANADA)
Completely liquidated 2/24/70
Each share Capital Stock no par exchanged for first and final distribution of (0.25) share Tontine Mining Ltd. Capital Stock no par
Tontine Mining Ltd. merged into Coldstream Mines Ltd. 1/13/72
(See Coldstream Mines Ltd.)

MCWATTERS MNG INC (QC)
Each share old Class A Common no par exchanged for (0.33333333) share new Class A Common no par 06/30/1997
Plan of reorganization under the Companies' Creditors Arrangement Act effective 04/08/2002
Each share Conv. Preferred exchanged for (1.29388) shares Common no par and (1.29388) Rights expiring 05/03/2002
Each share new Class A Common no par exchanged for (0.28122) share Common no par and (0.28122) Right expiring 05/03/2002
Each share Common no par exchanged for (1) share Class A Preferred no par 06/02/2008
Class A Preferred no par called for redemption at $0.000535 on 03/05/2014
Note: Distribution will be made only to holders entitled to $2 or more
Public interest eliminated

MCWHORTER TECHNOLOGIES INC (DE)
Merged into Eastman Chemical Co. 7/14/2000
Each share Common 1¢ par exchanged for $19.70 cash

MCWILLIAMS DREDGING CO. (DE)
Reincorporated 12/31/1955
Each share Common no par exchanged for (2) shares Common $10 par 00/00/1953
State of incorporation changed from (IL) to (DE) 12/31/1955
Name changed to Williams-McWilliams Industries, Inc. 03/13/1956
Williams-McWilliams Industries, Inc. merged into Zapata Off-Shore Co. 04/12/1968 which name changed to Zapata Norness Inc. 11/25/1968 which name changed to Zapata Corp. (DE) 02/15/1972 which reincorporated in Nevada 04/30/1999 which reincorporated in Delaware as Harbinger Group Inc. 12/23/2009 which name changed to HRG Group, Inc. 03/11/2015 which recapitalized as Spectrum Brands Holdings, Inc. (New) 07/16/2018

MCWILLYS ENTERPRISES (UT)
Involuntarily dissolved for failure to file annual reports 02/01/1989

MD HEALTHSHARES CORP (LA)
Assets seized for benefit of creditors 07/21/1999
Stockholders' equity unlikely

MD HLDGS CORP (NV)
Each share old Common $0.001 par exchanged for (0.05) share new Common $0.001 par 10/27/2008
New Common $0.001 par split (3.5) for (1) by issuance of (2.5) additional shares payable 11/04/2009 to holders of record 11/02/2009 Ex date - 11/05/2009
Name changed to Guanwei Recycling Corp. 12/28/2009

MD MULTIMEDIA INC (CANADA)
Dissolved for non-compliance 09/26/2008

MD TECHNOLOGIES INC (DE)
Each share Common $0.0001 par exchanged for (0.25) share Common $0.0004 par 09/26/2003
Completely liquidated 02/05/2015
Each share Common $0.0004 par exchanged for first and final distribution of $0.024 cash

MDC CORP (PA)
Name changed to Bouton Corp. (PA) 07/14/1982
Bouton Corp. (PA) reincorporated in Delaware 06/29/1992
(See Bouton Corp.)

MDC CORP INC (ON)
Recapitalized 05/27/1996
Name changed 05/28/1999
Recapitalized from MDC Corp. to MDC Communication Corp. 05/27/1996
Each share Class A Subordinate no par exchanged for (1/6) share Class A Subordinate no par
Name changed from MDC Communication Corp. to MDC Corp. Inc. 05/28/1999
Name changed to MDC Partners Inc. (ONT) 01/01/2004
MDC Partners Inc. (ONT) reincorporated in Canada 06/28/2004

MDC FINL INC (BC)
Delisted from Vancouver Stock Exchange 05/11/1990

MDC PARTNERS INC (ON)
Reincorporated under the laws of Canada 06/28/2004

MDCORP (NV)
Name changed to Qian Yuan Baixing Inc. 05/01/2018

MDE EXPLS LTD (BC)
Reincorporated under the laws of Delaware as Puff Pac Industries Inc. 12/01/1989
Puff Pac Industries Inc. name changed to Air Packaging Technologies Inc. 09/01/1992
(See Air Packaging Technologies Inc.)

MDI ENTMT INC (DE)
Merged into Scientific Games International, Inc. 1/22/2003
Each share Common $0.001 par exchanged for $1.60 cash

MDI INC (DE)
Each share old Common 1¢ par exchanged for (0.1) share new Common 1¢ par 08/25/2009
Chapter 7 bankruptcy proceedings terminated 10/10/2012
No stockholders' equity

MDI MOBILE DATA INTL LTD (CANADA)
Reincorporated 12/10/1984
Place of incorporation changed from (BC) to (Canada) 12/10/1984
Acquired by Motorola Canada Ltd. 07/22/1988
Each share Common no par exchanged for $13.50 cash

MDI TECHNOLOGIES INC (DE)
Merged into Logibec Groupe Informatique Ltd. 06/30/2005
Each share Common $0.001 par exchanged for $2.60 cash

MDL INFORMATION SYS INC (DE)
Merged into Elsevier N.V. 04/25/1997
Each share Common 1¢ par exchanged for $32 cash

MDM VASCULAR SYS INC (NV)
Reorganized as Casinolive.Com Corp. 3/9/99
Each share Common $0.001 par exchanged for (2) shares Common $0.001 par

MDN INC (QC)
Recapitalized as Niobay Metals Inc. 09/21/2016
Each share Common no par exchanged for (0.2) share Common no par

MDP WORLDWIDE ENTMT INC (CANADA)
Name changed to M8 Entertainment Inc. 04/14/2004

MDR SWITCHVIEW GLOBAL NETWORKS INC (CANADA)
Name changed to Avotus Corp. 5/14/2002
(See Avotus Corp.)

MDRNA INC (DE)
Recapitalized as Marina Biotech, Inc. 07/22/2010
Each share Common $0.006 par exchanged for (0.25) share Common $0.006 par
Marina Biotech, Inc. name changed to Adhera Therapeutics, Inc. 10/09/2018

MDS HEALTH GROUP LTD (ON)
8% Conv. Class A Preference $5 par reclassified as Class C Preferred $5 par 09/22/1980
Common no par reclassified as Conv. Class A Common no par and (1) share Class B Preferred no par distributed 09/30/1980
Each share Class B Preferred no par exchanged for (1) share Class B no par 06/04/1981
Class C Preferred called for redemption 07/00/1981
Conv. Class A Common no par split (2) for (1) by issuance of (1) additional share 07/15/1983
Class B no par split (2) for (1) by issuance of (1) additional share 07/15/1983
Conv. Class A Common no par split (2) for (1) by issuance of (1) additional share 03/15/1990
Class B no par split (2) for (1) by issuance of (1) additional share 03/15/1990
Name changed to MDS Inc. 10/31/1996
MDS Inc. name changed to Nordion Inc. 11/01/2010
(See Nordion Inc.)
(1st Ent. 07/10/1973 - Orig. Pros.)

MDS INC (ON)
Class A Common no par split (2) for (1) by issuance of (1) additional share payable 11/21/1996 to holders of record 11/15/1996
Each share Class A Common no par reclassified as (1.05) shares Common no par 03/03/2000
Class B Common no par reclassified as Common no par 03/03/2000
Common no par split (2) for (1) by issuance of (1) additional share payable 10/10/2000 to holders of record 09/26/2000 Ex date - 10/11/2000
Common no par split (2) for (1) by issuance of (1) additional share payable 02/26/2001 to holders of record 01/26/2001 Ex date - 02/27/2001
Name changed to Nordion Inc. 11/01/2010
(See Nordion Inc.)

MDS INDS INC (NY)
Charter cancelled and proclaimed dissolved for failure to pay taxes 12/20/1977

MDSI MOBILE DATA SOLUTIONS INC (CANADA)
Merged into Vista Equity Partners 09/23/2005
Each share Common no par exchanged for $8 cash

MDT CORP (DE)
Merged into Getinge Acquisition Corp. 07/29/1996
Each share Common $1.25 par exchanged for $5.50 cash

MDU COMMUNICATIONS INTL INC (DE)
Reincorporated 04/20/1999
State of incorporation changed from (CO) to (DE) and Common no par changed to $0.001 par 04/20/1999
Each share old Common $0.001 par exchanged for (0.1) share new Common $0.001 par 12/14/2010
SEC revoked common stock registration 07/25/2016

MDU RES GROUP INC (DE)
11% Preferred $100 par called for redemption 10/01/1989
4.5% Preferred $100 par called for redemption at $105 on 04/01/2017
4.7% Preferred $100 par called for redemption at $102 on 04/01/2017
5.1% Preferred $100 par called for redemption at $102 on 04/01/2017
(Additional Information in Active)

MDX MED INC (BC)
Each share old Common no par exchanged for (0.2) share new Common no par 11/08/2002
Name changed to Urodynamix Technologies Ltd. 06/21/2006
Urodynamix Technologies Ltd. recapitalized as Venturi Ventures Inc. 08/29/2011
(See Venturi Ventures Inc.)

MEACON BAY RES INC (ON)
Recapitalized as Advantex Marketing International Inc. 9/16/91
Each share Common no par exchanged for (0.66) share Common no par
Preference not affected except for change of name

MEAD CORP (OH)
$5.5 Preferred Ser. B no par called for redemption 09/01/1946
6% Preferred Ser. A no par called for redemption 09/01/1946
4% 2nd Preferred called for redemption 12/01/1951
4.3% 2nd Preferred $50 par called for redemption 11/01/1956
4.25% Preferred $100 par called for redemption 03/30/1979
5% Preferred $100 par called for redemption 03/30/1979
6% Preferred $100 par called for redemption 03/30/1979
$2.80 Conv. Preferred no par called for redemption 03/15/1984
$2.80 Conv. Vtg. Preferred 1968 Ser. no par called for redemption 03/15/1984
Common no par changed to $25 par 02/09/1955
Common $25 par changed to $5 par and (1) additional share issued 06/01/1956
Common $5 par changed to no par 05/31/1966
Common no par split (2) for (1) by issuance of (1) additional share 06/02/1969
Common no par split (3) for (2) by issuance of (0.5) additional share 06/01/1976
Common no par split (2) for (1) by issuance of (1) additional share 06/01/1987
Common no par split (2) for (1) by issuance of (1) additional share payable 12/01/1997 to holders of record 11/12/1997 Ex date - 12/02/1997
Merged into MeadWestvaco Corp. 01/29/2002
Each share Common no par exchanged for (1) share Common 1¢ par and $1.20 cash
MeadWestvaco Corp. merged into WestRock Co. 07/01/2015

MEAD FIBRE CO.
Acquired by Mead Corp. 00/00/1930
Details not available

MEAD JOHNSON & CO. (IN)
Each share 7% Preferred $10 par exchanged for (10) shares 4% Preferred $1 par in 1945
Each share Common no par exchanged for (10) shares Common $1 par in 1945
4% Preferred $1 par changed to 33-1/3¢ par and (2) additional shares issued 5/24/62
Common $1 par split (3) for (1) by issuance of (2) additional shares 5/24/62
Merged into Bristol-Myers Co. 12/22/67
Each share 4% Preferred 33-1/3¢ par exchanged for (0.008866) share $2 Conv. Preferred $1 par
Each share Common $1 par exchanged for (0.2) share $2 Conv. Preferred $1 par and (0.39) share Common $1 par
Bristol-Myers Co. name changed to Bristol-Myers Squibb Co. 10/4/89

MEAD JOHNSON NUTRITION CO (DE)
Class A Common 1¢ par reclassified as Common 1¢ par 01/07/2010
Acquired by Reckitt Benckiser Group PLC 06/15/2017
Each share Common 1¢ par exchanged for $90 cash

MEAD PAPER BOARD CORP.
Merged into Mead Corp. 00/00/1930
Details not available

MEAD PULP & PAPER CO.
Merged into Mead Corp. 00/00/1930
Details not available

MEADE INSTRS CORP (DE)
Old Common 1¢ par split (2) for (1) by issuance of (1) additional share payable 06/19/2000 to holders of record 05/22/2000
Each share old Common 1¢ par exchanged for (0.05) share new Common 1¢ par 08/10/2009
Acquired by Sunny Optics Inc. 09/13/2013
Each share Common 1¢ par exchanged for $4.50 cash

MEADFIELD MNG CORP (BC)
Merged into Keith Resources Ltd. 07/16/1991
Each share Common no par exchanged for (0.11111111) share Common no par
Keith Resources Ltd. recapitalized as Avalon Ventures Ltd. 09/30/1994 which name changed to Avalon Rare Metals Inc. (BC) 02/18/2009 which reincorporated in Canada 02/09/2011 which name changed to Avalon Advanced Materials Inc. 03/03/2016

MEADOW BAY CAP CORP (BC)
Each share old Common no par exchanged for (1/3) share new Common no par 02/10/2010
Name changed to Meadow Bay Gold Corp. 04/04/2011

MEADOW BROOK NATIONAL BANK (WEST HEMPSTEAD, NY)
Under plan of merger name changed to National Bank of North America (West Hempstead, NY) 05/08/1967
(See National Bank of North America (West Hempstead, NY))

MEADOW BROOK NATIONAL BANK OF NASSAU COUNTY (WEST HEMPSTEAD, NY)
Under plan of merger name changed to Meadow Brook National Bank (West Hempstead, NY) 11/14/1960
Meadow Brook National Bank (West Hempstead, NY) name changed to National Bank of North America (West Hempstead, NY) 05/08/1967
(See National Bank of North America (West Hempstead, NY))

exchanged for approximately (284.38) shares new Class A Common 1¢ par
Each share Conv. Preferred Ser. E exchanged for approximately (284.38) shares new Class A Common 1¢ par
Each share old Class A Common 1¢ par exchanged for (0.05854) share new Class A Common 1¢ par
Note: Unexchanged certificates were cancelled and became without value 04/16/2003
Plan of reorganization under Chapter 11 Federal Bankruptcy Code effective 01/06/2006
No stockholders' equity
Merged into PAETEC Holding Corp. 02/08/2008
Each share Common 1¢ par exchanged for (1.3) shares Common 1¢ par
PAETEC Holding Corp. merged into Windstream Corp. 12/01/2011 which name changed to Windstream Holdings, Inc. 09/03/2013

MCLOONE METAL GRAPHICS INC (WI)
Merged into JSJ Corp. 07/31/1980
Each share Common 10¢ par exchanged for $35 cash

MCLOUGHLIN TEXTILE CORP.
In process of liquidation in 1936

MCLOUTH STL CORP (MI)
Each share Common no par exchanged for (2) shares Common $5 par in 1945
Each share Common $5 par exchanged for (2) shares Common $2.50 par in 1948
5% Preferred $100 par called for redemption 2/19/59
Common $2.50 par split (2) for (1) by issuance of (1) additional share 5/6/60
5-1/4% Preferred called for redemption 3/31/61
Common $2.50 par split (3) for (2) by issuance of (0.5) additional share 9/20/74
Stock Dividends - 100% 9/29/50; 25% 10/1/53; 25% 4/10/56
Reorganized under Chapter 11 Federal Bankruptcy Code as MLX Corp. 12/11/84
Each share Common $2.50 par exchanged for (0.063816) share Common 1¢ par
Note: Unexchanged shares became valueless 12/11/89
MLX Corp. merged into Morton Industrial Group Inc. 1/20/98

MCM CAP GROUP INC (DE)
Issue Information - 2,500,000 shares COM offered at $10 per share on 07/08/1999
Name changed to Encore Capital Group, Inc. 4/2/2002

MCM CAP ONE INC (ON)
Name changed to Enerdynamic Hybrid Technologies Corp. 09/11/2014

MCM CORP (NC)
Each (3,000) shares old Common $1 par exchanged for (1) share new Common $1 par 7/20/2000
Note: In effect holders received $2.31 cash per share and public interest was eliminated

MCM SPLIT SHARE CORP (ON)
Preferred reclassified as Priority Equity Shares 12/12/2007
Completely liquidated
Each Priority Equity Share received first and final distribution of $13.1874 cash payable 03/31/2011 to holders of record 03/31/2011
No equity for Class A Shares

MCMANN INVTS INC (NV)
Name changed to Bulls On The Run Productions, Corp. 06/15/1988

Bulls On The Run Productions, Corp. name changed to China Treasure, Inc. 04/18/1994 which name changed to China Pacific, Inc. 01/25/1996
(See China Pacific, Inc.)

MCMANUS RED LAKE GOLD MINES LTD (ON)
Recapitalized as New McManus Red Lake Gold Mines Ltd. 09/13/1977
Each share Capital Stock $1 par exchanged for (0.1) share Common no par
New McManus Red Lake Gold Mines Ltd. recapitalized as Milestone Resource Corp. 08/26/1987 which reorganized as Horizontal Petroleum Exploration Ltd. 07/26/1990
(See Horizontal Petroleum Exploration Ltd.)

MCMANUS STEEL & IRON CO.
Bankrupt in 1930

MCMARMAC RED LAKE GOLD MINES LTD (ON)
Charter cancelled for failure to pay taxes and file returns 03/14/1978

MCMARTIN INC (CA)
Charter suspended for failure to file reports and pay fees 9/3/91

MCMILLAN GOLD MINES LTD. (ON)
Charter cancelled and declared dissolved for failure to pay taxes and file returns 4/10/79

MCMILLAN RADIATION LABS INC (MA)
Adjudicated bankrupt 11/15/1973
Stockholders' equity unlikely

MCMILLEN CO.
Acquired by Allied Mills, Inc. 00/00/1929
Details not available

MCMILLEN CORP (DE)
Merged into Peninsular Life Insurance Co. (New) 9/30/76
Each share Common $3 par exchanged for (1) share Common $3 par
Peninsular Life Insurance Co. (New) merged into McM Corp. 8/20/79
(See McM Corp.)

MCMORAN EXPLORATION CO. OLD (DE)
Reincorporated 03/31/1978
State of incorporation changed from (UT) to (DE) 03/31/1978
Name changed to McMoRan Oil & Gas Co. (Old) 01/31/1979
McMoRan Oil & Gas Co. (Old) merged into Freeport-McMoRan Inc. 04/07/1981 which merged into IMC Global Inc. 12/22/1997 which merged into Mosaic Co. (Old) 10/22/2004 which merged into Mosaic Co. (New) 05/25/2011

MCMORAN EXPLORATION CO NEW (DE)
Each share 5% Conv. Preferred exchanged for (5.1975) shares Common 1¢ par 06/30/2007
Each share 6.75% Mandatory Conv. Preferred automatically became (6.7204) shares Common 1¢ par 11/15/2010
Merged into Freeport-McMoRan Copper & Gold Inc. 06/03/2013
Each share Common 1¢ par exchanged for (1.15) Gulf Coast Ultra Deep Royalty Trust Royalty Trust Units and $14.75 cash (Additional Information in Active)

MCMORAN OIL & GAS CO NEW (DE)
Merged into McMoRan Exploration Co. 11/17/1998
Each share Common 1¢ par exchanged for (0.2) share Common 1¢ par
(See McMoRan Exploration Co.)

MCMORAN OIL & GAS CO OLD (DE)
Common no par split (2) for (1) by issuance of (1) additional share 05/19/1980
Merged into Freeport-McMoRan Inc. 04/07/1981
Each share Common $1 par exchanged for (1) share Common $1 par
Freeport-McMoRan Inc. merged into IMC Global Inc. 12/22/1997 which merged into Mosaic Co. (Old) 10/22/2004 which merged into Mosaic Co. (New) 05/25/2011

MCMS INC (DE)
Plan of reorganization under Chapter 11 Federal Bankruptcy Code effective 1/13/2004
No stockholders' equity

MCN ENERGY GROUP INC (MI)
Name changed 4/28/97
Common 1¢ par split (2) for (1) by issuance of (1) additional share 1/23/89
Common 1¢ par split (2) for (1) by issuance of (1) additional share 11/28/94
Name changed from MCN Corp. to MCN Energy Group Inc. 4/28/97
Each share 8.75% Preferred Increased Dividend Equity no par exchanged for (0.255) share Common 1¢ par 4/30/99
Each Income Pride exchanged for (1.7241) shares Common 1¢ par 5/16/2000
Merged into DTE Energy Co. 5/31/2001
Each share Common 1¢ par exchanged for either (0.715) share Common no par or $24 cash
Note: Option to receive stock expired 5/31/2001

MCN FING I (DE)
8.625% Trust Originated Preferred Securities called for redemption at $25 on 02/21/2002

MCN FING II (DE)
8.75% Guaranteed Trust Preferred Securities called for redemption at $25 on 1/15/2004

MCN FING III (DE)
Issue Information - 2,300,000 GTD TR PFD SECS 7.25% offered at $50 per share on 03/19/1997
7.25% Guaranteed Trust Preferred Securities called for redemption at $50 on 05/16/2002

MCN MICH LTD PARTNERSHIP (MI)
9.375% Preferred Ser. A called for redemption at $25 on 2/21/2002

MCN MULTICAST NETWORKS INC (NV)
Each share old Common $0.001 par exchanged for (0.25) share new Common $0.001 par 3/7/2005
Name changed to Downtown America Funding Corp. 9/8/2005
Downtown America Funding Corp. name changed to Savior Energy Corp. 12/22/2006

MCNAB CREEK GOLD CORP (NV)
Name changed to Utah Uranium Corp. 04/27/2007
Utah Uranium Corp. name changed to Universal Potash Corp. 06/16/2008

MCNAUGHTON APPAREL GROUP INC (DE)
Merged into Jones Apparel Group, Inc. 06/19/2001
Each share Common 1¢ par exchanged for (0.282) share Common 1¢ par and $10.50 cash
Jones Apparel Group, Inc. name changed to Jones Group Inc. 10/18/2010
(See Jones Group Inc.)

MCNEIL CORP (OH)
Common no par split (2) for (1) by issuance of (1) additional share 12/16/1968
Merged into Pentair, Inc. 09/02/1986

Each share Common no par exchanged for $39 cash

MCNEIL MACHINE & ENGINEERING CO. (OH)
Common $5 par changed to no par and (1) additional share issued 8/8/59
5% Preferred Ser. A $40 par called for redemption 4/1/61
Stock Dividend - 10% 8/31/54
Name changed to McNeil Corp. 12/28/64
(See McNeil Corp.)

MCNEIL REAL ESTATE FUND LTD (CA)
Merged into a private company 1/31/2000
Each Unit of Limited Partnership Int. Ser. IX exchanged for $429.13 cash
Each Unit of Limited Partnership Int. Ser. X exchanged for $234.37 cash
Each Unit of Limited Partnership Int. Ser. XI exchanged for $221.39 cash
Each Unit of Limited Partnership Int. Ser. XII exchanged for $73.17 cash
Each Unit of Limited Partnership Int. Ser. XV exchanged for $161.75 cash
Each Unit of Limited Partnership Int. Ser. XXI exchanged for $99.46 cash
Each Unit of Limited Partnership Int. Ser. XXII exchanged for $0.27 cash
Each Unit of Limited Partnership Int. Ser. XXIII exchanged for $0.27 cash
Each Unit of Limited Partnership Int. Ser. XXIV exchanged for $357.13 cash
Note: Above amounts include special cash distributions payable 1/31/2000

MCNEIL REAL ESTATE FUND XX L.P. (CA)
Merged into a private company 02/15/2000
Each Unit of Ltd. Partnership Int. received $105 cash
Note: Above amount includes special cash distribution payable 02/15/2000

MCNEIL REAL ESTATE FD XXVII LP (DE)
Merged into a private company 01/20/2000
Each Unit of Ltd. Partnership Int. exchanged for $10.98 cash
Note: Amount includes special cash distribution payable 01/20/2000

MCNELLEN RES INC (BC)
Common no par split (2) for (1) by issuance of (1) additional share 01/27/1987
Merged into Golden Goose Resources Inc. 09/30/1996
Each share Common no par exchanged for (0.04395604) share Common no par
Golden Goose Resources Inc. merged into Kodiak Exploration Ltd. 12/16/2010 which name changed to Prodigy Gold Inc. 01/04/2011 which merged into Argonaut Gold Inc. 12/11/2012

MCNELLEY MINES (1937) LTD. (ON)
Acquired by Barymin Explorations Ltd. 07/15/1966
Each share Capital Stock $1 par exchanged for (2) shares Capital Stock 50¢ par
(See Barymin Explorations Ltd.)

MCNICKEL INC (ON)
Recapitalized as Sahelian Goldfields Inc. 09/09/1996
Each share Common no par exchanged for (0.125) share Common no par
Sahelian Goldfields Inc. recapitalized as Sage Gold Inc. 03/03/2005

MCO CAP INC (QC)
Recapitalized as IOU Financial Inc. 02/28/2011
Each share Class B Common no par exchanged for (0.25) share Class B Common no par

exchanged for second and final distribution of (1) E & J Properties, Ltd. Unit of Limited Partnership Int. and $4.75 cash 10/26/1981
(See E & J Properties, Ltd.)

MCKESSON & ROBBINS, INC. (MD)
Common no par changed to $5 par 00/00/1932
Each share 7% Preference $50 par exchanged for (1.25) shares $3 Preference no par, (0.5) share Common $5 par and 50¢ cash 00/00/1935
Each share $3 Preference no par exchanged for (2.3) shares Common $18 par 00/00/1941
Each share Common $5 par exchanged for (0.25) share Common $18 par 00/00/1941
Common $18 par changed to $9 par and (1) additional share issued 08/10/1959
Stock Dividend - 10% 07/23/1951
Merged into Foremost-McKesson, Inc. 07/19/1967
Each share Common $9 par exchanged for (1) share $1.80 Conv. Preferred Ser. A $35 par and (0.75) share Common $2 par
Foremost-McKesson, Inc. name changed to McKesson Corp. (MD) 07/27/1983 which reincorporated in Delaware 07/31/1987
(See McKesson Corp. (Old) (DE))

MCKESSON & ROBBINS LTD.
Dissolved in 1941

MCKESSON CORP NEW (DE)
Common 1¢ par split (2) for (1) by issuance of (1) additional share payable 1/2/98 to holders of record 12/1/97 Ex date - 1/5/98
Under plan of merger name changed to McKesson HBOC Inc. 1/12/99
McKesson HBOC Inc. name changed to McKesson Corp. 7/30/2001

MCKESSON CORP OLD (DE)
Reincorporated 07/31/1987
Common $2 par split (2) for (1) by issuance of (1) additional share 10/01/1986
State of incorporation changed from (MD) to (DE) 07/31/1987
$1.80 Conv. Preferred Ser. A $35 par called for redemption 08/29/1994
Merged into ECO Acquisition Corp. 11/30/1994
Each share Common $2 par exchanged for $76 cash

MCKESSON FING TR (DE)
Issue Information - 3,500,000 TR CONV PFD SECS 5% offered at $50 per share on 02/13/1997
5% Trust Conv. Preferred Securities called for redemption at $50.50 plus $0.145833 accrued dividends on 6/22/2005

MCKESSON HBOC INC (DE)
Name changed to McKesson Corp. 07/30/2001

MCKINLEY DARRAGH SAVAGE MINES OF COBALT LTD.
Sold to McKinley Mines Securities Co. Ltd. on a (0.25) for (1) basis in 1928
McKinley Mines Securities Co. was acquired by Argus Interests Ltd. in 1939 which liquidated in 1943

MCKINLEY MINES SECURITIES CO. LTD.
Acquired by Argus Interests Ltd. in 1939 which liquidated in 1943

MCKINNEY GOLD HOLDINGS LTD.
Dissolved in 1948

MCKINNEY GOLD MINES LTD. (BC)
Recapitalized as Continental McKinney Mines Ltd. 3/10/67
Each share Capital Stock no par exchanged for (0.2) share Capital Stock no par
Continental McKinney Mines Ltd. recapitalized as Chandalar Resources Ltd. 6/13/73 which merged into International Park West Financial Corp. 6/20/78
(See International Park West Financial Corp.)

MCKINNEY MFG CO (PA)
Common $10 par changed to old Common $1 par 00/00/1939
Each share old Common $1 par exchanged for (5) shares new Common $1 par 00/00/1947
Stock Dividend - 100% 06/00/1950
Completely liquidated 12/29/1971
Each share 5% Preferred $100 par exchanged for first and final distribution of $100 cash
Each share new Common $1 par exchanged for first and final distribution of $2.65 cash

MCKINNEY RES INC (BC)
Recapitalized as Consolidated McKinney Resources, Inc. 09/03/1986
Each share Common no par exchanged for (0.4) share Common no par
Consolidated McKinney Resources, Inc. recapitalized as AZTEK Technologies Inc. 12/09/1996 which recapitalized as Aztek Resource Development Inc. 11/19/2004
(See Aztek Resource Development Inc.)

MCKINNON INDUSTRIES LTD.
Acquired by General Motors Corp. 00/00/1929
Details not available

MCKITTRICK OIL CO. (CA)
Completely liquidated 07/31/1964
Each (51.73734) shares Capital Stock $1 par exchanged (1) share Shell Oil Co. Common $1 par
(See Shell Oil Co.)

MCKONE TIRE & RUBBER CO.
Property sold 00/00/1928
Details not available

MCL CAP INC (ON)
Recapitalized as Feel Good Cars Corp. 02/02/2006
Each share Common no par exchanged for (0.33333333) share Common no par
Feel Good Cars Corp. name changed to Zenn Motor Co. Inc. which name changed to EEStor Corp. 04/06/2015

MCLACHLEN BANCSHARES CORP. (DC)
Merged into Citizens Bancorp (MD) 10/13/87
Each share Capital Stock $10 par exchanged for (0.95) share Common $10 par
Citizens Bancorp (MD) merged into Crestar Financial Corp. 12/31/96 which merged into SunTrust Banks, Inc. 12/31/98

MCLACHLEN BANKING CORP. (DC)
Each share Capital Stock $50 par exchanged for (2) shares Capital Stock $25 par 1/10/61
Stock Dividend - 12.5% 1/16/64
Name changed to McLachlen National Bank (Washington, DC) 7/5/68
McLachlen National Bank (Washington, DC) reorganized as McLachlen Bancshares Corp. 6/27/87 which merged into Citizens Bancorp (MD) 10/13/87 which merged into Crestar Financial Corp. 12/31/96 which merged into SunTrust Banks, Inc. 12/31/98

MCLACHLEN NATL BK (WASHINGTON, DC)
Capital Stock $25 par changed to $10 par and (1.5) additional shares issued 2/27/70
Under plan of reorganization each share Capital Stock $10 par automatically became (1) share McLachlen Bancshares Corp. Capital Stock $10 par 6/27/87
McLachlen Bancshares Corp. merged into Citizens Bancorp (MD) 10/13/87 which merged into Crestar Financial Corp. 12/31/96 which merged into SunTrust Banks, Inc. 12/31/98

MCLAIN GROCERY CO (OH)
Common $100 par split (4) for (3) by issuance of (1/3) additional share 9/20/57
Common $100 par changed to $10 par 11/1/62
Common $10 par changed to $5 par 9/1/65
Common $5 par changed to no par 6/21/71
Stock Dividends - 100% 2/27/52; 50% 9/1/65; 100% 6/21/71; 10% 10/28/75
Merged into Fleming Companies, Inc. 12/19/81
Each share Common no par exchanged for (1.5513) shares Common $2.50 par
(See Fleming Companies, Inc.)

MCLAREN CONSOLIDATED CONE CORP.
Acquired by National Biscuit Co. 00/00/1931
Details not available

MCLAREN PERFORMANCE TECHNOLOGIES INC (DE)
Name changed 4/20/2000
Name changed from McLaren Automotive Group, Inc. to McLaren Performance Technologies, Inc. 04/20/2000
Merged into Linamar Corp. 09/26/2003
Each share Common $0.00001 par exchanged for $0.8875 cash

MCLEAN BANK (MCLEAN, VA)
Name changed to McLean Bank N.A. (McLean, VA) 01/01/1987
McLean Bank N.A. (McLean, VA) name changed to Madison National Bank of Virginia (McLean, VA) 04/01/1988
(See Madison National Bank of Virginia (McLean, VA))

MCLEAN BANK N.A. (MCLEAN, VA)
Name changed to Madison National Bank of Virginia (McLean, VA) 04/01/1988
(See Madison National Bank of Virginia (McLean, VA))

MCLEAN INDS INC (DE)
Ctfs. dated prior to 05/13/1969
Common 1¢ par changed to Class A Common 1¢ par 06/03/1957
Stock Dividend - 500% 11/16/1955
$3 Preferred $5 par called for redemption 05/13/1969
$4 Preferred $5 par called for redemption 05/13/1969
Merged into Reynolds (R.J.) Tobacco Co. (NJ) 05/13/1969
Each share Class A Common 1¢ par or Class B Common 1¢ par exchanged for (1) share $2.25 Conv. Preferred no par
Reynolds (R.J.) Tobacco Co. (NJ) reincorporated in Delaware as Reynolds (R.J.) Industries, Inc. 06/29/1970 which name changed to RJR Nabisco, Inc. 04/25/1986 which merged into RJR Holdings Group, Inc. 04/28/1989
(See RJR Holdings Group, Inc.)

MCLEAN INDS INC NEW (DE)
Incorporated 00/00/1976
Plan of reorganization under Chapter 11 Federal Bankruptcy proceedings confirmed 05/16/1989
No stockholders' equity

MCLEAN SECURITIES CORP. (DE)
Name changed to McLean Industries, Inc. 07/06/1955
McLean Industries, Inc. merged into Reynolds (R.J.) Tobacco Co. (NJ) 05/13/1969 which reincorporated in Delaware as Reynolds (R.J.) Industries, Inc. 06/29/1970 which name changed to RJR Nabisco, Inc. 04/25/1986 which merged into RJR Holdings Group, Inc. 04/28/1989
(See RJR Holdings Group, Inc.)

MCLEAN TRUCKING CO (NC)
Class A Common $1 par reclassified as Common $1 par 12/31/56
6% Preferred called for redemption 9/1/57
Common $1 par changed to 50¢ par and (1) additional share issued 2/11/72
Common 50¢ par split (2) for (1) by issuance of (1) additional share 8/1/76
Stock Dividend - 25% 8/1/57
Merged into Meridian Express Co. 9/1/82
Each share Common 50¢ par exchanged for $18 cash

MCLELLAN GOLD MINES LTD.
Merged into Dyno Mines Ltd. 00/00/1953
Each share Capital Stock $1 par exchanged for (0.25) share Capital Stock $1 par
Dyno Mines Ltd. recapitalized as Canadian Dyno Mines Ltd. 12/06/1956 which merged into International Mogul Mines Ltd. 11/20/1968 which merged into Conwest Exploration Co. Ltd. (Old) (ON) 08/27/1982 which merged into Conwest Exploration Co. Ltd. (New) (AB) 09/01/1993 which merged into Alberta Energy Co. Ltd. 01/31/1996 which merged into EnCana Corp. 01/03/2003

MCLELLAN LONG LAC GOLD MINES LTD.
Acquired by McLellan Gold Mines Ltd. 00/00/1940
Details not available

MCLELLAN STORES CO. (DE)
Recapitalized 00/00/1935
Each share Class A & B Preferred $100 par exchanged for (1) share 6% Preferred $100 par and (1.5) shares Common $1 par
Common no par changed to $1 par
Merged into McCrory-McLellan Stores Corp. on a (1.25) for (1) basis
McCrory-McLellan Stores Corp. name changed to McCrory Corp. 07/16/1960
(See McCrory Corp.)

MCLEOD COPPER LTD (BC)
Recapitalized as MCP Resources Corp. 08/31/1977
Each share Capital Stock $1 par exchanged for (0.25) share Capital Stock no par
MCP Resources Corp. recapitalized as Petro-American Energy Inc. 07/06/1981
(See Petro-American Energy Inc.)

MCLEODUSA INC (DE)
Name changed 05/29/1997
Secondary Offering - 5,200,000 shares CL A offered at $28 per share on 11/15/1996
Name changed from McLeod Inc. to McLeodUSA Inc. 05/29/1997
Class A Common 1¢ par split (2) for (1) by issuance of (1) additional share payable 07/26/1999 to holders of record 07/12/1999
Class A Common 1¢ par split (3) for (1) by issuance of (2) additional shares payable 04/24/2000 to holders of record 04/04/2000
Plan of reorganization under Chapter 11 Federal Bankruptcy Code effective 04/16/2002
Each share 6.75% Conv. Preferred Ser. A exchanged for approximately (29.32) shares new Class A Common 1¢ par
Each share Conv. Preferred Ser. D

MCGRAW TIRE & RUBBER CO. (OH)
Charter cancelled for failure to pay taxes 2/14/25

MCGREGOR CAP CORP (AB)
Name changed to Canadian Platinum Corp. 11/22/2011

MCGREGOR CAP CORP (CO)
Name changed to Ultima International Corp. 10/14/1988

MCGREGOR CORP (NY)
Merged into Rapid-American Corp. 03/13/1985
Each share Common 1¢ par exchanged for $23 cash

MCGREGOR DONIGER INC (NY)
Class A $1 par split (3) for (2) by issuance of (0.5) additional share 06/04/1969
Class B $1 par split (3) for (2) by issuance of (0.5) additional share 06/04/1969
Merged into Rapid-American Corp. (DE) 05/01/1979
Each share Class A $1 par exchanged for $2 cash
Each share Class B $1 par exchanged for $2 cash

MCGUIRE BONDS (MI)
Dissolved 4/28/55

MCGUIRE CHRIS INC (FL)
Proclaimed dissolved for failure to file reports and pay fees 12/05/1978

MCGUIRE WTR CONDITIONING CORP (MO)
Charter forfeited for failure to file reports 01/01/1970

MCI CAP I (DE)
Plan of reorganization under Chapter 11 Federal Bankruptcy Code effective 4/20/2004
Each 8% Guaranteed Quarterly Income Preferred Security received initial distribution of $10.90 cash
Note: Distributions of less than $100 will not be made, unless requested in writing

MCI COMMUNICATIONS CORP (DE)
$2.64 Conv. Preferred 10¢ par called for redemption 3/14/80
Conv. Preferred Ser. B 10¢ par called for redemption 11/1/80
$1.80 Conv. Sr. Preferred 10¢ par called for redemption 5/8/81
$1.84 Conv. Preferred 10¢ par called for redemption 11/18/81
Common 10¢ par split (2) for (1) by issuance of (1) additional share 8/19/83
Common 10¢ par split (2) for (1) by issuance of (1) additional share 7/9/93
Stock Dividend - 100% 9/10/82
Merged into MCI WorldCom, Inc. 9/14/98
Each share Common 10¢ par exchanged for (1.2439) shares Common 1¢ par
MCI Communications, Inc. name changed to WorldCom Inc. (New) 5/1/2000
(See WorldCom Inc. (New))

MCI INC (GA)
Merged into Verizon Communications Inc. 1/6/2006
Each share Common 1¢ par exchanged for (0.5743) share Common 10¢ par and $2.738 cash

MCI LIQUIDATING CO., INC. (KY)
Liquidation completed
Each share Common no par exchanged for initial distribution of $13.75 cash 5/3/79
Each share Common no par received second and final distribution of $0.65 cash 3/3/86

MCI WORLDCOM INC (GA)
Common 1¢ par split (3) for (2) by issuance of (0.5) additional share payable 12/30/99 to holders of record 12/15/99
$2.25 Conv. Exchangeable Preferred Ser. C 1¢ par called for redemption at $50.75 plus $0.55625 accrued dividends on 1/14/2000
Name changed to WorldCom Inc. (New) 5/1/2000
(See WorldCom Inc. (New))

MCI WORLDCOM SYNERGIES MGMT INC
Plan of reorganization under Chapter 11 Federal Bankruptcy Code effective 4/20/2004
No stockholders' equity

MCINTOSH & SEYMOUR CORP.
Acquired by American Locomotive Co. in 1929
Details not available

MCINTOSH BANCSHARES INC (GA)
Common $2.50 par split (5) for (4) by issuance of (0.25) additional share payable 03/01/2001 to holders of record 02/15/2001 Ex date - 03/02/2001
Common $2.50 par split (5) for (4) by issuance of (0.25) additional share payable 06/01/2005 to holders of record 05/15/2005 Ex date - 06/02/2005
Common $2.50 par split (2) for (1) by issuance of (1) additional share payable 06/01/2007 to holders of record 05/15/2007 Ex date - 06/04/2007
Common $2.50 par changed to $1 par 06/07/2010
Stock Dividends - 10% payable 03/01/1999 to holders of record 02/15/1999; 10% payable 03/01/2000 to holders of record 02/15/2000
Principal asset placed in receivership 06/17/2011
Stockholders' equity unlikely

MCINTOSH CORP (DE)
Merged into Norris Industries, Inc. 06/30/1977
Each share Common $1 par exchanged for (0.8) share Common 50¢ par
(See Norris Industries, Inc.)

MCINTOSH (J.R.C.), INC. (NV)
Out of business in November 1963
Common stock is worthless

MCINTOSH LAB INC (DE)
Each share Common $10 par exchanged for (20) shares Common 50¢ par 10/10/1969
Merged into CCL Acquisition Co. 07/13/1990
Each share 6% Preferred $10 par exchanged for $159.78 cash
Each share Common 50¢ par exchanged for $159.78 cash

MCINTYRE MINES LTD (ON)
Name changed 5/31/74
Name changed from McIntyre Porcupine Mines Ltd. to McIntyre Mines Ltd. 5/31/74
Merged into Falconbridge Ltd. 1/24/89
Each share Common no par exchanged for (2.5186) shares Common no par
(See Falconbridge Ltd.)

MCIVOR DRILLING CO. LTD. (AB)
Name changed to Hi-Tower Drilling Co. Ltd. 00/00/1954
Hi-Tower Drilling Co. Ltd. name changed to Bow Valley Industries Ltd. 06/01/1962 which name changed to Bow Valley Energy Inc. 05/07/1993 which was acquired by Talisman Energy Inc. 08/11/1994
(See Talisman Energy Inc.)

MCK COMMUNICATIONS INC (DE)
Merged into Verso Technologies, Inc. 09/26/2003
Each share Common $0.001 par exchanged for (0.8517) share Common 1¢ par
(See Verso Technologies, Inc.)

MCK DISTRIBUTION CO. (WA)
Liquidation completed
Each share Class A $3 par or Class B $3 par exchanged for initial distribution of $10 cash 1/4/65
Each share Class A $3 par or Class B $3 par received second and final distribution of $5.13 cash 10/15/65

MCK MNG CORP (ON)
Name changed to PhosCan Chemical Corp. (ON) 08/01/2006
PhosCan Chemical Corp. (ON) reincorporated in Canada 10/19/2006
(See PhosCan Chemical Corp.)

MCKALE'S CORP. (WA)
Each share Common no par exchanged for (2) shares Class A $3 par and (1) share Class B $3 par 00/00/1949
Name changed to MCK Distribution Co. 11/17/1964
(See MCK Distribution Co.)

MCKALE'S INC. (WA)
Name changed to McKale's Corp. in 1950
McKale's Corp. name was changed to MCK Distribution Co. 11/17/64 which completed liquidation 10/15/65

MCKAY CO (PA)
Merged into Teledyne, Inc. 10/30/1969
Details not available

MCKAY CORMACK HLDGS LTD (BC)
Placed in receivership 04/29/1970
No stockholders' equity

MCKAY MACHINE CO. (OH)
Stock Dividends - 20% 1/20/50; 10% 11/16/53; 25% 2/1/55; 10% 2/3/58; 10% 2/3/61; 10% 2/5/62; 10% 1/31/66
Merged into Wean Industries, Inc. 5/1/67
Each share Common no par exchanged for (2.333333) shares 5-1/4% Conv. Preferred $24 par

MCKEE ARTHUR G & CO (DE)
Each share Class B no par exchanged for (2) shares Common no par in 1952
Common no par split (2) for (1) by issuance of (1) additional share 10/9/59
Common no par split (3) for (2) by issuance of (0.5) additional share 12/17/73
Common no par split (2) for (1) by issuance of (1) additional share 6/14/76
Stock Dividend - 200% 10/24/47
Under plan of reorganization each share Common no par automatically became (1) share McKee Corp. Common no par 9/1/77
(See McKee Corp.)

MCKEE CORP (DE)
Merged into Davy Corp. Ltd. 11/28/1978
Each share Common no par exchanged for $33 cash

MCKEE ROBERT E INC (NV)
Merged into Santa Fe Industries, Inc. 01/16/1973
Each share Common $5 par exchanged for either (A) $16.50 prinicipal amount of 6-1/4% Conv. Subord. Debentures due 08/01/1998 or (B) (0.542) share Common $10 par
Option to receive (B) expired 01/16/1973
Santa Fe Industries, Inc. merged into Santa Fe Southern Pacific Corp. 12/23/1983 which name changed to Santa Fe Pacific Corp. 04/25/1989 which merged into Burlington Northern Santa Fe Corp. 09/22/1995
(See Burlington Northern Santa Fe Corp.)

MCKEESPORT NATL BK (MCKEESPORT, PA)
Common $10 par changed to $5 par and (1) additional share issued 4/6/77
Stock Dividends - 10% 8/31/73; 10% 5/31/78
Reorganized as McKeesport National Corp. 6/30/84
Each share Common $5 par exchanged for (1) share Common no par
McKeesport National Corp. merged into USBANCORP, Inc. 12/1/85 which name changed to AmeriServ Financial, Inc. 5/7/2001

MCKEESPORT NATL CORP (PA)
Stock Dividend - 10% 08/15/1984
Merged into USBANCORP, Inc. 12/01/1985
Each share Common no par exchanged for (0.375) share Common $2.50 par
USBANCORP, Inc. name changed to AmeriServ Financial, Inc. 05/07/2001

MCKEESPORT OIL & DRILLING CO. (DE)
Charter cancelled and declared inoperative and void for non-payment of taxes 3/16/27

MCKEESPORT TIN PLATE CO.
Merged into McKeesport Tin Plate Corp. on a (2) for (1) basis in 1937
McKeesport Tin Plate Corp. name changed to National Can Corp. in 1941
(See National Can Corp.)

MCKEESPORT TIN PLATE CORP.
Name changed to National Can Corp. in 1941
(See National Can Corp.)

MCKELVEY G M CO (OH)
Acquired by Higbee Co. 07/03/1969
Each share Common no par exchanged for (1.2) shares Common $1 par
(See Higbee Co.)

MCKENZIE BAY INTL LTD (DE)
Recapitalized as CGE Energy, Inc. 09/14/2015
Each share Common $0.001 par exchanged for (0.04) share Common $0.001 par

MCKENZIE RED LAKE GOLD MINES LTD. (ON)
Merged into Little Long Lac Gold Mines Ltd. (Old) 6/15/66
Each share Capital Stock $1 par exchanged for (0.05) share Capital Stock no par
Little Long Lac Gold Mines Ltd. (Old) merged into Little Long Lac Gold Mines Ltd (The) 4/27/67 which merged into Little Long Lac Mines Ltd. 1/8/71 which name changed to Little Long Lac Gold Mines Ltd. 7/3/75 which merged into LAC Minerals Ltd. 7/29/85 which was acquired by American Barrick Resources Corp. 10/17/94 which name changed to Barrick Gold Corp. 1/18/95

MCKENZIE ST BK (SPRINGFIELD, OR)
Merged into Umpqua Holdings Corp. 12/31/2001
Each share Class A Common exchanged for (1.3) shares Common 83-1/3¢ par

MCKEON CONSTR (CA)
Name changed to McKeon Liquidating Co. 04/16/1981
(See McKeon Liquidating Co.)

MCKEON LIQUIDATING CO. (CA)
Liquidation completed
Each share Common $1 par received initial distribution of $3.58 cash 04/16/1981
Each share Common $1 par

MCDONOUGH MINING SYNDICATE (1940), LTD. (CANADA)
Charter surrendered 04/10/1964

MCDOUGALL MINES LTD.
Dissolved 00/00/1930
Details not available

MCDOUGALL-SEGUR EXPLORATION CO. OF CANADA LTD. (CANADA)
Acquired by Pathfinder Petroleums Ltd. 00/00/1954
Each share Capital Stock no par exchanged for (0.25) share Capital Stock 50¢ par
Pathfinder Petroleums Ltd. merged into Medallion Petroleums Ltd. 09/11/1956 which merged into Canadian Industrial Gas & Oil Ltd. 03/08/1965 which merged into Norcen Energy Resources Ltd. (AB) 10/28/1975 which reincorporated in Canada 04/15/1977
(See Norcen Energy Resources Ltd.)

MCDOWELL & CO LTD (INDIA)
Name changed to United Spirits Ltd. 11/14/2006

MCDOWELL ENTERPRISES INC (TN)
Common no par split (4) for (3) by issuance of (0.33333333) additional share 05/15/1979
Common no par changed to $1 par 05/06/1980
Stock Dividends - 10% 01/04/1974; 25% 01/04/1978
Name changed to Maxpharma, Inc. 08/20/1987
(See Maxpharma, Inc.)

MCDOWELL NATL BK (SHARON, PA)
Capital Stock $10 par split (4) for (3) by issuance of (0.33333333) additional share 06/22/1981
Stock Dividend - 150% 00/00/1952
Merged into Union National Corp. 09/01/1983
Each share Capital Stock $10 par exchanged for $53.65 cash

MCDOWELL WELLMAN ENGR CO (OH)
Through purchase offer 100% acquired by Helix Technology Corp. 00/00/1978
Public interest eliminated

MCDUFFIE BK & TR (THOMSON, GA)
Under plan of reorganization each share Common $0.001 par automatically became (1) share Georgia-Carolina Bancshares, Inc. Common $0.001 par 06/06/1997
Georgia-Carolina Bancshares, Inc. merged into State Bank Financial Corp. 01/01/2015

MCEG STERLING INC (DE)
Merged into Metromedia International Group, Inc. 11/01/1995
Each share Common $0.001 par exchanged for (0.04627) share Common $1 par
(See Metromedia International Group, Inc.)

MCELWAIN (J.F.) CO.
Merged into Melville Shoe Corp. 00/00/1939
Each share Preferred exchanged for (1.05) shares new Preferred
Each share Common exchanged for (354726/1047260) share Preferred and (1-4762/104726) shares new Common
Melville Shoe Corp. name changed to Melville Corp. (NY) 04/14/1976 which reorganized in Delaware as CVS Corp. 11/20/1996 which name changed to CVS/Caremark Corp. 03/22/2007 which name changed to CVS Caremark Corp. 05/10/2007 which name changed to CVS Health Corp. 09/04/2014

MCENANEY GOLD MINES LTD. (ON)
Charter cancelled and company declared dissolved by default 4/30/62

MCEWEN KNITTING CO.
Merged into May Hosiery Mills, Inc. on a (23.288) for (1) basis in 1940
May Hosiery Mills, Inc. name changed to May, McEwen, Kaiser Co. in January 1941 which was acquired by Burlington Mills Corp. 7/14/48 which name was changed to Burlington Industries, Inc. 2/3/55
(See Burlington Industries, Inc.)

MCEWEN MNG MINERA ANDES ACQUISITION CORP (AB)
Each Exchangeable Share exchanged for (1) share McEwen Mining Inc. Common no par 08/22/2016

MCF CORP (DE)
Each share old Common $0.0001 par exchanged for (1/7) share new Common $0.0001 par 11/16/2006
Name changed to Merriman Curhan Ford Group, Inc. 05/20/2008
Merriman Curhan Ford Group, Inc. recapitalized as Merriman Holdings, Inc. 08/16/2010

MCF ENTERPRISES INC (BC)
Name changed to Online Consortium Corp. 02/09/2001
Online Consortium Corp. name changed to Equicap Financial Corp. 07/10/2003 which name changed to Zecotek Medical Systems, Inc. 02/10/2005 which name changed to Zecotek Photonics Inc. 11/26/2007

MCFADDEN STORES, INC. (CA)
Out of business 00/00/1954
Details not available

MCFARLAND ENERGY INC (CA)
Merged into Monterey Resources, Inc. 7/24/97
Each share Common no par exchanged for $18.55 cash

MCFARLANE, SON & HODGSON LTD. (CANADA)
6-1/2% 1st Preferred $50 par called for redemption 9/18/78
Public interest eliminated

MCFINLEY MINES LTD (ON)
Reorganized 07/20/1984
Each (10) shares Capital Stock $1 par exchanged for (4.25) shares McFinley Red Lake Mines Ltd. Common no par and (5) shares Redaurum Red Lake Mines Ltd. Common no par
(See each company's listing)

MCFINLEY RED LAKE GOLD MINES LTD. (ON)
Recapitalized as McFinley Mines Ltd. 01/31/1971
Each share Capital Stock $1 par exchanged for (0.2) share Capital Stock no par
(See McFinley Mines Ltd.)

MCG CAP CORP (DE)
Merged into PennantPark Floating Rate Capital Ltd. 08/18/2015
Each share Common 1¢ par exchanged for (0.32044) share Common $0.001 par and $0.30595 cash

MCG DIVERSIFIED INC (FL)
Name changed to Electro Energy Inc. 06/09/2004
(See Electro Energy Inc.)

MCGAW INC (DE)
Merged into IVAX Corp. 3/25/94
Each share Common $0.001 par exchanged for (0.523) share Common 10¢ par
(See IVAX Corp.)

MCGEARY SMITH LABORATORIES, INC. (DE)
Name changed to Capital Film Laboratories, Inc. in 1954
(See Capital Film Laboratories, Inc.)

MCGILL MFG INC (IN)
Each share Common no par exchanged for (2) shares Common $50 par 10/09/1953
Each share Common $50 par exchanged for (3) shares Common no par 10/09/1959
Common no par split (5) for (4) by issuance of (0.25) additional share 10/26/1965
Common no par split (2) for (1) by issuance of (1) additional share 10/26/1973
Common no par split (2) for (1) by issuance of (1) additional share 09/29/1978
Stock Dividend - 20% 03/05/1965
Preferred Stock Purchase Rights declared for Common stockholders of record 10/23/1989 were redeemed at $0.01 per right 02/28/1990 for holders of record 02/14/1990
Merged into Emerson Electric Co. 04/04/1990
Each share Common no par exchanged for $93 cash

MCGILL METAL PRODS CO (IL)
Name changed 05/27/1987
Name changed from Mc Gill Metal Products Co. to Mc Gill Metal Products Co. of Marengo 05/27/1987
Voluntarily dissolved 12/24/1990
Details not available

MCGILLIVARY CREEK COAL & COKE CO. LTD. (CANADA)
Acquired by Coleman Collieries Ltd. 00/00/1952
Each (1,000) shares Capital Stock $1 par exchanged for (19.8) shares new Common $1 par, $682 in Bonds and $180 cash
(See Coleman Collieries Ltd.)

MCGINN GOLD MINES LTD. (ON)
Charter revoked for failure to file reports and pay fees 12/2/65

MCGLEN INTERNET GROUP INC (DE)
Recapitalized as Northgate Innovations, Inc. 03/20/2002
Each share Common 3¢ par exchanged for (0.1) share Common 3¢ par
Northgate Innovations, Inc. name changed to Digital Lifestyles Group, Inc. 06/25/2004 which name changed to TN-K Energy Group Inc. 10/29/2009

MCGOWEN GLASS FIBERS CORP (NJ)
Name changed to Wyndmoor Industries, Inc. 03/05/1971

MCGOWEN RES INC (UT)
Each (3.5) shares old Common $0.001 par exchanged for (1) share new Common $0.001 par 3/7/96
Name changed to Trek Resources Inc. (UT) 6/15/2000
Trek Resources Inc. (UT) reincorporated in Delaware 2/7/2001

MCGRATH CORP (WA)
Adjudicated bankrupt 03/23/1972
Stockholders' equity unlikely

MCGRATH ST PAUL CO (MN)
Each share Preferred $5 par exchanged for (2) shares Common 50¢ par 01/31/1969
Common 50¢ par changed to 1¢ par 10/24/1969
Recapitalized as Budget Systems Corp. 02/07/1973
Each share Common 1¢ par exchanged for (0.2) share Common 5¢ par

MCGRAW EDISON CO (DE)
Common $1 par split (2) for (1) by issuance of (1) additional share 05/21/1965
Merged into Cooper Industries, Inc. (OH) 05/30/1985
Each share Common $1 par exchanged for $65 cash

MCGRAW ELECTRIC CO. (DE)
Each share Common $5 par exchanged for (2) shares Common $1 par in 1937
Common $1 par split (2) for (1) by issuance of (1) additional share in 1955
Name changed to McGraw Edison Co. and (1) additional share issued 1/31/57
(See McGraw-Edison Co.)

MCGRAW F H & CO (NJ)
Common 10¢ par changed to $2 par 00/00/1949
Common $2 par changed to 10¢ par 11/30/1964
Adjudicated bankrupt 02/06/1970
Stockholders' equity unlikely

MCGRAW HILL FINL INC (NY)
Name changed 04/28/1995
Name changed 05/02/2013
Common $1 par split (2) for (1) by issuance of (1) additional share 07/17/1967
Class A $1 par called for redemption 03/01/1968
$5.50 Conv. Preferred $10 par called for redemption 04/05/1971
Common $1 par split (2) for (1) by issuance of (1) additional share 06/01/1983
Name changed from McGraw-Hill, Inc. to McGraw-Hill Companies, Inc. 04/28/1995
Common $1 par split (2) for (1) by issuance of (1) additional share payable 04/26/1996 to holders of record 03/28/1996
Common Stock Purchase Rights declared for holders of record 11/06/1989 were redeemed at $0.005 per right 08/27/1998 for holders of record 08/14/1998
Common $1 par split (2) for (1) by issuance of (1) additional share payable 03/08/1999 to holders of record 02/24/1999 Ex date - 03/09/1999
Common $1 par split (2) for (1) by issuance of (1) additional share payable 05/17/2005 to holders of record 05/06/2005 Ex date - 05/18/2005
$1.20 Conv. Preference $10 par called for redemption at $40 on 08/30/2002
Name changed from McGraw-Hill Companies, Inc. to McGraw Hill Financial, Inc. 05/02/2013
Name changed to S&P Global Inc. 04/28/2016

MCGRAW-HILL PUBLISHING CO., LTD. (NY)
Common no par changed to $5 par and (1) additional share issued 00/00/1953
Common $5 par changed to $3 par and (2) additional shares issued 08/08/1956
Common $3 par changed to $1 par and (2) additional shares issued 03/17/1961
Name changed to McGraw-Hill, Inc. 01/02/1964
McGraw-Hill, Inc. name changed to McGraw-Hill Companies, Inc. 04/28/1995 which name changed to McGraw Hill Financial, Inc. 05/02/2013 which name changed to S&P Global Inc. 04/28/2016

MCGRAW HILL RYERSON LTD (ON)
Acquired by McGraw-Hill Global Education Holdings, LLC 06/18/2014
Each share Common no par exchanged for $50 cash
Note: Unexchanged certificates will be cancelled and become without value 06/18/2020

MCCORMICK CAP INC (DE)
Merged into McCormick Acquisition Corp. 07/01/1993
Each share Common 1¢ par exchanged for $1.25 cash

MCCORMICK (CHAS. R.) LUMBER CO.
Assets sold 00/00/1938
No stockholders' equity

MCCORMICK MTG INVS FLA (FL)
Completely liquidated 03/01/1984
Each Share of Bene. Int. 10¢ par exchanged for first and final distribution of $11.79 cash

MCCORMICK OIL & GAS CO (DE)
Assets transferred to McCormick Oil & Gas Partnership 01/31/1984
Each share Common 10¢ par exchanged for (1) Depositary Receipt for Unit of Ltd. Partnership
McCormick Oil & Gas Partnership name changed to Graham-McCormick Oil & Gas Partnership 06/28/1985
(See Graham-McCormick Oil & Gas Partnership)

MCCORMICK OIL & GAS PARTNERSHIP (TX)
Name changed to Graham-McCormick Oil & Gas Partnership 06/28/1985
(See Graham-McCormick Oil & Gas Partnership)

MCCORMICK SELPH ASSOCIATES INC. (CA)
Acquired by Teledyne, Inc. 07/10/1964
Each share Common no par exchanged for (0.16666666) share Common $1 par

MCCORMICK STEEL CO. (TX)
Acquired by Ducommun Metals & Supply Co. 9/6/60
Each share Common $2 par exchanged for (0.5) share Common $2 par and $20 in cash
Ducommun Metals & Supply Co. name changed to Ducommun, Inc. (CA) 7/1/62 which reincorporated in Delaware 12/31/70

MCCORMICK'S LTD.
Merged into George Weston Ltd. 00/00/1937
Each $50 of Preferred exchanged for $25 of Bonds

MCCOY BROS INC (AB)
Name changed to McCoy Corp. 06/16/2005
McCoy Corp. name changed to McCoy Global Inc. 07/10/2014

MCCOY CORP (AB)
Name changed to McCoy Global Inc. 07/10/2014

MCCOY CORP (DE)
Charter cancelled and declared inoperative and void for non-payment of taxes 03/01/1975

MCCOY GOLD MINES, LTD. (ON)
Charter cancelled for failure to file reports and pay taxes 00/00/1953

MCCOY INDS INC (CO)
Adjudicated bankrupt 06/26/1983
Stockholders' equity unlikely

MCCRORY CORP (DE)
Merged into Rapid-American Corp. 03/12/1976
Each share Common 50¢ par exchanged for (0.5) share Common $1 par
(See Rapid-American Corp.)
3.5% Conv. Preferred $100 par called for redemption 05/29/1978
Chapter 11 Bankruptcy proceedings dismissed 08/06/1997
No stockholders' equity

MCCRORY-MCLELLAN STORES CORP. (DE)
Under plan of merger name changed to McCrory Corp. 07/16/1960
(See McCrory Corp.)

MCCRORY STORES CORP. (DE)
Reorganized 05/05/1936
Each share 6% Conv. Preferred $100 par exchanged for (1) share 6% Preferred $100 par
Each share Common no par exchanged for (1) share Common $1 par
Common $1 par changed to 50¢ par and (1) additional share issued 04/26/1951
Under plan of merger name changed to McCrory-McLellan Stores Corp. 01/30/1959
McCrory-McLellan Stores Corp. name changed to McCrory Corp. 07/16/1960
(See McCrory Corp.)

MCCULLOCH AIRCRAFT CORP (CA)
Name changed to Aero Resources, Inc. 11/30/1972
(See Aero Resources, Inc.)

MCCULLOCHS CDN BEVERAGES INC (BC)
Recapitalized as MCB Investments Corp. 10/06/1994
Each share Common no par exchanged for (0.2) share Common no par
(See MCB Investments Corp.)

MCD RES LTD (AB)
Recapitalized as Norpet Resources Ltd. 09/01/1987
Each share Common no par exchanged for (0.14285714) share Common no par
Norpet Resources Ltd. merged into HCO Energy Co. Ltd. 04/07/1989 which recapitalized as Consolidated HCO Energy Ltd. 04/12/1989 which name changed to HCO Energy Ltd. (New) 06/18/1993 which merged into Pinnacle Resources Ltd. (New) 10/20/1997 which merged into Renaissance Energy Ltd. 07/16/1998 which merged into Husky Energy Inc. 08/25/2000

MCDANIEL AUSTIN CORP (WA)
Recapitalized as Chinatek Inc. 11/16/1993
Each share Common $0.001 par exchanged for (0.4) share Common $0.001 par
(See Chinatek Inc.)

MCDANIEL EQUIPMENT, INC. (CA)
Charter suspended for failure to pay franchise taxes 10/01/1964

MCDATA CORP (DE)
Acquired by Brocade Communications Systems, Inc. 01/29/2007
Each share Class A Common 1¢ par exchanged for (0.75) share Common $0.001 par
Each share Class B Common 1¢ par exchanged for (0.75) share Common $0.001 par
(See Brocade Communications Systems, Inc.)

MCDC CASINO CORP (MN)
Name changed to Grand Gaming Corp. 08/03/1994
Grand Gaming Corp. merged into Grand Casinos, Inc. 11/30/1995 which merged into Park Place Entertainment Corp. 12/31/1998 which name changed to Caesars Entertainment, Inc. 01/05/2004
(See Caesars Entertainment, Inc.)

MCDERMOTT (J RAY) S A (PANAMA)
$2.25 Preferred Ser. B Preferred 1¢ par called for redemption at $26.60 on 10/16/1995
Merged into McDermott International, Inc. 07/30/1999
Each share Common 1¢ par exchanged for $35.62 cash

MCDERMOTT GOLD MINES LTD. (ON)
Acquired by McDermott Mines Ltd. 00/00/1949
Each share Capital Stock exchanged for (0.33333333) share Capital Stock
(See McDermott Mines Ltd.)

MCDERMOTT INC (DE)
Name changed 8/15/80
Common $1 par split (3) for (2) by issuance of (0.5) additional share 3/29/62
Common $1 par split (3) for (2) by issuance of (0.5) additional share 3/31/67
Common $1 par split (2) for (1) by issuance of (1) additional share 7/18/75
Common $1 par split (2) for (1) by issuance of (1) additional share 1/16/78
Stock Dividends - 10% 3/12/59; 10% 3/13/60
Name changed from McDermott (J. Ray) & Co., Inc. to McDermott Inc. 8/15/80
Merged into McDermott International, Inc. 3/15/83
Each share Common $1 par exchanged for (1) share Common $1 par and $0.10 cash
$2.60 Preferred Ser. B no par called for redemption at $31.25 on 7/17/98
$2.20 Conv. Preferred Ser. A $1 par called for redemption at $31.25 on 9/11/98

MCDERMOTT INTL INC (PANAMA)
Accredited Dollar Conv. Preferred Ser. C no par called for redemption at $51.73 plus $0.1677 accrued dividends on 04/21/1998
Each 6.25% Tangible Equity Unit automatically became (3.5496) shares Common $1 par 04/03/2017
(Additional Information in Active)

MCDERMOTT MINES LTD. (ON)
Company went private 00/00/1985
Details not available

MCDONALD & CO INVTS INC (DE)
Stock Dividend - 20% 08/20/1993
Merged into Keycorp (New) 10/23/1998
Each share Common $1 par exchanged for (1.06) shares Common $1 par

MCDONALD J M CO (DE)
Merged into Gamble-Skogmo, Inc. 07/29/1968
Each share Common $5 par exchanged for (0.8) share Common $5 par
Gamble-Skogmo, Inc. merged into Wickes Companies, Inc. 01/26/1985 which name changed to Collins & Aikman Group Inc. 07/17/1992
(See Collins & Aikman Group Inc.)

MCDONALD MICRADATA SVCS INC (NY)
Name changed to Turning Basin Inc. 05/26/1979
(See Turning Basin Inc.)

MCDONALD MONEY MKT FD INC (MD)
Merged into Gradison U.S. Government Reserves 09/27/1993
Details not available

MCDONALD-WILLIAMS FINANCIAL SERVICES, INC. (CA)
Name changed to Dynamic Capitalism, Inc. 12/28/1970
(See Dynamic Capitalism, Inc.)

MCDONALDS CORP (DE)
Non-Voting Adjustable Preferred no par called for redemption 6/15/87
Conv. Preferred Ser. B ESOP called for redemption 12/28/95
Conv. Preferred Ser. C ESOP called for redemption 12/28/95
7.72% Preferred Ser. E ESOP called for redemption 12/3/97
7.72% Depositary Preferred Ser. E called for redemption at $25 plus $0.107 accrued dividend on 12/3/97
(Additional Information in Active)

MCDONNELL AIRCRAFT CORP. (MD)
Each share Common $1 par exchanged for (2) shares Common $5 par in 1950
Common $5 par split (2) for (1) by issuance of (1) additional share 10/20/55
Common $5 par changed to $2.50 par and (1) additional share issued 5/26/60
Common $2.50 par changed to $1.25 par and (1) additional share issued 7/17/64
Common $1.25 par split (2) for (1) by issuance of (1) additional share 7/2/66
Name changed to McDonnell Co. 9/30/66
McDonnell Co. name changed to McDonnell Douglas Corp. 4/28/67

MCDONNELL CO. (MD)
Under plan of merger name changed to McDonnell Douglas Corp. 4/28/67 plus a 12% stock dividend paid 5/18/67
McDonnell Douglas Corp. merged into Boeing Co. 8/1/97

MCDONNELL DOUGLAS CORP (MD)
Common $1.25 par changed to $1 par and (0.25) additional share issued 05/18/1973
Common $1 par split (3) for (1) by issuance of (2) additional shares 01/03/1995
Common $1 par split (2) for (1) by issuance of (1) additional share payable 05/31/1996 to holders of record 05/10/1996 Ex date - 06/03/1996
Merged into Boeing Co. 08/01/1997
Each share Common $1 par exchanged for (1.3) shares Common $5 par

MCDONNELL FD INC (NY)
Name changed to Businessman's Fund, Inc. 01/14/1970
Businessman's Fund, Inc. merged into MagnaCap Fund Inc. 09/22/1972 which name changed to Pilgrim MagnaCap Fund, Inc. 06/20/1985 which merged into Pilgrim Investment Funds, Inc. 07/03/1992 which name changed to Pilgrim America Investment Funds, Inc. 07/14/1995 which name changed back to Pilgrim Investment Funds, Inc. 11/16/1998 which name changed to ING Investment Funds, Inc. 03/01/2002

MCDONOUGH CO (DE)
Each share Common no par exchanged for (0.06666666) shares Common $1 par 05/06/1966
Common $1 par split (2) for (1) by issuance of (1) additional share 03/09/1973
5% Preferred $25 par called for redemption 04/01/1977
Merged into Hanson Trust Ltd. 01/30/1981
Each share Common $1 par exchanged for $45 cash

MCDONOUGH MINING SYNDICATE LTD. (CANADA)
Succeeded by McDonough Mining Syndicate (1940) Ltd. in 1940
Each share exchanged for (1) share McDonough Mining Syndicate (1940) Ltd., (0.844) share Madsen Red Lake Gold Mines Ltd. and (0.368) share Cobalt Products Ltd.
(See each company's listing)

similar shares share for share
Each share Common $5 par
exchanged for (0.875) share
Common $1 par
Royal-McBee Corp. merged into
Litton Industries, Inc. 2/28/65
(See Litton Industries, Inc.)

MCBINE PORCUPINE GOLD MINES LTD. (ON)
Charter surrendered 12/21/70
No stockholders' equity

MCBRIDE TEMP STAFFING SVCS (NV)
Charter revoked for failure to file reports and pay fees 10/1/2002

MCBRIDES INDS INC (NY)
Recapitalized as Electro-Heat Resources Corp. 03/03/1980
Each share Common 1¢ par exchanged for (0.25) share Common 1¢ par
(See Electro-Heat Resources Corp.)

MCBRIDGE OIL & GAS CORP. (DE)
No longer in existence having become inoperative and void for non-payment of taxes 04/01/1958

MCBRINE L LTD (ON)
Placed in bankruptcy 06/00/1970
No stockholders' equity

MCBRYDE SUGAR LTD (HI)
Capital Stock $16 par changed to $10 par 00/00/1928
Each share Capital Stock $10 par exchanged for (2) shares Capital Stock $5 par 00/00/1931
Merged into Alexander & Baldwin, Inc. (Old) 07/01/1968
Each share Capital Stock $5 par exchanged for (0.4) share Common no par
Alexander & Baldwin, Inc. (Old) name changed to Alexander & Baldwin Holdings, Inc. 06/06/2012 which name changed to Matson, Inc. 06/29/2012

MCC CATERING INC (DE)
Recapitalized as Anything2ship, Inc. 06/28/2002
Each share Common $0.001 par exchanged for (0.4) share Common $0.001 par
(See Anything2ship, Inc.)

MCC HLDGS INC (CO)
Name changed to Beechport Capital Inc. (CO) 01/16/1996
Beechport Capital Inc. (CO) reorganized in Delaware as ITec Environmental Group, Inc. 10/11/2002 which name changed to Eco2 Plastics, Inc. 03/26/2007
(See Eco2 Plastics, Inc.)

MCC PRESIDENTIAL INC (NJ)
Name changed to Renault Winery, Inc. 02/27/1974 which name changed back to MCC-Presidential, Inc. 05/05/1977
Merged into First Montauk Financial Corp. 11/16/1987
Each share Common no par exchanged for (1) share Common no par
(See First Montauk Financial Corp.)

MCCABE GRAIN LTD (CANADA)
Class A no par and Class B no par reclassified as old Common no par 01/26/1959
Each share old Common no par exchanged for (5) shares new Common no par 05/28/1964
Acquired by National Grain Co. Ltd. 04/11/1969
Each share new Common no par exchanged for $11.50 cash

MCCAFFREY & MCCALL INC (NY)
Common $1 par split (3) for (1) by issuance of (2) additional shares 11/18/1975
Merged into M&M Advertising, Inc. 09/07/1978

Each share Common $1 par exchanged for $7.65 cash

MCCAHAN (W.J.) SUGER REFINING & MOLASSES CO.
Assets acquired by American Sugar Refining Co. 00/00/1944
Details not available

MCCALL CORP. (DE)
Each share Common $100 par exchanged for (4) shares Common no par 00/00/1926
Common no par split (3) for (2) by issuance of (0.5) additional share 06/01/1961
Common no par split (3) for (2) by issuance of (0.5) additional share 12/23/1963
Merged into Simon (Norton), Inc. 07/17/1968
Each share Common no par exchanged for (0.3125) share $1.60 Conv. Preferred Ser. A $5 par and (0.6875) share Common $1 par
Simon (Norton), Inc. merged into Esmark, Inc. (Inc. 03/14/1969) 09/09/1983
(See Esmark, Inc. (Inc. 03/14/1969))

MCCALLUM HOSIERY CO.
Merged into Propper-McCallum Hosiery Co., Inc. 00/00/1930
Details not available

MCCANDLESS CORP (DE)
Name changed to Food Resources, Inc. 10/06/1969
(See Food Resources, Inc.)

MCCARTHY (GLENN), INC. (DE)
Name changed to Tex N Petroleum Corp. 10/00/1961
(See Tex N Petroleum Corp.)

MCCARTHY CO (CA)
Merged into CBIS, Inc. 03/24/1980
Each share Common $1 par exchanged for $6 cash

MCCARTHY CORP PLC (UNITED KINGDOM)
Company Voluntary Arrangement proposed 06/19/2003
Stockholders' equity unlikely

MCCARTHY MILLING CO., LTD. (ON)
98% acquired by Weston (George) Ltd. through purchase offer 00/00/1972
Public interest eliminated

MCCARVILL CORP (ON)
Name changed to Rockwater Capital Corp. 06/28/2002
(See Rockwater Capital Corp.)

MCCASKEY REGISTER CO. (OH)
Common $100 par changed to no par 00/00/1932
Common no par changed to $1 par 00/00/1945
Common $1 par changed to $5 par 00/00/1947
Merged into Victor Adding Machine Co. 00/00/1953
Each share 4.50% Preferred $12.50 par exchanged for (1) share Victor Adding Machine Co. 4.50% Preferred $12.50 par
Each share Common $5 par exchanged for (1) share Atlantic Register Co. Common $1 par and $14.30 cash
Victor Adding Machine Co. merged into Victor Comptometer Corp. 10/30/1961 which merged into Kidde (Walter) & Co., Inc. (DE) 07/15/1977 which name changed to Kidde, Inc. 04/18/1980
(See Kidde, Inc.)

MCCAULEY ENTERPRISES INC (MN)
Out of business prior to 12/31/1973
No stockholders' equity

MCCAW CELLULAR COMMUNICATIONS INC (DE)
Merged into AT&T Corp. 09/19/1994
Each share Class A Common 1¢ par exchanged for (1) share Common $1 par
AT&T Corp. merged into AT&T Inc. 11/18/2005

MCCLAIN INDS INC (MI)
Common no par split (5) for (4) by issuance of (0.25) additional share 10/30/1985
Common no par split (5) for (4) by issuance of (0.25) additional share 05/16/1986
Common no par split (4) for (3) by issuance of (0.33333333) additional share 04/30/1987
Common no par split (4) for (3) by issuance of (0.33333333) additional share 06/15/1988
Common no par split (4) for (3) by issuance of (0.33333333) additional share 03/30/1995
Voluntarily dissolved 09/10/2004
Details not available

MCCLANAHAN OIL CO. (MI)
Name changed to Great Lakes Oil & Chemical Co. 05/08/1950
Great Lakes Oil & Chemical Co. name changed to Great Lakes Chemical Corp. (MI) 05/12/1960 which reincorporated in Delaware 09/16/1970 which merged into Chemtura Corp. 07/01/2005
(See Chemtura Corp.)

MCCLANAHAN REFINERIES, INC.
Acquired in reorganization by Leonard Refineries, Inc. 00/00/1939
Details not available

MCCLAREN RUBBER CO.
Merged into Ajax Rubber Co., Inc. 00/00/1927
Details not available

MCCLATCHY NEWSPAPERS INC (DE)
Class A Common 1¢ par split (5) for (4) by issuance of (0.25) additional share payable 01/02/1997 to holders of record 12/16/1996
Under plan of merger each share Class A Common 1¢ par and Class B Common 1¢ par automatically became (1) share McClatchy Co. Class A Common 1¢ par 03/19/1998

MCCLEARY STATE BANK (MCCLEARY, WA)
Name changed to Harbor Security Bank (McCleary, Wash.) 11/19/79

MCCLENDON TRANSN GROUP INC (NV)
Recapitalized as Nevada Stock Exchange, Inc. 03/10/2006
Each share Common $0.001 par exchanged for (0.001) share Common $0.001 par
Nevada Stock Exchange, Inc. name changed to SearchPath HCS, Inc. 02/23/2010

MCCLINTIC-MARSHALL CONSTRUCTION CO.
Acquired by Bethlehem Steel Corp. (NJ) 00/00/1931
Details not available

MCCLINTIC-MARSHALL CORP.
Acquired by Bethlehem Steel Corp. (NJ) 00/00/1931
Details not available

MCCLINTOCK (O.B.) CO.
Bankrupt 00/00/1947
No stockholders' equity

MCCLOUD RIVER LUMBER CO. (MN)
Each share Common $100 par exchanged for (9) shares Common $25 par to effect a (4) for (1) split and a 125% stock dividend in 1937
Liquidation completed
Each share Common $25 par exchanged for initial distribution of $15 cash 10/21/63
Each share Common $25 par received second distribution of $100 cash 1/15/64
Each share Common $25 par received third distribution of $2.50 cash 8/10/64
Each share Common $25 par received fourth and final distribution of $1.323 cash 11/15/65

MCCOMBE MINING & EXPLORATION LTD. (ON)
Charter revoked for failure to file reports and pay fees 11/30/1964

MCCOMBS CORP (CA)
Chapter 7 Federal Bankruptcy proceedings terminated 10/25/1994
Stockholders' equity unlikely

MCCONNELL PEEL RES LTD (BC)
Merged into Coast Falcon Resources Ltd. (BC) 07/07/1992
Each share Common no par exchanged for (0.1) share Common no par
Coast Falcon Resources Ltd. (BC) reorganized in Yukon as Inside Holdings Inc. 10/06/2000 which name changed to SHEP Technologies Inc. 10/07/2002
(See SHEP Technologies Inc.)

MCCONWAY & TORLEY CO.
Properties sold 00/00/1931
Details not available

MCCORD CORP (ME)
Common no par changed to $3 par and (1) additional share issued 12/13/48
$2.50 Preferred no par changed to $50 par 12/13/48
Common $3 par split (2) for (1) by issuance of (1) additional share 9/21/62
$2.50 Preferred $50 par called for redemption 5/29/64
Conv. Preferred $25 par called for redemption 7/31/68
Common $3 par split (3) for (2) by issuance of (0.5) additional share 6/15/72
Common $3 par split (3) for (2) by issuance of (0.5) additional share 6/14/76
Merged into Ex-Cell-O Corp. 1/27/78
Each share Common $3 par exchanged for (1.22) shares Common $3 par
(See Ex-Cell-O Corp.)

MCCORD MANUFACTURING CO., INC. (NY)
Each share 7% Preferred $100 par exchanged for (1) share Class A 7% Preferred $100 par and (1) share Debenture stock no par 00/00/1926
Liquidation for cash completed 05/05/1948
Note: Unexchanged certificates were cancelled and became without value 06/30/1956

MCCORD RADIATOR & MANUFACTURING CO. (ME)
Name changed to McCord Corp. 09/12/1944
McCord Corp. merged into Ex-Cell-O Corp. 01/27/1978
(See Ex-Cell-O Corp.)

MCCORMICK & SCHMICKS SEAFOOD RESTAURANTS INC (DE)
Issue Information - 6,000,000 shares COM offered at $12 per share on 07/20/2004
Acquired by Landry's, Inc. 01/03/2012
Each share Common $0.001 par exchanged for $8.75 cash

MCCORMICK-ARMSTRONG CO., INC. (KS)
Under plan of voluntary recapitalization each share Common $5 par exchanged for (0.31) share Litton Industries, Inc. Conv. Preference Part. Ser. $2.50 par and $1.25 cash 04/11/1968
All but (3) holders surrendered shares
Public interest eliminated

approximately $0.1439 cash 12/28/2005

MBPXL CORP (DE)
Stock Dividends - 10% 03/25/1976; 10% 02/17/1977; 10% 02/22/1978
Merged into Cargill Holdings, Inc. 03/01/1979
Each share Common $1 par exchanged for $27 cash

MBS ADJ RATE INCOME FD (ON)
Merged into Sentry Select MBS Adjustable Rate Income Fund II 4/5/2007
Each Trust Unit no par received (0.978) Unit

MBS INDS INC (FL)
Proclaimed dissolved for failure to file reports and pay fees 09/03/1976

MBS SOFTWARE INC (BC)
Struck from the register and dissolved 8/5/94

MBS TEXTBOOK EXCHANGE INC (DE)
Acquired by an investment group 6/30/89
Each share Common 1¢ par exchanged for $10 cash

MBSL GROUP INC (FL)
Name changed to InterSearch Group, Inc. 11/03/2004
InterSearch Group, Inc. name changed to Banks.com, Inc. 11/28/2007 which merged into Remark Media, Inc. 07/06/2012 which name changed to Remark Holdings, Inc. 04/11/2017

MBT INTL INC (NV)
Common $0.001 par split (3.16) for (1) by issuance of (2.16) additional shares 03/12/1998
Recapitalized as Strategic Resources International, Inc. 07/16/2007
Each share Common $0.001 par exchanged for (0.01) share Common $0.001 par

MBWM CAP TR I (DE)
9.60% Preferred Securities called for redemption at $10 on 09/17/2004

MC BRIDES LAB & SURGICAL SUPPLY CORP (NY)
Name changed to McBrides Industries, Inc. 09/21/1970
McBrides Industries, Inc. recapitalized as Electro-Heat Resources Corp. 03/03/1980
(See Electro-Heat Resources Corp.)

MC COLL FRONTEAC OIL LTD (CANADA)
Common no par exchanged (2) for (1) in 1947
Name changed to Texaco Canada Ltd. 2/2/59
Texaco Canada Ltd. name changed to Texaco Canada Ltd.-Texaco Canada Ltee. 7/14/75 which name changed to Texaco Canada Inc. 7/25/78 which merged into Imperial Oil Ltd.-Compagnie Petroliere Imperial Ltee. 4/19/89

MC CULLOCH OIL CORP (DE)
Common 50¢ par split (2) for (1) by issuance of (1) additional share 05/12/1971
Name changed to MCO Holdings, Inc. 06/19/1980
MCO Holdings, Inc. name changed to MAXXAM Inc. 10/06/1988
(See MAXXAM Inc.)

MC CULLOCH OIL CORP CALIF (DE)
Each share Common 10¢ par exchanged for (0.2) share Common 50¢ par 05/31/1963
Name changed to McCulloch Oil Corp. 05/09/1969
McCulloch Oil Corp. name changed to MCO Holdings, Inc. 06/19/1980 which name changed to MAXXAM Inc. 10/06/1988
(See MAXXAM Inc.)

MC-EVOY CO.
Liquidated in 1952

MC INC (KS)
Stock Dividend - 10% 02/22/1978
Acquired by Chandler Corp. 02/01/1980
Details not available

MC INFORMATICS INC (CA)
Ceased operations 04/06/2001
Stockholders' equity unlikely

MC LAUGHLIN S B ASSOC LTD (ON)
Name changed to Mascan Corp. 10/26/81
(See Mascan Corp.)

MC LIQUIDATING CORP. (NY)
Dissolved 01/25/1990
Details not available

MC PARTNERS INC (BC)
Name changed to bioMmune Technologies Inc. 05/29/2013
bioMmune Technologies Inc. name changed to Pascal Biosciences Inc. 03/31/2017

MC SHIPPING INC (LIBERIA)
Stock Dividends - 5% payable 04/30/2004 to holders of record 04/16/2004 Ex date - 04/14/2004; 5% payable 04/28/2006 to holders of record 04/14/2006 Ex date - 04/11/2006
Merged into Bear Stearns Companies Inc. 09/12/2007
Each share Common 1¢ par exchanged for $14.25 cash

MC WOOD CORP (DE)
6% Preferred $100 par called for redemption 2/20/67
Completely liquidated 3/3/67
Each share Common 25¢ par exchanged for (0.412) share Occidental Petroleum Corp. (Calif.) Capital Stock 20¢ par
Occidental Petroleum Corp. (Calif.) reincorporated in Delaware 5/21/86

MCA FINL CORP (MI)
Plan of reorganization under Chapter 11 Federal Bankruptcy Code effective 9/5/2000
Stockholders' equity unlikely

MCA INC (DE)
Common no par split (3) for (2) by issuance of (0.5) additional share 06/19/1968
$1.50 Conv. Preferred no par called for redemption 07/15/1968
Common no par split (2) for (1) by issuance of (1) additional share 05/21/1976
Common no par split (5) for (4) by issuance of (0.25) additional share 10/24/1978
Common no par split (2) for (1) by issuance of (1) additional share 01/17/1983
Common no par split (3) for (2) by issuance of (0.5) additional share 09/16/1985
Preferred Stock Purchase Rights declared for Common stockholders of record 07/27/1987 were redeemed at $0.02 per right 01/14/1991 for holders of record 12/28/1990
Merged into Matsushita Electric Industrial Co., Ltd. 01/03/1991
Each share Common no par exchanged for (0.2) share Pinelands, Inc. Common 1¢ par and $66 cash
Note: An additional payment of $0.02226968 cash per share was made in settlement of litigation to holders who tendered or exchanged their certificates at time of merger 03/18/1994

MCADAM MNG LTD (ON)
Common $1 par changed to no par 02/16/1977
Recapitalized as Flanagan McAdam Resources Inc. 12/12/1983
Each share Common no par exchanged for (0.33333333) share Common no par
Flanagan McAdam Resources Inc. merged into Golden Goose Resources Inc. 09/30/1996 which merged into Kodiak Exploration Ltd. 12/16/2010 which name changed to Prodigy Gold Inc. 01/04/2011 which merged into Argonaut Gold Inc. 12/11/2012

MCADAM RES INC (ON)
Recapitalized as Boulder Mining Corp. (ON) 05/09/1995
Each share Common no par exchanged for (0.33333333) share Common no par
Each share Class A Ser. I no par exchanged for (1) share Class A Ser. I no par
Boulder Mining Corp. (ON) reincorporated in British Columbia as Opal Energy Corp. 01/09/2007 which name changed to Versus Systems Inc. 07/13/2016

MCAFEE ASSOCS INC (DE)
Common 1¢ par split (3) for (2) by issuance of (0.5) additional share 10/31/1995
Common 1¢ par split (3) for (2) by issuance of (0.5) additional share payable 05/16/1996 to holders of record 04/29/1996
Common 1¢ par split (3) for (2) by issuance of (0.5) additional share payable 10/17/1996 to holders of record 10/07/1996
Name changed to Network Associates, Inc. 12/01/1997
Network Associates, Inc. name changed to McAfee, Inc. 06/30/2004
(See McAfee, Inc.)

MCAFEE COM CORP (DE)
Issue Information - 6,250,000 shares CL A offered at $12 per share on 12/01/1999
Merged into Networks Associates, Inc. 09/13/2002
Each share Class A $0.001 par exchanged for (0.675) share Common 1¢ par and $8 cash
Network Associates, Inc. name changed to McAfee, Inc. 06/30/2004
(See McAfee, Inc.)

MCAFEE INC (DE)
Acquired by Intel Corp. 02/28/2011
Each share Common 1¢ par exchanged for $48 cash

MCALEER MANUFACTURING CO.
Name changed to Higbie Manufacturing Co. in 1950
Higbie Manufacturing Co. merged into International Telegraph & Telephone Corp. 3/2/72 which name changed to ITT Corp. (DE) 12/31/83 which reorganized in Indiana as ITT Industries, Inc. 12/19/95 which name changed to ITT Corp. 7/1/2006

MCALLISTER TOWING LTD. (CANADA)
99.99% acquired by Genstar Ltd. through purchase offer which expired 02/01/1972
Public interest eliminated

MCAP INC (CANADA)
Name changed to MCAN Mortgage Corp. 9/15/2006

MCARTHUR DEVELOPMENT, INC. (UT)
Recapitalized as Holiday Services, Inc. 02/24/1987
Each share Common $0.001 par exchanged for (0.05) share Common $0.001 par
(See Holiday Services, Inc.)

MCARTHUR/GLEN RLTY CORP (DE)
Merged into HGI Realty, Inc. 7/14/95
Each share Common 1¢ par exchanged for (0.64) share Common 1¢ par

HGI Realty, Inc. name changed to Horizon Group, Inc. 6/14/96 which merged into Prime Retail, Inc. 6/15/98
(See Prime Retail, Inc.)

MCAVOY DIAMOND DRILLING & DEVELOPMENT CO. LTD. (CANADA)
Deemed not to be a subsisting company by the Dominion Secretary of State 10/12/1960

MCB BK LTD (PAKISTAN)
Sponsored 144A GDR's for Ordinary split (2) for (1) by issuance of (1) additional GDR payable 04/10/2008 to holders of record 03/03/2008 Ex date - 02/28/2008
Sponsored Reg. S GDR's for Ordinary split (2) for (1) by issuance of (1) additional GDR payable 04/10/2008 to holders of record 03/03/2008
Basis changed from (1:4) to (1:2) 04/10/2008
Stock Dividends - In 144A GDR's for Ordinary payable to holders of 144A GDR's for Ordinary 15% payable 04/09/2007 to holders of record 03/20/2007; 10% payable 04/07/2009 to holders of record 03/13/2009 Ex date - 03/11/2009; 10% payable 05/04/2010 to holders of record 03/18/2010 Ex date - 03/16/2010; 10% payable 04/15/2011 to holders of record 03/21/2011 Ex date - 03/17/2011; 10% payable 04/11/2012 to holders of record 03/15/2012 Ex date - 03/13/2012; 10% payable 04/10/2013 to holders of record 03/14/2013 Ex date - 03/12/2013; 10% payable 04/08/2014 to holders of record 03/17/2014 Ex date - 03/13/2014
In Reg. S GDR's for Ordinary payable to holders of Reg. S GDR's for Ordinary 10% payable 04/07/2009 to holders of record 03/13/2009; 10% payable 05/04/2010 to holders of record 03/18/2010; 10% payable 04/15/2011 to holders of record 03/21/2011; 10% payable 04/11/2012 to holders of record 03/15/2012; 10% payable 04/10/2013 to holders of record 03/14/2013 Ex date - 03/12/2013; 10% payable 04/08/2014 to holders of record 03/17/2014 Ex date - 03/13/2014
GDR agreement terminaed 01/25/2017
Each Sponsored 144A GDR for Ordinary exchanged for (2) shares Ordinary
Each Sponsored Reg. S GDR for Ordinary exchanged for (2) shares Ordinary

MCB FINL CORP (CA)
Common no par split (4) for (3) by issuance of (1/3) additional share payable 2/20/98 to holders of record 2/10/98
Stock Dividend - 5% payable 9/24/99 to holders of record 9/10/99
Merged into Business Bancorp (New) 12/31/2001
Each share Common no par exchanged for (1.1763) shares Common no par
(See Business Bancorp (New))

MCB INVTS CORP (BC)
Delisted from Canadian Venture Exchange 03/27/2002

MCBEE CO. (OH)
Each share Common $50 par exchanged for (10) shares Common $5 par in 1945
Stock Dividend - 30% 3/14/50
Merged into Royal-McBee Corp. in 1954
Each share 5%, 5-1/2% & 6% Preferred $100 par exchanged for

MAZAL PLT PHARMACEUTICALS INC (NV)
Charter revoked for failure to file reports and pay taxes 11/30/2011

MAZARIN MNG INC (QC)
Name changed to Mazarin Inc. 9/26/2000

MAZEL STORES INC (OH)
Issue Information - 2,574,000 shares Common offered at $16 per share on 11/21/1996
Name changed to Odd Job Stores, Inc. 6/19/2002
(See Odd Job Stores, Inc.)

MAZORRO RES INC (CANADA)
Each share old Common no par exchanged for (0.5) share new Common no par 06/23/2014
Name changed to GrowPros Cannabis Ventures Inc. 01/05/2015
GrowPros Cannabis Ventures Inc. name changed to Tetra Bio-Pharma Inc. 09/28/2016

MAZZAL HLDG CORP (NV)
Common $0.0001 split (10) for (1) by issuance of (9) additional shares payable 03/02/2015 to holders of record 03/02/2015
Name changed to Znergy, Inc. 08/05/2016

MB ASSOCIATES (CA)
Name changed to MBAssociates and Capital Stock no par changed to $1 par 6/16/70
MBAssociates acquired by Tracor, Inc. (Del.) 9/3/80
(See Tracor, Inc. (Del.))

MB CAP I (DE)
8.75% Guaranteed Trust Preferred Securities called for redemption at $10 on 4/1/2003

MB-CARADON PLC (ENGLAND)
Name changed 11/12/1990
Name changed from MB Group PLC to MB-Caradon PLC 11/12/1990
Name changed to Caradon PLC 10/29/1993
Caradon PLC name changed to Novar PLC 01/03/2001
(See Novar PLC)

MB COMMUNICATIONS INC (DE)
Name changed to Black Box Corp. 8/9/94

MB FINL CAP TR I (DE)
8.60% Guaranteed Trust Preferred Securities called for redemption at $25 on 10/02/2007

MB FINL INC (DE)
Merged into MB Financial, Inc. (MD) 11/7/2001
Each share Common 1¢ par exchanged for (1) share Common 1¢ par

MB FINL INC (MD)
8% Perpetual Non-Cum. Preferred Ser. A 1¢ par called for redemption at $25 on 02/15/2018
(Additional Information in Active)

MB SOFTWARE CORP (CO)
Reorganized under the laws of Texas 06/24/2002
Each share Common $0.001 par exchanged for (0.01) share Common $0.001 par
MB Software Corp. (TX) name changed to Wound Management Technologies, Inc. 06/12/2008

MB SOFTWARE CORP (TX)
Name changed to Wound Management Technologies, Inc. 06/12/2008

MB TECH INC (NV)
SEC revoked commmon stock registration 11/18/2008

MBA GOLD CORP (CANADA)
Common no par split (2) for (1) by issuance of (1) additional share payable 07/16/2003 to holders of record 07/15/2003
Name changed to MBA Resources Corp. 10/14/2005
MBA Resources Corp. name changed to Thunderbird Energy Corp. 07/27/2006 which recapitalized as Gordon Creek Energy Inc. 10/24/2013

MBA LICENSING CORP (DE)
Name changed to Internet Gaming Technologies, Inc. 06/21/1996
Internet Gaming Technologies, Inc. name changed to Virtual Gaming Technologies, Inc. 02/22/1997 which name changed to VirtGame.com Corp. 09/28/1999 which name changed to VirtGame Corp. 02/25/2002 which merged into Mikohn Gaming Corp. 10/07/2005 which name changed to Progressive Gaming International Corp. 04/03/2006
(See Progressive Gaming International Corp.)

MBA RES CORP (CANADA)
Name changed to Thunderbird Energy Corp. 07/27/2006
Thunderbird Energy Corp. recapitalized as Gordon Creek Energy Inc. 10/24/2013

MBAC FERTILIZER CORP (CANADA)
Reorganized under the laws of Cayman Islands 11/07/2016
Each share Common no par exchanged for (0.01) share Ordinary CAD $0.001 par
MBAC Fertilizer Corp. (Cayman Islands) name changed to Itafos 01/06/2017

MBAC FERTILIZER CORP (CAYMAN ISLANDS)
Name changed to Itafos 01/06/2017

MBANK FORT WORTH EAST (FORT WORTH, TX)
Acquired by MBank Fort Worth, N.A. (Fort Worth, TX) 07/01/1987
Details not available

MBASE COMMERCE INC (AB)
Name changed 7/5/2002
Name changed from mBase.com Inc. to mBase Commerce Inc. 7/5/2002
Recapitalized as Bri-Chem Corp. 1/11/2007
Each share Common no par exchanged for (0.2) share Common no par

MBASSOCIATES (CA)
Capital Stock $1 par split (2) for (1) by issuance of (1) additional share 05/10/1971
Acquired by Tracor, Inc. (DE) 09/03/1980
Each share Capital Stock $1 par exchanged for (0.3125) share Common 33-1/3¢ par
(See Tracor, Inc. (DE))

MBC CORP (CA)
Acquired by California Bancshares Inc. 03/31/1994
Each share Common no par exchanged for (0.7271) share Common $2.50 par
California Bancshares Inc. merged into U.S. Bancorp (OR) 06/06/1996 which merged into U.S. Bancorp 08/01/1997

MBC FOOD CORP (CO)
Recapitalized as Concorde America, Inc. 6/30/2004
Each share Common no par exchanged for (0.001) share Common no par

MBC HLDG CO (MN)
Filed a petition under Chapter 11 Federal Bankruptcy Code 2/21/2002
Stockholders' equity unlikely

MBEACH SOFTWARE INC (FL)
Common $0.0001 par split (13) for (1) by issuance of (12) additional shares payable 06/04/2010 to holders of record 06/03/2010
Ex date - 06/07/2010
SEC revoked common stock registration 11/06/2014

MBF HEALTHCARE ACQUISITION CORP (DE)
Issue Information - 18,750,000 UNITS consisting of (1) share COM and (1) WT offered at $8 per Unit on 04/17/2007
In process of liquidation
Each Unit exchanged for initial distribution of $8.23880432 cash 04/22/2009
Each share Common $0.0001 par exchanged for initial distribution of $8.23880432 $8.23880432 cash 04/22/2009
Each Unit received second distribution of $0.02015683 cash payable 08/24/2010 to holders of record 04/22/2009
Each share Common $0.0001 par received second distribution of $0.02015683 cash payable 08/24/2010 to holders of record 04/22/2009
Each Unit received third and final distribution of $0.00194365 cash payable 06/15/2011 to holders of record 04/22/2009
Each share Common $0.0001 par received third and final distribution of $0.00194365 cash payable 06/15/2011 to holders of record 04/22/2009

MBF HLDGS BERHAD (AUSTRALIA)
Each old Sponsored ADR for Ordinary exchanged for (0.05) new Sponsored ADR for Ordinary 12/10/2003
ADR agreement terminated 10/10/2013
Each new Sponsored ADR for Ordinary exchanged for $8.992946 cash

MBF USA INC (MD)
Reorganized 12/18/95
Reorganized from Oklahoma to under the laws of Maryland 12/18/95
Each share old Common 1¢ par exchanged for (0.1) share new Common 1¢ par
Name changed to WRP Corp. 6/23/98
WRP Corp. name changed to AHPC Holdings, Inc. 5/14/2004

MBHI CAP TR I (DE)
10% Trust Preferred Securities called for redemption at $$25 on 6/7/2005

MBI BUSINESS CTRS INC (MD)
Chapter 11 bankruptcy proceedings converted to Chapter 7 on 12/22/1987
No stockholders' equity

MBI CAP TR I (DE)
Accredited Investors Floating Rate Guaranteed Trust Preferred Securities called for redemption 9/7/2006
Accredited Investors Floating Rate Guaranteed Trust Preferred Securities called for redemption 9/7/2006

MBI FINL INC (NV)
SEC revoked common stock registration 12/06/2013

MBIA CAP / CLAYMORE MANAGED DURATION INVT GRADE MUN FD (DE)
Name changed to Managed Duration Investment Grade Municipal Fund 05/20/2010
(See Managed Duration Investment Grade Municipal Fund)

MBIA INC (CT)
6.95% Senior Quarterly Income Debt Securities called for redemption at $25 on 12/24/2004

(Additional Information in Active)

MBLA FINL CORP (DE)
Merged into Citizens Bancshares Co. 10/13/99
Each share Common exchanged for $25.18 cash

MBMI RES INC (BC)
Reincorporated 11/15/2005
Place of incorporation changed from (YT) to (BC) 11/15/2005
Each share Common no par received distribution of (0.1) share Garson Resources Ltd. no par payable 09/27/2006 to holders of record 01/06/2006 Ex date - 01/04/2006
Reorganized under the laws of Ontario 06/22/2012
Each share Common no par exchanged for (0.1) share Common no par

MBNA CAP D (DE)
8.125% Trust Preferred Securities Ser. D called for redemption at $25 plus $0.135417 accrued dividends on 07/25/2012

MBNA CAP E (DE)
8.10% Trust Originated Preferred Securities Ser. E called for redemption at $25 plus $0.39375 accrued dividends on 07/25/2012

MBNA CAP B (DE)
Floating Rate Capital Securities Ser. B called for redemption at $1,000 plus $3.15805 accrued dividends on 06/06/2018

MBNA CAP C (DE)
8.25% Trust Originated Preferred Securities called for redemption at $25 on 09/20/2006

MBNA CORP (MD)
7.5% Ser. A Preferred 1¢ par called for redemption at $25 plus $0.09896 accrued dividends on 11/3/2005
Adjustable Rate Ser. B Preferred 1¢ par called for redemption at $25 plus $0.0726 accrued dividends on 11/3/2005
Common 1¢ par split (2) for (1) by issuance of (1) additional share 2/12/93
Common 1¢ par split (3) for (2) by issuance of (0.5) additional share 2/14/94
Common 1¢ par split (3) for (2) by issuance of (0.5) additional share payable 2/16/96 to holders of record 2/2/96
Common 1¢ par split (3) for (2) by issuance of (0.5) additional share payable 1/1/97 to holders of record 12/16/96
Common 1¢ par split (3) for (2) by issuance of (0.5) additional share payable 10/1/97 to holders of record 9/15/97 Ex date - 10/2/97
Common 1¢ par split (3) for (2) by issuance of (0.5) additional share payable 10/1/98 to holders of record 9/15/98 Ex date - 10/2/98
Common 1¢ par split (3) for (2) by issuance of (0.5) additional share payable 7/15/2002 to holders of record 7/1/2002 Ex date - 7/16/2002
Merged into Bank of America Corp. 1/1/2006
Each share Common 1¢ par exchanged for (0.5009) share Common 1¢ par and $4.125 cash

MBO PPTYS INC
Assets transferred to MBOP Liquidating Trust 08/10/2001
(See MBOP Liquidating Trust)

MBOP LIQUIDATING TR
Liquidation completed
Each Trust Certificate received initial distribution of $1.05 cash payable 12/27/2002 to holders of record 12/17/2002 Ex date - 1/6/2003
Each Trust Certificate exchanged for second and final distribution of

MEADOW GROUP INC (NY)
Each share Common $0.001 par exchanged for (0.025) share Common 1¢ par 08/16/1990
Dissolved by proclamation 09/27/1995

MEADOW LANE GARDEN APTS CORP (IL)
Charter revoked for failure to file reports and pay fees 03/28/1968

MEADOW MTN RES LTD (BC)
Name changed to First Impression Singles Network Ltd. 09/11/1989
First Impression Singles Network Ltd. name changed to Global Explorations Corp. 05/29/1997 which merged into Trincomali, Ltd. 10/15/1999 which recapitalized as Malers, Inc. 05/17/2005 which name changed to Dot VN, Inc. 08/07/2006

MEADOW VY CORP (NV)
Acquired by Phoenix Parent Corp. 02/02/2009
Each share Common $0.001 par exchanged for $11.25 cash

MEADOW VY RANCHOS INC (NV)
Charter permanently revoked 09/01/2003

MEADOWBROOK GOLF & COUNTRY CLUB, INC. (NY)
Charter cancelled and proclaimed dissolved for failure to pay taxes 12/15/1949

MEADOWBROOK GOLF GROUP INC (DE)
Merged into Apollo Real Estate Investment Fund II, L.P. 07/25/2007
Each share Common no par exchanged for $0.08 cash

MEADOWBROOK GOLF INC (UT)
Reorganized under the laws of Delaware as Meadowbrook Golf Group Inc. 03/17/1997
Each share Common no par exchanged for (0.1) share Common no par
(See Meadowbrook Golf Group Inc.)

MEADOWBROOK INC (MI)
Merged into MDBK, Inc. 09/15/1981
Each share Common $1 par exchanged for $2 cash

MEADOWBROOK INS GROUP INC (MI)
Acquired by Fosun International Ltd. 07/07/2015
Each share Common 1¢ par exchanged for $8.65 cash

MEADOWBROOK REHABILITATION GROUP INC (DE)
Each share old Class A Common 1¢ par exchanged for (0.33333333) share new Class A Common 1¢ par 04/22/1996
New Class A Common 1¢ par split (3) for (2) by issuance of (0.5) additional share payable 04/22/1998 to holders of record 04/08/1998
Name changed to Cambio Inc. 10/22/1998
Cambio Inc. name changed to Telynx, Inc. 11/28/2000
(See Telynx, Inc.)

MEADOWCRAFT INC (DE)
Merged into SRB-MWI, LLC 06/30/1999
Each share Common 1¢ par exchanged for $10 cash

MEADOWLANDS INVTS INC (FL)
Proclaimed dissolved 10/13/1989

MEADOWS (HANK), INC. (MN)
Adjudicated bankrupt 08/04/1971

MEADOWS SPRINGS INC (NV)
Reorganized under the laws of Delaware as Earth Biofuels, Inc. 11/14/2005
Each share Common $0.001 par exchanged for (6) shares Common $0.001 par
Earth Biofuels, Inc. name changed to Evolution Fuels, Inc. 06/16/2009 which name changed to SC Holdings Corp. 06/20/2014

MEADOWVALE DEVELOPMENTS LTD. (ON)
Liquidation completed
Each share Capital Stock no par received initial distribution of $2.3225 cash 08/24/1965
Each share Capital Stock no par exchanged for second and final distribution of (0.82) share Markborough Properties Ltd. Common no par 01/24/1966
(See Marlborough Properties Ltd.)

MEADVILLE TEL CO (PA)
Stock Dividend - 10% 12/15/1955
Merged into Mid-Continent Telephone Corp. 07/31/1968
Each share 5% Preferred $25 par exchanged for (1) share 5-1/2% Preferred Ser. F $25 par
Each share Common $25 par exchanged for (7) shares Common no par
Note: Until 07/31/1970 unexchanged ctfs. could be exchanged for stock; after that date and until 07/31/1972 unexchanged ctfs. could be exchanged for cash and after 07/31/1972 unexchanged ctfs. became void
Mid-Continent Telephone Corp. name changed to Alltel Corp. (OH) 10/25/1983 which reincorporated in Delaware 05/15/1990
(See Alltel Corp.)

MEADWESTVACO CORP (DE)
Each share Common 1¢ par received distribution of (0.32986547) share ACCO Brands Corp. Common 1¢ par payable 04/30/2012 to holders of record 04/24/2012 Ex date - 05/01/2012
Merged into WestRock Co. 07/01/2015
Each share Common 1¢ par exchanged for (0.78) share Common 1¢ par

MEAKER (C.G.) CO., INC.
In process of liquidation 00/00/1946
Details not available

MEANS (F.W.) & CO. (IL)
Common no par split (5) for (1) by issuance of (4) additional shares 01/10/1961
7% Conv. Preference no par called for redemption 08/16/1962
Common no par split (3) for (1) by issuance of (2) additional shares 12/01/1965
Name changed to Means Services, Inc. 07/02/1979
(See Means Services, Inc.)

MEANS SVCS INC (IL)
Merged into ARA Services, Inc. 08/17/1982
Each share Common no par exchanged for $37 cash

MEARES RES INC (BC)
Name changed to Templar Mining Corp. 4/8/82
(See Templar Mining Corp.)

MEASUREGRAPH CO (DE)
Preferred $100 par called for redemption 08/01/1970
Name changed to MEPR Corp. 01/02/1981
(See MEPR Corp.)

MEASUREMENT SPECIALTIES INC (NJ)
Common no par split (2) for (1) by issuance of (1) additional share payable 10/20/2000 to holders of record 10/03/2000 Ex date - 10/23/2000
Acquired by TE Connectivity Ltd. 10/09/2014
Each share Common no par exchanged for $86 cash

MEASUREMENT SYS INC (CT)
Merged into Dover Corp. 11/12/1982
Each share Common $1 par exchanged for $110 cash

MEASUREMENTS GAME TECHNOLOGY INC (ID)
Charter forfeited for failure to file annual reports 00/00/1984

MEASUREMENTS SPECTRUM, INC. (CA)
Adjudicated bankrupt 11/13/62
No stockholders' equity

MEASUREX CORP (DE)
Reincorporated 6/18/84
Common no par split (2) for (1) by issuance of (1) additional share 1/24/84
State of incorporation changed from (CA) to (DE) and Common no par changed to 1¢ par 6/18/84
Common 1¢ par split (2) for (1) by issuance of (1) additional share 3/11/87
Merged into Honeywell Inc. 3/7/97
Each share Common 1¢ par exchanged for $35 cash

MEATS & TREATS SUPERMARKETS INC (NY)
Name changed to Freedco International, Inc. 11/15/1982
Freedco International, Inc. name changed to Radon Resources, Inc. 01/19/1983 which name changed to Industrial Technical Concepts, Inc. 08/25/1983 which name changed to ITC Integrated Systems, Inc. 10/03/1985
(See ITC Integrated Systems, Inc.)

MEBCO INDS INC (DE)
Adjudicated bankrupt 06/19/1979
Stockholders' equity unlikely

MEC HLDGS CDA INC (ON)
Each Exchangeable Share no par exchanged for (1) share Magna Entertainment Corp. Class A Subordinate no par 12/30/2002
(See Magna Entertainment Corp.)

MECA SOFTWARE INC (DE)
Merged into Block (H & R), Inc. 11/29/93
Each share Common 1¢ par exchanged for $6.625 cash

MECACHROME INTL INC (CANADA)
Issue Information - 14,687,500 SUB VTG SHS offered at $14 per share on 10/11/2007
Plan of arrangement under Companies' Creditors Arrangement Act effective 12/17/2009
No stockholders' equity

MECANAIR INC (MA)
Name changed to Perception Ventures Inc. 09/09/1969
(See Perception Ventures Inc.)

MECASERTO INC (FL)
Recapitalized as National Business Holdings, Inc. 5/25/2004
Each share Common $0.0001 par exchanged for (0.025) share Common $0.0001 par
National Business Holdings, Inc. name changed to Union Dental Holdings, Inc. 1/21/2005

MECCA COMPUTER SYSTEMS, INC. (NM)
Reincorporated under the laws of Delaware as Mecca Corp. and Common $1 par changed to 50¢ par 12/30/1970
Mecca Corp. name changed to Landco, Inc. 08/31/1972 which name changed to Milbrook Financial Corp. 01/17/1984
(See Milbrook Financial Corp.)

MECCA CORP (DE)
Name changed to Landco, Inc. 08/31/1972
Landco, Inc. name changed to Milbrook Financial Corp. 01/17/1984
(See Milbrook Financial Corp.)

MECCA MEDI-TECH INC (BC)
Name changed to Pheromone Sciences Corp. (BC) 2/28/2000
Pheromone Sciences Corp. (BC) reincorporated under the laws of Canada 5/29/2001 which name changed to Sernova Corp. 9/20/2006

MECCA MINERALS LTD (BC)
Delisted from Vancouver Stock Exchange 06/05/1987

MECH FINL INC (CT)
Merged into Webster Financial Corp. 6/26/2000
Each share Common 1¢ par exchanged for (1.52) shares Common 1¢ par

MECH-TRON INDUSTRIES, INC. (CO)
Adjudicated bankrupt 10/3/63
No stockholders' equity

MECHANEX CORP (CO)
Acquired by Tenneco Inc. 12/3/68
Each share Common 50¢ par exchanged for (0.285714) share Common $5 par
Tenneco Inc. merged into El Paso Natural Gas Co. 12/12/96 which reorganized as El Paso Energy Corp. 8/1/98 which name changed to El Paso Corp. 2/5/2001

MECHANICAL DYNAMICS INC (MI)
Merged into MSC.Software Corp. 5/10/2002
Each share Common no par exchanged for $18.85 cash

MECHANICAL ENTERPRISES INC (VA)
Common 50¢ par changed to 16-2/3¢ par and (2) additional shares issued 08/20/1962
Common 16-2/3¢ par changed to 5-5/9¢ par and (2) additional shares issued 09/16/1971
Charter cancelled and proclaimed dissolved for failure to file reports 09/30/2001

MECHANICAL HANDLING SYSTEMS, INC. (MI)
Each share Common $5 par exchanged for (6) shares Common $1 par in 1953
Merged into American Chain & Cable Co., Inc. 1/2/68
Each share Common $1 par exchanged for (0.4) share Common $1 par
(See American Chain & Cable Co., Inc.)

MECHANICAL IMPROVEMENT CORP (FL)
Dissolved by proclamation 9/16/36

MECHANICAL PIN RESETTER CO. LTD. (AB)
Recapitalized as Troymin Resources Ltd. 08/31/1983
Each share Common no par exchanged for (0.66666666) share Common no par
Troymin Resources Ltd. merged into Santoy Resources Ltd. (AB) (New) 04/24/2003 which reorganized in British Columbia as Virginia Energy Resources Ltd. (Old) 07/24/2009 which reorganized as Anthem Resources Inc. 09/28/2012 which merged into Boss Power Corp. 07/23/2015 which name changed to Eros Resources Corp. 07/29/2015

MECHANICKS NATL BK (CONCORD, NH)
Merged into Bank of New Hampshire, N.A. (Manchester, NH) 1/30/69
Each share Capital Stock $10 par exchanged for (1) share Common Capital Stock $10 par
Bank of New Hampshire, N.A. (Manchester, NH) reorganized as Bank of New Hampshire Corp.

4/30/80 which merged into Peoples Heritage Financial Group, Inc. 4/2/96 which name changed to Banknorth Group, Inc. (ME) 5/10/2000 which merged into TD Banknorth Inc. 3/1/2005
(See TD Banknorth Inc.)

MECHANICS & FMRS BK (ALBANY, NY)
Each share Capital Stock $100 par exchanged for (20) shares Capital Stock $10 par to effect a (10) for (1) split and a 100% stock dividend 02/29/1952
Merged into Bank of New York Co., Inc. 05/29/1969
Each share Capital Stock $10 par exchanged for $67.50 principal amount of 6-1/4% Conv. Debentures due 09/01/1994 and (0.25) share Common $15 par
Bank of New York Co., Inc. merged into Bank of New York Mellon Corp. 07/01/2007

MECHANICS & FMRS BK (DURHAM, NC)
Under plan of reorganization each share Common $5 par automatically became (1) share M&F Bancorp, Inc. Common no par 09/28/1999

MECHANICS BANCORP INC (MA)
Merged into Multibank Financial Corp. 01/01/1973
Each share Common $1 par exchanged for (1.8) shares Common $6.25 par
Multibank Financial Corp. acquired by Bank of Boston Corp. 07/13/1993 which name changed to BankBoston Corp 04/25/1997 which merged into Fleet Boston Corp. 10/01/1999 which name changed to Boston Financial Corp. 04/18/2000 which merged into Bank of America Corp. 04/01/2004

MECHANICS BK (RICHMOND, CA)
Preferred $50 par called for redemption 1/15/64
(Additional Information in Active)

MECHANICS BK (WATER VALLEY, MS)
Under plan of reorganization each share Common $1 par automatically became (1) share Mechanics Banc Holding Co. Common $1 par 4/10/2003

MECHANICS FIN CO (NJ)
8% Preferred $10 par called for redemption 7/1/87
(Additional Information in Active)

MECHANICS INSURANCE CO.
Dissolved in 1939

MECHANICS NATL BK (WORCESTER, MA)
Capital Stock $100 par changed to $10 par and (9) incorporation shares issued plus a 100% stock dividend paid 02/20/1964
Reorganized as Mechanics Bancorp, Inc. 04/06/1969
Each share Capital Stock $10 par exchanged for (1) share Common $1 par
Mechanics Bancorp, Inc. merged into Multibank Financial Corp. 01/01/1973 which was acquired by Bank of Boston Corp. 07/13/1993 which name changed to BankBoston Corp. 04/25/1997 which merged into Fleet Boston Corp. 10/01/1999 which name changed to FleetBoston Financial Corp. 04/18/2000 which merged into Bank of America Corp. 04/01/2004

MECHANICS NATL BK BURLINGTON CNTY (BURLINGTON, NJ)
Merged into First National State Bancorporation 12/31/1973
Each share Capital Stock $5 par exchanged for (1) share Common $6.25 par
First National State Bancorporation name changed to First Fidelity Bancorporation (Old) 05/01/1985 which merged into First Fidelity Bancorporation (New) 02/29/1988 which merged into First Union Corp. 01/01/1996 which name changed to Wachovia Corp. (Ctfs. dated after 09/01/2001) 09/01/2001 which merged into Wells Fargo & Co. (New) 12/31/2008

MECHANICS NATL BK HUNTINGTON PARK CALIF (PARAMOUNT, CA)
Common $10 par changed to $5 par and (1) additional share issued 8/11/69
Location changed from Huntington Park, CA to Paramount, CA 1/9/80
Bank closed by California Superintendent of Banks 4/1/94
No stockholders' equity

MECHANICS SVGS BK (HARTFORD, CT)
Under plan of reorganization each share Common 1¢ par automatically became (1) share MECH Financial, Inc. Common 1¢ par 1/1/98
MECH Financial, Inc. merged into Webster Financial Corp. 6/26/2000

MECHEL OAO (RUSSIA)
Name changed 08/24/2005
Name changed from Mechel Steel Group OAO to Mechel OAO 08/24/2005
Old Sponsored ADR's for Ordinary split (3) for (1) by issuance of (2) additional ADR's payable 05/19/2008 to holders of record 05/16/2008 Ex date - 05/20/2008
Basis changed from (1:3) to (1:1) 05/19/2008
Each old Sponsored ADR for Ordinary exchanged for (0.5) new Sponsored ADR for Ordinary 01/12/2016
Basis changed from (1:1) to (1:2) 01/12/2016
Name changed to Mechel PAO 07/01/2016

MECHMETAL TRONICS INC (DE)
Common 20¢ par changed to 10¢ par 5/10/60
Charter cancelled and declared inoperative and void for non-payment of taxes 3/1/94

MECHTRON CORP (FL)
Name changed to Mechtron-Genco Corp. (FL) 12/04/1968
Mechtron-Genco Corp. (FL) reincorporated in Delaware 09/26/1969 which name changed to Mechtron International Corp. 05/18/1970 which name changed to Gencor Industries Inc. 01/04/1988

MECHTRON GENCO CORP (DE)
Reincorporated 09/26/1969
State of incorporation changed from (FL) to (DE) 09/26/1969
Name changed to Mechtron International Corp. 05/18/1970
Mechtron International Corp. name changed to Gencor Industries Inc. 01/04/1988

MECHTRON INTL CORP (DE)
Common 10¢ par split (5) for (4) by issuance of (0.25) additional share 7/2/84
Common 10¢ par split (3) for (2) by issuance of (0.5) additional share 8/15/84
Name changed to Gencor Industries Inc. 1/4/88

MECK (JOHN) INDUSTRIES, INC.
Merged into Scott Radio Laboratories, Inc. 00/00/1951
Each share Common $1 par exchanged for (1.3) shares Common $1 par
Scott Radio Laboratories, Inc. name changed to Electrovision Corp.
00/00/1959 which merged into Monogram Precision Industries, Inc. 05/11/1962 which name changed to Monogram Industries Inc. (CA) 12/03/1962 which reincorporated in Delaware 11/28/1969 which merged into Nortek, Inc. (RI) 08/26/1983 which reincorporated in Delaware 04/23/1987 which reorganized as Nortek Holdings, Inc. 11/20/2002
(See Nortek Holdings, Inc.)

MECKLERMEDIA CORP NEW (DE)
Voluntarily dissolved 03/07/2016
No stockholders' equity

MECKLERMEDIA CORP OLD (DE)
Common 1¢ par split (2) for (1) by issuance of (1) additional share 09/19/1995
Merged into Penton Media Inc. 11/24/1998
Each share Common 1¢ par exchanged for $29 cash

MECON INC (DE)
Merged into General Electric Co. 2/11/2000
Each share Common $0.001 par exchanged for (0.081) share Common 16¢ par

MECOX LANE LTD (CAYMAN ISLANDS)
Each old Sponsored ADR for Ordinary exchanged for (0.2) new Sponsored ADR for Ordinary 02/01/2013
Basis changed from (1:7) to (1:35) 02/01/2013
Acquired by Minat Associated Co., Ltd. 04/14/2016
Each new Sponsored ADR for Ordinary exchanged for $3.95 cash

MED ASSIST INC (MA)
Out of business 08/26/1976
No stockholders' equity

MED-CANNABIS PHARMA INC (NV)
Name changed to Mansfield-Martin Exploration Mining, Inc. 03/14/2017

MED CARE CORP (NV)
Each share old Common $0.001 par exchanged for (0.2) share new Common $0.001 par 05/24/1989
Each share new Common $0.001 par exchanged for (0.5) share Common $0.002 par 06/01/1990
Name changed to Envirofil, Inc. (NV) 01/31/1991
Envirofil, Inc. (NV) reincorporated in Delaware 03/26/1993 which merged into USA Waste Services Inc. 05/27/1994 which merged into Waste Management, Inc. 07/16/1998

MED-CHEM HEALTH CARE LTD (ON)
Discharged from bankruptcy 07/00/2005
No stockholders' equity

MED-CHEM PRODS INC (MA)
Name changed 04/01/1986
Stock Dividend - 100% 09/01/1983
Name changed from Med-Chem Products, Inc. to MedChem Products, Inc. 04/01/1986
Merged into Bard (C.R.), Inc. 09/28/1995
Each share Common 1¢ par exchanged for (0.3082477) share Common 25¢ par
Bard (C.R.), Inc. merged into Becton, Dickinson & Co. 12/29/2017

MED CTL INC (NV)
Name changed to AmbiCom Holdings, Inc. 02/23/2010

MED DATA, INC. (WI)
Administratively dissolved 6/14/88

MED-DESIGN CORP (DE)
Issue Information - 1,500,000 shares COM offered at $7 per share on 06/06/1995
Common 1¢ par split (2) for (1) by issuance of (1) additional share payable 02/26/1996 to holders of record 02/12/1996
Merged into Specialized Health Products International, Inc. 06/02/2006
Each share Common 1¢ par exchanged for (1.25863) shares Common 2¢ par
(See Specialized Health Products International, Inc.)

MED DIVERSIFIED INC (NV)
Plan of reorganization under Chapter 11 Federal Bankruptcy Code effective 09/17/2004
No stockholders' equity

MED-EMERG INTL INC (ON)
Acquired by AIM Health Group Inc. 01/30/2009
Each share Common no par exchanged for (0.78091) share Common no par
(See AIM Health Group Inc.)

MED GEN INC (MN)
Name changed to Remedco, Inc. 01/12/1982
(See Remedco, Inc.)

MED GEN INC (NV)
Each share old Common $0.001 par exchanged for (0.0125) share new Common $0.001 par 02/03/2003
New Common $0.001 par split (4) for (1) by issuance of (3) additional shares payable 11/17/2003 to holders of record 11/10/2003
Ex date - 11/18/2003
Each share new Common $0.001 par exchanged again for (0.05) share new Common $0.001 par 09/06/2005
Each share new Common $0.001 par exchanged again for (0.005) share new Common $0.001 par 06/02/2008
Recapitalized as Northstar Global Business Services, Inc. (NV) 08/04/2010
Each share new Common $0.001 par exchanged for (0.33333333) share Common $0.001 par
Northstar Global Business Services, Inc. (NV) reincorporated in Wyoming as MedGen, Inc. 07/06/2015

MED INDEX INC (NV)
Name changed to Venmark, Inc. 09/11/1987
(See Venmark, Inc.)

MED LAB SYS INC (MN)
Statutorily dissolved 10/11/91

MED MARK INC (UT)
Merged into Healthgarde Corp. 11/08/1974
Each share Common $0.001 par exchanged for (1.25) shares Common 1¢ par
Healthgarde Corp. name changed to Allscope Resources International, Inc. 04/09/1982
(See Allscope Resources International, Inc.)

MED MOBILE INC (NJ)
Name changed to Bio-Reference Laboratories, Inc. 11/10/1989
Bio-Reference Laboratories, Inc. merged into OPKO Health, Inc. 08/20/2015

MED NET INTL LTD (BERMUDA)
Each share Ordinary 10¢ par exchanged for (1/3) share Ordinary 30¢ par 10/06/1999
Completely liquidated
Each share Ordinary 30¢ par received first and final distribution of (0.1) share LaserNet Ltd. Common payable 09/28/2005 to holders of record 08/29/2005
Note: Certificates were not required to be surrendered and are without value

MED PAK CORP (WV)
Bankruptcy proceedings converted from Chapter 11 to Chapter 7 on 7/8/81

FINANCIAL INFORMATION, INC.

MED-MED

No stockholders' equity
MED SEARCH INC (DE)
Recapitalized as Prospect Medical Holdings, Inc. 02/10/1998
Each (44) shares Common 1¢ par exchanged for (1) share Common 1¢ par
(See Prospect Medical Holdings, Inc.)

MED TECH PRODS INC (DE)
Name changed to U.S. Health Resources Corp. 02/05/1986
(See U.S. Health Resources Corp.)

MED-TECH SOLUTIONS INC (NV)
Common $0.001 par split (10) for (1) by issuance of (9) additional shares payable 11/02/2006 to holders of record 10/26/2006 Ex date - 11/03/2006
Recapitalized as Four Rivers BioEnergy Inc. 01/29/2008
Each share Common $0.001 par exchanged for (0.05882352) share Common $0.001 par
(See Four Rivers BioEnergy Inc.)

MED TECH SYS INC (BC)
Struck off register and declared dissolved for failure to file returns 07/15/1994

MED-TEMPS INC (CO)
Name changed to International Nursing Services Inc. 02/16/1990
International Nursing Services Inc. name changed to Medix Resources, Inc. (CO) 02/18/1998 which reincorporated in Delaware as Ramp Corp. 12/19/2003
(See Ramp Corp.)

MED TEST SYS INC (DE)
Common 10¢ par changed to 1¢ par 08/00/1983
Recapitalized as Enxuta Corp. of America 06/10/1992
Each share Common 1¢ par exchanged for (0.1) share Common 1¢ par

MED-TEX CORP (NV)
Recapitalized as Opal Technologies Inc. 7/7/97
Each share Common $0.001 par exchanged for (0.1) share Common $0.001 par

MED VENTURE INC (MN)
Out of business 10/25/1991
Details not available

MED/WASTE INC (DE)
Filed a petition under Chapter 7 Federal Bankruptcy Code 2/13/2002
No stockholders' equity

MED-X SYS INC (NV)
SEC revoked common stock registration 03/06/2017

MEDA AB (SWEDEN)
ADR agreement terminated 04/03/2017
Each ADR for Ordinary exchanged for $18.305909 cash
Note: Each ADR for Ordinary received an additional distribution of $0.213531 cash payable 12/07/2017 to holders of record 04/03/2017

MEDA INC (DE)
Name changed to PML, Inc. 2/24/97
(See PML, Inc.)

MEDAC INC (CO)
Name changed to Lifeline Healthcare Group, Ltd. (CO) 04/25/1988
Lifeline Healthcare Group, Ltd. (CO) reorganized in Delaware 09/02/1988
(See Lifeline Healthcare Group, Ltd. (DE))

MEDACO INC (DE)
Acquired by Medical Dimensions, Inc. 2/25/75
Each share Common 5¢ par exchanged for (0.629999) share Common 10¢ par
(See Medical Dimensions, Inc.)

MEDAID, INC. (DE)
Name changed to LFI Capital Corp. in June, 1989

MEDALION SVCS INC (DE)
Name changed to Orex Gold Mines Corp. 3/4/99
Orex Gold Mines Corp. name changed to Orex Corp. 11/8/99 which name changed to EarthNet.Tv, Inc. 12/11/2000 which name changed to Nocera Inc. 2/8/2002

MEDALIST FDS (MA)
Name changed to Virtus Funds 2/15/95

MEDALIST INDS INC (WI)
Common $4 par changed to $2 par 5/14/69
Common $2 par changed to $1 par 5/5/72
Stock Dividends - 20% 1/31/73; 10% 1/15/75; 10% 10/15/77
Merged into Illinois Tool Works Inc. 5/30/96
Each share Common $1 par exchanged for (0.2143) share Common no par

MEDALLIANCE INC (TN)
Liquidation completed
Each share Common 1¢ par exchanged for initial distribution of $4.20 cash payable 11/10/95 to holders of record 11/10/95
Each share Common 1¢ par received second distribution of $0.50 cash payable 9/20/96 to holders of record 11/10/95
Each share Common 1¢ par received third and final distribution of $0.10 cash payable 1/8/98 to holders of record 11/10/95

MEDALLION BOOKS LTD (BC)
Dissolved 01/26/1990
Details not available

MEDALLION CREST MGMT INC (FL)
Reincorporated under the laws of Delaware as CepTor Corp. 12/13/2004
(See CepTor Corp.)

MEDALLION EXPLS LTD (BC)
Recapitalized as Compass Resources Ltd. 07/14/1987
Each share Common no par exchanged for (0.33333333) share Common no par
Compass Resources Ltd. recapitalized as United Compass Resources Ltd. 06/09/1993 which recapitalized as Tartan Energy Inc. (BC) 10/02/1998 which reincorporated in Alberta 08/01/2001
(See Tartan Energy Inc.)

MEDALLION GROUP INC (DE)
$0.10 Conv. Preferred Ser. E no par called for redemption 8/15/78
Merged into Health-Chem Corp. 12/31/79
Each share Common $1 par exchanged for (1-1/3) shares Common 1¢ par
(See Health-Chem Corp.)

MEDALLION LEISURE CORP (DE)
Merged into Medallion Group, Inc. 11/06/1975
Each share Common 1¢ par exchanged for (1) share $0.10 Conv. Preferred Ser. E no par
(See Medallion Group, Inc.)

MEDALLION MINES LTD. (ON)
Charter cancelled for failure to pay taxes and file returns in March, 1968

MEDALLION MORTGAGE CORP. LTD. (AB)
Struck off register for failure to file annual returns 06/01/1982

MEDALLION NATIONAL INSURANCE CO. (MO)
Merged into Missouri General Insurance Co. 12/31/70

Missouri General Insurance Co. charter forfeited 1/1/77

MEDALLION PETROLEUMS LTD. (AB)
Merged into Canadian Industrial Gas & Oil Ltd. 03/08/1965
Each share Common $1.25 par exchanged for (0.47619047) share Capital Stock $2.50 par
Canadian Industrial Gas & Oil Ltd. merged into Norcen Energy Resources Ltd. (AB) 10/28/1975 which reincorporated in Canada 04/15/1977 which merged into Union Pacific Resources Group Inc. 04/17/1998 which merged into Anadarko Petroleum Corp. 07/14/2000

MEDALLION PICTURES CORP. (DE)
Each share Class A 10¢ par or Class B 10¢ par exchanged for (0.2) share Common 50¢ par 8/25/58
Stock Dividends - 10% 8/15/63; 50% 2/25/64; 10% 5/14/65
Name changed to Broadcast Industries Corp. 11/14/66
Broadcast Industries Corp. adjudicated bankrupt 6/12/78

MEDAMICUS INC (MN)
Name changed to Enpath Medical, Inc. 02/02/2004
(See Enpath Medical, Inc.)

MEDAPHIS CORP (DE)
Common 1¢ par split (2) for (1) by issuance of (1) additional share 5/31/95
Name changed to Per-Se Technologies, Inc. 8/16/99
(See Per-Se Technologies, Inc.)

MEDAR INC (MI)
Name changed to Integral Vision Inc. 6/30/99

MEDAREX INC (NJ)
Common 1¢ par split (2) for (1) by issuance of (1) additional share payable 10/18/2000 to holders of record 09/27/2000
Merged into Bristol-Myers Squibb Co. 09/01/2009
Each share Common 1¢ par exchanged for $16 cash

MEDART (FRED) MANUFACTURING CO.
Acquired by Medart Co. in 1947

MEDASORB TECHNOLOGIES CORP (NV)
Name changed to CytoSorbents Corp. (NV) 05/07/2010
CytoSorbents Corp. (NV) reorganized in Delaware 12/05/2014

MEDASSETS INC (DE)
Acquired by Magnitude Parent Holdings, LLC 01/27/2016
Each share Common 1¢ par exchanged for $31.35 cash

MEDATA COMPUTER SYS INC (DE)
Name changed to Europa Hair Inc. 10/4/71
Europa Hair Inc. name changed to Europa Group, Inc. 1/29/73
(See Europa Group, Inc.)

MEDBOX INC (NV)
Stock Dividend - 100% payable 02/03/2014 to holders of record 12/18/2013
Name changed to Notis Global, Inc. 02/22/2016

MEDBROADCAST CORP (CANADA)
Reorganized under the laws of Alberta as Rock Energy Inc. 02/18/2014
Each share Common no par exchanged for (0.03333333) share Common no par
Note: Holders of (1,000) or fewer pre-split shares received $0.1129 cash per share
Rock Energy Inc. merged into Raging River Exploration Inc. 07/26/2016

which merged into Baytex Energy Corp. 08/27/2018

MEDCAN INC (NV)
Merged into Diagnostek, Inc. 3/28/85
Each (11) shares Common $0.001 par exchanged for (1) share Common 1¢ par
Diagnostek, Inc. merged into Value Health, Inc. 7/28/95
(See Value Health, Inc.)

MEDCAP CORP (ON)
Reorganized under the laws of Nevada as Fortune Market Media, Inc. 11/13/2007
Each share Common no par exchanged for (0.001) share Common $0.001 par
(See Fortune Market Media, Inc.)

MEDCARE TECHNOLOGIES INC (DE)
Reincorporated 10/04/1996
State of incorporation changed from (UT) to (DE) 10/04/1996
Reincorporated under the laws of Nevada as Enterprise Technologies, Inc. and Common $0.001 par changed to $0.00001 par 11/16/2001
Enterprise Technologies, Inc. name changed to PhytoMedical Technologies, Inc. 09/02/2004 which recapitalized as Ceres Ventures, Inc. 12/12/2011

MEDCATH INC (NC)
Issue Information - 2,000,000 shares COM offered at $14 per share on 12/06/1994
Merged into MedCath Holdings, Inc. 7/31/98
Each share Common 1¢ par exchanged for $19 cash

MEDCLEAN TECHNOLOGIES INC (DE)
Each share old Common $0.0001 par exchanged for (0.01) share new Common $0.0001 par 04/05/2013
SEC revoked common stock registration 05/13/2015

MEDCO CONTAINMENT SVCS INC (DE)
Common 1¢ par split (5) for (2) by issuance of (1.5) additional shares 11/04/1987
Common 1¢ par split (5) for (2) by issuance of (1.5) additional shares 01/20/1992
Merged into Merck & Co., Inc. (Old) 11/18/1993
Each share Common 1¢ par exchanged for $39 cash

MEDCO GROUP INC (DE)
Each share old Common 10¢ par exchanged for (0.2) share new Common 10¢ par 11/4/83
Reincorporated under the laws of Pennsylvania as Sklar Corp. 7/3/92
(See Sklar Corp.)

MEDCO HEALTH CARE SVCS INC (CO)
Name changed to Cine-Chrome Video Corp. 10/21/1985
Cine-Chrome Video Corp. name changed to Network 4, Inc. 06/25/1986 which recapitalized as CEEE Group Corp. (CO) 05/00/1987 which reorganized in Delaware as Atlantic International Entertainment, Ltd. 11/26/1996 which name changed to Online Gaming Systems, Ltd. 10/01/1999 which name changed to Advanced Resources Group Ltd. 02/15/2007

MEDCO HEALTH CORP (NV)
SEC revoked common stock registration 12/04/2009

MEDCO HEALTH SOLUTIONS INC (DE)
Common 1¢ par split (2) for (1) by issuance of (1) additional share payable 01/24/2008 to holders of record 01/10/2008 Ex date - 01/25/2008

Merged into Express Scripts Holding Co. 04/02/2012
Each share Common 1¢ par exchanged for (0.81) share Common 1¢ par and $28.80 cash

MEDCO INC (MO)
Reincorporated under the laws of Delaware as Medco Jewelry Corp. 7/3/69
Medco Jewelry Corp. (DE) name changed to Medco Group Inc. (DE) 5/16/83 which reincorporated in Pennsylvania as Sklar Corp. 7/3/92
(See Sklar Corp.)

MEDCO JEWELRY CORP (DE)
Class A Common 10¢ par reclassified as Common 10¢ par 8/8/72
Name changed to Medco Group Inc. (DE) 5/16/83
Medco Group Inc. (DE) reincorporated in Pennsylvania as Sklar Corp. 7/3/92
(See Sklar Corp.)

MEDCO RESH INC (DE)
Reincorporated 05/11/1995
State of incorporation changed from (CA) to (DE) 05/11/1995
Common no par split (2) for (1) by issuance of (1) additional share 10/02/1987
Merged into King Pharmaceuticals, Inc. 02/25/2000
Each share Common no par exchanged for (0.6757) share Common no par
(See King Pharmaceuticals, Inc.)

MEDCOM INC (DE)
Reincorporated 6/30/72
Common 10¢ par split (3) for (2) by issuance of (0.5) additional share 7/1/72
State of incorporation changed from (MA) to (DE) 6/30/72
Merged into Baxter Travenol Laboratories, Inc. 5/14/82
Each share Common 10¢ par exchanged for $35 cash

MEDCOM MEDICAL COMPUTER CO. LTD. (CANADA)
Name changed to Ivey Medical Systems Ltd. 1/5/72
Ivey Medical Systems Ltd. proclaimed dissolved 12/16/80

MEDCOM USA INC (DE)
Each share old Common $0.0001 par exchanged for (0.2) share new Common $0.0001 par 05/09/2001
Each share Common $0.001 par received distribution of (1) share Card Activation Technologies, Inc. Restricted Common $0.001 par payable 03/01/2007 to holders of record 12/15/2006
SEC revoked common stock registration 01/17/2014

MEDCOMSOFT INC (ON)
Notice of Intention filed under Bankruptcy & Insolvency Act 11/03/2008
No stockholders' equity

MEDCOR INC (MA)
Chapter 11 converted to Chapter 7 bankruptcy proceedings 10/01/1981
No stockholders' equity

MEDCORE HLDGS INC (FL)
Recapitalized as Advanced Defense Technologies, Inc. 06/01/2010
Each share Common $0.001 par exchanged for (0.002) share Common $0.001 par
Advanced Defense Technologies, Inc. recapitalized as Star Jets International, Inc. 02/12/2018

MEDCROSS INC (FL)
Each share old Common $0.001 par exchanged for (0.14285714) share new Common $0.001 par 10/23/1992
Name changed to I-Link Inc. 10/13/1997

I-Link Inc. name changed to Acceris Communications Inc. 11/30/2003 which name changed to C2 Global Technologies Inc. 08/15/2005 which name changed to Counsel RB Capital Inc. 02/04/2011 which name changed to Heritage Global Inc. 08/29/2013

MEDE AMER CORP (DE)
Issue Information - 4,615,400 shares COM offered at $13 per share on 02/01/1999
Merged into Healtheon/WebMD Corp. 11/11/99
Each share Common 1¢ par exchanged for (0.7494) share Common $0.0001 par
Healtheon/WebMD Corp. name changed to WebMD Corp. 9/12/2000 which name changed to Emdeon Corp. 10/17/2005 which name changed to HLTH Corp. 5/21/2007

MEDECI CORP (NV)
Name changed to Therapy Lasers Inc. 02/27/1995
Therapy Lasers Inc. name changed to SpectraSource Corp. 08/17/2000 which recapitalized as China Yibai United Guarantee International Holding, Inc. 06/17/2009

MEDECISION INC (PA)
Issue Information - 4,700,000 shares COM offered at $10 per share on 12/13/2006
Acquired by Health Care Service Corp. 08/15/2008
Each share Common no par exchanged for $7 cash

MEDEFILE INTL INC (NV)
Old Common $0.0001 par split (15) for (1) by issuance of (14) additional shares payable 01/20/2006 to holders of record 01/16/2006
Ex date - 01/23/2006
Each share old Common $0.0001 par exchanged for (0.0002) share new Common $0.0001 par 10/09/2012
Each share new Common $0.0001 par exchanged again for (0.05) share new Common $0.0001 par 07/06/2015
Recapitalized as Tech Town Holdings Inc. 11/02/2017
Each share new Common $0.0001 par exchanged for (0.005) share Common $0.0001 par
Tech Town Holdings Inc. name changed to Hash Labs Inc. 03/06/2018

MEDELECTRON INC (DE)
Charter cancelled and declared inoperative and void for non-payment of taxes 04/15/1973

MEDENCO INC (DE)
Common 1¢ par split (5) for (4) by issuance of (0.25) additional share 12/30/1977
Common 1¢ par split (5) for (4) by issuance of (0.25) additional share 12/29/1978
Name changed to Lifemark Corp. 04/26/1979
Lifemark Corp. merged into American Medical International, Inc. 01/20/1984 which merged into American Medical Holdings, Inc. 04/12/1991 which merged into National Medical Enterprises, Inc. 02/28/1995 which name changed to Tenet Healthcare Corp. 06/23/1995

MEDENTA CORP (DE)
Name changed to Well Renewal, Inc. 04/11/2006
Well Renewal, Inc. recapitalized as Lighthouse Petroleum, Inc. 10/15/2008 which name changed to Supurva Healthcare Group, Inc. 06/30/2015

MEDEOREX INC (NY)
Name changed to Karver International, Inc. 11/15/2005

(See Karver International, Inc.)

MEDEQUIP CORP (MD)
Assets assigned for benefit of creditors 07/21/1976
No stockholders' equity

MEDERA LIFE SCIENCE CORP (CANADA)
Name changed to Medbroadcast Corp. (Canada) 01/04/2000
Medbroadcast Corp. (Canada) reorganized in Alberta as Rock Energy Inc. 02/18/2004 which merged into Raging River Exploration Inc. 07/26/2016 which merged into Baytex Energy Corp. 08/27/2018

MEDESTO EXPL LTD (AB)
Recapitalized as Cochrane Oil & Gas Ltd. 04/26/1978
Each share Common no par exchanged for (1/3) share Common no par
Cochrane Oil & Gas Ltd. recapitalized as Co-Maxx Energy Group Inc. 02/10/1988 which was acquired by NuGas Ltd. 05/01/1995 which merged into Q Energy Ltd. 09/16/1997
(See Q Energy Ltd.)

MEDEVA PLC (ENGLAND)
Sponsored ADR's for Ordinary 10p par split (5) for (2) by issuance of (1.5) additional ADR's 03/26/1992
Merged into Celltech Group PLC 01/26/2000
Each Sponsored ADR for Ordinary 10p par exchanged for (0.68) Sponsored ADR for Ordinary
(See Celltech Group PLC)

MEDEVCO (CA)
Merged into DCM Acquisiton Corp. 04/26/1983
Each share Common 13-1/3¢ par exchanged for $4 cash

MEDEX CORP (NV)
Name changed to Aussie Apparel Group, Ltd. 10/29/2002
Aussie Apparel Group, Ltd. name changed to Bluetorch Inc. 11/03/2003 which name changed to Pacific Crest Investments 04/25/2005 which name changed to Pacific Peak Investments 05/16/2005 which name changed to Global Beverage Solutions, Inc. 10/26/2005 which recapitalized as Real Brands, Inc. 10/22/2013

MEDEX INC (NV)
Old Common $0.001 par split (4) for (1) by issuance of (3) additional shares payable 02/25/2010 to holders of record 02/22/2010
Ex date - 02/26/2010
Each share old Common $0.001 par exchanged for (0.001) share new Common $0.001 par 10/03/2012
Charter revoked 06/30/2014

MEDEX INC (OH)
Common 1¢ par split (5) for (2) by issuance of (1.5) additional shares 10/5/79
Common 1¢ par split (3) for (2) by issuance of (0.5) additional share 10/7/80
Common 1¢ par split (4) for (3) by issuance of (1/3) additional share 9/28/81
Common 1¢ par split (3) for (2) by issuance of (0.5) additional share 3/15/83
Stock Dividends - 10% 10/13/78; 10% 4/14/89
Merged into Furon Co. 1/17/97
Each share Common 1¢ par exchanged for $23.50 cash

MEDFAX INC (DE)
Charter cancelled and declared inoperative and void for non-payment of taxes 03/01/1979

MEDFIELD CORP (FL)
Stock Dividends - 10% 11/05/1975; 10% 11/29/1976; 10% 11/28/1977
Merged into National Medical Enterprises, Inc. 02/28/1979
Each share Common 40¢ par exchanged for (0.193) share Ser. A Preferred 5¢ par and (0.86688) share Common 5¢ par
National Medical Enterprises, Inc. name changed to Tenet Healthcare Corp. 06/23/1995

MEDFORD BANCORP INC (MA)
Common 50¢ par split (2) for (1) by issuance of (1) additional share payable 9/15/98 to holders of record 8/17/98
Merged into Citizens Financial Group, Inc. 10/16/2002
Each share Common 50¢ par exchanged for $35 cash

MEDFORD CORP (DE)
Each share Capital Stock no par exchanged for (4) shares Capital Stock $10 par 00/00/1945
Capital Stock $10 par changed to $2 par and (4) additional shares issued 05/02/1963
Capital Stock $2 par changed to $1 par and (1) additional share issued 04/30/1970
Capital Stock $1 par split (2) for (1) by issuance of (1) additional share 10/16/1978
Stock Dividend - 25% 09/30/1977
Merged into Amalgamated Sugar Co. 02/01/1985
Each share Capital Stock $1 par exchanged for $44 cash

MEDFORD SVGS BK (MEDFORD, MA)
Reorganized under the laws of Delaware as Regional Bancorp, Inc. 8/4/87
Each share Common 10¢ par exchanged for (1) share Common 10¢ par
Regional Bancorp, Inc. name changed to Medford Savings Bank (New) (Medford, MA) 7/22/93 which recapitalized as Medford Bancorp, Inc. 11/26/97
(See Medford Bancorp, Inc.)

MEDFORD SVGS BK NEW (MEDFORD, MA)
Common 10¢ par split (2) for (1) by issuance of (1) additional share 10/15/94
Recapitalized as Medford Bancorp, Inc. 11/26/97
Each share Common 10¢ par exchanged for (1) share Common 50¢ par
(See Medford Bancorp, Inc.)

MEDGENICS INC (DE)
Each share old Common $0.0001 par exchanged for (0.02857142) share new Common $0.0001 par 02/14/2011
Name changed to Aevi Genomic Medicine, Inc. 12/16/2016

MEDGROUP INC (CA)
Each share old Common no par exchanged for (1/6) share new Common no par 01/11/1993
Filed a petition under Chapter 7 Federal Bankruptcy Code 03/14/1997
No stockholders' equity

MEDGRUP CORP (CO)
Merged into Provider HealthNet Services Inc. 6/21/2002
Each share Common $0.001 par exchanged for $2.2465 cash

MEDHEALTH SVC CORP (FL)
Each share old Common 1¢ par exchanged for (0.33333333) share new Common 1¢ par 10/18/1991
Each share new Common 1¢ par exchanged for (0.02) share Common $0.001 par 07/21/1993

Administratively dissolved 08/26/1994

MEDI CARD INC (DE)
Reported insolvent and no longer in operation 00/00/1970
Charter subsequently cancelled and declared inoperative and void for non-payment of taxes 04/15/1972

MEDI CLINIC CORP LTD (SOUTH AFRICA)
Name changed to Mediclinic International Ltd. 09/05/2011
(See Mediclinic International Ltd.)

MEDI-HUT INC (NV)
Reincorporated 2/27/98
Reincorporated 10/31/2001
State of incorporation changed from (UT) to (DE) 2/27/98
State of incorporation changed from (DE) to (NV) 10/31/2001
Name changed to Scivanta Medical Corp. 1/4/2007
Each share Common $0.001 par exchanged for (1) share Common $0.001 par

MEDI INC (DE)
Merged into Delmed, Inc. 3/19/81
Each share Common 5¢ par exchanged for (1) share Common 10¢ par
Delmed, Inc. recapitalized as Fresenius USA, Inc. 12/30/91 which merged into Fresenius Medical Care AG 9/30/96 which name changed to Fresenius Medical Care AG & Co. KGaA 2/10/2006

MEDI-JECT CORP (MN)
Each share old Common 1¢ par exchanged for (0.2) share new Common 1¢ par 1/29/99
Name changed to Antares Pharma, Inc. (MN) 2/1/2001
Antares Pharma, Inc. (MN) reincorporated in Delaware 4/30/2005

MEDI-MAIL INC (NV)
Name changed to Mednet, MPC Corp. 06/30/1995
(See Mednet, MPC Corp.)

MEDI QUIP INC (DE)
Each share Common $0.00005 par exchanged for (0.04) share Common $0.0001 par 11/22/89
Charter dissolved 10/14/2003

MEDI-RX AMER INC (DE)
Charter cancelled and declared inoperative and void for non-payment of taxes 3/1/90

MEDIA & ENTMT COM INC (NV)
Name changed to Winsonic Digital Media Group, Ltd. 11/23/2004

MEDIA & ENTMT HLDGS INC (DE)
Issue Information - 10,800,000 UNITS consisting of (1) share COM and (1) WT offered at $8 per Unit on 03/09/2007
Completely liquidated
Each Unit exchanged for initial distribution of $7.81302755 cash 06/12/2009
Each share Common $0.0001 par exchanged for initial distribution of $7.81302755 cash 06/12/2009
Each Unit received second and final distribution of $0.10197339 cash payable 11/13/2009 to holders of record 06/12/2009
Each share Common $0.0001 par received second and final distribution of $0.10197339 cash payable 11/13/2009 to holders of record 06/12/2009

MEDIA ANALYTICS CORP (FL)
Old Common $0.0001 par split (3) for (1) by issuance of (2) additional shares payable 11/10/2014 to holders of record 11/10/2014
Ex date - 11/12/2014
Each share old Common $0.0001 par exchanged for (0.03333333) share new Common $0.0001 par 03/30/2016
Recapitalized as Jade Global Holdings, Inc. 03/06/2017
Each share new Common $0.0001 par exchanged (0.05) share Common $0.0001 par

MEDIA ARTS GROUP INC (DE)
Merged into Thomas Kinkade Co. 01/29/2004
Each share Common 1¢ par exchanged for $4 cash

MEDIA AWARENESS INTL INC NEW (NV)
Recapitalized as Cloud Technologies, Inc. 06/17/2009
Each share Common $0.001 par exchanged for (0.01) share Common $0.001 par

MEDIA AWARENESS INTL INC OLD (NV)
Reorganized as Golfsmart Media, Inc. 06/02/2008
Each share Common $0.0001 par exchanged for (5) shares Common $0.0001 par
Golfsmart Media, Inc. name changed to Media Awareness International, Inc. (New) 08/29/2008 which recapitalized as Cloud Technologies, Inc. 06/17/2009

MEDIA CITY CORP (DE)
Name changed to Effective Control Transport, Inc. 12/04/2007

MEDIA CLASSICS GROUP INTL INC (DE)
Recapitalized as Global Gaming Network, Inc. (DE) 08/29/2005
Each share Common $0.0001 par exchanged for (0.0001) share Common $0.0001 par
Global Gaming Network, Inc. (DE) reincorporated in Washington as Innovativ Media Group, Inc. 07/27/2015 which name changed to Demand Brands, Inc. 10/24/2018

MEDIA COMMUNICATIONS GROUP INC (DE)
Name changed to Floor Decor, Inc. 08/02/2001
Floor Decor, Inc. name changed to Tiger Telematics, Inc. 06/06/2002

MEDIA CORP AMER (NY)
Common 1¢ par split (3) for (1) by issuance of (2) additional shares 08/07/1970
Filed a petition under Chapter 11 Federal Bankruptcy Code 00/00/1981
Attorney opined no stockholders' equity

MEDIA CREATIONS LTD (DE)
Completely liquidated 05/30/1975
Each share Common 1¢ par exchanged for first and final distribution of (1) share Federated Communications Corp. Class C Conv. Preferred $3 par
(See Federated Communications Corp.)

MEDIA DRUG CO.
Acquired by Sun Ray Drug Co. 00/00/1946
Details not available

MEDIA ENTMT INC (NV)
Name changed to Internet Media Corp. 07/24/1998
Internet Media Corp. name changed to USURF America Inc. 07/09/1999 which name changed to Cardinal Communications, Inc. 06/24/2005
(See Cardinal Communications, Inc.)

MEDIA EXCHANGE GROUP INC (NV)
Name changed to Intellicell Biosciences, Inc. 07/07/2011
(See Intellicell Biosciences, Inc.)

MEDIA FILM GROUP INC (UT)
Recapitalized as Royal Net, Inc. 4/26/96
Each (265) shares Common $0.001 par exchanged for (1) share Common $0.001 par
Note: No shareholder will receive fewer than (50) shares
Royal Net, Inc. (UT) reorganized in Nevada as Seychelle Environmental Technologies, Inc. 1/30/98

MEDIA FORUM INTL INC (FL)
Name changed to Advanced Communications Technologies, Inc. 06/28/1999
Advanced Communications Technologies, Inc. name changed to Encompass Group Affiliates, Inc. 05/20/2008
(See Encompass Group Affiliates, Inc.)

MEDIA GEN INC NEW (VA)
Merged into Nexstar Media Group, Inc. 01/18/2017
Each share Common no par exchanged for (0.1249) share Class A Common 1¢ par, (1) Contingent Value Right and $10.55 cash

MEDIA GEN INC OLD (VA)
Stock Dividend - 100% 09/08/1975
$5 Conv. Preferred Ser. A $5 par converted into Class A Common $5 par 00/00/1979
Non-Vtg. Class A Common $5 par split (2) for (1) by issuance of (1) additional share 12/04/1986
Class B Common $5 par split (2) for (1) by issuance of (1) additional share 12/04/1986
Non-Vtg. Class A Common $5 par split (2) for (1) by issuance of (1) additional share 06/12/1987
Class B Common $5 par split (2) for (1) by issuance of (1) additional share 06/12/1987
Non-Vtg. Class A Common $5 par reclassified as Common no par 11/12/2013
Class B Common $5 par reclassified as Common no par 11/12/2013
Under plan of merger each share Common no par automatically became (1) share Media General, Inc. (New) Common no par 12/22/2014 which merged into Nexstar Media Group, Inc. 01/18/2017

MEDIA GROUP SOUTH INC (NV)
Name changed to Montgomery Real Estate Service, Inc. 03/25/2008
Montgomery Real Estate Service, Inc. recapitalized as Man Shing Agricultural Holdings, Inc. 09/02/2009

MEDIA HORIZONS INC (NY)
Each share Class A Common 10¢ par exchanged for (0.005) share Class A Common $50 par 7/11/86
Dissolved by proclamation 9/27/95

MEDIA IMAGE CORP (CO)
Each share old Common $0.0001 par exchanged for (0.5) share new Common $0.0001 par 9/22/93
Name changed to Image Marketing Group, Inc. 10/8/93

MEDIA INTL CONCEPTS INC (NV)
Recapitalized as Microart, Inc. 9/19/2005
Each share Common $0.001 par exchanged for (0.002) share Common $0.001 par

MEDIA INVT CO (OH)
Merged into Scripps (E.W.) Co. 07/27/1978
Each share Capital Stock $1 par exchanged for $58 cash

MEDIA LOGIC INC (MA)
Common 1¢ par split (2) for (1) by issuance of (1) additional share 03/23/1993
Proclaimed dissolved for failure to file reports and pay taxes 05/31/2007

MEDIA MECHANICS INC (NV)
Common $0.001 par split (30) for (1) by issuance of (29) additional shares payable 09/12/2013 to holders of record 09/09/2013
Ex date - 09/13/2013
Name changed to Gawk Inc. 09/19/2013

MEDIA METRIX INC (DE)
Issue Information - 3,000,000 shares OC-COM offered at $17 per share on 05/07/1999
Name changed to Jupiter Media Metrix, Inc. 9/20/2000
Jupiter Media Metrix, Inc. name changed to JMXI, Inc. 4/1/2003
(See JMXI, Inc.)

MEDIA 100 INC (DE)
Plan of reorganization under Chapter 11 Federal Bankruptcy Code effective 1/9/2006
No stockholders' equity

MEDIA PRODS INC (DE)
Common 1¢ par split (2) for (1) by issuance of (1) additional share 12/19/88
Charter cancelled and declared inoperative and void for non-payment of taxes 3/1/90

MEDIA RES INC (NV)
Name changed to Chewie Newgett Inc. 11/01/1985
(See Chewie Newgett Inc.)

MEDIA SCIENCES INTL INC (DE)
Each share old Common $0.001 par exchanged for (1) share new Common $0.001 par to reflect a (1) for (125) reverse split followed by a (125) for (1) forward split 06/29/2012
Note: Holders of (124) or fewer pre-split will receive $0.145 cash per share
Completely liquidated
Each share new Common $0.001 par received first and final distribution of $0.14 cash payable 03/31/2014 to holders of record 03/21/2014
Ex date - 04/01/2014

MEDIA SCRIPT MARKETING INC (BC)
Reorganized under the laws of Canada as Pivotal Therapeutics Inc. 05/19/2011
Each share Common no par exchanged for (0.5) share Common no par

MEDIA SVCS GROUP INC (NV)
Name changed to MSGI Security Solutions, Inc. 02/09/2005
(See MSGI Security Solutions, Inc.)

MEDIA SOURCE INC (DE)
Merged into MSI Merger Corp. 9/22/2003
Each share Common 1¢ par exchanged for $24 cash

MEDIA SYS CORP (AZ)
Charter revoked for failure to file reports or pay fees 09/05/1974

MEDIA III INC (CO)
Administratively dissolved 01/01/1995

MEDIA U S A INC (CO)
Recapitalized as Life Medical Technologies Inc. (CO) 02/21/1994
Each (73.331) shares Common no par exchanged for (1) share Common no par
Life Medical Technologies Inc. (CO) reincorporated in Delaware 08/29/1994 which recapitalized as I-Sim International Inc. 06/04/1999 which name changed back to Life Medical Technologies Inc. 01/26/2000 which name changed to iBonZai.com, Inc. 05/12/2000 which name changed to IbonZi.com, Inc. (DE) 01/10/2002 which reorganized in Nevada as China Global Development, Inc. 01/23/2002 which recapitalized as Arizona Ventures,

MED-MED   **FINANCIAL INFORMATION, INC.**

Inc. 11/18/2002 which name changed to Fox River Holdings, Inc. 10/13/2003 which name changed to Zynex Medical Holdings, Inc. 12/23/2003 which name changed to Zynex, Inc. 07/08/2008

MEDIA USA COM INC (NV)
Reincorporated under the laws of Delaware as Java Detour, Inc. 12/22/2006
(See Java Detour, Inc.)

MEDIA VENTURES CORP (ON)
Name changed to Bassett Media Group Corp. 08/31/2009

MEDIA VIDEOTEX CORP (BC)
Recapitalized as New Century Resources Ltd. 05/20/1987
Each share Class A Common no par exchanged for (0.2) share Class A Common no par
Each share Non-Vtg. Class B Common no par exchanged for (0.2) share Non-Vtg. Class B Common no par
New Century Resources Ltd. name changed to A.I. Software Inc. 09/04/1990 which name changed to Network Gaming International Corp. 07/02/1996 which recapitalized as Network Exploration Ltd. 06/22/2004 which name changed to Ynvisible Interactive Inc. 01/12/2018

MEDIA VISION INC (DE)
Name changed to Media Vision Technology Inc. (Old) 11/09/1992
(See Media Vision Technology Inc. (Old))

MEDIA VISION PRODUCTIONS INC (DE)
Name changed to eCONTENT, Inc. 10/1/99
eCONTENT, Inc. name changed to Earthworks Entertainment, Inc. 1/15/2004

MEDIA VISION TECHNOLOGY INC NEW (DE)
Name changed to Aureal Semiconductor Inc. 05/17/1996
Aureal Semiconductor Inc. name changed to Aureal Inc. 06/10/1999
(See Aureal Inc.)

MEDIA VISION TECHNOLOGY INC OLD (DE)
Plan of reorganization under Chapter 11 Federal Bankruptcy proceedings confirmed 12/12/1994
No stockholders' equity

MEDIABAY INC (FL)
Each share old Common no par exchanged for (0.16666666) share new Common no par 10/25/2005
Administratively dissolved 09/14/2007

MEDIABIN INC (GA)
Each share old Common 1¢ par exchanged for (0.1) share new Common 1¢ par 12/23/2002
Merged into Interwoven, Inc. 06/27/2003
Each share new Common 1¢ par exchanged for $0.52 cash

MEDIABISTRO INC (DE)
Name changed to Mecklermedia Corp. (New) 08/25/2014
(See Mecklermedia Corp. (New))

MEDIABUS NETWORKS INC (FL)
Name changed to Presidion Corp. 02/28/2003
(See Presidion Corp.)

MEDIACOM COMMUNICATIONS CORP (DE)
Acquired by JMC Communications LLC 03/07/2011
Each share Class A Common 1¢ par exchanged for $8.75 cash

MEDIACOM COMMUNICATIONS INC (NV)
Name changed to Duraco Industries, Inc. 09/15/1990

MEDIACOM ENTMT INC (DE)
Charter cancelled and declared inoperative and void for non-payment of taxes 03/01/2003

MEDIACOM INDS INC (DE)
Common 10¢ par changed to 2¢ par 08/06/1983
Reorganized under Chapter 11 bankruptcy proceedings as Applause Networks Inc. 07/08/1998
Each share Common 2¢ par exchanged for (0.0076923) share Common 2¢ par and (0.0076923) Common Stock Purchase Warrant expiring 01/11/2000
Applause Networks Inc. recapitalized as Internet Broadcast Networks Inc. 06/10/1999 which name changed to Mediacom Entertainment Inc. 08/10/2001
(See Mediacom Entertainment Inc.)

MEDIACONCEPTS INC (NV)
Name changed to High Road International, Inc. 04/05/2004
High Road International, Inc. name changed to Global IT Holdings, Inc. 07/05/2005
(See Global IT Holdings, Inc.)

MEDIAGENIC (CA)
Each share old Common no par exchanged for (0.1) share new Common no par 01/17/1989
Recapitalized back as Activision, Inc. (CA) 08/03/1992
Each share new Common no par exchanged for (0.1) share Common no par
Activision, Inc. (CA) reincorporated in Delaware 12/15/1992 which name changed to Activision Blizzard, Inc. 07/09/2008

MEDIAL SAUDE S A (BRAZIL)
Acquired by Amil Participacoes S.A. 01/29/2010
Each 144A ADR for Ordinary exchanged for $6.559373 cash
Each Reg. S ADR for Ordinary exchanged for $6.559373 cash

MEDIALINK WORLDWIDE INC (DE)
Acquired by NewsMarket, Inc. 09/25/2009
Each share Common 1¢ par exchanged for $0.20 cash

MEDIAMAX TECHNOLOGY CORP (NV)
Recapitalized as Exchange Media Corp. 10/01/2008
Each share Common $0.001 par exchanged for (0.0005) share Common $0.001 par
Exchange Media Corp. name changed to Empire Oil Refineries Corp. 03/31/2011

MEDIAMIND TECHNOLOGIES INC (DE)
Issue Information - 5,000,000 shares COM offered at $11.50 per share on 08/10/2010
Acquired by DG FastChannel, Inc. 07/26/2011
Each share Common $0.001 par exchanged for $22 cash

MEDIAN MTG INVS (MA)
Acquired by First Mortgage Investors 10/31/1973
Each Share of Bene. Int. no par exchanged for (0.666667) Share of Bene. Int. no par
First Mortgage Investors reorganized as FMI Financial Corp. 12/30/1980 which name changed to American Communications Co. (Old) 10/12/1987 which reorganized as Great American Communications Co. (New) 12/28/1993 which name changed to Citicasters Inc. 06/08/1994
(See Citicasters Inc.)

MEDIANET GROUP TECHNOLOGIES INC (NV)
Name changed to DubLi, Inc. 09/27/2012
DubLi, Inc. name changed to Ominto, Inc. 07/01/2015

MEDIAONE FIN TR I (DE)
9.30% Trust Originated Preferred called for redemption at $25 on 09/11/2000

MEDIAONE FIN TR II (DE)
9.50% Trust Originated Preferred Securities called for redemption at $25 on 03/04/2002

MEDIAONE FIN TR III (DE)
9.04% Guaranteed Trust Originated Preferred called for redemption at $25 on 10/28/2003

MEDIAONE FING A (DE)
7.96% Trust Originated Preferred Securities called for redemption at $25 on 03/04/2002

MEDIAONE FING B (DE)
8.25% Trust Originated Preferred Securities called for redemption at $25 on 03/04/2002

MEDIAONE GROUP INC (DE)
Each share 7.625% DECS Preferred exchanged for (1.695) shares Enhance Financial Services Group, Inc. Common 10¢ par 12/15/1998
(See Enhance Financial Services Group, Inc.)
Conv. Preferred Ser. D $1 par called for redemption at (0.744) share Common on 11/15/1999
Merged into AT&T Corp. 06/15/2000
Each share Common 1¢ par exchanged for either (a) (0.95) share Common 1¢ par and $36.27 cash, (b) (1.4912) shares Common 1¢ par and $8.50 cash, or (c) (0.8955) share Common 1¢ par and $39.06 cash
Note: Option to receive (b) or (c) expired 07/14/2000
Each 6.25% Premium Income Exchangeable Security received an undetermined amount of Vodafone Group PLC ADR's for Ordinary and cash 08/15/2001
AT&T Corp. merged into AT&T Inc. 11/18/2005

MEDIAPLEX INC (DE)
Merged into ValueClick, Inc. 10/22/2001
Each share Common $0.0001 par exchanged for (0.4113) share Common $0.001 par
ValueClick, Inc. name changed to Conversant, Inc. 02/05/2014 which merged into Alliance Data Systems Corp. 12/11/2014

MEDIAREADY INC (FL)
Recapitalized as China Logistics Group, Inc. 03/12/2008
Each share Common $0.001 par exchanged for (0.025) share Common $0.001 par

MEDIASET S P A (ITALY)
ADR agreement terminated 07/05/2005
Each 144A Sponsored ADR for Ordinary exchanged for (10) shares Ordinary

MEDIASHIFT INC (NV)
Chapter 11 bankrutpcy proceedings dismissed 09/21/2016
Stockholders' equity unlikely

MEDIATELEVISION TV INC (DE)
Name changed to Digital Color Print, Inc. (DE) 05/24/2004
Digital Color Print, Inc. (DE) reorganized in Florida as Bell Buckle Holdings, Inc. 06/29/2007

MEDIATRICS INC (DE)
Charter cancelled and declared inoperative and void for non-payment of taxes 03/01/1980

MEDIAVEST INC (NJ)
Common $0.0001 par split (5) for (2) by issuance of (1.5) additional shares payable 08/17/2006 to holders of record 08/10/2006
Ex date - 08/18/2006
Reincorporated under the laws of Delaware as Mandalay Media, Inc. 11/21/2007
Mandalay Media, Inc. name changed to NeuMedia, Inc. 06/21/2010 which name changed to Mandalay Digital Group, Inc. 02/28/2012 which name changed to Digital Turbine, Inc. 01/20/2015

MEDIAWORX INC (WY)
Administratively dissolved for failure to pay taxes 06/04/2008

MEDIC COMPUTER SYS INC (NC)
Common 1¢ par split (2) for (1) by issuance of (1) additional share payable 07/09/1996 to holders of record 06/24/1996
Acquired by Misys PLC 11/25/1997
Each share Common 1¢ par exchanged for $35 cash

MEDIC HOME DEVELOPERS INC (NY)
Name changed to Medic-Home Enterprises Inc. 02/28/1969
Medic-Home Enterprises Inc. name changed to Ganot Corp. 05/16/1980
(See Ganot Corp.)

MEDIC HOME ENTERPRISES INC (NY)
Stock Dividends - 10% 03/20/1978; 10% 01/25/1979; 15% 03/21/1980
Name changed to Ganot Corp. 05/16/1980
(See Ganot Corp.)

MEDIC HOME LEASING CORP (DE)
Name changed to Delicias International, Inc. 03/19/1971
(See Delicias International, Inc.)

MEDIC MEDIA INC (DE)
Name changed to AMAC, Inc. 04/00/1999
AMAC, Inc. recapitalized as Auto Data Network Inc. 10/16/2001
(See Auto Data Network Inc.)

MEDICA USA INC (DE)
Common 10¢ par changed to $0.0001 par 10/21/1981
Name changed to Pacific Realm, Inc. 07/06/1984
Pacific Realm, Inc. name changed to aeroTelesis, Inc. 10/22/2003
(See aeroTelesis, Inc.)

MEDICADE (NV)
Name changed to Sassoon International, Inc. 02/20/1986
(See Sassoon International, Inc.)

MEDICAGO INC (QC)
Acquired by Mitsubishi Tanabe Pharma Corp. 09/19/2013
Each share Common no par exchanged for $1.16 cash
Note: Unexchanged certificates will be cancelled and become without value 09/19/2019

MEDICAL ACTION INDS INC (DE)
Reincorporated 11/05/1987
State of incorporation changed from (NY) to (DE) 11/05/1987
Common $0.001 par split (3) for (2) by issuance of (0.5) additional share payable 02/08/2007 to holders of record 01/23/2007 Ex date - 02/09/2007
Acquired by Owens & Minor, Inc. (New) 10/01/2014
Each share Common $0.001 par exchanged for $13.80 cash

MEDICAL ADVISORY SYS INC (DE)
Name changed to Digital Angel Corp. (Old) 04/02/2002
Digital Angel Corp. (Old) merged into Applied Digital Solutions, Inc. 12/31/2007 which name changed to

MED-MED

Digital Angel Corp. (New) 06/20/2008 which recapitalized as VeriTeQ Corp. 10/22/2013

MEDICAL ALARM CONCEPTS HLDG INC (NV)
Each share old Common $0.0001 par exchanged for (0.00125) share new Common $0.0001 par 02/24/2014
Name changed to Wearable Health Solutions, Inc. 06/03/2016

MEDICAL ALLIANCE INC (TX)
Each share Conv. Preferred Ser. B no par converted into (1) share Common $0.002 par 10/01/1996
Name changed to MAII Holdings Inc. 01/08/2001
(See MAII Holdings Inc.)

MEDICAL ANALYTICS INC (DE)
Common 1¢ par changed to $0.005 par and (1) additional share issued 11/3/71
Common $0.005 par split (1.5) for (1) by issuance of (0.5) additional share 8/1/72
Charter cancelled and declared inoperative and void for non-payment of taxes 4/15/73

MEDICAL ANCILLARY SVCS INC (CO)
Each share old Common no par exchanged for (0.02) share new Common no par 4/25/88
Each share new Common no par exchanged again for (1) share new Common no par 11/3/89
Proclaimed dissolved for failure to file reports 4/3/95

MEDICAL ARTS BLDG CORP (IA)
Liquidation completed
Each share Class A no par exchanged for initial distribution of $43 cash 12/19/69
Each share Class A no par received second and final distribution of $6 cash 8/14/74
No equity for holders of Class B no par

MEDICAL ARTS BLDG LTD (MB)
Name changed to MABL Holdings Ltd. 05/15/2006
(See MABL Holdings Ltd.)

MEDICAL ASSURN INC (DE)
Common $1 par split (2) for (1) by issuance of (1) additional share payable 9/22/97 to holders of record 9/2/97 Ex date - 9/23/97
Stock Dividends - 5% payable 2/6/98 to holders of record 1/6/98; 10% payable 2/5/99 to holders of record 1/4/99; 5% payable 2/15/2000 to holders of record 1/7/2000
Under plan of reorganization each share Common $1 par automatically became (1) share ProAssurance Corp. Common 1¢ par 6/27/2001

MEDICAL AUSTRALIA LTD (AUSTRALIA)
ADR agreement terminated 08/22/2017
Each Sponsored ADR for Ordinary exchanged for $3.200369 cash

MEDICAL BILLING ASSISTANCE INC (CO)
Reorganized under the laws of Delaware as First Choice Healthcare Solutions, Inc. 04/04/2012
Each share Common $0.001 par exchanged for (0.25) share Common $0.001 par

MEDICAL BUSINESS SYS INC (MT)
Involuntarily dissolved for failure to file annual reports 12/29/1980

MEDICAL CARE AMER INC (DE)
Common Stock Purchase Rights declared for Common stockholders of record 07/30/1992 were redeemed at $0.01 per right 09/16/1994

Merged into Columbia/HCA Healthcare Corp. 09/16/1994
Each share Common 1¢ par exchanged for (0.7042) share Common 1¢ par
Columbia/HCA Healthcare Corp. name changed to HCA - The Healthcare Co. 05/25/2000 which name changed to HCA Inc. (Ctfs. dated after 06/29/2001) 06/29/2001
(See HCA Inc. (Ctfs. dated after 03/29/2001))

MEDICAL CARE INTL INC (DE)
Preferred Stock Purchase Rights redeemed at $0.01 per right 06/23/1992 for holders of record 05/20/1992
Merged into Medical Care America, Inc. 09/09/1992
Each share Common 1¢ par exchanged for (1) share Common 1¢ par
Medical Care America, Inc. merged into Columbia/HCA Healthcare Corp. 09/16/1994 which name changed to HCA - The Healthcare Co. 05/25/2000 which name changed to HCA Inc. (Ctfs. dated after 06/29/2001) 06/29/2001
(See HCA Inc. (Ctfs. dated after 06/29/2001))

MEDICAL CAREER COLLEGES (NV)
Name changed to BodyScan Corp. 12/16/2003
(See BodyScan Corp.)

MEDICAL CENTER BANK (HOUSTON, TX)
Stock Dividend - 10.88% 3/1/73
Name changed to Med Center Bank (Houston, Tex.) 1/1/83

MEDICAL COMMUNICATIONS INC (MA)
Name changed to Medcom, Inc. (MA) 07/09/1970
Medcom, Inc. (MA) reincorporated in Delaware 06/30/1972
(See Medcom, Inc. (DE))

MEDICAL COMMUNICATIONS INC NEW (DE)
Each share Common 1¢ par exchanged for (0.025) share Common $0.001 par 3/17/94
Recapitalized as 1-800-Consumer International Inc. 4/29/97
Each share Common $0.001 par exchanged for (0.1) share Common $0.001 par
1-800-Consumer International Inc. recapitalized as ISA Internationale Inc. 5/9/98

MEDICAL COMPUTER SYS INC (TX)
Merged into Trans Union Corp. 05/11/1978
Each share Common 10¢ par exchanged for (0.15) share Common $1 par
(See Trans Union Corp.)

MEDICAL CTR NATL BK (HOUSTON, TX)
Common $10 par changed to $1.25 par and (7) additional shares issued 02/12/1970
Name changed to Medical Center Bank (Houston, TX) 04/12/1971
Each share Common $1.25 par exchanged for (1) share Common $1.25 par
Medical Center Bank (Houston, TX) name changed to Med Center Bank (Houston, TX) 01/01/1983

MEDICAL DATA SYSTEMS CORP. (OH)
Acquired by General Computer Corp. 11/25/87
Each share Common no par exchanged for (0.0909855) share Common 10¢ par, (1) 3-year Common Stock Purchase Warrant exercisable at $17 per share and (1) 3-year Common Stock Purchase Warrant exercisable at $22 per share
(See General Computer Corp.)

MEDICAL DEFENSE HLDG CO (MO)
$1 Preferred called for redemption at $1 on 11/30/1998
Name changed to Missouri Physicians Group Holding Co. 05/04/2000
Missouri Physicians Group Holding Co. name changed to Bush-O'Donnell & Co. Inc. 05/09/2001

MEDICAL DEPOT INC (DE)
Charter cancelled and declared inoperative and void for non-payment of taxes 3/1/94

MEDICAL DESIGN STUDIOS INC (NV)
Each share old Common $0.001 par exchanged for (0.5) share new Common $0.001 par 03/24/2008
New Common $0.001 par split (5) for (1) by issuance of (4) additional shares payable 11/25/2008 to holders of record 11/21/2008 Ex date - 11/26/2008
Each share new Common $0.001 par exchanged again for (0.28571428) share new Common $0.001 par 04/06/2009
Name changed to Dynastar Holdings, Inc. 11/02/2011

MEDICAL DEV CORP (UT)
Capital Stock $1 par changed to 50¢ par 10/09/1978
Name changed to C.D.M. Liquidating Co. 08/30/1979
(See C.D.M. Liquidating Co.)

MEDICAL DEVICE TECHNOLOGIES INC (UT)
Each share old Common 15¢ par exchanged for (0.5) share new Common 15¢ par 06/20/1996
Each share 6% Conv. Preferred Ser. A 1¢ par exchanged for (4) shares new Common 15¢ par 07/03/1997
Each (35) shares new Common 15¢ par exchanged again for (1) share new Common 15¢ par 03/06/1998
Name changed to Miracor Diagnostics Inc. 10/12/1999
(See Miracor Diagnostics Inc.)

MEDICAL DEVICES INC (MN)
Name changed to Rehabilicare Inc. 11/16/94
Rehabilicare Inc. name changed to Compex Technologies, Inc. 12/16/2002 which merged into Encore Medical Corp. 2/24/2006
(See Encore Medical Corp.)

MEDICAL DIAGNOSTIC PRODUCTS, INC. (CO)
Proclaimed dissolved for failure to file reports and pay fees 11/1/98

MEDICAL DIAGNOSTICS INC (DE)
Merged into Advanced NMR Systems, Inc. 08/31/1995
Each share Common 1¢ par exchanged for (2.861) shares Common 1¢ par and (1) Common Stock Purchase Warrant expiring 08/30/2000
Advanced NBR Systems, Inc. merged into Caprius, Inc. 11/10/1997
(See Caprius, Inc.)

MEDICAL DIMENSIONS INC (TX)
Charter forfeited for failure to pay franchise taxes 03/17/1980

MEDICAL DISCOVERIES INC (UT)
Name changed to Global Clean Energy Holdings, Inc. (UT) 02/29/2008
Global Clean Energy Holdings, Inc. (UT) reincorporated in Delaware 07/19/2010

MEDICAL DISPENSING SYS INC (NV)
Charter revoked for failure to file reports and pay fees 10/01/1985

MEDICAL DYNAMICS INC (CO)
Each share Common 1¢ par exchanged for (0.04) share Common $0.001 par 10/12/88
Merged into VitalWorks, Inc. 8/8/2001
Each share Common $0.001 par exchanged for (0.06873) share Common $0.001 par and (0.07558) share PracticeWorks Corp. Conv. Preferred Ser. B and (0.017183) share Common 1¢ par
Note: Holders of (100) shares or fewer received $0.75 cash per share
(See each company's listing)

MEDICAL ELECTROSCIENCE & PHARMACEUTICALS INC (DE)
Name changed to Elkins-Sinn Corp. 05/01/1975
Elkins-Sinn Corp. name changed to CSE Liquidating Corp. 09/30/1976
(See CSE Liquidating Corp.)

MEDICAL ELECTROSCIENCE INC (NY)
Conv. Preferred $50 par called for redemption 03/11/1969
Reincorporated under the laws of Delaware as Medical Electroscience & Pharmaceuticals, Inc. and Class A 10¢ par reclassified as Common 10¢ par 08/06/1969
Medical Electroscience & Pharmaceuticals, Inc. name changed to Elkins-Sinn Corp. 05/01/1975 which name changed to CSE Liquidating Corp. 09/30/1976
(See CSE Liquidating Corp.)

MEDICAL ELECTRS CORP AMER (CO)
Each share Common $0.001 par exchanged for (0.05) share Common 2¢ par 1/3/84
Declared dissolved for failure to file reports and pay fees 1/1/93

MEDICAL ELECTRS INVT CO (OR)
Completely liquidated 07/01/1982
Details not available

MEDICAL ELECTRS RESH CORP (MA)
Stock Dividend - 100% 06/30/1972
Name changed to Medcor, Inc. 07/27/1972
(See Medcor, Inc.)

MEDICAL ENTERPRISES INC (DE)
Charter forfeited for failure to maintain a registered agent 3/29/2001

MEDICAL EQUITIES CORP (NY)
Charter cancelled and proclaimed dissolved for failure to pay taxes 3/24/93

MEDICAL EXCHANGE INC (NV)
Name changed to IDO Security, Inc. 06/19/2007

MEDICAL FACS CORP (BC)
Reincorporated 05/16/2005
Place of incorporation changed from (ON) to (BC) 05/16/2005
Each Income Participation Security consisting of $5.90 principal amount of 12.5% Subordinated Notes due 03/29/2014 and (1) share Common automatically became (1) share Common no par 06/01/2011
(Additional information in Active)

MEDICAL FIDUCIARIES INC (DE)
Name changed to Global Health Services, Inc. 9/20/76
Global Health Services, Inc. name changed to American West Financial, Inc. 5/28/86
(See American West Financial, Inc.)

MEDICAL FOUNDATION INVESTMENT CORP. (TX)
Charter revoked for failure to file reports and pay fees 1/2/59

MEDICAL FRONTIERS INC (DE)
Name changed to MF Industries Inc. in 1986
(See MF Industries Inc.)

MED-MED

MEDICAL GRAPHICS CORP (MN)
Common 5¢ par split (3) for (2) by issuance of (0.5) additional share payable 06/08/1998 to holders of record 05/26/1998
Merged into Angeion Corp. 12/22/1999
Each share Common 5¢ par exchanged for $2.15 cash

MEDICAL GROWTH INDS (CA)
Preferred $100 par called for redemption 9/30/69
Common $5 par changed to $1 par and (2) additional shares issued 12/4/69
6% Conv. Preferred Ser. A $100 par called for redemption 3/31/70
Name changed to National Community Builders 8/26/71
(See National Community Builders)

MEDICAL HEALTH INDS INC (DE)
Merged into Marzet Inc. 10/8/76
Each share Common 10¢ par exchanged for $0.55 cash

MEDICAL HOME PRODS INC (FL)
Each share old Common no par exchanged for (0.2) share new Common no par 10/12/2004
New Common no par split (5) for (1) by issuance of (4) additional shares payable 03/17/2005 to holders of record 03/08/2005 Ex date - 03/18/2005
Name changed to Sequoia Asset Management Group, Inc. 02/15/2006
Sequoia Asset Management Group, Inc. name changed to Platcom, Inc. 11/09/2007
(See Platcom, Inc.)

MEDICAL HOME SUPPLIES INC (NV)
Name changed to ADS Systems, Ltd. 05/10/2004
ADS Systems, Ltd. recapitalized as Remington Ventures, Inc. 11/18/2004
(See Remington Ventures, Inc.)

MEDICAL HOMECARE INC (DE)
Recapitalized as Gateway Medical Systems, Inc. 07/01/1986
Each share Common 1¢ par exchanged for (0.1) share Common 10¢ par

MEDICAL IMAGING CTRS AMER INC (CA)
Common no par split (3) for (2) by issuance of (0.5) additional share 12/9/85
Each share old Common no par exchanged for (0.2) share new Common no par 10/16/95
Merged into U.S. Diagnostic Inc. 11/12/96
Each share new Common no par exchanged for $11.75 cash

MEDICAL INDS AMER INC (FL)
Each share old Common no par exchanged for (0.05) share new Common no par 11/01/1996
Reorganized as Cyber-Care, Inc. 08/26/1999
Each share new Common no par exchanged for (1) share Common $0.0025 par
Cyber-Care, Inc. name changed to CyberCare, Inc. 06/26/2001
(See CyberCare, Inc.)

MEDICAL INNOVATIONS INC (CO)
Merged into Horizon/CMS Healthcare Corp. 07/11/1996
Each share Common $0.0075 par exchanged for $1.85 cash

MEDICAL INSTL SVCS CORP (NV)
Recapitalized as National Pharmaceuticals Corp. 12/04/2009
Each share Common $0.0001 par exchanged for (0.001) share Common $0.0001 par
National Pharmaceuticals Corp. recapitalized as Ghana Gold Corp. 07/11/2012 which name changed to BrightRock Gold Corp. 11/11/2013

MEDICAL INSTL SVCS HLDGS INC (NV)
Name changed to In Control Security, Inc. 09/10/2008
In Control Security, Inc. recapitalized as Envirotek 10/28/2009 which name changed to Suffer 06/21/2010 which recapitalized as Ophir Resources Co. 01/23/2013
(See Ophir Resources Co.)

MEDICAL INTL INC (UT)
Reincorporated under the laws of Nevada as Giguere Industries Inc. 9/16/81
(See Giguere Industries Inc.)

MEDICAL INVT CORP (MN)
Common $7 par changed to 70¢ par and (9) additional share issued 02/00/1961
Common 70¢ par changed to 1¢ par 04/21/1969
Name changed to Wirtz Productions Ltd. 08/30/1977
(See Wirtz Productions Ltd.)

MEDICAL LASER TECHNOLOGIES INC (CO)
Recapitalized as MLT International Inc. (CO) 08/22/2000
Each (30) shares Common $0.001 par exchanged for (1) share Common $0.001 par
MLT International Inc. (CO) reincorporated in Delaware as SkyMark Holdings, Inc. 07/26/2004
(See SkyMark Holdings, Inc.)

MEDICAL LEASING CORP (DE)
Common 5¢ par split (2) for (1) by issuance of (1) additional share 11/10/71
Name changed to Medimark Group, Inc. 10/29/74
(See Medimark Group, Inc.)

MEDICAL LICENSING INTL CORP (DE)
Name changed to EmergenSys Corp. 11/18/2003
EmergenSys Corp. recapitalized as Spencer Pharmaceutical, Inc. 10/05/2009

MEDICAL MAKEOVER CORP AMER (DE)
Each share old Common $0.0001 par exchanged for (0.0001) share new Common $0.0001 par 07/12/2012
SEC revoked common stock registration 07/25/2016

MEDICAL MGMT AMER INC (DE)
Each share old Common 1¢ par exchanged for (1/3) share new Common 1¢ par 09/11/1990
Merged into New MMA, Inc. 05/17/1991
Each share new Common 1¢ par exchanged for $2.50 principal amount of 10% Mortgaged Bonds due 06/01/1993 and $5.75 cash

MEDICAL MGMT CORP (DE)
Merged into Urgent Care Centers of America, Inc. 04/29/1985
Each share Common 1¢ par exchanged for (0.1236) share Common no par
Urgent Care Centers of America, Inc. name changed to ReadiCare, Inc. 07/12/1985 which merged into HealthSouth Corp. 12/02/1996 which name changed to Encompass Health Corp. 01/02/2018

MEDICAL MGMT INC (NY)
Merged into Complete Management Inc. 1/3/96
Each share Common $0.001 par exchanged for (0.79) share Common $0.001 par
(See Complete Management Inc.)

MEDICAL MGMT SYS INC (CO)
Each share old Common no par exchanged for (0.01) share new Common no par 01/19/1999
Reincorporated under the laws of Delaware as Dominix, Inc. and Common no par changed to $0.0001 par 07/26/2000
Dominix, Inc. recapitalized as 110 Media Group, Inc. 06/04/2004 which name changed to Web2 Corp. 07/31/2006 which recapitalized as Full Motion Beverage, Inc. 12/08/2008

MEDICAL MANAGER CORP NEW (DE)
Merged into WebMD Corp. 09/12/2000
Each share Common 1¢ par exchanged for (2.5) shares Common $0.001 par
WebMD Corp. name changed to Emdeon Corp. 10/17/2005 which name changed to HLTH Corp. 05/21/2007 which merged into WebMD Health Corp. 10/23/2009
(See WebMD Health Corp.)

MEDICAL MANAGER CORP OLD (DE)
Merged into Medical Manager Corp. (New) 07/23/1999
Each share Common 1¢ par exchanged for (0.625) share Common 1¢ par
Medical Manager Corp. (New) merged into WebMD Corp. 09/12/2000 which name changed to Emdeon Corp. 10/17/2005 which name changed to HLTH Corp. 05/21/2007 which merged into WebMD Health Corp. 10/23/2009
(See WebMD Health Corp.)

MEDICAL MKTG GROUP INC (DE)
Merged into Medco Containment Services, Inc. 04/06/1994
Each share Common 1¢ par exchanged for $27.25 cash

MEDICAL MONITORS INC (DE)
Recapitalized as World Collectibles Inc. 07/26/2000
Each (135) shares Common 1¢ par exchanged for (1) share Common 1¢ par
World Collectibles Inc. name changed to Designer & Decorator House Holdings, Inc. 11/24/2000
(See Designer & Decorator House Holdings, Inc.)

MEDICAL MTG INVS (MA)
Name changed to Security Mortgage Investors (New) (MA) 5/2/72
Security Mortgage Investors (New) (MA) reorganized in Delaware as Security Capital Corp. 1/23/80
(See Security Capital Corp.)

MEDICAL NUTRITION INC (NJ)
Name changed to MNI Group Inc. 02/05/1992
MNI Group Inc. name changed to Gender Sciences Inc. (NJ) 10/23/2000 which reincorporated in Delaware as Medical Nutrition USA, Inc. 04/22/2003
(See Medical Nutrition USA, Inc.)

MEDICAL NUTRITION USA INC (DE)
Acquired by Danone North America, Inc. 07/22/2010
Each share Common $0.001 par exchanged for $4 cash

MEDICAL PATHWAYS INTL INC (CANADA)
Dissolved for non-compliance 06/10/2004

MEDICAL PEOPLE HLDGS INC (NY)
Charter cancelled and proclaimed dissolved for failure to pay taxes 06/23/1993

MEDICAL POLYMERS TECHNOLOGIES INC (BC)
Recapitalized as U.S. Medical Systems, Inc. 12/19/1996
Each share Common no par exchanged for (0.14285714) share Common 1¢ par
U.S. Medical Systems, Inc. recapitalized as Sharps Compliance Corp. 07/24/1998

MEDICAL PPTYS INC (MD)
SEC revoked common stock registration 12/01/2009

MEDICAL PROFESSIONAL BLDG. CORP. (TX)
Name changed to Portland Harbor Corp. 4/5/83

MEDICAL RESH INVT FD INC (MD)
Name changed to EV Traditional Worldwide Health Sciences Fund, Inc. 08/30/1996
(See EV Traditional Worldwide Health Sciences Fund, Inc.)

MEDICAL RESORTS INTL INC (ON)
Recapitalized as Medical Services International Inc. 2/20/2001
Each (15) shares Common no par exchanged for (1) share Common no par

MEDICAL RESOURCE COS AMER (CA)
Shares of Bene. Int. no par reclassified as old Common no par 05/31/1991
Each share old Common no par exchanged for (0.2) share new Common no par 12/01/1995
Name changed to Greenbriar Corp. 03/27/1996
Greenbriar Corp. name changed to CabelTel International Corp. 02/10/2005 which name changed to New Concept Energy, Inc. 06/03/2008

MEDICAL RES INC (DE)
Common 1¢ par split (3) for (2) by issuance of (0.5) additional share 8/19/93
Each share old Common 1¢ par exchanged for (1/3) share new Common 1¢ par 7/24/98
Plan of reorganization under Chapter 11 Federal Bankruptcy Code effective 2/26/2001
No stockholders' equity

MEDICAL RES MGMT INC (NV)
Merged into Emergent Group Inc. 07/06/2001
Each share Common $0.001 par exchanged for (0.37) share Common $0.001 par
(See Emergent Group Inc.)

MEDICAL RES TECHNOLOGIES LTD (NV)
Name changed to Coinless Systems Inc. 08/12/1999
Coinless Systems Inc. recapitalized as NHS Health Solutions, Inc. (NV) 07/11/2007 which reincorporated in Florida 02/28/2012
(See NHS Health Solutions, Inc.)

MEDICAL SAFETEC INC (IN)
Administratively dissolved 8/12/98

MEDICAL SCIENCE BUILDING CO. (OH)
Completely liquidated 12/1/66
Each share Common no par exchanged for first and final distribution of $41.25 cash

MEDICAL SCIENCE SYS INC (TX)
Name changed to Interleukin Genetics, Inc. (TX) 08/23/1999
Interleukin Genetics, Inc. (TX) reincorporated in Delaware 07/12/2000
(See Interleukin Genetics, Inc.)

MEDICAL SCIENTIFIC INTL CORP (DE)
Each share Common 10¢ par exchanged for (0.2) share Common 1¢ par 7/28/77
Charter cancelled and declared inoperative and void for non-payment of taxes 3/1/84

MEDICAL SECS FD INC (DE)
Name changed to Capital Income Fund, Inc. 02/17/1965
Capital Income Fund, Inc. name changed to Capamerica Fund, Inc. 09/03/1969 which name changed to Bull & Bear Equity-Income Fund, Inc. 05/02/1983 which merged into Bull & Bear Financial News Composite Fund, Inc. 09/00/1992 which merged into Bull & Bear Funds I, Inc. 01/21/1994 which name changed to Midas U.S. & Overseas Fund Ltd. 06/28/1999
(See Midas U.S. & Overseas Fund Ltd.)

MEDICAL SVCS CORP (MD)
Merged into Newco 10/22/1975
Each share Common 10¢ par exchanged for $4 principal amount of Medical Services Corp. 12% Subord. Debentures Ser. A or Ser. B due 10/15/1987
Note: Holders of (125) shares or less who failed to make an election received $4 cash per share
Holders of more than (125) shares who failed to make an election received Ser. A Debentures

MEDICAL SOLUTIONS MGMT INC (NV)
Charter revoked 07/31/2015

MEDICAL STAFFING NETWORK HLDGS INC (DE)
Issue Information - 7,812,500 shares COM offered at $19 per share on 04/17/2002
Plan of reorganization under Chapter 11 Federal Bankruptcy proceedings effective 04/11/2011
No stockholders' equity

MEDICAL STAFFING SOLUTIONS INC (NV)
Common $0.001 par split (15) for (1) by issuance of (14) additional shares payable 10/08/2003 to holders of record 09/29/2003
Ex date - 10/14/2003
Chapter 7 bankruptcy proceedings terminated 10/20/2016
Stockholders' equity unlikely

MEDICAL STERILIZATION INC (NY)
Name changed to SSI Surgical Services Inc. 11/2/99
(See SSI Surgical Services Inc.)

MEDICAL TECHNOLOGY & INNOVATIONS INC (FL)
Each share old Common no par exchanged for (0.04) share new Common no par 12/04/2001
Reincorporated under the laws of Delaware as itLinkz Group, Inc. and Common no par changed to $0.001 par 04/05/2007
itLinkz Group, Inc. recapitalized as China YCT International Group, Inc. 11/26/2007 which name changed to Spring Pharmaceutical Group, Inc. 08/31/2018

MEDICAL TECHNOLOGY SYS INC (DE)
Each share old Common 1¢ par exchanged for (0.5) share new Common 1¢ par 10/06/1987
Each share new Common 1¢ par exchanged again for (0.25) share new Common 1¢ par 01/03/1992
Each share new Common 1¢ par exchanged again for (0.4) share new Common 1¢ par 12/08/2000
Name changed to MTS Medication Technologies, Inc. 09/17/2004
(See MTS Medication Technologies, Inc.)

MEDICAL TESTING SYS INC (CA)
Reincorporated 8/24/81
Stock Dividend - 100% 4/14/72
State of incorporation changed from (NY) to (CA) 8/24/81
Name changed to Ultra Medical Devices 11/10/81
(See Ultra Medical Devices)

MEDICAL 21 CORP (DE)
Under plan of merger name changed to Medical Care International, Inc. 03/07/1984
Medical Care International, Inc. merged into Medical Care America, Inc. 09/09/1992 which merged into Columbia/HCA Healthcare Corp. 09/16/1994 which name changed to HCA - The Healthcare Co. 05/25/2000 which name changed to HCA Inc. (Ctfs. dated after 06/29/2001) 06/29/2001
(See HCA Inc. (Ctfs. dated after 06/29/2001))

MEDICAL VENTURES CORP (CANADA)
Reincorporated 04/19/2002
Place of incorporation changed from (BC) to (Canada) 04/19/2002
Recapitalized as Neovasc Inc. 07/02/2008
Each share Common no par exchanged for (0.05) share Common no par

MEDICAL WELLNESS TECHNOLOGIES INC (MN)
Involuntarily dissolved for failure to file reports 11/13/91

MEDICALAB MGMT CORP (CA)
Name changed to HMO International 04/25/1972
HMO International merged into INA Corp. 12/19/1978 which merged into Cigna Corp. 04/01/1982

MEDICALCONTROL INC (DE)
Name changed to Avidyn, Inc. 2/1/2001
Avidyn, Inc. merged into Fiserv, Inc. 1/13/2003

MEDICALCV INC (MN)
Each share old Common 1¢ par exchanged for (0.1) share new Common 1¢ par 06/01/2006
Recapitalized as Dalton Industries Inc. (MN) 12/05/2013
Each share new Common 1¢ par exchanged for (0.01) share Common $0.00001 par
Dalton Industries Inc. (MN) reincorporated in Nevada as Universal Media Group, Inc. 01/11/2016

MEDICALLY MINDED INC (NV)
Name changed to Sixty Six Oilfield Services, Inc. 05/08/2017

MEDICALODGES INC (DE)
Merged into Health Care Lodges, Inc. 10/31/1980
Each share Common 50¢ par exchanged for $6.94 cash

MEDICALOGIC/MEDSCAPE INC (OR)
Name changed 5/19/2000
Issue Information - 5,900,000 shares OC-COM offered at $17 per share on 12/9/1999
Name changed from Medicalogic Inc. to MedicaLogic/Medscape, Inc. 5/19/2000
Plan of reorganization under Chapter 11 Federal Bankruptcy Code effective 4/2/2003
Each share Common no par received initial distribution of $0.20 cash
Each share Common no par received second distribution of $0.205965 cash payable 9/30/2004 to holders of record 09/22/2002
Each share Common no par received third and final distribution of $0.0013047 cash payable 7/18/2006 to holders of record 12/20/2002
Ex date - 7/21/2006
Note: Certificates were not required to be surrendered and are without value

MEDICALS INC (DE)
Name changed to Medi, Inc. 3/13/72
Medi, Inc. merged into Delmed, Inc. 3/19/81 which recapitalized as Fresenius USA, Inc. 12/30/91 which merged into Fresenius Medical Care AG 9/30/96 which name changed to Fresenius Medical Care AG & Co. KGaA 2/10/2006

MEDICARE GLASER CORP (MO)
Merged into Superx Corp. 03/15/1989
Each share Common 50¢ par exchanged for $6 cash

MEDICENTERS AMER INC (TN)
Common $1 par split (2) for (1) by issuance of (1) additional share 12/15/67
Name changed to Merit Corp. 9/29/76
Merit Corp. name changed to Hillhaven Corp. 3/31/78
(See Hillhaven Corp.)

MEDICEO PALTAC HLDGS CO LTD (JAPAN)
Name changed to Medipal Holdings Corp. 10/06/2009

MEDICHEM LIFE SCIENCES INC (DE)
Issue Information - 6,400,000 shares COM offered at $7 per share on 10/25/2000
Merged into deCODE genetics, Inc. 03/15/2002
Each share Common 1¢ par exchanged for (0.3099) share Common $0.001 par
(See deCODE genetics, Inc.)

MEDICINE BOW URANIUM CO., INC. (UT)
Charter revoked for failure to file reports and pay fees 10/15/58

MEDICINE SHOPPE INTL INC (DE)
Common 1¢ par split (3) for (2) by issuance of (0.5) additional share 03/23/1987
Common 1¢ par split (3) for (2) by issuance of (0.5) additional share 12/04/1989
Merged into Cardinal Health, Inc. 11/13/1995
Each share Common 1¢ par exchanged for (0.8289) share Common 1¢ par

MEDICIS PHARMACEUTICAL CORP (DE)
Secondary Offering - 2,800,000 shares CL A offered at $30 per share on 10/02/1996
Additional Offering - 4,000,000 shares CL A offered at $48.25 per share on 02/01/1998
Each (14) shares old Class A Common $0.001 par exchanged for (1) share new Class A Common $0.014 par 10/23/1995
New Class A Common $0.014 par split (3) for (2) by issuance of (0.5) additional share payable 08/02/1996 to holders of record 07/22/1996
New Class A Common $0.014 par split (3) for (2) by issuance of (0.5) additional share payable 03/28/1997 to holders of record 03/17/1997
Ex date - 03/31/1997
New Class A Common $0.014 par split (3) for (2) by issuance of (0.5) additional share payable 02/16/1999 to holders of record 01/29/1999
New Class A Common $0.014 par split (2) for (1) by issuance of (1) additional share payable 01/23/2004 to holders of record 01/12/2004
Ex date - 01/26/2004
Acquired by Valeant Pharmaceuticals International, Inc. 12/11/2012
Each share new Class A Common $0.014 par exchanged for $44 cash

MEDICLINIC INTL LTD (SOUTH AFRICA)
ADR agreement terminated 03/10/2016
Each ADR for Ordinary issued by Bank of New York exchanged for $38.459593 cash
Note: Due to ADR's being unsponsored exchange rate may vary dependent upon depositary agent

MEDICO-DENTAL BUILDING CO. (CA)
Liquidated in 1945

MEDICO-DENTAL BUILDING CORP. (CA)
Liquidated 1/26/56

MEDICOM INTL INC (DE)
Charter cancelled and declared inoperative and void for non-payment of taxes 03/01/1989

MEDICON INC (DE)
Name changed to Medicals, Inc. 7/14/71
Medicals, Inc. name changed to Medi, Inc. 3/13/72 which merged into Delmed, Inc. 3/19/81 which recapitalized as Fresenius USA, Inc. 12/30/91 which merged into Fresenius Medical Care AG 9/30/96 which name changed to Fresenius Medical Care AG & Co. KGaA 2/10/2006

MEDICON INC (MN)
Name changed to Aequitron Medical Inc. 6/1/83
Aequitron Medical Inc. merged into Nellcor Puritan Bennett Inc. 12/5/96 which merged into Mallinckrodt Inc. (NY) 8/29/97 which merged into Tyco International Ltd. (New) 10/17/2000

MEDICONSULT COM INC (DE)
Secondary Offering - 5,000,000 shares COM offered at $13 per share on 04/06/1999
Merged into Andrx Corp. (DE) 4/3/2001
Each share Common $0.001 par exchanged for (0.143) share Andrx Group Common $0.001 par
(See Andrx Corp. (DE))

MEDICOR LTD (DE)
Plan of reorganization under Chapter 11 Federal Bankruptcy proceedings effective 11/24/2010
No stockholders' equity

MEDICORE INC (FL)
Merged into Dialysis Corp. of America 09/21/2005
Each share Common 1¢ par exchanged for (0.68) share Common 1¢ par
(See Dialysis Corp. of America)

MEDICORP INC (UT)
Proclaimed dissolved for failure to pay taxes 11/1/88

MEDICORP TECHNOLOGY LTD. (ON)
Merged into North American Combustion Technology Corp. 08/19/1980
Each share Capital Stock no par exchanged for (1) share Common no par
(See North American Combustion Technology Corp.)

MEDICSIGHT INC (DE)
Each share old Common $0.001 par exchanged for (0.33333333) share new Common $0.001 par 12/31/2002
Name changed to MGT Capital Investments, Inc. 01/24/2007

MEDICUS SYS CORP NEW (DE)
Merged into QuadraMed Corp. 05/27/1998
Each share Common 1¢ par exchanged for either (0.3125) share Common 1¢ par, $7.50 cash, or a combination thereof
Note: Non-electing holders received stock only
(See QuadraMed Corp.)

MED-MED

MEDICUS SYS CORP OLD (DE)
Each share Common 1¢ par received distribution of (1/3) share Medicus Systems Corp. (New) Common 1¢ par 3/1/96
Name changed to Managed Care Solutions, Inc. 3/1/96
Managed Care Solutions, Inc. name changed to Lifemark, Corp. 7/12/99 which merged into UnitedHealth Group Inc. 2/9/2001

MEDIENT STUDIOS INC (NV)
Acquired by FONU2 Inc. 02/10/2015 Holders were to receive a combination of stock and cash
Note: Although company amended its articles of incorporation to change its name to Moon River Studios, Inc. and effect a (1) for (1,000) reverse split 09/30/2014 regulatory approval was not received
SEC revoked common stock registration 12/21/2016

MEDIFAST INC (DE)
8% Preferred Ser. A $0.001 par called for redemption at $2 on 06/30/2002
(Additional Information in Active)

MEDIFAX INC (MO)
Merged into MedQuist Inc. 12/08/1998
Each share Common no par exchanged for (0.5163) share Common no par
MedQuist Inc. merged into MedQuist Holdings Inc. 10/18/2011 which name changed to MModal Inc. 01/25/2012
(See MModal Inc.)

MEDIFLEX SYS CORP (DE)
Merged into HBO & Co. 02/28/1985
Each share Common 1¢ par exchanged for (1) share Common 5¢ par
HBO & Co. merged into McKesson HBOC Inc. 01/12/1999 which name changed to McKesson Corp. 07/30/2001

MEDIFOR INC (WA)
Merged into Allscripts, Inc. 04/17/2000
Each share Common exchanged for (0.09798) share Common 1¢ par
Allscripts, Inc. merged into Allscripts Healthcare Solutions, Inc. 01/08/2001 which name changed to Allscripts-Misys Healthcare Solutions, Inc. 10/10/2008 which name changed back to Allscripts Healthcare Solutions, Inc. 08/23/2010

MEDIFY SOLUTIONS LTD (DE)
Old Common $0.0001 par split (4) for (1) by issuance of (3) additional shares payable 03/15/2005 to holders of record 03/11/2005
Ex date - 03/16/2005
Each share old Common $0.0001 par exchanged for (0.08333333) share new Common $0.0001 par 09/20/2006
New Common $0.0001 par split (5) for (4) by issuance of (0.25) additional share payable 12/15/2006 to holders of record 11/30/2006
Ex date - 12/18/2006
Name changed to Petel Inc. 05/08/2007
Petel Inc. recapitalized as Gleeworks, Inc. 12/14/2009 which name changed to Capital Art, Inc. 05/09/2011 which name changed to Globe Photos, Inc. 06/25/2018

MEDIGRAPH CORP (DE)
Recapitalized as Westwells Corp. 10/12/73
Each share Common 10¢ par exchanged for (1/3) share Common 1¢ par
(See Westwells Corp.)

MEDILASE INDS INC (BC)
Delisted from Vancouver Stock Exchange 05/04/1994

MEDIMARK GROUP INC (DE)
Adjudicated bankrupt 11/14/1977
Stockholders' equity unlikely

MEDIMMUNE INC (DE)
Common 1¢ par split (2) for (1) by issuance of (1) additional share payable 12/31/1998 to holders of record 12/15/1998
Common 1¢ par split (3) for (1) by issuance of (2) additional shares payable 06/02/2000 to holders of record 05/18/2000
Merged into AstraZeneca PLC 06/18/2007
Each share Common 1¢ par exchanged for $58 cash

MEDINA COFFEE INC (NV)
Name changed to China BAK Battery, Inc. 02/14/2005
China BAK Battery, Inc. name changed to CBAK Energy Technology, Inc. 01/17/2017

MEDINA CNTY BK (LODI, OH)
Merged into BancOhio Corp. 04/28/1976
Each share Capital Stock $25 par exchanged for $140 cash

MEDINA ENERGY RES CORP (ON)
Recapitalized as Meenreco Energy Corp. 1/19/84
Each share Common no par exchanged for (0.5) share Common no par
Meenreco Energy Corp. name changed to Millers Cove Resources Inc. 8/30/84
(See Millers Cove Resources Inc.)

MEDINA INTL CORP (NV)
Each share old Common $0.001 par exchanged for (7) shares new Common $0.001 par 02/07/2006
Name changed to ACRO Inc. 05/04/2006
ARCO Inc. recapitalized as TransAtlantic Capital Inc. 08/08/2014

MEDINA INTL HLDGS INC (CO)
Recapitalized as Medical Innovation Holdings, Inc. 09/15/2016
Each share Common $0.0001 par exchanged for (0.1) share Common $0.0001 par

MEDINAH ENERGY INC (NV)
Each share old Common $0.001 par exchanged for (0.02) share new Common $0.001 par 11/30/96
Name changed to Medinah Mining Inc. 5/5/99
Medinah Mining Inc. recapitalized as Medinah Minerals Inc. 3/1/2001

MEDINAH MNG INC (NV)
Recapitalized as Medinah Minerals Inc. 3/1/2001
Each share Common $0.001 par exchanged for (0.990099) share Common $0.001 par

MEDINET INC (DE)
Charter cancelled and declared inoperative and void for non-payment of taxes 3/1/93

MEDINEX SYS INC (DE)
Each share old Common 1¢ par exchanged for (0.01) share new Common 1¢ par 10/28/2003
Note: Holders of (99) or fewer pre-split shares will receive $0.05 cash per share
Name changed to Maxus Technology Corp. 04/07/2004
(See Maxus Technology Corp.)

MEDIOLANUM SPA (ITALY)
ADR agreement terminated 01/22/2016
Each ADR for Ordinary exchanged for $13.861544 cash
Note: Due to ADR's being unsponsored exchange rate may vary dependent upon agent

MEDIPAK CORP. (NV)
Charter revoked for failure to file reports and pay fees 7/1/90

MEDIPAK CORP (DE)
Recapitalized as Advanced Laser Products Inc. 02/10/1995
Each share Common $0.001 par exchanged for (0.125) share Common $0.001 par
Advanced Laser Products Inc. recapitalized as Digs Inc. 10/16/1998 which name changed to iVideoNow, Inc. (DE) 06/15/2000 which reorganized in Florida as 99 Cent Stuff, Inc. 09/15/2003
(See 99 Cent Stuff, Inc.)

MEDIPAK LTD (ON)
Recapitalized as Crown-Meakins Inc. 02/14/1975
Each share Capital Stock no par exchanged for (1/3) share Capital Stock no par
Crown-Meakins Inc. reorganized as Medicorp Technology Ltd. 01/05/1976 which merged into North American Combustion Technology Corp. 08/19/1980
(See North American Combustion Technology Corp.)

MEDIPATTERN CORP (ON)
Discharged from receivership 07/15/2013
Stockholders' equity unlikely

MEDIPLACE INC (TX)
Name changed to Virogen Inc. 10/07/2008
Virogen Inc. recapitalized as Small Business Development Group, Inc. 09/05/2013

MEDIPLEX CORP (DE)
Recapitalized as Lawton-York Corp. 09/16/1974
Each share Common $0.001 par exchanged for (0.33333333) share Common $0.001 par
Lawton-York Corp. name changed to AuctionAnything.Com Inc. 03/03/1999 which name changed to Disease Sciences Inc. 07/16/2001 which name changed to IceWEB, Inc. 05/30/2002 which recapitalized as UnifiedOnline, Inc. 01/05/2015

MEDIPLEX GROUP INC NEW (MA)
Merged into Sun Healthcare Group, Inc. (Old) 06/23/1994
Each share Common 10¢ par exchanged for (1.28) shares Common 1¢ par and $11 cash
(See Sun Healthcare Group, Inc. (Old))

MEDIPLEX GROUP INC OLD (MA)
Common 10¢ par split (3) for (2) by issuance of (0.5) additional share 3/7/85
Common 10¢ par split (3) for (2) by issuance of (0.5) additional share 8/26/85
Acquired by Avon Products, Inc. 4/22/86
Each share Common 10¢ par exchanged for $27.50 cash

MEDIPLEX INC (OH)
Name changed to MPX Investments, Inc. 12/31/81
MPX Investments, Inc. name changed to Amerigold Inc. 1/24/84
(See Amerigold Inc.)

MEDIQ INC (DE)
Each share Depositary Preferred $1 par exchanged for (1) share Conv. Preferred Ser. A 50¢ par 07/24/1986
Common $1 par split (3) for (2) by issuance of (0.5) additional share 06/21/1982
Common $1 par split (2) for (1) by issuance of (1) additional share 08/26/1983
Common $1 par split (3) for (2) by issuance of (0.5) additional share 01/07/1986
Stock Dividends - 10% 04/07/1983; In Depositary Preferred to holders of Common - 100% 05/21/1986
Each share Preferred Ser. A 50¢ par exchanged for (0.075) share 13% Preferred Ser. A $0.001 par and $13.75 cash 05/29/1998
Each share Common $1 par exchanged for (0.075) share 13% Preferred Ser. A $0.001 par and $13.75 cash 05/29/1998
Plan of reorganization under Chapter 11 Federal Bankruptcy proceedings effective 06/13/2001
No stockholders' equity

MEDIQUAL SYS INC (DE)
Merged into Cardinal Health, Inc. 2/19/98
Each share Common no par exchanged for (0.075) share Common no par
Note: An additional (0.0052) share is being held in escrow for later distribution

MEDIQUIK SVCS INC NEW (DE)
Name changed to SureCare, Inc. 06/03/2002
(See SureCare, Inc.)

MEDIQUIK SVCS INC OLD (DE)
Merged into Mediquik Services, Inc. (New) 12/31/1998
Each share Common $0.001 par exchanged for (1.0725) share Common $0.001 par
Mediquik Services, Inc. (New) name changed to SureCare, Inc. 06/03/2002
(See SureCare, Inc.)

MEDIQUIP HLDGS INC (NV)
Name changed to Deep Down, Inc. 12/18/2006
Each share Common $0.001 par exchanged for (1) share Common $0.001 par

MEDIRECT LATINO INC (FL)
Administratively dissolved 09/25/2009

MEDIRISK INC (DE)
Issue Information - 2,300,000 shares COM offered at $11 per share on 01/28/1997
Name changed to Caredata.com, Inc. 6/2/99
(See Caredata.com, Inc.)

MEDIS EL LTD (ISRAEL)
Merged into Medis Technologies Ltd. 06/05/2000
Each share Ordinary ILS 0.1 par exchanged for (1.37) shares Common 1¢ par

MEDIS TECHNOLOGIES LTD (DE)
SEC revoked common stock registration 02/27/2013

MEDISAFE 1 TECHNOLOGIES CORP (DE)
Common $0.0001 par split (5) for (1) by issuance of (4) additional shares payable 09/20/2010 to holders of record 09/17/2010 Ex date - 09/21/2010
SEC revoked common stock registration 07/25/2016

MEDISCIENCE INC (CO)
Reincorporated under the laws of Delaware as Cardis Corp. and Common 75¢ par changed to 1¢ par 4/3/84
(See Cardis Corp.)

MEDISCIENCE TECHNOLOGY CORP (NJ)
Recapitalized as SensiVida Medical Technologies, Inc. 05/18/2009
Each share Common 1¢ par exchanged for (0.1) share Common 1¢ par
(See SensiVida Medical Technologies, Inc.)

MEDISENSE INC (MA)
Issue Information - 4,500,000 shares COM offered at $12 per share on 06/30/1994
Merged into Abbott Laboratories 8/7/96
Each share Common 1¢ par exchanged for $45 cash

MEDISOLUTION LTD (ON)
Merged into Brookfield Asset Management Inc. 05/08/2009
Each share Common no par exchanged for $0.30 cash

MEDISTEM INC (NV)
Recapitalized 08/11/2008
Recapitalized from Medistem Laboratories, Inc. to Medistem Inc. 08/11/2008
Each share Common $0.0001 par exchanged for (0.04) share Common $0.0001 par
Merged into Intrexon Corp. 03/07/2014
Each share Common $0.0001 par exchanged for (0.0392) share Common no par and $0.27 cash

MEDISWIPE INC (DE)
Each share old Common 1¢ par received distribution of (0.0066908) share 800 Commerce, Inc. Common $0.001 par payable 09/04/2013 to holders of record 09/03/2013 Ex date - 09/03/2013
Each share old Common 1¢ par exchanged for (0.1) share new Common $0.0001 par 12/11/2013
Name changed to Agritek Holdings, Inc. 05/20/2014

MEDISYS CORP (DE)
08/28/2007
Charter revoked 09/23/2011

MEDISYS HEALTH GROUP INC (QC)
Recapitalized as Medisys Health Group Income Fund 01/04/2005
Each share Subordinate no par exchanged for (0.4) Trust Unit no par
(See Medisys Health Group Income Fund)

MEDISYS HEALTH GROUP INCOME FD (QC)
Acquired by Persistence Capital Partners LP 03/28/2008
Each Trust Unit no par received $8.50 cash

MEDISYS INC (DE)
Merged into Coram Healthcare Corp. 7/8/94
Each share Common 1¢ par exchanged for (0.243) share Common $0.001 par
(See Coram Healthcare Corp.)

MEDISYSTEM TECHNOLOGIES INC (ON)
Acquired by Shoppers Drug Mart Corp. 10/23/2006
Each share Common no par exchanged for $3.80 cash

MEDITECH ENERGY & ENVIRONMENTAL CORP (MA)
Creditor foreclosed on assets 11/21/1973
No stockholders' equity

MEDITECH MGMT INC (DE)
Charter cancelled and declared inoperative and void for non-payment of taxes 3/1/95

MEDITECH PHARMACEUTICALS INC (NV)
Each share old Common $0.001 par exchanged for (0.001) share new Common $0.001 par 01/12/2005
Recapitalized as Deli Solar (USA), Inc. 08/15/2005
Each share new Common $0.001 par exchanged for (1/6) share Common $0.001 par
Deli Solar (USA), Inc. name changed to China Solar & Clean Energy Solutions, Inc. 11/05/2007

MEDITERRANEAN FUND, INC. (MA)
Merged into GPM Fund, Inc. 05/19/1978
Each (4.79039) shares Common $1 par received (1) share Common $1 par
Note: Certificates were not required to be surrendered and are without value
(See GPM Fund, Inc.)

MEDITERRANEAN MINERALS CORP (BC)
Recapitalized as Mediterranean Resources Ltd. 12/19/2005
Each share Common no par exchanged for (0.1) share Common no par
Mediterranean Resources Ltd. merged into Transeastern Power Trust 11/02/2015 which name changed to Blockchain Power Trust 01/04/2018

MEDITERRANEAN OIL CORP (NV)
Recapitalized as Zmax Corp. (NV) 07/23/1996
Each share Common $0.001 par exchanged for (0.0125) share Common $0.001 par
Zmax Corp. (NV) reincorporated in Delaware 12/12/1997

MEDITERRANEAN PETROLEUM CORP. (PANAMA)
Name changed to Israel-Mediterranean Petroleum, Inc. 00/00/1954
Israel-Mediterranean Petroleum, Inc. merged into Magellan Petroleum Corp. (Panama) 07/02/1959 which reincorporated in Delaware 10/23/1967
(See Magellan Petroleum Corp. (DE))

MEDITERRANEAN RES LTD (BC)
Each share old Common no par exchanged for (0.1) share new Common no par 12/17/2014
Merged into Transeastern Power Trust 11/02/2015
Each share new Common no par exchanged for (0.247) Trust Unit and (0.247) Trust Unit Purchase Warrant expiring 11/02/2018
Note: Unexchanged certificates will be cancelled and become without value 11/02/2018
Transeastern Power Trust name changed to Blockchain Power Trust 01/04/2018

MEDITRUST CORP (DE)
Merged 11/5/97
Additional Offering - 8,750,000 SHS BEN INT offered at $30.125 per share on 03/17/1995
Shares of Bene. Int. no par split (3) for (2) by issuance of (0.5) additional share 12/31/86
Under plan of merger each Share of Bene. Int. no par automatically became (1) Paired Certificate consisting of (1) Meditrust Share of Bene. Int. no par and (1) Meditrust Acquisition Co. Share of Bene. Int. no par 10/3/97
Merged from Meditrust into Meditrust Corp. 11/5/97
Each Paired Certificate exchanged for (1.2016) Paired Certificates consisting of (1) share Meditrust Corp. Common 10¢ par and (1) share Meditrust Operating Co. Common 10¢ par
Name changed to La Quinta Properties, Inc. 6/20/2001
La Quinta Properties, Inc. reorganized as La Quinta Corp. 1/2/2002
(See La Quinta Corp.)

MEDIUM MINING & MANUFACTURING CO. (WV)
Charter revoked for failure to file reports and pay fees in 1933

MEDIUM4 COM INC (DE)
Name changed to IA Global, Inc. 1/3/2003

MEDIVATION INC (DE)
Common 1¢ par split (2) for (1) by issuance of (1) additional share payable 09/21/2012 to holders of record 09/07/2012 Ex date - 09/24/2012
Common 1¢ par split (2) for (1) by issuance of (1) additional share payable 09/15/2015 to holders of record 08/13/2015 Ex date - 09/16/2015
Acquired by Pfizer Inc. 09/28/2016
Each share Common 1¢ par exchanged for $81.50 cash

MEDIVATORS INC (MN)
Merged into Cantel Industries, Inc. 3/15/96
Each share Common 1¢ par exchanged for (0.2571) share Common 1¢ par
Cantel Industries, Inc. name changed to Cantel Medical Corp. 4/7/2000

MEDIVEST INC (UT)
Each (43.74) shares old Common 1¢ par exchanged for (1) share new Common 1¢ par 10/12/95
Each (18) shares new Common 1¢ par exchanged for (1) share Common $0.001 par 10/9/98
Name changed to Empire Energy Corp. (UT) 6/8/99
Empire Energy Corp. (UT) reorganized in Nevada as Empire Energy Corp. International 4/26/2004

MEDIVIR AB (SWEDEN)
ADR agreement terminated 05/21/2018
No ADR's remain outstanding

MEDIVISOR INC (DE)
Name changed to Blast Applications, Inc. 08/12/2009
Blast Applications, Inc. name changed to Italian Food & Beverage Corp. 03/17/2015

MEDIVISOR MARKETING INC (DE)
Name changed to ChemTrak, Inc. (New) 8/30/2006

MEDIVIX INC (DE)
Charter cancelled and declared inoperative and void for non-payment of taxes 03/01/1990

MEDIWARE INFORMATION SYS INC (NY)
Acquired by Thoma Bravo, LLC 11/09/2012
Each share Common 10¢ par exchanged for $22 cash

MEDIX INC (DE)
Common 10¢ par split (3) for (1) by issuance of (2) additional shares 12/31/1969
Adjudicated bankrupt 10/27/1970
Stockholders' equity unlikely

MEDIX RES INC (CO)
Reincorporated under the laws of Delaware as Ramp Corp. 12/19/2003
(See Ramp Corp.)

MEDIZONE CDA LTD (UT)
Each (243) shares old Common $0.001 par exchanged for (1) share new Common $0.001 par 06/10/1998
Each share new Common $0.001 par exchanged again for (4) shares new Common $0.001 par 04/26/1999
Name changed to One World Online.com Inc. 07/01/1999
(See One World Online.com Inc.)

MEDJET INC (DE)
Name changed to For The Earth Corp. 02/28/2011

MEDL MOBILE HLDGS INC (NV)
Name changed to With, Inc. 11/04/2015

MEDLEY CR ACCEP CORP (DE)
Name changed to Finantra Capital Inc. 08/11/1998
(See Finantra Capital Inc.)

MEDLINE INDS INC (IL)
Reacquired in 1977
Each share Common $1 par exchanged for $13 cash

MEDLINK TECHNOLOGIES INC (NV)
Name changed to Cambridge Resources Corp. 06/21/2006
(See Cambridge Resources Corp.)

MEDMARCO INC (UT)
Name changed to THC HomeCare, Inc. 10/28/1996
(See THC HomeCare, Inc.)

MEDMASTER SYS INC (DE)
Common 1¢ par split (3) for (1) by issuance of (2) additional shares 01/28/1988
Each share old Common 1¢ par exchanged for (0.08333333) share new Common 1¢ par 03/26/1999
Name changed to Omega Dynamics, Inc. 04/14/1999
(See Omega Dynamics, Inc.)

MEDNET MPC CORP (NV)
Chapter 11 bankruptcy proceedings closed 04/22/2004
No stockholders' equity

MEDORA CORP (NV)
Name changed to Xumanii 09/07/2012
Xumanii name changed to Xumanii International Holdings Corp. 07/30/2013 which recapitalized as Imerjn Inc. 11/19/2014

MEDORO RES LTD (YT)
Each share old Common no par exchanged for (0.14285714) share new Common no par 05/25/2006
Each share new Common no par exchanged again for (0.33333333) share new Common no par 08/04/2010
Merged into Gran Colombia Gold Corp. 06/14/2011
Each share new Common no par exchanged for (1.2) shares Common no par and (0.5) Common Stock Purchase Warrant expiring 08/24/2015
Note: Unexchanged certificates were cancelled and became without value 06/14/2017

MEDPARTNERS INC NEW (DE)
Issue Information - 18,929,577 THRESHOLD APPREC PRICE SECS 6-1/5% offered at $22.1875 on 09/15/1997
Name changed to Caremark Rx, Inc. 09/13/1999
Each 6.5% Threshold Appreciation Price Security exchanged for (1) share Caremark Rx, Inc. Common $0.001 par 02/01/2000
Caremark Rx, Inc. merged into CVS/Caremark Corp. 03/22/2007 which name changed to CVS Caremark Corp. 05/10/2007

MEDPARTNERS INC OLD (DE)
Merged into Medpartners/Mullikin, Inc. 03/12/1996
Each share Common $0.001 par exchanged for (1) share Common $0.001 par
Medpartners/Mullikin, Inc. name changed to MedPartners, Inc. (New) 09/05/1996 which name changed to Caremark Rx, Inc. 09/13/1999 which merged into CVS/Caremark Corp. 03/22/2007 which name changed to CVS Caremark Corp. 05/10/2007

MEDPARTNERS/MULLIKIN INC (DE)
Under plan of merger name changed to MedPartners, Inc. (New) 9/5/96

MedPartners, Inc. (New) name changed to Caremark Rx, Inc. 9/13/99 which merged into CVS/Caremark Corp. 3/22/2007 which name changed to CVS Caremark Corp. 5/10/2007

MEDPHONE CORP (DE)
Charter cancelled and declared inoperative and void for non-payment of taxes 3/1/94

MEDPLUS CORP (DE)
Each share old Common $0.001 par exchanged for (1/3) share new Common $0.001 par 05/09/1997
Recapitalized as Atlantis Business Development Corp. 08/25/2003
Each share new Common $0.001 par exchanged for (0.1) share Common $0.001 par
Atlantis Business Development Corp. reorganized as Atlantis Technology Group 10/11/2007

MEDPLUS INC (OH)
Issue Information - 1,100,000 shares COM offered at $4.50 per share on 05/24/1994
Merged into Quest Diagnostics Inc. 11/1/2001
Each share Common no par exchanged for $2 cash

MEDPRO GROUP INC (MN)
Name changed to Ultimap International Corp. 06/10/1988
Ultimap International Corp. reorganized as Ultimap Corp. 07/08/1991
(See Ultimap Corp.)

MEDQUIST HLDGS INC (DE)
Name changed to MModal Inc. 01/25/2012
(See MModal Inc.)

MEDQUIST INC (NJ)
Common no par split (3) for (2) by issuance of (0.5) additional share payable 09/09/1997 to holders of record 08/25/1997
Common no par split (2) for (1) by issuance of (1) additional share payable 06/15/1998 to holders of record 06/01/1998
Merged into MedQuist Holdings Inc. 10/18/2011
Each share Common no par exchanged for (1) share Common 10¢ par
MedQuist Holdings Inc. name changed to MModal Inc. 01/25/2012
(See MModal Inc.)

MEDRAD INC (PA)
Merged into Berlin Acquisition Co. 10/2/95
Each share Common 10¢ par exchanged for $28 cash

MEDREC SUPPLIES INC (NV)
Name changed to All Asia Licensing, Inc. 12/06/2007
All Asia Licensing, Inc. name changed to Recruits, Inc. 03/06/2014 which name changed to FlexWeek, Inc. 12/16/2015 which name changed to Holy Grail Co. 03/24/2017

MEDRELEAF CORP (ON)
Merged into Aurora Cannabis Inc. 07/26/2018
Each share Common no par exchanged for (3.575) shares Common no par and $0.000001 cash
Note: Unexchanged certificates will be cancelled and become without value 07/26/2018

MEDSAFE PRODS INTL LTD (CO)
Charter suspended for failure to file annual reports 09/30/1989

MEDSANA MED SYS INC (BC)
Recapitalized as Connect Inter-Tel Media Inc. 01/22/1996
Each share Common no par exchanged for (0.25) share Common no par
(See Connect Inter-Tel Media Inc.)

MEDSCAPE INC (OR)
Merged into MedicaLogic/Medscape, Inc. 5/19/2000
Each share Common no par exchanged for (0.323) share Common no par

MEDSEARCH INC (NV)
Reincorporated under the laws of Delaware as Medsearch Technologies Inc. 08/11/1999
(See Medsearch Technologies Inc.)

MEDSEARCH TECHNOLOGIES INC (DE)
SEC revoked common stock registration 09/11/2009

MEDSECURE GROUP INC (MA)
Proclaimed dissolved for failure to file reports and pay taxes 12/31/90

MEDSERCO INC (MN)
Plan of reorganization under Chapter 11 Federal Bankruptcy proceedings confirmed 10/16/1987
No stockholders' equity

MEDSONIC INC (NY)
Name changed to Misonix, Inc. 12/21/93

MEDSONIX INC (MN)
Statutorily dissolved 12/31/93

MEDSOURCE SYS INC (BC)
Recapitalized as Inter-Med Technologies Inc. 10/03/1995
Each share Common no par exchanged for (0.2) share Common no par
Inter-Med Technologies Inc. recapitalized as Botex Industries Corp. 08/07/1998 which name changed to Radical Elastomers Inc. 08/02/2001
(See Radical Elastomers Inc.)

MEDSOURCE TECHNOLOGIES INC (DE)
Issue Information - 8,340,000 shares OC-COM offered at $12 per share on 03/26/2002
Merged into Medical Device Manufacturing, Inc. 6/30/2004
Each share Common 1¢ par exchanged for $7.10 cash

MEDSPAS OF AMER INC (NV)
Each share old Common $0.001 par exchanged for (0.0005) share new Common $0.001 par 06/05/2007
Recapitalized as i Brands Corp. 03/16/2009
Each share Common $0.001 par exchanged for (0.002) share Common $0.001 par

MEDSTAT GROUP INC (MI)
Merged into Steam Acquisition Corp. 12/28/94
Each share Common 1¢ par exchanged for $27 cash

MEDSTAT SYSTEMS, INC. (MI)
Common 1¢ par split (2) for (1) by issuance of (1) additional share 3/2/92
Name changed to MEDSTAT Group, Inc. 2/25/93
(See MEDSTAT Group, Inc.)

MEDSTONE INTL INC NEW (DE)
Each share Common $0.004 par received distribution of (1) share Endocare Inc. Common $0.001 par and (1) share Urogen Corp. Common $0.001 par payable 01/15/1996 to holders of record 12/29/1995
Merged into Prime Medical Services, Inc. (New) 02/20/2004
Each share Common $0.004 par exchanged for (0.9559) share Common 1¢ par
Prime Medical Services, Inc. (New) merged into HealthTronics, Inc. 11/10/2004
(See HealthTronics, Inc.)

MEDSTONE INTL INC OLD (DE)
Name changed to Cytocare, Inc. 01/16/1991
Cytocare, Inc. name changed to Medstone International, Inc. (New) 09/25/1995 which merged into Prime Medical Services, Inc. (New) 02/20/2004 which merged into HealthTronics, Inc. 11/10/2004
(See HealthTronics, Inc.)

MEDSTRETCH INC (NV)
Name changed to Pride Business Development Holdings, Inc. 08/24/2004
(See Pride Business Development Holdings, Inc.)

MEDSTRONG INTL CORP (DE)
Each share old Common $0.001 par exchanged for (0.01333333) share new Common $0.001 par 11/02/2006
Name changed to VOIS, Inc. (DE) 03/30/2007
VOIS, Inc. (DE) reincorporated in Florida 03/18/2009 which reorganized in Nevada as Mind Solutions, Inc. 10/31/2013

MEDSURGE MED PRODS CORP (BC)
Name changed to CRH Medical Corp. 4/28/2006

MEDTECH DIAGNOSTICS INC (DE)
Recapitalized as 4networld.com Inc. 05/17/2000
Each share Common $0.00001 par exchanged for (0.02) share Common $0.00001 par
4networld.com Inc. name changed to 4net Software, Inc. 03/08/2001 which name changed to Regional Brands Inc. 06/01/2016

MEDTECH INC (NV)
Common $0.001 par split (5) for (1) by issuance of (4) additional shares payable 1/11/99 to holders of record 1/4/99
Name changed to e-MedSoft.com 2/16/99
e-Medsoft.com name changed to Med Diversified, Inc. 1/9/2002
(See Med Diversified, Inc.)

MEDTECH INTL INC (UT)
Proclaimed dissolved for failure to pay taxes 4/30/87

MEDTINO INC (DE)
Name changed to IntelaKare Marketing, Inc. 03/01/2011

MEDTOX SCIENTIFIC INC (DE)
Each share old Common 15¢ par exchanged for (0.05) share new Common 15¢ par 02/23/1999
New Common 15¢ par split (3) for (2) by issuance of (0.5) additional share payable 08/20/2004 to holders of record 08/10/2004 Ex date - 08/23/2004
Stock Dividends - 10% payable 11/09/2001 to holders of record 10/26/2001 Ex date - 10/24/2001; 10% payable 07/05/2002 to holders of record 05/22/2002 Ex date - 05/20/2002
Acquired by Laboratory Corp. of America Holdings 07/31/2012
Each share new Common 15¢ par exchanged for $27 cash

MEDTRAK ELECTRONICS INC (NV)
SEC revoked common stock registration 12/01/2009
Stockholders' equity unlikely

MEDTRONIC INC (MN)
Common 10¢ par split (2) for (1) by issuance of (1) additional share 08/16/1967
Stock Dividend - 100% 01/17/1969
Common 10¢ par split (2) for (1) by issuance of (1) additional share 09/29/1972
Common 10¢ par split (2) for (1) by issuance of (1) additional share 07/31/1980
Common 10¢ par split (2) for (1) by issuance of (1) additional share 08/30/1989
Common 10¢ par split (2) for (1) by issuance of (1) additional share 08/29/1991
Common 10¢ par split (2) for (1) by issuance of (1) additional share 09/29/1994
Common 10¢ par split (2) for (1) by issuance of (1) additional share 09/28/1995
Common 10¢ par split (2) for (1) by issuance of (1) additional share payable 09/12/1997 to holders of record 08/29/1997 Ex date - 09/15/1997
Common 10¢ par split (2) for (1) by issuance of (1) additional share payable 09/24/1999 to holders of record 09/10/1999 Ex date - 09/27/1999
Reincorporated under the laws of Ireland as Medtronic PLC and Common 10¢ par reclassified as Ordinary EUR 1 par 01/27/2015

MEDUSA CORP OLD (OH)
Name changed 3/31/72
6% Preferred $100 par called for redemption 1/1/47
Common no par changed to $15 par and (1) additional share issued in 1954
Common $15 par changed to no par and (1) additional share issued 1/5/59
Stock Dividends - 25% 7/15/50; 25% 1/29/54; 50% 1/30/56
Name changed from Medusa Portland Cement Co. to Medusa Corp. (Old) 3/31/72
Merged into Crane Co. 10/2/87
Each share Common no par exchanged for $50 cash
New Common no par split (3) for (2) by issuance of (0.5) additional share 10/18/93
Merged into Southdown Inc. 6/30/98
Each share new Common no par exchanged for (0.88) share Common $1.25 par
(See Southdown Inc.)

MEDUSA STYLE CORP (NV)
Common $0.00001 par split (3) for (1) by issuance of (2) additional shares payable 04/12/2007 to holders of record 04/10/2007 Ex date - 04/13/2007
Name changed to En2Go International, Inc. 09/19/2007
En2Go International, Inc. name changed to Lyynks Inc. (NV) 05/14/2012 which reincorporated in Delaware as Vancord Capital Inc. 01/06/2015

MEDWAVE INC (DE)
Reincorporated 08/01/2003
State of incorporation changed from (MN) to (DE) and Common no par changed to 1¢ par 08/01/2003
Completely liquidated
Each share Common 1¢ par received first and final distribution of $0.02779 cash payable 08/21/2013 to holders of record 03/01/2013

MEDWELL CAP CORP (AB)
Each share old Class A Common no par received distribution of approximately (0.6) share Spectral Diagnostics Inc. Common no par payable 09/09/2011 to holders of record 09/09/2011 Ex date - 09/07/2011
Each share old Class A Common no par exchanged for (0.05) share new Class A Common no par 09/26/2012
Each share new Class A Common no

par received distribution of (2.25) shares Spectral Diagnostics Inc. Common no par payable 01/02/2015 to holders of record 12/15/2014
Ex date - 01/05/2015
Note: Holders defined as "U.S. Persons" will receive cash from the sale of shares
Reorganized under the laws of Canada as GDI Integrated Facility Services Inc. 05/14/2015
Each share new Class A Common no par exchanged for (0.09615384) Subordinate Share no par

MEDWORTH ACQUISITION CORP (DE)
Name changed to MergeWorthRx Corp. 12/02/2013
(See MergeWorthRx Corp.)

MEDWORXX SOLUTIONS INC (CANADA)
Each share old Class A Common no par exchanged for (0.25) share new Class A Common no par 08/17/2015
Acquired by Aptean Parent Co. SARL 10/16/2015
Each share new Class A Common no par exchanged for $0.5656 cash
Note: Unexchanged certificates will be cancelled and become without value 10/16/2021

MEDXLINK CORP (NV)
Name changed to Particle Drilling Technologies, Inc. 02/09/2005
(See Particle Drilling Technologies, Inc.)

MEDYA HLDG A S (TURKEY)
ADR agreement terminated 04/17/2009
No ADR's remain outstanding

MEDYTOX SOLUTIONS INC (NV)
Merged into Rennova Health, Inc. 11/03/2014
Each share Common $0.0001 par exchanged for (0.40963774) share Common 1¢ par

MEDYX INC (ON)
Recapitalized as Alterra Resources Inc. 04/15/1996
Each share Common no par exchanged for (0.2) share Common no par
(See Alterra Resources Inc.)

MEDZED INC (NV)
Name changed to First Resources Corp. 09/28/2010
First Resources Corp. name changed to Graphite Corp. 06/22/2012

MEE INDS INC (CA)
Merged into Mee Acquisitions, Inc. 5/6/94
Each share Common 5¢ par exchanged for $0.105 cash

MEEHAN-TOOKER CO., INC. (NY)
Name changed to Metinco Corp. 2/28/63

MEEM-HASKINS COAL CORP.
Liquidated in 1953

MEEMIC HLDGS INC (MI)
Merged into ProNational Insurance Co. 1/30/2003
Each share Common no par exchanged for $29 cash

MEENAN OIL INC (DE)
Common $1 par split (3) for (2) by issuance of (0.5) additional share 3/21/80
Common $1 par split (3) for (2) by issuance of (0.5) additional share 3/19/81
Stock Dividend - 30% 3/19/79
Merged into KOV Corp. 12/8/83
Each share Common $1 par exchanged for $12 cash

MEENRECO ENERGY CORP (ON)
Name changed to Millers Cove Resources Inc. 8/30/84
(See Millers Cove Resources Inc.)

MEERES, INC. (PANAMA)
Completely liquidated
Each share Common 10¢ par exchanged for initial distribution of (1/41,240) Ctf. of Bene. Int. no par and $79.52 cash 12/03/1962
Each (1/41,240) Ctf. of Bene. Int. no par exchanged for second and final distribution of $24.61 cash 08/05/1966

MEES MASONRY CORP (NV)
Name changed to MC Endeavors, Inc. 11/15/2010

MEESCHAERT CAP ACCUMULATION TR (MA)
Name changed to Anchor Capital Accumulation Trust 12/05/1990
Anchor Capital Accumulation Trust name changed to Progressive Capital Accumulation Trust 01/21/1999
(See Progressive Capital Accumulation Trust)

MEESCHAERT CAPITAL ACCUMULATION FUND, INC. (MA)
Reorganized as Meeschaert Capital Accumulation Trust and Common $1 par reclassified as Shares of Bene. Int. $1 par 01/00/1986
Meeschaert Capital Accumulation Trust name changed to Anchor Capital Accumulation Trust 12/05/1990 which name changed to Progressive Capital Accumulation Trust 01/21/1999
(See Progressive Capital Accumulation Trust)

MEESCHAERT INTL BD TR (MA)
Name changed to Anchor International Bond Trust 12/5/90
(See Anchor International Bond Trust)

MEETINGHOUSE BANCORP INC (MD)
Acquired by Meridian Bancorp, Inc. 12/29/2017
Each share Common 1¢ par exchanged for $26 cash

MEETME INC (DE)
Name changed to Meet Group, Inc. 04/10/2017

MEEWOOD YELLOWKNIFE MINES, LTD. (ON)
Charter cancelled for failure to file reports and pay taxes in 1952

MEG ATHLETIC CORP (NV)
Recapitalized as Pure H2O Inc. 05/10/2006
Each share Common $0.001 par exchanged for (1/9) share Common $0.001 par
Pure H2O Inc. recapitalized as Newron Sport 10/03/2008

MEG PETROLEUM DRILLERS LTD.
Acquired by New Meg Oils Ltd. in 1951
Each share Capital Stock $1 par exchanged for (10) shares Common $1 par
New Meg Oils Ltd. acquired by Oil Selections Ltd. in 1953 which was acquired by Quonto Petroleums Ltd. in 1957 which name changed to Quonto Explorations Ltd. 7/27/62
(See Quonto Explorations Ltd.)

MEGA BANK (ST ANN, MO)
Name changed 10/29/1993
Name changed from Mega Bank of St. Ann (St. Ann, MO) to Mega Bank (St. Ann, MO) 10/29/1993
Merged into Magna Bank of Missouri (Brentwood, MO) 02/18/1994
Details not available

MEGA BRANDS INC (CANADA)
Name changed 07/27/2006
Name changed from MEGA Bloks Inc. to MEGA Brands Inc. 07/27/2006
Each share old Common no par exchanged for (0.05) share new Common no par 06/15/2011
Acquired by Mattel, Inc. 05/01/2014
Each share new Common no par exchanged for $17.75 cash
Note: Unexchanged certificates were cancelled and became without value 05/02/2016

MEGA BRDG INC (NV)
Name changed to HypGen Inc. 08/01/2017

MEGA CAP INVTS INC (BC)
Name changed to MAG Silver Corp. 4/22/2003

MEGA COM GROUP INC (DE)
Name changed to X-Stream Network, Inc. 7/28/98
(See X-Stream Network, Inc.)

MEGA CORP (DE)
Reincorporated 10/23/77
Stock Dividend - 100% 10/23/77
State of incorporation changed from (CO) to (DE) 5/5/78
Charter cancelled and declared inoperative and void for non-payment of taxes 3/1/86

MEGA DIAL COMMUNICATIONS LTD (ON)
Name changed to Faleck & Margolies Ltd. 09/03/1987
(See Faleck & Margolies Ltd.)

MEGA DYNE INDL CORP (BC)
Recapitalized as International Mega-Dyne Industrial Corp. 11/08/1989
Each share Common no par exchanged for (0.4) share Common no par
International Mega-Dyne Industrial Corp. name changed to ESC Envirotech Systems Corp. 07/12/1991 which recapitalized as SWI Steelworks Inc. 03/29/1999
(See SWI Steelworks Inc.)

MEGA ENERGY CORP (DE)
Name changed to Megatron Holding Corp. and Common 1¢ par changed to $0.001 par 06/09/1983
Megatron Holding Corp. name changed to Republic International Corp. 05/08/1992 which recapitalized as Investek Corp. 03/12/1997
(See Investek Corp.)

MEGA GOLD INC (OR)
Recapitalized as Gold Dome Mining Co. 7/11/88
Each share Class A Common no par exchanged for (0.25) share Common no par
Gold Dome Mining Co. name changed to American Development Corp. 4/17/91
(See American Development Corp.)

MEGA GOLD RES LTD (BC)
Struck from register and declared dissolved for failure to file returns 3/4/94

MEGA GROUP INC (NY)
Each share Common $0.002 par exchanged for (0.125) share Common $0.016 par 06/26/1992
Charter cancelled and proclaimed dissolved for failure to pay taxes 12/29/2004

MEGA-MART INC (DE)
Recapitalized as Auric Mining Corp. 09/01/1994
Each share Common 1¢ par exchanged for (0.2) share Common no par
Auric Mining Corp. recapitalized as Pinnacle Oil International Inc. 02/05/1996 which name changed to Energy Exploration Technologies (NV) 06/15/2000 which reincorporated in Alberta 10/24/2003 which name changed to NXT Energy Solutions Inc. 09/22/2008

MEGA MEDIA GROUP INC (NV)
Chapter 7 bankruptcy proceedings terminated 06/14/2013
No stockholders' equity

MEGA MICRO TECHNOLOGIES GROUP (NV)
Each share Common $0.001 par received distribution of (1) share Restricted Common payable 04/28/2000 to holders of record 04/28/2000
Chapter 7 bankruptcy proceedings terminated 08/17/2015
Stockholders' equity unlikely

MEGA MOLY INC (BC)
Recapitalized as Terreno Resources Corp. 08/23/2010
Each share Common no par exchanged for (0.2) share Common no par

MEGA PRECIOUS METALS INC (ON)
Merged into Yamana Gold Inc. 06/24/2015
Each share Common no par exchanged for (0.02092) share Common no par and $0.001 cash
Note: Unexchanged certificates will be cancelled and become without value 06/24/2021

MEGA SILVER INC (BC)
Reincorporated under the laws of Ontario as Mega Precious Metals Inc. 09/14/2009
Mega Precious Metals Inc. merged into Yamana Gold Inc. 06/24/2015

MEGA WIN INVTS INC (BC)
Name changed to Invech Holdings, Inc. 08/07/2018

MEGA WORLD FOOD HLDG CO (NV)
Name changed to Liberated Energy, Inc. 02/15/2013

MEGABANK FINL CORP (MI)
Issue Information - 1,450,000 shares COM offered at $11 per share on 11/16/1998
Merged into Compass Bancshares, Inc. 04/20/2000
Each share Common no par exchanged for (0.4357677) share Common $2 par
Compass Bancshares, Inc. merged into Banco Bilbao Vizcaya Argentaria, S.A. 09/07/2007

MEGABIOS CORP (DE)
Issue Information - 2,500,000 shares COM offered at $12 per share on 09/15/1997
Name changed to Valentis, Inc. 05/05/1999
Valentis, Inc. name changed to Urigen Pharmaceuticals, Inc. 07/30/2007

MEGACARDS INC (MO)
Each share Common 1¢ par exchanged for (0.33333333) share Common 3¢ par 11/16/1994
Recapitalized as Bentley International, Inc. 07/05/1996
Each share Common 3¢ par exchanged for (0.16666666) share Common 3¢ par
(See Bentley International, Inc.)

MEGACHAIN COM LTD (DE)
Each share old Common $0.001 par exchanged for (0.05) share new Common $0.001 par 1/4/2001
Each share new Common $0.001 par exchanged for (0.25) share Common $0.0001 par 8/17/2001
Name changed to Acola Corp. 10/22/2001
Acola Corp. name changed to Teda Travel Group Inc. 4/21/2004 which name changed to Network CN, Inc. 8/15/2006

MEGACOM INC (FL)
Involuntarily dissolved 11/5/87

MEGADATA CORP. (NY)
Name changed 10/18/1976
Common 1¢ par split (2) for (1) by

issuance of (1) additional share 07/02/1973
Name changed from Megadata Computer & Communications Corp. to Megadata Corp. 10/18/1976
Common 1¢ par split (2) for (1) by issuance of (1) additional share 12/06/1984
Name changed to PASSUR Aerospace, Inc. 05/06/2008

MEGADYNE ELECTRONICS, INC. (DE)
Charter revoked for non-payment of taxes 7/1/63

MEGADYNE INDS INC (NY)
Dissolved by proclamation 12/15/1975

MEGAFOODS STORES INC (NV)
Chapter 11 bankruptcy proceedings terminated 11/15/2001
Stockholders' equity unlikely

MEGAGOLD CORP (UT)
Reincorporated under the laws of Washington as MGC Ventures, Inc. 07/16/2001

MEGAHERTZ CORP (UT)
Merged into U.S. Robotics Corp. 02/22/1995
Each share Common $0.001 par exchanged for (0.3375) share Common 1¢ par
U.S. Robotics Corp. merged into 3Com Corp. 06/12/1997
(See 3Com Corp.)

MEGAL CAP CORP (BC)
Name changed to Gourmet Ocean Products Inc. 02/25/2014

MEGALINE RES LTD (BC)
Recapitalized as International Megaline Resources Ltd. 03/27/1985
Each share Common no par exchanged for (0.2) share Common no par
International Megaline Resources Ltd. name changed to Dyonix Greentree Technologies Inc. 07/08/1986
(See Dyonix Greentree Technologies Inc.)

MEGAMANIA INTERACTIVE INC (NV)
Recapitalized as Latin Television, Inc. (Old) 02/09/2006
Each share Common 1¢ par exchanged for (0.01) share Common $0.001 par
Latin Television, Inc. (Old) name changed to The League Publishing Inc. 09/07/2007 which name changed to Good Life China Corp. 04/08/2008

MEGAMATION INC (DE)
Merged into MI Merger Corp. 6/19/96
Each share Common 1¢ par exchanged for $0.10 cash

MEGAMEDIA NETWORKS INC (DE)
SEC revoked common stock registration 06/04/2007
Stockholders' equity unlikely

MEGAPHONE INTL INC (DE)
Reincorporated 1/15/87
State of incorporation changed from (NV) to (DE) 1/15/87
Acquired by Votrax, Inc. 1/19/89
Each share new Common 1¢ par exchanged for (0.16583747) share Common 1¢ par
(See Votrax, Inc.)

MEGAPRO TOOLS INC (NV)
Name changed to Spear & Jackson, Inc. 11/12/2002
(See Spear & Jackson, Inc.)

MEGASOL CORP (CANADA)
Recapitalized as Clonus Corp. 09/17/1996
Each share Common no par exchanged for (0.05) share Common no par
Clonus Corp. name changed to San-Mar Environmental Corp. 09/22/1997 which recapitalized as Pure Zinc Technologies, Inc. 08/21/1998 which name changed to Charityville.com International Inc. 08/27/1999 which name changed to eNblast productions inc. 06/14/2000
(See eNblast productions inc.)

MEGASTAR VENTURES LTD (BC)
Recapitalized as Megastar Development Corp. 11/3/2000
Each share Common no par exchanged for (1/3) share Common no par

MEGASYSTEMS INC (NY)
Adjudicated bankrupt 2/6/73
No stockholders' equity

MEGATEL INC (DE)
Incorporated in 1993
Charter cancelled and declared inoperative and void for non-payment of taxes 7/16/95

MEGATEST CORP (DE)
Merged into Teradyne Inc. 12/1/95
Each share Common $0.001 par exchanged for (0.9091) share Common $0.001 par

MEGATRON HLDG CORP (DE)
Common $0.001 par split (10) for (1) by issuance of (9) additional shares 06/09/1983
Each share Common $0.001 par exchanged for (0.05) share Common 1¢ par 02/27/1987
Name changed to Republic International Corp. 05/08/1992
Republic International Corp. recapitalized as Investek Corp. 03/12/1997
(See Investek Corp.)

MEGATRONICS INC (AZ)
Charter revoked for failure to file reports and pay fees 5/10/95

MEGAVEST INDS INC (NV)
Reorganized under the laws of Delaware as National TechTeam, Inc. 08/20/1987
Each (35) shares Common $0.001 par exchanged for (1) share Common 1¢ par
National TechTeam, Inc. name changed to TechTeam Global, Inc. 05/17/2002
(See TechTeam Global, Inc.)

MEGAWEST ENERGY CORP (AB)
Reincorporated 02/12/2008
Place of incorporation changed from (BC) to (AB) 02/12/2008
Recapitalized as Gravis Oil Corp. (AB) 06/20/2011
Each share Common no par exchanged for (0.1) share Common no par
Gravis Oil Corp. (AB) reincorporated in Delaware 09/11/2012 which name changed to Petro River Oil Corp. 03/20/2013

MEGAWHEELS INC (CANADA)
Name changed 7/4/2001
Name changed from Megawheels.com, Inc. to Megawheels Inc. 7/4/2001
Recapitalized as Megawheels Technologies Inc. 2/28/2002
Each share Common no par exchanged for (0.5) share Common no par

MEGAWORLD INC (DE)
Each share old Common $0.0001 par exchanged for (0.08333333) share new Common $0.0001 par 03/16/1998
Recapitalized as Power Sports Factory, Inc. 07/01/2005
Each share new Common $0.0001 par exchanged for (0.0025) share Common $0.0001 par
Power Sports Factory, Inc. name changed to Heringrat 478, Inc. 07/14/2006 which name changed to United Music & Media Group, Inc. 06/23/2010 which recapitalized as New Generation Consumer Group, Inc. 10/07/2014

MEGO FINL CORP (DE)
Name changed 06/11/1992
Name changed from Mego Corp. to Mego Financial Corp. 06/11/1992
Class B Common 1¢ par reclassified as Common 1¢ par 06/24/1992
Class A Common 1¢ par reclassified as Common 1¢ par 06/24/1992
Each share Common 1¢ par received distribution of (0.473) share Mego Mortgage Corp. Common 1¢ par payable 09/02/1997 to holders of record 08/27/1997
Each share old Common 1¢ par exchanged for (1/6) share new Common 1¢ par 09/09/1999
Chapter 11 bankruptcy proceedings converted to Chapter 7 on 02/03/2006
Stockholders' equity unlikely

MEGO INTL INC (DE)
Common 10¢ par split (3) for (2) by issuance of (0.5) additional share 06/27/1975
Merged into Mego Corp. 12/02/1983
Each share Common 10¢ par exchanged for (0.1089) share Class B Common 1¢ par
Mego Corp. name changed to Mego Financial Corp. 06/11/1992
(See Mego Financial Corp.)

MEGO MTG CORP (DE)
Recapitalized as Altiva Financial Corp. 3/27/99
Each share Common 1¢ par exchanged for (0.1) share Common 1¢ par
(See Altiva Financial Corp.)

MEGOWEN-EDUCATOR FOOD CO. (MA)
Recapitalized 00/00/1943
Class A no par changed to $10 par
Common no par changed to $1 par
Name changed to Educator Biscuit Co., Inc. 07/05/1962
(See Educator Biscuit Co., Inc.)

MEHADRIN PLANTATIONS, INC. (NY)
Dissolved 1/22/60

MEHL / BIOPHILE INTL CORP (DE)
Name changed to Hamilton-Biophile Companies (DE) 05/12/2000
Hamilton-Biophile Companies (DE) reincorporated in Nevada 11/26/2001 which recapitalized as Brampton Crest International, Inc. 10/04/2004

MEI CORP (DE)
Common 10¢ par changed to 5¢ par and (1) additional share issued 11/15/1982
Acquired by PepsiCo, Inc. (DE) 05/30/1986
Each share Common 5¢ par exchanged for (1) share MEI Diversified Inc. Common 5¢ par and $35 cash
(See MEI Diversified Inc.)

MEI CORP (NV)
Each share old Common $0.001 par exchanged for (0.25) share new Common $0.001 par 11/1/96
Name changed to Space Propulsion Systems Inc. 1/13/2004

MEI DIVERSIFIED INC (DE)
Plan of reorganization under Chapter 11 Federal Bankruptcy proceedings confirmed 09/27/1994
Stockholders will receive 10% of the net recovery from litigation

MEICOR (DE)
Charter cancelled and declared inoperative and void for non-payment of taxes 3/1/93

MEIER & FRANK CO., INC. (OR)
Merged into May Department Stores Co. 7/27/66
Each share Common $10 par or Depositary Receipt for Common $10 par exchanged for for (1) share $1.80 Conv. Preference no par
(See May Department Stores Co.)

MEIER WORLDWIDE INTERMEDIA INC (NV)
Each share old Common $0.001 par exchanged for (0.05) share new Common $0.001 par 10/24/2002
Recapitalized as QuadTech International, Inc. 3/31/2006
Each share new Common $0.001 par exchanged for (0.1) share Common $0.001 par
(See QuadTech International, Inc.)

MEIJI SEIKA KAISHA LTD (JAPAN)
Merged into Meiji Dairies Corp. 04/01/2009
Each ADR for Common 50 Yen par exchanged for $32.12034 cash

MEISEL PHOTOCHROME CORP. (TX)
Completely liquidated 06/13/1974
Each share Common no par exchanged for first and final distribution of (0.449) share Dun & Bradstreet Companies, Inc. Common $1 par
Dun & Bradstreet Companies, Inc. name changed to Dun & Bradstreet Corp. 04/17/1979 which name changed to R.H. Donnelley Corp. 07/01/1998
(See R.H. Donnelley Corp.)

MEISENHEIMER CAP INC (DE)
SEC revoked common stock registration 09/22/2009

MEISTER BRAU INC (DE)
Adjudicated bankrupt 02/15/1973
Stockholders' equity unlikely

MEKJU PROCESSING INC (DE)
Reincorporated under the laws of Nevada as Axium Technologies Inc. and Common 1¢ par changed to $0.001 par 11/24/2006
Axium Technologies Inc. name changed to Wincash Resources, Inc. 01/05/2016 which name changed to Fovea Jewelry Holdings, Ltd. 02/06/2018

MEKONG INTL DEV CORP (BC)
Recapitalized as Everest Mines & Minerals Ltd. 12/29/95
Each share Common no par exchanged for (0.125) share Common no par
Everest Mines & Minerals Ltd. recapitalized as First Narrows Resources Corp. 4/4/2000

MELA SCIENCES INC (DE)
Each share old Common $0.001 par exchanged for (0.1) share new Common $0.001 par 07/10/2014
Name changed to STRATA Skin Sciences, Inc. 01/05/2016

MELABS INC (CA)
Capital Stock no par split (3) for (1) by issuance of (2) additional shares 12/21/1967
Completely liquidated 03/27/1969
Each share Capital Stock no par exchanged for first and final distribution of (1/3) share SCM Corp. Common $5 par
(See SCM Corp.)

MELAMINE CHEMS INC (DE)
Merged into Borden Chemical, Inc. 11/14/97
Each share Common 1¢ par exchanged for $20.50 cash

MELARD MINING LTD. (BC)
Reorganized as Geo-Star Resources Ltd. 03/27/1972
Each share Common no par exchanged for (1) share Common no par
Geo-Star Resources Ltd. recapitalized as Northern Energy Corp. 05/03/1977 which recapitalized as United Northern Petroleum Corp.

03/24/1986 which name changed to UNP Industries Ltd. 11/06/1989 which recapitalized as International UNP Holdings Ltd. (BC) 11/29/1990 which reincorporated in Canada 08/04/1993
(See International UNP Holdings Ltd.)

MELBOURNE EQUITIES CORP (DE)
Each share old Common 1¢ par exchanged for (0.05) share new Common 1¢ par 2/21/74
Charter cancelled and declared inoperative and void for non-payment of taxes 3/1/75

MELBOURNE FUTURES FUND L.P. (DE)
Fund liquidated
Details not available

MELCHERS DISTILLERIES LTD (QC)
Recapitalized in 1937
Each share Class A no par exchanged for (1.25) shares 6% Preferred $10 par and $3.50 cash
Each share Class B no par exchanged for (1.25) shares Common no par
Each share 6% Preferred $10 par exchanged for (2) shares 7% Preferred $5 par and (0.3) share Common no par distributed 1/30/62
7% Preferred $5 par called for redemption 11/30/65
Common no par split (5) for (1) by issuance of (4) additional shares 7/15/68
Assets sold for benefit of creditors
No stockholders' equity

MELCHIOR ENGR CORP (DE)
Capital Stock $1 par changed to 20¢ par and (4) additional shares issued 6/17/59
Charter cancelled and declared inoperative and void for non payment of taxes 3/1/78

MELCO CHINA RESORTS HLDG LTD (BC)
Name changed to Mountain China Resorts (Holding) Ltd. 10/22/2010

MELCO CROWN ENTMT LTD (CAYMAN ISLANDS)
Name changed 06/30/2008
Name changed from Melco PBL Entertainment (Macau) Ltd. to Melco Crown Entertainment Ltd. 06/30/2008
Name changed to Melco Resorts & Entertainment Ltd. 04/06/2017

MELDEX INTL PLC (ENGLAND & WALES)
ADR agreement terminated 03/09/2015
No ADR holders' equity

MELEDANDRI ENTERPRISES INC (NY)
Name changed to Sunray Industries, Inc. 12/22/1975
(See Sunray Industries, Inc.)

MELETRON CORP (CA)
Completely liquidated 09/03/1970
Each share Common $1 par exchanged for first and final distribution of (1/3) share Transamerica Corp. Common $1 par
Tranamerica Corp. merged into Aegon N.V. 07/21/1999

MELIA HOTELS INTL S A (SPAIN)
ADR agreement terminated 08/09/2017
Each 144A Sponsored ADR for Ordinary exchanged for (0.5) share Ordinary
Each Reg. S Sponsored ADR for Ordinary exchanged for (0.5) share Ordinary
Note: Unexchanged ADR's will be sold and the proceeds, if any, held for claim after 08/13/2018

MELIA INVERSIONES AMERICANAS N V (SPAIN)
ADR agreement terminated 05/24/2006
Each 144A Sponsored ADR for Ordinary exchanged for (0.5) Ordinary share
Each Reg. S ADR for Ordinary exchanged for (0.5) Ordinary share
Note: Unexchanged ADR's will be sold and proceeds, if any, held for claim after 05/24/2007

MELINGA RES LTD (BC)
Recapitalized as Milagro Minerals Inc. 12/08/1993
Each share Common no par exchanged for (1/3) share Common no par
Milagro Minerals Inc. recapitalized as Geomaque Explorations Ltd./Explorations Geomaque Ltee. 01/10/1997 which merged into Defiance Mining Corp. 06/25/2003 which merged into Rio Narcea Gold Mines, Ltd. 09/03/2004
(See Rio Narcea Gold Mines, Ltd.)

MELISSA RES INC (BC)
Name changed to Bauska Manufacturing (B.C.) Ltd. 06/15/1987
(See Bauska Manufacturing (B.C.) Ltd.)

MELITA INTL CORP (GA)
Issue Information - 3,500,000 shares COM offered at $10 per share on 06/04/1997
Under plan of merger name changed to eShare Technologies Inc. 10/4/99
eShare Technologies Inc. name changed to eShare Communications Inc. 6/8/2000 which merged into divine, inc. 10/23/2001
(See divine, inc.)

MELJAN INDS INC (DE)
Charter cancelled and declared inoperative and void for non-payment of taxes 03/01/2003

MELLIN INDS INC (FL)
Each share old Common $0.001 par exchanged for (0.1) share new Common $0.001 par 10/5/93
Administratively dissolved for failure to file annual reporst 9/21/2001

MELLIN'S FOOD CO. OF NORTH AMERICA (DE)
Charter cancelled and declared inoperative and void for non-payment of taxes 12/23/68

MELLON BK CORP (PA)
$2.80 Preferred Ser. A $1 par called for redemption 07/19/1991
Fixed/Adjustable Rate Preferred Ser. G $1 par called for redemption 11/15/1991
Stated Rate Auction Preferred Ser. C-2 $1 par called for redemption 11/16/1992
6.75% Conv. Preferred Ser. B $1 par called for redemption 12/01/1993
10.40% Preferred Ser. H $1 par called for redemption 03/01/1995
9.60% Preferred Ser. I $1 par called for redemption 12/16/1996
8.50% Preferred Ser. J $1 par called for redemption 02/18/1997
8.20% Preferred Ser. K $1 par called for redemption at $25 on 02/17/1998
Common 50¢ par split (3) for (2) by issuance of (0.5) additional share 11/15/1994
Common 50¢ par split (2) for (1) by issuance of (1) additional share payable 06/02/1997 to holders of record 05/01/1997 Ex date - 06/03/1997
Common 50¢ par split (2) for (1) by issuance of (1) additional share payable 05/17/1999 to holders of record 05/03/1999 Ex date - 05/18/1999
Name changed to Mellon Financial Corp. 10/17/1999
Mellon Financial Corp. merged into Bank of New York Mellon Corp. 07/01/2007

MELLON FINL CORP (PA)
Merged into Bank of New York Mellon Corp. 07/01/2007
Each share Common 50¢ par exchanged for (1) share Common 1¢ par

MELLON INSTL FDS INVT TR (MA)
Trust terminated 09/26/2003
Each share Standish Tax-Sensitive Equity Fund received net asset value
Name changed to Dreyfus Investment Funds 12/01/2008

MELLON NATL BK & TR CO (PITTSBURGH, PA)
Each share Capital Stock $100 par exchanged for (4) shares Capital Stock $25 par 00/00/1954
Capital Stock $25 par changed to $10 par and (1.5) additional shares issued 02/05/1962
Stock Dividend - 50% 02/10/1969
Reorganized as Mellon National Corp. 11/28/1972
Each share Capital Stock $10 par exchanged for (1) share Common $1 par
Mellon National Corp. name changed to Mellon Bank Corp. 09/30/1984 which name changed to Mellon Financial Corp. 10/17/1999 which merged into Bank of New York Mellon Corp. 07/01/2007

MELLON NATIONAL BANK (PITTSBURGH, PA)
Merged into Mellon National Bank & Trust Co. (Pittsburgh, PA) 09/23/1946
Each share Capital Stock exchanged for (2) shares Capital Stock $100 par
Mellon National Bank & Trust Co. (Pittsburgh, PA) reorganized as Mellon National Corp. 11/28/1972 which name changed to Mellon Bank Corp. 09/30/1984 which name changed to Mellon Financial Corp. 10/17/1999 which merged into Bank of New York Mellon Corp. 07/01/2007

MELLON NATL CORP (PA)
Common $1 par changed to 50¢ par and (1) additional share issued 05/15/1978
Name changed to Mellon Bank Corp. 09/30/1984
Mellon Bank Corp. name changed to Mellon Financial Corp. 10/17/1999 which merged into Bank of New York Mellon Corp. 07/01/2007

MELLON PART MTG TR COML PPTYS SER 85/10 (MA)
Name changed to Vinings Investment Properties Trust 3/26/96
(See Vinings Investment Properties Trust)

MELLON RESH INC (AZ)
Name changed to Paychest, Inc. 2/7/2006

MELO BIOTECHNOLOGY HLDGS INC (ON)
Name changed to First Asia Holdings Ltd. 03/09/2011

MELO SONICS CORP (DE)
Out of business 00/00/1995
No stockholders' equity

MELONES MINING CO.
Liquidated in 1927

MELPAR INC (DE)
Merged into American Standard Inc. 06/06/1969
Each share Capital Stock $1 par exchanged for (0.25) share Common $5 par

(See American Standard Inc.)

MELPOMENE REALTY CORP.
Dissolved in 1929

MELRIDGE INC (WA)
Common 1¢ par split (2) for (1) by issuance of (1) additional share 07/27/1986
Plan of reorganization under Chapter 11 Federal Bankruptcy proceedings confirmed 01/30/1989
No stockholders' equity

MELRIDGE INCOME PARTNERS II LIMITED PARTNERSHIP (DE)
Charter forfeited for failure to maintain a registered agent 12/22/1995

MELROSE CORP. (CA)
Charter suspended for non-payment of taxes 01/02/1964

MELROSE ENERGY PLC (UNITED KINGDOM)
Name changed to Pentex Energy PLC 05/07/1997
(See Pentex Energy PLC)

MELROSE HOTEL CO. (TX)
Each share Capital Stock no par exchanged for (10) shares Capital Stock $1 par in 1943
Liquidation completed
Each share Capital Stock $1 par exchanged for initial distribution of $40 cash 6/30/66
Each share Capital Stock $1 par received second and final distribution of $3.04 cash 12/11/70

MELROSE INDS PLC (UNITED KINGDOM)
Name changed 12/14/2012
Name changed from Melrose PLC to Melrose Industries PLC 12/14/2012
ADR agreement terminated 10/24/2018
No ADR's remain outstanding

MELTDOWN MASSAGE & BODY WKS INC (NV)
Name changed to Pro-Tech Industries, Inc. 06/10/2009

MELTON DRILLING & EXPL CO (TX)
Recapitalized as Double River Oil & Gas Co. 10/19/1988
Each share Common no par exchanged for (0.04) share Common $0.001 par
(See Double River Oil & Gas Co.)

MELTON PETROLEUMS LTD. (AB)
Recapitalized as Trans-Canada Mortgage Corp. (Western) Ltd. 12/3/62
Each share Capital Stock no par exchanged for (0.1) share Capital Stock no par
Trans-Canada Mortgage Corp. (Western) Ltd. acquired by Melton Real Estate Ltd. 11/29/68 which name changed to Melcor Developments Ltd. 6/11/76

MELTON REAL ESTATE LTD (AB)
Name changed to Melcor Developments Ltd. 06/11/1976

MELTRONIX INC (CA)
Assets foreclosed upon 10/04/2002
Stockholders' equity unlikely

MELVILLE CORP (NY)
4% Preferred Ser. B $100 par called for redemption 10/11/1996
Common $1 par split (2) for (1) by issuance of (1) additional share 05/02/1983
Common $1 par split (2) for (1) by issuance of (1) additional share 03/14/1989
Each share Common $1 par received distribution of (0.2879) share Footstar, Inc. Common 1¢ par payable 10/15/1996 to holders of record 10/02/1996 Ex date - 10/16/1996
Reorganized under the laws of Delaware as CVS Corp. 11/20/1996

Each share Common $1 par exchanged for (1) share Common $1 par
CVS Corp. name changed to CVS/Caremark Corp. 03/22/2007 which name changed to CVS Caremark Corp. 05/10/2007 which name changed to CVS Health Corp. 09/04/2014

MELVILLE SHOE CORP (NY)
Each share old Common no par exchanged for (4) shares new Common no par 00/00/1928
Reorganized 00/00/1939
Each share Preferred $5 par exchanged for (0.055) share 4% Preferred $100 par
Each share new Common no par exchanged for (2) shares Common $1 par and (0.1) share 4% Preferred $100 par
4.75% Preferred Ser. A $100 par called for redemption 03/01/1965
Common $1 par split (2) for (1) by issuance of (1) additional share 04/26/1968
Common $1 par split (2) for (1) by issuance of (1) additional share 05/04/1970
Common $1 par split (2) for (1) by issuance of (1) additional share 04/28/1972
Stock Dividend - 100% 08/30/1946
Name changed to Melville Corp. (NY) 04/14/1996
Melville Corp. (NY) reorganized in Delaware as CVS Corp. 11/20/1996 which name changed to CVS/Caremark Corp. 03/22/2007 which name changed to CVS Caremark Corp. 05/10/2007 which name changed to CVS Health Corp. 09/04/2014

MEM FINL SOLUTIONS INC (FL)
Each share old Common $0.001 par exchanged for (0.005) share new Common $0.001 par 04/11/2005
Recapitalized as Sebastian River Holdings, Inc. 04/05/2006
Each share new Common $0.001 par exchanged for (0.0025) share Common $0.001 par
Sebastian River Holdings, Inc. recapitalized as Novacab International Inc. 11/12/2013 which name changed to Global Pole Trusion Group Corp. 07/24/2017

MEM INC (NY)
Common 5¢ par split (5) for (4) by issuance of (0.25) additional share 5/15/72
Common 5¢ par split (3) for (2) by issuance of (0.5) additional share 6/3/77
Common 5¢ par split (2) for (1) by issuance of (1) additional share 8/30/85
Merged into Renaissance Acquisition 12/4/96
Each share Common 5¢ par exchanged for $7.50 cash

MEMBERS FINL SVC BUR INC (CO)
Recapitalized as Shared Use Network Services, Inc. 8/25/95
Each (30) shares Common $1 par exchanged for (1) share Common $1 par
Shared Use Network Services, Inc. name changed to Evergreen Network.Com Inc. 4/7/2000

MEMBERS INS CO (CA)
Each share Common $3.50 par exchanged for (0.00035) share Common $10,000 par 12/28/1973
Note: In effect holders received 10¢ per share and public interest was eliminated

MEMBERS SVC CORP (CO)
Each share old Common 1¢ par exchanged for (1/3) share new Common 1¢ par 05/31/1990
Each share new Common 1¢ par exchanged for (0.2) share Common 5¢ par 12/14/1990
Each share Common 5¢ par exchanged for (0.1) share Common 50¢ par 11/22/1991
Each share old Common 50¢ par exchanged for (0.02) share new Common 50¢ par 02/18/1994
Each share new Common 50¢ par exchanged again for (0.025) share new Common 50¢ par 05/18/1994
Out of business 00/00/1997
Stockholders' equity unlikely

MEMBERWORKS INC (DE)
Name changed to Vertrue Inc. 11/18/2004
(See Vertrue Inc.)

MEMC ELECTR MATLS INC (DE)
Name changed to SunEdison, Inc. 06/03/2013
(See SunEdison, Inc.)

MEMCO SOFTWARE LTD (ISRAEL)
Issue Information - 3,365,000 ORD shs. offered at $15 per share on 10/15/1996
Merged into Platinum Technology International Inc. 03/29/1999
Each share Ordinary ILS 0.01 par exchanged for (0.836) share Common $0.001 par
(See Platinum Technology International Inc.)

MEMCOR, INC. (IN)
Merged into LTV Electrosystems, Inc. 4/19/67
Each share 6% Preferred $25 par exchanged for (1) share 6% Preferred Ser. B $25 par
Each share Common no par exchanged for (0.7) share Common 50¢ par
LTV Electrosystems, Inc. name changed to E-Systems Inc. 4/27/72
(See E-Systems Inc.)

MEMOREX CORP (CA)
Merged into Burroughs Corp. (MI) 12/03/1981
Each share Common $1 par exchanged for $14 cash

MEMOREX TELEX CORP (DE)
Reorganized under Chapter 11 Federal Bankruptcy proceedings 02/18/1992
Each share Exchangeable Preferred Ser. A 1¢ par exchanged for (0.035) Memorex Telex N.V. (Old) ADR for Common
(See Memorex Telex N.V. (Old))

MEMOREX TELEX N V NEW (NETHERLANDS)
ADR agreement terminated 11/06/2000
No stockholders' equity

MEMOREX TELEX N V OLD (NETHERLANDS)
Prepackaged plan of reorganization under Chapter 11 Federal Bankruptcy proceedings effective 03/24/1994
Each ADR for Common 0.10 Gldr par exchanged for (0.01) Memorex Telex N.V. (New) Common Stock Purchase Warrant expiring 03/24/2001

MEMORIAL CHAPEL FUNERAL HOME, INC. (SC)
Charter forfeited for failure to maintain a registered agent 10/13/64

MEMORIAL DRIVE BANK (SHEBOYGAN, WI)
Merged into Associated Banc-Corp 3/7/86
Each share Capital Stock $20 par held by Wisconsin residents exchanged for (6) shares Common 10¢ par
Each share Capital Stock $20 par held by non-residents exchanged for $93 cash

MEMORIAL HOSPITAL OF SOUTHERN CALIFORNIA (CA)
Merged into General Health Services, Inc. 02/13/1969
Each share Capital Stock $20 par exchanged for (5) shares Common $1 par
(See General Health Services, Inc.)

MEMORIAL OAKS INC (TX)
Each share old Common 10¢ par exchanged for (0.0001) share new Common 10¢ par 03/01/1973
Note: In effect holders received $1.80 cash per share public interest was eliminated

MEMORIAL PRODTN PARTNERS LP (DE)
Plan of reorganization under Chapter 11 Federal Bankruptcy proceedings effective 05/04/2017
Each Common Unit received distribution of (0.00597288) share Amplify Energy Corp. Common $0.0001 par, (0.02596904) Common Stock Purchase Warrant expiring 05/04/2022 and $0.01493217 cash

MEMORIAL RESOURCE DEV CORP (DE)
Merged into Range Resources Corp. 09/16/2016
Each share Common 1¢ par exchanged for (0.375) share Common 1¢ par

MEMORY MAGNETICS INC. (UT)
Proclaimed dissolved for failure to pay taxes 06/01/1988

MEMORY METALS INC (DE)
Name changed to Memry Corp. 06/06/1989
(See Memry Corp.)

MEMORY PHARMACEUTICALS CORP (DE)
Issue Information - 5,000,000 shares COM offered at $7 per share on 04/05/2004
Acquired by Hoffmann-La Roche Inc. 01/05/2009
Each share Common $0.001 par exchanged for $0.61 cash

MEMORY PROTN DEVICES INC (NY)
Name changed to Bogen Corp. 09/18/1987

MEMORY SCIENCES CORP (DE)
Name changed to Corporate Development Strategies, Inc. 2/26/2004
Corporate Development Strategies, Inc. name changed to Irwin Energy Inc. 12/8/2004 which recapitalized as Irwin Resources Inc. 11/20/2006

MEMORY SYSTEMS OF MISSOURI, INC. (MO)
Merged into Gale Industries, Inc. 05/06/1968
Each share Common no par exchanged for (1) share Common 50¢ par
(See Gale Industries, Inc.)

MEMORY TECHNOLOGY INC. (MA)
Each share Common no par exchanged for (50) shares Common $1 par 6/30/71
Adjudicated bankrupt 3/6/75
No stockholders' equity

MEMOTEC COMMUNICATIONS INC (CANADA)
Acquired by Kontron Communications Inc. 7/1/2001
Each share Common no par exchanged for (0.03377) share Exchangeable Preferred no par

MEMOTEC DATA INC (CANADA)
Class A Common no par reclassified as Common no par 10/3/85
Name changed to Teleglobe Inc. 8/12/91
Teleglobe Inc. acquired by BCE Inc. 11/1/2000

MEMPHIS GARAGES, INC. (MI)
Liquidation for cash completed 1/12/60

MEMPHIS NATURAL GAS CO.
Merged into Texas Gas Transmission Corp. on a (1.125) for (1) basis in 1948
Texas Gas Transmission Corp. reorganized as Texas Gas Corp. 1/1/83 which name changed to Texas Gas Resources Corp. 5/12/83 which merged into CSX Corp. 9/30/83

MEMPHIS POWER & LIGHT CO.
Dissolved in 1939

MEMPHIS STEAM LAUNDRY-CLEANER, INC. (TN)
Completely liquidated 4/26/68
Each share Preferred $100 par exchanged for first and final distribution of $100 cash

MEMPHIS STREET RAILWAY CO. (TN)
Each share 4% Preferred $100 par exchanged for (16) shares Common $5 par and $38 in cash 00/00/1949
Name changed to Memphis Transit Co. 04/01/1958
(See Memphis Transit Co.)

MEMPHIS TRANSIT CO. (TN)
Liquidation completed
Each share Common $5 par stamped to indicate initial distribution of $4 cash 02/06/1961
Each share Stamped Common $5 par stamped to indicate second distribution of $0.25 cash 12/01/1961
Each share Stamped Common $5 par stamped to indicate third distribution of $0.50 cash 12/16/1962
Each share Stamped Common $5 par exchanged for fourth and final distribution of $0.735 cash 04/06/1966

MEMPHIS TR CO (TN)
Each share Common $5 par exchanged for (0.002) share Common $2,500 par 4/10/79
Public interest eliminated

MEMREG INC (NV)
Name changed to ORHub, Inc. 02/10/2017

MEMRY CORP (DE)
Each share old Common 1¢ par exchanged for (0.1) share new Common 1¢ par 08/08/1994
Merged into SAES Getters S.p.A. 09/29/2008
Each share Common 1¢ par exchanged for $2.53 cash

MEMS USA INC (NV)
Name changed to Convergence Ethanol, Inc. 12/13/2006
(See Convergence Ethanol, Inc.)

MEMSIC INC (DE)
Issue Information - 6,000,000 shares COM offered at $10 per share on 12/13/2007
Acquired by MZ Investment Holdings Ltd. 09/17/2013
Each share Common $0.00001 par exchanged for $4.225 cash

MEMSOG MINING CO. LTD. (ON)
Declared dissolved 6/1/64
No stockholders' equity

MEMTEC LTD (AUSTRALIA)
Each old Sponsored ADR for Ordinary exchanged for (0.5) new Sponsored ADR for Ordinary 12/01/1992
Acquired by United States Filter Corp. (New) 02/20/1998
Each new Sponsored ADR for Ordinary exchanged for $35.95 cash

MEMTEK CORP (MA)
Merged into Horsehead Resource Development Co., Inc. 4/19/91

Each share Common 1¢ par exchanged for $0.0775 cash

MENA RES INC (AB)
Merged into Rusoro Mining Ltd. 3/5/2007
Each share Common no par exchanged for (0.58823529) share Common no par

MENASCO MFG CO (CA)
Merged into Colt Industries Inc. (PA) 05/20/1977
Each share Common $1 par exchanged for (0.475) share Common $1 par
(See Colt Industries Inc. (PA))

MENASHA PRINTING & CARTON CO.
Acquired by Marathon Paper Mills Co. 00/00/1927
Details not available

MENATEP BK (RUSSIA)
ADR agreement terminated due to bankruptcy 11/5/2002
No ADR holders' equity

MENDELL-DENVER CORP (CO)
Merged into Sunlight Systems, Ltd. 07/22/1996
Each share Common $0.001 par exchanged for (0.2) share Common $0.001 par
Sunlight Systems, Ltd. recapitalized as NanoPierce Technologies Inc. 02/27/1998 which recapitalized as VYTA Corp. (NV) 01/31/2006 which reincorporated in Delaware 08/20/2010 which recapitalized as Bio Lab Naturals, Inc. 11/05/2010

MENDOCINO RES INC (CANADA)
Name changed to EMR Microwave Technology Corp. 02/01/1995
(See EMR Microwave Technology Corp.)

MENDON LEASING CORP (NY)
Merged into CLM Merger Corp. 05/22/1979
Each share Common 5¢ par exchanged for $6 cash

MENDON RESEARCH & DEVELOPMENT CO., INC. (NY)
Dissolved 12/16/65
No stockholders' equity

MENDOSOMA TIMBER CO.
Dissolution approved in 1946

MENGEL CO. (NJ)
Each share Common $100 par exchanged for (4) shares Common no par in 1928
Common no par changed to $1 par in 1932
Each share 7% Preferred $100 par exchanged for (2) shares 5% Preferred $50 par and (3) shares Common $1 par in 1937
Merged into Container Corp. of America on a (2) for (1) basis 11/15/60
Container Corp. of America merged into Marcor Inc. 11/1/68 which merged into Mobil Corp. 7/1/76 which merged into Exxon Mobil Corp. 11/30/99

MENGOLD RES INC (QC)
Recapitalized as MGold Resources Inc. (QC) 09/22/2010
Each share Common no par exchanged for (0.125) share Common no par
MGold Resources Inc. (QC) reincorporated in Alberta 07/25/2013 which name changed to Tanager Energy Inc. 09/23/2013

MENIFEE URANIUM MINES LTD. (ON)
Charter cancelled by the Province of Ontario by default in November 1962

MENIKA MNG LTD (BC)
Common $1 par changed to no par 07/09/2007
Each share old Common no par exchanged for (0.025) share new Common no par 12/09/2013
Name changed to American Lithium Corp. 04/18/2016

MENLEY & JAMES INC (DE)
Completely liquidated 2/23/2000
Each share Common 1¢ par exchanged for first and final distribution of $2.13 cash

MENLO ACQUISITION CORP (DE)
Merged into Menlo Holding, Inc. 3/28/2002
Each share Common 1¢ par exchanged for $1 cash

MENLO CAP CORP (DE)
Name changed to Carstar International Inc. 09/12/1988

MENOMINEE RIVER SUGAR CO.
Out of existence 00/00/1937
Details not available

MENORA RES INC (QC)
Name changed 04/28/1983
Name changed from Menorah Mines Ltd. to Menora Resources Inc. 04/28/1983
Recapitalized as Mengold Resources Inc. 12/04/2003
Each share Common no par exchanged for (0.125) share Common no par
Mengold Resources Inc. recapitalized as MGold Resources Inc. (QC) 09/22/2010 which reincorporated in Alberta 07/25/2013 which name changed to Tanager Energy Inc. 09/23/2013

MENS MED CTRS AMER INC (FL)
Administratively dissolved for failure to maintain a registered agent 8/5/98

MENS WEARHOUSE INC (TX)
Common 1¢ par split (3) for (2) by issuance of (0.5) additional share 08/06/1993
Common 1¢ par split (3) for (2) by issuance of (0.5) additional share 11/15/1995
Common 1¢ par split (3) for (2) by issuance of (0.5) additional share payable 06/19/1998 to holders of record 06/12/1998
Common 1¢ par split (3) for (2) by issuance of (0.5) additional share payable 06/13/2005 to holders of record 05/31/2005 Ex date - 06/14/2005
Name changed to Tailored Brands, Inc. 02/01/2016

MENSH CORP (DE)
Name changed to Linden Corp. 01/01/1969
(See Linden Corp.)

MENSH INVT & DEV ASSOC INC (DE)
Name changed to Mensh Corp. 9/26/62
Mensh Corp. name changed to Linden Corp. 1/1/69
(See Linden Corp.)

MENSILVO MINES, LTD. (ON)
Charter cancelled 6/1/64

MENTAL HEALTH BENEFITS CORP (DE)
Name changed to Managed Health Benefits Corp. 11/22/88
Managed Health Benefits Corp. name changed to Avitar, Inc. (New) 5/19/95

MENTAL HEALTH MGMT INC (DE)
Reincorporated 10/28/1994
State of incorporation changed from (VA) to (DE) 10/28/1994
Name changed to MHM Services, Inc. 05/22/1996
(See MHM Services, Inc.)

MENTERGY LTD (ISRAEL)
Each share Ordinary ILS 1 exchanged for (0.25) share Ordinary ILS 0.04 par 12/24/2001
Placed in receivership and operations ceased 02/00/2003
Stockholders' equity unlikely

MENTOR CAP INC (CA)
Reincorporated under the laws of Delaware and Common no par changed to $0.0001 par 09/24/2015

MENTOR CORP (CO)
Assets awarded in out of court settlement 12/03/1990
No stockholders' equity

MENTOR CORP (MN)
Common 10¢ par split (3) for (1) by issuance of (2) additional shares 04/01/1983
Common 10¢ par split (2) for (1) by issuance of (1) additional share 02/24/1987
Common 10¢ par split (2) for (1) by issuance of (1) additional share payable 10/13/1995 to holders of record 09/27/1995
Common 10¢ par split (2) for (1) by issuance of (1) additional share payable 01/17/2003 to holders of record 12/31/2002 Ex date - 01/21/2003
Stock Dividend - 200% 12/21/1973
Merged into Johnson & Johnson 01/23/2009
Each share Common 10¢ par exchanged for $31 cash

MENTOR CORP (OK)
Liquidation completed 06/26/1975
Each share Common $1 par exchanged for first and final distribution of $2.592 cash

MENTOR EXPL & DEV LTD (ON)
Each share Capital Stock $5 par exchanged for (10) shares Capital Stock 50¢ par 01/00/1955
Capital Stock 50¢ par changed to no par 06/09/1971
Each share Common no par received distribution of (1.2753303) share Sudbury Contact Mines, Ltd. Common no par payable 10/24/2001 to holders of record 10/17/2001
Merged into Agnico-Eagle Mines Ltd. 10/17/2001
Each share Common no par exchanged for (0.21) share Common no par
Agnico-Eagle Mines Ltd. name changed to Agnico Eagle Mines Ltd. 04/30/2013

MENTOR GRAPHICS CORP (OR)
Common no par split (2) for (1) by issuance of (1) additional share 08/14/1989
Acquired by Siemens A.G. 03/30/2017
Each share Common no par exchanged for $37.25 cash

MENTOR INCOME FD INC (VA)
Name changed to American Income Fund, Inc. 03/15/2001
American Income Fund, Inc. name changed to Nuveen Multi-Market Income Fund, Inc. (VA) 09/08/2014 which reincorporated in Massachusetts as Nuveen Multi-Market Income Fund 11/19/2014

MENTOR ON CALL INC (NV)
Recapitalized as Platinum SuperYachts, Inc. 10/08/2002
Each share Common $0.001 par exchanged for (0.01) share Common $0.001 par
Platinum SuperYachts, Inc. name changed to Royal Quantum Group, Inc. 02/01/2006 which recapitalized as MineralRite Corp. 10/18/2012

MENTORTECH INC (DE)
Each share old Common 1¢ par exchanged for (0.125) share new Common 1¢ par 03/03/1998 exchanged for (0.25) share Ordinary ILS 0.04 par 12/24/2001

Company terminated registration of common stock and is no longer public as of 05/05/1999
Details not available

MENU FOODS INCOME FD (ON)
Acquired by Simmons Foods, Inc. 11/04/2010
Each Unit received $4.80 cash

MENU-MATICS, INC. (DE)
Voluntarily dissolved 10/10/72
Details not available

MENZIES SHOE CO.
Bankrupt in 1928

MEO AUSTRALIA LTD (AUSTRALIA)
ADR agreement terminated 12/07/2016
Each ADR for Ordinary exchanged for $0.119834 cash

MEOTA RES CORP (CANADA)
Class A Common no par reclassified as Common no par 06/09/2000
Acquired by Provident Energy Trust 10/02/2002
Each share Common no par exchanged for (0.415) Trust Unit no par
Provident Energy Trust reorganized as Provident Energy Ltd. (New) 01/03/2011 which merged into Pembina Pipeline Corp. 04/02/2012

MEPC CAP CORP (DE)
Dutch Auction Rate Preferred Ser. A no par called for redemption at $100,000 on 05/11/1998
Dutch Auction Rate Preferred Ser. B no par called for redemption at $100,000 on 06/01/1998

MEPC CAP CORP II (NV)
Auction Preferred Ser. D no par called for redemption at $100,000 on 04/28/1998
Auction Preferred Ser. A no par called for redemption at $100,000 on 05/19/1998
Auction Preferred Ser. B no par called for redemption at $100,000 on 05/26/1998
Auction Preferred Ser. C no par called for redemption at $100,000 on 06/09/1998

MEPC INTL CAP L P (DE)
Issue Information - 8,000,000 GTD QUARTERLY INCOME PFD SECS A 9.125% offered at $25 per share on 09/18/1995
9.125% Guaranteed Quarterly Income Preferred Securities called for redemption at $25 plus $0.52595 accrued dividends on 9/21/2005

MEPR CORP. (DE)
Shares reacquired by company 2/15/81
Each share Common no par exchanged for $105.47 cash

MERA PETES INC (AB)
Issue Information - 1,000,000 shares COM offered at $0.20 per share on 07/13/1993
Recapitalized as West Isle Energy Inc. 10/14/2004
Each share Common no par exchanged for (0.25) share Common no par

MERABANK FED SVGS BK (PHOENIX, AZ)
Merged into AZP Group, Inc. 12/16/1986
Each share Common 1¢ par exchanged for $51.084 cash

MERADA INDS INC (DE)
Reincorporated 4/11/69
State of incorporation changed from (FL) to (DE) 4/11/69
Name changed to First Quality Corp. 9/30/70
(See First Quality Corp.)

MERADA MED SUPPLY CORP (FL)
Charter cancelled for non-payment of taxes 12/01/1977

MERAFE RES LTD (SOUTH AFRICA)
ADR agreement terminated 10/19/2016
Each ADR for Ordinary exchanged for $3.770353 cash

MERANT PLC (ENGLAND)
Acquired by Serena Software, Inc. 06/30/2004
Each Sponsored ADR for Ordinary 10p par exchanged for (0.2483) share Common $0.001 par and $12.4247 cash
(See Serena Software, Inc.)

MERANTO TECHNOLOGY LTD (ON)
Recapitalized as World Sports Merchandising Inc. 02/01/1998
Each share Common no par exchanged for (0.25) share Common no par
World Sports Merchandising Inc. name changed to World Sales & Merchandising Inc. 02/22/2000
(See World Sales & Merchandising Inc.)

MERBANK CAP CORP (BC)
Reincorporated 06/13/1995
Place of incorporation changed from (ONT) to (BC) 06/13/1995
Merged into Gran Colombia Resources Inc. 07/11/1995
Each share Common no par exchanged for (0.1) share Common no par
Gran Colombia Resources Inc. name changed to Wavve Telecommunications, Inc. 10/29/1999
(See Wavve Telecommunications, Inc.)

MERC INTL MINERALS INC (ON)
Name changed to Nighthawk Gold Corp. 05/01/2012

MERCADO MKTG CORP (DE)
Name changed to COFIS International Corp. 06/05/1991
COFIS International Corp. recapitalized as U.S. Bridge Corp. 04/29/1994 which name changed to USABG Corp. 01/13/1998
(See USABG Corp.)

MERCANA INDS LTD (ON)
Reincorporated 06/28/1995
Place of incorporation changed from (BC) to (ONT) 06/28/1995
Cease trade order effective 05/14/1997
Stockholders' equity unlikely

MERCANTILE ACCEPTANCE CORP. OF CALIFORNIA (DE)
Class A Common $5 par and Class B Common $1 par changed to Common $5 par in 1944
Name changed to Laurentide Finance Corp. of California 11/30/61
Laurentide Finance Corp. of California merged into Eliminator, Inc. for cash 6/1/67

MERCANTILE ALTERNATIVE DEFD INVS TEDI LLC (DE)
Name changed to PNC Alternative Strategies TEDI Fund LLC 09/27/2007

MERCANTILE ALTERNATIVE STRATEGIES FD LLC (DE)
Name changed to PNC Mercantile Alternative Strategies Fund LLC 09/28/2007

MERCANTILE BANCORP INC (DE)
Common $6.25 par changed to $1.25 par and (4) additional shares issued payable 05/31/2002 to holders of record 05/15/2002 Ex date - 06/03/2002
Common $1.25 par changed to $0.4167 par and (2) additional shares issued payable 06/20/2006 to holders of record 06/05/2006 Ex date - 06/21/2006
Common $0.4167 par split (3) for (2) by issuance of (0.5) additional share payable 12/28/2007 to holders of record 12/17/2007 Ex date - 12/31/2007
Plan of reorganization under Chapter 11 Federal Bankruptcy proceedings effective 06/30/2014
No stockholders' equity

MERCANTILE BANCORP INC (IN)
Merged into Bank of Montreal (Montreal, QC) 12/30/2004
Each share Common exchanged for approximately $210 cash

MERCANTILE BANCORP INC (TX)
Merged into Colonial BancGroup, Inc. 03/28/2002
Each share Common $5 par exchanged for (3.4808) shares Common $2.50 par
(See Colonial BancGroup, Inc.)

MERCANTILE BANCORPORATION INC (MO)
Common $5 par split (3) for (2) by issuance of (0.5) additional share 04/09/1984
Common $5 par split (3) for (2) by issuance of (0.5) additional share 04/08/1986
Common $5 par split (3) for (2) by issuance of (0.5) additional share 04/11/1994
Common $5 par changed to 1¢ par 04/25/1997
Common 1¢ par split (3) for (2) by issuance of (0.5) additional share payable 10/01/1997 to holders of record 09/10/1997 Ex date - 10/02/1997
Merged into Firstar Corp. (New) 09/20/1999
Each share Common 1¢ par exchanged for (2.091) shares Common 1¢ par
Firstar Corp. (New) merged into U.S. Bancorp (New) 02/27/2001

MERCANTILE BANK & TRUST CO. (NEW YORK, NY)
Closed by New York State Banking Dept. and liquidated 04/12/1933
No stockholders' equity

MERCANTILE BK & TR CO (GRETNA, LA)
Name changed to Gulf South Bank & Trust Co. (Gretna, LA) 06/07/1974
(See Gulf South Bank & Trust Co. (Gretna, LA))

MERCANTILE BK & TR CO (KANSAS CITY, MO)
Each share Capital Stock $100 par exchanged for (5) shares Capital Stock $25 par to effect a (4) for (1) split and 25% stock dividend 06/17/1949
Stock Dividends - 50% 02/27/1953; 33-1/3% 02/25/1958; 50% 02/25/1963; 33-1/3% 02/26/1968
100% acquired by Mercantile Bancorporation Inc. through exchange offer which expired 12/10/1971
Public interest eliminated

MERCANTILE BK (HOUSTON, TX)
Merged into Allied Bancshares, Inc. (TX) 12/31/1979
Each share Common $2 par exchanged for $18.75 principal amount of 9-1/2% Restricted Debentures due 12/01/1989 plus $6.25 cash or $18.75 principal amount of 9-1/2% Unrestricted Debentures due 12/01/1989 plus $6.25 cash
Note: Option to receive Unrestricted Debentures expired 01/30/1980

MERCANTILE BK (SACRAMENTO, CA)
Merged into SierraWest Bancorp 6/30/97
Each share Common $5 par exchanged for (0.993346) share Common no par
SierraWest Bancorp merged into BancWest Corp. (New) 7/1/99
(See BancWest Corp. (New))

MERCANTILE BK CDA (MONTREAL, QC)
Common $10 par changed to $5 par and (1) additional share issued 01/31/1972
Merged into National Bank of Canada (Montreal, QC) 02/13/1986
Each share Floating Rate Preferred Class A Ser. 2 no par exchanged for (1) share 1st Preferred Ser. 7 no par
Each share $2.6875 Preferred Class A Ser. 1 no par exchanged for (1) share 1st Preferred Ser. 6 no par
Each share Common $5 par exchanged for (0.3) share Common $2 par

MERCANTILE BANKSHARES CORP (MD)
Common no par changed to $2 par and (5) additional shares issued 12/29/1970
$3 Conv. Class A Preferred no par called for redemption 08/01/1983
Common $2 par split (2) for (1) by issuance of (1) additional share 12/31/1985
Common $2 par split (2) for (1) by issuance of (1) additional share 12/31/1989
Common $2 par split (3) for (2) by issuance of (0.5) additional share 09/30/1993
Common $2 par split (3) for (2) by issuance of (0.5) additional share payable 06/30/1997 to holders of record 06/20/1997
Common $2 par split (3) for (2) by issuance of (0.5) additional share payable 01/27/2006 to holders of record 01/20/2006 Ex date - 01/30/2006
Merged into PNC Financial Services Group, Inc. 03/02/2007
Each share Common $2 par exchanged for (0.4184) share Common $5 par and $16.45 cash

MERCANTILE DISCOUNT CORP. (DE)
Name changed to Mercantile Financial Corp. 6/1/62
(See listing for Mercantile Financial Corp.)

MERCANTILE FACTORING CR ONLINE CORP (NV)
Name changed to Incitations Inc. 10/03/2000
Incitations Inc. recapitalized as Osprey Gold Corp. 05/16/2003 which recapitalized as Gilla Inc. 03/30/2007

MERCANTILE FINANCE CORP. (DE)
Charter cancelled and declared inoperative and void for non-payment of taxes 4/1/38

MERCANTILE FINANCE CORP. OF AMERICA (DE)
Charter cancelled and declared inoperative and void for non-payment of taxes 4/1/40

MERCANTILE FINANCIAL CORP. (DE)
5-3/4% Class A 1st Preferred $100 par reclassified as 5-3/4% Preferred 1963 Ser. $100 par 12/28/64
5-3/4% Class A 1st Preferred 2nd Ser. $100 par reclassified as 5-3/4% Preferred 1964 Ser. $100 par 12/28/64
6% 1st Preferred Ser. A $100 par reclassified as 6% Preferred 1959 Ser. $100 par 12/28/64
6% 1st Preferred Ser. C $100 par reclassified as 6% Preferred 1961 Ser. $100 par 12/28/64
Each share 4% 2nd Preference $100 par exchanged for (0.007407) share Common $2 par 12/28/64
Merged into Mercantile Industries, Inc. 12/30/70
Each share Common $2 par exchanged for (1) share Common $2 par

MERCANTILE GOLD CO (WY)
Reincorporated 09/23/2005
State of incorporation changed from (DE) to (WY) 09/23/2005
Recapitalized as Anglo Andean Mining Co. 02/07/2006
Each share Common $0.001 par exchanged for (0.001) share Common $0.001 par
Anglo Andean Mining Co. name changed to MGM Mineral Resources Inc. 04/28/2006 which recapitalized as Brownstone Resources, Inc. 10/05/2007 which recapitalized as Pomsta Group, Inc. 10/12/2010 which name changed to Oidon Co., Ltd. 12/31/2010

MERCANTILE GOLD CORP (BC)
Struck from the register and dissolved 11/10/94

MERCANTILE HOME BANK & TRUST CO. (KANSAS CITY, MO)
Stock Dividends - 50% 2/25/44; 33-1/3% 2/27/45
Name changed to Mercantile Bank & Trust Co. (Kansas City, MO) 6/17/49
(See Mercantile Bank & Trust Co. (Kansas City, MO))

MERCANTILE INDS INC (DE)
Merged into Bowater Holdings Inc. 03/01/1978
Each share Common $2 par exchanged for $2 cash

MERCANTILE LIQUIDATING CO. (MO)
Completely liquidated 4/27/72
Each share Capital Stock no par exchanged for first and final distribution of $0.63 cash

MERCANTILE LONG-SHORT MANAGER FD LLC (DE)
Name changed to PNC Long-Short Master Fund LLC 09/28/2007

MERCANTILE NATIONAL BANK (ATLANTA, GA)
Liquidated 06/30/1976
No stockholders' equity

MERCANTILE NATL BK (CHICAGO, IL)
Each share Common $100 par exchanged for (5) shares Common $20 par 00/00/1944
Stock Dividends - 10% 09/20/1955; (1) for (7-1/3) 09/18/1958
Completely liquidated 01/01/1980
Each share Common $20 par exchanged for first and final distribution of $3 cash

MERCANTILE NATL BK (CORPUS CHRISTI, TX)
Merged into Southwest Bancshares, Inc. 04/12/1982
Each share Common $5 par exchanged for (0.98999) share Common $5 par
Southwest Bancshares, Inc. merged into MCorp 10/11/1984
(See MCorp)

MERCANTILE NATL BK (DALLAS, TX)
Each share Capital Stock $20 par exchanged for (2.2) shares Capital Stock $10 par to effect a (2) for (1) split and a 10% stock dividend 00/00/1954
Each share Capital Stock $10 par exchanged for (2) shares Capital Stock $5 par 03/21/1972
Stock Dividends - 10% 01/31/1956; 10% 02/16/1959; 10% 02/01/1962; 14-2/7% 01/27/1970
Under plan of reorganization each share Capital Stock $5 par

automatically became (1) share Mercantile National Corp. (TX) Common $5 par 07/31/1975
Mercantile National Corp. (TX) reorganized in Delaware as Mercantile Texas Corp. 04/12/1976 which name changed to MCorp 10/11/1984
(See MCorp)

MERCANTILE NATL BK (LOS ANGELES, CA)
Reorganized as National Mercantile Bancorp 05/31/1984
Each share Common $5 par exchanged for (1) share Common no par
National Mercantile Bancorp merged into First California Financial Group, Inc. 03/12/2007 which merged into PacWest Bancorp 05/31/2013

MERCANTILE NATL BK (MIAMI BEACH, FL)
Each share Common $100 par exchanged for (10) shares Common $10 par 4/14/47
Each share Common $10 par exchanged for (2) shares Common $5 par 2/1/66
Stock Dividend - 50% 5/24/54
Merged into Atico Financial Corp. in 1972
Each share Common $5 par exchanged for $26 cash

MERCANTILE NATIONAL BANK (TULSA, OK)
Name changed to Mercantile Bank & Trust Co. (Tulsa, OK) 04/01/1971

MERCANTILE NATL BK IND (HAMMOND, IN)
Name changed 03/15/1969
Capital Stock $25 par changed to $10 par and (1.5) additional shares issued plus a 50% stock dividend paid 01/30/1964
Stock Dividends - 50% 01/27/1959; 33-1/3% 12/20/1960
Name changed from Mercantile National Bank (Hammond, IN) to Mercantile National Bank of Indiana (Hammond, IN) 03/15/1969
Capital Stock $10 par changed to $5 par and (1) additional share issued plus a 50% stock dividend paid 11/03/1969
Acquired by Mercantile Bancorp, Inc. (IN) 01/25/1983
Each share Common $5 par exchanged for (1) share Common $5 par
(See Mercantile Bancorp, Inc. (IN))

MERCANTILE NATL CORP (TX)
Reorganized under the laws of Delaware as Mercantile Texas Corp. 04/12/1976
Each share Common $5 par exchanged for (1) share Common $5 par
Mercantile Texas Corp. name changed to MCorp 10/11/1984
(See MCorp)

MERCANTILE PROPERTIES, INC. (NY)
Liquidation completed in 1949

MERCANTILE RES LTD (NV)
Recapitalized as Sharewell Capital Group, Inc. 03/25/2011
Each share Common $0.001 par exchanged for (0.03333333) share Common $0.001 par
Sharewell Capital Group, Inc. name changed to Artemis Energy Holdings Inc. 04/11/2013 which name changed to Findit, Inc. 02/20/2015

MERCANTILE SAFE DEP & TR CO (BALTIMORE, MD)
Capital Stock $20 par changed to $10 par and (1) additional share issued 01/31/1962
Reorganized as Mercantile Bankshares Corp. 09/01/1970

Each share Capital Stock $10 par exchanged for (0.83333) share $3 Conv. Class A Preferred no par and (0.5) share Common no par
Mercantile Bankshares Corp. merged into PNC Financial Services Group, Inc. 03/02/2007

MERCANTILE SEC LIFE INS CO (TX)
Capital Stock $10 par changed to $5 par 03/08/1960
Capital Stock $5 par changed to $1-2/3 par and (2) additional shares issued 03/10/1964
Merged into Republic National Life Insurance Co. 04/22/1971
Each share Capital Stock $1-2/3 par exchanged for (1.1) shares Capital Stock $1 par
Republic National Life Insurance Co. merged into Gulf United Corp. 04/06/1981
(See Gulf United Corp.)

MERCANTILE SECURITY CORP.
Out of business in 1932
No stockholders' equity

MERCANTILE STORES INC (DE)
Common no par changed to $3.66-2/3 par in 1947
Common $3.66-2/3 par changed to $1.83-1/3 par and (1) additional share issued 2/20/62
Common $1.83-1/3 par changed to 91-2/3¢ par and (1) additional share issued 6/14/73
Common 91-2/3¢ par changed to 36-2/3¢ par and (1.5) additional shares issued 6/15/83
Common 36-2/3¢ par changed to 14-2/3¢ par and (1.5) additional shares issued 6/15/87
Stock Dividend - 900% 12/27/45
Merged into Dillard's Inc. 8/18/98
Each share Common 14-2/3¢ par exchanged for $80 cash

MERCANTILE TEX CORP (DE)
Common $5 par split (4) for (3) by issuance of (1/3) additional share 06/01/1979
Common $5 par split (3) for (2) by issuance of (0.5) additional share 02/27/1981
$3 Conv. Preferred Ser. A $50 par called for redemption 03/11/1983
Under plan of merger name changed to MCorp 10/11/1984
(See MCorp)

MERCANTILE TR & SVGS BK (QUINCY, IL)
Each share Capital Stock $100 par exchanged for (4) shares Capital Stock $50 par to effect a (2) for (1) split and a 100% stock dividend 01/31/1955
Each share Capital Stock $50 par exchanged for (2.5) shares Capital Stock $25 par to effect a (2) for (1) split and a 25% stock dividend 01/26/1959
Capital Stock $25 par changed to $12.50 par and (0.5) additional share issued 02/22/1973
Capital Stock $12.50 par changed to $6.25 par and (2) additional shares issued to provide for a (2) for (1) split plus a 50% stock dividend 03/15/1982
Stock Dividends - 20% 02/03/1964; 25% 02/15/1967; 33-1/3% 02/18/1971
Reorganized as Mercantile Bancorp, Inc. 12/31/1983
Each share Capital Stock $6.25 par exchanged for (1) share Common $6.25 par
(See Mercantile Bancorp, Inc.)

MERCANTILE TRUST CO. (SAN FRANCISCO, CA)
Name changed to American Trust Co. (San Francisco, CA) 12/31/26
American Trust Co. (San Francisco, CA) merged into Wells Fargo Bank

American Trust Co. (San Francisco, CA) 3/25/60 which name changed to Wells Fargo Bank (San Francisco, CA) 1/31/62 which name changed to Wells Fargo Bank, N.A. (San Francisco, CA) 8/15/68 which reorganized as Wells Fargo & Co. (Old) (CA) 2/28/69 which reincorporated in Delaware 6/30/87 which merged into Wells Fargo & Co. (New) 11/2/98

MERCANTILE TRUST CO. (ST. LOUIS, MO)
Common $25 par changed to $12.50 par and (1) additional share issued 01/25/1960
Stock Dividend - 10% 03/25/1955
Name changed to Mercantile Trust Co. N.A. (St. Louis, MO) 12/28/1964
Mercantile Trust Co. N.A. (St. Louis, MO) reorganized as Mercantile Bancorporation Inc. 03/11/1971 which merged into Firstar Corp. (New) 09/20/1999 which merged into U.S. Bancorp 02/27/2001

MERCANTILE TR CO NATL ASSN (ST LOUIS, MO)
Common $12.50 par changed to $6.25 par and (1) additional share issued 07/28/1967
Common $6.25 par changed to $5 par and (0.25) additional share issued 05/09/1969
Under plan of reorganization each share Common $5 par automatically became (1) share Mercantile Bancorporation, Inc. Common $5 par 03/11/1971
Mercantile Bancorporation, Inc. merged into Firstar Corp. (New) 09/20/1999 which merged into U.S. Bancorp (DE) 02/27/2001

MERCARI ACQUISITION CORP (ON)
Recapitalized as Concordia Healthcare Corp. 12/24/2013
Each share Common no par exchanged for (0.02079866) share Common no par
Concordia Healthcare Corp. name changed to Concordia International Corp. (ON) 06/30/2016 which reincorporated in Canada 06/22/2018

MERCARI COMMUNICATIONS GROUP LTD (CO)
Each share old Common $0.00001 par exchanged for (0.00111111) share new Common $0.00001 par 08/03/2004
Each share new Common $0.00001 par exchanged again for (0.28571428) share new Common $0.00001 par 06/02/2008
Note: No holder will receive fewer than (100) post-split shares
Name changed to AiXin Life International, Inc. 02/01/2018

MERCAST CORP. (DE)
Name changed to Mertronics Corp. 6/28/60
Mertronics Corp. name changed to G & H Technology, Inc. 6/30/67
(See G & H Technology, Inc.)

MERCATOR GOLD PLC (UNITED KINGDOM)
Name changed to Electrum Resources PLC 10/05/2010
Electrum Resources PLC name changed to ECR Minerals PLC 01/10/2011
(See ECR Minerals PLC)

MERCATOR PARTNERS ACQUISITION CORP (DE)
Issue Information - 5,100,000 UNITS 500,000 Ser. A Units consisting of (2) shares COM, (5) CL W WTS and (5) CL Z WTS and 4,600,000 Ser. B Units consisting of (2) shares CL B COM, (1) CL W WT and (1) CL Z WT on 04/11/2005
Class B Common $0.0001 par

reclassified as Common $0.0001 par 11/29/2006
Name changed to Global Telecom & Technology, Inc. 11/29/2006
Global Telecom & Technology, Inc. name changed to GTT Communications, Inc. 01/02/2014

MERCATOR RESOURCE CORP (CANADA)
Recapitalized as Arimetco International, Inc. 03/14/1990
Each share Common no par exchanged for (1/3) share Common no par
(See Arimetco International, Inc.)

MERCATOR SOFTWARE INC (DE)
Merged into Ascential Software Corp. 9/12/2003
Each share Common 1¢ par exchanged for $3 cash

MERCEDES EXPLORATION CO. LTD. (ON)
Charter cancelled by the Province of Ontario for default 9/18/61

MERCER CONTROLS CORP. (NJ)
Liquidation completed 8/10/60

MERCER COUNTY NATIONAL BANK (HARRODSBURG, KY)
Each share Common $100 par exchanged for (20) shares Common $10 par 3/10/72
Merged into Citizens Fidelity Corp. 12/29/86
Each share Common $10 par exchanged for $400 cash

MERCER FUND, INC. (NY)
Completely liquidated 11/2/67
Each share Capital Stock $1 par exchanged for first and final distribution of (0.81724) share Steadman American Industry Fund, Inc. Common $1 par
Steadman American Industry Fund, Inc. name changed to Ameritor Industry Fund 9/23/98
(See Ameritor Industry Fund)

MERCER GOLD CORP (NV)
Each share old Common $0.001 par exchanged for (0.25) share new Common $0.001 par 05/12/2011
Name changed to Tresoro Mining Corp. 11/04/2011
(See Tresoro Mining Corp.)

MERCER INS GROUP INC (PA)
Acquired by United Fire & Casualty Co. 03/28/2011
Each share Common no par exchanged for $28.25 cash

MERCERSBURG FINL CORP (PA)
Common no par split (2) for (1) by issuance of (1) additional share payable 04/10/2000 to holders of record 04/10/2000
Merged into Orrstown Financial Services, Inc. 10/01/2018
Each share Common no par exchanged for (1.5291) shares Common no par

MERCHANDISE CREATIONS INC (NV)
Each share old Common $0.0001 par exchanged for (20) shares new Common $0.001 par 12/11/2006
Name changed to Intelligentias, Inc. 01/03/2007
(See Intelligentias, Inc.)

MERCHANDISE ENTMT TELEVISION HLDGS INC (DE)
Recapitalized as World Sports Licensing Corp. 11/29/99
Each share Common $0.00001 par exchanged for (0.01) share Common $0.00001 par
World Sports Licensing Corp. reorganized as Choice Sports Network, Inc. 3/14/2000 which name changed to Sports Entertainment & Learning Network Inc. 9/15/2000

MERCHANDISE NATL BK (CHICAGO, IL)
Each share Capital Stock $100 par exchanged for (5) shares Capital Stock $40 par to effect a (5) for (2) split and a 100% stock dividend 00/00/1946

Each share Capital Stock $40 par exchanged for (6) shares Capital Stock $10 par to effect a (4) for (1) split and a 50% stock dividend 00/00/1953

Stock Dividends - 10% 12/11/1956; 11-1/9% 12/14/1960; 10% 11/07/1963; 13.6363% 12/14/1965; 20% 07/01/1968

Merged into Edgewood Bancshares Inc. 12/30/1988

Each share Capital Stock $10 par exchanged for $56.75 cash

MERCHANT BK CALIF (BEVERLY HILLS, CA)
Stock Dividend - 25% 6/1/84
Placed in receivership 6/8/90
No stockholders' equity

MERCHANT BK CORP (GA)
Merged into Bank South Corp. 3/11/94

Each share Common no par exchanged for (0.5949) share Common $5 par

Bank South Corp. merged into NationsBank Corp. 1/9/96 which reincorporated in Delaware as BankAmerica Corp. (Old) 9/25/98 which merged into BankAmerica Corp. (New) 9/30/98 which name changed to Bank of America Corp. 4/28/99

MERCHANT CAP ENTERPRISES INC (DE)
Name changed to International Telecom Services, Inc. 01/25/1993
International Telecom Services, Inc. name changed to Bullet Sports International, Inc. 03/31/1995
(See Bullet Sports International, Inc.)

MERCHANT CAP GROUP INC (ON)
Each share old Common no par exchanged for (0.14285714) share new Common no par 11/22/2000
Delisted from the Toronto Venture Stock Exchange 04/20/2004

MERCHANT PRINCE CORP (DE)
Charter cancelled and declared inoperative and void for non-payment of taxes 3/1/77

MERCHANT PRIVATE LTD (ON)
Name changed to Connor Clark Ltd. 5/26/97
(See Connor Clark Ltd.)

MERCHANT RES INC (AB)
Recapitalized as Osprey Energy Ltd. 8/10/90
Each share Common no par exchanged for (0.5) share Common no par
(See Osprey Energy Ltd.)

MERCHANT ONLINE COM INC (FL)
Common $0.001 par split (2) for (1) by issuance of (1) additional share payable 05/22/2000 to holders of record 05/01/2000
Chapter 7 bankruptcy proceedings terminated 12/10/2004
Stockholders' equity unlikely

MERCHANTS & FARMERS BANK (MERIDIAN, MS)
Merged into Deposit Guaranty National Bank (Jackson, MS) 12/1/84
Each share Capital Stock $10 par exchanged for $150 cash

MERCHANTS & FMRS BK (PORTSMOUTH, VA)
Merged into Dominion Banksharcs Corp. 05/01/1974
Each share Capital Stock $30 par exchanged for (2.625) shares Common $5 par

Dominion Bankshares Corp. merged into First Union Corp. 03/01/1993 which name changed to Wachovia Corp. (Ctfs. dated after 09/01/2001) 09/01/2001 which merged into Wells Fargo & Co. (New) 12/31/2008

MERCHANTS & MANUFACTURERS FIRE INSURANCE CO.
Merged into Merchants & Manufacturers Insurance Co. of New York on a share for share basis in 1939

Merchants & Manufacturers Insurance Co. of New York merged into American Equitable Assurance Co. of New York 12/31/60 which merged into Reliance Insurance Co. 6/30/65
(See Reliance Insurance Co.)

MERCHANTS & MANUFACTURERS INSURANCE CO. OF NEW YORK (NY)
Merged into American Equitable Assurance Co. of New York on a (0.72) for (1) basis 12/31/60
American Equitable Assurance Co. of New York merged into Reliance Insurance Co. 6/30/65
(See Reliance Insurance Co.)

MERCHANTS & MANUFACTURERS SECURITIES CO.
Merged into Domestic Industries, Inc. in 1943

Each share Preferred exchanged for (0.85) share Preferred $25 par and (2) shares Class A Common $1 par
Class A & B Common exchanged share for share

Domestic Industries Inc. name changed to Domestic Credit Corp. in 1946 which name was changed to Domestic Finance Corp. (Del.) (New) which merged into American Investment Co. of Illinois which name was changed to American Investment Co. 11/30/63
(See American Investment Co.)

MERCHANTS & MFRS BANCORPORATION INC (WI)
Common $1 par split (3) for (2) by issuance of (0.5) additional share payable 04/13/1998 to holders of record 04/01/1998
Stock Dividends - 10% payable 10/15/1998 to holders of record 10/01/1998; 10% payable 12/15/2003 to holders of record 12/01/2003
Merged into Bank of Montreal (Montreal, QUE) 02/29/2008
Each share Common $1 par exchanged for $37.30 cash

MERCHANTS & MINERS TRANSPORTATION CO.
Liquidation completed in 1952

MERCHANTS & PLANTERS NATL BK (SHERMAN, TX)
Each share Common $50 par exchanged for (5) shares Common $10 par 3/8/60
Stock Dividends - 11-1/9% 2/15/66; 100% 4/15/80
Merged into Mercantile Texas Corp. 9/14/82
Each share Common $10 par exchanged for (3.025) shares Common $5 par
Mercantile Texas Corp. name changed to MCorp 10/11/84
(See MCorp)

MERCHANTS ACCEPTANCE CORP. (MA)
Each share 8% Preferred exchanged for (2) shares Class A no par 00/00/1936 which was redeemed 00/00/1948
Each share old Common no par exchanged for (2) shares new Common no par 00/00/1948
$1.50 Cv. Preferred no par called for redemption 10/01/1968

Acquired by Transamerica Corp. 11/04/1968
Each share Class A Common no par exchanged for (0.2051) share $4.80 Conv. Preferred $100 par
Each share new Common no par exchanged for (1.1524) shares Common $2 par
Transamerica Corp. merged into Aegon N.V. 07/21/1999

MERCHANTS BAKERY, INC. (VA)
Completely liquidated 3/4/77
Each share Common $1 par exchanged for first and final distribution of $29.37 cash

MERCHANTS BANCORP (OR)
Common $1 par split (2) for (1) by issuance of (1) additional share payable 08/15/2003 to holders of record 07/31/2003 Ex date - 08/18/2003
Stock Dividends - 10% payable 02/23/2001 to holders of record 01/31/2001 Ex date - 01/29/2001; 10% payable 02/23/2002 to holders of record 01/31/2002 Ex date - 01/30/2002; 10% payable 02/28/2003 to holders of record 01/31/2003 Ex date - 01/29/2003; 10% payable 03/15/2004 to holders of record 02/29/2004 Ex date - 02/25/2004; 10% payable 02/28/2005 to holders of record 02/15/2005 Ex date - 02/11/2005; 10% payable 02/28/2006 to holders of record 02/15/2006 Ex date - 02/13/2006; 10% payable 02/28/2007 to holders of record 02/16/2007 Ex date - 02/14/2007
Name changed to Sortis Holdings, Inc. 07/03/2017

MERCHANTS BANCORP INC (CT)
Common $1.25 par split (2) for (1) by issuance of (1) additional share 09/01/1986
Stock Dividend - 10% 10/02/1989
Charter forfeited 07/31/1992

MERCHANTS BANCORP INC (DE)
Common $15 par split (2) for (1) by issuance of (1) additional share 09/30/1987
Common $15 par changed to $1 par and (2) additional shares issued 05/13/1993
Common $1 par split (2) for (1) by issuance of (1) additional share payable 09/30/1997 to holders of record 09/15/1997
Merged into Old Kent Financial Corp. 02/11/2000
Each share Common $1 par exchanged for (0.83) share Common $1 par
Old Kent Financial Corp. merged into Fifth Third Bancorp 04/02/2001

MERCHANTS BANCORP INC (PA)
Common $3 par split (2) for (1) by issuance of (1) additional share 08/14/1985
Conv. Class A Preferred $3 par called for redemption 09/30/1986
Acquired by Fidelcor, Inc. 12/31/1986
Each share Common $3 par exchanged for (1.163) shares Common $1 par
Fidelcor, Inc. merged into First Fidelity Bancorporation (New) 02/29/1988 which merged into First Union Corp. 01/01/1996 which name changed to Wachovia Corp. (Ctfs. dated after 09/01/2001) 09/01/2001 which merged into Wells Fargo & Co. (New) 12/31/2008

MERCHANTS BANCORPORATION (KS)
Merged into MidAmerican Corp. 08/29/1989
Each share Common $10 par exchanged for (1) share Common $5 par
MidAmerican Corp. merged into Mercantile Bancorporation, Inc.

01/04/1993 which merged into Firstar Corp. (New) 09/20/1999 which merged into U.S. Bancorp (New) 02/27/2001

MERCHANTS BANCSHARES INC (DE)
Common 1¢ par split (3) for (2) by issuance of (0.5) additional share payable 12/14/2001 to holders of record 11/30/2001 Ex date - 12/17/2001
Merged into Community Bank System, Inc. 05/12/2017
Each share Common 1¢ par exchanged for (0.6741) share Common $1 par and $12 cash

MERCHANTS BANCSHARES INC (MS)
Merged into Whitney Holding Corp. 04/18/1997
Each share Common no par exchanged for (7.7879) shares Common no par
Whitney Holding Corp. merged into Hancock Holding Co. 06/04/2011 which name changed to Hancock Whitney Corp. 05/25/2018

MERCHANTS BANCSHARES INC (TX)
Merged into Union Planters Corp. 07/31/1998
Each share Common $1 par exchanged for (1.0345) shares Common $5 par
Union Planters Corp. merged into Regions Financial Corp. (New) 07/01/2004

MERCHANTS BK & TR CO (NORWALK, CT)
Each share old Capital Stock $25 par exchanged for (0.25) share new Capital Stock $25 par 12/05/1933
Capital Stock $25 par changed to $10 par and (2) additional shares issued 07/01/1958
Capital Stock $10 par changed to $2.50 par and (3) additional shares issued 06/01/1970
Capital Stock $2.50 par changed to $1.25 par and (1) additional share issued 07/15/1983
Stock Dividends - 100% 06/01/1945; 10% 01/01/1964; 20% 04/01/1968
Under plan of reorganization each share Capital Stock $1.25 par automatically became (1) share Merchants Bancorp, Inc. Common $1.25 par 12/31/1984
(See Merchants Bancorp, Inc.)

MERCHANTS BK (BURLINGTON, VT)
Capital Stock $5 par changed to $2.50 par and (1) additional share issued 09/15/1981
Reorganized as Merchants Bancshares, Inc. (DE) 01/27/1984
Each share Capital Stock $2.50 par exchanged for (1) share Common 1¢ par
Merchants Bancshares, Inc. merged into Community Bank System, Inc. 05/12/2017

MERCHANTS BK (GRESHAM, OR)
Common $1 par split (4) for (1) by issuance of (3) additional shares payable 06/30/1999 to holders of record 06/15/1999
Stock Dividend - 10% payable 02/15/2000 to holders of record 12/31/1999
Under plan of reorganization each share Common $1 par automatically became (1) share Merchants Bancorp Common $1 par 06/15/2000
Merchants Bancorp name changed to Sortis Holdings, Inc. 07/03/2017

MERCHANTS BK (PORT ARTHUR, TX)
Reorganized as Allied Bancshares, Inc. (TX) 12/29/1972
Each share Capital Stock $2.50 par

exchanged for (1) share Common $1 par
Allied Bancshares, Inc. (TX) reincorporated in Delaware 04/22/1987 which merged into First Interstate Bancorp 01/29/1988 which merged into Wells Fargo & Co. (Old) 04/01/1996 which merged into Wells Fargo & Co. (New) 11/02/1998

MERCHANTS BANK BUILDING, INC.
Liquidated in 1943

MERCHANTS BK NEW YORK (NEW YORK, NY)
Each share Common $100 par exchanged for (4) shares Common $25 par in 1946
Common $25 par changed to $12.50 par and (1) additional share issued 10/20/58
Common $12.50 par changed to $6.25 par and (1) additional share issued 12/28/62
Common $6.25 par changed to $3.125 par and (1) additional share issued 4/30/73
Common $3.125 par changed to $2.604167 par and (0.2) additional share issued 4/15/87
Common $2.604167 par changed to $2.0833336 par and (0.25) additional share issued 7/20/88
Common $2.0833336 par changed to $1.389 par and (0.5) additional share issued 5/30/90
Stock Dividends - 25% 12/10/45; 10% 12/29/81; 10% 12/28/82; 10% 12/23/83; 10% 12/21/84; 10% 12/21/85
Under plan of reorganization each share Common $1.389 par automatically became (1) share Merchants New York Bancorp, Inc. Common $1.389 par 7/1/93

MERCHANTS BLDG MAINTENANCE CO (CA)
Under plan of merger each share Common 10¢ par exchanged for $2.50 cash

MERCHANTS CAP CORP (DE)
Charter cancelled and declared inoperative and void for non-payment of taxes 3/1/91

MERCHANTS CAP CORP (MS)
Merged into BancorpSouth Inc. 12/04/1998
Each share Common no par exchanged for (3.768) shares Common $2.50 par
BancorpSouth Inc. reorganized as BancorpSouth Bank (Tupelo, MS) 11/01/2017

MERCHANTS CO OPERATIVE BK (BOSTON, MA)
Name changed to MerchantsBank of Boston A Co-Operative Bank (Boston, MA) 9/19/85
MerchantsBank of Boston, A Co-Operative Bank (Boston, MA) reorganized as Merchants Capital Corp. 8/6/87
(See Merchants Capital Corp.)

MERCHANTS CORP. (ME)
Liquidated for shares of Merchants National Bank (Bangor, Me.) and cash 12/28/91
(See Merchants National Bank (Bangor, Me.))

MERCHANTS DISTILLING CORP. (IN)
Reorganized 9/10/57
No stockholders' equity

MERCHANTS FAST MOTOR LINES, INC. (DE)
Name changed to Merchants Inc. 9/30/68
(See Merchants Inc.)

MERCHANTS GROUP INC (DE)
Acquired by American European Group, Inc. 3/30/2007
Each share Common 1¢ par exchanged for $33.2438 cash

MERCHANTS HLDG CO (MN)
Common 10¢ par split (3) for (1) by issuance of (2) additional shares payable 12/20/99 to holders of record 10/22/99
Name changed to Merchants Financial Group Inc. 11/4/99

MERCHANTS ICE & COLD STORAGE CO (CA)
Preferred $10 par called for redemption 08/31/1967
Liquidated and subsequently dissolved 03/19/1976
Details not available

MERCHANTS ICE & COLD STORAGE CO (KY)
Each share Common $25 par exchanged for (5) shares Common $5 par 05/15/1956
Reacquired 00/00/1980
Details not available

MERCHANTS INC (DE)
Common $1 par split (3) for (2) by issuance of (0.5) additional share 07/30/1971
Stock Dividend - 50% 07/28/1972
Liquidation completed
Each share Common $1 par exchanged for initial distribution of $26.50 cash 08/20/1979
Each share Common $1 par received second and final distribution of $0.1280407 cash 12/12/1979

MERCHANTS INDS INC (DE)
Charter cancelled and declared inoperative and void for non-payment of taxes 03/01/1993

MERCHANTS INSURANCE CO. OF PROVIDENCE (RI)
Merged into Rhode Island Insurance Co. share for share in 1940
(See Rhode Island Insurance Co.)

MERCHANTS INTL CORP (UT)
Recapitalized as In-Tec International (U.S.A.), Inc. (UT) 6/18/84
Each share Common 1¢ par exchanged for (0.05) share Common 1¢ par
In-Tec International (U.S.A.), Inc. (UT) reincorporated in Delaware as Seed Products International, Inc. 6/25/87

MERCHANTS LACLEDE SECURITIES CO.
Liquidated in 1942

MERCHANTS MORTGAGE CO., INC. (MA)
Name changed back to Farragut Mortgage Co., Inc. 3/4/91

MERCHANTS N Y BANCORP INC (NY)
Common $0.001 par split (2) for (1) by issuance of (1) additional share 10/2/95
Common $0.001 par split (2) for (1) by issuance of (1) additional share payable 10/7/97 to holders of record 9/19/97
Common $0.001 par split (2) for (1) by issuance of (1) additional share payable 10/1/99 to holders of record 9/21/99
Merged into Valley National Bancorp, Inc. 1/19/2001
Each share Common $0.001 par exchanged for (0.7634) share Common no par

MERCHANTS NATIONAL BANK & TRUST CO. (FARGO, ND)
Name changed to First Bank of North Dakota N.A. (Fargo, ND) 05/05/1977
(See First Bank of North Dakota N.A. (Fargo, ND))

MERCHANTS NATL BK & TR CO (INDIANAPOLIS, IN)
Stock Dividends - 10% 11/04/1957; 10% 07/14/1959; 10% 10/09/1961; 16% 07/19/1963; 100% 03/03/1969
Under plan of reorganization each share Common $10 par automatically became (1) share Merchants National Corp. Common no par 01/03/1972
Merchants National Corp. merged into National City Corp. 05/02/1992 which was acquired by PNC Financial Services Group, Inc. 12/31/2008

MERCHANTS NATL BK & TR CO (SYRACUSE, NY)
Each share Capital Stock $20 par exchanged for (2) shares Capital Stock $10 par 00/00/1950
99% acquired through exchange offer by Charter New York Corp. as of 12/31/1970
Public interest eliminated

MERCHANTS NATL BK (ALLENTOWN, PA)
Each share Capital Stock $25 par exchanged for (3) shares Capital Stock $12.50 par to effect a (2) for (1) split and a 50% stock dividend 01/14/1958
Capital Stock $12.50 par changed to $10 par and a 20% stock dividend paid 10/22/1962
Capital Stock $10 par changed to $5 par and (1) additional share issued 04/01/1972
Capital Stock $5 par changed to $3 par and (2/3) additional share issued 05/01/1981
Stock Dividend - 10% 03/01/1967
Under plan of reorganization each share Capital Stock $3 par automatically became (1) share Merchants Bancorp, Inc. (PA) Common $3 par 06/01/1982
Merchants Bancorp, Inc. (PA) acquired by Fidelcor, Inc. 12/31/1986 which merged into First Fidelity Bancorporation (New) 02/29/1988 which merged into First Union Corp. 01/01/1996 which name changed to Wachovia Corp. (Ctfs. dated after 09/01/2001) 09/01/2001 which merged into Wells Fargo & Co. (New) 12/31/2008

MERCHANTS NATL BK (AURORA, IL)
Capital Stock $0.66666666 par changed to $100 par 00/00/1943
Each share Capital Stock $100 par exchanged for (5) shares Capital Stock $25 par to effect a (4) for (1) split and a 25% stock dividend 00/00/1945
Capital Stock $25 par changed to $15 par and (1) additional share issued 03/10/1970
Stock Dividend - 100% 03/15/1966
Reorganized as Merchants Bancorp, Inc. 05/03/1982
Each share Capital Stock $15 par exchanged for (1) share Common $15 par
Merchants Bancorp, Inc. merged into Old Kent Financial 02/11/2000

MERCHANTS NATL BK (BANGOR, ME)
Each share Capital Stock $100 par exchanged for (5) shares Capital Stock $20 par 12/19/1961
Merged into Maine National Bank (Portland, ME) 02/12/1982
Each share Capital Stock $20 par exchanged for (3.5) shares Capital Stock $10 par
Maine National Bank (Portland, ME) reorganized as Maine National Corp. 02/18/1983 which merged into Bank of New England Corp. 12/18/1985
(See Bank of New England Corp.)

MERCHANTS NATL BK (BANGOR, PA)
Under plan of reorganization each share Common $25 par automatically became (1) share MNB Corp. Common $25 par 9/28/94

MERCHANTS NATIONAL BANK (BOSTON, MA)
Each share Capital Stock $100 par exchanged for (10) shares Capital Stock $10 par 06/09/1955
Stock Dividend - 14.28571428% 02/15/1960
Merged into New England Merchants National Bank (Boston, MA) 12/31/1960
Each share Capital Stock $10 par exchanged for (1) share Capital Stock $10 par
New England Merchants National Bank (Boston, MA) reorganized in Delaware as New England Merchants Co., Inc. 06/18/1970 which reincorporated in Massachusetts 03/31/1971 which name changed to Bank of New England Corp. 05/01/1982
(See Bank of New England Corp.)

MERCHANTS NATL BK (BURLINGTON, VT)
Capital Stock $10 par changed to $5 par and (1) additional share issued 03/01/1972
Name changed to Merchants Bank (Burlington, VT) 09/06/1974
Merchants Bank (Burlington, VT) reorganized as Merchants Bancshares, Inc. (DE) 01/27/1984 which merged into Community Bank System, Inc. 05/12/2017

MERCHANTS NATL BK (CEDAR RAPIDS, IA)
Stock Dividends - 100% 06/21/1955; 100% 05/26/1967
Reorganized as Banks of Iowa, Inc. 09/02/1969
Each share Capital Stock $100 par exchanged for (20) shares Common $5 par
Banks of Iowa, Inc. merged into Firstar Corp. (Old) 04/29/1991 which merged into Firstar Corp. (New) 11/20/1998 which merged into U.S. Bancorp (DE) 02/27/2001

MERCHANTS NATIONAL BANK (CHICAGO, IL)
Each share Capital Stock $100 par exchanged for (7.5) shares Capital Stock $20 par to effect a (5) for (1) split and 50% stock dividend 00/00/1946
Stock Dividends - 50% 04/10/1945; 33-1/3% 01/26/1953; 25% 10/25/1954; 25% 01/26/1959
Merged into Central National Bank (Chicago, IL) 03/09/1962
Each share Capital Stock $20 par exchanged for (1.5) shares Capital Stock $10 par
Central National Bank (Chicago, IL) reorganized as Central National Chicago Corp. 09/30/1969 which merged into Exchange International Corp. 08/21/1982 which name changed to Exchange Bancorp, Inc. 05/17/1988
(See Exchange Bancorp, Inc.)

MERCHANTS NATL BK (FORT SMITH, AR)
Stock Dividends - 10% 12/00/1949; 100% 05/31/1958
Acquired by Deposit Guaranty Corp. 08/11/1997
Details not available

MERCHANTS NATL BK (HILLSBORO, OH)
Reorganized as Merchants Bancorp, Inc. 12/31/96
Each share Common no par exchanged for (10) shares Common no par

MERCHANTS NATIONAL BANK (INDIANAPOLIS, IN)
Each share Capital Stock $100 par exchanged for (15) shares Capital Stock $10 par to effect a (10) for (1)

split and a 50% stock dividend 00/00/1948
Merged into Merchants National Bank & Trust Co. (Indianapolis, IN) 09/30/1953
Each share Capital Stock $10 par exchanged for (1) share Capital Stock $10 par
Merchants National Bank & Trust Co. (Indianapolis, IN) reorganized as Merchants National Corp. 01/03/1972 which merged into National City Corp. 05/02/1992 which was acquired by PNC Financial Services Group, Inc. 12/31/2008

MERCHANTS NATL BK (MOBILE, AL)
Capital Stock $20 par changed to $10 par and (1) additional share issued 02/17/1960
Capital Stock $10 par changed to $2.50 par and (3) additional shares issued 02/23/1973
Stock Dividends - 20% 01/25/1954; 16-2/3% 02/18/1955; 10% 03/05/1970
Merged into Southland Bancorporation 02/28/1975
Each share Capital Stock $2.50 par exchanged for (1) share Common $2.50 par
Southland Bancorporation name changed to Colonial BancGroup, Inc. 12/31/1981
(See Colonial BancGroup, Inc.)

MERCHANTS NATL BK (MUNCIE, IN)
Capital Stock $100 par changed to $10 par and (9) additional shares issued plus a 33-1/3% stock dividend paid 02/19/1959
Stock Dividends - 66-2/3% 11/19/1946; 20% 11/20/1963; 25% 02/01/1966; 33-1/3% 02/01/1968; 15% 02/27/1970
Under plan of reorganization each share Capital Stock $10 par automatically became (1) share First Merchants Corp. Common no par 06/14/1983

MERCHANTS NATL BK (NEW BEDFORD, MA)
Capital Stock $20 par changed to $10 par and (1) additional share issued plus a 100% stock dividend paid 02/07/1956
Stock Dividend - 20% 01/17/1946
Name changed to Baybank Merchants, N.A. (New Bedford, MA) 02/02/1976

MERCHANTS NATL BK (PORT ARTHUR, TX)
Capital Stock $50 par changed to $10 par and a (5) for (1) stock split effected 00/00/1956
Stock Dividends - 16-2/3% 02/14/1958; 14-2/7% 03/18/1960
Recapitalized as Merchants Bank (Port Arthur, TX) 04/19/1971
Each share Capital Stock $10 par exchanged for (4.4) shares Capital Stock $2.50 par to effect a (4) for (1) split plus a 10% stock dividend
Merchants Bank (Port Arthur, TX) reorganized as Allied Bancshares, Inc. (TX) 12/29/1972 which reincorporated in Delaware 04/22/1987 which merged into First Interstate Bancorp 01/29/1988 which merged into Wells Fargo & Co. (Old) 04/01/1996 which merged into Wells Fargo & Co. (New) 11/02/1998

MERCHANTS NATL BK (SHENANDOAH, PA)
Reorganized as Merchants of Shenandoah Ban-Corp 10/15/1984
Each share Common $100 par exchanged for (10) shares Common no par
Merchants of Shenandoah Ban-Corp merged into First Leesport Bancorp, Inc. 07/01/1999 which name changed to Leesport Financial Corp. 04/01/2002 which name changed to VIST Financial Corp. 03/03/2008 which merged into Tompkins Financial Corp. 08/01/2012

MERCHANTS NATL BK (TERRE HAUTE, IN)
Each share Capital Stock $100 par exchanged for (4) shares Capital Stock $25 par plus a 50% stock dividend paid 09/15/1959
Under plan of reorganization each share Capital Stock $25 par automatically became (1) share Merchants Republic Corp. Common no par 08/31/1984
(See Merchants Republic Corp.)

MERCHANTS NATL BK (TOPEKA, KS)
Each share Capital Stock $100 par exchanged for (4) shares Capital Stock $25 par 00/00/1950
Capital Stock $25 par changed to $10 par and (1.5) additional shares issued 01/29/1963
Stock Dividends - 50% 12/21/1943; 50% 11/01/1950; 25% 10/18/1958; 12-1/2% 12/08/1960; 11-1/9% 01/16/1962; 20% 03/02/1966; 10% 03/01/1968; 21.21% 02/15/1971; 25% 04/02/1974
Reorganized as Merchants Bancorporation 07/01/1982
Each share Capital Stock $10 par exchanged for (1) share Common $10 par
Merchants Bancorporation merged into MidAmerican Corp. 08/29/1989 which merged into Mercantile Bancorporation, Inc. 01/04/1993 which merged into Firstar Corp. (New) 09/20/1999 which merged into U.S. Bancorp (DE) 02/27/2001

MERCHANTS NATL BK (WINONA, MN)
Stock Dividends - 20% 01/28/1960; 25% 02/10/1964; 50% 03/05/1970
Under plan of reorganization each share Common $50 par automatically became (1) share Merchants Holding Co. Common 10¢ par 11/01/1984
Merchants Holding Co. name changed to Merchants Financial Group Inc. 11/04/1999

MERCHANTS NATL CORP (IN)
Common no par split (2) for (1) by issuance of (1) additional share 05/21/1973
Common no par split (3) for (2) by issuance of (0.5) additional share 06/17/1985
Common no par split (2) for (1) by issuance of (1) additional share 05/23/1986
Merged into National City Corp. 05/02/1992
Each share Common no par exchanged for (1.12) shares Common $4 par
National City Corp. acquired by PNC Financial Services Group, Inc. 12/31/2008

MERCHANTS PETE CO (CA)
Capital Stock $1 par changed to 25¢ par 4/12/57
Merged into Damson Oil Corp. 3/28/79
Each share Capital Stock 25¢ par exchanged for (0.565) share Common 40¢ par
(See Damson Oil Corp.)

MERCHANTS PRODUCE BK (KANSAS CITY, MO)
99.9% acquired by Merchants Bancorp, Inc. through exchange offer which expired 06/04/1969
Public interest eliminated

MERCHANTS REFRIGERATING CO (NY)
Common no par changed to Class B no par 00/00/1945
Each share Class A no par or Class B no par exchanged for (2) shares Common $1 par 00/00/1956
Merged into Pet Inc. 09/17/1969
Each share Common $1 par exchanged for (0.6) share $1 Conv. 2nd Preferred no par and (1) share Common no par
(See Pet Inc.)

MERCHANTS REP CORP (IN)
Merged into Old National Bancorp 09/30/1985
Each share Common no par exchanged for $110.32 cash

MERCHANTS SVGS BK (MANCHESTER, NH)
Name changed to Numerica Savings Bank, FSB (Manchester, NH) 04/01/1985
Numerica Savings Bank, FSB (Manchester, NH) reorganized as Numerica Financial Corp. 10/03/1985
(See Numerica Financial Corp.)

MERCHANTS SHENANDOAH BAN CORP (PA)
Stock Dividend - 5% payable 07/01/1998 to holders of record 06/17/1998
Merged into First Leesport Bancorp, Inc. 07/01/1999
Each share Common no par exchanged for (1.5854) shares Common $5 par
First Leesport Bancorp, Inc. name changed to Leesport Financial Corp. 04/01/2002 which name changed to VIST Financial Corp. 03/03/2008 which merged into Tompkins Financial Corp. 08/01/2012

MERCHANTS WELCOME SERVICE, INC. (DE)
Name changed to Auto-Data Systems, Inc. 8/9/72
Auto-Data Systems, Inc. charter cancelled 3/1/80

MERCHANTSBANK BOSTON CO-OPERATIVE BK (BOSTON, MA)
Common $1 par reclassified as Conv. Class B Common $1 par 06/30/1986
Class A Common $1 par split (3) for (2) by issuance of (0.5) additional share 03/31/1987
Reorganized under the laws of Delaware as Merchants Capital Corp. 08/06/1987
Each share Class A Common $1 par exchanged for (1) share Class A Common 10¢ par
Each share Conv. Class B Common $1 par exchanged for (1) share Conv. Class B Common 10¢ par
(See Merchants Capital Corp.)

MERCIER MINES LTD.
Dissolved in 1948

MERCK & CO INC NEW (NJ)
Each share 6% Conv. Preferred $1 par exchanged for (4.6719) shares Common 50¢ par and $85.06 cash 08/13/2010
(Additional Information in Active)

MERCK & CO INC OLD (NJ)
8% Preferred $100 par reclassified as 6% Preferred $100 par 00/00/1935
6% Preferred $100 par reclassified as 5-1/4% Preferred $100 par 00/00/1941
4-1/4% Preferred no par called for redemption 06/17/1946
5-1/4% Preferred $100 par called for redemption 06/17/1946
Each share Common $1 par exchanged for (2) shares Common 50¢ par 00/00/1949
$4 2nd Preferred no par called for redemption 10/31/1950
Each share Common 50¢ par exchanged for (3) shares Common 16-2/3¢ par 00/00/1951
$4.25 2nd Preferred no par called for redemption 02/02/1956
$4 Conv. 2nd Preferred no par called for redemption 10/24/1958
Common 16-2/3¢ par changed to 5-5/9¢ par and (2) additional shares issued 05/26/1964
Common 5-5/9¢ par changed to 2-7/9¢ par and (1) additional share issued 05/31/1972
$3.50 Preferred no par called for redemption 08/25/1980
Common 2-7/9¢ par changed to no par and (1) additional share issued 05/23/1986
Common no par split (3) for (1) by issuance of (2) additional shares 05/25/1988
Common no par split (3) for (1) by issuance of (2) additional shares 05/22/1992
Common no par changed to 1¢ par and (1) additional share issued payable 02/16/1999 to holders of record 01/25/1999 Ex date - 02/17/1999
Each share Common 1¢ par received distribution of (0.1206) share Medco Health Solutions, Inc. Common 1¢ par payable 08/19/2003 to holders of record 08/12/2003 Ex date - 08/20/2003
Under plan of merger each share Common 1¢ par automatically became (1) share Merck & Co., Inc. (New) Common 50¢ par 11/03/2009

MERCK CORP.
Recapitalized as Merck & Co., Inc. (Old) 00/00/1934
Details not available

MERCK SERONO S A (SWITZERLAND)
Acquired by Merck KGaA 03/07/2008
Each Sponsored ADR for Ordinary exchanged for $22.75076 cash

MERCO ENTERPRISES INC (NY)
Merged into Capitol Industries, Inc. 03/31/1970
Each share Class A 10¢ par exchanged for (0.7275) share Common 10¢ par
Capitol Industries, Inc. name changed to Capitol Industries-EMI, Inc. 01/02/1974
(See Capitol Industries-EMI, Inc.)

MERCOM INC (MI)
Merged into Mercom Acquisition 3/26/99
Each share Common $1 par exchanged for $12 cash

MERCRISTO DEVS INC (DE)
Recapitalized as Addison Industries Inc. (DE) 01/11/1999
Each share Common $0.001 par exchanged for (1/6) share Common $0.001 par
Addison Industries Inc. (DE) reorganized in Nevada as Bonanza Land Holdings, Inc. 05/16/2006 which name changed to VLinx Technology, Inc. 11/08/2011 which name changed to Vision Plasma Systems, Inc. 04/03/2012

MERCULITE DISTRG INC (NV)
Name changed to Blackcraft Cult, Inc. 03/27/2014

MERCUR DOME GOLD MINING CO. (UT)
Name changed to Strategic Automated Systems International, Inc. (UT) 2/14/69
Strategic Automated Systems International Inc. (UT) reincorporated in Delaware 3/7/72 which name changed to Superblock Industries Inc. 6/30/78 which recapitalized as Trilogy Gaming

Corp. 3/7/96 which name changed to TELnet go 2000, Inc. 1/1/2000

MERCUR DOME GOLD MNG INC (UT)
Reorganized as International Products Inc. 04/03/1980
Each share Common 1¢ par exchanged for (3) shares Common no par
(See International Products Inc.)

MERCUR ENTERPRISES INC (FL)
Name changed to Auto Metreks Inc. 01/13/1997
Auto Metreks Inc. recapitalized as Online Hearing.com Co. 04/06/1999 which name changed to Rompus Interactive Corp. 07/30/1999
(See Rompus Interactive Corp.)

MERCURIA INDS LTD (BC)
Struck off register and declared dissolved for failure to file returns 05/28/1979

MERCURY & CHEMICALS CORP. (DE)
No longer in existence having become inoperative and void for non-payment of taxes 4/1/59

MERCURY ACQUISITIONS INC (NV)
Name changed to Vista Technologies Inc. 03/30/1994
(See Vista Technologies Inc.)

MERCURY AIR GROUP INC (DE)
Reincorporated 3/1/2001
Common 25¢ par changed to 1¢ par 4/30/91
8% Conv. Preferred Ser. A 1¢ par called for redemption 1/28/94
Common 1¢ par split (5) for (4) by issuance of (0.25) additional share payable 4/11/97 to holders of record 3/27/97 Ex date - 4/14/97
Stock Dividend - 10% 6/16/95; 10% payable 5/1/96 to holders of record 4/17/96
State of incorporation changed from (NY) to (DE) 3/1/2001
Each share old Common 1¢ par exchanged for (0.5) share new Common 1¢ par 6/18/2003
Each share new Common 1¢ par exchanged again for (1) share new Common 1¢ par to reflect a (1) for (501) reverse split immediately followed by a (501) for (1) forward split 9/16/2005
Note: Holders of (500) or fewer pre-split shares received $4 cash per share
Each (750,000) shares new Common 1¢ par exchanged again for (1) share new Common 1¢ par 9/25/2006
Note: In effect holders received $3.70 cash per share and public interest was eliminated

MERCURY AVIATION COS (OH)
Name changed 02/05/1973
Name changed from Mercury Aviation Corp. to Mercury Aviation Companies 02/05/1973
Charter cancelled by operation of law 01/01/2001

MERCURY CAP CORP (OK)
Each share old Common 20¢ par exchanged for (0.0025) share new Common 20¢ par 2/8/91
Merged into MCC Acquisition Corp. 6/17/94
Each share new Common 20¢ par exchanged for $1 cash

MERCURY CAP LTD (ON)
Reorganized as Canada Coal Inc. 02/29/2012
Each share Common no par exchanged for (1) share Common no par

MERCURY CAP II LTD (ON)
Name changed to Revive Therapeutics Ltd. 01/08/2014

MERCURY CAS CO (CA)
Name changed to Mercury General Corp. 11/30/1968
(See Mercury General Corp.)

MERCURY CHEMICAL CORP. (NJ)
Name changed to Chemical & Pollution Sciences, Inc. 12/1/68
Chemical & Pollution Sciences, Inc. name changed to CPS Chemical Co., Inc. 12/20/79
(See CPS Chemical Co., Inc.)

MERCURY CHIPMAN CO. LTD. (CANADA)
Merged into Dynacore Enterprises Ltd. 07/15/1967
Each share Common no par exchanged for (0.08) share Common no par
Dynacore Enterprises Ltd. recapitalized as Dynaco Resources Ltd. 02/09/1971
(See Dynaco Resources Ltd.)

MERCURY-CHIPMAN KNIT LTD. (CANADA)
Reorganized as Mercury Chipman Co., Ltd. 06/00/1960
Each share Common no par exchanged for (1) share Common no par
Mercury Chipman Co., Ltd. merged into Dynacore Enterprises Ltd. 07/15/1967 which recapitalized as Dynaco Resources Ltd. 02/09/1971
(See Dynaco Resources Ltd.)

MERCURY COMPUTER SYS INC (MA)
Common 1¢ par split (2) for (1) by issuance of (1) additional share payable 12/20/1999 to holders of record 12/06/1999
Name changed to Mercury Systems, Inc. 11/13/2012

MERCURY CONSOLIDATED MINERALS CO. (NV)
Charter revoked 3/6/61 for failure to comply with Nevada corporation laws

MERCURY ELECTRONICS CORP. (NY)
Each share old Common 5¢ par exchanged for (0.1) share new Common 5¢ par 01/10/1977
New Common 5¢ par changed to 1¢ par 03/16/1977
Each share Common 1¢ par exchanged for (7) shares new Common 1¢ par 12/15/1977
Name changed to Airnado, Inc. 11/28/1983
(See Airnado, Inc.)

MERCURY ELECTRS CORP (DE)
Recapitalized as Mercury Industries, Inc. 04/25/1974
Each share Common 1¢ par exchanged for (0.1) share Common 1¢ par
(See Mercury Industries, Inc.)

MERCURY ENTMT CORP (DE)
Each share old Common $0.001 par exchanged for (0.05) share new Common $0.001 par 04/20/1989
Acquired by a private investor 01/20/1992
Each share new Common $0.001 par exchanged for $0.07 cash

MERCURY EXPLS LTD (BC)
Charter cancelled in April 1977

MERCURY FIN CO (DE)
Common $1 par split (4) for (3) by issuance of (1/3) additional share 12/28/89
Common $1 par split (4) for (3) by issuance of (1/3) additional share 10/31/90
Common $1 par split (4) for (3) by issuance of (1/3) additional share 6/10/91
Common $1 par split (4) for (3) by issuance of (1/3) additional share 12/4/91
Common $1 par split (2) for (1) by issuance of (1) additional share 6/18/92
Common $1 par split (4) for (3) by issuance of (1/3) additional share 6/21/93
Common $1 par split (3) for (2) by issuance of (0.5) additional share 10/31/95
Reorganized under Chapter 11 Federal Bankruptcy Code as MFN Financial Corp. 3/10/99
Each share Common $1 par exchanged for (0.00293179) share Common 1¢ par, (0.00340088) Common Stock Purchase Warrant Ser. A expiring 3/23/2002, (0.00340088) Common Stock Purchase Warrant Ser. B expiring 3/23/2003, and (0.00340088) Common Stock Purchase Warrant Ser. C expiring 3/23/2004
(See MFN Financial Corp.)

MERCURY GEN CORP (CA)
Ctfs. dated prior to 01/03/1979
Common $2 par changed to $1 par and (1) additional share issued 06/10/1971
Merged into California General Management, Inc. 01/03/1979
Each share Common $1 par exchanged for $28 cash

MERCURY GOLD MINES, LTD. (ON)
Charter cancelled 12/9/70

MERCURY INDUSTRIES, INC. (DE)
Charter cancelled and declared inoperative and void for non-payment of taxes 6/25/87

MERCURY INTERACTIVE CORP (DE)
Common $0.002 par split (2) for (1) by issuance of (1) additional share payable 02/26/1999 to holders of record 02/12/1999
Common $0.002 par split (2) for (1) by issuance of (1) additional share payable 02/11/2000 to holders of record 01/28/2000
Acquired by Hewlett-Packard Co. 11/07/2006
Each share Common $0.002 par exchanged for $52 cash

MERCURY METALS INC (UT)
Merged into Rial Oil Co. 03/07/1977
Each share Common 3¢ par exchanged for (0.04) share Common 75¢ par
Rial Oil Co. name changed to Sage Energy Co. 06/27/1980
(See Sage Energy Co.)

MERCURY MILLS, LTD. (CANADA)
Each share 6% Preference $100 par exchanged for (3.5) shares new Common no par 00/00/1940
Each share old Common no par exchanged for (0.1) share new Common no par 00/00/1940
Name changed to Mercury-Chipman Knit Ltd. 10/00/1954
Mercury-Chipman Knit Ltd. reorganized as Mercury-Chipman Co. Ltd. 06/00/1960 which merged into Dynacore Enterprises 07/15/1967 which recapitalized as Dynaco Resources Ltd. 02/09/1971
(See Dynaco Resources Ltd.)

MERCURY NATL LIFE INS CO (OK)
Stock Dividends - 10% 5/20/74; 10% 5/5/78
Merged into Mercury Capital Corp. 1/8/81
Each share Common 20¢ par exchanged for (1) share Common 20¢ par
(See Mercury Capital Corp.)

MERCURY OILS LTD. (CANADA)
Merged into Mill City Petroleums Ltd. on a (1) for (0.5) basis 6/15/55
Mill City Petroleums Ltd. liquidated for Pan Ocean Oil Corp. 1/1/72
(See Pan Ocean Oil Corp.)

MERCURY PARTNERS & CO INC (YT)
Name changed to Black Mountain Capital Corp. 05/02/2005
Black Mountain Capital Corp. recapitalized as Grand Peak Capital Corp. (YT) 11/20/2007 which reincorporated in British Columbia 04/27/2010

MERCURY PHOTO CORP. (DE)
Adjudicated bankrupt 4/2/64
Class A & B stocks worthless

MERCURY SAVINGS, A FEDERAL SAVINGS & LOAN ASSOCIATION (CA)
Name changed back to Mercury Savings & Loan Association and Common $1 par reclassified as Guarantee Stock $1 par 8/1/83

MERCURY SVGS & LN ASSN HUNTINGTON BEACH (CA)
Each share Guarantee Stock $10 par exchanged for (39) shares Guarantee Stock $3.33-1/3 par 04/10/1969
Guarantee Stock $3.33-1/3 par changed to $2 par and (2/3) additional share issued 08/12/1971
Guarantee Stock $2 par changed to $1 par and (1) additional share issued 11/10/1972
Name changed to Mercury Savings, a Federal Savings & Loan Association and Guarantee Stock $1 par reclassified as Common $1 par 09/03/1981 which name changed back to Mercury Savings & Loan Association and Common $1 par reclassified as Guarantee Stock $1 par 08/01/1983
Guarantee Stock $1 par reclassified as Common $1 par 07/26/1989
Placed in conservatorship 02/22/1990
No stockholders' equity

MERCURY SCHEDULING SYS INC (BC)
Name changed to Aventine Ventures Inc. 7/8/2003
Aventine Ventures Inc. recapitalized as Pacific Northwest Partners Ltd. (BC) 4/30/2004 which reincorporated in Canada as Enablence Technologies Inc. 7/24/2007

MERCURY SOFTWARE (NV)
Recapitalized as MedEx Corp. 04/15/2002
Each share new Common $0.001 par exchanged for (0.1) share Common $0.001 par
MedEx Corp. name changed to Aussie Apparel Group, Ltd. 10/29/2002 which name changed to Bluetorch Inc. 11/03/2003 which name changed to Pacific Crest Investments 04/25/2005 which name changed to Pacific Peak Investments 05/16/2005 which name changed to Global Beverage Solutions, Inc. 10/26/2005 which recapitalized as Real Brands, Inc. 10/22/2013

MERCURY WASTE SOLUTIONS INC (MN)
Issue Information - 1,000,000 shares COM offered at $5 per share on 02/28/1997
Each share old Common 1¢ par exchanged for (0.00001) share new Common 1¢ par 10/4/2004
Note: In effect holders received $0.104 cash per share and public interest was eliminated

MEREDITH (N.H.) LINEN MILLS
Liquidation approved in 1941

MEREDITH ENTERPRISES INC (DE)
Merged into Meredith Property Trust LLC 07/26/2006
Each share Common 1¢ par exchanged for $15 cash

MEREDITH PUBLISHING CO. (IA)
Common $1 par changed to $10 par 00/00/1948
Each share Common $10 par exchanged for (2) shares Common $5 par 00/00/1953
Stock Dividend - 100% 10/29/1965
Name changed to Meredith Corp. 10/17/1967 10/17/67

MERENDON CDA INC (AB)
Recapitalized as Richfield Explorations Inc. 03/08/2000
Each share Common no par exchanged for (1/3) share Common no par
(See Richfield Explorations Inc.)

MERET INC (OH)
Charter forfeited for failure to maintain a registered agent 12/26/1995

MERFIN INTL INC. (BC)
Name changed 5/25/87
Name changed 8/22/96
Name changed from Merfin Resources Ltd. to Merfin Hygienic Products Ltd. 5/25/87
Name changed from Merfin Hygienic Products Ltd. to Merfin International Inc. 8/22/96
Merged into Buckeye Acquisition Corp. 5/27/97
Each share Common no par exchanged for $7.50 cash

MERGE CEDARA EXCHANGECO LTD (ON)
Each Non-Vtg. Exchangeable Share no par exchanged for (1) share Merge Healthcare Inc. Common 1¢ par 04/15/2009
(See Merge Healthcare Inc.)

MERGE HEALTHCARE INC (DE)
Reincorporated 12/05/2008
State of incorporation changed from (WI) to (DE) 12/05/2008
Acquired by International Business Machines Corp. 10/13/2015
Each share Common 1¢ par exchanged for $7.13 cash

MERGE TECHNOLOGIES INC (WI)
Name changed to Merge Healthcare Inc. (WI) 02/22/2008
Merge Healthcare Inc. (WI) reincorporated in Delaware 12/05/2008
(See Merge Healthcare Inc.)

MERGECORP INC (AB)
Struck off register and declared dissolved for failure to file returns 4/1/90

MERGENTHALER LINOTYPE CO (NY)
Each share Capital Stock $100 par exchanged for (2) shares Capital Stock no par 00/00/1926
Capital Stock no par changed to $1 par 01/20/1958
Capital Stock $1 par changed to 25¢ par and (3) additional shares issued 03/28/1961
Stock Dividend - 100% 01/18/1951
Merged into Eltra Corp. 06/28/1963
Each share Capital Stock 25¢ par exchanged for (1) share Common 25¢ par
(See Eltra Corp.)

MERGER MINES CORP (AZ)
Capital Stock 1¢ par changed to old Common 10¢ par 00/00/1936
Each share old Common 10¢ par exchanged for (0.001) share new Common 10¢ par 08/19/2014
Note: In effect holders received $0.05 cash per share and public interest was eliminated

MERGER OIL CO. (AZ)
Charter revoked for failure to file reports or fees 12/13/23

MERGERS R US INC (FL)
Name changed to Life Petroleum Inc. 09/00/1989
Life Petroleum Inc. recapitalized as TAG Group, Inc. 08/07/2003
(See TAG Group, Inc.)

MERGEWORTHRX CORP (DE)
Completely liquidated 12/31/2014
Each share Common $0.0001 par exchanged for first and final distribution of $8.36 cash

MERICAN CAP VENTURES INC (CANADA)
Name changed to Encore Tickets Ltd. 12/30/92
(See Encore Tickets Ltd.)

MERICLE OIL CO (AZ)
Name changed to Energy Reserve, Inc. 8/4/75
Energy Reserve, Inc. name changed to Cox Technologies, Inc. (AZ) 3/31/98 which reincorporated in North Carolina 12/31/2000
(See Cox Technologies, Inc.)

MERICOL INC (NV)
Common $0.001 par split (11.68) for (1) by issuance of (10.68) additional shares payable 08/27/2012 to holders of record 08/10/2012
Ex date - 08/28/2012
Name changed to Maxwell Resources, Inc. 09/05/2012

MERIDEN ELECTRIC LIGHT CO.
Merged into Connecticut Light & Power Co. in 1926
(See Connecticut Light & Power Co.)

MERIDEN ENERGY CORP (AB)
Name changed to Triumph Energy Corp. 8/4/94
Triumph Energy Corp. acquired by Baytex Energy Ltd. 5/30/2001
(See Baytex Energy Ltd.)

MERIDEN GAS LIGHT CO.
Merged into Connecticut Light & Power Co. 00/00/1926
Details not available

MERIDEN INDUSTRIAL BANK (MERIDEN, CT)
Name changed to National Industrial Bank of Connecticut (Meriden, CT) 5/1/73
Each share Common $5 par exchanged for (1) share Common $5 par
(See National Industrial Bank of Connecticut (Meriden, CT))

MERIDEN SMOKELESS COAL CO.
Property sold in 1927
No stockholders' equity

MERIDEX NETWORK CORP (BC)
Recapitalized as Meridex Software Corp. 02/13/2003
Each share Common no par exchanged for (0.1) share Common no par
Meridex Software Corp. name changed to Cannabis Technologies Inc. 05/21/2014 which name changed to InMed Pharmaceuticals Inc. 10/21/2014

MERIDEX SOFTWARE CORP (BC)
Each share old Common no par exchanged for (0.06666666) share new Common no par 12/31/2009
Name changed to Cannabis Technologies Inc. 05/21/2014
Cannabis Technologies Inc. name changed to InMed Pharmaceuticals Inc. 10/21/2014

MERIDIAN & MARYLAND REALTY CO. INC. (IN)
Liquidation completed
Each share Preferred no par exchanged for first and final distribution of $103 cash 12/12/73
Each share Common no par exchanged for initial distribution of $30 cash 12/12/73
Each share Common no par received second and final distribution of $4.51 cash 7/5/74

MERIDIAN BANCORP INC (PA)
Common $5 par split (3) for (2) by issuance of (0.5) additional share 06/03/1985
Common $5 par split (2) for (1) by issuance of (1) additional share 08/25/1986
$2.50 Conv. Preferred Ser. A $25 par called for redemption 09/07/1989
Merged into CoreStates Financial Corp 04/09/1996
Each share Common $5 par exchanged for (1.225) shares Common $5 par
CoreStates Financial Corp merged into First Union Corp. 04/28/1998 which name changed to Wachovia Corp. (Ctfs. dated after 09/01/2001) 09/01/2001 which merged into Wells Fargo & Co. (New) 12/31/2008

MERIDIAN BANK ((ELDRED, IL))
Placed in receivership 10/10/2008
Stockholders' equity unlikely

MERIDIAN BK (MALVERN, PA)
Under plan of reorganization each share Common $1 par automatically became (1) share Meridian Corp. Common $1 par 08/27/2018

MERIDIAN CONCEPTS LTD (CANADA)
Each share old Common no par exchanged for (1/6) share new Common no par 7/4/79
Name changed to Meridian Technologies Inc. 7/22/82
(See Meridian Technologies Inc.)

MERIDIAN DATA INC (DE)
Reincorporated 5/27/97
State of incorporation changed from (CA) to (DE) 5/29/97
Merged into Quantum Corp. 9/10/99
Each share Common no par exchanged for (0.4425) share DSSG Common 1¢ par and (0.2212) share HDDG Common 1¢ par

MERIDIAN DIAGNOSTICS INC (OH)
Common no par split (3) for (2) by issuance of (0.5) additional share 3/27/92
Common no par split (3) for (2) by issuance of (0.5) additional share 10/2/95
Name changed to Meridian Bioscience, Inc. 1/23/2001

MERIDIAN ELECTRS INC (VA)
89.8% owned by Sterling Electronics Corp. as of 00/00/1977
Public interest eliminated

MERIDIAN ENERGY CORP (BC)
Reincorporated 9/96/96
Place of incorporation changed from (ALTA) to (BC) 9/9/96
Each share Class A Common no par exchanged for (0.5) share Common no par 5/28/2003
Merged into True Energy Inc. 3/29/2005
Each share Common no par exchanged for (0.91) share Common no par
(See True Energy Inc.)

MERIDIAN ENERGY INC (UT)
Recapitalized as Android Corp. 9/23/91
Each share Common $0.001 par exchanged for (0.5) share Common $0.001 par
Android Corp. name changed to Appliance Parts Plus International, Inc. 2/16/93 which name changed to International Equity Resources, Inc. 10/25/93 which name changed to International Protection Technologies, Inc. 7/27/98 which name changed to HyperSecur Corp. 3/4/99

MERIDIAN FAST FOOD SVCS INC (DE)
Name changed to Radiation Service Associates Inc. 05/01/1972
(See Radiation Service Associates Inc.)

MERIDIAN FD INC (MD)
Name changed to Founders Income Fund, Inc. 10/23/1970
Founders Income Fund, Inc. name changed to Founders Equity Income Fund, Inc. 07/23/1986

MERIDIAN GOLD INC (CANADA)
Merged into Yamana Gold Inc. 12/31/2007
Each share Common no par exchanged for (2.235) shares Common no par and $7 cash

MERIDIAN HLDGS INC (FL)
Stock Dividend - 10% payable 10/14/99 to holders of record 9/30/99
Name changed to Meridian USA Holdings, Inc. 12/3/99
Meridian USA Holdings, Inc. name changed to ChampionLyte Products, Inc. 10/1/2001 which name changed to ChampionLyte Holdings, Inc. 3/26/2003 which name changed to Cargo Connection Logistics Holding, Inc. 5/26/2005

MERIDIAN INDL TR INC (MO)
Secondary Offering - 3,400,000 shares COM offered at $18.25 per share on 11/19/1996
Merged into ProLogis Trust 03/30/1999
Each share 8.75% Preferred Ser. D $0.001 par exchanged for (1) Preferred Share of Bene. Int. Ser. E 1¢ par
Each share Common $0.001 par exchanged for (1.1) Shares of Bene. Int. 1¢ par and $2 cash
ProLogis Trust name changed to ProLogis 05/23/2002 which merged into Prologis, Inc. 06/03/2011

MERIDIAN INDS INC (DE)
Each share old Common 10¢ par exchanged for (0.33333333) share new Common 10¢ par 11/22/1971
Filed a petition under Chapter 7 Bankruptcy Code 10/26/1981
No stockholders' equity

MERIDIAN INS GROUP INC (IN)
Stock Dividends - 10% payable 1/6/99 to holders of record 12/21/98; 10% payable 1/11/2000 to holders of record 12/27/99
Merged into State Automobile Mutual Insurance Co. 6/1/2001
Each share Common no par exchanged for $30 cash

MERIDIAN INTST BANCORP INC (MA)
Reorganized under the laws of Maryland as Meridian Bancorp, Inc. 07/29/2014
Each share Common no par exchanged for (2.4484) shares Common 1¢ par

MERIDIAN INVESTING & DEV CORP (DE)
Merged into Donaldson, Lufkin & Jenrette, Inc. 05/07/1981
Each share Common $1 par exchanged for (1) share Common 10¢ par
(See Donaldson, Lufkin & Jenrette, Inc.)

MERIDIAN LIFE INSURANCE CO. (NV)
Merged into Madison National Life Insurance Co., Inc. of Wisconsin 7/18/74
Each share Capital Stock $1 par exchanged for (0.125) share Common $1 par
Madison National Life Insurance Co., Inc. of Wisconsin reorganized as Madison Co. 12/1/75 which merged into Independence Holding Co. (Old) 8/9/83 which name changed to Stamford Capital Group, Inc. 11/4/87

which name changed to Independence Holding Co. (New) 9/10/90

MERIDIAN LIFE INS CO (IN)
Class A Common $7 par reclassified as Common Capital Stock $7 par 8/2/73
Common Capital Stock $7 par split (2) for (1) by issuance of (1) additional share 11/24/76
Acquired by Meridian Mutual Insurance Co. 6/4/79
Details not available

MERIDIAN MED TECHNOLOGIES INC (DE)
Merged into King Pharmaceuticals, Inc. 1/9/2003
Each share Common 10¢ par exchanged for $44.50 cash

MERIDIAN MNG & EXPL LTD (CANADA)
Name changed to Meridian Concepts Ltd.- Concepts Meridien Ltee. 11/22/78
Meridian Concepts Ltd.- Concepts Meridian Ltee. changed name to Meridian Technologies Inc. 7/22/82
(See Meridian Technologies Inc.)

MERIDIAN NATL CORP (DE)
Each share $0.375 Conv. Preferred Ser. B $0.001 par received distribution of (1.05405) shares Common $0.001 par 08/17/1992
Each share $0.375 Conv. Preferred Ser. B $0.001 par received distribution of (1.6) shares Common $0.001 par 02/01/1993
Each share $0.375 Conv. Preferred Ser. B $0.001 par received distribution of (0.53608) share Common $0.001 par 08/02/1993
Each share Common $0.001 par exchanged for (0.1) share Common 1¢ par 08/18/1993
Each share $0.375 Conv. Preferred Ser. B $0.001 par received distribution of (0.05821) share Common 1¢ par 02/01/1994
Each share $0.375 Conv. Preferred Ser. B $0.001 par received distribution of (0.113578) share Common $0.001 par 08/01/1995
Company ceased operations 03/09/2001
Stockholders' equity unlikely

MERIDIAN OIL N L (AUSTRALIA)
ADR program terminated 03/27/1998
Underlying shares worthless
No ADR holders' equity

MERIDIAN PEAK RES CORP NEW (YT)
Recapitalized as Arcata Resources Corp. 09/26/2001
Each share Common no par exchanged for (0.25) share Common no par
Arcata Resources Corp. recapitalized as Goldrush Resources Ltd. (YT) 05/14/2003 which reincorporated in British Columbia 08/10/2006 which merged into First Mining Finance Corp. 01/11/2016 which name changed to First Mining Gold Corp. 01/11/2018

MERIDIAN PEAK RES CORP OLD (CANADA)
Reincorporated 05/12/1997
Place of incorporation changed from (QC) to (Canada) 05/12/1997
Under plan of reorganization name changed to Meridian Peak Resources Corp. (New) (Canada) 06/23/1999
Meridian Peak Resources Corp. (New) (Canada) reincorporated in Yukon 10/04/1999 which recapitalized as Arcata Resources Corp. 09/26/2001 which recapitalized as Goldrush Resources Ltd. (YT) 05/14/2003 which reincorporated in British Columbia 08/10/2006 which merged into First Mining Finance Corp. 01/11/2016 which name changed to First Mining Gold Corp. 01/11/2018

MERIDIAN PT RLTY TR 83 (CA)
Reorganized under the laws of Maryland as Liberty Self-Stor, Inc. 12/29/99
Each Share of Bene. Int. no par exchanged for (1) share Common no par
Liberty Self-Stor, Inc. name changed to John D. Oil & Gas Co. 6/27/2005

MERIDIAN PT RLTY TR IV CO (MO)
Merged into Meridian Industrial Trust, Inc. 02/23/1996
Each share Common no par exchanged for (0.1431) share Common no par
Meridian Industrial Trust, Inc. merged into ProLogis Trust 03/30/1999 which name changed to ProLogis 05/23/2002 which merged into Prologis, Inc. 06/03/2011

MERIDIAN PT RLTY TR VI CO (MO)
Merged into Meridian Industrial Trust, Inc. 02/23/1996
Each share 7% Preferred no par exchanged for (0.3419) share 7% Preferred no par
Each share Common no par exchanged for (0.07598) share Common no par and (0.07598) Common Stock Purchase Warrant expiring 02/23/1999
Meridian Industrial Trust, Inc. merged into ProLogis Trust 03/30/1999 which name changed to ProLogis 05/23/2002 which merged into Prologis, Inc. 06/03/2011

MERIDIAN PT RLTY TR VII CO (MO)
Merged into Meridian Industrial Trust, Inc. 02/23/1996
Each share Adjustable Dividend Preferred $0.001 par exchanged for (0.33498) share Common $0.001 par
Each share Common $0.001 par exchanged for (0.07444) share Common $0.001 par and (0.07444) Common Stock Purchase Warrant expiring 02/23/1999
Meridian Industrial Trust, Inc. merged into ProLogis Trust 03/30/1999 which name changed to ProLogis 05/23/2002 which merged into Prologis, Inc. 06/03/2011

MERIDIAN PT RLTY TR VIII CO (MO)
Merged into EastGroup Properties, Inc. 6/1/98
Each share Adjustable Dividend Preferred $0.001 par exchanged for $10 cash
Each share Common $0.001 par exchanged for $8.50 cash

MERIDIAN PRODTNS INC (DE)
Name changed to New Castle Communications, Inc. 1/14/86

MERIDIAN RESOURCE CORP (TX)
Conv. Preferred Ser. C called for redemption at $100 on 03/28/2005
Acquired by Alta Mesa Holdings LP 05/13/2010
Each share Common 1¢ par exchanged for $0.33 cash

MERIDIAN RES LTD (BC)
Recapitalized as International Meridian Resources Ltd. 01/19/1984
Each share Capital Stock 50¢ par exchanged for (0.5) share Capital Stock no par
International Meridian Resources Ltd. merged into Meridor Resources Ltd. 04/01/1985 which merged into Hughes Lang Corp. 08/01/1989 which merged into CanGold Resources Inc. (BC) 01/31/1994 which reorganized in Ontario as Amalgamated CanGold Inc. 07/31/1995 which merged into Central Asia Goldfields Corp. 01/08/1996
(See Central Asia Goldfields Corp.)

MERIDIAN RESV INC (DE)
Plan of reorganization under Chapter 11 Federal Bankruptcy proceedings confirmed 12/21/1989
No stockholders' equity

MERIDIAN SPORTS INC (DE)
Merged into National Health Care Group 5/13/99
Each share Common no par exchanged for $0.75 cash

MERIDIAN TECHNOLOGIES INC (CANADA)
Each (1,849,923) shares old Common no par exchanged for (1) share new Common no par 10/14/98
Note: In effect holders received $11 cash per share and public interest was eliminated

MERIDIAN USA HLDGS INC (FL)
Name changed to ChampionLyte Products, Inc. 10/1/2001
ChampionLyte Products, Inc. name changed to ChampionLyte Holdings, Inc. 3/26/2003 which name changed to Cargo Connection Logistics Holding, Inc. 5/26/2005

MERIDIAN VENTURE CORP (NJ)
Reorganized under the laws of Delaware as Meridian National Corp. 10/10/1985
Each share Common $0.00001 par exchanged for (0.01) share Common $0.001 par
(See Meridian National Corp.)

MERIDIAN WASTE SOLUTIONS INC (NY)
Each share old Common $0.025 par exchanged for (0.05) share new Common $0.025 par 11/03/2016
Name changed to Attis Industries Inc. 05/01/2018

MERIDOR RES LTD (BC)
Merged into Hughes Lang Corp. 08/01/1989
Each share Common no par exchanged for (0.1623) share Class B Subordinate no par
Hughes Lang Corp. merged into CanGold Resources Inc. (BC) 01/31/1994 which reorganized in Ontario as Amalgamated CanGold Inc. 07/31/1995 which merged into Central Asia Goldfields Corp. 01/08/1996
(See Central Asia Goldfields Corp.)

MERILUS INC (NV)
Each share old Common $0.001 par exchanged for (0.05) share new Common $0.001 par 07/30/2007
Note: Holders of between (100) and (1,999) shares received (100) shares
Holders of (99) shares or fewer were not affected
Recapitalized as Zendex Holdings, Inc. 06/18/2015
Each share Common $0.001 par exchanged for (0.1) share Common $0.001 par
Note: No holder of (100) or more pre-split shares will receive fewer than (100) shares
Zendex Holdings, Inc. name changed to Kingsmen Capital Group Ltd. 09/20/2016

MERINO YELLOWKNIFE MINES, LTD. (ON)
Charter cancelled for failure to file reports and pay taxes March 1957

MERIS LABS INC (CA)
Assets sold for benefit of creditors 11/5/98
No stockholders' equity

MERISEL INC (DE)
Each share old Common 1¢ par exchanged for (0.1) share new Common 1¢ par 02/14/2001
Acquired by Merisel Saints Newco, Inc. 07/31/2013
Each share Common 1¢ par exchanged for $0.17 cash

MERISTAR HOSPITALITY CORP (DE)
Merged into Blackstone Group 5/2/2006
Each share Common 1¢ par exchanged for $10.45 cash

MERISTAR HOTELS & RESORTS INC (DE)
Merged into Interstate Hotels & Resorts, Inc. 07/31/2002
Each share Common 1¢ par exchanged for (0.2) share Common 1¢ par
(See Interstate Hotels & Resorts, Inc.)

MERIT ASSOC INC (NY)
Stock Dividend - 10% 12/30/1963
Bankruptcy proceedings closed 01/22/1968
No stockholders' equity

MERIT CLOTHING CO (KY)
Charter revoked for failure to file annual reports 2/5/85

MERIT CORP (TN)
Under plan of merger each share Common $1 par automatically became (1) share Hillhaven Corp. Common $1 par 03/31/1978
(See Hillhaven Corp.)

MERIT DIVERSIFIED INTL INC (NV)
Reincorporated 08/09/1994
State of incorporation changed from (UT) to (NV) 08/09/1994
Each share old Common no par exchanged for (0.05) share new Common no par 05/30/1996
Name changed to Allied Artists Entertainment Group, Inc. 09/15/2000
Allied Artists Entertainment Group, Inc. recapitalized as International Synergy Holding Co. Ltd. 07/10/2001 which name changed to Along Mobile Technologies, Inc. 12/27/2005
(See Along Mobile Technologies, Inc.)

MERIT ENERGY CORP (CO)
Each share old Common no par exchanged for (1/1,500,000) share new Common no par 03/09/1987
Note: In effect holders received $0.01 cash per share and public interest was eliminated

MERIT ENERGY LTD (AB)
Declared bankrupt 09/22/2000
No stockholders' equity

MERIT GOLD MINES, LTD. (ON)
Charter cancelled and company declared dissolved for default in filing returns in 1955

MERIT GROWTH OPPORTUNITIES FD INC (MD)
Name changed to Meritor Growth Opportunities Fund, Inc. 04/18/1988
(See Meritor Growth Opportunities Fund, Inc.)

MERIT HLDG CORP (GA)
Merged into Synovus Financial Corp. 10/1/99
Each share Common $2.50 par exchanged for (1.2533) shares Common $1 par

MERIT HOSIERY CO., INC.
Assets sold in 1932
No stockholders' equity

MERIT INDS INC CDA (BC)
Recapitalized as Ialta Industries Ltd. 07/02/2002
Each share Common no par exchanged for (1/3) share Common no par
(See Ialta Industries Ltd.)

MERIT MNG CORP (BC)
Each share old Common no par

MER-MER   **FINANCIAL INFORMATION, INC.**

exchanged for (0.02) share new Common no par 09/16/2009
Name changed to Huakan International Mining Inc. 12/23/2010
(See Huakan International Mining Inc.)

MERIT MONEY MKT FD INC (MD)
Name changed to Meritor Money Market Fund, Inc. 04/18/1988
(See Meritor Money Market Fund, Inc.)

MERIT OILS LTD (AB)
Capital Stock 50¢ par changed to no par 10/15/1963
Merged into Pacific Asbestos Ltd. 06/24/1968
Each share Capital Stock no par exchanged for (0.25) share Capital Stock no par
Pacific Asbestos Ltd. name changed to Woodsreef Minerals Ltd. 07/26/1972 which recapitalized as Transpacific Asbestos, Inc. 04/30/1981 which name changed to Transpacific Resources Inc. 09/06/1984
(See Transpacific Resources Inc.)

MERIT PA TAX FREE TR (PA)
Name changed to Meritor Pennsylvania Tax-Free Trust 04/22/1988
Meritor Pennsylvania Tax-Free Trust name changed to Sigma Pennsylvania Tax-Free Trust 12/29/1988 which name changed to ProvidentMutual Pennsylvania Tax-Free Trust 03/06/1990 which name changed to Sentinel Pennsylvania Tax-Free Trust 07/03/1992 which merged into Federated Municipal Securities Fund, Inc. 07/21/2006

MERIT PHARMACEUTICAL CO., INC. (TX)
Charter forfeited for failure to pay franchise taxes 3/17/80

MERIT SAVINGS & LOAN ASSOCIATION (CA)
Merged into Charter Savings Bank (Los Angeles, CA) 8/1/88
Each share Common $4 par exchanged for $7.90 cash

MERIT STUDIOS INC (DE)
Name changed 9/14/96
Name changed from Merit Software, Inc. to to Merit Studios, Inc. 9/14/94
Each share 4% Conv. Preferred no par exchanged for (2) shares Common no par 7/26/2000
Each Common no par received distribution of (0.167) Braodband Wireless International Corp. Common 1-1/4¢ payable 10/4/2002 to holders of record 8/30/2002 Ex date - 10/28/2002
Petition filed under Chapter 11 bankruptcy proceedings dismissed 3/1/2005
Stockholders' equity unlikely

MERIT TAX FREE FD INC (MD)
Name changed to Sigma Tax-Free Moneyfund, Inc. and Class A Common $0.001 par, Class B Common $0.001 par reclassified as Capital Stock $0.001 par 12/29/88
Sigma Tax-Free Moneyfund, Inc. name changed to ProvidentMutual Tax-Free Moneyfund, Inc. 3/1/90

MERIT TECHNOLOGIES LTD (BC)
Name changed 7/21/86
Name changed from Merit Resources Ltd. to Merit Technologies Ltd. 7/21/86
Each share new Common no par exchanged again for (0.25) share new Common no par 5/29/96
Name changed to Systech Retail Systems Inc. (BC) 1/16/98
Systech Retail Systems Inc. (BC) reincorporated in Ontario as Systech Retail Systems Corp. 9/24/2002

(See Systech Retail Systems Corp. (ONT))

MERIT U S GOVT FD INC (MD)
Name changed to Meritor U.S. Government Fund, Inc. 04/22/1988
Meritor U.S. Government Fund, Inc. name changed to Sigma U.S. Government Fund, Inc. 12/29/1988 which name changed to ProvidentMutual U.S. Government Fund for Income, Inc. 03/01/1990
(See ProvidentMutual U.S. Government Fund for Income, Inc.)

MERITAGE CORP (MD)
Common 1¢ par split (2) for (1) by issuance of (1) additional share payable 4/26/2002 to holders of record 4/12/2002 Ex date - 4/29/2002
Name changed to Meritage Homes Corp. 9/14/2004

MERITOR AUTOMOTIVE INC (DE)
Merged into ArvinMeritor, Inc. 07/07/2000
Each share Common $1 par exchanged for (0.75) share Common $1 par
ArvinMeritor, Inc. name changed to Meritor, Inc. 03/30/2011

MERITOR CAP CORP (DE)
Dutch Auction Rate Transferable Securities Preferred $1 par called for redemption 2/13/89
Public interest eliminated

MERITOR FIN INC (DE)
Dutch Auction Rate Transferable Secutities Preferred $1 par called for redemption 3/27/89

MERITOR GROWTH OPPORTUNITIES FD INC (MD)
Merged into Sigma Special Fund, Inc. 12/30/1988
Details not available

MERITOR II FIN INC (DE)
Dutch Auction Rate Transferable Securities Preferred $1 par called for redemption 02/24/1989
Public interest eliminated

MERITOR MONEY MKT FD INC (MD)
Merged into Sigma Moneyfund, Inc. 12/30/1988
Details not available

MERITOR PA TAX FREE TR (PA)
Name changed to Sigma Pennsylvania Tax-Free Trust 12/29/1988
Sigma Pennsylvania Tax-Free Trust name changed to ProvidentMutual Pennsylvania Tax-Free Trust 03/06/1990 which name changed to Sentinel Pennsylvania Tax-Free Trust 07/03/1992 which merged into Federated Municipal Securities Fund, Inc. 07/21/2006

MERITOR SVGS BK (PHILADELPHIA, PA)
United States Court of Federal Claims Final Order issued 12/15/2011
Each share Common $1 par received initial distribution of $4.3113531 cash 03/01/2012
Each share Common $1 par received second distribution of $0.15101556 cash 04/08/2014
Each share Common $1 par received third and final distribution of $0.06649669 cash 12/19/2016
Note: Distributions were made to holders of record who filed a claim prior to 12/31/2012

MERITOR III FIN INC (DE)
Dutch Auction Rate Transferable Securities Preferred $1 par called for redemption 3/6/89
Public interest eliminated

MERITOR U S GOVT FD INC (MD)
Name changed to Sigma U.S. Government Fund, Inc. 12/29/1988
Sigma U.S. Government Fund, Inc.

name changed to ProvidentMutual U.S. Government Fund for Income, Inc. 03/01/1990
(See ProvidentMutual U.S. Government Fund for Income, Inc.)

MERITRUST FED SVGS BK (MORGAN CITY, LA)
Merged into Whitney Holding Corp. 04/24/1998
Each share Common $1 par exchanged for (1.352) shares Common no par
Whitney Holding Corp. merged into Hancock Holding Co. 06/04/2011 which name changed to Hancock Whitney Corp. 05/25/2018

MERIWETHER BK SHS INC
Merged into Greenville Banking Co. 12/2/98
Each share Common exchanged for $61.38 cash

MERIX CORP (OR)
Common no par split (3) for (2) by issuance of (0.5) additional share payable 08/25/2000 to holders of record 08/10/2000
Merged into Viasystems Group, Inc. 02/16/2010
Each share Common no par exchanged for (0.1119086) share new Common 1¢ par
Viasystems Group, Inc. merged into TTM Technologies, Inc. 05/31/2015

MERK GOLD TR (NY)
Name changed to Van Eck Merk Gold Trust and Shares of Bene. Int. reclassified as Gold Shares 10/26/2015
Van Eck Merk Gold Trust name changed to VanEck Merk Gold Trust 04/29/2016

MERKERT AMERN CORP (DE)
Issue Information - 4,400,000 shares COM offered at $15 per share on 12/15/1998
Name changed to Marketing Specialists Corp. 8/18/99
(See Marketing Specialists Corp.)

MERL HOLDINGS INC COM (TN)
Name changed 03/01/1999
Name changed from Merl Industries of Tennessee to Merl Holdings Inc.com 03/01/1999
Name changed to Relm Holdings Inc. 03/17/2008

MERLAND EXPLS LTD (CANADA)
Capital Stock no par split (3) for (1) by issuance of (2) additional shares 6/16/80
Merged into North Canadian Oils Ltd. 7/2/86
Each share Conv. 1st Preferred Ser. B no par exchanged for (1) share Class B Preferred Ser. 7 no par
Each share $2 Conv. 1st Preferred Ser. A no par exchanged for (1) share Class B Preferred Ser. 6 no par
Each (5.75) shares Common no par exchanged for (1) share Common no par
(See North Canadian Oils Ltd.)

MERLAND OIL CDA LTD (CANADA)
Name changed to Merland Explorations Ltd. 2/25/70
Merland Explorations Ltd. merged into North Canadian Oils Ltd. 7/2/86
(See North Canadian Oils Ltd.)

MERLE NORMAN COSMETICS INC (CA)
Merged into MNC, Inc. 08/12/1975
Each share Common no par exchanged for $13 cash

MERLIN BAINES & CO INC (DE)
Charter cancelled and declared inoperative and void for non-payment of taxes 3/1/91

MERLIN CAP CDA INC (BC)
Struck off register and declared

dissolved for failure to file returns 5/26/95

MERLIN MINES LTD. (ON)
Completely liquidated 12/5/69
No stockholders' equity

MERLIN MNG CO (DE)
Each share old Common $0.0001 par exchanged for (0.1) share new Common $0.0001 par 11/23/1992
Name changed to European American Resources Inc. 01/19/1996
(See European American Resources Inc.)

MERLIN PRODUCTS CORP. (DE)
No longer in existence having become inoperative and void for non-payment of taxes 4/1/32

MERLIN RES INC (BC)
Struck off register and declared dissolved for failure to file returns 6/12/98

MERLIN RES LTD (BC)
Name changed to Merlin Capital (Canada) Inc. 9/27/89
(See Merlin Capital (Canada) Inc.)

MERLIN SOFTWARE TECHNOLOGIES HLDGS INC (UT)
Name changed to Optika Investment Co. Inc. (NV) 1/25/2000
Optika Investment Co. Inc. (NV) reincorporated in Delaware as USA Broadband, Inc. 7/10/2001

MERLIN SOFTWARE TECHNOLOGIES INC (NV)
Charter permanently revoked 06/30/2004

MERLIN SOFTWARE TECHNOLOGIES INTL INC (NV)
Ceased operations 11/06/2002
Stockholders' equity unlikely

MERNAT TRADING CO., INC.
Liquidated in 1944

MERRELL (WILLIAM S.) CO.
Acquired by Vick Chemical Co. 00/00/1938
Each share Common exchanged for (3) shares Capital Stock $5 par
Vick Chemical Co. name changed to Richardson-Merrell Inc. 10/21/1960 which merged into Dow Chemical Co. 03/10/1981 which merged into DowDuPont Inc. 09/01/2017

MERRELL-SOULE CO.
Acquired by Borden Co. 00/00/1928
Details not available

MERREX GOLD INC (BC)
Each share Common no par received distribution of (0.20964361) share Frontline Gold Corp. Common no par payable 05/01/2010 to holders of record 04/15/2010 Ex date - 04/13/2010
Merged into IAMGOLD Corp. 03/01/2017
Each share Common no par exchanged for (0.0433) share Common no par
Note: Unexchanged certificates will be cancelled and become without value 03/01/2023

MERREX RES INC (BC)
Name changed to Merrex Gold Inc. 05/25/2006
Merrex Gold Inc. merged into IAMGOLD Corp. 03/01/2017

MERRIAM (G. & C.) CO. (MA)
Common $100 par split (10) for (1) by issuance of (9) additional shares 3/6/62
Acquired by Encyclopedia Britannica, Inc. at $36 for each share Common $100 par 10/26/64

MERRICAN INTERNATIONAL INDUSTRIES LTD. (BC)
Struck off register and declared dissolved for failure to file returns 11/22/76

MERRICAN INTERNATIONAL MINES LTD. (BC)
Name changed to Merrican International Industries Ltd. 07/12/1971
(See Merrican International Industries Ltd.)

MERRICK INDUSTRIES INC. (HI)
Proclaimed dissolved for failure to file annual reports 7/17/80

MERRILL BANKSHARES CO (ME)
Common $20 par changed to $4 par and (4) additional shares issued 11/5/71
Common $4 par changed to $2 par and (1) additional share issued 4/14/83
Common $2 par split (3) for (2) by issuance of (0.5) additional share 1/17/85
Acquired by Fleet Financial Group, Inc. (Old) 3/17/86
Each share Common $2 par exchanged for (0.59) share Common $1 par
Fleet Financial Group, Inc. (Old) merged into Fleet/Norstar Financial Group, Inc. 1/1/88 which name changed to Fleet Financial Group, Inc. (New) 4/15/92 which name changed to Fleet Boston Corp. 10/1/99 which name changed to FleetBoston Financial Corp. 4/18/2000 which merged into Bank of America Corp. 4/1/2004

MERRILL (CHARLES E.) BOOKS, INC. (DE)
Completely liquidated 8/31/67
Each share Common $1 par exchanged for first and final distribution of (0.4307) share Bell & Howell Co. (Ill.) Common no par
Bell & Howell Co. (Ill.) reincorporated in Delaware 5/6/77
(See Bell & Howell Co. (Del.))

MERRILL CORP (MN)
Common 1¢ par split (2) for (1) by issuance of (1) additional share 3/6/92
Common 1¢ par split (2) for (1) by issuance of (1) additional share payable 10/15/97 to holders of record 9/30/97
Merged into Viking Merger Sub 11/23/99
Each share Common 1¢ par exchanged for $22 cash

MERRILL ISLAND MNG LTD (QC)
Recapitalized as Canadian Merrill Ltd. 8/16/71
Each share Capital Stock $1 par exchanged for (0.2) share Capital Stock no par
Canadian Merrill Ltd. merged into Francana Oil & Gas Ltd. 3/31/80 which was acquired by Sceptre Resources Ltd. 5/14/82 which merged into Canadian Natural Resources Ltd. 8/15/96

MERRILL LYNCH, PIERCE, FENNER & SMITH, INC. (DE)
Under plan of reorganization each share Common $1.33-1/3 par automatically became (1) share Merrill Lynch & Co., Inc. Common $1.33-1/3 par 05/16/1973
Merrill Lynch & Co., Inc. acquired by Bank of America Corp. 01/02/2009

MERRILL LYNCH & CO CDA LTD (ON)
Each Exchangeable Share no par exchanged for (1) share Merrill Lynch & Co., Inc. Common $1.33-1/3 par 12/12/2008
Merrill Lynch & Co., Inc. acquired by Bank of America Corp. 01/02/2009

MERRILL LYNCH & CO INC (DE)
Common $1.33-1/3 par split (2) for (1) by issuance of (1) additional share 06/27/1983
Common $1.33-1/3 par split (2) for (1) by issuance of (1) additional share 11/24/1993
Remarketed Preferred Variable 7 Day Book Entry called for redemption 01/22/1997
Remarketed Preferred Ser. F 49 Day Book Entry called for redemption 01/22/1997
Remarketed Preferred Ser. G 49 Day Book Entry called for redemption 01/28/1997
Remarketed Preferred Ser. A 49 Day Book Entry called for redemption 02/04/1997
Remarketed Preferred Ser. B 49 Day Book Entry called for redemption 02/11/1997
Remarketed Preferred Ser. C 49 Day Book Entry called for redemption 02/19/1997
Remarketed Preferred Ser. D 49 Day Book Entry called for redemption 02/25/1997
Remarketed Preferred Ser. E 49 Day Book Entry called for redemption 03/04/1997
Common $1.33-1/3 par split (2) for (1) by issuance of (1) additional share payable 05/30/1997 to holders of record 05/02/1997 Ex date - 06/02/1997
Each Structured Yield Product Exchangeable Security exchanged for (1.6666) shares MGIC Investment Corp. Common $1 par 08/15/1998
Common $1.33-1/3 par split (2) for (1) by issuance of (1) additional share payable 08/31/2000 to holders of record 08/04/2000 Ex date - 09/01/2000
Each 7.875% Structured Yield Product Exchangeable for Stock exchanged for (2.1052) shares Ciber, Inc. Common 1¢ par 02/01/2001
9% Preferred Ser. A $1 par called for redemption at $10,000 on 12/30/2004
9% Depositary Shares Ser. A called for redemption at $25 on 12/30/2004
Acquired by Bank of America Corp. 01/02/2009
Each share Depositary Preferred Ser. 1 exchanged for (1) share Depositary Preferred Ser. 1
Each share Depositary Preferred Ser. 2 exchanged for (1) share Depositary Preferred Ser. 2
Each share Depositary Preferred Ser. 3 exchanged for (1) share Depositary Preferred Ser. 3
Each share Depositary Preferred Ser. 4 exchanged for (1) share Depositary Preferred Ser. 4
Each share Depositary Preferred Ser. 5 exchanged for (1) share Depositary Preferred Ser. 5
Each share Depositary Preferred Ser. 6 exchanged for (1) share Depositary Preferred Ser. 6
Each share Depositary Preferred Ser. 7 exchanged for (1) share Depositary Preferred Ser. 7
Each share Depositary Preferred Ser. 8 exchanged for (1) share Depositary Preferred Ser. 8
Each share Common $1.33-1/3 par exchanged for (0.8595) share Common 1¢ par
Bear Market Strategic Accelerated Redemption Securities called for redemption at $10.74 on 03/17/2009

MERRILL LYNCH & CO INC (DE)
Callable Stock Return Income called for redemption at $14.6289 on 10/10/2003
Callable Stock Return Income called for redemption at $37.0001 on 10/10/2003
Callable Stock Return Income called for redemption at $24.1974 on 10/15/2003
Callable Stock Return Income called for redemption at $31.21313 on 11/5/2003
Callable Stock Return Income called for redemption at $26.4465 on 2/5/2004
Callable Stock Return Income called for redemption at $37.2322 on 2/9/2004
Callable Stock Return Income called for redemption at $27.164 on 2/9/2004
Callable Stock Return Income called for redemption at $27.1523 on 2/11/2005

MERRILL LYNCH BALANCED CAP FD INC (MD)
Reincorporated 07/29/1987
Name changed 07/01/2000
State of incorporation changed from (DE) to (MD) 07/29/1987
Name changed from Merrill Lynch Capital Fund, Inc. to Merrill Lynch Balanced Capital Fund, Inc. 07/01/2000
Class A Common 10¢ par reclassified as Class I Common 10¢ par 04/14/2003
Class D Common 10¢ par reclassified as Class A Common 10¢ par 04/14/2003
Name changed to BlackRock Balanced Capital Fund, Inc. and Class A Common 10¢ par, Class B Common 10¢ par, Class C Common 10¢ par and Class I Common 10¢ par reclassified as Investor A Shares 10¢ par, Investor B Shares 10¢ par, Investor C Shares 10¢ par and Institutional Shares respectively 09/29/2006

MERRILL LYNCH BK & TR CO (PLAINSBORO, NJ)
Callable Market Participation DEPS S&P 500 Index called for redemption at $11.50 on 8/28/2000

MERRILL LYNCH CAP TR I (DE)
Each 6.45% Trust Preferred Security automatically became $25 principal amount of Bank of America Corp. Income Capital Obligations Notes due 12/15/2066 on 10/18/2018

MERRILL LYNCH CAP TR II (DE)
6.45% Trust Preferred Securities called for redemption at $25 plus $0.268749 accrued dividends on 08/15/2016

MERRILL LYNCH CAP TR III (DE)
Trust Preferred Securities called for redemption at $25 plus $0.4148438 accrued dividends on 06/06/2018

MERRILL LYNCH CONV FD INC (MD)
Merged into Merrill Lynch Balanced Capital Fund, Inc. 12/15/2000
Each share Class A Common 10¢ par exchanged for (0.346931) share Class A Common
Each share Class B Common exchanged for (0.35731) share Class B Common
Each share Class C Common exchanged for (0.362458) share Class C Common
Each share Class D Common exchanged for (0.348803) share Class D Common

MERRILL LYNCH EMERGING MKTS DEBT FD INC (MD)
Name changed 09/18/2000
Name changed from Merrill Lynch Americas Income Fund Inc. to Merrill Lynch Emerging Markets Debt Fund Inc. 09/18/2000
Merged into Merrill Lynch World Income Fund, Inc. 02/24/2003
Each share Class A 10¢ par exchanged for (1.291533) shares Class A
Each share Class B 10¢ par exchanged for (1.289296) shares Class B
Each share Class C 10¢ par exchanged for (1.289984) shares Class C
Each share Class D 10¢ par exchanged for (1.288048) shares Class D
Merrill Lynch World Income Fund, Inc. name changed to BlackRock World Income Fund, Inc. 09/26/2006

MERRILL LYNCH EMERGING TIGERS FD INC (MD)
Merged into Merrill Lynch Dragon Fund, Inc. 5/19/2000
Each share Class A 10¢ par exchanged for (0.770741) share Class A 10¢ par

MERRILL LYNCH FINL ASSETS INC (CANADA)
Each S&P 500 Backed Upside Linked Liquid Security received $9.85 cash 12/12/2001

MERRILL LYNCH FOCUS TWENTY FUND INC (MD)
Name changed to BlackRock Focus Twenty Fund, Inc. 09/29/2006
BlackRock Focus Twenty Fund, Inc. name changed to BlackRock Focus Growth Fund, Inc. 12/17/2007

MERRILL LYNCH FOCUS VALUE FD INC (MD)
Name changed to BlackRock Focus Value Fund, Inc. 09/29/2006

MERRILL LYNCH GLOBAL UTIL FD INC (MD)
Name changed to Merrill Lynch Utility & Telecommunications Fund, Inc. 8/21/2000

MERRILL LYNCH HIGH INCOME MUN BD FD INC (MD)
Reorganized as MuniAssets Fund, Inc. 11/19/2001
Each share Common 10¢ par exchanged for (0.0720689) share Common 10¢ par
MuniAssets Fund, Inc. name changed to BlackRock MuniAssets Fund, Inc. 10/2/2006

MERRILL LYNCH MTG LNS INC (CANADA)
Name changed to Merrill Lynch Financial Assets Inc. 03/15/2001
(See Merrill Lynch Financial Assets Inc.)

MERRILL LYNCH MUN STRATEGY FD INC (MD)
Reorganized as MuniYield Fund, Inc. 11/19/2001
Each share Auction Market Preferred Ser. A exchanged for (1) share Auction Market Preferred Ser. F
Each share Common 10¢ par exchanged for (0.685697) share Common 10¢ par
MuniYield Fund, Inc. name changed to BlackRock MuniYield Fund, Inc. 10/2/2006

MERRILL LYNCH PFD CAP TR I (DE)
7.75% Trust Originated Preferred Securities called for redemption at $25 on 12/30/2006

MERRILL LYNCH PFD CAP TR II (DE)
8% Trust Originated Preferred Securities called for redemption at $25 on 03/30/2007

MERRILL LYNCH PFD CAP TR III (DE)
7% Trust Originated Preferred Securities called for redemption at $25 plus $0.145833 accrued dividends on 01/29/2016

MERRILL LYNCH PFD CAP TR IV (DE)
7.12% Trust Originated Preferred Securities called for redemption at $25 plus $0.148333 accrued dividends on 01/29/2016

MERRILL LYNCH PFD CAP TR V (DE)
7.28% Trust Originated Preferred

MERRILL LYNCH PRIME FD INC (MD)
Securities called for redemption at $25 plus $0.151666 accrued dividends on 01/29/2016
Name changed to Merrill Lynch Senior Floating Rate Fund 3/11/94

MERRILL LYNCH READY ASSETS TR (MA)
Name changed to Ready Assets Prime Money Fund 05/04/2009

MERRILL LYNCH WORLD INCOME FD INC (MD)
Name changed to BlackRock World Income Fund, Inc. 09/26/2006

MERRILL MERCHANTS BANCSHARES INC (ME)
Issue Information - 600,000 shares COM offered at $12.75 per share on 08/10/1998
Stock Dividends - 5% payable 03/15/1999 to holders of record 02/26/1999; 3% payable 02/29/2000 to holders of record 02/15/2000; 3% payable 03/07/2001 to holders of record 02/28/2001; 3% payable 04/11/2002 to holders of record 03/28/2002; 3% payable 04/10/2003 to holders of record 03/27/2003 Ex date - 03/25/2003; 3% payable 04/12/2004 to holders of record 03/29/2004 Ex date - 03/25/2004; 3% payable 04/08/2005 to holders of record 03/28/2005 Ex date - 03/23/2005; 3% payable 04/07/2006 to holders of record 03/31/2006 Ex date - 03/29/2006
Merged into Chittenden Corp. 05/31/2007
Each share Common $1 par exchanged for (0.6814) share Common $1 par and $10.29 cash
(See Chittenden Corp.)

MERRILL PETROLEUMS LTD. (AB)
Merged into Pacific Petroleums Ltd. on a (0.5) for (1) basis 1/24/58
(See Pacific Petroleums Ltd.)

MERRILL TR CO (BANGOR, ME)
Common $20 par changed to $30 par in 1945
Common $30 par changed to $40 par in 1954
Common $40 par changed to $20 par and (4) additional shares issued 1/5/63
Reorganized as Merrill Bankshares Co. 10/24/68
Each share Common $20 par exchanged for (1) share Common $20 par
Merrill Bankshares Co. acquired by Fleet Financial Group, Inc. (Old) 3/17/86 which merged into Fleet/Norstar Financial Group, Inc. 1/1/88 which name changed to Fleet Financial Group, Inc. (New) 4/15/92 which name changed to Fleet Boston Corp. 10/1/99 which name changed to FleetBoston Financial Corp. 4/18/2000 which merged into Bank of America Corp. 4/1/2004

MERRIMAC CHEMICAL CO.
Acquired by Monsanto Chemical Works 00/00/1929
Details not available

MERRIMAC HAT CORP. (MA)
Common no par exchanged (4) for (1) 03/31/1937
Name changed to India Corp. 02/11/1959
(See India Corp.)

MERRIMAC INDS INC (DE)
Reincorporated 07/14/1994
Reincorporated 02/22/2001
Common 50¢ par split (5) for (4) by issuance of (0.25) additional share 04/15/1988
Stock Dividends - 10% 05/15/1989; 10% payable 06/05/1998 to holders of record 05/15/1998 Ex date - 05/13/1998
State of incorporation changed from (NY) to (NJ) 07/14/1994
State of incorporation changed from (NJ) to (DE) and Common 50¢ par changed to 1¢ par 02/22/2001
Acquired by Crane Co. 02/03/2010
Each share Common 1¢ par exchanged for $16 cash

MERRIMAC MILLS CO.
Bankrupt in 1950

MERRIMAC VALLEY POWER & BUILDING CO.
Sold to Amesbury Electric Light Co. 00/00/1939
Details not available

MERRIMACK BANCORP INC MASS (DE)
Assets taken over by Banking Commissioner 08/30/1991
No stockholders' equity

MERRIMACK-ESSEX ELECTRIC CO. (MA)
Common acquired by New England Electric System on a (1.5) for (1) basis 6/30/59
5.52% Preferred $100 par called for redemption 9/27/62
(See New England Electric System)

MERRIMACK FMRS EXCHANGE INC (NH)
Liquidation completed
Each share Capital Stock $25 par received initial distribution of $30 cash 09/17/1980
Each share Capital Stock $25 par received second distribution of $40 cash 09/01/1981
Each share Capital Stock $25 par received third and final distribution of $17.37 cash 09/17/1982

MERRIMACK MANUFACTURING CO.
Name changed to Lowell Liquidation Corp. for purpose of liquidation in 1946 and completely liquidated 3/25/59

MERRIMACK VALLEY COMMUNICATION INC (MA)
Foreclosed by creditors and went out of business 10/12/73
No stockholders' equity

MERRIMAN CURHAN FORD GROUP INC (DE)
Recapitalized as Merriman Holdings, Inc. 08/16/2010
Each share Common $0.0001 par exchanged for (1/7) share Common $0.0001 par

MERRITECH DEV CORP (BC)
Recapitalized as Dencam Development Corp. 08/17/1992
Each share Common no par exchanged for (0.33333333) share Common no par
Dencam Development Corp. recapitalized as Consolidated Dencam Development Corp. 01/19/1994 which name changed to Equinox Exploration Corp. 03/13/2009 which name changed to Equinox Copper Corp. 02/01/2013 which recapitalized as Anfield Resources Inc. 09/23/2013 which recapitalized as Anfield Energy Inc. 12/27/2017

MERRITT CHAPMAN & SCOTT CORP (DE)
6-1/2% Preferred Ser. A $100 par called for redemption 03/01/1951
Common no par changed to $12.50 par 00/00/1951
Stock Dividends - 40% 10/16/1950; 25% 01/11/1954
Liquidation completed
Each share Common $12.50 par received initial distribution of $6 cash 08/29/1968
Each share Common $12.50 par received second distribution of $3 cash 01/31/1969
Each share Common $12.50 par received third distribution of $2 cash 05/21/1969
Each share Common $12.50 par received fourth distribution of $4 cash 12/10/1969
Each share Common $12.50 par received fifth distribution of $3 cash 10/08/1970
Each share Common $12.50 par received sixth distribution of $4.50 cash 01/28/1971
Each share Common $12.50 par received seventh distribution of $1 cash 03/08/1972
Each share Common $12.50 par received eighth distribution of $2.50 cash 09/06/1972
Each share Common $12.50 par received ninth distribution of $1 cash 05/10/1973
Each share Common $12.50 par received tenth distribution of $4 cash 06/12/1973
Each share Common $12.50 par received eleventh distribution of $1.50 cash 04/02/1974
Each share Common $12.50 par received twelfth distribution of $1.50 cash 04/10/1975
Each share Common $12.50 par received thirteenth distribution of $1.50 cash 08/12/1975
Each share Common $12.50 par received fourteenth distribution of $2 cash 01/10/1977
Each share Common $12.50 par received fifteenth distribution of $1 cash 01/09/1979
Each share Common $12.50 par received sixteenth and final distribution of $1.552 cash 11/21/1980
Note: Holders of (1,000) or more shares also received (0.001) share new Common $100 par 11/21/1980
Each share Common $100 par received distribution of $500 cash 02/20/1986

MERRITT COPPER CO. LTD. (BC)
Name changed to National Nickel Ltd. 2/21/68
National Nickel Ltd. recapitalized as Aberdeen Minerals Ltd. 2/9/73
(See Aberdeen Minerals Ltd.)

MERRITT MINING EXPLORATIONS LTD. (BC)
Name changed to Banff Mines Ltd. 9/28/66
Banff Mines Ltd. merged into Camela Mines & Oils Ltd. in July 1971
(See Camela Mines & Oils Ltd.)

MERRITT VENTURES CORP (NV)
Name changed to Ireland, Inc. 12/19/2005

MERRY BROTHERS BRICK & TILE CO. (GA)
Name changed to Merry Companies, Inc. 5/7/68
(See Merry Companies, Inc.)

MERRY COS INC (GA)
Stock Dividends - 10% 09/15/1976; 10% 03/25/1977; 10% 09/15/1977; 10% 03/15/1978; 10% 09/15/1978; 10% 03/15/1979; 10% 09/15/1979; 10% 03/15/1980; 10% 09/15/1980
Merged into Boral Ltd. 02/06/1981
Each share Common $2.50 par exchanged for $18 cash

MERRY GO ROUND ENTERPRISES INC (MD)
Common 1¢ par split (3) for (2) by issuance of (0.5) additional share 6/29/84
Common 1¢ par split (3) for (2) by issuance of (0.5) additional share 5/1/87
Common 1¢ par split (3) for (2) by issuance of (0.5) additional share 8/26/89
Common 1¢ par split (4) for (3) by issuance of (1/3) additional share 3/16/90
Common 1¢ par split (3) for (2) by issuance of (0.5) additional share 1/4/91
Common 1¢ par split (3) for (2) by issuance of (0.5) additional share 7/5/91
Bankruptcy proceedings converted from Chapter 11 to Chapter 7 on 3/1/96
No stockholders' equity

MERRY LD & INVT INC (GA)
Common no par split (5) for (4) by issuance of (0.25) additional share 6/28/85
Common no par split (5) for (4) by issuance of (0.25) additional share 6/30/86
Common no par split (5) for (4) by issuance of (0.25) additional share 3/15/87
Each share Common no par received distribution of (0.05) share of Merry Land Properties Inc. Common no par payable 10/16/98 to holders of record 10/15/98
Merged into Equity Residential Properties Trust 10/19/98
Each share $1.75 Conv. Preferred Ser. A no par exchanged for (1) share $1.75 Conv. Preferred Ser. H 1¢ par
Each share 144A Conv. Ser. B no par exchanged for (0.6417) 9.125% Preferred Share of Bene. Int. Ser. B 1¢ par
Each share $2.15 Conv. Ser. C no par exchanged for (1) share Preferred Ser. C 1¢ par
Each share 8.29% Conv. Preferred Ser. D 1¢ par exchanged for (1) share 8.29% Preferred Ser. K 1¢ par
Each share 7.625% Preferred Ser. E no par exchanged for (1) share 7.625% Preferred Ser. L 1¢ par
Each share Common no par exchanged for (1) Share of Bene. Int. 1¢ par
Equity Residential Properties Trust name changed to Equity Residential 5/15/2002

MERRY LD PPTYS INC (GA)
Merged into Cornerstone Income Realty Trust, Inc. 05/28/2003
Each share Common no par exchanged for (0.22) share Conv. Preferred Ser. B no par and (1.818) shares Common no par
Cornerstone Income Realty Trust, Inc. merged into Colonial Properties Trust 04/01/2005 which merged into Mid-America Apartment Communities, Inc. 10/01/2013

MERRYMACK CORP (UT)
Recapitalized as Concept Technologies Inc. (UT) 04/11/1990
Each share Common $0.001 par exchanged for (0.1) share Common $0.001 par
Concept Technologies Inc. (UT) reincorporated in Nevada as Concept Holding Corp. 02/10/2015 which name changed to M101 Corp. 11/01/2017

MERSEY PAPER CO. LTD. NEW (NS)
Name changed to Bowaters Mersey Paper Co. Ltd. 02/11/1959
Bowaters Mersey Paper Co. Ltd. name changed to Bowater Mersey Paper Co. Ltd. 03/01/1976
(See Bowater Mersey Paper Co. Ltd.)

MERSEY PAPER CO. LTD. OLD (NS)
Assets sold and liquidation approved 7/17/56
Details not available

MERSICK INDS INC (CT)
Merged into Swift Industries, Inc. 5/16/69
Each share Class A Common $1 par exchanged for (0.5) share Common no par

MER-MES

(See Swift Industries, Inc.)

MERSINGTON CAP INC (CANADA)
Recapitalized as Prime Meridian Resources Corp. 2/28/2007
Each share Common no par exchanged for (0.5) share Common no par

MERTEN CO. (OH)
Liquidation completed 07/28/1961
Details not available

MERTIVA AKTIEBOLAG (SWEDEN)
ADR agreement terminated 08/09/2013
Each Sponsored ADR for Class B exchanged for $2.163972 cash

MERTRONICS CORP. (DE)
Name changed to G & H Technology, Inc. 6/30/67
(See G & H Technology, Inc.)

MERU NETWORKS INC (DE)
Acquired by Fortinet, Inc. 07/08/2015
Each share Common $0.0005 par exchanged for $1.63 cash

MERUELO MADDUX PPTYS INC (DE)
Each share old Common 1¢ par exchanged for (0.2) share new Common 1¢ par 07/29/2011
Name changed to EVOQ Properties, Inc. 03/05/2012
(See EVOQ Properties, Inc.)

MERUS LABS INTL INC NEW (BC)
Acquired by Norgine B.V. 07/20/2017
Each share Common no par exchanged for $1.65 cash
Note: Unexchanged certificates will be cancelled and become without value 07/20/2023

MERUS LABS INTL INC OLD (BC)
Merged into Merus Labs International Inc. (New) 12/22/2011
Each share Common no par exchanged for (0.25) share Common no par
Note: Unexchanged certificates were cancelled and became without value 12/22/2017
(See Merus Labs International Inc. (New))

MERVYN S (CA)
Common $1 par split (3) for (2) by issuance of (0.5) additional share 04/28/1972
Stock Dividends - 100% 09/11/1975; 100% 01/13/1978
Merged into Dayton-Hudson Corp. 05/28/1978
Each share Common $1 par exchanged for (0.8) share Common $1 par
Dayton-Hudson Corp. name changed to Target Corp. 01/31/2000

MESA AIR GROUP INC (NV)
Plan of reorganization under Chapter 11 Federal Bankruptcy proceedings effective 03/01/2011
No stockholders' equity
(Additional Information in Active)

MESA AIRLS INC (NM)
Common no par split (3) for (2) by issuance of (0.5) additional share 01/28/1992
Common no par split (3) for (2) by issuance of (0.5) additional share 08/18/1992
Common no par split (2) for (1) by issuance of (1) additional share 03/26/1993
Reincorporated under the laws of Nevada as Mesa Air Group, Inc. 09/27/1996
(See Mesa Air Group, Inc.)

MESA BIOMEDICAL INC (BC)
Reincorporated under the laws of Alberta as Meteor Minerals Inc. 12/18/96
Meteor Minerals Inc. name changed to Meteor Technologies Inc. 10/13/99 which name changed to ThoughtShare Communications Inc. 11/8/2001 which recapitalized as Qumana Software Inc. 12/6/2004

MESA CONTRACT MNG INC (CO)
Recapitalized as Gold Hill Corp. 05/07/1990
Each (30) shares Common $0.001 exchanged for (1) share Common $0.002 par

MESA ENERGY HLDGS INC (DE)
Merged into Armada Oil, Inc. 03/28/2013
Each share Common $0.0001 par exchanged for (0.4) share Common $0.001 par

MESA GOLD INC (NV)
Name changed to Private Trading Systems, Inc. and (2) additional shares issued 01/18/2005
(See Private Trading Systems, Inc.)

MESA INC (TX)
Merged into Pioneer Natural Resources Co. 08/07/1997
Each share 8% Conv. Preferred Ser. A 1¢ par exchanged for (0.1785714) share Common 1¢ par
Each share Common 1¢ par exchanged for (0.1428571) share Common 1¢ par

MESA LTD PARTNERSHIP (DE)
Depositary Units reclassified as Common Depositary Units 06/30/1986
Reorganized under the laws of Texas as Mesa Inc. 12/31/1991
Each Preference Depositary Unit exchanged for (0.27) share Common 1¢ par
Each Common Depositary Unit exchanged for (0.2) share Common 1¢ par
Mesa Inc. merged into Pioneer Natural Resources Co. 08/07/1997

MESA MED INC (CO)
Name changed to Mesa Laboratories, Inc. 10/21/92

MESA OFFSHORE TR (TX)
Liquidation completed
Each Unit of Bene. Int. received initial distribution of $0.116328 cash payable 03/24/2010 to holders of record 02/22/2010 Ex date - 03/25/2010
Each Unit of Bene. Int. received second and final distribution of $0.012984 cash payable 12/02/2010 to holders of record 02/22/2010
Note: Certificates were not required to be surrendered and are without value

MESA OIL & GAS VENTURES, INC. (CO)
Acquired by Elgin Gas & Oil Co. 06/05/1959
Details not available

MESA OIL CO., INC. (KS)
Name changed to Mesa Petroleum Co., Inc. in 1954
(See Mesa Petroleum Co.)

MESA PETE CO (DE)
Capital Stock $1 par reclassified as Common $1 par 9/27/67
Each share $2.50 Conv. Preferred $1 par exchanged for (1) share $2.20 Conv. Preferred $1 par 5/1/69
$2.20 Conv. Preferred $1 par called for redemption 11/1/71
Common $1 par split (2) for (1) by issuance of (1) additional share 12/7/73
$2.20 Conv. Senior Preferred $1 par called for redemption 10/18/76
$1.60 Conv. Preferred $1 par called for redemption 7/11/77
Common $1 par split (2) for (1) by issuance of (1) additional share 5/16/80
Common $1 par split (2) for (1) by issuance of (1) additional share 4/1/81
Stock Dividends - 10% 3/1/67; 10% 1/9/68; 10% 6/30/72
Under plan of reorganization each share Common $1 par received initial distribution of (1) Mesa Limited Partnership Depositary Unit 12/30/85
Each share Common $1 par received second and final distribution of (0.22834718) Mesa Limited Partnership Depositary Unit 2/2/87
Note: Certificates were not required to be surrendered and are without value
Mesa Limited Partnership reorganized as Mesa Inc. 12/31/91 which merged into Pioneer Natural Resources Co. 8/7/97

MESA PETROLEUM CO., INC. (KS)
Each share Common no par exchanged for (4) shares Common 25¢ par 7/2/56
Charter revoked for failure to file reports and pay fees 10/1/63

MESA RES INC (BC)
Merged into LongBow Energy Corp. (New) 02/25/2004
Each share Common no par exchanged for (1) share Common no par
LongBow Energy Corp. (New) recapitalized as LongBow Resources Inc. 04/01/2007
(See LongBow Resources Inc.)

MESA RES LTD (BC)
Name changed to Mesa Biomedical Inc. (BC) 9/28/93
Mesa Biomedical Inc. (BC) reincorporated in Alberta as Meteor Minerals Inc. 12/18/96 which name changed to Meteor Technologies Inc. 10/13/99 which name changed to ThoughtShare Communications Inc. 11/8/2001 which recapitalized as Qumana Software Inc. 12/6/2004

MESA URANIUM CORP. (DE)
Merged into Consolidated Uranium Mines, Inc. on a (0.2) for (1) basis in 1957
(See Consolidated Uranium Mines, Inc.)

MESA URANIUM CORP (BC)
Each share old Common no par exchanged for (1/3) share new Common no par 09/16/2008
Name changed to Mesa Exploration Corp. 03/30/2011

MESABA AVIATION INC (MN)
Under plan of reorganization each share Common 1¢ par automatically became (1) share Airtran Corp. Common 1¢ par 09/01/1988
Airtran Corp. name changed to Mesaba Holdings, Inc. 08/29/1995 which name changed to MAIR Holdings, Inc. 08/25/2003

MESABA HLDGS INC (MN)
Name changed to MAIR Holdings, Inc. 08/25/2003

MESABI IRON CO. (DE)
Capital Stock no par changed to $1 par in 1932
Stock Dividend - 10% 5/1/59
Completely liquidated 7/27/61
Each share Capital Stock $1 par exchanged for (10) Units of Bene. Int. no par of Mesabi Trust

MESHTECH WIRELESS INC (NV)
Name changed to Sleep Healers Holdings, Inc. 08/17/2006
Sleep Healers Holdings, Inc. name changed to Sleep Holdings, Inc. 10/09/2006 which name changed to ALL-Q-TELL Corp. 11/03/2010
(See ALL-Q-TELL Corp.)

MESON ELECTRS INC (NY)
Name changed to Stellex Industries, Inc. 11/4/74
(See Stellex Industries, Inc.)

MESQUITE CTRY INC (DE)
Each share old Common $0.001 par exchanged for (0.05) share new Common $0.001 par 07/05/1993
Each share new Common $0.001 par exchanged again for (0.05) share new Common $0.001 par 08/19/1993
Name changed to Gimmeabid.com, Inc. 10/14/1999
(See Gimmeabid.com, Inc.)

MESQUITE ENERGY INC (AB)
Recapitalized as Mesquite Exploration Inc. 06/07/2000
Each share Common no par exchanged for (0.33333333) share Common no par
Mesquite Exploration Inc. merged into High Point Resources Inc. 06/19/2002 which merged into Enterra Energy Trust 08/17/2005 which reorganized as Equal Energy Ltd. 06/03/2010
(See Equal Energy Ltd.)

MESQUITE EXPL INC (AB)
Merged into High Point Resources Inc. 06/19/2002
Each share Common no par exchanged for (1) share Common no par
High Point Resources Inc. merged into Enterra Energy Trust 08/17/2005 which reorganized as Equal Energy Ltd. 06/03/2010
(See Equal Energy Ltd.)

MESQUITE GOLD & COPPER MINING CO. (AZ)
Charter expired by time limitation 4/21/27

MESQUITE MINING INC (DE)
Common $0.0001 par split (14) for (1) by issuance of (13) additional shares payable 08/04/2009 to holders of record 07/20/2009 Ex date - 08/05/2009
Name changed to Mesa Energy Holdings, Inc. 08/05/2009
Mesa Energy Holdings, Inc. merged into Armada Oil, Inc. 03/28/2013

MESQUITE RES INC (AB)
Recapitalized as Mesquite Energy Inc. 06/21/1999
Each share Common no par exchanged for (0.33333333) share Common no par
Mesquite Energy Inc. recapitalized as Mesquite Exploration Inc. 06/07/2000 which merged into High Point Resources Inc. 06/19/2002 which merged into Enterra Energy Trust 08/17/2005 which reorganized as Equal Energy Ltd. 06/03/2010
(See Equal Energy Ltd.)

MESSAGEMEDIA INC (DE)
Merged into DoubleClick Inc. 1/22/2002
Each share Common $0.001 par exchanged for (0.01454) share Common $0.001 par
(See DoubleClick Inc.)

MESSENGER CORP. (IL)
Common no par changed to $1 par in 1938
Reincorporated under the laws of Indiana 5/15/68
(See Messenger Corp. (Ind.))

MESSENGER CORP. (IN)
Completely liquidated 3/1/77
Each share Common $1 par exchanged for first and final distribution of $40 cash

MESSENGER PUBLISHING CORP.
Succeeded by Messenger Corp. (Ill.) in 1930
Messenger Corp. (Ill.) reincorporated under the laws of Indiana 5/15/68
(See Messenger Corp. (Ind.))

MESSER OIL CORP (NY)
Merged into Amax Inc. 07/01/1980
Each share Capital Stock no par

MES-MET

exchanged for (0.21612) share
Common $1 par
Amax Inc. merged into Cyprus Amax
Minerals Co. 11/15/1993 which
merged into Phelps Dodge Corp.
12/02/1999 which merged into
Freeport-McMoRan Copper & Gold
Inc. 03/19/2007 which name
changed to Freeport-McMoRan Inc.
07/14/2014

MESSIDOR LTD (NV)
Recapitalized as Framewaves Inc.
12/29/2000
Each share Common $0.001 par
exchanged for (0.01) share Common
$0.001 par
Note: Above ratio applies to holders
of (10,000) or more shares
Holdings of between (10,000) and
(100) shares will receive (100)
shares only
Holdings of (99) or fewer shares will
receive a like number of shares
Framewaves Inc. name changed to
Sigma Labs, Inc. 10/14/2010

MESSINA DIAMOND CORP (ON)
Name changed to MineGem Inc.
7/10/2000
(See MineGem Inc.)

MESSINA LTD (SOUTH AFRICA)
Acquired by Lonmin PLC 02/06/2006
Details not available

MESSINA MEAT PRODS INC (UT)
Proclaimed dissolved for failure to
pay taxes 1/8/82

MESSINA MINERALS INC (BC)
Each share old Common no par
exchanged for (0.2) share new
Common no par 02/20/2013
Merged into Canadian Zinc Corp.
12/20/2013
Each share new Common no par
exchanged for (0.16949) share
Common no par
Note: Unexchanged certificates will
be cancelled and become without
value 12/20/2019
Canadian Zinc Corp. name changed
to NorZinc Ltd. 09/11/2018

MESSINA TRANSVAAL DEV LTD (SOUTH AFRICA)
Name changed to Messina Ltd.
01/28/1982
Each ADR for Ordinary Rand-50 par
exchanged for (1) ADR for Ordinary
Rand-50 par
(See Messina Ltd.)

MESTA MACH CO (PA)
Each share Common no par
exchanged for (6-2/3) shares
Common $5 par in 1929
Under plan of reorganization each
share Common $5 par automatically
became (1) share Mestek, Inc.
Common no par 10/22/84

MESTON LAKE RES INC (QC)
Merged into Campbell Resources Inc.
(New) 12/08/1987
Each share Common no par
exchanged for (2.35) shares
Common no par
(See Campbell Resources Inc. (New))

MESUR MATIC ELECTRS CORP (DE)
Each share Common 10¢ par
exchanged for (1/3) share Common
2¢ par 03/15/1971
Common 2¢ par reclassified as Class
A Common 10¢ par 00/00/1975
Charter cancelled and declared
inoperative and void for
non-payment of taxes 03/01/1995

MET COIL SYS CORP (DE)
Merged into Formtek, Inc. 6/1/2000
Each share Common 1¢ par
exchanged for $7.10 cash

MET-ED CAP L P (DE)
9% Guaranteed Monthly Income
Preferred Securities Ser. A no par
called for redemption at $25 on
12/29/99

MET ED CAP TR (DE)
7.35% Trust Preferred Securities
called for redemption at $25 on
6/1/2004

MET FOOD CORP (NY)
Name changed to White Rose Food
Corp. 1/1/74
(See White Rose Food Corp.)

MET PRO CORP (PA)
Name changed 05/21/1974
Reincorporated 07/31/2003
Class A 10¢ par reclassified as
Common 10¢ par 05/12/1971
Class B 10¢ par reclassified as
Common 10¢ par 05/12/1971
Common 10¢ par split (2) for (1) by
issuance of (1) additional share
05/26/1971
Name changed from Met-Pro Water
Treatment Corp. to Met-Pro Corp.
05/21/1974
Common 10¢ par split (3) for (2) by
issuance of (0.5) additional share
01/28/1983
Common 10¢ par split (3) for (2) by
issuance of (0.5) additional share
05/05/1989
Common 10¢ par split (3) for (2) by
issuance of (0.5) additional share
05/12/1995
Common 10¢ par split (3) for (2) by
issuance of (0.5) additional share
payable 07/08/1996 to holders of
record 06/17/1996
Stock Dividend - 25% 04/25/1980
State of incorporation changed from
(DE) to (PA) 07/31/2003
Common 10¢ par split (4) for (3) by
issuance of (0.33333333) additional
share payable 10/15/2003 to holders
of record 10/01/2003 Ex date -
10/16/2003
Common 10¢ par split (4) for (3) by
issuance of (0.33333333) additional
share payable 11/15/2005 to holders
of record 11/01/2005 Ex date -
11/16/2005
Common 10¢ par split (4) for (3) by
issuance of (0.33333333) additional
share payable 11/14/2007 to holders
of record 11/01/2007 Ex date -
11/15/2007
Merged into CECO Environmental
Corp. 08/27/2013
Each share Common 10¢ par
exchanged for for (1.0843) shares
Common 1¢ par

MET SPORTS CTRS INC (NY)
Name changed to Antares Resources
Corp. 12/20/1982
(See Antares Resources Corp.)

META COM INC (MN)
Merged into Sicom, Inc. 03/07/1984
Each share Common 1¢ par
exchanged for $4 cash

META COMMUNICATIONS GROUP INC (BC)
Acquired by International Movie
Group Inc. (BC) 6/19/89
Each (15) shares Common no par
exchanged for (1) share Common
no par
International Movie Group Inc. (BC)
reincorporated in Canada 12/31/90
which reincorporated in Delaware
5/16/91 which merged into Lions
Gate Entertainment Corp. 6/30/98

META GOLD INC (NV)
Common $0.001 par split (155) for (1)
by issuance of (154) additional
shares payable 07/18/2013 to
holders of record 07/18/2013
Recapitalized as Silverton Energy,
Inc. 01/26/2015
Each share Common $0.001 par
exchanged for (0.5) share Common
$0.001 par

META GROUP INC (DE)
Common 1¢ par split (3) for (2) by
issuance of (0.5) additional share
payable 6/11/98 to holders of record
5/22/98
Merged into Gartner Inc. 4/1/2005
Each share Common 1¢ par
exchanged for $10 cash

META HEALTH SVCS INC (AB)
Reorganized under the laws of British
Columbia as Brookwater Ventures
Inc. 12/22/2009
Each share Common no par
exchanged for (0.5) share Common
no par
Brookwater Ventures Inc. (BC)
reincorporated in Ontario
09/27/2013 which name changed to
Blue Sky Energy Inc. 07/15/2016

META-SOFTWARE INC (CA)
Merged into Avant! Corp. 10/29/96
Each share Common no par
exchanged for (0.438) share
Common $0.0001 par
Avant! Corp. merged into Synopsys,
Inc. 6/6/2002

META SYS INC (CA)
Each share Common 1¢ par
exchanged for (1/3) share Common
3¢ par 9/12/81
Merged into Millicom Inc. 10/21/82
Each share Common 3¢ par
exchanged for (1) share Common
1¢ par
Millicom Inc. merged into Millicom
International Inc. 12/31/93

META URANIUM MINES LTD (ON)
Recapitalized as Metina
Developments Inc. 08/24/1978
Each share Capital Stock $1 par
exchanged for (0.1) share Capital
Stock no par
Metina Developments Inc.
reorganized as Olympus Holdings
Ltd. (BC) 11/05/1992 which
recapitalized as Olympus Pacific
Minerals Inc. (BC) 11/29/1996 which
reincorporated in Yukon 11/17/1997
which reincorporated in Canada
07/13/2006 which name changed to
Besra Gold Inc. 11/23/2012

METABASIS THERAPEUTICS INC (DE)
Issue Information - 5,000,000 shares
COM offered at $7 per share on
06/15/2004
Acquired by Ligand Pharmaceuticals
Inc. 01/27/2010
Each share Common $0.001 par
exchanged for (1) General
Contingent Value Right, (1)
Glucagon Contingent Value Right,
(1) Roche Contingent Value Right,
(1) TR Beta Contingent Value Right
and $0.045741 cash
Note: Each share Common $0.001
par received distribution of $0.076
cash from Roche Contingent Value
Right 07/01/2010

METABOLIC PHARMACEUTICALS LTD (AUSTRALIA)
ADR agreement terminated
11/01/2010
Each Sponsored ADR for Ordinary
exchanged for $0.64284 cash

METABOLIX INC (DE)
Each share old Common 1¢ par
exchanged for (0.16666666) share
new Common 1¢ par 05/27/2015
Name changed to Yield10 Bioscience,
Inc. 01/09/2017

METACREATIONS CORP (DE)
Name changed to Viewpoint Corp.
12/01/2000
Viewpoint Corp. name changed to
Enliven Marketing Technologies
Corp. 01/01/2008 which merged into
DG FastChannel, Inc. 10/02/2008
which name changed to Digital
Generation, Inc. 11/07/2011 which
merged into Sizmek Inc. 02/07/2014
(See Sizmek Inc.)

METADYNE VENTURES INC (CO)
Name changed to Megapix Corp.
07/25/1987

METAFRAME CORP (DE)
Common $1 par changed to 50¢ par
and (1) additional share issued
10/10/1967
Common 50¢ par split (3) for (2) by
issuance of (0.5) additional share
08/23/1968
Acquired by Mattel, Inc. 12/15/1969
Each share Common 50¢ par
exchanged for (0.45) share Common
$1 par

METAGRAPHIC SYS INC (DE)
Charter cancelled and declared
inoperative and void for
non-payment of taxes 3/1/84

METAHOST NET TECHNOLOGIES INC (BC)
Name changed to Network
Technology Professionals Inc.
07/30/2001
(See Network Technology
Professionals Inc.)

METAIRIE BK & TR CO (METAIRIE, LA)
Name changed 05/28/1970
Name changed from Metairie Savings
Bank & Trust Co. (Metairie, LA) to
Metairie Bank & Trust Co. (Metairie,
LA) 05/28/1970
Under plan of reorganization each
share Common $1 par automatically
became (1) share MBT Bancshares,
Inc. Common $1 par 05/16/2018

METAL & MINING SHARES, INC. (MD)
Charter revoked for failure to file
reports and pay fees 2/10/33

METAL & THERMIT CORP. (NJ)
Common no par exchanged (4) for (1)
in 1940
7% Preferred $100 par changed to
$50 par and (1) additional share
issued 12/6/55
Common no par changed to $5 par
and (1) additional share issued
12/6/55
Merged into American Can Co.
12/19/62
Each share 7% Preferred $50 par
exchanged for (2) shares 7%
Preferred $25 par
Each share Common $5 par
exchanged for (0.75) share Common
$12.50 par
American Can Co. name changed to
Primerica Corp. (NJ) 4/28/87 which
was acquired by Primerica Corp.
(DE) 12/15/88 which name changed
to Travelers Inc. 12/31/93 which
name changed to Travelers Group
Inc. 4/16/95 which name changed to
Citigroup Inc. 10/8/98

METAL AMALGAMATIONS LTD. (CANADA)
Deemed not to be a subsisting
company by the Dominion Secretary
of State 12/30/39

METAL BELLOWS CORP (MA)
Completely liquidated 6/12/68
Each share Common no par
exchanged for first and final
distribution of (0.28) share Zurn
Industries, Inc. Common 50¢ par
Zurn Industries, Inc. merged into U.S.
Industries, Inc. (Holding Co.) 6/11/98

METAL BOX PLC (ENGLAND)
Name changed 12/20/1974
Stock Dividends - 100% 07/13/1950;
10% 07/16/1954; 100% 07/15/1955;
50% 07/17/1959; 10% 07/21/1960;
10% 07/18/1963; 25% 07/23/1964;
25% 07/22/1966
Name changed from Metal Box Co.
Ltd. to Metal Box PLC 12/20/1974
7% Preference £1 par reclassified as
4.9% Preference £1 par 07/22/1976
4% 2nd Preference £1 par

reclassified as 2.8% 2nd Preference £1 par 07/22/1976
Each share Ordinary Stock £1 par exchanged for (4) shares Ordinary Stock 25p par 08/06/1986
Each ADR for Ordinary £1 par exchanged for (8) ADR's for Ordinary 25p par 08/06/1986
Note: Common Market regulation required all publicly held British companies to replace LTD with PLC in 1982
Name changed to MB Group PLC 09/30/1988
MB Group PLC name changed to MB-Caradon PLC 11/12/1990 which name changed to Caradon PLC 10/29/1993 which name changed to Novar PLC 01/03/2001
(See Novar PLC)

METAL CLOSURES (CANADA) LTD. (ON)
Name changed to Metcan Products Ltd. 6/30/66
Metcan Products Ltd. name changed to Alcan Ingot Ltd. 3/1/69

METAL DOOR & TRIM CO.
Name changed to La Porte Corp. 00/00/1944
(See La Porte Corp.)

METAL FINISHING RESEARCH CORP.
Acquired by Parker Rust-Proof Co. 00/00/1935
Details not available

METAL FLO CORP. (MI)
Merged into AO Industries, Inc. 09/01/1971
Each share Common $1 par exchanged for (0.4) share Common 1¢ par
AO Industries, Inc. name changed to Aegis Corp. 06/01/1974
(See Aegis Corp.)

METAL FORMING CORP. (ON)
Common $1 par exchanged (2) for (1) 00/00/1948
Assets sold to Vanadium-Alloys Steel Co. on a (1) for (5.6) basis 09/10/1958
Vanadium-Alloys Steel Co. name changed to Vasco Metals Corp. 06/08/1965 which was acquired by Teledyne, Inc. 06/30/1966 which merged into Allegheny Teledyne Inc. 08/15/1996 which name changed to Allegheny Technologies Inc. 11/29/1999

METAL GOODS CORP (MO)
Stock Dividends - 10% 06/15/1964; 10% 03/15/1966
Acquired by Alcan Aluminum Ltd. (Old) 01/03/1969
Each share Common $3.75 par exchanged for (1.1) shares Common no par
Alcan Aluminum Ltd. (Old) merged into Alcan Aluminum Ltd. (New) 07/24/1987 which name changed to Alcan Inc. 03/01/2001
(See Alcan Inc.)

METAL HYDRIDES, INC. (MA)
Name changed to Ventron Corp. 3/23/65
(See Ventron Corp.)

METAL MGMT INC (DE)
Plan of reorganization under Chapter 11 Federal Bankruptcy Code effective 06/29/2001
Each share old Common 1¢ par exchanged for (0.00148148) share new Common 1¢ par and (0.01111111) Common Stock Purchase Warrant Ser. A expiring 06/29/2006
Note: Unexchanged certificates were cancelled and became without value 06/29/2003
New Common 1¢ par split (2) for (1) by issuance of (1) additional share payable 04/20/2004 to holders of record 04/05/2004 Ex date - 04/21/2004
Merged into Sims Group Ltd. 03/14/2008
Each share new Common 1¢ par exchanged for (2.05) Sponsored ADR's for Ordinary A$0.50 par
Sims Group Ltd. name changed to Sims Metal Management Ltd. 11/26/2008

METAL MARKING INDUSTRIES, INC. (CO)
Name changed to Markon Manufacturing, Inc. 1/24/64
(See Markon Manufacturing, Inc.)

METAL MINES INC (NV)
SEC revoked common stock registration 02/18/2010

METAL MINES LTD. (QC)
Merged into Consolidated Canadian Faraday Ltd. 05/04/1967
Each share Capital Stock $1 par exchanged for (0.5) share Capital Stock no par
Consolidated Canadian Faraday Ltd. name changed to Faraday Resources Inc. 08/02/1983 which merged into Conwest Exploration Co. Ltd. (New) (AB) 09/01/1993 which merged into Alberta Energy Co. Ltd. 01/31/1996 which merged into EnCana Corp. 01/03/2003

METAL PACKAGE CORP.
Name changed to National Can Co. in 1935
National Can Co. merged into McKeesport Tin Plate Corp. in 1937 which name was changed to National Can Corp. in 1941
(See National Can Corp.)

METAL PRODUCTS HOLDING CORP. (NV)
Charter revoked for failure to file reports and pay fees 3/7/60

METAL RECOVERY CORP. (TX)
Charter forfeited for failure to pay taxes 5/8/72

METAL RECOVERY TECHNOLOGIES INC (DE)
Chapter 11 bankruptcy proceedings dismissed 02/23/2009
No stockholders' equity

METAL RES CORP (FL)
Name changed to Orexana Corp. 02/01/1990
Orexana Corp. name changed to Advent Technologies, Inc. 05/14/1993 which recapitalized as Newreach Communications Inc. 09/26/1996 which name changed to Henley Group, Inc. (FL) 04/02/1997 which name changed to CIS.com, Inc. 05/27/1999 which name changed to InterAmerican Resources, Inc. 08/13/2001 which name changed to Allixon Corp. 06/04/2004 which recapitalized as Simcoe Mining Resources Corp. 01/16/2008

METAL SAFETY RAILWAY TIE CO. (DE)
Reincorporated 07/03/1923
State of incorporation changed from (UT) to (DE) 07/03/1923
Charter cancelled and declared inoperative and void for non-payment of taxes 04/01/1932

METAL SHINGLE & SIDING CO., LTD.
Acquired by Eastern Steel Products, Ltd. 00/00/1927
Details not available

METAL STORM LTD (AUSTRALIA)
ADR agreement terminated 10/31/2014
ADR holders' equity unlikely

METAL TEXTILE CORP. (DE)
Participating Preference no par changed to $15 par in 1938
Common no par changed to 25¢ par in 1938
Assets sold to General Cable Corp. on a (4) for (9) basis 7/10/57
General Cable Corp. name changed to GK Technologies, Inc. 4/25/79
(See GK Technologies, Inc.)

METALASTIC MFG CORP (NJ)
Dissolved 11/14/84

METALBANC CORP (FL)
Recapitalized as Carom Capital Corp. 5/3/90
Each share Common $0.001 par exchanged for (0.25) share Common $0.001 par
Carom Capital Corp. name changed to Jillian's Entertainment Corp. 11/13/91
(See Jillian's Entertainment Corp.)

METALCLAD CORP (DE)
Reincorporated 11/24/1993
State of incorporation changed from (AZ) to (DE) 11/24/1993
Each share old Common 10¢ par exchanged for (0.1) share new Common 10¢ par 07/01/1999
Name changed to Entrx Corp. 06/24/2002
Entrx Corp. name changed to Entrprize Corp. (DE) 06/04/2012 which reincorporated in Indiana as Tprize, Inc. 08/18/2016

METALCOAT INTL CORP (ON)
Reorganized as Wycliffe Resources Inc. 7/4/2003
Each share Common no par exchanged for (2) shares Common no par
Wycliffe Resources Inc. name changed to Renforth Resources Inc. 7/28/2006

METALCRAFT INC (NY)
Common 10¢ par changed to 5¢ par and (1) additional share issued 06/22/1968
Adjudicated bankrupt 08/02/1972

METALCRAFTERS SPECIALTIES INC (NY)
Liquidation completed
Each share Common 10¢ par exchanged for initial distribution of $1.837 cash 03/10/1975
Each share Common 10¢ par received second and final distribution of $0.342 cash 08/25/1976

METALDYNE PERFORMANCE GROUP INC (DE)
Merged into American Axle & Manufacturing Holdings, Inc. 04/06/2017
Each share Common $0.001 par exchanged for (0.5) share Common 1¢ par and $13.50 cash

METALEX RES INC (NV)
Common $0.00001 par split (14) for (1) by issuance of (13) additional shares payable 1/30/2006 to holders of record 01/30/2006 Ex date - 01/31/2006
Name changed to Rancher Energy Corp. (NV) 04/18/2006
Rancher Energy Corp. (NV) reorganized in Colorado as T-Rex Oil, Inc. 10/29/2014

METALFAB INC (WI)
Common $1 par reclassified as Class B Common $1 par 12/11/1967
Each share old Class B Common $1 par exchanged for (0.002) share new Class B Common $1 par 01/31/1975
Note: In effect holders received $12 cash per share public interest was eliminated

METALICO INC (DE)
Acquired by Total Merchant Ltd. 09/11/2015
Each share Common $0.001 par exchanged for $0.60 cash

METALINE & PINE CREEK CONSOLIDATED MINING CO. (WA)
Acquired by Metaline Contact Mines 5/4/64
Each share Common 10¢ par exchanged for (0.25) share Common 5¢ plus $0.19 cash

METALINE METALS CO.
Assets purchased by Pend Oreille Mines & Metals Co. 00/00/1945
Details not available

METALINE MNG & LEASING CO (WA)
Reincorporated under the laws of Nevada as HuntMountain Resources and Common no par changed to $0.001 par 08/03/2005
HuntMountain Resources (NV) reincorporated in Washington as HuntMountain Resources Ltd. 08/19/2008

METALIZED CERAMICS CORP (RI)
97% acquired by Rosenthal Technik U.S.A. through purchase offer which expired 08/31/1977
Public interest eliminated

METALL MNG CORP (CANADA)
Name changed to Inmet Mining Corp. 05/04/1995
Inmet Mining Corp. acquired by First Quantum Minerals Ltd. 04/09/2013

METALLA RTY & STREAMING LTD (CANADA)
Reincorporated under the laws of British Columbia 11/16/2017

METALLGESELLSCHAFT CDA INVTS LTD (CANADA)
Floating Rate Retractable Class B Preferred Ser. 1 no par called for redemption 7/31/90
Public interest eliminated

METALLIC VENTURES GOLD INC (ON)
Name changed 07/11/2003
Name changed from Metallic Ventures Inc. to Metallic Ventures Gold Inc. 07/11/2003
Merged into International Minerals Corp. 03/03/2010
Each share Common no par exchanged for (0.1635) share Common no par and USD $0.4615 cash
(See International Minerals Corp.)

METALLICA RES INC (ON)
Merged into New Gold Inc. 06/30/2008
Each share Common no par exchanged for (0.9) share Common no par and $0.0001 cash
Note: Unexchanged certificates were cancelled and became without value 06/30/2014

METALLINE MNG INC (NV)
Name changed to Silver Bull Resources, Inc. 05/02/2011

METALLINE RESOURCE CORP (BC)
Name changed to Direct Choice T.V. Inc. (BC) 3/14/95
Direct Choice T.V. Inc. (BC) reincorporated in Canada as Star Choice Communications Inc. 12/11/96 which merged into Canadian Satellite Communications 8/31/99 which was acquired by Shaw Communications Inc. 4/2/2001

METALLUM RES INC (ON)
Recapitalized as Torrent Capital Ltd. 02/06/2017
Each share Common no par exchanged for (0.33333333) share Common no par

METALLURG INC (DE)
Acquired by Safeguard International Fund LP 7/13/98
Each share Common 1¢ par exchanged for $30 cash

METALLURGICAL INDS INC (NJ)
Name changed 7/1/79
Class A Common 10¢ par split (3) for (2) by issuance of (0.5) additional share 6/15/79
Name changed from Metallurgical International Inc. to Metallurgical Industries Inc. 7/1/79
Stock Dividend - 25% 6/15/84
Class A Common 10¢ par split (3) for (2) by issuance of (0.5) additional share 12/22/89
Each share old Class A Common 10¢ par exchanged for (0.025) share new Class A Common 10¢ par 2/1/95
Name changed to Bria Communications Corp. 4/3/95
Bria Communications Corp. name changed to Tianrong Internet Products & Services Inc. 4/9/99

METALLURGICAL PROCESSING CORP (NY)
Common 10¢ par split (5) for (4) by issuance of (0.25) additional share 3/20/68
Stock Dividend - 25% 3/21/67
Completely liquidated 3/5/80
Each share Class A Common 10¢ par received first and final distribution of $0.25 cash
Note: Certificates were not required to be surrendered and are without value

METALLURGICAL RES INC (DE)
Charter cancelled and declared inoperative and void for non-payment of taxes 3/1/75

METALORE MINING CORP. LTD. (QC)
Acquired by New Metalore Mining Co. Ltd. on a (1) for (3) basis 00/00/1950
New Metalore Mining Co. Ltd. recapitalized as Metalore Resources Ltd. 10/22/1976

METALPHOTO CORP (NJ)
Merged into Horizons Research Inc. 12/31/1969
Each share Capital Stock 1¢ par exchanged for (0.5) share 2¢ Conv. Preferred Ser. A no par and (0.25) share Common no par
(See Horizons Research Inc.)

METALQUEST MINERALS INC (BC)
Recapitalized as Canada Gold Corp. 09/01/2009
Each share Common no par exchanged for (0.33333333) share Common no par
Canada Gold Corp. name changed to STEM 7 Capital Inc. 07/12/2013 which name changed to South Star Mining Corp. 12/22/2017

METALS & CHEMICALS CORP. (DE)
No longer in existence having become inoperative and void for non-payment of taxes 4/1/55

METALS & CONTROLS CORP. (MA)
Common $5 par split (3) for (1) by issuance of (2) additional shares 2/21/57
Merged into Texas Instruments, Inc. on a (0.75) for (1) basis 4/17/59

METALS DEVELOPMENTS LTD.
Properties acquired by Hudson-Patricia Gold Mines Ltd. in 1934 which became bankrupt in 1937

METALS EXPLORATION CORP. (NV)
Charter revoked for failure to file reports and pay fees 3/6/61

METALS PLUS INCOME CORP (ON)
Trust terminated 02/26/2016
Each Class A Share received $2.9363 cash

METALS RESH CORP AMER (UT)
Name changed to Metals Research Group Corp. 12/15/97

METALS SCIENCE & PROCESSING, INC. (PA)
Common 10¢ par changed to 5¢ par 11/25/63
Placed in receivership 9/27/65
Assets sold to pay taxes; no stockholders equity

METALS TECHNOLOGIES INTL INC (CO)
Charter suspended for failure to file annual reports 09/30/1981

METALS USA HLDGS CORP (DE)
Acquired by Reliance Steel & Aluminum Co. 04/12/2013
Each share Common 1¢ par exchanged for $20.65 cash

METALS USA INC (DE)
Issue Information - 5,900,000 shares COM offered at $10 per share on 07/11/1997
Plan of reorganization under Chapter 11 Federal Bankruptcy Code effective 10/31/2002
Each share old Common 1¢ par will receive approximately (0.1) Common Stock Purchase Warrant
Note: Exchange of certificates required by 10/31/2004 to receive distribution
Merged into Flag Holdings Corp. 11/30/2005
Each share new Common 1¢ par exchanged for $22 cash

METALS X LTD (AUSTRALIA)
ADR agreement terminated 12/30/2014
No ADR's remain outstanding

METALSMITH MINES LTD.
Dissolved 00/00/1947
Details not available

METALTEC CORP. (NJ)
Merged into Technology General Corp. 9/2/87
Each share Common 10¢ par exchanged for (2) shares Common 10¢ par

METALTECH CORP (OR)
Name changed to Enerphaze Corp. 12/13/2001
(See Enerphaze Corp.)

METALUX INDS INC (DE)
Each share old Common 5¢ par exchanged for (0.1) share new Common 5¢ par 5/1/73
Voluntarily dissolved 7/1/94
Details not available

METALWARES CORP.
Acquired by Service Stations, Ltd. in 1929 which name changed to International Metal Industries Ltd. in 1934 which name changed to Wood (John) Industries, Ltd. 5/15/57
Wood (John) Industries Ltd. acquired by Wood (John) Co. 12/3/62 which was acquired by Anthes Imperial Ltd. in March 1964

METAMEDIA CAP CORP (AB)
Reorganized under the laws of Canada as Brea Resources Corp. 08/10/2010
Each share Common no par exchanged for (0.1) share Common no par
Brea Resources Corp. recapitalized as Goldstream Minerals Inc. 09/21/2012

METAMOR WORLDWIDE INC (DE)
Merged into PSINet Inc. 6/15/2000
Each share Common 1¢ par exchanged for (0.9) share Common 1¢ par
(See PSINet Inc.)

METANA MINERALS N L (AUSTRALIA)
Acquired by Gold Mines of Australia 04/07/1994
Each Sponsored ADR for Ordinary AUD $0.25 par exchanged for $2.155 cash

METANOR RES INC (CANADA)
Each share old Common no par exchanged for (0.1) share new Common no par 04/13/2017
Merged into BonTerra Resources Inc. 09/24/2018
Each share new Common no par exchanged for (1.6039) shares new Common no par
Note: Unexchanged certificates will be cancelled and become without value 09/24/2024

METAPATH SOFTWARE INTL INC
Merged into Marconi plc 06/15/2000
Each share Common no par exchanged for $17.50 cash

METAPHOR CORP (NV)
Each share old Common $0.0001 par exchanged for (0.04) share new Common $0.0001 par 02/18/2005
Note: Holders of (101) to (2,500) shares received (100) shares only
Holders of (100) or fewer shares were not affected
Name changed to China Media Networks International, Inc. 08/25/2005
China Media Networks International, Inc. name changed to Medical Solutions Management Inc. 08/04/2006
(See Medical Solutions Management Inc.)

METARUNNER INC (WA)
Charter expired 06/30/2006

METASOLUTIONS INC (NV)
Name changed to Biotricity Inc. 02/01/2016

METASOLV INC (DE)
Merged into Oracle Corp. 12/18/2006
Each share Common 1¢ par exchanged for $4.10 cash

METASOLV SOFTWARE INC (DE)
Name changed to MetaSolv Inc. 01/02/2001
(See MetaSolv Inc.)

METASOURCE GROUP INC (NV)
Each share old Common $0.001 par exchanged for (1.1) shares new Common $0.001 par 11/26/2002
SEC revoked common stock registration 12/04/2009

METASUN ENTERPRISES INC (NV)
Old Common $0.001 par split (5.322687957) for (1) by issuance of (4.322687957) additional shares payable 01/12/2005 to holders of record 01/12/2005
Name changed to Pure Biofuels Corp. 08/07/2006
(See Pure Biofuels Corp.)

METATEC INC (OH)
Reincorporated 4/30/99
Name changed 5/30/2003
Class A Common 10¢ par reclassified as Common 10¢ par 5/20/93
Reincorporated from Metatec Corp. (FL) to Metatec International Inc. (OH) 4/30/99
Name changed from Metatec International Inc. to Metatec, Inc. 5/30/2003
Plan of reorganization under Chapter 11 Federal Bankruptcy Code effective 9/25/2004
No stockholders' equity

METATOOLS INC (DE)
Under plan of merger name changed to MetaCreations Corp. 05/29/1997
MetaCreations Corp. name changed to Viewpoint Corp. 12/01/2000 which name changed to Enliven Marketing Technologies Corp. 01/01/2008 which merged into DG FastChannel, Inc. 10/02/2008 which name changed to Digital Generation, Inc. 11/07/2011 which merged into Sizmek Inc. 02/07/2014
(See Sizmek Inc.)

METATRON INC OLD (DE)
Each share old Common $0.001 par exchanged for (0.0001) share new Common $0.001 par 06/24/2015
Reorganized as Metatron Inc. (New) 02/01/2017
Each share new Common $0.001 par exchanged for (0.01282051) share Common $0.001 par

METATRONICS MFG CORP (NY)
Charter cancelled and proclaimed dissolved for failure to pay taxes 12/23/92

METAVANTE TECHNOLOGIES INC (WI)
Merged into Fidelity National Information Services, Inc. 10/01/2009
Each share Common 1¢ par exchanged for (1.35) shares Common 1¢ par

METAWAVE COMMUNICATIONS CORP (DE)
Issue Information - 6,250,000 shares OC-COM offered at $9 per share on 04/26/2000
Plan of reorganization under Chapter 11 Federal Bankruptcy proceedings confirmed 01/09/2004
Stockholders' equity unlikely

METAXA RES LTD (BC)
Struck off register and declared dissolved for failure to file returns 10/30/92

METCALF & EDDY COS INC (MA)
Merged into Air & Water Technologies Corp. 10/31/91
Each share Common 1¢ par exchanged for (0.875) share Class A Common $0.001 par
Air & Water Technologies Corp. name changed to Aqua Alliance, Inc. 10/13/98
(See Aqua Alliance, Inc.)

METCALF FARMS HAWAII INC (UT)
Charter suspended for failure to file reports 12/31/1975

METCAN PRODUCTS LTD. (ON)
Name changed to Alcan Ingot Ltd. 3/1/69

METCASH TRADING LTD (AUSTRALIA)
Name changed to Metcash Ltd. 07/29/2005

METCO RES INC (QC)
Merged into Breakwater Resources Ltd. 04/15/2008
Each share Common no par exchanged for (0.0546448) share Common no par
(See Breakwater Resources Ltd.)

METCOM INC. (NV)
Name changed to Digital Metcom, Inc. 3/26/86

METCOM INC (DE)
Name changed to Omni-Wave Electronics Corp. 8/10/72
(See Omni-Wave Electronics Corp.)

METEOR AIR TRANSPORT, INC. (DE)
Stock Dividend - 10% 4/15/56
No longer in existence having become inoperative and void for non-payment of taxes 4/1/60

METEOR CREEK RES INC (BC)
Ceased operations 05/30/2003
Stockholders' equity unlikely

METEOR INDS INC (CO)
Reincorporated under the laws of Minnesota as Active IQ Technologies Inc. 04/30/2001
Active IQ Technologies Inc. name changed to Wits Basin Precious Minerals Inc. 07/10/2003

METEOR MNG LTD (BC)
Name changed to Tesla Explorations Ltd. 09/24/1979
(See Tesla Explorations Ltd.)

METEOR MOTOR CAR CO. (OH)
Name changed to Miami Manufacturing Co. 01/27/1954
(See Miami Manufacturing Co.)

METEOR TECHNOLOGIES INC (AB)
Name changed 10/13/99
Name changed from Meteor Minerals Inc. to Meteor Technologies Inc. 10/13/99
Name changed to ThoughtShare Communications Inc. 11/8/2001
Thoughtshare Communications Inc. recapitalized as Qumana Software Inc. 2/6/2004

METER DYNAMICS INC (UT)
Proclaimed dissolved for failure to pay taxes 12/31/86

METER MAID INDS INC (DE)
Adjudicated bankrupt 9/24/70
Charter subsequently cancelled and declared inoperative and void for non-payment of taxes 4/15/71

METEX CORP (DE)
Common 25¢ par split (3) for (2) by issuance of (0.5) additional share 06/06/1985
Merged into United Capital Corp. 03/03/1989
Each share Common 25¢ par exchanged for (1.538) shares Common 10¢ par
(See United Capital Corp.)

METEX ELECTRONICS CORP. (NJ)
Merged into Ferrodynamics Corp. (DE) 07/01/1964
Each share Capital Stock 20¢ par exchanged for (0.125) share Common 25¢ par
Ferrodynamics Corp. (DE) name changed to Metex Corp. 03/08/1966 which merged into United Capital Corp. 03/03/1989
(See United Capital Corp.)

METHA ENERGY SOLUTIONS INC (DE)
Name changed to China Network Media Inc. 12/13/2012

METHANOGEN FUELS CORP (DE)
Merged into NET Information Systems, Inc. 12/8/86
Each share Common 1¢ par exchanged for $0.90 cash

METHOD PRODS CORP NEW (FL)
Each share old Common $0.0001 par exchanged for (0.1) share new Common $0.0001 par 02/04/2002
Recapitalized as Alchemy Creative, Inc. 11/15/2007
Each share Common $0.0001 par exchanged for (0.01) share Common $0.0001 par

METHOD PRODS CORP OLD (FL)
Reorganized as Method Products Corp. (New) 10/06/2000
Each share Common $0.0001 par exchanged for (1) share Common $0.0001 par
Method Products Corp. (New) recapitalized as Alchemy Creative, Inc. 11/15/2007

METHODE ELECTRS INC OLD (DE)
Common $1 par reclassified as Class B Common 50¢ par 9/23/82
Each share Class B Common 50¢ par received distribution of (1) share Class A Common 50¢ par 10/15/82
Class B Common 50¢ par split (2) for (1) by issuance of (1) additional share 10/14/83
Each share Conv. Class B Common 50¢ par received distribution of (1) share Class A Common 50¢ par 1/15/93
Class B Common 50¢ par split (3) for (2) by issuance of (0.5) additional share 10/31/95
Each share Class B Common 50¢ par received distribution of (1.511303) shares Stratos Lightwave, Inc. Common 1¢ par payable 4/28/2001 to holders of record 4/5/2001 Ex date - 4/30/2001
Plan of merger effective 1/9/2004
Each share Conv. Class B Common 50¢ par exchanged for $23.55 cash
(Additional Information in Active)

METHYLGENE INC (CANADA)
Reorganized under the laws of Delaware as Mirati Therapeutics, Inc. 07/03/2013
Each share Common no par exchanged for (0.02) share Common $0.001 par

METHYLGENE INC (QC)
Issue Information - 4,710,000 shares COM offered at $4.25 per share on 06/18/2004
Reincorporated under the laws of Canada 05/21/2010
MethylGene Inc. (Canada) reorganized in Delaware as Mirati Therapeutics, Inc. 07/03/2013

METINA DEVS INC (ON)
Reorganized under the laws of British Columbia as Olympus Holdings Ltd. 11/05/1992
Each share Common no par exchanged for (0.22222222) share Common no par
Olympus Holdings Ltd. recapitalized as Olympus Pacific Minerals Inc. (BC) 11/29/1996 which reincorporated in Yukon 11/17/1997 which reincorporated in Canada 07/13/2006 which name changed to Besra Gold Inc. 11/23/2012

METISCAN INC (DE)
Recapitalized as Aclor International, Inc. 01/04/2012
Each share Common $0.0001 par exchanged for (0.0005) share Common $0.0001 par
(See Aclor International, Inc.)

METKA INDUSTRIAL-CONSTRUCTION S A (GREECE)
Name changed 08/01/2016
Name changed from Metka S.A. to Metka Industrial Construction S.A. 08/01/2016
ADR agreement terminated 07/28/2017
Each ADR for Ordinary exchanged for $9.395364 cash

METLIFE INC (DE)
Each 6.75% Common Equity Unit automatically became (0.294) share Common 1¢ par 02/17/2009
6.5% Preferred Ser. B 1¢ par called for redemption at $25 plus $0.036111 accrued dividends on 07/01/2015
(Additional Information in Active)

METLIFE ST STR EQUITY TR (MA)
Capital Appreciation Fund Shares of Bene. Int. $0.001 par split (2) for (1) by issuance of (1) additional share 10/30/1992
Name changed to State Street Research Equity Trust 11/03/1995
(See State Street Research Equity Trust)

METLIFE ST STR FINL TR (MA)
Name changed 09/01/1993
Name changed from MetLife-State Street Fixed Income Trust to MetLife-State Street Financial Trust 09/01/1993
Name changed to State Street Research Financial Trust 03/15/1996
(See State Street Research Financial Trust)

METLIFE ST STR INCOME TR (MA)
Name changed to State Street Research Income Trust 08/04/1995
(See State Street Research Income Trust)

METLIFE ST STR MONEY MKT TR (MA)
Name changed to State Street Research Money Market Trust 08/04/1995
(See State Street Research Money Market Trust)

METLIFE ST STR TAX EXEMPT TR (MA)
Name changed to State Street Research Tax-Exempt Trust 05/25/1995
(See State Street Research Tax-Exempt Trust)

METLOX MFG CO (CA)
Reported out of business 00/00/1989
Details not available

METOIL RES LTD (AB)
Name changed to Mohave Gold Inc. and Class A Common no par reclassified as Common no par 04/01/1986
(See Mohave Gold Inc.)

METONIC MINES LTD.
Dissolved in 1934

METOREX LTD (SOUTH AFRICA)
Acquired by Jinchuan Group Ltd. 01/16/2012
Each Sponsored ADR for Ordinary exchanged for $1.054835 cash

METOZ HLDGS LTD (SOUTH AFRICA)
Name changed 11/26/2004
Stock Dividends - 1.8% payable 01/12/2001 to holders of record 12/22/2000 Ex date - 12/26/2000; 1.3% payable 01/25/2002 to holders of record 01/04/2002 Ex date - 01/02/2002; 2% payable 07/17/2002 to holders of record 07/05/2002 Ex date - 07/02/2002; 1.7% payable 01/30/2003 to holders of record 01/10/2003 Ex date - 01/08/2003
Name changed from Metro Cash & Carry Ltd. to Metoz Holdings Ltd. 11/26/2004
GDR agreement terminated 04/25/2005
Each 144A GDR for Ordinary exchanged for $1.753 cash
Each Reg. S GDR for Ordinary shares exchanged for $1.753 cash

METPATH INC (NY)
Common 10¢ par split (2) for (1) by issuance of (1) additional share 2/27/81
Acquired by Corning Glass Works 2/26/82
Each share Common 10¢ par exchanged for (0.4488) share Common $5 par
Corning Glass Works name changed to Corning Inc. 4/28/89

METRA BIOSYSTEMS INC (CA)
Second Offering - 3,000,000 shares COM offered at $10 per share on 06/30/1995
Merged into Quidel Corp. 8/5/99
Each share Common $0.001 par exchanged for $1.78 cash

METRA ELECTRS CORP (NY)
Reincorporated 03/30/1991
Stock Dividend - 100% 11/15/1976
State of incorporation changed from (NY) to (FL) 03/30/1991
Company went private 10/30/1992
Details not available

METRETEK TECHNOLOGIES INC (DE)
Name changed to PowerSecure International, Inc. 08/22/2007
(See PowerSecure International, Inc.)

METRIC RES CORP (CA)
Merged into Trans Union Corp. 05/13/1977
Each share Common 5¢ par exchanged for (0.0946074) share Common $1 par
(See Trans Union Corp.)

METRICOM INC (DE)
Secondary Offering - 2,200,000 shares COM offered at $30.25 per share on 03/17/1994
Plan of reorganization under Chapter 11 Federal Bankruptcy Code effective 9/14/2002
No stockholders' equity

METRIDATA COMPUTING INC (KY)
Name changed to MCI Liquidating Co., Inc. 02/02/1979
(See MCI Liquidating Co., Inc.)

METRIKA SYS CORP (DE)
Issue Information - 2,000,000 shares COM offered at $15.50 per share on 06/20/1997
Merged into Thermo Instrument Systems Inc. 5/3/2000
Each share Common 1¢ par exchanged for $9 cash

METRIS COS INC (DE)
Issue Information - 2,833,333 shares COM offered at $16 per share on 10/25/1996
Common 1¢ par split (2) for (1) by issuance of (1) additional share payable 6/15/99 to holders of record 6/1/99 Ex date - 6/16/99
Common 1¢ par split (3) for (2) by issuance of (0.5) additional share payable 6/15/2000 to holders of record 6/1/2000
Merged into HSBC Finance Corp. 11/30/2005
Each share Common 1¢ par exchanged for $15 cash

METRISA INC (DE)
Name changed to P.A. Instruments Inc. 10/27/2003

METRIX DATA SYS INC (NY)
Ceased operations 07/00/1975
No stockholders' equity

METRIX INC (DE)
Name changed to Aristek Corp. 3/1/77
Aristek Corp. name changed to Aristek Communities, Inc. 12/28/81 which name changed to Homefree Village Resorts, Inc. 11/5/86
(See Homefree Village Resorts, Inc.)

METRO AG (GERMANY)
Each ADR for Ordinary received distribution of $4.073636 cash payable 08/14/2017 to holders of record 08/07/2017 Ex date - 08/15/2017
Name changed to Cecomony AG 08/25/2017

METRO AIRLS INC (DE)
Common 10¢ par split (3) for (2) by issuance of (0.5) additional share 03/22/1985
Common 10¢ par split (3) for (2) by issuance of (0.5) additional share 01/15/1987
Reorganized under Chapter 11 Federal Bankruptcy Code 12/28/1993
Each (26.5) shares old Common 10¢ par exchanged for (1) share new Common 10¢ par
Company terminated registration of common stock and is no longer public as of 03/26/1998

METRO BANCHOLDING CORP (MO)
Through exchange offer 99.9% of $3.25 Conv. Preference Class A 1st Ser. $5 par, $3.25 Conv. Preference Class A 2nd Ser. $5 par and Common $1 par acquired by Boatmen's Bancshares, Inc. as of 11/30/1983
8% Preferred Ser. A $10 par called for redemption 03/00/1984
Public interest eliminated

METRO BANCORP, INC. (MA)
Merged into Central Co-Operative Bank (Somerville, MA) 12/09/1994
Details not available

METRO BANCORP INC (PA)
Merged into F.N.B. Corp. 02/12/2016

MET-MET

Each share Common $1 par exchanged for (2.373) shares Common 1¢ par

METRO BANCORPORATION (IA)
Merged into Mercantile Bancorporation, Inc. 01/03/1994
Each share Common $5 par exchanged for (2.0967) shares $5 par
Mercantile Bancorporation, Inc. merged into Firstar Corp. (New) 09/20/1999 which merged into U.S. Bancorp (DE) 02/27/2001

METRO BANCSHARES INC (DE)
Common 1¢ par split (3) for (2) by issuance of (0.5) additional share 8/14/92
Common 1¢ par split (3) for (2) by issuance of (0.5) additional share 9/16/93
Merged into North Fork Bancorporation, Inc. 11/30/94
Each share Common 1¢ par exchanged for (1.645) shares Common $2.50 par
North Fork Bancorporation, Inc. merged into Capital One Financial Corp. 12/1/2006

METRO BK (ATLANTA, GA)
Each share Common $3 par exchanged for (2) shares Common $1.50 par 10/27/88
Reorganized as Metro Financial Corp. 4/2/90
Each share Common $1.50 par exchanged for (1) share Common $1 par
Metro Financial Corp. merged into Regions Financial Corp. (Old) 1/31/96 which merged into Regions Financial Corp. (New) 7/1/2004

METRO BANK (ST. LOUIS, MO)
Acquired by Boatmen's Bancshares, Inc. 11/01/1983
Details not available

METRO BK FINL SVCS INC (FL)
Chapter 7 bankruptcy proceedings terminated 08/28/2014
No stockholders' equity

METRO CABLE CORP (CO)
Each share Common $0.001 par exchanged for (0.04) share Common 1¢ par 12/05/1988
Reincorporated under the laws of Wyoming as Metro Capital Corp. 03/31/1992
Metro Capital Corp. name changed to American Rivers Oil Co. 11/29/1995 which merged into AROC Inc. 12/08/1999
(See AROC Inc.)

METRO CAP CORP (WY)
Name changed to American Rivers Oil Co. 11/29/1995
American Rivers Oil Co. merged into AROC Inc. 12/08/1999
(See AROC Inc.)

METRO-COUNTY BK VA INC (MECHANICSBURG, VA)
Common $4 par split (2) for (1) by issuance of (1) additional share payable 06/01/1998 to holders of record 05/20/1998
Common $4 par split (5) for (4) by issuance of (0.25) additional share payable 06/01/1999 to holders of record 05/14/1999
Stock Dividends - 10% payable 06/02/2000 to holders of record 05/19/2000; 10% payable 06/04/2001 to holders of record 05/18/2001 Ex date - 06/19/2001
Merged into Southern Financial Bancorp, Inc. 08/14/2002
Each share Common $4 par exchanged for (0.15058) share Common 1¢ par and $2.90 cash
Southern Financial Bancorp, Inc. merged into Provident Bankshares Corp. 04/30/2004 which was acquired by M&T Bank Corp. 05/26/2009

METRO DEV INC (UT)
Reorganized under the laws of Nevada as First Fidelity Acceptance Corp. 11/2/88
Each share Common $0.001 par exchanged for (0.05) share Common $0.001 par
(See First Fidelity Acceptance Corp.)

METRO DRUG LTD. (CANADA)
Declared bankrupt 7/12/66
No stockholders' equity

METRO ENERGY INC (UT)
Each share Common no par exchanged for (0.2) share Common 5¢ par 9/11/81
Recapitalized as Whisky Barrel Cooker Inc. 6/18/93
Each share Common 5¢ par exchanged for (0.25) share Common 5¢ par

METRO ENERGY LTD (BC)
Struck off register and declared dissolved for failure to file returns 3/15/96

METRO FINL CORP (GA)
Stock Dividends - 10% 9/17/93; 10% 3/15/94; 10% 5/15/95
Merged into Regions Financial Corp. (Old) 1/31/96
Each share Common $1 par exchanged for (0.431) share Common $1 par
Regions Financial Corp. (Old) merged into Regions Financial Corp. (New) 7/1/2004

METRO GLOBAL MEDIA INC (FL)
Reincorporated under the laws of Delaware 11/8/96

METRO GOLD MINES, LTD. (ON)
Charter surrendered for failure to file reports and pay taxes in 1951

METRO GOLDWYN MAYER FILM CO (DE)
Name changed to MGM/UA Entertainment Co. 4/12/82
MGM/UA Entertainment Co. acquired by Turner Broadcasting System, Inc. 3/25/86 which merged into Time Warner Inc. 10/10/96

METRO-GOLDWYN-MAYER INC NEW (DE)
Issue Information - 9,000,000 shares COM offered at $20 per share on 11/12/1997
Merged into LOC Acquisition Corp. 4/8/2005
Each share Common 1¢ par exchanged for $12 cash

METRO GOLDWYN MAYER INC OLD (DE)
Common no par split (2) for (1) by issuance of (1) additional share 7/8/66
Common no par split (5) for (2) by issuance of (1.5) additional shares 3/25/75
Common no par split (2) for (1) by issuance of (1) additional share 1/31/79
Name changed to MGM Grand Hotels, Inc. 5/30/80
(See MGM Grand Hotels, Inc.)

METRO INC (DE)
Stock Dividends - 300% 11/28/1955; 100% 02/01/1957; 25% 04/30/1969
Merged into U.S. Industries, Inc. 12/16/1969
Each share Preferred $10 par exchanged for $10.50 cash
Each share Common $1 par exchanged for $24 cash

METRO INFORMATION SVCS INC (DE)
Issue Information - 3,100,000 shares COM offered at $16 per share on 01/29/1997
Merged into Keane, Inc. 12/3/2001

Each share Common 1¢ par exchanged for (0.48) share Common 10¢ par
(See Keane, Inc.)

METRO MATCH INC (NV)
Charter revoked for failure to file reports and pay fees 9/1/2002

METRO MEAT PACKING INC (MN)
Adjudicated bankrupt 04/11/1975
Stockholders' equity unlikely

METRO MINERALS LTD. (ON)
Charter cancelled by Province of Ontario by default in 1957

METRO MOBILE CTS INC (DE)
Each share Common 10¢ par exchanged for (0.25) share Conv. Class A Common 10¢ par and (1/3) share Class B Common 10¢ par 5/4/88
Conv. Class A Common 10¢ par changed to 3-1/3¢ par 5/15/90
Class B Common 10¢ par changed to 3-1/3¢ par 5/15/90
Each share Conv. Class A Common 3-1/3¢ par received distribution of (2) shares Class B Common 3-1/3¢ par 5/25/90
Each share Class B Common 3-1/3¢ par received distribution of (2) shares Class B Common 3-1/3¢ par 5/25/90
Stock Dividend - 10% 4/13/87
Merged into Bell Atlantic Corp. 4/30/92
Each share Conv. Class A Common 3-1/3¢ par exchanged for (0.5193) share Common $1 par
Each share Class B Common 3-1/3¢ par exchanged for (0.5193) share Common $1 par
Bell Atlantic Corp. name changed to Verizon Communications Inc. 6/30/2000

METRO MORTGAGE CORP. LTD. (AB)
Name changed to Medallion Mortgage Corp. Ltd. 03/10/1967
Each share Capital Stock no par exchanged for (1) share Capital Stock no par
(See Medallion Mortgage Corp. Ltd.)

METRO NETWORKS INC (DE)
Merged into Westwood One, Inc. (Old) 09/22/1999
Each share Common $0.001 par exchanged for (1.5) shares Common 1¢ par
Westwood One, Inc. (Old) name changed to Dial Global, Inc. 12/12/2011 which name changed to Westwood One, Inc. (New) 11/25/2013
(See Westwood One, Inc. (New))

METRO RESOURCES INC. (BC)
Name changed to Metro Industrial Corp. 5/27/83

METRO RES LTD (YT)
Merged into Asia Pacific Resources Ltd. 01/18/1999
Each share Common no par exchanged for (0.44) share Common no par
(See Asia Pacific Resources Ltd.)

METRO RICHELIEU INC (QC)
Name changed to Metro, Inc. 1/25/2000

METRO SVGS BK F S B (WOOD RIVER, IL)
Merged into Mercantile Bancorporation, Inc. 03/07/1996
Each share Common $1 par exchanged for (1.0286) shares Common $1 par
Mercantile Bancorporation, Inc. merged into Firstar Corp. (New) 09/20/1999 which merged into U.S. Bancorp (DE) 02/27/2001

METRO SYS INC (NV)
Common $0.001 par split (5) for (1) by issuance of (4) additional shares 12/28/1987
Recapitalized as Adelaide Holdings, Inc. 07/30/1991
Each share Common $0.001 par exchanged for (0.02) share Common $0.001 par
Adelaide Holdings, Inc. name changed to Tasty Fries, Inc. 09/28/1993
(See Tasty Fries, Inc.)

METRO TEL CORP (DE)
Common 10¢ par changed to $0.025 par and (3) additional shares issued 04/19/1968
Common $0.025 par split (5) for (4) by issuance of (0.25) additional share 07/29/1983
Name changed to Dryclean USA, Inc. 11/10/1999
Dryclean USA, Inc. name changed to EnviroStar, Inc. 12/01/2009

METRO URBAN INVT CORP (UT)
Recapitalized as Metro International, Inc. 10/10/1976
Each share Capital Stock $0.001 par exchanged for (0.05) share Capital Stock 1¢ par

METRO WIRELESS INTERACTIVE CORP (NV)
Old Common $0.001 par split (3) for (1) by issuance of (2) additional shares 02/02/1994
Each share old Common $0.001 par exchanged for (0.04) share new Common $0.001 par 11/28/1994
Name changed to Red Rock International Corp. (NV) 04/01/1996
Red Rock International Corp. (NV) reorganized in Kentucky as Page International Inc. 11/05/1997 which reincorporated in Nevada 12/31/1997 which name changed to China TianRen Organic Food, Inc. 06/14/2007

METROBANC FED SVGS BK (GRAND RAPIDS, MI)
Common $1 par split (3) for (2) by issuance of (0.5) additional share 5/15/86
Merged into Comerica Inc. 7/24/87
Each share Common $1 par exchanged for (0.43) share $4.32 Preferred Ser. B no par

METROBANCORP (IN)
Stock Dividends - 5% payable 4/6/98 to holders of record 3/18/98; 10% payable 2/8/99 to holders of record 1/19/99; 5% payable 2/7/2000 to holders of record 1/20/2000; 5% payable 3/12/2001 to holders of record 3/1/2001; 5% payable 3/12/2002 to holders of record 3/1/2002
Merged into First Indiana Corp. 1/13/2003
Each share Common no par exchanged for $17 cash

METROBANK (LOS ANGELES, CA)
Name changed 11/1/88
Common $2.50 par changed to $1.66-2/3 par and (0.5) additional share issued 5/19/82
Under plan of reorganization name changed from Metrobank, N.A. (Los Angeles, CA) to Metrobank (Los Angeles, CA) and Common $1.66-2/3 par changed to no par 11/1/88
Merged into Comerica Inc. 1/17/96
Each share Common no par exchanged for (0.791) share Common no par

METROBANK FINL GROUP INC (DE)
Liquidating plan of reorganization under Chapter 7 Federal Bankruptcy proceedings effective 10/02/1992
Each share Common 10¢ par received $0.58 cash
Note: Certificates were not required to

FINANCIAL INFORMATION, INC.   MET-MET

be surrendered and are without value

METROBRIDGE NETWORKS INTL INC (CANADA)
Each share old Common no par exchanged for (0.1) share new Common no par 09/15/2009
Name changed to Clemson Resources Corp. (Canada) 12/06/2011.
Clemson Resources Corp. (Canada) reincorporated in British Columbia 10/22/2012 which name changed to Oyster Oil & Gas Ltd. 04/16/2013

METROCALL HLDGS INC (DE)
Common 1¢ par split (5) for (1) by issuance of (4) additional shares payable 10/16/2003 to holders of record 10/06/2003 Ex date - 10/17/2003
Preferred Ser. A 1¢ par called for redemption at $11.129028 on 05/17/2004
Merged into USA Mobility, Inc. 11/16/2004
Each share Common 1¢ par exchanged for (1.876) shares Common $0.0001 par
USA Mobility, Inc. name changed to Spok Holdings, Inc. 07/09/2014

METROCALL INC (DE)
Plan of reorganization under Chapter 11 Federal Bankruptcy code effective 10/8/2002
No stockholders' equity

METROCARE ENTERPRISES, INC. (DE)
Name changed to Metrocare, Inc. 11/16/72
(See Metrocare, Inc.)

METROCARE INC (DE)
Merged into Landmark Ventures, Inc. 03/13/1986
Each share Common 10¢ par exchanged for $28.75 cash

METROCONNECT INC (NV)
SEC revoked common stock registration 08/25/2011

METROCORP BANCSHARES INC (TX)
Common $1 par split (3) for (2) by issuance of (0.5) additional share payable 09/01/2006 to holders of record 08/18/2006 Ex date - 09/05/2006
Merged into East West Bancorp, Inc. 01/17/2014
Each share Common $1 par exchanged for (0.2985) share Common $0.001 par and $4.78 cash

METRODYNAMICS CORP (NJ)
Adjudicated bankrupt 12/19/1977
Stockholders' equity unlikely

METRODYNE CORP (DE)
Each share Common 1¢ par exchanged for (0.2) share Common 5¢ par 07/28/1978
Charter cancelled and declared inoperative and void for non-payment of taxes 03/01/1998

METROGAS S A (ARGENTINA)
Stock Dividend - 11.05% payable 05/02/1997 to holders of record 04/24/1997
ADR agreement terminated 09/07/2017
Each Sponsored ADR for Class B Shares exchanged for $24.625141 cash

METROGOLF INC (CO)
Merged into Family Golf Centers, Inc. 2/24/98
Each share Common no par exchanged for $1.50 cash

METROLAND DEVELOPMENT CORP. LTD. (CANADA)
Name changed to Oceanic Films & Enterprises Ltd. 07/25/1961

(See Oceanic Films & Enterprises Ltd.)

METROLINK GROUP INC (NY)
Charter cancelled and proclaimed dissolved for failure to pay taxes 09/29/1993

METROLOGIC INSTRS INC (NJ)
Issue Information - 1,500,000 shares COM offered at $9.50 per share on 09/29/1994
Common 1¢ par split (3) for (2) by issuance of (0.5) additional share payable 7/3/2003 to holders of record 6/23/2003 Ex date - 7/7/2003
Common 1¢ par split (2) for (1) by issuance of (1) additional share payable 10/30/2003 to holders of record 10/20/2003 Ex date - 10/31/2003
Merged into Francisco Partners 12/21/2006
Each share Common 1¢ par exchanged for $18.50 cash

METROMAIL CORP NEW (DE)
Merged into Great Universal Stores, P.L.C. 4/17/98
Each share Common 1¢ par exchanged for $34.50 cash

METROMAIL CORP OLD (DE)
Acquired by Donnelley (R.R.) & Sons Co. 8/14/87
Each share Common 40¢ par exchanged for $29.75 cash

METROMATION INC (DE)
Adjudicated bankrupt 05/20/1980
Stockholders' equity unlikely

METROMEDIA FIBER NETWORK INC (DE)
Issue Information - 7,920,000 shares CL A offered at $16 per share on 10/28/1997
Class A Common 1¢ par split (2) for (1) by issuance of (1) additional share payable 08/28/1998 to holders of record 08/07/1998
Class A Common 1¢ par split (2) for (1) by issuance of (1) additional share payable 12/22/1998 to holders of record 12/08/1998
Class A Common 1¢ par split (2) for (1) by issuance of (1) additional share payable 05/19/1999 to holders of record 05/03/1999
Class A Common 1¢ par split (2) for (1) by issuance of (1) additional share payable 04/17/2000 to holders of record 03/14/2000
Plan of reorganization under Chapter 11 Federal Bankruptcy Code effective 09/08/2003
No stockholders' equity

METROMEDIA INC (DE)
Common $1 par split (2) for (1) by issuance of (1) additional share 06/13/1968
Common $1 par split (10) for (1) by issuance of (9) additional shares 08/15/1983
Acquired by a group of private investors 06/21/1984
Each share Common $1 par exchanged for $22.50 principal amount of Metromedia, Inc. 16% Subordinated Discount Debentures due 07/01/1998, (0.5) Debenture Purchase Warrant due 07/01/2009 and $30 cash
Note: Holdings of (44) or fewer shares will not receive Discount Debentures

METROMEDIA INTL GROUP INC (DE)
Common $1 par changed to 1¢ par 11/05/2009
Merged into CaucusCom Ventures L.P. 08/22/2007
Each share Common 1¢ par exchanged for $1.80 cash

METROMODULAR SYS INC (DE)
Adjudicated bankrupt 12/19/1974
Stockholders' equity unlikely

METRON TECHNOLOGY N V (NETHERLANDS)
Issue Information - 3,750,000 shares COM offered at $13 per share on 11/19/1999
Name changed to Nortem N.V. 09/16/1999
(See Nortem N.V.)

METRONET COMMUNICATIONS CO (NV)
Name changed to FlashPoint International Inc. 10/26/2001
FlashPoint International Inc. name changed to Navitrak International Corp. 05/28/2004 which recapitalized as VECTr Systems, Inc. 05/21/2007

METRONET COMMUNICATIONS CORP (CANADA)
Issue Information - 7,500,000 shares CL B NON VTG offered at $16.23 per share on 12/03/1997
Merged into AT&T Canada Corp. 6/2/99
Each share Non-Vtg. Class B no par exchanged for (1) Class B Depositary Receipt no par
(See AT&T Canada Corp.)

METROPACIFIC BK (IRVINE, CA)
Placed in receivership 06/26/2009
Stockholders' equity unlikely

METROPANE INC (MN)
Name changed to Intermountain Ventures Inc. 08/28/2007
Intermountain Ventures Inc. name changed to Voice One Corp. 01/11/2011

METROPCS COMMUNICATIONS INC (DE)
Issue Information - 50,000,000 shares COM offered at $23 per share on 04/18/2007
Recapitalized as T-Mobile US, Inc. 04/30/2013
Each share Common $0.0001 par exchanged for (0.5) share Common $0.00001 par

METROPLEX RLTY TR (MA)
Merged into Vista Mortgage & Realty Inc. 10/31/80
Each Share of Bene. Int. no par exchanged for (0.1) share Common 10¢ par
(See Vista Mortgage & Realty Inc.)

METROPOLIS BOWLING CENTERS, INC. (NY)
Name changed to Met Sports Centers, Inc. 06/20/1963
Met Sports Centers, Inc. name changed to Antares Resources Corp. 12/20/1983
(See Antares Resources Corp.)

METROPOLIS TECHNOLOGIES CORP (NV)
Recapitalized as Impact E-Solutions Corp. 02/08/2007
Each share Common $0.001 par exchanged for (0.01) share Common $0.001 par
(See Impact E-Solutions Corp.)

METROPOLITAN 5 TO 50¢ STORES, INC. (DE)
No longer in existence having become inoperative and void for non-payment of taxes 4/1/34

METROPOLITAN ASSET MGMT CORP (NY)
Name changed to Diamond Laser International, Ltd. (NY) 12/04/1996
Diamond Laser International Ltd. (NY) reorganized in Nevada as Access TradeOne.Com, Inc. 06/11/1999
(See Access TradeOne.Com, Inc.)

METROPOLITAN ATLANTA REAL ESTATE INVT TR (GA)
Completely liquidated 10/31/2000
Each Share of Bene. Int. exchanged for first and final distribution of $4.90 cash

METROPOLITAN BANCORP (WA)
Stock Dividend - 10% 08/01/1994
Merged into Washington Federal, Inc. 11/29/1996
Each share Common $1 par exchanged for (0.738) share Common $1 par

METROPOLITAN BANCORP INC (OH)
Common $5 par split (2) for (1) by issuance of (1) additional share 4/22/86
Common $5 par split (3) for (2) by issuance of (0.5) additional share 3/3/87
Common $5 par split (4) for (3) by issuance of (1/3) additional share 2/10/88
Stock Dividends - 10% 3/25/85; 20% 2/15/89
Acquired by Banc One Corp. 3/30/90
Each share Common $5 par exchanged for (1.4575) shares Common no par
Banc One Corp. merged into Bank One Corp. 10/2/98 which merged into J.P. Morgan Chase & Co. 12/31/2000 which name changed to JPMorgan Chase & Co. 7/20/2004

METROPOLITAN BANCORPORATION (FL)
Stock Dividend - 10% 2/16/81
Name changed to Allied Banks, Inc. 8/3/82
Allied Banks, Inc. merged into Holiday Bank (Holiday, FL) which name changed to Florida State Bank (Holiday, FL) 2/21/89
(See Florida State Bank (Holiday, FL))

METROPOLITAN BANCSHARES INC (DE)
Charter cancelled and declared inoperative and void for non-payment of taxes 3/1/94

METROPOLITAN BANK & TRUST CO. (BRIDGEPORT, CT)
Liquidation completed
Each share Common $5 par exchanged for initial distribution of $9.30 cash 1/10/77
Each share Common $5 par received second and final distribution of $0.30 cash 11/3/80

METROPOLITAN BANK & TRUST CO. (MELROSE, MA)
Reorganized as Metro Bancorp, Inc. 11/14/1984
Each share Common $1 par exchanged for (10) shares Common $1 par
(See Metro Bancorp, Inc.)

METROPOLITAN BK & TR CO (TAMPA, FL)
99.82% held by Metropolitan Bancorporation as of 08/30/1979
Public interest eliminated

METROPOLITAN BANK (HOLLYWOOD, CA)
Voting Trust Agreement terminated 8/3/64
Each VTC for Capital Stock $10 par exchanged for (1) share Capital Stock $10 par
Merged into Bank of California, N.A. (San Francisco, CA) 9/25/67
Each share Capital Stock $10 par exchanged for (0.363636) share Common Capital Stock $10 par
Bank of California, N.A. (San Francisco, CA) reorganized as BanCal Tri-State Corp. 5/1/72
(See BanCal Tri-State Corp.)

METROPOLITAN BK (LIMA, OH)
Reorganized as Metropolitan Bancorp, Inc. 2/19/82
Each share Capital Stock $5 par exchanged for (1) share Common $5 par
Metropolitan Bancorp, Inc. acquired by Banc One Corp. 3/30/90 which merged into Bank One Corp.

MET-MET   **FINANCIAL INFORMATION, INC.**

10/2/98 which merged into J.P. Morgan Chase & Co. 12/31/2000 which name changed to JPMorgan Chase & Co. 7/20/2004

METROPOLITAN BANK (MIAMI, FL)
Capital Stock $15 par changed to $10 par and (0.5) additional share issued 01/02/1959
Stock Dividend - 10% 02/18/1960
Name changed to Capital National Bank (Miami, FL) 04/03/1964
Capital National Bank (Miami, FL) name changed to Peoples Downtown National Bank (Miami, FL) 06/01/1972
(See Peoples Downtown National Bank (Miami, FL))

METROPOLITAN BANK (OAK GROVE, OR)
Merged into United Bank of Oregon (Oak Grove, Ore.) 1/1/83
Each share Common $5 par exchanged for (.01) shares Common $1 par

METROPOLITAN BK JEFFERSON (METAIRIE, LA)
Name changed to First Metropolitan Bank (Metairie, LA) 04/01/1971
(See First Metropolitan Bank (Metairie, LA))

METROPOLITAN BRICK, INC. (OH)
Name changed to Metropolitan Industries, Inc. 5/1/67
(See Metropolitan Industries, Inc.)

METROPOLITAN BROADCASTING CORP. (DE)
Name changed to Metromedia, Inc. 03/29/1961
(See Metromedia, Inc.)

METROPOLITAN BROADCASTING CORP. OF CALIFORNIA (CA)
Name changed to KOVR Broadcasting Co. 09/09/1964
(See KOVR Broadcasting Co.)

METROPOLITAN BUFFALO INVESTORS, INC. (NY)
Dissolved 12/13/77

METROPOLITAN CAP TR I (DE)
8.60% Trust Preferred Securities called for redemption at $10 on 10/15/2003

METROPOLITAN CAP TR II (DE)
9.50% Guaranteed Trust Preferred Securities called for redemption at $10 on 6/30/2004

METROPOLITAN CHAIN STORES, INC. (DE)
Bankrupt in 1932

METROPOLITAN CIRCUITS INC (DE)
Charter forfeited for failure to maintain a registered agent 12/8/92

METROPOLITAN COMMERCIAL CORP. (NY)
Although transfers were effected until sometime in 1971 this company has not been operating for many years
The brokerage firm which had previously maintained a market revealed the securities are valueless

METROPOLITAN COMMUNICATIONS INC (NY)
Name changed to Dynatek Industries, Inc. 9/12/68
(See Dynatek Industries, Inc.)

METROPOLITAN COMPACTORS INC (NJ)
Charter revoked for failure to file annual reports 4/6/95

METROPOLITAN CONS INDS INC (DE)
Name changed to United Capital Corp. 03/03/1989
(See United Capital Corp.)

METROPOLITAN CREDIT & DISCOUNT CORP. (DE)
Charter cancelled and declared inoperative and void for non-payment of taxes 5/1/35

METROPOLITAN DAIRY PRODUCTS, INC.
Out of business 00/00/1933
Details not available

METROPOLITAN DEV CORP (DE)
Merged into First City Development Corp. of California 03/26/1979
Each share Capital Stock $1 par exchanged for $14.25 cash

METROPOLITAN DISCOUNT CO.
In process of liquidation in 1945

METROPOLITAN EDISON CO (PA)
$6 Prior Preferred no par called for redemption 1/1/45
$7 Prior Preferred no par called for redemption 1/1/45
$5 Preferred no par called for redemption 1/1/45
$6 Preferred no par called for redemption 1/1/45
$7 Preferred no par called for redemption 1/1/45
3.80% Preferred $100 par, 3.85% Preferred $100 par, 3.90% Preferred $100 par, 4.35% Preferred $100 par, 4.45% Preferred $100 par, 7.68% Preferred Ser. G $100 par, 8.12% Preferred $100 par, 8.12% Preferred Ser. I $100 par, 8.32% Preferred Ser. H $100 par, 8.32% Preferred Ser. J $100 par changed to no par 7/30/76
8.32% Preferred Ser. H no par called for redemption 9/9/93
8.32% Preferred Ser. J no par called for redemption 9/9/93
8.12% Preferred no par called for redemption 9/17/93
8.12% Preferred Ser. I no par called for redemption 9/17/93
7.68% Preferred Ser. G no par called for redemption 10/1/94
3.80% Ser. Preferred Ser. no par called for redemption at $104.70 plus $0.517 accrued dividends on 2/19/99
3.85% Ser. Preferred no par called for redemption at $104 plus $0.524 accrued interest on 2/19/99
3.90% Ser. Preferred no par called for redemption at $105.625 plus $0.531 accrued interest on 2/19/99
4.35% Ser. Preferred no par called for redemption at $104.25 plus $0.592 accrued interest on 2/19/99
4.45% Ser. Preferred no par called for redemption at $104.25 plus $0.606 accrued interest on 2/19/99
Public interest eliminated

METROPOLITAN ENTMT CORP AMER INC (MN)
Statutorily dissolved 6/15/95

METROPOLITAN FED BK (FARGO, ND)
Name changed 07/11/1984
Name changed from Metropolitan Federal Savings & Loan Association of Fargo to Metropolitan Federal Bank, F.S.B. (Fargo, ND) 07/11/1984
Under plan of reorganization each share Common 1¢ par automatically became (1) share Metropolitan Financial Corp. (DE) Common 1¢ par 03/01/1985
Metropolitan Financial Corp. merged into First Bank System, Inc. 01/24/1995 which name changed to U.S. Bancorp 08/01/1997

METROPOLITAN FED BK A FED SVGS BK (NASHVILLE, TN)
Reorganized 03/01/1991
Common $1 par split (3) for (2) by issuance of (0.5) additional share 09/05/1986
Under plan of reorganization each share Metropolitan Federal Savings & Loan Association Common $1 par automatically became (1) share Metropolitan Federal Bank, A Federal Savings Bank (Nashville, TN) Common $1 par 03/01/1991
Placed in receivership with FDIC 03/27/1992
Stockholders' equity unlikely

METROPOLITAN FED SVGS & LN ASSN BETHSEDA (MD)
Stock Dividend - 15% 10/15/1980
Acquired by Metropolitan Holding Co., Inc. 01/08/1986
Each share Common $1 par exchanged for $10 principal amount of 10% Subord. Debentures Ser. A due 01/08/1996 and $25 cash

METROPOLITAN FED SVGS & LN ASSN SEATTLE (WA)
Under plan of reorganization each share Common $1 par automatically became (1) share Metropolitan Bancorp Common 1¢ par 7/23/93
Metropolitan Bancorp merged into Washington Federal Inc. 11/29/95

METROPOLITAN FINL CORP (DE)
Common 1¢ par split (3) for (2) by issuance of (0.5) additional share 02/28/1986
Common 1¢ par split (6) for (5) by issuance of (0.2) additional share 10/04/1991
$2 Conv. Preferred Ser. A 1¢ par called for redemption 04/20/1992
Common 1¢ par split (2) for (1) by issuance of (1) additional share 06/22/1992
Stock Dividends - 10% 04/30/1985; 10% 07/11/1988; 10% 03/09/1989; 10% 03/12/1990; 10% 07/12/1993
Merged into First Bank System, Inc. 01/24/1995
Each share $2.875 Preferred Ser. B 1¢ par exchanged for $27 cash
Each share Common 1¢ par exchanged for (0.6803) share Common $1.25 par
First Bank System, Inc. name changed to U.S. Bancorp 08/01/1997

METROPOLITAN FINL CORP (OH)
Common no par split (2) for (1) by issuance of (1) additional share payable 12/10/1997 to holders of record 11/24/1997
Stock Dividend - 10% payable 12/29/1998 to holders of record 12/15/1998
Merged into Sky Financial Group, Inc. 04/30/2003
Each share Common no par exchanged for $4.70 cash

METROPOLITAN GAS & ELECTRIC CO.
Dissolution approved in 1937

METROPOLITAN GREETINGS INC. (NY)
Charter cancelled and proclaimed dissolved for failure to pay taxes 12/15/72

METROPOLITAN GREETINGS INC (MA)
Common 10¢ par split (3) for (2) by issuance of (0.5) additional share 05/12/1972
Reincorporated under the laws of Delaware as Metropolitan Consolidated Industries, Inc. 12/30/1980
Metropolitan Consolidated Industries, Inc. name changed to United Capital Corp. 03/03/1989
(See United Capital Corp.)

METROPOLITAN HEALTH CARE INC (NY)
Charter cancelled and proclaimed dissolved for failure to pay taxes 03/26/1980

METROPOLITAN HEALTH NETWORKS INC (FL)
Acquired by Humana Inc. 12/21/2012
Each share Common $0.001 par exchanged for $11.25 cash

METROPOLITAN HLDGS LTD (SOUTH AFRICA)
Name changed to MMI Holdings Ltd. 12/07/2010

METROPOLITAN HOSIERY & KNITTING MLS INC (NY)
Name changed to Multiway Industries, Inc. 12/31/1973
(See Multiway Industries, Inc.)

METROPOLITAN INDUSTRIES, INC. (TX)
Voluntarily dissoved 11/25/86
Details not available

METROPOLITAN INDUSTRIES CO. (DE)
6% Cum. Preferred $100 par changed to $55 par and $45 per share distributed in 1939 6% Cum. Preferred $55 par changed to $45 par and $10 per share distributed in 1943
Liquidation completed 10/28/46

METROPOLITAN INDS INC (OH)
Merged into MI Newco Corp. 12/20/90
Each share Common $4 par exchanged for $11.60 cash

METROPOLITAN INVESTMENT CO. (OK)
Merged into Progress Life & Accident Insurance Co. 08/08/1977
Each share Capital Stock 50¢ par exchanged for (1) share Common 50¢ par
(See Progress Life & Accident Insurance Co.)

METROPOLITAN INVESTMENT TRUST (LA)
Merged into First Metropolitan Bank (Metairie, La.) 4/3/73
Each share Capital Stock $50 par exchanged for (2) shares Capital Stock $10 par
(See First Metropolitan Bank (Metairie, La.))

METROPOLITAN INVESTMENTS, INC.
Dissolved in 1938

METROPOLITAN MAINTENANCE CO (NJ)
Each share old Common 1¢ par exchanged for (0.1) share new Common 1¢ par 10/31/1977
Each share new Common 1¢ par exchanged for (1/3,000) share new Common 1¢ par 06/28/1984
Note: In effect holders received $37 cash per share and public interest was eliminated

METROPOLITAN MNG INC (BC)
Each share old Common no par exchanged for (0.33333333) share new Common no par 10/24/2011
Name changed to Metropolitan Energy Corp. 02/02/2012

METROPOLITAN MTG & SECURITIES INC (WA)
Plan of reorganization under Chapter 11 Federal Bankruptcy proceedings effective 02/13/2006
No stockholders' equity

METROPOLITAN MOTORS INC. (DE)
Charter cancelled and declared inoperative and void for non-payment of taxes 03/19/1919

METROPOLITAN NATIONAL BANK (RICHMOND, VA)
Under plan of merger name changed to Dominion Bankshares Corp. 03/25/1977
Dominion Bankshares Corp. merged into First Union Corp. 03/01/1993 which name changed to Wachovia Corp. (Ctfs. dated after 09/01/2001) 09/01/2001 which merged into Wells Fargo & Co. (New) 12/31/2008

METROPOLITAN NATL BK (SYRACUSE, NY)
Capital Stock $10 par changed to

$6.67 par and (0.5) additional share issued 03/15/1968
Merged into Bank of New York Co., Inc. 05/29/1969
Each share Capital Stock $6.67 par exchanged for $21 principal amount of 6-1/4% Conv. Debentures due 09/01/1994 and (0.0833) share Common $15 par
Bank of New York Co., Inc. merged into Bank of New York Mellon Corp. 07/01/2007

METROPOLITAN NATL BK (WHEATON, MD)
Merged into Union Trust Co. of Maryland (Baltimore, MD) 10/19/1970
Each share Common $15 par exchanged for (1) share Capital Stock $10 par
Union Trust Co. of Maryland (Baltimore, MD) reorganized as Union Trust Bancorp 07/03/1972 which was acquired by Bank of Virginia Co. 12/31/1985 which name changed to Signet Banking Corp. 07/14/1986 which merged into First Union Corp. 11/28/1997 which name changed to Wachovia Corp. (Ctfs. dated after 09/01/2001) 09/01/2001 which merged into Wells Fargo & Co. (New) 12/31/2008

METROPOLITAN OIL & GAS CO. LTD. (AB)
Proclaimed dissolved and struck from register 9/30/67

METROPOLITAN PATHOLOGY LAB INC (NY)
Name changed to Metpath Inc. 05/28/1971
Metpath Inc. acquired by Corning Glass Works 02/26/1982 which name changed to Corning Inc. 04/28/1989

METROPOLITAN PAVING BRICK CO.
Name changed to Metropolitan Brick, Inc. in 1949
Metropolitan Brick, Inc. name changed to Metropolitan Industries, Inc. 5/1/67
(See Metropolitan Industries, Inc.)

METROPOLITAN PERSONAL LOAN CORP.
Name changed to Metropolitan Discount Co. in 1943
(See Metropolitan Discount Co.)

METROPOLITAN PLAYHOUSES INC (NY)
Merged into United Artists Communications, Inc. 12/21/84
Details not available

METROPOLITAN POWER CO.
Merged into Metropolitan Edison Co. 00/00/1926
Details not available

METROPOLITAN QUARTERBACK INC (DE)
Adjudicated bankrupt 07/23/1970
Stockholders' equity unlikely

METROPOLITAN REALTY, INC.
Liquidated in 1935

METROPOLITAN RLTY CORP (MI)
Reorganized under the laws of Delaware as Metropolitan Realty Corp., LLC 12/6/96
Each (50,000) shares Common 1¢ par exchanged for (1) Class A Membership Int.
Note: In effect holders received $9.06 cash per share and public interest was eliminated

METROPOLITAN RES INC (DE)
Name changed to International Telecharge, Inc. 5/9/86
(See International Telecharge, Inc.)

METROPOLITAN RTY CORP (DE)
Company became private 00/00/1985
Details not available

METROPOLITAN SVGS ASSN FARMINGTON HILLS (MI)
Declared insolvent 02/11/1983
No stockholders' equity

METROPOLITAN SEC INC (DC)
Liquidation completed
Each share Class A Capital Stock $1 par exchanged for initial distribution of $3.50 cash 02/15/1974
Each share Class A Capital Stock $1 par received second and final distribution of $0.3295 cash 10/29/1974

METROPOLITAN ST BK (MONTVILLE, NJ)
Merged into Lakeland Bancorp, Inc. 02/20/1998
Each share Common $5 par exchanged for (0.941) share Common no par

METROPOLITAN STORAGE WHSE CO (MA)
Capital Stock no par changed to $20 par and $5 cash per share distributed in 1940
In process of liquidation
Each share Capital Stock $20 par exchanged for initial distribution of $80 cash 9/20/62
Each share Capital Stock $20 par received second distribution of $9.17 cash 1/4/63
Note: Details on subsequent distributions, if any, are not available

METROPOLITAN STORES CDA LTD (CANADA)
Common no par split (3) for (1) by issuance of (2) additional shares 09/29/1971
Common no par reclassified as Conv. Class A Common no par 09/08/1975
Merged into General Distributors of Canada Ltd. 12/08/1977
Each share Conv. Class A Common no par exchanged for (1) Common Stock Purchase Warrant expiring 05/31/1982 and $11 cash
Each share Conv. Class B Common no par exchanged for (1) Common Stock Purchase Warrant expiring 05/31/1982 and $11 cash
$1.30 Preferred 1961 Ser. $20 par called for redemption 11/28/1983
$1.30 Preferred 1967 Ser. $20 par called for redemption 11/28/1983
Public interest eliminated

METROPOLITAN TELECOMMUNICATIONS CORP. (NY)
Name changed to Grow Corp. 12/29/61
Grow Corp. name changed to Grow Chemical Corp. 10/19/64 which name changed to Grow Group, Inc. 4/20/79
(See Grow Group, Inc.)

METROPOLITAN TOBACCO CO. (NY)
Each share Common $100 par exchanged for (4) shares Common $25 par 00/00/1949
Name changed to Metobco, Inc. which completely liquidated 2/28/64

METROPOLITAN TR CO (TORONTO, ONT)
Each share Common $25 par exchanged for (2.5) shares Common $10 par 04/05/1968
Under plan of merger each share Common $10 par exchanged for (1) share Common $10 par 06/27/1968
Common $10 par changed to no par 06/11/1974
Merged into Victoria Grey Metro Trust Co. (Stratford, ONT) 10/31/1979
Each share Common no par exchanged for (2) shares Common $3 par
Victoria Grey Metro Trust Co. (Stratford, ONT) name changed to Victoria & Grey Trust Co. (Stratford, ONT) 04/07/1980 which merged into National Victoria & Grey Trust Co. (Toronto, ONT) 08/31/1984 which name changed to National Trust Co. (Toronto, ONT) 10/28/1985
(See National Trust Co. (Toronto, ONT))

METROTRANS CORP (GA)
Issue Information - 1,500,000 shares COM offered at $8.50 per share on 06/08/1994
Plan of reorganization under Chapter 11 Federal Bankruptcy proceedings confirmed 09/08/2000
Each share Common 1¢ par received first and final distribution of $0.1512 cash payable 10/09/2003 to holders of record 06/30/2000 Ex date - 11/05/2003
Note: Certificates not required to be surrendered and are without value

METROVISION NORTH AMER INC (NY)
Issue Information - 800,000 UNITS consisting of (6) shares COM and (1) WT CL B offered at $5 per Unit on 11/02/1993
Each share old Common $0.001 par exchanged for (0.2173913) share new Common $0.001 par 04/01/1997
Charter cancelled and proclaimed dissolved for failure to pay taxes 12/27/2000

METROWERKS INC (CANADA)
Merged into Motorola Canada Acquisition 9/24/99
Each share Common no par exchanged for $6.25 cash

METROWEST BK (FRAMINGHAM, MA)
Acquired by Banknorth Group, Inc. (ME) 11/01/2001
Each share Common 10¢ par exchanged for $11.50 cash

METSA BRD CORP (FINLAND)
ADR agreement terminated 12/26/2017
No ADR's remain outstanding

METTRUM HEALTH CORP (ON)
Merged into Canopy Growth Corp. 02/02/2017
Each share Common no par exchanged for (0.7132) share Common no par
Note: Unexchanged certificates will be cancelled and become without value 02/02/2023

METU BRANDS INC (NV)
Name changed to American BriVision (Holding) Corp. 01/14/2016

METZ BREWING CO. (DE)
Name changed to Metz Industries, Inc. 7/9/62
Metz Industries, Inc. name changed to Continental Western Corp. 6/24/66
(See Continental Western Corp.)

METZ INDUSTRIES, INC. (DE)
Name changed to Continental Western Corp. 06/24/1966
(See Continental Western Corp.)

METZLER GROUP INC (DE)
Common $0.001 par split (3) for (2) by issuance of (0.5) additional share payable 4/1/98 to holders of record 3/18/98
Name changed to Navigant Consulting, Inc. 7/16/99

MEVC DRAPER FISHER JURVETSON FD I INC (DE)
Name changed to MVC Capital 11/27/2002
MVC Capital name changed to MVC Capital, Inc. 7/30/2004

MEX INC (UT)
Name changed to Drusilla Seafood Restaurants, Inc. 05/22/1987
Drusilla Seafood Restaurants, Inc. name changed to Life Signs Group, Inc. 08/29/1991
(See Life Signs Group, Inc.)

MEX TRANS SEAFOOD CONSULTING INC (TX)
Reorganized under the laws of Nevada as PCSupport.com, Inc. 05/27/1999
Each share Common $0.0001 par exchanged for (0.06666666) share Common $0.001 par
PCSupport.com, Inc. recapitalized as Nova Energy, Inc. 06/06/2005 which name changed to Savanna East Africa, Inc. 07/13/2010 which recapitalized as Algae International Group, Inc. (NV) 05/17/2013 which reincorporated in Wyoming as North American Cannabis Holdings, Inc. 06/10/2015

MEXGOLD RES INC (ON)
Acquired by Gammon Lake Resources Inc. 08/08/2006
Each share Common no par exchanged for (0.47) share Common no par
Gammon Lake Resources Inc. name changed to Gammon Gold Inc. (QC) 06/19/2007 which reincorporated in Ontario as AuRico Gold Inc. 06/14/2011 which merged into Alamos Gold Inc. (New) 07/06/2015

MEXICAN CRUDE RUBBER CO.
Liquidated in 1929

MEXICAN GOLD & SILVER MINING CO. (CA)
Out of business in 1980
Details not available

MEXICAN GULF SULPHUR CO. (DE)
Declared insolvent 00/00/1958
Details not available

MEXICAN INVESTMENT CO., INC.
Name changed to Venezuelan-Mexican Oil Corp. 00/00/1926
Venezuelan-Mexican Oil Corp. name changed to Wichita River Oil Corp. (VA) (Old) 00/00/1939 which name changed to Wichita Industries, Inc. 01/08/1969 which merged into Wichita River Oil Corp. (VA) (New) 11/04/1987 which reincorporated in Delaware 03/30/1990
(See Wichita River Oil Corp. (DE))

MEXICAN LT & PWR LTD (CANADA)
Ordinary $100 par changed to no par 00/00/1927
Each $100 par amount of 6% Income Debenture Stock exchanged for (7.2) shares Preferred $13.50 par and (6) shares Common no par
Each share 7% Preference $100 par exchanged for (10.4) shares Common no par
Each (20) shares 4% Preference $5 par exchanged for (4.6) shares Common no par
Each share Ordinary no par exchanged for (1) share Common no par
Stock Dividends - 10% 11/01/1966; 10% 08/01/1968; 10% 11/01/1969
Completely liquidated 09/24/1991
Each share Preferred $13.50 par exchanged for $5 cash
Each share Common no par exchanged for $1 cash
Note: In order to receive payment holders must file a Proof of Claim Form on or before 09/24/1992

MEXICAN PACIFIC CANNING CO. (DE)
No longer in existence having become inoperative and void for non-payment of taxes 3/19/24

MEXICAN PATIO CAFES INC (DE)
SEC revoked common stock registration 04/12/2010

MEXICAN PETROLEUM CO. LTD. OF DELAWARE
Dissolved 00/00/1936
Details not available

MEXICAN RESTAURANTS INC (TX)
Acquired by Williston Holding Co., Inc. 05/09/2014
Each share Common 1¢ par exchanged for $4.06 cash

MEXICAN SEABOARD OIL CO.
Name changed to Seaboard Oil Co. of Delaware in 1931
Seaboard Oil Co. of Delaware name changed to Seaboard Oil Co. in 1954 which merged into Texas Co. (New) 6/2/58 which name changed to Texaco Inc. 5/1/59 which merged into ChevronTexaco Corp. 10/9/2001 which name changed to Chevron Corp. 5/9/2005

MEXICAN SILVER MINES LTD (AB)
Name changed to Rio Alto Mining Ltd. 07/24/2009
Rio Alto Mining Ltd. merged into Tahoe Resources Inc. 04/01/2015

MEXICAN TELEPHONE & TELEGRAPH CO.
Liquidated 00/00/1950
Details not available

MEXICANA EXPLORATIONS LTD. (ON)
Charter cancelled and dissolved 7/1/63
Capital Stock valueless

MEXICO EQUITY & INCOME FD (MD)
Each share Preferred $0.001 par received distribution of (0.8295357) share Common $0.001 par payable 01/28/2014 to holders of record 12/30/2013 Ex date - 12/26/2013
Preferred $0.001 par called for redemption at $11.27 on 02/10/2016
(Additional Information in Active)

MEXICO INVESTMENT CORP (UT)
Name changed to Baja Pacific International, Inc. 02/26/1996
Baja Pacific International, Inc. name changed to Taig Ventures, Inc. 10/07/1998 which recapitalized as Viper Networks, Inc. (UT) 01/11/2001 which reincorporated in Nevada 05/18/2005

MEXICO-OHIO OIL CO.
Dissolved 00/00/1943
Details not available

MEXICO OIL CORP. (ME)
Charter suspended 00/00/1930

MEXICO REFRACTORIES CO. (MO)
Each share Common $20 par exchanged for (4) shares Common no par in 1937
Common no par changed to $5 par in 1944
Stock Dividends - 20% 5/10/55; 100% 7/25/55
Merged into Kaiser Aluminum & Chemical Corp. 5/1/59
Each share Common $5 par exchanged for (0.17404) share 4-3/4% Conv. Preference $100 par and (0.34808) share Common 33-1/3¢ par
(See Kaiser Aluminum & Chemical Corp.)

MEXICO TRAMWAYS CO. (CANADA)
Name changed to Magnum Fund Ltd. and Common $100 par changed to $10 par 6/30/58
Magnum Fund Ltd. reincorporated under the laws of the Netherlands 12/13/71
(See Magnum Fund Ltd. (Netherlands))

MEXIGOLD CORP (BC)
Recapitalized as Savannah Gold Corp. 08/22/2016
Each share Common no par exchanged for (0.5) share Common no par
Savannah Gold Corp. name changed to E3 Metals Corp. 05/19/2017

MEXNORWEST HOLDING COMPANY, LTD.
Charter surrendered for failure to file reports and pay taxes in 1949

MEXORO MINERALS LTD (CO)
Reincorporated under the laws of Delaware as Pan American Goldfields Ltd. and Common no par changed to 1¢ par 07/22/2010

MEXTOR MINERALS LTD (ON)
Name changed to ICI Industrial Minerals Ltd. 03/11/1985
ICI Industrial Minerals Ltd. name changed to Commercial Industrial Minerals Ltd. 07/12/1985 which recapitalized as ICV Integrated Commercial Ventures Inc. 10/31/1994 which recapitalized as Blue Gold International, Inc. 12/23/1997
(See Blue Gold International, Inc.)

MEXUS INC (DE)
Name changed to Wittcomm Inc. 04/29/1997
(See Wittcomm Inc.)

MEXUSCAN DEV LTD (BC)
Charter cancelled 6/24/74

MEYER BLANKE CO (DE)
Reincorporated 08/12/1974
Stock Dividend - 100% 12/00/1946
State of incorporation changed from (MO) to (DE) 08/12/1974
Merged into Stout Industries, Inc. 06/26/1984
Each share Common no par exchanged for $20.33 cash

MEYER FRED INC (OR)
Class A Common no par split (2) for (1) by issuance of (1) additional share 06/13/1972
Class A Common no par reclassified as Common no par 05/01/1979
Merged into Kohlberg, Kravis, Roberts & Co. 12/11/1981
Each share Common no par exchanged for $55 cash

MEYER FRED INC NEW (DE)
Common 1¢ par split (2) for (1) by issuance of (1) additional share payable 9/30/97 to holders of record 9/19/97 Ex date - 10/1/97
Merged into Kroger Co. 5/27/99
Each share Common 1¢ par exchanged for (1) share Common $1 par

MEYER FRED INC OLD (DE)
Under plan of merger name changed to Meyer (Fred), Inc. (New) 9/9/97

MEYER (GEO. J.) MANUFACTURING CO. (WI)
Merged into Automatic Sprinkler Corp. of America (OH) 03/29/1968
Each share Common $5 par exchanged for (1.64425) shares Common 10¢ par
Automatic Sprinkler Corp. of America (OH) name changed to A-T-O Inc. 10/29/1969 which name changed to Figgie International Inc. (OH) 06/01/1981 which reorganized in Delaware as Figgie International Holdings Inc. 07/18/1983 which name changed to Figgie International Inc. 12/31/1986 which name changed to Scott Technologies, Inc. 05/20/1998 which merged into Tyco International Ltd. (Bermuda) 05/03/2001 which reincorporated in Switzerland 03/17/2009 which merged into Johnson Controls International PLC 09/06/2016

MEYER-KISER CORP.
In receivership in 1934
Stock has no value

MEYERCORD CO (DE)
Reincorporated 01/14/1971
Each share Common no par exchanged for (10) shares Common $5 par 00/00/1946
State of incorporation changed from (IL) to (DE) 01/14/1971
100% acquired by Johnson, Mattey & Co. Ltd. through purchase offer which expired 02/23/1979
Public interest eliminated

MEYERLAND BK (HOUSTON, TX)
Name changed 2/15/72
Stock Dividend - 16-2/3% 2/15/68
Name changed from Meyerland State Bank (Houston, TX) to Meyerland Bank (Houston, TX) 2/15/72
Merged into National Bancshares Corp. of Texas 1/31/78
Each share Common $10 par exchanged for (3) shares Common $10 par
(See National Bancshares Corp. of Texas)

MEYERS PKG SYS INC (DE)
Common 10¢ par split (2) for (1) by issuance of (1) additional share 6/19/84
Stock Dividend - 10% 4/10/87
Merged into MPS Acquisition Corp. 9/22/88
Each share Common 10¢ par exchanged for $29.50 cash

MEZEY HOWARTH RACING STABLES INC (NV)
Recapitalized as Forterus Inc. 08/04/2008
Each share Common $0.001 par exchanged for (0.02) share Common $0.001 par
Forterus Inc. recapitalized as American Addiction Centers, Inc. which merged into AAC Holdings, Inc. 11/10/2014

MEZUMA INC (AB)
Name changed to How To Web TV Inc. 2/16/2001

MEZZI HLDGS INC (BC)
Each share old Common no par exchanged for (0.1) share new Common no par 08/18/2017
Name changed to Omni Commerce Corp. 04/13/2018

MF GLOBAL HLDGS LTD (DE)
Plan of reorganization under Chapter 11 Federal Bankruptcy proceedings effective 06/04/2013
Holders may receive an undetermined amount of cash

MF GLOBAL LTD (BERMUDA)
Issue Information - 97,379,765 shares COM offered at $30 per share on 07/18/2007
Reincorporated under the laws of Delaware as MF Global Holdings Ltd. 01/05/2010
(See MF Global Holdings Ltd.)

MF INDUSTRIES INC. (DE)
Charter cancelled and declared inoperative and void for non-payment of taxes 3/1/88

MF MEDIA CORP. (AB)
Delisted from Toronto Venture Stock Exchange 6/5/2002

MFA FINL INC (MD)
8.50% Preferred Ser. A 1¢ par called for redemption at $25 plus $0.27153 accrued dividends on 05/16/2013
(Additional Information in Active)

MFA MTG INVTS INC (MD)
Issue Information - 2,000,000 shares PFD SER A 8.5% offered at $25 per share on 04/22/2004
Name changed to MFA Financial, Inc. 01/01/2009

MFB CORP (IN)
Merged into MutualFirst Financial, Inc. 07/18/2008
Each share Common no par exchanged for (2.59) shares Common 1¢ par

MFC BANCORP LTD (BC)
Reincorporated 11/03/2004
Each share old Common no par exchanged for (1) share new Common no par to reflect a (1) for (100) reverse split followed by a (100) for (1) forward split 07/17/2000
Note: Holders of (99) or fewer pre-split shares received $7.25 cash per share
Each share new Common no par received distribution of (0.95) share Mymetics Corp. Common 1¢ par payable 08/13/2002 to holders of record 08/09/2002 Ex date - 08/14/2002
Place of incorporation changed from (YT) to (BC) 11/03/2004
Each share Common no par received distribution of (1) share Blue Earth Refineries Inc. Common no par payable 12/30/2004 to holders of record 12/14/2004
Name changed to KHD Humboldt Wedag International Ltd. 11/01/2005
KHD Humboldt Wedag International Ltd. reorganized as Terra Nova Royalty Corp. 03/30/2010 which name changed to MFC Industrial Ltd. 09/30/2011 which name changed to MFC Bancorp Ltd. (BC) 02/16/2016
(See MFC Bancorp Ltd. (BC))

MFC BANCORP LTD (BC)
Name changed 02/16/2016
Name changed from MFC Industrial Ltd. to MFC Bancorp Ltd. 02/16/2016
Reorganized under the laws of Cayman Islands 07/14/2017
Each share Common no par exchanged for (0.2) share Common USD $0.001 par and USD$0.0001 cash to reflect a (1) for (100) reverse split followed by a (20) for (1) forward split
Notes: Holders of (99) or fewer pre-split shares received USD$1.772 cash per share
Unexchanged certificates will be cancelled and become without value 07/14/2020
Distributions of less than $10 will not be made

MFC DEV CORP (DE)
Stock Dividend - 35% payable 08/24/2005 to holders of record 08/08/2005 Ex date - 08/25/2005
Name changed to Vertical Branding, Inc. 11/17/2006
(See Vertical Branding, Inc.)

MFC INC (ON)
Name changed to Municipal Bankers Corp. 05/22/1998
Municipal Bankers Corp. merged into Newco Bancorp Inc. 10/01/2000
(See Newco Bancorp Inc.)

MFC MNG FIN CORP (BC)
Merged into MinVen Gold Corp. 08/12/1988
Each share Common no par exchanged for (0.66666666) share Common no par
MinVen Gold Corp. reorganized as Dakota Mining Corp. 09/15/1993
(See Dakota Mining Corp.)

MFIC CORP (DE)
Name changed to Microfluidics International Corp. (New) 06/18/2008
(See Microfluidics International Corp. (New))

MFN FINL CORP (DE)
Merged into Consumer Portfolio Services, Inc. 3/8/2002
Each share Common 1¢ par exchanged for $10 cash

M45 MNG RES INC (NV)
Name changed to Neuro-Biotech Corp. 06/17/2010
Neuro-Biotech Corp. recapitalized as Institute of BioMedical Research Corp. 04/28/2014

MFP FINANCIAL SVCS LTD (ON)
Name changed to Clearlink Capital Corp. 10/01/2004
Clearlink Capital Corp. name changed to Renasant Financial Partners Ltd. 04/03/2006
(See Renasant Financial Partners Ltd.)

MFRI INC (DE)
Name changed to Perma-Pipe International Holdings, Inc. 03/21/2017

MFS CALIF MUN BD FD (MA)
Reorganized as MFS Municipal Series Trust 09/07/1993
Details not available

MFS CALIF MUN FD (MA)
Name changed 10/01/2010
Name changed from MFS California Insured Municipal Fund to MFS California Municipal Fund 10/01/2010
Municipal Auction Rate Preferred Ser. TH no par called for redemption at $25,000 on 11/20/2012
(Additional Information in Active)

MFS COMMUNICATIONS INC (DE)
Common 1¢ par split (2) for (1) by issuance of (1) additional share payable 4/16/96 to holders of record 4/16/96 Ex date - 5/1/96
Merged into WorldCom, Inc. 12/31/96
Each Depositary Preferred Ser. A exchanged for (1) Depositary Preferred Ser. A
Each share 8% Dividend Enhanced Conv. Preferred Ser. A 1¢ par exchanged for (1) share Dividend Enhanced Conv. Ser. A 8% 1¢ par
Each share Conv. Preferred Ser. B 1¢ par exchanged for (1) share Conv. Preferred Ser. B 1¢ par
Each share Common 1¢ par exchanged for (2.1) shares Common 1¢ par
WorldCom, Inc. name changed to MCI WorldCom, Inc. 9/14/98 which name changed to WorldCom Inc. (New) 5/1/2000
(See WorldCom Inc. (New))

MFS FINL INC (MD)
Name changed to Mutualfirst Financial, Inc. 4/27/2000

MFS GOVT MTG FD (DE)
Name changed 08/03/1992
Name changed 03/01/1993
Name changed from MFS Government Income Plus Trust to MFS Government Income Plus Fund 08/03/1992
Name changed from MFS Government Income Plus Fund to MFS Government Mortgage Fund 03/01/1993
Reorganized as MFS Series Trust X 06/02/1995
Details not available

MFS HIGH INCOME MUN TR (MA)
Auction Rate Preferred Ser. T no par called for redemption at $25,000 on 04/25/2016
Auction Rate Preferred Ser. W no par called for redemption at $25,000 on 04/26/2016
(Additional Information in Active)

MFS HIGH YIELD MUN TR (MA)
Auction Rate Preferred Ser. F no par called for redemption at $25,000 on 04/28/2016
(Additional Information in Active)

MFS INCOME & OPPORTUNITY FD (MA)
Name changed 08/03/1992
Name changed from MFS Income & Opportunity Trust to MFS Income & Opportunity Fund 08/03/1992
Reorganized as MFS Series Trust VIII 09/07/1993
Details not available

MFS INTERMARKET INCOME TR I (MA)
Completely liquidated
Each Share of Bene. Int. no par received first and final distribution of $8.6784 cash payable 09/25/2015 to holders of record 09/09/2015

MFS INVT GRADE MUN TR (MA)
Auction Rate Preferred Ser. M no par called for redemption at $25,000 on 04/29/2016
(Additional Information in Active)

MFS MANAGED CALIF TAX EXEMPT TR (MA)
Name changed to MFS California Municipal Bond Fund 08/03/1992
(See MFS California Municipal Bond Fund)

MFS MANAGED MUN BD TR (MA)
Name changed to MFS Municipal Bond Fund 8/3/92

MFS MULTIMARKET TOTAL RETURN TR (MA)
Acquired by Massachusetts Financial Bond Fund, Inc. 12/23/1991
Each Share of Bene. Int. no par exchanged for (1) share Common $1 par
(See Massachusetts Financial Bond Fund, Inc.)

MFS MUN INCOME TR (MA)
Auction Rate Preferred Ser. T no par called for redemption at $25,000 on 04/25/2016
Auction Rate Preferred Ser. TH no par called for redemption at $25,000 on 04/27/2016
(Additional Information in Active)

MFS RESH FD (MA)
Completely liquidated 04/21/1995
Details not available

MFS WORLDWIDE TOTAL RETURN TR (MA)
Name changed to MFS Worldwide Total Return Fund 8/3/92

MFY INDS INC (KS)
Stock Dividend - 100% 03/19/1976
Merged into Retail Management Corp. 08/19/1983
Each share Common 25¢ par exchanged for $9 cash

MG DIVIDEND & INCOME FD (ON)
Merged into YIELDPLUS Income Fund 09/27/2007
Each Trust Unit received (0.64565196) Trust Unit
YIELDPLUS Income Fund merged into MINT Income Fund 03/21/2017

MGC COMMUNICATIONS INC (NV)
Issue Information - 3,500,000 shares COM offered at $17 per share on 05/11/1998
Common $0.001 par split (3) for (2) by issuance of (0.5) additional share payable 8/28/2000 to holders of record 7/31/2000
Name changed to Mpower Communications Corp. (NV) 8/28/2000
Mpower Communications Corp. (NV) reincorporated in Delaware as Mpower Holding Corp. 6/28/2001
(See Mpower Holding Corp.)

MGC DIAGNOSTICS CORP (MN)
Acquired by MGC Parent LLC 12/28/2017
Each share Common 10¢ par exchanged for $11.03 cash

MGC LIQUIDATING CORP. (OH)
Liquidation completed
Each share Common no par exchanged for initial distribution of (0.409) share Grace (W.R.) & Co. (CT) Common $1 par 12/14/1971
Note: Option to receive (0.5108) share of Grace (W.R.) & Co. (CT) Common $1 par as first and final distribution expired 11/18/1971
Each share Common no par received second distribution of (0.077465) share Grace (W.R.) & Co. (CT) Common $1 par 00/00/1973
Each share Common no par received third distribution of (0.094346) share Grace (W.R.) & Co. (CT) Common $1 par 00/00/1974
Each share Common no par received fourth and final distribution of (0.282969) share Grace (W.R) & Co. (CT) Common $1 par 08/11/1975
Grace (W.R.) & Co. (CT) reincorporated in New York 05/19/1988
(See Grace (W.R.) & Co.)

MGCC INVT STRATEGIES INC (NV)
Each share old Common $0.0001 par exchanged for (0.05) share new Common $0.0001 par 02/13/2006
New Common $0.0001 par split (2.448719) for (1) by issuance of (1.448719) additional shares payable 07/25/2006 to holders of record 07/25/2006 Ex date - 07/26/2006
Name changed to Wonder Auto Technology, Inc. 09/05/2006
(See Wonder Auto Technology, Inc.)

MGF OIL CORP (DE)
Stock Dividend - 100% 01/19/1981
Plan of reorganization under Chapter 11 Federal Bankruptcy Code confirmed 12/02/1987
No Common stockholders' equity
Merged into a privately held company 03/29/1990
Each share new Common 1¢ par exchanged for $0.07429 cash

MGI INDS INC (AR)
Charter revoked for failure to pay taxes 01/07/1993

MGI PHARMA INC (MN)
Common 1¢ par split (2) for (1) by issuance of (1) additional share payable 06/09/2004 to holders of record 06/02/2004 Ex date - 06/10/2004
Merged into Eisai Co., Ltd. 01/28/2008
Each share Common 1¢ par exchanged for $41 cash

MGI PPTYS (MA)
In process of liquidation
Each share Common $1 par received initial distribution of $0.33 cash payable 1/19/99 to holders of record 1/8/99
Each share Common $1 par received second distribution of $0.33 cash payable 4/16/99 to holders of record 4/6/99
Each share Common $1 par received third distribution of $19 cash payable 7/30/99 to holders of record 7/16/99
Each share Common $1 par received fourth distribution of $4.50 cash payable 11/23/99 to holders of record 11/15/99
Each share Common $1 par received fifth distribution of $3 cash payable 4/13/2000 to holders of record 4/4/2000
Each share Common $1 par received sixth distribution of $1.85 cash payable 9/28/2000 to holders of record 9/14/2000
Each share Common $1 par received seventh distribution of $0.45 cash payable 4/12/2001 to holders of record 4/4/2001
Assets transferred to MGI Properties Liquidating Trust 9/28/2000
(See MGI Properties Liquidating Trust)

MGI PROPERTIES LIQUIDATING TRUST (MA)
Liquidation completed
Each share Common $1 par received first and final distribution of $0.455 cash payable 9/17/2002 to holders of record 8/28/2002
Note: Certificates were not required to be surrendered and are without value

MGI SOFTWARE INC (ON)
Merged into Roxio, Inc. 02/01/2002
Each share Common no par exchanged for (0.0505) share Common $0.001 par
Roxio, Inc. name changed to Napster, Inc. 12/23/2004
(See Napster, Inc.)

MGIC INVT CORP (WI)
Reincorporated 04/30/1976
Common $2 par split (3) for (2) by issuance of (0.5) additional share 05/14/1971
Common $2 par split (2) for (1) by issuance of (1) additional share 05/08/1972
State of incorporation changed from (DE) to (WI) and Common $2 par changed to $1 par 04/30/1976
Acquired by Baldwin-United Corp. 03/09/1982
Each share Common $1 par exchanged for $52 cash

MGM ENERGY CORP (AB)
Merged into Paramount Resources Ltd. 06/16/2014
Each share Common no par exchanged for (0.00333333) share Class A Common no par
Note: Unexchanged certificates were cancelled and became without value 06/16/2018

MGM GRAND HOTELS INC (DE)
Merged into Bally Manufacturing Corp. 04/25/1986
Each share 44¢ Ser. A Preferred $1 par exchanged for $14 cash
Each share Common no par exchanged for $18 cash

MGM MINERAL RES INC (WY)
Recapitalized as Brownstone Resources, Inc. 10/05/2007
Each share Common no par exchanged for (0.0002) share Common no par
Brownstone Resources, Inc. recapitalized as Pomsta Group, Inc. 10/12/2010 which name changed to Oidon Co., Ltd. 12/31/2010

MGM MIRAGE (DE)
Name changed 08/01/2000
Common 1¢ par split (2) for (1) by issuance of (1) additional share payable 02/25/2000 to holders of record 02/10/2000
Name changed from MGM Grand, Inc. to MGM Mirage 08/01/2000
Common 1¢ par split (2) for (1) by issuance of (1) additional share payable 05/18/2005 to holders of record 05/04/2005 Ex date - 05/19/2005
Name changed to MGM Resorts International 06/15/2010

MGM RESOURCE CORP (BC)
Recapitalized as Precision Petroleum Services Inc. 04/06/1989
Each share Common no par exchanged for (0.25) share Common no par
Precision Petroleum Services Inc. name changed to American Wellhead Services Inc. 01/23/1991 which recapitalized as Coronado Resources Inc. 05/13/1994 which recapitalized as Habanero Resources Inc. 10/27/1997 which recapitalized as Sienna Resources Inc. 01/24/2014

MGM UA COMMUNICATIONS CO (DE)
Merged into Pathe Communications Corp. 11/1/90
Each share Common $1 par exchanged for $17.50 cash

MGM UA ENTMT CO (DE)
Acquired by Turner Broadcasting System, Inc. 03/25/1986
Each share Common $1 par exchanged for (1) share Preferred Ser. A 10¢ par and $20 cash
(See Turner Broadcasting System, Inc.)

MGM UA HOME ENTMT GROUP INC (DE)
Merged into MGM/UA Entertainment Co. 06/14/1985
Each share Common 10¢ par exchanged for $27.8595 cash

MGN TECHNOLOGIES INC (BC)
SEC revoked common stock registration 02/21/2017

MGOLD RES INC (AB)
Reincorporated 07/25/2013
Place of incorporation changed from (QC) to (AB) 07/25/2013
Name changed to Tanager Energy Inc. 09/23/2013

MGP ASIA CAP INC (BC)
Recapitalized as Insular Explorations Ltd. 07/15/1991
Each share Common no par exchanged for (0.2) share Common no par
Insular Explorations Ltd. name changed to Masuparia Gold Corp. 09/01/1999 which name changed to MAS Gold Corp. 04/09/2018

MGP INGREDIENTS INC OLD (KS)
Common no par split (2) for (1) by issuance of (1) additional share payable 07/15/2004 to holders of record 06/30/2004 Ex date - 07/16/2004
Under plan of reorganization each share Common no par automatically became (1) share MGP Ingredients, Inc. (New) Common no par 01/04/2012

MGPX VENTURES INC (NV)
Name changed to Contango Oil & Gas Co. (NV) 10/7/99
Contango Oil & Gas Co. (NV) reorganized in Delaware 12/1/2000

MH STUDIOS INC (NY)
Recapitalized under the laws of Delaware as Science, Systems & Technology, Ltd. 3/30/70
Each share Common 1¢ par exchanged for (1) share Common 1¢ par
(See Science, Systems & Technology, Ltd.)

MH&SC INC (DE)
Name changed to Juhl Wind, Inc. and Common $0.000001 par changed to $0.0001 par 06/25/2008
Juhl Wind, Inc. name changed to Juhl Energy, Inc. 01/02/2013

MHB RES LTD (BC)
Name changed to Genoveva Resources Inc. 10/1/82
(See Genoveva Resources Inc.)

MHI GROUP INC (FL)
Each share Common 10¢ par exchanged for (0.25) share Common 40¢ par 11/19/93
Merged into SPRT Corp. 10/19/95
Each share Common 40¢ par exchanged for $10.25 cash

MHI HOSPITALITY CORP (MD)
Issue Information - 6,000,000 shares COM offered at $10 per share on 12/16/2004
Name changed to SoTHERLY Hotels Inc. 04/22/2013

MHI TELECOMMUNICATIONS INC (DE)
Charter cancelled and declared inoperative and void for non-payment of taxes 03/01/1985

MHM SVCS INC (DE)
Each share old Common 1¢ par exchanged for (0.002) share new Common 1¢ par 03/21/2000
Note: Holders of (499) or fewer pre-split shares received $0.45 cash per share
Merged into Centene Corp. 04/02/2018
Each share new Common 1¢ par exchanged for (85.46006367) shares Common $0.001 par and $1,325.88944 cash

MHP MACHS INC (DE)
Name changed to Applied Machining Technology, Inc. 10/30/1991
(See Applied Machining Technology, Inc.)

MHR EXCHANGECO CORP (AB)
Each Exchangeable Share exchanged for (1) share Magnum Hunter Resources Corp. Common 1¢ par 06/30/2013
(See Magnum Hunter Resources Corp.)

MI DEVS INC (ON)
Class A Subordinate no par reclassified as Common no par 07/04/2011
Each share Class B no par received (1.2) shares Common no par 07/04/2011
Note: Class B cancelled and certificates have no value
Reincorporated under the laws of Quebec as Granite Real Estate Inc. 06/18/2012
Granite Real Estate Inc. (QC) reorganized in Ontario as Granite Real Estate Investment Trust 01/03/2013

MI FD INC (NY)
Merged into Oppenheimer Tax-Free Bond Fund, Inc. 3/30/94
Each share Common 10¢ par exchanged for (1.898294) Shares of Bene. Int. $1 par
Oppenheimer Tax-Free Bond Fund, Inc. name changed to Oppenheimer Municipal Bond Fund 11/22/2002 which name changed to Oppenheimer AMT-Free Municipals 10/27/2003

MI LO HEALTH & BEAUTY AIDS LTD (BC)
Acquired by EFW Corp. 00/00/1980
Each share Common no par exchanged for $1.75 principal amount of 12% bonds due 00/00/1995

MI SOFTWARE CORP (BC)
Struck off register and declared dissolved for failure to file returns 06/10/1994

MIAD SYS LTD (ON)
Recapitalized as Melo Biotechnology Holdings Inc. 11/20/2006
Each share Common no par exchanged for (0.33333333) share Common no par
Melo Biotechnology Holdings Inc. name changed to First Asia Holdings Ltd. 03/09/2011

MIAMI AIR CONDITIONING CO (FL)
Proclaimed dissolved for failure to file reports and pay fees 12/05/1978

MIAMI BEACH FIRST NATIONAL BANK (MIAMI BEACH, FL)
Each share Common $100 par exchanged for (40) shares Common $10 par to effect a (10) for (1) split and a 300% stock dividend 00/00/1947
Stock Dividend - 200% 05/19/1965
Name changed to Flagship First National Bank (Miami Beach, FL) 11/08/1974
Flagship First National Bank (Miami Beach, FL) name changed to Flagship National Bank of Miami (Miami Beach, FL) 05/01/1979 which location was changed to (Miami, FL) 03/18/1980 which name changed to Sun Bank/Miami, N.A., (Miami, FL) 04/01/1985 which name changed to SunTrust Bank, Miami, N.A. (Miami, FL) 10/06/1995
(See SunTrust Bank, Miami, N.A. (Miami, FL))

MIAMI BRICK & STONE FLA INC (FL)
Class A Common $1 par changed to 10¢ par 08/21/1969
Name changed to MBS Industries, Inc. 02/15/1972
(See MBS Industries, Inc.)

MIAMI BRIDGE CO.
Capital Stock no par changed to $1 par in 1945
Liquidation completed in 1951

MIAMI CTZNS BANCORP (OH)
Common no par split (2) for (1) by issuance of (1) additional share 6/20/86
Stock Dividends - 10% 4/30/85; 10% 1/31/86; 10% 12/12/86
Under plan of merger name changed to C&H Bancorp 12/31/86
C&H Bancorp acquired by Fifth Third Bancorp 4/1/88

MIAMI CTZNS NATL BK & TR CO (PIQUA, OH)
Reorganized as Miami Citizens Bancorp 07/01/1984
Each share Common $10 par exchanged for (1) share Common no par
Miami Citizens Bancorp name changed to C&H Bancorp 12/31/1986 which was acquired by Fifth Third Bancorp 04/01/1988

MIAMI COMPUTER SUPPLY CORP (OH)
Issue Information - 1,000,000 shares COM offered at $8.50 per share on 11/11/1996
Secondary Offering - 2,100,000 shares COM offered at $16 per share on 06/29/1998
Common no par split (3) for (2) by issuance of (0.5) additional share payable 04/24/1998 to holders of record 04/10/1998
Reincorporated under the laws of Maryland as MCSi, Inc. 05/17/2000
(See MCSi, Inc.)

MIAMI COPPER CO. (DE)
Acquired by Tennessee Corp. and each share Capital Stock $5 par exchanged for (0.7) share Common $1.25 par and $45 in cash 6/17/60
Tennessee Corp. acquired by Cities Service Co. 6/14/63 which merged into Occidental Petroleum Corp. 12/3/82

MIAMI DATA PROCESSING CENTER, INC. (FL)
Stock Dividends - 10% 9/1/62; 10% 12/15/66
Under plan of merger name changed to Data Dynamics, Inc. 3/29/68

MIAMI DAYS CORP. (NV)
Name changed to Life Stem Genetics Inc. 09/20/2013

MIAMI EXTRUDERS, INC. (OH)
Completely liquidated 12/31/68
Each share Common 10¢ par exchanged for first and final distribution of (1) share Russell Aluminum Corp. Common $1 par
(See Russell Aluminum Corp.)

MIAMI INDUSTRIES, INC. (OH)
Merged into MSL Industries, Inc. (Minn.) 5/22/62
Each share Class A Common $1 par exchanged for (0.5) share Common no par
Each share Class B Common $1 par exchanged for (0.4) share Common no par
MSL Industries, Inc. (Minn.) reincorporated under the laws of Delaware 6/1/73
(See MSL Industries, Inc. (Del.))

MIAMI JOCKEY CLUB, INC.
Name changed to Hialeah Race Course, Inc. in 1944
(See Hialeah Race Course, Inc.)

MIAMI MANUFACTURING CO. (OH)
Liquidation completed
Each share Common no par exchanged for initial distribution of $0.50 cash 12/19/57
Each share Common no par received second distribution of $0.50 cash 5/15/58
Each share Common no par received third distribution of $0.75 cash 11/3/58
Each share Common no par received fourth distribution of $0.50 cash 4/22/59
Each share Common no par received fifth distribution of $0.50 cash 11/2/59
Each share Common no par received sixth and final distribution of $0.21221 cash 12/12/61

MIAMI NATL BK (MIAMI, FL)
Capital Stock $7.20 par changed to $1.80 par and (3) additional shares issued 05/28/1964
Stock Dividend - 10% 05/01/1962
Each (32,200) shares old Capital Stock $1.80 par exchanged for (1) share new Capital Stock $1.80 par 01/14/1988
Note: In effect holders received $0.90 cash per share and public interest was eliminated

MIAMI PAPER CO.
Acquired by Oxford Paper Co. 00/00/1926
Details not available

MIAMI SCREW INC (FL)
Adjudicated bankrupt 05/27/1971
No stockholders' equity

MIAMI SUBS CORP (FL)
Each share old Common 1¢ par exchanged for (0.25) share new Common 1¢ par 1/8/99
Merged into Nathan's Famous, Inc. 10/1/99
Each share new Common 1¢ par exchanged for (0.5) share Common 1¢ par and (1) Common Stock Purchase Warrant expiring 9/29/2004

MIAMI TILE & TERRAZO INC (FL)
Name changed to Mosaic Tile Co. of Florida 08/20/1968
(See Mosaic Tile Co. of Florida)

MIAMI VALLEY BK (LAKEVIEW, OH)
Placed in receivership 10/04/2007
Stockholders' equity unlikely

MIAMI WINDOW CORP (FL)
Each share 70¢ Conv. Preferred $8 par exchanged for (8) shares Common 50¢ par 2/24/64
Each share 16¢ Preferred $2 par exchanged for (2) shares Common 50¢ par 2/24/64
Each share Common 50¢ par exchanged for (0.2) share Common $1 par 7/22/64
Name changed to Russell Aluminum Corp. 6/14/66
(See Russell Aluminum Corp.)

MIB DIGITAL INC (FL)
Reorganized under the laws of Nevada as Cahaba Pharmaceuticals, Inc. 09/15/2010
Each share Common $0.0001 par exchanged for (8.33333333) shares Common $0.0001 par

FINANCIAL INFORMATION, INC.   MIC-MIC

Cahaba Pharmaceuticals, Inc. name changed to Visual Network Design, Inc. 07/21/2011 which name changed to Rackwise, Inc. 10/27/2011

MIC-MAC MINES LTD. (QC)
Acquired by United Mic Mac Mines Ltd. on a (1) for (3) basis 00/00/1947
United Mic Mac Mines Ltd. merged into Indian Lake Mines Ltd. 00/00/1956 which merged into Hydra Explorations Ltd. 11/16/1959 which name changed to HydraCapital Ltd. 12/30/1992 which name changed to Waterford Capital Management Inc. 11/12/1996 which merged into CPI Plastics Group Ltd. 09/21/1998

MIC MAC OILS (1963) LTD. (AB)
5.5% Preferred $4.50 par called 03/31/1964
Public interest eliminated

MIC MAC OILS LTD. (AB)
Merged into Consolidated Mic Mac Oils Ltd. and each (4.5) shares Common no par exchanged for (1) share new Common no par 00/00/1953
(See Consolidated Mic Mac Oils Ltd.)

MICA & MINERALS CORP. OF AMERICA (DE)
Charter cancelled and declared inoperative and void for non-payment of taxes 03/01/1977

MICA CORP. OF AMERICA (NV)
Name changed to Rep Corp. 4/22/69
Rep Corp. merged into Little Chef Food Products, Inc. 7/1/69

MICA PRODS CORP AMER (DE)
Charter cancelled and declared inoperative and void for non-payment of taxes 3/1/82

MICAMATIX CORP (DE)
Adjudicated bankrupt 11/03/1971
No stockholders' equity

MICC INVTS LTD (CANADA)
Common no par split (2) for (1) by issuance of (1) additional share 01/04/1974
Preferred Ser. A $25 par reclassified as 10% 1st Preferred Ser. A $25 par 04/17/1978
Preferred Ser. C $25 par reclassified as 8-5/8% 1st Preferred Ser. C $25 par 04/17/1978
8% Conv. 2nd Preferred Ser. A no par called for redemption 08/21/1987
Plan of arrangement effective 05/19/1998
Each share 10% 1st Preferred Ser. A $25 par and 8.625% 1st Preferred Ser. C $25 par received pro rata distribution of $3,209 assigned value of Participation Units and $8,920 cash
Note: Certificates were not required to be surrendered and are without value
Merged into CIGL Holdings Ltd. 03/27/2008
Each share Common no par exchanged for $2.55 cash

MICEL CORP (NY)
Each share old Common $0.001 par exchanged for (0.1) share new Common $0.001 par 11/25/1996
SEC revoked common stock registration 12/04/2009

MICHAEL ANTHONY JEWELERS INC (DE)
Each (1,500) shares old Common $0.001 par exchanged for (1) share new Common $0.001 par 12/15/2004
Note: In effect holders received $2.17 cash per share and public interest was eliminated

MICHAEL BAKER, JR., INC. (PA)
See - Baker (Michael), Jr., Inc.

MICHAEL FOODS INC (DE)
Common 1¢ par split (3) for (2) by issuance of (0.5) additional share 7/6/88
Common 1¢ par split (3) for (2) by issuance of (0.5) additional share 5/9/91
Merged into Michael Foods, Inc. (New) 2/28/97
Each share Common 1¢ par exchanged for (1) share Common 1¢ par
(See Michael Foods, Inc. (New))

MICHAEL FOODS INC NEW (MN)
Merged into Vestar Capital Partners 4/10/2001
Each share Common 1¢ par exchanged for $30.10 cash

MICHAEL LAMBERT INC (NV)
Name changed to Mass Hysteria Entertainment Co., Inc. 07/31/2009

MICHAEL PAGE INTL PLC (UNITED KINGDOM)
Name changed to PageGroup PLC 09/07/2018

MICHAEL RES LTD (BC)
Struck off register and declared dissolved for failure to file returns 04/15/1994

MICHAELS BROTHERS, INC. (NY)
Name changed to Sleahcim Corp. in 1954 which liquidated for cash in 1954

MICHAELS J INC (NY)
Common $1 par split (3) for (2) by issuance of (0.5) additional share 6/6/83
Stock Dividend - 100% 12/2/68
Merged into Siebert Financial Corp. 11/8/96
Each share Common $1 par exchanged for (0.14285714) share Common 1¢ par

MICHAELS STERN & CO., INC. (NY)
Each share Preferred $50 par exchanged for $31.50 principal amount of 5% Serial Notes and $18.50 cash 01/09/1964
Note: Holders of (19) or fewer shares received $50 cash per share
Each share $4.50 Preferred $100 par exchanged for $73 principal amount of 5% Serial Notes and $27 cash
Each share Class A Common $1 par or Class B Common $1 par exchanged for (10) shares Common 10¢ par 02/17/1972
100% reacquired through purchase offer as of 12/00/1974
Public interest eliminated

MICHAELS STORES INC (DE)
Common 10¢ par split (2) for (1) by issuance of (1) additional share payable 11/26/2001 to holders of record 11/12/2001 Ex date - 11/27/2001
Common 10¢ par split (2) for (1) by issuance of (1) additional share payable 10/12/2004 to holders of record 9/27/2004 Ex date - 10/13/2004
Merged into Bain Capital Partners LLC 10/31/2006
Each share Common 10¢ par exchanged for $44 cash

MICHAELY SILVER LEAD MINES LTD. (BC)
Declared dissolved and struck off register for failure to file reports and pay taxes 5/8/69

MICHAM EXPL INC (BC)
Recapitalized as International Micham Resources Inc. (BC) 12/17/1990
Each share Common no par exchanged for (1/3) share Common no par
International Micham Resources Inc.

(BC) reorganized in Ontario as Link Mineral Ventures Ltd. 05/29/1996
(See Link Mineral Ventures Ltd.)

MICHAUD PORCUPINE GOLD MINES, LTD. (ON)
Charter cancelled for failure to file reports and pay taxes in 1956

MICHEL OILS LTD.
Merged into Bailey Selburn Oil & Gas Ltd. and each (15) shares Common no par exchanged for (1) share Class A $1 par in 1952
(See Bailey Selburn Oil & Gas Ltd.)

MICHELIN CAP LTD (NS)
Floating Rate Retractable Class A Preferred no par called for redemption at $25 plus $0.148 accrued dividend on 6/4/97
Public interest eliminated

MICHELLE ENTERPRISES LTD (NV)
Recapitalized as America's Beautiful Cities 9/1/71
Each share Capital Stock $1 par exchanged for (0.1) share Capital Stock $1 par
(See America's Beautiful Cities)

MICHIGAN ABRASIVE CO (DE)
Reincorporated 7/18/68
6% Conv. Preferred called for redemption 7/1/65
State of incorporation changed from (MI) to (DE) 7/18/68
Name changed to Michigan General Corp. (Old) 4/15/88
Michigan General Corp. (Old) reorganized as Michigan General Corp. (New) 4/15/88
(See Michigan General Corp. (New))

MICHIGAN ASSOCIATED TELEPHONE CO.
Each share Common $100 par exchanged for (5) shares Common $20 par 1/23/50
Name changed to General Telephone Co. of Michigan in 1952
General Telephone Co. of Michigan merged into GTE MTO Inc. 3/31/87 which name changed to GTE North Inc. 1/1/88
(See GTE North Inc.)

MICHIGAN AVE FINL GROUP INC (DE)
Common $10 par split (2) for (1) by issuance of (1) additional share 1/1/69
Common $10 par changed to $1 par 7/17/69
Common $1 par split (6) for (5) by issuance of (0.2) additional share 7/24/70
Stock Dividend - 10% 8/1/69
Liquidation completed
Each share Common $1 par exchanged for initial distribution of $10.05 cash 12/7/84
Each share Common $1 par received second distribution of $0.07 cash 12/31/84
Each share Common $1 par received third and final distribution of $0.0653 cash 3/25/85

MICHIGAN AVE NATL BK (CHICAGO, IL)
Capital Stock $100 par changed to $20 par and (4) additional shares issued plus a 10% stock dividend paid 01/20/1961
Capital Stock $20 par changed to $10 par and (1) additional share issued 02/15/1968
Stock Dividends - 20% 04/25/1954; 25% 06/29/1956; 10% 07/05/1962; 12% 08/28/1963; 10.465% 06/30/1965; 10% 06/30/1967; 10% 07/31/1968
All shares excluding directors' shares acquired by Michigan Avenue Financial Group, Inc. through exchange offer as of 03/31/1971

MICHIGAN BAKERIES INC (MI)
$7 Preferred $100 par changed to no par 00/00/1933
Each share $7 Preferred no par exchanged for (1) share Prior Preference no par and $1 cash 00/00/1936
Each share Class A no par exchanged for (3) shares Common $1 par 00/00/1936
Each share Class B no par exchanged for (0.5) share Common $1 par 00/00/1936
Stock Dividend - 50% 10/25/1948
Charter cancelled for failure to file reports and pay fees 05/15/1973

MICHIGAN BK N A (DETROIT, MI)
Name changed to Michigan National Bank (Detroit, MI) 01/22/1973
(See Michigan National Bank (Detroit, MI))

MICHIGAN BREWERY, INC. (MI)
Ctfs. dated prior to 5/25/66
Adjudicated bankrupt 5/25/66
No stockholders' equity

MICHIGAN BREWERY INC (MI)
Ctfs. dated after 6/30/96
Name changed to Big Buck Brewery & Steakhouse, Inc. 9/30/97
(See Big Buck Brewery & Steakhouse, Inc.)

MICHIGAN BREWING CO. (MI)
Acquired by Fox (Peter) Brewing Co. 12/19/1940
Details not available

MICHIGAN BUMPER CORP. (MI)
Common $1 par exchanged (1) for (4) in 1944
Stock Dividend - 25% 12/20/49
Name changed to Michigan Plating & Stamping Co. 11/8/55
Michigan Plating & Stamping Co. name changed to Gulf & Western Corp. 11/6/58 which name changed to Gulf & Western Industries, Inc. (MI) 8/2/60 which reincorporated in Delaware 7/12/67 which name changed to Gulf + Western Inc. 5/1/86 which name changed to Paramount Communications Inc. 6/5/89 which merged into Viacom Inc. (Old) 7/7/94
(See Viacom Inc. (Old))

MICHIGAN CARTON CO (MI)
Each share Common no par exchanged for (2) shares Common $10 par 00/00/1951
Stock Dividend - 33-1/3% 01/15/1968
Through exchange offer all but (60) shares were acquired by St. Regis Paper Co. as of 05/06/1974
Public interest eliminated

MICHIGAN CENT RR CO (MI)
Merged into Penn Central Corp. 10/24/78
Each share Capital Stock $100 par exchanged for $925.13 cash
Note: a) distribution is certain only for certificates surrendered prior to 5/1/85 b) distribution may also be made for certificates surrendered between 5/1/85 and 12/31/86 c) no distribution will be made for certificates surrendered after 12/31/86
Penn Central Corp. name changed to American Premier Underwriters, Inc. 3/25/94 which merged into American Premier Group, Inc. 4/3/95 which name changed to American Financial Group, Inc. 6/9/95 which merged into American Financial Group, Inc. (Holding Co.) 12/2/97

MICHIGAN CHEM CORP (MI)
Each share Common 25¢ par exchanged for (0.05) share Common $1 par 00/00/1938
Each share Class A $2.50 par exchanged for $2.50 principal amount of 5-1/2% Debentures 00/00/1939

COPYRIGHTED MATERIAL   1719   NO UNAUTHORIZED REPRODUCTION

Common $1 par split (2) for (1) by issuance of (1) additional share 08/16/1968
Merged into Northwest Chemco, Inc. 12/26/1974
Each share Common $1 par exchanged for $22.50 cash

MICHIGAN CITIES NAT GAS CO (MI)
Liquidation completed
Each share Capital Stock $1 par exchanged for initial distribution of $0.25 cash 11/15/1968
Each share Capital Stock $1 par received second and final distribution of $0.122 cash 09/05/1969

MICHIGAN CMNTY BANCORP LTD (MI)
Completely liquidated
Each share Common no par received first and final distribution of approximately $0.0735 cash payable 01/27/2012 to holders of record 01/26/2012
Note: Certificates were not required to be surrendered and are without value

MICHIGAN CONS GAS CO (MI)
$3.19 Preference $1 par called for redemption 04/25/1985
Under plan of reorganization each share Common $1 par automatically became (1) share MCN Corp. Common 1¢ par 01/03/1989
$2.05 Preferred $1 par called for redemption 01/31/1996
MCN Corp. name changed to MCN Energy Group Inc. 04/28/1997
(See MCN Energy Group Inc.)

MICHIGAN COPPER & BRASS CO.
Merged into Republic Brass Corp. 00/00/1928
Details not available

MICHIGAN DAILY TAX FREE INCOME FD INC (MD)
Completely liquidated 10/23/2000
Details not available

MICHIGAN DAVIS CO.
Dissolution approved in 1937

MICHIGAN DIAMOND OIL & REFINING CO. (SD)
Charter expired by time limitations 4/8/22

MICHIGAN DIE CASTING CO. (MI)
Under plan of merger name changed to Gerity-Michigan Die Casting Co. 3/4/46
Gerity-Michigan Die Casting Co. name changed to Gerity-Michigan Corp. 10/1/47 which merged into Hoover Ball & Bearing Co. (Mich.) 12/28/56 which reincorporated under the laws of Delaware 12/31/68 then State of Incorporation changed back to Michigan 8/1/76 then name changed to Hoover Universal Inc. 1/17/78 which merged into Johnson Controls, Inc. 5/12/85

MICHIGAN ELECTRIC RAILWAY CO.
Acquired by Michigan Electric Shares Corp. in 1929 which dissolved in 1934

MICHIGAN ELECTRIC SHARES CORP.
Dissolved in 1934

MICHIGAN ENERGY RES CO (MI)
Merged into UtiliCorp United Inc. 05/26/1989
Each share Common $2.50 par exchanged for (1.0949) shares $1.775 Conv. Preference no par UtiliCorp United Inc. name changed to Aquila, Inc. (New) 03/15/2002 which was acquired by Great Plains Energy Inc. 07/14/2008 which merged into Evergy, Inc. 06/05/2018

MICHIGAN EQUITY CORP. (MI)
Completely liquidated 7/18/67
Each share Capital Stock $1 par exchanged for first and final distribution of $5.25 cash

MICHIGAN FINL CORP (MI)
Common $1 par changed to no par 08/01/1994
Common no par split (2) for (1) by issuance of (1) additional share 10/20/1994
Stock Dividends - 5% payable 06/20/1997 to holders of record 06/05/1997; 5% payable 06/22/1998 to holders of record 06/05/1998; 5% payable 06/21/1999 to holders of record 06/04/1999
Merged into Wells Fargo & Co. 03/30/2000
Each share Common no par exchanged for (0.682234) share Common $1-2/3 par

MICHIGAN GAS & ELEC CO (MI)
Each share Common $10 par exchanged for (7) shares Common $2 par 08/13/1966
Each share Common $2 par exchanged for $16.43 cash 02/25/1969
Name changed to Michigan Power Co. 02/28/1969
(See Michigan Power Co.)

MICHIGAN GAS & OIL CORP.
Out of existence 00/00/1941
Details not available

MICHIGAN GAS UTILS CO (MI)
Common $5 par changed to $2.50 par and (1) additional share issued 06/15/1960
Stock Dividends - 50% 02/29/1952; 25% 05/01/1963
Under plan of reorganization each share Common $2.50 par automatically became (1) share Michigan Energy Resources Co. Common $2.50 par 08/19/1980
Michigan Energy Resources Co. merged into UtiliCorp United Inc. 05/26/1989 which name changed to Aquila, Inc. (New) 03/15/2002 which was acquired by Great Plains Energy Inc. 07/14/2008 which merged into Evergy, Inc. 06/05/2018

MICHIGAN GEN CORP NEW (DE)
Charter cancelled and declared inoperative and void for non-payment of taxes 6/17/93

MICHIGAN GEN CORP OLD (DE)
$7 Conv. Preferred no par called for redemption 7/2/69
Reorganized under Chapter 11 Federal Bankruptcy Code as Michigan General Corp. (New) 4/15/88
Each share $2.50 Conv. Preferred $1 par exchanged for (1.25) shares Common 5¢ par and (0.25) Common Stock Purchase Warrant expiring 12/31/93
Each share Common $1 par exchanged for (0.25) share Common 5¢ par and (0.5) Common Stock Purchase Warrant expiring 12/31/93
(See Michigan General Corp. (New))

MICHIGAN GOLD MINES, INC.
Dissolved in 1936

MICHIGAN GOLD MNG INVTS INC (DE)
Reincorporated under the laws of Nevada as Sarissa Resources Inc. 03/23/2007

MICHIGAN HERITAGE BANCORP INC (MI)
Secondary Offering - 500,000 shares COM offered at $6 per share on 07/30/1999
Stock Dividend - 10% payable 06/15/1998 to holders of record 04/30/1998
Company's sole asset placed in receivership 04/24/2009
Stockholders' equity unlikely

MICHIGAN INTL SPEEDWAY INC (DE)
Common no par split (3) for (1) by issuance of (2) additional shares 1/10/69
Name changed to American Raceways, Inc. 6/30/69

MICHIGAN LIFE INS CO (MI)
Each share Capital Stock $50 par exchanged for (1/1200) share Capital Stock $60,000 par 02/23/1979
Note: In effect holders received $875 cash per share and public interest eliminated

MICHIGAN MOBILE HOMES CORP (MI)
Charter declared inoperative and void for failure to file reports 05/15/1978

MICHIGAN MUSHROOM CO. (MI)
Merged into Green Giant Co. (Minn.) 11/1/60
Each share 6% Preferred $10 par exchanged for (0.1) share 5% Preferred $100 par
Each share Common no par exchanged for (3.2) shares new Common no par
Green Giant Co. (Minn.) reincorporated under the laws of Delaware 11/1/73 which was acquired by Pillsbury Co. 3/9/79
(See Pillsbury Co.)

MICHIGAN NATIONAL BANK (DETROIT, MI)
Thru voluntary exchange offer over 99% acquired by Michigan National Corp. in 1972
Public interest eliminated

MICHIGAN NATL BK (LANSING, MI)
Stock Dividends - 33-1/3% 01/18/1944; 25% 01/17/1946; 20% 01/27/1947; 33-1/3% 01/17/1949; 25% 01/18/1952; 20% 01/15/1954; 25% 05/02/1956; 33-1/3% 01/16/1958; 20% 01/15/1960; 25% 01/25/1963; 20% 01/27/1965; 11.1% 06/30/1967; 10% 03/31/1969; 10% 04/30/1975
99.86% acquired by Michigan National Corp. through offer which expired 11/03/1972
Public interest eliminated

MICHIGAN NATL CORP (MI)
Reincorporated 4/20/83
6% Preferred $10 par called for redemption 1/2/74
Stock Dividends - 12% 6/5/73; 15% 6/25/75; 12% 1/26/76; 22% 5/10/77; 14% 7/28/78; 20% 5/31/79
State of incorporation changed from (DE) to (MI) 4/20/83
Merged into National Australia Bank Ltd. 11/2/95
Each share Common $10 par exchanged for $110 cash

MICHIGAN PLATING & STAMPING CO. (MI)
Stock Dividend - 10% 1/25/56
Name changed to Gulf & Western Corp. 11/6/58
Gulf & Western Corp. name changed to Gulf & Western Industries, Inc. (MI) 8/2/60 which reincorporated in Delaware 7/12/67 which name changed to Gulf + Western Inc. 5/1/86 which name changed to Paramount Communications Inc. 6/5/89 which merged into Viacom Inc. (Old) 7/7/94
(See Viacom Inc. (Old))

MICHIGAN PWR CO (MI)
4.40% Preferred $100 par called for redemption 07/31/1978
4.90% Preferred $100 par called for redemption 07/31/1978
Public interest eliminated

MICHIGAN PUBLIC SERVICE CO.
Acquired by Consumers Power Co. (ME) on a (0.45) for (1) basis in 1950
Consumers Power Co. (ME) reincorporated under the laws of Michigan 6/6/68
(See Consumers Power Co.)

MICHIGAN RACING ASSOCIATION, INC. (MI)
Common $100 par changed to $2 par 10/31/1955
Voting Trust Agreement expired 02/30/1960
Name changed to Detroit Race Course, Inc. 05/22/1961
(See Detroit Race Course, Inc.)

MICHIGAN RIVET CORP (MI)
Each share Common 20¢ par exchanged for (0.2) share Common $1 par 05/14/1982
Merged into MRC Industrial Group, Inc. 09/08/2003
Details not available

MICHIGAN ROTARY PRESS INC (MI)
Voluntarily dissolved 1/14/76
Details not available

MICHIGAN SCREW CO.
Acquired by Federal Screw Works 00/00/1929
Details not available

MICHIGAN SEAMLESS TUBE CO (DE)
Reincorporated 07/01/1968
Each share Common no par exchanged for (3) shares Common $5 par 00/00/1947
Common $5 par split (2) for (1) by issuance of (1) additional share 06/29/1959
Common $5 par split (2) for (1) by issuance of (1) additional share 12/20/1966
State of incorporation changed from (MI) to (DE) 07/01/1968
Common $5 par split (3) for (2) by issuance of (0.5) additional share 01/23/1976
Stock Dividends - 100% 10/26/1956; 10% 12/18/1964; 10% 12/20/1965
Name changed to Quanex Corp. 02/24/1977
(See Quanex Corp.)

MICHIGAN SMELTING & REFINING CO.
Acquired by Bohn Aluminum & Brass Corp. 00/00/1928
Details not available

MICHIGAN STEEL CASTING CO. (MI)
Liquidation completed 00/00/1959
Details not available

MICHIGAN STEEL CORP.
Acquired by National Steel Corp. 00/00/1930
Details not available

MICHIGAN STEEL TUBE PRODUCTS CO. (MI)
Each share Common no par exchanged for (2) shares Common $2.50 par 00/00/1936
Merged into Standard Tube Co. share for share 01/31/1958
Standard Tube Co. merged into Michigan Seamless Tube Co. (DE) 07/01/1968 which name changed to Quanex Corp. 02/24/1977
(See Quanex Corp.)

MICHIGAN SUGAR CO (MI)
Common no par changed to $1 par 12/14/54
Each share Preferred $10 par exchanged for $5 principal amount of 6% Subord. Income Debentures, (1) share 6% Preferred $4 par, (0.5) share new Common $1 par and $5 cash 7/31/64
Each share old Common $1 par exchanged for (1) share new Common $1 par 7/31/64
Stock Dividends - 25% 6/16/76; 25% 12/4/80

Merged into Savannah Foods & Industries, Inc. 7/19/84
Each share Common $1 par exchanged for $43.50 cash
6% Preferred $4 par called for redemption 12/20/89
Public interest eliminated

MICHIGAN SURETY CO. (MI)
Each share Capital Stock $50 par exchanged for (2) shares Capital Stock $25 par and (1) additional share issued in 1945
Stock Dividends - 11-1/9% 7/15/53; 20% 11/14/56
Declared insolvent 2/27/62
No stockholders' equity

MICHIGAN TERMINAL WAREHOUSE CO.
Reorganized as Warehouse & Terminals Corp. in 1943
No stockholders' equity

MICHIGAN UNITED OIL CO. (MI)
Charter dissolved for failure to file annual reports 8/31/41

MICHIGAN VENTURES INC (DE)
Name changed to Amerimark Corp. 11/02/1987
Amerimark Corp. recapitalized as Amerishop Corp. 07/10/1992
(See Amerishop Corp.)

MICHIGAN WIS PIPE LINE CO (DE)
Name changed to ANR Pipeline Co. 01/01/1984
(See ANR Pipeline Co.)

MICKELBERRY COMMUNICATIONS INC (DE)
Name changed 4/19/73
Name changed 5/10/94
Each share $3.50 Preferred $40 par exchanged for (1) share $2.40 Preferred $20 par and (3) shares Common $1 par in 1937
Name changed from Mickelberry's Food Products Co. to Mickelberry Corp. 4/19/73
Common $1 par split (3) for (2) by issuance of (0.5) additional share 6/5/81
Common $1 par split (2) for (1) by issuance of (1) additional share 12/31/82
Common $1 par split (3) for (2) by issuance of (0.5) additional share 7/2/84
Stock Dividends - 25% 8/19/75; 25% 3/10/78
Name changed from Mickelberry Corp. to Mickelberry Communications Inc. 5/10/94
Merged into Mickelberry Acquisition Corp. 9/29/95
Each share 30¢ Preferred Ser. A $1 par exchanged for $4.25 cash
Each share Common $1 par exchanged for $4.25 cash

MICO ENTERPRISES LTD (QC)
Acquired by National Hees Enterprises Ltd. in 1980
Each share 7% Class A Preference $2.50 par exchanged for (1.5) shares Common no par
Each share Common no par exchanged for (1.5) shares Common no par
National Hees Enterprises Ltd. name changed to Hees International Corp. 5/1/83 which name changed to Hees International Bancorp Inc. 5/6/88 which name changed to Edper Group Ltd. (New) 1/1/97 which merged into EdperBrascan Corp. 8/1/97 which name changed to Brascan Corp. 4/28/2000 which name changed to Brookfield Asset Management, Inc. 11/10/2005

MICO INSURANCE CO. (OK)
Name changed to Progress Life & Accident Insurance Co. 04/08/1966
(See Progress Life & Accident Insurance Co.)

MICO INVESTMENT CO. (OK)
Merged into Progress Life & Accident Insurance Co. 10/31/1967
Each share Common 50¢ par exchanged for (0.25) share Common 50¢ par
(See Progress Life & Accident Insurance Co.)

MICOM, INC. (MO)
Adjudicated bankrupt 1/30/65
Class A & B Common Stocks are worthless

MICOM COMMUNICATIONS CORP (DE)
Merged into Northern Telecom Ltd.-Northern Telecom Ltee. 06/21/1996
Each share Common $0.0000001 par exchanged for $12 cash

MICOM CORP. (MN)
Each share Common 50¢ par exchanged for (0.2) share Common 50¢ par 10/6/78
Through purchase offer 100% acquired by a private company
Public interest eliminated

MICOM SYS INC (DE)
Reincorporated 8/7/87
Common no par split (2) for (1) by issuance of (1) additional share 3/11/83
State of incorporation changed from (CA) to (DE) and Common no par changed to 1¢ par 8/7/87
Acquired by MSI Acquisition Corp. 9/28/88
Each share Common 1¢ par exchanged for $16 cash

MICON GOLD INC (ON)
Merged into Jubilee Gold Exploration Ltd. 01/25/2013
Each share Class A no par exchanged for (1.035) shares Common no par

MICONICS INDS INC (NY)
Merged into Bell Industries, Inc. 05/27/1981
Each share Common 1¢ par exchanged for $6.76 cash

MICREL INC (CA)
Common no par split (2) for (1) by issuance of (1) additional share payable 08/19/1997 to holders of record 08/04/1997
Common no par split (2) for (1) by issuance of (1) additional share payable 09/15/1999 to holders of record 08/30/1999
Common no par split (2) for (1) by issuance of (1) additional share payable 06/27/2000 to holders of record 06/06/2000
Acquired by Microchip Technology Inc. 08/03/2015
Each share Common no par exchanged for $14 cash

MICREX CORP (GA)
Proclaimed dissolved for failure to file annual reports 5/13/88

MICREX INTL CORP (AB)
Recapitalized as Micrex Development Corp. 12/13/1989
Each share Common no par exchanged for (0.1) share Common no par

MICRION CORP (MA)
Merged into FEI Co. 08/16/1999
Each share Common no par exchanged for (1) share Common no par and $6 cash
(See FEI Co.)

MICRO-ASI INTL INC (NV)
Name changed to McHenry Metals Golf Corp. 4/1/97

MICRO BIO-MEDICAL WASTE SYS INC (NV)
Each (30) shares old Common $0.001 par exchanged for (1) share new Common $0.001 par 8/19/2004

Name changed to Crown Equity Holdings Inc. 10/5/2006

MICRO BIO MEDICS INC (NY)
Each share old Common 1¢ par exchanged for (1/3) share new Common 1¢ par 6/28/91
Merged into Schein (Henry), Inc. 8/1/97
Each share new Common 1¢ par exchanged for (0.62) share Common 1¢ par

MICRO BOOK INTL INC (FL)
Administratively dissolved 09/25/2015

MICRO-BOOKS INTL INC (NV)
Name changed to Kwikscan, Inc. 06/13/1989

MICRO CAP CORP (DE)
SEC revoked common stock registration 11/30/2007

MICRO CARE INC (NY)
Recapitalized as Micro Holding Corp. 6/18/96
Each share Common $0.001 par exchanged for (0.01) share Common $0.001 par
Micro Holding Corp. name changed to Greenwood Acquisition Corp. 2/24/2004

MICRO CELLULAR COMMUNICATIONS INC (FL)
Common $0.0001 par split (5) for (1) by issuance of (4) additional shares 12/28/87
Proclaimed dissolved for failure to file reports and pay fees 10/9/92

MICRO COMPONENT TECHNOLOGY INC (MN)
Reincorporated 11/06/1996
State of incorporation changed from (DE) to (MN) 11/06/1996
Chapter 7 bankruptcy proceedings terminated 05/20/2010
No stockholders' equity

MICRO COMPUTER CORP (NY)
Common 2¢ par changed to 1¢ par 1/10/73
Name changed to Biotech Patent Inc. 11/24/2000
(See Biotech Patent Inc.)

MICRO CONCEPTS INC (BC)
Struck off register and declared dissolved for failure to file returns 11/26/1993

MICRO COPPER CORP (DE)
Reincorporated under the laws of Nevada 5/8/85
Each share Common 4¢ par exchanged for (1) share Common 4¢ par

MICRO CTL PRODS INC (CO)
Proclaimed dissolved for failure to file annual reports 1/1/87

MICRO CURL DISPLAY TECHNOLOGY INC (DE)
Charter cancelled and declared inoperative and void for non-payment of taxes 3/1/88

MICRO D INC (CA)
Merged into Ingram Acquisition Corp. 03/21/1989
Each share Common 1¢ par exchanged for $14.75 cash

MICRO DESIGN INC (TN)
Administratively dissolved 6/21/96

MICRO DISPLAY SYS INC (UT)
Each share Common 1¢ par exchanged for (0.125) share Common 8¢ par 12/02/1985
Name changed to Genius Technologies, Inc. 11/12/1990
(See Genius Technologies, Inc.)

MICRO-ECONOMICS INC (NV)
Name changed to E Med Future, Inc. 4/4/2003

MICRO ELECTRONICS CORP. (CO)
Declared defunct and inoperative for failure to pay franchise taxes 10/15/65

MICRO ENERGY INC (UT)
Name changed to Daystar Communications, Ltd. 9/22/83
Daystar Communications, Inc. recapitalized as Daystar International Holdings, Inc. 4/2/87 which name changed to BDI Systems, Inc. 5/25/95

MICRO ENHANCEMENT INTL INC (WA)
Reorganized 09/27/1995
Reorganized from (UT) to under the laws of Washington 09/27/1995
Each share Common 1¢ par exchanged for (0.25) share Common 1¢ par
Each share old Common 1¢ par exchanged for (0.00014285) share new Common 1¢ par
Note: In effect holders received an undetermined amount of cash per share and public interest was eliminated

MICRO-ERGICS INC (NV)
Name changed to MEI Corp. 10/21/91
MEI Corp. name changed to Space Propulsion Systems Inc. 1/13/2004

MICRO FOCUS GROUP PLC (ENGLAND)
Each Unsponsored ADR for Ordinary 10p par exchanged for (1) Sponsored ADR for Ordinary 10p par 06/04/1990
Name changed to Merant PLC 02/16/1999
Merant PLC was acquired by Serena Software, Inc. 06/30/2004
(See Serena Software, Inc.)

MICRO GEN CORP (DE)
Reincorporated 07/01/1988
State of incorporation changed from (UT) to (DE) 07/01/1988
Each share old Common 10¢ par exchanged for (0.2) share new Common 5¢ par 12/31/1992
Stock Dividend - 10% payable 06/01/2001 to holders of record 05/18/2001
Merged into Fidelity National Information Solutions, Inc. 07/10/2002
Each share new Common 5¢ par exchanged for (0.696) share Common 1¢ par
Fidelity National Information Solutions, Inc. merged into Fidelity National Financial, Inc. 09/30/2003 which merged into Fidelity National Information Services, Inc. 11/09/2006

MICRO HEALTHSYSTEMS INC (DE)
Common 1¢ par split (2) for (1) by issuance of (1) additional share 4/4/91
Name changed to US Servis, Inc. 11/18/95
US Servis, Inc. merged into HBO & Co. 10/1/98 which merged into McKesson HBOC Inc. 1/12/99 which name changed to McKesson Corp. 7/30/2001

MICRO HLDG CORP (NY)
Each share Common $0.001 par exchanged for (0.5) share Common $0.002 par 07/27/1997
Reincorporated under the laws of Delaware as Greenwood Acquisition Corp. 02/24/2004

MICRO-HYDRO PWR INC (DE)
Reincorporated 01/29/1998
State of incorporation changed from (UT) to (DE) 01/29/1998
Each share old Common $0.00001 par exchanged for (0.01) share new Common $0.00001 par 09/20/1996
Name changed to Kingsley Coach, Inc. 01/25/1999
(See Kingsley Coach, Inc.)

MICRO IMAGING SYS INC (DE)
Charter cancelled and declared inoperative and void for non-payment of taxes 6/24/92

MICRO INKS LTD (INDIA)
ADR agreement terminated 12/29/2006
No 144A GDR's for Equity shares remain outstanding
No Reg. S GDR for Equity shares remain outstanding

MICRO-INTEGRATION CORP (DE)
SEC revoked common stock registratiion 09/08/2008

MICRO INVESTMENT CORP. (UT)
Recapitalized as Century American Corp. 11/25/74
Each share Common $0.001 par exchanged for (0.01) share Common 10¢ par

MICRO-JET GENERAL CORP. (UT)
Recapitalized as E.P. Enterprises, Inc. 01/12/1987
Each share Common $0.001 par exchanged for (0.1) share Common $0.001 par
E.P. Enterprises, Inc. name changed to F/X Bio-Med, Inc. 03/05/1987
(See F/X Bio-Med, Inc.)

MICRO LABS INC (NV)
SEC revoked common stock registration 07/14/2010

MICRO LECTRIC INC (NY)
Dissolved by proclamation 12/15/75

MICRO LINEAR CORP (DE)
Acquired by Sirenza Microdevices, Inc. 10/31/2006
Each share Common $0.001 par exchanged for (0.365) share Common $0.001 par
Sirenza Microdevices, Inc. merged into RF Micro Devices, Inc. 11/13/2007 which merged into Qorvo, Inc. 01/02/2015

MICRO-LITE TELEVISION (NV)
Name changed to Superior Wireless Communications, Inc. 11/1/96
Superior Wireless Communications, Inc. recapitalized as JustWebit.Com, Inc. 8/16/99 which name changed to Synthetic Turf Corp. of America 11/12/2002 which recapitalized as City Capital Corp. 12/15/2004

MICRO MAMMOUTH SOLUTIONS INC (NV)
Name changed to Atlas Capital Holdings, Inc. 05/20/2010
Atlas Capital Holdings, Inc. name changed to Home Health International Inc. 03/26/2012 which recapitalized as American Transportation Holdings, Inc. 04/29/2014

MICRO MASK INC (DE)
Reincorporated 4/3/87
Common $1 par split (3) for (2) by issuance of (0.5) additional share 12/8/80
Stock Dividends - 25% 8/31/78; 25% 5/16/79; 10% 12/8/82
State of incorporation changed from (CA) to (DE) 4/3/87
Merged into Hoya Corp. USA 8/21/89
Each share Common $1 par exchanged for $10 cash

MICRO-MEDIA SOLUTIONS INC (UT)
Name changed to MSI Holdings, Inc. (UT) 10/14/1998
MSI Holdings, Inc. (UT) reorganized in Delaware as Aperian, Inc. 09/11/2000 which name changed to Fourthstage Technologies, Inc. 08/20/2001
(See Fourthstage Technologies, Inc.)

MICRO METALS CORP. (NJ)
Charter revoked for failure to file reports and pay fees 02/03/1965

MICRO METALS INC (MN)
Believed out of business 00/00/1986
Details not available

MICRO-MOISTURE CONTROLS, INC. (DE)
Charter revoked for non-payment of taxes 4/1/58

MICRO PHONICS TECHNOLOGY INTL CORP (BC)
Recapitalized as Var Computer Solutions Corp. 05/24/1989
Each share Common no par exchanged for (0.2) share Common no par
Var Computer Solutions Corp. name changed to Econ Ventures Ltd. 06/05/1995 which recapitalized as Richcor Resources Ltd. (BC) 09/12/2000 which reincorporated in Canada 07/24/2001 which name changed to Bioxel Pharma Inc. 08/13/2001
(See Bioxel Pharma Inc.)

MICRO PRECISION CORP (NY)
Name changed to MPC Educational Systems Inc. 11/27/1968
MPC Educational Systems Inc. name changed to PM&E Inc. 09/08/2001
(See PM&E Inc.)

MICRO SCAN SYS INC (NY)
Recapitalized as Keystone Micro Scan, Inc. (NY) 02/08/1971
Each share Common 1¢ par exchanged for (0.4) share Common 2-1/2¢ par
Keystone Micro Scan, Inc. (NY) reincorporated in Delaware 07/02/1971
(See Keystone Micro Scan, Inc.)

MICRO-TECH IDENTIFICATION SYS INC (NV)
Each share old Common $0.001 par exchanged for (0.025) share new Common $0.001 par 06/25/2007
Note: Holders of between (100) and (3,999) shares received (100) shares
Holders of (99) shares or fewer were not affected
Name changed to Amnutria Dairy, Inc. 10/10/2007
Amnutria Dairy, Inc. name changed to Emerald Dairy Inc. 01/28/2008
(See Emerald Dairy Inc.)

MICRO TECH INDS INC (NV)
Each share old Common $0.001 par exchanged for (0.05) share new Common $0.001 par 08/29/1988
Recapitalized as Next Generation Media Corp. 04/01/1997
Each share new Common $0.001 par exchanged for (0.1) share Common 1¢ par
Next Generation Media Corp. name changed to Next Generation Energy Corp. 07/28/2010 which name changed to Next Generation Management Corp. 06/19/2014

MICRO TECHNOLOGIES INDIA LTD (INDIA)
GDR agreement terminated 06/21/2013
No GDR's remain outstanding

MICRO TEMPUS INC (CANADA)
Each share old Common no par exchanged for (0.1) share new Common no par 11/13/1992
Name changed to Surefire Commerce Inc. 02/04/2000
Surefire Commerce Inc. name changed to Terra Payments Inc. 09/25/2003 which merged into Optimal Group Inc. 04/06/2004
(See Optimal Group Inc.)

MICRO TENNA CORP (FL)
Name changed to Data Computer Systems, Inc. 02/06/1970
(See Data Computer Systems, Inc.)

MICRO THERAPEUTICS INC (DE)
Incorporated 10/14/68
Charter cancelled and declared inoperative and void for non-payment of taxes 3/1/82

MICRO THERAPEUTICS INC (DE)
Incorporated 07/00/1996
Issue Information - 1,600,000 shares COM offered at $6 per share on 02/18/1997
Merged into ev3 Inc. 01/06/2006
Each share Common $0.001 par exchanged for (0.476289) share Common 1¢ par
(See ev3 Inc.)

MICRO THERMOLOGY CORP (UT)
Name changed to Designers International Corp. 01/12/1985
(See Designers International Corp.)

MICRO VENTURES LTD (BC)
Name changed to Diveresified Entertainment Inc. 12/29/1988
(See Diversified Entertainment Inc.)

MICRO WHSE INC (DE)
Common 1¢ par split (2) for (1) by issuance of (1) additional share 4/15/94
Merged into Bridgeport Holdings Inc. 2/3/2000
Each share Common 1¢ par exchanged for $19 cash

MICRO Z CORP (CA)
Reorganized as Brajdas Corp. 4/24/84
Each (5.822) shares 8% Non-Cum. Conv. Preferred Ser. B $10 par exchanged for (1) share Common 10¢ par
Each (29.412) shares Common $0.001 par exchanged for (1) share Common 10¢ par
Brajdas Corp. reorganized as Richey Electronics, Inc. 12/30/93
(See Richey Electronics, Inc.)

MICROACCEL INC (UT)
Each share old Common $0.001 par exchanged for (0.5) share new Common $0.001 par 08/15/2000
Each share new Common $0.001 par exchanged for (0.5) share Common $0.001 par 12/21/2001
Name changed to Health Anti-Aging Lifestyle Options, Inc. 03/18/2002
Health Anti-Aging Lifestyle Options, Inc. name changed to Previsto International Holdings, Inc. 12/07/2010

MICROAGE INC (DE)
Common 1¢ par split (3) for (2) by issuance of (0.5) additional share 01/13/1994
Plan of reorganization under Chapter 11 Federal Bankruptcy proceedings effective 07/31/2001
No stockholders' equity

MICROAMERICA INC (DE)
Merged into Softsel Computer Products, Inc. 04/09/1990
Each share Common 1¢ par exchanged for (0.9) share Common 1¢ par and $1.27 cash
Softsel Computer Products, Inc. name changed to Merisel, Inc. 08/28/1990
(See Merisel, Inc.)

MICROBEST INC (MN)
SEC revoked common stock registration 09/14/2006

MICROBIAL SOLUTIONS INC (NV)
Name changed to Skinvisible Inc. 3/2/99

MICROBILT CORP (GA)
Common no par split (3) for (2) by issuance of (0.5) additional share 07/15/1988
Merged into First Financial Management Corp. 12/15/1989
Each share Common no par exchanged for (0.435) share Common 10¢ par

First Financial Management Corp. merged into First Data Corp. (Old) 10/27/1995
(See First Data Corp. (Old))

MICROBIOLOGICAL RESH CORP (DE)
Recapitalized as General Biometrics Inc. 08/01/1987
Each share Capital Stock 10¢ par exchanged for (0.3076923) share Capital Stock 1¢ par
General Biometrics Inc. recapitalized as Syntello, Inc. 08/10/1993 which reorganized as Maxim Pharmaceuticals, Inc. 10/09/1996 which merged into EpiCept Corp. 01/05/2006 which recapitalized as Immune Pharmaceuticals Inc. 08/21/2013

MICROBIOLOGICAL SCIENCES INC (DE)
Name changed to Microbiological Research Corp. 11/16/1970
Microbiological Research Corp. recapitalized as General Biometrics Inc. 08/01/1987 which recapitalized as Syntello, Inc. 08/10/1993 which reorganized as Maxim Pharmaceuticals, Inc. 10/09/1996 which merged into EpiCept Corp. 01/05/2006 which recapitalized as Immune Pharmaceuticals Inc. 08/21/2013

MICROBIOLOGICAL SCIENCES INC (NY)
Common 10¢ par changed to 5¢ par and (1) additional share issued 3/15/83
Chapter 11 bankruptcy proceedings converted to Chapter 7 on 1/11/93
Stockholders' equity unlikely

MICROBYX CORP (DE)
Charter cancelled and declared inoperative and void for non-payment of taxes 03/01/2002

MICROCAP FD INC (MD)
Each share Common 1¢ par received distribution of (0.2) share Conv. Preferred Ser. A 1¢ par 3/20/95
In process of liquidation
Each share Conv. Preferred Ser. A 1¢ par received initial distribution of $4.375 cash payable 8/30/96 to holders of record 8/15/96
Each share Common 1¢ par received initial distribution of $3.50 cash payable 8/30/96 to holders of record 8/15/96
Assets transferred to MicroCap Liquidating Trust and each share Conv. Preferred Ser. A 1¢ par and Common 1¢ par automatically became (1.25) and (1) Unit of Bene. Int. respectively 2/24/97
(See MicroCap Liquidating Trust)

MICROCAP FINL SVCS INC (CO)
Name changed to GlobalNet Financial.Com, Inc. 4/16/99
(See GlobalNet Financial.Com, Inc.)

MICROCAP INC (UT)
Merged into Microsemi Corp. 08/30/1985
Each share Common $0.001 par exchanged for $0.0771111 cash

MICROCAP LIQUIDATING TR (MD)
Liquidation completed
Each Unit of Undivided Int. 1¢ par received initial distribution of $1 cash payable 7/15/97 to holders of record 6/30/97
Each Unit of Undivided Int. 1¢ par received second distribution of $0.75 cash payable 8/28/98 to holders of record 8/14/98
Each Unit of Undivided Int. 1¢ par received third distribution of $0.75 cash payable 3/31/99 to holders of record 3/16/99
Each Unit of Undivided Int. 1¢ par received fourth distribution of $0.40

cash payable 1/28/2000 to holders of record 1/14/2000
Each Unit of Undivided Int. 1¢ par received fifth distribution of $0.40 cash payable 8/15/2000 to holders of record 7/31/2000
Each Unit of Undivided Int. 1¢ par exchanged for sixth and final distribution of $0.15 cash 8/23/2001

MICROCARB INC (DE)
Name changed to Antex Biologics Inc. 9/3/96

MICROCELL TELECOMMUNICATIONS INC (CANADA)
Acquired by Rogers Wireless Communications Inc. 11/12/2004
Each share Restricted Class A no par exchanged for $35 cash
Each share Non-Vtg. Class B no par exchanged for $35 cash

MICROCHEMICAL SPECIALTIES CO (CA)
Name changed to Misco Dissolution Corp. 03/19/1971
(See Misco Dissolution Corp.)

MICROCIDE PHARMACEUTICALS INC (DE)
Name changed to Essential Therapeutics, Inc. 10/25/2001
(See Essential Therapeutics, Inc.)

MICROCOAL TECHNOLOGIES INC (CANADA)
Reorganized as Targeted Microwave Solutions Inc. 05/22/2015
Each share Common no par exchanged for (1) Common no par

MICROCOM INC (MA)
Common 1¢ par split (2) for (1) by issuance of (1) additional share 04/28/1989
Merged into Compaq Computer Corp. 06/26/1997
Each share Common 1¢ par exchanged for $16.25 cash

MICROCOMM CORP (MN)
Chapter 11 bankruptcy proceedings converted to Chapter 7 on 1/3/86
Stockholders' equity unlikely

MICRODATA CORP (CA)
Merged into McDonnell Douglas Corp. 11/02/1979
Each share Common no par exchanged for $32 cash

MICRODOT INC (DE)
Reincorporated 07/02/1971
Capital Stock no par reclassified as Common no par 10/24/1967
Common no par split (3) for (2) by issuance of (0.5) additional share 02/28/1968
State of incorporation changed from (CA) to (DE) 07/02/1971
Merged into Northwest Industries, Inc. 06/11/1976
Each share Common no par exchanged for $21 cash

MICRODYNE CORP (MD)
Common 10¢ par split (5) for (4) by issuance of (0.25) additional share 11/5/79
Stock Dividend - 50% 12/22/80
Merged into L-3 Communications Corp. 2/22/99
Each share Common 10¢ par exchanged for $5 cash

MICROELECTRONIC PACKAGING INC (CA)
Issue Information - 1,600,000 shares COM offered at $5 per share on 04/21/1994
Name changed to Meltronix, Inc. 11/01/1999
(See Meltronix, Inc.)

MICROELECTRONICS TECHNOLOGY INC (TAIWAN)
Old Reg. S GDR's for Common split (10) for (1) by issuance of (9) additional GDR's payable 08/22/1997 to holders of record 06/27/1997
Old 144A GDR's for Common split (10) for (1) by issuance of (9) additional GDR's payable 08/22/1997 to holders of record 06/30/1997
Each old Reg. S GDR for Common exchanged for (0.65351604) new Reg. S GDR for Common 04/04/2013
Each old 144A GDR for Common exchanged for (0.65351604) new 144A GDR for Common 04/04/2013
Stock Dividends - 10% payable 07/17/1996 to holders of record 05/23/1996; 19.4304% payable 09/22/2000 to holders of record 06/01/2000 Ex date - 09/02/2000; 18.68307% payable 08/08/2001 to holders of record 05/30/2001 Ex date - 05/25/2001; 10% payable 08/19/2002 to holders of record 06/12/2002 Ex date - 06/10/2002; 1.1% payable 08/31/2009 to holders of record 07/15/2009 Ex date - 07/13/2009
GDR agreement terminated 10/08/2013
Each new Reg. S GDR for Common exchanged for $2.312011 cash
Each new GDR 144A for Common exchanged for $2.312011 cash

MICROENERGY INC (DE)
Each (360) shares Common $0.001 par exchanged for (1) share Common 1¢ par 05/13/1996
Assets sold for the benefit of creditors 09/09/1999
Stockholders' equity unlikely

MICROFIELD GROUP INC (OR)
Name changed 05/13/2003
Name changed from Microfield Graphics, Inc. to Microfield Group, Inc. 05/13/2003
Name changed to EnergyConnect Group, Inc. 09/25/2008
(See EnergyConnect Group, Inc.)

MICROFILM UNLTD INC (NY)
Name changed to Micro Medical Industries, Inc. 12/15/72

MICROFINANCIAL INC (MA)
Acquired by MF Parent L.P. 01/23/2015
Each share Common 1¢ par exchanged for $10.20 cash

MICROFLUIDICS INTL CORP NEW (DE)
Acquired by IDEX Corp. 03/11/2011
Each share Common 1¢ par exchanged for $1.35 cash

MICROFLUIDICS INTL CORP OLD (DE)
Name changed to MFIC Corp. 06/25/1999
MFIC Corp. name changed to Microfluidics International Corp. (New) 06/18/2008
(See Microfluidics International Corp. (New))

MICROFORM DATA SYS INC (DE)
Name changed to Icot Corp. 12/19/80
Icot Corp. name changed to Amati Communications Corp. 11/28/95
(See Amati Communications Corp.)

MICROFORUM INC (ON)
Recapitalized as Homeserve Technologies Inc. 09/08/2003
Each share Common no par exchanged for (0.04) share Common no par
(See Homeserve Technologies Inc.)

MICROFRAME INC (NJ)
Each share old Common $0.001 par exchanged for (0.2) share new Common $0.001 par 09/20/1993
Reincorporated under the laws of Delaware as ION Networks, Inc. 04/01/1999
ION Networks, Inc. name changed to HealthWarehouse.com, Inc. 08/05/2009

MICROFUEL SYS INC (BC)
Name changed to Teranet IA Inc. 02/17/1992
Teranet IA Inc. name changed to Triant Technologies Inc. 05/06/1996 which recapitalized as Triant Holdings, Inc. 12/12/2005
(See Triant Holdings, Inc.)

MICROGENIX CDA INC (CANADA)
Reincorporated under the laws of Nevada as US BioTec, Inc. and Common no par changed to $0.001 par 06/30/2004

MICROGENIX FILTRATION SYS INC (WY)
Reincorporated 01/30/2006
Each share old Preferred no par exchanged for (0.01) share new Preferred no par 02/02/2004
Each share old Common no par exchanged for (0.01) share new Common no par 02/02/2004
Place of incorporation changed from (Canada) to (WY) 01/30/2006
New Common no par split (3) for (1) by issuance of (2) additional shares payable 01/31/2006 to holders of record 01/28/2006 Ex date - 02/01/2006
Recapitalized as Amerossi EC Inc. 05/09/2006
Each share new Common no par exchanged for (0.0004) share Common no par
Amerossi EC Inc. recapitalized as Nanotech Industries, Inc. 10/25/2007
(See Nanotech Industries, Inc.)

MICROGRAFX INC (TX)
Common 1¢ par split (3) for (2) by issuance of (0.5) additional share 4/15/92
Merged into Corel Corp. 10/30/2001
Each share Common 1¢ par exchanged for (0.4299) share Common no par and (1) Participation Right
Note: Holders received $1.0187 cash for each Participation Right 11/4/2002
(See Corel Corp.)

MICROHELIX INC (OR)
Issue Information - 2,000,000 UNITS consisting of (1) share COM, (1) CL A WT and (1) CL B WT offered at $6 per Unit on 11/16/2001
Each share old Common no par exchanged for (0.33333333) share new Common no par 12/09/2003
Each share new Common no par exchanged again for (0.06666666) share new Common no par 11/19/2008
Recapitalized as CarePayment Technologies, Inc. 04/27/2010
Each share new Common no par exchanged for (0.1) share Class A Common no par

MICROISLET INC (NV)
Chapter 11 bankruptcy proceedings converted to Chapter 7 on 02/25/2009
No stockholders' equity

MICROKEY COMMUNICATIONS SYS INC (BC)
Cease trade order effective 05/06/1998

MICROLAB FXR (NJ)
Merged into New Jersey Microwave, Inc. 12/20/1978
Each share Common 10¢ par exchanged for $4.50 cash

MICROLAB ONLINE INC (ON)
Name changed to Axios Mobile Assets Corp. 03/18/2010
(See Axios Mobile Assets Corp.)

MICROLEAGUE MULTIMEDIA INC (PA)
Plan of reorganization under Chapter 11 Federal Bankruptcy proceedings confirmed 09/17/1998
Each share Common 1¢ par received (0.0142) right to purchase Units of Ablesoft, Inc. (a private company) consisting of (1) share Preferred Ser. C and (40.0641) shares Common

MICROLOG CORP (VA)
Reincorporated under the laws of Delaware as Nutroganics, Inc. 09/25/2013

MICROLOGIX BIOTECH INC (BC)
Name changed to Migenix Inc. 09/20/2004
Migenix Inc. reorganized as BioWest Therapeutics Inc. 03/19/2010 which name changed to Carrus Capital Corp. 08/22/2011 which name changed to Global Blockchain Technologies Corp. 10/05/2017

MICROLYTICS INC (DE)
Reorganized under Chapter 11 Federal Bankruptcy Code as Santi Group, Inc. 4/30/98
Each share Common 1¢ par exchanged for (0.0025) share Common 1¢ par and (0.00125) Common Stock Purchase Warrant expiring 12/31/2001
Note: No holder will receive fewer than (100) Common shares
Santi Group, Inc. name changed to Earthcare Co. 9/25/98
(See Earthcare Co.)

MICROMATIC HONE CORP. (MI)
Stock Dividends - 25% 12/5/52; 10% 6/11/56
Acquired by Ex-Cell-O Corp. 12/2/63
Each share Common $1 par exchanged for (1/3) share Common $3 par
(See Ex-Cell-O Corp.)

MICROMATION SYS INC (MD)
Charter cancelled for failure to file annual reports 4/18/73

MICROMATION TECHNOLOGY CORP (DE)
Completed liquidated 4/13/71
Each share Common 1¢ par exchanged for first and final distribution of (0.16) share Computer Communications, Inc. Common $1 par
Computer Communications, Inc. recapitalized as Trendsetter Solar Products, Inc. 6/12/2006

MICROMEDICAL INDS LTD (AUSTRALIA)
Name changed to Ventracor Ltd. 07/08/2002
(See Ventracor Ltd.)

MICROMEDX INC (NV)
Name changed to Reno Gold Corp. 12/02/2004
(See Reno Gold Corp.)

MICROMET INC (DE)
Acquired by Amgen Inc. 03/07/2012
Each share Common $0.00004 par exchanged for $11 cash

MICROMINT INC (NV)
Charter permanently revoked 05/30/2008

MICROMUSE INC (DE)
Issue Information - 3,200,000 shares COM offered at $12 per share on 02/12/1998
Common 1¢ par split (2) for (1) by issuance of (1) additional share payable 2/22/2000 to holders of record 2/3/2000
Common 1¢ par split (2) for (1) by issuance of (1) additional share payable 12/19/2000 to holders of record 12/5/2000 Ex date - 12/20/2000

Merged into International Business Machines Corp. 2/15/2006
Each share Common 1¢ par exchanged for $10 cash

MICRON CORP. (UT)
Each share Common 2¢ par exchanged for (0.1) share Common 20¢ par 2/24/72
Ceased operations 8/4/76
No stockholders' equity

MICRON ELECTRONICS INC (MN)
Under plan of merger name changed to Interland, Inc. 08/06/2001
Interland, Inc. name changed to Web.com, Inc. 03/20/2006 which merged into Website Pros, Inc. 10/01/2007 which name changed to Web.com Group, Inc. 10/27/2008
(See Web.com Group, Inc.)

MICRON ENVIRO SYS INC (NV)
Each share old Common $0.001 par exchanged for (3) shares new Common $0.001 par 06/26/2006
Each share new Common $0.001 par exchanged again for (3) shares new Common $0.001 par 09/09/2009
Recapitalized as Britannia Mining, Inc. 05/31/2013
Each share new Common $0.001 par exchanged for (0.01666666) share Common $0.001 par
Note: No holder will receive fewer than (333) post-split shares

MICRON INDS INC (NY)
Name changed to Satra Corp. 6/15/71
(See Satra Corp.)

MICRON INDS LTD (BC)
Recapitalized as Lakewood Forest Products Ltd. 07/23/1987
Each share Common no par exchanged for (0.5) share Common no par
(See Lakewood Forest Products Ltd.)

MICRON INSTRS INC (CA)
Completely liquidated
Each share Capital Stock 10¢ par exchanged for first and final distribution of $1.22 cash 01/30/1981

MICRON METALS CDA CORP (AB)
Each share old Common no par exchanged for (2) shares new Common no par 10/10/1989
Name changed to USA Video Corp. (AB) 04/03/1992
USA Video Corp. (AB) reorganized in Wyoming as USA Video Interactive Corp. 02/23/1995 which recapitalized as Oculus VisionTech Inc. 01/26/2012

MICRON PLASTICS CORP. (NY)
Name changed to Micron Industries, Inc. 4/29/66
Micron Industries, Inc. name changed to Satra Corp. 6/15/71
(See Satra Corp.)

MICRON PRODS INC (MA)
Merged into Arrhythmia Research Technology, Inc. 11/25/1992
Each share Common 10¢ par exchanged for (0.05) share new Common 1¢ par
Arrhythmia Research Technology, Inc. name changed to Micron Solutions, Inc. 03/27/2017

MICRON RESOURCES LTD. (BC)
Name changed to Micron Industries Ltd. 04/01/1986
Micron Industries Ltd. recapitalized as Lakewood Forest Products Ltd. 07/23/1987
(See Lakewood Forest Products Ltd.)

MICRON SOLUTIONS INC (NV)
Common $0.001 par split (2) for (1) by issuance of (1) additional share payable 9/15/2001 to holders of record 9/10/2001 Ex date - 9/28/2001

Recapitalized as PanaMed Corp. 3/1/2002
Each share Common $0.001 par exchanged for (0.1) share Common $0.001 par
PanaMed Corp. name changed to Endexx Corp. 7/8/2005

MICRONAS SEMICONDUCTOR HLDG AG (SWITZERLAND)
ADR agreement terminated 09/21/2017
No ADR's remain outstanding

MICRONESIAN MINERAL RESOURCE LTD (BC)
Merged into DRX, Inc. 03/07/1989
Each share Common no par exchanged for (0.5) share Common 10¢ par
(See DRX, Inc.)

MICRONET ENERTEC TECHNOLOGIES INC (DE)
Name changed to MICT, Inc. 07/16/2018

MICRONETIC CORP (DE)
Adjudicated bankrupt 5/31/68
Trustee's opinion: Common Stock is worthless

MICRONETIC SYS INC (DE)
Charter cancelled and declared inoperative and void for non-payment of taxes 04/15/1973

MICRONETICS INC (DE)
Name changed 11/06/2002
Name changed from Micronetics Wireless, Inc. to Micronetics, Inc. 11/06/2002
Acquired by Mercury Computer Systems, Inc. 08/08/2012
Each share Common 1¢ par exchanged for $14.80 cash

MICRONETICS INC (NY)
Name changed to National Micronetics, Inc. (NY) 06/21/1971
National Micronetics, Inc. (NY) reincorporated in Delaware 01/25/1982
(See National Micronetics, Inc.)

MICRONETICS INC (UT)
Recapitalized as Praxis Pharmaceuticals, Inc. (UT) 07/08/1998
Each share Common $0.001 par exchanged for (0.00844238) share Common $0.001 par
Praxis Pharmaceuticals, Inc. (UT) reincorporated in Nevada as Patch International Inc. 06/15/2004 which reincorporated in Alberta 08/29/2008
(See Patch International Inc.)

MICRONETICS INC NEW (DE)
Name changed to Micronetics Wireless, Inc. 11/28/1995 which name changed back to Micronetics, Inc. 11/06/2002
(See Micronetics, Inc.)

MICRONICS, INC. (MN)
Merged into Electro-Med, Inc. 12/31/1961
Electro-Med, Inc. recapitalized as Knapic Electro-Physics, Inc. 03/12/1962
(See Knapic Electro-Physics, Inc.)

MICRONICS COMPUTERS INC (DE)
Reincorporated 11/26/93
State of incorporation changed from (CA) to (DE) and Common no par changed to 1¢ par 11/26/93
Merged into Diamond Multimedia Systems, Inc. 7/9/98
Each share Common 1¢ par exchanged for $2.45 cash

MICRONICS INTL INC (DE)
Recapitalized as Premier Enterprises Holdings, Inc. 2/22/99
Each share Common $0.0001 par exchanged for (1/30) share Common $0.001 par
Premier Enterprises Holdings, Inc. name changed to Hawaiilove.com,

Inc. 1/20/2000 which name changed to Ornate Solutions Inc. 8/2/2001 which recapitalized as Ornate Holdings Inc. 9/20/2001 which name changed to Absolute Health & Fitness, Inc. 5/14/2004

MICROPAC INDS INC (TX)
Reincorporated under the laws of Delaware 3/3/69

MICROPHONICS TECHNOLOGY CORP (WA)
Charter cancelled and proclaimed dissolved for failure to pay fees 10/22/1990

MICROPIN CORP (CA)
Name changed to Annandale Corp. 03/28/1983
(See Annandale Corp.)

MICROPOINT INC (DE)
Name changed to Flexpoint Sensor System, Inc. 6/18/99

MICROPOLIS CORP (DE)
Reincorporated 04/00/1987
State of incorporation changed from (CA) to (DE) and Common no par changed to $1 par 04/00/1987
Name changed to StreamLogic Corp. 03/29/1996
(See StreamLogic Corp.)

MICROPRO INTL CORP (CA)
Name changed to Wordstar International Inc. 06/15/1989
Wordstar International Inc. merged into SoftKey International Inc. 02/04/1994 which name changed to Learning Co. Inc. 10/24/1996 which merged into Mattel, Inc. 05/13/1999

MICROPROBE CORP (DE)
Name changed to Epoch Pharmaceuticals Inc. 12/4/95
Epoch Pharmaceuticals Inc. name changed to Epoch Biosciences Inc. 8/17/2000 which merged into Nanogen, Inc. 12/17/2004

MICROPROSE INC NEW (DE)
Merged into Hasbro, Inc. 9/14/98
Each share Common $0.001 par exchanged for $6 cash

MICROPROSE INC OLD (MD)
Merged into Spectrum HoloByte, Inc. 12/14/93
Each share Common $0.001 par exchanged for (1.666) shares Common $0.001 par
Spectrum Holobyte, Inc. name changed to MicroProse, Inc. (New) 9/22/97
(See MicroProse, Inc. (New))

MICRORESEARCH CORP (NV)
Merged into Insight Management Corp. 06/29/2009
Each share Common $0.001 par exchanged for (1.5) shares Common $0.001 par
Insight Management Corp. recapitalized as Striper Energy, Inc. 04/20/2016

MICROS SYS INC (MD)
Common $0.025 par split (2) for (1) by issuance of (1) additional share payable 06/22/1998 to holders of record 05/22/1998
Common $0.025 par changed to $0.0125 par and (1) additional share issued payable 02/01/2005 to holders of record 01/17/2005 Ex date - 02/02/2005
Common $0.0125 par changed to $0.00625 par and (1) additional share issued payable 02/05/2008 to holders of record 01/22/2008 Ex date - 02/06/2008
Common $0.00625 par changed to $0.025 par 07/10/2010
Acquired by Oracle Corp. 09/08/2014
Each share Common $0.025 par exchanged for $68 cash

MICROS TO MAINFRAMES INC (NY)
Name changed to MTM Technologies, Inc. 05/27/2004
(See MTM Technologies, Inc.)

MICROSCIENCE INTL CORP (CA)
Charter suspended for failure to file reports and pay fees 6/1/94

MICROSCINT INC (NV)
Name changed to World Mobile Holdings, Inc. 11/03/2009

MICROSEMI CORP (DE)
Name changed 02/10/1983
Name changed from Microsemiconductor Corp. to Microsemi Corp. 02/10/1983
Common 20¢ par split (5) for (4) by issuance of (0.25) additional share 07/08/1985
Common 20¢ par split (2) for (1) by issuance of (1) additional share payable 08/28/2001 to holders of record 08/14/2001 Ex date - 08/29/2001
Common 20¢ par split (2) for (1) by issuance of (1) additional share payable 02/20/2004 to holders of record 02/06/2004 Ex date - 02/23/2004
Acquired by Microchip Technology Inc. 05/29/2018
Each share Common 20¢ par exchanged for $68.78 cash

MICROSIGNAL CORP (NV)
Name changed to NanoSignal Corp. 11/10/2003
NanoSignal Corp. recapitalized as Nano Global Inc. 04/03/2006
(See Nano Global Inc.)

MICROSIZE INC (UT)
Proclaimed dissolved for failure to file annual reports 3/1/91

MICROSOFT CORP (DE)
Reincorporated 00/00/1986
Reincorporated 11/01/1993
State of incorporation changed from (WA) to (DE) 00/00/1986
Common $0.001 par split (2) for (1) by issuance of (1) additional share 09/18/1987
Common $0.001 par split (2) for (1) by issuance of (1) additional share 04/16/1990
Common $0.001 par split (3) for (2) by issuance of (0.5) additional share 06/26/1991
Common $0.001 par split (3) for (2) by issuance of (0.5) additional share 06/12/1992
State of incorporation changed from (DE) to (WA) 11/01/1993
Issue Information - 10,954,616 shares 2-3/4% PFD SER A CONV offered at $79.875 per share on 12/17/1996
Each share 2-3/4% Conv. Exchangeable Preferred Ser. A 1¢ par exchanged for (1.1273) shares Common $0.001 par 12/15/1999
(Additional Information in Active)

MICROSOLVE COMPUTER CAP INC (QC)
Name changed to Homebank Technologies Inc. 12/20/2000
Homebank Technologies Inc. name changed to Selient Inc. 06/15/2005
(See Selient Inc.)

MICROSONICS, INC. (MA)
Merged into Sangamo Electric Co. (Del.) 7/1/68
Each share Common no par exchanged for (0.181818) share Common $5 par

MICROSONICS CORP (WA)
Merged into Natural Organics, Inc. 5/15/84
Each share Common 10¢ par exchanged for (0.5) share Common 1¢ par
Natural Organics, Inc. name changed to I.H.V. Corp. 1/16/86 which name

changed to California Beach Restaurants, Inc. 7/10/90

MICROSTAR SOFTWARE LTD (CANADA)
Acquired By 3557855 Canada Inc. 9/24/99
Each share Common no par exchanged for $2.10 cash

MICROSTAT DEV CORP (BC)
Name changed to International Chess Enterprises Inc. 03/30/1992
International Chess Enterprises Inc. recapitalized as Grandmaster Technologies Inc. 06/22/1994 which recapitalized as EM Net Corp. (BC) 08/31/1998 which reincorporated in Canada as T & E Theatre.com Inc. 11/25/1999 which recapitalized as Manele Bay Ventures Inc. 02/28/2002 which name changed to MBA Gold Corp. 07/15/2003 which name changed to MBA Resources Corp. 10/14/2005 which name changed to Thunderbird Energy Corp. 07/27/2006 which recapitalized as Gordon Creek Energy Inc. 10/24/2013

MICROSURE INC (DE)
Recapitalized as 9A Investment Holding Corp. 08/31/2001
Each share Common 1¢ par exchanged for (0.03571428) share Common 1¢ par
9A Investment Holding Corp. name changed to Viking Power Services, Inc. 07/03/2006

MICROSYSTEMS INTL LTD (CANADA)
Acquired by Northern Electric Co. Ltd. 06/10/1975
Each share Common no par exchanged for (1/7) share Common no par
Northern Electric Co., Ltd. name changed to Northern Telecom Ltd.-Northern Telecom Ltee. 03/01/1976 which name changed to Nortel Networks Corp. (Old) 04/30/1999 which reorganized as Nortel Networks Corp. (New) 05/01/2000
(See Nortel Networks Corp. (New))

MICROTEC DEV INC (CO)
Charter suspended for failure to file annual reports 7/1/93

MICROTEC RESH INC (DE)
Merged into Mentor Graphics Corp. 01/31/1996
Each share Common $0.001 par exchanged for (0.6930693) share Common $0.001 par
(See Mentor Graphics Corp.)

MICROTECH MED SYS INC (CO)
Name changed to Eclipse Corp. 11/15/96

MICROTEK MED HLDGS INC (GA)
Merged into Ecolab Inc. 11/12/2007
Each share Common $0.001 par exchanged for $6.30 cash

MICROTEK MED INC (DE)
Acquired by Isolyser Inc. 08/30/1996
Each share Common 1¢ par exchanged for (1.65) shares Common $0.001 par
Isolyser Inc. name changed to Microtek Medical Holdings, Inc. 07/01/2002
(See Microtek Medical Holdings, Inc.)

MICROTEL FRANCHISE & DEV CORP (NY)
Name changed to Hudson Hotels Corp. 06/13/1996
(See Hudson Hotels Corp.)

MICROTEL INTL INC (DE)
Each share old Common $0.0033 par exchanged for (0.2) share new Common $0.0033 par 08/29/1996
Name changed to EMRISE Corp. 09/15/2004

MICROTERRA INC (DE)
Each share old Common 1¢ par exchanged for (0.05) share new Common 1¢ par 11/10/1994
Name changed to Atlantis Group, Inc. (Ctfs. dated after 11/02/1995) 11/02/1995
(See Atlantis Group, Inc. (Ctfs. dated after 11/02/1995))

MICROTEST INC (DE)
Merged into Danaher Corp. 8/9/2001
Each share Common $0.001 par exchanged for $8.15 cash

MICROTHERM NATIONAL CORP. (NY)
Charter cancelled and proclaimed dissolved for failure to pay taxes 12/16/74

MICROTHERMAL APPLICATIONS INC (DE)
Charter cancelled and declared inoperative and void for non-payment of taxes 4/15/72

MICROTOUCH SYS INC (MA)
Common 1¢ par split (2) for (1) by issuance of (1) additional share 11/01/1994
Merged into Minnesota Mining & Manufacturing Co. 02/15/2001
Each share Common 1¢ par exchanged for $21 cash

MICROTRAK INC (NV)
Name changed to Tracking Corp. 09/10/2007
Tracking Corp. recapitalized as H-D International Group 01/05/2018

MICROTRON INDS INC (CO)
Common 10¢ par changed to 1¢ par 7/10/72
Each share Common 1¢ par exchanged for (0.1) share Common no par 12/17/75
Merged into 614 North Beltline, Inc. 6/15/94
Details not available

MICROTUNE INC (DE)
Acquired by Zoran Corp. 12/01/2010
Each share Common $0.001 par exchanged for $2.92 cash

MICROVISION INC (DC)
Charter revoked for failure to file reports 9/13/76

MICROVISION INC (WA)
Reincorporated under the laws of Delaware and Common no par changed to $0.001 par 12/20/2003

MICROWARE SYS CORP (IA)
Merged into RadiSys Corp. 8/27/2001
Each share Common no par exchanged for $0.68 cash

MICROWAVE ASSOC INC (MA)
Name changed to M/A-Com, Inc. 04/01/1978
M/A-Com, Inc. merged into AMP Inc. 06/30/1995 which merged into Tyco International Ltd. (Bermuda) 04/01/1999 which reincorporated in Switzerland 03/17/2009 which merged into Johnson Controls International PLC 09/06/2016

MICROWAVE COMPONENTS SYS CORP (UT)
Charter suspended for failure to file reports and pay taxes 12/31/1975

MICROWAVE CORP AMER (DE)
Each share Common 10¢ par exchanged for (1/3) share Capital Stock 1¢ par 06/09/1967
Charter forfeited for failure to maintain a registered agent 01/20/1978

MICROWAVE ELECTRONIC TUBE CO., INC. (DE)
Name changed to Metcom, Inc. in 1960
Metcom, Inc. name changed to Omni-Wave Electronics Corp. 8/10/72
(See Omni-Wave Electronics Corp.)

MICROWAVE ELECTRONICS CORP. (DE)
Acquired by Teledyne, Inc. 09/20/1965
Each share Common 10¢ par exchanged for (0.14285714) share Common $1 par
Teledyne, Inc. merged into Allegheny Teledyne, Inc. 08/15/1996 which name changed to Allegheny Technologies Inc. 11/29/1999

MICROWAVE LABS INC (DE)
SEC revoked common stock registration 09/24/2010

MICROWAVE PWR DEVICES INC (DE)
Merged into Ericsson Inc. 11/28/2000
Each share Common 1¢ par exchanged for $8.70 cash

MICROWAVE PWR DEVICES INC (NY)
Stock Dividends - 100% 10/10/1978; 50% 09/20/1979; 50% 09/15/1980
Acquired by M/A-Com, Inc. 02/10/1981
Each share Common 10¢ par exchanged for (0.41172849) share Common $1 par
M/A-Com, Inc. merged into AMP Inc. 06/30/1995 which merged into Tyco International Ltd. (Bermuda) 04/01/1999 which reincorporated in Switzerland 03/17/2009 which merged into Johnson Controls International PLC 09/06/2016

MICROWAVE SEMICONDUCTOR & INSTRUMENTS INC. (DE)
Name changed to MSI Electronics, Inc. 02/14/1962
(See MSI Electronics, Inc.)

MICROWAVE SEMICONDUCTOR CORP (DE)
Merged into Siemens A.G. 11/02/1979
Each share Common 50¢ par exchanged for $14 cash

MICROWAVE SYS INC (NY)
Merged out of existence 05/02/1983
Details not available

MICROWAVE TRANSMISSION SYS INC (TX)
Acquired by CJGKC Acquisition Corp. 12/15/2004
Each share Common $0.001 par exchanged for $0.48 cash

MICRUS ENDOVASCULAR CORP (DE)
Issue Information - 3,250,000 shares COM offered at $11 per share on 06/16/2005
Acquired by Johnson & Johnson 09/27/2010
Each share Common 1¢ par exchanged for $23.40 cash

MID AM INC (OH)
Common no par split (3) for (2) by issuance of (0.5) additional share 10/10/1993
Conv. Preferred Ser. A no par called for redemption 06/26/1997
Stock Dividends - 10% 09/29/1989; 10% 09/07/1990; 10% 08/14/1992; 10% 10/31/1994; 10% 05/17/1995; 10% payable 09/30/1996 to holders of record 09/10/1996; 10% payable 09/15/1997 to holders of record 09/02/1997
Merged into Sky Financial Group, Inc. 10/02/1998
Each share Common no par exchanged for (0.77) share Common no par
Sky Financial Group, Inc. merged into Huntington Bancshares Inc. 07/02/2007

MID-AMER APT CMNTYS INC (TN)
Issue Information - 1,750,000 shares PFD SER A 9.5% offered at $25 per share on 10/10/1996
9-3/8% Preferred Ser. C called for redemption at $25 on 08/12/2003
9.5% Preferred Ser. A called for redemption at $25 on 08/12/2003
Issue Information - 1,875,000 shares PFD SER B 8-7/8% offered at $25 per share on 11/14/1997
8-7/8% Preferred Ser. B 1¢ par called for redemption at $25 on 08/18/2003
9.25% Preferred Ser. F 1¢ par called for redemption at $25 plus $0.0995 accrued dividends on 10/16/2007
8.30% Preferred Ser. H 1¢ par called for redemption at $25 plus $0.37215 accrued dividends on 08/05/2010
(Additional Information in Active)

MID-AMER RACING STABLES INC (OK)
Name changed to Basin Industries, Inc. 03/18/1991
(See Basin Industries, Inc.)

MID AMER BANCORP (KY)
Common no par split (3) for (1) by issuance of (2) additional shares 3/30/84
Stock Dividends - 11% 10/21/85; 12.5% 6/10/88; 15% 6/9/89; 10% 6/7/90; 10% 1/3/92; 3% payable 12/13/96 to holders of record 12/3/96 Ex date - 11/29/96; 3% payable 12/12/97 to holders of record 12/1/97 Ex date - 11/26/97; 3% payable 12/18/98 to holders of record 12/2/98; 3% payable 12/17/99 to holders of record 12/3/99; 3% payable 12/15/2000 to holders of record 12/4/2000 Ex date - 11/30/2000
Merged into BB&T Corp. 3/8/2002
Each share Common no par exchanged for (0.7187) share Common $5 par and $8.34 cash

MID AMER BANCSHARES INC (TN)
Merged into Pinnacle Financial Partners, Inc. 11/30/2007
Each share Common $1 par exchanged for (0.4655) share Common $1 par and $1.50 cash

MID AMER CAP CORP II (DE)
Market Auction Preferred no par called for redemption 12/02/1991

MID-AMERICA CORP. (OK)
Name changed to Doric Corp. (OK) 04/02/1964
Doric Corp. (OK) reincorporated in Delaware 09/26/1967 which merged into Esmark, Inc. (Inc. 03/14/1969) 04/24/1975
(See Esmark, Inc. (Inc. 03/14/1969))

MID AMER DRILLING & EXPL INC (CO)
Name changed to Prairie States Exploration Inc. 4/14/83
Prairie States Exploration Inc. reorganized as Prairie States Energy Co. 9/9/85 which recapitalized as Spindletop Oil & Gas Co. 7/13/90

MID AMER FID CORP (MI)
Merged into American Bankcorp, Inc. 04/30/1975
Each share Common $10 par exchanged for (1.36982) shares Common $10 par
American Bankcorp, Inc. merged into First American Bank Corp. 02/13/1978 which name changed to First of America Bank Corp. 01/14/1983 which merged into National City Corp. 03/31/1998 which was acquired by PNC Financial Services Group, Inc. 12/31/2008

MID-AMERICA FOODS, INC. (IA)
Merged into DeKalb AgResearch Inc. 10/17/80
Each share Common no par exchanged for $4.75 cash

MID AMER GREAT PLAINS CORP (MO)
Name changed 12/16/1981
Name changed from Mid-America

Great Plains Financial Corp. to Mid-America/Great Plains Corp. 12/16/1981
Charter forfeited for failure to file reports 01/01/1987

MID AMER INDS INC (DE)
Stock Dividends - 10% 01/17/1975; 15% 01/16/1976
Merged into MAI Acquisition Inc. 08/19/1988
Each share Common $1 par exchanged for $8.50 cash

MID AMER INS CO (MO)
Common $1 par changed to $1.66-2/3 par 01/27/1965
Completely liquidated 01/02/1969
Each share Common $1.66-2/3 par exchanged for first and final distribution of (1.2505) shares Mid-America Great Plains Financial Corp. Common no par
Mid-America Great Plains Financial Corp. name changed to Mid-America/Great Plains Corp. 12/16/1981
(See Mid-America/Great Plains Corp.)

MID AMER INS INVS CORP (IA)
Common $1 par changed to 50¢ par and (1) additional share issued 06/30/1972
Name changed to United America Group, Inc. 01/18/1974
(See United America Group, Inc.)

MID AMER LD CO (FL)
Name changed to Myler International Corp. 03/29/1996
Myler International Corp. name changed to Micro Book International Inc. 12/15/1997
(See Micro Book International Inc.)

MID AMER LEASING INC (WI)
Merged into Association Corp. 5/28/70
Each share Common 10¢ par exchanged for (1) share Common 30¢ par
Association Corp. merged into International Harvester Co. (DE) 3/9/73 which name changed to Navistar International Corp. 2/21/86

MID AMER LIFE ASSURN CO (MI)
Each share Common $1 par exchanged for (0.25) share Common $4 par 1/31/86
Each (5,000) shares Common $4 par exchanged for (1) share Common $4 par 1/17/89
Note: In effect holders received $7 cash per share and public interest was eliminated

MID-AMERICA LIFE INSURANCE CO. (OK)
Common 25¢ par changed to 15¢ par 12/17/63
Merged into National Empire Life Insurance Co. on a (1) for (9.5) basis 1/1/65
National Empire Life Insurance Co. merged into Empire Life Insurance Co. of America (AL) 6/30/66
(See Empire Life Insurance Co. of America (AL))

MID-AMERICA MINERALS INC. (DE)
Class A Common $1 par and Class B Common $1 par reclassified as Common $1 par 05/25/1959
Merged into Calvert Exploration Co. 12/31/1964
Each share 6% Conv. Preferred $100 par exchanged for (1) share 6% Conv. Preferred $100 par
Each share Common $1 par exchanged for (1) share Common 10¢ par
Calvert Exploration Co. merged into Sun Oil Co. (PA) 07/31/1974 which name changed to Sun Co. Inc. 04/27/1976 which name changed to Sunoco, Inc. 11/06/1998 which merged into Energy Transfer Partners, L.P. (Old) 10/05/2012 which which merged into Energy Transfer Partners, L.P. (New) 05/01/2017 which merged into Energy Transfer L.P. 10/19/2018

MID AMER NATL BK (CHICAGO, IL)
Acquired by Associated Bank of Chicago (Chicago, IL) 7/31/96
Each share Common $10 par exchanged for $9.43 cash

MID AMER NURSING CTRS INC (KS)
Company liquidated in 1983
Holders received approximately $4 cash per share
Note: Certificates were not required to be surrendered and are without value

MID AMER PETE INC (CO)
Plan of reorganization under Chapter 11 Federal Bankruptcy proceedings confirmed 02/16/1989
No stockholders' equity

MID AMER PIPELINE CO (DE)
Name changed to Mapco Inc. 05/14/1968
Mapco Inc. merged into Williams Companies, Inc. 03/28/1998

MID-AMERICA RLTY INVTS INC (MD)
Merged into Bradley Real Estate, Inc. 08/06/1998
Each share Common 1¢ par exchanged for (0.42) share 8.4% Conv. Preferred Ser. A 1¢ par
(See Bradley Real Estate, Inc.)

MID-AMERICA RESEARCH CORP. (DE)
Name changed to Marco Mfg. Co. 12/14/1953
(See Marco Mfg. Co.)

MID-AMERICAN INVESTORS LIFE INSURANCE CO. (OK)
Merged into Investors Life Insurance Co. 11/14/72
Each share Common $1 par exchanged for (20) shares Common 5¢ par
Investors Life Insurance Co. name changed to Investors Life Investment Co. 12/15/75
(See Investors Life Investment Co.)

MID AMERN LINES INC (MO)
Common 50¢ par changed to no par 9/23/83
Administratively dissolved 7/2/93
No stockholders' equity

MID AMERN NATL BK & TR CO BOWLING GREEN OHIO (NORTHWOOD, OH)
Common $10 par split (2) for (1) by issuance of (1) additional share 03/31/1987
Stock Dividend - 20% 08/12/1985
Merged into Mid Am, Inc. 03/04/1988
Each share Common $10 par exchanged for (1) share Common no par
Mid Am, Inc. merged into Sky Financial Group, Inc. 10/02/1998 which merged into Huntington Bancshares Inc. 07/02/2007

MID AMERICAN OIL & GAS CO. (IL)
Involuntarily dissolved in Superior Court Cook County, Illinois 12/22/61

MID-AMERN WASTE SYS INC (DE)
Common $1 par split (3) for (2) by issuance of (0.5) additional share 06/17/1991
Plan of reorganization under Chapter 11 Federal Bankruptcy proceedings confirmed 09/17/1997
No stockholders' equity

MID ATLANTIC BANKCORP (MD)
Merged into Fulton Financial Corp. 7/29/94
Each share Common $5 par exchanged for (2.06) shares Common $2.50 par

MID-ATLANTIC COMMUNITY BANKGROUP INC (VA)
Common $5 par split (2) for (1) by issuance of (1) additional share payable 3/16/98 to holders of record 3/9/98
Under plan of merger name changed to Atlantic Financial Corp. 12/1/98
Atlantic Financial Corp. merged into F & M National Corp. 2/26/2001 which merged into BB&T Corp. 8/9/2001

MID-ATLANTIC MARINAS INC (MD)
Each share 7% Preferred Ser. A $3.50 par exchanged for $3.50 principal amount of 7% Bonds due 10/1/92 and (1) share Common 1¢ par 2/28/72

MID ATLANTIC MED SVCS INC (DE)
Common 1¢ par split (3) for (2) by issuance of (0.5) additional share 11/19/1993
Common 1¢ par split (2) for (1) by issuance of (1) additional share 08/05/1994
Merged into UnitedHealth Group Inc. (MN) 02/10/2004
Each share Common 1¢ par exchanged for (0.82) share Common 1¢ par and $18 cash
UnitedHealth Group Inc. (MN) reincorporated in Delaware 07/01/2015

MID ATLANTIC REAL ESTATE INVT TR (MD)
Charter forfeited for failure to file annual reports 10/08/1985

MID-ATLANTIC RLTY TR (MD)
Issue Information - 3,000,000 SHS BEN INT offered at $10.50 per share on 08/31/1993
Merged into Kimco Realty Corp. 10/01/2003
Each Share of Bene. Int. 1¢ par exchanged for $21 cash

MID-CADDO OIL CO. (DE)
No longer in existence having become inoperative and void for non-payment of taxes 3/18/25

MID CAN EXPL LTD (SK)
Name changed to St. John's Petroleum Ltd. 5/17/82
St. John's Petroleum Ltd. merged into Westgrowth Petroleums Ltd. (ALTA) 7/11/85 which recapitalized as Canadian Westgrowth Ltd. 10/14/86 which merged into Ulster Petroleums Ltd. 10/27/87 which merged into Anderson Exploration Ltd. 5/23/2000
(See Anderson Exploration Ltd.)

MID CDA GOLD & COPPER MINES LTD (QC)
Merged into Consolidated Abitibi Resources Ltd. 05/31/1989
Each share Common $1 par exchanged for (0.21460609) share Common no par
Consolidated Abitibi Resources Ltd. merged into Aur Resources Inc. 11/22/1999 which was acquired by Teck Cominco Ltd. 09/28/2007 which name changed to Teck Resources Ltd. 04/27/2009

MID CAROLINA BK (BURLINGTON, NC)
Common $5 par split (5) for (4) by issuance of (0.25) additional share payable 02/15/1999 to holders of record 02/01/1999
Stock Dividend - 20% payable 06/15/2001 to holders of record 06/01/2001 Ex date - 05/30/2001
Under plan of reorganization each share Common $5 par automatically became (1) share MidCarolina Financial Corp. Common no par 05/31/2002
MidCarolina Financial Corp. merged into American National Bankshares Inc. 07/01/2011

MID CENT PPTYS LTD (NY)
In process of liquidation
Each share Common 1¢ par stamped to indicate initial distribution of $4.50 cash 12/12/77
Each share Stamped Common 1¢ par exchanged for second distribution of $0.50 cash 5/23/79
Amount or number of subsequent distributions, if any, are unavailable

MID CHIBOUGAMAU MINES LTD (QC)
Name changed to Mid Industries Ltd. 12/01/1970
Mid Industries Ltd. name changed to Mid Industries & Explorations Ltd. 09/10/1971
(See Mid Industries & Explorations Ltd.)

MID CITCO INC (DE)
Name changed to MidCity Financial Corp. 04/18/1995
MidCity Financial Corp. merged into MB Financial, Inc. (MD) 11/07/2001

MID CITY BANCORP (CA)
Assets placed in receivership with FDIC 10/21/1993
Stockholders' equity unlikely

MID CITY NATL BK (CHICAGO, IL)
Stock Dividends - 25% 12/20/1948; 50% 05/29/1952; 33-1/3% 10/23/1953; 25% 12/13/1955; 20% 07/26/1960; 33-1/3% 09/13/1961; 25% 05/12/1967; 20% 06/20/1969; 16-2/3% 08/26/1971; 14-1/2% 02/13/1975; 12-1/2% 02/10/1977; (1) for (9) 02/08/1979
Reorganized as Mid-Citco Inc. 02/17/1982
Each share Capital Stock $100 par exchanged for (1) share Capital Stock $20 par
Mid-Citco Inc. name changed to MidCity Financial Corp. 04/18/1995 which merged into MB Financial, Inc. (MD) 11/07/2001

MID-COAST BANCORP INC (DE)
Merged into Union Bankshares Co. 08/31/2000
Each share Common 1¢ par exchanged for $15.875 cash

MID-COLOMBIA OIL & DEVELOPMENT CO.
Dissolved in 1931

MID CON INC (DE)
5% Conv. Preferred 1965 Ser. $25 par called for redemption 06/16/1969
6% Conv. Preferred 1967 Ser. $25 par called for redemption 06/16/1969
Merged into A-T-O Inc. 10/29/1969
Each share Conv. Preferred 1968 Ser. $1 par exchanged for (1) share Conv. Preference 4th Ser. $1 par
Each share Common $1 par exchanged for (1) share Conv. Preference 3rd Ser. $1 par and (0.55) share Common 10¢ par
A-T-O Inc. name changed to Figgie International, Inc. (OH) 06/01/1981 which reorganized in Delaware as Figgie International Holdings Inc. 07/18/1983 which name changed to Figgie International Inc. 12/31/1986 which name changed to Scott Technologies, Inc. 05/20/1998 which merged into Tyco International Ltd. (Bermuda) 05/03/2001 which reincorporated in Switzerland 03/17/2009 which merged into Johnson Controls International PLC 09/06/2016

MID-CONTINENT AIRLINES, INC. (DE)
Merged into Braniff Airways, Inc. (Okla.) in 1952
Each share Common $1 par exchanged for (0.666666) share Common $2.50 par
Braniff Airways, Inc. (Okla.)

reincorporated under the laws of Nevada 8/31/66 which reorganized as Braniff International Corp. 11/28/73 which reorganized as Dalfort Corp. 12/15/83
(See Dalfort Corp.)

MID CONTINENT BANCSHARES INC (IL)
Merged into General Bancshares Corp. 11/1/82
Each share Common $5 par exchanged for (1.845) shares Common $2 par
General Bancshares Corp. merged into Boatmen's Bancshares, Inc. 3/29/86 which merged into NationsBank Corp. 1/7/97 which reincorporated in Delaware as BankAmerica Corp. (Old) 9/25/98 which merged into BankAmerica Corp. (New) 9/30/98 which name changed to Bank of America Corp. 4/28/99

MID CONTINENT BANCSHARES INC (KS)
Merged into Commercial Federal Corp. 2/27/98
Each share Common 10¢ par exchanged for (1.3039) shares Common $0.001 par
(See Commercial Federal Corp.)

MID CONTINENT BOTTLERS INC (IA)
Common $2 par changed to $1 par and (1) additional share issued 4/30/69
Name changed to Mid-Continent Industries, Inc. 4/8/70
Mid-Continent Industries, Inc. merged into Universal Foods Corp. 6/30/78 which name changed to Sensient Technologies Corp. 11/6/2000

MID-CONTINENT CAREY TRUST
Acquired by Prugh Petroleum Co. 12/31/53
Each Unit of Bene. Int. no par exchanged for (2.59) shares Common $5 par
Prugh Petroleum Co. merged into Livingston Oil Co. 9/1/56 which name changed to LVO Corp. 9/24/69 which merged into Utah International Inc. 10/31/74 which merged into General Electric Co. 12/20/76

MID-CONTINENT CASUALTY CO. (MO)
Under plan of merger reincorporated under the laws of Oklahoma in 1956
(See Mid-Continent Casualty Co. (Okla.))

MID-CONTINENT CASUALTY CO. (OK)
Merged into FMI Financial Corp. 10/7/83
Each share Common $4 par exchanged for $117.33 cash
Each share Common $4 par received additional and final distribution of $24 cash 5/1/86

MID-CONTINENT CORP. (CO)
Thru 1971 purchase offer all but (110) shares acquired by private party as of 4/15/74
Public interest eliminated

MID CONTINENT CORP (TN)
Name changed to Mid-Continent International Corp. 7/8/69
Mid-Continent International Corp. name changed to Amcon International, Inc. 1/15/70
(See Amcon International, Inc.)

MID CONTINENT ENERGY CORP (BC)
Merged into Eldorado Minerals & Petroleum Corp. 12/31/1981
Each share Common no par exchanged for (1) share Common no par
(See Eldorado Minerals & Petroleum Corp.)

MID-CONTINENT FINANCIAL CORP. (NE)
Reincorporated under the laws of Colorado as Mid-Continent Corp. 4/22/66

MID CONTINENT INC (AR)
Merged into Mid-Continent, Inc. (DE) 06/06/1974
Each share Common 2-1/2¢ par exchanged for (1.2523) shares Common 4¢ par
Mid-Continent, Inc. (DE) name changed to Mid Continent Systems, Inc. 09/24/1976
(See Mid Continent Systems, Inc.)

MID CONTINENT INC (DE)
Name changed to Mid Continent Systems, Inc. 09/24/1976
(See Mid Continent Systems, Inc.)

MID CONTINENT INDS INC (IA)
5% Preferred $10 par called for redemption 3/23/78
Merged into Universal Foods Corp. 6/30/78
Each share Common $1 par exchanged for (0.5411) share Common 10¢ par
Universal Foods Corp. name changed to Sensient Technologies Corp. 11/6/2000

MID CONTINENT INTL CORP (TN)
Name changed to Amcon International, Inc. 1/15/70
(See Amcon International, Inc.)

MID-CONTINENT LAUNDRIES, INC. (DE)
Each share Part. Class A no par exchanged for (1) share new Common no par in 1931
Each share old Common no par exchanged for (0.1) share new Common no par in 1931
New Common no par changed to $1 par in 1940
Liquidation completed
Each share Common $1 par received initial distribution of $5.40 cash 5/4/54
Each share Common $1 par received second distribution of $2 cash 6/23/54
Each share Common $1 par exchanged for third and final distribution of $1.15 cash 6/29/54

MID CONTINENT LIFE INS CO (OK)
Merged into Florida Progress Corp. 12/04/1986
Each share Capital Stock $1 par exchanged for $56 cash

MID-CONTINENT MANUFACTURING CO. (OH)
6% Preferred 1954 Ser. $25 par called for redemption 06/01/1965
Common $1 par split (3) for (2) by issuance of (0.5) additional share 07/18/1967
Reincorporated under the laws of Delaware as Mid-Con Inc. 10/31/1968
Mid-Con Inc. merged into A-T-O Inc. 10/29/1969 which name changed to Figgie International Inc. (OH) 06/01/1981 which reorganized in Delaware as Figgie International Holdings Inc. 07/18/1983 which name changed to Figgie International Inc. 12/31/1986 which name changed to Scott Technologies, Inc. 05/20/1998 which merged into Tyco International Ltd. (Bermuda) 05/03/2001 which reincorporated in Switzerland 03/17/2009 which merged into Johnson Controls International PLC 09/06/2016

MID CONTINENT MNG CORP (CO)
Each share new Common 1¢ par exchanged for (0.2) share new Common 1¢ par 06/10/1996
Reorganized under the laws of Delaware as Sherwood Ventures Inc. 02/12/1997
Each share new Common 1¢ par exchanged for (0.005) share Common 1¢ par
Sherwood Ventures Inc. name changed to Sherwood Forest Ventures, Inc. 05/30/2007

MID CONTINENT OIL & GAS LTD. (AB)
Recapitalized as Midcon Oil & Gas Ltd. 00/00/1953
Each share Capital Stock no par exchanged for (0.2) shares Capital Stock no par
Midcon Oil & Gas Ltd. merged into Discovery West Corp. 03/01/1987
(See Discovery West Corp.)

MID-CONTINENT OIL & REFINING CO. LTD. (CANADA)
Deemed not to be subsisting as of 12/00/1933
Charter dissolved for failure to file annual reports 12/16/1980

MID-CONTINENT PETROLEUM CORP. (DE)
Capital Stock no par changed to $10 par 00/00/1934
Merged into Sunray Mid-Continent Oil Co. 05/16/1955
Each share Capital Stock $10 par exchanged for (3) shares Common $1 par, (1) share 4.5% Preferred Ser. A $25 par and (0.5) share 5.5% Conv. 2nd Preferred 1955 Ser. $30 par
Sunray Mid-Continent Oil Co. name changed to Sunray DX Oil Co. 04/27/1962 which merged into Sun Oil Co. (NJ) 10/25/1968 which reincorporated in Pennsylvania 09/30/1971 which name changed to Sun Co., Inc. 04/27/1976
(See Sun Co., Inc.)

MID CONTINENT SYS INC (DE)
Each share Common 4¢ par exchanged for (0.25) share Common 16¢ par 09/30/1976
Each share Common 16¢ par exchanged for (0.002) share Common $80 par 12/23/1983
Charter forfeited for failure to maintain a registered agent 02/25/1999

MID-CONTINENT TAB CARD CO. (NE)
Recapitalized as Data Documents, Inc. 2/4/66
Each share Common $25 par exchanged for (100) shares Common $1 par
(See Data Documents, Inc.)

MID CONTINENT TEL CORP (OH)
Under plan of merger name changed to Alltel Corp. (OH) 10/25/1983
Alltel Corp. (OH) reincorporated in Delaware 05/15/1990
(See Alltel Corp.)

MID-CONTINENT TELEPHONE CO.
Name changed to Mid-West States Utilities Co. in 1929
(See Mid-West States Telephone Co.)

MID-CONTINENT URANIUM CORP. (CO)
Name changed to Mid-Continent Mining Corp. 06/01/1966
Mid-Continent Mining Corp. reorganized in Delaware as Sherwood Ventures Inc. 02/12/1997 which name changed to Sherwood Forest Ventures, Inc. 05/30/2007

MID CONTL RLTY CORP (DE)
Merged into Reynolds Development Co. 10/02/1973
Each share Common no par exchanged for $17.50 cash

MID EAST DEVS LTD (AB)
Name changed to Promed Technology Inc. 01/01/1982
Each share Common no par exchanged for (1) share Common no par
Promed Technology, Inc. name changed to Zavitz Technology, Inc. 06/21/1983 which recapitalized as Zavitz Petroleum Inc. 08/31/1993 which name changed to Jaguar Petroleum Corp. 11/21/1994 which merged into Probe Exploration Inc. 05/09/1997
(See Probe Exploration Inc.)

MID EAST MINERALS LTD (AUSTRALIA)
Name changed 06/23/1988
Each ADR for Ordinary AUD $0.20 par exchanged for (0.2) ADR for Ordinary AUD $1 par 12/20/1982
ADR's for Ordinary AUD $1 par changed to AUD $0.50205 par 11/24/1983
Name changed from Mid-East Minerals N.L. to Mid-East Minerals Ltd. 06/23/1988
Each ADR for Ordinary AUD $0.50205 par exchanged for (0.330033) ADR for Ordinary AUD $0.25 par 02/08/1991
ADR agreement terminated 11/06/2000
Each ADR for Ordinary AUD $0.25 par exchanged for $0.542 cash
Note: Due to ADR's being unsponsored exchange rate may vary dependent upon depositary agent

MID-EASTERN ELECTRONICS, INC. (NJ)
Name changed to Mid-Eastern Industries, Inc. 5/18/66
Mid-Eastern Industries, Inc. completely liquidated for Eanco, Inc. 6/26/67 which name changed to E.I. Liquidating Corp. 11/30/78
(See E.I. Liquidating Corp.)

MID-EASTERN INDUSTRIES, INC. (NJ)
Completely liquidated 6/26/67
Each share Common 10¢ par exchanged for first and final distribution of (0.166666) share Eanco, Inc. Common $1 par
Eanco, Inc. name changed to E.I. Liquidating Corp. 11/30/78
(See E.I. Liquidating Corp.)

MID-ERIE ACCEPTANCE CORP. LTD. (ON)
Bankrupt in March 1963
No stockholders' equity

MID-HUDSON NATURAL GAS CORP. (DE)
Acquired by Consolidated Emjay Petroleums Ltd. share for share 8/5/57
Consolidated Emjay Petroleums Ltd. recapitalized as New Emjay Petroleums Ltd. 2/4/66
(See New Emjay Petroleums Ltd.)

MID HUDSON SVGS BK FSB (FISHKILL, NY)
Common $1 par split (3) for (2) by issuance of (0.5) additional share 5/22/89
Reorganized under the laws of Delaware as First Inter-Bancorp Inc. 12/20/89
Each share Common $1 par exchanged for (1) share Common $1 par
(See First Inter-Bancorp Inc.)

MID-ILLINOIS GAS CO. (DE)
Merged into Northern Illinois Gas Co. 12/30/70
Each share Common $5 par exchanged for (1) share $1.90 Conv. Preference no par
Northern Illinois Gas Co. reorganized as Nicor Inc. 4/30/76

MID INDS & EXPLS LTD (QC)
Common $1 par changed to no par 07/24/1972

Merged into Mid Industries & Explorations Inc. 06/10/1980
Each share Common no par exchanged for $0.50 cash

MID INDUSTRIES LTD. (QC)
Name changed to Mid Industries & Explorations Ltd. 9/10/71
(See Mid Industries & Explorations Ltd.)

MID-IOWA FINL CORP (DE)
Common 1¢ par split (6) for (5) by issuance of (0.2) additional share 2/25/94
Common 1¢ par split (2) for (1) by issuance of (1) additional share 2/24/95
Common 1¢ par split (2) for (1) by issuance of (1) additional share payable 1/25/96 to holders of record 1/8/96
Merged into First Federal Bankshares 4/13/99
Each share Common 1¢ par exchanged for $15 cash

MID-IOWA LAKES CORP. (IA)
Charter cancelled for failure to file annual report 11/22/76

MID-KIRK GOLD MINES, LTD. (ON)
Charter revoked for failure to file reports and pay fees 02/18/1965

MID MAINE SVGS BK F S B (AUBURN, ME)
Merged into Peoples Heritage Financial Group, Inc. 07/31/1994
Each share Common 1¢ par exchanged for (0.835) share Common 1¢ par
Peoples Heritage Financial Group, Inc. name changed to Banknorth Group, Inc. (ME) 05/10/2000 which merged into TD Banknorth Inc. 03/01/2005
(See TD Banknorth Inc.)

MID MTN MNG LTD (BC)
Struck off register and declared dissolved for failure to file returns 2/10/89

MID NORTH RES LTD (AB)
Name changed 10/28/1980
Reincorporated 11/05/1986
Name changed from Mid-North Uranium Ltd. to Mid-North Resources Ltd. 10/28/1980
Place of incorporation changed from (MB) to (AB) 11/05/1986
Reorganized under the laws of Ontario as Bison Gold Exploration Inc. 12/28/2005
Each share Common no par exchanged for (0.25) share Common no par
Bison Gold Exploration Inc. recapitalized as Bison Gold Resources Inc. 05/11/2009 which merged into Klondex Mines Ltd. 10/20/2017
(See Klondex Mines Ltd.)

MID OCEAN LTD (CAYMAN ISLANDS)
Merged into EXEL Ltd. 08/07/1998
Each share Class A Ordinary 20¢ par exchanged for (1.0215) shares Ordinary 1¢ par
EXEL Ltd. name changed to XL Capital Ltd. (Cayman Islands) 02/01/1999 which reorganized in Ireland as XL Group PLC 07/01/2010 which reincorporated in Bermuda as XL Group Ltd. 07/25/2016
(See XL Group Ltd.)

MID OHIO BANC SHS INC (OH)
Common no par split (5) for (4) by issuance of (0.25) additional share 7/26/71
Merged into Centran Bancshares Corp. 6/30/72
Each share Common no par exchanged for (1.1) shares Common $8 par

Centran Bancshares Corp. name changed to Centran Corp. 4/5/74
(See Centran Corp.)

MID PAC AIR CORP (HI)
Merged into KOA Holdings Inc. 03/15/1990
Each share Common 1¢ par exchanged for $1.75 cash

MID PAC AIRLS INC (HI)
Under plan of reorganization each share Common 1¢ par automatically became (1) share Mid Pacific Air Corp. Common 1¢ par 08/03/1984
(See Mid Pacific Air Corp.)

MID PATAPEDIA MINES LTD (ON)
Capital Stock $1 par changed to no par 11/23/1971
Charter cancelled for failure to pay taxes and file returns 06/23/1980

MID PENINSULA BANCORP (CA)
Merged into Greater Bay Bancorp 11/29/1996
Each share Common no par exchanged for (1.1) shares Common no par
Greater Bay Bancorp merged into Wells Fargo & Co. (New) 10/01/2007

MID PENN BK (MILLERSBURG, PA)
Capital Stock $10 par changed to $5 par and (1) additional share issued 1/31/75
Each share Capital Stock $5 par exchanged for (5) shares Capital Stock $1 par 5/22/86
Under plan of reorganization each share Common $1 par automatically became (1) share Mid Penn Bancorp, Inc. 12/31/91

MID-PLAINS INC (WI)
Name changed 4/29/96
Common $10 par changed to $3.33-1/3 par and (2) additional shares issued 5/18/90
Stock Dividends - 10% 5/1/68; 20% 8/1/73; 20% 6/1/77; 10% 5/1/79; 20% 6/1/85
Name changed from Mid-Plains Telephone, Inc. to Mid-Plains Inc. 4/29/96
Name changed to Chorus Communications Group Ltd. 6/1/97
(See Chorus Communications Group Ltd.)

MID POWER SVC CORP (NV)
Reincorporated 07/31/2001
State of incorporation changed from (DE) to (NV) 07/31/2001
Reorganized as Caldera Corp. 03/05/2007
Each share Common $0.001 par exchanged for (1) share Common $0.001 par
Note: Holders of (99) or fewer pre-split shares received $1 cash per share
(See Caldera Corp.)

MID-SOUTH COTTON OIL CO.
Liquidated in 1943

MID SOUTH INC (AL)
Completely liquidated 01/05/1978
Each share Common 40¢ par exchanged for first and final distribution of $4.25 cash

MID SOUTH INS CO (NC)
Common $1 par split (6) for (5) by issuance of (0.2) additional share 4/17/91
Common $1 par split (6) for (5) by issuance of (0.2) additional share 9/28/92
Common $1 par split (6) for (5) by issuance of (0.2) additional share 11/12/93
Common $1 par split (6) for (5) by issuance of (0.2) additional share 11/22/94
Stock Dividends - 20% 12/1/82; 20% 1/4/85

Merged into Blue Cross Blue Shield 2/29/96
Each share Common $1 par exchanged for $15.67 cash

MID SOUTH LIFE INSURANCE CO., INC. (TN)
Merged into American Family Life Assurance Co. of Columbus 5/1/68
Details not available

MID-SOUTH OIL CORP. (DE)
No longer in existence having become inoperative and void for non-payment of taxes 4/1/53

MID-SOUTHERN INDIANA BANCORP (IN)
Merged into Merchants National Corp. 12/22/1986
Each share Capital Stock $10 par exchanged for (1.9133) shares Common no par
Merchants National Corp. merged into National City Corp. 05/02/1992 which was acquired by PNC Financial Services Group, Inc. 12/31/2008

MID-SOUTHERN SVGS BK FSB (SALEM, IN)
Reorganized as Mid-Southern Bancorp, Inc. 07/12/2018
Each share Common $1 par exchanged for (2.3462) shares Common 1¢ par

MID ST BANCORP INC (PA)
Merged into Keystone Financial, Inc. 12/31/84
Each share Common $2 par exchanged for (1.601334) shares Common $2 par
Keystone Financial, Inc. merged into M&T Bank Corp. 10/6/2000

MID-ST BANCSHARES (CA)
Common no par split (2) for (1) by issuance of (1) additional share payable 2/26/2001 to holders of record 1/26/2001 Ex date - 2/27/2001
Acquired by Rabobank, N.A. 5/1/2007
Each share Common no par exchanged for $37 cash

MID ST BK & TR CO (ALTOONA, PA)
Each share Capital Stock $10 par exchanged for (5) shares Capital Stock $2 par 10/16/67
Under plan of reorganization each share Capital Stock $2 par automatically became (1) share Mid-State Bancorp Inc. Common $2 par 1/12/82
Mid-State Bancorp Inc. merged into Keystone Financial, Inc. 12/31/84 which merged into M&T Bank Corp. 10/6/2000

MID ST BK (ARROYO GRANDE, CA)
Common $4 par changed to $1.33-1/3 par and (2) additional shares issued 4/30/76
Common $1.33-1/3 par changed to 44¢ par and (2) additional shares issued 6/6/83
Common 44¢ par split (3) for (1) by issuance of (2) additional shares 7/14/89
Stock Dividend - 5% payable 1/23/98 to holders of record 12/31/97
Merged into Mid-State Bancshares 7/10/98
Each share Common 44¢ par exchanged for (1.0123) shares Common no par
(See Mid-State Bancshares)

MID ST FED SVGS BK (OCALA, FL)
Reorganized 4/28/89
Under plan of reorganization name changed from Mid-State Federal Savings & Loan Association (U.S.A.) to Mid-State Federal Savings Bank (Ocala, FL) 4/28/89
Merged into AmSouth Bancorporation 12/9/93
Each share Common $1 par

exchanged for (0.8965) share Common $1 par and $13.90 cash
AmSouth Bancorporation merged into Regions Financial Corp. 11/4/2006

MID STATES BANCSHARES, INC. (DE)
Merged into Banc One Corp 6/9/94
Each share Common $5 par exchanged for (2.917) shares Common no par
Banc One Corp. merged into Bank One Corp. 10/2/98 which merged into J.P. Morgan Chase & Co. 12/31/2000 which name changed to JPMorgan Chase & Co. 7/20/2004

MID-STATES BUSINESS CAPITAL CORP. (MO)
Liquidation completed
Each share Common $1 par stamped to indicate initial distribution of $3 cash 8/20/64
Each share Stamped Common $1 par stamped to indicate second distribution of (0.339818) share Henry's Drive-In, Inc. Common no par; (0.0688) share Parkview Drugs, Inc. Common $1 par and $3 cash 3/5/65
Each share Stamped Common $1 par exchanged for third and final distribution of $1.428 cash 12/27/67
(See each company's listing)

MID-STATES EQUIPMENT CO. (DE)
Bankrupt in 1953

MID STS ENTERPRISES INC (IA)
Merged into MSE, Inc. 12/31/1973
Each share Common $2 par exchanged for $3.85 cash

MID STS PLC (UNITED KINGDOM)
ADR agreement terminated 8/31/97
Each Sponsored ADR for Ordinary 10p par exchanged for $2.6302 cash

MID STS STL & WIRE CO (IN)
Common $25 par changed to no par 00/00/1937
Merged into Keystone Consolidated Industries, Inc. 12/31/1968
Each share Common no par exchanged for $78 cash

MID-TEX COMMUNICATIONS SYS INC (TX)
Merged into Central Telephone & Utilities Corp. 12/16/1975
Each share Common $1 par exchanged for (0.9) share Common $2.50 par
Central Telephone & Utilities Corp. name changed to Centel Corp. 04/30/1982 which was acquired by Sprint Corp. (KS) 03/09/1993 which name changed to Sprint Nextel Corp. 08/12/2005 which merged into Sprint Corp. (DE) 07/10/2013

MID TEX TEL CO (TX)
6% Preferred called for redemption 09/15/1976
Public interest eliminated

MID-TEXAS TRUST & INSURANCE SECURITIES CORP. (TX)
Charter forfeited for failure to pay taxes 3/22/74

MID TRANSPORTATION SERVICES LTD. (ON)
Acquired by a controlling shareholder group 7/29/86
Each share Common no par received $0.65 cash
Note: Certificates were not required to be surrendered and are now valueless

MID VY BK (RED BLUFF, CA)
Stock Dividends - 10% payable 03/02/2001 to holders of record 02/14/2001 Ex date - 02/12/2001; 10% payable 03/01/2002 to holders of record 02/13/2002
Merged into PremierWest Bancorp 01/23/2004
Each share Common no par

exchanged for either (2.2622) shares Common no par or (0.7119) share Common no par and $15.3458 cash
Note: Option to receive stock and cash expired 02/23/2004
(See PremierWest Bancorp)

MID-VALLEY BK (WOODBURN, OR)
Common split (2) for (1) by issuance of (1) additional share payable 09/15/2004 to holders of record 8/31/2004 Ex date - 09/16/2004
Merged into West Coast Bancorp (New) 06/26/2006
Each share Common no par exchanged for (0.63656358) share Common no par and $1.38518 cash
(See West Coast Bancorp (New))

MID-WAY MED & DIAGNOSTIC CTR INC (FL)
Reorganized as under the laws of Nevada as Ciro International, Inc. 12/01/1997
Each share Common $0.001 par exchanged for (2.5) shares Common $0.001 par
Ciro International, Inc. name changed to Advanced Bio/Chem, Inc. 06/30/2003 which name changed to Industrial Enterprises of America, Inc. 12/09/2004
(See Industrial Enterprises of America, Inc.)

MID-WAY RECREATION, INC. (NY)
Voluntarily dissolved 6/30/76
Details not available

MID-WEST ABRASIVE CO. (DE)
Stock Dividend - 20% 12/3/56
Name changed to MWA Co. and Common 50¢ par changed to $5 par 10/21/68
(See MWA Co.)

MID WEST COPPER & URANIUM MINES LTD. (BC)
Recapitalized as Mid-West Mines Ltd. 10/20/64
Each share Capital Stock 50¢ par exchanged for (0.2) share Capital Stock no par
Mid-West Mines Ltd. recapitalized as Cardigan Development Co. Ltd. 9/20/72 which recapitalized as United Cardigan Development Ltd. 8/15/75
(See United Cardigan Development Ltd.)

MID WEST ENERGY INC (BC)
Recapitalized as Millrock Development Corp. 11/19/84
Each share Class A Capital Stock no par exchanged for (0.25) share Class A Capital Stock no par
Millrock Development Corp. recapitalized as Delta Gold Mining Corp. 9/5/91 which merged into Chase Resource Corp. (New) 5/30/97
(See Chase Resource Corp. (New))

MID WEST MINES LTD (BC)
Recapitalized as Cardigan Development Co. Ltd. 9/20/72
Each share Capital Stock no par exchanged for (0.2) share Capital Stock no par
Cardigan Development Co. Ltd. recapitalized as United Cardigan Development Ltd. 8/15/75
(See Cardigan Development Co. Ltd.)

MID-WEST MINING CORP. LTD. (SK)
Name changed to Viscount Oil & Gas Ltd. 00/00/1958
Viscount Oil & Gas Ltd. acquired by Bison Petroleum & Minerals Ltd. 09/15/1960 which recapitalized as United Bison Resources Ltd. 12/22/1987 which merged into Nalcap Holdings Inc. 04/25/1991 which recapitalized as Arbatax International Inc. (Canada) 03/28/1996 which reincorporated in Yukon 08/06/1996 which name changed to MFC Bancorp Ltd. (YT) 03/03/1997 which reincorporated in British Columbia 11/03/2004 which name changed to KHD Humboldt Wedag International Ltd. 11/01/2005 which reorganized as Terra Nova Royalty Corp. 03/30/2010 which name changed to MFC Industrial Ltd. 09/30/2011 which name changed to MFC Bancorp Ltd. (BC) 02/16/2016
(See MFC Bancorp Ltd. (BC))

MID-WEST NATIONAL CORP. (TN)
Liquidation completed
Each share Common $1 par exchanged for initial distribution of $7.05 cash 5/21/74
Each share Common $1 par received second and final distribution of $1.3456547 cash 11/24/75

MID WEST NATL FIRE & CAS INS CO (MO)
Name changed to Medallion National Insurance Co. 5/19/70
Medallion National Insurance Co. merged into Missouri General Insurance Co. 12/31/70
(See Missouri General Insurance Co.)

MID WEST NATL LIFE INS CO (MO)
Stock Dividends - 100% 4/13/64; 20% 4/20/65
Under plan of merger name changed to Progressive National Life Insurance Co. 12/31/70
Progressive National Life Insurance Co. merged into I.C.H. Corp. 11/4/82 which name changed to Southwestern Life Corp. (New) 6/15/94 which name changed to I.C.H. Corp. (New) 10/10/95
(See I.C.H. Corp. (New))

MID WEST NATL LIFE INS CO TENN (TN)
Common $5 par changed to $1 par and (1) additional share issued 4/15/67
Stock Dividends - 20% 6/30/71; 25% 6/30/72
Under plan of reorganization each share Common $1 par automatically became (1) share Mid-West National Corp. Common $1 par 5/17/73
(See Mid-West National Corp.)

MID-WEST REFINERIES, INC. (MI)
Stock Dividends - 10% 9/15/48; 10% 9/21/53
Merged into Leonard Refineries, Inc. on a (0.5) for (1) basis 11/30/55
Leonard Refineries, Inc. merged into Total Petroleum (North America) Ltd. 10/2/70 which merged into Ultramar Diamond Shamrock Corp. 9/25/97 which merged into Valero Energy Corp. (New) 12/31/2001

MID-WEST SPRING MFG CO (DE)
Company terminated registration of common stock and is no longer public as of 12/30/1996
Details not available

MID-WEST STATES TELEPHONE CO.
Acquired by General Telephone Corp. on a (1) for (5) basis in 1946
General Telephone Corp. name changed to General Telephone & Electronics Corp. 3/5/59 which name changed to GTE Corp. 7/1/82 which merged into Verizon Communications Inc. 6/30/2000

MID-WEST STATES UTILITIES CO.
Reorganized as Mid-West States Telephone Co. in 1936
No stockholders' equity

MID WEST STL FABRICATING CORP (TX)
Recapitalized as Tomanet Financial Corp. 04/18/1978
Each share Common $1 par exchanged for (0.2) share Common $5 par
Tomanet Financial Corp. name changed to Texana Capital Corp. 08/02/1984
(See Texana Capital Corp.)

MID WEST VIDEO SYS INC (OK)
Name changed to Telesell, Ltd. 07/27/1973
(See Telesell, Ltd.)

MID-WESTERN INDUSTRIAL GAS, LTD. (AB)
Merged into Canadian Industrial Gas & Oil Ltd. 03/08/1965
Each share Common no par exchanged for (0.30303030) share Common no par
Canadian Industrial Gas & Oil Ltd. merged into Norcen Energy Resources Ltd. (AB) 10/28/1975 which reincorporated in Canada 04/15/1977 which merged into Union Pacific Resources Group Inc. 04/17/1998 which merged into Anadarko Petroleum Corp. 07/14/2000

MID-WESTN LIFE INS CO (OK)
Charter cancelled for failure to pay taxes 10/30/96

MID-WIS BANKSHARES, INC. (WI)
Name changed to United Banks of Wisconsin, Inc. 7/10/72
(See United Banks of Wisconsin, Inc.)

MID-WISCONSIN FINL SVCS INC (WI)
Merged into Nicolet Bankshares, Inc. 04/26/2013
Each share Common 10¢ par exchanged for (0.3727) share Common 1¢ par
Note: Holders of (200) or fewer shares will receive $6.15 cash

MIDAMERICA BANCSYSTEM INC (MO)
Merged into Landmark Bancshares Corp. 11/27/86
Each share Common $1 par exchanged for (0.183) share Common no par and $12.68 cash
Note: An amount approximate to $0.50 per share of the cash portion of the purchase price was placed in escrow for possible future distribution
Landmark Bancshares Corp. merged into Magna Group, Inc. 12/20/91 which merged into Union Planters Corp. 7/1/98 which merged into Regions Financial Corp. (New) 7/1/2004

MIDAMERICA BK & TR CO EDGEMONT (ST LOUIS, IL)
Reorganized as MidAmerica BancSystem, Inc. 8/31/82
Each share Common $5 par exchanged for (2.98) shares Common $1 par
MidAmerica BancSystem, Inc. merged into Landmark Bancshares Corp. 11/27/86 which merged into Magna Group, Inc. 12/20/91 which merged into Union Planters Corp. 7/1/98 which merged into Regions Financial Corp. (New) 7/1/2004

MIDAMERICA HIGH GROWTH FD INC (MD)
Merged into Aegon USA Managed Portfolios, Inc. 12/01/1990
Details not available

MIDAMERICA OIL & GAS INC (NV)
Name changed to Sounds 24-7, Inc. 1/15/2004
Sounds 24-7, Inc. recapitalized as Allied Energy Corp. 1/26/2006

MIDAMERICA RES INC (DE)
Name changed to Seaboard Oil Co. 9/15/92
(See Seaboard Oil Co.)

MIDAMERICAN CORP (KS)
Merged into Mercantile Bancorporation, Inc. 01/04/1993
Each share Common $5 par exchanged for (0.75) share Common $5 par
Mercantile Bancorporation, Inc. merged into Firstar Corp. (New) 09/20/1999 which merged into U.S. Bancorp (DE) 02/27/2001

MIDAMERICAN ENERGY CO (IA)
Under plan of reorganization each share Common $1 par automatically became (1) share MidAmerican Energy Holdings Co. Common no par 12/02/1996
(See MidAmerican Energy Holdings Co.)
$1.7375 Preferred no par called for redemption at $25.695 on 01/12/1997
$5.25 Preferred no par called for redemption at $100 on 11/01/2001
$7.80 Preferred no par called for redemption at $103.90 on 05/01/2002
$3.30 Preferred no par called for redemption at $101.50 plus $0.348333 accrued dividends on 04/08/2013
$3.75 Preferred no par called for redemption at $102.75 plus $0.395833 accrued dividends on 04/08/2013
$3.90 Preferred no par called for redemption at $105 plus $0.411666 accrued dividends on 04/08/2013
$4.20 Preferred no par called for redemption at $103.439 plus $0.443333 accrued dividends on 04/08/2013
$4.35 Preferred no par called for redemption at $102 plus $0.459166 accrued dividends on 04/08/2013
$4.40 Preferred no par called for redemption at $101.50 plus $0.464444 accrued dividends on 04/08/2013
$4.80 Preferred no par called for redemption at $102.70 plus $0.506666 accrued dividends on 04/08/2013

MIDAMERICAN ENERGY FING I (IA)
7.98% Guaranteed Quarterly Income Preferred Securities called for redemption at $25 plus $0.3934583 accrued dividend on 3/11/2002

MIDAMERICAN ENERGY HLDGS CO (OLD) (IA)
Merged into CalEnergy Co., Inc. 03/12/1999
Each share Common no par exchanged for $27.15 cash

MIDAMERICAN ENERGY HLDGS CO NEW (IA)
Merged into Teton Acquisition Corp. 03/14/2000
Each share Common no par exchanged for $35.05 cash

MIDAS CAP CORP (ON)
Delisted from Toronto Stock Exchange 09/24/1999

MIDAS ENTMT INC (DE)
Each share old Common $0.00001 par exchanged for (20) shares new Common $0.00001 par 08/31/2005
Recapitalized as Textechnologies, Inc. 08/01/2006
Each share new Common $0.00001 par exchanged for (0.01) share Common $0.00001 par
Textechnologies, Inc. name changed to We-R-You Corp. 04/25/2008

MIDAS FD INC (MD)
Under plan of reorganization each share Common 1¢ par automatically became (1) share Midas Series Trust (DE) Midas Fund 10/12/2012

MIDAS GOLD INC (WA)
Name changed to Gold Coin Mining Inc. 8/22/85
Gold Coin Mining Inc. merged into Canaveral International Corp. 12/1/92

MIDAS INC (DE)
Acquired by TBC Corp. (New) 04/30/2012
Each share Common $0.001 par exchanged $11.50 cash

MIDAS INTL CORP (DE)
Class A Common $1 par and Class B Common $1 par split (2) for (1) respectively by issuance of (1) additional share 08/09/1968
Merged into Illinois Central Industries, Inc. 01/25/1972
Each share Class A Common $1 par or Class B Common (Series 1 thru 5) $1 par exchanged for (0.6568) share Common no par
Illinois Central Industries, Inc. name changed to IC Industries, Inc. 05/21/1975 which name changed to Whitman Corp. (Old) 12/01/1988 which name changed to Whitman Corp. (New) 11/30/2000 which name changed to PepsiAmericas, Inc. (DE) 01/24/2001 which merged into PepsiCo, Inc. 02/26/2010

MIDAS INTL INC (NV)
Capital Stock 20¢ par changed to $0.005 par 12/14/73
Each share Capital Stock $0.005 par exchanged for (2) shares Capital Stock $0.001 par 3/1/81
Name changed to MII 12/14/82
MII recapitalized as Pathfinder Corp. 8/1/90 which name changed to Pegasus Industries Inc. 3/9/95

MIDAS INVS LTD (MD)
Under plan of merger each share Common 1¢ par automatically became Midas Fund, Inc. (MD) Common 1¢ par on a net asset basis 11/16/2001
Midas Fund, Inc. (MD) reorganized in Delaware as Midas Series Trust 10/12/2012

MIDAS MAGIC INC NEW (MD)
Name changed 05/01/2006
04/29/2011
Name changed from Midas Special Equities Fund, Inc. to Midas Special Fund, Inc. 05/01/2006
Name changed from Midas Special Fund, Inc. to Midas Magic, Inc. (New) 04/29/2011
Under plan of reorganization each share Common 1¢ par automatically became (1) share Midas Series Trust (DE) Midas Magic 10/12/2012

MIDAS MAGIC INC OLD (MD)
Completely liquidated 04/30/2001
Each share Common 1¢ par received net asset value

MIDAS MINERALS INC (ON)
Name changed to Midas Capital Corp. 09/21/1994
(See Midas Capital Corp.)

MIDAS MINING CO., LTD. (ON)
Charter cancelled for failure to file reports and pay taxes in 1968

MIDAS PERP PORTFOLIO INC (MD)
Under plan of reorganization each share Common 1¢ par automatically became (1) share Midas Series Trust (DE) Midas Perpetual Portfolio 10/12/2012

MIDAS RES LTD (AB)
Recapitalized as Scorpion Energy Corp. 07/28/1998
Each share Common no par exchanged for (0.33333333) share Common no par
Scorpion Energy Corp. name changed to Gauntlet Energy Corp. 10/12/1999
(See Gauntlet Energy Corp.)

MIDAS RES LTD (BC)
Recapitalized as Continental Silver Corp. 03/14/1977
Each share Capital Stock no par exchanged for (0.2) share Capital Stock no par

Continental Silver Corp. merged into Arizona Silver Corp. 08/01/1985 which recapitalized as ASC Industries Ltd. 06/06/1995 which name changed to Acero-Martin Exploration Inc. 11/24/2004 which name changed to AM Gold Inc. 06/08/2010
(See AM Gold Inc.)

MIDAS U S & OVERSEAS FD LTD (MD)
Merged into Midas Special Equities Fund, Inc. 11/16/2001
Details not available

MIDASCO GOLD CORP (ON)
Name changed to Midasco Capital Corp. 07/17/2001

MIDASTRADE COM INC (NV)
Charter revoked for failure to file reports and pay taxes 04/01/2013

MIDBURN OIL CO. LTD.
Merged into Bailey Selburn Oil & Gas Ltd. and each (1.5) old shares exchanged for (1) share Class A $1 par in 1952
(See Bailey Selburn Oil & Gas Ltd.)

MIDCAMP MINES LTD. (ON)
Liquidation completed 5/5/59

MIDCAROLINA FINL CORP (NC)
Common no par split (6) for (5) by issuance of (0.2) additional share payable 08/15/2003 to holders of record 08/01/2003 Ex date - 07/30/2003
Common no par split (6) for (5) by issuance of (0.2) additional share payable 01/14/2005 to holders of record 12/15/2004
Common no par split (5) for (4) by issuance of (0.25) additional share payable 11/15/2005 to holders of record 10/14/2005 Ex date - 11/16/2005
Common no par split (5) for (4) by issuance of (0.25) additional share payable 01/19/2007 to holders of record 01/05/2007 Ex date - 01/22/2007
Stock Dividends - 10% payable 08/15/2002 to holders of record 08/01/2002; 10% payable 06/15/2006 to holders of record 05/22/2006 Ex date - 05/18/2006
Merged into American National Bankshares Inc. 07/01/2011
Each share Common no par exchanged for (0.33) share Common $1 par

MIDCITY FINL CORP (DE)
Merged into MB Financial, Inc. (MD) 11/07/2001
Each share Common $20 par exchanged for (230.32955) shares Common 1¢ par

MIDCO OIL CORP.
Dissolved 10/28/52

MIDCOAST ENERGY PARTNERS L P (DE)
Acquired by Enbridge Inc. 04/27/2017
Each Class A Common Unit exchanged for $8 cash

MIDCOAST ENERGY RES INC (TX)
Reincorporated 09/24/1999
Common 1¢ par split (5) for (4) by issuance of (0.25) additional share payable 03/01/1999 to holders of record 02/11/1999 Ex date - 03/02/1999
Stock Dividend - 10% payable 03/02/1998 to holders of record 02/13/1998 Ex date - 02/11/1998
State of incorporation changed from (NV) to (TX) 09/24/1999
Merged into Enbridge Inc. 05/14/2001
Each share Common 1¢ par exchanged for $27 cash

MIDCOM COMMUNICATIONS INC (DE)
Issue Information - 5,376,250 shares

COM offered at $11 per share on 07/06/1995
Plan of reorganization under Chapter 11 Federal Bankruptcy Code effective 7/21/98
No stockholders' equity

MIDCON CORP (DE)
Merged into Occidental Petroleum Corp. (CA) 04/01/1986
Each share Common no par exchanged for (2.2472) shares Common 20¢ par
Occidental Petroleum Corp. (CA) reincorporated in Delaware 05/21/1986

MIDCON INDS INC (DE)
Under plan of merger each share Common 1¢ par exchanged for $4.25 principal amount of GIT Industries, Inc. 12% Subordinated Debentures due 09/30/2001 on 09/02/1981

MIDCON OIL & GAS LTD (AB)
Merged into Discovery West Corp. 03/01/1987
Each share Capital Stock no par exchanged for (1.8) shares Conv. Vtg. Common no par
(See Discovery West Corp.)

MIDCONN BK (KENSINGTON, CT)
Merged into Eagle Financial Corp. 5/31/97
Each share Common $1 par exchanged for (0.86) share Common 1¢ par
Eagle Financial Corp. merged into Webster Financial Corp. 4/15/98

MIDD FINL CORP (BC)
Delisted from Vancouver Stock Exchange 10/31/94

MIDD-PERSHING GOLD MINES LTD. (ON)
Dissolved in 1958

MIDDLE AMERICA CORP. (KY)
Completely liquidated 8/30/66
Each share Common $1 par exchanged for first and final distribution of $1 cash

MIDDLE ATLANTIC CREDIT CORP. (PA)
Name changed to Middle Atlantic Financial Corp. 4/10/63

MIDDLE ATLANTIC FINL CORP (PA)
99.9% acquired by Management Data Corp. as of 02/20/1968
Public interest eliminated

MIDDLE ATLANTIC INVESTMENT CO. (DE)
Charter cancelled for non-payment of taxes 4/1/63

MIDDLE ATLANTIC UTILS CO (DE)
Name changed to U.S. Land & Utilities Co. 12/4/70
U.S. Land & Utilities Co. name changed to Dynastar Corp. 4/19/74
(See Dynastar Corp.)

MIDDLE BAY MINES, LTD. (ON)
Charter revoked for failure to file reports and pay fees 1/26/67

MIDDLE BAY OIL INC (DE)
Each share old Common 1¢ par exchanged for (0.5) share new Common 2¢ par 07/14/1995
Reincorporated under the laws of Delaware as 3TEC Energy Corp. 12/07/1999
3TEC Energy Corp. merged into Plains Exploration & Production Co. 06/04/2003 which merged into Freeport-McMoRan Copper & Gold Inc. 05/31/2013 which name changed to Freeport-McMoRan Inc. 07/14/2014

MIDDLE EAST ENGINEERING & SCIENTIFIC INTERNATIONAL, INC. (DE)
Charter cancelled and declared

inoperative and void for non-payment of taxes 3/1/77

MIDDLE EAST OIL CORP (UT)
Charter expired 06/24/2014

MIDDLE GA BK (PEACH CNTY, GA)
Merged into First Liberty Financial Corp. 11/15/96
Each share Common 1¢ par exchanged for (5.204) shares Common 1¢ par
First Liberty Financial Corp. merged into BB&T Corp. 11/19/99

MIDDLE KINGDOM ALLIANCE CORP (DE)
Issue Information - 198,000 UNITS consisting of (1) share COM and (5) CL A WTS offered at $8 per Unit on 12/13/2006
Issue Information - 3,300,000 UNITS consisting of (1) share COM and (1) CL B WT offered at $8 per Unit on 12/13/2006
Reincorporated under the laws of Cayman Islands as Pypo China Holdings Ltd. and Common $0.001 par and Class B Common $0.001 par reclassified as Ordinary $0.001 par 07/10/2009
Pypo China Holdings Ltd. name changed to Funtalk China Holdings Ltd. 12/15/2009
(See Funtalk China Holdings Ltd.)

MIDDLE KINGDOM PARADISO CORP (ON)
Name changed to Mega View Digital Entertainment Corp. 07/20/2009

MIDDLE SOUTH UTILS INC (FL)
Common no par changed to $10 par in 1954
Common $10 par split (2) for (1) by issuance of (1) additional share 3/7/60
Common $10 par changed to $5 par and (1) additional share issued 2/28/66
Name changed to Entergy Corp. (FL) 5/19/89
Entergy Corp. (FL) reincorporated in Delaware 12/31/93

MIDDLE STATES OIL CORP. (DE)
Reorganized as Middle States Petroleum Corp. 7/29/29
Each share Capital Stock $10 par exchanged for Certificates of Deposit which in turn were exchangeable for VTC's for Class B no par
Under the reorganization agreement the last day to exercise right to exchange, after which date stock and/or Certificate of Deposit became worthless was 12/19/30
Middle States Petroleum Corp. merged into Tennessee Gas Transmission Co. for cash 7/31/59

MIDDLE STATES PETROLEUM CORP. (DE)
Class A & B no par changed to $1 par in 1939
Class B $1 par redesignated as Common $1 par in 1949
Merged into Tennessee Gas Transmission Co. at $13.25 per share 7/31/59

MIDDLE STATES SECURITIES CORP.
Liquidation completed in 1942
Details not available

MIDDLE STATES TELEPHONE CO. OF ILLINOIS (IL)
6% Preferred Ser. B called for redemption 12/22/61
Common $10 par split (6) for (5) by issuance of (0.2) additional share 9/29/62
Preferred Ser. A $20 par called for redemption 12/29/62
Common $10 par split (11) for (10) by issuance of (0.1) additional share 6/29/63
Common $10 par split (5) for (4) by

issuance of (0.25) additional share 6/30/64
Stock Dividends - 150% 4/28/49; 30% 8/10/53; 40% 6/30/60
Name changed to Central Telephone Co. of Illinois 5/1/67
Central Telephone Co. of Illinois merged into Central Telephone Co. (New) 12/1/71
(See Central Telephone Co. (New))

MIDDLE STATES UTILITIES, INC. (DE)
Assets sold and company liquidated 8/22/56

MIDDLE STATES UTILITIES CO.
Reorganized as Middle States Utilities, Inc. in 1945
Each share 7% Series A and 6% Series B Preferred exchanged for (2) shares Common no par and (1) Common Stock Purchase Warrant
(See Middle States Utilities, Inc.)

MIDDLE TENN BK (COLUMBIA, TN)
Merged into First American Corp. (TN) 9/30/98
Each share Common no par exchanged for (7.768) shares Common $5 par
First American Corp. (TN) merged into AmSouth Bancorporation 10/1/99 which merged into Regions Financial Corp. 11/4/2006

MIDDLE WEST CORP.
Liquidation completed 12/29/55

MIDDLE WEST UTILITIES CO.
Reorganized as Middle West Corp. in 1936 which was completely liquidated 12/29/55

MIDDLE WESTERN TELEPHONE CO.
Dissolved in 1945

MIDDLE WITWATERSRAND WESTN AREAS LTD (SOUTH AFRICA)
ADR's for Ordinary Rand 25 par split (25) for (1) by issuance of (24) additional ADR's 09/25/1989
Name changed to Avmin Ltd. 11/30/1996
(See Avmin Ltd.)

MIDDLEBOROUGH TR CO (MIDDLEBORO, MA)
Merged into Independent Bank Corp. (MA) 01/31/1986
Each share Capital Stock $20 par exchanged for (4) shares Common 1¢ par

MIDDLEBROOK PHARMACEUTICALS INC (DE)
Plan of reorganization under Chapter 11 Federal Bankruptcy proceedings effective
Each share Common 1¢ par received initial distribution of $0.0916 cash payable 12/20/2011 to holders of record 01/03/2011

MIDDLEBURG & SCHOHARIE R.R. CO.
Operations discontinued 00/00/1936
Stockholders' equity unlikely

MIDDLEBURG FINL CORP (VA)
Common $5 par changed to $2.50 par and (1) additional share issued payable 10/17/2003 to holders of record 10/02/2003 Ex date - 10/20/2003
Merged into Access National Corp. 03/31/2017
Each share Common $2.50 par exchanged for (1.3314) shares Common $0.835 par

MIDDLEBURY ELECTRIC CO.
Acquired by New England Public Service Co. 00/00/1928
Details not available

MIDDLEFIELD BANCORP LTD (ON)
Merged into Middlefield Tactical Energy Corp. 02/23/2012
Each share Common no par exchanged for (0.16688754) share Common no par
Middlefield Tactical Energy Corp. name changed to MBN Corp. 02/27/2012

MIDDLEFIELD EQUAL SECTOR INCOME FD (ON)
Merged into INDEXPLUS Income Fund 05/26/2008
Each Trust Unit no par exchanged for (0.70861783) Unit
INDEXPLUS Income Fund reorganized as Middlefield Mutual Funds Ltd. 06/05/2017

MIDDLEFIELD INCOME PLUS II CORP (ON)
Under plan of merger each Equity Share automatically became (0.70239004) share Middlefield Mutual Funds Ltd. Income Plus Class Ser. A 03/03/2014

MIDDLEFIELD TACTICAL ENERGY CORP (ON)
Name changed to MBN Corp. 02/27/2012

MIDDLEGATE RES INC (BC)
Recapitalized as Banner Industries Inc. (BC) 10/02/1985
Each share Common no par exchanged for (0.4) share Common no par
Banner Industries Inc. (BC) name changed to Banner Entertainment Inc. 09/25/1987 which recapitalized as Windsor Court Holdings Inc. 06/15/1990 which recapitalized as Teledata Ventures Corp. (BC) 10/01/1996 which reincorporated in Yukon as CTF Technologies Inc. 04/06/1998 which reincorporated in British Columbia 08/11/2008
(See CTF Technologies Inc.)

MIDDLESBORO FED SVGS BK FSB (MIDDLESBORO, KY)
Under plan of reorganization each share Common $1 par automatically became (1) share Cumberland Mountain Bancshares, Inc. Common 1¢ par 03/31/1997
(See Cumberland Mountain Bancshares, Inc.)

MIDDLESEX & BOSTON STR RY CO (MA)
Liquidation completed
Each share Capital Stock $10 par exchanged for initial distribution of $25 cash 12/11/1973
Each share Capital Stock $10 par received second distribution of $2.90 cash 12/13/1973
Each share Capital Stock $10 par received third distribution of $2.50 cash 12/12/1974
Each share Capital Stock $10 par received fourth and final distribution of $4.50 cash 10/20/1978

MIDDLESEX BANK, N.A. (EVERETT, MA)
Location changed to Middlesex Bank, N.A. (Burlington, Mass.) 12/18/72
Middlesex Bank, N.A. (Burlington, Mass.) name changed to BayBank Middlesex, N.A. (Burlington, Mass.) 2/3/76 which merged into BayBank Middlesex (Burlington,Mass.) 11/9/79 which name changed to BayBank Trust Co. (Burlington, Mass.) 6/30/83 which name changed back to BayBank Middlesex (Burlington, Mass.) 12/8/83

MIDDLESEX BK N A (BURLINGTON, MA)
Name changed to BayBank Middlesex, N.A. (Burlington, MA) 02/03/1976
BayBank Middlesex N.A. (Burlington, MA) merged into BayBank Middlesex (Burlington, MA) 11/09/1979 which name changed to BayBank Trust Co. (Burlington, MA) 06/30/1983 which name changed back to BayBank Middlesex (Burlington, MA) 12/08/1983

MIDDLESEX CNTY BK (NORTH BRUNSWICK, NJ)
Stock Dividends - 10% 01/21/1971; 10% 04/24/1972; 10% 03/15/1973; 10% 03/15/1974
Name changed to First County Bank of New Jersey (North Brunswick, NJ) 12/27/1978
First County Bank of New Jersey (North Brunswick, NJ) merged into First Jersey National Corp. 12/03/1984
(See First Jersey National Corp.)

MIDDLESEX COUNTY NATIONAL BANK (EVERETT, MA)
Stock Dividends - 12-1/2% 2/8/56; 11-1/9% 2/10/58; 25% 2/12/62; 20% 3/16/67
Name changed to Middlesex Bank, N.A. (Everett, Mass.) 9/3/68
Middlesex Bank, N.A. (Everett, Mass.) changed location to Middlesex Bank, N.A. (Burlington, Mass.) 12/18/72 which name changed to BayBank Middlesex, N.A. (Burlington, Mass.) 2/3/76 which merged into BayBank Middlesex (Burlington, Mass.) 11/9/79 which name changed to BayBank Trust Co. (Burlington, Mass.) 6/30/83 which name changed back to BayBank Middlesex (Burlington, Mass.) 12/8/83

MIDDLESEX PRODUCTS CORP. (MA)
Each share Capital Stock $100 par exchanged for (4) shares new Capital Stock $20 par in 1937
Liquidation completed for cash in 1961

MIDDLETON DOLL CO (WI)
Each share old Common 6-2/3¢ par exchanged for (1) share new Common 6-2/3¢ par to reflect a (1) for (1,000) reverse split followed by a (1,000) for (1) forward split 01/16/2009
Note: Holders of (999) or fewer pre-split shares received $0.50 cash per share
Each share Adjustable Rate Preferred Ser. A 1¢ par exchanged for (37.96) shares new Common 6-2/3¢ par 02/18/2011
Recapitalized as FirsTime Design Ltd. 02/22/2011
Each share new Common 6-2/3¢ par exchanged for (0.1) share Common 6-2/3¢ par
Note: Holders of (9) or fewer pre-split shares received $0.20 cash per share

MIDDLETOWN & UNIONVILLE R.R. CO.
Bankrupt in 1946

MIDDLETOWN BK CO (MIDDLETOWN, NJ)
Capital Stock $5 par changed to $2.50 par and (1) additional share issued 02/17/1970
Stock Dividends - 10% 01/15/1969; 10% 01/16/1970; 10% 01/21/1971; 10% 01/14/1972
Merged into Community State Bank & Trust Co. (Linden, NJ) 11/20/1972
Each share Capital Stock $2.50 par exchanged for (0.5) share Common $12.50 par
(See Community State Bank & Trust Co. (Linden, NJ))

MIDDLETOWN GAS LIGHT CO. (CT)
Acquired by Connecticut Light & Power Co. 00/00/1927
Details not available

MIDDLETOWN NATIONAL CORP.
Merged into Connecticut Investment Management Corp. 00/00/1931
Details not available

MIDEAST ALUMINUM CORP. (NJ)
Merged into Mideast Aluminum Industries Corp. 3/1/69
Each share Capital Stock $2 par exchanged for (1) share Capital Stock $2.50 par
Mideast Aluminum Industries Corp. name changed to MAI Liquidating Co. 5/25/77
(See MAI Liquidating Co.)

MIDEAST ALUMINUM INDUSTRIES CORP. (NJ)
Name changed to MAI Liquidating Co. 5/25/77
(See MAI Liquidating Co.)

MIDEPSA INC. (CANADA)
Recapitalized as Midepsa International Inc. 08/14/1984
Each share Capital Stock no par exchanged for (0.25) share Common no par
Midepsa International Inc. name changed to Henlys Group Ltd.-Groupe Henlys Ltee. 11/18/1985 which name changed to Sechura Inc. (Canada) 10/05/1989 which reincorporated in Bermuda as Aaxis Ltd. 08/30/1996 which was acquired by BHI Corp. 03/31/1998 which name changed to Carlisle Holdings Ltd. 06/02/1999 which name changed to BB Holdings Ltd. 08/18/2005
(See BB Holdings Ltd.)

MIDEPSA INDUSTRIES LTD. (CANADA)
Name changed to Midepsa Inc. 12/02/1980
Midepsa Inc. recapitalized as Midepsa International Inc. 08/14/1984 which recapitalized as Henlys Group Ltd.-Groupe Henlys Ltee. 11/18/1985 which name changed to Sechura Inc. (Canada) 10/05/1989 which reincorporated in Bermuda as Aaxis Ltd. 08/30/1996 which was acquired by BHI Corp. 03/31/1998 which name changed to Carlisle Holdings Ltd. 06/02/1999 which name changed to BB Holdings Ltd. 08/18/2005
(See BB Holdings Ltd.)

MIDEPSA INTL INC (CANADA)
Recapitalized as Henlys Group Ltd.-Groupe Henlys Ltee. 11/18/1985
Each share Conv. Preferred no par exchanged for (1) share Conv. Preferred no par
Each share Common no par exchanged for (1) share Common no par
Henlys Group Ltd.-Groupe Henlys Ltee. name changed to Sechura Inc. (Canada) 10/05/1989 which reincorporated in Bermuda as Aaxis Ltd. 08/30/1996 which was acquired by BHI Corp. 03/31/1998 which name changed to Carlisle Holdings Ltd. 06/02/1999 which name changed to BB Holdings Ltd. 08/18/2005
(See BB Holdings Ltd.)

MIDEX GOLD CORP (WY)
Reincorporated 09/15/2010
Old Common $0.001 par split (5) for (1) by issuance of (4) additional shares payable 09/02/2009 to holders of record 09/02/2009
Each (30) shares old Common $0.001 par exchanged for (1) share new Common $0.001 par 08/11/2010
State of incorporation changed from (NV) to (WY) and new Common $0.001 par changed to $0.00000001 par 09/15/2010
Each share old Common $0.00000001 par exchanged for (0.0001) share new Common $0.00000001 par 10/16/2012
Name changed to Promithian Global Ventures, Inc. 05/14/2013

MIDGARDXXI INC (DE)
Involuntary petition filed under Chapter 7 Federal Bankruptcy Code 12/15/2006
No stockholders' equity

MIDISOFT CORP (WA)
Name changed to recordLab Corp. 10/19/1999
(See recordLab Corp.)

MIDLAND & PACIFIC GRAIN CORP. LTD. (CANADA)
7% Preferred $100 par called for redemption 01/09/1940
Each share old Common no par exchanged for (5) new shares Common no par 04/17/1961
Name changed to M P G Investment Corp. Ltd. 05/26/1965
(See M P G Investment Corp. Ltd.)

MIDLAND BAKERIES CO. (DE)
Common no par changed to $5 par 00/00/1948
Acquired by Consolidated Foods Corp. 12/31/1967
Each share 4% Preferred $100 par exchanged for $137 cash
Each share Common $5 par exchanged for $1.52 cash

MIDLAND BANCORP INC (DE)
Name changed to Unibancorp, Inc. 4/25/84
Unibancorp, Inc. acquired by Old Kent Financial Corp. 10/18/88 which merged into Fifth Third Bancorp 4/2/2001

MIDLAND BANCORPORATION INC (NJ)
Merged into Valley National Bancorp 3/1/97
Each share Common $15 par exchanged for (30) shares Common $1 par

MIDLAND BK & TR CO (PARAMUS, NJ)
Each share Common $5 par exchanged for (1/3) share Common $15 par 5/6/75
Common $25 par changed to $5 par and (4) additional shares issued 11/27/77
Reorganized as Midland Bancorporation, Inc. 7/31/85
Each share Common $15 par exchanged for (1) share Common $15 par
Midland Bancorporation, Inc. merged into Valley National Bancorp 3/1/97

MIDLAND BANK (PARAMUS, NJ)
Name changed to Midland Bank & Trust Co. (Paramus, NJ) 4/20/67
Midland Bank & Trust Co. (Paramus, NJ) reorganized as Midland Bancorporation, Inc. 7/31/85 which merged into Valley National Bancorp 3/1/97

MIDLAND BK PLC (ENGLAND & WALES)
Name changed to HSBC Bank PLC 10/18/99
(See HSBC Bank PLC)

MIDLAND BARING FINL GROUP LTD (DE)
Recapitalized as Level Vision Electronics, Ltd. 01/07/2009
Each share Common $0.001 par exchanged for (1/6) share Common $0.001 par

MIDLAND BUILDING CORP.
Property sold and Company dissolved 00/00/1948
Details not available

MIDLAND CAP CORP (DE)
Plan of reorganization under Chapter 11 Federal Bankruptcy proceedings confirmed 04/24/1990
No stockholders' equity

MIDLAND CAP CORP (NY)
Reorganized under the laws of Delaware 12/31/1981
Each share Common $1 par exchanged for (1) share Common $1 par
(See Midland Capital Corp. (DE))

MIDLAND CO (OH)
Common no par split (2) for (1) by issuance of (1) additional share 05/07/1987
Common no par split (3) for (1) by issuance of (2) additional shares payable 05/21/1998 to holders of record 04/30/1998 Ex date - 05/22/1998
Common no par split (2) for (1) by issuance of (1) additional share payable 07/16/2002 to holders of record 07/08/2002 Ex date - 07/17/2002
Stock Dividend - 10% 10/10/1972
Merged into Munich-American Holding Corp. 04/03/2008
Each share Common no par exchanged for $65 cash

MIDLAND COUNTIES PUBLIC SERVICE CORP.
Properties acquired by Pacific Gas & Electric Co. 00/00/1938
Details not available

MIDLAND DOHERTY FINL CORP (CANADA)
Merged into Midland Walwyn Inc. 06/01/1990
Each share Common no par exchanged for (0.5) share Common no par
Midland Walwyn Inc. merged into Merrill Lynch & Co., Inc. 08/27/1998 which was acquired by Bank of America Corp. 01/02/2009

MIDLAND ENERGY CORP (BC)
Name changed to Midland Gold Corp. 2/1/88
Midland Gold Corp. recapitalized as Minera Rayrock Inc. 7/19/89 which merged into Rayrock Yellowknife Resources Inc. 5/27/98 which name changed to Rayrock Resources Inc. 11/27/98
(See Rayrock Resources Inc.)

MIDLAND ENTERPRISES INC (NY)
Reincorporated 11/28/56
State of incorporation changed from (WV) to (NY) and Common $5 par changed to Capital Stock $1 par 11/28/56
Acquired by Eastern Gas & Fuel Associates 8/22/61
Each share Capital Stock $1 par exchanged for (1.25) shares Common $10 par
Eastern Gas & Fuel Associates name changed to Eastern Enterprises 4/28/89
(See Eastern Enterprises)

MIDLAND FED SVGS & LN ASSN BRIDGEVIEW (USA)
Under plan of reorganization each share Common 1¢ par automatically became (1) share Midland Capital Holding Corp. (DE) Common 1¢ par 7/23/98

MIDLAND FINL GROUP INC (TN)
Merged into Progressive Corp. 3/7/97
Each share Common no par exchanged for $9 cash

MIDLAND GLASS INC (DE)
Stock Dividends - 10% 02/20/1976; 10% 09/07/1979
Merged into Wesray Corp. 03/01/1984
Each share Common $1 par exchanged for $12.50 cash

MIDLAND GOLD CORP. (BC)
Recapitalized as Minera Rayrock Inc. 7/19/89
Each share Common no par exchanged for (0.25) share Common no par
Minera Rayrock Inc. merged into Rayrock Yellowknife Resources Inc. 5/27/98 which name changed to Rayrock Resources Inc. 11/27/98
(See Rayrock Resources Inc.)

MIDLAND GUARDIAN CO (OH)
100% acquired by Midland Co. through exchange offer which expired 11/30/1968
Public interest eliminated

MIDLAND HOLLAND INC (YT)
Reincorporated 03/11/1999
Place of incorporation changed from (Canada) to (YT) 03/11/1999
Name changed to Mercury Partners & Co. Inc. 02/22/2000
Mercury Partners & Co. Inc. name changed to Black Mountain Capital Corp. 05/02/2005 which recapitalized as Grand Peak Capital Corp. (YT) 11/20/2007 which reincorporated in British Columbia 04/27/2010

MIDLAND INC (CO)
Class A Preferred 40¢ par split (3) for (2) by issuance of (0.5) additional share payable 07/06/1998 to holders of record 05/29/1998
SEC revoked preferred and common stock registration 09/04/2007

MIDLAND INTL CORP (NV)
Name changed to Lumonall, Inc. 08/17/2007
(See Lumonall, Inc.)

MIDLAND INTL SALES INC (DE)
Charter cancelled and declared inoperative and void for non-payment of taxes 04/15/1973

MIDLAND MINING CO. (ID)
Charter forfeited for failure to file reports 11/30/40

MIDLAND MTG INVS TR (MA)
Each Share of Bene. Int. no par exchanged for (0.5) share Conv. Preferred no par and (0.5) share Common no par 11/07/1980
Under plan of reorganization each share Conv. Preferred no par and Common no par automatically became (1) share Centennial Group, Inc. Conv. Preferred $3 par and Common 10¢ par respectively 08/10/1981
Centennial Group, Inc. acquired by Investors Savings Bank (Richmond, VA) 12/31/1986
(See Investors Savings Bank (Richmond, VA))

MIDLAND NATIONAL BANK (MIDLAND, TX)
Each share Capital Stock $100 par exchanged for (5) shares Capital Stock $20 par 01/08/1957
Capital Stock $20 par changed to $10 par and (1) additional share issued 02/03/1964
Merged into First City Bancorporation of Texas, Inc. (TX) 04/30/1972
Each share Capital Stock $10 par exchanged for (1/3) share Common $6.50 par
(See First City Bancorporation of Texas, Inc. (TX))

MIDLAND NATL BK (MILWAUKEE, WI)
Common $15 par changed to $7.50 par and (1) additional share issued 02/24/1967
Common $7.50 par changed to $2.50 par and (2) additional shares issued 04/05/1974
Stock Dividend - 10% 01/31/1968
Liquidation completed
Each share Common $2.50 par received initial distribution of $7.50 cash 08/04/1977
Each share Common $2.50 par exchanged for second and final distribution of $2.052 cash 11/18/1977

MIDLAND NATL CORP (NV)
Completely liquidated 4/5/72

5/27/98 which name changed to Rayrock Resources Inc. 11/27/98
Each share Common no par exchanged for first and final distribution of (1/3) share First City Bancorporation of Texas, Inc. (TX) Common $10 par
(See First City Bancorporation of Texas, Inc. (TX))

MIDLAND NATURAL GAS CO.
Succeeded by Northeastern Natural Gas Co. 00/00/1932
Details not available

MIDLAND NICKEL LTD (ON)
Charter cancelled for failure to pay taxes and file returns 03/13/1979

MIDLAND OIL CO. (WY)
Merged into Consolidated Oil & Gas, Inc. (CO) on a (0.9) for (1) basis 02/16/1961
Consolidated Oil & Gas, Inc. (CO) acquired by Hugoton Energy Corp. 09/07/1995 which merged into Chesapeake Energy Corp. 03/10/1998

MIDLAND OIL CORP (DE)
Common no par changed to $1 par in 1935
Common $1 par changed to 25¢ par in 1943
Each share $2 Preferred no par exchanged for (1) share $1 Preferred no par and (2) shares new Common 25¢ par in 1946
Each share old Common 25¢ par exchanged for (1) share new Common 25¢ par in 1946
New Common 25¢ par changed to 10¢ par and (1.5) additional shares issued 3/14/69
Common 10¢ par changed to 5¢ par in November 1972
Each share Common 5¢ par exchanged for (0.05) share Common $1 par 1/8/74
Charter cancelled and declared inoperative and void for non-payment of taxes 3/1/76

MIDLAND PETES LTD (BC)
Merged into Davenport Oil & Mining Ltd. 02/29/1972
Each share Common no par exchanged for (0.1) share Capital Stock 50¢ par
Davenport Oil & Mining Ltd. name changed to Davenport Industries Ltd. 11/01/1973 which recapitalized as DVO Industries Ltd. 08/19/1991
(See DVO Industries Ltd.)

MIDLAND PETROL & GAS CO.
Liquidated in 1947

MIDLAND PROPERTIES, INC. (NY)
Completely liquidated 4/21/55
Each share Preferred $100 par exchanged for first and final distribution of $100 principal amount of 2% 30-year Debentures due in 1985 of Metropolitan Buffalo Investors, Inc.
Each share Common $10 par exchanged for first and final distribution of $0.30 cash

MIDLAND REALIZATION CO. (DE)
Liquidation completed 09/16/1955
Details not available

MIDLAND RES INC (NY)
Under plan of merger name changed to American Midland Corp. and Common 50¢ par changed to 1¢ par 07/06/1984
(See American Midland Corp.)

MIDLAND RES INC NEW (TX)
Merged into Vista Energy Resources, Inc. 10/28/98
Each share Common $0.001 par exchanged for (1) share Common 1¢ par
Vista Energy Resources, Inc. recapitalized as Prize Energy Corp. 2/9/2000 which merged into Magnum Hunter Resources, Inc.

3/15/2002 which merged into Cimarex Energy Co. 6/7/2005

MIDLAND ROSS CORP (OH)
5-1/2% 1st Preferred $100 par called for redemption 2/28/64
Common $5 par split (2) for (1) by issuance of (1) additional share 5/15/64
Common $5 par split (2) for (1) by issuance of (1) additional share 5/27/66
Common $5 par split (2) for (1) by issuance of (1) additional share 6/30/78
$5 Conv. Preferred Ser. B no par called for redemption 5/22/81
$4.75 Conv. Preferred Ser. A no par called for redemption 12/6/83
Merged into Forstmann Little & Co. 9/11/86
Each share Common $5 par exchanged for $28 cash

MIDLAND ROYALTY CORP.
Name changed to Midland Oil Corp. 00/00/1936
(See Midland Oil Corp.)

MIDLAND SECURITIES CO.
Liquidated in 1929

MIDLAND SHOE CO. (MO)
Common no par changed to $1 par 01/05/1954
Acquired by Craddock-Terry Shoe Corp. 04/18/1966
Each share Capital Stock $1 par exchanged for (3) shares Common $1 par
(See Craddock-Terry Shoe Corp.)

MIDLAND SOUTHWEST CORP (TX)
Merged into Hanna (M.A.) Co. (New) 12/31/1987
Each share Common $1 par exchanged for $0.375 cash

MIDLAND STEAMSHIP LINE, INC. (DE)
Liquidation for cash completed 9/30/63

MIDLAND STEEL PRODUCTS CO. (OH)
Each share Part. Preferred $100 par exchanged for (1) share 8% 1st Preferred $100 par and (2) shares Common no par in 1930
Each share Common no par exchanged for (2) shares $2 Preferred no par and (1) share new Common no par in 1930
Each share Common no par exchanged for (2) shares Common $5 par in 1949
Merged into Midland-Ross Corp. 12/7/57
Each share 8% 1st Preferred $100 par exchanged for (1.5) shares 5-1/2% 1st Preferred $100 par
Each share $2 Preferred no par exchanged for (2/3) share Common $5 par
Each share Common $5 par exchanged for (1) share new Common $5 par
(See Midland-Ross Corp.)

MIDLAND STL CORP (SC)
Involuntarily dissolved for failure to pay taxes 8/5/87

MIDLAND UNITED CO. (DE)
Reorganized 4/7/45
Each share $3 Preferred exchanged for (1) share Midland Realization Co. Capital Stock $1 par, (1) share Public Service Co. of Indiana, Inc. Common no par and $1.25 cash
Each share $6 Preferred exchanged for (2) shares Midland Realization Co. Capital Stock $1 par, (2) shares Public Service Co. of Indiana, Inc. Common no par and $2.50 cash
No equity for Common
(See each company's listing)

MIDLAND URANIUM, INC. (UT)
Merged into Mountain Mesa Uranium Corp. 05/11/1955
Each share Common $1 par exchanged for (0.2) share Common 5¢ par
Mountain Mesa Uranium Corp. merged into Hidden Splendor Mining Co. (DE) 10/19/1959 which merged into Atlas Corp. 08/17/1962
(See Atlas Corp.)

MIDLAND UTILITIES CO. (DE)
Reorganized 04/07/1945
Each share 6% and 7% Prior Lien Preferred $100 par exchanged for (0.5) share Capital Stock $1 par of Midland Realization Co.
No equity for holders of 6% and 7% Class A Preferred or Common
(See Midland Realization Co.)

MIDLAND VALLEY RAILROAD CO. (AR)
5% Preferred $50 par called 4/1/65
All Common Stock owned by Texas & Pacific Railway Co.

MIDLAND WALWYN INC (CANADA)
Merged into Merrill Lynch & Co., Inc. 08/27/1998
Each share Common no par exchanged for either (0.24) share Common no par or (0.24) Merrill Lynch & Co., Canada Ltd. Exchangeable Share no par
Note: Shares held by Non-Canadian residents will receive Common
Merrill Lynch & Co., Inc. acquired by Bank of America Corp. 01/02/2009

MIDLANDS ELECTRICITY PLC (UNITED KINGDOM)
ADR agreement terminated 08/22/1996
Each 144A ADR for Ordinary Final Instalment 50p par exchanged for $65 cash
Each 144A Sponsored ADR for Ordinary Final Instalment 50p par exchanged for $13 cash

MIDLANDS ENERGY CO (DE)
Merged into Freeport-McMoRan Inc. 12/04/1984
Each share Common 1¢ par exchanged for $27.50 principal amount of 10-1/2% 30-yr. Conv. Subord. S.F. Debentures due 12/04/2014

MIDLANDS MINERALS CORP (ON)
Recapitalized as Rosita Mining Corp. 07/28/2015
Each share Common no par exchanged for (0.1) share Common no par

MIDLANDS NATL BK (PROSPERITY, SC)
Acquired by Carolina First Corp. 6/30/95
Each share Common $5 par exchanged for $1.65 cash

MIDLANTIC BKS INC (NJ)
Common $10 par changed to $6-2/3 par and (0.5) additional share issued 11/19/1981
$2 Conv. Preferred 1st Ser. no par called for redemption 12/29/1983
$2 Conv. Preferred 2nd Ser. no par called for redemption 12/29/1983
Common $6-2/3 par changed to $3 par and (1) additional share issued 05/08/1984
Merged into Midlantic Corp. 01/30/1987
Each share Common $3 par exchanged for (1) share Common $3 par
Midlantic Corp. merged into PNC Bank Corp. 12/31/1995 which name changed to PNC Financial Services Group, Inc. 03/15/2000

MIDLANTIC CORP (NJ)
Merged into PNC Bank Corp. 12/31/1995
Each share Common $3 par exchanged for (2.05) shares Common $3 par
PNC Bank Corp. name changed to PNC Financial Services Group, Inc. 03/15/2000

MIDNAPORE 1979 RES INC (BC)
Name changed 1/22/86
Name changed from Midnapore Resources Inc. to Midnapore (1979) Resources Inc. 1/22/86
Each share Common no par exchanged for (4) shares Common no par
Struck off register and declared dissolved for failure to file returns 11/30/90

MIDNET INC (DE)
SEC revoked common stock registration 09/08/2011

MIDNIGHT CANDLE CO (NV)
Each share old Common $0.001 par exchanged for (30) shares new Common $0.001 par 10/15/2008
Name changed to SEFE, Inc. 09/30/2010

MIDNIGHT CONS MINES LTD (BC)
Struck off register and declared dissolved for failure to file returns 06/24/1974

MIDNIGHT GOLD & SILVER (UT)
Proclaimed dissolved for failure to pay taxes 09/30/1975

MIDNIGHT OIL & GAS LTD (AB)
Plan of arrangement effective 11/30/2004
Each share Common no par exchanged for (1) Daylight Energy Trust, Trust Unit and (0.5) share Midnight Oil Exploration Ltd. Common no par
(See each company's listing)

MIDNIGHT OIL EXPL LTD (AB)
Recapitalized as Pace Oil & Gas Ltd. 07/05/2010
Each share Common no par exchanged for (0.1) share Common no par
Pace Oil & Gas Ltd. reorganized as Spyglass Resources Corp. 04/04/2013

MIDNIGHT SUN CAP CORP (BC)
Name changed to Midnight Sun Mining Corp. 02/07/2011

MIDNITE MINES INC (WA)
Charter cancelled and proclaimed dissolved for failure to file reports 3/20/2000

MIDRANGE MARKETING SOLUTIONS INC (DE)
Recapitalized as Millennium Broadcast Corp. 9/20/99
Each share Common 1¢ par exchanged for (0.01) share Common $0.001 par
Millennium Broadcast Corp. recapitalized as Diversified Media Holdings Inc. 3/13/2003 which recapitalized as TPI International, Inc. 1/3/2006

MIDRIM MNG LTD (ON)
Capital Stock $1 par changed to no par 06/16/1971
Merged into Plasma Environmental Technologies, Inc. 05/31/1996
Each share Capital Stock no par exchanged for (1) share Common no par
Plasma Environmental Technologies, Inc. recapitalized as Blue Vista Technologies Inc. 08/17/2007 which recapitalized as Arbitrage Exploration Inc. 01/16/2015 which name changed to Argo Gold Inc. 09/22/2016

MIDSOUTH BANCORP INC (LA)
Conv. Preferred Ser. A $14.25 par called for redemption at $14.33 on 8/1/2001

(Additional Information in Active)
MIDSOUTH BK (MURFREESBORO, TN)
Merged into Franklin Financial Network, Inc. 07/01/2014
Each share Common $1 par exchanged for for (0.425926) share Common no par

MIDSOUTH CORP (DE)
Ser. A Common 20¢ par reclassified as Common 20¢ par in February 1987
Acquired by Kansas City Southern Industries, Inc. 6/10/93
Each share Common 20¢ par exchanged for $20.50 cash

MIDSOUTH GAS CO. (AR)
Stock Dividends - 25% 6/22/54; 40% 6/14/57
Merged into Arkansas Louisiana Gas Co. on a (0.5) for (1) basis 10/31/61
Arkansas Louisiana Gas Co. name changed to Arkla, Inc. 11/23/81 which name changed to NorAm Energy Corp. 5/11/94 which merged into Houston Industries Inc. 8/6/97 which name changed to Reliant Energy Inc. 2/8/99 which reorganized as CenterPoint Energy, Inc. 8/31/2002

MIDSTATE BANCORP INC (DE)
Merged into Shore Bancshares, Inc. 4/1/2004
Each share Common exchanged for (0.8732) share Common 1¢ par and $31 cash

MIDSTATES PETE CO INC (DE)
Each share old Common 1¢ par exchanged for (0.1) share new Common 1¢ par 08/04/2015
Plan of reorganization under Chapter 11 Federal Bankruptcy proceedings effective 10/21/2016
No stockholders' equity
(Additional Information in Active)

MIDSWANA DIAMOND EXPL CORP (ON)
Recapitalized as Vertex Ventures Inc. 03/29/1999
Each share Common no par exchanged for (0.2) share Common no par
Vertex Ventures Inc. name changed to First Strike Diamonds Inc. 02/23/2000
(See First Strike Diamonds Inc.)

MIDTEX INC (MN)
Each share Common 10¢ par exchanged for (0.1) share $1.65 Preferred $1 par or (1) share Common $1 par 03/14/1978
Note: Option to receive Common $1 par expired 04/21/1978
$1.65 Preferred $1 par called for redemption 01/04/1980
Merged into Midland-Ross Corp. 02/05/1980
Each share Common $1 par exchanged for $123.87 cash
Each share Common $1 par received initial distribution of $11.175 cash from escrow 02/05/1982
Each share Common $1 par received second and final distribution of $7.89 cash from escrow 02/05/1983

MIDTOWN ENTERPRISES, INC.
Liquidated in 1949

MIDTOWN MOTORS, INC. (PA)
Liquidation completed
Each share Common no par exchanged for initial distribution of $35 cash 5/4/64
Each share Common no par received second distribution of $7.94 cash 12/15/64
Each share Common no par received third and final distribution of $1.90 cash 12/22/66

MIDVALE CO. (DE)
Name changed to General Industrial Enterprises, Inc. 12/30/1955
General Industrial Enterprises, Inc. merged into Baldwin Securities Corp. (DE) 09/30/1965
(See Baldwin Securities Corp.)

MIDVALE MNG CO (WA)
Charter cancelled and proclaimed dissolved for failure to pay fees 01/04/2010

MIDVALE PETES LTD (BC)
Merged into Reigate Resources (Canada) Ltd. 1/31/83
Each share Common no par exchanged for (1/3) share Class A Stock no par
(See Reigate Resources (Canada) Ltd.)

MIDWAY AIRLS CORP (DE)
Issue Information - 4,200,000 shares COM offered at $15.50 per share on 12/04/1997
Chapter 11 Federal Bankruptcy proceedings converted to Chapter 7 on 10/30/2003
Stockholders' equity unlikely

MIDWAY AIRLS INC (DE)
Conv. Exchangeable Preferred Ser. B 1¢ par called for redemption 02/25/1987
Chapter 11 bankruptcy proceedings converted to Chapter 7 on 11/27/1991
Stockholders' equity unlikely

MIDWAY BANK (TAMPA, FL)
Name changed to Midway Marine Bank (Tampa, Fla.) 11/15/71
Midway Marine Bank (Tampa, Fla.) name changed to Flagship Bank of Town 'N Country (Tampa, Fla.) 11/10/74

MIDWAY ENERGY LTD (AB)
Merged into Whitecap Resources Inc. 04/26/2012
Each share Common no par exchanged for (0.4470426) share Common no par and $0.33488884 cash

MIDWAY ENTERPRISES, INC. (CO)
Name changed to Pike's Peak Turf Club, Inc. 04/17/1968
Pike's Peak Turf Club, Inc. name changed to Pike's Peak American Corp. 06/28/1974 which recapitalized as Transmedia Network, Inc. (CO) 09/01/1984 which reincorporated in Delaware 07/20/1987 which name changed to iDine Rewards Network Inc. 02/01/2002 which name changed to Rewards Network Inc. 12/09/2003
(See Rewards Network Inc.)

MIDWAY GAMES INC (DE)
Plan of reorganization under Chapter 11 Federal Bankruptcy proceedings effective 06/11/2010
No stockholders' equity

MIDWAY GAS CO.
Acquired by Southern California Gas Co. 00/00/1927
Details not available

MIDWAY GOLD CORP (BC)
Plan of reorganization under Chapter 11 Federal Bankruptcy proceedings effective 12/07/2017
No stockholders' equity

MIDWAY MARINE BANK (TAMPA, FL)
Name changed to Flagship Bank of Town 'N Country (Tampa, Fla.) 11/10/74

MIDWAY NATL BK (ST. PAUL, MN)
Acquired by Dakota Bancshares, Inc. 09/14/2002
Each share Common $10 par exchanged for approximately $712.72 cash

MIDWAY OIL CORP.
Liquidated in 1929

MIDWAY PORCUPINE MINES LTD.
Liquidation completed in 1938

MIDWAY TERMINALS LTD. (BC)
Name changed to National Forest Products 7/19/60
National Forest Products struck off register and dissolved 1/23/69

MIDWESCO FILTER RES INC (DE)
Merged into MFRI, Inc. 01/28/1994
Each share Common 1¢ par exchanged for (1) share Common 1¢ par
MFRI, Inc. name changed to Perma-Pipe International Holdings, Inc. 03/21/2017

MIDWEST & GULF OIL CORP. (DE)
Charter cancelled and declared inoperative and void for non-payment of taxes 3/17/26

MIDWEST ABRASIVE CO. (MI)
Reincorporated under the laws of Delaware as Mid-West Abrasive Co. 00/00/1936
Mid-West Abrasive Co. name changed to MWA Co. 10/21/1968
(See MWA Co.)

MIDWEST AIR GROUP INC (WI)
Reincorporated 04/22/1996
Name changed 01/01/2004
Issue Information - 4,500,000 shares COM offered at $18 per share on 09/22/1995
State of incorporation changed from (DE) to (WI) 04/22/1996
Common 1¢ par split (3) for (2) by issuance of (0.5) additional share payable 05/28/1997 to holders of record 05/12/1997 Ex date - 05/29/1997
Common 1¢ par split (3) for (2) by issuance of (0.5) additional share payable 05/27/1998 to holders of record 05/11/1998 Ex date - 05/28/1998
Name changed from Midwest Express Holdings Inc. to Midwest Air Group, Inc. 01/01/2004
Merged into Midwest Air Partners, LLC 01/31/2008
Each share Common 1¢ par exchanged for $17 cash

MIDWEST ART STUDIOS INC (DE)
Name changed to Systematic Tax, Inc. 07/06/1970
Systematic Tax, Inc. reorganized as Physiodata, Inc. 09/09/1975 which recapitalized as Petro Nicholas, Inc. 06/30/1980 which name changed to Mariah Oil & Gas Corp. 01/01/1981
(See Mariah Oil & Gas Corp.)

MIDWEST BANC HLDGS INC (DE)
Common 1¢ par split (3) for (2) by issuance of (0.5) additional share payable 07/09/2002 to holders of record 07/01/2002 Ex date - 07/10/2002
Plan of reorganization under Chapter 11 Federal Bankruptcy proceedings effective 06/03/2011
No stockholders' equity

MIDWEST BANCORPORATION INC (MO)
Name changed to Laurel Bancshares, Inc. 03/25/1974
Laurel Bancshares, Inc. merged into Ameribanc, Inc. 06/30/1982
(See Ameribanc, Inc.)

MIDWEST BANCORPORATION OHIO INC (OH)
Stock Dividend - 100% 07/20/1972
Completely liquidated 10/01/1982
Each share Common 10¢ par exchanged for $40 principal amount of Provident Bancorp, Inc. 17% Installment Notes due 11/30/1995

MIDWEST BANCSHARES INC (DE)
Common $10 par split (3) for (1) by issuance of (2) additional shares payable 11/19/1997 to holders of record 11/04/1997
Merged into Mahaska Investment Co. 09/30/1999
Each share Common $10 par exchanged for (1) share Common $5 par
Mahaska Investment Co. name changed to MidWestOne Financial Group, Inc. (Old) 05/09/2003 which merged into MidWestOne Financial Group, Inc. (New) 03/14/2008

MIDWEST BANCSHARES INC (OH)
Merged into Peoples Bancorp Inc. 05/30/2014
Each share Common no par exchanged for (2.6626) shares Common no par

MIDWEST BK & TR CO (CLEVELAND, OH)
Common $100 par changed to $10 par and (9) additional shares issued 07/01/1969
Reorganized as Midwest Bancorporation (of Ohio), Inc. 11/08/1971
Each share Common $10 par exchanged for (1) share Common 10¢ par
(See Midwest Bancorporation (of Ohio), Inc.)

MIDWEST BK & TR CO (ELMWOOD PK, IL)
Reorganized as First Midwest Corp. of Delaware 01/31/1984
Each share Common $5 par exchanged for (1) share Common $5 par
First Midwest Corp. of Delaware name changed to Midwest Banc Holdings, Inc. 02/17/1998
(See Midwest Banc Holdings, Inc.)

MIDWEST BEST WTR SALES INC (MN)
Statutorily dissolved 12/31/92

MIDWEST COMM CORP (IN)
Merged into NBD Bancorp, Inc. 6/30/86
Each share Common no par exchanged for $57.43 cash

MIDWEST COMMODITIES INC (IA)
Merged into Nevaco Systems, Inc. 10/09/1982
Each share Common 10¢ par exchanged for (1) share Common 10¢ par

MIDWEST COMMUNICATIONS CORP (DE)
Filed petition under Chapter 11 Federal Bankruptcy Code 06/26/1991
No stockholders' equity

MIDWEST CONSOLIDATED URANIUM CORP. (CO)
Merged into COG Minerals Corp. 05/01/1956
Each share Common exchanged for (0.05) share Common
(See COG Minerals Corp.)

MIDWEST CORP (WV)
Merged into Unarco Industries, Inc. 02/03/1978
Each share Common 50¢ par exchanged for (0.2) share Common $2.50 par
Unarco Industries, Inc. reorganized as UNR Industries, Inc. 09/30/1980 which name changed to ROHN Industries, Inc. 12/17/1997 which name changed to Frankfort Tower Industries, Inc. 02/17/2004
(See Frankfort Tower Industries, Inc.)

MIDWEST E S W T CORP (NV)
Name changed to DM Products, Inc. 03/02/2006
DM Products, Inc. name changed to New Asia Holdings, Inc. 02/13/2015

MIDWEST ENERGY CO (IA)
Common $5 par split (2) for (1) by issuance of (1) additional share 06/02/1986
Merged into Midwest Resources Inc. 11/07/1990
Each share Common $5 par exchanged for (1.08) shares Common no par
Midwest Resources Inc. merged into MidAmerican Energy Co. 07/01/1995
(See MidAmerican Energy Co.)

MIDWEST ENERGY CORP (NM)
Reorganized as Swab-Fox Companies 09/23/1983
Each share Class A Common no par exchanged for (30) shares Common 10¢ par
Preferred not affected except for change in name
Swab-Fox Companies name changed to Tribune/Swab Fox Companies, Inc. 10/01/1984
(See Tribune/Swab Fox Companies, Inc.)

MIDWEST ENGINE CORP. (DE)
Charter cancelled for non-payment of taxes in 1925

MIDWEST EXPL INC (DE)
Charter cancelled and declared inoperative and void for non-payment of taxes 03/01/1996

MIDWEST FED FINL CORP (WI)
Common 1¢ par split (3) for (2) by issuance of (0.5) additional share 05/19/1995
Common 1¢ par split (2) for (1) by issuance of (1) additional share payable 05/28/1996 to holders of record 05/10/1996
Merged into AMCORE Financial, Inc. 03/27/1998
Each share Common 1¢ par exchanged for (1.174) shares Common 22¢ par
(See AMCORE Financial, Inc.)

MIDWEST FINL CORP ONE (DE)
Dutch Auction Rate Transferable Securities Preferred no par called for redemption 3/29/89
Public interest eliminated

MIDWEST FINL GROUP INC (DE)
Merged into First of America Bank Corp. 11/01/1989
Each share Common $5 par exchanged for (1.01) shares Common $10 par
First of America Bank Corp. merged into National City Corp. 03/31/1998 which was acquired by PNC Financial Services Group, Inc. 12/31/2008

MIDWEST GAS CO.
Merged into Consolidated Gas Utilities Co. in 1928
Details not available

MIDWEST GRAIN PRODS INC (KS)
Common no par split (3) for (2) by issuance of (0.5) additional share 07/15/1992
Name changed to MGP Ingredients, Inc. (Old) 10/10/2002
MGP Ingredients, Inc. (Old) reorganized as MGP Ingredients, Inc. (New) 01/04/2012

MIDWEST INCOME TR (OH)
Name and state of incorporation changed from Midwest Income Investment Co. (OH) to Midwest Income Trust (MA) 12/29/1980
Completely liquidated 01/10/1987
Each share Cash Management Fund no par received net asset value
Completely liquidated 05/29/1992
Each share Money Market Fund no par received net asset value
Adjustable Rate U.S. Government Fund Class C no par reclassified as Adjustable Rate U.S. Government

Securities Fund Class C no par 11/25/1992
Intermediate Term Government Fund no par reclassified as Intermediate Term Government Income Fund Class A no par 02/01/1993
Institutional Government Fund no par reclassified as Institutional Government Income Fund no par 02/01/1993
Name changed to Countrywide Investment Trust 02/28/1997
Countrywide Investment Trust name changed to Touchstone Investment Trust 05/01/2000

MIDWEST INVESTMENT CO. (MO)
Liquidation completed
Each Special Reserve Fund Receipt no par received initial distribution of $0.30 cash 11/10/61
Each Special Reserve Fund Receipt no par received second distribution of $0.50 cash 4/12/62
Each Special Reserve Fund Receipt no par received third distribution of $0.20 cash 3/15/63
Each Special Reserve Fund Receipt no par received fourth distribution of $0.20 cash 7/15/65
Each Special Reserve Fund Receipt no par exchanged for fifth and final distribution of $0.1575 cash 8/1/66
Each share Common $5 par exchanged for initial distribution of (1.06377) shares Fidelity Fund, Inc. Capital Stock $1 par 6/19/67
Each share Common $5 par received second and final distribution of $0.2056 cash 12/8/71
Fidelity Fund, Inc. reorganized as Fidelity Fund 1/1/85

MIDWEST INVESTORS FUND, INC. (MN)
Completely liquidated 07/01/1963
Each share Common 1¢ par exchanged for first and final distribution of (0.224379) share Federated Growth Fund, Inc. Capital Stock $1 par
Federated Growth Fund, Inc. name changed to Pligrowth Fund, Inc. 01/01/1971 which merged into Plitrend Fund, Inc. 07/23/1982 which name changed to U.S. Trend Fund, Inc. (PA) 02/00/1986 which reincorporated in Maryland as Capstone U.S. Trend Fund, Inc. 05/11/1992 which name changed to Capstone Growth Fund, Inc. 08/26/1994 which name changed to Capstone Series Fund, Inc. 01/22/2002

MIDWEST LIFE INS CO (NE)
Capital Stock $100 par changed to $10 par and (9) additional shares issued plus a 100% stock dividend paid 03/01/1961
Capital Stock $10 par split (2) for (1) by issuance of (1) additional share 05/01/1968
Capital Stock $10 par changed to $4 par and (1.5) additional shares issued 05/20/1971
100% acquired by Illinois Central Industries, Inc. through purchase offer which expired 11/16/1973
Public interest eliminated

MIDWEST MGMT CORP (DE)
Merged into MMC Elmore Holdings 03/18/1993
Each share Common 50¢ par exchanged for $0.21 cash

MIDWEST NATIONAL CORP. (IN)
Merged into Irwin Union Corp. 01/02/1986
For holdings of (99) shares or fewer each share Common $1 par exchanged for $15 cash
For holdings of (100) shares or more each share Common $1 par exchanged for $5 principal amount of 11% Subord. Debentures due 01/02/1993 and $10 cash

MIDWEST NO-JOINT CONCRETE PIPE CO. (CO)
Name changed to U.S. No-Joint Concrete Pipe Co. 1/11/60
U.S. No-Joint Concrete Pipe Co. merged into Mancos Corp. 7/10/70 which was acquired by Union Oil Co. of California 11/27/78 which reorganized as Unocal Corp. 4/25/83 which merged into Chevron Corp. 8/10/2005

MIDWEST OIL CO.
Merged into Midwest Oil Corp. 00/00/1951
Each share 8% Preferred $1 par exchanged (0.21) share new Common $10 par
Each share Common $10 par exchanged for (1.465) shares new Common $10 par
Midwest Oil Corp. merged into Standard Oil Co. (IN) 04/15/1974 which name changed to Amoco Corp. 04/23/1985 which merged into BP Amoco p.l.c. 12/31/1998 which name changed to BP PLC 05/01/2001

MIDWEST OIL CORP (NV)
Merged into Standard Oil Co. (IN) 04/15/1974
Each share Common $10 par exchanged for (1.978) shares Capital Stock $12.50 par
Standard Oil Co. (IN) name changed to Amoco Corp. 04/23/1985 which merged into BP Amoco p.l.c. 12/31/1998 which name changed to BP PLC 05/01/2001

MIDWEST PACKAGING CORP (IA)
Merged into Hoerner Waldorf Corp. 5/31/72
Each share Common 25¢ par exchanged for (0.1827) share Common 50¢ par
Hoerner Waldorf Corp. merged into Champion International Corp. 2/24/77 which merged into International Paper Co. 6/20/2000

MIDWEST PACKAGING MATLS CO (MO)
Merged into MPM Co. 12/17/1984
Each share 5% Conv. Preferred $10 par exchanged for $20 cash
Each share Common $1 par exchanged for $20 cash

MIDWEST PIPING & SUPPLY CO., INC. (MO)
Stock Dividend - 100% 7/13/46
Recapitalized as Midwest Piping Co., Inc. 2/18/53
Each share Common no par exchanged for (2) shares Common $5 par
Midwest Piping Co., Inc. name changed to Midwest Investment Co.
(See Midwest Investment Co.)

MIDWEST PIPING CO., INC. (MO)
Name changed to Midwest Investment Co. 4/5/61
(See Midwest Investment Co.)

MIDWEST PWR SYS INC (IA)
7.64% Preferred no par called for redemption 12/10/1993
8.08% Preferred no par called for redemption 12/10/1993
$8.32 Class A Preferred no par called for redemption 12/10/1993
$8.52 Class A Preferred no par called for redemption 12/10/1993
Merged into MidAmerican Energy Co. 07/01/1995
Each share 3.30% Preferred no par exchanged for (1) share 3.30% Preferred no par
Each share 3.75% Preferred no par exchanged for (1) share 3.75% Preferred no par
Each share 3.90% Preferred no par exchanged for (1) share 3.90% Preferred no par
Each share 4.20% Preferred no par exchanged for (1) share 4.20% Preferred no par
Each share 4.35% Preferred no par exchanged for (1) share 4.35% Preferred no par
Each share 4.40% Preferred no par exchanged for (1) share 4.40% Preferred no par
Each share 4.80% Preferred no par exchanged for (1) share 4.80% Preferred no par
(See MidAmerican Energy Co.)
Preferred no par called for redemption at $25.695 on 01/12/1997
Public interest eliminated

MIDWEST PRESTRESSED CORP (OH)
Name changed to American Housing Systems Corp. 09/30/1971
American Housing Systems Corp. name changed to Ambina Corp. 07/09/1974
(See Ambina Corp.)

MIDWEST REAL ESTATE SHOPPING CTR L P (DE)
Partnership dissolved 7/28/98
Each Unit of Ltd. Partnership Int. exchanged for first and final distribution of $0.2825 cash

MIDWEST REALTY INVESTMENTS (OH)
Acquired by American Fidelity Investments 3/31/74
Each Share of Bene. Int. no par exchanged for (0.7) Shares of Bene. Int. no par
American Fidelity Investments merged into Leader Development Corp. 1/4/83 which name changed to Clinton Gas Systems Inc. 12/31/87
(See Clinton Gas Systems Inc.)

MIDWEST REFINING CO.
Dissolved in 1932

MIDWEST RES INC (IA)
Merged into MidAmerican Energy Co. 07/01/1995
Each share Common no par exchanged for (1) share Common no par
(See MidAmerican Energy Co.)

MIDWEST RUBR RECLAIMING CO (DE)
Reorganized 03/13/1946
Reorganized from (MO) to under the laws of Delaware 03/13/1946
Each share Common $5 par exchanged for (2) shares Common $2.50 par
4-1/2% Preferred $50 par called for redemption 04/01/1964
Stock Dividends - 25% 11/20/1958; 25% 01/01/1969
Under plan of merger each share Common $2.50 par exchanged for $45 principal amount of Midwest Rubber Reclaiming Co. 10% Subord. Debentures due 03/01/1998 on 03/16/1978

MIDWEST SVGS BK (BOLINGBROOK, IL)
Merged into Hemlock Federal Financial Corp. 6/9/2000
Each share Common no par exchanged for $16.75 cash

MIDWEST SECS INVT INC (DE)
6% Preferred $25 par called for redemption 11/16/61
Liquidation completed
Each share Common $25 par received initial distribution of $40 cash 12/1/75
Each share Common $25 par received second distribution of $10 cash 3/1/76
Each share Common $25 par received third distribution of $30 cash 4/30/76
Each share Common $25 par exchanged for fourth distribution of $10 cash 8/16/76
Each share Common $25 par received fifth distribution of $2 cash 12/21/78
Each share Common $25 par received sixth distribution of $1 cash 12/18/79
Each share Common $25 par received seventh and final distribution of $1 cash 9/15/80

MIDWEST SECURITIES, INC. (OH)
Reincorporated under the laws of Delaware as Midwest Securities Investment, Inc. 6/15/59
(See Midwest Securities Investment, Inc.)

MIDWEST SPORTS COLLECTIBLES INC (IL)
Recapitalized as Omni Oil & Gas Inc. 07/17/2006
Each share Common $0.001 par exchanged for (0.1) share Common $0.001 par
Omni Oil & Gas Inc. name changed to American Gold Resources Corp. 10/19/2009
(See American Gold Resources Corp.)

MIDWEST TECHNICAL DEVELOPMENT CORP. (MN)
Completely liquidated 2/11/66
Each share Common $1 par received first and final distribution of (1) share Midtex, Inc. Common 10¢ par
Certificates were not retired and are now without value

MIDWEST TELEVISION SYS INC (MN)
Sylvania Electric Products Inc. became sole holder through acquisitions of stock between 00/00/1964 and 00/00/1968
Public interest eliminated

MIDWEST TOOL & MANUFACTURING CO.
Name changed to Sheldrick Manufacturing Co. in 1949
(See Sheldrick Manufacturing Co.)

MIDWEST URANIUM CO. (UT)
Merged into Midwest Consolidated Uranium Corp. on a (0.125) for (1) basis 06/10/1955
Midwest Consolidated Uranium Corp. merged into COG Minerals Corp. 05/01/1956
(See COG Minerals Corp.)

MIDWEST URANIUM CORP (NV)
Old Common $0.001 par split (68) for (1) by issuance of (67) additional shares payable 08/30/2007 to holders of record 08/30/2007
Each share old Common $0.001 par exchanged for (0.01960784) share new Common $0.001 par 03/20/2009
Name changed to American Patriot Corp. 04/15/2009
(See American Patriot Corp.)

MIDWEST VENTURE GROUP INC (DE)
Recapitalized as Automated Vending Technologies, Inc. (DE) 09/28/2005
Each (11) shares Common 1¢ par exchanged for (1) share Common 1¢ par
Automated Vending Technologies, Inc. (DE) reorganized in Nevada as AVT, Inc. 01/17/2008
(See AVT, Inc.)

MIDWEST VENTURE HLDGS INC (NV)
Each share old Common $0.001 par exchanged for (0.02857142) share new Common $0.001 par 08/26/2002

Name changed to Inspiration
Products Group, Inc. 02/03/2003
Inspiration Products Group, Inc. name
changed to M-B Tech, Inc.
05/18/2003
(See M-B Tech, Inc.)

MIDWEST VESSEL CORP.
Liquidation completed in 1944

MIDWESTERN ACCEPTANCE CO., INC. (OK)
Class A Common $1 par reclassified as Common $1 par 7/31/62
Merged into Commercial Finance Co. 1/27/66
Each share Common $1 par exchanged for (1/9) share Common $5 par
Commercial Finance Co. dissolved 10/29/76

MIDWESTERN CAS & SURETY CO (IA)
Name changed to Midwestern Life Insurance Co. 11/30/1983
(See Midwestern Life Insurance Co.)

MIDWESTERN CORP. (OH)
Merged into Midwestern National Life Insurance Co. of Ohio 6/30/66
Each share Common $1 par exchanged for (1) share Common $1.50 par
(See Midwestern National Life Insurance Co. of Ohio)

MIDWESTERN COS (NV)
Chapter 11 Federal Bankruptcy proceedings converted to Chapter 7 on 03/17/1986
Stockholders' equity unlikely

MIDWESTERN COS INC (IN)
Stock Dividends - 10% 12/15/65; 10% 11/22/66; 10% 11/22/67; 10% 11/20/68
Name changed to Transcontinental Motor Inns, Inc. 10/20/70
Transcontinental Motor Inns, Inc. merged into United Inns, Inc. 12/8/72
(See United Inns, Inc.)

MIDWESTERN DISTR INC (KS)
Merged into Leaseway Transportation Corp. 05/12/1982
Each share Class A Common no par exchanged for $14.50 cash

MIDWESTERN EXPRESS, INC. (KS)
Class A Common no par split (2) for (1) by issuance of (1) additional share 2/16/72
Class A Common no par split (2) for (1) by issuance of (1) additional share 10/31/72
Name changed to Midwestern Distribution, Inc. 5/30/73
(See Midwestern Distribution, Inc.)

MIDWESTERN FID CORP (OH)
Stock Dividends - 50% 3/10/78; 50% 5/18/79
Merged into Guardian Royal Exchange Assurance Ltd. 2/5/80
Each share Common $1.66-2/3 par exchanged for $27 cash

MIDWESTERN FINANCIAL CORP. OF KANSAS, INC. (KS)
Liquidation completed
Each share Common 30¢ par exchanged for initial distribution of (0.69860) share ERC Corp. Common $2.50 par 06/06/1974
Each share Common 30¢ par received second and final distribution of (0.00776229) share ERC Corp. Common $2.50 par and $0.126 cash 06/17/1977
(See ERC Corp.)

MIDWESTERN FINL CORP NEW (CO)
Common $2.50 par split (3) for (2) by issuance of (0.5) additional share 3/8/71
Merged into Security Pacific Corp. 5/15/74
Each share Common $2.50 par exchanged for (0.6058) share Common $10 par
Security Pacific Corp. merged into BankAmerica Corp. (Old) 4/22/92 which merged into BankAmerica Corp. (New) 9/30/98 which name changed to Bank of America Corp. 4/28/99

MIDWESTERN FINL CORP OHIO (OH)
Recapitalized as Midwestern Fidelity Corp. 06/14/1971
Each share Common $5 par exchanged for (3) shares Common $1.66-2/3 par
(See Midwestern Fidelity Corp.)

MIDWESTERN FINL CORP OLD (CO)
Common $1 par changed to 50¢ par and (1) additional share issued 6/23/61
Stock Dividend - 50% 4/16/62
Reorganized 3/31/69
Each share Common 50¢ par exchanged for (0.2) share Midwestern Financial Corp. (New) Common $2.50 par and (0.2) share First S & L Shares, Inc. Common $2.50 par
(See each company's listing)

MIDWESTERN FUELS SYS INC (NV)
Name changed to Midwestern Companies, Inc. 05/25/1983
(See Midwestern Companies, Inc.)

MIDWESTERN GAS TRANSMISSION CO (DE)
Merged into Tenneco Inc. 5/31/77
Each share Common $5 par exchanged for (0.75) share Common $5 par
Tenneco Inc. merged into El Paso Natural Gas Co. 12/12/96 which reorganized as El Paso Energy Corp. 8/1/98 which name changed to El Paso Corp. 2/5/2001

MIDWESTERN INDEMNITY CO. (OH)
Stock Dividends - 10% 9/1/59; 10% 12/1/60; 10% 1/15/62; 10% 2/5/64
Thru voluntary exchange offer of (1) share Common $5 par for each share Common $5 par, 100% was acquired by Midwestern Financial Corp. of Ohio as of 11/7/68

MIDWESTERN INSTRUMENTS, INC. (DE)
Completely liquidated 06/11/1962
Each share Common $1 par exchanged for first and final distribution of (0.444444) share Telex, Inc. Common $1 par and (0.444444) share Data Products Corp. Common 10¢ par
(See each company's listing)

MIDWESTERN INVESTMENT CORP. (IN)
Stock Dividend - 10% 2/15/61
Name changed to Midwestern Companies, Inc. 7/30/63
Midwestern Companies, Inc. name changed to Transcontinental Motor Inns, Inc. 10/20/70 which merged into United Inns, Inc. 12/8/72
(See United Inns, Inc.)

MIDWESTERN LIFE INSURANCE CO. (IA)
Administratively dissolved 09/14/1990

MIDWESTERN NATL LIFE INS CO (OH)
Each share Common $1.50 par exchanged for (0.01) share Common $150 par 4/26/77
Merged into MCEquities Corp. 2/20/97
Each share Common $150 par exchanged for $1,379.81 cash

MIDWESTERN OIL & GAS CORP. (ID)
Completely liquidated 3/13/64
Each share Common 5¢ par exchanged for first and final distribution of (0.017) share Coast Exploration Co. Common $1 par Coast Exploration Co. completed liquidation 12/14/66

MIDWESTERN RES INC (OK)
Recapitalized as Potomac Energy Corp. 06/17/1998
Each (41.40846) shares Common $0.001 par exchanged for (1) share Common $0.001 par
(See Potomac Energy Corp.)

MIDWESTERN UTD LIFE INS CO (IN)
Stock Dividends - 20% 04/03/1957; 10% 03/20/1958; 10% 03/19/1959; 20% 05/15/1961; 10% 05/01/1963; 10% 05/07/1964; 10% 05/07/1965; 10% 05/05/1967; 10% 05/03/1968; 10% 06/11/1971; 10% 06/11/1973
Merged into Nationale-Nederlanden N.V. 11/24/1983
Each share Common $1 par exchanged for $16.30 cash

MIDWESTONE FINL GROUP INC OLD (IA)
Merged into MidWestOne Financial Group, Inc. (New) 03/14/2008
Each share Common $5 par exchanged for (0.95) share Common $1 par

MIEHLE GOSS DEXTER INC (DE)
Common $7.50 par changed to $3.75 par and (1) additional share issued 09/15/1964
Common $3.75 par changed to $1.875 par and (1) additional share issued 03/01/1968
Acquired by North American Rockwell Corp. 09/12/1969
Each share Common $1.875 par exchanged for (1) share $1.35 Conv. Preferred Ser. B no par
North American Rockwell Corp. merged into Rockwell International Corp. (Old) 02/16/1973
(See Rockwell International Corp. (Old))

MIEHLE PRINTING PRESS & MANUFACTURING CO. (DE)
Each share Common no par exchanged for (4) shares Class A Common $15 par and (1) share Class B Common $15 par 00/00/1948
Class A Common $15 par and Class B Common $15 par changed to $7.50 par respectively and (1) additional share issued 01/19/1956
Under plan of merger name changed to Miehle-Goss-Dexter, Inc. and Class A Common par and Class B Common $7.50 par reclassified as Common $7.50 par 01/31/1957
Miehle-Goss-Dexter, Inc. acquired by North American Rockwell Corp. 09/12/1969 which merged into Rockwell International Corp. (Old) 02/16/1973
(See Rockwell International Corp. (Old))

MIERACLE CORP (DE)
Reorganized as Akal International Inc. 4/8/92
Each share Common $0.001 par exchanged for (2) shares Common $0.001 par

MIFFLIN MCCAMBRIDGE CO (DE)
Completely liquidated 04/30/1976
Each share Common $1 par exchanged for first and final distribution of $5.50 cash

MIGAO CORP (ON)
Acquired by 2521416 Ontario Inc. 09/09/2016
Each share Common no par exchanged for $0.75 cash
Note: Unexchanged certificates will be cancelled and become without value 09/09/2022

MIGENIX INC (BC)
Plan of arrangement effective 03/19/2010
Each share Common no par exchanged for (0.1) share BioWest Therapeutics Inc. Class A Common no par and (0.02) share Metro Vancouver Properties Corp. Class B Common no par
BioWest Therapeutics Inc. name changed to Carrus Capital Corp. 08/22/2011 which name changed to Global Blockchain Technologies Corp. 10/05/2017

MIGENT SOFTWARE CORP (CANADA)
Reincorporated 3/18/88
Place of incorporation changed from (BC) to (Canada) 3/18/88
Delisted from Vancouver Stock Exchange 10/6/89

MIGHTY BEAUT MINERALS INC (YT)
Reincorporated 08/30/2000
Place of incorporation changed from (BC) to (YT) 08/30/2000
Recapitalized as MBMI Resources Inc. (YT) 12/20/2002
Each (5.5) shares Common no par exchanged for (1) share Common no par
MBMI Resources Inc. (YT) reincorporated in British Columbia 11/15/2005 which reorganized in Ontario 06/22/2012

MIGHTY MACK USA LTD (CO)
Each share old Common no par exchanged for (0.005) share new Common no par 12/23/2005
Name changed to Sao Luis Mining, Inc. (CO) 05/26/2006
Sao Luis Mining, Inc. (CO) reorganized in Nevada as Brazilian Mining Corp. 03/26/2009 which name changed to Sierra Desert Holdings Inc. 10/18/2010 which recapitalized as Telefix Communications Holdings, Inc. 03/12/2012

MIGHTY PWR USA INC (DE)
Recapitalized as Globenet International Inc. 4/17/97
Each share Common $0.001 par exchanged for (0.14285714) share Common $0.001 par
Globenet International Inc. name changed to Royal Bodycare Inc. 10/19/99 which name changed to RBC Life Sciences, Inc. 6/19/2006

MIGHTY STAR LTD (NV)
Name changed to Shao Tong Chuan Health Vegetarian Foods (USA) Holdings Ltd. (NV) 06/13/2003
Shao Tong Chuan Health Vegetarian Foods (USA) Holdings Ltd. (NV) reorganized in Delaware as Standard Commerce, Inc. 01/29/2007 which recapitalized as China Jianye Fuel, Inc. 01/18/2008
(See China Jianye Fuel, Inc.)

MIGO SOFTWARE INC (DE)
Assets foreclosed upon and operations ceased 04/17/2008
Stockholders' equity unlikely

MIGRATEC INC (DE)
Reincorporated 08/11/2000
State of incorporation changed from (FL) to (DE) 08/11/2000
SEC revoked common stock registration 11/18/2005

MIH LTD (BRITISH VIRGIN ISLANDS)
Issue Information - 9,075,000 shares CL A ORD offered at $18 per share on 04/13/1999
Merged into Naspers Ltd. 12/20/2002
Each share Class A Ordinary no par exchanged for (0.35) Sponsored ADR's for Class N

MII (NV)
Recapitalized as Pathfinder Corp. 8/1/90
Each share Capital Stock $0.001 par exchanged for (0.01) share Capital Stock $0.001 par

Pathfinder Corp. name changed to Pegasus Industries Inc. 3/9/95

MIIX GROUP INC (DE)
Issue Information - 3,000,000 shares COM offered at $13.50 per share on 07/30/1999
Plan of reorganization under Chapter 11 Federal Bankruptcy Code effective 02/24/2006
No stockholders' equity

MIJA CORP. (FL)
Proclaimed dissolved for failure to file reports and pay fees 07/11/1972

MIJA MINES LTD (ON)
Charter cancelled for failure to pay taxes and file returns 10/18/1978

MIKA TECHNOLOGY INC (AB)
Merged into Imaging Dynamic Co. Ltd. 11/29/2002
Each share Common no par exchanged for (0.25657924) share Common no par and (0.25657924) Common Stock Purchase Warrant expiring 5/31/2003

MIKADO RES LTD (BC)
Recapitalized as Silver Peak Resources Ltd. 12/02/1994
Each share Common no par exchanged for (1/3) share Common no par
(See Silver Peak Resources Ltd.)

MIKASA INC (DE)
Merged into J.G. Durand Industries, S.A. 1/12/2001
Each share Common 1¢ par exchanged for $16.50 cash

MIKE HENRY CONSOLIDATED INC. (DE)
Charter forfeited for failure to pay taxes 1/23/24

MIKE HENRY OIL CO. (WY)
See - Henry (Mike) Oil Co.

MIKE THE PIKE PRODUCTIONS INC (NV)
Reorganized under the laws of Wyoming 03/03/2011
Each share Common $0.001 par exchanged for (0.01) share Common $0.0001 par

MIKES ORIG INC (DE)
Recapitalized as New Yorker Marketing Corp. 02/26/1999
Each share Common $0.001 par exchanged for (0.2) share Common $0.001 par
(See New Yorker Marketing Corp.)

MIKES RESTAURANTS INC (ON)
Acquired by Pizza Delight Corp. 12/21/2000
Each share Common no par exchanged for $4.35 cash

MIKES SUBMARINES INC (ON)
Name changed to M-Corp Inc. 8/1/85
M-Corp Inc. name changed to Mikes Restaurants Inc. 12/8/98
(See Mikes Restaurants Inc.)

MIKOHN GAMING CORP (NV)
Name changed to Progressive Gaming International Corp. 04/03/2006
(See Progressive Gaming International Corp.)

MIKOJO INC (DE)
SEC revoked common stock registration 10/27/2015

MIKOTEL NETWORKS INC (ON)
Recapitalized as Wabi Exploration Inc. 3/4/2005
Each share Common no par exchanged for (0.5) share Common no par

MIKRON INFRARED INC (NJ)
Name changed 6/11/2002
Common 1¢ par split (2) for (1) by issuance of (1) additional share 10/20/89
Name changed from Mikron Instrument Co., Inc. to Mikron Infrared, Inc. 6/11/2002
Acquired by LumaSense Technologies, Inc. 5/7/2007
Each share Common 1¢ par exchanged for $11.50 cash

MIL-CENT BUILDING, INC.
Liquidated 00/00/1945
Details not available

MILACRON INC (DE)
Common $1 par changed to 1¢ par 06/09/2004
Each share old 4% Preferred $100 par exchanged for (0.1) share new 4% Preferred $100 par 05/16/2007
Each share old Common 1¢ par exchanged for (0.1) share new Common 1¢ par 05/16/2007
Assets sold for the benefit of creditors 06/30/2009
No stockholders' equity

MILADO MINES (1957) LTD. (QC)
Charter annulled for failure to file annual reports 4/30/77

MILAGRO ENERGY INC (AB)
Acquired by Second Wave Petroleum Inc. 08/29/2008
Each share Common no par exchanged for (0.0298) share Common no par and (0.0298) Common Stock Purchase Warrant expiring 08/28/2009
(See Second Wave Petroleum Inc.)

MILAGRO HLDGS INC (NY)
SEC revoked common stock registration 03/27/2007

MILAGRO MINERALS INC (BC)
Recapitalized as Geomaque Explorations Ltd./Explorations Geomaque Ltee. 01/10/1997
Each share Common no par exchanged for (0.25) share Common no par
Geomaque Explorations Ltd./Explorations Geomaque Ltee. merged into Defiance Mining Corp. 06/25/2003 which merged into Rio Narcea Gold Mines, Ltd. 09/03/2004
(See Rio Narcea Gold Mines, Ltd.)

MILAM PROPERTIES, INC.
Property sold 00/00/1943
Details not available

MILAN RES & EXPLS LTD (BC)
Recapitalized as Golden Bear Minerals Inc. 7/9/92
Each share Common no par exchanged for (0.25) share Common no par
Golden Bear Minerals Inc. recapitalized as West Coast Forest Products Ltd. 5/21/93

MILANO ASSICURAZIONI (ITALY)
ADR agreement terminated 02/10/2014
No ADR's remain outstanding

MILASTAR CORP (DE)
Common 5¢ par reclassified as Class A Common 5¢ par 09/15/1988
Class A Common 5¢ par split (4) for (3) by issuance of (1/3) additional share 04/01/1991
Merged into Easton Southpaw Inc. 07/30/2007
Each share Class A Common 5¢ par exchanged for $3.50 cash

MILBROOK FINL CORP (DE)
Charter cancelled and declared inoperative and void for non-payment of taxes 03/01/1992

MILBURN INDS INC (DE)
Charter cancelled and declared inoperative and void for non-payment of taxes 04/15/1973

MILBURN MNG CO (NY)
Merged into Milburn Industries, Inc. 07/22/1970
Each share Common 2¢ par exchanged for (1) share Common 1¢ par
(See Milburn Industries, Inc.)

MILE 18 MINES LTD (ON)
Charter cancelled for failure to file reports and pay taxes 11/04/1970

MILE HIGH KENNEL CLUB (CO)
Acquired by MHKC Mergerco, Inc. 07/29/1991
Each share Class A Common $1 par exchanged for $26 cash
Each share Class B Common $1 par exchanged for $31 cash

MILE HIGH OIL CO. (CO)
Each share Common $0.001 par exchanged for (0.1) share Common 1¢ par 00/00/1956
Name changed to U.S. Beryllium Corp. 09/14/1959
(See U.S. Beryllium Corp.)

MILE MARKER INTL INC (FL)
Reincorporated 11/22/2000
State of incorporation changed from (NY) to (FL) 11/22/2000
Each share old Common 1¢ par exchanged for (1) share new Common 1¢ par to reflect a (1) for (15) reverse split followed by a (15) for (1) forward split 07/09/2003
Note: Holders of (14) or fewer pre-split shares received approximately $0.81 cash per share
Chapter 11 bankruptcy proceedings terminated 02/13/2015
No stockholders' equity

MILES-DETROIT THEATRE
Name changed to Griswold Building, Inc. 00/00/1944
(See Griswold Building, Inc.)

MILES HOMES INC (DE)
Name changed to DeGeorge Financial Corp. 11/08/1996
DeGeorge Financial Corp. acquired by American Home Partners Inc. 03/15/2001

MILES LABS INC (IN)
Common $2 par split (3) for (1) by issuance of (2) additional shares 2/2/62
4-1/2% Preferred $25 par called for redemption 6/28/63
Merged into Rhinechem Laboratories, Inc. 2/8/79
Each share Common $2 par exchanged for $47 cash

MILES RED LAKE MINES LTD (ON)
Merged into Antelope Resources Inc. 02/28/1989
Each share Capital Stock $1 par exchanged for (0.5) share Common no par
(See Antelope Resources Inc.)

MILES SHOES, INC. (NY)
Merged into Melville Shoe Corp. in 1952
Each share 4-3/4% Preferred $100 par exchanged for (1) share $4.75 Preferred A $100 par
Each share Common $1 par exchanged for (1) share new Common $1 par

MILESTONE APTS REAL ESTATE INVT TR (ON)
Trust terminated 04/28/2017
Each Unit received USD$16.30041 cash

MILESTONE CAP INC (CO)
Reorganized under the laws of Delaware as Telestone Technologies Corp. 08/26/2004
Each share Common no par exchanged for (0.00121654) share Common $0.001 par
(See Telestone Technologies Corp.)

MILESTONE EXPL LTD (ON)
Merged into Jubilee Gold Inc. 01/01/2010
Each share Common no par exchanged for (1.749) shares Common no par
Jubilee Gold Inc. merged into Jubilee Gold Exploration Ltd. 01/25/2013

MILESTONE INTL CORP (NV)
Name changed to HashingSpace Corp. 06/15/2015
(See HashingSpace Corp.)

MILESTONE MINES LTD. (ON)
Merged into Milestone Exploration Ltd. 07/23/1968
Each share Capital Stock $1 par exchanged for (0.038520) share Capital Stock no par
Milestone Exploration Ltd. merged into Jubilee Gold Inc. 01/01/2010 which merged into Jubilee Gold Exploration Ltd. 01/25/2013

MILESTONE MINES LTD (BC)
Acquired by Cairn Petroleums Ltd. 05/08/1975
Each share Capital Stock no par exchanged for (0.5) share Common 50¢ par
(See Cairn Petroleums Ltd.)

MILESTONE PPTYS INC (DE)
Each share $0.78 Conv. Preferred Ser. A 1¢ par exchanged for $3 cash 03/05/1999
Merged into Concord Assets Group, Inc. 08/08/2001
Each share new $0.78 Conv. Preferred Ser. A 1¢ par exchanged for $2.91 cash
Each share Common 1¢ par exchanged for $2.65 cash

MILESTONE RESOURCE CORP (ON)
Reorganized as Horizontal Petroleum Exploration Ltd. 07/26/1990
Each share Common no par exchanged for (0.2) share Common no par
15% Preference $5 par was not affected except for change of name
(See Horizontal Petroleum Exploration Ltd.)

MILFORD CO OPERATIVE BK (MILFORD, NH)
Merged into CFX Corp. 07/01/1996
Each share Common $1 par exchanged for (2.6446) shares Common $0.66-2/3 par
CFX Corp. merged into Peoples Heritage Financial Group, Inc. 04/10/1998 which name changed to Banknorth Group, Inc. (ME) 05/10/2000 which merged into TD Banknorth Inc. 03/01/2005
(See TD Banknorth Inc.)

MILGATE MINES LTD. (ON)
Merged into Alchib Developments Ltd. 07/10/1969
Each share Capital Stock $1 par exchanged for (0.4) share Capital Stock no par
Alchib Developments Ltd. merged into Kalrock Developments Ltd. 10/23/1978 which merged into Kalrock Resources Ltd. 08/08/1990 which merged into Cercal Minerals Corp. 07/09/1993
(See Cercal Minerals Corp.)

MILGER INVT & DEV LTD (ON)
Charter cancelled for failure to pay taxes and file returns 11/29/1982

MILGO ELECTR CORP (FL)
Common $1 par split (2) for (1) by issuance of (1) additional share 4/13/70
Stock Dividend - 75% 2/7/59
Merged into Racal Electronics Ltd. 8/11/77
Each share Common $1 par exchanged for $36 cash

MILGRAY ELECTRS INC (NY)
Common 25¢ par split (2) for (1) by issuance of (1) additional share 6/14/93
Common 25¢ par split (2) for (1) by

issuance of (1) additional share 9/23/94
Common 25¢ par split (2) for (1) by issuance of (1) additional share payable 10/19/95 to holders of record 9/28/95
Merged into Bell Industries, Inc. 1/15/97
Each share Common 25¢ par exchanged for $14.77 cash

MILGRIM (H.) & BROS., INC. (NY)
Proclaimed dissolved for non-compliance with corporation laws 12/16/63

MILINX BUSINESS GROUP INC (DE)
Name changed 04/13/2000
Name changed from Milinx Marketing Group Inc. to Milinx Business Group, Inc. 04/13/2000
SEC revoked preferred and common stock registration 10/15/2008

MILITARY COMMUNICATIONS TECHNOLOGIES INC (DE)
Each share old Common $0.001 par exchanged for (0.0005) share new Common $0.001 par 5/31/2006
Name changed to Carbon Race Corp. 10/16/2006

MILITARY INTL LTD (AB)
Cease trade order 02/21/2003

MILITARY PUBLISHING INSTITUTE, INC. (NY)
Dissolved 3/5/63
No stockholders' equity

MILITARY PUR SYS INC (NY)
Name changed to MPS International Corp. 10/29/1971
(See MPS International Corp.)

MILITARY RESALE GROUP INC (NY)
SEC revoked common stock registration 04/08/2010

MILK CAP CORP (BC)
Name changed to Prescient Mining Corp. 09/08/2010
Prescient Mining Corp. name changed to Aurora Cannabis Inc. 12/16/2014

MILKYWAY NETWORKS CORP (CANADA)
Merged into SLM Software Inc. 10/1/98
Each share Common no par exchanged for (0.0711740) share Common no par and $0.80 cash
SLM Software Inc. recapitalized as Slmsoft.Com Inc. 7/23/99 which name changed to SLMsoft Inc. 6/14/2002

MILL ALL CO. (IL)
Involuntarily dissolved for failure to pay taxes 12/22/61

MILL BASIN TECHNOLOGIES LTD (NV)
Name changed to Huiheng Medical, Inc. 10/02/2007
(See Huiheng Medical, Inc.)

MILL BAY VENTURES INC (BC)
Each share old Common no par exchanged for (0.1) share new Common no par 06/17/2010
Recapitalized as Great Thunder Gold Corp. 04/16/2013
Each share Common no par exchanged for (0.33333333) share Common no par

MILL CITY GOLD CORP (BC)
Each share old Common no par exchanged for (0.05882352) share new Common no par 06/10/2013
New Common no par split (2) for (1) by issuance of (1) additional share payable 09/03/2014 to holders of record 09/03/2014 Ex date - 08/29/2014
Name changed to FPS Pharma Inc. 09/10/2015

MILL CITY INTL CORP (AB)
Plan of arrangement effective 09/01/2004
Each share Common no par exchanged for (1) share Mill City Gold Corp. Common no par
Note: Holders of (499) or fewer shares will receive $0.20 cash per share after 10/01/2004
Cash payments of less than $10 will not be made
Unexchanged certificates were cancelled and became without value 09/01/2010
Mill City Gold Corp. name changed to FPS Pharma Inc. 09/10/2015

MILL CITY INTL INC (CANADA)
Reorganized 12/14/88
Name changed 1/8/98
Reorganized from Mill City Gold Inc. to Mill City Gold Mining Corp. 12/14/88
Each share Common no par exchanged for (0.1) share Common no par
Name changed from Mill City Gold Mining Corp. to Mill City International Inc. 1/8/98
Recapitalized as E3 Energy Inc. 12/23/2002
Each (12) shares new Common no par exchanged for (1) share Common no par
(See E3 Energy Inc.)

MILL CITY OILS LTD.
Acquired by Mill City Petroleums Ltd. in 1929
Mill City Petroleums Ltd. liquidated for Pan Ocean Oil Corp. 1/1/72
(See Pan Ocean Oil Corp.)

MILL CITY PETES LTD (CANADA)
Each share Common $1 par exchanged for (4) shares Common no par 00/00/1929
Completely liquidated 01/01/1972
Each share Common no par exchanged for first and final distribution of (0.193) share Pan Ocean Oil Corp. Common 1¢ par
(See Pan Ocean Oil Corp.)

MILL CREEK & MINE HILL NAVIGATION & RAILROAD CO.
Merged into Reading Co. 2/28/50
Each share Capital Stock exchanged for (1.25) shares 1st Preferred $50 par
Reading Co. merged into Reading Entertainment Inc. (DE) 10/15/96 which reincorporated in Nevada 12/29/99 which merged into Reading International, Inc. 12/31/2001

MILL FACTORS CORP (DE)
Each share Class A $50 par or Class B $50 par exchanged for (20) shares Common $2.50 par 04/05/1960
Liquidation completed
Each share Common $2.50 par exchanged for initial distribution of (1.501153) shares Talcott (James), Inc. Jr. Preferred Ser. A, 50¢ par 07/29/1971
Each share Common $2.50 par received second and final distribution of $0.27 cash 12/30/1971
(See Talcott (James), Inc.)

MILL-ROCK MINES, LTD. (ON)
Charter cancelled and declared dissolved for failure to file returns and pay fees in March 1976

MILLAGRO INTL CORP (TX)
Name changed to Telatinos Inc. 11/08/2004
Telatinos Inc. name changed to Netco Investments, Inc. 11/04/2020
(See Netco Investments, Inc.)

MILLBREN COPPER MINES LTD. (ON)
Charter cancelled and company declared dissolved by default 10/7/57

MILLBROOK PRESS INC (DE)
Plan of reorganization under Chapter 11 Federal Bankruptcy Code effective 02/07/2005
Each share Common 1¢ par received $0.464 cash payable 12/02/2005 to holders of record 10/31/2005
Name changed to MPLC, Inc. 08/16/2006
MPLC, Inc. recapitalized as New Motion, Inc. 05/03/2007 which name changed to Atrinsic, Inc. 06/26/2009 which recapitalized as Protagenic Therapeutics, Inc. 07/27/2016

MILLBURN SHORT HILLS BK (MILLBURN, NJ)
Merged into Midlantic Banks Inc. 03/31/1974
Each share Capital Stock $10 par exchanged for (0.583) share Common $10 par
Midlantic Banks Inc. merged into Midlantic Corp. 01/30/1987 which merged into PNC Bank Corp. 12/31/1995 which name changed to PNC Financial Services Group, Inc. 03/15/2000

MILLCREST PRODS CORP (NY)
Reincorporated under the laws of Delaware as Vestro Foods Inc. and Common 10¢ par changed to 1¢ par 7/14/87
Vestro Foods Inc. name changed to Vestro Natural Foods Inc. 7/12/94 which name changed to Westbrae Natural Inc. 7/7/97
(See Westbrae Natural Inc.)

MILLDALE MINERALS LTD. (ON)
Charter cancelled and company declared dissolved for failure to file returns 8/24/64

MILLDALE URANIUM MINES LTD. (ON)
Name changed to Milldale Minerals Ltd. 6/30/60
(See Milldale Minerals Ltd.)

MILLE LACS INDS INC (MN)
Name changed to MLI, Inc. 03/30/1973
MLI, Inc. name changed to EDP of California Inc. 03/02/1990
(See EDP of California Inc.)

MILLEA HLDGS INC (JAPAN)
ADR's for Common split (5) for (2) by by issuance of (1.5) additional ADR's payable 10/12/2006 to holders of record 09/28/2006 Ex date - 10/13/2006
Name changed to Tokio Marine Holdings, Inc. 07/01/2008

MILLENIA CORP (NV)
Each share old Common $0.001 par exchanged for (0.05) share new Common $0.001 par 11/29/1997
Name changed to Internet Multi-Media Corp. 01/25/2000
Internet Multi-Media Corp. recapitalized as AmEurotech Corp. (NV) 12/18/2000 which reincorporated in Florida 04/18/2007 which recapitalized as Scott Contracting Holdings, Inc. 07/11/2007 and name changed to Liverpool Group, Inc. 04/29/2008

MILLENIA HOPE INC (DE)
Each share old Common $0.0001 par exchanged for (0.14285714) share new Common $0.0001 par 11/09/2009
SEC revoked common stock registration 09/18/2013

MILLENIUM BIOLOGIX CORP (CANADA)
Placed in receivership and all officers resigned 05/08/2007
Stockholders' equity unlikely

MILLENIUM CELLULAR INC (NV)
Name changed to Thrive Development Inc. 1/28/2002
Thrive Development Inc. name changed to Green Parts International, Inc. 5/25/2005

MILLENIUM HLDG GROUP INC (NV)
Old Common $1 par split (5) for (1) by issuance of (4) additional shares payable 03/20/2000 to holders of record 03/13/2000
Each share new Common $1 par received distribution of (0.063298) share Pacific First Corp. Restricted Common payable 12/21/2007 to holders of record 12/14/2007
SEC revoked common stock registration 01/17/2014

MILLENIUM ISTEC INC (NV)
Each share old Common $0.001 par exchanged for (0.01) share new Common $0.001 par 06/24/2000
Charter revoked for failure to file reports and pay fees 03/31/2008

MILLENIUM QUEST INC (DE)
Recapitalized as American Lorain Corp. (DE) 07/25/2007
Each shares Common $0.001 par exchanged for (0.03045066) share Common $0.001 par
American Lorain Corp. (DE) reincorporated in Nevada 11/09/2009 which recapitalized as Planet Green Holdings Corp. 10/01/2018

MILLENNIA FOODS INC (AB)
Struck from the register 12/1/95

MILLENNIA INC (NV)
Reincorporated 02/23/2005
Each share Common $0.000025 par received distribution of (0.25) share Omni Doors, Inc. Common no par payable 04/22/1998 to holders of record 04/17/1998 Ex date - 04/23/1998
Each share Common $0.000025 par exchanged for (0.01) share Common $0.0002 par 11/27/1998
State of incorporation changed from (DE) to (NV) and Common $0.0002 par changed to $0.001 par 02/23/2005
Common $0.001 par split (3) for (1) by issuance of (2) additional shares payable 11/15/2007 to holders of record 11/12/2007 Ex date - 11/16/2007
Name changed to Bonamour Pacific, Inc. 08/11/2011
Bonamour Pacific, Inc. name changed to TexStar Oil Corp. 12/03/2012

MILLENNIA TEA MASTERS INC (TX)
Name changed to VoIP, Inc. 04/15/2004
(See VoIP, Inc.)

MILLENNIAL MEDIA INC (DE)
Acquired by AOL Inc. 10/23/2015
Each share Common $0.001 par exchanged for $1.75 cash

MILLENNIUM & COPTHORNE HOTELS PLC (UNITED KINGDOM)
ADR agreement terminated 3/19/2004
Each Sponsored ADR for Ordinary 25p par exchanged for (4) Ordinary Shares
Each 144A Sponsored ADR for Ordinary exchanged for (4) Ordinary Shares

MILLENNIUM BK (MALVERN, PA)
Merged into Harleysville National Corp. 04/30/2004
Each share Common no par exchanged for (0.402744) share Common $1 par and $5.69962 cash
Harleysville National Corp. merged into First Niagara Financial Group, Inc. (New) 04/09/2010 which merged into KeyCorp (New) 08/01/2016

**MILLENNIUM BK
(SAN FRANCISCO, CA)**
Merged into First Banks America, Inc. 12/29/2000
Each share Common no par exchanged for $8.10 cash

MILLENNIUM BIOTECHNOLOGIES GROUP INC (DE)
Name changed to Inergetics, Inc. 05/06/2010

MILLENNIUM BROADCAST CORP (DE)
Recapitalized as Diversified Media Holdings Inc. 3/13/2003
Each share Common 1¢ par exchanged for (0.02) share Common 1¢ par
Diversified Media Holdings Inc. recapitalized as TPI International, Inc. 1/3/2006

MILLENNIUM CELL INC (DE)
Chapter 7 bankruptcy proceedings terminated 06/24/2014
No stockholders' equity

MILLENNIUM CHEMICALS INC (DE)
Merged into Lyondell Chemical Co. 12/01/2004
Each share Common 1¢ par exchanged for (0.95) share Common $1 par
(See Lyondell Chemical Co.)

MILLENNIUM COMMUNICATIONS INC (AB)
Recapitalized as Strategy Web Communications Inc. 3/31/2000
Each share Common no par exchanged for (1/6) share Common no par

MILLENNIUM DIRECT INC (DE)
Each share old Common $0.0001 par exchanged for (0.0833333) share new Common $0.0001 par 07/23/2000
New Common $0.0001 par split (2) for (1) by issuance of (1) additional share payable 03/05/2001 to holders of record 02/26/2001 Ex date - 03/06/2001
Recapitalized as Viyon Corp. 05/17/2004
Each share new Common $0.0001 par exchanged for (0.01) share Common $0.0001 par
Viyon Corp. name changed to First Guardian Financial Corp. 07/22/2005 which name changed to New Capital Funding Corp. 05/07/2007 which recapitalized as Ulysses Holding Corp. 10/29/2007 which name changed to Ulysses Diversified Holdings Corp. 05/08/2008 which name changed to JNS Holdings Corp. 02/16/2012

MILLENNIUM ELECTRONICS INC (NV)
Reorganized under the laws of Utah as Speaking Roses International, Inc. 2/17/2004
Each (16.859) shares Common $0.001 par exchanged for (1) share Common $0.001 par

MILLENNIUM ENERGY CORP (NV)
SEC revoked common stock registration 06/17/2013

MILLENNIUM ENERGY INC (AB)
Recapitalized as Bear Creek Energy Ltd. 7/24/2003
Each (15) shares Common no par exchanged for (1) share Common no par
(See Bear Creek Energy Ltd.)

MILLENNIUM GOLD CORP (NV)
Name changed to Prairie Oil & Gas Inc. 04/01/2005
Prairie Oil & Gas Inc. recapitalized as Prairie Energy Inc. 07/10/2007
(See Prairie Energy Inc.)

MILLENNIUM GROUP HLDGS INC (DE)
Each (35) shares old Common $0.001 par exchanged for (1) share new Common $0.001 par 03/25/1999
Each share new Common $0.001 par exchanged again for (0.5) share new Common $0.001 par 11/07/2000
Recapitalized as Ronn Motor Co. 04/22/2008
Each (900) shares Common $0.001 par exchanged for (1) share Common $0.001 par
Ronn Motor Co. recapitalized as Vydrotech, Inc. 04/02/2012

MILLENNIUM INDIA ACQUISITION CO INC (DE)
Units separated 08/05/2010
Name changed to Millennium Investment & Acquisition Co. Inc. 03/04/2015

MILLENNIUM MULTI MEDIA COM CORP (UT)
Name changed to Voxcorp Inc. 02/13/2002

MILLENNIUM NATL EVENTS INC (NV)
Recapitalized as Extensions, Inc. 08/24/2007
Each share Common $0.001 par exchanged for (0.001) share Common $0.001 par
(See Extensions, Inc.)

MILLENNIUM PHARMACEUTICALS INC (DE)
Common $0.001 par split (2) for (1) by issuance of (1) additional share payable 04/18/2000 to holders of record 03/28/2000
Common $0.001 par split (2) for (1) by issuance of (1) additional share payable 10/18/2000 to holders of record 09/27/2000
Acquired by Takeda Pharmaceutical Co. Ltd. 05/14/2008
Each share Common $0.001 par exchanged for $25 cash

MILLENNIUM PLASTICS CORP (NV)
Recapitalized as EnerJex Resources, Inc. 08/16/2006
Each share Common $0.001 par exchanged for (0.00394555) share Common $0.001 par
EnerJex Resources, Inc. recapitalized as AgEagle Aerial Systems, Inc. 03/27/2018

MILLENNIUM PROGRESS FD INC (UKRAINE)
GDR agreement terminated 01/23/2015
No GDR's remain outstanding

MILLENNIUM RES INC (BC)
Recapitalized as Calais Resources Inc. 03/19/1992
Each share Common no par exchanged for (0.2) share Common no par
(See Calais Resources Inc.)

MILLENNIUM SOFTWARE INC (NV)
SEC revoked common stock registration 10/14/2010
Stockholders' equity unlikely

MILLENNIUM SPORTS MGMT INC (NJ)
Each share old Common no par exchanged for (0.1) share new Common no par 01/04/1999
Completely liquidated
Each share new Common no par received first and final distribution of $0.3922918 cash payable 01/29/2014 to holders of record 01/28/2014

MILLENNIUM VENTURES LTD (BC)
Acquired by Verb Exchange Inc. 06/24/2003
Each share Common no par exchanged for (0.49) share Common no par
Verb Exchange Inc. recapitalized as Seymour Ventures Corp. 07/05/2010 which name changed to Rare Earth Industries Ltd. 07/13/2011 which recapitalized as Ackroo Inc. 10/10/2012

MILLEPEDE INTL LTD (AUSTRALIA)
ADR agreement terminated 12/12/2012
No ADR's remain outstanding

MILLER (G.E.) & CO. (TX)
Completely liquidated 9/10/63
Each share Common $5 par exchanged for first and final distribution of (1) share Radio KPCN, Inc. Capital Stock $1 par; (1) share Radio KBUY, Inc. Capital Stock $1 par; (1.5) shares Legal Security Life Insurance Co. Capital Stock no par and (1) share Gemco, Inc. Capital Stock $1 par
(See each company's listing)

MILLER & HART, INC. (DE)
Each share $3.50 Preference no par exchanged for (1) share $2 Preference $24 par which could be retained with rights to unpaid dividends or exchanged for (2) shares $1 Prior Preferred $10 par and (4) shares Common Vtg. Tr. Ctfs. $1 par in 1941
Each share Common no par exchanged for (1) share Common $1 par in 1941
Merged into Mount Vernon Co. 10/13/55
Each share $1 Prior Preferred exchanged for (2) shares $0.50 Preferred $5 par and (0.5) share Common $1 par
Each share Common $1 par exchanged for (1) share new Common $1 par
(See Mount Vernon Co.)

MILLER & RHOADS, INC. (VA)
Each share Common $100 par exchanged for (5) shares Common $20 par 03/14/1955
Completely liquidated 10/02/1967
Each share 4-3/4% Preferred $100 par exchanged for first and final distribution of (1) share Garfinckel (Julius) & Co., Inc. $5.75 Preference Ser. A $5 par
Each share Common $20 par exchanged for first and final distribution of (3) shares Garfinckel (Julius) & Co., Inc. Common 50¢ par
Garfinckel (Julius) & Co., Inc. name changed to Garfinckel, Brooks Brothers, Miller & Rhoads, Inc. 12/05/1967
(See Garfinckel, Brooks Brothers, Miller & Rhoads, Inc.)

MILLER (I.) & SONS, INC. (NY)
Acquired by General Shoe Corp. for cash 9/10/54

MILLER & VAN WINKLE CO (NJ)
Charter declared void for non-payment of taxes 2/8/71

MILLER APARTMENTS, INC. (IL)
Liquidation completed 6/24/60

MILLER BLDG SYS INC (DE)
Merged into Coachmen Industries, Inc. 11/1/2000
Each share Common 1¢ par exchanged for $8.40 cash
Note: Each share Common 1¢ par received an additional distribution of $0.079 cash 11/18/2004

MILLER BOX & LUMBER CO.
Out of business 00/00/1927
Stockholders' equity unlikely

MILLER BROS HAT INC (NY)
Name changed to Miller Bros. Industries, Inc. 04/01/1971
(See Miller Bros. Industries, Inc.)

MILLER BROS INDS INC (NY)
Common $1 par split (4) for (3) by issuance of (1/3) additional share 4/15/71
Merged into Miller Bros. Holdings, Inc. 7/31/84
Each share Common $1 par exchanged for $9 cash

MILLER COPPER MINES, LTD. (QC)
Acquired by New Miller Copper Mines, Ltd. on a (1) for (6) basis 7/6/61
New Miller Copper Mines, Ltd. name changed to New Miller Pipe Lines & Mining Exploration Ltd. 12/2/63 which name changed to Consolidated Miller Mining Co. Ltd. in 1981

MILLER DIVERSIFIED CORP (NV)
Each share Common $0.001 par exchanged for (10) shares Common $0.0001 par 12/19/1988
Each share Common $0.0001 par exchanged for (0.004) share Common $0.001 par 01/24/1990
Recapitalized as Vapor Corp. (NV) 02/10/2010
Each share Common $0.001 par exchanged for (0.4) share Common $0.001 par
Vapor Corp. (NV) reorganized in Delaware 12/27/2013 which name changed to Healthier Choices Management Corp. 03/06/2017

MILLER ED & COMMUNICATIONS CORP (AZ)
Name changed to Miller Technology & Communications Corp. 03/27/1981
Miller Technology & Communications Corp. name changed to Hospitality Capital Corp. 03/31/1987 which name changed to International Environmental Corp. 07/02/1991 which recapitalized as International Fibercom, Inc. 06/06/1994
(See International Fibercom, Inc.)

MILLER ENERGY RES INC (TN)
Plan of reorganization under Chapter 11 Federal Bankrutpcy proceedings effective 03/29/2016
No stockholders' equity

MILLER ESTHER CREATIONS INC (NY)
Adjudicated bankrupt 11/10/1976
Stockholders' equity unlikely

MILLER EXPL CO (DE)
Issue Information - 5,750,000 shares COM offered at $8 per share on 02/04/1998
Each share old Common 1¢ par exchanged for (0.1) share new Common 1¢ par 10/11/2002
Merged into Edge Petroleum Corp. 12/04/2003
Each share new Common 1¢ par exchanged for (1.22342) shares Common 1¢ par
(See Edge Petroleum Corp.)

MILLER FLORENCE COSMETICS INC (TX)
Charter forfeited for failure to pay taxes 03/19/1979

MILLER H & SONS INC (FL)
Common 1¢ par split (2) for (1) by issuance of (1) additional share 3/22/83
Acquired by Lennar Corp. 10/31/84
Each share Common 1¢ par exchanged for $24 cash

MILLER HENRY S RLTY TR (MA)
In process of liquidation
Each Share of Bene. Int. $1 par received initial distribution of $20.30 cash 01/11/1983
Each Share of Bene. Int. $1 par received second distribution of $0.50 cash 03/24/1983
Each Share of Bene. Int. $1 par received third distribution of $6 cash 08/03/1983
Assets transferred to Bryan Street Trust 09/22/1983

Each Share of Bene. Int. $1 par exchanged for (1) Non-Negotiable Receipt
(See Bryan Street Trust)

MILLER HERMAN INC (DE)
Common 20¢ par split (2) for (1) by issuance of (1) additional share 10/31/81
Stock Dividends - 25% 12/31/76; 25% 12/27/77; 25% 12/31/79
Reincorporated under the laws of Michigan 10/31/81

MILLER HILL MNG CO (UT)
Charter expired 07/11/2001

MILLER-LORRAIN MINES LTD. (ON)
Charter cancelled for failure to pay taxes and file returns 5/6/80

MILLER MANUFACTURING CO. (MI)
Conv. Class A Preferred called for redemption 08/15/1963
Name changed to Rellim Liquidating Co. 12/21/1964
(See Rellim Liquidating Co.)

MILLER (C.R.) MANUFACTURING CO.
Property sold 00/00/1929
Details not available

MILLER MED ELECTRS INC (AZ)
Charter revoked for failure to file reports or pay fees 08/10/1983

MILLER-MORGAN GARAGE CO. (IL)
Liquidation completed 2/6/57

MILLER OIL CO (CO)
Recapitalized as Mexco Energy Corp. 04/30/1980
Each share Capital Stock 1¢ par exchanged for (0.02) share Common 50¢ par

MILLER PETE INC (TN)
Name changed to Miller Energy Resources, Inc. 04/12/2011
(See Miller Energy Resources, Inc.)

MILLER PETER APPAREL GROUP INC (ON)
Name changed to PMG Financial Inc. 06/23/1989
PMG Financial Inc. name changed to Printera Corp. 05/08/1996
(See Printera Corp.)

MILLER PYRCZ PETROLEUMS LTD. (AB)
Merged into Campo United Petroleums Ltd. on a (4) for (13) basis 00/00/1952
(See Campo United Petroleums Ltd.)

MILLER RUBBER CO.
Acquired by Goodrich (B.F.) Co. 00/00/1930
Details not available

MILLER SHOE INDS INC (DE)
Recapitalized as Apparel America Inc. 1/11/89
Each share Common 10¢ par exchanged for (0.2) share Common 5¢ par
(See Apparel America Inc.)

MILLER SIGNAL CO. (IL)
Proclaimed dissolved for failure to pay taxes and file reports 11/17/1920

MILLER (I.) SONS CO., INC. (DE)
Merged into Miller (I.) & Sons, Inc. (New York) share for share in 1947 which was acquired by General Shoe Corp. for cash 9/10/54

MILLER TECHNOLOGY & COMMUNICATIONS CORP (AZ)
Name changed to Hospitality Capital Corp. 03/31/1987
Hospitality Capital Corp. name changed to International Environmental Corp. 07/02/1991 which recapitalized as International Fibercom, Inc. 06/06/1994
(See International Fibercom, Inc.)

MILLER TOOL & MANUFACTURING CO.
Name changed to Miller Manufacturing Co. 00/00/1944
Miller Manufacturing Co. name changed to Rellim Liquidating Co. 12/21/1964
(See Rellim Liquidating Co.)

MILLER WHOLESALE DRUG CO. (OH)
Acquired by American Home Products Corp. on a (0.415) for (1) basis 12/01/1941
American Home Products Corp. name changed to Wyeth 03/11/2002 which was acquired by Pfizer Inc. 10/15/2009

MILLER WOHL INC (DE)
Each share Common $1 par exchanged for (2) shares Common 50¢ par in 1946
5% Conv. Preferred $50 par called for redemption 5/1/46
4-1/2% Conv. Preferred $50 par called for redemption 5/1/75
Common 50¢ par split (2) for (1) by issuance of (1) additional share 9/29/75
Common 50¢ par split (2) for (1) by issuance of (1) additional share 6/30/76
Common 50¢ par split (2) for (1) by issuance of (1) additional share 1/3/78
Common 50¢ par split (2) for (1) by issuance of (1) additional share 8/10/83
Merged into Petrie Stores Corp. 7/30/84
Each share Common 50¢ par exchanged for $21 cash

MILLERFIELDS SILVER CORP. LTD. (ON)
Charter cancelled and declared dissolved for failure to file returns and pay fees 8/20/75

MILLERS COVE RES INC (ON)
Cease trade order effective 7/11/90
Stockholders' equity unlikely

MILLERS FALLS CO. (MA)
Common no par changed to $16 par 00/00/1953
Common $16 par changed to $8 par and (1) additional share issued 12/21/1955
Merged into Ingersoll-Rand Co. (NJ) on a (1) for (3.4) basis 07/17/1962
Ingersoll-Rand Co. (NJ) reorganized in Bermuda as Ingersoll-Rand Co. Ltd. 12/31/2001 which reincorporated in Ireland as Ingersoll-Rand PLC 07/01/2009

MILLERS INTL INC (OR)
Name changed to Agri-Seal, Inc. 8/10/83
Agri-Seal, Inc. name changed to Mega Gold, Inc. 11/6/86 which recapitalized as Gold Dome Mining Co. 7/11/88 which name changed to American Development Corp. 4/17/91
(See American Development Corp.)

MILLERS ROGER KING OF THE RD ENTERPRISES INC (TN)
Name changed to King of the Road Enterprises, Inc. 04/25/1973
(See King of the Road Enterprises, Inc.)

MILLFELD TRADING INC (DE)
Recapitalized as Candie's Inc. 2/23/93
Each (4.5) shares Common 1¢ par exchanged for (1) share Common $0.001 par
Candie's Inc. name changed to Iconix Brand Group, Inc. 7/1/2005

MILLICOM INC (DE)
Common 1¢ par split (2) for (1) by issuance of (1) additional share 7/10/89
Merged into Millicom International Cellular S.A. 12/31/93
Each share Common 1¢ par exchanged for (1.28742236) shares Common $2 par
An additional distribution of (0.05971372) share Common $2 par per share will be made upon surrender of certificate(s)

MILLIGAN & HIGGINS CORP. (NY)
Name changed to M & H Liquidating Corp. 04/28/1962
(See M & H Liquidating Corp.)

MILLIKEN (D.B.) CO. (CA)
Completely liquidated 10/03/1967
Each share Capital Stock no par exchanged for first and final distribution of (0.118) share Teledyne, Inc. Common $1 par
Teledyne, Inc. merged into Allegheny Teledyne Inc. 08/15/1996 which name changed to Allegheny Technologies Inc. 11/29/1999

MILLIKEN LAKE URANIUM MINES LTD. (ON)
Merged into Rio Algom Mines Ltd. 6/30/60
Each share Capital Stock $1 par exchanged for (0.14) share Capital Stock no par
Rio Algom Mines Ltd. name changed to Rio Algom Ltd. 4/30/75
(See Rio Algom Ltd.)

MILLIKIN BANCSHARES INC (DE)
Merged into Magna Group, Inc. 10/26/84
Each share Common no par exchanged for (2.1) shares Common $2 par
Magna Group, Inc. merged into Union Planters Corp. 7/1/98 which merged into Regions Financial Corp. (New) 7/1/2004

MILLIKIN NATL BK (DECATUR, IL)
Capital Stock $100 par changed to $25 par and (4) additional shares issued 1/28/58
Capital Stock $25 par changed to $10 par and (1.5) additional shares issued 10/10/70
Stock Dividends - 50% 12/31/46; 33-1/3% 2/6/56; 50% 1/31/67; 25% 1/31/73
Reorganized as Millikin Bancshares, Inc. 8/1/77
Each share Capital Stock $10 par exchanged for (1) share Common no par
Millikin Bancshares, Inc. merged into Magna Group, Inc. 10/26/84 which merged into Union Planters Corp. 7/1/98 which merged into Regions Financial Corp. (New) 7/1/2004

MILLIKIN TRUST CO. (DECATUR, IL)
Merged into Millikin National Bank (Decatur, IL) 12/31/69
Each share Capital Stock $100 par exchanged for (4) shares Capital Stock $25 par
Millikin National Bank (Decatur, IL) reorganized as Millikin Bancshares, Inc. 8/1/77 which merged into Magna Group, Inc. 10/26/84 which merged into Union Planters Corp. 7/1/98 which merged into Regions Financial Corp. (New) 7/1/2004

MILLIONAIRE COM (NV)
SEC revoked common stock registration 11/24/2010
Stockholders' equity unlikely

MILLIONAIRE'S MANUAL, INC. (NV)
Name changed to Sound Money Investors Inc. in February 1989
(See Sound Money Investors Inc.)

MILLIPORE CORP (MA)
Name changed 10/20/1966
Name changed from Millipore Filter Corp. to Millipore Corp. 10/20/1966
Common $1 par changed to 33-1/3¢ par and (2) additional shares issued 11/10/1966
Common 33-1/3¢ par changed to 16-2/3¢ par and (1) additional share issued 05/15/1972
Common 16-2/3¢ par changed to 8-1/3¢ par and (1) additional share issued 05/20/1976
Common 8-1/3¢ par changed to $1 par 00/00/1980
Common $1 par split (2) for (1) by issuance of (1) additional share 04/16/1986
Common $1 par split (2) for (1) by issuance of (1) additional share 07/21/1995
Each share Common $1 par received distribution of (0.6768132) share Mykrolis Corp. Common 1¢ par payable 02/27/2002 to holders of record 02/13/2002 Ex date - 02/28/2002
Acquired by Merck KGaA 07/14/2010
Each share Common $1 par exchanged for $107 cash

MILLIRON'S (CA)
Common $5 par changed to $1 par 6/16/54
Completely liquidated 3/20/60
Each share Common $1 par exchanged for first and final distribution of $3.20 cash

MILLKIRK CHIBOUGAMAU MINES LTD (ON)
Charter cancelled and declared dissolved for failure to file returns and pay fees 04/05/1975

MILLMASTER ONYX CORP (NY)
Merged into Kewanee Industries, Inc. 01/31/1976
Each share Common $1 par exchanged for $18.55 cash

MILLMORE PRODUCTS LTD. (ON)
Adjudicated bankrupt 5/4/71
No stockholders' equity

MILLROCK DEV CORP (BC)
Recapitalized as Delta Gold Mining Corp. 09/05/1991
Each share Class A Capital Stock no par exchanged for (0.33333333) share Class A Capital Stock no par Delta Gold Mining Corp. name changed to Chase Resource Corp. (New) 05/30/1997
(See Chase Resource Corp. (New))

MILLROCK RES INC (CANADA)
Reincorporated under the laws of British Columbia 07/24/2008

MILLS ALLOYS, INC.
Dissolved in 1949

MILLS CORP (DE)
Issue Information - 14,380,000 shares COM offered at $23.50 per share on 04/14/1994
Merged into Simon Property Group, Inc. 04/03/2007
Each share Common 1¢ par exchanged for $25.25 cash
Completely liquidated 08/01/2007
Each share 6.75% Conv. Preferred Ser. F 1¢ par exchanged for first and final distribution of $1,067.50 cash
Each share 8.75% Preferred Ser. E 1¢ par exchanged for first and final distribution of $27.1875 cash
Each share 9% Preferred Ser. B 1¢ par exchanged for first and final distribution of $27.25 cash
Each share 9% Preferred Ser. C 1¢ par exchanged for first and final distribution of $27.25 cash
Each share 7.875% Depository Preferred Ser. G exchanged for first and final distribution of $2,696.88 cash

MILLS JENNINGS CO (NV)
Common 4¢ par changed to 2¢ par and (1) additional share issued 7/15/86

FINANCIAL INFORMATION, INC.   MIL-MIN

Charter revoked for failure to file reports and pay fees 5/1/98

MILLS RED LAKE MINES LTD (ON)
Charter cancelled for failure to pay taxes and file returns 09/29/1980

MILLS VALUE FUND, INC. (VA)
Charter cancelled and proclaimed dissolved for failure to file reports 03/31/1998

MILLSAP OIL & GAS CO. (DE)
Common 10¢ par changed to 2¢ par and (4) additional shares issued 01/01/1959
Charter cancelled and declared inoperative and void for non-payment of taxes 04/01/1962

MILLSTADT BANCSHARES, INC. (DE)
Acquired by Central Bancompany, Inc. 06/13/2007
Details not available

MILLSTREAM ACQUISITION CORP (DE)
Name changed to NationsHealth, Inc. 08/31/2004
(See NationsHealth, Inc.)

MILLSTREAM II ACQUISITION CORP (DE)
Issue Information - 4,000,000 UNITS consisting of (1) share COM and (2) WTS offered at $6 per Unit on 12/23/2004
Completely liquidated 04/11/2007
Each share Common $0.0001 par exchanged for first and final distribution of $5.5548091 cash

MILLSTREAM VENTURES INC (NV)
Reorganized under the laws of Delaware as American Sands Energy Corp. 10/28/2011
Each share Common $0.001 par exchanged for (0.5) share Common $0.001 par

MILLSTREET DEV CORP (AB)
Recapitalized as Millstreet Industries Inc. 07/03/2001
Each share Common no par exchanged for (0.1) share Common no par
Millstreet Industries Inc. name changed to Kingsland Energy Corp. 12/23/2011

MILLSTREET INDS INC (AB)
Name changed to Kingsland Energy Corp. 12/23/2011

MILLTRONICS LTD (CANADA)
Merged into Siemens Canada Ltd. 3/7/2000
Each share Common no par exchanged for $21 cash

MILLVILLE MANUFACTURING CO. (NJ)
Name changed to Wawa, Inc. and Common $10 par changed to $1 par 9/3/74

MILMAR-ISLAND METALS & HOLDINGS LTD. (ON)
Charter cancelled for failure to pay taxes and file returns 2/20/80

MILMAR-ISLAND MINES LTD. (ON)
Name changed to Milmar-Island Metals & Holdings Ltd. 12/22/1970
(See Milmar-Island Metals & Holdings Ltd.)

MILNOR, INC.
Liquidation completed in 1946

MILNOR CORP. (PA)
Liquidation completed in 1953

MILO COMPONENTS INC (NY)
Filed petition under Chapter 11 Federal Bankruptcy Code 8/21/90
Case closed 4/2/98
No stockholders' equity

MILO ELECTRS CORP (NY)
6.50% Conv. Preferred $10 par called for redemption 03/07/1968
Adjudicated bankrupt 03/01/1974

Stockholders' equity unlikely

MILO OIL CO. (CO)
Charter dissolved for failure to pay taxes and file annual reports 01/01/1920

MILSTEAD MANUFACTURING CO.
Merged into Callaway Mills in 1932 which was liquidated in 1947

MILTON BRADLEY CO (MA)
Each share Common $1 par exchanged for (1.5) shares Common $1 par in 1951
Common $1 par split (10) for (1) by issuance of (9) additional shares 9/1/61
5% Prior Preferred $50 par called for redemption 5/1/64
Common $1 par split (2) for (1) by issuance of (1) additional share 5/2/68
Common $1 par split (5) for (3) by issuance of (2/3) additional share 4/24/72
Merged into Hasbro Bradley, Inc. 9/10/84
Each share Common $1 par exchanged for (0.4) share 8% Conv. Preference $2.50 par and (0.764) share Common 50¢ par
Hasbro Bradley, Inc. name changed to Hasbro Inc. 6/6/85

MILTON BRICK (1937), LTD.
Name changed to Milton Brick Co., Ltd. in 1938
Milton Brick Co., Ltd. name changed to Milton Group Ltd. 12/11/72
(See Milton Group Ltd.)

MILTON BRICK LTD (ON)
Name changed to Milton Group Ltd. 12/11/1972
(See Milton Group Ltd.)

MILTON CO., INC. (MA)
Proclaimed dissolved for failure to file reports and pay fees 10/19/1983

MILTON FED FINL CORP (OH)
Merged into BancFirst Ohio Corp. 6/20/2000
Each share Common no par exchanged for (0.444) share Common no par and $6.80 cash
BanFirst Ohio Corp. merged into Unizan Financial Corp. 3/8/2002 which merged into Huntington Bancshares Inc. 3/1/2006

MILTON GOLD MINING CO. LTD.
Dissolved in 1948

MILTON GROUP LTD (ON)
Reorganized under the bankruptcy act 10/25/1979
Each share Capital Stock no par exchanged for $0.45 principal amount of 10% Secured Income Debenture due 00/00/1987

MILTON ICE CO.
Name changed to Milton Co., Inc. 00/00/1947
(See Milton Co., Inc.)

MILTON J. WERSHOW ENTERPRISES (CA)
See - Wershow (Milton J.) Enterprises

MILTON MANOR APARTMENTS LIQUIDATION TRUST
Trust terminated and liquidated 00/00/1951
Details not available

MILTON MANUFACTURING CO.
Dissolved in 1946

MILTON ROY CO (PA)
7% Preferred $50 par called for redemption 9/22/62
5-1/4% Preferred $50 par called for redemption 5/31/67
Common no par changed to $1 par 5/3/71
Common $1 par split (3) for (2) by issuance of (0.5) additional share 3/27/80
Common $1 par split (4) for (3) by

issuance of (1/3) additional share 3/31/82
Common $1 par split (3) for (2) by issuance of (0.5) additional share 3/18/83
Stock Dividends - 100% 3/22/66; 100% 3/13/67
Merged into Sundstrand Merging Corp. 1/8/91
Each share Common $1 par exchanged for $28.02 cash

MILTOPE GROUP INC (DE)
Merged into Vision Technologies Kinetics, Inc. 12/29/2003
Each share Common 1¢ par exchanged for $5.78 cash and (1) Contingent Value Right

MILWAUKEE AVENUE NATIONAL BANK (CHICAGO, IL)
Name changed to Manufacturers National Bank (Chicago, IL) 02/01/1946
(See Manufacturers National Bank (Chicago, IL))

MILWAUKEE BRAVES, INC. (DE)
Name changed to Atlanta Braves, Inc. 10/14/1965
(See Atlanta Braves, Inc.)

MILWAUKEE CO. (WI)
Each share Common $50 par exchanged for (2) shares Common no par 00/00/1930
Each share Common no par exchanged for (2) shares Class A Common $17.50 par or Class B Common $17.50 par 02/03/1960
Class A Common $17.50 par and Class B Common $17.50 par changed to $3.50 par and (4) additional shares issued respectively 01/06/1965
Class A Common $3.50 par and Class B Common $3.50 par split (5) for (1) by issuance of (4) additional shares respectively 01/24/1969
Class A Common $3.50 par and Class B Common $3.50 par reclassified as Common $3.50 par respectively 10/26/1978
Merged out of existence 12/30/1988
Details not available

MILWAUKEE CNTY BK (WEST ALLIS, WI)
Each share Common $100 par exchanged for (10) shares Common $10 par 2/1/50
Each share Common $10 par exchanged for (2) shares Common $5 par 2/6/56
Common $5 par split (2) for (1) by issuance of (1) additional share 2/10/58
Stock Dividend - 12-1/2% 5/10/58
Merged into M&I Marshall & Ilsley Bank (Milwaukee, WI) 1/28/85
Each share Common $5 par exchanged for $67 cash

MILWAUKEE ELECTRIC RAILWAY & LIGHT CO.
Merged into Wisconsin Electric Power Co. share for share in 1939

MILWAUKEE EQUITY FD INC (DE)
Acquired by Supervised Investors Growth Fund, Inc. 11/14/1975
Each share Common $1 par exchanged for (0.62425) share Common 50¢ par
Supervised Investors Growth Fund, Inc. name changed to Kemper Growth Fund, Inc. (MD) 02/17/1977 which reincorporated in Massachusetts as Kemper Growth Fund 01/31/1986 which name changed to Scudder Growth Fund 06/25/2001 which name changed to Scudder Growth Trust 01/15/2003
(See Scudder Growth Trust)

MILWAUKEE INS GROUP INC (WI)
Reincorporated 11/16/90
State of incorporation changed from (DE) to (WI) 11/16/90

Acquired by Unitrin Inc. 10/2/95
Each share Common no par exchanged for $22 cash

MILWAUKEE IRON ARENA FOOTBALL INC (NV)
Each share old Common $0.001 par exchanged for (0.02) share new Common $0.001 par 07/19/2010
Name changed EV Charging USA, Inc. 12/05/2014

MILWAUKEE LD CO (DE)
Name changed to Heartland Technology, Inc. 10/31/1997
(See Heartland Technology, Inc.)

MILWAUKEE MINES, INC. (ID)
Name changed to Westar Corp. 8/31/82
Westar Corp. name changed to Pan American Corp. 9/29/95
(See Pan American Corp.)

MILWAUKEE NORTHERN RAILWAY
Merged into Milwaukee Electric Railway & Light Co. in 1928 which merged into Wisconsin Electric Power Co. in 1939

MILWAUKEE PROFESSIONAL SPORTS & SVCS INC (WI)
Under plan of merger each share Common 10¢ par received $12 cash 12/28/79
Certificates were not required to be surrendered and are now valueless

MILWAUKEE TERMINALS, INC.
Liquidated in 1946

MILWAUKEE WESTN BK (MILWAUKEE, WI)
Each share Common $20 par exchanged for (0.00025) share Common $100,000 par 06/08/1981
Note: In effect holders received $119 cash per share and public interest was eliminated

MILWAUKEE WESTN CORP (DE)
Common 5¢ par split (5) for (1) by issuance of (4) additional shares 07/29/1983
Stock Dividends - 100% 07/02/1976; 25% 01/15/1979
Name changed to Milastar Corp. 08/26/1983
(See Milastar Corp.)

MIM CORP (DE)
Under plan of merger name changed to BioScrip, Inc. 3/12/2005

MIM MUT FDS INC (MD)
Reorganized as Riverfront Funds, Inc. 09/29/1995
Details not available

MIMLIC MONEY MKT FD INC (MN)
Name changed to Advantus Money Market Fund, Inc. 03/01/1995
Advantus Money Market Fund, Inc. merged into Ivy Funds, Inc. 12/08/2003

MIMLIC MTG SECS INCOME FD INC (MN)
Common 1¢ par reclassified as Class A 1¢ par 08/19/1994
Name changed to Advantus Mortgage Securities Fund, Inc. 03/01/1995
(See Advantus Mortgage Securities Fund, Inc.)

MIMVI INC (NV)
Common $0.001 par split (30) for (1) by issuance of (29) additional shares payable 05/26/2010 to holders of record 05/26/2010
Name changed to Adaptive Medias, Inc. 11/19/2013

MIN ORE MINES LTD (ON)
Charter cancelled and proclaimed dissolved 10/29/1994

MIN TEX ENERGY CORP (NV)
Charter revoked for failure to file reports and pay fees 07/01/1987

MINA-NOVA MINES LTD. (ON)
Charter cancelled 6/24/65

MINA RES LTD (BC)
Stock is valueless
Name changed to Anaconda Uranium Corp. (BC) 04/28/1997
Anaconda Uranium Corp. (BC) reorganized in Ontario as Anaconda Gold Corp. 08/16/2002 which recapitalized as Anaconda Mining Inc. 04/18/2007

MINACS WORLDWIDE INC (AB)
Each share old Common no par exchanged for (0.125) share new Common no par 6/1/2001
Acquired by TransWorks Information Services Ltd. 9/12/2006
Each share new Common no par exchanged for $5.50 cash

MINAEAN INTL CORP (AB)
Reorganized under the laws of British Columbia as Minaean SP Construction Corp. 08/28/2015
Each share Common no par exchanged for (0.5) share Common no par

MINARET INVTS INC (CA)
Name changed to IT Financial and Common $10 par changed to $5 par 04/19/1973
IT Financial name changed to First Investors Bancorp 12/31/1982

MINAS DE CERRO DORADO LTD (BC)
Recapitalized as Windarra Minerals Ltd. 11/13/1979
Each share Capital Stock 50¢ par exchanged for (0.2) share Common no par par
Windarra Minerals Ltd. merged into Wesdome Gold Mines Ltd. 10/03/2013

MINAS NOVAS GOLD CORP (CO)
Name changed to Cool Entertainment, Inc. (CO) 03/01/1999
Cool Entertainment, Inc. (CO) reorganized in Delaware as E-Trend Networks, Inc. 02/22/2001 which name changed to Wilmington Rexford Inc. 02/19/2002 which recapitalized as China Pharmaceuticals Corp. (DE) 03/25/2004 which reincorporated in British Virgin Islands as China Pharmaceuticals International Corp. 08/26/2004 which recapitalized as China Heli Resource Renewable Inc. 11/07/2008
(See China Heli Resource Renewable Inc.)

MINATERRA MINERALS LTD (BC)
Recapitalized as Golden Cariboo Resources Ltd. 8/31/2000
Each share Common no par exchanged for (1/3) share Common no par

MINBANC CAP CORP (DE)
Under plan of merger each share Common $1 par automatically became (1) Minbanc Foundation, Inc. Membership Int. 09/28/1999

MINBANCO CORP (DE)
Liquidation completed
Each share Common 1¢ par received initial distribution of (0.55) share Abitibi Asbestos Mining Co. Ltd. Common $1 par 08/20/1971
Each share Common 1¢ par received second and final distribution of (0.1) share Jetlands Corp. Common 1¢ par 07/20/1972
(See each company's listing)

MINCO AMERN CORP (NV)
Name changed 11/02/1987
Name changed from Minco, Inc. to Minco American Corp. 11/02/1987
Each share Common 1¢ par exchanged for (0.1) share old Common no par
Each share old Common no par exchanged for (0.025) share new Common no par 08/01/1997
Name changed to Cyber Village, Inc. 05/02/2000
Cyber Village, Inc. merged into neXstage Corp. 09/30/2000
(See neXstage Corp.)

MINCO MNG & METALS CORP (BC)
Name changed to Minco Gold Corp. 2/1/2007

MINCOM CAP INC (CANADA)
Name changed to Braille Energy Systems Inc. 07/27/2018

MINCOMP CORP (CO)
Charter suspended for failure to file annual reports 09/30/1988

MINCOR RES INC (QC)
Struck off register 05/06/2005

MINCORP N L (AUSTRALIA)
Name changed 10/13/1982
Name changed 03/09/1992
Name changed from Mincorp Ltd. to Mincorp Petroleum N.L. 10/13/1982
Name changed from Mincorp Petroleum N.L. to Mincorp N.L. 03/09/1992
Each old Sponsored ADR for Ordinary AUD $0.20 par exchanged for (0.25) new Sponsored ADR for Ordinary AUD $0.20 par 01/28/1993
Company liquidated 00/00/2002
Ordinary shares deemed worthless

MIND TECHNOLOGIES INC (NV)
Stock Dividend - 2% payable 03/01/2013 to holders of record 02/01/2013
Each share Common $0.0001 par received distribution of (0.02040816) share VOIS, Inc. Common $0.001 par payable 03/05/2013 to holders of record 02/01/2013
Each share Common $0.0001 par received distribution of (0.08333333) share VOIS, Inc. Restricted Common $0.001 par payable 06/03/2013 to holders of record 06/01/2013
Note: Holders of (11) or fewer shares did not receive distribution
Voluntarily dissolved 06/28/2013

MINDA-SCOTIA MINES LTD. (ON)
Recapitalized as New Minda-Scotia Mines Ltd. 06/09/1955
Each share Capital Stock exchanged for (0.25) share Capital Stock
New Minda-Scotia Mines Ltd. merged into Andover Mining & Exploration Ltd. 09/19/1958 which was recapitalized as Andover Resources Ltd. 05/31/1971 which name changed to Andover Telecommunications Inc. 10/02/1986 which name changed to Kennecom Inc. 06/02/1989 which recapitalized as Deltona Industries Inc. 01/25/1995
(See Deltona Industries Inc.)

MINDAMAR ENERGY RES LTD (ON)
Charter cancelled for failure to pay taxes and file returns 04/02/1984

MINDAMAR METALS CORP., LTD. (ON)
Recapitalized as United Mindamar Metals Ltd. 9/14/61
Each share Capital Stock no par exchanged for (1/3) share Capital Stock no par
United Mindamar Metals Ltd. name changed to Mindamar Energy Resources Ltd. 7/13/73
(See Mindamar Energy Resources Ltd.)

MINDANAO MOTHER LODE MINES, INC. (PHILIPPINES)
Stock Dividend - 50% 1/15/51
Declared insolvent 7/24/65
No stockholders' equity

MINDARROW SYS INC (DE)
Merged into Avalon Digital Marketing Systems, Inc. 10/01/2002
Each share Common $0.001 par exchanged for (0.1) share Common $0.001 par

MINDCARE CORP (NV)
Recapitalized as Proactive Computer Services Inc. 06/08/2000
Each share Common $0.001 par exchanged for (0.5) share Common $0.001 par
Proactive Computer Services Inc. name changed to CortDev, Inc. 04/05/2004 which recapitalized as Fansfrenzy Corp. 12/05/2017

MINDEN BANCORP INC (LA)
Merged into Business First Bancshares, Inc. 01/02/2018
Each share Common 1¢ par exchanged for $23.20 cash

MINDEN BANCORP INC (USA)
Reorganized under the laws of Louisiana 01/05/2011
Each share Common 1¢ par exchanged for (1.7427) shares Common 1¢ par
(See Minden Bancorp, Inc. (LA))

MINDEN BANCSHARES INC (LA)
Merged into Regions Financial Corp. (Old) 12/31/99
Each share Common exchanged for (8.847) shares Common $0.625 par
Regions Financial Corp. (Old) merged into Regions Financial Corp. (New) 7/1/2004

MINDEN OIL & GAS INC (DE)
Name changed to Castle Energy Corp. 11/16/1986
Castle Energy Corp. merged into Delta Petroleum Corp. 05/01/2006
(See Delta Petroleum Corp.)

MINDENAO GOLD MNG CORP (OR)
Reincorporated under the laws of British Columbia as Grand Pacaraima Gold Corp. 03/13/2006
Grand Pacaraima Gold Corp. name changed to First Bitcoin Capital Corp. 08/15/2016

MINDESTA INC (DE)
Each share Common $0.0001 par received distribution of (1) share Northern Graphite Corp. Common no par payable 01/25/2012 to holders of record 01/05/2012
Ex date - 01/26/2012
Recapitalized as CTT Pharmaceutical Holdings, Inc. 08/28/2015
Each share Common $0.0001 par exchanged for (0.1) share Common $0.0001 par

MINDFLIGHT CORP (CANADA)
Name changed to RDM Corp. 06/19/1998
(See RDM Corp.)

MINDFULEYE INC (NV)
Each share old Common $0.001 par exchanged for (0.001) share new Common $0.001 par 06/18/2008
Note: No holder will receive fewer than (100) post-split shares
Each share new Common $0.001 par exchanged again for (0.00066666) share new Common $0.001 par 09/21/2009
Name changed to Medbox, Inc. 10/28/2011
Medbox, Inc. name changed to Notis Global, Inc. 02/22/2016

MINDRAY MED INTL LTD (CAYMAN ISLANDS)
Acquired by Excelsior Union Ltd. 03/08/2016
Each Sponsored ADR for Class A Ordinary exchanged for $27.95 cash

MINDREADY SOLUTIONS INC (CANADA)
Issue Information - 2,500,000 shares COM offered at $12 per share on 12/11/2000
Assets sold for the benefit of creditors 02/27/2008
Stockholders' equity unlikely

MINDSCAPE INC (DE)
Merged into Software Toolworks, Inc. 03/16/1990
Each share Common $0.00001 par exchanged for (0.4375) share Common 1¢ par
(See Software Toolworks, Inc.)

MINDSET INTERACTIVE CORP (NV)
Reincorporated under the laws of Delaware as DeGreko, Inc. 12/07/2005
DeGreko, Inc. name changed to VOIP 5000, Inc. 06/06/2006 which name changed to Target Development Group, Inc. (DE) 04/30/2007 which reincorporated in Wyoming 04/13/2009 which name changed to Hannover House, Inc. 04/03/2012

MINDSPEED TECHNOLOGIES INC (DE)
Each share old Common 1¢ par exchanged for (0.2) share new Common 1¢ par 07/01/2008
Acquired by M/A-COM Technology Solutions Holdings, Inc. 12/18/2013
Each share Common 1¢ par exchanged for $5.05 cash

MINDSPRING ENTERPRISES INC (DE)
Common 1¢ par split (3) for (1) by issuance of (2) additional shares payable 07/24/1998 to holders of record 07/09/1998
Common 1¢ par split (2) for (1) by issuance of (1) additional share payable 06/25/1999 to holders of record 06/11/1999
Under plan of merger name changed to EarthLink, Inc. 02/04/2000
EarthLink, Inc. name changed to EarthLink Holdings Corp. 01/02/2014 which merged into Windstream Holdings, Inc. 02/27/2017

MIND2MARKET INC (CO)
Each share old Common $0.001 par exchanged for (0.02) share new Common $0.001 par 04/20/2005
Name changed to Health Partnership, Inc. 05/25/2005
Health Partnership, Inc. name changed to Naerodynamics, Inc. 04/17/2008

MINDUS CORP. LTD. (ON)
Under Plan of Consolidation each (20) shares Capital Stock no par exchanged for (2) shares Common no par and (1) Warrant of Mindustrial Corp. Ltd. 11/14/1955
(See Mindustrial Corp. Ltd.)

MINDUSTRIAL LTD (ON)
Merged into Guthrie Corp. Ltd. 09/21/1978
Each share Common no par exchanged for $10.50 cash

MINDY EXPLS LTD (BC)
Name changed to International Telepool Corp. 09/09/1985
International Telepool Corp. name changed to U.S. Pay-Tel, Inc. (BC) 08/11/1986 which reincorporated in Delaware as U.S. Long Distance Corp. 09/29/1987 which name changed to USLD Communications Corp. 08/19/1997 which merged into LCI International Inc. 12/22/1997 which merged into Qwest Communications International Inc. 06/05/1998 which merged into CenturyLink, Inc. 04/01/2011

MINE-A-MAX CORP (NV)
Each share old Common $0.001 par exchanged for (0.01) share new Common $0.001 par 02/26/1999
Name changed to Peabody's Coffee, Inc. 03/15/1999
(See Peabody's Coffee, Inc.)

MINE CLEARING CORP (NV)
Recapitalized as ClickStream Corp. 06/19/2014

Each share Common $0.001 par exchanged for (0.00333333) share Common $0.001 par

MINE SAFETY APPLIANCES CO (PA)
Common $10 par changed to $3.33333333 par and (2) additional shares issued 05/06/1968
Common $3.33333333 par changed to $1.66666667 par and (1) additional share issued 05/09/1977
Common $1.66666667 par changed to $0.83333333 par and (1) additional share issued 05/15/1980
Common $0.83333333 par changed to no par and (1) additional share issued 09/10/1985
Common no par split (3) for (1) by issuance of (2) additional shares payable 05/24/2000 to holders of record 05/12/2000
Common no par split (3) for (1) by issuance of (2) additional shares payable 01/28/2004 to holders of record 01/16/2004
Name changed to MSA Safety Inc. 03/11/2014

MINEBEA LTD (JAPAN)
Each Unsponsored ADR for Common exchanged for (2.5) Sponsored ADR's for Common 03/27/1997
Name changed to Minebea Mitsumi Inc. 01/27/2017

MINECORE INTL INC (NV)
Reincorporated 04/09/2008
State of incorporation changed from (DE) to (NV) 04/09/2008
SEC revoked common stock registration 01/26/2010

MINECORP ENERGY LTD (BC)
Each share old Common no par exchanged for (0.1) share new Common no par 10/16/2015
Name changed to Freedom Energy Inc. 05/29/2017

MINEDEL MINES LTD (ON)
Name changed 00/00/1938
Name changed from Minedel Mining & Development Co. Ltd. to Minedel Mines Ltd. 00/00/1938
Name changed to Havelock Energy & Resources Inc. 05/01/1980
Havelock Energy & Resources Inc. recapitalized as Municipal Ticket Corp. 03/04/1994 which recapitalized as I.D. Investments Inc. 11/18/1994 which recapitalized as BioLink Corp. 03/12/1997 which recapitalized as First Empire Entertainment.com Inc. 03/31/2000 which recapitalized as First Empire Corp. 08/14/2003 which reorganized as Noble House Entertainment Inc. (ON) 11/01/2004 which reincorporated in Canada as LiveReel Media Corp. 12/01/2006

MINEFIELDS EXPL N L (AUSTRALIA)
Completely liquidated 12/05/1990
No ADR holder's equity

MINEFINDERS LTD (ON)
Merged into Pan American Silver Corp. 04/02/2012
Each share Common no par exchanged for (0.55) share Common no par and $1.84 cash
Note: Unexchanged certificates were cancelled and became without value 04/02/2018

MINEFINDERS', LTD. (CANADA)
Completely liquidated 03/31/1959
Each share Capital Stock no par exchanged for first and final distribution of $0.47 cash

MINEGEM INC (ON)
Acquired by European Diamonds PLC in December 2003
Each share Common no par exchanged for (0.1) share Ordinary 5p par

MINEMAKERS LTD (AUSTRALIA)
Each share Ordinary received distribution of (0.22026431) share TNT Mines Ltd. Ordinary payable 07/19/2011 to holders of record 07/14/2011
Name changed to Avenira Ltd. 12/24/2015
(See Avenira Ltd.)

MINEOLA BOND & MORTGAGE CO.
Liquidated in 1935

MINER INC (DE)
Charter cancelled and declared inoperative and void for non-payment of taxes 04/15/1972

MINER INDS INC (DE)
Each share old Common 1¢ par exchanged for (0.5) share new Common 1¢ par 1/7/80
Chapter 11 bankruptcy proceedings converted to Chapter 7 on 10/23/85
Stockholders' equity unlikely

MINER INTERNET TECHNOLOGIES & COMMUNICATIONS INC (NV)
Name changed to Imsure Network, Inc. 6/15/2000
(See Imsure Network, Inc.)

MINER RIV RES LTD (AB)
Merged into Eagle Plains Resources Ltd. 05/12/1999
Each share Common no par exchanged for (1.2) shares Common no par

MINERA ANDES INC (AB)
Preferred Stock Purchase Rights declared for Common stockholders of record 06/23/2005 were redeemed at $0.001 per right 02/07/2006 for holders of record 02/07/2006
Merged into McEwen Mining - Minera Andes Acquisition Corp. 01/27/2012
Each share Common no par exchanged for (0.45) Exchangeable Share no par
Note: Unexchanged certificates were cancelled and became without value 01/27/2018
McEwen Mining - Minera Andes Acquisition Corp. exchanged for McEwen Mining Inc. 08/22/2016

MINERA CAP CORP (BC)
Reincorporated 9/24/2004
Place of incorporation changed from (Yukon) to (BC) 9/24/2004
Recapitalized as Coronado Resources Ltd. 9/23/2005
Each share Common no par exchanged for (0.2) share Common no par

MINERA CORTEZ RES LTD (BC)
Name changed to Western Wind Energy Corp. 02/18/2002
(See Western Wind Energy Corp.)

MINERA DELTA INC NEW (CANADA)
Name changed to Vector Wind Energy Inc. 11/26/2004
(See Vector Wind Energy Inc.)

MINERA DELTA INC OLD (CANADA)
Recapitalized as Whitmore Resource Corp. 7/20/99
Each share Common no par exchanged for (0.2) share Common no par
Whitmore Resource Corp. name changed to Minera Delta Inc. (New) 10/15/2001 which name changed to Vector Wind Energy Inc. 11/26/2004
(See Vector Wind Energy Inc.)

MINERA RAYROCK INC (BC)
Each share Common no par exchanged for (0.5) Multiple Share no par and (0.5) Subordinate Share no par 6/25/93
Merged into Rayrock Yellowknife Resources Inc. 5/27/98
Each Multiple Share no par exchanged for $0.30 cash
Each Subordinate Share no par exchanged for $0.30 cash

MINERA SIERRA MADRE INC (AB)
Name changed to MSA Capital Corp. 07/24/2000
MSA Capital Corp. name changed to Coronation Minerals Inc. (AB) 10/29/2002 which reincorporated in Ontario 04/23/2004 which name changed to Guyana Precious Metals Inc. 08/18/2009 which name changed to GPM Metals Inc. 08/29/2013

MINERAL ACCEP CORP (DE)
Reincorporated under the laws of New Jersey 1/1/97

MINERAL CONCENTRATES & CHEM INC (CO)
Proclaimed dissolved 01/01/1986

MINERAL DEPOSITS LTD. (AUSTRALIA)
Issue Information - 45,500,000 ORD shares offered at $1.10 per share on 12/12/2007
Each share old Ordinary exchanged for (0.1) share new Ordinary 11/25/2010
Holdings transferred to the Australian register 07/27/2012

MINERAL DEV INC (TX)
Each share old Common 1¢ par exchanged for (0.1) share new Common 1¢ par 2/10/92
Recapitalized as Exco Resources Inc. 7/18/96
Each share new Common 1¢ par exchanged for (0.2) share Common 1¢ par
(See Exco Resources Inc.)

MINERAL DEVELOPMENT CO.
Capital Stock $67 par reduced to $62 par by payment of $5 in 1941 and to $47 par by payment of $15 in 1947
In process of liquidation in 1956

MINERAL ESTATES, LTD. (ON)
Charter cancelled for failure to file reports and pay taxes in September 1962

MINERAL EXPL LTD (QC)
Declared dissolved for failure to file reports or pay fees 10/00/1974

MINERAL KING BANCORP INC (CA)
Merged into ValliCorp Holdings, Inc. 12/16/94
Each share Common no par exchanged for (2.0103) shares Common 1¢ par
ValliCorp Holdings, Inc. merged into Westamerica Bancorporation 4/12/97

MINERAL MINING & POWER CO. (DE)
Charter cancelled and declared inoperative and void for non-payment of taxes in 1938

MINERAL MNG CORP (DE)
Common $1 par changed to 10¢ par 05/01/1947
Merged into MMC Holding Inc. 05/31/1989
Details not available

MINERAL MOUNTAIN MINING CO. (UT)
Incorporated 3/16/09
Charter revoked for failure to file reports and pay fees 11/9/74

MINERAL MOUNTAIN MINING CO. (UT)
Incorporated 4/7/50
Charter revoked for failure to file reports and pay fees 11/9/74

MINERAL MOUNTAIN MINING CO. (UT)
Incorporated 7/8/54
Charter revoked for failure to file reports and pay fees 10/10/58

MINERAL MOUNTAIN MINING CO. (UT)
Incorporated 2/26/69
Charter revoked for failure to file reports and pay fees 12/31/74

MINERAL MT MNG LTD (BC)
Recapitalized as Mid Mountain Mining Ltd. 12/15/75
Each share Capital Stock no par exchanged for (0.2) share Capital Stock no par
(See Mid Mountain Mining Ltd.)

MINERAL PK MNG CORP (BC)
Recapitalized as I.M.P. Industrial Park Mining Corp. 03/02/1994
Each (4.5) shares Common no par exchanged for (1) share Common no par
I.M.P. Industrial Park Mining Corp. name changed to Crystal Graphite Corp. 11/06/2000
(See Crystal Graphite Corp.)

MINERAL RESEARCH LTD. (BC)
Struck off register and declared dissolved for failure to file reports 4/1/67

MINERAL RESEARCH LTD. (SK)
No longer in business; struck off register 9/27/57

MINERAL RESOURCES, INC. (NY)
Ctfs. dated prior to 12/15/72
Charter cancelled and proclaimed dissolved for failure to pay taxes and file reports 12/15/72

MINERAL RES CORP (ON)
Each share old Common no par exchanged for (0.02) share new Common no par 03/27/1997
Name changed to Minroc Mines Inc. 06/10/1998
Minroc Mines Inc. name changed to Cassiar Mines & Metals, Inc. 06/10/1999 which name changed to Cassiar Magnesium Inc. 04/25/2000 which name changed to Cassiar Resources Inc. 07/25/2001 which name changed to Troutline Investments Inc. (ONT) 06/30/2003 which reorganized in Alberta as Innova Exploration Ltd. 04/16/2004
(See Innova Exploration Ltd.)

MINERAL RES INC (UT)
Reorganized 11/22/1976
Reorganized from (NY) to under the laws of (UT) 11/22/1976
Each share Common 1¢ par exchanged for (0.2) share Common 1¢ par
Proclaimed dissolved for failure to pay taxes 12/31/1980

MINERAL RES INTL LTD (ON)
Merged into Conwest Exploration Co. Ltd. (ONT) 6/1/90
Each share Capital Stock no par exchanged for (0.42553191) share Class B no par
Conwest Exploration Co. Ltd. (ONT) merged into Conwest Exploration Co. Ltd. (New) (ALTA) 9/1/93 which merged into Alberta Energy Co. Ltd. 1/31/96 which merged into EnCana Corp. 1/3/2003

MINERAL RESOURCES LTD. (AB)
Charter revoked for failure to file reports and pay fees 10/14/61

MINERAL VENTURES CO. (NV)
Merged into Globe Minerals, Inc. 3/7/69
Each share Capital Stock 1¢ par exchanged for (1) share Common no par
Globe Minerals, Inc. recapitalized as Globe Inc. 10/16/70
(See Globe Inc.)

MINERALS & CHEMICALS CORP. OF AMERICA (MD)
Name changed to Minerals & Chemicals-Philipp Corp. 7/21/60
Minerals & Chemical-Philipp Corp.

merged into Engelhard Minerals & Chemicals Corp. 9/27/67 which name changed to Phibro Corp. 5/20/81 which name changed to Phibro-Salomon Inc. 5/20/82 which name changed to Salomon Inc. 5/7/86 which merged into Travelers Group Inc. 11/28/97 which name changed to Citigroup Inc. 10/28/98

MINERALS & CHEMICALS-PHILIPP CORP. (MD)
Class B $1 par reclassified as Common $1 par 7/21/62
Merged into Engelhard Minerals & Chemicals Corp. 9/27/67
Each share Common $1 par exchanged for (0.177) share $4.25 Conv. Preferred no par and (1.094) shares Common $1 par
Engelhard Minerals & Chemicals Corp. name changed to Phibro Corp. 5/20/81 which name changed to Phibro-Salomon Inc. 5/20/82 which name changed to Salomon Inc. 5/7/86 which merged into Travelers Group Inc. 11/28/97 which name changed to Citigroup Inc. 10/8/98

MINERALS & INDS INC (DE)
Name changed to Techno-Design, Ltd. 06/22/1987

MINERALS & RESOURCES CORP., LTD. (BERMUDA)
Reincorporated under the laws of Luxembourg as Minorco 11/27/1987
(See Minorco)

MINERALS ANODOR INC (CANADA)
Recapitalized as Nora Exploration Inc. 3/8/91
Each share Common no par exchanged for (0.25) share Common no par
Nora Exploration Inc. name changed to Afri-Can Marine Minerals Corp. 3/24/2000

MINERALS CORP. OF AMERICA (DE)
Charter revoked for non-payment of taxes 4/1/64

MINERALS ENGR CO (CO)
Common $1 par changed to no par 07/07/1970
Each share Common no par exchanged for (0.2) share Common 1¢ par 04/10/1974
Name changed to CoCa Mines Inc. 12/31/1986
CoCa Mines Inc. merged into Hecla Mining 06/26/1991

MINERALS INTL INC (AZ)
Merged into Mansion Industries, Inc. 08/16/1972
Each share Capital Stock $1 par exchanged for (0.05) share Common 16-2/3¢ par
Mansion Industries, Inc. merged into Netcoast Communications, Inc. 03/18/1996 which recapitalized as SmartData, Inc. 10/26/2004 which name changed to Coastal Technologies Inc. 10/10/2005 which recapitalized as Cyclone Power Technologies, Inc. 07/02/2007

MINERALS MNG CORP (CO)
Recapitalized as Grand American International Corp. 4/1/86
Each share Common 1¢ par exchanged for (1/3) share Common $0.003 par
Grand American International Corp. name changed to Continental Wellness Casinos, Inc. 12/23/95 which name changed to Continental Wellness Casinos Trust R.E.I.T. 12/22/97 which name changed to Countryland Wellness Resorts, Inc. 9/22/99 which recapitalized as Minerals Mining Corp. 11/6/2000

MINERALS PROCESSING CO., INC. (WA)
Charter cancelled and proclaimed dissolved for failure to pay fees in 1976

MINERALS PROCESSING CO. (DE)
Bankrupt 7/11/57

MINERALS REFINING CO. (NV)
Liquidation completed 9/29/61

MINERALS SEPARATION NORTH AMERICAN CORP. (MD)
Name changed to Attapulgus Minerals & Chemicals Corp. 12/10/52
Attapulgus Minerals & Chemicals Corp. merged into Minerals & Chemicals Corp. of America 6/23/54 which name changed to Minerals & Chemicals-Philipp Corp. 7/21/60 which merged into Engelhard Minerals & Chemicals Corp. 9/27/67 which name changed to Phibro Corp. 5/20/81 which name changed to Phibro-Salomon Inc. 5/20/82 which name changed to Salomon Inc. 5/7/86 which merged into Travelers Group Inc. 11/28/97 which name changed to Citigroup Inc. 10/8/98

MINERALS TECHNOLOGY CORP (MN)
Statutorily dissolved 9/26/91

MINERALS WEST INC (UT)
Involuntarily dissolved 07/01/1999

MINERCO RES INC (NV)
Old Common $0.001 par split (6) for (1) by issuance of (5) additional shares payable 05/21/2010 to holders of record 05/21/2010
Each share old Common $0.001 par exchanged for (0.00666666) share new Common $0.001 par 02/13/2012
Recapitalized as Minerco, Inc. 10/02/2015
Each share new Common $0.001 par exchanged for (0.01) share Common $0.001 par

MINEREX RES LTD (BC)
Merged into Canada Tungsten Inc. 01/01/1993
Each share Common no par exchanged for (0.5) share Common no par
Canada Tungsten Inc. merged into Aur Resources Inc. 01/01/1997 which was acquired by Teck Cominco Ltd. 09/28/2007 which name changed to Teck Resources Ltd. 04/27/2009

MINERIA Y EXPLORACIONES OLYMPIA INC (NV)
Name changed to XLI Technologies, Inc. 12/02/2015

MINERS & MERCHANTS BANK (CHARLESTON, SC)
Merged into First National Bank of South Carolina (Columbia, SC) 06/01/1984
Details not available

MINERS BK (LYKENS, PA)
Merged into Mid Penn Bancorp, Inc. 7/10/98
Each share Common $5 par exchanged for (10) shares Common $1 par

MINERS COAL CO., INC. (MD)
Charter forfeited for failure to file reports and pay taxes 4/18/25

MINERS GOLD MINING CO. (NV)
Name changed to North American Resources Corp. (NV) 12/6/56
North American Resources Corp. (NV) name changed to National American Industries 3/13/69 which name changed to Vaportech Corp. 7/1/71

MINERS NATL BANCORP INC (PA)
Capital Stock $5 par split (3) for (1) by issuance of (2) additional shares 07/31/1986
Common $5 par split (5) for (4) by issuance of (0.25) additional share 04/16/1993
Stock Dividend - 25% 04/27/1994
Under plan of merger name changed to Heritage Bancorp Inc. 03/01/1995
Heritage Bancorp Inc. merged into Main Street Bancorp, Inc. 05/01/1998 which merged into Sovereign Bancorp, Inc. 03/08/2002 which merged into Banco Santander, S.A. 01/30/2009

MINERS NATL BK (POTTSVILLE, PA)
Each share Capital Stock $50 par exchanged for (2.5) shares Capital Stock $20 par 00/00/1952
Capital Stock $20 par changed to $10 par and (1) additional share issued plus a 25% stock divdend paid 09/13/1971
Capital Stock $10 par changed to $5 par and (1) additional share issued 07/15/1971
Under plan of reorganization each share Capital Stock $5 par automatically became (1) share Miners National Bancorp, Inc. Capital Stock $5 par 09/01/1983
Miners National Bancorp, Inc. name changed to Heritage Bancorp Inc. 03/01/1995 which merged into Main Street Bancorp, Inc. 05/01/1998 which merged into Sovereign Bancorp, Inc. 03/08/2002 which merged into Banco Santander, S.A. 01/30/2009

MINERS NATL BK (WILKES-BARRE, PA)
Each share Capital Stock $50 par exchanged for (5) shares Capital Stock $10 par 05/17/1955
Merged into United Penn Corp. 07/01/1969
Each share Capital Stock $10 par exchanged for (2) shares Common no par
United Penn Corp. merged into Continental Bancorp, Inc. 08/17/1984 which merged into Midlantic Corp. 01/30/1987 which merged into PNC Bank Corp. 12/31/1995 which name changed to PNC Financial Services Group, Inc. 03/15/2000

MINERS SVGS BK (PITTSTON, PA)
Stock Dividend - 60% 08/20/1969
Acquired by First Eastern Corp. 12/03/1986
Each share Capital Stock $25 par exchanged for (12.5) shares Common $10 par
(See First Eastern Corp.)

MINERVA ELECTRONICS INDUSTRIES, INC. (TN)
Name changed to Minerva International, Inc. 08/07/1972
(See Minerva International, Inc.)

MINERVA GOLD MINES LTD (BC)
Recapitalized as Consolidated Minerva Gold Mines Ltd. 02/19/1996
Each share Common no par exchanged for (1/3) share Common no par
Consolidated Minerva Gold Mines Ltd. name changed to El Misti Gold Ltd. (BC) 06/03/1996 which reincorporated in New Brunswick 12/06/1996 which recapitalized as Andean American Mining Corp. (NB) 10/21/1999 which reincorporated in British Columbia 08/22/2005 which name changed to Andean American Gold Corp. 09/07/2010 which merged into Lupaka Gold Corp. 10/01/2012

MINERVA INTL INC (TN)
Adjudicated bankrupt 09/30/1977
No stockholders' equity

MINERVA MINERALS LTD (CANADA)
Recapitalized as Greywacke Exploration Ltd. 05/28/2013
Each share Common no par exchanged for (0.5) share Common no par
Greywacke Exploration Ltd. name changed to Green River Gold Corp. 09/08/2017

MINERVA WAX PAPER CO. (OH)
Acquired by Alco Standard Corp. 12/29/1967
Details not availble

MINES D OR VA INC NEW (CANADA)
Merged into Virginia Mines Inc. 03/31/2006
Each share Common no par exchanged for (0.5) share Common no par and (0.4) share Goldcorp Inc. (New) Common no par
(See each company's listing)

MINES D OR VA INC OLD (CANADA)
Merged into Mines d'or Virginia Inc.-Virginia Gold Mines Inc. (Canada) 06/01/1996
Each share Common no par exchanged for (0.82) share Common no par and (0.1) share of Majescor Resources Inc. a wholly owned subsidiary
(See Mines d'or Virginia Inc.-Virginia Gold Mines Inc. (Canada))

MINES DYNACOR INC (QC)
Name changed to Malaga Inc. 07/17/2007
(See Malaga Inc.)

MINES MGMT INC (ID)
Merged into Hecla Mining Co. 09/14/2016
Each share Common $0.001 par exchanged for (0.2218) share Common 25¢ par

MINES MESSEGUAY INC (CANADA)
Recapitalized as Melkior Resources Inc. 1/10/94
Each share Common no par exchanged for (0.1) share Common no par

MINES METALS & EXPLORATION CO. LTD.
Dissolved 00/00/1933
Details not available

MINES ROY ROSS, INC. (QC)
Charter annulled for failure to file reports or pay fees 1/13/79

MINETA RES LTD (BC)
Recapitalized as Star of Mineta Ltd. 02/21/1992
Each share Common no par exchanged for (0.25) share Common no par
Star of Mineta Ltd. recapitalized as International Star Resources Ltd. 08/24/1995
(See International Star Resources Ltd.)

MINETWORK GROUP INC (NV)
Reincorporated 04/21/2004
Common $0.001 par split (4) for (1) by issuance of (1) additional share payable 03/10/2004 to holders of record 03/05/2004 Ex date - 03/11/2004
State of incorporation changed from (TN) to (NV) 04/21/2004
Each share old Common $0.001 par exchanged for (0.002) share new Common $0.001 par 07/16/2007
Name changed to Green Earth Technologies, Inc. 08/08/2007

MINEWORKS RES CORP (BC)
Name changed to Tower Energy Ltd. 07/25/2005
Tower Energy Ltd. recapitalized as Tower Resources Ltd. 09/20/2011

MINEX DEV LTD (BC)
Recapitalized as New Minex Resources Ltd. 2/11/74
Each share Capital Stock no par exchanged for (0.2) share Capital Stock no par
(See New Minex Resources Ltd.)

FINANCIAL INFORMATION, INC.   MIN-MIN

MINEX MINERALS INC (FL)
Each share old Common 1¢ par exchanged (0.01) share new Common 1¢ par 01/25/1999
Name changed to Redmond Capital Corp. (FL) 02/25/1999
Redmond Capital Corp. (FL) reincorporated in Delaware as Windsor Resource Corp. 02/06/2008 which name changed to Kleangas Energy Technologies, Inc. 02/25/2013

MINEX RES INC (WY)
SEC revoked common stock registration 02/27/2009

MING FINL CORP (AB)
Name changed to Eastern Meridian Mining Corp. 10/28/1997
Eastern Meridian Mining Corp. recapitalized as New Meridian Mining Corp. 11/22/2000 which name changed to Phillppine Metals Inc. (AB) 04/07/2010 which reincorporated in British Columbia 04/17/2018

MING MINES LTD (BC)
Struck off register and declared dissolved for failure to file returns 08/06/1993

MINGHUA GROUP INTL HLDGS LTD (NY)
Recapitalized as China Longyi Group International Holdings Ltd. 12/12/2007
Each share Common 1¢ par exchanged for (0.05) share Common 1¢ par

MINHAS ENERGY CONSULTANTS INC (NV)
Common $0.001 par split (14) for (1) by issuance of (13) additional shares payable 08/18/2008 to holders of record 08/18/2008
Name changed to American Exploration Corp. 08/19/2008
American Exploration Corp. recapitalized as Spotlight Innovation Inc. 12/19/2013

MINI COMPUTER SYS INC (DE)
Name changed to Americus Management Corp. 11/01/1990
(See Americus Management Corp.)

MINI INDS INC (UT)
Name changed to Caffe Ribs Inc. 05/28/1986

MINI INTL CORP (FL)
Proclaimed dissolved for failure to file reports and pay fees 11/14/1986

MINI MART CORP OLD (DE)
Common 10¢ par changed to 5¢ par and (1) additional share issued 3/27/74
Stock Dividend - 20% 4/14/72
Merged into Mini Mart Corp. (New) 10/4/84
Each share Common 5¢ par exchanged for $1 principal amount of Floating Rate Subordinated Installment Notes due 10/4/92 and $8 cash

MINI-MART PROPERTIES, INC. (FL)
Proclaimed dissolved for failure to pay taxes 6/10/68

MINI SYS INC (MN)
Statutorily dissolved 10/7/91

MINIATURE INSTRS INC (MN)
Assets sold at auction by Small Business Administration 5/1/74

MINIATURE PRECISION BEARINGS, INC. (NH)
5% Preferred called for redemption 01/01/1960
Each share Class A Common $2 par or Class B Common $2 par exchanged for (1) share Common $2 par 09/15/1965
Stock Dividend - 150% 03/30/1960

Name changed to MPB Corp. (NH) 06/28/1967
MPB Corp. (NH) reincorporated in Delaware 06/30/1969
(See MPB Corp. (DE))

MINICHROME, INC. (MN)
Ceased doing business and liquidated in November 1962
No stockholders' equity

MINIMALLY INVASIVE SURGERY CORP (DE)
Name changed to eCare Solutions, Inc. 03/23/2000

MINIMATIC IMPLANT TECHNOLOGY INC (DE)
Each share Common $0.001 par exchanged for (0.1) share Common 1¢ par 4/12/93
Name changed to American Bio-Dental Corp. 4/12/95
American Bio-Dental Corp. name changed to BioLok International Inc. 8/7/96
(See BioLok International Inc.)

MINIMED INC (DE)
Issue Information - 3,350,000 shares COM offered at $13 per share on 07/24/1995
Common 1¢ par split (2) for (1) by issuance of (1) additional share payable 04/16/1999 to holders of record 04/01/1999
Common 1¢ par split (2) for (1) by issuance of (1) additional share payable 08/18/2000 to holders of record 08/02/2000 Ex date - 08/21/2000
Merged into Medtronic, Inc. 08/28/2001
Each share Common 1¢ par exchanged for $48 cash

MINING & ALLIED SUPPLIES CDA LTD (ON)
Name changed to Bearing Power (Canada) Ltd. 3/28/94
(See Bearing Power (Canada) Ltd.)

MINING & OIL SHALE DEVELOPMENT CORP. (CA)
Merged into Consolidated General Corp. 04/28/1969
Each share Capital Stock $1 par exchanged for (1) share Common $1 par
Consolidated General Corp. name changed to Chisholm Resources Inc. (NV) 03/24/1998
(See Chisholm Resources Inc.)

MINING CORP. OF CANADA LTD. (CANADA)
Common $5 par changed to no par in 1931
Acquired by Noranda Mines Ltd. 11/15/63
Each share Capital Stock no par exchanged for (0.5) share Capital Stock no par plus $1 cash
Noranda Mines Ltd. name changed to Noranda Inc. 5/28/84 which name changed Falconbridge Ltd. (New) 2005 on 7/1/2005
(See Falconbridge Ltd. (New) 2005)

MINING CORP (NV)
Name changed to Latin American Resources, Inc. 10/14/93

MINING ENDEAVOR CO. LTD. (ON)
Charter revoked for failure to file reports and pay fees 11/30/1964

MINING FUTURES & HOLDINGS LTD. (ON)
Charter cancelled for failure to pay taxes and file returns 5/30/79

MINING HOUSES AUSTRALIA LTD (AUSTRALIA)
Name changed to Eastern Resources of Australia Ltd. 05/10/1984
Eastern Resources of Australia Ltd. recapitalized as Firstpac Ltd. 01/31/1990
(See Firstpac Ltd.)

MINING MINERALS MEXICO CORP (NV)
Recapitalized as Aurum Resource & Asset Management, Inc. 07/17/2014
Each share Common $0.001 par exchanged for (0.01) share Common $0.001 par
Aurum Resource & Asset Management, Inc. name changed to Innovest Global, Inc. 01/30/2017

MINING ROYALTY CORP. (DE)
Name changed to First U.S. Southern Corp. 10/10/1960
(See First U.S. Southern Corp.)

MINING SVCS INTL CORP (UT)
Each share Common $0.001 par exchanged for (0.2) share Common $0.001 par 06/15/1987
Stock Dividends - 10% payable 10/18/1996 to holders of record 09/20/1996; 15% payable 12/13/1996 to holders of record 12/10/1996
Name changed to Nevada Chemicals, Inc. 11/08/2001
(See Nevada Chemicals, Inc.)

MINING TECHNOLOGY & RES INC (UT)
Name changed to Marathon Holdings Corp. 01/05/1989

MININGCO COM INC (DE)
Issue Information - 3,000,000 shares COM offered at $25 per share on 03/24/1999
Name changed to About.com Inc. 05/17/1999
About.com Inc. merged into Primedia Inc. 02/28/2001
(See Primedia Inc.)

MINISCRIBE CORP (DE)
Chapter 11 bankruptcy proceedings converted to Chapter 7 on 04/26/1991
Stockholders' equity unlikely

MINISTOR PERIPHERALS INTL LTD (BERMUDA)
Filed a petition under Chapter 11 Federal Bankruptcy Code 04/14/1995
Stockholders' equity unlikely

MINITONE ELECTRONICS, INC. (DE)
No longer in existence having become inoperative and void for non-payment of taxes 4/1/65

MINITRONICS, INC. (NY)
Merged into Electro-Air Corp. 06/30/1964
Each share Class A 20¢ par exchanged for (0.25) share Common 10¢ par
Each share Class B 5¢ par exchanged for (0.05) share Common 10¢ par
(See Electro-Air Corp.)

MINK GOLD MINES LTD.
Acquired by Joburke Gold Mines Ltd. on a (1) for (5) basis 00/00/1952
Joburke Gold Mines Ltd. recapitalized as New Joburke Explorations Ltd. 08/21/1973 which name changed to Cenex Ltd. 08/16/1977
(See Cenex Ltd.)

MINK INTL RES CORP (BC)
Name changed 01/16/1997
Name changed from Mink Mineral Resources Inc. to Mink International Resources Corp. 01/16/1997
Delisted from Toronto Venture Stock Exchange 03/20/2002

MINMETALS RES LTD (HONG KONG)
Name changed to MMG Ltd. 12/23/2016
(See MMG Ltd.)

MINN SHS INC (DE)
Each share old Common $0.0001 par exchanged for (0.02) share new Common $0.0001 par 04/07/2017
Name changed to EVO Transportation & Energy Services, Inc. 09/06/2017

MINN SHS INC (MN)
Each share Common 1¢ par received initial partial liquidating distribution of approximately $0.0128932 cash 00/00/2005
Each share Common 1¢ par received second partial liquidating distribution of approximately $0.0020988 cash 00/00/2007
Each share Common 1¢ par received third partial liquidating distribution of approximately $0.0033528 cash 00/00/2009
Plan of dissolution and liquidation cancelled 00/00/2009
Reorganized under the laws of Delaware 12/01/2010
Each share Common 1¢ par exchanged for (0.1) share Common $0.0001 par
Minn Shares Inc. (DE) name changed to EVO Transportation & Energy Services, Inc. 09/06/2017

MINNEAPOLIS, ST. PAUL & SAULT STE. MARIE RAILWAY CO.
Reorganized as Minneapolis, St. Paul & Sault Ste. Marie Railroad Co. in 1944
No stockholders' equity

MINNEAPOLIS & ST. LOUIS R.R. CO.
Reorganized as Minneapolis & St. Louis Railway Co. in 1943
No stockholders' equity

MINNEAPOLIS & ST. LOUIS RAILWAY CO. (MN)
Stock Dividends - 300% 11/15/1946; 33-1/3% 07/28/1954
Certain assets sold 11/01/1960, liquidating distribution made 11/25/1960 and name changed to MSL Industries, Inc. (MN) 11/30/1960
MSL Industries, Inc. (MN) reincorporated in Delaware 06/01/1973
(See MSL Industries, Inc. (DE))

MINNEAPOLIS AREA DEVELOPMENT CORP. (MN)
99.5% held by North Star Research & Development Institute when dissolved 2/11/65
No public interest for details

MINNEAPOLIS ASSOCIATES, INC. (MN)
Name changed to Imperial Financial Services, Inc. 02/24/1961
Imperial Financial Services, Inc. name changed to Imperial Investment Management Co. 04/02/1969 which name changed to St. Paul Advisors, Inc. 11/01/1976 which name changed to AMEV Advisers, Inc. 04/01/1985 which name changed to Fortis Advisers, Inc. 02/22/1992
(See Fortis Advisers, Inc.)

MINNEAPOLIS BLACK SHEEP CLUB, INC. (MN)
Forced out of business by mortgage foreclosure 10/12/63
Stock is worthless

MINNEAPOLIS BREWING CO. (MN)
Name changed to Grain Belt Breweries, Inc. 4/25/67
Grain Belt Breweries, Inc. name changed to Minneapolis Shareholders Co. 4/5/75
(See Minneapolis Shareholders Co.)

MINNEAPOLIS ENGINEERING CO., INC. (MN)
Adjudicated bankrupt 11/22/65
No stockholders' equity

MINNEAPOLIS GAS CO (DE)
6% Preferred $100 par called for redemption 07/30/1948
Stock Dividend - 50% 08/18/1972
Under plan of merger name changed to Minnesota Gas Co. 05/10/1974
(See Minnesota Gas Co.)

COPYRIGHTED MATERIAL   **NO UNAUTHORIZED REPRODUCTION**

MINNEAPOLIS GAS LIGHT CO.
Acquired by Minneapolis Gas Co. 7/30/48
Each share $5 Preferred $100 par exchanged for (1) share $5 Preferred $100 par
Each share $5.10 Preferred $100 par exchanged for (1) share $5.10 Preferred $100 par
Each share $5.50 Preferred $100 par exchanged for (1) share $5.50 Preferred $100 par
Minneapolis Gas Co. name changed to Minnesota Gas Co. 5/10/74
(See Minnesota Gas Co.)

MINNEAPOLIS HONEYWELL REGULATOR CO (DE)
Each share Common no par exchanged for (2) shares Common $3 par in 1944
Each share Common $3 par exchanged for (2) shares Common $1.50 par in 1950
Common $1.50 par split (2) for (1) by issuance of (1) additional share 5/6/55
Name changed to Honeywell Inc. 4/29/64
Honeywell Inc. merged into Honeywell International Inc. 12/1/99

MINNEAPOLIS-MOLINE CO. (MN)
Name changed to Motec Industries, Inc. 02/21/1961
Motec Industries, Inc. name changed to Dolly Madison Foods, Inc. 09/27/1963 which name changed to Dolly Madison Industries, Inc. (MN) 02/15/1966 which reincorporated in Delaware 03/13/1969
(See Dolly Madison Industries, Inc. (DE))

MINNEAPOLIS-MOLINE POWER IMPLEMENT CO. (DE)
Recapitalized under the laws of Minnesota as Minneapolis-Moline Co. 02/21/1949
Each share $6.50 Preferred no par exchanged for (1) share $5.50 1st Preferred $100 par, (1) share $1.50 2nd Preferred $25 par and (1) share Common $1 par
Each share Common $1 par exchanged for (1) share new Common $1 par
Minneapolis-Moline Co. name changed to Motec Industries, Inc. 02/21/1961 which name changed to Dolly Madison Foods, Inc. 09/27/1963 which name changed to Dolly Madison Industries, Inc. (MN) 02/15/1966 which reincorporated in Delaware 03/13/1969
(See Dolly Madison Industries, Inc. (DE))

MINNEAPOLIS REAL ESTATE ASSOCIATES (MN)
Merged into Bradley Real Estate Trust 02/01/1961
Details not available

MINNEAPOLIS SCIENTIFIC CONTROLS CORP. (MN)
Common 50¢ par changed to 10¢ par 10/16/1964 Declared insolvent 07/10/1967
No stockholders' equity

MINNEAPOLIS SHAREHOLDERS CO (MN)
Liquidation completed
Each share Capital Stock 50¢ par exchanged for initial distribution of $5.38 cash 12/27/1978
Each share Capital Stock 50¢ par received second and final distribution of $0.56 cash 02/14/1980

MINNEAPOLIS ST PAUL & SAULT STE MARIE RR CO (MN)
Merged into Soo Line Railroad Co. 12/30/60
Each share Common no par exchanged for (1) share Common no par
Soo Line Railroad Co. reorganized as Soo Line Corp. 12/31/84
(See Soo Line Corp.)

MINNEAPOLIS STEEL & MACHINERY CO.
Merged into Minneapolis-Moline Power Implement Co. 03/30/1929
Details not available

MINNEAPOLIS THRESHING MACHINE CO. (MN)
Merged into Minneapolis-Moline Power Implement Co. 03/30/1929
Details not available

MINNEAPOLIS TOWER CO.
Liquidation completed
Each share Capital Stock no par received initial distribution of $175 cash 12/29/64
Each share Capital Stock exchanged for second and final distribution of $43.62 cash 5/25/65

MINNEGASCO INC (MN)
$5 Preferred $100 par called for redemption 11/15/1990
$5.10 Preferred $100 par called for redemption 11/15/1990
$5.50 Preferred $100 par called for redemption 11/15/1990
Public interest eliminated

MINNEHOMA FINL CO (DE)
Merged into New Minnehoma Co. 8/1/72
Each share Common $3 par exchanged for $9 cash

MINNESOTA & ONTARIO PAPER CO. (ME)
Reorganized as Minnesota & Ontario Paper Co. (Minn.) in 1941
No stockholders' equity

MINNESOTA & ONTARIO PAPER CO. (MN)
Common $5 par changed to $2.50 par and (1) additional share issued 02/29/1956
Acquired by Boise Cascade Corp. 01/29/1965
Each share Common $2.50 par exchanged for (1) share $1.40 Conv. Preferred no par
(See Boise Cascade Corp.)

MINNESOTA AMERN INC (MN)
Name changed to Corvu Corp. 1/18/2000
(See Corvu Corp.)

MINNESOTA ASSD PPTYS INC (MN)
Name changed to Fuel Corp. of America (MN) 06/01/1982
Fuel Corp. of America (MN) reincorporated in Nevada 02/21/1991 which name changed to flexSCAN, Inc. 09/20/2005 which name changed to Aperture Health, Inc. 03/03/2008

MINNESOTA BANKERS LIFE INSURANCE CO. (MN)
Name changed to Bankers Capital Life Insurance Co. 10/27/67
Bankers Capital Life Insurance Co. liquidated for Pacific Standard Life Co. (Ariz.) 9/30/71 which reincorporated in Delaware 5/13/74
(See Pacific Standard Life Co. (Del.))

MINNESOTA BREWING CO (MN)
Issue Information - 1,450,000 shares COM offered at $4.50 per share on 10/26/1993
Name changed to MBC Holding Co. 12/31/99
(See MBC Holding Co.)

MINNESOTA CAPITAL CORP. (MN)
Liquidation completed
Each share Common 10¢ par received initial distribution of $0.45 cash 5/13/64
Each share Common 10¢ par received second distribution of $0.25 cash 7/6/65
Each share Common 10¢ par received third distribution of $0.13 cash 8/29/67
Each share Common 10¢ par received fourth distribution of $0.06 cash 10/31/69
Each share Common 10¢ par received fifth and final distribution of $0.1044 cash 7/12/71
Note: Certificates were not required to be surrendered and are without value

MINNESOTA EDL COMPUTING CORP (MN)
Common 1¢ par split (3) for (2) by issuance of (0.5) additional share 06/30/1995
Merged into SoftKey International Inc. 05/17/1996
Each share Common 1¢ par exchanged for (1.14286) shares Common 1¢ par
SoftKey International Inc. name changed to Learning Co. Inc. 10/24/1996 which merged into Mattel, Inc. 05/13/1999

MINNESOTA ELECTRIC DISTRIBUTING CO.
Liquidated in 1927

MINNESOTA ELECTRIC LIGHT & POWER CO.
Dissolved 00/00/1927
Details not available

MINNESOTA ELECTRONICS CO. (MN)
Adjudicated bankrupt 12/5/66
No stockholders' equity

MINNESOTA ENTERPRISES INC (MN)
5% Conv. Prior Preferred $50 par called for redemption 11/30/64
Common no par split (2) for (1) by issuance of (1) additional share 2/28/67
Reincorporated under the laws of Delaware as MEI Corp. and Common no par changed to 10¢ par 2/20/70
(See MEI Corp.)

MINNESOTA EQUITIES CORP. (MN)
Name changed to Interfinancial Corp. 9/30/69
Interfinancial Corp. merged into El Dorado International, Inc. 2/28/73 which name changed to Westamerica Inc. (Minn.) 6/30/87 which reincorporated in California 6/28/88

MINNESOTA EQUITY CORP. (MN)
Completely liquidated 12/27/68
Each share Common 10¢ par exchanged for first and final distribution of (1) share Minnesota Equities Corp. Common 10¢ par
Minnesota Equities Corp. name changed to Interfinancial Corp. 9/30/70 which merged into El Dorado International, Inc. 2/28/73 which name changed to Westamerica Inc. (Minn.) 6/30/87 which reincorporated in California 6/28/88

MINNESOTA FABRICS INC (MN)
Common 10¢ par changed to 5¢ par and (2) additional shares issued 4/29/71
Common 5¢ par split (3) for (2) by issuance of (0.5) additional share 7/30/82
Merged into Hancock Textile Co., Inc. 2/5/85
Each share Common 5¢ par exchanged for $11.50 cash
Each share Common 5¢ par received second and final distribution of $1.78 cash 7/19/91

MINNESOTA FUND, INC. (MN)
Name changed to Imperial Capital Fund, Inc. 03/29/1960
Imperial Capital Fund, Inc. name changed to St. Paul Capital Fund, Inc. 03/30/1977 which name changed to AMEV Capital Fund, Inc. 05/01/1985 which reorganized as Fortis Equity Portfolios Inc. 02/22/1992
(See Fortis Equity Portfolios Inc.)

MINNESOTA GAS CO (DE)
Reincorporated under the laws of Minnesota as Minnegasco, Inc. 07/28/1982
Under plan of reorganization each share Common $1 par automatically became (1) share Diversified Energies, Inc. Common $1 par 07/28/1982
(See each company's listing)

MINNESOTA INVESTMENT TRUST (MN)
Completely liquidated 7/15/66
Each share Capital Stock 10¢ par exchanged for first and final distribution $0.14 cash

MINNESOTA INVESTORS CORP. (DE)
Dissolved in 1954

MINNESOTA MNG & MFG CO (DE)
$4 Preferred no par called for redemption 12/12/1958
Capital Stock no par reclassified as Common no par 00/00/1947
Common no par split (2) for (1) by issuance of (1) additional share 06/22/1956
Common no par split (3) for (1) by issuance of (2) additional shares 06/10/1960
Common no par split (2) for (1) by issuance of (1) additional share 06/15/1972
Common no par split (2) for (1) by issuance of (1) additional share 06/15/1987
Common no par split (2) for (1) by issuance of (1) additional share 04/08/1994
Common no par changed to 1¢ par 05/19/2000
Stock Dividends - 100% 11/26/1945; 300% 01/08/1951
Name changed to 3M Co. 04/08/2002

MINNESOTA MUN INCOME PORTFOLIO INC (MN)
Remarketed Preferred Ser. M called for redemption at $25,000 plus $0.94 accrued dividends on 05/06/2014
Remarketed Preferred Ser. W called for redemption at $25,000 on 05/08/2014
Merged into Nuveen Minnesota Municipal Income Fund 10/06/2014
Each 144A Variable Rate MuniFund Term Preferred Share Ser. 2017 1¢ par exchanged for (1) 144A Variable Rate MuniFund Term Preferred Share Ser. 2017 1¢ par
Each Common Share of Bene. Int. 1¢ par exchanged for (1) Common Share of Bene. Int. 1¢ par
Nuveen Minnesota Municipal Income Fund name changed to Nuveen Minnesota Quality Municipal Income Fund 12/28/2016

MINNESOTA MUN TERM TR INC (MA)
Remarketed Preferred called for redemption at $25 on 9/5/2001
Trust terminated 4/10/2002
Each share Common 1¢ par exchanged for $10.183 cash

MINNESOTA MUN TERM TR INC II (MN)
Remarketed Preferred called for redemption at $25,000 on 10/25/2002
Completely liquidated 4/7/2003
Each share Common 1¢ par exchanged for first and final distribution of $10.2713 cash

MINNESOTA NAT GAS CO (MN)
Common $10 par split (3) for (2) by

issuance of (0.5) additional share 10/01/1968
Stock Dividend - 10% 06/10/1970
Merged into Minnesota Gas Co. 05/10/1974
Each share Common $10 par exchanged for (1) share Common $1 par
(See Minnesota Gas Co.)

MINNESOTA NATL LIFE INS CO (MN)
Merged into International Telephone & Telegraph Corp. 12/30/1971
Each share Common $2 par exchanged for (0.1713) share Common $1 par
International Telephone & Telegraph Corp. name changed to ITT Corp. (DE) 12/31/1983 which reorganized in Indiana as ITT Industries, Inc. 12/19/1995 which name changed to ITT Corp. 07/01/2006

MINNESOTA NORTHERN POWER CO.
Merged into Montana-Dakota Utilities Co. (MN) 00/00/1935
Details not available

MINNESOTA PHARMACEUTICAL LABORATORIES, INC. (MN)
Merged into Ivey Corp. 06/13/1964
Each share Common 50¢ par exchanged for (0.04) share Common 1¢ par
Ivey Corp. acquired by Academic Systems & Management Corp. 10/11/1968
(See Academic Systems & Management Corp.)

MINNESOTA POWER CO.
Merged into Northern States Power Co. (MN) 00/00/1926
Details not available

MINNESOTA PWR INC (MN)
Name changed 5/27/98
6% Preferred $100 par called for redemption 6/30/44
Each share 7% Preferred $100 par exchanged for (1) share 5% Preferred $100 par and $10 cash 7/1/45
Each share $6 Preferred no par exchanged for (1) share 5% Preferred $100 par and $5 cash 7/1/45
$8.90 Preferred no par called for redemption 4/22/87
$7.36 Preferred no par called for redemption 5/13/96
Name changed from Minesota Power & Light Co. to Minnesota Power, Inc. 5/27/98
Common no par split (2) for (1) by issuance of (1) additional share payable 3/2/99 to holders of record 2/16/99
5% Preferred $100 par called for redemption at $102.50 on 8/24/2000
Name changed to Allete 9/1/2000
Allete name changed to Allete, Inc. 5/7/2001

MINNESOTA ROWSER'S INC. (MN)
Name changed to Home Builders of America, Inc. 6/10/71
(See Home Builders of America, Inc.)

MINNESOTA SCIENTIFIC CORP. (MN)
Name changed to Minnesota Capital Corp. 11/22/61
Minnesota Capital Corp. liquidation completed 7/12/71

MINNESOTA SMALL BUSINESS INVESTMENT CO. (MN)
Name changed to Northeast Fidelity Investment Co. 10/7/75
Northeast Fidelity Investment Co. acquired by Fidelity Securities & Investment Co. 3/29/76

MINNESOTA TITLE FINL CORP (MN)
Merged into Old Republic International Corp. 08/09/1978
Each share Common $1.25 par exchanged for (1.18) shares Common $1 par or $30 cash
Note: Option to receive cash expired 08/25/1978

MINNESOTA VALLEY CANNING CO. (MN)
Class B Common no par split (5) for (1) by issuance of (4) additional shares 1/1/47
Name changed to Green Giant Co. (Minn.) in May 1950
Green Giant Co. (Minn.) reincorporated under the laws of Delaware 11/1/73 which was acquired by Pillsbury Co. 3/9/79
(See Pillsbury Co.)

MINNESOTA VALLEY NATURAL GAS CO. (MN)
Each share Common no par exchanged for (5) shares Common $10 par 5/12/52
Name changed to Minnesota Natural Gas Co. 9/29/65
Minnesota Natural Gas Co. merged into Minnesota Gas Co. 5/10/74
(See Minnesota Gas Co.)

MINNETONKA CORP (DE)
Common $1 par split (2) for (1) by issuance of (1) additional share 5/26/87
Merged into CKCC Acquisition Corp. 8/11/89
Each share Common $1 par exchanged for $22.86 cash

MINNETONKA INC. (MN)
Common 10¢ par changed to 3-1/3¢ par and (2) additional shares issued 2/12/81
Stock Dividend - 100% 8/22/80
Reincorporated under the laws of Delaware as Minnetonka Corp. and Common 3-1/3¢ par changed to $1 par 9/29/86
(See Minnetonka Corp. (Del.))

MINNETONKA LABORATORIES, INC. (MN)
Common 10¢ par split (2) for (1) by issuance of (1) additional share 4/14/72
Name changed to Minnetonka Inc. (MN) 5/4/77
Minnetonka Inc. (MN) reincorporated in Delaware as Minnetonka Corp. 9/29/86
(See Minnetonka Corp. (DE))

MINNETONKA MLS INC (MN)
Company merged after 1976
Details not available

MINNIE PEARLS CHICKEN SYS INC (TN)
Name changed to Performance Systems, Inc. 02/06/1969
Performance Systems, Inc. recapitalized as DSI Corp. 09/29/1978
(See DSI Corp.)

MINNITAKI IRON RANGE LTD. (ON)
Charter cancelled for failure to pay taxes and file returns 3/10/76

MINNOVA INC (QC)
Merged into Metall Mining Corp. 05/05/1993
Each share Common no par exchanged for (1.43) shares Common no par
Metall Mining Corp. name changed to Inmet Mining Corp. 05/04/1995 which was acquired by First Quantum Minerals Ltd. 04/09/2013

MINNTECH CORP (MN)
Common 5¢ par split (5) for (4) by issuance of (0.25) additional share 6/28/89
Common 5¢ par split (3) for (2) by issuance of (0.5) additional share 2/11/91
Common 5¢ par split (3) for (2) by issuance of (0.5) additional share 8/16/91
Merged into Cantel Medical Corp. 9/6/2001
Each share Common 5¢ par exchanged for (0.2216) share Common 10¢ par and $6.25 cash

MINOLTA-QMS INC (DE)
Merged into Minolta Co., Ltd. 11/13/2000
Each share Common 1¢ par exchanged for $6 cash

MINORCA RES INC (CANADA)
Each share old Common no par exchanged for (0.5) share new Common no par 08/07/1997
Merged into McWatters Mining Inc. 10/26/1998
Each share new Common no par exchanged for (0.555) share Class A Common no par
(See McWatters Mining Inc.)

MINORCA RES LTD (QC)
Under plan of merger name changed to Minorca Resources Inc. 12/30/1994
Minorca Resources Inc. merged into McWatters Mining Inc. 10/26/1998
(See McWatters Mining Inc.)

MINORCO (LUXEMBOURG)
Each Unsponsored ADR for Ordinary $1.40 par exchanged for (1) Sponsored ADR for Ordinary $1.40 par 09/26/1994
ADR agreement terminated 06/04/1999
Each Sponsored ADR for Ordinary $1.40 par exchanged for $23.3975 cash

MINORCO CDA LTD (ON)
6.25% Preferred Ser. B $100 par called for redemption 03/01/1999

MINORITY BUSINESS ENTERPRISES INC (DE)
Charter cancelled and declared inoperative and void for non-payment of taxes 03/01/1990

MINORPLANET SYS USA INC (DE)
Each share old Common 1¢ par exchanged for (0.2) share new Common 1¢ par 12/3/2003
Reorganized under Chapter 11 Federal Bankruptcy Code as Remote Dynamics, Inc. 7/2/2004
Each share new Common 1¢ par exchanged for (0.31) share Common 1¢ par
Note: Unexchanged certificates were cancelled and became valueless 7/2/2005

MINOTAUR EXPLS LTD (BC)
Common no par split (5) for (1) by issuance of (4) additional shares 03/17/1993
Name changed to China Growth Enterprises Corp. (BC) 09/15/1994
China Growth Enterprises Corp. (BC) reincorporated in Ontario as T S Telecom Ltd. 02/27/1996 which reorganized in British Columbia as Quanta Resources Inc. 03/09/2009

MINOTAUR OIL & GAS CORP. LTD. (ON)
Charter revoked for failure to file reports and pay fees 12/29/66

MINOTOLA NATL BK (VINELAND, NJ)
Location changed 08/28/1974
Location changed from (Minotola, NJ) to (Vineland, NJ) 08/28/1974
Merged into Susquehanna Bancshares, Inc. 04/21/2006
Each share Common $10 par exchanged for (104.10192) shares Common $2 par and $719.8832928 cash
Susquehanna Bancshares, Inc. merged into BB&T Corp. 08/01/2015

MINOX CHEMICAL CORP. (DE)
Charter cancelled and declared inoperative and void for non-payment of taxes 04/01/1934

MINPETRO LTD (DE)
Charter cancelled and declared inoperative and void for non-payment of taxes 03/01/1996

MINRAD INTL INC (DE)
Reincorporated 04/25/2005
State of incorporation changed from (NV) to (DE) 04/25/2005
Acquired by Piramal Healthcare, Inc. 02/27/2009
Each share Common 1¢ par exchanged for $0.12 cash

MINRES RES INC (YT)
Name changed to Geoinformatics Exploration Inc. 02/11/2005
Geoinformatics Exploration Inc. recapitalized as Kiska Metals Corp. 08/05/2009 which name changed to AuRico Metals Inc. 03/14/2017
(See AuRico Metals Inc.)

MINROC MINES INC (ON)
Name changed to Cassiar Mines & Metals, Inc. 06/10/1999
Cassiar Mines & Metals, Inc. name changed to Cassiar Magnesium Inc. 04/25/2000 which name changed to Cassiar Resources Inc. 07/25/2001 which name changed to Troutline Investments Inc. (ONT) 06/30/2003 which reorganized in Alberta as Innova Exploration Ltd. 04/16/2004
(See Innova Exploration Ltd.)

MINSHALL ORGAN & ELECTRS INC (VT)
Name changed 06/07/1960
Name changed from Minshall Organ, Inc. to Minshall Organ & Electronics, Inc. 06/07/1960
Charter revoked for failure to file reports and pay fees 02/28/1967

MINSTAR INC (DE)
Reincorporated 8/31/85
Class A Common 10¢ par split (2) for (1) by issuance of (1) additional share 3/16/84
Class A Common 10¢ par reclassified as Common 10¢ par in May, 1984
State of incorporation changed from (MN) to (DE) 8/31/85
Each share Class A Common 10¢ par exchanged for (1) share Common 10¢ par
Merged into IJ Holdings Corp. 11/10/88
Each share Common 10¢ par exchanged for $31.50 principal amount of Minstar, Inc. Subordinated Debentures due 11/9/2000

MINSTER CAP CORP (CANADA)
Merged into Capital Markets West Inc. 09/21/1989
Each (13.5) shares Common no par exchanged for (1) share Common no par
(See Capital Markets West Inc.)

MINT CARDS & DISTR INC (FL)
Name changed to UniTransact Business Solutions Inc. 01/27/1999
UniTransact Business Solutions Inc. name changed to MoneyFocus USA.com Inc. 04/03/2000 which name changed to Amnis Energy Inc. 03/22/2002 which name changed to Homeland Security Group International, Inc. 10/10/2005 which recapitalized as Domestic Energy Corp. 04/07/2008
(See Domestic Energy Corp.)

MINT CONDITION INC (NY)
Common 1¢ par split (2) for (1) by issuance of (1) additional share 2/27/87
Dissolved by proclamation 3/24/93

MINT-ORE MINES LTD.
Dissolved in 1936

MINT TECHNOLOGY CORP (AB)
Each share old Common no par exchanged for (0.05) share new Common no par 03/04/2008
Recapitalized as Mint Corp. 08/12/2013
Each share Common no par exchanged for (0.1) share Common no par

MINTARO SLATE & FLAGSTONE LTD (AUSTRALIA)
Name changed to Independent Resources Ltd. 08/15/1983
(See Independent Resources Ltd.)

MINTEK RES LTD (BC)
Recapitalized as Coast Diamond Ventures Ltd. 10/19/1992
Each share Common no par exchanged for (0.33333333) share Common no par
Coast Diamond Ventures Ltd. recapitalized as Avcan Global Systems Inc. 07/04/1994 which recapitalized as ASC Avcan Systems Corp. 04/21/1999 which recapitalized as Avcan Systems Inc. (BC) 09/07/2001 which reincorporated in Canada as Optimal Geomatics Inc. 10/09/2003 which merged into Aeroquest International Ltd. 09/30/2009
(See Aeroquest International Ltd.)

MINTEL INTL DEV CORP (BC)
Recapitalized as Golden Trump Resources Ltd. 04/05/1989
Each share Common no par exchanged for (0.2) share Common no par
Golden Trump Resources Ltd. recapitalized as Golden Triumph Resources Ltd. 09/11/2002
(See Golden Triumph Resources Ltd.)

MINTERRA RES CORP (BC)
Delisted from NEX 06/08/2010

MINTO EXPLS LTD (BC)
Acquired by Sherwood Mining Corp. 06/08/2005
Each share Common no par exchanged for (1) share Non-Vtg. Ser. 1 Preferred no par and (2.5) shares Common no par
Sherwood Mining Corp. recapitalized as Sherwood Copper Corp. 09/12/2005 which merged into Capstone Mining Corp. 11/25/2008

MINTO GOLD MINES LTD. (BC)
Dissolved in 1948

MINTO RES LTD (ON)
Reincorporated 00/00/1981
Place of incorporation changed from (BC) to (ON) 00/00/1981
Delisted from Vancouver Stock Exchange 03/04/1991

MINTROCK MINES LTD.
Bankrupt in 1946

MINTRON ENTERPRISES LTD (ON)
Delisted from Alberta Stock Exchange 02/28/1992

MINUTE APPROVED CR PLAN INC (NY)
Adjudicated bankrupt 03/06/1973
Stockholders' equity unlikely

MINUTE MAID CORP. (FL)
Common 10¢ par changed to $1 par 2/9/56
Merged into Coca Cola Co. on a (1) for (2.2) basis 12/30/60

MINUTE MAN AMER INC (AR)
Stock Dividend - 50% 09/24/1973
Recapitalized as Tone Products, Inc. 10/25/1996
Each share Common 10¢ par exchanged for (0.25) share Common 10¢ par
(See Tone Products, Inc.)

MINUTE TAPIOCA CO., INC.
Acquired by Postum Cereal Co., Inc. 00/00/1926

Details not available

MINUTEMAN INTL INC (IL)
Merged into Hako-Werke International GmbH 11/9/2004
Each share Common no par exchanged for $13.75 cash

MINVEN GOLD CORP (BC)
Plan of arrangement effective 09/15/1993
Each share Common no par exchanged for (0.08042127) Dakota Mining Corp. Unit consisting of (1) share Common no par and (0.5) Common Stock Purchase Warrant expiring 09/15/1995
(See Dakota Mining Corp.)

MINVITA ENTERPRISES LTD (BC)
Name changed to Silver Grail Resources Ltd. 2/27/2006

MIO DIO URANIUM CORP. (CO)
Declared defunct and inoperative for non-payment of franchise taxes 10/11/61

MIOCENE METALS LTD (ON)
Recapitalized as Carube Copper Corp. 07/07/2015
Each share Common no par exchanged for (0.1) share Common no par

MIOCENE RES INC (NV)
Ceased operations 2/24/92
Details not available

MIP PPTYS INC (MD)
Acquired by J.E.R. Partners L.L.C. 10/6/95
Each share Common 1¢ par exchanged for $2.475 cash

MIPS COMPUTER SYS INC (CA)
Merged into Silicon Graphics, Inc. 6/29/92
Each share Common no par exchanged for (0.52) share Common $0.001 par
(See Silicon Graphics, Inc.)

MIPS TECHNOLOGIES INC (DE)
Common $0.001 par reclassified as Class A Common $0.001 par 03/31/1999
Class A Common $0.001 par reclassified as Common $0.001 par 11/14/2003
Class B Common $0.001 par reclassified as Common $0.001 par 11/14/2003
Merged into Imagination Technologies Group PLC 02/07/2013
Each share Common $0.001 par exchanged for $8.01 cash

MIPSOLUTIONS INC (NV)
Name changed to AWG International Water Corp. 06/18/2012
AWG International Water Corp. name changed to Ambient Water Corp. 07/01/2014

MIRA IV ACQUISITION CORP (ON)
Recapitalized as Profound Medical Corp. 06/08/2015
Each share Common no par exchanged for (0.07333367) share Common no par

MIRA HOLDING CORP. (NY)
Dissolved by proclamation 12/23/92

MIRA-MAR HOTEL BUILDING CORP. (IL)
Liquidated 5/16/58

MIRA IX ACQUISITION CORP (ON)
Recapitalized as Nuuvera Inc. 01/09/2018
Each share Common no par exchanged for (0.05999999) share Common no par
Nuuvera Inc. merged into Aphria Inc. 03/27/2018

MIRA PPTYS LTD (BC)
Recapitalized as Resolve Venture, Inc. 08/19/2003
Each share Common no par

exchanged for (0.2) share Common no par

MIRA RES CORP (BC)
Recapitalized as Serrano Resources Ltd. 06/08/2015
Each share Common no par exchanged for (0.02) share Common no par

MIRA VII ACQUISITION CORP (ON)
Recapitalized as Goodfood Market Corp. 06/07/2017
Each share Common no par exchanged for (0.04500004) share Common no par

MIRA VI ACQUISITION CORP (ON)
Recapitalized as Perk.com Inc. 07/15/2015
Each share Common no par exchanged for (0.02399998) share Common no par
Perk.com Inc. name changed to Perk Inc. 06/28/2016

MIRA III ACQUISITION CORP (BC)
Recapitalized as Northern Power Systems Corp. 04/22/2014
Each share Common no par exchanged for (0.02875) share Common no par

MIRA II ACQUISITION CORP (ON)
Recapitalized as Element Financial Corp. 12/16/2011
Each share Common no par exchanged for (0.03095237) share Common no par
Element Financial Corp. name changed to Element Fleet Management Corp. 10/04/2016

MIRABEAU 88 LTD (AB)
Recapitalized 10/6/88
Recapitalized from Mirabeau Resources Ltd. to Mirabeau 88 Ltd. 10/6/88
Each share Common no par exchanged for (0.2) share Common no par
Name changed to Xenotech Inc. 8/12/94
Xenotech Inc. recapitalized as Dynamic Digital Depth, Inc. 10/19/98
(See Dynamic Digital Depth, Inc.)

MIRABEL QUICKSILVER CO.
Dissolved in 1947

MIRACLE ADHESIVES CORP (NY)
Merged into Pratt & Lambert, Inc. 12/30/1986
Each share Common $1 par exchanged for $10 cash
Note: An additional $1.45 per share is being held in escrow

MIRACLE APPLICATIONS CORP (NV)
Name changed to Outfront Companies 01/26/2011
(See Outfront Companies)

MIRACLE MART INC (DE)
Merged into Kings Department Stores, Inc. 02/02/1974
Each share Common $1 par received $10 cash

MIRACLE MILE OPTICIANS, INC. (FL)
Charter cancelled and company declared dissolved for non-payment of taxes 4/25/58

MIRACLE PET PRODS INC (NY)
Adjudicated bankrupt 01/12/1973
Stockholders' equity unlikely

MIRACLE REC EQUIP CO (IA)
Merged into Miracle Acquisition Corp. 12/28/1991
Each share Common $1 par exchanged for $8 cash

MIRACLE YELLOWKNIFE MINES LTD. (ON)
Charter cancelled 00/00/1957

MIRACOM CORP (NV)
Name changed to Parts.com, Inc. 01/05/2000
(See Parts.com, Inc.)

MIRACOM INDS INC (NV)
Recapitalized as Axesstel Inc. 09/16/2002
Each share Common $0.0001 par exchanged for (0.03448275) share Common $0.0001 par

MIRACOR DIAGNOSTICS INC (UT)
SEC revoked common stock registration 07/07/2010

MIRACULINS INC (CANADA)
Each share old Common no par exchanged for (0.1) share new Common no par 01/27/2014
Recapitalized as Luminor Medical Technologies Inc. 04/14/2016
Each share new Common no par exchanged for (0.04) share Common no par
Luminor Medical Technologies Inc. name changed to RISE Life Science Corp. 03/14/2018

MIRADO NICKEL MINES LTD (ON)
Merged into Micon Gold Inc. 01/01/2011
Each share Common $1 par exchanged for (0.4185) share Class A no par
Micon Gold Inc. merged into Jubilee Gold Exploration Ltd. 01/25/2013

MIRADOR DIVERSIFIED SVCS INC (NV)
Charter permanently revoked 06/30/2003

MIRADOR INC (NV)
Recapitalized as VWAY International 7/5/2004
Each share Common no par exchanged for (0.002) share Common no par
VWAY International name changed to WorldWide Cannery & Distribution, Inc. 2/8/2006 which name changed to Global Diamond Exchange Inc. 9/22/2006

MIRADOR MINES LTD. (ON)
Charter cancelled and declared dissolved for failure to file returns and pay fees 3/15/76

MIRAE BANCORP (CA)
Company's sole asset placed in receivership 06/26/2009
Stockholders' equity unlikely

MIRAE BK (LOS ANGELES, CA)
Common no par split (3) for (2) by issuance of (0.5) additional share payable 12/15/2004 to holders of record 11/30/2004 Ex date - 12/16/2004
Common no par split (3) for (2) by issuance of (0.5) additional share payable 09/30/2005 to holders of record 09/15/2005 Ex date - 10/03/2005
Under plan of reorganization each share Common no par automatically became (1) share Mirae Bancorp Common no par 06/15/2006
(See Mirae Bancorp)

MIRAE CORP (KOREA)
Stock Dividend - 20% payable 11/18/2003 to holders of record 10/22/2003 Ex date - 10/20/2003
ADR agreement terminated 07/07/2008
Each Sponsored ADR for Common Won 100 par exchanged for $0.52551 cash

MIRAGE CAP CORP (NV)
Charter revoked 06/30/2016

MIRAGE COMPUTERS INC (NV)
Name changed to Mega Micro Technologies Group 04/14/2000
(See Mega Micro Technologies Group)

MIRAGE ENERGY LTD (AB)
Merged into Sahara Energy Ltd. 03/31/2008
Each share Common no par

MIRAGE HLDGS INC (NV)
exchanged for (0.5) share Common no par
Name changed to Netsol International, Inc. 5/21/99
Netsol International, Inc. name changed to NetSol Technologies, Inc. 3/20/2002

MIRAGE RESORTS INC (NV)
Merged into MGM Grand Inc. 5/31/2000
Each share Common $0.008 par exchanged for $21 cash

MIRAGE RESOURCE CORP (BC)
Merged into Dayton Mining Corp. 04/06/2000
Each share Common no par exchanged for (0.03335) share Common no par
Dayton Mining Corp. merged into Pacific Rim Mining Corp. 04/11/2002 which merged into OceanaGold Corp. 12/02/2013

MIRALTA ENERGY CORP (AB)
Merged into CanEuro Resources Ltd. 7/9/90
Each share Common no par exchanged for (1.15) shares Class A Common no par
CanEuro Resources Ltd. merged into Attock Oil Corp. 2/4/91 which recapitalized as Attock Energy Corp. 8/2/95
(See Attock Energy Corp.)

MIRAMAR ENERGY CORP (BC)
Name changed to Miramar Mining Corp. 07/17/1989
(See Miramar Mining Corp.)

MIRAMAR LABS INC (DE)
Merged into Sientra, Inc. 07/25/2017
Each share Common $0.001 par exchanged for (1) Contingent Value Right and $0.3149 cash

MIRAMAR MARINE CORP (TX)
Plan of reorganization under Chapter 11 Federal Bankruptcy proceedings confirmed 11/18/1991
No stockholders' equity

MIRAMAR MNG CORP (BC)
Merged into Newmont Mining Corp. 03/17/2008
Each share Common no par exchanged for $6.25 cash

MIRAMAR RES INC (DE)
Recapitalized as Franklin Credit Management Corp. (Old) 12/15/1994
Each share Common 1¢ par exchanged for (0.05) share Common 1¢ par
Franklin Credit Management Corp. (Old) name changed to Franklin Credit Holding Corp. 04/03/2009
(See Franklin Credit Holding Corp.)

MIRAMICHI MINES LTD. (ON)
Completely liquidated 9/29/67
Each share Capital Stock $1 par exchanged for first and final distribution $0.0063 cash

MIRANDA DIAMOND CORP (BC)
Name changed to Miranda Gold Corp. 3/4/2003

MIRANDA INDS INC (BC)
Recapitalized as Thrush Industries Inc. 8/3/2001
Each share Common no par exchanged for (0.2) share Common no par
Thrush Industries Inc. name changed to Miranda Diamond Corp. 3/15/2002 which name changed to Miranda Gold Corp. 3/4/2003

MIRANDA MNG CORP (YT)
Merged into Wheaton River Minerals Ltd. 10/31/2003
Each share Common no par exchanged for $0.53637 cash

MIRANDA TECHNOLOGIES INC (QC)
Acquired by Belden Inc. (New) 07/31/2012
Each share Common no par exchanged for $17 cash

MIRANT CORP NEW (DE)
Merged into GenOn Energy, Inc. 12/03/2010
Each share Common 1¢ par exchanged for (2.835) shares Common $0.001 par
GenOn Energy, Inc. merged into NRG Energy, Inc. 12/14/2012

MIRANT CORP OLD (DE)
Plan of reorganization under Chapter 11 Federal Bankruptcy Code effective 01/03/2006
Each share Common 1¢ par exchanged for (0.02710087) share Mirant Corp. (New) Common 1¢ par and (0.0870239) Common Stock Purchase Warrant Ser. A
Note: Each share Common 1¢ par received an initial distribution of $0.12504149 cash from designated net litigation payable 09/18/2009 to holders of record 01/03/2006
Each share Common 1¢ par received second distribution of $0.03229534 cash payable 03/30/2012 to holders of record 01/03/2006
Each share Common 1¢ par received third distribution of $0.04932453 cash payable 02/03/2014 to holders of record 01/03/2006
Mirant Corp. (New) merged into GenOn Energy, Inc. 12/03/2010 which merged into NRG Energy, Inc. 12/14/2012

MIRANT TR I (DE)
Plan of reorganization under Chapter 11 Federal Bankruptcy Code effective 01/03/2006
Each 6.25% Guaranteed Trust Conv. Conv. Preferred Security Ser. A 1¢ par exchanged for approximately (1.48) shares Mirant Corp. (New) Common 1¢ par and (2.55) Common Stock Purchase Warrants Ser. B expiring 01/03/2011
Each 6.25% Guaranteed Trust Conv. Conv. Preferred Security Ser. A 1¢ par received an initial additional distribution of $0.47156118 cash payable 10/06/2009 to holders of record 01/03/2006
Each 6.25% Guaranteed Trust Conv. Conv. Preferred Security Ser. A 1¢ par received a second additional distribution of $0.12510608 cash payable 04/19/2012 to holders of record 01/03/2006
Each 6.25% Guaranteed Trust Conv. Conv. Preferred Security Ser. A 1¢ par received a third additional distribution of $0.18947362 cash payable 05/02/2014 to holders of record 01/03/2006

MIRAPLAST INC (DE)
Charter cancelled and declared inoperative and void for non-payment of taxes 3/1/85

MIRATEL ELECTRONICS CO. (MN)
Completely liquidated 6/7/67
Each share Common 5¢ par exchanged for first and final distribution of $2.2273 cash

MIRATEL ELECTRS INC (MN)
Completely liquidated 12/06/1966
Each share Common 30¢ par exchanged for first and final distribution of (0.5) share K & M Electronics, Inc. Common no par and (0.5) share Miratel Electronics Co. Common 5¢ par
(See each company's listing)

MIRAVANT MED TECHNOLOGIES (DE)
Company terminated registration of common stock and is no longer public as of 03/31/2006

MIRAX CORP (NV)
Common $0.001 par split (1.185763) for (1) by issuance of (0.185763) additional share payable 07/07/2015 to holders of record 07/06/2015
Ex date - 07/08/2015
Name changed to ViewRay, Inc. (NV) 07/20/2015
ViewRay, Inc. (NV) reincorporated in Delaware 07/21/2015

MIRCAN INDS LTD (ON)
Recapitalized as MCR Capital Inc. 03/31/1985
Each share Common no par exchanged for (1) share 2nd Preferred Ser. Y no par and (2) shares Common no par
MCR Capital Inc. recapitalized as Covesco Capital Corp. 10/22/1993 which merged into Magra Computer Technologies Corp. 08/14/1996
(See Magra Computer Technologies Corp.)

MIRIVAL GOLD MINES, LTD. (ON)
Charter cancelled 00/00/1953

MIRNA THERAPEUTICS INC (DE)
Recapitalized as Synlogic, Inc. 08/28/201 08/28/2017
Each share Common $0.001 par exchanged for (0.14285714) share Common $0.001 par

MIRO MINES LTD (ON)
Capital Stock $1 par changed to no par 07/21/1971
Charter cancelled and declared dissolved for failure to file returns and pay fees 03/16/1976

MIROMIT SOLAR CORP (BC)
Struck off register and declared dissolved for failure to file returns 5/6/83

MIRON CO. LTD. (QC)
Each share 6% Preferred $10 par exchanged for (1) share Class A no par 6/9/71
Acquired by Genstar Ltd. 5/2/74
Each share 7% Conv. Preferred Ser. A $10 par exchanged for (0.647059) share $1.10 Conv. Preferred Ser. A $20 par
Each share Class A no par exchanged for (0.294118) share $1.20 Non-Cum. Conv. Preferred Ser. B $20 par
Genstar Ltd. name changed to Genstar Corp. 6/15/81
(See Genstar Corp.)

MIRRO ALUMINUM CO. (NJ)
Capital Stock $10 par changed to $5 par and (1) additional share issued 05/10/1973
Name changed to Mirro Corp. 05/01/1979
(See Mirro Corp.)

MIRRO CORP (NJ)
Merged into Newell Companies, Inc. 07/15/1983
Each share Capital Stock $5 par exchanged for $18 principal amount of 8.75% Conv. Subordinated Debentures due 07/15/2003

MIRROR ME INC (NV)
Name changed to Twinlab Consolidated Holdings, Inc. 08/18/2014

MIRROR TECHNOLOGIES INC (MN)
Name changed to Global Maintech Corp. (Old) 05/15/1995
Global Maintech Corp. (Old) name changed to Singlepoint Systems Corp. 08/14/2000 which name changed to Global Maintech Corp. (New) 03/07/2001
(See Maintech Corp. (New))

MIRTONE INTL INC (ON)
Reorganized as International Mirtone Inc. 02/21/1988
Each share Conv. Class A Non-Vtg. no par exchanged for (0.5) share Preference Ser. 1 no par
Each share Common no par exchanged for (0.5) share Common no par
International Mirtone Inc. name changed to Mirtronics Inc. 03/09/1990 which merged into Genterra Inc. 12/31/2003 which merged into Genterra Capital Inc. (New) 05/10/2010 which merged into Gencan Capital Inc. 10/30/2015

MIRTRONICS INC (ON)
Each share $0.026 Preferred Ser. 1 no par exchanged for (1) share Non-Vtg. Class B Preference no par 05/15/1997
Merged into Genterra Inc. 12/31/2003
Each share Non-Vtg. Class B Preference no par exchanged for (1) share Class C Preferred no par
Each share Common no par exchanged for (1.25) shares Class A Subordinate no par
Genterra Inc. merged into Genterra Capital Inc. (New) 05/10/2010 which merged into Gencan Capital Inc. 10/30/2015

MIS INTL INC (DE)
Reincorporated 07/01/1997
Reincorporated from MIS Multimedia Interactive Services Inc. (BC) to MIS International, Inc. (DE) and Common no par changed to $0.001 par 07/01/1997
Name changed to Cosmoz.Com, Inc. 12/07/1998
Cosmoz.Com, Inc. name changed to Cozmoz Infrastructure Solutions, Inc. 04/16/2001 which recapitalized as FinancialContent, Inc. 11/13/2001
(See FinancialContent, Inc.)

MIS SOLUTIONS INC (DE)
Recapitalized as Solutions Software Inc. 03/10/1999
Each share Common $0.001 par exchanged for (0.01) share Common $0.001 par
Solutions Software Inc. recapitalized as Solutions Software 2001 Inc. 04/20/2001 which recapitalized as EMC Development Corp. 01/14/2003 which recapitalized as EM International Enterprises Corp. 01/24/2008
(See EM International Enterprises Corp.)

MISCERAMIC TILE INC (MS)
Class A Common $1 par reclassified as Common $1 par 07/17/1961
Acquired by Banner Industries, Inc. (MO) 06/05/1969
Each share Common $1 par exchanged for (1/3) share Common 10¢ par
Banner Industries, Inc. (MO) reincorporated in Delaware 11/13/1970 which name changed to Fairchild Corp. 11/15/1990
(See Fairchild Corp.)

MISCHER CORP (DE)
Reincorporated 8/31/72
State of incorporation changed from (TX) to (DE) and each share Common no par exchanged for (1) share Common $1 par 8/31/72
Name changed to Southern Investors Service Co., Inc. 5/21/93
(See Southern Investors Service Co., Inc.)

MISCHIEF ENTERPRISES LTD (BC)
Name changed to CV Sportsmark International Inc. 07/15/1985
(See CV Sportsmark International Inc.)

MISCO DISSOLUTION CORP. (CA)
Completely liquidated 03/19/1971
Each share Common $1 par exchanged for (0.1508) share LST Electronics Inc. Common no par

MISCOR GROUP LTD (IN)
Each share old Common no par exchanged for (0.04) share new Common no par 01/14/2008
Merged into Integrated Electrical Services, Inc. 09/13/2013
Each share Common no par exchanged for (0.3118) share Common no par
Integrated Electrical Services, Inc. name changed to IES Holdings, Inc. 05/25/2016

MISECURITYPLUS INC (WY)
Reincorporated 5/23/2003
Place of incorporation changed from (ONT) to (WY) 5/23/2003
Each share old Common no par exchanged for (0.004) share new Common no par 6/25/2004
Name changed to WayPoint Biomedical Holdings, Inc. 5/24/2005

MISES CAP CORP (AB)
Name changed to Saha Petroleum Ltd. 04/25/2008
Saha Petroleum Ltd. name changed to Western Plains Petroleum Ltd. 08/26/2009
(See Western Plains Petroleum Ltd.)

MISHIBISHU GOLD CORP (BC)
Recapitalized as Messina Minerals Inc. 04/07/2003
Each share Common no par exchanged for (0.33333333) share Common no par
Messina Minerals Inc. merged into Canadian Zinc Corp. 12/20/2013 which name changed to NorZinc Ltd. 09/11/2018

MISHIBISHU RES LTD (BC)
Merged into Mishibishu Gold Corp. 10/27/1989
Each share Common no par exchanged for (0.6278) share Common no par
Mishibishu Gold Corp. recapitalized as Messina Minerals Inc. 04/07/2003 which merged into Canadian Zinc Corp. 12/20/2013 which name changed to NorZinc Ltd. 09/11/2018

MISR INTL BK SAE (EGYPT)
144A GDR's for Ordinary split (2) for (1) by issuance of (1) additional GDR payable 9/8/2004 to holders of record 9/1/2004
Regulation S GDR's for Ordinary split (2) for (1) by issuance of (1) additional GDR payable 9/8/2004 to holders of record 9/1/2004
Stock Dividend - 25% payable 11/5/2001 to holders of record 10/30/2001 Ex date - 10/26/2001
Merged into National Societe Generale Bank 11/30/2006
Each 144A GDR for Ordinary exchanged for $2.26221 cash
Each Regulation S GDR for Ordinary exchanged for $2.26221 cash

MISS ELLIETTE INC (DE)
Name changed to Continental Alliance Corp. 04/15/1969
(See Continental Alliance Corp.)

MISS-LA-TEX OIL & GAS CORP. (MS)
Charter suspended for failure to file reports and pay taxes 01/31/1967

MISS PAT (CA)
Common no par changed to 10¢ par 00/0/1972
Name changed to Beno's 05/27/1976
(See Beno's)

MISSI ENERGY LTD (AB)
Recapitalized 06/01/1990
Recapitalized from Missi Resources Ltd. to Missi Energy Ltd. 06/01/1990
Each share Common no par exchanged for (0.05) share Common no par
Name changed to Torino Oil & Gas Ltd. 02/09/1993
(See Torino Oil & Gas Ltd.)

MISSILE COMPONENTS CORP (NY)
Dissolved by proclamation 12/16/68

MISSILE SITES, INC. (DE)
Name changed to MSI Corp. 10/22/62
(See MSI Corp.)

MISSILE SYSTEMS CORP. (DE)
Name changed to Baifield Industries, Inc. 06/01/1964
Baifield Industries, Inc. liquidated for Automatic Sprinkler Corp. of America (OH) 07/12/1967 which name changed to A-T-O Inc. 10/29/1969 which name changed to Figgie International Inc. (OH) 06/01/1981 which reorganized in Delaware as Figgie International Holdings Inc. 07/18/1983 which name changed to Figgie International Inc. 12/31/1986 which name changed to Scott Technologies, Inc. 05/20/1998 which merged into Tyco International Ltd. (Bermuda) 05/03/2001 which reincorporated in Switzerland 03/17/2009 which merged into Johnson Controls International PLC 09/06/2016

MISSILE-TRONICS CORP. (NJ)
Charter forfeited for non-payment of taxes 2/3/65

MISSILES-JETS & AUTOMATION FUND, INC. (DE)
Acquired by Axe Science & Electronics Corp. 08/22/1960
Each share Capital Stock $1 par exchanged for (0.9544) share Capital Stock $1 par plus $0.044 cash
Axe Science & Electronics Corp. name changed to Axe Science Corp. 01/30/1964 which merged into Axe-Houghton Stock Fund, Inc. (MD) 12/09/1974 which reorganized as Axe-Houghton Funds, Inc. Growth Fund 10/31/1990
(See Axe-Houghton Funds, Inc.)

MISSIMER & ASSOC INC (FL)
Name changed to ViroGroup, Inc. 10/16/92
(See ViroGroup, Inc.)

MISSION APPLIANCE CORP. (CA)
Merged into Gaffers & Sattler Corp. 5/31/63
Each share Common $5 par exchanged for (0.756) share Common $1 par
(See Gaffers & Sattler Corp.)

MISSION BK (BAKERSFIELD, CA)
Stock Dividend - 5% payable 03/01/2000 to holders of record 02/15/2000
Under plan of reorganization each share Common no par automatically became (1) share Mission Bancorp Common no par 06/14/2002

MISSION BK (EL TORO, CA)
Merged into Southwest Bank (Vista, CA) 7/29/77
Each share Common $2.50 par exchanged for (1.75) shares Common $1.50 par
Southwest Bank (Vista, CA) reorganized as Southwest Bancorp 10/31/81 which was acquired by Security Pacific Corp. 10/19/89 which merged into BankAmerica Corp. (Old) 4/22/92 which merged into BankAmerica Corp. (New) 9/30/98 which name changed to Bank of America Corp. 4/28/99

MISSION BANK (RIVERSIDE, CA)
Acquired by Riverside National Bank (Riverside, CA) 05/06/1988
Details not available

MISSION CAP L P (DE)
9.875% Monthly Income Preferred Securities A no par called for redemption at $25 on 1/25/2005
8.50% Monthly Income Preferred Securities B no par called for redemption at $25 on 1/25/2005

MISSION CHEMICAL CO. (TX)
Name changed to Tex-Ag Co. 7/9/69
Each share Common $1 par exchanged for (1) share Common $1 par
Tex-Ag Co. merged into Tanger Industries 6/30/71 which name changed to Verit Industries (CA) 4/2/73 which reincorporated in Delaware as Verit Industries, Inc. 1/2/92
(See Verit Industries, Inc.)

MISSION CMTY BANCORP (CA)
Merged into Heritage Oaks Bancorp 02/28/2014
Each share Common $5 par exchanged for (0.8477) share Common no par and $0.2817 cash
Heritage Oaks Bancorp merged into Pacific Premier Bancorp, Inc. 03/31/2017

MISSION CMNTY BK N A (SAN LUIS OBISPO, CA)
Under plan of reorganization each share Common $5 par automatically became (1) share Mission Community Bancorp Common $5 par 12/18/2000
Mission Community Bancorp merged into Heritage Oaks Bancorp 02/28/2014 which merged into Pacific Premier Bancorp, Inc. 03/31/2017

MISSION CORP (NV)
Common no par changed to $10 par 00/00/1938
Common $10 par changed to $1 par and (2) additional shares issued 00/00/1951
Merged into Getty Oil Co. 01/31/1977
Each share Common $1 par exchanged for (1.4771) shares Common $4 par
(See Getty Oil Co.)

MISSION CRITICAL SOFTWARE INC (DE)
Merged into NetIQ Corp. 05/15/2000
Each share Common $0.001 par exchanged for (0.9413) share Common $0.001 par
(See NetIQ Corp.)

MISSION DEVELOPMENT CO. (DE)
Merged into Getty Oil Co. 9/30/67
Each share Capital Stock $5 par exchanged for (1.6688) shares Common $4 par
(See Getty Oil Co.)

MISSION DRY CORP. (DE)
Acquired by Cott Beverage Corp. 5/15/56
Each share Common $1 par exchanged for $6 principal amount of 5% Conv. Debentures due 1/1/76

MISSION EQUITIES CORP (CA)
Capital Stock no par split (3) for (2) by issuance of (0.5) additional share 1/24/73
Capital Stock no par reclassified as Common no par 5/22/73
Name changed to Mission Insurance Group, Inc. 5/19/77
Mission Insurance Group, Inc. reorganized as Danielson Holding Corp. (CA) 8/15/90 which reincorporated in Delaware 5/1/92 which name changed to Covanta Holding Corp. 9/20/2005

MISSION FINL LTD (ON)
Merged into H.R.S. Industries, Inc. 05/21/1982
Each share Common no par exchanged for (2) shares Class B Common no par
H.R.S. Industries, Inc. merged into International H.R.S. Industries Inc. 05/15/1984 which name changed to Glenex Industries Inc. 05/25/1987 which merged into Quest Investment Corp. 07/04/2002 which merged into Quest Capital Corp. (BC) 06/30/2003 which reincorporated in Canada 05/27/2008 which name changed to Sprott Resource Lending Corp. 09/10/2010 which merged into Sprott Inc. 07/24/2013

MISSION GOLD LTD (BC)
Merged into Northern Dynasty Minerals Ltd. 12/24/2015
Each share Common no par exchanged for (0.5467) share Common no par
Note: Unexchanged certificates will be cancelled and become without value 12/24/2021

MISSION INDEMNITY CO. (CA)
Common $1 par changed to 65¢ par 6/15/53
Name changed to Mission Insurance Co. 5/1/59

MISSION INS CO (CA)
10% Preferred called for redemption 11/09/1960
Common 65¢ par changed to $1.30 par 12/06/1960
Common $1.30 par changed to $1 par 07/17/1963
Each share Common $1 par exchanged for (0.00125) share Common $800 par 05/11/1972
Note: In effect holders received $24 cash per share public interest was eliminated

MISSION INS GROUP INC (CA)
Common no par split (3) for (2) by issuance of (0.5) additional share 10/25/78
Common no par split (3) for (2) by issuance of (0.5) additional share 10/25/79
Common no par split (3) for (2) by issuance of (0.5) additional share 4/26/82
Reorganized under Chapter 11 Federal Bankruptcy Code as Danielson Holding Corp. (CA) 8/15/90
Each share Common no par exchanged for approximately (0.0053) share Common 10¢ par
Danielson Holding Corp. (CA) reincorporated in Delaware 5/1/92 which name changed to Covanta Holding Corp. 9/20/2005

MISSION INVT TR (CA)
Under plan of reorganization each Share of Bene. Int. $1 par automatically became (1) share Mission West Properties (CA) Common no par 07/22/1982
Mission West Properties (CA) reorganized in Maryland as Mission West Properties, Inc. 12/28/1998 which liquidated for Mission West Liquidating Trust 12/28/2012
(See Mission West Liquidating Trust)

MISSION MNG & DEV LTD (BC)
Name changed 5/27/75
Name changed from Mission Mining Ltd. to Mission Mining & Development Ltd. 5/27/75
Struck off register and declared dissolved for failure to file returns 9/21/84

MISSION NATIONAL BANK (LOS ANGELES, CA)
Completely liquidated 1/23/67
Each share Capital Stock $15 par exchanged for first and final distribution of $27.07 cash

MISSION NATL BK (SAN FRANCISCO, CA)
Under plan of reorganization each share Common $5 par automatically became (1) share MNB Holdings Corp. Common no par 12/12/2002

MISSION OAKS BANCORP (CA)
Stock Dividends - 5% payable 01/31/2007 to holders of record

01/15/2007 Ex date - 01/10/2007; 5% payable 01/31/2008 to holders of record 01/15/2008 Ex date - 01/11/2008
Acquired by AltaPacific Bancorp 05/02/2014
Each share Common $5 par exchanged for $0.30 cash

MISSION OAKS NATL BK (TEMECULA, CA)
Common no par split (2) for (1) by issuance of (1) additional share payable 04/08/2004 to holders of record 04/01/2004 Ex date - 04/12/2004
Reorganized as Mission Oaks Bancorp 09/01/2005
Each share Common no par exchanged for (2) shares Common $5 par
(See Mission Oaks Bancorp)

MISSION OIL & GAS INC (AB)
Merged into Crescent Point Energy Trust 02/14/2007
Each share Common no par exchanged for (0.695) Trust Unit no par and $0.78 cash
Crescent Point Energy Trust reorganized as Crescent Point Energy Corp. 07/07/2009

MISSION OIL CO.
Liquidation completed in 1953

MISSION PK CORP (CA)
98% acquired by First Canadian Development Co. through purchase offer which expired 00/00/1980
Public interest eliminated

MISSION READY SVCS INC (BC)
Name changed to Mission Ready Solutions Inc. 06/05/2018

MISSION RESH CORP (DE)
Acquired by Alliant Techsystems Inc. 05/00/2004
Details not available

MISSION RESOURCE PARTNERS L P (DE)
Liquidation completed
Each Unit of Ltd. Partnership Int. received initial distribution of $8.54 cash 2/14/91
Each Unit of Ltd. Partnership Int. received second distribution of $0.425 cash 6/14/91
Each Unit of Ltd. Partnership Int. received third distribution of $0.18 cash 12/31/91
Each Unit of Ltd. Partnership Int. received fourth and final distribution of $22 cash 5/18/92

MISSION RES CORP (DE)
Merged into Petrohawk Energy Corp. 7/28/2005
Each share Common 1¢ par exchanged for $8.2752 cash

MISSION SAVINGS & LOAN ASSOCIATION (CA)
Acquired by LFC Financial Corp. 12/20/1968
Each share Guarantee Stock no par exchanged for (1.925949) shares Capital Stock $1 par
LFC Financial Corp. merged into Great Western Financial Corp. 12/22/1970 which merged into Washington Mutual Inc. 07/01/1997
(See Washington Mutual, Inc.)

MISSION STATE BANK & TRUST CO. (MISSION, KS)
Stock Dividend - 20% 02/16/1971
Declared insolvent and closed by the Kansas Bank Commissioner 08/08/1980
Stockholders' equity unlikely

MISSION VALLEY BANCORP (CA)
Common no par split (3) for (2) by issuance of (0.5) additional share 11/27/1989
Merged into California Bancshares Inc. 07/01/1991

Each share Common no par exchanged for (1) share Common $2.50 par
California Bancshares Inc. merged into U.S. Bancorp (OR) 06/06/1996 which merged into U.S. Bancorp 08/01/1997

MISSION VY BK (SUN VALLEY, CA)
Common no par split (5) for (4) by issuance of (0.25) additional share payable 4/15/2003 to holders of record 4/7/2003 Ex date - 4/16/2003
Common no par split (3) for (2) by issuance of (0.5) additional share payable 4/1/2005 to holders of record 3/18/2005 Ex date - 4/4/2005
Under plan of reorganization each share Common no par automatically became (1) share Mission Valley Bancorp Common no par 9/1/2005

MISSION WEST LIQUIDATING TR (MD)
Liquidation completed
Each Unit of Bene. Int. received initial distribution of $9.18 cash payable 01/15/2013 to holders of record 12/28/2012
Each Unit of Bene. Int. received second and final distribution of $0.1701 cash payable 09/18/2013 to holders of record 12/28/2012

MISSION WEST PPTYS (CA)
Each share old Common no par exchanged for (1/30) share new Common no par 11/10/1997
Reorganized under the laws of Maryland as Mission West Properties, Inc. 12/28/1998
Each share new Common no par exchanged for (1) share Common $0.001 par
Mission West Properties, Inc. liquidated for Mission West Liquidating Trust 12/28/2012
(See Mission West Liquidating Trust)

MISSION WEST PPTYS INC (MD)
Assets transferred to Mission West Liquidating Trust and Common $0.001 par reclassified as Units of Bene. Int. 12/28/2012
(See Mission West Liquidating Trust)

MISSISQUOI STONE & MARBLE CO. LTD. (QC)
Went into bankruptcy in 1956 and woundup 4/27/62
Preference and Common Stocks are valueless

MISSISSIPPI BK (JACKSON, MS)
Name changed 03/08/1976
Name changed from Mississippi Bank & Trust Co. (Jackson, MS) to Mississippi Bank (Jackson, MS) 03/08/1976
Stock Dividend - 25% 03/17/1978
Bank failed 05/12/1984
No stockholders' equity

MISSISSIPPI CENT RR CO (MS)
Preferred $10 par called for redemption 04/28/1967
Liquidation completed
Each share Common $100 par exchanged for initial distribution of $8.70 cash 05/23/1967
Each share Common $100 par received second and final distribution of $0.35 cash 04/25/1968

MISSISSIPPI CHEM CORP NEW (MS)
Reorganized 07/01/1994
Each share Nitrogen Ser. I Common $30 par, Nitrogen Ser. II Common $15 par, Nitrogen Ser. III Common $2 par, Mixed Ser. IV Common $15 par, and Mixed Ser. V Common $15 par exchanged for (1) share new Common 1¢ par
Plan of reorganization under Chapter 11 Federal Bankruptcy Code effective 12/21/2004
Each share new Common 1¢ par received approximately

(0.01030927) share Terra Industries Inc. Common no par
Note: Certificates were not required to be surrendered and are without value
Terra Industries Inc. merged into CF Industries Holdings, Inc. 04/15/2010

MISSISSIPPI CHEMICAL CORP. OLD (MS)
Recapitalized 07/01/1966
Special Common $75 par changed to $45 par
Common $5 par changed to $3 par
Merged into Mississippi Chemical Corp. (New) 06/30/1972
Each share Special Common $45 par exchanged for (1) share Nitrogen Ser. III Common $2 par
Each share Common $3 par exchanged for (1) share Nitrogen Ser. I Common $30 par
Mississippi Chemical Corp. (New) reorganized as Terra Industries Inc. 12/21/2004 which merged into CF Industries Holdings, Inc. 04/15/2010

MISSISSIPPI GLASS CO. (NY)
Each share Capital Stock $100 par exchanged for (4) shares Capital Stock $25 par in 1929
Capital Stock $25 par reclassified as Class A $25 par in 1932
Each share Class A $25 par exchanged for (1) share 4% Preferred $15 par and (1) share Common no par in 1942
Each share Class B $25 par exchanged for (1) share Common no par in 1942
4% Preferred $15 par called for redemption 4/1/55
Common no par changed to $10 par and (1) additional share issued 5/17/55
Stock Dividend - 10% 2/9/62
Acquired by Combustion Engineering, Inc. 2/29/68
Each share Common $10 par exchanged for (1) share $1.70 Conv. Preferred Ser. A no par
(See Combustion Engineering, Inc.)

MISSISSIPPI INDS INC (MS)
Name changed to Hood Industries, Inc. 11/04/1969
Hood Industries, Inc. acquired by Masonite Corp. 06/16/1970
(See Masonite Corp.)

MISSISSIPPI PWR & LT CO (MS)
Reincorporated 05/01/1963
State of incorporation changed from (FL) to (MS) 05/01/1963
17% Preferred $100 par called for redemption 11/01/1986
16.16% Preferred $100 par called for redemption 11/01/1993
9% Preferred $100 par called for redemption 07/01/1995
12% Preferred $100 par called for redemption 05/01/1996
Name changed to Entergy Mississippi, Inc. 04/22/1996

MISSISSIPPI PWR CAP TR II (DE)
7.20% Trust Originated Preferred Securities called for redemption at $25 on 4/6/2007

MISSISSIPPI PWR CO (MS)
Reincorporated 12/21/1972
State of incorporation changed from (ME) to (MS) 12/21/1972
10.2% Preferred $100 par called for redemption 06/28/1991
8.44% Preferred $100 par called for redemption 09/27/1993
8.8% Preferred $100 par called for redemption 09/00/1993
7.25% Depositary Preferred called for redemption at $25 on 08/04/1997
6.32% Preferred $100 par called for redemption at $102 plus $0.052666 accrued dividends on 04/05/2004
6.32% Depositary Preferred called for redemption at $25 on 04/05/2004

6.65% Depositary Preferred called for redemption at $25 on 04/05/2004
7% Preferred $100 par called for redemption at $103.20 on 04/05/2004
4.4% Preferred $100 par called for redemption at $104.32 plus $0.268889 accrued dividends on 10/23/2018
4.6% Preferred $100 par called for redemption at $107 plus $0.281111 accrued dividends on 10/23/2018
4.72% Preferred $100 par called for redemption at $102.25 plus $0.2888444 accrued dividends on 10/23/2018
5.25% Depositary Preferred called for redemption at $25 plus $0.080208 accrued dividends on 10/23/2018

MISSISSIPPI RIVER CORP (DE)
Common $10 par changed to $5 par and (1) additional share issued 06/04/1965
Name changed to Missouri Pacific Corp. 05/27/1976
Missouri Pacific Corp. merged into Union Pacific Corp. 12/22/1982

MISSISSIPPI RIVER FUEL CORP (DE)
Capital Stock $10 par reclassified as Common $10 par in 1951
Common $10 par split (2) for (1) by issuance of (1) additional share 6/1/55
Stock Dividend - 10% 12/27/50
Name changed to Mississippi River Corp. 5/28/65
Mississippi River Corp. name changed to Missouri Pacific Corp. 5/27/76 which merged into Union Pacific Corp. 12/22/82

MISSISSIPPI RIVER POWER CO.
Merged into Union Electric Co. of Missouri in 1945
Each share 6% Preferred exchanged for (1) share $4.50 Preferred and $2.82 in cash
Each share Common exchanged for (0.75) share $4.50 Preferred
Union Electric Co. of Missouri name changed to Union Electric Co. 4/24/56

MISSISSIPPI RIVER TRANSMISSION CORP (DE)
Merged into Mississippi River Corp. 07/01/1974
Each share Common $1 par exchanged for $20 principal amount of 8% Conv. Subord. Debentures due 07/01/1994

MISSISSIPPI SHIPPING CO., INC. (LA)
Each share Capital Stock $100 par exchanged for (10) shares new Capital Stock $10 par 00/00/1940
Each share Capital Stock $10 par exchanged for (2) shares new Capital Stock $5 par 00/00/1946
Stock Dividends - 20% 11/19/1947; 11-1/9% 12/30/1948; 12-1/2% 12/14/1951
Name changed to Delta Steamship Lines, Inc. 04/23/1962
(See Delta Steamship Lines, Inc.)

MISSISSIPPI STL CORP (MS)
Name changed to Magna Corp. 4/11/69
(See Magna Corp.)

MISSISSIPPI VY AIRLS INC (DE)
Merged into Air Wis Services, Inc. 5/17/85
Each share Common 10¢ par exchanged for (0.4621) share Common 10¢ par
Air Wis Services, Inc. merged into UAL Corp. 1/27/92
(See UAL Corp.)

MISSISSIPPI VY BANCSHARES INC (MO)
Common $1 par split (2) for (1) by issuance of (1) additional share

payable 1/1/98 to holders of record 12/15/97
Merged into Marshall & Ilsley Corp. 10/1/2002
Each share Common $1 par exchanged for (1.1622) shares Common $1 par and $17.48 cash

MISSISSIPPI VALLEY BARGE LINE CO (DE)
Common no par changed to $1 par 00/00/1939
Merged into Chromalloy American Corp. (NY) 06/04/1968
Each share Common $1 par exchanged for (0.4359) share $5 Conv. Preferred $1 par
Chromalloy American Corp. (NY) reincorporated in Delaware 10/31/1968 which merged into Sun Chemical Corp. 12/23/1986 which name changed to Sequa Corp. 05/08/1987
(See Sequa Corp.)

MISSISSIPPI VALLEY GAS CO (MS)
Common $5 par split (3) for (2) by issuance of (0.5) additional share 03/30/1966
Common $5 par split (5) for (4) by issuance of (0.25) additional share 05/01/1979
Stock Dividends - 25% 06/03/1955; 10% 11/18/1964; 10% 07/31/1970; 10% 07/30/1976
Through purchase offer majority of shares acquired by Yazoo Investment Corp. as of 05/04/1984
Public interest eliminated

MISSISSIPPI VALLEY HELICOPTERS, INC. (MO)
Out of business 2/3/64
No stockholders' equity

MISSISSIPPI VALLEY PORTLAND CEM CO (MS)
Name changed to Valley Cement Industries, Inc. 12/15/69
(See Valley Cement Industries, Inc.)

MISSISSIPPI VALLEY PUBLIC SERVICE CO. (WI)
Each share Common $100 par exchanged for (5) shares Common $10 par in 1949
Stock Dividends - 10% 1/31/55; 10% 8/31/56
Assets sold to Northern States Power Co. (MN) on a (1.65) for (1) basis 2/1/60
5% Preferred called for redemption 3/1/60
Northern States Power Co. (MN) name changed to Xcel Energy Inc. 8/18/2000

MISSISSIPPI VALLEY STRUCTURAL STL CO (IL)
Reincorporated under the laws of Delaware as Debron Corp. 6/15/72
(See Debron Corp.)

MISSISSIPPI VY TITLE INS CO (MS)
Each share Common no par exchanged for (0.002) share Common $500 par 1/11/80
Note: In effect holders received $31 cash per share and public interest was eliminated

MISSISSIPPI VALLEY UTILITIES INVESTMENT CO.
Liquidation completed in 1940

MISSISSIPPI VIEW HLDG CO (MN)
Merged into MIVI Acquisition Corp. 12/15/2004
Each share Common 10¢ par exchanged for $25.75 cash

MISSOURI BANCSHARES INC (MO)
Name changed to United Missouri Bancshares, Inc. 09/01/1971
United Missouri Bancshares, Inc. name changed to UMB Financial Corp. 04/22/1994

MISSOURI BEEF PACKERS INC (MO)
Common $10 par changed to $4 par and (1.5) additional shares issued 02/07/1968
6% Preferred $100 par called for redemption 04/01/1969
Merged into MBPXL Corp. 09/03/1974
Each share Common $4 par exchanged for (1) share Common $1 par
(See MBPXL Corp.)

MISSOURI EDISON CO (MO)
Stock Dividend - 12-1/2% 12/26/50
Merged into Union Electric Co. 12/30/83
Each share Common $5 par exchanged for (1) share $5.50 Preferred no par

MISSOURI FID UN TR LIFE INS CO (MN)
Merged into National Western Life Insurance Co. (CO) 10/15/1970
Each share Common $1 par exchanged for (0.357142) share Class A Common $1 par
National Western Life Insurance Co. (CO) reincorporated in Delaware as National Western Life Group, Inc. 10/02/2015

MISSOURI FIDELITY LIFE INSURANCE CO. (MO)
Merged into Missouri Fidelity/Union Trust Life Insurance Co. 12/31/1965
Each share Common $1 par exchanged for (1) share Common $1 par
Missouri Fidelity/Union Trust Life Insurance Co. merged into National Western Life Insurance Co. (CO) 10/15/1970 which reincorporated in Delaware as National Western Life Group, Inc. 10/02/2015

MISSOURI GAS & ELECTRIC SERVICE CO.
Merged into Missouri Public Service Co. (New) 00/00/1951
Each share Common no par exchanged for (5) shares new Common no par
Missouri Public Service Co. (New) name changed to UtiliCorp United Inc. (MO) 05/02/1985 which reincorporated in Delaware 04/01/1987 which name changed to Aquila, Inc. (New) 03/15/2002 which was acquired by Great Plains Energy Inc. 07/14/2008 which merged into Evergy, Inc. 06/05/2018

MISSOURI GENERAL INSURANCE CO. (MO)
Charter forfeited for failure to file reports 1/1/77

MISSOURI ILL MNG INC (UT)
Involuntarily dissolved 03/01/1989

MISSOURI-ILLINOIS BRIDGE CO.
Reorganized as Champ Clark Bridge Co. 00/00/1936
(See Champ Clark Bridge Co.)

MISSOURI ILLINOIS STORES CO.
Acquired by Kroger Grocery & Baking Co. in 1928 which name was changed to Kroger Co. 3/11/46

MISSOURI INSURANCE CO. (MO)
Name changed to Life Insurance Co. of Missouri 4/30/56 which was completely liquidated 6/30/57

MISSOURI KANS PIPELINE CO (DE)
Merged into Panhandle Eastern Pipe Line Co. 4/21/71
Each share Common $1 par exchanged for (4.72346) shares Common no par
Each share Class B $1 par exchanged for (0.236173) share Common no par
Panhandle Eastern Pipe Line Co. reorganized as Panhandle Eastern Corp. 5/22/81 which merged into Duke Energy Corp. (NC) 6/18/97 which merged into Duke Energy Corp. (DE) 4/3/2006

MISSOURI KANS TEX RR CO (DE)
Reincorporated 07/01/1960
Recapitalized 12/31/1958
Each share 7% Preferred Ser. A $100 par exchanged for (1) share Common $5 par, $100 principal amount of 5-1/2% Debentures and $110 principal amount of Non-Interest Bearing Ctfs.
Common no par changed to $5 par
State of incorporation changed from (MO) to (DE) 07/01/1960
Through exchange offer 98% of Common $5 par acquired by Katy Industries, Inc. as of 05/09/1968
Note: Shares not tendered exchanged for $52.26 cash
Non-Interest Bearing Certificates called for redemption at $110 on 03/15/2002
Public interest eliminated

MISSOURI LINCOLN TR CO (ST. LOUIS, MO)
Liquidation completed
Each share Capital Stock $50 par exchanged for initial distribution of (1) Missouri-Lincoln Trust Co. Unit of Net Profits Interest in Royalty and $88.217 cash 3/30/73
Note: Details on subsequent distributions, if any, are not available

MISSOURI-MC KEE MINES (CANADA) LTD.
Dissolved in 1938

MISSOURI MED INS CO (MO)
Each share Class A Common $1 par exchanged for (0.00002) share Common $3,000 par 12/09/1989
Note: In effect holders received $2.375 cash per share and public interest was eliminated

MISSOURI NAT GAS CO (MO)
Each share Capital Stock $5 par exchanged for (2) shares Capital Stock $2.50 par 02/01/1955
Merged into Laclede Gas Co. 02/29/1972
Each share Capital Stock $2.50 par exchanged for (0.5) share Common $4 par
Laclede Gas Co. reorganized as Laclede Group, Inc. 10/01/2001 name changed to Spire Inc. 04/29/2016

MISSOURI NATIONAL LIFE INSURANCE CO. (MO)
Incorporated 5/29/29
Dissolution ordered and charter forfeited for failure to file reports 1/1/37

MISSOURI NATL LIFE INS CO (MO)
Incorporated 09/15/1953
Declared insolvent 06/29/1989
Details not available

MISSOURI PAC CORP (DE)
Merged into Union Pacific Corp. 12/22/1982
Each share Common $5 par exchanged for (0.275) share $7.25 Conv. Preferred Ser. A no par and (1.1) shares Common $2.50 par

MISSOURI PAC RR CO (MO)
Each share Preferred $100 par exchanged for (2.645) shares Class A no par 3/15/56
Each share Common $100 par exchanged for (0.05) share Class B no par 3/15/56
Last date to exchange old securities for new securities under the 1956 plan was 3/1/62, after which date old securities became entitled to receive cash only
Last date to exchange old securities for cash under the 1956 plan was 3/1/68, after which date all unexchanged old stock became void for all purposes
Each share Class A no par exchanged for (1) share $5 Conv. Preferred no par 1/21/74
Each share Class B no par exchanged for (16) shares Common no par and $850 cash 1/21/74
Each share $5 Conv. Preferred no par exchanged for (5) shares $1 Conv. Preferred no par 7/5/74
Common no par split (5) for (1) by issuance of (4) additional shares 7/5/74
$1 Conv. Preferred no par called for redemption 1/17/77
Merged into Missouri Pacific Corp. 11/1/78
Each share Common no par exchanged for (0.95) share Common $5 par
Missouri Pacific Corp. merged into Union Pacific Corp. 12/22/82

MISSOURI PHYSICIANS GROUP HLDG CO (MO)
Name changed to Bush-O'Donnell & Co. Inc. 5/9/2001

MISSOURI PORTLAND CEM CO (DE)
Reincorporated 08/01/1972
Capital Stock $25 par changed to $12.50 par and (1) additional share issued 07/28/1955
Capital Stock $12.50 par changed to $6.25 par and (1) additional share issued 08/14/1959
Stock Dividend - 20% 11/26/1954
State of incorporation changed from (MO) to (DE) 08/01/1972
Capital Stock $6.25 par split (5) for (4) by issuance of (0.25) additional share 01/18/1974
Merged into Porter (H.K.), Inc. 05/25/1977
Each share Capital Stock $6.25 par exchanged for $30 principal amount of Missouri Portland Cement Co. 10% 20 yr. Subordinated Debentures due 05/15/1997

MISSOURI PWR & LT CO (MO)
Each share Common $20 par exchanged for (4) shares Common $5 par 00/00/1948
Merged into Union Electric Co. 12/30/1983
Each share 3.90% Preferred $100 par exchanged for (1) share $4.30 Preferred no par
Each share 4.30% Preferred $100 par exchanged for (1) share $4.75 Preferred no par

MISSOURI PUB SVC CO NEW (MO)
Each share old Common no par exchanged for (3) shares new Common no par 00/00/1951
4.375% Preferred $100 par called for redemption 09/30/1954
4.9% Preferred $100 par called for redemption 09/30/1954
New Common no par split (3) for (1) by issuance of (2) additional shares 04/19/1955
New Common no par changed to $1 par 06/24/1957
Name changed to UtiliCorp United Inc. (MO) 05/02/1985
UtiliCorp United Inc. (MO) reincorporated in Delaware 04/01/1987 which name changed to Aquila, Inc. (New) 03/15/2002 which was acquired by Great Plains Energy Inc. 07/14/2008 which merged into Evergy, Inc. 06/05/2018

MISSOURI PUBLIC SERVICE CO. OLD (MO)
Reorganized as Missouri Public Service Corp. in 1937
No stockholders' equity

MISSOURI PUBLIC SERVICE CORP. (MO)
Merged into Missouri Public Service Co. (New) share for share 00/00/1950
Missouri Public Service Co. (New) name changed to UtiliCorp United

Inc. (MO) 05/02/1985 which
reincorporated in Delaware
04/01/1987 which name changed to
Aquila, Inc. (New) 03/15/2002 which
was acquired by Great Plains
Energy Inc. 07/14/2008

MISSOURI RESH LABS INC (MO)
5% Conv. Preferred $5 par called for
redemption 6/1/62
Name changed to MRL, Inc. 6/18/91
(See MRL, Inc.)

MISSOURI RIV & GOLD GEM CORP (NV)
Reincorporated 07/26/2002
State of incorporation changed from
(MT) to (NV) 07/26/2002
Name changed to EntreMetrix Corp.
05/06/2004
EntreMetrix Corp. name changed to
NeoTactix Corp. 01/07/2008
(See NeoTactix Corp.)

MISSOURI RIV GOLD & GEM CORP (MT)
Recapitalized as American Dental
Products Corp. 8/7/86
Each share Common $0.001 par
exchanged for (0.05) share Common
$0.001 par
(See American Dental Products Corp.)

MISSOURI RIVER SVCS INC (DE)
Charter forfeited for failure to maintain
a registered agent 07/29/1990

MISSOURI RIVER SIOUX CITY BRIDGE CO.
Dissolved in 1938

MISSOURI ROLLING MILL CORP (MO)
100% acquired by Delaware Leggett
& Platt, Inc. through purchase offer
which expired 06/22/1979
Public interest eliminated

MISSOURI SHOE CO. (MO)
Charter cancelled for failure to file
reports 1/1/74

MISSOURI ST BK & TR CO (ST. LOUIS, MO)
Each share Common $10 par
exchanged for (0.001) share
Common $10,000 par 05/31/1994
Note: Unexchanged certificate holders received
$10.28 cash per share and public
interest was eliminated

MISSOURI STATE LIFE INSURANCE CO.
Assets acquired by General American
Life Insurance Co. in 1933. Stock
books closed August 31, 1948.
Stockholders to receive net
earnings, if any, after policies are
paid in full
General American Life Insurance Co.
completed mutualization in 1946

MISSOURI TELEPHONE CO. (MO)
Name changed to General Telephone
Co. of Missouri 12/1/56
(See listing for General Telephone Co. of Missouri)

MISSOURI THEATRE BUILDING CORP.
Capital Stock sold in 1948
Voting Trust Certificate holders
received $15 a share

MISSOURI UNION CORP. (MO)
Charter revoked for failure to file
reports and pay fees 1/1/64

MISSOURI URANIUM CORP. (MO)
Name changed to National
Consolidated Mining Corp. in 1956
National Consolidated Mining Corp.
charter revoked 1/1/58

MISSOURI UTILS CO (MO)
Acquired by Union Electric Co.
12/14/1977
Each share Common $1 par
exchanged for (1.1) shares Common
$5 par
Note: Unexchanged certificates were
cancelled and became without value
12/13/1992
Stock Dividends - 30% 05/00/1947;
50% 06/05/1961
Merged into Union Electric Co.
12/30/1983
Each share 5% Preferred $100 par
exchanged for (1) share $5.50
Preferred Ser. A no par
Each share 5% Preferred 1950 Ser.
$100 par exchanged for (1) share
$5.50 Preferred Ser. B no par
Each share 5.70% Preferred $100 par
exchanged for (1) share $6.30
Preferred no par

MISSOURI VALLEY PUBLIC SERVICE CO.
Assets acquired by bondholders in
1936

MIST INC (CANADA)
Name changed to NBS Technologies
Inc. (New) 3/16/2004
(See NBS Technologies Inc. (New))

MISTANGO CONS RES LTD (ON)
Recapitalized 11/05/1981
Common $1 par changed to no par
12/04/1970
Recapitalized from Mistango River
Mines Ltd. to Mistango Consolidated
Resources Ltd. 11/05/1981
Each share Common no par
exchanged for (0.2) share Common
no par
Recapitalized as Canadian Black
River Petroleum Ltd. (ON)
04/30/1989
Each share Common no par
exchanged for (0.1) share Common
no par
Canadian Black River Petroleum Ltd.
(ON) reorganized in Alberta as
Uruguay Goldfields Inc. 02/13/1998
which reincorporated in Yukon as
Uruguay Mineral Exploration Inc.
02/11/2002 which name changed to
Orosur Mining Inc. 01/08/2010

MISTASSINI LEAD CORP. LTD. (QC)
Charter annulled for failure to file
annual reports 5/4/74

MR BUILD INDS INC (BC)
Recapitalized as Canadian Mr. Build
Industries Inc. 01/22/1990
Each share Common no par
exchanged for (0.125) share
Common no par
Canadian Mr. Build Industries Inc.
name changed to Socal Capital
Corp. 02/18/1992 which name
changed to Empyrean Diagnostics
Ltd. (BC) 08/05/1993 which
reincorporated in Wyoming
12/31/1996 which name changed to
Empyrean Bioscience, Inc. (WY)
02/08/1999 which reincorporated in
Delaware 03/21/2001
(See Empyrean Bioscience, Inc. (DE))

MR BULB CO (DE)
Name changed to ENCON Systems,
Inc. 06/10/1993
(See ENCON Systems, Inc.)

MR COFFEE INC (DE)
Acquired by Health O Meter Products,
Inc. 8/16/94
Each share Common 1¢ par
exchanged for $15.50 cash

MR GASKET CO OLD (OH)
Ctfs. dated prior to 12/14/1971
Name changed to MGC Liquidating
Corp. 12/14/1971
(See MGC Liquidating Corp.)

MR GASKET CO NEW (OH)
Ctfs. dated after 10/28/83
Name changed to Performance
Industries, Inc. 5/4/93
(See Performance Industries, Inc.)

MR GOODBUYS CORP
Plan of reorganization under Chapter
11 Federal Bankruptcy proceedings
confirmed 02/21/1992
No stockholders' equity

MR HANGER INC (NY)
Disssolved by proclamation 3/25/92

MR JAX FASHIONS INC (BC)
Acquired by Koret Canada Inc. 2/7/95
Each share Common no par
exchanged for $1.40 cash

MISTER JAY FASHIONS INTL INC (DE)
Common 1¢ par split (3) for (1) by
issuance of (2) additional shares
3/20/95
Name changed to United Textiles &
Toys Corp. 3/24/97
United Textiles & Toys Corp. name
changed to U.S. Biomedical Corp.
5/23/2002

MR JOHN INC (DE)
Merged into M.J.I. Acquisition Inc.
07/29/1988
Each share Common 1¢ par
exchanged for $2.75 cash

MR MAN INC (FL)
Name changed to Ben-Tam, Inc.
9/25/85
(See Ben-Tam, Inc.)

MR QUICK INC (DE)
Charter cancelled and declared
inoperative and void for
non-payment of taxes 03/01/1984

MR ROLLER BOOGIES INC (FL)
Name changed to KeyClub.net, Inc.
5/17/99
KeyClub.net, Inc. recapitalized as
Global Wide Web, Inc. 3/16/2001
which name changed to TIE
Technologies, Inc. 4/5/2002

MR ROOTER CORP (OK)
Each share old Common 10¢ par
exchanged for (0.5) share new
Common 10¢ par 6/14/93
Name changed to Dwyer Group Inc.
7/30/93
(See Dwyer Group Inc.)

MR STEAK INC (CO)
Common no par split (3) for (1) by
issuance of (2) additional shares
3/24/84
Name changed to JAMCO Ltd.
3/24/87
(See JAMCO Ltd.)

MR SWISS AMER INC (DE)
Completely liquidated 08/24/1971
Each share Common no par
exchanged for first and final
distribution of (0.05) share First
World Corp. Class A Common 15¢
par and (0.45) share First World
Corp. Class B Common 15¢ par
(See First World Corp.)

MR SWISS EAST INC (NY)
Name changed to Deli Tree, Inc.
4/29/72
(See Deli Tree, Inc.)

MR TUBE STEAK CDA INC (AB)
Delisted from Alberta Stock Exchange
12/02/1998

MR WIGGS DEPT STORES INC OLD (OH)
Merged into Mr. Wiggs Department
Stores, Inc. (New) 09/30/1974
Each share Common no par
exchanged for (0.01) share Common
no par
Note: Holders of (99) shares or fewer
received $7 cash per share

MISTRAL PHARMA INC (CANADA)
Declared bankrupt 09/26/2008
No stockholders' equity

MISTRAL RES LTD (BC)
Struck off register and declared
dissolved for failure to file returns
4/12/90

MISTY MTN GOLD INC (BC)
Recapitalized 11/10/1995
Recapitalized from Misty Mountain
Gold Ltd. to Misty Mountain Gold
Inc. 11/10/1995
Each share Common no par
exchanged for (0.1) share Common
no par
Recapitalized as Continental Minerals
Corp. (Incorporated 02/07/1962)
10/18/2001
Each share Common no par
exchanged for (1) share
Redeemable Preferred and (0.1)
share Common no par
(See Continental Minerals Corp. (Incorporated 02/07/1962))

MITCHEL ALAN FURS INC (NY)
Name changed to Teleworld
Enterprises, Ltd. (NY) 08/07/1992
Teleworld Enterprises, Ltd. (NY)
reorganized under the laws of
Nevada as 1Twoe.Com, Inc.
08/05/1999 which recapitalized as
DMT Energy Inc. 06/23/2003
(See DMT Energy Inc.)

MITCHELL (J.S.) & CO. LTD. (QC)
Each share old Common no par
exchanged for (4) shares new
Common no par 00/00/1952
Completely liquidated 08/28/1964
Each share new Common no par
exchanged for first and final
distribution of $35 cash

MITCHELL BANCORP INC (NC)
Merged into First Western Bank
(Burnsville, NC) 12/31/98
Each share Common 1¢ par
exchanged for (1.6) shares Common
1¢ par
First Western Bank (Burnsville, NC)
merged into MountainBank Financial
Corp. 12/31/2001 which merged into
South Financial Group, Inc.
10/3/2003

MITCHELL (HARRY) BREWING CO. (TX)
Each share Common $25 par
exchanged for (25) shares Common
$1 par in 1951
Acquired by Falstaff Brewing Corp.
and each (25) shares Common $1
par exchanged for $100 principal
amount of 4-1/2% Debentures in
1956

MITCHELL (ROBERT) CO., LTD./LA COMPAGNIE MITCHELL (ROBERT) LTEE. (CANADA)
Name changed to Mitchell (Robert)
Inc. 4/17/79
(See Mitchell (Robert) Inc.)

MITCHELL (ROBERT) CO., LTD. (CANADA)
Common no par exchanged (3) for (1)
in 1954
Each share Common no par
exchanged for (1) share Class A no
par and (1) share Class B no par
5/20/55
Name changed to Mitchell (Robert)
Co., Ltd./La Compagnie Mitchell
(Robert) Ltee. 5/12/75
Mitchell (Robert) Co., Ltd./La
Compagnie Mitchell (Robert) Ltee.
name changed to Mitchell (Robert)
Inc. 4/17/79
(See Mitchell (Robert) Inc.)

MITCHELL ENERGY & DEV CORP (TX)
Common 10¢ par split (5) for (4) by
issuance of (0.25) additional share
8/16/76
Common 10¢ par split (4) for (3) by
issuance of (1/3) additional share
5/30/77
Common 10¢ par split (3) for (2) by
issuance of (0.5) additional share
5/15/78
Common 10¢ par split (4) for (3) by
issuance of (1/3) additional share
9/7/79
Common 10¢ par split (2) for (1) by
issuance of (1) additional share
4/30/80
Common 10¢ par split (4) for (3) by

issuance of (1/3) additional share 3/9/81
Each share Common 10¢ par exchanged for (0.5) share Class A Common 10¢ par and (0.5) share Non-Vtg. Class B Common 10¢ par 6/25/92
Class B Common 10¢ par reclassified as Class A Common 10¢ par 6/29/2000
Stock Dividend - 10% 8/9/74
Merged into Devon Energy Corp. (New) 1/24/2002
Each share Class A Common 10¢ par exchanged for (0.585) share Common 10¢ par and $31 cash

MITCHELL-HEARST GOLD MINES LTD. (ON)
Charter cancelled for failure to pay taxes and file returns 1/10/73

MITCHELL LANE INC (WA)
Believed out of business 00/00/1986
Details not available

MITCHELL RES LTD (BC)
Each share old Common no par exchanged for (0.5) share new Common no par 07/06/2016
Name changed to Hannan Metals Ltd. 01/10/2017

MITCHELL ROBERT INC (CANADA)
Conv. Class A no par split (3) for (1) by issuance of (2) additional shares 5/8/81
Class B no par split (3) for (1) by issuance of (2) additional shares 5/8/81
Conv. Class A no par split (2) for (1) by issuance of (1) additional share 6/15/88
Class B no par split (2) for (1) by issuance of (1) additional share 6/15/88
Merged into Marshall-Barwick Properties Inc. 11/9/2000
Each share Conv. Class A no par exchanged for $11 cash
Each share Class B no par exchanged for for $11 cash

MITCHELLS & BUTLERS PLC (UNITED KINGDOM)
Each old Sponsored ADR for Ordinary exchanged for (0.70588235) new Sponsored ADR for Ordinary and $1.1751 cash 12/2/2003
ADR agreement terminated 7/19/2005
Each new Sponsored ADR for Ordinary exchanged for $6.57469 cash

MITCHUM TULLY PARTICIPATIONS, INC. MITCHUM TULLY PARTICIPATIONS, INC. NO. 2
Merged into Consolidated Assets Co. in 1936
Details not available

MITE CORP (DE)
Capital Stock $1 par reclassified as Common $1 par 06/11/1968
Conv. Preferred Ser. A called for redemption 07/13/1979
Merged into Emhart Corp. 06/27/1985
Each share Common $1 par exchanged for $63.50 cash

MITEC CORP (UT)
Name changed to Baldwin Aircraft International Inc. 10/30/1986
(See Baldwin Aircraft International Inc.)

MITEC TECHNOLOGIES INC (CANADA)
Each share old Common no par exchanged for (0.00000019) share new Common no par 09/30/2016
Note: In effect holders received $0.02 cash per share and public interest was eliminated

MITEC TELECOM INC (CANADA)
Recapitalized as Mitec Technologies Inc. 02/26/2013
Each share Common no par exchanged for (0.025) share Common no par

MITEK INDL CORP (BC)
Recapitalized as International Mitek Computer Inc. 03/27/1987
Each share Common no par exchanged for (0.25) share Common no par
(See International Mitek Computer Inc.)

MITEK SURGICAL PRODS INC (DE)
Acquired by Johnson & Johnson 4/5/95
Each share Common 1¢ par exchanged for (0.5041) share Common 1¢ par

MITEK SYS INC (UT)
Each (50) shares old Common $0.001 par exchanged for (1) share new Common $0.001 par 08/01/1986
Reincorporated under the laws of Delaware 09/11/1987

MITEL CORP (CANADA)
Common no par split (3) for (1) by issuance of (2) additional shares payable 10/31/1980
$2 Preferred 1983 R&D Ser. no par conversion privilege expired 12/31/1988
Name changed to Zarlink Semiconductor Inc. 07/25/2001
(See Zarlink Semiconductor Inc.)

MITMOR OIL & GAS LTD.
Recapitalized as Canadian Pipe Lines Producers Ltd. 00/00/1954
Each share Capital Stock $1 par exchanged for (0.16666666) share Capital Stock $1 par
Canadian Pipe Lines Producers Ltd. acquired by Canadian Pipelines & Petroleums Ltd. 00/00/1954 which merged into Scurry-Rainbow Oil Ltd. 05/09/1957 which was acquired by Home Oil Co. Ltd. (New) 11/08/1993 which merged into Anderson Exploration Ltd. 09/07/1995
(See Anderson Exploration Ltd.)

MITOPHARM CORP (FL)
Old Common $0.001 par split (7) for (2) by issuance of (2.5) additional shares payable 09/19/2007 to holders of record 09/14/2007
Ex date - 09/19/2007
Each share old Common $0.001 par exchanged for (0.002) share new Common $0.001 par 11/15/2007
Charter revoked for failure to file reports and pay fees 09/26/2008

MITRA ENERGY INC (BC)
Name changed to Jadestone Energy Inc. 12/07/2016

MITRAL MED INTL INC (CO)
Common 1¢ par changed to $0.006-2/3 par and (0.5) additional share issued 12/22/1980
Common $0.006-2/3 par changed back to 1¢ par 00/00/1983
Name changed to Matrix Medica, Inc. 04/27/1987
Matrix Medica, Inc. name changed to Matrix Membranes, Inc. 06/02/1989
(See Matrix Membranes, Inc.)

MITRE INDS INC (TX)
Each share old Common 5¢ par exchanged for (0.1) share new Common 5¢ par 12/17/1973
Merged into Flick of Texas, Inc. 06/24/1975
Each share new Common 5¢ par exchanged for $0.57 cash

MITRON RESH & DEV CORP (DE)
Charter cancelled and declared inoperative and void for non-payment of taxes 3/1/75

MITRON TECHNOLOGIES INC (ON)
Recapitalized as Interactive Digital Systems Corp. 06/20/1994
Each share Common no par exchanged for (0.1) share Common no par
Interactive Digital Systems Corp. recapitalized as CRM Capital Inc. 05/23/1996 which recapitalized as Active Control Technology Inc. 04/01/1997
(See Active Control Technology Inc.)

MITSUBISHI BK LTD (JAPAN)
Each Unsponsored ADR for Common 50 Yen par exchanged for (10) Sponsored ADR's for Common 50 Yen par 9/19/89
Under plan of merger name changed to Bank of Tokyo-Mitsubishi Ltd. 4/1/96
Bank of Tokyo-Mitsubishi Ltd. merged into Mitsubishi Tokyo Financial Group Inc. 4/2/2001 which name changed to Mitsubishi UFJ Financial Group, Inc. 9/30/2005

MITSUBISHI CHEM CORP (JAPAN)
ADR agreement terminated 9/23/2005
Each ADR for Common 50 Yen par exchanged for $30.63086 cash

MITSUBISHI CHEM INDS LTD (JAPAN)
Name changed to Mitsubishi Kasei Corp. 6/1/88
Mitsubishi Kasei Corp. name changed to Mitsubishi Chemical Corp. 10/1/94

MITSUBISHI HEAVY INDS LTD (JAPAN)
Old ADR agreement terminated 02/28/1978
Details not available
New ADR agreement terminated 07/21/2010
No ADR's remain outstanding

MITSUBISHI KASEI CORP (JAPAN)
Stock Dividend - 10% 6/5/91
Name changed to Mitsubishi Chemical Corp. 10/1/94
(See Mitsubishi Chemical Corp.)

MITSUBISHI MATLS CORP (JAPAN)
ADR agreement terminated 03/04/2010
No ADR's outstanding

MITSUBISHI RAYON CO LTD (JAPAN)
Merged into Mitsubishi Chemical Holdings Corp. 09/28/2010
Each ADR for Common exchanged for $19.9081 cash

MITSUBISHI TOKYO FINL GROUP INC (JAPAN)
Name changed to Mitsubishi UFJ Financial Group, Inc. 9/30/2005

MITSUBISHI TR & BKG CORP (JAPAN)
Merged into Mitsubishi Tokyo Financial Group Inc. 4/2/2001
Each ADR for Common exchanged for (0.125) Sponsored ADR for Common
Mitsubishi Tokyo Financial Group Inc. name changed to Mitsubishi UFJ Financial Group, Inc. 9/30/2005

MITSUI BK LTD (JAPAN)
Under plan of merger name changed to Mitsui Taiyo Kobe Bank, Ltd. 4/1/90
Mitsui Taiyo Kobe Bank, Ltd. name changed to Sakura Bank, Ltd. 4/1/92 which merged into Sumitomo Mitsui Banking Corp. 6/12/91 which merged into Sumitomo Mitsui Financial Group, Inc. 1/15/2003

MITSUI ENGR & SHIPBUILDING CO LTD (JAPAN)
Basis changed from (1:10) to (1:1) 10/02/2017
Name changed to Mitsui E&S Holdings Co., Ltd. 04/02/2018

MITSUI SUMITOMO INS CO (JAPAN)
Name changed 11/30/2001
Name changed from Mitsui Marine & Fire Insurance Co., Ltd. to Mitsui Sumitomo Insurance Co. 11/30/2001
Reorganized as Mitsui Sumitomo Insurance Group Holdings, Inc. 04/01/2008
Each ADR for Common JPY 50 par exchanged for (6) ADR's for Common JPY 50 par
Mitsui Sumitomo Insurance Group Holdings, Inc. name changed to MS&AD Insurance Group Holdings, Inc. 04/01/2010

MITSUI SUMITOMO INS GROUP HLDGS INC (JAPAN)
Under plan of merger name changed to MS&AD Insurance Group Holdings, Inc. 04/01/2010

MITSUI TAIYO KOBE BK LTD (JAPAN)
Name changed to Sakura Bank, Ltd. 4/1/92
Sakura Bank, Ltd. merged into Sumito Mitsui Banking Corp. 6/12/2001 which merged into Sumito Mitsui Financial Group, Inc. 1/15/2003

MITSUI TR & BKG LTD (JAPAN)
Merged into Chou Trust & Banking Co. Ltd. 4/1/2000
Details not available

MITSUKOSHI LTD OLD (JAPAN)
Stock Dividends - 10% 5/21/73; 10% 5/21/74; 10% 6/1/76
Merged into Mitsukoshi, Ltd. 11/18/2003
Each Sponsored ADR for Ordinary 50 Yen par exchanged for $31.928 cash
Note: Due to ADR's being unsponsored exchange rate may vary among agents

MITTAL STL CO N V (NETHERLANDS)
Name changed to ArcelorMittal (Netherlands) 01/30/2007
ArcelorMittal (Netherlands) reincorporated in Luxembourg 09/03/2007 which merged into ArcelorMittal S.A. 11/13/2007

MITTAL STL SOUTH AFRICA LTD (SOUTH AFRICA)
Name changed to ArcelorMittal South Africa 11/02/2007

MITTEN BANK SECURITIES CORP.
Name changed to Transit Investment Corp. in 1938 which liquidated in 1948

MITY ENTERPRISES INC (UT)
Name changed 08/31/2000
Common 1¢ par split (3) for (2) by issuance of (0.5) additional share payable 09/23/1999 to holders of record 09/09/1999
Name changed from Mity-Lite Inc. to Mity Enterprises, Inc. 08/31/2000
Merged into Sorenson Capital Partners L.P. 07/17/2007
Each share Common 1¢ par exchanged for $21.50 cash

MIU INDS LTD (BC)
Recapitalized as Secured Communication Canada 95 Inc. 05/08/1995
Each share Common no par exchanged for (0.2) share Common no par
(See Secured Communication Canada 95 Inc.)

MIVA INC (DE)
Name changed to Vertro, Inc. 06/09/2009
Vertro, Inc. merged into Inuvo, Inc. 03/01/2012

MIVI BIOMEDICAL TECHNOLOGIES INC (NV)
Common $0.001 par split (2) for (1) by issuance of (1) additional share payable 7/28/2000 to holders of record 7/20/2000

FINANCIAL INFORMATION, INC.

MIW-MLP

Name changed to Last Company Clothing, Inc. (New) 12/4/2000
Last Company Clothing, Inc. (New) name changed to Premier Axiom ASP, Inc. 3/27/2001 which name changed to Core Solutions Inc. 7/15/2002 which recapitalized as Sunshine Ventures Inc. 5/12/2003 which name changed to Christine's Precious Petals Inc. 7/14/2003 which name changed to Global Business Markets, Inc. 9/5/2003 which name changed to GREM USA 3/3/2005

MIW INVS WASH (MD)
Name changed to Ameribanc Investors Group 6/16/86
(See Ameribanc Investors Group)

MIX RES LTD (BC)
Name changed to Rococco Resources Ltd. 12/3/84
(See Rococco Resources Ltd.)

MIXED ENTMT INC (MN)
Name changed to Conscious Co. 08/30/2006
Conscious Co. name changed to American Environmental Energy, Inc. 05/06/2008

MIZA ENTERPRISES INC (BC)
Common no par split (3) for (1) by issuance of (2) additional shares payable 01/03/2017 to holders of record 12/30/2016 Ex date - 01/04/2017
Name changed to BQ Metals Corp. 06/21/2017
BQ Metals Corp. name changed to BeMetals Corp. 04/18/2018

MIZAR ENERGY (CO)
Reincorporated under the laws of Florida as HBOA Holdings, Inc. 11/10/2000
HBOA Holdings, Inc. name changed to Kirshner Entertainment & Technologies, Inc. 07/17/2003 which name changed to Linkwell Corp. 08/17/2005
(See Linkwell Corp.)

MIZAR INC (DE)
Name changed to Blue Wave Systems Inc. 04/27/1998
Blue Wave Systems Inc. merged into Motorola, Inc. 07/02/2001 which recapitalized as Motorola Solutions, Inc. 01/04/2011

MIZATI LUXURY ALLOY WHEELS INC (CA)
Each share old Common $0.0001 par exchanged for (0.0001) share new Common $0.0001 par 07/23/2008
New Common $0.0001 par split (9,842) for (1) by issuance of (9,841) additional shares payable 08/28/2008 to holders of record 07/24/2008 Ex date - 08/29/2008
Each share new Common $0.0001 par exchanged again for (0.025) share new Common $0.0001 par 07/12/2010
Chapter 7 bankruptcy proceedings terminated 11/27/2013
No stockholders' equity

MIZEL DEV CORP (CO)
Name changed to M.D.C. Corp. (CO) 08/12/1977
M.D.C. Corp. (CO) reincorporated in Delaware as M.D.C. Holdings, Inc. 06/20/1985

MIZEL PETRO RES INC (DE)
Merged into M.D.C. Corp. (CO) 02/07/1985
Each share Common 1¢ par exchanged for (0.1209) share Common 1¢ par
M.D.C. Corp. (CO) reincorporated in Delaware as M.D.C. Holdings, Inc. 06/20/1985

MIZLOU COMMUNICATIONS INC (DE)
Name changed 12/23/88
Name changed from Mizlou Programming Inc. to Mizlou Communications Co., Inc. 12/23/88
Chapter 11 bankruptcy proceedings converted to Chapter 7 on 7/1/91
No stockholders' equity

MIZNER/1ST UTD BANCORP (FL)
Name changed to 1st United Bancorp 06/01/1993
1st United Bancorp merged into Wachovia Corp. (New) (Ctfs. dated between 05/20/1991 and 09/01/2001) 11/11/1997 which merged into Wachovia Corp. (Ctfs. dated after 09/01/2001) 09/01/2001 which merged into Wells Fargo & Co. (New) 12/31/2008

MIZPAH DIVIDE MINING CO. (NV)
Name changed to Coastal Plains Oil Co. 10/11/1957
Coastal Plains Oil Co. recapitalized as Western Oil Corp. 07/25/1960
(See Western Oil Corp.)

MIZUHO ASSET TR & BKG LTD (JAPAN)
ADR agreement terminated 8/25/2003
Each ADR for Ordinary 50 Yen par exchanged for $17.714 cash
Note: Due to ADR's being unsponsored exchange rate may vary dependent upon depositary agent

MJ OPPORTUNITY CORP (ON)
Recapitalized as Lift & Co. Corp. 09/17/2018
Each share Common no par exchanged for (0.41666666) share Common no par

MJB RES INC (FL)
Name changed to Universal Rehabilitation Centers of America, Inc. 8/25/98
Universal Rehabilitation Centers of America, Inc. name changed to Universal Medical Concepts Inc. 12/28/99

MJP INTL LTD (NV)
Recapitalized as Bionovate Technologies Corp. 12/21/2017
Each share Common $0.0001 par exchanged for (0.02) share Common $0.0001 par

MK & A HLDGS INC (FL)
Name changed to Castleguard Energy Inc. 11/30/1998
(See Castleguard Energy Inc.)

MK AUTOMOTIVE INC (NV)
Name changed to Clikia Corp. 07/19/2017

MK GOLD CO (DE)
Name changed to MK Resources Co. 06/08/2004
MK Resources Co. merged into Leucadia National Corp. 08/19/2005 which name changed to Jefferies Financial Group Inc. 05/24/2018

MK RAIL CORP (DE)
Issue Information - 6,000,000 shares COM offered at $16 per share on 04/26/1994
Name changed to MotivePower Industries, Inc. 1/1/97
MotivePower Industries, Inc. merged into Westinghouse Air Brake Co. (New) 11/19/99

MK RES CO (DE)
Merged into Leucadia National Corp. 08/19/2005
Each share Common 1¢ par exchanged for (0.0317) share Common $1 par
Each share Common 1¢ par received distribution of (1) Uncertificated Deferred Value Right payable 09/22/2005 to holders of record 08/18/2005 Ex date - 08/16/2005
Leucadia National Corp. name changed to Jefferies Financial Group Inc. 05/24/2018

MKA CAP INC (NV)
Name changed to Sancon Resources Recovery, Inc. 08/04/2006
Sancon Resources Recovery, Inc. recapitalized as IGS Capital Group Ltd. 06/09/2017

MKM RES LTD (BC)
Name changed to Sunward Resources Ltd. 03/05/2010
Sunward Resources Ltd. merged into NovaCopper Inc. 06/24/2015 which name changed to Trilogy Metals Inc. 09/08/2016

MKR HLDGS (UT)
Liquidation completed
Each share Common 1¢ par received initial distribution of $0.155 cash payable 5/10/2002 to holders of record 5/7/2002
Each share Common 1¢ par received second and final distribution of $0.00405532 cash payable 3/31/2003 to holders of record 5/7/2002 Ex date - 4/1/2003
Note: Certificates were not required to be surrendered and are without value

MKS INC (ON)
Each share old Common no par exchanged for (0.2) share new Common no par 07/29/2009
Acquired by Parametric Technology Corp. 06/01/2011
Each share new Common no par exchanged for $26.20 cash
Note: Unexchanged certificates were cancelled and became without value 06/01/2017

MKTG INC (DE)
Acquired by Aegis Lifestyle, Inc. 08/27/2014
Each share Common $0.001 par exchanged for $2.80 cash

MKTG SVCS INC (NV)
Each share old Common 1¢ par exchanged for (0.125) share new Common 1¢ par 01/27/2003
Name changed to Media Services Group, Inc. 12/26/2003
Media Services Group, Inc. name changed to MSGI Security Solutions, Inc. 02/09/2005
(See MSGI Security Solutions, Inc.)

ML BANCORP INC (PA)
Merged into Sovereign Bancorp 02/27/1998
Each share Common no par exchanged for (1.62) shares Common no par
Sovereign Bancorp, Inc. merged into Banco Santander, S.A. 01/30/2009

ML CONV SECS INC (MD)
Name changed to Convertible Holdings, Inc. 01/23/1987
Convertible Holdings, Inc. reorganized as Merrill Lynch Convertible Fund, Inc. 08/04/1997 which merged into Merrill Lynch Balanced Capital Fund, Inc. 12/15/2000

ML DIRECT INC (DE)
Charter cancelled and declared inoperative and void for non-payment of taxes 03/01/2000

ML MACADAMIA ORCHARDS L P (DE)
Name changed to Royal Hawaiian Orchards, L.P. 10/15/2012
Royal Hawaiian Orchards, L.P. name changed to Hawaiian Macadamia Nut Orchards, L.P. 10/17/2018

ML MEDIA PARTNERS L P (DE)
Completely liquidated 12/28/2004
Each Unit of Ltd. Partnership received first and final distribution of $103.53 cash

ML TR GOVT GTD SECS (MA)
Trust terminated 03/05/1998
Details not available

MLB INDS INC (CANADA)
Reorganized under the laws of Alberta as Blue Horizon Industries Inc. 09/14/2011
Each share Common no par exchanged for (0.03448275) share Common no par

MLC HLDGS INC (DE)
Issue Information - 1,000,000 shares COM offered at $8.75 per share on 11/14/1996
Name changed to ePlus inc. 10/19/1999

MLC LIFE LTD
Single Point Indexed Rate 144A Capital Securities called for redemption at $25 on 7/14/2004

MLF BANCORP INC (PA)
Common no par split (2) for (1) by issuance of (1) additional share payable 09/06/1996 to holders of record 08/09/1996
Name changed to ML Bancorp, Inc. 08/21/1996
ML Bancorp, Inc. merged into Sovereign Bancorp, Inc. 02/27/1998 which merged into Banco Santander, S.A. 01/30/2009

MLH INCOME RLTY PARTNERSHIP (NY)
Trust terminated 12/20/95
Each Unit of Limited Partnership Int. exchanged for $851.49 cash

MLH INCOME RLTY PARTNERSHIP II (NY)
Trust terminated 11/30/95
Each Unit of Limited Partnership Int. exchanged for $1,184.61 cash

MLH INCOME RLTY PARTNERSHIP III (NY)
Trust terminated 6/27/96
Each Unit of Limited Partnership Int. exchanged for $1,149.52 cash

MLH INCOME RLTY PARTNERSHIP IV (NY)
Trust terminated 12/20/96
Each Unit Limited Partnership Int. exchanged for $1,068.14 cash

MLH INCOME RLTY PARTNERSHIP V (NY)
Trust terminated 12/20/96
Each Class A Depositary Unit exchanged for $1,190.73 cash
Each Class B Depositary Unit exchanged for $1,190.73 cash

MLI INC (MN)
Name changed to EDP of California Inc. 03/02/1990
(See EDP of California Inc.)

MLIGHT TECH INC (FL)
Common $0.0001 par split (20) for (1) by issuance of (19) additional shares payable 02/27/2013 to holders of record 02/26/2013 Ex date - 02/28/2013
Reorganized under the laws of Nevada as CX Network Group, Inc. 07/12/2017
Each share Common $0.0001 par exchanged for (0.06666666) share Common $0.0001 par

MLM WORLD NEWS TODAY INC (NV)
Name changed to Presidential Air Corp. 08/06/2002
Presidential Air Corp. recapitalized as Safe Travel Care, Inc. 05/02/2003 which recapitalized as Titan Energy Worldwide, Inc. 12/28/2006
(See Titan Energy Worldwide, Inc.)

MLP & STRATEGIC EQUITY FD INC (MD)
Issue Information - 13,250,000 shares COM offered at $20 per share on 06/26/2007

Merged into Nuveen Energy MLP Total Return Fund 08/27/2012
Each share Common $0.001 par exchanged for (1.02955584) shares Common 1¢ par

MLS INDS INC (DE)
Name changed to Monterey Life Systems, Inc. 12/10/73
Monterey Life Systems, Inc. merged into Berkeley Bio-Engineering Inc. (CA) 12/17/75 which reincorporated in Delaware as Berkeley Bio-Medical, Inc. 2/14/77
(See Berkeley Bio-Medical, Inc.)

MLT INTL INC (CO)
Reincorporated under the laws of Delaware as SkyMark Holdings, Inc. 07/26/2004
(See SkyMark Holdings, Inc.)

MLW WORTHINGTON LTD (CANADA)
Name changed to Bombardier-MLW Ltd.- Bombardier-MLW-Ltee. 9/28/76
Bombardier-MLW Ltd.-Bombardier-MLW Ltee. name changed to Bombardier Inc. 7/20/78

MLX CORP (MI)
Each share old Common 1¢ par exchanged for (0.1) share new Common 1¢ par 6/25/93
Merged into Morton Industrial Group Inc. 1/20/98
Each share new Common 1¢ par exchanged for (1) share Class A Common 1¢ par
(See Morton Industrial Group Inc.)

MM COS INC (DE)
Name changed to George Foreman Enterprises, Inc. 8/24/2005

MM G INTL INC (ON)
Name changed to Stratas Corp. Ltd. 9/30/83
(See Stratas Corp. Ltd.)

MMA MEDIA INC (DE)
Common $0.001 par split (40) for (1) by issuance of (39) additional shares payable 06/07/2007 to holders of record 06/05/2007 Ex date - 06/08/2007
Recapitalized as China Energy Recovery, Inc. 02/05/2008
Each share Common $0.001 par exchanged for (1/9) share Common $0.001 par

MMAX MEDIA INC (NV)
Recapitalized as PayMeOn, Inc. 05/17/2013
Each share Common $0.001 par exchanged for (0.01449275) share Common $0.001 par

MMC ENERGY INC (DE)
Reincorporated 09/22/2006
State of incorporation changed from (NV) to (DE) 09/22/2006
Each share old Common $0.001 par exchanged for (0.1) share new Common $0.001 par 04/20/2007
Liquidation completed
Each share new Common $0.001 par exchanged for initial distribution of $1.35 cash 10/07/2009
Each share new Common $0.001 par received second distribution of $0.15 cash payable 01/06/2010 to holders of record 10/07/2009
Each share new Common $0.001 par received third distribution of $0.057 cash payable 11/17/2010 to holders of record 10/07/2009
Each share new Common $0.001 par received fourth and final distribution of $0.0058 cash payable 08/12/2013 to holders of record 10/07/2009

MMC NETWORKS INC (DE)
Merged into Applied Micro Circuits Corp. 10/25/2000
Each share Common no par exchanged for (1.238) shares Common 1¢ par
Applied Micro Circuits Corp. merged into MACOM Technology Solutions Holdings, Inc. 01/26/2017

MMC VIDEO ONE CDA LTD (BC)
Merged into Standard Broadcasting (British Columbia) Ltd. 9/29/88
Each share Common no par exchanged for $2.90 cash

MME SOLAR SYS INC (NV)
Charter revoked for failure to file annual reports and pay fees 04/01/1989

MMEX MNG CORP (NV)
Each share old Common $0.001 par exchanged for (0.1) share new Common $0.001 par 05/27/2011
Name changed to MMEX Resources Corp. 06/03/2016

MMG LTD (HONG KONG)
ADR agreement terminated 01/24/2018
No ADR's remain outstanding

MMH HLDGS INC (DE)
Plan of reorganization under Chapter 11 Federal Bankruptcy Code effective 9/28/2001
No stockholders' equity

MMI COS INC (DE)
Merged into St. Paul Companies, Inc. 04/18/2000
Each share Common 10¢ par exchanged for $10 cash

MMI MED INC (CA)
Stock Dividend - 10% 4/5/93
Name changed to InnoServ Technologies, Inc. 9/19/95
(See InnoServ Technologies, Inc.)

MMODAL INC (DE)
Acquired by Legend Parent, Inc. 08/17/2012
Each share Common 10¢ par exchanged for $14 cash

MMO2 PLC (ENGLAND & WALES)
Each Sponsored ADR for Ordinary received distribution of (1) BT Group PLC ADR for Ordinary payable 11/19/2001 to holders of record 11/16/2001
ADR agreement terminated 3/14/2005
Each Sponsored ADR for Ordinary exchanged for $21.81677 cash
Note: Holders of (99) or fewer ADR's received $24.6175 cash per ADR

MMR HLDG CORP (DE)
Plan of reorganization under Chapter 11 Federal Bankruptcy proceedings confirmed 11/04/1992
No stockholders' equity

MMR INFORMATION SYS INC (DE)
Name changed to MMRGlobal, Inc. 08/16/2010

MMT RES LTD (BC)
Struck off register and declared dissolved for failure to file reports 4/3/92

MM2 GROUP INC (NJ)
SEC revoked common stock registration 09/01/2011

MMX VENTURES INC (BC)
Name changed to IP Applications Corp. 06/23/2000
IP Applications Corp. name changed to Monexa Technologies Corp. 10/28/2009 which name changed to Santa Rosa Resources Corp. 04/03/2012

MNB BANCSHARES INC (DE)
Common 1¢ par split (2) for (1) by issuance of (1) additional share payable 02/09/1998 to holders of record 01/28/1998
Stock Dividends - 5% payable 08/12/1996 to holders of record 07/29/1996; 5% payable 05/15/1997 to holders of record 04/30/1997; 5% payable 08/10/1998 to holders of record 07/29/1998; 5% payable 08/16/1999 to holders of record 08/03/1999; 5% payable 08/14/2000 to holders of record 08/01/2000 Ex date - 07/28/2000
Merged into Landmark Bancorp, Inc. (DE) 10/09/2001
Each share Common 1¢ par exchanged for (0.523) share Common 1¢ par

MNC FINL INC (MD)
Common $2.50 par split (2) for (1) by issuance of (1) additional share 10/04/1989
Merged into NationsBank Corp. (NC) 10/01/1993
Each share Adjustable Rate Preferred Ser. CC $5 par exchanged for (1) share Common no par
Each share Adjustable Rate Preferred Ser. DD $5 par exchanged for (1) share Common no par
Each share Common $2.50 par exchanged for $15.17 cash
Note: Option to receive stock in lieu of cash expired 10/08/1993
NationsBank Corp. (NC) reincorporated in Delaware as BankAmerica Corp. (Old) 09/25/1998 which merged into BankAmerica Corp. (New) 09/30/1998 which name changed to Bank of America Corp. 04/28/1999

MNC MEDIA INVT LTD (CAYMAN ISLANDS)
ADR agreement terminated 04/25/2017
Each ADR for Ordinary exchanged for (10) shares Ordinary
Note: Unexchanged ADR's will be sold and the proceeds, if any, held for claim after 10/25/2017

MNI GROUP INC (NJ)
Name changed to Gender Sciences Inc. (NJ) 10/23/2000
Gender Sciences Inc. (NJ) reincorporated in Delaware as Medical Nutrition USA, Inc. 04/22/2003
(See Medical Nutrition USA, Inc.)

MNI NUTRACEUTICALS INC (NV)
Each share old Common $0.001 par exchanged for (0.0005) share new Common $0.001 par 09/23/2008
Recapitalized as Green Hygienics, Inc. 05/20/2011
Each share new Common $0.001 par exchanged for (0.0001) share Common $0.001 par

MNT LTD (ON)
Capital Shares no par split (2) for (1) by issuance of (1) additional share 8/31/93
Equity Dividend Shares no par split (2) for (1) by issuance of (1) additional share 8/31/93
Capital Shares no par called for redemption 6/30/97
Equity Dividend Shares no par called for redemption 6/30/97

MNX INC (MO)
Common 10¢ par split (3) for (2) by issuance of (0.5) additional share 3/4/87
Name changed to Mark VII, Inc. (MO) 6/7/94
Mark VII, Inc. (MO) reincorporated in Delaware 5/22/96
(See Mark VII, Inc. (DE))

MO-BILE INDS INC (NY)
Charter cancelled and proclaimed dissolved for failure to pay taxes 09/29/1982

MO-PARK INDS INC (DE)
Under plan of merger each share Common 1¢ par exchanged for $1.35 cash 09/07/1983

MOAB KING, INC. (NV)
Charter revoked for failure to file reports and pay fees 3/4/57

MOAB NATIONAL BANK (MOAB, UT)
Name changed to First Western National Bank (Moab, UT) 08/01/1972
(See First Western National Bank (Moab, UT))

MOAB URANIUM CO. (UT)
Name changed to Tower Enterprises, Inc. 4/9/63
Tower Enterprises, Inc. merged into Excalibur Industries 5/25/71

MOAB VALLEY URANIUM CO. (UT)
Charter revoked for failure to file reports and pay fees 3/31/59

MOAMCO CORP (MN)
Proclaimed dissolved for failure to file reports and pay taxes 10/5/91

MOBERLEY YELLOWKNIFE GOLD MINES LTD. (ON)
Name changed to Red Colley Gold Mines Ltd. in 1944
(See Red Colley Gold Mines Ltd.)

MOBICLEAR INC (PA)
Each share old Common $0.0001 par exchanged for (0.004) share new Common $0.0001 par 07/21/2008
Each share new Common $0.0001 par exchanged again for (0.00166666) share new Common $0.0001 par 10/20/2009
Name changed to Intelligent Communication Enterprise Corp. 12/22/2009
Intelligent Communication Enterprise Corp. name changed to One Horizon Group, Inc. (PA) 01/31/2013 which reorganized in Delaware 08/29/2013

MOBICOM COMMUNICATIONS INC (WY)
Each (15) shares old Common no par exchanged for (1) share new Common no par 06/19/2006
Recapitalized as Resource Group International, Inc. 11/08/2007
Each share Common no par exchanged for (0.000002) share Common no par

MOBICOM CORP (NV)
SEC revoked common stock registration 08/25/2011

MOBIEYES SOFTWARE INC (FL)
Reorganized as Resource Exchange of America Corp. 03/19/2010
Each share Common $0.0001 par exchanged for (25) shares Common $0.0001 par
Resource Exchange of America Corp. name changed to Allerayde SAB, Inc. 04/30/2013 which name changed to Stragenics, Inc. 04/28/2014

MOBIFORM SOFTWARE INC (DE)
Name changed to B-Scada Inc. 10/19/2012

MOBIKO MINES LTD. (ON)
Charter cancelled for failure to pay taxes and file returns 3/16/76

MOBIL CORP (DE)
Common $7.50 par changed to $3.75 par and (1) additional share issued 06/22/1979
Common $3.75 par changed to $2 par and (1) additional share issued 06/29/1981
Common $2 par changed to $1 par and (1) additional share issued payable 06/24/1997 to holders of record 05/20/1997 Ex date - 06/25/1997
Merged into Exxon Mobil Corp. 11/30/99
Each share Common $1 par exchanged for (1.32015) shares Common no par

MOBIL OIL CORP (NY)
Capital Stock $15 par changed to $7.50 par and (1) additional share issued 6/30/66
Capital Stock $7.50 par reclassified as Common $7.50 par 5/30/75

Under plan of reorganization each share Common $7.50 par automatically became (1) share Mobil Corp. Common $7.50 par 6/21/76
Mobil Corp. merged into Exxon Mobil Corp. 11/30/99

MOBILCRAFT INDUSTRIES, INC. (UT)
Declared bankrupt and involuntarily dissolved by the District Court of Salt Lake County, Utah 7/22/66

MOBILE & OHIO RAILROAD CO. (AL)
Reorganized as Gulf, Mobile & Ohio Railroad Co. 9/13/40
No stockholders' equity

MOBILE AIRWAVES CORP (CO)
Each share old Common no par exchanged for (18) shares new Common no par 09/26/2006
Recapitalized as American Community Development, Inc. 11/04/2009
Each share new Common no par exchanged for (0.00133333) share Common no par
American Community Development, Inc. recapitalized as UMF Group Inc. 02/23/2017

MOBILE AMER CORP (FL)
Common 10¢ par split (2) for (1) by issuance of (1) additional share 8/15/72
Each share Common 10¢ par exchanged for (1/3) share Common 30¢ par 7/25/80
Each share Common 30¢ par exchanged for (3) shares Common 10¢ par 9/25/87
Each share Common 10¢ par exchanged for (2) shares Common 5¢ par 10/1/92
Each share Common 5¢ par exchanged for (2) shares Common $0.025 par 9/24/93
Stock Dividend - 15% payable 7/11/97 to holders of record 6/23/97
Name changed to Fortune Financial Inc. 6/27/2000
(See Fortune Financial Inc.)

MOBILE AMER INC (NM)
Charter revoked 12/05/1988

MOBILE AMERICANA CORP (MN)
Common $2 par changed to $1.33-1/3 par and (0.5) additional share issued 3/2/70
Name changed to MoAmCo Corp. and Common $1.33-1/3 par changed to $1.06-2/3 par 2/15/72
(See MoAmCo. Corp.)

MOBILE ASSETS CORP (NV)
Recapitalized as Sunland Media Group 07/09/2008
Each share Common $0.001 par exchanged for (0.0005) share Common $0.001 par
Sunland Media Group name changed to Homestead Gold & Silver Ltd. 09/09/2011

MOBILE BROADCASTING HLDG INC (NV)
Name changed to Medically Minded, Inc. 03/02/2016
Medically Minded, Inc. name changed to Sixty Six Oilfield Services, Inc. 05/08/2017

MOBILE CLIMATE CTL INDS INC (ON)
Merged into Gunnar Mannerheim Holdco. 03/24/2004
Each share Common no par exchanged for $0.22 principal amount of 6% Unsecured Promissory Notes due 12/10/2005 and $0.22 cash
Each share Common no par received an additional distribution of $0.18861926 cash from escrow 01/28/2005

MOBILE COMMUNICATIONS CORP AMER (DE)
Common 1¢ par changed to 30¢ par 5/30/80
Common 30¢ par changed to $1 par 5/21/82
Common $1 par reclassified as Class B Common $1 par 3/1/83
Acquired by BellSouth Corp. 4/4/89
Each share Class A Common $1 par exchanged for (0.693) share Common $1 par
Each share Class B Common $1 par exchanged for (0.693) share Common $1 par
Note: Additional distribution of (0.01265822) share Common $1 par was made pursuant to a class action settlement to registered holders only 9/25/92
BellSouth Corp. merged into AT&T Inc. 12/29/2006

MOBILE COMPONENTS INC (KS)
Name changed to M.C. Inc. 01/19/1973
(See M.C. Inc.)

MOBILE COMPUTING CORP (ON)
Reincorporated under the laws of Canada as Canada West Capital Inc. 10/21/2003
Each share Common no par exchanged for (0.03703703) share Common no par
Canada West Capital Inc. (Canada) reorganized in Alberta as Canadian Sub-Surface Energy Services Corp. 02/14/2006 which merged into Pure Energy Services Ltd. 06/25/2009
(See Pure Energy Services Ltd.)

MOBILE CTRY CLUB (CA)
Common $10 par changed to $5 par 10/15/66
Liquidation completed
Each share Common $5 par exchanged for initial distribution of $8.25 cash 7/14/70
Each share Common $5 par received second and final distribution of $1.93 cash 5/31/72

MOBILE DATA CORP (NV)
Name changed to GeoTraq Inc. and Common $0.001 par changed to $0.0001 par 04/03/2014
GeoTraq Inc. name changed to GoTraq Inc. 11/01/2016 which name changed to MJ Venture Partners, Inc. 04/10/2018

MOBILE DESIGN CONCEPTS INC (NV)
Recapitalized as BioAccelerate Holdings, Inc. 09/23/2004
Each (3.5) shares Common $0.001 par exchanged for (1) share Common $0.001 par
BioAccelerate Holdings, Inc. name changed to Gardant Pharmaceuticals, Inc. 04/11/2006
(See Gardant Pharmaceuticals, Inc.)

MOBILE GAMING INTL CORP (NV)
Name changed to 3D Pioneer Systems, Inc. 10/29/2013

MOBILE GAS CO.
Assets acquired by Mobile Gas Service Corp. in 1933

MOBILE GAS SVC CORP (AL)
Common no par changed to $5 par and (1) additional share issued 00/00/1953
Common $5 par split (5) for (4) by issuance of (0.25) additional share 07/15/1955
Common $5 par changed to $2.50 par and (1) additional share issued 05/22/1964
Common $2.50 par split (2) for (1) by issuance of (1) additional share 01/31/1979
Common $2.50 par split (3) for (2) by issuance of (0.5) additional share 07/31/1987

4.90% Preferred $100 par called for redemption 12/01/1993
Stock Dividend - 10% 03/01/1963
Reorganized as EnergySouth, Inc. (AL) 02/01/1998
Each share Common $2.50 par exchanged for (1.5) shares Common 1¢ par
EnergySouth, Inc. (AL) reincorporated in Delaware 02/01/2007
(See EnergySouth, Inc. (DE))

MOBILE HOME CMNTYS (CO)
Reorganized under the laws of Delaware as Mobile Home Communities, Inc. 10/05/1973
Each Share of Bene. Int. no par exchanged for (1) share Common 1¢ par
(See Mobile Home Communities, Inc. (DE))

MOBILE HOME CMNTYS INC (DE)
Each share Common 1¢ par exchanged for (0.0005) share Common $20 par 12/21/1979
Note: In effect holders received $41.86 cash per share and public interest was eliminated

MOBILE HOME DYNAMICS INC (FL)
Name changed to Dycom Industries, Inc. 01/01/1982

MOBILE HOME INDS INC (FL)
Common $1 par split (2) for (1) by issuance of (1) additional share 3/7/72
Stock Dividend - 100% 7/21/69
Name changed to MHI Group, Inc. and Common $1 par changed to 10¢ par 1/16/87
(See MHI Group, Inc.)

MOBILE INTEGRATED SYS INC (NV)
Common $0.0001 par split (5) for (1) by issuance of (4) additional shares payable 03/27/2012 to holders of record 03/27/2012
Name changed to Epcylon Technologies, Inc. 08/08/2013

MOBILE KNOWLEDGE INC (CANADA)
Assets sold for the benefit of creditors 3/14/2003
No stockholders' equity

MOBILE LOTTERY SOLUTIONS INC (BC)
Name changed to NuMedia Games Inc. 09/27/2007
NuMedia Games Inc. recapitalized as Brandgamz Marketing Inc. 06/04/2008

MOBILE MEDIA UNLIMITED HLDGS INC (DE)
Recapitalized as EnableTS, Inc. 04/18/2011
Each share Common $0.0001 par exchanged for (0.001) share Common $0.0001 par

MOBILE MOTELS AMER INC (FL)
Proclaimed dissolved for failure to file reports and pay fees 06/28/1971

MOBILE MULTIMEDIA PRODUCTIONS INC (WY)
Name changed to Ekwan-X, Inc. 11/30/2004

MOBILE NATION INC (NV)
Each share old Common $0.001 par exchanged for (10) shares new Common $0.001 par 12/09/2003
Each share new Common $0.001 par exchanged again for (0.1) share new Common $0.001 par 03/03/2005
Name changed to AuraSource, Inc. 09/09/2008

MOBILE NATL CORP (DE)
Name changed to South Alabama Bancorporation Inc. (New) 09/30/1993
South Alabama Bancorporation Inc. (New) name changed to BancTrust Financial Group, Inc. 05/15/2002

which merged into Trustmark Corp. 02/15/2013

MOBILE OF MARYSVILLE, INC. (MI)
Charter declared inoperative and void for failure to file reports 5/15/66

MOBILE PET SYS INC (DE)
Name changed to Molecular Imaging Corp. 05/01/2003
(See Molecular Imaging Corp.)

MOBILE PRESENCE TECHNOLOGIES INC (DE)
Name changed to China Shandong Industries, Inc. 01/04/2010
(See China Shandong Industries, Inc.)

MOBILE REACH INTL INC (DE)
Each share old Common $0.001 par exchanged for (0.0125) share new Common $0.001 par 07/29/2005
Name changed to Crystal International Travel Group, Inc. 05/22/2006
(See Crystal International Travel Group, Inc.)

MOBILE RENTALS CORP. (CA)
Acquired by National General Corp. 2/11/63
Each share Common no par exchanged for (1) share Common $1 par
National General Corp. merged into American Financial Corp. 3/14/74

MOBILE SELF STORAGE INC (NV)
Charter revoked for failure to file reports and pay taxes 06/30/2003

MOBILE SVCS INTL CORP (DE)
Recapitalized as International Communications & Technologies Corp. 03/15/1996
Each share Common $0.0001 par exchanged for (0.01) share Common $0.0001 par
International Communications & Technologies Corp. recapitalized as GBS Com-Tech Corp. 05/15/1997
(See GBS Com-Tech Corp.)

MOBILE SYS INC (OH)
Charter cancelled for failure to pay taxes 08/15/1977

MOBILE TELECOMMUNICATION TECHNOLOGIES CORP (DE)
Name changed to Skytel Communications Inc. 5/22/98
Skytel Communications Inc. merged into MCI Worldcom, Inc. 10/1/99 which name changed to WorldCom Inc. (New) 5/1/2000
(See WorldCom Inc. (New))

MOBILE TELESYSTEMS PJSC (RUSSIA)
Sponsored ADR's for Common split (4) for (1) by issuance of (3) additional ADR's payable 12/31/2004 to holders of record 12/27/2004 Ex date - 01/03/2005
144A GDR's for Common split (4) for (1) by issuance of (3) additional GDR's payable 01/03/2005 to holders of record 12/29/2004
Reg. S GDR's for Common split (4) for (1) by issuance of (3) additional GDR's payable 01/03/2005 to holders of record 12/29/2004
Basis changed from (1:20) to (1:5) 01/02/2005
Sponsored ADR's for Common split (5) for (2) by issuance of (1.5) additional ADR's payable 04/30/2010 to holders of record 04/28/2010 Ex date - 05/03/2010
Basis changed from (1:5) to (1:2) 05/03/2010
144A GDR's for Common split (5) for (2) by issuance of (1.5) additional ADR's payable 05/10/2010 to holders of record 04/28/2010 Ex date - 05/11/2010
Reg. S GDR's for Common split (5) for (2) by issuance of (1.5) additional ADR's payable

05/10/2010 to holders of record 04/28/2010 Ex date - 05/11/2010
Name changed from Mobile TeleSystems OJSC to Mobile TeleSystems PJSC 07/07/2015
GDR agreement terminated 05/23/2018
Each 144A GDR for Common exchanged for (2) shares Common
Each Reg. S GDR for Common exchanged for (2) shares Common
Note: Unexchanged GDR's will be sold and the proceeds, if any, held for claim after 11/23/2018
(Additional Information in Active)

MOBILE TOWNES AMER INC (OR)
Reincorporated under the laws of Washington as MTA, Inc. 02/27/1978

MOBILE URANIUM & OIL CO. (UT)
Name changed to Monada Petroleum Corp. 10/31/1956
Monada Petroleum Corp. recapitalized as Diversified Energy Corp. 07/01/1977 which name changed to Diversified Enterprises, Inc. 11/25/2008

MOBILE VIDEO TAPES, INC. (CA)
Name changed to MVT Industries, Inc., 07/31/1962
(See MVT Industries, Inc.)

MOBILE WASTE CTLS INC (DE)
Reincorporated 08/14/1972
State of incorporation changed from (AR) to (DE) 08/14/1972
Merged into SCA Services, Inc. 10/26/1973
Each share Common 50¢ par exchanged for (0.6839) share Common $1 par
(See SCA Services, Inc.)

MOBILE WIRELESS SEC INC (NV)
Each share old Common $0.0001 par exchanged for (0.001) share new Common $0.0001 par 11/14/2005
Name changed to Hightowers Petroleum Holdings Ltd. 06/13/2006
Hightowers Petroleum Holdings Ltd. name changed to International Oil & Gas Holdings Corp. 07/19/2006 which name changed to Inscor, Inc. 05/26/2011 which recapitalized as Oicintra, Inc. 01/14/2016

MOBILEMAIL US INC (NV)
Name changed to MobiVentures, Inc. 08/02/2007
(See MobiVentures, Inc.)

MOBILMEDIA CORP (DE)
Issue Information - 8,000,000 shares CL A offered at $18.50 per share on 06/29/1995
Reorganized under Chapter 11 Federal Bankruptcy proceedings 06/03/1999
Each share Class A Common $0.001 par exchanged for an undetermined amount of Arch Communications Group Inc. Common Stock Purchase Warrants expiring 09/01/2001

MOBILEONE LTD (SINGAPORE)
Name changed to M1 Ltd. 04/16/2012

MOBILESTREAM INC (DE)
Name changed to Mobilestream Oil, Inc. 03/31/2006

MOBILEVEST INC (FL)
Name changed to Prime Capital Resources, Inc. (FL) 7/25/2002
Prime Capital Resources, Inc. (FL) reorganized in Nevada as ViaDux Health, Inc. 9/26/2005 which name changed to Solos Endoscopy, Inc. 3/14/2006

MOBILEX DEV LTD (ON)
Dissolved 10/11/77
Details not available

MOBILEYE N V (NETHERLANDS)
97.3% acquired by Intel Corp. 08/21/2017

Each share Ordinary EUR 0.01 par exchanged for $63.54 cash
Note: Remaining 2.7% acquired for $63.54 plus $0.86 interest per share through Squeeze-out 05/03/2018

MOBILIFE CORP. (DE)
Completely liquidated for cash 3/8/65

MOBILIFT INC (AB)
Delisted from Toronto Venture Stock Exchange 06/05/2002

MOBILIS RELOCATION SVCS INC (NV)
Name changed to Magnolia Solar Corp. 02/08/2010
Magnolia Solar Corp. recapitalized as Ecoark Holdings, Inc. 03/28/2016

MOBILITY ELECTRONICS INC (DE)
Issue Information - 4,000,000 shares COM offered at $12 per share on 06/30/2000
Name changed to iGo, Inc. 05/21/2008

MOBILITY INC (MN)
Merged into Fertilizer Equipment Co. 02/22/1977
Each share Common 1¢ par exchanged for $0.75 cash

MOBILTEK CORP (NV)
Recapitalized as Ten & 10, Inc. 09/20/2006
Each share Common $0.001 par exchanged for (0.02) share Common $0.001 par
Ten & 10, Inc. recapitalized as Globalite Group, Inc. 05/14/2007 which recapitalized as Language 2 Language Universal Holdings, Inc. 11/04/2008

MOBINETIX SYS INC (DE)
Name changed to @POS.com Inc. 6/29/99
(See @POS.com Inc.)

MOBISTAR SA (BELGIUM)
Name changed to Orange Belgium S.A. 07/11/2016

MOBIUS MGMT SYS INC (DE)
Issue Information - 3,300,000 shares COM offered at $14.50 per share on 04/27/1998
Merged into Allen Systems Group, Inc. 06/15/2007
Each share Common $0.0001 par exchanged for $10.05 cash

MOBIUS RES INC (AB)
Under plan of merger name changed to Sintana Energy Inc. 08/10/2015

MOBIVENTURES INC (NV)
Charter permanently revoked 05/02/2011

MOBLEY ENVIRONMENTAL SVCS INC (DE)
Each share new Common 1¢ par exchanged for (0.00002) share new Common 1¢ par 10/15/99
Note: In effect holders received $0.25 cash per share and public interest was eliminated

MOBOT CORP (CA)
Reincorporated under the laws of Delaware as Advanced Manufacturing Systems, Inc. and Common no par changed to 1¢ par 3/31/86
(See Advanced Manufacturing Systems, Inc.)

MOBRIDGE EXPLORATIONS INC (NV)
Name changed to PetroSouth Energy Corp. 05/01/2007
PetroSouth Energy Corp. name changed to West Canyon Energy Corp. 04/11/2008

MOBRUN COPPER LTD. (QC)
Name changed to Mobrun Copper Inc. 3/1/81

MOCCASIN FARMERS ELEVATOR CO. (MT)
Charter expired by time limitation 7/18/50

MOCCASIN MINES LTD.
Liquidated in 1950

MOCHE RES INC (BC)
Struck off register and declared dissolved for failure to file returns 1/22/93

MOCK, JUDSON, VOEHRINGER CO., INC.
Name changed to Mojud Hosiery Co., Inc. 00/00/1944
Mojud Hosiery Co., name changed to Mojud Co., Inc. 00/00/1953 which name changed to Martinall Industries, Inc. 01/25/1961 which liquidated for Bates Manufacturing Co., Inc. 01/03/1967
(See Bates Manufacturing Co., Inc.)

MOCON INC (MN)
Acquired by AMETEK, Inc. (New) 06/22/2017
Each share Common 10¢ par exchanged for $30 cash

MOD HOSPITALITY INC (NV)
Recapitalized as Stakool, Inc. 12/16/2009
Each share Common $0.001 par exchanged for (0.00066666) share Common $0.001 par
Stakool, Inc. name changed to Fresh Promise Foods, Inc. 11/12/2013

MOD-PAC CORP (NY)
Acquired by Rosalia Capital LLC 09/30/2013
Each share Common 1¢ par exchanged for $9.25 cash
Each share Class B 1¢ par exchanged for $9.25 cash

MOD U KRAF HOMES INC (VA)
Merged into Coachmen Industries, Inc. 6/22/2000
Each share Common $1 par exchanged for $11.75 cash

MODACAD INC (CA)
Name changed to Styleclick.Com, Inc. 07/19/1999
Styleclick.Com, Inc. merged into Styleclick, Inc. 07/27/2000
(See Styleclick, Inc.)

MODAMI SVCS INC (DE)
Name changed to AppleTree Companies, Inc. 07/11/1994
(See AppleTree Companies, Inc.)

MODATECH SYS INC (BC)
Each share Common no par exchanged for (1) share Class A Preferred no par 10/30/2004
Class A Preferred no par called for redemption at $0.025 on 07/16/2008

MODAVOX INC (DE)
Name changed to Augme Technologies, Inc. 03/23/2010
Augme Technologies, Inc. name changed to Hipcricket, Inc. 08/26/2013
(See Hipcricket, Inc.)

MODCO INC. (UT)
Name changed to General Automotive Corp. 11/07/1985
General Automotive Corp. recapitalized as Simondy Corp. 02/14/1989 which name changed to Pacific General, Inc. 03/15/1989
(See Pacific General, Inc.)

MODE PRODS INC (BC)
Delisted from Vancouver Stock Exchange 03/05/1993

MODEL ENGINEERING & MANUFACTURING CO., INC. (IN)
Name changed to Model Engineering & Manufacturing Corp. 8/9/60
Model Engineering & Manufacturing Corp. name changed to Memcor, Inc. 8/12/65 which merged into LTV Electrosystems, Inc. 4/19/67 which

name changed to E-Systems Inc. 4/27/72
(See E-Systems Inc.)

MODEL ENGINEERING & MANUFACTURING CORP. (IN)
Name changed to Memcor, Inc. 8/12/65
Memcor, Inc. merged into LTV Electrosystems, Inc. 4/10/67 which name changed to E-Systems Inc. 4/27/72
(See E-Systems Inc.)

MODEL IMPERIAL INC (FL)
Issue Information - 2,000,000 shares COM offered at $8 per share on 06/17/1994
Plan of reorganization under Chapter 11 Federal Bankruptcy proceedings confirmed 09/07/1997
Each share Common 1¢ par received $0.05 cash
Note: Certificates were not required to be surrendered and are without value

MODEL OILS LTD. (CANADA)
Recapitalized as Canadian Pipe Lines Producers Ltd. 00/00/1954
Each share Capital Stock $1 per exchanged for (0.5) share Capital Stock $1 par
Canadian Pipe Lines Producers Ltd. acquired by Canadian Pipelines & Petroleums Ltd. 00/00/1954 which merged into Scurry-Rainbow Oil Ltd. 05/09/1957 which was acquired by Home Oil Co. Ltd. (New) 11/08/1993 which merged into Anderson Exploration Ltd. 09/07/1995
(See Anderson Exploration Ltd.)

MODEL VENDING, INC. (PA)
Name changed to MVC Industries, Inc. 9/9/68
MVC Industries, Inc. name changed to Lyceum Companies, Inc. 1/27/69 which name changed back to MVC Industries, Inc. 9/15/69
(See MVC Industries, Inc.)

MODELE INC (FL)
Each share Common 1¢ par exchanged for (0.25) share Common 4¢ par 08/29/1969
Adjudicated bankrupt 01/26/1974
Stockholders' equity unlikely

MODEM MEDIA INC (DE)
Name changed 6/6/2000
Issue Information - 2,600,000 shares CL A offered at $16 per share on 02/04/1999
Class A Common $0.001 par split (2) for (1) by issuance of (1) additional share payable 3/1/2000 to holders of record 2/16/2000
Name changed from Modem Media.Poppe Tyson, Inc. to Modem Media Inc. 6/6/2000
Merged into Digitas Inc. 10/15/2004
Each share Class A Common $0.001 par exchanged for (0.7) share Common 1¢ par
(See Digitas Inc.)

MODENA I INC (DE)
Name changed to Alveron Energy Corp. 05/26/2010
Alveron Energy Corp. name changed to Safebrain Systems, Inc. 07/26/2012

MODER-RATE HOMES, INC. (DE)
Liquidation completed 7/13/62

MODERN AMERN LIFE INS CO (MO)
Stock Dividends - 100% 11/5/66; 20% 6/30/68; 20% 11/30/68; 10% 6/30/69; 10% 11/30/69; 10% 11/30/70; 10% 12/30/71
Merged into I.C.H. Corp. 11/3/82
Each share Common $1 par exchanged for (0.3589) share Common $1 par
I.C.H. Corp. name changed to Southwestern Life Corp. (New)

6/15/94 which name changed to I.C.H. Corp. (New) 10/10/95
(See I.C.H. Corp. (New))

MODERN AMERICAN MORTGAGE CORP. (AR)
Common $1 par changed to 50¢ par 12/21/1965
Completely liquidated 09/06/1977
Each share Common 50¢ par exchanged for (1) Non-Transferable Unit of Ltd. Partnership Int. of Modern Properties Ltd. and $1.25 cash

MODERN BAG CO.
Liquidation completed in 1950

MODERN BANKING DEVICE CO. (DE)
Charter cancelled and declared inoperative and void for non-payment of taxes 02/07/1912

MODERN CITY ENTMT INC (WA)
SEC revoked common stock registration 01/21/2016

MODERN COMMUNITY DEVELOPERS, INC. (NJ)
Merged into Planned Communities, Inc. 12/30/66
Each share Common $100 par exchanged for (6) shares Common $5 par
Planned Communities, Inc. completely liquidated 12/15/72

MODERN CONTAINERS, LTD. (ON)
Each share Common no par exchanged for (2) shares Class A no par and (2) shares Common no par in 1946
Merged into Metal Closures (Canada) Ltd. 7/15/63
Each share Class A no par exchanged for (15) shares Common no par
Each share Common no par exchanged for (12) shares Common no par
Metal Closures (Canada) Ltd. name changed to Metcan Products, Ltd. 6/30/66 which name changed to Alcan Ingot Ltd. 3/1/69

MODERN CTLS INC (MN)
Common 10¢ par split (2) for (1) by issuance of (1) additional share 10/16/1972
Common 10¢ par split (3) for (1) by issuance of (2) additional shares 08/27/1976
Common 10¢ par split (3) for (2) by issuance of (0.5) additional share 09/28/1990
Common 10¢ par split (3) for (2) by issuance of (0.5) additional share 08/23/1991
Common 10¢ par split (3) for (2) by issuance of (0.5) additional share payable 09/12/1997 to holders of record 08/22/1997
Name changed to MOCON, Inc. 06/01/1999
(See MOCON, Inc.)

MODERN DATA TECHNIQUES INC (DE)
Charter cancelled and declared inoperative and void for non-payment of taxes 4/15/72

MODERN DIVERSIFIED INDS INC (FL)
Merged into JHC, Inc. 02/03/1982
Each share Common no par exchanged for $0.40 cash

MODERN DIXIE CORP. (MS)
Name changed to Dixie National Corp. 11/05/1969
Dixie National Corp. name changed to Ethika Corp. 08/13/1996 which recapitalized as Tradequest International, Inc. (MS) 04/16/2001 which reincorporated in Nevada 10/11/2005
(See Tradequest International, Inc.)

MODERN ENERGY CORP (DE)
Name changed to Titan Energy Corp. 07/16/1982
(See Titan Energy Corp.)

MODERN FIN CO
Preferred called for redemption at $105 on 4/30/97

MODERN FOODS INC (FL)
Stock Dividends - 10% 09/12/1969; 10% 08/21/1970
Merged into Katy Towing Co., Inc. 12/31/1974
Each share Common $1 par exchanged for $5 cash

MODERN FOODS INC (MN)
Company reported out of business 02/28/1983
Details not available

MODERN HOMES CONSTR CO (FL)
Name changed to Modern Diversified Industries, Inc. 05/28/1969
(See Modern Diversified Industries, Inc.)

MODERN HOMES CORP. (MI)
Charter revoked for failure to file reports and pay fees 5/15/60

MODERN INCOME LIFE INS CO (IL)
Common $1 par split (1.8) for (1) by issuance of (0.8) additional share 00/00/1968
Stock Dividends - 25% 11/00/1969; 10% 09/00/1970; 10% 11/30/1971; 15% 10/30/1973
Each (62,434) shares Common $1 par exchanged for (1) share Common $62,434 par 05/29/1985
Note: In effect holders received $6.30 cash per share and public interest was eliminated

MODERN INDUSTRIAL BANK (NEW YORK, NY)
Name changed to Commercial State Bank & Trust Co. (New York, NY) 1/2/53
Commercial State Bank & Trust Co. (New York, NY) merged into Commercial Bank of North America (New York, NY) 9/5/58 which name changed to Bank of North America (New York, NY) (New)
(See Bank of North America (New York, NY) (New))

MODERN INDS INC (DE)
Recapitalized as Energy Development Corp. 10/16/95
Each share Common $0.001 par exchanged for (1/3) share Common $0.001 par

MODERN INVESTORS LIFE INSURANCE CO. (AR)
Merged into Roosevelt National Investment Co. (IL) 12/05/1974
Each share Capital Stock $1 par exchanged for (2) shares Class A Common $1 par
Roosevelt National Investment Co. (IL) reorganized in Delaware as Universal Guaranty Investment Co. 06/14/1990
(See Universal Guaranty Investment Co.)

MODERN LIFE INSURANCE CO. OF MINNESOTA
Name changed to North Central Life Insurance Co. in 1950
(See North Central Life Insurance Co.)

MODERN LIFE INS CO (NY)
Name changed to ITT Life Insurance Co. 04/11/1968
(See ITT Life Insurance Co.)

MODERN LN CO (KY)
6% Preferred $10 par called for redemption 07/21/1977
Liquidation completed
Each share Common $1 par exchanged for initial distribution of $5 cash 07/21/1977
Each share Common $1 par received second distribution of $3 cash 01/06/1978
Each share Common $1 par received third and final distribution of $0.12 cash 01/12/1980

MODERN MAID, INC. (TN)
Acquired by McGraw-Edison Co. 12/20/1972
Details not available

MODERN MAID FOOD PRODS INC (NY)
Stock Dividend - 10% 01/31/1977
Merged into Spillers Ltd. 02/06/1978
Each share Common $1 par exchanged for $16.70 cash

MODERN MFG SVCS INC (NV)
Each share old Common 5¢ par exchanged for (0.05) share new Common 5¢ par 8/6/2001
Name changed to Radix Marine Inc. 5/12/2003

MODERN MATLS CORP (MI)
Common $1 par split (5) for (4) by issuance of (0.25) additional share 5/14/64
Stock Dividend - 25% 9/30/68
Merged into American Forest Products Corp. 3/2/70
Each share Common $1 par exchanged for (0.2963) share Common no par
(See American Forest Products Corp.)

MODERN MERCHANDISING INC (MN)
Stock Dividends - 25% 04/30/1976; 100% 04/11/1977
Merged into Best Products Co., Inc. 09/16/1982
Each share Common 1¢ par exchanged for (0.73) share Common $1 par
(See Best Products Co., Inc.)

MODERN METAL PRODS CO
Merged into MMP Merger Co. 4/28/2000
Each share Common no par exchanged for $177.50 cash
Note: Each share Common no par received an initial distribution of approximately $0.768 cash payable 12/13/2002 to holders of record 4/28/2000
Each share Common no par received a second and final distribution of approximately $5.07 cash payable 6/24/2002 to holders of record 4/28/2000

MODERN METALCRAFT, INC. (MN)
Adjudicated bankrupt 4/22/70

MODERN MINERALS CORP (UT)
Proclaimed dissolved for failure to pay taxes 11/09/1974

MODERN MNG & MLG INC (UT)
Recapitalized as Copper Mountain Energy, Inc. 12/1/78
Each share Common 1¢ par exchanged for (1/3) share Common 1¢ par
(See Copper Mountain Energy, Inc.)

MODERN PIONEERS LIFE INS CO (AZ)
Merged into Patriot Subsidiary Corp. 09/18/1987
Each share Common $1 par exchanged for $3 principal amount of Surplus Debentures due 09/18/1999

MODERN PLASTIC LTD (QC)
Name changed 04/20/1977
Name changed from Modern Plastics Co. Ltd. to Modern Plastics Ltd./Les Plastiques Modernes Ltee. 04/20/1977
Name changed to Coronet Housewares Inc. 00/00/1980
(See Coronet Housewares Inc.)

MODERN RENEWABLE TECHNOLOGIES INC (NV)
Each share old Common $0.001 par exchanged for (0.01) share new Common $0.001 par 10/04/2010
Name changed to Eco Ventures Group, Inc. 05/16/2011
Eco Ventures Group, Inc. recapitalized as Petlife Pharmaceuticals, Inc. (Old) 08/12/2014 which reorganized as Petlife Pharmaceuticals, Inc. (New) 09/12/2016

MODERN SEC LIFE INS CO (MO)
Stock Dividends - 100% 4/28/64; 50% 5/10/65; 20% 5/23/66; 20% 6/30/67; 25% 6/30/68
Merged into I.C.H. Corp. 11/4/82
Each share Common $1 par exchanged for (0.1858) share Common $1 par
I.C.H. Corp. name changed to Southwestern Life Corp. (New) 6/15/94 which name changed to I.C.H. Corp. (New) 10/10/95
(See I.C.H. Corp. (New))

MODERN SPORTS ENTERPRISES, INC. (NY)
Dissolved 10/31/60

MODERN STAMPING & MANUFACTURING CO.
Acquired by Parker-Wolverine Co. on a (0.25) for (1) basis in 1938
Parker-Wolverine Co. merged into Udylite Co. in 1946 which merged into Hooker Chemical Corp. 1/2/68 which was acquired by Occidental Petroleum Corp. (Calif.) 7/24/68
(See Occidental Petroleum Corp. (Calif.))

MODERN TECHNOLOGY CORP (NV)
Each share old Common $0.0001 par received distribution of (0.02) share OmniComm Systems, Inc. Common $0.001 par payable 02/17/2000 to holders of record 10/04/1999
Each share old Common $0.0001 par received distribution of (0.02) share Scientio Inc. Common $0.001 par payable 10/13/2001 to holders of record 09/24/2001
Each share old Common $0.0001 par exchanged for (0.06666666) share new Common $0.0001 par 07/31/2004
Each share new Common $0.0001 par exchanged again for (0.05) share new Common $0.0001 par 05/15/2006
Charter permanently revoked 08/31/2011

MODERN TIMES GROUP MTG AB (SWEDEN)
Each Sponsored ADR for B shares received distribution of (1.5) Class A and (3.5) Class B shares of Metro International SA payable 08/21/2000 to holders of record 08/18/2000
Sponsored ADR's for Class B split (5) for (1) by issuance of (4) additional ADR's payable 03/08/2002 to holders of record 03/07/2002
Ex date - 03/11/2002
ADR basis changed from (1:5) to (1:1) 03/08/2002
ADR agreement terminated 02/13/2004
Each Sponsored ADR for Class B shares exchanged for $33.3257 cash

MODERN VENTURES CORP (NV)
Reincorporated under the laws of Michigan as Financial Equity Group, Inc. 06/11/1984

MODERN WORLD MEDIA INC (DE)
Name changed to Polaris International Holdings, Inc. 11/08/2007

MODERNCARE INC (DE)
Charter cancelled and declared

inoperative and void for non-payment of taxes 3/1/91

MODERNGROOVE ENTMT INC (NV)
Name changed to Immediatek, Inc. 12/9/2002

MODESTO COMM BK (MODESTO, CA)
Common no par split (3) for (2) by issuance of (0.5) additional share payable 4/15/2000 to holders of record 3/31/2000
Under plan of reorganization each share Common no par automatically became (1) share Central Valley Bancorp Common no par 10/6/2000
(See Central Valley Bancorp)

MODGLIN CO., INC. (CA)
Voluntarily dissolved 3/20/75
Details not available

MODICO INDS LTD (QC)
Name changed to Annabelle, Inc. 11/10/1997
Annabelle, Inc. name changed to Waitsfield Capital Inc. 10/22/1999
(See Waitsfield Capital Inc.)

MODIGENE INC (NV)
Common $0.00001 par split (4.3650792) for (1) by issuance of (3.3650792) additional shares payable 03/23/2007 to holders of record 03/16/2007 Ex date - 03/26/2007
Name changed to PROLOR Biotech, Inc. 06/12/2009
PROLOR Biotech, Inc. merged into OPKO Health, Inc. 08/29/2013

MODIGLASS FIBERS, INC. (NY)
Merged into Reichhold Chemicals, Inc. 12/31/63
Each share Capital Stock 10¢ par exchanged for (17/44) share Common $1 par
(See Reichhold Chemicals, Inc.)

MODIGLIANI GLASS FIBERS, INC. (NY)
Name changed to Modiglass Fibers, Inc. 3/28/57
Modiglass Fibers, Inc. merged into Reichhold Chemicals, Inc. 12/31/63
(See Reichhold Chemicals, Inc.)

MODINE MFG CO (WI)
Preferred Stock Purchase Rights declared for Common stockholders of record 10/27/1986 were redeemed at $0.0125 per right 09/05/2002 for holders of record 08/23/2002
(Additional Information in Active)

MODIS PROFESSIONAL SVCS INC (FL)
Name changed to MPS Group, Inc. 01/01/2002
(See MPS Group, Inc.)

MODOC OILS LTD. (CANADA)
Recapitalized as Canadian Chieftain Petroleums Ltd. 01/31/1956
Each share Capital Stock no par exchanged for (0.2) share Capital Stock no par
(See Canadian Cheiftan Petroleums Ltd.)

MODTECH HLDGS INC (DE)
Chapter 11 bankruptcy proceedings converted to Chapter 7 on 10/06/2011
Stockholders' equity unlikely

MODTECH INC (CA)
Merged into Modtech Holdings, Inc. 02/16/1999
Each share Common 1¢ par exchanged for (0.8508) share Common 1¢ par and $3.7293 cash
(See Modtech Holdings, Inc.)

MODULAIRE INDS (CA)
Stock Dividend - 10% 4/21/86
Merged into Waste Management, Inc. (Old) 7/31/87
Each share Common no par exchanged for (0.394) share Common $1 par
Waste Management, Inc. (Old) name changed to WMX Technologies Inc. 5/14/93 which name changed to Waste Management, Inc. (New) 5/12/97 which merged into Waste Management, Inc. 7/16/98

MODULAR AMBULANCE CORP (TX)
Stock Dividend - 100% 01/17/1977
Name changed to Amtech Group Ltd. 03/02/1982
(See Amtech Group Ltd.)

MODULAR COMPONENTS SYS INC (DE)
Charter cancelled and declared inoperative and void for non-payment of taxes 4/15/72

MODULAR COMPUTER SYS INC (FL)
Merged into AEG AG 7/11/86
Each share Common 5¢ par exchanged for $9 cash

MODULAR CONCEPTS INC (NY)
Assets assigned for benefit of creditors 08/00/1974
No stockholders' equity

MODULAR CORRECTIONAL SYS INC (NY)
Each share old Common $0.00001 par exchanged for (0.1) share new Common $0.00001 par 10/27/87
Charter cancelled and proclaimed dissolved for failure to pay taxes 12/29/93

MODULAR DESIGNED HOMES INC (WA)
Adjudicated bankrupt 08/02/1972
Stockholders' equity unlikely

MODULAR DIMENSIONS INC (DE)
Charter cancelled and declared inoperative and void for non-payment of taxes 4/15/72

MODULAR DYNAMICS INC (DE)
Charter cancelled and declared inoperative and void for non-payment of taxes 04/01/1973

MODULAR HSG SYS INC (DE)
Adjudicated bankrupt 09/20/1973
Stockholders' equity unlikely

MODULAR INDS INC (FL)
Proclaimed dissolved for non-payment of taxes 7/2/73

MODULAR SCIENCES INC (GA)
Name changed to Valley Forge Corp. (GA) 04/28/1971
Valley Forge Corp. (GA) reincorporated in Delaware 06/12/1997
(See Valley Forge Corp.)

MODULAR STRUCTURES INC (MN)
Adjudicated bankrupt 03/02/1973
Stockholders' equity unlikely

MODULAR SYS INC (GA)
Ceased operations 00/00/1974
No stockholders' equity

MODULAR TECHNOLOGY CORP (IL)
Proclaimed dissolved for failure to file reports and pay taxes 12/1/80

MODULAR TECHNOLOGY INC (DE)
Name changed to Miller Building Systems, Inc. 11/1/88
(See Miller Building Systems, Inc.)

MODULE RES INC (BC)
Name changed to New Carolin Gold Corp. 10/18/2011

MODULE SYS & DEV CORP (DE)
Charter cancelled and declared inoperative and void for non-payment of taxes 3/1/79

MODULEARN INC (UT)
Name changed to Micro General Corp. (UT) 01/25/1982
Micro General Corp. (UT) reincorporated in Delaware 07/01/1988 which merged into Fidelity National Information Solutions, Inc. 07/10/2002 which merged into Fidelity National Financial, Inc. 09/30/2003 which merged into Fidelity National Information Services, Inc. 11/09/2006

MODULINE INTL INC (WA)
Common no par split (5) for (4) by issuance of (0.25) additional share 08/19/1976
Merged into Champion Enterprises, Inc. 02/27/1988
Each share Common no par exchanged for $1.50 cash

MODUMATIC INDS INC (NY)
Common 1¢ par split (2) for (1) by issuance of (1) additional share 10/22/1971
Adjudicated bankrupt 06/13/1973
Stockholders' equity unlikely

MODUSLINK GLOBAL SOLUTIONS INC (DE)
Each share old Common 1¢ par exchanged for (1) share new Common 1¢ par to reflect a (1) for (100) reverse split followed by a (100) for (1) forward split 01/20/2015
Note: Holders of (99) or fewer pre-split shares received $3.62 cash per share
Name changed to Steel Connect, Inc. 02/27/2018

MOE LIGHT, INC. (WI)
Merged into Thomas Industries Inc. in 1953
Each share 5% Preferred $10 par exchanged for (1) share 5% Preferred Ser. B $10 par
Each share Common $1 par exchanged for (2.85714285) shares Common $1 par
(See Thomas Industries Inc.)

MOET HENNESSY S A (FRANCE)
Stock Dividend - 20% 3/7/86
Merged into LVMH Moet Hennessey Louis Vuitton 10/22/87
Each ADR for Ordinary 50 Frs. par exchanged for (1.2) Sponsored ADR's for Ordinary 50 Frs. par
(See LVMH Moet Hennessey Louis Vuitton)

MOEX INDS LTD (BC)
Struck off register 09/20/1985

MOFFAT COMMUNICATIONS LTD (BC)
Common no par reclassified as Conv. Class A Common no par 5/13/74
Conv. Class A Common no par split (3) for (2) by issuance of (0.5) additional share 8/21/78
Conv. Class B Common no par split (3) for (2) by issuance of (0.5) additional share 8/21/78
Conv. Class A Common no par split (2) for (1) by issuance of (1) additional share 11/1/83
Conv. Class B Common no par split (2) for (1) by issuance of (1) additional share 11/1/83
Conv. Class A Common no par reclassified as Common no par 2/22/84
Conv. Class B Common no par reclassified as Common no par 2/22/84
Common no par split (2) for (1) by issuance of (1) additional share payable 10/14/97 to holders of record 10/10/97
Common no par split (2) for (1) by issuance of (1) additional share payable 4/16/99 to holders of record 4/12/99
Merged into Shaw Communications Inc. 1/29/2001
Each share Common no par exchanged for (1.0508) Non-Vtg. Class B $0.0167 no par and $0.05 cash

MOFFATT-HALL GOLD MINES, LTD.
Acquired by Moffatt-Hall Mines, Ltd. in 1928
Details not available

MOFFATT-HALL MINES, LTD.
Assets acquired by Moffatt-Hall Mining Co., Ltd. in 1936
Details not available

MOFFATT-HALL MINING CO., LTD. (ON)
Charter cancelled and company declared dissolved for default in filing returns 2/10/58

MOGADOR MINES LTD. (QC)
Recapitalized as Consolidated Mogador Mines Ltd. on a (1) for (4) basis 5/4/62
(See Consolidated Mogador Mines Ltd.)

MOGAR MINES LTD (ON)
Charter cancelled for failure to file reports and pay fees 02/28/1973

MOGEN DAVID KOSHER MEAT PRODS CORP (NY)
Plan of reorganization under Chapter 11 Federal Bankruptcy Code effective 9/26/97
Each share Common 10¢ par exchanged for $0.75 cash

MOGGLE INC (DE)
Name changed to Virtual Piggy, Inc. 09/14/2011
Virtual Piggy, Inc. name changed to Rego Payment Architectures, Inc. 03/16/2017

MOGUL CORP (OH)
Stock Dividend - 20% 09/30/1975
Merged into Dexter Corp. 05/09/1977
Each share Common no par exchanged for (1) share Common $1 par
Dexter Corp. merged into Invitrogen Corp. 09/14/2000 which name changed to Life Technologies Corp. 11/21/2008
(See Life Technologies Corp.)

MOGUL INTL INC (NV)
Recapitalized as Las Vegas International, Inc. 11/16/87
Each share Common 1¢ par exchanged for (0.1) share Common 1¢ par
Las Vegas International, Inc. name changed to Rising Star International Inc. 2/14/97

MOGUL MINES LTD. (ON)
Merged into International Mogul Mines Ltd. 11/20/1968
Each share Capital Stock $1 par exchanged for (0.25) share Capital Stock no par
International Mogul Mines Ltd. merged into Conwest Exploration Co. Ltd. (ON) (Old) 08/27/1982 which merged into Conwest Exploration Co. Ltd. (New) (AB) 09/01/1993 which merged into Alberta Energy Co. Ltd. 01/31/1996 which merged into EnCana Corp. 01/03/2003

MOGUL MINING CORP. LTD. (ON)
Recapitalized as Consolidated Mogul Mines Ltd. on a (1) for (5) basis 3/24/58
Consolidated Mogul Mines Ltd. name changed to Mogul Mines Ltd. 7/27/67 which merged into International Mogul Mines Ltd. 11/20/68 which merged into Conwest Exploration Co. Ltd. (Old) (ONT) 8/27/82 which merged into Conwest Exploration Co. Ltd. (New) (ALTA) 9/1/93 which merged into Alberta Energy Co. Ltd. 1/31/96 which merged into EnCana Corp. 1/3/2003

MOHASCO CORP (NY)
Common $5 par split (3) for (2) by

issuance of (0.5) additional share 9/29/86
Common $5 par split (3) for (2) by issuance of (0.5) additional share 9/29/87
3-1/2% Preferred $100 par called for redemption 8/30/89
4.20% Preferred $100 par called for redemption 8/30/89
Merged into MHS Holdings Corp. 9/22/89
Each share Common $5 par exchanged for $36.50 principal amount of 16.875% Pay-In-Kind Subordinated Debentures due 9/22/2004 and (1) Class A Common Stock Purchase Warrant expiring 9/22/94
Stock Dividend - 10% 10/15/59
Name changed to Mohasco Corp. 5/3/74
(See Mohasco Corp.)

MOHAVE GOLD INC (AB)
Cease trade order effective 5/1/90
Stockholders' equity unlikely

MOHAVE MINERALS INC (CO)
Charter suspended for failure to file annual reports 09/30/1987

MOHAVE ST BK (LAKE HAVASU CITY, AZ)
Under plan of reorganization each share Common no par automatically became (1) share State Bank Corp. Common no par 3/31/2004

MOHAWK AIRLS INC (NY)
Merged into Allegheny Airlines, Inc. 4/12/72
Each share Capital Stock $1 par exchanged for (0.235294) share Common $1 par and (0.156863) Common Stock Purchase Warrant expiring 4/12/79
Allegheny Airlines, Inc. name changed to U S Air, Inc. 10/29/79 which reorganized as USAir Group, Inc. 2/1/83 which name changed to US Airways Group, Inc. 2/21/97
(See US Airways Group, Inc.)

MOHAWK BUSINESS MACHS CORP (MD)
Recapitalized 10/6/59
Each share Preferred $1 par exchanged for (0.25) share Preferred $4 par
Each share Common 10¢ par exchanged for (0.25) share Common 40¢ par
Name changed to Mohawk Electronics Corp. 7/7/61 which was adjudicated bankrupt 9/15/65

MOHAWK CDA LTD (CANADA)
Acquired by HB Acquisition Inc. 08/21/1998
Each share Common no par exchanged for $7.25 cash

MOHAWK CARPET MILLS, INC. (NY)
Capital Stock no par changed to $20 par in 1933
Merged into Mohasco Industries, Inc. 12/31/55
Each share Common $20 par exchanged for (4) shares Common $5 par
Mohasco Industries, Inc. name changed to Mohasco Corp. 5/3/74
(See Mohasco Corp.)

MOHAWK DATA SCIENCES CORP (NY)
Common 25¢ par changed to 10¢ par and (1) additional share issued 8/15/66
Common 10¢ par split (2) for (1) by issuance of (1) additional share 7/30/68
Name changed to Qantel Corp. 9/17/87
(See Qantel Corp.)

MOHAWK ELECTRONICS CORP. (MD)
Adjudicated bankrupt 9/15/65

MOHAWK FIRE INSURANCE CO.
Merged into Importers & Exporters Insurance Co. of New York in 1934
Details not available

MOHAWK HUDSON POWER CORP.
Merged into Niagara Hudson Power Corp. in 1937
Each share 1st Preferred exchanged for (1) share new 5% 1st Preferred $100 par and $4 in cash
Each share 2nd Preferred exchanged for (1) share new 5% 2nd Preferred $100 par
Each share Common exchanged for (1.0625) shares new Common $10 par and a Class A option warrant
Niagara Hudson Power Corp. recapitalized as Niagara Mohawk Power Corp. 1/5/50

MOHAWK INDS LTD (BC)
Placed in receivership 11/24/1977
No stockholders' equity

MOHAWK INS CO (NY)
Merged into Knickerbocker Insurance Co. 09/30/1968
Each share Class A Common $5 par exchanged for (0.35) share Class A Common $2 par
(See Knickerbocker Insurance Co.)

MOHAWK INVESTMENT CORP.
Acquired by State Street Investment Corp. 00/00/1933
Details not available

MOHAWK LIQUEUR CORP (MI)
Each share Common $1 par exchanged for (0.002) share Common $500 par 03/27/1973
Note: In effect holders received $115 cash per share and public interest was eliminated

MOHAWK MINES LTD (QC)
Charter cancelled for failure to file reports and pay fees 08/03/1974

MOHAWK NATL BK (SCHENECTADY, NY)
Common $10 par changed to $13.50 par 02/00/1941
Common $13.50 par changed to $15 par 05/00/1971
Common $15 par changed to $17.50 par 00/00/1942
Common $17.50 par changed to $18 par 05/00/1943
Common $18 par changed to $18.50 par 11/11/1943
Common $18.50 par changed to $20 par 00/00/1944
Common $20 par changed to $22 par 00/00/1945
Common $22 par changed to $25 par 00/00/1946
Common $25 par changed to $12.50 par and (1) additional share issued 02/15/1961
Common $12.50 par changed to $6.25 par and (1) additional share issued 02/01/1971
Merged into Security New York State Corp. 01/29/1982
Each share Common $6.25 par exchanged for (1.7238) shares $1.44 Conv. Preferred Ser. B $5 par and $30.42 principal amount of 10% 10-Yr. Subordinated Notes due 01/29/1992
Note: Above ratio applies to 60% of holdings exchanged for Preferred Ser. B and 40% exchanged for Notes
(See Security New York State Corp.)

MOHAWK PETE CORP (CA)
Completely liquidated 09/24/1969
Each share Capital Stock $1 par exchanged for first and final distribution of (1) share Reserve Oil & Gas Co. 5-1/2% Conv. Preferred Ser. D $25 par and (3.452) shares Common $1 par
(See Reserve Oil & Gas Co.)

MOHAWK PORCUPINE GOLD MINES LTD. (ON)
Dissolved 12/16/57

MOHAWK RUBR CO (OH)
Each share Preferred $100 par exchanged for (5) shares new Common no par in 1938
Each share old Common no par exchanged for (0.2) share new Common no par in 1938
New Common no par changed to $1 par 3/3/58
Common $1 par split (2) for (1) by issuance of (1) additional share 12/19/59
Common $1 par split (6) for (5) by issuance of (0.2) additional share 12/22/61
Common $1 par split (3) for (2) by issuance of (0.5) additional share 5/22/81
Stock Dividends - 30% 12/20/58; 20% 9/15/71
Merged into Equity Group Holdings 1/19/84
Each share Common $1 par exchanged for $40 cash

MOHAWK SHARE CO.
Absorbed by M. & T. Securities Corp. in 1929 which dissolved in 1937

MOHAWK SILVER-LEAD MINING CO. (ID)
Merged into Yreka United, Inc. (ID) 06/07/1957
Each share Common exchanged for (0.2) share Common 50¢ par
Yreka United, Inc. (ID) reorganized in Nevada as Southern Home Medical Equipment, Inc. 10/23/2006 which name changed to Southern Home Medical, Inc. 07/27/2012

MOHAWK URANIUM CORP. (UT)
Charter suspended for non-payment of taxes 3/21/56

MOHAWK VY CMNTY CORP (NY)
Name changed to Library Bureau, Inc. 02/19/1981
Library Bureau, Inc. name changed to LBI Manufacturing, Inc. 07/11/1995
(See LBI Manufacturing, Inc.)

MOHER YELLOWKNIFE GOLD MINES LTD. (ON)
Charter surrendered 11/5/76
No stockholders' equity

MOHICAN CORP (NY)
Recapitalized 5/7/62
5% Preferred $14 par changed to $10 par
Common $1 par changed to 10¢ par
Merged into Fab Industries, Inc. 10/23/68
Each share Common 10¢ par exchanged for (0.125) share Common 20¢ par
(See Fab Industries, Inc.)

MOHICAN STORES, INC. (NY)
Name changed to Mohican Corp. 5/13/59
Mohican Corp. merged into Fab Industries, Inc. 10/23/68
(See Fab Industries, Inc.)

MOIIBUS RES CORP (AB)
Name changed 2/26/96
Name changed from Moiibus Environmental Corp. to Moiibus Resource Corp. 2/26/96
Merged into Transglobe Energy Corp. (BC) 4/28/99
Each share Common no par exchanged for (0.615) share Common no par
Transglobe Energy Corp. (BC) reincorporated in Alberta 6/9/2004

MOIMSTONE CORP (BC)
Name changed to Apivio Systems Inc. 05/23/2014

(See Apivio Systems Inc.)

MOIR HOTEL CO.
Reorganized as Morrison Hotel Corp. (Del.) in 1938
No stockholders' equity

MOIRS, LTD. (NS)
Name changed to Ben's Holdings Ltd. 12/28/67

MOJAVE ACQUISITIONS INC (CO)
Name changed to Sorensen Industries Corp. 6/1/88
Sorensen Industries Corp. merged into Amglobal Corp. 3/17/89
(See Amglobal Corp.)

MOJAVE DESERT BK NATL ASSN (MOJAVE, CA)
Stock Dividends - 3% payable 01/14/2000 to holders of record 12/31/1999; 5% payable 01/15/2002 to holders of record 12/31/2001 Ex date - 12/27/2001; 5% payable 01/23/2004 to holders of record 01/09/2004 Ex date - 01/07/2004; 5% payable 01/18/2006 to holders of record 12/31/2005 Ex date - 12/28/2005; 5% payable 01/17/2007 to holders of record 12/29/2006 Ex date - 12/28/2006; 5% payable 01/16/2008 to holders of record 12/31/2007 Ex date - 12/27/2007; 5% payable 01/21/2009 to holders of record 12/31/2008 Ex date - 12/29/2008; 5% payable 01/20/2010 to holders of record 12/31/2009 Ex date - 01/20/2010; 5% payable 01/19/2011 to holders of record 12/31/2010 Ex date - 01/20/2011
Merged into Mission Bancorp 01/25/2013
Each share Common $5 par exchanged for (0.32135) share Common no par and $8.3091 cash

MOJAVE SOUTHN INC (NV)
Common $0.001 par split (28) for (1) by issuance of (27) additional shares payable 07/23/2002 to holders of record 07/22/2002 Ex date - 07/24/2002
Name changed to New York Medical, Inc. 08/20/2002
New York Medical, Inc. name changed to Critical Home Care, Inc. 09/26/2002 which name changed to Arcadia Resources, Inc. 12/01/2004

MOJAVE URANIUM CO. (NV)
Name changed to U.S. Silver & Mining Corp. 7/6/68
U.S. Silver & Mining Corp. recapitalized as Diversified Resources Corp. 9/1/72

MOJO SHOPPING INC (DE)
Name changed to Mojo Ventures, Inc. 05/09/2011
Mojo Ventures, Inc. name changed to Mojo Organics, Inc. 03/09/2012

MOJO VENTURES INC (DE)
Common $0.001 par split (25) for (1) by issuance of (24) additional shares payable 05/09/2011 to holders of record 05/09/2011
Name changed to Mojo Organics, Inc. 03/09/2012

MOJONNIER BROS CO (IL)
Acquired by FMC Corp. 05/23/1980
Each share Common no par exchanged for $113.25 cash

MOJUD CO., INC. (DE)
Name changed to Martinall Industries, Inc. 01/25/1961
Martinall Industries, Inc. liquidated for Bates Manufacturing Co., Inc. 01/03/1967
(See Bates Manufacturing Co., Inc.)

MOJUD HOSIERY CO., INC. (DE)
Each share Common $2.50 par exchanged for (2) shares Common $1.25 par 00/00/1946
Name changed to Mojud Co., Inc. 00/00/1953

MOK-MOL

Mojud Co., Inc. name changed to Martinall Industries, Inc. 01/25/1961 which liquidated for Bates Manufacturing Co., Inc. 01/03/1967
(See Bates Manufacturing Co., Inc.)

MOKI OIL & RARE METALS CO (NM)
Merged into Magna Oil Corp. 12/31/68
Each share Common 5¢ par exchanged for (1/3) share Common 50¢ par
Magna Oil Corp. merged into Triton Oil & Gas Corp. 4/28/72 which name changed to Triton Energy Corp. (TX) 12/1/81 which reincorporated in Delaware 5/12/95

MOKITA INC (NV)
Common $0.001 par split (10) for (1) by issuance of (9) additional shares payable 09/23/2013 to holders of record 09/23/2013
Name changed to MediJane Holdings Inc. 03/10/2014

MOKO SOCIAL MEDIA LTD (AUSTRALIA)
Name changed 09/24/2013
Name changed from MOKO.mobi Ltd. to MOKO Social Media Ltd.09/24/2013
Each old Sponsored ADR for Ordinary exchanged for (0.5) new Sponsored ADR for Ordinary 06/16/2014
Basis changed from (1:20) to (1:40) 06/16/2014
ADR agreement terminated 06/18/2018
No ADR holders' equity

MOL GLOBAL INC (CAYMAN ISLANDS)
ADR agreement terminated 05/01/2017
Each Sponsored ADR for Ordinary exchanged for $1.4614 cash

MOLCO INDS LTD (CANADA)
Reincorporated 07/01/1980
Each share old Capital Stock no par exchanged for (3) shares new Capital Stock no par 11/22/1979
Place of incorporation changed from (ONT) to (Canada) 07/01/1980
Company reported out of business 00/00/1986
Stockholders' equity not determined

MOLDED FIBER GLASS BODY CO. (OH)
Name changed to Molded Fiber Glass Companies, Inc. 8/7/68
Molded Fiber Glass Companies, Inc. merged into North American Rockwell Corp. 4/8/70 which merged into Rockwell International Corp. (Old) 2/16/73 which merged into Boeing Co. 12/6/96

MOLDED FIBER GLASS COS INC (OH)
Merged into North American Rockwell Corp. 04/08/1970
Each share Common $3 par exchanged for (0.3) share $4.75 Conv. Preferred Ser. A no par and (0.55) share Common $1 par
North American Rockwell Corp. merged into Rockwell International Corp. (Old) 02/16/1973 which merged into Boeing Co. 12/06/1996

MOLDED LATEX PRODUCTS, INC. (NJ)
Name changed to Kaysam Corp. of America 5/17/56
(See Kaysam Corp. of America)

MOLDFLOW CORP (DE)
Issue Information - 3,000,000 shares COM offered at $13 per share on 03/27/2000
Merged into Autodesk, Inc. 06/25/2008
Each share Common 1¢ par exchanged for $22 cash

MOLECULAR BIOSYSTEMS INC (DE)
Merged into Alliance Pharmaceutical Corp. 12/29/2000
Each share Common 1¢ par exchanged for (0.0410307) share Common 1¢ par
(See Alliance Pharmaceutical Corp.)

MOLECULAR DEVICES CORP (DE)
Merged into MDS Inc. 03/28/2007
Each share Common $0.001 par exchanged for $35.50 cash

MOLECULAR DIAGNOSTICS INC (DE)
Name changed to CytoCore, Inc. 08/17/2006
CytoCore, Inc. name changed to Medite Cancer Diagnostics, Inc. 12/11/2014

MOLECULAR DYNAMICS INC (DE)
Merged into Nycomed Amersham PLC 9/16/98
Each share Common 1¢ par exchanged for $20.50 cash

MOLECULAR ENERGY CORP (DE)
Class A 4¢ par changed to 1¢ par 01/30/1984
Recapitalized as Universal Medtech, Inc. 04/12/1984
Each share Class A 1¢ par exchanged for (1.5) shares Class A 1¢ par
Universal Medtech, Inc. recapitalized as Consolidated Travel Systems, Inc. 11/30/1987 which recapitalized as Knobias, Inc. 11/17/2004
(See Knobias, Inc.)

MOLECULAR GENETICS INC (MN)
Name changed to MGI Pharma, Inc. 05/17/1990
(See MGI Pharma, Inc.)

MOLECULAR IMAGING CORP (DE)
Plan of reorganization under Chapter 11 Federal Bankruptcy proceedings effective 06/28/2010
No stockholders' equity

MOLECULAR INSIGHT PHARMACEUTICALS INC (MA)
Issue Information - 5,000,000 shares COM offered at $14 per share on 02/01/2007
Plan of reorganization under Chapter 11 Federal bankruptcy proceedings effective 05/20/2011
No stockholders' equity

MOLECULAR RESH INC (FL)
Class A Common 30¢ par reclassified as Common 30¢ par 03/04/1965
Name changed to MRI Properties, Inc. 06/05/1973
(See MRI Properties, Inc.)

MOLECULAR ROBOTICS INC (DE)
SEC revoked common stock registration 10/01/2008

MOLECULAR SIMULATIONS INC (DE)
Acquired by Pharmacopeia, Inc. (Old) 06/12/1998
Each share Common $0.001 par exchanged for (0.5292) share Common $0.0001 par
Pharmacopeia, Inc. (Old) name changed to Accelrys, Inc. 05/12/2004
(See Accelrys, Inc.)

MOLECULAR SYS CORP (DE)
Charter cancelled and declared inoperative and void for non-payment of taxes 04/15/1968

MOLECULAR SYS INC (CA)
Charter suspended for failure to file reports and pay fees 08/01/1989

MOLECULAR TECHNOLOGY INC (UT)
Proclaimed dissolved for failure to file annual report 12/31/77

MOLECULON BIOTECH, INC. (DE)
Name changed to Moleculon, Inc. 4/4/86

Moleculon, Inc. name changed to Purepac Inc. 11/2/92 which name changed to Faulding Inc. 3/1/96
(See Faulding Inc.)

MOLECULON INC (DE)
Name changed to Purepac Inc. 11/2/92
Purepac Inc. name changed to Faulding Inc. 3/1/96
(See Faulding Inc.)

MOLESKINE S P A (ITALY)
ADR agreement terminated 02/03/2017
Each ADR for Common issued by Bank of New York exchanged for $10.242161 cash

MOLEX INC (DE)
Common 5¢ par split (2) for (1) by issuance of (1) additional share 01/25/1984
Class B Common 5¢ par split (2) for (1) by issuance of (1) additional share 01/25/1984
Common 5¢ par split (5) for (4) by issuance of (0.5) additional share 04/27/1987
Each share Common 5¢ par received distribution of (1) share Non-Vtg. Class A Common 5¢ par 07/25/1990
Each share Class B Common 5¢ par received distribution of (1) share Non-Vtg. Class A Common 5¢ par 07/25/1990
Common 5¢ par split (5) for (4) by issuance of (0.25) additional share 11/30/1992
Non-Vtg. Class A Common 5¢ par split (5) for (4) by issuance of (0.25) additional share 11/30/1992
Common 5¢ par split (5) for (4) by issuance of (0.25) additional share 11/28/1994
Non-Vtg. Class A Common 5¢ par split (5) for (4) by issuance of (0.25) additional share 11/28/1994
Common 5¢ par split (5) for (4) by issuance of (0.25) additional share payable 04/25/1997 to holders of record 03/31/1997
Non-Vtg. Class A Common 5¢ par split (5) for (4) by issuance of (0.25) additional share payable 04/25/1997 to holders of record 03/31/1997
Each share Class B Common 5¢ par received distribution of (0.25) share Common 5¢ par payable 04/25/1997 to holders of record 03/31/1997
Common 5¢ par split (5) for (4) by issuance of (0.25) additional share payable 12/01/1997 to holders of record 11/10/1997
Non-Vtg. Class A Common 5¢ par split (5) for (4) by issuance of (0.25) additional share payable 12/01/1997 to holders of record 11/10/1997
Common 5¢ par split (5) for (4) by issuance of (0.25) additional share payable 03/06/2000 to holders of record 02/14/2000
Non-Vtg Class A Common 5¢ par split (5) for (4) by issuance of (0.25) additional share payable 03/06/2000 to holders of record 02/14/2000
Stock Dividends - 50% 06/22/1978; 25% 06/02/1980; 50% 03/23/1981; 50% 04/25/1983; 25% 09/15/1995; 25% payable 04/25/1997 to holders of record 03/31/1997
Acquired by Koch Industries, Inc. 12/09/2013
Each share Common 5¢ par exchanged for $38.68 cash
Each share Non-Vtg Class A Common 5¢ par exchanged for $38.68 cash
Each share Class B Common 5¢ par exchanged for $38.68 cash

MOLI ENERGY LTD (BC)
Placed in receivership 02/27/1990
No stockholders' equity

MOLICHEM MEDICINES INC (DE)
Name changed to Medical Licensing International Corp. 06/25/2003
Medical Licensing International Corp. name changed to EmergenSys Corp. 11/18/2003 which recapitalized as Spencer Pharmaceutical, Inc. 10/05/2009

MOLIJEVIS GOLD MINES, LTD. (ON)
Charter cancelled 00/00/1957

MOLINE IMPLEMENT CO. (IL)
Merged into Minneapolis-Moline Power Implement Co. 03/30/1929
Details not available

MOLINE NATL BK (MOLINE, IL)
Capital Stock $100 par changed to $25 par and (3) additional shares issued plus a 25% stock dividend paid 05/18/1960
Capital Stock $25 par changed to $6.25 par and (3) additional shares issued 12/28/1964
Stock Dividends - 25% 01/29/1963; 20% 09/02/1969
Reorganized under the laws of Delaware as First Security Bancorp., Inc. 07/01/1981
Each share Capital Stock $6.25 par exchanged for (1) share Common $6.25 par
(See First Security Bancorp., Inc.)

MOLIRIS CORP (FL)
Each share old Common $0.001 par exchanged for (0.05) share new Common $0.001 par 04/14/2005
Name changed to Digifonica International Corp. 08/03/2006
Digifonica International Corp. merged into Digifonica International Inc. (AB) 10/26/2007 which reincorporated in British Columbia as Dominion Energy Inc. 12/09/2013 which name changed to Dynamic Oil & Gas Exploration Inc. 06/30/2014 which recapitalized as Darien Business Development Corp. 03/14/2017

MOLLER TEXTILE CORP. (DE)
Acquired by Moller Textile (Israel) 1961 Ltd. 6/15/64
Each share Capital Stock $1 par exchanged for (0.2) share Ordinary I£10 par
Moller Textile (Israel) 1961 Ltd. name changed to Moller Textile Ltd. 7/14/65 which name changed to Galil Industries & Development (Nahariya) Ltd. 1/15/81

MOLLER TEXTILE LTD. (ISRAEL)
Name changed 07/14/1965
Name changed from Moller Textile (Israel) 1961 Ltd. to Moller Textile Ltd. 07/14/1965
Ordinary I£10 par changed to IS1 par per currency change 10/01/1980
Name changed to Delta Galil Industries Ltd. 01/15/1981

MOLLIE MAC MINES LTD (BC)
Capital Stock 50¢ par changed to no par 05/01/1970
Recapitalized as Kandahar Resources Ltd. 06/05/1973
Each (7-1/2) shares Capital Stock no par exchanged for (1) share Capital Stock no par
Kandahar Resources Ltd. recapitalized as First Allied Resources Corp. 07/16/1985
(See First Allied Resources Corp.)

MOLLUSCA OILS LTD (AB)
Recapitalized as Lochiel Exploration Ltd. 08/25/1969
Each share Common 10¢ par exchanged for (0.1) share Common no par
(See Lochiel Exploration Ltd.)

MOLLY CORP. (DE)
Name changed to Maklaw Corp. 12/15/64
(See Maklaw Corp.)

FINANCIAL INFORMATION, INC.   MOL-MON

MOLLY MURPHYS INC (OK)
Name changed to Sterling Diversified Holdings, Inc. 1/26/94

MOLLY-O CORP.
Dissolved 00/00/1947
Details not available

MOLLY RIVER MINES LTD. (ON)
Merged into Bayfor Corp. Inc. 05/00/1972
Each share Capital Stock no par exchanged for (0.25) share Capital Stock no par
(See Bayfor Corp. Inc.)

MOLNAR CAP CORP (BC)
Name changed to Star Properties Inc. 5/13/98

MOLONEY ELECTRIC CO. (DE)
Merged into Central Transformer Corp. 10/7/65
Each share Class A no par or Class B no par exchanged for (1) share 5% 2nd Preferred $55 par and (2) shares Common $1 par
Central Transformer Corp. merged into Colt Industries Inc. (DE) 11/4/68 which reincorporated in Pennsylvania 5/6/76
(See Colt Industries Inc. (PA))

MOLSON BREWERIES LTD. (CANADA)
5-1/2% Preferred $40 par called for redemption 4/1/63
Class A no par and Class B no par split (2) for (1) by issuance of (1) additional share respectively 7/29/66
Recapitalized 8/15/68
Class A no par reclassified as Class A Common no par
Class B no par reclassified as Class B Common no par
Name changed to Molson Industries Ltd. 9/5/68
Molson Industries Ltd. name changed to Molson Companies Ltd. 8/17/73 which name changed to Molson Inc. 6/29/99 which merged into Molson Coors Brewing Co. 2/9/2005

MOLSON INC (CANADA)
Name changed 8/17/73
Name changed 6/29/99
Name changed from Molson Industries Ltd. to Molson Companies Ltd. 8/17/73
Class A Conv. Common no par reclassified as Class A Common no par 1/2/79
Class B Conv. Common no par reclassified as Class B Common no par 1/2/79
Class C Conv. Common no par reclassified as Class B Common no par 1/2/79
Class D Conv. Common no par reclassified as Class A Common no par 1/2/79
Class A Common no par split (2) for (1) by issuance of (1) additional share 7/22/83
Class B Common no par split (2) for (1) by issuance of (1) additional share 7/22/83
Class A Common no par split (3) for (2) by issuance of (0.5) additional share 7/23/91
Class B Common no par split (3) for (2) by issuance of (0.5) additional share 7/23/91
Name changed from Molson Companies Ltd. to Molson Inc. 6/29/99
Merged into Molson Coors Brewing Co. 2/9/2005
Each share Class A Common no par exchanged for (0.36) share Class B Common 1¢ par and $5.44 cash
Note: Non-electing Canadian residents will receive (0.36) Molson Coors Canada Inc. Class B Exchangeable share and $5.44 cash
Each share Class B Common no par exchanged for (0.126) share Non-Vtg. Class A Common 1¢ par, (0.234) share Class B Common 1¢ par and $5.44 cash
Note: Non-electing Canadian residents will receive (0.126) Molson Coors Canada Inc. Class A Exchangeable share, (0.234) Class B Exchangeable share and $5.44 cash

MOLSON M FUND LTD.-LE FONDS MOLSON M LTEE. (CANADA)
Name changed to Planned Resources Fund Ltd.-Fonds de Planification des Ressources Ltee. 10/17/69

MOLSON'S BREWERY LTD. (CANADA)
Each share Common no par exchanged for (1) share Class A no par and (1) share Class B no par in 1950
Recapitalized 11/12/58
Each share old Class A no par exchanged for (2) shares new Class A no par
Each share old Class B no par exchanged for (2) shares new Class B no par
Name changed to Molson Breweries Ltd. 3/1/62
Molson Breweries Ltd. name changed to Molson Industries Ltd. 9/5/68 which name changed to Molson Companies Ltd. 8/17/73 which name changed to Molson Inc. 6/29/99 which merged into Molson Coors Brewing Co. 2/9/2005

MOLTEN METAL TECHNOLOGY INC (DE)
Secondary Offering - 2,675,000 shares COM offered at $21.75 per share on 12/15/1993
Plan of reorganization under Chapter 11 Federal Bankruptcy proceedings confirmed 02/13/2006
No stockholders' equity

MOLY MINERALS INC (UT)
Recapitalized as Samantha Petroleum Corp. 09/15/1981
Each share Common 1¢ par exchanged for (0.2) share Common 1¢ par
(See Samantha Petroleum Corp.)

MOLY MITE MINES INC (BC)
Merged into Moly Mite Resources Inc. 03/16/1982
Each share Common no par exchanged for (1) share Common no par
Moly Mite Resources Inc. recapitalized as Macrotrends Ventures Inc. 07/02/1986 which merged into Macrotrends International Ventures Inc. 08/17/1988 which was recapitalized as Global Election Systems Inc. 11/22/1991 which was acquired by Diebold, Inc. 01/22/2002 which name changed to Diebold Nixdorf Inc. 12/12/2016

MOLY MITE RES INC (BC)
Recapitalized as Macrotrends Ventures Inc. 07/02/1986
Each share Common no par exchanged for (0.22222222) share Common no par
Macrotrends Ventures Inc. merged into Macrotrends International Ventures Inc. 08/17/1988 which recapitalized as Global Election Systems Inc. 11/22/1991 which was acquired by Diebold, Inc. 01/22/2002 which name changed to Diebold Nixdorf Inc. 12/12/2016

MOLY ORE MINES LTD (ON)
Name changed to Molco Industries Ltd. (ON 12/07/1978
Molco Industries Ltd. (ON) reincorporated in Canada 07/01/1980
(See Molco Industries Ltd. (Canada))

MOLY WIN MNG LTD (BC)
Name changed to Goodco International Ltd. 10/04/1974
(See Goodco International Ltd.)

MOLYBDENITE CORP CDA LTD (QC)
Each share Capital Stock $1 par exchanged for (0.2) share Capital Stock $5 par 10/01/1969
Adjudicated bankrupt 11/30/1973
No stockholders' equity

MOLYBDENUM CORP. OF AMERICA (DE)
Capital Stock $1 par split (2) for (1) by issuance of (1) additional share 9/29/55
Stock Dividend - 10% 12/18/51
Name changed to Molycorp, Inc. 4/29/74
Molycorp, Inc. merged into Union Oil Co. of California 7/29/77 which reorganized as Unocal Corp. 4/25/83 which merged into Chevron Corp. 8/10/2005

MOLYCOR GOLD CORP (BC)
Name changed to Nevada Clean Magnesium Inc. 04/17/2012

MOLYCORP INC NEW (DE)
Each share 5.5% Mandatory Conv. Preferred Ser. A $0.001 par exchanged for (2) shares Common $0.001 par 03/01/2014
Plan of reorganization under Chapter 11 Federal Bankruptcy proceedings effective 08/31/2016
No stockholders' equity

MOLYCORP INC OLD (DE)
$2.50 Conv. Preferred $1 par called for redemption 07/28/1977
Merged into Union Oil Co. of California 07/29/1977
Each share Common $1 par exchanged for (1.035) shares Common $8-1/3 par
Union Oil Co. of California reorganized as Unocal Corp. 04/25/1983

MOLYMINE EXPLS LTD (BC)
Merged into Seneca Developments Ltd. 12/08/1972
Each share Common 50¢ par exchanged for (0.111111) share Common no par
Seneca Developments Ltd. recapitalized as Award Resources Ltd. 02/08/1982 which recapitalized as Tomco Developments Inc. 06/16/1990

MOM N POPS HAM HOUSE INC (NC)
Name changed to Western Steer-Mom "N" Pop's, Inc. 6/24/81
Western Steer-Mom N Pop's, Inc. name changed to WSMP Inc. 7/6/88 which name changed to Fresh Foods Inc. 5/7/98 which name changed to Pierre Foods Inc. 7/27/2000
(See Pierre Foods Inc.)

MOM'S HOMEMADE ICE CREAM PARLORS, INC. (NV)
Name changed to Mom's Development Corp. 9/21/79
Mom's Development Corp. name changed to Resources Industries Inc. 6/11/81
(See Resources Industries Inc.)

MOMED HLDG CO (MO)
Common $1 par split (3) for (1) by issuance of (2) additional shares payable 1/22/96 to holders of record 11/8/95
Merged into MAIC Holdings Inc. 12/24/96
Each share Class A Common $1 par exchanged for $25.32 cash

MOMENTUM ADVANCED SOLUTIONS INC (ON)
Acquired by 2200821 Ontario Ltd. 04/30/2009
Each share Common no par exchanged for $0.22 cash

MOMENTUM BUSINESS APPLICATIONS INC (DE)
Merged into PeopleSoft, Inc. 4/9/2002
Each share Class A Common 1¢ par exchanged for $18.831 cash

MOMENTUM CORP (DE)
Name changed 9/1/93
Common $1 par split (3) for (1) by issuance of (2) additional shares 7/6/92
Name changed from Momentum Distribution Inc. to Momentum Corp. 9/1/93
Merged into PrimeSource Corp. 9/1/94
Each share Common $1 par exchanged for (0.71) share Common 1¢ par
(See PrimeSource Corp.)

MOMENTUM HLDGS CORP (DE)
Each share old Common no par exchanged for (0.01) share new Common no par 03/25/2002
Name changed to Cipher Holdings Corp. 11/25/2003
Cipher Holdings Corp. name changed to Imagin Molecular Corp. 07/05/2005
(See Imagin Molecular Corp.)

MOMENTUM INC (DE)
Name changed to Specialty Chemical Resources Inc. 12/12/1991
(See Specialty Chemical Resources Inc.)

MOMENTUM SOFTWARE CORP (NY)
Dissolved by proclamation 9/29/93

MOMS APPLE PIE ART PRODS INC (CA)
Charter suspended for failure to file reports and pay fees 09/04/1979

MOMS DEV CORP (NV)
Name changed to Resources Industries Inc. 06/11/1981
Resources Industries Inc. reorganized as Growth Resources, Inc. 10/01/1983

MOMS ONLINE INC (NV)
Name changed to BlockHold Capital Corp. 04/25/2018

MON-ART, INC. (MI)
Recapitalized 10/00/1962
Each share 6% Conv. Preferred $5 par exchanged for $5 principal amount of 6-1/2% Conv. Debentures due 06/01/1973

MONACO COACH CORP (DE)
Common 1¢ par split (3) for (2) by issuance of (0.5) additional share payable 04/16/1998 to holders of record 04/02/1998
Common 1¢ par split (3) for (2) by issuance of (0.5) additional share payable 11/30/1998 to holders of record 11/16/1998
Common 1¢ par split (3) for (2) by issuance of (0.5) additional share payable 07/07/1999 to holders of record 06/21/1999
Common 1¢ par split (3) for (2) by issuance of (0.5) additional share payable 09/07/2001 to holders of record 08/20/2001 Ex date - 09/10/2001
Chapter 11 bankruptcy proceedings converted to Chapter 7 on 06/30/2009
Stockholders' equity unlikely

MONACO FIN INC (CO)
Each share old Class A Common 1¢ par exchanged for (0.2) share new Class A Common 1¢ par 11/23/1998
SEC revoked common stock registration 06/22/2010

MONACO GROUP INC (ON)
Merged into Monaco Acquisition Corp. 02/03/1989
Each share Common no par exchanged for $8 cash

MONACO MOTORS & MODERN DEVICES, INC. (NY)
Charter revoked for failure to file reports and pay fees 12/16/35

MONADA PETE CORP (UT)
Recapitalized as Diversified Energy Corp. 07/01/1977
Each share Common 1¢ par exchanged for (0.125) share Common 8¢ par
Diversified Energy Corp. name changed to Diversified Enterprises, Inc. 11/25/2008

MONADNOCK BANCORP INC (MD)
Acquired by GFA Federal Credit Union 12/28/2012
Each share Common 1¢ par exchanged for approximately $5.50 cash

MONADNOCK BK (JAFFREY, NH)
Acquired by Cheshire Financial Corp. 05/31/1988
Each share Capital Stock $5 par exchanged for $110 cash

MONADNOCK CMNTY BANCORP INC (USA)
Reorganized under the laws of Maryland as Monadnock Bancorp, Inc. 06/28/2006
Each share Common 1¢ par exchanged for (1.3699) shares Common 1¢ par
(See Monadnock Bancorp, Inc.)

MONADNOCK MILLS
Liquidated in 1944

MONADNOCK NATIONAL BANK (JAFFREY, NH)
Reorganized as Monadnock Bank (Jaffrey, NH) 09/30/1976
Each share Capital Stock $100 par exchanged for (20) shares Capital Stock $5 par
(See Monadnock National Bank (Jaffrey, NH))

MONAHAN SUPPLY CORP., LTD. (CANADA)
97.5% acquired by Van Der Hout Associates Ltd. through purchase offer which expired 00/00/1975
Public interest eliminated

MONALTA RES INC (NV)
Reincorporated 07/20/2004
Place of incorporation changed from (BC) to (NV) and Common no par changed to $0.001 par 07/20/2004
Recapitalized as Ahchuk Furnishings, Inc. 11/10/2004
Each share Common $0.001 par exchanged for (0.005) share Common $0.001 par
Ahchuk Furnishings, Inc. name changed to China Datacom Corp. 05/05/2005 which name changed to Digital Paint International Holding Co. Ltd. 02/15/2008 which recapitalized as Direct Coating, Inc. 07/06/2009
(See Direct Coating, Inc.)

MONAMOTOR OIL CO.
Dissolved in 1936

MONARC, INC. (AR)
Charter revoked for failure to pay taxes 2/3/78

MONARC CORP (NV)
Recapitalized as Flexpower, Inc. 05/12/2014
Each share Common $0.0001 par exchanged for (0.0001) share Common $0.0001 par

MONARCH AVALON INC (DE)
Common 25¢ par split (3) for (2) by issuance of (0.5) additional share 1/31/86
Stock Dividends - 15% 2/18/81; 50% 9/4/81
Name changed to Monarch Services Inc. (DE) 10/23/98
Monarch Services Inc. (DE) reincorporated in Maryland 11/30/2000

MONARCH BANCORP (CA)
Each share Common no par exchanged for (0.2) share new Common no par 01/19/1994
Merged into Western Bancorp 06/04/1997
Each share new Common no par exchanged for (0.11764705) share Common no par
Western Bancorp merged into U.S. Bancorp 11/15/1999

MONARCH BK (CHESAPEAKE VA)
Common $5 par split (6) for (5) by issuance of (0.2) additional share payable 06/15/2004 to holders of record 05/17/2004
Stock Dividend - 10% payable 11/30/2005 to holders of record 11/10/2005 Ex date - 11/08/2005
Under plan of reorganization each share Common $5 par automatically became (1) share Monarch Financial Holdings, Inc. Common $5 par 06/01/2006
Monarch Financial Holdings, Inc. merged into TowneBank (Portsmouth, VA) 06/24/2016

MONARCH BANK (LAGUNA NIGUEL, CA)
Under plan of reorganization each share Common no par automatically became (1.5) shares Monarch Bancorp Common no par 06/28/1984
Monarch Bancorp merged into Western Bancorp 06/04/1997 which merged into U.S. Bancorp 11/15/1999

MONARCH CAP CORP (MA)
Reincorporated 12/22/1988
$3 Conv. Preferred $1 par called for redemption 05/08/1987
State of incorporation changed from (DE) to (MA) 12/22/1988
Chapter 11 Federal bankruptcy proceedings confirmed 02/05/1992
No stockholders' equity

MONARCH CMNTY BANCORP INC (MD)
Each share old Common 1¢ par exchanged for (0.2) share new Common 1¢ par 05/28/2013
Merged into Chemical Financial Corp. 04/01/2015
Each share new Common 1¢ par exchanged for (0.0982) share Common $1 par

MONARCH DENTAL CORP (DE)
Each share old Common 1¢ par exchanged for (0.16666666) share new Common 1¢ par 06/19/2001
Merged into Bright Now! Dental, Inc.
Each share new Common 1¢ par exchanged for $5.75 cash

MONARCH DEV CORP (ON)
Merged into Taylor Woodrow PLC 5/30/2000
Each share Common no par exchanged for $11.25 cash

MONARCH ELECTRS INTL INC (CA)
Reincorporated under the laws of Delaware as Westcalind Corp. 5/1/71
(See Westcaling Corp.)

MONARCH ENERGY LTD (BC)
Each share old Common no par exchanged for (0.57142857) share new Common no par 01/25/2011
Each share new Common no par exchanged again for (0.05) share new Common no par 07/07/2014
Reincorporated under the laws of Ontario as ChroMedX Corp. 09/18/2014
ChroMedX Corp. name changed to Relay Medical Corp. 07/09/2018

MONARCH ENTERPRISES INC (DE)
Reincorporated 11/5/70
State of incorporation changed from (NV) to (DE) 11/5/70
Merged into Uniflight, Inc. 6/2/71
Each share Common 25¢ par exchanged for (1) share Common 1¢ par
(See Uniflight, Inc.)

MONARCH FINL HLDGS INC (VA)
Each share 7.80% Conv. Perpetual Preferred Ser. B $5 par exchanged for (3.75) shares Common $5 par 03/08/2013
Stock Dividends - 25% payable 06/30/2006 to holders of record 06/09/2006 Ex date - 07/03/2006; 20% payable 11/01/2007 to holders of record 10/10/2007 Ex date - 10/05/2007; 20% payable 12/07/2012 to holders of record 11/09/2012 Ex date - 11/07/2012; 10% payable 12/04/2015 to holders of record 11/12/2015 Ex date - 11/09/2015
Merged into TowneBank (Portsmouth, VA) 06/24/2016
Each share Common $5 par exchanged for (0.883) share Common $1.667 par

MONARCH FINE FOODS LTD. (ON)
Name changed to M.F.F. Equities Ltd. 7/2/68
(See M.F.F. Equities Ltd.)

MONARCH FIRE INSURANCE CO. (OH)
Capital Stock $10 par changed to $5 par in 1933
Capital Stock $5 par changed to $4 par in 1934
Merged into Monarch Insurance Co. of Ohio on a (0.2) for (1) basis 7/1/56
(See listing for Monarch Insurance Co. of Ohio)

MONARCH GEN INC (NY)
Assets assigned for benefit of creditors 09/25/1975
No stockholders' equity

MONARCH GOLD MINES LTD (ON)
Charter cancelled and declared dissolved for failure to file returns and pay fees 3/16/76

MONARCH HLDGS INC (FL)
Recapitalized as ProConcept Marketing Group, Inc. 12/24/2007
Each share Common $0.001 par exchanged for (0.00033333) share Common $0.001 par
(See ProConcept Marketing Group, Inc.)

MONARCH IND INC (IN)
Common no par split (2) for (1) by issuance of (1) additional share 10/11/68
Charter revoked for failure to file annual reports 12/31/87

MONARCH INFORMATION SVCS INC (NY)
Reorganized as Sandsport Data Services, Inc. 12/31/86
Each share Common 1¢ par exchanged for (0.01) share Common $0.001 par
Sandsport Data Services, Inc. recapitalized as Sandata, Inc. 7/30/87 which name changed to Sandata Technologies, Inc. 11/21/2001
(See Sandata Technologies, Inc.)

MONARCH INSURANCE CO. OF OHIO (OH)
Each share Capital Stock $12.50 par exchanged for (0.015094) share Capital Stock $662.50 par 12/12/69

MONARCH INVT PPTYS INC (NV)
Charter revoked 06/01/2015

MONARCH INVTS LTD (ON)
Common no par split (6) for (1) by issuance of (5) additional shares 10/10/69
Common no par split (5) for (1) by issuance of (4) additional shares 11/17/72
Name changed to Monarch Development Corp. 8/18/89
(See Monarch Development Corp.)

MONARCH KNITTING CO., LTD. (ON)
Each share Common $100 par exchanged for (8) shares Common no par in 1946
Merged into Montex Apparel Industries Ltd. 7/2/65
Each share Common no par exchanged for (1) share Common no par
(See Montex Apparel Industries Ltd.)

MONARCH LIFE ASSURN CO (CANADA)
Each share Common $100 par exchanged for (10) shares Common $10 par 12/19/1958
Each share Common $10 par exchanged for (5) shares Common $2 par 12/01/1968
99.9% acquired by CanWest Capital Corp. through purchase offer which expired 11/24/1978
Public interest eliminated

MONARCH LIFE INS CO (MA)
Each share Capital Stock $100 par exchanged for (4) shares Capital Stock $25 par 00/00/1928
Capital Stock $25 par changed to $5 par and (4) additional shares issued 06/23/1956
Under plan of merger each share Capital Stock $5 par exchanged for (1.447) shares Capital Stock $2 par 05/28/1965
Capital Stock $2 par changed to $1 par and (1) additional share issued 05/09/1966
Stock Dividends - 100% 09/20/1944; 100% 05/28/1952; 100% 06/23/1956; 33-1/3% 07/19/1965
Acquired by Monarch Capital Corp. (DE) 04/25/1979
Each share Capital Stock $1 par exchanged for $31.95 cash

MONARCH LUMBER CO. (DE)
Merged into Boise Cascade Corp. 4/1/63
Each share Capital Stock $25 par exchanged for $40.41 cash
Boise Cascade Corp. name changed to OfficeMax Inc. 11/1/2004

MONARCH MACH TOOL CO (OH)
Common no par split (2) for (1) by issuance of (1) additional share 12/30/50
Common no par split (5) for (3) by issuance of (2/3) additional share 3/1/66
Common no par split (2) for (1) by issuance of (1) additional share 3/30/79
Common no par split (2) for (1) by issuance of (1) additional share 9/8/80
Name changed to Genesis Worldwide Inc. 9/1/99
(See Genesis Worldwide Inc.)

MONARCH MARKING SYS CO (OH)
Preferred called for redemption 01/15/1961
Common no par split (2) for (1) by issuance of (1) additional share 07/22/1963
Common no par split (2) for (1) by issuance of (1) additional share 05/15/1967
Merged into Pitney Bowes Inc. 05/15/1968
Each share Common no par exchanged for (0.62) share Common $2 par

MONARCH METAL MINES LTD (BC)
Recapitalized as Consolidated

Monarch Metal Mines Ltd.
06/19/1973
Each share Capital Stock no par exchanged for (0.33333333) share Capital Stock no par
Consolidated Monarch Metal Mines Ltd. recapitalized as San Rafael Resources Ltd. 11/15/1977 which recapitalized as Rafael Resources Ltd. 07/27/1984 which name changed to Biologix (B.C.) Ltd. 09/25/1986 which name changed to Biologix International Ltd. 05/01/1998
(See Biologix International Ltd.)

MONARCH MILLS (SC)
Each share Common $100 par exchanged for (10) shares Common $10 par 1/28/55
Merged into Pacolet Industries, Inc. on a (1.9) for (1) basis 12/3/62
Pacolet Industries, Inc. merged into Deering Milliken, Inc. for cash 10/1/67

MONARCH MINERALS & MNG INC (NV)
Acquired by Naturstein Beteiligungs AG 3/17/93
Each share Common $0.001 par exchanged for $3.85 in value of Naturstein stock

MONARCH MINERALS INC (MT)
Merged into International Retail Systems, Inc. 12/31/1972
Each share Common 1¢ par exchanged for (1) share Common 1¢ par

MONARCH MINES LTD.
Liquidated in 1941

MONARCH MNG CORP (UT)
Merged into Transportation Safety Systems, Inc. 12/29/1972
Each share Common 10¢ par exchanged for (1) share Common 25¢ par
(See Transportation Safety Systems, Inc.)

MONARCH MOLYBDENUM & RES INC (NV)
Ctfs. dated prior to 03/07/1988
Recapitalized as Mediacom Communications, Inc. 03/07/1988
Each (6) shares Common 10¢ par exchanged for (5) shares Common $0.001 par
Mediacom Communications, Inc. name changed to Duraco Industries, Inc. 09/15/1990

MONARCH MOLYBDENUM & RES INC (NV)
Ctfs. dated after 07/13/2007
Name changed to Thorium Energy, Inc. 01/07/2008
Thorium Energy, Inc. name changed to Monolith Ventures, Inc. 04/28/2008 which name changed to Zero Gravity Solutions, Inc. 03/13/2013

MONARCH MORTGAGE & INVESTMENTS LTD. (ON)
Each share Preference $10 par exchanged for (1) share new Common no par in 1948
Each (5) shares Common no par exchanged for (1) share new Common no par in 1948
Name changed to Monarch Investments Ltd. in 1959
Monarch Investments Ltd. name changed to Monarch Development Corp. 8/18/89

MONARCH N L (AUSTRALIA)
Each ADR for Ordinary AUD $2 par exchanged for (0.5) ADR for Ordinary AUD $0.20 par 05/15/1992
Merged into Black Hill Minerals Ltd. 03/08/1993
Each ADR for Ordinary AUD $0.20 par exchanged for $0.895 cash

MONARCH OIL & GAS CO. (SD)
Charter dissolved by proclamation in 1921

MONARCH OILS LTD. (AB)
Acquired by Oregon National Gas Reserves Ltd. on a (1) for (6.75) basis 00/00/1958
(See Oregon National Gas Reserves Ltd.)

MONARCH PRODUCTIONS, INC. (NV)
Merged into Aneth United, Inc. 4/30/69
Each share Common $1 par exchanged for (1) share Common 50¢ par

MONARCH RADIO & TELEVISION CORP.
Bankrupt in 1952

MONARCH RESOURCES N.L. (AUSTRALIA)
Name changed 04/09/1987
Name changed from Monarch Petroleum N.L. to Monarch Resources N.L. 04/09/1987
Recapitalized as Monarch N.L. 07/25/1988
Each ADR for Ordinary AUD$0.10 par exchanged for (0.05) ADR for Ordinary AUD$2 par
(See Monarch N.L.)

MONARCH ROYALTIES LTD.
Merged into Amalgamated Oils Ltd. in 1941 which was in process of liquidation in 1943

MONARCH ROYALTY CORP. (DE)
Assets sold and each share Class A Common $1 par exchanged for (0.5) share Aberdeen Petroleum Corp. Class A $1 par 7/17/59
(See Aberdeen Petroleum Corp.)

MONARCH RUBR CO (OH)
Common $10 par changed to no par 12/23/1966
Common no par split (2) for (1) by issuance of (1) additional share 09/10/1968
Completely liquidated 02/14/1969
Each share Common no par exchanged for first and final distribution of (0.142857) share Teledyne, Inc. $3.50 Conv. Preferred $1 par
(See Teledyne, Inc.)

MONARCH SVCS INC (DE)
Reincorporated under the laws of Maryland and Common 25¢ par changed to $0.001 par 11/30/2000

MONARCH STAFFING INC (NV)
Charter permanently revoked 10/01/2012

MONARCH TILE MANUFACTURING, INC. (TX)
Acquired by Dorchester Gas Producing Co. 10/1/64
Each share Common $5 par exchanged for (0.5) share 5-1/2% Preferred Ser. A $25 par
Dorchester Gas Producing Co. merged into Panoil Co. 11/26/68 which name changed to Dorchester Gas Corp. 2/1/72

MONARCH TILE MFG INC (DE)
Merged into Monarch Acquisition Inc. 06/15/1988
Each share Common $1 par exchanged for $8 cash

MONARCH URANIUM CO. (UT)
Name changed to International Silver Mining Corp. and Capital Stock 3¢ par changed to 1¢ par 05/05/1969
International Silver Mining Corp. recapitalized as Solar Dynamics Inc. 04/23/1977 which name changed to Goldynamics 03/27/1978 which name changed to Nugget Gold Mines, Inc. 10/25/1979
(See Nugget Gold Mines, Inc.)

MONARCH WEAR LTD (MB)
Receiver appointed 05/29/1981
Assets subsequently liquidated
No stockholders' equity

MONARCHY RES INC (NV)
Each share old Common $0.001 par exchanged for (0.01) share new Common $0.001 par 08/20/2014
Recapitalized as Monarchy Ventures Inc. 11/24/2014
Each share new Common $0.001 par exchanged for (0.33333333) share Common $0.001 par
Monarchy Ventures Inc. name changed to I-Wellness Marketing Group Inc. 02/11/2016

MONARCHY VENTURES INC (NV)
Name changed to I-Wellness Marketing Group Inc. 02/11/2016

MONARK BOAT CO (AR)
Out of business in 1978
Details not available

MONARO MNG NL (AUSTRALIA)
Name changed to Australian-American Mining Corp. NL 12/29/2010

MONARQUES RES INC (CANADA)
Name changed to Monarques Gold Corp. 01/21/2015

MONAT CAP CORP (MO)
Out of business in July 1989
Details not available

MONCHIK WEBER CORP (DE)
Merged into McGraw-Hill, Inc. 11/08/1984
Each share Common 1¢ par exchanged for $15 cash

MONCO INVT CORP (GA)
Proclaimed dissolved for failure to file annual reports and pay fees 04/29/1988

MONCOA CORP (CANADA)
Recapitalized as Monument Mining Ltd. 07/09/2007
Each share Common no par exchanged for (0.5) share Common no par

MONCOR INC (NM)
Plan of reorganization under Chapter 11 Federal Bankruptcy proceedings confirmed 08/04/1987
No stockholders' equity

MONCRIEFF URANIUM MINES LTD. (ON)
Name changed to Tombit Resources Ltd. 01/24/1983
Tombit Resources Ltd. name changed to Cliff Creek Resources Ltd. 04/26/1984 which name changed to Cliff Resources Corp. 00/00/1986 which name changed to Mineral Resources Corp. 09/13/1995 which name changed to Minroc Mines Inc. 06/10/1998 which name changed to Cassiar Mines & Metals, Inc. 06/10/1999 which name changed to Cassiar Resources Inc. 07/25/2001 which name changed to Troutline Investments Inc. (ONT) 06/30/2003 which reorganized in Alberta as Innova Exploration Ltd. 04/16/2004
(See Innova Exploration Ltd.)

MOND INDS INC (ON)
Name changed to Trailmobile Canada Ltd. 06/08/1999
(See Trailmobile Canada Ltd.)

MOND NICKEL CO.
Merged into International Nickel Co. of Canada Ltd. 00/00/1928
Details not available

MONDAKOTA RES INC (NV)
Charter revoked for failure to file reports and pay fees 08/01/1988

MONDANA VENTURES INC (BC)
Struck off register and declared dissolved for failure to file returns 8/27/93

MONDAS MINERALS CORP (DE)
Name changed to Consumer Capital Group Inc. 02/25/2011

MONDAVI RES LTD (BC)
Recapitalized as T.M.T. Resources Inc. 12/24/1991
Each share Common no par exchanged for (0.5) share Common no par
T.M.T. Resources Inc. recapitalized as Ladera Ventures Corp. 08/28/2017 which recapitalized as MedMen Enterprises Inc. 05/29/2018

MONDAVI ROBERT CORP (CA)
Merged into Constellation Brands, Inc. 12/22/2004
Each share Class A Common no par exchanged for $56.50 cash

MONDEV SR LIVING INC (AB)
Dissolved 05/07/2003
No stockholders' equity

MONDOPOLITAN INC (NV)
Recapitalized as CGT Resources, Inc. 03/31/2006
Each share Common $0.001 par exchanged for (0.001) share Common $0.001 par
CGT Resources, Inc. name changed to HealthSonix, Inc. 05/08/2006
(See HealthSonix, Inc.)

MONEDA LATAM FIXED INCOME FD (ON)
Trust terminated 06/20/2017
Each Class A Unit received $10.0688 cash
Each Class U Unit received USD$10.1271 cash

MONEDA LATAM GROWTH FD (ON)
Trust terminated 12/01/2016
Each Class A Unit received $7.06 cash

MONEDA RES LTD (AB)
Recapitalized as Canada Renewable Bioenergy Corp. (AB) 02/01/2012
Each share Common no par exchanged for (0.75471698) share Common no par
Canada Renewable Bioenergy Corp. (AB) reincorporated in British Columbia 09/27/2012

MONENCO LTD (AB)
Common no par reclassified as Conv. Class A Common no par 08/08/1975
Conv. Class A Common no par split (2) for (1) by issuance of (1) additional share 07/09/1976
Conv. Class B Common no par split (2) for (1) by issuance of (1) additional share 07/09/1976
Conv. Class B Common no par reclassified as Conv. Class A Common no par 06/05/1986
Conv. Class A Common no par reclassified as Common no par 10/21/1987
Acquired by AGRA Industries Ltd. 07/17/1992
Each share Common no par exchanged for $4.25 cash

MONET ENTMT GROUP LTD (CO)
Merged into Regatta Capital Partners, Inc. 08/01/2006
Each share Common no par exchanged for (0.2218333) share Common $0.001 par
(See Regatta Capital Partners, Inc.)

MONET GROUP HLDGS INC (DE)
Plan of reorganization under Chapter 11 Federal Bankruptcy Code effective 10/15/2001
No stockholders' equity

MONETA PORCUPINE MINES LTD. (ON)
Name changed to Moneta Porcupine Resources Ltd. 11/18/83
Moneta Porcupine Resources Ltd. name changed to Moneta Porcupine Mines Inc. 9/22/86

MONETA PORCUPINE RES LTD (ON)
Name changed to Moneta Porcupine Mines Inc. 9/22/86

MONETA RES INC (BC)
Name changed to Border Petroleum Inc. (BC) 08/08/2008
Border Petroleum Inc. (BC) reorganized in Alberta as Border Petroleum Corp. 09/14/2010 which recapitalized as Border Petroleum Ltd. 03/24/2014

MONETARY RLTY TR (OH)
Trust believed out of business 00/00/1986
Details not available

MONETARY RES INC (DE)
Charter cancelled and declared inoperative and void for non-payment of taxes 03/01/1989

MONEX BEANS HLDGS INC (JAPAN)
Name changed to Monex Group, Inc. 09/14/2009

MONEXA TECHNOLOGIES CORP (BC)
Name changed to Santa Rosa Resources Corp. 04/03/2012

MONEY CTRS AMER INC (DE)
Plan of reorganization under Chapter 11 Federal Bankruptcy proceedings effective 04/18/2017
No stockholders' equity

MONEY FD U S TREAS SECS INC (MD)
Name changed to PRO Money Fund, Inc. and Common 1¢ par reclassified as Treasury Portfolio Common 1¢ par 4/30/85
PRO Money Fund, Inc. name changed to AMA Money Fund, Inc. 7/31/86
(See AMA Money Fund, Inc.)

MONEY GROWTH INST INC (NY)
Merged into Money Growth Acquisition Corp. 01/09/1984
Each share Common 1¢ par exchanged for $1.50 cash

MONEY GUILD INC (NV)
Name changed to Vencap Holdings, Inc. 2/9/99
Vencap Holdings, Inc. name changed to Blue Planet Research & Technology, Inc. 4/22/2004

MONEY MGMT CORP (IN)
Merged into Banc One Corp. (DE) 07/01/1986
Each share 40¢ Conv. Preferred no par exchanged for (0.55) share Common no par
Each share Common $1 par exchanged for (0.825) share Common no par
Banc One Corp. (DE) reincorporated in Ohio 05/01/1989 which merged into Bank One Corp. 10/02/1998 which merged into J.P. Morgan Chase & Co. 12/31/2000 which name changed to JPMorgan Chase & Co. 07/20/2004

MONEY MGMT PLUS (MA)
Name changed to Calvert Cash Reserves (New) and Prime Portfolio reclassified as Institutional Prime Fund 06/30/1996

MONEY MKT MGMT (MD)
Reorganized 06/29/1982
Reorganized from Money Market Management, Inc. (MA) to under the laws of Maryland as Money Market Management and and Capital Stock 1¢ par reclassified as Shares of Bene. Int. 06/29/1982
Merged into Money Market Obligations Trust 02/01/2000
Each Share of Bene. Int. exchanged for Money Market Management shares on a net asset basis

MONEY MKT OBLIGS TR (MA)
Money Market Trust completely liquidated 08/26/2005
Details not available
(Additional Information in Active)

MONEY MKT OPTS INVTS INC (MA)
Voluntarily dissolved 10/02/1989
Details not available

MONEY MKT TR (MA)
Under plan of merger each Share of Bene. Int. automatically became Money Market Obligations Trust Money Market Trust on a net asset basis 02/01/2000
(See Money Market Obligations Trust)

MONEY RADIO INC (DE)
Each share old Common $0.0001 par exchanged for (0.9) share new Common $0.0001 par 12/01/1995
Chapter 11 bankruptcy proceedings dismissed 11/10/1998
Stockholders' equity unlikely

MONEY STORE INC (NJ)
Common no par split (3) for (2) by issuance of (0.5) additional share 03/16/1994
Common no par split (3) for (2) by issuance of (0.5) additional share 09/21/1995
Common no par split (5) for (2) by issuance of (1.5) additional shares 12/01/1995
Merged into First Union Corp. 06/30/1998
Each share Conv. Preferred no par exchanged for (0.5383) share Common no par
Each share Common no par exchanged for (0.5851) share Common $3.33-1/3 par
First Union Corp. name changed to Wachovia Corp. (Ctfs. dated after 09/01/2001) 09/01/2001 which merged into Wells Fargo & Co. (New) 12/31/2008

MONEY-TALKS CO., INC. (DE)
No longer in existence having become inoperative and void for non-payment of taxes 3/19/24

MONEY WKS INC (AB)
Recapitalized as CanArgo Energy Inc. 07/14/1997
Each share Common no par exchanged for (0.025) share Common no par
CanArgo Energy Inc. merged into CanArgo Energy Corp. 07/15/1998
(See CanArgo Energy Corp.)

MONEYFLAP CAP CORP (NV)
Recapitalized as Fortuna Gaming Corp. 07/06/2005
Each share Common $0.001 par exchanged for (0.1) share Common $0.001 par
Fortuna Gaming Corp. recapitalized as Principal Capital Group, Inc. (New) 11/21/2008 which name changed to Gazoo Energy Group, Inc. 09/11/2009
(See Gazoo Energy Group, Inc.)

MONEYFLOW SYS INTL INC (NV)
Each share old Common $0.001 par exchanged for (0.1) share new Common $0.001 par 07/19/2004
Recapitalized as Vault America, Inc. 03/10/2008
Each share Common $0.001 par exchanged for (0.02) share Common $0.001 par
Vault America, Inc. name changed to Green PolkaDot Box Inc. 04/23/2012

MONEYFOCUS USA COM INC (FL)
Name changed to Amnis Energy Inc. 03/22/2002
Amnis Energy Inc. name changed to Homeland Security Group International, Inc. 10/10/2005 which recapitalized as Domestic Energy Corp. 04/07/2008
(See Domestic Energy Corp.)

MONEY4GOLD HLDGS INC (DE)
Name changed to Upstream Worldwide Inc. 07/13/2010
Upstream Worldwide Inc. name changed to usell.com, Inc. 07/27/2012

MONEYGRAM PMT SYS INC (DE)
Issue Information - 14,463,750 shares COM offered at $12 per share on 12/11/1996
Merged into Viad Corp. 07/10/1998
Each share Common 1¢ par exchanged for $17.35 cash

MONEYLINE FINANCIAL GROUP, INC. (NV)
Name changed to Say Yes Foods Inc. 02/02/1996
Say Yes Foods Inc. recapitalized as CBP Carbon Industries, Inc. (NV) 03/27/2006 which reorganized in British Virgin Islands 02/14/2012

MONEYLOGIX GROUP INC (NV)
Name changed to Panacea Global, Inc. 06/16/2011

MONEYSWORTH & BEST SHOE CARE INC (ON)
Filed an assignment in bankruptcy and trustee appointed 7/11/2000
No stockholders' equity

MONEYWISE RES INC (BC)
Recapitalized as Stealth Ventures Inc. 10/01/1992
Each (3.5) shares Common no par exchanged for (1) share Common no par
Stealth Ventures Inc. name changed to Annova International Holdings Corp. 05/12/1994 which recapitalized as Annova Business Group Inc. 04/27/1995 which recapitalized as Capital Alliance Group Inc. 11/27/1998 which name changed to CIBT Education Group Inc. 11/14/2007

MONEYZONE COM (NV)
Each share old Common $0.001 par exchanged for (0.00666666) share new Common $0.001 par 03/30/2001
Reincorporated under the laws of Delaware as MoneyZone, Inc. 06/12/2001
MoneyZone.com, Inc. name changed to QT 5, Inc. 01/08/2003 which recapitalized as Addison-Davis Diagnostics, Inc. 11/18/2004
(See Addison-Davis Diagnostics, Inc.)

MONEYZONE COM INC (DE)
Name changed to QT 5, Inc. 01/08/2003
QT 5, Inc. recapitalized as Addison-Davis Diagnostics, Inc. 11/18/2004
(See Addison-Davis Diagnostics, Inc.)

MONFORT COLO INC (DE)
Merged into ConAgra, Inc. 05/13/1987
Each share Common $1 par exchanged for (2.5125) shares Common $5 par
ConAgra, Inc. name changed to ConAgra Foods, Inc. 09/28/2000 which name changed to Conagra Brands, Inc. 11/10/2016

MONGOLIA GOLD RES LTD (BC)
Recapitalized as Tyhee Development Corp. 08/16/1999
Each share Common no par exchanged for (0.05) share Common no par
Tyhee Development Corp. name changed to Tyhee Gold Corp. 02/01/2011

MONGOLIAN EXPLORATIONS LTD (NV)
Name changed to Knewtrino, Inc. 05/24/2006
Knewtrino, Inc. name changed to Vanguard Minerals Corp. 10/04/2007 which name changed to Zoned Properties, Inc. 10/25/2013

MONGOWIN SUDBURY EXPLS LTD (CANADA)
Completely liquidated 5/19/78
Each (3.647) shares Common no par exchanged for first and final distribution of (1) share Natural Resources Guardianship International, Inc. Capital Stock $0.001 par
Natural Resources Guardianship International, Inc. name changed to XRG International, Inc. 11/13/78
(See XRG International, Inc.)

MONICA RES LTD (BC)
Recapitalized as Fulham Explorations Inc. 02/06/1990
Each share Common no par exchanged for (0.5) share Common no par
(See Fulham Explorations Inc.)

MONICA SIMONE COSMETICS INC (NY)
Dissolved by proclamation 3/25/92

MONIQUE EXPL INC (QC)
Merged into Exploration SEG Inc./SEG Exploration Inc. 1/1/92
Each share Common no par exchanged for (0.18691588) share Common no par
Exploration SEG Inc./SEG Exploration Inc. name changed to West Africa Mining Exploration Inc. 7/6/95 which name changed to Semafo Inc. 5/13/97

MONITEK TECHNOLOGIES INC (DE)
Merged into Sentex Sensing Technology Inc. 11/27/1996
Each share Common 1¢ par exchanged for (6.897489) shares Common no par
(See Sentex Sensing Technology Inc.)

MONITERM CORP (MN)
Common 2-1/2¢ par split (3) for (1) by issuance of (2) additional shares 2/15/84
Filed a petition under Chapter 11 Federal Bankruptcy Code in November 1991
Details not available

MONITISE PLC (UNITED KINGDOM)
ADR agreement terminated 09/29/2017
Each ADR for Ordinary exchanged for $0.995081 cash

MONITOR EXPLORATION CO. (CO)
Proclaimed defunct and inoperative for non-payment of taxes 10/10/62

MONITOR LABS INC (DE)
Name changed to Monitor Technologies, Inc. 05/01/1986
(See Monitor Technologies, Inc.)

MONITOR RES LTD (BC)
Struck off register and declared dissolved for failure to file returns 6/13/86

MONITOR TECHNOLOGIES, INC. (DE)
Merged into LSMC Acquisition Corp. 8/25/89
Each share Common 1¢ par exchanged for $8 cash

MONITREND INVT MGMT INC (DE)
Company believed out of business 12/27/1996
Details not available

MONK AUSTIN INC (NC)
Merged into DIMON Inc. 04/01/1995
Each share Common 1¢ par exchanged for (1) share Common no par
DIMON Inc. name changed to Alliance One International, Inc. 05/13/2005 which name changed to Pyxus International, Inc. 09/12/2018

MONK GOLD & RES LTD (ON)
Name changed to Knomex Resources Inc. 10/25/1995
Knomex Resources Inc. recapitalized as Afitex Financial Services Inc. 11/10/1998
(See Afitex Financial Services Inc.)

MONMOUTH AIRLS INC (NJ)
Name changed to Ocean Airways, Inc. 5/8/79
Ocean Airways, Inc. merged into Regent Air Corp. 10/18/83
(See Regent Air Corp.)

MONMOUTH CAP CORP (NJ)
Stock Dividends - 25% 03/15/1966; 10% 07/20/1967; 10% 08/15/1968; 25% 11/29/1968
Merged into Monmouth Real Estate Investment Corp. 07/31/2007
Each share Common $1 par exchanged for (0.655) share Common 1¢ par

MONMOUTH CMNTY BANCORP (NJ)
Common 1¢ par split (6) for (5) by issuance of (0.2) additional share payable 07/30/2004 to holders of record 07/15/2004
Stock Dividends - 5% payable 12/31/2000 to holders of record 12/15/2000 Ex date - 12/13/2000; 5% payable 12/31/2001 to holders of record 12/15/2001 Ex date - 12/12/2001; 5% payable 12/31/2002 to holders of record 12/16/2002 Ex date - 12/12/2002; 5% payable 12/31/2003 to holders of record 12/15/2003
Under plan of merger name changed to Central Jersey Bancorp (Ctfs. dtd. after 01/01/2005) 01/01/2005
(See Central Jersey Bancorp (Ctfs. dtd. after 01/01/2005))

MONMOUTH CMNTY BK (LONG BRANCH, NJ)
Under plan of reorganization each share Common $5 par automatically became (1) share Monmouth Community Bancorp Common 1¢ par 08/31/2000
Monmouth Community Bancorp name changed to Central Jersey Bancorp (Ctfs. dtd. after 01/01/2005) 01/01/2005
(See Central Jersey Bancorp (Ctfs. dtd. after 01/01/2005))

MONMOUTH CNTY NATL BK (RED BK, NJ)
Under plan of merger name changed to Colonial First National Bank (Red Bank, NJ) 08/18/1972
Colonial First National Bank (Red Bank, NJ) merged into Fidelity Union Bancorporation 06/28/1974 which merged into First National State Bancorporation 04/05/1984 which name changed to First Fidelity Bancorporation (Old) 05/01/1985 which merged into First Fidelity Bancorporation (New) 02/29/1988 which merged into First Union Corp. 01/01/1996 which name changed to Wachovia Corp. (Ctfs. dated after 09/01/2001) 09/01/2001 which merged into Wells Fargo & Co. (New) 12/31/2008

MONMOUTH ELECTRIC CO., INC. (NJ)
Name changed to Monmouth Industries, Inc. 10/7/69
(See Monmouth Industries, Inc.)

MONMOUTH INDS INC (NJ)
Charter declared void for non-payment of taxes 3/1/77

MONMOUTH PARK JOCKEY CLUB (NJ)
5% Preferred $50 par called for redemption 12/19/55
Voting Trust Agreement of 1954 terminated 9/19/64
Each VTC for Common 1¢ par exchanged for (1) VTC Ser. 1974 for Common 1¢ par or (1) share Common 1¢ par
Voting Trust Agreement of 1964 terminated 9/20/74
Each VTC for Common 1¢ par exchanged for (1) share Common 1¢ par
Merged into New Jersey Sports & Exposition Authority 9/24/85
Each share Common 1¢ par exchanged for $58 cash

MONMOUTH PARK RACING ASSOCIATION
Suspended for non-payment of taxes 00/00/1945

MONMOUTH REAL ESTATE INVT CORP (MD)
Reorganized 10/01/1990
Reincorporated 05/15/2003
Shares of Bene. Int. no par split (3) for (1) by issuance of (2) additional shares 09/30/1987
Reorganized from Monmouth Real Estate Investment Trust (NJ) to Monmouth Real Estate Investment Corp. (DE) and Shares of Bene. Int. no par reclassified as Class A Common 1¢ par 10/01/1990
State of incorporation changed from (DE) to (MD) and Class A Common 1¢ par reclassified as Common 1¢ par 05/15/2003
7.625% Preferred Ser. A 1¢ par called for redemption at $25 plus $0.23299 accrued dividends on 10/14/2016
7.875% Preferred Ser. B 1¢ par called for redemption at $25 plus $0.032813 accrued dividends on 06/07/2017
(Additional Information in Active)

MONO GOLD MINES INC (BC)
Recapitalized as Canadian Mono Mines Inc. 02/12/1991
Each share Common no par exchanged for (1/3) share Common no par
(See Canadian Mono Mines Inc.)

MONO-KEARSARGE CONSOLIDATED MINING CO. (UT)
Recapitalized as Kashmir Oil Inc. 08/30/1963
Each share Common 10¢ par exchanged for (0.2) share Common 50¢ par
(See Kashmir Oil Inc.)

MONO RES INC (WA)
Proclaimed dissolved for non-payment of fees 07/01/1974

MONO SERVICE CO.
Assets acquired by Continental Can Co., Inc. 00/00/1944
Details not available

MONOCACY BANCSHARES INC (MD)
Stock Dividends - 10% payable 01/26/1996 to holders of record 01/12/1996; 10% payable 02/17/1998 to holders of record 02/02/1998
Merged into F&M Bancorp 11/30/1998
Each share Common $5 par exchanged for (1.251) shares Common $5 par
F&M Bancorp merged into Mercantile Bankshares Corp. 08/12/2003 which merged into PNC Financial Services Group, Inc. 03/02/2007

MONOCLONAL ANTIBODIES INC (DE)
Reincorporated 06/23/1987
State of incorporation changed from (CA) to (DE) and Common no par changed to 1¢ par 06/23/1987
Name changed to Quidel Corp. 01/31/1991

MONOCLONAL INTL TECHNOLOGY INC (DE)
Each share old Common $0.0001 par exchanged for (0.005) share new Common $0.0001 par 6/30/92
Recapitalized as Concord Energy Inc. 12/1/95
Each share Common $0.0001 par exchanged for (0.2) share Common $0.0001 par

MONOCLONAL MED INC (NV)
SEC revoked common stock registration 08/31/1992

MONOCOUPE AEROPLANE & ENGINE CORP.
Name changed to Universal Moulded Products Corp. 00/00/1942
(See Universal Moulded Products Corp.)

MONOGEN INC (CANADA)
Filed an assignment in bankruptcy 12/30/2008
No stockholders' equity

MONOGRAM BIOSCIENCES INC (DE)
Each Contingent Value Right received first and final distribution of $0.88 cash 06/11/2006
Each share old Common $0.001 par exchanged for (0.16666666) share new Common $0.001 par 11/04/2008
Acquired by Laboratory Corp. of America Holdings 08/04/2009
Each share Common $0.001 par exchanged for $4.55 cash

MONOGRAM DEVS LTD (BC)
Common 50¢ par changed to no par 10/16/78
Name changed to Monogram Oil & Gas, Inc. 11/30/81
(See Monogram Oil & Gas, Inc.)

MONOGRAM ENERGY INC (PA)
Each share old Common $0.001 par exchanged for (0.005) share new Common $0.001 par 03/31/2008
Reorganized as Marquis Tech Holdings, Inc. 07/19/2011
Each share new Common $0.001 par exchanged for (1.03) shares Common $0.001 par
Marquis Tech Holdings, Inc. recapitalized as Tritent Int'l Agriculture, Inc. 07/11/2012

MONOGRAM INDUSTRIES, INC. (IL)
Involuntarily dissolved 12/1/75

MONOGRAM INDS INC (DE)
Reincorporated 11/28/1969
Each share Common $1 par exchanged for (0.25) share Common $4 par 05/14/1965
Common $4 par changed to $1.33333333 par and (2) additional shares issued 11/15/1967
State of incorporation changed from (CA) to (DE) and Common $1.33333333 par changed to $1 par 11/28/1969
Merged into Nortek, Inc. 08/26/1983
Each share Common $1 par exchanged for (2) shares Common $1 par and $34.90 cash
(See Nortek, Inc.)

MONOGRAM OIL & GAS INC (BC)
Struck off register and declared dissolved for failure to file returns 6/28/91

MONOGRAM PETROLEUMS LTD. (ON)
Charter cancelled for failure to pay taxes and file returns 12/21/59

MONOGRAM PICTURES CORP. (DE)
Stock Dividend - 10% 7/10/53
Name changed to Allied Artists Pictures Corp. in 1953
Allied Artists Pictures Corp. merged into Allied Artists Industries, Inc. 1/20/76
(See Allied Artists Industries, Inc.)

MONOGRAM PICTURES INC (NV)
Each share old Common $0.001 par exchanged for (0.1) share new Common $0.001 par 05/09/2001
Name changed to Vitalabs, Inc. 05/20/2002
Vitalabs, Inc. name changed to America Asia Corp. (NV) 10/19/2004 which reincorporated in Washington as America Asia Energy Corp. 11/08/2005 which name changed to Renegade Energy Corp. 09/14/2006 which recapitalized as Carson Development Corp. 10/20/2008
(See Carson Development Corp.)

MONOGRAM PRECISION INDUSTRIES, INC. (CA)
Name changed to Monogram Industries, Inc. (CA) 12/03/1962
Monogram Industries, Inc. (CA) reincorporated in Delaware 11/28/1969 which merged into Nortek, Inc. (RI) 08/26/1983 which reincorporated in Delaware 04/23/1987 which reorganized as Nortek Holdings, Inc. 11/20/2002
(See Nortek Holdings, Inc.)

MONOGRAM RESIDENTIAL TR INC (MD)
Acquired by Greystar Growth & Income Fund, L.P. 09/19/2017
Each share Common $0.0001 par exchanged for $12 cash

MONOGRAM URANIUM & OIL CO. (CO)
Merged into Four Corners Uranium Corp. on a (1) for (3) basis 12/01/1958
Four Corners Uranium Corp. name changed to Four Corners Oil & Minerals Co. 06/00/1959 which was acquired by Consolidated Oil & Gas, Inc. (CO) 12/07/1967 which was acquired by Hugoton Energy Corp. 09/07/1995 which merged into Chesapeake Energy Corp. 03/10/1998

MONOLITE INDS INC (NV)
Recapitalized as Country World Casinos, Inc. 8/9/93
Each (35) shares Common $0.005 par exchanged for (1) share Common $0.001 par
(See Country World Casinos, Inc.)

MONOLITH PORTLAND CEM CO (NV)
Under plan of reorganization each share Common no par automatically became (1) share Common $1 par and (9) additional shares issued 08/31/1987
Merged into CBR Acquisition Corp. 03/30/1989
Each share 8% Preferred $10 par exchanged for $11.745 cash
Each share Common $1 par exchanged for $6.25 cash

MONOLITH PORTLAND MIDWEST CO (NV)
Merged into Monolith Portland Cement Co. 12/30/1977
Each share 8% Preferred $10 par exchanged for $20.55 cash

MONOLITH VENTURES INC (NV)
Name changed to Zero Gravity Solutions, Inc. 03/13/2013

MONOLITHIC MEMORIES INC (DE)
Reincorporated 03/14/1987
Common 4¢ par changed to 2¢ par and (1) additional share issued 06/17/1983
State of incorporation changed from (CA) to (DE) and Common 2¢ par changed to 1¢ par 03/14/1987
Merged into Advanced Micro Devices, Inc. 08/13/1987
Each share Common 1¢ par exchanged for (0.875) share Common 1¢ par

MONOLITHIC SYS TECHNOLOGY INC (DE)
Issue Information - 5,000,000 shares COM offered at $10 per share on 06/27/2001
Name changed to MoSys, Inc. 06/05/2006

MONOMAC SPINNING CO.
Acquired by Arlington Mills 00/00/1955
Details not available

MONON COAL CO., INC. (IN)
Ctfs. prior to 6/28/57
Reorganized 6/28/57
Certificates dated prior to 6/28/57 are valueless

MONON RR (IN)
Class B Common no par split (2) for (1) by issuance of (1) additional share 6/21/65
Class B Common no par reclassified as Common no par 5/31/68
Merged into Louisville & Nashville Railroad Co. 7/31/71
Each share Common no par exchanged for (1) share $2.10 Conv. Preferred Ser. A $35 par
Louisville & Nashville Railroad Co. merged into Seaboard Coast Line Industries, Inc. (DE) 11/10/72 which merged into CSX Corp. 11/1/80

MONONGAH GLASS CO.
Dissolved in 1932

MONONGAH GLASS CORP.
Properties sold 00/00/1936
Details not available

MONONGAHELA INCLINED PLANE CO. (PA)
Capital Stock $50 par changed to $25 par in 1936
Liquidation completed
Each share Capital Stock $25 par exchanged for initial distribution of $40 cash 5/19/64
Each share Capital Stock $25 par received second distribution of $8 cash 1/2/65
Each share Capital Stock $25 par received third and final distribution of $1.14 cash 11/10/65

MONONGAHELA LT & PWR CO (PA)
99% acquired by Duquesne Light Co. through purchase offer which expired 00/00/1989
Public interest eliminated

MONONGAHELA PWR CO (OH)
Reincorporated 01/01/1966
State of incorporation changed from (WV) to (OH) 01/01/1966
$15 Preferred Ser. K $100 par called for redemption 07/11/1986
$9.64 Preferred Ser. F $100 par called for redemption 11/20/1992
7.36% Preferred Ser. E $100 par called for redemption 07/17/1995
$7.92 Preferred Ser. H $100 par called for redemption 07/17/1995
$7.92 Preferred Ser. I $100 par called for redemption 07/17/1995
$8.60 Preferred Ser. J $100 par called for redemption 07/17/1995
8.80% Preferred Ser. G $100 par called for redemption 07/17/1995
7.73% Preferred Ser. L $100 par called for redemption at $100 on 10/31/2005
4.40% Preferred $100 par called for redemption at $106.50 on 09/04/2007
4.50% Preferred Ser. C $100 par called for redemption at $103.50 on 09/04/2007
4.80% Preferred Ser. B $100 par called for redemption at $105.25 on 09/04/2007
6.28% Preferred Ser. D $100 par called for redemption at $102.86 on 09/04/2007
Public interest eliminated

MONONGAHELA STREET RAILWAY CO.
Merged into Pittsburgh Railways Co. for cash 9/30/50

MONONGAHELA VY BK INC (FAIRMONT, WV)
Stock Dividend - 5% payable 6/1/2001 to holders of record 5/1/2001 Ex date - 6/20/2001
Under plan of reorganization each share Common $1 par automatically became (1) share MVB Financial Corp. Common $1 par 1/1/2004

MONONGAHELA WEST PENN PUBLIC SERVICE CO.
Name changed to Monongahela Power Co. (WV) 00/00/1945
Monongahela Power Co. (WV) reincorporated in Ohio 01/01/1966
(See Monongahela Power Co.)

MONOPOLY CAP CORP (UT)
Name changed to American Premier Financial Corp. 08/25/1988
(See American Premier Financial Corp.)

MONORAIL, INC. (TX)
Charter revoked for failure to file reports and pay fees 8/7/67

MONORE METALS CORP (BC)
Recapitalized as Julia Resources Corp. 2/5/79
Each share Common no par exchanged for (1/3) share Common no par
Julia Resources Corp. merged into Spokane Resources Ltd. 10/31/91 which recapitalized as SKN Resources Ltd. 7/26/2001 which name changed to Silvercorp Metals Inc. 5/2/2005

MONOREX INC (DE)
Charter cancelled and declared inoperative and void for non-payment of taxes 3/1/88

MONOSAIC, INC. (MI)
Adjudicated bankrupt 3/13/70

MONOSIL INC (CA)
Name changed to Citel Inc. 04/19/1983
(See Citel Inc.)

MONOWALL HOMES, INC. (MD)
Acquired by Heidler Corp. 01/25/1971
Each share Common 10¢ par exchanged for (0.1) share Common 10¢ par
(See Heidler Corp.)

MONPAS MINES LTD. (QC)
Recapitalized as Consolidated Monpas Mines Ltd. on a (1) for (2) basis 11/2/56
Consolidated Monpas Mines Ltd. merged into Albarmont Mines Corp. 10/12/71 which recapitalized as Albarmont (1985) Inc. 7/19/85
(See Albarmont (1985) Inc.)

MONPRE IRON MINES LTD (ON)
Recapitalized as Techoldmin Ltd. 11/23/1998
Each share Common no par exchanged for (1/3) share Common no par
Techoldmin Ltd. merged into Enviro Waste Technologies Inc. 02/25/2000 which merged into Compressario Corp. 03/07/2002
(See Compressario Corp.)

MONPRE MINING CO. LTD. (ON)
Recapitalized as Monpre Iron Mines Ltd. 7/28/67
Each share Capital Stock $1 par exchanged for (0.2) share Capital Stock $1 par
Monpre Iron Mines Ltd. recapitalized as Techoldmin Ltd. 11/23/98 which merged into Enviro Waste Technologies Inc. 2/25/2000 which merged into Compressario Corp. 3/7/2002

MONPRE URANIUM EXPLORATION LTD. (ON)
Name changed to Monpre Mining Co. Ltd. 11/30/66 which was recapitalized as Monpre Iron Mines Ltd. 7/28/67

MONRO MUFFLER BRAKE INC (NY)
Common 1¢ par split (3) for (2) by issuance of (0.5) additional share payable 10/31/2003 to holders of record 10/21/2003 Ex date - 11/03/2003
Common 1¢ par split (3) for (2) by issuance of (0.5) additional share payable 10/01/2007 to holders of record 09/21/2007 Ex date - 10/02/2007
Common 1¢ par split (3) for (2) by issuance of (0.5) additional share payable 12/23/2010 to holders of record 12/13/2010 Ex date - 12/27/2010
Stock Dividends - 5% payable 08/05/1996 to holders of record 06/21/1996; 5% payable 08/04/1997 to holders of record 06/20/1997; 5% payable 06/18/1998 to holders of record 06/08/1998
Name changed to Monro, Inc. 08/21/2017

MONROC INC (DE)
Merged into U.S. Aggregates, Inc. 06/15/1998
Each share Common 1¢ par exchanged for $10.771 cash

MONROE ABSTRACT & TITLE CORP (NY)
Name changed to Monroe Title Insurance Co. 1/1/93
(See Monroe Title Insurance Co.)

MONROE AUTO EQUIP CO (MI)
Common no par changed to $5 par in 1941
Common $5 par changed to $1 par in 1945
Common $1 par split (3) for (1) by issuance of (2) additional shares 2/18/60
Common $1 par split (2) for (1) by issuance of (1) additional share 3/30/62
Common $1 par split (2) for (1) by issuance of (1) additional share 6/27/69
Common $1 par split (2) for (1) by issuance of (1) additional share 9/30/71
Stock Dividends - 125% 6/45; 10% 7/15/59
5% Preferred $50 par called for redemption 1/1/60
Merged into Tenneco Inc. 7/29/77
Each share Common $1 par exchanged for (0.3846) share Common $5 par
Tenneco Inc. merged into El Paso Natural Gas Co. 12/12/96 which reorganized as El Paso Energy Corp. 8/1/98 which name changed to El Paso Corp. 2/5/2001

MONROE BANCORP (IN)
Stock Dividend - 10% payable 11/17/2005 to holders of record 11/07/2005 Ex date - 11/03/2005
Merged into Old National Bancorp 01/03/2011
Each share Common no par exchanged for (1.216) shares Common no par

MONROE BK & TR CO (MI)
Common $6.25 par changed to $3.125 par and (1) additional share issued 02/09/1969
Common $3.125 par split (2) for (1) by issuance of (1) additional share 06/11/1990
Common $3.125 par split (2) for (1) by issuance of (1) additional share payable 06/10/1998 to holders of record 04/03/1998
Stock Dividends - 25% 04/10/1973; 25% 06/10/1992; 100% 06/10/1994
Preferred $100 par called for redemption at $100 on 02/29/2000
Reorganized as MBT Financial Corp. 07/01/2000
Each share Common $3.125 par exchanged for (2) shares Common no par

MONROE BROADCASTING CO. (WA)
Charter cancelled and proclaimed dissolved for failure to pay fees 11/5/81

MONROE CHEM CO (MD)
$3.50 Preference no par called for redemption 08/19/1955
Name changed to Putnam Dyes, Inc. 11/09/1966
(See Putnam Dyes, Inc.)

MONROE COMBINING CORP (NY)
Name changed to Monroe Group, Inc. (NY) 05/04/1970
Monroe Group, Inc. (NY) reincorporated in Delaware 06/01/1972
(See Monroe Group, Inc.)

MONROE FINL INC (DE)
Acquired by First Community Bancshares, Inc. (NV) 11/30/2002
Each share Common 10¢ par exchanged for $41.06 cash

MONROE GASKET & MANUFACTURING CO. INC. (NY)
Charter revoked for failure to file reports and pay fees 12/15/52

MONROE GOLD & SILVER MINING CO. (NY)
Charter cancelled and proclaimed dissolved for failure to pay taxes 3/31/24

MONROE GROUP INC (DE)
Reincorporated 06/01/1972
State of incorporation changed from (NY) to (DE) 06/01/1972
Charter forfeited for failure to maintain a resident agent 01/18/1981

MONROE JAMES BK (ARLINGTON CNTY, VA)
Under plan of reorganization each share Common $1 par automatically became (1) share James Monroe Bancorp Inc. Common $1 par 07/01/1999
James Monroe Bancorp Inc. merged into Mercantile Bankshares Corp. 07/17/2006 which merged into PNC Financial Services Group, Inc. 03/02/2007

MONROE LOAN SOCIETY, INC. (DE)
Recapitalized 00/00/1936
Each share 7% Preferred Ser. A exchanged for (20) shares Class A Common no par
Each share Common exchanged for (0.9) share Class A Common no par and (0.1) share Class B Common no par
Recapitalized 00/00/1937
Class A Common no par and Class B Common no par changed to $1 par
Merged into Seaboard Finance Co. on a (1) for (3.7) basis 10/31/1956
(See Seaboard Finance Co.)

MONROE MINERALS INC (AB)
Recapitalized as Kirrin Resources Inc. 05/26/2009
Each share Common no par exchanged for (0.1) share Common no par
(See Kirrin Resources Inc.)

MONROE SEC BK & TR CO (STROUDSBURG, PA)
Common $11 par changed to $17 par 03/05/1968
Name changed to Security Bank & Trust Co. (Stroudsburg, PA) 08/00/1973
Security Bank & Trust Co. (Stroudsburg, PA) merged into Continental Bancorp, Inc. 06/01/1985 which merged into Midlantic Corp. 01/30/1987 which merged into PNC Bank Corp. 12/31/1995 which name changed to PNC Financial Services Group, Inc. 03/15/2000

MONROE STATE SAVINGS BANK (MONROE, MI)
Recapitalized as Monroe Bank & Trust Co. (Monroe, MI) 2/9/68
Each share Common $25 par exchanged for (4) shares Common $6.25 par
Monroe Bank & Trust Co. (Monroe, MI) reorganized as MBT Financial Corp. 7/1/2000

MONROE TITLE INS CO (NY)
Common $5 par split (4) for (1) by issuance of (3) additional shares 10/19/94
Merged into Stewart Information Services Corp. 2/3/2006
Each share Common $5 par exchanged for $21.15 cash
Note: Each share Common $5 par received an initial distribution of $0.7137 cash from escrow 7/7/2006
Each share Common $5 par received second and final distribution of $1.1698 cash from escrow 12/12/2006

MONSANTO CHEMICAL CO. (DE)
Common no par changed to $10 par in 1933
Each share Common $10 par exchanged for (3) shares Common $5 par in 1946
Common $5 par changed to $2 par and (2) additional shares issued 7/26/55
Stock Dividend - 100% 4/30/34
Name changed to Monsanto Co. (Old) 4/1/64
Monsanto Co. (Old) name changed to Pharmacia Corp. 3/31/2000 which merged into Pfizer Inc. 4/16/2003

MONSANTO CHEMICAL WORKS (MO)
Common no par split (2) for (1) by issuance of (1) additional share 7/19/29
Reincorporated in Delaware as Monsanto Chemical Co. and Common no par changed to $10 par 4/19/33
Monsanto Chemical Co. name changed to Monsanto Co. (Old) 4/1/64 which name changed to Pharmacia Corp. 3/31/2000 which merged into Pfizer Inc. 4/16/2003

MONSANTO CO NEW (DE)
Common 1¢ par split (2) for (1) by issuance of (1) additional share payable 07/28/2006 to holders of record 07/07/2006 Ex date - 07/31/2006
Acquired by Bayer AG 06/07/2018
Each share Common 1¢ par exchanged for $128 cash

MONSANTO CO OLD (DE)
Common $2 par split (2) for (1) by issuance of (1) additional share 06/06/1984
$2.75 Conv. Preferred no par called for redemption 10/15/1984
Common Stock Purchase Rights declared for Common stockholders of record 02/03/1986 were redeemed at $0.05 per right 02/28/1990 for holders of record 02/05/1990
Common $2 par split (2) for (1) by issuance of (1) additional share 06/06/1990
Common $2 par split (5) for (1) by issuance of (4) additional shares payable 06/05/1996 to holders of record 05/15/1996 Ex date - 06/06/1996
Each share Common $2 par received distribution of (0.2) share Solutia Inc. Common 1¢ par payable 09/02/1997 to holders of record 08/20/1997 Ex date - 09/03/1997
Under plan of merger name changed to Pharmacia Corp. 03/31/2000
Pharmacia Corp. merged into Pfizer Inc. 04/16/2003

MONSTER BEVERAGE CORP OLD (DE)
Common $0.005 par split (2) for (1) by issuance of (1) additional share payable 02/15/2012 to holders of record 02/06/2012 Ex date - 02/16/2012
Under plan of reorganization each share Common $0.005 par automatically became (1) share Monster Beverage Corp. (New) Common $0.005 par 06/15/2015

MONSTER COPPER CORP (YUKON)
Merged into Mega Uranium Ltd. 06/06/2007
Each share Common no par exchanged for (0.16666666) share Common no par and (0.08333333) Common Stock Purchase Warrant expiring 06/06/2012

MONSTER DIGITAL INC (DE)
Recapitalized as Innovate Biopharmaceuticals, Inc. 02/01/2018
Each share Common $0.0001 par exchanged for (0.1) share Common $0.0001 par

MONSTER MNG CORP (BC)
Each share old Common no par exchanged for (0.1) share new Common no par 05/25/2016
Name changed to Metallic Minerals Corp. 09/13/2016

MONSTER MTRS INC (NV)
Each (60) shares old Common $0.001 par exchanged for (1) share new Common $0.001 par 10/19/2007
Name changed to Eco2 Forests, Inc. 09/08/2009
Eco2 Forests, Inc. recapitalized as International Display Advertising, Inc. 03/20/2013

MONSTER OFFERS (NV)
Each share old Common $0.001 par exchanged for (0.00333333) share new Common $0.001 par 04/09/2012
Stock Dividend - 50% payable 12/02/2010 to holders of record 12/01/2010 Ex date - 12/03/2010
Name changed to Monster Arts Inc. 07/19/2013

MONSTER WORLDWIDE INC (DE)
Acquired by Randstad Holding N.V. 11/01/2016
Each share Common $0.001 par exchanged for $3.40 cash

MONSTERDAATA INC (DE)
Name changed 12/07/2000
Name changed from Monsterdaata.Com Inc. to Monsterdaata Inc. 12/07/2000
Each share old Common 1¢ par exchanged for (0.2) share new Common 1¢ par 03/26/2001
Each share new Common 1¢ par received distribution of (1) share Monstertech Ltd. Restricted Common payable 03/19/2007 to holders of record 02/28/2007
Recapitalized as Enviro Global Corp. 08/08/2007
Each share new Common 1¢ par exchanged for (0.05) share Common 1¢ par

MONT BLANC RES INC (BC)
Name changed to Sonora Gold & Silver Corp. 07/17/2008

MONT BLANC RES INC (NY)
Common $0.001 par split (3) for (1) by issuance of (2) additional shares 4/14/88
Name changed to Grafix Time Corp. 12/19/89
Grafix Time Corp. recapitalized as Grafix Corp. 8/1/98 which recapitalized as Player (Gary) Direct Inc. 4/9/99
(See Player (Gary) Direct Inc.)

MONT LAURIER URANIUM MINES INC (QC)
Name changed to Great Laurier Uranium Mines Ltd. 8/28/70
(See Great Laurier Uranium Mines Ltd.)

MONT ROUGE RES INC (NY)
Each share old Common $0.0001 par exchanged for (0.25) share new Common $0.0001 par 10/10/1992
Reincorporated under the laws of Wyoming as American Digital Communications, Inc. 07/28/1993
American Digital Communications, Inc. name changed to TrackPower, Inc. 09/20/1999 which reorganized in Nevada as Gate to Wire Solutions, Inc. 09/26/2008
(See Gate to Wire Solutions, Inc.)

MONT STE. ANNE MINES LTD. (ON)
Charter cancelled for failure to pay taxes and file returns 12/26/83

MONT ST SAUVEUR INTL INC (QC)
Acquired by a private company 4/28/2005
Each share Class A Subordinate no par exchanged for $2.50 cash

MONT SOUTH CORP (CO)
Name changed to National Media Holding Co. 07/12/1988

MONTACAL OIL CO. (MT)
Completely liquidated 9/16/70
Each share Capital Stock $1 par received first and final distribution of $0.0122 cash
Certificates were not required to be surrendered and are now valueless

MONTAGE PRODTNS INC (NY)
Common 4¢ par changed to 2¢ par and (1) additional share issued 05/07/1971
Charter cancelled and proclaimed dissolved for failure to pay taxes 06/24/1981

MONTAGE TECHNOLOGY GROUP LTD (CAYMAN ISLANDS)
Acquired by Shanghai Pudong Science & Technology Investment Co., Ltd. 11/19/2014
Each share Ordinary $0.0125 par exchanged for $22.60 cash

MONTAGU RES CORP (NV)
Old Common $0.00001 par split (25) for (1) by issuance of (24) additional shares payable 03/15/2007 to holders of record 03/15/2007
Reorganized as Uranium 308 Corp. 07/02/2007
Each share new Common $0.00001 par exchanged for (1.5) shares Common $0.00001 par
(See Uranium 308 Corp.)

MONTAGUE CITY ROD CO.
Name changed to Montague Rod & Reel Co. in 1927
Montague Rod & Reel Co. merged into Montague-Ocean City Rod & Reel Co. 8/1/55 which name was changed to American Tackle & Equipment Co. 6/1/57 which merged into True Temper Corp. 4/30/58 which merged into Allegheny Ludlum Steel Corp. 7/31/67 which name changed to Allegheny Ludlum Industries, Inc. 4/24/70 which name changed to Allegheny International Inc. 4/29/81
(See Allegheny International Inc.)

MONTAGUE GOLD MINES LTD.
Bankrupt in 1939
No stockholders' equity

MONTAGUE-OCEAN CITY ROD & REEL CO. (PA)
Name changed to American Tackle & Equipment Co. 6/1/57
American Tackle & Equipment Co. merged into True Temper Corp. 4/30/58 which merged into Allegheny Ludlum Steel Corp. 7/31/67 which name changed to Allegheny Ludlum Industries, Inc. 4/24/70 which name changed to Allegheny International Inc. 4/29/81
(See Allegheny International Inc.)

MONTAGUE ROD & REEL CO. (MA)
Merged into Montague-Ocean City Rod & Reel Co. 8/1/55
Each share Preferred $100 par exchanged for (2) shares $1.50 Preferred $30 par
Each share Common no par exchanged for (0.04) share $1.50 Preferred $30 par
Montague-Ocean City Rod & Reel Co. name changed to American Tackle & Equipment Co. 6/1/57 which merged into True Temper Corp. 4/30/58 which merged into Allegheny Ludlum Steel Corp. 7/31/67 which name changed to Allegheny Ludlum Industries, Inc. 4/24/70 which name changed to Allegheny International Inc. 4/29/81
(See Allegheny International Inc.)

MONTAN CAP CORP (BC)
Merged into Montan Mining Corp. 03/09/2015
Each share Common no par exchanged for (1) share Common no par

MONTANA ALPHA BUILDING CORP. OF SIGMA PHI EPSILON (MT)
Charter expired by time limitation 2/8/61

MONTANA-CANADIAN OIL CORP. (DE)
Merged into Pan-American Petroleum & Sulphur Corp. share for share 05/25/1956
Pan-American Petroleum & Sulphur Corp. name changed to Petroleum & Sulphur Development Co. 01/03/1957 which recapitalized as Mining Royalty Corp. 02/01/1958 which name changed to First U.S. Southern Corp. 10/10/1960
(See First U.S. Southern Corp.)

MONTANA CHEMICAL & MILLING CORP. (DE)
Charter revoked for non-payment of taxes 4/1/61

MONTANA CITIES GAS CO.
Merged into Montana-Dakota Utilities Co. in 1936
Each (3) shares Common no par exchanged for (1) share Common $10 par
Montana-Dakota Utilities Co. name changed to MDU Resources Group, Inc. 4/25/85

MONTANA CONSOLIDATED GAS & OIL CO. (WA)
Charter revoked for failure to file reports and pay fees 7/1/28

MONTANA CONSOLIDATED MINES CORP. (MT)
Adjudicated bankrupt in 1941
No stockholders' equity

MONTANA-DAKOTA POWER CO.
Merged into Montana-Dakota Utilities Co. in 1936
Each share Common no par exchanged for (1) share Common $10 par
Montana-Dakota Utilities Co. name changed to MDU Resources Group, Inc. 4/25/85

MONTANA DAKOTA UTILS CO (DE)
Common no par changed to $10 par 00/00/1935
Each share 7% Preferred $100 par exchanged for (1) share 6% Preferred $100 par and (0.2) share 5% Preferred $100 par 00/00/1936
Each share old 6% Preferred $100 par exchanged for (1.2) shares 5% Preferred $100 par 00/00/1936
Each share 6% Preferred $100 par

exchanged for (1.1) shares 5%
Preferred $100 par 10/01/1943
Common $10 par changed to $5 par
08/31/1945
5% Preferred $100 par redesignated
as 4.20% Preferred $100 par
04/01/1947 and then redesignated
as 4.20% Preferred $100 par
00/00/1951
Common $5 par changed to $15 par
04/27/1964
Common $15 par changed to $20 par
04/23/1974
Common $20 par changed to $10 par
and (1) additional share issued
01/31/1978
Name changed to MDU Resources
Group, Inc. 04/25/1985

MONTANA DE ORO CORP. (UT)
Recapitalized as Gyro Sensors
International, Inc. 11/08/1982
Each share Common $0.001 par
exchanged for (0.04) share Common
$0.001 par
(See Gyro Sensors International, Inc.)

MONTANA FLOUR MLS CO (MT)
Stock Dividends - 100% 04/20/1951;
18% 10/07/1958
100% acquired by Nebraska
Consolidated Mills as of 06/16/1971
Public interest eliminated

MONTANA GOLD MNG CO INC (ON)
Name changed to Peloton Minerals
Corp. 07/18/2016

MONTANA MINES CORP. (MT)
Name changed to Montana
Consolidated Mines Corp.
05/25/1932
(See Montana Consolidated Mines Corp.)

MONTANA MINES LTD (BC)
Recapitalized as Chatham Resources
Ltd. 10/3/73
Each share Capital Stock 50¢ par
exchanged for (0.25) share Capital
Stock no par
Chatham Resources Ltd. recapitalized
as Westmount Resources Ltd. (Old)
7/25/77
(See Westmount Resources Ltd. (Old))

MONTANA MINING LOAN & INVESTMENT CO. (MT)
Charter expired by time limitation
1/4/12

MONTANA MLS BREAD INC (DE)
Merged into Krispy Kreme
Doughnuts, Inc. 04/07/2003
Each share Common $0.001 par
exchanged for (0.1501) share
Common no par
(See Krispy Kreme Doughnuts, Inc.)

MONTANA MUTUAL COAL CO. (MT)
Charter expired 4/21/68

MONTANA NATS INTL INC (MT)
Merged into Vitamin Specialties Corp.
08/10/1994
Each share Common $0.001 par
exchanged for (0.21628) share
Common $0.001 par
Vitamin Specialties Corp. name
changed to Healthrite, Inc.
07/17/1995 which name changed to
Medifast, Inc. 02/05/2001

MONTANA OIL & GAS INC (NV)
Recapitalized as Falcon Energy Inc.
4/3/2006
Each share Common $0.0001 par
exchanged for (0.01) share Common
$0.0001 par
Falcon Energy Inc. recapitalized as
Red Truck Entertainment Inc.
2/12/2007

MONTANA PWR CAP I (DE)
Under Chapter 11 Plan of
Reorganization each 8.45%
Guaranteed Quarterly Income
Preferred Security received initial
distribution of (0.19445807) share
NorthWestern Corp. new Common
1¢ par and (0.36096384) Common
Stock Purchase expiring 11/01/2007
payable 11/01/2004 to holders of
record 10/20/2004
Each 8.45% Guaranteed Quarterly
Income Security received second
and final distribution of $3.6734242
cash payable 12/16/2008 to holders
of record 07/24/2008

MONTANA PWR CO (MT)
Reincorporated 11/30/61
Each share Common $100 par
exchanged for (5) shares Common
no par in 1929
Common no par split (3) for (1) by
issuance of (2) additional shares
6/26/59
State of incorporation changed from
(NJ) to (MT) 11/30/61
Common no par split (2) for (1) by
issuance of (1) additional share
1/31/90
Common no par split (2) for (1) by
issuance of (1) additional share
payable 8/9/99 to holders of record
7/16/99 Ex date - 8/10/99
$2.15 Preferred no par called for
redemption 12/16/96
Reorganized under the laws of
Delaware as Touch America
Holdings, Inc. 2/13/2002
Each share $6.875 Preferred no par
exchanged for (1) share $6.875
Preferred 1¢ par
Each share Common no par
exchanged for (1) share Common
1¢ par
$4.20 Preferred no par called for
redemption at $103 on 2/14/2002
$6 Preferred no par called for
redemption at $110 on 2/14/2002
(See Touch America Holdings, Inc.)

MONTANA PRECISION MNG LTD (WA)
Name changed to MPM Technologies,
Inc. 8/14/95

MONTANA SERVICE CORP.
Liquidated in 1949

MONTANA SPINDLE TOP OIL CO. (MT)
Charter expired by time limitation
10/20/56

MONTANA WESTN OIL & GAS CO (NV)
Common 10¢ par changed to 1¢ par
03/28/1969
Merged into International
Management & Research Corp.
12/20/1971
Each share Common 1¢ par
exchanged for (0.033333) share
Common 5¢ par
(See International Management & Research Corp.)

MONTANA-WYOMING GAS PIPE LINE CO. (DE)
Stock Dividends - 10% 12/31/51; 10%
12/31/52; 10% 12/31/53; 10%
12/31/54; 10% 9/30/55
Merged into Montana-Dakota Utilities
Co. 12/31/55
Each share Common $5 par
exchanged for (1) share Common
$5 par
Montana-Dakota Utilities Co. name
changed to MDU Resources Group,
Inc. 4/25/85

MONTARIO EXPLORATION LTD. (ON)
Charter cancelled 00/00/1957

MONTAUBAN MINES LTD. (ON)
Acquired by United Montauban Mines
Ltd. in 1953
Each share Capital Stock no par
exchanged for (0.5) share Capital
Stock $1 par
United Montauban Mines Ltd.
recapitalized as Satellite Metal
Mines Ltd. 7/30/58 which
recapitalized as Satellite
Consolidated Metals Ltd. 6/23/83
which name changed to Phoenix
Gold Mines Ltd. 6/30/86
(See Phoenix Gold Mines Ltd.)

MONTAUK BEACH DEVELOPMENT CORP.
Reorganized as Montauk Beach Co.,
Inc. in 1938
No stockholders' equity

MONTAUK BEACH INC (NY)
Voluntarily dissolved 7/7/97
Details not available

MONTCALM RES INC (QC)
Name changed to Pacific Tiger
Energy Inc. 06/12/1997
Pacific Tiger Energy Inc. recapitalized
as Tiger Petroleum Inc. 12/30/2004
(See Tiger Petroleum Inc.)

MONTCALM VINTNERS INC (DE)
Name changed to Filice Winery, Inc.
06/18/1975
Filice Winery, Inc. name changed to
Crown Companies, Inc. 03/04/1986
which name changed to Crown Gold
Companies Group, Ltd. 09/25/1987
which recapitalized as Tigershark
Enterprises Inc. 10/28/1997 which
name changed to Great White
Marine & Recreation, Inc.
05/14/1998
(See Great White Marine & Recreation, Inc.)

MONTCLAIR BANCORP INC (DE)
Acquired by Collective Bancorp., Inc.
4/1/93
Each share Common 1¢ par
exchanged for $24.15 cash

MONTCLAIR NATL BK & TR CO (MONCLAIR, NJ)
Common $10 par changed to $5 par
and (1) additional share issued
01/29/1963
Stock Dividends - 12% 01/30/1961;
100% 05/12/1969
Merged into American National Bank
& Trust (Montclair, NJ) 07/10/1970
Each share Common $5 par
exchanged for (1.2) shares Common
$4 par
American National Bank & Trust
(Montclair, NJ) reorganized as
Princeton American Bancorp
01/01/1972 which name changed to
Horizon Bancorp 12/31/1973
(See Horizon Bancorp)

MONTCLAIR SVGS BK (MONTCLAIR, NJ)
Reorganized under the laws of
Delaware as Montclair Bancorp, Inc.
3/1/89
Each share Common $2 par
exchanged for (1) share Common
1¢ par
(See Montclair Bancorp, Inc.)

MONTCLAIR TRUST CO. (MONTCLAIR, NJ)
Stock Dividend - 10% 2/17/55
Merged into Montclair National Bank
& Trust Co. (Montclair, N.J.)
12/20/57
Each share Capital Stock $10 par
exchanged for (1-1/11) share Capital
Stock $10 par
Montclair National Bank & Trust Co.
(Montclair, N.J.) merged into
American National Bank & Trust
(Montclair, N.J.) 7/10/70 which
reorganized as Princeton American
Bancorp 1/1/72 which name
changed to Horizon Bancorp
12/31/73
(See Horizon Bancorp)

MONTCLERG MINES LTD. (ON)
Recapitalized as Consolidated
Montclerg Mines Ltd. 02/23/1966
Each share Capital Stock $1 par
exchanged for (1/3) share Capital
Stock $1 par
Consolidated Montclerg Mines Ltd.
recapitalized as Montclerg
Resources Ltd. 11/25/1986 which
recapitalized as Prospectors Alliance
Corp. 09/17/1996 which
recapitalized as Explorers Alliance
Corp. 10/13/2000
(See Explorers Alliance Corp.)

MONTCLERG RES LTD (ON)
Recapitalized as Prospectors Alliance
Corp. 09/17/1996
Each share Common no par
exchanged for (0.5) share Common
no par
Prospectors Alliance Corp.
recapitalized as Explorers Alliance
Corp. 10/13/2000
(See Explorers Alliance Corp.)

MONTCO COPPER CORP. LTD. (ON)
Declared dissolved 12/18/61
No stockholders' equity

MONTDONO GOLD MINES, LTD. (ON)
Charter cancelled 00/00/1959

MONTE CARLO GOLD MINES LTD (ON)
Reincorporated 10/31/1987
Place of incorporation changed from
(AB) to (ON) 10/31/1987
Recapitalized as Exxadon Technology
Corp. 07/12/1993
Each share Common no par
exchanged for (0.1) share Common
no par
Exxadon Technology Corp. name
changed to EWMC International Inc.
12/03/1996 which name changed to
Environmental Waste International
Inc. 09/27/2001

MONTE CARLO RES LTD (BC)
Name changed to Provini (C.R.)
Financial Services Corp. 5/17/89
Provini (C.R.) Financial Services
Corp. recapitalized as DataWave
Vending Inc. 1/24/94 which name
changed to DataWave Systems Inc.
(BC) 1/15/97 which reincorporated in
Yukon 9/19/2000 which
reincorporated in Delaware
2/23/2005
(See DataWave Systems Inc.)

MONTE CHRISTO RES LTD (BC)
Name changed to International
Display Corp. 1/31/86
(See International Display Corp.)

MONTE CRISTO CORP (AZ)
Reincorporated under the laws of
Nevada as Savings Network, Inc.
04/06/1987
Savings Network, Inc. name changed
to Woodington Group, Inc.
08/30/1989
(See Woodington Group, Inc.)

MONTE CRISTO CORP (NV)
Charter revoked for failure to file
reports and pay fees 03/04/1974

MONTE CRISTO URANIUM CORP. (NV)
Recapitalized as Monte Cristo Corp.
08/14/1962
Each share Common 1¢ par
exchanged for (0.1) share Common
10¢ par
(See Monte Cristo Corp.)

MONTE GRANDE EXPLS LTD (AB)
Merged into MSR Exploration Ltd.
(AB) 05/27/1981
Each share Common no par
exchanged for (0.66666666) share
Common no par
MSR Exploration Ltd. (AB)
reincorporated in Delaware
10/31/1997 which merged into MSR
Exploration Ltd. (New) 10/31/1997
which merged into Quicksilver
Resources Inc. 03/04/1999
(See Quicksilver Resources Inc.)

MONTEAGLE EXPLS LTD (QC)
Declared dissolved for failure to file
reports or pay fees in 1978

MONTEAGLE MINERALS LTD (ON)
Common $1 par changed to no par 9/27/71
Reorganized under the laws of Quebec as Monteagle Explorations Ltd. 12/22/71
Each share Common no par exchanged for (1) share Common no par
(See Monteagle Explorations Ltd.)

MONTEBELLO FURNITURE INDS LTD (NY)
Dissolved by proclamation 6/23/93

MONTEBELLO RES LTD (BC)
Recapitalized as First American Capital Group Inc. (BC) 10/7/92
Each share Common no par exchanged for (0.2) share Common no par
First American Capital Group Inc. (BC) reincorporated in Wyoming as Rosetta Technologies Inc. 6/23/93 which name changed to Tanisys Technology, Inc. 7/11/94
(See Tanisys Technology, Inc.)

MONTEC HLDGS INC (CANADA)
Name changed to Datex Technologies Corp. 09/02/2009
(See Datex Technologies Corp.)

MONTECATINI EDISON S P A (ITALY)
Each (40) old ADR's for Unsponsored Capital Stock exchanged for (7) new Unsponsored ADR's for Capital Stock 06/19/1984
Stock Dividend - 10% 08/30/1985
Recapitalized as Montedison S.p.A. 06/19/1987
Each new Unsponsored ADR for Capital Stock exchanged for (0.1) Sponsored ADR for Ordinary
(See Montedison S.p.A.)

MONTECATINI SOCIETA GENERALE PER L'INDUSTRIA MINERARIA E CHIMICA ANONIMA (ITALY)
Stock Dividend - 20% 06/12/1962
Merged into Montecatini Edison S.p.A. 07/07/1966
Each ADR for Capital Stock 5000 Lire par exchanged for (6.5) ADR's for Capital Stock 1000 Lire par
Montecatini Edison S.P.A. recapitalized as Montedison S.p.A. 06/19/1987
(See Montedison S.p.A.)

MONTEDISON S P A (ITALY)
Each old Sponsored ADR for Ordinary 1000 Lire par exchanged for (0.74) new Sponsored ADR for Ordinary 1000 Lire par 7/22/96
Each old Sponsored ADR for Savings Shares 1000 Lire par exchanged for (0.74) new Sponsored ADR for Savings Shares 1000 Lire par 7/22/96
Each new Sponsored ADR for Ordinary 1000 Lire par exchanged for (0.74) Sponsored ADR for Ordinary 1000 Lire par 6/21/99
Each new Sponsored ADR for Savings Shares 1000 Lire par exchanged for (0.74) Sponsored ADR for Ordinary 1000 Lire par 6/21/99
Merged into Compart S.P.A. 1/5/2001
Each Sponsored ADR for Ordinary 1000 Lire par exchanged for $26.2463 cash
Each Sponsored ADR for Savings Shares 1000 Lire par exchanged for $13.9375 cash

MONTEGO CORP (NV)
Name changed to Calkins Industries, Inc. 06/30/1986
Calkins Industries, Inc. recapitalized as Compliance Industries, Inc. 11/23/1993 which recapitalized as Vintage Properties Inc. 04/03/1995 which name changed to Xecom Corp. 10/24/1995 which name changed to AirStar Technologies, Inc. 04/28/1998
(See AirStar Technologies, Inc.)

MONTEGO MINES LTD (ON)
Charter cancelled and declared dissolved for failure to file returns and pay fees 12/26/1973

MONTEGO RES LTD (AB)
Name changed to Canadian Majestic Resources Ltd. 01/05/1988
Canadian Majestic Resources Ltd. merged into Chancellor Energy Resources Inc. 12/05/1988 which merged into HCO Energy Ltd. 04/02/1996 which merged into Pinnacle Resources Ltd. (New) 10/20/1997 which merged into Renaissance Energy Ltd. 07/16/1998 which merged into Husky Energy Inc. 08/25/2000

MONTEJAS ENERGY RES INC (CO)
Merged into Seahawk Oil International, Inc. 02/24/1984
Each share Common $0.001 par exchanged for approximately (0.01867762) share Common no par
Seahawk Oil International, Inc. name changed to Seahawk Capital Corp. 11/28/1989 which name changed to Dynamicweb Enterprises Inc. 05/14/1996 which name changed to eB2B Commerce, Inc. 04/18/2000 which reorganized as Mediavest, Inc. (NJ) 02/08/2005 which reincorporated in Delaware as Mandalay Media, Inc. 11/21/2007 which name changed to NeuMedia, Inc. 06/21/2010 which name changed to Mandalay Digital Group, Inc. 02/28/2012 which name changed to Digital Turbine, Inc. 01/20/2015

MONTEK ASSOCIATES, INC. (UT)
Merged into Model Engineering & Manufacturing Corp. 8/9/60
Each share Common $1 par exchanged for (0.097540) share Common no par
Model Engineering & Manufacturing Corp. name changed to Memcor, Inc. 8/12/65 which merged into LTV Electrosystems, Inc. 4/19/67 which name changed to E-Systems Inc. 4/27/72
(See E-Systems Inc.)

MONTEMOR RES INC (ON)
Name changed to European Gold Resources Inc. (ONT) 8/11/97
European Gold Resources Inc. (ONT) reincorporated in Canada as Galantas Gold Corp. 5/10/2004

MONTERAY MNG GROUP LTD (AUSTRALIA)
Name changed 09/26/2011
Name changed from Monteray Group Ltd. to Monteray Mining Group Ltd. 09/26/2011
Name changed to Norwood Systems Ltd. 03/31/2016

MONTEREY BAY BANCORP INC (DE)
Common 1¢ par split (5) for (4) by issuance of (0.25) additional share payable 07/31/1998 to holders of record 07/09/1998
Merged into UnionBanCal Corp. (CA) 06/30/2003
Each share Common 1¢ par exchanged for (0.5875) share Common no par and $1.6557 cash
UnionBanCal Corp. (CA) reincorporated in Delaware 09/30/2003
(See UnionBanCal Corp. (DE))

MONTEREY BAY TECH INC (NV)
Name changed to SecureLogic Corp. 05/20/2005
(See SecureLogic Corp.)

MONTEREY CAP CORP (CO)
Name changed to O'Deli Corp. 09/14/1988
O'Deli Corp. name changed to Culinary Capital Corp. 11/29/1990 which recapitalized as Centra Capital Corp. (CO) 04/12/1996 which reincorporated in Delaware 04/24/1996 which reincorporated in Nevada 07/02/1998
(See Centra Capital Corp.)

MONTEREY CAP INC (QC)
Merged into Nymox Pharmaceutical Corp. (Canada) 12/18/1995
Each share Common no par exchanged for (0.5) share Common no par
Nymox Pharmaceutical Corp. (Canada) reincorporated in Bahamas 11/20/2015

MONTEREY CNTY BK (MONTEREY, CA)
Common $6.75 par changed to $4.50 par and (0.5) additional share issued 12/14/1980
Common $4.50 par changed to no par 09/00/1987
Under plan of reorganization each share Common no par automatically became (1) share Northern California Bancorp Common no par 12/29/1995

MONTEREY ENERGY CORP (AB)
Acquired by Constellation Oil & Gas Ltd. 06/04/1999
Each share Class A Common no par exchanged for (1.1) shares Class A Common no par
Constellation Oil & Gas Ltd. recapitalized as International Sovereign Energy Corp. (AB) 05/31/2000 which reorganized in Canada as Wi2Wi Corp. 02/05/2013

MONTEREY ENTERPRISES INC (CA)
Common $1 par changed to 50¢ par and (1) additional share issued 03/03/1972
Assets foreclosed on 04/02/1977
No stockholders' equity

MONTEREY EXPL LTD (AB)
Merged into Pengrowth Corp. 09/15/2010
Each share Common no par exchanged for either (0.8298) Exchangeable Share no par or (0.8298) Pengrowth Energy Trust Trust Unit no par
Note: Unexchanged certificates were cancelled and became without value 09/15/2014
(See each company's listing)

MONTEREY FARMING CORP (CA)
Acquired by MFC Acquisition Corp. 03/09/1988
Each share Common no par exchanged for $6.50 cash

MONTEREY GOURMET FOODS INC (DE)
Reincorporated 08/07/1996
Name changed 12/15/2004
State of incorporation changed from (CA) to (DE) and Common no par changed to $0.001 par 08/07/1996
Name changed from Monterey Pasta Co. to Monterey Gourmet Foods, Inc. 12/15/2004
Acquired by Pulmuone U.S.A., Inc. 12/14/2009
Each share Common $0.001 par exchanged for $2.70 cash

MONTEREY HOMES CORP (MD)
Name changed to Meritage Corp. 9/16/98
Meritage Corp. name changed to Meritage Homes Corp. 9/14/2004

MONTEREY LIFE SYS INC (DE)
Name changed to MLS Industries, Inc. 12/7/72 which name changed back to Monterey Life Systems, Inc. 12/10/73
Merged into Berkeley Bio-Engineering, Inc. (CA) 12/17/75
Each share Common 10¢ par exchanged for (1.2) shares Common 5¢ par
Berkeley Bio-Engineering, Inc. (CA) reincorporated in Delaware as Berkeley Bio-Medical, Inc. 2/14/77
(See Berkeley Bio-Medical, Inc.)

MONTEREY MINING CO. LTD. (BC)
Charter cancelled in 1968

MONTEREY MTG CO (CA)
Charter suspended for failure to file reports and pay fees 04/01/1981

MONTEREY NURSING INNS INC (DE)
Name changed to Monterey Life Systems, Inc. 5/13/70
Monterey Life Systems, Inc. name changed to MLS Industries, Inc. 12/7/72 which name changed back to Monterey Life Systems, Inc. 12/10/73 which merged into Berkeley Bio-Engineering, Inc. (CA) 12/17/75 which reincorporated in Delaware as Berkeley Bio-Medical, Inc. 2/14/77
(See Berkeley Bio-Medical, Inc.)

MONTEREY OIL CO. (DE)
Liquidation completed
Each share Common $1 par received initial distribution of $34 cash 1/18/61
Each share Common $1 par received second distribution of $7 cash 3/13/61
Each share Common $1 par exchanged for third and final distribution of $1.0465 cash 8/31/61

MONTEREY PARK LD CORP (CA)
Liquidated 2/26/85
Details not available

MONTEREY PETE 1971 LTD (AB)
Recapitalized 11/15/1971
Recapitalized from Monterey Petroleum Corp. Ltd. to Monterey Petroleum Corp. (1971) Ltd. 11/15/1971
Each share Capital Stock no par exchanged for (0.1) share Class A Stock no par
Struck off register for failure to file annual returns 04/30/1981

MONTEREY PROPERTIES CO. (CA)
Incorporated 05/27/1957
Charter suspended for failure to file reports and pay taxes 10/01/1969

MONTEREY RES INC (DE)
Merged into Texaco Inc. 11/4/97
Each share Common 1¢ par exchanged for (0.3471) share Common $6.25 par
Texaco Inc. merged into ChevronTexaco Corp. 10/9/2001 which name changed to Chevron Corp. 5/9/2005

MONTEREY RY LT & PWR CO (CANADA)
Involuntarily dissolved 12/16/1980

MONTEREY URANIUM CORP. (DE)
Acquired by Aneth Corp. 08/26/1957
Each share Common 10¢ par exchanged for (0.01) share Common 50¢ par
Aneth Corp. merged into Aneth United, Inc. 04/30/1969
(See Aneth United, Inc.)

MONTEX APPAREL INDS LTD (ON)
Common no par split (3) for (1) by issuance of (2) additional shares 7/18/66
In receivership 5/8/70 and all operations ceased 7/17/70
No Preference or Common stockholders' equity per receivers opinion 3/25/71

MONTEX HOLDINGS LTD. (ON)
Merged into Montex Apparel Industries Ltd. 7/2/65
Each share 5-1/2% Conv. 1st Preference $8 par exchanged for (1) share 5-1/2% Conv. 1st Preference $8 par
(See Montex Apparel Industries Ltd.)

MONTEX OIL & GAS CORP. (DE)
No longer in existence having become inoperative and void for non-payment of taxes 10/1/59

MONTEZUMA MINING CO. (CO)
Merged into Fall River Industries, Inc. 12/18/70
Each share Common 1¢ par exchanged for (2.0291) shares Capital Stock 1¢ par
Fall River Industries, Inc. proclaimed dissolved 1/31/77

MONTEZUMA URANIUM, INC. (CO)
Merged into Lisbon Valley Uranium Co. on a (1) for (4) basis in 1955
Lisbon Valley Uranium Co. recapitalized as Ocean Data Industries, Inc. 12/20/68 which name changed to Universal Investment Properties, Inc. 10/18/72
(See Universal Investment Properties, Inc.)

MONTGARY EXPLORATIONS LTD. (ON)
Name changed 06/23/1955
Name changed from Montgary Petroleums Corp. Ltd. to Montgary Explorations Ltd. 06/23/1955
Recapitalized as Chemalloy Minerals Ltd. 01/06/1960
Each share Capital Stock $1 par exchanged for (0.4) share Capital Stock $1 par
Chemalloy Minerals Ltd. recapitalized as International Chemalloy Corp. 11/21/1974 which recapitalized as Denbridge Capital Corp. (ON) 01/20/1986 which reincorporated in Canada 02/24/1994 which recapitalized as Atlantis Systems Corp. 06/11/2001
(See Atlantis Systems Corp.)

MONTGOMERY BANCORP INC (DE)
Stock Dividend - 25% 1/3/89
Name changed to Allegiance Banc Corp. 6/26/91
Allegiance Banc Corp. merged into F & M National Corp. 10/1/96 which merged into BB&T Corp. 8/9/2001

MONTGOMERY BKG & TR CO (ROCKVILLE, MD)
Merged into University National Bank (Rockville, MD) 07/06/1970
Each share Capital Stock $10 par exchanged for (1.2) shares Capital Stock $8 par
(See University National Bank (Rockville, MD))

MONTGOMERY-BROOKS CO., INC. (MA)
State charter of incorporation cancelled for failure to pay annual taxes 3/3/27

MONTGOMERY CO (CT)
Preferred Ser. A $100 par called for redemption 04/30/1964
Common $10 par reclassified as Class A Common $20 par 04/30/1969
Name change to M Corp. 01/06/1989
(See M Corp.)

MONTGOMERY COUNTY BANK & TRUST CO. (NORRISTOWN, PA)
Merged into Continental Bank & Trust Co. (Norristown, PA) 08/02/1965
Each share Capital Stock $10 par exchanged for (1.875) shares Capital Stock $5 par
Continental Bank & Trust Co. (Norristown, PA) name changed to Continental Bank (Norristown, PA) 07/17/1969 which name changed to Continental Bancorp, Inc. 05/01/1982 which merged into Midlantic Corp. 01/30/1987 which merged into PNC Bank Corp. 12/31/1995 which name changed to PNC Financial Services Group, Inc. 03/15/2000

MONTGOMERY COUNTY TRUST CO. (AMSTERDAM, NY)
Common $25 par changed to $6.25 par and (3) additional shares issued 04/28/1970
Acquired by Bankers Trust New York Corp. 03/01/1973
Each share Common $6.25 par exchanged for (1.5071) shares Common $10 par
Bankers Trust New York Corp. name changed to Bankers Trust Corp. 04/23/1998
(See Bankers Trust Corp.)

MONTGOMERY FINL CORP (IN)
Merged into Union Community Bancorp 01/02/2002
Each share Common 1¢ par exchanged for $15 cash

MONTGOMERY LD INVT & DEV CORP (MD)
Charter annulled by proclamation 1/28/75

MONTGOMERY NATL BK (ROCKY HILL, NJ)
Bank failed 06/30/1990
Stockholders' equity unlikely

MONTGOMERY REAL ESTATE SVC INC (NV)
Recapitalized as Man Shing Agricultural Holdings, Inc. 09/02/2009
Each share Common $0.001 par exchanged for (0.01) share Common $0.001 par

MONTGOMERY STR INCOME SECS INC (DE)
Completely liquidated 12/30/2015
Each share Common $1 par exchanged for first and final distribution of $17.741 cash

MONTGOMERY WARD & CO INC (IL)
Common $10 par changed to no par in 1927
Common no par split (2) for (1) by issuance of (1) additional share 5/31/56
Merged into Marcor Inc. 11/1/68
Each share Class A no par exchanged for $140 principal amount of 6-1/2% Subord. Debentures due 1988
Each share Common no par exchanged for (1) share Common $1 par
Marcor Inc. merged into Mobil Corp. 7/1/76 which merged into Exxon Mobil Corp. 11/30/99

MONTHLY INCOME SHS INC (MD)
Name changed to Bullock Monthly Income Shares, Inc. 1/14/85
Bullock Monthly Income Shares, Inc. reorganized as Alliance Bond Fund (MA) 3/13/87 which reorganized in Maryland as Alliance Bond Fund, Inc. 12/7/87 which name changed to AllianceBernstein Bond Fund, Inc. 3/31/2003

MONTICELLO LIFE INS CO (IL)
Acquired by National Capitol Life Insurance Co. (PA) 12/1/66
Each share Common $1.60 par exchanged for (0.24003) share Capital Stock $1 par
National Capitol Life Insurance Co. (PA) acquired by National Capitol Life Insurance Co. (AL) 4/8/68
(See National Capitol Life Insurance Co. (AL))

MONTICELLO TOBACCO CO., INC. (NY)
Charter revoked for failure to file reports and pay fees 12/15/50

MONTOCO PETROLEUMS LTD. (ON)
Recapitalized as Southern Union Oils Ltd. on a (0.2) for (1) basis 1/20/55
Southern Union Oils Ltd. charter cancelled in April 1975

MONTORO GOLD INC (BC)
Merged into Pegasus Gold Inc. 8/20/84
Each (2-2/3) shares Common no par exchanged for (1) share Common no par
(See Pegasus Gold Inc.)

MONTORO RES INC (BC)
Common no par split (2) for (1) by issuance of (1) additional share 1/9/89
Recapitalized as International Montoro Resources Inc. 10/12/2005
Each share Common no par exchanged for (0.2) share Common no par

MONTOUR BK (DANVILLE, PA)
Merged into Omega Financial Corp. 8/1/95
Each share Common $5 par exchanged for $12 cash

MONTPELIER & BARRE LIGHT & POWER CO.
Dissolved in 1927

MONTPELIER RE HLDGS LTD (BERMUDA)
8.875% Non-Cum. Preferred Ser. A $0.16666666 par called for redemption at $26 plus $0.554688 accrued dividends on 06/29/2015
Merged into Endurance Specialty Holdings Ltd. 07/31/2015
Each share Common $0.16666666 par exchanged for (0.472) share Ordinary $1 par
(See Endurance Specialty Holdings Ltd.)

MONTREAL AIRCRAFT INDUSTRIES, LTD.
Liquidation completed in 1944

MONTREAL CITY & DIST SVGS BK (MONTREAL, QUE)
Common $100 par changed to $10 par and (9) additional shares issued 9/1/44
Common $10 par changed to $1 par and (9) additional shares issued 12/13/63
Common $1 par changed to no par and (1) additional share issued 8/31/83
Common no par split (2) for (1) by issuance of (1) additional share 2/19/87
Name changed to Laurentian Bank of Canada (Montreal, QUE) 9/28/87

MONTREAL COTTONS LTD.
Acquired by Dominion Textile Co., Ltd. on a share for share basis in 1948
Dominion Textile Co., Ltd. name changed to Dominion Textile Ltd.-Dominion Textile Ltee. 10/31/69 which name changed to Dominion Textile Inc. 1/2/79
(See Dominion Textile Inc.)

MONTREAL LIGHT HEAT & POWER CONSOLIDATED
Acquired by Quebec Hydro-Electric Commission at a price of $25 per share 1947

MONTREAL LOAN & MORTGAGE CO.
Acquired by Canada Permanent Mortgage Corp. 00/00/1946
Details not available

MONTREAL LOCOMOTIVE WORKS, LTD. (CANADA)
Name changed to MLW-Worthington Ltd.-MLW-Worthington Ltee. 6/7/68
MLW-Worthington Ltd.-MLW-Worthington Ltee. name changed to Bombardier-MLW Ltd.-Bombardier-MLW Ltee. 9/28/76 which name changed to Bombardier Inc. 7/20/78

MONTREAL REFRIGERATING & STORAGE LTD (CANADA)
Each share $3 Preferred no par exchanged for (1) share 5% 1st

Preferred $30 par and (1) share 2nd Preferred $20 par in 1944 2nd Preferred $20 par called for redemption 8/11/47
5% 1st Preferred $30 par called for redemption 11/15/49
5% Preferred $10 par called for redemption 12/31/52
Common no par reclassified as Class B no par plus a stock dividend of (1) share 6-1/2% Class A $22 par paid 12/31/59
Class B no par reclassified as Common no par 11/25/63
6-1/2% Class A $22 par called for redemption 12/17/63
Dissolved 12/6/91
Details not available

MONTREAL SVCS CO (NV)
Name changed to iMetrik M2M Solutions Inc. 09/22/2010
iMetrik M2M Solutions Inc. name changed to Wiless Controls Inc. 02/28/2013 which name changed to Next Galaxy Corp. 08/19/2014

MONTREAL TELEGRAPH CO. (QC)
Liquidation completed 7/20/55

MONTREAL TRAMWAYS CO.
Acquired by Montreal Transportation Commission at a price of $60 per share in 1951

MONTREAL TR CO (MONTREAL, QUE)
Each share Capital Stock $25 par exchanged for (5) shares Capital Stock $5 par in 1951
Capital Stock $5 par changed to $1 par and (4) additional shares issued 2/19/65
Merged into Montreal Trustco Inc. 11/19/82
Each share Capital Stock $1 par exchanged for (2.5) shares Common Ser. A no par
(See Montreal Trustco Inc.)

MONTREAL TRUSTCO INC (QC)
Common Ser. A no par reclassified as Common no par 05/10/1920
Subordinate Ser. B no par reclassified as Common no par 05/10/1985
Common no par split (2) for (1) by issuance of (1) additional share 07/11/1986
Merged into BCE Inc. 06/01/1989
Each share Common no par exchanged for $23.50 cash
Adjustable Rate Preferred Ser. B no par called for redemption 07/30/1996
Public interest eliminated

MONTREAL WATER & POWER CO.
Acquired by City of Montreal in 1929

MONTREUX CAP CORP (BC)
Each share old Common no par exchanged for (0.4) share new Common no par 04/16/2014
Each share new Common no par exchanged again for (0.5) share new Common no par 09/29/2016
Reorganized under the laws of Nevada as Assure Holdings Corp. 05/29/2017
Each share new Common no par exchanged for (0.33333333) share Common $0.001 par

MONTROSE CHEMICAL CO. (DE)
Reincorporated 03/01/1961
State of incorporation changed from (NJ) to (DE) 03/01/1961
Merged into Baldwin-Montrose Chemical Co., Inc. 06/26/1961
Each share Common $1 par exchanged for (0.7) share $1 Conv. Preferred no par
Baldwin-Montrose Chemical Co., Inc. merged into Chris-Craft Industries, Inc. 06/19/1968 which merged into News Corp., Ltd. 07/31/2001 which reorganized as News Corp. (Old) 11/03/2004 which name changed to

Twenty-First Century Fox, Inc. 07/01/2013

MONTROSE ENERGY LTD (BC)
Recapitalized as Lunar Resources Ltd. 01/20/1984
Each share Common no par exchanged for (0.2) share Common no par
(See Lunar Resources Ltd.)

MONTROSE-IRVING CORP. (IL)
Dissolved 10/4/57

MONTROSE NATL PARTNERS INC (TX)
Name changed to Cross Atlantic Life & Science Technology Inc. 8/19/2005
Science Technology Inc. name changed to Deep Earth Resources, Inc. 5/5/2006

MONTROSE VENTURES INC (DE)
Name changed to Java Group, Inc. 08/25/1993
Java Group, Inc. name changed to Consolidated General Corp. 04/05/2005 which recapitalized as GoldCorp Holdings, Co. 08/17/2007 which name changed to Goldland Holdings, Co. 10/20/2010 which name changed to Bravo Multinational Inc. 04/07/2016

MONTRUSCO BOLTON INC (CANADA)
Name changed 6/1/99
Name changed from Montrusco Associates Inc. to Montrusco Bolton Inc. 6/1/99
Merged into First International Asset Management Inc. 11/8/2000
Each share Common no par exchanged for $14.25 cash

MONTRUSCO BOLTON INCOME & GROWTH FD (ON)
Name changed to First Asset Income & Growth Fund 09/20/2007
First Asset Income & Growth Fund merged into Criterion Global Dividend Fund 12/29/2009 which name changed to First Asset Global Dividend Fund 06/04/2012

MONTT INTL CORP (NY)
SEC revoked common stock registration 09/08/2008
Stockholders' equity unlikely

MONTZONE MINES, LTD. (ON)
Charter cancelled 3/10/58
Stock is valueless

MONUMENT ENERGY SVCS INC (TX)
Recapitalized 09/19/1980
Recapitalized from Monument Energy Corp. to Monument Energy Services, Inc. 09/19/1980
Each share Common 1¢ par exchanged for (0.5) share Common 1¢ par
Merged into Alliance Well Service, Inc. 09/28/1984
Each share Common 1¢ par exchanged for (1.1631) shares Common 1¢ par
Alliance Well Service, Inc. recapitalized as Alliance Northwest Industries, Inc. 07/30/1993
(See Alliance Northwest Industries, Inc.)

MONUMENT NATL BK (RIDGE CREST, CA)
Acquired by a private investor 7/3/97
Each share Common $5 par exchanged for $6 cash

MONUMENT RES INC (BC)
Recapitalized as Westwin Ventures Inc. 03/03/1992
Each share Common no par exchanged for (0.25) share Common no par
Westwin Ventures Inc. recapitalized as New Westwin Ventures Inc. 01/06/1995 which name changed to Arimex Mining Corp. 07/29/1997

which recapitalized as International Arimex Resources Inc. 02/22/1999 which name changed to WestCan Uranium Corp. 09/10/2007

MONUMENTAL CORP (MD)
Common $5 par and Class B Common $5 par split (3) for (2) by issuance of (0.5) additional share respectively 11/05/1971
Common $5 par and Class B Common $5 par changed to $3.50 par and (0.5) additional share issued respectively 06/04/1973
Under plan of partial liquidation each share old Common $3.50 par exchanged for (0.48) share new Common $3.50 par and (0.52) Monumental Properties Trust Unit of Bene. Int. no par 06/30/1978
Under plan of partial liquidation each share old Class B Common $3.50 par exchanged for (0.48) share new Class B Common $3.50 par and (0.52) Monumental Properties Trust Unit of Bene. Int. no par 06/30/1978
Under plan of partial liquidation each share old Common $3.50 par exchanged for (0.48) share new Common $3.50 par and (0.52) Monumental Properties Trust Unit of Bene. Int. no par 06/30/1978
New Class B Common $3.50 par reclassified as new Common $3.50 par 12/31/1979
$2 Conv. Preferred Ser. A $10 par called for redemption 07/15/1986
Merged into Aegon N.V. 09/03/1986
Each share new Common $3.50 par exchanged for $56 cash

MONUMENTAL LIFE INS CO (MD)
Capital Stock $10 par changed to $5 par and (1) additional share issued plus a 25% stock dividend paid 04/14/1964
Stock Dividends - 50% 07/25/1944; 33-1/3% 08/09/1949; 25% 08/14/1952; 20% 08/19/1955; 33-1/3% 08/19/1958; 25% 08/29/1961; 20% 06/09/1967
Each share Capital Stock $5 par exchanged for (0.001) share Common $1,000 par 04/24/1970
Public interest eliminated

MONUMENTAL MARKETING INC (WY)
Reincorporated under the laws of Nevada as Safer Shot, Inc. (NV) 02/08/2008
Safer Shot, Inc. (NV) reincorporated in Florida 03/02/2015

MONUMENTAL PPTYS TR (MD)
In process of liquidation
Each Unit of Bene. Int. no par received initial distribution of $10 cash 8/15/79
Each Unit of Bene. Int. no par received second distribution of $20 cash 9/15/79
Each Unit of Bene. Int. no par received third distribution of $35 cash 10/15/79
Each Unit of Bene. Int. no par received fourth distribution of $4 cash 1/15/80
Each Unit of Bene. Int. no par received fifth distribution of $1.50 cash 6/25/81
Each Unit of Bene. Int. no par received sixth distribution of $1 cash 7/21/82
Each Unit of Bene. Int. no par received seventh distribution of $0.80 cash 5/15/85
Each Unit of Bene. Int. no par exchanged for eighth and final distribution of $0.09 cash 12/15/85

MONUMENTAL RADIO CO. (MD)
Each share Common no par exchanged for (8) shares Common $1 par in 1935
Liquidation completed 10/10/57

MONVERT FINL CORP (NV)
Name changed to Transworld Network Corp. 05/14/1987
(See Transworld Network Corp.)

MONY FD INC (NY)
Merged into Massachusetts Financial Development Fund, Inc. 12/29/1981
Each share Capital Stock $1 par exchanged for (1.032914) shares Common $1 par
Massachusetts Financial Development Fund, Inc. name changed to MFS Research Fund 02/01/1992
(See MFS Research Fund)

MONY GROUP INC (DE)
Merged into AXA Financial Inc. 07/08/2004
Each share Common 1¢ par exchanged for $31 cash

MONY MORTGAGE INVESTORS (MA)
Shares of Bene. Int. no par changed to 50¢ par 8/24/72
Shares of Bene. Int. 50¢ par reclassified as Common 50¢ par 11/10/76
Name changed to Mony Real Estate Investors 11/4/85
Mony Real Estate Investors assets transferred to MYM Liquidating Trust 12/1/90
(See MYM Liquidating Trust)

MONY REAL ESTATE INVS (MA)
Liquidation completed
Each share Common 50¢ par received initial distribution of $0.18 cash 1/16/89
Each share Common 50¢ par received second distribution of $0.18 cash 4/17/89
Each share Common 50¢ par received third distribution of $0.18 cash 7/17/89
Each share Common 50¢ par received fourth distribution of $0.18 cash 10/16/89
Each share Common 50¢ par received fifth distribution of $0.29 cash 1/15/90
Each share Common 50¢ par received sixth distribution of $2 cash 4/16/90
Each share Common 50¢ par received seventh distribution of $1 cash 7/20/90
Each share Common 50¢ par received eighth distribution of $1 cash 10/15/90
Assets transferred to MYM Liquidating Trust and each share Common 50¢ par reclassified as Units of Bene. Int. no par 12/1/90
(See MYM Liquidating Trust)

MONZA CAP CORP (CO)
Name changed to Touchfon Int'l 04/19/1989
(See Touchfon Int'l)

MONZA VENTURES INC (NV)
Common $0.001 par split (7) for (1) by issuance of (6) additional shares payable 05/12/2011 to holders of record 05/02/2011 Ex date - 05/13/2011
Name changed to Imogo Mobile Technologies Corp. 02/24/2012

MOOCK ELECTRIC SUPPLY CO. (OH)
Name changed to Moock Investment Corp. 10/1/60 which completed liquidation 1/16/61

MOOCK INVESTMENT CORP. (OH)
Completely liquidated 1/16/61
Each share Common $50 par exchanged for first and final distribution of $107.74 cash

MOOD MEDIA CORP (CANADA)
Acquired by private entities 06/28/2017
Each share Common no par exchanged for $0.17 cash

MOODUS SVGS BK (MOODUS, CT)
Name changed to Hometown Bank (Moodus, CT) 8/24/98
(See Hometown Bank (Moodus, CT))

MOODY (MATTHEW) & SONS CO. LTD.
Bankrupt in 1930

MOODY MINING CORP. (NV)
Charter revoked for failure to file reports and pay taxes 3/7/60

MOODY'S INVESTORS SERVICE (NJ)
Acquired by Dun & Bradstreet, Inc. 03/30/1962
Each share Part. Preference no par exchanged for (1) share Common $1 par
Each share Common no par exchanged for (1/3) share Common $1 par
Dun & Bradstreet, Inc. name changed to Dun & Bradstreet Companies, Inc. 05/31/1973 which name changed to Dun & Bradstreet Corp. 04/17/1979 which name changed to R.H. Donnelley Corp. 07/01/1998
(See R.H. Donnelley Corp.)

MOOG INC (NY)
Each share 9% Conv. Preferred Ser. B $1 par automatically became (0.128775) share Class A $1 par 01/02/2004
(Additional Information in Active)

MOOG SERVOCONTROLS, INC. (NY)
Name changed to Moog Inc. 10/1/65

MOON LAKE URANIUM MINES LTD. (ON)
Merged into Consolidated Frederick Mines Ltd. on a (1) for (39) basis 9/9/57
Consolidated Frederick Mines Ltd. completed liquidation 10/23/61

MOON MOTOR CAR CO.
Property sold in 1936
No stockholders' equity

MOONCOR OIL & GAS CORP (ON)
Recapitalized as Sensor Technologies Inc. 10/24/2018
Each share Common no par exchanged for (0.03333333) share Common no par

MOONDUST VENTURES INC (BC)
Recapitalized as Global Metals Ltd. 01/26/1993
Each share Common no par exchanged for (0.2) share Common no par
Global Metals Ltd. name changed to Global Petroleum Inc. 01/09/1998 which recapitalized as Stellar Pacific Ventures Inc. (BC) 06/15/2000 which reincorporated in Canada 04/24/2006 which recapitalized as AfricaGold Inc. 04/01/2013

MOONEY AEROSPACE GROUP LTD (DE)
Plan of reorganization under Chapter 11 Federal Bankruptcy Code effective 12/15/2004
Each share Class A Common no par exchanged for (0.00031026) share Common no par
Note: Holdings of (3,224) shares or fewer will receive $0.0013999379 cash
Merged into Mag Holding Corp. 10/30/2006
Each share Common no par exchanged for $0.35 cash

MOONEY AIRCRAFT INC (TX)
Adjudicated bankrupt 02/17/1969
Assets sold for benefit of creditors
No stockholders' equity

MOONEY BROADCASTING CORP (TN)
Stock Dividend - 10% 03/20/1973
Name changed to Sungroup, Inc. 04/19/1983
(See Sungroup, Inc.)

MOONEY CORP. (TX)
Adjudicated bankrupt 2/17/69
Assets sold for benefit of creditors
No stockholders' equity

MOONGOLD RES INC (BC)
Struck off register and declared dissolved for failure to file returns 11/6/92

MOONIE OIL LTD (AUSTRALIA)
Name changed to TMOC Resources Ltd. 11/27/1986
(See TMOC Resources Ltd.)

MOONLIGHT INTL CORP (DE)
Each share old Common $0.0001 par exchanged for (0.02) share new Common $0.0001 par 11/13/1995
Charter cancelled and declared inoperative and void for non-payment of taxes 11/26/1998

MOONSHINE PRODTNS LTD (BC)
Name changed 04/26/1984
Name changed from Moonshine Resources Ltd. to Moonshine Productions Ltd. 04/26/1984
Name changed to Vanex Resources Ltd. 10/01/1986
Vanex Resources Ltd. recapitalized as Poplar Resources Ltd. 07/15/1991 which merged into Nordic Diamonds Ltd. 11/24/2003 which recapitalized as Western Standard Metals Ltd. 06/12/2009 which merged into Terraco Gold Corp. (AB) 01/25/2011 which reincorporated in British Columbia 06/08/2011

MOONSHOOT CAP CORP (AB)
Name changed to Cematrix Corp. 06/02/2006

MOONSTONE INC (CO)
Name changed to Entity Inc. 06/21/1989
Entity Inc. recapitalized as Boundless Motor Sports Racing, Inc. (CO) 08/12/2003 which reincorporated in Delaware as Dirt Motor Sports, Inc. 07/08/2005 which name changed to World Racing Group, Inc. 01/31/2008

MOORCO INTL INC (DE)
Preferred Stock Purchase Rights declared for Common stockholders of record 11/18/1994 were redeemed at $0.01 per right for holders of record 06/26/1995
Merged into FMC Corp. 06/30/1995
Each share Common 1¢ par exchanged for $28 cash

MOORE - MCCORMACK LINES INC (DE)
Each share Common $10 par exchanged for (2) shares Common $5 par 12/1/47
$2.50 Preferred $50 par called for redemption 12/31/47
Common $5 par changed to $12 par 4/10/52
Common $12 par changed to $5 par 10/31/63
Stock Dividend - 25% 11/15/51
Name changed to Moore & McCormack Co., Inc. 2/25/65
Moore & McCormack Co., Inc. name changed to Moore McCormack Resources Inc. 2/8/74
(See Moore McCormack Resources Inc.)

MOORE & MCCORMACK INC (DE)
Name changed to Moore McCormack Resources Inc. 02/08/1974
(See Moore McCormack Resources Inc.)

MOORE-ALBACH GOLD MINES LTD. (ON)
Name changed to Sherry Lee Gold Mines Ltd. in 1947
(See Sherry Lee Gold Mines Ltd.)

MOORE AUSTRALASIA HLDGS LTD (AUSTRALIA)
ADR agreement terminated 11/09/2015
No ADR's remain outstanding

MOORE BENJAMIN & CO (NJ)
Common $10 par split (3) for (1) by issuance of (2) additional shares payable 8/2/99 to holders of record 7/1/99
Merged into Berkshire Hathaway Inc. 1/1/2001
Each share Common $10 par exchanged for $37.82 cash

MOORE CLEAR CO (OR)
Each share Common no par received $4 cash and public interest was eliminated 05/30/1979
Note: Certificates were not required to be surrendered and are now without value

MOORE CORP.
Merged into Conlon-Moore Corp. 00/00/1947
Each share Preferred exchanged for (1) share Preferred $50 par
Each share Common exchanged for (5) shares Common $1 par
(See Conlon-Moore Corp.)

MOORE CORP LTD (CANADA)
Name changed 6/7/76
Reincorporated 6/3/2002
Common no par exchanged (4) for (1) in 1950
Common no par split (3) for (1) by issuance of (2) additional shares 5/29/59
Common no par split (4) for (1) by issuance of (3) additional shares 5/27/67
Name changed from Moore Corp. Ltd. to Moore Corp. Ltd.-Corporation Moore Ltee. 6/7/76
Common no par split (3) for (1) by issuance of (2) additional shares 5/3/85
Place of incorporation changed from (ONT) to (Canada) 6/3/2002
Name changed to Moore Wallace Inc. 5/15/2003
Moore Wallace Inc. acquired by Donnelley (R.R.) & Sons Co. 2/27/2004

MOORE DROP FORGING CO (MA)
Each share Class B no par exchanged for (5) shares Common $1 par 00/00/1945
4.75% Conv. Preferred $50 par called for redemption 03/06/1969
Merged into Eastern Stainless Steel Corp. 03/24/1969
Each share Common $1 par exchanged for (1) share $2.25 Conv. Preferred 1968 Ser. B $1 par
Eastern Stainless Steel Corp. name changed to Easco Corp. 04/29/1969
(See Easco Corp.)

MOORE E R CO (IL)
Merged into Beatrice Foods Co. 06/30/1969
Each share Common no par exchanged for (0.6) share Common no par
Beatrice Foods Co. name changed to Beatrice Companies, Inc. 06/05/1984
(See Beatrice Companies, Inc.)

MOORE FINANCIAL CORP. (DE)
Out of business 12/31/1986
Details not available

MOORE FINL GROUP INC (ID)
Stock Dividend - 10% 10/31/1984
Name changed to West One Bancorp 04/21/1989
West One Bancorp merged into U.S. Bancorp (OR) 12/26/1995 which merged into U.S. Bancorp (Old) (DE) 08/01/1997 which merged into U.S. Bancorp 02/27/2001

MOORE-HANDLEY, INC. (AL)
Name changed to Pelham Corp. 05/31/1968
Pelham Corp. liquidated for Scudder, Stevens & Clark Balanced Fund, Inc. 12/31/1973 which name changed to Scudder Income Fund, Inc. 03/02/1977 which name changed to Scudder Income Fund 12/31/1984
(See Scudder Income Fund)

MOORE-HANDLEY HARDWARE CO., INC. (AL)
Name changed to Moore-Handley, Inc. 02/28/1961
Moore-Handley, Inc. name changed to Pelham Corp. 05/31/1968 which was liquidated for Scudder, Stevens & Clark Balanced Fund, Inc. 12/31/1973 which name changed to Scudder Income Fund, Inc. 03/02/1977 which name changed to Scudder Income Fund 12/31/1984
(See Scudder Income Fund)

MOORE HANDLEY INC (DE)
Chapter 7 bankruptcy proceedings terminated 06/28/2012
No stockholders' equity

MOORE MCCORMACK RES INC (DE)
Each share Common $5 par exchanged for (2) shares Common $2.50 par 11/5/75
Common $2.50 par split (3) for (2) by issuance of (0.5) additional share 5/28/77
Common $2.50 par split (3) for (2) by issuance of (0.5) additional share 5/28/81
Depositary Conv. Preferred called for redemption 6/30/87
Merged into Southdown, Inc. 5/19/88
Each share $3.6875 Conv. Exchangeable Preferred $100 par exchanged for $66.80 cash
Each share $10 Conv. Preferred $100 par exchanged for $80.80 cash
Each share Common $2.50 par exchanged for $40.40 cash

MOORE MED CORP (DE)
Common 1¢ par split (3) for (1) by issuance of (2) additional shares 5/23/85
Merged into McKesson Corp. 4/2/2004
Each share Common 1¢ par exchanged for $12 cash

MOORE MOTOR VEHICLE CO. (SD)
Charter expired by time limitation 7/13/41

MOORE PRODS CO (PA)
Common $1 par split (5) for (1) by issuance of (4) additional shares 12/1/67
Merged into Siemens A.G. 2/24/2000
Each share 5% Conv. Preferred Ser. A $1 par exchanged for $21.88 cash
Each share Common $1 par exchanged for $54.71 cash

MOORE RANE MFG CO (OR)
Name changed to Moore Clear Co. 05/25/1971
(See Moore Clear Co.)

MOORE SAMUEL & CO (OH)
Common no par split (3) for (2) by issuance of (0.5) additional share 06/30/1972
Common no par split (2) for (1) by issuance of (1) additional share 10/15/1974
Merged into Eaton Corp. 08/28/1978
Each share Common no par exchanged for $20 cash

MOORE WALLACE INC (CANADA)
Acquired by Donnelley (R.R.) & Sons Co. 2/27/2004
Each share Common no par exchanged for (0.63) share Common $1.25 par

MOORE WILLIAM S INC (OH)
Completely liquidated 04/05/1977

No stockholders' equity

MOORES FOOD PRODS INC (WI)
Merged into Clorox Co. (CA) 02/10/1978
Each share Common 50¢ par exchanged for $9.75 cash

MOORES SEAFOOD PRODS INC (WI)
Name changed to Moore's Food Products, Inc. 09/28/1971
(See Moore's Food Products, Inc.)

MOORESVILLE COTTON MILLS (NC)
Name changed to Mooresville Mills in 1946, which merged into Burlington Industries, Inc. 4/29/55
(See Burlington Industries, Inc.)

MOORESVILLE MILLS (NC)
Merged into Burlington Industries, Inc. (Old) on a (1) for (2) basis 04/29/1955
(See Burlington Industries, Inc. (Old))

MOORHEAD PLASTICS, INC. (MN)
Name changed to Silverline, Inc. 1/22/68
Silverline, Inc. acquired by Arctic Enterprises, Inc. 3/8/70 which name changed to Minstar Inc. (Minn.) 12/14/82 which reorganized in Delaware 8/31/85
(See Minstar, Inc. (Del.))

MOORMAN MFG CO (IL)
Acquired by Archer-Daniels-Midland Co. 12/30/1997
Each share Common $1 par exchanged for (254.7545) shares Common no par

MOOSE FLAT PLACERS LTD.
Dissolved in 1950

MOOSE JAW ELECTRIC RWY. LTD.
Assets sold in 1934

MOOSEWOOD GOLD MINES, LTD. (ON)
Charter cancelled 08/06/1957

MOOSHLA GOLD MINES LTD (ON)
Charter cancelled for failure to pay taxes and file returns 08/27/1984

MOOTER MEDIA LTD (AUSTRALIA)
Each Sponsored ADR Ordinary received distribution of $0.010233 cash payable 09/29/2011 to holders of record 09/19/2011 Ex date - 09/15/2011
ADR agreement terminated 05/09/2016
Each Sponsored ADR for Ordinary exchanged for (200) shares Ordinary
Note: Unexchanged ADR's will be sold and the proceeds, if any, held for claim after 09/06/2016

MOOVIES INC (DE)
Merged into Video Update, Inc. 3/4/98
Each share Common $0.001 par exchanged for (0.75) share Class A Common 1¢ par
(See Video Update, Inc.)

MOQIZONE HLDG CORP (DE)
Name changed to Balincan USA, Inc. 09/30/2015

MOR-CAP, INC. (UT)
Name changed to Roseland Oil & Gas, Inc. (UT) and Common 1¢ par changed to no par 04/14/1980
Roseland Oil & Gas, Inc. (UT) reincorporated in Oklahoma 08/16/1991 which reincorporated in Texas as Cubic Energy, Inc. 10/04/1999
(See Cubic Energy, Inc.)

MOR FLO INDS INC (OH)
Acquired by SABH (U.S.) Inc. 07/01/1992
Each share Common no par exchanged for $7.90 cash
Each share Class B no par exchanged for $7.90 cash

MOR SYS INTL INC (NV)
Charter permanently revoked 05/31/2000

MORAGA CORP (DE)
Charter cancelled and declared inoperative and void for non-payment of taxes 03/01/1985

MORAGA RES LTD (BC)
Acquired by Jordex Resources Inc. (BC) 11/21/1991
Each share Common no par exchanged for (0.33333333) share Common no par
Jordex Resources Inc. (BC) reincorporated in Yukon 07/27/1998 which name changed to iTech Capital Corp. 03/10/2000 which name changed to Sirit Inc. 05/05/2003
(See Sirit Inc.)

MORAN BROS., INC. (TX)
Stock Dividends - 10% 12/15/1976; 10% 12/15/1978; 10% 03/12/1980
Name changed to Moran Energy Inc. 09/29/1980
Moran Energy Inc. merged into Kaneb Services, Inc. 03/20/1984 which name changed to Xanser Corp. 08/07/2001 which name changed to Furmanite Corp. 05/17/2007 which merged into Team, Inc. 02/29/2016

MORAN ENERGY INC (TX)
Stock Dividends - 100% 11/10/1980; 10% 12/14/1981
Merged into Kaneb Services, Inc. 03/20/1984
Each share Common 25¢ par exchanged for (1.14) shares Common no par
Kaneb Services, Inc. name changed to Xanser Corp. 08/07/2001 which name changed to Furmanite Corp. 05/17/2007 which merged into Team, Inc. 02/29/2016

MORAN J T FINL CORP (DE)
Charter cancelled and declared inoperative and void for non-payment of taxes 6/26/90

MORAN PPTYS INC (CA)
Company went private 00/00/1981
Details not available

MORAN RES CORP (BC)
Recapitalized as Stornaway Resources Corp. 03/25/1985
Each share Common no par exchanged for (0.5) share Common no par
Stornaway Resources Corp. name changed to Stornaway Capital Development Corp. 01/07/1988
(See Stornaway Capital Development Corp.)

MORDEN & HELWIG GROUP INC (CANADA)
Name changed to Lindsey Morden Group Inc. 07/24/1995
Lindsey Morden Group Inc. name changed to Cunningham Lindsey Group Inc. 04/13/2006
(See Cunningham Lindsey Group Inc.)

MORE CREATIVE MERGERS INC (NV)
Name changed to ATS Money Systems, Inc. 9/6/88
(See ATS Money Systems, Inc.)

MORE MINES LTD (MB)
Merged into Nufort Resources Inc. 8/20/74
Each share Capital Stock $1 par exchanged for (1/3) share Capital Stock no par
Nufort Resources Inc. name changed to Mikotel Networks Inc. 5/9/2000 which recapitalized as Wabi Exploration Inc. 3/4/2005

MORE RES INC (BC)
Name changed to General Diamond Corp. 08/11/1992

General Diamond Corp. recapitalized as Consolidated General Diamond Corp. 09/25/1995 which recapitalized as Exxel Energy Corp. 10/15/2001 which recapitalized as XXL Energy Corp. 05/30/2008

MOREHOUSE BARLOW INC (WI)
Stock Dividend - 100% 09/15/1959
6% Conv. Preferred $50 par called for redemption 07/01/1964
Majority of Common $50 par reacquired by the company 00/00/1989
Public interest eliminated

MOREHOUSE-GORHAM CO. (WI)
Name changed to Morehouse-Barlow Co., Inc. 8/21/59

MOREHOUSE INDS INC (CA)
Common no par split (5) for (4) by issuance of (0.25) additional share 8/15/83
Stock Dividend - 20% 3/27/81
Recapitalized as Summa Industries 12/22/93
Each share Common no par exchanged for (0.25) share Common no par
(See Summa Industries)

MORELAND LATCHFORD PRODTNS LTD (ON)
Charter cancelled for failure to pay taxes and file reports 05/31/1982

MORELAND MOTOR TRUCK CO.
Liquidated in 1942

MORELAND OIL & GAS LTD (AB)
Merged into Sugar Creek Oil & Gas Inc. 06/01/1990
Each share Common no par exchanged for (0.623) share Common no par
Sugar Creek Oil & Gas Inc. merged into Petrostar Petroleums Inc. (New) 06/11/1992 which merged into Crestar Energy Inc. 06/07/1996 which was acquired by Gulf Canada Resources Ltd. 11/13/2000
(See Gulf Canada Resources Ltd.)

MORELAND OIL CO.
Acquired by Vacuum Oil Co. 00/00/1930
Details not available

MORENCI CORP (NV)
Name changed to Esportbike.com, Inc. 05/11/2000
Esportbike.com, Inc. recapitalized as Red Butte Energy, Inc. 04/10/2002 which name changed to Canglobe International, Inc. 01/31/2003 which name changed to Globetech Environmental, Inc. 11/07/2005 which recapitalized as Global Gold Corp. 03/09/2009 which recapitalized as Fernhill Corp. 01/20/2012

MORENGO RES INC (BC)
Struck off register and declared dissolved for failure to file returns 2/21/92

MORENO URANIUM CORP (CO)
Name changed 00/00/1954
Name changed from Moreno Cripple Creek Corp. to Moreno Uranium Corp. 00/00/1954
Recapitalized as Envirosearch Corp. 04/14/1970
Each share Common 10¢ par exchanged for (0.1) share Common $1 par
Envirosearch Corp. name changed to Evro Financial Corp. (CO) 09/26/1986 which reincorporated in Florida as Evro Corp. 03/01/1994 which name changed to Channel America Broadcasting, Inc. 10/25/1996 which recapitalized as DTG Industries, Inc. 03/22/2004 which name changed to DTG Multimedia, Inc. (FL) 06/04/2004 which reorganized in Nevada as Amazing Technologies Corp.

12/23/2004 which name changed to Mvive, Inc. 08/24/2007
(See Mvive Inc.)

MORENO VENTURES INC (BC)
Recapitalized as Niogold Mining Corp. 09/24/2002
Each share Common no par exchanged for (0.4) share Common no par
Niogold Mining Corp. merged into Oban Mining Corp. 03/11/2016 which name changed to Osisko Mining Inc. 06/21/2016

MORFEE WHEEL MFG INC (BC)
Recapitalized as Transtech Industries Inc. 12/12/1991
Each share Common no par exchanged for (0.25) share Common no par
Transtech Industries Inc. recapitalized as International Transtech Inc. 09/23/1999 which recapitalized as North American Vanadium Inc. 09/02/2005 which name changed to Veraz Petroleum Ltd. (BC) 06/26/2007 which reincorporated in Alberta 01/24/2008 which name changed to AlkaLi3 Resources Inc. 08/16/2016

MORGAIN MINERALS INC (BC)
Merged into Castle Gold Corp. 08/28/2007
Each share Common no par exchanged for (0.5) share Common no par
(See Castle Gold Corp.)

MORGAN (J.P.) & CO. INC. (NY)
Stock Dividends - 25% 10/25/51; 20% 11/8/54
Merged into Morgan Guaranty Trust Co. (New York, NY) 4/24/59
Each share Capital Stock $100 par exchanged for (4.4) shares Capital Stock $25 par
Morgan Guaranty Trust Co. (New York, NY) reorganized as Morgan (J.P.) & Co. Inc. (DE) 4/1/69 which merged into J.P. Morgan Chase & Co. 12/31/2000 which name changed to JPMorgan Chase & Co. 7/20/2004

MORGAN (HENRY) & CO. LTD. (CANADA)
Acquired by Hudson's Bay Co. (England) 5/19/61
Each share Common no par exchanged for (1) share Ordinary £1 par and $13.75 cash
4.75% Preferred $100 par called for redemption 7/1/62
Hudson's Bay Co. (England) reincorporated in Canada 5/27/70
(See Hudson's Bay Co.)

MORGAN & FENTRESS RAILWAY CO.
Operations discontinued 00/00/1934
Details not available

MORGAN ADHESIVES CO (OH)
Each (24,000) shares old Common 10¢ par exchanged for (1) share new Common 10¢ par 1/6/2000
Note: In effect holders received $126.75 cash per share and public interest was eliminated

MORGAN ADVANCED MATLS PLC (UNITED KINGDOM)
ADR agreement terminated 05/21/2018
No ADR's remain outstanding

MORGAN BANK & TRUST (SPARTANBURG, SC)
Merged into Southern Bancorporation, Inc. 10/31/77
Each share Common $5 par exchanged for (1) share $6.28 Conv. Preferred $100 par
(See Southern Bancorporation, Inc.)

MORGAN BEAUMONT INC (NV)
Recapitalized as nFinanSe Inc. 12/26/2006

Each share Common $0.001 par exchanged for (0.05) share Common $0.001 par

MORGAN COOPER INC (DE)
SEC revoked common stock registration 07/21/2005

MORGAN CREEK ENERGY CORP (NV)
Old Common $0.001 par split (2) for (1) by issuance of (1) additional share payable 05/22/2006 to holders of record 05/22/2006 Ex date - 05/23/2006
Old Common $0.001 par split (2) for (1) by issuance of (1) additional share payable 08/08/2006 to holders of record 08/08/2006 Ex date - 08/09/2006
Each share old Common $0.001 par exchanged for (0.33333333) share new Common $0.001 par 04/22/2008
New Common $0.001 par split (2) for (1) by issuance of (1) additional share payable 07/31/2009 to holders of record 07/14/2009 Ex date - 08/03/2009
Name changed to TagLikeMe Corp. 06/15/2012

MORGAN CREEK MINES LTD. (ON)
Merged into Garrison Creek Consolidated Mines Ltd. on a (1) for (15) basis 12/09/1954
Garrison Creek Consolidated Mines Ltd. merged into QSR Ltd. 09/07/1993 which name changed to Coniagas Resources Ltd. 06/25/1999 which name changed to Lithium One Inc. 07/23/2009
(See Lithium One Inc.)

MORGAN CRUCIBLE CO PLC (UNITED KINGDOM)
Name changed to Morgan Advanced Materials PLC 08/15/2013
(See Morgan Advanced Materials PLC)

MORGAN ENGR CO (OH)
Recapitalized 00/00/1930
Each share 8% Preferred $100 par exchanged for (2) shares Class A Preferred no par and (1) share Class B Preferred no par
Each share Common $100 par exchanged for (3) shares Common no par
Recapitalized 00/00/1941
Each share Class A Preferred no par exchanged for (1.5) shares Prior Preferred no par, (0.5) share Common $1 par and $2 cash
Each share Common no par exchanged for (2) shares Common $1 par
Stock Dividends - 100% 09/17/1945; 10% 12/10/1957
100% of Prior Preferred no par and Common $1 par stock acquired by United Industrial Syndicate Inc. through purchase offer 04/29/1966
Public interest eliminated

MORGAN EQUITIES CORP (CA)
Capital Stock no par split (5) for (1) by issuance of (4) additional shares 04/28/1971
Name changed to California Casket Co. 00/00/1978
(See California Casket Co.)

MORGAN EQUITIES GROUP INC
Each share old Common $0.001 par exchanged for (0.05) share new Common $0.001 par 03/08/2006
Name changed to Deaf-Talk, Inc. 09/14/2010
(See Deaf-Talk, Inc.)

MORGAN FINL CORP (CO)
Reincorporated 02/16/1996
Common 1¢ par split (2) for (1) by issuance of (1) additional share 12/18/1995
State of incorporation changed from (DE) to (CO) 02/16/1996

Acquired by Mid-America Financial
Corp. 10/03/2017
Each share Common 1¢ par
exchanged for $20.73 cash

MORGAN FINL CORP (ON)
Conv. Retractable 1st Preferred Ser.
B no par called for redemption
3/31/87
Each share $1.75 Conv. 1st Preferred
Ser. C no par exchanged for (45)
shares Common no par 12/11/91
Common no par called for redemption
1/23/98

MORGAN FUNSHARES INC (OH)
Common no par split (2) for (1) by
issuance of (1) additional share
payable 3/25/98 to holders of record
3/2/98
Each share Common no par received
initial distribution of $3.1175 cash
payable 11/14/2003 to holders of
record 11/7/2003
Completely liquidated
Each share Common no par received
first and final distribution of $3.1175
cash payable 11/14/2003 to holders
of record 11/7/2003
Note: Certificates were not required to
be exchanged and are without value

MORGAN GAS & OIL CO (UT)
Each share old Common 5¢ par
exchanged for (0.00008264) share
new Common 5¢ par 05/16/2016
Note: In effect holders received $2.03
cash per share and public interest
was eliminated

MORGAN (J.H.) GAS & OIL CO. (UT)
Name changed to Morgan Gas & Oil
Co. 03/20/1961
(See Morgan Gas & Oil Co.)

MORGAN GRAMPIAN LTD (ENGLAND)
Acquired by Trafalgar House Ltd.
00/00/1978
Details not available

MORGAN GRENFELL SMALLCAP FD INC (MD)
Name changed to SmallCap Fund
Inc. 9/28/2000
SmallCap Fund Inc. name changed to
Investors First Fund, Inc. 10/16/2003
which merged into Cornerstone
Strategic Value Fund, Inc. 6/28/2004

MORGAN GROUP INC (DE)
Chapter 11 bankruptcy petition
dismissed 03/31/2008
No stockholders' equity

MORGAN GTY TR CO (NEW YORK, NY)
Stock Dividends - 10% 2/21/63; 10%
4/15/65
Reorganized under the laws of
Delaware as Morgan (J.P.) & Co.
Inc. 4/1/69
Each share Capital Stock $25 par
exchanged for (2) shares Common
$5 par
Morgan (J.P.) & Co. Inc. merged into
J.P. Morgan Chase & Co.
12/31/2000 which name changed to
JPMorgan Chase & Co. 7/20/2004

MORGAN HYDROCARBONS INC (QC)
9-1/2% Conv. 2nd Preferred Ser. B
$25 par called for redemption
8/12/88
Acquired by Stampeder Explorations
Ltd. 10/15/96
Each share Common no par
exchanged for (0.85) share Common
no par
Stampeder Explorations Ltd. acquired
by Gulf Canada Resources Ltd.
9/10/97
(See Gulf Canada Resources Ltd.)

MORGAN J P & CO INC (DE)
Common $5 par changed to $2.50 par
and (1) additional share issued
4/23/73
Common $2.50 par split (2) for (1) by
issuance of (1) additional share
1/15/85
Common $2.50 par split (2) for (1) by
(1) additional share 1/5/87
Each Exchangeable share exchanged
for (1.5) shares Ethan Allen Interiors
Inc. Common 1¢ par 7/21/2000
Merged into J.P. Morgan Chase & Co.
12/31/2000
Each share Variable Preferred Ser. B
no par exchanged for (1) share
Variable Preferred Ser. B no par
Each share Variable Preferred Ser. C
no par exchanged for (1) share
Variable Preferred Ser. C no par
Each share Variable Preferred Ser. D
no par exchanged for (1) share
Variable Preferred Ser. D no par
Each share Variable Preferred Ser. E
no par exchanged for (1) share
Variable Preferred Ser. D no par
Each share Variable Preferred Ser. F
no par exchanged for (1) share
Variable Preferred Ser. F no par
Each 6.625% Depositary Preferred
Ser. H exchanged for (1) 6.625%
Depositary Preferred Ser. H
Each share 6.625% Preferred Ser. H
no par exchanged for (1) share
6.625% Preferred Ser. H no par
Each share Common $2.50 par
exchanged for (3.7) shares Common
$1 par
J.P. Morgan Chase & Co. name
changed to JPMorgan Chase & Co.
7/20/2004

MORGAN KEEGAN & CO INC (TN)
Under plan of reorganization each
share Common $0.625 par
automatically became (1) share
Morgan Keegan, Inc. Common
$0.625 par 3/9/84
Morgan Keegan, Inc. merged into
Regions Financial Corp. (Old)
3/30/2001 which merged into
Regions Financial Corp. (New)
7/1/2004

MORGAN KEEGAN INC (TN)
Common $0.625 par split (3) for (2)
by issuance of (0.5) additional share
4/30/86
Common $0.625 par split (4) for (3)
by issuance of (1/3) additional share
9/12/91
Common $0.625 par split (3) for (2)
by issuance of (0.5) additional share
3/13/92
Common $0.625 par split (3) for (2)
by issuance of (0.5) additional share
6/11/93
Common $0.625 par split (3) for (2)
by issuance of (0.5) additional share
6/9/95
Common $0.625 par split (3) for (2)
by issuance of (0.5) additional share
payable 9/11/97 to holders of record
9/3/97 Ex date - 9/12/97
Merged into Regions Financial Corp.
(Old) 3/30/2001
Each share Common $0.625 par
exchanged for (0.96) share Common
$0.625 par
Regions Financial Corp. (Old) merged
into Regions Financial Corp. (New)
7/1/2004

MORGAN LITHOGRAPH CO.
Liquidated in 1934
Details not available

MORGAN MED HLDGS INC (CO)
Each share old Common no par
exchanged for (0.01) share new
Common no par 3/20/91
Merged into NMR of America Inc.
9/14/95
Each share new Common no par
exchanged for (0.3330886) share
Common no par
NMR of America Inc. merged into
Medical Resources Inc. 8/30/96

MORGAN MEDIA CAP CORP (AB)
Name changed to Global Consumer
Technologies Inc. 01/02/2001
(See Global Consumer Technologies Inc.)

MORGAN OLMSTEAD KENNEDY & GARDNER CAP CORP (DE)
Merged into Enden Holdings Inc.
11/3/88
Details not available

MORGAN PETE INC (BC)
Recapitalized as Mortlock Resources
Corp. 05/28/1993
Each share Common no par
exchanged for (0.2) share Common
no par
Mortlock Resources Corp. name
changed to NovaDx International
Inc. 01/20/1995 which recapitalized
as NovaDx Ventures Corp.
12/02/2004
(See NovaDx Ventures Corp.)

MORGAN PRODS LTD (DE)
Secondary Offering - 3,400,000
shares COM offered at $6.50 per
share on 11/13/1996
Merged into Anderson Windows Inc.
7/29/99
Each share Common 10¢ par
exchanged for $4 cash

MORGAN RES CORP (ON)
Name changed to Leviathan
Cannabis Group Inc. 04/16/2018

MORGAN STANLEY (DE)
Stock Participation Accreting
Redemption Quarterly Pay
Securities called for redemption at
$22.9006 on 09/02/2003
Stock Participation Accreting
Redemption Quarterly Pay
Securities called for redemption at
$15.1946 on 09/02/2003
Stock Participation Accreting
Redemption Exchangeable called for
redemption at $9.4913 on
10/01/2003
Stock Participation Accreting
Redemption Quarterly Pay
Securities called for redemption at
$41.356 on 11/21/2003
Stock Participation Accreting
Redemption Quarterly Pay
Securities called for redemption at
$21.1891 on 03/01/2004
Stock Participation Accreting
Redemption Quarterly Pay
Securities called for redemption at
$22.2663 plus $0.4053 accrued
dividends on 04/30/2004
Stock Participation Accreting
Redemption Quarterly Pay
Securities called for redemption at
$15.2383 plus $0.0664 accrued
dividends on 11/08/2006
Stock Participation Accreting
Redemption Quarterly Pay
Securities called for redemption at
$18.2499 on 11/27/2006
Redeemable Equity Linked Securities
called for redemption at $113.50 on
02/28/2007
Stock Participation Accreting
Redemption Quarterly Pay
Securities called for redemption at
$43.8955 on 03/05/2007
Stock Participation Accreting
Redemption Quarterly Pay
Securities called for redemption at
$33.3157 on 05/14/2007
Stock Participation Accreting
Redemption Quarterly Pay
Securities called for redemption at
$17.5436 on 05/14/2007
Stock Participation Accreting
Redemption Quarterly Pay
Securities called for redemption at
$19.6773 on 05/21/2007
Stock Participation Accreting
Redemption Quarterly Pay
Securities called for redemption at
$18.8749 plus $0.01 accrued
dividends on 06/22/2007
Bear Market Auto-Callable Securities
based on KBW Mortgage Finance
Index called for redemption at
$10.41 on 09/07/2007
Stock Participation Accreting
Redemption Quarterly Pay
Securities called for redemption at
$13.5873 plus $0.1371 accrued
dividends on 10/08/2007
Stock Participation Accreting
Redemption Quarterly Pay
Securities called for redemption at
$25.5756 on 11/13/2007
Mandatorily Exchangeable Shares
called for redemption at $54.6628
on 11/19/2007
Stock Participation Accreting
Redemption Quarterly Pay
Securities called for redemption at
$19.2785 on 12/21/2007
Pharmaceutical Basket Opportunity
Exchangeable Securities called for
redemption 03/12/2009

MORGAN STANLEY AFRICA INVT FD INC (MD)
Issue Information - 9,250,000 shares
COM offered at $15 per share on
02/03/1994
Name changed to Morgan Stanley
Dean Witter Africa Investment Fund
Inc. 6/21/99 which name changed
back to Morgan Stanley Africa
Investment Fund, Inc. 5/1/2001
Liquidation completed
Each Common 1¢ par exchanged for
initial distribution of $9 cash
4/24/2002
Each share Common 1¢ par received
second and final distribution of
$0.0471 cash payable 7/18/2003 to
holders of record 7/18/2003

MORGAN STANLEY CAP TR II (DE)
7.25% Capital Securities called for
redemption at $25 on 5/21/2007

MORGAN STANLEY CAP TR III (DE)
6.25% Capital Securities called for
redemption at $25 plus $0.334201
accrued dividends on 08/18/2016

MORGAN STANLEY CAP TR IV (DE)
6.25% Capital Securities called for
redemption at $25 plus $0.203993
accrued dividends on 08/18/2016

MORGAN STANLEY CAP TR V (DE)
5.75% Capital Securities called for
redemption at $25 plus $0.131771
accrued dividends on 08/18/2016

MORGAN STANLEY CAP TR VI (DE)
6.6% Capital Securities called for
redemption at $25 plus $0.119166
accrued dividends on 05/27/2015

MORGAN STANLEY CAP TR IV (DE)
Capital Securities called for
redemption at $25 plus $0.12375
accrued dividends on 05/12/2015

MORGAN STANLEY CAP TR VIII (DE)
6.45% Capital Securities called for
redemption at $25 plus $0.080625
accrued dividends on 08/18/2016

MORGAN STANLEY DEAN WITTER & CO (DE)
Name changed 3/24/98
Common $1 par split (2) for (1) by
issuance of (0.5) additional share
2/27/89
Common $1 par split (2) for (1) by
issuance of (1) additional share
8/27/91
Market Auction Preferred Ser. C no
par called for redemption 4/15/92
Market Auction Preferred Ser. D no
par called for redemption 4/22/92
Market Auction Preferred Ser. A no
par called for redemption 5/21/92
Market Auction Preferred Ser. B no
par called for redemption 5/28/92
Common $1 par split (2) for (1) by
issuance of (1) additional share
payable 1/26/96 to holders of record
1/16/96 Ex date - 1/29/96
9.36% Preferred no par called for
redemption 6/24/96

8.88% Preference no par called for redemption 1/3/97
8.75% Preferred no par called for redemption 5/30/97
Name changed from Morgan Stanley Group Inc. to Morgan Stanley, Dean Witter, Discover & Co. 5/31/97
Name changed from Morgan Stanley, Dean Witter, Discover & Co. to Morgan Stanley Dean Witter & Co. 3/24/98
7.375% Depositary Preferred called for redemption at $25 on 8/31/98
New Common $1 par split (2) for (1) by issuance of (1) additional share payable 1/26/2000 to holders of record 1/12/2000
7.75% Depositary Preferred called for redemption at $50 on 8/30/2001
Ser. A Fixed Adjustable Depositary Preferred called for redemption at $50 on 12/3/2001
Name changed to Morgan Stanley 6/20/2002

MORGAN STANLEY DEAN WITTER AMERN OPPORTUNITIES FD (MD)
Name changed 3/12/99
Name changed from Morgan Stanley Dean Witter American Value Fund to Morgan Stanley Dean Witter American Opportunities Fund 3/12/99
Name changed to Morgan Stanley American Opportunities Fund 6/18/2001

MORGAN STANLEY DEAN WITTER ASIA-PAC FD INC (MD)
Name changed back to Morgan Stanley Asia-Pacific Fund, Inc. 5/1/2001

MORGAN STANLEY DEAN WITTER EMERGING MKTS DEBT FD INC (MD)
Name changed back to Morgan Stanley Emerging Markets Debt Fund Inc. 5/1/2001

MORGAN STANLEY DEAN WITTER EMERGING MKTS FD INC (MD)
Name changed back to Morgan Stanley Emerging Markets Fund Inc. 5/1/2001

MORGAN STANLEY DEAN WITTER INDIA INVT FD INC (MD)
Name changed back to Morgan Stanley India Investment Fund Inc. 5/1/2001

MORGAN STANLEY DEAN WITTER PRIME INCOME TR (MA)
Name changed to Morgan Stanley Prime Income Trust 6/18/2001

MORGAN STANLEY DEAN WITTER U S GOVT SECS TR (MA)
Name changed to Morgan Stanley U.S. Government Securities Trust 6/18/2001

MORGAN STANLEY EASTN EUROPE FD INC (MD)
Name changed 05/01/2001
Name changed from Morgan Stanley Dean Witter Eastern Europe Fund, Inc. to Morgan Stanley Eastern Europe Fund, Inc. 05/01/2001
Completely liquidated 03/27/2015
Each share Common 1¢ par exchanged for $15.1844 cash

MORGAN STANLEY FD INC (MA)
Name changed to Van Kampen Series Fund, Inc. 8/28/98

MORGAN STANLEY FIN PLC (DE)
7.82% Capital Units called for redemption 2/28/99
8.20% Capital Units called for redemption at $25.025 on 11/30/2000
8.40% Capital Units called for redemption at $25.025 on 11/30/2000

MORGAN STANLEY FRONTIER EMERGING MKTS FD INC (DE)
Under plan of reorganization each share Common $0.001 par automatically became (1) share Morgan Stanley Institutional Fund, Inc. Frontier Emerging Markets Portfolio Class I $0.001 par 09/17/2012

MORGAN STANLEY GLOBAL OPPORTUNITY BD FD INC (MD)
Issue Information - 3,200,000 shares COM offered at $15 per share on 05/19/1994
Name changed to Morgan Stanley Dean Witter Global Opportunity Bond Fund, Inc. 06/21/1999 which name changed back to Morgan Stanley Global Opportunity Bond Fund, Inc. 05/01/2001
Merged into Morgan Stanley Emerging Markets Debt Fund, Inc. 02/01/2010
Each share Common 1¢ par exchanged for (0.66727599) share Common 1¢ par

MORGAN STANLEY HIGH YIELD FD INC (MD)
Name changed 06/21/1999
Name changed 05/01/2001
Name changed from Morgan Stanley Dean Witter High Yield Fund, Inc. 06/21/1999 which name changed back to Morgan Stanley High Yield Fund Inc. 05/01/2001
Name changed to Invesco High Yield Investments Fund, Inc. 06/01/2010
Invesco High Yield Investments Fund, Inc. merged into Invesco Van Kampen High Income Trust II 08/27/2012 which name changed to Invesco High Income Trust II 12/03/2012

MORGAN STANLEY HIGH YIELD SECS INC (MD)
Name changed 06/18/2001
Name changed from Morgan Stanley Dean Witter High Yield Securities Inc. to Morgan Stanley High Yield Securities Inc. 06/18/2001
Class D 1¢ par reclassified as Class I 1¢ par 03/31/2008
Under plan of merger each share Class A 1¢ par, Class B 1¢ par, Class C 1¢ par and Class I 1¢ par automatically became (1) share Aim Investment Securities Funds (Invesco Investment Securities Funds) (DE) Invesco High Yield Securities Fund Class A, Class B, Class C or Class Y respectively 06/01/2010

MORGAN STANLEY INSTL FD INC (MD)
European Equity Portfolio $0.001 par reclassified as European Value Equity Portfolio Class A $0.001 par 04/30/2001
Global Equity Portfolio $0.001 par reclassified as Global Value Equity Portfolio Class I $0.001 par 04/30/2001
Completely liquidated 05/20/2002
Each share Fixed Income Portfolio Class A $0.001 par received net asset value
Each share Fixed Income Portfolio Class B $0.001 par received net asset value
Completely liquidated 10/31/2002
Each share Global Fixed Income Portfolio Class A $0.001 par received net asset value
Each share Global Fixed Income Portfolio Class B $0.001 par received net asset value
Completely liquidated 05/27/2004
Each share European Value Equity Portfolio Class A $0.001 par received net asset value
Value Equity Portfolio Class A $0.001 par reclassified as Large Cap Relative Value Portfolio $0.001 par 01/02/2005
Completely liquidated 04/25/2006
Each share Municipal Money Market Portfolio $0.001 par received net asset value
Completely liquidated 08/25/2006
Each share Money Market Portfolio $0.001 par received net asset value
Large Cap Relative Value Portfolio $0.001 par reclassified as Large Cap Relative Value Portfolio Class I $0.001 par 01/02/2008
Completely liquidated 01/20/2010
Each share Global Value Equity Portfolio Class I $0.001 par automatically became shares of Global Franchise Portfolio Class I $0.001 par on a net asset basis
Completely liquidated 07/28/2010
Each share Large Cap Relative Value Portfolio Class I $0.001 par received net asset value
Under plan of merger each share Balanced Portfolio $0.001 par automatically became shares of Morgan Stanley Institutional Fund Trust Global Strategist Portfolio $0.001 par on a net asset basis 07/16/2012
(Additional Information in Active)

MORGAN STANLEY RUSSIA & NEW EUROPE FD INC (MD)
Name changed to Morgan Stanley Dean Witter Eastern Europe Fund, Inc. 05/07/1999
Morgan Stanley Dean Witter Eastern Europe Fund, Inc. name changed to Morgan Stanley Eastern Europe Fund, Inc. 05/01/2001
(See Morgan Stanley Eastern Europe Fund, Inc.)

MORGAN STANLEY TRUSTS (MA)
Name changed 12/20/2001
Name changed from Morgan Stanley Dean Witter to Morgan Stanley Trusts 12/20/2001
Under plan of merger each share High Income Advantatge Trust 1¢ par, High Income Advantatge Trust II 1¢ par and High Income Advantage Trust III 1¢ par automatically became Morgan Stanley High Yield Securities Inc. Class D 1¢ par on a net asset basis 12/13/2002
Merged into Morgan Stanley U.S. Government Securities Trust 03/26/2007
Each Government Income Trust Share of Bene. Int. 1¢ par received (1.071111) Class D Shares of Bene. Int. 1¢ par
Name changed from California Insured Municipal Income Trust to Invesco California Insured Municipal Income Trust 06/01/2010
Name changed from California Quality Municipal Securities to Invesco California Quality Municipal Securities 06/01/2010
Name changed from Insured California Municipal Securities to Invesco Insured California Municipal Securities 06/01/2010
Name changed from Insured Municipal Bond Trust to Invesco Insured Municipal Bond Trust 06/01/2010
Name changed from Insured Municipal Income Trust to Invesco Insured Municipal Income Trust 06/01/2010
Name changed from Insured Municipal Securities to Invesco Insured Municipal Securities 06/01/2010
Name changed from Insured Municipal Trust to Invesco Insured Municipal Trust 06/01/2010
Name changed from Quality Municipal Income Trust to Invesco Quality Municipal Income Trust 06/01/2010
Name changed from Municipal Income Opportunities Trust to Invesco Municipal Income Opportunities Trust 06/01/2010
Name changed from Municipal Income Opportunities Trust II to Invesco Municipal Income Opportunities Trust II 06/01/2010
Name changed from Municipal Income Opportunities Trust III to Invesco Municipal Income Opportunities Trust III 06/01/2010
Name changed from Municipal Premium Income Trust to Invesco Municipal Premium Income Trust 06/01/2010
Name changed from New York Quality Municipal Securities to Invesco New York Quality Municipal Securities 06/01/2010
Name changed from Quality Municipal Investment Trust to Invesco Quality Municipal Investment Trust 06/01/2010
Name changed from Quality Municipal Securities to Invesco Quality Municipal Securities 06/01/2010
(See each company's listing)
Merged into Morgan Stanley Institutional Fund Trust 06/01/2018
Each share Income Securities Inc. exchanged for approximately (1.58) share Morgan Stanley Institutional Fund Trust Corporate Bond Portfolio Cl I

MORGAN W L GROWTH FD (MD)
Reincorporated 04/01/1973
State of incorporation changed from (DE) to (MD) 04/01/1973
Stock Dividend - 50% 02/15/1979
Name changed to Vanguard/Morgan Growth Fund, Inc. (MD) 05/07/1990
Vanguard/Morgan Growth Fund, Inc. (MD) reorganized in Delaware as Vanguard Morgan Growth Fund 06/30/1998

MORGAN WINDSOR LTD (DE)
Name changed to Health-Pak Inc. 5/9/91
Health-Pak Inc. name changed to Life Energy & Technology Holdings, Inc. (DE) 12/19/2000 which reincorporated in Bahamas as Global Environmental Energy Corp. 8/30/2004

MORGANS FOODS INC (OH)
Each share old Common no par exchanged for (0.16666666) share new Common no par 07/14/1997
Acquired by Apex Restaurant Management, Inc. 05/27/2014
Each share new Common no par exchanged for $5 cash

MORGANS HOTEL GROUP CO (DE)
Acquired by SBEEG Holdings, LLC 12/01/2016
Each share Common 1¢ par exchanged for $2.25 cash

MORGANS RESTAURANTS INC (OH)
Name changed to Mortronics Inc. 06/30/1982
Mortronics Inc. name changed to Morgan's Foods, Inc. 09/19/1986
(See Morgan's Foods, Inc.)

MORGANTON FURNITURE CO. (DE)
Stock Dividend - 100% 5/30/46
Acquired by Drexel Furniture Co. on a (0.75) for (1) basis 1/7/57
Drexel Furniture Co. name changed to Drexel Enterprises, Inc. 11/1/60 which was acquired by U.S. Plywood-Champion Papers Inc. 7/9/68 which name changed to Champion International Corp. 5/12/72 which merged into International Paper Co. 6/20/2000

MORGRO CHEM CO (UT)
Each share old Common $0.005 par exchanged for (0.06666666) share

new Common $0.005 par 08/29/1990
Name changed to Global Casinos, Inc. 11/19/1993
Global Casinos, Inc. name changed to Global Healthcare REIT, Inc. 10/07/2013

MORGUARD REAL ESTATE INVT TR (ON)
Each Installment Receipt no par exchanged for (1) Trust Unit no par 10/14/98
(Additional Information in Active)

MORGUARD SUNSTONE REAL ESTATE INCOME FD (BC)
Trust terminated 06/21/2013
Each Class A Unit received approximately $11.48 cash
Each Class F Unit received approximately $12.06 cash

MORI SEIKI CO LTD (JAPAN)
Name changed to DMG Mori Seiki Co., Ltd. 11/08/2013
DMG Mori Seiki Co., Ltd. name changed to DMG Mori Co., Ltd. 07/02/2015

MORIE YELLOWKNIFE GOLD MINES, LTD. (ON)
Charter cancelled 00/00/1954

MORINO ASSOCIATES, INC. (DE)
Common 1¢ par split (3) for (2) by issuance of (0.5) additional share 06/17/1987
Name changed to Morino, Inc. 11/18/1988
Morino, Inc. merged into Legent Corp. 03/20/1989
(See Legent Corp.)

MORINO INC (DE)
Merged into Legent Corp. 03/20/1989
Each share Common 1¢ par exchanged for (0.8684) share Common 1¢ par
(See Legent Corp.)

MORITZ ENERGY CORP (CO)
Recapitalized 5/15/90
Recapitalized from Moritz Mining Co., Inc. to Moritz Energy Corp. 5/15/90
Each share old Common 10¢ par exchanged for (0.1) share new Common 10¢ par
Declared defunct and inoperative for failure to pay taxes and file annual reports 4/1/2002

MORLAN INTL INC (DE)
Merged into Service Corp. International 11/06/1987
Each share Common 1¢ par exchanged for (1/3) share Common $1 par

MORLAN PAC CORP (CA)
Common $5 par changed to $2.50 par and (1) additional share issued 08/05/1969
Merged into Credithrift Financial Corp. 11/04/1971
Each share Common $2.50 par exchanged for (0.95) share Common $1 par
Credithrift Financial Corp. name changed to American General Finance Corp. 03/20/1989
(See American General Finance Corp.)

MORLEX INC NEW (CO)
Each share old Common $0.0001 par exchanged for (0.001927) share new Common $0.001 par 12/05/2000
Reincorporated under the laws of Delaware as Superfly Advertising, Inc. 11/20/2008
(See Superfly Advertising, Inc.)

MORLEX INC OLD (CO)
Name changed to America Online, Inc. 07/15/1987
America Online, Inc. name changed to Morlex, Inc. (New) (CO) 06/02/1988 which reincorporated in Delaware as Superfly Advertising, Inc. 11/20/2008
(See Superfly Advertising, Inc.)

MORMAC ENERGY CORP (TX)
Name changed to Encino Energy & Development Corp. 10/28/83
Encino Energy & Development Corp. merged into Houston Oil Fields Co. (DE) 8/24/84 which merged into Plains Resources Co. 4/22/87
(See Plains Resources Co.)

MORNEAU SOBECO INCOME FD (ON)
Under plan of reorganization each Unit no par automatically became (1) share Morneau Shepell Inc. Common no par 01/04/2011

MORNING COFFEE, INC. (CA)
Name changed to Courtesy Products Corp. 3/9/62
(See Courtesy Products Corp.)

MORNING GLORY MINES, INC. (WA)
Bankrupt in 1951

MORNING STAR (FAIRVIEW) GOLD MINES LTD.
Liquidated in 1937

MORNING STAR HLDGS INC (NV)
Name changed to China Gold Corp. 01/06/2006
(See China Gold Corp.)

MORNING STAR INDS INC (DE)
Each share old Common $0.0001 par exchanged for (0.02) share new Common $0.0001 par 05/03/1996
Recapitalized as Eat at Joe's Ltd. 10/07/1996
Each share new Common $0.0001 par exchanged for (0.25) share Common $0.0001 par
Eat at Joe's Ltd. name changed to SPYR, Inc. 03/12/2015

MORNING STAR MINING CO. (WA)
Involuntarily dissolved by law for non-payment of corporate fees 7/1/23

MORNING STAR RES LTD (BC)
Name changed 04/27/1982
Name changed from Morning Star Mines Ltd. to Morning Star Resources Ltd. 04/27/1982
Recapitalized as Ballad Enterprises Ltd. 02/04/1991
Each share Common no par exchanged for (1/3) share Common no par
Ballad Enterprises Ltd. recapitalized as Ballad Ventures Ltd. 11/16/2001 which recapitalized as Ballad Gold & Silver Ltd. 07/21/2003 which recapitalized as Goldbank Mining Corp. 01/14/2009

MORNING SUN URANIUM, INC. (WA)
Merged into Daybreak Uranium, Inc. share for share 10/11/55
Daybreak Uranium, Inc. name changed to Daybreak Mines Inc. 4/18/64 which name changed to Daybreak Oil & Gas, Inc. 10/26/2005

MORNINGDALE MINES LTD. (ON)
Charter revoked for failure to file reports and pay fees 1/5/67

MORNINGSTAR, NICOL, INC. (DE)
Name changed to Morningstar-Paisley, Inc. 12/31/1957
Morningstar-Paisley, Inc. name changed to Paisley Products Inc. 03/30/1967
(See Paisley Products Inc.)

MORNINGSTAR GROUP INC (DE)
Merged into Suiza Foods Corp. 11/26/1997
Each share Common 1¢ par exchanged for (0.85) share Common 1¢ par
Suiza Foods Corp. name changed to Dean Foods Co. (New) 12/21/2001

MORNINGSTAR INDL HLDGS CORP (NV)
Name changed to New World Entertainment Corp. 05/01/2006
New World Entertainment Corp. name changed to Aultra Gold, Inc. 01/19/2007 which name changed to Shamika 2 Gold, Inc. 02/02/2011
(See Shamika 2 Gold, Inc.)

MORNINGSTAR INVESTMENTS, INC. (UT)
Reincorporated under the laws of Nevada as ZZZZ Best Co., Inc. 1/21/86
(See ZZZZ Best Co., Inc.)

MORNINGSTAR PAISLEY INC (DE)
Name changed to Paisley Products Inc. 03/30/1967
(See Paisley Products Inc.)

MORNORTH MTG HLDGS INC (NM)
Each share Common 20¢ par received distribution of (1/3) share St. George Metals, Inc. Common 1¢ par payable 08/08/2003 to holders of record 08/06/2003
Recapitalized as Westlake Canyon International, Inc. 09/09/2005
Each (35.22) shares Common 20¢ par exchanged for (1) share Common 20¢ par 09/09/2005
Westlake Canyon International, Inc. name changed to Vision International, Inc. 04/26/2006 which name changed to Exlites Holdings International, Inc. 09/19/2008

MOROCCO EXPLS INC (BC)
Recapitalized as Mask Resources Inc. 09/02/1998
Each share Common no par exchanged for (0.33333333) share Common no par
Mask Resources Inc. name changed to American Nevada Gold Corp. 10/01/2002 which recapitalized as Northern Canadian Minerals Inc. 08/06/2004 which name changed to Northern Canadian Uranium Inc. 04/09/2007 which merged into Bayswater Uranium Corp. (New) 12/21/2007 which recapitalized as Green Thumb Industries Inc. 06/13/2018

MOROCCO MINES LTD. (BC)
Recapitalized as Remar Resources Ltd. 10/30/1972
Each share Common 50¢ par exchanged for (0.25) share Common no par
Remar Resources Ltd. recapitalized as Golden Shamrock Resources Ltd. 07/17/1975 which merged into Colt Exploration Ltd. (BC) 07/08/1982 which reorganized in Alberta as Colt Exploration (Western) Ltd. 05/17/1983 which recapitalized as Colt Exploration (1988) Ltd. 06/30/1988 which reorganized as Stampede Oils Inc. 12/29/1988
(See Stampede Oils Inc.)

MORRELL (JOHN) & CO. (ME)
Reincorporated 12/31/1936
State of incorporation changed from (DE) to (ME) 12/31/1936
Capital Stock no par split (2) for (1) by issuance of (1) additional share 04/03/1947
Capital Stock no par changed to $10 par 03/19/1956
Capital Stock $10 par split (5) for (4) by issuance of (0.25) additional share 02/15/1960
Merged into AMK Corp. 12/31/1967
Each share Capital Stock $10 par exchanged for (0.25) share $3.20 Conv. Preference no par and (0.5) share Common $2 par
AMK Corp. merged into United Brands Co. 06/30/1970 which name changed to Chiquita Brands International, Inc. 03/20/1990

(See Chiquita Brands International, Inc.)

MORRIA BIOPHARMACEUTICALS PLC (ENGLAND & WALES)
Name changed to Celsus Therapeutics PLC 07/17/2013
Celsus Therapeutics PLC name changed to Akari Therapeutics PLC 09/18/2015

MORRIS & ESSEX RAILROAD CO.
Merged into Delaware, Lackawanna & Western Railroad Co. and each share Capital Stock exchanged for $50 principal amount of bonds in 1945

MORRIS (LEWIS) APARTMENTS, INC. (NY)
Liquidation completed 4/1/59

MORRIS (PHILIP) CONSOLIDATED, INC.
Liquidated in 1935

MORRIS CNTY SVGS BK (MORRISTOWN, NJ)
Merged into First Fidelity Bancorporation (Old) 06/09/1986
Each share Common $2 par exchanged for $52 cash

MORRIS FINANCE CO.
Merged into Associates Investment Co. (Ind.) in 1940
Each share Class A Common exchanged for (5) shares Common
Each share Class B Common exchanged for (1) share Common
Associates Investment Co. (Ind.) reincorporated under the laws of Delaware 6/26/69
(See Associates Investment Co. (Del.))

MORRIS HOMES CORP (TN)
Charter revoked for non-payment of taxes 09/30/1974

MORRIS (WILLIAM S.) INC. (NY)
Name changed to National Arbitrage Corp. 2/11/66
National Arbitrage Corp. name changed to Geosearch, Inc. 7/16/76
(See Geosearch, Inc.)

MORRIS (PHILIP) INC. (VA)
See - Philip Morris Inc

MORRIS INDS INC (DE)
Adjudicated bankrupt 05/23/1978
Stockholders' equity unlikely

MORRIS KIRKLAND GOLD MINES LTD.
Bankrupt in 1941

MORRIS PAPER MILLS (IL)
Merged into Federal Paper Board Co., Inc. (NY) 8/11/56
Each share Common $10 par exchanged for (1) share 4.6% Preferred $25 par and (0.4) share Common $5 par
Federal Paper Board Co., Inc. (NY) reincorporated in (NC) 4/20/94
(See Federal Paper Board Co., Inc.)

MORRIS PLAN BANK (CLEVELAND, OH)
Name changed to Bank of Ohio Co. (Cleveland, Ohio) in 1946
Bank of Ohio Co. (Cleveland, Ohio) completed liquidation 6/14/57

MORRIS PLAN BANK OF VIRGINIA (RICHMOND, VA)
Name changed to Bank of Virginia (Richmond, VA) 12/31/1945
(See Bank of Virginia (Richmond, VA))

MORRIS PLAN CO. OF CALIFORNIA (CA)
Name changed to Morris Plan Co. 12/31/1963
Morris Plan Co. name changed to Morlan Pacific Corp. 04/15/1969 which merged into Credithrift Financial Corp. 11/04/1971 which

name changed to American General Finance Corp. 03/20/1989
(See American General Finance Corp.)

MORRIS PLAN CO (CA)
Capital Stock $10 par changed to $5 par and (1) additional share issued 01/15/1964
Name changed to Morlan Pacific Corp. 04/15/1969
Morlan Pacific Corp. merged into Credithrift Financial Corp. 11/04/1971 which name changed to American General Finance Corp. 03/20/1989
(See American General Finance Corp.)

MORRIS PLAN CORP. OF AMERICA (VA)
Common $1 par changed to 25¢ par in 1934
Each share Common 25¢ par exchanged for (0.05) share Common $5 par in 1940
6% Preferred Ser. 1931 $10 par called for redemption 10/1/45
Under plan of merger each share Common $5 par exchanged for (4) shares Common 10¢ par 10/30/45
Stock Dividend - 10% 11/15/54
Name changed to Financial General Corp. 4/25/56
Financial General Corp. name changed to Financial General Bankshares, Inc. 4/29/70 which name changed to First American Bankshares, Inc. 8/12/82
(See First American Bankshares, Inc.)

MORRIS PLAN INSURANCE SOCIETY (NY)
Name changed to Bankers Security Life Insurance Society in 1946
Bankers Security Life Insurance Society merged into United Services Life Insurance Co. 12/20/79 which reorganized in Virginia as USLICO Corp. 8/15/84 which merged into NWNL Companies, Inc. 1/17/95 which name changed to ReliaStar Financial Corp. 2/13/95
(See ReliaStar Financial Corp.)

MORRIS PLAN SVGS BK INC (BURLINGTON, NC)
Reorganized 09/15/1997
Reorganized from Morris Plan Industrial Bank (Burlington, NC) to Morris Plan Savings Bank (Burlington, NC) 09/15/1997
Each share Common no par exchanged for (100) shares Common no par
Merged into Randolph Bank & Trust Co. (Asheboro, NC) 05/31/2002
Each share Common no par exchanged for (0.6746) share Common no par
Randolph Bank & Trust Co. (Asheboro, NC) merged into BNC Bancorp 10/01/2013 which merged into Pinnacle Financial Partners, Inc. 06/16/2017

MORRIS PLAN SHARES CORP.
Name changed to Industrial Bancshares Corp. in 1929
Industrial Bancshares Corp. recapitalized as General Contract Corp. in 1950 which name changed to General Bancshares Corp. 11/6/58 which merged into Boatmen's Banchshares, Inc. 3/29/86 which merged into NationsBank Corp. 1/7/97 which reincorporated in Delaware as BankAmerica Corp. (Old) 9/25/98 which merged into BankAmerica Corp. (New) 9/30/98 which name changed to Bank of America Corp. 4/28/99

MORRIS RUN COAL MNG CO (PA)
5% Preferred $100 par changed to $50 par and $50 in cash distributed in 1950
5% Preferred $50 par changed to $45 par and $5 in cash distributed in 1951
5% Preferred $45 par changed to $40 par and $5 in cash distributed in 1953
5% Preferred $40 par changed to $35 par and $5 in cash distributed 8/20/56
5% Preferred $35 par changed to $30 par and $5 in cash distributed 11/20/57
5% Preferred $30 par changed to $25 par and $5 in cash distributed 6/20/58
5% Preferred $25 par changed to $20 par and $5 in cash distributed 4/10/59
5% Preferred $20 par changed to $1 par and $19 in cash distributed 6/30/60
Completely liquidated 4/16/99
Each share Common $100 par exchanged for first and final distribution of $304.2917 cash
Details on Preferred not available

MORRIS SHELL HOMES INC (TN)
Name changed to Morris Homes Corp. 01/00/1963
(See Morris Homes Corp.)

MORRIS SUMMIT GOLD MINES LTD (BC)
Recapitalized as Scottie Gold Mines Ltd. 02/01/1979
Each share Common $1 par exchanged for (1) share Class A Common no par
Scottie Gold Mines Ltd. recapitalized as Royal Scot Resources Ltd. 06/02/1987 which merged into Tenajon Resources Corp. 08/01/1991 which merged into Creston Moly Corp. 08/26/2009 which merged into Mercator Minerals Ltd. 06/21/2011

MORRIS T. BAKER CO.
See - Baker (Morris T.) Co.

MORRISON BRASS CORP. LTD. (CANADA)
Recapitalized 12/30/44
Each share Preferred $50 par exchanged for (3) shares Capital Stock no par
Each share Common no par exchanged for (0.2) share Capital Stock no par
Reorganized 3/31/61
Each share Capital Stock no par exchanged for (1) share Morrison (James) Brass Manufacturing Co. Ltd. Capital Stock no par and (1) share Fidelitron Corp. Common 1¢ par
(See each company's listing)

MORRISON (JAMES) BRASS MANUFACTURING CO. LTD. (CANADA)
Name changed to Jamob Corp. Ltd. 10/1/65
Jamob Corp. Ltd. completed liquidation 9/1/69

MORRISON CAFETERIAS CONSOLIDATED, INC. (FL)
7% Preferred $100 par called for redemption 10/1/64
Stock Dividend - 100% 4/15/66
Under plan of merger name changed to Morrison Inc. (FL) 3/11/68
Morrison Inc. (FL) reincorporated in Delaware 10/1/87 which name changed to Morrison Restaurants Inc. 10/1/92 which merged into Piccadilly Cafeterias, Inc. 7/31/98
(See Piccadilly Cafeterias, Inc.)

MORRISON CAFETERIAS CONSOLIDATED INC. (LA)
Merged into Morrison Cafeterias Consolidated, Inc. (FL) 12/28/54
Each share Preferred $100 par exchanged for (1) share Preferred $100 par
Each share Common no par exchanged for (4) shares Common $5 par
Morrison Cafeterias Consolidated, Inc. (FL) name changed to Morrison Inc. (FL) 3/11/68 which reincorporated in Delaware 10/1/87 which name changed to Morrison Restaurants Inc. 10/1/92 which merged into Piccadilly Cafeterias, Inc. 7/31/98
(See Piccadilly Cafeterias, Inc.)

MORRISON CORP. (DE)
Charter cancelled and declared inoperative and void for non-payment of taxes 3/19/24

MORRISON FACS INCOME FD (AB)
Name changed to Western Facilities Fund 05/10/1999
Western Facilities Fund recapitalized as Acclaim Energy Trust 04/20/2001
(See Acclaim Energy Trust)

MORRISON FRESH COOKING INC (GA)
Name changed to Morrison Restaurants Inc. 9/5/97
Morrison Restaurants Inc. merged into Piccadilly Cafeterias, Inc. 7/31/98
(See Piccadilly Cafeterias, Inc.)

MORRISON GREY ENTERPRISES LTD (BC)
Name changed to MGP Asia Capital Inc. 05/01/1989
MGP Asia Capital Inc. recapitalized as Insular Explorations Ltd. 07/15/1991 which name changed to Masuparia Gold Corp. 09/01/1999 which name changed to MAS Gold Corp. 04/09/2018

MORRISON HEALTH CARE INC (GA)
Name changed to Morrison Management Specialists Inc. 6/30/99
(See Morrison Management Specialists Inc.)

MORRISON HOTEL CORP. (DE)
Completely liquidated 10/28/63
Each share Common no par exchanged for first and final distribution of $20 cash

MORRISON INC (DE)
Reincorporated 10/1/87
Common $5 par changed to $2 par and (2) additional shares issued 11/5/76
Stock Dividends - 100% 10/15/68; 25% 5/26/72; 25% 9/30/75
State of incorporation changed from (FL) to (DE) 10/1/87
Common $2 par changed to 1¢ par and (1/3) additional share issued 12/4/87
Common 1¢ par split (3) for (2) by issuance of (0.5) additional share 4/30/92
Name changed to Morrison Restaurants Inc. 10/1/92
Morrison Restaurants Inc. merged into Piccadilly Cafeterias, Inc. 7/31/98
(See Piccadilly Cafeterias, Inc.)

MORRISON KNUDSEN CORP NEW (DE)
Name changed to Washington Group International, Inc. 9/15/2000
(See Washington Group International, Inc.)

MORRISON KNUDSEN CORP OLD (DE)
Common $3.33-1/3 par changed to $1.67 par and (1) additional share issued 5/26/92
Reorganized as Morrison Knudsen Corp. (New) 9/11/96
Each share Common $1.67 par exchanged for (1) share Common 1¢ par, (0.075) Common Stock Purchase Warrant expiring 3/11/2003, and (1) Non-transferable Right

MORRISON KNUDSEN INC (DE)
Each share Common $10 par exchanged for (10) shares Common $10 par in 1946
Series E thru N Preferred called for redemption 11/28/46
$5 Preferred $50 par called for redemption 5/21/51
Common $10 par changed to $6.66-2/3 par and (0.5) additional share issued 6/9/78
Common $6.66-2/3 par changed to $3.33-1/3 par and (1) additional share issued 6/6/80
Stock Dividends - 15% 1/20/52; 100% 2/1/55; 10% 3/15/68
Under plan of reorganization each share Common $3.33-1/3 par automatically became (1) share Morrison Knudsen Corp. (Old) Common $3.33-1/3 par 5/6/85
Morrison Knudsen Corp. (Old) reorganized as Morrison Knudsen Corp. (New) 9/11/96

MORRISON LAMOTHE FOODS LTD (CANADA)
Name changed 6/19/70
Common no par reclassified as Class B Common no par 11/25/64
Name changed from Morrison-Lamothe Bakery Ltd. to Morrison Lamothe Foods Ltd. 6/19/70
Name changed to Morrison Lamothe Inc. 7/10/78

MORRISON MGMT SPECIALISTS INC (GA)
Stock Dividend - 10% payable 5/19/2000 to holders of record 5/1/2000
Merged into Compass Group PLC 4/5/2001
Each share Common 1¢ par exchanged for $40 cash

MORRISON MIDDLEFIELD RES LTD (AB)
Reincorporated 00/00/1995
Place of incorporation changed from (Canada) to (AB) 00/00/1995
Common no par split (2) for (1) by issuance of (1) additional share payable 06/13/1997 to holders of record 06/06/1997 Ex date - 06/04/1997
Plan of Arrangement effective 07/29/1999
Each share Common no par received (1) share 2M Energy Corp. Common no par and $5.50 cash
Note: Certificates were not required to be surrendered and are without value
(See 2M Energy Corp.)

MORRISON MINERALS LTD (ON)
Merged into OGY Petroleums Ltd. (ALTA) 11/1/92
Each share Common no par exchanged for (0.45) share Common no par
(See OGY Petroleums Ltd. (ALTA))

MORRISON MINES LTD. (ON)
Acquired by New Morrison Mines Ltd. on a (1) for (3.6) basis in 1951
New Morrison Mines Ltd. recapitalized as Consolidated Morrison Explorations Ltd. 5/11/55 which name changed to Morrison Petroleums Ltd. 10/22/80 which merged into Northstar Energy Corp. 3/14/97 which merged into Devon Energy Corp. (OK) 12/11/98 which merged into Devon Energy Corp. (New) (DE) 8/17/99

MORRISON MINES LTD (BC)
Under plan of merger name changed to Ronoco Resources Inc. and Capital Stock 50¢ par changed to no par 01/24/1977

(See Ronoco Resources Inc.)

MORRISON PETES LTD (ON)
Capital Stock no par split (2) for (1) by issuance of (1) additional share 12/8/89
Common no par split (3) for (1) by issuance of (2) additional shares 5/31/93
Merged into Northstar Energy Corp. 3/14/97
Each share Common no par exchanged for (0.7) share Common no par
Northstar Energy Corp. merged into Devon Energy Corp. (OK) 12/11/98 which merged into Devon Energy Corp. (New) (DE) 8/17/99

MORRISON RESTAURANTS INC (DE)
Common 1¢ par split (3) for (2) by issuance of (0.5) additional share 10/29/1983
Reorganized under the laws of Georgia as Ruby Tuesday, Inc. 03/09/1996
Each share Common 1¢ par exchanged for (0.5) share Common 1¢ par, distribution of (0.25) share Morrison Fresh Cooking, Inc. Common 1¢ par and distribution of (0.33333333) share Morrison Health Care, Inc. Common 1¢ par
(See each company's listing)

MORRISON RESTAURANTS INC (GA)
Merged into Piccadilly Cafeterias, Inc. 07/31/1998
Each share Common 1¢ par exchanged for $5 cash

MORRISTOWN SECURITIES CORP.
Dissolved in 1941

MORRISTOWN TRUST CO. (MORRISTOWN, NJ)
Capital Stock $15 par changed to $20 par in 1946
Merged into Trust Co. of Morris County (Morristown, N.J.) 12/19/58
Each share Capital Stock $20 par exchanged for (1) share Capital Stock $20 par
Trust Co. of Morris County (Morristown, N.J.) name changed to Trust Co. National Bank (Morristown, N.J.) 1/27/67 which merged into American National Bank & Trust (Montclair, N.J.) 7/10/70 which reorganized as Princeton American Bancorp 1/1/72 which name changed to Horizon Bancorp 12/31/73
(See Horizon Bancorp)

MORRISVILLE BK (MORRISVILLE, PA)
Merged into Bucks County Bank & Trust Co. (Perkasie, PA) 12/31/1981
Each share Common $20 par exchanged for (4.8) shares Common $2.50 par
Bucks County Bank & Trust Co. (Perkasie, PA) reorganized as Independence Bancorp, Inc. (PA) 11/01/1982 which merged into CoreStates Financial Corp 06/27/1994 which merged into First Union Corp. 04/28/1998 which name changed to Wachovia Corp. (Ctfs. dated after 09/01/2001) 09/01/2001 which merged into Wells Fargo & Co. (New) 12/31/2008

MORRO BAY CAP LTD (AB)
Name changed to Morro Bay Resources Ltd. (AB) 01/28/2014
Morro Bay Resources Ltd. (AB) reorganized in Canada as Viridium Pacific Group Ltd. 10/10/2017

MORRO BAY RES LTD (AB)
Each share old Common no par exchanged for (0.1) share new Common no par 05/09/2017
Reorganized under the laws of Canada as Viridium Pacific Group Ltd. 10/10/2017

Each share new Common no par exchanged for (0.27751128) share Common no par

MORROW SCREW & NUT LTD.
98.5% acquired by Ingersoll Machine & Tool Co. 00/00/1968
Public interest eliminated

MORROW SNOWBOARDS INC (OR)
Reincorporated under the laws of California as Granite Bay Technologies, Inc. 11/01/2000
Granite Bay Technologies, Inc. (CA) reincorporated in Delaware as International DisplayWorks, Inc. 10/11/2001 which merged into Flextronics International Ltd. 11/30/2006 which name changed to Flex Ltd. 09/28/2016

MORSE PAINT MANUFACTURING LTD. (ON)
Liquidation completed
Each share Common no par received initial distribution of $34 cash 8/21/64
Each share Common no par received second distribution of $4 cash 11/19/65
Each share Common no par received third distribution of $6 cash 8/22/66
Each share Common no par received fourth and final distribution of $2.43 cash 12/11/67
Certificates were not required to be surrendered and are now valueless

MORSE ROBERT LTD (CANADA)
Acquired by General Tire & Rubber Co. 8/23/74
Each share Class A Common no par exchanged for $18.50 cash
Each share Class B Common no par exchanged for $18.50 cash
5-1/2% Conv. Preferred Ser. A $50 par called for redemption 8/4/75
5-1/2% Conv. Preferred Ser. B $50 par called for redemption 8/4/75
Public interest eliminated

MORSE SHOE INC NEW (DE)
Acquired by Baker (J), Inc. 1/30/93
Each share Common 1¢ par exchanged for (0.17091) share Common 50¢ par
Baker (J), Inc. name changed to Casual Male Corp. 2/26/2001
(See Casual Male Corp.)

MORSE SHOE INC OLD (DE)
Common $1 par split (3) for (2) by issuance of (0.5) additional share 01/05/1968
Common $1 par split (4) for (3) by issuance of (1/3) additional share 07/15/1976
Common $1 par split (4) for (3) by issuance of (1/3) additional share 07/06/1978
Merged into Moacq Holdings Corp. 03/30/1988
Each share Common $1 par exchanged for $47 cash
Merged into Morse Shoe, Inc. (New) 01/15/1992
Each share 20% Sr. Exchangeable Preferred 1¢ par exchanged for $1.598 principal amount of Sr. Conv. Subordinated Notes due 01/15/2002 and (0.32) share Common 1¢ par
Morse Shoe, Inc. (New) acquired by Baker (J), Inc. 01/30/1993 which name changed to Casual Male Corp. 02/26/2001
(See Casual Male Corp.)

MORSEMERE FINL GROUP INC (DE)
Name changed to Metrobank Financial Group, Inc. 05/08/1989
(See Metrobank Financial Group, Inc.)

MORT LAKE MINES LTD. (BC)
Struck off register and declared dissolved for failure to pay fees or file reports 5/15/69

MORTBON CORP. OF NEW YORK
Acquired by Telfair Stockton & Co., Inc. on a share for share basis in 1945
Telfair Stockton & Co., Inc. merged into Stockton, Whatley, Davin & Co. in 1952 which was acquired by General American Oil Co. of Texas 5/19/64
(See General American Oil Co. of Texas)

MORTCORP ENTERPRISES INC (BC)
Recapitalized as Licefa International Inc. 10/03/1994
Each share Common no par exchanged for (0.2) share Common no par
Licefa International Inc. recapitalized as Continuum Arts Inc. 12/24/1996 which recapitalized as Continuum Resources Ltd. 05/13/1999 which was acquired by Fortuna Silver Mines Inc. 03/06/2009

MORTGAGE & CONTRACT CO.
Merged into Detroit Mortgage & Realty Co. (MI) 00/00/1946
Each share Common exchanged for (1.7) shares Common $1 par
Detroit Mortgage & Realty Co. (MI) reorganized in Nevada as Boundary Bay Resources, Inc. 09/24/2007 which recapitalized as Wave Technology Group Inc. 05/06/2010 which name changed to eMamba International Corp. 07/27/2011

MORTGAGE & DEVELOPMENT CORP. (VA)
Liquidation completed
Each share Common $3 par exchanged for initial distribution of $0.80 cash 7/18/77
Each share Common $3 par received second distribution of $0.50 cash 12/20/77
Each share Common $3 par received third and final distribution of $1.30 cash 4/14/78

MORTGAGE & RLTY TR (MD)
Name changed to Value Property Trust 10/27/1995
Value Property Trust merged into Wellsford Real Properties, Inc. 02/23/1998 which name changed to Reis, Inc. 06/01/2007
(See Reis, Inc.)

MORTGAGE & SECURITIES CO.
Liquidated in 1931

MORTGAGE ACQUISITION CORP (FL)
Name changed to American Lending & Acquisition Group, Inc. 03/16/1998
American Lending & Acquisition Group, Inc. recapitalized as Exosphere Aircraft Co., Inc. 06/19/2006 which name changed to Business Continuity Solutions Inc. 07/14/2011 which name changed to Tall Trees LED Co. 08/05/2016 which recapitalized as Light Engine Design Corp. 12/21/2016

MORTGAGE AMER FINL CORP (FL)
Name changed to Loan America Financial Corp. 1/10/85
(See Loan America Financial Corp.)

MORTGAGE ASSISTANCE CTR CORP (FL)
SEC revoked common stock registration 03/06/2013

MORTGAGE ASSOC INC (WI)
Common $1 par split (2) for (1) by issuance of (1) additional share 9/26/69
Common $1 par split (2) for (1) by issuance of (1) additional share 8/31/71
Merged into Industrial National Corp. 3/15/74
Each share Common $1 par exchanged for (0.5) share Common $1 par

Industrial National Corp. name changed to Fleet Financial Group, Inc. (Old) 4/14/82 which merged into Fleet/Norstar Financial Group, Inc. 1/1/88 which name changed to Fleet Financial Group, Inc. (New) 4/15/92 which name changed to Fleet Boston Corp. 10/1/99 which name changed to FleetBoston Financial Corp. 4/18/2000 which merged into Bank of America Corp. 4/1/2004

MORTGAGE BANKERS HLDG CORP (NY)
Name changed to National Institute Companies of America 04/12/2000
(See National Institute Companies of America)

MORTGAGE BANKERS SVC CORP N.A. (OR)
Name changed to Harcourt-Symes Ltd. (OR) 05/03/1996
Harcourt-Symes Ltd. (OR) reincorporated in Nevada as Nordic American Inc. 06/09/1997 which reorganized in Delaware as Stark Beneficial, Inc. 02/08/2008 which name changed to China Greenstar Corp. 01/22/2015

MORTGAGE BLDG. CORP. (DE)
Liquidation completed 7/20/62

MORTGAGE BOND & GUARANTY CORP.
Merged into Mortgage Security Corp. of America in 1927
Details not available

MORTGAGE-BOND CO. OF NEW YORK
Reorganized as Mortbon Corp. of New York 00/00/1935
Details not available

MORTGAGE BROKERS NETWORK INC (MN)
Name changed to Plenum Communications Inc. 11/22/1991
Plenum Communications Inc. name changed to LION, Inc. (MN) 08/20/1999 which reincorporated in Washington 12/15/2000
(See LION, Inc.)

MTG CAP CORP (DE)
Recapitalized as Continuum Group Inc. 12/09/1991
Each share Common $0.001 par exchanged for (0.1) share Common $0.001 par
Continuum Group Inc. reorganized as NuWeb Solutions, Inc. 05/04/2000 which recapitalized as Pensador Resources Inc. 05/30/2008

MORTGAGE COM INC (FL)
Placed in receivership under Chapter 727 Florida Statutes 05/08/2001
Stockholders' equity unlikely

MORTGAGE DISCOUNT CORP. (CO)
Charter revoked for failure to file reports and pay fees 10/15/65

MORTGAGE GROWTH INVS (MA)
Shares of Bene. Int. $1 par reclassified as Common $1 par 5/21/75
Name changed to MGI Properties 2/10/88
(See MGI Properties)

MORTGAGE GTY INS CORP (WI)
99.9% acquired by MGIC Investment Corp. through exchange offer which expired 10/14/1968
Public interest eliminated

MORTGAGE GUARANTEE CO. (CA)
Liquidated in 1947

MORTGAGE GUARANTEE CO. OF BALTIMORE
Reorganized in 1941
No stockholders' equity

MORTGAGE INS CO CDA (CANADA)
Acquired by Holborough Investments Ltd. 00/00/1969
Each share Common no par

exchanged for (0.1) share Common no par
Holborough Investments Ltd. recapitalized as MICC Investments Ltd. 05/04/1972
(See MICC Investments Ltd.)

MORTGAGE INVT GROUP (CA)
Name changed to Continental Illinois Realty 03/31/1971
(See Continental Illinois Realty)

MORTGAGE INVS WASH (MD)
Name changed to MIW Investors of Washington 8/28/81
MIW Investors of Washington name changed to Ameribanc Investors Group 6/16/86
(See Ameribanc Investors Group)

MORTGAGE INVTS PLUS INC (MD)
Name changed to MIP Properties, Inc. 6/14/90
(See MIP Properties, Inc.)

MORTGAGE LIQUIDITY FD INC (MD)
Merged into Ryland Securities, Inc. 07/01/1991
Details not available

MORTGAGE SECS TR (NY)
Units of Undivided Int. Collateral Mortgage Obligation Ser. 8 Short Intermediate Portfolio Monthly called for redemption 3/10/97
Units of Undivided Int. Collateral Mortgage Obligation Ser. 10 Short Intermediate Portfolio Monthly called for redemption 3/10/97
Units of Undivided Int. Collateral Mortgage Obligation Ser. 11 Short Intermediate Portfolio Monthly called for redemption 3/10/97

MORTGAGE SECURITY CORP. OF AMERICA
Reorganized as A-NY & B-NY Realizing Corp. 00/00/1935
Details not available

MORTGAGE SERVICE CO.
Name changed to Mortgage Oil Corp. in 1948

MORTGAGE TR AMER (CA)
Name changed to Transamerica Realty Investors 11/17/1980
Transamerica Realty Investors merged into Transamerica Corp. 09/30/1986 which merged into Aegon N.V. 07/21/1999

MORTGAGE XPRESS INC (DE)
Recapitalized as Alternative Energy Technology Center, Inc. 01/18/2008
Each share Common $0.001 par exchanged for (0.02) share Common $0.001 par
Alternative Energy Technology Center, Inc. recapitalized as Alternative Energy Technology Inc. 08/04/2008

MORTGAGEBANQUE INC (TX)
In process of liquidation
Each share Common $1 par exchanged for initial distribution of $2.50 cash 04/28/1978
Each share Common $1 par received second distribution of $0.25 cash 09/29/1978
Each share Common $1 par received third distribution of $0.25 cash 11/15/1978
Note: Details on additional distributions, if any, are not available

MORTGAGEBROKERS COM HLDGS INC (DE)
Old Common $0.0001 par split (15) for (1) by issuance of (14) additional shares payable 03/28/2005 to holders of record 03/21/2005
Ex date - 03/29/2005
Each (30) shares old Common $0.0001 par exchanged for (1) share new Common $0.0001 par 11/14/2011
Name changed to MoPals.com, Inc. 04/11/2013

MORTGAGEIT HLDGS INC (MD)
Merged into Deutsche Bank AG 01/02/2007
Each share Common 1¢ par exchanged for $14.75 cash

MORTGAGES, INC. (CO)
Name changed to Republic Financial Corp. 10/13/61
Republic Financial Corp. charter revoked 10/26/64

MORTICE KERN SYS INC (ON)
Name changed to MKS Inc. 10/10/2001
(See MKS Inc.)

MORTIMER & WALLING SECURITIES CORP. (NY)
Acquired by Johnston Mutual Fund Inc. on a (2.53) for (1) basis in 1959
Johnston Mutual Fund Inc. reincorporated in Massachusetts as Johnston Capital Appreciation Fund 8/1/79 which name changed to Boston Co. Capital Appreciation Fund 5/1/81

MORTLOCK RESOURCE CORP (BC)
Name changed to NovaDx International Inc. 01/20/1995
NovaDx International Inc. recapitalized as NovaDx Ventures Corp. 12/02/2004
(See NovaDx Ventures Corp.)

MORTLOCK VENTURES INC (NV)
Each share old Common $0.001 par exchanged for (16) shares new Common $0.001 par 02/14/2007
Name changed to China Tel Group Inc. 04/24/2008
China Tel Group Inc. name changed to VelaTel Global Communications, Inc. 07/25/2011
(See VelaTel Global Communications, Inc.)

MORTON B C FD INC (DE)
Stock Distribution - All Series 100% 5/15/62
Name changed to Admiralty Fund 1/23/70
Admiralty Fund merged into Oppenheimer A.I.M. Fund, Inc. 12/7/76 which name changed to Oppenheimer Global Fund 2/1/87

MORTON B C RLTY TR (MA)
Name changed to Transco Realty Trust 06/23/1971

MORTON COS INC (MA)
Proclaimed dissolved for failure to file reports and pay fees 12/31/90

MORTON FED SVGS BK (MORTON, IL)
Name changed to Bankplus FSB (Morton, IL) 01/31/1996
(See Bankplus FSB (Morton, IL))

MORTON FOODS, INC. (TX)
Common & Class B Common $5 par changed to $1.50 par and (2) additional shares issued 1/19/62
Acquired by General Mills, Inc. 2/28/64
Each share Common $1.50 par exchanged for (0.25) share Common $3 par
Each (4.45877) shares Class B Common $1.50 par exchanged for (1) share Common $3 par

MORTON GREGORY CORP.
Name changed to Gregory Industries, Inc. in 1951
Gregory Industries, Inc. merged into TRW Inc. 1/31/69 which merged into Northrop Grumman Corp. 12/11/2002

MORTON INDL GROUP INC (GA)
Merged into MMC Precision Holdings Corp. 8/25/2006
Each share Class A Common 1¢ par exchanged for $10 cash

MORTON INTL INC (DE)
Merged into Morton-Norwich Products, Inc. (NY) 4/25/69
Each share Common no par exchanged for (1.15) shares Common 31-1/4¢ par
Morton-Norwich Products, Inc. (NY) reincorporated in Delaware 11/28/69 which merged into Morton Thiokol, Inc. 9/24/82 which reorganized as Thiokol Corp. (DE) (New) 7/1/89 which name changed to Cordant Technologies Inc. 5/7/98
(See Cordant Technologies Inc.)

MORTON INTL INC (IN)
Common $1 par split (3) for (1) by issuance of (2) additional shares 8/17/94
Merged into Autoliv, Inc. 5/1/97
Each share Common $1 par exchanged for (0.341) share Common $1 par

MORTON INTL INC NEW (IN)
Merged into Rohm & Haas Co. 06/21/1999
Each share Common $1 par exchanged for (0.368776) share Common $2.50 par and $24.55 cash
(See Rohm & Haas Co.)

MORTON MANUFACTURING CORP. (VA)
4-1/2% Preferred called for redemption 11/24/1958
Each share Common $10 par exchanged for (10) shares Common $1 par 12/01/1958
Merged into Robins (A.H.) Co., Inc. 11/29/1963
Each share Common $1 par exchanged for (0.75) share Common $1 par
Robins (A.H.) Co. Inc. merged into American Home Products Corp. 12/15/1989 which name changed to Wyeth 03/11/2002 which was acquired by Pfizer Inc. 10/15/2009

MORTON NORWICH PRODS INC (DE)
Reincorporated 11/28/69
State of incorporation changed from (NY) to (DE) and Common 31-1/4¢ par changed to $1 par 11/28/69
Under plan of merger name changed to Morton Thiokol, Inc. 9/24/82
Morton Thiokol, Inc. reorganized as Thiokol Corp. (DE) (New) 7/1/89 which name changed to Cordant Technologies, Inc. 5/7/98
(See Cordant Technologies Inc.)

MORTON OIL CO. (WY)
Merged into Inland Oil & Uranium Corp. share for share in 1956
Inland Oil & Uranium Corp. recapitalized as Inland Development Corp. 6/1/56 which merged into American Industries, Inc. 8/1/62 which was acquired by Empire Petroleum Co. 11/16/66 which name changed to Empire International, Inc. 7/15/70 which was adjudicated bankrupt 5/9/73

MORTON PACKING CO. (KY)
Dissolved 11/1/56

MORTON SALT CO. (DE)
Name changed to Morton International, Inc. 5/11/65
Morton International, Inc. merged into Morton-Norwich Products, Inc. (NY) 4/25/69 which reincorporated in Delaware 11/28/69 which merged into Morton Thiokol, Inc. 9/24/82 which reorganized as Thiokol Corp. (DE) (New) 7/1/89 which name changed to Cordant Technologies Inc. 5/7/98
(See Cordant Technologies Inc.)

MORTON SHOE COS INC (MA)
Under plan of reorganization each share Common $1 par automatically became (1) share Morton Companies, Inc. Class A Common 1¢ par 08/01/1983
(See Morton Companies, Inc.)

MORTON THIOKOL INC (DE)
Common $1 par split (3) for (1) by issuance of (2) additional shares 11/16/84
Reorganized as Thiokol Corp. (New) 7/1/89
Each share Common $1 par exchanged for (0.4) share Common $1 par
Thiokol Corp. (New) name changed to Cordant Technologies Inc. 5/7/98
(See Cordant Technologies Inc.)

MORTON WOOLSEY CONSOLIDATED MINES LTD. (BC)
Struck off register and declared dissolved for failure to file returns 1/23/41

MORTONS RESTAURANT GROUP INC NEW (DE)
Issue Information - 9,465,000 shares COM offered at $17 per share on 02/08/2006
Conv. Preferred Ser. A 1¢ par called for redemption at $5 on 01/23/2012
Acquired by Fertitta Morton's Restaurants, Inc. 02/01/2012
Each share Common 1¢ par exchanged for $6.90 cash

MORTONS RESTAURANT GROUP INC OLD (DE)
Merged into Castle Harlan Partners III, L.P. 7/25/2002
Each share Common 1¢ par exchanged for $17 cash

MORTONS SHOE STORES INC (MA)
Name changed to Morton Shoe Companies, Inc. 12/22/78
Morton Shoe Companies, Inc. reorganized as Morton Companies, Inc. 8/1/83
(See Morton Companies, Inc.)

MORTRONICS INC (OH)
Name changed to Morgan's Foods, Inc. 09/19/1986
(See Morgan's Foods, Inc.)

MORUMBI RES INC (ON)
Each share old Common no par exchanged for (0.33333333) share new Common no par 06/19/2014
Recapitalized as Ascendant Resources Inc. 12/21/2016
Each share new Common no par exchanged for (0.2) share Common no par

MORUYA GOLD MINES 1983 N L (AUSTRALIA)
Acquired by United Coin Mines Ltd. 04/11/1990
Each share Ordinary AUD$0.20 par exchanged for (0.18867925) share Common no par
United Coin Mines Ltd. name changed to Winstaff Ventures Ltd. 06/25/1993 which merged into Romarco Minerals Inc. (ON) 07/11/1995 which reincorporated in British Columbia 06/16/2006 which merged into OceanaGold Corp. 10/01/2015

MOSAIC CAP CORP (AB)
Non-Vtg. Preferred Ser. A called for redemption at $10 plus $0.1096 accrued dividends on 02/10/2017
(Additional Information in Active)

MOSAIC CO OLD (DE)
Each share 7.50% Mandatory Conv. Preferred 1¢ par exchanged for (6.444) shares Common 1¢ par 07/01/2006
Merged into Mosaic Co. (New) 05/25/2011
Each share Common 1¢ par exchanged for (1) share Common 1¢ par

MOSAIC GROUP INC (CANADA)
Reincorporated 5/29/2002
Additional Offering - 12,000,000 shares COM offered at $3.80 per share on 03/11/2002
Place of incorporation changed from (ONT) to (Canada) 5/29/2002
Assets sold for the benefit of creditors 7/15/2003
No stockholders' equity

MOSAIC MAPPING CORP (AB)
Acquired by Pulse Data Inc. 05/25/2004
Each share Common no par exchanged for (0.1176) share Common no par and $0.05 cash
Pulse Data Inc. name changed to Pulse Seismic Inc. 05/28/2009

MOSAIC MULTISOFT CORP (NV)
Each share old Common $0.001 par exchanged for (0.25) share new Common $0.001 par 12/5/94
Charter revoked for failure to file reports and pay fees 3/1/96

MOSAIC NUTRACEUTICALS CORP (NV)
Name changed 02/15/2005
Name changed from Mosaic Nutriceuticals Corp. to Mosaic Nutraceuticals Corp. 02/15/2005
Charter permanently revoked 03/30/2007

MOSAIC TAX-FREE TR (MA)
Merged into Tax-Free National Fund 06/19/2001
Each Maryland Tax-Free Fund Share of Bene. Int. no par received approximately (0.92625) Share of Bene. Int. no par
Tax-Free Money Market Shares of Bene. Int. no par completely liquidated 12/18/2003
Details not available
Merged into Tax-Free National Fund 06/22/2006
Each Missouri Tax-Free Fund Share of Bene. Int. no par received approximately (0.982844) Share of Bene. Int. no par
Merged into Tax-Free National Fund 07/20/2006
Each Arizona Tax-Free Fund Share of Bene. Int. no par received approximately (0.943309) Share of Bene. Int. no par
Name changed to Madison Mosaic Tax-Free Trust 11/01/2006

MOSAIC TECHNOLOGIES CORP (CANADA)
Name changed 05/30/1990
Name changed 08/11/1997
Reincorporated 11/27/1997
Name changed from Mosaic Resources Ltd. to Mosaic Recycled Paper Ltd. 5/30/90
Name changed from Mosaic Recycled Paper Ltd. to Mosaic Technologies Corp. 08/11/1997
Place of incorporation changed from (BC) to (Canada) 11/27/1997
Dissolved 02/09/2006
Details not available

MOSAIC TILE CO. (OH)
Common $100 par changed to $10 par and (9) additional shares issued 05/01/1964
Acquired by Marmon Group, Inc. (DE) (Ctfs. dated prior to 12/14/1967) 03/02/1967
Details not available

MOSAIC TILE CO FLA (FL)
Proclaimed dissolved for failure to file reports and pay taxes 10/21/74

MOSAIC TRAVEL & TOURS INC (AB)
Name changed to Bookfortravel.com Inc. 04/27/2000
(See Bookfortravel.com Inc.)

MOSAID TECHNOLOGIES INC (ON)
Acquired by Sterling Fund Management, L.L.C. 12/23/2011
Each share Common no par exchanged for $46 cash
Note: Unexchanged certificates were cancelled and became without value 12/23/2017

MOSAIX INC (WA)
Merged into Lucent Technologies Inc. 7/15/99
Each share Common 1¢ par exchanged for (0.19273) share Common no par
Lucent Technologies Inc. merged into Alcatel-Lucent S.A. 11/30/2006

MOSAM CAP CORP (BC)
Name changed to Pan Global Resources Inc. 12/22/2009

MOSCOM CORP (DE)
Name changed to Veramark Technologies, Inc. 06/15/1998
(See Veramark Technologies, Inc.)

MOSCOW CABLECOM CORP (DE)
Merged into Renova Media Enterprises, Ltd. 07/19/2007
Each share Conv. Preferred Ser. A no par exchanged for $39.4095 cash
Each share Common 1¢ par exchanged for $12.90 cash

MOSCOW CANDY FACTORY RED OCTOBER OJSC (RUSSIA)
GDR agreement terminated 04/19/2018
No GDR's remain outstanding

MOSCOW CITY TEL NETWORK (RUSSIA)
Sponsored ADR's for Ordinary split (5) for (1) by issuance of (4) additional ADR's payable 04/27/2000 to holders of record 04/27/2000 Ex date - 04/25/2000
Name changed to PJSC Moscow City Telephone Network 03/07/2016

MOSEDA TECHNOLOGIES INC (BC)
Name changed to Reliq Health Technologies Inc. 05/10/2016

MOSEL VITELIC INC (TAIWAN)
Each old Sponsored Reg. S GDR for Common exchanged for (0.580747) new Sponsored Reg. S GDR for Common 05/07/2004
Each old Sponsored 144A GDR for Common exchanged for (0.580747) new Sponsored 144A GDR for Common 05/07/2004
Each new Sponsored Reg. S GDR for Common exchanged again for (0.4074) new Sponsored Reg. S GDR for Common 06/02/2005
Each new Sponsored 144A GDR for Common exchanged again for (0.4074) new Sponsored 144A GDR for Common 06/02/2005
Each new Sponsored Reg. S GDR for Common exchanged again for (0.545) new Sponsored Reg. S GDR for Common 10/20/2009
Each new Sponsored 144A GDR for Common exchanged again for (0.545) new Sponsored 144A GDR for Common 10/20/2009
Each new Sponsored Reg. S GDR for Common exchanged again for (0.5504) new Sponsored Reg. S GDR for Common 10/26/2012
Each new Sponsored 144A GDR for Common exchanged again for (0.5504) new Sponsored 144A GDR for Common 10/26/2012
Stock Dividends - 11.6129% payable 10/26/2000 to holders of record 07/20/2000; 10% payable 07/18/2001 to holders of record 06/28/2001 Ex date - 06/26/2001; 3% payable 10/23/2007 to holders of record 08/16/2007
GDR agreement terminated 10/29/2015
Each new Sponsored Reg. S GDR for Common exchanged for $0.984741 cash
Each new Sponsored 144A GDR for Common exchanged for $0.984741 cash

MOSELEY, HALLGARTEN, ESTABROOK & WEEDEN HOLDING CORP. (NV)
Name changed to Moseley Holding Corp. 05/01/1986
(See Moseley Holding Corp.)

MOSELEY HLDG CORP (NV)
Plan of liquidation under Chapter 11 Federal Bankruptcy proceedings confirmed 06/26/1990
No stockholders' equity

MOSHER INC (TX)
Common $20 par changed to $1 par and (14) additional shares issued 1/16/81
Reorganized as AIM Funds Group Municipal Bond Fund Class A Shares 7/28/97

MOSHER LONG LAC GOLD MINES LTD.
Each share Capital Stock $1 par exchanged for (0.15) share Newlund Mines Ltd. Capital Stock $1 par and (1) share New Mosher Longlac Mines Ltd. Capital Stock $1 par in 1950
(See each company's listing)

MOSINEE PAPER CORP (WI)
Common $5 par changed to $2.50 par and (1) additional share issued 01/24/1979
Common $2.50 par split (3) for (2) by issuance of (0.5) additional share 05/22/1986
Common $2.50 par split (4) for (3) by issuance of (0.33333333) additional share payable 05/15/1996 to holders of record 05/01/1996
Common $2.50 par split (3) for (2) by issuance of (0.5) additional share payable 05/15/1997 to holders of record 05/01/1997
Stock Dividends - 20% 05/23/1974; 10% 05/20/1976; 100% 02/17/1977; 20% 05/18/1978; 10% 05/20/1982; 10% 05/17/1984; 10% 05/18/1995
Merged into Wausau-Mosinee Paper Corp. 12/17/1997
Each share Common $2.50 par exchanged for (1.4) shares Common no par
Wausau-Mosinee Paper Corp. name changed to Wausau Paper Corp. 05/12/2005
(See Wausau Paper Corp.)

MOSINEE PAPER MLS CO (WI)
Each share Common $10 par exchanged for (0.33333333) share Common no par 00/00/1936
Common no par changed to $10 par 00/00/1951
Common $10 par changed to $5 par and (1) additional share issued 10/15/1965
Stock Dividend - 100% 11/21/1969
Name changed to Mosinee Paper Corp. 01/01/1971
Mosinee Paper Corp. merged into Wausau-Mosinee Paper Corp. 12/17/1997 which name changed to Wausau Paper Corp. 05/12/2005
(See Wausau Paper Corp.)

MOSLER SAFE CO. (NY)
Stock Dividend - 10% 01/15/1964
Merged into A-S Capital Corp. 03/15/1968
Each share Common $1 par exchanged for $38.50 cash

MOSPORT PK CORP (QC)
Recapitalized as Mosport Park Entertainment Corp. 11/3/94
Each share Common no par exchanged for (0.5) share Common no par

MOSQUITO CONS GOLD MINES LTD (BC)
Name changed to American Cumo Mining Corp. 01/07/2013

MOSQUITO CREEK GOLD MNG LTD (BC)
Recapitalized as Mosquito Consolidated Gold Mines Ltd. 11/05/1987
Each share Common 50¢ par exchanged for (0.2) share Common no par
Mosquito Consolidated Gold Mines Ltd. name changed to American Cumo Mining Corp. 01/07/2013

MOSS GOLD MINES LTD.
Reorganized as Ardeen Gold Mines Ltd. 00/00/1937
Details not available

MOSS LAKE GOLD MINES LTD (ON)
Merged into Wesdome Gold Mines Ltd. 04/01/2014
Each share Common no par exchanged for (0.25974025) share Common no par

MOSS MINES LTD.
Name changed to Moss Gold Mines Ltd. 00/00/1930
(See Moss Gold Mines Ltd.)

MOSS-PWR RES INC (ON)
Recapitalized as WisCan Resources Ltd. 02/14/1991
Each share Common no par exchanged for (1/7) share Common no par
(See WisCan Resources Ltd.)

MOSS RES INC (ON)
Name changed to Asset Management Software Systems Inc. 05/24/2000
(See Asset Management Software Systems Inc.)

MOSS RES LTD (BC)
Merged into Moss Resources Ltd. (ONT) 4/22/88
Each share Common no par exchanged for (1.1) shares Common no par
Moss Resources Ltd. (ONT) merged into Moss-Power Resources Inc. 2/28/90 which recapitalized as WisCan Resources Ltd. 2/14/91
(See WisCan Resources Ltd.)

MOSS RES LTD NEW (ON)
Merged into Moss-Power Resources Inc. 2/28/90
Each share Common no par exchanged for (1.5) shares Common no par
Moss-Power Resources Inc. recapitalized as WisCan Resources Ltd. 2/14/91
(See WisCan Resources Ltd.)

MOSSBERG (FRANK) CO.
Merged into Apco-Mossberg Corp. in 1927
Details not available

MOSSER (J.K.) LEATHER CORP.
Dissolved in 1937

MOSSIMO INC (DE)
Merged into Iconix Brand Group, Inc. 11/1/2006
Each share Common $0.001 par exchanged for (0.2271139) share Common $0.001 par, (1) Contingent Share Right and $4.25 cash

MOST HOME CORP (NV)
SEC revoked common stock registration 01/10/2014

MOSTEK CORP (DE)
Stock Dividend - 100% 01/19/1973
Merged into United Technologies Corp. 01/11/1980
Each share Common 10¢ par exchanged for $62 cash

MOSTOSTAL EXPT CORP (POLAND)
ADR agreement terminated 10/14/2013
Each Sponsored ADR for Ordinary exchanged for $0.036663 cash

MOTAPA DIAMONDS INC (BC)
Reincorporated 11/19/2008
Place of incorporation changed from (NB) to (BC) 11/19/2008
Acquired by Lucara Diamond Corp. 07/03/2009
Each share Common no par exchanged for (0.9055) share Common no par

MOTCH & MERRYWEATHER MACHY CO (OH)
Stock Dividends - 10% 12/20/1974; 10% 12/26/1975
Merged into Oerlikon U.S. Holdings, Inc. 08/14/1979
Each share Common no par exchanged for $40 cash

MOTCO INC (MN)
Common $2 par changed to 10¢ par 01/26/1972
Adjudicated bankrupt 04/29/1977
Stockholders' equity unlikely

MOTEC INDUSTRIES, INC. (MN)
Name changed to Dolly Madison Foods, Inc. 09/27/1963
Dolly Madison Foods, Inc. name changed to Dolly Madison Industries, Inc. (MN) 02/15/1966 which reincorporated in Delaware 03/13/1969
(See Dolly Madison Industries, Inc. (DE))

MOTEL CO. OF GASTONIA, INC. (NC)
7% Preferred $100 par called 1/1/68

MOTEL CO. OF ROANOKE, INC. (VA)
Name changed to American Motor Inns, Inc. 12/6/62
(See American Motor Inns, Inc.)

MOTEL MANAGERS TRAINING SCH INC (DE)
Capital Stock 10¢ par changed to 5¢ par and (1) additional share issued 07/15/1969
Name changed to Diversified Educational Systems, Inc. 11/24/1969
(See Diversified Educational Systems, Inc.)

MOTEL 6 L P (DE)
Acquired by Accor S.A. 9/17/90
Each Depositary Unit exchanged for $22.50 cash

MOTEL TRAILER DISTRS INC (NY)
Charter cancelled and proclaimed dissolved for failure to pay taxes and file reports 12/15/1972

MOTH AIRCRAFT CORP.
Merged into Curtiss-Wright Corp. in 1929

MOTHER LODE BK (PLACERVILLE, CA)
Stock Dividend - 10% 12/05/1969
Merged into Security Pacific National Bank (Los Angeles, CA) 06/29/1975
Each share Capital Stock $3 par exchanged for $40 cash

MOTHER LODE BK (SONORA, CA)
Common no par split (2) for (1) by issuance of (1) additional share payable 10/14/2005 to holders of record 10/03/2005 Ex date - 10/17/2005
Acquired by Oak Valley Bancorp 12/23/2015
Each share Common no par exchanged for $1.65 cash

MOTHER LODE COALITION MINES CO.
Liquidation completed in 1946

MOTHER LODE GOLD MINES CONS (CA)
Stock Dividend - 10% 03/30/1984
SEC revoked common stock registration 07/08/2008

MOTHER LODE SAVINGS BANK (SACRAMENTO, CA)
Merged into U.S. Bancorp 08/23/1990
Each share Common $10 par exchanged for $27.59 cash

MOTHER LODE URANIUM CO. (UT)
Merged into Comstock Uranium & Oil Corp. on a (1) for (20) basis 04/27/1956
Comstock Uranium & Oil Corp. recapitalized as Cochise Enterprises, Inc. 05/12/1960 which merged into Bella Vista Ranches, Inc. 10/08/1975
(See Bella Vista Ranches, Inc.)

MOTHER'S COOKIE CO. (KY)
Completely liquidated 1/3/68
Each share Common no par exchanged for first and final distribution of (0.119116) share Beatrice Foods Co. Common no par
Beatrice Foods Co. name changed to Beatrice Companies, Inc. 6/5/84
(See Beatrice Companies, Inc.)

MOTHERHOOD MATERNITY SHOPS INC (CA)
Merged into MMS of Delaware, Inc. 07/12/1977
Each share Common 10¢ par exchanged for $18 cash

MOTHERNATURE COM INC (DE)
Issue Information - 4,100,000 shares OC-COM offered at $13 per share on 12/10/1999
Liquidation completed
Each share Common 1¢ par received initial distribution of $0.85 cash payable 12/30/2000 to holders of record 12/27/2000 Ex date - 1/2/2001
Each share Common 1¢ par received second distribution of $0.20 cash payable 3/21/2002 to holders of record 3/7/2002 Ex date - 3/22/2002
Each share Common 1¢ par received third distribution of $0.08 cash payable 12/31/2002 to holders of record 12/23/2002 Ex date - 1/2/2003
Each share Common 1¢ par received fourth and final distribution of $0.03 cash payable 11/30/2004 to holders of record 11/15/2004 Ex date - 12/1/2004
Note: Certificates were not required to be surrendered and are without value

MOTHERS RESTAURANTS LTD (ON)
Merged into MFC Acquisition Inc. 10/08/1986
Each share Common no par exchanged for $12.25 cash

MOTHERS WK INC (DE)
Name changed to Destination Maternity Corp. 12/08/2008

MOTIENT CORP (DE)
Plan of reorganization under Chapter 11 Federal Bankruptcy Code effective 05/01/2002
Each share old Common 1¢ par exchanged for (0.02613) Common Stock Purchase Warrant expiring 05/02/2004
Name changed to TerreStar Corp. 08/16/2007
(See TerreStar Corp.)

MOTION CTL TECHNOLOGY INC (CO)
Plan of reorganization under Chapter 11 Federal Bankruptcy proceedings confirmed 04/22/1991
Stockholders' equity undetermined

MOTION DNA CORP (NV)
Each share old Common $0.001 par exchanged for (0.1) share new Common $0.001 par 08/30/2004
Each share new Common $0.001 par exchanged again for (0.02) share new Common $0.001 par 04/15/2005
New Common $0.001 par split (2) for (1) by issuance of (1) additional share payable 08/04/2005 to holders of record 07/28/2005 Ex date - 08/05/2005
Name changed to Sports Concepts, Inc. 11/17/2006
(See Sports Concepts, Inc.)

MOTION INDS INC (DE)
Stock Dividends - 33.33333333% 04/06/1973; 10% 09/02/1975
Merged into Genuine Parts Co. 12/10/1976
Each share Common $1 par exchanged for (0.7) share Common $1 par

MOTION INTL INC (CANADA)
Merged into TVA Group Inc 05/12/2000
Each share Class A Multiple no par exchanged for $5.45 cash

MOTION PICTURE ADVERTISING SERVICE CO., INC. (LA)
Name changed to Motion Picture Alexander Corp. 3/2/63 which name changed to Motion Picture Advertising Corp. 2/3/65

MOTION PICTURE ALEXANDER CORP. (LA)
Name changed to Motion Picture Advertising Corp. 2/3/65

MOTION PICTURE CAPITAL CORP.
Merged into Investors Equity Co., Inc. in 1929
Details not available

MOTION PICTURE HALL OF FAME INC (NV)
Recapitalized as Beverly Hills Group, Inc. 07/08/2014
Each share Common $0.001 par exchanged for (0.03333333) share Common $0.001 par
Beverly Hills Group, Inc. name changed to Full Alliance Group, Inc. 04/11/2017

MOTION PICTURE INVESTORS, INC. (MO)
Dissolved 4/17/67

MOTION WKS GROUP LTD (BC)
Name changed 08/08/1995
Name changed from Motion Works Corp. to Motion Works Group Ltd. 08/08/1995
Each share old Common no par exchanged for (0.1) share new Common no par 02/06/1998
Cease trade order effective 12/07/2001
Stockholders' equity unlikely

MOTIONCAST TELEVISION CORP AMER (NV)
Common $0.001 par split (5) for (1) by issuance of (4) additional shares payable 11/02/1998 to holders of record 10/22/1998
Each share old Common $0.001 par exchanged for (0.04) share new Common $0.001 par 03/10/1999
Name changed to BrowseSafe.com, Inc. 07/28/1999
BrowseSafe.com, Inc. name changed to PlanetGood Investments, Inc. 07/20/2000 which name changed to American Diamond Corp. 06/02/2004 which recapitalized as All American Coffee & Beverage, Inc. 03/21/2006
(See All American Coffee & Beverage, Inc.)

MOTIONSPHERE CAP INC (CANADA)
Name changed to Colba.Net Telecom Inc. 10/01/2010
(See Colba.Net Telecom Inc.)

MOTIVATIONAL LEARNING SYS (UT)
Merged into Standard Silver Corp. 05/11/1972
Each share Capital Stock 2¢ par exchanged for (0.1) share Capital Stock 1¢ par
Standard Silver Corp. name changed to Texas Rare Earth Resources Corp. (NV) 09/29/2010 which reincorporated in Delaware 08/24/2012 which name changed to Texas Mineral Resources Corp. 03/21/2016

MOTIVATIONAL SYS INC (NY)
Dissolved by proclamation 3/24/93

MOTIVE INC (DE)
Issue Information - 5,000,000 shares COM offered at $10 per share on 06/24/2004
Acquired by Alcatel-Lucent S.A. 10/07/2008
Each share Common $0.001 par exchanged for $2.23 cash

MOTIVEPOWER INDS INC (DE)
Common 1¢ par split (3) for (2) by issuance of (0.5) additional share payable 4/2/99 to holders of record 3/17/99 Ex date - 4/5/99
Merged into Westinghouse Air Brake Co. (New) 11/19/99
Each share Common 1¢ par exchanged for (0.66) share Common 1¢ par

MOTIVISION AMER INC (NY)
Charter cancelled and proclaimed dissolved for failure to pay taxes 06/27/2001

MOTIVUS INC (ON)
Merged into Cundari Group Ltd. 6/8/2004
Each share Common no par exchanged for $0.03 cash

MOTO GOLDMINES LTD (BC)
Merged into Randgold Resources Ltd. 10/15/2009
Each share Common no par exchanged for either (0.07061) share Ordinary for Canadian and non-U.S. residents or (0.07061) ADR for Ordinary for U.S. residents
Note: Unexchanged certificates were cancelled and became without value 10/15/2015

MOTO GUZZI CORP (DE)
Name changed to Centerpoint Corp. 08/11/2000
(See Centerpoint Corp.)

MOTO METER GAUGE & EQUIPMENT CORP.
Acquired by Electric Auto-Lite Co. in 1935, which merged into Eltra Corp. 6/28/63
(See Eltra Corp.)

MOTO PHOTO INC (DE)
Reincorporated 9/9/83
State of incorporation changed from (OK) to (DE) 9/9/83
Common 1¢ par split (2) for (1) by issuance of (1) additional share 2/20/84
$1.20 Conv. Preferred 1¢ par called for redemption 1/17/95
Plan of reorganization under Chapter 11 Federal Bankruptcy Code effective 7/16/2004
No stockholders' equity

MOTOR BANKERS CORP.
Liquidated in 1945

MOTOR BUYERS, INC.
Merged into Union Investment Co. 00/00/1927
Details not available

MOTOR CAR SECURITIES CORP.
Acquired by Mercantile Discount Corp. 00/00/1928
Details not available

MOTOR CARGO INDS INC (UT)
Issue Information - 2,230,000 shares COM offered at $12 per share on 11/24/1997
Merged into Union Pacific Corp. 2/15/2002
Each share Common no par exchanged for $12.10 cash

MOTOR CARS AUTO GROUP INC (FL)
Ceased operations 03/31/2003
Stockholders' equity unlikely

MOTOR CLUB AMER (NJ)
Class A Common 50¢ par reclassified as Common 50¢ par 3/25/66
Common 50¢ par split (2) for (1) by issuance of (1) additional share 6/14/72
Name changed to Preserver Group, Inc. 6/6/2001
(See Preserver Group, Inc.)

MOTOR CLUB AMER INS CO (NJ)
Common $10 par changed to $12 par 6/27/67
Common $12 par changed to $15 par 6/26/68
Common $15 par changed to $5 par and (2) additional shares issued plus a 33-1/3% stock dividend paid 4/20/70
Common $5 par changed to $2.50 par and (1) additional share issued 3/31/71
Common $2.50 par changed to $1.25 par and (1) additional share issued 7/28/71
Common $1.25 par split (3) for (2) by issuance of (0.5) additional share 5/17/72
Each share Common $1.25 par exchanged for (2/3) share Common $1 par 7/22/76
Common $1 par changed to $1.15 par 7/30/82
Acquired by Motor Club of America 2/12/88
Each share Common $1.15 par exchanged for $12.50 cash

MOTOR COACH INDS INTL INC (DE)
Merged into Consorcio G Grupo Dina, S.A. de C.V. 8/8/94
Option to receive either $16.72 principal amount of 8% Conv. Subordinated Debentures due 2004 or (1.236) Sponsored ADR's for Ser. L no par for each share Common 1¢ par exchanged expired 8/4/94
Non-electing holders of (5,000) shares or more will receive in exchange 70% in Ser. L ADR's and 30% in Debentures
Non-electing holders of (4,999) shares or fewer will receive in exchange a percentage determined by lot
(See Consorcio G Grupo Dina, S.A. de C.V.)

MOTOR COACH INDS LTD (CANADA)
Acquired by Motor Coach Industries International, Inc. 3/10/94
Each share Common no par exchanged for $17 cash

MOTOR COILS MFG CO (PA)
Common 50¢ par changed to 1¢ par 07/17/1972
Stock Dividend - 20% 07/01/1981
Acquired by MCG Investment Co. 01/16/1985
Each share Common 1¢ par exchanged for $5 cash

MOTOR DEALERS ACCEPTANCE CO. LTD. (SK)
Name changed to Orion Petroleum Ltd. 2/5/80
(See Orion Petroleum Ltd.)

MOTOR DISCOUNT, INC.
Acquired by National Discount Corp. 00/00/1927
Details not available

MOTOR FIN CORP (NJ)
$5 Preferred no par called for redemption 08/15/1962
Liquidation completed
Each share Common $5 par exchanged for initial distribution of $325 cash 01/12/1984
Each share Common $5 par received second and final distribution of $11.55 cash 01/23/1986

MOTOR FUELS CORP. (UT)
Each share Common $0.001 par exchanged for (0.2) share new Common $0.001 par 08/01/1986
Name changed to Denham Pullitz Co. 11/19/1987

MOTOR HOMES AMER INC (FL)
Reacquired 12/31/1984
Each share Common 10¢ par exchanged for $2.50 cash

MOTOR IMPROVEMENTS, INC.
Name changed to Purolator Products, Inc. in 1940
Purolator Products, Inc. name changed to Purolator, Inc. (Del.) 4/16/68 which reincorporated in New York as Purolator Courier Corp. 7/1/84
(See Purolator Courier Corp. (N.Y.))

MOTOR MAN INC (NV)
Charter revoked for failure to file reports and pay fees 11/01/1991

MOTOR MART GARAGE CO (MA)
Completely liquidated 01/13/1970
Each share Common $1 par exchanged for first and final distribution of $13.56 cash

MOTOR MART TRUST (MA)
Liquidation completed 10/31/55

MOTOR PRODUCTS CORP. (NY)
Common no par changed to $10 par in 1950
Common $10 par changed to $5 par and (1) additional share issued 11/17/59
Stock Dividend - 100% 3/11/59
Name changed to Nautec Corp. 11/2/60
(See Nautec Corp.)

MOTOR PRODUCTS CORP. OF CANADA LTD. (ON)
Assets sold 9/3/59
No stockholders' equity

MOTOR PTS INDS INC (NY)
Merged into Anglo Industries, Inc. 07/15/1975
Each share Class A 10¢ par exchanged for $7 cash

MOTOR SICH (UKRAINE)
GDR agreement terminated 08/15/2011
Each Reg. S Sponsored GDR for Ordinary exchanged for (0.2) share Ordinary
Note: Unexchanged GDR's will be sold and the proceeds, if any, held for claim after 02/15/2012

MOTOR SYS INC (MN)
Statutorily dissolved 10/7/91

MOTOR TRANSIT CO.
Merged into Jacksonville Coach Co. 10/16/46
Each share Common $10 par exchanged for (0.2) share Common no par
Jacksonville Coach Co. acquired by City Coach Lines, Inc. in 1952

MOTOR TRANSIT CORP. (DE)
Name changed to Greyhound Corp. (DE) in 1930
Greyhound Corp. (DE) reincorporated in Arizona 3/3/78 which name changed to Greyhound Dial Corp. 5/8/90 which name changed to Dial Corp. (AZ) 5/14/91 which reincorporated in (DE) 3/18/92 which name changed to Viad Corp. 8/15/96

MOTOR TRAVEL SVCS INC (MN)
Name changed to Graphics Diversified, Inc. 01/11/1974
(See Graphics Diversified, Inc.)

MOTOR VALET INDS INC (DE)
Assets sold for benefit of creditors 08/27/1974
No stockholders' equity

MOTOR WHEEL CORP. (MI)
Common no par changed to $5 par in 1933
Acquired by Goodyear Tire & Rubber Co. on a (2/3) for (1) basis 1/17/64

MOTORAMP GARAGES OF MARYLAND, INC. (MD)
Charter revoked for failure to file reports and pay fees 10/22/62

MOTORCADE INDS LTD (ON)
Name changed 8/10/78
Name changed from Motorcade Stores Ltd. to Motorcade Industries Ltd. 8/10/78
Acquired by Winter Privatizing Corp. 1/2/2002
Each share Common no par exchanged for $9.50 cash

MOTORCAR PTS & ACCESSORIES INC (NY)
Issue Information - 1,050,000 shares COM offered at $6 per share on 03/23/1994
Name changed to Motorcar Parts of America, Inc. 1/27/2004

MOTORCYCLE CTRS AMER INC (NV)
Each share old Common $0.001 par exchanged for (0.05) share new Common $0.001 par 4/1/99
Name changed to eUniverse, Inc. (NV) 4/27/99 eUniverse, Inc. (NV) reincorporated in Delaware 1/9/2003 which name changed to Intermix Media, Inc. 7/12/2004
(See Intermix Media, Inc.)

MOTORMASTER SVC SYS INC (NY)
Name changed to Motorpro Service Systems Inc. 11/07/1973

MOTOROLA CAP TR I (DE)
6.68% Guaranteed Trust Originated Preferred Securities called for redemption at $25 plus $0.039894 accrued dividend on 3/26/2004

MOTOROLA INC (DE)
Reincorporated 05/18/1973
Common $3 par split (2) for (1) by issuance of (1) additional share 07/15/1960
Common $3 par split (3) for (2) by issuance of (0.5) additional share 05/25/1965
Common $3 par split (2) for (1) by issuance of (1) additional share 05/25/1970
Stock Dividends - 10% 01/29/1951; 100% 07/30/1952
State of incorporation changed from (IL) to (DE) 05/18/1973
Common $3 par split (2) for (1) by issuance of (1) additional share 06/01/1973
Common $3 par split (3) for (1) by issuance of (2) additional shares 06/01/1984
Common $3 par split (2) for (1) by issuance of (1) additional share 01/15/1993
Common $3 par split (2) for (1) by issuance of (1) additional share 04/18/1994
Common $3 par split (3) for (1) by issuance of (2) additional shares payable 06/01/2000 to holders of record 05/15/2000 Ex date - 06/02/2000
Each 7% Equity Security Unit received (2.89109254) shares Common $3 par 11/16/2004
Each share Common $3 par received distribution of (0.110415) share Freescale Semiconductor, Inc. Class B Common 1¢ par payable 12/02/2004 to holders of record 11/26/2004 Ex date - 12/03/2004
Common $3 par changed to 1¢ par 05/05/2009
Each share Common 1¢ par received distribution of (0.125) share Motorola Mobility Holdings, Inc. Common 1¢ par payable 01/04/2011 to holders of record 12/21/2010
Recapitalized as Motorola Solutions, Inc. 01/04/2011
Each share Common 1¢ par exchanged for (1/7) share Common 1¢ par

MOTOROLA MOBILITY HLDGS INC (DE)
Acquired by Google Inc. 05/22/2012
Each share Common 1¢ par exchanged for $40 cash

MOTORS LIQ CO (DE)
Plan of reorganization under Chapter 11 Federal Bankruptcy proceedings effective 03/31/2011
No stockholders' equity

MOTORS METAL MANUFACTURING CO. (MI)
Each share Common $10 par exchanged for (2) shares Common $5 par in 1948
Merged into Abrasive & Metal Products Co. and each share Common $5 par exchanged for (0.16) share 5% Preferred $25 par and (1) share Common $1 par in 1954
Abrasive & Metal Products Co. name changed to Wakefield Corp. 4/28/61
Wakefield Corp. name changed to 729 Meldrum Corp. 2/24/66 which completed liquidation 10/22/66

MOTORS MORTGAGE CORP.
Liquidated in 1941

MOTORSPORTS EMPORIUM INC (NV)
Each share old Common $0.001 par exchanged for (0.00444444) share new Common $0.001 par 11/01/2006
Name changed to International Building Technologies Group, Inc. 08/16/2007
(See International Building Technologies Group, Inc.)

MOTORSPORTS USA INC (DE)
Name changed to Vast Technologies Holding Corp. 06/02/2000
Vast Technologies Holding Corp. name changed to Accelerated Learning Languages Inc. 11/13/2000 which recapitalized as Integrated Enterprises Inc. 06/20/2001 which recapitalized as SeaLife Corp. (DE) 12/20/2002 which reincorporated in Nevada 10/06/2016

MOTORVAC TECHNOLOGIES INC (DE)
Company terminated common stock registration and is no longer public as of 08/03/2000

MOTRICITY INC (DE)
Issue Information - 6,000,000 shares COM offered at $10 per share on 06/17/2010
Reorganized as Voltari Corp. 04/10/2013
Each share 13% Preferred Ser. J $0.001 par exchanged for (1) share 13% Preferred Ser. J $0.001 par
Each share Common $0.001 par exchanged for (1) share Common $0.001 par

MOTRLUBE INC (CANADA)
Name changed to MLB Industries Inc. (Canada) 09/20/1996
MLB Industries Inc. (Canada) reorganized in Alberta as Blue Horizon Industries Inc. 09/14/2011

MOTRONICS CORP. (NY)
Name changed to MC Liquidating Corp. 10/17/1988
(See MC Liquidating Corp.)

MOTTS HLDGS INC (CT)
Merged into NMI Acquisition Inc. 5/25/99
Each share Common $1 par exchanged for $8.50 cash

MOTTS SUPER MKTS INC (CT)
Stock Dividends - 25% 11/6/69; 10%

4/3/78; 10% 2/28/79; 25% 6/5/81; 25% 6/1/82; 25% 6/1/83
Reorganized as Mott's Holdings Inc. 5/25/89
Each share Common $1 par exchanged for (1) share Common $1 par
(See Mott's Holdings Inc.)

MOULDED PRODS INC (MN)
Certificates dated prior to 07/03/1973
Reorganized under Chapter X bankruptcy provision 07/03/1973
No stockholders' equity

MOULDINGS INC (OR)
Common $1 par split (2) for (1) by issuance of (1) additional share 5/9/69
Common $1 par split (2) for (1) by issuance of (1) additional share 11/7/69
Under plan of merger each share Common $1 par exchanged for $3.25 cash 11/21/78

MOUND CITY TR CO (ST LOUIS, MO)
Capital Stock $20 par changed to $10 par and (1) additional share issued plus a 300% stock dividend paid 6/21/60
Name changed to Commerce Bank of Mound City (St. Louis, MO) 3/15/76
(See Commerce Bank of Mound City (St. Louis, MO))

MT. AGNES MINES LTD. (BC)
Name changed to Lower Valley Mines Ltd. 07/15/1969
Lower Valley Mines Ltd. recapitalized as Groton Minerals Ltd. 07/22/1974
(See Groton Minerals Ltd.)

MOUNT ALLARD RES LTD (BC)
Recapitalized as Protection Technology Inc. 07/05/1991
Each share Common no par exchanged for (1/3) share Common no par
(See Protection Technology Inc.)

MT. ATTITASH LIFT CORP. (NH)
Acquired by LBO Holding Inc. 7/19/94
Details not available

MT BAKER BK SVGS (BELLINGHAM, WA)
Common $5 par split (2) for (1) by issuance of (1) additional share 06/28/1985
Common $5 par split (3) for (2) by issuance of (0.5) additional share 02/03/1986
Common $5 par split (4) for (3) by issuance of (1/3) additional share 02/02/1987
Acquired by U.S. Bancorp 06/30/1988
Each share Common $5 par exchanged for $16 cash

MT. BAKER PLYWOODS LTD. (BC)
Acquired by Canadian Collieries Resources Ltd. 3/3/62
Each share Common $1 par exchanged for (1.1) shares 5% Preferred Ser. G $1 par
(See listing for Canadian Collieries Resources Ltd.)

MOUNT BURGESS GOLD MNG CO N L (AUSTRALIA)
Stock Dividends - 12.5% 09/03/1987; 10% 09/07/1993
ADR agreement terminated 12/06/2001
Each ADR for Ordinary exchanged for $0.36 cash

MT CALVERY RES LTD (BC)
Recapitalized as Triumph Resources Ltd. 08/22/1989
Each share Common no par exchanged for (0.25) share Common no par
Triumph Resources Ltd. recapitalized as Jericho Resources Ltd. 10/02/1992 which name changed to Regia Resources Ltd. (BC) 04/18/1995 which reincorporated in Canada 07/07/1995

(See Regia Resources Ltd.)

MOUNT CARBON & PORT CARBON RAILROAD CO.
Merged into Reading Co. 12/31/49
Each share Capital Stock exchanged for (1.25) shares 1st Preferred $50 par
Reading Co. merged into Reading Entertainment Inc. (DE) 10/15/96 which reincorporated in Nevada 12/29/99 which merged into Reading International, Inc. 12/31/2001

MOUNT CLEMENS CORP (DE)
Charter cancelled and declared inoperative and void for non-payment of taxes 04/15/1970

MOUNT CLEMENS INDUSTRIES, INC. (DE)
Reincorporated 01/29/1965
State of incorporation changed from (MI) to (DE) 01/29/1965
6% Preferred $4 par called for redemption 03/10/1965
Merged into Riverside, Inc. 04/28/1967
Each share Common $1 par exchanged for $10 cash

MT. CLEMENS METAL PRODUCTS CO. (MI)
Under plan of merger each share Common $10 par exchanged for (18) shares Common $1 par 00/00/1953
Name changed to Mount Clemens Industries, Inc. (MI) 03/08/1962
Mount Clemens Industries, Inc. (MI) reincorporated in Delaware 01/29/1965
(See Mount Clemens Industries, Inc. (DE))

MOUNT COSTIGAN MINES LTD. (ON)
Recapitalized as New Mount Costigan Mines Ltd. 6/28/67
Each share Preferred $1 par exchanged for (1) share 5% Preference $1 par
Each share Common no par exchanged for (0.6) share Common no par

MOUNT DAKOTA ENERGY CORP (CANADA)
Reincorporated under the laws of British Columbia 08/07/2015

MT DIABLO BANCSHARES (CA)
Merged into Greater Bay Bancorp 01/31/2000
Each share Common no par exchanged for (0.9532) share Common no par
Greater Bay Bancorp merged into Wells Fargo & Co. (New) 10/01/2007

MT. DIABLO CO. (CA)
Acquired by Standard Oil Co. of California on a (1) for (6.2679) basis 7/30/64
Standard Oil Co. of California name changed to Chevron Corp. 7/1/84 which name changed to ChevronTexaco Corp. 10/9/2001 which name changed back to Chevron Corp. 5/9/2005

MT DIABLO NATL BK (DANVILLE, CA)
Reorganized as Mt. Diablo Bancshares 07/01/1998
Each share Common $5 par exchanged for (1.5) shares Common no par
Mt. Diablo Bancshares merged into Greater Bay Bancorp 01/31/2000 which merged into Wells Fargo & Co. (New) 10/01/2007

MOUNT DIABLO OIL, MINING & DEVELOPMENT CO. (CA)
Name changed to Mount Diablo Co. 8/5/49
Mount Diablo Co. acquired by Standard Oil Co. of California 7/30/64 which name changed to Chevron Corp. 7/1/84 which name changed to ChevronTexaco Corp. 10/9/2001 which name changed back to Chevron Corp. 5/9/2005

MT EMILY EXPL LTD (BC)
Recapitalized as Brookings Resources Ltd. 12/02/1991
Each share Common no par exchanged for (0.5) share Common no par
Brookings Resources Ltd. name changed to Cognoscente Software International Inc. 06/24/1993
(See Cognoscente Software International Inc.)

MT EXPEDITOR RES LTD (BC)
Name changed to Envirowaste Industries Inc. 03/29/1990
Envirowaste Industries Inc. recapitalized as Consolidated Envirowaste Industries Inc. 03/24/1992
(See Consolidated Envirowaste Industries Inc.)

MT. FOREST FUR FARMS OF AMERICA, INC. (DE)
Name changed to Vermilion Bayland LLC 12/29/99
(See Vermilion Bayland LLC)

MT GRANT MINES LTD (BC)
Name changed to Venezuelan Goldfields Ltd. (BC) 01/13/1993
Venezuelan Goldfields Ltd. (BC) reincorporated under the laws of Canada as Vengold Inc. 05/13/94 which name changed to itemus inc. 04/26/2000
(See itemus inc.)

MOUNT GRANT MINES LTD. (AB)
Struck off register for failure to file annual returns 6/15/78

MOUNT HAMILTON LAND & OIL CO. (SD)
Charter expired by time limitation in 1920

MOUNT HOLLY WTR CO (NJ)
100% acquired by Elizabethtown Water Co. through exchange offer which expired 09/14/1969
Public interest eliminated

MOUNT HOPE BRIDGE CO.
Succeeded by Mount Hope Bridge Corp. in 1932 which was completely liquidated 9/16/57

MOUNT HOPE BRIDGE CORP. (RI)
Each share Class B no par exchanged for (4) shares Capital Stock no par in 1953
Liquidation completed 9/16/57

MOUNT HOPE RES CORP (AB)
Issue Information - 2,000,000 shares COM offered at $0.10 per share on 03/12/1997
Name changed to 3Net Media Corp. 2/29/2000
3Net Media Corp. recapitalized as Everton Resources Inc. (ALTA) 11/4/2002 which reincorporated in Canada 4/16/2004

MOUNT HOPE SPINNING CO.
Liquidated in 1928

MT HYLAND MINES LTD (BC)
Recapitalized as Consolidated Mt. Hyland Mines & Resources Ltd. 05/16/1975
Each share Capital Stock no par exchanged for (0.2) share Capital Stock no par
Consolidated Mt. Hyland Mines & Resources Ltd. name changed to Avance International Inc. 01/26/1976 which recapitalized as Avance Venture Corp. 10/21/1999 which recapitalized as Santa Cruz Ventures Inc. 02/09/2004 which name changed to Lignol Energy Corp. 01/23/2007

Chevron Corp. 7/1/84 which name changed to ChevronTexaco Corp. 10/9/2001 which name changed back to Chevron Corp. 5/9/2005

MOUNT ISA MINES LTD (AUSTRALIA)
Stock Dividend - 150% 09/24/1963
Reorganized as M.I.M. Holdings Ltd. 10/05/1970
Each ADR for Ordinary AUD $0.50 par received (1) ADR's for Ordinary AUD $0.50 par
(See M.I.M. Holdings Ltd.)

MOUNT JAMIE MINES LTD (AB)
Merged into Jamie Frontier Resources Inc. 02/15/1984
Each share Common $1 par exchanged for (0.25) share Common no par
(See Jamie Frontier Resources Inc.)

MOUNT JAMIE MINES LTD (ON)
Completely liquidated 11/26/1970
Each share Capital Stock $1 par exchanged for first and final distribution of (1) share Mount Jamie Mines (Quebec) Ltd. (QUE) Common $1 par
Mount Jamie Mines (Quebec) Ltd. (QUE) liquidated for Mount Jamie Mines Ltd. (ALTA) 12/11/1979 which merged into Jamie Frontier Resources Inc. 02/15/1984
(See Jamie Frontier Resources Inc.)

MOUNT JAMIE MINES QUE LTD (QC)
Completely liquidated 12/11/1979
Each share Common $1 par exchanged for first and final distribution of (1/3) share Mount Jamie Mines Ltd. (ALTA) Common $1 par
Mount Jamie Mines Ltd. (ALTA) merged into Jamie Frontier Resources Inc. 02/15/1984
(See Jamie Frontier Resources Inc.)

MT. KEARSARGE MINERALS INC. (ON)
Recapitalized as Sino-Forest Corp. (ON) 03/11/1994
Each share Common no par exchanged for (0.1) share Common no par
Sino-Forest Corp. (ON) reincorporated in Canada 06/25/2002
(See Sino-Forest Corp.)

MOUNT KENO MINES LTD (ON)
Recapitalized as Keno Industries Inc. 03/26/1996
Each share Common no par exchanged for (0.5) share Common no par
Keno Industries Inc. recapitalized as Dayak Goldfields Corp. 06/03/1996 which merged into International Pursuit Corp. 05/22/1997 which recapitalized as Apollo Gold Corp. (ON) 06/24/2002 which reincorporated in Yukon 05/28/2003 which recapitalized as Brigus Gold Corp. (YT) 06/25/2010 which reincorporated in Canada 06/09/2011
(See Brigus Gold Corp.)

MOUNT KNOWLEDGE HLDGS INC (NV)
Old Common $0.0001 par split (22) for (1) by issuance of (21) additional shares payable 02/09/2010 to holders of record 02/09/2010
Each share old Common $0.001 par exchanged for (0.1) share new Common $0.001 par 12/22/2014
Name changed to Cybergy Holdings, Inc. 01/21/2015

MOUNT LEYLAND COLLIERIES, LTD. (BC)
Advised 2/19/64 that company is inactive and stock is worthless

MT LEYSHON GOLD MINES LTD (AUSTRALIA)
Name changed to Normandy Mount Leyshon Ltd. 10/20/1997
Normandy Mount Leyshon Ltd. name

changed to Leyshon Resources Ltd. 12/05/2001
(See Leyshon Resources Ltd.)

MT. MARSHALL MINES, LTD. (ID)
Charter forfeited for failure to file reports and pay taxes 11/30/23

MT MCKINLEY GOLD INC (WA)
Reorganized under the laws of Nevada as Venturenet.com Inc. 04/11/2000
Each share Common no par exchanged for (0.1) share Common $0.001 par
Venturenet.com Inc. name changed to Venture Media Communications Inc. 06/21/2000 which name changed to Global Debit Cash Card, Inc. 12/26/2003 which name changed to 1st Global Financial Corp. 03/27/2006 which recapitalized as Incorporated Productions 08/01/2013

MOUNT NEBO FOODS, INC. (UT)
Charter revoked for failure to file reports 9/2/75

MT. OGDEN MINES LTD. (BC)
Charter cancelled and declared dissolved for failure to file returns and pay fees 1/31/77

MOUNT OLIVE & STAUNTON COAL CO. (IL)
Voluntarily dissolved for failure to pay taxes and file reports 6/27/78

MOUNT OLIVER INCLINE RAILWAY CO.
Merged into Pittsburgh Railways Co. for cash 9/30/50

MT OLYMPUS ENTERPRISES INC NEW (UT)
Reorganized under the laws of Delaware as Recom Managed Systems, Inc. 11/11/1998
Each (43) shares Common $0.001 par exchanged for (1) share Common $0.001 par
Recom Managed Systems, Inc. name changed to Signalife Inc. 11/15/2005 which name changed to Heart Tronics Inc. 06/10/2009

MOUNT PEALE CORP. (UT)
Recapitalized as Hawk Enterprises, Inc. 06/26/1967
Each share Common 3¢ par exchanged for (0.05) share Common no par
Hawk Enterprises, Inc. recapitalized as Amco Energy Corp. 12/16/1974 which name changed to Amcole Energy Corp. 07/12/1978
(See Amcole Energy Corp.)

MOUNT PEALE URANIUM CORP. (UT)
Name changed to Mount Peale Corp. 12/10/1956
Mount Peale Corp. recapitalized as Hawk Enterprises, Inc. 06/26/1967 which recapitalized as Amco Energy Corp. 12/16/1974 which name changed to Amcole Energy Corp. 07/12/1978
(See Amcole Energy Corp.)

MOUNT PLEASANT MINES LTD (ON)
5% Preference 50¢ par called for redemption 5/31/62
Name changed to Mount Pleasant Resources, Inc. 7/30/84
Mount Pleasant Resources, Inc. name changed to Pleasant Realty & Financial Corp. 7/27/90
(See Pleasant Realty & Financial Corp.)

MOUNT PLEASANT RES INC (ON)
Each (14) shares old Common no par exchanged for (1) share new Common no par 9/13/85
Name changed to Pleasant Realty & Financial Corp. 7/27/90
(See Pleasant Realty & Financial Corp.)

MOUNT PROSPECT ST BK (MOUNT PROSPECT, IL)
Stock Dividend - 10% 06/13/1975
Reorganized under the laws of Delaware as MPSBancorp, Inc. 07/18/1980
Each share Common $10 par exchanged for (1) share Common $10 par
MPSBancorp, Inc. merged into First United Financial Services, Inc. 05/31/1985
(See First United Financial Services, Inc.)

MOUNT REAL CORP (CANADA)
Reincorporated 07/10/1998
Name changed from Mount Real Financial Corp. to Mount Real Corp. 08/25/1995
Place of incorporation changed from (AB) to (Canada) 07/10/1998
Each share old Common no par exchanged for (1/3) share new Common no par 05/08/2001
Filed a petition under Chapter 15 U.S. Bankruptcy Code 08/09/2006
Stockholders' equity unlikely

MOUNT ROYAL DAIRIES & CO LTD (QC)
Name changed to Laiteries Papineau Inc. 04/28/1973
(See Laiteries Papineau Inc.)

MOUNT ROYAL DAIRY STORES, INC.
Liquidated in 1929

MOUNT ROYAL HOTEL CO. LTD.
Acquired by Cardy Corp. Ltd. and each share Capital Stock exchanged for $6 in Debentures, (1) share Class A and $2.03 in cash in 1947
Cardy Corp. Ltd. name changed to Sheraton Ltd. in 1950
(See Sheraton Ltd.)

MOUNT ROYAL RICE MLS LTD (CANADA)
Common no par split (4) for (1) by issuance of (3) additional shares 07/24/1961
Common no par reclassified as Conv. Class A Common no par 02/15/1977
Name changed to MRRM, Inc. and 5.80% Preferred $25 par reclassified as $1.45 Preferred no par, Conv. Class A Common no par and Conv. Class B no par reclassified as Common no par 07/30/1979
(See MRRM, Inc.)

MOUNT SICKER MINES LTD (BC)
Name changed to Peppa Resources Ltd. and Capital Stock $1 par changed to no par 5/21/80
(See Peppa Resources Ltd.)

MOUNT STERLING NATL HLDG CORP (KY)
Reorganized 00/00/1987
Under plan of reorganization each share Mount Sterling National Bank (Mount Sterling, KY) Capital Stock $10 par automatically became (1) share Mount Sterling National Holding Corp. Common $10 par 00/00/1987
Merged into Whitaker Bank Corp. 03/15/1996
Each share Common $10 par exchanged for $220.75 cash

MT TOM MINERALS CORP (BC)
Name changed to Global Net Entertainment Corp. 10/14/1999
Global Net Entertainment Corp. recapitalized as Guildhall Minerals Ltd. 02/21/2006 which name changed to Edge Edge Resources Inc. 07/28/2009
(See Edge Resources Inc.)

MOUNT TOM SULPHITE PULP CO.
Acquired by San-Nap-Pack Manufacturing Co., Inc. in 1947 which name changed to Doeskin Products, Inc. in 1949 which completely liquidated 9/29/67

MOUNT UNION BK (ALLIANCE, OH)
Merged into United National Bank & Trust Co. (Canton, OH) 10/2/72
Each share Common $25 par exchanged for (0.76) share Common $20 par
United National Bank & Trust Co. (Canton, OH) reorganized as UNB Corp. 10/1/84 which name changed to Unizan Financial Corp. 3/8/2002 which merged into Huntington Bancshares Inc. 3/1/2006

MOUNT UNION INDS INC (NV)
Each share Capital Stock 3¢ par exchanged for (0.01) share Capital Stock $1 par 01/23/1970
Charter revoked for failure to file reports and pay fees 03/01/1976

MT. UNION MINES, INC. (NV)
Name changed to Mt. Union Uranium, Inc. 8/31/55
Mt. Union Uranium, Inc. name changed to Mt. Union Industries, Inc. 7/13/61
(See Union Industries, Inc.)

MT. UNION URANIUM, INC. (NV)
Name changed to Mt. Union Industries, Inc. and Capital Stock 10¢ par changed to 3¢ par 7/13/61
Mt. Union Industries, Inc. charter revoked 3/1/76

MOUNT VERNON BANK & TRUST CO. (ALEXANDRIA, VA)
Name changed to Mount Vernon National Bank & Trust Co. of Fairfax County (Annandale, VA) 3/31/62
Mount Vernon National Bank & Trust Co. of Fairfax County (Annandale, VA) merged into First Virginia Bankshares Corp. 9/5/69 which name changed to First Virginia Banks, Inc. 9/1/78 which merged into BB&T Corp. 7/1/2003

MOUNT VERNON CO (OH)
Voluntarily dissolved 7/29/77
Details not available

MT VERNON FINL CORP (DE)
Merged into Colonial BancGroup, Inc. 10/20/1995
Each share Common $2.50 par exchanged for (0.6712) share Common $2.50 par
(See Colonial BancGroup, Inc.)

MT. VERNON INSURANCE CO. (SC)
Merged into Triton Insurance Co. 10/03/1967
Each share Common $2 par exchanged for (0.5) share Class A Common $1 par
Triton Insurance Co. reorganized as Triton Corp. 03/01/1968
(See Triton Corp.)

MOUNT VERNON MLS INC (MD)
Stock Dividends - 20% 6/30/65; 20% 6/30/66
Merged into R.B. Pamplin Corp. 5/28/82
Each share 7% Preferred $100 par exchanged for $103.05 cash
Each share Common $2.50 par exchanged for $53 cash

MOUNT VERNON NATIONAL BANK & TRUST CO. OF FAIRFAX COUNTY (ANNANDALE, VA)
Merged into First Virginia Bankshares Corp. 9/5/69
Each share Capital Stock $25 par exchanged for (9) shares Common $1 par
First Virginia Bankshares Corp. name changed to First Virginia Banks, Inc. 9/1/78 which merged into BB&T Corp. 7/1/2003

MOUNT VERNON NATIONAL LIFE INSURANCE CO. (VA)
Completely liquidated 3/31/67
Each share Common $4 par exchanged for first and final distribution of (1) share 5% Conv. Preferred $10 par and (0.333333) share Common $1 par of First Virginia Corp.

MOUNT VERNON PORCUPINE GOLD MINES LTD. (ON)
Bankrupt in 1949

MT. VERNON SURETY CORP. (SC)
Name changed to Mt. Vernon Insurance Co. 11/10/1965
Mt. Vernon Insurance Co. merged into Triton Insurance Co. 10/03/1967 which reorganized as Triton Corp. 03/01/1968
(See Triton Corp.)

MOUNT VERNON TEL CORP (OH)
7% Preferred $100 par changed to 6% Preferred $100 par in 1937
4-1/4% Preferred $100 par called for redemption 9/30/65
5% Preferred $100 par called for redemption 9/30/65
6% Preferred $100 par called for redemption 9/30/65

MOUNT VERNON TRUST CO. (MOUNT VERNON, NY)
Merged into County Trust Co. (White Plains, NY) 03/31/1952
Each share Common $10 par exchanged for (1.125) shares Capital Stock $16 par
County Trust Co. (White Plains, NY) merged into Bank of New York Co., Inc. 05/29/1969 which merged into Bank of New York Mellon Corp. 07/01/2007

MOUNT VERNON-WOODBERRY MILLS, INC. (MD)
Each share Common $100 par exchanged for (1.25) shares Common $20 par 00/00/1945
Each share Common $20 par exchanged for (4) shares Common $5 par 00/00/1948
Each share Common $5 par exchanged for (2) shares Common $2.50 par 00/00/1952
Name changed to Mount Vernon Mills, Inc. 03/28/1956
(See Mount Vernon Mills, Inc.)

MOUNT VISTA GOLD & SILVER MINING CO. (NY)
Charter revoked for failure to file reports and pay fees 4/2/24

MOUNT WASHINGTON COPPER LTD (BC)
Recapitalized as Alawas Gold Corp. 05/29/1986
Each share Capital Stock $1 par exchanged for (0.2) share Common no par
Alawas Gold Corp. merged into Kaaba Resources Inc. 04/13/1989 which recapitalized as International Kaaba Gold Corp. 04/17/1990
(See International Kaaba Gold Corp.)

MOUNT WRIGHT IRON MINES LTD (ON)
Name changed to Mantaur Goldfields Corp. 04/30/1996
Mantaur Goldfields Corp. name changed to Mantaur Petroleum Corp. 06/25/1997 which merged into Videoflicks.com Inc. 03/24/1999
(See Videoflicks.com Inc.)

MOUNT ZEBALLOS GOLD MINES LTD.
Liquidated in 1943

MOUNTAIN & GULF OIL CO.
Dissolved in 1936

MOUNTAIN ASHE INC (CO)
Name changed to Holographic Systems, Inc. (CO) 9/23/87
Holographic Systems, Inc. (CO) reorganized in Nevada 2/7/2000 which name changed to Emission Control Devices Inc. 1/25/2001 which recapitalized as Rocky Mountain Energy Corp. (NV) 6/5/2002

(See Rocky Mountain Energy Corp. (NV))

MOUNTAIN BANCSHARES INC (GA)
Merged into GB&T Bancshares, Inc. 04/28/2006
Each share Common $5 par exchanged for (0.8911) share Common no par and $8.40 cash
GB&T Bancshares, Inc. merged into SunTrust Banks, Inc. 05/01/2008

MOUNTAIN BK HLDG CO (WA)
Merged into Columbia Banking System, Inc. 07/23/2007
Each share Common no par exchanged for (0.4231) share Common no par and $11.25 cash

MOUNTAIN BKS LTD (DE)
Common $5 par split (4) for (3) by issuance of (1/3) additional share 12/15/1978
Liquidation completed
Each share Common $5 par received initial distribution of $37.25 cash 02/12/1982
Each share Common $5 par exchanged for second distribution of $20.70 cash 10/21/1982
Each share Common $5 par received third and final distribution of $0.5437 cash 10/02/1985

MOUNTAIN BEAVER RES LTD (ON)
Merged into East Asia Gold Corp. 5/17/96
Each share Common no par exchanged for (0.05) share Common no par
East Asia Gold Corp. recapitalized as EAGC Ventures Corp. 5/28/2001 which merged into Bema Gold Corp. 2/14/2003 which merged into Kinross Gold Corp. 2/27/2007

MOUNTAIN CAP INC (BC)
Name changed to First Lithium Resources Inc. 05/14/2009
First Lithium Resources Inc. recapitalized as Golden Virtue Resources Inc. 10/11/2012 which name changed to Moseda Technologies, Inc. 04/23/2015 which name changed to Reliq Health Technologies Inc. 05/10/2016

MOUNTAIN CHEF INC (NV)
Reorganized as IVP Technology Corp. 11/11/1994
Each share Common $0.001 par exchanged for (20) shares Common $0.001 par
IVP Technology Corp. recapitalized as ActiveCore Technologies, Inc. 03/01/2005
(See ActiveCore Technologies, Inc.)

MOUNTAIN CITY COPPER CO.
Liquidation completed in 1951

MOUNTAIN COPPER CO. LTD. (ENGLAND)
Through voluntary tender offer of (0.095744) share Common $5 par and USD $1.50 cash all shares Capital Stock 6s par acquired by Stauffer Chemical Co. 07/04/1967

MOUNTAIN CORP (NV)
Company believed out of business 00/00/1990
Details not available

MOUNTAIN CREST INC (NV)
Recapitalized as Greyfield Capital Inc. (NV) 05/02/2002
Each share Common $0.001 par exchanged for (0.02) share Common $0.001 par
(See Greyfield Capital Inc.)

MOUNTAIN CREST INVTS INC (UT)
Involuntarily dissolved 07/01/1989

MOUNTAIN CREST MINES LTD.
Bankrupt in 1952

MOUNTAIN ELECTRONICS CO., INC. (WV)
Name changed to Mountain National Corp. 06/16/1965
Mountain National Corp. name changed to Midwest Corp. 06/30/1971 which merged into Unarco Industries, Inc. 02/03/1978 which reorganized as UNR Industries, Inc. 09/30/1980 which name changed to ROHN Industries, Inc. 12/19/1997 which name changed to Frankfort Tower Industries, Inc. 02/17/2004
(See Frankfort Tower Industries, Inc.)

MOUNTAIN ENERGY INC (NV)
Filed a petition under Chapter 7 Federal Bankruptcy Code 10/18/2000
Stockholders' equity unlikely

MOUNTAIN EQUITIES INC (DE)
Each share Class A $1 par or Class B 1¢ par exchanged for (1.05) shares Common 10¢ par 12/9/68
Adjudicated bankrupt 1/30/75
Stockholders' equity unlikely

MOUNTAIN FINL CO (TN)
Merged into First Tennessee National Corp. 04/30/1983
Each share Common $10 par exchanged for $105.75 cash

MOUNTAIN 1ST BK & TR CO (HENDERSONVILLE, NC)
Common $5 par split (5) for (4) by issuance of (0.25) additional share payable 02/14/2005 to holders of record 01/14/2005 Ex date - 02/15/2005
Common $5 par split (5) for (4) by issuance of (0.25) additional share payable 12/01/2005 to holders of record 11/01/2005 Ex date - 12/02/2005
Common $5 par split (5) for (4) by issuance of (0.25) additional share payable 12/5/2006 to holders of record 11/20/2006 Ex date - 12/06/2006
Reorganized as 1st Financial Services Corp. 06/02/2008
Each share Common $5 par exchanged for (1) share Common $5 par
(See 1st Financial Services Corp.)

MOUNTAIN FRONTIER EXPLS LTD (ON)
Merged into Castlestar Capital Developments Corp. 03/30/1990
Each share Common no par exchanged for (1.8) shares Common no par
Castlestar Capital Developments Corp. recapitalized as Southern Frontier Resources Inc. 11/11/1993
(See Southern Frontier Resources Inc.)

MOUNTAIN FUEL SUPPLY CO (UT)
Common $10 par changed to $5 par and (1) additional share issued 12/06/1974
Common $5 par changed to $2.50 par and (1) additional share issued 09/08/1983
Under plan of reorganization each share Common $2.50 par automatically became (1) share Questar Corp. Common no par 10/02/1984
8% Preferred no par called for redemption at $101 on 07/01/1997
(See Questar Corp.)

MOUNTAIN GOLD RES LTD (BC)
Recapitalized as Iron Tank Resources Corp. 04/20/2011
Each share Common no par exchanged for (0.06666666) share Common no par
Iron Tank Resources Corp. name changed to Spriza Media Inc. 03/01/2016 which name changed to Fanlogic Interactive Inc. 03/29/2017

MOUNTAIN HIGH INC (CO)
Name changed to MTH, Inc. 03/23/1983

MOUNTAIN LAKE RES INC (BC)
Merged into Marathon Gold Corp. 07/16/2012
Each share Common no par exchanged for (0.4) share Common no par and (0.4) share Mountain Lake Minerals Inc. Common no par
Note: Unexchanged certificates were cancelled and became without value 07/16/2018

MOUNTAIN MED EQUIP INC (DE)
Common 10¢ par split (2) for (1) by issuance of (1) additional share 02/25/1983
Merged into Cryogenic Associates, Inc. 07/30/1993
Each share Common 10¢ par exchanged for (0.005) share Common 1¢ par

MOUNTAIN MESA URANIUM CORP. (WY)
Each share Common 5¢ par exchanged for (0.2) share Common 25¢ par 07/25/1955
Merged into Hidden Splendor Mining Co. (DE) 10/19/1959
Each share Common 25¢ par exchanged for (0.01) share Common $1 par
Hidden Splendor Mining Co. (DE) merged into Atlas Corp. 08/17/1962
(See Atlas Corp.)

MOUNTAIN MINERALS LTD (BC)
Merged into Highwood Resources Ltd. 8/12/96
Each share Common no par exchanged for (0.284) share Common no par

MOUNTAIN MINES CO. (UT)
Charter forfeited 8/31/55

MOUNTAIN MODULAR MFG INC (CO)
Declared defunct and inoperative for failure to pay taxes and file annual reports 01/01/1986

MOUNTAIN NATL BANCSHARES INC (TN)
Stock Dividends - 5% payable 02/10/2004 to holders of record 12/31/2003 Ex date - 01/07/2004; 5% payable 01/31/2005 to holders of record 01/07/2005 Ex date - 01/05/2005; 5% payable 06/23/2006 to holders of record 06/01/2006 Ex date - 05/30/2006; 5% payable 02/28/2007 to holders of record 02/15/2007 Ex date - 02/13/2007; 5% payable 03/07/2008 to holders of record 02/15/2008 Ex date - 03/24/2008
Principal asset placed in receivership 06/07/2013
Stockholders' equity unlikely

MOUNTAIN NATL BK (GALAX, VA)
Stock Dividends - 10% payable 07/31/2000 to holders of record 06/30/2000 Ex date - 08/18/2000; 10% payable 07/31/2001 to holders of record 06/30/2001; 10% payable 07/31/2002 to holders of record 06/28/2002 Ex date - 07/29/2002
Merged into Carter Bank & Trust (Martinsville, VA) 12/29/2006
Each share Common $5 par exchanged for (3.981) shares Common

MOUNTAIN NATL CORP (WV)
Name changed to Midwest Corp. 06/30/1971
Each share Common 50¢ par exchanged for (1) share Common 50¢ par
Midwest Corp. merged into Unarco Industries, Inc. 02/03/1978 which reorganized as UNR Industries, Inc. 09/30/1980 which name changed to ROHN Industries, Inc. 12/17/1997

which name changed to Frankfort Tower Industries, Inc. 02/17/2004
(See Frankfort Tower Industries, Inc.)

MOUNTAIN OIL INC (UT)
Name changed to Dental Patient Care America, Inc. 8/25/2004

MOUNTAIN PAC INVT CO (CO)
Company went private 00/00/1985
Details not available

MOUNTAIN PKS FINL CORP (DE)
Merged into Community First Bancshares, Inc. 12/18/96
Each share Common $0.001 par exchanged for (1.275) shares Common 1¢ par
(See Community First Bancshares, Inc.)

MOUNTAIN PRODUCERS CORP.
Merged into Midwest Oil Corp. 00/00/1951
Each share Capital Stock $10 par exchanged for (1) share Common $10 par
Midwest Oil Corp. merged into Standard Oil Co. (IN) 04/15/1974 which name changed to Amoco Corp. 04/23/1985 which merged into BP Amoco p.l.c. 12/31/1998 which name changed to BP PLC 05/01/2001

MOUNTAIN PROVINCE MNG INC NEW (BC)
Merged 11/03/1997
Merged from Mountain Province Mining Inc. (Old) into Mountain Province Mining Inc. (New) 11/03/1997
Each share Common no par exchanged for (1) share Common no par
Name changed to Mountain Province Diamonds Inc. 10/16/2000

MOUNTAIN RENEWABLES INC (NV)
Name changed to Arcis Resources Corp. 12/21/2010

MOUNTAIN STATE MORTGAGE CO. INC. (WV)
Name changed to Radlon Inc. 12/10/1970
(See Radlon Inc.)

MOUNTAIN STS DEV CO (UT)
Proclaimed dissolved for failure to pay taxes 11/09/1974

MOUNTAIN STS FINL CORP (NM)
Liquidation completed
Each share Common $1 par exchanged for initial distribution of $21.31 cash 10/01/1984
Each share Common $1 par received second and final distribution of $0.53875 cash 10/31/1984
Note: Holders who did not surrender their certificates prior to 11/01/1984 have to apply to the Treasurer of the State of New Mexico to obtain payment

MOUNTAIN STATES LIFE INSURANCE CO. (CO)
Merged into Rocky Mountain Life Insurance Co. on a (5/6) for (1) basis 12/31/59
Rocky Mountain Life Insurance Co. merged into National American Life Insurance Co. 2/27/62
(See National American Life Insurance Co.)

MOUNTAIN STS OVERTHRUST OIL & GAS INC (UT)
Each share old Common no par exchanged for (0.1) share new Common no par 05/17/1982
Name changed to Peregrine Entertainment Ltd. 02/01/1984
(See Peregrine Entertainment Ltd.)

MOUNTAIN STATES PETROLEUM CORP. (UT)
Charter revoked for failure to file reports and pay fees 4/1/63

MOUNTAIN STATES POWER CO. (DE)
Each share 7% Preferred $100 par exchanged for (1) share 5% Preferred $50 par and (2) shares Common no par in 1940
Each (20) shares Common no par exchanged for (1) share new Common no par in 1940
Each share Common no par exchanged for (3) shares Common $7.25 par in 1951
Merged into Pacific Power & Light Co. in 1954
Each (2) shares 5% Preferred $50 par exchanged for (1) share 5% Preferred $100 par
Each share Common $7.25 par exchanged for (0.9) share Common $6.50 par
Pacific Power & Light Co. name changed to PacifiCorp (Me.) 6/15/84 which reincorporated in Oregon 1/9/89

MOUNTAIN STS RES LTD (BC)
Merged into MSR Exploration Ltd. (AB) 05/27/1981
Each share Capital Stock no par exchanged for (1) share Common no par
MSR Exploration Ltd. (AB) reincorporated in Delaware 10/31/1997 which merged into MSR Exploration Ltd. (New) 10/31/1997 which merged into Quicksilver Resources Inc. 03/04/1999
(See Quicksilver Resources Inc.)

MOUNTAIN STS TEL & TELEG CO (CO)
Capital Stock $100 par changed to $12.50 par and (7) additional shares issued 8/25/60
Merged into American Telephone & Telegraph Co. 12/22/80
Each share Capital Stock $12.50 par exchanged for (0.555) share Common $16-2/3 par
American Telephone & Telegraph Co. name changed to AT&T Corp. 4/20/94 which merged into AT&T Inc. 11/18/2005

MOUNTAIN STATES URANIUM, INC. (CO)
Proclaimed defunct and inoperative for failure to pay taxes 10/28/60

MOUNTAIN STS HLDGS INC (CO)
Recapitalized as Better Biodiesel, Inc. 09/21/2006
Each share Common no par exchanged for (0.5) share Common no par
Better Biodiesel, Inc. name changed to GeoBio Energy, Inc. 02/15/2008

MOUNTAIN STS RES CORP (UT)
Each share old Common 10¢ par exchanged for (0.01) share new Common 10¢ par 09/27/1996
Name changed to Micro-Media Solutions Inc. 09/29/1997
Micro-Media Solutions Inc. name changed to MSI Holdings, Inc. (UT) 10/14/1998 which reorganized in Delaware as Aperian, Inc. 09/11/2000 which name changed to Fourthstage Technologies, Inc. 08/20/2001
(See Fourthstage Technologies, Inc.)

MOUNTAIN SURGICAL CTRS INC (NV)
Name changed to CUSA Technologies, Inc. 7/26/94
CUSA Technologies, Inc. merged into Fiserv, Inc. 4/30/98

MOUNTAIN TOP MINING & MILLING CO. (CO)
Merged into Giant Resources, Inc. on a (1) for (10) basis 10/22/56
(See Giant Resources, Inc.)

MOUNTAIN TR BK (ROANOKE, VA)
Each share Capital Stock $100 par exchanged for (10) shares Capital Stock $10 par in 1948
Stock Dividends - 20% 12/31/61; 10% 10/15/64; 10% 1/15/69
Merged into First & Merchants Corp. 9/30/73
Each share Capital Stock $10 par exchanged for (2.25) shares Common $7.50 par
First & Merchants Corp. merged into Sovran Financial Corp. 12/31/83 which merged into C&S/Sovran Corp. 9/1/90 which merged into NationsBank Corp. 12/31/91 which reincorporated in Delaware as BankAmerica Corp. (Old) 9/25/98 which merged into BankAmerica Corp. (New) 9/30/98 which name changed to Bank of America Corp. 4/28/99

MOUNTAIN VALLEY OIL CORP. (OK)
Dissolved 6/27/60

MOUNTAIN VALLEY URANIUM CORP. (UT)
Merged into King Silver Corp. 3/19/69
Each share Common 1¢ par exchanged for (1) share Common 1¢ par
King Silver Corp. name changed to Altex Oil Corp. 5/17/72 which reorganized in Delaware as Altex Industries Inc. 10/30/85

MOUNTAIN VENTURES INC (NV)
Recapitalized as A.G.C. Management Enterprises Inc. 05/23/1994
Each share Common $0.0001 par exchanged for (0.008333) share Common $0.0001 par
(See A.G.C. Management Enterprises Inc.)

MOUNTAIN VIEW INVT CORP (WA)
Reincorporated under the laws of Delaware as Maratech Corp. and Common no par changed to $0.001 par 03/19/1987

MOUNTAIN VIEW MNG CO (UT)
Merged into North Lily Mining Co. 12/1/76
Each share Capital Stock 10¢ par exchanged for (0.0033) share Capital Stock 10¢ par
(See North Lily Mining Co.)

MOUNTAIN VIEW VENTURES (CANADA)
Recapitalized as Blackrun Ventures Inc. 04/08/1997
Each share Common no par exchanged for (0.25) share Common no par
Blackrun Ventures Inc. recapitalized as Blackrun Minerals Inc. 06/10/1999 which name changed to Diversified Industries Ltd. 03/29/2000
(See Diversified Industries Ltd.)

MOUNTAIN WEST AIRLS INC (ID)
Petition under Chapter 7 of the Federal Bankruptcy code filed 4/16/81
No stockholders' equity

MOUNTAIN WEST BK (COEUR D'ALENE, ID)
Name changed 8/1/98
Name changed from Mountain West Savings Bank F.S.B. to Mountain West Bank (Coeur D'Alene, ID) 8/1/98
Stock Dividend - 10% payable 8/21/98 to holders of record 7/31/98
Merged into Glacier Bancorp, Inc. 2/4/2000
Each share Common $2.50 par exchanged for (1.18) shares Common 1¢ par

MOUNTAIN WEST BUSINESS SOLUTIONS INC (NV)
Name changed to Sunshine Biopharma, Inc. 11/25/2009

MOUNTAIN WEST FINL CORP (MT)
Common no par split (10) for (1) by issuance of (9) additional shares payable 07/20/2007 to holders of record 06/22/2007 Ex date - 07/23/2007
Merged into First Interstate BancSystem, Inc. 07/31/2014
Each share Common no par exchanged for (0.2552) share Class A Common no par and $7.125 cash

MOUNTAIN WEST RES INC (BC)
Name changed to Mountainstar Gold Inc. 04/02/2012

MOUNTAIN WEST SVGS BK F S B (COEUR D'ALENE, ID)
Stock Dividend - 10% 10/20/89
Acquired by Security Pacific Bancorporation Northwest 8/27/90
Each share Common $1 par exchanged for $18.0272 cash

MOUNTAIN WORLD ENTMT LTD (BC)
Discharged from bankruptcy 10/10/2001
No stockholders' equity

MOUNTAINBANK (HENDERSONVILLE, NC)
Stock Dividends - 20% payable 1/20/99 to holders of record 1/6/99; 20% payable 1/15/2000 to holders of record 12/20/99
Under plan of reorganization each share Common $5 par automatically became (1.25) shares MountainBank Financial Corp. Common 1¢ par 3/30/2001
MountainBank Financial Corp. merged into South Financial Group, Inc. 10/3/2003

MOUNTAINBANK FINL CORP (NC)
Stock Dividend - 20% payable 4/1/2002 to holders of record 3/11/2002 Ex date - 3/7/2002
Merged into South Financial Group, Inc. 10/3/2003
Each share 6% Conv. Accredited Investors Preferred Ser. A no par exchanged for (1.581) shares Common $1 par
Each share Common $4 par exchanged for (1.318) shares Common $1 par

MOUNTAINEER BANKSHARES W VA INC (WV)
Stock Dividends - 100% 07/30/1986; 10% 10/31/1988
Merged into One Valley Bancorp of West Virginia, Inc. 01/28/1994
Each share Common $2.50 par exchanged for (1.5) shares Common $10 par
One Valley Bancorp of West Virginia, Inc. name changed to One Valley Bancorp Inc. 04/30/1996 which name changed to BB&T Corp. 07/06/2000

MOUNTAINEER MINES LTD (BC)
Recapitalized as Canadian Mineral Corp. 09/22/1980
Each share Common no par exchanged for (0.5) share Common no par
Canadian Mineral Corp. recapitalized as Canadian United Minerals Inc. 07/14/1983 which recapitalized as Mansfield Minerals Inc. 09/10/1990 which name changed to Goldrock Mines Corp. 01/22/2013 which merged into Fortuna Silver Mines Inc. 07/28/2016

MOUNTAINS WEST EXPL INC (NM)
Each share old Common $0.001 par exchanged for (0.02) share new Common $0.001 par 05/03/2005
Name changed to Secured Digital Storage Corp. 02/20/2008
(See Secured Digital Storage Corp.)

MOUNTAINTOP CORP (DE)
Name changed to New Mountaintop Corp. and Common 1¢ par changed to $0.0001 par 02/21/2003
New Mountaintop Corp. recapitalized as Trust Licensing, Inc. 08/24/2004 which name changed to Connected Media Technologies, Inc. 05/23/2005

MOUNTAINVIEW ENERGY LTD (BC)
Reincorporated under the laws of Alberta 05/24/2012

MOUNTAINVILLE DEV INC (UT)
Name changed to Agri World Trade Development Corp. 5/5/87
Agri World Trade Development Corp. recapitalized as Industrial Ecosystems, Inc. 3/7/94
(See Industrial Ecosystems, Inc.)

MOUNTAINWEST EXPLORATION INC. (UT)
Name changed to Plateau West Exploration, Inc. 11/20/1981
Plateau West Exploration, Inc. recapitalized as Kendall Management Corp. (UT) 02/07/1995 which reincorporated in Nevada as Medical Resources Management Inc. 08/20/1996 which merged into Emergent Group Inc. 07/06/2001
(See Emergent Group Inc.)

MOUNTASIA ENTMT INTL INC (GA)
Name changed to Malibu Entertainment Worldwide, Inc. 4/29/97

MOUNTBATTEN INC (PA)
Issue Information - 1,000,000 shares COM offered at $5 per share on 09/01/1994
Merged into F&B Merger Sub Inc. 8/5/98
Each share Common $0.001 par exchanged for $14.60 cash

MOUNTEX MINERALS CORP. (CO)
Proclaimed defunct and inoperative for non-payment of taxes 11/30/59

MOUNTFORT WEBB OIL INC (CO)
Name changed to Bennett Petroleum Corp. 12/14/1973
Bennett Petroleum Corp. merged into Abraxas Petroleum Corp. 08/14/1992

MOUNT10 INC (DE)
Merged into Mount10 Holding AG 5/3/2001
Each share Common $0.001 par exchanged for an undetermined amount of cash

MOVARIE CAP LTD (BC)
Name changed to Wellness Lifestyles Inc. 06/01/2017
Wellness Lifestyles Inc. name changed to WELL Health Technologies Corp. 07/13/2018

MOVE INC (DE)
Each share old Common $0.001 par exchanged for (0.25) share new Common $0.001 par 11/21/2011
Acquired by News Corp. (New) 11/14/2014
Each share Common $0.001 par exchanged for $21 cash

MOVEITONLINE INC (AB)
Name changed to Producers Oilfield Services Inc. 05/13/2003
(See Producers Oilfield Services Inc.)

MOVENTIS CAP INC (DE)
SEC revoked common stock registration 01/21/2014

MOVIE DISTR INCOME FD (ON)
Merged into Edgestone Capital Partners, Inc. 08/16/2007
Each Unit received $10 cash

MOVIE GALLERY INC (DE)
Issue Information - 3,000,000 shares COM offered at $14 per share on 08/02/1994
Common $0.001 par split (3) for (2) by issuance of (0.5) additional share payable 08/31/2001 to holders of record 08/17/2001 Ex date - 09/04/2001
Common $0.001 par split (3) for (2) by issuance of (0.5) additional share

payable 01/03/2002 to holders of record 12/17/2001 Ex date - 01/04/2002
Plan of reorganization under Chapter 11 Federal Bankruptcy Code effective 05/20/2008
No old Common stockholders' equity
Chapter 11 bankruptcy proceedings effective 11/18/2010
No new Common stockholders' equity

MOVIE GREATS NETWORK INC (NV)
Name changed to Program Entertainment Group, Inc. 8/4/92
Program Entertainment Group, Inc. recapitalized as Santa Maria Resources Inc. 8/5/97 which recapitalized as FantastiCon, Inc. 10/17/2000 which recapitalized as USCorp 3/6/2002

MOVIE STAR INC (NY)
Recapitalized as Frederick's of Hollywood Group Inc. 01/29/2008
Each share Common 1¢ par exchanged for (0.5) share Common 1¢ par
(See Frederick's of Hollywood Group Inc.)

MOVIE SUPERSTORE INC (AZ)
Charter revoked for failure to file reports or pay fees 12/10/93

MOVIE SYS INC (IA)
Common 25¢ par changed to $0.1875 par and (0.33333333) additional share issued 08/15/1983
Filed a petition under Chapter 11 Federal Bankruptcy Code 12/13/1985
No stockholders' equity

MOVIE TRAILER GALAXY INC (NV)
Each share old Common $0.0001 par exchanged for (560) shares new Common $0.0001 par 10/16/2012
Name changed to Brookfield Resources Inc. 11/15/2012
Brookfield Resources Inc. name changed to Broadcast Live Digital Corp. 08/02/2013

MOVIEFONE INC (DE)
Merged into America Online, Inc. 05/21/1999
Each share Class A Common 1¢ par exchanged for (0.3339) share Common 1¢ par
America Online, Inc. merged into AOL Time Warner Inc. 01/11/2001 which name changed to Time Warner Inc. (New) 10/16/2003 which merged into AT&T Inc. 06/15/2018

MOVIELAB FILM LABORATORIES, INC. (NY)
Name changed to Movielab, Inc. 4/23/62
(See Movielab, Inc.)

MOVIELAB INC (NY)
Class A Common $1 par reclassified as Common $1 par 5/5/64
Common $1 par split (3) for (2) by issuance of (0.5) additional share 4/27/65
Common $1 par split (3) for (2) by issuance of (0.5) additional share 12/15/65
Common $1 par changed to 50¢ par 5/13/66
Common 50¢ par split (5) for (4) by issuance of (0.25) additional share 4/10/68
Stock Dividends - 10% 1/20/67; 10% 9/20/67; 10% 10/31/79
Dissolved by proclamation 6/23/93

MOVING BOX INC (DE)
Name changed to Barfresh Food Group Inc. 02/29/2012

MOVING BYTES INC (CANADA)
Recapitalized as China International Enterprises Inc. (Canada) 03/23/2006
Each share Common no par exchanged for (0.03125) share Common no par

China International Enterprises Inc. (Canada) reincorporated in Delaware as China Software Technology Group Co., Ltd. 11/16/2006 which recapitalized as American Wenshen Steel Group, Inc. 10/12/2007
(See American Wenshen Steel Group, Inc.)

MOVIT MEDIA CORP (BC)
Each share old Common no par exchanged for (0.02) share new Common no par 01/19/2017
Reorganized under the laws of Ontario as Ether Capital Corp. 04/19/2018
Each share new Common no par exchanged for (0.08) share Common no par

MOVITO HLDGS LTD (NV)
Name changed to Silver Star Energy Inc. and (11) additional shares issued 11/20/2003

MOXA ENERGY CORP (NV)
Merged into MAZE Exploration Inc. 04/05/1985
Each share Common 10¢ par exchanged for $0.40 cash

MOXHAM BK CORP (PA)
Common $4 par changed to $2 par and (1) additional share issued 5/1/87
Stock Dividend - 10% 12/30/94
Merged into BT Financial Corp. 6/25/96
Each share Common $2 par exchanged for (1.15) shares Common $5 par
BT Financial Corp. name changed to Promistar Financial Corp. 11/15/2000 which merged into F.N.B. Corp. (FL) 1/18/2002

MOXHAM NATL BK (JOHNSTOWN, PA)
Common $100 par changed to $10 par and (9) additional shares issued plus a 50% stock dividend paid 7/15/64
Common $10 par changed to $12 par 2/14/67
Under plan of reorganization each share Common $12 par automatically became (1) share Moxham Bank Corp. Common $4 par 4/11/86
Moxham Bank Corp. merged into BT Financial Corp. 6/25/96 which name changed to Promistar Financial Corp. 11/15/2000 which merged into F.N.B. Corp. (FL) 1/18/2002

MOXIAN CHINA INC (NV)
Common $0.001 par split (60) for (1) by issuance of (59) additional shares payable 12/13/2013 to holders of record 12/13/2013
Name changed to Moxian, Inc. 07/29/2015

MOXIAN GROUP HLDGS INC (FL)
Common $0.0001 par split (20) for (1) by issuance of (19) additional shares payable 04/16/2013 to holders of record 04/16/2013
Recapitalized as Inception Technology Group, Inc. 07/23/2014
Each share Common $0.0001 par exchanged for (0.2) share Common $0.0001 par
Inception Technology Group, Inc. recapitalized as Rebel Group, Inc. 12/05/2014

MOXIE CO. OF AMERICA
Merged into Moxie Co. 00/00/1931
Details not available

MOXIE CO (MA)
Each share Class A no par exchanged for (2) shares Conv. Preferred no par and (1) share new Class B no par 00/00/1938
Each share old Class B no par exchanged for (0.25) share new Class B no par 00/00/1938
New Class B no par reclassified as Common no par 00/00/1947
Common no par changed to $1 par 12/27/1957
Conv. Preferred no par called for redemption 04/13/1962
Name changed to Moxie-Monarch-NuGrape Co. 04/28/1970
Moxie-Monarch-NuGrape Co. name changed to Moxie Industries, Inc. 05/19/1972 which merged into SPI Acquisition Corp. 08/11/1988
(See SPI Acquisition Corp.)

MOXIE EXPL LTD (AB)
Acquired by Endev Energy Inc. 07/25/2003
Each share Common no par exchanged for (0.070478) share Common no par and $0.341113 cash
Endev Energy Inc. merged into Penn West Energy Trust 07/22/2008 which reorganized as Penn West Petroleum Ltd. (New) 01/03/2011 which name changed to Obsidian Energy Ltd. 06/29/2017

MOXIE INDS INC (MA)
Name changed 5/19/72
Name changed from Moxie-Monarch-NuGrape Co. to Moxie Industries, Inc. 5/19/72
Merged into SPI Acquisition Corp. 8/11/88
Each share Common $1 par exchanged for (0.056497) share Common 1¢ par

MOXIE INVESTMENTS, INC. (UT)
Name changed to Worldtron International, Inc. 8/22/85
Worldtron International, Inc. recapitalized as POS Systems Inc. 12/10/85

MOXIE PETROLEUM LTD (AB)
Acquired by Richland Petroleum Corp. 12/23/1999
Each share Common no par exchanged for (0.18) share Common no par, (0.7) share Moxie Exploration Ltd. Common no par and $1.135 cash
(See each company's listing)

MOXON INC (CA)
Reorganized under Chapter 11 Federal Bankruptcy Code 03/03/1981
Each share Common 10¢ par received $0.001 cash
Note: Certificates were not required to be surrendered and are without value

MOYA OVERVIEW INC (CO)
Assets fraudently transferred to Devo General Partnership 10/00/1991
No stockholders' equity

MOYCO TECHNOLOGIES INC (PA)
Name changed 12/6/95
Common $0.025 par changed to $0.005 par and (5) additional shares issued 5/26/87
Name changed from Moyco Industries, Inc. to Moyco Technologies Inc. 12/6/95
Stock Dividends - 10% payable 9/30/98 to holders of record 9/18/98; 10% payable 11/24/99 to holders of record 11/13/99
Each (170,000) shares old Common $0.005 par exchanged for (1) share new Common $0.005 par on 8/29/2003
Note: In effect holders received $0.045 cash per share and public interest was eliminated

MOYDOW MINES INTL INC (BC)
Reincorporated 12/18/2006
Place of incorporation changed from (ON) to (BC) 12/18/2006

Merged into Franco-Nevada Corp. 01/27/2010
Each share Common no par exchanged for (0.02863) share Common no par

MOZART GOLD MINES, LTD. (ON)
Charter cancelled for failure to file reports and pay taxes May 1960

MP WESTN PPTYS INC (CANADA)
Merged into Madison Pacific Properties Inc. 07/07/2011
Each share Class A Common no par exchanged for $0.06 cash
Each share Class B Common no par exchanged for $0.06 cash
Note: Unexchanged certificates were cancelled and became without value 07/07/2017

MP&L CAP I (DE)
Name changed to Allete Capital I 9/1/2000
(See Allete Capital I)

MPA ASSOCS INC (UT)
Involuntarily dissolved for failure to file annual reports 10/01/1988

MPAC INDS CORP (YUKON)
Reincorporated under the laws of British Columbia 7/28/2006

MPAC RES CORP (NV)
Name changed 04/30/2004
Name changed from MPAC Corp. to MPAC Resources Corp. 04/30/2004
Recapitalized as American United Gold Corp. 10/04/2004
Each share Common $0.001 par exchanged for (0.5) share Common $0.001 par
(See American United Gold Corp.)

MPACT IMMEDIA CORP (CANADA)
Name changed to BCE Emergis Inc. 01/21/1999
BCE Emergis Inc. name changed to Emergis Inc. 12/01/2004
(See Emergis Inc.)

MPATH INTERACTIVE INC (DE)
Name changed to HearMe 01/31/2000
(See HearMe)

MPB CORP (DE)
Reincorporated 06/30/1969
State of incorporation changed from (NH) to (DE) and Common $2 par changed to $1 par 06/30/1969
Merged into Wheelabrator-Frye Inc. 11/16/1976
Each share Common $1 par exchanged for $26.50 cash

MPC CORP (CO)
Plan of reorganization under Chapter 11 Federal Bankruptcy proceedings effective 05/12/2011
No stockholders' equity

MPC EDL SYS INC (NY)
Name changed to PM&E Inc. 09/08/2001
(See PM&E Inc.)

MPD DEV CORP (DE)
Recapitalized as Astor Explorations Corp. 05/19/2010
Each share Common $0.001 par exchanged for (1/6) share Common $0.001 par

MPEG SUPER SITE INC (CO)
Reincorporated under the laws of Nevada as Modern Manufacturing Services, Inc. 7/6/2001
Modern Manufacturing Services, Inc. name changed to Radix Marine Inc. 5/12/2003

MPEL HLDGS CORP (NY)
SEC revoked common stock registration 07/07/2010
Stockholders' equity unlikely

MPG OFFICE TR INC (MD)
Merged into Brookfield DTLA Fund Office Trust Investor Inc. 10/15/2013
Each share 7.625% Ser. A Preferred 1¢ par exchanged for (1) share

7.625% Ser. A Preferred Stock 1¢ par
Each share Common 1¢ par exchanged for $3.15 cash

MPH VENTURES CORP (BC)
Each share old Common no par exchanged for (0.1) share new Common no par 06/04/2014
Name changed to Cuba Ventures Corp. 03/21/2016
Cuba Ventures Corp. name changed to CUV Ventures Corp. 03/01/2018

MPI HLDGS INC (WY)
Reincorporated 06/24/1994
Place of incorporation changed from (BC) to (WY) 06/24/1994
Administratively dissolved 06/24/1994

MPI INDS INC (DE)
Reincorporated 04/05/1968
Voting Trust Agreement terminated 02/01/1966
Each VTC for Common $1 par exchanged for (1) share Common $1 par
Stock Dividend - 100% 04/27/1966
State of incorporation changed from (IL) to (DE) 04/05/1968
Merged into DeSoto, Inc. 11/03/1969
Each share Common $1 par exchanged for (0.731) share Common $1 par
DeSoto, Inc. merged into Keystone Consolidated Industries Inc. 09/26/1996
(See Keystone Consolidated Industries, Inc.)

MPL COMMUNICATIONS INC (AB)
Delisted from Toronto Venture Stock Exchange 07/11/2010

MPLC INC (DE)
Recapitalized as New Motion, Inc. 05/03/2007
Each share Common 1¢ par exchanged for (0.00333333) share Common 1¢ par
Note: Holders of between (100) and (29,999) shares will receive (100) shares
Holders of (99) or fewer shares were not affected by the reverse split
New Motion, Inc. name changed to Atrinsic, Inc. 06/26/2009 which recapitalized as Protagenic Therapeutics, Inc. 07/27/2016

MPO VIDEOTRONICS INC (NY)
Class A $1 par reclassified as Common $1 par 03/10/1969
Stock Dividend - 10% 04/12/1968
Merged into Montauk Corp. 02/18/1982
Each share Common $1 par exchanged for $7 cash

MPOWER COMMUNICATIONS CORP (NV)
Reincorporated under the laws of Delaware as Mpower Holding Corp. 6/28/2001
(See Mpower Holding Corp.)

MPOWER HLDG CORP (DE)
Plan of reorganization under Chapter 11 Federal Bankruptcy Code effective 7/30/2002
Each share 7.25% Conv. Preferred Ser. D exchanged for approximately (2.3) shares new Common $0.001 par
Each share old Common $0.001 par exchanged for (0.01636739) share new Common $0.001 par
Acquired by U.S. TelePacific Holdings Corp. 8/4/2006
Each share new Common $0.001 par exchanged for $1.92 cash

MPS GROUP INC (FL)
Acquired by Adecco, Inc. 01/19/2010
Each share Common 1¢ par exchanged for $13.80 cash

MPS INTL CORP (NY)
Adjudicated bankrupt 05/26/1978
Stockholders' equity unlikely

MPSBANCORP INC (DE)
Common $10 par split (2) for (1) by issuance of (1) additional share 9/30/83
Merged into First United Financial Services, Inc. 5/31/85
Each share Common $10 par exchanged for (2.365) shares Common $5 par
(See First United Financial Services, Inc.)

MPSI SYS INC (DE)
Name changed 10/24/1983
Name changed from MPSI Group Inc. to MPSI Systems 10/24/1983
Common 5¢ par split (3) for (2) by issuance of (0.5) additional share 02/24/1984
Each share old Common 5¢ par exchanged for (0.1) share new Common 5¢ par 11/18/1993
Each share new Common 5¢ par exchanged again for (0.01) share new Common 5¢ par 08/13/2004
Note: Holders of (99) or fewer pre-split shares received $0.30 cash per share
Name changed to Market Planning Solutions Inc. 04/16/2007
(See Market Planning Solutions Inc.)

MP3 COM INC (DE)
Issue Information - 12,347,233 shares COM offered at $28 per share on 07/21/1999
Merged into Vivendi Universal S.A. 8/28/2001
Each share Common $0.001 par exchanged for $5 cash

MPTV INC (NV)
Common 5¢ par changed to 1¢ par 11/05/1999
Each share old Common 1¢ par exchanged for (0.1) share new Common 1¢ par 01/11/2002
SEC revoked common stock registration 08/03/2005
Stockholders' equity unlikely

MP2 TECHNOLOGIES INC (DE)
Recapitalized as The Kiley Group, Inc. 11/03/2009
Each share Common $0.001 par exchanged for (0.001) share Common $0.001 par

MPV INC (UT)
Name changed to Optimum Source International (UT) 09/14/1989
Optimum Source International (UT) reincorporated in Nevada as Optimum Source International, Ltd. 06/29/1990

MPVC INC (CANADA)
Each share old Common no par exchanged for (0.2) share new Common no par 06/07/2013
Name changed to Northern Uranium Corp. 06/27/2014

MPW INDL SVCS GROUP INC (OH)
Issue Information - 3,750,000 shares COM offered at $9 per share on 12/02/1997
Merged into Black Family Trust 9/26/2006
Each share Common no par exchanged for $2.55 cash

MPX ENERGIA S A (BRAZIL)
Sponsored ADR's for Common split (4) for (1) by issuance of (3) additional ADR's payable 07/24/2009 to holders of record 07/22/2009 Ex date - 07/27/2009
ADR basis changed from (1:0.2) to (1:1) 07/24/2009
Sponsored ADR's for Common split (3) for (1) by issuance of (2) additional ADR's payable 08/23/2012 to holders of record 08/20/2012 Ex date - 08/24/2012
Name changed to Eneva S.A. 10/22/2013

MPX INVESTMENTS, INC. (OH)
Name changed to Amerigold Inc. 1/24/84
Amerigold Inc. charter cancelled 12/15/93

MRC METALL RESOURCES CORP (BC)
Reincorporated under the laws of Canada as Mount Dakota Energy Corp. 08/24/1998
Mount Dakota Energy Corp. (Canada) reincorporated in British Columbia 08/07/2015

MRC TECHNOLOGIES INC (AB)
Name changed to Telkwa Gold Corp. (ALTA) 09/17/1996
Telkwa Gold Corp. (ALTA) reincorporated in Ontario as Honey Badger Exploration Inc. 06/23/2008

MRF 2005 RESOURCE LTD PARTNERSHIP (ON)
Completely liquidated 05/15/2007
Each Unit of Ltd. Partnership exchanged for first and final distribution of (1.75193872) shares Middlefield Mutual Funds Ltd. Canadian Growth Class Ser. A

MRFY CORP (MN)
Filed for Chapter 7 Federal Bankruptcy Code 2/26/87
No stockholders' equity

MRI LIQUIDATING, INC. (NY)
Liquidation completed
Each share Common 10¢ par exchanged for initial distribution of $0.10 cash 4/13/79
Each share Common 10¢ par received second and final distribution of $0.03 cash 11/29/79

MRI MGMT ASSOC INC (NY)
Name changed to Medical Management, Inc. 1/3/95
Medical Management, Inc. merged into Complete Management Inc. 1/3/96
(See Complete Management Inc.)

MRI MED DIAGNOSTICS INC (CO)
Each share old Common no par exchanged for (0.2) share new Common no par 7/15/97
Recapitalized as HomeZipR Corp. (CO) 9/6/2000
Each (18.85077263) shares new Common no par exchanged for (1) share Common no par
HomeZipR Corp. (CO) reorganized in Delaware as Advansys Companies, Inc. 12/28/2006

MRI MED TECHNOLOGIES INC (BC)
Recapitalized as Tri-National Development Corp. (BC) 12/07/1992
Each share Common no par exchanged for (0.2) share Common no par
Tri-National Development Corp. (BC) reincorporated in Wyoming 02/25/1997
(See Tri-National Development Corp.)

MRI PPTYS INC (FL)
Merged into CAM Corp. 05/31/1983
Each share Common 30¢ par exchanged for $0.25 cash

MRL INC (MO)
Dissolved 00/00/2000
Stockholders' equity unlikely

MRLD HLDGS INC (TX)
Name changed to Taj Systems, Inc. 10/24/2005

MRO SOFTWARE INC (MA)
Merged into International Business Machines Corp. 10/6/2006
Each share Common 1¢ par exchanged for $25.80 cash

MRP WASTE MGMT CORP (ON)
Name changed 8/18/89
Name changed from MRP Petroleums Inc. to MRP Waste Management Corp. 8/18/89

Charter cancelled for failure to pay taxes and file returns 9/17/94

MRRM INC (CANADA)
$1.45 Preferred no par called for redemption 01/30/1987
Common no par split (10) for (1) by issuance of (9) additional shares payable 07/23/2003 to holders of record 07/18/2003
Acquired by Marbour S.A.S. 04/02/2015
Each share Common no par exchanged for $4.45 cash
Note: Unexchanged certificates will be cancelled and become without value 04/02/2021

MRS. TUCKER'S FOODS, INC.
Merged into Anderson, Clayton & Co. 00/00/1952
Each share Common $2.50 par exchanged for (0.33333333) share Common $21.80 par
(See Anderson, Clayton & Co.)

MRS SMITHS PIE CO (DE)
Merged into Kellogg Co. 08/17/1976
Each share Common $1 par exchanged for (0.9) share Common 50¢ par

MRS TECHNOLOGY INC (MA)
Chapter 11 bankruptcy proceedings converted to Chapter 7 on 02/18/1999
No stockholders' equity

MR3 SYS INC (DE)
SEC revoked common stock registration 07/07/2010
Stockholders' equity unlikely

MRU HOLDINGS INC (DE)
Filed a petition under Chapter 7 Federal Bankruptcy Code 02/06/2009
Stockholders' equity unlikely

MRV COMMUNICATIONS INC (DE)
Common 1¢ changed to $0.0067 par and (0.5) additional share issued 04/02/1996
Common $0.0067 par changed to $0.0034 par and (1) additional share issued 07/31/1996
Common $0.0034 par changed to $0.0017 par and (1) additional share issued 05/26/2000
Each share old Common $0.0017 par exchanged for (0.05) share new Common $0.0017 par 12/27/2012
Acquired by ADVA Optical Networking SE 08/14/2017
Each share new Common $0.0017 par exchanged for $10 cash

MRV ENGENHARIA PARTICIPACOES SA (BRAZIL)
Sponsored ADR's for Ordinary split (3) for (1) by issuance of (2) additional ADR's payable 01/05/2010 to holders of record 12/17/2009 Ex date - 01/06/2010
ADR agreement terminated 05/29/2018
Each Sponsored ADR for Ordinary exchanged for (2) shares Ordinary
Note: Unexchanged ADR's will be sold and the proceeds, if any, held for claim after 10/01/2018

MS DIVERSIFIED CORP (MS)
Merged into American Bankers Insurance Group, Inc. 10/28/98
Each share Common $1 par exchanged for $10.556 cash

MS FINL INC (MS)
Issue Information - 2,400,000 shares COM offered at $12 per share on 07/21/1995
Merged into Search Financial Services Inc. 7/31/97
Each share Common $0.001 par exchanged for (0.3515) share Common 2¢ par
(See Search Financial Services Inc.)

MSA CAP CORP (AB)
Name changed to Coronation Minerals Inc. (AB) 10/29/2002
Coronation Minerals Inc. (AB) reincorporated in Ontario 04/23/2004 which name changed to Guyana Precious Metals Inc. 08/18/2009 which name changed to GPM Metals Inc. 08/29/2013

MSA PETE LTD (BC)
Merged into Tygas Resource Corp. 01/04/1989
Each share Common no par exchanged for (0.5) share Common no par
Tygas Resource Corp. merged into Alberta Oil & Gas Ltd. 08/02/1990 which recapitalized as Alberta Oil & Gas Petroleum Corp. 11/19/1997 which recapitalized as Edge Energy Inc. 04/14/1998 which merged into Ventus Energy Ltd. 08/11/2000 which name changed to Navigo Energy Inc. 05/24/2002
(See Navigo Energy Inc.)

MSA RLTY CORP (IN)
Merged into Simon Property Group, Inc. 9/1/94
Each share Common $1 par exchanged for (0.31) share Common $0.0001 par

MSB BANCORP INC (DE)
Merged into HUBCO, Inc. 05/29/1998
Each share Common 1¢ par exchanged for (1.0209) shares Common no par
HUBCO, Inc. name changed Hudson United Bancorp 04/21/1999 which merged into TD Banknorth Inc. 01/31/2006
(See TD Banknorth Inc.)

MSB FINL CORP (USA)
Reorganized under the laws of Maryland 07/16/2015
Each share Common 10¢ par exchanged for (1.1397) shares Common 1¢ par

MSB FINL INC (DE)
Common 1¢ par split (2) for (1) by issuance of (1) additional share payable 08/07/1997 to holders of record 07/22/1997
Stock Dividend - 10% payable 08/31/1998 to holders of record 08/10/1998
Merged into Monarch Community Bancorp, Inc. 04/15/2004
Each share Common 1¢ par exchanged for (0.2381) share Common 1¢ par and $15.04 cash
Monarch Community Bancorp, Inc, merged into Chemical Financial Corp. 04/01/2015

MSC SOFTWARE CORP (DE)
Acquired by Maximus Holdings Inc. 10/14/2009
Each share Common 1¢ par exchanged for $8.40 cash

MSDW CAP TR I (DE)
Issue Information - 16,000,000 CAP SECS 7.10% offered at $25 per share on 03/05/1998
7.10% Capital Securities split (3) for (2) by issuance of (0.5) additional share payable 1/2/2002 to holders of record 12/14/2001
7.10% Capital Securities called for redemption at $25 on 8/11/2003

MSE ECOENGINE INC (DE)
Name changed to MSE Enviro-Tech Corp. 2/21/2007

MSGI SEC SOLUTIONS INC (NV)
Common 1¢ par split (2) for (1) by issuance of (1) additional share payable 03/08/2005 to holders of record 02/22/2005 Ex date - 03/09/2005
SEC revoked common stock registration 12/18/2015

MSI CORP (DE)
Charter cancelled and declared inoperative and void for non-payment of taxes 06/27/1975

MSI DATA CORP (DE)
Reincorporated 9/15/80
State of incorporation changed from (CA) to (DE) 9/15/80
Common $1 par split (3) for (2) by issuance of (0.5) additional share 4/7/88
Merged into Symbol Technologies, Inc. 11/10/88
Each share Common $1 par exchanged for $23 cash

MSI ELECTRS INC (DE)
Common 3¢ par split (2) for (1) by issuance of (1) additional share 01/16/1984
Charter cancelled and declared inoperative and void for non-payment of taxes 03/01/2003

MSI ENERGY SVCS INC (AB)
Acquired by Willbros Group, Inc. (Panama) 10/17/2001
Each share Common no par exchanged for $0.95 cash

MSI HLDGS INC (UT)
Reorganized under the laws of Delaware as Aperian, Inc. 9/11/2000
Each share Common 10¢ par exchanged for (1/3) share Common 1¢ par
Aperian, Inc. name changed to Fourthstage Technologies, Inc. 8/20/2001
(See Fourthstage Technologies, Inc.)

MSL INDS INC (DE)
Reincorporated 6/1/73
State of incorporation changed from (MN) to (DE) and Common no par changed to $1 par 06/01/1973
Merged into Alleghany Corp. (MD) 09/25/1975
Each share Common $1 par exchanged for $50 cash

MSM JEWELRY CORP (NV)
Each share old Common 1¢ par exchanged for (0.008) share new Common 1¢ par 5/22/2003
Name changed to GEMZ Corp. 10/27/2003

MSM SYS INC (OR)
Filed for Chapter 7 Bankruptcy proceedings 12/07/1984
No stockholders' equity

MSN INDS LTD (CANADA)
Acquired by Resources Services Group Ltd. 10/18/1974
Each share Common no par exchanged for $8.83 cash

MSP MAXXUM TR (ON)
Merged into Mackenzie Maxxum Dividend Class 06/26/2009
Each Trust Unit no par received (0.4884) Ser. B no par

MSR EXPL LTD NEW (DE)
Merged into Quicksilver Resources Inc. 03/04/1999
Each share Common 1¢ par exchanged for (0.1) share Common 1¢ par
(See Quicksilver Resources Inc.)

MSR EXPL LTD OLD (DE)
Reincorporated 10/31/1997
Place of incorporation changed from (AB) to (DE) and Common no par changed to 1¢ par 10/31/1997
Merged into MSR Exploration Ltd. (New) 10/31/1997
Each share Common 1¢ par exchanged for (1) share Common 1¢ par
MSR Exploration Ltd. (New) merged into Quicksilver Resources Inc. 03/04/1999
(See Quicksilver Resources Inc.)

MSR FOODS, INC. (DE)
Each (30,000) shares old Common 10¢ par exchanged for (1) share new Common 10¢ par 3/15/91
Note: In effect holders received $5.50 cash per share and public interest was eliminated

MSS INFORMATION CORP (NY)
Dissolved by proclamation 3/26/80

MSTI HLDGS INC (DE)
SEC revoked common stock registration 01/21/2014

MSU DEVICES INC (DE)
Name changed 7/17/2001
Name changed from MSU Corp. to MSU Devices Inc. and state of incorporation changed from (FL) to (DE) 7/17/2001
Plan of reorganization under Chapter 11 Federal Bankruptcy Code effective 7/1/2003
No stockholders' equity

MSV RES INC (QC)
Class A no par reclassified as Common no par 06/20/1994
Each share Common no par received distribution of (0.1) share Arca Explorations Inc. Common no par payable 11/25/1997 to holders of record 11/25/1997
Merged into Campbell Resources Inc. (New) 06/30/2001
Each share Common no par exchanged for (0.24390243) share new Common no par
(See Campbell Resources Inc. (New))

MSZ RES LTD (NB)
Reorganized under the laws of Alberta as Corrida Oils Ltd. 02/08/1982
Each share Common no par exchanged for (0.33333333) share Common no par
(See Corrida Oils Ltd.)

MT ULTIMATE HEALTHCARE CORP (NV)
Old Common $0.001 par split (80) for (1) by issuance of (79) additional shares payable 09/02/2003 to holders of record 09/02/2003
Each share old Common $0.001 par exchanged for (0.25) share new Common $0.001 par 09/29/2003
Recapitalized as Monarch Staffing, Inc. 03/31/2006
Each share new Common $0.001 par exchanged for (0.01111111) share Common $0.001 par
(See Monarch Staffing, Inc.)

MTC ELECTR TECHNOLOGIES LTD (BC)
Each share old Common no par exchanged for (0.25) share new Common no par 10/29/1991
Name changed to GrandeTel Technologies Inc. (BC) 09/08/1995
GrandeTel Technologies Inc. (BC) reincorporated in Canada 09/28/1995
(See GrandeTel Technologies Inc.)

MTC LIQUIDATING CORP. (TX)
Liquidation completed
Each share Common $1 par exchanged for initial distribution of $26 cash 12/18/73
Each share Common $1 par received second distribution of $2.50 cash 9/20/74
Each share Common $1 par received third and final distribution of $0.73 cash 12/21/77

MTC MTG INVT CORP (ON)
Name changed to MCAP Inc. 1/6/2000
MCAP Inc. name changed to MCAN Mortgage Corp. 9/15/2006

MTC TECHNOLOGIES INC (DE)
Issue Information - 5,000,000 shares COM offered at $17 per share on 06/27/2002
Merged into BAE Systems plc 06/09/2008

Each share Common $0.001 par exchanged for $24 cash

MTECH CORP (DE)
Merged into EDS Acquisition Corp. 06/27/1988
Each share Common 1¢ par exchanged for $30 cash

MTGE INVT CORP (MD)
Merged into Annaly Capital Management, Inc. 09/07/2018
Each share 8.125% Preferred Ser. A 1¢ par exchanged for (1) share 8.125% Preferred Ser. H 1¢ par
Each share Common 1¢ par exchanged for (0.9519) Common 1¢ par and $9.82 cash

MTI GLOBAL INC (ON)
Name changed to Zuni Holdings Inc. (New) 07/15/2010
Zuni Holdings Inc. (New) merged into Pacific Safety Products Inc. 01/04/2011

MTI SYS CORP (NY)
Acquired by Ducommun, Inc. 10/12/1984
Each share Common 1¢ par exchanged for $3 cash

MTI TECHNOLOGY CORP (DE)
Issue Information - 5,700,000 shares COM offered at $9 per share on 04/07/1994
Plan of reorganization under Chapter 11 Federal Bankruptcy proceedings effective 09/27/2010
Stockholders' equity unlikely

MTL INC (FL)
Merged into Apollo Management L.P. 6/9/98
Each share Common 1¢ par exchanged for $40 cash

MTM TECHNOLOGIES INC (NY)
Each share old Common $0.001 par exchanged for (0.06666666) share new Common $0.001 par 06/26/2008
Acquired by MTM Holding, Inc. 10/02/2015
Each share new Common $0.001 par exchanged for $0.25 cash

MTN HLDGS INC (NV)
Each share old Common $0.001 par exchanged for (0.01) share new Common $0.001 par 07/16/2001
Each share new Common $0.001 par exchanged again for (0.00105263) share new Common $0.001 par 11/08/2001
Each share new Common $0.001 par exchanged again for (0.0005) share new Common $0.001 par 04/09/2002
Recapitalized as Nextronics II Inc. 02/18/2005
Each share new Common $0.001 par exchanged for (0.1) share Common $0.001 par
Nextronics II Inc. name changed to Ukraine Financial Services, Inc. 06/12/2008 which name changed to National Investment Corporation, Real Estate Holdings 06/23/2008
(See National Investment Corporation, Real Estate Holdings)

MTR CORP LTD (HONG KONG)
ADR agreement terminated 02/13/2017
Each Sponsored ADR for Ordinary exchanged for $57.697912 cash

MTR GAMING GROUP INC (DE)
Merged into Eldorado Resorts, Inc. 09/19/2014
Each share Common $0.00001 par exchanged for (1) share Common $0.00001 par

MTS INTL SVCS INC (ON)
Name changed 10/06/1971
Name changed from MTS International Services Ltd. to MTS

International Services Inc. 10/06/1971
Reincorporated under the laws of Canada as Epitek International Inc. 12/07/1981
Epitek International Inc. recapitalized as International Epitek Inc. 08/01/1987 which name changed to CompAS Electronics Inc. 07/29/1993 which was acquired by AIM Safety Co., Inc. 12/08/1997 which name changed to AimGlobal Technologies Co., Inc. 01/29/1999
(See AimGlobal Technologies Co., Inc.)

MTS MEDICATION TECHNOLOGIES INC (DE)
Acquired by MedPak Holdings, Inc. 12/22/2009
Each share Common 1¢ par exchanged for $5.75 cash

MTU AERO ENGINES HLDGS AG (GERMANY)
Name changed to MTU Aero Engines AG 06/21/2013

MTU INVTS INC (AB)
Merged into Prospectus Group Inc. (ALTA) 12/9/97
Each share Common no par exchanged for (0.5) share Common no par
Prospectus Group Inc. (ALTA) reincorporated in Ontario as Route1 Inc. 10/21/2004

MTV NETWORKS INC (DE)
Acquired by Viacom International, Inc. 03/31/1986
Each share Common 1¢ par exchanged for $33.50 cash

MTX INTL INC (CO)
Administratively dissolved 5/1/99

MTX INTL INC (FL)
Name changed to AmeriNet Financial Systems, Inc. 10/31/95

MUEHLEBACH (GEORGE) BREWING CO. (MO)
Liquidation completed 11/14/58

MUEHLHAUSEN SPRING CORP.
Acquired by Standard Steel Spring Co. in 1940
Details not available

MUELLER BRASS CO. (MI)
Stock Dividend - 100% 2/10/47
Merged into United States Smelting Refining & Mining Co. (Me.) (New) 9/24/65
Each share Common $1 par exchanged for (0.42) share $5.50 Preferred $5 par
United States Smelting Refining & Mining Co. (Me.) (New) name changed to UV Industries, Inc. 6/9/72 which name changed to UV Industries, Inc. Liquidating Trust 3/25/80
(See UV Industries, Inc. Liquidating Trust)

MUELLER (L.J.) FURNACE CO. (WI)
Each share Common no par received (1) share 4-1/2% Preferred $50 par and (2) additional shares Common no par in 1949
Acquired by Worthington Corp. in 1954
Each share 4-1/2% Preferred $50 par exchanged for (1.666666) shares Common no par
Each share Common no par exchanged for (1.4) shares Common no par
Worthington Corp. merged into Studebaker- Worthington, Inc. 11/27/67

MUELLER MED INTL INC (ON)
Recapitalized as Vasogen Inc. 04/21/1994
Each share Common no par exchanged for (1/7) share Common no par

Vasogen Inc. merged into IntelliPharmaCeutics International Inc. 10/22/2009

MUIRFIELD INVT CORP (BC)
Recapitalized as First Western Minerals Inc. 04/05/1994
Each share Common no par exchanged for (1/3) share Common no par
First Western Minerals Inc. name changed to Augusta Metals Inc. 07/04/1997 which name changed to CyberCom Systems Inc. 09/14/2000
(See CyberCom Systems Inc.)

MUKUBA RES LTD (ON)
Each share old Common no par exchanged for (0.25) share new Common no par 09/06/2012
Each share new Common no par exchanged again for (0.03333333) share new Common no par 08/12/2016
Recapitalized as FogChain Corp. 05/29/2018
Each share new Common no par exchanged for (0.60240963) share Common no par

MUL-PACIFIC COPPER MINES LTD. (ON)
Charter revoked for failure to file reports and pay fees 6/3/65

MULESOFT INC (DE)
Merged into salesforce.com, inc. 05/02/2018
Each share Class A Common $0.000025 par exchanged for (0.0711) share Common $0.001 par and $36 cash

MULFORD (H.K.) CO.
Acquired by Sharp & Dohme, Inc. 00/00/1929
Details not available

MULFORD SECURITIES CORP. (DE)
Merged into New York Venture Fund, Inc. 10/12/90
Each share Capital Stock $25 par exchanged for (181.65866) shares Capital Stock $1 par
New York Venture Fund, Inc. name changed to Davis New York Venture Fund, Inc. 10/1/95

MULKA INC (DE)
Name changed to Entertainment Corp. of America 09/15/1989
Entertainment Corp. of America recapitalized as CAC Homes Corp. (DE) 01/27/2006 which reincorporated in Wyoming as Ostashkov Industrial Inc. 11/20/2013
(See Ostashkov Industrial Inc.)

MULLAN SILVER LEAD CO (ID)
Completely liquidated 11/03/1970
Each share Capital Stock 10¢ par exchanged for first and final distribution of (0.749) share Alice Consolidated Mines, Inc. Common 10¢ par

MULLEN CO LTD PARTNERSHIP (AB)
Reorganized as Mullen Group Ltd. 05/08/2009
Each Class B Unit exchanged for (1) share Common no par
Note: Unexchanged certificates were cancelled and became without value 05/08/2015

MULLEN GROUP INCOME FD (AB)
Each Trust Unit no par received distribution of (0.2878) share Horizon North Logistics Inc. Common no par and (0.2025) Common Stock Purchase Warrant payable 06/01/2006 to holders of record 06/01/2006 Ex date - 06/02/2006
Reorganized as Mullen Group Ltd. 05/08/2009
Each Trust Unit no par exchanged for (1) share Common no par

MULLEN TRANSN INC (AB)
Each share Common no par received distribution of (1) share Moveitonline Inc. Common no par payable 06/08/2001 to holders of record 06/08/2001
Reorganized as Mullen Group Income Fund 07/07/2005
Each share Common no par exchanged for (3) Trust Units no par
Note: Canadian residents' option to receive Mullen Co. L.P. Class B Units in lieu Trust Units expired 06/24/2005
Mullen Group Income Fund reorganized as Mullen Group Ltd. 05/08/2009

MULLEN TRUCKING LTD (AB)
Name changed to Mullen Transportation Inc. 01/01/1997
Mullen Transportation Inc. reorganized as Mullen Group Income Fund 07/07/2005 which reorganized as Mullen Group Ltd. 05/08/2009

MULLER BAKERIES, INC.
Name changed to Michigan Bakeries, Inc. in 1934
Michigan Bakeries, Inc. charter cancelled 5/15/73

MULLER (MAUD) CANDY CO. (OH)
Common no par changed to $1 par in 1944
Insolvent in 1965
No stockholders' equity

MULLER MEDIA INC (NV)
Each share old Common $0.001 par exchanged for (0.05) share new Common $0.001 par 12/19/2002
New Common $0.001 par split (3) for (1) by issuance of (2) additional shares payable 07/14/2006 to holders of record 07/14/2006
Each share new Common $0.001 par exchanged again for (0.001) share new Common $0.001 par 04/27/2007
Recapitalized as China Jiangsu Golden Horse Steel Ball, Inc. 10/05/2007
Each share new Common $0.001 exchanged for (0.0002) share Common $0.001 par
China Jiangsu Golden Horse Steel Ball, Inc. recapitalized as Santana Mining Inc. 12/24/2008
(See Santana Mining Inc.)

MULLIGAN CAPITAL CORP (BC)
Name changed to Blue Sky Uranium Corp. 02/07/2007

MULLINS BODY CORP. (NY)
Name changed to Mullins Manufacturing Corp. in 1927
Mullins Manufacturing Corp. merged into American Radiator & Standard Sanitary Corp. 1/30/56 which name changed to American Standard Inc. 6/1/67
(See American Standard Inc.)

MULLINS MANUFACTURING CORP. (NY)
Each share old $7 Preferred no par exchanged for (1) share new $7 Preferred no par and (2) shares Class A Common $7.50 par in 1935
Each share Common no par exchanged for (1) share Class B Common $1 par in 1935
Class B Common $1 par reclassified as Common $1 par in 1948
$7 Preferred no par called for redemption 10/11/48
Common $1 par split (2) for (1) by issuance of (1) additional share 10/21/48
Stock Dividend - Class B Common 100% 7/20/37
Merged into American Radiator & Standard Sanitary Corp. on a (1.1) for (1) basis 1/30/56
American Radiator & Standard

Sanitary Corp. name changed to American Standard Inc. 6/1/67
(See American Standard Inc.)

MULTAPLEX CORP (MN)
Common 5¢ par split (20) for (1) by issuance of (19) additional shares 4/11/84
Merged into Advance Circuits, Inc. 9/3/85
Each share Common 5¢ par exchanged for $5 cash

MULTEX COM INC (DE)
Merged into Reuters Group PLC 03/31/2003
Each share Common 1¢ par exchanged for $7.35 cash

MULTI AMP CORP (NJ)
Name changed 7/15/64
Name changed from Multi-Amp Electronics Corp. to Multi-Amp Corp. 7/15/64
Merged into M A Tex Corp. 7/26/78
Details not available

MULTI CHOICE COMMUNICATIONS INC (ON)
Delisted from Canadian Dealer Network 01/03/1995

MULTI COLOR INC (AZ)
Recapitalized as Phototron Corp. (AZ) 08/28/1973
Each share Common $2 par exchanged for (0.25) share Common 10¢ par
Phototron Corp. (AZ) reincorporated in Delaware 06/17/1976
(See Phototron Corp. (DE))

MULTI COLORTYPE CO (OH)
Merged into Georgia-Pacific Corp. 1/8/69
Each share Common no par exchanged for (0.646) share Common 80¢ par
(See Georgia-Pacific Corp.)

MULTI-CORP INC (AB)
Name changed to Zi Corp. 06/19/1997
Zi Corp. merged into Nuance Communications, Inc. (New) 04/09/2009

MULTI-ENERGIES DEVS LTD (AB)
Name changed to Sunalta Energy Inc. 6/20/94
(See Sunalta Energy Inc.)

MULTI EQUITIES INC (DE)
Common 10¢ par changed to 1¢ par 11/13/1973
Name changed to Jetfilm Corp. 04/16/1980

MULTI-FINELINE ELECTRONIX INC (DE)
Acquired by Suzhou Dongshan Precision Precision Manufacturing Co., Ltd. 07/27/2016
Each share Common $0.0001 par exchanged for $23.95 cash

MULTI-FUND INCOME TR (ON)
Each Instalment Receipt plus final payment of $8 cash received (1) Trust Unit prior to 04/30/1998
Acquired by Amalgamated Income L.P. 02/15/2007
Each Trust Unit received (0.18) new Unit of Ltd. Partnership Int.
(See Amalgamated Income L.P.)

MULTI-GLASS INTL CORP (AB)
Merged into 2044278 Ontario Inc. 4/28/2006
Each share Common no par exchanged for $0.03 cash

MULTI-GLASS INTL INC (AB)
Recapitalized as Multi-Glass International Corp. 10/28/2002
Each share Common no par exchanged for (0.2) share Common no par
(See Multi-Glass International Corp.)

MULTI-I-INC (OR)
Involuntarily dissolved for failure to file reports and pay fees 5/1/93

MULTI-LINK TELECOMMUNICATIONS INC (CO)
Issue Information - 1,200,000 UNITS consisting of (1) share COM and (1) WT offered at $6 per Unit on 05/14/1999
Reorganized under the laws of Delaware as Auriga Laboratories, Inc. 07/20/2006
Each (15) shares Common no par exchanged for (1) share Common no par
Note: Holders of between (100) and (1,500) shares received (100) shares
(See Auriga Laboratories, Inc.)

MULTI LOC MEDIA CORP (DE)
Merged into NUMLM Holdings Inc. 12/01/1988
Each share Common 1¢ par exchanged for $14.25 cash

MULTI-MANAGER LTD PARTNERSHIP I (ON)
Completely liquidated
Each Unit of Ltd. Partnership received first and final distribution of $0.23 cash payable 11/05/2012 to holders of record 11/05/2012

MULTI MEDIA BARTER LTD (DE)
Filed petition under Chapter 7 Federal Bankruptcy Code 8/2/89
No stockholders' equity

MULTI MEDIA INC (IA)
Voluntarily dissolved 08/29/1978
Details not available

MULTI-MEDIA INDS CORP (UT)
Recapitalized as Worldnet Resources Group Inc. 02/14/2000
Each share Common $0.001 par exchanged (0.08333333 share Common $0.001 par
Worldnet Resources Group Inc. recapitalized as Asset Equity Group, Inc. 12/12/2001
(See Asset Equity Group, Inc.)

MULTI-MEDIA TUTORIAL SVCS INC (DE)
Each share old Common 1¢ par exchanged for (0.1) share new Common 1¢ par 05/24/1999
New Common 1¢ par changed to Common $0.0001 par 05/24/2004
Company terminated common stock registration and is no longer public as of 05/28/2009

MULTI-MKT RADIO INC (DE)
Merged into SFX Broadcasting, Inc. 11/22/1996
Each share Class A Common 1¢ par exchanged for (0.2983) share Class A Common 1¢ par
(See SFX Broadcasting, Inc.)

MULTI OPERATIONS INC (NV)
Each share Common $0.001 par exchanged for (0.01) share Common $1 par 12/31/81
Completely liquidated 6/1/95
Each share Common $0.001 par exchanged for first and final distribution of $0.86 cash

MULTI PACKAGING SOLUTIONS INTERNATIONAL LTD (BERMUDA)
Acquired by WestRock Co. 06/07/2017
Each share Common $1 par exchanged for $18 cash

MULTI-PLATFORM INTEGRATIONS INC (DE)
Charter cancelled and declared inoperative and void for non-payment of taxes 03/01/2004

MULTI SCREEN CORP (AB)
Recapitalized as Cephalon Resource Corp. 6/29/93
Each share Common no par exchanged for (0.2) share Common no par
(See Cephalon Resource Corp.)

MULTI SELECT INCOME TR (ON)
Merged into Sentry Select Canadian Income Fund 06/12/2009
Each Preferred Security no par received approximately $10 cash
Each Capital Unit no par received (0.3819) Ser. A Unit no par

MULTI SOFT INC (NJ)
Each share old Common $0.001 par exchanged for (0.33333333) share new Common $0.001 par 02/01/1995
Reorganized under the laws of Florida as Multi Soft II, Inc. 09/29/2011
Each share new Common $0.001 par exchanged for (0.02) share Common $0.001 par

MULTI SOLUTIONS INC (NJ)
Reorganized under the laws of Florida as Multi Solutions II, Inc. 09/28/2011
Each share Common $0.001 par exchanged for (0.02) share Common $0.001 par

MULTI-SPECTRUM GROUP INC (UT)
Recapitalized as MedCare Technologies, Inc. (UT) 08/11/1995
Each share Common $0.001 par exchanged for (0.0008333) share Common $0.001 par
MedCare Technologies, Inc. (UT) reincorporated in Delaware 10/04/1996 which reincorporated in Nevada as Enterprise Technologies, Inc. 11/16/2001 which name changed to PhytoMedical Technologies, Inc. 09/02/2004 which recapitalized as Ceres Ventures, Inc. 12/12/2011

MULTI STEP INDS INC (BC)
Delisted from Vancouver Stock Exchange 1/10/90

MULTI STEP PRODS INC (ON)
Name changed to Tarxien International Inc. 05/15/1987
Tarxien International Inc. recapitalized as Tarxien Corp. 01/31/1989
(See Tarxien Corp.)

MULTI TECH CORP (DE)
Common 1¢ par split (2) for (1) by issuance of (1) additional share 12/31/82
Recapitalized as DNA Dynamics, Inc. 8/4/2006
Each share Common 1¢ par exchanged for (0.01) share Common $0.001 par

MULTI-TECH INTL CORP (NV)
Recapitalized as Australian Forest Industries 10/21/2004
Each share Common $0.001 par exchanged for (0.005) share Common $0.001 par
Australian Forest Industries recapitalized as Lone Pine Holdings, Inc. 02/11/2009 which name changed to Flux Power Holdings, Inc. 06/11/2012

MULTI-TEK TECHNOLOGIES INC (AB)
Name changed to Tactex Controls Inc. 08/04/2000
(See Tactex Controls Inc.)

MULTI-TEX PRODUCTS CORP. (NV)
Name changed to Multi-Operations, Inc. 9/5/80
(See Multi-Operations, Inc.)

MULTI-TOOL TECHNOLOGIES INC (DE)
Charter cancelled and declared inoperative and void for non-payment of taxes 03/01/1991

MULTI WAY INDS INC (NY)
Company believed out of business 00/00/1975
Details not available

MULTIACTIVE SOFTWARE INC (CANADA)
Reincorporated 05/07/1999
Place of incorporation changed from (ON) to (Canada) 05/07/1999
Name changed to Maximizer Software Inc. 12/11/2002
(See Maximizer Software Inc.)

MULTIBANC FINL CORP (CANADA)
Retractable Participating Preferred no par called for redemption 3/6/2000
Public interest eliminated

MULTIBANC NT FINL CORP (CANADA)
Capital Shares no par called for redemption at $81.14 on 03/06/2000

MULTIBANCO BG - BANCO DE GUAYAQUIL S A (ECUADOR)
Stock Dividends - 13.10205% payable 04/25/2008 to holders of record 02/15/2008 Ex date - 02/13/2008; 14.04558% payable 05/12/2010 to holders of record 02/16/2010 Ex date - 02/11/2010; 16.02564% payable 04/18/2011 to holders of record 02/14/2011 Ex date - 02/10/2011; 37.75161% payable 05/09/2012 to holders of record 02/27/2012 Ex date - 05/10/2012; 6.73306% payable 06/12/2013 to holders of record 06/10/2013 Ex date - 06/06/2013; 9.44382% payable 05/15/2014 to holders of record 05/12/2014 Ex date - 05/08/2014; 7.87859% payable 11/30/2015 to holders of record 11/23/2015 Ex date - 11/19/2015
ADR agreement terminated 08/03/2016
Each Sponsored ADR for Ordinary exchanged for (4) shares Ordinary
Note: Unexchanged ADR's will be sold and the proceeds, if any, held for claim after 02/03/2017

MULTIBAND CORP (MN)
Each share old Common no par received distribution of (0.05) share URON Inc. Common no par payable 08/10/2006 to holders of record 05/01/2006
Each share old Common no par exchanged exchanged for (0.2) share new Common no par 08/07/2007
Acquired by Goodman Networks Inc. 08/30/2013
Each share new Common no par exchanged for $3.25 cash

MULTIBANK FINL CORP (MA)
Common $6.25 par split (3) for (2) by issuance of (0.5) additional share 01/05/1984
Common $6.25 par split (3) for (2) by issuance of (0.5) additional share 01/07/1985
Common $6.25 par split (3) for (2) by issuance of (0.5) additional share 01/03/1986
Stock Dividends - 10% 05/25/1982; 50% 01/14/1983
Acquired by Bank of Boston Corp. 07/13/1993
Each share Common $6.25 par exchanged for (1.125) shares Common $2.25 par
Bank of Boston Corp. name changed to BankBoston Corp. 04/25/1997 which merged into Fleet Boston Corp. 10/01/1999 which name changed to FleetBoston Financial Corp. 04/18/2000 which merged into Bank of America Corp. 04/01/2004

MULTIBANK WEST (PITTSFIELD, MA)
Acquired by First National Bank (Boston, MA) 06/10/1994
Details not available

MULTIBESTOS CO.
Acquired by Dewey & Almy Chemical Co. in 1929
Details not available

MULTICANAL PARTICIPACOES S A (BRAZIL)
Name changed to Globo Cabo S.A. 09/09/1998
Globo Cabo S.A. recapitalized as NET Servicos de Comunicacao S.A. 06/17/2002
(See NET Servicos de Comunicacao S.A.)

MULTICARE COS INC (DE)
Secondary Offering - 3,000,000 shares Common offered at $18.50 per share on 10/24/1996
Common 1¢ par split (3) for (2) by issuance of (0.5) additional share payable 5/28/96 to holders of record 5/8/96 Ex date - 5/29/96
Merged into Genesis ElderCare Acquisition Corp. 10/10/97
Each share Common 1¢ par exchanged for $28 cash

MULTICAST INTERACTIVE CORP (DE)
Recapitalized as MPD Development Corp. 03/15/2007
Each (30) shares Common $0.001 par exchanged for (1) share Common $0.001 par
MPD Development Corp. recapitalized as Astor Explorations Corp. 05/19/2010

MULTICOM CORP (PA)
Each share old Common 10¢ par exchanged for (0.2) share new Common 10¢ par 11/19/1973
New Common 10¢ par split (5) for (1) by issuance of (4) additional shares 08/13/1976
Name changed to Great Western Systems, Inc. and Common 10¢ par changed to 1¢ par 01/31/1983
(See Great Western Systems, Inc.)

MULTICOM PUBG INC (WA)
Issue Information - 1,100,000 shares COM offered at $6.50 per share on 06/05/1996
Assets sold for the benefit of creditors 02/02/1998
Stockholders' equity unlikely

MULTIEMEDIA LTD (AUSTRALIA)
Name changed to NewSat Ltd. 01/29/2007

MULTIFAB MANUFACTURING CORP. (OK)
Out of business 5/29/73
No stockholders' equity

MULTIGRAPHICS INC (DE)
Merged into Paragon Corporate Holdings, Inc. 1/27/2000
Each share Common 1¢ par exchanged for $1.25 cash

MULTILINK TECHNOLOGIES INC (AB)
Reorganized under the laws of Ontario as Airesurf Networks Holdings Inc. 09/18/2003
Each share Class A Common no par exchanged for (0.25) share Class A Common no par
Airesurf Networks Holdings Inc. merged into IsoEnergy Ltd. 10/19/2016

MULTILINK TECHNOLOGY CORP (CA)
Each share old Class A Common $0.0001 par exchanged for (0.1) share new Class A Common $0.0001 par 09/10/2002
Merged into Vitesse Semiconductor Corp. 08/21/2003
Each share new Class A Common $0.0001 par exchanged for (0.5493) share Common 1¢ par
(See Vitesse Semiconductor Corp.)

MULTIMEDIA ACCESS CORP (DE)
Issue Information - 1,400,000 shares COM offered at $4.50 per share on 02/04/1997
Name changed to Viewcast.Com Inc. 4/8/99

MULTIMEDIA COMMUNICATIONS GROUP, INC. (DE)
Name changed to Satellite Communication Corp. 10/14/1994
(See Satellite Communication Corp.)

MULTIMEDIA CONCEPTS INTL INC (DE)
Charter cancelled and declared inoperative and void for non-payment of taxes 3/1/97

MULTIMEDIA ED INC (DE)
Charter cancelled and declared inoperative and void for non-payment of taxes 3/1/75

MULTIMEDIA GAMES HLDG CO INC (TX)
Name changed 04/05/2011
Common 1¢ par split (3) for (2) by issuance of (0.5) additional share payable 02/11/2002 to holders of record 01/25/2002 Ex date - 02/12/2002
Common 1¢ par split (2) for (1) by issuance of (1) additional share payable 02/27/2004 to holders of record 02/16/2004 Ex date - 03/01/2004
Name changed from Multimedia Games Inc. to Multimedia Games Holding Co., Inc. 04/05/2011
Acquired by Global Cash Access Holdings, Inc. 12/19/2014
Each share Common $0.001 par exchanged for $36.50 cash

MULTIMEDIA INC NEW (SC)
Common 10¢ par split (3) for (1) by issuance of (2) additional shares 04/29/1991
Merged into Gannett Co., Inc. (Old) 12/04/1995
Each share Common 10¢ par exchanged for $45.25 cash

MULTIMEDIA INC OLD (SC)
Common $1 par split (3) for (2) by issuance of (0.5) additional share 1/15/73
Common $1 par split (3) for (2) by issuance of (0.5) additional share 2/15/78
Common $1 par split (3) for (2) by issuance of (0.5) additional share 2/15/80
Stock Dividend - 50% 2/15/83
Merged into MultiMedia, Inc. (New) 10/1/85
Each share Common $1 par exchanged for (0.527) share Common 10¢ par and $47.19 cash

MULTIMEDIA K I D INC (DE)
Recapitalized as SYCO, Inc. (DE) 12/28/2006
Each share Common $0.001 par exchanged for (0.002) share Common $0.001 par
SYCO, Inc. (DE) reincorporated in Colorado as Marine Exploration, Inc. 05/11/2007 which recapitalized as In Ovations Holdings Inc. 10/15/2013

MULTIMEDIA NOVA CORP (ON)
Recapitalized 06/23/1992
Name changed 01/01/2002
Recapitalized from Multimedia Capital Corp. to Multimedia WTM Corp. 06/23/1992
Each share Common no par exchanged for (0.4) share old Class A Subordinate no par
Each share old Class A Subordinate no par exchanged for (0.25) share new Class A Subordinate no par 06/30/1997
Name changed from Multimedia WTM Corp. to Multimedia Nova Corp. 01/01/2002
Placed in receivership 05/27/2013
Stockholders' equity unlikely

MULTINATIONAL RES INC (BC)
Reorganized under the laws of Yukon as New Guinea Gold Corp. 6/4/96
Each share Common no par exchanged for (0.2) share Common no par
New Guinea Gold Corp. (Yukon) reincorporated in British Columbia 10/20/2005

MULTINET INTL CORP INC (NV)
Name changed to Showintel Networks, Inc. 10/15/2002
Showintel Networks, Inc. name changed to Limelight Media Group, Inc. 11/05/2003 which recapitalized as Impart Media Group, Inc. 12/22/2005
(See Impart Media Group, Inc.)

MULTIPHONIC CORP (DE)
Reincorporated 10/2/86
State of incorporation changed from (UT) to (DE) 10/2/86
Charter cancelled and declared inoperative and void for non-payment of taxes 3/1/90

MULTIPLAYER ONLINE DRAGON INC (NV)
Old Common $0.0001 par split (8) for (1) by issuance of (7) additional shares payable 11/05/2010 to holders of record 09/30/2010 Ex date - 11/08/2010
Each share old Common $0.0001 par exchanged for (0.1) share new Common $0.0001 par 10/29/2014
Name changed to NaturalShrimp Inc. 03/03/2015

MULTIPLE ACCESS LTD (CANADA)
Acquired by CFCF Inc. 08/31/1979
Each share Common no par exchanged for $8.50 cash

MULTIPLE EQUITY INVTS CORP (CO)
Name changed to PowerStar, Inc. 12/11/1986
(See PowerStar, Inc.)

MULTIPLE MNG DEV LTD (AB)
Name changed to Madre Mining Ltd. 12/20/1979
Madre Mining Ltd. recapitalized as Cortez Corp. 03/19/1986 which recapitalized as Cortez International Ltd. 06/02/1986
(See Cortez International Ltd.)

MULTIPLE ZONES INC (WA)
Name changed 10/30/2000
Name changed from Multiple Zones International, Inc. to Multiple Zones Inc. 10/30/2000
Name changed to Zones, Inc. 05/10/2001
(See Zones, Inc.)

MULTIPLEX TECHNOLOGIES INC (BC)
Name changed 11/06/1991
Name changed from Multiplex Resources Ltd. to Multiplex Technologies Inc. 11/06/1991
Delisted from Toronto Venture Stock Exchange 06/05/2002

MULTIPLIED MEDIA CORP (AB)
Name changed to Poynt Corp. 10/27/2010
(See Poynt Corp.)

MULTIPRESS INTL INC (NY)
Charter cancelled and proclaimed dissolved for failure to pay taxes 12/27/2000

MULTIREAL PPTYS INC (ON)
Recapitalized as XPF Development Inc. 06/09/1992
Each share Common no par exchanged for (0.6666666) share Common no par
XPF Development Inc. recapitalized as GolfNorth Properties Inc. 1/12/98
(See GolfNorth Properties Inc.)

MULTISYS LANGUAGE SOLUTIONS INC (NV)
Common $0.001 par split (3) for (1) by issuance of (2) additional shares payable 06/24/2010 to holders of record 06/24/2010 Ex date - 06/25/2010
Name changed to Bakken Resources, Inc. 12/17/2010

MULTITECH BROKERAGE SOLUTIONS INC (FL)
Name changed to MBSL Group, Inc. 11/14/2000
MBSL Group, Inc. name changed to InterSearch Group, Inc. 11/03/2004 which name changed to Banks.com, Inc. 11/28/2007 which merged into Remark Media, Inc. 07/06/2012 which name changed to Remark Holdings, Inc. 04/11/2017

MULTITECH INC (DE)
Charter cancelled and declared inoperative and void for non-payment of taxes 04/15/1973

MULTIVEST INC (DE)
Merged into Multivest Acquisition Corp. 07/15/1983
Each share Common 1¢ par exchanged for $15.50 cash

MULTIVEST REAL ESTATE LTD SER (MI)
Terminated registration of Ltd. Partnership Interests and is no longer public as of 03/28/1997

MULTIVISION COMMUNICATIONS CORP (YT)
Reincorporated 10/02/2000
Reorganized 01/24/2011
Place of incorporation changed from (BC) to (YT) 10/02/2000
Reorganized from (YT) to (BC) 01/24/2011
Each share Common no par exchanged for (0.2) share Common no par
Name changed to ZoomAway Travel Inc. 10/05/2016

MULTIVISIONS CORP (DE)
Common 1¢ par split (4) for (3) by issuance of (1/3) additional share 10/15/1972
Stock Dividend - 33.33333333% 10/15/1973
Charter cancelled and declared inoperative and void for non-payment of taxes 03/01/1993

MULTIVOX CORP AMER (NY)
Dissolved by proclamation 3/24/93

MULTIWIN EXPLORATIONS LTD. (ON)
Charter revoked for failure to file reports and pay fees 6/3/65

MULTNOMAH CO (OH)
Name changed to General Color Graphics, Inc. 12/10/1969
(See General Color Graphics, Inc.)

MULTNOMAH FUND (OR)
Trust agreement terminated 3/25/77
Each share Class B Voting $1 par exchanged for (1) share Multnomah Kennel Club Class B Common $1 par

MULTNOMAH KENNEL CLUB (OR)
Merged into Cerberus Acquisition Corp. 02/04/1992
Each share Class A Common $1 par exchanged for $17.40 cash
Each share Class B Common $1 par exchanged for $17.40 cash

MULTRONICS INC (MD)
Adjudicated bankrupt 06/06/1980
Stockholders' equity unlikely

MULVEN LAKE GOLD MINES LTD. (ON)
Charter cancelled by Province of Ontario for default 12/26/60

MULVIHILL PRO AMS 100 PLUS CDN$ TR (ON)
Completely liquidated 09/29/2008
Each Trust Unit no par received first and final distribution of $20.1673 cash

MULVIHILL PRO AMS 100 PLUS US$ TR (ON)
Completely liquidated 09/29/2008
Each Trust Unit no par received first and final distribution of $16.9049 cash

MULVIHILL PRO-AMS RSP SPLIT SH CORP (ON)
Issue Information - 6,000,000 SHS CL A and 6,000,000 SHS CL B offered at $10 per CL A and $20 per CL B on 02/26/2002
Class A Shares called for redemption at $8.484 on 10/29/2010
Class B Shares called for redemption at $18.8627 on 10/29/2010

MUNCIE MALLEABLE FOUNDRY CO. (DE)
Acquired by Albion Malleable Iron Co. 2/1/60
Each share 7% Preferred $100 par exchanged for (10) shares Common $1 par
Each share Common no par exchanged for (1) share Common $1 par
Albion Malleable Iron Co. merged into Hayes-Albion Corp. (Mich.) 8/14/67 which reincorporated under the laws of Delaware 12/11/68 then state of incorporation changed back to Michigan 12/31/79
(See Hayes-Albion Corp. (Mich.))

MUNCY BK & TR CO (MUNCY, PA)
Under plan of reorganization each share Common $2.50 par automatically became (1) share Muncy Bank Financial Inc. Common $0.86666666 par 01/03/1989

MUNDEE MINES LTD (BC)
Recapitalized as AGM Capital Corp. (BC) 06/26/1992
Each share Common no par exchanged for (1/3) share Common no par
AGM Capital Corp. (BC) reincorporated in Yukon as Dueling Grounds Thoroughbred Racing Corp. 09/22/1993 which reincorporated in Delaware as Dueling Grounds Entertainment Corp. 12/20/1995
(See Dueling Grounds Entertainment Corp.)

MUNDORO MNG INC (BC)
Reincorporated 06/14/2005
Place of incorporation changed from (Yukon) to (BC) 06/14/2005
Reorganized as Mundoro Capital Inc. 04/16/2008
Each share Common no par exchanged for (1) share Common no par

MUNDUS BREWING CO.
Acquired by Albert Brewing Co. in 1936 which was declared insolvent in 1939

MUNDUS ENVIRONMENTAL PRODS INC (NV)
Name changed to Mundus Group Inc. 8/28/2006

MUNFORD INC (GA)
Common $1 par split (5) for (4) by issuance of (0.25) additional share 6/3/83
4% Conv. Preferred $10 par called for redemption 10/14/83
Stock Dividend - 12-1/2% 6/15/84
Acquired by Alabama Acquisition Corp. 11/29/88
Each share Common $1 par exchanged for $17 cash

MUNI FDG CO AMER LLC (DE)
Merged into Tiptree Financial Partners, L.P. 06/30/2011
Each Reg. S Share no par exchanged for $1.70 cash

MUNI INTER DURATION FD INC (MD)
Issue Information - 33,350,000 shares

COM offered at $15 per share on 07/29/2003
Name changed to BlackRock Muni Intermediate Duration Fund, Inc. 10/2/2006

MUNI NEW YORK INTER DURATION FD INC (MD)
Issue Information - 4,000,000 shares COM offered at $15 per share on 07/29/2003
Name changed to BlackRock Muni New York Intermediate Duration Fund, Inc. 10/2/2006

MUNIASSETS FD INC (MD)
Name changed to BlackRock MuniAssets Fund, Inc. 10/2/2006

MUNIBOND INCOME FD INC (MD)
Merged into MuniAssets Fund, Inc. 4/21/95
Each share Common 10¢ par exchanged for (0.97994) share Common 10¢ par
MuniAssets Fund, Inc. name changed to BlackRock MuniAssets Fund, Inc. 10/2/2006

MUNICIPAL ADVANTAGE FD INC (MD)
Name changed to PIMCO Municipal Advantage Fund, Inc. 03/30/2007
(See PIMCO Municipal Advantage Fund, Inc.)

MUNICIPAL BANKERS CORP (ON)
1st Retractable Preference Ser. B $10 par called for redemption at $10 plus $0.0876 accrued dividends on 07/31/2000
Merged into Newco Bancorp Inc. 10/01/2000
Each share Retractable 1st Preference Ser. A $10 par exchanged for (0.8) share 1st Preference Ser. A and $2 cash
Each share Class A no par exchanged for (0.8) share Non-Voting Class A no par and $0.55 cash
Each share Common no par exchanged for (0.8) share Common no par and $0.55 cash
(See Newco Bancorp Inc.)

MUNICIPAL DEV CORP (DE)
Voluntarily dissolved 01/29/1993
Details not available

MUNICIPAL FD FOR TEMP INVT (MD)
Under plan of reorganization each MuniFund Portfolio $0.001 par automatically became Provident Institutional Funds MuniFund Cash Management Shares on a net asset value basis 2/10/99
Provident Institutional Funds name changed to BlackRock Provident Institutional Funds 1/29/2001 which name changed to BlackRock Liquidity Funds 11/19/2003

MUNICIPAL FINANCIAL CORP.
Bankrupt 00/00/1931
No stockholders' equity

MUNICIPAL FINL CORP (ON)
Common no par reclassified as Conv. Common no par 05/08/1986
Each share Conv. Common no par received distribution of (1) share Non-Vtg. Class A Common no par 05/13/1986
Name changed to MFC Inc. 08/22/1996
MFC Inc. name changed to Municipal Bankers Corp. 06/05/1998 which merged into Newco Bancorp Inc. 10/01/2000
(See Newco Bancorp Inc.)

MUNICIPAL GAS CO.
Merged into New York Power & Light Corp. 00/00/1927
Details not available

MUNICIPAL HIGH INCOME FD INC (MD)
Name changed to Western Asset Municipal High Income Fund Inc. 10/9/2006

MUNICIPAL INCOME OPPORTUNITIES TR (MA)
Name changed to Morgan Stanley Dean Witter 12/21/1998
Morgan Stanley Dean Witter name changed to Morgan Stanley Trusts 12/20/2001
(See Morgan Stanley Trusts)

MUNICIPAL INCOME OPPORTUNITIES TR II (MA)
Name changed to Morgan Stanley Dean Witter 12/21/1998
Morgan Stanley Dean Witter name changed to Morgan Stanley Trusts 12/20/2001 which name changed to Morgan Stanley Funds 12/16/2002

MUNICIPAL INCOME OPPORTUNITIES TR III (MA)
Name changed to Morgan Stanley Dean Witter 12/21/1998
Morgan Stanley Dean Witter name changed to Morgan Stanley Trusts 12/20/2001 which name changed to Morgan Stanley Funds 12/16/2002

MUNICIPAL INCOME TR (MA)
Name changed to Morgan Stanley Dean Witter 12/21/1998
Morgan Stanley Dean Witter name changed to Morgan Stanley Trusts 12/20/2001
(See Morgan Stanley Trusts)

MUNICIPAL INCOME TR II (MA)
Name changed to Morgan Stanley Dean Witter 12/21/1998
Morgan Stanley Dean Witter name changed to Morgan Stanley Trusts 12/20/2001
(See Morgan Stanley Trusts)

MUNICIPAL INCOME TR III (MA)
Name changed to Morgan Stanley Dean Witter 12/21/1998
Morgan Stanley Dean Witter name changed to Morgan Stanley Trusts 12/20/2001
(See Morgan Stanley Trusts)

MUNICIPAL INVESTMENT TRUST FUND (NY)
First Pennsylvania Series completely liquidated 5/5/70
Each Unit of Undivided Int. no par exchanged for $484.45 cash

MUNICIPAL MTG & EQUITY L L C (DE)
Preferred Ser. I no par called for redemption 03/00/2002
Preferred Ser. II no par called for redemption 03/00/2002
Preferred Ser. I Capital Distribution Shares no par called for redemption 03/00/2002
Preferred Ser. II Distribution Shares no par called for redemption 03/00/2002
Recapitalized as MMA Capital Management LLC 09/29/2014
Each share Common no par exchanged for (0.2) share Common no par

MUNICIPAL PARTNERS FD INC (MD)
Name changed to Salomon Brothers Municipal Partners Fund Inc. 04/21/2003
Salomon Brothers Municipal Partners Fund Inc. 10/09/2006 name changed to Western Asset Municipal Partners Fund, Inc. 10/09/2006

MUNICIPAL PARTNERS FD II INC (MD)
Name changed to Salomon Brothers Municipal Partners Fund II Inc. 04/21/2003
Salomon Brothers Municipal Partners Fund II Inc. name changed to Western Asset Municipal Partners Fund II, Inc. 10/09/2006 which merged into Western Asset Municipal Partners Fund, Inc. 07/23/2007

MUNICIPAL PMT SYS INC (NV)
Reorganized under the laws of Wyoming as Victura Construction Group, Inc. 07/21/2014
Each share Common $0.001 par exchanged for (0.005) share Common $0.001 par

MUNICIPAL PREM INCOME TR (MA)
Name changed to Morgan Stanley Dean Witter 12/21/1998
Morgan Stanley Dean Witter name changed to Morgan Stanley Trusts 12/20/2001
(See Morgan Stanley Trusts)

MUNICIPAL SVGS & LN CORP (ON)
99.6% acquired by Municipal Financial Corp. through voluntary exchange offer which expired 6/30/82
(See Municipal Financial Corp.)
9.75% Preferred Ser. A $10 par called for redemption 9/23/96
Public interest eliminated

MUNICIPAL SECS INCOME TR (MA)
Name changed to Federated Municipal Securities Income Trust 11/01/1999

MUNICIPAL SERVICE CORP. LTD.
Succeeded by Consolidated Utilities Ltd. in 1931 which was merged into City Gas & Electric Corp. Ltd. in 1933

MUNICIPAL SOLUTIONS GROUP INC (BC)
Each share old Common no par exchanged for (0.125) share new Common no par 04/06/2005
Reorganized as CloudBench Applications, Inc. 07/21/2008
Each share Common no par exchanged for (1) share Common no par and approximately $0.06 cash
Note: An additional amount of approximately $0.031 cash per share was placed in escrow for future distribution
CloudBench Applications, Inc. name changed to BasicGov Systems, Inc. 12/24/2009 which name changed to Pedro Resources Ltd. 09/30/2010

MUNICIPAL SYS INC (NV)
Recapitalized as New Systems, Inc. 3/10/99
Each share Common $0.001 par exchanged for (0.004) share Common $0.001 par
New Systems, Inc. name changed to Tremor Entertainment Inc. 12/4/2001 which name changed to Durham Marketing Corp. 8/25/2003

MUNICIPAL TELEPHONE & UTILITIES CO.
Bankrupt in 1932

MUNICIPAL TICKET CORP (ON)
Recapitalized as I.D. Investments Inc. 11/18/1994
Each share Common no par exchanged for (0.25) share Common no par
I.D. Investments Inc. recapitalized as BioLink Corp. 03/12/1997 which recapitalized as First Empire Entertainment.com Inc. 03/31/2000 which recapitalized as First Empire Corp. 08/14/2003 which reorganized as Noble House Entertainment Inc. (ON) 11/01/2004 which reincorporated in Canada as LiveReel Media Corp. 12/01/2006

MUNICIPLEX INC (NJ)
Name changed to Paragon Securities Co. and Common no par reclassified as Class A Common 1¢ par 11/03/1972
(See Paragon Securities Co.)

MUNIENHANCED FD INC (MD)
Name changed to BlackRock MuniEnhanced Fund, Inc. 10/2/2006

MUNIHOLDINGS CALIF INSD FD INC (MD)
Reorganized as MuniHoldings California Insured Fund II, Inc. 03/06/2000
Each share Auction Market Preferred Ser. A exchanged for (1) share Auction Market Preferred Ser. C
Each share Auction Market Preferred Ser. B exchanged for (1) share Auction Market Preferred Ser. C
Each share Common 10¢ par exchanged for (1.039211) shares Common 10¢ par
MuniHoldings California Insured Fund II, Inc. name changed to BlackRock MuniHoldings California Insured Fund, Inc. 10/02/2006 which name changed to BlackRock MuniHoldings California Quality Fund, Inc. 11/09/2010

MUNIHOLDINGS CALIF INSD FD II INC (MD)
Name changed 02/01/2000
Name changed from MuniHoldings California Insured Fund, Inc. to MuniHoldings California Insured Fund II, Inc. 02/01/2000
Name changed to BlackRock MuniHoldings California Insured Fund, Inc. 10/02/2006
BlackRock MuniHoldings California Insured Fund, Inc. name changed to BlackRock MuniHoldings California Quality Fund, Inc. 11/09/2010

MUNIHOLDINGS CALIF INSD FD III INC (MD)
Reorganized as MuniHoldings California Insured Fund II, Inc. 03/06/2000
Each share Auction Market Preferred Ser. A 10¢ par exchanged for (1) share Auction Market Preferred Ser. D
Each share Auction Market Preferred Ser. B 10¢ par exchanged for (1) share Auction Market Preferred Ser. D
Each share Common 10¢ par exchanged for (0.960822) share Common 10¢ par
MuniHoldings California Insured Fund II, Inc. name changed to BlackRock MuniHoldings California Insured Fund, Inc. 10/02/2006 which name changed to BlackRock MuniHoldings California Quality Fund, Inc. 11/09/2010

MUNIHOLDINGS CALIF INSD FD IV INC (MD)
Reorganized as MuniHoldings California Insured Fund II, Inc. 03/06/2000
Each share Auction Market Preferred Ser. A exchanged for (1) share Auction Market Preferred Ser. E
Each share Auction Market Preferred Ser. B exchanged for (1) share Auction Market Preferred Ser. E
Each share Common 10¢ par exchanged for (0.957902) share Common 10¢ par
MuniHoldings California Insured Fund II, Inc. name changed to BlackRock MuniHoldings California Insured Fund, Inc. 10/02/2006 which name changed to BlackRock MuniHoldings California Quality Fund, Inc. 11/09/2010

MUNIHOLDINGS CALIF INSD FD V INC (MD)
Reorganized as MuniHoldings California Insured Fund II, Inc. 03/05/2001
Each share Auction Market Preferred Ser. A exchanged for Auction Market Preferred Ser. B on a dollar-for-dollar basis
Each share Common 10¢ par exchanged for (1.076219) shares Common 10¢ par
MuniHoldings California Insured Fund

II, Inc. name changed to BlackRock MuniHoldings California Insured Fund, Inc. 10/02/2006 which name changed to BlackRock MuniHoldings California Quality Fund, Inc. 11/09/2010

MUNIHOLDINGS FLA INSD FD (MA)
Name changed to BlackRock MuniHoldings Florida Insured Fund, Inc. 10/02/2006
BlackRock MuniHoldings Florida Insured Fund, Inc. name changed to BlackRock MuniHoldings Insured Investment Fund 09/16/2008 which name changed to BlackRock MuniHoldings Investment Quality Fund 11/09/2010

MUNIHOLDINGS FLA INSD FD II (MA)
Reorganized as MuniHoldings Florida Insured Fund, Inc. 02/07/2000
Each Common Share of Bene. Int. 10¢ par exchanged for (0.974012) Common Share of Bene. Int. 10¢ par
MuniHoldings Florida Insured Fund, Inc. name changed to BlackRock MuniHoldings Florida Insured Fund, Inc. 10/02/2006 which name changed to BlackRock MuniHoldings Insured Investment Fund 09/16/2008 which name changed to BlackRock MuniHoldings Investment Quality Fund 11/09/2010

MUNIHOLDINGS FLA INSD FD III (MA)
Reorganized as MuniHoldings Florida Insured Fund, Inc. 02/07/2000
Each Share of Bene. Int. 10¢ par exchanged for (0.943619) Common Share of Bene. Int. 10¢ par
MuniHoldings Florida Insured Fund, Inc. name changed to BlackRock MuniHoldings Florida Insured Fund, Inc. 10/02/2006 which name changed to BlackRock MuniHoldings Insured Investment Fund 09/16/2008 which name changed to BlackRock MuniHoldings Investment Quality Fund 11/09/2010

MUNIHOLDINGS FLA INSD FD IV (MA)
Reorganized as MuniHoldings Florida Insured Fund, Inc. 02/07/2000
Each Share of Bene. Int. 10¢ par exchanged for (0.935642) Common Share of Bene. Int. 10¢ par
MuniHoldings Florida Insured Fund, Inc. name changed to BlackRock MuniHoldings Florida Insured Fund, Inc. 10/02/2006 which name changed to BlackRock MuniHoldings Insured Investment Fund 09/16/2008 which name changed to BlackRock MuniHoldings Investment Quality Fund 11/09/2010

MUNIHOLDINGS FLA INSD FD V (MD)
Reorganized as MuniHoldings Florida Insured Fund, Inc. 03/05/2001
Each share Auction Market Preferred Ser. A exchanged for Auction Market Preferred Ser. B on a dollar-for-dollar basis
Each share Common 10¢ par exchanged for (1.040429) shares Common 10¢ par
MuniHoldings Florida Insured Fund, Inc. name changed to BlackRock MuniHoldings Florida Insured Fund, Inc. 10/02/2006 which name changed to BlackRock MuniHoldings Insured Investment Fund 09/16/2008 which name changed to BlackRock MuniHoldings Investment Quality Fund 11/09/2010

MUNIHOLDINGS FD INC (MD)
Name changed to BlackRock MuniHoldings Fund, Inc. 10/02/2006

MUNIHOLDINGS FD II INC (MD)
Name changed to BlackRock MuniHoldings Fund II, Inc. 10/2/2006

MUNIHOLDINGS INSD FD INC (NJ)
Name changed to BlackRock MuniHoldings Insured Fund, Inc. 10/02/2006
BlackRock MuniHoldings Insured Fund, Inc. name changed to BlackRock MuniHoldings Quality Fund, Inc. 11/09/2010

MUNIHOLDINGS INSURED FD II INC (MD)
Name changed to BlackRock MuniHoldings Insured Fund II, Inc. 10/02/2006
BlackRock MuniHoldings Insured Fund II, Inc. name changed to BlackRock MuniHoldings Quality Fund II, Inc. 11/09/2010

MUNIHOLDINGS INSD FD III INC (MD)
Reorganized as MuniHoldings Insured Fund II, Inc. 08/14/2000
Each share Auction Market Preferred Ser. A exchanged for (1) share Auction Market Preferred Ser. C
Each share Common 10¢ par exchanged for (1.04969) shares Common 10¢ par
MuniHoldings Insured Fund II, Inc. name changed to BlackRock MuniHoldings Insured Fund II, Inc. 10/02/2006 which name changed to BlackRock MuniHoldings Quality Fund II, Inc. 11/09/2010

MUNIHOLDINGS INSD FD IV INC (MD)
Reorganized as MuniHoldings Insured Fund II, Inc. 08/14/2000
Each share Auction Market Preferred Ser. A exchanged for (1) share Auction Market Preferred Ser. C
Each share Common 10¢ par exchanged for (1.218029) shares Common 10¢ par
MuniHoldings Insured Fund II, Inc. name changed to BlackRock MuniHoldings Insured Fund II, Inc. 10/02/2006 which name changed to BlackRock MuniHoldings Quality Fund II, Inc. 11/09/2010

MUNIHOLDINGS MICH INSD FD INC (MD)
Reorganized as MuniYield Michigan Insured Fund, Inc. 03/06/2000
Each share Auction Market Preferred Ser. A exchanged for Auction Market Preferred Ser. C on a dollar-for-dollar basis
Each share Common 10¢ par exchanged for (0.888936) share Common 10¢ par
MuniYield Michigan Insured Fund, Inc. name changed to BlackRock MuniYield Michigan Insured Fund, Inc. 10/02/2006 which name changed to BlackRock MuniYield Michigan Quality Fund, Inc. 11/09/2010

MUNIHOLDINGS MICH INSD FD II INC (MD)
Reorganized as MuniYield Michigan Insured Fund II, Inc. 6/3/2002
Each Auction Market Preferred Ser. A exchanged for (1) Auction Preferred Ser. A
Each Common 10¢ par exchanged for (1.140441) shares Common 10¢ par
MuniYield Michigan Insured Fund II Inc. name changed to BlackRock MuniYield Michigan Insured Fund II Inc. 10/2/2006

MUNIHOLDINGS N Y FD INC (MD)
Reorganized as MuniHoldings New York Insured Fund, Inc. 03/06/2000
Each share Auction Rate Preferred Ser. A exchanged for (1) Auction Rate Preferred Ser. C
Each share Auction Rate Preferred Ser. B exchanged for (1) share Auction Rate Preferred Ser. C
Each share Common 10¢ par exchanged for (0.948547) share Common 10¢ par
MuniHoldings New York Insured Fund, Inc. name changed to BlackRock MuniHoldings New York Insured Fund, Inc. 10/02/2006 which name changed to BlackRock MuniHoldings New York Quality Fund, Inc. 11/09/2010

MUNIHOLDINGS NEW JERSEY INSD FD INC (MD)
Name changed to BlackRock MuniHoldings New Jersey Insured Fund, Inc. 10/02/2006
BlackRock MuniHoldings New Jersey Insured Fund, Inc. name changed to BlackRock MuniHoldings New Jersey Quality Fund, Inc. 11/09/2010

MUNIHOLDINGS NEW JERSEY INSD FD II INC (MD)
Reorganized as MuniHoldings New Jersey Insured Fund, Inc. 03/06/2000
Each share Auction Market Preferred Ser. A exchanged for Auction Market Preferred Ser. C on a dollar-for-dollar basis
Each share Auction Market Preferred Ser. B exchanged for Auction Market Preferred Ser. C on a dollar-for-dollar basis
Each share Common 10¢ par exchanged for (0.962319) share Common 10¢ par

MUNIHOLDINGS NEW JERSEY INSD FD III INC (MD)
Reorganized as MuniHoldings New Jersey Insured Fund, Inc. 03/06/2000
Each share Auction Market Preferred Ser. A exchanged for Auction Market Preferred Ser. D on a dollar-for-dollar basis
Each share Common 10¢ par exchanged for (0.962319) share Common 10¢ par

MUNIHOLDINGS NEW JERSEY INSD FD IV INC (MD)
Reorganized as MuniHoldings New Jersey Insured Fund, Inc. 03/05/2001
Each share Auction Market Preferred Ser. A exchanged for Auction Market Preferred Ser. E on a dollar-for-dollar basis
Each share Common 10¢ par exchanged for (1.074602) shares Common 10¢ par

MUNIHOLDINGS N Y INSD FD INC (MD)
Name changed to BlackRock MuniHoldings New York Insured Fund, Inc. 10/02/2006
BlackRock MuniHoldings New York Insured Fund, Inc. name changed to BlackRock MuniHoldings New York Quality Fund, Inc. 11/09/2010

MUNIHOLDINGS NEW YORK INSD FD II INC (MD)
Reorganized as MuniHoldings New York Insured Fund, Inc. 03/06/2000
Each share Auction Market Preferred Ser. A exchanged for (1) share Auction Market Preferred Ser. D
Each share Auction Market Preferred Ser. B exchanged for (1) share Auction Market Preferred Ser. D
Each share Common 10¢ par exchanged for (0.895706) share Common 10¢ par
MuniHoldings New York Insured Fund, Inc. name changed to BlackRock MuniHoldings New York Insured Fund, Inc. 10/02/2006 which name changed to BlackRock MuniHoldings New York Quality Fund, Inc. 11/09/2010

MUNIHOLDINGS NEW YORK INSD FD III INC (MD)
Reorganized as MuniHoldings New York Insured Fund, Inc. 03/06/2000
Each share Auction Market Preferred Ser. A exchanged for (1) share Auction Market Preferred Ser. B
Each share Common 10¢ par exchanged for (0.894808) share Common 10¢ par
MuniHoldings New York Insured Fund, Inc. name changed to BlackRock MuniHoldings New York Insured Fund, Inc. 10/02/2006 which name changed to BlackRock MuniHoldings New York Quality Fund, Inc. 11/09/2010

MUNIHOLDINGS NEW YORK INSD FD IV INC (MD)
Reorganized as MuniHoldings New York Insured Fund, Inc. 03/05/2001
Each share Auction Market Preferred Ser. A exchanged for (1.018991) shares Auction Market Preferred Ser. B
Each share Common 10¢ par exchanged for (1.018991) shares Common 10¢ par
MuniHoldings New York Insured Fund, Inc. name changed to BlackRock MuniHoldings New York Insured Fund, Inc. 10/02/2006 which name changed to BlackRock MuniHoldings New York Quality Fund, Inc. 11/09/2010

MUNIINSURED FD INC (MD)
Merged into MuniYield Insured Fund, Inc. 06/07/2004
Each share Common 1¢ exchanged for (0.643807) share Common 10¢ par
MuniYield Insured Fund, Inc. name changed to BlackRock MuniYield Insured Fund, Inc. 10/02/2006 which name changed to BlackRock Muniyield Quality Fund III, Inc. 11/09/2010

MUNISING CORP (DE)
Charter cancelled and declared inoperative and void for non-payment of taxes 4/25/99

MUNISING PAPER CO. (OH)
Recapitalized in 1937
Each share 6% Preferred $100 par exchanged for (7) shares 5% Preferred $20 par and (1.5) shares Common $5 par
Each share Common no par exchanged for (1) share Common $5 par
Acquired by Kimberly-Clark Corp. in 1951

MUNISING WOOD PRODUCTS CO., INC. (DE)
Name changed to Munising Corp. in October 1962
(See Munising Corp.)

MUNIVEST CALIF INSD FD INC (MD)
Merged into MuniYield California Insured Fund II, Inc. 1/24/97
Each share Common 10¢ par exchanged for (0.903899) share Common 10¢ par
Note: Preferred not affected except for change of name
MuniYield California Insured Fund II, Inc. name changed to MuniYield California Insured Fund, Inc. 4/16/2002 which name changed to BlackRock MuniYield California Insured Fund, Inc. 10/2/2006

MUNIVEST FLA FD (MA)
Reorganized as MuniYield Florida Fund 02/07/2000
Each Common Share of Bene. Int. 10¢ par exchanged for (0.928075) Common Share of Bene. Int. 10¢ par
MuniYield Florida Fund name changed to BlackRock MuniYield Florida Fund 10/02/2006 which

name changed to BlackRock MuniYield Investment Fund 09/16/2008

MUNIVEST FD INC (MD)
Name changed to BlackRock MuniVest Fund, Inc. 10/02/2006

MUNIVEST FD II INC (MD)
Name changed to BlackRock MuniVest Fund II, Inc. 10/02/2006

MUNIVEST MICH INSD FD INC (MD)
Reorganized as MuniYield Michigan Insured Fund, Inc. 03/06/2000
Each share Auction Market Preferred 5¢ par exchanged for (1) share Auction Market Preferred Ser. B
Each share Common 10¢ par exchanged for (0.915186) share Common 10¢ par
MuniYield Michigan Insured Fund, Inc. name changed to BlackRock MuniYield Michigan Insured Fund, Inc. 10/02/2006 which name changed to BlackRock MuniYield Michigan Quality Fund, Inc. 11/09/2010

MUNIVEST N J FD INC (MD)
Reorganized as MuniYield New Jersey Fund, Inc. 2/7/2000
Each Common Share of Bene. Int. 10¢ par exchanged for (0.920584) Common Share of Bene. Int. 10¢ par
MuniYield New Jersey Fund, Inc. name changed to BlackRock MuniYield New Jersey Fund, Inc. 10/2/2006

MUNIVEST N Y INSD FD (MD)
Merged into MuniYield New York Insured Fund II, Inc. 01/24/1997
Each share Common 10¢ par exchanged for (0.896284) share Common 10¢ par
Note: Preferred not affected except for change of name
MuniYield New York Insured Fund II, Inc. reorganized as MuniYield New York Insured Fund, Inc. 03/06/2000 which name changed to BlackRock MuniYield New York Insured Fund, Inc. 10/02/2006 which name changed to BlackRock MuniYield New York Quality Fund, Inc. 11/09/2010

MUNIVEST PA INSD FD (MA)
Reorganized as MuniYield Pennsylvania Insured Fund 2/8/2000
Each Common Share of Bene. Int. 10¢ par exchanged for (0.913641) Common Share of Bene. Int. 10¢ par
MuniYield Pennsylvania Insured Fund name changed to BlackRock MuniYield Pennsylvania Insured Fund 10/2/2006

MUNIYIELD ARIZ FD INC NEW (MD)
Name changed 4/21/95
Name changed from MuniYield Arizona Fund II, Inc. to MuniYield Arizona Fund, Inc. (New) 4/21/95
Name changed to BlackRock MuniYield Arizona Fund, Inc. 10/2/2006

MUNIYIELD ARIZ FD INC OLD (MD)
Acquired by MuniYield Arizona Fund II, Inc. 3/27/95
Each Auction Market Preferred 5¢ par exchanged for (1) Auction Market Preferred Ser. B 10¢ par
Each share Common 10¢ par exchanged for (1) share Common 10¢ par
MuniYield Arizona Fund II, Inc. name changed to MuniYield Arizona Fund, Inc. (New) 4/21/95 which name changed to BlackRock MuniYield Arizona Fund, Inc. 10/2/2006

MUNIYIELD CALIF FD INC (MD)
Name changed to BlackRock MuniYield California Fund, Inc. 10/02/2006

MUNIYIELD CALIF INSD FD INC (MD)
Merged into MuniYield California Insured Fund II, Inc. 02/14/2002
Each Auction Market Preferred Ser. A 10¢ par exchanged for (0.966162) Auction Market Preferred Ser. D 10¢ par
Each Auction Market Preferred Ser. B 10¢ par exchanged for (0.966162) Auction Market Preferred Ser. E 10¢ par
Each share Common 10¢ par exchanged for (0.966162) share Common 10¢ par
MuniYield California Insured Fund II, Inc. name changed to MuniYield California Insured Fund, Inc. 04/16/2002 which name changed to BlackRock MuniYield California Insured Fund, Inc. 10/02/2006 which name changed to BlackRock MuniYield California Quality Fund, Inc. 11/09/2010

MUNIYIELD CALIF INSD FD INC (MD)
Name changed 4/16/2002
Name changed from MuniYield California Insured Fund II, Inc. to MuniYield California Insured Fund, Inc. 4/16/2002
Name changed to BlackRock MuniYield California Insured Fund, Inc. 10/2/2006

MUNIYIELD FD INC (MD)
Name changed to BlackRock MuniYield Fund, Inc. 10/2/2006

MUNIYIELD FLA FD (MA)
Name changed to BlackRock MuniYield Florida Fund 10/02/2006
BlackRock MuniYield Florida Fund name changed to BlackRock MuniYield Investment Fund 09/16/2008

MUNIYIELD FLA INSD FD (MA)
Name changed to BlackRock MuniYield Florida Insured Fund Inc. 10/02/2006
BlackRock MuniYield Florida Insured Fund Inc. name changed to BlackRock MuniYield Insured Investment Fund 09/16/2008 which name changed to BlackRock MuniYield Investment Quality Fund 11/09/2010

MUNIYIELD INSD FD INC (MD)
Name changed to BlackRock MuniYield Insured Fund, Inc. 10/02/2006
BlackRock MuniYield Insured Fund, Inc. name changed to BlackRock Muniyield Quality Fund III, Inc. 11/09/2010

MUNIYIELD MICH INSD FD INC (MD)
Name changed to BlackRock MuniYield Michigan Insured Fund, Inc. 10/02/2006
BlackRock MuniYield Michigan Insured Fund, Inc. name changed to BlackRock MuniYield Michigan Quality Fund, Inc. 11/09/2010

MUNIYIELD MICH INSD FD II INC (MD)
Name changed 06/02/2002
Name changed from MuniYield Michigan Fund Inc. to MuniYield Michigan Insured Fund II, Inc. 06/03/2002
Name changed to BlackRock MuniYield Michigan Insured Fund II, Inc. 10/02/2006
BlackRock MuniYield Michigan Insured Fund II, Inc. name changed to BlackRock MuniYield Michigan Quality Fund II, Inc. 11/09/2010 which merged into BlackRock MuniYield Michigan Quality Fund, Inc. 09/14/2015

MUNIYIELD N J FD INC (MD)
Name changed to BlackRock MuniYield New Jersey Fund, Inc. 10/2/2006

MUNIYIELD N J INSD FD INC (MD)
Name changed to BlackRock MuniYield New Jersey Insured Fund, Inc. 10/02/2006
BlackRock MuniYield New Jersey Insured Fund, Inc. name changed to BlackRock MuniYield New Jersey Quality Fund, Inc. 11/09/2010 which merged into BlackRock MuniHoldings New Jersey Quality Fund, Inc. 04/13/2015

MUNIYIELD N Y INSD FD INC (MD)
Name changed to BlackRock MuniYield New York Insured Fund, Inc. 10/02/2006
BlackRock MuniYield New York Insured Fund, Inc. name changed to BlackRock MuniYield New York Quality Fund, Inc. 11/09/2010

MUNIYIELD N Y INDS FD II INC (MD)
Reorganized as MuniYield New York Insured Fund, Inc. 03/06/2000
Each share Auction Market Preferred exchanged for Auction Market Preferred Ser. C on a dollar-for-dollar basis
Each share Auction Market Preferred Ser. B exchanged for Auction Market Preferred Ser. D on a dollar-for-dollar basis
Each share Auction Market Preferred Ser. C exchanged for Auction Market Preferred Ser. E on a dollar-for-dollar basis
Each share Auction Market Preferred Ser. D exchanged for Auction Market Preferred Ser. E on a dollar-for-dollar basis
Each share Common 10¢ par exchanged for Common 10¢ par on a dollar-for-dollar basis
MuniYield New York Insured Fund, Inc name changed to BlackRock MuniYield New York Insured Fund, Inc. 10/02/2006 which name changed to BlackRock MuniYield New York Quality Fund, Inc. 11/09/2010

MUNIYIELD PA INSD FD (MA)
Name changed 02/01/2000
Name changed from MuniYield Pennsylvania Fund to MuniYield Pennsylvania Insured Fund 02/01/2000
Name changed to BlackRock MuniYield Pennsylvania Insured Fund 10/02/2006
BlackRock MuniYield Pennsylvania Insured Fund name changed to BlackRock MuniYield Pennsylvania Quality Fund 11/09/2010

MUNIYIELD QUALITY FD INC (MD)
Name changed to BlackRock MuniYield Quality Fund, Inc. 10/02/2006

MUNIYIELD QUALITY FD II INC (MD)
Name changed to BlackRock MuniYield Quality Fund II, Inc. 10/2/2006

MUNRO COPPER MINES LTD. (ON)
Into receivership 4/4/68
Assets sold to benefit of bondholders
No stockholders' equity

MUNRO GAMES INC (DE)
Merged into Servotronics, Inc. 05/16/1983
Each (11.13) shares Common 5¢ par exchanged for (1) share Common 20¢ par

MUNRO SYS CORP (PA)
Each share old Common 10¢ par exchanged for (0.1) share new Common 10¢ par 12/6/71
Name changed to General Hydraulics Corp. 3/28/74
(See General Hydraulics Corp.)

MUNSINGWEAR INC (DE)
Each share Capital Stock no par exchanged for (2) shares Capital Stock $5 par in 1946
Capital Stock $5 par reclassified as Common $5 par in 1951
Common $5 par split (2) for (1) by issuance of (1) additional share 9/20/60
5-1/2% Preferred $20 par called for redemption 1/15/63
Common $5 par split (3) for (2) by issuance of (0.5) additional share 12/18/68
Common $5 par changed to $1 par and (1) additional share issued 5/24/85
Common $1 par split (3) for (2) by issuance of (0.5) additional share 7/31/86
Under plan of reorganization each share Common $1 par exchanged for (0.03331761) share Common 1¢ par 10/29/91
Name changed to PremiumWear, Inc. 9/6/96
(See PremiumWear, Inc.)

MUNSON GEOTHERMAL INC (DE)
Each share Common $0.001 par exchanged for (0.1) share Common no par 12/16/1985
Under plan of reorganization name changed to Nevada Energy Inc. 11/20/1990
Nevada Energy Inc. recapitalized as PowerTel USA Inc. 01/31/1997 which name changed to Worldcall Corp. 11/25/1998
(See Worldcall Corp.)

MUNSON LINE, INC. (MD)
Recapitalized in 1946
Each share Class A Preferred no par exchanged for (3) shares Capital Stock $1 par
Each share Class C Preferred no par exchanged for (1) share Capital Stock $1 par
Each share Common no par exchanged for (0.1) share Capital Stock $1 par
Liquidation completed 2/1/61

MUNSON STEAMSHIP LINE
Reorganized as Munson Line, Inc. in 1939
No stockholders' equity

MUNSTON ELECTRONIC MANUFACTURING CORP. (NY)
Merged into Comspace Corp. 11/01/1965
Each share Common 10¢ par exchanged for (4/15) share Common 10¢ par
(See Comspace Corp.)

MUNTZ CDA LTD (CANADA)
Adjudicated bankrupt 05/10/1977
No stockholders' equity

MUNTZ TV INC. (DE)
Stock Dividend - 10% 12/28/51
Name changed to Television Manufacturers of America Co. 1/1/67
Television Manufacturers of America Co. name changed to TMA Co. 1/26/70 which was adjudicated bankrupt 7/28/72

MUNYON REMEDY CO.
Assets sold in 1930
No stockholders' equity

MUNZIG INTL INC (DE)
Voluntarily dissolved 1/2/79
No stockholders' equity

MURALS BY MAURICE INC (FL)
Recapitalized as Decor Products International, Inc. (FL) 07/24/2009
Each share Common $0.001 par exchanged for (0.25) share Common $0.001 par
Decor Products International, Inc. (FL) reorganized in Nevada 05/25/2010 which recapitalized as ViaDerma, Inc. 05/06/2014

MURDOCK ACCEP CORP (TN)
Stock Dividend - 50% 8/1/72
Adjudicated bankrupt 4/30/79
Stockholders' equity unlikely

MUR-MUR   **FINANCIAL INFORMATION, INC.**

MURDOCK CAP CORP (CO)
Each share old Common $0.0001 par exchanged for (0.002) share new Common $0.0001 par 9/18/95
Each share new Common $0.0001 par exchanged again for (0.2) share new Common $0.0001 par 6/3/96
Proclaimed dissolved for failure to file annual reports 4/10/98

MURDOCK COMMUNICATIONS CORP (IA)
Issue Information - 800,000 shares COM offered at $10.01 per share on 10/21/1996
Reorganized under the laws of Delaware as Polar Molecular Holding Corp. 07/14/2003
Each share Common no par exchanged for (1) share Common 1¢ par
(See Polar Molecular Holding Corp.)

MURDOCK CORP (MA)
Involuntarily dissolved 12/31/1990

MURDOCK FLA BK (MURDOCK, FL)
Merged into American Bancshares, Inc. 03/23/1998
Each share Common $10 par exchanged for (2.4) shares Common $1.175 par
American Bancshares, Inc. merged into Gold Banc Corp., Inc. 03/20/2000 which merged into Marshall & Ilsley Corp. (Old) 04/01/2006
(See Marshall & Ilsley Corp. (Old))

MURDOCK GROUP HLDG CORP (UT)
Name changed 02/08/2001
Name changed from Murdock Group Career Satisfaction Corp. to Murdock Group Holding Corp. 02/08/2001
Each share old Class A Common no par exchanged for (0.07142857) share new Class A Common no par 07/09/2001
SEC revoked common stock registration 01/10/2011

MURDOCK SVGS BK (MURDOCK, FL)
Name changed to Murdock Florida Bank (Murdock, FL) 12/12/1992
Murdock Florida Bank (Murdock, FL) merged into American Bancshares, Inc. 03/23/1998 which merged into Gold Banc Corp., Inc. 03/20/2000 which merged into Marshall & Ilsley Corp. (Old) 04/01/2006
(See Marshall & Ilsley Corp. (Old))

MUREX CLINICAL TECHNOLOGIES CORP (BC)
Recapitalized as International Murex Technologies Corp. 12/12/90
Each (7) shares Common no par exchanged for (1) share Common no par
(See International Murex Technologies Corp.)

MURFREESBORO BANCORP INC (TN)
Merged into First South Bancorp 06/10/2003
Each share Common $5 par exchanged for $21.25 cash

MURGOLD RES INC (BC)
Recapitalized as Arimathaea Resources Inc. (BC) 02/01/1991
Each share Common no par exchanged for (0.1) share Common no par
Arimathaea Resources Inc. (BC) reincorporated in Bermuda as Van Diemen's Co. Ltd. 06/29/1992 which recapitalized as VDC Corp. Ltd. 07/17/1995 which merged into VDC Communications, Inc. 11/06/1998
(See VDC Communications, Inc.)

MURGOR EXPLS LTD (ON)
Recapitalized as Advance Murgor Explorations Ltd. 06/07/1976

Each share Common $1 par exchanged for (0.2) share Common no par
Advance Murgor Explorations Ltd. recapitalized as Murgor Resources Ltd.- Les Ressources Murgor Inc. (ON) 07/23/1985 which reincorporated in Canada 09/22/1989 which merged into Alexandria Minerals Corp. 03/12/2015

MURGOR RES INC (CANADA)
Reincorporated 09/22/1989
Place of incorporation changed from (ON) to (Canada) 09/22/1989
Each share old Common no par exchanged for (0.16666666) share new Common no par 11/26/2007
Merged into Alexandria Minerals Corp. 03/12/2015
Each share Common no par exchanged for for (0.5) share Common no par
Note: Unexchanged certificates will be cancelled and become without value 03/12/2021

MURKY FAULT METAL MINES LTD (ON)
Merged into Indian Mountain Metal Mines Ltd. 06/24/1971
Each share Capital Stock $1 par exchanged for (1) share Capital Stock $1 par
Indian Mountain Metal Mines Ltd. merged into Initiative Explorations Inc. 02/13/1980 which merged into Canhorn Chemical Corp. 04/26/1995 which merged into Nayarit Gold Inc. 05/02/2005 which merged into Capital Gold Corp. 08/02/2010 which merged into Gammon Gold Inc. (QC) 04/08/2011 which reincorporated in Ontario as AuRico Gold Inc. 06/14/2011 which merged into Alamos Gold Inc. (New) 07/06/2015

MURMAC LAKE ATHABASKA MINES LTD (ON)
Charter cancelled for failure to pay taxes and file returns 03/16/1976

MURMONT MINING & EXPLORATION LTD. (ON)
Charter revoked for failure to file reports and pay fees 3/30/67

MURPHY (GEORGE) & ASSOCIATES ENTERTAINMENT INDUSTRIES, INC. (AZ)
Charter revoked for failure to file reports or pay fees 8/3/70

MURPHY (A.A.) & CO., INC. (MN)
5-1/2% Prior Preferred 1947 Ser. $50 par redesignated as 6% Prior Preferred 1947 Ser. $50 par in 1952
Name changed to Murphy Finance Co. 12/1/59
Murphy Finance Co. name changed to GAC Finance Inc. 10/21/70 which name changed to Finance Corp. of Minnesota Inc. 10/1/74

MURPHY CHAIR CO. (KY)
Reincorporated under laws of Massachusetts as Marshfield Corp. 1/10/61
Marshfield Corp. merged into Kilburn Mill 8/29/61
(See Kilburn Mill)

MURPHY CONTAINER CORP. (MA)
Charter revoked for failure to file reports and pay fees 12/13/61

MURPHY CORP. (LA)
Reincorporated under laws of Delaware as Murphy Oil Corp. 1/1/64

MURPHY FIN CO (MN)
6% Prior Preferred 1947 Ser. $50 par called for redemption 8/31/63
6% Preferred 1956 Ser. $50 par called for redemption 8/31/63
Name changed to GAC Finance Inc. 10/21/70

GAC Finance Inc. name changed to Finance America Corp. of Minnesota Inc. 10/1/74
(See Finance America Corp. of Minnesota Inc.)

MURPHY G C CO (PA)
Each share old Common no par exchanged for (3) shares new Common no par in 1936
5% Preferred called for redemption 12/2/42
New Common no par changed to $1 par and (3) additional shares issued in 1946
4-3/4% Preferred $100 par called for redemption 5/13/55
Common $1 par split (2) for (1) by issuance of (1) additional share 10/1/62
Merged into Ames Department Stores, Inc. 8/6/85
Each share Common $1 par exchanged for $48 cash

MURPHY G W INDS INC (TX)
Common $5 par changed to $2.50 par and (1) additional share issued 03/22/1968
Stock Dividends - 10% 05/23/1967; 20% 12/15/1970
Name changed to Reed Tool Co. 09/15/1972
Reed Tool Co. merged into Baker Oil Tools, Inc. 11/26/1975 which name changed to Baker International Corp. (CA) 01/28/1976 which reincorporated in Delaware 01/27/1983 which merged into Baker Hughes Inc. 04/03/1987 which merged into Baker Hughes, a GE company 07/05/2017

MURPHY HOT SPRINGS LAND CORP. (NV)
Charter revoked for failure to file reports and pay fees 03/07/1966

MURPHY INDS INC (DE)
Plan of reorganization under Chapter 11 Federal Bankruptcy proceedings confirmed 01/19/1988
No stockholders' equity

MURPHY MINES LTD. (CANADA)
Acquired by Queenston Gold Mines Ltd. (ON) 00/00/1941
Each (100) shares Capital Stock $1 par exchanged for (13.5) shares Common $1 par
Queenston Gold Mines Ltd. (ON) reincorporated in Alberta 00/00/1981 which reincorporated in Canada 04/23/1985 which merged into Queenston Mining Inc. 01/02/1990 which merged into Osisko Mining Corp. 01/02/2013
(See Osisko Mining Corp.)

MURPHY MTR FGHT LINES INC (MN)
Statutorily dissolved 10/8/91

MURPHY OIL CORP (DE)
4.90% Conv. Preference $100 par called for redemption 06/03/1968
5.20% Ser. Conv. Preference $100 par called for redemption 12/15/1972
(Additional Information in Active)

MURPHY OIL LTD (CANADA)
5-3/4% Conv. Preferred Ser. $25 par called for redemption 3/1/72
Common $1 par changed to no par and (1) additional share issued 10/16/72
Common no par split (2) for (1) by issuance of (1) additional share 5/20/83
Merged into Murphy Oil Corp. 10/2/87
Each share Common no par exchanged for $32 cash

MURPHY PAC MARINE SALVAGE CO (CA)
Common no par reclassified as Class B Common no par 03/22/1974
Charter suspended for failure to file reports and pay fees 05/01/1980

MURPHY VARNISH CO.
Acquired by Interchemical Corp. in 1944
Interchemical Corp. name changed to Inmont Corp. 4/15/69 which merged into Carrier Corp. 12/27/77 which was acquired by United Technologies Corp. 7/6/79

MURRAY BODY CORP.
Assets and properties acquired by Murray Corp. of America in 1927
Murray Corp. of America name was changed to Wallace-Murray Corp. 9/1/65
(See Wallace-Murray Corp.)

MURRAY CO. (TX)
Reincorporated under the laws of Delaware as Murray Co. of Texas, Inc. and each share Common $100 par exchanged for (10) shares Common $10 par in 1948
Murray Co. of Texas, Inc. merged into Rockwell-Standard Corp. (DE) 12/1/65 which merged into North American Rockwell Corp. 9/22/67 which merged into Rockwell International Corp. (Old) 2/16/73 which merged into Boeing Co. 12/6/96

MURRAY CO. OF TEXAS, INC. (DE)
Each share Common $10 par exchanged for (2) shares Common $5 par in 1949
Common $5 par changed to $2.50 par and (1) additional share issued 3/25/60
Stock Dividend - 100% 9/1/55
Merged into Rockwell-Standard Corp. (DE) 12/1/65
Each share Common $2.50 par exchanged for (1) share Common $5 par
Rockwell-Standard Corp. (DE) merged into North American Rockwell Corp. 9/22/67 which merged into Rockwell International Corp. (Old) 2/16/73 which merged into Boeing Co. 12/6/96

MURRAY CORP. OF AMERICA (DE)
Common no par changed to $10 par in 1932
Recapitalized 12/11/63
Each share Common $10 par exchanged for (1) share Common $7.50 par plus $14 cash
Under plan of merger name changed to Wallace-Murray Corp. 9/1/65 and holders of Common $7.50 par of record 9/1/65 received (0.1) share $1.70 Convertible Preferred no par by distribution 9/2/65
(See Wallace-Murray Corp.)

MURRAY HILL FD INC (NY)
Name changed to Shiff Hedge Fund, Inc. 11/04/1968
Shiff Hedge Fund, Inc. name changed to Integrated Growth Fund, Inc. 11/28/1969
(See Integrated Growth Fund, Inc.)

MURRAY MACHINERY INC (DE)
Name changed 4/28/66
Reincorporated 10/6/86
Each share Common no par exchanged for (2.5) shares Common $10 par in 1952
Stock Dividend - 60% 6/16/52
Name changed from Murray (D.J.) Manufacturing Co. to Murray Machinery, Inc. (WI) 4/28/66
State of incorporation changed from (WI) to (DE) 10/6/86
Charter cancelled and declared inoperative and void for non-payment of taxes 12/30/88

MURRAY MANUFACTURING CORP. (NY)
Merged into Arrow-Hart, Inc. 03/12/1969
Details not available

MURRAY MINING CORP. LTD. (QC)
Acquired by Asbestos Corp. Ltd. on a (0.0625) for (1) basis 3/27/64

MURRAY MTG INVS (MA)
In process of liquidation
Each Share of Bene. Int. no par received initial distribution of $1 cash 08/17/1982
Each Share of Bene. Int. no par received second distribution of $1 cash 11/17/1982
Each Share of Bene. Int. no par received third distribution of $1 cash 05/17/1983
Each Share of Bene. Int. no par received fourth distribution of $2 cash 08/17/1983
Details on subsequent distributions, if any, are not available

MURRAY OHIO MFG CO (OH)
Each share Common no par exchanged for (2) shares Common $5 par 00/00/1950
Each share Common $5 par exchanged for (2) shares Common $2.50 par 03/30/1962
Common $2.50 par split (2) for (1) by issuance of (1) additional share 04/15/1968
Common $2.50 par split (3) for (2) by issuance of (0.5) additional share 04/21/1969
Common $2.50 par split (3) for (2) by issuance of (0.5) additional share 08/31/1977
Merged into Tomkins PLC 08/04/1988
Each share Common $2.50 par exchanged for $56 cash

MURRAY ST BK (MURRAY, UT)
Acquired by Commercial Security Bank (Ogden, UT) 03/31/1973
Details not available

MURRAY STATE INVESTMENT, INC. (UT)
Merged into Emdeko International, Inc. 2/28/69
Each share Capital Stock $1 par exchanged for (0.266666) share Common no par
(See Emdeko International, Inc.)

MURRAY UTD DEV CORP (DE)
Name changed to American Metal & Technology, Inc. 6/11/2007

MURRAY WATTS EXPLORATIONS LTD. (ON)
Merged into Assembly Mines Ltd. 12/30/1977
Details not available

MURRITT BUSINESS MACHINES LTD. (ON)
Name changed to Murritt Photofax Ltd. 06/11/1971
Murritt Photofax Ltd. name changed to Devant Holdings Ltd. 02/18/1974 which liquidated for Nashua Corp. (DE) 04/29/1974 which reincorporated in Massachusetts 06/12/2002 which was acquired by Cenveo, Inc. 09/15/2009
(See Cenveo, Inc.)

MURRITT PHOTOFAX LTD (ON)
Name changed to Devant Holdings Ltd. 02/18/1974
Devant Holdings Ltd. liquidated for Nashua Corp. (DE) 04/29/1974 which reincorporated in Massachusetts 06/12/2002 which was acquired by Cenveo, Inc. 09/15/2009
(See Cenveo, Inc.)

MURTO RED LAKE MINES, LTD. (ON)
Charter cancelled 04/01/1957

MURWELL RES LTD (AB)
Acquired by Icon Energy Ltd. 02/02/1996
Each share Common no par exchanged for (0.5) share Common no par
Icon Energy Ltd. merged into Lexxor Energy Inc. 04/03/2000 which reorganized as Find Energy Ltd. 09/05/2003 which was acquired by Shiningbank Energy Income Fund 09/22/2006 which merged into PrimeWest Energy Trust 07/13/2007
(See PrimeWest Energy Trust)

MUSCATO GROUP INC (NV)
Each share old Common $0.0001 par exchanged for (0.00000222) share new Common $0.0001 par 07/02/2012
Note: In effect holders of (449,999) shares or fewer received $0.02 cash per share and public interest was eliminated

MUSCLE FLEX INC (DE)
Name changed to Bravada International, Ltd. 07/19/2010

MUSCLE SHOALS NAT GAS CO (AL)
In process of liquidation
Each share Capital Stock $1 par exchanged for initial distribution of $80.4833 cash 9/29/72
Each share Capital Stock $1 par received second distribution of $8 cash 6/8/73
Details on subsequent distributions, if any, are not available

MUSCLE WARFARE INTL INC (NV)
Common $0.001 par split (3) for (1) by issuance of (2) additional shares payable 01/21/2014 to holders of record 01/07/2014 Ex date - 01/22/2014
Name changed to Cannabusiness Group, Inc. 02/18/2014

MUSCOCHO EXPLS LTD (QC)
Each share 68¢ Conv. Preferred $4 par exchanged for (4) shares Common $1 par 12/31/1986
Merged into Golden Goose Resources Inc. 09/30/1996
Each share Common $1 par exchanged for (0.25) share Common $1 par
Golden Goose Resources Inc. merged into Kodiak Exploration Ltd. 12/16/2010 which name changed to Prodigy Gold Inc. 01/04/2011 which merged into Argonaut Gold Inc. 12/11/2012

MUSE AIR CORP (TX)
Common 10¢ par changed to $1 par 06/30/1982
Acquired by Southwest Airlines Co. 06/25/1985
Each share Common $1 par exchanged for (0.125) share Common $1 par, (0.125) Common Stock Purchase Warrant expiring 06/25/1990 and $6 cash

MUSE TECHNOLOGIES INC (DE)
Issue Information - 1,200,000 UNITS consisting of (1) share COM and (0.5) WT offered at $8 per Unit on 11/16/1998
Filed a petition under Chapter 7 Federal Bankruptcy Code 11/13/2002
Stockholders' equity unlikely

MUSEBECK SHOE CO (IL)
Chapter 7 bankruptcy proceedings converted to a Liquidating Chapter 11 on 10/4/92
No stockholders' equity

MUSGROVE MINERALS CORP (BC)
Each share old Common no par exchanged for (0.2) share new Common no par 04/26/2012
Each share new Common no par exchanged again for (0.2) share new Common no par 03/05/2014
Each share new Common no par exchanged again for (0.33333333) share new Common no par 06/16/2015
Recapitalized as RewardStream Solutions Inc. 08/04/2016
Each share new Common no par exchanged for (0.5) share Common no par

MUSIC & ENTMT INC (DE)
Name changed to Wallichs Music & Entertainment Co., Inc. 07/09/1970
Wallichs Music & Entertainment Co., Inc. name changed to National Industrial Security Corp. 11/01/1983 which recapitalized as NPS International Corp. 11/06/1998 which name changed to OneClass Synergy Corp. 12/21/2000 which recapitalized as ABCI Holdings Inc. (DE) 08/13/2001 which reorganized in Nevada as Metaphor Corp. 01/06/2005 which name changed to Medical Solutions Management Inc. 08/04/2006
(See Medical Solutions Management Inc.)

MUSIC & ENTMT NETWORK INC (NV)
Each share old Common $0.001 par exchanged for (0.0005) share new Common $0.001 par 01/26/1998
Reorganized under the laws of Delaware as Informatix Holdings, Inc. 06/30/1998
Each share new Common $0.001 par exchanged for (0.2) share Common $0.0001 par
Informatix Holdings, Inc. recapitalized as Autologous Wound Therapy, Inc. 11/08/1999 which name changed to Cytomedix, Inc. 03/30/2000 which name changed to Nuo Therapeutics, Inc. 11/14/2014

MUSIC FAIR ENTERPRISES INC (PA)
Conv. Preferred $5 par called for redemption 01/29/1963
Class B Common 50¢ par reclassified as Common 50¢ par 01/28/1971
Merged into Music Fair Group, Inc. 10/13/1982
Each share Common 50¢ par exchanged for (0.04) share 8% Preferred $1 par
(See Music Fair Group, Inc.)

MUSIC FAIR GROUP INC (PA)
Company went private 00/00/1989
Details not available

MUSIC MAKERS GROUP INC (DE)
Merged into Leigh Group, Inc. 03/14/1973
Each share Common 10¢ par exchanged for $3 cash

MUSIC MASTER CORP. (DE)
Charter forfeited and declared inoperative and void for non-payment of taxes in 1930

MUSIC RTY CORP (NY)
Name changed to National Growth Industries Inc. 04/14/1969
(See National Growth Industries Inc.)

MUSIC SHOP INC (IL)
Name changed to Property Solutions-USA-Inc. 02/22/1989
Property Solutions-USA-Inc. name changed to Bright Star Corp. 11/09/1991
(See Bright Star Corp.)

MUSIC THEATRE INC (CA)
Each share Common $100 par exchanged for (20) shares Common $5 par 03/15/1965
Adjudicated bankrupt 06/21/1968
No stockholders' equity

MUSIC TONES LTD (CO)
Name changed to Simplex Medical Systems, Inc. 03/28/1997
Simplex Medical Systems, Inc. name changed to SMLX Technologies, Inc. 08/21/1998
(See SMLX Technologies, Inc.)

MUSICIANS EXCHANGE (NV)
Common $0.001 par split (10) for (1) by issuance of (9) additional shares payable 04/06/2010 to holders of record 03/14/2010 Ex date - 04/07/2010
Name changed to Voice Assist, Inc. 10/18/2010

MUSICLAND GROUP INC (DE)
Merged into Musicland Stores Corp. 8/25/88
Each share Common 10¢ par exchanged for $36 cash

MUSICLAND STORES CORP (DE)
Merged into Best Buy Co., Inc. 1/31/2001
Each share Common 1¢ par exchanged for $12.55 cash

MUSICMAKER COM INC (DE)
Issue Information - 8,400,000 shares COM offered at $14 per share on 07/06/1999
Each share old Common 1¢ par exchanged for (0.1) share new Common 1¢ par 11/3/2000
Each share new Common 1¢ par received distribution of $3 cash payable 3/9/2001 to holders of record 3/1/2001
Reorganized as MM Companies, Inc. 7/12/2002
Each share new Common 1¢ par exchanged for (1) share Common 1¢ par
Note: Holders of (99) shares or fewer received $1.35 cash per share
MM Companies, Inc. name changed to George Foreman Enterprises, Inc. 8/24/2005

MUSICRAFT RECORDING CORP.
Merged into Musicraft Records, Inc. in 1947 which filed a bankruptcy petition in 1950

MUSICRAFT RECORDS, INC.
Bankruptcy petition filed in 1950

MUSICRYPT INC (ON)
Name changed to Yangaroo Inc. 07/18/2007

MUSICSOURCE U S A INC (DE)
Each share old Common 1¢ par exchanged for (0.1) share new Common 1¢ par 10/21/1994
Charter forfeited for failure to maintain a registered agent 01/02/1997

MUSKEGON BK & TR CO (MUSKEGON, MI)
Each share Common $20 par exchanged for (3) shares Common $6.66-2/3 par 02/01/1968
Stock Dividends - 20.2% 02/01/1960; 10% 02/05/1965; 10% 02/03/1967; 25% 03/14/1969
Acquired by American Bankcorp, Inc. 05/31/1977
Details not available

MUSKEGON MOTOR SPECIALTIES CO. (DE)
Class A no par changed to $20 par in 1951
Reorganized 1/25/65
No stockholders' equity

MUSKEGON PISTON RING CO. (MI)
Under plan of merger each share old Common exchanged for (1.5) shares Common $2.50 par 00/00/1936
Common $2.50 par changed to $1.25 par and (1) additional share issued 06/01/1965
Stock Dividends - 100% 07/10/1947; 10% 10/31/1963
Name changed to AP Parts Corp. and Common $1.25 par changed to $2.50 par 04/11/1966
AP Parts Corp. merged into Dunhill International, Inc. 10/31/67 which name changed to Questor Corp. 12/01/1968
(See Questor Corp.)

MUSKOGEE CO. (DE)
Each share old Common no par exchanged for (2) shares new Common no par 00/00/1930

New Common no par changed to $10 par 00/00/1942
Liquidation completed
Each share Common $10 par exchanged for initial distribution of $55 cash 09/29/1964
Each share Common $10 par received second distribution of $2.50 cash 01/11/1965
Each share Common $10 par received third and final distribution of $1.5125 cash 05/15/1967

MUSKOX MINERALS CORP (AB)
Recapitalized as Prize Mining Corp. 3/29/2005
Each share Common no par exchanged for (0.2) share Common no par

MUSKRAT MINERALS INC (AB)
Name changed to Metalo Manufacturing Inc. 12/16/2015

MUSSENS CANADA LTD. (CANADA)
Name changed to Mussens Ltd. 8/6/63
Mussens Ltd. name changed to M S N Industries Ltd. 11/6/69 which was acquired by Resources Services Group Ltd. 10/18/74

MUSSENS LTD (CANADA)
Common no par split (3) for (1) by issuance of (2) additional shares 10/5/65
Name changed to M S N Industries Ltd. 11/6/69
(See M S N Industries Ltd.)

MUSTANG COM INC (CA)
Merged into Quintus Corp. 5/18/2000
Each share Common no par exchanged for (0.793) share Common $0.001 par
(See Quintus Corp.)

MUSTANG COS INC (KS)
Merged into Gulf Resources Corp. 08/30/1990
Each share Common no par exchanged for $0.85 cash

MUSTANG DRILLING & EXPLORATION, INC. (KS)
Name changed to Mustang Cos., Inc. 6/3/86
(See Mustang Cos., Inc.)

MUSTANG GEOTHERMAL CORP (NV)
Recapitalized as Dakota Territory Resource Corp. 09/26/2012
Each share Common $0.001 par exchanged for (0.1) share Common $0.001 par

MUSTANG GOLD CORP (ON)
Recapitalized as Mustang Minerals Corp. 03/11/1999
Each share Common no par exchanged for (0.33333333) share Common no par
Mustang Minerals Corp. name changed to Grid Metals Corp. 06/08/2018

MUSTANG INVT CORP (MN)
Name changed to Information Dialogues Inc. and Common 10¢ par changed to 1¢ par 12/30/76
Information Dialogues Inc. name changed to GHC Inc. 1/24/77
(See GHC Inc.)

MUSTANG LUBRICANTS, INC. (CO)
Declared defunct and inoperative for non-payment of taxes 10/19/64

MUSTANG MINERALS CORP (ON)
Each share old Common no par exchanged for (0.1) share new Common no par 10/26/2017
Name changed to Grid Metals Corp. 06/08/2018

MUSTANG RES CORP (DE)
Reorganized under Chapter 11 Federal Bankruptcy Code 11/14/1989
Each share Common 40¢ par received either (1) share Common 1¢ par or $0.20 cash
Note: Option to receive stock expired 01/05/1990
Name changed to Blue Dolphin Energy Co. 01/05/1990

MUSTANG RES INC (AB)
Plan of arrangement effective 7/12/2005
Each share Class A Common no par exchanged for (0.55) Thunder Energy Trust, Trust Unit no par, (0.36666666) share Alberta Clipper Energy Inc. Common no par and (0.08333333) share Ember Resources Inc. Common no par
Each share Class B Common no par exchanged for (0.55) Thunder Energy Trust, Trust Unit no par, (0.36666666) share Alberta Clipper Energy Inc. Common no par and (0.08333333) share Ember Resources Inc. Common no par
(See each company's listing)

MUSTANG RES INC (BC)
Recapitalized as Fairlane Transportation Inc. 12/4/91
Each share Common no par exchanged for (1/3) share Common no par
Fairlane Transportation Inc. recapitalized as Excellerated Resources Inc. 11/24/98 which recapitalized as Consolidated Excellerated Resources Inc. 2/28/2000 which name changed to Amarillo Gold Corp. 11/21/2003

MUSTANG SOFTWARE INC (CA)
Issue Information - 1,250,000 shares COM offered at $6.50 per share on 04/05/1995
Name changed to Mustang.com Inc. 10/12/99
Mustang.com Inc. merged into Quintus Corp. 5/18/2000
(See Quintus Corp.)

MUSTANG VENTURES INC (NV)
Each share old Common $0.001 par exchanged for (3) shares new Common $0.001 par 03/03/2000
Name changed to Self Help Zone Inc. 08/02/2000
Self Help Zone Inc. name changed to U.S. Petroleum Corp. 08/30/2001 which recapitalized as Emergent Energy Corp. 07/29/2008

MUSTO EXPLS LTD (BC)
Reincorporated 3/7/79
Place of incorporation changed from (ONT) to (BC) 3/7/79
Recapitalized as International Musto Explorations Ltd. 10/21/91
Each share Common no par exchanged for (0.05) share Common no par
(See International Musto Explorations Ltd.)

MUTAPA COPPER & COBALT INC (BC)
Recapitalized as Springbank Ventures Inc. 07/04/2003
Each share Common no par exchanged for (0.25) share Common no par
Springbank Ventures Inc. name changed to Ondine Biopharma Corp. 04/02/2004 which recapitalized as Ondine Biomedical Inc. 10/14/2010
(See Ondine Biomedical Inc.)

MUTAPA GOLD CORP (BC)
Name changed to Mutapa Copper & Cobalt Inc. 12/08/1998
Mutapa Copper & Cobalt Inc. recapitalized as Springbank Ventures Inc. 07/04/2003 which name changed to Ondine Biopharma Corp. 04/02/2004 which recapitalized as Ondine Biomedical Inc. 10/14/2010
(See Ondine Biomedical Inc.)

MUTER CO (DE)
Reincorporated 05/15/1969
Stock Dividend - 10% 01/15/1951
State of incorporation changed from (IL) to (DE) 05/15/1969
Merged into Pemcor, Inc. 07/01/1971
Each share Common 50¢ par exchanged for (0.4) share Common $1 par
Pemcor, Inc. merged into Esmark, Inc. (Inc. 03/14/1969) 09/28/1978
(See Esmark, Inc. (Inc. 03/14/1969))

MUTUAL & HOME SAVINGS ASSOCIATION (OH)
Voluntarily dissolved 9/30/33
Details not available

MUTUAL ACCUMULATING FD (BC)
Shares no par split (4) for (1) by issuance of (3) additional shares in 1953
Shares no par split (5) for (2) by issuance of (1.5) additional shares 3/1/62
Reincorporated under the laws of Ontario as Guardian Canadian Fund 4/20/83
Guardian Canadian Fund reorganized as Guardian Group of Funds Ltd. Growth Equity Fund Class B no par in December 1994

MUTUAL ASSURN INC (AL)
Recapitalized as MAIC Holdings Inc. 9/1/95
Each share Common $1 par exchanged for (1) share Common $1 par
MAIC Holdings Inc. name changed to Medical Assurance, Inc. 6/1/97

MUTUAL BANCOMPANY INC (MO)
Merged into Roosevelt Financial Group, Inc. 10/25/1996
Each share Common 1¢ par exchanged for (1.3235) shares Common 1¢ par
Roosevelt Financial Group, Inc. merged into Mercantile Bancorporation, Inc. 07/01/1997 which merged into Firstar Corp. (New) 09/20/1999 which merged into U.S. Bancorp (DE) 02/27/2001

MUTUAL BD FD (ON)
Merged 3/31/70
Reincorporated in 1973
Mutual Bond Income Fund merged into Mutual Bond Fund 3/31/70
Each Unit no par exchanged for $4.54015 value of Unit no par
Place of incorporation changed from (BC) to (ONT) in 1973
Mutual Bond Fund name changed to Guardian Security Income Fund 4/28/75 which name changed to Guardian Short Term Money Fund 7/3/81 which reorganized as Guardian Group of Funds Ltd. Canadian Money Market Fund no par in September 1993

MUTUAL BEACON FD INC (MA)
Under plan of merger each share Common $0.001 par automatically became (1) share Mutual Series Fund Inc. Beacon Fund Common $0.001 par 02/19/1988
Mutual Series Fund Inc. name changed to Franklin Mutual Series Fund Inc. (MD) which reorganized in Delaware as Franklin Mutual Series Funds 05/01/2008

MUTUAL BENEFIT INCOME PARTNERS L P (RI)
Terminated registration of Units of Ltd. Partnership and is no longer public as of 08/09/1996
Details not available

MUTUAL BENEFIT MTG INVS L P (RI)
Completely liquidated 11/01/1996
Each Unit of Ltd. Partnership received first and final distribution of an undetermined amount of cash and a pro-rata share of Class 4 claim in the Rehabilitation of the Mutual Benefit Life Insurance Co.

MUTUAL BUILDING & INVESTMENT CO.
Reorganized as Mutual Mortgage & Investment Co. in 1939
Details not available

MUTUAL CREAMERY CO.
Assets acquired by Creameries of America, Inc. 00/00/1945
Details not available

MUTUAL DRUG CO. (OH)
Recapitalized as Forest City Industries, Inc. 00/00/1952
Each share Prior Preference no par exchanged for (1) share Common $2 par
Each share Class A Common $100 par exchanged for (5) shares Common $2 par
Each share Class B Common $100 par exchanged for (0.1) share Common $2 par
Forest City Industries, Inc. name changed to Parsons & Co., Inc. 05/10/1957
(See Parsons & Co., Inc.)

MUTUAL ENTERPRISES INC (DE)
Name changed to First Mutual Inc. 01/18/1988
(See First Mutual Inc.)

MUTUAL EXCHANGE INTL INC (FL)
Reorganized under the laws of Delaware as Avenue Exchange Corp. 07/16/2008
Each share Common $0.001 par exchanged for (0.1) share Common $0.000001 par
Avenue Exchange Corp. name changed to Eyes on the Go, Inc. 06/27/2011

MUTUAL EXPL FDS INC (DE)
Merged into Hershey Oil Corp. 12/13/88
Details not available

MUTUAL FD BUYERS GUIDE INC (NY)
Dissolved by proclamation 12/20/77

MUTUAL FD INVESTING USG SECS INC (MD)
Name changed to Fund for U.S. Government Securities, Inc. 10/25/1971
Fund for U.S. Government Securities, Inc. name changed to Federated Fund for U.S. Government Securities, Inc. 03/31/1996 which reorganized as Federated Income Securirties Trust 10/07/2002

MUTUAL FED SVGS & LN ASSN ELKIN N C (USA)
Stock Dividend - 10% 09/30/1989
Merged into Southern National Corp. 08/31/1990
Each share Common $1 par exchanged for (1.15603) shares Common $5 par
Southern National Corp. name changed to BB&T Corp. 05/19/1997

MUTUAL FED SVGS BK (MIAMISBURG, OH)
Merged into Fifth Third Bancorp 1/20/95
Each share Common $1 par exchanged for (0.6298) share Common no par

MUTUAL FED SVGS BK A STK CORP ZANESVILLE OHIO (USA)
Merged into Park National Corp. 08/31/1990
Each share Common $1 par exchanged for (0.2086) share Common $6.25 par

MUTUAL FINANCE CORP.
Merged into General Investors Trust 00/00/1932
Details not available

MUTUAL FINANCE CORP., LTD. (ON)
Liquidation completed 03/15/1962
Preferred holders received cash
Common Stock adjudicated worthless

MUTUAL FRANCHISE CORP (DE)
Name changed to Mutual Enterprises Inc. 04/29/1970
Mutual Enterprises Inc. name changed to First Mutual Inc. 01/18/1988
(See First Mutual Inc.)

MUTUAL GROWTH FD (BC)
Name changed to Guardian North American Fund (BC) 4/28/74
Guardian North American Fund (BC) reincorporated in Ontario in 1973 which reorganized as Guardian Group of Funds Ltd. American Equity Fund no par in July 1994

MUTUAL HOME FED SVGS BK (GRAND RAPIDS, MI)
Name changed to PrimeBank Federal Savings Bank (Grand Rapids, MI) 4/22/86
(See PrimeBank Federal Savings Bank (Grand Rapids, MI))

MUTUAL INCOME FD INC (TX)
Completely liquidated 04/22/1969
Each share Common $1 par exchanged for first and final distribution of $12.40 cash

MUTUAL INCOME FOUNDATION (MI)
Shares of Bene. Int. no par changed to $1 par 01/11/1957
Name changed to Mutual Investing Foundation 01/03/1961
Mutual Investing Foundation name changed to Nationwide Investing Foundation 11/01/1982
(See Nationwide Investing Foundation)

MUTUAL INCOME FUND (BC)
Merged into Mutual Accumulating Fund (BC) 09/21/1979
Each Share no par exchanged for (0.933409) Share no par
Mutual Accumulating Fund (BC) reincorporated in Ontario as Guardian Canadian Fund 04/30/1983 which reorganized as Guardian Group of Funds Ltd. Growth Equity Fund Class B no par 12/00/1994

MUTUAL INVESTING FNDTN (MI)
MIF Fund Shares of Bene. Int. $1 par split (2) for (1) by issuance of (1) additional share 07/28/1969
Name changed to Nationwide Investing Foundation and MIF Fund Shares of Bene. Int. $1 par, MIF Growth Fund Shares $1 par reclassified as Nationwide Fund Shares of Bene. Int. and Nationwide Growth Fund Shares respectively 11/01/1982
(See Nationwide Investing Foundation)

MUTUAL INVESTMENT & TRUST CORP. (AZ)
Merged into Flori Investment Co. 3/28/68
Each share Common $1 par exchanged for (0.390625) share Capital Stock $1 par
Flori Investment Co. name changed to Flori Corp. (Ariz.) 7/21/69 which reincorporated under the laws of Delaware 7/6/70
(See Flori Corp. (Del.))

MUTUAL INVESTMENT CO. OF AMERICA (DE)
Name changed to Capital Investors Growth Fund, Inc. 10/10/1966
Capital Investors Growth Fund, Inc. merged into Capital Shares, Inc. 12/27/1974 which name changed to Bull & Bear Capital Growth Fund 05/02/1983 which name changed to Bull & Bear Special Equities Fund 06/00/1992 which name changed to Midas Special Equities Fund 06/30/1999 which name changed to Midas Special Fund, Inc. 05/01/2006 which name changed to Midas Magic, Inc. (New) 04/29/2011 which reorganized as Midas Series Trust 10/12/2012

MUTUAL INVESTMENT FUND, INC. (MD)
Capital Stock $1 par split (2) for (1) by issuance of (1) additional share 01/15/1954
Name changed to First Investors Stock Fund, Inc. 04/13/1966
First Investors Stock Fund, Inc. name changed to First Investors Fund, Inc. 06/18/1968 which name changed to First Investors Natural Resources Fund, Inc. 04/29/1981 which merged into First Investors International Securities Fund, Inc. 11/30/1987
(See First Investors International Securities Fund, Inc.)

MUTUAL INVESTMENT FUND (NJ)
Reincorporated under the laws of Maryland as Mutual Investment Fund, Inc. 02/10/1941
Mutual Investment Fund, Inc. name changed to First Investors Stock Fund, Inc. 04/13/1966 which name changed to First Investors Fund, Inc. 06/18/1968 which name changed to First Investors Natural Resources Fund, Inc. 04/29/1981 which merged into First Investors International Securities Fund, Inc. 11/30/1987
(See First Investors International Securities Fund, Inc.)

MUTUAL INVESTMENT TRUST (NY)
Reincorporated under the laws of New Jersey as Mutual Investment Fund 10/00/1935
Mutual Investment Fund (NJ) reincorporated in Maryland as Mutual Investment Fund, Inc. 02/10/1941 which name changed to First Investors Stock Fund, Inc. 04/13/1966 which name changed to First Investors Fund, Inc. 06/18/1968 which name changed to First Investors Natural Resources Fund, Inc. 04/29/1981 which merged into First Investors International Securities Fund, Inc. 11/30/1987
(See First Investors International Securities Fund, Inc.)

MUTUAL INVESTORS CORP. OF NEW YORK (DE)
Dissolved 1/13/60
Details not available

MUTUAL LIFE INSURANCE OF BALTIMORE (MD)
Each share Capital Stock $100 par exchanged for (10) shares Capital Stock $10 par 07/00/1931
Stock Dividends - 100% 08/01/1931; 100% 04/10/1934
Name changed to Monumental Life Insurance Co. 07/00/1935
(See Monumental Life Insurance Co.)

MUTUAL MANAGEMENT CO. (DE)
Merged into First Investors Management Co., Inc. 5/25/66
Each share Common 10¢ par exchanged for (0.1) share $1.50 Preferred $25 par

MUTUAL MORTGAGE & INVESTMENT CO. (OH)
Liquidation completed 8/26/60

MUTUAL NATIONAL BANK (CHICAGO, IL)
Stock Dividends - 25% 12/20/43; 20% 12/15/49; 25% 12/10/53
Each share Capital Stock $100 par exchanged for (13-1/3) shares Capital Stock $10 par to effect a (10) for (1) split and 33-1/3% stock dividend 10/21/58
Merged into La Salle National Bank (Chicago, Ill.) 8/14/67
Each share Capital Stock $10 par exchanged for (0.5) share 5.75% Preferred $60 par and $56 cash

MUTUAL OIL & GAS CO. (DE)
Charter cancelled and declared inoperative and void for non-payment of taxes 1/26/26

MUTUAL OIL AMER INC (DE)
Common 10¢ par split (5) for (4) by issuance of (0.25) additional share 10/31/80
Common 10¢ par split (3) for (1) by issuance of (2) additional shares 5/1/81
Charter cancelled and declared inoperative and void for non-payment of taxes 11/11/90

MUTUAL OIL CO. LTD. (AB)
Acquired by Flag Oils Ltd. 10/11/60
Each share Common no par exchanged for (0.2) share Common no par
Flag Oils Ltd. name changed to Flag Resources Ltd. 1/4/82 which recapitalized as Flag Resources (1985) Ltd. 2/18/85

MUTUAL OMAHA AMER FD INC (NE)
Name changed to Pioneer America Fund, Inc. 12/1/93
Pioneer America Fund, Inc. merged into Pioneer American Income Trust 7/5/94

MUTUAL OMAHA CASH RESV FD INC (NE)
Under plan of merger each share Common 1¢ par automatically became (1) share Mutual of Omaha Money Market Account, Inc. Common 1¢ par 02/22/1991
Mutual of Omaha Money Market Account, Inc. name changed to Pioneer Money Market Account, Inc. 12/01/1993 which merged into Pioneer Money Market Trust (MA) 06/30/1994 which reincorporated in Delaware 03/31/1995

MUTUAL OMAHA GROWTH FD INC (NE)
Reincorporated under the laws of Delaware as Pioneer Growth Shares 12/01/1993
Pioneer Growth Shares reorganized as Pioneer Independence Fund 12/07/2007

MUTUAL OMAHA INCOME FD INC (NE)
Name changed to Pioneer Income Fund, Inc. (NE) 12/01/1993
Pioneer Income Fund, Inc. reincorporated in Delaware as Pioneer Income Fund 06/30/1994 which name changed to Pioneer Balanced Fund 02/01/1997 which merged into Pioneer Series Trust IV 11/10/2006

MUTUAL OMAHA INT SHS INC (NE)
Name changed to Pioneer Interest Shares, Inc. (NE) 12/01/1993
Pioneer Interest Shares, Inc. (NE) reincorporated in Delaware as Pioneer Interest Shares 08/01/1996 which merged into Pioneer Bond Fund 10/19/2007

MUTUAL OMAHA MONEY MKT ACCOUNT INC (NE)
Name changed to Pioneer Money Market Account, Inc. 12/01/1993
Pioneer Money Market Account, Inc. merged into Pioneer Money Market Trust (MA) 06/30/1994 which reincorporated in Delaware 03/31/1995

MUTUAL OMAHA TAX FREE INCOME FD INC (NE)
Reincorporated under the laws of Delaware as Pioneer Tax-Free Income Fund, Inc. 12/01/1993
Pioneer Tax-Free Income Fund, Inc. name changed to Pioneer Tax Free Income Fund 06/30/1994

MUTUAL PHARMACAL CO., INC.
Completely liquidated 07/01/1964
Each share Capital Stock $10 par exchanged for first and final distribution of $6.52 cash

MUTUAL QUALIFIED INCOME FD INC (NY)
Under plan of merger each share Common 1¢ par automatically became (1) share Mutual Series Fund Inc. Qualified Income Fund Common $0.001 par 02/19/1988
Mutual Series Fund Inc. name changed to Franklin Mutual Series Fund Inc. (MD) which reorganized in Delaware as Franklin Mutual Series Funds 05/01/2008

MUTUAL REAL ESTATE INVT TR (NY)
Stock Dividend - 250% 02/07/1969
Reorganized under the laws of Delaware as InterGroup Corp. 12/09/1985
Each Share of Bene. Int. $1 par exchanged for (1) share Common 1¢ par

MUTUAL RES LTD (BC)
Merged into Golden Knight Resources Inc. 10/6/95
Each share Common no par exchanged for (0.15625) share Common no par and (0.15625) Common Stock Purchase Warrant expiring 10/6/96

MUTUAL RISK MGMT LTD (BERMUDA)
Common 1¢ par split (3) for (2) by issuance of (0.5) additional share 10/20/1993
Common 1¢ par split (4) for (3) by issuance of (1/3) additional share payable 06/19/1996 to holders of record 05/31/1996 Ex date - 06/20/1996
Common 1¢ par split (2) for (1) by issuance of (1) additional share payable 10/10/1997 to holders of record 09/26/1997 Ex date - 10/14/1997
SEC revoked common stock registration 07/07/2010
Stockholders' equity unlikely

MUTUAL SVGS & LN ASSN VA A FED STK CORP (DANVILLE, VA)
Merged into American National Bankshares Inc. 03/14/1996
Each share Common $1 par exchanged for (0.705) share Common $1 par

MUTUAL SVGS BK FSB (BAY CITY, MI)
Common 1¢ par split (2) for (1) by issuance of (1) additional share 9/8/93
Merged into Independent Bank Corp. 9/16/99
Each share Common 1¢ par exchanged for (0.8) share Common $1 par

MUTUAL SVGS LIFE INS CO (AL)
Stock Dividends - 100% 3/10/45; 100% 1/12/48; 50% 9/15/50; 100% 3/1/54; 10% 5/12/58; 10% 7/13/59; 10% 7/25/60; 20% 5/15/66
Merged into Primesco Inc. 12/4/98
Each share Common $1 par exchanged for $57.40 cash

MUTUAL SECS FD BOSTON (MA)
Stock Dividend - 200% 8/12/68
Name changed to Mutual Trust 1/3/77
(See Mutual Trust)

MUTUAL SER FD INC (MD)
Name changed to Franklin Mutual Series Fund Inc. (MD) and Beacon Fund $0.001 par, Discovery Fund $0.001 par, European Fund $0.001 par, Qualified Income Fund $0.001 par and Shares Fund $0.001 par reclassified as Mutual Beacon Fund Class Z $0.001 par, Mutual Global

Discovery Fund $0.001 par, Mutual European Fund Class Z $0.001 par, Mutual Quest Fund Class Z $0.001 par or Mutual Shares Fund Class Z $0.001 par respectively 11/01/1996
Franklin Mutual Series Fund Inc. (MD) reorganized as Franklin Mutual Series Funds (DE) 05/01/2008

MUTUAL SHS CORP (NY)
Each share Common no par exchanged for (10) shares Common $1 par 00/00/1950
Under plan of merger each share Common $1 par automatically became (1) share Mutual Series Fund Inc. Shares Fund Common $0.001 par 02/19/1988
Mutual Series Fund Inc. name changed to Franklin Mutual Series Fund Inc. (MD) which reorganized in Delaware as Franklin Mutual Series Funds 05/01/2008

MUTUAL STORES, INC.
Acquired by MacMarr Stores, Inc. 00/00/1929
Details not available

MUTUAL SYSTEM, INC. (DE)
Each share Common no par exchanged for (3) shares Common $1 par in 1934
Preferred $25 par called for redemption 11/1/66
Merged into Ritter Finance Co., Inc. 11/1/66
Each share Common $1 par exchanged for (0.1) share 5-1/2% Conv. Preferred Ser. B $50 par and (1) share Class B Common $1 par
Each share Founders Stock 25¢ par exchanged for (0.5) share 5-1/2% Conv. Preferred Ser. B $50 par and (0.5) share Class B Common $1 par
Ritter Finance Co., Inc. reorganized as Ritter Financial Corp. 9/25/69 which was acquired by Manufacturers Hanover Corp. 1/3/75 which merged into Chemical Banking Corp. 12/31/91

MUTUAL TEL CO (HI)
Name changed to Hawaiian Telephone Co. in 1954
Hawaiian Telephone Co. merged into General Telephone & Electronics Corp. 5/17/67 which name changed to GTE Corp. 7/1/82 which merged into Verizon Communications Inc. 6/30/2000

MUTUAL TELEPHONE CO. (PA)
Name changed to Pennsylvania Telephone Corp. in 1931
Pennsylvania Telephone Corp. name changed to General Telephone Co. of Pennsylvania in 1952 which merged into GTE MTO Inc. 3/31/87 which name changed to GTE North Inc. 1/1/88
(See GTE North Inc.)

MUTUAL TRUST, MTG 1
Liquidated in 1953

MUTUAL TR (MA)
In process of liquidation
Each share of Bene. Int. $1 par exchanged for initial distribution of $0.08 cash 6/26/78
Note: Details on subsequent distributions, if any, are not available

MUTUAL TR (MO)
Each Share of Bene. Int. $1 par exchanged for (4) Shares of Bene. Int. 25¢ par 09/30/1955
Name changed to Babson (D.L.) Income Trust 09/30/1975
Babson (D.L.) Income Trust name changed to Babson (D.L.) Bond Trust 02/14/1984
(See Babson (D.L.) Bond Trust)

MUTUALOAN CORP (WY)
Name changed to Nexus Enterprise Solutions, Inc. 02/27/2012

MUTZ CORP (IN)
Common no par split (2) for (1) by issuance of (1) additional share 03/31/1978
Stock Dividends - 10% 08/29/1975; 10% 07/20/1976; 10% 07/01/1977
Merged into Excepticon, Inc. 03/31/1981
Each share Common no par exchanged for (1.55) shares Capital Stock no par
Excepticon, Inc. merged into Forum Group, Inc. 09/08/1981
(See Forum Group, Inc.)

MUX LAB INC (CANADA)
Class A Subordinate no par reclassified as Common no par 04/07/1988
Merged into National Hav-Info Communications Inc. (BC) 11/23/1990
Each share Common no par exchanged for (0.2) share Common no par
National Hav-Info Communications Inc. (BC) reincorporated in Canada 08/13/1993 which name changed to NHC Communications Inc. 02/02/1995
(See NHC Communications Inc.)

MVBI CAP TR (DE)
Floating Rate Trust Preferred Securities called for redemption $25 on 7/31/2003

MVC CAP (DE)
Name changed to MVC Capital, Inc. 7/30/2004

MVC INDS INC (PA)
Name changed to Lyceum Companies, Inc. 01/27/1969 which name changed back to MVC Industries, Inc. 09/15/1969
Merged into MVC Acquisition Co. 07/18/1986
Each share Common $1 par exchanged for $0.03 cash

MVD INC (DE)
Name changed to NT Media Corp. of California, Inc. 04/24/2001
NT Media Corp. of California, Inc. name changed to Global Health Voyager, Inc. 08/10/2011

MVE CAP CORP (BC)
Merged into Range Capital Corp. (New) 08/06/2009
Each share Common no par exchanged for (1.55) shares Common no par
Range Capital Corp. (New) name changed to Open Gold Corp. 11/08/2010 which recapitalized as betterU Education Corp. (BC) 03/08/2017 which reincorporated in Canada 10/13/2017

MVIVE INC (NV)
Common $0.001 par split (2) for (1) by issuance of (1) additional share payable 08/24/2007 to holders of record 08/22/2007 Ex date - 08/27/2007
Charter permanently revoked 12/31/2008

MVP CAP CORP (ON)
Recapitalized as LatinGold Inc. 10/23/96
Each share new Common no par exchanged for (0.05) share Common no par
LatinGold Inc. name changed to Travelbyus.Com Ltd. 6/11/99
(See Travelbyus.Com Ltd.)

MVP NETWORK INC (NV)
Common 5¢ par changed to $0.001 par and (3.177) additional shares issued payable 04/02/2007 to holders of record 04/02/2007
SEC revoked common stock registration 03/06/2013

MVS CAP CORP (BC)
Recapitalized as CY Oriental Holdings Ltd. 2/26/2007
Each share Common no par exchanged for (0.2) share Common no par

MVS MODULAR VEH SYS LTD (BC)
Recapitalized as Cobra Pacific Systems Inc. 03/28/1996
Each share Common no par exchanged for (0.4) share Common no par
Cobra Pacific Systems Inc. name changed to Marathon Foods Inc. 02/16/1998
(See Marathon Foods Inc.)

MVSI INC (DE)
Name changed to Socrates Technologies Corp. 12/11/1998
(See Socrates Technologies Corp.)

MVT INDUSTRIES, INC. (CA)
Foreclosed and assets liquidated for benefit of creditors 11/16/66
No stockholders' equity

MW CAP RES CORP (ON)
Recapitalized 09/14/1990
Name changed from MW Resources Ltd. to MW Capital Resources Corp. 09/14/1990
Each share Capital Stock no par exchanged for (0.05) share Common no par
Reorganized under the laws of Alberta as Oro Nevada Resources Inc. 08/31/1996
Each share Common no par exchanged for (1.093) shares Common no par
Oro Nevada Resources Inc. name changed to Martlet Venture Management Ltd. 09/02/1999
(See Martlet Venture Management Ltd.)

MW COS INC (DE)
Name changed to Caldera, Inc. 09/14/1988
Caldera, Inc. recapitalized as Unistar Financial Service Corp. 08/17/1998
(See Unistar Financial Service Corp.)

MW INTL (CA)
Adjudicated bankrupt 11/15/1976
Stockholders' equity unlikely

MW MED INC (NV)
Recapitalized as Davi Skin, Inc. 06/04/2004
Each share Common $0.001 par exchanged for (0.002) share Common $0.001 par
(See Davi Skin, Inc.)

MWA CO (DE)
Stock Dividend - 10% 10/02/1972
Merged into Mitchell Corp. 06/22/1979
Each share Common $5 par exchanged for $8.75 cash

MWI VETERINARY SUPPLY INC (DE)
Acquired by AmerisourceBergen Corp. 02/24/2015
Each share Common 1¢ par exchanged for $190 cash

MWP CAP CORP (AB)
Name changed to Shear Wind Inc. 06/27/2006
(See Shear Wind Inc.)

MXC ACQUISITION, INC. (FL)
Name changed to Maxxima Corp. 6/26/86
(See Maxxima Corp.)

MY CATALOGS ONLINE INC (NV)
Recapitalized as Bright Mountain Holdings, Inc. 11/30/2012
Each share Common $0.001 par exchanged for (0.1) share Common $0.001 par
Bright Mountain Holdings, Inc. name changed to Wall Street Media Co, Inc. 09/10/2013

MY CLOUDZ INC (NV)
Name changed to Gridiron BioNutrients, Inc. 12/19/2017

MY GROUP INC (NV)
Name changed to Royale Group Holding, Inc. 03/12/2013
Royale Group Holding, Inc. name changed to Royale Globe Holding Inc. 01/09/2014

MY MARIJUANA CDA INC (BC)
Name changed to MYM Nutraceuticals Inc. 02/29/2016

MY MEDS EXPRESS COM INC (DE)
Charter cancelled and declared inoperative and void for non-payment of taxes 3/1/2002

MY POOL LEAKS INC (FL)
Recapitalized as Hydromedix Group, Inc. 06/30/2006
Each share Common $0.001 par exchanged for (0.001) share Common 1¢ par
(See Hydromedix Group, Inc.)

MY QUOTE ZONE INC (NV)
Name changed to China 9D Construction Group 11/01/2007
(See China 9D Construction Group)

MY RITT RED LAKE GOLD MINES LTD (ON)
Recapitalized as Metalcoat International Corp. 5/31/2002
Each share Common no par exchanged for (0.1) share Common no par
Metalcoat International Corp. reorganized as Wycliffe Resources Inc. 7/4/2003 which name changed to Renforth Resources Inc. 7/28/2006

MY SOCIAL INCOME INC (WY)
Reincorporated 07/30/2014
Each share old Common $0.001 par exchanged for (0.001) share new Common $0.001 par 05/11/2011
Each share new Common $0.001 par exchanged again for (0.00133333) share new Common $0.001 par 04/14/2014
State of incorporation changed from (NV) to (WY) and Common $0.001 par changed to $0.00001 par 07/30/2014
Each share old Common $0.00001 par exchanged for (0.001) share Common $0.00001 par 01/28/2015
Each share new Common $0.00001 par exchanged again for (0.0004) share Common $0.00001 par 06/24/2016
Name changed to PDX Partners, Inc. 06/02/2017

MY TOY INC (NY)
Stock Dividend - 100% 6/30/72
Charter cancelled and proclaimed dissolved for failure to pay taxes 9/24/80

MY VENTURE INC (BC)
Name changed to Avantec Technologies Inc. and (3) additional shares issued 07/18/2003
Avantec Technologies Inc. recapitalized as Harmony Gold Corp. 08/17/2009 which name changed to Pure Energy Minerals Ltd. 10/22/2012

MY VINTAGE BABY INC (FL)
Assets transferred to secured lenders 11/16/2010
Stockholders' equity unlikely

MY WEB INC COM (NV)
Merged out of existence 10/30/2007
Details not available

MYCOGEN CORP (CA)
State of incorporation changed from (DE) to (CA) 10/26/1995
Merged into Dow Chemical Co. 10/30/1998
Each share Common no par exchanged for $28 cash

MYCOM GROUP INC (NV)
Each share old Common 1¢ par exchanged for (0.1) share new Common 1¢ par 05/16/2005
Each share new Common 1¢ par exchanged again for (0.03333333) share new Common 1¢ par 02/20/2007
Each share new Common 1¢ par exchanged again for (0.2) share new Common 1¢ par 06/04/2007
Name changed to SARS Corp. 10/08/2007
(See SARS Corp.)

MYDAS FD (AB)
Issue Information - 10,000,000 TR UNITS offered at $25 per Trust Unit on 01/28/2002
Trust Units split (2) for (1) by issuance of (1) additional Unit payable 11/15/2005 to holders of record 11/15/2005 Ex date - 11/10/2005
Merged into Citadel Premium Income Fund 07/20/2006
Each Trust Unit no par exchanged for (1.22) Trust Units no par
Citadel Premium Income Fund merged into Citadel Income Fund 12/02/2009

MYER-BRIDGES CO.
In process of liquidation in 1950

MYERS (F.E.) & BRO. CO. (OH)
Liquidation completed 4/3/61

MYERS (L.E.) CO. (OLD) (DE)
Under plan of reorganization each share Common $1 par exchanged for (1) Non-Separable Unit of (1) share Myers (L.E.) Co. (New) Common $1 par and (1) share Myers (L.E.) Co. International, Ltd. Common 10¢ par 12/29/77
Myers (L.E.) Co. (New) reorganized as Myers (L.E.) Co. Group 4/28/82 which name changed to MYR Group Inc. 12/15/95
(See MYR Group Inc.)

MYERS EMPORIUM LTD (AUSTRALIA)
Stock Dividends - 50% 01/21/1974; 20% 01/29/1982
Merged into Coles (G.J.) & Coy, Ltd. 00/00/1985
Details not available

MYERS L E CO GROUP (DE)
Units terminated 6/29/84
Each Unit consisting of (1) share Myers (L.E.) Co. Group old Common $1 par and (1) share Myers (L.E.) Co. International Ltd. Common 10¢ par exchanged for (1.18) shares Myers (L.E.) Co. Group new Common $1 par
Common $1 par split (4) for (3) by issuance of (1/3) additional share 2/15/95
Name changed to MYR Group Inc. 12/15/95
(See MYR Group Inc.)

MYERS L E CO NEW (DE)
Issued in Non-Separable Units of (1) share Myers (L.E.) Co. (New) Common $1 par and (1) share Myers (L.E.) Co. International Ltd. Common 10¢ par
Under plan of reorganization each Unit automatically became (1) Non-Separable Unit of (1) share Myers (L.E.) Co. Group Common $1 par and (1) share Myers (L.E.) Co. International Ltd. Common 10¢ par 4/28/82
Myers (L.E.) Co. Group name changed to MYR Group Inc. 12/15/95
(See MYR Group Inc.)

MYERS (FRED C.) LTD. (BC)
Common acquired by McLennam, McFeely & Prior Ltd. for cash 3/8/63

MYERS MILLS, INC.
Merged into Textiles, Inc. in 1931
Textiles, Inc. name changed to Ti-Caro Inc. 9/30/78
(See Ti-Caro Inc.)

MYERS-SPALTI MANUFACTURING CO. (TX)
Merged into Olive-Myers-Spalti Manufacturing Co. 5/2/55
Each share Common $10 par exchanged for (1) share Common $10 par
Olive-Myers-Spalti Manufacturing Co. name changed to Mathes Manufacturing Co. 4/22/58 which name changed to Mathes (Curtis) Manufacturing Co. 8/28/59 which merged into Mathes (Curtis) Corp. 1/19/70

MYEZSMOKES INC (NV)
Name changed to Icon Vapor, Inc. 02/06/2014

MYGLOBAL CONCIERGE COM INC (FL)
Reincorporated under the laws of Delaware 08/21/2008

MYKROLIS CORP (DE)
Issue Information - 7,000,000 shares COM offered at $15 per share on 08/09/2001
Merged into Entegris, Inc. 08/06/2005
Each share Common 1¢ par exchanged for (1.39) shares Common 1¢ par

MYLAKE MINES LTD (ON)
Charter cancelled for failure to pay taxes and file returns 11/07/1978

MYLAMAQUE MINES LTD. (ON)
Acquired by New Mylamaque Explorations Ltd. on a (1) for (4) basis 00/00/1953
New Mylamaque Explorations Ltd. name changed to New Mylamaque Mining & Smelting Ltd. 10/11/1960 which recapitalized as Mymar Mining & Reduction Ltd. 12/22/1969 which merged into Dynamar Energy Ltd. 08/24/1977
(See Dynamar Energy Ltd.)

MYLAN INC (PA)
Name changed 10/02/2007
Common 50¢ par split (2) for (1) by issuance of (1) additional share 06/30/1983
Common 50¢ par split (3) for (2) by issuance of (0.5) additional share 03/01/1984
Common 50¢ par split (3) for (2) by issuance of (0.5) additional share 07/31/1984
Common 50¢ par split (2) for (1) by issuance of (1) additional share 02/15/1985
Common 50¢ par split (3) for (2) by issuance of (0.5) additional share 08/01/1986
Common 50¢ par split (2) for (1) by issuance of (1) additional share 07/31/1992
Common 50¢ par split (3) for (2) by issuance of (0.5) additional share 08/15/1995
Common 50¢ par split (3) for (2) by issuance of (0.5) additional share payable 01/27/2003 to holders of record 01/17/2003 Ex date - 01/28/2003
Common 50¢ par split (3) for (2) by issuance of (0.5) additional share payable 10/08/2003 to holders of record 09/30/2003 Ex date - 10/09/2003
Stock Dividends - 25% 08/15/1979; 100% 11/13/1981
Name changed from Mylan Laboratories Inc. to Mylan Inc. 10/02/2007
Each share Common 6.50% Mandatory Conv. Preferred 50¢ exchanged for (58.548) shares Common 50¢ par 11/15/2010
Merged into Mylan N.V. 02/27/2015
Each share Common 50¢ par exchanged for (1) share Ordinary EUR 0.01 par

MYLAN VENTURES LTD (WY)
Reincorporated 09/10/1996
Place of incorporation changed from (BC) to (WY) 09/10/1996
Administratively dissolved 06/25/1999

MYLEE DIGITAL SCIENCES INC (MO)
Merged into Mylee Holdings, Inc. 01/19/1989
Each share Capital Stock no par exchanged for $0.08 cash

MYLER INTL CORP (FL)
Name changed to Micro Book International Inc. 12/15/1997
(See Micro Book International Inc.)

MYLER PLASTICS CORP. (NY)
Out of business 12/22/1954
Details not available

MYLES LEE CORP (NY)
Each share Common 10¢ par exchanged for (0.5) share Common 20¢ par 04/20/1979
Merged out of existence 02/25/1988
Details not available

MYLES STANDISH CO.
Liquidated in 1950

MYLEX CORP (FL)
Merged into International Business Machines Corp. 9/29/99
Each share Common 1¢ par exchanged for $12 cash

MYM LIQUIDATING TR (MA)
Each Unit of Bene. Int. no par received initial distribution of $0.50 cash 2/15/91
Each Unit of Bene. Int. no par received second distribution of $0.50 cash 5/15/91
Each Unit of Bene. Int. no par received third distribution of $0.25 cash 2/17/92
Each Unit of Bene. Int. no par received fourth distribution of $0.25 cash 5/15/92
Each Unit of Bene. Int. no par received fifth distribution of $0.35 cash 8/17/92
Each Unit of Bene. Int. no par received sixth distribution of $0.50 cash 11/16/92
Each Unit of Bene. Int. no par received seventh and final distribution of $0.375 cash 12/21/92
Note: Certificates were not required to be surrendered and are without value

MYMAR MNG & REDUCTION LTD (ON)
Merged into Dynamar Energy Ltd. 08/24/1977
Each share Capital Stock no par exchanged for (1) share Common no par
(See Dynamar Energy Ltd.)

MYMEDICALCD LTD (WY)
Each share old Common $0.0001 par received distribution of (1) share Interactive Solutions International Restricted Common $0.0001 par payable 01/29/2005 to holders of record 09/24/2004
Each share old Common $0.0001 par exchanged for (43) shares new Common $0.0001 par 01/25/2005
Recapitalized as United Treatment Centers, Inc. 01/30/2009
Each share new Common $0.0001 par exchanged for (0.00025) share Common $0.0001 par
United Treatment Centers, Inc. name changed to PotNetwork Holdings, Inc. (WY) 07/24/2015 which reincorporated in Colorado 03/03/2017

MYND CORP (SC)
Merged into Computer Sciences Corp. 12/27/2000
Each share Common 1¢ par exchanged for $16 cash

MYNEWPEDIA CORP (OR)
Name changed to Club Vivanet, Inc. 06/11/2008
Club Vivanet, Inc. name changed to Medical Marijuana, Inc. 04/28/2009

MYO-TECH CORP (DE)
Name changed to Microterra, Inc. 02/14/1992
Microterra, Inc. name changed to Atlantis Group, Inc. (Ctfs. dated after 11/02/1995) 11/02/1995
(See Atlantis Group, Inc. (Ctfs. dated after 11/02/1995))

MYOGEN INC (DE)
10/29/2003
Acquired by Gilead Sciences, Inc. 11/17/2006
Each share Common $0.001 par exchanged for $52.50 cash

MYOS CORP (NV)
Each share old Common $0.001 par exchanged for (0.02) share new Common $0.001 par 02/10/2014
Name changed to MYOS RENS Technology Inc. 03/22/2016

MYOTHERCOUNTRYCLUB COM (NV)
Name changed to Jameson Stanford Reources Corp. 05/23/2012
Jameson Stanford Reources Corp. name changed to Star Mountain Resources, Inc. 12/15/2014

MYPHOTOPIPE COM INC (NV)
Chapter 7 bankruptcy proceedings terminated 01/17/2014
No stockholders' equity

MYPOINTS COM INC (DE)
Merged into United New Ventures, Inc. 07/19/2001
Each share Common $0.001 par exchanged $2.60 cash

MYR GROUP INC OLD (DE)
Merged into GPU, Inc. 04/26/2000
Each share Common $1 par exchanged for $30.10 cash

MYRIAD CONCEPTS LTD (BC)
Delisted from Vancouver Stock Exchange 07/07/1989

MYRIAD GROUP INC (NY)
Merged into Micron Products Inc. 01/28/1988
Each share Common 1¢ par exchanged for (4) shares Common 10¢ par
Micron Products Inc. merged into Arrhythmia Research Technology, Inc. 11/25/1992

MYRIAD INTL CORP (NV)
Name changed to Aura Bio Corp. 12/04/2009
Aura Bio Corp. name changed to Global Resource Energy, Inc. 12/10/2010

MYRIAD INTL INC (DE)
Name changed 12/29/1995
Name changed from Myriad Industries Inc. to Myriad International, Inc. 12/29/1995
Each (15) shares old Common $0.001 par exchanged for (1) share new Common $0.001 par 07/16/1998
Charter cancelled and declared inoperative and void for non-payment of taxes 03/01/2002

MYRIAD PHARMACEUTICALS INC (DE)
Name changed to Myrexis, Inc. 07/01/2010

MYRIENT INC (NV)
SEC revoked common stock registration 12/12/2008
Stockholders' equity unlikely

MYRTLE GROVE CORP. (VA)
Voluntarily dissolved 9/20/85
Details not available

MYSHARES TR (DE)
Name changed to FocusShares Trust 11/16/2007
(See FocusShares Trust)

MYSKIN INC (CA)
Common $0.001 par split (4) for (1) by issuance of (3) additional shares payable 03/21/2014 to holders of record 03/19/2014 Ex date - 03/24/2014
Reincorporated under the laws of Colorado as United Cannabis Corp. and Common $0.001 par changed to no par 05/14/2014

MYSOFTWARE CO (DE)
Issue Information - 2,000,000 shares COM offered at $11 per share on 06/15/1995
Name changed to ClickAction, Inc. 09/16/1999
(See ClickAction, Inc.)

MYSTARU COM INC (DE)
Recapitalized as Subaye, Inc. 10/26/2009
Each share Common $0.001 par exchanged for (0.01) share Common $0.001 par

MYSTIC FINL INC (DE)
Merged into Brookline Bancorp, Inc. 1/7/2005
Each share Common 1¢ par exchanged for either (1.9433243) shares Common 1¢ par and $10.7055 cash or $39 cash
Note: Option to receive stock and cash expired 1/4/2005

MYSTIC VALLEY GAS CO (MA)
Completely liquidated 12/28/1973
Each share Common $25 par exchanged for first and final distribution of $39.64 cash

MYSTICA CANDLE CORP (NV)
Common $0.001 par split (3.031578) for (1) by issuance of (2.031578) additional shares payable 07/28/2008 to holders of record 07/21/2008 Ex date - 07/29/2008
Name changed to NanoDynamics Holdings, Inc. 07/29/2008
NanoDynamics Holdings, Inc. name changed to Li3 Energy, Inc. 11/18/2009 which merged into Bearing Lithium Corp. (Old) 09/28/2017 which reorganized as Bearing Lithium Corp. (New) 07/20/2018

MYSTIQUE DEVS INC (WY)
Name changed to Colorado Wyoming Reserve Co. 10/17/1997
(See Colorado Wyoming Reserve Co.)

MYSTIQUE ENERGY INC (AB)
Recapitalized as Bella Resources Inc. 10/28/2011
Each share Common no par exchanged for (0.1) share Common no par
Bella Resources Inc. recapitalized as Angel Bioventures Inc. (AB) 08/28/2013 which reorganized in British Columbia as AbraPlata Resource Corp. 03/28/2017

MYTEC TECHNOLOGIES INC (CANADA)
Name changed to Bioscrypt Inc. 04/06/2001
Bioscrypt Inc. acquired by L-1 Identity Solutions Inc. 03/05/2008
(See L-1 Identity Solutions, Inc.)

MYTOLON CHEMS INC (ON)
Merged into Elkins Productions of Canada Ltd. in 1972
Each share Common no par exchanged for (0.04) share Common no par
Elkins Productions of Canada Ltd.
merged into Life Investors Ltd. in June 1973 which merged into Life Investors International Ltd. 7/14/73
(See Life Investors International Ltd.)

MYTRAVELGUIDE COM INC (NV)
Name changed to Prime Holdings & Investments, Inc. 08/15/2001
(See Prime Holdings & Investments, Inc.)

MYTURN COM (DE)
Chapter 11 bankruptcy proceedings converted to Chapter 7 on 04/30/2001
No stockholders' equity

MZT HLDGS INC (DE)
Liquidation completed
Each share Common 1¢ par received initial distribution of $0.15 cash payable 08/25/2008 to holders of record 04/04/2008 Ex date - 08/26/2008
Each share Common 1¢ par received second and final distribution of $0.049087 cash payable 05/10/2012 to holders of record 04/04/2008
Note: Certificates were not required to be surrendered and are without value

N

N. P. G. GROWTH FUND, INC. (NY)
Voluntarily dissolved 6/14/77
Details not available

N & W INDUSTRIES, INC. (VA)
Each share Common no par exchanged for (4) shares Common $1 par 00/00/1950
Merged into Williamson-Dickie Manufacturing Co. 12/28/1968
Each share 5% Preferred $25 par exchanged for (1) share 6% Preferred $25 par
Each share Common $1 par exchanged for (0.129032) share 6% Preferred $25 par

N A C INDS CORP (DE)
Charter cancelled and declared inoperative and void for non-payment of taxes 3/1/89

N B COOK LTD (BC)
Common no par split (2) for (1) by issuance of (1) additional share 01/15/1981
Struck off register and declared dissolved for failure to file returns 08/07/1993

N B CORP (VA)
Common $5 par changed to $2.50 par and (1) additional share issued 05/15/1972
Stock Dividend - 10% 04/30/1971
Merged into Jefferson Bankshares, Inc. 12/31/1979
Each share Common $2.50 par exchanged for (1) share Common $2.50 par
Jefferson Bankshares, Inc. merged into Wachovia Corp. (New) (Ctfs. dated between 05/20/1991 and 09/01/2001) 10/31/1997 which merged into Wachovia Corp. (Ctfs. dated after 09/01/2001) 09/01/2001 which merged into Wells Fargo & Co. (New) 12/31/2008

N.B.P. ENTERPRISES (UT)
Reorganized as Hart Industries, Inc. (UT) 06/23/1983
Each share Common $0.001 par exchanged for (3) shares Common $0.001 par
Hart Industries, Inc. (UT) reorganized in Nevada 03/08/1994 which name changed to H-Entertainment, Inc. 08/24/2001
(See H-Entertainment, Inc.)

N B S INC (WI)
Liquidation completed
Each share Common $2.50 par or VTC for Common $2.50 par received initial distribution of (0.3337) share Universal Foods Corp. $4.40 Conv. Preferred Ser. B no par 01/06/1969
Each share Common $2.50 par or VTC for Common $2.50 par received second distribution of (0.0554) share Universal Foods Corp. $4.40 Conv. Preferred Ser. B no par 06/29/1971
Each share Common $2.50 par or VTC for Common $2.50 par exchanged for third and final distribution of $0.56 cash 06/06/1972

N B W P INC (PA)
Merged into First Philson Financial Corp. 1/2/91
Each share Common $10 par exchanged for (1) share Common $10 par
First Philson Financial Corp. merged into BT Financial Corp. 7/14/99 which name changed to Promistar Financial Corp. 11/15/2000 which merged into F.N.B. Corp. (FL) 1/18/2002

N D L PRODS INC (DE)
Name changed to Normans Sporting Aids, Inc. 2/16/95
(See Normans Sporting Aids, Inc.)

N D V INDS INC (NY)
Name changed to Audio Visual Electronics Corp. 10/12/85
(See Audio Visual Electronics Corp.)

N E C PPTYS INC (NV)
Name changed to March Indy International, Inc. 11/10/1999
March Indy International, Inc. name changed to Bancorp International Group 08/08/2001 which reorganized as Energy Source, Inc. 06/27/2008
(See Energy Source, Inc.)

N E O G HLDG CO (DE)
Charter cancelled and declared inoperative and void for non-payment of taxes 3/1/88

N.I. LIQUIDATING CORP. (DE)
Liquidation completed
Each share Common $0.025 par exchanged for initial distribution of $1.023 cash 10/15/1975
Each share Common $0.025 par received second distribution of $0.17 cash 02/21/1978
Each share Common $0.025 par received third and final distribution of $0.049032 cash 06/27/1979

N I S HLDGS CORP (NV)
Each share old Common $0.00025 par exchanged for (0.01) share new Common $0.00025 par 10/28/2011
Name changed to E-Rewards Network Inc. 08/16/2013
E-Rewards Network Inc. name changed to Rewards Nexus Inc. 10/02/2013 which recapitalized as One Step Vending, Corp. 04/06/2015

N-L, INC. (MN)
Liquidation completed
Each share Common 20¢ par exchanged for initial distribution of $2.50 cash 2/1/66
Each share Common 20¢ par received second and final distribution of $0.90 cash 11/29/66

N.M.S. CORP. (DE)
Completely liquidated 12/31/73
Each share Common $1 par exchanged for first and final distribution of $6.50 cash

N N INVS LIFE INS INC (WI)
Each share Common $1 par exchanged for (0.00002) share Common $50,000 par 07/24/1975
Note: In effect holders received $4 cash per share and public interest was eliminated

N P U CORP (NY)
Dissolved by proclamation 9/25/91

N R G ENTMT INC (NV)
Each share old Common $0.001 par exchanged for (0.25) share new Common $0.001 par 11/26/1999
Each share new Common $0.001 par exchanged again for (0.03333333) share new Common $0.001 par 03/20/2001
Each share new Common $0.001 par exchanged again for (0.01) share new Common $0.001 par 10/26/2002
Each share new Common $0.001 par exchanged again for (0.008) share new Common $0.001 par 04/21/2003
Name changed to Trim Image, Inc. 08/20/2004
Trim Image, Inc. recapitalized as Karrington Holding Corp. 02/24/2005 which name changed to World Wide Energy Corp. 03/23/2006 which recapitalized as Czech Republic Resource Corp. 10/30/2007 which name changed to Global Senior Enterprises Inc. 04/26/2013 which recapitalized as World Financial Holding Group 05/01/2018

N R G INC (TX)
Name changed to XRG Inc. 10/14/1975
XRG Inc. name changed to Doran Energy Corp. 01/20/1981 which name changed to Wright Brothers Energy Inc. 10/30/1985

N S BANCORP INC (DE)
Merged into MAF Bancorp, Inc. 05/30/1996
Each share Common 1¢ par exchanged for (0.8529) share Common 1¢ par and $20.1799 cash
MAF Bancorp, Inc. merged into National City Corp. 09/01/2007 which was acquired by PNC Financial Services Group, Inc. 12/31/2008

N.S.I., INC. (DE)
Liquidation completed
Each share Common $1 par exchanged for initial distribution of (0.171) share of Towle Manufacturing Co. Common no par and $2 cash 5/21/82
Each share Common $1 par received second distribution of $1.25 cash 5/26/83
Each share Common $1 par received third and final distribution of $0.10 cash 7/25/84

N S PWR HLDGS INC (NS)
Name changed to Emera Inc. 7/17/2000

N.T.C. LIQUIDATING CORP. (NY)
Completely liquidated 7/15/70
Each share Common 10¢ par exchanged for first and final distribution of (0.1) share Display Sciences, Inc. Common 1¢ par
(See Display Sciences, Inc.)

N T M INC (UT)
Name changed to Biolog, Inc. and Common 5¢ par changed to $0.001 par 12/15/2004

N TANDEM TR (CA)
Acquired by Chateau Communities, Inc. 06/23/2003
Details not available

N TONE INTL LTD (BC)
Cease trade order effective 10/18/1990

N TRIPLE C INC (NE)
Merged into MCI Communications Corp. 9/25/81
Each share Common $2 par

FINANCIAL INFORMATION, INC.   N2K-NAC

exchanged for (0.5) share Common 10¢ par
MCI Communications Corp. merged into MCI WorldCom, Inc. 9/14/98 which name changed to WorldCom Inc. (New) 5/1/2000
(See WorldCom Inc. (New))

N2K INC (DE)
Merged into CDnow, Inc. (DE) 03/17/1999
Each share Common $0.001 par exchanged for (0.83) share Common no par
(See CDnow, Inc. (New))

N U PIZZA HLDG CORP (NV)
Each share old Common $0.001 par exchanged for (0.02) share new Common $0.001 par 12/15/2000
SEC revoked common stock registration 08/10/2009
Stockholders' equity unlikely

N V KONINKLIJKE KNP BT (NETHERLANDS)
Reorganized as Buhrmann NV 08/31/1998
Each Sponsored ADR for Ordinary 2.50 Gldrs. par exchanged for (0.8) Sponsored ADR for Ordinary 2.50 Gldrs. par and $5.7939 cash
Buhrmann NV name changed to Corporate Express N.V. 04/19/2007
(See Corporate Express N.V.)

N V VERENIGD BEZIT VNU (NETHERLANDS)
Name changed to VNU N.V. 7/28/98
(See VNU N.V.)

N-VIRO RECOVERY INC (NV)
Name changed to Synagro Technologies Inc. (NV) 11/3/94
Synagro Technologies Inc. (NV) reincorporated in Delaware 5/28/96
(See Synagro Technologies Inc.)

N VISION INC (DE)
Issue Information - 1,300,000 shares COM offered at $5 per share on 05/29/1996
Each share old Common 1¢ par exchanged for (0.5) share new Common 1¢ par 11/27/98
Merged into Advanced Technology Systems, Inc. 3/7/2000
Each share new Common 1¢ par exchanged for $0.50 cash

N-VISION TECHNOLOGY INC (DE)
Reorganized under the laws of Nevada as Rapid Fire Marketing, Inc. 07/05/2007
Each share Common 1¢ par exchanged for (0.01) share Common $0.001 par

N W GROUP INC (DE)
Under plan of recapitalization each share Common 1¢ par exchanged for (0.5) share Common 2¢ par 06/06/1990
Name changed to Glenayre Technologies, Inc. 11/10/1992
Glenayre Technologies, Inc. name changed to Entertainment Distribution Co., Inc. 05/11/2007 which recapitalized as EDCI Holdings, Inc. 08/26/2008
(See EDCI Holdings, Inc.)

N W P RES LTD (BC)
Recapitalized 06/17/1981
Recapitalized from N.W.P. Developments Ltd. to N.W.P. Resources Ltd. 06/17/1981
Each share Capital Stock no par exchanged for (0.16666666) share Capital Stock no par
Merged into Golden North Resource Corp. 09/11/1984
Each share Capital Stock no par exchanged for (0.3667) share Common no par
Golden North Resource Corp. merged into Caledonia Mining Corp. (BC) 02/04/1992 which reincorporated in Canada 03/29/1995 which reincorporated in Jersey as Caledonia Mining Corp. PLC 03/24/2016

NA AMERN TECHNOLOGIES INC (DE)
Name changed to JSX Energy, Inc. 8/30/2006

NA CHURS INTL LTD (ON)
Common no par split (3) for (1) by issuance of (2) additional shares 12/31/1971
Common no par split (2) for (1) by issuance of (1) additional share 2/8/74
6% Class A Preference $10 par called for redemption 9/30/77
6% Non-Vtg. Class B Preference 45¢ par called for redemption 9/30/77
Liquidation completed
Each share Common no par received initial distribution of $7.90 cash 5/5/78
Each share Common no par received second and final distribution of $0.60 cash 11/10/78
Certificates were not required to be surrendered and are now valueless

NAAC CORP. (PA)
Completely liquidated 08/03/1963
Each share Class A Common $1 par exchanged for (1/9) share Transcontinental Investing Corp. Class A Common $1 par
Transcontinental Investing Corp. merged into Omega-Alpha, Inc. 03/07/1972
(See Omega-Alpha, Inc.)

NAALEHU RANCH & DAIRY, INC. (HI)
Merged into Hawaiian Ranch Co., Inc. on a (1.5) for (1) basis 7/30/62
Hawaiian Ranch Co., Inc. merged into Brewer (C.) & Co., Ltd. 6/16/64 which merged into IU International Corp. 8/14/78
(See IU International Corp.)

NAB ASSET CORP (TX)
Each share Common 1¢ par exchanged for (0.75) share Common 10¢ par and $3.64 cash 6/5/96
Plan of reorganization under Chapter 11 Federal Bankruptcy Code effective 12/6/2001
Each share Common 10¢ par received $0.106 cash payable 1/4/2002 to holders of record 12/6/2001
Note: Certificates were not required to be surrendered and are without value

NAB EXCHANGEABLE PFD TR (DE)
$2 Trust Unit Exchangeable Preference Shares called for redemption at $25 on 1/22/2004

NABCO INC (CO)
Each share old Common $0.001 par exchanged for (0.05) share new Common $0.001 par 8/11/97
Reincorporated under the laws of Nevada as Motorcycle Centers of America, Inc. 6/18/98
Motorcycle Centers of America, Inc. name changed to eUniverse, Inc. (NV) 4/27/99 which reincorporated in Delaware 1/9/2003 which name changed to Intermix Media, Inc. 7/12/2004
(See Intermix Media, Inc.)

NABCO LIQUIDATING CO.
Liquidation completed in 1944

NABCO MANGANESE MINING CO. LTD.
Acquired by Regent Mines Ltd. on a (3) for (1) basis in 1943
(See Regent Mines Ltd.)

NABCOR INC (PA)
Company believed out of business 00/00/1981
Details not available

NABESNA MINING CORP. (AK)
Charter revoked for failure to file reports and pay fees 1/2/62

NABI (DE)
Name changed to Nabi Biopharmaceuticals 03/05/2002
Nabi Biopharmaceuticals recapitalized as Biota Pharmaceuticals, Inc. 11/09/2012 which name changed to Aviragen Therapeutics, Inc. 04/13/2016 which recapitalized as Vaxart, Inc. 02/14/2018

NABI BIOPHARMACEUTICALS (DE)
Recapitalized as Biota Pharmaceuticals, Inc. 11/09/2012
Each share Common 10¢ par exchanged for (0.16666666) share Common 10¢ par
Biota Pharmaceuticals, Inc. name changed to Aviragen Therapeutics, Inc. 04/13/2016 which recapitalized as Vaxart, Inc. 02/14/2018

NABIS FINE ARTS INC (NY)
Adjudicated bankrupt 8/22/74
Stockholders' equity unlikely

NABISCO BRANDS INC (DE)
Merged into Reynolds (R.J.) Industries, Inc. 09/10/1985
Each share Common $2 par exchanged for $42.50 principal amount of 11.2% Notes due 08/01/1997 and (0.34) share $12.96 Preferred Ser. C no par
$3.50 Preferred $1 par called for redemption 09/15/1994
Public interest eliminated

NABISCO BRANDS LTD (CANADA)
Acquired by Nabisco Brands Investments Ltd. 05/11/1988
Each share Common no par exchanged for $45 cash

NABISCO GROUP HLDGS CAP TR II (DE)
Each 9.50% Trust Originated Preferred Security exchanged for $25 principal amount of 9.20% Jr. Subordinated Debentures due 9/30/2047 on 11/21/2000

NABISCO GROUP HLDGS CORP (DE)
Merged into Reynolds (R.J.) Tobacco Holdings, Inc. 12/11/2000
Each share Common 1¢ par exchanged for $30 cash

NABISCO HLDGS CORP (DE)
Issue Information - 45,000,000 shares CL A offered at $24.50 per share on 01/19/1995
Acquired by Morris (Philip) Companies Inc. 12/11/2000
Each share Class A Common 1¢ par exchanged for $55 cash

NABISCO INC (NJ)
Common $5 par changed to $2.50 par and (1) additional share issued 06/01/1978
Merged into Nabisco Brands, Inc. 07/06/1981
Each share Common $2.50 par exchanged for (1.04) shares Common $2 par
(See Nabisco Brands, Inc.)

NABO INC (NV)
Reorganized as Star Resorts Development Inc. 04/19/2007
Each share Common $0.001 par exchanged for (7) shares Common $0.001 par

NABORS DRILLING LTD (AB)
Common no par split (2) for (1) by issuance of (1) additional share 1/16/70
Common no par split (2) for (1) by issuance of (1) additional share 9/10/76
Merged into Anglo Nabors Ltd. 5/1/79
Each share Common no par exchanged for $56 cash

NABORS EXCHANGECO CDA INC (CANADA)
Exchangeable Shares split (2) for (1) by issuance of (1) additional share payable 04/21/2006 to holders of record 04/20/2006 Ex date - 04/18/2006
Each Exchangeable Share exchanged for (1) share Nabors Industries Ltd. Common 10¢ par 07/31/2009

NABORS INDS INC (DE)
Reincorporated under the laws of Bermuda as Nabors Industries Ltd. and Common 10¢ par changed to $0.001 par 06/24/2002

NABRIVA THERAPEUTICS AG (AUSTRIA)
Each Sponsored ADR for Common exchanged for (1) share Nabriva Therapeutics PLC Ordinary USD $0.01 par 06/26/2017

NABU MFG CORP (CANADA)
Name changed to Computer Innovations Distribution Inc. 01/23/1984
(See Computer Innovations Distribution Inc.)

NABU NETWORK CORP (CANADA)
Placed in receivership in December 1986
No stockholders' equity

NABUFIT GLOBAL INC (DE)
Each share old Common $0.0001 par exchanged for (0.03333333) share new Common $0.0001 par 07/13/2017
Note: Holders of (29) or fewer pre-split shares will receive $0.20 cash per share
Name changed to NewBridge Global Ventures, Inc. 12/12/2017

NAC CHARGE PLAN & NORTHERN ACCEPTANCE CORP. (MD)
Completely liquidated 09/01/1965
Each share Class A Common 30¢ par exchanged for (0.0178571) share Korvette (E.J.), Inc. Common $1 par
Korvette (E.J.), Inc. merged into Spartans Industries, Inc. (NY) 09/25/1966 which merged into Arlen Realty & Development Corp. 02/26/1971 which name changed to Arlen Corp. 10/16/1985
(See Arlen Corp.)

NAC INC (DE)
Recapitalized as Seal Inc. 11/02/1981
Each share Common 1¢ par exchanged for (0.1) share Common 10¢ par
(See Seal Inc.)

NAC RE CORP (DE)
Common 10¢ par split (3) for (2) by issuance of (0.5) additional share 07/06/1989
Common 10¢ par split (3) for (2) by issuance of (0.5) additional share 08/16/1991
Merged into XL Capital Ltd. (Cayman Islands) 06/18/1999
Each share Common 10¢ par exchanged for (0.915) share Class A Ordinary 1¢ par
XL Capital Ltd. (Cayman Islands) reorganized in Ireland as XL Group PLC 07/01/2010 which reincorporated in Bermuda as XL Group Ltd. 07/25/2016
(See XL Group Ltd.)

NACASA VENTURES INC (BC)
Name changed to Molnar Capital Corp. 8/16/93
Molnar Capital Corp. name changed to Star Properties Inc. 5/13/98

NACHMAN CORP (IL)
Common no par split (2) for (1) by issuance of (1) additional share 11/9/46
Common no par changed to $10 par in 1947

Common $10 par changed to $5 par and (1) additional share issued 11/3/58
Stock Dividend - 10% 11/5/69
Each share Common $5 par exchanged for (1/30,000) share new Common $5 par 6/10/83
Note: In effect holders received $2.50 cash per share and public interest was eliminated

NACHMAN SPRINGFILLED CORP.
Name changed to Nachman Corp. in 1943
(See Nachman Corp.)

NACO INDS INC (UT)
Class A Ser. 1 Preferred 1¢ par called for redemption at $6 on 1/1/2006

NACO LTD. (AB)
Recapitalized as Western Naco Petroleums Ltd. on a (0.25) for (1) basis 00/00/1955
Western Naco Petroleums Ltd. merged into Provo Gas Producers Ltd. 03/02/1961 which was acquired by Dome Petroleum Ltd. 06/28/1967
(See Dome Petroleum Ltd.)

NACOMA CONS INDS INC (DE)
Each share old Common $0.001 par exchanged for (0.5) share new Common $0.001 par 12/06/1991
Each share new Common $0.001 par exchanged for (0.05) share new Common $0.001 par 11/02/1992
Filed a petition under Chapter 11 Federal Bankruptcy Code 11/00/1994
Stockholders' equity unlikely

NACOZARI CONSOLIDATED COPPER CO. (AZ)
Charter expired by time limitation 08/14/1932

NACT TELECOMMUNICATIONS INC (DE)
Issue Information - 3,000,000 shares COM offered at $10 per share on 02/26/1997
Merged into World Access Inc. 10/28/98
Each share Common 1¢ par exchanged for (1.0469) shares Common 1¢ par
(See World Access Inc.)

NADEL COMMUNICATIONS CORP (DE)
Each share Common $0.001 par exchanged for (10) shares Common $0.0001 par 9/1/84
Name changed to First Commonwealth Financial Corp. 6/28/86
First Commonwealth Financial Corp. name changed to Global-Tron, Inc. 1/8/87
(See Global-Tron, Inc.)

NADINA EXPLS LTD (BC)
Recapitalized as New Nadina Explorations Ltd. 04/17/1978
Each share Common no par exchanged for (0.25) share Common no par

NADIR ENERGY & MNG CORP (WY)
Administratively dissolved for failure to pay taxes 11/10/2011

NADIRA MINES LTD. (BC)
Struck off the register and declared dissolved for failure to file reports 5/15/69

NADOLI CAP INC (QC)
Name changed to Komet Manufacturers Inc. 06/29/2007
Komet Manufacturers Inc. name changed to Komet Resources Inc. 12/19/2013

NADRO S A DE CV (MEXICO)
ADR agreement terminated 03/04/2003
Each Sponsored ADR for Ser. B exchanged for $7.86664 cash

NAEGELE ADVERTISING COMPANIES, INC. (MN)
Liquidation completed
Each share Common 10¢ par stamped to indicate initial distribution of $6 cash 9/10/69
Each share Stamped Common 10¢ par stamped to indicate second and final distribution of $10 cash 1/20/70
Certificates were not required to be surrendered and are now valueless

NAESS & THOMAS SPL FD INC (MD)
Name changed to Vanguard Small Capitalization Stock Fund, Inc. 9/11/89

NAF LIQUIDATING TRUST (DE)
Liquidation Completed
Each Ctf. of Bene. Int. received initial distribution of $0.69 cash 10/30/87
Each Ctf. of Bene. Int. received second and final distribution of $4 cash 12/30/88
(See New America Fund, Inc. for previous distributions)

NAFCO FINL GROUP INC (FL)
Stock Dividends - 10% 03/30/1984; 10% 03/31/1986; 10% 03/31/1987
Name changed to BancFlorida Financial Corp. 03/06/1989
BancFlorida Financial Corp. merged into First Union Corp. 08/01/1994 which name changed to Wachovia Corp. (Ctfs. dated after 09/01/2001) 09/01/2001 which merged into Wells Fargo & Co. (New) 12/31/2008

NAFI CORP. (DE)
Name changed to Chris-Craft Industries, Inc. 4/30/62
Chris-Craft Industries, Inc. merged into News Corp., Ltd. 7/31/2001 which reorganized in Delaware as News Corp. 11/3/2004

NAFTA TRADING INC (AB)
Name changed to AutoTradeCenter Canada Ltd. 9/22/2003
(See AutoTradeCenter Canada Ltd.)

NAFTEX ENERGY CORP (YUKON)
Reincorporated 09/16/1998
Place of incorporation changed from (ON) to (YT) 09/16/1998
Each share old Common no par exchanged for (0.00000029) share new Common no par 06/05/2006
Note: In effect holders received $0.66 cash per share and public interest was eliminated

NAFTOKHIMIK PRYKARPATTYA REFINERY JSC (UKRAINE)
GDR agreement terminated 01/16/2009
No GDR's remain outstanding

NAGANTA MNG & DEV LTD (QC)
Merged into Brominco Inc. 06/01/1976
Each share Capital Stock $1 par exchanged for (0.25) share Capital Stock no par and $0.10 cash
Brominco Inc. merged into Aur Resources Inc. 05/16/1985 which was acquired by Teck Cominco Ltd. 08/30/2007

NAGARJUNA CONSTR CO LTD (INDIA)
Sponsored 144A GDR's for Equity Shares split (2) for (1) by issuance of (1) additional GDR payable 10/12/2006 to holders of record 09/21/2006
Name changed to NCC Ltd. 03/14/2011

NAGLER HELICOPTER INC (DE)
Reorganized as Medical Enterprises, Inc. 2/7/72
Each (15) shares Common 1¢ par exchanged for (1) share Common 1¢ par
(See Medical Enterprises, Inc.)

NAGOYA RR LTD (JAPAN)
ADR agreement terminated 12/09/2011
No ADR's remain outstanding

NAHAMA & WEAGANT ENERGY CO (CA)
Each share old Common no par exchanged for (0.5) share new Common no par 01/17/1992
SEC revoked common stock registration 08/10/2009
Stockholders' equity unlikely

NAHANNI MINES LTD (ON)
Recapitalized as RG Properties Ltd. 2/3/94
Each share Common no par exchanged for (0.08) share Restricted Vtg. Shares no par
(See RG Properties Ltd.)

NAHATLATCH RES LTD (BC)
Merged into Seadrift Resources Ltd. 11/14/78
Each share Common no par exchanged for (1/3) share Common no par
Seadrift Resources Ltd. recapitalized as Pacific Seadrift Resources Ltd. (BC) 8/13/80 which reincorporated in Alberta 6/3/82 which recapitalized as Seadrift International Exploration Ltd. 6/1/85 which merged into Deak International Resources Corp. 12/30/88 which name changed to Deak Resources Corp. 3/27/89 which name changed to AJ Perron Gold Corp. 10/7/94
(See AJ Perron Gold Corp.)

NAHC INC (DE)
Merged into J.L. Halsey Corp. 06/18/2002
Each share Common 1¢ par exchanged for (1) share Common 1¢ par
J.L. Halsey Corp. name changed to Lyris, Inc. 11/15/2007
(See Lyris, Inc.)

NAHDREE GROUP LTD (DE)
Chapter 11 bankruptcy proceedings closed 10/14/2003
Stockholders' equity unlikely

NAI TECHNOLOGIES INC (NY)
Common 10¢ par split (3) for (2) by issuance of (0.5) additional share 09/17/1993
Merged into DRS Technologies, Inc. 02/11/1999
Each share Common 10¢ par exchanged for (0.25) share Common 1¢ par
(See DRS Technologies, Inc.)

NAIC GROWTH FD INC (MD)
Common $0.001 par split (2) for (1) by issuance of (1) additional share payable 10/01/1997 to holders of record 09/12/1997
Stock Dividend - 15% payable 05/23/2005 to holders of record 05/13/2005 Ex date - 05/11/2005
Name changed to Eagle Capital Growth Fund, Inc. 06/02/2008

NAIDA-VALE BUILDING CORP. (IL)
Liquidated in 1942

NAIL-TONE, INC. (FL)
Name changed to Forward Industries, Inc. 2/5/63
(See Forward Industries, Inc.)

NAILDRIVER MNG CO (UT)
Involuntarily dissolved 01/01/1996

NAINA CAP CORP (BC)
Name changed to Sierra Iron Ore Corp. 05/17/2011
Sierra Iron Ore Corp. name changed to Crystal Lake Mining Corp. 07/14/2016

NAK (E J) MATTRESS CO (UT)
SEC revoked common stock registration 10/15/2008
Stockholders' equity unlikely

NAKED BRAND GROUP INC (NV)
Each share old Common $0.001 par exchanged for (0.025) share new Common $0.001 par 08/10/2015
Merged into Naked Brand Group Ltd. 06/20/2018
Each share new Common $0.001 par exchanged for (0.2) share Ordinary

NAKUSP RES LTD (BC)
Name changed to Western Canadian Land Corp. 12/18/1985
Western Canadian Land Corp. recapitalized as King George Development Corp. (BC) 11/29/1996 which reincorporated in Canada as Allied Hotel Properties Inc. 10/21/1999 which reincorporated in British Columbia 06/22/2009

NAL ENERGY CORP (AB)
Merged into Pengrowth Energy Corp. 06/05/2012
Each share Common no par exchanged for (0.86) share Common no par
Note: Unexchanged certificates were cancelled and became without value 06/05/2015

NAL FINL GROUP INC (DE)
Secondary Offering - 2,500,000 shares COM offered at $7.50 per share on 12/23/1996
Plan of reorganization under Chapter 11 Federal Bankruptcy Code effective 10/30/98
No stockholders' equity

NAL OIL & GAS TR (AB)
Reorganized as NAL Energy Corp. 01/06/2011
Each Trust Unit no par exchanged for (1) share Common no par
Note: Unexchanged certificates were cancelled and became without value 01/06/2014
NAL Energy Corp. merged into Pengrowth Energy Corp. 06/05/2012

NALCAP HLDGS INC (CANADA)
Each share old Common no par exchanged exchanged for (5) shares new Common no par 08/31/1990
Recapitalized as Arbatax International Inc. (Canada) 03/28/1996
Each share new Common no par exchanged for (2.5) shares Common no par
Arbatax International Inc. (Canada) reincorporated in Yukon 08/06/1996 which name changed to MFC Bancorp Ltd. (YT) 03/03/1997 which reincorporated in British Columbia 11/03/2004 which name changed to KHD Humboldt Wedag International Ltd. 11/01/2005 which reorganized as Terra Nova Royalty Corp. 03/30/2010 which name changed to MFC Industrial Ltd. 09/30/2011 which name changed to MFC Bancorp Ltd. (BC) 02/16/2016
(See MFC Bancorp Ltd. (BC))

NALCO CHEM CO (DE)
Common $2.50 par changed to $1.25 par and (1) additional share issued 5/18/60
Common $1.25 par changed to 62-1/2¢ par and (1) additional share issued 8/18/64
Common 62-1/2¢ par changed to $1.50 par and (1) additional share issued 5/18/67
Common $1.50 par changed to 75¢ par and (1) additional share issued 5/14/73
Common 75¢ par changed to $0.375 par and (1) additional share issued 5/14/82
Common $0.375 par changed to $0.1875 par and (1) additional share issued 6/7/91
Merged into Suez Lyonnaise des Eaux 12/20/99
Each share Common $0.1875 par exchanged for $53 cash

NALCO HLDG CO (DE)
Issue Information - 44,444,444 shares COM offered at $15 per share on 11/10/2004
Merged into Ecolab Inc. 12/01/2011
Each share Common 1¢ par exchanged for either approximately (0.65847) share Common $1 par and $2.238 cash or $38.80 cash
Note: Option to receive stock and cash expired 12/07/2011

NALCUS RES LTD (BC)
Name changed to Trasco Wind-Force Technologies Inc. 01/05/1988
(See Trasco Wind-Force Technologies Inc.)

NALGAR NICKEL MINES LTD. (ON)
Declared dissolved 9/19/60
No stockholders' equity

NALLEY'S, INC. (WA)
Common $1.25 par changed to 62-1/2¢ par and (1) additional share issued 09/30/1961
Merged into Grace (W.R.) & Co. (CT) 06/25/1966
Each share Common 62-1/2¢ par exchanged for (0.533186) share Common $1 par
Grace (W.R.) & Co. (CT) reincorporated in New York 05/19/1988
(See Grace (W.R.) & Co.)

NALOS RES CORP (BC)
Name changed 07/06/1981
Name changed from Nalos Mining Corp. to Nalos Resources Corp. 07/06/1981
Recapitalized as Salon Resources Corp. 01/13/1986
Each share Common no par exchanged for (0.41666666) share Common no par
Salon Resources Corp. name changed to Salon Resources Corp.-Corporation Miniere Salon 04/28/1986 which name changed to Corptech Industries Inc. 09/23/1987 which recapitalized as Forefront Ventures Ltd. 07/15/1992 which recapitalized as First Echelon Ventures Inc. 02/16/1999 which name changed to Aumega Discoveries Ltd. 12/12/2003 which recapitalized as Fortress Base Metals Corp. 01/10/2007 which name changed to Lions Gate Metals Inc. 07/21/2008 which name changed to Block X Capital Corp. 01/25/2018

NAM CORP (DE)
Name changed to clickNsettle.com, Inc. 06/19/2000
clickNsettle.com, Inc. name changed to Cardo Medical, Inc. 11/26/2008 which name changed to Tiger X Medical, Inc. 07/13/2011 which name changed to BioCardia, Inc. 10/26/2016

NAM TAI ELECTRS INC (VIRGIN ISLANDS)
Each share Common $0.0001 par exchanged for (0.005) share Common 2¢ par 11/19/1990
Common 2¢ par changed to 1¢ par and (1) additional share issued 07/16/1992
Common 1¢ par split (3) for (1) by issuance of (2) additional shares payable 07/07/2003 to holders of record 06/30/2003 Ex date - 07/08/2003
Name changed to Nam Tai Property Inc. 04/22/2014

NAMA CREEK MINES LTD. (ON)
Recapitalized as Big Nama Creek Mines Ltd. 06/08/1964
Each share Capital Stock $1 par exchanged for (0.25) share Capital Stock $1 par
Big Nama Creek Mines Ltd. recapitalized as York Consolidated Exploration Ltd. 07/29/1977 which name changed to Amco Industrial Holdings Ltd. 09/09/1983 which recapitalized as International Amco Corp. (ON) 11/04/1985 which reorganized in England & Wales as Amco Corp. PLC 11/10/1989 which name changed to Billington Holdings Plc 03/31/2009

NAME BRAND SALES INC (ON)
Name changed to Tele-Find Technologies Corp. 1/1/2002

NAME DYNAMICS INC (DE)
Name changed to UBL Interactive, Inc. 07/03/2012

NAME INC (ON)
Acquired by itemus inc. 06/08/2001
Each share Common no par exchanged for (0.9155) share Common no par
(See itemus inc.)

NAMIBIA RARE EARTHS INC (CANADA)
Name changed to Namibia Critical Metals Inc. 05/30/2018

NAMIBIAN COPPER MINES LTD (DE)
Name changed to American Southwest Holdings Inc. 06/09/2000
(See American Southwest Holdings Inc.)

NAMIBIAN MINERALS CORP (YT)
Struck off register and declared dissolved for failure to file reports 05/31/2005

NAMIC U S A CORP (DE)
Merged into Pfizer Inc. 3/16/95
Each share Common 10¢ par exchanged for (0.24599) share Common 10¢ par

NAMM-LOESER'S INC. (NY)
Stock Dividend - 10% 1/22/63
Name changed to Hughes & Hatcher, Inc. 5/15/63
Hughes & Hatcher, Inc. name changed to Widener Place Fund, Inc. 9/28/77 which liquidated for Dreyfus Tax Exempt Bond Fund, Inc. 7/16/81 which name changed to Dreyfus Municipal Bond Fund Inc. 2/9/93

NAMM'S, INC. (NY)
Name changed to Namm-Loeser's Inc. 5/12/62
Namm-Loeser's Inc. name changed to Hughes & Hatcher, Inc. 5/15/63 which name changed to Widener Place Fund, Inc. 9/28/77 which liquidated for Dreyfus Tax Exempt Bond Fund, Inc. 7/16/81 which name changed to Dreyfus Municipal Bond Fund Inc. 2/9/93

NAMOCO MORTGAGE CO., INC. (KS)
Common $1 par changed to 95¢ par and (1/19) additional share issued 9/15/65
Common 95¢ par changed to 90¢ par and (1) additional share issued 9/15/66
Recapitalized as First Home Investment Corp. of Kansas, Inc. 4/18/67
Each share Common 90¢ par exchanged for (0.2) share Common $4.50 par
First Home Investment Corp. of Kansas, Inc. name changed to First Kansas Financial, Inc. 4/26/76 which merged into Central National Bancshares, Inc. 8/11/77 which name changed to United Central Bancshares Inc. 4/16/81 which name changed to First Interstate of Iowa, Inc. 6/24/85 which merged into Boatmen's Bancshares, Inc. 4/1/92 which merged into NationsBank Corp. 1/7/97 which reincorporated in Delaware as BankAmerica Corp. (Old) 9/25/98 which merged into BankAmerica Corp. (New) 9/30/98 which name changed to Bank of America Corp. 4/28/99

NAMSCO CORP (UT)
SEC revoked common stock registration 08/10/2009
Stockholders' equity unlikely

NANAIMO-DUNCAN UTILITIES LTD.
Liquidation completed in 1952

NANCY LEE MINES INC (ID)
Voluntarily dissolved 06/19/2006
Details not available

NANECO MINERALS LTD (AB)
Reincorporated 12/01/1983
Recapitalized 06/28/1991
Place of incorporation changed from (ONT) to (ALTA) 12/01/1983
Recapitalized from Naneco Resources Ltd. to Naneco Minerals Ltd. 06/28/1991
Each share Common no par exchanged for (1/3) share Common no par
Recapitalized as Southpoint Resources Ltd. 03/28/2002
Each share Common no par exchanged for (1/6) share Common no par
Southpoint Resources Ltd. name changed to E4 Energy Inc. 08/23/2005 which merged into Twin Butte Energy Ltd. 02/08/2008

NANERGY INC (DE)
Name changed to Xacord Corp. 07/07/2006
Xacord Corp. recapitalized as Empire Minerals, Corp. 01/22/2007 which name changed to Dominion Minerals Corp. 02/14/2008

NANIKA RES INC (BC)
Recapitalized as Goldbar Resources Inc. 07/06/2012
Each share Common no par exchanged for (0.1) share Common no par

NANKIN EXPRESS INC (MN)
Each share old Common no par exchanged for (0.1) share new Common no par 09/30/1986
Name changed to Bush Acquisition Corp. 01/14/1992
(See Bush Acquisition Corp.)

NANNACO INC (TX)
Each share old Common $0.001 par exchanged for (0.000001) share new Common $0.001 par 3/10/2000
Note: Holders of (999,999) or fewer pre-split shares received $0.00185 cash per share
Each share new Common $0.001 par exchanged again for (0.01) share new Common $0.001 par 10/18/2004
Each share new Common $0.001 par exchanged again for (0.025) share new Common $0.001 par 1/3/2005
Each share new Common $0.001 par exchanged again for (0.0025) share new Common $0.001 par 9/20/2005
Name changed to Oncology Med, Inc. 8/15/2006
Oncology Med, Inc. recapitalized as Haz Holdings, Inc. (TX) 2/22/2007 which reincorporated in Delaware 3/15/2007

NANO CAP CORP (AB)
Name changed to Z-Gold Exploration Inc. 03/16/2010
Z-Gold Exploration Inc. name changed to Brunswick Resources Inc. 05/22/2014

NANO CHEM SYS HLDGS INC (NV)
Recapitalized as PanGenex Corp. 04/08/2008
Each share Common $0.001 par exchanged for (0.05882352) share Common $0.001 par
PanGenex Corp. recapitalized as Virtual Sourcing, Inc. 08/31/2012

NANO DIMENSIONS INC (DE)
Name changed to Legal Life Plans, Inc. 02/07/2012
(See Legal Life Plans, Inc.)

NANO GLOBAL INC (NV)
SEC revoked common stock registration 06/19/2009
Stockholders' equity unlikely

NANO HLDGS INTL INC (DE)
Common $0.001 par split (30.30303) for (1) by issuance of (29.30303) additional shares payable 11/21/2008 to holders of record 11/19/2008 Ex date - 11/24/2008
Name changed to Nevada Gold Holdings, Inc. 11/24/2008
Nevada Gold Holdings, Inc. name changed to HK Battery Technology Inc. 09/06/2013

NANO-JET INC (NV)
Name changed to Hitor Group, Inc. 01/09/2008

NANO MASK INC (NV)
Recapitalized as NMI Health, Inc. 06/05/2013
Each share Common $0.001 par exchanged for (0.1) share Common $0.001 par

NANO-PROPRIETARY INC (TX)
Name changed to Applied Nanotech Holdings, Inc. (TX) 07/01/2008
Applied Nanotech Holdings, Inc. (TX) reincorporated in Delaware as PEN Inc. 09/03/2014

NANO SUPERLATTICE TECHNOLOGY INC (DE)
SEC revoked common stock registration 04/11/2012

NANO WORLD PROJS CORP (DE)
Each share old Common 1¢ par exchanged for (0.01) share new Common 1¢ par 06/17/2002
SEC revoked common stock registration 05/20/2003

NANOANTIBIOTICS INC (NV)
Name changed to BioVie, Inc. 08/08/2016

NANOASIA LTD (NV)
Name changed to Ad Systems Communications Inc. 04/09/2010
(See Ad Systems Communications Inc.)

NANOBAC PHARMACEUTICALS INC (FL)
Administratively dissolved 09/23/2011

NANODYNAMICS HLDGS INC (NV)
Name changed to Li3 Energy, Inc. 11/18/2009
Li3 Energy, Inc. merged into Bearing Lithium Corp. (Old) 09/28/2017 which reorganized as Bearing Lithium Corp. (New) 07/20/2018

NANOGEN INC (DE)
Chapter 11 bankruptcy proceedings converted to Chapter 7 on 12/01/2009
No stockholders' equity

NANOMETER STORAGE CORP (CO)
Each share old Common $0.001 par exchanged for (0.01) share new Common $0.001 par 05/23/2011
Name changed to Success Holding Group Corp. USA 01/09/2013

NANOMETRICS INC (CA)
Reincorporated under the laws of Delaware and Common no par changed to $0.001 par 9/29/2006

NANOPIERCE TECHNOLOGIES INC (NV)
Recapitalized as VYTA Corp. (NV) 01/31/2006
Each share Common $0.0001 par exchanged for (0.05) share Common $0.0001 par
VYTA Corp. (NV) reincorporated in Delaware 08/20/2010 which

recapitalized as Bio Lab Naturals, Inc. 11/05/2010

NANOSCIENCE TECHNOLOGIES INC (NV)
Name changed to American Films, Inc. 03/07/2012

NANOSECOND SYS INC (DE)
Adjudicated bankrupt 3/28/72
Trustee opined that there is no stockholders' equity

NANOSIGNAL CORP (NV)
Recapitalized as Nano Global Inc. 04/03/2006
Each share Common $0.001 par exchanged for (0.0001) share Common $0.0001 par
(See Nano Global Inc.)

NANOSPHERE INC (DE)
Each share old Common 1¢ par exchanged for (0.05) share new Common 1¢ par 04/09/2015
Acquired by Luminex Corp. 06/30/2016
Each share new Common 1¢ par exchanged for $1.70 cash

NANOSTART AG (GERMANY)
Name changed to Coreo AG 07/15/2016
(See Coreo AG)

NANOSTRUCK TECHNOLOGIES INC (BC)
Name changed to Fineqia International Inc. 11/01/2016

NANOTEC CDA INC (CANADA)
Company reported out of business 00/00/1987
Details not available

NANOTECH INDS INC (WY)
Administratively dissolved 03/14/2009

NANOTEK INC (BC)
Name changed to Minterra Resource Corp. 10/25/2002
(See Minterra Resource Corp.)

NANTAHALA BK & TR CO (FRANKLIN, NC)
Reorganized as Nantahala Bancshares, Inc. 12/21/2009
Each share Common $5 par exchanged for (1) share Common $1 par

NANTICOKE FINANCIAL SERVICES INC. (PA)
Merged into Guaranty Bancshares Corp. (PA) 7/11/86
Each share Common $2.50 par exchanged for (0.6) share Common no par
(See Guaranty Bancshares Corp. (PA))

NANTICOKE NATL BK (NANTICOKE, PA)
Under plan of reorganization each share Common $2.50 par automatically became (1) share Nanticoke Financial Services Inc. Common $2.50 par 1/8/85
Nanticoke Financial Services Inc. merged into Guaranty Bancshares Corp. (PA) 7/11/86
(See Guaranty Bancshares Corp. (PA))

NANTON NICKEL CORP (BC)
Name changed to Eyecarrot Innovations Corp. 07/13/2015

NANTUCKET ELEC CO (MA)
Merged into New England Electric System 3/26/96
Each share Common $25 par exchanged for (3.4646) shares Common $25 par
(See New England Electric System)

NANTUCKET GAS & ELECTRIC CO. (MA)
Each share Common $100 par exchanged for (4) shares Common $25 par in 1931

Name changed to Nantucket Electric Co. 5/17/73
Nantucket Electric Co. merged into New England Electric System 3/26/96
(See New England Electric System)

NANTUCKET INDS INC (DE)
Each share old Common 10¢ par exchanged for (0.1) share new Common 10¢ par 01/25/2002
Stock Dividends - 25% 02/29/1980; 33-1/3% 09/05/1980; 15% 05/01/1981; 25% 05/31/1983; 15% 06/02/1986
Name changed to Comprehensive Healthcare Solutions, Inc. 08/19/2004
Comprehensive Healthcare Solutions, Inc. name changed to Hybrid Energy Holdings, Inc. 11/12/2009

NANUET NATL BK (NANUET, NY)
Merged into Charter New York Corp. 05/07/1973
Each share Common $5 par exchanged for (1.6616) shares Common $10 par
Charter New York Corp. name changed to Irving Bank Corp. 10/17/1979 which merged into Bank of New York Co., Inc. 12/30/1988 which merged into Bank of New York Mellon Corp. 07/01/2007

NANYA TECHNOLOGY CORP (TAIWAN)
GDR agreement terminated 05/08/2017
Each 144A Sponsored GDR's for Ordinary exchanged for (10) shares Ordinary
Note: Unexchanged GDR's will be sold and the proceeds, if any, held for claim after 11/08/2017

NAP ENTERPRISES INC (ON)
Name changed to HTTL Enterprises Inc. 03/30/1989
(See HTTL Enterprises Inc.)

NAPA NATL BANCORP (CA)
Merged into Wells Fargo & Co. (New) 03/17/2000
Each share Common no par exchanged for (0.7775) share Common $1-2/3 par

NAPA RES INC (BC)
Name changed to Zurfund International Ltd. 12/13/88
Zurfund International Ltd. recapitalized as Atacama Resources Ltd. 2/2/90 which merged into KAP Resources Ltd. 11/14/90
(See KAP Resources Ltd.)

NAPA VY BANCORP (CA)
Common no par split (4) for (3) by issuance of (1/3) additional share 10/24/86
Acquired by Westamerica Bancorporation 4/15/93
Each share Common no par exchanged for (0.6323) share Common no par

NAPAR CHEM CORP (PA)
Merged into La-Co, Inc. 4/30/69
Each share Common 1¢ par exchanged for (1) share Common 10¢ par
(See La-Co, Inc.)

NAPCO GRAPHIC ARTS INC (WI)
Administratively dissolved 8/31/90

NAPCO INDS INC (IN)
Common $1 par split (5) for (4) by issuance of (0.25) additional share 06/12/1978
Common $1 par split (6) for (5) by issuance of (0.2) additional share 02/14/1979
Common $1 par split (5) for (4) by issuance of (0.25) additional share 09/29/1980
Common $1 par split (3) for (2) by issuance of (0.5) additional share 01/28/1982

Name changed to Mass Merchandisers, Inc. (IN) 05/11/1984
Mass Merchandisers, Inc. (IN) acquired by McKesson Corp. (MD) 10/29/1985 which reincorporated in Delaware 07/31/1987
(See McKesson Corp. (Old) (DE))

NAPCO INTL INC (MN)
Name changed to Venturian Corp. 6/15/87
(See Venturian Corp.)

NAPCO SEC SYS INC (DE)
Common 1¢ par split (3) for (2) by issuance of (0.5) additional share 01/04/1982
Common 1¢ par split (3) for (2) by issuance of (0.5) additional share 02/05/1985
Common 1¢ par split (3) for (2) by issuance of (0.5) additional share 08/20/1985
Common 1¢ par split (2) for (1) by issuance of (1) additional share payable 04/27/2004 to holders of record 04/13/2004 Ex date - 04/28/2004
Common 1¢ par split (3) for (2) by issuance of (0.5) additional share payable 12/28/2005 to holders of record 12/14/2005 Ex date - 12/29/2005
Common 1¢ par split (3) for (2) by issuance of (0.5) additional share payable 06/07/2006 to holders of record 05/24/2006 Ex date - 06/08/2006
Stock Dividends - 100% 02/06/1981; 100% 06/30/1981; 20% payable 12/06/2004 to holders of record 11/22/2004 Ex date - 11/18/2004
Name changed to NAPCO Security Technologies, Inc. 01/09/2009

NAPEC INC (CANADA)
Acquired by Oaktree Capital Management, L.P. 02/15/2018
Each share Common no par exchanged for $1.95 cash
Note: Unexchanged certificates will be cancelled and become without value 02/15/2024

NAPHTHALENE MANUFACTURING CORP. (WV)
Merged into Educational Sciences Programs, Inc. 04/10/1968
Each share Common $0.002 par exchanged for (1) share Common 10¢ par
Educational Sciences Programs, Inc. name changed to Delehanty Educational Systems, Inc. 01/05/1971
(See Delehanty Educational Systems, Inc.)

NAPIER CO (CT)
7% Preferred no par called for redemption at $26.52 on 3/11/99

NAPIER ENVIRONMENTAL TECHNOLOGIES INC (BC)
Name changed 01/03/2001
Name changed from Napier International Technologies Inc. to Napier Environmental Technologies Inc. 01/03/2001
Merged into I.C.T.C. Holdings Corp. 12/31/2009
Each share Common no par exchanged for $0.01 cash
Note: Unexchanged certificates were cancelled and became without value 12/31/2012

NAPLES CAP CORP (CANADA)
Name changed to Takara Resources Inc. 11/20/2007
Takara Resources Inc. name changed to Castle Silver Resources Inc. 11/28/2016 which name changed to Canada Cobalt Works Inc. 02/23/2018

NAPLES CO., INC. (IN)
Liquidation completed
Each share Class A $5 par

exchanged for initial distribution of $9.39 cash 11/24/75
Each share Class A $5 par received second distribution of $1.25 cash 5/20/76
Each share Class A $5 par received third distribution of $0.40 cash 9/10/76
Each share Class A $5 par received fourth and final distribution of $1.0072817 cash 4/26/77

NAPLES FED SVGS & LN ASSN (FL)
Stock Dividends - 10% 03/29/1982; 10% 04/01/1983
Reorganized as NAFCO Financial Group, Inc. 04/01/1983
Each share Common 1¢ par exchanged for (1) share Common 1¢ par
Nafco Financial Group, Inc. name changed to BancFlorida Financial Corp. 03/06/1989 which merged into First Union Corp. 08/01/1994 which name changed to Wachovia Corp. (Ctfs. dated after 09/01/2001) 09/01/2001 which merged into Wells Fargo & Co. (New) 12/31/2008

NAPLES FORT MYERS KENNEL CLUB INC (FL)
Merged into Southwest Florida Enterprises, Inc. 05/01/1969
Each share Common $1 par exchanged for (0.1) share Preferred $10 par and (0.6) share Common 10¢ par
(See Southwest Florida Enterprises, Inc.)

NAPOLEON EXPL LTD (BC)
Name changed to Argentina Gold Corp. 6/28/93
Argentina Gold Corp. merged into HomeStake Mining Co. 4/28/99 which merged into Barrick Gold Corp. 12/14/2001

NAPOLI ENTERPRISES INC (CO)
Each share old Common $0.001 par exchanged for (0.02) share new Common $0.001 par 12/24/2002
Name changed to Lion-Gri International, Inc. 10/20/2004
Lion-Gri International, Inc. recapitalized as Promotora Valle Hermoso, Inc. 07/24/2006 which name changed to UNR Holdings, Inc. 10/15/2009

NAPRO BIOTHERAPEUTICS INC (DE)
Name changed to Tapestry Pharmaceuticals, Inc. 05/04/2004
(See Tapestry Pharmaceuticals, Inc.)

NAPRODIS INC (NV)
Name changed to Sibannac, Inc. 01/26/2015

NAPSTER INC (DE)
Acquired by Best Buy Co., Inc. 10/30/2008
Each share Common $0.001 par exchanged for $2.65 cash

NAPTAU GOLD CORP (DE)
Name changed to 1st NRG Corp. 5/1/2007

NAPUDA TECHNOLOGIES INC (NV)
Recapitalized as Cabriolet Corp. 12/10/2003
Each share Common $0.001 par exchanged for (0.001) share Common $0.001 par
(See Cabriolet Corp.)

NAR RES LTD (ON)
Name changed to Titanium Corporation Inc. (ONT) 07/24/2001
Titanium Corporation Inc. (ONT) reincorporated in Canada 03/19/2009

NARA BANCORP INC (DE)
Common $0.001 par split (2) for (1) by issuance of (1) additional share payable 03/17/2003 to holders of

record 03/03/2003 Ex date - 03/18/2003
Common $0.001 par split (2) for (1) by issuance of (1) additional share payable 06/15/2004 to holders of record 05/31/2004 Ex date - 06/16/2004
Under plan of merger name changed to BBCN Bancorp, Inc. 12/01/2011
BBCN Bancorp, Inc. name changed to Hope Bancorp, Inc. 08/01/2016

NARA BANK N A
(LOS ANGELES, CA)
Stock Dividends - 5% payable 05/17/1999 to holders of record 05/10/1999; 8% payable 05/10/2000 to holders of record 04/14/2000
Under plan of reorganization each share Common no par automatically became (1) share Nara Bancorp, Inc. Common $0.001 par 02/05/2001
Nara Bancorp, Inc. name changed to BBCN Bancorp, Inc. 12/01/2011 which name changed to Hope Bancorp, Inc. 08/01/2016

NARAEWIN CO LTD (KOREA)
ADR basis changed from (1:20) to (1:1) 08/14/2007
Name changed to G Learning Corp. 09/14/2012
(See G Learning Corp.)

NARCO SCIENTIFIC INC (DE)
Reincorporated 03/29/1968
Name changed 08/30/1978
State of incorporation changed from (NJ) to (DE) 03/29/1968
Name changed from Narco Scientific Industries, Inc. to Narco Scientific, Inc. 08/30/1978
Merged into Healthdyne, Inc. 01/27/1983
Each share Common $1 par exchanged for (1.2) shares Common 1¢ par
Healthdyne, Inc. merged into Matria Healthcare, Inc. 03/08/1996 which merged into Inverness Medical Innovations, Inc. 05/09/2008 which name changed to Alere Inc. 07/14/2010
(See Alere Inc.)

NARDA MICROWAVE CORP (NY)
Common 10¢ par changed to $1 par 2/23/62
Common $1 par split (3) for (2) by issuance of (0.5) additional share 9/2/80
Merged into Loral Corp. 6/6/83
Each share Common $1 par exchanged for (0.599) share Common 25¢ par
(See Loral Corp.)

NARDA ULTRASONICS CORP. (NY)
Each share Common 10¢ par exchanged for (0.2) share Common 50¢ par 12/19/1960
Name changed to Dynasonics Corp. (NY) 08/07/1961
(See Dynasonics Corp. (NY))

NARDIS DALLAS INC (DE)
Stock Dividend - 20% 02/12/1971
Merged into Akard Co. 05/24/1974
Each share Common 10¢ par exchanged for $6.50 cash

NARNIA CORP (NV)
Name changed to Neologic Animation Inc. 05/11/2012
(See Neologic Animation Inc.)

NARRAGANSETT CAP CORP (RI)
Capital Stock $1 par split (1.75) for (1) by issuance of (0.75) additional share 12/31/1980
Stock Dividends - 10% 03/02/1970; 10% 12/15/1978; 10% 12/17/1979
Completely liquidated 12/23/1986
Each share Capital Stock $1 par exchanged for first and final distribution of $54.98 cash

NARRAGANSETT ELEC CO (RI)
6.95% Preferred called for redemption at $51.74 on 08/01/2003
4.64% Preferred $50 par called for redemption at $52.125 on 12/31/2007
(Additional Information in Active)

NARRAGANSETT ELECTRIC LIGHTING CO.
Acquired by Narragansett Electric Co. in 1927

NARRAGANSETT RACING ASSN INC (RI)
Completely liquidated 06/23/1980
Each share Common $1 par exchanged for first and final distribution of $3.75 cash

NARROW FABRIC CO. (PA)
Name changed to Wyomissing Corp. 12/26/63
(See Wyomissing Corp.)

NARROWSTEP INC (DE)
Company terminated common stock registration and is no longer public as of 04/13/2009

NARTICO RES LTD (ON)
Name changed to Privatel Inc. 2/23/88
(See Privatel Inc.)

NASCO, INC. (DE)
Merged into Gamble-Skogmo, Inc. in 1946
Each share 6% Preferred no par exchanged for (1) share 5% Preferred $50 par
Each share Common no par exchanged for (1.75) shares Common $5 par
Gamble-Skogmo, Inc. merged into Wickes Companies, Inc. 1/26/85 which name changed to Collins & Aikman Group Inc. 7/17/92
(See Collins & Aikman Group Inc.)

NASCO, INC. (WI)
Merged into Johnson Hill's Inc. 10/28/61
Each share Class A Common $2 par exchanged for (1) share Common $1 par

NASCO COBALT SILVER MINES LTD (ON)
Name changed to Frankfield Explorations Ltd. 01/14/1974
Frankfield Explorations Ltd. recapitalized as Frankfield Consolidated Corp. 08/19/1992 which name changed to Lagasco Corp. (ON) 04/05/1994 which reincorporated in British Columbia as El Condor Minerals Inc. 08/04/2010 which recapitalized as Worldwide Resources Corp. 06/08/2015

NASCO INDS INC (WI)
Class A Common $1 par reclassified as Common $1 par 06/30/1966
Common $1 par changed to 33-1/3¢ par and (2) additional shares issued 12/06/1968
Name changed to Weatherby/Nasco, Inc. 04/01/1971
Weatherby/Nasco, Inc. name changed to Nasco International, Inc. 08/08/1974
(See Nasco International, Inc.)

NASCO INTL INC (WI)
Merged into Stannet Capital Corp. 08/31/1977
Each share Common 25¢ par exchanged for $8 cash

NASCO METAL MINES LTD. (ON)
Name changed to Nasco Cobalt Silver Mines Ltd. 00/00/1951
Nasco Cobalt Silver Mines Ltd. name changed to Frankfield Explorations Ltd. 01/14/1974 which recapitalized as Frankfield Consolidated Corp. 08/19/1992 which name changed to Lagasco Corp. (ON) 04/05/1994

which reincorporated in British Columbia as El Condor Minerals Inc. 08/04/2010 which recapitalized as Worldwide Resources Corp. 06/08/2015

NASDAQ-100 TR (NY)
Ser. 1 Units split (2) for (1) by issuance of (1) additional Unit payable 03/17/2000 to holders of record 02/28/2000 Ex date - 03/20/2000
Name changed to PowerShares QQQ Trust 03/21/2007
PowerShares QQQ Trust name changed to Powershares QQQ Trust 06/04/2018

NASDAQ PREM INCOME & GROWTH FD INC (MD)
Under plan of merger each share Common $0.001 par automatically became (1) share Nuveen NASDAQ 100 Dynamic Overwrite Fund Common Shares of Bene. Int. 1¢ par 12/22/2014

NASDAQ STK MKT INC (DE)
Name changed to NASDAQ OMX Group, Inc. 02/27/2008

NASH (A.) CO.
Assets sold 00/00/1944
Details not available

NASH (J.M.) CO., INC. (WI)
Recapitalized as Medalist Industries, Inc. 7/5/67
Each share Common $1 par exchanged for (0.25) share Common $4 par
Medalist Industries, Inc. merged into Illinois Tool Works Inc. 5/30/96

NASH F C & CO (CA)
Assets assigned for benefit of creditors 06/09/1979
No stockholders' equity

NASH FINCH CO (DE)
5% Preferred $100 par called for redemption 06/30/1964
Common $10 par changed to $3.33333333 par and (2) additional shares issued 05/19/1972
Common $3.33333333 par changed to $1.66666666 par and (1) additional share issued 05/29/1978
Common $1.66666666 par split (3) for (2) by issuance of (0.5) additional share 09/20/1983
Common $1.66666666 par split (2) for (1) by issuance of (1) additional share 06/12/1987
Merged into Spartan Stores Inc. 11/19/2013
Each share Common $1.66666666 par exchanged for (1.2) shares Common no par
Spartan Stores Inc. name changed to SpartanNash Co. 05/29/2014

NASH-KELVINATOR CORP. (MD)
Merged into American Motors Corp. 00/00/1954
Each share Capital Stock $5 par exchanged for (1) share Capital Stock $5 par
American Motors Corp. merged into Chrysler Corp. 08/05/1987 which merged into DaimlerChrysler AG 11/12/1998 which name changed to Daimler AG 10/19/2007

NASH MOTORS CO.
Merged into Nash-Kelvinator Corp. on a share for share basis 00/00/1936
Nash-Kelvinator Corp. merged into American Motors Corp. 00/00/1954 which merged into Chrysler Corp. 08/05/1987 which merged into DaimlerChrysler AG 11/12/1998 which name changed to Daimler AG 10/19/2007

NASHAWENA MILLS (MA)
Dissolved in 1952

NASHUA & LOWELL RAILROAD CO.
Acquired by Boston & Maine Railroad

Co. and each share Common received $110 in cash in 1944

NASHUA CORP (MA)
Reincorporated 12/31/1957
Reincorporated 06/12/2002
Common $5 par changed to Class A Common $5 par 03/22/1956
Stock Dividend - 100% Class B Common 04/05/1956
State of incorporation changed from (MA) to (DE) 12/31/1957
Class A Common $5 par and Class B Common $5 par changed to $1.66-2/3 par respectively and (2) additional shares issued 08/29/1960
Class A Common $1.66-2/3 par reclassified as Common $1.66-2/3 par 05/03/1963
Common $1.66-2/3 par changed to $1.50 par and (0.5) additional share issued 05/20/1966
Each share $4.50 Conv. Preferred no par exchanged for (3.33) shares Common $1.50 par 07/26/1968
Common $1.50 par changed to $1 par and (1) additional share issued 12/02/1968
Common $1 par split (2) for (1) by issuance of (1) additional share 07/02/1986
Common Stock Purchase Rights declared for Common stockholders of record 09/02/1996 were redeemed at $0.01 per right 05/12/2000 for holders of record 05/09/2000
State of incorporation changed from (DE) to (MA) 06/12/2002
Acquired by Cenveo, Inc. 09/15/2009
Each share Common $1 par exchanged for (1.265) shares Common 1¢ par and $0.75 cash
(See Cenveo, Inc.)

NASHUA EXPLORATION & MINING LTD. (ON)
Charter cancelled and declared dissolved for failure to file returns and pay fees 4/9/75

NASHUA GUMMED & COATED PAPERCO. (MA)
Reorganized as Nashua Corp. (MA) 00/00/1952
Each share Common no par exchanged for (1) share Common $5 par
Nashua Corp. (MA) reincorporated in Delaware 12/31/1957 which reincorporated in Massachusetts 06/12/2002 which was acquired by Cenveo, Inc. 09/15/2009
(See Cenveo, Inc.)

NASHUA MANUFACTURING CO.
Name changed to Textron, Inc. (NH) 12/00/1947
(See Textron, Inc. (NH))

NASHUA STREET RAILWAY CO.
Operations discontinued 00/00/1932
Details not available

NASHUA TR CO (NASHUA, NH)
Capital Stock $25 par changed to $5 par and (4) additional shares issued 4/10/70
Stock Dividend - 10% 1/31/75
Reorganized as NTC Corp. 4/30/84
Each share Capital Stock $5 par exchanged for (3) shares Common $1 par
NTC Corp. acquired by Amoskeag Bank Shares, Inc. 7/31/87
(See Amoskeag Bank Shares, Inc.)

NASHVILLE, CHATTANOOGA & ST. LOUIS RAILWAY (TN)
Merged into Louisville & Nashville Railroad Co. 9/3/57
Each share Capital Stock $100 par exchanged for (1.5) shares Capital Stock $50 par
Louisville & Nashville Railroad Co. merged into Seaboard Coast Line Industries, Inc. (DE) 11/10/72 which merged into CSX Corp. 11/1/80

NASHVILLE ALPS SKI RESORT INC (IN)
Administratively dissolved 12/31/1987

NASHVILLE BK & TR CO NEW (NASHVILLE, TN)
Reorganized as NBT Holdings Inc. 07/24/2009
Each share Common no par exchanged for (1) share Common no par
NBT Holdings Inc. name changed to Truxton Corp. 10/10/2013

NASHVILLE BK & TR CO OLD (NASHVILLE, TN)
Merged into Third National Bank (Old) (Nashville, TN) 8/18/64
Each share Common $100 par exchanged for (4.5) shares Capital Stock $10 par
Third National Bank (Old) (Nashville, TN) merged into NLT Corp. (DE) 12/31/68 which reincorporated in Tennessee 1/1/81 which merged into American General Corp. 11/4/82 which merged into American International Group, Inc. 8/29/2001

NASHVILLE BREEKO BLOCK CO. (TN)
Name changed to Breeko Industries, Inc. 3/13/62
(See Breeko Industries, Inc.)

NASHVILLE CITY BK & TR CO (NASHVILLE, TN)
Each share Common $2 par exchanged for (0.4875) share Common $4 par 11/10/1976
Common $4 par split (3) for (2) by issuance of (0.5) additional share 08/15/1985
Common $4 par changed to $2 par 11/21/1985
Stock Dividends - 20% 11/14/1980; 20% 05/17/1982; 50% 02/28/1983; 20% 07/27/1984; 20% 01/24/1985
Merged into Dominion Bankshares Corp. 01/30/1987
Each share Common $2 par exchanged for (1.108) shares Common $5 par
Dominion Bankshares Corp. merged into First Union Corp. 03/01/1993 which name changed to Wachovia Corp. (Ctfs. dated after 09/01/2001) 09/01/2001 which merged into Wells Fargo & Co. (New) 12/31/2008

NASHVILLE CTRY CLUB INC (TN)
Reincorporated under the laws of Delaware as TBA Entertainment Corp. 9/8/97
(See TBA Entertainment Corp.)

NASHVILLE ELECTRONICS INC. (TN)
Name changed to Whale Electronics, Inc. 6/30/67
Whale Electronics, Inc. name changed to Whale, Inc. 1/31/69
(See Whale, Inc.)

NASHVILLE FREE PRESS, INC. (TN)
Charter revoked for non-payment of taxes 3/9/38

NASHVILLE GAS & HEATING CO.
Reorganized in 1937
No stockholders' equity

NASHVILLE RAILWAY & LIGHT CO.
Merged into Tennessee Electric Power Co. in 1926
Details not available

NASHVILLE RECORDS INC OLD (NV)
Each share old Common $0.001 par exchanged for (0.0005) share new Common $0.001 par 08/25/2008
Name changed to Welltek, Inc. (Ctfs. dated prior to 11/05/2009) 09/10/2008
Welltek, Inc. (Ctfs. dated prior to 11/05/2009) name changed to Nashville Records, Inc. (New) 11/05/2009

NASHVILLE SAVINGS & LOAN CORP. (TN)
Charter surrendered 12/31/1970

NASSAU & SUFFOLK LIGHTING CO.
Merged into Long Island Lighting Co. 00/00/1950
Each share 7% Preferred $100 par exchanged for (6.7) shares new Common no par
Long Island Lighting Co. merged into MarketSpan Corp. 05/29/1998 which name changed to KeySpan Energy 09/10/1998 which name changed to KeySpan Corp. 05/20/1999
(See KeySpan Corp.)

NASSAU BAY NATIONAL BANK (NASSAU BAY, TX)
Acquired by First International Bancshares, Inc. 12/31/75
Each share Common Capital Stock $10 par exchanged for (1.93) shares Common $5 par
First International Bancshares, Inc. name changed to InterFirst Corp. 12/31/81 which merged into First RepublicBank Corp. 6/6/87
(See First RepublicBank Corp.)

NASSAU BAY NATL BK CLEAR LAKE (HOUSTON, TX)
Stock Dividends - 11.111% 4/1/73; 25% 4/1/74
Merged into First International Bancshares, Inc. 12/31/75
Each share Common $10 par exchanged for (1.93) shares Common $5 par
First International Bancshares, Inc. name changed to InterFirst Corp. 12/31/81 which merged into First RepublicBank Corp. 6/6/87
(See First RepublicBank Corp.)

NASSAU-BEEKMAN REALTY CORP. (NY)
Dissolved 5/12/66
No stockholders' equity

NASSAU DEV CORP (CO)
Recapitalized as Primo's Holdings, Inc. 11/17/1989
Each share Common no par exchanged for (0.01) share Common no par

NASSAU ELECTRIC RAILROAD CO.
Acquired by the City of New York in 1940

NASSAU FD (NJ)
Acquired by Windsor Fund, Inc. (MD) 05/07/1979
Each share Common $1 par exchanged for (1.067) shares Capital Stock $1 par
Windsor Fund, Inc. (MD) reincorporated in Pennsylvania 01/02/1985 which reincorporated in Maryland as Windsor Funds, Inc. 12/30/1985 which name changed to Vanguard/Windsor Funds, Inc. (MD) 04/30/1993 which reincorporated in Delaware as Vanguard Windsor Funds 05/29/1998

NASSAU TROTTING ASSOCIATION, INC. (NY)
Merged into Roosevelt Raceway, Inc. 11/23/54
Each share Common $1 par exchanged for (0.4) share Common $3 par
Roosevelt Raceway, Inc. merged into Madison Square Garden Corp. (Mich.) 12/21/73
(See Madison Square Garden Corp. (Mich.))

NASSAU TR CO (GLEN COVE, NY)
Common $5 par changed to $2.50 par and (1) additional share issued 6/30/67
Stock Dividend - 100% 4/15/70
Merged into Norstar Bancorp Inc. 8/1/83
Each share Common $2.50 par exchanged for (0.7) share Common $5 par
Norstar Bancorp Inc. merged into Fleet/Norstar Financial Group, Inc. 1/1/88 which name changed to Fleet Financial Group, Inc. (New) 4/15/92 which name changed to Fleet Boston Corp. 10/1/99 which name changed to FleetBoston Financial Corp. 4/18/2000 which merged into Bank of America Corp. 4/1/2004

NASSAU VENTURES INC (DE)
Name changed to Megaworld Inc. 03/26/1997
Megaworld Inc. recapitalized as Power Sports Factory, Inc. 07/01/2005 which name changed to Heringrat 478, Inc. 07/14/2006 which name changed to United Music & Media Group, Inc. 06/23/2010 which recapitalized as New Generation Consumer Group, Inc. 10/07/2014

NASSCO MARINE CO. (CA)
6% Preferred $10 par called for redemption 7/20/60
Common $10 par changed to $1 par 10/11/60
Completely liquidated 10/18/60
Each share Common $1 par received first and final distribution of (1) share Westgate-California Corp. Class A Common $10 par
Certificates were not surrendered and are now valueless
(See Westgate-California Corp.)

NASSDA CORP (DE)
Issue Information - 5,000,000 shares COM offered at $11 per share on 12/12/2001
Merged into Synopsys, Inc. 5/11/2005
Each share Common $0.001 par exchanged for $7 cash
Note: Each share Common $0.001 par received an additional distribution of $0.15 cash from escrow 12/15/2005

NAST (NAT), INC (DE)
See - Nat Nast Inc

NASTA INTL INC (DE)
Merged into Tyco Toys, Inc. 10/15/90
Each share Common 1¢ par exchanged for $1.25 cash

NASTECH PHARMACEUTICAL INC (DE)
Each share Common $0.00001 par exchanged for (0.005) share Common $0.002 par 01/02/1990
Each share Common $0.002 par exchanged for (0.33333333) share Common $0.006 par 11/08/1993
Name changed to MDRNA, Inc. 06/11/2008
MDRNA, Inc. recapitalized as Marina Biotech, Inc. 07/22/2010 which name changed to Adhera Therapeutics, Inc. 10/09/2018

NASUS CONSULTING INC (NV)
Common $0.001 par split (20) for (1) by issuance of (19) additional shares payable 07/06/2009 to holders of record 07/01/2009
Ex date - 07/07/2009
Name changed to National Asset Recovery Corp. 10/06/2010

NAT NAST INC (DE)
Each share Class A Common 25¢ par exchanged for (0.1) share Common $2.50 par 10/06/1967
Stock Dividend - 100% 06/06/1972
Merged into Beatrice Foods Co. 01/25/1973
Each share Common $2.50 par exchanged for (1.0552) shares Common no par
Beatrice Foods Co. name changed to Beatrice Companies, Inc. 06/05/1984
(See Beatrice Companies, Inc.)

NATALMA INDS INC (NV)
Recapitalized as Tactical Air Defense Services, Inc. 9/14/2005
Each share Common no par exchanged for (1/3) share Common $0.001 par

NATAN RES LTD (BC)
Each share old Common no par exchanged for (0.1) share new Common no par 05/11/2016
Name changed to Enforcer Gold Corp. 03/02/2017

NATCHEZ, COLUMBIA & MOBILE RAILROAD CO.
Road abandoned in 1934

NATCO CORP. (PA)
Stock Dividends - 10% 04/30/1954; 10% 04/30/1955
Name changed to Fuqua Industries, Inc. (PA) 02/13/1967
Fuqua Industries, Inc. (PA) reincorporated in Delaware 05/06/1968 which name changed to Actava Group Inc. 07/21/1993 which name changed to Metromedia International Group, Inc. 11/01/1995
(See Metromedia International Group, Inc.)

NATCO GROUP INC (DE)
Class A Common 1¢ par reclassified as Common 1¢ par 01/01/2002
Acquired by Cameron International Corp. 11/18/2009
Each share Common 1¢ par exchanged for (1.185) shares Common 1¢ par
Cameron International Corp. merged into Schlumberger Ltd. 04/01/2016

NATCO INDS INC (DE)
Reorganized under Chapter 11 Federal Bankruptcy Code 12/10/1985
Each share Common 1¢ par received $1.50 cash
Note: Certificates were not required to be surrendered and are now valueless

NATCO INTERNATIONAL INC (DE)
Name changed to P2 Solar, Inc. 04/16/2009

NATCONTAINER CORP (DE)
Each share old Common 1¢ par exchanged for (0.0008) share new Common 1¢ par 02/18/1981
Note: In effect holders received $4.83 cash per share and public interest was eliminated

NATEC RES INC (UT)
Voluntarily dissolved 8/24/95
Details not available

NATEK CORP (DE)
Charter dissolved 5/24/82

NATEL ELECTR INDS INC (CA)
Common no par split (2) for (1) by issuance of (1) additional share 6/19/69
Name changed to MW International 1/1/74
(See MW International)

NATEL ENGR CO (CA)
Name changed to Natel Electronic Industries, Inc. 10/28/1968
Natel Electronic Industries, Inc. name changed to MW International 01/01/1974
(See MW International)

NATEX CORP (UT)
Name changed to Powerball International Inc. 05/26/2000
Powerball International Inc. name changed to Apollo Resources International, Inc. 02/03/2005
(See Apollo Resources International, Inc.)

NATEXCO CORP (NV)
Common $0.001 par split (4) for (1) by issuance of (3) additional shares payable 12/28/2001 to holders of

record 12/27/2001 Ex date - 01/04/2002
Name changed to Diomed Holdings, Inc. (NV) 02/14/2002
Diomed Holdings, Inc. (NV) reincorporated in Delaware 05/13/2002
(See Diomed Holdings, Inc.)

NATHAN HALE INVT CORP (IL)
Reverted to a private company 00/00/1982
Each share Class A Common $1 par exchanged for $0.11 cash

NATHAN HALE LIFE INSURANCE CO. (IL)
See - Hale (Nathan) Life Insurance Co.

NATHAN HALE LIFE INS CO N Y (NY)
Capital Stock $2 par changed to $1.60 par 12/31/1966
Acquired by Washington National Corp. 06/20/1972
Each share Capital Stock $1.60 par exchanged for $6.69 cash

NATHAN MINERALS INC (AB)
Delisted from Alberta Stock Exchange 03/30/1993

NATHANIEL ENERGY CORP NEW (DE)
Name changed to Vista International Technologies, Inc. 12/20/2007

NATHANIEL ENERGY CORP OLD (DE)
Under plan of reorganization each share Common $0.001 par automatically became (1) share Nathaniel Energy Corp. (New) Common $0.001 par 12/00/1998
Nathaniel Energy Corp. (New) name changed to Vista International Technologies, Inc. 12/20/2007

NATHANS FAMOUS INC (NY)
Common 10¢ par split (2) for (1) by issuance of (1) additional share 05/12/1969
Acquired by Equi-Cor Group Ltd. 07/23/1987
Each share Common 10¢ par exchanged for $8.50 cash

NATICK CHEMICAL INDUSTRIES, INC. (DE)
Charter cancelled and declared inoperative and void for non-payment of taxes 5/25/71

NATICK INDUSTRIES CORP. (MA)
Recapitalized under the laws of Delaware as Natick Chemical Industries, Inc. in 1955
Each share Common $1 par exchanged for (5) shares Common 1¢ par
Natick Chemical Industries, Inc. charter cancelled 5/21/71

NATICK TR CO (NATICK, MA)
Each share Common $100 par exchanged for (6) shares Common $25 par to effect a (4) for (1) split plus a 50% stock dividend 01/01/1952
Common $25 par changed to $10 par 03/01/1965
Stock Dividends - 33-1/3% 04/15/1960; 60% 03/10/1965; 25% 03/01/1968; 25% 03/02/1970; 20% 03/01/1974; 10% 05/01/1980; 10% 03/01/1982
98% acquired by UST Corp. through purchase offer which expired 03/05/1984
Public interest eliminated

NATION ENERGY INC (DE)
Reincorporated under the laws of Wyoming 6/13/2003

NATION LAKE MINES LTD (BC)
Recapitalized as Can-Nation Resources Ltd. 5/12/77
Each share Common 50¢ par exchanged for (1/3) share Common no par
(See Can-Nation Resources Ltd.)

NATION WIDE AUTO AUCTION LTD (NY)
Stock Dividend - 200% 12/31/1969
Adjudicated bankrupt 08/24/1971
Stockholders' equity unlikely

NATION WIDE CHECK CORP (MD)
Under plan of reorganization each share Common 25¢ par automatically became (1) share of Nation-Wide Diversified Corp. Common 25¢ par 12/21/76
Nation-Wide Diversified Corp. name changed to Monarch Avalon, Inc. 9/25/80 which name changed to Monarch Services Inc. (DE) 10/23/98 which reincorporated in Maryland 11/30/2000

NATION WIDE DIVERSIFIED CORP (DE)
Name changed to Monarch Avalon, Inc. 9/25/80
Monarch Avalon, Inc. name changed to Monarch Services Inc. (DE) 10/23/98 which reincorporated in Maryland 11/30/2000

NATION WIDE RES INC (AB)
Voluntarily dissolved 04/30/2009
Details not available

NATION WIDE SECURITIES CO. (CO)
Series A Trust Agreement terminated and liquidated 00/00/1945
Series B Trust Agreement terminated and liquidated 00/00/1950
Details not available

NATION WIDE SECURITIES CO. (MD)
Recapitalized as Nation-Wide Securities Co., Inc. in 1945
Each share Capital Stock 25¢ par exchanged for (0.1) share Capital Stock $1 par
Nation-Wide Securities Co., Inc. name changed to Bullock Balanced Shares, Inc. 1/14/85

NATION WIDE SECS INC (MD)
Stock Dividend - 100% 4/1/65
Name changed to Bullock Balanced Shares, Inc. 1/14/85
Bullock Balanced Shares, Inc. name changed to Alliance Balanced Shares, Inc. 3/13/87 which name changed to AllianceBernstein Balanced Shares, Inc. 3/31/2003

NATIONAL ACADEMY COMPUTER PROGRAMMING INC (NJ)
Name changed to Career Guidance Corp. 04/21/1972
(See Career Guidance Corp.)

NATIONAL ACCEPTANCE CORP. (DC)
Charter revoked for failure to file reports and pay fees 9/11/67

NATIONAL ACCIDENT & HEALTH INSURANCE CO. OF PHILADELPHIA (PA)
Name changed to Integrity National Life Insurance Co. 5/28/65
(See Integrity National Life Insurance Co.)

NATIONAL ACCOMODATIONS INC (CA)
Merged into NAI Newco 04/11/1977
Each share Common 10¢ par exchanged for $3.30 cash

NATIONAL ACME CO. (OH)
Capital Stock $10 par changed to $1 par in 1933
Capital Stock $1 par split (2) for (1) by issuance of (1) additional share 4/23/65
Under plan of merger name changed to Acme-Cleveland Corp. 10/25/68
(See Acme-Cleveland Corp.)

NATIONAL ACQUISITION CORP (MN)
Merged into Garment Graphics Inc. 05/25/1993
Each share Common no par exchanged for (0.25) share Common $0.001 par and (0.125) Common Stock Purchase Warrant expiring 05/26/1996
(See Garment Graphics Inc.)

NATIONAL ACQUISITIONS CORP (CO)
Recapitalized as Resaca, Inc. 01/17/1986
Each (15) shares Common $0.001 par exchanged for (1) share Common $0.001 par

NATIONAL AERONAUTICAL CORP. (NJ)
Each share Common no par exchanged for (5) shares Common $1 par 03/31/1958
Common $1 par split (2) for (1) by issuance of (1) additional share 08/06/1959
Name changed to Narco Scientific Industries, Inc. (NJ) 05/01/1967
Narco Scientific Industries, Inc. (NJ) reincorporated in Delaware 03/29/1968 which name changed to Narco Scientific, Inc. 03/30/1978 which merged into Healthdyne, Inc. 01/27/1983 which merged into Matria Healthcare, Inc. 03/08/1996 which merged into Inverness Medical Innovations, Inc. 05/09/2008 which name changed to Alere Inc. 07/14/2010
(See Alere Inc.)

NATIONAL AFFILIATED CORP (LA)
Class B Common no par reclassified as Common no par 4/27/90
Name changed to Lifeone Inc. 7/31/98
(See Lifeone, Inc.)

NATIONAL AGGRESSIVE GROWTH FD INC (MA)
Name changed to National Worldwide Opportunities Fund and Common $1 par reclassified as Shares of Bene. Int. $1 par 12/17/90
(See National Worldwide Opportunities Fund)

NATIONAL AGROL CO.
Out of existence 00/00/1951
Details not available

NATIONAL AIR CORP (NV)
Each share old Common $0.001 par exchanged for (0.05) share new Common $0.001 par 07/31/1996
Name changed to Berens Industries, Inc. 08/02/1999
Berens Industries, Inc. recapitalized as Crescent Communications, Inc. 09/25/2001 which recapitalized as Bluegate Corp. 11/23/2004 which recapitalized as Logicquest Technology, Inc. 03/19/2015

NATIONAL AIR TRANSPORT, INC.
Acquired by United Air Lines Transport Corp. in 1935
Details not available

NATIONAL AIRLS INC (FL)
Common $1 par changed to 50¢ par and (1) additional share issued 11/23/1965
Common 50¢ par changed to 25¢ par and (1) additional share issued 11/21/1967
Stock Dividends - 33-1/3% 04/29/1944; 20% 01/15/1946
Merged into Pan American World Airways, Inc. 01/07/1980
Each share Common 25¢ par exchanged for $50 cash

NATIONAL AIROIL BURNER CO. (DE)
Company became private 00/00/1971
Details not available

NATIONAL ALFALFA DEHYDRATING & MLG CO (DE)
Recapitalized 07/24/1957
Each share 5% Preferred $50 par exchanged for $50 principal amount of 5% Debentures and a warrant to purchase (0.5) share Common $3 par
Common $1 par changed to $3 par Merged into Bass Brothers Enterprises, Inc. 05/17/1976
Each share Common $3 par exchanged for $6.45 cash

NATIONAL ALUMINATE CORP. (DE)
Common $2.50 par split (2) for (1) by issuance of (1) additional share 5/11/55
Name changed to Nalco Chemical Co. 4/30/59

NATIONAL AMERN BANCORP INC (PA)
Acquired by Keystone Financial, Inc. 12/29/95
Each share Common $5 par exchanged for (2) shares Common $5 par
Keystone Financial, Inc. merged into M&T Bank Corp. 10/6/2000

NATIONAL AMERICAN CO., INC.
Bankrupt in 1935

NATIONAL AMERICAN CORP. (LA)
Merged into First Colonial Corp. of America 8/31/65
Each share Preferred $10 par exchanged for either (1) share Preferred $10 par or (1.769) shares Common $1 par
Each share Common no par exchanged for (2.818) shares Common $1 par
(See First Colonial Corp. of America)

NATIONAL AMERN CORP (DE)
Name changed to NAC Industries Corp. 1/26/82
(See NAC Industries Corp.)

NATIONAL AMERICAN ENTERPRISES INC. (ID)
Charter forfeited for failure to file reports 11/30/78

NATIONAL AMERN INDS (NV)
Incorporated 07/25/1932
Ctfs. dated after 03/12/1969
Each share old Common 10¢ par exchanged for (0.2) share new Common 10¢ par 09/25/1969
Name changed to Vaportech Corp. 07/01/1971

NATIONAL AMERICAN INDUSTRIES (NV)
Incorporated 11/22/1957
Ctfs. dated prior to 03/13/1969
Each share Common 10¢ par exchanged for (0.166666) share Common 60¢ par 08/11/1960
Charter revoked for failure to file reports and pay fees 03/04/1963

NATIONAL AMERN INS CO (NE)
Acquired by Ahmanson (H.F.) & Co. 11/09/1974
Each share Capital Stock $50 par exchanged for $1,139 cash

NATIONAL AMERN LIFE INS CO (LA)
Each share Common 10¢ par exchanged for (0.2) share Common 50¢ par 04/22/1963
Each share Common 50¢ par exchanged for (0.5) share Common $1 par 04/17/1972
Stock Dividend - 10% 10/01/1965
Merged into NALICO Insurance Co. 06/30/1981
Each share Common $1 par exchanged for $0.50 cash

NATIONAL ANESTHESIA CORP. (DE)
No longer in existence having become inoperative and void for non-payment of taxes 4/1/63

NATIONAL ANN ARBOR CORP (MI)
Stock Dividends - 50% 4/21/77; 10% 4/20/79
Merged into NBD Bancorp, Inc. 6/1/81
Each share Common $10 par exchanged for $65.25 principal amount of NBD Bancorp, Inc. 12% Installment Notes due 1984-1988 or $65.25 cash

NATIONAL ANNUITY LIFE INSURANCE CO. (AZ)
Receivership terminated 12/30/96
No stockholders' equity

NATIONAL APEX INDUSTRIES CORP. (OH)
Out of business in 1964
No stockholders' equity

NATIONAL APPAREL CORP (DE)
Name changed to NAC Inc. and Common 33-1/3¢ par changed to 1¢ par 06/23/1978
NAC Inc. recapitalized as Seal Inc. 11/02/1981
(See Seal Inc.)

NATIONAL ARBITRAGE CORP (NY)
Class A 5¢ par changed to 3-1/3¢ par and (0.5) additional share issued 9/18/68
Class A 3-1/3¢ par split (2) for (1) by issuance of (1) additional share 3/17/70
Name changed to Geosearch Inc. 7/16/76
(See Geosearch, Inc.)

NATIONAL ASSET BK (HOUSTON, TX)
Liquidation completed
Each share Common 1¢ par received initial distribution of $0.15 cash 02/15/1989
Each share Common 1¢ par received second distribution of $0.15 cash 08/31/1989
Each share Common 1¢ par received third distribution of $0.15 cash 02/28/1990
Each share Common 1¢ par received fourth distribution of $0.15 cash 12/27/1990
Each share Common 1¢ par received fifth and final distribution of (0.1) share NAB Asset Corp. Common 1¢ par 07/25/1991
Note: Certificates were not required to be surrendered and are without value
(See NAB Asset Corp.)

NATIONAL ASSET RESV (MA)
Merged into Phoenix Asset Reserve Fund 12/31/1993
Details not available

NATIONAL ASSETS CORP.
Bankrupt in 1932

NATIONAL ASSOCIATED INVESTORS
Liquidation completed in 1938

NATIONAL ASSOCIATION LIFE INSURANCE CO., INC. (DE)
Merged into American Association Old Line Life Insurance Co. 10/15/65
Each share Common $1 par exchanged for (2) shares Common $1 par
American Association Old Line Life Insurance Co. merged into American Pyramid Companies Inc. 12/10/69 which merged into American Consolidated Corp. 2/28/77 which merged into I.C.H. Corp. 4/18/85 which name changed to Southwestern Life Corp. (New) 6/15/94 which name changed to I.C.H. Corp. (New) 10/10/95
(See I.C.H. Corp. (New))

NATIONAL ATLANTIC HLDGS CORP (NJ)
Issue Information - 6,650,000 shares COM offered at $12 per share on 04/20/2005
Merged into Palisades Safety & Insurance Association 08/01/2008
Each share Common no par exchanged for $6.25 cash

NATIONAL ATTORNEYS TITLE INS CO (NY)
Capital Stock $5 par changed to $7.50 par 12/31/1983
Name changed to New York TRW Title Insurance Co. 02/12/1990
(See New York TRW Title Insurance Co.)

NATIONAL AUSTRALIA BK LTD (AUSTRALIA)
7.875% Exchangeable Capital Units called for redemption at $25 plus $0.4648 accrued dividends on 04/18/2007
(Additional Information in Active)

NATIONAL AUTO BROKERS CORP (PA)
Name changed to Nabcor, Inc. 04/02/1974
(See Nabcor, Inc.)

NATIONAL AUTO CR INC NEW (DE)
Name changed to iDNA, Inc. 03/08/2006
(See iDNA, Inc.)

NATIONAL AUTO CR INC OLD (DE)
Stock Dividend - 10% payable 04/30/1996 to holders of record 04/15/1996
Under plan of reorganization each share Common 5¢ par automatically became (1) share National Auto Credit Inc. (New) 12/28/1995
National Auto Credit Inc. name changed to iDNA, Inc. 03/08/2006
(See iDNA, Inc.)

NATIONAL AUTO FIN INC (DE)
Issue Information - 2,000,000 shares COM offered at $8.50 per share on 01/29/1997
Name changed to National Auto Receivables Liquidation, Inc. 1/8/2001
National Auto Receivables Liquidation, Inc. recapitalized as Cobra Energy, Inc. 3/4/2005

NATIONAL AUTO RECEIVABLES LIQ INC (DE)
Recapitalized as Cobra Energy, Inc. 3/4/2005
Each share Common 1¢ par exchanged for (0.001) share Common 1¢ par

NATIONAL AUTO SVC CTRS INC (FL)
Recapitalized as National Automotive Industries, Inc. 10/1/74
Each share Common 1¢ par exchanged for (2) shares Common 1¢ par
National Automotive Industries, Inc. name changed to General Energy Development, Inc. 8/21/78 which reincorporated in Delaware as Beck Group, Inc. 11/22/85
(See Beck Group, Inc.)

NATIONAL AUTOMATIC VENDING LTD (ON)
Name changed to Navco Food Services Ltd. 7/4/69
Navco Food Services Ltd. name changed to Canvedo Industries Ltd. 4/1/72 which recapitalized as Corporate Master Ltd. 11/19/73
(See Corporate Master Ltd.)

NATIONAL AUTOMATION SVCS INC (NV)
Each share old Common $0.001 par exchanged for (0.005) share new Common $0.001 par 12/11/2014
Name changed to National Energy Services, Inc. 07/15/2015

NATIONAL AUTOMOTIVE FIBRES, INC. (DE)
Recapitalized in 1930
Preferred no par exchanged for new Preferred no par
Common no par exchanged for Class A no par
Recapitalized in 1937
Each share Class A no par exchanged for (2) shares new Common $1 par
Recapitalized in 1949
Common $1 par redesignated as Capital Stock $1 par
Stock Dividend - 10% 12/1/55
Name changed to Nafi Corp. 4/27/59
Nafi Corp. name changed to Chris-Craft Industries, Inc. 4/30/62 which merged into News Corp., Ltd. 7/31/2001 which reorganized as News Corp. 11/3/2004

NATIONAL AUTOMOTIVE INDS INC (FL)
Name changed to General Energy Development, Inc. 8/21/78
General Energy Development, Inc. reincorporated in Delaware as Beck Group, Inc. 11/22/82
(See Beck Group, Inc.)

NATIONAL AVIATION & TECHNOLOGY CORP (NY)
Capital Stock $5 par split (4) for (1) by issuance of (3) additional shares 06/13/1980
Merged into AFA Funds, Inc. 05/01/1990
Each share Capital Stock $5 par exchanged for (1) share National Aviation & Technology Fund Common $1.25 par
AFA Funds, Inc. name changed to Hancock (John) Technology Series, Inc. 12/20/1991
(See Hancock (John) Technology Series, Inc.)

NATIONAL AVIATION CORP. (NY)
Capital Stock no par changed to $5 par 00/00/1938
Name changed to National Aviation & Technology Corp. 03/26/1976
National Aviation & Technology Corp. merged into AFA Funds, Inc. 05/01/1990 which name changed to Hancock (John) Technology Series, Inc. 12/20/1991
(See Hancock (John) Technology Series, Inc.)

NATIONAL AVIATION UNDERWRITERS INC (MO)
Common 50¢ par changed to 25¢ par and (1) additional share issued 08/24/1965
Stock Dividend - 100% 10/15/1971
Name changed to Navco Corp. 05/16/1980
(See Navco Corp.)

NATIONAL BAGASSE PRODUCTS CORP. (DE)
No longer in existence having become inoperative and void for non-payment of taxes 4/1/66

NATIONAL BAKING CO.
Name changed to Omar, Inc. in 1938
Omar, Inc. name changed to Ramo Investment Co. 11/29/58 which name changed to Ramo, Inc. 11/21/60 which merged into Telecom Corp. 11/23/71 which name changed to TCC Industries, Inc. 6/1/94
(See TCC Industries, Inc.)

NATIONAL BANC COMM CO (WV)
Common $5 par split (2) for (1) by issuance of (1) additional share 03/20/1984
Common $5 par changed to $2.50 par and (1) additional share issued 04/17/1986
Common $2.50 par changed to $1.25 par and (1) additional share issued 08/26/1986
Common $1.25 par changed to $1 par and (0.5) additional share issued 05/09/1988
Name changed to Commerce Banc Corp. 04/21/1992
Commerce Banc Corp. merged into Huntington Bancshares Inc. 09/24/1993

NATIONAL BANCORP (IN)
Merged into CNB Bancshares Inc. 8/3/98
Each share Common $5 par exchanged for (3.45) shares Common no par
CNB Bancshares Inc. merged into Fifth Third Bancorp 10/29/99

NATIONAL BANCORP ALASKA INC (DE)
Common $10 par split (4) for (3) by issuance of (1/3) additional share 10/07/1983
Common $10 par split (5) for (4) by issuance of (0.25) additional share 10/04/1985
Common $10 par split (4) for (3) by issuance of (1/3) additional share 05/04/1990
Common $10 par changed to $2.50 par and (3) additional shares issued payable 04/10/1998 to holders of record 04/03/1998
Stock Dividend - 20% 10/02/1987
Merged into Wells Fargo & Co. (New) 07/14/2000
Each share Common $2.50 par exchanged for (0.896303) share Common $1-2/3 par

NATIONAL BANCORPORATION OF AMERICA, INC.
Out of existence 00/00/1933
Details not available

NATIONAL BANCSERVICE CORP.
Dissolved in 1940
No Common stockholders' equity

NATIONAL BANCSHARES CORP (DE)
Acquired by Worthen Banking Corp. 04/03/1989
Details not available

NATIONAL BANCSHARES CORP (OH)
Common $10 par split (5) for (4) by issuance of (0.25) additional share payable 12/15/1995 to holders of record 11/30/1995 Ex date - 12/18/1995
Common $10 par changed to no par and (1) additional share issued payable 05/29/1998 to holders of record 05/15/1998
Merged into Farmers National Banc Corp. 06/19/2015
Each share Common no par exchanged for (1.730292) shares Common no par and $18.366127 cash

NATIONAL BANCSHARES CORP TEX (TX)
Common $10 par changed to $5 par and (1) additional share issued 05/29/1981
Stock Dividends - 20% 11/15/1973; 25% 07/15/1976; 25% 12/15/1978; 10% 12/12/1980; 15% 11/29/1985
Plan of reorganization under Chapter 11 Federal Bankruptcy proceedings effective 05/26/1992
No stockholders' equity for Common $5 par
Each share old Common 1¢ par exchanged for (0.125) share new Common 1¢ par 09/12/1994
Preferred Ser. A called for redemption 12/01/1995
Merged into International Bancshares Corp. 12/31/2001
Each share new Common 1¢ par exchanged for $24.75 cash

NATIONAL BANK & TRUST CO. (CHARLOTTESVILLE, VA)
Common $12.50 par changed to $5 par and (1.5) additional shares issued 07/11/1961
Stock Dividends - 66-2/3% 03/02/1942; 50% 01/11/1957; 33-1/3% 03/31/1965; 10% 01/31/1969
Reorganized as N B Corp. 05/01/1969
Each share Common $5 par exchanged for (1) share Common $5 par
N B Corp. merged into Jefferson Bankshares, Inc. 12/31/1979 which merged into Wachovia Corp. (New) (Ctfs. dated between 05/20/1991 and 09/01/2001) 10/31/1997 which

merged into Wachovia Corp. (Ctfs. dated after 09/01/2001) 09/01/2001 which merged into Wells Fargo & Co. (New) 12/31/2008

NATIONAL BANK & TRUST CO. (COLUMBUS, GA)
Merged into Trust Co. of Georgia 8/17/78
Each share Capital Stock $10 par exchanged for (0.5771) share Common $5 par
Trust Co. of Georgia merged into SunTrust Banks, Inc. 7/1/85

NATIONAL BK & TR CO (ANN ARBOR, MI)
Common $20 par changed to $10 par and (1) additional share issued plus a 10% stock dividend paid 03/10/1968
Stock Dividends - 25% 11/15/1965; 15% 01/28/1971; 25% 03/22/1973
Merged into National Ann Arbor Corp. 03/18/1974
Each share Common $10 par exchanged for (1) share Common $10 par
(See National Ann Arbor Corp.)

NATIONAL BK & TR CO (KENNETT SQUARE, PA)
Stock Dividend - 100% 04/17/1972
Acquired by American Bancorp, Inc. 03/26/1982
Each share Capital Stock $10 par exchanged for (8.25) shares Capital Stock $5 par
American Bancorp, Inc. merged into Meridian Bancorp, Inc. 06/30/1983 which merged into CoreStates Financial Corp 04/09/1996 which merged into First Union Corp. 04/28/1998 which name changed to Wachovia Corp. (Ctfs. dated after 09/01/2001) 09/01/2001 which merged into Wells Fargo & Co. (New) 12/31/2008

NATIONAL BK & TR CO (NORWICH, NY)
Capital Stock $20 par changed to $5 par and (3) additional shares issued 10/01/1973
Stock Dividends - 25% 00/00/1946; 20% 03/05/1952; 11-1/9% 02/23/1955; 10% 02/23/1960; 10% 12/15/1983; 10% 12/14/1984
Reorganized as NBT Bancorp Inc. 05/17/1986
Each share Capital Stock $5 par exchanged for (1) share Common $0.0001 par

NATIONAL BK & TR CO (SOUTH BEND, IN)
Capital Stock $10 par split (2) for (1) by issuance of (1) additional share 04/18/1986
Stock Dividends - 11-1/9% 12/27/1945; 25% 03/22/1965; 40% 10/06/1967; 20% 04/26/1971; 15% 05/31/1974; 10% 12/05/1979
Name changed to First Interstate Bank of Northern Indiana, N.A. (South Bend, IN) 06/30/1986
(See First Interstate Bank of Northern Indiana, N.A. (South Bend, IN))

NATIONAL BK & TR CO CENT PA (YORK, PA)
Merged into National Central Bank (Lancaster, PA) 12/07/1970
Each share Capital Stock $10 par exchanged for (1.1) shares Common $10 par
National Central Bank (Lancaster, PA) reorganized as National Central Financial Corp. 12/31/1972 which merged into CoreStates Financial Corp 05/02/1983 which merged into First Union Corp. 04/28/1998 which name changed to Wachovia Corp. (Ctfs. dated after 09/01/2001) 09/01/2001 which merged into Wells Fargo & Co. (New) 12/31/2008

NATIONAL BK & TR CO GLOUCESTER CNTY (WOODBURY, NJ)
Capital Stock $10 par changed to $5 par and (1) additional share issued plus a 100% stock dividend paid 12/18/1972
Reorganized as Community Bancshares Corp. 10/01/1975
Each share Capital Stock $5 par exchanged for (1) share Common $5 par
Community Bancshares Corp. merged into First Fidelity Bancorporation (Old) 09/28/1985 which merged into First Fidelity Bancorporation (New) 02/29/1988 which merged into First Union Corp. 01/01/1996 which name changed to Wachovia Corp. (Ctfs. dated after 09/01/2001) 09/01/2001 which merged into Wells Fargo & Co. (New) 12/31/2008

NATIONAL BK (CAMBRIDGE, MD)
Under plan of reorganization each share Common 1¢ par automatically became (1) share Delmarva Bancshares, Inc. Common 1¢ par 09/01/1998

NATIONAL BK ALASKA (ANCHORAGE, AK)
Each share Capital Stock $50 par exchanged for (10) shares Capital Stock $10 par to effect a (5) for (1) split and 100% stock dividend 04/01/1960
Stock Dividends - 40% 01/21/1959; 25% 12/07/1965; 33-1/3% 11/27/1967; 25% 08/25/1969; 16.505% 03/15/1972; 50% 06/16/1972; 33-1/3% 09/14/1973; 29.65964% 10/10/1975; 24.872% 11/11/1977; 25% 08/17/1979; 20% 05/15/1981
Reorganized as National Bancorp of Alaska, Inc. 12/01/1982
Each share Capital Stock $10 par exchanged for (1) share Common $10 par
National Bancorp of Alaska, Inc. merged into Wells Fargo & Co. (New) 07/14/2000

NATIONAL BK ALBANY (ALBANY, GA)
Name changed to First National Bank (Albany, GA) 11/15/1972
First National Bank (Albany, GA) merged into Trust Co. of Georgia 07/01/1977 which merged into SunTrust Banks, Inc. 07/01/1985

NATIONAL BK ALBANY PARK (CHICAGO, IL)
Each share Capital Stock $14 par exchanged for (1.163636) shares Capital Stock $12.50 par which includes a 4% stock dividend 7/10/57
Voting Trust Agreement terminated 5/11/62
Each VTC for Capital Stock $12.50 par exchanged for (1) share Capital Stock $12.50 par
Stock Dividends - 10% 7/23/56; 10% 12/10/67; 10% 12/10/69
Name changed to Albany Bank & Trust Co., N.A. (Chicago, IL) 5/15/77
(See Albany Bank & Trust Co., N.A. (Chicago, IL))

NATIONAL BK AUSTIN (CHICAGO, IL)
Capital Stock $50 par changed to $10 par and (4) additional shares issued 02/28/1972
Stock Dividends - 25% 07/16/1957; 25% 07/01/1960; 25% 07/01/1964; 11-1/9% 02/13/1967; 25% 02/14/1969
Name changed to Austin Bank (Chicago, IL) 07/02/1979
(See Austin Bank (Chicago, IL))

NATIONAL BK AUSTRALASIA LTD (MELBOURNE, AUSTRALIA)
Stock Dividends - 10% 11/25/64; 10% 11/24/65; 10% 11/30/66; 10% 11/30/67; 11% 11/28/68; 11% 11/27/69; 12% 11/26/70; 12% 12/16/71; 11.5% 12/14/72; 12% 12/20/73; 13% 12/19/74; 13-1/2% 12/19/75; 14% 12/20/76; 14-1/2% 12/19/77; 15% 12/18/78; 15% 12/18/79; 18% 12/18/80
Name changed to National Commercial Banking Corp. of Australia Ltd. 1/4/83
National Commercial Banking Corp. of Australia Ltd. name changed to National Australia Bank Ltd. 10/4/84

NATIONAL BK BEAVER CNTY (MONACA, PA)
Merged into Century National Bank & Trust Co. (Rochester, PA) 12/09/1985
Each share Capital Stock $25 par exchanged for (1) share Common $5 par
Century National Bank & Trust Co. (Rochester, PA) reorganized as Century Financial Corp. 06/01/1988 which merged into Citizens Bancshares, Inc. 05/12/1998 which name changed to Sky Financial Group, Inc. 10/02/1998 which merged into Huntington Bancshares Inc. 07/02/2007

NATIONAL BK BOYERTOWN (BOYERTOWN, PA)
Stock Dividend - 100% 11/17/1972
Under plan of reorganization each share Capital Stock $5 par automatically became (1) share National Penn Bancshares, Inc. Common $5 par 10/01/1982
National Penn Bancshares, Inc. merged into BB&T Corp. 04/01/2016

NATIONAL BK CALIF (LOS ANGELES, CA)
Under plan of reorganization each share Common $5 par automatically became (1) share NCAL Bancorp Common no par 09/29/2000
(See NCAL Bancorp)

NATIONAL BK CDA (MONTREAL, QC)
Conv. Class A Preferred $31 par called for redemption 11/01/1985
15% 1st Preferred Ser. 4 no par called for redemption 02/17/1987
1st Preferred Ser. 6 no par called for redemption 01/01/1993
Adjustable Dividend 1st Preferred Ser. 9 no par called for redemption 10/16/1995
Floating Rate 1st Preferred Ser. 7 no par called for redemption at $25 plus $0.198 accrued dividends on 10/15/1998
Adjustable Rate 1st Preferred Ser. 8 no par called for redemption at $25 plus $0.1898 accrued dividends on 10/15/1998
Adjustable Dividend 1st Preferred Ser. 10 no par called for redemption at $25 on 11/16/2001
Adjustable Dividend 1st Preferred Ser. 11 no par called for redemption at $25 plus $0.50 accrued dividends on 02/15/2002
Adjustable Dividend 1st Preferred Ser. 12 no par called for redemption at $25 plus $0.40625 accrued dividends on 05/15/2003
1st Preferred Ser. 13 no par called for redemption at $25 plus $0.40 accrued dividends on 08/15/2005
Fixed Rate 1st Preferred Ser. 15 no par called for redemption at $25 plus $0.24442 accrued dividends on 01/15/2013
Non-Cum. 5 Year Rate Reset 1st Preferred Ser. 21 no par called for redemption at $25 plus $0.0335940 accrued dividends on 08/16/2013
5 Year Rate Reset 1st Preferred Ser. 24 no par called for redemption at $25 on 02/15/2014
Non-Cum. 5 Year Rate Reset 1st Preferred Ser. 26 no par called for redemption at $25 on 02/15/2014
4.85% 1st Preferred Ser. 16 no par called for redemption at $25 on 11/15/2014
Non-Cum. Fixed Rate 1st Preferred Ser. 20 no par called for redemption at $25.50 on 11/15/2015
5 Year Rate Reset 1st Preferred Ser. 28 no par called for redemption at $25 on 11/15/2017
(Additional Information in Active)

NATIONAL BK CHESTER CNTY & TR CO (WEST CHESTER, PA)
Each share Capital Stock $100 par exchanged for (10) shares Capital Stock $10 par 01/24/1956
Stock Dividend - 25% 02/02/1961
Merged into Southeast National Bank of Pennsylvania (Chester, PA) 01/01/1970
Each share Capital Stock $10 par exchanged for (3.75) shares Common $3.33-1/3 par and $3 cash
Southeast National Bank of Pennsylvania (Chester, PA) reorganized as Southeast National Bancshares of Pennsylvania 01/04/1982 which merged into Fidelcor, Inc. 06/30/1983 which merged into First Fidelity Bancorporation (New) 02/29/1988
(See First Fidelity Bancorporation (New))

NATIONAL BK COMM (BIRMINGHAM, AL)
Common $5 par changed to $2.50 par 11/19/1974
Under plan of reorganization each share Common $2.50 par automatically became (1) share National Commerce Corp. Common $2.50 par 12/26/1979
National Commerce Corp. merged into Alabama National BanCorporation (DE) 01/03/1996 which merged into Royal Bank of Canada (Montreal, QUE) 02/22/2008

NATIONAL BK COMM (CHARLESTON, WV)
Reorganized as National Banc of Commerce Co. 05/02/1983
Each share Capital Stock $100 par exchanged for (1) share Common $5 par
National Banc of Commerce Co. name changed to Commerce Banc Corp. 04/21/1992 which merged into Huntington Bancshares Inc. 09/24/1993

NATIONAL BK COMM (DALLAS, TX)
Common $100 par changed to $10 par and (9) additional shares issued plus a 33-1/3% stock dividend paid 5/21/61
Common $10 par changed to $7.50 par and (1/3) additional share issued 2/25/66
Common $7.50 par changed to $1 par 3/2/76
6% Conv. Preferred $22 par called for redemption 9/29/78
Stock Dividends - 100% 1/22/58; 25% 2/14/62; 10% 2/19/71
Reorganized as Commerce Southwest Inc. 3/16/79
Each share Class A Conv. Preferred $8 par exchanged for (1) share Class A Conv. Preferred $8 par
Each share Common $1 par exchanged for (1) share Common $1 par
Commerce Southwest Inc. name changed to BancTEXAS Group Inc. 8/31/82 which recapitalized as First Banks America, Inc. 8/31/95

NATIONAL BK COMM (LINCOLN, NE)
Each share Capital Stock $100 par

NAT-NAT   FINANCIAL INFORMATION, INC.

exchanged for (5.625) shares
Capital Stock $20 par to effect a (5)
for (1) split and 12-1/2% stock
dividend 11/23/53
Stock Dividends - 42.9% 12/4/44;
20% 12/4/47; 20% 10/4/51; 15%
10/31/55; 10% 12/3/57; 10% 1/19/60
Merged into National Bank of
Commerce Trust & Savings
Association (Lincoln, NE) 9/8/61
Each share Capital Stock $20 par
exchanged for (1) share Capital
Stock $20 par
National Bank of Commerce Trust &
Savings Association (Lincoln, NE)
reorganized as NBC Co. 3/24/69
which name changed to Commerce
Group, Inc. 5/22/78 which merged
into First Commerce Bancshares,
Inc. 9/30/87 which merged into
Wells Fargo & Co. 6/16/2000

**NATIONAL BK COMM
(MEMPHIS, TN)**
Each share Capital Stock $100 par
exchanged for (4) shares Capital
Stock $25 par 00/00/1948
Each share Capital Stock $25 par
exchanged for (2.5) shares Capital
Stock $10 par 00/00/1951
Stock Dividends - 15% 02/20/1967;
100% 03/02/1969
98.70% held by United Tennessee
Bancshares Corp. as of 05/10/1971
Public interest eliminated

**NATIONAL BK COMM
(NEW ORLEANS, LA)**
Each share Common $20 par
exchanged for (2.2) shares Common
$10 par to effect a (2) for (1) split
and a 10% stock dividend 1/14/58
Stock Dividends - 20% 2/12/45; 20%
1/20/55; 10% 2/12/60; 10% 2/14/64;
10% 1/31/66
Under plan of reorganization each
share Common $10 par
automatically became (1) share First
Commerce Corp. (DE) Common $10
par 1/1/71
First Commerce Corp. (DE)
reincorporated in Louisiana 5/21/74

**NATIONAL BK COMM
(PINE BLUFF, AR)**
Each share old Capital Stock $100
par exchanged for (2) shares new
Capital Stock $100 par 02/21/1948
Each share new Capital Stock $100
par exchanged for (10) shares
Capital Stock $10 par 01/25/1955
Stock Dividends - 50% 02/26/1948;
50% 05/22/1950; 20% 06/26/1957;
25% 04/19/1962; 21.7% 03/01/1968;
33-1/3% 11/27/1972
Reorganized under the laws of
Delaware as National Bancshares
Corp. 12/31/1974
Each share Capital Stock $10 par
exchanged for (1) share Common
$10 par
(See National Bancshares Corp.)

**NATIONAL BK COMM
(SAN ANTONIO, TX)**
Each share Common Capital Stock
$100 par exchanged for (5) shares
Common Capital Stock $20 par
00/00/1946
Each share Common Capital Stock
$20 par exchanged for (2) shares
Common Capital Stock $10 par
03/31/1961
Stock Dividends - (0.68) for (5)
01/30/1940; 42.86% 12/31/1943;
35% 06/28/1946; 13-1/3%
04/01/1953; 50% 03/15/1955; 20%
03/01/1966
Under plan of reorganization each
share Common Capital Stock $10
par automatically became (1) share
National Bancshares Corp. of Texas
Common $10 par 04/03/1972
(See National Bancshares Corp. of
Texas)

**NATIONAL BK COMM FAIRFAX
CNTY SEVEN CORNERS VA
(FALLS CHURCH, VA)**
Through exchange offer Virginia
Commonwealth Bankshares, Inc.
acquired all but (1,504) shares
00/00/1967
Public interest eliminated

**NATIONAL BK COMM JEFFERSON
PARISH NEW ORLEANS LA
(JEFFERSON, LA)**
Common Capital Stock $10 par
changed to $5 par and (1) additional
share issued 12/31/78
Stock Dividends - 10% 2/28/69; 10%
3/6/70; 10% 3/5/71; 10% 3/15/72;
10% 3/15/73; 10% 3/22/74; 10%
3/21/75; 10% 5/22/76; 10% 3/25/77;
10% 6/2/78; 10% 6/30/79; 10%
9/30/80
Under plan of reorganization each
share Common Capital Stock $5 par
automatically became (1) share
NBC Bancshares, Inc.
Common $5 par 2/22/82
(See NBC Bancshares, Inc.)

**NATIONAL BK COMM TR & SVGS
ASSN (LINCOLN, ME)**
Each share Capital Stock $20 par
exchanged for (2.2) shares Capital
Stock $10 par to effect a (2) for (1)
split and 10% stock dividend 2/21/68
Reorganized as NBC Co. 3/24/69
Each share Capital Stock $10 par
exchanged for (2) shares Common
$5 par
NBC Co. name changed to
Commerce Group, Inc. 5/22/78
which merged into First Commerce
Bancshares, Inc. 9/30/87 which
merged into Wells Fargo & Co.
6/16/2000

**NATIONAL BK COMWLTH
(INDIANA, PA)**
Under plan of reorganization each
share Common $5 par automatically
became (1) share First
Commonwealth Financial Corp.
Common $5 par 04/29/1983

**NATIONAL BK DETROIT
(DETROIT, MI)**
Common $10 par changed to $12.50
par 1/30/59
Stock Dividends - 21.2122%
12/12/41; 20% 2/1/47; 19.732%
11/16/53; 11-1/2% 12/1/55; 10.444%
2/26/59; 12-1/2% 2/28/61; 11-1/9%
2/24/64; 20% 4/21/67; 25% 4/17/70
Reorganized as National Detroit Corp.
1/1/73
Each share Common $12.50 par
exchanged for (1) share Common
$12.50 par
National Detroit Corp. name changed
to NBD Bancorp, Inc. 4/30/81 which
name changed to NBD Bancorp, Inc.
12/1/95 which merged into Bank
One Corp. 10/2/98 which merged
into J.P. Morgan Chase & Co.
12/31/2000 which name changed to
JPMorgan Chase & Co. 7/20/2004

**NATIONAL BK FAIRFAX
(FAIRFAX, VA)**
Each share Common Capital Stock
$10 par exchanged for (1.1) shares Capital
Stock $5 par to effect a (2) for (1)
split plus a 10% stock dividend
8/11/72
Merged into First & Merchants Corp.
7/1/81
Each share Capital Stock $5 par
exchanged for (1.08) shares $2.37
Conv. Preferred Ser. A $25 par and
(0.75) share Common $7.50 par
First & Merchants Corp. merged into
Sovran Financial Corp. 12/31/83
which merged into C&S/Sovran
Corp. 9/1/90 which merged into
NationsBank Corp. 12/31/91 which
reincorporated in Delaware as
BankAmerica Corp. (Old) 9/25/98
which merged into BankAmerica

Corp. (New) 9/30/98 which name
changed to Bank of America Corp.
4/28/99

**NATIONAL BK FAR ROCKAWAY
NEW YORK N Y
(FAR ROCKAWAY, NY)**
Acquired by C.I.T. Financial Corp.
10/16/72
Each share Capital Stock $100 par
exchanged for (6.25) shares
Common no par
C.I.T. Financial Corp. merged into
RCA Corp. 1/31/80
(See RCA Corp.)

**NATIONAL BK FORT BENNING
(FORT BENNING, GA)**
Common $5 par changed to $2.50 par
and (1) additional share issued
12/6/68
Name changed to Fort Benning
National Bank (Fort Benning, GA)
7/1/81
(See Fort Benning National Bank
(Fort Benning, GA))

**NATIONAL BK FREDERICKSBURG
(FREDERICKSBURG, VA)**
Under plan of reorganization each
share Common $4 par automatically
became (1) share Fredericksburg
National Bancorp, Inc. Common $4
par 01/01/1983
Fredericksburg National Bancorp, Inc.
merged into Mercantile Bankshares
Corp. 12/01/1994 which merged into
PNC Financial Services Group, Inc.
03/02/2007

**NATIONAL BK FT SAM HOUSTON
(SAN ANTONIO, TX)**
Capital Stock $100 par changed to
$25 par and (3) additional shares
issued 01/12/1966
Capital Stock $25 par changed to $5
par and (4) additional shares issued
02/08/1968
Stock Dividends - 200% 05/06/1953;
100% 04/24/1958; 100%
04/18/1962; 100% 02/10/1971
Reorganized as Fort Sam Houston
Bankshares, Inc. 06/11/1975
Each share Capital Stock $5 par
exchanged for (1) share Common
$5 par
Fort Sam Houston Bankshares, Inc.
merged into Republic of Texas Corp.
01/01/1981 which name changed to
RepublicBank Corp. 06/30/1982
which merged into First
RepublicBank Corp. 06/06/1987
(See First RepublicBank Corp.)

NATIONAL BK GA (ATLANTA, GA)
Capital Stock $10 par changed to $5
par and (1) additional share issued
12/27/1972
Stock Dividends - 17.646%
09/01/1966; 10% 05/17/1967; 10%
04/22/1968; 10% 11/20/1975
Merged into GRP, Inc. 05/21/1982
Each share Capital Stock $5 par
exchanged for $11 cash

**NATIONAL BK GREECE S A
(GREECE)**
Sponsored GDR Reg. S for Ordinary
split (4) for (1) by issuance of (3)
additional GDR's payable
02/09/1999 to holders of record
02/04/1999
144A Sponsored GDR's for Ordinary
split (4) for (1) by issuance of (3)
additional GDR's payable
02/09/1999 to holders of record
02/04/1999
Each Sponsored GDR Reg. S for
Ordinary exchanged for (1)
Sponsored ADR for Ordinary
10/18/1999
GDR agreement terminated
04/05/2002
Each 144A Sponsored GDR for
Ordinary exchanged for $3.7641
cash
Each old Sponsored ADR for

Common exchanged for (0.2) new
Sponsored ADR for for Common
11/28/2011
Basis changed from (1:0.2) to (1:1)
11/28/2011
Each new Sponsored ADR for
Common exchanged again for (0.1)
new Sponsored ADR for Common
05/30/2013
Each new Sponsored ADR for
Common exchanged again for
(0.06666666) new Sponsored ADR
for Common 12/03/2015
Each ADR for Ser. A Preference
exchanged for (23.631723) new
Sponsored ADR's for Common
12/14/2015
Stock Dividends - in Sponsored
ADR's for Common to holders of
Sponsored ADR's for Common 40%
payable 05/19/2000 to holders of
record 05/08/2000 Ex date -
05/19/2000; 10% payable
06/10/2003 to holders of record
05/30/2003; 30% payable
06/22/2004 to holders of record
06/14/2004 Ex date - 06/23/2004;
4% payable 05/27/2008 to holders of
record 05/23/2008 Ex date -
05/21/2008
ADR agreement terminated
03/15/2018
Each new Sponsored ADR for
Common exchanged for $0.300697
cash

**NATIONAL BK HASTINGS
(HASTINGS, MI)**
Stock Dividend - 50% 04/27/1972
Merged into Sand Ridge Bank
(Highland, IN) 11/15/2002
Details not available

**NATIONAL BK JACKSON
(JACKSON, MI)**
Common $10 par changed to $15 par
00/00/1953
Common $15 par changed to $5 par
and (2) additional shares issued
01/28/1964
Stock Dividends - 50% 12/22/1941;
33-1/3% 11/06/1946; 25%
10/19/1949; 10% 01/31/1961; 20%
09/03/1965; 15% 01/29/1968; 10%
03/16/1970; 15% 04/02/1973; 10%
05/05/1975; 15% 06/15/1977; 15%
06/15/1979
Acquired by Comerica, Inc.
09/01/1982
Each share Common $5 par
exchanged for (1.2246305) shares
Common $5 par

**NATIONAL BK KEYSER
(KEYSER, WV)**
Common $10 par changed to $5 par
and (1) additional share issued
1/13/76
Reorganized as Potomac Bancorp,
Inc. in September 1983
Each share Common $5 par
exchanged for (1) share Common
$1 par
Potomac Bancorp, Inc. merged into
WM Bancorp which was acquired by
Keystone Financial, Inc. 1/7/94
which merged into M&T Bank Corp.
10/6/2000

**NATIONAL BK LEBANON
(LEBANON, NH)**
Common $10 par changed to $5 par
and (1) additional share issued
03/10/1976
Acquired by First NH Banks, Inc.
05/31/1985
Each share Common $5 par
exchanged for (1) share Conv.
Preferred Ser. I no par and (6.5)
shares Common $1 par
(See First NH Banks, Inc.)

NATIONAL BK LOGAN (LOGAN, WV)
Merged into Key Bancshares of West
Virginia, Inc. 10/8/84
Each share Capital Stock $25 par

exchanged for (1.75) shares Common $3 par
Key Bancshares of West Virginia, Inc. merged into Key Centurion Bancshares, Inc. 11/30/85 which merged into Banc One Corp. 5/3/93 which merged into Bank One Corp. 10/2/98 which merged into J.P. Morgan Chase & Co. 12/31/2000 which name changed to JPMorgan Chase & Co. 7/20/2004

NATIONAL BK LOGANSPORT (LOGANSPORT, IN)
Each share Common $100 par exchanged for (8) shares Common $25 par to effect a (4) for (1) split and 100% stock dividend 01/22/1952
Common $25 par changed to $10 par and (1.5) additional shares issued plus a 20% stock dividend paid 03/01/1968
Stock Dividends - 50% 01/31/1957; 33-1/3% 01/29/1960; 10% 03/01/1967; 10% 02/15/1971; 20% 03/15/1976
Name changed to First National Bank (Logansport, IN) 01/01/1978
First National Bank (Logansport, IN) reorganized as First National Bankshares, Inc. (IN) 05/31/1983
(See First National Bankshares, Inc. (IN))

NATIONAL BK MIDDLEBURY (MIDDLEBURY, VT)
Reorganized as Middlebury National Corp. 11/06/1985
Each share Common $2.50 par exchanged for (1) share Common no par

NATIONAL BK N J (NEW BRUNSWICK, NJ)
Common $25 par changed to $30 par 03/09/1943
Common $30 par changed to $35 par 11/23/1943
Common $35 par changed to $40 par 06/13/1944
Common $40 par changed to $45 par 10/13/1944
Common $45 par changed to $50 par 06/22/1945
Common $50 par changed to $55 par 12/01/1945
Common $55 par changed to $60 par 06/30/1946
Common $60 par changed to $65 par 12/02/1946
Common $65 par changed to $72.50 par 06/30/1948
Common $72.50 par changed to $87.50 par 04/29/1949
Common $87.50 par changed to $100 par 01/16/1950
Each share Common $100 par exchanged for (4) shares Common $25 par 01/27/1953
Common $25 par changed to $10 par and (1.5) additional shares issued 02/05/1957
Common $10 par changed to $5 par and (1) additional share issued 02/26/1965
Stock Dividends - 10% 02/03/1959; 10% 02/03/1961; 10% 02/04/1963
Reorganized as Fidelity Union Bancorporation 01/04/1971
Each share Common $5 par exchanged for (1.3) shares Common $5 par
Fidelity Union Bancorporation merged into First National State Bancorporation 04/05/1984 which name changed to First Fidelity Bancorporation (Old) 05/01/1985 which merged into First Fidelity Bancorporation (New) 02/29/1988 which merged into First Union Corp. 01/01/1996 which name changed to Wachovia Corp. (Ctfs. dated after 09/01/2001) 09/01/2001 which merged into Wells Fargo & Co. (New) 12/31/2008

NATIONAL BK NEW YORK CITY (FLUSHING, NY)
Each share old Common $10 par exchanged for (0.001) share new Common $10 par 12/29/2000
Note: In effect holders received $336 cash per share and public interest was eliminated

NATIONAL BK NORTH AMER (WEST HEMPSTEAD, NY)
Acquired by C.I.T. Financial Corp. 10/16/1972
Each share Capital Stock $5 par exchanged for $43 cash

NATIONAL BK NORTH EVANSTON (EVANSTON, IL)
Name changed to American National Bank of Evanston (Evanston, IL) 06/01/1987
American National Bank of Evanston (Evanston, IL) name changed to First Chicago Bank of Evanston, N.A. (Evanston, IL) 04/10/1989
(See First Chicago Bank of Evanston, N.A. (Evanston, IL))

NATIONAL BK NORTH KANSAS CITY (NORTH KANSAS CITY, MO)
Each share Capital Stock $100 par exchanged for (5) shares Capital Stock $20 par 2/2/61
Stock Dividend - 13.63% 03/11/1968
All but (75) shares held by directors or First Union, Inc. as of 03/31/1973
Public interest eliminated

NATIONAL BK NORTHN N Y (WATERTOWN, NY)
Merged into Key Banks Inc. 11/28/1980
Each share Common $10 par exchanged for $55 principal amount 10% 10-Yr. Promissory Installment Notes due 00/00/1980-00/00/1990, (3.5) shares
Common $5 par or $50 cash
Key Banks Inc. name changed to KeyCorp (NY) 08/28/1985 which merged into KeyCorp (New) (OH) 03/01/1994

NATIONAL BANK OF ARIZONA (SCOTTSDALE, AZ)
Bank failed 09/29/1989
No stockholders' equity

NATIONAL BANK OF BERKELEY (BERKELEY, CA)
Liquidation completed
Each share Common $10 par received initial distribution of $7 cash 7/5/67
Each share Common $10 par received second distribution of $7 cash 11/22/68
Each share Common $10 par exchanged for third and final distribution of $2.81 cash 12/7/72

NATIONAL BANK OF CHAMBERSBURG (CHAMBERSBURG, PA)
Merged into National Valley Bank & Trust Co. (Chambersburg, PA) 8/3/63
Each share Capital Stock $10 par exchanged for (1.275) shares Capital Stock $10 par
National Valley Bank & Trust Co. (Chambersburg, PA) reorganized as National Valley Corp. 12/31/69 which name changed to Valley Bancorp, Inc. 4/3/80 which was acquired by Dauphin Deposit Corp. 1/1/94 which merged into Allied Irish Banks, P.L.C. 7/8/97

NATIONAL BANK OF COMMERCE (CHICAGO, IL)
Capital Stock $100 par changed to $20 par and (4) additional shares issued 01/27/1959
Stock Dividends - 100% 06/30/1945; 25% 06/30/1950; 11.11111111% 01/15/1954
Merged into Central National Bank (Chicago, IL) 07/18/1964
Each share Capital Stock $20 par exchanged for (2.5) shares Capital Stock $10 par
Central National Bank (Chicago, IL) reorganized as Central National Chicago Corp. 09/30/1969 which merged into Exchange International Corp. 08/21/1982 which name changed to Exchange Bancorp, Inc. 05/17/1988
(See Exchange Bancorp, Inc.)

NATIONAL BANK OF COMMERCE (HOUSTON, TX)
Each share Common $100 par exchanged for (5) shares Common $20 par 00/00/1945
Common $20 par changed to $10 par and (1) additional share issued 01/16/1961
Stock Dividends - 25% 10/13/1955; 10% 01/20/1958; 17.806721% 01/24/1964
Merged into Texas National Bank of Commerce (Houston, TX) 01/17/1964
Each share Common $10 par exchanged for (1) share Capital Stock $10 par
Texas National Bank of Commerce (Houston, TX) name changed to Texas Commerce Bank N.A. (Houston, TX) 01/20/1970 which reorganized as Texas Commerce Bancshares, Inc. 07/07/1971 which was acquired by Chemical New York Corp. 05/01/1987 which name changed to Chemical Banking Corp. 04/29/1988 which name changed to Chase Manhattan Corp. (New) 03/31/1996 which name changed to J.P. Morgan Chase & Co. 12/31/2000 which name changed to JPMorgan Chase & Co. 07/20/2004

NATIONAL BANK OF COMMERCE (LAKE CHARLES, LA)
Merged into Premier Bancorp Inc. 4/30/94
Each share Common 25¢ par exchanged for (1.6) shares Common no par
Premier Bancorp Inc. merged into Banc One Corp. 1/2/96 which merged into Bank One Corp. 10/2/98 which merged into J.P. Morgan Chase & Co. 12/31/2000 which name changed to JPMorgan Chase & Co. 7/20/2004

NATIONAL BANK OF COMMERCE (LOS ANGELES, CA)
Under plan of merger name changed to Republic National Bank of California (Los Angeles) and Capital Stock $10 par reclassified as Common $10 par 2/29/68
Republic National Bank of California (Los Angeles) recapitalized as Republic National Bank & Trust Co. (Los Angeles) 7/15/70

NATIONAL BANK OF COMMERCE (NORFOLK, VA)
Each share Capital Stock $100 par exchanged for (5) shares Capital Stock $20 par in 1949
Each share Capital Stock $20 par exchanged for (2) shares Capital Stock $10 par 11/4/57
Merged into Virginia National Bank (Norfolk, VA) 4/26/63
Each share Capital Stock $10 par exchanged for (1) share Common $5 par
Virginia National Bank (Norfolk, VA) reorganized as Virginia National Bankshares, Inc. 7/10/72 which merged into Sovran Financial Corp. 12/31/83 which merged into C&S/Sovran Corp. 9/1/90 which merged into NationsBank Corp. 12/31/91 which reincorporated in Delaware as BankAmerica Corp.

(Old) 9/25/98 which merged into BankAmerica Corp. (New) 9/30/98 which name changed to Bank of America Corp. 4/28/99

NATIONAL BANK OF COMMERCE (WASHINGTON, DC)
Reorganized under the laws of Delaware as Commerce Bancorp, Inc. 1/31/85
Each share Common $4 par exchanged for (1) share Common $4 par
(See Commerce Bancorp, Inc. (Del.))

NATIONAL BANK OF DAYTON (DAYTON, OH)
Common $12.50 par changed to $6.25 par and (1) additional share issued 01/21/1964
Stock Dividends - 11-1/9% 01/21/1963; 15% 03/07/1966
Name changed to First National Bank (Dayton, OH) 05/26/1966
First National Bank (Dayton, OH) acquired by National City Corp. 12/29/1977 which was acquired by PNC Financial Services Group, Inc. 12/31/2008

NATIONAL BANK OF EASTERN ARKANSAS (FORREST CITY, AR)
Stock Dividend - 100% 3/8/51
Name changed to First National Bank of Eastern Arkansas (Forrest City, Ark.) 3/15/63

NATIONAL BANK OF HYDE PARK (CHICAGO, IL)
Name changed to Hyde Park Bank & Trust Co. (Chicago, Ill.) 1/1/66

NATIONAL BANK OF LA JOLLA (LA JOLLA, CA)
Under plan of reorganization each share Common $5 par automatically became (1) share National Bankshares of La Jolla Common no par 8/11/83
National Bankshares of La Jolla merged into First National Corp. (CA) 5/29/87 which reorganized as Boatracs, Inc. 1/12/95 which name changed to Advanced Remote Communication Solutions Inc. 7/26/99
(See Advanced Remote Communication Solutions Inc.)

NATIONAL BANK OF MELBOURNE & TRUST CO. (MELBOURNE, FL)
Name changed to Flagship Bank of Melbourne, N.A. (Melbourne, Fla.) 11/8/74

NATIONAL BANK OF MONMOUTH (MONMOUTH, IL)
Reorganized as West Central Illinois Bancorp, Inc. 12/31/1984
Each share Capital Stock $20 par exchanged for (1) share Common $20 par
(See West Central Illinois Bancorp, Inc.)

NATIONAL BANK OF PLYMOUTH COUNTY (BROCKTON, MA)
Name changed to First County National Bank (Brockton, Mass.) 9/12/66
First County National Bank (Brockton, Mass.) name changed to Shawmut First County Bank, N.A. (Brockton, Mass.) 4/1/75

NATIONAL BK ST PETERSBURG (ST. PETERSBURG, FL)
Stock Dividend - 10% 2/20/70
Acquired by American Bancshares, Inc. 1/15/72
Details not available

NATIONAL BK S C (SUMTER, SC)
Each share Common Capital Stock $100 par exchanged for (4) shares Common Capital Stock $25 par 1/25/54
Common Capital Stock $25 par changed to $5 par and (4) additional

shares issued plus a 50% stock dividend paid 2/2/65
Stock Dividends - 50% 2/2/59; 33-1/3% 2/2/62; 20% 2/6/68; 25% 3/1/71; 25% 3/1/72; 50% 4/1/75; 25% 4/1/77
Merged into NBSC Corp. 8/10/83
Each share Common Capital Stock $5 par exchanged for (2) shares Common $5 par
NBSC Corp. merged into Synovus Financial Corp. 2/28/95

NATIONAL BANK OF THE REDWOODS (SANTA ROSA, CA)
Under plan of reorganization each share Common no par automatically became (1) share Redwood Empire Bancorp Common no par 01/24/1989
Redwood Empire Bancorp merged into Westamerica Bancorporation 03/01/2005

NATIONAL BANK OF TOLEDO (TOLEDO, OH)
Stock Dividends - 25% 6/30/55; 20% 2/5/59; 10% 8/14/63; 10% 9/22/64
Name changed to First National Bank (Toledo, Ohio) 6/7/65
First National Bank (Toledo, Ohio) reorganized as First Ohio Bancshares, Inc. 7/1/80 which merged into Fifth Third Bancorp 11/30/89

NATIONAL BANK OF TULSA (TULSA, OK)
Stock Dividends - 11-1/9% 04/10/1944; 16-2/3% 10/18/1954; 14-2/7% 10/18/1955; 25% 10/18/1956
Reorganized under the laws of Delaware as NBT Corp. 02/11/1969
Each share Common $10 par exchanged for (1) share Common $10 par
NBT Corp. name changed to BancOklahoma Corp. 07/01/1975
(See BancOklahoma Corp.)

NATIONAL BANK OF WEST VIRGINIA (WHEELING, WV)
Each share Capital Stock $100 par exchanged for (5) shares Capital Stock $20 par 3/26/51
Merged into Security National Bank & Trust Co. (Wheeling, WV) 6/29/62
Each share Capital Stock $20 par exchanged for (1) share Capital Stock $20 par
Security National Bank & Trust Co. (Wheeling, WV) reorganized as Spectrum Financial Corp. 6/1/84 which merged into Key Centurion Bancshares, Inc. 1/31/91 which merged into Banc One Corp. 5/3/93 which merged into Bank One Corp. 10/2/98 which merged into J.P. Morgan Chase & Co. 12/31/2000 which name changed to JPMorgan Chase & Co. 7/20/2004

NATIONAL BANK OF YORK COUNTY (YORK, PA)
Merged into National Bank & Trust Co. of Central Pennsylvania (York, PA) 10/13/1961
Each share Capital Stock $10 par exchanged for (1.374) shares Capital Stock $10 par
National Bank & Trust Co. of Central Pennsylvania (York, PA) merged into National Central Bank (Lancaster, PA) 12/07/1970 which reorganized as National Central Financial Corp. 12/31/1972 which merged into CoreStates Financial Corp 05/02/1983 which merged into First Union Corp. 04/28/1998 which name changed to Wachovia Corp. (Ctfs. dated after 09/01/2001) 09/01/2001 which merged into Wells Fargo & Co. (New) 12/31/2008

NATIONAL BK PALISADES PARK (PALISADES PARK, NJ)
Stock Dividends - 100% 08/01/1942; 100% 02/01/1961; 100% 08/03/1970
Completely liquidated 04/16/1973
Each share Common $20 par exchanged for first and final distribution of $120 cash

NATIONAL BK RISING SUN MD (RISING SUN, MD)
Reorganized as Rising Sun Bancorp 02/15/1991
Each share Common $1 par exchanged for (1) share Common $10 par

NATIONAL BK ROCHESTER (ROCHESTER, MI)
Acquired by Northern States Bancorporation, Inc. 3/8/74
Each share Common $10 par exchanged for $42 cash

NATIONAL BK ROYAL OAK (ROYAL OAK, MI)
Reorganized as Royal Bank Group, Inc. 09/05/1984
Each share Common $10 par exchanged for (1) share Common $10 par
Royal Bank Group, Inc. acquired by Citizens Banking Corp. 10/01/1993 which name changed to Citizens Republic Bancorp, Inc. 04/26/2007

NATIONAL BK SECAUCUS (SECAUCUS, NJ)
Name changed to Plaza National Bank (Secaucus, NJ) 01/16/1971
(See Plaza National Bank (Secaucus, NJ))

NATIONAL BK SOUTHFIELD (SOUTHFIELD, MI)
Over 99% acquired by Manufacturers National Corp. as of 01/29/1977
Public interest eliminated

NATIONAL BK STAMFORD (STAMFORD, NY)
Under plan of reorganization each share Common $5 par automatically became (1) share Stamford Bank Corp. Common $5 par 04/10/1991
(See Stamford Bank Corp.)

NATIONAL BK SUSSEX CNTY (BRANCHVILLE, NJ)
Reorganized as High Point Financial Corp. 4/1/83
Each share Capital Stock $10 par exchanged for (1) share Common no par
High Point Financial Corp. merged into Lakeland Bancorp, Inc. 7/15/99

NATIONAL BK TAMPA (TAMPA, FL)
Name changed to Ellis National Bank of Tampa (Tampa, FL) 04/01/1970
Ellis National Bank of Tampa (Tampa, FL) name changed to Ellis National Bank of Central Florida (Tampa, FL) 10/08/1982
(See Ellis National Bank of Central Florida (Tampa, FL))

NATIONAL BK WALTON CNTY (MONROE, GA)
Under plan of reorganization each share Common $5 par automatically became (1) share NBWC Corp. Common $5 par 11/30/82
(See NBWC Corp.)

NATIONAL BK WASH (TACOMA, WA)
Each share Common $100 par exchanged for (8) shares Common $12.50 par in 1944
Stock Dividends - 100% 4/1/55; 16% 12/6/57; 20% 2/27/68
Under plan of merger name changed to Pacific National Bank of Washington (Seattle, WA) 8/17/70
Pacific National Bank of Washington (Seattle, WA) merged into Western Bancorporation 1/1/81 which name changed to First Interstate Bancorp 6/1/81 which merged into Wells Fargo & Co. (Old) 4/1/96 which merged into Wells Fargo & Co. (New) 11/2/98

NATIONAL BK WASHINGTON (WASHINGTON, DC)
Each share Capital Stock $100 par exchanged for (10) shares Capital Stock $10 par in 1950
Stock Dividends - 11.5658% 12/11/67; 10% 4/15/77; 25% 4/16/79
Reorganized under the laws of Delaware as Washington Bancorporation and Capital Stock $10 par reclassified as Common $10 par 8/24/83
(See Washington Bancorporation)

NATIONAL BK WATERLOO (WATERLOO, IA)
Capital Stock $100 par changed to $50 par and (1) additional share issued plus a 100% stock dividend paid 1/10/67
Stock Dividend - 20% 9/18/52
Merged into Iowa National Bankshares Corp. 12/31/81
Each share Capital Stock $50 par exchanged for (6) shares Common $50 par
Iowa National Bankshares Corp. name changed to Homeland Bankshares Corp. 12/31/94 which merged into Magna Group, Inc. 3/1/97 which merged into Union Planters Corp. 7/1/98 which merged into Regions Financial Corp. (New) 7/1/2004

NATIONAL BK WESTCHESTER (WHITE PLAINS, NY)
Capital Stock $10 par changed to $5 par and (1) additional share issued 2/3/55
Stock Dividends - 25% 3/29/65; 10% 3/27/68
Merged into Lincoln First Banks Inc. 9/26/69
Each share Capital Stock $5 par exchanged for (1) share $1.05 Conv. Preferred $4.50 par and (0.2692) share Common $10 par
Lincoln First Banks Inc. merged into Chase Manhattan Corp. (Old) 7/1/84 which merged into Chase Manhattan Corp. (New) 3/31/96 which name changed to J.P. Morgan Chase & Co. 12/31/2000 which name changed to JPMorgan Chase & Co. 7/20/2004

NATIONAL BK WESTFIELD (WESTFIELD, NJ)
Merged into Central Jersey Bank & Trust Co. (Freehold, NJ) 12/31/1969
Each share Common $10 par exchanged for (6) shares Capital Stock $2.50 par
Central Jersey Bank & Trust Co. (Freehold, NJ) reorganized as Central Jersey Bancorp (Ctfs. dtd. prior to 01/14/1995) 05/31/1985 which merged into National Westminster Bank PLC (London, England) 01/14/1995

NATIONAL BK WESTN PA (BERLIN, PA)
Reorganized as N.B.W.P., Inc. 12/13/85
Each share Common $10 par exchanged for (1) share Common $10 par
N.B.W.P., Inc. merged into First Philson Financial Corp. 1/2/91 which merged into BT Financial Corp. 7/14/99 which name changed to Promistar Financial Corp. 11/15/2000 which merged into F.N.B. Corp. (FL) 1/18/2002

NATIONAL BK WHITTIER (WHITTIER, CA)
Stock Dividend - 10% 03/01/1980
Merged into S C Bancorp 10/01/1981
Each share Capital Stock $10 par exchanged for (4.3) shares Common no par
S C Bancorp Merged into Western Bancorp 10/10/1997 which into U.S. Bancorp 11/15/1999

NATIONAL BK YPSILANTI (YPSILANTI, MI)
Capital Stock $10 par changed to $5 par and (1) additional share issued 2/26/71
Stock Dividends - 25% 2/25/71; 10% 4/15/74
Reorganized as Universal Corp. (MI) 8/1/85
Each share Capital Stock $5 par exchanged for (1) share Common $5 par
Universal Corp. merged into Banc One Corp. (DE) 4/1/88 which reincorporated in Ohio 5/1/89 which merged into Bank One Corp. 10/2/98 which merged into J.P. Morgan Chase & Co. 12/31/2000 which name changed to JPMorgan Chase & Co. 7/20/2004

NATIONAL BANKERS LIFE INS CO (TX)
Placed in permanent receivership and charter cancelled 12/14/81

NATIONAL BANKSHARES OF LA JOLLA (CA)
Merged into First National Corp. (CA) 5/29/87
Each share Common no par exchanged for (0.7) share Common no par
First National Corp. (CA) reorganized as Boatracs, Inc. 1/12/95 which name changed to Advanced Remote Communication Solutions Inc. 7/26/99
(See Advanced Remote Communication Solutions Inc.)

NATIONAL BANNER CORP. (DE)
Name changed to Turbo Cast Industries, Inc. 7/20/67
(See Turbo Cast Industries, Inc.)

NATIONAL BARTER SVCS INC (DE)
Name changed to Stratford Financial Group, Ltd. 12/30/1986
Stratford Financial Group, Ltd. name changed to SFG Corp. 01/19/1993 which name changed to SFG Financial Corp. 08/04/2000
(See SFG Financial Corp.)

NATIONAL BATTERY CO.
Name changed to Gould-National Batteries, Inc. in 1950
Gould-National Batteries, Inc. merged into Gould Inc. 7/31/69
(See Gould Inc.)

NATIONAL BEARING METALS CORP. (NY)
7% Preferred called for redemption 11/01/1944
Merged into American Brake Shoe Co. 12/30/1944
Each share Common no par exchanged for (0.5) share Common no par
American Brake Shoe Co. name changed to Abex Corp. 05/05/1966 which merged into Illinois Central Industries, Inc. 12/26/1968 which name changed to IC Industries, Inc. 05/21/1975
(See IC Industries, Inc.)

NATIONAL BEAUTY CORP (NV)
Each share old Common $0.001 par exchanged for (0.005) share new Common $0.001 par 07/30/2001
Recapitalized as Hairmax International, Inc. 08/01/2003
Each share new Common $0.001 par exchanged for (0.02) share Common $0.001 par
Hairmax International, Inc. name changed to China Digital Media Corp. 03/31/2005
(See China Digital Media Corp.)

NATIONAL BEAUTY INC (DE)
Merged into NB Holding Corp. 7/29/92
Each share Common 10¢ par exchanged for $0.4413 cash

NATIONAL BEEF PACKING CO (DE)
Under plan of merger name changed to Idle Wild Foods, Inc. and Common no par changed to $1 par 05/13/1974
(See Idle Wild Foods, Inc.)

NATIONAL BELLAS HESS CO., INC. (NY)
Liquidation completed in 1936

NATIONAL BELLAS HESS INC (DE)
Adjudicated bankrupt 2/10/76
No stockholders' equity

NATIONAL BENEFIT LIFE INSURANCE CO. (NY)
Under plan of acquisition each share Common $1 par exchanged for $28.75 cash 12/15/82

NATIONAL BERYL & MINING CORP. (CO)
Proclaimed defunct and inoperative for non-payment of taxes 10/13/64

NATIONAL BERYLLIA CORP (NJ)
Common $1 par split (3) for (2) by issuance of (0.5) additional share 1/3/83
Common $1 par split (5) for (4) by issuance of (0.25) additional share 1/3/84
Name changed to General Ceramics Inc. 11/15/84
(See General Ceramics Inc.)

NATIONAL BEVERAGES, INC. (UT)
Each share Common 20¢ par exchanged for (0.2) share Common $1 par 2/17/58
Recapitalized 2/23/62
Each share 6% Preferred $1 par exchanged for (0.1) share Common no par
Each share Common $1 par exchanged for (16) shares Common no par
Merged into American Properties, Inc. 5/29/64
Each share Common no par exchanged for $1 of 6% five year Debentures

NATIONAL BIRMINGHAM GARAGES, INC. (AL)
Liquidation completed 1/9/63

NATIONAL BISCUIT CO (NJ)
Each share Common $25 par exchanged for (2.5) shares Common $10 par 00/00/1930
Recapitalized 04/12/1962
Each share 7% Preferred $100 par exchanged for $175 cash or $175 principal amount of 4.75% Subord. Debentures due 04/01/1987
Note: Option to receive Debentures expired 05/15/1962
Common $10 par changed to $5 par and (1) additional share issued 05/11/1962
Name changed to Nabisco Inc. 04/27/1971
Nabisco Inc. merged into Nabisco Brands, Inc. 07/06/1981
(See Nabisco Brands, Inc.)

NATIONAL BLANK BOOK CO. (MA)
Common $25 par changed to $10 par in 1958
Stock Dividend - 50% 9/25/62
Merged into Dennison Manufacturing Co. (NV) 5/26/67
Each share Common $10 par exchanged for (1) share $1 Conv. Preferred $10 par
Dennison Manufacturing Co. (NV) merged into Avery Dennison Corp. 10/16/90

NATIONAL BLDG SUPPLY INC (NV)
Chapter 11 bankruptcy proceedings terminated 08/04/1997
Stockholders' equity unlikely

NATIONAL BLVD BK (CHICAGO, IL)
Each share Capital Stock $100 par exchanged for (5) shares Capital Stock $20 par 00/00/1947
Stock Dividends - 50% 12/28/1943; 50% 10/14/1958; 16-2/3% 07/10/1961; 14-2/7% 01/18/1963; 25% 10/25/1965; 20% 07/20/1967; 16-2/3% 01/15/1971; 14% 02/23/1973
Reorganized under the laws of Delaware as Boulevard Bancorp, Inc. 06/30/1985
Each share Capital Stock $20 par exchanged for (1) share Common $1 par
Boulevard Bancorp, Inc. merged into First Bank System, Inc. 03/25/1994 which name changed to U.S. Bancorp 08/01/1997

NATIONAL BOND & INVESTMENT CO.
Name changed to Nabco Liquidating Co. in 1941 which was liquidated in 1944

NATIONAL BOND & SHARE CORP.
Name changed to National Shares Corp. in 1948
National Shares Corp. name changed to Dominick Fund, Inc. 3/4/59 which merged into Putnam Investors Fund, Inc. 10/15/74

NATIONAL BOSTON MED INC (NV)
Each share old Common $0.001 par exchanged for (0.25) share new Common $0.001 par 10/29/1998
Each share new Common $0.001 par exchanged again for (0.03125) share new Common $0.001 par 05/01/2001
Holdings of (101) shares or more were reduced to (100) shares exactly
Recapitalized as Storage Innovation Technologies, Inc. (NV) 05/21/2004
Each share new Common $0.001 par exchanged for (0.001) share Common $0.001 par
Storage Innovation Technologies, Inc. (NV) reorganized in Florida as Connectyx Technologies Holdings Group, Inc. 10/29/2007

NATIONAL BOSTON MONTANA MINES CORP. (MT)
Charter expired by time limitation 5/17/73

NATIONAL BOWL-O-MAT CORP. (NJ)
Name changed to NBO Industries 1/2/69
NBO Industries name changed to Treadway Companies, Inc. 8/10/71
(See Treadway Companies, Inc.)

NATIONAL BOWLING LANES, INC. (DE)
Name changed to National Banner Corp. 12/11/63
National Banner Corp. name changed to Turbo Cast Industries, Inc. 7/20/67 which charter was revoked 4/15/70 and subsequently adjudicated bankrupt 7/24/70

NATIONAL BRANDS, INC. (DE)
Incorporated 2/3/30
No longer in existence having become inoperative and void for non-payment of taxes 4/1/34

NATIONAL BRANDS INC (DE)
Incorporated 06/28/1955
Merged into Chamberlain Manufacturing Co. 03/29/1982
Each share Common 15¢ par exchanged for $1.50 cash

NATIONAL BREWERIES LTD.
Name changed to Dow Brewery Ltd. in 1952
Dow Brewery Ltd. merged into Carling O'Keefe Ltd. 6/28/74
(See Carling O'Keefe Ltd.)

NATIONAL BREWING CO. OF MICHIGAN (MI)
Merged into National Brewing Co. (Md.) 5/1/67
Each share Common $1 par exchanged for (1) share 6% Preferred $8 par
National Brewing Co. (Md.) name changed to O-W Fund, Inc. 10/31/75 which merged into New York Venture Fund, Inc. 12/14/88

NATIONAL BREWING CO (MD)
Name changed to O-W Fund, Inc. 10/31/1975
O-W Fund, Inc. merged into New York Venture Fund, Inc. 12/14/1988 which name changed to Davis New York Venture Fund, Inc. 10/01/1995

NATIONAL BROACH & MACHINE CO. (MI)
Acquired by Lear Siegler, Inc. 1/10/68
Each share Common $1 par exchanged for (0.878) share $4.50 Conv. Preferred no par and (2.45) shares Common $1 par
(See Lear Siegler, Inc.)

NATIONAL BRONZE & ALUMINUM FOUNDRY CO. (OH)
Each share Common no par exchanged for (2) shares Common $1 par 00/00/1945
Name changed to National Apex Industries Corp. and Common $1 par changed to 50¢ par 05/26/1955
(See National Apex Industries Corp.)

NATIONAL BUSINESS COMMUNICATIONS CORP (FL)
Plan of reorganization under Chapter 11 Federal Bankruptcy proceedings confirmed 12/03/1986
No stockholders' equity

NATIONAL BUSINESS HLDGS INC (FL)
Name changed to Union Dental Holdings, Inc. 1/21/2005

NATIONAL BUSINESS LISTS INC (DE)
Acquired by private investors 06/15/1984
Each share Common 1¢ par exchanged for $10 cash

NATIONAL BUSINESS PROMOTIONS INC (FL)
Administratively dissolved 09/26/2008

NATIONAL BUSINESS SYS INC (CANADA)
Common no par split (2) for (1) by issuance of (1) additional share 8/18/86
Recapitalized as Consolidated NBS Inc. 4/18/90
Each share Common no par exchanged for (0.1) share Common no par
Consolidated NBS Inc. name changed to SBN Systems, Inc. 5/14/92 which name changed to NBS Technologies Inc. (Old) 4/14/94 which name changed to Mist Inc. 11/1/2000 which name changed to NBS Technologies Inc. (New) 3/16/2004
(See NBS Technologies Inc. (New))

NATIONAL BY PRODS INC (IA)
Common $1 par split (2) for (1) by issuance of (1) additional share 6/27/66
Common $1 par split (2) for (1) by issuance of (1) additional share 6/27/73
Stock Dividends - 40% 9/1/45; 100% 8/15/46
Merged into Federal Co. 4/12/78
Each share Common $1 par exchanged for (1) share Common $12 par
Federal Co. name changed to Holly Farms Corp. 9/10/87
(See Holly Farms Corp.)

NATIONAL CABLE SERVICE CORP. (DE)
Name changed to National Communication Service Corp. 6/4/69
National Communication Service Corp. merged into Continental Telephone Corp. 12/31/70 which name changed to Continental Telecom Inc. 5/6/82 which name changed to Contel Corp. 5/1/86 which merged into GTE Corp. 3/14/91 which merged into Verizon Communications Inc. 6/30/2000

NATIONAL CALIF TAX EXEMPT BDS INC (MA)
Merged into Phoenix California Tax-Exempt Bonds, Inc. 12/31/1993
Details not available

NATIONAL CAN CO.
Merged into McKeesport Tin Plate Corp. on a (2) for (1) basis in 1937
McKeesport Tin Plate Corp. name changed to National Can Corp. in 1941
(See National Can Corp.)

NATIONAL CAN CORP (DE)
Common $10 par changed to $5 par and (1) additional share issued 06/30/1970
60¢ Conv. Preferred Ser. B $10 par changed to $5 par and (1) additional share issued 06/30/1970
60¢ Conv. Preferred Ser. B $5 par called for redemption 06/19/1985
$1.50 Conv. Preferred Ser. A $10 par called for redemption 06/19/1985
Merged into Triangle Industries, Inc. 06/28/1985
Each share Common $5 par exchanged for $42 cash

NATIONAL CANDY CO., INC. (NJ)
Each share Common $25 par exchanged for (3) shares Common $8-1/3 par 00/00/1945
Merged into National Candy Co. 00/00/1945
Details not available

NATIONAL CANDY CO. (DE)
Merged into Clinton Industries, Inc. share for share 2/4/46
Clinton Industries, Inc. name changed to Clinton Foods, Inc. in 1949 which name changed to C.N.I. Liquidating Co. 4/30/56
(See C.N.I. Liquidating Co.)

NATIONAL CAP FINL (AZ)
Charter revoked for failure to file reports or pay fees 5/10/77

NATIONAL CAP INC (NV)
SEC revoked common stock registration 09/17/2008
Stockholders' equity unlikely

NATIONAL CAP LIFE INS CO (AZ)
Capital Stock 25¢ par changed to 15¢ par 06/26/1968
Each share old Capital Stock 15¢ par exchanged for (0.5) share new Capital Stock 15¢ par 08/11/1972
Name changed to National Capital Financial 12/04/1974

NATIONAL CAP MGMT CORP (DE)
Reorganized 02/25/1988
Reorganized from National Capital Real Estate Trust (CA) to National Capital Management Corp. (DE) 02/25/1988
Each Share of Bene. Int. no par exchanged for (1) share Common no par
Each share old Common no par exchanged for (1/3) share new Common no par 07/11/1995
Name changed to Fragrancenet.Com, Inc. 07/28/1999

NATIONAL CAPITAL CORP. (FL)
Charter cancelled for non-payment of taxes 6/28/65

NAT-NAT — FINANCIAL INFORMATION, INC.

NATIONAL CAPITAL GUN CLUB, INC. (MD)
Charter annulled for failure to file annual reports 10/14/82

NATIONAL CAPITOL LIFE INSURANCE CO. (AL)
Placed in receivership 09/20/1969
No stockholders' equity

NATIONAL CAPITOL LIFE INSURANCE CO. (PA)
Completely liquidated 04/08/1968
Each share Capital Stock $1 par exchanged for first and final distribution of (0.612369) share Washington Trust Insurance Co. Common $1 par
Washington Trust Insurance Co. name changed to National Capitol Life Insurance Co. (AL) 04/15/1968
(See National Capitol Life Insurance Co. (AL))

NATIONAL CAR RENT SYS INC (NV)
Common $1 par changed to 20¢ par and (4) additional shares issued 04/05/1968
Merged into Household Finance Corp. 01/11/1974
Each share Common 20¢ par exchanged for $2.50 cash
Each share Special Class A 20¢ par exchanged for $2.731817 cash

NATIONAL CASH CREDIT CORP.
Merged into Franklin Plan Corp. in 1931
Details not available

NATIONAL CASH REGISTER CO (MD)
Each share Class A no par received (0.2) share Class A no par in 1933
Each share Class B no par exchanged for (0.5) share Class C no par in 1933
Class A no par and Class C no par reclassified as Common no par in 1934
Common no par changed to $5 par and (2) additional shares issued 2/10/55
Common $5 par split (2) for (1) by issuance of (1) additional share 5/14/70
Stock Dividends - 10% 12/20/48; 10% 12/20/50; 10% 12/15/53
Name changed to NCR Corp. 5/10/74
NCR Corp. merged into American Telephone & Telegraph Co. 9/19/91 which name changed to AT&T Corp. 4/20/94 which merged into AT&T Inc. 11/18/2005

NATIONAL CASKET INC (NY)
7% Preferred no par called for redemption 3/31/56
Common no par split (3) for (1) by issuance of (2) additional shares 4/16/56
Common no par changed to $5 par 10/17/56
Name changed to Walco National Corp. 5/4/70
(See Walco National Corp.)

NATIONAL CASTINGS CO. (OH)
Merged into Midland-Ross Corp. 4/23/65
Each share Common Stock no par exchanged for (0.45) share $4.75 Conv. Preferred Ser. A no par
(See Midland-Ross Corp.)

NATIONAL CASUALTY CO. (MI)
Each share Common $50 par exchanged for (5) shares Common $10 par in 1927
Stock Dividends - 33-1/3% 12/15/41; 50% 12/15/45; 33-1/3% 2/25/55
Each share Common $10 par exchanged for (2,000) shares Common $2,000 par 11/30/48
Note: In effect holders received $150 cash per share and public interest eliminated

NATIONAL CELLULOSE CORP. (NY)
Dissolved 10/11/56

NATIONAL CENT BK (LANCASTER, PA)
Under plan of reorganization each share Common $10 par automatically became (1) share National Central Financial Corp. Common $10 par 12/31/1972
National Central Financial Corp. merged into CoreStates Financial Corp 05/02/1983 which merged into First Union Corp. 04/28/1998 which name changed to Wachovia Corp. (Ctfs. dated after 09/01/2001) 09/01/2001 which merged into Wells Fargo & Co. (New) 12/31/2008

NATIONAL CENT FINL CORP (PA)
Common $10 par changed to $5 par and (1) additional share issued 05/31/1973
Stock Dividend - 10% 06/20/1979
Merged into CoreStates Financial Corp 05/02/1983
Each share Common $5 par exchanged for (0.645) share Preferred Ser. A no par and (0.43) share Common $1 par
CoreStates Financial Corp merged into First Union Corp. 04/28/1998 which name changed to Wachovia Corp. (Ctfs. dated after 09/01/2001) 09/01/2001 which merged into Wells Fargo & Co. (New) 12/31/2008

NATIONAL CENT LIFE INS CO (MO)
Acquired by Pennsylvania Life Co. (DE) 12/31/1969
Each share Common $1 par exchanged for $30 cash

NATIONAL CHALLENGE SYS INC (CANADA)
Reincorporated 09/30/2003
Place of incorporation changed from (BC) to (Canada) 09/30/2003
Name changed to Organic Resource Management Inc. 07/04/2007
(See Organic Resource Management Inc.)

NATIONAL CHEM CORP (KY)
Name changed to Orbit Gas Co. 11/1/74
Orbit Gas Co. name changed to Orco, Inc. 4/13/92
(See Orco, Inc.)

NATIONAL CHEMICAL & MANUFACTURING CO. (IL)
Merged into Luminall Paints, Inc. on a (2) for (1) basis 8/21/63
(See Luminall Paints, Inc.)

NATIONAL CHEMICAL & MINERALS CORP. (NV)
Charter revoked for failure to file reports and pay fees 3/4/63

NATIONAL CHEMICAL CORP. (ME)
Charter suspended for non-payment of taxes in 1943

NATIONAL CHEMSEARCH CORP (DE)
Common $1 par split (2) for (1) by issuance of (1) additional share 3/15/71
Common $1 par split (2) for (1) by issuance of (1) additional share 12/28/73
Stock Dividend - 100% 8/15/67
Name changed to NCH Corp. 7/31/78
(See NCH Corp.)

NATIONAL CHLOROPHYLL & CHEMICAL CO. (DE)
Name changed to Hofmann Industries, Inc. and Common $1 par changed to 25¢ par 8/2/55

NATIONAL CINEMA CORP (DE)
Name changed to Convaire International, Inc. 12/21/1983
(See Convaire International, Inc.)

NATIONAL CITRUS CORP. (FL)
Completely liquidated 2/28/65
Each share Class A Common $2 par exchanged for first and final distribution of $1.49564 cash

NATIONAL CITY BANCORPORATION (IA)
Stock Dividends - 10% 05/21/1982; 10% 05/20/1983; 10% 05/18/1984; 10% 05/24/1985; 10% 05/23/1986; 10% 05/22/1987; 10% 05/27/1988; 10% 05/26/1989; 10% 06/07/1990; 10% 06/06/1991; 10% 06/04/1992; 10% 06/03/1993; 10% 06/06/1994; 10% 06/05/1995; 10% payable 05/29/1996 to holders of record 04/29/1996; 10% payable 06/05/1997 to holders of record 05/05/1997; 10% payable 06/08/1998 to holders of record 05/06/1998
Merged into Marshall & Ilsley Corp. (Old) 08/01/2001
Each share Common $1.25 par exchanged for (0.53636) share Common $1 par
(See Marshall & Ilsley Corp. (Old))

NATIONAL CITY BANCSHARES INC (IN)
Common $10 par changed to $3.33-1/3 par and (2) additional shares issued 01/21/1987
Common $3.33-1/3 par split (2) for (1) by issuance of (1) additional share payable 04/19/1996 to holders of record 04/08/1996
Stock Dividends - 10% 02/15/1989; 5% payable 12/09/1996 to holders of record 11/25/1996; 5% payable 12/08/1997 to holders of record 11/24/1997; 5% payable 12/07/1998 to holders of record 11/21/1998; 5% payable 12/07/1999 to holders of record 11/21/1999
Name changed to Integra Bank Corp. 05/22/2000
(See Integra Bank Corp.)

NATIONAL CITY BK (BALTIMORE, MD)
Merged into Suburban Trust Co. (Hyattsville, MD) 9/14/70
Each share Common $10 par exchanged for (0.5) share Capital Stock $10 par
Suburban Trust Co. (Hyattsville, MD) reorganized as Suburban Bancorporation 7/1/72 which name changed to Suburban Bancorp 12/31/81 which merged into Sovran Financial Corp. 3/31/86 which merged into C&S/Sovran Corp. 9/1/90 which merged into NationsBank Corp. 12/31/91 which reincorporated in Delaware as BankAmerica Corp. (Old) 9/25/98 which merged into BankAmerica Corp. (New) 9/30/98 which name changed to Bank of America Corp. 4/28/99

NATIONAL CITY BK (CLEVELAND, OH)
Common $20 par changed to $16 par 00/00/1944
Common $16 par changed to $8 par and (1) additional share issued 02/17/1961
Stock Dividends - 11-1/9% 02/04/1946; 14-2/7% 02/04/1955; 10% 02/13/1959; 10% 02/17/1960; 10% 12/12/1963; 10% 12/11/1964; 10% 02/10/1971
Reorganized as National City Corp. 04/30/1973
Each share Common $8 par exchanged for (2) shares Common $4 par
National City Corp. acquired by PNC Financial Services Group, Inc. 12/31/2008

NATIONAL CITY BK (EVANSVILLE, IN)
Each share Common $100 par exchanged for (12) shares Common $10 par to effect a (10) for (1) split and a 20% stock dividend 00/00/1951
Stock Dividends - 50% 07/06/1965; 20% 02/21/1968; 11.1% 02/18/1970; 25% 03/23/1973; 20% 03/23/1976; 25% 04/24/1979; 20% 04/24/1984
Reorganized as National City Bancshares, Inc. 05/06/1985
Each share Common $10 par exchanged for (1) share Common $10 par
National City Bancshares, Inc. name changed to Integra Bank Corp. 05/22/2000
(See Integra Bank Corp.)

NATIONAL CITY BK (MARION, OH)
Capital Stock $33-1/3 par changed to $50 par 00/00/1946
Capital Stock $50 par changed to $20 par and (2) additional shares issued 04/23/1955
Capital Stock $20 par changed to $10 par and (1) additional share issued plus a 10% stock dividend paid 03/14/1969
Stock Dividend - 25% 01/18/1950
Acquired by National City Corp. 12/10/1979
Each share Capital Stock $10 par exchanged for $80 cash

NATIONAL CITY BANK (MINNEAPOLIS, MN)
Each share Capital Stock $10 par exchanged for (2.5) shares Capital Stock $5 par to effect a (2) for (1) split and a 25% stock dividend 06/30/1971
Stock Dividends - 100% 06/30/1972; 26% 03/28/1979; 20% 06/04/1982
97.88% held by National City Bancorporation as of 00/00/1982
Public interest eliminated

NATIONAL CITY CAP TR II (DE)
6.625% Trust Preferred Securities called for redemption at $25 on 11/15/2011

NATIONAL CITY CAP TR III (DE)
Trust Preferred Securities called for redemption at $25 on 05/25/2012

NATIONAL CITY CAP TR IV (DE)
Enhanced Trust Preferred Securities called for redemption at $25 on 07/30/2012

NATIONAL CITY CORP (DE)
Common $4 par split (3) for (2) by issuance of (0.5) additional share 01/20/1984
Common $4 par split (3) for (2) by issuance of (0.5) additional share 01/20/1986
$3.70 Conv. Preferred Ser. A no par called for redemption 03/03/1986
Common $4 par split (3) for (2) by issuance of (0.5) additional share 01/15/1987
Adjustable Rate Preferred no par called for redemption 03/01/1988
Common $4 par split (2) for (1) by issuance of (1) additional share 07/23/1993
8% Depositary Preferred called for redemption 05/01/1996
Common $4 par split (2) for (1) by issuance of (1) additional share payable 07/26/1999 to holders of record 07/09/1999 Ex date - 07/27/1999
6% Conv. Preferred Ser. 1 no par called for redemption at $50 plus $0.50137 accrued dividend on 08/30/2002
Acquired by PNC Financial Services Group, Inc. 12/31/2008
Each share Common $4 par exchanged for (0.0392) share Common $5 par

NATIONAL CITY LINES INC (DE)
Each share old Common $1 par exchanged for (2) shares old Common 50¢ par 00/00/1934
Each share Class A $10 par

exchanged for (3.25) shares old Common 50¢ par 00/00/1945
Each share old Common 50¢ par exchanged for (2) shares new Common $1 par 00/00/1946
New Common $1 par changed to 50¢ par and (1) additional share issued 02/25/1969
Merged into Contran Corp. 04/08/1985
Each share Common 50¢ par exchanged for $22 principal amount of 15.25% Subord. Debentures due 01/01/2000

NATIONAL CLEAN FUELS INC (TX)
Common $0.001 par split (4) for (1) by issuance of (3) additional shares payable 06/16/2010 to holders of record 06/02/2010 Ex date - 06/17/2010
Recapitalized as Quantum International Corp. 01/20/2012
Each share Common $0.001 par exchanged for (0.002) share Common $0.001 par

NATIONAL CLEANING CONTRACTORS, INC. (NY)
Merged into Kinney National Service, Inc. 08/12/1966
Each share Common $1 par exchanged for (1.05) shares Conv. Preferred 1966 Ser. A $1 par
Kinney National Service, Inc. name changed to Kinney Services, Inc. 02/17/1971
(See Kinney Services, Inc.)

NATIONAL CLEVELAND CORP (OH)
Adjudicated bankrupt 03/10/1972
Stockholders' equity unlikely

NATIONAL CLOAK & SUIT CO.
Merged into National Bellas Hess Co., Inc. in 1927
Details not available

NATIONAL CO., INC. (MA)
Common $1 par split (2) for (1) by issuance of (1) additional share 8/2/59
Name changed to National Radio Co., Inc. 3/22/68
(See National Radio Co., Inc.)

NATIONAL COAL CORP (FL)
Each share old Common $0.0001 par exchanged for (0.25) share new Common $0.0001 par 01/13/2005
Each share new Common $0.0001 par exchanged again for (0.25) share new Common $0.0001 par 06/22/2010
Acquired by Ranger Energy Investments, L.L.C. 12/15/2010
Each share new Common $0.0001 par exchanged for $1 cash

NATIONAL COLOR CORP (NJ)
Name changed to Studio Color Corp. 10/24/1978

NATIONAL COLOR LABS INC (DE)
Stock Dividends - 20% 01/05/1979; 20% 01/07/1980; 20% 01/07/1981; 20% 01/07/1982; 20% 02/01/1983
Acquired by an investor group 12/27/1984
Each share Common 10¢ par exchanged for $4.50 cash

NATIONAL COLUMBUS BANCORP INC PROVIDENCE (RI)
Acquired by Rhode Island Hospital Trust Corp. 9/2/82
Details not available

NATIONAL COMM BANCORPORATION (TN)
Common $2 par split (3) for (2) by issuance of (0.5) additional share 7/2/85
Common $2 par split (3) for (2) by issuance of (0.5) additional share 9/1/86
Common $2 par split (3) for (2) by issuance of (0.5) additional share 1/2/92
Common $2 par split (3) for (2) by issuance of (0.5) additional share 10/29/93
Common $2 par split (2) for (1) by issuance of (1) additional share payable 5/16/97 to holders of record 5/5/97
Common $2 par split (2) for (1) by issuance of (1) additional share payable 7/1/98 to holders of record 6/5/98
Stock Dividends - 10% 12/27/84; 10% 1/4/88; 10% 1/3/89
Name changed to National Commerce Financial Corp. 4/25/2001
National Commerce Financial Corp. merged into SunTrust Banks, Inc. 10/1/2004

NATIONAL COMM CAP TR II (DE)
7.70% Guaranteed Trust Preferred Securities called for redemption at $25 plus $0.48125 accrued dividends on 12/15/2006

NATIONAL COMMERCE CORP. (AL)
Merged into Alabama National BanCorporation (DE) 01/03/1996
Each share Common $2.50 par exchanged for (348.14) shares Common $1 par
Alabama National BanCorporation (DE) merged into Royal Bank of Canada (Montreal, QUE) 02/22/2008

NATIONAL COMMERCE CORP. (MS)
Merged into Union Planters Corp. 11/30/89
Each share Common $5 par exchanged for (7.164179) shares Common $5 par
Union Planters Corp. merged into Regions Financial Corp. (New) 7/1/2004

NATIONAL COMM FINL CORP (TN)
Merged into SunTrust Banks, Inc. 10/1/2004
Each share Common $2 par exchanged for (0.063972) share Common $1 par and $30.0073 cash

NATIONAL COML BK & TR CO (ALBANY, NY)
Each share Common $100 par exchanged for (5) shares Common $20 par 00/00/1946
Common $20 par changed to $7.50 par and (2) additional shares issued 01/31/1957
Stock Dividends - 100% 01/27/1953; 10% 09/09/1955; 10% 03/15/1971
Reorganized as First Commercial Banks Inc. 12/31/1971
Each share Common $7.50 par exchanged for (2.25) shares Common $5 par
First Commercial Banks, Inc. name changed to Key Banks Inc. 04/23/1979 which name changed to KeyCorp (NY) 08/28/1985 which merged into KeyCorp (New) (OH) 03/01/1994

NATIONAL COML BKG CORP AUSTRALIA LTD (AUSTRALIA)
Name changed to National Australia Bank Ltd. 10/04/1984

NATIONAL COMMERCIAL TITLE & MORTGAGE GUARANTY CO. (NJ)
Common $10 par changed to $1 par in 1938
Liquidation completed 3/23/55

NATIONAL COMMUNICATION INDS CO (DE)
Name changed to Petroleum Resources Corp. 09/16/1981
Petroleum Resources Corp. name changed to PRC Corp. 01/21/1986
(See PRC Corp.)

NATIONAL COMMUNICATION SERVICE CORP. (DE)
Merged into Continental Telephone Corp. 12/31/70
Each share Common $1 par exchanged for (0.111111) share Common $1 par
Continental Telephone Corp. name changed to Continental Telecom Inc. 5/6/82 which name changed to Contel Corp. 5/1/86 which merged into GTE Corp. 3/14/91 which merged into Verizon Communications Inc. 6/30/2000

NATIONAL COMMUNICATIONS GROUP INC (NY)
Name changed to Schulman Coin & Mint Inc. 04/09/1971
(See Schulman Coin & Mint Inc.)

NATIONAL CMNTY BK N J (RUTHERFORD, NJ)
Name changed 02/07/1975
Common $12.50 par changed to $6.25 par and (1) additional share issued 01/28/1969
Name changed from National Community Bank to National Community Bank of New Jersey (Rutherford, NJ) 02/07/1975
Common $6.25 par changed to $1.5625 par and (3) additional shares issued 05/19/1987
Under plan of reorganization each share Common $1.5625 par automatically became (1) share National Community Banks, Inc. Common $2 par 02/28/1989
National Community Banks, Inc. merged into Bank of New York Co., Inc. 08/11/1993 which merged into Bank of New York Mellon Corp. 07/01/2007

NATIONAL CMNTY BKS INC (NJ)
Merged into Bank of New York Co., Inc. 08/11/1993
Each share 7.75% Conv. Preferred Ser. B $2 par exchanged for (1) share 7.75% Conv. Preferred $2 par
Each share Common $2 par exchanged for (0.96) share Common $7.50 par
Bank of New York Co., Inc. merged into Bank of New York Mellon Corp. 07/01/2007

NATIONAL CMNTY BLDRS (CA)
Charter suspended for failure to file reports and pay taxes 05/03/1976

NATIONAL COMPACTOR & TECHNOLOGY SYS INC (DE)
Name changed to International Baler Corp. (Old) 10/09/1979
International Baler Corp. (Old) merged into Waste Technology Corp. 06/27/1997 which name changed to International Baler Corp. (New) 03/16/2009

NATIONAL COMPREHENSIVE SVCS INC (NV)
Name changed to HMO America, Inc. 12/21/1984
HMO America, Inc. merged into United HealthCare Corp. 08/31/1993 which name changed to UnitedHealth Group Inc. (MN) 03/01/2000 which reincorporated in Delaware 07/01/2015

NATIONAL COMPUTER ANALYSTS INC (DE)
Common 10¢ par split (5) for (2) by issuance of (1.5) additional shares 12/13/68
Merged into M Tech New England Corp. 6/20/86
Each share Common 10¢ par exchanged for $1.74 cash

NATIONAL COMPUTER CORP (DE)
Charter cancelled and declared inoperative and void for non-payment of taxes 03/01/1981

NATIONAL COMPUTER FRANCHISE CORP (DE)
Name changed to National-American Corp. 11/10/70
National-American Corp. name changed to NAC Industries Corp. 1/26/82
(See NAC Industries Corp.)

NATIONAL COMPUTER PRODS INC (AB)
Name changed to Cambridge Colleges Ltd. 10/14/1998
Cambridge Colleges Ltd. name changed to Cambridge Colleges Inc. 02/10/1999
(See Cambridge Colleges Inc.)

NATIONAL COMPUTER SVCS CORP (NY)
Charter cancelled and proclaimed dissolved for failure to pay taxes 12/15/1975

NATIONAL COMPUTER SYS INC (MN)
Merged into Pearson PLC 9/19/2000
Each share Common 3¢ par exchanged for $73 cash

NATIONAL CONNECTOR CORP (MN)
Name changed to Butler National Corp. (DE) 11/21/69
Butler National Corp. (DE) reincorporated in Kansas 1/29/2002

NATIONAL CONSOLIDATED MINING CORP. (MO)
Charter revoked for failure to file reports and pay fees 1/1/58

NATIONAL CONSOLIDATED OIL CORP. (DE)
No longer in existence having become inoperative and void for non-payment of taxes 3/19/24

NATIONAL CONSTR INC (ON)
Name changed to E.G. Capital Inc. 03/16/2005
E.G. Capital Inc. recapitalized as Quantum International Income Corp. 03/14/2014

NATIONAL CONSUMER FINANCE CORP. (DE)
Name changed to Guardian Consumer Finance Corp. 11/21/55
Guardian Consumer Finance Corp. merged into Liberty Loan Corp. 4/4/60 which name changed to LLC Corp. 3/14/80 which name changed to Valhi, Inc. 3/10/87

NATIONAL CONTAINER CORP. (DE)
Stock Dividends - 100% 9/12/44; 10% 1/15/46; 200% 7/31/47
Merged into Owens-Illinois Glass Co. 10/4/56
Each share $1.25 Preferred $25 par exchanged for (0.352) share 4% Preferred $100 par and (0.44) share Common $6.25 par
Each share Common $1 par exchanged for (0.2) share 4% Preferred $100 par and (0.25) share Common $6.25 par
Owens-Illinois Glass Co. name changed to Owens-Illinois, Inc. 4/28/65
(See Owens-Illinois, Inc.)

NATIONAL CONTAINER CORP. (NY)
Acquired by National Container Corp. (Del.) on a share for share basis in 1937
National Container Corp. merged into Owens-Illinois Glass Co. 10/4/56 which name changed to Owens-Illinois, Inc. 4/28/65
(See Owens-Illinois, Inc.)

NATIONAL CONTAINERS LTD (QC)
Acquired by Plant Industries, Inc. (DE) 9/23/69
Each share Common $1 par exchanged for (0.5) share Common 50¢ par
(See Plant Industries, Inc. (DE))

NATIONAL CONTROLS CORP. (AZ)
Charter revoked for failure to file reports or pay fees 9/5/74

NATIONAL CONTROLS (CANADA) LTD. (ON)
Charter cancelled and declared dissolved for failure to file reports 4/14/66

NATIONAL CONVENIENCE STORES INC (DE)
Reincorporated 12/31/1979
Common $1-2/3 par changed to 83-1/3¢ par and (1) additional share issued 11/04/1968
$1.20 Preferred no par called for redemption 09/01/1975
Common 83-1/3¢ par changed to 41-2/3¢ par and (1) additional share issued 12/15/1978
State of incorporation changed from (TX) to (DE) 12/31/1979
Common 41-2/3¢ par changed to 31-1/4¢ par and (1/3) additional share issued 09/26/1980
Common 31-1/4¢ par split (5) for (4) by issuance of (0.25) additional share 10/15/1982
Common 31-1/4¢ par split (3) for (2) by issuance of (0.5) additional share 10/21/1983
Common 31-1/4¢ par split (5) for (4) by issuance of (0.25) additional share 10/15/1984
Stock Dividends - 20% 12/05/1977; 20% 10/13/1981
Preferred Stock Purchase Rights declared for Common stockholders of record 06/16/1986 were redeemed at $0.01 per right 04/23/1990 for holders of record 04/16/1990
Plan of reorganization under Chapter 11 Federal Bankruptcy Code effective 03/09/1993
Each share Common 31-1/4¢ par exchanged for (0.00374354) share Common 1¢ par
Preferred Stock Purchase Rights declared for Common stockholders of record 09/11/1995 were redeemed at $0.01 per right 01/03/1996 for holders of record 12/13/1995
Merged into Diamond Shamrock Inc. 12/18/1995
Each share Common 1¢ par exchanged for $27 cash

NATIONAL COTTONSEED PRODUCTS CORP.
Assets acquired by Mid-South Cotton Oil Co. in 1936 which was liquidated in 1943

NATIONAL CRANBERRY ASSOCIATION (DE)
Name changed to Ocean Spray Cranberries, Inc. 8/28/59

NATIONAL CSS INC (DE)
Common 2¢ par split (2) for (1) by issuance of (1) additional share 11/4/77
Completely liquidated 4/11/80
Each share Common 2¢ par exchanged for first and final distribution of $47.35 cash

NATIONAL CTLS INC (DE)
Acquired by Weigh-Tronix, Inc. (IA) 12/23/1986
Each share Common $1 par exchanged for $7.25 cash

NATIONAL CUBA HOTEL CORP. (DE)
Liquidation completed 1/23/56

NATIONAL CULTURAL INDS INC (NY)
Name changed to Big Rock Oil & Gas Co., Inc. 09/09/1974
Big Rock Oil & Gas Co., Inc. name changed to Resort Resource Group, Inc. 10/03/1986 which name changed to Asia American Industries, Inc. 03/20/1990
(See Asia American Industries, Inc.)

NATIONAL CYLINDER GAS CO (DE)
Name changed to Chemetron Corp. 5/6/58
Chemetron Corp. merged into Allegheny Ludlum Industries, Inc. 11/30/77 which name changed to Allegheny International Inc. 4/29/81
(See Allegheny International Inc.)

NATIONAL DAIRY PRODS CORP (DE)
Common no par changed to $10 par 00/00/1953
Common $10 par changed to $5 par 04/20/1954
Common $5 par split (2) for (1) by issuance of (1) additional share 09/14/1954
Common $5 par changed to $2.50 par and (1) additional share issued 05/27/1966
Name changed to Kraftco Corp. 04/18/1969
Kraftco Corp. name changed to Kraft, Inc. (Old) 10/27/1976 which reorganized as Dart & Kraft, Inc. 09/25/1980 which name changed to Kraft, Inc. (New) 11/21/1986
(See Kraft, Inc. (New))

NATIONAL DATA COMMUNICATIONS INC (DE)
Common 50¢ par changed to 10¢ par 8/24/84
Each share Common 10¢ par exchanged for (0.1) share Common 1¢ par 5/6/87
Stock Dividend - 25% 2/27/81
Name changed to Libra Systems, Inc. 4/11/88
(See Libra Systems, Inc.)

NATIONAL DATA CORP (DE)
Common $1.25 par changed to $0.3125 par and (3) additional shares issued 07/09/1971
Common $0.3125 par changed to $0.125 par and (1.5) additional shares issued 10/16/1972
Common $0.125 par split (3) for (2) by issuance of (0.5) additional share 03/20/1995
Each share Common $0.125 par received distribution of (0.8) share Global Payments Inc. Common no par payable 01/31/2001 to holders of record 01/19/2001 Ex date - 02/01/2001
Stock Dividend - 100% 02/27/1981
Name changed to NDCHealth Corp. 10/25/2001
NDCHealth Corp. merged into Per-Se Technologies, Inc. 01/06/2006
(See Per-Se Technologies, Inc.)

NATIONAL DATA PROCESSING CORP (IA)
Name changed to Network Data Processing Corp. 11/21/69
Network Data Processing Corp. merged into Fiserv, Inc. 4/14/98

NATIONAL DATACOMPUTER INC (DE)
Each share old Common $0.0002 par exchanged for (0.01) share new Common $0.0002 par 10/17/1994
Each share new Common $0.0002 par exchanged for (0.25) share Common 8¢ par 12/18/1996
Common 8¢ par changed to $0.001 par 03/30/2007
Each share old Common $0.001 par exchanged for (0.06666666) share new Common $0.001 par 07/31/2008
SEC revoked common stock registration 02/27/2013

NATIONAL DENTEX CORP (MA)
Common 1¢ par split (3) for (2) by issuance of (0.5) additional share payable 12/31/2004 to holders of record 12/20/2004 Ex date - 01/03/2005
Acquired by GDC Holdings, Inc. 07/29/2010

Each share Common 1¢ par exchanged for $17 cash

NATIONAL DEPARTMENT STORES, INC. (DE)
Reorganized as National Department Stores Corp. 1/30/36
Each share 1st Preferred exchanged for (3.5) shares Common no par
Each share 2nd Preferred exchanged for (1.5) shares Common no par
Each share Common exchanged for (0.25) share Common no par
National Department Stores Corp. name changed to International Mining Corp. 6/6/58
(See International Mining Corp.)

NATIONAL DEPARTMENT STORES CORP. (DE)
Common no par changed to $5 par and (0.5) additional share distributed 6/12/46
Name changed to International Mining Corp. 6/6/58
(See International Mining Corp.)

NATIONAL DETECTION CLINICS LTD (NV)
Name changed to TGC Ventures International, Inc. 10/11/2005

NATIONAL DETROIT CORP (DE)
Common $12.50 par changed to $6.25 par and (1) additional share issued 10/12/76
Name changed to NBD Bancorp, Inc. 4/30/81
NBD Bancorp, Inc. name changed to First Chicago NBD Corp. 12/1/95 which merged into Bank One Corp. 10/2/98 which merged into J.P. Morgan Chase & Co. 12/31/2000 which name changed to JPMorgan Chase & Co. 7/20/2004

NATIONAL DEV CORP (NC)
Charter suspended for failure to pay taxes 04/28/1978

NATIONAL DIAGNOSTICS INC (FL)
Recapitalized as American Enterprise.com Corp. 03/03/2000
Each share Common no par exchanged for (0.25) share Common no par
American Enterprises.com Corp. name changed to Nanobac Pharmaceuicals, Inc. 06/17/2003
(See Nanobac Pharmaceuticals, Inc.)

NATIONAL DISC BROKERS GROUP INC (DE)
Merged into Deutsche Bank AG 11/30/2000
Each share Common 1¢ par exchanged for $49 cash

NATIONAL DISCOUNT CORP. (IN)
Common $100 par changed to no par in 1927
Each share Common no par exchanged for (2) shares Common $10 par in 1947
Merged into Heller (Walter E.) & Co. in 1953
Each share 5% Preferred $100 par exchanged for (1) share 5-1/2% Preferred $100 par
Each share Common $10 par exchanged for (1) share 5-1/2% Preferred $100 par, (1.26) shares Common $2 par and a Trust Certificate for (1) Unit of Interest
Heller (Walter E.) & Co. reorganized as Heller (Walter E.) International Corp. 7/28/69 which name changed to Amerifin Corp. 1/26/84
(See Amerifin Corp.)

NATIONAL DISCOUNT CORP. OF PHILADELPHIA
Merged into Finance Co. of America 00/00/1931
Details not available

NATIONAL DISTILLERS & CHEM CORP (VA)
4-1/2% Preferred $50 par conversion privilege expired 05/03/1965

Common $5 par changed to $2.50 par and (1) additional share issued 05/05/1969
4-1/4% Preferred 1951 Ser. $100 par called for redemption 05/05/1987
4-1/2% Preferred $50 par called for redemption 05/05/1987
$1.85 Preference $1 par called for redemption 05/19/1977
Name changed to Quantum Chemical Corp. 01/04/1988
Quantum Chemical Corp. merged into Hanson PLC (Old) 10/01/1993 which reorganized as Hanson PLC (New) 10/15/2003
(See Hanson PLC (New))

NATIONAL DISTILLERS LTD.
Liquidation completed in 1934

NATIONAL DISTILLERS PRODS CORP (VA)
Common no par exchanged (3) for (1) 00/00/1933
Common no par changed to $5 par 00/00/1951
Stock Dividend - 200% 07/31/1946
Name changed to National Distillers & Chemical Corp. 05/01/1957
National Distillers & Chemical Corp. name changed to Quantum Chemical Corp. 01/04/1988 which merged into Hanson PLC (Old) 10/01/1993 which reorganized as Hanson PLC (New) 10/15/2003
(See Hanson PLC (New))

NATIONAL DISTRG INC (GA)
Merged into NDC, Inc. 09/15/1978
Each share Common 10¢ par exchanged for $12.40 cash

NATIONAL DISTRG PPTYS INC (MD)
Liquidation completed
Each share Common $10 par exchanged for initial distribution of $47 cash 04/13/1982
Each share Common $10 par received second distribution of $6.50 cash 03/16/1984
Each share Common $10 par received third and final distribution of $7.57 cash 11/20/1984

NATIONAL DIVERSIFIED CORP. (DE)
Charter cancelled and declared inoperative and void for non-payment of taxes 04/01/1932

NATIONAL DIVERSIFIED CORP. (OH)
Reorganized under the laws of Delaware as National Fast Food Corp. 08/14/1969
Each share Class A Common no par or Class B Common no par exchanged for (1) share Common 10¢ par
National Fast Food Corp. name changed to NFF Corp. 01/18/1971 which name changed to Orange-co, Inc. 08/29/1973 which name changed to Stoneridge Resources, Inc. 04/29/1987 which recapitalized as Acceptance Insurance Companies Inc. 12/22/1992
(See Acceptance Insurance Companies Inc.)

NATIONAL DIVERSIFIED INDS INC (DE)
Each share Common 10¢ par exchanged for (0.1) share Common $1 par 05/17/1967
Charter cancelled and declared inoperative and void for non-payment of taxes 03/01/1974

NATIONAL DIVERSIFIED SVCS INC (DE)
Recapitalized as Certo Group Corp. 11/10/2005
Each share Common $0.001 par exchanged for (0.2) share Common $0.001 par

NATIONAL DRIVE-IN GROCERY CORP. (TX)
Name changed to National Convenience Stores Inc. 11/28/67

National Convenience Stores Inc. reincorporated under the laws of Delaware 12/31/79

NATIONAL DRUG & CHEMICAL CO. OF CANADA LTD. (CANADA)
Recapitalized in 1946
Each share 6% Preference 15s par exchanged for (0.4) share 60¢ Conv. Preferred $5 par and (0.33) share new Common $5 par
Each share old Common $5 par exchanged for (0.4) share 60¢ Conv. Preferred $5 par and (0.6) share new Common $5 par
New Common $5 par changed to no par 12/11/58
Name changed to National Drug Ltd./Compagnie National Drug Ltee. 7/16/80
(See National Drug Ltd./Compagnie National Drug Ltee.)

NATIONAL DRUG CO. (PA)
Merged into Vick Chemical Co. 03/15/1956
Each share Common $50 par exchanged for (1) share Capital Stock $2.50 par
Vick Chemical Co. name changed to Richardson-Merrell Inc. 10/21/1960 which merged into Dow Chemical Co. 03/10/1981 which merged into DowDuPont Inc. 09/01/2017

NATIONAL DRUG LTD (CANADA)
Merged into Provigo Inc. 2/16/81
Each share 60¢ Conv. Preferred $5 par exchanged for $16 cash
Each share Common no par exchanged for $16 cash

NATIONAL DYEING & PRINTING CO.
Dissolved in 1948

NATIONAL EARLY WARNING SYS INC (FL)
Proclaimed dissolved for failure to file reports and pay fees 10/13/1989

NATIONAL ED CORP (DE)
Common no par split (2) for (1) by issuance of (1) additional share 4/1/83
Common no par changed to 1¢ par 5/23/83
Common 1¢ par split (3) for (2) by issuance of (0.5) additional share 2/17/84
Common 1¢ par split (3) for (2) by issuance of (0.5) additional share 5/9/86
Stock Dividends - 10% 4/24/79; 10% 4/17/80; 10% 4/2/81; 10% 3/31/82
Merged into Harcourt General, Inc. 6/10/97
Each share Common 1¢ par exchanged for $21 cash

NATIONAL EDUCATION SYSTEMS CORP. (DE)
Charter cancelled and declared inoperative and void for non-payment of taxes 3/1/76

NATIONAL EDUCATORS LIFE INS CO (TX)
Merged into United Fidelity Life Insurance Co. 12/31/69
Each share Common Capital Stock $1 par exchanged for (0.714285) share Common $5 par
(See United Fidelity Life Insurance Co.)

NATIONAL ELEC WELDING MACHS CO (MI)
Reincorporated under the laws of Delaware as Newcor, Inc. 5/1/69
(See Newcor, Inc.)

NATIONAL ELECTRIC POWER CO.
Bankrupt in 1933

NATIONAL ELECTRO PROCESS CORP. (DE)
No longer in existence having become inoperative and void for non-payment of taxes 4/1/61

NATIONAL ELECTRODYNAMICS CORP. (CA)
Charter suspended for non-payment of taxes 10/01/1962

NATIONAL ELECTRONIC AUTO-WASH SYSTEMS, INC. (MN)
Name changed to Northern National Forests, Inc. 5/11/72

NATIONAL ELECTRONIC SYSTEMS, INC. (IN)
Charter revoked for failure to file annual reports 6/1/70

NATIONAL ELECTRONIC TUBE CORP. (NY)
Completely liquidated 08/09/1967
Each share Common 5¢ par exchanged for first and final distribution of (0.5) share Intercontinental Trailsea Corp. (NY) Common 1¢ par
Intercontinental Trailsea Corp. (NY) reincorporated in Delaware 07/18/1969
(See Intercontinental Trailsea Corp. (DE))

NATIONAL EMPIRE LIFE INSURANCE CO. (TX)
Merged into Empire Life Insurance Co. of America (AL) 06/30/1966
Each share Common $1 par exchanged for (1) share Class A Common $1 par
(See Empire Life Insurance Co. of America (AL))

NATIONAL ENAMELING & STAMPING CO. (NJ)
Name changed to Nesco, Inc. 6/28/50
Nesco, Inc. merged into New York Shipbuilding Corp. 4/23/54 which merged into Merritt-Chapman & Scott Corp. 10/23/70
(See Merritt-Chapman & Scott Corp.)

NATIONAL ENERGY CAP CORP (NY)
Dissolved by proclamation 12/24/91

NATIONAL ENERGY CORP (CO)
Reorganized under the laws of Tennessee as Aaminex Gold Corp. 04/01/1975
Each share Common 20¢ par exchanged for (1) share Common 20¢ par
Aaminex Gold Corp. (TN) reincorporated in Nevada 01/29/1981 which name changed to Aaminex Capital Corp. 12/23/1986
(See Aaminex Capital Corp.)

NATIONAL ENERGY CORP (NV)
Charter revoked for failure to file reports and pay fees 03/05/1973

NATIONAL ENERGY GROUP INC (DE)
Each share old Class A Common 1¢ par exchanged for (0.01960784) share new Class A Common 1¢ par 06/29/1992
New Class A Common 1¢ par split (51) for (1) by issuance of (50) additional shares 06/29/1992
New Class A Common 1¢ par reclassified as old Common 1¢ par 08/29/1996
Plan of reorganization under Chapter 11 Federal Bankruptcy Code effective 08/04/2000
Each share old Common 1¢ par received (1) share new Common 1¢ par 08/04/2000
Note: Certificates were not required to be surrendered and are without value
Liquidation completed
Each share new Common 1¢ par received initial distribution of $1.15 cash payable 09/03/2010 to holders of record 03/25/2008
Each share new Common 1¢ par exchanged for second and final distribution of $3.63 cash 04/19/2011

NATIONAL ENERGY SVCS INC (NV)
Name changed to NX Global, Inc. 10/06/2010

NATIONAL ENTERPRISE BK (WASHINGTON, DC)
Name changed to First Interstate Bank of Washington, DC (Washington, DC) 10/6/87
First Interstate Bank of Washington, DC (Washington, D.C.) reorganized as Franklin Bancorporation, Inc. 10/31/89 which merged into BB&T Corp. 7/1/98

NATIONAL ENTERPRISES INC (DC)
Merged into American Water Works Co., Inc. 06/25/1999
Each share Common exchanged for (14.937) shares Common $1.25 par
(See American Water Works Co., Inc.)

NATIONAL ENTERPRISES INC (IN)
Name changed to Empire Gold Inc. 09/30/1997
(See Empire Gold Inc.)

NATIONAL ENTMT CORP (NV)
Recapitalized as Major Video Corp. 3/16/87
Each share Common $0.001 par exchanged for (0.04) share Common $0.025 par
Major Video Corp. merged into Blockbuster Entertainment Corp. 1/17/89 which merged into Viacom Inc. (Old) 9/30/94
(See Viacom Inc. (Old))

NATIONAL ENVIRONMENT CORP (NV)
Common $1 par changed to 50¢ par and (1) additional share issued 09/27/1968
Filed petition for Chapter X bankruptcy proceedings 10/09/1974
No stockholders' equity

NATIONAL ENVIRONMENTAL CTLS INC (DE)
Each share Common 1¢ par received distribution of (0.2) share Chemfix Technologies, Inc. Common 1¢ par 04/15/1982
SEC revoked common stock registration 09/17/2008
Stockholders' equity unlikely

NATIONAL ENVIRONMENTAL GROUP INC (MD)
Reorganized as Key Energy Group, Inc. 12/04/1992
Each share 14% Conv. Preferred 10¢ par exchanged for (1.04) shares Common 10¢ par
Each share Common 10¢ par exchanged for (0.0178) share Common 10¢ par
Key Energy Group, Inc. name changed to Key Energy Services Inc. (MD) 12/09/1998
(See Key Energy Services Inc. (MD))

NATIONAL ENVIRONMENTAL SVC CO (OK)
Name changed to Nesco, Inc. 12/27/99
(See Nesco, Inc.)

NATIONAL EQUIP RENT LTD (DE)
Common $1 par changed to 33-1/3¢ par and (2) additional shares issued 3/19/68
Merged into American Export Industries, Inc. 8/8/69
Each share Common 33-1/3¢ par exchanged for (0.8625) share Common 40¢ par
American Export Industries, Inc. name changed to Aeicor, Inc. 3/31/78 which name changed to Doskocil Companies Inc. 9/30/83 which name changed to Foodbrands America Inc. 5/15/95 which merged into IBP, Inc. 5/7/97 which merged into Tyson Foods, Inc. 9/28/2001

NATIONAL EQUIP SVCS INC (DE)
Issue Information - 7,000,000 shares COM offered at $13.50 per share on 07/13/1998
Reorganized under Chapter 11 Federal Bankruptcy Code as NES Rentals Holdings, Inc. 2/11/2004
Each share Common 1¢ par exchanged for (0.00505882) share Common 1¢ par
Note: Unexchanged certificates were cancelled and became without value 2/11/2005
(See NES Rentals Holdings, Inc.)

NATIONAL EQUIPMENT CO. (MA)
Acquired by Van Norman Machine Tool Co. 10/28/1940
Each share Preferred exchanged for $13 cash
No Common stockholders' equity

NATIONAL EQUIPMENT CORP.
Assets acquired by Koehring Co. in 1937
(See Koehring Co.)

NATIONAL EQUITABLE INVESTMENT CO., INC.
Succeeded by American National Finance Corp. 00/00/1930
Details not available

NATIONAL EQUITIES HLDGS INC (DE)
Each share old Common $0.001 par exchanged for (1/7) share new Common $0.001 par 09/15/1995
Each share new Common $0.001 par exchanged again for (0.1) share new Common $0.001 par 11/06/2003
Each share new Common $0.001 par exchanged again for (0.2) share new Common $0.001 par 06/14/2004
Each (60) shares new Common $0.001 par exchanged again for (1) share new Common $0.001 par 10/31/2005
Note: Holders between (100) and (5,999) shares received (100) shares
Holders of (99) shares or fewer were not affected by reverse split
Name changed to Skye Petroleum, Inc. 04/05/2010

NATIONAL EQUITIES INC (NY)
Common $10 par changed to $3.33-1/3 par and (2) additional shares issued 05/03/1968
Common $3.33-1/3 par changed to 83-1/3¢ par and (3) additional shares issued 09/16/1971
Stock Dividend - 10% 02/21/1966
Reincorporated under the laws of Delaware as NEI Corp. 04/01/1973
NEI Corp. merged into Rockwood National Corp. 07/13/1977
(See Rockwood National Corp.)

NATIONAL EQUITY LIFE INSURANCE CO. (OK)
Merged into Norin Corp. (Del.) 10/31/72
Each share Common 14¢ par exchanged for (0.016) share Common $1 par
Norin Corp. (Del.) reorganized in Florida 5/31/79
(See Norin Corp. (Fla.))

NATIONAL ERIE CO.
Reorganized as National Erie Corp. in 1935 which was dissolved in January 1954

NATIONAL ERIE CORP. (PA)
Each share Common no par exchanged for (2) shares Common $1.50 par in 1948
Dissolved in January 1954

NATIONAL EXHIB CO (NJ)
5% Non-Cum. Preferred $40 par called for redemption 06/28/1976
Liquidation completed
Each share Common $60 par received initial distribution of $293 cash 06/28/1976
Each share Common $60 par

received second distribution of $220 cash 01/10/1977
Each share Common $60 par received third distribution of $80 cash 01/05/1978
Each share Common $60 par received fourth and final distribution of $93 cash 02/28/1978
Note: Certificates were not required to be surrendered and are without value

NATIONAL EXPLORATIONS LTD. (BC)
Completely liquidated 9/11/67
Each share Common no par exchanged for first and final distribution of (0.166666) share First National Uranium Mines Ltd. Capital Stock $1 par
First National Uranium Mines Ltd. acquired by Groundstar Resources Ltd. (BC) 8/31/73 which reincorporated in Alberta 10/28/2005

NATIONAL FABRICS INC (DE)
Charter forfeited for failure to maintain a registered agent 11/30/90

NATIONAL FACTORS INC (OH)
Name changed to NFD Inc. 10/31/1977
(See NFD Inc.)

NATIONAL FAMILY STORES, INC.
Bankrupt in 1931

NATIONAL FAST FOOD CORP. (DE)
Name changed to NFF Corp. 01/18/1971
NFF Corp. name changed to Orange-Co, Inc. 08/29/1973 which name changed to Stoneridge Resources, Inc. 04/29/1987 which recapitalized as Acceptance Insurance Companies Inc. 12/22/1992
(See Acceptance Insurance Companies Inc.)

NATIONAL FASTENER CORP. (NY)
Dissolved by proclamation 6/23/93

NATIONAL FEATURES LTD (QC)
Acquired by National Telepix, Inc. in 1963
Each share Capital Stock $1 par exchanged for (0.9) share Common 1¢ par
National Telepix, Inc. name changed to American Diversified Industries Corp. 11/18/68 which name changed to Brewer Alcohol Fuels Corp. 8/29/80 which recapitalized as National Gas & Power Co., Inc. 11/21/83
(See National Gas & Power Co., Inc.)

NATIONAL FED SECS TR (NY)
Merged into Phoenix Series Fund 12/31/93
Each Share of Bene. Int. $1 par exchanged for (1.004082827) U.S. Government Securities Fund shares $10 par

NATIONAL FEEDERS LTD. (SK)
Name changed to National Investment Corp. Ltd. 12/17/65

NATIONAL FERRO CORP (NJ)
Merged into Continental Art Galleries, Ltd. 10/1/68
Each share Common 1¢ par exchanged for (0.1) share Capital Stock 1¢ par
Continental Art Galleries, Ltd. name changed to Quest Systems, Inc. 3/17/80
(See Quest Systems, Inc.)

NATIONAL FIBRETECH INC (ON)
Trustee discharged 1/22/2004
No stockholders' equity

NATIONAL FID LIFE INS CO (MO)
Stock Dividends - 100% 12/20/1945; 150% 12/29/1950; 100% 05/20/1955; 100% 03/02/1964; 25% 06/10/1966; 25% 06/29/1969
Merged into ERC Corp. 07/01/1970

Each share Common $2 par exchanged for (0.3125) share Common $2.50 par
(See ERC Corp.)

NATIONAL FILING AGENTS INC (NV)
Name changed to Bonanza Oil & Gas, Inc. 01/10/2008
(See Bonanza Oil & Gas, Inc.)

NATIONAL FILM STUDIOS, INC. (DC)
Each share Common 1¢ par exchanged for (0.1) share new Common in 1964
Declared bankrupt 12/24/64
Common Stock valueless

NATIONAL FILTRONICS INC (AL)
Proclaimed dissolved for failure to file reports and pay fees 12/1/83

NATIONAL FIN LIFE UNDERWRITERS INC (KS)
Name changed to Farm & Ranch Financial, Inc. 06/02/1970
(See Farm & Ranch Financial, Inc.)

NATIONAL FINANCE CO. (MI)
Merged into Liberty Loan Corp. 9/15/60
Each share 68¢ Conv. Preferred $10 par exchanged for (0.47619) share 5-3/4% Preference 1960 Series $25 par
Each share 6-1/4% Preferred with attached Common Stock Purchase Warrants $10 par exchanged for (0.380952) share 5-3/4% Preference 1960 Ser. $25 par
Each share 6-1/4% Preferred without attached Common Stock Purchase Warrants $10 par exchanged for (0.358243) share 5-3/4% Preference 1960 Ser. $25 par
Each share Common $1 par exchanged for (0.105147) share new Common $1 par
Liberty Loan Corp. name changed to LLC Corp. 3/14/80 which name changed to Valhi, Inc. 3/10/87

NATIONAL FINL PARTNERS CORP (DE)
Issue Information - 9,066,978 shares COM offered at $23 per share on 09/17/2003
Acquired by Patriot Parent Corp. 07/01/2013
Each share Common 10¢ par exchanged for $25.35 cash

NATIONAL FINL RLTY TR (IN)
Administratively dissolved 2/9/96

NATIONAL FIRE & MARINE INSURANCE CO.
Acquired by Industrial Insurance Co. and liquidated in 1946

NATIONAL FIRE INSURANCE CO. OF HARTFORD (CT)
Each share Capital Stock $100 par exchanged for (10) shares Capital Stock $10 par in 1929
Each share old Capital Stock $10 par exchanged for (0.005) share new Capital Stock $10 par 4/14/83
Note: In effect holders of Capital Stock $10 par received $355.91 cash per share and public interest eliminated

NATIONAL FIRE PROOFING CO.
Acquired by National Fireproofing Corp. share for share 00/00/1929
Unexchanged shares escheated by Pennsylvania 00/00/1955
National Fireproofing Corp. name changed to Natco Corp. 12/08/1952 which name changed to Fuqua Industries, Inc. (PA) 02/13/1967 which reincorporated under the laws of Delaware 05/06/1968 which name changed to Actava Group Inc. 07/21/1993 which name changed to Metromedia International Group, Inc. 11/01/1995
(See Metromedia International Group, Inc.)

NATIONAL FIRE PROTN INC (CA)
Charter suspended for failure to file reports and pay fees 04/01/1977

NATIONAL FIREPROOFING CORP. (PA)
Name changed to Natco Corp. 12/08/1952
Natco Corp. name changed to Fuqua Industries, Inc. (PA) 02/13/1967 which reincorporated in Delaware 05/06/68 which which name changed to Actava Group Inc. 07/21/1993 which name changed to Metromedia International Group, Inc. 11/01/1995
(See Metromedia International Group, Inc.)

NATIONAL FNDTN LIFE INS CO NEW (OK)
Reorganized under the laws of Delaware as Westbridge Capital Corp. and each share Common $1 par automatically became (1) share Common 10¢ par 9/8/82
Westbridge Capital Corp. reorganized as Ascent Assurance, Inc. 3/24/99 which name changed to USHEALTH Group, Inc. 3/3/2005
(See USHEALTH Group, Inc.)

NATIONAL FOLDING BOX CO., INC. (CT)
Reorganized 00/00/1946
Each share Common $100 par exchanged for (4) shares Common $25 par 00/00/1937
Reorganized from (NJ) to under the laws of Connecticut 00/00/1946
Each (3) shares Common $25 par exchanged for (4) shares Common $25 par
Acquired by Federal Paper Board Co. Inc. (NY) 00/00/1953
Details not available

NATIONAL FOOD MARKETERS INC (NJ)
Charter declared void for non-payment of taxes 5/31/74

NATIONAL FOOD PRODUCTS CORP. (MD)
Recapitalized in 1932
Class A (Original Issue) no par changed to $1 par
Class B no par changed to 50¢ par
Reorganized in 1938
Each share Class A (Series of 1932) $1 par exchanged for (0.433333) share Class B $1 par
Each share Class A (Original Issue) $1 par exchanged for (0.666666) share Class B $1 par
Class B 50¢ par declared worthless
Class B $1 par changed to Common $1 par and (4) additional shares issued in 1946
Common $1 par split (2) for (1) by issuance of (1) additional share 11/6/56
Stock Dividend - 25% 5/22/53
Completely liquidated 12/16/69
Each share Common $1 par exchanged for first and final distribution of (1.274) shares Colonial Stores, Inc. Common $2.50 par
(See Colonial Stores, Inc.)

NATIONAL FOODLINE CORP (NV)
Stock Dividend - 25% 12/31/1975
Charter revoked for failure to file reports and pay fees 03/02/1981

NATIONAL FOODS CORP. (DE)
Name changed to Quaker States Foods Corp. 6/16/65
Quaker States Foods Corp. charter revoked 4/15/68

NATIONAL FOREST PRODUCTS (BC)
Struck off register and declared dissolved for failure to file returns 1/23/69

NATIONAL FOUNDATION LIFE INSURANCE CO. OLD (OK)
Each share Common 5¢ par exchanged for (0.1) share Common $1 par 08/01/1969
Merged into NFC Corp. 11/27/1972
Each share Common $1 par exchanged for (1) share Common 10¢ par
NFC Corp. merged into National Foundation Life Insurance Co. (New) (OK) 01/16/1981 which reorganized in Delaware as Westbridge Capital Corp. 09/08/1982 which reorganized as Ascent Assurance, Inc. 03/24/1999 which name changed to USHEALTH Group, Inc. 03/03/2005
(See USHEALTH Group, Inc.)

NATIONAL FOUNDERS CORP. (TX)
Liquidated 1/3/67

NATIONAL FOUNDERS LIFE INSURANCE CO. (TX)
Name changed to American Investors Life Insurance Co. 00/00/1956
American Investors Life Insurance Co. merged into American Investors Corp. 07/03/1959 which reincorporated in Delaware as AIC Corp. 12/31/1964 which name changed to Crutcher Resources Corp. 12/31/1968
(See Crutcher Resources Corp.)

NATIONAL FSI INC (TX)
Acquired by SEI Corp. 5/12/89
Each share Common 1¢ par exchanged for $6.17 cash

NATIONAL FUEL GAS CO (NJ)
9.20% Preferred $25 par called for redemption 7/25/86
(Additional Information in Active)

NATIONAL FUELCORP LTD (BC)
Recapitalized as Fuelcorp International Ltd. 07/31/1991
Each share Common no par exchanged for (0.2) share Common no par
Fuelcorp International Ltd. name changed to Specialty Retail Concepts Inc. 05/27/1994 which recapitalized as Altoro Gold Corp. 01/09/1997 which merged into Solitario Resources Corp. 10/18/2000 which name changed to Solitario Exploration & Royalty Corp. 06/17/2008 which name changed to Solitario Zinc Corp. 07/18/2017

NATIONAL GAMING CORP (DE)
Name changed to National Lodging Corp. 1/12/96
National Lodging Corp. name changed to Chartwell Leisure, Inc. 8/8/96
(See Chartwell Leisure, Inc.)

NATIONAL GAS & ELECTRIC CORP.
Dissolved pursuant to Public Utility Holding Company Act 12/31/1949
Each share Common exchanged for (1) share National Gas & Oil Corp. Common $1 par and (0.5) share National Utilities Co. of Michigan Common $1 par
(See each company's listing)

NATIONAL GAS & OIL CO (OH)
Common $1 par split (3) for (2) by issuance of (0.5) additional share 12/19/94
Stock Dividends - 3% payable 12/23/96 to holders of record 12/2/96 Ex date - 11/27/96; 2% payable 12/22/97 to holders of record 12/1/97
Merged into Licking Rural Electrification, Inc. 10/22/98
Each share Common $1 par exchanged for $13 cash

NATIONAL GAS & OIL CORP (OH)
Common $5 par changed to $1 par 1/2/69
Common $1 par split (2) for (1) by

issuance of (1) additional share 12/22/80
Stock Dividend - 10% 12/27/78
Under plan of reorganization each share Common $1 par automatically became (1) share National Gas & Oil Co. Common $1 par 9/1/81
(See National Gas & Oil Co.)

NATIONAL GAS & PWR INC (DE)
Charter cancelled and declared inoperative and void for non-payment of taxes 3/1/89

NATIONAL GAS CO.
Assets sold 00/00/1934
Details not available

NATIONAL GAS TEK CORP (DE)
Charter cancelled and declared inoperative and void for non-payment of taxes 03/01/1989

NATIONAL GEN CORP (DE)
Merged into American Financial Corp. 03/14/1974
Each share Common $1 par exchanged for $44.75 principal amount of 9.5% Debentures due 03/14/1989

NATIONAL GERIATRIC CTRS INC (DE)
Name changed to National Living Centers, Inc. 08/03/1970
National Living Centers, Inc. merged into ARA Services, Inc. 09/21/1973
(See ARA Services, Inc.)

NATIONAL GLASS CASKET CO. (CO)
Charter dissolved for failure to file annual reports 1/1/29

NATIONAL GLASS INC (RI)
6% Preferred $10 par called for redemption 03/00/1971
Charter revoked for failure to file reports and pay fees 12/16/1977

NATIONAL GOLD & NICKEL RES INC (BC)
Struck off register and declared dissolved for failure to file returns 3/3/95

NATIONAL GOLD CORP (BC)
Reincorporated 01/24/2003
Place of incorporation changed from (AB) to (BC) 01/24/2003
Merged into Alamos Gold Inc. (Old) 02/20/2003
Each share Common no par exchanged for (0.42517006) share Common no par
Alamos Gold Inc. (Old) merged into Alamos Gold Inc. (New) 07/06/2015

NATIONAL GOLD DISTRS LTD (DE)
Chapter 11 Federal Bankruptcy Code converted to Chapter 7 on 9/16/86
Stockholders' equity unlikely

NATIONAL GOLF EMPORIUM INC (NV)
Common $0.001 par split (23) for (1) by issuance of (22) additional shares payable 09/02/2009 to holders of record 09/01/2009
Ex date - 09/03/2009
Name changed to Idle Media, Inc. 04/15/2010

NATIONAL GOLF PPTYS INC (MD)
Reincorporated 8/31/95
State of incorporation changed from (DE) to (MD) 8/31/95
Merged into NGP LLC 2/6/2003
Each share Common 1¢ par exchanged for $12 cash

NATIONAL GRANGE FIRE INSURANCE CO. (NH)
Stock Dividends - 60% 10/1/51; 25% 6/30/53; 10% 12/1/55
Assets sold to National Grange Mutual Liability Co. and liquidation completed 3/2/59

NATIONAL GRID TRANSCO PLC (ENGLAND & WALES)
Name changed 10/21/2002
Stock Dividend - 70% payable 02/09/1998 to holders of record 02/06/1998
Name changed from National Grid Group plc to National Grid Transco plc 10/21/2002
Under plan of reorganization each Sponsored ADR for Ordinary 10p par automatically became (0.877551) National Grid plc Sponsored ADR for Ordinary 07/29/2005

NATIONAL GROCERS LTD (ON)
100% acquired by Loblaw Groceterias Co. Ltd. as of 05/15/1977
Public interest eliminated

NATIONAL GROCERY CO. (NJ)
Called for redemption 3/31/76
Public interest eliminated

NATIONAL GROCERY CO. (WA)
Reorganized as Lang & Co. 00/00/1948
Each share Common $2 par exchanged for (2) shares Common $1 par
Lang & Co. liquidated for Safeco Income Fund, Inc. (WA) 03/10/1981 which reincorporated in Delaware 09/30/1993
(See Safeco Income Fund, Inc.)

NATIONAL GROWTH CORP (CO)
Charter revoked for failure to pay taxes 10/15/1965

NATIONAL GROWTH INDS INC (NY)
Charter cancelled and proclaimed dissolved for failure to pay taxes 12/15/1975

NATIONAL GTY INS CO (OK)
Company reported out of business 04/08/1994
Details not available

NATIONAL GUARANTEE CREDIT CORP. (DE)
Company liquidated in 1936
Each share Class A Capital Stock no par and Class B Capital Stock no par received $0.39 cash

NATIONAL GUARANTY FIRE INSURANCE CO.
Liquidated in 1937

NATIONAL GUARDIAN CORP (DE)
Merged into Lep Group plc 09/29/1988
Each share Common 10¢ par exchanged for (1.044) Sponsored ADR's for Ordinary 2p par
(See Lep Group plc)

NATIONAL GYPSUM CO NEW (DE)
Merged into Delcor Inc. (DE) 9/21/95
Each share Common 1¢ par exchanged for $54 cash

NATIONAL GYPSUM CO OLD (DE)
Class A Common no par changed to $5 par 00/00/1935
Class B Common no par changed to $1 par 00/00/1935
Each share Class A Common $5 par exchanged for (4) shares Common $1 par 00/00/1937
Each share Class B Common $1 par exchanged for (6) shares Common $1 par 00/00/1937
Common $1 par changed to 50¢ par and (1) additional share issued 05/15/1969
$4.50 Preferred no par called for redemption 03/01/1975
Common 50¢ par split (3) for (2) by issuance of (0.5) additional share 10/01/1985
Acquired by Aancor Holdings, Inc. 04/29/1986
Each share Common 50¢ par exchanged for $44 principal amount of National Gypsum Co. 18-Yr.
Subord. Discount Debentures due 06/30/2004 and $46 cash

NATIONAL HARDGOODS DISTRS INC (MA)
Common 10¢ par split (3) for (2) by issuance of (0.5) additional share 10/9/84
Stock Dividends - 25% 4/24/84; 10% 10/15/86
Name changed to NHD Stores Inc. 7/12/88
(See NHD Stores Inc.)

NATIONAL HARDWOOD CO. (DE)
Charter cancelled and declared inoperative and void for non-payment of taxes 3/17/26

NATIONAL HAV-INFO COMMUNICATIONS INC (CANADA)
Reincorporated 08/13/1993
Place of incorporation changed from (BC) to (Canada) 08/13/1993
Each share old Common no par exchanged for (0.2) share new Common no par 12/09/1993
Name changed to NHC Communications Inc. 02/02/1995
(See NHC Communications Inc.)

NATIONAL HEADHUNTERS INC (NV)
Stock Dividend - 12.5% payable 04/30/2002 to holders of record 04/12/2002 Ex date - 04/10/2002
Name changed to Heritage Companies, Inc. 05/15/2002
Heritage Companies, Inc. name changed to Songzai International Holding Group, Inc. 11/10/2003 which name changed to U.S. China Mining Group, Inc. 07/27/2010

NATIONAL HEALTH & SAFETY CORP (UT)
Old Common 1¢ par changed to new Common 1¢ par 01/22/2001
Recapitalized as ADS Media Group, Inc. 02/06/2003
Each share new Common 1¢ par exchanged for (0.01) share Common $0.001 par
(See ADS Media Group, Inc.)

NATIONAL HEALTH CARE SYS INC (CA)
Acquired by Foundation Health Corp. 12/27/91
Each share Common no par exchanged for (0.0985) share Common 1¢ par
Foundation Health Corp. merged into Foundation Health Systems, Inc. 4/1/97 which name changed to Health Net, Inc. 11/6/2000

NATIONAL HEALTH CORP (TN)
Common no par split (2) for (1) by issuance of (1) additional share 06/21/1985
Reincorporated under the laws of Delaware as National Healthcorp L.P. and Common no par reclassified as Units of Ltd. Partnership 12/31/1986
National Healthcorp L.P. name changed to National Healthcare, L.P. 01/01/1995 which name changed to National HealthCare Corp. 12/31/1997

NATIONAL HEALTH ENHANCEMENT SYS INC (DE)
Common $0.001 par split (2) for (1) by issuance of (1) additional share payable 02/09/1996 to holders of record 01/25/1996
Merged into HBO & Co. 12/29/1997
Each share Common $0.001 par exchanged for (0.3084) share Common 5¢ par
HBO & Co. merged into McKesson HBOC Inc. 01/12/1999 which name changed to McKesson Corp. 07/30/2001

NATIONAL HEALTH ENTERPRISES INC (DE)
Each share old Common 80¢ par exchanged for (0.2) share new Common 80¢ par 03/31/1977
New Common 80¢ par split (2) for (1) by issuance of (1) additional share 02/20/1981
New Common 80¢ par split (2) for (1) by issuance of (1) additional share 12/11/1981
Stock Dividend - 400% 01/21/1969
Acquired by National Medical Enterprises, Inc. 09/01/1982
Each share new Common 80¢ par exchanged for $22.50 cash

NATIONAL HEALTH INST INC (NY)
Name changed to International Buyers Club Corp. 08/17/1983
International Buyers Club Corp. name changed to Medical People Holdings, Inc. 06/19/1989
(See Medical People Holdings, Inc.)

NATIONAL HEALTH INVS INC (MD)
Each share 8.5% Conv. Preferred 1¢ par exchanged for (0.905) share Common 1¢ par 02/09/1994
(Additional Information in Active)

NATIONAL HEALTH LABS HLDGS INC (DE)
Merged into Laboratory Corp. of America Holdings 4/28/95
Each share Common 1¢ par exchanged for (0.72) share old Common 1¢ par and $5.60 cash

NATIONAL HEALTH LABS INC (DE)
Under plan of reorganization each share Common 1¢ par automatically became (1) share National Health Laboratories Holdings Inc. Common 1¢ par 6/7/94
National Health Laboratories Holdings Inc. merged into Laboratory Corp. of America Holdings 4/28/95

NATIONAL HEALTH RLTY INC (MD)
Merged into National HealthCare Corp. 10/31/2007
Each share Common 1¢ par exchanged for (1) share Conv. Preferred Ser. A 1¢ par and $9 cash

NATIONAL HEALTH SCAN INC (NV)
Each share old Common $0.001 par exchanged for (0.01) share new Common $0.001 par 02/09/2006
Name changed to Gaensel Energy Group, Inc. 02/24/2015

NATIONAL HEALTH SVCS INC (DE)
Name changed to Carex International, Inc. 04/01/1974
Carex International, Inc. name changed to Medica USA, Inc. 09/13/1980 which name changed to Pacific Realm, Inc. 07/06/1984 which name changed to aeroTelesis, Inc. 10/22/2003
(See aeroTelesis, Inc.)

NATIONAL HEALTHCARE ALLIANCE INC (NV)
Name changed to Berman Holdings, Inc. 11/07/2007
Berman Holdings, Inc. name changed to Prepaid Card Holdings Inc. 05/16/2008 which name changed to PrepaYd, Inc. 05/12/2011

NATIONAL HEALTHCARE CORP (DE)
Conv. Preferred Ser. A 1¢ par called for redemption at $15.75 plus $0.04 accrued dividends on 11/03/2015
(Additional Information in Active)

NATIONAL HEALTHCARE EXCHANGE SVCS INC (DE)
Liquidation completed
Each share Common 1¢ par exchanged for initial distribution of $0.0088 cash 06/29/2012
Each share Common 1¢ par received second distribution of $0.0037 cash payable 11/13/2013 to holders of record 11/12/2013
Each share Common 1¢ par received third and final distribution of $0.0017 cash payable 04/07/2015 to holders of record 03/18/2015

NATIONAL HEALTHCARE INC (DE)
Name changed to Hallmark Healthcare Corp. 12/23/91
Hallmark Healthcare Corp. merged into Community Health Systems Inc. 10/5/94
(See Community Health Systems Inc.)

NATIONAL HEALTHCARE L P (DE)
Name changed 01/01/1995
Each Unit of Ltd. Partnership Int. received distribution of (1) share National Health Investors, Inc. Common 1¢ par 10/16/1991
Name changed from National Healthcorp L.P. to National Healthcare, L.P. 01/01/1995
Each Unit of Ltd. Partnership Int. received distribution of (1) share National Health Realty, Inc. Common 1¢ par payable 01/02/1998 to holders of record 12/31/1997
Name changed to National HealthCare Corp. and Units of Ltd. Partnership Int. reclassified as Common 1¢ par 12/31/1997

NATIONAL HEALTHCARE TECHNOLOGY INC (CO)
Each share old Common $0.001 par exchanged for (0.01) share new Common $0.001 par 10/07/2004
Reincorporated under the laws of Nevada as Brighton Oil & Gas, Inc. 06/05/2007
Brighton Oil & Gas, Inc. recapitalized as Gulf Onshore Inc. 04/04/2008 which name changed to Cannabis Science, Inc. 05/07/2009

NATIONAL HEES ENTERPRISES LTD (ON)
Stock Dividend - 100% 11/30/82
Name changed to Hees International Corp. 5/16/83
Hees International Corp. name changed to Hees International Bancorp Inc. 5/6/88 which name changed to Edper Group Ltd. (New) 1/1/97 which merged into EdperBrascan Corp. 8/1/97 which name changed to Brascan Corp. 4/28/2000 which name changed to Brookfield Asset Management, Inc. 11/10/2005

NATIONAL HEES INDS LTD (CANADA)
Acquired by National Hees Enterprises Ltd. 5/10/73
Each share Common no par exchanged for (1) share Common no par
National Hees Enterprises Ltd. name changed to Hees International Corp. 5/16/83 which name changed to Hees International Bancorp Inc. 5/6/88 which name changed to Edper Group Ltd. (New) 1/1/97 which merged into EdperBrascan Corp. 8/1/97 which name changed to Brascan Corp. 4/28/2000 which name changed to Brookfield Asset Management, Inc. 11/10/2005

NATIONAL HERITAGE INC (GA)
Common 1¢ par split (3) for (2) by issuance of (0.5) additional share 8/14/87
Recapitalized as Evergreen Healthcare Inc. 6/30/93
Each share Common 1¢ par exchanged for (0.2) share Common 1¢ par
Evergreen Healthcare Inc. merged into GranCare, Inc. 7/20/95 which merged into Vitalink Pharmacy Services, Inc. 2/12/97 which merged into Genesis Health Ventures, Inc. 8/28/98
(See Genesis Health Ventures, Inc.)

NATIONAL HERITAGE INDS INC (NV)
Plan of reorganization under Chapter 11 Federal Bankruptcy Code effective 3/18/96
Each share old Common 3¢ par exchanged for (0.001) share new Common 3¢ par
Note: Holdings of (46) shares or fewer did not participate and are without value
Unexchanged certificates became valueless 3/18/97
(Additional Information in Active)

NATIONAL HERITAGE LIFE INS CO (IL)
Under plan of reorganization each share Common $1 par automatically became (1) share National Heritage Management Corp. Common $1 par 12/13/73
National Heritage Management Corp. merged into I.C.H. Corp. 10/14/82 which name changed to Southwestern Life Corp. (New) 6/15/94 which name changed to I.C.H. Corp. (New) 10/10/95
(See I.C.H. Corp. (New))

NATIONAL HERITAGE MGMT CORP (DE)
Merged into I.C.H. Corp. 10/14/82
Each share Common $1 par exchanged for (0.3678) share Common $1 par
I.C.H. Corp. name changed to Southwestern Life Corp. (New) 6/15/94 which name changed to I.C.H. Corp. (New) 10/10/95
(See I.C.H. Corp. (New))

NATIONAL HMO CORP (DE)
Name changed to National Home Health Care Corp. 12/24/1991
(See National Home Health Care Corp.)

NATIONAL HOLDING CORP. (NM)
Charter forfeited for non-payment of franchise taxes 10/2/64

NATIONAL HOME CTRS INC (AR)
Merged into Newman Family, LLC 2/12/2002
Each share Common 1¢ par exchanged for $1.40 cash

NATIONAL HOME HEALTH CARE CORP (DE)
Stock Dividends - 6% payable 12/04/1996 to holders of record 11/08/1996; 3% payable 12/08/1997 to holders of record 11/06/1997; 5% payable 03/23/2001 to holders of record 03/16/2001; 5% payable 05/17/2002 to holders of record 05/10/2002 Ex date - 05/08/2002
Merged into AG Home Health LLC 11/21/2007
Each share Common $0.001 par exchanged for $12.75 cash

NATIONAL HOME LIFE ASSURN CO (MO)
99.4% owned by National Liberty Corp. through exchange offer which expired 01/06/1970
Public interest eliminated

NATIONAL HOME PRODS INC (DE)
Incorporated 10/08/1963
Name changed to Damson Oil Corp. 02/04/1969
(See Damson Oil Corp.)

NATIONAL HOME PRODS INC (DE)
Ctfs. dated after 04/01/1974
Merged into New NHP Inc. 08/11/1977
Each share Common $1 par exchanged for $9 cash

NATIONAL HOMES CORP (IN)
Each share Common $1 par exchanged for (1) share Class A Common 50¢ par and (1) share Class B Common 50¢ par in 1954
Class A Common 50¢ par split (2) for (1) by issuance of (1) additional share 6/1/59
Class B Common 50¢ par split (2) for (1) by issuance of (1) additional share 6/1/59
Class A Common 50¢ par and Class B Common 50¢ par reclassified as Common 50¢ par 8/15/63
Stock Dividends - 10% 12/1/49; 50% 9/1/50; 20% 10/1/52; 20% 1/1/53; 10% 10/1/54; 20% 10/1/55; 20% 10/1/56; 20% 10/1/57
Name changed to National Enterprises, Inc. 6/3/86
National Enterprises, Inc. name changed to Empire Gold Inc. 9/30/97
(See Empire Gold Inc.)

NATIONAL HOSIERY MILLS LTD. (ON)
Each share Common no par exchanged for (1) share old Class A no par and (0.5) share old Class B no par 00/00/1946
Each share old Class A no par exchanged for (3) shares new Class A no par 00/00/1951
Each share old Class B no par exchanged for (3) shares new Class B no par 00/00/1951
Recapitalized as Phantom Industries Ltd. 06/07/1961
Each share new Class A no par exchanged for (1) share Common no par
Each share new Class B no par exchanged for (1) share Common no par
Phantom Industries Ltd. recapitalized as Consolidated Phantom Industries Ltd. 10/21/1966 which name changed to In. Mark Corp. Ltd. 07/30/1971 which name changed to Gemini Food Corp. 03/30/1984
(See Gemini Food Corp.)

NATIONAL HOSP CORP (DE)
Common 25¢ par split (3) for (1) by issuance of (2) additional shares 10/3/68
Liquidation completed
Each share Common 25¢ par received initial distribution of $2.70 principal amount of American Medicorp, Inc. 12% Subord. Debentures due 1981 plus $0.108 cash 10/15/71
Each share Common 25¢ par received second distribution of $0.0675 cash 11/26/71
Each share Common 25¢ par received third and final distribution of $0.50 principal amount 6% Conv. Subord. Debentures due 1987, (0.5) share Common no par plus (0.3) Common Stock Purchase Warrant expiring 12/14/79 all of Oil Resources, Inc. 12/14/72
Certificates were not required to be surrendered and are now valueless

NATIONAL HOSP MGMT SVCS LTD (BC)
Name changed to National Nursing Homes Ltd. 4/7/70
National Nursing Homes Ltd. name changed to Cook (N.B.) Corp. Ltd. 11/8/72
(See Cook (N.B.) Corp. Ltd.)

NATIONAL HOSPITAL SUPPLY, INC. (DE)
Reincorporated 11/18/1968
State of incorporation changed from (NY) to (DE) 11/18/1968
Name changed to Caldwell Industries, Inc. 07/18/1969
(See Caldwell Industries, Inc.)

NATIONAL HOSPITAL SUPPLY CO., INC. (NY)
Name changed to National Hospital Supply, Inc. (NY) in 1967
National Hospital Supply, Inc. (NY) reincorporated under the laws of Delaware 11/18/68 which name changed to Caldwell Industries, Inc. 7/18/69
(See Caldwell Industries, Inc.)

NATIONAL HOSPITALITY GROUP INC (DE)
Name changed to Corporate Mortgage Solutions, Inc. 02/23/2005
Corporate Mortgage Solutions, Inc. name changed to Big Apple Worldwide, Inc. 11/25/2005 which name changed to Fusion Restaurant Group, Inc. 02/24/2011

NATIONAL HOTEL OF CUBA CORP.
Name changed to National Cuba Hotel Corp. in 1940 which was completely liquidated 1/23/56

NATIONAL HSG INDS INC (DE)
Completely liquidated 10/31/1978
Each share Class A Common 5¢ par received first and final distribution of $0.50 cash
Note: Certificates were not required to be surrendered and are without value

NATIONAL HYDROCARBONS LTD. (BC)
Name changed to Auspex Gold Ltd. 09/17/1987
Auspex Gold Ltd. name changed to Auspex Minerals Ltd. 12/04/1995 which merged into EuroZinc Mining Corp. 04/21/1999 which merged into Lundin Mining Corp. 11/01/2006

NATIONAL HYGIENICS INC (DE)
Charter cancelled and declared inoperative and void for non-payment of taxes 3/1/86

NATIONAL HYPERBARIC REHAB CTR INC (NV)
Recapitalized as SanCuro Corp. 02/07/2008
Each share Common 1¢ par exchanged for (0.002) share Common 1¢ par
SanCuro Corp. name changed to Kendall Square Research Corp. 09/08/2009

NATIONAL ICE CREAM CO.
Merged into Golden State Milk Products Co. 00/00/1929
Details not available

NATIONAL IMAGING AFFILIATES INC (DE)
Merged into HealthSouth Corp. 07/22/1998
Each share Common exchanged for (1.0972) shares Common 1¢ par
HealthSouth Corp. name changed to Encompass Health Corp. 01/02/2018

NATIONAL IMAGING INC (FL)
Chapter 11 Federal Bankruptcy proceedings converted to Chapter 7 on 02/19/1992
No stockholders' equity

NATIONAL INCOME & GROWTH FD (MA)
Merged into Phoenix Income & Growth Fund 12/31/93
Details not available

NATIONAL INCOME RLTY TR (CA)
Each old Share of Bene. Int. no par exchanged for (1/3) new Share of Bene. Int. no par 03/26/1990
Share of Bene. Int. Purchase Rights were redeemed at $0.03 per right for holders of record 01/15/1992
Merged into Tarragon Realty Investors Inc. 10/21/1998
Each new Share of Bene. Int. no par exchanged for (1.97) shares Common no par
Tarragon Realty Investors Inc. name changed to Tarragon Corp. 07/01/2004
(See Tarragon Corp.)

NATIONAL INDEMNITY CO. (NE)
Acquired by Berkshire Hathaway Inc. (Mass.) 3/15/67
Each share Common $10 par exchanged for $49 cash

NATIONAL INDL BANCORP INC (CT)
Class A Common $0.001 par changed to 1¢ par and (1) additional share issued 05/26/1987
Filed a petition under Chapter 7 Federal Bankruptcy Code 12/18/1989
No stockholders' equity

NATIONAL INDL BK (MIAMI, FL)
Name changed to Capital Bank of Miami, N.A. (Miami, FL) 12/1/75
Capital Bank of Miami, N.A. (Miami, FL) merged into Capital Bank (North Bay Village, FL) 12/30/77 which was acquired by Capital Bancorp in September 1982 which merged into Union Planters Corp. 12/31/97 which merged into Regions Financial Corp. (New) 7/1/2004

NATIONAL INDUSTRIAL BANK OF CONNECTICUT (MERIDEN, CT)
Closed by Office of the Comptroller of the Currency 11/8/89
Stockholders' equity unlikely

NATIONAL INDUSTRIAL BANKERS, INC.
Dissolved in 1940
Details not available

NATIONAL INDL PRODS CO (OH)
Each share Common $12.50 par exchanged for (2.5) shares Common $5 par 05/05/1960
Recapitalized 07/01/1966
Each share 5% Non-Cum. Preferred $50 par exchanged for (1) share Keever Co. 5% Non-Cum. Preferred $50 par
Each share 5% Preferred $100 par exchanged for (1) share Keever Co. 5% Preferred $100 par
Each share Common $5 par exchanged for (0.7) share Keever Co. Common $5 par and (0.3) share Exact Weight Scale Corp. Common $5 par
(See each company's listing)

NATIONAL INDL SEC CORP (DE)
Recapitalized as NPS International Corp. 11/06/1998
Each share Common $0.16666666 par exchanged for (0.33333333) share Common $0.16666666 par
NPS International Corp. name changed to OneClass Synergy Corp. 12/21/2000 which recapitalized as ABCI Holdings Inc. (DE) 08/13/2001 which reorganized in Nevada as Metaphor Corp. 01/06/2005 which name changed to Medical Solutions Management Inc. 08/04/2006
(See Medical Solutions Management Inc.)

NATIONAL INDL SVCS CORP (NY)
Common 10¢ par split (3) for (2) by issuance of (0.5) additional share 5/3/71
Stock Dividend - 50% 8/2/76
Name changed to Capital Market Services Corp. 12/21/83
(See Capital Market Services Corp.)

NATIONAL INDUSTRIES, INC. (DE)
Charter revoked for non-payment of taxes 4/1/64

NATIONAL INDS INC (KY)
Merged into Fuqua Industries, Inc. 01/03/1978
Each share 60¢ Conv. Preferred Ser. A $1 par exchanged for (1) share 60¢ Conv. Preferred Ser. A $1 par or $14 cash
Each share $1.25 Conv. Preferred Ser. B $1 par exchanged for (1) share $1.25 Conv. Preferred Ser. B $1 par or $7.50 cash
Each share Common $1 par exchanged for (1) share Common $1 par or $10 cash
Note: Option to receive cash expired 01/31/1978
Fuqua Industries, Inc. name changed to Actava Group Inc. 07/21/1993 which name changed to Metromedia International Group, Inc. 11/01/1995
(See Metromedia International Group, Inc.)

NATIONAL INDUSTRIES SHARES SERIES A
Liquidated in 1932

NATIONAL INFORMATION CONSORTIUM INC (CO)
Issue Information - 13,000,000 shares COM offered at $12 per share on 07/15/1999
Name changed to NIC Inc. (CO) 05/14/2002
NIC Inc. (CO) reincorporated in Delaware 05/07/2009

NATIONAL INFORMATION GROUP (CA)
Merged into First American Financial Corp. (CA) 05/14/1999
Each share Common no par exchanged for (0.67) share Common $1 par
First American Financial Corp. (CA) name changed to First American Corp. (CA) 05/19/2000 which reincorporated in Delaware as CoreLogic, Inc. 06/01/2010

NATIONAL INFORMATION SVCS INC (MA)
Proclaimed dissolved for failure to file reports and pay fees 10/19/83

NATIONAL INFORMATION SYS CORP (PA)
Merged into National Liberty Corp. 5/14/74
Each share Common no par exchanged for $1.25 cash

NATIONAL INST COMPUTER PROFESSIONS INC (MD)
Merged into Delta Automated Systems, Inc. 10/01/1970
Each share Common 1¢ par exchanged for (0.222222) share Common 10¢ par
(See Delta Automated Systems, Inc.)

NATIONAL INST COS AMER (NY)
SEC revoked common stock registration 06/08/2005
Stockholders' equity unlikely

NATIONAL INST OF CAREERS INC (FL)
Proclaimed dissolved for failure to maintain a registered agent 12/12/1988

NATIONAL INSTRUMENT CORP.
Bankrupt in 1950
Details not available

NATIONAL INSTRUMENT LABORATORIES, INC. (MD)
Completely liquidated 7/26/68
Each share Capital Stock 10¢ par exchanged for first and final distribution of (0.381679) share General Kinetics, Inc. Common 25¢ par

NATIONAL INSURANCE AGENCY (AZ)
Liquidation completed 12/14/55

NATIONAL INSURANCE CAPITAL CORP. (DE)
Acquired by Mayflower Investors, Inc. (IL) 8/31/65
Each share Common 50¢ par exchanged for (1.5) shares Common 50¢ par
Mayflower Investors, Inc. (IL) reincorporated under the laws of Delaware 6/18/70 which recapitalized as Seago Group, Inc. 9/2/76
(See Seago Group, Inc.)

NATIONAL INS CO AMER (ND)
Each share Preferred $10 par exchanged for (1.5) shares Class A Common $1 par 04/09/1964
Stock Dividend - Paid in Class A Common to holders of Class A and B Common 100% 04/15/1964
Completely liquidated 12/01/1976
Each share Class A Common $1 par received first and final distribution of $8.50 cash
Each share Class B Common $1 par received first and final distribution of $8.50 cash
Note: Certificates were not required to be surrendered and are without value

NATIONAL INS GROUP (CA)
Name changed to National Information Group 06/15/1998
National Information Group merged into First American Financial Corp. (CA) 05/14/1999 which name changed to First American Corp. (CA) 05/19/2000 which reincorporated in Delaware as CoreLogic, Inc. 06/01/2010

NATIONAL INTEGRATED FOOD SERVICE CORP (NV)
Charter revoked for failure to file reports and pay fees 01/01/2000

NATIONAL INTEGRATED INDS INC (DE)
Company advised it is private 10/05/2009
Details not available

NATIONAL INTELLIGENCE ASSN INC (NV)
Old Common $0.001 par split (4) for (1) by issuance of (3) additional shares payable 11/01/2010 to holders of record 11/01/2010
Each share old Common $0.001 par exchanged for (0.02) share new Common $0.001 par 09/18/2012
Name changed to Acceleritas Corp. 03/20/2013
Acceleritas Corp. name changed to Hollywall Entertainment Inc. 12/24/2013

NATIONAL INTERGROUP INC (DE)
Preferred Stock Purchase Rights declared for Common stockholders of record 03/31/1986 were redeemed at $0.05 per right 06/10/1992 for holders of record 06/01/1992
Under plan of merger name changed to FoxMeyer Health Corp. 10/12/1994
FoxMeyer Health Corp. name changed to Avatex Corp. 03/07/1997
(See Avatex Corp.)

NATIONAL INTST CORP (OH)
Acquired by American Financial Group, Inc. 11/10/2016
Each share Common 1¢ par exchanged for $32 cash

NATIONAL INVESTMENT CO. (CA)
Incorporated January 16, 1901
Charter suspended for failure to file reports and pay fees 12/14/1905

NATIONAL INVT CORP REAL ESTATE HLDGS (NV)
Charter permanently revoked 02/01/2010

NATIONAL INVT INC (KS)
Each (750) shares Common $1 par exchanged for (1) share Common $1 par 7/24/80
Note: In effect holders received cash per share and public interest was eliminated
Certificates were not required to be surrendered and without value

NATIONAL INVT MANAGERS INC (FL)
Acquired by Stonehenge Opportunity Fund III, L.P. 03/21/2011
Each share Common $0.001 par exchanged for $0.02 cash

NATIONAL INVT TR (POLAND)
Magna Polonia GDR agreement terminated 12/23/2010

Details not available
(Additional Information in Active)

NATIONAL INVESTORS CORP. (NY)
Merged into National Investors Corp. (MD) in 1937
Each share Preferred exchanged for (10.13) shares new Capital Stock $1 par and $13.69 cash
Each share Common exchanged for (0.4) share new Capital Stock $1 par
National Investors Corp. (MD) name changed to Seligman Growth Fund, Inc. 5/1/82

NATIONAL INVS CORP (MD)
Capital Stock $1 par split (2) for (1) by issuance of (1) additional share 03/31/1956
Capital Stock $1 par split (3) for (1) by issuance of (2) additional shares 03/30/1966
Name changed to Seligman Growth Fund, Inc. 05/01/1982

NATIONAL INVESTORS FIRE & CASUALTY INSURANCE CO. (AR)
Merged into Norin Corp. (DE) 11/1/72
Each share Common 10¢ par exchanged for (0.016) share Common $1 par
Norin Corp. (DE) reorganized in Florida 5/31/79
(See Norin Corp. (FL))

NATIONAL INVESTORS LIFE INSURANCE CO. (OK)
Merged into National Investors Life Insurance Co. (Ark.) 6/30/65
Each share Common 10¢ par exchanged for (1/6) share Common $1 par
National Investors Life Insurance Co. (Ark.) merged into Norin Corp. (Del.) 10/31/72 which reorganized in Florida 5/31/79
(See Norin Corp. (Fla.))

NATIONAL INVESTORS LIFE INSURANCE CO. OF ALABAMA (AL)
Merged into Norin Corp. (Del.) 10/31/72
Each share Common $1 par exchanged for (0.114) share Common $1 par
Norin Corp. (Del.) reorganized in Florida 5/31/79
(See Norin Corp. (Fla.))

NATIONAL INVESTORS LIFE INSURANCE CO. OF ARIZONA (AZ)
Merged into Norin Corp. (Del.) 10/31/72
Each share Common 10¢ par exchanged for (0.032) share Common $1 par
Norin Corp. (Del.) reorganized in Florida 5/31/79
(See Norin Corp. (Fla.))

NATIONAL INVESTORS LIFE INSURANCE CO. OF KENTUCKY (KY)
Name changed to Investors Heritage Life Insurance Co. 12/29/1964
Investors Heritage Life Insurance Co. merged into Kentucky Investors Inc. 12/31/1999 which name changed to Investors Heritage Capital Corp. 06/01/2009

NATIONAL INVS LIFE INS CO (AR)
Merged into Norin Corp. (DE) 10/31/1972
Each share Common $1 par exchanged for (0.2) share Common $1 par
Norin Corp. (DE) reorganized in Florida 05/31/1979
(See Norin Corp. (FL))

NATIONAL INVS LIFE INS CO COLO (CO)
Common 10¢ par changed to 12¢ par 05/10/1966
Merged into Norin Corp. (DE) 10/31/1972
Each share Common 12¢ par

NAT-NAT

FINANCIAL INFORMATION, INC.

exchanged for (0.05) share Common $1 par
Norin Corp. (DE) reorganized in Florida 05/31/1979
(See Norin Corp. (FL))

NATIONAL INVS LIFE INS CO GA (GA)
Merged into Norin Corp. (DE) 12/31/1972
Each share Common $1 par exchanged for (0.1) share Common $1 par
Norin Corp. (DE) reorganized in Florida 05/31/1979
(See Norin Corp. (FL))

NATIONAL INVS LIFE INS CO NEB (NE)
Merged into Norin Corp. (DE) 10/31/1972
Each share Common Capital Stock 10¢ par exchanged for (0.055) share Common $1 par
Norin Corp. (DE) reorganized in Florida 05/31/1979
(See Norin Corp. (FL))

NATIONAL IRON BK (SALISBURY, CT)
Under plan of reorganization each share Common $200 par automatically became (1) share Iron Bancshares Inc. Common $1 par 12/30/1997

NATIONAL IRON WORKS
Name changed to National Steel & Shipbuilding Corp. in 1949
National Steel & Shipbuilding Corp. name changed to Nassco Marine Co. 1/4/60
(See Nassco Marine Co.)

NATIONAL IRRON RES LTD (BC)
Struck off register and declared dissolved for failure to file returns 10/30/79

NATIONAL KEY CO. (OH)
Name changed to Cole National Corp. 12/31/1960
(See Cole National Corp.)

NATIONAL KINNEY CORP (NY)
Common $1 par split (2) for (1) by issuance of (1) additional share 6/23/72
Name changed to Andal Corp. 11/7/83
(See Andal Corp.)

NATIONAL LAMPOON INC (DE)
Common $0.0001 par split (2) for (1) by issuance of (1) additional share payable 09/30/2004 to holders of record 09/15/2004 Ex date - 10/01/2004
Company terminated common stock registration and is no longer public as of 10/22/2009

NATIONAL LAMPOON INC (NY)
Acquired by J2 Communications (CA) 10/24/1990
Each share Common 10¢ par exchanged for (0.66666666) share Common no par and (1) Common Stock Purchase Warrant expiring 12/31/1995
J2 Communications (CA) reincorporated in Delaware as National Lampoon, Inc. 11/05/2002
(See National Lampoon, Inc. (DE))

NATIONAL LAND TITLE CORP. (MI)
Adjudicated bankrupt 2/23/71

NATIONAL LASER SYSTEMS, INC. (NV)
Name changed to End Rust USA, Inc. 6/14/88
End Rust USA, Inc. recapitalized as Wray-Tech Instruments Inc. 3/25/91

NATIONAL LD CORP (UT)
Stock Dividend - 20% 09/30/1968
Recapitalized as Dyna-Flex Corp. 04/30/1970
Each share Class A Common $1 par or Class B Common $1 par exchanged for (1) share Class A Common $1 par or Class B Common $1 par respectively
Dyna-Flex Corp. name changed to Dynamic American Corp. 12/31/1974
(See Dynamic American Corp.)

NATIONAL LEAD CO (NJ)
Each share Common $100 par exchanged for (10) shares Common $10 par 00/00/1939
Each share Common $10 par exchanged for (3) shares Common $5 par 00/00/1951
Recapitalized 04/19/1963
Each share Class A Preferred $100 par exchanged for $177.50 cash
Each share Class B Preferred $100 par exchanged for $152.50 cash
Common $5 par changed to $2.50 par and (1) additional share issued 05/16/1969
Name changed to N L Industries, Inc. 04/16/1971

NATIONAL LEARNING CORP (NY)
Company went private in 1993
Details not available

NATIONAL LEASING CO., INC. (IN)
Charter revoked for failure to file reports and pay fees 2/28/69

NATIONAL LEASING CO. (DE)
Charter cancelled and declared inoperative and void for non-payment of taxes 03/17/1920

NATIONAL LEISURE CORP (DE)
Charter cancelled and declared inoperative and void for non-payment of taxes 03/01/1983

NATIONAL LIBERTY CORP (PA)
Common $1 par split (6) for (5) by issuance of (0.2) additional share 6/3/69
Common $1 par split (4) for (3) by issuance of (1/3) additional share 5/10/71
Common $1 par split (3) for (2) by issuance of (0.5) additional share 7/6/72
Stock Dividend - 25% 6/4/70
Completely liquidated 1/26/81
Each share Common $1 par exchanged for approximately $22.28237 principal amount of Capital Holding Corp. 12.75% Ser. A Debentures due 1/15/2006 and $3.705 cash

NATIONAL LIBERTY INSURANCE CO. OF AMERICA
Merged into Home Insurance Co. 00/00/1948
Each share Capital Stock $2 par exchanged for (0.249) share Common $5 par
(See Home Insurance Co.)

NATIONAL LICORICE CO (NY)
6% Preferred $100 par and Common $100 par changed to $10 par respectively and (9) additional shares issued 12/4/64
Each share 6% Preferred $10 par exchanged for (1) share Common $3 par 11/23/66
Common $10 par changed to $3 par and (2.5) additional shares issued 12/5/66
Name changed to Y & S Candies Inc. 5/1/68
Y & S Candies Inc. merged into Hershey Foods Corp. 11/30/77 which name changed to Hershey Co. 4/19/2005

NATIONAL LIFE & ACCIDENT INSURANCE CO. (TN)
Each share Capital Stock $100 par exchanged for (10) shares Capital Stock $10 par 3/1/31
Each share Capital Stock $10 par exchanged for (2) shares Capital Stock $5 par 2/13/62
Stock Dividends - 20% 3/3/30; 33-1/3% 3/1/38; 25% 2/21/40; 100% 12/28/43; 50% 2/24/47; 33-1/3% 12/20/50; 25% 3/1/54; 20% 3/1/58; 20% 3/1/62; 50% 4/1/66; 40% 4/5/68
Reorganized as NLT Corp. (DE) 12/23/68
Each share Capital Stock $5 par exchanged for (1) share Common $5 par
NLT Corp. (DE) reincorporated in Tennessee 1/1/81 which merged into American General Corp. 11/4/82 which merged into American International Group, Inc. 8/29/2001

NATIONAL LIFE & CASUALTY INSURANCE CO. (AZ)
Merged into National Producers Life Insurance Co. 12/31/1964
Each share Common $1 par exchanged for (1) share Common 50¢ par
National Producers Life Insurance Co. name changed to NPL Corp. 03/27/1981
(See NPL Corp.)

NATIONAL LIFE FLA CORP (FL)
Name changed to Voyager Group, Inc. 07/01/1980
(See Voyager Group, Inc.)

NATIONAL LIFE INSURANCE CO. OF FLORIDA (FL)
Reorganized as National Life of Florida Corp. 10/31/1968
Each share Common $1 par exchanged for (1) share Common $1 par
National Life of Florida Corp. name changed to Voyager Group, Inc. 07/01/1980
(See Voyager Group, Inc.)

NATIONAL LINEN SERVICE CORP. (DE)
Name changed to National Service Industries, Inc. 12/14/64
(See National Service Industries, Inc.)

NATIONAL LITHOGRAPHERS & PUBLISHERS INC (FL)
Proclaimed dissolved for failure to file reports and pay fees 09/22/2000

NATIONAL LIVING CTRS INC (DE)
Stock Dividend - 10% 10/14/1971
Merged into ARA Services, Inc. 09/21/1973
Each share Common 1¢ par exchanged for (0.0854) share Common 50¢ par
(See ARA Services, Inc.)

NATIONAL LMBR & SUPPLY INC (CA)
Chapter 11 bankruptcy proceedings converted to Chapter 7 on 8/28/90
Stockholders' equity unlikely

NATIONAL LN BK (HOUSTON, TX)
Liquidation completed
Each share Common 1¢ par received initial distribution of $0.30 cash 2/15/88
Each share Common 1¢ par received second distribution of $0.25 cash 6/17/88
Each share Common 1¢ par received third distribution of $0.35 cash 8/17/88
Each share Common 1¢ par received fourth distribution of $0.35 cash 12/24/88
Each share Common 1¢ par received fifth distribution of $0.25 cash 6/7/89
Each share Common 1¢ par received sixth distribution of $0.30 cash 11/8/89
Each share Common 1¢ par received seventh distribution of $0.20 cash 1/23/90
Each share Common 1¢ par received eighth distribution of $0.15 cash 8/9/90
Each share Common 1¢ par received ninth distribution of $0.15 cash 12/13/90
Each share Common 1¢ par received tenth distribution of $0.15 cash 5/22/91
Each share Common 1¢ par received eleventh distribution of $0.20 cash 10/23/91
Each share Common 1¢ par received twelfth distribution of $0.15 cash 2/5/92
Each share Common 1¢ par received thirteenth distribution of $0.25 cash 12/11/92
Each share Common 1¢ par received fourteenth distribution of $0.20 cash 2/18/93
Each share Common 1¢ par received fifteenth distribution of $0.15 cash 7/9/93
Each share Common 1¢ par received sixteenth distribution of $0.15 cash 12/13/93
Each share Common 1¢ par exchanged for seventeenth and final distribution of of $0.156317 cash 2/15/94

NATIONAL LOCK CO. (DE)
Each share old Common no par exchanged for (50) shares new Common no par 9/20/46
Merged into Keystone Steel & Wire Co. 7/31/68
Each share new Common no par exchanged for $14.50 cash

NATIONAL LOCK WASHER CO. (NJ)
Merged into American Seal-Kap Corp. of Delaware 06/30/1956
Each (3-1/3) shares Common $20 par exchanged for (1) share 5% Preferred 2nd Ser. $100 par
(See American Seal-Kap Corp. of Delaware)

NATIONAL LODGING CORP (DE)
Name changed to Chartwell Leisure, Inc. 8/8/96
(See Chartwell Leisure, Inc.)

NATIONAL LUGGAGE INC (FL)
Stock Dividend - 100% 09/08/1971
Name changed to Bentley National Corp. 01/23/1973
Bentley National Corp. name changed to Sunshine Resources International, Inc. 09/24/1975
(See Sunshine Resources International, Inc.)

NATIONAL LUMBER & CREOSOTING CO.
Dissolved in 1938

NATIONAL LUMBERMAN'S BANK (MUSKEGON, MI)
Stock Dividends - 100% 11/20/44; 50% 8/1/45; 33-1/3% 12/20/46; 25% 2/9/54; 40% 12/31/62
Name changed to National Lumberman's Bank & Trust Co. (Muskegon, MI) 2/1/66
National Lumberman's Bank & Trust Co. (Muskegon, MI) merged into First Michigan Bank Corp. 1/31/79 which merged into Huntington Bancshares Inc. 9/30/97

NATIONAL LUMBERMANS BK & TR CO (MUSKEGON, MI)
Common $10 par changed to $5 par and (1) additional share issued 1/30/70
Stock Dividends - 14-2/7% 9/30/68; 10% 9/30/70
Merged into First Michigan Bank Corp. 1/30/79
Each share Common $5 par exchanged for (2.3) shares Common $1 par
First Michigan Bank Corp. merged into Huntington Bancshares Inc. 9/30/97

NATIONAL MALARTIC GOLD MINES LTD (QC)
Each share old Capital Stock $1 par exchanged for (0.2) share new Capital Stock $1 par and (0.5) share Barnat Mines Ltd. Capital Stock $1 par 00/00/1949

(See Barnat Mines Ltd.)
Acquired by Consolidated Marbenor Mines Ltd. 06/12/1970
Each share Capital Stock $1 par exchanged for (0.6) share Capital Stock $1 par
Consolidated Marbenor Mines Ltd. merged into Canhorn Mining Corp. 01/09/1986 which merged into Canhorn Chemical Corp. 04/26/1995 which merged into Nayarit Gold Inc. 05/02/2005 which merged into Capital Gold Corp. 08/02/2010 which merged into Gammon Gold Inc. (QC) 04/08/2011 which reincorporated in Ontario as AuRico Gold Inc. 06/14/2011

NATIONAL MALLEABLE & STEEL CASTINGS CO. (OH)
Stock Dividends - 10% 3/9/56; 10% 1/6/58
Name changed to National Castings Co. 7/1/61
National Castings Co. merged into Midland-Ross Corp. 4/23/65
(See Midland-Ross Corp.)

NATIONAL MALLINSON FABRICS CORP.
Acquired by Burlington Mills Corp. share for share 5/2/52, which name was changed to Burlington Industries, Inc. 2/3/55
(See Burlington Industries, Inc.)

NATIONAL MGMT CONSULTING INC (DE)
Name changed to Genio Group, Inc. 09/11/2003
Genio Group, Inc. recapitalized as Millennium Prime, Inc. 10/29/2009

NATIONAL MANGANESE CO., INC. (PA)
Liquidated for benefit of creditors in 1959
No stockholders' equity

NATIONAL MANUFACTURE & STORES CORP (DE)
Recapitalized 00/00/1936
Each share 7% Preferred $100 par exchanged for (1-1/3) shares $5.50 Prior Preferred no par
Each share Class A $100 par exchanged for (1) share Class A no par and (3) shares new Common no par
Each share old Common no par exchanged for (1) share new Common no par
Recapitalized 00/00/1945
Common no par changed to $1 par
Stock Dividends - 25% 08/31/1951; 10% 12/01/1955
Name changed to N.M.S. Corp. 08/31/1967
(See N.M.S. Corp.)

NATIONAL MFG TECHNOLOGIES INC (CA)
Common no par split (3) for (2) by issuance of (0.5) additional share payable 06/18/2001 to holders of record 06/04/2001 Ex date - 06/19/2001
SEC revoked common stock registration 07/02/2008
Stockholders' equity unlikely

NATIONAL MARINE TERM INC (CA)
Charter suspended for failure to file reports and pay fees 02/01/1979

NATIONAL MED CARE INC (DE)
Common 20¢ par split (3) for (2) by issuance of (0.5) additional share 8/16/78
Common 20¢ par split (5) for (4) by issuance of (0.25) additional share 5/16/79
Common 20¢ par split (2) for (1) by issuance of (1) additional share 11/12/80
Acquired by NMC Holding Corp. 12/20/84

Each share Common 20¢ par exchanged for $19.25 cash

NATIONAL MED EMERGENCY CARD INC (MD)
Name changed to National Pubs, Inc. 08/19/1986
National Pubs, Inc. recapitalized as Banyantree Healthcare Corp. 04/15/1995
(See Banyantree Healthcare Corp.)

NATIONAL MED ENTERPRISES INC (NV)
Reincorporated 01/09/1976
Class A Common 30¢ par split (3) for (2) by issuance of (0.5) additional share 08/18/1972
State of incorporation changed from (CA) to (NV) and Class A Common 30¢ par reclassified as Common 5¢ par 01/09/1976
Common 5¢ par split (5) for (4) by issuance of (0.25) additional share 12/15/1977
Common 5¢ par split (3) for (2) by issuance of (0.5) additional share 03/19/1979
Common 5¢ par split (3) for (2) by issuance of (0.5) additional share 11/03/1980
Ser. A Preferred 5¢ par changed to $0.025 par and (1) additional share issued 04/29/1981
Common 5¢ par changed to $0.025 par and (1) additional share issued 04/29/1981
Ser. A Preferred $0.025 par changed to 2¢ par and (0.25) additional share issued 04/26/1983
Common $0.025 par changed to 2¢ par and (0.25) additional share issued 04/26/1983
Ser. A Preferred 2¢ par called for redemption 05/31/1984
Common 2¢ par changed to $0.075 par and (1) additional share issued 09/13/1991
Stock Dividends - 10% 06/20/1975; 10% 06/16/1976; 10% 06/15/1977; 10% 06/15/1978
Name changed to Tenet Healthcare Corp. 06/23/1995

NATIONAL MED FINL SVCS CORP (NV)
Common 1¢ par split (2) for (1) by issuance of (1) additional share payable 02/24/1997 to holders of record 02/17/1997
Each share old Common 1¢ par exchanged for (0.1) share new Common 1¢ par 02/10/1998
Company terminated registration of common stock and is no longer public as of 11/13/1998
Details not available

NATIONAL MED GROWTH CORP (MN)
Name changed to Pharmacy Corp. of America, Inc. 11/20/82
Pharmacy Corp. of America, Inc. merged into Beverly Enterprises (CA) 5/22/86 which reorganized in Delaware as Beverly Enterprises, Inc. 7/31/87
(See Beverly Enterprises, Inc.)

NATIONAL MED HEALTH CARD SYS INC (DE)
Reincorporated 02/15/2002
Each share old Common $0.001 par exchanged for (0.12784617) share new Common $0.001 par 05/25/1999
State of incorporation changed from (NY) to (DE) 02/15/2002
Acquired by SXC Health Solutions Corp. 04/30/2008
Each share Common $0.001 par exchanged for (0.217) share Common no par and $7.70 cash
SXC Health Solutions Corp. name changed to Catamaran Corp. 07/11/2012
(See Catamaran Corp.)

NATIONAL MED PRODS INC (DE)
Charter cancelled and declared inoperative and void for non-payment of taxes 3/1/76

NATIONAL MED WASTE INC (DE)
Merged into BioMedical Waste Systems, Inc. 05/27/1994
Each share Common 1¢ par exchanged for (0.2927) share Common $0.001 par
(See BioMedical Waste Systems, Inc.)

NATIONAL MEDIA CORP (DE)
Name changed to e4L, Inc. 02/25/1999
e4L, Inc. recapitalized as Holographic Storage Ltd. 11/25/2005
(See Holographic Storage Ltd.)

NATIONAL MEDPLEX CORP (NY)
Charter cancelled and proclaimed dissolved for failure to pay taxes 09/25/1991

NATIONAL MERCANTILE BANCORP (CA)
Common no par split (5) for (4) by issuance of (0.25) additional share 06/15/1989
Each share old Common no par exchanged for (0.110011) share new Common no par 06/20/1997
New Common no par split (2) for (1) by issuance of (1) additional share payable 02/13/1998 to holders of record 02/04/1998
Each share 6.50% Conv. Preferred no par converted into (2) shares new Common no par 06/23/2005
New Common no par split (5) for (4) by issuance of (0.25) additional share payable 04/14/2006 to holders of record 03/31/2006 Ex date - 04/18/2006
Stock Dividend - 10% 08/15/1988
Merged into First California Financial Group, Inc. 03/12/2007
Each share new Common no par exchanged for (1) share Common 1¢ par
First California Financial Group, Inc. merged into PacWest Bancorp 05/31/2013

NATIONAL MERCANTILE CORP. (NJ)
Each share old Common 10¢ par exchanged for (0.025) share new Common 10¢ par 03/27/1961
Reincorporated under the laws of Delaware as NMC Corp. 01/25/1968
NMC Corp. name changed to Regent Group, Inc. 09/15/1997 which reorganized as Millennium Biotechnologies Group, Inc. 04/01/2002 which name changed to Inergetics, Inc. 05/06/2010

NATIONAL MERIDIAN SVCS INC (DE)
Name changed to Trexar Corp. 06/29/1978
(See Trexar Corp.)

NATIONAL MICRONETICS INC (DE)
Reincorporated 01/25/1982
State of incorporation changed from (NY) to (DE) 01/25/1982
Common 10¢ par split (7) for (5) by issuance of (0.4) additional share 02/19/1982
Common 10¢ par split (3) for (2) by issuance of (0.5) additional share 06/30/1983
Completely dissolved 09/20/1999
No stockholders' equity

NATIONAL MINE SVC CO (WV)
Common $10 par changed to $2.50 par and (3) additional shares issued 06/20/1969
Common $2.50 par changed to $1 par and (1.5) additional shares issued 06/25/1971
Stock Dividend - 100% 04/30/1976
Merged into Anderson Mavor Investments Ltd. 05/23/1990
Each share Common $1 par exchanged for $8.875 cash

NATIONAL MINI THEATRES INC (PA)
Name changed to Atlantic General Corp. 10/15/1974
(See Atlantic General Corp.)

NATIONAL MINING, TUNNEL & LAND CO. (CO)
Charter dissolved for failure to file annual reports 1/1/1919

NATIONAL MOBILE CONCRETE CORP (MI)
Each share old Common no par exchanged for (1/33,013) share new Common no par 03/30/1983
Note: In effect holders received $8.50 cash per share and public interest was eliminated

NATIONAL MOBILE DEV CO (DE)
Reincorporated under the laws of Nevada 4/3/73

NATIONAL MOBILE HEALTH CARE INC (MN)
Common 10¢ par changed to 1¢ par 01/13/1972
Adjudicated bankrupt 06/28/1974
Stockholders' equity unlikely

NATIONAL MOBILE HOME CITIES CORP. (IA)
Under plan of merger each share Common $2 par automatically became (1) share Leisure Time Products, Inc. Common no par

NATIONAL MOBILE INDS INC (CA)
Each share old Common no par exchanged for (0.1) share new Common no par 9/27/71
Charter cancelled for failure to file reports and pay taxes 5/3/76

NATIONAL MOBILE PKS INC (KS)
Name changed to National Ventures & Equities, Inc. 12/12/1973
(See National Ventures & Equities, Inc.)

NATIONAL MODULAR CONCEPTS INC (DE)
Name changed to Kruth Associates, Inc. 04/25/1977
(See Kruth Associates, Inc.)

NATIONAL MODULAR HSG COMPONENTS INC (DE)
Charter cancelled and declared inoperative and void for non-payment of taxes 4/15/73

NATIONAL MODULAR SYS INC (DE)
Name changed to Bon-Aire Industries, Inc. 6/26/72
(See Bon-Aire Industries, Inc.)

NATIONAL MONEY CORP.
Merged into Seaboard Finance Co. 00/00/1946
Each share Preference exchanged for (1) share Class B Preferred
No equity for holders of Common
(See listing for Seaboard Finance Co.)

NATIONAL MORTGAGE & DISCOUNT CO.
Out of business 00/00/1933
Details not available

NATIONAL MTG & INVT CORP (DE)
Common $10 par changed to no par in 1934; to $1 par in October, 1953; then to $25 par 9/19/61
Each share 8% Cum. Preferred $10 par exchanged for (1) share 5% Non-Cum. Preferred $7 par in March, 1939
Name changed to National Mortgage Corp. 11/1/63
(See National Mortgage Corp.)

NATIONAL MORTGAGE CORP. (DE)
Name changed to Federated Mortgage Corp. of Delaware 00/00/1956
Federated Mortgage Corp. of Delaware name changed to Federated Corp. of Delaware 00/00/1959 which name changed to Norma Industries, Inc. 12/01/1966

NAT-NAT

which name changed to Gal Friday
Services, Inc. 05/12/1968
(See Gal Friday Services, Inc.)

NATIONAL MTG CORP (DE)
Merged into FAB Holding Corp.
12/21/1984
Each share 5% Non-Cum. Preferred
$7 par exchanged for $10 cash
Each share Common $25 par
exchanged for $18 cash

NATIONAL MTG FD (NY)
Reorganized under the laws of
Delaware as Highlands-National,
Inc. 06/21/1985
Each Share of Bene. Int. $1 par
exchanged for (1) share Common
$1 par
(See Highlands-National, Inc.)

**NATIONAL MOTOR BEARING CO.,
INC. (CA)**
Each share Capital Stock no par
exchanged for (2) shares Capital
Stock $1 par 00/00/1950
Merged into Federal-Mogul-Bower
Bearings, Inc. on a (0.7) for (1)
basis 07/27/1956
Federal-Mogul-Bower Bearings, Inc.
name changed to Federal-Mogul
Corp. (MI) 04/30/1965
(See Federal-Mogul Corp. (MI))

NATIONAL MOTOR CASTINGS CO.
Acquired by Campbell, Wyant &
Cannon Foundry Co. 00/00/1929
Details not available

**NATIONAL MTR CONVERSIONS
CORP (DE)**
Name changed to National Gas Tek
Corp. 06/14/1983
(See National Gas Tek Corp.)

NATIONAL MTR INN CORP (IA)
Name changed to National Properties
Corp. 7/1/73
National Properties Corp. merged into
Commercial Net Lease Realty, Inc.
6/16/2005 which name changed to
National Retail Properties, Inc.
5/1/2006

**NATIONAL MULTI-SECTOR FIXED
INCOME FD INC (MA)**
Merged into Phoenix Multi-Sector
Fixed Income Fund 12/31/93
Basis not available

NATIONAL MUN TR (NY)
Units of Undivided Int. Insured
Monthly Ser. 37 called for
redemption at $107.35 per $1,000
principal amount on 3/25/99
Units of Undivided Int. Insured
Quarterly Ser. 37 called for
redemption at $107.35 per $1,000
principal amount on 3/25/99
Units of Undivided Int. Insured Semi
Annual Ser. 37 called for redemption
at $107.35 per $1,000 principal
amount on 3/25/99
(Additional Information in Active)

NATIONAL MUSITIME CORP (DE)
Charter cancelled and declared
inoperative and void fon
non-payment of taxes 3/1/75

**NATIONAL NEWARK & ESSEX BK
(NEWARK, NJ)**
Stock Dividend - 10% 03/07/1969
Reorganized as Midlantic Banks Inc.
06/12/1970
Each share Capital Stock $10 par
exchanged for (1) share Common
$10 par
Midlantic Banks Inc. merged into
Midlantic Corp. 01/30/1987 which
merged into PNC Bank Corp.
12/31/1995 which name changed to
PNC Financial Services Group, Inc.
03/15/2000

**NATIONAL NEWARK & ESSEX
BANKING CO. (NEWARK, NJ)**
Each share Capital Stock $100 par
exchanged for (4) shares Capital
Stock $25 par 00/00/1951

Stock Dividend - 16-2/3% 06/20/1952
Name changed to National Newark &
Essex Bank (Newark, NJ)
03/30/1962
National Newark & Essex Bank
(Newark, NJ) reorganized as
Midlantic Banks Inc. 06/12/1970
which merged into Midlantic Corp.
01/30/1987 which merged into PNC
Bank Corp. 12/31/1995 which name
changed to PNC Financial Services
Group, Inc. 03/15/2000

NATIONAL NICKEL LTD (BC)
Recapitalized as Aberdeen Minerals
Ltd. 02/09/1973
Each share Common no par
exchanged for (0.33333333) share
Common no par
(See Aberdeen Minerals Ltd.)

NATIONAL NON METALIC INC (WA)
Each share old Common $0.0001 par
exchanged for (0.05) share new
Common $0.0001 par 10/28/85
Recapitalized as Global Games
International, Inc. 11/12/85
Each share new Common $0.0001
par exchanged for (0.5) share
Common $0.001 par
(See Global Games International,
Inc.)

**NATIONAL NOVA MARKETING INC
(BC)**
Delisted from Vancouver Stock
Exchange for failure to file financial
statements 10/19/94

**NATIONAL NURSING HOMES LTD
(BC)**
Name changed to Cook (N.B.) Corp.
Ltd. 11/8/72
(See Cook (N.B.) Corp. Ltd.)

NATIONAL OATS CO. (IL)
Stock Dividend - 50% 2/11/50
Completely liquidated 10/4/67
Each share Common no par
exchanged for first and final
distribution of (0.444444) share
Liggett & Myers Tobacco Co.
Common $25 par
Liggett & Myers Tobacco Co. name
changed to Liggett & Myers Inc.
5/31/68 which name changed to
Liggett Group Inc. 4/28/76
(See Liggett Group Inc.)

**NATIONAL OIL CO. OF DELAWARE
(DE)**
Charter cancelled and declared
inoperative and void for
non-payment of taxes 4/1/31

NATIONAL OIL CO (CA)
Acquired by Shell Oil Co. 10/31/1974
Each share Capital Stock $5 par
exchanged for (4.5) shares Common
$1 par
(See Shell Oil Co.)

NATIONAL OIL PRODUCTS CO.
Name changed to Nopco Chemical
Co. in 1947
Nopco Chemical Co. merged into
Diamond Alkali 5/1/67 which merged
into Diamond Shamrock Corp.
12/19/67 which name changed to
Maxus Energy Corp. 4/30/87
(See Maxus Energy Corp.)

NATIONAL OIL REFINING CO. (AZ)
Charter expired in 1926
No known value

NATIONAL-OILWELL INC (DE)
Common 1¢ par split (2) for (1) by
issuance of (1) additional share
payable 11/18/1997 to holders of
record 11/10/1997
Name changed to National Oilwell
Varco, Inc. 03/11/2005

NATIONAL OLD LINE INS CO (AR)
Each share Capital Stock $1 par
exchanged for (0.2) share Common
$5 par 11/16/1954
Each share Common $5 par
exchanged for (5) shares Class A

Common $2 par and (5) shares
Class B Common $2 par 11/23/1955
Each share Class A Common $2 par
exchanged for (2) shares Class AA
Common $1 par and (1) share Class
BB Common $1 par 09/20/1957
Each share Class B Common $2 par
exchanged for (3) shares Class BB
Common $1 par 09/20/1957
Stock Dividends - Paid in Class BB
Common to holders of Class AA
Common and/or Class BB
Common - 50% 06/15/1959; 20%
07/18/1960; 20% 01/08/1962; 20%
05/15/1963; 20% 07/15/1964; 10%
04/15/1969
Merged into Ennia N.V. 12/22/1981
Each share Class AA Common $1 par
exchanged for $67.80 cash
Each share Class BB Common $1 par
exchanged for $28.2367 cash

**NATIONAL OLYMPIC SOLAR CORP
(DE)**
Merged into Olympic Solar Corp.
9/18/80
Each share Common 1¢ par
exchanged for (1) share Common
1¢ par
Olympic Solar Corp. name changed
to Olymco Inc. 7/18/85
(See Olymco Inc.)

**NATIONAL OTC CLEARING CORP.
(DE)**
Merged into National Clearing Corp.
9/25/70
Each share Common no par
exchanged for $2,193.82 principal
amount of 8-1/2% Subord. Notes
due 7/31/75 or $2,193.82 cash

**NATIONAL OUTDOOR
ADVERTISING, INC. (MS)**
Charter revoked for failure to pay
taxes 6/19/65

NATIONAL OXYGEN CO.
Acquired by National Cylinder Gas
Co. 00/00/1937
Details not available

**NATIONAL PACIFIC TANK & MILL
CO. (CA)**
Liquidation completed in 1951

NATIONAL PACKAGING CORP. (IN)
Charter revoked for failure to file
annual reports 02/09/1968

NATIONAL PACKAGING CORP (MN)
Name changed to NPC Packaging
Corp. 09/01/1976
(See NPC Packaging Corp.)

NATIONAL PAPER & TYPE CO. (NJ)
Recapitalized 00/00/1936
Each share Preferred $100 par
exchanged for (1) share 5%
Preferred $50 par and (4) shares
Common $1 par
Common $100 par changed to $1 par
Stock Dividend - 100% 12/31/1948
Merged into Otis, McAllister & Co.
00/00/1954
Each share 5% Preferred $50 par
exchanged for (2.5) shares new
Common $1 par Old Common $1
par exchanged for new Common $1
par
(See Otis, McAllister & Co.)

NATIONAL PARAGON CORP (NY)
Common 10¢ par split (3) for (2) by
issuance of (0.5) additional share
11/15/1971
Reincorporated under the laws of
Delaware as National Media Corp.
and Common 10¢ par changed to 1¢
par 07/10/1987
National Media Corp. name changed
to e4L, Inc. 02/25/1999 which
recapitalized as Holographic
Storage Ltd. 11/25/2005
(See Holographic Storage Ltd.)

**NATIONAL PARKING GARAGES,
INC.**
Bankrupt in 1933

NATIONAL PARKS AIRWAYS, INC.
Merged into Western Air Express
Corp. in 1937
Each share Capital Stock $1 par
exchanged for (1) share Capital
Stock $1 par
Western Air Express Corp. name
changed to Western Air Lines, Inc.
3/11/41 which was acquired by Delta
Air Lines, Inc. 12/18/86
(See Delta Air Lines, Inc.)

NATIONAL PASSTIMES INC (DE)
Recapitalized as First American
Equity Corp. (DE) 05/30/1972
Each share Common 1¢ par
exchanged for (0.7) share Common
1¢ par
First American Equity Corp. (DE)
reincorporated in Pennsylvania
11/15/1974
(See First American Equity Corp.)

**NATIONAL PATENT DEV CORP NEW
(DE)**
Name changed to Wright Investors'
Service Holdings, Inc. 02/14/2013

**NATIONAL PATENT DEV CORP OLD
(DE)**
Common 1¢ par split (5) for (2) by
issuance of (1.5) additional shares
5/14/71
Common 1¢ par split (5) for (2) by
issuance of (1.5) additional shares
3/31/72
Each share old Common 1¢ par
exchanged for (0.25) share new
Common 1¢ par 10/6/95
Name changed to GP Strategies
Corp. 3/9/98

NATIONAL PAY TEL CORP (NV)
Each share old Common $0.001 par
exchanged for (0.1) share new
Common $0.001 par 04/22/1986
Name changed to Dynamic Sciences
International, Inc. 07/10/1987
(See Dynamic Sciences International,
Inc.)

**NATIONAL PENN BANCSHARES INC
(PA)**
Common $5 par split (2) for (1) by
issuance of (1) additional share
09/26/1986
Common $5 par changed to $2.50 par
and (1) additional share issued
10/30/1992
Common $2.50 par changed to
$1.875 par and (0.33333333)
additional share issued payable
07/31/1997 to holders of record
07/15/1997
Common $1.875 par changed to no
par and (0.25) additional share
issued payable 07/31/1998 to
holders of record 07/15/1998
Common no par split (5) for (4) by
issuance of (0.25) additional share
payable 09/30/2004 to holders of
record 09/10/2004 Ex date -
10/01/2004
Common no par split (5) for (4) by
issuance of (0.25) additional share
payable 09/30/2005 to holders of
record 09/09/2005 Ex date -
10/03/2005
Stock Dividends - 100% 07/08/1983;
5% payable 10/31/1996 to holders of
record 09/27/1996; 5% payable
12/22/1999 to holders of record
12/06/1999; 5% payable 12/20/2000
to holders of record 12/08/2000
Ex date - 12/06/2000; 3% payable
12/27/2001 to holders of record
12/11/2001 Ex date - 12/07/2001;
5% payable 12/27/2002 to holders of
record 12/06/2002 Ex date -
12/04/2002; 5% payable 09/30/2003
to holders of record 09/12/2003
Ex date - 09/10/2003; 3% payable
09/30/2006 to holders of record
09/08/2006 Ex date - 09/06/2006;
3% payable 09/28/2007 to holders of
record 09/07/2007 Ex date -
09/05/2007

Merged into BB&T Corp. 04/01/2016
Each share Common no par
  exchanged for (0.3206) share
  Common $5 par

NATIONAL PEPSI-COLA CORP.
Assets sold 00/00/1931
Details not available

NATIONAL PERIODICAL PUBLICATIONS, INC. (NY)
Merged into Kinney National Service, Inc. 03/26/1968
Each share Common $1 par
  exchanged for (0.25) share $4.25
  Conv. Preferred Ser. B $1 par and
  (0.39) share Common $1 par
Kinney National Service, Inc. name changed to Kinney Services, Inc. 02/17/1971 which reincorporated in Delaware as Warner Communications Inc. 02/11/1972 which merged into Time Warner Inc. (Old) 01/10/1990 which merged into AOL Time Warner Inc. 01/11/2001 which name changed to Time Warner Inc. (New) 10/16/2003 which merged into AT&T Inc. 06/15/2018

NATIONAL PETROLEUM CORP. (NV)
Charter revoked for failure to file reports and pay taxes 3/5/79

NATIONAL PETROLEUM CORP. (UT)
Charter cancelled for non-payment of corporate taxes 9/30/57

NATIONAL PHARMACEUTICALS CORP (NV)
Recapitalized as Ghana Gold Corp. 07/11/2012
Each share Common $0.0001 par
  exchanged for (0.001) share
  Common $0.0001 par
Ghana Gold Corp. name changed to BrightRock Gold Corp. 11/11/2013

NATIONAL PHOENIX INDUSTRIES, INC. OLD (DE)
Ctfs. dated prior to 4/29/54
Merged into C & C Super Corp. share for share 4/29/54
C & C Super Corp. name changed to C & C Television Corp. 8/5/57 which recapitalized as Television Industries, Inc. 6/18/58 which name changed to Trans-Beacon Corp. 5/5/66
(See Trans-Beacon Corp.)

NATIONAL PHOENIX INDUSTRIES INC. NEW (DE)
Ctfs. dated after 7/31/57
Each share Common 10¢ par
  exchanged for (0.25) share Common
  25¢ par 6/1/58
Merged into Great American Industries, Inc. 9/25/61
Each share Common 25¢ par
  exchanged for (2.25) shares Capital
  Stock 10¢ par
(See Great American Industries, Inc.)

NATIONAL PICTURE & FRAME CO (DE)
Merged into Colonnade Capital, L.L.C. 10/16/97
Each share Common 1¢ par
  exchanged for $12 cash

NATIONAL PIGEONHOLE PARKING, INC. (ID)
Dissolved in 1955

NATIONAL PIZZA CO (KS)
Common 1¢ par split (4) for (3) by issuance of (1/3) additional share 5/1/86
Common 1¢ par split (3) for (2) by issuance of (0.5) additional share 10/25/88
Common 1¢ par reclassified as Class A Common 1¢ par 7/31/91
Each share Class A Common 1¢ par received distribution of (1) share Non-Vtg. Class B Common 1¢ par 8/9/91
Name changed to NPC International, Inc. 7/12/94
(See NPC International, Inc.)

NATIONAL PIZZA CORP (DE)
Ctfs. dated prior to 7/17/86
Name changed to United Satellite Associates, Inc. and Common 10¢ par changed to 1¢ par 7/17/86
United Satellite Associates, Inc. name changed to United Satellite America, Inc. 2/8/88 which name changed to United Satellite/America, Inc. 6/23/89
(See United Satellite/America, Inc.)

NATIONAL PIZZA CORP (DE)
Ctfs. dated after 9/7/2001
Name changed to BSP Onelink, Inc. 9/10/2002
BSP Onelink, Inc. name changed to One Link 4 Travel, Inc. 1/20/2004 which name changed to OneLink Corp. 3/15/2006

NATIONAL PKG SYS INC (NV)
Each share old Common $0.001 par exchanged for (4) shares new Common $0.001 par 10/20/2005
Name changed to BioStem, Inc. 11/18/2005
BioStem, Inc. recapitalized as Joytoto USA, Inc. 10/31/2007 which recapitalized as Pollex, Inc. 10/24/2008 which name changed to eMARINE Global Inc. 09/12/2017

NATIONAL POLE & TREATING CO.
Dissolved in 1946

NATIONAL POOL EQUIP CO (AL)
Common $1 par changed to no par 10/7/64
Recapitalized as National Filtronics, Inc. 12/2/68
Each share Common no par
  exchanged for (0.25) share Common
  no par
(See National Filtronics, Inc.)

NATIONAL POSTAL SYS INC (UT)
Name changed to Sound & Visual Education, Inc. 05/11/1973
Sound & Visual Education, Inc. name changed to Tanner Petroleum, Inc. 05/28/1974 which recapitalized as Solar Design Systems, Inc. 10/13/1978 name changed to Biopetrol, Inc. (UT) 06/15/1981 which reincorporated in Nevada as Kensington International, Inc. 04/17/1996
(See Kensington International, Inc.)

NATIONAL POWDER EXTINGUISHER CORP. (DE)
Dissolved 3/16/62
No Preferred or Common stockholders' equity

NATIONAL POWER & LIGHT CO. (NJ)
Merged into National Phoenix Industries, Inc. (Old) in 1951
Each share Common no par
  exchanged for (0.5) share Common
  10¢ par
National Phoenix Industries, Inc. (Old) merged into C & C Super Corp. 4/29/54 which name changed to C & C Television Corp. 8/5/57 which recapitalized as Television Industries, Inc. 6/18/58 which name changed to Trans-Beacon Corp. 5/5/66 which was adjudicated bankrupt 3/22/71

NATIONAL POWER CORP. (UT)
Reincorporated under the laws of Michigan as World Wide Motion Pictures Corp. 03/19/1984
World Wide Motion Pictures Corp. name changed to Buckeye Ventures, Inc. (MI) 04/27/2006 which reincorporated in Nevada 10/29/2007 which name changed to Energy King, Inc. 02/26/2008 which name changed to Godfather Media, Inc. 10/18/2011 which name changed to Embark Holdings, Inc. 08/20/2012 which name changed to Muscle Warfare International, Inc. 06/28/2013 which name changed to Cannabusiness Group, Inc. 02/18/2014

NATIONAL PWR PLC (UNITED KINGDOM)
Each Sponsored ADR for Final Instalment 50p par exchanged for (1) Sponsored ADR for 1st Instalment 1995 50p par 03/03/1995
Each Sponsored ADR for 1st Instalment 1995 50p par exchanged for (1) Sponsored ADR for 2nd Instalment 1995 50p par 02/06/1996
Each Sponsored ADR for 2nd Instalment 1995 50p par exchanged for (1) new Sponsored ADR for Final Instalment 50p par 09/18/1996
Name changed to International Power PLC 10/02/2000
(See International Power PLC)

NATIONAL PPTYS CORP (IA)
Merged into Commercial Net Lease Realty, Inc. 06/16/2005
Each share Common $1 par
  exchanged for (4) shares Common
  1¢ par
Commercial Net Lease Realty, Inc. name changed to National Retail Properties, Inc. 05/01/2006

NATIONAL PPTYS INC (FL)
Each share Common 1¢ par
  exchanged for (0.25) share Common
  10¢ par 02/07/1972
Reorganized under the laws of Delaware as Delaware National Corp. 05/24/1983
Each share Common 10¢ par
  exchanged for (3) shares Common
  1¢ par
Delaware National Corp. merged into Biscayne National Corp. 11/27/1991
(See Biscayne National Corp.)

NATIONAL PPTYS INVT TR (MA)
SEC revoked common stock registration 07/21/2008
Stockholders' equity unlikely

NATIONAL PRESSURE COOKER CO. (WI)
Stock Dividends - 100% 8/31/46; 100% 2/23/48
Name changed to National Presto Industries, Inc. in 1953

NATIONAL PRIORITIES CORP (DE)
Charter cancelled and declared inoperative and void for non-payment of taxes 03/01/1985

NATIONAL PROCESSING INC (OH)
Merged into Bank of America Corp. 10/15/2004
Each share Common no par
  exchanged for $26.60 cash

NATIONAL PRODUCERS LIFE INS CO (AZ)
Name changed to NPL Corp. 03/27/1981
(See NPL Corp.)

NATIONAL PROPANE CORP (DE)
Common $1 par changed to 10¢ par and (4) additional shares issued 11/15/1971
Merged into D W G Corp. 05/29/1975
Each share Common 10¢ par
  exchanged for $4.25 cash
5% 2nd Preferred Ser. A $25 par called for redemption 06/21/1994
5% 2nd Preferred Ser. B $25 par called for redemption 06/21/1994
Public interest eliminated

NATIONAL PROPANE PARTNERS L P (DE)
Merged into Columbia Propane Corp. 7/19/99
Each share Common no par
  exchanged for $12 cash

NATIONAL PPTY INVS (CA)
Units of Ltd. Partnership II registration terminated 03/21/1997
Details not available
Units of Ltd. Partnership 7 registration terminated 03/28/2007
Details not available
Merged into AIMCO Properties, L.P. 02/11/2011
Each Unit of Ltd. Partnership III received $57.24 cash
Merged into AIMCO Properties, L.P. 02/21/2012
Each Unit of Ltd. Partnership 4 received either (6.68) Common Units or $167.15 cash
Note: California residents will receive cash
(Additional Information in Active)

NATIONAL PROPERTY INVESTORS I (CA)
Limited Partnership closed in 1990
Details not available

NATIONAL PROTECTIVE COMPANIES
Acquired by Loyal Protective Life Insurance Co. and liquidated in 1944
(See Loyal Protective Life Insurance Co.)

NATIONAL PUB SVC INS CO (WA)
Common $10 par changed to $5 par and (1) additional share issued 04/01/1964
Common $5 par changed to $2.50 par and (1) additional share issued 04/18/1969
Stock Dividends - 10% 03/01/1960; 10% 03/01/1962; 10% 03/25/1965; 10% 04/25/1967; 10% 04/24/1970; 10% 06/08/1972
Merged into California-Western States Life Insurance Co. 11/26/1979
Each share Common $2.50 par exchanged for $90 cash

NATIONAL PUBLIC SERVICE CORP. (VA)
Bankrupt in 1932

NATIONAL PUBLIC UTILITIES CORP.
Reorganized in 1940
No stockholders' equity

NATIONAL PUBS INC (MD)
Recapitalized as Banyantree Healthcare Corp. 04/15/1995
Each share Common 1¢ par
  exchanged for (0.1) share Common
  1¢ par
(See Banyantree Healthcare Corp.)

NATIONAL PUMPS CORP.
Acquired by Tokheim Oil Tank & Pump Co. on a (1) for (2.6) basis in 1947
Tokheim Oil Tank & Pump Co. name changed to Tokheim Corp. in 1953
(See Tokheim Corp.)

NATIONAL QUICK LUBE LTD (BC)
Common no par reclassified as Class A Common no par 6/3/93
Recapitalized as NQL Drilling Tools Inc. 6/14/94
Each share Class A Common no par exchanged for (0.25) share Common no par
NQL Drilling Tools Inc. name changed to NQL Energy Services Inc. 7/11/2005
(See NQL Energy Services Inc.)

NATIONAL QUICK START INC (UT)
Involuntarily dissolved 11/01/1988

NATIONAL QUOTES INC (ON)
Reincorporated under the laws of Florida as Natquote Financial, Inc. and Class A Common no par reclassified as Common no par 04/30/1997
Natquote Financial, Inc. name changed to Contact Capital Group Inc. 04/28/2003
(See Contact Capital Group Inc.)

NATIONAL R V HLDGS INC (DE)
Common 1¢ par split (3) for (2) by issuance of (0.5) additional share payable 05/16/1996 to holders of record 05/06/1996
Common 1¢ par split (3) for (2) by

issuance of (0.5) additional share payable 07/24/1998 to holders of record 07/10/1998
Plan of reorganization under Chapter 11 Federal Bankruptcy Code effective 12/22/2008
Each share Common 1¢ par received initial distribution of approximately $0.015 cash payable 01/05/2012 to holders of record 12/22/2008
Each share Common 1¢ par received second and final distribution of $0.017892 cash payable 01/11/2013 to holders of record 12/22/2008

NATIONAL RADIAC, INC. (NJ)
Merged into Delta Instrument Corp. (N.J.) share for share 7/16/62 which was adjudged insolvent 3/8/63

NATIONAL RADIATOR CO. (MD)
Each share Common $10 par exchanged for (2.5) shares Common $4 par in 1946
Merged into National-U.S. Radiator Corp. 4/1/55
Each share Common $4 par exchanged for (1.625) shares Common $1 par
National-U.S. Radiator Corp. name changed to Natus Corp. 2/1/60 which name changed to Kirkeby-Natus Corp. 6/30/61 which name changed to United Ventures, Inc. 6/24/66 which merged into Federated Development Co. 7/31/70
(See Federated Development Co.)

NATIONAL RADIATOR CORP. (DE)
Acquired by National Radiator Corp. (MD) 09/27/1932
Each share $7 Preferred no par exchanged for (1) share Common no par
Each share Common no par exchanged for (1/3) Common Stock Purchase Warrant expiring 07/01/1941
(See National Radiator Corp. (MD))

NATIONAL RADIATOR CORP. (MD)
Reorganized as National Radiator Co. 5/19/39
No stockholders' equity

NATIONAL RADIO INC (MA)
Adjudicated bankrupt 09/07/1973
No stockholders' equity

NATIONAL RE CORP (DE)
Name changed 5/26/92
Name changed from National Re Holdings to National Re Corp. 5/26/92
Merged into General Re Corp. 10/3/96
Each share Common no par exchanged for (0.37262) share Common 50¢ par
General Re Corp. merged into Berkshire Hathaway Inc. 12/21/98

NATIONAL REAL ESTATE FD (CA)
Fund liquidated in 1976
Distribution amounts and dates not available

NATIONAL REAL ESTATE LIMITED PARTNERSHIP-VI (WI)
Certificate of Cancellation filed 12/23/1993
Details not available

NATIONAL REAL ESTATE LTD PARTNERSHIP INCOME PPTYS (WI)
In process of liquidation and certificate of cancellation filed 10/15/2002
Details not available

NATIONAL REAL ESTATE STK FD (MA)
Name changed to National Real Estate Trust 12/19/1986
National Real Estate Trust merged into Templeton Real Estate Securities Fund 12/14/1990 which name changed to Templeton Global Real Estate Fund 05/15/1996

(See Templeton Global Real Estate Fund)

NATIONAL REAL ESTATE TR (MA)
Merged into Templeton Real Estate Securities Fund 12/14/1990
Each Income Fund Share of Bene. Int. 1¢ par exchanged for (1.385) Share of Bene. Int. 1¢ par
Each Stock Fund Share of Bene. Int. 1¢ par exchanged for (1.385) Share of Bene. Int. 1¢ par
Templeton Real Estate Securities Fund name changed to Templeton Global Real Estate Fund 05/15/1996
(See Templeton Global Real Estate Fund)

NATIONAL RLTY & MTG INC (NV)
Each shares old Common $0.0000001 par exchanged for (0.00333333) share new Common $0.0000001 par 12/19/2005
New Common $0.0000001 par changed to $0.001 par 10/24/2006
Recapitalized as Sunway Global Inc. 02/07/2008
Each share Common $0.001 par exchanged for (0.01158701) share Common $0.0000001 par
(See Sunway Global Inc.)

NATIONAL REALTY CORP. (MD)
Liquidation completed
Each Ctf. of Participation no par exchanged for initial distribution of $7.06 cash 03/26/1965
Each Ctf. of Participation no par received second distribution of $8.88 cash 05/31/1966
Each Ctf. of Participation no par received third and final distribution of $83.64 cash 03/01/1968

NATIONAL RLTY INVS (MA)
Acquired by United National Corp. (DE) 02/28/1973
Each Bene. Ctf. for Common no par exchanged for $5.50 principal amount of 7-1/2% Subord. S.F. Debentures due 02/29/1988, (0.2) share Common $1 par and (1) Common Stock Purchase Warrant expiring 05/28/1978
United National Corp. (DE) merged into Goldome National Corp. 05/13/1983
(See Goldome National Corp.)

NATIONAL RLTY L P (DE)
Each old Unit of Ltd. Partnership Int. exchanged for (0.2) new Unit of Ltd. Partnership Int. 1/20/89
Each new Unit of Ltd. Partnership Int. exchanged again for (0.25) new Unit of Ltd. Partnership Int. 1/1/91
New Units of Ltd. Partnership Int. split (3) for (1) by issuance of (2) additional Units payable 1/15/96 to holders of record 1/2/96 Ex date - 1/16/96
Merged into American Realty Investors Inc. 8/2/2000
Each new Unit of Ltd. Partnership Int. exchanged for (1) share Common 1¢ par

NATIONAL REALTY TRUST (MA)
Reorganized in 1953
Last date to participate was 6/19/62 and unexchanged Certificates of Beneficial Interest $25 par became worthless after that date

NATIONAL REC INDS INC (DE)
Name changed to NRI, Inc. 00/00/1983
(See NRI, Inc.)

NATIONAL REC PRODS INC (DE)
Merged into Fuqua Industries, Inc. 12/29/1978
Each share Common $1 par exchanged for $9.25 cash

NATIONAL RECORD MART INC (DE)
Plan of reorganization under Chapter 11 Federal Bankruptcy Code effective 06/16/2003

No stockholders' equity

NATIONAL RECORDING PUMP CO.
Name changed to National Pumps Corp. in 1930
National Pumps Corp. acquired by Tokheim Oil Tank & Pump Co. in 1947 which name was changed to Tokheim Corp. in 1953
(See Tokheim Corp.)

NATIONAL RECYCLED CONTAINERS CORP (DE)
Name changed to Natcontainer Corp. 12/01/1974
(See Natcontainer Corp.)

NATIONAL REFERENCE PUBG INC (DE)
Name changed to NRP Inc. 7/13/88
NRP Inc. name changed to ATC Communications Inc. 4/30/96 which name changed to Aegis Communications Group, Inc. 7/9/98

NATIONAL REFRIGERATION CORP.
Name changed to General Refrigeration Corp. in 1930
General Refrigeration Corp. merged into Yates-American Machine Co. in 1940
(See Yates-American Machine Co.)

NATIONAL REGISTRY INC (DE)
Each share old Common 1¢ par exchanged for (1/6) share new Common 1¢ par 05/27/1998
Name changed to Saflink Corp. 11/12/1999
Saflink Corp. recapitalized as IdentiPHI, Inc. 02/19/2008
(See IdentiPHI, Inc.)

NATIONAL REHAB PPTYS INC (NV)
Each share old Common $0.001 par exchanged for (0.1) share new Common $0.001 par 01/15/1999
Name changed to National Residential Properties, Inc. 12/22/2000
National Residential Properties, Inc. name changed to National Realty & Mortgage, Inc. 10/20/2005 which recapitalized as Sunway Global Inc. 02/07/2008
(See Sunway Global Inc.)

NATIONAL REHABILITATION CTRS INC (TN)
Name changed to Rehability Corp. 6/1/93
Rehability Corp. merged into Living Centers of America, Inc. 6/30/95 which merged into Paragon Health Network, Inc. 11/4/97 which name changed to Mariner Post-Acute Network, Inc. 7/31/98
(See Post-Acute Network, Inc.)

NATIONAL REINVESTING CORP.
Liquidated in 1937

NATIONAL REP BK (CHICAGO, IL)
Merged into NR Interim Bank 12/31/98
Each share Common exchanged for $2.73 cash

NATIONAL REPUBLIC INVESTMENT TRUST
Liquidated in 1938

NATIONAL RESEARCH & DEVELOPMENT CORP. (GA)
Class A Common 10¢ par reclassified as Common 10¢ par plus a 300% stock dividend paid which was effected by an exchange of (1) share Class A Common 10¢ par for (4) shares Common 10¢ par 2/2/62
Assets sold for benefit of creditors in 1962
No equity for Common Stockholders

NATIONAL RESEARCH CORP. (MA)
Stock Dividend - 200% 3/31/52
Merged into Norton Co. 5/7/63
Each share Common $1 par exchanged for (0.6) share Common $10 par
(See Norton Co.)

NATIONAL RESERVE LIFE INSURANCE CO. (KS)
Merged into National Reserve Life Insurance Co. (SD) 10/11/51
Each (0.3) share Capital Stock $10 par exchanged for (1) share Common $10 par
(See National Reserve Life Insurance Co. (SD))

NATIONAL RESH & DEV INC (UT)
Involuntarily dissolved 05/01/1987

NATIONAL RESH ASSOC INC (NV)
Reincorporated 09/26/1968
State of incorporation changed from (MD) to (NV) and Capital Stock no par changed to Common 25¢ par 09/26/1968
Charter revoked for failure to file reports and pay fees 03/01/1979

NATIONAL RESIDENTIAL PPTYS INC (NV)
New Common $0.001 par split (3) for (1) by issuance of (2) additional shares payable 02/01/2001 to holders of record 01/22/2001 Ex date - 02/02/2001
Stock Dividend - 10% payable 01/10/2002 to holders of record 11/19/2001 Ex date - 12/10/2001
Name changed to National Realty & Mortgage, Inc. and new Common $0.001 par changed to $0.0000001 par 10/20/2005
National Realty & Mortgage, Inc. recapitalized as Sunway Global Inc. 02/07/2008
(See Sunway Global Inc.)

NATIONAL RESOURCE EXPLS LTD (BC)
Merged into NIM Petroleum Corp. 6/1/90
Each share Common no par exchanged for (0.117647) share Common no par
NIM Petroleum Corp. name changed to Petrorep Resources Ltd. 8/26/92
(See Petrorep Resources Ltd.)

NATIONAL RES CORP (AZ)
Charter revoked for failure to file reports and pay fees 06/20/1967

NATIONAL RES GROUP INC (NV)
Charter permanently revoked 11/01/2005

NATIONAL RESTAURANT GROUP INC (DE)
Each share old Common 10¢ par exchanged for (0.1) share new Common 10¢ par 7/26/96
Name changed to Galconda Corp. (New) 8/2/96
Galconda Corp. (New) recapitalized as Jax International Inc. 12/3/96
(See Jax International Inc.)

NATIONAL RESV LIFE INS CO (SD)
Common $10 par reclassified as Class A Common $10 par 05/03/1961
Class A Common $10 par changed to $1 par and (9) additional shares issued 02/20/1963
Class A-1 Preferred Ser. 1 $10 par called for redemption 06/30/1968
Class A-1 Preferred Ser. 2 $10 par called for redemption 01/20/1969
Stock Dividends - Class A & AA Common - 10% 06/10/1964; 10% 06/10/1965; 10% 06/15/1966; 10% 06/06/1969; 50% 06/05/1972; 100% 03/15/1978
Merged into Kansas City Life Insurance Co. 11/09/1984
Each share Class A Common $1 par exchanged for $31 cash
Each share Class AA Common $1 par exchanged for $31 cash

NATIONAL RETAIL PPTYS INC (MD)
Preferred Ser. A 1¢ par called for redemption at $25 plus $0.20625 accrued dividends on 01/02/2007
7.375% Depositary Preferred Ser. C

called for redemption at $25 plus $0.107552 accrued dividends on 03/15/2012
6.625% Depositary Preferred Ser. D called for redemption at $25 plus $0.312847 accrued dividends on 02/23/2017
(Additional Information in Active)

NATIONAL RETIREMENT INS CO (MI)
Each share Common $1 par exchanged for (0.0002) share Common $5,000 par 03/27/1986
Note: Holders of Common $1 par received and undetermined amount of cash and public interest was eliminated

NATIONAL ROLL & FOUNDRY CO.
Merged into General Steel Castings Corp. on a (1) for (4.69) basis 12/5/55 which name was changed to General Steel Industries, Inc. 5/1/61

NATIONAL ROLLING MILLS CO. (PA)
Common $1 par split (5) for (4) by issuance of (0.25) additional share 12/16/63
Common $1 par split (5) for (4) by issuance of (0.25) additional share 12/21/64
Common $1 par split (5) for (4) by issuance of (0.25) additional share 2/8/66
Completely liquidated 3/17/67
Each share Common $1 par exchanged for first and final distribution of (0.5) share Bundy Corp. Common $5 par
(See Bundy Corp.)

NATIONAL RTY CORP (OK)
Reincorporated under the laws of Delaware as Pacer Energy Corp. 9/19/88
(See Pacer Energy Corp.)

NATIONAL RUBBER MACHINERY CO. (OH)
Common no par changed to $10 par 00/00/1948
Common $10 par changed to $5 par and (1) additional share issued 04/26/1963
Name changed to NRM Corp. 05/01/1964
NRM Corp. merged into AMK Corp. 07/03/1967 which merged into United Brands Co. 06/30/1970 which name changed to Chiquita Brands International, Inc. 03/20/1990
(See Chiquita Brands International, Inc.)

NATIONAL RUBBER PRODUCTS CORP. (DE)
No longer in existence having become inoperative and void for non-payment of taxes 3/17/26

NATIONAL RURAL UTILS COOP FIN CORP (DC)
8% Quarterly Income Capital Securities Preferred called for redemption at $25 on 12/31/2001
Quarterly Income Capital Securities called for redemption at $25 plus $0.153646 accrued dividends on 10/15/2003
Quarterly Income Capital Securities Ser. NRY called for redemption at $25 plus $0.476562 accrued dividends on 6/15/2006
7.4% Quarterly Income Capital Securities Ser. NRS called for redemption at $25 plus $0.154167 accrued dividends on 6/1/2007

NATIONAL RY PUBN CO (PA)
Name changed to NRP Co. Liquidating Ltd. 7/20/81
(See NRP Co. Liquidating Ltd.)

NATIONAL RY UTILIZATION CORP (SC)
Name changed to NRUC Corp. 6/5/84
NRUC Corp. name changed to Emergent Group Inc. 8/24/91 which name changed to Homegold Financial Inc. 7/1/98
(See Homegold Financial Inc.)

NATIONAL SAFETY BANK & TRUST CO. (NEW YORK, NY)
Stock Dividend - 12% 4/1/44
Merged into Chemical Bank & Trust Co. (New York, NY) 3/19/51
Each share Common $12.50 par exchanged for (0.25) share Capital Stock $10 par plus $128 cash
Chemical Bank & Trust Co. (New York, NY) merged into Chemical Corn Exchange Bank (New York, NY) 10/18/54 which merged into Chemical Bank New York Trust Co. (New York, NY) 9/8/59 which reorganized as Chemical New York Corp. 2/17/69 which name changed to Chemical Banking Corp. 4/29/88 which name changed to Chase Manhattan Corp. (New) 3/31/96 which name changed to J.P. Morgan Chase & Co. 12/31/2000 which name changed to JPMorgan Chase & Co. 7/20/2004

NATIONAL SAN SUPPLY CO (DE)
Merged into Unisource Worldwide, Inc. 9/30/97
Each share Common no par exchanged for $21 cash

NATIONAL SASH WEIGHT CORP (MD)
$3.50 Conv. Preferred no par called for redemption at $57.50 on 02/02/1998
Charter dissolved 06/08/1999

NATIONAL SVGS & TR CO (WASHINGTON, DC)
Each share Capital Stock $100 par exchanged for (10) shares Capital Stock $10 par 00/00/1952
Stock Dividends - 100% 01/16/1962; 50% 10/07/1966
Reorganized under the laws of Delaware as NS&T Bankshares, Inc. 11/16/1981
Each share Capital Stock $10 par exchanged for (3) shares Common $5 par
(See NS&T Bankshares, Inc.)

NATIONAL SVGS BK (ALBANY, NY)
Common $1 par split (3) for (2) by issuance of (0.5) additional share 5/12/92
Stock Dividend - 10% 8/30/91
Acquired by KeyCorp (NY) 2/26/93
Each share Common $1 par exchanged for (0.883) share Common $5 par
KeyCorp (NY) merged into KeyCorp (New) (OH) 3/1/94

NATIONAL SVGS CORP (TN)
Reorganized 03/14/1969
Under plan of reorganization each share National Savings Life Insurance Co. automatically became (1) share National Savings Corp. Common $1 par 03/14/1969
Stock Dividend - 20% 03/01/1971
Merged into Western Preferred Corp. 12/10/1982
Each share Common $1 par exchanged for $25 cash

NATIONAL SVGS LIFE INS CO (AR)
Acquired by National Savings Corp. (AR) 08/11/1989
Each share Common no par exchanged for $0.116 cash

NATIONAL SCIENTIFIC CORP (TX)
Recapitalized as Cipherloc Corp. 03/23/2015
Each share Common 1¢ par exchanged for (0.01) share Common 1¢ par

NATIONAL SCIENTIFIC PRODS CORP (BC)
Delisted from Vancouver Stock Exchange 03/02/1990

NATIONAL SCREW & MFG CO (OH)
Each share Common $100 par exchanged for (4) shares Common $1 par 00/00/1941
Stock Dividend - 100% 02/20/1953
Through voluntary purchase offer Monogram Industries Inc. acquired 99.8% as of 00/00/1967
Public interest eliminated

NATIONAL SEA PRODS LTD (NS)
5-1/2% Preferred $5 par reclassified as 5-1/2% Class C Conv. Preference $5 par 8/31/72
Old Common no par reclassified as Conv. Class A Common no par 8/31/72
Conv. Class A Common no par split (3) for (1) by issuance of (2) additional shares 11/13/78
Conv. Class B Common no par split (3) for (1) by issuance of (2) additional shares 11/13/78
Conv. Class A Common no par reclassified as new Common no par 1/28/86
Conv. Class B Common no par reclassified as new Common no par 1/28/86
New Common no par reclassified as Conv. Common no par 8/15/86
Each share Conv. Common no par received distribution of (1) share Non-Vtg. Equity Stock no par 8/18/86
Each share Non-Vtg. Equity Stock no par exchanged for (1) share Conv. Common no par 6/19/91
Each share Conv. Common no par exchanged for (0.25) share Common no par 5/10/95
Name changed to High Liner Foods Inc. 1/28/99

NATIONAL SEASTAR CORP (BC)
Recapitalized as Pacific National Seafarms Ltd. (BC) 1/16/90
Each share Common no par exchanged for (0.5) share Common no par
Pacific National Seafarms Ltd. (BC) reorganized in Delaware as Starbase Corp. 10/21/92
(See Starbase Corp.)

NATIONAL SEC INS CO (AL)
Common $1 par changed to 50¢ par 02/27/1964
Common 50¢ par changed to $1 par 07/18/1968
Stock Dividends - 100% 00/00/1954; 10% 00/00/1956; 10% 00/00/1957; 15% 00/00/1958; 10% 02/04/1960; 10% 03/01/1961; 10% 07/01/1968; 10% 07/01/1969; 10% 08/30/1972; 10% 07/20/1973; 20% 12/01/1977; 25% 06/19/1978
Reorganized under the laws of Delaware as National Security Group, Inc. 09/28/1990
Each share Common $1 par exchanged for (2) shares Common $1 par

NATIONAL SECS & RESH CORP (NY)
Each share Capital Stock $1 par exchanged for (2) shares Capital Stock 50¢ par 00/00/1940
Capital Stock 50¢ par changed to 25¢ par and (2) additional shares issued 07/09/1956
Capital Stock 25¢ par changed to 8-1/3¢ par 03/01/1959
Merged into Aitken Hume Holding plc 03/06/1984
Each share Capital Stock 8-1/3¢ par exchanged for $27 cash

NATIONAL SECS CORP (WA)
Each share old Common 1¢ par exchanged for (0.25) share new Common 1¢ par 03/09/1992
Each share new Common 1¢ par exchanged for (2) shares Common 2¢ par 02/15/1994
Stock Dividends - 5% payable 06/14/1996 to holders of record 06/04/1996; 5% payable 02/10/1997 to holders of record 01/27/1997
Reincorporated under the laws of Delaware as Olympic Cascade Financial Corp. 02/07/1997
Olympic Cascade Financial Corp. name changed to National Holdings Corp. 03/20/2006

NATIONAL SECS FDS (NY)
Name changed 08/25/1971
Speculative Series reclassified as Dividend Series 10/05/1955
Growth Stock Series shares $1 par split (3) for (1) by issuance of (2) additional shares 10/05/1955
Name changed from National Securities Series to National Securities Funds and Bond Series, Dividend Series, Income Series, Preferred Stock Series and Stock Series reclassified as Bond Fund, Dividend Fund, Income Fund, Preferred Fund and Stock Fund respectively 08/25/1971
Dividend Fund reclassified as Total Return Fund 11/06/1981
Bond Fund merged into Phoenix High Yield Fund 12/31/1993
Each share $1 par exchanged for (0.231664) share Common $1 par
Income Fund reorganized as National Total Income Fund Inc. 06/27/1986
Each share $1 par exchanged for (1) share Class A Common $1 par
Stock Fund merged into Phoenix Equity Opportunities Fund 12/31/1993
Details not available
Total Return Fund merged into Phoenix Total Return Fund Inc. 12/31/1993
Each share $1 par exchanged for (0.343429848) share Common $1 par
(See each company's listing)

NATIONAL SECS HLDG CORP (CO)
Recapitalized as New Frontier Media Inc. 09/15/1995
Each share Common $0.0001 par exchanged for (0.00049148) share Common $0.0001 par
(See New Frontier Media Inc.)

NATIONAL SECS TAX EXEMPT BDS INC (MD)
Merged into Phoenix Multi-Portfolio Fund 11/12/1993
Each share 1¢ par exchanged for (0.902689566) share Tax-Exempt Bond Portfolio $1 par
(See Phoenix Multi-Portfolio Fund)

NATIONAL SECURITIES CORP. (VA)
Bankrupt in 1930
No stockholders' equity

NATIONAL SECURITIES INC. (AZ)
Reincorporated under the laws of Colorado 06/30/1964

NATIONAL SECURITIES INVESTMENT CO.
Dissolved 00/00/1935
Details not available

NATIONAL SECURITY INSURANCE CO.
Merged into Insurance Co. of North America in 1946
Insurance Co. of North America acquired by INA Corp. 5/29/68 which merged into Cigna Corp. 4/1/82

NATIONAL SECURITY LIFE INSURANCE CO., INC. (WI)
Recapitalized as Madison National Life Insurance Co., Inc. 8/26/63
Each share Common 40¢ par exchanged for (0.4) share Common $1 par
Madison National Life Insurance Co., Inc. name changed to Madison National Life Insurance Co., Inc. of Wisconsin 8/17/64 which reorganized as Madison Co. 12/1/75 which merged into Independence Holding Co. (Old) 8/9/83 which

name changed to Stamford Capital Group, Inc. 11/4/87 which name changed to Independence Holding Co. (New) 9/10/90

NATIONAL SECURITY LIFE INSURANCE CO. (IN)
Merged into United Home Life Insurance Co. 6/28/65
Each share Capital Stock $1 par exchanged for (1/13) share Common $1 par
(See United Home Life Insurance Co.)

NATIONAL SECURITY LIFE INSURANCE CO. (NM)
Each share Common $1 par exchanged for (2) shares Common 30¢ par 11/8/63
Name changed to International Properties, Inc. (NM) 1/26/66
(See International Properties, Inc.)

NATIONAL SEMICONDUCTOR CORP (DE)
Common 50¢ par split (2) for (1) by issuance of (1) additional share 04/07/1972
Common 50¢ par split (3) for (1) by issuance of (2) additional shares 01/25/1974
Common 50¢ par split (3) for (2) by issuance of (0.5) additional share 03/17/1980
Common 50¢ par split (3) for (1) by issuance of (2) additional shares 11/29/1983
Conv. Depositary Preferred called for redemption 04/21/1994
$40 Conv. Exchangeable Preferred 50¢ par called for redemption 04/21/1994
$32.50 Conv. Depositary Preferred called for redemption 12/01/1995
$32.50 Conv. Preferred 50¢ par called for redemption 12/01/1995
Common 50¢ par split (2) for (1) by issuance of (1) additional share payable 05/13/2004 to holders of record 04/29/2004 Ex date - 05/14/2004
Acquired by Texas Instruments Inc. 09/23/2011
Each share Common 50¢ par exchanged for $25 cash

NATIONAL SERVICE COMPANIES (MA)
Common no par changed to $1 par in 1935
Assets transferred to Northeast Equities, Inc. 6/1/62
Each share $4 Preferred no par exchanged for (1.2) shares Common $1 par
Each share $3 Preferred no par exchanged for (1) share Common $1 par
Common $1 par exchanged on a (0.002) for (1) basis
After 8/1/62 only Preferred remained exchangeable; Common became worthless
Northeast Equities, Inc. name changed to Northeast Petroleum Industries, Inc. 10/29/69
(See Northeast Petroleum Industries, Inc.)

NATIONAL SVC INDS INC (DE)
Common $1 par split (4) for (3) by issuance of (0.33333333) additional share 01/11/1965
Common $1 par split (4) for (3) by issuance of (0.33333333) additional share 01/04/1968
Common $1 par split (2) for (1) by issuance of (1) additional share 10/02/1969
Common $1 par split (4) for (3) by issuance of (0.33333333) additional share 01/11/1983
Common $1 par split (3) for (2) by issuance of (0.5) additional share 01/20/1984
Common $1 par split (4) for (3) by issuance of (0.33333333) additional share 01/21/1986
Common $1 par split (3) for (2) by issuance of (0.5) additional share 01/27/1987
Each share Common $1 par received distribution of (1) share Acuity Brands, Inc. Common 1¢ par payable 11/30/2001 to holders of record 11/16/2001 Ex date - 12/03/2001
Each share old Common $1 par exchanged for (0.25) share new Common $1 par 01/07/2002
Merged into California Investment Fund, LLC 06/12/2003
Each share new Common $1 par exchanged for $10 cash

NATIONAL SEWER PIPE CO., LTD. (ON)
Name changed to National Sewer Pipe Ltd. in 1953

NATIONAL SHAREDATA CORP (DE)
Merged into Western Union Corp. (Old) 08/13/1973
Each share Common 5¢ par exchanged for (0.387) share Common $2.50 par
Western Union Corp. (Old) merged into Western Union Corp. (New) 12/31/1987 which name changed to New Valley Corp. 04/22/1991 which reorganized in Delaware 07/29/1996 which was acquired by Vector Group Ltd. 12/13/2005

NATIONAL SHAREHOLDERS CORP.
Common no par changed to $1 par in 1935
Voluntarily dissolved 2/26/65
Details not available

NATIONAL SHARES CORP. (DE)
Capital Stock no par changed to $1 par and (1) additional share issued 3/2/55
Name changed to Dominick Fund, Inc. 3/4/59
Dominick Fund, Inc. merged into Putnam Investors Fund, Inc. 10/15/74

NATIONAL SHAWMUT BANK (BOSTON, MA)
Merged into Shawmut Association, Inc. 5/6/65
Each share Capital Stock $12.50 par exchanged for (1.4) shares Common no par
Shawmut Association, Inc. name changed to Shawmut Corp. 4/24/75 which merged into Shawmut National Corp. 2/29/88 which merged into Fleet Financial Group Inc. (New) 11/30/95 which name changed to Fleet Boston Corp. 10/1/99 which name changed to FleetBoston Financial Corp. 4/18/2000 which merged into Bank of America Corp. 4/1/2004

NATIONAL SHIP COPPER PLATING CO. (ME)
Excused by State of Maine having ceased to transact business 00/00/1904
Details not available

NATIONAL SHIRT SHOPS OF DELAWARE, INC. (DE)
Each share Common no par exchanged for (6) shares Common $1 par 07/00/1946
Merged into McCrory Corp. 12/22/1960
Each share Common $1 par exchanged for (0.18) share 5-1/2% Conv. Preference Ser. B $100 par 12/22/1960
(See McCrory Corp.)

NATIONAL SHOES INC (NY)
Acquired by Shoecliff Corp. 7/10/85
Each share Common $1 par exchanged for $13 cash

NATIONAL SHOWMANSHIP SVCS INC (NY)
Stock Dividends - 10% 3/25/80; 10% 4/1/81
Dissolved by proclamation 12/23/92

NATIONAL SILK DYEING CO.
Name changed to National Dyeing & Printing Co. in 1934 which was dissolved in 1948

NATIONAL SILVER INDS INC (DE)
Name changed to N.S.I., Inc. 05/14/1982
(See N.S.I., Inc.)

NATIONAL SKYWAY FREIGHT CORP.
Name changed to Flying Tiger Line Inc. in 1947
Flying Tiger Line Inc. name changed to Flying Tiger Corp. 6/30/70 which name changed to Tiger International, Inc. 7/1/74
(See Tiger International, Inc.)

NATIONAL SOFTWARE & COMMUNICATIONS INC (DE)
Charter cancelled and declared inoperative and void for non-payment of taxes 3/1/88

NATIONAL SORBENTS INC (NV)
Reincorporated 01/18/2000
Each (3.324) shares old Class A no par exchanged for (1) share new Class A Common no par 01/19/1996
Each share new Class A Common no par exchanged for (0.5) share Class A Common $0.001 par 09/09/1998
State of incorporation changed from (OH) to (NV) 01/18/2000
SEC revoked common stock registration 07/31/2008
Stockholders' equity unlikely

NATIONAL SPINNING CO (NY)
Merged into NSC Merger, Inc. 01/06/1981
Each share Common $1 par exchanged for $12 cash

NATIONAL SPORTS CENTERS, INC. (DE)
Name changed to Federal Bowling Centers, Inc. 6/23/60
(See Federal Bowling Centers, Inc.)

NATIONAL SPORTS CLUB, INC. (FL)
Name changed to Job Stores, Inc. 10/16/80
(See Job Stores, Inc.)

NATIONAL SPORTS ENTERPRISES LTD (NY)
Dissolved by proclamation 9/26/90

NATIONAL ST BK (BOULDER, CO)
Merged into First National Bancorporation, Inc. 01/19/1982
Each share Common $10 par exchanged for (5.408) shares Common $10 par
First National Bancorporation, Inc. name changed to IntraWest Financial Corp. 10/01/1982 which merged into United Banks of Colorado, Inc. 04/30/1987 which merged into Norwest Corp. 04/19/1991 which name changed to Wells Fargo & Co. (New) 11/02/1998

NATIONAL ST BK (ELIZABETH, NJ)
Each share Common $25 par exchanged for (2.5) shares Common $10 par 08/10/1959
Each share Common $10 par exchanged for (2) shares Common $5 par 01/14/1964
Under plan of merger a stock distribution of (19) for (225) paid 09/17/1962
Common $5 par changed to $3 par and (1) additional share issued 10/10/1969
Common $3 par changed to $4 par 03/22/1971
Common $4 par changed to $5 par 03/11/1974
Common $5 par changed to $6 par 03/15/1976
Common $6 par changed to $7 par 03/22/1977
Common $7 par changed to $10 par 04/11/1983
Stock Dividends - 100% 08/15/1945; 25% 01/24/1955; 50% 06/03/1957; 20% 01/12/1962; 25% 02/14/1966
Reorganized as Constellation Bancorp 03/08/1985
Each share Common $10 par exchanged for (1) share Common no par
Constellation Bancorp merged into CoreStates Financial Corp 03/16/1994 which merged into First Union Corp. 04/28/1998 which name changed to Wachovia Corp. (Ctfs. dated after 09/01/2001) 09/01/2001 which merged into Wells Fargo & Co. (New) 12/31/2008

NATIONAL ST BK (NEWARK, NJ)
Each share Common $100 par exchanged for (4) shares Common $25 par 10/19/1954
Each share Common $25 par exchanged for (2) shares Common $12.50 par 05/04/1956
Common $12.50 par changed to $6.25 par and (1) additional share issued 01/09/1962
Stock Dividends - 100% 01/14/1947; 33-1/3% 01/08/1952; 25% 10/19/1954
Name changed to First National State Bank of New Jersey (Newark, NJ) 12/15/1965
First National State Bank of New Jersey (Newark, NJ) reorganized as First National State Bancorporation 01/15/1970 which name changed to First Fidelity Bancorporation (Old) 05/01/1985 which merged into First Fidelity Bancorporation (New) 02/29/1988 which merged into First Union Corp. 01/01/1996 which name changed to Wachovia Corp. (Ctfs. dated after 09/01/2001) 09/01/2001 which merged into Wells Fargo & Co. (New) 12/31/2008

NATIONAL STAMPING CO. (MI)
Merged into Mt. Clemens Metal Products Co. in 1953
Each share Common $2 par exchanged for (0.666666) share 6% Preferred $4 par and (0.333333) share Common $1 par
Mt. Clemens Metal Products Co. name changed to Mount Clemens Industries, Inc. (Mich.) 3/8/62 which reincorporated under the laws of Delaware 1/29/65
(See Riverside, Inc.)

NATIONAL STANDARD ELECTRONICS, INC. (DE)
Name changed to Standard Electronics Research Corp. 3/8/61
(See Standard Electronics Research Corp.)

NATIONAL STARCH & CHEM CORP (DE)
Common 50¢ par split (3) for (2) by issuance of (0.5) additional share 03/30/1965
Common 50¢ par split (3) for (2) by issuance of (0.5) additional share 03/28/1969
Merged into National Starch & Chemical Holding Corp. 08/16/1978
Each share Common 50¢ par exchanged for $73.50 cash

NATIONAL STARCH & CHEM HLDG CORP (DE)
Merged into Unilever U.S. 04/00/1990
Details not available

NATIONAL STARCH PRODUCTS, INC. (DE)
Common $1 par split (2) for (1) by issuance of (1) additional share in 1954
Stock Dividends - 10% 3/25/57; 10% 3/25/58

Name changed to National Starch & Chemical Corp. 5/7/59 and Common $1 par changed to 50¢ par and (1) additional share issued 5/20/59
(See National Starch & Chemical Corp.)

NATIONAL STD CO (IN)
Reincorporated 9/30/55
Reincorporated 1/31/94
Each share Common no par exchanged for (2) shares Common $10 par in 1937
Stock Dividends - 25% 8/1/47; 50% 8/15/52
State of incorporation changed from (MI) to (DE) 9/30/55
Common $10 par changed to no par and (1) additional share issued 1/10/66
Common no par changed to $1 par 2/6/67
Common $1 par split (3) for (2) by issuance of (0.5) additional share 1/15/69
State of incorporation changed from (DE) to (IN) 1/31/94
Stock Dividends - 25% 8/1/47; 50% 8/15/52; 50% 9/26/56; 33-1/3% 11/30/59
Merged into Heico Holding, Inc. 9/25/2000
Each share Common 1¢ par exchanged for $1 cash

NATIONAL STD INVT CORP (FL)
Merged into Capital Holding Corp. 7/30/70
Each share Capital Stock $1 par exchanged for (1) share 24¢ Conv. Preferred Ser. A $5 par
Capital Holding Corp. name changed to Providian Corp. 5/12/94 which merged into Aegon N.V. 6/10/97

NATIONAL STD LIFE INS CO (FL)
Each share Capital Stock $10 par exchanged for (10) shares Capital Stock $1 par 03/13/1962
Stock Dividends - 100% 07/16/1956; 50% 09/21/1959; 11-1/9% 09/18/1962; 10% 09/04/1963; 20% 09/21/1964; 16-2/3% 09/20/1965; 20% 09/19/1966; 10% 09/18/1967; 10% 06/17/1968
Reorganized as National Standard Investment Corp. 12/31/1969
Each share Capital Stock $1 par exchanged for (1) share Capital Stock $1 par
National Standard Investment Corp. merged into Capital Holding Corp. 07/30/1970 which name changed to Providian Corp. 05/12/1994 which merged into Aegon N.V. 06/10/1997

NATIONAL STEEL & SHIPBUILDING CORP. (CA)
Each share Common $1 par exchanged for (0.1) share Common $10 par 01/31/1957
Name changed to Nassco Marine Co. 01/04/1960
(See Nassco Marine Co.)

NATIONAL STEEL CAR CORP. LTD. (CANADA)
Common no par exchanged (4) for (1) in 1943
Acquired by Dominion Foundries & Steel, Ltd. on a (1) for (3) basis 7/16/62
Dominion Foundries & Steel, Ltd. name changed to Dofasco Inc. 10/17/80
(See Dofasco Inc.)

NATIONAL STL CORP (DE)
Capital Stock no par changed to $25 par 00/00/1933
Each share Capital Stock $25 par exchanged for (3) shares Capital Stock $10 par 03/31/1950
Capital Stock $10 par changed to $5 par and (1) additional share issued 02/13/1962

Capital Stock $5 par reclassified as Common $5 par 04/27/1977
Stock Dividend - 10% 12/17/1948
Under plan of reorganization each share $5 Conv. Preferred $5 par and Common $5 par automatically became (1) share National Intergroup, Inc. $5 Conv. Preferred $5 par and Common $5 par respectively 09/13/1983
National Intergroup, Inc. name changed to FoxMeyer Health Corp. 10/12/1994 which name changed to Avatex Corp. 03/07/1997
(See Avitex Corp.)
Plan of reorganization under Chapter 11 Federal Bankruptcy Code effective 12/19/2003
No Class B stockholders' equity

NATIONAL STEM CELL HLDG INC (DE)
Name changed to Proteonomix, Inc. 08/19/2008

NATIONAL STK YDS NATL BK NATIONAL CITY ILL (NATIONAL STOCK YARDS, IL)
Liquidated 11/10/77
Details not available

NATIONAL STORAGE CO., INC. (PA)
Name changed to National Underground Storage, Inc. 5/3/72
(See National Underground Storage, Inc.)

NATIONAL STORM MGMT INC (NV)
Charter revoked for failure to file reports and pay fees 09/30/2013

NATIONAL STUDENT MARKETING CORP (DE)
Reincorporated 4/1/70
Common 5¢ par changed to 2-1/2¢ par and (1) additional share issued 12/31/68
Common 2-1/2¢ par changed to 1¢ par 10/8/69
Common 1¢ par split (2) for (1) by issuance of (1) additional share 1/30/70
State of incorporation changed from (DC) to (DE) and Common 1¢ par changed to $1 par 4/1/70
Liquidation completed
Each share Common $1 par exchanged for initial distribution of $6.95 cash 3/6/81
Each share Common $1 par received second distribution of $0.04 cash 6/5/81
Each share Common $1 par received third distribution of $0.10 cash 1/7/82
Each share Common $1 par received fourth distribution of $0.11 cash 7/15/82
Each share Common $1 par received fifth distribution of $0.06 cash 1/13/83
Each share Common $1 par received sixth distribution of $0.49 cash 7/28/83
Each share Common $1 par received seventh distribution of $0.36 cash 1/27/84
Each share Common $1 par received eighth distribution of $0.11 cash 6/29/84
Each share Common $1 par received ninth and final distribution of $0.06 cash 12/28/84

NATIONAL SUGAR MFG CO (CO)
Each share Preferred no par exchanged for (1) share new Common no par 00/00/1936
Each share old Common no par exchanged for (0.5) share new Common no par
Each share new Common no par exchanged for (0.25) share Common $1 par 00/00/1950
Declared defunct and inoperative for failure to pay taxes and file reports 10/15/1973

NATIONAL SUGAR REFINING CO. OF NEW JERSEY
Name changed to National Sugar Refining Co. in 1937
National Sugar Refining Co. name changed to R.S.N. Projects, Inc. 12/24/75
(See R.S.N. Projects, Inc.)

NATIONAL SUGAR REFNG CO (NJ)
Capital Stock no par reclassified as Common no par 01/31/1966
Name changed to R.S.N. Projects, Inc. 12/24/1975
(See R.S.N. Projects, Inc.)

NATIONAL SUPERSTARS INC (NV)
Reorganized under the laws of Delaware as MSO Holdings, Inc. 06/01/2005
Each share Common $0.005 par exchanged for (0.005) share Common $0.005 par
Note: No holder will receive fewer than (100) post-split shares

NATIONAL SUPPLY CO. (PA)
$2 Ten-Year Preference $40 par automatically became Common $10 par 00/00/1947
Common $10 par changed to $5 par and (1) additional share issued 02/05/1957
Merged into Armco Steel Corp. on a (0.85) for (1) basis 04/30/1958
Armco Steel Corp. name changed to Armco Inc. 07/01/1978 which merged into AK Steel Holding Corp. 09/30/1999

NATIONAL SUPPLY CO. OF DELAWARE
Merged into National Supply Co. (PA) in 1937
Each share Preferred exchanged for (1) share Prior Preferred and (1) share $2 Preference
Each share Common exchanged for (1) share new Common
National Supply Co. merged into Armco Steel Corp. 4/30/58 which name changed to Armco Inc. 7/1/78

NATIONAL SURETY CO. (NY)
Assets acquired by National Surety Corp. in 1933
No stockholders' equity

NATIONAL SURETY CORP (NV)
Reincorporated 04/30/1989
State of incorporation changed from (UT) to (NV) 04/30/1989
Name changed to Stratum International Holdings, Inc. 07/02/1990

NATIONAL SURGERY CTRS INC (DE)
Common 1¢ par split (3) for (2) by issuance of (0.5) additional share payable 05/31/1996 to holders of record 05/15/1996
Common 1¢ par split (3) for (2) by issuance of (0.5) additional share payable 08/29/1997 to holders of record 08/15/1997
Merged into HealthSouth Corp. 07/22/1998
Each share Common 1¢ par exchanged for (1.0972) shares Common 1¢ par
HealthSouth Corp. name changed to Encompass Health Corp. 01/02/2018

NATIONAL SWEEPSTAKES CORP (UT)
Proclaimed dissolved for failure to pay taxes 11/9/74

NATIONAL SWEEPSTAKES INC (FL)
Name changed to Natural Fuels Inc. 1/1/94
Natural Fuels Inc. name changed to CBR Brewing Co., Inc. (FL) 3/15/95 which reincorporated in British Virgin Islands as High Worth Holdings Ltd. 3/3/2003

NATIONAL SWR PIPE LTD (ON)
Preferred $15 par called for redemption 12/15/69
(Additional Information in Active)

NATIONAL SYS ANALYSTS INC (DE)
Name changed to NSA, Inc. 01/30/1975
(See NSA, Inc.)

NATIONAL SYS CORP (DE)
Reincorporated 6/29/72
Capital Stock $1 par changed to 66-2/3¢ par and (0.5) additional share issued 12/18/67
Capital Stock 66-2/3¢ par changed to no par and (0.5) additional share issued 7/30/68
Capital Stock no par split (3) for (2) by issuance of (0.5) additional share 5/5/69
State of incorporation changed from (CA) to (DE) and Capital Stock no par automatically became Common no par 6/29/72
Name changed to National Education Corp. 7/1/78
National Education Corp. merged into Harcourt General, Inc. 6/10/97
(See Harcourt General, Inc.)

NATIONAL TANK CO. (NV)
Stock Dividends - 50% 11/30/48; 50% 6/3/52; 100% 4/4/55
Completely liquidated 6/27/66
Each share Common $1 par exchanged for first and final distribution of $35.50 cash

NATIONAL TAPE CORP (DE)
Charter cancelled and declared inoperative and void for non-payment of taxes 03/01/1975

NATIONAL TAX EXEMPT BD TR (CA)
Completely liquidated 00/00/1990
Details not available

NATIONAL TEA CO (IL)
Each share old Common no par exchanged for (4) shares new Common no par 02/25/1929
New Common no par changed to $10 par 00/00/1945
Common $10 par changed to $5 par and (1) additional share issued 00/00/1950
Common $5 par changed to $4 par and (2) additional shares issued 04/10/1959
Merged into Loblaw Companies Ltd. 01/27/1982
Each share Common $4 par exchanged for $8 principal amount of National Tea Co. 15.898% 90-day Promissory Notes

NATIONAL TECHNICAL SYS INC (CA)
Name changed 06/24/1981
Name changed 11/15/1987
Reincorporated 01/31/1997
Common 10¢ par split (5) for (3) by issuance of (0.66666666) additional share 04/30/1981
Name changed from National Technical Services, Inc. (CA) to National Technical Systems (CA) 06/24/1981
Stock Dividend - 60% 02/05/1982
Common 10¢ par split (4) for (3) by issuance of (0.33333333) additional share 10/03/1985
Name changed from National Technical Systems (CA) to National Technical Systems, Inc. (DE) 11/15/1987
Common 1¢ par split (3) for (2) by issuance of (0.5) additional share 04/14/1988
State of incorporation changed from (DE) back to (CA) and Common 1¢ par changed to no par 01/31/1997
Acquired by Nest Parent, Inc. 11/22/2013
Each share Common no par exchanged for $23 cash

NATIONAL TECHNOLOGIES INC (DE)
Charter cancelled and declared inoperative and void for non-payment of taxes 3/1/89

NATIONAL TECHTEAM INC (DE)
Name changed to TechTeam Global, Inc. 05/17/2002
(See TechTeam Global, Inc.)

NATIONAL TEL COMMUNICATIONS INC (NV)
Merged into Incomnet, Inc. 10/27/94
Each share Common $0.001 par exchanged for (0.1) share new Common no par
(See Incomnet, Inc.)

NATIONAL TEL INC (CT)
Common no par split (2) for (1) by issuance of (1) additional share 02/14/1973
Plan of arrangement under Chapter X Federal Bankruptcy Act confirmed 06/15/1978
No stockholders' equity

NATIONAL TEL TRONICS CORP (NY)
Merged into Eastern Air Devices, Inc. 8/4/71
Each share Common 10¢ par exchanged for (1/3) share Common $1 par
Eastern Air Devices, Inc. name changed to Electro Audio Dynamics, Inc. 12/19/74
(See Electro Audio Dynamics, Inc.)

NATIONAL TELCOM SOLUTIONS INC (BC)
Cease trade order effective 05/29/2002
Stockholders' equity unlikely

NATIONAL TELECOMMUNICATIONS & TECHNOLOGY FD INC (MD)
Merged into AFA Funds, Inc. 05/01/1990
Each share Common 20¢ par exchanged for (1) share National Telecommunications & Technology Fund Common 20¢ par
AFA Funds, Inc. name changed to Hancock (John) Technology Series, Inc. 12/20/1991
(See Hancock (John) Technology Series, Inc.)

NATIONAL TELEFILM ASSOC INC (NY)
Reorganized under the laws of Delaware as Republic Pictures Corp. 12/28/1984
Each share Common 10¢ par exchanged for (0.1) share Class A Common 1¢ par
(See Republic Pictures Corp. (DE))

NATIONAL TELEPHONE & TELEGRAPH CORP.
Assets acquired by Anglo-Canadian Telephone Co. in 1935

NATIONAL TELEPIX INC (DE)
Name changed to American Diversified Industries Corp. 11/18/68
American Diversified Industries Corp. name changed to Brewer Alcohol Fuels Corp. 8/29/80 which recapitalized as National Gas & Power Co., Inc. 11/21/83
(See National Gas & Power Co., Inc.)

NATIONAL TERMS CORP (DE)
Each share 7% Preferred $25 par exchanged for (2) shares Common $5 par in 1934
Each share Preference no par exchanged for (1) share Common $5 par in 1934
Each share Common no par exchanged for (0.2) share Common $5 par in 1934
6% Preferred $100 par called for redemption 10/10/46
Merged into NTC Holdings Co. 3/25/83
Each share Common $5 par exchanged for $20 cash

NATIONAL THEATRE SUPPLY CO.
Acquired by General Theatres Equipment, Inc. in 1929
Details not available

NATIONAL THEATRES & TELEVISION, INC. (DE)
Name changed to National General Corp. 3/1/62
National General Corp. merged into American Financial Corp. 3/14/74

NATIONAL THEATRES INC (DE)
Name changed to National Theatres & Television, Inc. 9/1/59
National Theatres & Television, Inc. name changed to National General Corp. 3/1/62 which merged into American Financial Corp. 3/14/74

NATIONAL THOROUGHBRED CORP (NY)
Name changed to NTC Holdings Inc. (NY) 04/29/1998
NTC Holdings Inc. (NY) reorganized in Nevada as MedXLink Corp. 07/24/2002 which name changed to Particle Drilling Technologies, Inc. 02/09/2005
(See Particle Drilling Technologies, Inc.)

NATIONAL THRIFT CORP. OF AMERICA
Bankrupt in 1933

NATIONAL TILE & MFG CO (OH)
Merged into Mor-Flo Industries, Inc. 08/13/1969
Each share Common $1 par exchanged for (1) share Common no par
(See Mor-Flo Industries, Inc.)

NATIONAL TILE CO.
Name changed to National Tile & Manufacturing Co. and Capital Stock no par changed to Common $1 par in 1945
National Tile & Manufacturing Co. merged into Mor-Flo Industries, Inc. 8/13/69
(See Mor-Flo Industries, Inc.)

NATIONAL TIN CO. (DE)
Charter cancelled and declared inoperative and void for non-payment of taxes 4/1/32

NATIONAL TIRE SVCS INC (MN)
Statutorily dissolved 9/25/98

NATIONAL TITLE GUARANTY CO.
Liquidated in 1935

NATIONAL TITLE INSURANCE CO. (CA)
Merged into Title Insurance & Trust Co. in 1948
Title Insurance & Trust Co. name changed to TI Corp. (of California) 6/28/68 which name changed to Ticor 4/27/77
(See Ticor)

NATIONAL TITLE INSURANCE CO. (UT)
Merged into Plastronics Corp. 07/20/1971
Each share Common $1 par exchanged for (2.3) shares Common no par
Plastronics Corp. name changed to Continental Benefit Corp. 04/13/1987
(See Continental Benefit Corp.)

NATIONAL TOLL BRIDGE CO.
Sold to State of Kentucky in 1937
No stockholders' equity

NATIONAL TOOL CO. (OH)
Each share Preferred $100 par exchanged for (10) shares Common $1 par 00/00/1937
Each share Common $50 par exchanged for (1) share Common $1 par 00/00/1937
Name changed to National Cleveland Corp. 04/29/1959
(See National Cleveland Corp.)

NATIONAL TOTAL INCOME FD INC (MA)
Merged into Phoenix Income & Growth Fund Inc. 12/31/1993
Details not available

NATIONAL TRADE JOURNALS, INC.
Assets sold in 1931
No stockholders' equity

NATIONAL TRAINING RINKS CORP (AB)
Delisted from Alberta Stock Exchange 06/22/2003

NATIONAL TRANSACTION NETWORK INC (DE)
Reincorporated 2/17/88
Each share old Common no par exchanged for (0.2) share new Common no par 12/12/86
State of incorporation changed from (TX) to (DE) 2/17/88
Each (15) shares new Common no par exchanged for (1) share Common 15¢ par 10/20/93
Merged into IVI Checkmate Corp. 6/14/2000
Each share Common 15¢ par exchanged for (0.0956) share Common 1¢ par
(See IVI Checkmate Corp.)

NATIONAL TRANSFER & REGISTER CORP (CO)
Each share old Common $0.0001 par exchanged for (0.1) share new Common $0.0001 par 2/23/93
Recapitalized as Leather Factory Inc. (CO) 7/14/93
Each (24) shares new Common $0.0001 par exchanged for (1) share Common $0.0024 par
Leather Factory Inc. (CO) reincorporated in Delaware 6/17/94 which name changed to Tandy Leather Factory, Inc. 5/25/2005

NATIONAL TRANSIT CO. (OLD) (PA)
Ctfs. dated prior to 9/15/47
Each share Capital Stock $12.50 par exchanged for (1) share National Transit Co. (New) Capital Stock $1 par, (1) share National Transit Pump & Machine Co. Capital Stock $5 par and $6 cash 9/15/47
(See each company's listing)

NATIONAL TRANSIT CO. NEW (PA)
Ctfs. dated after 9/14/47
Acquired by Pennzoil Co. (PA) (New) 3/22/65
Each share Capital Stock $1 par exchanged for (0.147058) share Common $2.50 par
Pennzoil Co. (PA) (New) merged into Pennzoil United, Inc. 4/1/68 which name changed to Pennzoil Co. (DE) 6/1/72 which name changed to PennzEnergy Co. 12/30/98

NATIONAL TRANSIT PUMP & MACHINE CO. (PA)
Liquidation completed 2/23/55

NATIONAL TRANSTECH CORP (DE)
Charter cancelled and declared inoperative and void for non-payment of taxes 03/01/1997

NATIONAL TREASURE MINES CO (UT)
Each share Common 1¢ par exchanged for (0.2) share Common 5¢ par 08/02/1971
Name changed to N. T. M., Inc. 12/02/1986
N. T. M., Inc. name changed to Biolog, Inc. 12/15/2004

NATIONAL TR CO (TORONTO, ONT)
5.35% Preferred Ser. A $50 par called for redemption at $50.50 plus $0.66875 accrued dividends on 10/30/1997

NATIONAL TR LIFE INS CO AMER (FL)
Merged into Community National Life Insurance Co. 12/31/67
Each share Capital Stock $1 par exchanged for (0.4) share Class A Common $1 par
(See Community National Life Insurance Co.)

NATIONAL TR LTD (TORONTO, ONT)
Each share Capital Stock $100 par exchanged for (10) shares Capital Stock $10 par 00/00/1946
Each share Capital Stock $10 par exchanged for (5) shares Capital Stock $2 par 07/26/1962
Each share Capital Stock $2 par exchanged for (2) shares Capital Stock $1 par 08/10/1973
Capital Stock $1 par changed to no par 01/12/1979
Capital Stock no par reclassified as Common no par 03/05/1982
Merged into National Victoria & Grey Trust Co. (Toronto, ONT) 08/31/1984
Each share Common no par exchanged for (1.45) shares Common no par
National Victoria & Grey Trust Co. (Toronto, ONT) name changed to National Trust Co. (Toronto, ONT) 10/28/1985
(See National Trust Co. (Toronto, ONT))

NATIONAL TRUSTCO INC (ON)
Merged into Bank of Nova Scotia (Halifax, NS) 08/15/1997
Each share Common $3 par exchanged for (0.125) share Common no par and $26.475 cash

NATIONAL TUNGSTEN CORP. (NV)
Recapitalized as Sunburst Petroleum Corp. (NV) on a (29) for (1000) basis in 1958
Sunburst Petroleum Corp. (NV) name changed to Sunburst Industries, Inc. 3/6/70
(See Sunburst Industries, Inc.)

NATIONAL TUNNEL & MINES CO.
Bankrupt in 1948

NATIONAL-U.S. RADIATOR CORP. (MD)
Name changed to Natus Corp. 02/01/1960
Natus Corp. name changed to Kirkeby-Natus Corp. 06/30/1961 which name change to United Ventures, Inc. 06/24/1966 which merged into Federated Development Co. 07/31/1970
(See Federated Development Co.)

NATIONAL UN BK (DOVER, NJ)
Each share Common $100 par exchanged for (5) shares Common $20 par 01/25/1956
Common $20 par changed to $10 par and (1) additional share issued 01/13/1966
Common $10 par changed to $5 par and (1) additional share issued 09/24/1968
Stock Dividends - 25% 01/18/1957; 20% 10/23/1958; 10% 11/24/1964; 10% 11/06/1969
Name changed to National Union Bank of New Jersey (Dover, NJ) 09/01/1971
National Union Bank of New Jersey (Dover, NJ) merged into National Community Bank (Rutherford, NJ) 04/01/1973 which name changed to National Community Bank of New Jersey (Rutherford, NJ) 02/07/1975 which reorganized as National Community Banks, Inc. 02/28/1989 which merged into Bank of New York, Inc. 08/11/1993 which merged into Bank of New York Mellon Corp. 07/01/2007

NATIONAL UN BK (KINDERHOOK, NY)
Under plan of reorganization each share Common $10 par automatically became (1) share

Kinderhook Bank Corp. Common 83¢ par 06/06/1997

NATIONAL UN BK N J (DOVER, NJ)
Merged into National Community Bank (Rutherford, NJ) 04/01/1973
Each share Common $5 par exchanged for (1.1) shares Common $6.25 par
National Community Bank (Rutherford, NJ) name changed to National Community Bank of New Jersey (Rutherford, NJ) 02/07/1975 which reorganized as National Community Banks, Inc. 02/28/1989 which merged into Bank of New York Co., Inc. 08/11/1993 which merged into Bank of New York Mellon Corp. 07/01/2007

NATIONAL UN ELEC CORP (DE)
Each share Common 30¢ par exchanged for (0.2) share Common $1 par 05/08/1964
Merged into Aktiebolaget Electrolux 08/01/1975
Each share Common $1 par exchanged for $28 cash

NATIONAL UN FIRE INS CO PITTSBURGH (PA)
Capital Stock $100 par changed to $50 par 00/00/1931
Capital Stock $50 par changed to $20 par 00/00/1932
Each share Capital Stock $20 par exchanged for (4) shares Capital Stock $5 par 00/00/1947
Through purchase offer 99.7% held by American International Group Inc. as of 11/03/1972
Public interest eliminated

NATIONAL UN LIFE INS CO PITTSBURGH (PA)
Name changed to Life Insurance Co. of New Hampshire 01/15/1971
(See Life Insurance Co. of New Hampshire)

NATIONAL UNDERGROUND STORAGE INC (PA)
Merged into Iron Mountain Inc. 7/1/98
Each share $25 par exchanged for $2,804.57 cash
Each share Common $25 par received an additional distribution of $172.75 cash from escrow payable 7/29/99 to holders of record 7/1/98

NATIONAL UNI CARE HEALTH SYS LTD (BC)
Name changed to Snaper Patent Technologies Inc. 10/31/1991
Snaper Patent Technologies Inc. recapitalized as Emerging Growth Technologies Inc. 05/19/1992 which name changed to Mandorin Goldfields, Inc. (BC) 04/23/1996 which reincorporated in Yukon 06/11/1999 which name changed to Sphere Resources Inc. 11/27/2007

NATIONAL UNION LIFE INSURANCE CO. (AL)
Merged into National Empire Life Insurance Co. on a (1.6) for (1) basis 12/31/1963
National Empire Life Insurance Co. merged into Empire Life Insurance Co. of America (AL) 06/30/1966
(See Empire Life Insurance Co. of America (AL))

NATIONAL UNION RADIO CORP. (DE)
Common no par changed to $1 par in 1932 and to 30¢ par in 1940
Name changed to National Union Electric Corp. in 1954
(See National Union Electric Corp.)

NATIONAL URANIUM CORP. (ID)
Charter forfeited for failure to pay taxes and file reports 12/01/1959

NATIONAL URANIUM CORP. (UT)
Name changed to Industries & Mines Inc. 01/27/1956
Industries & Mines Inc. merged into General Utilities & Industries, Inc. 08/29/1960 which recapitalized as General Utilities, Inc. (FL) 05/04/1962
(See General Utilities, Inc. (FL))

NATIONAL UTILITIES CO. OF MICHIGAN (MI)
Name changed to Michigan Gas Utilities Co. and Common $1 par changed to $5 par 09/01/1951
Michigan Gas Utilities Co. reorganized as Michigan Energy Resources Co. 08/19/1980 which merged into UtiliCorp United Inc. 05/26/1989 which name changed to Aquila, Inc. (New) 03/15/2002 which was acquired by Great Plains Energy Inc. 07/14/2008 which merged into Evergy, Inc. 06/05/2018

NATIONAL UTILS & INDS CORP (NJ)
Name changed to NUI Corp. (Old) 4/4/83
NUI Corp. (Old) reorganized as NUI Corp. (New) 3/1/2001
(See NUI Corp. (New))

NATIONAL VY BK & TR CO (CHAMBERSBURG, PA)
Reorganized as National Valley Corp. 12/31/1969
Each share Capital Stock $10 par exchanged for (2) shares Common $5 par
National Valley Corp. name changed to Valley Bancorp, Inc. 04/03/1980 which was acquired by Dauphin Deposit Corp. 01/01/1994 which merged into Allied Irish Banks, PLC 07/08/1997

NATIONAL VY CORP (PA)
Name changed to Valley Bancorp, Inc. 04/03/1980
Valley Bancorp, Inc. acquired by Dauphin Deposit Corp. 01/01/1994 which merged into Allied Irish Banks, PLC 07/08/1997

NATIONAL VALUE FD INC (MD)
Completely liquidated 02/10/1992
Each share Common 20¢ par received first and final distribution of $11.80 cash
Note: Certificates were not required to be surrendered and are without value

NATIONAL VALVE & MFG CO (DE)
Reincorporated 06/06/1955
State of incorporation changed from (PA) to (DE) 06/06/1955
Merged into Austin Industries, Inc. 06/15/1983
Each share Common $1 par exchanged for $74.50 cash

NATIONAL VENTURE CORP N L (AUSTRALIA)
Name changed to Doral Mineral Industries Ltd. 03/28/1991
(See Doral Mineral Industries Ltd.)

NATIONAL VENTURE GROUP INC (CO)
Name changed to CRTC, Inc. 01/13/1987
(See CRTC, Inc.)

NATIONAL VENTURES & EQUITIES, INC. (KS)
Adjudicated bankrupt 1/22/75

NATIONAL VENTURES INC. (FL)
Name changed to Auto-Mission, Inc. 9/11/69
Auto-Mission, Inc. proclaimed dissolved 7/11/72

NATIONAL VICTORIA & GREY TR CO (TORONTO, ONT)
Name changed to National Trust Co. (Toronto, ONT) 10/28/1985
(See National Trust Co. (Toronto, ONT))

NATIONAL VICTORIA & GREY TRUSTCO LTD (ON)
Name changed to National Trustco Inc.-Trustco National Inc. 03/22/1989
National Trustco Inc.-Trustco National Inc. merged into Bank of Nova Scotia (Halifax, NS) 08/15/1997

NATIONAL VIDEO CORP. (NV)
Name changed to Unidyne Corp. 1/14/83
(See Unidyne Corp.)

NATIONAL VIDEO CORP (IL)
(Common 25¢ par endorsed to show proportional interest in Rico Electronics, Inc.)
Class A $1 par changed to 50¢ par and (1) additional share issued 10/06/1961
Class A 50¢ par reclassified as Common 25¢ par and (1) additional share issued 10/28/1965
Completely liquidated 06/07/1974
Each share Common 25¢ par (Endorsed) exchanged for initial distribution of $0.227855 cash
Note: Unexchanged certificates were cancelled and became without value 12/01/1979
Each share Common 25¢ par (Endorsed) received second and final distribution of $0.04 cash 06/30/1980
Note: Qualifying holders who did not receive their distribution and did not report their current address prior to 08/28/1980 were barred from receiving the second distribution

NATIONAL VIDEO CTRS INC (NY)
Under plan of reorganization name changed to Corporation For Entertainment & Learning, Inc. 04/12/1984
Corporation For Entertainment & Learning, Inc. name changed to CEL Communications, Inc. 12/13/1985
(See CEL Communications, Inc.)

NATIONAL VIDEO INC (OR)
Name changed to Rentrak Corp. 09/21/1988
Rentrak Corp. merged into comScore, Inc. 01/29/2016

NATIONAL VISION ASSOC LTD (GA)
Common 1¢ par split (3) for (2) by issuance of (0.5) additional share 9/26/92
Name changed to Vista Eyecare, Inc. 12/31/98
(See Vista Eyecare, Inc.)

NATIONAL VISION INC (GA)
Merged into Vision Holding Corp. 9/15/2005
Each share Common 1¢ par exchanged for $7.25 cash

NATIONAL VISION SVCS INC (DE)
Name changed to NBS National Benefit Services, Inc. 12/19/1989
NBS National Benefit Services, Inc. name changed to Avesis Inc. 12/07/1990
(See Avesis Inc.)

NATIONAL VITAMIN CORP (NY)
Recapitalized as Vend-A-Phone, Inc. 1/20/85
Each share Common 1¢ par exchanged for (0.25) share Common 1¢ par
(See Vend-A-Phone, Inc.)

NATIONAL VULCANIZED FIBRE CO. (DE)
Name changed to NVF Co. 4/26/65
(See NVF Co.)

NATIONAL WASTE CONVERSION CORP. (FL)
Name changed to Ecology, Inc. 1/16/69
Ecology, Inc. charter cancelled 4/15/73

NATIONAL WATER WORKS CORP.
Reorganized as Delaware Valley Utilities Co. in 1931
(See Delaware Valley Utilities Co.)

NATIONAL WEEKLY INC. (NY)
Dissolved 5/6/66
No stockholders' equity

NATIONAL WESTMINSTER BK PLC (LONDON, ENGLAND)
ADR's for Ordinary 1p par split (2) for (1) by issuance of (1) additional share 06/19/1989
Issue Information - 20,000,000 shares CAP SECS EXCHANGEABLE SER A offered at $25 per share on 10/28/1993
ADR's for Preference Ser. A called for redemption at $25.90 on 10/16/1998
Acquired by Royal Bank of Scotland Group PLC 05/23/2000
Each ADR for Ordinary £1 par exchanged for (5.808) new Ordinary shares 25p par and $35.904 cash or proceeds from the sale of (5.808) new Ordinary shares and $35.3904 cash
Note: Option to receive cash and shares expired 05/23/2002
Exchangeable Capital Securities Ser. A called for redemption at $25 on 01/16/2006
ADR for Preference Ser. B called for redemption at $25 on 01/16/2007
(Additional Information in Active)

NATIONAL WESTN DEV CORP (DE)
Charter cancelled and declared inoperative and void for non-payment of taxes 3/1/83

NATIONAL WESTN FD INC (DE)
Name changed to Apollo Fund, Inc. and Common $1 par reclassified as Capital Stock $1 par 10/01/1969
Apollo Fund, Inc. name changed to Founders Special Fund, Inc. 10/20/1970 which reorganized as Founders Funds, Inc. 08/31/1987 which name changed to Dreyfus Founders Funds, Inc. 12/31/1999 which name changed to Dreyfus Discovery Fund 12/01/2008

NATIONAL WESTN LIFE INS CO (CO)
Common $1 par changed to 40¢ par 05/27/1960
Common 40¢ par changed to 10¢ par 11/12/1963
Each share Common 10¢ par exchanged for (0.33333333) share Class A Common $1 par 07/31/1965
Reincorporated under the laws of Delaware as National Western Life Group, Inc. and Class A Common $1 par changed to 1¢ par 10/02/2015

NATIONAL WESTN MOBILE PKS & MODULAR HOMES INC (DE)
Name changed to National Western Development Corp. 2/20/73
(See National Western Development Corp.)

NATIONAL WIND SOLUTIONS INC (TX)
Recapitalized as National Clean Fuels Inc. 03/17/2010
Each (300) shares Common $0.001 par exchanged for (1) share Common $0.001 par
National Clean Fuels Inc. recapitalized as Quantum International Corp. 01/20/2012

NATIONAL WIRE PRODUCTS CORP. OF MARYLAND (MD)
Merged into Niagara Lockport Industries, Inc. 04/06/1987
Details not available

NATIONAL WIRELESS HLDGS INC (DE)
Name changed to NWH, Inc. 02/07/2002
(See NWH, Inc.)

NATIONAL WORK-CLOTHES RENTAL (NJ)
Name changed to Servisco 10/18/68
(See Servisco)

NATIONAL WORLDWIDE OPPORTUNITIES FD (MA)
Merged into Phoenix Worldwide Opportunities Fund 12/31/93
Basis not available

NATIONS BALANCED TARGET MAT FD INC (MD)
Liquidation completed
Each share Common $0.001 par received initial distribution of $0.247 cash payable 12/30/2003 to holders of record 12/19/2003
Each share Common $0.001 par received second distribution of $0.11 cash payable 3/30/2004 to holders of record 3/19/2004
Each share Common $0.001 par received third distribution of $0.11 cash payable 6/29/2004 to holders of record 6/18/2004
Each share Common $0.001 par received fourth and final distribution of $9.446804 cash payable 10/1/2004 to holders of record 9/30/2004
Note: Certificates were not required to be surrendered and are without value

NATIONS FD (MA)
Name changed to Nations Fund Trust 9/22/92

NATIONS FLOORING INC (DE)
Plan of reorganization under Chapter 11 Federal Bankruptcy Code effective 12/29/2003
No stockholders' equity

NATIONS GOVT INCOME TERM TR 2003 INC (MD)
Trust terminated 10/1/2003
Each share Common $0.001 par exchanged for $10 cash

NATIONS GOVT INCOME TERM TR 2004 INC (MD)
Trust terminated 4/1/2004
Each share Common $0.001 par exchanged for $10.02 cash

NATIONS OIL REFINERIES LTD.
Liquidated in 1936

NATIONS RX INC (NV)
Name changed to Lifespan Inc. 04/06/2006
(See Lifespan Inc.)

NATIONSBANK CORP (NC)
Perpetual Conv. Preferred Ser. B no par called for redemption 10/05/1992
Adjustable Rate Preferred Ser. CC no par called for redemption 03/31/1994
Adjustable Rate Preferred Ser. DD no par called for redemption 03/31/1994
7% Depositary Preferred Class A called for redemption 03/31/1997
Adjustable Rate Preferred Ser. A no par called for redemption at $25 plus $0.58333 accrued dividends on 03/31/1998
Common no par split (2) for (1) by issuance of (1) additional share payable 02/27/1997 to holders of record 02/07/1997 Ex date - 02/28/1997
Reincorporated under the laws of Delaware as BankAmerica Corp. (Old) 09/25/1998
BankAmerica Corp. (Old) merged into BankAmerica Corp. (New) 09/30/1998 which name changed to Bank of America Corp. 04/28/1999

NATIONSBANK N A (SOUTH ATLANTA, GA)
Merged into NationsBank Corp. 6/1/97
Each share 8.50% Preferred Ser. H exchanged for $25 cash
Each share 8.75% Preferred Ser. 1993-A exchanged for $27.1875 cash

NATIONSBANK OF FLORIDA, N.A. (TAMPA, FL)
Acquired by NationsBank, N.A. (Atlanta, GA) 12/30/1995
Details not available

NATIONSHEALTH INC (DE)
Acquired by NationsHealth Acquisition Corp. 07/23/2009
Each share Common $0.0001 par exchanged for $0.12 cash

NATIONSMARK NEXTGEN (NV)
Name changed to NationsMark Nexgen 05/12/2017

NATIONSMART CORP (MO)
SEC revoked common stock registration 10/19/2009
Stockholders' equity unlikely

NATIONSRENT INC (DE)
Issue Information - 13,000,000 shares COM offered at $8 per share on 08/07/1998
Plan of reorganization under Chapter 11 Federal Bankruptcy Code effective 6/13/2003
No stockholders' equity

NATIONSTAR MTG HLDGS INC (DE)
Merged into WMIH Corp. 07/31/2018
Each share Common 1¢ par exchanged for (12.7793) shares Common $0.00001 par
WMIH Corp. recapitalized as Mr. Cooper Group Inc. 10/11/2018

NATIONWIDE AUTO LEASING SYS INC (DC)
Name changed to Nationwide Resources, Inc. 12/01/1970
(See Nationwide Resources, Inc.)

NATIONWIDE BROKERAGE INC (NV)
Charter revoked for failure to file reports and pay fees 01/04/1971

NATIONWIDE CAP CORP (NV)
SEC revoked common stock registration 10/19/2009
Stockholders' equity unlikely

NATIONWIDE CELLULAR SVC INC (DE)
Reincorporated 11/12/87
Stock Dividend - 100% 5/8/89
State of incorporation changed from (NY) to (DE) 11/12/87
Merged into MCI Communications Corp. 9/20/95
Each share Common 1¢ par exchanged for $18.50 cash

NATIONWIDE CONSUMER SVCS INC (OH)
99.97% held by Nationwide Mutual Insurance Co. and Nationwide Mutual Fire Insurance Co. as of 11/05/1974
Public interest eliminated

NATIONWIDE CORP (OH)
Class A Common $5 par changed to $2.50 par and (1) additional share issued 09/14/1962
Merged into Nationwide Mutual Insurance Co. 03/30/1983
Each share Class A Common $2.50 par exchanged for $42.50 cash

NATIONWIDE FDG INC (CO)
Name changed to Capvest Internationale Ltd. 9/27/88
(See Capvest Internationale Ltd.)

NATIONWIDE FINL SVCS CAP TR II (DE)
7.10% Trust Preferred Securities called for redemption at $25 on 9/28/2005

NATIONWIDE FINL SVCS INC (DE)
Acquired by Nationwide Mutual Insurance Co. 01/02/2009
Each share Class A Common 1¢ par exchanged for $52.25 cash

NATIONWIDE FINL SOLUTIONS INC (NV)
Name changed to Clear Choice Financial, Inc. 04/04/2006
(See Clear Choice Financial, Inc.)

NATIONWIDE HEALTH PPTYS INC (MD)
Common 10¢ par split (2) for (1) by issuance of (1) additional share payable 03/08/1996 to holders of record 02/16/1996 Ex date - 03/11/1996
7.677% Step-Up REIT Preferred Ser. A $1 par called for redemption at $100 plus $1.91925 accrued dividends on 10/01/2007
7.75% Conv. Preferred Ser. B $1 par called for redemption at $103.875 plus $0.3875 accrued dividends on 01/18/2010
Merged into Ventas, Inc. 07/01/2011
Each share Common 10¢ par exchanged for (0.7866) share Common 25¢ par

NATIONWIDE HOME EQUIPMENT CORP. (DE)
No longer in existence having become inoperative and void for non-payment of taxes 4/1/53

NATIONWIDE HOMES INC (VA)
Stock Dividends - 25% 4/9/75; 25% 4/9/76
Merged into Insilco Corp. 6/4/79
Each share Common 50¢ par exchanged for $16 cash

NATIONWIDE INDS INC (DE)
Common 10¢ par split (5) for (2) by issuance of (1.5) additional shares 09/30/1968
Merged into Jupiter Corp. 12/30/1980
To holdings of (153) shares or fewer each share Common 10¢ par exchanged for $0.60 cash
To holdings of (154) shares or more each share Common 10¢ par exchanged for $0.65 principal amount of 14-1/2% Debentures due 11/01/2000

NATIONWIDE INTERIORS, INC. (MD)
Charter annulled for failure to file reports and pay taxes 11/9/65

NATIONWIDE INVESTING FNDTN (MI)
Merged into Nationwide Mutual Funds 05/09/1998
Details not available

NATIONWIDE LAND CORP. (MN)
Name changed to Metco Development Corp. 4/6/72

NATIONWIDE LEASING SYS INC (MN)
Voluntarily dissolved 1/21/76
No stockholders' equity

NATIONWIDE LEGAL SVCS INC (NJ)
Charter revoked for failure to file reports and pay fees 6/6/95

NATIONWIDE LIFE INS CO (OH)
Common $10 par changed to $1 par and (9) additional shares issued plus a 50% stock dividend paid 10/22/1964
Under plan of merger each share Common $1 par exchanged for $85 cash 05/10/1983

NATIONWIDE MARKETING ASSOC INC (DE)
Charter cancelled and declared inoperative and void for non-payment of taxes 04/15/1972

NATIONWIDE MINERALS LTD. (ON)
Charter cancelled for failure to pay taxes and file returns 04/15/1965

NATIONWIDE MOTORIST ASSOCIATION, INC. (DE)
Common 50¢ par split (2) for (1) by issuance of (1) additional share 8/25/64
No longer in existence having become inoperative and void for non-payment of taxes 4/15/69

NATIONWIDE MOTORIST ASSOCIATION OF NORTH CAROLINA, INC. (NC)
Charter revoked for failure to file reports and pay fees 2/15/66

NATIONWIDE NURSING CTRS INC (FL)
Proclaimed dissolved for failure to file reports and pay fees 11/13/1987

NATIONWIDE PETROLEUM, INC. (MN)
Name changed to Nationwide Land Corp. 11/3/69
Nationwide Land Corp. name changed to Metco Development Corp. 4/6/72

NATIONWIDE PWR CORP (DE)
Merged into Brooks Satellite Inc. 5/29/86
Each share Common 1¢ par exchanged for (1) share Common 1¢ par and (1) Common Stock Purchase Warrant Ser. B expiring 5/29/91
(See Brooks Satellite Inc.)

NATIONWIDE REAL ESTATE INVS (OH)
Acquired by Old Stone Corp. 02/20/1981
Each Share of Bene. Int. no par exchanged for (1) share 12% Conv. Preferred Ser. B $1 par
(See Old Stone Corp.)

NATIONWIDE RESOURCES, INC. (DC)
Charter revoked for failure to file reports 9/9/74

NATIONWIDE RES CORP (DE)
Name changed to Baseball Card Society, Inc. 10/12/88
(See Baseball Card Society, Inc.)

NATIONWIDE RES INC (DE)
Recapitalized as Dotwap.com Holdings Corp. 12/22/1999
Each share Common $0.001 par exchanged for (1/6) share Common $0.001 par
(See Dotwap.com Holdings Corp.)

NATIONWIDE SAFE T PROPANE INC (NV)
Recapitalized as EMP Solutions Inc. 03/10/2015
Each share Common $0.001 par exchanged for (0.03333333) share Common $0.001 par

NATIONWIDE SAFETY CENTERS, INC. (CA)
Merged into Nationwide Safety Centers 10/31/61
Each share Common 50¢ par exchanged for (0.75) share Class A 50¢ par and (0.5) share Class B 50¢ par
Nationwide Safety Centers charter cancelled 7/3/67

NATIONWIDE SAFETY CENTERS (CA)
Charter cancelled for failure to file reports and pay taxes 7/3/67

NATIONWIDE TABULATING CORP. (DE)
Merged into Financial Data Corp. 2/1/63
Each share Common 10¢ par exchanged for (1) share Common 10¢ par
Financial Data Corp. merged into Indiana Industries Inc. 12/22/65 which name changed to Bankshares of Indiana, Inc. 5/4/72 which name changed to Money Management Corp. 12/31/75 which merged into Banc One Corp. (DE) 7/1/86 which reincorporated in Ohio 5/1/89 which merged into Bank One Corp. 10/2/98 which merged into J.P. Morgan Chase & Co. 12/31/2000 which name changed to JPMorgan Chase & Co. 7/20/2004

NATIVE AMERN ENERGY GROUP INC (NV)
Common $0.001 par split (20) for (1) by issuance of (19) additional shares payable 09/18/2006 to holders of record 09/07/2006 Ex date - 09/19/2006
Merged into Native American Energy Group, Inc. (DE) 12/18/2009
Each share Common $0.001 par exchanged for (0.0001) share Common $0.001 par

NATIVE MINERALS LTD (AB)
Struck off register for failure to file annual returns 08/31/1976

NATIVE STRATEGIC INVTS LTD (BC)
Recapitalized as NSI Strategic Investments Ltd. 05/08/2001
Each share Common no par exchanged for (0.125) share Common no par
(See NSI Strategic Investments Ltd.)

NATIXIS CASH MGMT TR (MA)
Trust terminated 02/16/2011
Each share Money Market Series Class A no par received $1 cash
Each share Money Market Series Class B no par received $1 cash
Each share Money Market Series Class C no par received $1 cash

NATMAR INC (OH)
Name changed to Antex Corp. 04/01/1985 which name changed back to Natmar, Inc. 07/05/1985
Company went private 00/00/1989
Details not available

NATOL PETE CORP (OH)
Acquired by Damson Oil Corp. 12/3/69
Each share Common $1 par exchanged for (1) share Common 40¢ par
(See Damson Oil Corp.)

NATOMAS CO. OF CALIFORNIA
Reorganized as Natomas Co. in 1928
(See Natomas Co.)

NATOMAS CO (CA)
Each share old Capital Stock no par exchanged for (10) shares new Capital Stock no par in 1934
New Capital Stock no par changed to $1 par 7/22/55
Capital Stock $1 par split (3) for (2) by issuance of (0.5) additional share 5/20/75
Capital Stock $1 par reclassified as Common $1 par 5/7/76
$1.60 Conv. Preferred Ser. A $1 par called for redemption 9/27/79
Common $1 par split (2) for (1) by issuance of (1) additional share issued 10/26/79
Common $1 par split (2) for (1) by issuance of (1) additional share 9/18/80
$4 Conv. Preferred Ser. B $1 par called for redemption 9/29/80
Stock Dividends - 10% 6/10/74; 10% 5/18/77
Merged into Diamond Shamrock Corp. 8/31/83
Each share $4 Conv. Preferred Ser. C $1 par exchanged for (1) share $4 Conv. Preferred $1 par
Each share Common $1 par exchanged for (1.05) shares Common $1 par
Diamond Shamrock Corp. name changed to Maxus Energy Corp. 4/30/87
(See Maxus Energy Corp.)

NATPAC INC (DE)
Reincorporated 10/31/69
Stock Dividends - 25% 10/11/1963; 25% 06/17/1964; 25% 10/20/1965; 25% 10/06/1966
State of incorporation changed from (NY) to (DE) 10/31/1969
Charter cancelled and declared inoperative and void for non-payment of taxes 03/01/1985

NATQUOTE FINL INC (FL)
Each share old Common no par exchanged for (0.14285714) share new Common no par 02/02/1999
Name changed to Contact Capital Group Inc. 04/28/2003
(See Contact Capital Group Inc.)

NATRACEUTICALS INC (CANADA)
Name changed to Nu-Life Corp. 02/25/2000
(See Nu-Life Corp.)

NATROL INC (DE)
Issue Information - 3,940,000 shares COM offered at $15 per share on 07/22/1998
Merged into Plethico Pharmaceuticals Ltd. 12/28/2007
Each share Common 1¢ par exchanged for $4.40 cash

NATRUSCO COM SH FD LTD (ON)
Fund terminated 04/30/1990
Details not available

NATTEM USA INC (NM)
Name changed to Comtec International, Inc. 10/26/95

NATTO MINING CORP. LTD. (ON)
Charter revoked for failure to file reports and pay fees 8/19/65

NATUNOLA AGRITECH INC (CANADA)
Acquired by 8716137 Canada Inc. 02/07/2014
Each share Common no par exchanged for $0.0068 cash
Note: Unexchanged certificates will be cancelled and become without value 02/07/2020

NATUNOLA HEALTH BIOSCIENCES INC (AB)
Merged into Botaneco Corp. 10/14/2011
Each share Common no par exchanged for (1.1875) shares Common no par
Botaneco Corp. name changed to Natunola AgriTech Inc. 07/09/2013
(See Natunola AgriTech Inc.)

NATURA ENERGY CORP (CO)
Each share Common no par exchanged for (0.05) share Common 5¢ par 06/25/1985
Plan of reorganization under Chapter 11 Federal Bankruptcy proceedings effective 06/17/1990
Shareholders received (400) shares LAZ Financial Corp. Common no par in exchange for their holdings
Note: Unexchanged certificates were cancelled and became without value 11/07/1991
LAZ Financial Corp. name changed to American Teletronics, Inc. 05/16/1994 which recapitalized as Shine Holdings, Inc. 03/13/2006
(See Shine Holdings, Inc.)

NATURADE INC (DE)
Reorganized under Chapter 11 Federal Bankruptcy Code 7/8/91
Each share old Common $0.001 par exchanged for (1) share new Common $0.001 par, (0.14285714) Common Stock Purchase Warrant, Class A expiring 12/4/91 and (0.14285714) Common Stock Purchase Warrrant, Class B expiring 6/4/93
Note: Unexchanged certificates were cancelled and became valueless 9/2/91
(Additional Information in Active)

NATURAL ALTERNATIVES INTL INC (CO)
Name changed 4/22/88
Name changed from Natural Alternatives, Inc. to Natural Alternatives International, Inc. 4/22/88
Reincorporated under the laws of Delaware 12/8/89

NATURAL BEAUTY LANDSCAPING INC (UT)
Name changed to Octagon Capital Corp. 06/30/1986
Octagon Capital Corp. name changed to AC&C Systems Corp. (UT) 04/29/1988 which reorganized in Oklahoma as Environmental Remediation Services, Inc. 12/15/1989
(See Environmental Remediation Services, Inc.)

NATURAL BORN CARVERS INC (CO)
Name changed to Carv Industries, Inc. 06/12/1998
Carv Industries, Inc. recapitalized as Carv.com, Inc. (CO) 12/14/1998 which reincorporated in Nevada as PacificTrading Post.Com, Inc. 02/26/1999 which recapitalized as IDC Technologies Inc. 11/23/2001 which name changed to Jill Kelly Productions Holding, Inc. 08/20/2003 which name changed to eWorldCompanies, Inc. 03/13/2007

NATURAL BRDG VA INC (VA)
Acquired by Bridge Associates, Inc. 04/04/1988
Each share Common $5 par exchanged for $42 cash

NATURAL CARBONIC HOLDING CORP. (DE)
No longer in existence having become inoperative and void for non-payment of taxes 4/1/47

NATURAL CHILD CARE INC (DE)
Common $0.005 par split (6) for (5) by issuance of (0.2) additional share 09/30/1993
Name changed to Winners All International, Inc. 11/01/1993
Winners All International, Inc. name changed to Urecoats Industries, Inc. 02/12/1999 which name changed to Lapolla Industries, Inc. 11/08/2005
(See Lapolla Industries, Inc.)

NATURAL DISCOVERY RESH INC (UT)
Recapitalized as Global Vision Unlimited, Inc. 7/23/91
Each share Common $0.001 par exchanged for (0.05) share Common $0.001 par
Global Vision Unlimited, Inc. name changed to DHS Industries Inc. 6/7/96 which name changed to Glenhills Corp. 4/2/98 which name changed to Millennium Multi-Media.com Corp. 7/6/2000 which name changed to Voxcorp Inc. 2/13/2002

NATURAL EARTH TECHNOLOGIES INC (DE)
Name changed to U.S. Home & Garden Inc. 07/28/1995
U.S. Home & Garden Inc. name changed to Ionatron, Inc. 04/30/2004 which name changed to Applied Energetics, Inc. 02/20/2008

NATURAL ENERGY CORP (DE)
Name changed to National Olympic Solar Corp. 07/17/1979
National Olympic Solar Corp. merged into Olympic Solar Corp. 09/18/1980 which name changed to Olymco Inc. 07/18/1985
(See Olymco Inc.)

NATURAL FOODS CO., INC. (FL)
Name changed to Zephyr Products, Inc. 06/25/1965
(See Zephyr Products, Inc.)

NATURAL FUELS INC (FL)
Each share old Common $0.0001 par exchanged for (0.045) share new Common $0.0001 par 12/7/94
Name changed to CBR Brewing Co., Inc. (FL) 3/15/95
CBR Brewing Co., Inc. (FL) reincorporated in British Virgin Islands as High Worth Holdings Ltd. 3/3/2003

NATURAL GAS & OIL CORP. (DE)
Merged into Mississippi River Fuel Corp. in 1954
Each share Common $5 par exchanged for (1/3) share Common $10 par
Mississippi River Fuel Corp. name changed to Mississippi River Corp. 5/28/65 which name changed to Missouri Pacific Corp. 5/27/76 which merged into Union Pacific Corp. 12/22/82

NATURAL GAS PIPELINE CO AMER (DE)
5-3/4% Preferred $100 par called for redemption 07/01/1965
5-1/2% Preferred $100 par called for redemption 10/28/1965
9.20% Preferred $100 par called for redemption 12/31/1989
7.10% Preferred $100 par called for redemption 03/31/1992
7.90% Preferred $100 par called for redemption 03/31/1992
8.12% Preferred $100 par called for redemption 03/31/1992

NATURAL GAS SERVICE CO. OF ARIZONA (AZ)
Merged into Southwest Gas Corp. 08/20/1957
Each (1.536) shares Class A or B Common $5 par exchanged for (1) share $1.20 Prior Preferred $9 par
(See Southwest Gas Corp.)

NATURAL GAS SVC CO (VA)
Merged into Commonwealth Natural Gas Corp. 12/29/67
Each share Common $1 par exchanged for $6 cash

NATURAL GAS SYS INC (NV)
Name changed to Evolution Petroleum Corp. 7/17/2006

NATURAL GOLF CORP (IL)
Issue Information - 2,500,000 shares COM offered at $5 per share on 12/11/2003
Chapter 11 bankruptcy proceedings converted to Chapter 7 on 02/08/2006
Stockholders' equity unlikely

NATURAL HARMONY FOODS INC (FL)
Administratively dissolved 09/25/2009

NATURAL HEALTH TRENDS CORP (FL)
Old Common 1¢ par split (2) for (1) by issuance of (1) additional share 10/30/95
Each share old Common 1¢ par exchanged for (0.025) share new Common 1¢ par 4/6/98
Each share new Common 1¢ par exchanged for (0.01) share Common $0.001 par 3/19/2003
Reincorporated under the laws of Delaware 6/29/2005

NATURAL MICROSYSTEMS CORP (DE)
Common 1¢ par split (2) for (1) by issuance of (1) additional share payable 11/22/1996 to holders of record 11/07/1996
Common 1¢ par split (2) for (1) by issuance of (1) additional share payable 08/07/2000 to holders of record 07/24/2000
Name changed to NMS Communications Corp. 05/07/2001
NMS Communications Corp. name changed to LiveWire Mobile, Inc. 12/08/2008 which name changed to Live Microsystems, Inc. 08/29/2013

NATURAL NUTRITION INC (NV)
Each share old Common $0.001 par exchanged for (1.25) shares new Common $0.001 par 02/15/2008

Recapitalized as AppTech Corp. 11/16/2009
Each share new Common $0.001 par exchanged for (0.05) share Common $0.001 par

NATURAL ORGANICS CORP (CA)
Reorganized as Classic Auto Accessories 11/18/1987
Each share Common exchanged for (1) share Common
Classic Auto Accessories name changed to FCR Automotive Group, Inc. (CA) 07/27/1988 which reorganized in Delaware as Simco America Inc. 10/18/2005 which name changed to Leo Motors, Inc. 11/05/2007

NATURAL ORGANICS INC (CA)
Name changed to I.H.V. Corp. 1/16/86
I.H.V. Corp. name changed to California Beach Restaurants, Inc. 7/10/90

NATURAL POWER CORP. OF AMERICA (DE)
No longer in existence having become inoperative and void for non-payment of taxes 4/1/58

NATURAL PURE BEVERAGE CORP (ON)
Reincorporated under the laws of Nevada as E Com Force Corp. and Common no par changed to $0.001 par 08/05/2003
E Com Force Corp. name changed to Personal Portals Online, Inc. 02/09/2004 which recapitalized as E Trade Systems, Inc. 09/15/2005 which name changed to Enterprise Traders, Inc. 11/23/2005 which name changed to Micromint, Inc. 01/16/2007
(See Micromint, Inc.)

NATURAL RESOURCE HLDGS (ISRAEL)
Name changed to Blockchain Mining Ltd. 01/11/2018
(See Blockchain Mining Ltd.)

NATURAL RESOURCE MANAGEMENT CORP. (DE)
Name changed to Edisto Resources Corp. 6/29/89
Edisto Resources Corp. merged into Forcenergy Inc. 10/22/97 which merged into Forest Oil Corp. 12/7/2000

NATURAL RESOURCE PARTNERS L P (DE)
Each old Subordinate Unit exchanged for (0.25) Common Unit and (0.75) new Subordinate Unit 11/14/2005
Each new Subordinate Unit exchanged for (1/3) Common Unit and (2/3) new Subordinate Unit 11/14/2006
New Subordinate Units split (2) for (1) by issuance of (1) additional Unit payable 04/18/2007 to holders of record 04/09/2007 Ex date - 04/19/2007
Each new Subordinate Unit exchanged for (1) Common Unit 11/14/2007
(Additional Information in Active)

NATURAL RESOURCE SERVICES (AZ)
Charter revoked for failure to file reports or pay fees 6/28/76

NATURAL RES & LD DEV CORP (DE)
Charter cancelled and declared inoperative and void for non-payment of taxes 3/1/88

NATURAL RES DEV CORP (DE)
Name changed to Intercontinental Energy Corp. 9/29/72
Intercontinental Energy Corp. merged into Greenwood Holdings, Inc. 12/17/87 which name changed to Packaging Research Corp. 2/3/93

NATURAL RESOURCES FUND, INC. (DE)
Name changed to International Resources Fund, Inc. 9/1/55
International Resources Fund, Inc. acquired by Investment Co. of America 6/28/65

NATURAL RES GROWTH FD LTD (CANADA)
Special Shares $1 par changed to 60¢ par and (2/3) additional share issued 08/08/1973
Reincorporated under the laws of Canada and Special Shares 60¢ par changed to no par 02/01/1980
Name changed to All-Canadian Resources Corp. 12/30/1992
(See All-Canadian Resources Corp.)

NATURAL RES GUARDIANSHIP INTL INC (NJ)
Name changed to XRG International, Inc. 11/13/78
(See XRG International, Inc.)

NATURAL RESOURCES OF CANADA FUND, INC. (DE)
Merged into International Resources Fund, Inc. on the basis of (0.671351148) for (1) 9/1/55
International Resources Fund, Inc. acquired by Investment Co. of America 6/28/65

NATURAL RES RECOVERY INC (FL)
Name changed to Rare Earth Metals, Inc. (FL) 3/13/92
Rare Earth Metals, Inc. (FL) reorganized in Delaware as Americare Health Group Inc. 3/3/93 which name changed to Zagreus Inc. 3/26/99

NATURAL RES USA CORP (UT)
Acquired by Green SEA Resources Inc. 12/28/2011
Each share Common 1¢ par exchanged for $0.57 cash

NATURAL SOLUTIONS CORP (NV)
SEC revoked common stock registration 07/02/2008
Stockholders' equity unlikely

NATURAL SOLUTIONS LTD (NV)
Recapitalized as Highseas Entertainment & Casinos Ltd. 02/22/1994
Each share Common $0.001 par exchanged for (0.2) share Common $0.001 par
Highseas Entertainment & Casino Ltd. name changed to Phoenix Media Group Ltd. 03/24/1994 which recapitalized as TecScan International, Inc. 06/23/2003 which name changed to Bio-Life Labs, Inc. 05/19/2004
(See Bio-Life Labs, Inc.)

NATURAL WAY TECHNOLOGIES INC (NV)
Recapitalized as eSoftBank.com, Inc. 04/01/2000
Each share Common $0.001 par exchanged for (0.2) share new Common $0.001 par
eSoftBank.com, Inc. name changed to Broadengate Systems Inc. 11/17/2001 which name changed to Otter Lake Resources, Inc. 11/06/2006
(See Otter Lake Resources, Inc.)

NATURAL WONDERS INC (CA)
Plan of reorganization under Chapter 11 Federal Bankruptcy Code effective 08/00/2001
No stockholders' equity

NATURALLY ADVANCED TECHNOLOGIES INC (BC)
Name changed to Crailar Technologies Inc. 10/31/2012

NATURALLY IOWA INC (NV)
Name changed to Totally Green, Inc. 11/04/2010

NATURALLY NIAGARA BEVERAGE CORP (NV)
Merged into Millenia Corp. 06/01/1998
Each share Common $0.001 par exchanged for (2) shares Common $0.001 par
Millenia Corp. name changed to Internet Multi-Media Corp. 01/25/2000 which recapitalized as AmEurotech Corp. (NV) 12/18/2000 which reincorporated in Florida 04/18/2007 which recapitalized as Scott Contracting Holdings, Inc. 07/11/2007 which name changed to Liverpool Group, Inc. 04/29/2008

NATURALLY NIAGARA INC (BC)
Recapitalized as Northern Gaming Inc. 1/22/96
Each share Common no par exchanged for (1/6) share Common no par
Northern Gaming Inc. recapitalized as Icon Laser Eye Centers Inc. 9/1/99

NATURALNANO INC (NV)
Old Common $0.001 par split (2) for (1) by issuance of (1) additional share payable 02/09/2006 to holders of record 02/08/2006 Ex date - 02/10/2006
Each share old Common $0.001 par exchanged for (0.05882352) share new Common $0.001 par 06/14/2012
Each share new Common $0.001 par exchanged again for (0.00333333) share new Common $0.001 par 12/23/2014
Name changed to Omni Shrimp, Inc. 05/03/2017

NATURE COAST BK (HERNANDO, FL)
Common $5 par changed to $1 par 10/31/2011
Acquired by Drummond Community Bank (Chiefland, FL) 01/25/2017
Each share Common $1 par exchanged for $6.37 cash

NATURE FOOD CTRS INC (MD)
Acquired by General Nutrition Companies, Inc. 9/20/94
Each share Common $0.001 par exchanged for $12 cash

NATURE GENETIKS CAP INC (CANADA)
Name changed to Mercator Transport Group Corp. 01/30/2007

NATURE OF BEAUTY LTD (NV)
Name changed to Bio-Clean, Inc. and (8) additional shares issued 10/16/2009
Bio-Clean, Inc. name changed to Global NuTech, Inc. 10/08/2010 which name changed to Texas Gulf Energy, Inc. 03/07/2012

NATURE VISION INC
Name changed to Swordfish Financial, Inc. 10/13/2009
Swordfish Financial, Inc. recapitalized as SoOum, Corp. 10/01/2015

NATURES BOUNTY INC (DE)
Common 1¢ par changed to $0.002 par and (4) additional shares issued 12/31/1980
Each share Common $0.002 par exchanged for (0.25) share Common $0.008 par 07/12/1988
Common $0.008 par split (2) for (1) by issuance of (1) additional share 05/08/1992
Common $0.008 par split (3) for (1) by issuance of (2) additional shares 11/02/1992
Common $0.008 par split (2) for (1) by issuance of (1) additional share 08/23/1993
Stock Dividend - 100% 03/30/1973
Name changed to NBTY, Inc. 05/26/1995
(See NBTY, Inc.)

NATURES CALL BRANDS INC (NV)
Common $0.001 par split (21) for (1) by issuance of (20) additional shares payable 11/08/2010 to holders of record 11/07/2010 Ex date - 11/09/2010
Name changed to Sonora Resources Corp. 03/02/2011

NATURES ELEMENTS HLDG CORP (DE)
Charter cancelled and declared inoperative and void for non-payment of taxes 3/1/96

NATURES GIFT INC (UT)
Name changed to Imall Inc. 1/16/96
Imall Inc. merged into At Home Corp. 10/27/99
(See At Home Corp.)

NATURES PREF INC (NY)
Charter cancelled and proclaimed dissolved for failure to pay taxes 12/23/92

NATUREWELL INC (DE)
Reincorporated 10/25/2001
State of incorporation changed from (CA) to (DE) and Common no par changed to 1¢ par 10/25/2001
Common 1¢ par changed to $0.00001 par 04/03/2006
Recapitalized as Brazil Interactive Media, Inc. 05/30/2013
Each share Common $0.00001 par exchanged for (0.00011786) share Common $0.00001 par
Brazil Interactive Media, Inc. name changed to American Cannabis Co., Inc. 10/10/2014

NATURIZER INC (OK)
Reorganized 09/20/1960
Reorganized from Naturizer Co. to Naturizer Inc. 09/20/1960
Each share Class A Common $1 par exchanged for (5) shares Class A Common 20¢ par
Each share Class B Common $1 par exchanged for (5) shares Class B Common 20¢ par
Each share Class A Common 20¢ par exchanged for (5) shares Class A Common 4¢ par 03/01/1962
Each share Class B Common 20¢ par exchanged for (5) shares Class B Common 4¢ par 03/01/1962
Chapter 11 bankruptcy proceedings terminated 12/17/1991
Holders may have received shares in SuperCorp, Inc. but details are not available

NATUROL HLDGS LTD (DE)
Name changed to Integrated Environmental Technologies, Ltd. (DE) 04/23/2004
Integrated Environmental Technologies, Ltd. (DE) reincorporated in Nevada 01/11/2008

NATUS CORP. (MD)
Name changed to Kirkeby-Natus Corp. 06/30/1961
Kirkeby-Natus Corp. name changed to United Ventures, Inc. 06/24/1966 which merged into Federated Development Co. 07/31/1970
(See Federated Development Co.)

NATVAN INC (UT)
Name changed to Prime Multimedia, Inc. 07/02/2003
Prime Multimedia, Inc. recapitalized as Eagle Rock Enterprises Inc. 07/01/2008 which name changed to Worldwide Food Services, Inc. 08/19/2009 which name changed to Global Holdings, Inc. 10/29/2013 which name changed to Element Global, Inc. 08/06/2015

NAUGATUCK VY FINL CORP (MD)
Acquired by Liberty Bank (Middletown, CT) 01/15/2016
Each share Common 1¢ par exchanged for $11 cash

NAUGATUCK VY FINL CORP (USA)
Reorganized under the laws of Maryland 06/30/2011
Each share Common 1¢ par exchanged for (0.9978) share Common 1¢ par
(See Naugatuck Valley Financial Corp. (MD))

NAUGATUCK WATER CO. (CT)
Merged into Connecticut Water Co. 7/24/56
Each share Common $25 par exchanged for (2) shares Common no par
Connecticut Water Co. merged into Connecticut Water Service, Inc. 4/10/75

NAUGLES INC (CA)
Common no par split (4) for (3) by issuance of (0.33333333) additional share 10/29/1982
Merged into Collins Foods International, Inc. (DE) 04/30/1987
Each share Common no par exchanged for (0.2326) share Common 10¢ par
Collins Foods International, Inc. (DE) merged into PepsiCo, Inc. 03/18/1991

NAUM BROS INC (NY)
Common 40¢ par split (3) for (2) by issuance of (0.5) additional share 11/10/76
Common 40¢ par split (4) for (3) by issuance of (1/3) additional share 10/20/77
Merged into HRR, Inc. 10/31/78
Each share Common 40¢ par exchanged for $7 cash

NAUMKEAG COPPER CO.
Acquired by Copper Range Co. 00/00/1931
Details not available

NAUMKEAG STEAM COTTON CO. (MA)
Each share Capital Stock $100 par exchanged for (5) shares Capital Stock $20 par 00/00/1945
Merged into Indian Head Mills, Inc. (MA) 02/18/1955
Each share Capital Stock $20 par exchanged for (1) share $1.25 Preferred $20 par which was subsequently called for redemption 6/30/65

NAUMKEAG TR CO (SALEM, MA)
Each share Common $100 par exchanged for (10) shares Common $10 par 07/09/1929
Stock Dividends - 20% 03/01/1961; 10% 06/01/1968
Merged into Eastern Savings Bank (Lynn, MA) 09/30/1983
Each share 5% Preferred $10 par exchanged for $20 cash
Each share Common $10 par exchanged for $333.33 cash

NAUTEC CORP. (NY)
Liquidation completed
Each share Common $5 par exchanged for initial distribution of (0.237059) share Whittaker Corp. Common $1 par 9/4/68
Note: Details on subsequent distributions, if any, are not available

NAUTICA ENTERPRISES INC (DE)
Common 10¢ par split (3) for (2) by issuance of (0.5) additional share 11/15/93
Common 10¢ par split (2) for (1) by issuance of (1) additional share payable 5/28/96 to holders of record 5/13/96
Merged into VF Corp. 8/28/2003
Each share Common 10¢ par exchanged for $17 cash

NAUTILOID CORP (DE)
Merged into Electric Lady Studios 7/25/96
Each share Common 1¢ par exchanged for $0.25 cash

NAUTILUS ENVIROMEDICAL SYS INC (DE)
Chapter 11 Federal Bankruptcy Code converted to Chapter 7 on 9/3/87
Stockholders' equity unlikely

NAUTILUS FD INC (MA)
Common $1 par changed to 50¢ par and (1) additional share 4/25/85
Voluntarily dissolved 3/18/93
Details not available

NAUTILUS GROUP INC (WA)
Name changed to Nautilus, Inc. 03/14/2005

NAUTILUS MARINE ACQUISITION CORP (MARSHALL ISLANDS)
Combined Units separated 08/29/2011
Acquired by Nautilus Shareholdings Ltd. 10/28/2013
Each share Common $0.0001 par exchanged for $10.25 cash

NAUTILUS RES LTD (BC)
Recapitalized as New Leather Corp. 06/14/1994
Each share Common no par exchanged for (1/3) share Common no par
New Leather Corp. name changed to Global Focus Resources Ltd. 11/02/1995
(See Global Focus Resources Ltd.)

NAV ENERGY TR (AB)
Under plan of reorganization name changed to Sound Energy Trust 08/14/2006
Sound Energy Trust merged into Advantage Energy Income Fund 09/06/2007 which reorganized as Advantage Oil & Gas Ltd. 07/09/2009

NAV MASTER TECHNOLOGIES INC (BC)
Recapitalized as Starpoint Systems Inc. 02/23/1994
Each share Common no par exchanged for (0.2) share Common no par
Starpoint Systems Inc. name changed to Starpoint Goldfields Inc. 05/27/1996
(See Starpoint Goldfields Inc.)

NAVA INDS INC (BC)
Recapitalized as BIT Integration Technology Inc. 04/30/1996
Each share Common no par exchanged for (1/3) share Common no par
BIT Integration Technology Inc. name changed to Smartcardesolutions.com Ltd. 09/21/2000
(See Smartcardesolutions.com Ltd.)

NAVA LEISURE USA INC (ID)
Recapitalized as Senesco Technologies, Inc. (ID) 01/21/1999
Each share Common $0.0015 par exchanged for (0.33333333) share Common $0.0015 par
Senesco Technologies, Inc. (ID) reincorporated in Delaware 10/25/1999 which name changed to Sevion Therapeutics, Inc. 10/03/2014 which recapitalized as Eloxx Pharmaceuticals, Inc. 12/20/2017

NAVA RES INC (NV)
Name changed to Blox, Inc. 07/31/2013

NAVAJO BANCORPORATION, INC. (AZ)
Merged into Great Western Corp. (Del.) 10/24/68
Each share Common $2 par exchanged for (0.25) share Common $1 par
Great Western Corp. (Del.) name changed to Patagonia Corp. 6/9/70
(See Patagonia Corp.)

NAVAJO FGHT LINES INC (NM)
Stock Dividends - 10% 8/29/69; 10% 9/9/71; 10% 9/7/72; 10% 6/28/74
Merged into United Transportation Investment Co. 12/31/78
Each share Common $1 par exchanged for $20.35 cash

NAVAJO NATURAL GAS CORP. (TX)
Liquidated 12/15/59

NAVAJO OIL CO.
Merged into Navajo Production Co. in 1939 which name was changed to Navajo Natural Gas Corp. in 1947 which was liquidated 12/15/59

NAVAJO PRODUCTION CO. (TX)
Name changed to Navajo Natural Gas Corp. in 1947 which was liquidated 12/15/59

NAVAL STORES HOLDING CO., INC.
Liquidation completed in 1947

NAVAL STORES INVESTMENT CO.
Dissolved in 1944

NAVARRE CORP (MN)
Common no par split (2) for (1) by issuance of (1) additional share payable 06/21/1996 to holders of record 06/05/1996
Name changed to Speed Commerce, Inc. 09/09/2013
(See Speed Commerce, Inc.)

NAVARRE DEP BK CO (OH)
Merged into Citizens Bancshares, Inc. 10/11/1996
Each share Common no par exchanged for (1.8106) shares Common no par
Citizens Bancshares, Inc. name changed to Sky Financial Group, Inc. 10/02/1998 which merged into Huntington Bancshares Inc. 07/02/2007

NAVARRE RES CORP (BC)
Recapitalized as Ameridex Minerals Corp. 08/27/1998
Each (13.8) shares Common no par exchanged for (1) share Common no par
Ameridex Minerals Corp. name changed to Rocher Deboule Minerals Corp. 09/15/2006 which name changed to American Manganese Inc. 01/20/2010

NAVASOTA RES LTD (BC)
Name changed to Anglo Aluminum Corp. 01/26/2010
Anglo Aluminum Corp. recapitalized as Navasota Resources Inc. 07/12/2013

NAVCO CORP (MO)
Merged into Crum & Forster 01/04/1984
Each share Common 25¢ par exchanged for $31 cash

NAVCO ELECTRONIC INDUSTRIES, INC. (CA)
Name changed to Beta Engineering Corp. 6/10/63
Beta Engineering Corp. acquired by Aero-Chatillon Corp. 4/12/68 which merged into Macrodyne-Chatillon Corp. 4/1/69 which merged into Macrodyne Industries, Inc. 1/1/74
(See Macrodyne Industries, Inc.)

NAVCO FOOD SVCS LTD (ON)
Name changed to Canvedo Industries Ltd. 4/1/72
Canvedo Industries Ltd. recapitalized as Corporate Master Ltd. 11/19/73
(See Corporate Master Ltd.)

NAVES LODGES, INC. (AK)
Voluntarily dissolved 12/19/75
Details not available

NAVICUS INC (DE)
Name changed to Super Nova Resources, Inc. 11/13/2008

NAVIDEC FINL SVCS INC (CO)
Name changed to Two Rivers Water Co. 01/15/2010
Two Rivers Water Co. name changed to Two Rivers Water & Farming Co. 03/19/2013

NAVIDEC INC (CO)
Each share old Common no par exchanged for (0.05555555) share new Common no par 12/04/2002
Each share new Common no par received distribution of (1) share Navidec Financial Services, Inc. Common $0.001 par payable 01/31/2005 to holders of record 09/09/2004
Name changed to BPZ Energy, Inc. (CO) 02/04/2005
BPZ Energy, Inc. (CO) reincorporated in Texas as BPZ Resources, Inc. 10/17/2007
(See BPZ Resources, Inc.)

NAVIGANT INTL INC (DE)
Issue Information - 2,000,000 shares COM offered at $9 per share on 06/09/1998
Merged into Carlson Wagonlit B.V. 8/8/2006
Each share Common $0.001 par exchanged for $16.50 cash

NAVIGATION COMPUTER CORP. (PA)
Completely liquidated 9/4/68
Each share Common no par exchanged for first and final distribution of (0.307692) share KDI Corp. Common 35¢ par
(See KDI Corp.)

NAVIGATO INTL INC (DE)
Name changed to Businessnet International Inc. 06/10/1996
Businessnet International Inc. recapitalized as Businessnet Holdings Corp. 08/28/1998 which name changed to Invicta Corp. 06/30/2000 which name changed to Executive Hospitality Corp. 05/02/2005 which recapitalized as Forest Resources Management Corp. 08/09/2006
(See Forest Resources Management Corp.)

NAVIGATOR EXPL CORP (AB)
Issue Information - 1,500,000 shares COM offered at $0.50 per share on 11/07/1997
Acquired by Strongbow Resources Inc. (BC) 5/3/2004
Each share Common no par exchanged for (0.7) share Common no par
Strongbow Resources Inc. (BC) reorganized in Canada as Strongbow Exploration Inc. 5/3/2004

NAVIGATOR VENTURES INC (NV)
Common $0.001 par split (9) for (1) by issuance of (8) additional shares payable 11/22/2002 to holders of record 11/20/2002 Ex date - 11/25/2002
Company terminated common stock registration and is no longer public as of 12/11/2006

NAVIGO ENERGY INC (AB)
Plan of arrangement effective 12/29/2003
Each share Common no par exchanged for (0.33333333) share C1 Energy Ltd. Common no par and (0.33333333) NAV Energy Trust Unit no par
(See each company's listing)

NAVINA GLOBAL RESOURCE FD (ON)
Units reclassified as Class A Units 07/05/2010
Name changed to Aston Hill Global Resource Fund (Old) 01/12/2011
(See Aston Hill Global Resource Fund (Old))

NAVISITE INC (DE)
Old Common 1¢ par split (2) for (1) by issuance of (1) additional share payable 04/05/2000 to holders of record 03/22/2000
Each share old Common 1¢ par exchanged for (0.06666666) share new Common 1¢ par 01/08/2003
Acquired by Time Warner Cable Inc. 04/20/2011
Each share new Common 1¢ par exchanged for $5.50 cash

NAVISTAR INTL CORP NEW (DE)
Common Stock Purchase Rights declared for holders of record 05/03/1999 were redeemed at $0.01 per right 11/15/2001 for holders of record 10/26/2001
(Additional Information in Active)

NAVISTAR INTL CORP OLD (DE)
$5.76 Conv. Preferred Ser. C no par changed to $1 par 12/19/1986
Common no par changed to $1 par 12/19/1986
Each share $5.76 Conv. Preferred Ser. C $1 par exchanged for (1.6) shares $6 Conv. Preferred Ser. G $1 par 01/15/1987
Reorganized 06/30/1993
Each share $6 Conv. Preferred Ser. G $1 par exchanged for (1) share $6 Conv. Preferred Ser. G $1 par (Legend Ctf.)
Each share Common $1 par exchanged for (0.1) share Navistar International Corp. (New) Common 10¢ par
Note: No consideration of fractional shares were made for certificates surrendered after 09/03/1993
$6 Conv. Preferred Ser. G $1 par (Legend Ctf.) called for redemption at $50 plus $0.85 accrued dividend on 03/06/1998
(Additional Information in Active)

NAVITRAK INTL CORP (NV)
Common $0.001 par split (2) for (1) by issuance of (1) additional share payable 06/01/2004 to holders of record 05/28/2004 Ex date - 06/02/2004
Common $0.001 par split (2) for (1) by issuance of (1) additional share payable 08/29/2005 to holders of record 08/26/2005 Ex date - 08/30/2005
Recapitalized as VECTr Systems, Inc. 05/21/2007
Each share Common $0.001 par exchanged for (0.01) share Common $0.001 par
(See VECTr Systems, Inc.)

NAVITRAK INTL CORP (ON)
Delisted from Toronto Venture Stock Exchange 10/03/2006

NAVSAT SYS INC (NV)
Capital Stock $1 par changed to 10¢ par 00/00/1974
Charter revoked for failure to file reports and pay fees 03/05/1979

NAVSTAR MEDIA HLDGS INC (NV)
Recapitalized as Rodobo International, Inc. 11/12/2008
Each share Common $0.001 par exchanged for (0.02673796) share Common $0.001 par

NAVSTAR TECHNOLOGIES INC (NV)
Each share old Common $0.001 par exchanged for (0.1) share new Common $0.001 par 08/19/2008
Each (150) shares new Common $0.001 par exchanged again for (1) share new Common $0.001 par 12/16/2009
Each share new Common $0.001 par exchanged again for (0.01) share new Common $0.001 par 08/29/2011
Stock Dividend - 10% payable 10/14/2009 to holders of record 09/30/2009

Recapitalized as Energy Revenue America, Inc. 08/01/2012
Each share new Common $0.001 par exchanged for (0.01538461) share Common $0.001 par

NAVTECH INC (DE)
Merged into Cambridge Information Group II LLC 11/28/2007
Each share Common $0.001 par exchanged for $2.50 cash

NAVTEQ CORP (DE)
Issue Information - 40,000,000 shares COM offered at $22 per share on 08/06/2004
Merged into Nokia Corp. 07/10/2008
Each share Common $0.001 par exchanged for $78 cash

NAWILIWILI CANNING CO., LTD. (HI)
Common $1 par changed to 1¢ par 5/31/56
Dissolved 10/15/62
No stockholders' equity

NAXOS RES LTD (CANADA)
Reorganized under the laws of Nevada as Franklin Lake Resources Inc. 01/09/2002
Each share Common no par exchanged for (0.1) share Common $0.001 par
Franklin Lake Resources Inc. recapitalized as Seen On Screen TV Inc. 03/19/2009

NAYARIT GOLD INC (ON)
Merged into Capital Gold Corp. 08/02/2010
Each share Common no par exchanged for (0.134048) share Common $0.0001 par
Note: Unexchanged certificates were cancelled and became without value 08/02/2016
Capital Gold Corp. merged into Gammon Gold Inc. (QC) 04/08/2011 which reincorporated in Ontario as AuRico Gold Inc. 06/14/2011 which merged into Alamos Gold Inc. (New) 07/06/2015

NAYBOB (1945) GOLD MINES LTD.
Succeeded by Logan Porcupine Mines Ltd. on a (1) for (3) basis in 1948
(See Logan Porcupine Mines Ltd.)

NAYBOB GOLD MINES, LTD.
Reorganized as Naylor Mines, Ltd. on a (0.1) for (1) basis in August 1943
(See Naylor Mines, Ltd.)

NAYLOR INDS INC (DE)
Reincorporated 06/16/1992
State of incorporation changed from (TX) to (DE) 06/16/1992
Merged into Insituform Technologies, Inc. 07/14/1993
Each share Common 1¢ par exchanged for $5.15 cash

NAYLOR MINES LTD.
Succeeded by Naybob (1945) Gold Mines Ltd. share for share in 1945
(See Naybob (1945) Gold Mines Ltd.)

NAYLOR PIPE CO (IL)
Prior Preferred $10 par called for redemption 6/29/56
(Additional Information in Active)

NAYNA NETWORKS INC (NV)
SEC revoked common stock registration 09/01/2011

NAZARETH CEM CO (PA)
Common no par changed to $10 par 00/00/1950
Stock Dividend - 100% 05/06/1955
Merged into Coplay Cement Manufacturing Co. 06/01/1968
Each share Common $10 par exchanged for $15 cash

NAZARETH NATL BK & TR CO (NAZARETH, PA)
Capital Stock $20 par changed to $5 par and (3) additional shares issued 02/21/1974

Stock Dividend - 200% 03/13/1980
Under plan of reorganization each share Capital Stock $5 par automatically became (1) share First Colonial Group, Inc. Common $5 par 11/26/1983
First Colonial Group, Inc. merged into KNBT Bancorp, Inc. 10/31/2003 which merged into National Penn Bancshares, Inc. 02/01/2008

NB & T FINL GROUP INC (OH)
Merged into Peoples Bancorp Inc. 03/06/2015
Each share Common no par exchanged for (0.9319) share Common no par and $7.75 cash

NB CAP CORP (MD)
8.35% Exchangeable Depositary Preferred Ser. A 1¢ par called for redemption at $25.94 plus $0.521875 accrued dividends on 09/30/2008

NB CAP TR I (DE)
Issue Information - 24,000,000 TR ORIGINATED PFD SECS 7.84% offered at $25 per share on 11/27/1996
7.84% Trust Originated Preferred Securities called for redemption at $25 on 3/15/2002

NB DESIGN & LICENSING INC (NV)
Name changed to Organic Alliance, Inc. 06/11/2008

NB MFG INC (NV)
Common $0.0001 par split (8) for (1) by issuance of (7) additional shares payable 03/05/2012 to holders of record 03/01/2012 Ex date - 03/06/2012
Name changed to Xhibit Corp. 11/13/2012
(See Xhibit Corp.)

NB SPLIT CORP (ON)
Class A Preferred Shares called for redemption at $$32.72 on 02/15/2012
Capital Shares called for redemption at $21.97 on 02/15/2012

NB TELECOM INC (NV)
Recapitalized as China XD Plastics Co. Ltd. 02/06/2009
Each (124.1) shares Common $0.0001 par exchanged for (1) share Common $0.0001 par

NBB BANCORP (WA)
Merged into Kitsap Bank (Port Orchard, WA) 1/13/97
Each share Common no par exchanged for $48 cash

NBB BANCORP INC (DE)
Merged into Fleet Financial Group, Inc. (New) 1/27/95
Each share Common 10¢ par exchanged for either (1.457) shares Common $1 par and (0.28) Common Stock Purchase Warrant expiring 1/27/2001 or (0.28) Common Stock Purchase Warrant expiring 1/27/2001 and $48.50 cash
Note: Option to elect to receive Warrants and cash expired 2/21/95
Fleet Financial Group, Inc. (New) name changed to Fleet Boston Corp. 10/1/99 which name changed to FleetBoston Financial Corp. 4/18/2000 which merged into Bank of America Corp. 4/1/2004

NBC BANCSHARES INC (LA)
Stock Dividend - 10% 03/31/1982
Acquired by Whitney Holding Corp. 01/07/1985
Each share Common $5 par exchanged for $85 cash

NBC BK CORP (AR)
Merged into Simmons First National Corp. 7/9/99
Each share Common $1 par exchanged for (4.164) shares Class A Common $1 par

NBC CAP CORP (MI)
Common $1 par split (4) for (3) by issuance of (0.33333333) additional share payable 09/09/2002 to holders of record 08/16/2002 Ex date - 09/12/2002
Name changed to Cadence Financial Corp. 06/28/2006
(See Cadence Financial Corp.)

NBC CO (NE)
Stock Dividends - 10% 1/4/71; 10% 5/21/73; 20% 11/5/75
Name changed to Commerce Group, Inc. 5/22/78
Commerce Group, Inc. merged into First Commerce Bancshares, Inc. 9/30/87 which merged into Wells Fargo & Co. 6/16/2000

NBC INTERNET INC (DE)
Merged into National Broadcasting Co., Inc. 8/13/2001
Each share Class A Common $0.0001 par exchanged for $2.19 cash

NBD BANCORP INC (DE)
Common $6.25 par changed to $2.50 par 05/16/1984
Common $2.50 par split (2) for (1) by issuance of (1) additional share 05/31/1985
Common $2.50 par split (3) for (2) by issuance of (0.5) additional share 10/17/1986
Common $2.50 par changed to $1 par 02/19/1987
Common $1 par split (3) for (2) by issuance of (0.5) additional share 06/30/1989
Common $1 par split (3) for (2) by issuance of (0.5) additional share 01/06/1992
Name changed to First Chicago NBD Corp. 12/01/1995
First Chicago NBD Corp. merged into Bank One Corp. 10/02/1998 which merged into J.P. Morgan Chase & Co. 12/31/2000 which name changed to JPMorgan Chase & Co. 07/20/2004

NBG RADIO NETWORK INC (NV)
Common $0.001 par split (3) for (1) by issuance of (2) additional shares payable 08/03/1998 to holders of record 07/31/1998
SEC revoked common stock registration 09/17/2008
Stockholders' equity unlikely

NBI INC (DE)
Common 10¢ par split (3) for (1) by issuance of (2) additional shares 03/09/1981
Plan of reorganization under Chapter 11 Federal Bankruptcy Code effective 02/03/1992
Each share old Common 10¢ par exchanged for (0.021191) share new Common 10¢ par
SEC revoked common stock registration 07/19/2010
Stockholders' equity unlikely

NBM BANCORP INC (OH)
Acquired by Rurban Financial Corp. 12/01/2008
Each share Common $2.50 par exchanged for $113.98 cash

NBM INC (DE)
Charter cancelled and declared inoperative and void for non-payment of taxes 3/1/77

NBO INDS (NJ)
Name changed to Treadway Companies, Inc. 08/10/1971
(See Treadway Companies, Inc.)

NBOG BANCORPORATION INC (GA)
Name changed to First Century Bancorp. 10/01/2007

NBP TRUECROSSING FDS (DE)
Completely liquidated 11/26/2002
Each share Growth Fund $3.48 par received net asset value

FINANCIAL INFORMATION, INC. NBS-NCH

Each share Technology Fund $3.48 par received net asset value

NBS FINL CORP (DE)
Name changed to NBSF Liquidating Trust and Common $10 par reclassified as Ctfs. of Bene. Int. 01/31/1977
NBSF Liquidating Trust completed liquidation for National Bank of Royal Oak (Royal Oak, MI) 04/06/1978
(See National Bank of Royal Oak (Royal Oak, MI))

NBS NATL BENEFIT SVCS INC (DE)
Name changed to Avesis Inc. 12/07/1990
(See Avesis Inc.)

NBS TECHNOLOGIES INC NEW (CANADA)
Merged into Brookfield Asset Management Inc. 12/29/2006
Each share Common no par exchanged for $1 cash
Note: Holders also received a Contigent Right to share in net litigation proceeds

NBS TECHNOLOGIES INC OLD (CANADA)
Name changed to Mist Inc. 11/1/2000
Mist Inc. name changed to NBS Technologies Inc. (New) 3/16/2004
(See NBS Technologies Inc. (New))

NBSC CORP (SC)
Common $5 par split (2) for (1) by issuance of (1) additional share 7/1/88
Merged into Synovus Financial Corp. 2/28/95
Each share Common $5 par exchanged for (1.6981) shares Common $1 par

NBSF LIQUIDATING TR (DE)
Liquidation completed
Each Ctf. of Bene. Int. received initial distribution of $1.50 cash 02/04/1977
Each Ctf. of Bene. Int. received second distribution of (1/3) share National Bank of Royal Oak (Royal Oak, MI) Common $10 par 11/25/1977
Each Ctf. of Bene. Int. received third and final distribution of $0.83 cash 04/06/1978
Note: Ctfs. of Bene. Int. were not required to be surrendered and are without value
National Bank of Royal Oak (Royal Oak, MI) reorganized as Royal Bank Group, Inc. 09/05/1984 which was acquired by Citizens Banking Corp. 10/01/1993

NBT CORP (DE)
Common $10 par changed to $4 par and (2) additional shares issued 02/10/1970
Name changed to BancOklahoma Corp. 07/01/1975
(See BancOklahoma Corp.)

NBT HLDGS INC (TN)
Name changed to Truxton Corp. 10/10/2013

NBT NORTHWEST BANCORP (WA)
Merged into Interwest Bancorp, Inc. 10/1/99
Each share Common $1 par exchanged for (0.88) share Common 20¢ par
Interwest Bancorp, Inc. name changed to Pacific Northwest Bancorp 9/1/2000 which merged into Wells Fargo & Co. (New) 11/3/2003

NBTY INC (DE)
Secondary Offering - 8,600,000 shares COM offered at $18 per share on 07/01/1998
Common $0.008 par split (3) for (1) by issuance of (2) additional shares payable 04/03/1998 to holders of record 03/23/1998

Acquired by TC Group, L.L.C. 10/01/2010
Each share Common $0.008 par exchanged for $55 cash

NBU MINES LTD (NB)
Merged into Dominion Explorers Inc. (Old) 7/19/85
Each (0.9) share Capital Stock $1 par exchanged for (1) share Subordinated no par
Dominion Explorers Inc. (Old) merged into Dominion Explorers Inc. (New) 12/31/94 which merged into Neutrino Resources Inc. 2/28/97
(See Neutrino Resources Inc.)

NBWC CORP (GA)
Merged into Synovus Financial Corp. 3/28/90
Details not available

NBWL INC (NV)
Charter revoked for failure to file reports and pay fees 07/31/2009

NC SALES CORP. (FL)
Proclaimed dissolved for failure to file reports and pay fees 08/25/1995

NC SCIENCES INC (DE)
Name changed to BGI Corp. 02/02/1971
BGI Corp. name changed to Frontier U.S.A. Corp. 06/07/1976

NC SOLAR INC (NV)
Name changed to Aqua Power Systems Inc. 08/12/2014

NCA CORP (CA)
Merged into ASK Computer Systems, Inc. 9/16/87
Each share Common no par exchanged for $8.50 cash

NCA MINERALS CORP (BC)
Struck off register and declared dissolved for failure to file returns 6/30/95

NCAL BANCORP (CA)
Common no par split (4) for (3) by issuance of (0.33333333) additional share payable 11/15/2002 to holders of record 10/30/2002 Ex date - 11/18/2002
Common no par split (2) for (1) by issuance of (1) additional share payable 02/28/2007 to holders of record 02/28/2007 Ex date - 03/01/2007
Acquired by CBC Bancorp 05/14/2018
Each share Common no par exchanged for $1.02 cash

NCB FINL CORP (PA)
Merged into Keystone Financial, Inc. 12/31/84
Each share Common $5 par exchanged for (3) shares Common $2 par
Keystone Financial, Inc. merged into M&T Bank Corp. 10/6/2000

NCBE CAP TR I (IN)
Name changed to Integra Capital Trust I 5/17/2000
(See Integra Capital Trust I)

NCC INDS INC (DE)
Reincorporated 01/06/1971
State of incorporation changed from (TN) to (DE) 01/06/1971
Chapter 11 bankruptcy procedings terminated 03/15/2005
Details not available

NCC LEASING INC (TN)
Name changed to NCC Industries, Inc. (TN) 07/02/1970
NCC Industries, Inc. (TN) reincorporated in Delaware 01/06/1971
(See NCC Industries, Inc.)

NCC MNG CORP (BC)
Recapitalized as BMA Mining Corp. 07/11/1997
Each share Common no par exchanged for (0.14285714) share Common no par

BMA Mining Corp. recapitalized as Dasher Energy Corp. 05/26/1999 which name changed to Dasher Resources Corp. 10/03/2002 which recapitalized as Dasher Exploration Ltd. 04/16/2003 which name changed to New World Resource Corp. 06/27/2005

NCD FINL INC (CA)
Company went private 00/00/1984
Details not available

NCE DIVERSIFIED FLOW-THROUGH 05 LTD PARTNERSHIP (ON)
Acquired by Sentry Select Corporate Class Ltd. 02/07/2007
Details not available

NCE DIVERSIFIED FLOW-THROUGH 05-2 LTD PARTNERSHIP (ON)
Acquired by Sentry Select Corporate Class Ltd. 02/07/2007
Details not available

NCE DIVERSIFIED INCOME TR (ON)
Name changed to Sentry Select Diversified Income Trust 03/01/2001
Sentry Select Diversified Income Trust name changed to Sentry Select Diversified Income Fund 01/08/2009

NCE ENERGY ASSETS 1993 FD (ON)
Acquired by Flock Resources Ltd. 06/30/2002
Each Unit of Limited Partnership no par exchanged for (119.03) shares Common no par
Flock Resources Ltd. name changed to Endev Energy Inc. 07/11/2002

NCE ENERGY ASSETS 1994 FD (ON)
Acquired by Flock Resources Ltd. 06/30/2002
Each Unit of Limited Partnership no par exchanged for (216.38) shares Common no par
Flock Resources Ltd. name changed to Endev Energy Inc. 07/11/2002

NCE ENERGY ASSETS 1995 FD (ON)
Acquired by Flock Resources Ltd. 06/30/2002
Each Unit of Limited Partnership no par exchanged for (340.75) shares Common no par
Flock Resources Ltd. name changed to Endev Energy Inc. 07/11/2002

NCE ENERGY ASSETS 1996 FD (ON)
Acquired by Flock Resources Ltd. 06/30/2002
Each Unit of Limited Partnership no par exchanged for (369.27) shares Common no par
Flock Resources Ltd. name changed to Endev Energy Inc. 07/11/2002

NCE ENERGY TR I (AB)
Merged into NCE Petrofund 05/31/2002
Each Trust Unit exchanged for (0.2325) new Trust Unit 2001
NCE Petrofund name changed to Petrofund Energy Trust 11/01/2003 which merged into Penn West Energy Trust 07/04/2006 which reorganized as Penn West Petroleum Ltd. (New) 01/03/2011 which name changed to Obsidian Energy Ltd. 06/29/2017

NCE FLOW THRU 2002-1 LTD PARTNERSHIP (ON)
Acquired by Sentry Select Canadian Resource Fund Ltd. 3/25/2004
Each Unit of Ltd. Partnership Int. no par exchanged for Common no par at $21.6413 net asset value

NCE FLOW THRU 2002-2 LTD PARTNERSHIP (ON)
Acquired by Sentry Select Canadian Resource Fund Ltd. 3/25/2004
Each Unit of Ltd. Partnership Int. no par exchanged for Common no par at $21.6413 net asset value

NCE OIL & GAS 1993 FD (ON)
Acquired by Flock Resources Ltd. 6/30/2002
Each Unit of Limited Partnership no par exchanged for (391.52) shares Common no par
Flock Resources Ltd. name changed to Endev Energy Inc. 7/11/2002

NCE OIL & GAS 1994 FD (ON)
Acquired by Flock Resources Ltd. 6/30/2002
Each Unit of Limited Partnership no par exchanged for (936.38) shares Common no par
Flock Resources Ltd. name changed to Endev Energy Inc. 7/11/2002

NCE OIL & GAS 1995 FD (ON)
Acquired by Flock Resources Ltd. 6/30/2002
Each Unit of Limited Partnership no par exchanged for (616.27) shares Common no par
Flock Resources Ltd. name changed to Endev Energy Inc. 7/11/2002

NCE OIL & GAS 1996 FD (ON)
Acquired by Flock Resources Ltd. 6/30/2002
Each Unit of Limited Partnership no par exchanged for (879.08) shares Common no par
Flock Resources Ltd. name changed to Endev Energy Inc. 7/11/2002

NCE OIL & GAS 1997 FD (ON)
Acquired by Flock Resources Ltd. 6/30/2002
Each Unit of Limited Partnership no par exchanged for (591.05) shares Common no par
Flock Resources Ltd. name changed to Endev Energy Inc. 7/11/2002

NCE PETROFUND (ON)
Name changed 07/04/1996
Each old Trust Unit exchanged for (0.1) new Trust Unit 10/05/1995
Name changed from NCE Petrofund I to NCE Petrofund 07/04/1996
Each new Trust Unit exchanged again for (0.33333333) new Trust Unit 2001 on 07/06/2001
Name changed to Petrofund Energy Trust 11/01/2003
Petrofund Energy Trust merged into Penn West Energy Trust 07/04/2006 which reorganized as Penn West Petroleum Ltd. (New) 01/03/2011 which name changed to Obsidian Energy Ltd. 06/29/2017

NCE STRATEGIC ENERGY FD (ON)
Name changed to Strategic Energy Fund 03/04/2003
Strategic Energy Fund reorganized as Sentry Select Energy Income Fund 02/24/2009

NCF FINL CORP (DE)
Merged into Community Bank Shares of Indiana, Inc. 05/06/1998
Each share Common 10¢ par exchanged for (0.935) share Common 10¢ par
Community Bank Shares of Indiana, Inc. name changed to Your Community Bankshares, Inc. 07/01/2015 which merged into WesBanco, Inc. 09/09/2016

NCH CORP (DE)
Merged into Ranger Holding LLC 2/13/2002
Each share Common $1 par exchanged for $52.50 cash

NCHANGA CONS COPPER MINES LTD (ZAMBIA)
ADR's for Ordinary £1 par split (4) for (1) by issuance of (3) additional shares 10/15/1959
Merged into Zambia Copper Investments Ltd. 06/25/1970
Each ADR for Ordinary KMZ 2 par exchanged for either (2) ADR's for Ordinary and (3.680261) Units of Loan Stock or $1.68 cash

COPYRIGHTED MATERIAL   NO UNAUTHORIZED REPRODUCTION

Note: Option to receive stock expired 08/31/1970
Zambia Copper Investments Ltd. name changed to ZCI Ltd. 05/24/2010

NCI HLDGS INC (NV)
Name changed to Dark Dynamite, Inc. 05/07/2004
Dark Dynamite, Inc. name changed to China International Tourism Holdings, Ltd. 10/26/2007 which name changed to China Logistics, Inc. (NV) 08/10/2009 which reorganized in British Virgin Islands as Hutech21 Co., Ltd. 03/21/2011

NCI INC (DE)
Acquired by Cloud Merger Sub, Inc. 08/15/2017
Each share Class A Common $0.019 par exchanged for $20 cash

NCL HLDG ASA (NORWAY)
Acquired by Star Cruises PLC 1/26/2001
Each Sponsored ADR for Ordinary 2.30 NOK par exchanged for $5.5835 cash

NCM SVCS INC (DE)
Each (3,456,315) shares old Common $0.001 par exchanged for (1) share new Common $0.001 par 09/25/2012
Note: In effect holders received $0.035 cash per share and public interest was eliminated

NCN EXPL & DEV CORP (BC)
Involuntarily dissolved 01/05/1990

NCNB CORP (NC)
Common $5 par changed to $2.50 par and (1) additional share issued 11/15/1972
Common $2.50 par split (2) for (1) by issuance of (1) additional share 11/20/1986
Name changed to NationsBank Corp. and Common $2.50 par changed to no par 12/31/1991
NationsBank Corp. (NC) reincorporated in Delaware as BankAmerica Corp. (Old) 09/25/1998 which merged into BankAmerica Corp. (New) 09/30/1998 which name changed to Bank of America Corp. 04/28/1999

NCNB NATIONAL BANK OF FLORIDA (TAMPA, FL)
Name changed to NationsBank of Florida, N.A. (Tampa, FL) 09/04/1992
(See NationsBank of Florida, N.A. (Tampa, FL))

NCO GROUP INC (PA)
Common no par split (3) for (2) by isauance of (0.5) additional share payable 12/05/1997 to holders of record 11/21/1997
Merged into Collect Holdings, Inc. 11/15/2006
Each share Common no par exchanged for $27.50 cash

NCO INVESTORS, INC. (TX)
Completely liquidated 4/30/65.
Each share Common exchanged for first and final distribution of (1) share Non-Commissioned Officers Life Insurance Co. Common no par
Non-Commissioned Officers Life Insurance Co. merged into Citizens Insurance Co. of America 2/3/78 which merged into Citizens, Inc. 12/1/88

NCO PORTFOLIO MGMT INC (DE)
Merged into NCO Group, Inc. 03/26/2004
Each share Common 1¢ par exchanged for (0.36187) share Common no par
(See NCO Group, Inc.)

NCOAT INC (DE)
Plan of reorganization under Chapter 11 Federal Bankruptcy proceedings effective 06/01/2012
No stockholders' equity

NCP INDS INC (NV)
Charter revoked for failure to file reports and pay taxes 03/01/1976

NCR CORP (MD)
Common $5 par split (4) for (1) by issuance of (3) additional shares 05/18/1984
$1.25 Conv. Preferred Ser. A $5 par called for redemption 08/14/1986
Preferred Stock Purchase Rights declared for Common stockholders of record 08/16/1986 were redeemed at $0.05 per right 09/30/1991 for holders of record 09/18/1991
Merged into American Telephone & Telegraph Co. 09/19/1991
Each share Common $5 par exchanged for (2.839) shares Common $1 par
American Telephone & Telegraph Co. name changed to AT&T Corp. 04/20/1994 which merged into AT&T Inc. 11/18/2005

NCRIC GROUP INC (DC)
Reorganized under the laws of Delaware 6/25/2003
Each share Common 1¢ par exchanged for (1.8665) share Common 1¢ par
NCRIC Group, Inc. (DE) merged into ProAssurance Corp. 8/3/2005

NCRIC GROUP INC (DE)
Merged into ProAssurance Corp. 8/3/2005
Each share Common 1¢ par exchanged for (0.25) share Common 1¢ par

NCS COMPUTING CORP (TX)
Recapitalized as Booth, Inc. 05/10/1973
Each share Common no par exchanged for (1/3) share Common 50¢ par
(See Booth, Inc.)

NCS HEALTHCARE INC (DE)
Merged into Omnicare, Inc. 01/16/2003
Each share Class A Common 1¢ par exchanged for $5.149 cash
Note: Each share Class A Common 1¢ par received an additional distribution of approximately $0.11 cash 06/00/2003

NCS HLDG CORP (DE)
Name changed to Compucharge, Inc. 12/10/69
(See Compucharge, Inc.)

NCT GROUP INC (DE)
Chapter 7 bankruptcy proceedings terminated 07/20/2009
Stockholders' equity unlikely

NCW CMNTY BK (WENATCHEE, WA)
Merged into Banner Corp. 10/10/2007
Each share Common exchanged for (0.7438) share Common 1¢ par and $14.22 cash

ND HLDGS INC (ND)
Reorganized as Integrity Mutual Funds Inc. 07/01/2002
Each share Common no par exchanged for (2) shares Common $0.0001 par
Integrity Mutual Funds Inc. name changed to Capital Financial Holdings, Inc. 09/10/2009

NDB ENERGY INC (NV)
Name changed to Armada Oil, Inc. 05/15/2012

NDC AUTOMATION INC (DE)
Each share old Common 1¢ par exchanged for (0.25) share new Common 1¢ par 03/06/1992
New Common 1¢ par split (3) for (2) by issuance of (0.5) additional share 03/15/1993
Name changed Transbotics Corp. 07/23/2002
(See Transbotics Corp.)

NDCHEALTH CORP (DE)
Merged into Per-Se Technologies, Inc. 1/6/2006
Each share Common $0.125 par exchanged for (0.2253) share new Common 1¢ par and $14.05 cash
(See Per-Se Technologies, Inc.)

NDE ENVIRONMENTAL CORP (DE)
Each share old Common $0.0001 par exchanged for (0.1) share new Common $0.0001 par 09/01/1994
Name changed to Tanknology-NDE International Inc. 08/06/1997
(See Tanknology-NDE International Inc.)

NDS GROUP PLC (ENGLAND & WALES)
Issue Information - 9,000,000 SPONSORED ADR'S offered at $20 per ADR on 11/22/1999
Acquired by News Corp. 02/05/2009
Each Sponsored ADR for Ser. A Ordinary 1¢ par exchanged for $62.95 cash

NDS SOFTWARE INC (NV)
Name changed to HomeSeekers.Com Inc. 7/1/98
(See HomeSeekers.Com Inc.)

NDT ENERGY LTD (BC)
Reorganized under the laws of Alberta as Pegasus Oil & Gas Inc. 06/23/2006
Each share Common no par exchanged for (0.0174256) share Class A Common no par
Pegasus Oil & Gas Inc. acquired by Harvest Energy Trust 08/17/2009
(See Harvest Energy Trust)

NDT VENTURES LTD (BC)
Reorganized as New Dimension Resources Ltd. 1/11/2006
Each share Common no par exchanged for (0.2) share Common no par and (0.05) share NDT Energy Ltd. Common no par
(See each company's listing)

NDU RES LTD (BC)
Merged into United Keno Hill Mines Ltd. 3/12/98
Each share Common no par exchanged for (1.35) shares Common no par
(See United Keno Hill Mines Ltd.)

NEA MUT FD INC (DE)
Merged into Mann (Horace) Fund, Inc. 01/06/1979
Each share Capital Stock $1 par exchanged for (0.514556) shares Common $1 par
Mann (Horace) Fund, Inc. name changed to Mann (Horace) Growth Fund, Inc. 10/31/1983

NEALON MINES LTD (ON)
Charter cancelled for failure to pay taxes and file returns 04/00/1975

NEARCTIC RES INC (ON)
Delisted from Canadian Dealer Network 01/03/1995

NEARMAP LTD (AUSTRALIA)
ADR agreement terminated 06/13/2018
No ADR's remain outstanding

NEARY RES CORP (BC)
Recapitalized as Red Emerald Resource Corp. 10/08/1999
Each share Common no par exchanged for (0.5) share Common no par
Red Emerald Resource Corp. name changed to Midway Gold Corp. 07/10/2002
(See Midway Gold Corp.)

NEASE CHEM INC (PA)
Common no par split (3) for (1) by issuance of (2) additional shares 12/30/58
Common no par split (3) for (1) by issuance of (2) additional shares 8/15/60
Common no par changed to $1 par 4/22/68
Merged into Rutgers Chemicals, Inc. 12/30/77
Each share Common $1 par exchanged for $7.75 cash

NEATT CORP (ON)
Ceased operations 05/28/2002
Stockholders' equity unlikely

NEBA INTERNATIONAL, INC. (FL)
Charter cancelled and proclaimed dissolved for non-payment of taxes 7/2/73

NEBEL (OSCAR) CO., INC.
Reorganized as Nebel (Oscar) Hosiery Corp. 00/00/1941
Each share Preferred exchanged for (1) share Common no par
No Common stockholders' equity
(See Nebel (Oscar) Hosiery Corp.)

NEBEL OSCAR HOSIERY CORP (VA)
Completely liquidated 07/08/1971
Each share Common $8 par exchanged for first and final distribution of $1.56 cash

NEBEX RES LTD (AB)
Struck off register 12/01/1999

NEBO CAP CORP (AB)
Name changed to Quisitive Technology Solutions Inc. 08/13/2018

NEBO PRODS INC (UT)
Reorganized under the laws of Delaware as Osage Enterprise Corp. 02/29/2008
Each share Common no par exchanged for (0.00333333) share Common no par
Osage Enterprise Corp. name changed to R'Vibrant, Inc. 03/11/2010 which name changed to Markray Corp. 02/16/2011

NEBRASKA CONS COMMUNICATIONS CORP (NE)
Name changed to N-Triple-C Inc. 12/28/73
N-Triple-C Inc. merged into MCI Communications Corp. 9/25/81 which merged into MCI WorldCom, Inc. 9/14/98 which name changed to WorldCom Inc. (New) 5/1/2000
(See WorldCom Inc. (New))

NEBRASKA CONS MLS CO (NE)
Common $10 par changed to $5 par and (1) additional share issued plus a 25% stock dividend paid 10/09/1963
Name changed to ConAgra, Inc. (NE) 02/25/1971
ConAgra, Inc. (NE) reincorporated in Delaware 01/12/1976 which name changed to Conagra Foods, Inc. 09/28/2000 which name changed to Conagra Brands, Inc. 11/10/2016

NEBRASKA CONTINENTAL TELEPHONE CO. (NE)
Name changed to General Telephone Co. of Nebraska 12/1/56
(See listing for General Telephone Co. of Nebraska)

NEBRASKA INSURANCE AGENCY, INC. (NE)
Name changed to Union Casualty Underwriters, Inc. 09/09/1968
(See Union Casualty Underwriters, Inc.)

NEBRASKA-IOWA BRIDGE CORP.
In process of liquidation in 1947

NEBRASKA-IOWA PACKING CO. (NE)
Liquidation completed in 1958

NEBRASKA MORTGAGE & INVESTMENT CO. (NE)
Charter cancelled and declared dissolved for non-payment of taxes 8/2/73

NEBRASKA NATL LIFE INS CO (NE)
Each share Common 50¢ par exchanged for (0.1) share Common $5 par 02/07/1964
Merged into United Security Life Co. 12/31/1968
Each share Common $5 par exchanged for (4) shares Common 25¢ par
(See United Security Life Co.)

NEBRASKA STATE BANK OF OMAHA (OMAHA, NE)
Acquired by Mutual of Omaha Bank (Omaha, NE) 11/02/2007
Details not available

NEC CORP (JAPAN)
Stock Dividends - 10% 11/16/1984; 400% payable 05/24/2001 to holders of record 05/18/2001
ADR agreement terminated 03/31/2010
Each ADR for Common JPY 50 par exchanged for $2.003255 cash

NEC ELECTRONICS CORP (JAPAN)
Name changed to Renesas Electronics Corp. 04/01/2010

NECHI CONSOLIDATED DREDGING LTD. (BC)
Acquired by Pato Consolidated Gold Dredging Ltd. (B.C.) in 1953
Each (8) shares Capital Stock $1 par exchanged for (1) new share Capital Stock $1 par
Pato Consolidated Gold Dredging Ltd. (B.C.) reincorporated in Bermuda 10/1/76
(See Pato Consolidated Gold Dredging Ltd. (Bermuda))

NECO ENERGY CORP (UT)
Charter expired 08/01/2006

NECO ENTERPRISES INC (RI)
Common no par changed to $1 par 03/28/1989
Common $1 par changed to 40¢ par and (1.5) additional shares issued 06/15/1990
Chapter 11 bankruptcy proceedings terminated 02/21/2001
Stockholders' equity unlikely

NEDCOR LTD (SOUTH AFRICA)
Stock Dividend - 0.77777% payable 4/20/2004 to holders of record 4/20/2004 Ex date - 3/30/2004
GDR agreement terminated 4/11/2005
Each GDR for 144A Ordinary exchanged for $11.7876 cash
Name changed to Nedbank Group Ltd. 5/16/2005

NEDERLAND MINES INC (DE)
Charter cancelled and declared inoperative and void for non-payment of taxes 03/01/1992

NEDICK'S STORES, INC. (DE)
Merged into ABC-Nedick's Inc. 10/1/65
Each share Common 20¢ par exchanged for $12.50 cash

NEDICKS CORP.
Assets sold in 1934
No stockholders' equity

NEDICKS INC.
Reorganized as Nedicks Corp. 00/00/1931
Details not available

NEEBO INC (DE)
Name changed to Nebraska Book Holdings, Inc. 07/02/2015

NEECO INC (MA)
Merged into JWP Inc. 5/22/90
Each share Common 1¢ par exchanged for (0.523) share Common 10¢ par
(See JWP Inc.)

NEEDCO COOLING SEMICONDUCTORS LTD. (CANADA)
Name changed to Needco Frigistors Ltd. 5/31/62
Needco Frigistors Ltd. name changed to Frigistors Ltd. in September 1963 which name changed to Termo Ltd. 7/29/67 which dissolved 3/20/72

NEEDCO FRIGISTORS LTD. (CANADA)
Name changed to Frigistors Ltd. in September 1963
Frigistors Ltd. name changed to Termo Ltd. 7/29/67 which dissolved 3/20/72

NEEDCO PARTNERS (TX)
Name changed to Great American Partners 6/12/84
Great American Partners reorganized as Eastern Petroleum Co. 11/1/89
(See Eastern Petroleum Co.)

NEEDHAM ENGINEERING, INC. (FL)
Proclaimed dissolved for failure to file reports and pay fees 6/28/71

NEEDHAM HARPER & STEERS INC (DE)
Class A Common 10¢ par reclassified as Common 10¢ par 04/18/1973
Merged into NHS Inc. 07/08/1977
Each share Common 10¢ par exchanged for $13.50 cash

NEEDHAM NATL BK (NEEDHAM, MA)
Name changed to Shawmut Needham Bank, N.A. (Needham, MA) 04/01/1975
(See Shawmut Needham Bank, N.A. (Needham, MA))

NEEDHAM PACKING INC (DE)
6% Preferred $25 par called for redemption 04/15/1965
Name changed to Flavorland Industries Inc. 07/17/1973
(See Flavorland Industries Inc.)

NEEDLE IN A HAYSTACK INC (MD)
Charter forfeited for failure to file reports and pay fees 10/5/92

NEEDLE POINT RES LTD (BC)
Name changed to Asian Canadian Resources Ltd. 4/7/86
Asian Canadian Resources Ltd. recapitalized as Victorian Enuretic Services Ltd. 7/15/90
(See Victorian Enuretic Services Ltd.)

NEEDLER GROUP LTD (ON)
Acquired by Blue Circle America Inc. 8/24/98
Each share Common no par exchanged for $1.90 cash

NEEMA INC (NV)
Name changed to Carbon Green Inc. 11/05/2009

NEENAH ENTERPRISES INC (DE)
Plan of reorganization under Chapter 11 Federal Bankruptcy proceedings effective 07/29/2010
No stockholders' equity

NEENAH PAPER INC (DE)
Recapitalized 03/13/2008
Holders of (49) or fewer shares exchanged for $24.99 cash per share
Name changed to Neenah, Inc. 01/02/2018

NEF ENTERPRISES INC (NV)
Name changed to Panther Biotechnology, Inc. 06/18/2014
Panther Biotechnology, Inc. name changed to ProBility Media Corp. 02/10/2017

NEFF CORP (DE)
Merged into Odyssey Investment Partners, LLC 06/03/2005
Each share Class A Common 1¢ par exchanged for $8.214 cash
Issue Information - 10,476,190 shares CL A COM offered at $15 per share on 11/20/2014
Acquired by United Rentals, Inc. 10/02/2017
Each share Class A Common 1¢ par exchanged for $25 cash

NEFFS NATL BK (NEFFS, PA)
Reorganized as Neffs Bancorp, Inc. 10/31/1986
Each share Common $100 par exchanged for (20) shares Common $5 par

NEGUS MINES LTD. (ON)
Recapitalized as Consolidated Negus Mines Ltd. 02/22/1955
Each share Capital Stock $1 par exchanged for (0.33333333) share Capital Stock $1 par
Consolidated Negus Mines Ltd. acquired by Groundstar Resources Ltd. (BC) 08/31/1973 which reincorporated in Alberta 10/28/2005

NEHAMA DATA CORP (MD)
Merged into International Gem Exchange, Inc. 06/16/1972
Each share Common no par exchanged for (0.5) share Common 1¢ par
(See International Gem Exchange, Inc.)

NEHI CORP. (DE)
Common no par changed to $1 par in 1950
Name changed to Royal Crown Cola Co. 3/30/59
Royal Crown Cola Co. name changed to Royal Crown Companies, Inc. 3/7/78
(See Royal Crown Companies, Inc.)

NEI CORP (DE)
Common 83-1/3¢ par changed to 41-2/3¢ par and (1) additional share issued 06/21/1973
Merged into Rockwood National Corp. 07/13/1977
Each share Common 41-2/3¢ par exchanged for (1.4) shares Common 25¢ par

NEI WEBWORLD INC (TX)
Issue Information - 1,000,000 shares COM offered at $5.50 per share on 05/21/1997
Chapter 7 bankruptcy proceedings terminated 11/07/2002
Stockholders' equity unlikely

NEIGHBORCARE INC (PA)
Each share 6% Conv. Preferred exchanged for (8.9375) shares Common 2¢ par 01/13/2004
Merged into Omnicare, Inc. 07/28/2005
Each share Common 2¢ par exchanged for $34.75 cash

NEIGHBORHOOD CONNECTIONS INC (NV)
Name changed to Lpath, Inc. (NV) and Common $0.001 par reclassified as Class A Common $0.001 par 12/09/2005
Lpath, Inc. (NV) reincorporated in Delaware 07/21/2014 which recapitalized as Apollo Endosurgery, Inc. 12/30/2016

NEIGHBORHOOD RLTY GROUP USA INC (NY)
Dissolved by proclamation 12/24/91

NEIGHBORS RES INC (ON)
Merged into Baitex Medical Technologies Inc. 3/11/92
Each share Common no par exchanged for (1/3) share Common no par
Baitex Medical Technologies Inc. recapitalized as Stockguard Corp. 11/10/94
(See Stockguard Corp.)

N8 CONCEPTS INC (CO)
Common $0.001 par split (10) for (1) by issuance of (9) additional shares payable 03/16/2009 to holders of record 03/06/2009 Ex date - 03/17/2009
Name changed to EcoBlu Products, Inc. 08/17/2009
EcoBlu Products, Inc. name changed to Eco Building Products, Inc. 07/15/2011

NEIMAN MARCUS CO (TX)
5% Preferred $100 par called for redemption 6/1/46
4-1/4% Preferred $100 par called for redemption 5/15/69
Stock Dividend - 15% 1/17/66
Completely liquidated 4/22/69
Each share Common $2 par exchanged for (1.05) shares Broadway-Hale Stores, Inc. (DE) $2 Conv. Preferred Ser. A $5 par
Broadway-Hale Stores, Inc. (DE) merged into Broadway-Hale Stores, Inc. (CA) 8/27/70 which name changed to Carter Hawley Hale Stores Inc. (CA) 5/30/74 which reincorporated in Delaware 7/26/84 which name changed to Broadway Stores, Inc. 6/17/94

NEIMAN-MARCUS GROUP INC (DE)
Common 1¢ par reclassified as Class A Common 1¢ par 9/22/99
Acquired by Newton Acquisition Inc. 10/6/2005
Each share Class A Common 1¢ par exchanged for $100 cash
Each share Class B Common 1¢ par exchanged for $100 cash

NEISNER BROS INC (NY)
Common no par changed to $1 par in 1937
Stock Dividend - 200% 9/46
Merged into Ames Department Stores, Inc. 11/16/78
Each share Common $1 par exchanged for (0.25) share $1.50 Conv. Preferred no par
(See Ames Department Stores, Inc.)

NEKOOSA EDWARDS PAPER CO (WI)
Each share Common $100 par exchanged for (4) shares Common $25 par 00/00/1945
Common $25 par changed to $10 par and (1) additional share issued 00/00/1954
Common $10 par reclassified as Class A Common $10 par 12/13/1957 and (1) share Class B Common $10 par distributed 12/17/1957
Class A Common $10 par and Class B Common $10 par reclassified as Common $10 par 04/29/1963
Stock Dividends - 10% 12/31/1948; 10% 12/02/1955; 10% 11/28/1956; 10% 12/01/1961
Merged into Great Northern Nekoosa Corp. 04/01/1970
Each share $5 Conv. Preferred Ser. A no par exchanged for (5) shares Conv. Preferred Ser. C no par
Each share 5% Conv. Preferred Ser. B no par exchanged for (5) shares Conv. Preferred Ser. D no par
Each share Common $10 par exchanged for (0.125) share Conv. Preferred Ser. B no par and (0.5) share Common $10 par
(See Great Northern Nekoosa Corp.)

NEL CASH MGMT ACCOUNT INC (MA)
Voluntarily dissolved 12/15/80
Details not available

NEL EQUITY FD INC (MA)
Under plan of merger each share Common $1 par automatically became (1) New England Funds Equity Income Fund Share of Bene. Int. no par 01/09/1987
New England Funds name changed to New England Funds Trust I 04/18/1994 which name changed to

NEL-NEN

Nvest Funds Trust I 02/01/2000 which name changed to CDC Nvest Funds Trust I 05/01/2001
(See CDC Nvest Funds Trust I)

NEL GROWTH FD INC (MA)
Under plan of merger each share Common $1 par automatically became (1) New England Funds Growth Fund Share of Bene. Int. no par 01/09/1987
New England Funds name changed to New England Funds Trust I 04/18/1994 which name changed to Nvest Funds Trust I 02/01/2000 which name changed to CDC Nvest Funds Trust I 05/01/2001
(See CDC Nvest Funds Trust I)

NEL INCOME FD INC (MA)
Under plan of merger each share Common $1 par automatically became (1) New England Funds Bond Income Fund Share of Bene. Int. no par 01/09/1987
New England Funds name changed to New England Funds Trust I 04/18/1994 which name changed to Nvest Funds Trust I 02/01/2000 which name changed to CDC Nvest Funds Trust I 05/01/2001
(See CDC Nvest Funds Trust I)

NEL RETIREMENT EQUITY FD INC (MA)
Under plan of merger each share Common $1 par automatically became (1) New England Funds Retirement Equity Fund Share of Bene. Int. no par 01/09/1987
New England Funds name changed to New England Funds Trust I 04/18/1994 which name changed to Nvest Funds Trust I 02/01/2000 which name changed to CDC Nvest Funds Trust I 05/01/2001
(See CDC Nvest Funds Trust I)

NEL TAX EXEMPT BD FD INC (MA)
Under plan of merger each share Common $1 par automatically became (1) New England Funds Tax Exempt Income Fund Share of Bene. Int. no par 01/09/1987
New England Funds name changed to New England Funds Trust I 04/18/1994 which name changed to Nvest Funds Trust I 02/01/2000 which name changed to CDC Nvest Funds Trust I 05/01/2001
(See CDC Nvest Funds Trust I)

NELA ALPHA ANTICIPATION CO.
Dissolved in 1941

NELA ALPHA INVESTING CO (ME)
Acquired by Massachusetts Investors Trust 12/18/1967
Each share Preferred $10 par exchanged for (0.574843) Ctf. of Bene. Int. 33-1/3¢ par
Each share Common $100 par exchanged for (34.714) Ctfs. of Bene. Int. 33-1/3¢ par

NELIO CHEMICALS, INC. (DE)
Name changed to Argyle Southern Co. 3/16/64
(See Argyle Southern Co.)

NELLCOR PURITAN BENNETT INC (DE)
Name changed 08/25/1995
Name changed from Nellcor Inc. to Nellcor Puritan Bennett Inc. 08/25/1995
Common $0.001 par split (2) for (1) by issuance of (1) additional share payable 06/28/1996 to holders of record 06/06/1996
Merged into Mallinckrodt Inc. 08/29/1997
Each share Common $0.001 par exchanged for $28.50 cash

NELLIE MEDA GOLD MINES (AZ)
Property sold at sheriff's sale 00/00/1938
Details not available

NELLO RES INC (ON)
Name changed 07/06/1982
Name changed from Nello Mining Ltd. to Nello Resources Inc. 07/06/1982
Each share Capital Stock no par exchanged for (0.33333333) share Class A Common no par 03/16/1984
Reincorporated under the laws of Alberta as Highridge Exploration Ltd. 08/03/1984
Highridge Exploration Ltd. merged into Talisman Energy Inc. 08/05/1999
(See Talisman Energy Inc.)

NELLY DON INC (MO)
Stock Dividend - 25% 02/01/1960
Reorganized under Chapter X bankruptcy act 11/29/1978
No stockholders' equity

NELSON, BAKER & CO.
Out of business 00/00/1950
Details not available

NELSON BROTHERS BOND & MORTGAGE CO. (IL)
Proclaimed dissolved for failure to pay taxes and file reports 6/25/34

NELSON (N.O.) CO. (MO)
Each share Preferred or Common $100 par exchanged for (10) shares Preferred or Common $10 par in 1948
Acquired by Bellanca Aircraft Corp. for cash 8/29/55

NELSON (HERMAN) CORP.
Merged into American Air Filter Co., Inc. in 1949
Each share Common $5 par exchanged for (1) share 5% Preference $15 par
(See American Air Filter Co., Inc.)

NELSON EXPL INC (KS)
Name changed to NELX, Inc. (KS) in October 1993
NELX, Inc. (KS) reincorporated in Delaware as Jacobs Financial Group, Inc. 12/27/2005

NELSON FINL CONCEPTS INC (UT)
Name changed to Zinetics Medical, Inc. 6/6/88
(See Zinetics Medical, Inc.)

NELSON GOLD LTD (BERMUDA)
Name changed to Nelson Resources Ltd. 10/31/2000
(See Nelson Resources Ltd.)

NELSON HLDGS INTL LTD (CANADA)
Reincorporated 09/18/1987
Place of incorporation changed from (BC) to (Canada) 09/18/1987
Recapitalized as NHI Nelson Holdings International Ltd. (Canada) 11/15/1989
Each share Common no par exchanged for (0.1) share Common no par
Preferred not affected except for change of name
NHI Nelson Holdings International Ltd. (Canada) reincorporated in Ontario 06/29/1993 which recapitalized as JPY Holdings Ltd. 07/26/1994 which reincorporated in Canada 11/09/2007

NELSON INDS INC (WI)
Merged into Cummins Engine Co., Inc. 1/8/98
Each share Common no par exchanged for $172.70 cash

NELSON L B CORP (CA)
Capital Stock $1 par reclassified as Common $1 par 04/26/1973
Stock Dividends - 10% 09/26/1977; 10% 07/28/1978; 10% 05/25/1979; 10% 05/14/1980; 10% 03/27/1981
Charter suspended for failure to file reports and pay fees 01/00/1994

NELSON (N.O.) MANUFACTURING CO.
Name changed to Nelson (N.O.) Co.

in 1942 which was acquired by Bellanca Aircraft Corp. for cash 8/29/55

NELSON OIL SYNDICATE, INC. (TX)
Completely liquidated 12/09/1968
Each share Capital Stock received first and final distribution of $0.010562 cash
Note: Certificates were not required to be surrendered and are without value

NELSON RESH & DEV CO (CA)
Common no par split (2) for (1) by issuance of (1) additional share 9/1/83
Acquired by Ethyl Corp. 3/23/87
Each share Common no par exchanged for $5.75 cash

NELSON RES CORP (DE)
Common 10¢ par changed to $1 par 12/11/1972
Chapter 11 bankruptcy proceedings closed 11/17/1981
No stockholders' equity

NELSON RES LTD (BERMUDA)
Merged into LUKOIL Overseas Holding Ltd. 12/05/2005
Each share Common no par exchanged for $2.19162 cash

NELSON SLOCAN CONSOLIDATED MINES, LTD. (BC)
Struck off the register and declared dissolved for failure to file returns 7/2/54

NELSON THOMAS INC (TN)
Common $1 par split (6) for (5) by issuance of (0.2) additional share 07/29/1976
Common $1 par split (4) for (3) by issuance of (1/3) additional share 07/29/1979
Common $1 par split (3) for (2) by issuance of (0.5) additional share 07/29/1983
Common $1 par split (3) for (2) by issuance of (0.5) additional share 09/30/1992
Class B Common $1 par split (3) for (2) by issuance of (0.5) additional share 09/30/1992
Common $1 par split (5) for (4) by issuance of (0.25) additional share 03/24/1995
Class B Common $1 par split (5) for (4) by issuance of (0.25) additional share 03/24/1995
Stock Dividends - 50% 06/28/1978; 25% 08/08/1980; 100% 06/05/1981; 20% 07/30/1982
Merged into InterMedia Partners, LP 06/12/2006
Each share Common $1 par exchanged for $29.85 cash
Each share Class B Common $1 par exchanged for $29.85 cash

NELSON TRADE & FIN LTD (BERMUDA)
Name changed to Nelson Gold Corp. Ltd. 6/22/95
Nelson Gold Corp. Ltd. name changed to Nelson Resources Ltd. 10/31/2000
(See Nelson Resources Ltd.)

NELSON VENDING TECHNOLOGY LTD (CANADA)
Reincorporated 7/23/87
Place of incorporation changed from (BC) to (Canada) 7/23/87
Acquired by Cinram Ltd. 7/31/93
Each share Common no par exchanged for (0.00169779) share Common no par
Cinram Ltd. name changed to Cinram International Inc. 6/12/97 which reorganized as Cinram International Income Fund 5/8/2006

NELVANA LTD (ON)
Acquired by Corus Entertainment Inc. 11/17/2000
Each share Subordinate no par exchanged for (1.147) shares Non-Vtg. Class B no par and $0.05 cash

NELWAY MINES LTD. (BC)
Struck off register and declared dissolved for failure to file returns 10/15/74

NELX INC (KS)
Reincorporated under the laws of Delaware as Jacobs Financial Group, Inc. 12/27/2005

NEMAHA OIL CO. (DE)
Acquired by Britalta Petroleums Ltd. 07/27/1962
Each share Capital Stock no par exchanged for (0.2) share Capital Stock no par
Britalta Petroleums Ltd. was acquired by Wilshire Oil Co. of Texas 10/12/1962 which name changed to Wilshire Enterprises, Inc. 07/01/2003
(See Wilshire Enterprises, Inc.)

NEMASKA EXPL INC (CANADA)
Each share Common no par received distribution of (0.05) share Monarques Resources Inc. Common no par payable 06/27/2011 to holders of record 06/22/2011
Ex date - 06/20/2011
Name changed to Nemaska Lithium Inc. 12/01/2011

NEMATRON CORP (MI)
Recapitalized as Sandston Corp. 4/6/2004
Each share Common no par exchanged for (0.2) share Common no par

NEMCO EXPL LTD (BC)
Name changed to Seaward Resources Ltd. 7/15/80
Seaward Resources Ltd. recapitalized as Seaquest Energy Ltd. (BC) 9/10/82 which reincorporated in Alberta 7/23/84 which recapitalized as Alta Petroleum Ltd. 1/13/87 which merged into CanEuro Resources Ltd. 4/4/89 which merged into Attock Oil Corp. 2/4/91 which recapitalized as Attock Energy Corp. 8/2/95
(See Attock Energy Corp.)

NEMDACO INC (CO)
Each share Common $0.0001 par received distribution of (0.25) share Woleko Industries Inc. Common $0.001 par payable 01/15/1997 to holders of record 12/15/1996
SEC revoked common stock registration 08/10/2009
Stockholders' equity unlikely

NEMI NORTHN ENERGY & MNG INC (AB)
Reincorporated 04/15/2010
Place of incorporation changed from (AB) to (BC) 04/15/2010
Each share old Common no par exchanged for (0.0000025) share new Common no par 08/16/2016
Note: In effect holders received $0.71 cash per share and public interest was eliminated
No distributions of less than $10 will be made

NEMO MINES LTD (ON)
Charter cancelled for failure to pay taxes and file returns 10/23/1979

NEMROD MNG LTD (QC)
Merged into Brominco Inc. 06/01/1976
Each share Capital Stock $1 par exchanged for (0.2) share Capital Stock no par and $0.10 cash
Brominco Inc. merged into Aur Resources Inc. 05/16/1985 which was acquired by Teck Cominco Ltd. 08/30/2007

NENDELS CORP (NV)
Name changed to Skylink

Telecommunications Corp. (NV) 2/20/96
Skylink Telecommunications Corp. (NV) reorganized in Oregon as Skylink Communications Corp. 6/15/98
(See Skylink Communications Corp.)

NEO ALLIANCE MINERALS INC (AB)
Name changed to Synergy Acquisition Corp. (AB) 12/20/2010
Synergy Acquisition Corp. (AB) reincorporated in Canada as Genius Properties Ltd. 02/13/2014 which name changed to Cerro de Pasco Resources Inc. 10/18/2018

NEO BIONICS INC (NV)
Charter revoked for failure to file reports and pay taxes 8/1/90

NEO FLASHER INDS INC (CA)
Charter cancelled for failure to file reports and pay taxes 11/3/75

NEO-LINE PRODUCTS CORP. (NY)
Each share Capital Stock $1 par exchanged for (2) shares Capital Stock 25¢ par 06/13/1956
Charter revoked for failure to file reports and pay fees 12/15/1961

NEO MATL TECHNOLOGIES INC (CANADA)
Merged into Molycorp, Inc. (New) 06/14/2012
Each share Common no par exchanged for (0.1984829) share Common $0.001 par and $6.01265778 cash
Note: Unexchanged certificates were cancelled and became without value 06/14/2018
(See Molycorp, Inc. (New))

NEO MODERN ENTMT CORP (CA)
Name changed to Chinawe.com Inc. 3/15/2001

NEO VISION CORP (DE)
Each share old Class A Common 50¢ par received distribution of (0.13) share LRNN Corp. Common $0.001 par payable 04/17/2002 to holders of record 04/03/2002
Each share old Class A Common 50¢ par exchanged for (0.004) share new Class A Common 50¢ par 04/04/2002
Each share new Class A Common 50¢ par received distribution of (0.01) share ANF Telecast, Inc. Common $0.001 par payable 08/23/2002 to holders of record 08/16/2002
Recapitalized as Storage Suites America, Inc. 11/07/2002
Each share new Class A Common 50¢ par exchanged for (0.01) share Class A Common 50¢ par
Storage Suites America, Inc. recapitalized as Bio-Matrix Scientific Group, Inc. 12/20/2004 which name changed to BMXP Holdings, Inc. 08/28/2006 which recapitalized as Freedom Environmental Services, Inc. 06/11/2008

NEOAX INC (DE)
Reincorporated 05/21/1987
State of incorporation changed from (OH) to (DE) 05/21/1987
Preferred Class C Ser. A 25¢ par called for redemption 06/15/1988
Exchangeable Preferred Class I Ser. B 25¢ par called for redemption 10/13/1989
Name changed to EnviroSource, Inc. 11/14/1989
EnviroSource, Inc. recapitalized as Envirosource, Inc. 06/22/1998
(See Envirosource, Inc.)

NEOCELL PRODUCTS CORP. (DE)
Dissolved 11/29/67

NEODONTICS INC (NV)
Common $0.001 par split (10) for (1) by issuance of (9) additional shares 11/30/84

Charter revoked for failure to file reports and pay fees 12/1/2003

NEODYM TECHNOLOGIES INC (BC)
Recapitalized as Neoteck Solutions Inc. 09/06/2012
Each share Common no par exchanged for (0.5) share Common no par
Neoteck Solutions Inc. recapitalized as Hello Pal International Inc. 05/13/2016

NEOFORMA INC (DE)
Recapitalized 8/27/2001
Issue Information - 7,000,000 shares COM offered at $13 per share on 01/24/2000
Recapitalized from Neoforma.com, Inc. to Neoforma Inc. 8/27/2001
Each share old Common $0.001 par exchanged for (0.1) share new Common $0.001 par
Merged into Global Healthcare Exchange, LLC 3/6/2006
Each share new Common $0.001 par exchanged for $10 cash

NEOHYDRO TECHNOLOGIES CORP (NV)
Name changed to Epoxy, Inc. 08/14/2014

NEOLENS INC (FL)
Merged into Sola International, Inc. 8/19/96
Each share Common $0.001 par exchanged for $1.14 cash

NEOLOGIC ANIMATION INC (NV)
SEC revoked common stock registration 08/19/2015

NEOMAR RES LTD (ON)
Name changed to Tarragon Oil & Gas Ltd. 06/29/1987
Tarragon Oil & Gas Ltd. merged into Marathon Oil Canada Ltd. 09/11/1998
(See Marathon Oil Canada Ltd.)

NEOMED INC (CO)
Merged into Rorer Group Inc. 01/16/1981
Each share Common 10¢ par exchanged for (0.4835) share Common no par
Rorer Group Inc. name changed to Rhone Poulenc-Rorer Inc. 07/31/1990
(See Rhone Poulenc-Rorer Inc.)

NEOMEDYX MED CORP (BC)
Name changed to Blue Marble Media Corp. 03/30/2010
Blue Marble Media Corp. name changed to KBridge Energy Corp. 01/31/2012

NEOMETRIX TECHNOLOGY GROUP INC (DE)
SEC revoked common stock registration 10/24/2006
Stockholders' equity unlikely

NEON COMMUNICATIONS GROUP INC (DE)
Merged into RCN Corp. 11/14/2007
Each share Common 1¢ par exchanged for $5.15 cash

NEON COMMUNICATIONS INC (DE)
Plan of reorganization under Chapter 11 Federal Bankruptcy Code effective 12/20/2002
No old Common stockholders' equity
Merged into Globix Corp. 03/08/2005
Each share 12% Preferred exchanged for (2.08333) shares 6% Conv. Preferred 1¢ par and $3.75 cash
Each share new Common 1¢ par exchanged for (1.2748) shares new Common 1¢ par
Globix Corp. name changed to NEON Communications Group, Inc. 03/01/2007
(See NEON Communications Group, Inc.)

NEON ENERGY LTD (AUSTRALIA)
ADR agreement terminated 12/26/2017
No ADR's remain outstanding

NEON PRODS CDA LTD (CANADA)
Common no par split (3) for (1) by issuance of (2) additional shares 9/25/64
Name changed to Neonex International Ltd. 3/24/69
(See Neonex International Ltd.)

NEON PRODUCTS INVESTMENT CORP. LTD.
Dissolved in 1939

NEON PRODUCTS OF WESTERN CANADA LTD. (CANADA)
Each share old Common no par exchanged for (4) shares new Common no par 03/15/1956
Name changed to Neon Products of Canada Ltd. 09/05/1956
Neon Products of Canada Ltd. name changed to Neonex International Ltd. 03/24/1969
(See Neonex International Ltd.)

NEON SYS INC (DE)
Merged into Progress Software Corp. 02/02/2006
Each share Common 1¢ par exchanged for $6.20 cash

NEONEX INTL LTD (CANADA)
Common no par split (2) for (1) by issuance of (1) additional share 4/30/69
Merged into Pattison (Jim) (British Columbia) Ltd. 11/1/77
Each share Common no par exchanged for (1) share 5-1/2% Preference no par or $3 cash
Note: Option not applicable to United States residents who received $3 cash per share

NEOPATH INC (WA)
Merged into TriPath Imaging, Inc. 9/30/99
Each share Common 1¢ par exchanged for (0.7903) share Common 1¢ par
(See TriPath Imaging, Inc.)

NEOPHARM INC (DE)
Common $0.000429 par changed to $0.0002145 par and (1) additional share issued payable 09/13/1996 to holders of record 08/26/1996
Stock Dividends - 10% payable 12/04/2001 to holders of record 11/27/2001 Ex date - 11/23/2001;
15% payable 06/10/2003 to holders of record 06/03/2003 Ex date - 05/30/2003
Name changed to Insys Therapeutics, Inc. 05/02/2011

NEOPROBE CORP (DE)
Name changed to Navidea Biopharmaceuticals, Inc. 01/05/2012

NEORX CORP (WA)
Each share old Common 2¢ par exchanged for (0.25) share new Common 2¢ par 12/14/93
Name changed to Poniard Pharmaceuticals, Inc. 6/19/2006

NEOSE TECHNOLOGIES INC (DE)
Liquidation completed
Each share Common 1¢ par received initial distribution of $0.33 cash payable 03/24/2009 to holders of record 03/02/2009 Ex date - 03/25/2009
Each share Common 1¢ par received second distribution of $0.20 cash payable 12/24/2009 to holders of record 03/02/2009 Ex date - 12/28/2009
Each share Common 1¢ par received third and final distribution of $0.0121 cash payable 06/16/2010 to holders of record 03/02/2009 Ex date - 06/17/2010
Note: Certificates were not required to

be surrendered and are without value

NEOSPHERE TECHNOLOGIES INC (NV)
Recapitalized as Microsmart Devices, Inc. 07/06/2004
Each (35) shares Common $0.001 par exchanged for (1) share Common $0.001 par

NEOSPORT INC (CA)
Charter suspended for failure to pay taxes 08/01/2000

NEOSTAR RETAIL GROUP INC (DE)
Petition under Chapter 11 Federal Bankruptcy Code dismissed 6/17/98
No stockholders' equity

NEOSTEM INC (DE)
Each share old Common $0.001 par exchanged for (0.1) share new Common $0.001 par 08/09/2007
Each share new Common $0.001 par exchanged again for (0.1) share new Common $0.001 par 07/16/2013
Name changed to Caladrius Biosciences, Inc. 06/08/2015

NEOTACTIX CORP (NV)
Ceased operations 05/00/2008
Stockholders' equity unlikely

NEOTEC CORP (DE)
Completely liquidated 07/29/1982
Each share Common 1¢ par exchanged for first and final distribution of $0.52 cash

NEOTECK SOLUTIONS INC (BC)
Recapitalized as Hello Pal International Inc. 05/13/2016
Each share Common no par exchanged for (0.66666666) share Common no par

NEOTEL INC (ON)
Recapitalized as Neotel International Inc. 04/05/2005
Each share Common no par exchanged for (0.33333333) share Common no par
Neotel International Inc. name changed to Tenth Power Technologies Corp. 10/01/2008
(See Tenth Power Technologies Corp.)

NEOTEL INTL INC (ON)
Name changed to Tenth Power Technologies Corp. 10/01/2008
(See Tenth Power Technologies Corp.)

NEOTERIC CORP. (NV)
Charter permanently revoked 4/1/2004

NEOTERIC GROUP INC (NV)
SEC revoked common stock registration 12/05/2002

NEOTERIK HEALTH TECHNOLOGIES INC (MD)
Merged into Global Neoterick 4/15/2005
Each share Common $0.015 par exchanged for $0.08 cash

NEOTHERAPEUTICS INC (DE)
Reincorporated 6/17/97
State of incorporation changed from (CO) to (DE) and Common no par changed to $0.001 par 6/17/97
Each share old Common $0.001 par exchanged for (0.04) share new Common $0.001 par 9/6/2002
Name changed to Spectrum Pharmaceuticals Inc. 12/11/2002

NEOTHETICS INC (DE)
Recapitalized as Evofem Biosciences, Inc. 01/18/2018
Each share Common $0.0001 par exchanged for (0.16666666) share Common $0.0001 par

NEOVIEW HLDGS INC (NV)
Name changed to Jingwei International Ltd. 06/01/2007
Jingwei International Ltd.

recapitalized as iSocialy, Inc. 01/25/2017

NEOWARE INC (DE)
Name changed 12/01/2005
Name changed from Neoware Systems, Inc. to Neoware, Inc. 12/01/2005
Merged into Hewlett-Packard Co. 10/01/2007
Each share Common $0.001 par exchanged for $16.25 cash

NEOZYME CORP (DE)
Completely liquidated 12/21/93
Each share Common 1¢ par exchanged for first and final distribution of $16.97 cash

NEPC INDIA LTD (INDIA)
Name changed 08/18/1998
Stock Dividend - 5.04648% payable 04/05/2002 to holders of record 07/16/1996
Name changed from NEPC-Micon Ltd. to NEPC India Ltd. 08/18/1998
GDR agreement terminated 07/10/2015
Each 144A GDR for Equity Shares exchanged for (1) Equity Share
Note: Unexchanged GDR's will be sold and the proceeds, if any, held for claim

NEPHROGENEX INC (DE)
Plan of reorganization under Chapter 11 Federal Bankruptcy proceedings effective 05/24/2017
No stockholders' equity

NEPIA INC (NV)
Name changed to Rich Pharmaceuticals, Inc. 09/03/2013

NEPTUNA CORP. (CA)
Name changed to Diversified Industries, Inc. 6/16/60 which was acquired by Tronchemics Research, Inc. 11/15/62

NEPTUNALIA SEAFOOD CO (GA)
Name changed to Gold King Frozen Foods, Inc. 07/31/1968
Gold King Frozen Foods, Inc. acquired by Seeman Brothers, Inc. 05/23/1969 which name changed to Seabrook Foods, Inc. 07/24/1970
(See Seabrook Foods, Inc.)

NEPTUNE CAP CORP (AB)
Merged into Vanguard Aviation Corp. 07/31/2003
Each share Common no par exchanged for (0.34013605) share Common no par and (0.34013605) Common Stock Purchase Warrant expiring 10/31/2005
(See Vanguard Aviation Corp.)

NEPTUNE CORP. (DE)
Name changed to Atlantic Beach Development Corp. 11/29/48
(See Atlantic Beach Development Corp.)

NEPTUNE GOLD MNG CO (DE)
Name changed to Neptune Mining Co. 05/09/1972
(See Neptune Mining Co.)

NEPTUNE INDS INC (FL)
Reorganized 04/12/2004
Each share old Common $0.001 par exchanged for (0.25) share new Common $0.001 par 10/04/2001
Reorganized from Neptune Aquaculture, Inc. to Neptune Industries, Inc. 04/12/2004
Each share new Common $0.001 par exchanged for (2) shares new Common $0.001 par
Each share new Common $0.001 par exchanged again for (0.16666666) share new Common $0.001 par 06/21/2005
SEC revoked common stock registration 09/01/2011

NEPTUNE INTL CORP (NJ)
Name changed 5/1/74
Class A Common no par and Class B Common no par reclassified as Common no par in March 1946
Common no par changed to $5 par in September 1946
Common $5 par changed to $2.50 par and (1) additional share issued in 1950
Common $2.50 par changed to $10 par in April 1954
Each share Common $10 par exchanged for (2) shares Common $5 par in December 1954
$2.40 Preferred $50 par called for redemption 2/15/64
Common $5 par split (2) for (1) by issuance of (1) additional share 3/10/69
Name changed from Neptune Meter Co. to Neptune International Corp. 5/1/74
Common $5 par split (3) for (2) by issuance of (0.5) additional share 2/24/77
Merged into Wheelabrator-Frye Inc. 1/4/79
Each share Common $5 par exchanged for (0.8) share Common 30¢ par
Wheelabrator-Frye Inc. merged into Signal Companies, Inc. 2/1/83 which merged into Allied-Signal Inc. 9/19/85 which name changed to AlliedSignal Inc. 4/26/93 which name changed to Honeywell International Inc. 12/1/99

NEPTUNE MARINE SVCS LTD (AUSTRALIA)
ADR agreement terminated 08/03/2017
No ADR's remain outstanding

NEPTUNE MNG CO (DE)
Voluntarily dissolved 03/22/2001
Details not available

NEPTUNE ORIENT LINES LTD (SINGAPORE)
ADR agreement terminated 07/06/2016
Each Sponsored ADR for Ordinary exchanged for $3.806994 cash

NEPTUNE RES CORP (BC)
Merged into ABM Gold Corp. 12/05/1989
Each share Capital Stock no par exchanged for (0.42857142) share Class A Common no par
ABM Gold Corp. reorganized as NorthWest Gold Corp. 06/01/1990 which merged into Northgate Exploration Ltd. (ON) 06/08/1993 which reincorporated in British Columbia 07/01/2001 which name changed to Northgate Minerals Corp. 05/20/2004 which merged into AuRico Gold Inc. 10/26/2011

NEPTUNE SOC INC (FL)
Each share Common $0.001 par exchanged for (0.5) share Common $0.002 par 5/19/2000
Each share Common $0.002 par exchanged for (0.25) share Common $0.008 par 3/22/2002
Merged into BG Capital Group Ltd. 11/22/2005
Each share Common $0.008 par exchanged for $2.68 cash

NEPTUNE TECHNOLOGIES & BIORESSOURCES INC (QC)
Each share Common no par received distribution of (0.03416467) share NeuroBioPharm Inc. Class A Subordinate no par and (0.06832934) Class A Share Purchase Warrant expiring 04/12/2014 payable 10/31/2012 to holders of record 10/15/2012
Ex date - 10/11/2012
Name changed to Neptune Wellness Solutions Inc. 09/21/2018

NERA AS (NORWAY)
Issue Information - 1,975,000 SPONSORED ADR's offered at $28.50 per ADR on on 06/27/1995
ADR agreement terminated 1/20/2004
Each Sponsored ADR for Ordinary NOK 10 par exchanged for $2.4164 cash

NERCO INC (OR)
Merged into RTZ America Inc. 6/2/93
Each share Common no par exchanged for $12 cash

NEROX ENERGY CORP (NV)
Each share Common $0.001 par exchanged for (0.02800022) share old Common $0.002 par 09/01/1995
Each share old Common $0.002 par exchanged for (0.4) share new Common $0.002 par 12/01/1998
Name changed to E*twoMedia.com 12/15/1998
E*twoMedia.com name changed to Exus Networks, Inc. 12/19/2000 which recapitalized as Exus Global, Inc. 09/12/2003 which recapitalized as StarInvest Group, Inc. 01/14/2005
(See StarInvest Group, Inc.)

NERTORN, INC. (MI)
Liquidation completed
Each share Common $1 par exchanged for initial distribution of $12 cash 6/16/67
Each share Common $1 par received second distribution of $2 cash 9/27/67
Each share Common $1 par received third distribution of $2.25 cash 4/12/68
Each share Common $1 par received fourth and final distribution of $0.38 cash 3/6/70

NES RENTALS HLDGS INC (DE)
Merged into Diamond Castle Holdings, LLC 7/21/2006
Each share Common 1¢ par exchanged for $18.75 cash

NESB CORP (DE)
Charter cancelled and declared inoperative and void for non-payment of taxes 03/01/1995

NESBETT FUND, INC.
Name changed to Dreyfus Fund Inc. in 1951

NESBITT (JOHN J.), INC. (PA)
Acquired by International Telephone & Telegraph Corp. (MD) 12/31/63
Each share Common 50¢ par exchanged for (0.4) share 4% Conv. Preferred Ser. E $100 par and (0.3) share Capital Stock no par
International Telephone & Telegraph Corp. (MD) reincorporated in Delaware 1/31/68 which name changed to ITT Corp. 12/31/83 which reorganized in Indiana as ITT Industries, Inc. 12/19/95 which name changed to ITT Corp. 7/1/2006

NESBITT LA BINE URANIUM MINES LTD. (ON)
Merged into Gunnar Mining Ltd. 11/30/60
Each share Capital Stock $1 par exchanged for (0.0125) share Capital Stock $1 par
Gunnar Mining Ltd. name changed to Bovis Corp. Ltd. 2/16/71
(See Bovis Corp. Ltd.)

NESBITT MNG & EXPL LTD (ON)
Recapitalized as Naneco Resources Ltd. (ONT) 08/17/1983
Each share Common no par exchanged for (1/3) share Common no par
Naneco Resources Ltd. (ONT) reincorporated in Alberta 12/01/1983 which recapitalized as Naneco Minerals Ltd. 06/28/1991 which recapitalized as Southpoint Resources Ltd. 03/28/2002 which name changed to E4 Energy Inc. 08/23/2005 which merged into Twin Butte Energy Ltd. 02/08/2008

NESBITT THOMPSON DEACON INC (CANADA)
Name changed 9/30/86
Name changed from Nesbitt, Thompson Inc. to Nesbitt, Thompson, Deacon Inc. 9/30/86
Acquired by Bank of Montreal (Montreal, QUE) in September 1997
Each share Class A Subordinate no par exchanged for $22 cash

NESCO, INC. (NJ)
Common $12.50 par changed to $5 par in 1950
Merged into New York Shipbuilding Corp. share for share 4/23/54
New York Shipbuilding Corp. merged into Merritt-Chapman & Scott Corp. 10/23/70
(See Merritt-Chapman & Scott Corp.)

NESCO INC (OK)
Plan of reorganization under Chapter 11 Federal Bankruptcy Code effective 6/14/2003
No stockholders' equity

NESCO INDS INC (NV)
Name changed to Aquamatrix, Inc. 4/16/2007

NESCO MINING CORP. (WA)
Name changed to Nesco Resources Inc. and Common 1-1/3¢ par changed to no par 6/1/82
(See Nesco Resources Inc.)

NESCO RES INC (WA)
Charter cancelled and proclaimed dissolved for failure to pay fees 2/9/88

NESHAMINY VY BK (CORNWELLS HEIGHTS, PA)
Merged into Industrial Valley Bank & Trust Co. (Jenkintown, PA) 12/31/1974
Each share Capital Stock $10 par exchanged for (0.4) share Common $5 par
Industrial Valley Bank & Trust Co. (Jenkintown, PA) reorganized as IVB Financial Corp. 01/01/1984
(See IVB Financial Corp.)

NESIKEP MINES LTD (BC)
Charter cancelled for failure to file returns in 1971

NESMONT INDL CORP (BC)
Recapitalized as International Nesmont Industrial Corp. 5/10/93
Each (3.5) shares Common no par exchanged for (1) share Common no par

NESS ENERGY INTL INC (TX)
Reincorporated 03/05/2008
State of incorporation changed from (WA) to (TX) 03/05/2008
SEC revoked common stock registration 06/14/2011

NESS TECHNOLOGIES INC (DE)
Acquired by Jersey Holding Corp. 10/11/2011
Each share Common 1¢ par exchanged for $7.75 cash

NESSCAP ENERGY INC (ON)
Voluntarily dissolved 05/03/2017
Each share Common no par received approximately (0.005) share Maxwell Technologies, Inc. Common 10¢ par

NESTE OIL OYJ (FINLAND)
Name changed to Neste OYJ 06/15/2015

NESTLE LE MUR CO (OH)
Each share Class A no par exchanged for (1.1) shares Common $1 par 00/00/1949
Each share Class B no par exchanged for (0.08) share Common $1 par 00/00/1949
Common $1 par split (2) for (1) by issuance of (1) additional share 08/10/1961

Stock Dividends - 50% 06/01/1956;
50% 12/23/1957
Merged into Kleer-Vu Industries, Inc.
01/09/1984
Each share Common $1 par
exchanged for (1.5) shares Common
10¢ par
Kleer-Vu Industries, Inc. recapitalized
as Calypso Wireless Inc. 11/08/2002
(See Calypso Wireless Inc.)

NESTLE S A (SWITZERLAND)
144A Sponsored ADR's for Ordinary
split (2) for (1) by issuance of (1)
additional ADR payable 06/15/2001
to holders of record 06/08/2001
ADR agreement terminated
07/26/2004
Each 144A Sponsored ADR for
Ordinary exchanged for $67.7801
cash
(Additional Information in Active)

NESTOR INC (DE)
Old Common 1¢ par split (2) for (1)
by issuance of (1) additional share
01/02/1986
7% Conv. Preferred Ser. D $1 par
called for redemption at $1.50 on
06/30/1998
Each share old Common 1¢ par
exchanged for (0.1) share new
Common 1¢ par 04/11/2003
SEC revoked common stock
registration 01/21/2014

NET COMMAND TECH INC (FL)
Reincorporated 02/01/2000
State of incorporation changed from
(DE) to (FL) 02/01/2000
Each share old Common $0.001 par
exchanged for (0.2) share new
Common $0.001 par 04/10/2000
SEC revoked common stock
registration 04/23/2007
Stockholders' equity unlikely

NET ELEMENT INC OLD (DE)
Merged into Net Element
International, Inc. 10/03/2012
Each share Common $0.001 par
exchanged for (0.025) share
Common $0.0001 par
Net Element International, Inc. name
changed to Net Element, Inc. (New)
12/09/2013

NET ELEMENT INTL INC (DE)
Name changed to Net Element, Inc.
(New) 12/09/2013

NET FORCE SYS INC
(ANTIGUA & BARBUDA)
Name changed to Sinovac Biotech
Ltd. 11/03/2003

NET GENESIS CORP (DE)
Issue Information - 4,250,000 shares
COM offered at $18 per share on
02/28/2000
Merged into SPSS Inc. 12/21/2001
Each share Common $0.001 par
exchanged for (0.097) share
Common 1¢ par
(See SPSS Inc.)

NET/GUARD TECHNOLOGIES INC (DE)
Charter forfeited for failure to maintain
a registered agent 01/01/2000

NET HLDGS COM INC (NV)
Each share old Common $0.001 par
exchanged for (0.025) share new
Common $0.001 par 12/20/99
Each share new Common $0.001 par
exchanged for (0.5) share new
Common $0.001 par 9/18/2000
Name changed to Global Acxess
Corp. 5/9/2001

NET HLDG INC (TURKEY)
Stock Dividends - 10% payable
12/30/98 to holders of record
6/22/98; 94% payable 10/29/99 to
holders of record 6/22/98; 25%
payable 11/5/99 to holders of record
8/2/99; 35% payable 6/20/2000 to
holders of record 6/1/2000; 13%
payable 12/18/2001 to holders of
record 12/6/2001 Ex date -
12/4/2001
ADR agreement terminated 6/16/2003
No ADR holders' equity

NET LNNX INC (PA)
Name changed to Printonthenet.com,
Inc. 08/27/1999
Printonthenet.com, Inc. name
changed to NexPub, Inc. 12/19/2000
(See NexPub, Inc.)

NET MASTER CONSULTANTS INC. (TX)
Each share old Common $0.0001 par
exchanged for (2) shares new
Common $0.0001 par 01/31/2000
Recapitalized as Sona Development
Corp. 10/18/2002
Each share new Common $0.0001
par exchanged for (0.1) share
Common $0.0001 par
Sona Development Corp. name
changed to Sibling Entertainment
Group Holdings, Inc. 06/15/2007
which recapitalized as Sibling Group
Holdings, Inc. 08/21/2012

NET NANNY SOFTWARE INTL INC (YUKON)
Reincorporated 11/15/2000
Place of incorporation changed from
(BC) to (Yukon) 11/15/2000
Filed a Notice of Intention pursuant to
the Bankruptcy and Insolvency Act
06/00/2002
Stockholders' equity unlikely

NET PERCEPTIONS INC (DE)
Issue Information - 3,650,000 shares
COM offered at $14 per share on
04/22/1999
Name changed to Stamford Industrial
Group, Inc. 09/13/2007
(See Stamford Industrial Group, Inc.)

NET PROFITS TEN INC (NV)
Common $0.0001 par split (181) for
(1) by issuance of (180) additional
shares payable 11/08/2012 to
holders of record 11/08/2012
Ex date - 11/09/2012
Name changed to World Moto, Inc.
11/15/2012

NET-QUOTE COM INC (ON)
Name changed to HYWY.Com Corp.
04/17/2000
HYWY.Com Corp. name changed to
HYWY Corp. 05/18/2000 which
recapitalized as HY Lake Gold Inc.
03/30/2006 which name changed to
West Red Lake Gold Mines Inc.
06/29/2012

NET RES INC (AB)
Name changed to BakBone Software
Inc. (AB) 03/13/2000
BakBone Software Inc. (AB)
reincorporated in Canada
08/11/2003
(See BakBone Software Inc.)

NET SVGS LINK INC (CO)
Reincorporated 02/28/2017
Each share old Common $0.001 par
exchanged for (0.06666666) share
new Common $0.001 par
05/13/2013
State of incorporation changed from
(NV) to (CO) 02/28/2017
Reincorporated under the laws of
Delaware 05/17/2017

NET SERVICOS DE COMUNICACAO S A (BRAZIL)
Each old Sponsored ADR for
Preferred exchanged for
(0.66666666) new Sponsored ADR
for Preferred 08/03/2006
ADR basis changed from (1:10) to
(1:1) 08/03/2006
ADR agreement terminated
01/20/2014
Each new Sponsored ADR for
Preferred exchanged for $10.319746
cash

NET SHEPHERD INC (AB)
Recapitalized as Flock Resources
Ltd. 05/09/2002
Each share Common no par
exchanged for (0.1) share Common
no par
Flock Resources Ltd. name changed
to Endev Energy Inc. 07/11/2002
which merged into Penn West
Energy Trust 07/22/2008 which
reorganized as Penn West
Petroleum Ltd. (New) 01/03/2011
which name changed to Obsidian
Energy Ltd. 06/29/2017

NET SOFT SYS INC (BC)
Recapitalized as Rhys Resources Ltd.
02/24/2011
Each share Common no par
exchanged for (0.1) share Common
no par
Rhys Resources Ltd. recapitalized as
Pacific Rim Cobalt Corp. 10/24/2017

NET/TECH INTL INC (DE)
Recapitalized as Return on
Investment Corp. 8/9/2000
Each share Common 1¢ par
exchanged for (0.05) share Common
1¢ par
Return on Investment Corp. name
changed to Tectonic Network, Inc.
3/10/2005

NET TEL INTL INC (UT)
Each share old Common $0.0005 par
exchanged for (0.01) share new
Common $0.0005 par 3/19/99
Charter expired for failure to file
renewal 8/1/2002

NET TELECOMMUNICATIONS INC (NV)
SEC revoked common stock
registration 08/10/2009
Stockholders' equity unlikely

NET WORLD MARKETING INC (NV)
Charter permanently revoked
10/31/2012

NET X AMER INC (OR)
Each share old Common $0.001 par
exchanged for (0.2) share new
Common $0.001 par 04/27/1998
Recapitalized as CB Scientific Inc.
02/16/2016
Each share Common $0.001 par
exchanged for (0.01333333) share
Common $0.001 par

NETAIR INTL CORP (CO)
Declared defunct and inoperative for
failure to pay taxes and file annual
reports 9/30/90

NETALCO CORP (AB)
Issue Information - 1,000,000 shares
COM offered at $0.30 per share on
03/21/1997
Recapitalized as Saddle Resources
Inc. 1/26/99
Each share Common no par
exchanged for (0.2) share Common
no par
(See Saddle Resources Inc.)

NETAMERICA.COM CORP (DE)
Name changed to RateXchange Corp.
04/20/2000
RateXchange Corp. name changed to
MCF Corp. 07/22/2003 which name
changed to Merriman Curhan Ford
Group, Inc. 05/20/2008 which
recapitalized as Merriman Holdings,
Inc. 08/16/2010

NETAMERICA CORP (DE)
Name changed to NetAmerica.com
Corp. 06/18/1999
NetAmerica.com Corp. name
changed to RateXchange Corp.
04/20/2000 which name changed to
MCF Corp. 07/22/2003 which name
changed to Merriman Curhan Ford
Group, Inc. 05/20/2008 which
recapitalized as Merriman Holdings,
Inc. 08/16/2010

NETBANK INC (GA)
Name changed 04/27/2000
Issue Information - 3,500,000 shares
COM offered at $12 per share on
07/28/1997
Common 1¢ par split (3) for (1) by
issuance of (2) additional shares
payable 05/14/1999 to holders of
record 04/23/1999
Name changed from Net.B@nk, Inc.
to NetBank, Inc. 04/27/2000
Plan of reorganization under Chapter
11 Federal Bankruptcy Code
effective 09/29/2008
No stockholders' equity

NETBANX COM CORP (NV)
Name changed to NetJ.com Corp.
11/05/1999
NetJ.com Corp. name changed to
ZooLink Corp. 11/20/2002 which
recapitalized as Action Energy Corp.
04/02/2009 which name changed to
SMC Recordings Inc. 09/03/2009
which recapitalized as SMC
Entertainment, Inc. 05/06/2011

NETBET INC (NV)
Name changed to Telemais
Telecommunications Inc. 05/17/2002
Telemais Telecommunications Inc.
recapitalized as WebSky, Inc.
01/20/2004

NETCARE HEALTH GROUP INC (DE)
Each share old Common 1¢ par
exchanged for (0.04) share new
Common 1¢ par 04/16/2002
SEC revoked common stock
registration 07/31/2008
Stockholders' equity unlikely

NETCENTIVES INC (DE)
Issue Information - 6,000,000 shares
COM offered at $12 per share on
10/13/1999
Plan of reorganization under Chapter
11 Federal Bankruptcy Code
effective 7/6/2002
No stockholders' equity

NETCERT INC (NV)
Name changed to Ise Blu Equity
Corp. 07/24/2006
(See Ise Blu Equity Corp.)

NETCHOICE INC (DE)
Recapitalized as Xstream Mobile
Solutions Corp. 1/31/2006
Each share Common 1¢ par
exchanged for (0.125) share
Common $0.001 par

NETCO ENERGY INC (AB)
Name changed to Netco Silver Inc.
(AB) 07/14/2011
Netco Silver Inc. (AB) reincorporated
in British Columbia as Brisio
Innovations Inc. 02/12/2014

NETCO INVTS INC (TX)
Each share old Common $0.0001 par
exchanged for (0.003003003) share
new Common $0.0001 par
01/13/2006
Each share old Common $0.0001 par
exchanged again for (0.00001942)
share new Common $0.0001 par
06/30/2006
SEC revoked common stock
registration 12/23/2014

NETCO INVTS INC (WA)
Reorganized as Syntec Biofuel Inc.
08/21/2006
Each share Common $0.0001 par
exchanged for (2) shares Common
$0.0001 par

NETCO SILVER INC (AB)
Each share old Common no par
exchanged for (0.2) share new
Common no par 08/26/2013
Reincorporated under the laws of
British Columbia as Brisio
Innovations Inc. 02/12/2014

NETCOAST COMMUNICATIONS INC (CA)
Each share old Common 16-2/3¢ par

exchanged for (1/3) share new Common 16-2/3¢ par 03/01/1999
Recapitalized as SmartData, Inc. 10/26/2004
Each share Common 16-2/3¢ par exchanged for (0.2) share Common 16-2/3¢ par
SmartData, Inc. name changed to Coastal Technologies Inc. 10/10/2005 which recapitalized as Cyclone Power Technologies, Inc. 07/02/2007

NETCOM AB (SWEDEN)
Name changed 10/15/1998
Name changed from Netcom Systems AB to Netcom AB 10/15/1998
Name changed to Tele2 AB 02/20/2001
(See Tele2 AB)

NETCOM ON-LINE COMMUNICATION SVCS INC (DE)
Issue Information - 1,850,000 shares COM offered at $13 per share on 12/15/1994
Merged into ICG Communications Inc. 1/21/98
Each share Common 1¢ par exchanged for (0.8628) share Common 1¢ par
(See ICG Communications, Inc.)

NETCOMMERCE INC (CO)
Each share Common no par received distribution of (1/9) share Easysearchresults.com Restricted Common payable 04/30/2001 to holders of record 02/16/2001
Charter permanently revoked 03/31/2003

NETCOR INC (CA)
Charter cancelled for failure to file reports and pay taxes 8/1/94

NETCREATIONS INC (NY)
Merged into SEAT Pagine Gialle S.p.A. 2/15/2001
Each share Common 1¢ par exchanged for $7 cash

NETCRUISE COM INC (NJ)
SEC revoked common stock registration 07/02/2008
Stockholders' equity unlikely

NETCURRENTS INC (DE)
Stock Dividends - in Common to holders of Preferred 0.05% payable 02/16/2000 to holders of record 02/04/2000; in Preferred to holders of Preferred 0.02% payable 08/24/2000 to holders of record 08/08/2000; in Preferred to holders of Preferred 0.02% payable 04/05/2001 to holders of record 03/21/2001
Reorganized as NetCurrents Information Services, Inc. 08/30/2001
Each share 8.50% Preferred Ser. A exchanged for (1) share 8.50% Preferred Ser. A
Each share Common $0.001 par exchanged for (1) share Common $0.001 par
(See NetCurrents Information Services, Inc.)

NETCURRENTS INFORMATION SVCS INC (DE)
SEC revoked securities registration 09/15/2005

NETDIMENSIONS HLDGS LTD (CAYMAN ISLANDS)
ADR agreement terminated 04/21/2017
Each Sponsored ADR for Ordinary exchanged for $6.855 cash

NETDRIVEN STORAGE SOLUTIONS INC (AB)
Name changed 03/30/2001
Name changed from NetDriven Solutions Inc. to NetDriven Storage Solutions Inc. 03/30/2001
Recapitalized as Cervus Financial Group Inc. 07/15/2004

Each share Common no par exchanged for (0.05) share Common no par
(See Cervus Financial Group Inc.)

NETEASE COM INC (CAYMAN ISLANDS)
Sponsored ADR's for Ordinary split (4) for (1) by issuance of (3) additional ADR's payable 03/27/2006 to holders of record 03/24/2006 Ex date - 03/28/2006
Name changed to NetEase, Inc. 04/12/2012

NETEC (NV)
Charter revoked for failure to file reports and pay fees 6/1/96

NETEGRITY INC (DE)
Common 1¢ par split (3) for (2) by issuance of (0.5) additional share payable 09/01/2000 to holders of record 08/18/2000
Merged into Computer Associates International, Inc. 11/24/2004
Each share Common 1¢ par exchanged for $10.75 cash

NETERGY NETWORKS INC (DE)
Name changed to 8x8, Inc. (New) 7/19/2001

NETEZZA CORP (DE)
Issue Information - 9,000,000 shares COM offered at $12 per share on 07/18/2007
Acquired by International Business Machines Corp. 11/10/2010
Each share Common $0.001 par exchanged for $27 cash

NETFABRIC HLDGS INC (DE)
Each share old Common $0.001 par exchanged for (0.00192105) share new Common $0.001 par 09/29/2011
Name changed to XCel Brands, Inc. 10/28/2011

NETFONE INC (NV)
Recapitalized as ITP Energy Corp. 03/21/2011
Each share Common no par exchanged for (0.41666666) share Common no par
ITP Energy Corp. name changed to Tristar Acquisition Group 02/26/2018

NET4MUSIC INC (MN)
Name changed to MakeMusic! Inc. 05/22/2002
MakeMusic! Inc. name changed to MakeMusic, Inc. 06/09/2006
(See MakeMusic, Inc.)

NETFRAME SYS INC (DE)
Merged into Micron Electronics, Inc. 08/28/1997
Each share Common $0.001 par exchanged for $1 cash

NETFRAN DEV CORP (FL)
Name changed to Ariel Way, Inc. 05/26/2005

NETGAIN DEV INC (CO)
SEC revoked common stock registration 07/31/2018
Stockholders' equity unlikely

NETGATES HLDGS INC (DE)
Name changed to Sustainable Energy Development, Inc. 09/05/2006
Sustainable Energy Development, Inc. recapitalized as United States Oil & Gas Corp. 04/17/2008

NETGATES INC (DE)
Recapitalized as Netgates Holdings, Inc. 06/29/2006
Each share Common $0.0001 par exchanged for (0.01) share Common $0.0001 par
Netgates Holdings, Inc. name changed to Sustainable Energy Development, Inc. 09/05/2006 which recapitalized as United States Oil & Gas Corp. 04/17/2008

NETGATEWAY INC (DE)
Recapitalized as iMergent, Inc. 07/02/2002
Each share Common $0.001 par exchanged for (0.1) share Common $0.001 par
iMergent, Inc. name changed to Crexendo, Inc. (DE) 05/23/2011 which reincorporated in Nevada 12/13/2016

NETGEN 2000 INC (FL)
Recapitalized as Royal Finance Inc. 11/21/2000
Each (30) shares Common 1¢ par exchanged for (1) share Common 1¢ par
Royal Finance Inc. recapitalized as Bio Standard Corp. 05/24/2002 which name changed to Nettel Holdings, Inc. 05/23/2003
(See Nettel Holdings, Inc.)

NETGO LTD (NY)
Name changed to Butler Capital Corp. 12/17/71
Butler Capital Corp. name changed to Butler Publishing Corp. 5/22/73 which name changed to Macro Communications, Inc. 1/27/77 which reincorporated in Nevada as First Capital Holdings Corp. 4/27/83
(See First Capital Holdings Corp.)

NETGRAPHE INC (QC)
Each share Common no par exchanged for (1.1) shares Subordinate no par 5/28/2001
Acquired by Quebecor Media Inc. 9/15/2004
Each share Subordinate no par exchanged for $0.63 cash
Each Multiple Share no par exchanged for $0.63 cash

NETGRAVITY INC (DE)
Issue Information - 3,000,000 shares COM offered at $9 per share on 06/11/1998
Merged into DoubleClick Inc. 10/27/99
Each share Common $0.001 par exchanged for (0.28) share Common $0.001 par
(See DoubleClick Inc.)

NETGURU INC (DE)
Under plan of partial liquidation each share old Common 1¢ par received distribution of $0.85 cash payable 01/27/2006 to holders of record 01/17/2006
Each (15) shares old Common 1¢ par exchanged for (1) share new Common 1¢ par 12/15/2006
Name changed to BPO Management Services, Inc. (DE) 12/18/2006
BPO Management Services, Inc. (DE) merged into BPO Management Services, Inc. (PA) 12/30/2008
(See BPO Management Services, Inc. (PA))

NETHERFIELD ENERGY CORP (AB)
Merged into Antrim Energy Inc. 09/29/1999
Each share Common no par exchanged for (0.25) share Common no par

NETI TECHNOLOGIES INC (BC)
Struck off register and declared dissolved for failure to file returns 7/9/93

NETIA HLDGS S A (POLAND)
Issue Information - 5,500,000 SPONSORED ADR'S offered at $22 per ADR on 07/29/1999
Each old Sponsored ADR for Ordinary exchanged for (0.25) new Sponsored ADR for Ordinary 7/30/2002
ADR agreement terminated 9/29/2003
Each new Sponsored ADR for Ordinary exchanged for $4.0263 cash

NETIQ CORP (DE)
Issue Information - 3,000,000 shares COM offered at $13 per share on 07/29/1999
Merged into Attachmate Corp. 6/30/2006
Each share Common $0.001 par exchanged for $12.20 cash

NETIVATION COM INC (DE)
Issue Information - 2,500,000 shares COM offered at $20 per share on 06/22/1999
Name changed to Medinex Systems Inc. 07/27/2000
Medinex Systems Inc. name changed to Maxus Technology Corp. 04/07/2004
(See Maxus Technology Corp.)

NETJ COM CORP (NV)
Old Common $0.001 par reclassified as Class A Common $0.001 par 10/11/2001
Each share Class A Common $0.001 par exchanged for (0.01) share new Common $0.001 par 09/30/2002
Note: Holders of between (100) and (10,000) shares received (100) shares
Holders of (99) or fewer shares were not affected by the reverse split
Name changed to ZooLink Corp. 11/20/2002
ZooLink Corp. recapitalized as Action Energy Corp. 04/02/2009 which name changed to SMC Recordings Inc. 09/03/2009 which recapitalized as SMC Entertainment, Inc. 05/06/2011

NETLIST CORP. OF FLORIDA (FL)
Dissolved for failure to file annual report 9/22/2000

NETLIVE COMMUNICATIONS INC (DE)
Recapitalized as Lindatech Inc. 05/18/1999
Each (3.4) shares Common $0.0001 par exchanged for (1) share Common $0.0001 par
(See Lindatech Inc.)

NETLOGIC MICROSYSTEMS INC (DE)
Issue Information - 5,775,000 shares COM offered at $12 per share on 07/08/2004
Common 1¢ par split (2) for (1) by issuance of (1) additional share payable 03/20/2010 to holders of record 03/05/2010 Ex date - 03/22/2010
Acquired by Broadcom Corp. 02/17/2012
Each share Common 1¢ par exchanged for $50 cash

NETLOJIX COMMUNICATIONS INC (DE)
Merged into NetLojix Acquisitions Corp. 6/27/2003
Each share Common $0.001 par exchanged for $0.02 cash

NETMANAGE INC (DE)
Old Common 1¢ par split (2) for (1) by issuance of (1) additional share 05/23/1994
Old Common 1¢ par split (2) for (1) by issuance of (1) additional share 04/03/1995
Each share old Common 1¢ par exchanged for (0.14285714) share new Common 1¢ par 09/04/2002
Merged into Micro Focus (US), Inc. 06/18/2008
Each share new Common 1¢ par exchanged for $7.20 cash

NETMASTER GROUP INC (UT)
Name changed to Zulu Tek, Inc. 1/15/98

NETMAXIMIZER COM INC (FL)
Common $0.001 par split (3) for (1) by issuance of (2) additional shares

payable 11/04/1999 to holders of record 11/01/1999
Recapitalized as Gentech Pharma Inc. 11/14/2005
Each share Common $0.001 par exchanged for (0.002) share Common $0.001 par
Gentech Pharma Inc. name changed to Fintech Group, Inc. 09/20/2006 which name changed to Capital Markets Technologies, Inc. 02/20/2007
(See Capital Markets Technologies, Inc.)

NETMEASURE TECHNOLOGY INC (NV)
Each share old Common $0.001 par exchanged for (0.02) share new Common $0.001 par 04/08/2002
Name changed to Sorell, Inc. 12/02/2005
Sorell, Inc. name changed to Emporia, Inc. 02/27/2008

NETMOVES CORP (DE)
Merged into Mail.Com, Inc. 02/09/2000
Each share Common 1¢ par exchanged for (0.385336) share Common 1¢ par
Mail.Com, Inc. name changed to EasyLink Services Corp. 04/03/2001
(See EasyLink Services Corp.)

NETMUSIC ENTMT CORP (DE)
Recapitalized as Enterayon, Inc. 03/22/2006
Each share Common exchanged for (0.1) share Common
Enterayon, Inc. recapitalized as North Bay Resources Inc. 02/07/2008

NETNATION COMMUNICATIONS INC (DE)
Each share old Common $0.0001 par exchanged for (0.4) share new Common $0.0001 par 6/13/2003
Merged into Hostway Corp. 8/22/2003
Each share new Common $0.0001 par exchanged for $1.65 cash

NETOBJECTS INC (DE)
Issue Information - 6,000,000 shares COM offered at $12 per share on 05/07/1999
Out of business in September 2001
Stockholders' equity unlikely

NETOPIA INC (DE)
Merged into Motorola, Inc. 2/7/2007
Each share Common $0.001 par exchanged for $7 cash

NETOPTIX CORP (DE)
Merged into Corning Inc. 5/12/2000
Each share Common 1¢ par exchanged for (0.9) share Common 50¢ par

NETOY COM CORP (DE)
Name changed to SafePay Solutions, Inc. 03/03/2006
SafePay Solutions, Inc. name changed to Emaji, Inc. 03/11/2008 whhich name changed to Broadside Enterprises, Inc. 12/01/2016

NETPARTS COM INC (NV)
Each share old Common $0.001 par exchanged for (0.1) share new Common $0.001 par 07/18/2003
Note: Holders of (100) or fewer shares were not affected by the reverse split
Holders of between (101) and (999) shares received (100) post split shares
Name changed to Turner Valley Oil & Gas, Inc. 08/20/2003

NETPLEX GROUP INC (NY)
Company terminated registration of common stock and is no longer public as of 08/14/2003

NETPLIANCE INC (DE)
Recapitalized as TippingPoint Technologies, Inc. 08/20/2001
Each (15) shares Common 1¢ par exchanged for (1) share Common 1¢ par
(See TippingPoint Technologies, Inc.)

NETRADIO CORP (MN)
Each share old Common 1¢ par exchanged for (0.22222222) share new Common 1¢ par 06/13/2001
Completely liquidated 04/02/2002
Each share new Common 1¢ par exchanged for first and final distribution of $0.064277 cash

NETRATINGS INC (DE)
Issue Information - 4,000,000 shares COM offered at $17 per share on 12/08/1999
Merged into Nielsen Co. 06/22/2007
Each share Common $0.001 par exchanged for $21 cash

NETREIT (CA)
Stock Dividend - 5% payable 01/02/2010 to holders of record 12/31/2009
Reincorporated under the laws of Maryland as NetREIT, Inc. and Common no par changed to 1¢ par 08/04/2010

NETRIX CORP (DE)
Name changed to NX Networks, Inc. 09/19/2000
(See NX Networks, Inc.)

NETRO CORP (DE)
Reincorporated 06/01/2001
Issue Information - 5,000,000 shares COM offered at $8 per share on 08/18/1999
State of incorporation changed from (CA) to (DE) 06/01/2001
Merged into SR Telecom Inc. 09/04/2003
Each share Common $0.001 par exchanged for (0.104727) share new Common no par
SR Telecom Inc. name changed to SRX Post Holdings Inc. 06/18/2008
(See SRX Post Holdings Inc.)

NETROM INC (CA)
Each share old Common no par exchanged for (0.2) share new Common no par 09/22/2000
Name changed to Tempest Trading Technologies, Inc. (CA) 08/01/2003
Tempest Trading Technologies, Inc. (CA) reorganized in Nevada as Humble Energy, Inc. 02/25/2009

NETRUE COMMUNICATIONS INC (AB)
Reincorporated under the laws of Delaware 4/19/2000

NETSALON CORP (TX)
Name changed to Military Communications Technologies, Inc. 4/17/2003
Military Communications Technologies, Inc. name changed to Carbon Race Corp. 10/16/2006

NETSCAPE COMMUNICATIONS CORP (DE)
Common $0.0001 par split (2) for (1) by issuance of (1) additional share payable 02/06/1996 to holders of record 01/23/1996
Merged into America Online, Inc. 03/17/1999
Each share Common $0.0001 par exchanged for (0.9) share Common $0.0001 par
America Online, Inc. merged into AOL Time Warner Inc. 01/11/2001 which name changed to Time Warner Inc. (New) 10/16/2003 which merged into AT&T Inc. 06/15/2018

NETSCOUT CAP CORP (AB)
Name changed to Scout Capital Corp. 10/30/2001
Scout Capital Corp. recapitalized as Birchcliff Energy Ltd. (Old) 1/20/2005 which merged into Birchcliff Energy Ltd. (New) 5/31/2005

NETSCREEN TECHNOLOGIES INC (DE)
Issue Information - 10,000,000 shares COM offered at $16 per share on 12/11/2001
Merged into Juniper Networks, Inc. 04/16/2004
Each share Common $0.001 par exchanged for (1.404) shares Common $0.00001 par

NETSEERS INTERNET INTL CORP (BC)
Recapitalized as 1st Anyox Resources Ltd. 12/2/2003
Each share Common no par exchanged for (0.1) share Common no par
1st Anyox Resources Ltd. name changed to Victory Resources Corp. 2/28/2005

NETSILICON INC (MA)
Issue Information - 5,250,000 shares COM offered at $7 per share on 09/14/1999
Merged into Digi International Inc. 2/13/2002
Each share Common 1¢ par exchanged for (0.65) share Common 1¢ par

NETSKY HLDGS INC (NV)
Each share old Common $0.0001 par exchanged for (0.001) share new Common $0.0001 par 02/05/2008
Recapitalized as Social Media Ventures, Inc. 05/28/2008
Each share Common $0.0001 par exchanged for (0.005) share Common $0.0001 par

NETSMART TECHNOLOGIES INC (DE)
Each share old Common 1¢ par exchanged for (1/3) share new Common 1¢ par 9/14/98
Merged into Insight Venture Partners 4/10/2007
Each share new Common 1¢ par exchanged for $16.50 cash

NETSOL INTL INC (NV)
Name changed to NetSol Technologies, Inc. 3/20/2002

NETSOLVE INC (DE)
Issue Information - 3,700,000 shares COM offered at $13 per share on 09/29/1999
Merged into Cisco Systems, Inc. 11/19/2004
Each share Common 1¢ par exchanged for $11 cash

NETSPACE INTL HLDGS INC (DE)
Recapitalized as Alternative Fuels Americas, Inc. 10/13/2010
Each share Common $0.001 par exchanged for (0.005) share Common $0.001 par
Alternative Fuels Americas, Inc. name changed to Kaya Holdings, Inc. 04/07/2015

NETSPAN CORP (NV)
Name changed to MDM Vascular Systems, Inc. 9/22/98
MDM Vascular Systems, Inc. recapitalized as Casinolive.Com Corp. 3/9/99

NETSPEAK CORP (FL)
Issue Information - 2,400,000 shares CDT-COM offered at $8.75 per share on 05/29/1997
Merged into Adir Technologies, Inc. 8/14/2001
Each share Common 1¢ par exchanged for $3.10 cash

NETSPEND HLDGS INC (DE)
Issue Information - 18,536,043 shares COM offered at $11 per share on 10/18/2010
Acquired by Total System Services, Inc. 07/01/2013
Each share Common $0.001 par exchanged for $16 cash

NETSTAFF INC (IN)
Reincorporated under the laws of Delaware as Financial Systems Group, Inc. 07/15/2002
(See Financial Systems Group, Inc.)

NETSTAR INC (MN)
Merged into Ascend Communications, Inc. 8/15/96
Each share Common no par exchanged for (0.35398) share Common no par
Ascend Communications, Inc. merged into Lucent Technologies Inc. 6/24/99 which merged into Alcatel-Lucent S.A. 11/30/2006

NETSUITE INC (DE)
Acquired by Oracle Corp. 11/07/2016
Each share Common 1¢ par exchanged for $109 cash

NETT WORKK INC (AB)
Struck off register and declared dissolved for failure to file returns 6/1/91

NETTAXI COM (NV)
Name changed 11/09/1999
Name changed from Nettaxi, Inc. to Nettaxi.com 11/09/1999
Reorganized under the laws of Delaware as RAE Systems Inc. 04/09/2002
Each (5.67) shares Common $0.001 par exchanged for (1) share Common $0.001 par
(See RAE Systems Inc.)

NETTEL HLDGS INC (FL)
Administratively dissolved 09/16/2005

NETTEL INC (NV)
Name changed to One Touch Total Communications Inc. 09/27/1999
One Touch Total Communications Inc. name changed to One Touch Total Development, Inc. 06/10/2004 which name changed to Carbon Jungle, Inc. 03/27/2006 which recapitalized as Global New Energy Industries Inc. 01/17/2013 which name changed to Coin Citadel 11/06/2014

NETTER DIGITAL ENTMT INC (DE)
Chapter 11 bankruptcy proceedings converted to Chapter 7 on 10/04/2002
Stockholders' equity unlikely

NETTIME SOLUTIONS INC (NV)
Name changed to Tempco, Inc. 10/14/2008
Tempco, Inc. name changed to Esio Water & Beverage Development Corp. 01/18/2013 which name changed to UPD Holding Corp. 03/01/2017

NETTLETON A E CO (NY)
5% Preferred $100 par called for redemption 00/00/1978
Public interest eliminated

NETTRON COM INC (AB)
Recapitalized as Valcent Products Inc. 05/03/2005
Each share Common no par exchanged for (0.33333333) share Common no par
Valcent Products Inc. name changed to Alterrus Systems Inc. 06/12/2012

NET2AUCTION INC (DE)
Recapitalized as Green Endeavors, Ltd. 08/03/2007
Each share Common $0.001 par exchanged for (0.2) share Common $0.001 par
Green Endeavors, Ltd. name changed to Green Endeavors Inc. 08/30/2010

NET2PHONE INC (DE)
Issue Information - 5,400,000 shares COM offered at $15 per share on 07/29/1999
Merged into IDT Corp. 3/13/2006
Each share Common 1¢ par exchanged for $2.05 cash

NET2000 COMMUNICATIONS INC (DE)
Issue Information - 10,000,000 shares COM offered at $20 per share on 03/06/2000
Assets sold for the benefit of creditors 1/21/2002
Stockholders' equity unlikely

NETVALUE HLDGS INC (DE)
Name changed to Stonepath Group, Inc. 09/25/2000

NETVALUE INC (DE)
Merged into Stonepath Group, Inc. 11/13/2000
Each share Common $0.001 par exchanged for (0.4) share Common $0.001 par

NETVANTAGE INC (DE)
Issue Information - 1,500,000 Units consisting of (1) share CL A, (1) WT CL A, and (1) WT CL B offered at $5 per Unit on 05/03/1995
Merged into Cabletron Systems, Inc. 9/25/98
Each share Class A Common $0.001 par exchanged for (0.6154) share Common 1¢ par
Each share Class B Common $0.001 par exchanged for (0.6154) share Common 1¢ par
Cabletron Systems, Inc. name changed to Enterasys Networks, Inc. 8/6/2001
(See Enterasys Networks, Inc.)

NETVENTORY SOLUTIONS INC (NV)
Name changed to OncoSec Medical Inc. 03/01/2011

NETVOICE TECHNOLOGIES CORP (NV)
Common $0.001 par split (2) for (1) by issuance of (1) additional share payable 03/13/2000 to holders of record 03/01/2000
SEC revoked common stock registration 06/19/2009
Stockholders' equity unlikely

NETWEB ONLINE COM INC (TX)
Reorganized under the laws of Florida as Spectrum Brands Corp. 05/16/2001
Each share Common $0.001 par exchanged for (0.05) share Common $0.001 par
(See Spectrum Brands Corp.)

NETWOLVES CORP (NY)
Plan of reorganization under Chapter 11 Federal Bankruptcy Code effective 09/01/2008
No stockholders' equity

NETWORD INC NEW (DE)
Recapitalized as Home Director, Inc. 12/18/2002
Each share Common $0.001 par exchanged for (0.025) share Common $0.001 par
(See Home Director, Inc.)

NETWORD INC OLD (DE)
Each share old Common 1¢ par exchanged for (0.1) share new Common 1¢ par 5/7/87
Each share new Common 1¢ par exchanged again for (0.00000613) share new Common 1¢ par 8/31/91
Note: In effect holders received $0.60 cash per share and public interest was eliminated

NETWORK ACCESS SOLUTIONS CORP (DE)
Issue Information - 7,500,000 shares COM offered at $12 per share on 06/03/1999
Plan of reorganization under Chapter 11 Federal Bankruptcy Code effective 9/16/2003
Stockholders' equity unlikely

NETWORK APPLIANCE INC (DE)
Reincorporated 11/01/2001
Common no par split (2) for (1) by issuance of (1) additional share payable 12/18/1997 to holders of record 12/08/1997
Common no par split (2) for (1) by issuance of (1) additional share payable 12/21/1998 to holders of record 12/11/1998
Common no par split (2) for (1) by issuance of (1) additional share payable 12/20/1999 to holders of record 12/10/1999
Common no par split (2) for (1) by issuance of (1) additional share payable 03/22/2000 to holders of record 03/10/2000
State of incorporation changed from (CA) to (DE) and Common no par changed to $0.001 par 11/01/2001
Name changed to NetApp, Inc. 03/10/2008

NETWORK ASSOCS INC (DE)
Common 1¢ par split (3) for (2) by issuance of (0.5) additional share payable 05/29/1998 to holders of record 05/12/1998
Name changed to McAfee, Inc. 06/30/2004
(See McAfee, Inc.)

NETWORK BUSINESS EXCHANGE INC (MI)
Automatically dissolved 05/15/1991

NETWORK COMM INC (WA)
Each share old Common $0.001 par exchanged for (0.06666666) share new Common $0.001 par 06/18/2001
Plan of reorganization under Chapter 11 Federal Bankruptcy Code effective 02/23/2004
No stockholders' equity

NETWORK COMPUTING DEVICES INC (DE)
Reincorporated 10/00/1998
State of incorporation changed from (CA) to (DE) and Common no par changed to $0.001 par 10/00/1998
Ceased operations 12/31/2004
No stockholders' equity

NETWORK CONNECTION INC (GA)
Issue Information - 1,000,000 shares COM offered at $5 per share on 05/11/1995
Chapter 7 bankruptcy proceedings closed 01/13/2016
Stockholders' equity unlikely

NETWORK CTL CORP (DE)
Company went out of business in 1988
Details not available

NETWORK DATA PROCESSING CORP (IA)
Each share Common no par exchanged for (0.01) share Common $100 par 6/19/87
Merged into Fiserv, Inc. 4/14/98
Each share Common $100 par exchanged for (36.68888) shares Common 1¢ par

NETWORK ENGINES INC (DE)
Issue Information - 6,500,000 shares COM offered at $17 per share on 07/13/2000
Acquired by UNICOM Systems, Inc. 09/18/2012
Each share Common 1¢ par exchanged for $1.45 cash

NETWORK EQUIP TECHNOLOGIES (DE)
Acquired by Sonus Networks, Inc. (Old) 08/24/2012
Each share Common 1¢ par exchanged for $1.35 cash

NETWORK EVENT THEATER INC (DE)
Merged into YouthStream Media Networks, Inc. 2/28/2000
Each share Common 1¢ par exchanged for (1) share Common 1¢ par
YouthStream Media Networks, Inc. name changed to ALJ Regional Holdings, Inc. 12/8/2006

NETWORK EXPL LTD (BC)
Each share old Class A Common no par exchanged for (0.16666666) share new Class A Common no par 06/23/2010
Each share new Class A Common no par exchanged again for (0.1) share new Class A Common no par 04/02/2014
Each share new Class A Common no par exchanged again for (0.25) share new Class A Common no par 01/20/2016
Each share new Class A Common no par exchanged again for (0.5) share new Class A Common no par 12/04/2017
Name changed to Ynvisible Interactive Inc. 01/12/2018

NETWORK EXPRESS INC (MI)
Merged into Cabletron Systems, Inc. 8/1/96
Each share Common $0.125 par exchanged for (0.1388) share Common $0.125 par
Cabletron Systems, Inc. name changed to Enterasys Networks, Inc. 8/6/2001
(See Enterasys Networks, Inc.)

NETWORK FINL SVCS INC (CO)
Name changed to Westmark Group Holdings Inc. 07/13/1994
Westmark Group Holdings Inc. recapitalized as Viking Consolidated, Inc. (DE) 05/15/2006 which reincorporated in Nevada as Tailor Aquaponics World Wide, Inc. 08/15/2006 which recapitalized as Diversified Acquisitions, Inc. 08/20/2007 which recapitalized as Vitalcare Diabetes Treatment Centers, Inc. 03/24/2008 which recapitalized as China Advanced Technology 06/23/2010 which name changed to Goliath Film & Media Holdings 01/20/2012

NETWORK 4 INC (CO)
Recapitalized as CEEE Group Corp. (CO) 05/00/1987
Each share Common $0.001 par exchanged for (0.3853249) share Common $0.001 par
CEEE Group Corp. (CO) reorganized in Delaware as Atlantic International Entertainment, Ltd. 11/26/1996 which name changed to Online Gaming Systems, Ltd. 10/01/1999 which name changed to Advanced Resources Group, Ltd. 02/15/2007

NETWORK GAMING INTL CORP (BC)
Recapitalized as Network Exploration Ltd. 06/22/2004
Each share Class A Common no par exchanged for (0.33333333) share Class A Common no par
Network Exploration Ltd. name changed to Ynvisible Interactive Inc. 01/12/2018

NETWORK GEN CORP (DE)
Common 1¢ par split (2) for (1) by issuance of (1) additional share payable 05/28/1996 to holders of record 05/13/1996
Stock Dividend - 100% 08/20/1990
Merged into Network Associates, Inc. 12/01/1997
Each share Common 1¢ par exchanged for (0.4167) share Common 1¢ par
Network Associates, Inc. name changed to McAfee, Inc. 06/30/2004
(See McAfee, Inc.)

NETWORK IMAGING CORP (DE)
Name changed to Treev, Inc. 05/08/1998
Treev, Inc. merged into CE Computer Equipment AG 01/22/2001 which name changed to Ceyoniq AG 03/02/2001
(See Ceyoniq AG)

NETWORK INSTALLATION CORP (NV)
Each share old Common $0.001 par exchanged for (2) shares new Common $0.001 par 09/20/2004
Name changed to Siena Technologies, Inc. 10/30/2006
Siena Technologies, Inc. recapitalized as XnE, Inc. 07/01/2009
(See XnE, Inc.)

NETWORK INV COMMUNICATIONS INC (NV)
Name changed to Category 5 Technologies Inc. 8/6/2001
Category 5 Technologies Inc. merged into Avalon Digital Marketing Systems, Inc. 10/1/2002

NETWORK LIFE SCIENCES INC (BC)
Each share old Common no par exchanged for (0.2) share new Common no par 05/18/2016
Name changed to ePlay Digital Inc. 11/23/2016

NETWORK LONG DISTANCE INC (DE)
Merged into IXC Communications Inc. 6/3/98
Each share Common $0.001 par exchanged for (0.2998) share Common 1¢ par
IXC Communications Inc. merged into Cincinnati Bell Inc. (Old) 11/9/99 which name changed to Broadwing Inc. 11/15/99 which name changed to Cincinnati Bell Inc. (New) 5/16/2003

NETWORK MGMT CORP (DE)
Merged into United States Land Resources, Inc. 12/28/1973
Each share Common 1¢ par exchanged for (0.39) share Conv. Preferred 1¢ par
(See United States Land Resources, Inc.)

NETWORK MGMT SVCS GROUP INC (MN)
Name changed to eBenX, Inc. 11/15/1999
(See eBenX, Inc.)

NETWORK ONCOLOGY INC (BC)
Recapitalized as Network Life Sciences Inc. 06/23/2015
Each share Common no par exchanged for (0.33333333) share Common no par
Network Life Sciences Inc. name changed to ePlay Digital Inc. 11/23/2016

NETWORK ONE HLDGS CORP (BC)
SEC revoked common stock registration 08/10/2009
Stockholders' equity unlikely

NETWORK ONE INC (UT)
Proclaimed dissolved for failure to pay taxes 12/31/1982

NETWORK-1 SEC SOLUTIONS INC (DE)
Name changed to Network-1 Technologies, Inc. 10/24/2013

NETWORK PERIPHERALS INC (DE)
Issue Information - 2,000,000 shares COM offered at $6 per share on 06/28/1994
Name changed to FalconStor Software, Inc. 8/23/2001

NETWORK PLUS CORP (DE)
Issue Information - 8,000,000 shares COM offered at $16 per share on 06/29/1999
13.50% 144A Preferred Ser. A called for redemption at $115.928 on 07/06/1999
Each Depositary Preferred Ser. A received distribution of (0.2855) share Common 1¢ par payable 04/02/2001 to holders of record 03/15/2001
Each Depositary Preferred Ser. A

received distribution of (0.8686992) share Common 1¢ par payable 01/02/2002 to holders of record 12/17/2001
Chapter 11 bankruptcy proceedings converted to Chapter 7 on 06/11/2003
No stockholders' equity

NETWORK REAL ESTATE CALIF INC (CO)
Each (150) shares old Common no par exchanged for (1) share new Common no par 02/25/1991
Name changed to Network Financial Services, Inc. 06/22/1992
Network Financial Services, Inc. name changed to Westmark Group Holdings Inc. 07/13/1994 which recapitalized as Viking Consolidated, Inc. (DE) 05/15/2006 which reincorporated in Nevada as Tailor Aquaponics World Wide, Inc. 08/15/2006 which recapitalized as Diversified Acquisitions, Inc. 08/20/2007 which recapitalized as Vitalcare Diabetes Treatment Centers, Inc. 03/24/2008 which recapitalized as China Advanced Technology 06/23/2010 which name changed to Goliath Film & Media Holdings 01/20/2012

NETWORK SEC CORP (TX)
Acquired by Inspectorate International S.A. 10/06/1987
Each share Common no par exchanged for $9 cash

NETWORK SIX INC (RI)
Name changed 2/1/94
Name changed from Network Solutions, Inc. to Network Six Inc. 2/1/94
Each share old Common 10¢ par exchanged for (0.25) share new Common 10¢ par 12/11/96
Merged into TRW Inc. 8/16/2001
Each share new Common 10¢ par exchanged for $3.60 cash

NETWORK SOLUTIONS INC (DE)
Issue Information - 3,300,000 shares CL A offered at $18 per share on 09/26/1997
Class A Common $0.001 par split (2) for (1) by issuance of (1) additional share payable 3/23/99 to holders of record 2/26/99
Class A Common $0.001 par reclassified as Common $0.001 par 6/17/99
Common $0.001 par split (2) for (1) by issuance of (1) additional share payable 3/10/2000 to holders of record 2/25/2000
Merged into VeriSign, Inc. 6/8/2000
Each share Common $0.001 par exchanged for (1.075) shares Common $0.001 par

NETWORK STORAGE CORP (MN)
Name changed to Virtual Technology Corp. 1/21/97
Virtual Technology Corp. name changed to Graphics Technologies Inc. 12/20/2000

NETWORK SYS CORP (DE)
Common 2¢ par split (5) for (4) by issuance of (0.25) additional share 04/15/1985
Stock Dividends - 100% 02/27/1981; 100% 04/27/1983
Merged into Storage Technology Corp. 03/07/1995
Each share Common 2¢ par exchanged for (0.26) share Common 10¢ par and $0.05 cash
(See Storage Technology Corp.)

NETWORK SYS INTL INC (NV)
144A Preferred Ser. A $0.001 par split (5) for (4) by issuance of (0.25) additional share payable 01/30/1998 to holders of record 01/16/1998
Common $0.001 par split (5) for (4) by issuance of (0.25) additional share payable 01/30/1998 to holders of record 01/16/1998 Ex date - 02/02/1998
Name changed to OnSpan Networking, Inc. 02/15/2001
OnSpan Networking, Inc. recapitalized as Double Eagle Holdings, Ltd. 04/02/2007 which name changed to Fuse Science, Inc. 11/03/2011

NETWORK TECHNOLOGY PROFESSIONALS INC (BC)
Ceased operations 11/01/2001
Stockholders' equity unlikely

NETWORK TELEMETRICS LTD (BC)
Name changed to Belvedere Resources Ltd. 10/14/97

NETWORK USA INC. (DE)
Charter cancelled and declared inoperative and void for non-payment of taxes 3/1/93

NETWORK USA INC (NV)
Each share old Common 1¢ par exchanged for (0.11111111) share new Common 1¢ par 03/31/2003
New Common 1¢ par split (6) for (1) by issuance of (5) additional shares payable 07/27/2004 to holders of record 07/27/2004 Ex date - 07/28/2004
Name changed to Sunwin International Neutraceuticals, Inc. 07/27/2004
Sunwin International Neutraceuticals, Inc. name changed to Sunwin Stevia International, Inc. 04/20/2012

NETWORK VIDEO INC (DE)
Each share old Common $0.001 par exchanged for (0.2) share new Common $0.001 par 10/25/1994
Name changed to NVID International, Inc. 05/26/1995
(See NVID International, Inc.)

NETWORK VIDEOTEX SYS INC (ID)
Name changed to Wessex International, Inc. 11/06/1989
Wessex International, Inc. name changed to Ocean Express Lines, Inc. (ID) 05/00/1991 which reincorporated in Nevada 03/02/2000 which name changed to American Thorium, Inc. 07/29/2003 which recapitalized as Cementitious Materials, Inc. 10/21/2003 which name changed to NaturalNano, Inc. 12/02/2005 which name changed to Omni Shrimp, Inc. 05/03/2017

NETWORKED PICTURE SYS INC (CA)
Each share old Common no par exchanged for (0.1) share new Common no par 10/15/1991
Charter suspended for failure to file reports and pay fees 11/00/1995

NETWORKS ELECTRS CORP (CA)
Common 25¢ par split (2) for (1) by issuance of (1) additional share 07/21/1981
Acquired by NE Holdco Corp. 10/14/1999
Each share Common 25¢ par exchanged for $7.50 cash

NETWORKS NORTH INC (NY)
Name changed to Chell Group Corp. 09/27/2000
(See Chell Group Corp.)

NETWORTH INC (DE)
Merged into Compaq Computer Corp. 12/19/1995
Each share Common 1¢ par exchanged for $42 cash

NETWORTH TECHNOLOGIES INC (DE)
Common 1¢ par split (10) for (1) by issuance of (9) additional shares payable 01/05/2006 to holders of record 12/29/2005 Ex date - 01/27/2006
Recapitalized as Solution Technology International, Inc. 08/22/2006
Each share Common 1¢ par exchanged for (0.00666666) share Common 1¢ par
Solution Technology International, Inc. recapitalized as Reinsurance Technologies Ltd. 06/01/2009
(See Reinsurance Technologies Ltd.)

NETWORTHUSA COM INC (FL)
Name changed to EBUX Inc. 10/6/2000
EBUX Inc. name changed to Petapeer Holdings Inc. 5/5/2001 which name changed to Studio Bromont Inc. 2/14/2002 which name changed to United American Corp. 3/1/2004

NETZEE INC (GA)
Issue Information - 4,448,155 shares COM offered at $14 per share on 11/09/1999
Each share old Common no par exchanged for (0.125) share new Common no par 5/16/2001
Completely liquidated
Each share new Common no par received first and final distribution of $0.50 cash payable 2/7/2003 to holders of record 2/6/2003 Ex date - 2/10/2003
Note: Certificates were not required to be surrendered and are without value

NETZERO INC (DE)
Merged into United Online, Inc. 09/25/2001
Each share Common $0.001 par exchanged for (0.2) share Common $0.001 par
(See United Online, Inc.)

NEU-FLAME (CANADA) LTD.
Business discontinued 00/00/1930
Stockholders' equity unlikely

NEUBERGER & BERMAN CASH RESVS (MA)
Reorganized as Neuberger & Berman Income Funds 07/02/1993
Details not available

NEUBERGER & BERMAN GOVT MONEY FD INC (MD)
Reorganized as Neuberger & Berman Income Funds 07/02/1993
Details not available

NEUBERGER & BERMAN LTD MAT BD FD (MA)
Reorganized as Neuberger & Berman Income Funds 07/02/1993
Details not available

NEUBERGER & BERMAN MONEY MKT PLUS (MA)
Name changed to Neuberger & Berman Ultra Short Bond Fund 03/01/1991
(See Neuberger & Berman Ultra Short Bond Fund)

NEUBERGER & BERMAN MUN MONEY FD (MA)
Name changed 05/00/1988
Name changed from Neuberger & Berman Tax Free Money Fund to Neuberger & Berman Municipal Money Fund 05/00/1988
Reorganized as Neuberger & Berman Income Funds 07/02/1993
Details not available

NEUBERGER & BERMAN ULTRA SHORT BD FD (MA)
Reorganized as Neuberger & Berman Income Funds 07/02/1993
Details not available

NEUBERGER BERMAN CALIF INTER MUN FD INC (MD)
Auction Market Preferred Ser. A called for redemption at $25,000 on 07/01/2014
Auction Market Preferred Ser. B called for redemption at $25,000 on 07/01/2014
(Additional Information in Active)

NEUBERGER BERMAN DIVID ADVANTAGE FD INC (MD)
Auction Market Preferred Ser. A $0.0001 par called for redemption at $25,000 on 10/29/2008
Auction Market Preferred Ser. B $0.0001 par called for redemption at $25,000 on 11/10/2008
Completely liquidated
Each share Common $0.0001 par received first and final distribution of $10.1945 cash payable 10/30/2009 to holders of record 10/26/2009
Note: Certificates were not required to be surrendered and are without value

NEUBERGER BERMAN HIGH YIELD STRATEGIES FD (DE)
Reincorporated under the laws of Maryland as Neuberger Berman High Yield Strategies Fund Inc. 08/06/2010

NEUBERGER BERMAN INC (DE)
Issue Information - 7,250,000 shares COM offered at $32 per share on 10/06/1999
Common 1¢ par split (3) for (2) by issuance of (0.5) additional share payable 08/16/2001 to holders of record 08/01/2001 Ex date - 08/17/2001
Merged into Lehman Brothers Holdings Inc. 10/31/2003
Each share Common 1¢ par exchanged for (0.4741) share Common 10¢ par
(See Lehman Brothers Holdings Inc.)

NEUBERGER BERMAN INCOME OPPORTUNITY FD INC (MD)
Auction Preferred Ser. A called for redemption at $25,000 on 10/27/2008
Auction Preferred Ser. B called for redemption at $25,000 on 11/12/2008
Merged into Neuberger Berman High Yield Strategies Fund Inc. 08/06/2010
Each share Common $0.0001 par exchanged for (0.577293) share Common $0.0001 par

NEUBERGER BERMAN INTER MUN FD INC (MD)
Auction Market Preferred Ser. A $0.0001 par called for redemption at $25,000 on 07/02/2014
Auction Market Preferred Ser. B $0.0001 par called for redemption at $25,000 on 07/02/2014
(Additional Information in Active)

NEUBERGER BERMAN N Y INTER MUN FD INC (MD)
Auction Market Preferred Ser. B $0.0001 par called for redemption at $25,000 on 07/03/2014
Auction Market Preferred Ser. A $0.0001 par called for redemption at $25,000 on 07/07/2014
(Additional Information in Active)

NEUBERGER BERMAN REAL ESTATE INCOME FD INC (MD)
Name changed to Denali Fund Inc. 10/26/2007
Denali Fund Inc. merged into Boulder Growth & Income Fund, Inc. 03/20/2015

NEUBERGER BERMAN REAL ESTATE SECS INCOME FD INC (MD)
Auction Market Preferred Ser. B reclassified as Auction Market Preferred Ser. C 03/10/2008
Auction Market Preferred Ser. C reclassified as Auction Market Preferred Ser. G 03/10/2008
Auction Market Preferred Ser. D reclassified as Auction Market Preferred Ser. H 03/10/2008
Auction Market Preferred Ser. E

called for redemption at $25,000 on 06/06/2012
Auction Market Preferred Ser. H called for redemption at $25,000 on 06/06/2012
Auction Market Preferred Ser. F called for redemption at $25,000 on 06/07/2012
Auction Market Preferred Ser. A called for redemption at $25,000 on 06/08/2012
Auction Market Preferred Ser. B called for redemption at $25,000 on 06/11/2012
Auction Market Preferred Ser. C called for redemption at $25,000 on 06/12/2012
Auction Market Preferred Ser. D called for redemption at $25,000 on 06/12/2012
Auction Market Preferred Ser. G called for redemption at $25,000 on 06/18/2012
(Additional Information in Active)

NEUBERGER BERMAN RLTY INCOME FD INC (MD)
Issue Information - 24,000,000 shares COM offered at $15 per share on 04/24/2003
Merged into Neuberger Berman Real Estate Securities Income Fund Inc. 03/10/2008
Ser. A Preferred reclassified as Auction Market Preferred Ser. B1
Ser. B Preferred reclassified as Auction Market Preferred Ser. D1
Ser. C Preferred reclassified as Auction Market Preferred Ser. E
Ser. D Preferred reclassified as Auction Market Preferred Ser. F
Each share Common $0.0001 par exchanged for (1.409) shares Common $0.0001 par

NEUER KAPITAL CORP (BC)
Name changed to Crescent Resources Corp. 08/03/2005
Crescent Resources Corp. recapitalized as Coventry Resources Inc. 01/09/2013
(See Coventry Resources Inc.)

NEUFELD BUILDING TRUST
Trust terminated in 1947
Details not available

NEUHOFF BROS PACKERS INC (TX)
Common $10 par split (5) for (4) by issuance of (0.25) additional share 12/28/64
Common $10 par changed to $5 par and (0.5) additional share issued 1/7/66
Common $5 par split (5) for (4) by issuance of (0.25) additional share 2/20/68
Stock Dividend - 10% 12/8/61
Name changed to Newcourt Industries, Inc. 6/26/79
Newcourt Industries, Inc. acquired by Mickelberry Corp. 10/27/82 which name changed to Mickelberry Communications Inc. 5/10/94
(See Mickelberry Communications Inc.)

NEULION INC (DE)
Reincorporated 12/01/2010
Place of incorporation changed from (Canada) to (DE) and Common no par changed to 1¢ par 12/01/2010
Acquired by WME Entertainment Parent, LLC 05/08/2018
Each share Common 1¢ par exchanged for $0.84 cash

NEUMED SYS CORP (BC)
Recapitalized as Reneaux Capital Inc. 3/19/88
Each share Common no par exchanged for (1/3) Common no par
Reneaux Capital Inc. name changed to Naturally Niagara, Inc. 6/29/93 which recapitalized as Northern Gaming Inc. 1/22/96 which recapitalized as Icon Laser Eye Centers Inc. 9/1/99

NEUMEDIA INC (DE)
Name changed to Mandalay Digital Group, Inc. 02/28/2012
Mandalay Digital Group, Inc. name changed to Digital Turbine, Inc. 01/20/2015

NEUREX CORP (DE)
Merged into Elan Corp., PLC 08/11/1998
Each share Common 1¢ par exchanged for (0.51) Sponsored ADR for Ordinary
Elan Corp., PLC merged into Perrigo Co. PLC 12/18/2013

NEURO BIOTECH CORP (NV)
Recapitalized as Institute of BioMedical Research Corp. 04/28/2014
Each share Common $0.001 par exchanged for (0.1) share Common $0.0001 par

NEURO-BIOTECH CORP (ON)
Name changed to DPC Biosciences, Corp. 10/31/2001
DPC Biosciences, Corp. name changed to iGaming Corp. 09/05/2006 which name changed to Big Stick Media Corp. 06/29/2007
(See Big Stick Media Corp.)

NEURO DATA INC (DE)
Charter cancelled and declared inoperative and void for non-payment of taxes 3/1/76

NEURO DISCOVERY INC (CANADA)
Reincorporated 06/28/2002
Place of incorporation changed from (BC) to (Canada) 06/28/2002
Name changed to Allon Therapeutics Inc. 09/29/2004
Each share Common no par exchanged for (1) share Common no par
(See Allon Therapeutics Inc.)

NEURO HITECH PHARMACEUTICALS INC (DE)
Name changed to Neuro-Hitech, Inc. 08/11/2006

NEURO NAVAGATIONAL CORP (DE)
Name changed to Kinetic Ventures Ltd. 04/30/1997
Kinetic Venture Ltd. recapitalized as Suite101.com, Inc. 12/04/1998 which name changed to GeoGlobal Resources Inc. 02/02/2004

NEURO PSYCHIATRIC & HEALTH SVCS INC (DE)
Name changed to Comprehensive Care Corp. 12/02/1972

NEUROCHEM INC (CANADA)
Name changed to BELLUS Health Inc. (Old) 04/21/2008
BELLUS Health Inc. (Old) reorganized as BELLUS Health Inc. (New) 05/29/2012

NEUROCHEMICAL RESH CORP (NV)
Each share old Common $0.001 par exchanged for (0.005) share new Common $0.001 par 01/12/2001
Name changed to Covenant Environmental Technologies Inc. (NV) 05/07/2001
Covenant Environmental Technologies Inc. (NV) reincorporated under the laws of Tennessee as Neurochemical Research Corp. 06/14/2001 which recapitalized as MiNetwork Group, Inc. (TN) 12/15/2003 which reincorporated in Nevada 04/21/2004 which name changed to Green Earth Technologies, Inc. 08/08/2007

NEUROCHEMICAL RESH CORP (TN)
Each share old Common $0.001 par exchanged for (1/6) share new Common $0.001 par 05/07/2002
Recapitalized as MiNetwork Group, Inc. (TN) 12/15/2003
Each share Common $0.001 par exchanged for (0.1) share Common $0.001 par
MiNetwork Group, Inc. (TN) reincorporated in Nevada 04/21/2004 which name changed to Green Earth Technologies, Inc. 08/08/2007

NEUROCHEMICAL RESH INTL INC (DE)
Name changed to Ultimate Sports Entertainment Inc. and (3) additional shares issued 4/12/99

NEUROCORP LTD (NV)
Charter revoked for failure to file reports and pay taxes 03/31/2002

NEURODERM LTD (ISRAEL)
Acquired by Mitsubishi Tanabe Pharma Corp. 10/18/2017
Each share Ordinary ILS 0.01 par exchanged for $39 cash

NEUROGEN CORP (DE)
Merged into Ligand Pharmaceuticals Inc. 12/23/2009
Each share Common $0.025 par exchanged for (0.0608355) share Common $0.001 par, (1) Aplindore Contingent Value Right, (1) H3 Contingent Value Right, (1) Merck Contingent Value Right, (1) Real Estate Contingent Value Right and $0.00869 cash

NEUROGESX INC (DE)
Assets sold for the benefit of creditors 07/08/2013
Stockholders' equity unlikely

NEUROKINE PHARMACEUTICALS INC (BC)
Recapitalized as Pivot Pharmaceuticals Inc. 04/20/2015
Each share Common no par exchanged for (0.1) share Common no par

NEUROLOGIX INC (DE)
Each share old Common $0.001 par exchanged for (0.04) share new Common $0.001 par 09/10/2004
Chapter 7 bankruptcy proceedings terminated 02/14/2017
No stockholders' equity

NEUROMEDICAL SYS INC (DE)
Liquidating plan of reorganization under Chapter 11 Federal Bankruptcy Code effective 3/15/2000
No stockholders' equity

NEUROMEDICAL TECHNOLOGIES INC (DE)
Charter cancelled and declared inoperative and void for non-payment of taxes 03/01/1994

NEUROSCIENCE THERAPY CORP (WA)
Reincorporated under the laws of Nevada as Nashville Records, Inc. (Old) 04/12/2007
Nashville Records, Inc. (Old) name changed to Welltek, Inc. (Ctfs. dated prior to 11/05/2009) 09/10/2008 which name changed to Nashville Records, Inc. (New) 11/05/2009

NEUROTECH DEVL CORP (DE)
Recapitalized 05/24/2002
Recapitalized from Neurotech Corp. to Neurotech Development Corp. 05/24/2002
Each share Common 1¢ par exchanged for (0.09090909) share Class A Common 1¢ par and (0.909090909) share Class B Ser. 1 1¢ par
Note: Unexchanged certificates were cancelled and became without value 07/01/2002
SEC revoked Class A Common and Class B Ser. 1 registration 05/17/2005
Stockholders' equity unlikely

NEUSTAR INC (DE)
Acquired by Aerial Topco, L.P. 08/08/2017
Each share Class A Common $0.001 par exchanged for $33.50 cash

NEUTRA CORP (FL)
Each share old Common $0.0001 par exchanged for (0.05) share new Common $0.0001 par 08/08/2012
Reorganized under the laws of Nevada 10/06/2015
Each share new Common $0.0001 par exchanged for (0.02) share Common $0.001 par
Note: No holder will receive fewer than (5) post-split shares

NEUTRAL POSTURE ERGONOMICS INC (TX)
Merged into Neutral Posture Ergonomics Merger Co., Inc. 4/30/2001
Each share Common 1¢ par exchanged for $2.27 cash

NEUTRAL TANDEM INC (DE)
Name changed to Inteliquent, Inc. 07/01/2013
(See Inteliquent, Inc.)

NEUTRINO RES INC (CANADA)
Merged into Southern Mineral Corp. 07/28/1998
Each share Common no par exchanged for $1.80 cash

NEUTRINO RESOURCES LTD. (CANADA)
Merged into Neutrino Resources Inc. 11/08/1995
Each share Common no par exchanged for (1.8) shares Common no par
(See Neutrino Resources Inc.)

NEUTROGENA CORP (DE)
Reincorporated 2/17/88
Common 50¢ par changed to no par and (1) additional share issued 3/6/81
Common no par split (2) for (1) by issuance of (1) additional share 1/6/84
Common no par split (3) for (2) by issuance of (0.5) additional share 1/17/85
Common no par split (3) for (2) by issuance of (0.5) additional share 1/16/86
Common no par split (3) for (2) by issuance of (0.5) additional share 3/12/87
Common no par split (3) for (2) by issuance of (0.5) additional share 1/15/88
Stock Dividend - 10% 1/17/83
State of incorporation changed from (CA) to (DE) and Common no par changed to $0.001 par 2/17/88
Merged into Johnson & Johnson 10/11/94
Each share Common $0.001 par exchanged for $35.25 cash

NEUTRON ENTERPRISES INC (NV)
Each share old Common $0.001 par exchanged for (10) shares new Common $0.001 par 06/30/2003
Name changed to Stock-Trak Group, Inc. 01/25/2008
Stock-Trak Group, Inc. name changed to Media Survivors, Inc. 09/02/2009

NEUWIRTH CENTY FD (DE)
Merged into Neuwirth Fund, Inc. 03/31/1975
Each share Common $1 par exchanged for (0.6657) share Common 50¢ par
Neuwirth Fund, Inc. reorganized as Winthrop Focus Funds 07/10/1992 which name changed to DLJ Winthrop Focus Funds 01/29/1999 which name changed to DLJ Focus Funds 08/01/2000 which reorganized as Credit Suisse

Warburg Pincus Capital Funds 01/18/2001 which name changed to Credit Suisse Capital Funds 12/12/2001

NEUWIRTH FD INC (DE)
Common $1 par changed to 50¢ par and (1) additional share issued 10/23/1970
Common 50¢ par split (3) for (2) by issuance of (0.5) additional share 06/19/1986
Under plan of reorganization each share Common 50¢ par automatically became (1) share Winthrop Focus Funds Aggressive Fund Class A 1¢ par 07/10/1992
Winthrop Focus Funds name changed to DLJ Winthrop Focus Funds 01/29/1999 which name changed to DLJ Focus Funds 08/01/2000 which reorganized as Credit Suisse Warburg Pincus Capital Funds 01/18/2001 which name changed to Credit Suisse Capital Funds 12/12/2001

NEUWIRTH INCOME DEVELOPMENT CORP. (DE)
Completely liquidated 9/13/74
Each share Common 10¢ par received first and final distribution of $8.57 cash
Note: Certificates were not required to be surrendered and are now valueless

NEV-TAH OIL & MINING CO. (UT)
Charter suspended for non-payment of corporate taxes 3/31/59

NEVA EQUITIES INC (NV)
Dissolved 07/18/2001
Details not available

NEVADA BANK OF COMMERCE (RENO, NV)
Name changed to Nevada National Bank of Commerce (Reno) 1/31/68
Nevada National Bank of Commerce (Reno) name changed to Nevada National Bank (Reno) 3/3/69
(See Nevada National Bank (Reno, Nev.))

NEVADA BKG CO (NV)
Common par split (2) for (1) by issuance of (1) additional share payable 2/27/98 to holders of record 2/20/98
Under plan of reorganization each share Common no par automatically became (1) share Xeon Financial Corp. Common no par 10/15/98
Xeon Financial Corp. merged into First Security Corp. 6/14/99 which merged into Wells Fargo & Co. (New) 10/26/2000

NEVADA BOBS GOLF INC (AB)
Name changed 10/5/99
Name changed from Nevada Bob's Canada Inc. to Nevada Bob's Golf Inc. 10/5/99
Assets sold for the benefit of creditors 3/1/2002
No stockholders' equity

NEVADA BOBS INTL INC (ON)
Each share old Common no par exchanged for (0.33333333) share new Common no par 05/06/2002
Name changed to Loncor Resources Inc. 12/02/2008

NEVADA-CALIFORNIA ELECTRIC CORP. (DE)
Common $100 par changed to $10 par in 1940
Recapitalized as California Electric Power Co. 6/30/41
Each share 7% Preferred $100 par exchanged for (0.8) share $3 Preferred $50 par and (6) shares Common $10 par
Holders also had option to receive an additional (0.2) share $3 Preferred plus $1 in cash in settlement of dividend arrears on each share of 7% Preferred
Common $10 par exchanged share for share
California Electric Power Co. merged into Southern California Edison Co. 12/31/63 which reorganized as SCEcorp 7/1/88

NEVADA CHEMICALS INC (UT)
Acquired by Calypso Acquisition Corp. 10/22/2008
Each share Common $0.001 par exchanged for $13.37 cash

NEVADA-COMMONWEALTH MINING & MILLING CO. (AZ)
Charter revoked for failure to file reports and pay fees 6/7/27

NEVADA CONSOLIDATED COPPER & GOLD MINING & MILLING CO. (ME)
Voluntarily dissolved 6/29/11
Details not available

NEVADA CONSOLIDATED COPPER CO.
Acquired by Kennecott Copper Corp. in 1933
Details not available

NEVADA CONSOLIDATED MINES, INC. (NV)
Charter revoked for failure to file reports and pay fees 3/6/67

NEVADA DEV INC (UT)
Name changed to Husky Developments, Ltd. 10/28/1987
(See Husky Developments, Ltd.)

NEVADA ENERGY INC (DE)
Each share old Class A Common no par exchanged for (0.25) share new Class A Common no par 07/09/1992
Name changed to PowerTel USA Inc 01/31/1997
PowerTel USA Inc. name changed to Worldcall Corp. 11/25/1998
(See Worldcall Corp.)

NEVADA GEOTHERMAL PWR INC (BC)
Recapitalized as Alternative Earth Resources Inc. 04/02/2013
Each share Common no par exchanged for (0.2) share Common no par
Alternative Earth Resources Inc. recapitalized as Black Sea Copper & Gold Corp. 09/28/2016

NEVADA GOLD CO (NV)
Charter revoked for failure to file reports and pay fees 5/1/96

NEVADA GOLD DEVELOPMENT CO. (NV)
Merged into Argus Resources, Inc. (NV) 12/27/72
Each share Common $1 par exchanged for (2) shares Common 20¢ par
Argus Resources, Inc. (NV) reincorporated in Delaware as 1st Global Petroleum Group, Inc. 3/31/2005 which name changed to Commonwealth American Financial Group, Inc. 5/13/2005 which name changed to James Monroe Capital Corp. 5/30/2006

NEVADA GOLD HLDGS INC (DE)
Old Common $0.001 par split (2) for (1) by issuance of (1) additional share payable 05/12/2009 to holders of record 05/08/2009 Ex date - 05/13/2009
Each share old Common $0.001 par exchanged for (0.06666666) share new Common $0.001 par 10/05/2010
Name changed to HK Battery Technology Inc. 09/06/2013

NEVADA GOLDFIELDS CONSOLIDATED MINES CO. (NV)
Charter revoked for failure to file reports and pay fees 3/7/60

NEVADA GOLDFIELDS CORP (CANADA)
Reincorporated 04/27/1989
Place of incorporation changed from (BC) to (Canada) 04/27/1989
Recapitalized as Consolidated Nevada Goldfields Corp. 05/01/1991
Each share Common no par exchanged for (1/6) share Common no par
Consolidated Nevada Goldfields Corp. recapitalized as Real Del Monte Mining Corp. 05/14/1998
(See Real Del Monte Mining Corp.)

NEVADA HEALTH SCAN INC (DE)
Common $0.0001 par split (5) for (1) by issuance of (4) additional shares payable 04/09/2014 to holders of record 04/07/2014 Ex date - 04/10/2014
Name changed to Americann, Inc. 04/17/2014

NEVADA HLDG GROUP INC (NV)
Recapitalized as New Life Scientific, Inc. 03/11/2005
Each (35) shares Common $0.001 par exchanged for (1) share Common $0.001 par
New Life Scientific, Inc. recapitalized as Applied Wellness Corp. 03/25/2008
(See Applied Wellness Corp.)

NEVADA IRON LTD (AUSTRALIA)
Shares transferred to Australian share register 08/24/2015

NEVADA KING CO. (NV)
Merged into Siskon Gold Corp. 12/24/1991
Details not available

NEVADA KING COPPER CO. (NV)
Name changed to Nevada King Co. 12/03/1971
(See Nevada King Co.)

NEVADA MAGIC HLDGS INC (UT)
Name changed to To4c Corp. (UT) 6/29/99
To4c Corp. (UT) reorganized in Nevada as Aplox Corp. 4/27/2001 which name changed to Mirador Inc. 7/25/2001 which recapitalized as VWAY International 7/5/2004 which name changed to WorldWide Cannery & Distribution, Inc. 2/8/2006 which name changed to Global Diamond Exchange Inc. 9/22/2006

NEVADA MANHATTAN GROUP INC (NV)
Charter revoked for failure to file reports and pay fees 3/1/2001

NEVADA MANHATTAN MNG INC (NV)
Incorporated 6/10/85
Each share old Common no par exchanged for (0.1) share new Common no par 7/25/95
Name changed to Nevada Manhattan Group, Inc. 12/11/98
(See Nevada Manhattan Group, Inc.)

NEVADA MANHATTAN MNG INC (NV)
Incorporated 03/04/1987
Name changed to Cozy Financial Corp. 04/06/1993
Cozy Financial Corp. name changed to Braintech, Inc. (New) 02/17/1994
(See Braintech, Inc. (New))

NEVADA MERCURY CORP. (NV)
Merged into United Mercury Corp. 2/27/57
Each share Common 1¢ par exchanged for (0.25) share Common 1¢ par
United Mercury Corp. name changed to Mercury Electronics Corp. (Del.) which recapitalized as Mercury Industries, Inc. 4/25/74

NEVADA METALS MINING CO.
Name changed to Nev-Tah Oil & Mining Co. in 1952
(See Nev-Tah Oil & Mining Co.)

NEVADA MINERALS & CONSTRUCTION, INC. (UT)
Merged into Emdeko International, Inc. 2/28/69
Each share Capital Stock 1¢ par exchanged for (2) shares Common no par
(See Emdeko International, Inc.)

NEVADA MINERALS & OIL CORP. (NV)
Charter revoked for failure to file reports and pay fees 3/4/63

NEVADA MONARCH CONSOLIDATED MINES CORP. (NV)
Charter revoked for failure to file reports and pay fees 3/6/67

NEVADA NATL BANCORPORATION (NV)
Common $1 par changed to 66-2/3¢ par and (0.5) additional share issued 06/29/1979
Merged into Security Pacific Corp. 01/05/1989
Each share $1.125 Conv. Preferred $1 par exchanged for $19.53 cash
Each share $1.3125 Preferred $1 par exchanged for $20.70 cash
Each share Common 66-2/3¢ par exchanged for $8.06 cash

NEVADA NATIONAL BANK (RENO, NV)
Name and location changed to Security Pacific Bank Nevada, N.A. (Las Vegas, NV) 01/05/1989
(See Security Pacific Bank Nevada, N.A. (Las Vegas, NV))

NEVADA NATIONAL BANK OF COMMERCE (RENO, NV)
Name changed to Nevada National Bank (Reno, NV) 3/3/69
(See Nevada National Bank (Reno, NV))

NEVADA NATURAL GAS PIPE LINE CO. (NV)
Stock Dividend - 200% 02/06/1956
Merged into Southwest Gas Corp. 03/23/1962
Each share $1.50 Preferred $21 par exchanged for (1) share $1.50 Preferred $25 par
Each share Common $1 par exchanged for (0.5) share $1 Conv. Preferred $5 par
Southwest Gas Corp. name changed to Southwest Gas Holdings, Inc. 01/03/2017

NEVADA NORTH RES INC (BC)
Name changed to Inca Pacific Resources, Inc. 12/02/1994
(See Inca Pacific Resources, Inc.)

NEVADA NORTHERN GAS CO. (NV)
Merged into Southwest Gas Corp. 12/31/1963
Each share Common $1 par exchanged for (0.6) share Common $1 par
Southwest Gas Corp. name changed to Southwest Gas Holdings, Inc. 01/03/2017

NEVADA NUCLEAR, INC. (NV)
Charter revoked for failure to file reports and pay fees 3/4/74

NEVADA OIL & GAS CO. (NV)
Recapitalized as Great Western Petroleum Corp. 3/15/54
Each share Common $1 par exchanged for (20) shares Common 5¢ par
(See Great Western Petroleum Corp.)

NEVADA PAC GOLD LTD (BC)
Acquired by US Gold Canadian Acquisition Corp. 06/28/2007
Each share Common no par exchanged for (0.23) Exchangeable Share no par
US Gold Canadian Acquisition Corp. exchanged for McEwen Mining Inc. 05/29/2012

NEVADA PACKING CO.
Out of business 00/00/1947
Details not available

NEVADA PWR CO (NV)
Common $1 par split (3) for (2) by issuance of (0.5) additional share 4/30/63
5-1/2% Preferred $20 par called for redemption 7/15/65
Common $1 par split (3) for (2) by issuance of (0.5) additional share 2/1/78
Common $1 par split (5) for (4) by issuance of (0.25) additional share 11/1/79
11.50% Preferred $20 par called for redemption 6/2/86
Common $1 par split (2) for (1) by issuance of (1) additional share 8/1/86
8% Preferred $20 par called for redemption 8/24/87
8.70% Preferred $20 par called for redemption 8/24/87
9.75% Preferred $20 par called for redemption 8/24/87
Each share Auction Market Preferred Ser. A exchanged for (1) share 9.90% Preferred $20 par 4/23/92
9.90% Preferred Units $20 par called for redemption at $105 on 4/1/97
4.70% Preferred $20 par called for redemption at $20.25 on 7/23/99
5.20% Preferred $20 par called for redemption at $21 on 7/23/99
5.40% Preferred $20 par called for redemption at $21 on 7/23/99
Merged into Sierra Pacific Resources (New) 7/28/99
Each share Common $1 par exchanged for either (1) share Common $1 par, $26 cash or a combination thereof 1/13/78
Note: Cash electors received 88.7% of total holdings in cash and the remaining 11.3% in stock
Holdings of (99) shares of fewer received cash

NEVADA PROCESSING SOLUTIONS INC (NV)
Name changed to MMax Media, Inc. 04/16/2010
MMax Media, Inc. recapitalized as PayMeOn, Inc. 05/17/2013

NEVADA REAL ESTATE INVESTMENT CORP. (NV)
Name changed to Harbor Resources, Inc. 4/20/72
Each share Common $1 par exchanged for (1) share Common $1 par
Harbor Resources, Inc. name changed to Western Smelting & Refining Inc. 2/12/79
(See Western Smelting & Refining Inc.)

NEVADA RESOURCE TECH INC (NV)
Reorganized under the laws of New Jersey as TCP Reliable, Inc. 01/24/1996
Each share Common $0.001 par exchanged for (0.26666666) share Common $0.001 par
(See TCP Reliable, Inc.)

NEVADA RES INC (NV)
Reincorporated under the laws of Delaware as Cadema Corp. 12/19/1986
(See Cadema Corp.)

NEVADA SVGS & LN ASSN (NV)
Permanent Stock $1 par changed to 80¢ par and (0.25) additional share issued 12/20/1976
Permanent Stock 80¢ par changed to 64¢ par and (0.25) additional share issued 12/20/1977
Permanent Stock 64¢ par changed to $0.512 par and (0.25) additional share issued 12/20/1978
Permanent Stock $0.512 par changed to $0.4096 par and (0.25) additional share issued 12/20/1979
Permanent Stock $0.4096 par changed to $0.32768 par and (0.25) additional share issued 12/22/1980
Permanent Stock $0.32768 par changed to $0.262144 par and (0.25) additional share issued 12/30/1982
Merged into Southwest Gas Corp. 12/30/1986
Each share Permanent Stock $0.262144 par exchanged for $25 cash

NEVADA SILVER HORN MINING CO. (NV)
Charter revoked for failure to file reports and pay fees 3/1/26

NEVADA SILVER REFINERY (NV)
Charter revoked for failure to file reports and pay fees 7/1/82

NEVADA SOUTHERN GAS CO. (NV)
Merged into Southwest Gas Corp. 03/15/1957
Each share 1st Preferred $20 par exchanged for $20 principal amount of 6% Debentures due 01/01/1977
Each share Common $1 par exchanged for (1) share Common $1 par
Southwest Gas Corp. name changed to Southwest Gas Holdings, Inc. 01/03/2017

NEVADA ST BK (LAS VEGAS, NV)
Capital Stock $25 par changed to $6.25 par and (3) additional shares issued 04/17/1973
Stock Dividend - 25% 09/17/1976
Acquired by Zions Utah Bancorporation 12/20/1985
Each share Capital Stock $6.25 par exchanged for $78.721 cash

NEVADA STAR MINING CO. (SD)
Charter expired by time limitation 4/10/26

NEVADA STAR RESOURCE CORP (YT)
Reincorporated 06/23/1998
Place of incorporation changed from (BC) to (YT) 06/23/1998
Recapitalized as Pure Nickel Inc. (YT) 03/30/2007
Each share Common no par exchanged for (0.2) share Common no par
Pure Nickel Inc. (YT) reincorporated in Canada 04/07/2009

NEVADA STATE GOLD MINES CO. (NV)
Each share old Common exchanged for (0.2) share new Common $1 par in 1936
Charter revoked for failure to file reports and pay fees 3/3/52

NEVADA STK EXCHANGE INC (NV)
Name changed to SearchPath HCS, Inc. 02/23/2010

NEVADA TUNGSTEN & COPPER INC (NV)
Charter revoked for failure to file reports and pay fees 03/06/1972

NEVADA-TUNGSTEN CORP. (DE)
No longer in existence having become inoperative and void for non-payment of taxes 7/1/61

NEVADA/UTAH GOLD INC (NV)
Name changed to Fenway International Inc. 09/11/1998

NEVADA-UTAH MINES & SMELTERS CORP. (ME)
Went bankrupt in February 1912
No stockholders' equity

NEVADA UTE MINING CO. (UT)
Name changed to Inter Chem Inc. 4/5/76
(See Inter Chem Inc.)

NEVADA WESTERN GOLD CORP., LTD. (NV)
Charter revoked for failure to file reports and pay fees 3/5/34

NEVADA-WYOMING MINES CO. (NV)
Name changed to Nevada-Wyoming Oil & Minerals Co. in 1952
Nevada-Wyoming Oil & Minerals Co. charter revoked 3/5/62

NEVADA-WYOMING OIL & MINERALS CO. (NV)
Charter revoked for failure to file reports and pay fees 3/5/62

NEVADABOBS COM INC (ON)
Name changed to Nevada Bob's International Inc. 08/27/2001
Nevada Bob's International Inc. name changed to Loncor Resources Inc. 12/02/2008

NEVADO VENTURE CAP CORP (CANADA)
Name changed to Nevado Resources Corp. 08/27/2010

NEVAEH ENTERPRISES LTD (NV)
Name changed to Pan Ocean Container Supplies Ltd. 05/05/2014

NEVARO CAP CORP OLD (CANADA)
Each share old Common no par exchanged for (0.05) share new Common no par to reflect a ( ) for (5,000) reverse split followed by a (250) for (1) forward split 09/15/2009
Note: Holders of (4,999) or fewer pre-split shares received $0.00825 cash per share
Merged into Nevaro Capital Corp. (New) 01/01/2010
Each share new Common no par exchanged for (1) share Common no par
Note: Unexchanged certificates were cancelled and became without value 01/01/2016

NEVARRO ENERGY INC (AB)
Issue Information - 2,000,000 shares COM offered at $0.10 per share on 10/20/1997
Recapitalized as Nevarro Energy Ltd. 09/20/2000
Each share Common no par exchanged for (1/3) share Common no par
(See Nevarro Energy Ltd.)

NEVARRO ENERGY LTD (AB)
Merged into Pearl Exploration & Production Ltd. 09/19/2006
Each share Common no par exchanged for (0.125) share Common no par, (0.5) share Serrano Energy Ltd. Common no par, (0.20866) Common Stock Purchase Warrant expiring 10/23/2006 and $1.875 cash
Note: Unexchanged certificates were cancelled and became without value 09/19/2012
(See each company's listing)

NEVCAL RES LTD (BC)
Recapitalized as Arapahoe Mining Corp. 12/03/1986
Each share Common no par exchanged for (0.5) share Common no par
Arapahoe Mining Corp. recapitalized as Salus Resource Corp. 05/06/1996 which name changed to Brandon Gold Corp. 12/04/1996 which recapitalized as Redmond Ventures Corp. 09/16/1999 which recapitalized as Crown Point Ventures Ltd. (BC) 03/12/2002 which reincorporated in Alberta as Crown Point Energy Inc. 07/31/2012

NEVCO BLUE JAY CORP (NV)
Charter revoked for failure to file reports and pay fees 03/05/1973

NEVCOR BUSINESS SOLUTIONS INC (NV)
Name changed to CPSM, Inc. 07/15/2014
CPSM, Inc. name changed to Astro Aerospace Ltd. 04/24/2018

NEVE DRUG STORES, INC.
Bankrupt in 1930

NEVER MISS A CALL INC (NV)
Reorganized under the laws of Florida as Intercallnet, Inc. 04/03/2001
Each share Common $0.001 par exchanged for (3.5) shares Common $0.001 par
(See Intercallnet, Inc.)

NEVEX GOLD INC (WA)
Merged into Canyon Resources Corp. 11/19/1987
Each share Common $0.0025 par exchanged for (0.14285714) share Common 1¢ par
Canyon Resources Corp. merged into Atna Resources Ltd. 03/19/2008
(See Atna Resources Ltd.)

NEVEX MINES LTD (BC)
Recapitalized as Wasp International Resources Inc. 6/25/80
Each share Common no par exchanged for (0.2) share Common no par
Wasp International Resources Inc. name changed to Plexus Resources Corp. 2/1/82 which merged into Kinross Gold Corp. 5/31/93

NEVGOLD RESOURCE CORP (CANADA)
Merged into Silver Predator Corp. 02/28/2012
Each share Common no par exchanged for (0.5) share Common no par
Note: Unexchanged certificates were cancelled and became without value 02/28/2018

NEVIS CAP CORP (NV)
Common $0.001 par split (10) for (1) by issuance of (9) additional shares payable 07/08/2013 to holders of record 07/08/2013
Recapitalized as ASC Biosciences, Inc. 05/10/2017
Each share Common $0.001 par exchanged for (0.0005) share Common $0.001 par

NEVIS ENERGY SVCS LTD (AB)
Acquired by Phoenix Technology Services Inc. 11/01/2002
Each share Class A Common no par exchanged for (0.5) share Common no par
Phoenix Technology Services Inc. recapitalized as Phoenix Technology Income Fund 07/01/2004 which reorganized as PHX Energy Services Corp. 01/06/2011

NEVIS PETE CORP (AB)
Acquired by AC Energy Inc. (ALTA) 10/16/2002
Each share Class A no par exchanged for $0.10 cash

NEVORO INC (CANADA)
Acquired by Starfield Resources, Inc. 10/08/2009
Each share Common no par exchanged for (0.87) share Common no par
Note: Unexchanged certificates were cancelled and became without value 10/08/2015

NEVSTAR CORP (NV)
Name changed 01/12/2006
Name changed from NevStar Gaming & Entertainment Corp. to NevStar Corp. 01/12/2006
Each share Common 1¢ par exchanged for (0.00333333) share Common 1¢ par
Name changed to Golden Elephant Glass Technology, Inc. 06/11/2008

(See Golden Elephant Glass Technology, Inc.)

NEVSTAR PRECIOUS METALS INC (DE)
Recapitalized as Deploy Technologies Inc. (DE) 11/06/2008
Each share Common $0.0001 par exchanged for (0.01) share Common $0.0001 par
Deploy Technologies Inc. (DE) reincorporated in Nevada 09/15/2010 which recapitalized as Body & Mind Inc. 12/07/2017

NEVSUR INC (DE)
Name changed to Worthcorp Inc. 9/9/87
(See Worthcorp Inc.)

NEW AEGIS RES LTD (BC)
Acquired by Norcan Resources Ltd. 08/19/1994
Each share Common no par exchanged for (0.75187969) share Common no par
Norcan Resources Ltd. recapitalized as Odyssey Exploration Inc. 06/07/2000 which recapitalized as Consolidated Odyssey Exploration Inc. 12/08/2000 which reorganized as Odyssey Petroleum Corp. 08/25/2005 which recapitalized as Petrichor Energy Inc. 03/03/2011

NEW AGE CITIES COM INC (ID)
Reincorporated under the laws of Florida as Genesis Technology Group, Inc. 10/15/2001
Genesis Technology Group, Inc. name changed to Genesis Pharmaceuticals Enterprises, Inc. 10/26/2007 which name changed to Jiangbo Pharmaceuticals, Inc. 05/12/2009
(See Jiangbo Pharmaceuticals, Inc.)

NEW AGE CORP (NV)
Name changed to Biomune Systems, Inc. 11/02/1992
Biomune Systems, Inc. name changed to Donlar Biosyntrex Corp. 06/15/2001 which merged into Donlar Corp. 03/05/2003
(See Donlar Corp.)

NEW AGE INDS INC (FL)
Administratively dissolved 11/09/1990

NEW AGE MEDIA FD INC (MD)
Name changed to Price (T. Rowe) Media & Telecommunications Fund, Inc. 7/28/97

NEW AGE TRANSLATION INC (NV)
Reorganized under the laws of Delaware as InfoLogix, Inc. 12/07/2006
Each share Common $0.00001 par exchanged for (3.18877518) shares Common $0.00001 par
(See InfoLogix, Inc.)

NEW AGE VENTURES INC (YT)
Recapitalized as Great Panther Inc. 01/01/1998
Each share Common no par exchanged for (0.1) share Common no par
Great Panther Inc. recapitalized as Great Panther Resources Ltd. (YT) 10/02/2003 which reincorporated in British Columbia 07/14/2004 which name changed to Great Panther Silver Ltd. 01/12/2010

NEW AINSWORTH BASE METALS LTD (BC)
Recapitalized as Angus River Mines Ltd. 01/27/1969
Each share Capital Stock no par exchanged for (0.1) share Capital Stock
Angus River Mines Ltd. acquired by Abco Mining Ltd. 07/23/1969 which name changed to Aselo Industries Ltd. 02/00/1971 which recapitalized as Fairmont Gas & Oil Corp. 10/15/1979 which recapitalized as Cater Energy, Inc. 05/23/1984 which recapitalized as Houston Metals Corp. 10/27/1986 which recapitalized as Pacific Houston Resources, Inc. 03/30/1989
(See Pacific Houston Resources, Inc.)

NEW ALGER MINES LTD (ON)
Charter cancelled for failure to pay taxes and file returns 11/01/1982

NEW ALLIED DEV CORP (CO)
Recapitalized as Consolidated Biofuels Inc. 8/1/2005
Each share Common no par exchanged for (0.1) share Common no oar

NEW ALMADEN CORP.
Liquidated in 1947
Details not available

NEW ALSTER ENERGY LTD (BC)
Recapitalized as Anacondo Explorations Inc. 03/26/1990
Each share Common no par exchanged for (0.25) share Common no par
Anacondo Explorations Inc. name changed to O-Tech Ventures Corp. 09/16/1992 which recapitalized as Bright Star Ventures Ltd. 06/26/1996
(See Bright Star Ventures Ltd.)

NEW ALTO DIVIDE MINING CO.
Name changed to Alto Development Co. in 1937
Alto Development Co. name changed to American Silver Corp. in 1946
(See American Silver Corp.)

NEW AMBASADOR DEVS LTD (ON)
Dissolved 02/20/1980
Details not available

NEW AMER FD INC (DE)
In process of liquidation
Each share Common $1 par received initial distribution of (0.323) share Triton Group Ltd. $1.20 Conv. Preferred Ser. C $1 par 4/19/85
Each share Common $1 par received second distribution of (0.845) share Lee Enterprises, Inc. Common $2 par 7/9/85
Each share Common $1 par received third distribution of (0.0636) share Welded Tube Co. of America Common $1 par 1/31/86
Each share Common $1 par received fourth distribution of (1) share Daily Journal Co. Common 1¢ par and $6.33 cash 2/3/86
Assets transferred to NAF Liquidating Trust 2/3/86
Each share Common $1 par exchanged for (1) Share of Bene. Int. no par
(See NAF Liquidating Trust)

NEW AMER GROUP INC (NJ)
Charter revoked for failure to file reports and pay fees 2/28/94

NEW AMER HIGH INCOME FD INC (MD)
Auction Term Preferred Ser. A $1 par called for redemption at $25,000 on 11/09/2012
Auction Term Preferred Ser. B $1 par called for redemption at $25,000 on 11/09/2012
Auction Term Preferred Ser. C $1 par called for redemption at $25,000 on 11/09/2012
Auction Term Preferred Ser. D $1 par called for redemption at $25,000 on 11/09/2012
(Additional Information in Active)

NEW AMER INDS INC (DE)
Name changed to Campanelli Industries, Inc. 5/29/73
Campanelli Industries, Inc. name changed to Realmark, Inc. (Old) 7/23/87
(See Realmark, Inc. (Old))

NEW AMERN HEALTHCARE CORP (DE)
Issue Information - 5,000,000 shares COM offered at $13 per share on 08/19/1998
Plan of reorganization under Chapter 11 Federal Bankruptcy Code effective 07/08/2003
No stockholders' equity

NEW AMERN SHOE INC (DE)
Charter cancelled and declared inoperative and void for non-payment of taxes 03/01/1991

NEW AMERICAN VIDEO, INC. (DE)
Recapitalized as Tropicana, Inc. 6/18/83
Each share Common 1¢ par exchanged for (0.2) share Common 5¢ par

NEW AMSTERDAM CASUALTY CO. (NY)
Capital Stock $10 par changed to $5 par in 1933
Capital Stock $5 par changed to $2 par in 1934
Capital Stock $2 par changed to $4 par 5/24/57
Merged into Security Insurance Co. of Hartford 6/30/66
Each share Capital Stock $4 par exchanged for (2.625) shares Common $10 par
Security Insurance Co. of Hartford name changed to Security Corp. 6/30/68 which was acquired by Textron Inc. 6/29/73

NEW AMSTERDAM GAS CO.
Merged into Consolidated Edison Co. of New York, Inc. 00/00/1937
Details not available

NEW ANACONDA CO (UT)
SEC revoked common stock registration 06/19/2009
Stockholders' equity unlikely

NEW ARCADIA RES LTD (BC)
Name changed 11/10/1992
Name changed from New Arcadia Explorations Ltd. to New Arcadia Resources Ltd. 11/10/1992
Cease trade order effective 07/18/2003
Stockholders' equity unlikely

NEW ARLINGTON MINES LTD. (BC)
Dissolved 3/12/64
Stock has no value

NEW ARNTFIELD MINES LTD (QC)
Charter annulled for failure to file annual reports 3/21/81

NEW ASIA ENERGY INC (CO)
Recapitalized as LNPR Group Inc. 01/17/2018
Each share Common $0.001 par exchanged for (0.025) share Common $0.001 par

NEW ASIA GOLD CORP (FL)
Recapitalized as New World Gold Corp. 05/08/2009
Each share Common $0.0001 par exchanged for (0.001) share Common $0.0001 par

NEW ASIA INC (NV)
Charter revoked for failure to file reports and pay fees 06/30/2010

NEW ASSOCIATED DEVELOPMENTS LTD. (QC)
Recapitalized as Consolidated Developments Ltd. 5/10/71
Each share Capital Stock $1 par exchanged for (0.2) share Common no par
(See Consolidated Developments Ltd.)

NEW ASTON RES INC (BC)
Merged into Atlantic Energy Corp. 11/03/1981
Each (1.5) shares Common no par exchanged for (1) share Common no par
Atlantic Energy Corp. merged into Bowtex Energy (Canada) Corp. 06/01/1987 which name changed to Luscar Oil & Gas Ltd. 10/21/1993 which merged into Encal Energy Ltd. 07/13/1994 which merged into Calpine Canada Holdings Ltd. 04/19/2001 which was exchanged for Calpine Corp. 05/27/2002
(See Calpine Corp.)

NEW ASTRAL MINING & RESOURCES LTD. (ON)
Charter revoked for failure to file reports and pay fees 10/02/1968

NEW ATHONA MINES LTD (ON)
Capital Stock $1 par changed to Common no par 10/06/1981
Recapitalized as Lakota Resources Inc. 11/21/1994
Each (3.5) shares Common no par exchanged for (1) share Common no par
Lakota Resources Inc. recapitalized as Tembo Gold Corp. 09/26/2011

NEW AUGARITA PORCUPINE MINES LTD. (ON)
Acquired by Augdome Explorations Ltd. in 1957
Each share Capital Stock $1 par exchanged for (0.2) share Capital Stock $1 par
Augdome Exploration Ltd. recapitalized as Augdome Corp. Ltd. 2/8/66
(See Augdome Corp. Ltd.)

NEW BAILEY MINES LTD. (ON)
Charter revoked for failure to file reports and pay fees in 1961

NEW BANCSHARES, INC. (KY)
Acquired by First National Cincinnati Corp. 03/31/1986
Each share Common $10 par exchanged for (13.72) shares Common $5 par
First National Cincinnati Corp. name changed to Star Banc Corp. 04/13/1990 which merged into Firstar Corp. (New) 11/20/1998 which merged into U.S Bancorp (DE) 02/27/2001

NEW BARBER-LARDER MINES LTD. (ON)
Charter surrendered 00/00/1953
No stockholders' equity

NEW BASTION DEV INC (PA)
SEC revoked common stock registration 06/25/2012

NEW BEDFORD & ONSET STREET RAILWAY CO.
Property sold in 1927
Details not available

NEW BEDFORD CORDAGE CO (MA)
Merged into Wall Rope Works, Inc. on a (0.4) for (1) basis 7/31/58
Wall Rope Works, Inc. name changed to Wall Industries, Inc. 4/13/60 which was acquired by Phillips Petroleum Co. 8/1/63 which name changed to ConocoPhillips 8/30/2002

NEW BEDFORD COTTON MILLS CORP.
Merged into Hoosac Mills Corp. in 1932
Details not available

NEW BEDFORD INVESTORS TRUST
Liquidated in 1936
Details not available

NEW BEDFORD RAYON CO. (DE)
Merged into Mohawk Carpet Mills, Inc. and each share Class A or B Common $25 par received $22.50 in cash 5/31/55

NEW BEGINNING GROWTH FD INC (MN)
Name changed to Sit New Beginning Growth Fund, Inc. 08/28/1987
Sit New Beginning Growth Fund, Inc. name changed to Sit Growth Fund Inc. 11/01/1993 which name changed to Sit Mid Cap Growth Fund, Inc. 10/23/1996

NEW BEGINNING INVT RESV FD INC (MN)
Name changed to Sit "New Beginning" Investment Reserve Fund 08/28/1987
Sit "New Beginning" Investment Reserve Fund name changed to Sit Money Market Fund 11/01/1993
(See Sit Money Market Fund)

NEW BEGINNING YIELD FD INC (MN)
Name changed to Sit "New Beginnning" Yield Fund Inc. 08/28/1987
Sit "New Beginning" Yield Fund Inc. name changed to Sit "New Beginning" Tax-Free Income Fund Inc. 09/29/1988 which name changed to Sit Tax-Free Income Fund 07/03/1992

NEW BETHSAIDA MINES LTD. (BC)
Completely liquidated 04/30/1964
Each share Common $1 par exchanged for first and final distribution of (1) share Western Beaver Lodge Mines Ltd. Capital Stock no par
Western Beaver Lodge Mines Ltd. recapitalized as Portcomm Communications Corp. Ltd. 08/19/1969 which name changed to Roach (Hal) Studios Corp. 11/01/1977 which merged into H.R.S. Industries, Inc. 05/21/1982 which merged into International H.R.S. Industries Inc. 05/15/1984 which name changed to Glenex Industries Inc. 05/25/1987 which merged into Quest Investment Corp. 07/04/2002 which merged into Quest Capital Corp. (BC) 06/30/2003 which reincorporated in Canada 05/27/2008 which name changed to Sprott Resource Lending Corp. 09/10/2010 which merged into Sprott Inc. 07/24/2013

NEW BIDLAMAQUE ENTERPRISES INC (CANADA)
Reincorporated 00/00/1987
Recapitalized 10/31/1995
Place of incorporation changed from (ON) to (Canada) 00/00/1987
Recapitalized from New Bidlamaque Gold Mines Ltd. to New Bidlamaque Enterprises Inc. 10/31/1995
Each share old Common no par exchanged for (0.1) share new Common no par
Reorganized under the laws of British Virgin Islands as Chivor Emerald Corp. Ltd. 06/05/1996
Each share new Common no par exchanged for (0.25) share Common no par
(See Chivor Emerald Corp. Ltd.)

NEW BINGHAM MARY MNG CO (UT)
Merged into BCC 1/1/98
Each share Common 10¢ par exchanged for $1.10 cash

NEW BISON, INC. (NY)
Liquidation completed
Each share Common 50¢ par exchanged for initial distribution of (0.075) share Roblin Steel Corp. $5 Conv. Preferred no par 9/11/67
Roblin Steel Corp. name changed to Roblin Industries, Inc. 4/17/68
Each share Common 50¢ par received second and final distribution of (0.0083) share Roblin Industries, Inc. $5 Conv. Preferred no par plus cash (which represents accrued dividends paid on shares while held in escrow) 8/7/68

NEW BLACK BAY MINERALS LTD (AB)
Acquired by Thomson Exploration Ltd. 3/3/75
Each share Common no par exchanged for $0.33 cash

NEW BLONDEAU NICKEL MINES LTD. (ON)
Charter cancelled and declared dissolved for failure to file returns and pay fees 5/15/74

NEW BLUE RIBBON RES LTD (BC)
Recapitalized as Blue Diamond Mining Corp. 01/28/2003
Each (15) shares Common no par exchanged for (1) share Common no par
Blue Diamond Mining Corp. recapitalized as Colossal Resources Corp. (BC) 06/07/2010 which reincorporated in Alberta as Top Strike Resources Corp. 12/13/2012

NEW BOBS LAKE GOLD MINES LTD. (ON)
Charter cancelled and company declared dissolved for default in filing returns 5/25/59

NEW BOSTON ARENA CO.
Merged into Boston Garden-Arena Corp. in 1936
Details not available

NEW BOSTON BK & TR CO (BOSTON, MA)
Declared insolvent 9/14/76

NEW BOSTON RAILROAD CO.
Dissolved in 1937
Details not available

NEW BRADFORD OIL CO.
Merged into Argo Oil Corp. on a share for share basis in 1936
(See Argo Oil Corp.)

NEW BRDG PRODS INC (NV)
Each share old Common $0.001 par exchanged for (1/3) share new Common $0.001 par 08/19/1998
Charter revoked for failure to file reports and pay fees 09/01/2004

NEW BRDG REORGN CORP (NV)
Recapitalized as Sweet Success Enterprises Inc. 11/25/2002
Each share Common exchanged for (0.125) share Common
(See Sweet Success Enterprises Inc.)

NEW BREED INC (DE)
Recapitalized as Genetic Research Laboratories, Inc. 11/25/85
Each share Common 1¢ par exchanged for (0.5) share Common 1¢ par
Genetic Research Laboratories, Inc. merged into Organo Med Products, Ltd. 5/28/87
(See Organo Med Products, Ltd.)

NEW BRIDGE DEV CORP (BC)
Cease trade order effective 09/25/1991
Stockholders' equity unlikely

NEW BRISTOL OILS LTD. (ON)
Common $1 par changed to 20¢ par 11/07/1957
Each share Common 20¢ par stamped to indicate a distribution of (0.3) share Bayview Oil Corp. Common 25¢ par
Merged into Able Land & Minerals Ltd. 09/16/1959
Each share Common 20¢ par exchanged for (0.2) share Capital Stock $1 par
Able Land & Minerals Ltd. acquired by Canaveral International Corp. 05/01/1963 which recapitalized as Madison Group Associates Inc. 02/02/1993
(See Madison Group Associates Inc.)

NEW BRITAIN BK & TR CO (NEW BRITAIN, CT)
Stock Dividend - 50% 11/15/66
Reorganized as Connecticut BancFederation, Inc. 12/28/73
Each share Common $10 par exchanged for (2.4241) shares Common $10 par
(See Connecticut BancFederation, Inc.)

NEW BRITAIN GAS LIGHT CO. (CT)
Merged into Connecticut Natural Gas Corp. 8/30/68
Each share 4.75% Preferred $100 par exchanged for (1) share 5.75% Preferred $100 par
Each share Common $25 par exchanged for (2) shares Common $12.50 par

NEW BRITAIN MACHINE CO. (CT)
Common no par changed to $10 par in 1954
Common $10 par split (4) for (3) by issuance of (1/3) additional share 7/15/66
Common $10 par split (5) for (4) by issuance of (0.25) additional share 7/14/67
Stock Dividends - 100% 4/15/54; 10% 10/25/65
Merged into Litton Industries, Inc. 12/31/68
Each share Common $10 par exchanged for (1.08787) shares $2 Conv. Preferred Ser. B $5 par
(See Litton Industries, Inc.)

NEW BRITAIN NATL BK (NEW BRITAIN, CT)
Each share Capital Stock $100 par exchanged for (6) shares Capital Stock $20 par to effect a (5) for (1) split and 20% stock dividend 00/00/1949
Capital Stock $20 par changed to $10 par and (1) additional share issued plus a 10% stock dividend paid 11/05/1963
Stock Dividends - 16-2/3% 01/20/1953; 14-2/7% 07/11/1955; 12-1/2% 01/23/1959; 11-1/9% 04/25/1960; (1) for (6.5) 08/12/1968
Through exchange offer First Connecticut Bancorp, Inc. held all but directors qualifying shares as of 12/29/1970

NEW BRITAIN TRUST CO. (NEW BRITAIN, CT)
Common $50 par changed to $12.50 par and (3) additional shares issued 2/2/59
Common $12.50 par changed to $10 par and (1) additional share issued 4/17/62
Stock Dividends - 10% 1/24/61; 25% 4/17/62
Name changed to New Britain Bank & Trust Co. (New Britain, CT) 2/15/65
New Britain Bank & Trust Co. (New Britain, CT) reorganized as Connecticut BancFederation, Inc. 12/28/73
(See Connecticut BancFederation, Inc.)

NEW BRITISH DOMINION OIL CO. LTD. (CANADA)
Name changed to Asamera Oil Corp. Ltd. 1/20/58
Asamera Oil Corp. Ltd. name changed to Asamera Inc. 10/1/80 which was acquired by Gulf Canada Resources Ltd. 8/4/88
(See Gulf Canada Resources Ltd.)

NEW BROS INC (GA)
Reorganized under Chapter 11 Federal Bankruptcy Code as Vidalia Sweets Brand, Inc. 5/8/89
Each share Common 1¢ par exchanged for (0.2) share Common 1¢ par

NEW BRUNSWICK FIRE INSURANCE CO.
Merged into Home Insurance Co. in 1948
Each share Capital Stock $10 par exchanged for (1.078) shares Common $5 par
(See Home Insurance Co.)

NEW BRUNSWICK LIGHT, HEAT & POWER CO.
Acquired by Public Service Electric & Gas Co. and stock exchanged for a like amount of First and Refunding Mortgage Bonds in 1938

NEW BRUNSWICK OILFIELDS LTD (NB)
Each share Capital Stock no par exchanged for (10) shares Capital Stock 40¢ par 3/14/55
Merged into Decalta Petroleum (1977) Ltd. 1/14/85
Each share Capital Stock 40¢ par exchanged for $0.81 cash

NEW BRUNSWICK SCIENTIFIC INC (NJ)
Common $0.125 par changed to $0.0625 par and (1) additional share issued 01/12/1981
Stock Dividends - 5% payable 05/15/1996 to holders of record 04/15/1996; 10% payable 05/15/1997 to holders of record 04/15/1997; 10% payable 05/15/1998 to holders of record 04/15/1998; 10% payable 05/14/1999 to holders of record 04/15/1999; 10% payable 05/15/2000 to holders of record 04/14/2000; 10% payable 05/15/2001 to holders of record 04/16/2001; 10% payable 05/15/2002 to holders of record 04/15/2002 Ex date - 04/11/2002; 10% payable 05/15/2003 to holders of record 04/18/2003 Ex date - 04/15/2003
Merged into Eppendorf Inc. 09/24/2007
Each share Common $0.0625 par exchanged for $11.50 cash

NEW BRUNSWICK TEL LTD (NB)
Capital Stock $10 par reclassified as Common $10 par 3/17/72
Common $10 par changed to no par and (1) additional share issued 3/27/84
Under plan of reorganization each share Common no par automatically became (1) share Bruncor Inc. Common no par 7/1/85
$1.85 Preferred $20 par called for redemption 3/15/90
$1.37 Preferred $20 par called for redemption 7/31/92
Bruncor Inc. merged into Aliant Inc. (Canada) 6/1/99 which reorganized in Ontario as Bell Aliant Regional Communications Income Fund 7/10/2006

NEW BRUNSWICK TR CO (NEW BRUNSWICK, NJ)
Preferred $10 par called for redemption 8/31/64
Common $10 par changed to $2 par and (4) additional shares issued 1/25/72
Stock Dividends - 10% 9/10/71; 20% 11/15/72; 20% 5/1/74
Merged into Brunswick Bank & Trust Co. (Manalapan, NJ) 11/3/75
Each share Common $2 par exchanged for (1.2) shares Common $2 par
Brunswick Bank & Trust Co. (Manalapan, NJ) reorganized as Brunswick Bancorp 1/15/86

NEW BRUNSWICK URANIUM METALS & MNG LTD (NB)
Name changed to NBU Mines Ltd. 9/1/71
NBU Mines Ltd. merged into Dominion Explorers Inc. (Old) 7/19/85 which merged into Dominion Explorers Inc. (New) 12/31/94 which merged into Neutrino Resources Inc. 2/28/97
(See Neutrino Resources Inc.)

NEW BULLET GROUP INC (BC)
Reincorporated under the laws of Ontario as Amerix Precious Metals Corp. 05/31/2004
Amerix Precious Metals Corp.

recapitalized as Eagle Graphite Inc. 01/22/2015

NEW CACHE PETES LTD (AB)
Each share old Common no par exchanged for (0.2) share new Common no par 5/29/95
Merged into Abraxas Petroleum Corp. 1/12/99
Each share new Common no par exchanged for $6.50 cash

NEW CALBRICO PETROLEUMS LTD. (AB)
Acquired by Thomson Drilling Ltd. 12/10/66
Each share Capital Stock no par exchanged for $0.475 cash

NEW CALUMET MINES LTD (QC)
Completely liquidated 8/6/75
Each share Capital Stock $1 par received first and final distribution of (0.321750) share Consolidated Professor Mines Ltd. Capital Stock no par
Note: Certificates were not required to be surrendered and are now valueless

NEW CAMPBELL ISLAND MINES LTD (CANADA)
Reincorporated 7/23/84
Place of incorporation changed from (ONT) to (Canada) and Capital Stock $1 par reclassified as Common no par 7/23/84
Recapitalized as Minera Delta Inc. (Old) 3/12/97
Each share Common no par exchanged for (0.25) share Common no par
Minera Delta Inc. (Old) recapitalized as Whitmore Resource Corp. 7/20/99 which name changed to Minera Delta Inc. (New) 10/15/2001 which name changed to Vector Wind Energy Inc. 11/26/2004
(See Vector Wind Energy Inc.)

NEW CANAAN BK & TR CO (NEW CANAAN, CT)
Common $10 par changed to $5 par and (1) additional share issued 5/30/86
Merged into Summit Bancorp 3/31/99
Each share Common $5 par exchanged for (3.4037) shares Common 80¢ par
Summit Bancorp merged into FleetBoston Financial Corp. 3/1/2001 which merged into Bank of America Corp. 4/1/2004

NEW CANAAN DEVELOPMENT CO. (CT)
Reincorporated under the laws of New York as New Canaan Development Co. of Northern Westchester, Inc. 12/21/73
(See New Canaan Development Co. of Northern Westchester, Inc.)

NEW CANAAN DEVELOPMENT CO. OF NORTHERN WESTCHESTER, INC. (NY)
Voluntarily dissolved 12/27/79
Details not available

NEW CANALASK MINERALS LTD. (ON)
Acquired by Thomson Resources Ltd. 04/01/1974
Each share Capital Stock no par exchanged for $0.175 cash

NEW CANAMIN RES LTD (BC)
Merged into Princeton Mining Corp. 7/3/95
Each share Common no par exchanged for (1.25) shares Common no par and (1) Common Stock Purchase Warrant expiring 8/31/97
(See Princeton Mining Corp.)

NEW CANDELA RES LTD (BC)
Recapitalized as Sherwood Petroleum Corp. (BC) 10/20/1999
Each share Common no par exchanged for (0.5) share Common no par
Sherwood Petroleum Corp. (BC) reincorporated in Alberta 07/20/2000 which name changed to Sherwood Mining Corp. 11/09/2001 which recapitalized as Sherwood Copper Corp. 09/12/2005 which merged into Capstone Mining Corp. 11/25/2008

NEW CANTECH VENTURES INC (BC)
Name changed to Nanika Resources Inc. 06/20/2008
Nanika Resources Inc. recapitalized as Goldbar Resources Inc. 07/06/2012

NEW CAP FDG CORP (DE)
Recapitalized as Ulysses Holding Corp. 10/29/2007
Each share Common $0.0001 par exchanged for (0.0125) share Common $0.0001 par
Ulysses Holding Corp. name changed to Ulysses Diversified Holdings Corp. 05/08/2008 which name changed to JNS Holdings Corp. 02/16/2012

NEW CASCADE MINERALS LTD. (BC)
Merged into Maloney Steel Crafts Ltd. 1/12/76
Each share Common no par exchanged for $0.23 cash

NEW CASTLE COMMUNICATIONS INC (DE)
Charter cancelled and declared inoperative and void for non-payment of taxes 3/1/91

NEW CASTLE ENERGY CORP (CO)
Declared defunct and inoperative for failure to pay taxes and file annual reports 11/1/92

NEW CAYZOR ATHABASKA MINES LTD (ON)
Charter cancelled for failure to pay taxes and file returns 3/31/81

NEW CENTURY CASUALTY CO.
Assets acquired by Citizens Casualty Co. of New York in 1941
Details not available

NEW CENTURY PRODUCTIONS, LTD. (DE)
Name changed to New Century Entertainment Corp. 7/3/86
New Century Entertainment Corp. name changed to New Visions Entertainment Corp. 8/8/88
(See New Visions Entertainment Corp.)

NEW CENTY BANCORP INC (NC)
Common $1 par split (3) for (2) by issuance of (0.5) additional share payable 07/01/2004 to holders of record 06/15/2004 Ex date - 06/14/2004
Common $1 par split (6) for (5) by issuance of (0.2) additional share payable 12/12/2006 to holders of record 11/28/2006 Ex date - 11/24/2006
Stock Dividends - 10% payable 10/24/2003 to holders of record 10/10/2003; 10% payable 08/10/2005 to holders of record 07/27/2005 Ex date - 08/11/2005
Under plan of merger name changed to Select Bancorp, Inc. (New) 07/28/2014

NEW CENTY BK (DUNN, NC)
Reorganized as New Century Bancorp, Inc. 09/19/2003
Each share Common $5 par exchanged for (1) share Common $1 par
New Century Bancorp, Inc. name changed to Select Bancorp, Inc. (New) 07/28/2014

NEW CENTY BK (PHOENIXVILLE, PA)
Reorganized as Customers Bancorp, Inc. 11/30/2011
Each share Common $1 par exchanged for (1/3) share Common $1 par

NEW CENTY COS INC (DE)
Each share old Common 10¢ par exchanged for (0.1) share new Common 10¢ par 12/26/2001
Name changed to U.S. Aerospace, Inc. 04/27/2010

NEW CENTY ENERGIES INC (CO)
Merged into Xcel Energy Inc. 8/18/2000
Each share Common $1 par exchanged for (1.55) shares Common $2.50 par

NEW CENTY ENERGY CORP (CO)
Plan of reorganization under Chapter 11 Federal Bankruptcy Code effective 06/12/2009
No stockholders' equity

NEW CENTY ENTMT CORP (DE)
Each share Conv. Preferred Ser. B $0.001 par exchanged for (1.3) shares Common $0.001 par 2/20/87
Name changed to New Visions Entertainment Corp. 8/8/88
(See New Visions Entertainment Corp.)

NEW CENTY EQUITY HLDS CORP (DE)
Name changed to Wilhelmina International, Inc. 02/19/2009

NEW CENTY FINL CORP (DE)
Common 1¢ par split (3) for (2) by issuance of (0.5) additional share payable 07/11/2003 to holders of record 06/12/2003 Ex date - 07/14/2003
Reincorporated under the laws of Maryland as New Century REIT, Inc. 10/01/2004
New Century REIT, Inc. name changed to New Century Financial Corp. 10/01/2004
(See New Century Financial Corp.)

NEW CENTY FINL CORP (MD)
Plan of reorganization under Chapter 11 Federal Bankruptcy Code effective 08/01/2008
No stockholders' equity

NEW CENTY MEDIA CORP (NV)
Reorganized under the laws of Delaware as International Diamond Corp. 1/14/98
Each share Common $0.001 par exchanged for (1/7) share Common $0.000001 par
International Diamond Corp. recapitalized as Diginet Systems Corp. 10/1/98

NEW CENTY MEDIA LTD (NV)
Name changed to LBU, Inc. 03/24/1995
(See LBU, Inc.)

NEW CENTY REIT INC (MD)
Name changed to New Century Financial Corp. 10/01/2004
(See New Century Financial Corp.)

NEW CENTY RES LTD (BC)
Name changed to A.I. Software Inc. 09/04/1990
A.I Software Inc. name changed to Network Gaming International Corp. 07/02/1996 which recapitalized as Network Exploration Ltd. 06/22/2004 which name changed to Ynvisible Interactive Inc. 01/12/2018

NEW CENTY TECHNOLOGIES CORP (UT)
Each share old Common $0.001 par exchanged for (0.1) share new Common $0.001 par 10/25/1994
Each share new Common $0.001 par exchanged again for (0.05) share new Common $0.001 par 03/10/1997
Name changed to Cybernet Internet Services International, Inc. (UT) 05/22/1997
Cybernet Internet Services International, Inc. (UT) reincorporated in Delaware 09/18/1998
(See Cybernet Internet Services International, Inc. (DE))

NEW CHAMBERLAIN PETROLEUMS LTD. (AB)
Under plan of merger name changed to Sarcee Petroleums Ltd. 3/9/59
(See Sarcee Petroleums Ltd.)

NEW CHARTER MINERALS INC (BC)
Name changed to Cambridge BioChemics Inc. 04/23/1992
Cambridge BioChemics Inc. name changed to Cambridge Softek Inc. 06/23/1993 which recapitalized as Alantra Venture Corp. 11/21/1994
(See Alantra Venture Corp.)

NEW CHEMCRUDE RES LTD (BC)
Struck off register and declared dissolved for failure to file returns 2/4/83

NEW CHEROKEE CORP (DE)
Acquired by Dan River Inc. (Old) 02/03/1997
Details not available

NEW CHESTER WATER CO.
Acquired by Chester Water Service Co. in 1927 which was sold to the City of Chester, Pa. in 1939

NEW CHIEF MINES LTD (BC)
Recapitalized as Sydney Development Corp. 5/10/78
Each share Capital Stock no par exchanged for (0.4) share Capital Stock no par
Sydney Development Corp. reorganized in Canada as SDC Sydney Development Corp. 9/18/86
(See SDC Sydney Development Corp.)

NEW CHINA GLOBAL INC (NV)
Reorganized under the laws of Wyoming as Globestar Industries 08/07/2014
Each share Common $0.001 par exchanged for (0.01) share Common $0.0000001 par
Globestar Industries name changed to Pineapple Express, Inc. 09/22/2015

NEW CHINA HOMES, LTD. (CAYMAN ISLANDS)
Issue Information - 2,000,000 shares COM offered at $5 per share on 03/09/2000
Acquired by Zhongshan Development Ltd. 04/24/2003
Each share Common $1 par exchanged for $0.22 cash

NEW CHINA RES LTD (BC)
Name changed to Sino Pac International Investments Inc. 2/6/91
Sino Pac International Investments Inc. recapitalized as Paron Resources Inc. 12/16/96

NEW CINCH URANIUM LTD (BC)
Struck off register and declared dissolved for failure to file returns 7/24/92

NEW CINEMA PARTNERS INC (NV)
Name changed to Witnet International, Inc. 08/28/2002
Witnet International, Inc. recapitalized as KSign International, Inc. 02/25/2004 which name changed to Columbus Geographics Systems (GIS) Ltd. 09/06/2007
(See Columbus Geographic Systems (GIS) Ltd.)

NEW CLAYMORE RES LTD (BC)
Reincorporated under the laws of

Alberta as Brazalta Resources Corp. 11/26/2004
Brazalta Resources Corp. name changed to Canacol Energy Ltd. 02/13/2009

NEW COMM BANCORP (SC)
Merged into SCBT Financial Corp. 04/11/2005
Each share Common no par exchanged for $18 cash

NEW CONCEPT TECHNOLOGIES INTL INC (BERMUDA)
Reincorporated 12/15/1994
Place of incorporation changed from (ONT) to (Bermuda) 12/15/1994
Name changed to NTI Resources Ltd. (Bermuda) 08/16/1996
NTI Resources Ltd. (Bermuda) reincorporated in Alberta 05/28/1997
(See NTI Resources Ltd.)

NEW CONCORD DEVELOPMENT CORP. LTD. (ON)
Charter revoked for failure to file reports and pay fees 01/03/1966

NEW CONGRESS RES LTD (BC)
Recapitalized as Levon Resources Ltd. (Old) 01/12/1983
Each share Capital Stock no par exchanged for (0.2) share Common no par
(See Levon Resources Ltd. (Old))

NEW CONTL OIL CO CDA LTD (AB)
Completely liquidated 1/1/72
Each share Capital Stock no par exchanged for first and final distribution of (0.0647) share Pan Ocean Oil Corp. Common 1¢ par
(See Pan Ocean Oil Corp.)

NEW COPPER MOUNTAIN MINES LTD. (BC)
Struck off register and declared dissolved for failure to file returns 01/10/1992

NEW CORNELIA COPPER CO.
Merged into Calumet & Arizona Mining Co. in 1929
Details not available

NEW CORNELIA EXTENSION COPPER CORP. (DE)
Recapitalized as Cornelia Corp. 5/26/67
Each share Common 10¢ par exchanged for (1/3) share Common 30¢ par
(See Cornelia Corp.)

NEW COSMIC INDUSTRIES LTD. (BC)
Name changed to Cosmic Industries Ltd. 8/8/77
(See Cosmic Industries Ltd.)

NEW CRONIN BABINE MINES LTD (ON)
Recapitalized as Sproatt Silver Mines Ltd. (ON) 06/26/1973
Each share Capital Stock $1 par exchanged for (0.25) share Capital Stock no par
Sproatt Silver Mines Ltd. (ON) reorganized in British Columbia as Hecate Gold Corp. 07/06/1977 which merged into Host Ventures Ltd. 06/29/1982 which recapitalized as Hot Resources Ltd. 04/30/1984 which name changed to Inter-Globe Resources Ltd. 04/16/1985
(See Inter-Globe Resources Ltd.)

NEW CTR ASSET TR
Money Market Certificate Ser. A called for redemption at $500,000 on 2/19/2003

NEW DARWIN GOLD MINES LTD. (ON)
Charter cancelled in 1949

NEW DAVIES PETES LTD (AB)
Capital Stock 50¢ par changed to no par 7/9/63
Recapitalized as Davoil Natural Resources Ltd. 3/20/72
Each share Capital Stock no par exchanged for (0.2) share Capital Stock no par
Davoil Natural Resources Ltd. (1976) merged into Ranchmen's Resources (1976) Ltd. 1/31/77 which name changed to Ranchmen's Resources Ltd. 5/31/85 which merged into Crestar Energy Inc. 10/11/95 which was acquired by Gulf Canada Resources Ltd. 11/13/2000
(See Gulf Canada Resources Ltd.)

NEW DAWN DEV LTD (NV)
Charter revoked for failure to file reports and pay fees 2/1/94

NEW DAWN MNG CORP (CANADA)
Reorganized 11/15/2007
Reorganized from (BC) to under the laws of Canada 11/15/2007
Each share Common 1¢ par exchanged for (4.7) shares old Common no par
Each share old Common no par exchanged for (0.00001) share new Common no par 12/06/2013
Note: In effect holders received $0.13 cash per share and public interest was eliminated

NEW DAY BEVERAGE INC (DE)
Name changed to Bev-Tyme, Inc. 01/05/1996
(See Bev-Tyme, Inc.)

NEW DELHI MINES LTD. (ON)
Recapitalized as Delhi Pacific Mines Ltd. on a (1) for (4) basis 05/23/1961
Delhi Pacific Mines Ltd. name changed to Delhi Pacific Resources Ltd. 01/12/1981
(See Delhi Pacific Resources Ltd.)

NEW DESIGN CABINETS INC (NV)
Each share old Common $0.001 par exchanged for (0.06666666) share new Common $0.001 par 10/11/2007
Name changed to Stratos Renewables Corp. 12/06/2007

NEW DEVILS ELBOW MINES LTD (ON)
Recapitalized as Lancer Resources Inc. 06/09/1978
Each share Capital Stock no par exchanged for (0.2) share Common no par
Lancer Resources Inc. recapitalized as V-Tech Diagnostics (Canada) Inc. 01/29/1991
(See V-Tech Diagnostics (Canada) Inc.)

NEW DEVON PETROLEUMS LTD. (AB)
Acquired by Nuco Petroleums Ltd. 00/00/1954
Each share Capital Stock no par exchanged for (0.125) share Capital Stock no par
Nuco Petroleums Ltd. was acquired by Kodiak Petroleums Ltd. 02/13/1963 which was acquired by Manhattan Continental Development Corp. 10/02/1969
(See Manhattan Continental Development Corp.)

NEW DICKENSON MINES, LTD. (ON)
Merged into Dickenson Mines Ltd. (Old) 10/14/1960
Each share Common $1 par exchanged for (1) share Common $1 par
Dickenson Mines Ltd. (Old) merged into Dickenson Mines Ltd. (New) 10/31/1980 which merged into Goldcorp Inc. (New) 03/31/1994

NEW DICTATYPE CO., INC. (DE)
Charter relinquished and declared inoperative and void for non-payment of taxes in 1956

NEW DIGBY DOME MINES LTD (ON)
Charter cancelled and declared dissolved for failure to file returns and pay fees 03/05/1975

NEW DIMENSION INDS CORP (WY)
Reincorporated 09/22/1983
Recapitalized 09/19/1989
Place of incorporation changed from (ON) to (WY) 09/22/1983
Recapitalized from New Dimension Resources Ltd. to New Dimension Industries Corp. 09/19/1989
Basis not available
Recapitalized as Toxic Disposal Corp. 02/15/1994
Each share Common no par exchanged for (0.2) share Common no par
Toxic Disposal Corp. recapitalized as Global Disposal Corp. 03/29/1996
(See Global Disposal Corp.)

NEW DIMENSION SOFTWARE LTD (ISRAEL)
Acquired by BMC Software, Inc. 04/14/1999
Each share Common NIS 0.01 par exchanged for $52.50 cash

NEW DIMENSIONS IN EDUCATION INC (DE)
Reported out of business 00/00/2001
Details not available

NEW DIMENSIONS LEARNING CORP (NJ)
Shares reacquired 05/04/2012
Each share Common no par exchanged for $0.87 cash

NEW DIMENSIONS MEDICINE INC (DE)
Liquidation completed
Each share Common no par exchanged for initial distribution of $4.3189 cash 2/29/96
Each share Common no par received second and final distribution of $0.1201 cash 4/23/96

NEW DIMENSIONS TECHNOLOGIES LTD (BC)
Recapitalized as NDT Ventures Ltd. 2/20/95
Each share Common no par exchanged for (0.2) share Common no par
NDT Ventures Ltd. reorganized as New Dimension Resources Ltd. 1/11/2006

NEW DIRECTIONS MFG INC (LA)
Reorganized under the laws of Nevada as American Soil Technologies Inc. 1/18/2000
Each (15) shares Common no par exchanged for (1) share Common $0.001 par

NEW DISCOVERIES PUBG CORP (NV)
Name changed to NWDP.com, Inc. 6/2/99
NWDP.com, Inc. name changed to Hop-On.com 7/18/2000 which recapitalized as Hop-On, Inc. 5/18/2005

NEW DOLLY VARDEN MINERALS INC (ON)
Each share old Common no par exchanged for (1) share new Common no par to reflect a (1) for (100) reverse split followed by a (100) for (1) forward split
Note: Holders of (99) or fewer pre-split shares received $0.30 cash per share 04/17/2000
Name changed to Dolly Varden Resources Inc. 04/17/2000
Dolly Varden Resources Inc. name changed to DV Resources Ltd. 01/31/2012 which name changed to DLV Resources Ltd. 11/27/2017

NEW DOMINION MINERALS DEVELOPMENT LTD. (AB)
Acquired by Bow Valley Industries Ltd. for cash 2/3/64

NEW DOMINION NICKEL MINES LTD. (ON)
Name changed to New Dominion Resources Ltd. 4/24/78
New Dominion Resources Ltd. name changed to Epping Resources Ltd. 10/13/82 which name changed to Tri-D Automotive Industries Ltd. 12/1/86
(See Tri-D Automotive Industries Ltd.)

NEW DOMINION RES LTD (ON)
Name changed to Epping Resources Ltd. 10/13/82
Epping Resources Ltd. name changed to Tri-D Automotive Industries Ltd. 12/1/86
(See Tri-D Automotive Industries Ltd.)

NEW DRAGON ASIA CORP (FL)
SEC revoked common stock registration 11/03/2014

NEW DYNAMIC MARKETING INC (FL)
Each (12) shares old Common $0.001 par exchanged for (0.08333333) share new Common $0.001 par 7/11/2006
Name changed to China Pet Pharmacy, Inc. 01/30/2007
China Pet Pharmacy, Inc. name changed to China M161 Network Co. 02/11/2008

NEW DYNASTY RESOURCES INC. (BC)
Name changed to International Dynasty Resources Inc. 06/22/1984
International Dynasty Resources Inc. name changed to Commander Resources Ltd. 10/23/1985 which name changed to Commander Technologies Corp. 05/15/1992 which recapitalized as SCS Solars Computing Systems Inc. 09/12/1995

NEW EAGLE MINING CORP. LTD. (BC)
Struck off register and declared dissolved for failure to file returns 8/19/74

NEW EAR INC (NV)
Recapitalized as Progressive Environmental Recovery Corp. 09/25/1997
Each share Common $0.001 par exchanged for (0.05) share Common $0.001 par
Progressive Environmental Recovery Corp. name changed to Advanced Encryption Technology of America Inc. 10/01/1997
(See Advanced Encryption Technology of America Inc.)

NEW EAST BANCORP (NC)
Merged into Triangle Bancorp, Inc. 12/23/93
Each share Common $1 par exchanged for (0.55) share Common $4 par
Triangle Bancorp, Inc. merged into Centura Banks, Inc. 2/18/2000 which merged into Royal Bank of Canada (Montreal, QC) 6/5/2001

NEW EGYPTIAN-PORTLAND CEMENT CO.
Merged into Peerless Egyptian Cement Co. in 1927
Details not available

NEW ELECTRA PORCUPINE GOLD MINES LTD. (ON)
Merged into Pardee Amalgamated Mines Ltd. 12/00/1954
Each share Capital Stock $1 par exchanged for (0.05714285) share Common $1 par
Pardee Amalgamated Mines Ltd. liquidated for Rio Algom Mines Ltd. 11/09/1961 which name changed to Rio Algom Ltd. 04/30/1975
(See Rio Algom Ltd.)

NEW ELECTRODYNAMICS CORP. (NY)
Charter revoked for failure to file reports and pay fees 12/15/59

NEW EMJAY PETROLEUMS LTD. (AB)
Acquired by Thomson Drilling Ltd. 11/01/1966
Each share Capital Stock no par exchanged for $0.071 cash

NEW ENERGY TECHNOLOGIES INC (NV)
Each share old Common $0.001 par exchanged for (0.33333333) share new Common $0.001 par 03/21/2011
Name changed to SolarWindow Technologies, Inc. 03/12/2015

NEW ENERGY WEST CORP (AB)
Acquired by Gastar Exploration Ltd. (AB) 11/20/2001
Each share Common no par exchanged for initial distribution of (0.01694586) share Common no par 02/16/2002
Each share Common no par received second distribution of (0.00847293) share Common no par 06/05/2002
Each share Common no par received third distribution of (0.00847293) share Common no par 08/16/2002
Each share Common no par received fourth distribution of (0.00847293) share Common no par 12/00/2002
Each share Common no par received fifth distribution of (0.00847293) share Common no par 03/00/2003
Each share Common no par received sixth distribution of (0.00847293) share Common no par payable 06/00/2003
Each share Common no par received seventh and final distribution of (0.00847293) share Common no par payable 09/00/2003
Gastar Exploration Ltd. (AB) reincorporated in Delaware as Gastar Exploration, Inc. (Old) 11/15/2013 which reorganized as Gastar Exploration, Inc. (New) 02/03/2014

NEW ENG ACQUISITIONS INC (FL)
Name changed to Atlantic Wine Agencies Inc. 01/13/2004
Atlantic Wine Agencies Inc. reorganized as Novo Energies Corp. 06/24/2009 which name changed to Immunovative, Inc. 05/08/2012 which name changed to Tauriga Sciences, Inc. 04/09/2013

NEW ENG CMNTY BANCORP INC (DE)
Stock Dividend - 10% payable 1/16/98 to holders of record 12/31/97
Merged into Webster Financial Corp. 12/1/99
Each share Common no par exchanged for (1.06) shares Common no par

NEW ENG INVT COS L P (DE)
Name changed to NVEST, L.P. 3/30/98
(See NVEST, L.P.)

NEW ENGLAND BANCORP INC (MA)
Common $1 par changed to $4 par 5/13/80
Common $4 par changed to 25¢ par and (14) additional shares issued 6/24/88
Stock Dividends - 10% 8/3/79; 10% 2/26/82
Taken over by the FDIC 11/13/92
Stockholders' equity undetermined

NEW ENGLAND BANCSHARES INC (MD)
Reorganized 12/28/2005
Reorganized from New England Bancshares Inc. (USA) to under the laws of Maryland as New England Bancshares Inc. 12/28/2005
Each share Common 1¢ par exchanged for (2.3683) shares Common 1¢ par
Merged into United Financial Bancorp, Inc. (MD) 11/19/2012
Each share Common 1¢ par exchanged for (0.9575) share Common 1¢ par
United Financial Bancorp, Inc. (MD) merged into United Financial Bancorp, Inc. (CT) 05/01/2014

NEW ENGLAND BANK & TRUST CO. (ENFIELD, CT)
Acquired by Olde Windsor Bancorp, Inc. 3/14/86
Each share Capital Stock $5 par exchanged for (0.66) share Common 10¢ par
Olde Windsor Bancorp, Inc. name changed to New England Community Bancorp, Inc. 9/27/94 which merged into Webster Financial Corp. 12/1/99

NEW ENGLAND BUSINESS SVC INC (DE)
Reincorporated 10/24/86
Common $1 par split (3) for (2) by issuance of (0.5) additional share 4/10/81
Common $1 par split (2) for (1) by issuance of (1) additional share 11/25/83
State of incorporation changed from (MA) to (DE) 10/24/86
Common $1 par split (2) for (1) by issuance of (1) additional share 11/21/86
Merged into Deluxe Corp. 6/25/2004
Each share Common $1 par exchanged for $44 cash

NEW ENGLAND CASH MGMT TR (MA)
Name changed to TNE Cash Management Trust 04/01/1992 which name changed back to New England Cash Management Trust 04/11/1994
Name changed to Nvest Cash Management Trust 02/01/2000
Nvest Cash Management Trust name changed to CDC Nvest Cash Management Trust 05/01/2001 which name changed to Ixis Advisor Cash Management Trust 04/05/2005 which name changed to Natixis Cash Management Trust 06/20/2007
(See Natixis Cash Management Trust)

NEW ENGLAND CO.
Liquidated in 1926
Details not available

NEW ENGLAND COMPRESSED GAS CO.
Purchased by Air Reduction Co. in 1927
Details not available

NEW ENGLAND CORP (CT)
Merged into New England Corp. (DE) 01/06/1987
Each share 80¢ Preferred no par exchanged for (1) share Class A Non-Vtg. no par
Each share Common 10¢ par exchanged for (1) share Class A Non-Vtg. no par
Note: No certificates of Class A shares will be issued. Holders received a Receipt evidencing their beneficial ownership of Class A shares which Receipt will be entitled to only cash

NEW ENGLAND CRITICAL CARE INC (DE)
Common 10¢ par split (2) for (1) by issuance of (1) additional share 3/31/90
Name changed to Critical Care America, Inc. 3/29/91
Critical Care America, Inc. merged into Medical Care America, Inc. 9/9/92 which merged into Columbia/HCA Healthcare Corp. 9/16/94 which name changed to HCA - The Healthcare Co. 5/25/2000 which name changed to HCA Inc. (Ctfs. dated after 6/29/2001) 6/29/2001
(See HCA Inc. (Ctfs. dated after 6/29/2001))

NEW ENGLAND DRESSED MEAT & WOOL CO.
Acquired by Swift & Co. (IL) in 1931
Details not available

NEW ENGLAND ELEC SYS (MA)
Common $20 par changed to $1 par in 1949
Common $1 par split (2) for (1) by issuance of (1) additional share 2/21/86
Merged into National Grid Group plc 3/22/2000
Each share Common $1 par exchanged for $54.207032 cash

NEW ENGLAND ELECTRIC SECURITIES CO.
Bankrupt in 1929
Details not available

NEW ENGLAND FISH CO (ME)
Each share Class B Common no par exchanged for (50) shares Common $1 par 12/16/69
Stock Dividends - 10% 6/15/73; 15% 6/24/74
Adjudicated bankrupt 5/5/80
Stockholders' equity unlikely

NEW ENGLAND FUEL OIL CO. OF MASSACHUSETTS
Name changed to New England Fuel Oil Corp. in 1929
(See New England Fuel Oil Corp.)

NEW ENGLAND FUEL OIL CORP.
In liquidation in 1945
Details not available

NEW ENGLAND FDS TR I (MA)
Name changed 04/18/1994
Bond Income Fund Shares of Bene. Int. no par split (3) for (1) by issuance of (2) additional shares 03/16/1987
Equity Income Fund Shares of Bene. Int. no par split (3) for (1) by issuance of (2) additional shares 03/16/1987
Growth Fund Shares of Bene. Int. no par split (3) for (1) by issuance of (2) additional shares 03/16/1987
Retirement Equity Fund Shares of Bene. Int. no par split (3) for (1) by issuance of (2) additional shares 03/16/1987
Tax Exempt Income Fund Shares of Bene. Int. no par split (3) for (1) by issuance of (2) additional shares 03/16/1987
Equity Income Fund Shares of Bene. Int. no par reclassified as Balanced Fund Shares of Bene. Int. no par 03/01/1990
Balanced Fund Shares of Bene. Int. no par reclassified as TNE Balanced Fund 04/01/1992
Bond Income Fund Shares of Bene. Int. no par reclassified as TNE Bond Income Fund Shares of Bene. Int. no par 04/01/1992
Global Government Fund Shares of Bene. Int. no par reclassified as TNE Global Government Fund Shares of Bene. Int. no par 04/01/1992
Government Securities Fund Shares of Bene. Int. no par reclassified as TNE Government Securities Fund Shares of Bene. Int. no par 04/01/1992
Growth Fund Shares of Bene. Int. no par reclassified as TNE Growth Fund Shares of Bene. Int. no par 04/01/1992
Retirement Equity Fund Shares of Bene. Int. no par reclassified as TNE Retirement Equity Fund Shares of Bene. Int. no par 04/01/1992
Tax Exempt Income Fund Shares of Bene. Int. no par reclassified as TNE Tax Exempt Income Fund Shares of Bene. Int. no par 04/01/1992
Name changed from New England Funds to New England Funds Trust I and TNE Balanced Fund no par, TNE Bond Income Fund no par, TNE Global Government Fund no par, TNE Government Securities Fund no par, TNE Growth Fund no par, TNE International Equity Fund no par, TNE Retirement Equity Fund no par and TNE Tax Exempt Income Fund no par reclassified as Balanced Fund no par, Bond Income Fund no par, Global Government Fund no par, Government Securities Fund no par, Growth Fund no par, International Equity Fund no par, Value Fund no par and Tax Exempt Income Fund no par respectively 04/18/1994
Name changed to Nvest Funds Trust I 02/01/2000
Nvest Funds Trust I name changed to CDC Nvest Funds Trust I 05/01/2001
(See CDC Nvest Funds Trust I)

NEW ENGLAND FDS TR II (MA)
Adjustable Rate U.S. Government Fund reclassified as Short Term Corporate Income Fund 12/01/1998
Name changed to Nvest Funds Trust II 02/01/2000
Nvest Funds Trust II name changed to CDC Nvest Funds Trust II 05/01/2001
(See CDC Nvest Funds Trust II)

NEW ENGLAND FDS TR III (MA)
Reorganized as Nvest Funds Trust III 02/01/2000
Details not available

NEW ENGLAND GAS & ELEC ASSN (MA)
Each share $5.50 Preferred no par exchanged for (8) Common Shares of Bene. Int. $8 par 00/00/1947
4.5% Preferred $100 par called for redemption 07/01/1959
Common Shares of Bene. Int. $8 par changed to $4 par and (1) additional Share issued 01/18/1966
Name changed to Commonwealth Energy System 05/11/1981
Commonwealth Energy System merged into NSTAR 08/25/1998 which merged into Northeast Utilities 04/10/2012 which name changed to Eversource Energy 02/19/2015

NEW ENGLAND GRAIN PRODUCTS CO. (ME)
Common no par changed to $5 par 00/00/1934
Common $5 par changed to $1 par 00/00/1934
Merged into Corn Products Refining Co. 05/20/1955
Each share Common $1 par exchanged for (2.1) shares Common $10 par
Corn Products Refining Co. merged into Corn Products Co. (NJ) 09/30/1958 which reincorporated in Delaware 04/30/1959 which name changed to CPC International Inc. 04/23/1969 which name changed to BestFoods 01/01/1998
(See BestFoods)

NEW ENGLAND INVESTMENT & SECURITY CO.
Merged into New York, New Haven & Hartford Railroad Co. under plan of reorganization on basis of (1) share Common no par for each $100 of allowed claims 5/26/48
(See New York, New Haven & Hartford Railroad Co.)

NEW ENGLAND INVESTMENT CO. (RI)
Charter forfeited for non-payment of taxes 10/15/1919

NEW ENGLAND INVESTMENT TRUST, INC.
Name changed to New England Investors Shares, Inc. which was then liquidated in 1929

NEW ENGLAND INVESTORS SHARES, INC.
Liquidated in 1929
Details not available

NEW ENGLAND LAUNDRIES INC (MA)
Reorganized in 1936
Each share Preferred $100 par exchanged for (4) shares new Common no par
Each share old Common no par exchanged for (0.3) share new Common no par
Liquidation completed
Each share Common no par exchanged for initial distribution of (2.47) shares Puritan Fund, Inc. (MA) Capital Stock $1 par 12/29/70
Each share Common no par received second distribution of $0.55 cash 12/28/71
Each share Common no par received third and final distribution of $1.50 cash 9/11/72
Puritan Fund, Inc. (MA) name changed to Fidelity Puritan Fund, Inc. 11/18/80

NEW ENGLAND LIFE GOVT SECS TR (MA)
Under plan of reorganization each Share of Bene. Int. no par automatically became (1) New England Funds Government Securities Fund Share of Bene. Int. no par 01/09/1987
New England Funds name changed to New England Funds Trust I 04/18/1994 which name changed to Nvest Funds Trust I 02/01/2000 which name changed to CDC Nvest Funds Trust I 05/01/2001
(See CDC Nvest Funds Trust I)

NEW ENGLAND LIFE SIDE FD INC (MA)
Name changed to NEL Retirement Equity Fund, Inc. 12/15/1977
NEL Retirement Equity Fund, Inc. merged into New England Funds 01/09/1987 which name changed to New England Funds Trust I 04/18/1994 which name changed to Nvest Funds Trust I 02/01/2000 which name changed to CDC Nvest Funds Trust I 05/01/2001
(See CDC Nvest Funds Trust I)

NEW ENGLAND LIME CO. (DE)
Recapitalized as New England Lime Co. (MA) in 1935
Details not available

NEW ENGLAND LIME CO. (MA)
Common no par changed to $5 par 4/1/54
Each share Common $5 par exchanged for (3) shares Common $2 par 4/15/55
Merged into Pfizer (Chas.) & Co., Inc. (DE) on a (1.5) for (1) basis 10/18/61
Pfizer (Chas.) & Co., Inc. (DE) name changed to Pfizer Inc. 4/27/70

NEW ENGLAND MERCHANTS INC (MA)
Reincorporated 03/31/1971
State of incorporation changed from (DE) to (MA) 03/31/1971
Name changed to Bank of New England Corp. 05/01/1982
(See Bank of New England Corp.)

NEW ENGLAND MERCHANTS NATL BK (BOSTON, MA)
Capital Stock $10 par changed to $5 par and (1) additional share issued 05/26/1969
Stock Dividend - 25% 02/20/1968
Under plan of reorganization each share Capital Stock $5 par automatically became (1) share of New England Merchants Co., Inc. (DE) Common $5 par 06/18/1970
New England Merchants Co., Inc. (DE) reincorporated in Massachusetts 03/31/1971 which name changed to Bank of New England Corp. 05/01/1982
(See Bank of New England Corp.)

NEW ENGLAND NATIONAL BANK (BOSTON, MA)
Merged into New England Merchants National Bank (Boston, MA) 12/31/60
Each share Capital Stock $10 par exchanged for (1) share Capital Stock $10 par
New England Merchants National Bank (Boston, MA) reorganized in Delaware as New England Merchants Co., Inc. 6/18/70 which reincorporated in Massachusetts 3/31/71 which name changed to Bank of New England Corp. 5/1/82
(See Bank of New England Corp.)

NEW ENGLAND NUCLEAR CORP (IN)
Reincorporated 12/05/1975
Each share Common no par exchanged for (4) shares Common $1 par 05/01/1967
State of incorporation changed from (MA) to (IN) 12/05/1975
Common $1 par split (2) for (1) by issuance of (1) additional share 06/23/1978
Common $1 par split (2) for (1) by issuance of (1) additional share 06/22/1979
Merged into Du Pont (E.I.) De Nemours & Co. 04/09/1981
Each share Common $1 par exchanged for (1.3) shares Common $1.66666666 par
Du Pont (E.I.) De Nemours & Co. merged into DowDuPont Inc. 09/01/2017

NEW ENGLAND PATRIOTS FOOTBALL CLUB INC (MA)
Merged into New Patriots Football Club, Inc. 1/31/77
Each share Common Non-Voting $1 par exchanged for $15 cash

NEW ENGLAND POWER ASSOCIATION (MA)
Reorganized as New England Electric System 6/3/47
Each share 6% Preferred $100 par exchanged for (5.4) shares Common $20 par
Each share $2 Preferred no par exchanged for (1.8) shares Common $20 par
Each share Common no par exchanged for (0.65) share Common $20 par
(See New England Electric System)

NEW ENGLAND PWR CO (MA)
5.52% Preferred $100 par called for redemption 1/10/63
11.04% Preferred $25 par called for redemption 7/16/86
13.48% Preferred $100 par called for redemption 9/1/87
8.40% Preferred $100 par called for redemption 9/1/93
8.68% Preferred $100 par called for redemption 9/1/93
7.24% Preferred $100 par called for redemption 5/1/96
4.56% Preferred $100 par called for redemption at $104.08 on 10/23/98
4.60% Preferred $100 par called for redemption at $101 on 10/23/98
4.64% Preferred $100 par called for redemption at $102.56 on 10/23/98
6.08% Preferred $100 par called for redemption at $102.34 on 10/23/98

NEW ENGLAND PUBLIC SERVICE CO. (ME)
Liquidated 00/00/1953
Each share $7 Preferred no par and Adjustment Series Preferred no par received (6) shares Central Maine Power Co. Common $10 par, (1.3) shares Central Vermont Public Service Corp. Common $6 par, (2.8) shares Public Service Co. of New Hampshire Common $10 par and a dividend adjustment of $0.8517 cash
Each share $6 Preferred no par received (5.25) shares Central Maine Power Co. Common $10 par, (1.15) shares Central Vermont Public Service Corp. Common $6 par, (2.45) shares Public Service Co. of New Hampshire Common $10 par and a dividend adjustment of $0.71779 cash
Each share Common $5 par received (0.19) share Central Maine Power Co. Common $10 par, (0.04) share Central Vermont Public Service Corp. Common $6 par and (0.09) share Public Service Co. of New Hampshire Common $10 par
(See each company's listing)

NEW ENGLAND REAL ESTATE TRUST
Dissolved in 1951
Details not available

NEW ENGLAND SVGS BK (NEW LONDON, CT)
Reorganized under the laws of Delaware as NESB Corp. and Common $1 par changed to 1¢ par 9/16/87
(See NESB Corp.)

NEW ENGLAND SOUTHERN CORP.
Bankrupt in 1933
Details not available

NEW ENGLAND SOUTHERN MILLS
Acquired by New England Southern Corp. in 1928
Details not available

NEW ENGLAND TAX EXEMPT MONEY MKT TR NEW (MA)
Name changed to Nvest Tax Exempt Money Market Trust 02/01/2000
Nvest Tax Exempt Money Market Trust name changed to CDC Nvest Tax Exempt Money Market Trust 05/01/2001
(See CDC Nvest Tax Exempt Money Market Trust)

NEW ENGLAND TAX EXEMPT MONEY MKT TR OLD (MA)
Name changed to TNE Tax Exempt Money Market Trust 04/01/1992
TNE Tax Exempt Money Market Trust name changed to New England Tax Exempt Money Market Trust (New) 04/18/1994 which name changed to Nvest Tax Exempt Money Market Trust 02/01/2000 which name changed to CDC Nvest Tax Exempt Money Market Trust 05/01/2001
(See CDC Nvest Tax Exempt Money Market Trust)

NEW ENGLAND TEL & TELEG CO (NY)
Capital Stock $100 par changed to $20 par and (4) additional shares issued 10/26/59
Merged into American Telephone & Telegraph Co. 12/22/80
Each share Capital Stock $20 par exchanged for (0.75) share Common $16-2/3 par
American Telephone & Telegraph Co. name changed to AT&T Corp. 4/20/94 which merged into AT&T Inc. 11/18/2005

NEW ENGLAND THEATRES OPERATING CORP.
Name changed to American Theatres Corp. in 1948
(See American Theatres Corp.)

NEW ENGLAND TRANSFORMER INC (MA)
Involuntarily dissolved 08/31/1998

NEW ENGLAND TRUST CO. (BOSTON, MA)
Each share Capital Stock $100 par exchanged for (5) shares Capital Stock $20 par in 1949
Each share Capital Stock $20 par exchanged for (4) shares Capital Stock $10 par to effect a (2) for (1) split and a 100% stock dividend 3/29/56
Name changed to New England National Bank (Boston, MA) 10/31/60
New England National Bank (Boston, MA) merged into New England Merchants National Bank (Boston, MA) 12/31/60 which reorganized in Delaware as New England Merchants Co., Inc. 6/10/70 which reincorporated in Massachusetts 3/31/71 which name changed to Bank of New England Corp. 5/1/82
(See Bank of New England Corp.)

NEW ENGLISH VENTURES LIMITED (ISRAEL)
Reincorporated under the laws of California as Enjoy Media Holdings Ltd. 05/09/2005
Enjoy Media Holdings Ltd. name changed to Square Inn Budget Hotels Management, Inc. 06/29/2007

NEW ENVIRONMENTAL SOLUTIONS INC (WA)
Each share old Common $0.001 par exchanged for (2) shares new Common new Common $0.001 par 10/16/2006
Charter expired 08/30/2009

NEW ENVIRONMENTAL TECHNOLOGIES INC (MN)
Name changed to Keystone Energy Services Inc. 3/8/97
(See Keystone Energy Services Inc.)

NEW ENVIRONMENTAL TECHNOLOGIES INC (NV)
Each share old Common $0.001 par exchanged for (0.004) share new Common $0.001 par 10/01/1995
Name changed to Victory Capital Holdings Corp. 04/28/2003
Victory Capital Holdings Corp. name changed to Victory Energy Corp. 05/11/2006 which name changed to Victory Oilfield Tech, Inc. 05/31/2018

NEW ENVOY INC (DE)
Name changed to Envoy Corp. (New) 7/12/95
Envoy Corp. (New) merged into Quintiles Transnational Corp. 3/30/99
(See Quintiles Transnational Corp.)

NEW ERA BK (SOMMERSET, NJ)
Merged into United National Bancorp 6/30/95
Each share Common $5 par exchanged for (0.7431) share Common $5 par
(See United National Bancorp)

NEW ERA DEVS LTD (BC)
Struck off register and declared dissolved for failure to file returns 4/22/94

NEW ERA ELECTRIC RANGE CO.
Merged into Armstrong Electric & Manufacturing Corp. in 1928
(See Armstrong Electric & Manufacturing Corp.)

NEW ERA INDS INC (UT)
Recapitalized 12/3/71
Recapitalized from New Era, Inc. to New Era Industries, Inc. 12/3/71
Each share Common 1¢ par exchanged for (0.05) share Common 1¢ par
Charter supended for failure to pay taxes 12/31/76

NEW ERA MARKETING INC (NV)
Common $0.001 par split (12) for (1) by issuance of (11) additional shares payable 11/20/2006 to holders of record 11/17/2006 Ex date - 11/21/2006
Name changed to Fearless International, Inc. 01/30/2007
(See Fearless International, Inc.)

NEW ERA MINES INC (ID)
Charter forfeited for failure to file reports 12/1/93

NEW ERA MINING CO. (DE)
Charter cancelled and declared inoperative and void for non-payment of taxes 03/01/1977

NEW ERA OF NETWORKS INC (DE)
Secondary Offering - 4,400,000 shares COM offered at $34 per share on 12/04/1998
Common $0.0001 par split (2) for (1) by issuance of (1) additional share payable 12/09/1998 to holders of record 11/23/1998
Merged into Sybase, Inc. 06/19/2001
Each share Common $0.0001 par exchanged for (0.3878) share Common $0.001 par
(See Sybase, Inc.)

NEW-ERA TECHNOLOGIES INTL INC (DE)
Recapitalized as Global Electronics Manufacturing Inc. 5/3/99
Each share Common $0.001 par exchanged for (0.005) share Common $0.001 par
Global Electronics Manufacturing Inc. name changed to ECS Industries Inc. 8/19/99 which recapitalized as Infoserve Global Holdings Corp. 2/6/2002

NEW FAMILY WELCOME KIT INC (NY)
Name changed to Sampling Research Corp. 3/18/71
Sampling Research Corp. name changed to Cable Holdings Inc. 8/19/75
(See Cable Holdings Inc.)

NEW FAR NORTH EXPL LTD (AB)
Charter cancelled 11/00/1977

NEW FAULKENHAM MINES LTD. (ON)
Acquired by Starratt Nickel Mines Ltd. 07/09/1963
Each free share Capital Stock $10 par exchanged for (0.1) free share and (0.9) escrowed share Capital Stock $1 par
Escrowed shares exchanged share for share Starratt Nickel Mines Ltd. recapitalized as Starratt Resources Ltd. 10/31/1994
(See Starratt Resources Ltd.)

NEW FEDERAL CHIBOUGAMAU MINES LTD. (ON)
Charter cancelled for failure to file reports and pay taxes 07/27/1976

NEW FENIMORE IRON MINES LTD (QC)
Acquired by Westburne Petroleum Services Ltd. 6/16/73
Each share Capital Stock no par exchanged for $0.20 cash

NEW FIBERS INTL LTD (BC)
Struck off register and declared dissolved for failure to file returns 2/25/94

NEW FIDELITY MINERALS LTD. (AB)
Acquired by Kenting Ltd. 05/00/1975
Each share Common no par exchanged for $0.105 cash

NEW FLYER INDS INC / NEW FLYER INDS CDA ULC (ON)
Note: Each IDS consists of (1) share Common and $55.30 principal amount of 14% Subordinated Notes of New Flyer Industries Canada ULC
Each new Income Deposit Security automatically became (0.1) new Income Deposit Security 10/05/2011
Under plan of reorganization each new Income Deposit Security automatically became (1) share New Flyer Industries Inc. Common no par and $58.065 cash 08/20/2012
New Flyer Industries Inc. name changed to NFI Group Inc. 05/18/2018

NEW FLYER INDS INC (ON)
Each share old Common no par automatically became (0.1) share new Common no par 10/05/2011
Name changed to NFI Group Inc. 05/18/2018

NEW FOCUS INC (DE)
Issue Information - 5,000,000 shares COM offered at $20 per share on 05/18/2000
Merged into Bookham Technology PLC (England & Wales) 03/08/2004
Each share Common $0.001 par exchanged for either (1.2015) Ordinary shares 1/3p par or (1.2015) Sponsored ADR's for Ordinary 1/3p par
Note: Option to receive Ordinary shares expired 05/10/2004
Bookham Technology PLC (England & Wales) reorganized in Delaware as Bookham, Inc. 09/10/2004 which name changed to Oclaro, Inc. 04/27/2009

NEW FORCE CRAG MINES LTD (ON)
Charter cancelled for failure to pay taxes and file returns 7/12/82

NEW FORMAQUE MINES LTD (QC)
Recapitalized as Sobiga Mines Ltd.-Les Mines Sobiga Ltee. 1/16/74
Each share Capital Stock $1 par exchanged for (0.1) share Capital Stock $1 par
(See Sobiga Mines Ltd.-Les Mines Sobiga Ltee.)

NEW FORTUNE MINES LTD. (ON)
Recapitalized as United New Fortune Mines Ltd. on a (1) for (4) basis 7/11/58
(See United New Fortune Mines Ltd.)

NEW FORTY FOUR MINES LTD (MB)
Merged into Canadian Gold Mines Ltd. 3/24/86
Each share Capital Stock no par exchanged for (1) share Common no par
Canadian Gold Mines Ltd. merged into Consolidated Canadian Fortune Resources Inc. 12/6/90 which name changed to Canadian Fortune Resources Inc. (New) 3/15/93 which merged into Fortune Energy Inc. 9/1/93
(See Fortune Energy Inc.)

NEW FOUND SHRIMP INC (FL)
Each share old Common $0.00001 par exchanged for (0.00002) share new Common $0.00001 par 12/28/2012
Name changed to Innovate Building Systems, Inc. 04/23/2014
Innovate Building Systems, Inc. name changed to Xterra Building Systems, Inc. 09/30/2014 which name changed to North America Frac Sand, Inc. 08/14/2015

NEW FRANKLIN OIL & REFINING CO. (CA)
Charter forfeited for failure to pay taxes 11/30/06

NEW FRONTIER EXPLORATION INC. (BC)
Name changed to New Frontier Petroleum, Inc. 4/7/81
New Frontier Petroleum, Inc. merged into New Frontier Petroleum Corp. 1/18/82 which recapitalized as PetroMac Energy Inc. 8/30/85
(See PetroMac Energy Inc.)

NEW FRONTIER MEDIA INC (CO)
Acquired by LFP Broadcasting, LLC 11/28/2012
Each share Common $0.0001 par exchanged for $2.06 cash

NEW FRONTIER MINING & MILLING CO., INC. (NM)
Charter forfeited for failure to pay taxes 10/11/62

NEW FRONTIER PETE CORP (BC)
Recapitalized as PetroMac Energy Inc. 8/30/85
Each share Common no par exchanged for (0.2) share Common no par
(See PetroMac Energy Inc.)

NEW FRONTIER PETE INC (BC)
Merged into New Frontier Petroleum Corp. 1/18/82
Each share Common no par exchanged for (1) share Common no par
New Frontier Petroleum Corp. recapitalized as PetroMac Energy Inc. 8/30/85
(See PetroMac Energy Inc.)

NEW GAS EXPLORATION CO. OF ALBERTA LTD. (AB)
Merged into Medallion Petroleums Ltd. 06/18/1958
Each share Capital Stock $1 par exchanged for (0.5) share Common $1.25 par
Medallion Petroleums Ltd. merged into Canadian Industrial Gas & Oil Ltd. 03/08/1965 which merged into Norcen Energy Resources Ltd. (AB) 10/28/1975 which reincorporated under the laws of Canada 04/15/1977 which merged into Union Pacific Resources Group Inc. 04/17/1998 which merged into Anadarko Petroleum Corp. 07/14/2000

NEW GAS LIGHT CO. OF JANESVILLE
Acquired by Wisconsin Power & Light Co. in 1927
Details not available

NEW GATEWAY OILS & MINERALS LTD (AB)
Merged into Killucan Resources Ltd. 9/30/81
Each share Capital Stock no par exchanged for (1) share Class A Common no par
Killucan Resources Ltd. merged into Skill Resources Ltd. 8/17/83 which recapitalized as Unicorp Resources Ltd. 6/27/84 which was acquired by Asamera Inc. 5/1/86 which was acquired by Gulf Canada Resources Ltd. 8/4/88
(See Gulf Canada Resources Ltd.)

NEW GENERATION BIOFUELS HLDGS INC (FL)
Administratively dissolved 09/28/2012

NEW GENERATION FOODS INC (NV)
Each share old Common 1¢ par exchanged for (0.125) share new Common 1¢ par 01/23/1992
Each share new Common 1¢ par exchanged again for (0.2) share new Common 1¢ par 11/01/1992
Name changed to CreditRiskMonitor.com Inc. 05/11/1999

NEW GENERATION HLDGS INC (DE)
Name changed 08/08/2000
Name changed from New Generation Plastic, Inc. to New Generation Holdings, Inc. 08/08/2000
Each share Common $0.001 par received distribution of (1) share Plastinum Corp. Common 1¢ par payable 02/20/2007 to holders of record 02/20/2007
Each share old Common $0.001 par exchanged for (0.1) share new Common $0.001 par 08/01/2008
SEC revoked common stock registration 01/21/2014

NEW GLACIER EXPLORERS LTD (ON)
Charter cancelled for failure to pay taxes and file returns 10/24/73

NEW GLOBAL VENTURES INTL LTD (BC)
Name changed to Auro Resources Corp. 10/15/2010
Auro Resources Corp. recapitalized as Tesoro Minerals Corp. 08/26/2013

NEW GLOBAL VENTURES LTD (BC)
Recapitalized as New Global Ventures International Ltd. 03/14/2008
Each share Common no par exchanged for (0.5) share Common no par
New Global Ventures International Ltd. name changed to Auro Resources Corp. 10/15/2010 which recapitalized as Tesoro Minerals Corp. 08/26/2013

NEW GOLD DLR MNG CO (CO)
Name changed to Tax Specialist, Inc. and Common 5¢ par changed to 1¢ par 7/23/71
(See Tax Specialist, Inc.)

NEW GOLD INC (NV)
Each share Common $0.001 par exchanged for (0.1) share Common 1¢ par 05/12/1989
Name changed to American Resource Corp., Inc. 08/19/1991
American Resource Corp., Inc. merged into Rea Gold Corp. 06/26/1996
(See Rea Gold Corp.)

NEW GOLD STAR MINES LTD (BC)
Recapitalized as Norwich Resources Ltd. 8/9/73
Each share Common no par exchanged for (0.2) share Common no par
Norwich Resources Ltd. recapitalized as Kelly Petroleum Inc. 1/29/80 which merged into New Frontier Petroleum Corp. 1/18/82 which recapitalized as PetroMac Energy Inc. 8/30/85
(See PetroMac Energy Inc.)

NEW GOLDBRAE DEVS LTD (BC)
Struck off register and declared dissolved for failure to file returns 5/13/94

NEW GOLDCORE VENTURES LTD (BC)
Recapitalized as Namex Explorations, Inc. 12/8/97
Each share Common no par exchanged for (1/7) share Common no par

NEW GOLDEN ROSE MINES LTD.
Liquidated in 1942
Details not available

NEW GOLDEN SCEPTRE MINERALS LTD (BC)
Delisted from Vancouver Stock Exchange 03/01/1999

NEW GOLDVUE MINES LTD (ON)
Capital Stock $1 par changed to no par 09/08/1971
Recapitalized as Lava Cap Resources Ltd. 04/06/1979
Each share Capital Stock no par exchanged for (0.2) share Capital Stock no par

NEW-NEW   FINANCIAL INFORMATION, INC.

Lava Cap Resources Ltd. name changed to Lava Capital Corp. 11/14/1985 which recapitalized as Samoth Capital Corp. 02/17/1988 which name changed to Sterling Financial Corp. 06/14/2000 which name changed to Sterling Centrecorp Inc. 06/08/2001
(See Sterling Centrecorp Inc.)

NEW GOLF CONCEPTS INC (CO)
Name changed to Innova Corp. 10/1/91

NEW GOLIATH MINERALS LTD (BC)
Merged into Hughes Lang Corp. 08/01/1989
Each share Common no par exchanged for (0.0812) share Class B Subordinate no par
Hughes Lang Corp. merged into CanGold Resources Inc. (BC) 01/31/1994 which reorganized in Ontario as Amalgamated CanGold Inc. 07/31/1995 which merged into Central Asia Goldfields Corp. 01/08/1996
(See Central Asia Goldfields Corp.)

NEW GRANDROY RES INC (ON)
Recapitalized as Hillsborough Exploration Ltd. 11/24/1980
Each share Capital Stock no par exchanged for (0.1) share Capital Stock no par
Hillsborough Exploration Ltd. name changed to Hillsborough Resources Ltd. (ON) 03/13/1987 which reincorporated in Canada 11/05/1997
(See Hillsborough Resources Ltd. (Canada))

NEW GREEN TECHNOLOGIES INC (FL)
Recapitalized as Spur Ranch, Inc. 08/25/2010
Each (3,500) shares Common $0.001 par exchanged for (1) share Common $0.001 par
Spur Ranch, Inc. name changed to Rounder, Inc. 01/24/2012 which name changed to Fortitude Group, Inc. 01/08/2013

NEW GROUSE CREEK MINES LTD (BC)
Merged into Westburne Petroleum Services Ltd. 09/18/1972
Each share Capital Stock no par exchanged for $0.0575 cash

NEW GUINEA ENERGY LTD (AUSTRALIA)
Basis changed from (1:50) to (1:2.5) 04/05/2017
ADR agreement terminated 07/18/2017
Each Sponsored ADR for Ordinary exchanged for $1.206171 cash

NEW GUINEA GOLD CORP (YUKON)
Reincorporated under the laws of British Columbia 10/20/2005

NEW HAMIL SILVER LEAD MINES LTD (BC)
Struck off register and declared dissolved for failure to file returns 5/4/72

NEW HAMPSHIRE BALL BEARINGS INC (NH)
Common $2 par split (2) for (1) by issuance of (1) additional share 12/01/1980
Stock Dividends - 10% 08/19/1966; 25% 08/18/1967
Acquired by Minebea Co. Ltd. 03/05/1985
Each share Common $2 par exchanged for $63.50 cash
Note: An additional and final distribution of $0.9091994 cash per share was made 08/29/1985

NEW HAMPSHIRE BANKSHARES INC (NH)
Class A Common $5 par and Class B Common $5 par reclassified as Common $5 par 4/25/63
Name changed to Indian Head Banks, Inc. 6/6/72
Indian Head Banks, Inc. acquired by Fleet/Norstar Financial Group, Inc. 12/21/88 which name changed to Fleet Financial Group, Inc. (New) 4/15/92 which name changed to Fleet Boston Corp. 10/1/99 which name changed to FleetBoston Financial Corp. 4/18/2000 which merged into Bank of America Corp. 4/1/2004

NEW HAMPSHIRE FIRE INSURANCE CO. (NH)
Each share Capital Stock $100 par exchanged for (10) shares Capital Stock $10 par in 1929
Name changed to New Hampshire Insurance Co. 9/30/59
New Hampshire Insurance Co. acquired by American International Group, Inc. 2/24/71

NEW HAMPSHIRE INS CO (NH)
Capital Stock $10 par changed to $5 par and (1) additional share issued 4/16/62
Acquired by American International Group, Inc. 2/24/71
Each share Capital Stock $5 par exchanged for (1) share $2 Conv. Preferred Ser. A $5 par

NEW HAMPSHIRE JOCKEY CLUB INC (NH)
Each 1965 Voting Trust Certificate exchanged for (1) 1975 Voting Trust Certificate in October 1975
Proclaimed dissolved 8/8/90

NEW HAMPSHIRE POWER CO.
Acquired by Public Service Co. of New Hampshire 00/00/1936
Details not available

NEW HAMPSHIRE RACING & BREEDERS ASSOCIATION
Name changed to New Hampshire Jockey Club, Inc. in 1934
(See New Hampshire Jockey Club, Inc.)

NEW HAMPSHIRE SVGS BK CORP (NH)
Common $1 par split (2) for (1) by issuance of (1) additional share 6/15/86
Closed by FDIC 10/10/91
No stockholders' equity

NEW HAMPSHIRE THRIFT BANCSHARES INC (DE)
Common 1¢ par split (2) for (1) by issuance of (1) additional share payable 02/28/2005 to holders of record 02/14/2005 Ex date - 03/01/2005
Name changed to Lake Sunapee Bank Group 06/01/2015
Lake Sunapee Bank Group merged into Bar Harbor Bankshares 01/13/2017

NEW HAMPSHIRE TRACTION CO. (NH)
Dissolved in 1933
Details not available

NEW HANA COPPER MNG LTD (BC)
Name changed to Handa Copper Corp. 04/25/2014
Handa Copper Corp. name changed to Handa Mining Corp. 06/13/2018

NEW HARDING GROUP INC (ON)
Name changed to Clarus Corp. 6/19/89
(See Clarus Corp.)

NEW HARRICANA MINES LTD (QC)
Charter cancelled for failure to file reports and pay fees 8/13/74

NEW HARVEST CAP CORP (DE)
Name changed to Azur Holdings, Inc. 01/23/2006
(See Azur Holdings, Inc.)

NEW HAVEN BANK, N.B.A. (NEW HAVEN, CT)
Each share Capital Stock $50 par exchanged for (2) shares Capital Stock $25 par 9/30/55
Stock Dividend - 25% 4/17/53
Merged into First New Haven National Bank (New Haven, CT) 9/27/57
Each share Capital Stock $25 par exchanged for (3.25) shares Common $10 par
First New Haven National Bank (New Haven, CT) name changed to First Bank of New Haven (New Haven, CT) 4/1/77 which reorganized as FirstBancorp, Inc. (CT) 2/1/79 which merged into Hartford National Corp. 3/30/84 which merged into Shawmut National Corp. 2/29/88 which merged into Fleet Financial Group Inc. (New) 11/30/95 which name changed to Fleet Boston Corp. 10/1/99 which name changed to FleetBoston Financial Corp. 4/18/2000 which merged into Bank of America Corp. 4/1/2004

NEW HAVEN BOARD & CARTON CO., INC. (CT)
Each share Common $12.50 par exchanged for (3) shares Common $10 par in 1954
Common $10 par changed to $1 par 2/28/64
Name changed to Simkins Industries, Inc. 9/1/67
(See Simkins Industries, Inc.)

NEW HAVEN CLOCK & WATCH CO. (CT)
Common no par changed to $1 par in 1947
Each share 4-1/2% Preferred $20 par exchanged for (1) share 50¢ Preferred no par and (1) share Common $1 par 9/30/55
Each share 50¢ Preferred no par exchanged for (0.5) share new Common $1 par 2/20/58
Each share old Common $1 par exchanged for (0.125) share new Common $1 par 2/20/58
Under plan of merger reincorporated under the laws of Delaware as Haven Industries, Inc. and Common $1 par changed to 10¢ par 4/30/62
Haven Industries, Inc. name changed to Federated Communications Corp. 4/29/75
(See Federated Communications Corp.)

NEW HAVEN CLOCK CO. (CT)
6-1/2% Preferred Ser. A $100 par called for redemption 4/20/46
Recapitalized as New Haven Clock & Watch Co. 5/1/46
Each share Common no par exchanged for (3) shares Common no par
New Haven Clock & Watch Co. reincorporated in Delaware as Haven Industries, Inc. 4/30/62 which name changed to Federated Communications Corp. 4/29/75
(See Federated Communications Corp.)

NEW HAVEN GAS CO. (CT)
Merged into Southern Connecticut Gas Co. 01/01/1967
Each share Common $25 par exchanged for (1) share Common $20 par
Southern Connecticut Gas Corp. reorganized as Connecticut Energy Corp. 05/01/1979 which merged into Energy East Corp. 02/08/2000
(See Energy East Corp.)

NEW HAVEN GAS LIGHT CO. (CT)
Name changed to New Haven Gas Co. 00/00/1953
New Haven Gas Co. merged into Southern Connecticut Gas Co. 01/01/1967 which reorganized as Connecticut Energy Corp. 05/01/1979 which merged into Energy East Corp. 02/08/2000
(See Energy East Corp.)

NEW HAVEN PULP & BOARD CO. (CT)
Each share Common $25 par exchanged for (2) shares Common $12.50 par in 1950
Name changed to New Haven Board & Carton Co. in 1953 which name changed to Simkins Industries, Inc. 9/1/67
(See Simkins Industries, Inc.)

NEW HAVEN SHORE LINE RAILWAY
Property sold to bondholders in 1934
Details not available

NEW HAVEN TRAP ROCK CO. (CT)
Common $50 par changed to no par and (2) additional shares issued 7/17/64
Completely liquidated 8/20/68
Each share Common no par exchanged for first and final distribution of (1.5) shares Ashland Oil & Refining Co. Common $1 par and $72.23 cash
Ashland Oil & Refining Co. name changed to Ashland Oil, Inc. 2/2/70 which name changed to Ashland Inc. (Old) 1/27/95
(See Ashland Inc. (Old))

NEW HAVEN WTR CO (CT)
Common Capital Stock $50 par changed to $25 par and (1) additional share issued 5/22/67
Merged into South Central Connecticut Regional Water Authority 8/26/80
Each share Common Capital Stock $25 par exchanged for $93 cash

NEW HEALTH TECHNOLOGIES INC (DE)
Name changed to Pubbs Worldwide, Inc. 09/09/1996
Pubbs Worldwide, Inc. recapitalized as Chasen's International Inc. 05/25/1999 which name changed to Tril-Medianet.Com, Inc. 07/21/1999 which name changed to Tec Factory, Inc. 11/28/2000

NEW HEALTH TECHNOLOGIES INC (UT)
Proclaimed dissolved for failure to pay taxes 10/21/1988

NEW HERITAGE BK (LAWRENCE, MA)
Closed by FDIC in 1994
Stockholders' equity unlikely

NEW HIBERNIAN RES INC (BC)
Name changed to E.C. Auto Centres Inc. 1/18/91
E.C. Auto Centres Inc. recapitalized as Python Oil & Gas Corp. 2/27/95 which recapitalized as Goldex Resources Corp. 7/4/2003

NEW HIGH RIDGE RES INC (BC)
Name changed to Newton Gold Corp. 02/07/2011
Newton Gold Corp. recapitalized as Chlormet Technologies Inc. 11/07/2013 which name changed to PUF Ventures Inc. 11/13/2015

NEW HIGHLAND VY MINES LTD (BC)
Merged into Great Manhattan Gold Corp. 08/21/1975
Each share Capital Stock no par exchanged for (1) share Capital Stock no par
(See Great Manhattan Gold Corp.)

NEW HIGHRIDGE MINING CO., LTD. (ON)
Recapitalized as Combined Metal Mines Ltd. 06/25/1958
Each share Capital Stock no par exchanged for (0.33333333) share Capital Stock no par
Combined Metal Mines Ltd. recapitalized as CME Resources Inc. 11/15/1979 which name

FINANCIAL INFORMATION, INC. **NEW-NEW**

changed to CME Capital Inc. 10/15/1986
(See CME Capital Inc.)

NEW HILARITY INC (NV)
Name changed 03/30/1999
Name, state of incorporation and par value changed from New Hilarity Mining Co. (ID) Common 10¢ par to New Hilarity Inc. (NV) Common $0.001 par 03/30/1999
Each share Common $0.001 par exchanged for (0.2) share Common $0.005 par 09/05/2000
Name changed to Orbit E-Commerce, Inc. 04/13/2001
(See Orbit E-Commerce, Inc.)

NEW HOLLAND, BLUE BALL & TERRE HILL STREET RAILWAY CO.
Merged into Conestoga Transportation Co. in 1932
Details not available

NEW HOLLAND FMRS NATL BK (NEW HOLLAND, PA)
Reorganized as Colonial Bancorp, Inc. (PA) 6/30/83
Each share Common $2.50 par exchanged for (1) share Common $2.50 par
Colonial Bancorp, Inc. (PA) merged into Dauphin Deposit Corp. 9/1/87 which merged into Allied Irish Banks, P.L.C. 7/8/97

NEW HOLLAND N V (NETHERLANDS)
Name changed to CNH Global N.V. 11/15/1999
CNH Global N.V. merged into CNH Industrial N.V. 09/29/2013

NEW HOMBRE RES LTD (BC)
Recapitalized as X.T.C. Resources Ltd. 03/20/1989
Each share Common no par exchanged for (0.4) share Common no par
(See X.T.C. Resources Ltd.)

NEW HOPE PORCUPINE GOLD MINES LTD (ON)
Charter cancelled and declared dissolved for failure to file returns and pay fees 07/27/1976

NEW HOPE RES CORP (BC)
Name changed to Hi Tech Ventures Inc. 01/31/1985
Hi Tech Ventures Inc. recapitalized as Pro-Tech Venture Corp. 09/07/1993
(See Pro-Tech Venture Corp.)

NEW HORIZON ED INC (UT)
Each share old Common 1¢ par exchanged for (0.02) share new Common 1¢ par 7/29/2000
Name changed to American Hospital Resources, Inc. 6/26/2002
American Hospital Resources, Inc. name changed to HAPS USA, Inc. 5/12/2005 which name changed to PGMI, Inc. 3/16/2006

NEW HORIZON GROUP INC (WY)
Administratively dissolved 05/10/2012

NEW HORIZON KIDS QUEST INC (MN)
Merged into New Horizon Acquisition Corp. 12/16/2004
Each share Common 1¢ par exchanged for $4 cash

NEW HORIZONS AWYS INC (NV)
Charter permanently revoked 10/31/2002

NEW HORIZONS CAP CORP (BC)
Completely liquidated 11/21/2003
Each share Common no par exchanged for first and final distribution of (0.8) share Chalk Media Corp. Common no par

NEW HORIZONS SVGS & LN ASSN (CA)
Guarantee Stock $10 par split (2) for (1) by issuance of (1) additional share 4/6/88
Stock Dividends - 10% 10/1/89; 10% 3/16/90; 10% 10/1/90; 10% 9/19/91; 15% 2/10/95
Merged into NHS Financial Inc. 12/1/95
Each share Common $10 par exchanged for (1) share Common no par
(See NHS Financial Inc.)

NEW HORIZONS WORLDWIDE INC (DE)
Old Common 1¢ par split (5) for (4) by issuance of (0.25) additional share payable 06/08/1999 to holders of record 05/18/1999
Each share old Common 1¢ par exchanged for (1) share new Common 1¢ par to reflect a (1) for (25) reverse split followed by a (25) for (1) forward split 09/17/2009
Note: Holders of (24) or fewer pre-split shares received $1.85 cash per share
Acquired by NWHW Holdings, Inc. 09/28/2012
Each share new Common 1¢ par exchanged for $2.17 cash

NEW HOSCO MINES LTD (ON)
Common $1 par changed to no par 02/29/1972
Charter cancelled for failure to pay taxes and file returns 11/07/1978

NEW HUGH MALARTIC MINES LTD. (ON)
Recapitalized as Alba Explorations Ltd. 08/12/1955
Each share Capital Stock $1 par exchanged for (0.25) share Capital Stock $1 par
Alba Explorations Ltd. was recapitalized as Accra Explorations Ltd. 12/21/1962 which merged into Xtra Developments Inc. 05/25/1972 which merged into Sumtra Diversified Inc. 08/30/1978

NEW IBERIA BANCORP INC (LA)
Common $10 par split (40) for (1) by issuance of (39) additional shares 8/29/95
Common $10 par split (3) for (2) by issuance of (0.5) additional share payable 9/24/96 to holders of record 9/10/96 Ex date - 9/25/96
Merged into Regions Financial Corp. (Old) 5/31/97
Each share Common $10 par exchanged for (0.72) share Common $0.625 par
Regions Financial Corp. (Old) merged into Regions Financial Corp. (New) 7/1/2004

NEW IBERIA NATIONAL BANK (NEW IBERIA, LA)
Reorganized as New Iberia National Bancorp, Inc. 5/1/84
Each share Common $10 par exchanged for (1) share Common $10 par
New Iberia National Bancorp, Inc. merged into Regions Financial Corp. (Old) 5/31/97 which merged into Regions Financial Corp. (New) 7/1/2004

NEW IDEA, INC.
Acquired by Aviation Corp. 11/30/46
Each share Common no par exchanged for (3.5) shares Common $3 par
Aviation Corp. name changed to Avco Manufacturing Corp. 3/25/47 which name changed to Avco Corp. 4/10/59
(See Avco Corp.)

NEW IDEA CORP. (NY)
Charter revoked for failure to file reports and pay fees 12/16/29

NEW IDEA MARKETERS, INC. (DE)
Name changed to Dolphin Marine Corp. and Class A Common $1 par and Class B Common no par reclassified as Common 10¢ par 03/02/1972
Dolphin Marine Corp. name changed to Med-Test Systems, Inc. 01/12/1983 which recapitalized as Enxuta Corp. of America 06/10/1992

NEW IDRIA INC (NV)
Merged into Buckhorn Inc. (DE) 12/22/1981
Each share Common 50¢ par exchanged for (0.25) share Conv. Preferred Ser. A $1 par and (0.113879) share Common $1 par
(See Buckhorn Inc. (DE))

NEW IDRIA MINING & CHEMICAL CO. (NV)
Name changed to New Idria, Inc. 11/5/75
New Idria, Inc. merged into Buckhorn Inc. (DE) 12/22/81
(See Buckhorn Inc. (DE))

NEW IDRIA QUICKSILVER MINES, INC.
Property acquired by New Idria Quicksilver Mining Co. 7/3/36
No stockholders' equity

NEW IDRIA QUICKSILVER MINING CO. (NV)
Recapitalized as New Idria Mining & Chemical Co. 5/19/51
Each share Class A and Class B $1 par exchanged for (20) shares Common 50¢ par

NEW IMAGE CONCEPTS INC (NV)
Common $0.001 par split (3) for (1) by issuance of (2) additional shares payable 06/02/2008 to holders of record 05/13/2008 Ex date - 06/03/2008
Common $0.001 par split (6.6) for (1) by issuance of (5.6) additional shares payable 10/23/2009 to holders of record 10/22/2009 Ex date - 10/26/2009
Name changed to Car Charging Group, Inc. 12/18/2009
Car Charging Group, Inc. recapitalized as Blink Charging Co. 08/29/2017

NEW IMAGE INDS INC (CA)
Merged into Dentsply International Inc. 03/10/1997
Each share Common $0.001 par exchanged for $2 cash

NEW IMPACT RES INC (BC)
Recapitalized as Consolidated Impact Resources Inc. 8/22/89
Each share Common no par exchanged for (0.4) share Common no par
Consolidated Impact Resources Inc. name changed to InContext Systems Inc. 7/22/92 which merged into EveryWare Development Canada Inc. 6/30/97
(See EveryWare Development Canada Inc.)

NEW IMPERIAL MINES LTD (AB)
Recapitalized as Whitehorse Copper Mines Ltd. 09/08/1971
Each share Capital Stock no par exchanged for (0.4) share Capital Stock no par
(See Whitehorse Copper Mines Ltd.)

NEW INDIAN MINES LTD (BC)
Recapitalized as Azure Resources Ltd. 05/11/1972
Each share Capital Stock no par exchanged for (0.2) share Capital Stock no par
Azure Resources Ltd. recapitalized as Consolidated Azure Resources Ltd. 04/23/1987 which name changed to Caltech Data Ltd. 02/05/1988 which recapitalized as Roraima Gold Corp. 09/14/1994 which recapitalized as International Roraima Gold Corp. 06/13/1996

(See International Roraima Gold Corp.)

NEW INDIGO RES INC (AB)
Merged into Tahera Corp. 03/01/1999
Each share Common no par exchanged for (2.43) shares Common no par
Tahera Corp. name changed to Tahera Diamond Corp. 06/23/2004
(See Tahera Diamond Corp.)

NEW INDL TECHNIQUES INC (FL)
Through exchange offer all but (1,400) shares held by Advanced Technology Systems, Inc. as of 08/27/1975
Public interest eliminated

NEW INSCO MINES LTD (QC)
Reorganized under the laws of British Columbia as Nuinsco Resources Ltd. 10/15/79
Each share Common $1 par exchanged for (1/3) share Common no par
Nuinsco Resources Ltd. (BC) reincorporated in Ontario 7/26/89

NEW INTL INFOPET SYS LTD (ON)
Name changed to SponsorsOne Inc. 01/13/2014

NEW INVERNESS EXPLORATIONS INC (NV)
Common $0.001 par split (5) for (1) by issuance of (4) additional shares payable 08/07/2006 to holders of record 08/07/2006 Ex date - 08/08/2006
Name changed to Ethanex Energy, Inc. 08/25/2006
(See Ethanex Energy, Inc.)

NEW IS MINERALS LTD (AB)
Recapitalized as New Island Resources Inc. 04/22/1997
Each share Common no par exchanged for (0.125) share Common no par

NEW JACK LAKE URANIUM MINES LTD. (ON)
Name changed to Equity Explorations Ltd. 10/10/1962
Equity Explorations Ltd. recapitalized as Eagle Gold Mines Ltd. 02/08/1967 which merged into Agnico-Eagle Mines Ltd. 06/01/1972 which name changed to Agnico Eagle Mines Ltd. 04/30/2013

NEW JACULET MINES LTD. (ON)
Recapitalized as Chibougamau Jaculet Mines Ltd. on a (1) for (2) basis 7/20/56
Chibougamau Jaculet Mines Ltd. was acquired by Copper Rand Chibougamau Mines Ltd. 8/29/60 which merged into Patino Mining Corp. 11/26/62 which reorganized as Patino N.V. 12/20/71
(See Patino N.V.)

NEW JASON MINES LTD (ON)
Charter cancelled for failure to pay taxes and file returns 05/00/1976

NEW JEFFERSON HOTEL CO.
Property sold in 1934
No stockholders' equity

NEW JERICHO DEV LTD (BC)
Recapitalized as Mt. Calvery Resources Ltd. 03/01/1982
Each share Capital Stock $1 par exchanged for (0.25) share Common no par
Mt. Calvery Resources Ltd. recapitalized as Triumph Resources Ltd. 08/22/1989 which recapitalized as Jericho Resources Ltd. 10/02/1992 which name changed to Regia Resources Ltd. (BC) 04/18/1995 which reincorporated in Canada 07/07/1995
(See Regia Resources Ltd.)

NEW-NEW   FINANCIAL INFORMATION, INC.

NEW JERSEY & HUDSON RIVER RAILWAY & FERRY CO.
Merged into Public Service Coordinated Transport in 1940
Details not available

NEW JERSEY ACCEPTANCE CORP.
Merged into Capital Securities Co., Inc. in 1928
Details not available

NEW JERSEY ALUM CO (NJ)
Acquired by Eastern Stainless Steel Corp. 01/22/1969
Each share Capital Stock $1 par exchanged for (0.1) share $2.25 Conv. Preferred 1968 Ser. B $1 par
Eastern Stainless Steel Corp. name changed to Easco Corp. 04/29/1969
(See Easco Corp.)

NEW JERSEY ALUMINUM EXTRUSION CO., INC. (NJ)
Stock Dividend - 100% 02/01/1967
Name changed to New Jersey Aluminum Co. and Class A Capital Stock $1 par reclassified as Capital Stock $1 par 05/05/1967
New Jersey Aluminum Co. acquired by Eastern Stainless Steel Corp. 01/22/1969 which name changed to Easco Corp. 04/29/1969
(See Easco Corp.)

NEW JERSEY BK & TR CO (CLIFTON, NJ)
Name changed to New Jersey Bank (N.A.) (Clifton, NJ) 04/03/1969
New Jersey Bank (N.A.) (Clifton, NJ) reorganized as Greater Jersey Bancorp. 04/13/1972 which merged into Midlantic Banks Inc. 08/12/1983 which merged into Midlantic Corp. 01/30/1987 which merged into PNC Bank Corp. 12/31/1995 which name changed to PNC Financial Services Group, Inc. 03/15/2000

NEW JERSEY BK N A (CLIFTON, NJ)
Capital Stock $11 par changed to $5.50 par and (1) additional share issued 04/15/1969
Reorganized as Greater Jersey Bancorp. 04/13/1972
Each share Capital Stock $5.50 par exchanged for (1) share Common $5.50 par
Greater Jersey Bancorp. merged into Midlantic Banks Inc. 08/12/1983 which merged into Midlantic Corp. 01/30/1987 which merged into PNC Bank Corp. 12/31/1995 which name changed to PNC Financial Services Group, Inc. 03/15/2000

NEW JERSEY BANKERS SECURITIES CO. (NJ)
Liquidated in 1936
Details not available

NEW JERSEY CASH CREDIT CORP.
Merged into Franklin Plan Corp. in 1932
Details not available

NEW JERSEY CMNTY BK (FREEHOLD, NJ)
Stock Dividends - 5% payable 05/31/2011 to holders of record 05/13/2011 Ex date - 05/11/2011; 5% payable 05/31/2012 to holders of record 05/18/2012 Ex date - 05/16/2012; 5% payable 05/31/2013 to holders of record 05/17/2013 Ex date - 05/15/2013
Merged into 1st Constitution Bancorp 04/12/2018
Each share Common $2 par exchanged for (0.1309) share Common no par and $1.39 cash
Note: An additional $0.21 cash per share has been placed in escrow pending outcome of litigation

NEW JERSEY FIDELITY & PLATE GLASS INSURANCE CO.
Liquidated in 1941
Details not available

NEW JERSEY GROWTH FUND, INC. (NY)
Name changed to Mercer Fund, Inc. 9/10/63
Mercer Fund, Inc. acquired by Steadman American Industry Fund, Inc. 11/2/67 which name changed to Ameritor Industry Fund 9/23/98
(See Ameritor Industry Fund)

NEW JERSEY INSURANCE CO.
Merged into Jersey Insurance Co. of New York in 1938
Details not available

NEW JERSEY INVESTING FUND, INC. (NY)
Name changed to New Jersey Growth Fund, Inc. 6/29/60
New Jersey Growth Fund, Inc. name changed to Mercer Fund, Inc. 9/10/63 which was acquired by Steadman American Industries Fund, Inc. 11/2/67 which name changed to Ameritor Industry Fund 9/23/98
(See Ameritor Industry Fund)

NEW JERSEY LAND & INVESTMENT CO. (NJ)
Charter declared void for non-payment of taxes 03/11/1914

NEW JERSEY LEAD MINES, INC. (ID)
Name changed to Zenith Pacific Mines, Inc. 11/28/1969
Zenith Pacific Mines, Inc. liquidated for Selectors, Inc. 07/06/1973 which reorganized as Source Capital Corp. 09/00/1991 which merged into Sterling Financial Corp. 09/28/2001 which merged into Umpqua Holdings Corp. 04/18/2014

NEW JERSEY LIFE CO (DE)
Merged into NJL Corp. 9/18/79
Each share Common $1 par exchanged for $2.45 cash

NEW JERSEY LIFE INS CO (NJ)
Acquired by New Jersey Life Co. 8/1/73
Each share Common 20¢ par exchanged for (1) share Common 1¢ par
(See New Jersey Life Co.)

NEW JERSEY MTG & TITLE CO (NJ)
Merged into Greater Jersey Bancorp. 7/2/73
Each share Common $25 par exchanged for (3) shares Common $5.50 par
Greater Jersey Bancorp. merged into merged into Midlantic Banks Inc. 8/12/83 which merged into Midlantic Corp. 1/30/87

NEW JERSEY NAT GAS CO (NJ)
Common $10 par changed to $5 par and (1) additional share issued 12/04/1959
Common $5 par split (2) for (1) by issuance of (1) additional share 07/22/1963
6% Preferred $20 par called for redemption 01/15/1965
Under plan of reorganization each share Common $5 par automatically became (1) share New Jersey Resources Corp. Common $5 par 01/29/1982
144A Preferred called for redemption at $101.72 on 10/26/1998
5.65% Preferred called for redemption at $102 on 11/12/2002

NEW JERSEY NATIONAL BANK & TRUST CO. (NEPTUNE, NJ)
Common $5 par changed to $2 par and (3) additional shares issued 07/01/1967
Merged into New Jersey National Bank (Trenton, NJ) 05/11/1970
Each share Common $2 par exchanged for (1/3) share Common $5 par
New Jersey National Bank (Trenton, NJ) reorganized as NJN Bancorporation 07/01/1971 which name changed to New Jersey National Corp. 03/21/1972 which was acquired by CoreStates Financial Corp 10/30/1986 which merged into First Union Corp. 04/28/1998 which name changed to Wachovia Corp. (Ctfs. dated after 09/01/2001) 09/01/2001 which merged into Wells Fargo & Co. (New) 12/31/2008

NEW JERSEY NATL BK (TRENTON, NJ)
Reorganized as NJN Bancorporation 07/01/1971
Each share Common $5 par exchanged for (1) share Common $5 par
NJN Bancorporation name changed to New Jersey National Corp. 03/21/1972 which was acquired by CoreStates Financial Corp 10/30/1986 which merged into First Union Corp. 04/28/1998 which name changed to Wachovia Corp. (Ctfs. dated after 09/01/2001) 09/01/2001 which merged into Wells Fargo & Co. (New) 12/31/2008

NEW JERSEY NATL CORP (NJ)
Common $5 par changed to $3.33-1/3 par and (0.5) additional share issued 02/18/1983
Common $3.33-1/3 par changed to $2.22-1/5 par and (0.5) additional share issued 05/21/1984
Common $2.22-1/5 par changed to $1.48148 par and (0.5) additional share issued 03/31/1986
Acquired by CoreStates Financial Corp 10/30/1986
Each share Common $1.48148 par exchanged for (0.993) share Common $1 par
CoreStates Financial Corp merged into First Union Corp. 04/28/1998 which name changed to Wachovia Corp. (Ctfs. dated after 09/01/2001) 09/01/2001 which merged into Wells Fargo & Co. (New) 12/31/2008

NEW JERSEY PWR & LT CO (NJ)
4% Preferred $100 par called for redemption 10/1/73
4.05% Preferred $100 par called for redemption 10/1/73
Public interest eliminated

NEW JERSEY RLTY CO (NJ)
Common $1 par split (3) for (1) by issuance of (2) additional shares 8/28/72
Acquired by Thompson (Noel) Enterprises, Inc. 9/4/84
Each share Common $1 par exchanged for $20 cash

NEW JERSEY SVGS BK (SOMERVILLE, NJ)
Under plan of reorganization each share Common $2 par automatically became (1) share Bancorp New Jersey, Inc. (DE) Common 1¢ par 6/6/88
Bancorp New Jersey, Inc. merged into UJB Financial Corp. 7/14/95 which name changed to Summit Bancorp 3/1/96 which merged into FleetBoston Financial Corp. 3/1/2001 which merged into Bank of America Corp. 4/1/2004

NEW JERSEY SHARES CORP.
Acquired by Bankinstocks Holdings Corp. in 1928
Details not available

NEW JERSEY STL CORP (DE)
Merged into Co-Steel Inc. 01/20/1998
Each share Common 1¢ par exchanged for $23 cash 05/20/1987
(Inc. 00/00/1976)

NEW JERSEY TRUST CO. (ASBURY PARK, NJ)
Name changed to New Jersey National Bank & Trust Co. (Neptune, NJ) 04/07/1964

New Jersey National Bank & Trust Co. (Neptune, NJ) merged into New Jersey National Bank (Trenton, NJ) 05/11/1970 which reorganized as NJN Bancorporation 07/01/1971 which name changed to New Jersey National Corp. 03/21/1972 which was acquired by CoreStates Financial Corp 10/30/1986 which merged into First Union Corp. 04/28/1998 which name changed to Wachovia Corp. (Ctfs. dated after 09/01/2001) 09/01/2001 which merged into Wells Fargo & Co. (New) 12/31/2008

NEW JERSEY WORSTED MILLS
Name changed to Gera Mills 00/00/1952
Gera Mills recapitalized as Gera Corp. (NJ) 00/00/1954 which merged into Gera Corp. (DE) 07/28/1964
(See Gera Corp. (DE))

NEW JERSEY ZINC CO. (NJ)
Each share Capital Stock $100 par exchanged for (4) shares Capital Stock $25 par in 1929
Capital Stock $25 par changed to $12.50 par and (1) additional share issued 11/27/64
Merged into Gulf & Western Industries, Inc. (MI) 2/25/66
Each share Capital Stock $12.50 par exchanged for (0.425) share $3.50 Conv. Preferred Ser. B $2.50 par
(See Gulf & Western Industries, Inc. (MI))

NEW JOBURKE EXPLS LTD (ON)
Common $1 par changed to no par 02/22/1977
Name changed to Cenex Ltd. 08/16/1977
(See Cenex Ltd.)

NEW JONSMITH EXPL LTD (AB)
Name changed to Chal-Bert Drilling (Western) Ltd. 4/27/77
(See Chal-Bert Drilling (Western) Ltd.)

NEW JORDAN PETE LTD (CANADA)
Name changed back to Jordan Petroleum Ltd. 05/07/1992
(See Jordan Petroleum Ltd.)

NEW KELORE MINES LTD (ON)
Merged into Orvana Minerals Corp. 2/24/92
Each share Capital Stock no par exchanged for (0.27247956) share Common no par

NEW KELVER RES LTD (BC)
Recapitalized as Access Resources Ltd. 03/31/1982
Each share Common no par exchanged for (1) share Common no par
(See Access Resources Ltd.)

NEW KENRELL RES INC (BC)
Reincorporated under the laws of Alberta as International Broadcasting Centre Ltd. 08/31/1987
International Broadcasting Centre Ltd. recapitalized as Ensel Corp. 10/13/1992 which name changed to Surge Resources Inc. 05/04/2005 which name changed to Eaglewood Energy Inc. 11/05/2007
(See Eaglewood Energy Inc.)

NEW KEY INDS LTD (BC)
Merged into Ambassador Industries Ltd. (Old) 6/1/78
Each share Common no par exchanged for (1) share Common no par
(See Ambassador Industries Ltd. (Old))

NEW KLONDIKE EXPL LTD (ON)
Company announced the resignation of all officers and directors 02/15/2017

NEW LAFAYETTE ASBESTOS CO. LTD. (QC)
Name changed to North American Asbestos Co. Ltd. 3/2/57
North American Asbestos Co. Ltd. name changed to Bishop Resources International Exploration Inc. 9/30/93 which recapitalized as Caldera Resources Inc. 11/30/95

NEW LAGUERRE MINES LTD. (ON)
Recapitalized as Can-Erin Mines Ltd. on a (1) for (6) basis 00/00/1956
Can-Erin Mines Ltd. recapitalized as Argosy Mining Corp. Ltd. 11/16/1964 which name changed to Argosy Capital Corp. 03/29/1989
(See Argosy Capital Corp.)

NEW LARDER U ISLAND MINES LTD. (ON)
Acquired by Anacon Lead Mines Ltd. on a (1) for (3) basis in January 1955
Anacon Lead Mines Ltd. was recapitalized as Key Anacon Mines Ltd. 2/14/64
(See Key Anacon Mines Ltd.)

NEW LAROSE MINING & SMELTING LTD. (ON)
Acquired by Silver-Miller Mines Ltd. on a (1) for (2.5) basis in 1953
Silver-Miller Mines Ltd. recapitalized as Silmil Explorations Inc. 9/20/72 which merged into Belle Aire Resource Explorations Ltd. 8/29/78 which name changed to Sprint Resources Ltd. 9/23/82 which name changed to Meacon Bay Resources Inc. 3/9/87 which recapitalized as Advantex Marketing International Inc. 9/16/91

NEW LAWRENCE HOTEL CO.
Liquidated in 1946
Details not available

NEW LEAF BRANDS INC (NV)
SEC revoked common stock registration 01/15/2016

NEW LEATHER CORP (BC)
Name changed to Global Focus Resources Ltd. 11/02/1995
(See Global Focus Resources Ltd.)

NEW LEGEND GROUP LTD (BERMUDA)
Recapitalized as Liuyang Fireworks Ltd. 06/24/2009
Each share Common CAD$0.02 par exchanged for (0.08333333) share Common CAD$0.02 par
(See Liuyang Fireworks Ltd.)

NEW LIFE SCIENTIFIC INC (NV)
Each share old Common $0.001 par exchanged for (1.1) shares new Common $0.001 par 01/25/2006
Recapitalized as Applied Wellness Corp. 03/25/2008
Each share Common $0.001 par exchanged for (0.02) share Common $0.001 par
(See Applied Wellness Corp.)

NEW LINE CINEMA CORP (DE)
Reincorporated 02/25/1987
State of incorporation changed from (NY) to (DE) 02/25/1987
Common 1¢ par split (5) for (4) by issuance of (0.25) additional share 07/18/1990
Common 1¢ par split (6) for (5) by issuance of (0.2) additional share 02/28/1991
Stock Dividend - 10% 12/01/1988
Merged into Turner Broadcasting Systems, Inc. 01/28/1994
Each share Common 1¢ par exchanged for (0.96386) share Class B Common $0.0625 par
Turner Broadcasting Systems, Inc. merged into Time Warner Inc. (Old) 10/10/1996 which merged into AOL Time Warner Inc. 01/11/2001 which name changed to Time Warner Inc.

(New) 10/16/2003 which merged into AT&T Inc. 06/15/2018

NEW LINTEX MINERALS LTD (BC)
Merged into Globaltex Industries Inc. 03/05/1993
Each share Common no par exchanged for (1) share Common no par
Globaltex Industries Inc. name changed to Pine Valley Mining Corp. 05/14/2003

NEW LONDON INC (TX)
Each share old Common 10¢ par exchanged for (0.5) share new Common 10¢ par 6/26/91
Acquired by New London Acquisition Corp. 8/7/92
Each share new Common 10¢ par exchanged for $4 cash

NEW LONDON NORTHERN RAILROAD CO.
Liquidated in 1952
Details not available

NEW LONDON SHIP & ENGINE CO.
Merged into Electric Boat Co. in 1928
Details not available

NEW LOOK EYEWEAR INC NEW (CANADA)
Name changed to New Look Vision Group Inc. and Common no par reclassified as Class A Common no par 06/01/2015

NEW LOOK EYEWEAR INC OLD (CANADA)
Each Exchangeable Share no par exchanged for (1) share New Look Eyewear Inc. (New) Common no par 03/04/2010
New Look Eyewear Inc. (New) name changed to New Look Vision Group Inc. 06/01/2015

NEW LORIE MINES LTD (ON)
Recapitalized as Lorie Resources Inc. 3/10/81
Each share Capital Stock $1 par exchanged for (0.1) share Common no par
Lorie Resources Inc. recapitalized as Theme Restaurants Inc. 12/30/86
(See Theme Restaurants Inc.)

NEW LOUVRE MINES LTD. (QC)
Name changed to Fano Mining & Exploration, Inc. 12/30/1955
Fano Mining & Exploration, Inc. recapitalized as Fanex Resources Ltd. 08/26/1971
(See Fanex Resources Ltd.)

NEW MAJESTIC MINING CO. (UT)
Name changed to Majestic Oil & Mining Co. 00/00/1952
Majestic Oil & Mining Co. recapitalized as American Mining Co. (UT) 05/05/1964 which merged into Toledo Mining Co. 09/16/1968 which name changed to Toledo Technology, Inc. 03/26/1984 which recapitalized as HIPP International Inc. 08/31/1994 which name changed to Assembly & Manufacturing Systems Corp. 04/12/1995 which recapitalized as American Ship Inc. 09/05/1997 which name changed to Petshealth, Inc. 05/20/1999
(See Petshealth, Inc.)

NEW MALARTIC GOLD MINES, LTD. (QC)
Dissolved 7/30/60
Details not available

NEW MALLEN RED LAKE MINES LTD. (ON)
Charter cancelled and company declared dissolved for default in filing returns 12/30/1970

NEW MANCO GOLD MINES, LTD. (ON)
Charter cancelled and declared dissolved for failure to file returns 10/4/54

NEW MANITOBA GOLD MINES LTD. (ON)
Name changed to New Manitoba Mining & Smelting Co. Ltd. 6/4/57
New Manitoba Mining & Smelting Co. Ltd. merged into Manoka Mining & Smelting Co. Ltd. 5/4/62 which recapitalized as Cat Lake Mines Ltd. 10/18/71 which merged into Fundy Chemical International Ltd. 3/16/73
(See Fundy Chemical International Ltd.)

NEW MANITOBA MINING & SMELTING CO. LTD. (ON)
Merged into Manoka Mining & Smelting Co. Ltd. share for share 5/4/62
Manoka Mining & Smelting Co. Ltd. recapitalized as Cat Lake Mines Ltd. 10/18/71 which merged into Fundy Chemical International Ltd. 3/16/73
(See Fundy Chemical International Ltd.)

NEW-MAR URANIUM CORP. (CO)
Acquired by Standard Uranium Corp. 04/15/1957
Each share Common exchanged for (17) shares Common
Standard Uranium Corp. name changed to Standard Metals Corp. 05/19/1960 which name changed to American Holdings, Inc. 11/22/2005
(See American Holdings, Inc.)

NEW MARLON GOLD MINES LTD. (ON)
Recapitalized as Marcon Mines Ltd. on a (1) for (2) basis 3/16/56
Marcon Mines Ltd. recapitalized as Conmar Explorations Ltd. 10/12/66
(See Conmar Explorations Ltd.)

NEW MARTINSVILLE BK (NEW MARTINSVILLE, WV)
Stock Dividend - 100% 3/15/69
Merged into Wesbanco, Inc. 10/1/84
Each share Common $25 par exchanged for (6.3636) shares Common $12.50 par

NEW MARVEL OILS LTD (CANADA)
Involuntarily dissolved for failure to file annual returns 12/16/1980

NEW MCMANUS RED LAKE GOLD MINES LTD (ON)
Recapitalized as Milestone Resource Corp. 08/26/1987
Each share Common no par exchanged for (0.25) share Common no par
15% Preference Stock $5 par not affected except for change of name
Milestone Resource Corp. reorganized as Horizontal Petroleum Exploration Ltd. 07/26/1990
(See Horizontal Petroleum Exploration Ltd.)

NEW MED TECHNIQUES INC (CT)
Each share old Common no par exchanged for (0.2) share new Common no par 7/6/73
Charter cancelled for failure to pay fees 10/25/91

NEW MEDIA CAP INC (AB)
Name changed to CSM Systems Corp. 06/22/2001
CSM Systems Corp. recapitalized as Visionstate Corp. 09/16/2014

NEW MEDIA LOTTERY SVCS INC (DE)
SEC revoked common stock registration 02/27/2013

NEW MEDIA SYS INC (BC)
Reorganized under the laws of Canada as Wavefront Energy & Environmental Services Inc. 10/01/2003
Each share Common no par exchanged for (0.8) share Common no par
Wavefront Energy & Environmental Services Inc. name changed to Wavefront Technology Solutions Inc. 03/27/2009

NEW MEDIUM ENTERPRISES INC (NV)
Common $0.001 par changed to Common $0.0001 par 01/14/2004
Recapitalized as Dukeshire Ventures Inc. 03/26/2013
Each share Common $0.0001 par exchanged for (0.001) share Common $0.0001 par
Dukeshire Ventures Inc. name changed to InterActive Leisure Systems, Inc. 06/06/2013

NEW MEG OILS LTD. (ON)
Acquired by Oil Selections Ltd. in 1953
Each share Common $1 par exchanged for (1/3) share Capital Stock no par
Oil Selections Ltd. acquired by Quonto Petroleums Ltd. in 1957 which name changed to Quonto Explorations Ltd. 7/27/62
(See Quonto Explorations Ltd.)

NEW MERCUR GOLD MINING CO. (UT)
Proclaimed dissolved for failure to pay taxes 11/9/74

NEW MERIDIAN MNG CORP (AB)
Each share old Common no par exchanged for (0.33333333) share new Common no par 09/27/2007
Recapitalized as Philippine Metals Inc. (AB) 04/07/2010
Each share new Common no par exchanged for (0.5) share Common no par
Philippine Metals Inc. (AB) reincorporated in British Columbia 04/17/2018

NEW METALORE MNG LTD (ON)
Recapitalized as Metalore Resources Ltd. 10/22/76
Each share Capital Stock $1 par exchanged for (0.25) share Common no par

NEW METALS CORP (CA)
Name changed to Hobson Oil Co., Inc. 8/3/71
Each share Capital Stock 10¢ par exchanged for (1) share Capital Stock 10¢ par
Hobson Oil Co., Inc. recapitalized as Arthritis Clinics International, Inc. 6/2/72
(See Arthritis Clinics International, Inc.)

NEW METALS MNG CORP (NV)
Charter revoked for failure to file reports and pay fees 01/31/2002

NEW METHOD FIN CORP (MA)
Class A no par and Class B no par changed to $5 par 11/21/1956
Proclaimed dissolved for failure to file reports and pay taxes 10/19/1983

NEW METHOD LAUNDRY CO. LTD. (ON)
Acquired by Canadian Corporate Management Co. Ltd. 5/15/69
Each share Common no par exchanged for $12.50 cash

NEW MEXICO & ARIZ LD CO (AZ)
Capital Stock $1 par changed to no par and (1) additional share issued 07/10/1978
Capital Stock no par split (6) for (5) by issuance of (0.2) additional share payable 07/10/1998 to holders of record 06/10/1998 Ex date - 07/13/1998
Capital Stock no par split (3) for (2) by issuance of (0.5) additional share payable 01/15/1999 to holders of record 12/31/1998 Ex date - 01/19/1999
Stock Dividends - 10% 06/02/1986; 10% 05/01/1995; 10% payable 07/18/1996 to holders of record 06/17/1996 Ex date - 06/13/1996;

10% payable 07/18/1997 to holders of record 06/16/1997 Ex date - 06/12/1997
Name changed to NZ Corp. 06/20/2000
NZ Corp. name changed to Lipid Sciences, Inc. (AZ) 11/29/2001 which reincorporated in Delaware 06/19/2002
(See Lipid Sciences, Inc.)

NEW MEXICO BANCORPORATION, INC. (NM)
Name changed to New Mexico Banquest Corp. 05/01/1980
(See New Mexico Banquest Corp.)

NEW MEXICO BANQUEST CORP (NM)
Merged out of existence 02/27/2002
Details not available

NEW MEXICO COPPER CORP (NM)
Each share old Common 25¢ par exchanged for (0.04) share new Common 25¢ par 03/28/1964
Charter forfeited for failure to file reports 10/10/1968

NEW MEXICO COPPER MINING CO.
Recapitalized as New Mexico Copper Corp. and Common 50¢ par changed to 25¢ par in 1952
(See New Mexico Copper Corp.)

NEW MEXICO EASTERN GAS CO.
Merged into Southern Union Gas Co. (DE) (New) 11/24/42
Preferred exchanged for a like par amount of 6% 25-year Debentures and cash for accrued dividends
Each share Common exchanged for (1-1/3) shares Common $1 par Southern Union Gas Co. (DE) (New) name changed to Southern Union Co. (Old) 5/7/76
(See Southern Union Co. (Old))

NEW MEXICO GAS CO.
Merged into Southern Union Gas Co. (DE) (New) 11/24/42
Preferred exchanged for a like par amount of 6% 25-year Debentures and cash for accrued dividends
Each share Common exchanged for (1.5) shares Common $1 par Southern Union Gas Co. (DE) (New) name changed to Southern Union Co. (Old) 5/7/76
(See Southern Union Co. (Old))

NEW MEXICO LIFE INSURANCE CO. (NM)
Merged into Sierra Life Insurance Co. on a (0.1333333) for (1) basis 09/30/1964
(See Sierra Life Insurance Co.)

NEW MEXICO OIL CO. (NM)
Charter cancelled in 1938

NEW MEXICO OSAGE COOPERATIVE ROYALTY CO. (NM)
Merged into Panhandle Royalty Co. 03/15/1988
Each share Common $1 par exchanged for (210) shares Class A Common 10¢ par
Panhandle Royalty Co. name changed to Panhandle Oil & Gas Inc. 04/03/2007

NEW MEXICO POTASH & CHEMICAL CO., INC. (NM)
Completely liquidated in 1958
Each share Capital Stock 25¢ par exchanged for first and final distribution of (0.7399912) share Three-States Natural Gas Co. Common $1 par and $0.0078 cash
Three-States Natural Gas Co. merged into Delhi-Taylor Oil Corp. 5/31/61
(See Delhi-Taylor Oil Corp.)

NEW MEXICO QUARTZ MFG. CO., INC. (NM)
Charter forfeited for failure to file reports and pay taxes 10/8/66

NEW MEXICO-SAN JUAN NATURAL GAS CO. (NM)
Charter forfeited for failure to pay taxes 10/10/68

NEW MEXICO SOFTWARE INC (NV)
Name changed to Net Medical Xpress Solutions, Inc. 01/10/2013

NEW MEXICO STATE BANK (ALBUQUERQUE, NM)
Name changed to Bank of New Mexico (Albuquerque, NM) in 1950
Bank of New Mexico (Albuquerque, NM) name changed to First Interstate Bank of Albuquerque (Albuquerque, NM) 6/1/81
(See First Interstate Bank of Albuquerque (Albuquerque, NM))

NEW MIC MAC MINES LTD.
Name changed to United Mic Mac Mines Ltd. 00/00/1949
United Mic Mac Mines Ltd. merged into Indian Lake Mines Ltd. 00/00/1956 which merged into Hydra Explorations Ltd. 11/16/1959 which name changed to Hydra Capital Corp. 12/30/1992 which name changed to Waterford Capital Management Inc. 11/12/1996 which merged into CPI Plastics Group Inc. 09/21/1998
(See CPI Plastics Group Inc.)

NEW MILFORD BK & TR CO (NEW MILFORD, CT)
Stock Dividend - 10% 6/19/92
Under plan of reorganization each share Common $5 par automatically became (1) share NMBT Corp. Common $1 par 11/25/97
NMBT Corp. merged into Summit Bancorp 3/29/2000 which merged into FleetBoston Financial Corp. 3/1/2001 which merged into Bank of America Corp. 4/1/2004

NEW MILFORD SVGS BK (NEW MILFORD, CT)
Reorganized under the laws of Delaware as NewMil Bancorp, Inc. 10/19/87
NewMil Bancorp, Inc. merged into Webster Financial Corp. 10/6/2006

NEW MILLENNIUM BK (NEW BRUNSWICK, NJ)
Old Common $2 par split (5) for (4) by issuance of (0.25) additional share payable 04/30/2003 to holders of record 04/04/2003 Ex date - 05/01/2003
Each share old Common $2 par exchanged for (0.25) share new Common $2 par 04/13/2015
Stock Dividends - 5% payable 03/28/2001 to holders of record 02/26/2001 Ex date - 03/27/2001; 5% payable 04/15/2002 to holders of record 04/05/2002 Ex date - 04/03/2002; 5% payable 04/26/2004 to holders of record 04/15/2004 Ex date - 04/13/2004; 5% payable 04/26/2005 to holders of record 04/15/2005 Ex date - 04/13/2005; 5% payable 04/25/2006 to holders of record 04/14/2006 Ex date - 04/11/2006; 5% payable 04/25/2007 to holders of record 04/16/2007 Ex date - 04/12/2007; 5% payable 04/28/2008 to holders of record 04/15/2008 Ex date - 04/11/2008; 5% payable 04/28/2009 to holders of record 04/15/2009 Ex date - 04/15/2009
Under plan of reorganization each share new Common $2 par automatically became (1) share NMB Financial Corp. Common no par 10/11/2017

NEW MILLENNIUM CAP CORP (AB)
Name changed to New Millennium Iron Corp. 06/15/2011

NEW MILLENNIUM COMMUNICATIONS CORP (FL)
Administratively dissolved for failure to file annual reports 09/24/1999

NEW MILLENNIUM DEV GROUP (NV)
Each share old Common $0.001 par exchanged for (0.01) share new Common $0.001 par 09/18/2003
Name changed to Millennium National Events, Inc. 10/05/2004
Millennium National Events, Inc. recapitalized as Extensions, Inc. 08/24/2007
(See Extensions, Inc.)

NEW MILLENNIUM MEDIA INTL INC (CO)
Each share old Common $0.001 par exchanged for (0.2) share new Common $0.001 par 05/18/2001
Name changed to OnScreen Technologies, Inc. 07/14/2004
OnScreen Technologies, Inc. name changed to Waytronx, Inc. 01/07/2008 which name changed to CUI Global, Inc. 01/04/2011

NEW MILLENNIUM METALS CORP (BC)
Merged into Platinum Group Metals Ltd. 2/19/2002
Each share Common no par exchanged for (0.6060606) share new Common no par

NEW MILLENNIUM TECHNOLOGY TR (ON)
Name changed to First Asset Opportunity Fund 06/20/2007
(See First Asset Opportunity Fund)

NEW MILLER COPPER MINES LTD. (QC)
Name changed to New Miller Pipe Lines & Mining Exploration Ltd. 12/2/63
New Miller Pipe Lines & Mining Exploration Ltd. name changed to Consolidated Miller Mining Co. Ltd. in 1981

NEW MILLER PIPE LINES & MNG EXPL LTD (QC)
Name changed to Consolidated Miller Mining Co. Ltd. in 1981

NEW MINDA-SCOTIA MINES LTD. (ON)
Merged into Andover Mining & Exploration Ltd. 09/19/1958
Each share Capital Stock exchanged for (0.4) share Capital Stock 25¢ par
Andover Mining & Exploration Ltd. recapitalized as Andover Resources Ltd. 05/31/1971 which name changed to Andover Telecommunications Inc. 10/02/1986 which name changed to Kennecom Inc. 06/02/1989 which recapitalized as Deltona Industries Inc. 01/25/1995
(See Deltona Industries Inc.)

NEW MINE SAPPHIRE SYNDICATE (MT)
Proclaimed dissolved for failure to file annual reports 7/27/70

NEW MINEX RES LTD (BC)
Struck off register and declared dissolved for failure to file returns 4/16/92

NEW MNG CORP LTD (SOUTH AFRICA)
Name changed to Matodzi Resources Ltd. 12/06/2002
Matodzi Resources Ltd. name changed to White Water Resources Ltd. 03/02/2009 which name changed to Goliath Gold Mining Ltd. 05/26/2011
(See Goliath Gold Mining Ltd.)

NEW MINOILS LTD. (ON)
Acquired by Oil Selections Ltd. in 1953
Each share Common $1 par exchanged for (1/3) share Capital Stock no par
Oil Selections Ltd. acquired by Quonto Petroleums Ltd. in 1957 which name changed to Quonto Explorations Ltd. 7/27/62
(See Quonto Explorations Ltd.)

NEW MKT CHINA INC (NV)
Name changed to China Crescent Enterprises, Inc. 07/03/2008

NEW MKT VENTURES INC (BC)
Reorganized as Russell Breweries Inc. 5/18/2005
Each share Common no par exchanged for (4) shares Common no par

NEW MONTE CRISTO MINING CO. (NV)
Charter revoked for failure to file reports and pay fees 3/3/30

NEW MORNING CORP (NV)
Name changed to Window Rock Capital Holdings, Inc. 10/28/2005
(See Window Rock Capital Holdings, Inc.)

NEW MORRISON MINES LTD. (ON)
Recapitalized as Consolidated Morrison Explorations Ltd. on a (1) for (2) basis 5/11/55
Consolidated Morrison Explorations Ltd. name changed to Morrison Petroleums Ltd. 10/22/80 which merged into Northstar Energy Corp. 3/14/97 which merged into Devon Energy Corp. (OK) 12/11/98 which merged into Devon Energy Corp. (New) (DE) 8/17/99

NEW MOSHER LONGLAC MINES LTD. (ON)
Recapitalized as Consolidated Mosher Mines Ltd. in 1954
Each (2) shares Capital Stock $1 par exchanged for (1) share Capital Stock $2 par
Consolidated Mosher Mines Ltd. merged into MacLeod Mosher Gold Mines Ltd. 6/15/67 which was acquired by Lake Shore Mines Ltd. 12/31/68 which merged into LAC Minerals Ltd. (New) 7/29/85 which was acquired by American Barrick Resources Corp. 10/17/94 which name changed to Barrick Gold Corp. 1/18/95

NEW MOTION INC (DE)
Name changed to Atrinsic, Inc. 06/26/2009
Atrinsic, Inc. recapitalized as Protagenic Therapeutics, Inc. 07/27/2016

NEW MOUNTAINTOP CORP (DE)
Recapitalized as Trust Licensing, Inc. 08/24/2004
Each share Common $0.0001 par exchanged for (0.1) share Common $0.0001 par
Trust Licensing, Inc. name changed to Connected Media Technologies, Inc. 05/23/2005

NEW MYLAMAQUE EXPLORATIONS LTD. (ON)
Name changed to New Mylamaque Mining & Smelting Ltd. 10/11/1960
New Mylamaque Mining & Smelting Ltd. recapitalized as Mymar Mining & Reduction Ltd. 12/22/1969 which merged into Dynamar Energy Ltd. 08/24/1977
(See Dynamar Energy Ltd.)

NEW MYLAMAQUE MNG & SMLT LTD (ON)
Recapitalized as Mymar Mining & Reduction Ltd. 12/22/1969
Each share Capital Stock $1 par exchanged for (1/9) share Capital Stock no par
Mymar Mining & Reduction Ltd. merged into Dynamar Energy Ltd. 08/24/1977
(See Dynamar Energy Ltd.)

NEW NATIONAL INDUSTRIES, INC. (DE)
Charter cancelled and declared inoperative and void for non-payment of taxes 4/1/30

NEW NEXUS PETE LTD (BC)
Dissolved and struck from the register for failure to file reports 5/8/92

NEW NIPIRON MINES LTD. (ON)
Acquired by New York Oils Ltd. (BC) 6/29/70
Each share Common no par exchanged for (0.25) share Capital Stock no par
New York Oils Ltd. (BC) reincorporated in Alberta 7/19/82 which was acquired by Sceptre Resources Ltd. 3/14/89 which merged into Canadian Natural Resources Ltd. 8/15/96

NEW NIQUERO SUGAR CO.
Out of existence in 1948
Details not available

NEW NORQUE MINES LTD (ON)
Charter cancelled for failure to pay taxes and file returns 3/16/76

NEW NORSEMAN MINES LTD.
Recapitalized as Norsewick Mines Ltd. 00/00/1953
Each share Capital Stock $1 par exchanged for (0.2) share Capital Stock $1 par
Norsewick Mines Ltd. name changed to Brunsman Mines Ltd. 00/00/1953 which merged into Hydra Explorations Ltd. 11/16/1959 which name changed to Hydra Capital Corp. 12/30/1992 which name changed to Waterford Capital Management Inc. 11/12/1996 which merged into CPI Plastics Group Ltd. 09/21/1998
(See CPI Plastics Group Ltd.)

NEW NORTH PACIFIC EXPLORATION LTD. (ON)
Name changed to Commonwealth Drilling (Northern) Ltd. 10/9/68
(See listing for Commonwealth Drilling (Northern) Ltd.)

NEW NORTH RES LTD (AB)
Acquired by 1080699 Alberta Inc. 4/5/2004
Each share Common no par exchanged for $0.47 cash

NEW NORTHCAL MINES LTD (AB)
Recapitalized as Venture Properties Ltd. 4/17/74
Each share Capital Stock no par exchanged for (0.5) share Common $1 par
Venture Properties Ltd. recapitalized as Allied Venture Properties Ltd. 9/2/75 which recapitalized as Buckingham International Holdings Ltd. 3/22/79
(See Buckingham International Holdings Ltd.)

NEW NORZONE MINES LTD. (ON)
Recapitalized as Diadem Mines Ltd. on a (1) for (7) basis 9/27/55
(See Diadem Mines Ltd.)

NEW NRG INC (DE)
SEC revoked common stock registration 08/12/2013

NEW OJI PAPER CO LTD (JAPAN)
Name changed to Oji Paper Co., Ltd. (New) 10/01/1996
Oji Paper Co., Ltd. (New) name changed to Oji Holdings Corp. 10/01/2012

NEW ORLEANS, TEXAS & MEXICO RAILWAY CO. (LA)
Capital Stock $100 par reclassified as Common $100 par 12/29/1955
Merged into Missouri Pacific Railroad Co. 03/15/1956
Each share Common $100 par exchanged for $58.7769 principal amount of 1st Mtge. 4.25% Ser. C Bonds due 01/01/2005, $135.4053 principal amount of Gen'l Mtge. 4.75% Ser. A Income Bonds due 01/01/2020 and $21.6657 principal amount of General Mtg. 4.75% Ser. B Income Bonds due 01/01/2030
Note: Last date to exchange old securities for new securities was 03/01/1962, after which date old securities became entitled to receive cash only
Last date to exchange old securities for cash under the 1956 plan was 03/01/1968; after which date all unexchanged old stock became void for all purposes

NEW ORLEANS BANCSHARES INC (LA)
Common $12.50 par changed to $4.25 par and (2) additional shares issued 5/1/72
Stock Dividends - 20% 1/2/81; 20% 10/1/81; 20% 10/1/82
Merged into First Commerce Corp. 5/23/83
Each share Common $4.25 par exchanged for (1.5) shares Common $5 par
First Commerce Corp. merged into Banc One Corp. 6/12/98 which merged into Bank One Corp. 10/2/98 which merged into J.P. Morgan Chase & Co. 12/31/2000 which name changed to JPMorgan Chase & Co. 7/20/2004

NEW ORLEANS GREAT NORTHN RY CO (MS)
Merged into Gulf, Mobile & Ohio Railroad Co. 09/13/1940
Each share Common exchanged for (0.25) share Common no par
Gulf, Mobile & Ohio Railroad Co. merged into Illinois Central Industries, Inc. 08/10/1972 which name changed to IC Industries, Inc. 05/21/1975
(See IC Industries, Inc.)

NEW ORLEANS PONTCHARTRAIN BRIDGE CO.
Purchased by the State of Louisiana in 1938
Details not available

NEW ORLEANS PUB SVC INC (LA)
Merged into Middle South Utilities Inc. 12/04/1961
Each share Common no par exchanged for (2.75) shares Common $10 par
Note: Unexchanged certificates were cancelled and became without value 12/05/1966
15.44% Preferred $100 par called for redemption 10/01/1995
Name changed to Entergy New Orleans, Inc. 04/22/1996

NEW ORLEANS RED RIVER OIL CO., INC. (LA)
Charter revoked for failure to file annual reports 5/13/82

NEW OTTAWA TELEPHONE CO.
Merged into Northern Ohio Telephone Co. in 1926
Details not available

NEW PAC HLDGS CORP (BC)
Name changed to New Pacific Metals Corp. (New) 07/24/2017

NEW PAC METALS CORP OLD (BC)
Name changed to New Pacific Holdings Corp. 07/04/2016
New Pacific Holdings Corp. name changed to New Pacific Metals Corp. (New) 07/24/2017

NEW PAC VENTURES INC (CO)
Each share old Common $0.001 par exchanged for (4) shares new Common $0.001 par 09/18/2006
Name changed to Tatonka Oil & Gas, Inc. 11/29/2006
(See Tatonka Oil & Gas, Inc.)

NEW PACALTA OILS CO. LTD. (ON)
Recapitalized as Wespac Petroleums Ltd. 5/27/55
Each share Capital Stock no par exchanged for (0.2) share Capital Stock no par
Wespac Petroleums Ltd. recapitalized as Canada Geothermal Oil Ltd. 9/7/71
(See Canada Geothermal Oil Ltd.)

NEW PACIFIC COAL & OILS LTD. (ON)
Common no par changed to 20¢ par 00/00/1955
Recapitalized as Consolidated New Pacific Ltd. 02/01/1960
Each share Common 20¢ par exchanged for (0.2) share Common $1 par
Consolidated New Pacific Ltd. name changed to Conuco Ltd. 12/22/1969 which merged into Brinco Ltd. 12/17/1979 which merged into Consolidated Brinco Ltd. 05/30/1986 which merged into Hillsborough Resources Ltd. (ON) 02/06/1992 which reincorporated in Canada 11/05/1997
(See Hillsborough Resources Ltd. (Canada))

NEW PALTZ CAP CORP (NV)
Common $0.001 par split (6) for (1) by issuance of (5) additional shares payable 09/22/2003 to holders of record 09/01/2003 Ex date - 10/06/2003
Name changed to FemOne, Inc. 10/02/2003
FemOne, Inc. name changed to ACTIS Global Ventures, Inc. 07/10/2006
(See ACTIS Global Ventures, Inc.)

NEW PARADIGM PRODUCTIONS INC (NV)
Each (7.5) shares old Common $0.001 par exchanged for (1) share new Common $0.001 par 09/25/2007
Name changed to China Marine Food Group Ltd. 01/22/2008

NEW PARADIGM STRATEGIC COMMUNICATIONS (NY)
Name changed 12/01/2000
Name changed from New Paradigm Software Corp. to New Paradigm Strategic Communications, Inc. 12/01/2000
Recapitalized as Brunton Vineyards Holdings, Inc. 02/05/2007
Each share Common 1¢ par exchanged for (0.005) share Common 1¢ par
(See Brunton Vineyards Holdings, Inc.)

NEW PARAHO CORP (CO)
Reincorporated under the laws of Nevada as NPC Holdings Inc. 07/12/2000
NPC Holdings Inc. name changed to Regent Energy Corp. 03/12/2001
(See Regent Energy Corp.)

NEW PARK MNG CO (NV)
Name changed to Newpark Resources, Inc. 6/9/72

NEW PASCALIS MINES LTD (CANADA)
Merged into Tiomin Resources Inc. 10/09/1992
Each share Common no par exchanged for (1/3) share Common no par
Tiomin Resources Inc. recapitalized as Vaaldiam Mining Inc. 03/26/2010
(See Vaaldiam Mining Inc.)

NEW PATRIOT TRANSN HLDG INC (FL)
Name changed to Patriot Transportation Holding, Inc. 02/06/2015

NEW PENINSULAR OIL LTD. (QC)
Charter cancelled for failure to file reports and pay fees 2/28/73

NEW PENN ENERGY CORP (NEW) (CANADA)
Reincorporated 1/29/82
Place of incorporation changed from (BC) to (Canada) 1/29/82
Under plan of merger New Penn Energy Corp. (Old) became New Penn Energy Corp. (New) and each share Common no par exchanged for (1) share Common no par 11/22/82
Merged into International Interlake Industries Inc. 12/31/86
Each (5.85) shares Common no par exchanged for (1) share Common no par
(See International Interlake Industries Inc.)

NEW PENN MTR EXPRESS INC (PA)
Reorganized as Arnold Industries, Inc. 4/1/82
Each share Common $1 par exchanged for (2) shares Common $1 par
(See Arnold Industries, Inc.)

NEW PERSPECTIVE FD INC (MD)
Common $1 par split (3) for (1) by issuance of (2) additional shares 08/25/1978
Stock Dividend - 10% 10/07/1980
Reincorporated under the laws of Delaware as New Perspective Fund and Common $1 par reclassified as Class A 12/01/2012

NEW PICTON URANIUM MINES LTD (ON)
Charter cancelled for failure to pay taxes and file returns 3/16/76

NEW PIONEER EXPLS LTD (BC)
Delisted from Vancouver Stock Exchange 03/02/1989

NEW PLAN EXCEL RLTY TR INC (MD)
8.50% Preferred Ser. A 1¢ par called for redemption 7/15/2002
Depositary Preferred Ser. B 1¢ par called for redemption at $25 plus $0.209635 accrued dividend on 5/5/2003
Merged into Centro Properties Ltd. 4/20/2007
Each Depositary Preferred Ser. D 1¢ par exchanged for $50.21667 cash
Each Depositary Preferred Ser. E 1¢ par exchanged for $25.12179 cash
Each share Common 1¢ par exchanged for $33.15 cash

NEW PLAN RLTY CORP (DE)
Completely liquidated 8/14/72
Each share Class A Common 50¢ par exchanged for (1) New Plan Realty Trust Share of Bene. Int. no par
New Plan Realty Trust merged into New Plan Excel Realty Trust, Inc. 9/28/98

NEW PLAN RLTY TR (MA)
Shares of Bene. Int. no par split (2) for (1) by issuance of (1) additional share 6/1/76
Shares of Bene. Int. no par split (3) for (2) by issuance of (0.5) additional share 12/1/78
Shares of Bene. Int. no par split (2) for (1) by issuance of (1) additional share 2/1/83
Shares of Bene. Int. no par split (3) for (2) by issuance of (0.5) additional share 4/1/86
Merged into New Plan Excel Realty Trust, Inc. 9/28/98
Each 7.80% Depositary Preferred Ser. A exchanged for (1) 7.80% Depositary Preferred Ser. D
Each Share of Bene. Int. no par exchanged for (1) share Common 1¢ par

NEW PLANET COPPER MNG CO (DE)
Charter cancelled and declared inoperative and void for non-payment of taxes 5/30/96

NEW PLYMOUTH VENTURES INC (BC)
Struck off register and declared dissolved for failure to file returns 8/14/92

NEW PRIVATEER MINE LTD (BC)
Recapitalized as Phrygian Mining Corp. 06/06/1995
Each share Common no par exchanged for (0.2) share Common no par
Phrygian Mining Corp. recapitalized as Crowflight Minerals Inc. (BC) 10/12/1998 which reincorporated in Ontario 07/31/2003 which reincorporated in British Columbia as CaNickel Mining Ltd. 06/23/2011

NEW PROCESS CO (DE)
Each share old Common no par exchanged for (5) shares new Common no par 09/17/1962
New Common no par split (3) for (1) by issuance of (2) additional shares 05/10/1968
New Common no par split (2) for (1) by issuance of (1) additional share 10/29/1969
New Common no par split (2) for (1) by issuance of (1) additional share 12/29/1970
New Common no par split (2) for (1) by issuance of (1) additional share 12/29/1971
Name changed to Blair Corp. 04/18/1989
(See Blair Corp.)

NEW PROCESS CORK CO., INC.
Merged into Crown Cork & Seal Co., Inc. (NY) 00/00/1927
Details not available

NEW PROCESS IRON & STEEL CO.
Merged into Crown Cork & Seal Co., Inc. (NY) 00/00/1927
Details not available

NEW PROCESS RAYON, INC.
Name changed to Imperial Rayon Corp. in 1939
(See Imperial Reyon Corp.)

NEW PROD DEV SVCS INC (MO)
Common 10¢ par split (5) for (2) by issuance of (1.5) additional shares 7/10/72
Each share old Common 10¢ par exchanged for (0.1) share new Common 10¢ par 1/3/87
Administratively dissolved 10/22/90

NEW PRODS CORP (UT)
Each share old Common 10¢ par exchanged for (0.33333333) share new Common 10¢ par 03/01/1975
Recapitalized as Commodore Resources Corp. 12/29/1978
Each share new Common 10¢ par exchanged for (0.2) share Common 10¢ par
Commodore Resources Corp. name changed to Commodore Environmental Services, Inc. (UT) 06/26/1987 which reincorporated in Delaware 08/00/1998
(See Commodore Environmental Services, Inc.)

NEW PRODUCE BUILDING CO. (IL)
Liquidated in 1953
Details not available

NEW PROVIDENCE DEV LTD (BAHAMAS)
Merged into Enaj International 2/14/2000
Each share Common B$1 par exchanged for $1.74 cash

NEW PRUDENTIAL PETROLEUMS LTD. (BC)
Name changed to Consolidated Prudential Mines Ltd. 12/23/1965
Consolidated Prudential Mines Ltd. merged into Davenport Oil & Mining Ltd. 02/29/1972 which name changed to Davenport Industries Ltd. 11/01/1973 which recapitalized as DVO Industries Ltd. 08/19/1991
(See DVO Industries Ltd.)

NEW PYRAMID GOLD MINES INC (BC)
Recapitalized as International Pyramid Mines Inc. 2/7/77
Each share Common no par exchanged for (0.2) share Common no par
International Pyramid Mines Ltd. merged into American Pyramid Resources Inc. 7/24/79
(See American Pyramid Resources Inc.)

NEW QUE RAGLAN MINES LTD (ON)
Capital Stock $1 par changed to Common no par 7/13/84
Merged into Falconbridge Ltd. 6/13/89
Each (5.5) shares Common no par exchanged for (1) share Common no par
(See Falconbridge Ltd.)

NEW QUINCY MNG CO (UT)
Completely liquidated 04/29/1998
Each share Common 10¢ par exchanged for first and final distribution of (0.146) share United Park City Mines Co. new Common 1¢ par
(See United Park City Mines Co.)

NEW RANCHMEN'S OIL CO. LTD. (AB)
Common no par changed to 10¢ par in 1951
Recapitalized as Ranchmen's Oils (1957) Ltd. 11/15/57
Each share Common 10¢ par exchanged for (0.1) share Common 10¢ par
Ranchmen's Oils (1957) Ltd. name changed to Ranchmen's Resources Ltd. 6/2/70 which merged into Ranchmen's Resources (1975) Ltd. 8/28/75 which merged into Ranchmen's Resources (1976) Ltd. 1/31/77 which name changed to Ranchmen's Resources Ltd. 5/31/85 which merged into Crestar Energy Inc. 10/11/95 which was acquired by Gulf Canada Resources Ltd. 11/13/2000
(See Gulf Canada Resources Ltd.)

NEW RANGE RES LTD (AB)
Recapitalized as Relentless Resources Ltd. 06/11/2010
Each share Common no par exchanged for (0.5) share Common no par

NEW REALM RES INC (ON)
Name changed to Direct Equity Corp. 05/15/1987
Direct Equity Corp. merged into Envirothermic Technologies Ltd. 10/01/1993 which recapitalized as Environmental Reclamation Inc. 06/22/1998 which was acquired by Therma Freeze Inc. 02/28/2001 which name changed to Enviro-Energy Corp. 07/03/2001
(See Enviro-Energy Corp.)

NEW REDWOOD GOLD MINES LTD (ON)
Charter cancelled for failure to file reports and pay taxes 3/25/91

NEW RESOURCE BANCORP (CA)
Merged into Amalgamated Bank (New York, NY) 05/18/2018
Each share Common no par exchanged for (0.0315) share Common $10 par

NEW RESOURCE BK (SAN FRANCISCO, CA)
Under plan of reorganization each share Common no par automatically became (1) share New Resource Bancorp Common no par 12/14/2017
New Resource Bancorp merged into Amalgamated Bank (New York, NY) 05/18/2018

NEW RETAIL CONCEPTS INC (DE)
Each share old Common $0.0001 par exchanged for (0.1) share new Common $0.0001 par 5/26/89
Merged into Candie's, Inc. 8/18/98
Each share Common $0.0001 par exchanged for (0.405) share Common $0.001 par
Candie's, Inc. name changed to Iconix Brand Group, Inc. 7/1/2005

NEW RIBAGO MINES LTD.
Each (10) shares Capital Stock exchanged for (1) share Capital Stock of Ribago Rouyn Mines Ltd. and (1) share Capital Stock of Continental Copper Mines Ltd. 00/00/1944
(See each company's listing)

NEW RICE LAKE GOLD MINES LTD (CANADA)
Recapitalized as Jagor Resources Ltd. 7/24/70
Each share Common no par exchanged for (0.25) share Common no par
Jagor Resources Ltd. acquired by Normandie Resource Corp. 9/12/85
(See Normandie Resource Corp.)

NEW RICHFIELD PETE LTD (CANADA)
Capital Stock $1 par changed to no par 04/22/1954
Recapitalized as Twin Richfield Oils Ltd. 02/06/1969
Each share Common no par exchanged for (0.1) share Common no par
(See Twin Richfield Oils Ltd.)

NEW RICHLAND OIL & GAS LTD. (AB)
Acquired by Boundary Drilling Ltd. 12/5/64
Each share Common no par exchanged for $0.1325 cash

NEW RICHMOND NATL BK (NEW RICHMOND, OH)
Reorganized as New Richmond Bancorporation 04/15/1980
Details not available

NEW RIDGE RES LTD (BC)
Name changed 03/19/1982
Name changed from New Ridge Mines Ltd. to New Ridge Resources Ltd. 03/19/1982
Recapitalized as Destiny Resources Ltd. 05/22/1987
Each share Common no par exchanged for (0.25) share Common no par
Destiny Resources Ltd. recapitalized as Double Down Resources Ltd. 06/12/1990 which recapitalized as Meteor Creek Resources Inc. 01/11/2001
(See Meteor Creek Resources Inc.)

NEW RIO RES LTD (BC)
Name changed to Southern Rio Resources Ltd. 08/23/1994
Southern Rio Resources Ltd. recapitalized as Silver Quest Resources Ltd. 12/15/2005
(See Silver Quest Resources Ltd.)

NEW RIV PHARMACEUTICALS INC (VA)
Common $0.001 par split (2) for (1) by issuance of (1) additional share payable 01/12/2006 to holders of record 12/30/2005 Ex date - 01/13/2006
Merged into Shire PLC 04/19/2007

Each share Common $0.001 par exchanged for $64 cash

NEW RIVER COLLIERIES CO.
Liquidated in 1941
Details not available

NEW RIVER CORP (UT)
Reincorporated under the laws of Kansas as Photo Images Inc. 7/14/86
(See Photo Images Inc.)

NEW ROOSEVELT HOTEL CO.
Liquidated in 1948
Details not available

NEW ROUYN EXPL LTD (QC)
Charter cancelled 6/18/77

NEW ROUYN MERGER MINES, LTD. (ON)
Recapitalized as Goldrim Mining Co. Ltd. 6/8/65
Each share Capital Stock $1 par exchanged for (0.2) share Capital Stock $1 par
(See Goldrim Mining Co. Ltd.)

NEW ROYRAN COPPER MINES LTD. (QC)
Merged into Copper Rand Chibougamau Mines Ltd. on a (21) for (40) basis 9/25/56
Copper Rand Chibougamau Mines Ltd. merged into Patino Mining Corp. 11/26/62 which reorganized as Patino N.V. 12/20/71
(See Patino N.V.)

NEW RUSSIAN KID MINING CO. LTD. (ON)
Name changed to Augmitto Explorations Ltd. 3/1/66
(See Augmitto Explorations Ltd.)

NEW RYAN LAKE MINES LTD. (ON)
Recapitalized as Min-Ore Mines Ltd. on a (1) for (3.5) basis 10/01/1955
(See Min-Ore Mines Ltd.)

NEW SABINA RES LTD (BC)
Reorganized as Sabina Resources Ltd. 12/23/1987
Each share Common no par exchanged for (2) shares Common no par
Sabina Resources Ltd. name changed to Sabina Silver Corp. 10/17/2005 which name changed to Sabina Gold & Silver Corp. 10/28/2009

NEW SAGE RES LTD (BC)
Recapitalized as Consolidated New Sage Resources Ltd. (BC) 01/30/2002
Each share Common no par exchanged for (0.5) share Common no par
Consolidated New Sage Resources Ltd. (BC) reincorporated in Canada 10/24/2003 which name changed to New Sage Energy Corp. 05/24/2007

NEW SANTIAGO MINES LTD. (BC)
Recapitalized as Santico Mining & Exploration Ltd. 8/10/70
Each share Capital Stock 50¢ par exchanged for (0.1) share Capital Stock 50¢ par
(See Santico Mining & Exploration Ltd.)

NEW SCOPE RES LTD (MB)
Reincorporated under the laws of Canada as Newscope Resources Ltd. 9/13/84
Newscope Resources Ltd. recapitalized as Canadian Newscope Resources Ltd. 12/13/90 which name changed back to Newscope Resources Ltd. 7/11/94 which changed to Denbury Resources Ltd. 12/21/95

NEW SENATOR ROUYN LTD (QC)
Name changed to NSR Resources Inc. 10/02/1980

NEW SEPHA MINES LTD (ON)
Charter cancelled for failure to pay taxes and file returns 6/30/80

NEW SHEEPROCK INVTS INC (NV)
Charter suspended for failure to pay taxes 04/30/1986

NEW SHOSHONI VENTURES LTD (BC)
Recapitalized as Shoshoni Gold Ltd. 05/09/2012
Each share Common no par exchanged for (0.2) share Common no par

NEW SIDNEYS INC (VA)
Charter cancelled for failure to file annual reports 9/1/94

NEW SIGNET RES INC (BC)
Recapitalized as Amir Ventures Corp. (BC) 6/29/93
Each share Common no par exchanged for (0.2) share Common no par
Amir Ventures Corp. (BC) reorganized in Yukon Territory as America Mineral Fields Inc. 8/8/95 which name changed to Adasta Minerals Inc. 5/12/2004

NEW SILVER BELL MINING CO., INC. (WA)
Charter revoked for failure to file reports and pay fees 7/1/65

NEW SKIES SATELLITES HLDGS LTD. (BERMUDA)
Issue Information - 11,900,000 shares COM offered at $16.50 per share on 05/09/2005
Merged into SES Global S.A. 03/30/2006
Each share Common 1¢ par exchanged for $22.52 cash

NEW SKIES SATELLITES N V (NETHERLANDS)
Acquired by Blackstone Group 11/19/2004
Each Sponsored ADR for Ordinary exchanged for $7.51 cash
Each Sponsored ADR for Ordinary received an initial additional distribution of $0.41 cash from escrow 03/07/2005
Each Sponsored ADR for Ordinary received a second and final additional distribution of $0.005278 cash from escrow 04/27/2005

NEW SKY COMMUNICATIONS INC (NY)
Each share Common $0.0001 par exchanged for (0.005) share Common 2¢ par 11/01/2001
Name changed to Document Security Systems, Inc. 02/03/2003

NEW SLEEPER GOLD CORP (CANADA)
Name changed to Reunion Gold Corp. 6/6/2006

NEW SOURCE ENERGY GROUP INC (DE)
Name changed to Encompass Energy Services, Inc. 04/19/2012

NEW SOUTH AFRICA FD INC (MD)
Issue Information - 3,800,000 shares COM offered at $15 per share on 03/04/1994
Liquidation completed
Each share Common $0.001 par exchanged for initial distribution of $10.22 cash payable 6/3/99 to holders of record 6/1/99
Each share Common $0.001 par received second and final distribution of $0.1682 cash payable 1/11/2000 to holders of record 6/1/99

NEW SOUTH CAP TR I (DE)
8.50% Trust Preferred Securities called for redemption at $10 on 3/5/2004

NEW SOUTH LIFE INS CO (SC)
Assets transferred to Citadel Life Insurance Co. of South Carolina by Court Order 12/29/78
No stockholders' equity

NEW SOUTHERN EUREKA MINING CO. (UT)
Merged into North Lily Mining Co. 12/1/76
Each share Common 10¢ par exchanged for (0.0161) share Capital Stock 10¢ par
(See North Lily Mining Co.)

NEW SOUTHLAND NATL INS CO (AL)
Common $1 par split (5) for (4) by issuance of (0.25) additional share 9/1/86
Stock Dividends - 10% 6/1/73; 25% 9/15/83
Name changed to Southland National Insurance Corp. 9/18/88
(See Southland National Insurance Corp.)

NEW SOUTHN BK (MACON, GA)
Under plan of reorganization each share Common $5 par automatically became (1) share NSB Holdings, Inc. Common $5 par 07/08/2005
NSB Holdings, Inc. name changed to Atlantic Southern Financial Group, Inc. 01/23/2006
(See Atlantic Southern Financial Group, Inc.)

NEW SPIRIT RESH & DEV CORP (BC)
Name changed to New Spirit Research & Development Corp. 12/22/88

NEW SPRING COULEE OIL & MINERALS LTD. (AB)
Recapitalized as Native Minerals Ltd. on a (1) for (4) basis 11/3/60
(See Native Minerals Ltd.)

NEW STAFFORD INDS LTD (BC)
Name changed to Grandcru Resources Corp. 07/10/2003
Grandcru Resources Corp. merged into Bell Copper Corp. (Old) 05/12/2008 which reorganized as Bell Copper Corp. (New) 07/23/2013

NEW STAR ENTMT INC (CA)
Chapter 11 bankruptcy proceedings converted to Chapter 7 on 10/26/90
Stockholders' equity unlikely

NEW STRATEGIC METALS INC (BC)
Name changed to P.S.M. Technologies Inc. 12/29/1986
(See P.S.M. Technologies Inc.)

NEW SUPERIOR OILS OF CANADA LTD. (AB)
Acquired by Canadian Petrofina Ltd. 06/29/1960
Each share Capital Stock $1 par exchanged for (0.055625) share 6% Preferred $10 par
Canadian Petrofina Ltd. name changed to Petrofina Canada Ltd. 08/01/1968 which name changed to Petro-Canada Enterprises Inc./Entreprises Petro-Canada Inc. 11/16/1981
(See Petro-Canada Enterprises Inc./Entreprises Petro-Canada Inc.)

NEW SURPASS PETROCHEMICALS LTD. (ON)
Name changed to Surpass Chemicals Ltd. 08/01/1968
Surpass Chemicals Ltd. merged into Witco Chemical Corp. 08/31/1979 which name changed to Witco Corp. 10/01/1985 which merged into CK Witco Corp. 09/01/1999 which name changed to Crompton Corp. 04/27/2000 which name changed to Chemtura Corp. 07/01/2005
(See Chemtura Corp.)

NEW SYRUS CAP CORP (BC)
Name changed to Player Petroleum Corp. (BC) 2/25/97
Player Petroleum Corp. (BC) reincorporated in Alberta 4/29/98
(See Player Petroleum Corp.)

NEW SYS INC (NV)
Common $0.001 par split (4) for (1) by issuance of (3) additional shares payable 03/16/2001 to holders of record 03/13/2001 Ex date - 03/19/2001
Name changed to Tremor Entertainment Inc. 12/04/2001
Tremor Entertainment Inc. name changed to Durham Marketing Corp. 08/25/2003
(See Durham Marketing Corp.)

NEW TAKU MINES LTD (ON)
Each share old Common no par exchanged for (0.2) share new Common no par 08/15/1974
Name changed to Rembrandt Gold Mines Ltd. (ON) 10/17/1974
Rembrandt Gold Mines Ltd. (ON) reincorporated in Canada 08/04/1992 which reincorporated in Cayman Islands 05/16/1996
(See Rembrandt Gold Mines Ltd.)

NEW TAOHUAYUAN CULTURE TOURISM CO LTD (NV)
Recapitalized as KYN Capital Group, Inc. 04/09/2015
Each share Common $0.001 par exchanged for (0.000625) share Common $0.001 par

NEW-TEK-NIC INDS LTD (NY)
Charter cancelled and proclaimed dissolved for failure to pay taxes and file reports 12/20/1977

NEW TEL LTD (AUSTRALIA)
ADR agreement terminated 05/01/2009
No stockholders' equity

NEW TELLURIDE GOLD MINES OF CANADA LTD. (ON)
Charter revoked for failure to file reports and pay fees 6/3/65

NEW TERRITORIAL URANIUM MINES LTD (BC)
Name changed to Mid-West Energy Inc. and Capital Stock no par reclassified as Class A Capital Stock no par 2/8/79
Mid-West Energy Inc. recapitalized as Millrock Development Corp. 11/19/84 which recapitalized as Delta Gold Mining Corp. 9/5/91 which merged into Chase Resource Corp. (New) 5/30/97
(See Chase Resource Corp. (New))

NEW TEX AMERN GROUP INC (TX)
Each share old Common 10¢ par exchanged for (0.0001) share new Common 10¢ par 06/05/2008
Recapitalized as Zana Acquisition Co. 06/26/2008
Each share Common 10¢ par exchanged for (0.0005) share Common 10¢ par

NEW TEXMONT EXPLS LTD (CANADA)
Reincorporated 03/19/1982
Place of incorporation changed from (ONT) to (Canada) 03/19/1982
Delisted from Alberta Stock Exchange 02/28/1992

NEW THOUGHT BROADCASTING INC (NV)
Name changed to Mundus Environmental Products Inc. and (5) additional shares issued 8/16/2004
Mundus Environmental Products Inc. name changed to Mundus Group Inc. 8/28/2006

NEW 360 (CA)
Name changed to Point.360 (New) 08/21/2007

NEW THURBOIS MINES LTD. (ON)
Name changed to Canadian Thorium Corp. Ltd. 10/10/56
Canadian Thorium Corp. recapitalized as Quebec Mattagami Minerals Ltd. 10/11/61 which name changed to Q.M.G. Holdings Inc. 10/3/77
(See Q.M.G. Holdings Inc.)

NEW TONOPAH DIVIDEND MINING CO. (NV)
Charter revoked for failure to file reports and pay fees 3/4/35

NEW TYEE RES LTD (BC)
Recapitalized as Alban Explorations Ltd. 01/24/1985
Each share Capital Stock no par exchanged for (0.2) share Common no par
Alban Explorations Ltd. recapitalized as Pacific Amber Resources Ltd. (BC) 05/19/1994 which reincorporated in Alberta 07/25/2002 which recapitalized as Grand Banks Energy Corp. 05/14/2003
(See Grand Banks Energy Corp.)

NEW ULM TELECOM INC (MN)
Common $5 par changed to $1.66 par and (2) additional shares issued payable 02/15/2002 to holders of record 01/10/2002 Ex date - 02/19/2002
Name changed to Nuvera Communications, Inc. 06/04/2018

NEW UNGAVA COPPER LTD (QC)
Name changed to Unergie Inc. 11/18/82
Unergie Inc. merged into Atlas Yellowknife Resources Ltd. 12/31/85 which recapitalized as Panatlas Energy Inc. 2/8/88 which was acquired by Velvet Exploration Ltd. 7/17/2000
(See Velvet Exploration Ltd.)

NEW UNI-WAY HLDGS LTD (BC)
Name changed to Full Riches Investments Ltd. 02/26/1998
Full Riches Investments Ltd. was acquired by Medoro Resources Ltd. 03/02/2004 which merged into Gran Colombia Gold Corp. 06/14/2011

NEW UNISPHERE RES LTD (AB)
Struck off register for failure to file annual reports 9/30/81

NEW UNIV HLDGS CORP (AB)
Reorganized under the laws of Ontario as ePals Corp. 08/09/2011
Each share Common no par exchanged for (0.41881308) share Common no par
ePals Corp. recapitalized as Cricket Media Group Inc. 07/10/2014
(See Cricket Media Group Ltd.)

NEW UNIVERSE URANIUM & DEV (NV)
Merged into Gulf Continental, Inc. 9/24/68
Each share Capital Stock 2¢ par exchanged for (1) share Common 2¢ par
(See Gulf Continental, Inc.)

NEW VA BANCORPORATION (VA)
Liquidation completed
Each share Common $1 par exchanged for first and final distribution of $20 cash 9/1/82

NEW VY CORP (DE)
Reorganized 07/29/1996
Reorganized from (NY) to under the laws of Delaware 07/29/1996
Each share Common $2.50 par exchanged for (0.05) share Common $2.50 par
Plan of recapitalization effective 06/04/1999
Each share Increasing Rate Sr. Preferred Class A 1¢ par exchanged for (20) shares Common 1¢ par and (1) Common Stock Purchase Warrant which expired 01/01/2004
Each share $3 Conv. Preferred Class

NEW-NEW

B 10¢ par exchanged for (1/3) share Common 1¢ par and (5) Common Stock Purchase Warrants which expired 01/01/2004
Each share new Common $2.50 par exchanged for (0.1) share Common 1¢ par and (1/3) Common Stock Purchase Warrant which expired 01/01/2004
Each share Common 1¢ par received distribution of (0.988) share Ladenburg Thalmann Financial Services, Inc. Common $0.001 par payable 12/20/2001 to holders of record 12/10/2001 Ex date - 12/21/2001
Acquired by Vector Group Ltd. 12/13/2005
Each share Common 1¢ par exchanged for (0.54) share Common 10¢ par

NEW VENORO GOLD CORP (CANADA)
Name changed to Vanteck (VRB) Technology Corp. and Class A Common no par reclassified as Common no par 06/20/2000
Vanteck (VRB) Technology Corp. name changed to VRB Power Systems Inc. 01/17/2003 which name changed to Nevaro Capital Corp. (Old) 08/24/2009
(See Nevaro Capital Corp. (Old))

NEW VENTURE CAP CORP (UT)
Recapitalized as Nut & Candy Kitchen, Inc. 6/17/85
Each share Common $0.001 par exchanged for (0.1) share Common 1¢ par
(See Nut & Candy Kitchen, Inc.)

NEW-VIEW INDS INC (AB)
Merged into Home Products, Inc. 09/28/1992
Each share Common no par exchanged for (0.125) share Common no par
(See Home Products, Inc.)

NEW VINRAY MINES LTD. (ON)
Recapitalized as Atlas Telefilm Ltd. 3/11/60
Each share Capital Stock $1 par exchanged for (0.25) share Capital Stock no par
Atlas Telefilm Ltd. recapitalized as Atlas Telemedia Ltd. 1/24/64
(See Atlas Telemedia Ltd.)

NEW VISIONS ENTMT CORP (DE)
Charter cancelled and declared inoperative and void for non-payment of taxes 5/30/96

NEW VISUAL CORP (UT)
Name changed 07/02/2001
Each share old Common $0.001 par exchanged for (0.25) share new Common $0.001 par 06/23/2000
Name changed from New Visual Entertainment, Inc. to New Visual Corp. 07/02/2001
Name changed to Rim Semiconductor Co. 09/19/2005
(See Rim Semiconductor Co.)

NEW WALCORO MINES LTD (ON)
Charter cancelled for failure to pay taxes and file returns 7/17/77

NEW WAVE ART INC (DE)
Name changed to One World Entertainment Corp. 05/06/1985
One World Entertainment Corp. name changed to Sun Scientific Group, Inc. 04/07/1987
(See Sun Scientific Group, Inc.)

NEW WAVE ENERGY INC (UT)
Name changed to Groen Brothers Aviation, Inc. 10/4/90

NEW WAVE HLDGS INC (NV)
Name changed to PAO Group, Inc. 06/29/2017

NEW WAVE MEDIA INC (WA)
Name changed to CA Goldfields, Inc. 04/08/2008
(See CA Goldfields, Inc.)

NEW WAVE MOBILE INC (WA)
Name changed to New Wave Media, Inc. 03/26/2007
Each share Common $0.001 par exchanged for (1) share Common $0.001 par
New Wave Media, Inc. name changed to CA Goldfields, Inc. 04/08/2008

NEW WAVE WINDMILLS INC (ON)
Reincorporated under the laws of Nevada as AirCharter Express Inc. 10/20/2004

NEW WAY LAUNDRY CORP.
Acquired by Consolidated Laundries Corp. in 1929
Details not available

NEW WELLINGTON MINES LTD. (BC)
Name changed to New Wellington Resources Ltd. and Capital Stock 50¢ par changed to no par 09/01/1970
New Wellington Resources Ltd. recapitalized as International Wellington Resources Ltd. 03/25/1976 which recapitalized as Wellington Resources Ltd. 12/12/1983 which name changed to First Hospitality (Canada) Corp. 09/24/1987 which recapitalized as Southern Pacific Development Corp. 11/05/1991 which recapitalized as Southern Pacific Resource Corp. (BC) 03/03/2006 which reincorporated in Alberta 11/17/2006

NEW WELLINGTON RES LTD (BC)
Recapitalized as International Wellington Resources Ltd. 03/25/1976
Each share Capital Stock no par exchanged for (0.2) share Capital Stock no par
International Wellington Resources Ltd. recapitalized as Consolidated Wellington Resources Ltd. 12/12/1983 which name changed to First Hospitality (Canada) Corp. 09/24/1987 which recapitalized as Southern Pacific Development Corp. 11/05/1991 which recapitalized as Southern Pacific Resource Corp. (BC) 03/03/2006 which reincorporated in Alberta 11/17/2006

NEW WEST AMULET MINES LTD. (QC)
Recapitalized as Waite Dufault Mines Ltd. 09/13/1966
Each share Common $1 par exchanged for (0.2) share Common $1 par
Waite Dufault Mines Ltd. recapitalized as KPI International Inc. 05/28/1996
(See KPI International Inc.)

NEW WEST BANCSHARES INC (CA)
Merged into Nuevaco 6/6/99
Each share Common $10 par exchanged for $0.50 cash

NEW WEST EYEWORKS INC (DE)
Merged into National Vision Associates, Ltd. 10/23/98
Each share Common 1¢ par exchanged for $11.50 cash

NEW WEST LD CORP (DE)
Common $1 par changed to 50¢ par 10/23/63
Name changed to Resource Reserves, Inc. and Common 50¢ par changed to 10¢ par 6/30/80
(See Resource Reserves, Inc.)

NEW WESTWIN VENTURES INC (BC)
Name changed to Arimex Mining Corp. 07/29/1997
Arimex Mining Corp. recapitalized as International Arimex Resources Inc. 02/22/1999 which name changed to WestCan Uranium Corp. 09/10/2007

NEW WINDSOR BANCORP INC (MD)
Common 1¢ par split (3) for (1) by issuance of (2) additional shares payable 03/13/2002 to holders of record 2/15/2002 02/15/2002 Ex date - 03/15/2002
Stock Dividend - 5% payable 02/13/2015 to holders of record 01/30/2015 Ex date - 01/28/2015
Merged into ACNB Corp. 07/01/2017
Each share Common 1¢ par exchanged for (0.708) share Common $2.50 par and $10.6914 cash

NEW WINDSOR ST BK (NEW WINDSOR, MD)
Reorganized as New Windsor Bancorp Inc. 02/08/1997
Each share Common 1¢ par exchanged for (0.25) share Common 1¢ par
New Windsor Bancorp Inc. merged into ACNB Corp. 07/01/2017

NEW WINE HAY & FEED INC (OK)
Name changed to GoBabyRacing, Inc. (OK) 11/11/2005
GoBabyRacing, Inc. (OK) reincorporated in Nevada as Heartland Energy Group, Inc. 05/15/2006 which name changed to Tritent International Corp. 01/20/2009

NEW WITS LTD (SOUTH AFRICA)
Each ADR for Ordinary R0.50 par exchanged for (2) ADR's for Ordinary R0.25 par 12/11/87
ADR agreement terminated 2/4/2002
Each ADR for Ordinary R0.25 par exchanged for $0.311 cash
Note: Actual amount received may vary based upon issuing depositary

NEW WITWATERSRAND GOLD EXPLORATION CO. LTD. (SOUTH AFRICA)
Name changed to New Wits Ltd. 10/11/82
(See New Wits Ltd.)

NEW WORLD CAP ADVISORS INC (DE)
Charter cancelled and declared inoperative and void for non-payment of taxes 3/1/99

NEW WORLD COFFEE MANHATTAN BAGEL INC (DE)
Name changed 11/04/1997
Name changed 04/09/1999
Name changed from New World Coffee Inc. to New World Coffee & Bagels, Inc. 11/04/1997
Name changed from New World Coffee & Bagels, Inc. to New World Coffee - Manhattan Bagel, Inc. 04/09/1999
Each share old Common $0.001 par exchanged for (0.5) share new Common $0.001 par 08/24/1999
Name changed to New World Restaurant Group, Inc. 09/25/2001
New World Restaurant Group, Inc. name changed to Einstein Noah Restaurant Group, Inc. 05/03/2007
(See Einstein Noah Restaurant Group, Inc.)

NEW WORLD COMMUNICATIONS GROUP INC (DE)
Merged into News Corp., Ltd. 01/22/1997
Each share Class A Common 1¢ par exchanged for (1.45) Sponsored ADR's for Ltd. Voting Preferred Ordinary AUD $0.50 par
Each share Class B Common 1¢ par exchanged for (1.45) Sponsored ADR's for Ltd. Voting Preferred Ordinary AUD $0.50 par
News Corp., Ltd. reorganized as News Corp. (Old) 11/03/2004 which name changed to Twenty-First Century Fox, Inc. 07/01/2013

NEW WORLD COMPUTER INC (NV)
Charter revoked for failure to file reports and pay fees 10/1/85

NEW WORLD ENTMT CORP (NV)
Name changed to Aultra Gold, Inc. 01/19/2007
Aultra Gold, Inc. name changed to Shamika 2 Gold, Inc. 02/02/2011
(See Shamika 2 Gold, Inc.)

NEW WORLD ENTMT LTD (DE)
Merged into Andrews Group Inc. 4/25/90
Each share Common 1¢ par exchanged for $8.95 cash

NEW WORLD FD INC (CA)
Merged into Investment Co. of America 1/23/81
Each (1.442827) shares Common $1 par exchanged for (1) share Common $1 par

NEW WORLD INDS INC (NV)
Charter cancelled and declared dissolved for failure to file reports 06/30/2003

NEW WORLD LIFE INSURANCE CO. (WA)
Name changed to Farmers New World Life Insurance Co. in 1954
Farmers New World Life Insurance Co. merged into Farmers Group, Inc. 12/21/77
(See Farmers Group, Inc.)

NEW WORLD OIL & URANIUM LTD. (AB)
Name changed in 1955
Name changed from New World Oil Ltd. to New World Oil & Uranium Ltd. in 1955
Merged into Sastex Oil & Gas Ltd. in 1956
Each share Common no par exchanged for (0.1) share Common no par
Sastex Oil & Gas Ltd. recapitalized as Sastex Petro-Minerals Ltd. 4/27/66
(See Sastex Petro-Minerals Ltd.)

NEW WORLD PICTURES LTD (DE)
Common 10¢ par changed to 1¢ par and (0.5) additional share issued 3/21/86
Name changed to New World Entertainment, Ltd. 7/28/87
(See New World Entertainment, Ltd.)

NEW WORLD PWR CORP (DE)
Each share old Common 1¢ par exchanged for (0.1) share new Common 1¢ par 10/19/1992
Each share new Common 1¢ par exchanged for (0.2) share Common 1¢ par 11/04/1996
Recapitalized as Distributed Power Inc. 10/24/2003
Each share Common 1¢ par exchanged for (0.01) share Common 1¢ par
Distributed Power Inc. name changed to Global Pay Solutions, Inc. 04/23/2007 which recapitalized as China National Appliance of North America Corp. 03/26/2009

NEW WORLD PUBG INC (CO)
Name changed to SonicPort.com, Inc. (CO) 10/18/1999
SonicPort.com, Inc. (CO) reincorporated in Nevada 02/00/2000 which name changed to SonicPort, Inc. 02/07/2001 which name changed to US Dataworks, Inc. 03/27/2002
(See US Dataworks, Inc.)

NEW WORLD RESTAURANT GROUP INC (DE)
Each share old Common $0.001 par exchanged for (0.01661044) share new Common $0.001 par to reflect a (1) for (100) reverse split followed by a (1.6610444) for (1) forward split 09/30/2003
Name changed to Einstein Noah Restaurant Group, Inc. 05/03/2007

(See Einstein Noah Restaurant Group, Inc.)

NEW WORLD VENTURES INC (AB)
Recapitalized as Digital Precision Imagery Corp. 12/02/1992
Each share Common no par exchanged for (1/3) share Common no par
Digital Precision Imagery Corp. recapitalized as Alava Ventures Inc. 12/04/1996
(See Alava Ventures Inc.)

NEW WORLD WINE GROUP LTD (NY)
Each share old Common 1¢ par exchanged for (0.005) share new Common 1¢ par 08/11/2006
New Common 1¢ par split (8) for (1) by issuance of (7) additional shares payable 08/27/2007 to holders of record 08/27/2007 Ex date - 08/28/2007
Reincorporated under the laws of Nevada as QX Bio Tech Group, Inc. and Common 1¢ par changed to $0.001 par 12/04/2007
QX Bio Tech Group, Inc. recapitalized as AcumedSpa Holdings, Inc. 09/18/2009 which recapitalized as Organic Plant Health, Inc. 02/02/2011

NEW XAVIER CAP CORP (BC)
Name changed to RET Internet Services Inc. 05/25/2001
RET Internet Services Inc. recapitalized as Terra Ventures Inc. 06/15/2004 which merged into Hathor Exploration Ltd. 08/05/2011
(See Hathor Exploration Ltd.)

NEW YARANDRY LTD (ON)
Name changed to Merbank Capital Corp. (ONT) 02/23/1988
Merbank Capital Corp. (ONT) reincorporated in British Columbia 06/13/1995 which merged into Gran Colombia Resources Inc. 07/11/1995 which name changed to Wavve Telecommunications, Inc. 10/29/1999
(See Wavve Telecommunications, Inc.)

NEW YORK, LACKAWANNA & WESTERN RAILWAY
Merged into Delaware, Lackawanna & Western Railroad Co. and each share Capital Stock $100 par exchanged for $60 of 1st and Refunding Mtge. Bonds Series C and $40 of Income Mtge. Bonds in 1945

NEW YORK, ONTARIO & WESTERN RAILWAY CO. (NY)
In receivership and sale of property completed 7/8/57
Only bondholders participated in plan of liquidating distribution which was confirmed by Federal Court 11/18/60
No stockholders' equity

NEW YORK, RIO & BUENOS AIRES LINES, INC. (DE)
Liquidation completed 10/6/31
Holders of record 10/15/30 received two liquidating distributions in shares of Aviation Corp. of the Americas
Note: Certificates were not required to be surrendered and are without value

NEW YORK & FOREIGN INVESTING CORP.
Liquidated in 1938
Details not available

NEW YORK & HAMBURG CORP.
Liquidated in 1936
Details not available

NEW YORK & HARLEM RR CO (NY)
Merged into American Premier Underwriters, Inc. 9/26/2006
Each share 10% Preferred $50 par exchanged for $462 cash
Each share Common $50 par exchanged for $462 cash

NEW YORK & HONDURAS ROSARIO MNG CO (NY)
Capital Stock $10 par changed to $3.33333333 par and (2) additional shares issued 02/18/1959
Capital Stock $3.33333333 par changed to $1 par and (2) additional shares issued 11/27/1963
Capital Stock $1 par split (2) for (1) by issuance of (1) additional share 02/27/1970
Name changed to Rosario Resources Corp. 04/27/1973
Rosario Resources Corp. merged into Amax Inc. 04/10/1980 which merged into Cyprus Amax Minerals Co. 11/15/1993 which merged into Phelps Dodge Corp. 12/02/1999 which merged into Freeport-McMoRan Copper & Gold Inc. 03/19/2007 which name changed to Freeport-McMoRan Inc. 07/14/2014

NEW YORK & NORTHEASTERN STRAWBERRY ASSN., INC. (NY)
Dissolved in 1957
Details not available

NEW YORK & PENNSYLVANIA RAILWAY CO.
Operations discontinued in 1936
Details not available

NEW YORK & QUEENS ELECTRIC LIGHT & POWER CO.
Merged into Consolidated Edison Co. of New York, Inc. in 1945
Each Preferred share received $108.625 cash
Each Common share received $115 cash

NEW YORK & QUEENS GAS CO.
Acquired by Consolidated Edison Co. of New York, Inc. and liquidated 00/00/1936
Details not available

NEW YORK & RICHMOND GAS CO. (NY)
Each share Common $100 par exchanged for (10) shares Common no par 00/00/1928
Common no par exchanged (1) for (10) 00/00/1940
Merged into Brooklyn Union Gas Co. on a (6) for (1) basis 01/15/1957
Brooklyn Union Gas Co. reorganized as KeySpan Energy Corp. 09/30/1997 which merged into MarketSpan Corp. 05/29/1998 which name changed to KeySpan Energy 09/10/1998 which name changed to KeySpan Corp. 05/20/1999
(See KeySpan Corp.)

NEW YORK AIR BRAKE CO. (NJ)
Each share Common no par exchanged for (2) shares Common $5 par in 1951
Common $5 par split (2) for (1) by issuance of (1) additional share 3/28/66
Merged into General Signal Corp. 9/20/67
Each share Common $5 par exchanged for (0.32) share $4 Conv. Preferred Ser. A $5 par and (0.2) share Common $6.67 par
General Signal Corp. merged into SPX Corp. 10/6/98

NEW YORK AIRLS INC (DE)
Acquired by Texas Air Corp. 8/28/85
Each share Common 1¢ par exchanged for $6.25 principal amount of 15.75% Senior Notes due 2/1/92

NEW YORK ALASKA GOLD DREDGING CORP (DE)
Capital Stock $2 par changed to 50¢ par and (3) additional shares issued 4/28/57
Stock Dividend - 10% 5/1/57
No longer in existence having become inoperative and void for non-payment of taxes 4/1/66

NEW YORK AMBASSADOR, INC. (NY)
Merged into Ambassador Hotel of New York, Inc. 12/31/54
Each share Common 10¢ par exchanged for (9/50) share 6% 2nd Preferred $50 par and (0.9) share Common $1 par
(See Ambassador Hotel of New York, Inc.)

NEW YORK AMERN BEVERAGE INC (NY)
Name changed to American Beverage Corp. (NY) 5/15/70
American Beverage Corp. (NY) assets transferred to American Beverage Trust 9/28/82
(See American Beverage Trust)

NEW YORK ASSET MGMT INC (DE)
Charter cancelled and declared inoperative and void for non-payment of taxes 3/1/74

NEW YORK AUCTION CO., INC. (NY)
Common no par split (5) for (4) by issuance of (0.25) additional share 09/15/1960
Merged into Standard Prudential United Corp. 07/12/1968
Each share Common no par exchanged for (1) share 10¢ Conv. Preferred no par and (0.5) share Common $1 par
Standard Prudential United Corp. name changed to Standard Prudential Corp. (New) 10/22/1968 which name changed to Sterling Bancorp (NY) 10/24/1978 which merged into Sterling Bancorp (DE) 11/01/2013

NEW YORK AWYS INC (DE)
Common $1 par changed to 2¢ par 10/30/73
Plan of arrangement under Chapter XI Federal Bankruptcy Act confirmed 7/23/85
No stockholders' equity

NEW YORK BAGEL ENTERPRISES INC (KS)
Plan of reorganization under Chapter 11 Federal Bankruptcy Code effective 10/25/2001
No stockholders' equity

NEW YORK BAGEL EXCHANGE INC (DE)
Name changed to Webboat.Com Inc. 02/04/1999
Webboat.Com Inc. name changed to Web4boats.Com Inc. 05/04/1999 which recapitalized as Federal Security Protection Services, Inc. 03/25/2002 which name changed to Platina Energy Group, Inc. 06/17/2005
(See Platina Energy Group, Inc.)

NEW YORK BANCORP INC (DE)
Common 1¢ par split (3) for (2) by issuance of (0.5) additional share 10/22/92
Common 1¢ par split (3) for (2) by issuance of (0.5) additional share 7/29/93
Common 1¢ par split (3) for (2) by issuance of (0.5) additional share payable 1/23/97 to holders of record 1/9/97
Common 1¢ par split (4) for (3) by issuance of (1/3) additional share payable 7/24/97 to holders of record 7/10/97 Ex date - 7/25/97
Stock Dividend - 10% 2/14/94
Merged into North Fork Bancorporation, Inc. 3/27/98
Each share Common 1¢ par exchanged for (1.19) shares Common $2.50 par
North Fork Bancorporation, Inc. merged into Capital One Financial Corp. 12/1/2006

NEW YORK BROKER DEUTSCHLAND AG (GERMANY)
Sponsored ADR's for Ordinary split (3) for (1) by issuance of (2) additional ADR's payable 05/27/1998 to holders of record 05/26/1998
ADR agreement terminated 12/01/2008
Each (30) Sponsored ADR's for Ordinary exchanged for (1) Ordinary share
Note: Unexchanged ADR's will be sold and the proceeds, if any, held for claim after 12/01/2009

NEW YORK-BUFFALO TRADING CORP.
Liquidated in 1941
Details not available

NEW YORK BUSINESS BLDGS. CORP. (NY)
Liquidated in 1950
Details not available

NEW YORK CANNERS, INC.
Name changed to Snider Packing Corp. in 1927
Snider Packing Corp. acquired by General Foods Corp. 7/7/73
(See General Foods Corp.)

NEW YORK CAPITAL FUND LTD. (CANADA)
Reincorporated under the laws of Maryland as Stein Roe & Farnham International Fund, Inc. 5/8/64
Stein Roe & Farnham International Fund, Inc. name changed to Stein Roe & Farnham Capital Opportunities Fund, Inc. 3/24/69 which merged into SteinRoe Equity Trust 12/31/87 which name changed to SteinRoe Investment Trust 6/30/89

NEW YORK CAPITAL FUND OF CANADA LTD. (CANADA)
Common $1 par changed to 34¢ par and (2) additional shares issued 7/17/59
Name changed to New York Capital Fund Ltd. (Canada) 11/7/60
New York Capital Fund Ltd. (Canada) reincorporated under the laws of Maryland as Stein Roe & Farnham International Fund Inc. 5/8/64 which name changed to Stein Roe & Farnham Capital Opportunities Fund, Inc. 3/24/69 which merged into SteinRoe Equity Trust 12/31/87 which name changed to SteinRoe Investment Trust 6/30/89

NEW YORK CASUALTY CO.
Merged into American Surety Co. in 1929
Details not available

NEW YORK CENT RR CO (DE)
Merged into Pennsylvania New York Central Transportation Co. 2/1/68
Each share Capital Stock $1 exchanged for (1.3) shares Capital Stock $10 par
Pennsylvania New York Central Transportation Co. name changed to Penn Central Co. 5/8/68 which reorganized as Penn Central Corp. 10/24/78 which name changed to American Premier Underwriters, Co. 3/25/94 which merged into American Premier Group, Inc. 4/3/95 which name changed to American Financial Group, Inc. 6/9/95 which merged into American Financial Group, Inc. (Holding Co.) 12/2/97

NEW YORK CENTRAL ELECTRIC CORP.
Merged into New York State Electric & Gas Corp. 00/00/1937
Details not available

NEW YORK CENTRAL RAILROAD CO. (NY, OH, IL, IN, PA & MI)
Capital Stock $100 par changed to no par in April 1934

Reincorporated under the laws of Delaware and Capital Stock no par changed to $1 par 2/28/61
New York Central Railroad Co. (DE) merged into Pennsylvania New York Central Transportation Co. 2/1/68 which name changed to Penn Central Co. 5/8/68 which reorganized as Penn Central Corp. 10/24/79 which name changed to American Premier Underwriters, Inc. 3/25/94 which merged into American Premier Group, Inc. 4/3/95 which name changed to American Financial Group, Inc. 6/9/95

NEW YORK CHICAGO & ST LOUIS RR CO (OH, NY, PA, IN & IL)
Each share Common $100 par exchanged for (5) shares Common $20 par in 1951
Common $20 par changed to $15 par and (1) additional share issued 6/15/56
Stock Dividend - 10% 8/7/53
Merged into Norfolk & Western Railway Co. on a (0.45) for (1) basis 10/16/64
Norfolk & Western Railway Co. merged into Norfolk Southern Corp. 6/1/82

NEW YORK CITY AIRPORT, INC.
Dissolved in 1931
Details not available

NEW YORK CITY INTERBOROUGH RAILWAY CO.
Merged into Third Avenue Transit Corp. on a share for share basis in 1942
(See Third Avenue Transit Corp.)

NEW YORK CITY OMNIBUS CORP. (NY)
Capital Stock no par changed to $10 par in 1954
Name changed to Fifth Avenue Coach Lines, Inc. 5/31/56
Fifth Avenue Coach Lines, Inc. name changed to South Bay Corp. 11/30/73 which assets tranferred to South Bay Corp. Liquidating Trust 3/31/79
(See South Bay Corp. Liquidating Trust)

NEW YORK CITY SHOES INC (DE)
Plan of reorganization under Chapter 11 Federal Bankruptcy proceedings confirmed 11/09/1988
No stockholders' equity

NEW YORK DOCK CO. (NY)
Recapitalized in 1937
Each share 5% Preferred $100 par exchanged for (1) share $5 Preferred no par
Each share Common $100 par exchanged for (1) share Common no par
Merged into Dunhill International, Inc. 12/31/58
Each share $5 Preferred no par exchanged for (10) shares Common $1 par
Each share Common no par exchanged for (8) shares Common $1 par
Dunhill International, Inc. name changed to Questor Corp. 12/1/68
(See Questor Corp.)

NEW YORK EDISON CO.
Merged into Consolidated Edison Co. of New York, Inc. 00/00/1937
Details not available

NEW YORK EQUITIES INC (NY)
Acquired by Gould Investors Trust 1/25/84
Each share Class A $1 par exchanged for $30 cash

NEW YORK FILM WKS INC (NY)
Each share old Common $0.001 par exchanged for (0.01) share new Common $0.001 par 12/31/2003

SEC revoked common stock registration 09/09/2009
Stockholders' equity unlikely

NEW YORK FINANCIAL & COMMUNITY CORP. (NY)
Charter revoked for failure to file reports and pay fees 12/16/40

NEW YORK FIRE INSURANCE CO. (NY)
Each share Capital Stock $5 par exchanged for (0.75) share Capital Stock $5 par in 1932
Capital Stock $5 par changed to $6 par 5/7/62
Merged into Reliance Insurance Co. 6/30/65
Each share Capital Stock $6 par exchanged for (1.45) shares Common $5 par
(See Reliance Insurance Co.)

NEW YORK FRUIT AUCTION CORP (NY)
Merged into Cayuga Corp. 11/10/72
Each share Class A no par or Class B no par exchanged for $45 cash

NEW YORK GLOBAL INNOVATIONS INC (DE)
Recapitalized as Artemis Therapeutics, Inc. 12/20/2016
Each share Common 1¢ par exchanged for (0.02) share Common 1¢ par

NEW YORK GUARANTEED MORTGAGE PROTECTION CO.
Liquidated in 1935
Details not available

NEW YORK HAMBURG CORP.
Dissolved in 1933
Details not available

NEW YORK HARBOR REALTY CORP. (NY)
Charter cancelled and proclaimed dissolved for failure to pay taxes and file reports 12/15/47

NEW YORK HEDGE FD INC (MD)
Liquidated 09/00/1976
Details not available

NEW YORK HOTEL STATLER CO., INC. (NY)
Acquired by Plaza Hotel Corp. at $52.50 a share 12/31/56

NEW YORK INTL COMM GROUP (NV)
Charter revoked for failure to file reports and pay fees 06/30/2003

NEW YORK INTL LOG & LMBR CO (NY)
Name changed to Green Energy Resources, Inc. 3/8/2005

NEW YORK INVESTORS, INC.
Bankrupt in 1938
Details not available

NEW YORK MAGAZINE INC (DE)
Class A $1 par and Class B $1 par reclassified as Common $1 par 05/15/1974
Merged into New York Post Corp. 01/30/1978
Each share Common $1 par exchanged for $8.25 cash

NEW YORK MAJESTIC CORP. (NY)
Under Plan of Reorganization Common $1 par declared valueless 6/7/60

NEW YORK MARINE & GEN INS CO (NY)
Common $1 par split (3) for (1) by issuance of (2) additional shares 03/24/1987
Name changed to NYMAGIC, INC. 10/02/1989
(See NYMAGIC, INC.)

NEW YORK MAUSOLEUM ASSOCIATION, INC. (NY)
Charter cancelled and proclaimed dissolved for failure to pay taxes and file reports 9/14/72

NEW YORK MED INC (NV)
Name changed to Critical Home Care, Inc. 09/26/2002
Critical Home Care, Inc. name changed to Arcadia Resources, Inc. 12/01/2004

NEW YORK MUTUAL TELEGRAPH CO. (NY)
Out of existence 11/21/57
Details not available

NEW YORK N-72 CORP. (NY)
Dissolved 4/18/60
No Common stockholders' equity

NEW YORK NEW HAVEN & HARTFORD RR CO (CT, MA & RI)
Reorganized in October 1947
No stockholders' equity
Common $100 par changed to no par 11/29/55 Declared insolvent 12/24/68
No stockholders' equity

NEW YORK OIL CO.
Dissolved in 1934
Details not available

NEW YORK OILS LTD (AB)
Reincorporated 7/19/82
Place of incorporation changed from (BC) to (ALTA) 7/19/82
Acquired by Sceptre Resources Ltd. 3/14/89
Each share Capital Stock no par exchanged for (0.053548) share Common no par
Sceptre Resources Ltd. merged into Canadian Natural Resources Ltd. 8/15/96

NY PA NJ UTILITIES CO.
Dissolved in 1947

NEW YORK PETROLEUM ROYALTY CORP.
Name changed to Michigan Gas & Oil Corp. 00/00/1931
(See Michigan Gas & Oil Corp.)

NEW YORK POWER & LIGHT CORP.
Merged into Niagara Mohawk Power Corp. 1/5/50
Each share 3.90% Preferred $100 par exchanged for like stock of new company

NEW YORK RAILWAYS CORP.
Reorganized as New York City Omnibus Corp. 00/00/1937
Preferred stockholders only received Option Warrants to purchase new stock

NEW YORK RAILWAYS PARTICIPATION CORP.
Dissolved in 1927
Details not available

NEW YORK RAPID TRANSIT CORP.
Acquired by the City of New York in 1940
Details not available

NEW YORK REALTY & IMPROVEMENT CO.
Assets sold at foreclosure in 1937
Details not available

NEW YORK REGL RAIL CORP (DE)
Voluntarily dissolved 02/07/2008
No stockholders' equity

NEW YORK SHIPBUILDING CORP (NY)
Participating Shares no par and Founders Shares no par changed to $1 par in 1932
Each Participating Share $1 par or Founders Share $1 par exchanged for (1) share Common $1 par in 1954
Stock Dividend - 50% 2/18/54
In process of liquidation
Each share Common $1 par received initial distribution of $5 cash 1/3/68
Each share Common $1 par received second distribution of $4 cash 5/15/68
Each share Common $1 par received third distribution of $2 cash 10/16/68

Each share Common $1 par received fourth distribution of $2 cash 3/14/69
Each share Common $1 par received fifth distribution of $1 cash 11/25/69
Merged into Merritt-Chapman & Scott Corp. 10/23/70
Each share Common $1 par exchanged for either (1) Unit of Participation and $3.89 cash or $11 cash
Note: Option to receive Units and cash expired 12/7/70

NEW YORK ST ELEC & GAS CORP (NY)
Name changed 00/00/1929
Name changed from New York State Gas & Electric Co. to New York State Electric & Gas Corp. 00/00/1929
5.10% Preferred $100 par called for redemption 03/13/1947
Common no par split (2.1) for (1) by issuance of (1.1) additional shares 11/10/1959
Common no par changed to $10 par 09/05/1969
Common $10 par changed to $6.66-2/3 par and (0.5) additional share issued 06/17/1977
8.50% Preferred $25 par called for redemption 07/01/1982
8.25% Preferred $100 par called for redemption 03/29/1985
15-3/8% Serial Preferred $100 par called for redemption 05/01/1986
15% Serial Preferred $25 par called for redemption 01/01/1987
9.10% Preferred $25 par called for redemption 07/01/1989
9% Preferred $100 par called for redemption 10/13/1993
Adjustable Rate Preferred Ser. A $25 par called for redemption 01/10/1994
8.80% Preferred $100 par called for redemption 01/18/1994
8.48% Preferred $25 par called for redemption 02/01/1994
8.95% Preferred $25 par called for redemption 01/01/1996
Under plan of reorganization each share Common $6.66-2/3 par automatically became (1) share Energy East Corp. Common 1¢ par 05/01/1998
(See Energy East Corp.)
6.48% Preferred $100 par called for redemption at $102 on 07/01/1998
Adjustable Rate Preferred Ser. B $25 par called for redemption at $25 on 02/01/1999
7.40% Preferred $25 par called for redemption at $25 on 02/01/1999
6.30% Preferred $100 par called for redemption at $102.52 on 12/10/1999
3.75% Preferred $100 par called for redemption at $104 on 06/22/2012
4.15% Preferred 1954 Ser. $100 par called for redemption at $104 on 06/22/2012
4.40% Preferred $100 par called for redemption at $102 on 06/22/2012
4.50% Preferred Ser. 1949 $100 par called for redemption at $103.75 on 06/22/2012

NEW YORK STATE FIRE INSURANCE CO. OF ALBANY
Merged into Richmond Insurance Co. of New York in 1932
Details not available

NEW YORK STATE RAILWAYS
Reorganized as Syracuse Transit Corp. in 1940
No stockholders' equity

NEW YORK STEAM CORP. (NY)
Merged into Consolidated Edison Co. 1/1/54
$6 & $7 Preferred Series A and Common no par exchanged for cash

FINANCIAL INFORMATION, INC.   NEW-NEW

NEW YORK STOCKS, INC.
Name changed to Diversified Funds, Inc. in 1951
Diversified Funds, Inc. merged into Diversified Growth Stock Fund, Inc. and Diversified Investment Fund, Inc. in 1954
(See Diversified Funds, Inc.)

NEW YORK STONE & MINERALS CORP (NY)
Charter cancelled and proclaimed dissolved for non-payment of taxes 12/16/68

NEW YORK SUGAR INDS INC (NY)
Completely liquidated 7/21/69
Each share Common 1¢ par received first and final distribution of (0.6) share Main Sugar Industries, Inc. Common $1.25 par
Certificates were not surrendered and are now without value

NEW YORK SUSQUEHANNA & WESTN RR CO (NJ)
Reorganized in 1953
No stockholders' equity
Petition for reorganization pursuant to Section 77 Bankruptcy Act filed 1/20/76
No stockholders' equity

NEW YORK TAX EXEMPT INCOME FD INC (MN)
Under plan of reorganization each share Common 1¢ par automatically became (1) Oppenheimer New York Municipal Fund (MA) Share of Bene. Int. Class A 1¢ par 2/18/99
Oppenheimer New York Municipal Fund name changed to Oppenheimer AMT-Free New York Municipal Fund 1/22/2003

NEW YORK TELECOIN CORP. (NY)
Charter revoked for failure to file reports and pay fees 12/15/59

NEW YORK TELECOMPUTING & VIDEOTEX CORP (NY)
Dissolved by proclamation 3/25/92

NEW YORK TESTING LABS INC (NY)
Common 25¢ par changed to $0.125 par and (1) additional share issued 06/06/1978
Common $0.125 par split (2) for (1) by issuance of (1) additional share 08/28/1987
Each share Common $0.125 par exchanged for (0.05) share Common 25¢ par 09/30/1993
Stock Dividends - 25% 07/30/1982; 25% 06/21/1983; 25% 06/28/1984; 25% 06/28/1985
Acquired by Integrated Resource Technologies Inc. 00/00/1995
Details not available

NEW YORK TIMES CO (NY)
1st Preferred $100 par called for redemption 10/1/57
2nd Preferred $100 par called for redemption 10/1/57
3rd Preferred $100 par called for redemption 10/1/57
4th Preferred $100 par called for redemption 10/1/57
5.50% Prior Preference $100 par called for redemption at $100 plus $1.375 accrued dividend on 10/1/97
(Additional Information in Active)

NEW YORK TITLE & MORTGAGE CO. (NY)
Liquidation completed 9/16/57
Guaranteed Mortgage Participation certificates exchanged for 28.8% of face value
No equity for Common stockholders

NEW YORK TITLE & MORTGAGE CORP. (DE)
Dissolved 10/8/34
No stockholders' equity

NEW YORK TOWERS, INC. (NY)
Class A Common no par recapitalized as Preferred no par in 1954
Liquidated in 1956
Details not available

NEW YORK TRANSFER CO.
Dissolved in 1946
Details not available

NEW YORK TRANSIT CO.
Merged into Buckeye Pipe Line Co. on a share for share basis in 1943
Buckeye Pipe Line Co. was acquired by Pennsylvania Co. 7/24/64
(See Pennsylvania Co.)

NEW YORK TRANSPORTATION CO.
Dissolved in 1936
Details not available

NEW YORK TRAP ROCK CORP. (NY)
Preferred no par called for redemption 3/31/61
Each share old Common no par exchanged for (5) shares new Common no par 5/16/61
Name changed to Old Mill Road Corp. 1/6/65
(See Old Mill Road Corp.)

NEW YORK TRUST CO. (NEW YORK, NY)
Capital Stock $25 par split (2) for (1) by issuance of (1) additional share in 1955
Merged into Chemical Bank New York Trust Co. (New York, NY) 9/8/59
Each share Capital Stock $25 par exchanged for (1.75) shares Capital Stock $12 par
Chemical Bank New York Trust Co. (New York, NY) reorganized as Chemical New York Corp. 2/17/69 which name changed to Chemical Banking Corp. 4/29/88 which name changed to Chase Manhattan Corp. (New) 3/31/96 which name changed to J.P. Morgan Chase & Co. 12/31/2000 which name changed to JPMorgan Chase & Co. 7/20/2004

NEW YORK TRW TITLE INSURANCE CO. (NY)
Acquired by Nations Holding Group 01/10/1994
Details not available

NEW YORK TUTOR CO (NV)
Name changed to African Copper Corp. 05/07/2013
(See African Copper Corp.)

NEW YORK VENTURE FD INC (MD)
Capital Stock $1 par split (3) for (2) issuance of (0.5) additional share 08/27/1971
Capital Stock $1 par split (2) for (1) by issuance of (1) additional share 02/23/1981
Capital Stock $1 par reclassified as Class A Common $1 par 00/00/1994
Name changed to Davis New York Venture Fund, Inc. 10/01/1995

NEW YORK WATER SERVICE CORP. (NY)
Each share Preferred $100 par exchanged for (1) share new Common no par in 1947
Each share Common no par exchanged for (8) shares Common $10 par in 1950
Each share Common $10 par exchanged for (5) shares Common $2 par 7/10/58
Name changed to Utilities & Industries Corp. (NY) 5/19/60
Utilities & Industries Corp. (NY) merged into Carter Group Inc. 11/19/74 which name changed to Utilities & Industries Corp. (DE) 11/20/74
(See Utilities & Industries Corp. (DE))

NEW YORK WIRE CLOTH CO. (DE)
Name changed to New York Wire Co. 4/9/63
(See New York Wire Co.)

NEW YORK WIRE CO (DE)
5% Preferred $100 par, 6% Preferred $100 par, Common $1 par and Class B Common $1 par all repurchased prior to 08/04/1967
Public interest eliminated

NEW YORK WOMAN, INC.
Liquidated in 1937
Details not available

NEW YORKER MAGAZINE INC (NY)
Each share Common no par exchanged for (3) shares Common $1 par in 1947
Common $1 par changed to $10 par in 1957
Common $10 par changed to $25 par 3/23/65
Common $25 par changed to $5 par and (4) additional shares issued 11/24/81
Merged into Advance Publications, Inc. 5/7/85
Each share Common $5 par exchanged for $200 cash

NEW YORKER MARKETING CORP (DE)
SEC revoked common stock registration 10/30/2006
Stockholders' equity unlikely

NEW ZEALAND PETE LTD (NEW ZEALAND)
Name changed 10/3/69
Name changed from New Zealand Petroleum Exploration Co. Ltd. to New Zealand Petroleum Co. Ltd. 10/3/69
ADR's for Ordinary N.Z.50¢ par changed to N.Z.25¢ par and (1) additional share issued 11/12/84
ADR agreement terminated 1/16/97
Each ADR for Ordinary N.Z.25¢ par exchanged for (1) Ordinary share N.Z.25¢ par

NEWAIR FLIGHT INC
Each share old Common 1¢ par exchanged for (0.1) share new Common 1¢ par 03/07/1988
Charter cancelled and declared inoperative and void for non-payment of taxes 03/01/1996

NEWAL INC (MA)
Reorganized as Waltham Precision Instruments, Inc. (MA) 12/06/1966
Each share Common $1 par exchanged for (0.0625) share Common 25¢ par
Waltham Precision Instruments, Inc. (MA) reincorporated in Delaware as Waltham Industries Corp. 01/17/1969
(See Waltham Industries Corp.)

NEWALL TECHNOLOGIES INC (UT)
Involuntarily dissolved 04/01/1988

NEWALLIANCE BANCSHARES INC (DE)
Merged into First Niagara Financial Group, Inc. (New) 04/15/2011
Each share Common 1¢ par exchanged for (0.16) share Common 1¢ par and $12.21 cash
First Niagara Financial Group, Inc. (New) merged into KeyCorp (New) 08/01/2016

NEWALTA CORP NEW (AB)
Name changed 01/22/2010
Name changed from Newalta Inc. to Newalta Corp. (New) 01/22/2010
Reorganized as Tervita Corp. 07/24/2018
Each share Common no par exchanged for (0.1467) share Common no par and (0.0307) Common Stock Purchase Right expiring 07/19/2020

NEWALTA CORP OLD (AB)
Name changed 07/07/1986
Name changed from Newalta Oil & Gas Ltd. to Newalta Corp. (Old) 07/07/1986
Recapitalized as Newalta Income Fund 03/10/2003
Each share Common no par exchanged for (0.5) Trust Unit no par
Newalta Income Fund reorganized as Newalta Inc. 12/31/2008 which name changed to Newalta Corp. (New) 01/22/2010 which reorganized as Tervita Corp. 07/24/2018

NEWALTA INCOME FD (AB)
Reorganized as Newalta Inc. 12/31/2008
Each Trust Unit no par exchanged for (1) share Common no par
Newalta Inc. name changed to Newalta Corp. (New) 01/22/2010 which reorganized as Tervita Corp. 07/24/2018

NEWALTA PETROLEUMS, LTD. (AB)
Stricken from Alberta register and dissolved 12/31/56
Common Stock is valueless

NEWARK & BLOOMFIELD R.R. CO.
Merged into Delaware, Lackawanna & Western Railroad Co. through payment of $55 per share in 1946

NEWARK & ESSEX SECURITIES CORP.
Liquidated in 1948

NEWARK CONSOLIDATED GAS CO.
Merged into Public Service Electric & Gas Co. and stock exchanged for a like amount of First and Refunding Mtge. Bonds in 1938

NEWARK DISTRIBUTING TERMINALS, INC.
Liquidation completed in 1949

NEWARK ELECTRS CORP (IL)
Merged into Premier Industrial Corp. 11/27/68
Each share Class A $2 par exchanged for (1) share 90¢ Conv. Preferred Ser. A no par
Premier Industrial Corp. merged into Farnell Electronics PLC 4/11/96 which name changed to Premier Farnell PLC 4/11/96
(See Premier Farnell PLC)

NEWARK PROVIDENT LOAN ASSOCIATION (NJ)
Each share Common $100 par exchanged for (5) shares Common $20 par 12/31/53
Acquired by Beneficial Finance Co. in 1956
Each share Common $20 par exchanged for $25 cash

NEWARK TEL CO (OH)
Common no par split (5) for (1) by issuance of (4) additional shares 1/3/73
Merged into Mid-Continent Telephone Corp. 9/21/79
Each share Preferred $100 par exchanged for $105 cash
Each share Common no par exchanged for $136 cash

NEWARK TRUST CO. (NEWARK, OH)
99% held by Citizens Financial Corp. as of August 1967
Public interest eliminated

NEWAVE INC (UT)
Each share old Common $0.001 par exchanged for (3) shares new Common $0.001 par 2/18/2005
Name changed to Commerce Planet, Inc. 6/22/2006

NEWAYGO PORTLAND CEMENT CO.
Merged into Medusa Portland Cement Co. 00/00/1929
Details not available

NEWBAR TELEVONICS INC (NV)
Recapitalized as Emerson Films Inc. 11/6/70
Each share Common $1 par exchanged for (0.05) share Common $1 par
(See Emerson Films Inc.)

NEWBEC MINES LTD.
Liquidated in 1944

NEWBERN HOTEL CO. (MO)
Charter forfeited for failure to file annual reports 1/1/40

NEWBERRY BANCORP INC (DE)
Each share Class A Common $0.001 par exchanged for (0.2) share Common $0.005 par 12/27/90
Each share Common $0.005 par exchanged for (0.5) share Common 1¢ par 5/15/92
Name changed to University Bancorp, Inc. 6/6/96

NEWBERRY J J CO (DE)
5% Preferred called for redemption 09/24/1945
Stock Dividend - 300% 12/28/1945
Merged into McCrory Corp. 09/01/1972
Each share Common no par exchanged for (0.7) share Common 50¢ par or $30 principal amount of 7-5/8% S.F. Subord. Debentures due 12/15/1997
Note: Holder's option expired 10/17/1972 after which form of distribution made at the discretion of McCrory Corp.
Details on 3.75% Preferred $100 par not available
(See McCrory Corp.)

NEWBERRY LUMBER & CHEMICAL CO.
Dissolved in 1946

NEWBERY CORP (AZ)
Name changed 1/7/86
Stock Dividends - 10% 6/1/77; 10% 11/30/81
Name changed from Newbery Energy Corp. to Newbery Corp. 1/7/86
Charter revoked for failure to file reports and pay fees 12/10/93

NEWBERY ELECTRIC CORP. OF ARIZONA (AZ)
Name changed to Newbery Energy Corp. 1/31/68
Newbery Energy Corp. name changed to Newbery Corp. 1/7/86
(See Newbery Corp.)

NEWBRIDGE BANCORP (NC)
Common $5 par reclassified as Class A Common no par 02/22/2013
Merged into Yadkin Financial Corp. 03/01/2016
Each share Class A Common no par exchanged for (0.5) share Common $1 par
Yadkin Financial Corp. merged into F.N.B. Corp. 03/11/2017

NEWBRIDGE CAP INC (BC)
Name changed to KazaX Minerals Inc. 03/16/2012
(See KazaX Minerals Inc.)

NEWBRIDGE CAP INC (NV)
Common $0.001 par split (5) for (1) by issuance of (4) additional shares payable 07/02/2001 to holders of record 06/01/2001 Ex date - 07/03/2001
Each share old Common $0.001 par exchanged for (0.01) share new Common $0.001 par 04/01/2003
Name changed to SeaHAVN Corp. 06/10/2005
SeaHAVN Corp. recapitalized as China Travel Resort Holdings, Inc. 10/01/2009

NEWBRIDGE NETWORKS CORP (CANADA)
Common no par split (2) for (1) by issuance of (1) additional share 06/30/1993
Common no par split (2) for (1) by issuance of (1) additional share payable 10/11/1996 to holders of record 09/30/1996 Ex date - 10/15/1996
Merged into Alcatel 05/25/2000
Each share Common no par exchanged for either (0.81) Sponsored ADR for Ordinary or (0.81) Newbridge Networks Corp. Exchangeable share
Note: Option to elect to receive Exchangeable Shares expired 05/12/2000
All Exchangeable Shares were converted into ADR's prior to 05/25/2005
Alcatel name changed to Alcatel-Lucent 11/30/2006
(See Alcatel-Lucent)

NEWBRIDGE RES LTD (AB)
Name changed to Lamplighter Energy Ltd. 11/15/1999
Lamplighter Energy Ltd. merged into Blackdog Resources Ltd. 01/12/2006 which name changed to StonePoint Energy Inc. 11/06/2014
(See StonePoint Energy Inc.)

NEWBURN MINES LTD. (ON)
Charter cancelled in September, 1962
Stock worthless

NEWBURY INTL VENTURES INC (BC)
Name changed 3/7/86
Name changed from Newbury Explorations Ltd. to Newbury International Ventures Inc. 3/7/86
Struck off register and declared dissolved for failure to file returns 12/4/92

NEWBURY STREET GARAGE CO. (MA)
Name changed to Sheraton Restaurants, Inc. in 1952 which was liquidated 4/30/56

NEWBURYPORT GAS & ELECTRIC CO.
Acquired by Haverhill Electric Co. 00/00/1926
Details not available

NEWCAN MINERALS LTD (AB)
Name changed to World Aquathemes Ltd. 06/20/1985
World Aquathemes Ltd. name changed to Telesis Corp. Inc. 09/02/1986 which recapitalized as P.C. Ventures Ltd. 02/23/1989
(See P.C. Ventures Ltd.)

NEWCARE HEALTH CORP (NV)
Chapter 11 bankruptcy proceedings converted to Chapter 7 on 03/18/2002
Stockholders' equity unlikely

NEWCASTLE ENERGY CORP (BC)
Each share old Common no par exchanged for (0.03333333) share new Common no par 08/25/2014
Name changed to Martello Technologies Group Inc. 09/12/2018

NEWCASTLE GOLD LTD (ON)
Merged into Equinox Gold Corp. 12/22/2017
Each share Common no par exchanged for (0.873) share Common no par
Note: Unexchanged certificates will be cancelled and become without value 12/22/2023

NEWCASTLE INVT CORP (MD)
Each share old Common 1¢ par received distribution of (1) share New Residential Investment Corp. Common 1¢ par payable 05/15/2013 to holders of record 05/06/2013 Ex date - 05/16/2013
Each share old Common 1¢ par received distribution of (0.07219481) share New Media Investment Group Inc. Common 1¢ par payable 02/13/2014 to holders of record 02/06/2014 Ex date - 02/14/2014
Each share old Common 1¢ par exchanged for (0.33333333) share new Common 1¢ par 08/19/2014
Each share new Common 1¢ par exchanged again for (0.5) share new Common 1¢ par 10/23/2014
Each share new Common 1¢ par received distribution of (1) share New Senior Investment Group Inc. Common 1¢ par payable 11/06/2014 to holders of record 10/27/2014 Ex date - 11/07/2014
Name changed to Drive Shack Inc. 12/29/2016

NEWCASTLE MARKET-NEUTRAL TR (ON)
Name changed to Northwater Market-Neutral Trust 2/1/2002

NEWCASTLE MINERALS LTD (BC)
Recapitalized as GoldON Resources Ltd. 03/07/2013
Each share Common no par exchanged for (0.2) share Common no par

NEWCASTLE MNG CO LTD (NB)
Charter forfeited for failure to file annual reports 12/13/1978

NEWCASTLE RES LTD (ON)
Reincorporated under the laws of British Columbia as RepliCel Life Sciences Inc. 07/01/2011

NEWCENTURY BK CORP (MI)
Merged into First of America Bank Corp. 12/31/86
Each share Common $5 par exchanged for (1) share 10% Conv. Preferred Ser. E $19 par
(See First of America Bank Corp.)

NEWCITY COMMUNICATIONS INC (DE)
Merged into Cox Radio, Inc. 4/2/97
Details not available

NEWCLARE OILS LTD. (AB)
Assets acquired by Vulcan Oils Ltd. in 1958 was recapitalized as Siscalta Oils Ltd. 8/15/58 which was acquired by Siscoe Mines Ltd. for cash 9/6/63

NEWCO BANCORP INC (ON)
1st Preference Ser. A called for redemption at $10 on 12/31/2003
Acquired by Munbancorp Realty Inc. 04/25/2016
Each share Non-Vtg. Class A Common no par exchanged for $0.39 cash
Each share Common no par exchanged for $0.39 cash
Note: Unexchanged certificates will be cancelled and become without value 04/25/2022

NEWCO FINL CORP (BC)
Each share old Common no par exchanged for (0.01) share new Common no par 12/12/1977
Note: In effect holders received $25 cash per share and public interest was eliminated

NEWCO SILVER MINES LTD. (ON)
Name changed to Great Pine Mines Ltd. 12/01/1965
(See Great Pine Mines Ltd.)

NEWCOAST SILVER MINES LTD (BC)
Recapitalized as Southern Silver Exploration Corp. 7/16/2004
Each share Common no par exchanged for (1/7) share Common no par

NEWCOM INC (DE)
SEC revoked common stock registration 07/30/2002
Stockholders' equity unlikely

NEWCOM INTL INC (NV)
Each share old Common $0.001 par exchanged for (0.02) share new Common $0.001 par 10/28/2003
Name changed to Skogan Foods, Inc. 10/28/2003
Skogan Foods, Inc. name changed to Sino Express Travel, Ltd. 11/1/2005

NEWCONEX HLDGS LTD (CANADA)
Reincorporated 01/18/1978
Place of incorporation changed from (ON) to (Canada) 01/18/1978
Under plan of merger each share Common $1 par exchanged for $8.40 cash 03/31/1978

NEWCOR INC (DE)
Common $1 par split (2) for (1) by issuance of (1) additional share 4/2/79
Common $1 par split (3) for (2) by issuance of (0.5) additional share 5/7/81
Common $1 par split (3) for (2) by issuance of (0.5) additional share 5/10/82
Common $1 par split (3) for (2) by issuance of (0.5) additional share 5/10/83
Common $1 par split (3) for (2) by issuance of (0.5) additional share 2/10/93
Stock Dividends - 10% 11/18/76; 10% 6/5/90; 5% payable 9/12/97 to holders of record 8/14/97
Plan of reorganization under Chapter 11 Federal Bankruptcy Code effective 1/31/2003
No stockholders' equity

NEWCOR MINING & REFINING LTD.
Acquired by Asfe Mines Ltd. in 1951
Each (5) shares Capital Stock no par exchanged for (1) share new Capital Stock $1 par
(See Asfe Mines Ltd.)

NEWCORP, INC. (IN)
Completely liquidated 08/31/1959
Details not available

NEWCORP INC (GA)
Name changed to Pier 1. Imports, Inc. (GA) 04/07/1980
Pier 1. Imports, Inc. name changed to Pier 1 Inc. 07/13/1984 which reincorporated in Delaware as Pier 1 Imports, Inc. 09/19/1986

NEWCOURT CR GROUP INC (ON)
Common no par split (2) for (1) by issuance of (1) additional share payable 04/18/1997 to holders of record 04/14/1997
Merged into CIT Group, Inc. 11/15/1999
Each share Common no par exchanged for (0.7) share Class A Common 1¢ par
CIT Group, Inc. merged into Tyco International Ltd. (Bermuda) 06/01/2001 which reincorporated in Switzerland 03/17/2009 which merged into Johnson Controls International PLC 09/06/2016

NEWCOURT INDS INC (TX)
Common $5 par split (3) for (1) by issuance of (2) additional shares 7/31/80
Acquired by Mickelberry Corp. 10/27/82
Each share Preferred Ser. A $5 par exchanged for (1) share Preferred Ser. A $1 par
Each share Common $5 par exchanged for (0.25) share Common $1 par
Mickelberry Corp. name changed to Mickelberry Communications Inc. 5/10/94
(See Mickelberry Communications Inc.)

NEWCREST DEVS LTD (ON)
Charter cancelled for failure to pay taxes and file returns 05/27/1985

NEWCREST MNG LTD (AUSTRALIA)
Delisted from Toronto Stock Exchange 09/04/2013

NEWDOMINION BK (CHARLOTTE, NC)
Common $4.50 par changed to $1.50 par 07/08/2011
Common $1.50 par changed to 25¢ par 07/01/2015
Merged into Park National Corp. 07/01/2018
Each share Common 25¢ par

exchanged for (0.00396487) share Common no par and $0.6614 cash

NEWELL ASSOCIATES, INC. (CA)
Name changed to Newell Industries, Inc. 06/03/1968
Newell Industries, Inc. name changed to American Videonetics Corp. 02/28/1973
(See American Videonetics Corp.)

NEWELL CO (DE)
Name changed 05/22/1985
Common $1 par split (2) for (1) by issuance of (1) additional share 03/18/1983
Name changed from Newell Companies, Inc. to Newell Co. 05/22/1985
Common $1 par split (2) for (1) by issuance of (1) additional share 08/29/1988
$2.08 Conv. Preferred Ser. A $1 par called for redemption 02/22/1989
Common $1 par split (2) for (1) by issuance of (1) additional share 12/01/1989
Common $1 par split (2) for (1) by issuance of (1) additional share 09/01/1994
Under plan of merger name changed to Newell Rubbermaid Inc. 03/24/1999
Newell Rubbermaid Inc. name changed to Newell Brands Inc. 04/18/2016

NEWELL FINL TR I (DE)
Each share 5.25% 144A Conv. Quarterly Income Preferred Securities exchanged for (1) share 5.25% Conv. Quarterly Income Preferred Securities 12/12/1999
5.25% Conv. Quarterly Income Preferred Securities called for redemption at $50 plus $0.313540 accrued dividends on 07/14/2012

NEWELL INDS INC (CA)
Name changed to American Videonetics Corp. 02/28/1973
(See American Videonetics Corp.)

NEWELL RUBBERMAID INC (DE)
Under plan of merger name changed to Newell Brands Inc. 04/18/2016

NEWEN ENTERPRISES INC (BC)
Recapitalized as Consolidated Newen Enterprises Inc. 11/02/1998
Each share Common no par exchanged for (0.2) share Common no par
Consolidated Newen Enterprises Inc. recapitalized as North American Gold Inc. 04/07/2003 which name changed to Northland Resources Inc. (BC) 09/07/2005 which reincorporated in Luxembourg as Northland Resources S.A. 06/14/2010

NEWERA CAP CORP (BC)
Name changed to ThrillTime Entertainment International, Inc. 8/12/97
ThrillTime Entertainment International, Inc. name changed to Advanced Proteome Therapeutics Corp. 10/25/2006

NEWFIELD FINL TR I (DE)
Quarterly Income Conv. Preferred Ser. AA called for redemption at $52.275 plus $0.3792 accrued dividend on 6/27/2003

NEWFIELD MINES LTD (ON)
Merged into Jonpol Explorations Ltd. 8/31/89
Each share Capital Stock $1 par exchanged for (2) shares Common no par
Jonpol Explorations Ltd. merged into Eastern Platinum Ltd. 4/26/2005

NEWFOUNDLAND CAP LTD (NL)
Reincorporated under the laws of Canada 03/04/1987

NEWFOUNDLAND EXPL LTD (NL)
Recapitalized as Drug Royalty Corp. Inc. 04/02/1993
Each share Common no par exchanged for (0.1) share Common no par
(See Drug Royalty Corp. Inc.)

NEWFOUNDLAND GULL LAKE MINES LTD (ON)
Charter cancelled for failure to file reports and pay taxes in 1969

NEWFOUNDLAND LT & PWR LTD (NL)
Ordinary Stock $10 par changed to no par and (9) additional shares issued 08/16/1963
Each share 5% Preference $100 par exchanged for (10) shares 5.25% Preference Ser. B $10 par 09/08/1966
Each share Ordinary Stock no par exchanged for (1) share Common no par 09/08/1966
Common no par reclassified as Conv. Class A Common no par 07/18/1975
Conv. Class A Common no par split (2) for (1) by issuance of (1) additional share 07/08/1985
Conv. Class B Common no par split (2) for (1) by issuance of (1) additional share 07/08/1985
14.25% 1st Preference Ser. I $10 par called for redemption 10/01/1986
Under plan of reorganization each share Conv. Class A Common no par and Conv. Class B Common no par automatically became (1) share Fortis Inc. Common no par 12/29/1987
6% 1st Preference Ser. C $10 par called for redemption 08/04/1992
9% 1st Preference Ser. E $10 par called for redemption 08/04/1992
9.84% 1st Preference Ser. F $10 par called for redemption 08/04/1992
7.4% Retractable 1st Preference Ser. J called for redemption 12/16/1993
Name changed to Newfoundland Power Inc. 10/01/1998

NEWFOUNDLAND TEL LTD (NL)
Ordinary $5 par reclassified as Common no par 06/14/1976
Under plan of reorganization each share Common no par automatically became (1) share NewTel Enterprises Ltd. Common no 10/15/1985
13.50% Redeemable Preferred Ser. D $20 par called for redemption 06/15/1988
7.25% Redeemable Preferred $20 par called redemption 01/15/1993
8.85% Redeemable Preferred Ser. C $20 par called for redemption 01/15/1993
9.75% Redeemable Preferred $20 par called for redemption 01/15/1993
NewTel Enterprises Ltd. merged into Aliant Inc. (Canada) 06/01/1999 which reorganized in Ontario as Bell Aliant Regional Communications Income Fund 07/10/2006 which reorganized in Canada as Bell Aliant Inc. 01/04/2011 which merged into BCE Inc. 10/31/2014

NEWGATE RES (AB)
Recapitalized as Para-Tech Energy Corp. 12/16/96
Each share Common no par exchanged for (0.1) share Common no par

NEWGATE RES LTD (BC)
Recapitalized as Consolidated Newgate Resources Ltd. 7/2/91
Each share Common no par exchanged for (0.25) share Common no par
Consolidated Newgate Resources Ltd. recapitalized as Antler Resources Ltd. 1/17/96 which merged into Winspear Resources Ltd. (New) 1/13/97

NEWGEN RESULTS CORP (DE)
Merged into TeleTech Holdings, Inc. 12/20/2000
Each share Common $0.001 par exchanged for (0.8) share Common 1¢ par
TeleTech Holdings, Inc. name changed to TTEC Holdings, Inc. 01/10/2018

NEWGEN TECHNOLOGIES INC (NV)
Charter revoked for failure to file reports and pay taxes 02/01/2010

NEWGOLD INC (DE)
Common $0.005 par split (3) for (2) by issuance of (0.5) additional share payable 06/17/1999 to holders of record 06/10/1999
Name changed to Firstgold Corp. 12/08/2006
(See Firstgold Corp.)

NEWGROWTH CORP (ON)
Equity Dividend share no par called for redemption on 06/26/1998
Capital Share no par called for redemption on 06/26/1998
Preferred no par called for redemption at $13.78 on 06/25/2004
Preferred Ser. 1 called for redemption at $18.25 on 06/26/2009
Class B Preferred Ser. 2 called for redemption at $13.70 on 06/26/2014
(Additional Information in Active)

NEWHALL INVT PPTYS (CA)
Charter cancelled 09/26/1988

NEWHALL LD & FARMING CO (DE)
Reincorporated 7/30/76
State of incorporation changed from (CA) to (DE) and Common no par changed to $1 par 07/30/1976
Common $1 par split (2) for (1) by issuance of (1) additional share 03/14/1980
Common $1 par changed to 75¢ par 03/09/1983
Under plan of partial liquidation each share Common 75¢ par received (0.5) Depositary Receipt of Newhall Investment Properties and (0.5) Depositary Receipt of Newhall Resources 03/28/1983
(See each company's listing)
Assets transferred to Newhall Land & Farming Co. (CA) (New) 01/08/1985
Each share Common 75¢ par exchanged for (1) Depositary Receipt
(See Newhall Land & Farming Co. (CA))

NEWHALL LD & FARMING CO NEW (CA)
Depositary Receipts split (2) for (1) by issuance of (1) additional Depositary Receipt 12/20/1985
Depositary Receipts split (2) for (1) by issuance of (1) additional Depositary Receipt 01/26/1990
Merged into Lennar Corp. 01/27/2004
Each Depositary Receipt exchanged for $40.50 cash

NEWHALL OIL CO. (AZ)
Charter expired by time limitation 4/16/25

NEWHALL RES (CA)
Liquidation completed
Each Depositary Receipt exchanged for initial distribution of $6.05 cash 2/17/89
Each Depositary Receipt received second and final distribution of $0.56 cash 12/11/89

NEWHAVEN MEDIA INC (AB)
Assets sold for the benefit of creditors in June 2002
No stockholders' equity

NEWHAWK GOLD MINES LTD (BC)
Merged into Silver Standard Resources Inc. 09/30/1999
Each share Common no par exchanged for (0.16666666) share Common no par

Silver Standard Resources Inc. name changed to SSR Mining Inc. 08/03/2017

NEWJAY RES LTD (BC)
Recapitalized as Consolidated Newjay Resources Ltd. 08/25/1993
Each share Common no par exchanged for (0.285714) share Common no par
Consolidated Newjay Resources Ltd. name changed to Indo-Pacific Energy Ltd. (BC) 05/09/1995 which reincorporated in Yukon 10/15/1997 which name changed to Austral Pacific Energy Ltd. (YT) 01/02/2004 which reincorporated in British Columbia 10/16/2006
(See Austral Pacific Energy Ltd.)

NEWKIDCO INTL INC (NB)
Chapter 11 bankruptcy proceedings dismissed 08/18/2005
No stockholders' equity

NEWKIRK MINING CORP. LTD. (ON)
Name changed to Continental Mining Exploration Ltd. 12/11/56
Continental Mining Exploration Ltd. merged into Augustus Exploration Ltd. 11/26/58 which merged into Consolidated Canadian Faraday Ltd. 5/4/67 which name changed to Faraday Resources Inc. 8/2/83 which merged into Conwest Exploration Co. Ltd. (New) (ALTA) 9/1/93 which merged into Alberta Energy Co. Ltd. 1/31/96 which merged into EnCana Corp. 1/3/2003

NEWKIRK RLTY TR INC (MD)
Issue Information - 15,000,000 shares COM offered at $16 per share on 11/01/2005
Merged into Lexington Realty Trust 12/31/2006
Each share Common 1¢ par exchanged for (0.8) share Common $0.0001 par

NEWLANDS OIL & GAS INC (NV)
Name changed to PC-EPhone, Inc. 12/18/2000
(See PC-EPhone, Inc.)

NEWLIFE PRODUCTIONS INC (UT)
Each share Common $0.001 par exchanged for (1,000) shares Bevex, Inc. Common $0.001 par 6/15/2005
Note: Above action taken due to lack of shareholder authorization to change name to NewLife Productions, Inc.

NEWLINE DEV CORP (BC)
Delisted from Vancouver Stock Exchange 10/06/1989

NEWLINE RES LTD (BC)
Name changed to Newline Development Corp. 03/28/1987
(See Newline Development Corp.)

NEWLOCK INC (DE)
Charter cancelled and declared inoperative and void for non-payment of taxes 3/1/2001

NEWLOOK CAP CORP (BC)
Recapitalized as Newlook Industries Corp. (BC) 05/17/2002
Each share Common no par exchanged for (0.5) share Common no par
Newlook Industries Corp. (BC) reincorporated in Ontario 02/03/2009

NEWLOOK INDS CORP (BC)
Reincorporated under the laws of Ontario 02/03/2009

NEWLUND MINES LTD (ON)
Recapitalized as Goldlund Mines Ltd. 06/06/1973
Each share Capital Stock $1 par exchanged for (0.4) share Capital Stock no par
Goldlund Mines Ltd. merged into Camreco Inc. 12/31/1986 which

merged into Environmental Technologies International Inc. 11/29/1991 which recapitalized as Eco Technologies International Inc. 04/24/1998
(See Eco Technologies International Inc.)

NEWMAN COMMUNICATIONS CORP. OLD (NM)
Reorganized under Chapter 11 Federal Bankruptcy Code as Newman Communications Corp. (New) 11/22/93
Stockholders of Common 1¢ par received, regardless of amount of stock held, (500) shares Common no par, (1,000) Common Stock Purchase Warrants, Class A expiring 11/22/94 (1,000) Common Stock Purchase Warrants, Class B expiring 11/22/95 and (1,000) Common Stock Purchase Warrants, Class C expiring 11/22/96
Note: Unexchanged certificates became valueless 3/22/94
Newman Communications Corp. (New) reorganized as Index Inc. 12/4/96 which recapitalized as DXP Enterprises, Inc. 5/12/97

NEWMAN COMMUNICATIONS INC (NEW) (NM)
Reorganized under the laws of Texas as Index Inc. 12/4/96
Each share Common no par exchanged for (0.25) share Common 1¢ par
Index Inc. recapitalized as DXP Enterprises, Inc. 5/12/97

NEWMAN ENERGY TECHNOLOGIES INC (NV)
Name changed to World Star Asia, Inc. 06/15/1998
World Star Asia, Inc. name changed to Comgen Corp. 11/16/1998 which name changed to Planet 411.com Corp. (NV) 02/11/1999 reincorporated in Delaware as Planet411.com Inc. 10/07/1999 which name changed to Ivany Mining, Inc. 07/27/2007 which name changed to Ivany Nguyen, Inc. 02/16/2010 which name changed to Myriad Interactive Media, Inc. 07/25/2011

NEWMARK & LEWIS INC (NC)
Common 5¢ par split (2) for (1) by issuance of (1) additional share 4/11/86
Chapter 11 Federal Bankruptcy proceedings converted to Chapter 7 on 2/20/92
Stockholders' equity unlikely

NEWMARK HOMES CORP (NV)
Reincorporated 03/23/2001
State of incorporation changed from (NV) to (DE) 03/23/2001
Name changed to Technical Olympic USA, Inc. 06/25/2002
Technical Olympic USA, Inc. name changed to TOUSA, Inc. 05/08/2007
(See TOUSA, Inc.)

NEWMARK MNG CORP (WA)
Recapitalized as New Environmental Solutions, Inc. 09/22/2006
Each share Common $0.001 par exchanged for (0.004) share Common $0.001 par
(See New Environmental Solutions, Inc.)

NEWMARK RES LTD (AB)
Recapitalized as Trinity Resources Ltd. 5/10/77
Each share Capital Stock no par exchanged for (1/3) share Capital Stock no par
Trinity Resources Ltd. merged into Ensor Corp. 7/8/91 which name changed to Rose Corp. 6/1/98
(See Rose Corp.)

NEWMARK VENTURES INC (DE)
Each share old Common $0.001 par exchanged for (0.25) share new Common $0.001 par 12/31/2004
New Common $0.001 par split (3) for (2) by issuance of (0.5) additional share payable 04/18/2005 to holders of record 04/04/2005 Ex date - 04/19/2005
Reorganized as Mangapets, Inc. 10/26/2005
Each share new Common $0.001 par exchanged for (1.5) shares Common $0.001 par
Mangapets, Inc. name changed to Intrepid Global Imaging 3D, Inc. 03/01/2007 which name changed to Spine Pain Management, Inc. 11/27/2009 which name changed to Spine Injury Solutions, Inc. 10/08/2015

NEWMARKET GOLD INC (BC)
Reorganized under the laws of Ontario 07/14/2015
Each share Common no par exchanged for (0.2) share Common no par
Newmarket Gold Inc. (ON) recapitalized as Kirkland Lake Gold Ltd. 12/06/2016

NEWMARKET GOLD INC (ON)
Recapitalized as Kirkland Lake Gold Ltd. 12/06/2016
Each share Common no par exchanged for (0.475) share Common no par

NEWMARKET LATIN AMER INC (DE)
SEC revoked common stock registration 11/21/2008
Stockholders' equity unlikely

NEWMARKET MANUFACTURING CO. (DE)
Acquired by Textron Inc. (R.I.) 7/12/54
Each share Common $2.50 par exchanged for (0.2) share 4% Preferred Ser. B $100 par and $1 cash
Textron Inc. (R.I.) name changed to Textron American, Inc. 2/24/55 which name changed back to Textron Inc. (R.I.) 5/15/56 which was reincorporated under the laws of Delaware 1/2/68

NEWMARKET MANUFACTURING CO. (MA)
Common $100 par changed to no par 00/00/1932
Common no par changed to $100 par 00/00/1944
Each share Common $100 par exchanged for (40) shares Common $2.50 par 00/00/1946
Reincorporated under the laws of Delaware 00/00/1951
Newmarket Manufacturing Co. (DE) acquired by Textron Inc. (RI) 07/12/1954 which name changed to Textron American, Inc. 02/24/1955 which name changed back to Textron Inc. (RI) 05/15/1956 which reincorporated in Delaware 01/02/1968

NEWMARKT CORP (NV)
Name changed to Ozop Surgical Corp. 05/21/2018

NEWMEX MINERALS INC (AB)
Name changed to Pearl Exploration & Production Ltd. 02/28/2006
Pearl Exploration & Production Ltd. name changed to BlackPearl Resources Inc. 05/14/2009

NEWMEX MNG LTD (ON)
Merged into Santa Cruz Gold Inc. (New) 09/09/1997
Each share Common no par exchanged for (2.2) shares Common no par
Santa Cruz Gold Inc. (New) merged into Queenstake Resources Ltd. (Yukon) 07/19/1999 which reincorporated in British Columbia 07/10/2006 which merged into Yukon-Nevada Gold Corp. 06/25/2007

NEWMEX URANIUM & DEVELOPMENT CORP. (NM)
Merged into Resource Ventures Corp. 2/28/56
Each share Common 3¢ par exchanged for (0.04) share Common $1 par
Resource Ventures Corp. merged into Petroleum Resources Corp. 6/30/65 which name changed to PRC Corp. 11/9/70 which name changed to Corterra Corp. 11/28/72 which assets were transferred to CorTerra Corp. Liquidating Corp. 10/8/80
(See CorTerra Corp. Liquidating Corp.)

NEWMIL BANCORP INC (DE)
Common $1 par changed to 50¢ par and (1) additional share issued 2/15/88
Merged into Webster Financial Corp. 10/6/2006
Each share Common 50¢ par exchanged for (0.8736) share Common 1¢ par

NEWMINE DEVELOPMENT LTD. (BC)
Recapitalized as Geoquest Resources Ltd. 5/18/71
Each share Common 50¢ par exchanged for (1) share Common 50¢ par
Geoquest Resources Ltd. recapitalized as Claytron Energy Corp. 12/13/76 which merged into International Interlake Industries Inc. 12/31/86
(See International Interlake Industries Inc.)

NEWMONT FIRST CAP CORP (DE)
Dutch Auction Rate Transferable Securities Preferred no par called for redemption 03/29/1988
Public interest eliminated

NEWMONT GOLD CO (DE)
Merged into Newmont Mining Corp. 10/7/98
Each share Common 1¢ par exchanged for (1.025) shares Common $1.60 par

NEWMONT MNG CORP (DE)
4% Conv. Preferred $100 par called for redemption 11/14/1968
$4.50 Conv. Preferred Ser. A $5 par called for redemption 09/15/1983
Depositary Shares called for redemption 12/14/1995
$3.25 Conv. Preferred $1 par called for redemption at $50.325 plus $0.8125 accrued dividends on 05/15/2002
(Additional Information in Active)

NEWMONT MNG CORP CDA LTD (BC)
Each Exchangeable Share exchanged for (1) share Newmont Mining Corp. Common $1.60 par 02/18/2014

NEWMONT MNG CORP CDA LTD (CANADA)
Merged into Newmont Mining Corp. 12/16/2011
Each Exchangeable Share exchanged for either (1) share Common $1.60 par or (1) Newmont Mining Corp. of Canada Ltd. (BC) Exchangeable Share
(See Newmont Mining Corp. of Canada Ltd. (BC))
Note: Unexchanged certificates were cancelled and became without value 12/16/2017

NEWNAN COTTON MILLS (GA)
Merged into Mount Vernon Mills, Inc. share for share 8/24/56
(See Mount Vernon Mills, Inc.)

NEWNAN COWETA BANCSHARES INC (GA)
Company's sole asset placed in receivership 06/26/2009
Stockholders' equity unlikely

NEWNAN COWETA BK (COWETA COUNTY, GA)
Reorganized as Newnan Coweta Bancshares, Inc. 10/01/2001
Each share Common $5 par exchanged for (1) share Common $5 par
(See Newnan Coweta Bancshares, Inc.)

NEWNAN FED SVGS & LN ASSN GA (USA)
Common $1 par split (2) for (1) by issuance of (1) additional share 05/25/1987
Name changed to Newnan Savings Bank, FSB (Newnan, GA) 10/01/1988
Newnan Savings Bank, FSB (Newnan, GA) recapitalized as Newnan Holdings Inc. 08/22/1996 which name changed to First Citizens Corp. 01/14/1997 which merged into BB&T Corp. 07/09/1999

NEWNAN HLDGS INC (GA)
Name changed to First Citizens Corp. 1/14/97
First Citizens Corp. merged into BB&T Corp. 7/9/99

NEWNAN SVGS BK FSB (NEWNAN, GA)
Stock Dividend - 10% 1/31/94
Under plan of reorganization each share Common $1 par automatically became (1) share Newnan Holdings Inc. Common $1 par 8/22/96
Newnan Holdings Inc. name changed to First Citizens Corp. 1/14/97 which merged into BB&T Corp. 7/9/99

NEWNORTH GOLD MINES LTD (ON)
Recapitalized as Canadian Newnorth Resources Ltd. 07/19/1982
Each share Capital Stock $1 par exchanged for (0.25) share Capital Stock $1 par
(See Canadian Newnorth Resources Ltd.)

NEWORE DEVELOPMENTS LTD. (ON)
Charter cancelled for failure to pay taxes and file returns 10/11/77

NEWORK CORP (AB)
Name changed to Talware Networx Inc. 06/27/2001
(See Talware Networx Inc.)

NEWORLD BANCORP INC (DE)
Acquired by Citizens Financial Group, Inc. 04/14/1994
Each share Common $1 par exchanged for $35.50 cash

NEWORLD BK FOR SVGS (BOSTON, MA)
Under plan of reorganization each share Common $1 par automatically became (1) share Neworld Bancorp, Inc. Common $1 par 04/20/1987
(See Neworld Bancorp, Inc.)

NEWPASS RES LTD (AB)
Recapitalized as First Class Entertainment & Filmworks Corp. 8/11/87
Each share Common no par exchanged for (0.1) share Common no par

NEWPATH CAP CORP (ON)
Recapitalized as Cyberplex Inc. 04/24/1997
Each share Common no par exchanged for for (0.66666666) share Common no par
Cyberplex Inc. recapitalized as EQ Inc. 06/19/2013

NEWPOINT FDS (MA)
Name changed to FirstMerit Funds 01/31/2000

(See FirstMerit Funds)

NEWPORT BALBOA SAVINGS & LOAN ASSOCIATION (CA)
Merged into International Telephone & Telegraph Corp. 05/20/1983
Each share Guarantee Stock $10 par exchanged for $52 cash
Note: An additional $15.98 cash per share was distributed 05/20/1985

NEWPORT BANCORP (CA)
Acquired by San Marino Savings & Loan Association 05/10/1983
Each share Common no par exchanged for $20 aggregate amount of Savings Account

NEWPORT BANCORP INC (MD)
Merged into SI Financial Group, Inc. 09/06/2013
Each share Common 1¢ par exchanged for (1.5129) shares Common 1¢ par

NEWPORT BUSINESS FORMS INC (VA)
Voluntarily dissolved 12/14/66
Details not available

NEWPORT CHEM INDS INC (DE)
Common $1 par changed to 10¢ par 05/27/1970
Name changed to Newport General Corp. 08/07/1972
(See Newport General Corp.)

NEWPORT CO.
Reorganized as Newport Industries, Inc. 00/00/1931
Details not available

NEWPORT CORP (NV)
Common 35¢ par changed to $0.1167 par and (2) additional shares payable 05/31/2000 to holders of record 05/17/2000
Stock Dividends - 50% 09/29/1981; 50% 10/18/1982; 50% 04/11/1983; 50% 04/18/1984
Acquired by MKS Instruments, Inc. 04/29/2016
Each share Common $0.1167 par exchanged for $23 cash

NEWPORT CTLS CORP (DE)
Name changed to California Leisure Products, Inc. 07/26/1977
(See California Leisure Products, Inc.)

NEWPORT ELEC CORP (RI)
Each share Common $100 par exchanged for (5) shares Common $20 par 00/00/1939
6% Preferred $100 par called for redemption 10/01/1946
Common $20 par changed to $10 par and (1) additional share issued 03/09/1956
Common $10 par split (2) for (1) by issuance of (1) additional share 05/07/1968
Common $10 par changed to no par 04/28/1981
Under plan of reorganization each share Common no par automatically became (1) share NECO Enterprises, Inc. Common no par 01/26/1987
(See NECO Enterprises, Inc.)
3.75% Preferred $100 par called for redemption at $103.50 on 03/28/2000

NEWPORT ELECTRS INC (CA)
Merged into N Merger Corp. 11/10/1992
Each share Common 1¢ par exchanged for $4 cash

NEWPORT GAS LT CO (RI)
Each share Common $100 par exchanged for (10) shares Common no par 00/00/1950
Completely liquidated 01/15/1975
Each share Capital Stock no par exchanged for first and final distribution of $10.30 cash

NEWPORT GEN CORP (DE)
Chapter 11 bankruptcy proceedings converted to Chapter 7 on 8/8/84
Stockholders' equity unlikely

NEWPORT INC (ON)
Name changed to Tuckamore Capital Management Inc. 07/05/2011
Tuckamore Capital Management Inc. name changed to ClearStream Energy Services Inc. 10/18/2016

NEWPORT INDUSTRIES, INC. (DE)
Capital Stock $1 par reclassified as Common $1 par in 1946
Merged into Heyden Newport Chemical Corp. on a (1.5) for (1) basis 1/9/57
Heyden Newport Chemical Corp. acquired by Tennessee Gas Transmission Co. 10/4/63 which name changed to Tenneco Inc. 4/11/66 which merged into El Paso Natural Gas Co. 12/12/96 which reorganized as El Paso Energy Corp. 8/1/98 which name changed to El Paso Corp. 2/5/2001

NEWPORT INTL GROUP INC (DE)
Each share old Common $0.0001 par exchanged for (0.05) share new Common $0.0001 par 12/0/2003
Name changed to Spare Backup, Inc. 08/16/2006
(See Spare Backup, Inc.)

NEWPORT INVT CORP (DE)
Charter cancelled and declared inoperative and void for non-payment of taxes 03/01/1992

NEWPORT INVTS INC (CO)
Recapitalized as Multibase Technologies Inc. 07/26/1991
Each share Common no par exchanged for (1/3) share Common no par

NEWPORT LABS INC (CA)
Name changed to Newport Electronics Inc. 06/27/1979
(See Newport Electronics Inc.)

NEWPORT LD INC (DE)
Charter dissolved 12/27/94

NEWPORT MANOR APARTMENTS
Property sold 00/00/1949
Details not available

NEWPORT MINING & LAND DEVELOPMENT LTD. (CANADA)
Declared dissolved for failure to file reports or pay fees 3/16/79

NEWPORT NATL BK (NEWPORT BEACH, CA)
Reorganized as Newport National Corp. 06/02/1969
Each share Common $10 par exchanged for (2) shares Common $5 par
Newport National Corp. merged into Southern California First National Corp. 09/23/1971
(See Southern California First National Corp.)

NEWPORT NATL CORP (CA)
Merged into Southern California First National Corp. 09/23/1971
Each share Common $5 par exchanged for (1.3) shares Common $5 par plus $11 cash
(See Southern California First National Corp.)

NEWPORT NEWS & HAMPTON RAILWAY GAS & ELECTRIC CO.
Merged into Virginia Public Service Co. 00/00/1927
Details not available

NEWPORT NEWS BK (NEWPORT NEWS, VA)
Name changed 02/11/1987
Name changed from Newport News Savings & Loan Association to Newport News Savings Bank (Newport News, VA) 02/11/1987

Name changed to Tidemark Bancorp, Inc. 01/01/1993
Tidemark Bancorp acquired by Crestar Financial Corp. 03/24/1995 which merged into SunTrust Banks, Inc. 12/31/1998

NEWPORT NEWS SHIPBUILDING & DRY DOCK CO. (VA)
Common $1 par split (2) for (1) by issuance of (1) additional share 11/29/57
Merged into Tenneco Inc. 9/4/68
Each share Common $1 par exchanged for $60 principal amount of 7% Debentures due 10/1/93 and (0.5) share Common $5 par
Tenneco Inc. merged into El Paso Natural Gas Co. 12/12/96 which reorganized as El Paso Energy Corp. 8/1/98 which name changed to El Paso Corp. 2/5/2001

NEWPORT NEWS SHIPBUILDING INC (DE)
Merged into Northrop Grumman Corp. 1/18/2002
Each share Common 1¢ par exchanged for (0.1743) share Common $1 par and $51.14 cash

NEWPORT OIL & GAS INC (NV)
Recapitalized as Intergem, Inc. 3/18/83
Each share Common 1¢ par exchanged for (0.1) share Common 1¢ par
Intergem, Inc. name changed to Excel InterFinancial Corp. 10/26/87
(See Excel InterFinancial Corp.)

NEWPORT PARTNERS INCOME FD (ON)
Under plan of reorganization each Unit no par automatically became (1) share Newport Inc. Common no par 04/05/2011
Newport Inc. name changed to Tuckamore Capital Management Inc. 07/05/2011 which name changed to ClearStream Energy Services Inc. 10/18/2016

NEWPORT PETE CORP (BC)
Merged into Hunt Oil Co. 6/14/2000
Each share Common no par exchanged for $5.50 cash

NEWPORT PETES INC (CO)
Merged into Mineral Development, Inc. 4/17/86
Each share Common no par exchanged for (1) share Common 1¢ par
Mineral Development, Inc. recapitalized as Exco Resources Inc. 7/18/96
(See Exco Resources Inc.)

NEWPORT PETES LTD (AB)
Merged into Stanford Resources Ltd. 12/05/1983
Each share Common no par exchanged for $1.32 cash

NEWPORT PHARMACEUTICALS INTL INC (DE)
Reincorporated 7/15/70
Reincorporated 11/30/87
Under plan of reorganization state of incorporation changed from (UT) to (CA) and each share Common 50¢ par exchanged for (2) shares Common 10¢ par 7/15/70
Common 10¢ par split (3) for (1) by issuance of (2) additional shares 9/16/71
State of incorporation changed from (CA) to (DE) 11/30/87
Name changed to Systemed Inc. 10/1/91
(See Systemed Inc. (DE))

NEWPORT STEEL CORP. (IN)
Name changed to Newcorp, Inc. (IN) 09/18/1956
(See Newcorp, Inc. (IN))

NEWPORT VENTURE ACQUISITIONS CORP (CO)
Name changed to Freight Services Group Inc. 10/31/1988

NEWPORT WATER CORP.
Property sold to City of Newport, R.I. in 1940
Liquidation completed in 1946

NEWPORT WESTN INC (CA)
Name changed to Pride N Joy Industries, Inc. 7/18/72
(See Pride N Joy Industries, Inc.)

NEWPORTER YACHTS INC. (NJ)
Assets sold for benefit of creditors 2/5/71
Capital Stock is valueless

NEWPOWER HLDGS INC (DE)
Plan of reorganization under Chapter 11 Federal Bankruptcy Code effective 10/9/2003
Each share Common 1¢ par received initial distribution of $0.59 cash payable 10/26/2004 to holders of record 10/12/2004
Each share Common 1¢ par received second distribution of $0.15 cash payable 12/14/2006 to holders of record 11/30/2006
Each share Common 1¢ par received third and final distribution of $0.0375 cash payable 5/8/2007 to holders of record 4/24/2007
Note: Certificates were not required to be surrendered and are without value

NEWQUARK INC (UT)
Involuntarily dissolved 03/31/1986

NEWQUEST ENERGY INC (AB)
Each share Class B Common no par exchanged for (10) shares Class A Common no par 12/20/99
Recapitalized as Ranchero Energy Inc. 9/1/2000
Each share Class A Common no par exchanged for (1/3) share Class A Common no par
Ranchero Energy Inc. merged into PrimeWest Energy Trust 5/29/2001

NEWQUEST VENTURES CORP (BC)
Recapitalized as Aster Ventures Corp. 05/26/1999
Each share Common no par exchanged for (0.5) share Common no par
Aster Ventures Corp. recapitalized as Knight Petroleum Corp. 03/22/2001 which name changed to Knight Resources Ltd. 03/07/2003 which recapitalized as Knight Metals Ltd. 05/25/2011 which name changed to Africa Hydrocarbons Inc. (BC) 02/02/2012 which reincorporated in Alberta 04/25/2013 which name changed to Blockchaink2 Corp. 05/30/2018

NEWREACH COMMUNICATIONS INC (FL)
Name changed to Henley Group, Inc. 04/02/1997
Henley Group, Inc. name changed to CIS.com, Inc. 05/27/1999 which name changed to InterAmerican Resources, Inc. 08/13/2001 which name changed to Allixon Corp. 06/04/2004 which recapitalized as Simcoe Mining Resources Corp. 01/16/2008

NEWRICH EXPLS LTD (ON)
Capital Stock $1 par changed to no par 7/2/71
Merged into Belle Aire Resource Explorations Ltd. 8/29/78
Each share Capital Stock no par exchanged for (0.12) share Common no par
Belle Aire Resource Explorations Ltd. name changed to Sprint Resources Ltd. 9/23/82 which name changed to Meacon Bay Resources Inc. 3/9/87

NEWRIDERS INC (NV)
Merged into EasyRiders, Inc. 09/23/1998
Each share Common $0.001 par exchanged for (0.5) share Common $0.001 par
(See EasyRiders, Inc.)

NEWROY GOLD MINES LTD. (ON)
Recapitalized as Newroy Mines Ltd. on a (0.2) for (1) basis in 1944
Newroy Mines Ltd. was acquired by Courville Mines Ltd. 12/31/64
(See Newroy Mines Ltd.)

NEWROY MINES LTD. (ON)
Acquired by Courville Mines Ltd. 12/31/1964
Each share Capital Stock $1 par exchanged for (0.05) share Capital Stock $1 par
(See Courville Mines Ltd.)

NEWS COMMUNICATIONS INC (NV)
Each share old Common 1¢ par exchanged for (0.33333333) share new Common 1¢ par 08/21/1990
Each share new Common 1¢ par exchanged again for (0.1) share new Common 1¢ par 05/12/1992
Each share new Common 1¢ par exchanged again for (0.33333333) share new Common 1¢ par 01/19/1999
Each share new Common 1¢ par exchanged again for (0.01) share new Common 1¢ par 11/16/2005
Note: Holders of (99) or fewer pre-split shares received $1.10 cash per share Acquired by CHM Holdings LLC 12/28/2015
Each share new Common 1¢ par exchanged for $148.20 cash

NEWS CORP LTD (AUSTRALIA)
ADR's for Ordinary AUD $0.50 par split (2) for (1) by issuance of (1) additional ADR 01/16/1987
Reorganized under the laws of Delaware as News Corp. (Old) 11/03/2004
Each Sponsored ADR for Ltd. Voting Preferred Ordinary exchanged for (2) shares Class A Common 1¢ par
Each ADR for Ordinary exchanged for (2) shares Class B Common 1¢ par
News Corp. (Old) name changed to Twenty-First Century Fox, Inc. 07/01/2013

NEWS CORP OLD (DE)
Each share Class A Common 1¢ par received distribution of (0.25) share News Corp. (New) Class A Common 1¢ par payable 06/28/2013 to holders of record 06/21/2013
Ex date - 07/01/2013
Each share Class B Common 1¢ par received distribution of (0.25) share News Corp. (New) Class B Common 1¢ par payable 06/28/2013 to holders of record 06/21/2013
Ex date - 07/01/2013
Name changed to Twenty-First Century Fox, Inc. 07/01/2013

NEWSBOY COPPER MINING CO. (WY)
Charter revoked for failure to pay taxes 7/19/27

NEWSCOPE RES LTD (CANADA)
Recapitalized as Canadian Newscope Resources Ltd. 12/13/90
Each share Common no par exchanged for (0.1) share Common no par
Canadian Newscope Resources Ltd. name changed back to Newscope Resources Ltd. 7/11/94 which name changed to Denbury Resources Ltd. 12/21/95

NEWSCOPE RES LTD (CANADA)
Name changed to Denbury Resources Inc. (Canada) 12/21/1995
Denbury Resources Inc. (Canada) reincorporated in Delaware 04/21/1999

NEWSCORP CAYMAN IS LTD (CAYMAN ISLANDS)
$3.50 Conv. Guaranteed Preferred 1¢ par called for redemption 7/15/94
Public interest eliminated

NEWSEARCH INC NEW (CO)
Reincorporated under the laws of Maryland as Global Clean Energy, Inc. 11/13/2007

NEWSEARCH INC OLD (CO)
Administratively dissolved 01/01/1990
Each share Common $0.001 par subsequently received distribution of (0.01) share Newsearch, Inc. (New) (CO) Common $0.001 par 12/03/1999
Newsearch, Inc. (New) (CO) reincorporated in Maryland as Global Clean Energy, Inc. 11/13/2007

NEWSEDGE CORP (DE)
Merged into Thompson Corp. 9/27/2001
Each share Common 1¢ par exchanged for $2.30 cash

NEWSGURUS COM INC (NV)
Recapitalized as Secure Enterprise Solutions Inc. 01/25/2002
Each share Common $0.001 par exchanged for (0.5) share Common $0.001 par
Secure Enterprise Solutions Inc. name changed to Edgetech Services Inc. 11/20/2002 which name changed to Inova Technology, Inc. 05/23/2007
(See Inova Technology, Inc.)

NEWSOUTH BANCORP INC (VA)
Reincorporated 03/29/1999
Common 1¢ par split (3) for (2) by issuance of (0.5) additional share payable 08/19/1998 to holders of record 07/31/1998
State of incorporation changed from (DE) to (VA) 03/29/1999
Name changed to First South Bancorp Inc. 02/17/2000
First South Bancorp Inc. merged into Carolina Financial Corp. (New) 11/01/2017

NEWSPAN INC (DE)
Each share old Common 25¢ par exchanged for (0.00008) share new Common no par 07/16/1985
Note: In effect holders received $2.50 cash per share and public interest was eliminated

NEWSPLAYER GROUP PLC (UNITED KINGDOM)
Name changed to Catalyst Media Group PLC 06/02/2004
(See Catalyst Media Group PLC)

NEWSTAR ENERGY INC (AB)
Recapitalized as Newstar Resources Inc. 6/28/95
Each share Class A no par exchanged for (1/7) share Class A no par

NEWSTAR FINL INC (DE)
Acquired by First Eagle Holdings, Inc. 12/22/2017
Each share Common 1¢ par exchanged for (1) Contingent Value Right and $11.44 cash
Note: Each Contingent Value Right received initial distribution of $0.04773 cash 03/12/2018

NEWSTAR MEDIA INC (CA)
Chapter 11 bankruptcy proceedings converted to Chapter 7 on 06/28/2001
Stockholders' equity unlikely

NEWSTATE HLDGS INC (DE)
Company terminated common stock registration and is no longer public as of 12/12/2001

NEWSTRIKE CAP INC (BC)
Common no par split (2) for (1) by issuance of (1) additional share payable 02/07/2007 to holders of record 02/01/2007
Merged into Timmins Gold Corp. 05/28/2015
Each share Common no par exchanged for (0.9) share Common no par and $0.0001 cash
Note: Unexchanged certificates will be cancelled and become without value 05/28/2021
Timmins Gold Corp. recapitalized as Alio Gold Inc. 05/16/2017

NEWSTRIKE RES LTD (ON)
Name changed to Newstrike Brands Ltd. 07/27/2018

NEWSYS SOLUTIONS INC (CANADA)
Reincorporated 03/07/2000
Place of incorporation changed from (AB) to Canada 03/07/2000
Name changed to InBusiness Solutions Inc. 09/22/2000
(See InBusiness Solutions Inc.)

NEWTEC INDS LTD (BC)
Struck off register and declared dissolved for failure to file returns 8/28/92

NEWTECH BRAKE CORP (DE)
SEC revoked common stock registration 05/22/2013

NEWTEK BUSINESS SVCS INC (NY)
Name changed 11/26/2002
Name changed from Newtek Capital Inc. to Newtek Business Services, Inc. 11/26/2002
Each share old Common 2¢ par exchanged for (0.2) share new Common 2¢ par 10/23/2014
Reincorporated under the laws of Maryland as Newtek Business Services Corp. 11/13/2014

NEWTEL ENTERPRISES LTD (NL)
Merged into Aliant Inc. (Canada) 06/01/1999
Each share Common no par exchanged for (1.567) shares Common no par
Aliant Inc. (Canada) reorganized in Ontario as Bell Aliant Regional Communications Income Fund 07/10/2006 which reorganized in Canada as Bell Aliant Inc. 01/04/2011 which merged into BCE Inc. 10/31/2014

NEWTON (GEO. B.) COAL CO.
Liquidation approved in 1945
No Common stockholders' equity

NEWTON-CONROE OIL CORP. (DE)
Dissolved and each (5.4688) share Common 1¢ par exchanged for (1) share Common $1 par of New Bristol Oils Ltd. 7/8/55
New Bristol Oils Ltd. merged into Able Land & Minerals Ltd. 9/16/59 which was acquired by Canaveral International Corp. 5/1/63 which recapitalized as Madison Group Associates Inc. 2/2/93
(See Madison Group Associates Inc.)

NEWTON ELKIN SHOES, INC. (PA)
Name changed to Henry (Edith) Shoes, Inc. 5/16/68
(See Henry (Edith) Shoes, Inc.)

NEWTON FINL CORP (NJ)
Common $5 par split (2) for (1) by issuance of (1) additional share payable 12/21/98 to holders of record 12/15/98
Merged into Lakeland Bancorp, Inc. 7/1/2004
Each share Common $5 par exchanged for $72.08 cash

NEWTON GAS CO.
Merged into New Jersey Power & Light Co. in 1926
Details not available

NEWTON GOLD CORP (BC)
Recapitalized as Chlormet Technologies Inc. 11/07/2013
Each share Common no par exchanged for (0.2) share Common no par
Chlormet Technologies Inc. name changed to PUF Ventures Inc. 11/13/2015

NEWTON GROWTH FD INC (MD)
Name changed 4/4/77
Common $1 par split (2) for (1) by issuance of (1) additional share 1/31/68
Name changed from Newton Fund, Inc. to Newton Growth Fund, Inc. 4/4/77
Voluntarily dissolved 9/17/93
Details not available

NEWTON INCOME FD INC (MD)
Name changed 04/29/1977
Name changed from Newton Investors Fund, Inc. to Newton Income Fund, Inc. 04/29/1977
Common $1 par reclassified as Income Fund Portfolio $1 par 10/19/1981
Money Fund Portfolio $1 par changed to 1¢ par 10/22/1982
Reorganized as Marshall Funds, Inc. 12/11/1992
Details not available

NEWTON INVESTMENT, INC. (UT)
Name changed to Price of His Toys, Inc. 07/24/1989
Price of His Toys, Inc. recapitalized as Buccaneer Casino & Hotel Corp. 01/22/1994 which name changed to Worthington Venture Fund Inc. (UT) 02/06/1995 which reincorporated in Delaware 06/03/1998 which name changed to Admax Technology Inc. 08/16/1998 which name changed to Aamaxan Transport Group, Inc. 08/28/1998

NEWTON NATIONAL BANK (NEWTON, MA)
Stock Dividend - 20% 02/23/1962
Merged into Community National Bank (Framingham, MA) 12/31/1971
Each share Capital Stock $10 par exchanged for (2.8) shares Common $5 par
Community National Bank (Framingham, MA) name changed to Shawmut Community Bank, N.A. (Framingham, MA) 04/01/1975
(See Shawmut Community Bank, N.A. (Framington, MA))

NEWTON-PHOENIX OIL CORP. (DE)
Merged into Newton-Conroe Oil Corp. share for share in 1954
Newton-Conroe Oil Corp. was liquidated by exchange for New Bristol Oils Ltd. 7/8/55 which merged into Able Land & Minerals Ltd. 9/16/59 which was acquired by Canaveral International Corp. 5/1/63 which recapitalized as Madison Group Associates Inc. 2/2/93
(See Madison Group Associates Inc.)

NEWTON SELECT FD INC (MD)
Reorganized as Newton Income Fund, Inc. 11/16/1977
Each share Capital Stock $1 par exchanged for (0.9858) share Common $1 par
(See Newton Income Fund, Inc.)

NEWTON STEEL CO.
Properties sold to Republic Steel Corp. 00/00/1937
Details not available

NEWTON VENTURES INC (BC)
Recapitalized as Rusoro Mining Ltd. 11/9/2006
Each share Common no par

exchanged for (0.600024) share Common no par

NEWTON WALTHAM BK & TR CO (WALTHAM, MA)
Stock Dividends - 51.5% 3/10/61; 100% 4/15/69
Name changed to BayBank Newton-Waltham Trust Co. (Waltham, MA) 2/2/76
BayBank Newton-Waltham Trust Co. (Waltham, MA) merged into BayBank Middlesex (Burlington, MA) 11/9/79 which name changed to BayBank Trust Co. (Burlington, MA) 6/30/83 which name changed back to BayBank Middlesex (Burlington, MA) 12/8/83

NEWVAN RES LTD (BC)
Recapitalized as Tricor Resources Ltd. 06/02/1977
Each share Capital Stock no par exchanged for (0.25) share Capital Stock no par
(See Tricor Resources Ltd.)

NEWVISION TECHNOLOGY INC (DE)
Name changed to Sight Resource Corp. 10/30/95
(See Sight Resource Corp.)

NEWWEST GOLD CORP (BC)
Acquired by Fronteer Development Group Inc. 09/24/2007
Each share Common no par exchanged for (0.26) share Common no par
Note: Unexchanged certificates were cancelled and became without value 09/24/2013
Fronteer Development Group Inc. name changed to Fronteer Gold Inc. 05/13/2010 which merged into Pilot Gold Inc. 04/08/2011 which name changed to Liberty Gold Corp. 05/12/2017

NEWZSTAND COM INC (NV)
Name changed to uAuthorize Corp. and (9) additional shares issued 6/4/2004
uAuthorize Corp. name changed to Ablaze Technologies, Inc. 4/4/2005

NEXAGEN INC (DE)
Issue Information - 2,000,000 shares COM offered at $11.50 per share on 01/28/1994
Under plan of merger name changed to Nexstar Pharmeceuticals Inc. 2/21/95

NEXAR TECHNOLOGIES INC (DE)
Issue Information - 2,500,000 shares COM offered at $9 per share on 04/08/1997
Filed a petition under Chapter 7 Federal Bankruptcy Code 12/17/98
Stockholders' equity unlikely

NEXC PARTNERS CORP (ON)
Under plan of merger each Class A Share automatically became (1) Purpose Enhanced Dividend Fund ETF Unit 01/02/2018

NEXCEN BRANDS INC (DE)
Liquidation completed
Each share Common 1¢ par received initial distribution of $0.06 cash payable 01/27/2012 to holders of record 09/13/2010
Each share Common 1¢ par exchanged for second and final distribution of $0.137498 cash 12/02/2013

NEXCORE HEALTHCARE CAP CORP (DE)
Each share Common $0.001 par received distribution of (1) share NexCore Real Estate LLC Restricted Common payable 12/26/2012 to holders of record 12/24/2012
Acquired by NexCore Group 12/19/2014
Each share Common $0.001 par exchanged for $0.31 cash

NEXELL THERAPEUTICS INC (DE)
Each share old Common $0.001 par exchanged for (0.25) share new Common $0.001 par 6/15/2000
Completely liquidated
Each share new Common $0.001 par received first and final distribution of $0.05 cash payable 12/23/2002 to holders of record 12/18/2002
Ex date - 12/24/2002
Note: Certificates were not required to be surrendered and are now valueless

NEXEN INC (CANADA)
9.75% Preferred Securities no par called for redemption at $25 plus $0.514583 accrued dividend on 12/15/2003
9.375% Preferred Securities no par called for redemption at $25 on 2/9/2004
Common no par split (2) for (1) by issuance of (1) additional share payable 05/17/2005 to holders of record 05/12/2005 Ex date - 05/18/2005
Common no par split (2) for (1) by issuance of (1) additional share payable 05/15/2007 to holders of record 05/10/2007 Ex date - 05/16/2007
Acquired by CNOOC Ltd. 02/25/2013
Each share Rate Reset Preferred Ser. 2 no par exchanged for $26 cash
Each share Common no par exchanged for USD $27.50 cash

NEXFOR INC (CANADA)
Name changed to Norbord Inc. 7/5/2004

NEXGEN APPLIED SOLUTIONS INC (NV)
Name changed to Bingo Nation, Inc. 11/08/2016

NEXGEN BIOFUELS LTD (ISRAEL)
Name changed to Laxai Pharma, Ltd. 04/01/2010

NEXGEN FINL CORP (ON)
Acquired by Natixis Global Asset Management, L.P. 12/24/2014
Each share Common no par exchanged for $7.25 cash
Note: Unexchanged certificates were cancelled and became without value 12/24/2016

NEXGEN INC (DE)
Issue Information - 3,550,000 shares COM offered at $15 per share on 05/24/1995
Merged into Advanced Micro Devices, Inc. 1/18/96
Each share Common $0.0001 par exchanged for (0.8) share Common $0.0001 par

NEXGEN PETROLEUM CORP (NV)
Recapitalized as Hubei Minkang Pharmaceutical Inc. 10/21/2010
Each share Common $0.001 par exchanged for (0.125) share Common $0.001 par

NEXGEN VISION INC (DE)
SEC revoked common stock registration 07/14/2009
Stockholders' equity unlikely

NEXHORIZON COMMUNICATIONS INC (DE)
Name changed to NX Capital Co. 09/16/2013
NX Capital Co. recapitalized as NX Uranium, Inc. 09/29/2014

NEXIA BIOTECHNOLOGIES INC (CANADA)
Each share Common no par received initial distribution of $0.72 cash payable 03/23/2005 to holders of record 03/23/2005
Reorganized under the laws of Alberta as Enseco Energy Services Corp. 10/24/2006
Each share Common no par exchanged for (0.08842) share

Common no par and (1) share Nexia Biotechnologies Ltd. Common no par
(See each company's listing)

NEXIA BIOTECHNOLOGIES LTD (AB)
Recapitalized as Symax Lift (Holding) Co. Ltd. (AB) 12/11/2009
Each share Common no par exchanged for (0.1) share Common no par
Symax Lift (Holding) Co. Ltd. (AB) reincorporated in British Columbia 10/05/2010
(See Symax Lift (Holding) Co. Ltd.)

NEXIA HLDGS INC (NV)
Each share old Common $0.001 par exchanged for (0.001) share new Common $0.001 par 11/01/2004
New Common $0.001 par changed to $0.0001 par 09/18/2006
Each share old Common $0.0001 par exchanged for (0.1) share new Common $0.0001 par 02/20/2007
Each share new Common $0.0001 par exchanged again for (0.01) share new Common $0.0001 par 12/14/2007
Each share new Common $0.0001 par exchanged again for (0.001) share new Common $0.0001 par 07/29/2008
Each share new Common $0.0001 par exchanged again for (0.0005) share new Common $0.0001 par 02/23/2010
Reincorporated under the laws of Utah as Sack Lunch Productions, Inc. 04/20/2015

NEXIASOFT INC (DE)
Recapitalized as SPI Worldwide, Inc. 04/18/2008
Each share Common $0.001 par exchanged for (0.01) share Common $0.001 par
SPI Worldwide, Inc. name changed to Talent Alliance, Inc. 06/30/2008 which name changed to Hire International, Inc. 09/24/2010 which recapitalized as TruLan Resources Inc. 11/20/2012 which recapitalized as Trinity Resources Inc. 09/18/2015

NEXICON INC (NV)
Each share old Common $0.001 par exchanged for (0.625) share new Common $0.001 par 04/29/2008
SEC revoked common stock registration 09/08/2011

NEXIENT LEARNING INC (NS)
Each share old Common no par exchanged for (0.25) share new Common no par 07/03/2008
Assets sold for the benefit of creditors 08/21/2009
No stockholders' equity

NEXIQ TECHNOLOGIES INC (NH)
Chapter 11 bankruptcy proceedings converted to Chapter 7 on 7/21/2003
Stockholders' equity unlikely

NEXIS INTL INDS INC (WA)
Charter expired 05/01/2009

NEXITY FINL CORP (DE)
Issue Information - 1,700,000 shares COM offered at $16 per share on 09/20/2005
Each share old Common 1¢ par exchanged for (0.25) share new Common 1¢ par 09/01/2005
Chapter 11 bankruptcy proceedings converted to Chapter 7 on 07/21/2011
Stockholders' equity unlikely

NEXJ SYS INC OLD (CANADA)
Each share Common no par received distribution of (1) share NexJ Health Holdings Inc. Common no par payable 01/25/2016 to holders of record 01/22/2016
Under plan of reorganization each share Common no par automatically became (1) share NexJ Systems

Inc. (New) Common no par 01/25/2016

NEXLAND INC (DE)
Reincorporated 9/13/2000
State of incorporation changed from (AZ) to (DE) 9/13/2000
Merged into Symantec Corp. 7/18/2003
Each share Common $0.0001 par exchanged for $0.5118 cash

NEXLE CORP (DE)
Recapitalized as Springfield Co., Inc. 03/07/2005
Each (45) shares Common $0.0001 par exchanged for (1) share Common $0.0001 par
(See Springfield Co., Inc.)

NEXMED INC (NV)
Each (15) shares old Common $0.001 par exchanged for (1) share new Common $0.001 par 06/21/2010
Name changed to Apricus Biosciences, Inc. 09/14/2010

NEXMEDIA TECHNOLOGIES INC (BC)
Cease trade order effective 06/03/2003
Stockholders' equity unlikely

NEXPOINT CR STRATEGIES FD (DE)
Each share old Common $0.001 par received distribution of (0.33333333) share NexPoint Residential Trust, Inc. Common 1¢ par payable 03/31/2015 to holders of record 03/23/2015 Ex date - 04/01/2015
Each share old Common $0.001 par exchanged for (0.25) share new Common $0.001 par 10/06/2015
Name changed to NexPoint Strategic Opportunities Fund 03/19/2018

NEXPRISE INC (DE)
Each share old Common $0.0002 par exchanged for (0.06666666) share new Common $0.0002 par 04/22/2002
Assets sold for the benefit of creditors 04/12/2011
Stockholders' equity unlikely

NEXPUB INC (PA)
SEC revoked common stock registration 11/07/2005
Stockholders' equity unlikely

NEXSTAGE CORP (NV)
SEC revoked common stock registration 10/09/2008
Stockholders' equity unlikely

NEXSTAR AUTOMATION INC (NL)
Merged into Zygo Corp. 09/12/1996
Each share Common no par exchanged for (22.0637) shares Common 10¢ par
(See Zygo Corp.)

NEXSTAR BROADCASTING GROUP INC (DE)
Under plan of merger name changed to Nexstar Media Group, Inc. 01/18/2017

NEXSTAR PHARMACEUTICALS INC (DE)
Merged into Gilead Sciences, Inc. 7/29/99
Each share Common 1¢ par exchanged for (0.3786) share Common $0.001 par

NEXT EDGE GLG EMERGING MKTS INCOME FD (ON)
Merged into Next Edge Theta Yield Fund 12/30/2014
Each Class A Unit automatically became (0.7) Class A1 Unit
Each Class F Unit automatically became (0.77) Class F1 Unit

NEXT ETFS TR (DE)
Name changed to Precidian ETFs Trust 05/16/2011
(See Precidian ETFs Trust)

NEXT GEN METALS INC (BC)
Each share old Common no par

exchanged for (0.5) share new Common no par 06/28/2010
Recapitalized as Namaste Technologies Inc. 03/02/2016
Each share new Common no par exchanged for (0.33333333) share Common no par

NEXT GENERATION ENERGY CORP (NV)
Common 1¢ par changed to $0.001 par 12/03/2012
Name changed to Next Generation Management Corp. 06/19/2014

NEXT GENERATION MEDIA CORP (NV)
Each share old Common 1¢ par exchanged for (0.001) share new Common 1¢ par 05/25/2010
Name changed to Next Generation Energy Corp. 07/28/2010
Next Generation Energy Corp. name changed to Next Generation Management Corp. 06/19/2014

NEXT GENERATION TECHNOLOGY HLDGS INC (DE)
Chapter 11 bankruptcy proceedings converted to Chapter 7 on 08/01/2007
No stockholders' equity

NEXT GROUP HLDGS INC (FL)
Recapitalized as Cuentas Inc. 08/13/2018
Each share Common $0.001 par exchanged for (0.00333333) share Common $0.001 par

NEXT INC (DE)
Liquidation completed
Each share Common $0.001 par exchanged for initial distribution of $0.02 cash 01/25/2011
Each share Common $0.001 par received second and final distribution of $0.0056741 cash payable 04/08/2011 to holders of record 01/25/2011

NEXT LEVEL COMMUNICATIONS INC (DE)
Merged into Motorola, Inc. 4/25/2003
Each share Common 1¢ par exchanged for $1.18 cash

NEXT MILLENNIUM COML CORP (CANADA)
Name changed to Roadrunner Oil & Gas Inc. 07/17/2008
Roadrunner Oil & Gas Inc. name changed to Bowood Energy Inc. 06/21/2010 which recapitalized as LGX Oil + Gas Inc. (Canada) 08/22/2012 which reincorporated in Alberta 06/27/2013

NEXT 1 INTERACTIVE INC (NV)
Each share old Common $0.00001 par exchanged for (0.002) share new Common $0.00001 par 05/22/2012
Recapitalized as Monaker Group, Inc. 06/25/2015
Each share new Common $0.00001 par exchanged for (0.02) share Common $0.00001 par

NEXTAIR INC (ON)
Recapitalized as NXA Inc. 02/23/2005
Each share Common no par exchanged for (0.1) share Common no par
NXA Inc. recapitalized as Ellipsiz Communications Ltd. 11/26/2015

NEXTCARD INC (DE)
Issue Information - 6,000,000 shares COM offered at $20 per share on 05/14/1999
Chapter 11 bankruptcy proceedings converted to Chapter 7 on 08/11/2003
No stockholders' equity

NEXTECH ENTERPRISES INTL INC (DE)
SEC revoked common stock registration 05/29/2007

Stockholders' equity unlikely

NEXTEL COMMUNICATIONS INC (DE)
Stock Dividends - in 13% Preferred to holders of 13% Preferred 3.25% payable 10/15/1999 to holders of record 10/05/1999; in 11.125% Preferred to holders of 11.125% Preferred 2.78125% payable 08/15/2000 to holders of record 08/04/2000 Ex date - 08/10/2000; in 13% Preferred to holders of 13% Preferred 3.25% payable 10/16/2000 to holders of record 10/05/2000; in 11.125% Preferred to holders of 11.125% Preferred 2.78125% payable 11/15/2000 to holders of record 11/03/2000; in 13% Preferred to holders of 13% Preferred 3.25% payable 07/16/2001 to holders of record 07/05/2001 Ex date - 07/17/2001; 3.25% payable 10/15/2002 to holders of record 10/04/2002 Ex date - 10/02/2002; 3.25% payable 01/15/2003 to holders of record 01/03/2003 Ex date - 12/31/2002; in 13% Preferred to holders of 13% Preferred 3.25% payable 04/15/2003 to holders of record 04/04/2003 Ex date - 04/02/2003
13% Exchangeable Preferred Ser. D $0.001 par called for redemption at $103.25 on 07/15/2003
11.125% Exchangeable Preferred Ser. E called for redemption at $105.5625 on 08/16/2003
Class A Common $0.001 par split (2) for (1) by issuance of (1) additional share payable 6/6/2000 to holders of record 05/26/2000
Merged into Sprint Nextel Corp. 08/12/2005
Each share Class A Common $0.001 par exchanged for (1.3) shares Common Ser. 1 $2 par
Sprint Nextel Corp. merged into Sprint Corp. (DE) 07/10/2013

NEXTEL PARTNERS INC (DE)
Issue Information - 23,500,000 shares CL A offered at $20 per share on 02/22/2000
Acquired by Sprint Nextel Corp. 6/27/2006
Each share Common $0.001 par exchanged for $28.50 cash

NEXTEL STRYPES TR (DE)
Issue Information - 7,168,587 EXCHANGEABLE STK offered at $14 per share on 03/04/1997
Each Exchangeable Structured Yield Product Security exchanged for (0.843) share Nextel Communications, Inc. Class A Common $0.001 par 05/15/2000
Nextel Communications, Inc. merged into Sprint Nextel Corp. 08/12/2005

NEXTERA ENERGY INC (FL)
Each Corporate Unit automatically became (0.7715) share Common 1¢ par 06/01/2012
Each Corporate Unit automatically became (0.7387) share Common 1¢ par 09/03/2013
Each Corporate Unit automatically became (0.655) share Common 1¢ par 06/01/2015
Each Corporate Unit automatically became (0.6287) share Common 1¢ par 09/01/2015
Each 5.799% Corporate Unit automatically became (0.5101) share Common 1¢ par 09/01/2016
Each 6.371% Corporate Unit automatically became (0.444) share Common 1¢ par 09/04/2018
(Additional Information in Active)

NEXTERA ENTERPRISES INC (DE)
Issue Information - 11,500,000 shares CL A offered at $10 per share on 05/21/1999

Charter voluntarily dissolved 09/02/2008
Details not available

NEXTERRA PPTY GROUP INC (AB)
Name changed to Mariah Energy Corp. 1/23/2003

NEXTEST SYS CORP (DE)
Issue Information - 5,400,000 shares COM offered at $14 per share on 03/21/2006
Merged into Teradyne, Inc. 01/24/2008
Each share Common $0.001 par exchanged for $20 cash

NEXTFIT INC (NV)
SEC revoked common stock registration 05/28/2014

NEXTGEN BIOSCIENCE INC (NV)
Common $0.001 par split (4) for (1) by issuance of (3) additional shares payable 10/29/2007 to holders of record 10/26/2007 Ex date - 10/30/2007
Recapitalized as Kalahari Greentech Inc. 12/09/2008
Each share Common $0.001 par exchanged for (0.0005) share Common $0.001 par
Kalahari Greentech Inc. recapitalized as PF Hospitality Group, Inc. 06/11/2015 which name changed to EXOlifestyle, Inc. 09/27/2016 which recapitalized as Sun Pacific Holding Corp. 10/13/2017

NEXTGEN COMMUNICATIONS CORP (DE)
Name changed to Home Solutions of America, Inc. 12/23/2002
(See Home Solutions of America, Inc.)

NEXTHEALTH INC (DE)
Merged into Anam LLC 3/25/2002
Each share Common 1¢ par exchanged for $5.10 cash

NEXTLEVEL SYS INC (DE)
Name changed to General Instrument Corp. (Ctfs. dtd. after 02/02/1998) 02/02/1998
General Instrument Corp. (Ctfs. dtd. after 02/02/1998) merged into Motorola Inc. 01/05/2000 which recapitalized as Motorola Solutions, Inc. 01/04/2011

NEXTLINK COMMUNICATIONS INC (WA)
Issue Information - 15,200,000 shares CL A offered at $17 per share on 09/26/1997
Class A Common 2¢ par split (2) for (1) by issuance of (1) additional share payable 8/27/99 to holders of record 8/18/99
Class A Common 2¢ par split (2) for (1) by issuance of (1) additional share payable 6/15/2000 to holders of record 6/1/2000
Stock Dividend - in Preferred to holders to Preferred 3.50% payable 11/1/99 to holders of record 10/15/99
Name changed to XO Communications, Inc. 10/26/2000
(See XO Communications, Inc.)

NEXTPATH TECHNOLOGIES INC (NV)
SEC revoked common stock registration 08/10/2009
Stockholders' equity unlikely

NEXTPHASE WIRELESS INC (NV)
Each share old Common $0.001 par exchanged for (0.05) share new Common $0.001 par 11/05/2007
Name changed to MetroConnect Inc. 02/02/2009
(See MetroConnect Inc.)

NEXTRA TECHNOLOGIES INC (AB)
Name changed to NUVO Network Management Inc. 06/27/1997

(See NUVO Network Management Inc.)

NEXTRON CORP (AB)
Acquired by PowerComm Inc. 10/24/2007
Each share Common no par exchanged for (0.06666666) share Common no par and $0.05 cash
PowerComm Inc. name changed to PetroCorp Group Inc. 12/23/2009

NEXTRONICS II INC (NV)
Name changed to Ukraine Financial Services, Inc. 06/12/2008
Ukraine Financial Services, Inc. name changed to National Investment Corporation, Real Estate Holdings 06/23/2008
(See National Investment Corporation, Real Estate Holdings)

NEXTSOURCE MATLS INC (MN)
Reincorporated under the laws of Canada and Common $0.001 par changed to no par 12/27/2017

NEXTTRIP COM TRAVEL INC (BC)
Recapitalized as WorldPlus Ventures Ltd. 05/26/2003
Each share Common no par exchanged for (0.1) share Common no par
WorldPlus Ventures Ltd. recapitalized as New Global Ventures Ltd. 06/07/2007 which recapitalized as New Global Ventures International Ltd. 03/14/2008 which name changed to Auro Resources Corp. 10/15/2010 which recapitalized as Tesoro Minerals Corp. 08/26/2013

NEXTWAVE SOFTWARE CORP (CANADA)
Recapitalized as Stox Infolink Systems Inc. 07/21/1994
Each share Common no par exchanged for (0.2) share Common no par
Stok Infolink Systems Inc. name changed to stox.com Inc. 02/24/1999
(See stox.com Inc.)

NEXTWAVE TELECOM INC (DE)
Plan of reorganization under Chapter 11 Federal Bankruptcy Code effective 04/13/2005
Each share Class B Common $0.0001 par exchanged for (1) NextWave Wireless LLC Equity Interest and $6.79 cash
Note: Equity Interests are not publicly traded
Distribution to holders entitled to less than (25) Equity Interests or less than $25 cash will not be made

NEXTWAVE WIRELESS INC (DE)
Each share old Common $0.001 par exchanged for (0.14285714) share Common $0.007 par 06/21/2010
Acquired by AT&T Inc. 01/24/2013
Each share new Common $0.007 par exchanged for $1 cash and (1) Contingent Payment Right
Each Contingent Payment Right received initial distribution of $0.393796 cash 02/12/2014
Each Contingent Payment Right received second and final distribution of $0.565246 cash 02/04/2015

NEX2U INC (FL)
Name changed to KMA Capital Partners, Inc. 6/9/2006

NEXUS ENERGY SVCS INC (NV)
Name changed to Illegal Restaurant Group, Inc. 06/02/2015
Illegal Restaurant Group, Inc. name changed back to Nexus Energy Services, Inc. 08/13/2015

NEXUS GROUP INTL INC (QC)
Cease trade order 06/21/2005

NEXUS INDS INC (DE)
Common $1 par split (2) for (1) by

issuance of (1) additional share 10/22/1980
Common $1 par changed to 1¢ par 00/00/1981
Reorganized as Shirt Shed, Inc. 12/19/1986
Each share Common 1¢ par exchanged for (0.1) share Common 1¢ par
Shirt Shed, Inc. merged into Signal Apparel Co., Inc. 07/22/1991
(See Signal Apparel Co., Inc.)

NEXUS MEDIA INC (NV)
Name changed to Dickson Media, Inc. 1/17/2006

NEXUS NANO ELECTRONICS INC (NV)
Recapitalized as International Merchant Advisors Inc. 06/30/2008
Each (300) shares Common $0.001 par exchanged for (1) share Common $0.001 par
International Merchant Advisors Inc. name changed to DHS Holding Co. 07/15/2011

NEXUS RESOURCE CORP (BC)
Recapitalized as Pacific Gold Corp. (BC) 07/05/1990
Each share Common no par exchanged for (1/6) share Common no par
Pacific Gold Corp. (BC) reincorporated under the laws of Alberta 05/12/1994 which reincorporated in Ontario 06/27/1995 which name changed to Worldtek (Canada) Ltd. 07/04/1996
(See Worldtek (Canada) Ltd.)

NEXUS TELOCATION SYS LTD (ISRAEL)
Each share Ordinary ILS 0.01 par exchanged for (0.33333333) share Ordinary ILS 0.03 par 04/03/2001
Each share Ordinary ILS 0.03 par exchanged for (0.01) share Ordinary ILS 3 par 08/10/2005
Name changed to Pointer Telocation Ltd. 02/21/2006

NEXVET BIOPHARMA PLC (IRELAND)
Acquired by Zoetis Inc. 07/31/2017
Each share Ordinary $0.125 par exchanged for $6.72 cash

NEXXLINK TECHNOLOGIES INC (CANADA)
Merged into BCE Inc. 04/07/2005
Each share Common no par exchanged for $6.05 cash

NEXXNOW INC (NY)
Name changed to InoLife Technologies, Inc. 01/20/2010

NEXXUS LTG INC (DE)
Name changed to Revolution Lighting Technologies, Inc. 11/15/2012

NEXXUS TECHNOLOGIES INC (OR)
Recapitalized as Eli Scientific Inc. 9/29/87
Each share Common $0.005 par exchanged for (0.1) share Common $0.005 par
Eli Scientific Inc. name changed to Lazarus Holdings, Inc. 8/31/89
(See Lazarus Holdings, Inc.)

NF ENERGY SAVING CORP AMER (DE)
Recapitalized as NF Energy Saving Corp. 08/26/2009
Each share Common $0.001 par exchanged for (1/3) share Common $0.001 par

NFA CORP (MA)
Acquired by a group of private investors 12/14/1984
Each share Common 10¢ par exchanged for $9.50 cash

NFC CORP (DE)
Stock Dividends - 15% 11/30/72; 100% 2/28/77
Merged into National Foundation Life Insurance Co. (New) (OK) 1/16/81
Each share Common 10¢ par exchanged for (0.32) share Common $1 par and $22.932 cash
National Foundation Life Insurance Co. (New) (OK) reorganized in Delaware as Westbridge Capital Corp. 9/8/82 which reorganized as Ascent Assurance, Inc. 3/24/99 which name changed to USHEALTH Group, Inc. 3/3/2005
(See USHEALTH Group, Inc.)

NFC PLC (UNITED KINGDOM)
Each old Sponsored ADR for Ordinary 5p par exchanged for (0.2) new Sponsored ADR for Ordinary 5p par 8/26/91
Each new Sponsored ADR for Ordinary 5p par exchanged again for (0.75) new Sponsored ADR for Ordinary 5p par 9/4/98
Name changed to Exel PLC 2/23/2000
(See Exel PLC)

NFD INC (OH)
Plan of reorganization under Chapter 11 Federal Bankruptcy proceedings confirmed 03/28/1986
No stockholders' equity

NFF CORP (DE)
Common 10¢ par split (2) for (1) by issuance of (1) additional share 03/04/1971
Name changed to Orange-co, Inc. 08/29/1973
Orange-co, Inc. name changed to Stoneridge Resources, Inc. 04/29/1987 which recapitalized as Acceptance Insurance Companies Inc. 12/22/1992
(See Acceptance Insurance Companies Inc.)

NFI HLDGS INC (NJ)
Reorganized as ICR Systems, Inc. 11/19/2002
Each share Common 10¢ par exchanged for (4) shares Common $0.001 par
ICR Systems, Inc. name changed to Redux Holdings, Inc. 5/30/2006

NFJ DIVID INT & PREM STRATEGY FD (MA)
Issue Information - 86,100,000 shares COM offered at $25 on 02/23/2005
Name changed to AllianzGI NFJ Dividend, Interest & Premium Strategy Fund 01/28/2013

NFO RESH INC (DE)
Common 1¢ par split (3) for (2) by issuance of (0.5) additional share 4/5/94
Common 1¢ par split (3) for (2) by issuance of (0.5) additional share payable 2/5/96 to holders of record 1/22/96
Common 1¢ par split (3) for (2) by issuance of (0.5) additional share payable 10/15/97 to holders of record 9/30/97
Name changed to NFO Worldwide, Inc. 10/24/97
NFO Worldwide, Inc. merged into Interpublic Group Companies, Inc. 4/20/2000

NFO WORLDWIDE INC (DE)
Merged into Interpublic Group Companies, Inc. 4/20/2000
Each share Common 1¢ par exchanged for (0.5503) share Common 10¢ par

NFRONT INC (GA)
Issue Information - 3,900,000 shares COM offered at $10 per share on 06/29/1999
Merged into Digital Insight Corp. 2/10/2000
Each share Common no par exchanged for (0.579) share Common $0.001 par
(See Digital Insight Corp.)

NFS FINL CORP (DE)
Merged into BayBanks Inc. 6/30/95
Each share Common 1¢ par exchanged for (0.1696) share Common 1¢ par and $20.15 cash
BayBanks Inc. merged into Bank of Boston Corp. 7/29/96 which name changed to BankBoston Corp. 4/25/97 which merged into Fleet Financial Corp. 10/1/99 which name changed to FleetBoston Financial Corp. 4/18/2000 which merged into Bank of America Corp. 4/1/2004

NFS FINANCIAL SERVICES, INC. (DE)
Name changed to NFS Services, Inc. 10/25/77
(See NFS Services, Inc.)

NFS SVCS INC (DE)
Merged into Swanton Corp. 4/27/82
Each share Common 1¢ par exchanged for $0.20 cash

NFS SVCS INC (UT)
Recapitalized as Walnut Financial Services Inc. 02/27/1995
Each share Common no par exchanged for (0.5) share Common $0.002 par
Walnut Financial Services Inc. name changed to THCG, Inc. (UT) 11/01/1999 which reincorporated in Delaware 05/16/2000 which name changed to THCG Liquidating Trust 07/16/2001
(See THCG Liquidating Trust)

NFT LIQUIDATING TRUST (NY)
Trust terminated 12/30/77
Each Unit of Bene. Int. exchanged for $1.184 cash

NFW CAP GROUP INC (DE)
Name changed to Portafone International Cellular Communications, Inc. 04/21/1990
Portafone International Cellular Communications, Inc. name changed to PNF Industries, Inc. 10/10/1991 which reorganized as No Fire Technologies, Inc. 08/11/1995

NFX GOLD INC (CO)
Under plan of merger name changed to Bear Lake Gold Ltd. 09/17/2008
Bear Lake Gold Ltd. merged into Kerr Mines Inc. 05/26/2014

NGAS RES INC (BC)
Merged into Magnum Hunter Resources Corp. 04/13/2011
Each share Common no par exchanged for (0.0846) share Common 1¢ par
(See Magnum Hunter Resources Corp.)

NGC CORP (CO)
Name changed to Dynegy Inc. (CO) 07/06/1998
Dynegy Inc. (CO) merged into Dynegy Inc. (IL) 02/01/2000 which merged into Dynegy Inc. (DE) (Old) 04/02/2007 which reorganized as Dynegy Inc. (DE) (New) 10/01/2012 which merged into Vistra Energy Corp. 04/09/2018

NGFC EQUITIES INC (FL)
Name changed to American Resources Corp. 03/13/2017

NGK INSULATORS LTD (JAPAN)
ADR agreement terminated 07/21/2010
No ADR's were outstanding

NGP CAP RES CO (MD)
Name changed to OHA Investment Corp. 10/03/2014

NGT ENTERPRISES INC (DE)
Recapitalized as IMN Financial Corp. 5/15/97
Each share Common $0.0001 par exchanged for (0.25) share Common $0.0001 par
IMN Financial Corp. name changed to Apponline.com Inc. 5/11/99
(See Apponline.com Inc.)

NH HOTEL GROUP S A (SPAIN)
Name changed 07/03/2015
Name changed from NH Hoteles, S.A. to NH Hotel Group, S.A. 07/03/2015
ADR agreement terminated 07/31/2017
Each Sponsored ADR for Ordinary exchanged for $14.251314

NHA INC (TX)
Adjudicated bankrupt 04/02/1976
Stockholders' equity unlikely

NHANCEMENT TECHNOLOGIES INC (DE)
Issue Information - 2,300,000 shares COM offered at $4 per share on 01/30/1997
Name changed to Appiant Technologies, Inc. 3/21/2001
(See Appiant Technologies, Inc.)

NHC COMMUNICATIONS INC (BC)
Court approved the sale of assets for the benefit of creditors 03/20/2007
Stockholders' equity unlikely

NHD STORES INC (MA)
Merged into ACO Inc. 5/31/95
Each share Common 10¢ par exchanged for $1.75 cash

NHI NELSON HLDGS INTL LTD (ON)
Reincorporated 06/29/1993
Each share Conv. 1st Preference Ser. 1 no par exchanged for (0.8) share Common no par 12/06/1991
Place of incorporation changed from (Canada) to (ONT) 06/29/1993
Recapitalized as JPY Holdings Ltd. (ONT) 07/26/1994
Each share Common no par exchanged for (0.2) share Common no par
JPY Holdings Ltd. (ONT) reincorporated in Canada 11/09/2007

NHP INC (DE)
Each share Common 1¢ par received distribution of (1/3) share WMF Group Ltd. Common 1¢ par payable 12/12/97 to holders of record 12/8/97
Merged into Apartment Investment & Management Co. 12/8/97
Each share Common 1¢ par exchanged for (0.74766) share Class A Common 1¢ par

NHP NATURAL HEALTH LTD (AB)
Name changed to Whats-Online.Com Inc. 03/16/1999
Whats-Online.Com Inc. recapitalized as Great Pacific International Inc. 10/16/2001 which recapitalized as WesCan Energy Corp. 10/04/2012

NHS FINL INC (CA)
Merged into Luther Burbank Savings & Loan Association 09/30/1996
Each share Common no par exchanged for $11.50 cash

NHS HEALTH SOLUTIONS INC (FL)
Reincorporated 02/28/2012
State of incorporation changed from (NV) to (FL) 02/28/2012
SEC revoked common stock registration 08/28/2013

NHTB CAP TR I (DE)
9.25% Capital Securities called for redemption at $10 on 9/30/2004

NI-AG-CO MINES LTD. (ON)
Charter cancelled in 1958

NI BANCSHARES CORP (DE)
Merged into First Midwest Bancorp, Inc. 03/09/2016
Each share Common $1.25 par exchanged for (2.8858) shares Common 1¢ par and $13.17 cash

NI CAL DEVS LTD (BC)
Capital Stock no par split (3) for (1) by issuance of (2) additional shares 05/25/1981
Reincorporated under the laws of

Delaware as Nickel Resources Development Corp. and Capital Stock no par changed to 1¢ par 12/29/1988
Nickel Resources Development Corp. recapitalized as Nycal Corp. 12/15/1989
(See Nycal Corp.)

NI INDS INC (DE)
Acquired by Nimas Corp. 03/08/1985
Each share Common 50¢ par exchanged for $22 cash

NIAGARA ALKALI CO. (NY)
Stock Dividends - 200% 8/47; 100% 1/15/54
Merged into Hooker Electrochemical Co. 11/30/55
Each share Common $10 par exchanged for (1.6) shares Common $5 par
Hooker Electrochemical Co. name changed to Hooker Chemical Corp. 5/29/58 which was acquired by Occidental Petroleum Corp. (Calif.) 7/24/68
(See Occidental Petroleum Corp. (Calif.))

NIAGARA ARBITRAGE CORP.
Liquidated 00/00/1931
Details not available

NIAGARA BANCORP INC (DE)
Name changed to First Niagara Financial Group, Inc. (Old) 05/16/2000
First Niagara Financial Group, Inc. (Old) merged into First Niagara Financial Group, Inc. (New) 01/17/2003 which merged into KeyCorp (New) 08/01/2016

NIAGARA CAP CORP (BC)
Delisted from Vancouver Stock Exchange 7/7/89

NIAGARA CORP (DE)
Each share old Common $0.001 par exchanged for (1) share new Common $0.001 par to reflect a (1) for (200) reverse split followed by a (200) for (1) forward split 01/07/2005
Note: Holders of (199) or fewer pre-split shares received $8.47 cash per share
Each share new Common $0.001 par exchanged again for (1) share new Common $0.001 par to reflect a (1) for (2) reverse split followed by a (2) for (1) forward split 01/03/2006
Note: Holders of less than (2) pre-split shares received $15.85 cash per share
Merged into Kohlberg & Co., LLC 09/07/2006
Each share new Common $0.001 par exchanged for $16 cash

NIAGARA CORP (FL)
Name changed to NC Sales Corp. 08/25/1995
(See NC Sales Corp.)

NIAGARA CREDIT CORP.
Liquidated in 1931

NIAGARA EXCHANGE CORP (DE)
Stock Dividends - 300% 04/10/1986; 10% 05/31/1989
Merged into Selective Insurance Group, Inc. 08/27/1992
Each share Common $1 par exchanged for $11.50 cash

NIAGARA FALLS HOTEL CORP. (NY)
Liquidation completed 7/14/60

NIAGARA FRONTIER SVCS INC (NY)
Merged into SB Investors, Inc. 05/05/1983
Each share Common $1 par exchanged for $37.77 cash

NIAGARA FRONTIER TRAN SYS INC (NY)
Common $10 par changed to 1¢ par 05/13/1974
Liquidation completed
Each share Common 1¢ par received initial distribution of $17.50 cash 05/31/1974
Each share Common 1¢ par received second distribution of $6.30 cash 03/11/1975
Assets transferred to NFT Liquidating Trust and Common 1¢ par reclassified as Units of Bene. Int. 02/28/1975
(See NFT Liquidating Trust)

NIAGARA HUDSON POWER CORP. (NY)
Recapitalized as Niagara Mohawk Power Corp. 1/5/50
Each share 1st Preferred $100 par exchanged for (4) shares Class A no par and $0.83-1/3 in cash
Each share 2nd Preferred $100 par exchanged for (3.9) shares Class A no par
Each share Common $1 par exchanged for (0.78) share Common no par

NIAGARA HUDSON PUBLIC SERVICE CORP.
Name changed to Central New York Power Corp. 07/31/1937
Central New York Power Corp. merged into Niagara Mohawk Power Corp. 01/05/1950

NIAGARA MNG & DEV INC (ID)
Reorganized under the laws of Delaware as Sanomedics International Holdings, Inc. 06/30/2009
Each share Common 1¢ par exchanged for (0.04) share Common $0.001 par
Sanomedics International Holdings, Inc. recapitalized as Sanomedics, Inc. 02/09/2015

NIAGARA MINING & DEVELOPMENT CORP. LTD. (BC)
Recapitalized as Tiki Development Corp. Ltd. 10/25/71
Each share Capital Stock 50¢ par exchanged for (0.1) share Capital Stock no par
Tiki Development Corp. Ltd. name changed to Beermaster Distributors Ltd. 8/13/73 which recapitalized as Sunatco Development Corp. 6/6/77 which recapitalized as International Sunatco Industries Ltd. 1/14/91

NIAGARA MOHAWK HLDGS INC (NY)
Merged into National Grid Group plc 01/31/2002
Each share Common $1 par exchanged for (0.5863) Sponsored ADR for Ordinary
National Grid Group plc name changed to National Grid Transco plc 10/21/2002 which reorganized as National Grid plc 07/29/2005

NIAGARA MOHAWK PWR CORP (NY)
$1.20 Class A called for redemption 06/30/1953
Common no par changed to $8 par and (1) additional share issued 05/28/1965
Common $8 par changed to $1 par 05/07/1975
11-3/4% Preferred $100 par called for redemption 08/31/1978
10.60% Preferred $100 par called for redemption 03/31/1992
8.75% Preferred $25 par called for redemption 12/31/1994
Secondary Offering - 22,399,248 shares COM offered at $14.125 per share on 06/01/1998
Under plan of reorganization each share Common $1 par automatically became (1) share Niagara Mohawk Holdings, Inc. Common $1 par 03/18/1999
9.50% Preferred $25 par called for redemption at $25 on 12/31/1999
7.85% Preferred $25 par called for redemption at $25 on 09/30/2001
Niagara Mohawk Holdings, Inc. merged into National Grid Group PLC 01/31/2002
6.10% Preferred $100 par called for redemption at $101 on 03/04/2002
7.72% Preferred $100 par called for redemption at $102.36 on 03/04/2002
Adjustable Rate Preferred Ser. A $25 par called for redemption at $25 on 03/04/2002
Adjustable Rate Preferred Ser. C $25 par called for redemption at $25 on 03/04/2002
Adjustable Rate Preferred Ser. B $25 par called for redemption at $25 on 03/04/2002
National Grid Group PLC name changed to National Grid Transco PLC 10/21/2002
Adjustable Rate Preferred Ser. D called for redemption at $50 on 12/31/2004
4.10% Preferred $100 par called for redemption at $102 on 12/31/2007
4.85% Preferred $100 par called for redemption at $102 on 12/31/2007
5.25% Preferred $100 par called for redemption at $102 on 12/31/2007
(Additional Information in Active)

NIAGARA SH CORP (MD)
6% Class A Preferred called for redemption 03/31/1945
4-1/2% Preferred $100 par called for redemption 03/07/1946
Class B Common $5 par reclassified as Common $5 par 00/00/1949
Common $5 par split (4) for (3) by issuance of (1/3) additional share 11/20/1964
Common $5 par changed to $1 par and (0.5) additional share issued 06/12/1969
Stock Dividends - 50% 03/14/1955; 50% 08/20/1959
Acquired by Scudder Growth & Income Fund 07/27/1992
Each share Common $1 par exchanged for (0.939606) share Capital Stock $1 par
(See Scudder Growth & Income Fund)

NIAGARA SHARE CORP. (DE)
Succeeded by Niagara Share Corp. of Maryland 06/18/1929
Details not available

NIAGARA SHARE CORP. OF DELAWARE (DE)
Acquired by Niagara Share Corp. of Maryland 12/31/1929
Details not available

NIAGARA SHARE CORP. OF MARYLAND (MD)
Name changed to Niagara Share Corp. 01/12/1945
Niagara Share Corp. acquired by Scudder Growth & Income Fund 07/27/1992
(See Scudder Growth & Income Fund)

NIAGARA STRUCTURAL STL LTD (ON)
Name changed to Tecsyn International Inc. 2/17/84
(See Tecsyn International Inc.)

NIAGARA VENTURES CORP (ON)
Each share old Common no par exchanged for (0.00000034) share new Common no par 04/19/2017
Notes: In effect holders received $0.015 cash per share and public interest was eliminated
Distributions of less than $10 will not be made
Unexchanged certificates will be cancelled and become without value 04/19/2020

NIASKI ENVIRONMENTAL INC (AB)
Recapitalized as Rimron Resources Inc. 11/22/2002
Each share Common no par exchanged for (1/3) share Common no par
Rimron Resources Inc. recapitalized as Caribou Resources Corp. 01/22/2004 which merged into JED Oil Inc. 07/31/2007
(See JED Oil Inc.)

NIB YELLOWKNIFE MINES LTD. (ON)
Recapitalized as Mining Endeavor Co. Ltd. on a (0.2) for (1) basis 3/28/56
(See Mining Endeavor Co. Ltd.)

NIBCO INC (IN)
Company advised privately held 00/00/1980
Details not available

NIBLACK MINERAL DEV INC (AB)
Merged into Heatherdale Resources Ltd. 01/23/2012
Each share Common no par exchanged for (0.5) share Common no par
Note: Unexchanged certificates were cancelled and became without value 01/23/2018

NIBLACK MNG CORP (BC)
Acquired by Committee Bay Resources Ltd. 10/01/2008
Each share Common no par exchanged for (1) share Common no par
Note: Unexchanged certificates were cancelled and became without value 10/03/2014
Committee Bay Resources Ltd. recapitalized as CBR Gold Corp. 03/02/2009 which name changed to Niblack Mineral Development Inc. 04/15/2010 which merged into Heatherdale Resources Ltd. 01/23/2012

NIBOT CORP. (IL)
Acquired by Valve Corp. of America in February 1970
Details not available

NIC INC (CO)
Reincorporated under the laws of Delaware and Common no par changed to $0.0001 par 05/07/2009

NIC-L-SILVER BATTERY CO. (CA)
Acquired by Instrument Systems Corp. (N.Y.) 10/1/66

NIC NIK RES LTD (BC)
Name changed to Transtel Communications Corp. 10/18/1989
Transtel Communications Corp. recapitalized as Consolidated T.C. Resources Ltd. 07/23/1990 which name changed to Cyclone Capital Corp. 05/20/1992 which recapitalized as Nikos Explorations Ltd. 06/04/1996 which name changed to Labrador Gold Corp. 12/19/2017

NICARAGUA RISING INC (NV)
Name changed to Ceelox, Inc. 09/30/2010

NICARAGUAN DEVELOPMENT CORP.
Dissolved in 1947

NICE SYS LTD (ISRAEL)
Sponsored ADR's for Ordinary split (2) for (1) by issuance of (1) additional ADR payable 06/06/2006 to holders of record 05/30/2006
Ex date - 05/31/2006
Name changed to NICE Ltd. 06/22/2016

NICER CDA CORP (BC)
Cease trade order 05/11/2009

NICHE BUSINESS GROUP INC (DE)
Name changed to Marbledge Group, Inc. 01/20/1993
Marbledge Group, Inc. recapitalized as AR Growth Finance Corp. 03/13/2007
(See AR Growth Finance Corp.)

FINANCIAL INFORMATION, INC.

NICHE PERIPHERALS INC (BC)
Recapitalized as Consolidated Niche Peripherals Inc. 10/31/1994
Each share Common no par exchanged for (2/3) share Common no par
(See Consolidated Niche Peripherals Inc.)

NICHE RES INC (NV)
Charter permanently revoked 04/30/2003

NICHOLAS & SHEPARD CO.
Merged into Oliver Farm Equipment Co. in 1929
Details not available

NICHOLAS-APPLEGATE CONV & INCOME FD (MA)
Issue Information - 60,000,000 shares COM offered at $15 per share on 03/26/2003
Name changed to AGIC Convertible & Income Fund 08/25/2010
AGIC Convertible & Income Fund name changed to AllianzGI Convertible & Income Fund 01/28/2013

NICHOLAS-APPLEGATE CONV & INCOME FD II (MA)
Name changed to AGIC Convertible & Income Fund II 08/25/2010
AGIC Convertible & Income Fund II name changed to AllianzGI Convertible & Income Fund II 01/28/2013

NICHOLAS-APPLEGATE EQUITY & CONV INCOME FD (MA)
Issue Information - 20,300,000 shares COM offered at $25 per share on 02/22/2007
Name changed to AGIC Equity & Convertible Income Fund 08/25/2010
AGIC Equity & Convertible Income Fund name changed to AllianzGI Equity & Convertible Income Fund 01/28/2013

NICHOLAS-APPLEGATE GLOBAL EQUITY & CONV INCOME FD (MA)
Issue Information - 7,000,000 shares COM offered at $25 per share on 09/25/2007
Name changed to AGIC Global Equity & Convertible Income Fund 08/25/2010
AGIC Global Equity & Convertible Income Fund name changed to AllianzGI Global Equity & Convertible Income Fund 01/28/2013 which merged into AllianzGI Equity & Convertible Income Fund 01/24/2014

NICHOLAS APPLEGATE GROWTH EQUITY FD INC (MD)
Name changed to Nicholas-Applegate Fund, Inc. and Common 1¢ par reclassified as Class A 1¢ par 06/10/1991

NICHOLAS-APPLEGATE INTL & PREM STRATEGY FD (MA)
Name changed to AGIC International & Premium Strategy Fund 08/25/2010
AGIC International & Premium Strategy Fund name changed to AllianzGI International & Premium Strategy Fund 01/28/2013
(See AllianzGI International & Premium Strategy Fund)

NICHOLAS-BEAZLEY AIRPLANE CO., INC.
Acquired by Air Associates, Inc. (NY) on a (0.2) for (1) basis in 1938
Air Associates, Inc. (NY) reincorporated under the laws of New Jersey 10/1/40 which name changed to Electronic Communications, Inc. 4/30/57 which merged into ECI Merger Corp. 12/29/71

NICHOLAS DATA SVCS LTD (BC)
Name changed to Nicholas Financial Inc. 8/9/93

NICHOLAS INCOME FD INC (MD)
Reincorporated in 1986
State of incorporation changed from (DE) to (MD) and Common $1 par changed to 1¢ par in 1986
Name changed to Nicholas High Income Fund, Inc. and Common 1¢ par reclassified as Class I 1¢ par 2/7/2005

NICHOLAS INVT INC (NV)
Each share old Common $0.001 par exchanged for (0.005) share new Common $0.001 par 11/13/2003
Acquired by YaSheng Group 7/16/2004
Each share new Common $0.001 par exchanged for (0.0117647) share Common par

NICHOLAS STRONG FD INC (MD)
Name changed to Nicholas Fund, Inc. 7/18/74

NICHOLL ACQUISITIONS INC (UT)
Name changed to Copymat Inc. 01/09/1989
Copymat Inc. recapitalized as Global Ecosystems, Inc. (UT) 10/03/1994 which reorganized in Delaware as Rose International Inc. 08/07/1995 which name changed to Securities Resolution Advisors, Inc. 07/14/1998 which name changed to Sales Online Direct, Inc. 03/16/1999 which name changed to Paid, Inc. 12/08/2003

NICHOLS COPPER CO.
Acquired by Phelps Dodge Corp. 00/00/1930
Details not available

NICHOLS ENGINEERING & RESEARCH CORP. (DE)
Merged into Neptune Meter Co. 12/10/68
Each share Common $10 par exchanged for (1.1875) shares Common $5 par
Neptune Meter Co. name changed to Neptune International Corp. 5/1/74 which merged into Wheelabrator-Frye Inc. 1/4/79 which merged into Signal Companies, Inc. 2/1/83 which merged into Allied-Signal Inc. 9/19/85 which name changed to AlliedSignal Inc. 4/26/93 which name changed to Honeywell International Inc. 12/1/99

NICHOLS HOMESHIELD INC (DE)
Merged into Quanex Corp. 08/22/1989
Each share Common 1¢ par exchanged for $15.48 cash
Note: An additional payment of $0.47 cash per share was made on 08/03/1993

NICHOLS INST (DE)
Common 10¢ par split (2) for (1) by issuance of (1) additional share 11/27/89
Conv. Class B Common 10¢ par split (2) for (1) by issuance of (1) additional share 11/27/89
Each share Conv. Preferred Ser. C 1¢ par exchanged for (4.116) shares Common 10¢ par 12/12/89
Each share old Common 10¢ par exchanged for (0.5) share new Common 10¢ par 6/4/91
Each share old Class B Common 10¢ par exchanged for (0.5) share new Class B Common 10¢ par 6/4/91
New Common 10¢ par reclassified as Class A Common 10¢ par 5/18/92
Stock Dividend - In Non-Vtg. Class C Common to holders of new Common 100% 6/4/91
Merged into Corning Inc. 8/31/94
Each share new Common 10¢ par exchanged for (0.431) share Common $1 par
Each share new Class B Common 10¢ par exchanged for (0.431) share Common $1 par
Each share Non-Vtg. Class C Common 10¢ par exchanged for (0.431) share Common $1 par

NICHOLS J C CO (MO)
Merged into Highwoods Properties Inc. 7/13/98
Each share Common 1¢ par exchanged for either (2.03) shares Common 1¢ par, $65 cash, or a combination of stock and cash
Note: Option to receive stock or stock and cash expired 6/24/98

NICHOLS RESH CORP (DE)
Reincorporated 06/29/1989
State of incorporation changed from (AL) to (DE) 06/29/1989
Common 1¢ par split (4) for (3) by issuance of (0.33333333) additional share 03/01/1991
Common 1¢ par split (3) for (2) by issuance of (0.5) additional share payable 11/04/1996 to holders of record 10/21/1996
Merged into Computer Sciences Corp. 11/17/1999
Each share Common 1¢ par exchanged for (0.423) share Common $1 par
Computer Sciences Corp. merged into DXC Technology Co. 04/03/2017

NICHOLS S E INC (NY)
Reorganized under Chapter 11 Federal Bankruptcy Code 12/24/91
Each share Common 10¢ par exchanged for (0.138) share Common 1¢ par
Stock Dividends - 10% 11/5/76; 10% 12/20/77; 10% 3/2/79; 10% 1/15/80; 10% 1/28/81
Recapitalized as Pharmhouse Corp. 4/1/93
Each (4.35) shares Common 1¢ par exchanged for (1) share Common 1¢ par
(See Pharmhouse Corp.)

NICHOLS WIRE & ALUMINUM CO. (MO)
Common $50 par changed to $10 par and (4) additional shares issued 11/28/1961
Acquired by ANTA Corp. 00/00/1973
Details not available

NICHOLS WIRE & STEEL CO. (MO)
Name changed to Nichols Wire & Aluminum Co. 00/00/1948
(See Nichols Wire & Aluminum Co.)

NICHOLS WIRE SHEET & HARDWARE CO. (MO)
Reorganized as Nichols Wire & Steel Co. 00/00/1937
Details not available

NICHOLSON CREEK MINING CORP. (WA)
No longer in existence having been declared defunct in 1964

NICHOLSON FILE CO (RI)
Each share Common $100 par exchanged for (6) shares Common no par 00/00/1929
Common no par changed to $1 par 04/14/1960
Merged into Cooper Industries, Inc. 10/31/1972
Each share Common $1 par exchanged for (1) share $2.50 Conv. Preferred Ser. B no par
(See Cooper Industries, Inc.)

NICHOLSON MINES LTD. (ON)
Recapitalized as Consolidated Nicholson Mines Ltd. 00/00/1951
Each share Capital Stock no par exchanged for (0.66666666) share Capital Stock no par
Consolidated Nicholson Mines Ltd. recapitalized as Auric Resources Ltd. 02/04/1975 which recapitalized as Chancellor Energy Resources Inc. 05/01/1978 which merged into HCO Energy Ltd. 04/02/1996 which merged into Pinnacle Resources Ltd. (New) 10/20/1997 which merged into Renaissance Energy Ltd. 07/16/1998 which merged into Husky Energy Inc. 08/25/2000

NICHOLSON TERM & DOCK CO (MI)
Preferred $100 par called for redemption 3/1/58
(Additional Information in Active)

NICKEL HILL MINES LTD (BC)
Recapitalized as Vantreal Resources Ltd. 03/18/1974
Each share Capital Stock 50¢ par exchanged for (0.25) share Capital Stock no par
Vantreal Resources Ltd. recapitalized as Caspian Resources Ltd. 04/11/1978
(See Caspian Resources Ltd.)

NICKEL LAKE MINES LTD (MB)
Charter cancelled and declared dissolved for failure to file returns 03/05/1979

NICKEL MINING & SMELTING CORP. (QC)
Recapitalized as Metal Mines Ltd. 12/31/1963
Each share Capital Stock $1 par exchanged for (0.2) share Capital Stock $1 par
Metal Mines Ltd. merged into Consolidated Canadian Faraday Ltd. 05/04/1967 which name changed to Faraday Resources Inc. 08/02/1983 which merged into Conwest Exploration Co. Ltd. (New) (AB) 09/01/1993 which merged into Alberta Energy Co. Ltd. 01/31/1996 which merged into EnCana Corp. 01/03/2003

NICKEL OFFSETS LTD (CANADA)
Merged into Canhorn Mining Corp. 01/09/1986
Each share Common no par exchanged for (0.08460236) share Common no par
Canhorn Mining Corp. merged into Canhorn Chemical Corp. 04/26/1995 which merged into Nayarit Gold Inc. 05/02/2005 which merged into Capital Gold Corp. 08/02/2010 which merged into Gammon Gold Inc. (QC) 04/08/2011 which reincorporated in Ontario as AuRico Gold Inc. 06/14/2011 which merged into Alamos Gold Inc. (New) 07/06/2015

NICKEL PETE RES LTD (CANADA)
Cease trade order effective 12/16/2005
Stockholders' equity unlikely

NICKEL RES DEV CORP (DE)
Recapitalized as Nycal Corp. 12/15/1989
Each share Common no par exchanged for (0.1) share Common no par
(See Nycal Corp.)

NICKEL RIM MINES LTD (ON)
Common $1 par changed to no par 09/24/1975
Delisted from Canadian Dealer Network 01/03/1995

NICKELODEON MINERALS INC (BC)
Name changed to Strongbow Resources Inc. (BC) 8/18/2000
Strongbow Resources Inc. (BC) reorganized in Canada as Strongbow Exploration Inc. 5/3/2004

NICKELODEON THEATER CO INC (CA)
Issue Information - 1,500,000 shares COM offered at $5 per share on 02/07/1995
Name changed to CinemaStar Luxury Theaters, Inc. (CA) 8/24/95
CinemaStar Luxury Theaters, Inc.

(CA) reorganized under the laws of Delaware 12/1/98
(See CinemaStar Luxury Theaters, Inc.)

NICKLAS MINING CO. (AZ)
Charter cancelled 7/26/27

NICKLEBYS COM INC (CO)
Reorganized under the laws of Delaware as FIIC Holdings, Inc. 03/02/2006
Each (2.00317) shares Common $0.0001 par exchanged for (1) share Common $0.001 par
(See FIIC Holdings, Inc.)

NICKLING RES INC (BC)
Recapitalized as Florin Resources Inc. 05/09/1989
Each share Common no par exchanged for (1/3) share Common no par
Florin Resources Inc. merged into Crimsonstar Mining Corp. 06/19/1991 which recapitalized as Mountain View Ventures Inc. 05/21/1993 which recapitalized as Blackrun Ventures Inc. 04/08/1997 which recapitalized as Blackrun Minerals Inc. 06/10/1999 which name changed to Diversified Industries Ltd. 03/29/2000
(See Diversified Industries Ltd.)

NICKLOS OIL & GAS CO (DE)
Stock Dividend - 50% 12/31/80
Chapter 11 bankruptcy proceedings converted to Chapter 7 on 7/7/86
No stockholders' equity

NICKOLODEON INDS CORP (BC)
Dissolved and struck off register 11/24/1989

NICO INC (DE)
Merged into Lehigh Valley Industries, Inc. 10/31/1985
Each share Common 1¢ par exchanged for (3) shares Common 50¢ par and $13.50 cash
Lehigh Valley Industries, Inc. name changed to LVI Group Inc. 06/04/1986 which name changed to Lehigh Group Inc. 01/27/1995 which recapitalized as First Medical Group, Inc. 11/13/1997
(See First Medical Group, Inc.)

NICO MNG LTD (ON)
Name changed to Red Crescent Resources Ltd. 11/11/2010

NICO TELECOM INC (NV)
Name changed to Far East Ventures Trading Co. 10/09/2007
(See Far East Ventures Trading Co.)

NICOA CORP (MA)
Reincorporated under the laws of Nevada as Agritherm Corp. 07/06/1994
Agritherm Corp. recapitalized as Infotex Holdings Ltd. 12/30/1997
(See Infotex Holdings Ltd.)

NICOHAL MINES LTD (ON)
Charter cancelled for failure to pay taxes and file returns 03/16/1976

NICOLA COPPER MINES LTD (BC)
Recapitalized as Buccaneer Resources Ltd. 02/07/1978
Each share Capital Stock $1 par exchanged for (0.2) share Capital Stock no par
(See Buccaneer Resources Ltd.)

NICOLET INSTR CORP (WI)
Stock Dividends - 50% 8/20/75; 50% 5/3/77; 50% 2/15/79; 50% 3/20/80
Merged into Thermo Acquisition Systems Inc. 12/29/92
Each share Common 25¢ par exchanged for $21 cash

NICOLLET HOTEL, INC.
Succeeded by Nicollet Hotel Co. in 1935 which property was sold to Hotel Nicollet Operating Co. and company dissolved in 1948

NICOLLET HOTEL CO.
Property sold to Hotel Nicollet Operating Co. and Company dissolved in 1948

NICOLLET PROCESS ENGR INC (MN)
Reincorporated under the laws of Delaware as Xbox Technologies Inc. 06/21/2000
Xbox Technologies Inc. name changed to Knowledge Mechanics Group, Inc. 10/16/2001
(See Knowledge Mechanics Group, Inc.)

NICOR INC (IL)
$1.90 Conv. Preference no par called for redemption 12/14/1992
4.48% Preferred $100 par changed to $50 par and (1) additional share issued 04/26/1993
5% Preferred $100 par changed to $50 par and (1) additional share issued 04/26/1993
Common $5 par changed to $2.50 par and (1) additional share issued 04/26/1993
5% Preferred $100 par called for redemption at $51 on 11/03/2005
4.48% Preferred $50 par called for redemption at $51.06 on 09/08/2010
5% Conv. Preferred $50 par called for redemption at $50 plus $0.13 accrued dividends on 01/18/2011
Merged into AGL Resources Inc. 12/09/2011
Each share Common $2.50 par exchanged for (0.8382) share Common $5 par and $21.20 cash

NICTAU COPPER MINES LTD. (NB)
Charter cancelled for failure to file reports in 1971

NIDO PETE LTD (AUSTRALIA)
Basis changed from (1:250) to (1:25) 07/30/2015
ADR agreement terminated 12/26/2017
No ADR's remain outstanding

NIELSEN A C CO (DE)
Common $1 par split (3) for (1) by issuance of (2) additional shares 08/24/1960
Common $1 par reclassified as Class B $1 par and (2) shares Class A Non-Vtg. $1 par issued 07/20/1965
Class A Non-Vtg. $1 par split (2) for (1) by issuance of (1) additional share 03/18/1983
Class B Vtg. $1 par split (2) for (1) by issuance of (1) additional share 03/18/1983
Stock Dividend - Class A & B - 100% 03/01/1973
Merged into Dun & Bradstreet Corp. 08/29/1984
Each share Class A Non-Vtg. $1 par exchanged for (0.875) share Common $1 par
Each share Class B Vtg. $1 par exchanged for (0.875) share Common $1 par
Dun & Bradstreet Corp. name changed to R.H. Donnelley Corp. 07/01/1998
(See R.H. Donnelley Corp.)

NIELSEN MEDIA RESH INC (DE)
Each share old Common 1¢ par exchanged for (1/3) share new Common 1¢ par 8/26/98
Merged into VNU N.V. 10/27/99
Each share new Common 1¢ par exchanged for $37.75 cash

NIELSEN N V (NETHERLANDS)
Name changed 05/07/2014
Name changed from Nielsen Holdings N.V. to Nielsen N.V. 05/07/2014
Reorganized under the laws of England & Wales as Nielsen Holdings PLC 08/31/2015
Each share Common EUR 0.07 par exchanged for (1) share Ordinary EUR 0.07 par

NIGADOO MINES LTD. (ON)
Recapitalized as Nigadoo River Mines Ltd. 7/8/64
Each share Capital Stock $1 par exchanged for (0.2222222) share Capital Stock no par
Nigadoo River Mines Ltd. recapitalized as Sullico Resources Ltd. 8/28/78 which name changed to Sullivan Resources Ltd. 6/23/82

NIGADOO RIV MINES LTD (ON)
Recapitalized as Sullico Resources Ltd. 8/28/78
Each share Capital Stock no par exchanged for (0.01) share Capital Stock no par
Sullico Resources Ltd. name changed to Sullivan Resources Ltd. 6/23/82

NIGHT FLIGHT ENTMT INC (NV)
Name changed to Ally Media Group, Inc. 04/19/1991
Ally Media Group, Inc. reorganized as Success Financial Services Group, Inc. 01/31/2001 which name changed to Consolidated American Industries Corp. 03/01/2005

NIGHT HAWK PENINSULAR MINES LTD.
Liquidated in 1953
No stockholders' equity

NIGHT HAWK RES LTD (BC)
Common no par split (4) for (1) by issuance of (3) additional shares 5/30/84
Under plan of merger each share Common no par automatically became (1) share Stratford American Corp. Common 1¢ par 5/24/88
(See Stratford American Corp.)

NIGHT VISION CORP (CA)
Each (100) shares old Common no par exchanged for (1) new Common Stock Purchase Warrant expiring 11/17/89 on 11/18/88
Note: Unexchanged old Common no par shares are now valueless
Charter cancelled for failure to file reports and pay taxes 10/1/92

NIGHTCULTURE INC (NV)
Old Common $0.001 par split (8) for (1) by issuance of (7) additional shares payable 09/20/2011 to holders of record 09/20/2011
Each share old Common $0.001 par exchanged for (1) share new Common $0.001 to reflect a (1) for (2,000,000) reverse split followed by a (2,000,000) for (1) forward split 02/27/2018
Note: In effect holders received $0.00125 cash per share and public interest was eliminated

NIGHTHAWK CAP INC (NV)
Name changed to Chancellor Group, Inc. 4/8/96

NIGHTHAWK ENERGY PLC (UNITED KINGDOM)
ADR agreement terminated 10/22/2018
ADR holders' equity unlikely

NIGHTHAWK GOLD MINES LTD. (BC)
Recapitalized as High Point Mines Ltd. 03/07/1966
Each share Common $1 par exchanged for (0.25) share Common no par
High Point Mines Ltd. recapitalized as Highhawk Mines Ltd. 05/18/1972 which recapitalized as Newhawk Gold Mines Ltd. 03/12/1979 which merged into Silver Standard Resources Inc. 09/30/1999 which name changed to SSR Mining Inc. 08/03/2017

NIGHTHAWK RADIOLOGY HLDGS INC (DE)
Issue Information - 6,300,000 shares COM offered at $16 per share on 02/08/2006
Acquired by Virtual Radiologic Corp. 12/22/2010
Each share Common $0.001 par exchanged for $6.50 cash

NIGHTHAWK RES INC (AB)
Struck from register and dissolved 12/01/1997

NIGHTHAWK SYS INC (NV)
Name changed to Video River Networks, Inc. 03/03/2011

NIGHTIME PEDIATRICS CLINICS INC. (UT)
Charter expired 04/11/2006

NIGHTINGALE INFORMATIX CORP (AB)
Name changed to Nexia Health Technologies Inc. 09/28/2016

NIGHTWATCH RES INC (BC)
Struck off register and declared dissolved for failure to file returns 2/25/83

NIGHTWING ENTERTAINMENT GROUP INC (NV)
Name changed 12/25/95
Name changed from Nightwing Group, Inc. to Nightwing Entertainment Group, Inc. 12/25/95
Name changed to Entertainment Arts Inc. 3/13/2000

NII HLDGS INC (DE)
Common $0.001 par split (3) for (1) by issuance of (2) additional shares payable 03/22/2004 to holders of record 03/12/2004 Ex date - 03/23/2004
Common $0.001 par split (2) for (1) by issuance of (1) additional share payable 11/21/2005 to holders of record 11/11/2005 Ex date - 11/22/2005
Plan of reorganization under Chapter 11 Federal Bankruptcy proceedings effective 06/26/2015
No old Common stockholders' equity
(Additional Information in Active)

NII NORSAT INTL INC (BC)
Name changed to Norsat International Inc. (New) 07/12/1999
(See Norsat International Inc. (New))

NIK CAP CORP (AB)
Recapitalized as H.L. International Inc. 05/18/1989
Each share Common no par exchanged for (0.33333333) share Common no par
H.L. International Inc. name changed to Maple Mark International Inc. 04/17/1996 which name changed to Linear Resources Inc. 10/15/1999 which name changed to Linear Gold Corp. (AB) 11/24/2003 which reincorporated in Canada 11/10/2004 which merged into Brigus Gold Corp. (YT) 06/25/2010 which reincorporated in Canada 06/09/2011
(See Brigus Gold Corp.)

NIKANA CAPITAL INC. (ON)
Name changed to Redruth Gold Mines Ltd. 10/17/1995
Redruth Gold Mines Ltd. recapitalized as Gemstar Communications Inc. 02/12/1996 which was acquired by SIRIT Technologies Inc. 09/06/2001 which was acquired by iTech Capital Corp. 11/01/2002 which name changed to Sirit Inc. 05/05/2003
(See Sirit Inc.)

NIKI LU INDS INC (FL)
Voluntarily dissolved 4/23/90
Details not available

NIKI SILVER-COBALT, LTD. (ON)
Acquired by Ni-Ag-Co Mines Ltd. 00/00/1946
Details not available

NIKKO CORDIAL CORP (JAPAN)
Name changed 10/01/2001
Stock Dividends - 10% 12/21/1973;

12% 12/26/1974; 10% 12/24/1975; 10% 12/23/1976; 20% 12/16/1980
Name changed from Nikko Securities Co., Ltd. to Nikko Cordial Corp. 10/01/2001
ADR's for Common 50 Yen par split (5) for (1) by issuance of (4) additional ADR's payable 09/08/2005 to holders of record 08/31/2005 Ex date - 09/09/2005
Merged into Citigroup Inc. 01/29/2008
Each ADR for Common 50 Yen par exchanged for $15.921902 cash

NIKOPOL FERROALLOY PLT JSC (UKRAINE)
GDR agreement terminated 04/21/2017
No GDR's remain outstanding

NIKOS EXPLORATIONS LTD (BC)
Each share old Common no par exchanged for (0.2) share new Common no par 01/23/2014
Name changed to Labrador Gold Corp. 12/19/2017

NIKU CORP (DE)
Each share old Common $0.0001 par exchanged for (0.1) share new Common $0.0001 par 11/21/2002
Merged into Computer Associates International, Inc. 07/29/2005
Each share new Common $0.0001 par exchanged for $21 cash

NILE THERAPEUTICS INC (DE)
Recapitalized as Capricor Therapeutics, Inc. 11/21/2013
Each share Common $0.001 par exchanged for (0.02) share Common $0.001 par

NILES-BEMENT-POND CO. (NJ)
Each share old Common no par exchanged for (4) shares new Common no par in 1941
Stock Dividend - 10% 12/15/51
Merged into Penn-Texas Corp. 9/30/55
Each share old Common no par exchanged for (1) share $1.60 Conv. Preferred $40 par and (1) share Common $10 par
Penn-Texas Corp. name changed to Fairbanks Whitney Corp. 5/29/59 which recapitalized as Colt Industries Inc. (Pa.) 5/15/64 which reincorporated in Delaware 10/17/68 then reincorporated in Pennsylvania 5/6/76
(See Colt Industries Inc. (Pa.))

NILES NATIONAL BANK & TRUST CO. (NILES, MI)
Merged into American National Holding Co. 1/8/73
Each share Common $10 par exchanged for (1) share Common $10 par
American National Holding Co. merged into Old Kent Financial Corp. 7/31/86 which merged into Fifth Third Bancorp 4/2/2001

NIM PETE CORP (BC)
Name changed to Petrorep Resources Ltd. 8/26/92
(See Petrorep Resources Ltd.)

NIMBLE STORAGE INC (DE)
Acquired by Hewlett Packard Enterprise Co. 04/17/2017
Each share Common $0.001 par exchanged for $12.50 cash

NIMBLE TECHNOLOGIES INTL INC (NV)
Recapitalized as CoreCare Systems Inc. (NV) 01/01/1995
Each share Common $0.001 par exchanged for (0.125) share Common $0.001 par
CoreCare Systems Inc. (NV) reincorporated in Delaware 01/27/1997
(See CoreCare Systems Inc.)

NIMBUS CD INTL INC (DE)
Merged into Carlton Communications Plc 7/27/98
Each share Common 1¢ par exchanged for $11.50 cash

NIMBUS GROUP INC (FL)
Name changed to Taylor Madison Corp. 04/01/2004
Taylor Madison Corp. recapitalized as Telzuit Medical Technologies, Inc. 08/19/2005
(See Telzuit Medical Technologies, Inc.)

NIMIN CAP CORP (AB)
Recapitalized as NiMin Energy Corp. 09/04/2009
Each share Common no par exchanged for (0.33333333) share Common no par
(See NiMin Energy Corp.)

NIMIN ENERGY CORP (AB)
Liquidation completed
Each share Common no par received initial distribution of USD$1.01 cash payable 10/22/2012 to holders of record 10/09/2012 Ex date - 10/23/2012
Each share Common no par received second and final distribution of USD$0.07 cash payable 04/28/2014 to holders of record 04/11/2014 Ex date - 04/09/2014

NIMROD RES LTD (AB)
Acquired by Atlas Yellowknife Resources Ltd. 00/00/1981
Each share Common no par exchanged for (6) shares Common no par and (4) Common Stock Purchase Warrants expiring 06/30/1982
Atlas Yellowknife Resources Ltd. recapitalized as Panatlas Energy Inc. 02/08/1988 which was acquired by Velvet Exploration Ltd. 07/17/2000
(See Velvet Exploration Ltd.)

NIMSLO INTL LTD (BERMUDA)
Name changed to Fairhaven International Ltd. 5/23/88
(See Fairhaven International Ltd.)

9A INVT HLDG CORP (DE)
Each share old Common 1¢ par exchanged for (0.001) share new Common 1¢ par 04/26/2006
Name changed to Viking Power Services, Inc. 07/03/2006

NINE HUNDRED EIGHTY THREE PARK AVE.
Liquidated in 1947

900 NORTH MAIN CO. (TX)
Completely liquidated 3/1/76
Each share Common $1.50 par exchanged for first and final distribution of $4.84 cash

NINE MILE MINING CO. (ID)
Acquired by Nine Corp. 12/13/67
Each share Capital Stock 10¢ par exchanged for (0.5) share Capital Stock 10¢ par

NINE MILE SOFTWARE INC (NV)
Each share old Common $0.001 par exchanged for (0.25) share new Common $0.001 par 05/06/2011
Name changed to SaveDaily, Inc. 09/06/2011
(See SaveDaily, Inc.)

NINE MUSES ENTMT INC (WY)
Name changed to Quotezy, Inc. 03/03/2006
Quotezy, Inc. recapitalized as Lord Tech, Inc. 04/23/2008
(See Lord Tech, Inc.)

999 (NV)
Reincorporated under the laws of Delaware as 999 Inc. 5/1/91

NINE SOUTH KEDZIE CORP. (DE)
Acquired by Madison-Kedzie Corp. 12/5/49

Each share Common no par exchanged for (1) share Preferred $20 par

935-1009 E. 63RD ST. BLDG. CORP. (IL)
Liquidation completed 10/4/57

920 OAKDALE BUILDING CORP. (IL)
Liquidation completed in 1944

9278 COMMUNICATIONS INC (DE)
Reincorporated 4/24/2000
State of incorporation changed from (NV) to (DE) 4/24/2000
Merged into Sajid Kapadia 6/3/2003
Each share Common $0.001 par exchanged for $0.10 cash

NINE WEST GROUP INC (DE)
Merged into Jones Apparel Group, Inc. 06/15/1999
Each share Common 1¢ par exchanged for (0.5011) share Common 1¢ par and $13 cash
Jones Apparel Group, Inc. name changed to Jones Group Inc. 10/18/2010
(See Jones Group Inc.)

1957 SUPERVISED EXECUTIVE FUND LTD. (CANADA)
Voluntarily dissolved 10/28/1965
Details not available

NINETEEN HUNDRED CORP.
Name changed to Whirlpool Corp. (N.Y.) in 1950 which merged into Whirlpool- Seeger Corp. 9/15/55 which name was changed to Whirlpool Corp. (Del.) 4/1/57

NINETEEN HUNDRED WASHER CO., INC.
Name changed to Nineteen Hundred Corp. in 1929 and to Whirlpool Corp. (N.Y.) in 1950 which was merged into Whirlpool Seeger Corp. 9/15/55 which name was changed to Whirlpool Corp. (Del.) 4/1/57

19101 NEWPORT CORP. (CA)
Completely liquidated 7/5/67
Each share Capital Stock 50¢ par exchanged for first and final distribution (0.1) share Larson Industries, Inc. Common 10¢ par
(See Larson Industries, Inc.)

NINETOWNS INTERNET TECHNOLOGY GROUP CO LTD (CAYMAN ISLANDS)
Name changed 10/03/2006
Name changed from Ninetowns Digital World Trade Holdings Ltd. to Ninetowns Internet Technology Group Co., Ltd. 10/03/2006
Acquired by Ninetowns Holdings Ltd. 05/30/2014
Each Sponsored ADR for Ordinary exchanged for $1.75 cash

NINETY-EIGHT GOLD MINING CO. (WA)
Charter revoked for failure to file reports and pay fees 7/1/23

9400 WEST FORT STREET LIQUIDATING CORP. (MI)
Liquidation completed
Each share Common $5 par exchanged for initial distribution of $70 cash 5/6/82
Each share Common $5 par received second distribution of $30 cash 6/24/82
Each share Common $5 par received third and final distribution of $19 cash 10/4/82

99 CAP CORP (BC)
Reincorporated 08/04/2010
Place of incorporation changed from (Canada) to (BC) 08/04/2010
Name changed to Giyani Gold Corp. 01/25/2011
Giyani Gold Corp. name changed to Giyani Metals Corp. 07/17/2017

99 CENT STUFF INC (FL)
SEC revoked common stock registration 04/22/2016

99 CENTS ONLY STORES (CA)
Secondary Offering - 3,500,000 shares COM offered at $38.125 per share on 04/29/1998
Common no par split (5) for (4) by issuance of (0.25) additional share payable 11/28/1997 to holders of record 11/17/1997 Ex date - 12/01/1997
Common no par split (5) for (4) by issuance of (0.25) additional share payable 11/12/1998 to holders of record 11/05/1998 Ex date - 11/13/1998
Common no par split (4) for (3) by issuance of (1/3) additional share payable 02/08/2000 to holders of record 01/28/2000 Ex date - 02/09/2000
Common no par split (3) for (2) by issuance of (0.5) additional share payable 03/20/2001 to holders of record 03/14/2001 Ex date - 03/21/2001
Common no par split (4) for (3) by issuance of (1/3) additional share payable 04/03/2002 to holders of record 03/25/2002 Ex date - 04/04/2002
Acquired by Number Holdings, Inc. 01/13/2012
Each share Common no par exchanged for $22 cash

99 DLR STORES INC (ID)
Name changed to InvestSource Communications, Inc. 1/17/2006
InvestSource Communications, Inc. name changed to United Resource Holdings Group, Inc. 2/5/2007

NINTH & ALAMEDA CO. (CA)
Liquidation completed for cash 2/12/65

NIOBRARA OIL, INC. (WY)
Merged into Crusader Oil & Uranium Co. 04/20/1955
Each share Capital Stock exchanged for (1) share Capital Stock 1¢ par
Crusader Oil & Uranium Co. merged into Crusader Oil & Gas Co. 02/06/1959 which merged into Old Empire Mining Co. 06/15/1968
(See Old Empire Mining Co.)

NIOGOLD MNG CORP (BC)
Merged into Oban Mining Corp. 03/11/2016
Each share Common no par exchanged for (0.4167) share Common no par
Note: Unexchanged certificates will be cancelled and become without value 03/11/2022
Oban Mining Corp. name changed to Osisko Mining Inc. 06/21/2016

NIPILAC GOLDFIELDS LTD.
Succeeded by Jellicoe Mines (1939) Ltd. on a (1) for (2) basis in 1939
Jellicoe Mines (1939) Ltd. recapitalized as Jelex Mines Ltd. 10/1/63 which recapitalized as Key Lake Explorations Ltd. 6/21/78
(See Key Lake Explorations Ltd.)

NIPIRON MINES LTD. (ON)
Name changed to New Nipiron Mines Ltd. and Common $1 par changed to no par 7/27/66
New Nipiron Mines Ltd. acquired by New York Oils Ltd. (BC) 6/29/70 which reincorporated in Alberta 7/19/82 which was acquired by Sceptre Resources Ltd. 3/14/89 which merged into Canadian Natural Resources Ltd. 8/15/96

NIPISSING MINES CO. LTD. (ON)
Capital Stock $5 par changed to $1 par in 1952
Merged into Patino Corp. Ltd. on a (0.2) for (1) basis 6/11/62
Patino Corp. Ltd. merged into Patino

NIPPON DENRO ISPAT LTD (INDIA)
Name changed to JSW ISPAT Steel Ltd. 07/14/2011
(See JSW ISPAT Steel Ltd.)

NIPPON ELEC LTD (JAPAN)
Each old ADR for Common 50 Yen par exchanged for (5) new ADR's for Common JPY 50 par 09/29/1982
Name changed to NEC Corp. 04/01/1983
(See NEC Corp.)

NIPPON INVTS CORP (BC)
Struck off register and declared dissolved for failure to file returns 08/12/1994

NIPPON KANGYO BK (JAPAN)
Merged into Dai-Ichi Kangyo Bank, Ltd. 12/1/71
Each ADR for Common 50 Yen par exchanged for (1) ADR for Common 50 Yen par
(See Dai-Ichi Kangyo Bank, Ltd.)

NIPPON KOKAN K K (JAPAN)
Name changed to NKK Corp. 6/8/88
(See NKK Corp.)

NIPPON MEAT PACKERS INC (JAPAN)
Name changed to NH Foods Ltd. 02/20/2015

NIPPON MINIATURE BEARING LTD (JAPAN)
Name changed to Minebea Co. Ltd. 10/01/1981
Minebea Co. Ltd. name changed to Minebea Mitsumi Inc. 01/27/2017

NIPPON MNG HLDGS INC (JAPAN)
ADR agreement terminated 04/27/2010
No ADR's remain outstanding

NIPPON OIL CORP (JAPAN)
ADR agreement terminated 04/02/2010
Each ADR for Common exchanged for (1.07) JX Holdings, Inc. ADR's for Common
JX Holdings, Inc. name changed to JXTG Holdings, Inc. 04/03/2017

NIPPON OPTICAL LTD (JAPAN)
Stock Dividends - 10% 12/22/1971; 10% 12/21/1973; 10% 07/14/1981; 10% 12/29/1983; 10% 12/28/1984; 13% 12/12/1985; 15% 12/29/1986
Name changed to Nikon Corp. 4/1/88

NIPPON SEIKO K K (JAPAN)
Name changed to NSK Corp. 8/8/94

NIPPON SHINPAN LTD (JAPAN)
Stock Dividends - 10% 06/15/1975; 15% 08/08/1984
Merged into Mitsubishi UFJ Financial Group, Inc. 08/01/2008
Each ADR for Common 50 Yen par exchanged for $29.239258 cash

NIPPON SHOKUBAI LTD (JAPAN)
Reorganized as Kabushiki Kaisha Nippon Shokubai 09/28/2009
Each Unsponsored ADR for Common 50 Yen par exchanged for (5) Sponsored ADR's for Common
Note: Unexchanged ADR's will be sold and proceeds, if any, held for claim after 03/25/2010

NIPPON STL CORP (JAPAN)
Merged into Nippon Steel & Sumitomo Metal Corp. 10/01/2012
Each Unsponsored ADR for Common exchanged for (1) Sponsored ADR for Common

NIPPONDENSO LTD (JAPAN)
Stock Dividend - 10% 5/25/90
Name changed to Denso Corp. 10/1/96

NIPSCO INDS INC (IN)
Common no par split (2) for (1) by issuance of (1) additional share payable 02/20/1998 to holders of record 01/30/1998 Ex date - 02/23/1998
Name changed to NiSource Inc. (IN) 04/14/1999
NiSource Inc. (IN) reincorporated in Delaware 11/01/2000

NIR DIAGNOSTICS INC (ON)
Discharged from receivership 05/21/2009
No stockholders' equity

NIRAVOICE INC (CA)
Name changed to Netcor, Inc. 1/2/90
(See Netcor, Inc.)

NIRENBERG M & SONS INC (NY)
Charter cancelled and proclaimed dissolved for failure to file reports and pay taxes 12/15/1973

NIRVANA INDS LTD (BC)
Name changed 10/06/1986
Name changed from Nirvana Oil & Gas Ltd. to Nirvana Industries Ltd. 10/06/1986
Recapitalized as Consolidated Nirvana Industries Ltd. 02/22/1989
Each share Common no par exchanged for (0.25) share Common no par
Consolidated Nirvana Industries Ltd. recapitalized as Navasota Resources Ltd. 06/02/1995 which name changed to Anglo Aluminum Corp. 01/26/2010 which recapitalized as Navasota Resources Inc. 07/12/2013

NIS GROUP (JAPAN)
ADR basis changed from (1:10) to (1:0.5) 08/31/2007
ADR agreement terminated 08/01/2012
Underlying shares subsequently declared worthless through bankruptcy proceedings
No ADR holders' equity

NISARC COMPUTERS LTD (NY)
Charter cancelled and proclaimed dissolved for failure to pay taxes 12/15/1975

NISE INC (UT)
Voluntarily dissolved 09/11/1995
Details not available

NISKA GAS STORAGE PARTNERS LLC (DE)
Acquired by Swan Holdings L.P. 07/19/2016
Each Common Unit exchanged for $4.225 cash

NISOURCE INC (DE)
Reincorporated 11/01/2000
State of incorporation changed from (IN) to (DE) and Common no par changed to 1¢ par 11/01/2000
Each Corporate Premium Income Equity Security no par exchanged for (1.9002) shares Common no par 02/19/2003
Each Stock Appreciation Income Linked Security exchanged for (0.12266465) share Common no par 11/01/2004
(Additional Information in Active)

NISSAN CHEM INDS LTD (JAPAN)
Name changed to Nissan Chemical Corp. 07/02/2018

NISSAN COPPER LTD (INDIA)
Basis changed from (1:5) to (1:50) 09/29/2010
GDR agreement terminated 12/14/2015
Each Sponsored Reg. S GDR for Equity Shares exchanged for (50) Equity Shares

NISSEN CORP (IA)
Name changed 3/14/62
Name changed from Nissen Trampoline Co. to Nissen Corp. 3/14/62
Merged into Victor Comptometer Corp. 10/31/72
Each share Common $1 par exchanged for (1.1726) shares Common $1 par
Victor Comptometer Corp. merged into Kidde (Walter) & Co., Inc. (DE) 7/15/77 which name changed to Kidde, Inc. 4/18/80 which merged into Hanson Trust p.l.c. 12/31/87 which name changed to Hanson Trust PLC (Old) 1/29/88 which reorganized as Hanson Trust PLC (New) 10/15/2003

NISSEN SPORTS ACADEMY INC (IA)
Administratively dissolved for failure to file annual reports 08/04/1995

NISSHIN STL HLDGS CO LTD (JAPAN)
Name changed to Nisshin Steel Co., Ltd. 06/20/2014

NISSHIN STL LTD (JAPAN)
ADR agreement terminated 11/02/2012
Each ADR for Common exchanged for approximately $20.328001 cash

NISSIN CO LTD (JAPAN)
Issue Information - 5,000,000 SPONSORED ADR'S offered at $12.39 per ADR on 08/01/2002
Old Sponsored ADR's for Common no par split (2) for (1) by issuance of (1) additional ADR payable 05/22/2003 to holders of record 03/28/2003 Ex date - 05/23/2003
Old Sponsored ADR's for Common no par split (2) for (1) by issuance of (1) additional ADR payable 05/25/2004 to holders of record 03/30/2004 Ex date - 05/26/2004
Old Sponsored ADR's for Common no par split (2) for (1) by issuance of (1) additional ADR payable 11/23/2004 to holders of record 09/29/2004 Ex date - 11/24/2004
Each old Sponsored ADR for Common no par exchanged for (0.4) new Sponsored ADR for Common no par 11/18/2005
New Sponsored ADR's for Common no par split (2) for (1) by issuance of (1) additional ADR payable 04/05/2006 to holders of record 03/30/2006 Ex date - 04/06/2006
Stock Dividend - 20% payable 05/27/2005 to holders of record 03/30/2005 Ex date - 03/28/2005
Name changed to NIS Group Co., Ltd. 10/02/2006
(See NIS Group Co., Ltd.)

NISSON MNG & DEV LTD (BC)
Struck off register and declared dissolved for failure to file returns 03/23/1979

NISTO MINES LTD. (ON)
Recapitalized as Canadian Nisto Mines Ltd. 08/19/1966
Each share Capital Stock $1 par exchanged for (0.5) share Capital Stock $1 par
(See Canadian Nisto Mines Ltd.)

NISUS VIDEO INC (NM)
Plan of reorganization under Chapter 11 Federal Bankruptcy proceedings confirmed 04/10/1992
Each share Common no par exchanged for (1,000) shares White Acquisition Group Inc. Common no par, (1,000) Class A Common Stock Purchase Warrants expiring 04/10/1993, (1,000) Class B Common Stock Purchase Warrants expiring 04/10/1994 and (1,000) Class C Common Stock Purchase Warrants expiring 04/10/1995
Note: Unexchanged certificates were cancelled and became without value 04/10/1993
White Acquisition Group Inc. recapitalized as Nattem USA Inc. 01/04/1993 which name changed to Comtec International, Inc. 10/26/1995

NITAR TECH CORP (DE)
Recapitalized as Winscon Electronics Co. Ltd. 10/13/2009
Each share Common $0.001 par exchanged for (0.06666666) share Common $0.001 par
Winscon Electronics Co. Ltd. name changed to Uniwell Electronic Corp. 09/16/2010 which name changed to Analytica Bio-Energy Corp. 09/19/2013

NITCHES INC (CA)
Common no par split (2) for (1) by issuance of (1) additional share payable 05/04/1998 to holders of record 04/17/1998
Common no par split (5) for (4) by issuance of (0.25) additional share payable 01/20/2006 to holders of record 01/03/2006 Ex date - 01/23/2006
Stock Dividend - 10% payable 03/29/2002 to holders of record 03/22/2002 Ex date - 03/20/2002
Reincorporated under the laws of Nevada and Common no par changed to $0.001 par 11/05/2008

NITE & DAY TECHNOLOGIES INC (NV)
Recapitalized as SDI Virtual Reality Corp. 11/2/93
Each (150) shares Common $0.001 par exchanged for (1) share Common $0.001 par

NITE-LITE USA LTD (CO)
Each share old Common no par exchanged for (0.1) share new Common no par 07/01/1996
Name changed to Concorde Strategies Group Inc. 11/01/1996
Concorde Strategies Group Inc. recapitalized as W3 Group, Inc. (CO) 10/01/1999 which reincorporated in Delaware 05/07/2003 which name changed to Aftersoft Group, Inc. 01/19/2006 which name changed to MAM Software Group, Inc. 05/27/2010

NITEAGLE SYS INC (NV)
Recapitalized as Alternative Green Technologies Inc. 12/12/2008
Each share Common $0.001 par exchanged for (0.00005) share Common $0.001 par

NITECAP WORLDWIDE COMMUNICATIONS, INC. (UT)
Proclaimed dissolved for failure to pay taxes 9/30/80

NITHEX EXPLORATION & DEVELOPMENT LTD. (BC)
Merged into Nithex Exploration Ltd. 6/8/76
Each share Capital Stock no par exchanged for (0.5) share Common no par
Nithex Exploration Ltd. merged into Lintex Minerals Ltd. 6/1/83 which recapitalized as New Lintex Minerals Ltd. 12/7/87 which merged into Globaltex Industries Inc. 3/5/93 which name changed to Pine Valley Mining Corp. 5/14/2003

NITHEX EXPL LTD (BC)
Merged into Lintex Minerals Ltd. 06/01/1983
Each share Common no par exchanged for (1) share Common no par
Lintex Minerals Ltd. recapitalized as New Lintex Minerals Ltd. 12/07/1987 which merged into Globaltex Industries Inc. 03/05/1993 which name changed to Pine Valley Mining Corp. 05/14/2003

NITINAT MINES, LTD. (BC)
Charter cancelled for failure to file returns 10/11/54

NITINOL MED TECHNOLOGIES INC (DE)
Name changed to NMT Medical, Inc. 06/03/1999
(See NMT Medical, Inc.)

NITRACELL CDA LTD (AB)
Recapitalized as Magnum Resources Ltd. 01/09/1975
Each share Common no par exchanged for (0.2) share Common no par
(See Magnum Resources Ltd.)

NITRAM INC (WY)
Recapitalized as Diversified Resources, Inc. 02/22/1982
Each share Common 1¢ par exchanged for (0.25) share Common 1¢ par
Diversified Resources, Inc. recapitalized Techtower Group, Inc. 07/20/1984
(See Techtower Group, Inc.)

NITRO DEVELOPMENTS INC. (ON)
Merged into Xtra Developments Inc. 5/25/72
Each share Capital Stock exchanged for (0.076923) share Capital Stock no par
Xtra Developments Inc. merged into Sumtra Diversified Inc. 8/30/78

NITRO LUBE INC (NV)
Old Common $0.001 par split (3) for (1) by issuance of (2) additional shares payable 01/22/2006 to holders of record 01/22/2006
Each share old Common $0.001 par exchanged for (3) shares new Common $0.001 par 01/22/2007
Each share new Common $0.001 par received distribution of (0.25) share Easy Phone, Inc. (New) Restricted Common $0.001 par payable 03/21/2007 to holders of record 03/20/2007
Each share new Common $0.001 par exchanged again for (0.0005) share new Common $0.001 par 10/17/2007
Name changed to Uranium City Mining Corp. 11/14/2007
Uranium City Mining Corp. name changed to U.S. Mine Makers, Inc. (NV) 01/28/2008 which reincorporated in Wyoming as Vid3G, Inc. 02/13/2014 which recapitalized as Argus Worldwide Corp. 11/14/2016

NITRO PETE INC (NV)
Each share old Common $0.001 par exchanged for (5) shares new Common $0.001 par 12/29/2006
Each share new Common $0.001 par exchanged again for (0.01) share new Common $0.001 par 11/01/2012
Merged into Core Resource Management, Inc. 03/26/2015
Each share new Common $0.001 par exchanged for (0.09523809) share Common $0.001 par

NITROGEN OIL WELL SERVICE CO. (TX)
Merged into Big Three Welding Equipment Co. 1/14/63
Each share Common $5 par exchanged for (1) share Capital Stock $5 par
Big Three Welding Equipment Co. recapitalized as Big Three Industrial Gas & Equipment Co. 11/6/64 which name changed to Big Three Industries Inc. 4/6/70
(See Big Three Industries Inc.)

NITROMED INC (DE)
Issue Information - 6,000,000 shares COM offered at $11 per share on 11/14/2003
Acquired by NTMD Acquisition Corp. 04/24/2009
Each share Common 1¢ par exchanged for $0.8585 cash

NITRON INC (CA)
Charter cancelled for failure to file reports and pay taxes 8/1/90

NITTANY FINL CORP (PA)
Common 10¢ par split (6) for (5) by issuance of (0.2) additional share payable 02/15/2003 to holders of record 01/31/2003 Ex date - 01/29/2003
Common 10¢ par split (6) for (5) by issuance of (0.2) additional share payable 03/31/2004 to holders of record 03/10/2004 Ex date - 03/08/2004
Stock Dividends - 10% payable 01/01/2001 to holders of record 12/01/2000 Ex date - 11/29/2000; 10% payable 01/15/2002 to holders of record 12/31/2001 Ex date - 01/02/2002
Merged into National Penn Bancshares, Inc. 01/27/2006
Each share Common 10¢ par exchanged for (1.994) shares Common $5 par
National Penn Bancshares, Inc. merged into BB&T Corp. 04/01/2016

NITTANY VENTURES INC (DE)
Name changed to Hauser Chemical Research Inc. (DE) 3/20/86
Hauser Chemical Research Inc. (DE) reincorporated in Colorado as Hauser, Inc. 12/3/96 which reincorporated in Delaware 12/6/99
(See Hauser, Inc. (DE))

NIUGINI MNG LTD (PAPUA NEW GUINEA)
Each Unsponsored ADR for Ordinary 10 Toea par exchanged for (1) Sponsored ADR for Ordinary 10 Toea par 3/18/91
Merged into Lihir Gold Ltd. 4/7/2000
Each Sponsored ADR for Ordinary 10 Toea par exchanged for $0.8778 cash

NIUSULE BIO PHARMACEUTICAL CORP (NV)
Charter revoked 04/30/2014

NIUSULE BIOTECH CORP (NV)
Name changed to Niusule Bio-pharmaceutical Corp. 09/30/2010
(See Niusule Bio-pharmaceutical Corp.)

NIVALIS THERAPEUTICS INC (DE)
Recapitalized as Alpine Immune Sciences, Inc. 07/25/2017
Each share Common $0.001 par exchanged for (0.25) share Common $0.001 par

NIX CO LTD (DE)
Name changed to Eco Hybrid Energy, Inc. 11/11/2003
Eco Hybrid Energy, Inc. name changed to Global Energy Resources, Inc. 06/08/2004
(See Global Energy Resources, Inc.)

NIX O TINE PHARMACEUTICALS LTD (BC)
Assets sold for the benefits of creditors in March 1993
No stockholders' equity

NIXON-BALDWIN CHEMICALS INC. (DE)
Acquired by Tennessee Gas Transmission Co. 1/3/66
Each share Common 10¢ par exchanged for (1/3) share Common $5 par
Tennessee Gas Transmission Co. name changed to Tenneco Inc. 4/11/66 which merged into El Paso Natural Gas Co. 12/12/96 which reorganized as El Paso Energy Corp. 8/1/98 which name changed to El Paso Corp. 2/5/2001

NIZHEGORODSVYAZINFORM AO (RUSSIA)
Name changed to VolgaTelecom Public JSC 07/30/2002

(See VolgaTelecom Public JSC)

NIZHNEDNEPROVSKY TUBE ROLLING PLT (UKRAINE)
Name changed to Interpipe Nyzhniodniprovsky Tube-Rolling Plant, JSC 03/21/2007
(See Interpipe Nizhnedneprovsky Tube-Rolling Plant JSC)

NIZHNEKAMSKNEFTEKHIM OAO (RUSSIA)
Name changed 11/13/2015
Basis changed from (1:0.5) to (1:10) 11/21/2001
Stock Dividend - 25% payable 11/21/2001 to holders of record 10/01/2001
Name changed from Nizhnekamskneftekhim OAO to Nizhnekamskneftekhim PJSC 11/13/2015
ADR agreement terminated 01/21/2016
Each Sponsored ADR for Ordinary exchanged for $7.745486 cash

NIZHNEKAMSKSHINA OAO (RUSSIA)
Name changed to Nizhnekamskshina PJSC 12/03/2015

NJB PRIME INVS (MA)
Name changed to Vyquest Trust (MA) 04/14/1980
Vyquest Trust (MA) reorganized in New Jersey as Vyquest Inc. 07/01/1981
(See Vyquest Inc.)

NJN BANCORPORATION (NJ)
Name changed to New Jersey National Corp. 03/21/1972
New Jersey National Corp. acquired by CoreStates Financial Corp 10/30/1986 which merged into First Union Corp. 04/28/1998 which name changed to Wachovia Corp. (Ctfs. dated after 09/01/2001) 09/01/2001 which merged into Wells Fargo & Co. (New) 12/31/2008

NJS ACQUISITION CORP (DE)
Name changed to KIWI Holdings Inc. 11/21/1997
KIWI Holdings Inc. name changed to Chariot International Holdings Inc. 04/30/1999
(See Chariot International Holdings Inc.)

NKK CORP (JAPAN)
ADR agreement terminated 1/30/2003
Each ADR for Common 50 Yen par exchanged for $8.9188 cash
Note: Due to ADR's being unsponsored exchange rate may vary dependent upon depositary agent

NKT HLDG AS (DENMARK)
Name changed to NKT A/S 06/23/2017

NKWE PLATINUM LTD (BERMUDA)
ADR agreement terminated 11/04/2015
Each Sponsored ADR for Ordinary exchanged for $0.754157 cash

NL INDS INC (NJ)
Each Depositary Preferred Ser. C exchanged for either (1) share Common 12-1/2¢ par or $15.66 cash 12/22/1988
Note: Non-electors received stock (Additional Information in Active)

NL ONE CORP (NV)
Recapitalized as Flagship Global Corp. 07/13/2016
Each share Common $0.0001 par exchanged for (0.125) share Common $0.0001 par

NLB CAP CORP (UT)
Recapitalized as Integrated Masonry Systems International 11/01/1997
Each share Common 2¢ par exchanged for (0.1) share Common $0.001 par

(See Integrated Masonry Systems International)

NLI CORP (TX)
Merged into National City Lines, Inc. 05/26/1983
Each share Common no par exchanged for (0.3077) share Common 50¢ par
(See National City Lines, Inc.)

NLT CORP (TN)
Reincorporated 1/1/81
Common $5 par split (2) for (1) by issuance of (1) additional share 4/23/73
State of incorporation changed from (DE) to (TN) 1/1/81
Merged into American General Corp. 11/4/82
Each share Common $5 par exchanged for (0.2875) share Adjustable Rate Preferred Ser. A $1.50 par, (0.2875) share Adjustable Rate Conv. Preferred Ser. B $1.50 par, $10.0625 principal amount of 11% Conv. Debs. due 11/4/2008 and $7.1875 cash
American General Corp. merged into American International Group, Inc. 8/29/2001

NLX RES INC (ON)
Charter cancelled for failure to file reports and pay taxes 2/14/94

NM HLDGS INC (MN)
Name changed to Stockwalk.com Group, Inc. 7/13/99
Stockwalk.com Group, Inc. name changed to Stockwalk Group, Inc. 1/1/2001
(See Stockwalk Group, Inc.)

NMBT CORP (DE)
Merged into Summit Bancorp 03/29/2000
Each share Common 1¢ par exchanged for (0.9503) share Common 1¢ par
Summit Bancorp merged into FleetBoston Financial Corp. 03/01/2001 which merged into Bank of America Corp. 04/01/2004

NMC CORP (DE)
Common 10¢ par changed to 6-2/3¢ par and (0.5) additional share issued 02/07/1968
Common 6-2/3¢ par split (5) for (4) by issuance of (0.25) additional share 04/14/1972
Each share old Common 6-2/3¢ par exchanged for (0.1) share new Common 6-2/3¢ par 04/17/1995
Name changed to Regent Group, Inc. 09/15/1997
Regent Group, Inc. reorganized as Millennium Biotechnologies Group, Inc. 04/01/2002 which name changed to Inergetics, Inc. 05/06/2010

NMC RESOURCE CORP (BC)
Each share old Common no par exchanged for (0.2) share new Common no par 12/15/2010
Acquired by Dong Won Corp. 02/17/2015
Each share Common no par exchanged for $0.20 cash
Note: Unexchanged certificates will be cancelled and become without value 02/17/2021

NMR AMER INC (PA)
Merged into Medical Resources Inc. 8/30/96
Each share Common no par exchanged for (0.6875) share Common 1¢ par

NMR CTRS INC (DE)
Name changed to American Health Services Corp. 5/11/87
American Health Services Corp. merged into InSight Health Services Corp. 6/26/96
(See InSight Health Services Corp.)

NMS COMMUNICATIONS CORP (DE)
Name changed to LiveWire Mobile, Inc. 12/08/2008
LiveWire Mobile, Inc. name changed to Live Microsystems, Inc. 08/29/2013

NMS INDS INC (NY)
Out of business in September 1975
No stockholders' equity

NMS PHARMACEUTICALS INC (DE)
Name changed to Biomerica, Inc. 10/20/1987

NMS REHABILITATION INC (FL)
Reorganized under the laws of Delaware as Amhealth Physical Care Inc. 10/28/1992
Each share Common $0.000001 par exchanged for (0.0285714) share Common 1¢ par
(See Amhealth Physical Care Inc.)

NMT MED INC (DE)
Assets assigned for the benefit of creditors 04/20/2011
No stockholders' equity

NMXS COM INC (DE)
Reincorporated under the laws of Nevada as New Mexico Software, Inc. 01/09/2006
New Mexico Software, Inc. name changed to Net Medical Xpress Solutions, Inc. 01/10/2013

NN BALL & ROLLER INC (DE)
Issue Information - 2,300,000 shares COM offered at $14 per share on 03/15/1994
Common 1¢ par split (3) for (2) by issuance of (0.5) additional share 3/6/95
Common 1¢ par split (3) for (2) by issuance of (0.5) additional share 12/5/95
Name changed to NN Inc. 6/9/2000

NN CORP (DE)
Common $5 par split (3) for (2) by issuance of (0.5) additional share 8/9/68
Stock Dividends - 50% 1/17/72; 50% 12/29/72; 50% 9/14/79
Merged into Armco Inc. 12/1/80
Each share Common $5 par exchanged for (1.5) shares Common $5 par $3.60 Preferred Ser. A called for redemption at $44 on 10/3/98
Public interest eliminated

NNZ AMER INC (DE)
Name changed to GTrade.Network, Inc. 04/20/1999
GTrade.Network, Inc. name changed to VS2, Inc. 01/12/2001 which recapitalized as EuroWork Global, Ltd. 11/08/2004 which name changed to Quintessence Holdings, Inc. 07/25/2007 which name changed to Terminus Energy, Inc. 12/04/2009

NO GLUG JUG CORP (DE)
Recapitalized as Jet Travel Services, Inc. 07/06/1973
Each share Common 1¢ par exchanged for (0.142857) share Common 1¢ par
(See Jet Travel Services, Inc.)

NO GOOD TV INC (GA)
Name changed to LB Center, Inc. 05/03/2005
LB Center, Inc. name changed to Berman Center, Inc. 09/16/2005
(See Berman Center, Inc.)

NO NAME STORES INC (DE)
Charter forfeited for failure to maintain a registered agent 3/1/97

NO-SAG SPRING CO. (MI)
Completely liquidated for cash 1/27/64

NO SHOW INC (NV)
Name changed to EnDev Holdings Inc. 03/26/2012

EnDev Holdings Inc. name changed to MeeMee Media Inc. 05/16/2013

NOAH ED HLDGS LTD (CAYMAN ISLANDS)
Acquired by Rainbow Education Holding Ltd. 07/30/2014
Each Sponsored ADR for Ordinary exchanged for $2.80 cash

NOARKO RES INC (CO)
Merged into Dillon Holding, Inc. 12/17/1987
Each share Common no par exchanged for $0.01 cash

NOBEL BIOCARE (SWITZERLAND)
ADR agreement terminated 07/07/2015
Each ADR for Ordinary exchanged for $9.11693 cash

NOBEL ED DYNAMICS INC (DE)
Each share old Common $0.001 par exchanged for (0.25) share new Common $0.001 par 09/28/1995
Name changed to Nobel Learning Communities, Inc. 11/19/1998
(See Nobel Learning Communities, Inc.)

NOBEL INS LTD (BERMUDA)
Stock Dividends - 15% 4/15/83; 15% 5/18/84
Common $1 par changed to 5¢ par 6/29/98
In process of liquidation
Each share Common 5¢ par received initial distribution of $13 cash payable 7/3/98 to holders of record 6/29/98
Note: Details on subsequent distributions, if any, are not available

NOBEL LEARNING CMNTYS INC (DE)
Conv. Preferred Ser. A called for redemption at $1 on 12/30/2004
Conv. Preferred Ser. C called for redemption at $1 on 12/30/2004
Common Stock Purchase Rights declared for Common stockholders of record 06/01/2000 were redeemed at $0.001 per right 11/30/2005 for holders of record 06/01/2000
Acquired by Academic Acquisition Corp. 08/09/2011
Each share Common $0.001 par exchanged for $11.75 cash

NOBEL REAL ESTATE INVT TR (QC)
Each old Trust Unit exchanged for (0.1) new Trust Unit 08/20/2014
Each new Trust Unit exchanged again for (0.2) new Trust Unit 08/21/2015
Merged into Nexus Real Estate Investment Trust 04/05/2017
Each new Trust Unit exchanged for (1.67) Trust Units
Note: Unexchanged certificates will be cancelled and become without value 04/05/2023

NOBLE AFFILIATES INC (DE)
Common $3.33-1/3 par split (2) for (1) by issuance of (1) additional share 12/27/1977
Common $3.33-1/3 par split (6) for (5) by issuance of (0.2) additional share 05/01/1979
Common $3.33-1/3 par split (2) for (1) by issuance of (1) additional share 05/15/1981
Stock Dividends - 10% 05/06/1976; 50% 02/01/1977; 50% 02/20/1980
Name changed to Noble Energy, Inc. 05/13/2002

NOBLE CHINA INC (AB)
Recapitalized 10/07/1993
Recapitalized from Noble China Corp. to Noble China Inc. 10/07/1993
Each share Common no par exchanged for (0.5) share Common no par
Delisted from Toronto Venture Stock Exchange 02/14/2003

NOBLE CONSOLIDATED INDUSTRIES CORP (NV)
SEC revoked common stock registration 03/19/2013

NOBLE CORP (CAYMAN ISLANDS)
Ordinary 10¢ par split (2) for (1) by issuance of (1) additional share payable 08/28/2007 to holders of record 08/07/2007 Ex date - 08/29/2007
Reorganized under the laws of Switzerland 03/27/2009
Each share Ordinary 10¢ par exchanged for (1) Registered Share CHF 5 par
Noble Corp. (Switzerland) reorganized in England & Wales as Noble Corp. PLC 11/20/2013

NOBLE CORP (SWITZERLAND)
Registered Shares CHF 5 par changed to CHF 4.90 par 08/07/2009
Registered Shares CHF 4.90 par changed to CHF 4.85 par 11/05/2009
Registered Shares CHF 4.85 par changed to CHF 4.80 par 02/16/2010
Registered Shares CHF 4.80 par changed to CHF 4.75 par 05/06/2010
Registered Shares CHF 4.75 par changed to CHF 4.06 par 08/05/2010
Registered Shares CHF 4.06 par changed to CHF 3.93 par 11/04/2010
Registered Shares CHF 3.93 par changed to CHF 3.80 par 02/10/2011
Registered Shares CHF 3.80 par changed to CHF 3.67 par 05/05/2011
Registered Shares CHF 3.67 par changed to CHF 3.54 par 08/18/2011
Registered Shares CHF 3.54 par changed to CHF 3.41 par 11/17/2011
Registered Shares CHF 3.41 par changed to CHF 3.28 par 02/23/2012
Registered Shares CHF 3.28 par changed to CHF 3.15 par 05/16/2012
Reorganized under the laws of England & Wales as Noble Corp. PLC 11/20/2013
Each share Common CHF 3.15 par exchanged for (1) share Ordinary USD $0.01 par

NOBLE DRILLING CORP (DE)
Common $1 par changed to 10¢ par 12/31/1987
$2.25 Conv. Exchangeable Preferred $1 par called for redemption 06/01/1995
$1.50 Conv. Preferred $1 par called for redemption 12/31/1996
Reincorporated under the laws of Cayman Islands as Noble Corp. and Common 10¢ par reclassified as Ordinary shares 04/30/2002
Noble Corp. (Cayman Islands) reorganized in Switzerland 03/27/2009 which reorganized in England & Wales as Noble Corp. PLC 11/20/2013

NOBLE ELECTRIC STEEL CO. (CA)
Charter revoked for failure to file reports and pay fees 3/8/32

NOBLE FINL GROUP INC (NV)
Recapitalized as Newman Energy Technologies Inc. 04/21/1998
Each share Common $0.001 par exchanged for (0.025) share Common $0.001 par
Newman Energy Technologies Inc. name changed to World Star Asia, Inc. 06/15/1998 which name changed to Comgen Corp. 11/16/1998 which name changed to

Planet 411.com Corp. (NV) 02/11/1999 which reincorporated in Delaware as Planet411.com Inc. 10/07/1999 which name changed to Ivany Mining, Inc. 07/27/2007 which name changed to Ivany Nguyen, Inc. 02/16/2010 which name changed to Myriad Interactive Media, Inc. 07/25/2011

NOBLE FIVE MINES LTD.
Acquired by Nelson Slocan Consolidated Mines Ltd. on a (1) for (10) basis in 1949
(See Nelson Slocan Consolidated Mines Ltd.)

NOBLE HSE COMMUNICATIONS INC (ON)
Each share old Common no par exchanged for (1/6) share new Common no par 02/24/1998
Name changed to Webengine Corp. (ON) 06/06/2000
Webengine Corp. (ON) reorganized in Canada as Foccini International Inc. 11/13/2003 which name changed to Arch Biopartners Inc. 05/07/2010

NOBLE HSE ENTMT INC (ON)
Each share old Common no par exchanged for (0.5) share new Common no par 11/23/2004
Reincorporated under the laws of Canada as LiveReel Media Corp. 12/01/2006
LiveReel Media Corp. name changed to CordovaCann Corp. 08/08/2018

NOBLE INDS INC (UT)
Involuntarily dissolved 05/01/1989

NOBLE INNOVATIONS INC (NV)
Each share old Common $0.001 par exchanged for (0.05) share new Common $0.001 par 05/20/2008
SEC revoked common stock registration 04/16/2013

NOBLE INTL LTD (DE)
Common $0.001 par split (3) for (2) by issuance of (0.5) additional share payable 02/03/2006 to holders of record 01/27/2006 Ex date - 02/06/2006
Plan of reorganization under Chapter 11 Federal Bankruptcy proceedings effective 11/30/2009
No stockholders' equity

NOBLE LMBR CORP (NY)
Dissolved by proclamation 12/27/2000

NOBLE MGMT INC (NV)
Recapitalized 5/31/91
Reorganized from (CO) to under the laws of (NV) 5/31/91
Each share Common no par exchanged for (0.1) share Common $0.001 par 5/31/91
Charter permanently revoked 1/1/2005

NOBLE METALS INC (WA)
Name changed to Intrex Inc. (WA) 10/29/1984
Intrex Inc. (WA) reincorporated in Nevada as Intrex.com, Inc. 05/19/1999 which name changed to Financial Commerce Network, Inc. 09/28/1999 which name changed to Regions Oil & Gas Inc. 01/23/2007 which recapitalized as American Green Group, Inc. 02/27/2008
(See American Green Group, Inc.)

NOBLE MINES & OILS LTD (AB)
Name changed to Noble China Corp. 07/08/1993
Noble China Corp. recapitalized as Noble China Inc. 10/07/1993
(See Noble China Inc.)

NOBLE MOTOR TRUCK CORP. (IN)
Charter revoked for failure to file annual reports 5/29/37

NOBLE OILS LTD. (AB)
Name changed to Noble Mines & Oils Ltd. 08/15/1969
Noble Mines & Oils Ltd. name

FINANCIAL INFORMATION, INC. NOB-NOM

changed to Noble China Corp.
07/08/1993 which recapitalized as
Noble China Inc. 10/07/1993
(See Noble China Inc.)

NOBLE ONIE INC (NV)
Name changed to National Capital
Companies Inc. 05/23/2000
(See National Capital Companies
Inc.)

NOBLE PEAK RES LTD (CANADA)
Reincorporated 03/04/1987
Place of incorporation changed from
(BC) to (Canada) 03/04/1987
Recapitalized as Vaaldiam Resources
Ltd. 08/21/1998
Each share Common no par
exchanged for (0.1) share Common
no par
Vaaldiam Resources Ltd. merged into
Vaaldiam Mining Inc. 03/26/2010
(See Vaaldiam Mining Inc.)

NOBLE QUESTS INC (NV)
Name changed to Legend Media, Inc.
02/25/2008

NOBLE RES INC (NV)
Name changed to Image Globe
Solutions Inc. 6/23/2000

**NOBLES ENGINEERING &
MANUFACTURING CO. (MN)**
Name changed to Nobles Industries,
Inc. 1/3/67

NOBLITT-SPARKS INDUSTRIES, INC.
Name changed to Arvin Industries,
Inc. 00/00/1950
Arvin Industries, Inc. merged into
ArvinMeritor, Inc. 07/07/2000 which
name changed to Meritor, Inc.
03/30/2011

NOCANA LTD (QC)
Name changed to Grandma Lee's Inc.
03/19/1979
Grandma Lee's Inc. name changed to
Heritage Concepts International Inc.
11/14/1997 which name changed to
NEXUS Group International Inc.
03/13/2001
(See NEXUS Group International Inc.)

NOCANA MINES LTD. (QC)
Common $1 par changed to no par
08/28/1973
Name changed to Nocana
Ltd.-Nocana Ltee. 12/29/1975
Nocana Ltd.-Nocana Ltee. name
changed to Grandma Lee's Inc.
03/19/1979 which name changed to
Heritage Concepts International Inc.
11/14/1997 which name changed to
NEXUS Group International Inc.
03/13/2001
(See NEXUS Group International Inc.)

NOCOPI INTL INC (MD)
Name changed to Nocopi
Technologies, Inc. 06/08/1992

NODAWAY VY CO (IA)
Name changed 06/05/1980
Name changed from Nodaway Valley
Packing Co. to Nodaway Valley Co.
06/05/1980
Stock Dividends - 33% 11/01/1978;
10% 04/12/1985; 10% 03/14/1986;
10% 03/13/1987
Merged into Whitestar Acquisition
Corp. 08/30/1989
Each share Common $2 par
exchanged for $11 cash

NODDINGS INVT TR (MA)
Trust terminated 12/28/92
Details not available

NODRAER LIQUIDATING CO. (MO)
Liquidation completed
Each share Common $1 par stamped
to indicate initial distribution of $9
cash 4/1/66
Each share Stamped Common $1 par
exchanged for second and final
distribution of $0.98 cash 12/12/66

NOEL GROUP INC (DE)
Each share Common 10¢ par
received distribution of (0.058824)
share Garnet Resources Corp.
Common 1¢ par, (0.257104) share
Global Natural Resources, Inc.
Common $1 par, and (0.068242)
share VISX, Inc. Common 1¢ par
09/21/1992
Each share Common 10¢ par
received distribution of (0.069448)
share Sylvan Foods Holdings Inc.
Common $0.001 par 12/06/1993
Each share Common 10¢ par
received distribution of (0.175434)
share Belding Heminway Co., Inc.
Common $1 par 02/28/1994
Units unstapled 12/15/1994
Each share Common 10¢ par
received (0.175434) share Belding
Heminway Co., Inc. (New) Ser. A
Common $1 par
In process of liquidation
Each share Common 10¢ par
received initial distribution of
(0.1838631) share HealthPlan
Services Corp. Common 1¢ par
payable 04/25/1997 to holders of
record 04/18/1997
Each share Common 10¢ par
received second distribution of
(0.02) share HealthPlan Services
Corp. Common 1¢ par payable
10/06/1997 to holders of record
09/29/1997
Each share Common 10¢ par
received third distribution of
(0.107246) share Carlyle Industries
Inc. Common $1 par payable
12/01/1997 to holders of record
11/21/1997
Each share Common 10¢ par
received fourth distribution of $0.70
cash payable 03/27/1998
Each share Common 10¢ par
received fifth distribution of $0.45
cash payable 04/30/1998 to holders
of record 04/22/1998
Each share Common 10¢ par
received sixth distribution of $0.92
cash payable 08/14/1998 to holders
of record 07/31/1998
Each share Common 10¢ par
received seventh distribution of (1)
CBI Distribution Trust Unit of Bene.
Int. payable 04/12/1999 to holders of
record 04/12/1999
Each share Common 10¢ par
received eighth distribution of (0.1)
share Career Blazers Inc. Common
1¢ par payable 04/15/1999 to
holders of record 04/15/1999
Each share Common 10¢ par
received ninth distribution of $0.146
cash payable 09/03/1999 to holders
of record 09/03/1999
Assets transferred to Noel Liquidating
Trust 09/03/1999
(See Noel Liquidating Trust)

NOEL INDS INC (NY)
Merged into Gitano 04/25/1988
Each share Common 10¢ par
exchanged for $1.70 cash

NOEL LIQUIDATING TR (DE)
In process of liquidation
Each Unit of Bene. Int. received initial
distribution of (0.307257) share
Carlyle Industries, Inc. Common $1
par payable 12/13/1999 to holders
of record 09/03/1999
Note: Details on subsequent
distributions, if any, are not available

NOFOG CORP. (NV)
Common $1 par changed to 50¢ par
in 1956
Common 50¢ par changed to 5¢ par
11/25/59
Name changed to Mark IX Industries
6/11/69

**NOGA ELECTRO MECHANICAL INDS
(1986) LTD (ISRAEL)**
Filed an application under Chapter 15
on 09/18/2002
Stockholders' equity unlikely

NOGAL ENERGY INC (NV)
Name changed to Novamex Energy,
Inc. 12/23/2014

NOGATECH INC (DE)
Merged into Zoran Corp. 10/25/2000
Each share Common $0.001 par
exchanged for (0.166) share
Common $0.001 par
Zoran Corp. merged into CSR PLC
08/31/2011
(See CSR PLC)

**NOISE CANCELLATION
TECHNOLOGIES INC (DE)**
Reincorporated 01/00/1987
State of incorporation changed from
(FL) to (DE) 01/00/1987
Name changed to NCT Group, Inc.
10/21/1998
(See NCT Group, Inc.)

NOISE COM INC (NJ)
Name changed to Wireless Telecom
Group, Inc. 9/12/94

NOISE MEDIA INC (BC)
Recapitalized as GFK Resources Inc.
(BC) 01/17/2008
Each share Common no par
exchanged for (0.25) share Common
no par
GFK Resources Inc. (BC)
reincorporated in Canada
07/13/2012 which name changed to
Opus One Resources Inc.
07/31/2017

NOKA RES INC (BC)
Each share old Common no par
exchanged for (0.1) share new
Common no par 12/11/2014
Name changed to Pacton Gold Inc.
04/27/2017

NOKOMIS, INC. (UT)
Name changed to Wall Street Capital
Corp. (Old) in 1992
Wall Street Capital Corp. (Old) name
changed to Silk Parade Inc. 4/8/93
which name changed to Wall Street
Capital Corp. (New) 4/8/94
(See Wall Street Capital Corp. (New))

NOLAN RES LTD (BC)
Recapitalized as Amble Resources
Ltd. 09/07/1984
Each share Common no par
exchanged for (0.33333333) share
Common no par
Amble Resources Ltd. acquired by
Valar Resources Ltd. 10/00/1986
(See Valar Resources Ltd.)

NOLAND CO (VA)
Name changed 5/10/65
Name from Noland Co., Inc. to
Noland Co. 5/10/65
Capital Stock $20 par split (4) for (3)
by issuance of (1/3) additional share
2/15/71
Capital Stock $20 par changed to $10
par and (1) additional share issued
7/7/76
Capital Stock $10 par split (3) for (2)
by issuance of (0.5) additional share
2/14/86
Merged into WinWholesale 5/19/2005
Each share Common $10 par
exchanged for $74 cash

NOLAND MINES LTD. (BC)
Recapitalized as Las Maderas Mining
& Petroleum Ltd. 7/6/71
Each share Capital Stock no par
exchanged for (0.1) share Capital
Stock no par
Las Maderas Mining & Petroleum Ltd.
struck off register and declared
dissolved 8/30/76

NOLEX CORP (CA)
Common 1¢ par split (2) for (1) by
issuance of (1) additional share
7/28/75
Merged into Hardie (James)
Industries Ltd. 4/1/86
Each share Common 1¢ par
exchanged for $5 cash

NOLIF CORP. (CA)
Liquidation completed
Each share Common 20¢ par
exchanged for initial distribution of
(0.14039) share 4% Conv. Preferred
Ser. B $100 par and (0.01706) share
Common $5 par of Standard Oil Co.
(Ohio) 3/17/66
Each share Common 20¢ par
received second distribution of $0.30
cash 4/19/66
Each share Common 20¢ par
received third distribution of $0.08
cash 2/8/67
Each share Common 20¢ par
received fourth and final distribution
of $0.051 cash 10/31/68
(See Standard Oil Co. (Ohio))

NOMA CORP (DE)
Incorporated 1/23/53
Merged into Ward Foods, Inc. 5/22/64
Each share Common $1 par
exchanged for (0.8) share Common
$1 par
(See Ward Foods, Inc.)

NOMA CORP (DE)
Incorporated 4/27/81
Charter cancelled and declared
inoperative and void for
non-payment of taxes 3/1/89

NOMA ELECTRIC CORP. (NY)
Common no par changed to $1 par in
1935
Stock Dividend - 25% 1/30/51
Name changed to Northeast Capital
Corp. in 1953
Northeast Capital Corp. merged into
Mack Trucks, Inc. 10/1/59 which
merged into Signal Oil & Gas Co.
9/1/67 which name changed to
Signal Companies, Inc. 5/1/68 which
merged into Allied-Signal Inc.
9/19/85 which name changed to
AlliedSignal Inc. 4/26/93 which
name changed to Honeywell
International Inc. 12/1/99

NOMA INDS LTD (ON)
Recapitalized 08/19/1981
Common no par reclassified as Conv.
Class A Common Special Stock no
par 06/15/1976
Conv. Class A Special no par
reclassified as Common no par
08/01/1980
Conv. Class B Special Stock no par
reclassified as Common no par
08/01/1980
Recapitalized from Noma Industries
Ltd. to Noma Industries Ltd.-
Industrial Noma Ltee. 08/19/1981
Each share Common no par
exchanged for (1.5) shares Class A
no par and (1) share Conv. Class B
no par
Class A no par split (2) for (1) by
issuance of (1) additional share
07/11/1984
Conv. Class B no par split (2) for (1)
by issuance of (1) additional share
07/11/1984
Class A no par split (2) for (1) by
issuance of (1) additional share
06/21/1985
Conv. Class B no par split (2) for (1)
by issuance of (1) additional share
06/21/1985
Class A no par split (2) for (1) by
issuance of (1) additional share
06/09/1986
Conv. Class B no par split (2) for (1)
by issuance of (1) additional share
06/09/1986
Merged into General Chemical Group
Inc. 04/06/1999
Each share Class A Common no par
exchanged for $9.25 cash
Each share Class B Common no par
exchanged for $9.25 cash

NOMA LITES, INC. (DE)
Name changed to Noma Corp.
7/24/62 which was merged into
Ward Foods, Inc. 5/22/64

(See Ward Foods, Inc.)

NOMAD ENERGY & RES LTD (BC)
Name changed 3/18/82
Name changed from Nomad Mines Ltd. to Nomad Energy & Resources Ltd. and Capital Stock 50¢ par reclassified as Common no par 3/18/82
Struck off register and declared dissolved for failure to file returns 8/14/87

NOMAD INTL INC (NV)
Recapitalized as iPackets International, Inc. 11/22/2005
Each share Common $0.0001 par exchanged for (0.02) share Common $0.0001 par

NOMAD VENTURES INC (BC)
Each share old Common no par exchanged for (0.05) share new Common no par 10/25/2016
Name changed to Bankers Cobalt Corp. 10/12/2017

NOMADIC COLLABORATION INTL INC (NV)
Each share old Common $0.001 par exchanged for (0.00666666) share new Common $0.001 par 01/23/2003
Name changed to LiquidGolf Holding Corp. (NV) 06/09/2003
LiquidGolf Holding Corp. (NV) reincorporated in Delaware 09/29/2003 which name changed to Horizon Holding Corp. 09/02/2004 which name changed to Inverted Paradigms Corp. 05/12/2006 which recapitalized as Transfer Technology International Corp. 12/07/2007 which name changed to Enviro-Serv, Inc. 04/23/2013

NOMAS CORP (CT)
Reincorporated under the laws of Nevada 3/30/99
(See Nomas Corp. (NV))

NOMAS CORP (NV)
Liquidation completed
Each share Common received first and final distribution of $0.55 cash payable 5/28/2003 to holders of record 5/22/2003 Ex date - 7/24/2003

NOMATTERWARE INC (NV)
SEC revoked common stock registration 09/28/2011

NOME-ANVIL GOLD MINING CO. (SD)
Charter expired by time limitation 01/02/1920

NOME EXPLORATION CO. (WA)
Charter revoked for failure to file reports and pay fees 7/1/23

NOME OIL INC (TX)
Name changed to EZUtilities Corp. 02/22/2001
EZUtilities Corp. name changed to Texas Commercial Resources, Inc. (TX) 09/18/2001 which reincorporated in Delaware as Petrosearch Corp. 08/28/2003 which reorganized in Nevada as Petrosearch Energy Corp. 12/31/2004 which merged into Double Eagle Petroleum Co. 08/06/2009

NOMURA CAP FD JAPAN INC (MD)
Name changed to Merrill Lynch Pacific Fund, Inc. 07/25/1980

NOMURA PAC BASIN FD INC (MD)
Common 10¢ par reclassified as Class Z 10¢ par 6/17/99
Completely liquidated 1/24/2002
Each share Class Z 10¢ par exchanged for net asset value

NOMURA SECS LTD (JAPAN)
Each old ADR for Common 50 Yen par exchanged for (2) new ADR's for Common 50 Yen par 7/25/77
Stock Dividends - 10% 12/21/72; 12% 12/27/73; 10% 12/29/76
Name changed to Nomura Holdings Inc. 10/9/2001

NON-COMMISSIONED OFFICERS LIFE INSURANCE CO. (TX)
Common no par changed to $1 par and (0.5) additional share issued 11/21/66
Merged into Citizens Insurance Co. of America 2/3/78
Each share Common $1 par exchanged for (1.2073) shares Class A Common $1 par
Citizens Insurance Co. of America merged into Citizens, Inc. 12/1/88

NON FERROUS METAL PRODUCTS LTD. (ENGLAND)
Name changed to Western Stockholders Investment Trust Ltd. 03/31/1955
Western Stockholders Investment Trust Ltd. merged into Border & Southern Stockholders Trust PLC which name changed to Govett Strategic Investment Trust PLC 01/29/1986
(See Govett Strategic Investment Trust P.L.C.)

NON-LETHAL WEAPONS INC (CA)
Reorganized under the laws of Nevada as Advanced Growing Systems, Inc. 06/22/2006
Each share Common no par exchanged for (0.0001) share Common $0.001 par
(See Advanced Growing Systems, Inc.)

NON PAR DEVS LTD (CANADA)
Reincorporated under the laws of British Columbia as Similkameen Hydro-Power Ltd. 08/17/1992
Similkameen Hydro-Power Ltd. recapitalized as Norte Resources Ltd. (BC) 07/25/1996 which reorganized in Yukon as Banks Ventures Ltd. 04/06/1998 which name changed to Banks Energy Inc. 07/26/2004 which merged into Arapahoe Energy Corp. (New) 10/20/2005 which name changed to Canadian Phoenix Resources Corp. 01/07/2008 which recapitalized as Knol Resources Corp. 03/11/2013

NONA MORELLIS II INC (CO)
Each share Common $0.001 par exchanged for (0.015) share Common 1¢ par 03/16/1992
Each share old Common 1¢ par exchanged for (0.1) share new Common 1¢ par 12/29/1993
Reincorporated under the laws of Nevada as NuOasis Resorts Inc. 01/20/1998
NuOasis Resorts Inc. recapitalized as Leonidas Films, Inc. 02/08/2006 which recapitalized as Consolidated Pictures Group, Inc. 06/09/2009
(See Consolidated Pictures Group, Inc.)

NONPAREIL MINING CO. (NV)
Charter revoked for failure to file reports and pay fees 3/3/24

NONQUITT MILLS
In process of liquidation in 1949

NONQUITT SPINNING CO.
Name changed to Nonquitt Mills in 1929 which was in process of liquidation in 1949

NOODLE KIDOODLE INC (DE)
Reincorporated 1/22/96
State of incorporation changed from (NY) to (DE) and Common 10¢ par changed to $0.001 par 1/22/96
Merged into Zany Brainy, Inc. 7/27/2000
Each share Common $0.001 par exchanged for (1.233) shares Common $0.001 par
(See Zany Brainy, Inc.)

NOONEY INCOME FD LTD L P (MO)
Merged into American Spectrum Realty, Inc. 10/19/2001
Each Unit of Limited Partnership Int. exchanged for (48.801989) shares Common 1¢ par
Each Unit of Limited Partnership Int. II exchanged for (59.163203) shares Common 1¢ par

NOONEY REAL PPTYS INVS - TWO (MO)
Merged into American Spectrum Realty, Inc. 10/19/2001
Each Unit of Limited Partnership Int. exchanged for (46.614083) shares Common 1¢ par

NOONEY RLTY TR INC (MO)
Name changed to Maxus Realty Trust Inc. 05/17/2000

NOORDUYN AVIATION, LTD.
Name changed to Nuclear Enterprises, Ltd. in 1946 which was acquired by Allied Enterprises Ltd. in 1954

NOPCO CHEMICAL CO. (NJ)
Each share Common $4 par exchanged for (2) shares Common $2 par in 1952
Common $2 par changed to $1 par and (1) additional share issued 4/24/59
4% Preferred Ser. A $100 par called for redemption 11/30/65
Stock Dividend - 10% 12/23/50
Merged into Diamond Alkali Co. 5/1/67
Each share Common $1 par exchanged for (1) share $2 Conv. Preferred Ser. C, no par
Diamond Alkali Co. merged into Diamond Shamrock Corp. 12/19/67 which name changed to Maxus Energy Corp. 4/30/87
(See Maxus Energy Corp.)

NOR ACME GOLD MINES LTD (CANADA)
Capital Stock no par changed to $1 par 00/00/1947
Capital Stock $1 par changed to no par 02/24/1971
Merged into High River Gold Mines Ltd. (Canada) 12/08/1988
Each share Capital Stock no par exchanged for (1.2) shares Common no par
High River Gold Mines Ltd. (Canada) reincorporated in Yukon 02/02/2011
(See High River Gold Mines Ltd.)

NOR CON EXPL LTD (BC)
Delisted from Vancouver Stock Exchange 03/02/1988

NOR-LAND DEV INC (ME)
Involuntarily dissolved 05/12/2006

NOR-PENN MINES, LTD. (ON)
Charter revoked for failure to file reports and pay fees 4/29/70

NOR QUEST RES LTD (BC)
Recapitalized as Western & Pacific Resources Corp. 04/22/1991
Each share Capital Stock no par exchanged for (0.1) share Common no par
Western & Pacific Resources Corp. recapitalized as Consolidated Western & Pacific Resources Corp. 07/05/1994 which name changed to Synergy Resource Technologies Inc. 07/02/1996 which recapitalized as Synergy Renewable Resources Inc. 01/09/1997
(See Synergy Renewable Resources Inc.)

NOR WEST KIM RES LTD (BC)
Struck off register and declared dissolved for failure to file returns in July 1978

NOR WESTER BREWING INC (OR)
Ceased operations 09/12/1997
Stockholders' equity unlikely

NOR'ANIUM MINERALS LTD. (SK)
Charter cancelled and struck off the register for failure to file returns 9/27/68

NORA EXPL INC (CANADA)
Name changed to Afri-Can Marine Minerals Corp. 3/24/2000

NORAC FINANCE CORP. LTD. (CANADA)
Acquired by Alliance Credit Corp. through cash purchase offer in 1964

NORAC INDS INC (AB)
Each share Common no par exchanged for (1) share Subordinate Stock no par 07/23/1990
Merged into ViRexx Medical Corp. 12/23/2003
Each share Common no par exchanged for (0.2244667) share Common no par
(See ViRexx Medical Corp.)

NORADCO MINES LTD (BC)
Struck off register and declared dissolved for failure to file returns 6/11/93

NORAH CAP CORP (AB)
Name changed to Ezenet Corp. 4/12/99
Ezenet Corp. merged into Cognicase Corp. 9/24/2001
(See Cognicase Corp.)

NORALMAC MINES LTD (CANADA)
Struck off register for failure to file annual reports 12/16/80

NORALYN PAPER MLS INC (LA)
Charter revoked for failure to file annual reports 05/13/1982

NORAM CAP HLDGS INC (DE)
SEC revoked common stock registration 09/16/2014

NORAM ENERGY CORP (DE)
Each share $3 Conv. Exchangeable Preferred Ser. A 10¢ par exchanged for $50 principal amount of 6% Conv. Subordinated Debentures due 03/15/2012 on 06/17/1996
Merged into Houston Industries Inc. 08/06/1997
Each share Common $0.625 par exchanged for either (0.74963) share Common no par or $16.3051 cash
Houston Industries Inc. name changed to Reliant Energy Inc. 02/08/1999 which reorganized as CenterPoint Energy, Inc. 08/31/2002

NORAM ENVIRONMENTAL SOLUTIONS INC (AB)
Reincorporated 02/27/1997
Place of incorporation changed from (BC) to (AB) 02/27/1997
Name changed to Alternative Fuel Systems Inc. 07/07/1997
(See Alternative Fuel Systems Inc.)

NORAM FING INC I (DE)
6.25% Trust Originated Conv. Preferred Securities called for redemption at $50 on 8/1/2005

NORAMCO, INC. (DE)
No longer in existence having become inoperative and void for non-payment of taxes 04/01/1959

NORAMCO, INC. (WI)
Adjudicated bankrupt 02/14/1967
No stockholders' equity

NORAMCO MNG CORP (BC)
Name changed to Quest Capital Corp. 01/03/1995
Quest Capital Corp. name changed to Quest Oil & Gas Inc. 11/15/1996 which merged into EnerMark Income Fund 04/18/1997 which merged into Enerplus Resources Fund 06/22/2001 which reorganized as Enerplus Corp. 01/03/2011

NORAMEX MINERALS INC (BC)
Recapitalized as Nacasa Ventures Inc. 12/29/92
Each share Common no par exchanged for (0.2) share Common no par
Nacasa Ventures Inc. name changed to Molnar Capital Corp. 8/16/93 which name changed to Star Properties Inc. 5/13/98

NORAND CORP (DE)
Merged into Western Atlas Inc. 03/05/1997
Each share Common 1¢ par exchanged for $33.50 cash

NORANDA FST INC (CANADA)
Name changed to Nexfor Inc. 12/30/98
Nexfor Inc. name changed to Norbord Inc. 7/5/2004

NORANDA INC (ON)
9-1/2% Conv. Preferred Ser. A $100 par called for redemption 09/15/1987
Floating Rate Preferred Ser. B no par called for redemption 10/15/1994
6% Conv. Preferred Ser. E $25 par called for redemption 12/15/1994
7.75% Conv. Preferred Ser. C $25 par called for redemption at $25 plus $0.163213 accrued dividends on 04/15/1998
Each share Common no par received distribution of (0.25) share Canadian Hunter Exploration Ltd. Common no par and (0.436) share Nexfor Inc. Common no par payable 01/08/1999 to holders of record 12/30/1998
Due to partial redemption each share old Jr. Preference Ser. 1 exchanged for new Jr. Preference Ser. 1 on a pro rata basis and US$25.25 per redeemed share 08/11/2005 for holders of record 07/01/2005
Due to partial redemption each share old Jr. Preference Ser. 2 exchanged for new Jr. Preference Ser. 2 on a pro rata basis and US$25.25 per redeemed share 08/11/2005 for holders of record 07/01/2005
Due to partial redemption each share old Jr. Preference Ser. 3 exchanged for new Jr. Preference Ser. 3 on a pro rata basis and US$25.25 per redeemed share 08/11/2005 for holders of record 07/01/2005
Name changed to Falconbridge Ltd. (New) 2005 on 07/01/2005
(See Falconbridge Ltd. (New) 2005)

NORANDA MINES LTD. (ON)
Capital Stock no par split (2) for (1) by issuance of (1) additional share 06/02/1955
Capital Stock no par split (2) for (1) by issuance of (1) additional share 06/20/1962
Capital Stock no par split (2) for (1) by issuance of (1) additional share 12/28/1968
Capital Stock no par reclassified as Conv. Class A no par 08/03/1973
Conv. Class A no par reclassified as Common no par 06/01/1979
Conv. Class B no par reclassified as Common no par 06/01/1979
Common no par split (3) for (1) by issuance of (2) additional shares 09/13/1979
8-1/2% Conv. Preferred Ser. A $100 par reclassified as 9-1/2% Conv. Preferred Ser. A $100 par 11/18/1981
Name changed to Noranda Inc. 05/28/1984
Noranda Inc. name changed to Falconbridge Ltd. (New) 2005 on 07/01/2005
(See Falconbridge Ltd. (New) 2005)

NORANDA OIL CORP (NJ)
Merged into Frontier Oil & Gas Co., Inc. 12/31/1970
Each share Common $1 par exchanged for $0.43 cash

NORART MINERALS LTD. (ON)
Merged into Angelus Petroleums (1965) Ltd. 7/8/67
Each share Capital Stock $1 par exchanged for (0.1) share Capital Stock no par
Angelus Petroleums (1965) Ltd. dissolved 11/28/78

NORART URANIUM & GOLD MINES LTD. (ON)
Name changed to Norart Minerals Ltd. in 1959
Norart Minerals Ltd. merged into Angelus Petroleums (1965) Ltd. 7/8/67 which dissolved 11/28/78

NORAVENA CAP CORP (CANADA)
Recapitalized as 3MV Energy Corp. 02/07/2012
Each share Common no par exchanged for (0.1) share Common no par
(See 3MV Energy Corp.)

NORBANK EXPLORATIONS LTD. (ON)
Charter dissolved 12/16/1970

NORBASKA MINES LTD (SK)
Merged into Dore-Norbaska Resources Inc. 12/23/1987
Each share Capital Stock no par exchanged for (3.5) shares Common no par
Dore-Norbaska Resources Inc. merged into Griffin Corp. 02/23/1998
(See Griffin Corp.)

NORBEAU MINES INC (ON)
Acquired by WMC Acquisition Corp. 06/03/1988
Each share Common no par exchanged for $0.22 cash

NORBEAU MINES LTD (QC)
Completely liquidated 01/08/1971
Each share Capital Stock $1 par exchanged for first and final distribution (0.08333333) share Lake Shore Mines, Ltd. Capital Stock $1 par
Lake Shore Mines, Ltd. merged into LAC Minerals Ltd. (New) 07/29/1985 which was acquired by American Barrick Resources Corp. 10/17/1994 which name changed to Barrick Gold Corp. 01/18/1995

NORBEC COPPER MINES LTD. (CANADA)
Merged into Lake Dufault Mines Ltd. 03/15/1955
Each share Capital Stock no par exchanged for (0.2) share Capital Stock $1 par
Lake Dufault Mines Ltd. merged into Falconbribge Copper Ltd. 12/16/1971 which name changed to Corporation Falconbridge Copper 07/09/1980 which name changed to Minnova Inc. 05/26/1987 which merged into Metall Mining Corp. 05/05/1993 which name changed to Inmet Mining Corp. 05/04/1995 which was acquired by First Quantum Minerals Ltd. 04/09/2013

NORBENITE MALARTIC MINES LTD.
Recapitalized as Norlartic Mines Ltd. 00/00/1949
Each share Capital Stock $1 par exchanged for (0.25) share Capital Stock $1 par
Norlartic Mines Ltd. merged into Willroy Mines Ltd. 05/31/1966 which merged into Lac Minerals Ltd. (Old) 12/31/1982 which merged into LAC Minerals Ltd. (New) 07/29/1985 which was acquired by American Barrick Resources Corp. 10/17/1994 which name changed to Barrick Gold Corp. 01/18/1995

NORBERT ACQUISITION CORP (CO)
Charter suspended for failure to file annual reports 08/01/1991

NORBERT SILVER MINES LTD. (ON)
Charter cancelled 2/18/52

NORBORD INC (CANADA)
Class A Preferred Ser. I no par called for redemption at $25 plus $0.146 accrued dividends on 5/20/2005
(Additional Information in Active)

NORBUTE CORP. (MN)
Capital Stock $2.50 par changed to 50¢ par 8/17/64
Acquired by Crescent Petroleum Corp. 8/6/58
Each share Common 50¢ par exchanged for (0.2) share 5% Preferred $25 par and (0.05) share Common $1 par
Crescent Petroleum Corp. name changed to Crescent Corp. 12/16/63 which merged into National Industries, Inc. (KY) 7/1/68 which merged into Fuqua Industries, Inc. 1/3/78 which name changed to Actava Group Inc. 7/21/93 which name changed to Metromedia International Group, Inc. 11/1/95

NORCAL CMNTY BANCORP (CA)
Common no par split (3) for (2) by issuance of (0.5) additional share payable 12/01/2003 to holders of record 11/05/2003 Ex date - 12/02/2003
Common no par split (3) for (2) by issuance of (0.5) additional share payable 12/07/2006 to holders of record 11/22/2006 Ex date - 12/08/2006
Acquired by Bank of Marin Bancorp 11/29/2013
Each share Common no par exchanged for $3.01 cash

NORCAL RES LTD (BC)
Recapitalized as Troon Ventures Ltd. (BC) 06/18/2002
Each share Common no par exchanged for (0.2) share Common no par
Troon Ventures Ltd. (BC) reorganized in Ontario as Grenville Strategic Royalty Corp. 02/21/2014 which merged into LOGiQ Asset Management Inc. (AB) 06/07/2018 which reorganized in British Columbia as Flow Capital Corp. 06/11/2018

NORCAN MINES LTD (BC)
Recapitalized as Accent Resources Ltd. 12/05/1972
Each share Capital Stock 50¢ par exchanged for (0.2) share Capital Stock 50¢ par
Accent Resources Ltd. recapitalized as Midas Resources Ltd. 03/10/1975 which recapitalized as Continental Silver Corp. 03/14/1977 which merged into Arizona Silver Corp. 08/01/1985 which recapitalized as ASC Industries Ltd. 06/06/1995 which name changed to Acero-Martin Exploration Inc. 11/24/2004 which name changed to AM Gold Inc. 06/08/2010
(See AM Gold Inc.)

NORCAN OILS LTD. (AB)
Merged into Gridoil Freehold Leases Ltd. 02/18/1963
Each share Common exchanged for (9) shares Common
Gridoil Freehold Leases Ltd. merged into Canadian Gridoil Ltd. 02/18/1966 which merged into Ashland Oil Canada Ltd. 09/14/1970 which name changed to Kaiser Petroleum Ltd. 03/23/1979
(See Kaiser Petroleum Ltd.)

NORCAN RES LTD (BC)
Recapitalized as Odyssey Exploration Inc. 06/07/2000
Each share Common no par exchanged for (0.2) share Common no par
Odyssey Exploration Inc. recapitalized as Consolidated Odyssey Exploration Inc. 12/08/2000 which reorganized as Odyssey Petroleum Corp. 08/25/2005 which recapitalized as Petrichor Energy Inc. 03/03/2011

NORCAP INC (CO)
Each (45) shares old Common no par exchanged for (1) share new Common no par 05/04/1989
Filed a petition under Chapter 11 Federal Bankruptcy Code 08/09/1989
Stockholders' equity unlikely

NORCAST INCOME FD (ON)
Acquired by Pala Investments Holdings Ltd. 3/27/2007
Each Unit no par received $9.30 cash

NORCEN ENERGY RES LTD (CANADA)
Reincorporated 04/15/1977
Place of incorporation changed from (ALTA) to (Canada) 04/15/1977
$1.50 1st Preference Ser. B $25 par conversion privilege expired 08/15/1977
$1.50 Conv. Jr. Preference 1st Ser. $50 par called for redemption 09/30/1979
$2.88 Conv. Jr. Preference 1979 Ser. $50 par called for redemption 09/01/1983
Common no par reclassified as Conv. Ordinary Stock no par 11/04/1983
Each share Conv. Ordinary Stock no par received distribution of (1) share Non-Vtg. Ordinary Stock no par 11/09/1983
7-3/4% Conv. Jr. Preference 1983 Ser. no par called for redemption 09/01/1987
$1.06 1st Preference Ser. A $25 par called for redemption 02/01/1988
$1.50 1st Preference Ser. B $25 par called for redemption 02/15/1988
8.12% 2nd Preference Ser. A no par reclassified as 8.12% 1st Preference Ser. A no par 04/25/1988
Conv. Ordinary no par reclassified as Multiple Ordinary no par 04/25/1988
Non-Vtg. Ordinary no par reclassified as Subordinate Ordinary no par 04/25/1988
Multiple Ordinary no par reclassified as Common no par 05/07/1993
Subordinate Ordinary no par reclassified as Common no par 05/07/1993
8.12% 1st Preference Ser. A no par called for redemption 03/31/1995
Common no par split (2) for (1) by issuance of (1) additional share payable 12/05/1997 to holders of record 12/01/1997
Merged into Union Pacific Resources Group Inc. 04/17/1998
Each share Common no par exchanged for $19.80 cash

NORCEN PIPELINES LTD. (MB)
Merged into Norcen Resources Ltd. 02/27/1981
Each share Common no par exchanged for $70 cash

NORCO CAP INC (QC)
Name changed to Nuvolt Corp. Inc. 08/31/2007

NORCO OIL CORP (MN)
Adjudicated bankrupt 09/23/1975
Stockholders' equity unlikely

NORCO RES LTD (BC)
Struck off register and declared dissolved for failure to file returns 6/15/90

NORCOLD, INC. (CA)
Liquidated 1/8/64

NORCRAFT COS INC (DE)
Acquired by Fortune Brands Home & Security, Inc. 05/12/2015
Each share Common 1¢ par exchanged for $25.50 cash

NORCROWN BK ROSELAND (ROSELAND, NJ)
Merged into Norcrown Bank Acquisition 6/18/96
Each share Common $2 par exchanged for $2.1913 cash

NORD ANGLIA ED INC (CAYMAN ISLANDS)
Acquired by Bach Finance Ltd. 09/01/2017
Each share Ordinary 1¢ par exchanged for $32.50 cash

NORD BUSINESS MACHINES CORP. (NY)
Merged into Meljan Industries, Inc. 07/25/1967
Each share Common 10¢ par exchanged for (1) share Common 10¢ par
(See Meljan Industries, Inc.)

NORD OIL INTL INC (FL)
Name changed to North West Oil Group, Inc. 11/16/2006

NORD PAC LTD (BERMUDA)
Common 5¢ par split (8) for (1) by issuance of (7) additional shares 02/16/1994
Each share Common 5¢ par exchanged for (0.2) Sponsored ADR for Common 5¢ par 03/10/1997
ADR agreement terminated 06/10/1997
ADR's for Common 5¢ par reclassified as Common 5¢ par
Reincorporated under the laws of New Brunswick 09/30/1998
Nord Pacific Ltd. (NB) merged into Allied Gold Ltd. (Australia) 09/20/2004 which reorganized in England and Wales as Allied Gold Mining PLC 06/30/2011
(See Allied Gold Mining PLC)

NORD PAC LTD (NB)
Merged into Allied Gold Ltd. (Australia) 09/20/2004
Each share Common 5¢ par exchanged for (1) share Ordinary Allied Gold Ltd. (Australia) reorganized in England and Wales as Allied Gold Mining PLC 06/30/2011
(See Allied Gold Mining PLC)

NORD PHOTOCOPY & BUSINESS EQUIPMENT CORP. (NY)
Name changed to Nord Photocopy & Electronics Corp. 09/28/1960
Nord Photocopy & Electronics Corp. name changed to Nord Business Machines Corp. 10/18/1962 which merged into Meljan Industries, Inc. 07/25/1967
(See Meljan Industries, Inc.)

NORD PHOTOCOPY & ELECTRONICS CORP. (NY)
Name changed to Nord Business Machines Corp. 10/18/1962
Nord Business Machines Corp. merged into Meljan Industries, Inc. 07/25/1967
(See Meljan Industries, Inc.)

NORDAC MNG CORP (BC)
Recapitalized as Big Creek Resources Ltd. 11/06/1987
Each share Common no par exchanged for (0.4) share Common no par
Big Creek Resources Ltd. merged into Pacific Sentinel Gold Corp. 12/01/1992 which merged into Great Basin Gold Ltd. 12/18/1997
(See Great Basin Gold Ltd.)

NORDAC RES LTD (BC)
Recapitalized as Strategic Metals Ltd. (Old) 06/22/2001
Each share Common no par exchanged for (0.25) share Common no par
Strategic Metals Ltd. (Old) reorganized as Strategic Metals Ltd. (New) 06/15/2017

NORDAIR LTD (CANADA)
Recapitalized 01/01/1985
Common no par reclassified as Conv. Class A Common no par 12/16/1976
Recapitalized from Nordair Ltd.-Nordair Ltee. to Nordair Inc. 01/01/1985
Each share Conv. Class A Common no par exchanged for (1.8888885) shares Common no par
Each share Conv. Class B Common no par exchanged for (1.8888885) shares Common no par
Public interest eliminated through exchange offer which expired 07/31/1986

NORDARM LONG LAC MINES LTD. (ON)
Charter cancelled for failure to pay taxes and file returns 8/9/72

NORDCO CORP. (WA)
Merged into International-United Corp. 4/1/70
Each share Common no par exchanged for (0.125) share Common 10¢ par
International-United Corp. adjudicated bankrupt 9/13/71

NORDEA BK AB (SWEDEN)
Unsponsored ADR's for Ordinary reclassified as Sponsored ADR's for Ordinary 01/19/2011
Merged into Nordea Bank Abp 10/01/2018
Each Sponsored ADR for Ordinary exchanged for (1) Sponsored ADR for Ordinary

NORDEAU MINING CO. LTD. (ON)
Acquired by Vauquelin Iron Mines Ltd. 10/8/63
Each share Capital Stock $1 par exchanged for (1/3) share Common no par
Vauquelin Iron Mines Ltd. name changed to Vauquelin Mines Ltd. in 1964 which name changed to Bridgepoint International Inc. 12/2/99 which was acquired by Afcan Mining Corp. 11/3/2003 which merged into Eldorado Gold Corp. (New) 9/13/2005

NORDEN-KETAY CORP. (IL)
Merged into United Aircraft Corp. on a (0.05) for (1) basis 7/1/58
United Aircraft Corp. name changed to United Technologies Corp. 4/30/75

NORDEN LABORATORIES (NE)
Acquired by Smith Kline & French Laboratories 1/12/60
Each share Common $25 par exchanged for (3.5) shares Common no par
Smith Kline & French Laboratories name changed to SmithKline Corp. 7/1/73 which name changed to SmithKline Beckman Corp. 3/4/82 which merged into SmithKline Beecham p.l.c. 7/26/89 which merged into GlaxoSmithKline PLC 12/27/2000

NORDEN LABORATORIES CORP. (CT)
Merged into Ketay Instrument Corp. on 2/4/55
Each (4) shares Common $1 par exchanged for (1) share Common 10¢ par
Each (2.7) shares Class B $1 par exchanged for (1) share Common 10¢ par
Name changed to Norden-Ketay Corp. 2/11/55
Norden-Ketay Corp. merged into United Aircraft Corp. 7/1/58 which name changed to United Technologies Corp. 4/30/75

NORDEV MINES LTD. (ON)
Merged into Nordev Resources Ltd. 03/24/1972
Each share Capital Stock $1 par exchanged for (0.2) share Common no par
Nordev Resources Ltd. recapitalized as Vedron Ltd. 06/05/1979 which recapitalized as Vedron Gold Inc. 01/04/1995 which name changed to VG Gold Corp. 08/07/2007 which merged into Lexam VG Gold Inc. 01/04/2011 which merged into McEwen Mining Inc. 05/01/2017

NORDEV RES LTD (ON)
Recapitalized as Vedron Ltd. 06/05/1979
Each share Common no par exchanged for (0.33333333) share Common no par
Vedron Ltd. recapitalized as Vedron Gold Inc. 01/04/1995 which name changed to VG Gold Corp. 08/07/2007 which merged into Lexam VG Gold Inc. 01/04/2011 which merged into McEwen Mining Inc. 05/01/2017

NORDEX EXPLOSIVES LTD (QC)
Acquired by Societe Anonyme d'Explosifs et de Produit Chimiques 08/25/2016
Each share Common no par exchanged for $0.25 cash

NORDIC AMERN INC (NV)
Each share old Common no par exchanged for (0.05) share new Common no par 01/26/2006
Reorganized under the laws of Delaware as Stark Beneficial, Inc. 02/08/2008
Each share Common no par exchanged for (0.05) share Common no par
Stark Beneficial, Inc. name changed to China Greenstar Corp. 01/22/2015

NORDIC AMERICAN OFFSHORE LTD (MARSHALL ISLANDS)
Reincorporated under the laws of Bermuda 09/27/2016

NORDIC AMERICAN TANKER SHIPPING LTD (BERMUDA)
Name changed to Nordic American Tankers Ltd. 07/06/2011

NORDIC DIAMONDS LTD (BC)
Recapitalized as Western Standard Metals Ltd. 06/12/2009
Each share Common no par exchanged for (0.1) share Common no par
Western Standard Metals Ltd. merged into Terraco Gold Corp. (AB) 01/25/2011 which reincorporated in British Columbia 06/08/2011

NORDIC EQUITY PARTNERS CORP (DE)
Charter cancelled and declared inoperative and void for non-payment of taxes 3/1/2001

NORDIC EXPLORATIONS LTD. (ON)
Name changed to Nordic Mines & Investments Ltd. 12/24/1968
Nordic Mines & Investments Ltd. recapitalized as Nordic Industries Ltd. 06/03/1969
(See Nordic Industries Ltd.)

NORDIC GOLD CORP (BC)
Name changed to Compass Gold Corp. (BC) 10/03/2008
Compass Gold Corp. (BC) reincorporated in Ontario 12/04/2017

NORDIC HOMES INC (MN)
Reported out of business 00/00/1974
No stockholders' equity

NORDIC INDS LTD (ON)
Recapitalized 06/03/1969
Recapitalized from Nordic Mines & Investments Ltd. to Nordic Industries Ltd. 06/03/1969
Each share Capital Stock $1 par exchanged for (1/3) share Capital Stock no par

Charter cancelled for failure to pay taxes and file returns 03/14/1978

NORDIC LTD INC (NV)
Reorganized 9/24/84
Reorganized from under the laws of (UT) to (NV) 9/24/84
Each share Common 1¢ par exchanged for (0.025) share Common 1¢ par
Charter revoked for failure to file reports and pay fees 6/1/2001

NORDIC NICKEL LTD (NV)
Name changed to Constitution Mining Corp. (NV) 11/15/2007
Constitution Mining Corp. (NV) reincorporated in Delaware 10/21/2009 which name changed to Goldsands Development Co. 04/01/2011

NORDIC TURBINES INC (NV)
Name changed to GC China Turbine Corp. 09/14/2009

NORDION INC (ON)
Acquired by Sterigenics International LLC 08/06/2014
Each share Common no par exchanged for $13 cash
Note: Unexchanged certificates will be cancelled and become without value 08/06/2020

NORDIX CORP. (TX)
Acquired by Certain-Teed Products Corp. 5/11/71
(See Certain-Teed Products Corp.)

NORDON CORP. LTD. (CANADA)
Acquired by Nordon Corp. Ltd. (DE) 00/00/1930
Details not available

NORDON LTD (DE)
Common $5 par changed to $1 par 00/00/1937
Each share Common $1 par exchanged for (0.1) share Common no par 07/05/1962
Common no par changed to 25¢ par 09/30/1963
Each share Common 25¢ par exchanged for (0.2) share Common $1.25 par 01/27/1967
Name changed to Texas International Petroleum Corp. and Common $1.25 par changed to 10¢ par 02/11/1969
Texas International Petroleum Corp. name changed to Texas International Co. 01/03/1972 which reorganized as Phoenix Resource Companies, Inc. 04/09/1990 which merged into Apache Corp. 05/20/1996

NORDSTROM BEST, INC. (WA)
Name changed to Nordstrom, Inc. 5/24/73

NORDTECH AEROSPACE INC (CANADA)
Name changed to ExelTech Aerospace Inc. 04/19/2005
(See ExelTech Aerospace Inc.)

NOREAGLE URANIUM MINES LTD. (ON)
Charter revoked for failure to file reports and pay fees 8/3/64

NOREL ELECTRS INDS INC (NY)
Name changed to Norelcom Industries, Inc. 11/17/1970
Norelcom Industries, Inc. name changed to Tri-Delta Corp. 12/23/1986
(See Tri-Delta Corp.)

NORELCOM INDS INC (NY)
Name changed to Tri-Delta Corp. 12/23/1986
(See Tri-Delta Corp.)

NOREX EXPL SVCS INC (AB)
Recapitalized as Tesla Exploration Ltd. 04/22/2010
Each share Common no par exchanged for (0.125) share Common no par

NOREX INDS INC (CAYMAN ISLANDS)
Name changed 07/23/1996
Name changed from Norex America, Inc. to Norex Industries Inc. 07/23/1996
Common $1 par changed to 25¢ par and (3) additional shares issued payable 06/20/1997 to holders of record 06/10/1997 Ex date - 06/23/1997
Name changed to Siem Industries Inc. 06/01/1998

NOREX MINES LTD. (ON)
Charter revoked for failure to file reports and pay fees 9/24/56

NOREX RES CORP (BC)
Name changed 05/29/1970
Name changed from Norex Uranium Ltd. to Norex Resources Ltd. 05/29/1970
Recapitalized as Consolidated Norex Resources Corp. 09/19/1983
Each share new Common no par exchanged for (0.125) share Common no par
Consolidated Norex Resources Corp. acquired by Morgan Hydrocarbons Inc. 05/15/1992 which was acquired by Stampeder Exploration Ltd. 10/15/1996 which was acquired by Gulf Canada Resources Ltd. 09/10/1997
(See Gulf Canada Resources Ltd.)

NORFAULT MINES, LTD. (ON)
Merged into Alchib Developments Ltd. 07/10/1969
Each share Capital Stock $1 par exchanged for (0.13) share Capital Stock no par
Alchib Developments Ltd. merged into Kalrock Developments Ltd. 10/23/1978 which merged into Kalrock Resources Ltd. 08/08/1990 which merged into Cercal Minerals Corp. 07/09/1993
(See Cercal Minerals Corp.)

NORFIN BUSINESS ADVISORS CORP (CANADA)
Name changed to Gopher Media Services Corp. 05/30/2003
(See Gopher Media Services Corp.)

NORFOLK & CAROLINA TEL & TELEG CO (NC)
Common $100 par and Class B Non-Vtg. Common $100 par changed to $20 par and (4) additional shares issued respectively 05/01/1974
Merged into Norfolk Carolina Telephone Co. 08/24/1976
Each share 6% Preferred Ser. A $100 par exchanged for (1) share 6% Preferred $100 par
Each share 6% Preferred Ser. B $100 par exchanged for (1) share 6% Preferred $100 par
Each share Common $20 par exchanged for (2) shares Common $1 par
Each share Class B Non-Vtg. Common $20 par exchanged for (2) shares Common $1 par
(See Norfolk Carolina Telephone Co.)

NORFOLK & WASHINGTON STEAMBOAT CO.
Dissolved in 1948

NORFOLK & WESTN RY CO (VA)
Each share 4% Adjusted Non-Cum. Preferred $100 par exchanged for (4) shares 4% Adjusted Non-Cum. Preferred $25 par 09/03/1947
Each share Common $100 par exchanged for (4) shares Common $25 par 09/03/1947
Recapitalized 11/15/1965
Each share 4% Adjusted Non-Cum. Preferred $25 par exchanged for $25 cash or $25 principal amount of 4.85% Debentures due 11/15/2015.
Option to receive Debentures expired 12/31/1965
Each share 6% Preferred $10 par exchanged for $15 cash or $15 principal amount of 4.85% Debentures due 11/15/2015. Option to receive Debentures expired 12/31/1965
Common $25 par changed to $8.33-1/3 par and (2) additional shares issued 10/26/1976
Merged into Norfolk Southern Corp. 06/01/1982
Each share Common $8.33-1/3 par exchanged for (1) share Common $1 par

NORFOLK CAROLINA TEL CO (VA)
Merged into United Telecommunications, Inc. 04/26/1978
Each share Common $1 par exchanged for (1.1) shares Common $2.50 par
6% Preferred Ser. A $100 par called for redemption 00/00/1979
Public interest eliminated

NORFOLK CNTY TR CO (DEDHAM, MA)
Name changed 00/00/1975
Stock Dividends - 25% 10/31/1955; (3) for (22) 02/10/1961; 25% 12/15/1964; 49-1/4% 02/24/1967; 100% 05/01/1972
Name changed from Norfolk County Trust Co. (Brookline, MA) to Norfolk County Trust Co. (Dedham, MA) 00/00/1975
Name changed to Baybank Norfolk County Trust Co. (Dedham, MA) 02/03/1976
(See Baybank Norfolk County Trust Co. (Dedham, MA))

NORFOLK INVESTMENT LTD. (UT)
Recapitalized as Merchants International Corp. 3/27/81
Each share Common $0.001 par exchanged for (0.1) share Common 1¢ par
Merchants International Corp. recapitalized as In-Tec International (U.S.A.), Inc. 6/18/84 which reincorporated in Delaware as Seed Products International, Inc. 6/25/87

NORFOLK PETE LTD (BC)
Recapitalized as International Norfolk Industries Ltd. 03/17/1993
Each share Common no par exchanged for (0.1) share Common no par
International Norfolk Industries Ltd. merged into Ventures Resources Corp. 11/20/1996 which merged into BrazMin Corp. 04/06/2005 which name changed to Talon Metals Corp. 07/09/2007

NORFOLK-PORTSMOUTH BRIDGE, INC.
Taken over by South Norfolk Bridge Commission, Inc. in 1944

NORFOLK-PORTSMOUTH BRIDGE CORP.
Reorganized as Norfolk-Portsmouth Bridge, Inc. in 1933 which was taken over by South Norfolk Bridge Commission, Inc. in 1944

NORFOLK RAILWAY & LIGHT CO.
Merged into Virginia Electric & Power Co. 00/00/1927
Details not available

NORFOLK SOUTHERN RAILROAD CO. (VA)
Reorganized as Norfolk Southern Railway Co. 1/21/42. Stockholders received 3-yr. Common Stock Purchase Warrants

NORFOLK SOUTHN RY CO (VA)
Common no par split (2) for (1) by issuance of (1) additional share 11/20/52
Common no par changed to $1 par 7/25/58
Merged into Southern Railway Co. 1/1/74
Each share Common $1 par exchanged for (0.7) share $3 3-Yr. Conv. Preference Ser A no par
Southern Railway Co. name changed to Norfolk Southern Railway Co. 12/31/90

NORFOLK SOUTHN RY CO (VA)
$2.60 Preferred Ser. A no par called for redemption at $50 plus $0.2066 accrued dividend on 12/29/2003
Name changed to Southern Railway Co. Mobile & Ohio RR Co. 09/09/2014

NORFORD PERSHING MINES, LTD. (ON)
Charter cancelled by the Province of Ontario for default 11/27/61

NORGOLD ENERGY & MINES LTD (CANADA)
Reorganized 03/30/1981
Reorganized from Norgold Mines Ltd. (ONT) to Norgold Energy & Mines Ltd. (Canada) 03/30/1981
Each share Capital Stock $1 par exchanged for (0.2) share Common no par
Reincorporated under the laws of Ontario Multi Choice Communications Inc. 04/14/1986
(See Multi Choice Communications Inc.)

NORGOLD RES INC (BC)
Acquired by Bema Gold Corp. (BC) 4/8/91
Each share Common no par exchanged for (0.4) share Common no par
Bema Gold Corp. (BC) reincorporated in (Canada) 7/19/2002 which merged into Kinross Gold Corp. 2/27/2007

NORHACK-ROUYN MINES LTD. (ON)
Charter cancelled and company declared dissolved by default 8/18/58

NORI AQUAFOOD SYS INC (BC)
Recapitalized as Royale Nori Foods Inc. 03/16/1990
Each share Common no par exchanged for (0.33333333) share Common no par
Royale Nori Foods Inc. name changed to Agrotech Greenhouses Inc. 11/05/1997 which recapitalized as Archer Petroleum Corp. 04/30/2010 which name changed to Atlas Engineered Products Ltd. 11/09/2017

NORILSK NICKEL (RUSSIA)
Name changed to JSC MMC Norilsk Nickel 10/05/2001
JSC MMC Norilsk Nickel name changed to MMC Norilsk Nickel PJSC 09/18/2015

NORIN CORP (FL)
Reorganized 05/31/1979
Stock Dividends - 10% 07/21/1977; 10% 07/07/1978
Reorganized from Delaware to under the laws of Florida 05/31/1979
Each share Common $1 par exchanged for (1) share Common $1 par
Note: Holdings of (35) shares or fewer received $10.725 cash per share
Merged into Canadian Pacific Enterprises Ltd. 07/10/1980
Each share $1.50 Preferred $1 par exchanged for $16.75 cash plus accrued dividends
Each share Common $1 par exchanged for $32 cash

NORITE EXPLORATIONS LTD. (ON)
Merged into Alchib Developments Ltd. 07/10/1969
Each share Capital Stock $1 par exchanged for (0.07) share Capital Stock no par
Alchib Developments Ltd. merged into Kalrock Developments Ltd. 10/23/1978 which merged into Kalrock Resources Ltd. 08/08/1990 which merged into Cercal Minerals Corp. 07/09/1993
(See Cercal Minerals Corp.)

NORLANA RES LTD (AB)
Recapitalized 12/2/97
Recapitalized from Norlana Energy Inc. to Norlana Resources Ltd. 12/2/97
Each share Common no par exchanged for (0.1) share Common no par
Delisted from Alberta Stock Exchange 5/4/98

NORLAND MED SYS INC (DE)
Common $0.0005 par split (3) for (2) by issuance of (0.5) additional share payable 6/14/96 to holders of record 6/13/96
Name changed to Orthometrix, Inc. 4/11/2002

NORLARTIC MINES LTD. (ON)
Merged into Willroy Mines Ltd. 05/31/1966
Each share Capital Stock $1 par exchanged for (0.05) share Capital Stock no par
Willroy Mines Ltd. merged into Lac Minerals Ltd. (Old) 12/31/1982 which merged into LAC Minerals Ltd. (New) 07/29/1985 which was acquired by American Barrick Resources Corp. 10/17/1994 which name changed to Barrick Gold Corp. 01/18/1995

NORLEX MINES LTD (ON)
Capital Stock $1 par changed to no par 12/8/71
Recapitalized as NLX Resources Inc. 10/7/87
Each share Capital Stock no par exchanged for (1/3) share Common no par
(See NLX Resources Inc.)

NORLIN CORP (PANAMA)
Name changed to Service Resources Corp. (Panama) 03/06/1986
Service Resources Corp. (Panama) reorganized in Delaware as Ameriscribe Corp. 07/24/1990 which merged into Pitney Bowes Inc. 10/29/1993

NORMA-HOFFMANN BEARINGS CORP. (NY)
Merged into Universal American Corp. for cash 12/31/62

NORMA INDUSTRIES, INC. (DE)
Name changed to Gal Friday Services, Inc. 5/12/68
Gal Friday Services, Inc. was adjudicated bankrupt 2/1/71

NORMABEC MNG RES LTD (QC)
Merged into First Majestic Silver Corp. 11/13/2009
Each share Common no par exchanged for (0.060425) share Common no par and (0.25) share Brionor Resources Inc. Common no par
(See each company's listing)

NORMALLOY EXPLORATIONS LTD. (ON)
Name changed to Normalloy Explorations & Holdings Ltd. 08/23/1963
(See Normalloy Explorations & Holdings Ltd.)

NORMALLOY EXPLS & HLDGS LTD (ON)
Charter cancelled for failure to pay taxes and file returns 02/26/1980

NORMAN, INC. TRUST
Trust terminated in 1941

NOR-NOR   FINANCIAL INFORMATION, INC.

Details not available

NORMAN BILL INTL INC (AR)
Charter revoked for failure to pay taxes 12/19/1991

NORMAN CAY DEV INC (NV)
Common $0.001 par split (15) for (1) by issuance of (14) additional shares payable 01/19/2011 to holders of record 01/19/2011
Name changed to Discovery Gold Corp. 07/16/2012

NORMAN RES LTD (BC)
Recapitalized as Golden Ring Resources Ltd. 04/05/1989
Each share Common no par exchanged for (0.2) share Common no par
Golden Ring Resources Ltd. recapitalized as Golden Gate Resources Ltd. 06/06/1994 which was acquired by Golden Gate Petroleum Ltd. 06/30/2003

NORMANCO GOLD MINES, LTD. (ON)
Charter cancelled and declared dissolved for failure to file returns 10/24/55

NORMANDIE NATIONAL SECURITES CORP.
Liquidated in 1940

NORMANDIE RESOURCE CORP (AB)
Each share Common no par exchanged for (0.5) share Class A no par 12/5/85
Merged into Argyll Energy Corp. 8/25/89
Each share Class A no par exchanged for $0.10 cash

NORMANDY MNG LTD (AUSTRALIA)
Each old Sponsored ADR for Ordinary A$0.20 par exchanged for (0.5) new Sponsored ADR for Ordinary A$0.20 par 11/24/1997
Acquired by Newmont Mining Corp. 06/26/2002
Each new Sponsored ADR for Ordinary A$0.20 par exchanged for (0.385) share Common $1.60 par and $5 cash

NORMANDY MT LEYSHON LTD (AUSTRALIA)
Name changed to Leyshon Resources Ltd. 12/05/2001
(See Leyshon Resources Ltd.)

NORMANDY OIL & GAS CO (NY)
Each share Common 1¢ par exchanged for (0.1) share Common 10¢ par 5/21/87
Reorganized under the laws of Delaware as Producers Pipeline Corp. 6/30/94
Each share Common 10¢ par exchanged for (0.01) share Class A $0.001 par

NORMANDY POSEIDON LTD (AUSTRALIA)
Name changed 06/05/1991
Under plan of merger name changed from Normandy Resources N.L. to Normandy Poseidon Ltd. 06/05/1991
Name changed to Normandy Mining Ltd. 06/20/1995
Normandy Mining Ltd. acquired by Newmont Mining Corp. 06/26/2002

NORMANDY PRODUCTIONS, INC. (NV)
Charter revoked for failure to file reports and pay fees 3/4/57

NORMANS SPORTING AIDS, INC. (DE)
Charter forfeited for failure to maintain a registered agent 2/25/98

NORMAR CORP (MN)
Chapter 11 Federal Bankruptcy Code converted to Chapter 7 on 12/22/86
Stockholders' equity unlikely

NORMAR GOLD MINES LTD (ON)
Charter cancelled for failure to file returns and pay fees 02/05/1980

NORMAR MINES LTD.
Succeeded by Normar Gold Mines Ltd. share for share in 1944

NORMETAL MNG LTD (CANADA)
Acquired by Kerr Addison Mines Ltd. 5/3/68
Each share Capital Stock no par exchanged for (0.3) share Capital Stock no par
Kerr Addison Mines Ltd. merged into Noranda Inc. 4/11/96 which name changed to Falconbridge Ltd. (New) 2005 on 7/1/2005
(See Falconbridge Ltd. (New) 2005)

NORMEX TECHNOLOGIES CORP (ON)
Recapitalized as Cygnal Technologies Corp. 04/07/1998
Each share Common no par exchanged for (0.025) share Common no par
(See Cygnal Technologies Corp.)

NORMEXSTEEL INC (FL)
Each share old Common no par exchanged for (0.002) share new Common no par 09/14/2005
Each share new Common no par exchanged again for (500) shares new Common no par 10/21/2005
Recapitalized as BioChem Solutions Inc. 07/07/2006
Each share new Common no par exchanged for (0.0001) share Common no par
BioChem Solutions Inc. name changed to Balmoral FX Systems Inc. 07/29/2010 which recapitalized as Amalgamated Gold & Silver, Inc. 08/01/2012 which recapitalized as Rainforest Resources Inc. 03/15/2016

NORMICK PERRON INC (QC)
Each share Common no par exchanged for (1.5) shares Class A Subordinate no par and (1.5) shares Conv. Class B no par 07/15/1986
Acquired by NPI Acquisition Inc. 10/13/1989
Each share Class A Subordinate no par exchanged for $7.63 cash
Each share Conv. Class B no par exchanged for $7.63 cash

NORMINCO DEVS LTD (CANADA)
Recapitalized as Sumburgh Developments Ltd. 10/17/1983
Each share Common no par exchanged for (0.2) share Common no par
Sumburgh Developments Ltd. recapitalized as Access Banking Network Inc. 09/24/1984 which recapitalized as Access ATM Network Inc. 05/24/1985 which merged into Ancom ATM International Inc. 01/18/1988
(See Ancom ATM International Inc.)

NORMINE RES LTD (BC)
Merged into Bema Gold Corp. (BC) 12/8/88
Each share Common no par exchanged for (0.5) share Common no par
Bema Gold Corp. (BC) reincorporated in Canada 7/19/2002 which merged into Kinross Gold Corp. 2/27/2007

NORMINGO MINES, LTD. (ON)
Charter revoked for failure to file reports and pay fees 8/3/64

NORMISKA CORP (ON)
Each share old Common no par exchanged for (0.2) share new Common no par 1/18/2006
Merged into 2129711 Ontario Ltd. 5/2/2007
Each share new Common no par exchanged for $0.15 cash

NOROCONA GOLD MINES LTD. (ON)
Charter revoked for failure to file reports and pay fees 11/30/64

NORPAC EXPL SVCS INC (DE)
Acquired by Petrolane, Inc. 09/07/1984
Each share Common 20¢ par exchanged for $3.85 cash

NORPAC TECHNOLOGIES INC (NV)
Name changed to Cellynx Group, Inc. 08/05/2008
(See Cellynx Group, Inc.)

NORPAX NICKEL MINES LTD (ON)
Name changed 08/28/1957
Name changed from Norpax Oils & Mines Ltd. to Norpax Nickel Mines Ltd. 08/28/1957
Charter cancelled for failure to pay taxes and file returns 03/06/1976

NORPET RES LTD (AB)
Merged into HCO Energy Co. Ltd. 04/07/1989
Each share Common no par exchanged for (2.894) shares Common no par
HCO Energy Co. Ltd. recapitalized as Consolidated HCO Energy Ltd. 04/12/1989 which name changed to HCO Energy Ltd. 06/18/1993 which merged into Pinnacle Resources Ltd. (New) 10/20/1997 which merged into Renaissance Energy Ltd. 07/16/1998 which merged into Husky Energy Inc. 08/25/2000

NORPICK GOLD MINES LTD. (ON)
Recapitalized as Norpax Oils & Mines Ltd. on a (1) for (3) basis 00/00/1952
Norpax Oils & Mines Ltd. name changed to Norpax Nickel Mines Ltd. 08/28/1957
(See Norpax Nickel Mines Ltd.)

NORPLEX CORP. (WI)
Common $1 par split (1.333) for (1) by issuance of (0.333) additional share 4/1/65
Completely liquidated 9/30/66
Each share Common $1 par exchanged for first and final distribution of (0.38461) share Universal Oil Products Co. Capital Stock $1 par
Universal Oil Products Co. name changed to UOP Inc. 7/15/75
(See UOP Inc.)

NORPOINT EXPLORATIONS LTD. (ON)
Completely liquidated 06/00/1968
Each share Common $1 par exchanged for first and final distribution of (0.01840) share Mission Financial Corp. Ltd. Common no par
Mission Financial Corp. Ltd. merged into H.R.S. Industries, Inc. 05/21/1982 which merged into International H.R.S. Industries Inc. 05/15/1984 which name changed to Glenex Industries Inc. 05/25/1987 which merged into Quest Investment Corp. 07/04/2002 which merged into Quest Capital Corp. (BC) 06/30/2003 which reincorporated in Canada 05/27/2008 which name changed to Sprott Resource Lending Corp. 09/10/2010 which merged into Sprott Inc. 07/24/2013

NORQUE COPPER MINES LTD. (ON)
Recapitalized as New Norque Mines Ltd. 3/18/68
Each share Common $1 par exchanged for (0.25) share Common $1 par
New Norque Mines Ltd. charter cancelled 3/16/76

NORRA CORP (AB)
Name changed to GC Greyhawke Corp. 12/31/1992
(See GC Greyhawke Corp.)

NORRELL CORP (GA)
Issue Information - 3,740,000 shares COM offered at $14 per share on 07/26/1994
Common no par split (2) for (1) by issuance of (1) additional share payable 07/08/1996 to holders of record 06/24/1996 Ex date - 07/09/1996
Merged into Interim Services Inc. 07/02/1999
Each share Common no par exchanged for (0.9) share Common no par
Interim Services Inc. name changed to Spherion Corp. 07/07/2000 which name changed to SFN Group, Inc. 03/01/2010
(See SFN Group, Inc.)

NORRIS COMMUNICATIONS INC (DE)
Reincorporated 09/17/1996
Place of incorporation changed from (BC) to (YT) 11/22/1994
Place of incorporation changed from (YT) to (DE) and Common no par changed to $0.001 par 09/17/1996
Name changed to e.Digital Corp. 01/13/1999

NORRIS COTTON MILLS CO. (SC)
Each share Common $100 par exchanged for (10) shares Common $10 par in 1948
Acquired by Woodside Mills for cash 9/30/59

NORRIS DISPENSERS INC (MN)
Liquidation completed
Each share Common $1 par exchanged for initial distribution of $3 cash 03/15/1973
Each share Common $1 par received second and final distribution of $1.62 cash 11/09/1973

NORRIS INDS INC (CA)
Common 50¢ par split (2) for (1) by issuance of (1) additional share 08/22/1966
Common 50¢ par split (3) for (2) by issuance of (0.5) additional share 04/01/1968
Common 50¢ par split (2) for (1) by issuance of (1) additional share 04/01/1977
Acquired by Kohlberg, Kravis, Roberts & Co. 12/08/1981
Each share Common 50¢ par exchanged for $43.05 cash

NORRIS OIL CO (NV)
Merged into Berry Petroleum Co. (DE) 06/26/1987
Each share Common $1 par exchanged for (0.0333) share Class A Common 1¢ par
Berry Petroleum Co. (DE) merged into LinnCo, LLC 12/16/2013
(See LinnCo, LLC)

NORRIS STAMPING & MANUFACTURING CO.
Name changed to Norris-Thermador Corp. in 1951
Norris-Thermador Corp. name changed to Norris Industries, Inc. 7/29/66
(See Norris Industries, Inc.)

NORRIS-THERMADOR CORP. (CA)
Common $1 par changed to 50¢ and (1) additional share issued 7/25/55
Name changed to Norris Industries, Inc. 7/29/66
(See Norris Industries, Inc.)

NORROCK RLTY FIN CORP (ON)
Acquired by Partners Real Estate Investment Trust 02/01/2012
Each share Ser. 1 Preferred no par exchanged for (13.72824) Trust Units and (1) Stock Appreciation Right
Each share Class A no par received distribution of (0.8236125) Partners Real Estate Investment Trust Trust

Unit payable 02/14/2012 to holders of record 02/08/2012
Name changed to Griffin Skye Corp. 01/22/2015
Griffin Skye Corp. recapitalized as ANB Canada Inc. 10/01/2016

NORSAT INTL INC NEW (BC)
Each share old Common no par exchanged for (0.1) share new Common no par 01/21/2015
Acquired by Hytera Communications Co., Ltd. 07/24/2017
Each share new Common no par exchanged for $14.57 cash
Note: Unexchanged certificates will be cancelled and become without value 07/24/2023

NORSAT INTL INC OLD (BC)
Recapitalized as NII Norsat International Inc. 09/27/1989
Each share Common no par exchanged for (0.2) share Common no par
NII Norsat International Inc. name changed to Norsat International Inc. (New) 07/12/1999
(See Norsat International Inc. (New))

NORSCO MINES LTD. (ON)
Merged into Jorsco Explorations Ltd. on a share for share basis 03/08/1961
(See Jorsco Explorations Ltd.)

NORSE ENERGY CORP ASA (NORWAY)
Each Sponsored ADR for Ordinary received distribution of $1.364279 cash payable 07/07/2010 to holders of record 06/29/2010 Ex date - 06/25/2010
ADR agreement terminated 06/13/2016
No ADR holders' equity

NORSEMAN BROADCASTING CORP (MN)
Merged into Putbrese Community 1/7/99
Each share Common $1 par exchanged for $1.4496 cash

NORSEMAN INDS INC (DE)
Merged into a private company 6/30/98
Each share Common 5¢ par exchanged for $4 cash

NORSEMAN MINES LTD.
Recapitalized as New Norseman Mines Ltd. on a (1) for (2) basis in 1950
New Norseman Mines Ltd. recapitalized as Norsewick Mines Ltd. in 1953 which name changed to Brunsman Mines Ltd. in 1953 which merged into Hydra Explorations Ltd. 11/16/59 which name changed to Hydra Capital Corp. 12/30/92 which name changed to Waterford Capital Management Inc. 11/12/96 which merged into CPI Plastics Group Ltd. 9/21/98

NORSEMAN MINES LTD (QC)
Merged into Grosmont Resources Ltd. 05/31/1982
Each share Capital Stock $1 par exchanged for (0.5571) share Capital Stock $1 par
(See Grosmont Resources Ltd.)

NORSEMAN NICKEL CORP. LTD. (ON)
Charter revoked for failure to file reports and pay fees 8/19/65

NORSEMONT MNG CORP (BC)
Recapitalized as International Norsemont Ventures Ltd. 10/24/1994
Each share Common no par exchanged for (0.1) share Common no par
International Norsemont Ventures Ltd. recapitalized as Consolidated Norsemont Ventures Ltd. 09/29/1999 which name changed to Norsemont Mining Inc. 01/27/2005 which was acquired by HudBay Minerals Inc. 07/05/2011

NORSEMONT MNG INC (BC)
Acquired by HudBay Minerals Inc. 07/05/2011
Each share Common no par exchanged for (0.2617) share Common no par and $0.001 cash

NORSEWICK MINES LTD. (ON)
Name changed to Brunsman Mines Ltd. 00/00/1953
Brunsman Mines Ltd. merged into Hydra Explorations Ltd. 11/16/1959 which name changed to Hydra Capital Corp. 12/30/1992 which name changed to Waterford Capital Management Inc. 11/12/1996 which merged into CPI Plastics Group Ltd. 09/21/1998
(See CPI Plastics Group Ltd.)

NORSK DATA A S (NORWAY)
ADR's for B Ordinary Kr. 20 par split (5) for (4) by issuance of (0.25) additional share 07/22/1985
Stock Dividend - 100% 07/07/1986
Reported out of business 00/00/1992
ADR holders' equity unlikely

NORSKE ENERGY CORP (DE)
Name changed to Ebaseone Corp. 06/02/1999
(See Ebaseone Corp.)

NORSKE SKOG CDA LTD (CANADA)
Reincorporated 08/27/2001
Place of incorporation changed from (BC) to Canada 08/27/2001
Name changed to Catalyst Paper Corp. (Old) 10/06/2005
(See Catalyst Paper Corp. (Old))

NORSTAN INC (MN)
Name changed 7/21/77
Name changed from Norstan Research & Development Co. to Norstan, Inc. 7/21/77
Common 1¢ par split (2) for (1) by issuance of (1) additional share payable 7/13/96 to holders of record 7/15/96
Stock Dividends - 10% 7/6/79; 10% 6/30/80; 50% 11/21/80
Merged into Black Box Corp. 1/25/2005
Each share Common 10¢ par exchanged for $5.60 cash

NORSTAR BANCORP INC (NY)
Common $5 par split (2) for (1) by issuance of (1) additional share 12/18/85
Conv. Preferred Ser. C $20 par called for redemption 12/15/87
Conv. Preferred Ser. E $20 par called for redemption 12/15/87
Stock Dividend - 10% 2/1/83
Merged into Fleet/Norstar Financial Group, Inc. 1/1/88
Each share Adjustable Rate Preferred $20 par exchanged for (1) share Adjustable Rate Preferred $20 par
Each share Common $5 par exchanged for (1.2) shares Common $1 par
Fleet/Norstar Financial Group, Inc. name changed to Fleet Financial Group, Inc. (New) 4/15/92 which name changed to Fleet Boston Corp. 10/1/99 which name changed to FleetBoston Financial Corp. 4/18/2000 which merged into Bank of America Corp. 4/1/2004

NORSTAR GROUP INC (UT)
Each share old Common 1¢ par exchanged for (0.2) share new Common 1¢ par 04/01/1998
Recapitalized as Gaming & Entertainment Group, Inc. 01/20/2004
Each (24.852732) shares new Common 1¢ par exchanged for (1) share Common 1¢ par
(See Gaming & Entertainment Group, Inc.)

NORSTAR VENTURES CORP (BC)
Name changed to Zongshen PEM Power Systems Inc. 07/30/2004

NORSUL OIL & MNG LTD (AB)
Struck off register and declared dissolved for failure to file returns 00/00/1999

NORSYNCO MINING & EXPLORATION LTD. (ON)
Assets sold to Norsyncomaque Mining Ltd. share for share 05/21/1957
Norsyncomaque Mining Ltd. recapitalized as Silvermaque Mining Ltd. 07/04/1961 which recapitalized as Geomaque Explorations Ltd./Explorations Geomaque Ltee. 09/19/1986 which merged into Defiance Mining Corp. 06/25/2003 which merged into Rio Narcea Gold Mines, Ltd. 09/03/2004
(See Rio Narcea Gold Mines, Ltd.)

NORSYNCOMAQUE MINING LTD. (QC)
Recapitalized as Silvermaque Mining Ltd. 07/04/1961
Each share Capital Stock $1 par exchanged for (0.25) share Common no par
Silvermaque Mining Ltd. recapitalized as Geomaque Explorations Ltd./Explorations Geomaque Ltee. 09/19/1986 which merged into Defiance Mining Corp. 06/25/2003 which merged into Rio Narcea Gold Mines, Ltd. 09/03/2004
(See Rio Narcea Gold Mines, Ltd.)

NORTE RES LTD (BC)
Reorganized under the laws of Yukon as Banks Ventures Ltd. 04/06/1998
Each share Common no par exchanged for (1/3) share Common no par
Banks Ventures Ltd. name changed to Banks Energy Inc. 07/26/2004 which merged into Arapahoe Energy Corp. (New) 10/20/2005 which name changed to Canadian Phoenix Resources Corp. 01/07/2008 which recapitalized as Knol Resources Corp. 03/11/2013

NORTEC VENTURES CORP (BC)
Name changed to Nortec Minerals Corp. 01/07/2010

NORTECH FOREST TECHNOLOGIES INC (DE)
Reincorporated 06/21/1995
State of incorporation changed from (CO) to (DE) and Common no par changed to 1¢ par 06/21/1995
Company terminated common stock registration and is no longer public as of 10/11/2000

NORTECH GEOMATICS INTL INC (AB)
Cease trade order effective 07/07/2000

NORTEK CAP CORP (BC)
Name changed 10/3/88
Common no par split (3) for (1) by issuance of (2) additional shares 4/1/81
Common no par reclassified as Class A Common no par 8/20/86
Name changed from Nortek Energy Corp. to Nortek Capital Corp. 10/3/88
Recapitalized as Brigdon Resources Inc. 11/5/91
Each share Class A Common no par exchanged for (0.05) share Class A Common no par
Brigdon Resources Inc. name changed to Tikal Resources Inc. 2/5/99 which merged into Tikal Resources Corp. 5/31/99 which was acquired by BelAir Energy Corp. 12/14/2001 which merged into Purcell Energy Ltd. (New) 9/4/2003
(See Purcell Energy Ltd. (New))

NORTEK ENGINES LTD. (BC)
Name changed to Nortek Energy Corp. 9/24/79
Nortek Energy Corp. name changed to Nortek Capital Corp. 10/3/88 which recapitalized as Brigdon Resources Inc. 11/5/91 which name changed to Tikal Resources Inc. 2/5/99 which merged into Tikal Resources Corp. 5/31/99 which was acquired by BelAir Energy Corp. 12/14/2001 which merged into Purcell Energy Ltd. (New) 9/4/2003
(See Purcell Energy Ltd. (New))

NORTEK HLDGS INC (DE)
Merged into Kelso & Co., L.P. 01/09/2003
Each share Common $1 par exchanged for $46 cash
Each share Special Common $1 par exchanged for $46 cash

NORTEK INC (DE)
Reincorporated 04/23/1987
Each share Common $1 par received distribution of (0.33333333) share Special Common $1 par 12/22/1986
State of incorporation changed from (RI) to (DE) 04/23/1987
Under plan of reorganization each share Common $1 par and Special Common $1 par automatically became (1) share Nortek Holdings, Inc. Common $1 par or Special Common $1 par respectively 11/20/2002
Acquired by Melrose Industries PLC 08/31/2016
Each share Common 1¢ par exchanged for $86 cash

NORTEL COMMUNICATIONS INC (BC)
Recapitalized as American Nortel Communications Inc. (BC) 05/11/1992
Each share Common no par exchanged for (0.1) share Common no par
American Nortel Communications Inc. (BC) reincorporated in Wyoming 02/09/1993 which reincorporated in Nevada 08/03/2007

NORTEL INVERSORA S A (ARGENTINA)
ADR agreement terminated 11/25/2013
No ADR's remain outstanding
Merged into Telecom Argentina S.A. 12/18/2017
Each Sponsored ADR for Ser. B Preferred exchanged for (1.34565053) Sponsored ADR for Class B Ordinary

NORTEL NETWORKS CORP NEW (CANADA)
Old Common no par split (2) for (1) by issuance of (1) additional share payable 05/08/2000 to holders of record 05/05/2000 Ex date - 05/09/2000
Each share old Common no par exchanged for (0.1) share new Common no par 12/01/2006
Plan of reorganization under Chapter 11 Federal Bankruptcy proceedings effective 05/08/2017
No stockholders' equity

NORTEL NETWORKS LTD (CANADA)
Name changed 05/01/2000
Common no par split (2) for (1) by issuance of (1) additional share payable 08/19/1999 to holders of record 08/17/1999 Ex date - 08/20/1999
Under plan of reorganization each share Common no par automatically became (1) share Nortel Networks Corp. (New) Common no par 05/01/2000
(See Nortel Networks Corp. (New))
Preferreds name changed from Nortel

Networks Corp. (Old) to Nortel Networks Ltd. 05/01/2000
Plan of reorganization under Chapter 11 Federal Bankruptcy proceedings effective 05/08/2017
Stockholders' equity unlikely

NORTEM N V (NETHERLANDS)
Liquidation completed
Each share Common EUR 0.44 par received initial distribution of $3.75 cash payable 03/11/2005 to holders of record 03/04/2005
Each share Common EUR 0.44 par received second and final distribution of $1.08 cash payable 06/01/2005 to holders of record 05/30/2005 Ex date - 06/03/2005
Note: Certificates were not required to be surrendered and are without value

NORTERRE MINES LTD. (QC)
Out of business 06/30/1959
Details not available

NORTEX OIL & GAS CORP (DE)
Each share $1.20 Conv. Preferred $1 par exchanged for (8) shares Common 15¢ par 6/16/67
Common $1 par changed to 15¢ par 6/16/67
Completely liquidated 2/8/71
Each share Common 15¢ par exchanged for (0.02365) share C & K Petroleum Inc. Common 10¢ par
(See C & K Petroleum Inc.)

NORTEX PETE LTD (AB)
Recapitalized as Seba Exploration Ltd. 03/05/1986
Each share Common no par exchanged for (0.2) share Common no par
Seba Exploration Ltd. name changed to Camrex Resources Ltd. 01/22/1991 which name changed to Crispin Energy Inc. 08/20/1996 which was acquired by Pengrowth Energy Trust 04/29/2005 which reorganized as Pengrowth Energy Corp. 01/03/2011

NORTH & JUDD MANUFACTURING CO. (CT)
Capital Stock $25 par changed to $12.50 par and (1) additional share issued 6/6/60
Stock Dividend - 20% 6/1/58
Acquired by Gulf & Western Industries, Inc. (DE) 7/12/67
Each share Capital Stock $12.50 par exchanged for (0.45) share $5.75 Preferred $2.50 par
Gulf & Western Industries, Inc. (DE) name changed to Gulf + Western Inc. 5/1/86 which name changed to Paramount Communications Inc. 6/5/89 which merged into Viacom Inc. (Old) 7/7/94
(See Viacom Inc. (Old))

NORTH & SOUTH AMERICAN CORP.
Dissolved in 1942

NORTH-AIR, INC. (AK)
Charter dissolved for failure to pay taxes and file reports 11/6/72

NORTH AMERICA ARMS CORP. LTD. (ON)
Bankrupt 4/6/62
No stockholders' equity

NORTH AMER ASSURN SOC VA INC (VA)
Stock Dividend - 20% 05/02/1973
Name changed to North American Insurance Co. 02/28/1978
North American Insurance Co. merged into North American Corp. (VA) 06/30/1981
(See North American Corp. (VA))

NORTH AMERICA BOWLING, INC. (MD)
Name changed to Bowl America, Inc. 1/15/62

NORTH AMERN & INTL PETE INC (UT)
Name changed to North American Petroleum, Inc. 10/8/82
North American Petroleum, Inc. name changed to North American Consolidated, Inc. 12/6/85

NORTH AMERN ACCEP CORP (DE)
Common $25 par changed to $10 par 00/00/1936
Common $10 par changed to $1 par and (9) additional shares issued 09/14/1961
Preferred $25 par called for redemption 02/20/1962
Liquidation completed
Each share Common $1 par exchanged for initial distribution of $7 cash 12/03/1968
Each share Common $1 par received second distribution of $1 cash 05/20/1969
Each share Common $1 par received third and final distribution of $0.39 cash 01/20/1970

NORTH AMERICAN ACCEPTANCE CORP. (PA)
Under plan of merger each share Class A $1 par exchanged for (1) share Class A Common $1 par 6/25/56
Name changed to NAAC Corp. 6/21/63
NAAC Corp. liquidated for Transcontinental Investing Corp. 8/3/63 which merged into Omega-Alpha, Inc. 3/7/72
(See Omega-Alpha, Inc.)

NORTH AMERN ACQUISITIONS INC (CO)
Name changed to RNB Entertainment Group Inc. 03/10/1988

NORTH AMERN ADVANCED MATLS CORP (WY)
Each share old Common no par exchanged for (0.33333333) share new Common no par 03/16/1994
Each share new Common no par exchanged for (0.5) share Common $0.001 par 05/16/1994
Merged out of existence 03/04/1994
Details not available

NORTH AMERN ADVANTAGED CONVERTIBLES FD (ON)
Name changed to First Asset North American Convertibles Fund 05/24/2016

NORTH AMERN AERO DYNAMICS LTD (BC)
Struck off register and declared dissolved for failure to file returns 01/22/1993

NORTH AMERN ASBESTOS LTD (QC)
Name changed to Bishop Resources International Exploration Inc. 9/30/93
Bishop Resources International Exploration Inc. recapitalized as Caldera Resources Inc. 11/30/95

NORTH AMERICAN AVIATION, INC. (DE)
Capital Stock no par changed to $5 par in 1932
Capital Stock $5 par changed to $1 par in 1933
Capital Stock $1 par split (2) for (1) by issuance of (1) additional share 8/24/56
Under plan of merger each share Capital Stock $1 par automatically became (1) share North American Rockwell Corp. Common $1 par 9/22/67
North American Rockwell Corp. merged into Rockwell International Corp. (DE) 2/16/73 which merged into Boeing Co. 12/6/96

NORTH AMERN BANCORPORATION INC (CT)
Capital Stock $5 par split (3) for (2) by issuance of (0.5) additional share 12/15/87
Stock Dividends - 10% 4/30/84; 10% 4/30/85; 10% 6/15/87
Under plan of reorganization each share Common $5 par automatically became (1) share North American Bank & Trust Co. (New) (Stratford, CT) Common $5 par 9/30/94
North American Bank & Trust Co. (New) (Stratford, CT) merged into Webster Financial Corp. 11/7/2003

NORTH AMERN BK & TR CO NEW (STRATFORD, CT)
Merged into Webster Financial Corp. 11/7/2003
Each share Common $5 par exchanged for (0.1503) share Common 1¢ par and $5.625 cash

NORTH AMERN BK & TR CO OLD (STRATFORD, CT)
Under plan of reorganization each share Capital Stock $5 par automatically became (1) share North American Bancorporation, Inc. Capital Stock $5 par 6/1/82
North American Bancorporation, Inc. reorganized as North American Bank & Trust Co. (New) (Stratford, CT) 9/30/94 which merged into Webster Financial Corp. 11/7/2003

NORTH AMERICAN BERYLLIUM CO., INC. (DE)
No longer in existence having become inoperative and void for non-payment of taxes 4/1/61

NORTH AMERN BINGO INC (NV)
Charter revoked for failure to file reports and pay fees 8/1/92

NORTH AMERN BIOLOGICALS INC (DE)
Name changed to Nabi 01/18/1996
Nabi name changed to Nabi Biopharmaceuticals 03/05/2002 which recapitalized as Biota Pharmaceuticals, Inc. 11/09/2012 which name changed to Aviragen Therapeutics, Inc. 04/13/2016 which recapitalized as Vaxart, Inc. 02/14/2018

NORTH AMERN BLDG TECHNOLOGY INC (DE)
Name changed to Perpetual Energy Products, Inc. 02/16/1978
(See Perpetual Energy Products, Inc.)

NORTH AMERICAN BOND TRUST CERTIFICATES
Trust terminated 00/00/1952
Details not available

NORTH AMERN BUS INDS RT (HUNGARY)
Name changed to Exbus Asset Management Nyrt. 7/6/2006
(See Exbus Asset Management Nyrt.)

NORTH AMERN CAR CORP (DE)
Reincorporated 9/30/64
Each share Common $20 par exchanged for (2) shares Common $10 par in 1950
5-3/8% Preferred called for redemption 8/30/58
Common $10 par changed to $5 par and (1) additional share issued 6/10/59
Common $5 par changed to $7 par and (1) additional share issued 4/27/62
State of incorporation changed from (IL) to (DE) 9/30/64
Merged into Flying Tiger Corp. 1/7/71
Each share Common $7 par exchanged for $1.20 Conv. Preferred $1 par and (1/3) Common Stock Purchase Warrant which expired 12/31/75
Plan of reorganization under Chapter 11 bankruptcy proceedings confirmed 11/30/90
Stockholders' equity unlikely

NORTH AMERICAN CEMENT CORP. (DE)
7% Preferred $100 par changed to $2 Preferred $1 par in 1933
Each (100) shares Common no par exchanged for (15) shares Class A Common $1 par in 1933
Each share Ser. A Preference $1 par exchanged for (1.2) shares Class A Common $10 par plus dividend of 50% on the new stock in 1952
Each share Ser. B Preference $1 par exchanged for (1.2) shares Class B Common $10 par plus dividend of 50% on the new stock in 1952
Each share Class A Common $1 par and Class B Common $1 par exchanged for (1.5) shares Class A Common $10 par or Class B Common $10 par respectively to effect a (2) for (1) split and a 50% stock stock dividend in 1952
Class A Common $10 par and Class B Common $10 par split (4) for (3) by issuance of (1/3) additional share respectively 3/23/55
Stock Dividends - 10% 12/18/53; 10% 9/1/54; 10% 12/15/55; 10% 12/18/57
Acquired by Marquette Cement Manufacturing Co. (IL) 1/31/61
Each share Class A Common $10 par and Class B Common $10 par exchanged for (0.8) share Common $4 par
Marquette Cement Manufacturing Co. (IL) reincorporated in Delaware 3/2/73 which name changed to Marquette Co. 5/30/75 which merged into Gulf & Western Industries, Inc. (DE) 9/16/76 which name changed to Gulf + Western Inc. 5/1/86 which name changed to Paramount Communications Inc. 6/5/89 which merged into Viacom Inc. (Old) 7/7/94
(See Viacom Inc. (Old))

NORTH AMERN CHEM CORP (CO)
Name changed to Golden Pharmaceuticals, Inc. 03/04/1994
Golden Pharmaceuticals, Inc. recapitalized as docsales.com, inc. 07/12/1999 which name changed to Docplanet.com Inc. 10/19/1999
(See Docplanet.com Inc.)

NORTH AMERICAN CIGARETTE MANUFACTURERS, INC. (DE)
Reincorporated 7/3/59
State of incorporation changed from (NY) to (DE) 7/3/59
Name changed to Meter Maid Industries, Inc. 2/19/68
(See Meter Maid Industries, Inc.)

NORTH AMERICAN CO. (NJ)
Common $10 par changed to no par 00/00/1927
Recapitalized 00/00/1939
Each share 6% Preferred $50 par exchanged for (1) share 6% Ser. Preferred $50 par
Common no par changed to $10 par
Completely liquidated
Each share Common $10 par received initial distribution of (0.1) share Union Electric Co. of Missouri Common $10 par paid 01/20/1953 to holders of record 12/22/1952
Each share Common $10 par received second distribution of (0.1) share Union Electric Co. of Missouri Common $10 par paid 01/21/1954 to holders of record 12/21/1953
Each share Common $10 par exchanged for third and final distribution of (1) share Union Electric Co. of Missouri Common $10 par 01/20/1955
Note: Unexchanged certificates were cancelled and became without value 01/20/1961
Union Electric Co. of Missouri name changed to Union Electric Co. 04/24/1956

NORTH AMERICAN COAL & COKE CO. (WV)
Dissolved 1/26/21

NORTH AMERN COAL CORP (OH)
Reorganized under the laws of Delaware as NACCO Industries, Inc. 06/06/1986
Each share Common $1 par exchanged for (2) shares Class A Common $1 par

NORTH AMERN COIN & CURRENCY LTD (AZ)
Name changed to Norcap Financial Corp. 06/10/1985

NORTH AMERN COMBUSTION TECHNOLOGY CORP (ON)
Struck off register and declared dissolved for failure to file returns in 1985

NORTH AMERN COMMUNICATIONS CORP (NV)
Acquired by Continental Telephone Corp. 1/15/70
Each share Preferred Ser. B. exchanged for (4-1/3) shares 80¢ Conv. Preferred Ser. C no par
Each share Common $1 par exchanged for (2/3) share 80¢ Conv. Preferred Ser. C no par
Continental Telephone Corp. name changed to Continental Telecom Inc. 5/6/82 which name changed to Contel Corp. 5/1/86 which merged into GTE Corp. 3/14/91 which merged into Verizon Communications Inc. 6/30/2000

NORTH AMERN COMMUNICATIONS CORP NEW (MN)
Acquired by Star Midwest, Inc. 3/1/88
Each share Common 1¢ par exchanged for $29.10 cash

NORTH AMERN COMPUTER & COMMUNICATIONS CO (DE)
Name changed to Compultility, Inc. 12/31/1971
(See Compultility, Inc.)

NORTH AMERN CONTRACTING CORP (MD)
Charter annulled for failure to file annual reports 07/03/1974

NORTH AMERN CORP (OH)
Merged into North American National Corp. 11/15/1974
Each share Common no par exchanged for (1) share Common no par
Note: Holdings of (19) shares or fewer exchanged for $3 cash per share but unexchanged certificates were cancelled and became without value 11/15/1978
(See North American National Corp.)

NORTH AMERN CORP (VA)
Completely liquidated 03/00/1983
Details not available

NORTH AMERN DATA SYS INC (NY)
Adjudicated bankrupt 10/26/1976
No stockholders' equity

NORTH AMERN DATACOM INC (DE)
Halted operations 03/31/2003
Stockholders' equity unlikely

NORTH AMERN DETECTORS INC (ON)
Delisted from Toronto Venture Stock Exchange 06/20/2003

NORTH AMERN DEV CORP (MA)
Name changed to Scotts Seaboard Corp. 07/03/1980
(See Scotts Seaboard Corp.)

NORTH AMERICAN EDISON CO.
Dissolved in 1939

NORTH-AMERICAN ELEVATORS, LTD. (CANADA)
Recapitalized in 1952
Each share 1st Preference $100 par or 2nd Preference $100 par exchanged for (1) share Preferred $100 par and (8) shares new Common no par
Each share old Common no par exchanged for (0.5) share new Common no par
Name changed to Sorel Elevators Ltd.-Les Elevateurs de Sorel Ltee. 9/17/74
(See Sorel Elevators Ltd.-Les Elevateurs de Sorel Ltee.)

NORTH AMERN ENCLOSURERS INC (NY)
Company no longer public as of 00/00/1995
Details not available

NORTH AMERN ENERGY INC (DE)
Reorganized as ORA Electronics, Inc. 12/20/1996
Each share Common 1¢ par exchanged for (0.01379) share Common $0.001 par, (0.02752) Common Stock Purchase Warrant Class A expiring 06/18/1997, (0.03770) Common Stock Purchase Warrant Class B expiring 06/20/1998, (0.03261) Common Stock Purchase Warrant Class C expiring 12/20/1999, and (0.0429) Common Stock Purchase Warrant, Class D expiring 12/20/2001

NORTH AMERN ENERGY PARTNERS INC. (CANADA)
Name changed to North American Construction Group Ltd. 04/16/2018

NORTH AMERN ENERGY RES INC (CO)
Each share old Common 1¢ par exchanged for (0.2) share new Common 1¢ par 3/4/82
Proclaimed dissolved for failure to file annual reports 1/1/91

NORTH AMERN ENERGY RES INC (NV)
Each share old Common $0.001 par exchanged for (0.02) share new Common $0.001 par 05/18/2009
Each share new Common $0.001 par exchanged again for (0.04347826) share new Common $0.001 par 03/31/2015
Name changed to KSIX Media Holdings, Inc. 08/03/2015
KSIX Media Holdings, Inc. name changed to Surge Holdings, Inc. 01/16/2018

NORTH AMERN ENVIRONMENTAL CORP (DE)
Merged into North American Technologies Group, Inc. 08/15/1996
Each share Common $0.001 par exchanged for (1) share Common $0.001 par
(See North American Technologies Group, Inc.)

NORTH AMERN EQUITABLE LIFE ASSURN CO (OH)
Common $2 par changed to $1 par 12/26/1963
Acquired by North American Corp. 12/31/1968
Each share Common $1 par received (1) share Common no par
Note: Certificates were not required to be surrendered and are without value
(See North American Corp.)

NORTH AMERN EQUITY CORP (BC)
Struck off register and declared dissolved for failure to file returns 5/1/92

NORTH AMERN FDG INC (CO)
Name changed to Video Ad Network, Inc. 8/7/87
(See Video Ad Network, Inc.)

NORTH AMERICAN FINANCE CO. (AZ)
Completely liquidated 3/22/72
Each share Class B Common $1 par exchanged for first and final distribution $0.75 cash

NORTH AMERN FINANCIALS CAP SECS TR (ON)
Under plan of merger name changed to Global Capital Securities Trust 02/04/2016
Global Capital Securities Trust name changed to Redwood Global Financials Income Fund 12/20/2017
(See Redwood Global Financials Income Fund)

NORTH AMERN FIRE GUARDIAN TECHNOLOGY INC (BC)
Recapitalized as Rival Technologies, Inc. (BC) 3/21/2000
Each share Common no par exchanged for (0.1) share Common no par
Rival Technologies, Inc. (BC) reincorporated in Nevada 10/28/2005

NORTH AMERN FOOD & BEVERAGE CORP (CO)
Name changed to Liquor Group Wholesale, Inc. 01/11/2008
(See Liquor Group Wholesale, Inc.)

NORTH AMERICAN FUND OF CANADA LTD. (CANADA)
Transfer of assets to Canada Growth Fund 12/31/1964
Each share Common $1 par exchanged for (2.3131) Certificates of Undivided Int. no par
Canada Growth Fund name changed to Bolton, Tremblay International Fund 04/14/1977
(See Bolton, Tremblay International Fund)

NORTH AMERICAN FUNDING, INC. (NC)
Charter suspended for failure to pay taxes 03/01/1973

NORTH AMERN GALVANIZING & COATINGS INC (DE)
Common 10¢ par split (3) for (2) by issuance of (0.5) additional share payable 06/08/2007 to holders of record 05/25/2007 Ex date - 06/11/2007
Common 10¢ par split (4) for (3) by issuance of (1/3) additional share payable 09/14/2008 to holders of record 08/31/2008 Ex date - 09/15/2008
Acquired by AZZ Inc. 08/03/2010
Each share Common 10¢ par exchanged for $7.50 cash

NORTH AMERN GAMING & ENTMT CORP (DE)
Reorganized under the laws of Nevada as China Changjiang Mining & New Energy Co., Ltd. 08/02/2010
Each share Common 1¢ par exchanged for (0.1) share Common $0.001 par

NORTH AMERICAN GAS & ELECTRIC CO.
Liquidated in 1944
No stockholders' equity

NORTH AMERN GAS CORP (CO)
Recapitalized as Synvion Corp. 10/1/97
Each share Common $0.001 par exchanged for (0.5) share Common $0.001 par

NORTH AMERN GAS LTD (QC)
Charter cancelled for failure to file reports and pay fees 08/18/1973

NORTH AMERICAN GEM INC (AB)
Recapitalized as Victory Mountain Ventures Ltd. 08/03/2012
Each share Common no par exchanged for (0.025) share Common no par

NORTH AMERN GEN RES CORP (NV)
Each share old Common $0.001 par exchanged for (0.04) share new Common $0.001 par 06/02/2004

Name changed to MoneyFlow Capital Corp. 12/08/2004
MoneyFlow Capital Corp. recapitalized as Fortuna Gaming Corp. 07/06/2005 which recapitalized as Principal Capital Group, Inc. (New) 11/21/2008 which name changed to Gazoo Energy Group, Inc. 09/11/2009
(See Gazoo Energy Group, Inc.)

NORTH AMERN GOLD & MINERALS FD (NV)
Common $0.001 par split (10) for (1) by issuance of (9) additional shares payable 10/15/2009 to holders of record 10/15/2009
Recapitalized as Nationsmark Nextgen 09/25/2015
Each share Common $0.001 par exchanged for (0.00025) share Common $0.001 par
Nationsmark Nextgen name changed to NationsMark Nexgen 05/12/2017

NORTH AMERN GOLD CORP (AB)
Name changed to North American Technologies Inc. 11/26/1991
North American Technologies Inc. merged into North American Technologies Group, Inc. 11/25/1993
(See North American Technologies Group, Inc.)

NORTH AMERN GOLD INC (BC)
Name changed to Northland Resources Inc. (BC) 09/07/2005
Northland Resources Inc. (BC) reincorporated in Luxembourg as Northland Resources S.A. 06/14/2010

NORTH AMERICAN GOLDFIELDS LTD. (BC)
Dissolved 11/16/52

NORTH AMERN GRAPHICS LTD (NV)
Name changed to Environmental Technology Systems Inc. 08/18/1997
Environmental Technology Systems Inc. recapitalized as Tombao Antiques & Art Group 04/05/2012

NORTH AMERN GROUP LTD (NV)
Assets sold for the benefit of creditors in September 1990
No stockholders' equity

NORTH AMERN GROWTH FD INC (CO)
Completely liquidated 12/31/1976
Each share Common $1 par received first and final distribution of $6.23 cash
Note: Certificates were not required to be surrendered and are without value

NORTH AMERN HEALTH & FITNESS CORP (ON)
Name changed to 1st Miracle Group Inc. 3/3/98 1st Miracle Group Inc. recapitalized as Miracle Entertainment, Inc. 11/16/2001

NORTH AMERN HITECH GROUP INC (UT)
Merged into Hitech Acquisition Inc. 02/26/1990
Each share Common $0.001 par exchanged for $0.90 cash

NORTH AMERICAN INDUSTRIES, INC. (NV)
Ctfs. dated prior to 04/26/1969
Name changed to Western American Industries, Inc. 04/26/1969
Western American Industries, Inc. name changed to Cardiodynamics, Inc. 09/29/1969 which name changed to Vida Medical Systems, Inc. 10/16/1974 which recapitalized as Oasis Oil Corp. 10/06/1997 which name changed to MVP Network, Inc. 09/07/2005

NORTH AMERN INDS INC (CT)
Charter forfeited 3/15/85

NORTH AMERN INDS INC (NV)
Charter revoked for failure to file reports and pay fees 06/02/2008

NORTH AMERN INDS INC (NV)
Ctfs. dated after 08/25/1972
Name changed to Colossus Corp. 08/27/1980
(See Colossus Corp.)

NORTH AMERN INS CO (VA)
Merged into North American Corp. (VA) 06/30/1981
Each share Capital Stock $5 par exchanged for (1/3) share Vtg. Common $1 par and (3) shares Non-Vtg. Common $1 par
(See North American Corp. (VA))

NORTH AMERN INS LEADERS INC (DE)
Issue Information - 12,500,000 UNITS consisting of (1) share COM and (1) WT offered at $8 per Unit on 03/22/2006
Completely liquidated
Each share Common $0.0001 par received first and final distribution of $7.9986753 cash payable 07/25/2008 to holders of record 07/21/2008
Note: Certificates were not required to be surrendered and are without value

NORTH AMERN INTEGRATED MKTG INC (DE)
Each (12) shares old Common $0.00001 par exchanged for (1) share new Common $0.00001 par 04/21/1997
Name changed to Directcom Inc. 04/09/1997
(See Directcom Inc.)

NORTH AMERICAN INVESTMENT & DEVELOPMENT CORP. (OH)
Completely liquidated 10/31/69
Each share Common no par exchanged for first and final distribution of (1) share Systems General Corp. Common 10¢ par

NORTH AMERICAN INVESTMENT CORP. (CA)
Recapitalized 00/00/1951
Each share 5-1/2% Preferred $100 par exchanged for (4) shares 5-1/2% Preferred $25 par
Each share 6% Preferred $100 par exchanged for (4) shares 6% Preferred $25 par
Each share Common $100 par exchanged for (4) shares Common $1 par
5-1/2% Preferred $25 par called for redemption 06/20/1963
Merged into Fund American Companies 01/04/1966
Each share 6% Preferred $25 par exchanged for (1) share 6% Conv. Preferred $25 par
Each share Common $1 par exchanged for (1.3) shares 4% Conv. Preferred $25 par
Fund American Companies acquired by American Express Co. 10/31/68

NORTH AMERICAN INVESTMENTS LTD. (ON)
Liquidation completed
Each share Class A no par exchanged for initial distribution of $5 cash 4/10/52
Each share Class A no par received second and final distribution of $6.43 cash 3/20/53
No stockholders' equity for Class B no par

NORTH AMERICAN INVESTORS CORP.
Merged into Liberty Share Corp. 00/00/1929
Details not available

NORTH AMERN INVS INC (GA)
Each share Common $0.005 par exchanged for (0.05) share Class A Common 10¢ par 01/31/1986
Administratively dissolved 07/17/1994

NORTH AMERN KARATE CONFERENCE INC (NV)
Name changed to KB Communications, Inc. 5/9/88
(See KB Communications, Inc.)

NORTH AMERICAN LAND & MINERALS LTD.
Name changed to Kelly-Kirkland Mines Ltd. 00/00/1937
(See Kelly-Kirkland Mines Ltd.)

NORTH AMERN LIABILITY GROUP INC (FL)
Each share old Common no par exchanged for (0.03333333) share new Common no par 07/14/2004
Each share new Common no par exchanged again for (0.1) share new Common no par 11/03/2004
Name changed to NorMexSteel, Inc. 04/13/2005
NorMexSteel, Inc. recapitalized as BioChem Solutions Inc. 07/07/2006 which name changed to Balmoral FX Systems Inc. 07/29/2010 which recapitalized as Amalgamated Gold & Silver, Inc. 08/01/2012 which recapitalized as recapitalized as Rainforest Resources Inc. 03/15/2016

NORTH AMERN LIFE & CAS CO (MN)
Each share Common $10 par exchanged for (25) shares Common $1 par to effect a (10) for (1) split and a 150% stock dividend 08/20/1962
Common $1 par split (3) for (2) by issuance of (0.2) additional share 05/15/1964
Common $1 par split (4) for (3) by issuance of (1/3) additional share 05/10/1965
Merged into Allianz Minnesota Life Insurance Co. 01/02/1981
Each share Common $1 par exchanged for $27.75 cash

NORTH AMERN LIFE INS CO CHICAGO (IL)
Capital Stock $5 par changed to $2 par 00/00/1936
Capital Stock $2 par reclassified as Common $2 par 03/21/1967
Stock Dividends - 50% 02/29/1956; 10% 03/14/1960; 10% 03/20/1961; 10% 03/20/1962
Acquired by USLIFE Corp. 04/26/1971
Each share Common $2 par exchanged for (0.57) share Common $2 par
USLIFE Corp. merged into American General Corp. 06/17/1997 which merged into American International Group, Inc. 08/29/2001

NORTH AMERICAN LIGHT & POWER CO. (DE)
Liquidated in 1948

NORTH AMERN MFG CO
Merged into Nevco 9/25/98
Each share Class A Common exchanged for either $2,950 principal amount of North American Manufacturing Co. Bonds due 2008 or $2,950 cash
Note: Option to receive cash expired 10/5/99

NORTH AMERICAN MATCH CORP.
Merged into Ohio Match Co. in 1936
(See Ohio Match Co.)

NORTH AMERN MED SVCS INC (YT)
Reincorporated 07/30/1992
Place of incorporation changed from (BC) to (YT) 07/30/1992
Reincorporated under the laws of British Columbia as KDR Industrials Ltd. 02/25/2013

NORTH AMERICAN MERCHANDISING CO. (DE)
Name changed to Williamsburg Greetings Corp. 3/5/62
Williamsburg Greetings Corp. charter revoked 4/1/67

NORTH AMERN METALS CORP.
Liquidated in 1935

NORTH AMERN METALS CORP (BC)
Merged into Wheaton River Minerals Ltd. 3/26/2004
Each share Common no par exchanged for $0.30 cash

NORTH AMERICAN MILK INDUSTRIES, INC. (FL)
Charter cancelled and proclaimed dissolved for non-payment of taxes 4/30/56

NORTH AMERICAN MINERALS, INC. (UT)
Proclaimed dissolved for non-payment of taxes 9/30/78

NORTH AMERN MINERALS CORP (UT)
Name changed to Tari Group, Inc. 3/18/86
Tari Group, Inc. name changed to Microshare Corp. 11/12/86

NORTH AMERN MINES INC (DE)
Each share Class A $10 par exchanged for (20) shares Common $1 par 00/00/1947
Each share Class B no par exchanged for (0.2) share Common $1 par 00/00/1947
Voluntarily dissolved 12/30/1988
Details not available

NORTH AMERN MTG CO (DE)
Merged into Dime Bancorp, Inc. (New) 10/15/1997
Each share Common 1¢ par exchanged for (1.37) shares Common 1¢ par
Dime Bancorp, Inc. (New) merged into Washington Mutual, Inc. 01/04/2002
(See Washington Mutual, Inc.)

NORTH AMERN MTG INVS (MA)
Shares of Bene. Int. no par reclassified as Common no par 06/07/1974
Merged into Southmark Corp. 05/10/1984
Each share Common no par exchanged for (0.2668) share Common $1 par
(See Southmark Corp.)

NORTH AMERN NAT GAS INC (WA)
Common $0.0001 par split (5) for (4) by issuance of (0.25) additional share payable 03/24/2003 to holders of record 03/17/2003 Ex date - 03/20/2003
Common $0.0001 par split (44) for (25) by issuance of (0.76) additional share payable 05/21/2008 to holders of record 05/19/2008 Ex date - 05/22/2008
Name changed to PureRay Corp. 08/27/2008

NORTH AMERN NAT RES (NV)
Recapitalized as PinkMonkey.com, Inc. 06/22/1998
Each share Common $0.002 par exchanged for (0.125) share Common $0.002 par
(See PinkMonkey.com, Inc.)

NORTH AMERN NATL CORP (DE)
Common 1¢ par split (5) for (4) by issuance of (0.25) additional share 10/14/83
Acquired by Liberty Corp. 2/23/94
Each share Common 1¢ par exchanged for $14.75 cash

NORTH AMERN NIPPON TECHNOLOGIES CORP (BC)
Common no par split (2) for (1) by issuance of (1) additional share 10/17/1986
Name changed to Agro International Holdings Inc. 10/02/1996
Agro International Holdings Inc. name changed to HOST International Holdings Inc. 06/01/2004
(See HOST International Holdings Inc.)

NORTH AMERN OIL & GAS CORP (NV)
SEC revoked common stock registration 10/04/2017

NORTH AMERN OIL & GAS INC (NV)
Name changed to Century Gold Ventures Inc. 05/01/2013
Century Gold Ventures Inc. name changed to Hub Deals Corp. 05/24/2018

NORTH AMERICAN OIL & REFINING CORP.
Property sold in 1926

NORTH AMERN OIL CO. (DE)
Charter cancelled and declared inoperative and void for non-payment of taxes 4/1/28

NORTH AMERN OIL CO. (MD)
Capital Stock $1 par changed to 25¢ par and distribution of 50¢ a share made in 1941
In process of liquidation in 1954

NORTH AMERICAN OIL CONSOLIDATED
Property sold to General American Oil Co. of Texas and dissolved in 1951

NORTH AMERN PALLADIUM LTD OLD (CANADA)
Reorganized as North American Palladium Ltd. (New) 08/10/2015
Each share Common no par exchanged for (0.0025) share Common no par

NORTH AMERN PETE INC (UT)
Name changed to North American Consolidated, Inc. 12/6/85

NORTH AMERICAN PETROLEUM CORP. (UT)
Charter suspended for failure to pay taxes 09/29/1961

NORTH AMERN PHILIPS CORP (DE)
Common $5 par split (2) for (1) by issuance of (1) additional share 04/03/1984
Merged into FGP Corp. 11/02/1987
Each share Common $5 par exchanged for $55.50 cash
Note: Due to settlement of litigation an additional $0.50 cash per share was distributed 03/02/1988

NORTH AMERN PLANNING CORP (NY)
Completely liquidated 11/9/76
No stockholders' equity

NORTH AMERN PLATINUM LTD (BC)
Struck off register and declared dissolved for failure to file returns 02/25/1983

NORTH AMERN PLATINUM LTD (BC)
Struck off register and declared dissolved for failure to file returns 04/24/1992

NORTH AMERN POTASH DEVS INC (BC)
Each share old Common no par exchanged for (0.1) share new Common no par 05/18/2016
Recapitalized as Barolo Ventures Corp. 09/20/2018
Each share new Common no par exchanged for (0.57142857) share Common no par

NORTH AMERN PWR PETES INC (BC)
Recapitalized as International North American Resources Inc. 09/18/1985
Each share Common no par exchanged for (0.2) share Common no par

International North American Resources Inc. recapitalized as Sonoma Resource Corp. (BC) 01/05/1990 which reincorporated in Wyoming as Biometric Security Corp. 10/09/1998 which recapitalized as Safeguard Biometric Corp. (WY) 12/29/1999 which reincorporated in British Columbia 11/30/2001 which name changed to Devon Ventures Corp. 02/11/2002 which name changed to Pender Financial Group Corp. 06/23/2004
(See Pender Financial Group Corp.)

NORTH AMERICAN PROPERTIES CORP. (DE)
No longer in existence having become inoperative and void for non-payment of taxes 4/1/61

NORTH AMERN PUBG CO (PA)
Each share Common 10¢ par exchanged for (1/15,000) share Common $1,500 par 7/21/81
Note: In effect holders received $9 cash per share and public interest was eliminated

NORTH AMERN RARE METALS LTD (ON)
Capital Stock $1 par changed to no par 11/13/1970
Reorganized 06/01/1994
Each share Common no par exchanged for (0.1) share NAR Resources Ltd. Common no par and (0.1) share Sunstate International Ltd. Common no par
(See each company's listing)

NORTH AMERN RECYCLING SYS INC (DE)
Charter cancelled and declared inoperative and void for non-payment of taxes 03/01/1996

NORTH AMERN REIT INCOME FD (ON)
Trust terminated 05/29/2017
Each Unit received $9.3342 cash

NORTH AMERICAN RESEARCH & DEVELOPMENT CORP. (UT)
Charter suspended for failure to pay taxes 03/02/1970

NORTH AMERN RESORT & GOLF INC (NV)
Name changed to MarketU Inc. 06/28/2000
MarketU Inc. name changed to Most Home Corp. 03/28/2002
(See Most Home Corp.)

NORTH AMERN RESORTS INC (CO)
Each share old Common no par exchanged for (0.1) share new Common no par 11/07/1995
Each share new Common no par exchanged for (0.001) share Common $0.001 par 06/20/2000
Name changed to Immulabs Corp. 09/15/2000
Immulabs Corp. name changed to Xerion EcoSolutions Group, Inc. (CO) 04/07/2003 which reorganized in Nevada as SINO-American Development Corp. 06/19/2006 which recapitalized as Harvest Bio-Organic International Co., Ltd. 12/07/2010
(See Harvest Bio-Organic International Co., Ltd.)

NORTH AMERN RESOURCE CAP LTD (ON)
Charter dissolved 09/03/1994

NORTH AMERICAN RESOURCES CORP. (NV)
Name changed to National American Industries (NV) (Incorporated 07/25/1932) 03/13/1969
National American Industries (NV) (Incorporated 07/25/1932) name changed to Vaportech Corp. 07/01/1971

NORTH AMERN ROCKWELL CORP (DE)
Under plan of merger name changed to Rockwell International Corp. (Old) 02/16/1973
Rockwell International Corp. (Old) merged into Boeing Co. 12/06/1996

NORTH AMERN RTYS INC (DE)
Each share 4% Preferred $100 par exchanged for (18) shares Common $1 par in 1953
Each share Common no par exchanged for (2.6) shares Common $1 par in 1953
Common $1 par split (2) for (1) by issuance of (1) additional share 1/30/81
Merged into RAN Merging Corp. 10/19/83
Each share Common $1 par exchanged for $19 cash
Preferred $5 par called for redemption 4/15/96

NORTH AMERN SVGS BK F S B (GRANDVIEW, MO)
Name changed 07/12/1990
Name changed 01/28/1992
Stock Dividends - 10% 09/30/1986; 10% 09/30/1987; 10% 09/29/1989
Name changed from North American Savings Association to North American Savings Bank (Grandview, MO) 07/12/1990
Name changed from North American Savings Bank (Grandview, MO) to North American Savings Bank F.S.B. (Grandview, MO) 01/28/1992
Under plan of reorganization each share Common $1 par automatically became (1) share NASB Financial, Inc. Common $1 par 04/01/1998

NORTH AMERN SCIENTIFIC INC (DE)
Reincorporated 05/03/1994
Reincorporated 04/20/1995
Place of incorporation changed from (BC) to (Canada) 05/03/1994
Place of incorporation changed from (Canada) to (DE) and Common no par changed to 1¢ par 04/20/1995
Common 1¢ par split (3) for (2) by issuance of (0.5) additional share payable 04/30/1998 to holders of record 04/20/1998
Each share old Common 1¢ par exchanged for (0.2) share new Common 1¢ par 05/01/2008
Chapter 11 Federal Bankruptcy proceedings terminated 10/11/2011
Stockholders' equity unlikely

NORTH AMERN SILVER CORP (ID)
Merged into NERCO, Inc. in 1990
Each (17) shares Common 10¢ par exchanged for (1) share Common no par
(See NERCO, Inc.)

NORTH AMERN SUGAR INDS INC (NJ)
Merged into Borden, Inc. 4/28/71
Each share Common $10 par exchanged for (1) share $1.32 Conv. Preferred Ser. B no par
(See Borden, Inc.)

NORTH AMERN SULPHUR HLDG CORP (UT)
Proclaimed dissolved for failure to file annual report 4/1/88

NORTH AMERN TECHNOLOGIES GROUP INC (DE)
Each share old Common $0.001 par exchanged for (0.1111111) share new Common $0.001 par 05/13/1998
Each share new Common $0.001 par exchanged again for (0.05) share new Common $0.001 par 09/07/2007
Chapter 11 bankruptcy proceedings dismissed 01/17/2012
No stockholders' equity

NORTH AMERN TECHNOLOGIES INC (AB)
Merged into North American Technologies Group, Inc. 11/25/1993
Each share Common no par exchanged for (0.5) share Common $0.0007 par
(See North American Technologies Group, Inc.)

NORTH AMERICAN TECHNOLOGY LTD. (BC)
Name changed to Yalakum Resources Ltd. 2/23/81
(See Yalakum Resources Ltd.)

NORTH AMERICAN TELEGRAPH CO.
Name changed to Postal Telegraph & Cable Corp. 00/00/1929
(See Postal Telegraph & Cable Corp.)

NORTH AMERICAN TIMBER CO.
Liquidation completed in 1948

NORTH AMERN TIRE RECYCLING LTD (BC)
Merged into Omnicorp Ltd. 04/08/1993
Each share Common no par exchanged for (1) share Common 1¢ par
(See Omnicorp Ltd.)

NORTH AMERICAN TITLE GUARANTY CO.
Liquidated in 1929

NORTH AMERN TR INC (MD)
Completely liquidated 10/16/1995
Each share Common 1¢ par exchanged for first and final distribution of approximately $5.69 cash
Note: An additional amount of approximately $0.24 cash per share was placed in escrow for possible future distribution

NORTH AMERICAN TRUST SHARES, SERIES 1958
Trust terminated 6/30/58
Details not available

NORTH AMERICAN URANIUM & OIL CORP. (DE)
Liquidation completed 8/1/57

NORTH AMERICAN UTILITY SECURITIES CORP. (MD)
Liquidated in 1952

NORTH AMERN VACCINE INC (CANADA)
Common no par split (2) for (1) by issuance of (1) additional share 1/29/92
Merged into Baxter International Inc. 6/26/2000
Each share Common no par exchanged for (0.1021) share Common $1 par and $0.03 cash

NORTH AMERN VAN LINES INC (IN)
Common no par split (2) for (1) by issuance of (1) additional share 05/09/1960
Stock Dividend - 10% 02/25/1963
Completely liquidated 06/26/1968
Each share Common no par exchanged for first and final distribution of (0.71428) share PepsiCo, Inc. (DE) Capital Stock 16-2/3¢ par
PepsiCo, Inc. (DE) reincorporated in North Carolina 12/04/1986

NORTH AMERN VANADIUM INC (BC)
Name changed to Veraz Petroleum Ltd. (BC) 06/26/2007
Veraz Petroleum Ltd. (BC) reincorporated in Alberta 01/24/2008 which name changed to AlkaLi3 Resources Inc. 08/16/2016

NORTH AMERICAN VENDING MANUFACTURING CORP. (DE)
No longer in existence having become inoperative and void for non-payment of taxes 4/1/66

NORTH AMERN VENTURES INC (MD)
Common $0.001 par split (3) for (1) by issuance of (2) additional shares 04/20/1987
Recapitalized as Butler International Inc. (MD) 06/29/1992
Each share Common $0.001 par exchanged for (1/6) share Common $0.001 par
(See Butler International Inc. (MD))

NORTH AMERN VENTURES LTD (BC)
Name changed to Newport Petroleum Corp. 6/1/92
(See Newport Petroleum Corp.)

NORTH AMERN WATCH CORP (NY)
Common 50¢ par reclassified as Class A Common 50¢ par 7/24/79
Class A Common 50¢ par changed to 1¢ par and (10.46) additional shares issued 9/27/93
Secondary Offering - 2,666,667 shares COM offered at $14 per share on 09/30/1993
Name changed to Movado Group, Inc. 4/15/96

NORTH AMERICAN WATER WORKS & ELECTRIC CORP.
Reorganized as Northeastern Public Service Co. and Northeastern Utilities Co. in 1931
(See each company's listing)

NORTH AMERICAN WATER WORKS CORP.
Name changed to North American Water Works & Electric Corp. in 1928
(See North American Water Works & Electric Corp.)

NORTH ARK BANCSHARES INC (TN)
Merged into Pocahontas Bancorp, Inc. 6/18/2002
Each share Common 1¢ par exchanged for (1.515) shares Common 1¢ par
Pocahontas Bancorp, Inc. merged into IBERIABANK Corp. 2/1/2007

NORTH ASIA INVT CORP (CAYMAN ISLANDS)
Issue Information - 5,000,000 UNITS consisting of (1) share ORD and (1) WT offered at $10 per Unit on 07/23/2008
In process of liquidation
Each Unit exchanged for initial distribution of $10.001 cash 08/18/2010
Each share Ordinary $0.0001 par exchanged for initial distribution of $10.001 cash 08/18/2010

NORTH ATLANTIC ACQUISITION CORP (DE)
Merged into Moto Guzzi Corp. 03/05/1999
Each share Class A Common 1¢ par exchanged for (1) share Class A Common 1¢ par
Each share Class B Common 1¢ par exchanged for (2) shares Class A Common 1¢ par and (2) Class A Common Stock Purchase Warrants expiring 08/22/2002
Moto Guzzi Corp. name changed to Centerpoint Corp. 08/11/2000
(See Centerpoint Corp.)

NORTH ATLANTIC AIRLS INC (DE)
Chapter 11 bankruptcy proceedings converted to Chapter 7 on 8/11/86
Stockholders' equity unlikely

NORTH ATLANTIC BANCORP (MA)
Common $1 par split (2) for (1) by issuance of (1) additional share 1/15/74
Completely liquidated 12/31/78
Each share Common $1 par exchanged for first and final distribution of (0.0909228) share University Bank & Trust Co.

(Chestnut Hill, MA) Common $10 par
(See University Bank & Trust Co. (Chestnut Hill, MA))

NORTH ATLANTIC CORP (PA)
Merged into Zemarc, Ltd. 9/15/71
Each share Common 25¢ par exchanged for (0.2527) share Common 25¢ par
(See Zemarc, Ltd.)

NORTH ATLANTIC DRILLING LTD (BERMUDA)
Each share Common $5 par exchanged for (0.1) share Common 10¢ par 12/31/2015
Plan of reorganization under Chapter 11 Federal Bankruptcy proceedings effective 07/02/2018
No stockholders' equity

NORTH ATLANTIC FISHERIES INC (NY)
Dissolved by proclamation 3/25/92

NORTH ATLANTIC INDS INC (NY)
Common 10¢ par split (3) for (2) by issuance of (0.5) additional share 03/11/1983
Common 10¢ par split (3) for (2) by issuance of (0.5) additional share 04/03/1984
Stock Dividend - 100% 10/29/1975
Name changed to NAI Technologies Inc. 04/28/1993
NAI Technologies Inc. merged into DRS Technologies, Inc. 02/11/1999
(See DRS Technologies, Inc.)

NORTH ATLANTIC LIFE INS CO AMER (NY)
Each share Common $100 par exchanged for (100) shares Common $2 par 06/28/1962
Common $2 par changed to $1 par 07/27/1966
Acquired by Northwestern National Life Insurance Co. 07/10/1979
Each share Common $1 par exchanged for $12.50 cash

NORTH ATLANTIC MARINE ENTERPRISES INC (DE)
Merged into Computer Facilities Corp. Ltd. 08/23/1971
Each share Common 10¢ par exchanged for (1) share Common no par
Computer Facilities Corp. name changed to Rotex Corp. 03/05/1973
(See Rotex Corp.)

NORTH ATLANTIC OYSTER FARMS, INC.
Acquired by General Foods Corp. in 1929
(See General Foods Corp.)

NORTH ATLANTIC RES LTD (BC)
Recapitalized as Damascus Resources Ltd. 08/04/1978
Each share Common no par exchanged for (0.25) share Common no par
Damascus Resources Ltd. recapitalized as International Damascus Resources Ltd. 07/16/1982 which recapitalized as Ravenhead Recovery Corp. 07/13/1998
(See Ravenhead Recovery Corp.)

NORTH ATLANTIC RES LTD (ON)
Name changed 06/04/2004
Name changed from North Atlantic Nickel Corp. to North Atlantic Resources Ltd. 06/04/2004
Each share Common no par exchanged for (1) share Common no par
Name changed to Legend Gold Corp. (ON) 02/18/2011
Legend Gold Corp. (ON) reincorporated in British Columbia 06/20/2014 which reorganized as Altus Strategies PLC 02/01/2018

NORTH ATLANTIC TECHNOLOGIES INC (MN)
Each share old Common no par exchanged for (1/3) share new Common no par 5/31/96
Company out of business in 1997
Details not available

NORTH ATLANTIC TRADING INC (DE)
Stock Dividends - 3.0667% payable 9/15/99 to holders of record 9/1/99; 3.0333% payable 3/15/2000 to holders of record 3/1/2000; 3.0333% payable 6/15/2000 to holders of record 6/1/2000; 3.0333% payable 9/15/2000 to holders of record 9/1/2000; 3.0667% payable 3/15/2001 to holders of record 3/1/2001; 3.0667% payable 6/15/2001 to holders of record 6/1/2001; 3.0667% payable 9/15/2001 to holders of record 9/1/2001 Ex date - 9/27/2001; 3.0667% payable 12/15/2001 to holders of record 12/1/2001 Ex date - 12/20/2001; 2.9667% payable 3/15/2002 to holders of record 3/1/2002 Ex date - 3/21/2002; 3.0333% payable 6/15/2002 to holders of record 6/1/2002 Ex date - 6/19/2002; 3% payable 9/16/2002 to holders of record 9/1/2002 Ex date - 9/6/2002; 3% payable 12/16/2002 to holders of record 12/1/2002 Ex date - 12/18/2002; 3% payable 3/15/2003 to holders of record 3/1/2003; 3% payable 6/15/2003 to holders of record 6/1/2003; 3% payable 9/15/2003 to holders of record 9/1/2003 Ex date - 9/8/2003; 3% payable 12/15/2003 to holders of record 12/1/2003 Ex date - 1/16/2004; 3% payable 3/15/2004 to holders of record 3/1/2004 Ex date - 3/5/2004
12% Senior Pay in Kind Preferred 1¢ par called for redemption at $22 plus $0.004211 accrued dividend on 3/18/2004

NORTH AUSTIN BUILDING CORP. (IL)
Liquidation completed 7/2/56

NORTH AUSTRALIAN DIAMONDS LTD (AUSTRALIA)
Name changed to Merlin Diamonds Ltd. 02/06/2013

NORTH AVENUE MARKET HOLDING CORP. (MD)
Name changed to North Avenue Market, Inc. 5/26/59
North Avenue Market, Inc. acquired by Center City, Inc. 3/29/62

NORTH AVENUE MARKET INC. (MD)
All shares acquired by Center City, Inc. for cash 3/29/62

NORTH BANCORP INC (MI)
Merged into Independent Bank Corp. 7/1/2004
Each share Common $1 par exchanged for (0.6488) share Common $1 par

NORTH BANCSHARES INC (DE)
Common 1¢ par split (3) for (2) by issuance of (1) additional share payable 12/29/97 to holders of record 12/8/97
Merged into Diamond Bancorp, Inc. 8/31/2004
Each share Common 1¢ par exchanged for $22.75 cash

NORTH BK CORP (MI)
Merged into Independent Bank Corp. 6/10/96
Each share Common no par exchanged for $32.50 cash

NORTH BATON ROUGE DEVELOPMENT CO., INC. (LA)
Merged into Kansas City Southern Industries, Inc. 3/10/71

Each share Capital Stock no par exchanged for $30 cash

NORTH BATTLEFORD BREWING CO. (SK)
Completely liquidated 06/30/1966
Each share Capital Stock no par exchanged for first and final distribution of $0.1619846 cash

NORTH BAY BANCORP (CA)
Common no par split (2) for (1) by issuance of (1) additional share 5/1/87
Merged into Westamerica Bancorporation 7/21/95
Each share Common no par exchanged for (0.2958) share Common no par

NORTH BAY BANCORP (CA)
Common no par split (3) for (2) by issuance of (0.5) additional share payable 12/16/2004 to holders of record 12/6/2004 Ex date - 2/17/2004
Stock Dividends - 5% payable 3/20/2000 to holders of record 3/1/2000; 5% payable 3/20/2001 to holders of record 3/1/2001 Ex date - 2/27/2001; 5% payable 3/22/2002 to holders of record 3/4/2002 Ex date - 2/28/2002; 5% payable 3/28/2003 to holders of record 3/10/2003 Ex date - 3/6/2003; 5% payable 3/29/2004 to holders of record 3/12/2004 Ex date - 3/10/2004; 5% payable 3/31/2005 to holders of record 3/18/2005 Ex date - 3/16/2005; 5% payable 4/12/2006 to holders of record 3/22/2006 Ex date - 3/20/2006
Merged into Umpqua Holdings Corp. 4/26/2007
Each share Common no par exchanged for (1.228) shares Common no par

NORTH BECK INDS INC (UT)
Recapitalized as Golden Phoenix Inc. (UT) 4/7/80
Each share Capital Stock 5¢ par exchanged for (1/3) share Capital Stock $0.005 par
Golden Phoenix Inc. (UT) name changed to Quantum Energy, Inc. 2/10/82 which name changed to Western Bell Communications, Inc. 5/20/85
(See Western Bell Communications, Inc.)

NORTH BECK MINING CO. (UT)
Recapitalized as North Beck Industries, Inc. 04/26/1973
Each share Capital Stock 10¢ par exchanged for (0.25) share Capital Stock 5¢ par
North Beck Industries, Inc. recapitalized as Golden Phoenix Inc. 04/07/1980 which name changed to Quantum Energy, Inc. 02/10/1982 which name changed to Western Bell Communications, Inc. 05/20/1985
(See Western Bell Communications, Inc.)

NORTH BLUFF CAPITAL CORP (BC)
Each share old Common no par exchanged for (0.5) share new Common no par 12/14/2017
Name changed to Sun Metals Corp. 05/08/2018

NORTH BORDULAC MINES LTD (ON)
Recapitalized as Gold Hawk Exploration Ltd. 10/31/1969
Each share Capital Stock $1 par exchanged for (0.5) share Capital Stock $1 par
(See Gold Hawk Exploration Ltd.)

NORTH BOSTON LIGHTING PROPERTIES
Recapitalized in 1927
Each share Preferred $100 par exchanged for (2) shares Preference $50 par

Each share old Common no par exchanged for (2) shares new Common no par
Merged into New England Electric System 6/3/47
Each share Preference $50 par exchanged for (1) share Common $20 par and $36 in cash
Each share Common no par exchanged for (2) shares Common $20 par
(See New England Electric System)

NORTH BRIAR MINES LTD (ON)
Charter cancelled for failure to pay taxes and file returns 03/16/1976

NORTH BROKEN HILL PEKO LTD (AUSTRALIA)
Name changed 12/01/1988
Stock Dividend - 20% 07/24/1987
Name changed from North Broken Hill Holdings Ltd. to North Broken Hill Peko Ltd. 12/01/1988
Each Unsponsored ADR for Ordinary exchanged for (0.2) Sponsored ADR for Ordinary 06/14/1989
Name changed to North Ltd. 12/29/1994
(See North Ltd.)

NORTH BUTTE MINING CO. (MN)
Capital Stock $10 par changed to $2.50 par in 1928
Name changed to Norbute Corp. in 1953
Norbute Corp. acquired by Crescent Petroleum Corp. 8/6/58 which name changed to Crescent Corp. 12/16/63 which merged into National Industries, Inc. (Ky.) 7/1/68

NORTH CDN OILS LTD (AB)
Common no par changed to 25¢ par in 1951
Common 25¢ par changed to no par 1/3/79
Common no par split (3) for (2) by issuance of (0.5) additional share 8/22/85
5-1/2% Preferred $50 par called for redemption 12/22/89
Class B Preferred Ser. 3 no par called for redemption 12/22/89
Class B Preferred Ser. 7 no par called for redemption 12/10/93
Class B Preferred Ser. 6 no par called for redemption 8/15/94
Merged into Norcen Energy Resources Ltd. 11/18/94
Each share Common no par exchanged for $14 cash

NORTH CAROLINA FED SVGS & LN ASSN (USA)
Common $1 par split (5) for (4) by issuance of (0.25) additional share 03/24/1986
Stock Dividend - 30% 05/26/1987
Under plan of reorganization each share Common $1 par automatically became (1) share NCF Financial Corp. Common 10¢ par 06/17/1988
NCF Financial Corp. merged into Community Bank Shares of Indiana, Inc. 05/06/1998 which name changed to Your Community Bankshares, Inc. 07/01/2015 which merged into WesBanco, Inc. 09/09/2016

NORTH CAROLINA LIFE COMPANIES, INC. (NC)
Name changed to United North Carolina Industries, Inc. 06/03/1969
United North Carolina Industries, Inc. name changed to United Group, Inc. 04/27/1976 which merged into Norwest Corp. 03/21/1997 which name changed to Wells Fargo & Co. (New) 11/02/1998

NORTH CAROLINA MORTGAGE CORP.
Dissolved in 1946

NORTH CAROLINA NAT ENERGY INC (FL)
Each share old Common $0.001 par exchanged for (0.0002) share new Common $0.001 par 03/14/2013
Name changed to Appalachian Mountain Brewery, Inc. 01/08/2014

NORTH CAROLINA NAT GAS CORP (DE)
Common $2.50 par split (2) for (1) by issuance of (1) additional share 03/16/1987
Common $2.50 par split (3) for (2) by issuance of (0.5) additional share 10/30/1992
Common $2.50 par split (3) for (2) by issuance of (0.5) additional share payable 02/20/1998 to holders of record 01/26/1998 Ex date - 02/23/1998
Merged into Carolina Power & Light Co. 07/15/1999
Each share Common $2.50 par exchanged for (0.8054) share Common no par
Carolina Power & Light Co. reorganized as CP&L Energy, Inc. 06/19/2000 which name changed to Progress Energy, Inc. 12/11/2000 which merged into Duke Energy Corp. 07/02/2012

NORTH CAROLINA NATL BK (CHARLOTTE, NC)
Stock Dividend - 20% 7/1/67
Reorganized as NCNB Corp. 11/4/68
Each share Common $5 par exchanged for (2) shares Common $5 par
NCNB Corp. name changed to NationsBank Corp. 12/31/91 which reincorporated in Delaware as BankAmerica Corp. (Old) 9/25/98 which merged into BankAmerica Corp. (New) 9/30/98 which name changed to Bank of America Corp. 4/28/99

NORTH CAROLINA RR CO (NC)
Each share Common $100 par exchanged for (0.01) share Common 50¢ par 00/00/1986
Merged into Beaufort & Morehead Railroad Co. 04/01/1998
Each share Common 50¢ par exchanged for $66 cash

NORTH CAROLINA TEL CO (NC)
Merged into Mid-Continent Telephone Corp. 09/30/1977
Each share 8% Conv. Preferred $1 par exchanged for $1.76 cash
Each share Common $1 par exchanged for $1.70 cash

NORTH CASCADES BANCSHARES INC (WA)
Common 1¢ par split (6) for (1) by issuance of (5) additional shares payable 04/25/2002 to holders of record 04/17/2002
Stock Dividend - 5% payable 03/11/2003 to holders of record 03/10/2003 Ex date - 04/30/2003
Acquired by Glacier Bancorp, Inc. 07/31/2013
Each share Common 1¢ par exchanged for $8.973 cash

NORTH CENT AIRLS INC (WI)
Common $1 par changed to 20¢ par and (4) additional shares issued 11/8/57
Common 20¢ par split (4) for (1) by issuance of (3) additional shares 12/30/61
Under plan of merger name changed to Republic Airlines, Inc. 7/1/79
(See Republic Airlines, Inc.)

NORTH CENT BANCSHARES INC (IA)
Acquired by Great Western Bancorporation, Inc. 06/22/2012
Each share Common 1¢ par exchanged for $30.58 cash

NORTH CENT COS INC (MN)
Each share Common $1 par exchanged for (0.01) share 10% Conv. Preferred no par 04/09/1980
10% Preferred no par called for redemption 09/21/1983
Merged into Financial Life Companies, Inc. 09/21/1983
Each share Common $100 par exchanged for $2,943 cash

NORTH CENT LIFE INS CO (MN)
Common $17 par changed to $25.50 par 01/10/1953
Common $25.50 par changed to $50 par 02/13/1962
Common $50 par changed to $62 par 11/22/1967
Common $62 par changed to $75 par 01/18/1972
Common $75 par changed to $100 par 08/10/1972
Reverted to a private company 04/00/1980
Each share Common $100 par exchanged for $20 cash

NORTH CENTRAL CO. (MN)
Stock Dividends - 10% 06/17/1964; 10% 06/28/1965
Name changed to North Central Companies, Inc. 07/25/1972
(See North Central Companies, Inc.)

NORTH CENTRAL DEVELOPMENT CORP. (IN)
Charter revoked for failure to file annual reports in 1970

NORTH CENTRAL TEXAS OIL CO., INC. (DE)
Common no par changed to $5 par in 1931
Liquidation completed 7/14/55

NORTH CHANNEL MINING & DEVELOPMENT CO., LTD. (ON)
Charter cancelled and company declared dissolved by default 2/18/63

NORTH CHINA HORTICULTURE INC (NV)
SEC revoked common stock registration 04/23/2014

NORTH CINCINNATI SVGS BK INC (BLUE ASH, OH)
Merged into Enterprise Federal Bancorp, Inc. 2/25/98
Each share Common $1 par exchanged for either (0.8409) share Common 1¢ par, $18.50 cash or a combination thereof
Note: Option to receive stock only or a combination of stock and cash expired 4/7/98
Enterprise Federal Bancorp, Inc. merged into Fifth Third Bancorp 6/4/99

NORTH COAST BK NATL ASSN (WINDSOR, CA)
Common $5 par changed to $4 par in 1999
Merged into American River Holdings 10/25/2000
Each share Common $4 par exchanged for (0.9644) share Common no par
American River Holdings name changed to American River Bankshares 6/2/2004

NORTH COAST ENERGY INC (DE)
Old Common 1¢ par split (2) for (1) by issuance of (1) additional share 9/24/91
Each share old Common 1¢ par exchanged for (0.2) share new Common 1¢ par 6/7/99
Ser. B Conv. Preferred 1¢ par called for redemption at $10 on 3/31/2002
6% Conv. Preferred Ser. A 1¢ par called for redemption at $10 on 7/31/2003
Stock Dividend - 15% 3/31/94
Merged into EXCO Resources, Inc. 1/28/2004
Each share new Common 1¢ par exchanged for $10.75 cash

NORTH COAST INDS LTD (BC)
Recapitalized as Consolidated North Coast Industries, Ltd. 08/14/1991
Each share Common no par exchanged for (0.25) share Common no par
Consolidated North Coast Industries Ltd. recapitalized as Great Basin Gold Ltd. 12/18/1997
(See Great Basin Gold Ltd.)

NORTH COAST LIFE INS CO (WA)
10% Conv. Preferred Ser. A $1 par called for redemption at $10 plus $8.41 accrued dividends on 11/26/2012
Acquired by Government Personnel Mutual Life Insurance Co. 12/31/2012
Each share Common $2 par exchanged for $7.66 cash

NORTH COAST PARTNERS INC (DE)
Common $0.001 par split (2) for (1) by issuance of (1) additional share payable 12/28/2007 to holders of record 12/27/2007 Ex date - 12/31/2007
Name changed to Montavo, Inc. 09/11/2008

NORTH COLDSTREAM MINES LTD (ON)
Merged into Coldstream Mines Ltd. 1/13/72
Each share Capital Stock no par exchanged for (0.25) share Capital Stock no par
(See Coldstream Mines Ltd.)

NORTH CONTINENT UTILITIES CORP. (IL)
Recapitalized 00/00/1935
Each share 7% Preferred $100 par exchanged for (1-1/6) shares $7 Preferred no par and (1) share new Common no par
Each share 6% Preferred $100 par exchanged for (1) share $7 Preferred no par and (1) share new Common no par
Each share Class A no par exchanged for (0.5) share new Common no par
Each share Common no par exchanged for (0.25) share new Common no par
Recapitalized 00/00/1950
Each share $7 Preferred no par exchanged for (1) share Common of Denver Ice & Cold Storage Co., (2) shares Great Falls Gas Co. Common, (1.1) shares North Shore Gas Co. Common, (1) share North Continent Utilities Corp. new Common $1 par, and $19.44 cash
Each share Common no par exchanged for (0.125) share new Common $1 par

NORTH CONTL ENERGY LTD (AB)
Recapitalized 06/30/1978
Common no par changed to 10¢ par 06/29/1939
Common 10¢ par changed to no par 06/29/1963
Recapitalized from North Continental Oil & Gas Corp. Ltd. to North Continental Energy Ltd. 06/30/1986
Each share Common no par exchanged for (0.25) share Common no par
Delisted from Alberta Stock Exchange 01/05/1996

NORTH COUNTRY URANIUM & MINERALS LTD. (AB)
Merged into Inland Resources Corp. on a (1) for (4) basis 8/24/56
Inland Resources Corp. merged into Universal Major Corp. 10/10/66 which name changed to Universal Major Industries Corp. 12/19/66
(See Universal Major Industries Corp.)

NORTH CNTY BANCORP (CA)
Common no par split (2) for (1) by issuance of (1) additional share payable 04/15/1997 to holders of record 03/14/1997
Stock Dividends - 5% payable 02/28/1997 to holders of record 01/31/1997; 5% payable 01/31/1998 to holders of record 12/31/1997; 5% payable 03/10/1999 to holders of record 02/10/1999
Merged into Wells Fargo & Co. (New) 01/27/2000
Each share Common no par exchanged for (0.541829) share Common $1-2/3 par

NORTH CREEK ASSOCS (TN)
Charter cancelled 01/16/2004

NORTH CRIPPLE CREEK MINING & MILLING CO. (CO)
Charter dissolved for failure to file annual reports 01/01/1917

NORTH CTRY FINL CORP (MI)
Recapitalized as Mackinac Financial Corp. 12/16/2004
Each share Common no par exchanged for (0.05) share Common no par

NORTH CTRY GOLD CORP (AB)
Merged into Auryn Resources Inc. 09/28/2015
Each share Common no par exchanged for (0.1) share Common no par
Note: Unexchanged certificates will be cancelled and become without value 09/28/2021

NORTH D'ARCY EXPLORATIONS LTD. (ON)
Merged into Tri-Bridge Consolidated Gold Mines Ltd. 10/13/1973
Each share Capital Stock $1 par exchanged for (0.1) share Common no par
Tri-Bridge Consolidated Gold Mines Ltd. merged into Lobo Gold & Resources Inc. 07/06/1983 which recapitalized as Lobo Capital Inc. 06/11/1992 which name changed to Q & A Communications Inc. 03/01/1993 which recapitalized as Q & A Capital Inc. 11/05/1997 which recapitalized as Leader Capital Corp. 08/17/1998
(See Leader Capital Corp.)

NORTH DAVID & ASSOC INC (NY)
Name changed to Abbey Medical Supply Corp. 12/01/1971
Abbey Medical Supply Corp. name changed to Abbey Group Inc. (NY) 05/27/1983 which reincorporated in Delaware as Power Phone, Inc. 06/16/1995 which name changed to TMC Agroworld Corp. 08/09/1996 which name changed to Dominican Cigar Corp. 08/22/1997 which name changed to DCGR International Holdings, Inc. 06/01/1998 which recapitalized as American Way Home Based Business Systems, Inc. 04/12/2004 which name changed to American Way Business Development Corp. (DE) 09/30/2004 which reincorporated in Florida as Harvard Learning Centers, Inc. 10/30/2006 which name changed to Americas Learning Centers, Inc. 09/25/2007 which recapitalized as Hackett's Stores, Inc. 01/26/2009 which recapitalized as WiseBuys, Inc. 06/17/2010 which name changed to Empire Pizza Holdings, Inc. 04/20/2011 recapitalized as Vestiage, Inc. 03/22/2013

NORTH DENISON MINES LTD. (ON)
Recapitalized as Consolidated Denison Mines Ltd. 00/00/1954
Each share Common no par exchanged for (0.28571428) share Common no par
Consolidated Denison Mines Ltd.

name changed to Denison Mines Ltd. 04/07/1960 which recapitalized as Denison Energy Inc. (ON) 05/30/2002 which reorganized in Alberta 03/08/2004 which name changed to Calfrac Well Services Ltd. 03/29/2004

NORTH DEVON MINES LTD. (ON)
Merged into Dynacore Enterprises Ltd. 07/15/1967
Each share Capital Stock $1 par exchanged for (0.090909) share Common no par
Dynacore Enterprises Ltd. recapitalized as Dynaco Resources Ltd. 02/09/1971
(See Dynaco Resources Ltd.)

NORTH EAST ELECTRIC CO.
Acquired by General Motors Corp. 00/00/1929
Details not available

NORTH EAST INS CO (ME)
Merged into Motor Club of America 9/24/99
Each share Common $1 par exchanged for either (0.19048) share Common 50¢ par, $3.30 cash, or a combination thereof
Motor Club of America name changed to Preserver Group, Inc. 6/6/2001
(See Preserver Group, Inc.)

NORTH EAST PENNSYLVANIA R.R. CO.
Merged into Reading Co. on a (0.04) for (1) basis 12/31/45
Reading Co. merged into Reading Entertainment Inc. (DE) 10/15/96 which reincorporated in Nevada 12/29/99 which merged into Reading International, Inc. 12/31/2001

NORTH EASTN ENERGY GROUP LTD (AB)
Recapitalized as Ensign Resource Service Group Inc. 01/28/1991
Each share Common no par exchanged for (0.2) share Common no par
Ensign Resource Service Group Inc. name changed to Ensign Energy Services Inc. 06/07/2005

NORTH ELECTRIC CO. (OH)
Merged into United Utilities, Inc. 12/29/1967
Each share Common $10 par exchanged for (2.75) shares Common $2.50 par
United Utilities, Inc. name changed to United Telecommunications, Inc. 06/02/1972 which name changed to Sprint Corp. (KS) 02/26/1992 which name changed to Sprint Nextel Corp. 08/12/2005 which merged into Sprint Corp. (DE) 07/10/2013

NORTH ELECTRIC MANUFACTURING CO. (OH)
Each share Common no par exchanged for (0.2) shares Common $10 par 00/00/1951
Name changed to North Electric Co. 04/22/1955
North Electric Co. merged into United Utilities, Inc. 12/29/1967 which name changed to United Telecommunications, Inc. 06/02/1972 which name changed to Sprint Corp. (KS) 02/26/1992 which name changed to Sprint Nextel Corp. 08/12/2005 which merged into Sprint Corp. (DE) 07/10/2013

NORTH EUROPEAN OIL CO (DE)
Reorganized as North European Oil Royalty Trust 09/12/1975
Each share Common $1 par exchanged for (2) Ctfs. of Bene. Int. and $1.45 cash

NORTH EUROPEAN OIL CORP. (DE)
Completely liquidated 10/28/1957
Each share Common exchanged for first and final distribution of (1) share North European Oil Co. Common $1 par
North European Oil Co. reorganized as North European Oil Royalty Trust 09/12/1975

NORTH EXPO MINES LTD. (ON)
Merged into Proto Explorations & Holdings Inc. 2/24/72
Each (5) shares Common $1 par exchanged for (1) share Common no par
Proto Explorations & Holdings Inc. name changed to Baxter Resources Corp. 6/26/81 which merged into Baxter Technologies Corp. 12/31/81 which name changed to Standard-Modern Technologies Corp. 10/8/85
(See Standard-Modern Technologies Corp.)

NORTH FACE INC (DE)
Secondary Offering - 2,500,000 shares COM offered at $23.50 per share on 11/15/1996
Merged into VF Corp. 8/14/2000
Each share Common $0.0025 par exchanged for $2 cash

NORTH FLA TEL CO (FL)
Class A $10 par and Class B $10 par changed to $5 par respectively and (1) additional share issued 05/20/1966
Merged into Mid-Continent Telephone Corp. 09/12/1979
Each share Class A $5 par exchanged for (1.43) shares Common no par
Each share Class B $5 par exchanged for (1.36) shares Common no par
Mid-Continent Telephone Corp. name changed to Alltel Corp. (OH) 10/25/1983 which reincorporated in Delaware 05/15/1990
(See Alltel Corp.)

NORTH FLORIDA HOTEL CO. (FL)
Dissolved 4/27/61

NORTH FORK BANCORPORATION INC N Y (DE)
Common $10 par changed to $5 par and (1) additional share issued 05/19/1982
Common $5 par changed to $2.50 par and (1) additional share issued 07/31/1985
Common $2.50 par split (2) for (1) by issuance of (1) additional share 11/03/1986
Common $2.50 par split (2) for (1) by issuance of (1) additional share payable 05/15/1997 to holders of record 04/25/1997 Ex date - 05/16/1997
Common $2.50 par split (3) for (2) by issuance of (0.5) additional share payable 05/15/1998 to holders of record 04/24/1998 Ex date - 05/18/1998
Common $2.50 par changed to 1¢ par 02/11/2000
Common 1¢ par split (3) for (2) by issuance of (0.5) additional share payable 11/15/2004 to holders of record 10/29/2004 Ex date - 11/16/2004
Merged into Capital One Financial Corp. 12/01/2006
Each share Common 1¢ par exchanged for (0.0169832) share Common 1¢ par and $26.849376 cash

NORTH FORK BK & TR CO (MATTITUCK, NY)
Capital Stock $10 par changed to $5 par and (1) additional share issued 07/15/1968
Capital Stock $5 par changed to $7.50 par 04/14/1972
Under plan of reorganization each share Capital Stock $7.50 par automatically became (1) share North Fork Bancorporation Inc. (DE) Common $10 par 12/17/1981
North Fork Bancorporation Inc. (DE) merged into Capital One Financial Corp. 12/01/2006

NORTH FORK MINING CO., INC. (ID)
Charter forfeited 11/30/70

NORTH FULTON BANCSHARES INC (GA)
Merged into Premier Bancshares, Inc. (New) 8/31/99
Each share Common no par exchanged for (0.8749) share Common $1 par
Premier Bancshares Inc. (New) merged into BB&T Corp. 1/13/2000

NORTH GODIVA CONSOLIDATED MINING CO. (UT)
Merged into North Lily Mining Co. 12/1/76
Each share Common 10¢ par exchanged for (0.003) share Capital Stock 10¢ par
(See North Lily Mining Co.)

NORTH GOLDCREST MINES LTD. (ON)
Merged into Crestland Mines Ltd. 05/04/1965
Each share Capital Stock $1 par exchanged for (0.5) share Capital Stock $1 par
Crestland Mines Ltd. merged into PYX Explorations Ltd. 07/30/1976 which merged into Discovery Mines Ltd. (Canada) 01/15/1982
(See Discovery Mines Ltd. (Canada))

NORTH GROUP FIN LTD (BC)
Each share old Common no par exchanged for (0.25) share new Common no par 08/22/2013
Each share new Common no par exchanged again for (0.001) share new Common no par 12/01/2014
Note: Holders of (999) or fewer pre-split shares received $0.10 cash per share
Unexchanged certificates will be cancelled and become without value 12/01/2020
Recapitalized as Peekaboo Beans Inc. 09/29/2016
Each share new Common no par exchanged for (0.33333333) share Common no par

NORTH GROUP LTD (CANADA)
Reincorporated under the laws of British Columbia as North Group Finance Ltd. 12/22/2005
North Group Finance Ltd. recapitalized as Peekaboo Beans Inc. 09/29/2016

NORTH HART RES LTD (BC)
Recapitalized as Calypso Developments Ltd. 08/20/1984
Each share Capital Stock no par exchanged for (0.33333333) share Common no par
Calypso Developments Ltd. recapitalized as Calypso Acquisition Corp. 11/18/2002 which name changed to Calypso Uranium Corp. 09/24/2007 which merged into U308 Corp. 05/15/2013

NORTH HATLEY CAP INC (CANADA)
Recapitalized as ORTHOsoft Holdings Inc. 08/31/2004
Each share Common no par exchanged for (0.14) share Common no par
ORTHOsoft Holdings Inc. name changed to ORTHOsoft Inc. 06/02/2005
(See ORTHOsoft Inc.)

NORTH HAVEN NATL BK (NORTH HAVEN, CT)
Merged into First New Haven National Bank (New Haven, CT) 8/31/76
Each share Common Capital Stock $5 par exchanged for $29.1243 cash

NORTH HAWK RES LTD (ON)
Recapitalized as ELI Eco Logic Inc. 03/25/1994
Each share Common no par exchanged for (0.025) share Common no par
ELI Eco Logic Inc. recapitalized as Global Development Resources Inc. 03/11/2005 which recapitalized as GDV Resources Inc. 12/21/2010 which name changed to Cardinal Capital Partners Inc. 09/13/2013

NORTH HILLS ELECTRIC CO., INC. (NY)
Name changed to North Hills Electronics, Inc. 6/23/60
(See North Hills Electronics, Inc.)

NORTH HILLS ELECTRS INC (NY)
Common 1¢ par split (2) for (1) by issuance of (1) additional share 11/5/82
Common 1¢ par split (2) for (1) by issuance of (1) additional share 3/15/83
Common 1¢ par split (3) for (2) by issuance of (0.5) additional share 8/5/83
Merged into PCS Acquisition Corp. 1/2/91
Each share Common 1¢ par exchanged for $2.50 cash

NORTH HILLS SIGNAL PROCESSING CORP (DE)
Each share old Common 1¢ par exchanged for (0.0005) share new Common 1¢ par 07/21/2014
Note: In effect holders received $5 cash per share and public interest was eliminated

NORTH HORIZON INC (NV)
Recapitalized as Innovus Pharmaceuticals, Inc. 12/06/2011
Each share Common $0.001 par exchanged for (0.1) share Common $0.001 par

NORTH HOUSTON BK (HOUSTON, TX)
Placed in receivership 10/30/2009
Stockholders' equity unlikely

NORTH INCA GOLD MINES LTD. (ON)
Recapitalized as Canadian North Inca Mines Ltd. on a (1) for (7) basis in February 1957
Canadian North Inca Mines Ltd. recapitalized as Southmark Petroleum Ltd. 11/20/68
(See Southmark Petroleum Ltd.)

NORTH IS MINES LTD (BC)
Recapitalized as Carnes Creek Explorations Ltd. 5/17/79
Each share Common 50¢ par exchanged for (0.2) share Common no par
Carnes Creek Explorations Ltd. recapitalized as Marathon Telecom Corp. 2/6/91
(See Marathon Telecom Corp.)

NORTH JERSEY CMNTY BANCORP INC (NJ)
Name changed to ConnectOne Bancorp, Inc. 11/26/2012

NORTH JERSEY NATL BK (JERSEY CITY, NJ)
Merged into Garden State National Bank (Hackensack, NJ) 2/1/71
Each share Common $10 par exchanged for (1) share Class A Common $5 par
Garden State National Bank (Hackensack, NJ) location changed to Garden State National Bank (Paramus, NJ) 11/15/74
(See Garden State National Bank (Hackensack, NJ))

NORTH JERSEY TITLE INSURANCE CO.
Insolvent 00/00/1937
Stockholders' equity unlikely

NORTH JERSEY TRUST CO. (RIDGEWOOD, NJ)
Merged into National Community Bank (Rutherford, NJ) 11/01/1966
Each share Common $12.50 par exchanged for (2.25) shares Common $12.50 par
National Community Bank (Rutherford, NJ) name changed to National Community Bank of New Jersey (Rutherford, NJ) 02/07/1975 which reorganized as National Community Banks, Inc. 02/28/1989 which merged into Bank of New York Co., Inc. 08/11/1993 which merged into Bank of New York Mellon Corp. 07/01/2007

NORTH KIRKLAND MINES LTD (AB)
Recapitalized as Seal Cove Corp. 11/2/87
Each share Common no par exchanged for (0.25) share Common no par
(See Seal Cove Corp.)

NORTH LAKE CORP (DE)
Reorganized 2/15/80
North Lake Corp. (PA) reorganized as North Lake Corp. (DE) 2/15/80
Holdings of more than (100) shares of Class A $1 par exchanged for (0.5) share Common $2 par per share
Note: Certificates surrendered after 2/28/82 will receive cash
Holdings of (100) shares or fewer of Class A $1 par exchanged for (0.5) share Common $2 par or $0.50 cash per share
Note: Option to receive Common $2 par expired 4/30/80
Each share Class B 10¢ par exchanged for (0.25) share Common $2 par or $0.25 cash
Note: Option to receive Common $2 par expired 4/30/80
Charter cancelled and declared inoperative and void for non-payment of taxes 3/1/94

NORTH LAND SVGS & LN ASSN ASHLAND (WI)
Name changed to NorthLand Bank of Wisconsin S.S.B. (Ashland, WI) 8/9/89
Northland Bank of Wisconsin S.S.B. (Ashland, WI) merged into First Financial Corp. (WI) 2/26/94 which merged into Associated Banc-Corp 10/29/97

NORTH LAWNDALE ECONOMIC DEV CORP (DE)
Name changed to Pyramidwest Development Corp. 10/14/1977
(See Pyramidwest Development Corp.)

NORTH LILY MNG CO (UT)
Each share old Common 10¢ par exchanged for (0.1) share new Common 10¢ par 12/08/1996
SEC revoked common stock registration 05/11/2006

NORTH LIME CORP (PA)
Stock Dividends - 100% 5/3/71; 40% 9/1/71
Name changed to AC & S Corp. 5/11/72
AC & S Corp. name changed to Irex Corp. 5/12/83
(See Irex Corp.)

NORTH LOUISIANA OIL & MINERAL CO., LTD (LA)
Charter revoked for failure to file annual reports 10/21/85

NORTH LTD (AUSTRALIA)
Acquired by Rio Tinto Ltd. 08/24/2000
Each Sponsored ADR for Ordinary exchanged for $14.2235 cash

NORTH MATTAGAMI MINES LTD. (QC)
Recapitalized as New Miller Copper Mines Ltd. on a (0.5) for (1) basis 7/6/61
New Miller Copper Mines Ltd. name changed to New Miller Pipe & Mining Exploration Ltd. 12/2/63 which name changed to Consolidated Miller Mining Co. Ltd. in 1981

NORTH MERRITT MINES LTD. (BC)
Recapitalized as Toronado Development Corp. 01/25/1971
Each share Capital Stock $1 par exchanged for (0.2) share Capital Stock no par
Toronado Development Corp. recapitalized as Cyclone Developments Ltd. 04/26/1977 which merged into Acheron Resources Ltd. 10/01/1982 which recapitalized as Abaddon Resources Inc. 09/12/1994 which recapitalized as Consolidated Abaddon Resources Inc. 01/31/2001 which name changed to Aben Resources Ltd. 01/13/2011

NORTH ORLANDO BK (ORLANDO, FL)
Name changed to Combank/Fairvilla (Orlando, FL) 02/28/1973
(See Combank/Fairvilla (Orlando, FL))

NORTH PA RR CO (PA)
Liquidation completed
Each share Capital Stock $50 par received initial distribution of $110 cash 4/19/82
Each share Capital Stock $50 par exchanged for (1) North Penn R.R. Liquidating Trust Non-Transferable Receipt of Bene. Int. and $45 cash 11/22/82
(See North Penn R.R. Liquidating Trust)

NORTH PAC GEOPOWER CORP (BC)
Recapitalized as Western GeoPower Corp. 10/09/2003
Each share Common no par exchanged for (0.1) share Common no par
Western GeoPower Corp. merged into Ram Power, Corp. 10/20/2009 which recapitalized as Polaris Infrastructure Inc. 05/19/2015

NORTH PAC INDS CORP (BC)
Struck off register and declared dissolved for failure to file returns 8/6/93

NORTH PAC MINES LTD (BC)
Merged into Initial Developers Ltd. 06/19/1974
Each share Capital Stock no par exchanged for (0.2) share Capital Stock 50¢ par
(See Initial Developers Ltd.)

NORTH PACIFIC CAPITAL CORP. (NV)
Name changed to Schoolweb Systems Inc. 12/19/2001
Schoolweb Systems Inc. name changed to Alternet Systems, Inc. 05/14/2002

NORTH PACIFIC EXPLORATION LTD. (ON)
Recapitalized as New North Pacific Exploration Ltd. 5/9/66
Each share Capital Stock 25¢ par exchanged for (0.01) share Common no par
New North Pacific Exploration Ltd. name changed to Commonwealth Drilling (Northern) Ltd. 10/9/68
(See listing for Commonwealth Drilling (Northern) Ltd.)

NORTH PACIFIC PAPER MILLS, INC.
Dissolution completed in 1947

NORTH PACIFIC PUBLIC SERVICE CO.
Acquired by Washington Gas & Electric Co. (Old) 00/00/1926
Details not available

NORTH PARK URANIUM CO., INC.
No longer in existence having been declared inoperative and void for non-payment of taxes 4/1/61

NORTH PEACE ENERGY CORP (AB)
Merged into Southern Pacific Resource Corp. 11/23/2010
Each share Common no par exchanged for (0.185) share Common no par
Note: Unexchanged certificates were cancelled and became without value 11/23/2012

NORTH PENN BANCORP INC (PA)
Each share old Common 10¢ par exchanged for (1.092) shares new Common 10¢ par 10/02/2007
Merged into Norwood Financial Corp. 05/31/2011
Each share new Common 10¢ par exchanged for (0.6829) share Common 10¢ par

NORTH PENN GAS CO (PA)
Prior Preferred no par called for redemption 07/15/1947
Merged into Penn Fuel System, Inc. 05/19/1977
Each share Capital Stock $5 par exchanged for $20.20 cash

NORTH PENN R.R. LIQUIDATING TRUST (PA)
Liquidation completed
Each Non-Transferable Receipt of Bene. Int. received initial distribution of $10 cash 2/24/86
Each Non-Transferable Receipt of Bene. Int. received second and final distribution of $9.54 cash 7/21/89
Note: Receipts were not required to be surrendered and are now valueless

NORTH PITTSBURGH SYS INC (PA)
Common $3.125 par changed to 62-1/2¢ par and (4) additional shares issued 12/19/1986
Common 62-1/2¢ par split (2) for (1) by issuance of (1) additional share 11/10/1992
Merged into Consolidated Communications Holdings, Inc. 12/31/2007
Each share Common 62-1/2¢ par exchanged for (1.1061947) shares Common 1¢ par

NORTH PITTSBURGH TEL CO (PA)
Common $25 par changed to $12.50 par and (1) additional share issued 06/27/1963
Common $12.50 par changed to $6.25 par and (1) additional share issued 01/24/1967
Common $6.25 par changed to $3.125 par and (1) additional share issued 06/04/1980
Under plan of reorganization each share Common $3.125 par automatically became (1) share North Pittsburgh Systems, Inc. Common $3.125 par 05/31/1985
4-1/2% Preferred Ser. A $100 par called for redemption 06/30/1992
4-1/2% Preferred $100 par called for redemption 06/30/1992
North Pittsburgh Systems, Inc. merged into Consolidated Communications Holdings, Inc. 12/31/2007

NORTH PK HLDGS INC (DE)
Name changed to Wyncrest Group, Inc. 2/22/2005

NORTH PLAINFIELD STATE BANK (NORTH PLAINFIELD, NJ)
Reorganized as Rock Financial Corp. 1/2/86
Each share Common $10 par exchanged for (1) share Common $10 par
Rock Financial Corp. merged into Valley National Bancorp 11/30/94

NORTH POINT PIER INC (CA)
Name changed to Pier 39, Inc. 03/15/1979
(See Pier 39, Inc.)

NORTH POINTE HLDGS CORP (MI)
Issue Information - 4,000,000 shares COM offered at $12 per share on 09/23/2005
Acquired by QBE Holdings, Inc. 04/30/2008
Each share Common no par exchanged for $16 cash

NORTH PT BANCSHARES INC (GA)
Merged into United Community Banks Inc. 7/26/2000
Each share Common $5 par exchanged for (2.2368) shares Common $1 par

NORTH RANKIN NICKEL MINES LTD (ON)
Recapitalized as Tontine Mining Ltd. 2/23/70
Each (6) shares Capital Stock $1 par exchanged for (1) share Capital Stock no par
Tontine Mining Ltd. merged into Coldstream Mines Ltd. 1/13/72
(See Coldstream Mines Ltd.)

NORTH RIV INS CO (NY)
Each share Capital Stock $25 par exchanged for (2.5) shares Capital Stock $10 par 00/00/1929
Each share Capital Stock $10 par exchanged for (1.612) shares Capital Stock $5 par 00/00/1931
Capital Stock $5 par changed to $2.50 par 00/00/1932
Acquired by Crum & Forster 10/07/1969
Each share Capital Stock $2.50 par exchanged for $86.02 cash

NORTH ROCK EXPLS LTD (ON)
Capital Stock $1 par changed to no par 10/28/70
Charter cancelled for failure to pay taxes and file returns 3/14/78

NORTH SCRANTON BK & TR CO (SCRANTON, PA)
Merged into First Eastern Bank, N.A. (Wilkes-Barre, PA) 09/19/1980
Each share Capital Stock $15 par exchanged for (3) shares Common $10 par
First Eastern Bank, N.A. (Wilkes-Barre, PA) reorganized as First Eastern Corp. 08/02/1982
(See First Eastern Corp.)

NORTH SHORE ACQUISITION CORP (DE)
Completely liquidated 12/09/2009
Each Unit exchanged for first and final distribution of $7.821999 cash
Each share Common $0.0001 par exchanged for first and final distribution of $7.821999 cash

NORTH SHORE BANK (MIAMI BEACH, FL)
Stock Dividend - 50% 1/20/53
Name changed to City National Bank (Miami Beach, Fla.) 10/1/63
(See City National Bank (Miami Beach, Fla.))

NORTH SHORE BK (SHOREWOOD, WI)
99.45% acquired by Citizens Bancorporation through exchange offer which expired 05/01/1978
Public interest eliminated

NORTH SHORE COKE & CHEMICAL CO.
Acquired by North Shore Gas Co. (IL) in 1942
Details not available

NORTH SHORE CMNTY BANCORP INC (IL)
Merged into Wintrust Financial Corp. 9/1/96
Each share Common no par

exchanged for (5.1618) shares Common no par

NORTH SHORE GAS CO (IL)
Each share 7% Preferred $100 par exchanged for (3) shares Common $15 par and $2.50 cash in 1942
Each share Common $15 par exchanged for (5) shares Common $5 par in 1/25/56
Common $5 par split (3) for (2) by issuance of (0.5) additional share 3/1/62
Acquired by Peoples Gas Light & Coke Co. on a (0.75) for (1) basis 12/20/63
Peoples Gas Light & Coke Co. acquired by Peoples Gas Co. 9/26/68 which name changed to Peoples Energy Corp. 2/1/80 which merged into Integrys Energy Group, Inc. 2/21/2007

NORTH SHORE GAS CO (MA)
Completely liquidated 12/28/1973
Each share Common $10 par exchanged for first and final distribution of $26.14 cash

NORTH SHORE GOLD FIELDS & MINES LTD. (ON)
Name changed to Northshore Goldfields Ltd. 3/29/60
Northshore Goldfields Ltd. charter cancelled in January 1971

NORTH SHORE NATL BK (CHICAGO, IL)
Common Capital Stock $15 par changed to $30 par 00/00/1943
Common Capital Stock $30 par changed to $40 par 00/00/1948
Common Capital Stock $40 par changed to $50 par 00/00/1949
Common Capital Stock $50 par changed to $60 par 00/00/1951
Common Capital Stock $60 par changed to $50 par and (1) additional share issued 00/00/1954
Common Capital Stock $50 par changed to $10 par and (4) additional shares issued 04/14/1960
Common Capital Stock $10 par changed to $5 par and (1) additional share issued 01/22/1964
Stock Dividends - 25% 09/07/1944; 25% 11/30/1944; 20% 12/28/1945; 25% 12/24/1949; 10% 06/21/1961; 10% 05/26/1969; 10% 02/25/1970; 10.19283% 02/26/1971
Acquired by LaSalle National Corp. 11/01/1990
Details not available

NORTH SHORE ST BK (SHOREWOOD, WI)
Name changed to North Shore Bank (Shorewood, WI) 08/18/1970
(See North Shore Bank (Shorewood, WI))

NORTH SHORE URANIUM CORP (QC)
Merged into Brominco Inc. 06/01/1976
Each share Capital Stock $1 par exchanged for (0.004) share Capital Stock no par
Brominco Inc. merged into Aur Resources Inc. 05/16/1985 which was acquired by Teck Cominco Ltd. 09/28/2007 which name changed to Teck Resources Ltd. 04/27/2009

NORTH SHORES GOLD MINES, LTD.
Acquired by North Shores Gold Mines (1936), Ltd. in 1936 which was dissolved 1/1/59

NORTH SHORES GOLD MINES (1936), LTD. (ON)
Dissolved 1/1/59

NORTH SIDE BANK (EVANSVILLE, IN)
Merged into Old National Bank (Evansville, Ind.) 8/28/50
Each share Capital Stock $100 par exchanged for (10) shares Common $10 par
Old National Bank (Evansville, Ind.) reorganized as Old National Bancorp 1/4/83

NORTH SIDE BANK (HOUSTON, TX)
Acquired by BancTexas Houston, N.A. (Houston, TX) 04/02/1987
Details not available

NORTH SIDE DEP BK (PITTSBURGH, PA)
Reorganized as NSD Bancorp Inc. 8/2/93
Each share Common $10 par exchanged for (1) share Common $1 par
(See NSD Bancorp Inc.)

NORTH SIDE SVGS BK (BRONX, NY)
Stock Dividend - 10% 11/22/88
Merged into North Fork Bancorporation, Inc. 12/31/96
Each share Common $1 par exchanged for (1.556) shares Common $2.50 par
North Fork Bancorporation, Inc. merged into Capital One Financial Corp. 12/1/2006

NORTH SIDE ST BK (HOUSTON, TX)
Name changed to North Side Bank (Houston, TX) 03/16/1976
(See North Side Bank (Houston, TX))

NORTH SIDE STATE BANK (SHEBOYGAN, WI)
Thru voluntary exchange offer of (8) shares Citizens Bancorporation Common $10 par for each share Common $5 par, all but (10) shares was acquired as of 10/7/70

NORTH SLAVE EXPLS LTD (BC)
Name changed to Calcorp Resources Ltd. and Capital Stock 50¢ par changed to no par 7/15/69
(See Calcorp Resources Ltd.)

NORTH SLOPE MINERALS INC (BC)
Recapitalized as Sino Pacific Development Ltd. 1/18/95
Each share Common no par exchanged for (0.25) share Common no par
Sino Pacific Development Inc. name changed to Prominex Resource Corp. 11/17/2005

NORTH SOUND BANK (POULSBO, WA)
Under plan of reorganization each share Common no par automatically became (1) share Liberty Bay Financial Corp. Common no par 10/1/85
Liberty Bay Financial Corp. merged into Frontier Fiancial Corp. 7/20/2000

NORTH SOUTH PETE CORP (BC)
Name changed to Advantage Lithium Corp. 07/05/2016

NORTH SOUTH RES LTD (BC)
Merged into Consolidated International Petroleum Corp. 6/1/85
Each (6.9) shares Common no par exchanged for (1) share Common no par
Consolidated International Petroleum Corp. name changed to International Petroleum Corp. 6/30/86 which was acquired by Sands Petroleum AB 1/15/98

NORTH ST BANCORP (NC)
Common $1 par changed to no par 05/04/2007
Stock Dividends - 10% payable 12/15/2002 to holders of record 11/15/2002 Ex date - 12/16/2002; 10% payable 12/15/2003 to holders of record 11/14/2003; 15% payable 10/20/2004 to holders of record 10/08/2004 Ex date - 10/06/2004; 20% payable 10/31/2005 to holders of record 10/17/2005 Ex date - 10/13/2005; 50% payable 08/28/2006 to holders of record 08/14/2006 Ex date - 08/29/2006; 50% payable 07/12/2007 to holders of record 06/28/2007 Ex date - 07/13/2007
Went private 11/24/2015
Each share Common no par exchanged for $9.75 cash

NORTH STANDARD MINING CO. (UT)
Recapitalized as North Standard Hotels, Inc. 12/14/61
Each share Common 10¢ par exchanged for (0.02) share Common $1 par
North Standard Hotels, Inc. name changed to International United Industries Inc. 11/30/77

NORTH STANDARD OF CANADA, INC. (NV)
Charter revoked for failure to file reports and pay fees 3/5/51

NORTH STAR ACCEP & INVT CORP (MN)
Stock Dividend - 25% 3/1/79
Name changed to Enstar Corp. (MN) 4/23/81
Enstar Corp. (MN) merged into North Star Universal Inc. 8/21/85 which merged into Michael Foods, Inc. (New) 2/28/97
(See Michael Foods, Inc. (New))

NORTH STAR APOLLO FD INC (MN)
Name changed to IAI Apollo Fund, Inc. 08/03/1987
(See IAI Apollo Fund, Inc.)

NORTH STAR BD FD INC (MN)
Name changed to IAI Bond Fund, Inc. 08/03/1987
(See IAI Bond Fund, Inc.)

NORTH STAR DIAMONDS INC (FL)
Each share Common $0.001 par received distribution of (1) share North Star Strategic Minerals, Inc. Common $0.001 par payable 11/21/2006 to holders of record 11/14/2006
Each share Common $0.001 par received distribution of (0.2) share North Star & Zale, Inc. Common $0.001 par payable 01/19/2007 to holders of record 01/05/2007
Each share Common $0.001 par received distribution of (0.1) share Black Sea Minerals, Inc. Restricted Common payable 03/02/2007 to holders of record 02/09/2007
Recapitalized as Chanaral Resources Inc. 04/23/2007
Each share Common $0.001 par exchanged for (0.0004) share Common $0.001 par
Chanaral Resources Inc. name changed to Alkane, Inc. 04/03/2009

NORTH STAR FD INC (MN)
Name changed to North Star Stock Fund, Inc. 04/27/1977
North Star Stock Fund, Inc. name changed to IAI Stock Fund, Inc. 08/03/1987
(See IAI Stock Fund, Inc.)

NORTH STAR FINL CORP (DE)
Merged into Marshall & Ilsley Corp. (Old) 04/20/2007
Each share Common no par exchanged for (0.0613) share Common $1 par
(See Marshall & Ilsley Corp. (Old))

NORTH STAR INC (ID)
Name changed to Arkansas Casino Corp. 4/28/97

NORTH STAR INSURANCE CO.
Name changed to North Star Reinsurance Corp. in 1939
North Star Reinsurance Corp. merged into General Reinsurance Corp. (NY) 6/30/56 which reincorporated in Delaware 12/31/72 which reorganized as General RE Corp. 10/31/80 which merged into Berkshire Hathaway Inc. 12/21/98

NORTH STAR INTL (NV)
Charter permanently revoked 07/31/2002

NORTH STAR INTL FD INC (MN)
Name changed to IAI International Fund, Inc. 08/03/1987
(See IAI International Fund, Inc.)

NORTH STAR MINES CO.
Sold to Empire Star Mines Co., Ltd. 00/00/1929
Details not available

NORTH STAR MINING & DEVELOPING CO. OF ALASKA (NJ)
Charter declared void for non-payment of taxes 1/10/02

NORTH STAR MINING CO. LTD.
Liquidated in 1931

NORTH STAR MINING CO. OF WONDER (NV)
Charter revoked for failure to file reports and pay fees 3/3/24

NORTH STAR OIL & REFINING CO., LTD.
Name changed to North Star Oil Ltd. 00/00/1929
(See North Star Oil Ltd.)

NORTH STAR OIL & URANIUM CORP. (DE)
Acquired by Consolidated Emjay Petroleums Ltd. share for share 8/5/57 which was recapitalized as New Emjay Petroleums Ltd. 2/4/66
(See New Emjay Petroleums Ltd.)

NORTH STAR OIL CO. (NV)
Each share Common 1¢ par exchanged for (0.1) share Common 10¢ par 02/27/1961
Merged into North Star Oil Corp. on a (1.5) for (1) basis 05/12/1961
North Star Oil Corp. acquired by Texam Oil Corp. 04/22/1964 which name changed to Energy Resources Corp. 10/23/1967 which merged into ENERTEC Corp. 05/04/1984
(See ENERTEC Corp.)

NORTH STAR OIL CORP. (DE)
Acquired by Texam Oil Corp. 04/22/1964
Each share Common 10¢ par exchanged for (0.18181818) share Common $1 par
Texam Oil Corp. name changed to Energy Resources Corp. 10/23/1967 which merged into ENERTEC Corp. 05/04/1984
(See ENERTEC Corp.)

NORTH STAR OIL LTD. (CANADA)
Each share old Common no par exchanged for (2) shares new Common no par 00/00/1952
Acquired by Shell Oil Co. of Canada Ltd. 05/10/1960
Each share Class A no par exchanged for $18.85 cash
Each share new Common no par exchanged for $34.10 cash
$2.50 Preferred 1956 Ser. $50 par called for redemption 08/08/1961

NORTH STAR PETE (NV)
Recapitalized as Gemstar Enterprises, Inc. 05/14/1990
Each share Common $0.001 par exchanged for (0.05) share Common 2¢ par
Gemstar Enterprises, Inc. recapitalized as CGI Holding Corp. 08/04/1997 which name changed to Think Partnership, Inc. 03/14/2006 which name changed to Kowabunga! Inc. 10/01/2008 which name changed to Inuvo, Inc. 07/30/2009

NORTH STAR REGL FD INC (MN)
Name changed to IAI Regional Fund, Inc. 08/03/1987
(See IAI Regional Fund, Inc.)

NORTH STAR REINSURANCE CORP. (NY)
Merged into General Reinsurance Corp. 6/30/56
Each share Common exchanged for $65.15 cash

NORTH STAR RESV FD INC (MN)
Name changed to IAI Reserve Fund, Inc. 01/31/1986
(See IAI Reserve Fund, Inc.)

NORTH STAR STK FD INC (MN)
Name changed to IAI Stock Fund, Inc. 08/03/1987
(See IAI Stock Fund, Inc.)

NORTH STAR TR CO (DE)
Reorganized as North Star Financial Corp. 06/30/2001
Each share Common no par exchanged for (1) share Common no par
North Star Financial Corp. merged into Marshall & Ilsley Corp. (Old) 04/20/2007
(See Marshall & Ilsley Corp. (Old))

NORTH STAR UNVL INC (MN)
Common 25¢ par split (3) for (1) by issuance of (2) additional shares 5/1/86
Common 25¢ par split (3) for (1) by issuance of (2) additional shares 5/29/87
$11 Preferred $100 par called for redemption 8/23/91
Each share Common 25¢ par received distribution of (1/3) share ENStar Inc. Common 1¢ par payable 2/28/97 to holders of record 2/27/97
Merged into Michael Foods, Inc. (New) 2/28/97
Each share Common 25¢ par exchanged for (0.562) share Common 1¢ par
(See Michael Foods, Inc. (New))

NORTH STAR URANIUM INC (WA)
Each share Common 10¢ par exchanged for (0.2) share Common $0.001 par 10/24/84
Name changed to West Coast Traders, Inc. 3/6/87
(See West Coast Traders, Inc.)

NORTH ST BK (BURLINGTON, NC)
Common $5 par changed to $2.50 par and (1) additional share issued 03/01/1969
Merged into Bancshares of North Carolina, Inc. 12/28/1972
Each share Common $2.50 par exchanged for (1.25) shares Common $5 par
Banshares of North Carolina, Inc. merged into NCNB Corp. 12/23/1982 which name changed to NationsBank Corp. 12/31/1991 which reincorporated in Delaware as BankAmerica Corp. (Old) 09/25/1998 which merged into BankAmerica Corp. (New) 09/30/1998 which name changed to Bank of America Corp. 04/28/1999

NORTH ST BK (RALEIGH, NC)
Stock Dividend - 10% payable 12/15/2001 of holders of record 11/15/2001
Under plan of reorganization each share Common $1 par automatically became (1) share North State Bancorp Common $1 par 06/28/2002
(See North State Bancorp)

NORTH ST FINL CORP (NC)
Assets and liabilities sold 07/21/1986
No stockholders' equity

NORTH ST NATL BK (CHICO, CA)
Stock Dividends - 5% payable 05/14/1996 to holders of record 04/16/1996; 10% payable 06/01/1998 to holders of record 04/21/1998; 10% payable 06/01/1999 to holders of record 04/20/1999
Merged into TriCo Bancshares 04/04/2003
Each share Common $2.50 par exchanged for (0.5861) share Common no par and $10.6043 cash

NORTH STATE SAVINGS & LOAN CORP. (NC)
Under plan of reorganization each share Common $6 par automatically became (1) share North State Financial Corp. Common $1 par 00/00/1983
(See North State Financial Corp.)

NORTH ST TEL CO (NC)
Under plan of reorganization each share 4% Preferred Ser. A $100 par, 4% Preferred Ser. B $100 par, 5% Preferred Ser. C $100 par, 5% Preferred Ser. D $100 par, 5% Preferred Ser. E $100 par, 8.25% Preferred Ser. F $100 par, Class A Common no par, and Non-Vtg. Class B Common no par automatically became (1) share North State Telecommunications Corp. 4% Preferred Ser. A $100 par, 4% Preferred Ser. B $100 par, 5% Preferred Ser. C $100 par, 5% Preferred Ser. D $100 par, 5% Preferred Ser. E $100 par, 8.25% Preferred Ser. F $100 par, Class A Common no par, and Non-Vtg. Class B Common no par respectively 01/01/1997

NORTH STD HOTELS INC (UT)
Name changed to International United Industries Inc. 11/30/1977

NORTH SULLIVAN CONTACT MINES LTD. (QC)
Charter cancelled for failure to pay taxes and file returns 11/7/75

NORTH SUMMIT EXPLORATIONS LTD. (ON)
Merged into Summit Explorations & Holdings Ltd. 9/19/69
Each share Capital Stock $1 par exchanged for (0.25) share Capital Stock no par
Summit Explorations & Holdings Ltd. name changed to Summit Diversified Ltd. 3/3/72 which merged into Sumtra Diversified Inc. 8/30/78

NORTH SUN INTERNATIONAL, INC. (NV)
Charter revoked for failure to file reports and pay fees 05/01/1987

NORTH SUN RES CO (NV)
Name changed to North Sun International, Inc. 06/19/1986
(See North Sun International, Inc.)

NORTH TAYLOR BUILDING CORP. (IL)
Liquidated 7/9/56

NORTH TEXAS CO.
Reorganized as Fort Worth Transit Co., Inc. in 1947
Each share Capital Stock $10 par exchanged for (2) shares Capital Stock $10 par and $10 principal amount of 4-1/2% 1st Mortgage Bonds
Fort Worth Transit Co., Inc. completed liquidation 8/15/74

NORTH TRINITY MINING CORP. (QC)
Recapitalized as Trinity Chibougamau Mines Ltd. on a (1) for (4) basis 10/30/56
Trinity Chibougamau Mines Ltd. name changed to Trinity Mines Inc. 3/26/82 which recapitalized as Harlake Capital Group, Inc. 1/12/90 which name changed to Madison Grant Resources Inc. (QUE) 10/11/90 which reorganized under the laws of Canada as Banro International Capital Inc. 3/2/95 which name changed to Banro Resources Corp. (Canada) 5/6/96 which reincorporated in Ontario 10/24/96 which recapitalized as Banro Corp. (ONT) 1/22/2001 which reincorporated in Canada 4/2/2004

NORTH VY BANCORP (CA)
Old Common no par split (2) for (1) by issuance of (1) additional share payable 10/30/1998 to holders of record 10/15/1998
Old Common no par split (3) for (2) by issuance of (0.5) additional share payable 05/15/2003 to holders of record 04/15/2003 Ex date - 05/16/2003
Each share old Common no par exchanged for (0.2) share new Common no par 12/29/2010
Merged into TriCo Bancshares 10/03/2014
Each share new Common no par exchanged for (0.9433) share Common no par

NORTH VALLEY BANK (REDDING, CA)
Common $5 par changed to $1.66666666 par and (2) additional shares issued 12/18/1978
Under plan of reorganization each share Common $1.66666666 par automatically became (1) share North Valley Bancorp Common no par 12/31/1981
North Valley Bancorp merged into TriCo Bancshares 10/03/2014

NORTH WAVE COMMUNICATIONS CORP (DE)
Recapitalized as Knoway Ventures Inc. 12/23/99
Each share Common $0.001 par exchanged for (0.05) share Common $0.0001 par
Knoway Ventures Inc. recapitalized as Olympus Mountain Gold Ltd. 8/5/2004

NORTH WEST BK (SEATTLE, WA)
Merged into Washington Bancshares, Inc. 09/25/1970
Each share Common $30 par exchanged for (3.75) shares Common $5 par
Washington Bancshares, Inc. name changed to Old National Bancorporation (WA) 06/21/1976 which reincorporated in Delaware 07/01/1977
(See Old National Bancorporation)

NORTH WEST CO FD (MB)
Trust Units no par split (3) for (1) by issuance of (2) additional Units payable 09/27/2006 to holders of record 09/20/2006 Ex date - 09/18/2006
Reorganized under the laws of Canada as North West Co. Inc. (New) 01/04/2011
Each Trust Unit no par exchanged for (1) share Common no par

NORTH WEST FARMS INC (WA)
Name changed to La Jolla Coffee Co. Inc. 06/04/1999
La Jolla Coffee Co. Inc. name changed to La Jolla Fresh Squeezed Coffee Co. Inc. (WA) 06/21/1999 which reincorporated in Delaware as Javo Beverage Co., Inc. 08/21/2002
(See Javo Beverage Co., Inc.)

NORTH WEST INC OLD (CANADA)
Reorganized under the laws of Manitoba as North West Co. Fund 03/27/1997
Each share Common no par exchanged for (1) Trust Unit no par
North West Co. Fund (MB) reorganized in Canada as North West Co. Inc. (New) 01/04/2011

NORTH WEST MNG N L (AUSTRALIA)
Acquired by Haoma North West NL 07/10/1982
Each ADR for Ordinary A$0.25 par exchanged for (0.7) share Ordinary A$0.25 par
Haoma North West NL name changed to Haoma Mining NL 07/12/1994

NORTH WEST PACIFIC DEVELOPMENTS LTD. (BC)
Recapitalized as N.W.P. Developments Ltd. 02/28/1966
Each share Capital Stock no par exchanged for (0.2) share Capital Stock no par
N.W.P. Developments Ltd. recapitalized as N.W.P. Resources Ltd. 06/17/1981 which merged into Golden North Resource Corp. 09/11/1984 which merged into Caledonia Mining Corp. (BC) 02/04/1992 which reincorporated in Canada 03/29/1995 which reincorporated in Jersey as Caledonia Mining Corp. PLC 03/24/2016

NORTH WEST TEL CO (WI)
Each share Common $100 par exchanged for (2) shares Common $50 par 00/00/1941
5-1/2% Preferred $100 par called for redemption 09/30/1963
Common $50 par changed to $5 par and (9) additional shares issued plus a 150% stock dividend paid 03/01/1971
Stock Dividends - 20% 12/15/1976; 10% 04/28/1978; 10% 05/15/1979; 10% 01/31/1980
Reincorporated under the laws of Nevada as North-West Telecommunications, Inc. 12/01/1982
North-West Telecommunications, Inc. merged into PacifiCorp 07/31/1990

NORTH-WEST TELECOM OPEN JT STK (RUSSIA)
Sponsored ADR's for Ordinary split (5) for (1) by issuance of (4) additional ADR's payable 07/31/2008 to holders of record 07/24/2008 Ex date - 08/01/2008
Merged into Rostelecom OJSC 04/13/2011
Each Sponsored ADR for Ordinary exchanged for $13.536797 cash

NORTH WEST TELECOMMUNICATIONS INC (NV)
Common $5 par split (3) for (2) by issuance of (0.5) additional share 06/20/1985
Common $5 par split (3) for (2) by issuance of (0.5) additional share 06/22/1987
Common $5 par split (3) for (2) by issuance of (0.5) additional share 06/22/1988
Common $5 par split (3) for (2) by issuance of (0.5) additional share 06/22/1989
Conv. Class B Common $5 par split (3) for (2) by issuance of (0.5) additional share 06/22/1989
Preferred Stock Purchase Rights declared for Class B Common stockholders of record 09/15/1989 were redeemed at $0.01 per right 08/15/1990 for holders of record 07/31/1990
Merged into PacifiCorp 07/31/1990
Each share Common $5 par exchanged for (1.97) shares Common $3.25 par and $4.41 cash
Each share Conv. Class B Common $5 par exchanged for (1.97) shares Common $3.25 par and $4.41 cash

NORTH WEST TR CO (EDMONTON, ALTA)
Each share 1st Part. Class A Preferred $10 par exchanged for (10) shares Class A Non-Vtg. $1 par 01/24/1986
Acquired by Canadian Western Bank (Edmonton, ALTA) 00/00/1994
Details not available

NORTH WEST UTILITIES CO.
Liquidated in 1948

NORTH WESTERN MINING & EXPLORATION CORP. (DE)
Became inoperative and void for non-payment of taxes 4/1/64

NORTH-WESTERN STANDARD OIL CO. (WY)
Charter forfeited for failure to pay taxes 7/19/27

NORTH WHITNEY RES LTD (CANADA)
Recapitalized 2/22/82
Recapitalized from North Whitney Mines Ltd. to North Whitney Resources Ltd. 2/22/82
Each share Capital Stock no par exchanged for (0.1) share Capital Stock no par
Charter dissolved 12/13/95

NORTHABIE MINES LTD. (ON)
Charter cancelled in 1970

NORTHAIR MINES LTD (BC)
Recapitalized as International Northair Mines Ltd. 08/15/1991
Each share Common no par exchanged for (0.2) share Common no par
International Northair Mines Ltd. name changed to Northair Silver Corp. 11/20/2014 which merged into Kootenay Silver Inc. 04/21/2016

NORTHAIR SILVER CORP (BC)
Merged into Kootenay Silver Inc. 04/21/2016
Each share Common no par exchanged for (0.35) share Common no par and (0.15) Common Stock Purchase Warrant expiring 04/21/2021
Note: Unexchanged certificates will be cancelled and become without value 04/21/2022

NORTHAMPTON GROUP INC (ON)
Acquired by 2425138 Ontario Inc. 09/29/2014
Each share Common no par exchanged for $1.40 cash
Note: Unexchanged certificates will be cancelled and become without value 09/29/2020

NORTHAMPTON INC (UT)
Recapitalized as Eurogas Inc. 09/06/1994
Each (24) shares Common $0.001 par exchanged for (1) share Common $0.001 par
(See Eurogas Inc.)

NORTHAMPTON NATL BK (NORTHAMPTON, MA)
Stock Dividend - 10% 04/06/1971
97.8% acquired by Multibank Financial Corp. through exchange offer as of 12/15/1978
Public interest eliminated

NORTHAMPTON STREET RY. CO.
In process of liquidation since 1951

NORTHBAY FINL CORP (DE)
Common 10¢ par split (3) for (2) by issuance of (0.5) additional share 11/18/91
Common 10¢ par split (6) for (5) by issuance of (0.2) additional share 10/28/94
Stock Dividends - 15% 7/31/92; 10% 1/29/93; 10% 6/24/94
Merged into Bank of the West (San Francisco, CA) 4/26/96
Each share Common 10¢ par exchanged for $15.75 cash

NORTHBRIDGE FINL CORP (CANADA)
Acquired by Fairfax Financial Holdings Ltd. 02/20/2009
Each share Common no par exchanged for $39 cash
Each share 144A Common no par exchanged for $39 cash

NORTHCAL MINES LTD (AB)
Recapitalized as New Northcal Mines Ltd. 09/08/1971
Each share Capital Stock no par exchanged for (0.1) share Capital Stock no par
New Northcal Mines Ltd. recapitalized as Venture Properties Ltd. 04/17/1974 which recapitalized as Allied Venture Properties Ltd. 09/02/1975 which recapitalized as Buckingham International Holdings Ltd. 03/22/1979
(See Buckingham International Holdings Ltd.)

NORTHCAL OILS LTD. (AB)
Name changed to Northcal Mines Ltd. 9/27/63
Northcal Mines Ltd. recapitalized as New Northcal Mines Ltd. 7/26/71 which recapitalized as Venture Properties Ltd. 4/17/74 which recapitalized as Allied Venture Properties Ltd. 9/2/75 which recapitalized as Buckingham International Holdings Ltd. 3/22/79
(See Buckingham International Holdings Ltd.)

NORTHCAL RES LTD (BC)
Recapitalized as Calnor Resources Ltd. 09/20/1985
Each share Common no par exchanged for (0.33333333) share Common no par
Calnor Resources Ltd. recapitalized as Norcal Resources Ltd. 08/23/1991 which recapitalized as Troon Ventures Ltd. (BC) 06/18/2002 which reorganized in Ontario as Grenville Strategic Royalty Corp. 02/21/2014 which merged into LOGiQ Asset Management Inc. (AB) 06/07/2018 which reorganized in British Columbia as Flow Capital Corp. 06/11/2018

NORTHCOR RES LTD (AB)
Recapitalized as Canadian Northcor Energy Inc. 01/10/1990
Each share Class A Common no par exchanged for (0.25) share Class A Common no par
Canadian Northcor Energy Inc. merged into Purcell Energy Ltd. (Old) 11/19/1993 which recapitalized as Purcell Energy Ltd. (New) 03/07/1997
(See Purcell Energy Ltd. (New))

NORTHCORP RLTY ADVISORS INC (DE)
Name changed to Crown Northcorp, Inc. 05/25/1995
(See Crown Northcorp, Inc.)

NORTHCOTT GOLD INC (ON)
Name changed to Laurion Gold Inc. 03/12/2004
Laurion Gold Inc. name changed to Laurion Mineral Exploration Inc. 11/03/2006

NORTHEAST AIRLS INC (MA)
Recapitalized in 1941
Each share Preferred $100 par exchanged for (22) shares Common $1 par
Each share Common $100 par exchanged for (86) shares Common $1 par
Merged into Delta Air Lines, Inc. 8/1/72
Each share Common $1 par exchanged for (0.1) share Common $3 par
(See Delta Air Lines, Inc.)

NORTHEAST AUTO ACCEP CORP (FL)
Reincorporated under the laws of Nevada as Northeast Automotive Holdings, Inc. and Common no par changed to $0.001 par 03/10/2008
Northeast Automotive Holdings, Inc. name changed to Kogeto, Inc. 03/11/2014
(See Kogeto, Inc.)

NORTHEAST AUTOMOTIVE HLDGS INC (NV)
Each share old Common $0.001 par exchanged for (0.03333333) share new Common $0.001 par 06/17/2008
Name changed to Kogeto, Inc. 03/11/2014
(See Kogeto, Inc.)

NORTHEAST BANCORP, INC. (TX)
Name changed to Northeast United Bancorp, Inc. of Texas 3/12/74
Northeast United Bancorp, Inc. of Texas name changed to Texas United Bancorp, Inc. 4/8/83 which merged into Allied Bancshares, Inc. (TX) 6/1/84 which reincorporated in Delaware 4/22/87 which merged into First Interstate Bancorp 1/29/88

NORTHEAST BANCORP INC (CT)
Common $5 par split (2) for (1) by issuance of (1) additional share 10/01/1985
Stock Dividends - 10% 03/10/1978; 10% 03/10/1979; 12-1/2% 03/10/1980
Merged into First Fidelity Bancorporation (New) 05/03/1993
Each share Common $5 par exchanged for (0.08408) share Common $1 par
First Fidelity Bancorporation (New) merged into First Union Corp. 01/01/1996 which name changed to Wachovia Corp. (Ctfs. dated after 09/01/2001) 09/01/2001 which merged into Wells Fargo & Co. (New) 12/31/2008

NORTHEAST BK N A LEWISTON & AUBURN (LEWISTON, ME)
99.96% held by Northeastern Bankshare Association as of 05/01/1980
Public interest eliminated

NORTHEAST BANKSHARE ASSN (ME)
Merged into Norstar Bancorp Inc. 6/1/83
Each share Common $5 par exchanged for (1.46) shares Common $5 par
Norstar Bancorp Inc. merged into Fleet/Norstar Financial Group, Inc. 1/1/88 which name changed to Fleet Financial Group, Inc. (New) 4/15/92 which name changed to Fleet Boston Corp. 10/1/99 which name changed to FleetBoston Financial Corp. 4/18/2000 which merged into Bank of America Corp. 4/1/2004

NORTHEAST CAP CORP (NY)
Stock Dividend - 10% 12/16/58
Merged into Mack Trucks, Inc. 10/1/59
Each share Common $1 par exchanged for (0.231) share 5-1/4% Preferred $50 par and (0.7) share Common $5 par
Mack Trucks, Inc. merged into Signal Oil & Gas Co. 9/1/67 which name changed to Signal Companies, Inc. 5/1/68 which merged into Allied-Signal Inc. 9/19/85 which name changed to AlliedSignal Inc. 4/26/93 which name changed to Honeywell International Inc. 12/1/99

NORTHEAST COLORADO NATIONAL BANK (DENVER, CO)
Merged into Colorado National Bankshares, Inc. 09/27/1982
Each share Common $12.50 par exchanged for (8.75) shares Common no par
Colorado National Bankshares, Inc. merged into First Bank System, Inc. 05/28/1993 which name changed to U.S. Bancorp 08/01/1997

NORTHEAST DAIRY COOPERATIVE FEDERATION, INC. (NY)
Plan of reorganization under Chapter 11 Federal Bankruptcy proceedings confirmed 01/26/1987
No stockholders' equity

NORTHEAST DIGITAL NETWORKS INC (DE)
Charter cancelled and declared inoperative and void for non-payment of taxes 03/01/2000

NORTHEAST ENERGY DEV CORP (CA)
Reincorporated under the laws of Delaware as Great American Resources Inc. 07/07/1982
(See Great American Resources Inc.)

NORTHEAST EQUITIES INC (DE)
Name changed to Northeast Petroleum Industries, Inc. 10/29/69
(See Northeast Petroleum Industries, Inc.)

NORTHEAST FED CORP (DE)
Each share $2.25 Preferred Ser. A 1¢ par exchanged for (4.75) shares Common 1¢ par 5/14/93
Merged into Shawmut National Corp. 6/12/95
Each share Common 1¢ par exchanged for (0.415) share Common 1¢ par
Shawmut National Corp. merged into Fleet Financial Corp. (New) 11/30/95 which name changed to Fleet Boston Corp. 10/1/99 which name changed to FleetBoston Financial Corp. 4/18/2000 which merged into Bank of America Corp. 4/1/2004

NORTHEAST FIDELITY INVESTMENT CO. (MN)
Acquired by Fidelity Securities & Investment Co. 3/29/76
Each share Common $5 par exchanged for $4.25 cash

NORTHEAST FINANCIAL CORP. (CT)
Voluntarily dissolved 9/2/80
Details not available

NORTHEAST FINL RES CORP (NV)
Adjustable Rate Preferred no par called for redemption 09/30/1989
Public interest eliminated

NORTHEAST INVS GROWTH FD INC (MA)
Under plan of reorganization each share Common $1 par automatically became (1) Northeast Investors Growth Fund Share of Bene. Int. no par 02/12/1987

NORTHEAST METALS INDUSTRIES, INC. (PA)
Merged into Vanguard Air & Marine Corp. on a (1) for (2) basis 8/1/60
(See Vanguard Air & Marine Corp.)

NORTHEAST MTG CORP (NV)
Charter revoked 08/01/2011

NORTHEAST NURSING HOME, INC. (MD)
Merged into Convalescent Care Centers, Inc. 9/26/68
Each share Common $1 par automatically became (1) share Common 25¢ par
Convalescent Care Centers, Inc. name changed to Medical Services Corp. 12/5/69
(See Medical Services Corp.)

NORTHEAST OHIO AXLE INC (OH)
Name changed to NEOAX, Inc. (OH) 5/13/86
NEOAX, Inc. (OH) reincorporated in Delaware 5/21/87 which name changed to EnviroSource, Inc. 11/14/89 which recapitalized as Envirosource, Inc. 6/22/98
(See Envirosource, Inc.)

NORTHEAST OPTIC NETWORK INC (DE)
Issue Information - 4,500,000 shares

COM offered at $12 per share on 07/30/1998
Under plan of reorganization each share Common 1¢ par automatically became (1) share Neon Communications, Inc. Common 1¢ par 9/15/2000
(See Neon Communications, Inc.)

NORTHEAST PA FINL CORP (DE)
Merged into KNBT Bancorp, Inc. 05/20/2005
Each share Common 1¢ par exchanged for (0.4441216) share Common 1¢ par and $16.744 cash
KNBT Bancorp, Inc. merged into National Penn Bancshares, Inc. 02/01/2008 which merged into BB&T Corp. 04/01/2016

NORTHEAST PETE INDS INC (DE)
$2.30 Preferred $1 par called for redemption 08/14/1972
Capital Stock $1 par changed to 10¢ par and (39) additional shares issued 10/13/1972
Merged into NPI, Inc. 05/12/1977
Each share Capital Stock 10¢ par exchanged for $20.50 cash

NORTHEAST POLLUTION CTL CORP (DE)
Charter cancelled and declared inoperative and void for non-payment of taxes 4/15/72

NORTHEAST SVGS F A HARTFORD CONN (USA)
Under plan of reorganization each share $2.25 Preferred Ser. A 1¢ par and Common 1¢ par automatically became (1) share Northeast Federal Corp. (DE) $2.25 Preferred Ser. A 1¢ par or Common 1¢ par respectively 07/09/1990
Northeast Federal Corp. merged into Shawmut National Corp. 06/12/1995 which merged into Fleet Financial Group Inc. (New) 11/30/1995 which name changed to Fleet Boston Corp. 10/01/1999 which name changed to FleetBoston Financial Corp. 04/18/2000 which merged into Bank of America Corp. 04/01/2004

NORTHEAST TELECOMMUNICATIONS, INC. (DE)
No longer in existence having become inoperative and void for non-payment of taxes 4/1/64

NORTHEAST UTD BANCORP INC TEX (TX)
Stock Dividend - 15% 09/30/1981
Name changed to Texas United Bancorp, Inc. 04/08/1983
Texas United Bancorp, Inc. merged into Allied Bancshares, Inc. (TX) 06/01/1984 which reincorporated in Delaware 04/22/1987 which merged into First Interstate Bancorp 01/29/1988 which merged into Wells Fargo & Co. (Old) 04/01/1996 Wells Fargo & Co. (Old) merged into Wells Fargo & Co. (New) 11/02/1998

NORTHEAST USA CORP (DE)
Name changed to Buy It Cheap.com, Inc. 12/13/1999
Buy It Cheap.com, Inc. recapitalized as Advanced Battery Technologies, Inc. 07/12/2004
(See Advanced Battery Technologies, Inc.)

NORTHEAST UTILS (MA)
Common $5 par split (2) for (1) by issuance of (1) additional share 07/01/1966
Name changed to Eversource Energy 02/19/2015

NORTHEASTERN AMUSEMENT RIDES & SVC CORP (NY)
Merged into Management Dynamics, Inc. 8/20/69
Each share Common 1¢ par exchanged for (1) share Common 1¢ par
(See Management Dynamics, Inc.)

NORTHEASTERN BANCORP INC (PA)
Common $10 par split (2) for (1) by issuance of (1) additional share 06/15/1984
Merged into PNC Financial Corp 01/30/1985
Each share $2.60 Preferred Ser. A $10 par exchanged for (1) share $2.60 Preferred Ser. E $1 par
Each share Common $10 par exchanged for (0.5) share $1.80 Conv. Preferred Ser. D $1 par and (0.45) share Common $5 par
PNC Financial Corp name changed to PNC Bank Corp. 02/08/1993 which name changed to PNC Financial Services Group, Inc. 03/15/2000

NORTHEASTERN BK PA (SCRANTON, PA)
Under plan of reorganization each share Capital Stock $10 par automatically became (1) share Northeastern Bancorp, Inc. Common $10 par 08/12/1981
Northeastern Bancorp, Inc. merged into PNC Financial Corp 01/30/1985 which name changed to PNC Bank Corp. 02/08/1993 which name changed to PNC Financial Services Group, Inc. 03/15/2000

NORTHEASTERN BANKSHARE ASSN (ME)
Name changed to Northeast Bankshare Association 3/23/71
Northeast Bankshare Association merged into Norstar Bancorp Inc. 6/1/83 which merged into Fleet/Norstar Financial Group, Inc. 1/1/88 which name changed to Fleet Financial Group, Inc. (New) 4/15/92 which name changed to Fleet Boston Corp. 10/1/99 which name changed to FleetBoston Financial Corp. 4/18/2000 which merged into Bank of America Corp. 4/1/2004

NORTHEASTERN COIN CORP. (DE)
Merged into United Professional Data Processing Corp. 03/30/1970
Details not available

NORTHEASTERN INS CO HARTFORD (CT)
Capital Stock $5 par changed to $3.33-1/3 par 00/00/1947
Stock Dividend - 100% 11/06/1972
Merged into Financial Security Group, Inc. 02/01/1978
Each share Capital Stock $3.33-1/3 par exchanged for $44 cash

NORTHEASTERN LIFE INS CO (NY)
Under plan of merger each share Class A $10 par or Class B $10 par exchanged for (0.5) share Common $4.50 par 01/31/1958
Involuntarily dissolved 08/03/1976
Stockholders' equity unlikely

NORTHEASTERN MTG INC (MA)
Stock Dividend - 10% 2/27/87
Merged into University Bank, N.A. (Newton, MA) 6/2/88
Each share Common 10¢ par exchanged for (0.5) share Common 30¢ par
(See University Bank, N.A (Newton, MA))

NORTHEASTERN NATL BK PA (SCRANTON, PA)
Capital Stock $20 par changed to $10 par and (1) additional share issued 03/23/1973
Name changed to Northeastern Bank of Pennsylvania (Scranton, PA) 01/02/1974
Northeastern Bank of Pennsylvania (Scranton, PA) reorganized as Northeastern Bancorp, Inc. 08/12/1981 which merged into PNC Financial Corp 01/30/1985 which name changed to PNC Bank Corp. 02/08/1993 which name changed to PNC Financial Services Group, Inc. 03/15/2000

NORTHEASTERN NATURAL GAS CO.
Merged into Northeastern Oil & Gas Co. in 1936 which was liquidated in 1942

NORTHEASTERN OHIO NATL BK (ASHTABULA, OH)
Common Capital Stock $25 par changed to $10 par and (1.5) additional shares issued 07/02/1973
Stock Dividend - 14.3% 06/01/1971
Merged into CleveTrust Corp. 11/25/1975
Each share Common Capital Stock $10 par exchanged for $46.75 cash

NORTHEASTERN OIL & GAS CO.
Liquidated in 1942

NORTHEASTERN PA NATL BK & TR CO (SCRANTON, PA)
Capital Stock $18 par changed to $20 par 02/07/1967
Name changed to Northeastern National Bank of Pennsylvania (Scranton, PA) 04/02/1971
Northeastern National Bank of Pennsylvania (Scranton, PA) name changed to Northeastern Bank of Pennsylvania (Scranton, PA) 01/02/1974 which reorganized as Northeastern Bancorp, Inc. 08/12/1981 which merged into PNC Financial Corp. 01/30/1985 which name changed to PNC Bank Corp. 02/08/1993 which name changed to PNC Financial Services Group, Inc. 03/15/2000

NORTHEASTERN PENNSYLVANIA BROADCASTING, INC. (PA)
Liquidation completed
Each share Class B Common no par or VTC for Class A Common no par exchanged for initial distribution of $0.52 cash 10/5/66
Each share Class B Common no par or VTC for Class A Common no par received second and final distribution of $0.07 cash 6/26/67

NORTHEASTERN PLASTICS INC (NY)
Merged into Teledata, Inc. 10/10/1969
Each share Common 10¢ par exchanged for (0.42595) share Common 10¢ par
Teledata, Inc. name changed to TDA Industries, Inc. 12/02/1970
(See TDA Industries, Inc.)

NORTHEASTERN POWER CORP.
Merged into Niagara Hudson Power Corp. in 1929
Details not available

NORTHEASTERN PUBLIC SERVICE CO.
Reorganized as Northeastern Water & Electric Corp. in 1934
(See Northeastern Water & Electric Corp.)

NORTHEASTERN STEEL CORP. (CT)
Reorganized 9/6/57
No stockholders' equity

NORTHEASTERN SURETY CO.
Acquired by Lloyds Casualty Co. in 1930
(See Lloyds Casualty Co.)

NORTHEASTERN UTILITIES CO. (DE)
No longer in existence having become inoperative and void for non-payment of taxes 4/1/35

NORTHEASTERN WATER & ELECTRIC CORP.
Merged into Northeastern Water Co. share for share in 1944
Northeastern Water Co. merged into American Water Works Co., Inc. 8/17/62
(See American Water Works Co., Inc.)

NORTHEASTERN WATER CO. (DE)
Each share $4 Prior Preferred no par exchanged for (1) share new $4 Prior Preferred no par 00/00/1947
Each share $2 Preferred no par exchanged for (1) share new $2 Preferred no par 00/00/1947
Each (2) shares Common $1 par exchanged for (1) share new $2 Preferred no par 00/00/1947
Recapitalized 11/15/1956
Each share Common $1 par exchanged for (1) share Class A Common $1 par and (2) shares Class B Common $1 par
Merged into American Water Works Co., Inc. 08/17/1962
Each share $4 Prior Preferred no par exchanged for (4) shares 5% Preference $25 par
Each share $2 Preferred no par exchanged for (2) shares 5% Preference $25 par
(See American Water Works Co., Inc.)

NORTHERN & CENT GAS LTD (ON)
Merged into Norcen Energy Resources Ltd. 10/28/1972
Each share $1.06 2nd Preference Ser. A $25 par exchanged for (1) share 1st Preference Ser. A $25 par
Each share $1.50 Conv. Jr. Preference 1st Ser. $25 par exchanged for (1) share $1.50 Conv. Jr. Preference 1st Ser. $25 par
Each share $1.50 Conv. 2nd Preference Ser. B $25 par exchanged for (1) share $1.50 Conv. 1st Preference Ser. B $25 par
Each share Common no par exchanged for (1) share Common no par
Note: The $2.60 1st Preference 1st Ser. $50 par and $2.70 1st Preference 2nd Ser. $50 par shares were not affected by the merger and remained outstanding
Name changed to ICG Utilities (Ontario) Ltd. 07/11/1986
ICG Utilities (Ontario) Ltd. name changed to Centra Gas Ontario Inc. 01/21/1991

NORTHERN & CENTRAL GAS CO. LTD. (ON)
Common no par split (2) for (1) by issuance of (1) additional share 7/11/66
Under plan of merger name changed to Northern & Central Gas Corp. Ltd. 1/1/68
All classes affected by change of name only with exception of $2.60 1st Preference 1965 Ser. $50 par which also automatically became $2.60 1st Preference 1st Ser. $50 par
(See Northern & Central Gas Corp. Ltd.)

NORTHERN ABITIBI MNG CORP (AB)
Reincorporated 07/14/2011
Place of incorporation changed from (QC) to (AB) 07/14/2011
Recapitalized as CANEX Metals Inc. 04/03/2017
Each share Common no par exchanged for (0.2) share Common no par

NORTHERN ACQUISITION CORP (AB)
Name changed to Ultra Pure Water Systems (Canada) Inc. 03/15/1994
(See Ultra Pure Water Systems (Canada) Inc.)

NORTHERN AERIAL MINERALS EXPLORATION, LTD.
Liquidated in 1935

NORTHERN AIR FGHT INC (WA)
Merged into Danzas AG 02/27/1989
Each share Common 1¢ par exchanged for $9.125 cash

NORTHERN AIRLINES, INC. (OH)
Charter cancelled for non-payment of taxes 9/30/71

NORTHERN ARIZ GOLD & SILVER MLG & MNG INC (DE)
Name changed to Dominion Resources, Inc. 03/08/1982
Dominion Resources, Inc. reorganized as Digital Imaging Resources Inc. 11/12/2004 which recapitalized as Boomerang Systems, Inc. 02/08/2008
(See Boomerang Systems, Inc.)

NORTHERN ASPECT RES LTD (AB)
Name changed to BTL Group Ltd. 11/06/2015

NORTHERN BAKERIES OF CANADA
Merged into Consolidated Bakeries of Canada Ltd. 00/00/1928
Details not available

NORTHERN BK COMM ORE (PORTLAND, OR)
Merged into Cowlitz Bancorporation 07/01/2000
Each share Common $1 par exchanged for $1.665 cash
Note: Each share Common $1 par received an additional distribution of approximately $0.02 cash 08/31/2001

NORTHERN BLIZZARD RES INC (AB)
Name changed to Cona Resources Ltd. 07/17/2017
(See Cona Resources Ltd.)

NORTHERN BORDER PARTNERS L P (DE)
Name changed to ONEOK Partners, L.P. 05/17/2006
ONEOK Partners, L.P. merged into ONEOK, Inc. (New) 06/30/2017

NORTHERN BULLION KENO LTD (BC)
Recapitalized as Jubilee Explorations Inc. 4/23/79
Each share Common no par exchanged for (1/3) share Common no par

NORTHERN CALIF CMNTY BANCORPORATION INC (DE)
Merged into California Bancshares Inc. 07/01/1991
Each share Common Capital $2.50 par exchanged for (1.163) shares Common $2.50 par
California Bancshares Inc. merged into U.S. Bancorp (OR) 06/06/1996 which merged into U.S. Bancorp 08/01/1997

NORTHERN CALIF DEVELOPERS INC (CA)
Capital Stock $10 par changed to $1 par 11/10/1970
Name changed to NCD Financial, Inc. 12/31/1973
(See NCD Financial, Inc.)

NORTHERN CALIF SVGS A FED SVGS & LN ASSN (CA)
Name changed 05/14/1982
Guarantee Stock no par split (3) for (2) by issuance of (0.5) additional share 11/30/1977
Name changed from Northern California Savings & Loan Association to Northern California Savings, A Federal Savings & Loan Association and Guarantee Stock no par reclassified as Common no par 05/14/1982
Merged into Great Western Financial Corp. 07/31/1982
Each share Common no par exchanged for (1) share Capital Stock $1 par
Great Western Financial Corp. merged into Washington Mutual Inc. 07/01/1997
(See Washington Mutual, Inc.)

NORTHERN CALIFORNIA GOLD MINES CO. (SD)
Charter expired by time limitation 5/4/25

NORTHERN CALIFORNIA MORTGAGE CO.
Acquired by Mercantile Acceptance Corp. of California 00/00/1929
Details not available

NORTHERN CALIFORNIA NATIONAL BANK (SAN MATEO, CA)
Liquidation completed
Each share Common $10 par exchanged for initial distribution of $15 cash 8/22/66
Each share Common $10 par received second distribution of $3.50 cash 12/15/66
Each share Common $10 par received third and final distribution of $2.89 cash 8/31/67

NORTHERN CDA MINES LTD (ON)
Common no par split (3) for (2) by issuance of (0.5) additional share payable 8/14/96 to holders of record 8/1/96
Merged into Hunter Brook Holdings Ltd. 1/1/99
Each share Common no par exchanged for $8.50 cash

NORTHERN CANADA MINING CORP. LTD.
Reorganized 03/21/1938
Each share Capital Stock exchanged for (0.4) share Capital Stock no par of Northern Canada Mines Ltd. and (0.4) share Capital Stock $1 par of Kirkland Lake Gold Mining Co. Ltd.
(See each company's listing)

NORTHERN CANADA POWER LTD.
Merged into Northern Ontario Power Co. Ltd. 00/00/1928
Details not available

NORTHERN CDN MINERALS INC (BC)
Name changed to Northern Canadian Uranium Inc. 04/09/2007
Northern Canadian Uranium Inc. merged into Bayswater Uranium Corp. (New) 12/21/2007 which recapitalized as Green Thumb Industries Inc. 06/13/2018

NORTHERN CDN URANIUM INC (BC)
Merged into Bayswater Uranium Corp. (New) 12/21/2007
Each share Common no par exchanged for (0.65) share Common no par
Bayswater Uranium Corp. (New) recapitalized as Green Thumb Industries Inc. 06/13/2018

NORTHERN CENT BK (WILLIAMSPORT, PA)
Under plan of merger each share Common $5 par automatically became (1) share NCB Financial Corp. Common $5 par 07/29/1983
NCB Financial Corp. merged into Keystone Financial, Inc. 12/31/1984 which merged into M&T Bank Corp. 10/06/2000

NORTHERN CENT RY CO (MD & PA)
Merged into Penn Central Corp. 10/24/78
Each share Capital Stock $50 par exchanged for $21 principal amount of non-interest bearing Ctf. of Bene. Int. no par and (0.73) share Common $1 par
Note: a) Distribution is certain only for certificates surrendered prior to 5/1/85 b) Distribution may also be made for certificates surrendered between 5/1/85 and 12/31/86 c) No distribution will be made for certificates surrendered after 12/31/86
Penn Central Corp. name changed to American Premier Underwriters, Inc. 3/25/94 which merged into American Premier Group, Inc. 4/3/95 which name changed to American Financial Group, Inc. 6/9/95 which merged into American Financial Group, Inc. (Holding Co.) 12/2/97

NORTHERN CENTRAL BANK & TRUST CO. (WILLIAMSPORT, PA)
Common $10 par changed to $5 par and (1) additional share issued plus a 50% stock dividend paid 8/1/74
Stock Dividend - 100% 5/19/70
Name changed to Northern Central Bank (Williamsport, PA) 7/1/75
Northern Central Bank (Williamsport, PA) merged into NCB Financial Corp. 7/29/83 which merged into Keystone Financial, Inc. 12/31/84 which merged into M&T Bank Corp. 10/6/2000

NORTHERN CHEM INDS INC (ME)
Liquidation completed
Each share Class A Common $50 par exchanged for first and final distribution of $50 cash 04/15/1970
Each share Class B Common no par exchanged for initial distribution of $8 cash 04/15/1970
Each share Class B Common no par received second and final distribution of $1.48 cash 10/09/1970

NORTHERN COAL MINES LTD (BC)
Recapitalized as Norco Resources Ltd. 1/19/76
Each share Capital Stock no par exchanged for (0.1) share Common no par
(See Norco Resources Ltd.)

NORTHERN CONN NATL BK (WINDSOR LOCKS, CT)
Stock Dividend - 25% 07/01/1981
Merged into CBT Corp. 02/11/1985
Each share Capital Stock $10 par exchanged for (2.319) shares Common $10 par
CBT Corp. merged into Bank of New England Corp. 06/14/1985
(See Bank of New England Corp.)

NORTHERN CONSOLIDATED AIRLINES, INC. (AK)
Stock Dividend - Paid in Non-Vtg. Common to holders of Common - 12% 4/25/68
Name changed to Wien Consolidated Airlines, Inc. 7/17/68
Wien Consolidated Airlines, Inc. name changed to Wien Air Alaska, Inc. 7/16/73
(See Wien Air Alaska, Inc.)

NORTHERN CONTL RES INC (BC)
Merged into Hathor Exploration Ltd. 11/23/2009
Each share Common no par exchanged for (0.1389) share Common no par
Note: Unexchanged certificates were cancelled and became without value 11/23/2015
(See Hathor Exploration Ltd.)

NORTHERN COPPER LTD (MB)
Charter cancelled and declared dissolved for failure to file returns 03/01/1973

NORTHERN COPPER RIDGE MINES LTD (BC)
Name changed to Ventec Resources Inc. 07/19/1982
(See Ventec Resources Inc.)

NORTHERN CORP (DE)
Charter cancelled and declared inoperative and void for non-payment of taxes 3/1/97

NORTHERN CROWN MINES LTD (BC)
Each share old Common no par exchanged for (0.1) share new Common no par 12/06/2001
Name changed to Canadian Empire Exploration Corp. 08/15/2002
Canadian Empire Exploration Corp. recapitalized as X-Terra Resources Corp. (BC) 02/23/2007 which reincorporated in Canada 09/04/2008 which name changed to Norvista Capital Corp. 07/03/2014

NORTHERN DANCER CORP (CO)
Recapitalized as U.S. Trucking, Inc. 9/7/98
Each (160) shares Common no par exchanged for (1) share Common no par
U.S. Trucking, Inc. recapitalized as Logistics Management Resources Inc. 2/12/2001 which name changed to American Business Corp. 6/28/2004

NORTHERN DANCER RES LTD (BC)
Struck off register and declared dissolved for failure to file returns 04/08/1994

NORTHERN DATA SYS INC (MA)
Merged into Continental Telecom Inc. 7/16/85
Each share Common $0.001 par exchanged for (0.455) share Common $1 par
Continental Telecom Inc. name changed to Contel Corp. 5/1/86 which merged into GTE Corp. 3/14/91 which merged into Verizon Communications Inc. 6/30/2000

NORTHERN DYNASTY EXPLS LTD (BC)
Recapitalized as Northern Dynasty Minerals Ltd. 12/09/1994
Each share Common no par exchanged for (0.33333333) share Common no par

NORTHERN EAGLE MINES, LTD. (ON)
Merged into Great Eagle Explorations & Holdings Ltd. 7/7/69
Each (9) shares Common no par exchanged for (4) shares Common no par
Great Eagle Explorations & Holdings Ltd. merged into Belle Aire Resource Explorations Ltd. 8/29/78 which name changed to Sprint Resources Ltd. 9/23/82 which name changed to Meacon Bay Resources Inc. 3/9/87 which recapitalized as Advantex Marketing International Inc. 9/16/91

NORTHERN EAGLE MINES LTD (BC)
Recapitalized as Bentley Resources Ltd. 07/19/1985
Each share Common no par exchanged for (0.2) share Common no par
(See Bentley Resources Ltd.)

NORTHERN ELEC LTD (CANADA)
Name changed to Northern Telecom Ltd.-Northern Telecom Ltee. 03/01/1976
Northern Telecom Ltd.-Northern Telecom Ltee. name changed to Nortel Networks Corp. (Old) 04/30/1999 which reorganized as Nortel Networks Corp. (New) 05/01/2000
(See Nortel Networks Corp. (New))

NORTHERN ELEC PLC (UNITED KINGDOM)
ADR agreement terminated 3/14/97
Each Final Installment Sponsored ADR for Ordinary 50p par exchanged for $10.54 cash

NORTHERN ELECTRIC STREET RAILWAY CO.
Property sold in 1932
No stockholders' equity

NORTHERN EMPIRE BANCSHARES (CA)
Common no par split (2) for (1) by issuance of (1) additional share payable 10/15/1998 to holders of record 09/30/1998
Common no par split (2) for (1) by issuance of (1) additional share

payable 12/15/2003 to holders of record 12/01/2003 Ex date - 12/16/2003
Stock Dividends - 5% payable 07/01/1996 to holders of record 06/14/1996; 5% payable 05/15/1998 to holders of record 05/01/1998; 5% payable 06/07/1999 to holders of record 05/18/1999; 5% payable 05/17/2000 to holders of record 05/03/2000; 5% payable 05/21/2001 to holders of record 05/04/2001 Ex date - 05/02/2001; 5% payable 05/17/2002 to holders of record 04/30/2002 Ex date - 04/26/2002; 5% payable 05/30/2003 to holders of record 05/09/2003 Ex date - 05/07/2003; 5% payable 05/31/2004 to holders of record 05/03/2004 Ex date - 04/29/2004; 5% payable 05/31/2005 to holders of record 05/02/2005 Ex date - 04/28/2005; 5% payable 05/19/2006 to holders of record 05/01/2006 Ex date - 04/27/2006
Merged into Sterling Financial Corp. 03/01/2007
Each share Common no par exchanged for (0.805) share Common $1 par and $2.71 cash
Sterling Financial Corp. merged into Umpqua Holdings Corp. 04/18/2014

NORTHERN EMPIRE ENERGY CORP (NV)
Name changed to SmartChase Corp. 12/03/2014

NORTHERN EMPIRE MINERALS LTD (BC)
Under plan of merger name changed to Stornoway Diamond Corp. (BC) 07/16/2003
Stornoway Diamond Corp. (BC) reincorporated in Canada 10/28/2011

NORTHERN EMPIRE MINES CO. LTD. (ON)
Liquidated 00/00/1954
Details not available

NORTHERN EMPIRE MINES LTD. (BC)
Completely liquidated 03/02/1972
Each share Common 50¢ par exchanged for first and final distribution of (1) share Northern Homestake Mines Ltd. Capital Stock no par
Northern Homestake Mines Ltd. recapitalized as Thunderwood Explorations Ltd. 05/31/1976 which recapitalized as International Thunderwood Explorations Ltd. (BC) 07/14/1983 which reincorporated in Canada 04/27/1987 which reorganized in Ontario as Thunderwood Resources Inc.-Les Ressources Thunderwood Inc. 06/01/1989 which merged into Thundermin Resources Inc. 11/01/1998 which merged into Rambler Metals & Mining PLC 01/12/2016

NORTHERN EMPIRE RES CORP (BC)
Each share old Common no par exchanged for (0.33333333) share new Common no par 05/31/2017
Merged into Coeur Mining, Inc. 10/01/2018
Each share new Common no par exchanged for (0.185) share Common 1¢ par
Note: Unexchanged certificates will be cancelled and become without value 10/01/2024

NORTHERN ENERGY CORP (BC)
Recapitalized as United Northern Petroleum Corp. 03/24/1986
Each share Common no par exchanged for (0.5) share Common no par
United Northern Petroleum Corp. name changed to UNP Industries Ltd. 11/06/1989 which recapitalized as International UNP Holdings Ltd. (BC) 11/29/1990 which reincorporated in Canada 08/04/1993
(See International UNP Holdings Ltd.)

NORTHERN ENGINEERED GOLD RES LTD (BC)
Name changed to Petrocel Industries Inc. 08/29/1983
(See Petrocel Industries Inc.)

NORTHERN ENGINEERING WORKS (MI)
Each share Common no par exchanged for (3) shares Common $1 par 00/00/1946
Name changed to Nertorn, Inc. 05/01/1967
(See Nertorn, Inc.)

NORTHERN ENTERPRISES INC (MN)
Merged into Kodiak, Inc. 09/30/1968
Each share Common no par exchanged for (194) shares Common 50¢ par
Kodiak, Inc. recapitalized as Kodicor, Inc. 05/10/1972
(See Kodicor, Inc.)

NORTHERN ESPINA RES LTD (BC)
Name changed to Erica Resources Ltd. 01/09/1981
(See Erica Resources Ltd.)

NORTHERN EXPL LTD (QC)
Recapitalized as Consolidated Northern Exploration Ltd. 11/17/1969
Each share Capital Stock $1 par exchanged for (1/3) share Capital Stock $1 par
(See Consolidated Northern Exploration Ltd.)

NORTHERN EXPLORATIONS LTD (NV)
Common $0.001 par split (6) for (1) by issuance of (5) additional shares payable 07/28/2008 to holders of record 07/16/2008 Ex date - 07/29/2008
Common $0.001 par split (3) for (1) by issuance of (2) additional shares payable 04/28/2009 to holders of record 03/30/2009 Ex date - 04/29/2009
Recapitalized as High Plains Gas, Inc. 09/30/2010
Each share Common $0.001 par exchanged for (0.005) share Common $0.001 par
(See High Plains Gas, Inc.)

NORTHERN EXPRESS AIRLS INC (DE)
Charter cancelled and declared inoperative and void for non-payment of taxes 3/1/90

NORTHERN EXTENSIONS LTD.
Acquired by Consolidated East Crest Oil Co. Ltd. 09/00/1954
Each share Common no par exchanged for (0.166666) share Capital Stock no par
Consolidated East Crest Oil Co. Ltd. liquidated for Pan Ocean Oil Corp. 01/01/1972
(See Pan Ocean Oil Corp.)

NORTHERN FIBERGLASS, INC. (MN)
Merged into Interplastic Corp. 5/1/62
Each share Capital Stock 25¢ par exchanged for (1) share Common 10¢ par
(See Interplastic Corp.)

NORTHERN FINL CORP (ON)
Each share old Common no par exchanged for (0.01) share new Common no par 11/02/2005
Recapitalized as Added Capital Inc. 07/23/2014
Each share new Common no par exchanged for (0.1) share Common no par

NORTHERN FOUNDERS INSURANCE CO. (ND)
Name changed to Northern National Life Insurance Co. 4/2/65
Northern National Life Insurance Co. name changed to Manhattan National Life Insurance Co. 1/1/82
(See Manhattan National Life Insurance Co.)

NORTHERN FREEGOLD RES LTD (BC)
Reincorporated 12/19/2011
Place of incorporation changed from (AB) to (BC) 12/19/2011
Each share old Common no par exchanged for (0.1) share new Common no par 10/09/2014
Name changed to Triumph Gold Corp. 01/25/2017

NORTHERN GAMING INC (BC)
Recapitalized as Icon Laser Eye Centers Inc. 9/1/99
Each share Common no par exchanged for (0.1) share Common no par

NORTHERN GEM MNG LTD (BC)
Name changed to Cepeda Minerals Inc. and Common $1 par changed to no par 08/11/1988
(See Cepeda Minerals Inc.)

NORTHERN GLACIER RES INC (AB)
Recapitalized as Basic Realty Investment Corp. 12/10/1999
Each share Common no par exchanged for (0.33333333) share Common no par
Basic Realty Investment Corp. recapitalized as Uni-Invest Ltd. 11/17/2000 which name changed to Homburg Invest Inc. 01/11/2001
(See Homburg Invest Inc.)

NORTHERN GOLD MNG INC (ON)
Merged into Oban Mining Corp. 12/24/2015
Each share Common no par exchanged for (0.01270168) share Common no par
Note: Unexchanged certificates will be cancelled and become without value 12/24/2021
Oban Mining Corp. name changed to Osisko Mining Inc. 06/21/2016

NORTHERN HEMISPHERE DEV CORP (BC)
Recapitalized as Hemisphere Energy Corp. 04/27/2009
Each share Common no par exchanged for (0.2) share Common no par

NORTHERN HLDG & DEV CO (MN)
Name changed to Medserco Inc. 06/16/1975
(See Medserco Inc.)

NORTHERN HOMESTAKE MINES LTD (BC)
Recapitalized as Thunderwood Explorations Ltd. 05/31/1976
Each share Capital Stock no par exchanged for (0.33333333) share Capital Stock no par
Thunderwood Explorations Ltd. recapitalized as International Thunderwood Explorations Ltd. (BC) 07/14/1983 which reincorporated in Canada 04/27/1987 which reorganized in Ontario as Thunderwood Resources Inc.-Les Ressources Thunderwood Inc. 06/01/1989 which merged into Thundermin Resources Inc. 11/01/1998 which merged into Rambler Metals & Mining PLC 01/12/2016

NORTHERN HORIZON RES CORP (BC)
Recapitalized as Golden Horizon Resource Corp. 10/3/85
Each share Common no par exchanged for (0.25) share Common no par
Golden Horizon Resource Corp. recapitalized as GHZ Resource Corp. 1/2/90 which name changed to Canadian Reserve Gold Corp. 6/10/94 which recapitalized as Christina Gold Resources Ltd. 4/18/96 which recapitalized as PowerHouse Energy Corp. 12/11/98 which recapitalized as International Powerhouse Energy Corp. 9/18/2001 which name changed to Sea Breeze Power Corp. 7/30/2003

NORTHERN ILL CORP (DE)
Merged into Associates Investment Co. (IN.) 1/2/68
Each share $1.50 Conv. Preferred no par exchanged for (1) share Common $5 par
Each share Common no par exchanged for (0.5771) share Common $5 par
Associates Investment Co. (IN) reincorporated under the laws of Delaware 6/26/69
(See Associates Investment Co. (DE))

NORTHERN ILL GAS CO (IL)
Common $5 par split (3) for (2) by issuance of (0.5) additional share 07/31/1964
5.50% Pfd. $100 par called for redemption 05/01/1965
Under plan of reorganization each share $1.90 Conv. Pref. no par, 4.48% Pfd. $100 par, 4.60% Conv. Pfd. $100 par, 5% Pfd. $100 par, 5% Cv. Pfd. 100 par and Common Common $5 par automatically became (1) share Nicor Inc. $1.90 Conv. Pref. no par, 4.48% Pfd. $100 par, 4.60% Conv. Pfd. $100 par, 5% Pfd. $100 par, 5% Conv. Pfd. $100 par and Common $5 par respectively 04/30/1976
Nicor Inc. merged into AGL Resources Inc. 12/09/2011

NORTHERN ILLINOIS FINANCE CORP.
Name changed to Northern Illinois Corp. in 1942
Northern Illinois Corp. merged into Associates Investment Co. (Ind.) 1/2/68 which reincorporated under the laws of Delaware 6/26/69
(See Associates Investment Co. (Del.))

NORTHERN IND FUEL & LT INC (IN)
Acquired by NIPSCO Industries Inc. 3/31/93
Each share Common no par exchanged for $109.8125 cash

NORTHERN IND PUB SVC CO (IN)
5-1/2% Preferred called for redemption 10/22/44
6% Preferred called for redemption 10/22/44
7% Preferred called for redemption 10/22/44
5% Preferred $100 par called for redemption 2/27/50
4-1/2% Preference $20 par called for redemption 5/6/55
4.56% Preference $25 par called for redemption 6/28/56
Common no par split (2) for (1) by issuance of (1) additional share 5/5/61
Common no par split (2) for (1) by issuance of (10 additional share 5/9/66
4.40% Preference $40 par called for redemption 8/15/72
Under plan of reorganization each share Common no par automatically became (1) share Nipsco Industries, Inc. Common no par 3/3/88
8.36% Preference $50 par called for redemption 8/22/88
11.64% Preference $50 par called for redemption 10/11/88
Adjustable Rate Preferred Ser. A no par called for redemption at $50 on 4/14/2006

4.22% Preferred $100 par called for redemption at $101.60 on 4/14/2006
4.25% Preferred $100 par called for redemption at $101.20 on 4/14/2006
4.50% Preferred $100 par called for redemption at $100 on 4/14/2006
4.88% Preferred $100 par called for redemption at $102 on 4/14/2006
7.44% Preferred $100 par called for redemption at $101 on 4/14/2006
7.50% Preferred $100 par called for redemption at $101 on 4/14/2006
Public interest eliminated

NORTHERN INDIANA GAS & ELECTRIC CO.
Merged into Northern Indiana Public Service Co. in 1926
Details not available

NORTHERN INDIANA RAILWAY, INC.
Reorganized as Northern Indiana Transit, Inc. in 1940
No stockholders' equity

NORTHERN INDIANA TELEPHONE CO.
Assets acquired by Indiana Associated Telephone Corp. 00/00/1950
Details not available

NORTHERN INDIANA TRANSIT, INC. (IN)
Acquired by National City Lines, Inc. 04/01/1956
Details not available

NORTHERN INDL MINERALS INC (NV)
Recapitalized as Provident Holdings Inc. 7/2/2002
Each (15) shares Common $0.001 par exchanged for (1) share Common $0.001 par
Provident Holdings Inc. name changed to QMAC Energy Inc. 1/14/2004

NORTHERN INDUSTRIES, LTD. (SK)
Charter revoked for failure to file reports and pay fees 9/28/62

NORTHERN INFORMATION TECHNOLOGY INC (DE)
Charter cancelled and declared inoperative and void for non-payment of taxes 6/27/89

NORTHERN INSTRS CORP (DE)
Reincorporated 01/30/1978
State of incorporation changed from (MN) to (DE) 01/30/1978
Name changed to Northern Technologies International Corp. 05/03/1993

NORTHERN INSTRUMENT CORP. (NY)
Charter cancelled and proclaimed dissolved for failure to pay taxes and file reports 12/16/74

NORTHERN INSTRUMENTS, INC. (MN)
Name changed to Northern Instruments Corp. (MN) 4/9/76
Northern Instruments Corp. (MN) reincorporated in Delaware 1/30/78 which name changed to Northern Technologies International Corp. 5/3/93

NORTHERN INSURANCE CO. OF NEW YORK (NY)
Each share Capital Stock $100 par exchanged for (4) shares Capital Stock $25 par in 1928
Capital Stock $25 par changed to $12.50 par in 1932
Capital Stock $12.50 par split (2) for (1) by issuance of (1) additional share 12/23/58
Stock Dividends - 100% 6/22/50; 10% 3/8/54; 10% 3/12/56
Each share Capital Stock $12.50 par exchanged for (0.002) share Capital Stock $6,250 par 8/28/68
Public interest eliminated

NORTHERN INVTS PPTYS (OH)
Merged into Northern Real Estate Trust 08/31/1974
Each Share of Bene. Int. no par held by Ohio residents exchanged for (1.2) Shares of Bene. Int. no par
Each Share of Bene. Int. no par held by non-Ohio residents exchanged for $8 cash
(See Northern Real Estate Trust)

NORTHERN IRON CORP (ON)
Name changed to Lithium Energy Products Inc. 12/08/2016

NORTHERN KYANITE MINES LTD. (ON)
Completely liquidated 8/14/64
Each share Capital Stock $1 par exchanged for first and final distribution of $0.007 cash

NORTHERN LEAD ZINC LTD.
Acquired by Pine Point Mines Ltd. 00/00/1951
Each (6.331) shares Capital Stock $1 par exchanged for (1) share Common no par
(See Pine Point Mines Ltd.)

NORTHERN LEHIGH BANCORP INC (PA)
Merged into Harleysville National Corp. 01/22/1999
Each share Common $10 par exchanged for (3.57) shares Common $1 par
Harleysville National Corp. merged into First Niagara Financial Group, Inc. (New) 04/09/2010 which merged into KeyCorp (New) 08/01/2016

NORTHERN LIBERTIES GAS CO. (PA)
Liquidation completed 7/16/56

NORTHERN LIFE INS CO (WA)
Common $100 par changed to $20 par and (4) additional shares issued plus a 100% stock dividend paid 03/15/1957
Each share Common $20 par exchanged for (4) shares Common $5 par 09/10/1965
Stock Dividend - 100% 09/17/1965
100% reacquired by company 10/31/1972
Details not available

NORTHERN LTS ACQUISITION CORP (AB)
Recapitalized as Iona Energy Inc. 06/08/2011
Each share Common no par exchanged for (0.34293552) share Common no par
(See Iona Energy Inc.)

NORTHERN LTS BIG GAME CORP (SK)
Delisted from Vancouver Stock Exchange 10/31/1994

NORTHERN LTS ETF TR (DE)
Name changed to Arrow ETF Trust 07/29/2014

NORTHERN LTS RES LTD (BC)
Recapitalized as Larch Resources Ltd. 03/25/1986
Each share Common no par exchanged for (0.2) share Common no par
Larch Resources Ltd. recapitalized as Manticore Petroleum Corp. 01/28/1987 which recapitalized as Dexx Energy Corp. 05/31/1988
(See Dexx Energy Corp.)

NORTHERN LTS SOFTWARE LTD (DE)
Name changed to Formquest International Ltd. 9/3/97
Formquest International Ltd. name changed to MegaChain.com, Ltd. 4/9/99 which name changed to Acola Corp. 10/22/2001 which name changed to Teda Travel Group Inc. 4/21/2004 which name changed to Network CN, Inc. 8/15/2006

NORTHERN MANUFACTURING CO. OF NEWARK
Acquired by National Union Radio Corp. 00/00/1929
Details not available

NORTHERN MINERALS, INC. (DE)
Dissolved 11/23/64
No stockholders' equity

NORTHERN MINERALS INC (NV)
Name changed to Raider Ventures Inc. 10/03/2012
Raider Ventures Inc. name changed to Integrated Electric Systems Corp. 04/01/2013 which name changed to KollagenX Corp. 07/30/2014

NORTHERN MINERALS LTD (AB)
Merged into Capilano International Inc. 02/11/1991
Each share Common no par exchanged for (0.25) share Common no par and (0.25) Common Stock Purchase Warrant expiring 11/30/1991
Capilano International Inc. name changed to Kelman Technologies Inc. 08/14/1996
(See Kelman Technologies Inc.)

NORTHERN MNG CORP N L (AUSTRALIA)
ADR agreement terminated 08/25/1982
Each ADR for Ordinary AUD $0.50 par exchanged for $3.69 cash

NORTHERN MNG EXPLORATIONS LTD (QC)
Name changed to MDN Inc. 07/13/2007
MDN Inc. recapitalized as Niobay Metals Inc. 09/21/2016

NORTHERN MTN HELICOPTERS GROUP INC (AB)
Bankruptcy trustee discharged 12/23/2004
No stockholders' equity

NORTHERN NAT GAS CO (DE)
Each share Common $20 par exchanged for (2) shares Common $10 par in 1947
Common $10 par split (2) for (1) by issuance of (1) additional share 4/11/58
Common $10 par split (2) for (1) by issuance of (1) additional share 11/21/75
Name changed to InterNorth, Inc. 3/28/80
InterNorth, Inc. name changed to Enron Corp. 5/12/86
(See Enron Corp.)

NORTHERN NATIONAL BANK (GRAYLING, MI)
Merged into Chemical Financial Corp. 8/31/84
Each share Common $12.50 par exchanged for (0.5) share Common $10 par

NORTHERN NATL BK (PRESQUE ISLE, ME)
Each share Common $100 par exchanged for (4) shares Common $25 par 01/14/1958
Common $25 par changed to $6.25 par and (3) additional shares issued 03/15/1967
Stock Dividends - 10% 03/15/1965; 10% 03/15/1966; 10% 03/15/1968
99.97% acquired by Casco-Northern Corp. through exchange offer as of 08/31/1972
Public interest eliminated

NORTHERN NATL CORP (NJ)
Stock Dividend - 10% 05/10/1982
Merged into Horizon Bancorp 10/01/1983
Each share Common $5 par exchanged for (0.92) share Adjustable Rate Preferred no par, (1.2) shares Common $4 par or $24 cash
(See Horizon Bancorp)

NORTHERN NATL LIFE INS CO (ND)
Name changed to Manhattan National Life Insurance Co. 01/01/1982
(See Manhattan National Life Insurance Co.)

NORTHERN NEW ENGLAND CO. (ME)
Liquidated in 1953
Each Share of Bene. Int. received (0.26) share Central Maine Power Co. Common $10 par, (0.05) share Central Vermont Public Service Corp. Common $6 par and (0.12) share Public Service Co. of New Hampshire Common $10 par

NORTHERN NEW YORK BANCORP INC (NY)
Common $10 par split (3) for (2) by issuance of (0.5) additional share payable 12/10/1999 to holders of record 12/01/1999
Acquired by Watertown Savings Bank (Watertown, NY) 06/13/2008
Each share Common $10 par exchanged for $85.16 cash

NORTHERN NEW YORK SECURITIES CORP. (NY)
Charter cancelled and proclaimed dissolved for failure to file reports and pay taxes 12/15/43

NORTHERN NEW YORK UTILITIES, INC.
Merged into Niagara Hudson Public Service Corp.
Details not available

NORTHERN NUCLEAR ENERGY LTD (AB)
Recapitalized as Gaslite Petroleum Ltd. 01/28/1980
Each share Common no par exchanged for (0.5) share Common no par
(See Gaslite Petroleum Ltd.)

NORTHERN NUCLEAR MINES LTD (ON)
Reincorporated under the laws of Alberta as Northern Nuclear Energy Ltd. 10/3/77
Northern Nuclear Energy Ltd. recapitalized as Gaslite Petroleum Ltd. 1/28/80
(See Gaslite Petroleum Ltd.)

NORTHERN OHIO BK (CLEVELAND, OH)
Common $7.50 par changed to $3.75 par and (1) additional share issued 03/26/1973
Stock Dividend - 10% 03/25/1974
Placed in receivership 02/14/1975
No stockholders' equity

NORTHERN OHIO POWER & LIGHT CO.
Merged into Ohio Edison Co. 7/5/30
Details not available

NORTHERN OHIO POWER CO.
Acquired by Penn-Ohio Edison Co. in 1928
Details not available

NORTHERN OHIO TEL CO (OH)
Each share Common $100 par exchanged for (10) shares Common $10 par in 1940
Common $10 par changed to no par in 1948
Common no par changed to $10 par in 1954
Common $10 par changed to $3.33-1/3 par and (2) additional shares issued 6/4/65
4-1/4% Preferred $100 par called for redemption 1/1/68
4-1/2% Preferred $100 par called for redemption 1/1/68
5% Preferred Class A $100 par called for redemption 1/1/68

5% Preferred Class B $100 par called for redemption 1/1/68
Stock Dividend - 33-1/3% 3/12/66
Merged into General Telephone & Electronics Corp. 8/15/68
Each share Common $3.33-1/3 par exchanged for (1) share Common $3.33-1/3 par
General Telephone & Electronics Corp. name changed to GTE Corp. 7/1/82 which merged into Verizon Communications Inc. 6/30/2000

NORTHERN OHIO TRACTION & LIGHT CO.
Name changed to Northern Ohio Power & Light Co. in 1926
(See Northern Ohio Power & Light Co.)

NORTHERN OIL & GAS INC (MN)
Reincorporated 06/30/2010
State of incorporation changed from (NV) to (MN) 06/30/2010
Reincorporated under the laws of Delaware 05/09/2018

NORTHERN OIL CO. LTD.
Liquidated in 1953

NORTHERN OKLAHOMA GAS CO. (DE)
Each share old Common $1 par exchanged for (3) shares new Common $1 par 00/00/1937
Common $1 par changed to $8 par 00/00/1946
Stock Dividends - 25% 11/01/1949; 20% 03/07/1955
Acquired by Oklahoma Natural Gas Co. (DE) 07/29/1960
Each share Common $8 par exchanged for (0.8) share Common $15 par
Oklahoma Natural Gas Co. (DE) name changed to ONEOK Inc. (DE) 12/10/1980 which merged into ONEOK, Inc. (New) 11/26/1997

NORTHERN OKLAHOMA OIL CO., INC. (KS)
Charter cancelled for failure to file reports and pay fees 10/15/58
Common stock is worthless

NORTHERN ONT NAT GAS LTD (ON)
6% Conv. Preference Ser. A $50 par called for redemption 5/14/65
Name changed to Northern & Central Gas Co. Ltd. 12/10/65
Northern & Central Gas Co. Ltd. name changed to Northern & Central Gas Corp. Ltd. 1/1/68
(See Northern & Central Gas Corp. Ltd.)

NORTHERN ONTARIO LIGHT & POWER CO. LTD.
Merged into Northern Ontario Power Co. Ltd. 00/00/1928
Details not available

NORTHERN ONTARIO POWER CO., LTD.
Acquired by Hydro Electric Power Commission of Ontario and liquidated in 1944

NORTHERN ORION EXPLS LTD (BC)
Recapitalized as Northern Orion Resources Inc. 06/24/2003
Each share Common no par exchanged for (0.1) share Common no par
Northern Orion Resources Inc. merged into Yamana Gold Inc. 10/13/2007

NORTHERN ORION RES INC (BC)
Merged into Yamana Gold Inc. 10/13/2007
Each share Common no par exchanged for (0.543) share Common no par and $0.001 cash

NORTHERN OSTRICH CORP (NV)
Name changed to Patriot Gold Corp. 6/11/2003

NORTHERN PAC RY CO (WI)
Capital Stock $100 par changed to no par 00/00/1954
Capital Stock no par changed to $5 par and (1) additional share issued 05/11/1956
Stock Dividend - 20% 12/24/1958
Merged into Burlington Northern Inc. 03/02/1970
Each share Capital Stock $5 par exchanged for (1) share Common no par
Burlington Northern Inc. name changed to Burlington Northern Santa Fe Corp. 09/22/1995
(See Burlington Northern Santa Fe Corp.)

NORTHERN PAPER MILLS (WI)
Acquired by Marathon Corp. in 1953
Each share 6% Preferred $100 par exchanged for (5) shares Common $6.25 par
Each share Common no par exchanged for (6) shares Common $6.25 par
Marathon Corp. acquired by American Can Co. 12/3/57 which name changed to Primerica Corp. (NJ) 4/28/87 which was acquired by Primerica Corp. (DE) 12/15/88 which name changed to Travelers Inc. 12/31/93 which name changed to Travelers Group Inc. 4/16/95 which name changed to Citigroup Inc. 10/8/98

NORTHERN PERU COPPER CORP (BC)
Merged into Jiangxi Copper Co. Ltd. 03/28/2008
Each share Common no par exchanged for $13.75 cash

NORTHERN PINE VENTURES INC (AB)
Reincorporated under the laws of British Columbia as Landmark Minerals Inc. 07/18/2005
Landmark Minerals Inc. merged into Ucore Uranium Inc. 08/17/2007 which name changed to Ucore Rare Metals Inc. 06/29/2010

NORTHERN PIPE LINE CO.
Merged into Buckeye Pipe Line Co. and each share Common exchanged for (1.1) shares Common no par and $3 cash in 1943
Buckeye Pipe Line Co. was acquired by Pennsylvania Co. 7/24/64
(See Pennsylvania Co.)

NORTHERN PLAINS BANCSHARES INC (ND)
Name changed to First Interstate of North Dakota, Inc. 02/16/1988
(See First Interstate of North Dakota, Inc.)

NORTHERN PLAINS OIL CORP (BC)
Reorganized under the laws of Alberta as Gopher Oil & Gas Ltd. 01/22/1997
Each share Common no par exchanged for (0.33333333) share Common no par
Gopher Oil & Gas Ltd. recapitalized as Ventus Energy Ltd. 12/31/1998 which name changed to Navigo Energy Inc. 05/24/2002
(See Navigo Energy Inc.)

NORTHERN PLASTICS CORP. (WI)
Common $1 par split (2) for (1) by issuance of (1) additional share 4/9/62
Stock Dividends - 10% 9/30/59; 50% 2/20/60; 20% 1/2/64
Name changed to Norplex Corp. 3/2/65
Norplex Corp. acquired by Universal Oil Products Co. 9/30/66 which name changed to UOP Inc. 7/15/75
(See UOP Inc.)

NORTHERN PLATINUM LTD (BC)
Merged into Prophecy Resource Corp. (New) 09/23/2010
Each share Common no par exchanged for (0.5) share Common no par and (0.1) Common Stock Warrant expiring 03/23/2012
Note: Unexchanged certificates were cancelled and became without value 09/23/2016
Prophecy Resource Corp. (New) reorganized as Prophecy Coal Corp. 06/13/2011

NORTHERN PRECISION LABS INC (NJ)
Filed petition under Chapter 7 Federal Bankruptcy Code 2/27/90
Stockholders' equity unlikely

NORTHERN PROPERTIES, INC. (NY)
Merged into United Improvement & Investing Corp. on a (2) for (1) basis 7/1/60
United Improvement & Investing Corp. name changed to U.I.P. Corp. 5/7/68 which merged into Eastmet Corp. 12/20/79
(See Eastmet Corp.)

NORTHERN PPTY REAL ESTATE INVT TR (AB)
Under plan of reorganization each Stapled Unit consisting of (1) Northern Property Real Estate Investment Trust, Trust Unit and (1) share NorSerCo Inc. Common automatically became (1) Northern Property Real Estate Investment Trust, Trust Unit 02/06/2014
Note: NorSerCo Inc. has been dissolved
Northern Property Real Estate Investment Trust name changed to Northview Apartment Real Estate Investment Trust 11/05/2015

NORTHERN PPTY REAL ESTATE INVT TR (AB)
Reorganized as Northern Property Real Estate Investment Trust/NorSerCo Inc. 01/06/2011
Each Trust Unit no par exchanged for (1) Stapled Unit no par
Note: Unexchanged certificates were cancelled and became without value 01/06/2017
Northern Property Real Estate Investment Trust/NorSerCo Inc. reorganized back as Northern Property Real Estate Investment Trust 02/06/2014
Under plan of merger name changed to Northview Apartment Real Estate Investment Trust 11/05/2015

NORTHERN QUE EXPLORERS LTD (QC)
Recapitalized as Northern Mineral Explorations Ltd.-Explorations Minieres du Nord Ltee. 07/26/1985
Each share Capital Stock $1 par exchanged for (0.4) share Capital Stock $2.50 par

NORTHERN QUE PWR LTD (CANADA)
Acquired by Quebec Hydro-Electric Commission 09/24/1963
Each share Common no par exchanged for $33 cash
Each share 5.5% 1st Preferred $50 par exchanged for $50 principal amount of 5.5% 10-year Debentures 11/05/1963

NORTHERN RAILROAD OF NEW JERSEY
Acquired by Erie Railroad Co. share for share plus $1 cash in 1943
Erie Railroad Co. name was changed to Erie-Lackawanna Railroad Co. 10/17/60 which merged into Dereco, Inc. 4/1/68
(See Dereco, Inc.)

NORTHERN RAND RESOURCE CORP (BC)
Name changed to Suparna Gold Corp. 06/09/2011
Suparna Gold Corp. name changed to Scientific Metals Corp. 05/09/2016 which name changed to US Cobalt Inc. 05/25/2017 which merged into First Cobalt Corp. (BC) 06/05/2018 which reincorporated in Canada 09/04/2018

NORTHERN RANGER MINERALS INC (ON)
Merged into Rockford Minerals Inc. 12/31/88
Each (1.3) shares Common no par exchanged for (1) share Common no par
Rockford Minerals Inc. recapitalized as Reclamation Management Ltd. 4/30/92 which name changed to Euro-Net Investments Ltd. 8/19/99

NORTHERN RANGER OIL & GAS LTD. (ON)
Name changed to Northern Ranger Minerals Inc. 7/15/87
Northern Ranger Minerals Inc. merged into Rockford Minerals Inc. 12/31/88 which recapitalized as Reclamation Management Ltd. 4/30/92 which name changed to Euro-Net Investments Ltd. 8/19/99

NORTHERN REACTOR DMB RES INC (AB)
Recapitalized as TMN Capital Corp. 2/10/95
Each share Common no par exchanged for (0.5) share Common no par
TMN Capital Corp. recapitalized as Mayfair Media Corp. 9/6/95 which name changed to MF Media Corp. 12/15/98
(See MF Media Corp.)

NORTHERN REAL ESTATE TR (OH)
Merged into Nucorp, Inc. (OH) 7/20/76
Each Share of Bene. Int. no par exchanged for (2/3) share Common no par and $3.50 principal amount of 8% Subordinated Debentures due 7/31/2001
Nucorp, Inc. (OH) name changed to Nucorp Energy, Inc. (Old) 5/23/80
(See Nucorp Energy, Inc. (Old))

NORTHERN REALTY SHARES (OH)
Name changed to Northern Real Estate Trust 12/29/1970
Northern Real Estate Trust merged into Nucorp Inc. (OH) 07/20/1976 which name changed to Nucorp Energy, Inc. (Old) 05/23/1980
(See Nucorp Energy, Inc. (Old))

NORTHERN REEF EXPL LTD (CANADA)
Acquired by Penn West Petroleum Ltd. (Old) 08/31/1995
Each share Common no par exchanged for $1.85 cash

NORTHERN RESH & ENGR CORP (MA)
Merged into NREC Inc. 02/24/1978
Each share Common 10¢ par exchanged for $1 cash

NORTHERN RES CORP (UT)
Merged into Tancor International Inc. 09/22/1972
Each share Common 10¢ par exchanged for (0.645161) share Common 2-1/2¢ par
(See Tancor International Inc.)

NORTHERN RESOURCES LTD. (AB)
Defunct; charter revoked 9/15/54

NORTHERN RESOURCES LTD. (DE)
No longer in existence having become inoperative and void for non-payment of taxes 4/1/61

NORTHERN RR (NH)
Merged into B & M Corp. 12/13/1987
Each share 6% Guaranteed Capital Stock $100 par exchanged for $100 cash

NORTHERN SVGS & LN CO (ELYRIA, OH)
Each share Common 25¢ par exchanged for (2) shares Common 25¢ par 08/11/1997
Common 25¢ par split (2) for (1) by issuance of (1) additional share payable 07/28/2003 to holders of record 07/21/2003 Ex date - 07/29/2003
Stock Dividends - 5% payable 12/26/2001 to holders of record 12/21/2001 Ex date - 12/19/2001; 5% payable 12/27/2002 to holders of record 12/20/2002 Ex date - 12/18/2002; 5% payable 12/27/2004 to holders of record 12/20/2004
Merged into First Place Financial Corp. 06/27/2006
Each share Common 25¢ par exchanged for either (1.14135277) shares Common 1¢ par or $29 cash
Note: Option to receive cash expired 08/31/2006
(See First Place Financial Corp.)

NORTHERN SCH SUPPLY CO (WI)
Class A Preferred no par called for redemption at $10,000 on 8/15/97
Public interest eliminated

NORTHERN SPIRIT RES INC (AB)
Recapitalized as Altura Energy Inc. 10/19/2015
Each share Common no par exchanged for (0.1) share Common no par

NORTHERN SPRINGS INC (DE)
Name changed to Vermont Pure Holdings, Ltd. (Old) 08/05/1993
Vermont Pure Holdings, Ltd. (Old) reorganized as Vermont Pure Holdings, Ltd. (New) 11/09/2000 which name changed to Crystal Rock Holdings, Inc. 05/03/2010
(See Crystal Rock Holdings, Inc.)

NORTHERN ST BK (TOWANDA, PA)
Merged into Legacy Bank (Harrisburg, PA) 1/1/2003
Each share Common exchanged for (1) share Common $5 par
Legacy Bank (Harrisburg, PA) merged into F.N.B. Corp. (FL) 5/26/2006

NORTHERN STAR INDS INC (NY)
Dissolved by proclamation 9/25/91

NORTHERN STAR MNG CORP (YUKON)
Reincorporated under the laws of British Columbia 07/17/2006

NORTHERN STAR RES INC CDA (AB)
Recapitalized as Odaat Inc. 3/9/2000
Each share Class A Common no par exchanged for (0.2) share Class A Common no par
Odaat Inc. recapitalized as Explor Resources Inc. 1/29/2004

NORTHERN STATES FINANCIAL CORP. (DE)
Incorporated 04/28/1971
Common $10 par changed to $5 par and (1) additional share issued 11/13/1972
Name changed to Northern States Bancorporation, Inc. 03/27/1973
Northern States Bancorporation, Inc. merged into First American Bank Corp. 10/09/1981 which name changed to First of America Bank Corp. 01/14/1983
(See First of America Bank Corp.)

NORTHERN STS LIFE INS CORP (WI)
Old Common $1 par changed to 55¢ par 07/18/1961
Each share Common 55¢ par exchanged for (0.55) share new Common $1 par 09/23/1965
Merged into Underwriters Investment Corp. 12/31/1968
Each share new Common $1 par exchanged for (0.45) share Class A Common $1 par and (1) 6-month Class A Common Stock Purchase Warrant
Underwriters Investment Corp. merged into Pan-Western Corp. 07/29/1980 which merged into North American National Corp. 08/30/1984
(See North American National Corp.)

NORTHERN STATES POWER CO. (DE)
Dissolved pursuant to Public Utility Holding Company Act 9/30/48 - Stock of Northern States Power Co. (MN) issued in exchange
Each share 7% Preferred $100 par exchanged for (10) shares Common no par
Each share 6% Preferred $100 par exchanged for (9) shares Common no par
Each share Class A Common $25 par exchanged for (5.25) shares Common no par
Northern States Power Co. (MN) name changed to Xcel Energy Inc. 8/18/2000

NORTHERN STS PWR CO (MN)
$3.60, $4.10 and $4.80 Ser. Preferred no par changed to $100 par in 1951
Common no par changed to $5 par in 1951
$4.80 Preferred $100 par called for redemption 9/30/54
Common $5 par changed to $2.50 par and (1) additional share issued 6/13/86
$10.36 Preferred $100 par called for redemption 7/1/86
Auction Preferred Stock Ser. C $100 par called for redemption 8/11/89
$8.80 Preferred $100 par called for redemption 4/30/92
$7.84 Preferred $100 par called for redemption 10/30/93
$6.80 Preferred $100 par called for redemption 2/27/97
$7 Preferred $100 par called for redemption 2/27/97
Adjustable Rate Preferred Ser. A $100 par called for redemption at $100 on 3/31/98
Adjustable Dividend Preferred Ser. B $100 par called for redemption at $100 on 3/31/98
Common $2.50 par split (2) for (1) by issuance of (1) additional share payable 6/1/98 to holders of record 5/18/98 Ex date - 6/2/98
Name changed to Xcel Energy Inc. 8/18/2000

NORTHERN STATES REALTY FUND (WI)
Completely liquidated 8/1/77
Each share Common $2.50 par exchanged for $0.5521 cash

NORTHERN STS BANCORPORATION INC (DE)
Merged into First American Bank Corp. 10/09/1981
Each share 6-1/2% Conv. Preferred no par exchanged for (2.28) shares 9% Conv. Preference $11 par
Each share $8.25 Preferred no par exchanged for (4.5) shares 9% Conv. Preference $11 par and $50 cash
Each share Common $5 par exchanged for (0.5) share 9% Conv. Preference $11 par
First American Bank Corp. name changed to First of America Bank Corp. 01/14/1983
(See First of America Bank Corp.)

NORTHERN STS MTG & RLTY INVS (OH)
Name changed to Monetary Realty Trust 01/17/1979
(See Monetary Realty Trust)

NORTHERN SUN EXPL CO INC (BC)
Recapitalized as Reparo Energy Partners Corp. 11/08/2013
Each share Common no par exchanged for (0.02) share Common no par

NORTHERN SUN HOLDINGS, INC. (UT)
Liquidation completed 5/1/90
Each share Common $0.001 par exchanged for first and final distribution of $0.02321

NORTHERN SUN MNG CORP (ON)
Acquired by Regal Silver Investments Ltd. 04/27/2016
Each share Common no par exchanged for $0.07 cash
Note: Unexchanged certificates will be cancelled and become without value 04/27/2022

NORTHERN TAR CHEM & WOOD LTD (ON)
Each share $1.70 Preference Ser. A $25 par exchanged for $25.04 cash 07/05/1974
99.9% acquired by Jannock Corp. as of 06/18/1974
Public interest eliminated

NORTHERN TEL LTD (ON)
Recapitalized 1/1/60
Recapitalized from Northern Telephone Co. Ltd. to Northern Telephone Ltd. and Common $1 par changed to no par 1/1/60
5.50% 1st Preference Ser. A $20 par called for redemption at $20 plus $0.4573 accrued dividend on 4/20/2001
5.50% 1st Preference Ser. B $20 par called for redemption at $20 plus $0.4573 accrued dividend on 4/20/2001
5.50% 1st Preference Ser. C $20 par called for redemption at $20 plus $0.4573 accrued dividend on 4/20/2001
5.50% 1st Preference Ser. D $20 par called for redemption at $20 plus $0.4573 accrued dividend on 4/20/2001
5% 2nd Preference Ser. A $20 par called for redemption at $20 plus $0.4521 accrued dividend on 4/20/2001
5.25% 2nd Preference Ser. B $20 par called for redemption at $20 plus $0.4521 accrued dividend on 4/20/2001
Merged into Bell Telephone Co. of Canada-La Compagnie de Telephone Bell Du Canada 06/01/2001
Each share Common no par exchanged for $17.50 cash

NORTHERN TELECOM LTD (CANADA)
Common no par split (3) for (1) by issuance of (2) additional shares 05/20/1983
$2.1875 Retractable Class A Preferred Ser. 1 no par called for redemption 04/27/1987
Common no par split (2) for (1) by issuance of (1) additional share 05/22/1987
$2.22 Retractable Class A Preferred Ser. 2 no par called for redemption 06/12/1987
Floating Rate Class A Preferred Ser. 3 no par called for redemption 12/10/1993
Common no par split (2) for (1) by issuance of (1) additional share payable 01/09/1998 to holders of record 01/07/1998 Ex date - 01/12/1998
Name changed to Nortel Networks Corp. (Old) 04/30/1999
Nortel Networks Corp. (Old) Preferred name changed to Nortel Networks Ltd. 05/01/2000
Nortel Networks Corp. (Old) Common reorganized as Nortel Networks Corp. (New) 05/01/2000
(See each company's listing)

NORTHERN TEXAS ELECTRIC CO.
Reorganized as North Texas Co. in 1938
Each (4) shares Preferred or $100 of scrip exchanged for (1) share Capital Stock
North Texas Co. reorganized as Fort Worth Transit Co., Inc. in 1947 which completed liquidation 8/15/74

NORTHERN TIER ENERGY LP (DE)
Merged into Western Refining, Inc. 06/23/2016
Each Common Unit exchanged for (0.2986) share Common 1¢ par and $15 cash
Western Refining, Inc. merged into Tesoro Corp. 06/01/2017 which name changed to Andeavor 08/01/2017 which merged into Marathon Petroleum Corp. 10/01/2018

NORTHERN TIGER RES INC (AB)
Each share old Class A Common no par exchanged for (0.5) share new Class A Common no par 01/25/2013
Recapitalized as Golden Predator Mining Corp. (AB) 04/17/2014
Each share new Class A Common no par exchanged for (0.14285714) share Class A Common no par
Golden Predator Mining Corp. (AB) reincorporated in British Columbia 10/21/2015

NORTHERN TIN MINES LTD. (ON)
Name changed to Tanaur Yellowknife Mines Ltd. 5/17/45
(See Tanaur Yellowknife Mines Ltd.)

NORTHERN TR CO (CHICAGO, IL)
Each share Capital Stock $100 par exchanged for (5) shares Capital Stock $20 par 09/15/1960
Stock Dividends - 100% 12/22/1952; 50% 12/20/1955; 11-1/9% 12/17/1957; 25% 05/27/1959; 20% 11/30/1962; 33-1/3% 06/22/1964; 25% 06/30/1966; 33-1/3% 12/29/1969; 25% 03/16/1971
Under plan of reorganization each share Capital Stock $20 par automatically became (1) share Nortrust Corp. Common $20 par 12/02/1971
Nortrust Corp. name changed to Northern Trust Corp. 3/8/78

NORTHERN TR CORP (DE)
Adjustable Rate Preferred Ser. A no par called for redemption 07/03/1987
$3.125 Preferred Stock Int. Ser. B no par called for redemption 12/00/1989
$6.25 Preferred Conv. Ser. B no par called for redemption 12/00/1989
Depositary Preferred Ser. E $50 par called for redemption 01/26/1996
Conv. Preferred Ser. E $50 par called for redemption 01/26/1996
Auction Preferred Stock Ser. C no par called for redemption at $100,000 on 05/21/2003
Flexible Auction Preferred Stock Ser. D no par called for redemption at $100,000 on 06/04/2003
(Additional Information in Active)

NORTHERN TURNBULL GOLD MINES, LTD. (ON)
Charter cancelled and proclaimed dissolved for failure to pay taxes and file returns 11/9/59

NORTHERN UN HLDGS CORP (OH)
Class A no par split (5) for (4) by issuance of (0.25) additional share 1/20/69
Class A no par split (2) for (1) by issuance of (1) additional share 6/2/72
Class A no par split (2) for (1) by issuance of (1) additional share 3/22/74
Name changed to Nucorp, Inc. (OH) 6/7/75

Nucorp, Inc. (OH) name changed to Nucorp Energy, Inc. (Old) 5/23/80
(See Nucorp Energy, Inc. (Old))

NORTHERN UTILITIES CO. (DE)
Reorganized as Northern Utilities Co. (Wyo.) in 1935 which liquidated for cash 12/31/62

NORTHERN UTILITIES CO. (WY)
Completely liquidated for cash 12/21/62

NORTHERN UTILS INC (ME)
Merged into Northern Utilities, Inc. (NH) 6/30/69
Each share 5% Preferred $100 par exchanged for (1) share 5% Preferred $100 par
Each share Common $5 par exchanged for (1) share Common $5 par
Northern Utilities, Inc. (NH) merged into Bay State Gas Co. (New) 10/30/79 which merged into Nipsco Industries, Inc. 2/12/99 which name changed to NiSource Inc. (IN) 4/14/99 which reincorporated in Delaware 11/1/2000

NORTHERN UTILS INC (NH)
Merged into Bay State Gas Co. (New) 10/30/79
Each share 5% Preferred $100 par exchanged for (1) share 5% Preferred $100 par
Each share 7.2% Preference $10 par exchanged for (0.2) share 7.2% Preferred $50 par
Each share Common $5 par exchanged for (0.4) share Common $10 par
Bay State Gas Co. (New) merged into Nipsco Industries, Inc. 2/12/99 which name changed to NiSource Inc. (IN) 4/14/99 which reincorporated in Delaware 11/1/2000

NORTHERN VA BK (SPRINGFIELD, VA)
Each share Common $10 par exchanged for (2) shares Common $5 par 04/30/1963
Each share Common $5 par exchanged for (5) shares Common $1 par 03/31/1969
Stock Dividends - 100% 04/23/1963; 10% 12/31/1968
Reorganized as New Virginia Bancorporation 04/01/1975
Each share Common $1 par exchanged for (1) share Common $1 par
(See New Virginia Bancorporation)

NORTHERN VA BANKSHARES INC (VA)
Liquidation completed
Each share Common $1 par exchanged for initial distribution of (0.25) share Central National Corp. (VA) Common $5 par and $10.75 cash 01/02/1975
Each share Common $1 par received second and final distribution of $0.50 cash 07/14/1975
Central National Corp. (VA) merged into Commonwealth Banks, Inc. 12/31/1978 which name changed to Central Fidelity Banks, Inc. 06/01/1979 which merged into Wachovia Corp. (New) (Ctfs. dated between 05/20/1991 and 09/01/2001) 12/15/1997 which merged into Wachovia Corp. (Ctfs. dated after 09/01/2001) 09/01/2001 which merged into Wells Fargo & Co. (New) 12/31/2008

NORTHERN VA DOCTORS HOSP CORP (VA)
Capital Stock 1¢ par changed to $4 par and (1) additional share issued 06/20/1966
Capital Stock $4 par changed to $1 par and (3) additional shares issued 02/15/1968
Capital Stock $1 par split (2) for (1) by issuance of (1) additional share 04/30/1971
Under plan of reorganization each share Capital Stock $1 par automatically became (1) share NVDH Corp. Common $1 par 10/01/1973
(See NVDH Corp.)

NORTHERN VA HOTEL CORP (VA)
Charter cancelled and proclaimed dissolved for failure to file reports 06/01/1974

NORTHERN VY MINES LTD (BC)
Name changed to Northern Valley Resources Ltd. 07/28/1975
Northern Valley Resources Ltd. recapitalized as Black Thunder Petroleum Corp. 07/20/1982 which recapitalized as Conley Resources Corp. 06/28/1990
(See Conley Resources Corp.)

NORTHERN VY RES LTD (BC)
Recapitalized as Black Thunder Petroleum Corp. 07/20/1982
Each share Common 50¢ par exchanged for (0.5) share Common no par
Black Thunder Petroleum Corp. recapitalized as Conley Resources Corp. 06/28/1990
(See Conley Resources Corp.)

NORTHERN VERMICULITE LTD. (ON)
Charter cancelled for failure to file reports and pay taxes in 1970

NORTHERN VERTEX CAP INC (BC)
Name changed to Northern Vertex Mining Corp. 02/16/2012

NORTHESK MINING CORP. LTD. (NB)
Charter cancelled for failure to file reports in 1968

NORTHEWAN MINERALS CORP (BC)
Name changed to Flotek Industries, Inc. (BC) 12/11/1992
Flotek Industries, Inc. (BC) reincorporated in Alberta 09/15/1995 which reorganized in Delaware 11/05/2001

NORTHFIELD BANCORP INC (MD)
Merged into Patapsco Bancorp Inc. 11/13/2000
Each share Common 1¢ par exchanged for (0.24) share 7.5% Conv. Perpetual Preferred Ser. A 1¢. par and $12.50 cash
(See Patapsco Bancorp Inc.)

NORTHFIELD BANCORP INC (USA)
Issue Information - 16,752,449 shares COM offered at $10 per share on 08/13/2007
Reorganized under the laws of Delaware 01/25/2013
Each share Common 1¢ par exchanged for (1.4029) shares Common 1¢ par

NORTHFIELD INC (ON)
Recapitalized as Northfield Metals Inc. 10/13/2006
Each share Common no par exchanged for (0.1) share Common no par
Northfield Metals Inc. name changed to Cartier Iron Corp. 01/16/2013

NORTHFIELD LABS INC (DE)
Plan of reorganization under Chapter 11 Federal Bankruptcy proceedings effective 09/25/2009
No stockholders' equity

NORTHFIELD METALS INC (ON)
Each share old Common no par exchanged for (0.25) share new Common no par 05/04/2012
Name changed to Cartier Iron Corp. 01/16/2013

NORTHFIELD MINERALS INC (ON)
Name changed to Northfield Inc. 07/23/1999
Northfield Inc. recapitalized as Northfield Metals Inc. 10/13/2006 which name changed to Cartier Iron Corp. 01/16/2013

NORTHFIELD MINES LTD.
Dissolved in 1948

NORTHFIELD RACEWAY INC (OH)
Liquidation completed
Each share Common no par exchanged for initial distribution of $3.69 cash 08/16/1972
Each share Common no par received second and final distribution of $0.54 cash 07/15/1977

NORTHFORK VENTURES LTD (BC)
Name changed to Medsana Medical Systems, Inc. 11/26/1993
Medsana Medical Systems, Inc. recapitalized as Connect Inter-Tel Media Inc. 01/22/1996
(See Connect Inter-Tel Media Inc.)

NORTHGANE MINERALS LTD (CANADA)
Name changed to General Minerals Corp. (Incorporated 09/18/1981) 10/29/1986
(See General Minerals Corp. (Incorporated 09/18/1981))

NORTHGATE INDS INC (MN)
Name changed to Northgate Computer Corp. 9/27/90
(See Northgate Computer Corp.)

NORTHGATE INNOVATIONS INC (DE)
Name changed to Digital Lifestyles Group, Inc. 06/25/2004
Digital Lifestyles Group, Inc. name changed to TN-K Energy Group Inc. 10/29/2009

NORTHGATE MINERALS CORP (BC)
Reincorporated 07/01/2001
Name changed 05/20/2004
Capital Stock $1 par reclassified as Common no par 00/00/1983
Place of incorporation changed from (ON) to (BC) 07/01/2001
Name changed from Northgate Exploration Ltd. to Northgate Minerals Corp. 05/20/2004
Merged into AuRico Gold Inc. 10/26/2011
Each share Common no par exchanged for (0.365) share Common no par
Note: Unexchanged certificates were cancelled and became without value 10/26/2017
AuRico Gold Inc. merged into Alamos Gold Inc. (New) 07/06/2015

NORTHHILL APARTMENTS LIQUIDATION TRUST
Trust liquidated in 1951

NORTHILL RES LTD (BC)
Merged into Canadian Continental Oil Corp. 4/19/84
Each share Common no par exchanged for (0.5) share Common no par
Canadian Continental Oil Corp. recapitalized as CBO Resources Corp. 3/25/87
(See CBO Resources Corp.)

NORTHLAND BK (WINNEPEG, MB)
Placed in liquidation 01/20/1986
No stockholders' equity

NORTHLAND BK WIS S S B (ASHLAND, WI)
Merged into First Financial Corp. (WI) 2/26/94
Each share Common $1 par exchanged for (1.899) shares Common $1 par
First Financial Corp. (WI) merged into Associated Banc-Corp 10/29/97

NORTHLAND CABLE PPTYS LTD PARTNERSHIP (WA)
Units of Ltd. Partnership Int.-7 completely liquidated 12/31/2014
Details not available
(Additional Information in Active)

NORTHLAND CABLE PROPERTIES FIVE LIMITED PARTNERSHIP (WA)
Partnership terminated 6/25/98
Unitholders received an undetermined amount of cash

NORTHLAND CABLE PROPERTIES FOUR LIMITED PARTNERSHIP (WA)
Partnership terminated 12/18/96
Unitholders received an undetermined amount of cash

NORTHLAND CRANBERRIES INC (WI)
Secondary Offering - 5,000,000 shares CL A offered at $14 per share on 06/25/1998
Old Class A Common 1¢ par split (2) for (1) by issuance of (1) additional share payable 9/2/96 to holders of record 8/15/96
Each share old Class A Common 1¢ par exchanged for (0.25) share new Class A Common 1¢ par 11/6/2001
Merged into New Harvest, Inc. 11/28/2005
Each share new Class A Common 1¢ par exchanged for $0.21 cash

NORTHLAND GOLD MINES LTD.
Succeeded by Northland Mines (1940) Ltd. on a (0.2) for (1) basis in 1940
Northland Mines (1940) Ltd. recapitalized as Consolidated Northland Mines Ltd. in 1954 which merged into Crestland Mines Ltd. 5/4/65 which merged into PYX Explorations Ltd. 7/30/76 which merged into Discovery Mines Ltd. (Canada) 1/15/82
(See Discovery Mines Ltd. (Canada))

NORTHLAND GREYHOUND LINES, INC. (DE)
Merged into Greyhound Corp. (DE) 7/2/56
Each share 3-3/4% Preferred $100 par exchanged for (1) share 4-1/4% Preferred $100 par
Each share Common no par exchanged for (1.5) shares Common $3 par
Greyhound Corp. (DE) reincorporated in (AZ) 3/3/78 which name changed to Greyhound Dial Corp. 5/8/90 which name changed to Dial Corp. (AZ) 5/14/91 which reincorporated in (DE) 3/18/92 which name changed to Viad Corp. 8/15/96

NORTHLAND MINES (1940) LTD. (ON)
Recapitalized as Consolidated Northland Mines Ltd. in 1954
Each (4.5) shares Capital Stock $1 par exchanged for (1) share Capital Stock $1 par
Consolidated Northland Mines Ltd. merged into Crestland Mines Ltd. 5/4/65 which merged into PYX Explorations Ltd. 7/30/76 which merged into Discovery Mines Ltd. (Canada) 1/15/82
(See Discovery Mines Ltd. (Canada))

NORTHLAND OILS LTD (AB)
Capital Stock no par changed to 20¢ par in 1952
Recapitalized as Consolidated Northland Oils Ltd. 10/23/89
Each (7) shares Capital Stock 20¢ par exchanged for (1) share Common 20¢ par
Consolidated Northland Oils Ltd. recapitalized as International Northland Resources Inc. (ALTA) 1/11/96 which reincorporated in Bahamas 9/10/97 which merged into Combined Logistics International Ltd. 11/3/97
(See Combined Logistics International Ltd.)

NORTHLAND PWR INCOME FD (ON)
Under plan of reorganization each Trust Unit no par automatically

became (1) share Northland Power Inc. Common no par 01/03/2011

NORTHLAND RES INC (BC)
Reincorporated under the laws of Luxembourg as Northland Resources S.A. and Common no par changed to CAD $1.65 par 06/14/2010

NORTHLAND SYS TRAINING INC (CANADA)
Dissolved 05/06/2005
Details not available

NORTHLINE ENERGY SVCS INC (AB)
Acquired by Trican Well Services Ltd. 02/14/2000
Each share Common no par exchanged for $1.05 cash

NORTHLINKS LTD (AB)
Name changed 02/01/1999
Name changed from Northlinks Capital Ltd. to Northlinks Ltd. 02/01/1999
Recapitalized as Ausam Energy Corp. 09/15/2004
Each share Common no par exchanged for (0.03333333) share Common no par
(See Ausam Energy Corp.)

NORTHLODE EXPL LTD (BC)
Struck off register and declared dissolved for failure to file returns 11/29/1976

NORTHLODGE COPPER MINES LTD (ON)
Ceased operations 00/00/1969
No stockholders' equity

NORTHMOUNT MINING CORP. LTD. (ON)
Charter cancelled for failure to pay taxes and file returns in March 1976

NORTHPOINT COMMUNICATIONS GROUP INC (DE)
Chapter 11 bankruptcy proceedings converted to Chapter 7 on 06/12/2001
Stockholders' equity unlikely

NORTHPOINT CORP (ON)
Dissolved 5/8/2000
Details not available

NORTHPOINT RES LTD (BC)
Recapitalized as Glacier Resources Ltd. 11/02/1998
Each share Common no par exchanged for (0.13333333) share Common no par
Glacier Resources Ltd. recapitalized as Bayfield Ventures Corp. 05/18/2001 which merged into New Gold Inc. 01/02/2015

NORTHPORT CAP INC (CO)
Reincorporated under the laws of Washington as Northport Network Systems, Inc. 12/17/2008

NORTHPORT INDS INC (NV)
SEC revoked Preferred and Common stock registration 11/29/2007

NORTHQUEST LTD (ON)
Acquired by Nord Gold SE 10/19/2016
Each share Common no par exchanged for $0.26 cash
Note: Unexchanged certificates will be cancelled and become without value 10/19/2022

NORTHQUEST VENTURES INC (ON)
Each share Conv. 1st Preference Ser. A no par exchanged for (1) share Class A no par 04/21/1993
Discharged from receivership 09/12/1997
No stockholders' equity

NORTHRICH PAC VENTURES INC (BC)
Delisted from Vancouver Stock Exchange 03/01/1999

NORTHRIDGE AMER CORP (NV)
Each share old Common 1¢ par exchanged for (0.5) share new Common 1¢ par 08/01/1992
Completely liquidated 11/18/1992
Each share new Common 1¢ par exchanged for first and final distribution of an undetermined amount of Tricom Corp. Common 1¢ par

NORTHRIDGE BANK (NORTHRIDGE, CA)
Name changed to Premier Bank (Northridge, CA) 6/1/83
(See Premier Bank (Northridge, CA))

NORTHRIDGE EXPL LTD (AB)
Merged into Chancellor Energy Resources Inc. 07/21/1995
Each share Common no par exchanged for (1) share Common no par
Chancellor Energy Resources Inc. merged into HCO Energy Ltd. 04/02/1996 which merged into Pinnacle Resources Ltd. (New) 10/20/1997 which merged into Renaissance Energy Ltd. 07/16/1998 which merged into Husky Energy Inc. 08/25/2000

NORTHRIDGE VENTURES INC (NV)
Name changed to UCP Holdings, Inc. 06/25/2013

NORTHRIM BK (ANCHORAGE, AK)
Common $1 par split (5) for (4) by issuance of (0.25) additional share 9/23/93
Stock Dividends - 5% payable 2/14/97 to holders of record 1/31/97; 5% payable 2/16/98 to holders of record 2/2/98; 5% payable 2/16/99 to holders of record 2/2/99; 5% payable 2/17/2000 to holders of record 2/3/2000; 10% payable 11/30/2001 to holders of record 11/15/2001 Ex date - 11/13/2001
Under plan of reorganization each share Common $1 par automatically became (1) share Northrim BanCorp, Inc. Common $1 par 1/2/2002

NORTHRIM MINES LTD (AB)
Company placed in receivership in 1979
Struck off register and declared dissolved in 1981

NORTHROCK RES INC (BC)
Each share old Common no par exchanged for (0.2) share new Common no par 11/09/2010
Name changed to Bama Gold Corp. 12/13/2011
Bama Gold Corp. recapitalized as Whattozee Networks Inc. 01/25/2017 which name changed to Chemistree Technology Inc. 08/04/2017

NORTHROCK RES LTD (AB)
Acquired by Unocal Corp. 07/17/2000
Each share Common no par exchanged for $10.10 cash

NORTHROP AIRCRAFT, INC. (CA)
Class A $1 par and Class B $1 par reclassified as Common $1 par in 1944
Common $1 par split (2) for (1) by issuance of (1) additional share in 1954
Stock Dividends - 10% 10/21/52; 10% 4/5/54
Name changed to Northrop Corp. (CA) 2/2/59
Northrop Corp. (CA) reincorporated in Delaware 6/18/85 which name changed to Northrop Grumman Corp. 5/18/94 which reorganized as Northrop Grumman Corp. (Holding Company) 4/2/2001

NORTHROP GRUMMAN CORP (DE)
Reincorporated 06/18/1985
Name changed 05/18/1994
Common $1 par split (2) for (1) by issuance of (1) additional share 01/12/1962
Common $1 par split (3) for (2) by issuance of (0.5) additional share 12/19/1975
$1.45 Preferred $1 par called for redemption 09/30/1976
Common $1 par split (2) for (1) by issuance of (1) additional share 06/18/1977
Common $1 par changed to no par 07/31/1979
Common no par split (3) for (1) by issuance of (2) additional shares 09/10/1984
State of incorporation changed from (CA) to (DE) 06/18/1985
Name changed from Northrop Corp. to Northrop Grumman Corp. 05/18/1994
Additional Offering - 6,000,000 EQUITY SECS UNITS offered at $100 per Unit on 11/15/2001
Each Equity Security Unit received (2.2598) shares Common $1 par 11/16/2004
Each share Conv. Preferred Ser. B exchanged for (1.299246) shares Common $1 par 04/04/2008

NORTHRUP KING & CO (MN)
Common $6.25 par changed to $1 par and (2) additional shares issued 8/4/71
Common $1 par split (2) for (1) by issuance of (1) additional share 6/21/72
Common $1 par changed to 50¢ par and (1) additional share issued 11/23/73
Merged into Sandoz Seed Co. 2/8/77
Each share Common 50¢ par exchanged for $19.40 cash

NORTHSHORE GOLDFIELDS, LTD. (ON)
Charter cancelled and company declared dissolved for default in filing returns 1/6/71

NORTHSIDE BANCSHARES, INC. (GA)
Under plan of reorganization each share Common $1 par automatically became (1) share Southern Bank Group Inc. 00/00/1989
Southern Bank Group Inc. merged into SouthTrust Corp. 06/30/1995 which merged into Wachovia Corp. (Ctfs. dated after 09/01/2001) 11/01/2004 which merged into Wells Fargo & Co. (New) 12/31/2008

NORTHSIDE BK (TAMPA, FL)
Capital Stock $10 par changed to $5 par and (1) additional share issued 12/10/1970
Stock Dividend - 50% 07/25/1972
100% acquired by Landmark Banking Corp. of Florida as of 02/28/1974
Public interest eliminated

NORTHSIDE GROUP INC (AB)
Name changed to Wittke Inc. 1/23/2002
Wittke Inc. merged into Federal Signal Corp. 10/3/2002

NORTHSIDE MINERALS INTL INC (AB)
Recapitalized 05/15/1995
Recapitalized from Northside Resources Ltd. to Northside Minerals International Inc. 05/15/1995
Each share Class A no par exchanged for (0.2) share Class A no par
Delisted from Canadian Venture Stock Exchange 05/31/2000

NORTHSPAN URANIUM MINES LTD. (ON)
Merged into Rio Algom Mines Ltd. 6/30/60
Each share Capital Stock $1 par exchanged for (0.13) share Capital Stock no par
Rio Algom Mines Ltd. name changed to Rio Algom Ltd. 4/30/75
(See Rio Algom Ltd.)

NORTHSTAR ACQUISITION CORP (CO)
Completely liquidated 5/31/94
Each share Common 1¢ par exchanged for first and final distribution of $0.038 cash

NORTHSTAR ADVANTAGE GROWTH FD (MA)
Name changed to Northstar Growth Fund 8/12/96
Northstar Growth Fund name changed to Pilgrim Growth Opportunities Fund 11/1/99 which name changed to ING Growth Opportunities Fund 3/1/2002

NORTHSTAR ADVANTAGE SPL FD (MA)
Name changed to Northstar Special Fund 8/12/96
Northstar Special Fund name changed to Pilgrim SmallCap Opportunities Fund 11/1/99 which name changed to ING SmallCap Opportunities Fund 3/1/2002

NORTHSTAR ADVANTAGE TR (MA)
Name changed 6/5/95
Name changed from Northstar Series Trust to Northstar Advantage Trust 6/5/95
Name changed to Northstar Trust 8/1/96
Northstar Trust name changed to Pilgrim Mayflower Trust 11/1/99 which name changed to ING Mayflower Trust 3/1/2002

NORTHSTAR AEROSPACE INC (ON)
Assets sold for the benefit of creditors 09/11/2012
Stockholders' equity unlikely

NORTHSTAR ASSET MGMT GROUP INC (DE)
Merged into Colony NorthStar, Inc. 01/10/2017
Each share Common 1¢ par exchanged for (1) share Class A Common 1¢ par
Colony NorthStar, Inc. name changed to Colony Capital, Inc. (New) 06/25/2018

NORTHSTAR COMPUTER FORMS INC (MN)
Merged into Ennis Business Forms, Inc. 6/6/2000
Each share Common 5¢ par exchanged for $14 cash

NORTHSTAR CORP. (OH)
Name changed to Leader National Corp. 4/6/64
(See Leader National Corp.)

NORTHSTAR DRILLING SYS INC (AB)
Merged into NQL Drilling Tools Inc. 5/31/2001
Each share Common no par exchanged for (0.2) share Common no par
NQL Drilling Tools Inc. name changed to NQL Energy Services Inc. 7/11/2005
(See NQL Energy Services Inc.)

NORTHSTAR ENERGY CORP (AB)
Common no par split (2) for (1) by issuance of (1) additional share 5/11/94
Merged into Devon Energy Corp. (OK) 12/11/98
Each share Common no par exchanged for (0.235) share Common 10¢ par
Devon Energy Corp. (OK) merged

into Devon Energy Corp. (New) (DE) 8/17/99

NORTHSTAR FINL CORP (WI)
Merged into Frontier Financial Corp. 2/1/2006
Each share Common no par exchanged for (1.754) shares Common no par

NORTHSTAR GLOBAL BUSINESS SVCS INC (NV)
Reincorporated under the laws of Wyoming as MedGen, Inc. 07/06/2015

NORTHSTAR GROWTH FUND (MA)
Name changed to Pilgrim Growth Opportunities Fund 11/1/99
Pilgrim Growth Opportunities Fund name changed to ING Growth Opportunities Fund 3/1/2002

NORTHSTAR HEALTH SVCS INC (DE)
Merged into Benchmark Medical 9/22/2000
Each share Common 1¢ par exchanged for $1.50 cash

NORTHSTAR HEALTHCARE INC (BC)
Name changed to Nobilis Health Corp. 12/10/2014

NORTHSTAR MINERALS INC (DE)
Chapter 11 Federal Bankruptcy Code converted to Chapter 7 on 4/10/89
Stockholders' equity unlikely

NORTHSTAR NETWORK INC (WA)
Each share old Common no par exchanged for (0.1) share new Common no par 03/30/2001
SEC revoked common stock registration 08/21/2002
Stockholders' equity unlikely

NORTHSTAR NEUROSCIENCE INC (WA)
Issue Information - 7,100,000 shares COM offered at $15 per share on 05/04/2006
Liquidation completed
Each share Common $0.001 par received initial distribution of $2.06 cash payable 07/15/2009 to holders of record 07/02/2009 Ex date - 07/16/2009
Each share Common $0.001 par received second distribution of $0.10 cash payable 12/15/2009 to holders of record 07/02/2009 Ex date - 12/17/2009
Each share Common $0.001 par received third and final distribution of $0.02859 cash payable 08/15/2012 to holders of record 07/02/2009
Note: Certificates were not required to be surrendered and are without value

NORTHSTAR RLTY FIN CORP (MD)
Each share old Common 1¢ par exchanged for (0.5) share new Common 1¢ par and (0.5) share NorthStar Asset Management Group Inc. Common 1¢ par 06/30/2014
Each share new Common 1¢ par received distribution of (0.16666666) share NorthStar Realty Europe Corp. Common 1¢ par payable 10/31/2015 to holders of record 10/22/2015 Ex date - 11/02/2015
Each share new Common 1¢ par exchanged again for (0.5) share new Common 1¢ par 11/02/2015
Merged into Colony NorthStar, Inc. 01/10/2017
Each share 8.25% Preferred Ser. B 1¢ par exchanged for (1) share 8.25% Preferred B 1¢ par
Each share 8.5% Preferred Ser. D 1¢ par exchanged for (1) share 8.5% Preferred Ser. D 1¢ par
(See Colony NorthStar, Inc.)
Each share 8.75% Preferred Ser. E 1¢ par exchanged for (1) share 8.75% Preferred Ser. E 1¢ par

Each share 8.875% Preferred Ser. C 1¢ par exchanged for (1) share 8.875% Preferred Ser. C 1¢ par
Each share new Common 1¢ par exchanged for (1.0996) shares Class A Common 1¢ par
Colony NorthStar, Inc. name changed to Colony Capital, Inc. (New) 06/25/2018

NORTHSTAR RES LTD (AB)
Each share 10% Conv. 1st Preferred Ser. A $10 par exchanged for (5) shares Common no par 12/13/1984
Recapitalized as Canadian Northstar Corp. 01/27/1986
Each share Common no par exchanged for (0.2) share Common no par
Canadian Northstar Corp. reorganized as First Chicago Investment Corp. 12/07/2001 which name changed to Graystone Corp. 02/25/2004 which merged into Pyxis Capital Inc. 02/27/2006
(See Pyxis Capital Inc.)

NORTHSTAR SPL FD (MA)
Name changed to Pilgrim SmallCap Opportunities Fund 11/1/99
Pilgrim SmallCap Opportunities Fund name changed to ING SmallCap Opportunities Fund 3/1/2002

NORTHSTAR TR (MA)
Name changed to Pilgrim Mayflower Trust 11/1/99
Pilgrim Mayflower Trust name changed to ING Mayflower Trust 3/1/2002

NORTHTECH CORP (NV)
Reorganized as Platinum Research Organization, Inc. (NV) 10/31/2006
Each share Common $0.001 par exchanged for (5) shares Common $0.001 par
Platinum Research Organization, Inc. (NV) reincorporated in Delaware 04/13/2007
(See Platinum Research Organization, Inc.)

NORTHUMBERLAND MINES LTD (ON)
Merged into NovaGold Resources Inc. (NS) 06/13/1988
Each (5.5) shares Common no par exchanged for (1) share Common no par
NovaGold Resources Inc. (NS) reincorporated in British Columbia 06/12/2013

NORTHUMBERLAND NATL BK (NORTHUMBERLAND, PA)
Under plan of reorganization each share Common $20 par automatically became (1) share Northumberland Bancorp Common 10¢ par 07/31/1997

NORTHUMBERLAND RES INC (NV)
Common $0.001 par split (20) for (1) by issuance of (19) additional shares payable 09/30/2011 to holders of record 09/15/2011 Ex date - 10/03/2011
Recapitalized as Supernova Energy, Inc. 06/25/2014
Each share Common $0.001 par exchanged for (0.5) share Common $0.001 par

NORTHUMBRIAN WTR GROUP PLC (UNITED KINGDOM)
ADR agreement terminated 10/24/2011
No ADR's remain outstanding

NORTHVIEW CORP (DE)
Reincorporated 6/14/85
State of incorporation changed from (CA) to (DE) 6/14/85
Acquired by Calmark Holding Corp. 12/30/87
Details not available

NORTHWARD VENTURES INC (NV)
Name changed to Bulldog Technologies Inc. 11/10/2003
Bulldog Technologies Inc. recapitalized as Next10, Inc. 03/25/2011

NORTHWATER FIVE-YEAR MKT NEUTRAL TR (ON)
Issue Information - 2,400,000 TR UNITS offered at $25 per Unit on 06/30/2004
Liquidation completed
Each Trust Unit received initial distribution of $3.87 cash payable 07/15/2009 to holders of record 06/30/2009 Ex date - 06/26/2009
Each Trust Unit received second distribution of $1.63 cash payable 11/26/2009 to holders of record 11/19/2009
Each Trust Unit received third distribution of $2.53 cash payable 01/29/2010 to holders of record 01/22/2010
Each Trust Unit received fourth and final distribution of $0.0779625 cash payable 03/26/2010 to holders of record 03/19/2010

NORTHWATER MARKET-NEUTRAL TR (ON)
Liquidation completed
Each Trust Unit received initial distribution of $3.14 cash payable 07/29/2009 to holders of record 06/30/2009
Each Trust Unit received second distribution of $1.54 cash payable 02/03/2010 to holders of record 01/27/2010
Each Trust Unit received third distribution of $0.50 cash payable 04/07/2010 to holders of record 03/31/2010
Each Trust Unit received fourth distribution of $0.17 cash payable 07/08/2010 to holders of record 06/30/2010
Each Trust Unit received fifth distribution of $0.06 cash payable 10/07/2010 to holders of record 09/30/2010
Each Trust Unit received sixth distribution of $0.05 cash payable 01/10/2011 to holders of record 12/31/2010
Each Trust Unit received seventh distribution of $0.07 cash payable 04/07/2011 to holders of record 03/31/2011
Each Trust Unit received eighth distribution of $0.05 cash payable 07/08/2011 to holders of record 06/30/2011
Each Trust Unit received ninth distribution of $0.07 cash payable 10/07/2011 to holders of record 09/30/2011
Each Trust Unit received tenth distribution of $0.53 cash payable 01/30/2012 to holders of record 01/23/2012
Each Trust Unit received eleventh and final distribution of $0.2100197 cash payable 06/28/2012 to holders of record 06/21/2012

NORTHWATER RES INC (NV)
Each share old Common $0.001 par exchanged for (0.01666666) share new Common $0.001 par 01/09/2008
Name changed to Dex-Ray Resources, Inc. 03/27/2008
(See Dex-Ray Resources, Inc.)

NORTHWATER TOP 75 INCOME TRS (ON)
Liquidation completed
Each Trust Unit no par received initial distribution of $1 cash payable 01/15/2010 to holders of record 12/31/2009
Each Trust Unit no par received second distribution of $1 cash

payable 01/29/2010 to holders of record 01/22/2010
Each Trust Unit no par received third and final distribution of $0.100441 cash payable 03/26/2010 to holders of record 03/19/2010

NORTHWAY (JOHN) & SON LTD. (ON)
Adjudicated bankrupt 2/63
No stockholders' equity

NORTHWAY EXPLS LTD (ON)
Name changed to Caspian Energy Inc. (ON) 09/10/2004
Caspian Energy Inc. (ON) reincorporated in British Columbia 02/25/2015
(See Caspian Energy Inc.)

NORTHWAY GESTALT CORP (CANADA)
Acquired by Spar Aerospace Ltd. 09/19/1981
Each share Common no par exchanged for (1) share Jr. Preferred Second Ser. no par, (0.09) share Common no par, (0.2) Common Stock Purchase Warrant expiring 02/28/1985 and $1 cash
(See Spar Aerospace Ltd.)

NORTHWAY MOTORS CORP.
Property sold in 1926
No stockholders' equity

NORTHWEST AIRLS CORP (DE)
Issue Information - 20,000,000 shares CL A offered at $13 per share on 03/18/1994
Plan of reorganization under Chapter 11 Federal Bankruptcy Code effective 05/31/2007
No Class A stockholders' equity
Merged into Delta Air Lines, Inc. 10/30/2008
Each share Common 1¢ par exchanged for (1.25) shares Common $0.0001 par

NORTHWEST AIRLS INC (MN)
Common $1 par changed to old Common no par 00/00/1936
Each share old Common no par exchanged for (10) shares new Common no par 00/00/1937
New Common no par changed to $10 par 00/00/1946
4.60% Preference $25 par called for redemption 12/31/58
5-1/4% Conv. Preferred $25 par called for redemption 02/14/1963
Common $10 par changed to $5 par and (1) additional share issued 06/09/1964
Common $5 par changed to $2.50 par and (1) additional share issued 06/08/1966
Common $2.50 par changed to $1.25 par and (1) additional share issued 06/06/1969
Under plan of reorganization each share Common $1.25 par automatically became (1) share NWA Inc. (DE) Common $2 par 11/20/1984
(See NWA Inc.)

NORTHWEST ARM CAP INC (CANADA)
Name changed to Antler Gold Inc. 01/04/2017

NORTHWEST BANCORP (OR)
Merged into KeyCorp (NY) 11/10/1986
Each share Common $1 par exchanged for (1.11) shares Common $5 par
KeyCorp (NY) merged into KeyCorp (New) (OH) 03/01/1994

NORTHWEST BANCORP INC (USA)
Reincorporated 06/29/2001
Place of incorporation changed from (PA) to (USA) 06/29/2001
Merged into Northwest Bancshares, Inc. 12/18/2009
Each share Common 10¢ par

exchanged for (2.25) shares Common 1¢ par

NORTHWEST BANCORPORATION (DE)
Common $50 par changed to no par 00/00/1932
Common no par changed to $10 par 00/00/1949
4.20% Preferred $50 par called for redemption 12/14/1956
Common $10 par changed to $3.33-1/3 par and (2) additional shares issued 04/22/1959
4.50% Conv. Preferred $100 par called for redemption 09/19/1963
Common $3.33-1/3 par changed to $1-2/3 par and (1) additional share issued 04/25/1969
Common $1-2/3 par split (2) for (1) by issuance of (1) additional share 06/17/1977
Name changed to Norwest Corp. 05/02/1983
Northwest Corp. name changed to Wells Fargo & Co. (New) 11/02/1998

NORTHWEST BANCORPORATION INC (WA)
Stock Dividends - 5% payable 06/12/2000 to holders of record 06/01/2000 Ex date - 07/05/2000; 5% payable 06/15/2001 to holders of record 05/15/2001 Ex date - 05/11/2001; 5% payable 06/14/2002 to holders of record 05/15/2002 Ex date - 05/13/2002; 5% payable 06/13/2003 to holders of record 05/15/2003 Ex date - 05/13/2003; 5% payable 06/15/2004 to holders of record 05/14/2004 Ex date - 05/12/2004; 5% payable 06/15/2005 to holders of record 05/16/2005 Ex date - 05/12/2005; 5% payable 06/15/2006 to holders of record 05/15/2006 Ex date - 05/11/2006; 5% payable 06/15/2007 to holders of record 05/14/2007 Ex date - 05/10/2007
Merged into First Interstate BancSystem, Inc. 08/16/2018
Each share Common no par exchanged for (0.516) share Common no par

NORTHWEST BANCSHARES LA INC (LA)
Acquired by Hibernia Corp. 1/1/98
Each share Common no par exchanged for (3.898) shares Common no par
Hibernia Corp. merged into Capital One Financial Corp. 11/16/2005

NORTHWEST BK & TR CO (DAVENPORT, IA)
Common $25 par changed to $5 par and (4) additional shares issued 3/1/73
Each share old Common $5 par exchanged for (0.01) share new Common $5 par 4/17/2000
Each (82) shares new Common $5 par exchanged again for (1) share new Common $5 par 11/20/2006
Note: In effect holders received $3,561 cash per share and public interest was eliminated

NORTHWEST BANK (DALLAS, TX)
Closed by the FDIC 1/21/88
Stockholders' equity undetermined

NORTHWEST BERYLLIUM CORP. (MD)
Charter annulled for failure to file reports and pay fees 12/15/71

NORTHWEST CANALASK NICKEL MINES LTD (ON)
Capital Stock $1 par changed to no par 8/17/71
Recapitalized as New Canalask Minerals Ltd. 8/30/73
Each share Capital Stock no par exchanged for (0.01) share Capital Stock no par
(See New Canalask Minerals Ltd.)

NORTHWEST CAP TR I (DE)
Stock Dividend - 5% payable 10/15/2002 to holders of record 10/1/2002 Ex date - 9/27/2002
8.75% Guaranteed Trust Preferred Securities called for redemption at $25 on 12/31/2006

NORTHWEST CATTLE & RES INC (OR)
Placed in receivership 12/2/71
No stockholders' equity

NORTHWEST CENT PIPELINE CORP (DE)
Name changed to Williams Natural Gas Co. 01/01/1987
(See Williams Natural Gas Co.)

NORTHWEST CHEMCO INC (WI)
5% Preferred Ser. A $100 par called for redemption 05/31/1974
Common no par changed to $10 par 05/31/1974
5% Preferred Ser. A $10 par called for redemption 07/01/1985
Merged into NWC, Inc. 07/23/1985
Each share Common $10 par exchanged for $93.85 cash

NORTHWEST CINEMA CORP (DE)
Merged into Midwest Cinema Corp. 02/02/1982
Each share Common 10¢ par exchanged for $0.20 cash

NORTHWEST COML BK (LAKEWOOD, WA)
Acquired by Heritage Financial Corp. 01/09/2013
Each share Common exchanged for $5.50 cash

NORTHWEST DEFENSE MINERALS, INC. (MD)
Name changed to Northwest Beryllium Corp. 3/16/62
(See Northwest Beryllium Corp.)

NORTHWEST DIGITAL LTD (BC)
Acquired by Hartco Enterprises Inc. 01/21/1994
Each share Common no par exchanged for $0.10 cash

NORTHWEST DISTILLERS, INC. (MN)
Merged into Honeywood, Inc. 3/12/82
Each share Common 5¢ par exchanged for (1) share Common 5¢ par

NORTHWEST DRUG LTD (AB)
Merged into Drug Trading Co. 8/24/93
Each share Common no par exchanged for $9.26 cash

NORTHWEST ELECTRONICS CORP. (MN)
Each share Common 50¢ par exchanged for (0.5) share Common 5¢ par 12/3/68
Name changed to NWE Corp. 3/25/69
(See NWE Corp.)

NORTHWEST ENERGY CO (UT)
Reincorporated 4/22/80
Each VTC for Common $1 par exchanged for (1) share Common $1 par 2/7/79
Unexchanged VTC's for Common $1 par became worthless 3/1/79
Note: Holders of VTC's for Common $1 par who were also holders of El Paso Co. Common $3 par through 2/28/79 received $29.126174 cash 3/23/79
Common $1 par split (2) for (1) by issuance of (1) additional share 6/8/79
State of incorporation changed from (DE) to (UT) 4/22/80
Common $1 par split (3) for (2) by issuance of (0.5) additional share 9/12/80
$2.125 Conv. Preference Ser. A $1 par called for redemption 11/23/83
Merged into Williams Companies 11/30/83
Each share Common $1 par exchanged for $39 cash

NORTHWEST ENGR CO (DE)
Each share Capital Stock no par exchanged for (1) share Class A no par and (1) share Class B no par in 1952
Class A no par reclassified as Common no par 10/29/73
Class B no par reclassified as Common no par 10/29/73
Common no par split (3) for (1) by issuance of (2) additional shares 12/1/73
Common no par changed to 1¢ par 2/27/87
Name changed to Terex Corp. 5/6/88

NORTHWEST EQUITY CORP (WI)
Merged into Bremer Financial Corp. 3/21/2000
Each share Common $1 par exchanged for $24.28 cash

NORTHWEST EXPLORATIONS INC (ON)
Recapitalized as CGX Energy, Inc. 10/26/98
Each share Common no par exchanged for (0.2) share Common no par

NORTHWEST FABRICS INC (WI)
Merged into Peavey Co. 02/23/1973
Each share Common 5¢ par exchanged for (0.4) share Common $2.50 par
Peavey Co. merged into ConAgra, Inc. 07/20/1982 which name changed to ConAgra Foods, Inc. 09/28/2000 which name changed to Conagra Brands, Inc. 11/10/2016

NORTHWEST GAS & OIL EXPL CO (DE)
Name changed to Yandel Northwest Petroleums Inc. 9/4/73
Yandel Northwest Petroleums Inc. name changed to Allerton Resources Inc. 8/17/78
(See Allerton Resources Inc.)

NORTHWEST GEN INC (UT)
Name changed to Meter Dynamics, Inc. 7/23/84
(See Meter Dynamics, Inc.)

NORTHWEST GOLD CORP (BC)
Merged into Northgate Exploration Ltd. (ON) 06/08/1993
Each (15) shares Class A Subordinate no par exchanged for (1) share Common no par
Northgate Exploration Ltd. (ON) reincorporated in British Columbia 07/01/2001 which name changed to Northgate Minerals Corp. 05/20/2004 which merged into AuRico Gold Inc. 10/26/2011

NORTHWEST GOLD INC (WY)
Each share old Common $0.001 par exchanged for (0.01) share new Common $0.001 par 05/22/2000
Reincorporated under the laws of Nevada as Pogo! Products, Ltd. 10/07/2003
(See Pogo! Products, Ltd.)

NORTHWEST HARDWOODS, INC. (NV)
Merged into Weyerhaeuser Co. 7/7/81
Each share Common 50¢ par exchanged for (0.1661) share Common $1.875 par or $5.52 cash

NORTHWEST HOMES CHEHALIS INC (WA)
Charter cancelled and proclaimed dissolved for failure to pay fees 4/30/99

NORTHWEST ILL BANCORP INC (DE)
Common $10 par changed to $5 par and (1) additional share issued 08/01/1982
Common $5 par split (2) for (1) by issuance of (1) additional share 05/01/1985
Common $5 par split (2) for (1) by issuance of (1) additional share 04/24/1987
Common $5 par split (3) for (2) by issuance of (0.5) additional share 02/18/1993
Name changed to Today's Bancorp Inc. 01/01/1995
Today's Bancorp Inc. merged into Mercantile Bancorporation, Inc. 11/07/1996 which merged into Firstar Corp. (New) 09/20/1999 which merged into U.S. Bancorp (DE) 02/27/2001

NORTHWEST INDUSTRIES, LTD. (AB)
Common no par exchanged (3) for (1) 10/2/59
Acquired by Canadian Aviation Electronics Ltd. for cash 3/1/63

NORTHWEST INDS INC (DE)
Common no par split (3) for (1) by issuance of (2) additional shares 06/06/1969
5% Conv. Preferred Ser. A $100 par called for redemption 03/04/1976
$4.20 Conv. Prior Preferred no par called for redemption 01/30/1978
Common no par split (2) for (1) by issuance of (1) additional share 07/21/1978
$5 Conv. Preferred Ser. C no par called for redemption 04/02/1979
Acquired by Farley Industries Inc. 07/31/1985
Each share Common no par exchanged for (2) shares Farley/Northwest Industries, Inc. 13-1/2% Exchangeable Preferred 1¢ par and (1) share Lone Star Steel Co. Common $1 par
(See each company's listing)

NORTHWEST INTL HEALTHCARE PPTYS REAL ESTATE INVT TR (ON)
Merged into NorthWest Healthcare Properties REIT 05/19/2015
Each Trust Unit exchanged for (0.208) Trust Unit
Note: Unexchanged certificates will be cancelled and become without value 05/19/2021

NORTHWEST LOUISIANA GAS CO., INC.
Reorganized in 1938
No stockholders' equity

NORTHWEST MILLS, INC. (WA)
Merged into International-United Corp. 4/1/70
Each share Common 1¢ par exchanged for (0.916666) share Common 10¢ par
International-United Corp. adjudicated bankrupt 9/13/71

NORTHWEST NAT GAS CO (OR)
5.72% Preferred $100 par called for redemption 07/31/1963
5.75% Preferred $100 par called for redemption 01/15/1964
Common $9.50 par changed to $3.16666666 par and (2) additional shares issued 05/28/1965
4.75% Preferred $100 par reclassified as $4.75 Preferred no par 05/28/1976
6.875% Preferred $100 par reclassified as $6.875 Preferred no par 05/28/1976
8% Preferred $100 par reclassified as $8 Preferred no par 05/28/1976
$2.42 Preferred no par called for redemption 01/29/1993
$8 Preferred no par called for redemption 01/29/1993
6.875% Preferred no par called for redemption 09/17/1993
$2.375 Conv. Preferred no par called for redemption 05/15/1995
Common $3.16666666 par split (3) for (2) by issuance of (0.5) additional share payable 09/06/1996 to holders of record 08/23/1996

$4.75 Preferred no par called for redemption 09/01/2000
$6.95 Preference no par called for redemption 12/31/2002
Common $3.16666666 par changed to no par 05/31/2006
Under plan of reorganization each share Common no par automatically became (1) share Northwest Natural Holding Co. Common no par 10/01/2018

NORTHWEST NATL BK (CHICAGO, IL)
Each share Capital Stock $100 par exchanged for (5) shares Capital Stock $20 par 00/00/1947
Capital Stock $20 par changed to $10 par and (1) additional share issued plus a 50% stock dividend paid 06/24/1966
Stock Dividends - 100% 07/22/1957; 100% 05/17/1961
Through purchase offer 00/00/1970 by Northwestco, Inc. held 100% as of 04/07/1971
Public interest eliminated

NORTHWEST NATURAL GAS CO. (DE)
No longer in existence having become inoperative and void for non-payment of taxes 4/1/57

NORTHWEST NITRO CHEMS LTD (AB)
5% Preferred $100 par called for redemption 00/00/1974
Merged into International Minerals & Chemical Corp. 05/19/1978
Each share Common 1¢ par exchanged for $2.45 cash

NORTHWEST NURSING HOME, INC. (MD)
Merged into Convalescent Care Centers, Inc. 9/26/68
Each share Common $1 par automatically became (1) share Common 25¢ par
Convalescent Care Centers, Inc. name changed to Medical Services Corp. 12/5/69
(See Medical Services Corp.)

NORTHWEST OHIO BANCSHARES INC (DE)
Stock Dividends - 25% 09/01/1972; 50% 11/03/1973; 20% 06/01/1975; 33-1/3% 07/01/1976; 25% 08/01/1977
Name changed to Toledo Trustcorp, Inc. 04/02/1979
Toledo Trustcorp, Inc. name changed to Trustcorp, Inc. 04/10/1986 which was acquired by Society Corp. 01/05/1990 which merged into KeyCorp (New) 03/01/1994

NORTHWEST OIL CO. (WY)
Proclaimed dissolved for failure to file reports and pay fees 5/23/78

NORTHWEST PA BK & TR CO (OIL CITY, PA)
Common $20 par changed to $10 par and (1) additional share issued 01/28/1965
Common $10 par changed to $5 par and (1) additional share issued 08/28/1970
Stock Dividend - 20% 11/20/1963
Under plan of reorganization each share Common $5 par automatically became (1) share Northwest Pennsylvania Corp. Common $5 par 07/01/1981
Northwest Pennsylvania Corp. merged into Mellon National Corp. 04/12/1984 which changed to Mellon Bank Corp. 09/30/1984 which name changed to Mellon Financial Corp. 10/17/1999 which merged into Bank of New York Mellon Corp. 07/01/2007

NORTHWEST PA CORP (PA)
Merged into Mellon National Corp. 04/12/1984
Each share Common $5 par exchanged for (0.7131) share $2.80 Preferred Ser. A $1 par and (0.8) share Common 50¢ par or $54 cash
Mellon National Corp. name changed to Mellon Bank Corp. 09/30/1984 which name changed to Mellon Financial Corp. 10/17/1999 which merged into Bank of New York Mellon Corp. 07/01/2007

NORTHWEST PAC ENTERPRISES INC (UT)
Proclaimed dissolved for failure to pay taxes 11/09/1974

NORTHWEST PAPER CO. (MN)
Class B Common no par reclassified as Common no par 00/00/1951
Each share Common no par exchanged for (3) shares Common $5 par 00/00/1957
Merged into Potlatch Forests, Inc. (DE) 05/28/1964
Each share Common $5 par exchanged for (1.25) shares Common $1 par
Potlatch Forests, Inc. (DE) name changed to Potlatch Corp. (Old) 04/27/1973 which reorganized as Potlatch Corp. (New) 02/03/2006 which name changed to PotlatchDeltic Corp. 02/23/2018

NORTHWEST PASSAGE NORTH AMER INC (NY)
Name changed to Advanced Environmental Systems Inc. 8/31/90
(See Advanced Environmental Systems Inc.)

NORTHWEST PASSAGE VENTURES LTD (NV)
Common $0.0001 par split (6) for (1) by issuance of (5) additional shares payable 06/03/2005 to holders of record 05/31/2005 Ex date - 06/06/2005
Common $0.0001 par split (4.195) for (1) by issuance of (3.195) additional shares payable 10/14/2005 to holders of record 10/11/2005 Ex date - 10/17/2005
Name changed to Americas Wind Energy Corp. 10/16/2006

NORTHWEST PIPELINE CORP (DE)
Under plan of reorganization each share Common $1 par or VTC for Common $1 par automatically became (1) share Northwest Energy Co. (DE) Common $1 par or VTC for Common $1 par respectively 02/28/1975
Northwest Energy Co. (DE) reincorporated in Utah 04/22/1980
(See Northwest Energy Co. (UT))
$2.50 Preferred $1 par called for called for redemption 01/01/1991
$2.36 Preferred $1 par called for redemption 07/01/1992

NORTHWEST PLASTICS INC (MN)
Common $2.50 par changed to $2 par 12/04/1964
Common $2 par changed to 50¢ par and (2) additional shares issued 06/14/1965
Stock Dividend - 25% 12/29/1964
Name changed to Norwesco, Inc. 03/27/1973
(See Norwesco, Inc.)

NORTHWEST PRODTN CORP (DE)
Merged into El Paso Co. 09/06/1977
Each share Common $1 par exchanged for $3 cash

NORTHWEST PUBLICATIONS INC. (DE)
Acquired by Ridder Publications, Inc. in 1969
(See Ridder Publications, Inc.)

NORTHWEST RES INC (NV)
Name changed to Cubed, Inc. 03/18/2014

NORTHWEST SVGS BK (WARREN, PA)
Common 10¢ par split (2) for (1) by issuance of (1) additional share payable 05/20/1996 to holders of record 05/03/1996
Common 10¢ par split (2) for (1) by issuance of (1) additional share payable 11/14/1997 to holders of record 11/01/1997
Under plan of reorganization each share Common 10¢ par automatically became (1) share Northwest Bancorp, Inc. (PA) Common 10¢ par 02/18/1998
Northwest Bancorp, Inc. (PA) reincorporated in United States 06/29/2001 which merged into Northwest Bancshares, Inc. 12/18/2009

NORTHWEST SHROOM INDS LTD (BC)
Cease trade order effective 08/16/1989
Stockholders' equity unlikely

NORTHWEST SILICA & GYPSUM CO (UT)
Name changed to Egbert & Backus Excavating Co. 02/23/1976
Each share Common 1¢ par exchanged for (1) share Common 1¢ par
(See Egbert & Backus Excavating Co.)

NORTHWEST SPORTS ENTERPRISES LTD (BC)
Merged into Orca BayHockey Holdings Inc. 11/9/2000
Each share Common no par exchanged for $14 cash

NORTHWEST STATES UTILITIES CO.
Merged into Montana-Dakota Utilities Co. in 1935
(See Montana-Dakota Utilities Co.)

NORTHWEST SYS CORP (MN)
Out of business and assets assigned to creditors 00/00/1971
Stockholders' equity unlikely

NORTHWEST TELEPHONE CO. (OR)
Merged into United Utilities, Inc. 07/01/2060
Each share Common $5 par exchanged for (1) share Common $10 par
United Utilities, Inc. name changed to United Telecommunications, Inc. 06/02/1972 which name changed to Sprint Corp. (KS) 02/26/1992 which name changed to Sprint Nextel Corp. 08/12/2005 which merged into Sprint Corp. (DE) 07/10/2013

NORTHWEST TELEPRODUCTIONS INC (MN)
Common 1¢ par split (3) for (2) by issuance of (0.5) additional share 01/18/1985
Common 1¢ par split (3) for (2) by issuance of (0.5) additional share 10/10/1986
Name changed to Broadview Media, Inc. 04/03/2000
Broadview Media, Inc. name changed to Broadview Institute, Inc. 08/15/2006
(See Broadview Institute, Inc.)

NORTHWEST TIMBER EXPT CO (WA)
Charter cancelled and proclaimed dissolved for failure to pay fees 12/24/90

NORTHWEST URANIUM MINES, INC. (ID)
Assets sold to Silver Buckle Mining Co., liquidation approved and non-negotiable evidence of interest issued in exchange for Capital Stock 6/23/58

NORTHWEST VENTURES LTD (BC)
Common 50¢ par changed to no par 07/10/1969
Merged into Stampede International Resources Inc. 05/31/1982
Each share Common no par exchanged for (0.25) share Class A Common no par
Stampede International Resources Inc. merged into International H.R.S. Industries Inc. 05/15/1984 which name changed to Glenex Industries Inc. 05/25/1987 which merged into Quest Investment Corp. 07/04/2002 which merged into Quest Capital Corp. (BC) 06/30/2003 which reincorporated in Canada 05/27/2008 which name changed to Sprott Resource Lending Corp. 09/10/2010 which merged into Sprott Inc. 07/24/2013

NORTHWESTERN BANCORP INC (MI)
Merged into Chemical Financial Corp. 11/03/2014
Each share Common no par exchanged for $568.59 cash

NORTHWESTERN BK (NORTH WILKESBORO, NC)
Each share Capital Stock $10 par exchanged for (2) shares Capital Stock $5 par 02/15/1960
Stock Dividends - 30% 11/01/1958; 10% 01/10/1964; 100% 02/10/1966
Reorganized as Northwestern Financial Corp. 07/31/1969
Each share Capital Stock $5 par exchanged for (2) shares Common $5 par
Northwestern Financial Corp. merged into First Union Corp. 12/02/1985 which name changed to Wachovia Corp. (Ctfs. dated after 09/01/2001) 09/01/2001 which merged into Wells Fargo & Co. (New) 12/31/2008

NORTHWESTERN BK CORP (MI)
Merged into First Michigan Bank Corp. 5/31/91
Each share Common $1 par exchanged for $244.26 principal amount of 10% Subordinated Debentures due 5/31/2001, (14.5476) shares Common $1 par and $16.49 cash
First Michigan Bank Corp. merged into Huntington Bancshares Inc. 9/30/97

NORTHWESTERN BARB WIRE CO.
Name changed to Northwestern Steel & Wire Co. in 1938
(See Northwestern Steel & Wire Co.)

NORTHWESTERN CAPITAL CORP. (NC)
Merged into NWFC Corp. 1/1/82
Each share Common $5 par exchanged for $7.97 cash

NORTHWESTERN CAP FING I (DE)
Under plan of reorganization each 7.20% Guaranteed Trust Preferred Security received (0.18901534) share NorthWestern Corp. new Common 1¢ par and (0.36215096) Common Stock Purchase Warrant expiring 11/1/2007 on 11/1/2004
Note: Each 7.20% Guaranteed Trust Preferred Security received an additional distribution of $0.00759057 cash payable 5/31/2006 to holders of record 10/20/2004

NORTHWESTERN CAP FING II (DE)
Under plan of reorganization each 8.25% Trust Preferred Security received (0.18955822) share NorthWestern Corp. new Common 1¢ par and (0.36319111) Common Stock Purchase Warrant expiring 11/1/2007 on 11/1/2004
Note: Each 8.25% Trust Preferred Security received an additional distribution of $0.00759057 cash

payable 5/31/2006 to holders of record 10/20/2004

NORTHWESTERN CAP FING III (DE)
Under plan of reorganization each 8.10% Trust Preferred Security received (0.18979083) share NorthWestern Corp. new Common 1¢ par and (0.36363679) Common Stock Purchase Warrant expiring 11/1/2007 on 11/1/2004
Note: Each 8.10% Trust Preferred Security received an additional distribution of $0.00759057 cash payable 5/31/2006 to holders of record 10/20/2004

NORTHWESTERN CO (WA)
Acquired by USLIFE Holding Corp. 7/10/69
Each share Class A Common no par or Class B Common no par exchanged for (1.333333) shares Common $2 par
USLIFE Holding Corp. name changed to USLIFE Corp. 5/22/70 which merged into American General Corp. 6/17/97 which merged into American International Group, Inc. 8/29/2001

NORTHWESTERN CORP (DE)
4.50% Preferred $100 par called for redemption at $110 on 07/31/2002
Plan of reorganization under Chapter 11 Federal Bankruptcy Code effective 11/01/2004
No Common $1.75 par stockholders' equity
(Additional Information in Active)

NORTHWESTERN DRUG CO (MN)
Acquired by Dohmen (F.) Co. 00/00/1992
Details not available

NORTHWESTERN ELECTRIC CO.
Merged into Pacific Power & Light Co. in 1947
Each share 6% and 7% Preferred exchanged for (1) share 5% Preferred $100 par
Note: Each share 7% Preferred also received $5 cash
Pacific Power & Light Co. name changed to PacifiCorp (Me.) 6/15/84 which reincorporated in Oregon 1/9/89

NORTHWESTERN FIN CO (NC)
Capital Stock $1 par split (4) for (3) by issuance of (1/3) additional share 08/01/1972
Merged into Northwestern Financial Corp. 12/31/1975
Each share Capital Stock $1 par exchanged for (0.572747) share Common $1 par
Note: An additional (0.108728) share Common $1 par was distributed 12/00/1976
Northwestern Financial Corp. merged into First Union Corp. 12/02/1985 which name changed to Wachovia Corp. (Ctfs. dated after 09/01/2001) 09/01/2001 which merged into Wells Fargo & Co. (New) 12/31/2008

NORTHWESTERN FINL CORP (IA)
Merged into American Federal Bank (East Grand Forks, MN) 8/2/96
Each share Common 1¢ par exchanged for $23.25 cash

NORTHWESTERN FINL CORP (NC)
Common $5 par changed to $1 par and (0.5) additional share issued 04/12/1972
Common $1 par split (2) for (1) by issuance of (1) additional share 04/01/1985
Stock Dividend - 10% 06/21/1976
Merged into First Union Corp. 12/02/1985
Each share Common $1 par exchanged for (0.77) share Common $3.33-1/3 par
First Union Corp. name changed to Wachovia Corp. (Ctfs. dated after 09/01/2001) 09/01/2001 which merged into Wells Fargo & Co. (New) 12/31/2008

NORTHWESTERN FINL INVS (SC)
Name changed to First Carolina Investors (SC) 06/30/1979
First Carolina Investors (SC) reorganized in Delaware as First Carolina Investors, Inc. 07/01/1987
(See First Carolina Investors, Inc.)

NORTHWESTERN FIRE & MARINE INSURANCE CO. (MN)
Each share Capital Stock $100 par exchanged for (10) shares Capital Stock $10 par in 1929
Capital Stock $10 par changed to $5 par 6/12/59
Stock Dividend - 25% 3/3/55
Under plan of merger name changed to Guaranty Security Insurance Co. 6/19/59
Guaranty Security Insurance Co. merged into Diversified Insurers Co. 1/29/68
(See Diversified Insurers Co.)

NORTHWESTERN GLASS CO. (WA)
Merged into Indian Head Inc. 4/11/68
Each share Common $5 par exchanged for (0.066666) share $4.50 Conv. Preferred Ser. A no par and (0.666666) share Common $1 par

NORTHWESTERN LEATHER CO. (MA)
Stock Dividend - 20% 12/24/47
Liquidation completed 11/18/55

NORTHWESTERN LEATHER CO. (MI)
Liquidation completed in 1958

NORTHWESTERN LIFE INS CO (WA)
Acquired by USLIFE Holding Corp. 9/2/69
Each share Common $10 par exchanged for (8) shares Common $2 par
USLIFE Holding Corp. name changed to USLIFE Corp. 5/22/70 which merged into American General Corp. 6/17/97 which merged into American International Group, Inc. 8/29/2001

NORTHWESTERN LIGHT & POWER CO. (DE)
Liquidation completed 11/8/54

NORTHWESTERN MINERAL VENTURES INC (ON)
Common no par split (2) for (1) by issuance of (1) additional share payable 09/09/2005 to holders of record 09/08/2005 Ex date - 09/06/2005
Name changed to NWT Uranium Corp. 08/03/2007
NWT Uranium Corp. name changed to Captor Capital Corp. 06/02/2017

NORTHWESTERN MUT LIFE MTG & RLTY INVS (MA)
Shares of Bene. Int. $1 par reclassified as Common $1 par 07/29/1974
Merged into Northwestern Mutual Life Insurance Co. 01/12/1983
Each share Common $1 par exchanged for $13.75 cash

NORTHWESTERN NATIONAL BANK OF SOUTH ST PAUL (SOUTH ST. PAUL, MN)
Acquired by Norwest Bank Minneapolis N.A. (Minneapolis, MN) 01/01/1988
Details not available

NORTHWESTERN NATIONAL INSURANCE CO. (WI)
Capital Stock $100 par changed to $25 par and 50% stock dividend paid in 1926
Each share Capital Stock $25 par exchanged for (4) shares Capital Stock $10 par in 1950
Capital Stock $10 par changed to $5 par and (1) additional share issued plus a 50% stock dividend paid 3/30/62
Each share Capital Stock $5 par exchanged for (0.001) share Capital Stock $5000 par 5/25/71
Public interest was eliminated

NORTHWESTERN NATL LIFE INS CO (MN)
Common $5 par changed to $7.50 par in 1940
Common $7.50 par changed to $10 par in 1947
Common $10 par changed to $20 par 10/27/58
Each share Common $20 par exchanged for (8) shares Common $2.50 par 5/1/63
Common $2.50 par changed to $1.25 par and (1) additional share issued 5/15/70
Stock Dividend - 100% 5/18/84
Reorganized under the laws of Delaware as NWNL Companies, Inc. and Common $1.25 par changed to no par 1/3/89
NWNL Companies, Inc. name changed to ReliaStar Financial Corp. 2/13/95
(See ReliaStar Financial Corp.)

NORTHWESTERN OIL & MINING CORP. (WY)
Charter revoked for failure to file reports and pay fees 2/19/60

NORTHWESTERN OILS INC. (NV)
Charter revoked for non-compliance with Nevada corporation laws 3/3/58

NORTHWESTERN PETROLEUM & REFINING CO. (DE)
Charter cancelled for failure to pay taxes in 1925

NORTHWESTERN PORTLAND CEMENT CO. (WA)
3% 2nd Preferred $38 par changed to $1.14 2nd Preferred no par in 1955
Acquired by Ideal Cement Co. 9/30/57
Each share 6% 1st Preferred $100 par exchanged for (1.5) shares Capital Stock $10 par
Each share $1.14 2nd Preferred no par exchanged for (0.543) share Capital Stock $10 par
Each share Common no par exchanged for (0.488) share Capital Stock $10 par
Ideal Cement Co. merged into Ideal Basic Industries, Inc. (CO) 12/31/67 which reincorporated in Delaware 5/15/87 which merged into Holnam Inc. 3/8/90
(See Holnam Inc.)

NORTHWESTERN POWER & LIGHT CO.
Merged into Crown Zellerbach Corp. in 1936
(See Crown Zellerbach Corp.)

NORTHWESTERN PUB SVC CO (DE)
6% Preferred $100 par called for redemption 3/20/47
7% Preferred $100 par called for redemption 3/20/47
Common $3 par changed to $7 par and (1/3) additional share issued 4/29/64
5-1/4% Preferred (1948) $100 par called for redemption in 1982
5-1/4% (1950) $100 par called for redemption 11/30/84
10-1/8% Preferred $100 par called for redemption 10/1/86
Common $7 par changed to $3.50 par and (1) additional share issued 6/13/88
7-5/8% Preferred $100 par called for redemption 1/2/92
8% Preferred $100 par called for redemption 1/2/92
5.25% Preferred $100 par called for redemption 1/1/96
Common $3.50 par changed to $1.75 par and (1) additional share issued payable 5/27/97 to holders of record 5/19/97 Ex date - 5/28/97
Name changed to Northwestern Corp. 5/6/98

NORTHWESTERN SVGS & LN ASSN (TRAVERSE CITY, MI)
Under plan of reorganization each share Common no par automatically became (1) share Northwestern Bancorp, Inc. Common no par 02/26/1996
(See Northwestern Bancorp, Inc.)

NORTHWESTERN SVC CORP (DE)
Each share Common 1¢ par exchanged for (0.01) share Common $1 par 10/12/1977
Company believed out of business 00/00/1989
Details not available

NORTHWESTERN STL & WIRE CO (IL)
Common $5 par split (5) for (1) by issuance of (4) additional shares 6/11/47
Common $5 par split (3) for (1) by issuance of (2) additional shares 5/14/56
Common $5 par split (3) for (1) by issuance of (2) additional shares 5/26/72
Under plan of merger each share Common $5 par exchanged for $6 principal amount of 13% Subordinated notes due 5/15/97 and $19 cash on 8/16/88
Chapter 11 bankruptcy proceedings converted to Chapter 7 on 7/12/2002
Stockholders' equity unlikely

NORTHWESTERN STS PORTLAND CEM CO (IA)
Each share Capital Stock no par exchanged for (2) shares Capital Stock $10 par 07/26/1955
Acquired by Dundee Cement Co. 01/19/1990
Each share Capital Stock $10 par exchanged for $22.50 cash

NORTHWESTERN TEL CO (IL)
Common $10 par changed to $15 par 7/26/61
Common $15 par changed to $20 par 4/14/65
Common $20 par changed to $40 par 5/17/72
Common $40 par changed to $15 par and (3) additional shares issued 10/27/76
Merged into Continental Telephone Corp. 3/20/80
Each share Common $15 par exchanged for (3.25) shares Common $1 par
Continental Telephone Corp. name changed to Continental Telecom Inc. 5/6/82 which name changed to Contel Corp. 5/1/86 which merged into GTE Corp. 3/14/91 merged into Verizon Communications Inc. 6/30/2000

NORTHWESTERN TEL SYS INC (OR)
5% Preferred called for redemption at $100 on 01/31/2011

NORTHWESTERN TELEGRAPH CO. (WI)
Acquired by Western Union Telegraph Co. and each share Capital Stock $50 par exchanged for $40 of Debentures in 1952

NORTHWESTERN TERM RR CO (NV)
Liquidation completed 01/02/1969
Each share Capital Stock no par exchanged for first and final distribution of $50 cash

NORTHWESTERN TERMINAL CO.
Liquidated in 1952
No stockholders' equity

NORTHWESTERN TERRA COTTA CORP. (IL)
Name changed to Spectra Industries, Inc. 1/13/67

Spectra Industries, Inc. name changed to Spectra Corp. 9/25/68 which merged into Spectra McIntosh Corp. 6/30/69 which name changed to McIntosh Corp. 9/27/73 which merged into Norris Industries, Inc. 6/30/77
(See Norris Industries, Inc.)

NORTHWESTERN URANIUM LTD. (AB)
Struck from Alberta Registrar of Companies and proclaimed dissolved 7/15/61

NORTHWESTERN UTILS LTD (CANADA)
Under plan of merger each share old 4% Preference $100 par exchanged for (1) share new 4% Preference $100 par 8/2/72
New 4% Preference $100 par called for redemption 12/30/96
Public interest eliminated

NORTHWESTERN YEAST CO.
Liquidated in 1947

NORTHWIND EXPLORATIONS, LTD. (ON)
Dissolved 10/10/61

NORTHWIND VENTURES LTD (BC)
Recapitalized as Sloane Petroleums, Inc. 07/10/1998
Each share Common no par exchanged for (1/3) share Common no par
Sloane Petroleums, Inc. merged into Gentry Resources Ltd. 03/01/2001 which merged into Crew Energy Inc. 08/22/2008

NORTHWOOD CORP. (NY)
Name changed to Allied Scale Corp. 2/16/86
Allied Scale Corp. name changed to InAmerica Corp. (N.Y.) 11/21/86 which reincorporated in Oklahoma 8/31/88

NORTHWOOD PRODS CORP (UT)
Recapitalized as Phoenix Companies, Inc. (UT) 12/13/1977
Each share Common 1¢ par exchanged for (0.1) share Common 10¢ par
Phoenix Companies, Inc. (UT) name changed to Tropical Development International, Inc. 00/00/1987 which recapitalized as Impulse Energy Systems, Inc. 04/02/1990
(See Impulse Energy Systems, Inc.)

NORTHWOOD SHOPPING CENTER INC. (MD)
Dissolved 10/30/59

NORTOBA MINES LTD. (ON)
Charter cancelled and company declared dissolved by default 4/22/65

NORTOBA NICKEL EXPLORATIONS LTD. (ON)
Name changed to Nortoba Mines Ltd. 8/14/58
(See Nortoba Mines Ltd.)

NORTON (T.M.) BREWING CO.
Dissolved in 1941

NORTON BSA INC (UT)
Name changed to Brooklyn Drink Co. Inc. 2/20/95
Brooklyn Drink Co. Inc. name changed to Net Tel International, Inc. 5/28/96
(See Net Tel International, Inc.)

NORTON CO (MA)
Common $10 par changed to $5 par and (1) additional share issued 12/06/1978
Merged into Compagnie de Saint-Gobain 09/18/1990
Each share Common $5 par exchanged for $90 cash

NORTON DRILLING SVCS INC (DE)
Each share old Common 1¢ par exchanged for (0.2) share new Common 1¢ par 02/02/1999
Merged into UTI Energy Corp. 06/26/1999
Each share Common 1¢ par exchanged for (0.2631578) share Common $0.001 par
UTI Energy Corp. merged into Patterson-UTI Energy, Inc. 05/09/2001

NORTON ENTERPRISES INC (DE)
Acquired by N Acquisition Corp. 09/02/1988
Each share Common 1¢ par exchanged for $13 cash

NORTON GROUP PLC (UNITED KINGDOM)
Acquired by Minty PLC 12/19/1989
Each Sponsored ADR for Ordinary 5p par exchanged for $0.25 cash

NORTON MCNAUGHTON INC (DE)
Name changed to McNaughton Apparel Group Inc. 02/09/1999
McNaughton Apparel Group Inc. merged into Jones Apparel Group, Inc. 06/19/2001 which name changed to Jones Group Inc. 10/18/2010
(See Jones Group Inc.)

NORTON MOTORCYCLES INC (CO)
Each share old Common no par exchanged for (0.02380952) share new Common no par 04/30/1999
Administratively dissolved 06/01/2004

NORTON PORTLAND CORP. (ME)
Charter suspended for non-payment of franchise tax 12/01/1962

NORTON SIMON INC (DE)
Common $1 par split (2) for (1) by issuance of (1) additional share 06/23/1972
$3 Conv. Preferred Ser. C $5 par called for redemption 11/09/1973
$1.60 Conv. Preferred Ser. A $5 par called for redemption 08/25/1983
Merged into Esmark, Inc. (Inc. 03/14/1969) 09/09/1983
Each share Common $1 par exchanged for (1) share $2.80 Conv. Class 2 Preferred Ser. B $1 par
(See Esmark, Inc. (Inc. 03/14/1969))

NORTRAN PHARMACEUTICALS INC (BC)
Name changed 06/24/1992
Common no par split (2) for (1) by issuance of (1) additional share 06/17/1991
Name changed from Nortran Resources Ltd. to Nortran Pharmaceuticals Inc. 06/24/1992
Name changed to Cardiome Pharma Corp. (BC) 06/25/2001
Cardiome Pharma Corp. (BC) reorganized in Canada 03/12/2002 which name changed to Correvio Pharma Corp. 05/17/2018

NORTRUST CORP (DE)
Common $20 par changed to $10 par and (1) additional share issued 12/13/1972
Name changed to Northern Trust Corp. 03/08/1978

NORVALIE MINES LTD. (ON)
Recapitalized as International Norvalie Mines Ltd. 12/20/65
Each share Capital Stock $1 par exchanged for (1/3) share Capital Stock $1 par

NORVELL WILDER SUPPLY CO (TX)
100% acquired by Mayeaux Industries, Inc. as of 04/10/1972
Public interest eliminated

NORVEX INC (DE)
Recapitalized as Capital Title Group Inc. 05/23/1996
Each share Common $0.001 par exchanged for (0.1) share Common $0.001 par
Capital Title Group Inc. merged into LandAmerica Financial Group, Inc. 09/08/2006
(See LandAmerica Financial Group, Inc.)

NORVEX MINING CO. LTD. (QC)
Dissolved in 1960
No stockholders' equity

NORWALK CO., INC. (DE)
Acquired by Union Corp. (NJ) 10/17/68
Each share Common $1 par exchanged for (1.875) shares Common 50¢ par
Union Corp. (NJ) reincorporated in Delaware 7/24/87
(See Union Corp. (DE))

NORWALK NATL BK (NORWALK, CT)
Name changed to Fairfield County National Bank (Norwalk, CT) in December 1969
Fairfield County National Bank (Norwalk, CT) merged into CBT Corp. 2/26/73 which merged into Bank of New England Corp. 6/14/85
(See Bank of New England Corp.)

NORWALK SVGS SOC (CT)
Stock Dividend - 10% payable 05/29/1997 to holders of record 05/14/1997
Recapitalized as NSS Bancorp, Inc. 10/01/1997
Each share Common 1¢ par exchanged for (1) share Common 1¢ par
NSS Bancorp, Inc. merged into Summit Bancorp 11/20/1998 which merged into FleetBoston Financial Corp. 03/01/2001 which merged into Bank of America Corp. 04/01/2004

NORWALK TANK CO., INC. (CT)
Name changed to Mersick Industries, Inc. 04/28/1960
Mersick Industries, Inc. merged into Swift Industries, Inc. 05/16/1969
(See Swift Industries, Inc.)

NORWALK TIRE & RUBBER CO. (CT)
Assets sold in 1950
No stockholders' equity

NORWALK TRUCK LINES, INC. OF DELAWARE (DE)
6% Preferred $10 par called 12/18/67

NORWALK TRUCK LINES INC. (OH)
Class B Common $1 par reclassified as Common $1 par 04/10/1961
Voting Trust Agreement terminated 04/03/1964
Each VTC for Class B Common $1 par exchanged for Common $1 par
Merged into United-Buckingham Freight Lines, Inc. 03/31/1974
Each share Common $1 par exchanged for (0.519751) share Class A Common $1 par
(See United-Buckingham Freight Lines, Inc.)

NORWALL GROUP INC (ON)
Each share old Common no par exchanged for (1) share new Common no par to reflect a (1) for (100) reverse split followed by a (100) for (1) forward split 05/31/2006
Note: Holders of (99) or fewer pre-split shares received $1.71 cash per share
Each share new Common no par exchanged again for (0.00000026) share new Common no par 12/08/2010
Note: In effect holders received $0.93 cash per share and public interest was eliminated

NORWEB PLC (UNITED KINGDOM)
Acquired by North West Water Group P.L.C. 8/3/2000
Details not available

NORWEGIAN AMER LINE (NORWAY)
Each share Capital Stock Kr. 200 par exchanged for (2) shares Capital Stock Kr. 100 par 07/10/1968
Ceased operations 00/00/1995
Details not available

NORWEGIAN CONSOLIDATED MINING CO. (AZ)
Charter expired in 1927
No known value

NORWESCO INC (MN)
Common 50¢ par split (2) for (1) by issuance of (1) additional share 6/10/83
Common 50¢ par changed to 10¢ par 11/15/83
Common 10¢ par split (2) for (1) by issuance of (1) additional share 6/15/84
Acquired by NWC Acquisition, Inc. 1/29/88
Each share Common 10¢ par exchanged for $8.75 cash

NORWEST BANK TEXAS, SOUTH, N.A. (SAN ANTONIO, TX)
Acquired by Norwest Corp. 10/11/1997
Details not available

NORWEST CORP (DE)
Adjustable Rate Preferred no par called for redemption 08/14/1987
Adjustable Rate Preferred Ser. B no par called for redemption 09/23/1987
Common $1-2/3 par split (3) for (2) by issuance of (0.5) additional share 06/30/1988
Dutch Auction Rate Transferable Securities Preferred no par called for redemption 04/25/1989
Common $1-2/3 par split (2) for (1) by issuance of (1) additional share 07/21/1989
Common $1-2/3 par split (2) for (1) by issuance of (1) additional share 06/28/1993
$3.50 Depositary Preferred Ser. B no par called for redemption 09/01/1995
$3.50 Conv. Preferred Ser. B no par called for redemption 09/01/1995
10.24% Depositary Preferred called for redemption 01/02/1996
Common $1-2/3 par split (2) for (1) by issuance of (1) additional share payable 10/10/1997 to holders of record 10/02/1997
Under plan of merger name changed to Wells Fargo & Co. (New) 11/02/1998

NORWESTECH INC (DE)
Name changed to Grandparents.com, Inc. 03/09/2012
(See Grandparents.com, Inc.)

NORWICH & WORCESTER RR CO (CT & MA)
Merged into Penn Central Corp. 12/28/83
Each share Preferred $100 par exchanged for (3.147) shares Common $1 par
Note: a) Distribution is certain only for certificates surrendered prior to 5/1/85 b) Distribution may also be made for certificates surrendered between 5/1/85 and 12/31/86 c) No distribution will be made for certificates surrendered after 12/31/86
Penn Central Corp. name changed to American Premier Underwriters, Inc. 3/25/94 which merged into American Premier Group, Inc. 4/3/95 which name changed to American Financial Group, Inc. 6/9/95 which merged into American Financial Group, Inc. (Holding Co.) 12/2/97

NORWICH FINL CORP (DE)
Merged into People's Bank (Bridgeport, CT) 2/23/98
Each share Common 1¢ par exchanged for either (0.80129058)

share Common no par or $32.14 cash
Note: Option to receive stock expired 2/17/98
People's Bank (Bridgeport, CT) reorganized as People's United Financial, Inc. 4/16/2007

NORWICH KNITTING CO. (NY)
Name changed to Norwich Mills Inc. 02/03/1954
Norwich Mills Inc. merged into Champion Products Inc. 03/14/1969
(See Champion Products Inc.)

NORWICH MILLS INC. (NY)
Merged into Champion Products Inc. 03/14/1969
Each share Common no par exchanged for (5.2489) shares Common $1 par
(See Champion Products Inc.)

NORWICH PHARMACAL CO (NY)
Each share Capital Stock no par exchanged for (4) shares Capital Stock $5 par 00/00/1934
Each share Capital Stock $5 par exchanged for (2) shares Capital Stock $2.50 par 00/00/1939
Capital Stock $2.50 par reclassified as Common $2.50 par 00/00/1950
Common $2.50 par changed to $1.25 par and (1) additional share issued 05/10/1957
Common $1.25 par changed to 62-1/2¢ par and (1) additional share issued 12/23/1959
Common 62-1/2¢ par changed to 31-1/4¢ par and (1) additional share issued 10/18/1967
Under plan of merger name changed to Morton-Norwich Products, Inc. (NY) 04/25/1969
Morton-Norwich Products, Inc. (NY) reincorporated in Delaware 11/28/1969 which merged into Morton Thiokol Corp. 09/24/1982 which reorganized as Thiokol Corp. (DE) (New) 07/01/1989 which name changed to Cordant Technologies Inc. 05/07/1998
(See Cordant Technologies Inc.)

NORWICH RES LTD (BC)
Recapitalized as Kelly Petroleum Inc. 01/29/1980
Each share Common no par exchanged for (0.2) share Common no par
Kelly Petroleum Inc. merged into New Frontier Petroleum Corp. 01/18/1982 which recapitalized as PetroMac Energy Inc. 08/30/1985
(See PetroMac Energy Inc.)

NORWICH SVGS SOC (NORWICH, CT)
Reorganized under the laws of Delaware as Norwich Financial Corp. and Common $1 par changed to 1¢ par 8/10/88
Norwich Financial Corp. merged into People's Bank (Bridgeport, CT) 2/23/98 which reorganized as People's United Financial, Inc. 4/16/2007

NORWICH VENTURES LTD (BC)
Delisted from Alberta Stock Exchange 02/08/1993

NORWOOD ABBEY LTD (AUSTRALIA)
Name changed to Sino-Excel Energy Ltd. 05/01/2012
(See Sino-Excel Energy Ltd.)

NORWOOD ARENA, INC. (MA)
Assets sold for benefit of creditors 7/26/76
No stockholders' equity

NORWOOD-HYDE PARK BANK & TRUST CO. (NORWOOD, OH)
Acquired by Fifth Third Union Trust Co. (Cincinnati, Ohio) 1/19/62
Each share Capital Stock $100 par exchanged for $620 cash

NORWOOD PROMOTIONAL PRODS INC (TX)
Merged into FPK, LLC 10/30/98
Each share Common no par exchanged for $20.70 cash

NORWOOD RES LTD (BC)
Filed an assignment in bankruptcy 01/21/2011
No stockholders' equity

NORWOOD URANIUM, INC. (CO)
Merged into Rimrock Tidelands, Inc. on a (1) for (40) basis 2/23/56 which merged into Husky Oil Co. for cash 2/28/67

NORZINC MINES LTD. (ON)
Charter cancelled by the Province of Ontario for default 00/00/1958

NORZONE ROUYN MINES LTD.
Acquired by New Norzone Mines Ltd. on a (1) for (2) basis in 1947
New Norzone Mines Ltd. recapitalized as Diadem Mines Ltd. 9/27/55
(See Diadem Mines Ltd.)

NOS SGPS (PORTUGAL)
ADR agreement terminated 08/19/2016
Each Sponsored ADR for Ordinary exchanged for $6.290992 cash

NOSTALGIA BROADCASTING CORP (NV)
Name changed to NBG Radio Network, Inc. 01/30/1998
(See NBG Radio Network, Inc.)

NOSTALGIA MOTORCARS INC (NV)
Recapitalized as Elution Technologies Inc. 06/26/2002
Each share Common $0.001 par exchanged for (0.1) share Common $0.001 par
Elution Technologies Inc. name changed to Tankless Systems Worldwide, Inc. 07/25/2003 which name changed to Skye International, Inc. 11/11/2005
(See Skye International, Inc.)

NOSTALGIA NETWORK INC (DE)
Reincorporated 10/09/1987
State of incorporation changed from (CO) to (DE) 10/09/1987
Each share old Common 4¢ par exchanged for (0.5) share new Common 4¢ par 11/02/1987
Acquired by NNI Acquisition Corp. 12/27/2000
Each share Common 4¢ par exchanged for $0.07 cash

NOSTALGIA RENT-A-CAR INC (NV)
Charter revoked for failure to file list of officers 2/1/95

NOSTRAD TELECOMMUNICATIONS INC (NV)
Each share old Common no par exchanged for (0.1) share new Common no par 02/17/2003
Name changed to Skunk Work Technologies, Inc. 05/07/2003
Skunk Work Technologies, Inc. name changed to Genoray Advanced Technologies Ltd. 02/29/2004 which recapitalized as Fennel Resources, Inc. 11/07/2005 which recapitalized as 3P Networks, Inc. 09/20/2006 which recapitalized as Kender Energy Inc. 10/07/2008 which recapitalized as Bettwork Industries Inc. 07/02/2014

NOSTRUM OIL & GAS LP (KAZAKHSTAN)
GDR agreement terminated 09/22/2014
No GDR holders' equity

NOTASEME HOSIERY CO.
Ceased operations in 1932
No stockholders' equity

NOTCH NOVELTY CO (CA)
Name changed to Atlantic Energy Solutions, Inc. 07/21/2008

NOTE BANKERS AMER INC (TX)
Reorganized under the laws of Nevada as Facit Group Holdings, Inc. 10/28/98
Each share Common $0.001 par exchanged for (0.25) share Common $0.001 par

NOTEBOOK CTR INC (DE)
Name changed to Universal Biotechnologies Inc. 1/25/94
Universal Biotechnologies Inc. recapitalized as Queen Sand Resources, Inc. 3/3/95 which name changed to Devx Energy Inc. 9/19/2000
(See Devx Energy Inc.)

NOTIFY CORP (CA)
Issue Information - 1,600,000 Units consisting of (1) share COM and (1) WT offered at $5 per Unit on 08/28/1997
Name changed to Notify Technology Corp. 8/26/98

NOTOX INC (NY)
Dissolved by proclamation 6/23/93

NOUVEAU INTL INC (DE)
Each share old Common $0.001 par exchanged for (0.01) share new Common $0.001 par 4/3/2007
Name changed to My Screen Mobile, Inc. 5/23/2007

NOUVEAU MONDE MNG ENTERPRISES INC (AB)
Name changed to Nouveau Monde Graphite Inc. 02/10/2017

NOUVEAUX CORP (CO)
Each (1,500) shares old Common no par exchanged for (1) share new Common no par 11/10/1997
Name changed to Persona Records, Inc. (CO) 04/29/1998
Persona Records, Inc. (CO) reincorporated in Nevada as HIV-VAC Inc. 03/08/1999 which name changed to Grupo International, Inc. 10/28/2010

NOVA BEAUCAGE RES LTD (ON)
Recapitalized 08/14/1996
Common $1 par split (7) for (1) by issuance of (6) additional shares 10/26/1983
Recapitalized from Nova Beaucage Mines Ltd. to Nova Beaucage Resources Ltd. 08/14/1996
Each share Common $1 par exchanged for (0.1) share new Common $1 par
Merged into Canuc Resources Corp. (New) 12/31/1996
Each share new Common $1 par exchanged for (0.2739726) share Common no par

NOVA BIOGENETICS INC (DE)
Charter cancelled and declared inoperative and void for non-payment of taxes 03/01/2007

NOVA BIOSOURCE FUELS INC (NV)
Chapter 11 bankruptcy proceedings dismissed 09/22/2010
No stockholders' equity

NOVA CDA ENTERPRISES LTD (BC)
Merged into Stepstone Enterprises Ltd. (New) 06/30/2003
Each share Common no par exchanged for (1) share Common no par
Stepstone Enterprises Ltd. (New) name changed to ACT360 Solutions Ltd. 09/03/2004 which recapitalized as Kona Bay Technologies Inc. 06/03/2016

NOVA CAP INC (NV)
Each share old Common 1¢ par exchanged for (0.04) share new Common 1¢ par 9/22/89
Name changed to Visual Equities Inc. 6/4/91
(See Visual Equities Inc.)

NOVA CHEMICALS CORP (CANADA)
Reincorporated 04/14/2004
9.04% Preferred Securities called for redemption at $25.37675 on 03/01/2004
9.50% Preferred Securities called for redemption at $25.39575 on 03/01/2004
Place of incorporation changed from (AB) to (Canada) 04/14/2004
Acquired by International Petroleum Investment Co. 07/06/2009
Each share Common no par exchanged for USD $6 cash

NOVA CO EXPL LTD (ON)
Recapitalized as Optical Data Corp. 07/17/1987
Each share Capital Stock $1 par exchanged for (0.16666666) share Capital Stock no par
Optical Data Corp. recapitalized as AVL Information Systems Inc. 03/20/1992 which recapitalized as AVL Information Systems Ltd. 07/31/1996 which recapitalized as AVL Ventures Inc. 02/17/2003
(See AVL Ventures Inc.)

NOVA COGESCO RES INC (CANADA)
Merged into CanGold Resources Inc. (BC) 01/31/1994
Each share Common no par exchanged for (0.4) share Common no par
CanGold Resources Inc. (BC) reorganized in Ontario as Amalgamated CanGold Inc. 07/31/1995 which merged into Central Asia Goldfields Corp. 01/08/1996
(See Central Asia Goldfields Corp.)

NOVA COMMUNICATIONS LTD (NV)
Each share old Common $0.001 par exchanged for (0.01) share new Common $0.001 par 10/8/2004
Name changed to Encompass Holdings, Inc. 1/31/2006

NOVA CONTL DEV CORP (NY)
Dissolved by proclamation 01/25/2012

NOVA CORP (GA)
Merged into U.S. Bancorp 7/24/2001
Each share Common 1¢ par exchanged for either (1.01341989) shares Common 1¢ par and $8.67163 cash or $31 cash
Note: Option to receive stock and cash expired 7/24/2001

NOVA CORP (VA)
Merged into Parkway Co. (TX) 06/30/1983
Each share Common 1¢ par exchanged for (0.52631579) share Common $1 par
Parkway Co. (TX) reincorporated in Maryland as Parkway Properties, Inc. 08/02/1996 which merged into Cousins Properties Inc. 10/06/2016

NOVA CORP NEW (AB)
Name changed to NOVA Chemicals Corp. (AB) 01/01/1999
NOVA Chemicals Corp. (AB) reincorporated in Canada 04/14/2004
(See NOVA Chemicals Corp. (Canada))

NOVA CORP OLD (AB)
Each share Common no par received distribution of (0.104) share Nova Corp. (New) Common no par payable 07/03/1998 to holders of record 07/02/1998
Merged into TransCanada PipeLines Ltd. 07/02/1998
Each share Common no par exchanged for (0.52) share Common no par
TransCanada PipeLines Ltd. reorganized as TransCanada Corp. 05/15/2003

NOVA ENERGY CORP (BC)
Name changed to Voir Energy Corp. 9/16/81
Voir Energy Corp. merged into Zone Petroleum Corp. 5/28/82
(See Zone Petroleum Corp.)

NOVA ENERGY INC (NV)
Each share old Common $0.001 par exchanged for (0.1) share new Common $0.001 par 04/22/2008
Name changed to Savanna East Africa, Inc. 07/13/2010
Savanna East Africa, Inc. recapitalized as Algae International Group, Inc. (NV) 05/17/2013 which reincorporated in Wyoming as North American Cannabis Holdings, Inc. 06/10/2015

NOVA EQUITY VENTURES INC (DE)
Reincorporated 1/30/95
State of incorporation changed from (NY) to (DE) 1/30/95
Charter cancelled and declared inoperative and void for non-payment of taxes 9/27/95

NOVA FD INC (MA)
Merged into AFA Funds, Inc. 02/17/1989
Each share Common $1 par exchanged for (0.82379) share National Telecommunications & Technology Fund Common 20¢ par
AFA Funds, Inc. name changed to Hancock (John) Technology Series Inc. 12/20/1991

NOVA GAS TRANSMISSION LTD (AB)
Name changed 09/01/1987
Name changed 05/10/1994
5-3/8% Preferred Ser. D $100 par called for redemption 02/15/1981
Class A Common $1.25 par changed to no par and (2) additional shares issued 02/27/1981
12% Conv. 2nd Preferred $25 par called for redemption 05/15/1987
15% 1st Preferred $25 par called for redemption 08/15/1987
6-1/2% Conv. 2nd Preferred $25 par called for redemption 08/24/1987
Class B Common no par called for redemption 09/01/1987
Name changed from Nova, An Alberta Corp. to Nova Corp. of Alberta, par value of all outstanding Preferreds changed to no par and Class A Common no par reclassified as Common no par 09/01/1987
11.24% 1st Preferred no par called for redemption 05/15/1988
4-3/4% Preferred Ser. C no par called redemption 11/15/1988
6-3/8% Conv. 2nd Preferred no par called for redemption 11/16/1988
Name changed from Nova Corp. of Alberta to Nova Gas Transmission Ltd. 05/10/1994
Under plan of reorganization each share Common no par automatically became (1) share Nova Corp. (Old) Common no par 05/10/1994
7.60% Preferred no par called for redemption 08/15/1994
7.75% Preferred no par called for redemption 08/15/1994
9.75% Preferred no par called for redemption 08/15/1994
9.76% Preferred no par called for redemption 08/15/1994
Fixed/Floating Rate 1st Preferred no par called for redemption 02/18/1995
Nova Corp. (Old) merged into TransCanada PipeLines Ltd. 07/02/1998 which reorganized as TransCanada Corp. 05/15/2003

NOVA GOLD CORP (UT)
Proclaimed dissolved for failure to file annual report 8/1/92

NOVA GROWTH CORP (ON)
Each share old Common no par exchanged for (0.33333333) share new Common no par 12/23/1998
Each share new Common no par exchanged again for (0.1) share new Common no par 02/13/2003
Acquired by 2155300 Ontario Inc. 05/15/2008
Each share new Common no par exchanged for $0.50 cash

NOVA INDS INC (NJ)
Merged into Hobart Brothers Co. 05/29/1984
Each share Common 1¢ par exchanged for $1.94 cash

NOVA INTL FILMS INC (DE)
Each share old Common $0.00001 par exchanged for (0.0625) share new Common $0.00001 par 11/22/2002
Name changed to China Cable & Communication, Inc. 7/10/2003

NOVA MARKETING LTD (BC)
Recapitalized as National Nova Marketing Inc. 07/24/1992
Each share Common no par exchanged for (0.33333333) share Common no par
(See National Nova Marketing Inc.)

NOVA MNG CORP (NV)
Common $0.00001 par split (5) for (1) by issuance of (4) additional shares payable 11/16/2011 to holders of record 11/11/2011 Ex date - 11/17/2011
Name changed to Radiant Creations Group, Inc. 07/26/2013

NOVA NAT RES CORP (CO)
Each share Common 10¢ par exchanged for (0.00033333) share Common 1¢ par 08/22/2003
Name changed to Greenestone Healthcare Corp. 05/21/2012
Greenestone Healthcare Corp. name changed to Ethema Health Corp. 07/12/2017

NOVA OIL INC (NV)
Common $0.001 par split (3) for (2) by issuance of (0.5) additional share payable 04/24/2006 to holders of record 04/10/2006 Ex date - 04/25/2006
Name changed to Nova Biosource Fuels, Inc. 11/01/2006
(See Nova Biosource Fuels, Inc.)

NOVA PETE CORP (CO)
Merged into Nova Natural Resources Corp. 09/29/1986
Each share Common no par exchanged for (0.10152284) share Common 10¢ par
Nova Natural Resources Corp. name changed to Greenestone Healthcare Corp. 05/21/2012 which name changed to Ethema Health Corp. 07/12/2017

NOVA PHARMACEUTICAL CORP (DE)
Merged into Scios-Nova Inc. 9/4/92
Each share Common 1¢ par exchanged for (0.39) share Common 1¢ par
Scios-Nova Inc. name changed back to Scios Inc. 3/26/96
(See Scios Inc.)

NOVA PHARMACEUTICAL INC (NV)
Recapitalized as GTP123, Inc. 02/08/2007
Each share Common $0.001 par exchanged for (0.1) share Common $0.001 par
GTP123, Inc. name changed to Dream Factory, Inc. 01/25/2008

NOVA REAL ESTATE INVT TR (VA)
Under plan of reorganization each Share of Bene. Int. no par automatically became (1) share Nova Corp. Common 1¢ par 05/31/1983
Nova Corp. merged into Parkway Co. (TX) 06/30/1983 which reincorporated in Maryland as Parkway Properties, Inc. 08/02/1996 which merged into Cousins Properties Inc. 10/06/2016

NOVA RES INC (NV)
Reincorporated 11/04/2004
State of incorporation changed from (CO) to (NV) 11/04/2004
Each share old Common $0.001 par exchanged for (6) shares new Common $0.001 par 01/11/2007
Name changed to Fox Petroleum, Inc. 02/05/2007
(See Fox Petroleum, Inc.)

NOVA SCOTIA GOLD MINES LTD.
Bankrupt in 1938

NOVA SCOTIA LT & PWR LTD (NS)
Each share old Ordinary no par exchanged for (6) shares new Ordinary no par 00/00/1947
New Ordinary no par split (3) for (1) by issuance of (2) additional shares 11/23/1955
New Ordinary no par split (3) for (1) by issuance of (2) additional shares 04/15/1966
Acquired by Nova Scotia Power Corp. 03/29/1973
Each share 4% Preference $100 par exchanged for $74.50 cash
Each share 4-1/2% Preference $100 par exchanged for $81 cash
Each share 5% Preference $100 par exchanged for $44 cash
Each share Ordinary no par exchanged for $13 cash

NOVA SCOTIA PWR INC (NS)
Name changed to NS Power Holdings Inc. 01/06/1999
NS Power Holdings Inc. name changed to Emera Inc. 07/17/2010
6% 1st Preferred Ser. A no par called for redemption at $25 on 10/01/2000
1st Preferred Ser. B called for redemption at $6.25 on 02/00/2002
1st Preferred Ser. C called for redemption at $25 on 04/01/2009
5.9% 1st Preferred Ser. D called for redemption at $25 on 10/15/2015

NOVA SCOTIA PUBLIC COLD STORAGE TERMINALS LTD.
Acquired by Halifax Harbour Commission in 1934

NOVA SCOTIA STEEL & COAL CO. LTD.
Acquired by Dominion Steel & Coal Corp., Ltd. under plan of reorganization in 1938
Each share 8% Preferred exchanged for (1) share Class B Common $25 par
Dominion Steel & Coal Corp., Ltd. acquired for cash by Sidbec 8/22/69

NOVA SCOTIA TRAMWAYS & POWER CO. LTD.
Succeeded by Nova Scotia Light & Power Co. in 1928
(See Nova Scotia Light & Power Co.)

NOVA SCOTIA TR CO (HALIFAX, NS)
Each share Capital Stock $100 par exchanged for (10) shares Capital Stock $10 par 00/00/1951
Merged into Central & Nova Scotia Trust Co. (Halifax, NS) 01/01/1974
Each share Capital Stock $10 par exchanged for (8.4) shares Common $1 par
Central & Nova Scotia Trust Co. (Halifax, NS) merged into Central & Eastern Trust Co. (Moncton, NB) 07/02/1976 which merged into Central Trust Co. (Moncton, NB) 03/01/1981

NOVA TECH INC (CA)
Adjudicated bankrupt 04/06/1971
Stockholders' equity unlikely

NOVA TECHNOLOGIES INC (DE)
Each share old Common 1¢ par exchanged for (2/3) share new Common 1¢ par 2/28/92

Name changed to Vivax Medical Corp. 6/3/97

NOVA TECHNOLOGY CORP (UT)
Involuntarily dissolved 4/1/89

NOVA URANIUM CORP (CANADA)
Name changed to Secova Metals Corp. 12/21/2009

NOVABAY PHARMACEUTICALS INC (CA)
Reincorporated under the laws of Delaware 06/29/2010

NOVACAB INTL INC (FL)
Name changed to Global Pole Trusion Group Corp. 07/24/2017

NOVACARE EMPLOYEE SVCS INC (DE)
Merged into Plato Holdings, Inc. 10/20/1999
Each share Common 1¢ par exchanged for $2.50 cash

NOVACARE INC (DE)
Common 1¢ par split (2) for (1) by issuance of (1) additional share 07/01/1991
Name changed to NAHC, Inc. 03/28/2000
NAHC, Inc. merged into J.L. Halsey Corp. 06/18/2002 which name changed to Lyris, Inc. 11/15/2007
(See Lyris, Inc.)

NOVACEA INC (DE)
Recapitalized as Transcept Pharmaceuticals, Inc. 02/02/2009
Each share Common $0.001 par exchanged for (0.2) share Common $0.001 par
Transcept Pharmaceuticals, Inc. recapitalized as Paratek Pharmaceuticals, Inc. 10/31/2014

NOVACON CORP (DE)
Recapitalized as NVCN Corp. 6/20/2002
Each (12) shares Common 1¢ par exchanged for (1) share Common 1¢ par

NOVACOPPER INC (BC)
Name changed to Trilogy Metals Inc. 09/08/2016

NOVADAQ TECHNOLOGIES INC (CANADA)
Acquired by Stryker Corp. 09/05/2017
Each share Common no par exchanged for USD$11.75 cash
Note: Unexchanged certificates will be cancelled and become without value 09/05/2023

NOVADEL-AGENE CORP. (DE)
Each share old Common no par exchanged for (3) shares new Common no par in 1934
Merged into Wallace & Tiernan Inc. in 1953
Each share new Common no par exchanged for (1) share Common $1 par
Wallace & Tiernan Inc. merged into Pennwalt Corp. 3/31/69
(See Pennwalt Corp.)

NOVADEL PHARMA INC (DE)
Completely liquidated 06/16/2017
Each share Common $0.001 par exchanged for first and final distribution of $0.01 cash

NOVADEL PROCESS CORP.
Merged into Novadel-Agene Corp. in 1928
(See Novadel-Agene Corp.)

NOVADIGM INC (DE)
Merged into Hewlett-Packard Co. 04/02/2004
Each share Common $0.001 par exchanged for $6.10 cash

NOVADX INTL INC (BC)
Recapitalized as NovaDx Ventures Corp. 12/02/2004
Each share Common no par exchanged for (0.03333333) share Common no par

NOVADX VENTURES CORP (BC)
(See NovaDx Ventures Corp.)
Assets sold for the benefit of creditors 07/14/2015
No stockholders' equity

NOVAFERON LABS INC (CO)
Company subject of SEC fraud investigation 08/16/1991
Stockholders' equity unlikely

NOVAGEN SOLAR INC (NV)
Name changed to Novagen Ingenium Inc. 04/30/2012

NOVAGOLD RES INC (NS)
Each share old Common no par exchanged for (0.1) share new Common no par 12/17/1997
Each share new Common no par received distribution of (0.16666667) share NovaCopper Inc. Common no par payable 04/30/2012 to holders of record 04/27/2012 Ex date - 05/01/2012
Reincorporated under the laws of British Columbia 06/12/2013

NOVAMED INC (DE)
Name changed 03/26/2004
Issue Information - 4,000,000 shares COM offered at $8 per share on 08/17/1999
Name changed from NovaMed Eyecare, Inc. to NovaMed, Inc. 03/26/2004
Each share old Common 1¢ par exchanged for (1/3) share new Common 1¢ par 06/01/2010
Acquired by Surgery Center Holdings, Inc. 05/04/2011
Each share new Common 1¢ par exchanged for $13.25 cash

NOVAMED INC (NV)
Each share old Common $0.001 par exchanged for (0.02) share new Common $0.001 par 05/06/2002
Name changed to WWA Group, Inc. 10/03/2003
WWA Group, Inc. recapitalized as Genie Gateway 09/09/2015

NOVAMERICAN STL INC (CANADA)
Issue Information - 2,200,000 shares COM offered at $14 per share on 10/30/1997
Acquired by Symmetry Holdings Inc. 11/15/2007
Each share Common no par exchanged for $56 cash

NOVAMERICAN STL INC (DE)
Name changed to Barzel Industries Inc. 02/13/2009
(See Barzel Industries Inc.)

NOVAMETRIX MED SYS INC (DE)
Common 1¢ par split (3) for (2) by issuance of (0.5) additional share 11/18/1982
Merged into Respironics, Inc. 04/15/2002
Each share Common 1¢ par exchanged for (0.2541) share Common 1¢ par
(See Respironics, Inc.)

NOVAMEX USA LTD (OR)
Recapitalized as Falcon Technologies, Inc. 06/04/2007
Each share Common no par exchanged for (0.01) share Common no par

NOVAMIN INC (QC)
Merged into Breakwater Resources Ltd. (BC) 05/18/1988
Each share Common no par exchanged for (0.5) share Common no par
Breakwater Resources Ltd. (BC) reincorporated in Canada 05/11/1992
(See Breakwater Resources Ltd.)

NOVAN ENERGY INC (DE)
Reincorporated 11/12/87
State of incorporation changed from (CO) to (DE) and Common no par changed to 10¢ par 11/12/87
Name changed to American Toxxic Control, Inc. 12/17/87
American Toxxic Control, Inc. name changed to United States Filter Corp. (New) 12/10/90
(See United States Filter Corp. (New))

NOVAR ELECTRS CORP (OH)
Common no par split (3) for (2) by issuance of (0.5) additional share 12/31/82
Common no par split (2) for (1) by issuance of (1) additional share 8/1/83
Merged into Pillar Electrical PLC 3/1/90
Each share Common no par exchanged for $9.50 cash

NOVAR INTL CORP (DE)
Charter cancelled and declared inoperative and void for non-payment of taxes 3/1/89

NOVAR PLC (UNITED KINGDOM)
Merged into Honeywell Acquisitions Ltd. 8/8/2005
Each ADR for Ordinary 27.7777p par exchanged for $3.33229 cash

NOVARAY MED INC (DE)
Company terminated common stock registration and is no longer public as of 04/30/2010

NOVASTAR FINL INC (MD)
Issue Information - 3,750,000 shares COM offered at $18 per share on 10/30/1997
Old Common 1¢ par split (2) for (1) by issuance of (1) additional share payable 12/01/2003 to holders of record 11/17/2003 Ex date - 12/02/2003
Each share old Common 1¢ par exchanged for (0.25) share new Common 1¢ par 07/30/2007
8.90% Preferred Ser. C 1¢ par called for redemption at $2.3741 on 07/05/2011
Name changed to Novation Companies, Inc. 05/25/2012

NOVASTAR RES LTD (NV)
Name changed to Thorium Power, Ltd. 10/10/2006
Thorium Power, Ltd. recapitalized as Lightbridge Corp. 09/29/2009

NOVATEK INTL INC (CO)
Each share old Common no par exchanged for (0.1) share new Common no par 9/4/91
Each share new Common no par exchanged for (0.1) share new Common no par 1/9/95
Name changed to Medical Diagnostic Products, Inc. 9/30/96
(See Medical Diagnostic Products, Inc.)

NOVATEK JT STK CO (RUSSIA)
ADR basis changed from (1:0.01) to (1:10) 08/03/2006
GDR agreement terminated 07/09/2012
Each 144A GDR for Ordinary exchanged for $111.6282 cash
(Additional Information in Active)

NOVATEL INC (CANADA)
Merged into Hexagon AB 12/20/2007
Each share Common no par exchanged for USD$50 cash

NOVATEL WIRELESS INC (DE)
Each share old Common $0.001 par exchanged for (0.66666666) share new Common $0.001 par 10/29/2002
Name changed to Inseego Corp. 11/09/2016

NOVATRON INC (MN)
Name changed to Assisted Care Corp. 07/19/1995
Assisted Care Corp. name changed to Quality One Wireless, Inc. 08/27/2002
(See Quality One Wireless, Inc.)

NOVAWEST RES INC (BC)
Each share Common no par received distribution of (0.2) share Pro Minerals Inc. Common no par payable 03/10/2008 to holders of record 03/04/2008
Name changed to Apella Resources Inc. 04/02/2008
Apella Resources Inc. name changed to PacificOre Mining Corp. 05/28/2012 which name changed to Vanadiumcorp Resource Inc. 11/22/2013

NOVAX CAP CORP (AB)
Recapitalized 02/16/1990
Recapitalized from Novax Equity Corp. to Novax Capital Corp. 02/16/1990
Each share Common no par exchanged for (0.2) share Common no par
Recapitalized as Northern Mountain Helicopters Group Inc. 05/06/1996
Each (2.63) shares Common no par exchanged for (1) share Common no par
(See Northern Mountain Helicopters Group Inc.)

NOVEDER INC (CANADA)
Recapitalized as Atlantis Exploration Inc. 10/11/2001
Each share Common no par exchanged for (0.1) share Common no par
Atlantis Exploration Inc. recapitalized as Noveko Echographs Inc. 2/4/2004 which name changed to Noveko International Inc. 1/11/2006

NOVEKO ECHOGRAPHS INC (CANADA)
Name changed to Noveko International Inc. 1/11/2006

NOVEL APPLIANCES, INC.
Liquidated in 1950

NOVEL DENIM HLDGS LTD. (BRITISH VIRGIN ISLANDS)
Issue Information - 4,250,000 ORD SHS offered at $18 per share on 07/23/1997
Merged into NDH Acquisition Ltd. 02/28/2005
Each share Orcinary $1 exchanged for $1.20 cash

NOVELIS INC (CANADA)
Acquired by Hindalco Industries Ltd. 05/15/2007
Each share Common no par exchanged for $44.93 cash

NOVELL INC (DE)
Common 10¢ par split (2) for (1) by issuance of (1) additional share 04/13/1987
Common 10¢ par split (2) for (1) by issuance of (1) additional share 08/17/1990
Common 10¢ par split (2) for (1) by issuance of (1) additional share 08/30/1991
Common 10¢ par split (2) for (1) by issuance of (1) additional share 09/25/1992
Acquired by Attachmate Corp. 04/27/2011
Each share Common 10¢ par exchanged for $6.10 cash

NOVELL PORCUPINE GOLD MINES, LTD. (ON)
Acquired by Consolidated Novell Mines Ltd. on a (1) for (8) basis 7/26/55
Consolidated Novell Mines Ltd. charter cancelled 3/16/76

NOVELLUS SYS INC (CA)
Common no par split (2) for (1) by issuance of (1) additional share 08/21/1990
Common no par split (2) for (1) by issuance of (1) additional share payable 10/13/1997 to holders of record 09/29/1997
Merged into Lam Research Corp. 06/04/2012
Each share Common no par exchanged for (1.125) shares Common $0.001 par

NOVELOS THERAPEUTICS INC (DE)
Each share old Common $0.00001 par exchanged for (0.00653594) share new Common $0.00001 par 04/11/2011
Name changed to Cellectar Biosciences, Inc. 02/12/2014

NOVEN PHARMACEUTICALS INC (DE)
Acquired by Hisamitsu Pharmaceutical Co., Inc. 08/27/2009
Each share Common $0.0001 par exchanged for $16.50 cash

NOVENTA LTD (CHANNEL ISLANDS)
Each share old Ordinary exchanged for exchanged for (0.05) share new Ordinary 03/11/2011
Delisted from Toronto Stock Exchange 03/08/2012
Shareholders on Canadian branch register were transferred to United Kingdom main register 03/14/2012

NOVERCO INC (QC)
Acquired by Corporation d'Acquisitions Energie Inc. 9/8/90
Each share Common no par exchanged for $15.25 cash

NOVEX SYS INTL INC (NY)
Recapitalized as American Home Food Products Inc. 06/08/2005
Each share Common $0.001 par exchanged for (1/7) share Common $0.001 par
American Home Food Products Inc. name changed to Artisanal Brands, Inc. 11/04/2010

NOVGORODTELECOM OPEN JT STK CO (RUSSIA)
Acquired by North-West Telecom Open Joint Stock Co. 10/31/2002
Details not available

NOVICOURT INC (QC)
1st Preferred Ser. A no par called for redemption at $5 plus $0.08777 accrued dividend on 12/15/97
Each share old Common no par exchanged for (0.5) share new Common and $1.30 cash 5/4/2005
Merged into Xstrata PLC 10/17/2006
Each share new Common no par exchanged for $2.30 cash

NOVIK INC (QC)
Acquired by 9293-3985 Quebec Inc. 02/19/2014
Each share Common no par exchanged for $0.85 cash

NOVINO CORP.
Out of business 00/00/1937
Details not available

NOVITAS ENERGY LTD (AB)
Acquired by Bonterra Energy Income Trust (New) 01/27/2005
Each share Common no par exchanged for (0.03636) Trust Unit
Bonterra Energy Income Trust (New) name changed to Bonterra Oil & Gas Ltd. 11/17/2008 which name changed to Bonterra Energy Corp. (New) 01/15/2010

NOVITRON INTL INC (DE)
Each share old Common 1¢ par exchanged for (1/3) share new Common 1¢ par 12/04/1996
Stock Dividends - 10% payable 03/27/1998 to holders of record 03/13/1998; 25% payable 09/10/2002 to holders of record 08/26/2002
Name changed to Clinical Data, Inc. (New) 10/07/2003
(See Clinical Data, Inc. (New))

NOVO CORP (NY)
Common $1 par changed to 10¢ par 08/00/1978
Common 10¢ par split (2) for (1) by issuance of (1) additional share 04/19/1982
Company merged out of existence 12/00/1988
Details not available

NOVO ENERGIES CORP (FL)
Name changed to Immunovative, Inc. 05/08/2012
Immunovative, Inc. name changed to Tauriga Sciences, Inc. 04/09/2013

NOVO INDUSTRI A S (DENMARK)
Name changed to Novo Nordisk A/S 01/01/1989

NOVO INDL CORP (NY)
Name changed to Novo Corp. 05/05/1969
(See Novo Corp.)

NOVO NETWORKS INC (DE)
Recapitalized as Berliner Communications, Inc. 09/19/2005
Each share Common $0.00002 par exchanged for (0.00333333) share Common $0.00002 par
Berliner Communications, Inc. name changed to UniTek Global Services, Inc. 07/06/2010
(See UniTek Global Services, Inc.)

NOVOGEN LIMITED (AUSTRALIA)
Each old Sponsored ADR for Ordinary exchanged for (0.2) new Sponsored ADR for Ordinary 01/03/2012
Basis changed from (1:5) to (1:25) 01/03/2012
Each new Sponsored ADR for Ordinary received distribution of (0.7142857) share MEI Pharma, Inc. Common $0.00000002 par payable 01/25/2013 to holders of record 11/19/2012 Ex date - 01/28/2013
Each new Sponsored ADR for Ordinary exchanged again for (0.25) new Sponsored ADR for Ordinary 07/14/2017
Basis changed from (1:25) to (1:100) 07/14/2017
Basis changed from (1:100) to (1:10) 11/21/2017
Name changed to Kazia Therapeutics Ltd. 11/24/2017

NOVOLIPETSK IRON & STL CORP (RUSSIA)
Name changed to Novolipetsk Steel PJSC 06/24/2016

NOVOPHARM BIOTECH INC (BC)
Name changed to Viventia Biotech Inc. 9/11/2000
(See Viventia Biotech Inc.)

NOVOPHARM BIOTECH INC (DE)
Merged into Novopharm Biotech Inc. (BC) 8/25/97
Each share Common no par exchanged for (1) share Common no par
Novopharm Biotech Inc. (BC) name changed to Viventia Biotech Inc. 9/11/2000
(See Viventia Biotech Inc.)

NOVORI INC (DE)
Old Common $0.0001 par split (2) for (1) by issuance of (1) additional share payable 02/16/2007 to holders of record 02/09/2007 Ex date - 02/20/2007
Old Common $0.0001 par split (2) for (1) by issuance of (1) additional share payable 03/30/2007 to holders of record 03/29/2007 Ex date - 04/02/2007
Each share old Common $0.0001 par exchanged for (0.05) share new Common $0.0001 par 12/08/2008
Name changed to Aeon Holdings Inc. 01/30/2009
Aeon Holdings Inc. name changed to BCM Energy Partners, Inc. 04/13/2011

NOVOSTE CORP (FL)
Each share old Common 1¢ par exchanged for (0.25) share new Common 1¢ par 11/04/2005
Reincorporated under the laws of Delaware as NOVT Corp. 11/27/2007

NOVUS ENERGY INC (AB)
Acquired by Yanchang Petroleum International Ltd. 01/23/2014
Each share Common no par exchanged for $1.18 cash

NOVUS ENVIRONMENTAL INC (DE)
Name changed to Wave Power.Net, Inc. 02/28/2000
Wave Power.Net, Inc. recapitalized as telcoBlue, Inc. (DE) 08/29/2002 which reincorporated in Wyoming 12/23/2004
(See telcoBlue, Inc.)

NOVUS GOLD CORP (BC)
Merged into PanTerra Gold Ltd. 04/19/2012
Each share Common no par exchanged for (0.33333333) share Common
Note: Unexchanged certificates were cancelled and became without value 04/19/2018

NOVUS LABS INC (DE)
Name changed to World Golf League, Inc. and (2.7) additional shares issued 02/12/2003
World Golf League, Inc. name changed to WGL Entertainment Holdings, Inc. 08/29/2006 which recapitalized as Heathrow Natural Food & Beverage Inc. 03/09/2009

NOVUS PPTY CO (MA)
Merged into American Realty Trust (DC) 10/31/1986
Each Share of Bene. Int. $1 par exchanged for (3.25) shares of Bene. Int. $1 par
American Realty Trust (DC) reorganized in Georgia as American Realty Trust, Inc. 06/24/1988 which merged into American Realty Investors Inc. 08/02/2000

NOW TECHNOLOGIES INC (MN)
Merged into ATMI, Inc. 08/04/1998
Each share Common exchanged for (0.865338) share Common 1¢ par
(See ATMI, Inc.)

NOWATA OIL & REFINING CO.
Dissolved in 1949

NOWAUTO GROUP INC (NV)
Company terminated common stock registration and is no longer public as of 10/13/2011

NOWSCO WELL SVC LTD (AB)
Common no par split (2) for (1) by issuance of (1) additional share 10/10/75
Common no par split (2) for (1) by issuance of (1) additional share 10/11/78
Common no par split (3) for (1) by issuance of (2) additional shares 5/14/80
Merged into BJ Services Co. 6/28/96
Each share Common no par exchanged for $35 cash

NOXA INC (FL)
Name changed to Lasertec International, Inc. (FL) 04/18/1997
Lasertec International, Inc. (FL) reorganized in Nevada as Chaichem Holdings Inc. 02/18/2005 which name changed to Excelsior Biotechnology, Inc. 05/16/2005 which name changed to Targetviewz, Inc. 03/03/2006 which recapitalized as Greenway Energy 11/15/2007 which name changed to Greenway Technology 09/19/2008

NOXE RES CORP (BC)
Name changed 11/04/1986
Name changed from Noxe Petroleum Corp. to Noxe Resource Corp. 11/04/1986
Cease trade order in effect 10/30/1989

NOXELL CORP (MD)
Non-Vtg. Class B Common $1 par split (3) for (1) by issuance of (2) additional shares 5/16/67
Common $1 par split (3) for (1) by issuance of (2) additional shares 5/16/67
Non-Vtg. Class B Common $1 par split (2) for (1) by issuance of (1) additional share 6/14/68
Common $1 par split (2) for (1) by issuance of (1) additional share 6/14/68
Non-Vtg. Class B Common $1 par split (2) for (1) by issuance of (1) additional share 8/17/71
Common $1 par split (2) for (1) by issuance of (1) additional share 8/17/71
Common $1 par split (2) for (1) by issuance of (1) additional share 3/4/83
Non-Vtg. Class B Common $1 par split (2) for (1) by issuance of (1) additional share 3/4/83
Non-Vtg. Class B Common $1 par split (2) for (1) by issuance of (1) additional share 3/4/86
Non-Vtg. Class B Common $1 par split (2) for (1) by issuance of (1) additional share 8/19/87
Acquired by Procter & Gamble Co. 11/30/89
Each share Common $1 par exchanged for (0.544) share Common no par
Each share Non-Vtg. Class B Common $1 par exchanged for (0.544) share Common no par

NOXSO CORP (VA)
Common 1¢ par split (2) for (1) by issuance of (1) additional share 06/02/1992
Plan of reorganization under Chapter 11 Federal Bankruptcy Code effective 05/25/2000
No stockholders' equity

NOXZEMA CHEMICAL CO. (MD)
Each share Class B Common $10 par exchanged for (10) shares Class B Common $1 par in 1936
Each share Common $10 par exchanged for (10) shares Common $1 par in 1936
Name changed to Noxell Corp. 7/15/66
Noxell Corp. acquired by Procter & Gamble Co. 11/30/89

NOXZEMA CHEMICAL CO. OF CANADA, LTD. (MD)
Acquired by Noxell Corp. 11/11/66
Each share Class A Common $10 par or Class B Common $1 par exchanged for $180 cash

NOYLY DEVELOPMENT CO. (PA)
Each share Common $100 par exchanged for (1,000) shares Common 10¢ par in 1952
Merged into Devonian Gas & Oil Co. (PA) in 1953
Each share Common 10¢ par exchanged for (0.5) share Capital Stock 10¢ par
Devonian Gas & Oil Co. (PA) merged into Devonian Gas & Oil Co. (DE) 12/20/57
(See Devonian Gas & Oil Co. (DE))

NP CAP CORP (DE)
Name changed to Solar Energy Initiatives, Inc. 09/24/2008

NPB CAP TR (DE)
9% Trust Preferred Securities called for redemption at $25 plus $0.193749 accrued dividends on 10/31/2002

NPB CAP TR (DE)
7.85% Trust Preferred Securities called for redemption at $25 plus $0.36 accrued dividends on 03/07/2013

NPC HLDGS INC (NV)
Each share old Common 1¢ par exchanged for (0.0033333) share new Common 1¢ par 10/11/2000
Name changed to Regent Energy Corp. 03/12/2001
(See Regent Energy Corp.)

NPC INTL INC (KS)
Each share Class A 1¢ par exchanged for (1) share Common 1¢ par 8/9/95
Each share Class B 1¢ par exchanged for (1) share Common 1¢ par 8/9/95
Merged into Mergeco, Inc. 8/31/2001
Each share Common 1¢ par exchanged for $11.55 cash

NPC PACKAGING CORP. (MN)
Liquidation completed
Each share Common 25¢ par received initial distribution of $7.50 cash 09/30/1976
Each share Common 25¢ par received second and final distribution of $0.8794 cash 08/05/1977
Note: Certificates were not required to be surrendered and are without value

NPI08 INC (DE)
Each share old Common $0.001 par exchanged for (0.01) share new Common $0.001 par 07/16/2008
Name changed to BlackStar Energy Group, Inc. 02/09/2010
BlackStar Energy Group, Inc. name changed to BlackStar Enterprise Group, Inc. 09/30/2016

NPL CORP (AZ)
Each share Common 50¢ par exchanged for (0.02) share Common $25 par 06/16/1981
Acquired by Lifeshares of Nebraska, Inc. 00/00/1981
Details not available

NPM HEALTHCARE PRODS INC (DE)
Name changed to American White Cross, Inc. 3/3/94
(See American White Cross, Inc.)

NPN INVT GROUP INC (ON)
Reincorporated under the laws of British Columbia as Alix Resources Corp. 12/05/2007
Alix Resources Corp. name changed to Infinite Lithium Corp. 12/06/2017

NPOWR DIGITAL MEDIA INC (NV)
Name changed to NPW Development, Inc. 07/28/2005
NPW Development, Inc. name changed to GreenZap, Inc. 11/07/2005 which name changed to Blue Star Opportunities Corp. 07/28/2008

NPS ALLELIX INC (ON)
Non-Voting Exchangeable Shares no par called for redemption on 07/04/2003

NPS INTL CORP (DE)
Name changed to OneClass Synergy Corp. 12/21/2000
OneClass Synergy Corp. recapitalized as ABCI Holdings Inc. (DE) 08/13/2001 which reorganized in Nevada as Metaphor Corp. 01/06/2005 which name changed to China Media Networks International, Inc. 08/25/2005 which name changed to Medical Solutions Management Inc. 08/04/2006
(See Medical Solutions Management Inc.)

NPS PHARMACEUTICALS INC (DE)
Acquired by Shire PLC 02/21/2015
Each share Common $0.001 par exchanged for $46 cash

NPS TECHNOLOGIES GROUP INC (DE)
Charter cancelled and declared inoperative and void for non-payment of taxes 03/01/1991

NPTEST HLDG CORP (DE)
Merged into Credence Systems Corp. 06/01/2004
Each share Common $0.001 par exchanged for (0.8) share Common $0.001 par and $5.75 cash
Credence Systems Corp. merged into LTX-Credence Corp. 08/29/2008 which name changed to Xcerra Corp. 05/22/2014 which merged into Cohu, Inc. 10/01/2018

NPW DEV INC (NV)
Name changed to GreenZap, Inc. 11/07/2005
GreenZap, Inc. name changed to Blue Star Opportunities Corp. 07/28/2008

NQ EXPL LTD (CANADA)
Each share Common no par received distribution of (0.19623876) share Imperial Mining Group Ltd. Common no par and (0.09811938) Common Stock Purchase Warrant expiring 12/28/2022 payable 12/22/2017 to holders of record 12/19/2017
Recapitalized as AM Resoures Corp. 05/15/2018
Each share Common no par exchanged for (0.02) share Common no par

NQ MOBILE INC (CAYMAN ISLANDS)
Name changed 05/01/2012
Name changed from NetQin Mobile Inc. to NQ Mobile Inc. 05/01/2012
Name changed to Link Motion Inc. 03/14/2018

NQL ENERGY SVCS INC (BC)
Name changed 7/11/2005
Name changed from NQL Drilling Tools Inc. to NQL Energy Services Inc. 7/11/2005
Acquired by National Oilwell Varco, Inc. 1/16/2007
Each share Common no par exchanged for $7.60 cash

NQL INC (DE)
Chapter 11 bankruptcy proceedings terminated 10/20/2005
No stockholders' equity

NQN MINES LTD (QC)
Declared dissolved for failure to file reports or pay fees 06/06/1981

NRCI NORTHN RESOURCE CAP INC (AB)
Struck off register for failure to file annual returns 12/01/1993

NRD MNG LTD (BC)
Recapitalized as Consolidated NRD Resources Ltd./Ressources Consolidees NRD Ltee. 03/13/1987
Each share Capital Stock no par exchanged for (0.2) share Common no par
(See Consolidated NRD Resources Ltd./ Ressources Consolidees NRD Ltee.)

NRDC ACQUISITION CORP (DE)
Issue Information - 36,000,000 UNITS consisting of (1) share COM and (1) WT offered at $10 per Unit on 10/17/2007
Name changed to Retail Opportunity Investments Corp. (DE) 10/22/2009
Retail Opportunity Investments Corp. (DE) reincorporated in Maryland 06/02/2011

NRG, INC. (UT)
Name changed to Synetix Group, Inc. (UT) 10/19/1983
Synetix Group, Inc. (UT) reincorporated in Nevada 12/31/2008
(See Synetix Group, Inc.)

NRG DYNAMICS INC (NV)
Recapitalized as Kastel Communications, Inc. 11/06/1985
Each share Common $0.0001 par exchanged for (0.1) share Common $0.001 par

NRG ENERGY INC (DE)
Merged into Xcel Energy Inc. 06/03/2002
Each share old Common 1¢ par exchanged for (0.5) share Common $2.50 par
Each Corp Unit 1¢ par exchanged for $25 principal amount of 6.5% Sr. Debentures due 05/05/2006 on 09/15/2003
Each share 5.75% Mandatory Conv. Preferred 1¢ par exchanged for (10.2564) shares new Common 1¢ par 03/16/2009
4% Conv. Preferred 1¢ par called for redemption at $1,000 on 01/21/2010 (Additional Information in Active)

NRG GENERATING U S INC (DE)
Name changed to Cogeneration Corp. of America 07/20/1998
(See Cogeneration Corp. of America)

NRG GROUP INC (ON)
Name changed to Welton Energy Corp. (Old) 09/02/2003
Welton Energy Corp. (Old) reorganized as Welton Energy Corp. (New) 08/04/2005 which merged into Churchill Energy Inc. 02/13/2009 which merged into Zargon Energy Trust 09/23/2009 which reorganized as Zargon Oil & Gas Ltd. (New) 01/07/2011

NRG INC (DE)
Each share Common $0.005 par exchanged for (0.05) share Common 10¢ par 12/19/1983
SEC revoked common stock registration 04/04/2013

NRG INC (MN)
Name changed to Scientific NRG, Inc. (MN) 12/08/1986
Scientific NRG, Inc. (MN) reorganized in Nevada as Newbridge Capital, Inc. 01/05/2000 which name changed to SeaHAVN Corp. 06/10/2005 which recapitalized as China Travel Resort Holdings, Inc. 10/01/2009

NRG INTL INC (UT)
Proclaimed dissolved for failure to pay taxes 7/1/92

NRG INVTS INC (BC)
Name changed to Bucking Horse Energy Inc. 03/03/2008

NRG RES LTD (BC)
Recapitalized as Vigor Resources Ltd. 04/07/1997
Each share Common no par exchanged for (1/3) share Common no par
Vigor Resources Ltd. merged into Biomax Technologies Inc. 03/25/1999
(See Biomax Technologies Inc.)

NRG YIELD INC (DE)
Each share old Class A Common 1¢ par exchanged for (1) share new Class A Common 1¢ par and (1) share Class C Common 1¢ par 05/15/2015
Name changed to Clearway Energy, Inc. 09/17/2018

NRI, INC. (DE)
Voluntarily dissolved 09/13/2001
Details not available

NRI ON-LINE INC (AB)
Acquired by Geophysical Micro Computer Applications (International) Ltd. 04/28/1999
Each share Common no par exchanged for (1/6) share Common no par
Geophysical Micro Computer Applications (International) Ltd. name changed to NetDriven Solutions Inc. 03/07/2000 which name changed to NetDriven Storage Solutions Inc. 03/30/2001 which recapitalized as Cervus Financial Group Inc. 07/15/2004
(See Cervus Financial Group Inc.)

NRM CORP. (OH)
Common $5 par changed to $2.50 par and (1) additional share issued 04/29/1966
Merged into AMK Corp. 07/03/1967
Each share Common $2.50 par exchanged for (0.25) share $3 Conv. Preferred no par and (0.25) share Common $2 par
AMK Corp. merged into United Brands Co. 06/30/1970 which name changed to Chiquita Brands International, Inc. 03/20/1990
(See Chiquita Brands International, Inc.)

NRM ENERGY CO LP (DE)
Merged into Edisto Resources Corp. 12/15/89
Each share $2 Conv. Acquisition Preferred Ser. A Units exchanged for (0.745) share Common 1¢ par
Each share $2.60 Sr. Conv. Preferred Depositary Units exchanged for (1) share $2.60 Sr. Conv. Preferred $1 par
Each Common Unit exchanged for (0.0668) share Common 1¢ par
Edisto Resources Corp. merged into Forcenergy Inc. 10/22/97 which merged into Forest Oil Corp. 12/7/2000

NRP CO. LIQUIDATING LTD. (PA)
In process of liquidation
Each share Common $25 par received initial distribution of $50 cash 9/11/81
Each share Common $25 par received second distribution of $50 cash 10/9/81
Each share Common $25 par received third distribution of $20 cash 1/8/82
Each share Common $25 par exchanged for fourth distribution of $2 cash 4/16/82
Each share Common $25 par received fifth distribution of $3 cash 1/15/83
Note: Details on subsequent distributions, if any, are not available

NRP INC (DE)
Name changed to ATC Communications Group Inc. 4/30/96
ATC Communications Group Inc. name changed to Aegis Communications Group, Inc. 7/9/98

NRT INDS INC (ON)
Name changed 01/20/1988
Name changed from NRT Research Technologies Inc. to NRT Industries Inc. 01/20/1988
Recapitalized as Cuda Consolidated Inc. 03/04/1991
Each share Common no par exchanged for (0.06) share Common no par
Cuda Consolidated Inc. name changed to FoodQuest Corp. 09/27/1994 which recapitalized as Foodquest International Corp. 11/30/1994 which recapitalized as Dealcheck.com Inc. 01/21/1999 which recapitalized as Bontan Corp. Inc. (ON) 04/17/2003 which reincorporated in British Virgin Islands as Portage Biotech Inc. 08/23/2013

NR2 RES CORP (AB)
Merged into Unitech Energy Resources Inc. 07/07/2006
Each share Common no par exchanged for (0.2966111) share Common no par
Unitech Energy Resources Inc. recapitalized as Jadela Oil Corp. 07/21/2011 which recapitalized as Tenth Avenue Petroleum Corp. 05/19/2015

NRUC CORP (SC)
Name changed to Emergent Group, Inc. 8/24/91
Emergent Group, Inc. name changed to Homegold Financial Inc. 7/1/98 (Homegold Financial Inc.)

NRX TECHNOLOGIES INC (DE)
Charter cancelled and declared inoperative and void for non-payment of taxes 3/1/83

NS & T BANKSHARES INC (DE)
Merged into United Virginia Bankshares, Inc. 12/27/1985
Each share Common $5 par exchanged for $86.98 cash

NS GROUP INC (KY)
Merged into IPSCO Inc. 12/01/2006
Each share Common no par exchanged for $66 cash

NS&L BANCORP INC (MO)
Stock Dividend - 20% payable 4/30/99 to holders of record 4/15/99
Merged into NS&L Acquisition Inc. 10/8/2003
Each share Common 1¢ par exchanged for $18 cash

NSA INC (DE)
Merged into Arms, Inc. 09/29/1987
Details not available

NSA INTL INC (TN)
Each (2,400) shares Common 5¢ par exchanged for (1) share Common $120 par 3/5/99
Note: In effect holders received $1.125 cash per share and public interest was eliminated

NSB HLDGS INC (GA)
Common $5 par split (3) for (2) by issuance of (0.5) additional share payable 09/30/2005 to holders of record 09/20/2005 Ex date - 10/03/2005
Name changed to Atlantic Southern Financial Group, Inc. 01/23/2006
(See Atlantic Southern Financial Group, Inc.)

NSC CORP (DE)
Merged into NSC Acquisition Inc. 6/22/99
Each share Common 1¢ par exchanged for $1.25 cash

NSC SVC GROUP INC (DE)
Name changed to Fibercorp International, Inc. 2/1/91
(See Fibercorp International, Inc.)

NSD BANCORP INC (PA)
Common $1 par split (3) for (2) by issuance of (0.5) additional share payable 12/31/1997 to holders of record 12/01/1997
Common Stock Purchase Rights declared for Common stockholders of record 09/30/2002 were redeemed at $0.001 per right 12/15/2004 for holders of record 12/01/2004
Stock Dividends - 5% payable 05/31/1996 holders of record 04/30/1996; 5% payable 05/30/1997 to holders of record 04/30/1997; 10% payable 03/03/1999 to holders of record 02/01/1999; 5% payable 05/31/2000 to holders of record 05/01/2000; 5% payable 05/31/2001 to holders of record 05/01/2001 Ex date - 04/27/2001; 5% payable 05/31/2002 to holders of record 05/01/2002 Ex date - 04/29/2002; 5% payable 05/15/2003 to holders of record 05/01/2003 Ex date - 04/29/2003; 5% payable 05/17/2004 to holders of record 05/03/2004
Merged into F.N.B. Corp. 02/21/2005
Each share Common $1 par

FINANCIAL INFORMATION, INC.

NSJ-NTS

exchanged for (1.8) shares Common 1¢ par

NSI GLOBAL INC (CANADA)
Name changed 08/31/2001
Name changed from NSI Communications Inc. to NSI Global Inc. 08/31/2001
Dissolved 02/09/2006
Details not available

NSI MARKETING LTD (CANADA)
Common no par reclassfied as Conv. 1st Preference no par 3/20/78
Conv. 1st Preference no par called for redemption 12/29/78

NSI STRATEGIC INVTS LTD (BC)
Voluntarily dissolved
Each share Common no par received first and final distribution of $0.076 cash payable 12/15/2016 to holders of record 12/12/2016

NSJ MTG CAP CORP (TX)
Recapitalized as Enviro-Recovery Inc. 04/23/1997
Each share Common $0.001 par exchanged for (0.25) share Common $0.0001 par
(See Enviro-Recovery Inc.)

NSJ-US CO LTD (NV)
Charter revoked 03/31/2014

NSP FING I (DE)
Issue Information - 8,000,000 TR ORIGINATED PFD SECS 7.875% offered at $25 per share on 01/28/1997
7.875% Trust Originated Preferred Securities called for redemption at $25 plus $0.1695 accrued dividend on 7/31/2003

NSP PHARMA CORP (CANADA)
Delisted from NEX 08/01/2008

NSS BANCORP INC (CT)
Merged into Summit Bancorp 11/20/98
Each share Common 1¢ par exchanged for (1.232) shares Common $1.20 par
Summit Bancorp merged into FleetBoston Financial Corp. 3/1/2001 which merged into Bank of America Corp. 4/1/2004

NSS RES INC (BC)
Name changed to Upco International Inc. 11/03/2017

NSTAR (MA)
Common $1 par split (2) for (1) by issuance of (1) additional share payable 06/03/2005 to holders of record 05/16/2005 Ex date - 06/06/2005
Merged into Northeast Utilities 04/10/2012
Each share Common $1 par exchanged for (1.312) shares Common $5 par
Northeast Utilities name changed to Eversource Energy 02/19/2015

NSTEIN TECHNOLOGIES INC (QC)
Each share old Common no par exchanged for (0.1) share new Common no par 06/13/2006
Merged into Open Text Corp. 04/01/2010
Each share new Common no par exchanged for $0.64805583 cash

NSTOR TECHNOLOGIES INC (DE)
Merged into Xyratex Ltd. 09/08/2005
Each share Common 5¢ par exchanged for $0.105 cash

NSU RES INC (NV)
Recapitalized as Hemcare Health Services Inc. 05/05/2015
Each share Common $0.001 par exchanged (0.02) share Common $0.001 par
Hemcare Health Services Inc. recapitalized as DLT Resolution Inc. 12/20/2017

NSX SILVER INC (BC)
Each share old Common no par exchanged for (0.1) share new Common no par 01/23/2015
Name changed to ViveRe Communities Inc. 08/23/2018

NT HLDG CORP (NV)
Recapitalized as HST Global, Inc. 07/07/2008
Each share Common $0.001 par exchanged for (0.04) share Common $0.001 par

NT MEDIA CORP CALIF INC (DE)
Each share Accredited Investors Common $0.001 par exchanged for (0.01) share Common $0.001 par 07/20/2007
Name changed to Global Health Voyager, Inc. 08/10/2011

NT MNG CORP (NV)
Common $0.001 par split (2) for (1) by issuance of (1) additional share payable 03/15/2010 to holders of record 03/10/2010 Ex date - 03/11/2010
Recapitalized as Sanwire Corp. (NV) 03/07/2013
Each share Common $0.001 par exchanged for (0.02) share Common $0.00001 par
Note: No holder will receive fewer than (100) post-split shares
Sanwire Corp. (NV) reincorporated in Wyoming 07/07/2015

NT NETWORK SYS INC (BC)
Recapitalized as Network Telemetrics Ltd. 1/12/96
Each share Common no par exchanged for (0.2) share Common no par
Network Telemetrics Ltd. name changed to Belvedere Resources Ltd. 10/14/97

NT TECHNOLOGIES INC (NV)
Name changed to NeXplore Corp. and Common $0.001 par changed to $0.00001 par 06/05/2007

NTC CAP CORP (BC)
Name changed to Sungold Gaming Inc. 03/01/1994
Sungold Gaming Inc. name changed to Sungold Gaming International Ltd. 05/26/1997 which name changed to Sungold Entertainment Corp. (BC) 03/20/2000 which reincorporated in Canada as Sungold International Holdings Corp. 12/12/2003

NTC CORP (NH)
Acquired by Amoskeag Bank Shares, Inc. 7/31/87
Each share Common $1 par exchanged for (4) shares Common $1 par
(See Amoskeag Bank Shares, Inc.)

NTC HLDGS INC (NY)
Reorganized under the laws of Nevada as MedXLink Corp. 07/24/2002
Each share Common $0.001 par exchanged for (0.01) share Common $0.001 par
MedXLink Corp. name changed to Particle Drilling Technologies, Inc. 02/09/2005
(See Particle Drilling Technologies, Inc.)

NTECH CORP (DE)
Recapitalized as Molecular Robotics Inc. 03/30/2000
Each share Common $0.0001 par exchanged for (0.1) share Common $0.0001 par
(See Molecular Robotics Inc.)

NTELOS HLDGS CORP (DE)
Each share old Common 1¢ par exchanged for (0.5) share new Common 1¢ par and (0.5) share Lumos Networks Corp. Common Networks Corp. Common 1¢ par 11/01/2011
Acquired by Shenandoah Telecommunications Co. 05/06/2016
Each share new Common 1¢ par exchanged for $9.25 cash

NTELOS INC (VA)
Plan of reorganization under Chapter 11 Federal Bankruptcy Code effective 9/9/2003
No stockholders' equity
Acquired by NTELOS Holdings Corp. 5/2/2005
Each share new Common 1¢ par exchanged for $40 cash

NTEX INC (ON)
Assets sold for the benefit of creditors 03/31/2002

NTI NEWMERICAL INC (AB)
Each share old Common no par exchanged for (0.00001) share new Common no par 01/05/2010
Note: In effect holders received $0.04 cash per share and public interest was eliminated

NTI RES LTD (AB)
Reincorporated 05/28/1997
Place of incorporation changed from (Bermuda) to (AB) 05/28/1997
Delisted from Alberta Stock Exchange 06/11/1999

NTL EUROPE INC (DE)
Each (50,000) shares old Common 1¢ par exchanged for (1) share new Common 1¢ par 1/29/2004
Note: In effect holders received $0.01 cash per share and public interest was eliminated

NTL INC (DE)
Ctfs. dated after 03/03/2006
Name changed to Virgin Media, Inc. 02/06/2007
Virgin Media, Inc. merged into Liberty Global PLC 06/10/2013

NTL INC NEW (DE)
Merged into NTL Inc. (Ctfs. dated after 03/03/2006) 03/03/2006
Each share Common 1¢ par exchanged for (2.5) shares Common 1¢ par
NTL Inc. (Ctfs. dated after 03/03/2006) name changed to Virgin Media, Inc. 02/06/2007 which merged into Liberty Global PLC 06/10/2013

NTL INC OLD (DE)
Common 1¢ par split (5) for (4) by issuance of (0.25) additional share payable 10/07/1999 to holders of record 10/04/1999
Common 1¢ par split (5) for (4) by issuance of (0.25) additional share payable 02/03/2000 to holders of record 01/31/2000
Stock Dividends - in 13% Sr. Exchangeable Pfd. to holders of 13% Sr. Exchangeable Pfd. 0.0325% payable 02/17/1998 to holders of record 02/05/1998; 3.25% payable 11/15/1999 to holders of record 11/05/1999; 3.25% payable 08/15/2000 to holders of record 08/04/2000 Ex date - 08/02/2000; 3.25% payable 11/15/2000 to holders of record 11/03/2000; 3.25% payable 08/15/2001 to holders of record 08/03/2001; 3.25% payable 11/15/2001 to holders of record 11/02/2001 Ex date - 10/31/2001
Plan of reorganization under Chapter 11 Federal Bankruptcy Code effective 01/10/2003
Each share Ser. A Jr. Participating Preferred 1¢ par exchanged for an undetermined amount of NTL Inc. Common Stock Purchase Warrant Ser. A expiring 01/13/2011
Each share 144A 13% Sr. Exchangeable Preferred 1¢ par exchanged for (3.493263) shares NTL Europe, Inc. Common 1¢ par and (4.075472) NTL Inc. Common Stock Purchase Warrants Ser. A expiring 01/13/2011
Each share 13% Accrued Investors Sr. Exchangeable Preferred 1¢ par exchanged for (3.493263) shares NTL Europe, Inc. Common 1¢ par and (4.075472) NTL Inc. Common Stock Purchase Warrants Ser. A expiring 01/13/2011
Each share 13% Sr. Exchangeable Preferred 1¢ par exchanged for (3.493263) shares NTL Europe, Inc. Common 1¢ par and (4.075472) NTL Inc. Common Stock Purchase Warrants Ser. A expiring 01/13/2011
Each share Common 1¢ par exchanged for (0.007436) share NTL Europe, Inc. Common 1¢ par and (0.008675) NTL Inc. Common Stock Purchase Warrants Ser. A expiring 01/13/2011
Note: Unexchanged certificates were cancelled and became without value 01/10/2005

NTN CDA INC (NY)
Each share Common $0.001 par exchanged for (0.1) share Common 1¢ par 08/31/1990
Each share Common 1¢ par exchanged for (1/7) share Common 4¢ par 09/30/1992
Common 4¢ par split (3) for (2) by issuance of (0.5) additional share payable 08/14/1996 to holders of record 08/01/1996
Name changed to Networks North Inc. 03/16/1998
Networks North Inc. name changed to Chell Group Corp. 09/28/2000
(See Chell Group Corp.)

NTN COMMUNICATIONS INC (DE)
Each share old Common $0.005 par exchanged for (0.05) share new Common $0.005 par 6/14/91
Each share Preferred Ser. A $0.005 par received distribution of (0.081755) share new Common $0.005 par payable 12/18/98 to holders of record 12/1/98 Ex date - 12/21/98
Each share Preferred Ser. A $0.005 par received distribution of (0.06504065) share new Common $0.005 par payable 6/24/99 to holders of record 6/1/99 Ex date - 8/17/99
Each share Preferred Ser. A $0.005 par received distribution of (0.015066) share new Common $0.005 par payable 12/29/99 to holders of record 12/1/99 Ex date - 1/25/2000
Each share Preferred Ser. A $0.005 par received distribution of (0.0418848) share new Common $0.005 par payable 12/1/2000 to holders of record 11/15/2000
Each share Preferred Ser. A $0.005 par received distribution of (0.0418848) share new Common $0.005 par payable 6/1/2001 to holders of record 5/15/2001 Ex date - 12/21/98
Each share Preferred Ser. A $0.005 par received distribution of (0.07331378) share new Common $0.005 par payable 12/1/2001 to holders of record 11/15/2001
Each share Preferred Ser. A $0.005 par received distribution of (0.035739) share new Common $0.005 par payable 6/1/2002 to holders of record 5/15/2002 Ex date - 7/25/2002
Each share Preferred Ser. A $0.005 par received distribution of (0.05) share new Common $0.005 par payable 12/1/2003 to holders of record 11/15/2003
Name changed to NTN Buzztime, Inc. 1/1/2006

NTR ACQUISITION CO (DE)
Issue Information - 24,000,000 UNITS

consisting of (1) share COM and (1) WT offered at $10 per Unit on 01/30/2007
Completely liquidated 02/12/2009
Each Unit exchanged for first and final distribution of $10.03 cash
Each share Common $0.001 par exchanged for first and final distribution of $10.03 cash

NTRR INC (NY)
Name changed to J.K.M. Industries, Inc. 7/23/69
(See J.K.M. Industries, Inc.)

NTS COMPUTER SYS LTD (BC)
Name changed to Brainium Technologies Inc. 06/21/2001
(See Brainium Technologies Inc.)

NTS INC (NV)
Acquired by T3 North Intermediate Holdings, LLC 06/06/2014
Each share Common $0.001 par exchanged for $2 cash

NTS-PPTYS LTD PARTNERSHIP (GA, KY, MD, & FL)
Merged into NTS Realty Holdings Limited Partnership 12/28/2004
Each Unit of Ltd. Partnership Int.-III exchanged for approximately (84.473) Partnership Units
Each Unit of Ltd. Partnership Int.-IV exchanged for approximately (72.048) Partnership Units
Each Unit of Ltd. Partnership Int.-V exchanged for approximately (48.848) Partnership Units
Each Unit of Ltd. Partnership Int.-VI exchanged for approximately (101.052) Partnership Units
Each Unit of Ltd. Partnership Int.-VII exchanged for approximately (1.812) Partnership Units
Note: The above Limited Partnerships are registered in the following states: LP III (GA), LP IV (KY), LP V (MD), LP VI (MD) & LP VII (FL)
(See NTS Realty Holdings Limited Partnership)

NTS-PPTYS PLUS LTD (FL)
Merged into ORIG, LLC 06/25/2002
Each Ltd. Partnership Int. exchanged for $1.30 cash

NTS RLTY HLDGS LTD PARTNERSHIP (DE)
Acquired by NTS Merger Parent, LLC 06/10/2014
Each Partnership Unit exchanged for $8.68 cash

NTS TECHNOLOGY INC (DE)
Name changed to Environmental Corp. of America 7/23/97

NTT DOCOMO INC (JAPAN)
ADR agreement terminated 04/29/2002
Each 144A Sponsored ADR for Ordinary no par exchanged for (200) Ordinary shares no par
(Additional Information in Active)

NTT MOBILE COMMUNICATIONS NETWORK INC (JAPAN)
Each Unsponsored ADR for Ordinary no par exchanged for (0.2) Sponsored ADR for Ordinary no par 6/29/99
Each 144A Unsponsored ADR for Ordinary no par exchanged for (0.2) 144A Sponsored ADR for Ordinary no par 06/29/1999
Name changed to NTT Docomo Inc. 04/01/2000

NTV OIL SVCS INDS INC (BC)
Delisted from Vancouver Stock Exchange 07/07/1989

N2AWARENESS COM (NV)
Name changed to Affiance, Inc. (New) 05/17/1999
Affiance, Inc. (New) reorganized as SMI Financial Group Inc. 11/14/2000 which name changed to AmeraMex International Inc. 05/30/2001

N2H2 INC (WA)
Issue Information - 5,000,000 shares COM offered at $13 per share on 07/29/1999
Merged into Secure Computing Corp. 10/15/2003
Each share Common no par exchanged for (0.0841) share Common 1¢ par
(See Secure Computing Corp.)

NU-AGE URANIUM MINES LTD. (ON)
Name changed to Haitian Copper Corp. Ltd. 7/23/56
(See Haitian Copper Corp. Ltd.)

NU-APEX ENERGY CORP (BC)
Recapitalized as Digital Ventures Inc. 01/04/2000
Each share Common no par exchanged for (0.2) share Common no par
Digital Ventures Inc. recapitalized as Castleworth Ventures Inc. 01/04/2002 which name changed to Pan-Nevada Gold Corp. 01/20/2006 which merged into Midway Gold Corp. 04/13/2007
(See Midway Gold Corp.)

NU-CYCLE URANIUM MINES LTD. (ON)
Charter revoked for failure to file reports and pay fees 2/9/67

NU D ZINE INC (FL)
Name changed 12/27/2000
Common $0.001 par split (3) for (1) by issuance of (2) additional shares payable 12/15/1999 to holders of record 12/08/1999 Ex date - 12/16/1999
Name changed from NU-D-Zine Bedding & Bath, Inc. to NU-D-Zine Inc. 12/27/2000
Name changed to XtraCard Corp. (FL) 01/07/2003
XtraCard Corp. (FL) reincorporated in Nevada as Hero International USA Holding Corp. 08/19/2008

NU DAWN RES INC (BC)
Name changed to World Ventures Inc. 6/28/99

NU DEAL VENDING CORP (NY)
Name changed to N.D.V. Industries, Inc. 12/18/75
N.D.V. Industries, Inc. name changed to Audio Visual Electronics Corp. 10/12/85
(See Audio Visual Electronics Corp.)

NU ELEC CORP (DE)
Name changed to Clean Water Technologies Inc. 4/2/2002
Clean Water Technologies Inc. name changed to SheerVision, Inc. 6/19/2006

NU-ENAMEL CORP. (DE)
Recapitalized as E Z Paintr Corp. 00/00/1952
Each share Common 25¢ par exchanged for (0.01) share Common $1 par
E Z Paintr Corp. merged into Newell Companies, Inc. 10/31/1974 which name changed to Newell Co. 05/22/1985 which name changed to Newell Rubbermaid Inc. 03/24/1999 which name changed to Newell Brands Inc. 04/18/2016

NU-ENAMEL OIL CORP. (DE)
Name changed to Transcontinental Oil Corp. (Old) 12/16/1949
Transcontinental Oil Corp. (Old) reorganized as Transcontinental Oil Corp. (New) 05/05/1980 which name changed to Transcontinental Energy Corp. 05/15/1981
(See Transcontinental Energy Corp.)

NU ENERGY DEV CORP (BC)
Name changed to Erickson Gold Mines Ltd. (BC) 02/25/1983
Erickson Gold Mines Ltd. (BC) reincorporated in Canada as Total Erickson Resources Ltd. 02/14/1986 which merged into TOTAL Energold Corp. 09/19/1988
(See TOTAL Energold Corp.)

NU ENERGY URANIUM CORP (BC)
Acquired by Mega Uranium Ltd. 08/14/2007
Each share Common no par exchanged for (2/3) share Common no par

NU ERA COINS INC (NJ)
Each share Common no par exchanged for (0.1) share Common 1¢ par 12/05/1984
Name changed to Cyttran International Inc. 07/27/1991

NU-ERA CORP. (MI)
Completely liquidated 07/21/1967
Each share Common no par exchanged for first and final distribution of (1/6) share Napco Industries, Inc. Common $1 par
Napco Industries, Inc. name changed to Mass Merchandisers, Inc. (IN) 05/11/1984 which merged into McKesson Corp. (MD) 10/29/1985 which reincorporated in Delaware 07/31/1987
(See McKesson Corp. (DE) (Old))

NU-GORD MINES LTD. (ON)
Charter cancelled for failure to pay taxes and file returns 1/27/66

NU GRO CORP (ON)
Merged into United Industries Corp. 4/30/2004
Each share Common no par exchanged for $11 cash

NU-HESIVE, INC.
Dissolved in 1948

NU HORIZONS ELECTRS CORP (DE)
Reincorporated 06/26/1989
State of incorporation changed from (NY) to (DE) 06/26/1989
Common 1¢ par changed to $0.0066 par and (0.5) additional share issued 09/30/1993
Common $0.0066 par split (3) for (2) by issuance of (0.5) additional share payable 10/23/2000 to holders of record 10/02/2000 Ex date - 10/03/2000
Stock Dividends - 10% 08/25/1987; 5% payable 11/19/1999 to holders of record 11/04/1999
Acquired by Arrow Electronics, Inc. 01/03/2011
Each share Common $0.0066 par exchanged for $7 cash

NU-IDA, INC. (ID)
Charter forfeited for non-payment of taxes 12/2/68

NU-KOTE HLDG INC (DE)
Class A Common 1¢ par split (2) for (1) by issuance of (1) additional share 8/15/95
Plan of reorganization under Chapter 11 Federal Bankruptcy Code effective 12/31/2000
No stockholders' equity

NU LADY GOLD MINES LTD (BC)
Delisted from Vancouver Stock Exchange 01/10/1990

NU-LIFE CORP (CANADA)
Charter dissolved for non-compliance 10/17/2008

NU-LINE INDUSTRIES, INC. (MN)
Name changed to N-L, Inc. 12/1/65 which completed liquidation 11/29/66

NU LITE INDS LTD (BC)
Name changed to Netseers Internet International Corp. 5/31/2000
Netseers Internet International Corp. recapitalized as 1st Anyox Resources Ltd. 12/2/2003 which name changed to Victory Resources Corp. 2/28/2005

NU MED INC (DE)
Reincorporated 11/17/86
State of incorporation changed from (CA) to (DE) and Common no par changed to 1¢ par 11/17/86
Reorganized as Progressions Health Systems, Inc. 9/30/94
Each share new Common 1¢ par exchanged for (0.0111122) share Common $0.012 par and $0.60066 cash
Note: Holders entitled to (99) or fewer shares will receive $0.80 cash per share
(See Progressions Health Systems, Inc.)

NU-MED SYSTEMS, INC. (CA)
Common no par split (2) for (1) by issuance of (1) additional share 2/23/81
Each share old Common no par exchanged for (0.5) share new Common no par 6/23/82
Name changed to Nu-Med, Inc. (CA) 7/7/83
Nu-Med, Inc. (CA) reincorporated in Delaware 11/17/86
(See Progressions Health Systems, Inc.)

NU-MEDIA INDS INTL INC (BC)
Recapitalized as Consolidated Nu-Media Industries Inc. (BC) 12/15/1994
Each share Common no par exchanged for (1/7) share Common no par
Consolidated Nu-Media Industries Inc. (BC) reincorporated in Yukon as Pan Asia Mining Corp. 10/08/1997 which name changed to China Diamond Corp. 01/02/2004
(See China Diamond Corp.)

NU-MEX URANIUM CORP (NV)
Common $0.001 par split (5) for (1) by issuance of (4) additional shares payable 06/07/2007 to holders of record 06/06/2007 Ex date - 06/08/2007
Name changed to Uranium International Corp. 03/11/2008
Uranium International Corp. name changed to Mercer Gold Corp. 06/09/2010 which name changed to Tresoro Mining Corp. 11/04/2011
(See Tresoro Mining Corp.)

NU MODE INDS INC (NY)
Dissolved by proclamation 06/16/1993

NU PAC RES LTD (BC)
Recapitalized as Iron Lady Resources Inc. 03/11/1988
Each share Common no par exchanged for (0.33333333) share Common no par
Iron Lady Resources Inc. recapitalized as Takepoint Ventures Ltd. (BC) 08/03/1994 which reorganized in Yukon as Consolidated Takepoint Ventures Ltd. 06/25/2002 which name changed to Lake Shore Gold Corp. (YT) 12/18/2002 which reincorporated in British Columbia 06/30/2004 which reincorporated in Canada 07/18/2008 which merged into Tahoe Resources Inc. 04/07/2016

NU-REALITY OILS LTD. (AB)
Acquired by Flag Oils Ltd. 10/11/60
Each share Capital Stock no par exchanged for (0.25) share Common no par
Flag Oils Ltd. name changed to Flag Resources Ltd. 1/4/82 which recapitalized as Flag Resources (1985) Ltd. 2/18/85

NU-RIDGEWAY PETROLEUMS LTD. (AB)
Name changed to Pere Marquette Petroleums Ltd. 3/20/63
Pere Marquette Petroleums Ltd. struck off register 6/30/77

NU-SILCO MINES LTD. (ON)
Charter cancelled for failure to pay taxes and file returns 11/21/78

NU SKIN ASIA PAC INC (DE)
Issue Information - 9,100,000 shares Class A Common offered at $24 per share on 11/21/1996
Name changed to Nu Skin Enterprises, Inc. 5/6/98

NU-SKY ENERGY INC (AB)
Acquired by Kinloch Resources Inc. 07/31/2003
Each share Common no par exchanged for $0.8275 cash

NU-SKY EXPL INC (BC)
Recapitalized as Consolidated Nu-Sky Exploration Inc. 5/22/91
Each share Common no par exchanged for (0.2) share Common no par
Consolidated Nu-Sky Exploration Inc. (BC) reorganized in (Alta) as Nu-Sky Energy Inc. 3/1/95
(See Nu-Sky Energy Inc.)

NU START RESOURCE CORP (BC)
Struck off register and declared dissolved for failure to file returns 8/9/91

NU-TECH BIO-MED INC (DE)
Recapitalized as United Diagnostic, Inc. 12/23/1998
Each share Common 1¢ par exchanged for (0.01428571) share Common 1¢ par
United Diagnostic, Inc. name changed to SPO Medical Inc. 04/21/2005 which recapitalized as SPO Global Inc. 10/07/2013

NU TECH INDS CORP (DE)
Each share Common 1¢ par exchanged for (1) share Class A Common 1¢ par and (3) shares Class B Common 1¢ par 03/27/1984
Note: Only Class A Common 1¢ par were issued and were considered as a Unit consisting of (1) share Class A Common 1¢ par and (3) shares Class B Common 1¢ par until 09/26/1984
Class B Common 1¢ par were issued in the above ratio 09/27/1984
Name changed to Numericom Inc. 11/01/1984
Numericom Inc. name changed to Infotex Holdings, Inc. 04/19/2005 which name changed to Integrated Camera Optics, Corp. 12/19/2005 which recapitalized as Global Healthcare & Education Management, Inc. 09/27/2007

NU-VISION INTL INC (FL)
Name changed to Highland Healthcare Corp. 05/31/1991
Highland Healthcare Corp. recapitalized as Systems Communications Inc. 09/09/1994 which recapitalized as Hitsgalore.com, Inc. 03/19/1999 which name changed to Diamond Hitts Production, Inc. (FL) 05/01/2001 which reincorporated in Nevada 09/04/2001
(See Diamond Hitts Production, Inc.)

NU-VISION RESOURCE CORP (BC)
Name changed to Vision Coatings Group Ltd. 02/16/2004
(See Vision Coatings Group Ltd.)

NU VU CORP (DE)
Charter cancelled and declared inoperative and void for non-payment of taxes 3/1/86

NU-WALL INDUSTRIES LTD.
Assets sold 00/00/1941
Details not available

NU-WAVE HEALTH PRODUCTS, INC. (FL)
Name changed to Dynamic Health Products, Inc. 06/15/1998
Dynamic Health Products, Inc. merged into GeoPharma, Inc. 10/17/2007
(See GeoPharma, Inc.)

NU-WEST ARIZONA, INC. (AZ)
Name changed to Nu-West, Inc. 12/31/1980
(See Nu-West, Inc.)

NU-WEST DEVELOPMENT CORP. OF ARIZONA (AZ)
Name changed to Nu-West Arizona, Inc. 6/27/80
Nu-West Arizona, Inc. name changed to Nu-West, Inc. 12/31/80
(See Nu-West, Inc.)

NU WEST GROUP LTD (AB)
Name changed 01/10/1980
Each share Common no par exchanged for (1.5) shares Conv. Class A Common no par 05/09/1974
Conv. Class A Common no par split (3) for (2) by issuance of (0.5) additional share 07/28/1976
Conv. Class B Common no par split (3) for (2) by issuance of (0.5) additional share 07/28/1976
Conv. Class A Common no par split (3) for (2) by issuance of (0.5) additional share 12/16/1977
Conv. Class B Common no par split (3) for (2) by issuance of (0.5) additional share 12/16/1977
Conv. Class A Common no par split (3) for (2) by issuance of (0.5) additional share 01/05/1979
Conv. Class B Common no par split (3) for (2) by issuance of (0.5) additional share 01/05/1979
Conv. Class A Common no par split (2) for (1) by issuance of (1) additional share 10/05/1979
Conv. Class B Common no par split (2) for (1) by issuance of (1) additional share 10/05/1979
Name changed from Nu-West Development Ltd. to Nu-West Group Ltd. 01/10/1980
Conv. Class A Common no par split (2) for (1) by issuance of (1) additional share 11/14/1980
Conv. Class B Common no par split (2) for (1) by issuance of (1) additional share 11/14/1980
Plan of Arrangement effective 11/19/1984
Each share 8-3/4% First Preferred Ser. A $20 par, 8.85% First Preferred Ser. B $20 par and 9% First Preferred Ser. C $20 par exchanged for (3.5) shares Class B Special Common no par respectively
Each share 8% Conv. Second Preferred Ser. A $20 par exchanged for (3) shares Class B Special Common no par
Each share Conv. Class A Common no par, Conv. Class B Common no par, Conv. Class C Common no par and Conv. Class D Common no par exchanged for (1) share Common no par respectively
Reincorporated under the laws of Delaware 01/29/1988
Nu-West Group Ltd. (DE) recapitalized as N-W Group, Inc. 02/24/1988 which name changed to Glenayre Technologies, Inc. 11/10/1992 which name changed to Entertainment Distribution Co., Inc. 05/11/2007 which recapitalized as EDCI Holdings, Inc. 08/26/2008
(See EDCI Holdings, Inc.)

NU WEST GROUP LTD NEW (DE)
Recapitalized as N-W Group, Inc. 02/24/1988
Each share Class A Special Common no par exchanged for (0.04) share Common no par
Each share Class B Special Common no par exchanged for (0.04) share Common no par
Each share Common no par exchanged for (0.04) share Common no par
N-W Group, Inc. name changed to Glenayre Technologies, Inc. 11/10/1992 which name changed to Entertainment Distribution Co., Inc. 05/11/2007 which recapitalized as EDCI Holdings, Inc. 08/26/2008

NU-WEST HOMES LTD. (AB)
Name changed to Nu-West Development Ltd. 06/14/1971
Nu-West Development Ltd. name changed to Nu-West Group Ltd. (AB) 01/10/1980 which reincorporated in Delaware 01/29/1988 which recapitalized as N-W Group, Inc. 02/24/1988 which name changed to Glenayre Technologies, Inc. 11/10/1992 which name changed to Entertainment Distribution Co., Inc. 05/11/2007 which recapitalized as EDCI Holdings, Inc. 08/26/2008
(See EDCI Holdings, Inc.)

NU WEST INC (AZ)
Merged into Nu-West Group Ltd. 03/11/1983
Each share Common no par exchanged for $1.50 cash

NU-WEST INDS INC (DE)
Each share old Common 1¢ par exchanged for (0.16666666) share new Common 1¢ par 12/12/1994
Merged into Agrium Inc. 10/06/1995
Each share Common 1¢ par exchanged for $10.50 cash
$11 Class A Preferred $15 par called for redemption 12/13/1996
Public interest eliminated

NU-WORLD URANIUM MINES LTD. (ON)
Charter revoked for failure to file reports and pay fees 1/27/66

NU XMP VENTURES LTD (BC)
Name changed to New Pacific Metals Corp. (Old) 11/04/2004
New Pacific Metals Corp. (Old) name changed to New Pacific Holdings Corp. 07/04/2016 which name changed to New Pacific Metals Corp. (New) 07/24/2017

NUANCE COMMUNICATIONS INC OLD (DE)
Issue Information - 4,500,000 shares COM offered at $17 per share on 04/12/2000
Merged into ScanSoft, Inc. 9/15/2005
Each share Common $0.001 par exchanged for (0.77) share Common $0.001 par and $2.20 cash
ScanSoft, Inc. name changed to Nuance Communications, Inc. (New) 11/21/2005

NUANCE RES CORP (NV)
Name changed to Force Energy Corp. 02/25/2008
Force Energy Corp. recapitalized as Force Minerals Corp. 06/28/2013

NUBAR MINES LTD. (ON)
Acquired by Tandem Mines Ltd. share for share in 1954
Tandem Mines Ltd. recapitalized as Halmon Mining & Processing Ltd. 4/3/58
(See Halmon Mining & Processing Ltd.)

NUBIO VENTURES INC (NV)
Recapitalized as County Line Resources Inc. 03/18/2005
Each share Common $0.001 par exchanged for (0.2) share Common $0.001 par
County Line Resources Inc. reorganized as County Line Energy Corp. 05/15/2006

NUC MED INC (NM)
Name changed to Summa Medical Corp. 01/20/1982
(See Summa Medical Corp.)

NUCAL RES LTD (BC)
Recapitalized as Captive Air International Inc. 06/30/1987
Each share Common no par exchanged for (0.2) share Common no par
Captive Air International Inc. recapitalized as Kik Tire Technologies Inc. 04/08/1996 which recapitalized as Kik Polymers Inc. 06/20/2006 which name changed to Edgewater Wireless Systems Inc. 02/01/2012

NUCANOLAN RES LTD (ON)
Name changed to Westchester Resources Inc. 09/25/2003
Westchester Resources Inc. name changed to WSR Gold Inc. 02/16/2007 which recapitalized as White Pine Resources Inc. 12/18/2008 which name changed to SBD Capital Corp. 09/15/2017

NUCELL ENERGY CDA INC (BC)
Cease trade order effective 04/15/1992
Stockholders' equity unlikely

NUCENTRIX BROADBAND NETWORKS INC (DE)
Plan of reorganization under Chapter 11 Federal Bankruptcy Code effective 6/10/2004
Each share Common $0.001 par exchanged for $2.25 cash
Each share Common $0.001 par received second and final distribution of $0.435 cash payable 6/13/2005 to holders of record 6/10/2004
Note: Unexchanged certificates were cancelled and became without value 12/31/2006

NUCKASEE MANUFACTURING CO.
Acquired by Union Buffalo Mills Co. in 1929

NUCLEAR & GENETIC TECHNOLOGY INC (DE)
Recapitalized as NGT Enterprises Inc. 11/30/89
Each share Common $0.0001 par exchanged for (0.005) share Common $0.0001 par
NGT Enterprises Inc. recapitalized as IMN Financial Corp. 5/15/97 which name changed to Apponline.com Inc. 5/11/99
(See Apponline.com Inc.)

NUCLEAR-CHICAGO CORP. (DE)
Common $1 par split (3) for (2) by issuance of (0.5) additional share 11/30/61
Stock Dividend - 100% 12/20/58
Completely liquidated 8/1/66
Each share Common $1 par exchanged for first and final distribution of (1) share Searle (G.D.) & Co. (Del.) Conv. Preferred $1 par
(See Searle (G.D.) & Co. (Del.))

NUCLEAR-CHICAGO CORP. (IL)
Reincorporated under the laws of Delaware 11/18/57
Nuclear-Chicago Corp. (Del.) acquired by Searle (G.D.) & Co. (Del.) 8/1/66
(See Searle (G.D.) & Co. (Del.))

NUCLEAR CORP AMER (DE)
Reincorporated 06/30/1958
Name, state of incorporation changed from from Nuclear Corp. of America, Inc. (MI) to Nuclear Corp. of America (DE) and Class A Common and Common no par changed to Common 10¢ par 06/30/1958
Recapitalized as Nucor Corp. 12/29/1971
Each share Common 10¢ par exchanged for (0.25) share Common 40¢ par

NUCLEAR DATA INC (DE)
Reincorporated 11/30/67
State of incorporation changed from (IL) to (DE) and Common no par changed to 50¢ par 11/30/67
Common 50¢ par split (5) for (4) by

NUC-NUC   FINANCIAL INFORMATION, INC.

issuance of (0.25) additional share 5/20/81
Name changed to Metropolitan Circuits, Inc. 7/31/89
(See Metropolitan Circuits, Inc.)

NUCLEAR DEVELOPMENT CORP. OF AMERICA (NY)
Acquired by United Nuclear Corp. (DE) 5/31/61
Each share Common $1 par exchanged for (1) share Common 20¢ par
United Nuclear Corp. (DE) reorganized in Virginia as UNC Resources, Inc. 8/31/78 which name changed to UNC Inc. (VA) 6/3/86 which reincorporated in Delaware 4/30/87
(See UNC Inc.)

NUCLEAR DYNAMICS (NV)
Under plan of merger each share Common 5¢ par exchanged for (1) share Common $0.025 par 6/29/70
Name changed to Power Alternatives, Inc. 1/13/78
Power Alternatives, Inc. name changed to New World Minerals, Inc. 4/15/82

NUCLEAR DYNAMICS INC (AZ)
Common 10¢ par split (1.5) for (1) by issuance of (0.5) additional share 11/25/75
Name changed to ND Resources, Inc. 12/4/80

NUCLEAR ELECTRONICS CORP. (PA)
Assets sold in 1961
No stockholders' equity

NUCLEAR ENGR INC (CA)
Stock Dividend - 10% 12/01/1970
Merged into Teledyne Nuclear Corp. 09/18/1975
Each share Common 33-1/3¢ par exchanged for $15 cash

NUCLEAR ENTERPRISES LTD. (CANADA)
Assets sold to Allied Enterprises Ltd. and each (10) shares Capital Stock no par exchanged for (1) share Capital Stock $1 par, $50 principal amount in 3% Notes and 80¢ in cash in 1954

NUCLEAR EXPL & DEV CO (WY)
Merged into Nedco of Oregon, Inc. 10/15/1980
Each share Common no par exchanged for $7.25 cash

NUCLEAR EXPLORATIONS LTD. (AB)
Dissolved 10/30/60

NUCLEAR INSTRUMENT & CHEMICAL CORP. (IL)
Stock Dividend - 10% 9/15/56
Name changed to Nuclear-Chicago Corp. (Ill.) 11/21/56
Nuclear-Chicago Corp. (Ill.) reincorporated under the laws of Delaware 11/18/57 which was acquired by Searle (G.D.) & Co. (Del.) 8/1/66
(See Searle (G.D.) & Co. (Del.))

NUCLEAR MATERIALS & EQUIPMENT CORP. (PA)
6% Preferred $10 par called for redemption 12/30/60
Completely liquidated 4/17/67
Each share Common no par exchanged for first and final distribution of (0.255) share Atlantic Richfield Co. (PA) Common $10 par
Atlantic Richfield Co. (PA) reincorporated in Delaware 5/7/85 which merged into BP Amoco p.l.c. 4/18/2000

NUCLEAR MED SYS INC (DE)
Each share Common 1¢ par exchanged for (0.25) share Common 4¢ par 01/30/1976

Stock Dividends - 10% 05/29/1978; 25% 06/27/1980; 50% 12/12/1980
Name changed to NMS Pharmaceuticals, Inc. 02/04/1983
NMS Pharmaceuticals, Inc. name changed to Biomerica, Inc. 10/20/1987

NUCLEAR METALS INC (MA)
Common 10¢ par split (2) for (1) by issuance of (1) additional share payable 4/7/97 to holders of record 3/3/97
Stock Dividend - 50% 11/17/80
Name changed to Starmet Corp. 10/1/97
(See Starmet Corp.)

NUCLEAR PHARMACY INC (DE)
Reincorporated 10/15/85
State of incorporation changed from (NM) to (DE) 10/15/85
Name changed to Syncor International Corp. 2/3/86 which merged into Cardinal Health, Inc. 1/3/2003

NUCLEAR PWR & ENERGY CO (WY)
Name changed to Nupec Resources Inc. 06/11/1981
(See Nupec Resources Inc.)

NUCLEAR RADIATION SHELTERS, INC. (DC)
Name changed to Continental Industries, Inc. (DC) 3/10/69
Continental Industries, Inc. (DC) reorganized as Ecological Recycling Co. 4/25/71
(See Ecological Recycling Co.)

NUCLEAR RESEARCH CHEMICALS, INC. (FL)
Liquidation completed
Each share Class A Common $1 par or Class B Common $1 par exchanged for initial distribution of $4.30 cash 1/19/67
Each share Class A Common $1 par or Class B Common $1 par received second and final distribution of $1.72 cash 10/28/70

NUCLEAR RESH ASSOC INC (DE)
Charter cancelled and declared inoperative and void for non-payment of taxes 3/1/81

NUCLEAR RESH CORP (PA)
Each share Common 1¢ par exchanged for (0.002) share Common no par 1/31/68
Merged into Aptec Acquisition Corp. 10/28/99
Each share Common no par exchanged for $224.02 cash

NUCLEAR RES CORP (UT)
Name changed to Unicept, Inc. 6/15/72
Each share Common Capital Stock 1¢ par exchanged for (1) share Common Capital Stock 1¢ par
Unicept, Inc. name changed to Power Train, Inc. 11/29/76 which name changed to Scanner Energy Exploration Corp. 8/28/80 which name changed to Odin-Phoenix, Ltd. 10/18/82

NUCLEAR SCIENCE & ENGINEERING CORP. (DE)
Completely liquidated 09/14/1967
Each share Common 25¢ par exchanged for first and final distribution of (0.0638) share International Chemical & Nuclear Corp. Common $5 par
International Chemical & Nuclear Corp. name changed to ICN Pharmaceuticals, Inc. (CA) 04/13/1973 which reincorporated in Delaware 10/03/1986 which merged into ICN Pharmaceuticals, Inc. (New) 11/10/1994 which name changed to Valeant Pharmaceuticals International 11/12/2003 which merged into Valeant Pharmaceuticals International, Inc.

(Canada) 09/28/2010 which reincorporated in British Columbia 08/09/2013

NUCLEAR SVCS CORP (CA)
Common 20¢ par changed to no par 07/19/1977
Stock Dividend - 30% 07/01/1974
Name changed to Quadrex Corp. 09/12/1978
(See Quadrex Corp.)

NUCLEAR SILVER CORP. (ID)
Reincorporated under the laws of Delaware as Technimed Corp. 01/31/1984
(See Technimed Corp.)

NUCLEAR SOLUTIONS INC (NV)
Name changed to U.S. Fuel Corp. 10/07/2011
(See U.S. Fuel Corp.)

NUCLEAR SUPPORT SVCS INC (VA)
Common $0.0025 par split (2) for (1) by issuance of (1) additional share 11/2/85
Reorganized under the laws of Delaware as Canisco Resources, Inc. 7/1/96
Each share Common $0.0025 par exchanged for (1) share Common $0.0025 par

NUCLEAR SYS INC (DE)
Each share Common 10¢ par exchanged for (0.008) share Common $12.50 par 10/15/1984
Note: In effect holders received $0.50 cash per share and public interest was eliminated

NUCLEAR TECHNOLOGY CORP (NY)
Name changed to N.T.C. Liquidating Corp. 7/10/70
N.T.C. Liquidating Corp. liquidated for Display Sciences, Inc. 7/15/70
(See Display Sciences, Inc.)

NUCLEONIC CONTROLS CORP. (MN)
Acquired by Analysts International Corp. 06/07/1966
Each share Common 10¢ par exchanged for (0.5) share Common 10¢ par
(See Analysts International Corp.)

NUCLEONIC INDS INC (AZ)
Charter revoked for failure to file reports and pay fees 12/26/1972

NUCLEONIC PRODS INC (DE)
Merged into Semiconductor Electronics Inc. 12/12/1975
Each share Common 25¢ par exchanged for $3.50 cash

NUCLEONICS, CHEMISTRY & ELECTRONICS SHARES, INC. (DE)
Merged into Research Investing Corp. 12/31/1964
Each share Capital Stock $1 par exchanged for (1.001) shares Capital Stock $1 par
Research Investing Corp. name changed to Lexington Research Investing Corp. 04/18/1967 which name changed to Lexington Research Fund, Inc. (NJ) 04/28/1969 which reincorporated in Maryland as Lexington Growth & Income Fund, Inc. 04/30/1991 which name changed to Pilgrim Growth & Income Fund, Inc. 07/26/2000 which name changed to ING Large Company Value Fund, Inc. 03/01/2002
(See ING Large Company Value Fund, Inc.)

NUCLEONICS CORP (CA)
Charter cancelled for failure to file reports and pay taxes 1/3/84

NUCLEUS BIOSCIENCE INC (BC)
Merged into SNB Capital Corp. 05/20/2003
Each share Common no par exchanged for (0.3319) share Common no par
SNB Capital Corp. name changed to

Protox Therapeutics Inc. 07/14/2004 which name changed to Sophiris Bio Inc. 04/05/2012

NUCLEUS INC (NV)
Reorganized under the laws of Delaware as eNucleus, Inc. 07/14/2000
Each share Common $0.001 par exchanged for (1) share Common $0.001 par
eNucleus, Inc. recapitalized as EC Development, Inc. 08/10/2010
(See EC Development, Inc.)

NUCO PETROLEUMS LTD. (AB)
Acquired by Kodiak Petroleum Ltd. 02/13/1963
Each share Capital Stock no par exchanged for (0.0280) share Common no par
Kodiak Petroleums Ltd. acquired by Manhattan Continental Development Corp. 10/02/1969
(See Manhattan Continental Development Corp.)

NUCO2 INC (FL)
Merged into Aurora Capital Group 05/28/2008
Each share Common $0.001 par exchanged for $30 cash

NUCON-RF INC (NV)
Name changed to NNRF, Inc. 09/10/2007

NUCONTEX CORP (ON)
Delisted from Toronto Venture Stock Exchange 11/14/2002

NUCORE RES LTD (BC)
Acquired by Norcan Resources Ltd. 08/19/1994
Each share Common no par exchanged for (0.56497175) share Common no par
Norcan Resources Ltd. recapitalized as Odyssey Exploration Inc. 06/07/2000 which recapitalized as Consolidated Odyssey Exploration Inc. 12/08/2000 which reorganized as Odyssey Petroleum Corp. 08/25/2005 which recapitalized as Petrichor Energy Inc. 03/03/2011

NUCORP ENERGY INC NEW (OH)
Merged into Nucorp Inc. (DE) 08/18/1988
Each share Common no par exchanged for (1) share Common 5¢ par
Nucorp Inc. (DE) name changed to Capsure Holdings Corp. 06/07/1993 which merged into CNA Surety Corp. 09/30/1997
(See CNA Surety Corp.)

NUCORP ENERGY INC OLD (OH)
Name changed 05/23/1980
Class A no par reclassified as Common no par 07/20/1976
Name changed from Nucorp Inc. to Nucorp Energy, Inc. (Old) 05/23/1980
Stock Dividend - 50% 06/15/1981
Plan of reorganization under Chapter 11 Federal Bankruptcy proceedings confirmed 07/31/1986
No stockholders' equity

NUCORP INC (DE)
Name changed to Capsure Holdings Corp. 06/07/1993
Capsure Holdings Corp. merged into CNA Surety Corp. 09/30/1997
(See CNA Surety Corp.)

NUCORR PETES LTD (CANADA)
Acquired by 168316 Canada Ltd. 03/01/1990
Each share Common no par exchanged for $0.0001 cash

NUCOTEC INC (NV)
Name changed to Tornado Gold International Corp. (NV) 07/07/2004
Tornado Gold International Corp. (NV) reincorporated in Delaware 02/28/2007

(See Tornado Gold International Corp.)

NUCRYST PHARMACEUTICALS CORP (AB)
Issue Information - 4,500,000 shares COM offered at $10 per share on 12/21/2005
Acquired by Westaim Corp. 02/09/2010
Each share Common no par exchanged for USD $1.77 cash

NUDULAMA MINES LTD (ON)
Recapitalized as Anglo Dominion Gold Exploration Ltd. 03/06/1979
Each share Capital Stock no par exchanged for (0.25) share Capital Stock no par
Anglo Dominion Gold Exploration Ltd. merged into QSR Ltd. 09/07/1993 which name changed to Coniagas Resources Ltd. 06/25/1999 which name changed to Lithium One Inc. 07/23/2009
(See Lithium One Inc.)

NUENERGY GROUP INC (DE)
Common $0.001 par split (2) for (1) by issuance of (1) additional share payable 08/20/2003 to holders of record 08/14/2003 Ex date - 08/21/2003
Recapitalized as Rising India Inc. 05/14/2009
Each share Common $0.001 par exchanged for (0.004) share Common $0.001 par
Rising India Inc. name changed to Rising Biosciences, Inc. 05/31/2018

NUEQUUS PETE CORP (BC)
Name changed to Equus Energy Corp. 11/28/2002
Equus Energy Corp. recapitalized as Habibi Resources Corp. 08/27/2008 which recapitalized as One World Investments Inc. 10/07/2009 which name changed to One World Minerals Inc. 02/28/2017 which name changed to One World Lithium Inc. 01/19/2018

NUEVO ENERGY CO (DE)
Merged into Plains Exploration & Production Co. 05/14/2004
Each share Common 1¢ par exchanged for (1.765) shares Common 1¢ par
Plains Exploration & Production Co. merged into Freeport-McMoRan Copper & Gold Inc. 05/31/2013 which name changed to Freeport-McMoRan Inc. 07/14/2014

NUEVO FING I (DE)
$2.875 Guaranteed Term Ser. A called for redemption at $50 on 6/29/2004

NUEVO GRUPO IUSACELL S A DE C V (MEXICO)
Name changed to Grupo Iusacell S.A. de C.V. (New) 5/8/2000
(See Grupo Iusacell S.A. de C.V. (New))

NUFCOR URANIUM LTD (GUERNSEY)
Name changed to Uranium Ltd. 09/21/2009
Uranium Ltd. merged into Uranium Participation Corp. 03/30/2010

NUFORT RES INC (UT)
Name changed to Mikotel Networks Inc. 5/9/2000
Mikotel Networks Inc. recapitalized as Wabi Exploration Inc. 3/4/2005

NUGAS LTD (CANADA)
Merged into Q Energy Ltd. 09/16/1997
Each share Common no par exchanged for (1) share Common no par and $3.60 cash
(See Q Energy Ltd.)

NUGGET EXPL INC (NV)
Each shares old Common 1¢ par exchanged for (0.0032258) share new Common 1¢ par 10/21/1998
Name changed to GoHealth.MD, Inc. 01/24/2000
GoHealth.MD, Inc. recapitalized as Tree Top Industries, Inc. 09/18/2006 which name changed to Global Tech Industries Group, Inc. 07/07/2016

NUGGET GOLD MINES INC (UT)
Involuntarily dissolved 08/01/1988

NUGGET INC (FL)
Name changed to Specialized Medical Services, Inc. 9/12/88
Specialized Medical Services, Inc. name changed to SMS Group Inc. 12/18/89 which name changed to Natural Resources Recovery Inc. 11/8/90 which name changed to Rare Earth Metals, Inc. (FL) 3/13/92 which reorganized in Delaware as Americare Health Group Inc. 3/3/93 which name changed to Zagreus Inc. 3/26/99

NUGGET OIL CORP (MN)
Reorganized under the laws of Nevada as Midcoast Energy Resources, Inc. 9/15/92
Each (750) shares Common 10¢ par exchanged for (1) share Common 1¢ par
Midcoast Energy Resources, Inc. (NV) reincorporated in Texas 9/24/99
(See Midcoast Energy Resources, Inc.)

NUGGET RES INC (AB)
Reorganized under the laws of British Columbia as Peninsula Resources Ltd. 05/09/2008
Each share Class A Common no par exchanged for (0.06666666) share Class A Common no par par
Peninsula Resources Ltd. (BC) reincorporated in Alberta as Zodiac Exploration Inc. 10/06/2010 which recapitalized as Mobius Resources Inc. 05/01/2014 which name changed to Sintana Energy Inc. 08/10/2015

NUGGET RES INC (NV)
Name changed to American Lithium Minerals, Inc. 03/20/2009

NUGOLD ENTERPRISES CORP (BC)
Merged into United Gold Corp. 11/20/1984
Each share Common no par exchanged for (0.2) share Common no par
United Gold Corp. merged into ABM Gold Corp. 11/17/1989 which reorganized as NorthWest Gold Corp. 06/01/1990 which merged into Northgate Exploration Ltd. (ON) 06/08/1993 which reincorporated in British Columbia 07/01/2001 which name changed to Northgate Minerals Corp. 05/20/2004 which merged into AuRico Gold Inc. 10/26/2011

NUI CORP NEW (NJ)
Merged into AGL Resources Inc. 11/30/2004
Each share Common no par exchanged for $13.70 cash

NUI CORP OLD (NJ)
Common $10 par changed to $7 par and (0.5) additional share issued 4/15/87
Under plan of reorganization each share Common no par automatically became (1) share NUI Corp. (New) Common no par 3/1/2001
(See NUI Corp. (New))

NUINSCO RES LTD (BC)
Reincorporated under the laws of Ontario 7/26/89

NUKO INFORMATION SYS INC (DE)
Reincorporated 1/8/97
Each share old Common 1¢ par exchanged for (1/3) share new Common 1¢ par 5/27/94
State of incorporation changed from (NY) to (DE) 1/8/97
Chapter 11 Federal Bankruptcy proceedings converted to Chapter 7 on 2/4/2003
Stockholders' equity unlikely

NULOCH RES INC (AB)
Merged into Magnum Hunter Resources Corp. 05/03/2011
Each share Class A Common no par exchanged for either (0.3304) share Common 1¢ par or (0.3304) MHR Exchangeco Corp. Exchangeable Share no par
Note: Canadian residents option to receive Exchangeable Shares expired 04/27/2011
Unexchanged certificates were cancelled and become without value 05/03/2016
(See each company's listing)

NUMAC ENERGY INC (AB)
Merged into Anderson Exploration Ltd. 2/14/2001
Each share Common no par exchanged for $8 cash

NUMAC OIL & GAS LTD (AB)
Common no par split (2) for (1) by issuance of (1) additional share 9/12/78
Common no par split (2) for (1) by issuance of (1) additional share 12/9/83
Merged into Numac Energy Inc. 8/31/93
Each share Common no par exchanged for (1) share Common no par
(See Numac Energy Inc.)

NUMALAKE MINES LTD. (ON)
Under plan of merger name changed to New Taku Mines Ltd. 04/22/1954
New Taku Mines Ltd. name changed to Rembrandt Gold Mines Ltd. (ON) 10/17/1974 which reincorporated in Canada 08/04/1992 which reincorporated in Cayman Islands 05/16/1996
(See Rembrandt Gold Mines Ltd.)

NUMAQUE MINING CO.
Acquired by Union Mining Corp. 00/00/1945
Each share Common exchanged for (0.33333333) share Common no par
Union Mining Corp. name changed to Union Gold Inc. 03/05/1993 which merged into Jubilee Gold Inc. 01/01/2010 which merged into Jubilee Gold Exploration Ltd. 01/25/2013

NUMAR CORP (PA)
Issue Information - 1,800,000 shares COM offered at $12.50 per share on 04/14/1994
Merged into Halliburton Co. 9/30/97
Each share Common 1¢ par exchanged for (0.9664) share Common $2.50 par

NUMBEER INC (NV)
Name changed to eFleets Corp. 02/10/2014

NUMBER NINE VISUAL TECHNOLOGY CORP (DE)
Recapitalized as International Precious Minerals Group, Inc. 5/5/2005
Each share Common 1¢ par exchanged for (0.01) share Common 1¢ par

NUMBER ONE BANCORP INC (PA)
Merged into Merchants Bancorp, Inc. (PA) 03/01/1985
Each share Common $2 par exchanged for (0.7) share Common $3 par
Merchants Bancorp, Inc. (PA) acquired by Fidelcor, Inc. 12/31/1986 which merged into First Fidelity Bancorporation (New) 02/29/1988 which merged into First Union Corp. 01/01/1996 which name changed to Wachovia Corp. (Ctfs. dated after 09/01/2001) 09/01/2001 which merged into Wells Fargo & Co. (New) 12/31/2008

NO 1 COUSIN ORGANIZATION INC (NV)
Name changed to J & J Research Inc. and Common $0.0001 par changed to $0.001 par 2/11/86

NUMBER 1 SPORTS FAN INC (FL)
Each share old Common $0.00001 par exchanged for (0.05) share new Common $0.00001 par 09/10/1989
Administratively dissolved 10/11/1991

NO 6 MOTEL LTD (BC)
Stock Dividend - 10% 09/30/1981
Name changed to Economy Inns, Inc. 11/18/1982
Economy Inns, Inc. name changed to Mintel International Development Corp. 11/01/1985 which recapitalized as Golden Trump Resources Ltd. 04/05/1989 which recapitalized as Golden Triumph Resources Ltd. 09/11/2002
(See Golden Triumph Resources Ltd.)

NUMED HOME HEALTH CARE INC (FL)
Each share old Common $0.001 par exchanged for (0.4) share new Common $0.001 par 04/29/1994
Name changed to White Knight SST, Inc. 01/27/2004
White Knight SST, Inc. name changed to Online Sales Strategies, Inc. 09/12/2005 which recapitalized as Growth Technologies International, Inc. 12/20/2007 which recapitalized as Alternafuels, Inc. 03/18/2011
(See Alternafuels, Inc.)

NUMED SURGICAL INC (NV)
Recapitalized as Nutriceuticals.com Corp. 4/6/99
Each share Common $0.001 par exchanged for (0.02) share Common no par
Nutriceuticals.com Corp. name changed to DrugMax.com, Inc. 1/11/2000 which recapitalized as DrugMax, Inc. 9/7/2001 which name changed to Familymeds Group, Inc. 7/10/2006

NUMEDIA GAMES INC (BC)
Recapitalized as Brandgamz Marketing Inc. 06/04/2008
Each share Common no par exchanged for (0.2) share Common no par

NUMERAX INC (DE)
Merged into McGraw-Hill, Inc. 06/10/1986
Each share Common 1¢ par exchanged for $12.62 cash

NUMEREX CORP (MN)
Merged into XYZ Opitcal Corp. Acquiring Co. 10/18/89
Each share Common 1¢ par exchanged for $4.25 cash

NUMEREX CORP (PA)
Reincorporated 06/21/1994
State of incorporation changed from (NY) to (PA) and Common $0.001 par reclassified as Class A Common $0.001 par 06/21/1994
Class A Common $0.001 par split (5) for (2) by issuance of (1.5) additional shares 10/28/1994
Merged into Sierra Wireless, Inc. 12/07/2017
Each share Class A Common $0.001 par exchanged for (0.18) Class A Common no par

NUMERIC DATA SYS INC (NY)
Liquidation completed
Each share Common 1¢ par exchanged for initial distribution of $0.41 cash 02/23/1981

Each share Common 1¢ par received second distribution of $0.38 cash 01/28/1982
Each share Common 1¢ par received third and final distribution of $0.46 cash 03/18/1983

NUMERIC ONE CORP (NV)
Charter revoked for failure to file reports and pay fees 06/01/1990

NUMERICA FINL CORP (NH)
Filed a petition under Chapter 7 Federal Bankruptcy Code 06/04/1996
Stockholders' equity unlikely

NUMERICA SVGS BK FSB (MANCHESTER, NH)
Reorganized as Numerica Financial Corp. 10/03/1985
Each share Common $1 par exchanged for (2) shares Common $1 par
(See Numerica Financial Corp.)

NUMERICAL CONTROL CORP. (CA)
Completely liquidated 3/2/66
Each share Capital Stock no par exchanged for first and final distribution of (1.136) shares Century Geophysical Corp. Common $1 par
(See Century Geophysical Corp.)

NUMERICAL CTL EDUCATION & CONSULTING INC (DE)
Name changed to NC Sciences, Inc. 10/27/1969
NC Sciences, Inc. name changed to BGI Corp. 02/02/1971 which name changed to Frontier U.S.A. Corp. 06/07/1976

NUMERICAL TECHNOLOGIES INC (DE)
Issue Information - 5,534,000 shares COM offered at $14 per share on 04/07/2000
Merged into Synopsys, Inc. 3/3/2003
Each share Common $0.0001 par exchanged for $7 cash

NUMERICOM INC (DE)
Class B Common 1¢ par reclassified as Class A Common 1¢ par 06/04/1986
Each share Class A Common 1¢ par exchanged for (1) share Common 1¢ par 07/21/1986
Each share Common 1¢ par exchanged for (0.1) share Common 10¢ par 06/12/1990
Name changed to Infotex Holdings, Inc. 04/19/2005
Infotex Holdings, Inc. name changed to Integrated Camera Optics, Corp. 12/19/2005 which recapitalized as Global Healthcare & Education Management, Inc. 09/27/2007

NUMEX CORP (DE)
Each share Common 1¢ par exchanged for (1/3) share Common 10¢ par 08/30/1985
Name changed to InternetMercado.com, Inc. 09/27/2000
InternetMercado.com, Inc. name changed to New Century Companies, Inc. 06/07/2001 which name changed to U.S. Aerospace, Inc. 04/27/2010

NUMINE RES LTD (BC)
Name changed to Sunset Cove Mining Inc. 12/13/2010
Sunset Cove Mining Inc. name changed to Manganese X Energy Corp. 12/02/2016

NUMISMATIC CORP. OF AMERICA (NY)
Name changed to Metropolitan Communications, Inc. 6/30/66
Metropolitan Communications, Inc. name changed to Dynatek Industries, Inc. 9/12/68
(See Dynatek Industries, Inc.)

NUMOBILE INC (NV)
Each share old Common $0.001 par exchanged for (0.02) share new Common $0.001 par 09/03/2010
Recapitalized as Priority Aviation, Inc. 01/06/2014
Each share new Common $0.001 par exchanged for (0.001) share Common $0.001 par

NUNAVIK NICKEL MINES LTD (BC)
Name changed to Val-d'Or Mining Corp. 08/01/2017

NUNN BUSH & WELDON SHOE CO.
Name changed to Nunn-Bush Shoe Co. in 1935
Nunn-Bush Shoe Co. name changed to N.B.S. Co., Inc. 8/31/67
(See N.B.S. Co., Inc.)

NUNN-BUSH SHOE CO. (WI)
Each share Capital Stock no par exchanged for (3) shares Common $2.50 par 00/00/1936
Name changed to N.B.S. Co., Inc. 08/31/1967
(See N.B.S. Co., Inc.)

NUNNALLY CO.
Name changed to Columbus Transportation Co. in 1943
Columbus Transportation Co. liquidation completed 8/4/69

NUOASIS GAMING INC (DE)
Name changed to Group V Corp. 06/12/1997
Group V Corp. name changed to TotalAxcess.com, Inc. 05/17/1999
(See TotalAxcess.com, Inc.)

NUOASIS PPTYS INC (NV)
Recapitalized as Northamerican Energy Group Corp. 4/18/2005
Each share Common $0.001 par exchanged for (0.5) share Common $0.001 par

NUOASIS RESORTS INC (NV)
Recapitalized as Leonidas Films, Inc. 02/08/2006
Each share Common 1¢ par exchanged for (0.02) share Common 1¢ par
Leonidas Films, Inc. recapitalized as Consolidated Pictures Group, Inc. 06/09/2009
(See Consolidated Pictures Group, Inc.)

NUOILCO INC (NV)
Name changed to System Controls Inc. 12/03/1992
(See System Controls Inc.)

NUPAC INTL INC (NV)
Each share old Common $0.001 par exchanged for (0.1) share new Common $0.001 par 01/28/2003
Recapitalized as International Mart Corp. 04/01/2003
Each share new Common $0.001 par exchanged for (0.1) share Common $0.001 par
International Mart Corp. recapitalized as Sycamore Development Group, Inc. 11/20/2006 which name changed to ReBuilder Medical Technologies, Inc. 03/20/2007 which name changed to Lion Gold Brazil, Inc. 08/23/2012 which recapitalized as Cannabiz Mobile, Inc. 06/24/2014

NUPACK CORP. (IA)
Charter revoked for failure to file reports and pay fees 11/22/63

NUPATHE INC (DE)
Issue Information - 5,000,000 shares COM offered at $10 per share on 08/05/2010
Merged into Teva Pharmaceutical Industries Ltd. 02/21/2014
Each share Common $0.001 par exchanged for (1) Contingent Value Right and $3.65 cash

NUPEC RES INC (WY)
Proclaimed dissolved for failure to file reports and pay fees 2/9/90

NUPRO INNOVATIONS INC (DE)
Recapitalized as SweetskinZ Holdings, Inc. 12/30/2005
Each (800) shares Common $0.001 par exchanged for (1) share Common $0.001 par
(See SweetskinZ Holdings, Inc.)

NUR ADVANCED TECHNOLOGIES LTD (ISRAEL)
Name changed to Nur Macroprinters Ltd. 11/16/1997
Nur Macroprinters Ltd. name changed to Ellomay Capital Ltd. 04/30/2008

NUR MACROPRINTERS LTD (ISRAEL)
Name changed to Ellomay Capital Ltd. 04/30/2008

NURESCELL INC (NV)
Each share old Common no par exchanged for (0.001) share new Common no par 04/22/2005
Name changed to House of Taylor Jewelry, Inc. 05/23/2005
(See House of Taylor Jewelry, Inc.)

NUROVYSN BIOTECH CORP (NV)
Dissolved 10/06/2006
Details not available

NURSE SOLUTIONS INC (NV)
Common $0.001 par split (5) for (1) by issuance of (4) additional shares payable 10/10/2008 to holders of record 09/15/2005 Ex date - 10/14/2008
Name changed to Sync2 Entertainment Corp. 10/14/2008
Sync2 Entertainment Corp. recapitalized as iGen Networks Corp. 06/30/2009

NURSES NETWORK COM INC (FL)
Reorganized under the laws of Delaware as Scandia Inc. 04/29/2008
Each share Common 1¢ par exchanged for (0.05) share Common 1¢ par

NURSING CTRS INC (FL)
Name changed to First Atlas Corp. 9/14/72
First Atlas Corp. recapitalized as First Allied Corp. 7/6/73
(See First Allied Corp.)

NURUN INC (CANADA)
Merged into Quebecor Media Inc. 02/27/2008
Each share Common no par exchanged for $4.75 cash

NUSPAR RES LTD (BC)
Struck off register and declared dissolved for failure to file returns 9/29/95

NUSRALA-BOWEN SHOE CO. (MO)
Name changed to Nusrala Shoe Co., Inc. 10/29/58

NUSSENTIALS HLDGS INC (NV)
Recapitalized as Alternate Energy Holdings, Inc. 09/20/2006
Each (67) shares Common $0.001 par exchanged for (1) share Common $0.001 par

NUSTAR GP HLDGS LLC (DE)
Merged into NuStar Energy L.P. 07/20/2018
Each Unit exchanged for (0.55) Common Unit

NUSTAR RES INC (BC)
Merged into Canstar Resources Inc. 4/7/2005
Each share Common no par exchanged for (1) share Common no par

NUSTATE ENERGY HLDGS INC (FL)
Reincorporated 10/28/2015
State of incorporation changed from (NV) to (FL) and Common $0.001 par changed to $0.0001 par 10/28/2015
Each share old Common $0.0001 par exchanged for (0.00066666) share new Common $0.0001 par 06/13/2016
Recapitalized as Visium Technologies, Inc. 04/25/2018
Each share new Common $0.0001 par exchanged for (0.00033333) share Common $0.0001 par

NUT & CANDY KITCHEN INC (UT)
Proclaimed dissolved for failure to pay taxes 06/03/1988

NUTEC TRANSMISSION LTD (TX)
Reincorporated under the laws of Delaware as Aster Development Enterprises Ltd. 06/01/1992
Aster Development Enterprises Ltd. name changed to P A N Environmental Services Inc. 04/00/1993 which name changed to PAN Environmental Corp. 02/22/1994 which name changed to Pan International Gaming Inc. 12/30/1998 which name changed to SearchHound.com, Inc. 06/07/2000 which recapitalized as Coach Industries Group, Inc. 08/25/2003
(See Coach Industries Group, Inc.)

NUTECH DIGITAL INC (CA)
Each share old Common no par exchanged for (0.01666666) share new Common no par 05/12/2008
Name changed to Interlink-US-Network, Ltd. 10/10/2008
(See Interlink-US-Network, Ltd.)

NUTEK CORP (DE)
Company declared bankrupt in 1994
No stockholders' equity

NUTEK INC (NV)
Each share Common $0.001 par received distribution of (0.00425531) share Allenergy Inc. Common $0.001 par payable 04/30/1998 to holders of record 12/31/1997
Each share Common $0.001 par received distribution of (0.01) share Nutek Oil Inc. Common $0.001 par payable 08/01/2001 to holders of record 08/01/2001
Name changed to Datascension, Inc. 01/26/2004
Each share Common $0.001 par exchanged for (1) share Common $0.001 par
Note: Unexchanged certificates were cancelled and became without value 04/25/2004
(See Datascension, Inc.)

NUTEK OIL INC (NV)
Name changed to South Texas Oil Co. 04/04/2005
(See South Texas Oil Co.)

NUTMEG FED SVGS & LN ASSN (CT)
Common $0.005 par split (4) for (3) by issuance of (1/3) additional share payable 12/8/97 to holders of record 12/1/97
Common $0.005 par split (5) for (4) by issuance of (0.25) additional share payable 12/8/98 to holders of record 12/1/98
Stock Dividends - 5% payable 1/31/2000 to holders of record 12/8/99
Merged into NewMil Bancorp Inc. 11/20/2000
Each share Preferred Ser. B $0.005 par exchanged for either (1.469) shares Common 50¢ par, $14.665 cash, or a combination thereof
Each share Common $0.005 par exchanged for either (0.8394) share Common 50¢ par, $8.38 cash, or a combination thereof
Note: Option to receive stock or stock and cash expired 11/20/2000
NewMil Bancorp, Inc. merged into Webster Financial Corp. 10/6/2006

NUTMEG INDS INC (FL)
Common 1¢ par split (5) for (4) by issuance of (0.25) additional share 1/21/87

Common 1¢ par split (5) for (4) by issuance of (0.25) additional share 9/26/88
Common 1¢ par split (3) for (2) by issuance of (0.5) additional share 1/24/92
Common 1¢ par split (3) for (2) by issuance of (0.5) additional share 6/1/92
Merged into V.F. Corp. 1/31/94
Each share Common 1¢ par exchanged for $17.50 cash

NUTONE, INC. (DE)
Merged into Scovill Manufacturing Co. 9/15/67
Each share $1.28 Conv. Preferred Ser. A $5 par exchanged for (0.54) share $2.50 Conv. Preferred Ser. A no par
Each share Common $1 par exchanged for (0.5) share $2.50 Conv. Preferred Ser. A no par
Scovill Manufacturing Co. name changed to Scovill Inc. 7/6/79
(See Scovill Inc.)

NUTRACEA (CA)
Each share old Common no par exchanged for (0.1) share new Common no par 11/12/2003
Name changed to RiceBran Technologies 10/26/2012

NUTRACEUTICAL CLINICAL LABORATORIES INTERNATIONAL INC (FL)
Name changed 10/12/2001
Name changed from Nutraceutical Clinical Labs Inc. to Nutraceutical Clinical Laboratories International Inc. 10/12/2001
Name changed to Preservation Sciences, Inc. 06/27/2003
Preservation Sciences, Inc. name changed to eFUEL EFN, Corp. 02/08/2008

NUTRACEUTICAL INTL CORP (DE)
Acquired by HGGC, LLC 08/23/2017
Each share Common 1¢ par exchanged for $41.80 cash

NUTRACEUTIX INC (DE)
Name changed to SCOLR, Inc. 7/31/2002
SCOLR, Inc. name changed to SCOLR Pharma, Inc. 7/31/2004

NUTRADYNE GROUP INC (DE)
Name changed to China Yongxin Pharmaceuticals Inc. 05/15/2008

NUTRAGENICS INC (NV)
Name changed to Bionutrics, Inc. 1/1/97
Bionutrics, Inc. name changed to Synovics Pharmaceuticals, Inc. 4/11/2006

NUTRALOGIX LABS INC (NV)
Stock Dividend - 10% payable 09/12/2006 to holders of record 08/25/2006 Ex date - 08/23/2006
Recapitalized as Matrix Denture Systems International, Inc. 10/09/2007
Each (300) shares Common $0.001 par exchanged for (1) share Common $0.001 par

NUTRAMAX PRODS INC (DE)
Each share old Common $0.001 par exchanged for (0.04) share new Common $0.001 par 06/19/1991
Plan of reorganization under Chapter 11 Federal Bankruptcy proceedings effective 02/02/2001
Each share new Common $0.001 par received (1) Common Stock Subscription Right expiring 12/18/2000
Note: Certificates were not required to be surrendered and are without value
Merged into First Boston Pharma, L.L.C. 01/20/2009
Each share new Common $0.001 par exchanged for $0.922 cash

NUTRAMED CAP CORP (YT)
Reorganized under the laws of British Columbia as Winwell Ventures Inc. 06/14/2006
Each share Common no par exchanged for (0.33333333) share Common no par
Winwell Ventures Inc. (BC) reorganized in Nevada as Contact Gold Corp. 06/15/2017

NUTRASTAR INC (CA)
Name changed to NutraCea 08/12/2003
NutraCea name changed to RiceBran Technologies 10/26/2012

NUTRI BERRY INDS INC (NV)
Charter revoked for failure to file reports and pay fees 8/1/2004

NUTRI BEVCO INC (NY)
Chapter 11 bankruptcy proceedings converted to Chapter 7 on 6/28/90
Stockholders' equity unlikely

NUTRI FOODS INTL INC (NY)
Acquired by Coca-Cola Co. 12/17/1985
Each share Common 1¢ par exchanged for $10 cash

NUTRI-LABORATORIES, INC. (DC)
Charter revoked by the District of Columbia for failure to file reports 9/9/63

NUTRI-PRODS INC (FL)
Merged into Phoenix Advanced Technology, Inc. 9/24/90
Each share Common $0.0001 par exchanged for (4.69) shares Common $0.0001 par
Phoenix Advanced Technology, Inc. name changed to Global TeleMedia International, Inc. 2/13/95 which recapitalized as Seacoast Holding Corp. 1/26/2004

NUTRI SOURCE INDS INC (WA)
Recapitalized as Newmark Mining Corp. 01/31/2005
Each share Common $0.001 par exchanged for (0.01) share Common $0.001 par
Newmark Mining Corp. recapitalized as New Environmental Solutions, Inc. 09/22/2006
(See New Environmental Solutions, Inc.)

NUTRI SYS INC (DE)
Name changed to NutriSystem, Inc. 5/13/2003

NUTRI SYS INC (PA)
Common 1¢ par split (2) for (1) by issuance of (1) additional share 8/28/81
Common 1¢ par split (3) for (2) by issuance of (0.5) additional share 8/6/82
Acquired by a group of investors 8/18/86
Each share Common 1¢ par exchanged for $2.12 principal amount of Nutri/System, Inc. Discount Debentures due 8/15/2001 and $6.13 cash

NUTRIBRANDS INC (NV)
Name changed to St. James Capital Holdings, Inc. 04/25/2005
(See St. James Capital Holdings, Inc.)

NUTRICEUTICALS COM CORP (NV)
Each share old Common no par exchanged for (0.02) share new Common no par 3/16/99
New Common no par split (2) for (1) by issuance of (1) additional share payable 4/29/99 to holders of record 4/26/99
Each share new Common no par exchanged for (0.5) share Common $0.001 par 10/29/99
Name changed to DrugMax.com, Inc. 1/11/2000
DrugMax.com, Inc. name changed to DrugMax, Inc. 9/7/2001 which name changed to Familymeds Group, Inc. 7/10/2006

NUTRIENT COSMETIC LTD (DE)
Common 1¢ par changed to $0.005 par and (1) additional share issued 05/31/1972
Name changed to Channel Industries Ltd. 03/01/1982
(See Channel Industries Ltd.)

NUTRIFEEDS TECHNOLOGIES INC (NV)
Each share old Common $0.001 par exchanged for (0.05) share new Common $0.001 par 7/18/2003
Name changed to Advanced Solutions & Technologies, Inc. 1/16/2004
(See Advanced Solutions & Technologies, Inc.)

NUTRILAWN INTL INC (CANADA)
Recapitalized as Plus International Corp. 02/13/2001
Each share Common no par exchanged for (1/6) share Common no par
(See Plus International Corp.)

NUTRINE CANDY CO. (IL)
Liquidation completed in 1952

NUTRIONE CORP (FL)
Administratively dissolved for failure to file annual reports 09/25/2009

NUTRIPURE COM (NV)
Company terminated common stock registration and is no longer public as of 11/02/2000

NUTRISYSTEM COM INC (DE)
Name changed to Nutri/System, Inc. 09/25/2000
Nutri/System, Inc. name changed to NutriSystem, Inc. 05/13/2003

NUTRITION CTRS INC (DE)
Charter cancelled and declared inoperative and void for non-payment of taxes 04/15/1973

NUTRITION EXPRESS CORP (UT)
Name changed 01/31/1990
Name changed from Nutrition for Life, Inc. to Nutrition Express Corp. 01/31/1990
Merged into Nutrition for Life International, Inc. 06/24/1994
Each share Common $0.001 par exchanged for (0.02631578) share Common $0.001 par
Nutrition for Life International, Inc. reorganized as Advanced Nutraceuticals Inc. 03/15/2000 which recapitalized as Bactolac Pharmaceutical, Inc. 09/11/2006
(See Bactolac Pharmaceutical, Inc.)

NUTRITION EXPRESS CORP COLO INC (CO)
Merged into Nutrition for Life International, Inc. 06/24/1994
Each share Common $0.0001 par exchanged for (0.03333333) share Common $0.001 par
Nutrition for Life International, Inc. reorganized as Advanced Nutraceuticals Inc. 03/15/2000 which recapitalized as Bactolac Pharmaceutical, Inc. 09/11/2006
(See Bactolac Pharmaceutical, Inc.)

NUTRITION FOR LIFE INTL INC (TX)
Each share Common $0.001 par exchanged for (0.6) share Common 1¢ par 07/10/1995
Common 1¢ par split (2) for (1) by issuance of (1) additional share 12/08/1995
Under plan of reorganization each share Common 1¢ par automatically became (1) share Advanced Nutraceuticals Inc. Common 1¢ par 03/15/2000
Advanced Nutraceuticals Inc. recapitalized as Bactolac Pharmaceutical, Inc. 09/11/2006
(See Bactolac Pharmaceutical, Inc.)

NUTRITION MED INC (MN)
Each share old Common no par exchanged for (0.25) share new Common no par 6/10/98
Name changed to NM Holdings, Inc. 12/30/98
NM Holdings, Inc. name changed to Stockwalk.com Group, Inc. 7/13/99 which name changed to Stockwalk Group, Inc. 1/1/2001
(See Stockwalk Group, Inc.)

NUTRITION NOW INC (DE)
Each share Common $0.00001 par exchanged for (0.002) share Common $0.001 par 7/1/97
Each share Common $0.001 par received distribution of (1) share Northwest Natural Products Inc. Common payable 1/24/2002 to holders of record 1/10/2002
Each (35,000) shares old Common $0.001 par exchanged for (1) share new Common $0.001 par 6/9/2003
Note: In effect holders received $0.32 cash per share and public interest was eliminated

NUTRITION PEOPLE INC (NY)
Name changed to Star Mining, Inc. 10/30/79
Star Mining, Inc. name changed to Tech-Star International Inc. 3/29/84
(See Tech-Star International Inc.)

NUTRITION RESEARCH PRODUCTS CO. INC. (IN)
Charter revoked for failure to file annual reports 6/1/70

NUTRITION WORLD INC (MN)
Stock Dividend - 10% 11/09/1982
Name changed to Atlantic Group, Inc. 01/19/1988

NUTRONICS CORP (NV)
Recapitalized as Hallmark Research Corp. 3/13/98
Each share Common $0.001 par exchanged for (0.002) share Common $0.001 par
(See Hallmark Research Corp.)

NUTRONICS INTL INC (DE)
Each share old Common 1¢ par exchanged for (0.11416606) share new Common 1¢ par 12/31/97
Name changed to Trimol Group, Inc. 1/26/98

NUTRTION 21 INC (NY)
Plan of reorganization under Chapter 11 Federal Bankruptcy proceedings effective 01/13/2012
No stockholders' equity

NUTS & BOLTS INTL INC (NV)
Reorganized as Trendmaker Inc. Ltd. 06/10/2016
Each share Common $0.0001 par exchanged for (2) shares Common $0.0001 par

NUTT SALES, INC. (DE)
Name changed to Computer & Data Components Corp. 10/30/68
Computer & Data Components Corp. name changed to Arts & Science Technology, Inc. 2/1/72 which reorganized as Litex Energy Inc. 11/17/95 which recapitalized as International Ostrich Corp. 12/11/97

NUTTING INDUSTRIES, LTD. (WI)
Assets sold for benefit of creditors 11/29/71
No stockholders' equity

NUUKFJORD GOLD LTD (BC)
Name changed to Revolution Resources Corp. 09/08/2010
Revolution Resources Corp. recapitalized as IDM Mining Ltd. 06/11/2014

NUUVERA INC (ON)
Merged into Aphria Inc. 03/27/2018
Each share Common no par exchanged for (0.3546) share Common no par and $0.62 cash
Note: Unexchanged certificates will

be cancelled and become without value 03/27/2020

NUVA PHARMACEUTICALS INC (BC)
Name changed to Vanc Pharmaceuticals Inc. 08/07/2014

NUVEEN AMT-FREE MUN INCOME FD (MA)
Name changed 01/03/2012
Municipal Auction Rate Preferred Ser. T 1¢ par called for redemption at $25,000 on 08/22/2011
Municipal Auction Rate Preferred Ser. W 1¢ par called for redemption at $25,000 on 08/23/2011
Municipal Auction Rate Preferred Ser. W2 1¢ par called for redemption at $25,000 on 08/23/2011
Name changed from Nuveen Insured Tax-Free Advantage Municipal Fund to Nuveen AMT-Free Municipal Income Fund 01/03/2012
MuniFund Term Preferred Ser. 2015 1¢ par called for redemption at $10 plus $0.015042 accrued dividends on 12/20/2013
Variable Rate MuniFund Term Preferred 1¢ par called for redemption at $100,000 plus $14.986301 accrued dividends on 01/06/2014
Name changed to Nuveen AMT-Free Quality Municipal Income Fund 09/12/2016

NUVEEN ARIZ PREM INCOME MUN FD (MA)
Name changed 04/08/2013
Municipal Auction Rate Preferred Ser. TH 1¢ par split (2) for (1) by issuance of (1) additional share 01/07/1994
Municipal Auction Rate Preferred Ser. TH 1¢ par called for redemption at $25,000 on 08/24/2011
Name and state of incorporation changed from Nuveen Arizona Premium Income Municipal Fund Inc. (MN) to Nuveen Arizona Premium Income Municipal Fund (MA) and Common 1¢ par reclassified as Common Shares of Bene. Int. 1¢ par 04/08/2013
2.05% MuniFund Term Preferred Ser. 2015 1¢ par called for redemption at $10 plus $0.010819 accrued dividends on 12/20/2013
2.9% MuniFund Term Preferred Ser. 2016 1¢ par called for redemption at $10 plus $0.015306 accrued dividends on 12/20/2013
Variable Rate MuniFund Term Preferred Ser. 2014 1¢ par called for redemption at $100,000 on 01/06/2014
Name changed to Nuveen Arizona Quality Municipal Income Fund 12/28/2016

NUVEEN ARIZ DIVID ADVANTAGE MUN FD (MA)
Municipal Auction Rate Preferred 1¢ par called for redemption at $25,000 on 11/08/2010
Merged into Nuveen Arizona Premium Income Municipal Fund 04/08/2013
Each 2.05% MuniFund Term Preferred Share Ser. 2015 1¢ par exchanged for (1) 2.05% MuniFund Term Preferred Share Ser. 2015 1¢ par
Each Common Share of Bene. Int. 1¢ par exchanged for (1.00237402) Common Shares of Bene. Int. 1¢ par
Nuveen Arizona Premium Income Municipal Fund name changed to Nuveen Arizona Quality Municipal Income Fund 12/28/2016

NUVEEN ARIZ DIVID ADVANTAGE MUN FD 2 (MA)
Municipal Auction Rate Preferred Ser. W 1¢ par called for redemption at $25,000 on 11/08/2010
Merged into Nuveen Arizona Premium Income Municipal Fund 04/08/2013
Each 2.05% MuniFund Term Preferred Share Ser. 2015 1¢ par exchanged for (1) 2.05% MuniFund Term Preferred Share Ser. 2015 1¢ par
Each Common Share of Bene. Int. 1¢ par exchanged for (1.02270691) Common Shares of Bene. Int. 1¢ par
Nuveen Arizona Premium Income Municipal Fund name changed to Nuveen Arizona Quality Municipal Income Fund 12/28/2016

NUVEEN ARIZ DIVID ADVANTAGE MUN FD 3 (MA)
Municipal Auction Rate Preferred Ser. M 1¢ par called for redemption at $25,000 on 03/25/2011
Merged into Nuveen Arizona Premium Income Municipal Fund 04/08/2013
Each 2.9% MuniFund Term Preferred Share Ser. 2016 1¢ par exchanged for (1) 2.9% MuniFund Term Preferred Share Ser. 2016 1¢ par
Each Common Share of Bene. Int. 1¢ par exchanged for (0.99153069) Common Share of Bene. Int. 1¢ par
Nuveen Arizona Premium Income Municipal Fund name changed to Nuveen Arizona Quality Municipal Income Fund 12/28/2016

NUVEEN CALIF AMT-FREE MUN INCOME FD (MA)
Name changed 05/07/2012
Municipal Auction Rate Preferred Ser. TH 1¢ par called for redemption at $25,000 on 09/05/2008
Each share Variable Rate Demand Preferred 1¢ par exchanged for (1) share new Variable Rate Demand Preferred Ser. 2 1¢ par 06/24/2010
Under plan of merger name changed from Nuveen Insured California Tax-Free Advantage Municipal Fund to Nuveen California AMT-Free Municipal Income Fund 05/07/2012
2% MuniFund Term Preferred Ser. 2015 1¢ par called for redemption at $10 on 12/29/2014
Name changed to Nuveen California AMT-Free Quality Municipal Income Fund 12/28/2016

NUVEEN CALIF INVT QUALITY MUN FD INC (MN)
Municipal Auction Rate Preferred Ser. M 1¢ par split (2) for (1) by issuance of (1) additional share 01/07/1994
Municipal Auction Rate Preferred Ser. M 1¢ par called for redemption at $25,000 on 01/07/2011
Municipal Auction Rate Preferred Ser. W 1¢ par called for redemption at $25,000 on 01/11/2011
Each share 144A Variable Rate Demand Preferred Ser. 1 1¢ par exchanged for (1) share Variable Rate Demand Preferred Ser. 2 1¢ par 12/20/2012
Merged into Nuveen California Dividend Advantage Municipal Fund 06/09/2014
Each Variable Rate Demand Preferred Share Ser. 2 1¢ par exchanged for (1) 144A Variable Rate Demand Preferred Share Ser. 4 1¢ par
Each share Common 1¢ par exchanged for (1.03165896) Common Shares of Bene. Int. 1¢ par
Nuveen California Dividend Advantage Municipal Fund name changed to Nuveen California Quality Municipal Income Fund 11/07/2016

NUVEEN CALIF MUN INCOME FD INC (MN)
Under plan of reorganization each share Common 1¢ par exchanged for (1.160451) share Nuveen California Municipal Value Fund, Inc. Common 1¢ par 01/08/1996

NUVEEN CALIF MUN MKT OPPORTUNITY FD INC (MN)
Municipal Auction Rate Preferred Ser. W 1¢ par split (2) for (1) by issuance of (1) additional share 01/07/1994
Municipal Auction Rate Preferred Ser. F 1¢ par called for redemption at $25,000 on 04/22/2010
Municipal Auction Rate Preferred Ser. W 1¢ par called for redemption at $25,000 on 04/27/2010
Merged into Nuveen California Dividend Advantage Municipal Fund 06/09/2014
Each 144A Variable Rate Demand Preferred Share 1¢ par exchanged for (1) 144A Variable Rate Demand Preferred Share Ser. 3 1¢ par
Each share Common 1¢ par exchanged for (1.04765986) Common Shares of Bene. Int. 1¢ par
Nuveen California Dividend Advantage Municipal Fund name changed to Nuveen California Quality Municipal Income Fund 11/07/2016

NUVEEN CALIF PERFORMANCE PLUS MUN FD INC (MN)
Money Market Preferred Ser. F 1¢ par split (2) for (1) by issuance of (1) additional share 01/07/1994
Money Market Preferred Ser. T 1¢ par split (2) for (1) by issuance of (1) additional share 01/07/1994
Money Market Preferred Ser. F 1¢ par called for redemption at $25,000 on 01/06/2011
Money Market Preferred Ser. T 1¢ par called for redemption at $25,000 on 01/10/2011
Money Market Preferred Ser. W 1¢ par called for redemption at $25,000 on 01/11/2011
Merged into Nuveen California Dividend Advantage Municipal Fund 06/09/2014
Each 144A Variable Rate Demand Preferred Share Ser. 1 1¢ par exchanged for (1) 144A Variable Rate Demand Preferred Share Ser. 2 1¢ par
Each share Common 1¢ par exchanged for (1.0161855) Common Shares of Bene. Int. 1¢ par
Nuveen California Dividend Advantage Municipal Fund name changed to Nuveen California Quality Municipal Income Fund 11/07/2016

NUVEEN CALIF PREM INCOME MUN FD (MA)
Municipal Auction Rate Preferred Ser. M 1¢ par called for redemption at $25,000 on 10/15/2010
Merged into Nuveen California AMT-Free Municipal Income Fund 06/09/2014
Each share MuniFund Term Preferred Ser. 2015 1¢ par exchanged for (1) share 2% MuniFund Term Preferred Ser. 2015 1¢ par
Each Common Share of Bene. Int. 1¢ par exchanged for (1.02299895) Common Shares of Bene. Int. 1¢ par

NUVEEN CALIF QUALITY INCOME MUN FD INC (MN)
Municipal Auction Rate Preferred Ser. F 1¢ par split (2) for (1) by issuance of (1) additional share 01/07/1994
Municipal Auction Rate Preferred Ser. W 1¢ par split (2) for (1) by issuance of (1) additional share 01/07/1994
Municipal Auction Rate Preferred Ser. F 1¢ par called for redemption at $25,000 on 09/09/2010
Municipal Auction Rate Preferred Ser. M 1¢ par called for redemption at $25,000 on 09/10/2010
Municipal Auction Rate Preferred Ser. W 1¢ par called for redemption at $25,000 on 09/14/2010
Merged into Nuveen California Dividend Advantage Municipal Fund 06/09/2014
Each Variable Rate Demand Preferred Share 1¢ par exchanged for (1) 144A Variable Rate Demand Preferred Share Ser. 6 1¢ par
Each share Common 1¢ par exchanged for (1.06123458) Common Shares of Bene. Int. 1¢ par
Nuveen California Dividend Advantage Municipal Fund name changed to Nuveen California Quality Municipal Income Fund 11/07/2016

NUVEEN CALIF SELECT QUALITY MUN FD INC (MN)
Municipal Auction Rate Preferred Ser. T 1¢ par split (2) for (1) by issuance of (1) additional share 01/07/1994
Municipal Auction Rate Preferred Ser. TH 1¢ par split (2) for (1) by issuance of (1) additional share 01/07/1994
Municipal Auction Rate Preferred Ser. TH 1¢ par called for redemption at $25,000 on 09/08/2010
Municipal Auction Rate Preferred Ser. T 1¢ par called for redemption at $25,000 on 09/13/2010
Municipal Auction Rate Preferred Ser. W 1¢ par called for redemption at $25,000 on 09/14/2010
Merged into Nuveen California Dividend Advantage Municipal Fund 06/09/2014
Each Variable Rate Demand Preferred Share 1¢ par exchanged for (1) 144A Variable Rate Demand Preferred Share Ser. 5 1¢ par
Each share Common 1¢ par exchanged for for (1.04696102) Common Shares of Bene. Int. 1¢ par
Nuveen California Dividend Advantage Municipal Fund name changed to Nuveen California Quality Municipal Income Fund 11/07/2016

NUVEEN CALIF TAX FREE FD INC (MD)
Merged into Nuveen Money Market Trust 06/25/1999
Details not available

NUVEEN CALIF DIVID ADVANTAGE MUN FD (MA)
Auction Rate Municipal Preferred Ser. F 1¢ par called for redemption at $25,000 on 07/21/2011
Auction Rate Municipal Preferred Ser. TH 1¢ par called for redemption at $25,000 on 07/27/2011
Name changed to Nuveen California Quality Municipal Income Fund 11/07/2016

NUVEEN CALIF DIVID ADVANTAGE MUN FD 2 (MA)
Municipal Auction Rate Preferred Ser. F 1¢ par called for redemption at $25,000 on 04/20/2011
Municipal Auction Rate Preferred Ser. M 1¢ par called for redemption at $25,000 on 04/21/2011
2.05% MuniFund Term Preferred Ser. 2015 1¢ par called for redemption at $10 on 09/09/2013
2.35% MuniFund Term Preferred Ser. 2014 1¢ par called for redemption at $10 on 09/09/2013
Merged into Nuveen California Quality Municipal Income Fund 11/07/2016
Each 144A Variable Rate Demand Preferred Share Ser. 1 1¢ par exchanged for (1) 144A Variable Rate Demand Preferred Share Ser. 7 1¢ par
Each Common Share of Bene. Int. 1¢ par exchanged for (1.00120709)

Common Shares of Bene. Int. 1¢ par

NUVEEN CALIF DIVID ADVANTAGE MUN FD 3 (MA)

Municipal Auction Rate Preferred Ser. TH 1¢ par called for redemption at $25,000 on 06/29/2011
Municipal Auction Rate Preferred Ser. M 1¢ par called for redemption at $25,000 on 06/30/2011
2.25% MuniFund Term Preferred Ser. 2014-1 1¢ par called for redemption at $10 plus $0.00375 accrued dividends on 10/07/2013
2.35% MuniFund Term Preferred Ser. 2014 1¢ par called for redemption at $10 plus $0.00391667 accrued dividends on 10/07/2013
2.95% MuniFund Term Preferred Ser. 2015 1¢ par called for redemption at $10 plus $0.00491667 accrued dividends on 10/07/2013
Merged into Nuveen California Quality Municipal Income Fund 11/07/2016
Each 144A Variable Rate Demand Preferred Share Ser. 1 1¢ par exchanged for (1) 144A Variable Rate Demand Preferred Share Ser. 8 1¢ par
Each Common Share of Bene. Int. 1¢ par exchanged for (0.92770435) Common Share of Bene. Int. 1¢ par

NUVEEN CONN DIVID ADVANTAGE MUN FD (MA)

Municipal Auction Rate Preferred Ser. T 1¢ par called for redemption at $25,000 on 04/26/2010
Merged into Nuveen Connecticut Premium Income Municipal Fund 07/09/2012
Each share 2.60% MuniFund Term Preferred Ser. 2015 1¢ par exchanged for (1) share 2.60% MuniFund Term Preferred Ser. 2015 1¢ par
Each share Common 1¢ par exchanged for (1.02226025) shares Common 1¢ par
Nuveen Connecticut Premium Income Municipal Fund name changed to Nuveen Connecticut Quality Municipal Income Fund 12/28/2016

NUVEEN CONN DIVID ADVANTAGE MUN FD 2 (MA)

Municipal Auction Rate Preferred Ser. W 1¢ par called for redemption at $25,000 on 04/27/2010
Merged into Nuveen Connecticut Premium Income Municipal Fund 07/09/2012
Each share 2.60% MuniFund Term Preferred Ser. 2015 1¢ par exchanged for (1) share 2.60% MuniFund Term Preferred Ser. 2015-1 1¢ par
Each share Common 1¢ par exchanged for (1.01134322) shares Common 1¢ par
Nuveen Connecticut Premium Income Municipal Fund name changed to Nuveen Connecticut Quality Municipal Income Fund 12/28/2016

NUVEEN CONN DIVID ADVANTAGE MUN FD 3 (MA)

Municipal Auction Rate Preferred Ser. F 1¢ par called for redemption at $25,000 on 03/04/2010
Merged into Nuveen Connecticut Premium Income Municipal Fund 07/09/2012
Each share 2.65% MuniFund Term Preferred Ser. 2015 1¢ par exchanged for (1) share 2.65% MuniFund Term Preferred Ser. 2015-1 1¢ par
Each share Common 1¢ par exchanged for (0.9921122) share Common 1¢ par
Nuveen Connecticut Premium Income Municipal Fund name changed to Nuveen Connecticut Quality Municipal Income Fund 12/28/2016

NUVEEN CONN PREM INCOME MUN FD (MA)

Municipal Auction Rate Preferred Ser. TH 1¢ par split (2) for (1) by issuance of (1) additional share 01/07/1994
Municipal Auction Rate Preferred Ser. TH 1¢ par called for redemption at $25,000 on 01/05/2011
2.55% MuniFund Term Preferred Ser. 2016 1¢ par called for redemption at $10 plus $0.001417 accrued dividends on 03/03/2014
2.6% MuniFund Term Preferred Ser. 2015 1¢ par called for redemption at $10 plus $0.001444 accrued dividends on 03/03/2014
2.6% MuniFund Term Preferred Ser. 2015 #1 1¢ par called for redemption at $10 plus $0.001444 accrued dividends on 03/03/2014
2.65% MuniFund Term Preferred Ser. 2015 1¢ par called for redemption at $10 plus $0.001472 accrued dividends on 03/03/2014
2.65% MuniFund Term Preferred Ser. 2015 #1 1¢ par called for redemption at $10 plus $0.001472 accrued dividends on 03/03/2014
Name changed to Nuveen Connecticut Quality Municipal Income Fund 12/28/2016

NUVEEN DIVERSIFIED COMMODITY FD (DE)

Completely liquidated
Each Common Unit of Bene. Int. received first and final distribution of $9.6223 cash payable 01/03/2017 to holders of record 12/30/2016

NUVEEN DIVERSIFIED CURRENCY OPPORTUNITIES FD (MA)

Name changed 10/10/2012
Name changed from Nuveen Multi-Currency Short-Term Government Income Fund to Nuveen Diversified Currency Opportunities Fund 10/10/2012
Merged into Nuveen Global High Income Fund 11/24/2014
Each Common Share of Bene. Int. 1¢ par exchanged for (0.58838) Common Share of Bene. Int. 1¢ par

NUVEEN DIVERSIFIED DIVID & INCOME FD (MA)

FundPreferred Shares Ser. W 1¢ par called for redemption at $25,000 on 09/17/2009
FundPreferred Shares Ser. T 1¢ par called for redemption at $25,000 on 09/23/2009
(Additional Information in Active)

NUVEEN DIVID ADVANTAGE MUN FD (MA)

Auction Rate Municipal Preferred Ser. M 1¢ par called for redemption at $25,000 on 08/19/2011
Auction Rate Municipal Preferred Ser. T 1¢ par called for redemption at $25,000 on 08/22/2011
Auction Rate Municipal Preferred Ser. TH 1¢ par called for redemption at $25,000 on 08/24/2011
2.7% MuniFund Term Preferred Ser. 2015 1¢ par called for redemption at $10 plus $0.01425 accrued dividends on 12/20/2013
Variable Rate MuniFund Term Preferred Ser. 2014 1¢ par called for redemption at $100,000 plus $14.986301 accrued dividends on 01/06/2014
Under plan of merger name changed to Nuveen Quality Municipal Income Fund 09/12/2016

NUVEEN DIVID ADVANTAGE MUN FD 2 (MA)

Municipal Auction Rate Preferred Ser. F 1¢ par called for redemption at $25,000 on 09/02/2008
Municipal Auction Rate Preferred Ser. M 1¢ par called for redemption at $25,000 on 09/02/2008
Municipal Auction Rate Preferred Ser. T 1¢ par called for redemption at $25,000 on 09/03/2008
Each 144A Variable Rate Demand Preferred Share 1¢ par exchanged for (1) 144A Variable Rate Demand Preferred Share Ser. 2 1¢ par 06/24/2010
Merged into Nuveen Enhanced Municipal Credit Opportunities Fund 04/11/2016
Each 144A Variable Rate Demand Preferred Share Ser. 2 1¢ par exchanged for (1) 144A Variable Rate Demand Preferred Share Ser. 3 1¢ par
Each share Common 1¢ par exchanged for (0.9917157) Common Share of Bene. Int. 1¢ par
Nuveen Enhanced Municipal Credit Opportunities Fund name changed to Nuveen Municipal Credit Income Fund 12/28/2016

NUVEEN ENHANCED AMT-FREE MUN CR OPPORTUNITIES FD (MA)

Name changed 01/03/2012
Name changed 04/11/2016
Municipal Auction Rate Preferred Ser. M 1¢ par called for redemption at $25,000 on 09/30/2011
Municipal Auction Rate Preferred Ser. T 1¢ par called for redemption at $25,000 on 10/03/2011
Municipal Auction Rate Preferred Ser. TH 1¢ par called for redemption at $25,000 on 10/05/2011
Name changed from Nuveen Insured Dividend Advantage Municipal Fund to Nuveen Dividend Advantage Municipal Income Fund 01/03/2012
2.95% MuniFund Term Preferred Ser. 2014 1¢ par called for redemption at $10 plus $0.018028 accrued dividends on 12/23/2013
Variable Rate MuniFund Term Preferred Ser. 2014 1¢ par called for redemption at $100,066.602735 on 12/23/2013
Name changed from Nuveen Dividend Advantage Municipal Income Fund to Nuveen Enhanced AMT-Free Municipal Credit Opportunities Fund 04/11/2016
Name changed to Nuveen AMT-Free Municipal Credit Income Fund 12/28/2016

NUVEEN ENHANCED MUN CR OPPORTUNITIES FD (MA)

Name changed 04/11/2016
Municipal Auction Rate Preferred Ser. F 1¢ par called for redemption at $25,000 on 09/29/2011
Municipal Auction Rate Preferred Ser. W 1¢ par called for redemption at $25,000 on 10/04/2011
Municipal Auction Rate Preferred Ser. TH 1¢ par called for redemption at $25,000 on 10/05/2011
Variable Rate MuniFund Term Preferred Ser. 2014 1¢ par called for redemption at $100,000 on 04/11/2014
2.8% MuniFund Term Preferred Ser. 2016 1¢ par called for redemption at $10 on 04/11/2014
Name changed from Nuveen Dividend Advantage Municipal Fund 3 to Nuveen Enhanced Municipal Credit Opportunities Fund 04/11/2016
Name changed to Nuveen Municipal Credit Income Fund 12/28/2016

NUVEEN EQUITY PREM & GROWTH FD (MA)

Name changed to Nuveen S&P 500 Dynamic Overwrite Fund 12/22/2014

NUVEEN EQUITY PREM ADVANTAGE FD (MA)

Under plan of merger each share Common 1¢ par automatically became (0.70225331) Nuveen NASDAQ 100 Dynamic Overwrite Fund Common Share of Bene. Int. 1¢ par 12/22/2014

NUVEEN EQUITY PREM INCOME FD (MA)

Under plan of merger name changed to Nuveen S&P 500 Buy/Write Income Fund 12/22/2014

NUVEEN EQUITY PREM OPPORTUNITY FD (MA)

Merged into Nuveen S&P 500 Buy/Write Income Fund 12/22/2014
Each Common Share of Bene. Int. 1¢ par exchanged for (0.97897104) Common Share of Bene. Int. 1¢ par

NUVEEN FLA INVT QUALITY MUN FD (MA)

Municipal Auction Rate Preferred Ser. F 1¢ par split (2) for (1) by issuance of (1) additional share 01/07/1994
Municipal Auction Rate Preferred Ser. T 1¢ par split (2) for (1) by issuance of (1) additional share 01/07/1994
Merged into Nuveen Premium Income Municipal Fund 2, Inc. 10/17/2009
Each share Municipal Auction Rate Preferred Ser. F 1¢ par exchanged for (1) share Municipal Auction Rate Preferred Ser. F3 1¢ par
Each share Municipal Auction Rate Preferred Ser. T 1¢ par exchanged for (1) share Municipal Auction Rate Preferred Ser. T2 1¢ par
Each share Common 1¢ par exchanged for (0.97404707) share Common 1¢ par
Nuveen Premium Income Municipal Fund 2, Inc. merged into Nuveen AMT-Free Quality Municipal Income Fund 09/12/2016

NUVEEN FLA QUALITY INCOME MUN FD (MA)

Municipal Auction Rate Preferred Ser. M 1¢ par split (2) for (1) by issuance of (1) additional share 01/07/1994
Municipal Auction Rate Preferred Ser. TH 1¢ par split (2) for (1) by issuance of (1) additional share 01/07/1994
Merged into Nuveen Premium Income Municipal Fund 2, Inc. 10/17/2009
Each share Municipal Auction Rate Preferred Ser. F 1¢ par exchanged for (1) share Municipal Auction Rate Preferred Ser. F4 1¢ par
Each share Municipal Auction Rate Preferred Ser. M 1¢ par exchanged for (1) share Municipal Auction Rate Preferred Ser. M2 1¢ par
Each share Municipal Auction Rate Preferred Ser. TH 1¢ par exchanged for (1) share Municipal Auction Rate Preferred Ser. TH2 1¢ par
Each share Common 1¢ par exchanged for (1.00062326) shares Common 1¢ par
Nuveen Premium Income Municipal Fund 2, Inc. merged into Nuveen AMT-Free Quality Municipal Income Fund 09/12/2016

NUVEEN FLAGSHIP MULTISTATE TR II (MA)

Name changed to Nuveen Multistate Trust II 06/27/2000

NUVEEN FLEXIBLE INVT INCOME FD (MA)

Merged into Nuveen Preferred Income Opportunities Fund 06/12/2017
Each Common Share of Bene. Int. 1¢ par exchanged for (1.73985578) Common Shares of Bene. Int. 1¢ par
Nuveen Preferred Income Opportunities Fund name changed to Nuveen Preferred & Income Opportunities Fund 09/29/2017

NUVEEN FLOATING RATE INCOME FD (MA)

FundPreferred Shares Ser. W 1¢ par called for redemption at $25,000 on 09/17/2009

FundPreferred Shares Ser. F 1¢ par called for redemption at $25,000 on 09/21/2009
FundPreferred Shares Ser. M 1¢ par called for redemption at $25,000 on 09/22/2009
FundPreferred Shares Ser. T 1¢ par called for redemption at $25,000 on 09/23/2009
(Additional Information in Active)

NUVEEN FLOATING RATE INCOME OPPORTUNITY FD (MA)
FundPreferred Shares Ser. TH 1¢ par called for redemption at $25,000 on 09/18/2009
FundPreferred Shares Ser. F 1¢ par called for redemption at $25,000 on 09/21/2009
FundPreferred Shares Ser. M 1¢ par called for redemption at $25,000 on 09/22/2009
144A Variable Rate Preferred Ser. C-4 1¢ par called for redemption at $100,000 plus $188.27907 accrued dividends on 12/28/2016
(Additional Information in Active)

NUVEEN GA PREM INCOME MUN FD (MA)
Municipal Auction Rate Preferred Ser. TH 1¢ par called for redemption at $25,000 on 03/17/2010
Merged into Nuveen Georgia Dividend Advantage Municipal Fund 2 on 07/09/2012
Each share 2.65% MuniFund Term Preferred Ser. 2015 1¢ par exchanged for (1) share 2.65% MuniFund Term Preferred Ser. 2015-1 1¢ par
Each share Common 1¢ par exchanged for (1.02315988) shares Common 1¢ par
Nuveen Georgia Dividend Advantage Municipal Fund 2 name changed to Nuveen Georgia Quality Municipal Income Fund 12/28/2016

NUVEEN GA DIVID ADVANTAGE MUN FD (MA)
Municipal Auction Rate Preferred Ser. M 1¢ par called for redemption at $25,000 on 03/19/2010
Merged into Nuveen Georgia Dividend Advantage Municipal Fund 2 on 07/09/2012
Each share 2.65% MuniFund Term Preferred Ser. 2015 1¢ par exchanged for (1) share 2.65% MuniFund Term Preferred Ser. 2015-2 1¢ par
Each share Common 1¢ par exchanged for (1.05933737) shares Common 1¢ par
Nuveen Georgia Dividend Advantage Municipal Fund 2 name changed to Nuveen Georgia Quality Municipal Income Fund 12/28/2016

NUVEEN GA DIVID ADVANTAGE MUN FD 2 (MA)
Municipal Auction Rate Preferred Ser. F 1¢ par called for redemption at $25,000 on 02/25/2010
2.65% MuniFund Term Preferred Ser. 2015 1¢ par called for redemption at $10 on 05/30/2014
2.65% MuniFund Term Preferred Ser. 2015#1 1¢ par called for redemption at $10 on 05/30/2014
2.65% MuniFund Term Preferred Ser. 2015 #2 1¢ par called for redemption at $10 on 05/30/2014
Name changed to Nuveen Georgia Quality Municipal Income Fund 12/28/2016

NUVEEN GLOBAL EQUITY INCOME FD (MA)
Name changed 01/24/2014
Name changed from Nuveen Global Value Opportunities Fund to Nuveen Global Equity Income Fund 01/24/2014
Under plan of merger each Common Share of Bene. Int. 1¢ par automatically became (0.47919923) share Nuveen Investment Trust NWQ Global Equity Income Fund Class A 1¢ par 10/17/2016

NUVEEN GLOBAL INCOME OPPORTUNITIES FD (MA)
Name changed 10/10/2012
Name changed from Nuveen Global Government Enhanced Income Fund to Nuveen Global Income Opportunities Fund 10/10/2012
Merged into Nuveen Global High Income Fund 11/24/2014
Each Common Share of Bene. Int. exchanged exchanged for (0.64662) Common Share of Bene. Int. 1¢ par

NUVEEN INSD CALIF SELECT TAX FREE INCOME PORTFOLIO (MA)
Name changed to Nuveen California Select Tax Free Income Portfolio 2/22/2002

NUVEEN INSD FLA TAX-FREE ADVANTAGE MUN FD (MA)
Merged into Nuveen Insured Tax-Free Advantage Municipal Fund 10/17/2009
Each share Municipal Auction Rate Preferred 1¢ par exchanged for (1) share Municipal Auction Rate Preferred Ser. W2 1¢ par
Each share Common 1¢ par exchanged for (0.96498795) share Common 1¢ par
Nuveen Insured Tax-Free Advantage Municipal Fund name changed to Nuveen AMT-Free Municipal Income Fund 01/03/2012 which name changed to Nuveen AMT-Free Quality Municipal Income Fund 09/12/2016

NUVEEN INSD N Y SELECT TAX FREE INCOME PORTFOLIO (MA)
Name changed to Nuveen New York Select Tax-Free Income Portfolio 2/22/2002

NUVEEN INSD TAX FREE BD FD INC (MN)
Massachusetts Value Fund and New York Value Fund merged into Nuveen Flagship Multistate Trust II 01/31/1997
Details not available
Municipal Bond Fund merged into Nuveen Flagship Municipal Trust 01/31/1997
Details not available

NUVEEN INSD CALIF DIVID ADVANTAGE MUN FD (MA)
Municipal Auction Rate Preferred Ser. F 1¢ par called for redemption at $25,000 on 07/21/2011
Municipal Auction Rate Preferred Ser. T 1¢ par called for redemption at $25,000 on 07/25/2011
Merged into Nuveen California AMT-Free Municipal Income Fund 05/07/2012
Each share Variable Rate Demand Preferred Ser. 1 1¢ par exchanged for (1) share Variable Rate Demand Preferred Ser. 5 1¢ par
Each share Common 1¢ par exchanged for (1.06786763) shares Common 1¢ par
Nuveen California AMT-Free Municipal Income Fund name changed to Nuveen California AMT-Free Quality Municipal Income Fund 12/28/2016

NUVEEN INSD CALIF PREM INCOME MUN FD INC (MA)
Municipal Auction Rate Preferred Ser. T 1¢ par split (2) for (1) by issuance of (1) additional share 01/07/1994
Municipal Auction Rate Preferred Ser. T 1¢ par called for redemption at $25,000 on 04/26/2010
Merged into Nuveen California AMT-Free Municipal Income Fund 05/07/2012
Each share 144A Variable Rate Demand Preferred Ser. 1 1¢ par exchanged for (1) share Variable Rate Demand Preferred Ser. 3 1¢ par
Each share Common 1¢ par exchanged for (1.02343823) shares Common 1¢ par
Nuveen California AMT-Free Municipal Income Fund name changed to Nuveen California AMT-Free Quality Municipal Income Fund 12/28/2016

NUVEEN INSD CALIF PREM INCOME MUN FD 2 INC (MN)
Municipal Auction Rate Preferred Ser. T 1¢ par split (2) for (1) by issuance of (1) additional share 01/07/1994
Municipal Auction Rate Preferred Ser. TH 1¢ par split (2) for (1) by issuance of (1) additional share 01/07/1994
Municipal Auction Rate Preferred Ser. T 1¢ par called for redemption at $25,000 on 01/24/2011
Municipal Auction Rate Preferred Ser. TH 1¢ par called for redemption at $25,000 on 01/26/2011
Merged into Nuveen California AMT-Free Municipal Income Fund 05/07/2012
Each share Preferred Ser. 1 1¢ par exchanged for (1) share Variable Rate Demand Preferred Ser. 4 1¢ par
Each share Common 1¢ par exchanged for (1.02555679) shares Common 1¢ par
Nuveen California AMT-Free Municipal Income Fund name changed to Nuveen California AMT-Free Quality Municipal Income Fund 12/28/2016

NUVEEN INSD FLA PREM INCOME MUN FD (MA)
Merged into Nuveen Insured Municipal Opportunity Fund, Inc. 10/17/2009
Each share Municipal Auction Rate Preferred Ser. TH 1¢ par exchanged for (1) share Municipal Auction Rate Preferred Ser. TH3 1¢ par
Each share Municipal Auction Rate Preferred Ser. W 1¢ par exchanged for (1) share Municipal Auction Rate Preferred Ser. W3 1¢ par
Each share Common 1¢ par exchanged for (1.01988494) shares Common 1¢ par
Nuveen Insured Municipal Opportunity Fund, Inc. name changed to Nuveen Municipal Opportunity Fund, Inc. 01/03/2012 which merged into Nuveen Enhanced AMT-Free Municipal Credit Opportunities Fund 04/11/2016 which name changed to Nuveen AMT-Free Municipal Credit Income Fund 12/28/2016

NUVEEN INSD FLA PREM INCOME MUN FD 2 (MA)
Municipal Auction Rate Preferred Ser. W 1¢ par split (2) for (1) by issuance of (1) additional share 01/07/1994
Reorganized as Nuveen Insured Florida Premium Income Municipal Fund 01/09/1995
Each share Municipal Auction Rate Preferred Ser. W 1¢ par exchanged for (1) share Municipal Auction Rate Preferred Ser. W 1¢ par
Each share Common 1¢ par exchanged for (0.935807) share Common 1¢ par
Nuveen Insured Florida Premium Income Municipal Fund merged into Nuveen Insured Municipal Opportunity Fund, Inc. 10/17/2009 which name changed to Nuveen Municipal Opportunity Fund, Inc. 01/03/2012 which merged into Nuveen Enhanced AMT-Free Municipal Credit Opportunities Fund 04/11/2016 which name changed to Nuveen AMT-Free Municipal Credit Income Fund 12/28/2016

NUVEEN INSD N Y PREM INCOME MUN FD 2 (MA)
Municipal Auction Rate Preferred Ser. T 1¢ par split (2) for (1) by issuance of (1) additional share 01/07/1994
Reorganized as Nuveen Insured New York Premium Income Municipal Fund, Inc. 12/07/1994
Each share Municipal Auction Rate Preferred Ser. T 1¢ par exchanged for (1) share Municipal Auction Rate Preferred Ser. T 1¢ par
Each share Common 1¢ par exchanged for (0.941145) share Common 1¢ par
Nuveen Insured New York Premium Income Municipal Fund, Inc. name changed to Nuveen New York Premium Income Municipal Fund, Inc. 01/03/2012

NUVEEN INVT QUALITY MUN FD INC (MN)
Municipal Auction Rate Preferred Ser. F 1¢ par split (2) for (1) by issuance of (1) additional share 01/07/1994
Municipal Auction Rate Preferred Ser. M 1¢ par split (2) for (1) by issuance of (1) additional share 01/07/1994
Municipal Auction Rate Preferred Ser. T 1¢ par split (2) for (1) by issuance of (1) additional share 01/07/1994
Municipal Auction Rate Preferred Ser. W 1¢ par split (2) for (1) by issuance of (1) additional share 01/07/1994
Municipal Auction Rate Preferred Ser. F 1¢ par called for redemption at $25,000 on 05/26/2011
Municipal Auction Rate Preferred Ser. M 1¢ par called for redemption at $25,000 on 05/26/2011
Municipal Auction Rate Preferred Ser. T 1¢ par called for redemption at $25,000 on 05/27/2011
Municipal Auction Rate Preferred Ser. W 1¢ par called for redemption at $25,000 on 05/31/2011
Municipal Auction Rate Preferred Ser. TH 1¢ par called for redemption at $25,000 on 06/01/2011
Merged into Nuveen Quality Municipal Income Fund 09/12/2016
Each share 144A Variable Rate Demand Preferred Ser. 1 1¢ par exchanged for (1) share 144A Variable Rate Demand Preferred Ser. 1 1¢ par
Each share 144A Variable Rate MuniFund Term Preferred Ser. 2017 1¢ par exchanged for (1) share 144A Variable Rate MuniFund Term Preferred Ser. 2017 1¢ par
Each share Common 1¢ par exchanged for (1.02891867) shares Common 1¢ par

NUVEEN INVTS INC (DE)
Merged into Windy City Investments, Inc. 11/13/2007
Each share Class A Common 1¢ par exchanged for $65 cash

NUVEEN LONG/SHORT COMMODITY TOTAL RETURN FD (DE)
Completely liquidated
Each Common Unit of Bene. Int. received first and final distribution of $13.9241 cash payable 01/03/2017 to holders of record 12/30/2016

NUVEEN MD DIVID ADVANTAGE MUN FD 1 (MA)
Municipal Auction Rate Preferred Ser. M 1¢ par called for redemption at $25,000 on 05/07/2010
Merged into Nuveen Maryland Premium Income Municipal Fund 08/06/2012
Each share 2.6% MuniFund Term Preferred Ser. 2015 1¢ par exchanged for (1) share 2.6% MuniFund Term Preferred Ser. 2015 1¢ par
Each share Common 1¢ par

exchanged for (0.97225976) share Common 1¢ par
Nuveen Maryland Premium Income Municipal Fund name changed to Nuveen Maryland Quality Municipal Income Fund 12/28/2016

NUVEEN MD DIVID ADVANTAGE MUN FD 2 (MA)
- Municipal Auction Rate Preferred Ser. F 1¢ par called for redemption at $25,000 on 05/06/2010
- Merged into Nuveen Maryland Premium Income Municipal Fund 08/06/2012
- Each share 2.6% MuniFund Term Preferred Ser. 2015 1¢ par exchanged for (1) share 2.6% MuniFund Term Preferred Ser. 2015-1 1¢ par
- Each share Common 1¢ par exchanged for (0.98257669) share Common 1¢ par
- Nuveen Maryland Premium Income Municipal Fund name changed to Nuveen Maryland Quality Municipal Income Fund 12/28/2016

NUVEEN MD DIVID ADVANTAGE MUN FD 3 (MA)
- Municipal Auction Rate Preferred Ser. T 1¢ par called for redemption at $25,000 on 02/14/2011
- Merged into Nuveen Maryland Premium Income Municipal Fund 08/06/2012
- Each share 2.65% MuniFund Term Preferred Ser. 2015 1¢ par exchanged for (1) share 2.65% MuniFund Term Preferred Ser. 2015-1 1¢ par
- Each share 2.85% MuniFund Term Preferred Ser. 2016 1¢ par exchanged for (1) share 2.85% MuniFund Term Preferred Ser. 2016 1¢ par
- Each share Common 1¢ par exchanged for (0.97394118) share Common 1¢ par
- Nuveen Maryland Premium Income Municipal Fund name changed to Nuveen Maryland Quality Municipal Income Fund 12/28/2016

NUVEEN MD PREM INCOME MUN FD (MA)
- Municipal Auction Rate Preferred Ser. TH 1¢ par split (2) for (1) by issuance of (1) additional share 01/07/1994
- Municipal Auction Rate Preferred Ser. W 1¢ par called for redemption at $25,000 on 04/05/2011
- Municipal Auction Rate Preferred Ser. TH 1¢ par called for redemption at $25,000 on 04/06/2011
- 2.6% MuniFund Term Preferred Ser. 2015 1¢ par called for redemption at $10 on 05/30/2014
- 2.6% MuniFund Term Preferred Ser. 2015 #1 1¢ par callled for redemption at $10 on 05/30/2014
- 2.65% MuniFund Term Preferred Ser. 2015 1¢ par callled for redemption at $10 on 05/30/2014
- 2.65% MuniFund Term Preferred Ser. 2015 #1 1¢ par callled for redemption at $10 on 05/30/2014
- 2.85% MuniFund Term Preferred Ser. 2016 1¢ par called for redemption at $10 on 05/30/2014
- 2.9% MuniFund Term Preferred Ser. 2016 1¢ par called for redemption at $10 on 05/30/2014
- Name changed to Nuveen Maryland Quality Municipal Income Fund 12/28/2016

NUVEEN MD PREM INCOME MUN FD 2 (MA)
- Municipal Auction Rate Preferred Ser. W 1¢ par split (2) for (1) by issuance of (1) additional share 01/07/1994
- Under plan of reorganization each share Municipal Auction Rate Preferred Ser. W 1¢ par and Common 1¢ par automatically became (1) share Nuveen Maryland Premium Income Municipal Fund Municipal Auction Rate Preferred Ser. W 1¢ par or (0.980428) share Common 1¢ par respectively 12/08/1994
- Nuveen Maryland Premium Income Municipal Fund name changed to Nuveen Maryland Quality Municipal Income Fund 12/28/2016

NUVEEN MASS AMT-FREE MUN INCOME FD (MA)
Name changed 05/24/2012
- Municipal Auction Rate Preferred Ser. W 1¢ par called for redemption at $25,000 on 03/09/2010
- Name changed from Nuveen Insured Massachusetts Tax-Free Advantage Municipal Fund to Nuveen Massachusetts AMT-Free Municipal Income Fund 05/24/2012
- Merged into Nuveen Massachusetts Premium Income Municipal Fund 06/09/2014
- Each share 2.65% MuniFund Term Preferred Ser. 2015 1¢ par exchanged for (1) share 2.65% MuniFund Term Preferred Ser. 2015 #1 1¢ par
- Each Common Share of Bene. Int. 1¢ par exchanged for (0.96093745) Common Share of Bene. Int. 1¢ par
- Nuveen Massachusetts Premium Income Municipal Fund name changed to Nuveen Massachusetts Quality Municipal Income Fund 12/28/2016

NUVEEN MASS DIVID ADVANTAGE MUN FD (MA)
- Municipal Auction Rate Preferred Ser. T 1¢ par called for redemption at $25,000 on 04/19/2010
- Merged into Nuveen Massachusetts Premium Income Municipal Fund 06/09/2014
- Each share 2.6% MuniFund Term Preferred Ser. 2015 1¢ par exchanged for (1) share 2.6% MuniFund Term Preferred Ser. 2015 1¢ par
- Each Common Share of Bene. Int. 1¢ par exchanged for (0.99141407) Common Share of Bene. Int. 1¢ par
- Nuveen Massachusetts Premium Income Municipal Fund name changed to Nuveen Massachusetts Quality Municipal Income Fund 12/28/2016

NUVEEN MASS PREM INCOME MUN FD (MA)
- Municipal Auction Rate Preferred Ser. TH 1¢ par called for redemption at $25,000 on 02/16/2011
- 2.6% MuniFund Term Preferred Ser. 2015 1¢ par called for redemption at $10 on 07/11/2014
- 2.65% MuniFund Term Preferred Ser. 2015 1¢ par called for redemption at $10 on 07/11/2014
- 2.65% MuniFund Term Preferred Ser. 2015#1 1¢ par called for redemption at $10 on 07/11/2014
- 2.75% MuniFund Term Preferred Ser. 2016 1¢ par called for redemption at $10 on 07/11/2014
- Name changed to Nuveen Massachusetts Quality Municipal Income Fund 12/28/2016

NUVEEN MICH DIVID ADVANTAGE MUN FD (MA)
- Municipal Auction Rate Preferred Ser. W 1¢ par called for redemption at $25,000 on 12/07/2010
- Merged into Nuveen Michigan Quality Income Municipal Fund 01/07/2013
- Each MuniFund Term Preferred Share of Bene. Int. 1¢ par exchanged for (1) 2.3% Preferred Share of Bene. Int. Ser. 2015 1¢ par
- Each Common Share of Bene. Int. 1¢ par exchanged for (0.95647566) Common Share of Bene. Int. 1¢ par
- Nuveen Michigan Quality Income Municipal Fund name changed to Nuveen Michigan Quality Municipal Income Fund 12/28/2016

NUVEEN MICH PREMIUM INCOME MUN FD INC (MN)
- Municipal Auction Rate Preferred Ser. TH 1¢ par split (2) for (1) by issuance of (1) additional share 01/07/1994
- Municipal Auction Rate Preferred Ser. M 1¢ par called for redemption at $25,000 on 08/19/2011
- Municipal Auction Rate Preferred Ser. TH 1¢ par called for redemption at $25,000 on 08/24/2011
- Merged into Nuveen Michigan Quality Income Municipal Fund 01/07/2013
- Each Variable MuniFund Term Preferred Share of Bene. Int. 1¢ par exchanged for (1) share Variable MuniFund Term Preferred Share of Bene. Int. Ser. 2 1¢ par
- Each share Common 1¢ par exchanged for (0.96503389) Common Share of Bene. Int. 1¢ par
- Nuveen Michigan Quality Income Municipal Fund name changed to Nuveen Michigan Quality Municipal Income Fund 12/28/2016

NUVEEN MICH QUALITY INCOME MUN FD (MA)
Reorganized 01/07/2013
- Municipal Auction Rate Preferred Ser. TH 1¢ par split (2) for (1) by issuance of (1) additional share 01/07/1994
- Municipal Auction Rate Preferred Ser. F 1¢ par called for redemption at $25,000 on 08/04/2011
- Municipal Auction Rate Preferred Ser. TH 1¢ par called for redemption at $25,000 on 08/10/2011
- Under plan of reorganization each share Nuveen Michigan Quality Income Municipal Fund, Inc. (MN) Variable Rate MuniFund Term Preferred 1¢ par and Common 1¢ par automatically became (1) share Nuveen Michigan Quality Income Municipal Fund (MA) Variable Rate MuniFund Term Preferred Share of Bene. Int. Ser. 2014 1¢ par or Common Share of Bene. Int. 1¢ par respectively 01/07/2013
- Each Variable Rate MuniFund Term Preferred Share of Bene. Int. Ser. 2014 1¢ par automatically became (1) 144A Variable Rate MuniFund Term Preferred Share of Bene. Int. Ser. 2016 1¢ par 12/20/2013
- 2.3% MuniFund Term Preferred Shares of Bene. Int. Ser. 2015 1¢ par called for redemption at $10 plus $0.012139 accrued dividends on 12/20/2013
- Variable Rate MuniFund Term Preferred Shares of Bene. Int. Ser. 2014 #1 1¢ par called for redemption at $100,000 plus $14.986301 accrued dividends on 01/06/2014
- Name changed to Nuveen Michigan Quality Municipal Income Fund 12/28/2016

NUVEEN MINN MUN INCOME FD (MA)
- Name changed to Nuveen Minnesota Quality Municipal Income Fund 12/28/2016

NUVEEN MO PREM INCOME MUN FD (MA)
- Municipal Auction Rate Preferred Ser. TH 1¢ par split (2) for (1) by issuance of (1) additional share 01/07/1994
- Municipal Auction Rate Preferred Ser. TH 1¢ par called for redemption at $25,000 on 12/01/2010
- 2.1% MuniFund Term Preferred Ser. 2015 1¢ par called for redemption at $10 plus $0.04666 accrued dividends on 02/09/2015
- Name changed to Nuveen Missouri Quality Municipal Income Fund 12/28/2016

NUVEEN MULTI-MKT INCOME FD INC (VA)
- Reincorporated under the laws of Massachusetts as Nuveen Multi-Market Income Fund and Common 1¢ par reclassified as Common Shares of Bene. Int. 1¢ par 11/19/2014

NUVEEN MULTI-STRATEGY INCOME & GROWTH FD 2 (MA)
Name changed 05/07/2007
- Issue Information - 135,000,000 shares COM offered at $15 per share on 06/25/2003
- Name changed from Nuveen Preferred & Convertible Income Fund 2 to Nuveen Multi-Strategy Income & Growth Fund 2 on 05/07/2007
- FundPreferred Shares Ser. W 1¢ par called for redemption at $25,000 on 09/17/2009
- FundPreferred Shares Ser. W2 1¢ par called for redemption at $25,000 on 09/17/2009
- FundPreferred Shares Ser. TH 1¢ par called for redemption at $25,000 on 09/18/2009
- FundPreferred Shares Ser. TH2 1¢ par called for redemption at $25,000 on 09/18/2009
- FundPreferred Shares Ser. F 1¢ par called for redemption at $25,000 on 09/21/2009
- FundPreferred Shares Ser. F2 1¢ par called for redemption at $25,000 on 09/21/2009
- FundPreferred Shares Ser. M 1¢ par called for redemption at $25,000 on 09/22/2009
- FundPreferred Shares Ser. M2 1¢ par called for redemption at $25,000 on 09/22/2009
- FundPreferred Shares Ser. T 1¢ par called for redemption at $25,000 on 09/23/2009
- FundPreferred Shares Ser. T2 1¢ par called for redemption at $25,000 on 09/23/2009
- Name changed to Nuveen Credit Strategies Income Fund 04/02/2012

NUVEEN MULTISTATE TAX FREE TR (MA)
- Arizona Tax Free Value Fund, Florida Tax Free Value Fund, Maryland Tax Free Value Fund, Pennsylvania Tax Free Value Fund and Virginia Tax Free Value Fund merged into Nuveen Flagship Multistate Trust I 01/31/1997
- Details not available
- Michigan Tax Free Value Fund merged into Nuveen Flagship Multistate Trust IV 01/31/1997
- Details not available
- New Jersey Tax Free Value Fund merged into Nuveen Flagship Multistate Trust II 01/31/1997
- Details not available

NUVEEN MUN ADVANTAGE FD INC (MN)
- Municipal Auction Rate Preferred Ser. F 1¢ par split (2) for (1) by issuance of (1) additional share 01/07/1994
- Municipal Auction Rate Preferred Ser. M 1¢ par split (2) for (1) by issuance of (1) additional share 01/07/1994
- Municipal Auction Rate Preferred Ser. T 1¢ par split (2) for (1) by issuance of (1) additional share 01/07/1994
- Municipal Auction Rate Preferred Ser. W 1¢ par split (2) for (1) by issuance of (1) additional share 01/07/1994
- Municipal Auction Rate Preferred Ser. F 1¢ par called for redemption at $25,000 on 04/08/2010

Municipal Auction Rate Preferred Ser. M 1¢ par called for redemption at $25,000 on 04/09/2010
Municipal Auction Rate Preferred Ser. T 1¢ par called for redemption at $25,000 on 04/12/2010
Municipal Auction Rate Preferred Ser. W 1¢ par called for redemption at $25,000 04/13/2010
Municipal Auction Rate Preferred Ser. TH 1¢ par called for redemption at $25,000 04/14/2010
Merged into Nuveen Enhanced Municipal Credit Opportunities Fund 04/11/2016
Each 144A Variable Rate Demand Preferred Share Ser. 1 1¢ par exchanged for (1) 144A Variable Rate Demand Preferred Share Ser. 1 1¢ par
Each share Common 1¢ par exchanged for (0.96192244) Common Share of Bene. Int. 1¢ par
Nuveen Enhanced Municipal Credit Opportunities Fund name changed to Nuveen Municipal Credit Income Fund 12/28/2016

NUVEEN MUN BD FD INC (MD)
Common 10¢ par reclassified as Class R 10¢ par 09/06/1994
Merged into Nuveen Flagship Municipal Trust 01/31/1997
Details not available

NUVEEN MUN HIGH INCOME OPPORTUNITY FD (MA)
Municipal Auction Rate Preferred Ser. M 1¢ par called for redemption at $25,000 on 06/17/2011
Municipal Auction Rate Preferred Ser. T 1¢ par called for redemption at $25,000 on 06/20/2011
Municipal Auction Rate Preferred Ser. W 1¢ par called for redemption at $25,000 on 06/21/2011
(Additional Information in Active)

NUVEEN MUN MKT OPPORTUNITY FD INC (MN)
Municipal Auction Rate Preferred Ser. F 1¢ par split (2) for (1) by issuance of (1) additional share 01/07/1994
Municipal Auction Rate Preferred Ser. M 1¢ par split (2) for (1) by issuance of (1) additional share 01/07/1994
Municipal Auction Rate Preferred Ser. T 1¢ par split (2) for (1) by issuance of (1) additional share 01/07/1994
Municipal Auction Rate Preferred Ser. F 1¢ par called for redemption at $25,000 on 04/22/2010
Municipal Auction Rate Preferred Ser. M 1¢ par called for redemption at $25,000 on 04/23/2010
Municipal Auction Rate Preferred Ser. T 1¢ par called for redemption at $25,000 on 04/26/2010
Municipal Auction Rate Preferred Ser. W 1¢ par called for redemption at $25,000 on 04/27/2010
Merged into Nuveen AMT-Free Quality Municipal Income Fund 09/12/2016
Each 144A Variable Rate Demand Preferred 1¢ par exchanged for (1) share 144A Variable Rate Demand Preferred Ser. 3 1¢ par
Each share Common 1¢ par exchanged for (1.0153817) shares Common 1¢ par

NUVEEN MUN OPPORTUNITY FD INC (MN)
Name changed 01/03/2012
Municipal Auction Rate Preferred Ser. F 1¢ par split (2) for (1) by issuance of (1) additional share 01/07/1994
Municipal Auction Rate Preferred Ser. M 1¢ par split (2) for (1) by issuance of (1) additional share 01/07/1994
Municipal Auction Rate Preferred Ser. T 1¢ par split (2) for (1) by issuance of (1) additional share 01/07/1994
Municipal Auction Rate Preferred Ser. TH-1 1¢ par split (2) for (1) by issuance of (1) additional share 01/07/1994
Municipal Auction Rate Preferred Ser. TH-2 1¢ par split (2) for (1) by issuance of (1) additional share 01/07/1994
Municipal Auction Rate Preferred Ser. W 1¢ par split (2) for (1) by issuance of (1) additional share 01/07/1994
Municipal Auction Rate Preferred Ser. F 1¢ par called for redemption at $25,000 on 01/20/2011
Municipal Auction Rate Preferred Ser. M 1¢ par called for redemption at $25,000 on 01/21/2011
Municipal Auction Rate Preferred Ser. T 1¢ par called for redemption at $25,000 on 01/24/2011
Municipal Auction Rate Preferred Ser. W 1¢ par called for redemption at $25,000 on 01/25/2011
Municipal Auction Rate Preferred Ser. W2 1¢ par called for redemption at $25,000 on 01/25/2011
Municipal Auction Rate Preferred Ser. W3 1¢ par called for redemption at $25,000 on 01/25/2011
Municipal Auction Rate Preferred Ser. TH-1 1¢ par called for redemption at $25,000 on 01/26/2011
Municipal Auction Rate Preferred Ser. TH-2 1¢ par called for redemption at $25,000 on 01/26/2011
Municipal Auction Rate Preferred Ser. TH-3 1¢ par called for redemption at $25,000 on 01/26/2011
Name changed from Nuveen Insured Municipal Opportunity Fund to Nuveen Municipal Opportunity Fund, Inc. 01/03/2012
Merged into Nuveen Enhanced AMT-Free Municipal Credit Opportunities Fund 04/11/2016
Each Preferred Share Ser. 1 1¢ par exchanged for (1) 144A Variable Rate Demand Preferred Share Ser. 3 1¢ par
Each share Common 1¢ par exchanged for (0.96279789) Common Share of Bene. Int. 1¢ par
Nuveen Enhanced AMT-Free Municipal Credit Opportunities Fund name changed to Nuveen AMT-Free Municipal Credit Income Fund 12/28/2016

NUVEEN MUN HIGH INCOME OPPORTUNITY FD 2 (MA)
Issue Information - 13,750,000 shares COM offered at $15 per share on 11/15/2007
Merged into Nuveen Municipal High Income Opportunity Fund 07/15/2013
Each share Variable Rate MuniFund Term Preferred Ser. 2016 exchanged for (1) share Variable Rate MuniFund Term Preferred Ser 2-2016
Each share Common 1¢ par exchanged for (0.97055385) share Common 1¢ par

NUVEEN MUN VALUE FD 2 (MA)
Issue Information - 11,500,000 shares COM offered at $15 per share on 02/24/2009
Name changed to Nuveen AMT-Free Municipal Value Fund 10/15/2012

NUVEEN N C PREM INCOME MUN FD (MA)
Municipal Auction Rate Preferred Ser. TH 1¢ par split (2) for (1) by issuance of (1) additional share 01/07/1994
Municipal Auction Rate Preferred Ser. TH 1¢ par called for redemption at $25,000 on 01/05/2011
2.6% MuniFund Term Preferred Ser. 2015 1¢ par called for redemption at $10 plus $0.001444 accrued dividends on 03/03/2014
2.6% MuniFund Term Preferred Ser. 2015 #1 1¢ par called for redemption at $10 plus $0.001444 accrued dividends on 03/03/2014
2.6% MuniFund Term Preferred Ser. 2016 1¢ par called for redemption at $10 plus $0.001444 accrued dividends on 03/03/2014
2.65% MuniFund Term Preferred Ser. 2015 1¢ par called for redemption at $10 plus $0.001472 accrued dividends on 03/03/2014
2.65% MuniFund Term Preferred Ser. 2015 #1 1¢ par called for redemption at $10 plus $0.001472 accrued dividends on 03/03/2014
Name changed to Nuveen North Carolina Quality Municipal Income Fund 12/28/2016

NUVEEN N J INVT QUALITY MUN FD INC (MN)
Municipal Auction Rate Ser. M 1¢ par split (2) for (1) by issuance of (1) additional share 01/07/1994
Municipal Auction Rate Ser. F 1¢ par called for redemption at $25,000 on 09/02/2010
Municipal Auction Rate Ser. M 1¢ par called for redemption at $25,000 on 09/02/2010
Municipal Auction Rate Ser. TH 1¢ par called for redemption at $25,000 on 09/08/2010
Merged into Nuveen New Jersey Dividend Advantage Municipal Fund 11/10/2014
Each share Variable Rate Demand Preferred Ser 2 1¢ par exchanged for (1) share 144A Variable Rate Demand Preferred Ser 2 1¢ par
Each share Common 1¢ par exchanged for (0.98422389) Common Share of Bene. Int. 1¢ par
Nuveen New Jersey Dividend Advantage Municipal Fund name changed to Nuveen New Jersey Quality Municipal Income Fund 12/28/2016

NUVEEN N J PREM INCOME MUN FD (MA)
Municipal Auction Rate Preferred Ser. T 1¢ par called for redemption at $25,000 on 09/03/2010
Municipal Auction Rate Preferred Ser. W 1¢ par called for redemption at $25,000 on 09/07/2010
Municipal Auction Rate Preferred Ser. TH 1¢ par called for redemption at $25,000 on 09/08/2010
Merged into Nuveen New Jersey Dividend Advantage Municipal Fund 11/10/2014
Each share Variable Rate Demand Preferred Ser. 2 1¢ par exchanged for (1) share 144A Variable Rate Demand Preferred Ser. 3 1¢ par
Each share Common 1¢ par exchanged for (1.00159044) Common Shares of Bene. Int. 1¢ par
Nuveen New Jersey Dividend Advantage Municipal Fund name changed to Nuveen New Jersey Quality Municipal Income Fund 12/28/2016

NUVEEN N J PREM INCOME MUN FD 2 (MA)
Municipal Auction Rate Preferred Ser. W 1¢ par split (2) for (1) by issuance of (1) additional share 1/7/94
Reorganized as Nuveen New Jersey Premium Income Municipal Fund, Inc. 2/6/95
Each share Municipal Auction Rate Preferred Ser. W 1¢ par exchanged for (1) share Municipal Auction Rate Preferred Ser. W 1¢ par
Each share Common 1¢ par exchanged for (0.929851) share Common 1¢ par

NUVEEN N J QUALITY INCOME MUN FD INC (MN)
Municipal Auction Rate Preferred Ser. TH 1¢ par split (2) for (1) by issuance of (1) additional share 01/07/1994
Under plan of reorganization each share Municipal Auction Rate Preferred Ser. TH 1¢ par and Common 1¢ par exchanged for (1) share Nuveen New Jersey Investment Quality Municipal Fund, Inc. Municipal Auction Rate Ser. M 1¢ par or (0.978289) share Common 1¢ par respectively 01/10/1995
Nuveen New Jersey Investment Quality Municipal Fund, Inc. merged into Nuveen New Jersey Dividend Advantage Municipal Fund 11/10/2014 which name changed to Nuveen New Jersey Quality Municipal Income Fund 12/28/2016

NUVEEN N Y INVT QUALITY MUN FD INC (MN)
Municipal Auction Rate Preferred Ser. F 1¢ par split (2) for (1) by issuance of (1) additional share 01/07/1994
Municipal Auction Rate Preferred Ser. T 1¢ par split (2) for (1) by issuance of (1) additional share 01/07/1994
Municipal Auction Rate Preferred Ser. F 1¢ par called for redemption at $25,000 on 09/09/2010
Municipal Auction Rate Preferred Ser. M 1¢ par called for redemption at $25,000 on 09/10/2010
Municipal Auction Rate Preferred Ser. T 1¢ par called for redemption at $25,000 on 09/13/2010
Merged into Nuveen New York AMT-Free Municipal Income Fund 03/11/2013
Each Variable Rate Demand Preferred Share 1¢ par exchanged for (1) Variable Rate Demand Preferred Share Ser. 1 1¢ par
Each share Common 1¢ par exchanged for (1.03463) shares Common 1¢ par
Nuveen New York AMT-Free Municipal Income Fund name changed to Nuveen New York AMT-Free Quality Municipal Income Fund 12/28/2016

NUVEEN N Y MUN INCOME FD INC (MN)
Under plan of reorganization each share Common 1¢ par exchanged for (1.098617) share Nuveen New York Municipal Value Fund, Inc. Common 1¢ par 1/8/96

NUVEEN N Y MUN MKT OPPORTUNITY FD INC (MN)
Municipal Auction Rate Preferred Ser. M 1¢ par split (2) for (1) by issuance of (1) additional share 01/07/1994
Under plan of reorganization each share Municipal Auction Rate Preferred Ser. M 1¢ par and Common 1¢ par exchanged for (1) share Nuveen New York Performance Plus Municipal Fund, Inc. Municipal Auction Rate Preferred Ser. M 1¢ par or (1.000453) shares Common 1¢ par respectively 01/10/1995
Nuveen New York Performance Plus Municipal Fund, Inc. merged into Nuveen New York Dividend Advantage Municipal Fund 06/08/2015 which name changed to Nuveen New York Quality Municipal Income Fund 12/28/2016

NUVEEN N Y PERFORMANCE PLUS MUN FD INC (MN)
Money Market Preferred 1¢ par split (2) for (1) by issuance of (1) additional share 01/07/1994
Municipal Auction Rate Preferred Ser. F 1¢ par called for redemption at $25,000 on 04/22/2010
Municipal Auction Rate Preferred Ser. M 1¢ par called for redemption at $25,000 on 04/23/2010
Municipal Auction Rate Preferred Ser.

T 1¢ par called for redemption at $25,000 on 04/26/2010
Municipal Auction Rate Preferred Ser. W 1¢ par called for redemption at $25,000 on 04/27/2010
Merged into Nuveen New York Dividend Advantage Municipal Fund 06/08/2015
Each share 144A Varible Rate Demand Preferred Ser. 1 1¢ par exchanged for (1) share 144A Variable Rate Demand Preferred Ser. 1 1¢ par
Each share Common 1¢ par exchanged for (1.03045469) Common Shares of Bene. Int. 1¢ par
Nuveen New York Dividend Advantage Municipal Fund name changed to Nuveen New York Quality Municipal Income Fund 12/28/2016

NUVEEN N Y SELECT QUALITY MUN FD INC (MN)
Municipal Auction Rate Preferred Ser. TH 1¢ par split (2) for (1) by issuance of (1) additional share 01/07/1994
Municipal Auction Rate Preferred Ser. W 1¢ par split (2) for (1) by issuance of (1) additional share 01/07/1994
Municipal Auction Rate Preferred Ser. TH 1¢ par called for redemption at $25,000 on 09/08/2010
Municipal Auction Rate Preferred Ser. T 1¢ par called for redemption at $25,000 on 09/13/2010
Municipal Auction Rate Preferred Ser. W 1¢ par called for redemption at $25,000 on 09/14/2010
Merged into Nuveen New York AMT-Free Municipal Income Fund 03/11/2013
Each Variable Rate Demand Preferred Share 1¢ par exchanged for (1) Variable Rate Demand Preferred Share Ser. 2 1¢ par
Each share Common 1¢ par exchanged for (1.055839) shares Common 1¢ par
Nuveen New York AMT-Free Municipal Income Fund name changed to Nuveen New York AMT-Free Quality Municipal Income Fund 12/28/2016

NUVEEN NEW JERSEY DIVID ADVANTAGE MUN FD (MA)
Municipal Auction Rate Preferred Ser. T 1¢ par called for redemption at $25,000 on 04/18/2011
2.3% MuniFund Term Preferred Ser. 2014 1¢ par called for redemption at $10 on 09/09/2013
2% MuniFund Term Preferred Ser. 2015 1¢ par called for redemption at $10 on 02/09/2015
Name changed to Nuveen New Jersey Quality Municipal Income Fund 12/28/2016

NUVEEN NEW JERSEY DIVID ADVANTAGE MUN FD 2 (MA)
Municipal Auction Rate Preferred Ser. W 1¢ par called for redemption at $25,000 on 10/26/2010
Merged into Nuveen New Jersey Dividend Advantage Municipal Fund 11/10/2014
Each share 2% MuniFund Term Preferred Ser. 2015 1¢ par exchanged for (1) share 2% MuniFund Term Preferred Ser. 2015 1¢ par
Each Common Share of Bene. Int. 1¢ par exchanged for (0.98199215) Common Share of Bene. Int. 1¢ par
Nuveen New Jersey Dividend Advantage Municipal Fund name changed to Nuveen New Jersey Quality Municipal Income Fund 12/28/2016

NUVEEN NEW YORK AMT-FREE MUN INCOME FD (MA)
Name changed 01/03/2012
Municipal Auction Rate Preferred Ser. TH 1¢ par called for redemption at $25,000 on 05/10/2010
Name changed from Nuveen Insured New York Tax-Free Advantage Municipal Fund to Nuveen New York AMT-Free Municipal Income Fund 01/03/2012
Variable Rate MuniFund Term Preferred Ser. 2014 1¢ par called for redemption at $100,000 on 04/11/2014
2.55% MuniFund Term Preferred Ser. 2015 1¢ par called for redemption at $10 on 04/11/2014
Name changed to Nuveen New York AMT-Free Quality Municipal Income Fund 12/28/2016

NUVEEN NEW YORK DIVID ADVANTAGE MUN INCOME FD (MA)
Name changed 01/03/2012
Municipal Auction Rate Preferred called for redemption at $25,000 on 09/05/2008
Each share Variable Rate Demand Preferred 1¢ par exchanged for (1) share 144A Variable Rate Demand Preferred Ser. 2 1¢ par 06/24/2010
Name changed from Nuveen Insured New York Dividend Advantage Municipal Fund to Nuveen New York Dividend Advantage Municipal Income Fund 01/03/2012
Merged into Nuveen New York AMT-Free Municipal Income Fund 03/11/2013
Each 144A Variable Rate Demand Preferred Share Ser. 2 1¢ par exchanged for (1) Variable Rate Demand Preferred Share Ser. 4 1¢ par
Each share Common 1¢ par exchanged for (1.031876) shares Common 1¢ par
Nuveen New York AMT-Free Municipal Income Fund name changed to Nuveen New York AMT-Free Quality Municipal Income Fund 12/28/2016

NUVEEN NY DIVID ADVANTAGE MUN FD (MA)
Municipal Auction Rate Preferred Ser. F 1¢ par called for redemption at $25,000 on 01/06/2011
2.5% MuniFund Term Preferred Ser. 2016 1¢ par called for redemption at $10 on 06/13/2014
2.7% MuniFund Term Preferred Ser. 2015 1¢ par called for redemption at $10 on 06/13/2014
Name changed to Nuveen New York Quality Municipal Income Fund 12/28/2016

NUVEEN NEW YORK DIVID ADVANTAGE MUN FD 2 (MA)
Municipal Auction Rate Preferred Ser. W 1¢ par called for redemption at $25,000 on 05/04/2010
2.55% MuniFund Term Preferred Ser. 2015 1¢ par called for redemption at $10 on 06/13/2014
Merged into Nuveen New York Dividend Advantage Municipal Fund 06/08/2015
Each share 144A Variable Rate MuniFund Term Preferred Ser. 2017 1¢ par exchanged for (1) share 144A Variable Rate MuniFund Term Preferred Ser. 2017 1¢ par
Each share Common 1¢ par exchanged for (0.97814859) Common Share of Bene. Int. 1¢ par
Nuveen New York Dividend Advantage Municipal Fund name changed to Nuveen New York Quality Municipal Income Fund 12/28/2016

NUVEEN N Y PREM INCOME MUN FD INC (MA)
Name changed 01/03/2012
Municipal Auction Rate Preferred Ser. M 1¢ par called for redemption at $25,000 on 09/30/2011
Municipal Auction Rate Preferred Ser. T 1¢ par called for redemption at $25,000 on 10/03/2011
Name changed from Nuveen Insured New York Premium Income Municipal Fund, Inc. to Nuveen New York Premium Income Municipal Fund, Inc. 01/03/2012
Merged into Nuveen New York AMT-Free Municipal Income Fund 03/11/2013
Each Variable MuniFund Preferred Share Ser. 1 1¢ par exchanged for (1) Variable Rate Demand Preferred Share Ser. 1-2014 1¢ par
Each share Common 1¢ par exchanged for (1.046608) shares Common 1¢ par
Nuveen New York AMT-Free Municipal Income Fund name changed to Nuveen New York AMT-Free Quality Municipal Income Fund 12/28/2016

NUVEEN NORTH CAROLINA DIVID ADVANTAGE MUN FD 1 (MA)
Municipal Auction Rate Preferred Ser. T 1¢ par called for redemption at $25,000 on 04/26/2010
Merged into Nuveen North Carolina Premium Income Municipal Fund 07/09/2012
Each share 2.60% MuniFund Term Preferred Ser. 2015 1¢ par exchanged for (1) share 2.60% MuniFund Term Preferred Ser. 2015 1¢ par
Each share Common 1¢ par exchanged for (1.03581226) shares Common 1¢ par

NUVEEN NORTH CAROLINA DIVID ADVANTAGE MUN FD 2 (MA)
Municipal Auction Rate Preferred Ser. F 1¢ par called for redemption at $25,000 on 04/22/2010
Merged into Nuveen North Carolina Premium Income Municipal Fund 07/09/2012
Each share 2.60% MuniFund Term Preferred Ser. 2015 1¢ par exchanged for (1) share 2.60% MuniFund Term Preferred Ser. 2015-1 1¢ par
Each share Common 1¢ par exchanged for (1.02649583) shares Common 1¢ par

NUVEEN NORTH CAROLINA DIVID ADVANTAGE MUN FD 3 (MA)
Municipal Auction Rate Preferred Ser. W 1¢ par called for redemption at $25,000 on 03/02/2010
Merged into Nuveen North Carolina Premium Income Municipal Fund 07/09/2012
Each share 2.65% MuniFund Term Preferred Ser. 2015 1¢ par exchanged for (1) share 2.65% MuniFund Term Preferred Ser. 2015-1 1¢ par
Each share Common 1¢ par exchanged for (1.00621968) shares Common 1¢ par

NUVEEN NY QUALITY INCOME MUN FD INC (MN)
Municipal Auction Rate Preferred Ser. M 1¢ par split (2) for (1) by issuance of (1) additional share 01/07/1994
Municipal Auction Rate Preferred Ser. TH 1¢ par split (2) for (1) by issuance of (1) additional share 01/07/1994
Municipal Auction Rate Preferred Ser. W 1¢ par split (2) for (1) by issuance of (1) additional share 01/07/1994
Municipal Auction Rate Preferred Ser. F 1¢ par called for redemption at $25,000 on 01/06/2011
Municipal Auction Rate Preferred Ser. M 1¢ par called for redemption at $25,000 on 01/07/2011
Municipal Auction Rate Preferred Ser. W 1¢ par called for redemption at $25,000 on 01/11/2011
Municipal Auction Rate Preferred Ser. TH 1¢ par called for redemption at $25,000 on 01/12/2011
Merged into Nuveen New York AMT-Free Municipal Income Fund 03/11/2013
Each 144A Variable Rate Demand Preferred Share Ser. 1 1¢ par exchanged for (1) Variable Rate Demand Preferred Share Ser. 3 1¢ par
Each share Common 1¢ par exchanged for (1.034102) shares Common 1¢ par
Nuveen New York AMT-Free Municipal Income Fund name changed to Nuveen New York AMT-Free Quality Municipal Income Fund 12/28/2016

NUVEEN OHIO DIVID ADVANTAGE MUN FD (MA)
Municipal Auction Rate Preferred Ser. W 1¢ par called for redemption at $25,000 on 04/12/2011
Merged into Nuveen Ohio Quality Income Municipal Fund 04/08/2013
Each 2.35% MuniFund Term Preferred Share Ser. 2015 1¢ par exchanged for (1) 2.35% MuniFund Term Preferred Share Ser. 2015 1¢ par
Each 2.95% MuniFund Term Preferred Share Ser. 2016 1¢ par exchanged for (1) 2.95% MuniFund Term Preferred Share Ser. 2016 1¢ par
Each Common Share of Bene. Int. 1¢ par exchanged for (0.92165228) Common Share of Bene. Int. 1¢ par
Nuveen Ohio Quality Income Municipal Fund name changed to Nuveen Ohio Quality Municipal Income Fund 12/28/2016

NUVEEN OHIO DIVID ADVANTAGE MUN FD 2 (MA)
Municipal Auction Rate Preferred Ser. F 1¢ par called for redemption at $25,000 on 04/28/2011
Merged into Nuveen Ohio Quality Income Municipal Fund 04/08/2013
Each 2.35% MuniFund Term Preferred Share Ser. 2014 1¢ par exchanged for (1) 2.35% MuniFund Term Preferred Share Ser. 2014 1¢ par
Each Common Share of Bene. Int. 1¢ par exchanged for (0.90047399) Common 1¢ par
Nuveen Ohio Quality Income Municipal Fund name changed to Nuveen Ohio Quality Municipal Income Fund 12/28/2016

NUVEEN OHIO DIVID ADVANTAGE MUN FD 3 (MA)
Municipal Auction Rate Preferred Ser. T 1¢ par called for redemption at $25,000 on 05/16/2011
Merged into Nuveen Ohio Quality Income Municipal Fund 04/08/2013
Each 2.35% MuniFund Term Preferred Share Ser. 2014 1¢ par exchanged for (1) 2.35% MuniFund Term Preferred Share Ser. 2014 1¢ par
Each Common Share of Bene. Int. 1¢ par exchanged for (0.91738582) Common Share of Bene. Int. 1¢ par
Nuveen Ohio Quality Income Municipal Fund name changed to Nuveen Ohio Quality Municipal Income Fund 12/28/2016

NUVEEN OHIO QUALITY INCOME MUN FD (MN)
Name changed 04/08/2013
Municipal Auction Rate Preferred Ser. TH 1¢ par split (2) for (1) by

issuance of (1) additional share 01/07/1994
Municipal Auction Rate Preferred Ser. M 1¢ par called for redemption at $25,000 on 08/05/2011
Municipal Auction Rate Preferred Ser. TH 1¢ par called for redemption at $25,000 on 08/10/2011
Municipal Auction Rate Preferred Ser. TH2 1¢ par called for redemption at $25,000 on 08/10/2011
Reincorporated from Nuveen Ohio Quality Income Municipal Fund, Inc. (MN) to under the laws of Massachusetts as Nuveen Ohio Quality Income Municipal Fund and Common 1¢ par reclassified as Common Shares of Bene. Int. 1¢ par 04/08/2013
Variable Rate MuniFund Term Preferred Ser. 2014 called for redemption at $100,000 plus $18.3014 accrued dividends on 10/07/2013
2.35% MuniFund Term Preferred Ser. 2014 1¢ par called for redemption at $10 plus $0.00391667 accrued dividends on 10/07/2013
2.35% MuniFund Term Preferred Ser. 2015 1¢ par called for redemption at $10 plus $0.00391667 accrued dividends on 10/07/2013
2.95% MuniFund Term Preferred Ser. 2016 1¢ par called for redemption at $10 plus $0.00491667 accrued dividends on 10/07/2013
Name changed to Nuveen Ohio Quality Municipal Income Fund 12/28/2016

NUVEEN PA INVT QUALITY MUN FD (MA)
Municipal Auction Rate Preferred Ser. W 1¢ par split (2) for (1) by issuance of (1) additional share 01/07/1994
Municipal Auction Rate Preferred Ser. T 1¢ par called for redemption at $25,000 on 09/03/2010
Municipal Auction Rate Preferred Ser. W 1¢ par called for redemption at $25,000 on 09/07/2010
Municipal Auction Rate Preferred Ser. TH 1¢ par called for redemption at $25,000 on 09/08/2010
Each share Variable Rate Demand Preferred Ser. 1 1¢ par exchanged for (1) share Variable Rate Demand Preferred Ser. 2 1¢ par 12/20/2012
2.1% MuniFund Term Preferred Ser. 2015 1¢ par called for redemption at $10 on 05/30/2014
2.15% MuniFund Term Preferred Ser. 2015 1¢ par called for redemption at $10 on 05/30/2014
Name changed to Nuveen Pennsylvania Quality Municipal Income Fund 12/28/2016

NUVEEN PA QUALITY INCOME MUN FD (MA)
Municipal Auction Rate Preferred Ser. TH 1¢ par split (2) for (1) by issuance of (1) additional share 01/07/1994
Under plan of reorganization each share Municipal Auction Rate Preferred Ser. TH 1¢ par and Common 1¢ par exchanged for (1) share Nuveen Pennsylvania Investment Quality Municipal Fund Municipal Auction Rate Preferred Ser. TH 1¢ par or (0.971687) share Common 1¢ par respectively 01/09/1995
Nuveen Pennsylvania Investment Quality Municipal Fund name changed to Nuveen Pennsylvania Quality Municipal Income Fund 12/28/2016

NUVEEN PA DIVID ADVANTAGE MUN FD (MA)
Municipal Auction Rate Preferred Ser. T 1¢ par called for redemption at $25,000 on 10/25/2010
Merged into Nuveen Pennsylvania Investment Quality Municipal Fund 02/10/2014
Each 2.1% MuniFund Term Preferred Share of Bene. Int. Ser. 2015 1¢ par exchanged for (1) 2.1% MuniFund Term Preferred Share of Bene. Int. Ser. 2015 1¢ par
Each Common Share of Bene. Int. 1¢ par exchanged for (0.98405061) Common Share of Bene. Int. 1¢ par
Nuveen Pennsylvania Investment Quality Municipal Fund name changed to Nuveen Pennsylvania Quality Municipal Income Fund 12/28/2016

NUVEEN PA DIVID ADVANTAGE MUN FD 2 (MA)
Municipal Auction Rate Preferred Ser. M 1¢ par called for redemption at $25,000 on 11/19/2010
Merged into Nuveen Pennsylvania Investment Quality Municipal Fund 02/10/2014
Each 2.15% MuniFund Term Preferred Share of Bene. Int. Ser. 2015 1¢ par exchanged for (1) 2.15% MuniFund Term Preferred Share of Bene. Int. Ser. 2015 1¢ par
Each Common Share of Bene. Int. 1¢ par exchanged for (0.9723462) Common Share of Bene. Int. 1¢ par
Nuveen Pennsylvania Investment Quality Municipal Fund name changed to Nuveen Pennsylvania Quality Municipal Income Fund 12/28/2016

NUVEEN PA PREM INCOME MUN FD (MA)
Municipal Auction Rate Preferred Ser. TH 1¢ par split (2) for (1) by issuance of (1) additional share 01/07/1994
Reorganized as Nuveen Pennsylvania Premium Income Municipal Fund 2 02/06/1995
Each share Common 1¢ par exchanged for (1.050861) shares Common 1¢ par
Municipal Auction Rate Preferred Ser. F 1¢ par called for redemption at $25,000 on 09/02/2010
Municipal Auction Rate Preferred Ser. M 1¢ par called for redemption at $25,000 on 09/02/2010
Municipal Auction Rate Preferred Ser. TH 1¢ par called for redemption at $25,000 on 09/08/2010
Nuveen Pennsylvania Premium Income Municipal Fund 2 merged into Nuveen Pennsylvania Investment Quality Municipal Fund 02/10/2014 which name changed to Nuveen Pennsylvania Quality Municipal Income Fund 12/28/2016

NUVEEN PA PREM INCOME MUN FD 2 (MA)
Each share Variable Rate Demand Preferred Ser. 1 1¢ par exchanged for (1) share Variable Rate Demand Preferred Ser. 2 1¢ par 12/20/2012
Merged into Nuveen Pennsylvania Investment Quality Municipal Fund 02/10/2014
Each share Variable Rate Demand Preferred Ser. 2 1¢ par exchanged for (1) share 144A Variable Rate Demand Preferred Ser. 3 1¢ par
Each share Common 1¢ par exchanged for (0.95999345) share Common 1¢ par
Nuveen Pennsylvania Investment Quality Municipal Fund name changed to Nuveen Pennsylvania Quality Municipal Income Fund 12/28/2016

NUVEEN PERFORMANCE PLUS MUN FD INC (MN)
Money Market Preferred Ser. F 1¢ par split (2) for (1) by issuance of (1) additional share 01/07/1994
Money Market Preferred Ser. M 1¢ par split (2) for (1) by issuance of (1) additional share 01/07/1994
Money Market Preferred Ser. T 1¢ par split (2) for (1) by issuance of (1) additional share 01/07/1994
Money Market Preferred Ser. W 1¢ par split (2) for (1) by issuance of (1) additional share 01/07/1994
Municipal Auction Rate Preferred Ser. F 1¢ par called for redemption at $25,000 on 03/17/2011
Municipal Auction Rate Preferred Ser. M 1¢ par called for redemption at $25,000 on 03/18/2011
Municipal Auction Rate Preferred Ser. T 1¢ par called for redemption at $25,000 on 03/21/2011
Municipal Auction Rate Preferred Ser. W 1¢ par called for redemption at $25,000 on 03/22/2011
Municipal Auction Rate Preferred Ser. TH 1¢ par called for redemption at $25,000 on 03/23/2011
Merged into Nuveen AMT-Free Quality Municipal Income Fund 09/12/2016
Each share 144A Variable Rate MuniFund Term Preferred Ser. 2018 1¢ par exchanged for (1) share 144A Variable Rate MuniFund Term Preferred Ser. 2018 1¢ par
Each share Common 1¢ par exchanged for (1.07649194) shares Common 1¢ par

NUVEEN PFD INCOME OPPORTUNITIES FD (MA)
Name changed 05/07/2007
Name changed 04/02/2012
Name changed from Nuveen Preferred & Convertible Income Fund to Nuveen Multi-Strategy Income & Growth Fund 05/07/2007
FundPreferred Shares Ser. W 1¢ par called for redemption at $25,000 on 09/17/2009
FundPreferred Shares Ser. TH 1¢ par called for redemption at $25,000 on 09/18/2009
FundPreferred Shares Ser. F 1¢ par called for redemption at $25,000 on 09/21/2009
FundPreferred Shares Ser. F2 1¢ par called for redemption at $25,000 on 09/21/2009
FundPreferred Shares Ser. M 1¢ par called for redemption at $25,000 on 09/22/2009
FundPreferred Shares Ser. T 1¢ par called for redemption at $25,000 on 09/23/2009
Name changed from Nuveen Multi-Strategy Income & Growth Fund to Nuveen Preferred Income Opportunities Fund 04/02/2012
Name changed to Nuveen Preferred & Income Opportunities Fund 09/29/2017

NUVEEN PFD SECS INCOME FD (MA)
Name changed 05/09/2016
FundPreferred Shares Ser. W 1¢ par called for redemption at $25,000 on 09/17/2009
FundPreferred Shares Ser. TH 1¢ par called for redemption at $25,000 on 09/18/2009
FundPreferred Shares Ser. TH2 1¢ par called for redemption at $25,000 on 09/18/2009
FundPreferred Shares Ser. F 1¢ par called for redemption at $25,000 on 09/21/2009
FundPreferred Shares Ser. M 1¢ par called for redemption at $25,000 on 09/22/2009
FundPreferred Shares Ser. T 1¢ par called for redemption at $25,000 on 09/23/2009
FundPreferred Shares Ser. T2 1¢ par called for redemption at $25,000 on 09/23/2009
Under plan of merger name changed from Nuveen Quality Preferred Income Fund 2 to Nuveen Preferred Securities Income Fund 05/09/2016
Name changed to Nuveen Preferred & Income Securities Fund 09/29/2017

NUVEEN PREMIER MUN INCOME FD INC (MN)
Municipal Auction Rate Preferred Ser. T 1¢ par split (2) for (1) by issuance of (1) additional share 01/07/1994
Municipal Auction Rate Preferred Ser. TH 1¢ par split (2) for (1) by issuance of (1) additional share 01/07/1994
Municipal Auction Rate Preferred Ser. M 1¢ par called for redemption at $25,000 on 05/26/2011
Municipal Auction Rate Preferred Ser. T 1¢ par called for redemption at $25,000 on 05/27/2011
Municipal Auction Rate Preferred Ser. TH 1¢ par called for redemption at $25,000 on 06/01/2011
Merged into Nuveen Quality Municipal Income Fund 09/12/2016
Each share 144A Variable Rate Demand Preferred 1¢ par exchanged for (1) share 144A Variable Rate Demand Preferred 1¢ par
Each share Common 1¢ par exchanged for (0.98481723) share Common 1¢ par

NUVEEN PREMIER MUN OPPORTUNITY FD INC (MN)
Name changed 01/03/2012
Municipal Auction Rate Preferred Ser. F 1¢ par split (2) for (1) by issuance of (1) additional share 01/07/1994
Municipal Auction Rate Preferred Ser. TH 1¢ par split (2) for (1) by issuance of (1) additional share 01/07/1994
Municipal Auction Rate Preferred Ser. F 1¢ par called for redemption at $25,000 on 01/06/2011
Municipal Auction Rate Preferred Ser. W 1¢ par called for redemption at $25,000 on 01/11/2011
Municipal Auction Rate Preferred Ser. TH 1¢ par called for redemption at $25,000 on 01/12/2011
Name changed from Nuveen Premier Insured Municipal Income Fund, Inc. to Nuveen Premier Municipal Opportunity Fund, Inc. 01/03/2012
Merged into Nuveen AMT-Free Municipal Income Fund 05/06/2013
Each 144A Variable Rate Demand Preferred Share Ser. 1 1¢ par exchanged for (1) 144A Variable Rate Demand Preferred Share Ser. 2 1¢ par
Each Common Share of Bene. Int. 1¢ par exchanged for (1.04762747) Common Shares of Bene. Int. 1¢ par
Nuveen AMT-Free Municipal Income Fund name changed to Nuveen AMT-Free Quality Municipal Income Fund 09/12/2016

NUVEEN PREM INCOME MUN OPPORTUNITY FD (MA)
Name changed 01/03/2012
Municipal Auction Rate Preferred Series F 1¢ par split (2) for (1) by issuance of (1) additional share 01/07/1994
Municipal Auction Rate Preferred Series M 1¢ par split (2) for (1) by issuance of (1) additional share 01/07/1994
Municipal Auction Rate Preferred Series W 1¢ par split (2) for (1) by issuance of (1) additional share 01/07/1994
Municipal Auction Rate Preferred Series F called for redemption at $25,000 on 09/02/2008
Municipal Auction Rate Preferred Series M called for redemption at $25,000 on 09/02/2008
Municipal Auction Rate Preferred

Series TH called for redemption at $25,000 on 09/05/2008
Municipal Auction Rate Preferred Series T called for redemption at $25,000 on 09/03/2008
Municipal Auction Rate Preferred Series W called for redemption at $25,000 on 09/04/2008
Each share Variable Rate Demand Preferred Ser. 1 1¢ par exchanged for (1) share 144A Variable Rate Demand Preferred Ser. 2 1¢ par 06/24/2010
Name changed from Nuveen Insured Premium Income Municipal Fund II, Inc. to Nuveen Premium Income Municipal Opportunity Fund 01/03/2012
Merged into Nuveen AMT-Free Municipal Income Fund 05/06/2013
Each 144A Variable Rate Demand Preferred Ser. 2 1¢ par exchanged for (1) 144A Variable Rate Demand Preferred Share Ser. 1 1¢ par
Each Common Share of Bene. Int. 1¢ par exchanged for (0.96847325) Common Share of Bene. Int. 1¢ par

NUVEEN PREM INCOME MUN FD 4 INC (MN)

Municipal Auction Rate Preferred Ser. F 1¢ par split (2) for (1) by issuance of (1) additional share 01/07/1994
Municipal Auction Rate Preferred Ser. T 1¢ par split (2) for (1) by issuance of (1) additional share 01/07/1994
Municipal Auction Rate Preferred Ser. TH 1¢ par split (2) for (1) by issuance of (1) additional share 01/07/1994
Municipal Auction Rate Preferred Ser. F 1¢ par called for redemption at $25,000 on 04/08/2010
Municipal Auction Rate Preferred Ser. F2 1¢ par called for redemption at $25,000 on 04/08/2010
Municipal Auction Rate Preferred Ser. M 1¢ par called for redemption at $25,000 on 04/09/2010
Municipal Auction Rate Preferred Ser. T 1¢ par called for redemption at $25,000 on 04/12/2010
Municipal Auction Rate Preferred Ser. T2 1¢ par called for redemption at $25,000 on 04/12/2010
Municipal Auction Rate Preferred Ser. W 1¢ par called for redemption at $25,000 on 04/13/2010
Municipal Auction Rate Preferred Ser. W2 1¢ par called for redemption at $25,000 on 04/13/2010
Municipal Auction Rate Preferred Ser. TH 1¢ par called for redemption at $25,000 on 04/14/2010
Merged into Nuveen Enhanced Municipal Credit Opportunities Fund 04/11/2016
Each 144A Variable Rate Demand Preferred Share Ser. 1 1¢ par exchanged for (1) 144A Variable Rate Demand Preferred Share Ser. 2 1¢ par
Each share Common 1¢ par exchanged for (0.89550894) Common Share of Bene. Int. 1¢ par

NUVEEN PREM INCOME MUN FD 5 (MA)

Municipal Auction Rate Preferred Ser. F 1¢ par split (2) for (1) by issuance of (1) additional share 01/07/1994
Municipal Auction Rate Preferred Ser. T 1¢ par split (2) for (1) by issuance of (1) additional share 01/07/1994
Trust terminated 11/30/1995
Details not available

NUVEEN PREM INCOME MUN FD INC (MN)

Remarketed Preferred Ser. E 1¢ par reclassified as Municipal Auction Rate Preferred Ser. W 1¢ par 08/21/1997
Remarketed Preferred Ser. D 1¢ par reclassified as Municipal Auction Rate Preferred Ser. F 1¢ par 08/29/1997
Remarketed Preferred Ser. A 1¢ par reclassified as Municipal Auction Rate Preferred Ser. M 1¢ par 09/08/1997
Remarketed Preferred Ser. B 1¢ par reclassified as Municipal Auction Rate Preferred Ser. T 1¢ par 09/09/1997
Remarketed Preferred Ser. D 1¢ par reclassified as Municipal Auction Rate Preferred Ser. TH 1¢ par 09/21/1997
Municipal Auction Rate Preferred Ser. F 1¢ par called for redemption at $25,000 on 03/17/2011
Municipal Auction Rate Preferred Ser. M 1¢ par called for redemption at $25,000 on 03/18/2011
Municipal Auction Rate Preferred Ser. M2 1¢ par called for redemption at $25,000 on 03/18/2011
Municipal Auction Rate Preferred Ser. T 1¢ par called for redemption at $25,000 on 03/21/2011
Municipal Auction Rate Preferred Ser. W 1¢ par called for redemption at $25,000 on 03/22/2011
Municipal Auction Rate Preferred Ser. TH 1¢ par called for redemption at $25,000 on 03/23/2011
Merged into Nuveen Quality Municipal Income Fund 09/12/2016
Each share 144A Variable Rate MuniFund Term Preferred Ser. 2018 1¢ par exchanged for (1) share 144A Variable Rate MuniFund Term Preferred Ser. 2018 1¢ par
Each share Common 1¢ par exchanged for (1.00361406) shares Common 1¢ par

NUVEEN PREM INCOME MUN FD 2 INC (MA)

Municipal Auction Rate Preferred Ser. F 1¢ par split (2) for (1) by issuance of (1) additional share 01/07/1994
Municipal Auction Rate Preferred Ser. M 1¢ par split (2) for (1) by issuance of (1) additional share 01/07/1994
Municipal Auction Rate Preferred Ser. TH 1¢ par split (2) for (1) by issuance of (1) additional share 01/07/1994
Municipal Auction Rate Preferred Ser. T 1¢ par split (2) for (1) by issuance of (1) additional share 01/07/1994
Municipal Auction Rate Preferred Ser. W 1¢ par split (2) for (1) by issuance of (1) additional share 01/07/1994
Municipal Auction Rate Preferred Ser. F 1¢ par called for redemption at $25,000 on 05/26/2011
Municipal Auction Rate Preferred Ser. F2 1¢ par called for redemption at $25,000 on 05/26/2011
Municipal Auction Rate Preferred Ser. F3 1¢ par called for redemption at $25,000 on 05/26/2011
Municipal Auction Rate Preferred Ser. F4 1¢ par called for redemption at $25,000 on 05/26/2011
Municipal Auction Rate Preferred Ser. M 1¢ par called for redemption at $25,000 on 05/26/2011
Municipal Auction Rate Preferred Ser. M2 1¢ par called for redemption at $25,000 on 05/26/2011
Municipal Auction Rate Preferred Ser. T 1¢ par called for redemption at $25,000 on 05/27/2011
Municipal Auction Rate Preferred Ser. T2 1¢ par called for redemption at $25,000 on 05/27/2011
Municipal Auction Rate Preferred Ser. W 1¢ par called for redemption at $25,000 on 05/31/2011
Municipal Auction Rate Preferred Ser. TH 1¢ par called for redemption at $25,000 on 06/01/2011
Municipal Auction Rate Preferred Ser. TH2 1¢ par called for redemption at $25,000 on 06/01/2011
Merged into Nuveen AMT-Free Quality Municipal Income Fund 09/12/2016
Each share 144A Variable Rate Demand Preferred Ser. 1 1¢ par exchanged for (1) share 144A 1 Variable Rate Demand Preferred Ser. 1 1¢ par
Each share Common 1¢ par exchanged for (1.02834601) shares Common 1¢ par

NUVEEN QUALITY INCOME MUN FD INC (MN)

Municipal Auction Rate Preferred Ser. F 1¢ par split (2) for (1) by issuance of (1) additional share 01/07/1994
Municipal Auction Rate Preferred Ser. M 1¢ par split (2) for (1) by issuance of (1) additional share 01/07/1994
Municipal Auction Rate Preferred Ser. T 1¢ par split (2) for (1) by issuance of (1) additional share 01/07/1994
Municipal Auction Rate Preferred Ser. TH 1¢ par split (2) for (1) by issuance of (1) additional share 01/07/1994
Municipal Auction Rate Preferred Ser. W1 1¢ par split (2) for (1) by issuance of (1) additional share 01/07/1994
Municipal Auction Rate Preferred Ser. W1 1¢ par called for redemption at $25,000 on 01/18/2011
Municipal Auction Rate Preferred Ser. W2 1¢ par called for redemption at $25,000 on 01/18/2011
Municipal Auction Rate Preferred Ser. TH 1¢ par called for redemption at $25,000 on 01/19/2011
Municipal Auction Rate Preferred Ser. F 1¢ par called for redemption at $25,000 on 01/20/2011
Municipal Auction Rate Preferred Ser. M 1¢ par called for redemption at $25,000 on 01/21/2011
Municipal Auction Rate Preferred Ser. T 1¢ par called for redemption at $25,000 on 01/24/2011
Merged into Nuveen Enhanced AMT-Free Municipal Credit Opportunities Fund 04/11/2016
Each Preferred Share Ser. 1 1¢ par exchanged for (1) 144A Variable Rate Demand Preferred Share Ser. 2 1¢ par
Each share Common 1¢ par exchanged for (0.9789377) Common Share of Bene. Int. 1¢ par
Nuveen Enhanced AMT-Free Municipal Credit Opportunities Fund name changed to Nuveen AMT-Free Municipal Credit Income Fund 12/28/2016

NUVEEN QUALITY MUN FD INC (MN)
Name changed 01/03/2012

Municipal Auction Rate Preferred Ser. F 1¢ par split (2) for (1) by issuance of (1) additional share 01/07/1994
Municipal Auction Rate Preferred Ser. M 1¢ par split (2) for (1) by issuance of (1) additional share 01/07/1994
Municipal Auction Rate Preferred Ser. T 1¢ par split (2) for (1) by issuance of (1) additional share 01/07/1994
Municipal Auction Rate Preferred Ser. W 1¢ par split (2) for (1) by issuance of (1) additional share 01/07/1994
Municipal Auction Rate Preferred Ser. F 1¢ par called for redemption at $25,000 on 03/17/2011
Municipal Auction Rate Preferred Ser. M 1¢ par called for redemption at $25,000 on 03/18/2011
Municipal Auction Rate Preferred Ser. T 1¢ par called for redemption at $25,000 on 03/21/2011
Municipal Auction Rate Preferred Ser. W 1¢ par called for redemption at $25,000 on 03/22/2011
Municipal Auction Rate Preferred Ser. TH 1¢ par called for redemption at $25,000 on 03/23/2011
Name changed from Nuveen Insured Quality Municipal Fund, Inc. to Nuveen Quality Municipal Fund, Inc. 01/03/2012
Each 144A Variable Rate Term Preferred Share Ser. 2014 1¢ par exchanged for (1) 144A Variable Rate Term Preferred Share Ser. 2015 1¢ par 10/31/2012
Each 144A Variable Rate Term Preferred Share Ser. 2015 1¢ par exchanged for (1) 144A Variable Rate Term Preferred Share Ser. 2018 1¢ par 05/19/2015
Merged into Nuveen Enhanced AMT-Free Municipal Credit Opportunities Fund 04/11/2016
Each 144A Variable Rate Term Preferred Share Ser. 2018 1¢ par exchanged for (1) 144A Variable Rate MuniFund Term Preferred Share Ser. 2018 1¢ par
Each share Common 1¢ par exchanged for (0.93635366) Common Share of Bene. Int. 1¢ par
Nuveen Enhanced AMT-Free Municipal Credit Opportunities Fund name changed to Nuveen AMT-Free Municipal Credit Income Fund 12/28/2016

NUVEEN QUALITY PFD INCOME FD (MA)

FundPreferred Shares Ser. W 1¢ par called for redemption at $25,000 on 09/17/2009
FundPreferred Shares Ser. TH 1¢ par called for redemption at $25,000 on 09/18/2009
FundPreferred Shares Ser. F 1¢ par called for redemption at $25,000 on 09/21/2009
FundPreferred Shares Ser. M 1¢ par called for redemption at $25,000 on 09/22/2009
FundPreferred Shares Ser. T 1¢ par called for redemption at $25,000 on 09/23/2009
Merged into Nuveen Preferred Securities Income Fund 05/09/2016
Each Common Share of Bene. Int. 1¢ par exchanged for (0.93255163) Common Share of Bene. Int. 1¢ par
Nuveen Preferred Securities Income Fund name changed to Nuveen Preferred & Income Securities Fund 09/29/2017

NUVEEN QUALITY PFD INCOME FD 3 (MA)

FundPreferred Shares Ser. TH 1¢ par called for redemption at $25,000 on 09/18/2009
FundPreferred Shares Ser. M 1¢ par called for redemption at $25,000 on 09/22/2009
Merged into Nuveen Preferred Securities Income Fund 05/09/2016
Each Common Share of Bene. Int. 1¢ par exchanged for (0.97616317) Common Share of Bene. Int. 1¢ par
Nuveen Preferred Securities Income Fund name changed to Nuveen Preferred & Income Securities Fund 09/29/2017

NUVEEN REAL ESTATE INCOME FD (MA)

Taxable Auctioned Preferred Ser. W 1¢ par called for redemption at $25,000 on 09/17/2009
Taxable Auctioned Preferred Ser. TH 1¢ par called for redemption at $25,000 on 09/18/2009
Taxable Auctioned Preferred Ser. F 1¢ par called for redemption at $25,000 on 09/21/2009
Taxable Auctioned Preferred Ser. M 1¢ par called for redemption at $25,000 on 09/22/2009
Taxable Auctioned Preferred Ser. T 1¢ par called for redemption at $25,000 on 09/23/2009
(Additional Information in Active)

NUVEEN SELECT QUALITY MUN FD INC (MN)

Municipal Auction Rate Preferred Ser.

NUV-NVE

F 1¢ par split (2) for (1) by issuance of (1) additional share 01/07/1994
Municipal Auction Rate Preferred Ser. M 1¢ par split (2) for (1) by issuance of (1) additional share 01/07/1994
Municipal Auction Rate Preferred Ser. T 1¢ par split (2) for (1) by issuance of (1) additional share 01/07/1994
Municipal Auction Rate Preferred Ser. W 1¢ par split (2) for (1) by issuance of (1) additional share 01/07/1994
Municipal Auction Rate Preferred Ser. F 1¢ par called for redemption at $25,000 on 05/26/2011
Municipal Auction Rate Preferred Ser. M 1¢ par called for redemption at $25,000 on 05/26/2011
Municipal Auction Rate Preferred Ser. T 1¢ par called for redemption at $25,000 on 05/27/2011
Municipal Auction Rate Preferred Ser. W 1¢ par called for redemption at $25,000 on 05/31/2011
Municipal Auction Rate Preferred Ser. TH 1¢ par called for redemption at $25,000 on 06/01/2011
Merged into Nuveen Quality Municipal Income Fund 09/12/2016
Each share 144A Variable Rate Demand Preferred 1¢ par exchanged for (1) share 144A Variable Rate Demand Preferred Ser. 2 1¢ par
Each share Common 1¢ par exchanged for (1.0200713) shares Common 1¢ par

NUVEEN SR FLOATING RATE INCOME FD (ON)
Under plan of merger each Unit no par automatically became (0.65053768) Fairway Diversified Income & Growth Trust Unit no par 09/12/2008
Fairway Diversified Income & Growth Trust merged into Crown Hill Fund 01/23/2009 which merged into Citadel Income Fund 12/02/2009

NUVEEN SR INCOME FD (MA)
Municipal Auction Rate Preferred Ser. TH 1¢ par called for redemption at $25,000 on 10/09/2009
144A Variable Rate Term Preferred Ser. C-4 1¢ par called for redemption at $100,000 plus $134.422667 accrued dividends on 11/22/2016
(Additional Information in Active)

NUVEEN TAX-ADVANTAGED DIVID GROWTH FD (MA)
FundPreferred Shares Ser. T 1¢ par called for redemption at $25,000 on 04/23/2008
(Additional Information in Active)

NUVEEN TAX ADVANTAGED FLOATING RATE FD (MA)
Issue Information - 13,000,000 shares COM offered at $15 per share on 03/28/2005
Auction Rate Preferred Securities Ser. TH called for redemption at $25,000 on 03/20/2009
Completely liquidated
Each share Common 1¢ par received first and final distribution of $2.59 cash payable 06/27/2012 to holders of record 06/27/2012

NUVEEN TAX-ADVANTAGED TOTAL RETURN STRATEGY FD (MA)
FundPreferred Shares Ser. W 1¢ par called for redemption at $25,000 on 09/17/2009
(Additional Information in Active)

NUVEEN TAX FREE BD FD INC (MN)
Massachusetts Value Fund 1¢ par reclassified as Massachusetts Value Fund Class R 1¢ par 09/06/1994
New York Value Fund 1¢ par reclassified as New York Value Fund Class R 1¢ par 09/06/1994
Ohio Value Fund 1¢ par reclassified as Ohio Value Fund Class R 1¢ par 09/06/1994
Massachusetts Value Fund and New York Value Fund merged into Nuveen Flagship Multistate Trust II 01/31/1997
Details not available
Ohio Value Fund merged into Nuveen Flagship Multistate Trust IV 01/31/1997
Details not available

NUVEEN TAX-FREE MONEY MKT FD INC (MD)
Merged into Nuveen Money Market Trust 06/25/1999
Details not available

NUVEEN TAXABLE FDS INC (MD)
Completely liquidated 10/31/2000
Each share Dividend & Growth Fund Class A received net asset value
Each share Dividend & Growth Fund Class B received net asset value
Each share Dividend & Growth Fund Class C received net asset value
Each share Dividend & Growth Fund Class R received net asset value

NUVEEN TEX QUALITY INCOME MUN FD (MA)
Municipal Auction Rate Preferred Ser. TH 1¢ par split (2) for (1) by issuance of (1) additional share 01/07/1994
Municipal Auction Rate Preferred Ser. TH 1¢ par called for redemption at $25,000 on 11/23/2010
Municipal Auction Rate Preferred Ser. M 1¢ par called for redemption at $25,000 on 11/26/2010
2.3% MuniFund Term Preferred Ser. 2015 1¢ par called for redemption at $10 plus $0.012139 accrued dividends on 04/20/2015
Name changed to Nuveen Texas Quality Municipal Income Fund 12/28/2016

NUVEEN VA PREM INCOME MUN FD (MA)
Municipal Auction Rate Preferred Ser. TH 1¢ par split (2) for (1) by issuance of (1) additional share 01/07/1994
Municipal Auction Rate Preferred Ser. T 1¢ par called for redemption at $25,000 on 04/04/2011
Municipal Auction Rate Preferred Ser. TH 1¢ par called for redemption at $25,000 on 04/06/2011
2.25% MuniFund Term Preferred Ser. 2014 1¢ par called for redemption at $10 on 09/09/2013
2.65% MuniFund Term Preferred Ser. 2015 1¢ par called for redemption at $10 on 09/09/2013
2.8% MuniFund Term Preferred Ser. 2014 1¢ par called for redemption at $10 on 09/09/2013
2.8% MuniFund Term Preferred Ser. 2014-1 1¢ par called for redemption at $10 on 09/09/2013
Name changed to Nuveen Virginia Quality Municipal Income Fund 12/28/2016

NUVEEN VA DIVID ADVANTAGE MUN FD 1 (MA)
Municipal Auction Rate Preferred Ser. W 1¢ par called for redemption at $25,000 on 12/15/2009
Merged into Nuveen Virginia Premium Income Municipal Fund 08/06/2012
Each share 2.8% MuniFund Term Preferred Ser. 2014 1¢ par exchanged for (1) share 2.8% MuniFund Term Preferred Ser. 2014 1¢ par
Each share Common 1¢ par exchanged for (0.98099322) share Common 1¢ par
Nuveen Virginia Premium Income Municipal Fund name changed to Nuveen Virginia Quality Municipal Income Fund 12/28/2016

NUVEEN VA DIVID ADVANTAGE MUN FD 2 (MA)
Municipal Auction Rate Preferred Ser. M 1¢ par called for redemption at $25,000 on 11/27/2009
Merged into Nuveen Virginia Premium Income Municipal Fund 08/06/2012
Each share 2.8% MuniFund Term Preferred Ser. 2014 1¢ par exchanged for (1) share 2.8% MuniFund Term Preferred Ser. 2014-1 1¢ par
Each share Common 1¢ par exchanged for (1.00043328) shares Common 1¢ par
Nuveen Virginia Premium Income Municipal Fund name changed to Nuveen Virginia Quality Municipal Income Fund 12/28/2016

NUVEEN WASH PREM INCOME MUN FD (MA)
Merged into Nuveen Premium Income Municipal Fund 4 Inc. 09/09/1999
Each share Municipal Auction Rate Preferred Ser. TH 1¢ par exchanged for (1) share Municipal Auction Rate Preferred Ser. TH 1¢ par
Each share Common 1¢ par exchanged for (1.013) shares Common 1¢ par
Nuveen Premium Income Municipal Fund 4 Inc. merged into Nuveen Enhanced Municipal Credit Opportunities Fund 04/11/2016

NUVEL HLDGS INC (FL)
Recapitalized as OrangeHook, Inc. 03/10/2017
Each share Common $0.001 par exchanged for (0.00000083) share Common $0.001 par

NUVELO INC (DE)
Reorganized 02/23/2004
Reorganized from under the laws of Nevada to Delaware 02/23/2004
Each share Common $0.001 par exchanged for (0.33333333) share Common $0.001 par
Recapitalized as ARCA biopharma, Inc. 01/28/2009
Each share Common $0.001 par exchanged for (0.05) share Common $0.001 par

NUVERRA ENVIRONMENTAL SOLUTIONS INC (DE)
Each share old Common $0.001 par exchanged for (0.1) share new Common $0.001 par 12/03/2013
Plan of reorganization under Chapter 11 Federal Bankruptcy proceedings effective 08/07/2017
No stockholders' equity
(Additional Information in Active)

NUVILEX INC (NV)
Stock Dividend - 0.002% payable 07/06/2009 to holders of record 06/30/2009
Name changed to PharmaCyte Biotech, Inc. 01/08/2015

NUVISION INC (MI)
Common 50¢ par split (3) for (2) by issuance of (0.5) additional share 12/16/1985
Merged into American Vision Centers, Inc. 06/02/1995
Each share Common 50¢ par exchanged for $7.60 cash

NUVO NETWORK MGMT INC (AB)
Each share old Common no par exchanged for (0.16666666) share new Common no par 03/17/2005
Acquired by Versata Enterprises, Inc. 02/22/2008
Each share Common no par exchanged for $0.57 cash

NUVO RESH INC (ON)
Each share old Common no par exchanged for (0.01538461) share new Common no par 05/09/2013
Each share new Common no par received distribution of (1) share Crescita Therapeutics Inc. Common no par payable 03/04/2016 to holders of record 03/03/2016
Ex date - 03/07/2016
Name changed to Nuvo Pharmaceuticals Inc. 03/07/2016

NUVOCI INC (NV)
Reorganized as Cyberhand Technologies International, Inc. 05/13/2005
Each share Common $0.001 par exchanged for (10) shares Common $0.001 par
Cyberhand Technologies International, Inc. name changed to ChromoCure, Inc. 07/09/2009

NUVOLA INC (NV)
Name changed to Modern Round Entertainment Corp. 02/11/2016

NUVONYX INC (NV)
Recapitalized as Tracker Financial Group Ltd. 05/15/2017
Each share Common $0.001 par exchanged for (0.02) share Common $0.001 par

NUWAVE TECHNOLOGIES INC (DE)
Common 1¢ par changed to $0.001 par 12/20/2002
Each share old Common $0.001 par exchanged for (0.02) share new Common $0.001 par 07/21/2003
Name changed to Emerge Capital Corp. (DE) 01/23/2006
Emerge Capital Corp. (DE) reincorporated in Nevada as Turnaround Partners, Inc. 01/03/2007 which recapitalized as Advanced Clean Technologies, Inc. 01/12/2009 which name changed to Act Clean Technologies, Inc. 12/09/2009

NUWAY MED INC (DE)
Name changed 10/29/2002
Name changed from NuWay Energy, Inc. to NuWay Medical, Inc. 10/29/2002
Recapitalized as BioLargo, Inc. 03/21/2007
Each share Common $0.00067 par exchanged for (0.04) share Common $0.00067 par

NUWEB SOLUTIONS INC (DE)
Recapitalized as Pensador Resources Inc. 05/30/2008
Each share Common $0.015 par exchanged for (0.005) share Common $0.015 par

NV ENERGY INC (NV)
Acquired by MidAmerican Energy Holdings Co. (New) 12/19/2013
Each share Common $1 par exchanged for $23.75 cash

NV HOMES L P (VA)
Units of Ltd. Partnership split (2) for (1) by issuance of (1) additional Unit 4/30/87
Under plan of merger name changed to NVRyan L.P. 6/23/87
NVRyan L.P. name changed to NVR L.P. 3/22/89 which reorganized as NVR Inc. 9/30/93

NVDH CORP (VA)
Liquidation completed
Each share Common $1 par exchanged for initial distribution of $18.75 cash 01/04/1984
Each share Common $1 par received second and final distribution of $0.797330 cash 10/23/1987

NVENTA BIOPHARMACEUTICALS CORP (BC)
Acquired by Akela Pharma Inc. 05/21/2009
Each share Common no par exchanged for (0.0355) share Common no par
(See Akela Pharma Inc.)

NVEST CASH MGMT TR (MA)
Name changed to CDC Nvest Cash Management Trust 05/01/2001

FINANCIAL INFORMATION, INC. — NVE-NYC

CDC Nvest Cash Management Trust name changed to Ixis Advisor Cash Management Trust 04/05/2005 which name changed to Natixis Cash Management Trust 06/20/2007
(See Natixis Cash Management Trust)

NVEST FDS TR I (MA)
Name changed to CDC Nvest Funds Trust I 05/01/2001
(See CDC Nvest Funds Trust I)

NVEST FDS TR II (MA)
Name changed to CDC Nvest Funds Trust II 05/01/2001
(See CDC Nvest Funds Trust II)

NVEST L P (DE)
Merged into Caisse des Depots Group 10/30/2000
Each share Common no par exchanged for $40 cash

NVEST TAX EXEMPT MONEY MKT TR (MA)
Name changed to CDC Nvest Tax Exempt Money Market Trust 05/01/2001
(See CDC Nvest Tax Exempt Money Market Trust)

NVF CO (DE)
Common $1 par split (2) for (1) by issuance of (1) additional share plus a 25% stock dividend paid 5/30/75
Common $1 par changed to 10¢ par 7/13/76
Common 10¢ par split (5) for (4) by issuance of (0.25) additional share 3/5/79
Common 10¢ par split (4) for (3) by issuance of (1/3) additional share 7/10/79
Common 10¢ par split (2) for (1) by issuance of (1) additional share 1/21/80
Stock Dividends - 15% 3/1/72; 20% 3/1/73; 20% 3/1/74; 20% 3/3/75; 20% 9/3/75; 25% 3/3/76; 10% 9/2/76; 10% 3/8/77; 10% 9/1/77; 10% 3/1/78; 10% 9/1/78; 10% 9/5/79; 10% 3/3/80; 10% 9/3/80
Plan of reorganization under Chapter 11 Federal Bankruptcy Code effective 6/12/96
No stockholders' equity

NV5 HLDGS INC (DE)
Units separated 09/27/2013
Name changed to NV5 Global, Inc. 12/09/2015

NVID INTL INC (DE)
SEC revoked common stock registration 06/18/2008
Stockholders' equity unlikely

NVIEW CORP (VA)
Stock Dividend - 100% 12/9/91
Charter cancelled and proclaimed dissolved for failure to file reports 7/31/2003

NVP CAP I (DE)
8.20% Guaranteed Quarterly Income Preferred Securities A called for redemption at $25 on 4/27/2006

NVP CAP III (DE)
7-3/4% Trust Preferred Securities called for redemption at $25 on 6/7/2006

NVR L P (VA)
Name changed 3/22/89
Name changed from NVRyan L.P. to NVR L.P. 3/22/89
Reorganized as NVR Inc. 9/30/93
Each Unit of Ltd. Partnership Int. exchanged for (1.0080808) shares Common 1¢ par and (0.0107041) Common Stock Purchase Warrant expiring 9/30/96

NVS ENTMT INC (NV)
Each share old Common $0.001 par exchanged for (0.01960784) share new Common $0.001 par 10/17/2005
Name changed to Pure Vanilla eXchange, Inc. 06/08/2006

(See Pure Vanilla eXchange, Inc.)

NW CDN FD LTD (AB)
Trust terminated 00/00/1991
Details not available

NW FINANCIAL FUND LTD. (AB)
Name changed to NW Canadian Fund Ltd. 08/23/1972
(See NW Canadian Fund Ltd.)

NW FINL LTD (BC)
Recapitalized as Newco Financial Corp. 01/13/1975
Each share Common no par exchanged for (0.1) share Common no par
(See Newco Financial Corp.)

NW GROWTH INVTS LTD (CANADA)
Name changed to Citco Growth Investments Ltd. (Canada) 06/01/1983
Citco Growth Investments Ltd. (Canada) reincorporated in British Columbia 05/31/1989 which name changed to First Global Investments Inc. 07/28/2005

NWA INC (DE)
Merged into Wings Holdings Inc. 08/04/1989
Each share Common $2 par exchanged for $121 cash

NWB FINL CORP (WA)
Merged into Pacific Continental Corp. 11/30/2005
Each share Common exchanged for (1.442592) shares Common no par and $8.9768 cash
Pacific Continental Corp. merged into Columbia Banking System, Inc. 11/01/2017

NWDP COM INC (NV)
Name changed to Hop-On.com 7/18/2000
Hop-On.com recapitalized as Hop-On, Inc. 5/18/2005

NWE CAP CORP (ON)
Each share old Common no par exchanged for (0.1) share new Common no par 07/27/1992
Name changed to Petersburg Long Distance Inc. 12/31/1992
Petersburg Long Distance Inc. name changed to PLD Telekom, Inc. (ON) 08/01/1996 which reincorporated in Delaware 02/28/1997 which merged into Metromedia International Group, Inc. 09/30/1999
(See Metromedia International Group, Inc.)

NWE CORP. (MN)
Out of business in 1972
No stockholders' equity

NWEST ENERGY CORP (CANADA)
Each share old Common no par exchanged for (0.14285714) share new Common no par 09/30/2016
Name changed to Ceylon Graphite Corp. 01/03/2017

NWEST ENERGY INC (CANADA)
Recapitalized as NWest Energy Corp. 11/04/2010
Each share Common no par exchanged for (0.1) share Common no par
NWest Energy Corp. name changed to Ceylon Graphite Corp. 01/03/2017

NWH INC (DE)
Merged into UnitedHealth Group Inc. 08/09/2006
Each share Common 1¢ par exchanged for $18.24 cash

NWL FINANCIAL CORP. LTD. (BC)
Name changed to NW Financial Corp. Ltd. 7/21/72
NW Financial Corp. Ltd. recapitalized as Newco Financial Corp. 1/13/75
(See Newco Financial Corp.)

NWM MNG CORP (ON)
Acquired by GFM Minera S.A.P.I. de C.V. 10/02/2015
Each share Common no par exchanged for $0.005 cash
Note: Unexchanged certificates were cancelled and became without value 10/02/2018

NWNL COS INC (DE)
Common no par split (2) for (1) by issuance of (1) additional share 05/21/1993
Name changed to ReliaStar Financial Corp. 02/13/1995
(See ReliaStar Financial Corp.)

NWPS CAP FING I (DE)
Under plan of reorganization each 8.125% Trust Capital Preferred Security received (0.18960547) share NorthWestern Corp. new Common 1¢ par and (0.36328164) Common Stock Purchase Warrant expiring 11/1/2007 payable 11/1/2004 to holders of record 10/24/2004
Note: Each 8.125% Trust Capital Preferred Security received an additional distribution of $0.00759057 cash payable 5/31/2006 to holders of record 10/20/2004

NWT URANIUM CORP (ON)
Name changed to Captor Capital Corp. 06/02/2017

NX CAP CO (DE)
Recapitalized as NX Uranium, Inc. 09/29/2014
Each share Common $0.0001 par exchanged for (0.06666666) share Common $0.0001 par

NX CAP CORP (AB)
Recapitalized as Newton Energy Corp. 02/18/2009
Each share Common no par exchanged for (0.05) share Common no par

NX NETWORKS INC (DE)
Plan of reorganization under Chapter 11 Federal Bankruptcy proceedings confirmed 09/18/2002
No stockholders' equity

NXA INC (ON)
Each share old Common no par exchanged for (0.06666666) share new Common no par 06/11/2012
Recapitalized as Ellipsiz Communications Ltd. 11/26/2015
Each share new Common no par exchanged for (0.1) share Common no par

NXGEN HLDGS INC (NV)
Name changed to Green Bridge Industries, Inc. 08/20/2009

NXTECH WIRELESS & CABLE SYS INC (NV)
Recapitalized as Chimera Technology Corp. 09/26/2002
Each share Common no par exchanged for (0.05) share Common no par
Chimera Technology Corp. recapitalized as Oriens Travel & Hotel Management Corp. 08/21/2007 which recapitalized as Pure Hospitality Solutions, Inc. 11/12/2014

NY COM INC (NY)
Name changed to NYCOM Information Services, Inc. 02/19/1989
NYCOM Information Services, Inc. name changed to Amnex, Inc. 08/05/1992
(See Amnex, Inc.)

NYAC ASSOCIATES, INC. (NY)
Liquidation completed 12/6/62

NYAH RES CORP (ON)
Recapitalized as Forbes & Manhattan Coal Corp. 09/27/2010
Each share Common no par exchanged for (0.02512562) share Common no par
Forbes & Manhattan Coal Corp. name changed to Buffalo Coal Corp. 07/21/2014

NYANZA MILLS
Liquidated in 1939

NYBD HLDG INC (FL)
Name changed to Pleasant Kids, Inc. 10/29/2014
Pleasant Kids, Inc. name changed to Next Group Holdings, Inc. 12/30/2015 which recapitalized as Cuentas Inc. 08/13/2018

NYC MODA INC. (NV)
Name changed to China Xuefeng Environmental Engineering, Inc. 12/14/2012

NYCAL CDA INC (YT)
Reincorporated 04/05/1995
Place of incorporation changed from (BC) to (Yukon) 04/05/1995
Delisted from Vancouver Stock Exchange 03/01/1999

NYCAL CORP (DE)
Charter cancelled and declared inoperative and void for non-payment of taxes 03/01/1994

NYCAN ENERGY CORP (AB)
Reorganized 06/01/1998
Reorganized from Nycan Petroleum Corp. to Nycan Energy Corp. 06/01/1998
Each share old Class A Common no par exchanged for (0.25) share new Class A Common no par
Acquired by APF Energy Trust 04/30/2003
Each share Common no par exchanged for $2.075 cash

NYCOM INFORMATION SVCS INC (NY)
Each share old Common $0.001 par exchanged for (0.125) share new Common $0.001 par 04/18/1991
Name changed to Amnex, Inc. 08/05/1992
(See Amnex, Inc.)

NYCOMED AMERSHAM PLC (UNITED KINGDOM)
Each Sponsored ADR for Class B exchanged for (1) Sponsored ADR for Ordinary 6/10/98
Name changed to Amersham PLC 7/12/2001
Amersham PLC merged into General Electric Co. 4/8/2004

NYCOMED ASA (NORWAY)
Acquired by Nycomed Amersham PLC 1/28/98
Each Sponsored ADR for Class A exchanged for £15.74 cash
Each Sponsored ADR for Class B exchanged for £15.22 cash
Nycomed Amersham PLC name changed to Amersham PLC 7/12/2001 which merged into General Electric Co. 4/8/2004

NYCOR INC (DE)
Under plan of recapitalization each share old Class B $1 par exchanged for (0.25) share new Class B $1 par and (0.25) share Class A $1 par 01/02/1991
Under plan of recapitalization each share old Common $1 par exchanged for (0.25) share new Common $1 par and (0.25) share Class A $1 par 01/02/1991
Each share $1.70 Conv. Exchangeable Preferred $1 par exchanged for $20 principal amount of 8-1/2% Conv. Subordinated Debentures due 06/15/2012 on 03/15/1996
Merged into Fedders Corp. 08/13/1996
Each share Class A Common $1 par

exchanged for (1) share Conv.
Preferred no par
Each share Class B Common $1 par
exchanged for (1) share Conv.
Preferred no par
Each share new Common $1 par
exchanged for (1) share Conv.
Preferred no par
(See Fedders Corp.)

NYE METALS INC (IN)
Voluntarily dissolved 3/20/92
Details not available

NYE ODORLESS INCINERATOR CORP.
Dissolved in 1934

NYE PRODUCTS, INC. (WA)
Completely liquidated 8/2/67
Each share Common $1 par exchanged for first and final distribution of (1) share Nye Systems, Inc. Common $1 par
Nye Systems, Inc. name changed to Columbia Nyematic Systems, Inc. 1/31/69 which name changed to Columbia Corp. 4/28/71
(See Columbia Corp.)

NYE SYS INC (WA)
Name changed to Columbia Nyematic Systems, Inc. 01/31/1969
Columbia Nyematic Systems, Inc. name changed to Columbia Corp. 04/28/1971
(See Columbia Corp.)

NY85 CAP INC (BC)
Name changed to Alchemist Mining Inc. 10/16/2012

NYER MED GROUP INC (FL)
Each share Common $0.0001 par received distribution of (0.16666666) share Genetic Vectors Inc. Common $0.001 par payable 01/31/1997 to holders of record 05/31/1996
Stock Dividend - 10% payable 01/28/2000 to holders of record 01/14/2000
Completely liquidated
Each share Common $0.0001 par received first and final distribution of $2.08 cash payable 05/20/2010 to holders of record 05/03/2010
Note: Certificates were not required to be surrendered and are without value

NYFIX INC (DE)
Reincorporated 12/16/2003
Common $0.001 par split (3) for (2) by issuance of (0.5) additional share payable 11/15/1999 to holders of record 11/01/1999
Common $0.001 par split (3) for (2) by issuance of (0.5) additional share payable 04/04/2000 to holders of record 03/24/2000
State of incorporation changed from (NY) to (DE) 12/16/2003
Acquired by NYSE Technologies, Inc. 11/30/2009
Each share Common $0.001 par exchanged for $1.675 cash

NYLACARB INC (DE)
Name changed to N.I. Liquidating Corp. 11/14/1974
(See N.I. Liquidating Corp.)

NYLACORE CORP (DE)
Each share Class A Common 10¢ par or Class B Common 10¢ par exchanged for (0.2) share Common 50¢ par 3/5/62
Common 50¢ par changed to 1¢ par in April 1970
Completely liquidated 7/15/71
Each share Common 1¢ par received first and final distribution of (0.2) share Living Industries, Inc. (NY) Common 1¢ par
Note: Certificates were not required to be surrendered and are now without value
Living Industries, Inc. (NY) merged into Living Industries, Inc. (DE) 11/2/77

NYLIFE RLTY INCOME PARTNERS L P (DE)
Completely liquidated 06/30/1997
No Unitholders' equity

NYLO THANE PLASTICS CORP (NY)
Name changed to Polymers Systems Inc. 12/21/1972
Polymers Systems Inc. recapitalized as Olan Laboratories International, Inc. 11/05/1981 which recapitalized as Mile Marker International, Inc. (NY) 12/28/1993 which reincorporated in Florida 11/22/2000
(See Mile Marker International, Inc.)

NYLON ENGR INC (MA)
Assets sold for benefit of creditors 10/00/1974
No stockholders' equity

NYLON MOLDED PRODUCTS CORP. (OH)
Name changed to Nymold, Inc. 9/23/68
Nymold, Inc. merged into VCA Corp. 6/1/70 which merged into Ethyl Corp. 10/30/74 which reorganized as NewMarket Corp. 6/18/2004

NYLONET CORP. (FL)
Reorganized 2/7/64
No stockholders' equity

NYMAGIC INC (NY)
Acquired by ProSight Specialty Insurance Holdings, Inc. 11/23/2010
Each share Common $1 par exchanged for $25.75 cash

NYMEX HLDGS INC (DE)
Issue Information - 6,500,000 shares COM offered at $59 per share on 11/16/2006
Merged into CME Group Inc. 08/22/2008
Each share Common 1¢ par exchanged for either (0.2164) share Common 1¢ par and $7.29 cash or $81.16 cash
Note: Option to receive stock and cash expired 08/20/2008

NYMOLD, INC. (OH)
Merged into VCA Corp. 6/1/70
Each share Common no par exchanged for (0.527) share 80¢ Conv. Preferred 1970 Ser. no par
VCA Corp. merged into Ethyl Corp. 10/30/74 which reorganized as NewMarket Corp. 6/18/2004

NYMOX PHARMACEUTICAL CORP (CANADA)
Reincorporated under the laws of Bahamas 11/20/2015

NYNEX CABLECOMMS GROUP PLC / NYNEX CABLECOMMS GROUP INC (DE)
Merged into Cable & Wireless Communications plc 2/9/98
Each ADR for Ordinary no par exchanged for (0.73492) Sponsored ADR for Ordinary 50p par 2/9/98
(See Cable & Wireless Communications plc)

NYNEX CORP (DE)
Common $1 par split (2) for (1) by issuance of (1) additional share 4/30/86
Common $1 par split (2) for (1) by issuance of (1) additional share 9/15/93
Merged into Bell Atlantic Corp. 8/14/97
Each share Common $1 par exchanged for (0.768) share Common $1 par
Bell Atlantic Corp. name changed to Verizon Communications Inc. 6/30/2000

NYPA GAS CORP. (NY)
Dissolved in 1959

NYSE EURONEXT (DE)
Merged into IntercontinentalExchange Group, Inc. 11/13/2013
Each share Common 1¢ par exchanged for (0.1703) share Common 1¢ par and $11.27 cash IntercontinentalExchange Group, Inc. name changed to Intercontinental Exchange, Inc. 06/02/2014

NYSE GROUP INC (DE)
Under plan of merger each share Common 1¢ par automatically became (1) share NYSE Euronext Common 1¢ par 04/04/2007
NYSE Euronext merged into IntercontinentalExchange Group, Inc. 11/13/2013 which name changed to Intercontinental Exchange, Inc. 06/02/2014

NYTEST ENVIRONMENTAL INC (DE)
Assets surrendered to creditor 02/24/1998
Stockholders' equity unlikely

NYTEX ENERGY HLDGS (DE)
Name changed to Sable Natural Resources Corp. 02/25/2015
(See Sable Natural Resources Corp.)

NYTRONICS INC (DE)
Reincorporated 01/04/1968
State of incorporation changed from (NJ) to (DE) 01/04/1968
Capital Stock $1 par changed to 50¢ par and (1) additional share issued 07/05/1968
Each share Capital Stock 50¢ par changed for (0.1) share Capital Stock 1¢ par 06/18/1973
Merged into Bastian Industries, Inc. 11/24/1980
Each share Capital Stock 1¢ par exchanged for (0.375) share Common 1¢ par
(See Bastian Industries, Inc.)

NYX GAMING GROUP LTD (GUERNSEY)
Acquired by Scientific Games Corp. 01/09/2018
Each share Ordinary no par exchanged for CAD$2.40 cash

NZ CORP (AZ)
Name changed to Lipid Sciences, Inc. (AZ) 11/29/2001
Lipid Sciences, Inc. (AZ) reincorporated in Delaware 06/19/2002
(See Lipid Sciences, Inc.)

NZCH CORP (NV)
Each share old Common $0.001 par exchanged for (1) share new Common $0.001 par to reflect a (1) for (500,000) reverse split followed by a (500,000) by (1) forward split 03/05/2018
Note: In effect holders received $0.02 cash per share and public interest was eliminated

O

O & R CORP. (NV)
Recapitalized as General Financial Industries, Inc. 12/29/1972
Each share Common 10¢ par exchanged for (3) shares Common 10¢ par
General Financial Industries, Inc. name changed to Monarch Molybdenum & Resources, Inc. (Ctfs. dated prior to 03/07/1988) 09/14/1978 which recapitalized as Mediacom Communications, Inc. 03/07/1988 which name changed to Duraco Industries, Inc. 09/15/1990

O & U, INC. (IA)
Charter cancelled for failure to file reports 11/21/73

O & W THUM CO.
Name changed to Tanglefoot Co. in 1942

O A K FINL CORP (MI)
Stock Dividends - 10% payable 05/31/2005 to holders of record 05/16/2005 Ex date - 05/12/2005; 10% payable 05/31/2006 to holders of record 05/15/2006 Ex date - 05/11/2006; 10% payable 05/31/2007 to holders of record 05/15/2007 Ex date - 05/11/2007
Merged into Chemical Financial Corp. 05/03/2010
Each share Common $1 par exchanged for (1.306) shares Common $1 par

O A O TATNEFT (RUSSIA)
Sponsored GDR's for Ordinary split (10) for (3) by issuance of (2.33333333) additional GDR's payable 05/08/2009 to holders of record 05/07/2009
Basis changed from (1:20) to (1:6) 05/08/2009
Name changed to Tatneft PJSC 12/08/2015

O BRIEN MED INC (DE)
Name changed 03/28/1982
Name changed from O'Brien Industries, Inc. to O'Brien Medical, Inc. 03/28/1982
Each share Common $0.0001 par exchanged for (0.1) share Common $0.001 par 07/15/1983
Company believed out of business 08/21/1990
Details not available

O C G OIL & GAS CO. (DE)
Charter cancelled and declared inoperative and void for non-payment of taxes 3/19/24

O C G TECHNOLOGY INC (DE)
Each share Common 1¢ par received distribution of (1) share PrimeCare Systems, Inc. Common $0.001 par payable 12/29/2005 to holders of record 12/29/2005 Ex date - 12/27/2005
Recapitalized as UraniumCore Co. 04/12/2006
Each share Common 1¢ par exchanged (0.00333333) share Common 1¢ par
UraniumCore Co. name changed to Horizon Health International Corp. 10/09/2009 which name changed to Horizons Holdings International, Corp. 04/16/2015

O C R SYS INC (PA)
Merged out of existence 09/16/1991
Details not available

O-CEL-O, INC. (NY)
Merged into General Mills, Inc. 00/00/1952
Each (3.5) shares Common $1 par exchanged for (1) share Common no par

O CHARLEYS INC (TN)
Common no par split (3) for (2) by issuance of (0.5) additional share 08/08/1994
Common no par split (3) for (2) by issuance of (0.5) additional share payable 06/01/1998 to holders of record 05/20/1998
Acquired by Fidelity National Financial, Inc. (New) 05/09/2012
Each share Common no par exchanged for $9.85 cash

O DELI CORP (CO)
Each share old Common no par exchanged for (0.005) share new Common no par 10/20/1989
Name changed to Culinary Capital Corp. 11/29/1990
Culinary Capital Corp. recapitalized as Centra Capital Corp. (CO) 04/12/1996 which reincorporated in Delaware 04/24/1996 which reincorporated in Nevada 07/02/1998
(See Centra Capital Corp.)

FINANCIAL INFORMATION, INC.

O DONNELL GROUP INC (ON)
Name changed to spyn corp.
01/29/2001
(See spyn corp.)

O DONNELL INVT MGMT CORP (ON)
Merged into Strategic Value Corp.
6/8/99
Each share Common no par exchanged for $4 cash

O E INC (CANADA)
Acquired by Canon Canada Inc.
03/22/1990
Each share Common no par exchanged for $15.95 cash

O E X ELECTROMAGNETIC INC (BC)
Delisted from Vancouver Stock Exchange 03/01/1989

O G CONSULTING CORP (NJ)
Recapitalized as Towers Financial Corp. 06/04/1986
Each share Common $0.00001 par exchanged for (0.02) share Common $0.001 par
(See Towers Financial Corp.)

O GARA CO (OH)
Name changed to Kroll O'Gara Co.
12/1/97
Kroll O'Gara Co. name changed to Kroll Inc. (OH) 8/23/2001 which reincorporated in Delaware 7/2/2002
(See Kroll Inc.)

O I CORP (OK)
Acquired by ITT Corp. 11/15/2010
Each share Common 10¢ par exchanged for $12 cash

O I F FD (CA)
Charter suspended for failure to file reports and pay taxes 01/02/1974

O J OIL & GAS CORP (BC)
Name changed to U.S. Oil & Gas Corp. 08/26/1996
U.S. Oil & Gas Corp. merged into U.S. Oil & Gas Resources Inc. 11/13/1997 which reorganized as Odyssey Petroleum Corp. 08/25/2005 which recapitalized as Petrichor Energy Inc. 03/03/2011

O-JAY FOODS INC (MN)
Plan of reorganization under Chapter 11 Federal Bankruptcy proceedings confirmed 02/12/1990
No stockholders' equity

O-JAY INC (MN)
Name changed to Omni International Trading, Inc. 4/13/93
(See Omni International Trading, Inc.)

O.K. RUBBER WELDERS, INC. (CO)
Name changed to O.K. Tire & Rubber Co. 3/20/64
O.K. Tire & Rubber Co. merged into Ashland Oil & Refining Co. 6/27/66 which name changed to Ashland Oil, Inc. 2/2/70 which name changed to Ashland Inc. (Old) 1/27/95
(See Ashland Inc. (Old))

O.K. TIRE & RUBBER CO. (CO)
Voting Trust Agreement terminated 5/14/64
Each VTC for Common Capital Stock $10 par exchanged for (1) share Common Capital Stock $10 par
Acquired by Ashland Oil & Refining Co. 6/27/66
Each share Common Capital Stock $10 par exchanged for (0.324) share $2.40 Conv. Preferred 1966 Ser. no par
Ashland Oil & Refining Co. name changed to Ashland Oil, Inc. 2/2/70 which name changed to Ashland Inc. (Old) 1/27/95
(See Ashland Inc. (Old))

O LEARY ADVANTAGED TACTICAL GLOBAL CORPORATE BD FD (ON)
Combined Units separated 07/14/2010
Under plan of reorganization each Trust Unit automatically became O'Leary Global Bond Yield Advantaged Fund Ser. X Units on a net asset basis 08/15/2011

O LEARY CDN DIVERSIFIED INCOME FD (ON)
Name changed to Canoe Canadian Diversified Income Fund 02/23/2016
Canoe Canadian Diversified Income Fund merged into Canoe GO CANADA! Fund Corp. 04/22/2016

O'LEARY CANADIAN DIVIDEND FUND (ON)
Name changed to Canoe Canadian Dividend Fund 02/17/2016

O LEARY CDN EQUITY INCOME FD (ON)
Combined Units separated 01/15/2010
Trust Units reclassified as Ser. X Units 12/01/2011
Merged into O'Leary Canadian High Income Fund 03/26/2012
Each Ser. A Unit received (0.99123418) Ser. A Unit
Each Ser. F Unit received (1.02842901) Ser. F Units
Each Ser. M Unit received (1.03877835) Ser. M Units
Each Ser. X Unit received (0.98173548) Ser. X Unit

O'LEARY CANADIAN HIGH INCOME FUND (ON)
Name changed to Canoe Canadian High Income Fund 06/25/2013

O LEARY CDN INCOME OPPORTUNITIES FD (ON)
Units reclassified as Ser. X Units 12/01/2011
Name changed to O'Leary Canadian High Income Fund 01/25/2012
O'Leary Canadian High Income Fund name changed to Canoe Canadian High Income Fund 06/25/2013

O LEARY CDN INCOME OPPORTUNITIES FD 2 (ON)
Merged into O'Leary Canadian High Income Fund 12/14/2012
Each Unit received (1) Ser. Y Unit
O'Leary Canadian High Income Fund name changed to Canoe Canadian High Income Fund 06/25/2013

O LEARY FOUNDERS SER INCOME & GROWTH FD (ON)
Issue Information - 12,500,000 TR UNITS consisting of (1) TR UNIT and (1) WT offered at $12 per Unit on 09/28/2009
Combined Units separated 11/12/2009
Trust Units reclassified as Founder's Ser. Units 11/01/2010
Note: Non-Canadian residents will receive cash
Name changed to O'Leary Strategic Yield Plus Fund 01/25/2011
O'Leary Strategic Yield Plus Fund name changed to O'Leary Global Growth & Income Fund 09/30/2013

O LEARY GLOBAL EQUITY INCOME FD (ON)
Merged into O'Leary Global Equity Yield Fund 03/04/2011
Each Trust Unit no par automatically became (1.012519) Ser. X Units no par
O'Leary Global Equity Yield Fund name changed to O'Leary Canadian Dividend Fund 06/25/2013 which name changed to Canoe Canadian Dividend Fund 02/17/2016

O'LEARY GLOBAL EQUITY YIELD FUND (ON)
Name changed to O'Leary Canadian Dividend Fund 06/25/2013
O'Leary Canadian Dividend Fund name changed to Canoe Canadian Dividend Fund 02/17/2016

O LEARY GLOBAL INCOME OPPORTUNITIES FD (ON)
Merged into O'Leary Global Yield Opportunities Fund 08/16/2010
Each Trust Unit received (1.196585) Ser. X Unit
O'Leary Global Yield Opportunities Fund merged into O'Leary Strategic Yield Plus Fund 12/14/2012 which name changed to O'Leary Global Growth & Income Fund 09/30/2013

O LEARY GLOBAL INFRASTRUCTURE FD (ON)
Combined Units separated 12/08/2008
Under plan of merger each Class A Trust Unit automatically became (1.098816) O'Leary Global Infrastructure Yield Fund Ser. X Units 06/04/2010

O'LEARY GLOBAL YIELD OPPORTUNITIES FUND (ON)
Merged into O'Leary Strategic Yield Plus Fund 12/14/2012
Each Ser. A Unit received (0.996163965) Ser. A Unit
Each Ser. F Unit received (1.011139104) Ser. F Unit
Each Ser. M Unit received (0.969679354) Ser. M Unit
Each Ser. X Unit received (1) Ser. X Unit
O'Leary Strategic Yield Plus Fund name changed to O'Leary Global Growth & Income Fund 09/30/2013

O LEARY RES INC (CANADA)
Recapitalized 05/07/1997
Recapitalized from O'Leary Malartic Mines, Ltd. to O'Leary Resources Inc. 05/07/1997
Each share Common no par exchanged for (0.25) share Common no par
Charter dissolved for non-compliance 02/11/2009

O'LEARY STRATEGIC YIELD PLUS FUND (ON)
Name changed to O'Leary Global Growth & Income Fund 09/30/2013

O LEARY U S STRATEGIC YIELD ADVANTAGED FD (ON)
Name changed to Canoe U.S. Strategic Yield Advantaged Fund 02/23/2016
Canoe U.S. Strategic Yield Advantaged Fund merged into Canoe 'GO CANADA!' Fund Corp. 05/20/2016

O LORI HLDGS LTD (BC)
Struck off register and declared dissolved for failure to file returns 3/18/83

O-M CO. (OH)
Liquidation completed
Each share Common $2 par received initial distribution of $5.89488 principal amount of Plymouth Corp. 6% Debentures due 5/1/82, (0.589488) Plymouth Corp. Common Stock purchase warrant and $8 cash 11/2/64
Each share Common $2 par received second distribution of $2 cash 2/23/66
Each share Common $2 par exchanged for third and final distribution of $1 cash 12/19/66

O MEDIA INC (DE)
Name changed to Original Media, Inc. 1/4/2000
Original Media, Inc. recapitalized as OMDA Oil & Gas Inc. 6/7/2002

O N E WORLD DISTRG INC (DE)
Name changed to Polythene Metro, Inc. 12/4/2006
Polythene Metro, Inc. name changed to Gold River Productions, Inc. 2/12/2007

O NEAL PETE INC (IL)
Merged into Strata Corp. (DE) 05/09/1984
Each share Common no par exchanged for (0.19802) share Class A Common no par
Strata Corp. (DE) name changed to B.T. Energy Corp. 09/07/1989
(See B.T. Energy Corp.)

O OKIEP COPPER LTD (SOUTH AFRICA)
Acquired by Metorex Properties Ltd. in 1998
Each ADR for Ordinary Rand-1 par exchanged for $4.94 cash

O.P. SKAGGS CO. (DE)
Name changed to Western Energy Empire Inc. 08/20/1981
Western Energy Empire Inc. name changed to Accurate Business Systems, Inc. 04/20/1987
(See Accurate Business Systems, Inc.)

O P RES LTD (BC)
Recapitalized as L.E.H. Ventures Ltd. 02/15/1994
Each (3.41) shares Common no par exchanged for (1) share Common no par
L.E.H. Ventures Ltd. name changed to Discovery PGM Exploration Ltd. 09/16/2005 which was acquired by Marathon PGM Corp. 06/13/2008
(See Marathon PGM Corp.)

O PETRO ENERGY CORP (OK)
Each share old Common $0.001 par exchanged for (0.01) share new Common $0.001 par 03/18/1985
Recapitalized as Primary Development Corp. 10/26/1989
Each share Common $0.001 par exchanged for (0.2) share Common $0.001 par
Primary Development Corp. name changed to Bingo & Gaming International, Inc. 08/28/1995 which name changed to BGI Inc. 10/19/1999

O REILLY AUTOMOTIVE INC OLD (MO)
Common 1¢ par split (2) for (1) by issuance of (1) additional share payable 08/31/1997 to holders of record 07/31/1997
Common 1¢ par split (2) for (1) by issuance of (1) additional share payable 11/30/1999 to holders of record 11/15/1999
Common 1¢ par split (2) for (1) by issuance of (1) additional share payable 06/15/2005 to holders of record 05/31/2005 Ex date - 06/16/2005
Under plan of reorganization each share Common 1¢ par automatically became (1) share O'Reilly Automotive, Inc. (New) Common 1¢ par 12/29/2010

O.T.C. GROWTH FUND INC. (NY)
Name changed to Taurus, Inc. 11/19/70

O T C CAP CORP (CO)
Recapitalized as Capital 2000 Inc. 03/27/1995
Each share Common $0.001 par exchanged for (0.004) share Common $0.001 par
Capital 2000 Inc. name changed to United Shields Corp. 05/19/1997
(See United Shields Corp.)

O-TECH VENTURES CORP (BC)
Recapitalized as Bright Star Ventures Ltd. 06/26/1996
Each share Common no par exchanged for (0.33333333) share Common no par
(See Bright Star Ventures Ltd.)

O TOOLES GROUP INC (ON)
Assets sold for the benefit of creditors in May 1992

O-W-OAK

No stockholders' equity

O.U. LIQUIDATION, INC. (DE)
Under plan of liquidation each share Common $1 par exchanged for (0.108313) share Filigree Foods, Inc. Common $1 par 06/23/1972
(See Filigree Foods, Inc.)

O-W FUND, INC. (MD)
Merged into New York Venture Fund, Inc. 12/14/1988
Each share Common $10 par exchanged for (63.6445) shares Capital Stock $1 par
New York Venture Fund, Inc. name changed to Davis New York Venture Fund, Inc. 10/01/1995

O&Y PPTYS CORP (ON)
Each share old Common no par exchanged for (1) share new Common no par to reflect a (1) for (25) reverse split followed by a (25) for (1) forward split 06/30/2003
Note: Holders of (24) shares or fewer received $5.35 cash per share
Merged into Brookfield Properties Corp. 10/21/2005
Each share new Common no par exchanged for $12.72 cash

O&Y REAL ESTATE INVT TR (ON)
Acquired by Brookfield Properties Corp. 11/29/2005
Each Unit exchanged for $16.25 cash

O'BRIEN ENVIRONMENTAL ENERGY INC. (DE)
Name changed 07/02/1991
Class A Common 1¢ par split (3) for (2) by issuance of (0.5) additional share 11/05/1986
Name changed from O'Brien Energy Systems, Inc. to O'Brien Environmental Energy, Inc. 07/02/1991
Name changed to NRG Generating (U.S.) Inc. and Class A Common 1¢ par reclassified as Common 1¢ par 04/16/1996
NRG Generating (U.S.) Inc. name changed to Cogeneration Corp. of America 07/20/1998
(See Cogeneration Corp. of America)

O'BRIEN'S OF CALIFORNIA, INC.
Merged into Chase Candy Co. 00/00/1948
Each (4) shares $1.35 Preferred $25 par exchanged for (5) shares 5% Preferred B $20 par
Chase Candy Co. name changed to Bunte Brothers Chase Candy Co. 00/00/1954 which name changed to Chase General Corp. 03/26/1962

O'CEDAR CORP. (IL)
Class A Common $10 par changed to no par in 1928
Each (10) shares Class A or B Common no par exchanged for (1) share Class A or B Common $5 par in 1930
Dissolved 1/29/55

O'CONNOR DRUG CO. (MI)
Acquired by Time Industries, Inc. 6/30/72
Each share Preferred $100 par exchanged for $106 cash

O'CONNOR MOFFATT & CO.
Acquired by Macy (R.H.) & Co., Inc. 00/00/1945
Each (4) shares Class B exchanged for (3) shares Common Class AA redeemed 00/00/1945
(See Macy (R.H.) & Co.)

O'DAY CORP. (MA)
Completely liquidated 8/26/66
Each share Capital Stock no par exchanged for first and final distribution of (0.2) share Bangor Punta Alegre Sugar Corp. Common $1 par
Bangor Punta Alegre Sugar Corp. name changed to Bangor Punta Corp. 1/20/67

(See Bangor Punta Corp.)

O'DONNELL MINES LTD. (ON)
Charter cancelled for failure to file reports and pay taxes in 1968

O'GARA COAL CO.
Reorganized as Sahara Coal Co. in 1935

O'MAHONY (JERRY), INC. (NJ)
Bankrupt in 1958

O'NEIL (GEO. F.) REALTY CORP. (NY)
Charter cancelled and proclaimed dissolved for failure to pay taxes and file reports 1/9/57

O'QUIN CORP. (DE)
No longer in existence having become inoperative and void for non-payment of taxes 4/1/59

O'SULLIVAN INDS HLDGS INC NEW (DE)
Plan of reorganization under Chapter 11 Federal Bankruptcy Code effective 3/16/2006
No stockholders' equity

O'SULLIVAN INDS HLDGS INC OLD (DE)
Issue Information - 14,764,000 shares COM offered at $22 per share on 01/26/1994
Merged into O'Sullivan Industries Holdings, Inc. (New) 11/30/99
Each share Common $1 par exchanged for (1) share 12% Sr. Preferred 1 par and $16.75 cash
(See O'Sullivan Industries Holdings, Inc. (New))

O'SULLIVAN RUBBER CO., INC. (DE)
Reincorporated under the laws of Virginia as O'Sullivan Rubber Corp. 9/22/45
O'Sullivan Rubber Corp. name changed to O'Sullivan Corp. 1/1/71
(See O'Sullivan Corp.)

O2 CAP INC (AB)
Name changed to Xianburg Data Systems Canada Corp. (AB) 11/26/2010
Xianburg Data Systems Canada Corp. (AB) reincorporated in British Columbia 08/15/2013

OACIS HEALTHCARE HLDGS CORP (DE)
Merged into Science Applications International Corp. 03/31/1999
Each share Common 1¢ par exchanged for $4.45 cash

OAHE INVTS INC (MN)
Stock Dividend - 100% 2/13/81
Name changed to Kinnard Investments, Inc. 5/25/83
Kinnard Investments, Inc. name changed to Stockwalk.com Group, Inc. 9/11/2000 which name changed to Stockwalk Group, Inc. 1/1/2001
(See Stockwalk Group, Inc.)

OAHU RAILWAY & LAND CO. (HI)
Merged into Dillingham Corp. 12/29/61
Each share Capital Stock $20 par exchanged for (1) share $1.35 Conv. Preferred no par and (2) shares Common no par
(See Dillingham Corp.)

OAHU SUGAR CO., LTD. (HI)
Merged into American Factors Ltd. 1/6/61
Each share Capital Stock $20 par exchanged for (1) share Capital Stock $20 par
American Factors Ltd. name changed to Amfac, Inc. 4/30/66
(See Amfac, Inc.)

OAK CLIFF BK & TR CO (DALLAS, TX)
Each share Capital Stock $20 par exchanged for (2) shares Capital Stock $10 par 01/25/1960
Capital Stock $10 par changed to $5

par and (1) additional share issued 09/29/1967
Stock Dividends - (1) for (7.5) 01/12/1960; 20% 11/02/1964; 10% 07/31/1969; 10% 11/30/1970; 10% 05/31/1973; 25% 04/30/1979
Merged into Republic of Texas Corp. 09/02/1980
Each share Capital Stock $5 par exchanged for (1.3) shares $2.125 Conv. Preferred Ser. A no par
Republic of Texas Corp. name changed to RepublicBank Corp. 06/30/1982 which merged into First RepublicBank Corp. 06/06/1987
(See First RepublicBank Corp.)

OAK CLIFF SVGS & LN ASSN (TX)
Through purchase offer First Texas Financial Corp. held all but (524) shares as of 04/30/1973
Public interest eliminated

OAK CREEK PARK, INC. (IA)
Charter cancelled for failure to file annual reports 11/24/75

OAK ELECTRO NETICS CORP (DE)
Common $1 par split (3) for (2) by issuance of (0.5) additional share 8/12/66
Name changed to Oak Industries, Inc. 5/5/72
Oak Industries, Inc. merged into Corning Inc. 1/28/2000

OAK HILL FINL INC (OH)
Common no par split (5) for (4) by issuance of (0.25) additional share payable 06/01/1998 to holders of record 05/01/1998
Merged into WesBanco, Inc. 11/30/2007
Each share Common no par exchanged for (1.256) shares Common $2.0833 par

OAK HILL INC (NV)
Name changed to ThermoView Industries Inc. (NV) 02/24/1998
ThermoView Industries Inc. (NV) reincorporated in Delaware 05/22/1998
(See ThermoView Industries Inc.)

OAK HILL SPORTSWEAR CORP (NY)
Name changed to Rexx Environmental Corp. 02/17/1998
Rexx Environmental Corp. recapitalized as Newtek Capital Inc. 09/19/2000 which name changed to Newtek Business Services, Inc. (NY) 11/26/2002 which reincorporated in Maryland as Newtek Business Services Corp. 11/13/2014

OAK HILL SPORTSWEAR INC (NY)
Stock Dividends - 50% 10/23/1975; 50% 04/15/1976
Completely liquidated 08/08/1979
Each share Common 1¢ par exchanged for first and final distribution of $10 cash

OAK INDS INC (DE)
Common $1 par split (3) for (2) by issuance of (0.5) additional share 12/8/78
$4.375 Conv. Preferred Ser. A no par called for redemption 3/28/80
$4.375 Conv. Preferred Ser. B no par called for redemption 3/28/80
Common $1 par split (2) for (1) by issuance of (1) additional share 3/26/81
$1.75 Conv. Preferred Ser. C $5 par called for redemption 6/16/86
Common $1 par changed to 1¢ par 6/4/92
Each share old Common 1¢ par exchanged for (0.2) share new Common 1¢ par 5/13/93
Merged into Corning Inc. 1/28/2000
Each share new Common 1¢ par exchanged for (0.83) share Common 1¢ par

OAK MANUFACTURING CO. (DE)
Reincorporated 4/30/60
Stock Dividend - 25% 9/15/55
State of incorporation changed from (IL) to (DE) 4/30/60
Name changed to Oak Electro/Netics Corp. 4/24/64
Oak Electro/Netics Corp. name changed to Oak Industries, Inc. 5/5/72 which merged into Corning Inc. 1/28/2000

OAK MOUNTAIN PROPERTY MANAGEMENT CO., INC. (CA)
Charter suspended for failure to file reports and pay fees 4/2/90

OAK PARK BANCORP INC (DE)
Merged into First United Financial Services, Inc. 05/31/1985
Each share Common $6 par exchanged for (2.781) shares Common $5 par
(See First United Financial Services, Inc.)

OAK PARK INC (DE)
Charter cancelled and declared inoperative and void for non-payment of taxes 3/1/75

OAK PARK NATL BK (OAK PARK, IL)
Each share Capital Stock $100 par exchanged for (2) shares Capital Stock $50 par plus a 50% stock dividend paid 00/00/1954
Stock Dividend - 100% 10/18/1960
Name changed to First Bank of Oak Park (Oak Park, IL) 10/01/1971
Each share Capital Stock $50 par exchanged for (1) share Capital Stock $50 par
(See First Bank of Oak Park (Oak Park, IL))

OAK PARK TR & SVGS BK (OAK PARK, IL)
Capital Stock $50 par changed to $16-2/3 par and (2) additional shares issued 07/22/1968
Stock Dividends - 25% 06/01/1955; 16-2/3% 03/01/1958; 20% 05/01/1961
Reorganized as Oak Park Bancorp, Inc. 12/28/1973
Each share Capital Stock $16-2/3 par exchanged for (3) shares Common $6 par
Oak Park Bancorp, Inc. merged into First United Financial Services, Inc. 05/31/1985
(See First United Financial Services, Inc.)

OAK RIDGE, INC. (FL)
Name changed to Pershing Industries, Inc. 10/22/68

OAK RIDGE ATOM INDS INC (TN)
Charter revoked for non-payment of taxes 12/31/1987

OAK RIDGE ENERGY TECHNOLOGIES INC (CO)
Name changed to Oakridge Global Energy Solutions, Inc. 11/07/2014

OAK RIDGE MICRO-ENERGY INC (CO)
Each share old Common $0.001 par exchanged for (0.1) share new Common $0.001 par 01/06/2003
Each share new Common $0.001 par exchanged again for (3) shares new Common $0.001 par 06/01/2004
Each share new Common $0.001 par exchanged again for (0.04545454) share new Common $0.001 par 09/30/2010
Name changed to Oak Ridge Energy Technologies, Inc. 08/28/2013
Oak Ridge Energy Technologies, Inc. name changed to Oakridge Global Energy Solutions, Inc. 11/07/2014

OAK TECHNOLOGY INC (DE)
Common $0.001 par split (2) for (1) by issuance of (1) additional share payable 03/28/1996 to holders of record 02/09/1996

Merged into Zoran Corp. 08/11/2003
Each share Common $0.001 par exchanged for (0.2323) share Common $0.001 par and $1.78 cash
Zoran Corp. merged into CSR PLC 08/31/2011
(See CSR PLC)

OAK TREE MED SYS INC (DE)
Recapitalized 8/1/94
Recapitalized from Oak Tree Construction Computers, Inc. to Oak Tree Medical Systems, Inc. 8/1/94
Each share Common 1¢ par exchanged for (0.125) share Common 1¢ par
Name changed to New World Brands, Inc. 12/21/2001

OAK TR & SVGS BK (CHICAGO, IL)
Name changed to Oak Bank (Chicago, IL) 12/01/1999

OAK VY CMNTY BK (OAKDALE, CA)
Common no par split (3) for (2) by issuance of (0.5) additional share payable 03/13/2000 to holders of record 02/29/2000
Common no par split (3) for (2) by issuance of (0.5) additional share payable 06/25/2003 to holders of record 06/16/2003 Ex date - 06/26/2003
Common no par split (3) for (2) by issuance of (0.5) additional share payable 01/13/2005 to holders of record 01/03/2005 Ex date - 01/14/2005
Common no par split (3) for (2) by issuance of (0.5) additional share payable 01/13/2006 to holders of record 01/03/2006 Ex date - 01/17/2006
Stock Dividend - 4% payable 02/20/1998 to holders of record 02/02/1998
Under plan of reorganization each share Common no par automatically became (1) share Oak Valley Bancorp Common no par 07/03/2008

OAKBROOK CONS INC (DE)
Preferred Ser. A $1 par called for redemption 05/17/1984
Each share Common $1 par exchanged for (0.01) share Common $100 par 05/17/1984
Merged into Obazs Corp. 01/15/1985
Each share Common $100 par exchanged for $2,000 cash

OAKES PRODUCTS CORP.
Merged into Houdaille-Hershey Corp. in 1929
Houdaille-Hershey Corp. name changed to Houdaille Industries, Inc. (Mich.) 11/30/55 which reincorporated under the laws of Delaware 4/1/68
(See Houdaille Industries, Inc. (Del.))

OAKHAM CAP CORP (BC)
Recapitalized as LSC Lithium Corp. 02/28/2017
Each share Common no par exchanged for (0.15384615) share Common no par

OAKHILL COMMUNICATIONS INC. (AB)
Delisted from Alberta Stock Exchange 12/10/91

OAKHURST INC (DE)
Name changed 08/23/1995
Name changed from Oakhurst Capital, Inc. to Oakhurst Co., Inc. 08/23/1995
Name changed to Sterling Construction Co., Inc. 11/13/2001

OAKITE PRODS INC (NY)
Each share Common $20 par exchanged for (4) shares Common $5 par 00/00/1952
Common $5 par changed to $1.66-2/3 par and (2) additional shares issued 03/15/1966
Common $1.66-2/3 par changed to $1.20 par and (0.5) additional share issued 10/04/1968
Merged into Carlyle Holding Corp. 01/24/1989
Each share Common $1.20 par exchanged for $45.50 cash

OAKLAND BK COMM (OAKLAND, CA)
Capital Stock $50 par changed to $5 par and (9) additional shares issued 04/01/1966
Acquired by Union Bancorp 04/25/1969
Each share Capital Stock $5 par exchanged for (1.16) shares Common $10 par
Union Bancorp name changed to Unionamerica, Inc. (CA) 05/09/1969
(See Unionamerica, Inc. (CA))

OAKLAND CONS CORP (MI)
Charter declared inoperative and void for failure to file reports 05/15/1979

OAKLAND RUBBER CO. (CA)
Dissolution completed 4/18/60

OAKLAND TITLE INSURANCE & GUARANTY CO. (CA)
Each share Capital Stock $100 par exchanged for (4) shares Capital Stock $25 par 00/00/1946
Name changed to Oakland Title Insurance Co. 00/00/1953
Oakland Title Insurance Co. merged into California Pacific Title Insurance Co. 10/01/1957 which merged into Title Insurance & Trust Co. 01/14/1959 which name changed to TI Corp. (of California) 06/28/1968 which name changed to Ticor 04/27/1977
(See Ticor)

OAKLAND TITLE INSURANCE CO. (CA)
Merged into California Pacific Title Insurance Co. share for share 10/1/57
California Pacific Title Insurance Co. merged into Title Insurance & Trust Co. 1/14/59 which name changed to TI Corp. (of California) 6/28/68 which name changed to Ticor 4/27/77
(See Ticor)

OAKLEY ECONOMY STORES CO.
Acquired by Kroger Grocery & Baking Co. 00/00/1939
Details not available

OAKLEY INC (WA)
Common 1¢ par split (2) for (1) by issuance of (1) additional share payable 10/10/1996 to holders of record 09/25/1996 Ex date - 10/11/1996
Merged into Luxottica Group S.p.A. 11/14/2007
Each share Common 1¢ par exchanged for $29.30 cash

OAKMONT ACQUISITION CORP (DE)
Name changed to Brooke Credit Corp. 07/18/2007
Brooke Credit Corp. name changed to Aleritas Capital Corp. 08/19/2008
(See Aleritas Capital Corp.)

OAKMONT CAP CORP (BC)
Name changed to Oakmont Minerals Corp. 07/08/2013
Oakmont Minerals Corp. recapitalized as GreenPower Motor Co. Inc. 12/30/2014

OAKMONT CORP. (TX)
Name changed to Oakmont Marine Corp. 9/12/75
Oakmont Marine Corp. name changed to Lorain Telecom Corp. (TX) 11/7/83 which reorganized in Delaware 4/10/85
(See Lorain Telecom Corp.)

OAKMONT MARINE CORP (TX)
Conv. Preference Ser. B $100 par called for redemption 6/15/77
Name changed to Lorain Telecom Corp. (TX) 11/7/83
Lorain Telecom Corp. (TX) reorganized in Delaware 4/10/85
(See Lorain Telecom Corp.)

OAKMONT MINERALS CORP (BC)
Recapitalized as GreenPower Motor Co. Inc. 12/30/2014
Each share Common no par exchanged for (0.5) share Common no par

OAKRIDGE ACQUISITIONS INC (CO)
Name changed to Child Care Centers of North America, Inc. 01/07/1992
(See Child Care Centers of North America, Inc.)

OAKRIDGE ENERGY INC (UT)
Name changed 10/22/1982
Each share Common 1¢ par exchanged for (0.25) share Common 4¢ par 08/18/1978
Name changed from Oakridge Exploration, Inc. to Oakridge Energy, Inc. 10/22/1982
Liquidation completed
Each share Common 4¢ par received initial distribution of $2.35 cash payable 07/07/2015 to holders of record 04/09/2015 Ex date - 07/10/2015
Each share Common 4¢ par received second and final distribution of $0.94 cash payable 07/20/2018 to holders of record 04/09/2015

OAKRIDGE HLDGS INC (MN)
Plan of reorganization under Chapter 11 Federal Bankruptcy proceedings effective 08/02/2018
No stockholders' equity

OAKRIDGE MINING CORP. LTD. (ON)
Charter cancelled 10/21/57

OAKRIDGE URANIUM MINES LTD. (ON)
Name changed to Oakridge Mining Corp. Ltd. in 1951
(See Oakridge Mining Corp. Ltd.)

OAKS INC (KY)
Voluntarily dissolved 10/31/2006
Details not available

OAKVILLE WOOD SPECIALTIES LTD (ON)
Voluntarily dissolved in 1993
Details not available

OAKWOOD DEP BK CO (OAKWOOD, OH)
Placed in receivership 02/01/2002
Stockholders' equity unlikely

OAKWOOD HOMES CORP (NC)
Common 50¢ par split (2) for (1) by issuance of (1) additional share 03/21/1983
Common 50¢ par split (5) for (4) by issuance of (0.25) additional share 11/29/1985
Common 50¢ par split (5) for (4) by issuance of (0.25) additional share 11/28/1986
Common 50¢ par split (5) for (4) by issuance of (0.25) additional share 03/26/1991
Common 50¢ par split (3) for (2) by issuance of (0.5) additional share 05/18/1992
Common 50¢ par split (2) for (1) by issuance of (1) additional share payable 05/31/1996 to holders of record 05/17/1996 Ex date - 06/03/1996
Each share old Common 50¢ par exchanged for (0.2) share new Common 50¢ par 06/18/2001
Stock Dividends - 10% 04/30/1976; 10% 08/05/1977; 10% 07/24/1978; 10% 04/01/1979; 10% 09/08/1980; 10% 10/21/1981; 10% 10/21/1982
Plan of reorganization under Chapter 11 Federal Bankruptcy proceedings effective 04/14/2004
Stockholders' equity unlikely
Note: Name changed to Reorganized Sale OKWD, Inc. 04/21/2004

OAKWOOD INTL PETE N L (AUSTRALIA)
Name changed to Winton Oil N.L. 03/12/1986
(See Winton Oil N.L.)

OAKWOOD MINES LTD. (ON)
Charter revoked for failure to file reports and pay fees 11/16/67

OAKWOOD NATIONAL BANK (WOODLAND HILLS, CA)
Name changed to National Bank of Commerce (Los Angeles) 10/15/65
National Bank of Commerce (Los Angeles) name changed to Republic National Bank of California (Los Angeles) 2/29/68 which recapitalized as Republic National Bank & Trust Co. (Los Angeles) 7/15/70

OAKWOOD PETES LTD (CANADA)
Old Common no par reclassified as new Common no par 4/15/83
Each share new Common no par received distribution of (1) share Class A no par 4/29/83
$1.90 1st Preferred Ser. A no par conversion privilege expired 9/1/88
Acquired by Sceptre Resources Ltd. 3/14/89
Each share $0.675 Retractable Preferred Ser. C no par exchanged for (0.270944) share Common no par and (0.338679) Common Stock Purchase Warrant expiring 3/14/94
Each share $0.96 Conv. Retractable Preferred Ser. D no par exchanged for (0.424658) share Common no par and (0.530823) Common Stock Purchase Warrant expiring 3/14/94
Each share $1.90 1st Preferred Ser. A no par exchanged for (0.878523) share Common no par and (1.098154) Common Stock Purchase Warrants expiring 3/14/94
Each share $2.78 Retractable Preferred Ser. B no par exchanged for (0.98649) share Common no par and (1.233112) Common Stock Purchase Warrants expiring 3/14/94
Each share Class A no par exchanged for (0.179258) share Common no par and (0.229982) Common Stock Purchase Warrant expiring 3/14/94
Each share new Common no par exchanged for (0.179258) share Common no par and (0.229982) Common Stock Purchase Warrant expiring 3/14/94
Spectre Resources Ltd. merged into Canadian Natural Resources Ltd. 8/15/96

OANDO ENERGY RES INC (CANADA)
Acquired by Oando PLC 05/16/2016
Each share Common no par exchanged for USD$1.20 cash

OAO BALTIKA BREWERY (RUSSIA)
GDR agreement terminated 02/29/2016
Each GDR for Preferred exchanged for (1) share Preferred
Each GDR for Ordinary exchanged for (1) share Ordinary
Note: Unexchanged GDR's will be sold and the proceeds, if any, held for claim after 08/29/2016

OAO KOSTROMSKAYA GRES (RUSSIA)
Acquired by Unified Energy System of Russia 12/00/2005
Details not available

OAO OPEN INVTS (RUSSIA)
Name changed to Joint Stock Company Open Investments 12/11/2006
Joint Stock Company Open

OAO-OBJ

Investments name changed to Open Investments PJSC 09/04/2015 which name changed to Ingrad PJSC 02/08/2018

OAO TECHNOLOGY SOLUTIONS INC (DE)
Issue Information - 6,720,000 shares COM offered at $5 per share on 10/21/1997
Merged into Terrapin Partners Subsidiary LLC 2/27/2004
Each share Common 1¢ par exchanged for $3.15 cash

OASIS DIAMOND EXPL INC (CANADA)
Recapitalized as Temoris Resources Inc. 03/27/2006
Each share Common no par exchanged for (1/6) share Common no par
Temoris Resources Inc. name changed to Glen Eagle Resources Inc. 09/10/2008

OASIS ENERGY CORP (AB)
Merged into Zargon Oil & Gas Ltd. (Old) 07/31/1997
Each share Common no par exchanged for (0.0125) share Common no par
Zargon Oil & Gas Ltd. (Old) reorganized as Zargon Energy Trust 07/21/2004 which reorganized as Zargon Oil & Gas Ltd. (New) 01/07/2011

OASIS ENTERTAINMENTS FOURTH MOVIE PROJ INC (NV)
Each share old Common $0.001 par exchanged for (0.01) share new Common $0.001 par 09/10/2001
Each share new Common $0.001 par exchanged again for (2) shares new Common $0.001 par 12/20/2001
Each share new Common $0.001 par exchanged again for (1/3) share new Common $0.001 par 09/18/2002
Note: Holders of (100) to (300) shares will receive (100) shares only
Holders of (99) shares or fewer were not affected by the reverse split
Each share new Common $0.001 par exchanged again for (0.02) share new Common $0.001 par 09/25/2003
Name changed to Family Healthcare Solutions, Inc. 10/10/2003
Family Healthcare Solutions, Inc. name changed to Mega Media Group, Inc. 08/24/2007
(See Mega Media Group, Inc.)

OASIS INFORMATION SYS INC NEW (NV)
Each share old Common $0.001 par exchanged for (0.1) share new Common $0.001 par 06/21/2002
Recapitalized as 777 Sports Entertainment, Corp. 02/07/2005
Each share Common $0.001 par exchanged for (0.00333333) share Common $0.001 par
Note: No holder will receive fewer than (100) shares
777 Sports Entertainment, Corp. recapitalized as NT Mining Corp. 11/04/2008 which recapitalized as Sanwire Corp. (NV) 03/07/2013 which reincorporated in Wyoming 07/07/2015

OASIS LAUNDERIES INC (CA)
Charter suspended for failure to file reports and pay fees 4/1/93

OASIS OIL CORP (NV)
Name changed to MVP Network, Inc. 09/07/2005
(See MVP Network, Inc.)

OASIS ONLINE TECHNOLOGIES CORP (MN)
Name changed to Capital Group Holdings, Inc. 11/01/2010

OASIS PARKS (CA)
Capital Stock $2 par changed to no par 01/01/1969
Name changed to Dental Dynamic Systems 02/13/1969
Dental Dynamic Systems name changed to Alto Communications, Inc. 06/11/1973
(See Alto Communications, Inc.)

OASIS RESIDENTIAL INC (NV)
Merged into Camden Property Trust 4/8/98
Each share $2.25 Conv. Preferred Ser. A 1¢ par exchanged for (1) share $2.25 Conv. Preferred Ser. A 1¢ par
Each share Common 1¢ par exchanged for (0.759) Share of Bene. Int. no par

OASIS RESORTS INTL INC (NV)
Each share old Common no par exchanged for (0.2) share new Common no par 03/03/2000
Each share new Common no par exchanged for (0.01666666) share Common $0.001 par 03/19/2001
SEC revoked common stock registration 07/30/2004
Stockholders' equity unlikely

OASIS RES INC (CANADA)
Recapitalized as Consolidated Oasis Resources Inc. 06/28/1990
Each (15) shares Common no par exchanged for (1) share Common no par
Consolidated Oasis Resources Inc. name changed to Oasis Diamond Exploration Inc. 06/18/2001 which recapitalized as Temoris Resources Inc. 03/27/2006 which name changed to Glen Eagle Resources Inc. 09/10/2008

OASYS MOBILE INC (DE)
Plan of reorganization under Chapter 11 Federal Bankruptcy Code effective 10/12/2007
No stockholders' equity

OATPOINT CAP CORP (BC)
Name changed to Richfield Ventures Corp. 11/26/2007
Richfield Ventures Corp. merged into New Gold Inc. 06/01/2011

OAXACA RES CORP (NV)
Name changed to Garmatex Holdings Ltd. 08/15/2016
Garmatex Holdings Ltd. recapitalized as Evolution Blockchain Group Inc. 02/28/2018

OBA FINL SVCS INC (MD)
Merged into F.N.B. Corp. 09/22/2014
Each share Common 1¢ par exchanged for (1.781) shares Common 1¢ par

OBABIKA MINES LTD. (ON)
Charter cancelled in 1962

OBAGI MED PRODS INC (DE)
Issue Information - 5,350,000 shares COM offered at $11 per share on 12/13/2006
Acquired by Valeant Pharmaceuticals International, Inc. 04/25/2013
Each share Common $0.001 exchanged for $24 cash

OBALSKI MINING CORP. (QC)
Recapitalized as Obalski (1945) Ltd. 00/00/1946
Each share Capital Stock exchanged for (0.2) share Capital Stock
Obalski (1945) Ltd. recapitalized as United Obalski Mining Co. Ltd. 11/13/1961 which merged into Allied Mining Corp. 09/22/1969 which merged into United Asbestos Inc. 06/29/173 wh merged into Campbell Resources Inc. (New) 06/08/1983
(See Campbell Resources Inc. (New))

OBALSKI (1945) LTD. (QC)
Recapitalized as United Obalski Mining 11/13/1961
Each share Capital Stock exchanged for (0.2) share Capital Stock $1 par United Obalski Mining Co. Ltd. merged into Allied Mining Corp. 09/22/1969 which merged into United Asbestos Inc. 06/29/1973 which merged into Campbell Resources Inc. (New) 06/08/1983
(See Campbell Resources Inc. (New))

OBAN MNG CORP (ON)
Each share old Common no par exchanged for (0.05) share new Common no par 08/27/2015
Name changed to Osisko Mining Inc. 06/21/2016

OBAN PETES INC (AB)
Name changed to Devlan Exploration Co. Ltd. 3/29/96
Devlan Exploration Co. recapitalized as Devlan Exploration Inc. 11/2/98
(See Devlan Exploration Inc.)

OBASKA LAKE MINES LTD (CANADA)
Recapitalized as International Obaska Mines Ltd. 9/14/70
Each share Capital Stock no par exchanged for (0.2) share Capital Stock no par
(See International Obaska Mines Ltd.)

OBAYASHI CORP (JAPAN)
ADR agreement terminated 09/17/2009
Each ADR for Common exchanged for $34.60224 cash

OBEAR-NESTER GLASS CO. (MO)
Merged into Indian Head Inc. 9/15/67
Each share Common no par exchanged for (0.4) share $4.50 Conv. Preferred Ser. A no par
(See Indian Head Inc.)

OBEATRO MINE CO. LTD. (BC)
Struck from British Columbia Registrar of Companies and proclaimed dissolved in December 1965

OBEES FRANCHISE SYS INC (GA)
Each share old Common $0.001 par exchanged for (30) shares new Common $0.001 par 07/23/2007
Each share new Common $0.001 par exchanged again for (0.01) share new Common $0.001 par 05/06/2008
Administratively dissolved 09/03/2012

OBERG INDS LTD (BC)
Recapitalized as Consolidated Oberg Industries Ltd. 8/21/90
Each share Common no par exchanged for (0.2) share Common no par
Consolidated Oberg Industries Ltd. name changed to Hytec Flow Systems Inc. 1/16/97
(See Hytec Flow Systems Inc.)

OBERLIN BANCSHARES INC (OH)
Acquired by Central Bancorporation, Inc. 11/30/1986
Each share Common $10 par exchanged for (1.188) shares Common $5 par
Central Bancorporation, Inc. merged into PNC Financial Corp 02/29/1988 which name changed to PNC Bank Corp. 02/08/1993 which name changed to PNC Financial Services Group, Inc. 03/15/2000

OBERLIN SVGS BK CO (OBERLIN, OH)
Stock Dividends - 10% 04/18/1977; 10% 04/20/1978
Reorganized as Oberlin Bancshares, Inc. 02/29/1984
Each share Capital Stock $10 par exchanged for (1) share Common $10 par
Oberlin Bancshares, Inc. acquired by Central Bancorporation, Inc.

11/30/1986 which merged into PNC Financial Corp. 02/29/1988 which name changed to PNC Bank Corp. 02/08/1993 which name changed to PNC Financial Services Group, Inc. 03/15/2000

OBERMAN & CO. (MO)
Name changed to Oberman Manufacturing Co. in 1952
(See Oberman Manufacturing Co.)

OBERMAN MFG CO (MO)
Voluntarily dissolved 11/19/68
Details not available

OBERON PETROLEUMS LTD. (ON)
Charter cancelled by Province of Ontario 8/29/60

OBERT (LOUIS) BREWING CO.
Bankrupt in 1936

OBIE MEDIA CORP (OR)
Common no par split (11) for (10) by issuance of (0.1) additional share payable 12/15/1997 to holders of record 11/21/1997
Common no par split (11) for (10) by issuance of (0.1) additional share payable 12/15/1998 to holders of record 11/21/1998
Stock Dividend - 10% payable 12/15/1999 to holders of record 11/22/1999
Merged into Lamar Advertising Co. (Old) 01/19/2005
Each share Common no par exchanged for (0.1665) share Class A Common $0.001 par
Lamar Advertising Co. (Old) merged into Lamar Advertising Co. (New) 11/19/2014

OBJ ENTERPRISES INC (FL)
Name change to MyGo Games Holding Co. 07/28/2014

OBJECT DESIGN INC (DE)
Name changed to eXcelon Corp. 01/27/2000
(See eXcelon Corp.)

OBJECT RECOGNITION SYS INC (DE)
Name changed to ORS Automation, Inc. 05/30/1985
ORS Automation, Inc. reorganized as Somerset International Group, Inc. 02/23/2004
(See Somerset International Group, Inc.)

OBJECTIVE COMMUNICATIONS INC (DE)
Issue Informaton - 1,800,000 shares COM offered at $5.50 per share on 04/03/1997
Each share old Common 1¢ par exchanged for (1/7) share new Common 1¢ par 4/15/99
Name changed to Video Network Communications, Inc. 9/10/99
Video Network Communications, Inc. name changed to TalkPoint Communications, Inc. 8/14/2003
(See TalkPoint Communications, Inc.)

OBJECTIVE SYS INTEGRATORS INC (DE)
Reincorporated 10/9/96
State of incorporation changed from (CA) to (DE) 10/9/96
Merged into Agilent Technologies, Inc. 1/5/2001
Each share Common $0.001 par exchanged for $17.75 cash

OBJECTSHARE INC (DE)
Merged into Starbase Corp. 4/14/2000
Each share Common no par exchanged for (0.09717) share Common no par
(See Starbase Corp.)

OBJECTSOFT (DE)
Each share old Common $0.001 par exchanged for (1/6) share new Common $0.001 par 10/13/1999

Recapitalized as Nanergy, Inc. 06/17/2005
Each share new Common $0.001 par exchanged for (0.01) share Common $0.0001 par
Nanergy, Inc. name changed to Xacord Corp. 07/07/2006 which recapitalized as Empire Minerals, Corp. 01/22/2007 which name changed to Dominion Minerals Corp. 02/14/2008

OBOLUS RES INC (BC)
Name changed to Cajun Oil & Gas Producers Inc. 05/16/1990
Cajun Oil & Gas Producers Inc. recapitalized as Alto Industries Inc. 01/21/1994 which name changed to Alto Minerals Inc. 04/07/1997 which recapitalized as Alto Ventures Ltd. 04/19/2002

OBRASCON HUARTE LAIN BRASIL S A (BRAZIL)
Name changed to Arteris S.A. 01/09/2013
(See Arteris S.A.)

OBRIEN ENERGY & RES LTD (QC)
Name changed 10/1/77
Capital Stock $1 par changed to no par 9/11/74
Name changed from O'Brien Gold Mines Ltd. to O'Brien Energy & Resources Ltd.-Energie & Ressources O'Brien Ltee. 10/1/77
Capital Stock no par split (3) for (2) by issuance of (0.5) additional share 11/5/86
Cease trade order effective 2/11/87
Stockholders' equity unlikely

OBSCENE JEANS CORP (FL)
Recapitalized as OBJ Enterprises, Inc. 11/13/2012
Each share Common $0.0001 par exchanged for (0.025) share Common $0.0001 par
OBJ Enterprises, Inc. name changed to MyGo Games Holding Co. 07/28/2014

OBSIDIAN ENTERPRISES INC (DE)
Each share old Common $0.001 par exchanged for (0.02) share new Common $0.001 par 2/18/2004
Merged into Black Rock Acquisition Corp. 3/17/2006
Each share new Common $0.001 par exchanged for $1.85 cash

OC ENERGY, INC. (UT)
Name changed to Sungold, Inc. 01/31/1986
(See Sungold, Inc.)

OC FINL INC (MD)
Merged into First Place Financial Corp. 06/30/2008
Each share Common 1¢ par exchanged for (0.9615) share Common 1¢ par
(See First Place Financial Corp.)

OCA INC (DE)
Plan of reorganization under Chapter 11 Federal Bankruptcy Code effective 01/26/2007
No stockholders' equity

OCAL INC (DE)
Merged into Thomas & Betts Corp. 1/5/99
Each share Common $0.001 par exchanged for $3.54139 cash

OCATA THERAPEUTICS INC (DE)
Acquired by Astellas Pharma Inc. 02/10/2016
Each share Common $0.001 par exchanged for $8.50 cash

OCB BANCORP (CA)
Stock Dividend - 5% payable 06/16/2014 to holders of record 05/09/2014 Ex date - 05/07/2014
Merged into Sierra Bancorp 10/02/2017
Each share Common no par exchanged for (0.55511) share Common no par

OCC LIQUIDATING CO. (GA)
In process of liquidation
Each share Class A Common 25¢ par exchanged for initial distribution of (0.232527) share Consolidated Foods Corp. Common $1.33-1/3 par 12/16/66
Each share Class A Common 25¢ par received second distribution of (0.01031) share Consolidated Foods Corp. Common $1.33-1/3 par 5/3/67
Each share Class A Common 25¢ par received third distribution of (0.02213) share Consolidated Foods Corp. Common $1.33-1/3 par 9/13/68
Each share Class A Common 25¢ par received fourth distribution of (0.0337) share Consolidated Foods Corp. Common $1.33-1/3 par 10/15/69
Note: Details on subsequent distributions, if any, are not available

OCCAM NETWORKS INC (DE)
Each share old Common $0.001 par exchanged for (0.025) share new Common $0.001 par 03/13/2006
Merged into Calix, Inc. 02/22/2011
Each share new Common $0.001 par exchanged for (0.2925) share Common $0.025 par and $3.8337 cash

OCCIDENT OIL PRODUCTION CO. (DE)
No longer in existence having become inoperative and'void for non-payment of taxes 3/17/26

OCCIDENTAL DEVELOPMENT FUND IV (CA)
Filed a petition under Chapter 11 Federal Bankruptcy Code 11/01/1995
Stockholders' equity unlikely

OCCIDENTAL DEVELOPMENT FUND V (CA)
Filed a petition under Chapter 11 Federal Bankruptcy Code 11/01/1995
Stockholders' equity unlikely

OCCIDENTAL FINL GROUP INC (DE)
Name changed 3/23/90
Name changed from Occidental Development Corp. to Occidental Financial Group Inc. 3/23/90
Filed petition under Chapter 11 Federal Bankruptcy Code 5/31/91
No stockholders' equity

OCCIDENTAL LIFE INSURANCE CO. (NC)
Stock Dividends - 100% 2/11/52; 50% 3/15/56
Name changed to Occidental Life Insurance Co. of North Carolina 8/9/56
Occidental Life Insurance Co. of North Carolina reorganized as McM Corp. 12/31/77
(See McM Corp.)

OCCIDENTAL LIFE INS CO N C (NC)
Stock Dividends - (1) for (3.878) 3/10/60; 25% 4/15/66
Reorganized as McM Corp. 12/31/77
Each share Capital Stock $1 par exchanged for (1) share Common $1 par
(See McM Corp.)

OCCIDENTAL NEB SVGS BK (OMAHA, NE)
Name changed 07/14/1989
Name changed from Occidental Nebraska Federal Savings Bank (Omaha, NE) to Occidental-Nebraska Savings Bank, F.S.B. (Omaha, NE) 07/14/1989
Bank failed 06/23/1990
No stockholders' equity

OCCIDENTAL PETE CORP (DE)
Reincorporated 5/21/86
Capital Stock $1 par changed to 20¢ par 12/29/55
Capital Stock 20¢ par reclassified as Common 20¢ par 5/11/67
Common 20¢ par split (3) for (1) by issuance of (2) additional shares 2/26/68
$15.50 Preferred $1 par called for redemption 12/3/85
$2.125 Preferred $1 par called for redemption 4/1/86
$2.16 Conv. Preferred $1 par called for redemption 4/1/86
$2.30 Preferred $1 par called for redemption 4/1/86
$2.50 Preferred $1 par called for redemption 4/1/82
$3.60 Conv. Preferred $1 par called for redemption 4/1/86
$4 Conv. Preferred $1 par called for redemption 4/1/86
State of incorporation changed from (CA) to (DE) 5/21/86
$14.625 Preferred $1 par called for redemption 10/20/86
6.25% Conv. Exchangeable Preferred $1 par called for redemption 10/1/87
$14 Preferred $1 par called for redemption 10/1/91
Issue Information - 10,250,000 PFD CONV CXY INDEXED $3.00 offered at $50 per share on 01/26/1994
$3.875 Conv. Preferred 144A 1993 $1 par called for redemption 3/13/98
$3 CXY Indexed Preferred $1 par called for redemption at $51.50 plus $0.625 accrued dividend on 9/16/99
(Additional Information in Active)

OCCIDENTAL PROPERTIES, INC. (UT)
Name changed to Uni-Trade Marketing, Inc. 6/2/77
Uni-Trade Marketing, Inc. recapitalized as Golden Gate Safety Products, Inc. 7/29/85

OCCIDENTAL RAND CORP (NV)
Name changed to Youticket.com, Inc. 8/27/99
Youticket.com, Inc. name changed to Weight Loss Forever International, Inc. 4/3/2002 which name changed to Beverly Hills Weight Loss & Wellness, Inc. (NV) 7/8/2004 which reorganized in Delaware as Cardiovascular Sciences, Inc. 5/30/2006

OCCULOGIX INC (DE)
Issue Information - 8,400,000 shares COM offered at $12 per share on 12/08/2004
Each share old Common $0.001 par exchanged for (0.04) share new Common $0.001 par 10/09/2008
Name changed to TearLab Corp. 05/17/2010

OCCUPATIONAL & MED INNOVATIONS LTD (AUSTRALIA)
Each old Sponsored ADR for Ordinary exchanged for (0.2) new Sponsored ADR for Ordinary 08/16/2010
Name changed to OMI Holdings Ltd. 12/07/2010

OCCUPATIONAL HEALTH & REHABILITATION INC (DE)
Merged into Concentra Operating Corp. 10/31/2005
Each share Common $0.001 par exchanged for $10.40153 cash

OCCUPATIONAL MED CORP AMER INC (CA)
Voluntarily dissolved 09/25/1997
Details not available

OCCUPATIONAL URGENT CARE HEALTH SYS INC (CA)
Common no par split (2) for (1) by issuance of (1) additional share 08/31/1989
Merged into HealthCare Compare Corp. 02/25/1992
Each share Common no par exchanged for (0.93) share Common 1¢ par
HealthCare Compare Corp. name changed to First Health Group Corp. 01/01/1998 which merged into Conventry Health Care, Inc. 01/28/2005 which merged into Aetna, Inc. 05/07/2013

OCCUSYSTEMS INC (DE)
Issue Information - 4,666,667 shares COM offered at $14 per share on 05/08/1995
Under plan of merger name changed to Concentra Managed Care, Inc. 8/29/97
(See Concentra Managed Care Inc.)

OCE INDS INC (DE)
Merged into Elliott Subsidiary Inc. 11/30/1973
Each share Common 10¢ par exchanged for $12 cash

OCE N V (NETHERLANDS)
Name changed 05/01/1997
ADR's for Ordinary 20 Gldrs. par changed to 4 Gldrs. par and (4) additional ADR's issued 05/09/1990
Name changed from Oce-van der Grinten N.V. to OCE N.V. 05/01/1997
ADR's for Ordinary 4 Gldrs. par split (4) for (1) by issuance of (3) additional ADR's payable 05/08/1998 to holders of record 05/01/1998
ADR's for Ordinary 4 Gldrs. par changed to EUR 0.50 04/08/1999
Acquired by Canon Inc. 03/01/2013
Each ADR for Ordinary EUR 0.50 par exchanged for $12.81559 cash

OCEAN AWYS INC (NJ)
Merged into Regent Air Corp. 10/18/83
Each share Conv. Preferred 50¢ par exchanged for (2.218) shares Common 1¢ par
Each share Common 10¢ par exchanged for (1) share Common 1¢ par
Regent Air Corp. charter cancelled 3/1/87

OCEAN CEM & SUPPLIES LTD (CANADA)
Liquidation completed
Each share Common no par exchanged for initial distribution of $25.92 cash 01/17/1972
Each share Common no par received second and final distribution of $3.08 cash 06/07/1972

OCEAN CITY AUTOMOBILE BRDG CO (NJ)
Preferred $100 par changed to $50 par 00/00/1935
Common no par changed to $1 par 00/00/1935
Each share Preference $1 par exchanged for (0.2) share Common $5 par 00/00/1951
Each share Preferred $50 par exchanged for (1) share Preferred $40 par 00/00/1951
Each share Common $1 par exchanged for (0.2) share Common $5 par 00/00/1951
Preferred $40 par called for redemption 01/02/1973
Liquidation completed
Each share Common $5 par exchanged for initial distribution of $10 cash 11/22/1977
Each share Common $5 par received second and final distribution of $5 cash 02/01/1978

OCEAN CITY COASTAL HIGHWAY BRIDGE CO.
Liquidated in 1947

OCEAN CITY LIFE INSURANCE CO. (SC)
Capital Stock $1 par changed to 50¢ par 04/27/1961

Merged into United Insurance Co. of America (IL) 03/12/1975
Each share Capital Stock 50¢ par exchanged for $9 cash

OCEAN CNTY NATL BK (POINT PLEASANT, NJ)
Merged into Summit Bancorporation 12/31/82
Each share Common $2.50 par exchanged for (0.75) share Common no par
Summit Bancorporation merged into Summit Bancorp 3/1/96 which merged into FleetBoston Financial Corp. 3/1/2001 which merged into Bank of America Corp. 4/1/2004

OCEAN DATA EQUIP CORP (RI)
Name changed to Odec, Inc. and Common 2¢ par changed to 1¢ par 06/09/1972
Odec, Inc. merged into Data 100 Corp. 12/04/1974
(See Data 100 Corp.)

OCEAN DATA INDS INC (CO)
Name changed to Universal Investment Properties, Inc. 10/18/1972
(See Universal Investment Properties, Inc.)

OCEAN DIAMOND MNG HLDGS LTD (SOUTH AFRICA)
ADR agreement terminated 4/28/2004
No ADR holders' equity

OCEAN DRILLING & EXPL CO (DE)
Each share 5% Preferred $100 par exchanged for (2) shares 5% Preferred $50 par 3/20/58
6% Preferred $50 par called for redemption 5/1/61
Common $1 par changed to 50¢ par and (1) additional share issued 5/14/65
Common 50¢ par split (2) for (1) by issuance of (1) additional share 11/22/71
6% Conv. Preferred $50 par called for redemption 8/1/72
5% Preferred $50 par called for redemption 11/15/78
6% Conv. Preferred $50 par called for redemption 11/15/78
Common 50¢ par split (4) for (1) by issuance of (3) additional shares 8/25/80
Merged into Murphy Oil Corp. 7/3/91
Each share Common 50¢ par exchanged for (0.55) share Common $1 par

OCEAN ENERGY INC (NV)
Name changed to Sino Cement, Inc. 09/20/2010
Sino Cement, Inc. name changed to Nevis Capital Corp. 07/08/2013 which recapitalized as ASC Biosciences, Inc. 05/10/2017

OCEAN ENERGY INC NEW (DE)
Reincorporated 05/09/2001
State of incorporation changed from (TX) to (DE) 05/09/2001
Merged into Devon Energy Corp. 04/25/2003
Each share Common 10¢ par exchanged for (0.414) share Common 10¢ par

OCEAN ENERGY INC OLD (DE)
Each share old Common 1¢ par exchanged for (2.34) shares new Common 1¢ par 03/27/1998
Merged into Ocean Energy Inc. (TX) 03/30/1999
Each share new Common 1¢ par exchanged (1) share Common 10¢ par
Ocean Energy Inc. (TX) reincorporated in Delaware 05/09/2001 which merged into Devon Energy Corp. 04/25/2003

OCEAN EXPRESS LINES INC (ID)
Reincorporated under the laws of Nevada 03/02/2000
Ocean Express Lines, Inc. (NV) name changed to American Thorium, Inc. 07/29/2003 which recapitalized as Cementitious Materials, Inc. 10/21/2003 which name changed to NaturalNano, Inc. 12/02/2005 which name changed to Omni Shrimp, Inc. 05/03/2017

OCEAN EXPRESS LINES INC (NV)
Each share old Common $0.0001 par exchanged for (0.1) share new Common $0.0001 par 05/15/2003
Name changed to American Thorium, Inc. 07/29/2003
American Thorium, Inc. recapitalized as Cementitious Materials, Inc. 10/21/2003 which name changed to NaturalNano, Inc. 12/02/2005 which name changed to Omni Shrimp, Inc. 05/03/2017

OCEAN FINL CORP (DE)
Common 1¢ par split (2) for (1) by issuance of (1) additional share payable 5/15/98 to holders of record 5/4/98
Name changed to OceanFirst Financial Corp. 9/13/99

OCEAN FIRST NATL BK (FORT LAUDERDALE, FL)
99% held by Consolidated Bankshares of Florida, Inc. as of 06/30/1972
Public interest eliminated

OCEAN FISHERIES INC (DE)
Merged into Star-Kist Foods, Inc. 09/03/1974
Each share Common $1 par exchanged for $11.50 cash

OCEAN FISHERIES LTD. (NS)
Name changed to National Sea Products Ltd. 3/1/67
National Sea Products Ltd. name changed to High Liner Foods Inc. 1/28/99

OCEAN FLOATING SAFE COMPANY (SD)
Charter expired by time limitations 12/4/41

OCEAN FRESH SEAFOOD MARKETPLACE INC (FL)
Name changed to International Builders Ltd., Inc. 03/23/2004
(See International Builders Ltd., Inc.)

OCEAN GROVE TITLE CORP.
Liquidation completed in 1945

OCEAN INDPT BK (OCEAN, NJ)
Merged into First State Financial Services, Inc. 10/21/1994
Each share Common $5 par exchanged for (1.271) shares Common no par
First State Financial Services, Inc. merged into Sovereign Bancorp, Inc. 02/18/1997 which merged into Banco Santander, S.A. 01/30/2009

OCEAN MARINE TECHNOLOGIES INC (BC)
Recapitalized as AGC Americas Gold Corp. (BC) 05/17/1994
Each share Common no par exchanged for (0.2) share Common no par
AGC Americas Gold Corp. (BC) reincorporated in Yukon as Timebeat.com Enterprises Inc. 10/04/1999 which reincorporated in Nevada 10/16/2001 which name changed to New Morning Corp. 09/30/2004 which name changed to Window Rock Capital Holdings, Inc. 10/28/2005
(See Window Rock Capital Holdings, Inc.)

OCEAN NATL BK (FORT LAUDERDALE, FL)
Name changed to Ocean First National Bank (Fort Lauderdale, FL) 07/01/1970
(See Ocean First National Bank (Fort Lauderdale, FL))

OCEAN OIL & GAS CO (DE)
Ser. A Common $1 par reclassified as Common $1 par 12/31/1976
Ser. B Common 1¢ par reclassified as Common $1 par 12/31/1976
Merged into Ocean Drilling & Exploration Co. 11/05/1980
Each share Common $1 par exchanged for (1.5) shares Common 50¢ par
Ocean Drilling & Exploration Co. merged into Murphy Oil Corp. 07/03/1991

OCEAN OPTIQUE DISTRS INC (FL)
Common no par split (6) for (5) by issuance of (0.2) additional share 03/15/1993
Each share old Common no par exchanged for (0.125) share new Common no par 05/11/1998
Recapitalized as Energy Finders, Inc. (FL) 06/15/2005
Each share new Common no par exchanged for (0.1) share Common $0.001 par
Energy Finders, Inc. (FL) reincorporated in Nevada 02/14/2006

OCEAN PK VENTURES CORP (BC)
Recapitalized as Dunnedin Ventures Inc. 08/06/2013
Each share Common no par exchanged for (0.1) share Common no par

OCEAN PWR CORP (ID)
Each share old Common $0.001 par exchanged for (0.1) share new Common $0.001 par 08/20/1999
Chapter 11 bankruptcy proceedings dismissed 05/27/2008
Stockholders' equity unlikely

OCEAN PWR TECHNOLOGIES INC (NJ)
Reorganized under the laws of Delaware 4/23/2007
Each share Common $0.001 par exchanged for (0.1) share Common $0.001 par

OCEAN PRODS INC (FL)
Each share Common $5 par exchanged for (6) shares Common $1 par 03/04/1963
Name changed to Treasure Isle, Inc. 11/08/1971
(See Treasure Isle, Inc.)

OCEAN RESH EQUIP INC (DE)
Each share old Common 5¢ par exchanged for (0.33333333) share new Common 5¢ par 01/16/1969
Completely liquidated 08/30/1982
Each share new Common 5¢ par exchanged for first and final distribution of $5.50 cash

OCEAN RES INC (DE)
SEC revoked common stock registration 10/14/2008
Stockholders' equity unlikely

OCEAN RIG UDW INC (MARSHALL ISLANDS)
Reincorporated under the laws of Cayman Islands 04/15/2016

OCEAN SCIENCE & ENGR INC (DE)
Recapitalized as Berry Industries Corp. (Old) 05/10/1978
Each share Common 10¢ par exchanged for (0.1) share Common $1 par
Berry Industries Corp. (Old) merged into Berry Industries Corp. (New) 07/01/1979 which name changed to Strata Search, Inc. 12/23/1987
(See Strata Search, Inc.)

OCEAN SCIENCE SERVICES, INC. (CA)
Charter suspended for failure to file reports and pay taxes 12/01/1970

OCEAN SHORE HLDG CO (NJ)
Merged into OceanFirst Financial Corp. 11/30/2016
Each share Common 1¢ par exchanged for (0.9667) share Common $1 par and $4.35 cash

OCEAN SHORE HLDG CO (USA)
Reorganized under the laws of New Jersey 12/18/2009
Each share Common 1¢ par exchanged for (0.8793) share Common 1¢ par
Ocean Shore Holding Co. (NJ) merged into OceanFirst Financial Corp. 11/30/2016

OCEAN SPRAY PRESERVING CO. (MA)
Name changed to United Cape Cod Cranberry Co. 00/00/1931
(See United Cape Cod Cranberry Co.)

OCEAN ST BK (NEPTUNE BEACH, FL)
Each share Common $10 par exchanged for (2) shares Common $5 par 5/23/77
Merged into Citizens & Southern Corp. 12/2/89
Each share Common $5 par exchanged for $321.072319 cash

OCEAN STATE BANK (SANTA MONICA, CA)
Merged into First Pacific Bank (Los Angeles, CA) (New) 10/31/77
Each share Common $5 par exchanged for (1) share Common $2.50 par
First Pacific Bank (Los Angeles, CA) (New) reorganized as First Pacific Bancorp, Inc. 10/1/82
(See First Pacific Bancorp, Inc.)

OCEAN TECHNOLOGY FD INC (DE)
Name changed to OTF Equities, Inc. 03/19/1975
(See OTF Equities, Inc.)

OCEAN VENTURES INC (AB)
Name changed to Digital Youth Network Corp. 07/28/2004
(See Digital Youth Network Corp.)

OCEAN VIEW PROPERTIES, INC. (CA)
Liquidation completed 6/15/55

OCEAN WEST HLDG CORP (DE)
Name changed to AskMeNow, Inc. 12/18/2006
(See AskMeNow, Inc.)

OCEANADA CORP (FL)
Merged into Interwest Corp. (UT) 05/13/1971
Each share Common no par exchanged for (1) share Common no par
(See Interwest Corp.)

OCEANARIUM INC (DE)
Name changed to Marineland of the Pacific, Inc. 06/16/1969
Marineland of the Pacific, Inc. liquidated for Hollywood Turf Club (CA) 11/10/1971 which reincorporated in Delaware as Hollywood Park, Inc. (Old) 01/31/1974 which reorganized as Hollywood Park Realty Enterprises, Inc. 04/13/1982 which reorganized as Hollywood Park, Inc. (New) 01/02/1992 which name changed to Pinnacle Entertainment, Inc. (Old) 02/23/2000 which merged into Gaming & Leisure Properties, Inc. 04/28/2016

OCEANAUT INC (MARSHALL ISLANDS)
Issue Information - 18,750,000 UNITS consisting of (1) share COM and (1) WT offered at $8 per Unit on 03/01/2007
Completely liquidated 04/14/2009
Each Unit exchanged for first and

FINANCIAL INFORMATION, INC.

OCE-OCT

final distribution of $8.26612866 cash
Each share Common $0.0001 par exchanged for first and final distribution of $8.26612866 cash

OCEANEX INCOME FD (ON)
Each Installment Receipt no par exchanged for (1) Trust Unit no par 01/06/1999
Merged into South Coast Partners LP 11/12/2007
Each Trust Unit no par exchanged for $19 cash

OCEANFREIGHT INC (MARSHALL ISLANDS)
Each share old Class A Common 1¢ par exchanged for (0.33333333) share new Class A Common 1¢ par 06/17/2010
Each share new Class A Common 1¢ par exchanged again for (0.05) share new Class A Common 1¢ par 07/06/2011
Merged into Ocean Rig UDW Inc. (Marshall Islands) 11/03/2011
Each share new Class A Common 1¢ par exchanged for (0.52326) share Common 1¢ par and USD$11.25 cash
Ocean Rig UDW Inc. (Marshall Islands) reincorporated in Cayman Islands 04/15/2016

OCEANIA GROUP INC (DE)
Name changed to Classic Video Theatre Inc. 3/22/92
Classic Video Theatre Inc. recapitalized as Seaton Group Inc. 5/10/96 which name changed to United Information Systems Inc. 12/5/97
(See United Information Systems Inc.)

OCEANIA RES INC (NV)
Name changed to Capital Diamond & Development Corp. 7/13/81
(See Capital Diamond & Development Corp.)

OCEANIC ELECTRS INC (CANADA)
In process of dissolution 12/1/90
Details not available

OCEANIC ENERGY, INC. (UT)
Name changed to Great American Health & Nutrition, Inc. 7/31/84
(See Great American Health & Nutrition, Inc.)

OCEANIC EXPL CO (DE)
Conv. Preferred $10 par called for redemption 5/3/74
(Additional Information in Active)

OCEANIC FILMS & ENTERPRISES LTD. (CANADA)
Voluntarily dissolved and charter subsequently cancelled 9/4/75

OCEANIC INSTRUMENTS, INC. (WA)
Defunct in 1963
No stockholders' equity

OCEANIC INSURANCE CO. LTD.
Liquidated in 1940

OCEANIC IRON ORE CDA LTD (ON)
Common no par changed to 35¢ par in 1955
Reorganized under the laws of Canada as Oceanic Electronics Corp. Inc./Oceanique, Societe D'Electronique Inc. 11/27/81
Each share Common 35¢ par exchanged for (0.2) share Class A Common no par
(See Ocean Electronics Corp. Inc./Oceanique, Societe D'Electronque Inc.)

OCEANIC LOBSTER CORP. (NY)
Charter cancelled and proclaimed dissolved for failure to file reports and pay taxes 12/15/70

OCEANIC OIL CO. (CA)
Assets sold to Producing Properties, Inc. on a (1) for (2.4962) basis 1/9/59

Producing Properties, Inc. completely liquidated 10/4/73

OCEANIC RESH & RECOVERY INC (NV)
Name changed to McCusker Holdings Corp. 11/13/2017

OCEANIC RES INC (DE)
Charter cancelled and declared inoperative and void for non-payment of taxes 3/1/79

OCEANIC TRADING INC (PANAMA)
Completely liquidated 07/02/1970
Each share Common 10¢ par exchanged for first and final distribution of $52.50 cash

OCEANICS INC (DE)
Charter cancelled and declared inoperative and void for non-payment of taxes 3/1/82

OCEANOGRAPHIC & GROWTH FD INC (DE)
Reincorporated under the laws of the District of Columbia as Steadman Oceanographic, Technology & Growth Fund and Common $1 par reclassified as Share of Bene. Int. $1 par 06/27/1979
(See Steadman Oceanographic, Technology & Growth Fund)

OCEANOGRAPHIC FUND, INC. (DE)
Name changed to Oceanographic & Growth Fund, Inc. 11/10/77
Oceanographic & Growth Fund, Inc. reincorporated under the laws of the District of Columbia as Steadman Oceanographic, Technology & Growth Fund 6/27/79

OCEANOGRAPHY DEV CORP (DE)
Charter cancelled and declared inoperative and void for non-payment of taxes 6/25/76

OCEANOGRAPHY INC (DE)
Common $1 par changed to 6-2/3¢ par and (14) additional shares issued 10/8/69
Charter cancelled and declared inoperative and void for non-payment of taxes 4/15/72

OCEANOGRAPHY INTL CORP (OK)
Name changed to O.I. Corp. 08/08/1980
(See O.I. Corp.)

OCEANOGRAPHY MARICULTURE INDS INC (DE)
Common 1¢ par split (5) for (4) by issuance of (0.25) additional share 10/06/1972
Stock Dividend - 100% 04/15/1970
Adjudicated bankrupt 12/17/1974
Stockholders' equity unlikely

OCEANOGRAPHY UNLIMITED INC (DE)
Name changed to O.U. Liquidation, Inc. 6/12/72
O.U. liquidation, Inc. liquidated for Filigree Foods, Inc. 6/23/72
(See Filigree Foods, Inc.)

OCEANOVA ENTMT GROUP INC (UT)
Each share old Common 1¢ par exchanged for (0.01) share new Common 1¢ par 12/17/96
Name changed to MIRP Inc. 1/1/97

OCEANS GEN INC (DE)
Completely liquidated 6/10/71
Each share Class A Common $1 par exchanged for (1) share Fairfield Communities Land Co. Common 30¢ par
Fairfield Communities Land Co. name changed to Fairfield Communities, Inc. 8/26/77
(See Fairfield Communities, Inc.)

OCEANSIDE BK (JACKSONVILLE BEACH, FL)
Under plan of reorganization each share Common $5 par automatically became (1) share Atlantic

BancGroup, Inc. Common 1¢ par 05/05/1999
Atlantic BancGroup, Inc. merged into Jacksonville Bancorp, Inc. 11/17/2010 which merged into Ameris Bancorp 03/11/2016

OCEANSIDE CAP CORP (BC)
Incorporated 02/05/2008
Each share old Common no par exchanged for (0.5) share new Common no par 09/02/2010
Reorganized under the laws of Ontario as Gaming Nation Inc. 06/15/2015
Each share Common no par exchanged for (0.5) share Common no par
(See Gaming Nation Inc.)

OCEANSIDE CAP CORP (BC)
Incorporated 03/23/2015
Recapitalized as Kootenay Zinc Corp. 10/05/2016
Each share Common no par exchanged for (0.5) share Common no par

OCEANUS INDS BAHAMAS LTD (ON)
Merged into Strean Investments Ltd. 09/07/1983
Each share Common no par exchanged for $5.15 cash

OCEANUS WTR PURITY INC (ON)
Recapitalized as Vena Resources Inc. 04/16/2004
Each share Common no par exchanged for (0.33333333) share Common no par
Vena Resources Inc. name changed to Forrester Metals Inc. 10/06/2016 which merged into Zinc One Resources Inc. 06/02/2017

OCELOT ENERGY INC (AB)
Reincorporated under the laws of Bermuda as Ocelot International Ltd. 05/31/1999
Ocelot International Ltd. (Bermuda) reincorporated in Channel Islands as PanAfrican Energy Corporation Ltd. 07/06/2000 which name changed to Pan-Ocean Energy Corporation Ltd. 08/14/2001 which reorganized as Pan-Ocean Energy Ltd. 08/31/2004
(See Pan-Ocean Energy Ltd.)

OCELOT INDS LTD (AB)
Each share Common no par exchanged for (1) share Conv. Class A Common no par and (1) share Class B Common no par 10/07/1976
Each share Conv. Class A Common no par received distribution of (0.5) share Ocelot Energy Inc. Class A Common no par 09/23/1991
Each share Class B Common no par received distribution of (0.5) share Ocelot Energy Inc. Class B Subordinate no par 09/23/1991
Conv. Class A Common no par reclassified as Common no par 09/23/1991
Class B Common no par reclassified as Common no par 09/23/1991
Name changed to Methanex Corp. 03/23/1992

OCELOT INTERNATIONAL LTD (BERMUDA)
Reincorporated under the laws of Channel Islands as PanAfrican Energy Corporation Ltd. 07/06/2000
PanAfrican Energy Corporation Ltd. name changed to Pan-Ocean Energy Corporation Ltd. 08/14/2001 which reorganized as Pan-Ocean Energy Corp. 08/31/2004
(See Pan-Ocean Energy Ltd.)

OCERA THERAPEUTICS INC (DE)
Acquired by Mallinckrodt PLC 12/11/2017
Each share Common $0.00001 par exchanged for (1) Contingent Value Right and $1.52 cash

OCI COMMUNICATIONS INC (ON)
Name changed to AXXENT Inc. 06/01/2000
(See AXXENT Inc.)

OCI N V (NETHERLANDS)
ADR agreement terminated 09/24/2018
Each Sponsored ADR for Ordinary exchanged for (1) share Ordinary
Note: Unexchanged ADR's will be sold and the proceeds, if any, held for claim after 01/25/2019

OCI PARTNERS LP (DE)
Acquired by OCI N.V. 07/17/2018
Each Common Unit exchanged for $11.50 cash

OCI RES LP (DE)
Name changed to Ciner Resources L.P. 11/06/2015

OCILLA INDS INC (DE)
Common 1¢ par split (3) for (2) by issuance of (0.5) additional share 7/20/84
Name changed to Allico Corp. 12/19/89
(See Allico Corp.)

OCIS CORP (NV)
Name changed to Ecology Coatings, Inc. 06/18/2007
Ecology Coatings, Inc. recapitalized as Metu Brands, Inc. 08/13/2015 which name changed to American BriVision (Holding) Corp. 01/14/2016

OCM LIQUIDATING CORP (DE)
Assets transferred to OCM Liquidating Trust 02/19/1986
Each share Common 20¢ par exchanged for initial distribution of $10 cash
(See OCM Liquidating Trust)

OCM LIQUIDATING TRUST (DE)
Liquidation completed
Each share Common 20¢ par received second distribution of $0.63 cash 05/28/1987
Each share Common 20¢ par received third and final distribution of $2.11 cash 03/23/1992
(See OCM Liquidating Corp. for previous distribution)

OCOM CORP (DE)
Name changed to International CableTel, Inc. 10/13/93
International CableTel, Inc. name changed to NTL Inc. 3/27/97 which reorganized as NTL Europe, Inc. 1/10/2003
(See NTL Europe, Inc.)

OCONN INDS CORP (NV)
Common $0.001 par split (4) for (1) by issuance of (3) additional shares payable 04/11/2014 to holders of record 03/31/2014 Ex date - 04/14/2014
Name changed to Diamante Minerals, Inc. 04/22/2014
Diamante Minerals, Inc. name changed to iMine Corp. 05/04/2018

OCOTILLO ENTERPRISES INC. (IDAHO)
Administratively dissolved 6/5/2002

OCS TECHNOLOGIES CORP (BC)
Placed in bankruptcy 01/19/1996
Stockholders' equity unlikely

OCTAGON ASSOC INC (DE)
Name changed to Consolin (U.S.) Inc. 08/27/1974
(See Consolin (U.S.) Inc.)

OCTAGON CAP CORP (UT)
Name changed to AC&C Systems Corp. 04/29/1988
AC&C Systems Corp. (UT) reorganized in Oklahoma as Environmental Remediation Services, Inc. 12/15/1989
(See Environmental Remediation Services, Inc.)

COPYRIGHTED MATERIAL — **NO UNAUTHORIZED REPRODUCTION**

OCT-ODY

OCTAGON INC (DE)
Merged into Numanco Acquisition Sub Inc. 9/25/97
Each share Common 1¢ par exchanged for $0.0502 cash

OCTAGON INDUSTRIES, INC. (DE)
Name changed to Octagon Associates, Inc. 07/30/1973
Octagon Associates, Inc. name changed to Consolin (U.S.) Inc. 08/27/1974 which merged into CHI (U.S.) Inc. 01/08/1975

OCTAGON INDS INC (BC)
Name changed to Lynx Opportunities Corp. 07/08/2009

OCTAN RES INC (AB)
Struck off register and declared dissolved for failure to file returns 3/1/92

OCTANE ENERGY SVCS LTD (AB)
Name changed to NX Capital Corp. 06/27/2005
NX Capital Corp. recapitalized as Newton Energy Corp. 02/18/2009

OCTEL COMMUNICATIONS CORP (DE)
Reincorporated 12/15/89
State of incorporation changed from (CA) to (DE) 12/15/89
Common $0.001 par split (2) for (1) by issuance of (1) additional share payable 5/10/96 to holders of record 4/5/96
Merged into Lucent Technologies Inc. 9/29/97
Each share Common $0.001 par exchanged for $31 cash

OCTEL CORP (DE)
Name changed to Innospec, Inc. 1/30/2006

OCTILLION CORP (NV)
Each share old Common $0.001 par exchanged for (3) shares new Common $0.001 par 09/01/2006
Each share new Common $0.001 par received distribution of (1) share MicroChannel Technologies Corp. Common $0.0001 par payable 12/24/2007 to holders of record 08/22/2007 Ex date - 12/21/2007
Name changed to New Energy Technologies, Inc. 01/14/2009
New Energy Technologies, Inc. name changed to SolarWindow Technologies, Inc. 03/12/2015

OCTO LTD (DE)
Common 10¢ par reclassified as Conv. Class A Common 10¢ par 7/24/86
Name changed to Informedia Corp. 8/21/87
Informedia Corp. name changed to Strategic Information, Inc. 12/15/88 which name changed to Strategic Distribution, Inc. 11/9/90
(See Strategic Distribution, Inc.)

OCTOBER OIL CO NEW (CO)
Declared defunct and inoperative for failure to pay taxes and file annual reports 10/1/94

OCTOBER OIL CO OLD (CO)
Common 1¢ par split (20) for (1) by issuance of (19) additional shares 5/5/80
Merged into October Oil Co. (New) 10/18/82
Each share Common 1¢ par exchanged for (0.125) share Common $0.001 par
(See October Oil Co. (New))

OCTOBER PROJ I CORP (FL)
Name changed to Indiginet, Inc. 10/22/2000
Indiginet, Inc. recapitalized as Winsted Holdings, Inc. 03/07/2005 which recapitalized as Aventura Equities, Inc. 11/03/2008

OCTOBER PROJ II CORP (FL)
Name changed to Nutraceutical Clinical Labs Inc. 07/19/2000
Nutraceutical Clinical Labs Inc. name changed to Nutraceutical Clinical Laboratories International Inc. 10/12/2001 which name changed to Preservation Sciences, Inc. 06/27/2003 which name changed to eFUEL EFN, Corp. 02/08/2008

OCTOBER PROJ III CORP (FL)
Name changed to Old Mission Assessment Corp. 01/16/2002
Old Mission Assessment Corp. recapitalized as Global Development & Enviromental Resources, Inc. 07/25/2005

OCTOBER PROJ IV CORP (FL)
Name changed to Legaldocumentscenter Inc. 09/29/2000
Legaldocumentscenter Inc. name changed to Seafood Harvest Group Inc. 09/17/2002 which name changed to Vision Media Technologies, Inc. 03/17/2004 which recapitalized as ASF Group, Inc. (FL) 08/01/2008 which reincorporated in Georgia as American Seniors Association Holding Group, Inc. 04/28/2010

OCTUS INC (NV)
Reincorporated 12/23/2003
Each share Common no par exchanged for (0.05) share Common no par 04/10/2002
State of incorporation changed from (CA) to (NV) and Common no par changed to $0.001 par 12/23/2003
Each share old Common $0.001 par exchanged for (2) shares new Common $0.001 par 06/21/2005
SEC revoked common stock registration 08/07/2014

OCULAR SCIENCES INC (DE)
Merged into Cooper Companies, Inc. 1/6/2005
Each share Common $0.001 par exchanged for (0.3879) share Common 10¢ par and $22 cash

OCULUS INC (NV)
Name changed to OneLife Technologies Corp. 06/13/2017

OCULUS INNOVATIVE SCIENCES INC (DE)
Each share old Common $0.0001 par exchanged for (0.14285714) share new Common $0.0001 par 04/01/2013
Each share new Common $0.0001 par exchanged again for (0.2) share new Common $0.0001 par 06/27/2016
Name changed to Sonoma Pharmaceuticals, Inc. 12/06/2016

OCULUS VENTURES CORP (BC)
Reincorporated 03/14/2011
Place of incorporation changed from (Canada) to (BC) 03/14/2011
Each share Class A Common no par exchanged for (0.25) share new Common no par
Reorganized under the laws of Alberta as SLYCE Inc. 07/21/2014
Each share Common no par exchanged for (0.57142857) share Common no par
SLYCE Inc. recapitalized as Pounce Technologies Inc. 01/30/2017

OCUMED GROUP INC (DE)
SEC revoked common stock registration 07/07/2004

OCUREST LABS INC (FL)
Issue Information - 1,200,000 Units consisting of (1) share of COM and (1) CL A WT offered at $4 per Unit on 11/12/1996
Proclaimed dissolved for failure to file reports and pay fees 10/16/98

OCUTEC HLDGS INC (DE)
Charter cancelled and declared inoperative and void for non-payment of taxes 03/01/1997

OCUTECH CDA INC (BC)
Struck off register and declared dissolved for failure to file returns 8/20/93

OCWEN ASSET INVT CORP (VA)
Issue Information - 15,000,000 shares COM offered at $16 per share on 05/14/1997
Merged into Ocwen Financial Corp. 10/7/99
Each share Common 1¢ par exchanged for (0.71) share Common 1¢ par

OCZ TECHNOLOGY GROUP INC (DE)
Plan of reorganization under Chapter 11 Federal Bankruptcy proceedings effective 08/18/2014
No stockholders' equity

ODAAT INC (AB)
Recapitalized as Explor Resources Inc. 1/29/2004
Each share Class A Common no par exchanged for (0.25) share Common no par

ODD JOB STORES INC (OH)
Merged into Amazing Savings Holdings LLC 11/14/2003
Each share Common no par exchanged for $3 cash

ODDS-N-ENDS INC NEW (DE)
Merged into 99¢ Only Stores 09/29/1998
Each share Common 1¢ par exchanged for $0.30 cash

ODDS-N-ENDS INC OLD (DE)
Reorganized as Odd's-N-End's, Inc. (New) 12/28/1994
Each share Common 1¢ par exchanged for (1/7) share Common 1¢ par
(See Odd's-N-End's, Inc. (New))

ODEC INC (RI)
Common 1¢ par split (2) for (1) by issuance of (1) additional share 06/30/1972
Merged into Data 100 Corp. 12/04/1974
Each share Common 1¢ par exchanged for (0.022272) share Preferred 1974 Ser. $1 par
(See Data 100 Corp.)

ODELL INC (DE)
Each share Common 25¢ par exchanged for (0.01) share 5% Conv. Preferred $100 par and (0.4) share Common 62-1/2¢ par 08/28/1967
Merged into Papercraft Corp. 03/26/1971
Each share 5% Conv. Preferred $100 par exchanged for (1) share $5 Non-Cum. Conv. Preferred $1 par
Each share Common 62-1/2¢ par exchanged for (0.25) share Common $1 par
(See Papercraft Corp.)

ODESA CABLE PLT ODESKABLE OJSC (UKRAINE)
GDR agreement terminated 04/21/2017
No GDR's remain outstanding

ODESSA EXPLS INC (BC)
Recapitalized as Amble Green Ventures Inc. 10/12/89
Each share Common no par exchanged for (0.2) share Common no par
Amble Green Ventures Inc. recapitalized as Western Logic Technologies Inc. 6/23/93 which name changed to Western Logic Resources Inc. 9/18/96

ODESSA FOODS INTL INC (DE)
SEC revoked common stock registration 10/22/2008
Stockholders' equity unlikely

ODESSA GOLD CORP (BC)
Recapitalized as Emerson Exploration Inc. 04/20/2005
Each share Common no par exchanged for (0.1) share Common no par
Emerson Exploration Inc. name changed to GBS Gold International, Inc. 09/19/2005

ODESSA INDS INC (AB)
Delisted from Canadian Venture Exchange 05/31/2000

ODESSA PETE CORP (BC)
Recapitalized as Aquarius Ventures Inc. (BC) 05/12/1999
Each share Common no par exchanged for (0.1) share Common no par
Aquarius Ventures Inc. (BC) reincorporated in Canada as Citotech Systems Inc. 10/30/2000 which recapitalized as SmartCool Systems Inc. 07/21/2004

ODETICS INC (DE)
Reincorporated 10/6/87
Common 10¢ par reclassified as Class B Common 10¢ par 9/21/84
Each share Class B Common 10¢ par received distribution of (1) share Class A Common 10¢ par 11/5/84
State of incorporation changed from (CA) to (DE) 10/6/87
Each share Class A 10¢ par received distribution of (1.1) shares ATL Products, Inc. Common $0.0001 par payable 10/31/97 to holders of record 10/31/97
Each share Class B 10¢ par received distribution of (1.1) shares ATL Products, Inc. Common $0.0001 par payable 10/31/97 to holders of record 10/31/97
Name changed to Iteris Holdings, Inc. 9/15/2003
Iteris Holdings, Inc. name changed to Iteris, Inc. 10/22/2004

ODFJELL ASA (NORWAY)
ADR agreement terminated 3/18/2005
Each Sponsored ADR for Ordinary NOK 10 par exchanged for $81.174259 cash

ODIN CIGAR CO.
Acquired by Deisel-Wemmer-Gilbert Corp. in 1929
Details not available

ODIN INDS LTD (BC)
Delisted from Toronto Venture Stock Exchange 03/26/2003

ODIN MNG & EXPL LTD (BC)
Each share old Common no par exchanged for (0.2) share new Common no par 06/04/2014
Under plan of merger name changed to Lumina Gold Corp. 11/01/2016

ODONTOPREV S A (BRAZIL)
ADR agreement terminated 01/30/2017
Each Sponsored ADR for Ordinary exchanged for $9.415676 cash

ODOR-RIDD CORP. OF AMERICA, INC. (NV)
Recapitalized as O & R Corp. 07/07/1972
Each share Common 10¢ par exchanged for (0.1) share Common 10¢ par
O & R Corp. recapitalized as General Financial Industries, Inc. 12/29/1972 which name changed to Monarch Molybdenum & Resources, Inc. (Ctfs. dated prior to 03/07/1988) 09/14/1978 which recapitalized as Mediacom Communications, Inc. 03/07/1988 which name changed to Duraco Industries, Inc. 09/15/1990

ODS NETWORKS INC (DE)
Name changed to Intrusion.com, Inc. 6/1/2000
Intrusion.com, Inc. name changed to Intrusion Inc. 11/1/2001

ODWALLA INC (CA)
Common no par split (3) for (2) by issuance of (0.5) additional share 5/1/95
Merged into Coca-Cola Co. 12/13/2001
Each share Common no par exchanged for $15.25 cash

ODYNE CORP (DE)
Assets sold for the benefit of creditors 01/20/2009
Stockholders' equity unlikely

ODYNO MINIERE INC (QC)
Reorganized in June 1980
Reorganized from Odyno Exploration & Development Ltee. to Odyno Miniere Inc. in June 1980
Each share Common no par exchanged for (5) shares Common no par
Acquired by Cambior Inc. 11/22/89
Each share Common no par exchanged for $5 cash

ODYSSEY CAP GRP LTD (NV)
Name changed to Print Data Corp. (NV) 08/13/2001
Print Data Corp. (NV) reorganized in Delaware 10/11/2002 which name changed to ACL Semiconductors Inc. 12/16/2003 which name changed to USmart Mobile Device Inc. 04/17/2013 which name changed to Eagle Mountain Corp. 05/06/2015

ODYSSEY ENERGY CORP (CANADA)
Dissolved for non-compliance 05/21/2008

ODYSSEY ENTMT LTD (NV)
Each share Common $0.003 par exchanged for (0.04) share Common 5¢ par 08/31/1988
Merged into Communications & Entertainment Corp. 09/06/1990
Each share Common 5¢ par exchanged for (1) share Conv. Class A 1¢ par
Communications & Entertainment Corp. name changed to Odyssey Pictures Corp. 01/21/1997
(See Odyssey Pictures Corp.)

ODYSSEY EXPL INC (BC)
Recapitalized as Consolidated Odyssey Exploration Inc. 12/08/2000
Each share Common no par exchanged for (0.5) share Common no par
Consolidated Odyssey Exploration Inc. reorganized as Odyssey Petroleum Corp. 08/25/2005 which recapitalized as Petrichor Energy Inc. 03/03/2011

ODYSSEY FILMPARTNERS LTD. (NV)
Name changed to Odyssey Entertainment Ltd. 10/30/1987
Odyssey Entertainment Ltd. merged into Communications & Entertainment Corp. 09/06/1990 which name changed to Odyssey Pictures Corp. 01/21/1997
(See Odyssey Pictures Corp.)

ODYSSEY HEALTHCARE INC (DE)
Common $0.001 par split (3) for (2) by issuance of (0.5) additional share payable 02/21/2003 to holders of record 02/06/2003 Ex date - 02/22/2003
Common $0.001 par split (3) for (2) by issuance of (0.5) additional share payable 08/12/2003 to holders of record 07/28/2003 Ex date - 08/13/2003
Acquired by Gentiva Health Services, Inc. 08/17/2010

Each share Common $0.001 par exchanged for $27 cash

ODYSSEY INC (DE)
Merged into Profile-United Industries Ltd. 01/13/1981
Each share Common $1 par exchanged for $10.75 cash

ODYSSEY OIL CO (CO)
Declared defunct and inoperative for failure to pay taxes and file annual reports 01/01/1996

ODYSSEY PETE CORP (BC)
Recapitalized as Petrichor Energy Inc. 03/03/2011
Each share Common no par exchanged for (0.05) share Common no par

ODYSSEY PETE CORP (CANADA)
Each share old Common no par exchanged for (1/3) share new Common no par 07/02/1997
Each share new Common no par exchanged again for (0.00000014) share new Common no par 09/22/1999
Note: In effect holders received $0.125 cash per share and public interest was eliminated

ODYSSEY PICTURES CORP (NV)
SEC revoked common stock registration 12/23/2016

ODYSSEY RE HLDGS CORP
Issue Information - 17,142,857 shares COM offered at $18 per share on 06/13/2001
Merged into Fairfax Financial Holdings Ltd. 10/28/2009
Each share Common 1¢ par exchanged for $65 cash
8.125% Preferred Ser. A 1¢ par called for redemption at $25 on 10/20/2010
Floating Rate Preferred Ser. B 1¢ par called for redemption at $25.375 on 10/20/2010
Public interest eliminated

ODYSSEY RES LTD (BARBADOS)
Reorganized under the laws of Ontario 05/08/2008
Each share Common no par exchanged for (0.1) share Common no par

ODYSSEY RES LTD (BC)
Struck off register and declared dissolved for failure to file returns 02/19/1993

ODYSSEY 2000 NA INC (NV)
Name changed to Celebrity Entertainment Group, Inc. (NV) 01/09/1996
Celebrity Entertainment Group, Inc. (NV) reincorporated in Wyoming 01/11/1996 which reincorporated in Delaware as Sharp Holding Corp. 04/19/2001 which recapitalized as Cooper Holding Corp. 10/28/2010 which recapitalized as Crednology Holding Corp. 05/03/2013

OEA INC (DE)
Common 10¢ par split (2) for (1) by issuance of (1) additional share 12/3/82
Common 10¢ par split (2) for (1) by issuance of (1) additional share 5/25/90
Common 10¢ par split (3) for (1) by issuance of (2) additional shares 2/13/92
Merged into Autoliv, Inc. 5/10/2000
Each share Common 10¢ par exchanged for $10 cash

OEC COMPRESSION CORP (OK)
Merged into Hanover Compressor Co. 03/19/2001
Each share Common 1¢ par exchanged for (0.0307692) share Common $0.001 par
Hanover Compressor Co. merged into Exterran Holdings, Inc. 08/20/2007 which name changed to Archrock, Inc. 11/04/2015

OEC MED SYS INC (DE)
Merged into General Electric Co. 11/29/1999
Each share Common 1¢ par exchanged for (0.262) share Common 16¢ par

OESI PWR CORP (DE)
Merged into OESI Merging Corp. 12/20/95
Each share Common 1¢ par exchanged for $0.125 cash

OF COUNSEL ENTERPRISES INC (TX)
Name changed to Co-Counsel, Inc. 05/24/1995
Co-Counsel, Inc. merged into Olsten Corp. 08/09/1996 which merged into Adecco S.A. 03/15/2000 which name changed to Adecco Group AG 06/03/2016

OFB CORP. (DE)
Liquidation completed
Each share Common $25 par stamped to indicate initial distribution of $45 cash 6/10/65
Each share Common $25 par exchanged for second distribution of $9 cash 4/14/66
Each share Common $25 par received third and final distribution of $5.32 cash 4/28/66

OFF TRACK BETTING CORP AMER INC (NV)
Recapitalized as Midwestern Fuel Systems, Inc. 05/08/1981
Each share Capital Stock 2¢ par exchanged for (0.25) share common 8¢ par
Midwestern Fuel Systems, Inc. name changed to Midwestern Companies, Inc. 05/25/1983
(See Midwestern Companies, Inc.)

OFFICE CLUB INC (CA)
Merged into Office Depot, Inc. 04/10/1991
Each share Common no par exchanged for (1.194) shares Common 1¢ par

OFFICE MANAGERS INC (NV)
Name changed to Omega Ventures Group, Inc. 11/11/2003

OFFICE PRODS AMER INC (DE)
Chapter 11 bankruptcy proceedings converted to Chapter 7 on 07/14/1991
No stockholders' equity

OFFICE SOLUTIONS INC (OR)
Involuntarily dissolved for failure to file reports and pay fees 03/11/1986

OFFICE SPECIALTY INC (ON)
Name changed to Inscape Corp. 10/2/2000

OFFICELAND INC (ON)
Common no par split (3) for (1) by issuance of (2) additional shares 02/23/1990
Each share old Common no par exchanged for (0.1) share new Common no par 05/07/1993
Filed an assignment under Bankruptcy and Insolvency Act 01/29/2001
Stockholders' equity unlikely

OFFICEMAX INC (DE)
Merged into Office Depot, Inc. 11/05/2013
Each share Common $2.50 par exchanged for (2.69) shares Common 1¢ par

OFFICEMAX INC (OH)
Common no par split (3) for (2) by issuance of (0.5) additional share 7/12/95
Common no par split (3) for (2) by issuance of (0.5) additional share payable 7/9/96 to holders of record 6/3/96 Ex date - 7/10/96
Merged into Boise Cascade Corp. 12/9/2003
Each share Common no par exchanged for $9.33 cash

OFFICIAL FILMS INC (DE)
Name changed to Official Industries, Inc. 11/28/1969
Official Industries, Inc. name changed to SwedishVegas, Inc. 01/18/2008

OFFICIAL INDS INC (DE)
Name changed to SwedishVegas, Inc. 01/18/2008
(See SwedishVegas, Inc.)

OFFICIAL PMTS CORP (DE)
Merged into Tier Technologies, Inc. 07/31/2002
Each share Common 1¢ par exchanged for $3 cash

OFFICIAL PMTS HLDGS INC (DE)
Acquired by ACI Worldwide, Inc. 11/05/2013
Each share Common 1¢ par exchanged for $8.35 cash

OFFICIAL SYSTEMS, INC. (DE)
Recapitalized as Air L.A., Inc. 06/21/1990
Each share Common 1¢ par exchanged for (1/3) share Common $0.001 par
(See Air L.A., Inc.)

OFFITBANK HLDGS INC (DE)
Merged into Wachovia Corp. (New) (Ctfs. dated between 05/20/1991 and 09/01/2001) 09/01/1999
Each share Common 1¢ par exchanged for (0.2284) share Common $5 par
Wachovia Corp. (New) (Ctfs. dated between 05/20/1991 and 09/01/2001) merged into Wachovia Corp. (Ctfs. dated after 09/01/2001) 09/01/2001 which merged into Wells Fargo & Co. (New) 12/31/2008

OFFLINE CONSULTING INC (DE)
Name changed to Kesselring Holding Corp. 06/08/2007

OFFSETTERS CLIMATE SOLUTIONS INC (BC)
Name changed to NatureBank Asset Management Inc. 10/20/2015

OFFSHORE CO (DE)
Merged into Southern Natural Resources, Inc. 04/10/1978
Each share Common 25¢ par exchanged for $34 cash

OFFSHORE CREATIONS INC (NV)
Name changed to Sustainable Power Corp. 02/16/2007
(See Sustainable Power Corp.)

OFFSHORE ENERGY DEVELOPMENT CORP (DE)
Issue Information - 3,682,000 shares COM offered at $12 per share on 11/01/1996
Merged into Titan Exploration Inc. 12/12/97
Each share Common 1¢ par exchanged for (0.63) share Common 1¢ par
Titan Exploration Inc. merged into Pure Resources Inc. 5/25/2000 which merged into Unocal Corp. 10/30/2002 which merged into Chevron Corp. 8/10/2005

OFFSHORE EXPL OIL CO (CA)
Name changed to Oxoco (CA) 11/12/1974
Oxoco (CA) reincorporated in Delaware as Oxoco Inc. 06/16/1983 which name changed to Ironstone Group, Inc. 09/15/1988

OFFSHORE LOGISTICS INC (DE)
Reincorporated 00/00/1988
Common no par split (3) for (2) by issuance of (0.5) additional share 08/15/1972

OFF-OHI

FINANCIAL INFORMATION, INC.

Common no par split (3) for (2) by issuance of (0.5) additional share 06/15/1976
Each share $2.4375 Conv. Preferred no par exchanged for (6) shares Common no par 12/31/1986
Each share $3.125 Conv. Exchangeable Preference Ser. A no par exchanged for (3) shares Common no par 12/31/1986
State of incorporation changed from (LA) to (DE) and Common no par changed to 1¢ par 00/00/1988
Name changed to Bristow Group, Inc. 02/01/2006

OFFSHORE NAV INC (DE)
Capital Stock no par split (2) for (1) by issuance of (1) additional share 3/12/69
Name changed to ONI International Inc. 4/28/94
(See ONI International Inc.)

OFFSHORE OIL & GAS LTD (WY)
Reincorporated 8/16/90
Place of incorporation changed from (BC) to (WY) 8/16/90
Charter revoked for failure to pay taxes 3/11/93

OFFSHORE OIL N L (AUSTRALIA)
Name changed to Petroz N.L. 01/15/1987
(See Petroz N.L.)

OFFSHORE PIPELINES INC (DE)
Merged into J. Ray McDermott S.A. 1/31/95
Each share Conv. Exchangeable Preferred 1¢ par exchanged for (1) share $2.25 Conv. Exchangeable Preferred Ser. B 1¢ par
Each share Common 1¢ par exchanged for (1) share Common 1¢ par

OFFSHORE SEA DEV CORP (NY)
Charter cancelled and proclaimed dissolved for failure to pay taxes 12/15/1975

OFFSHORE SYS INTL LTD (BC)
Name changed to OSI Geospatial Inc. 06/05/2006
(See OSI Geospatial Inc.)

OFI INCOME FD (ON)
Acquired by Compagnie de Saint-Gobain S.A. 01/30/2009
Each Unit no par received $3.17 cash

OG NATION INC (NV)
Common $0.001 par split (20) for (1) by issuance of (19) additional shares payable 07/27/2007 to holders of record 07/23/2007 Ex date - 07/30/2007
Name changed to Hall of Fame Beverages, Inc. 03/31/2008

OGAMA-ROCKLAND GOLD MINES, LTD. (MB)
Recapitalized as Realm Mining Corp. in 1959
Each share Common no par exchanged for (0.2) share Common no par
(See Realm Mining Corp. Ltd.)

OGDEN-AMERICAN ENERGY CORP. (UT)
Recapitalized as Mainline Holding Corp. 9/22/82
Each share Common 2¢ par exchanged for (0.25) share Common 1¢ par
Mainline Holding Corp. recapitalized as Tulsa Oil & Gas Co. 6/27/83

OGDEN CORP (DE)
5% Preferred called for redemption 5/23/40
Common $4 par changed to 50¢ par and $3 cash distributed in 1945
Common 50¢ par split (3) for (2) by issuance of (0.5) additional share 12/29/80
Common 50¢ par split (2) for (1) by issuance of (1) additional share 7/3/87
Name changed to Covanta Energy Corp. 3/14/2001
(See Covanta Energy Corp.)

OGDEN GOLF CO CORP (UT)
Name changed to Bio-Path Holdings, Inc. (UT) 02/27/2008
Bio-Path Holdings, Inc. (UT) reincorporated in Delaware 12/31/2014

OGDEN MCDONALD & CO (CO)
Name changed to WorldWide Petromoly, Inc. (CO) 10/16/96
WorldWide Petromoly, Inc. (CO) reorganized in Nevada as Small Town Radio, Inc. 5/12/2006 which recapitalized as Tombstone Western Resources, Inc. 5/12/2006 which name changed to Dutch Gold Resources, Inc. 12/12/2006

OGDEN PROJS INC (DE)
Merged into Ogden Corp. 12/29/94
Each share Common 50¢ par exchanged for (0.84) share Common 50¢ par
Ogden Corp. name changed to Covanta Energy Corp. 3/14/2001
(See Covanta Energy Corp.)

OGDEN TEL CO (NY)
7% Preferred called for redemption at $100 plus $2.90 accrued dividends on 11/27/1997
8% Preferred called for redemption at $100 plus $3.31 accrued dividends on 11/28/1997
Merged into Citizens Utilities Co. 12/31/1997
Each share Common no par exchanged for (17.61689) shares Ser. B Common 25¢ par
Citizens Utilities Co. name changed to Citizens Communications Co. 05/18/2000 which name changed to Frontier Communications Corp. 07/31/2008

OGDENSBURG TR CO (OGDENSBURG, NY)
Capital Stock $20 par changed to $10 par and (1) additional share issued 11/14/1963
Merged into Oneida National Bank & Trust Co. of Central New York (Utica, NY) 11/19/1976
Each share Capital Stock $10 par exchanged for $38.50 cash

OGE ENERGY CAP TR I (DE)
8.375% Guaranteed Preferred Securities called for redemption at $25 on 10/15/2004

OGILVIE FLOUR MILLS CO., LTD. (CANADA)
Common no par exchanged (8) for (1) in 1938
7% Preferred $100 par changed to $25 par and (3) additional shares issued 1/11/63
Common no par split (4) for (1) by issuance of (3) additional shares 1/25/63
Name changed to Ogilvie Mills Ltd./Les Minoteries Ogilvie Ltee. 9/15/75
(See Ogilvie Mills Ltd./Les Minoteries Ogilvie Ltee.)

OGILVIE MLS LTD (CANADA)
7% Preferred $25 par called for redemption 10/23/1981
Merged into Labatt (John) Ltd. 10/23/1981
Each share Common no par exchanged for $25 cash

OGILVY & MATHER INTERNATIONAL INC. (NY)
Common $2 par split (3) for (2) by issuance of (0.5) additional share 6/15/72
Common $2 par changed to $1 par 6/13/78
Common $1 par split (2) for (1) by issuance of (1) additional share 8/31/78
Common $1 par split (2) for (1) by issuance of (1) additional share 5/31/84
Name changed to Ogilvy Group, Inc. 5/14/85
(See Ogilvy Group, Inc.)

OGILVY GROUP INC (NY)
Common $1 par split (3) for (2) by issuance of (0.5) additional share 2/28/86
Merged into WPP Group plc 8/11/89
Each share Common $1 par exchanged for $54 cash

OGIVAR INC (QC)
Assets sold for the benefit of creditors 4/3/92
No stockholders' equity

OGK 6 JSC (RUSSIA)
Acquired by OGK 2 JSC 11/01/2011
Each Sponsored 144A GDR for Ordinary exchanged for $1.9319 cash
Each Sponsored Reg. S GDR for Ordinary exchanged for $1.9319 cash

OGK-1 OPEN JT STK CO (RUSSIA)
Each old Sponsored 144A GDR for Ordinary exchanged for (0.25) new Sponsored 144A GDR for Ordinary 09/03/2010
Each old Sponsored Reg. S GDR for Ordinary exchanged for (0.25) new Sponsored Reg. S GDR for Ordinary 09/03/2010
Basis changed from (1:50) to (1:200) 09/03/2010
Merged into Inter RAO UES 10/01/2012
Each new Sponsored 144A GDR for Ordinary exchanged for (0.48) Sponsored 144A GDR for Ordinary
Each new Sponsored Reg. S GDR for Ordinary exchanged for (0.48) Sponsored Reg. S GDR for Ordinary
Inter RAO UES name changed to Inter RAO UES PJSC 09/29/2015

OGK 3 OJSC (RUSSIA)
Merged into Inter RAO UES 10/01/2012
Each Sponsored 144A GDR for Ordinary exchanged for (0.2) Sponsored 144A GDR for Ordinary
Each Sponsored Reg. S GDR for Ordinary exchanged for (0.2) Sponsored Reg. S GDR for Ordinary
Inter RAO UES name changed to Inter RAO UES PJSC 09/29/2015

OGLEBAY NORTON CO (OH)
Reincorporated 04/30/2001
Common $1 par split (2) for (1) by issuance of (1) additional share payable 10/30/1997 to holders of record 10/10/1997
Stock Dividends - 100% 03/22/1976; 50% 03/23/1981
State of incorporation changed from (DE) to (OH) 04/30/2001
Plan of reorganization under Chapter 11 Federal Bankruptcy Code effective 01/31/2005
Each share old Common $1 par received distribution of (1) Common Stock Purchase Warrant expiring 03/02/2005
Note: Certificates were not required to be surrendered and are without value
14.8275% Conv. Preferred Ser. A 1¢ par called for redemption at $14.02 on 10/30/2006
Merged into Carmeuse Group 02/13/2008
Each share new Common $1 par exchanged for $36 cash

OGLESBY (W.B.) PAPER CO.
Merged into Sorg Paper Co. in 1930

OGLETHORPE FUND, INC. (GA)
Name changed to Southern Industries Fund, Inc. 10/7/52
Southern Industries Fund, Inc. name changed to Fund of America, Inc. (GA) 9/20/60 which reincorporated in New York 10/21/63 which name changed to American Capital Growth & Income Fund, Inc. (NY) 7/23/90 which reincorporated in Maryland 7/6/93 which reorganized in Delaware as Van Kampen American Capital Growth & Income fund 7/31/95 which name changed to Van Kampen Growth & Income Fund 7/14/98

OGLETHORPE LIFE INSURANCE CO. (GA)
Acquired by Coastal States Life Insurance Co. on a (1) for (4.27616) basis 10/17/60
Coastal States Life Insurance Co. reorganized as Coastal States Corp. 10/5/72
(See Coastal States Corp.)

OGX PETROLEO E GAS PARTICIPACOES S A (BRAZIL)
Sponsored GDR's for Common split (20) for (1) by issuance of (19) additional GDR's payable 12/29/2009 to holders of record 12/23/2009 Ex date - 12/30/2009
GDR basis changed from (1:0.2) to (1:1) 12/29/2009
Name changed to Oleo e Gas Participacoes S.A. 12/31/2013

OGX PETROLEO E GAS S A EM RECUPERACAO JUDICIAL (BRAZIL)
Name changed to Dommo Energia S.A. 10/10/2017

OGY PETES LTD NEW (AB)
Acquired by Baytex Energy Ltd. 5/22/2001
Each share Common no par exchanged for either (0.12574135) share Common no par and $1.411633 cash or $2.90 cash
Note: Option to receive stock and cash expired 6/15/2001
(See Baytex Energy Ltd.)

OGY PETROLEUMS LTD (BC)
Merged into OGY Petroleums Ltd. (ALTA) 11/1/92
Each share Common no par exchanged for (0.5) share Common no par
(See OGY Petroleums Ltd. (ALTA))

OHANA ENTERPRISES INC (DE)
Recapitalized as Vinoble, Inc. 11/19/2004
Each share Common $0.001 par exchanged for (0.002) share Common $0.001 par
Vinoble, Inc. name changed to Matrixx Resource Holdings, Inc. 07/14/2006
(See Matrixx Resource Holdings, Inc.)

OHARA RES LTD (BC)
Reorganized under the laws of Nevada 10/25/1990
Each share Common no par exchanged for (1) share Common $0.001 par
O'Hara Resources Ltd. recapitalized as Vision Energy Group, Inc. 03/10/2005 which name changed to Advanced Mineral Technologies, Inc. 04/30/2007
(See Advanced Mineral Technologies, Inc.)

OHARA RES LTD (NV)
Each share old Common $0.001 par exchanged for (0.1) share new Common $0.001 par 10/26/2001
Recapitalized as Vision Energy Group, Inc. 3/10/2005
Each share new Common $0.001 par exchanged for (0.025) share Common $0.001 par
Vision Energy Group, Inc. name changed to Advanced Mineral Technologies, Inc. 4/30/2007

OHARE BANC CORP (IL)
Merged into Northern Trust Corp. 05/14/1982
Each share Common $5 par exchanged for $32.61 cash

OHARE CHICAGO CORP (IL)
Voluntarily dissolved 10/4/84
Details not available

OHARE INTL BK N A (CHICAGO, IL)
Under plan of reorganization each share Common $5 par automatically became (1) share O'Hare Banc Corp. Common $5 par 10/21/1980
(See O'Hare Banc Corp.)

OHIO & SOUTHWESTN ENERGY CO (CO)
Each (300) shares old Common no par exchanged for (1) share new Common no par 9/26/95
Reincorporated under the laws of Delaware as Strategic Internet Investments, Inc. 10/8/2001

OHIO & WESTERN UTILITIES CO.
Acquired by Southern Ohio Electric Co. 00/00/1929
Details not available

OHIO AIR CONDITIONING CO. (DE)
No longer in existence having become inoperative and void for non-payment of taxes 4/1/40

OHIO-AMERICAN WTR CO (DE)
5.5% Preferred Ser. B no par called for redemption at $100 on 11/01/2010
Public interest eliminated

OHIO-AMERICAN WTR CO (OH)
5.5% Preferred Ser. B no par called for redemption at $100 on 11/01/2010
Public interest eliminated

OHIO ARIZONA CORP.
Dissolved in 1936

OHIO ASSOCIATED TELEPHONE CO.
Name changed to General Telephone Co. of Ohio in 1952
General Telephone Co. of Ohio merged into GTE MTO Inc. 3/31/87 which name changed to GTE North Inc. 1/1/88
(See GTE North Inc.)

OHIO BANCORP (OH)
Common $10 par split (2) for (1) by issuance of (1) additional share 4/15/86
Common $10 par split (3) for (2) by issuance of (0.5) additional share 8/4/89
Common $10 par split (3) for (2) by issuance of (0.5) additional share 5/15/92
Merged into National City Corp. 10/12/93
Each share Common $10 par exchanged for $28.25 cash

OHIO BK (FINDLAY, OH)
Merged into Sky Financial Group, Inc. 12/07/1998
Each share Class A Common no par exchanged for (69.575) shares Common no par
Each share Class B Common no par exchanged for (69.575) shares Common no par
Sky Financial Group, Inc. merged into Huntington Bancshares Inc. 07/02/2007

OHIO BAR LIABILITY INS CO (OH)
Class A called for redemption at $40 on 1/15/98

OHIO BODY & BLOWER CO., INC.
Bankrupt in 1927

OHIO BOXBOARD CO. (OH)
Each share Common $1000 par exchanged for (100) shares Common $10 par in 1952
Merged into Packaging Corp. of America on a (2.470598) for (1) basis 7/31/59
Packaging Corp. of America was acquired by Tennessee Gas Transmission Co. 6/8/65 which name changed to Tenneco Inc. 4/11/66 which merged into El Paso Natural Gas Co. 12/12/96 which reorganized as El Paso Energy Corp. 8/1/98 which name changed to El Paso Corp. 2/5/2001

OHIO BRASS CO (NJ)
Under plan of merger each share Class A or B Common no par exchanged for (2) shares Common $1 par 11/17/1958
Merged into Hubbell (Harvey), Inc. 08/25/1978
Each share Common $1 par exchanged for (2.92) shares $2.06 Conv. Preferred Ser. C no par or $73 cash
Note: Option to receive cash expired 07/24/1978
Hubbell (Harvey), Inc. name changed to Hubbell Inc. 05/12/1986

OHIO BREWERY, INC. (OH)
Charter revoked for failure to file reports and pay fees 10/15/49

OHIO BUS LINE CO (OH)
Name changed to Valley Industries Co. 08/05/1969
(See Valley Industries Co.)

OHIO CAP FD INC (OH)
Merged into Cardinal Fund Inc. 05/30/1975
Each share Common $1 par exchanged for (4.178) shares Common $1 par
(See Cardinal Fund Inc.)

OHIO CAS CORP (OH)
Common 50¢ par changed to 25¢ par and (1) additional share issued 01/24/1978
VTC's for Common 50¢ par changed to 25¢ par and (1) additional share issued 01/24/1978
VTC's for Common 50¢ par expired 01/15/1980
Common 25¢ par changed to 12-1/2¢ par and (1) additional share issued 01/23/1987
Common 12-1/2¢ par split (2) for (1) by issuance of (1) additional share 04/22/1994
Common 12-1/2¢ par split (2) for (1) payable 07/22/1999 to holders of record 07/01/1999
Merged into Liberty Mutual Insurance Co. 08/28/2007
Each share Common 12-1/2¢ par exchanged for $44 cash

OHIO CAS INS CO (OH)
Each share Capital Stock $50 par exchanged for (10) shares Capital Stock $5 par in 07/00/1937
Capital Stock $5 par changed to $1.25 par and (3) additional shares issued 07/12/1956
Capital Stock $1.25 par changed to 50¢ par and (1.5) additional shares issued 08/15/1969
Stock Dividends - 100% 12/31/1941; 25% 04/16/1947; 33-1/3% 11/07/1950; 25% 04/22/1953; 10% 07/01/1965
Reorganized as Ohio Casualty Corp. 01/01/1970
Each share Capital Stock 50¢ par exchanged for (1) share Common 50¢ par
(See Ohio Casualty Corp.)

OHIO CENTRAL TELEPHONE CORP. (OH)
Each share 7% Preferred $100 par exchanged for (1) share 3%-5% Preferred $100 par and (1) share Class A no par in 1936
Merged into United Utilities, Inc. 4/4/68
(See United Utilities, Inc.)

OHIO CHEMICAL & MANUFACTURING CO.
Acquired by Air Reduction Co., Inc. in 1940
Each share Capital Stock exchanged for (0.48) share Common no par
Air Reduction Co., Inc. name changed to Airco, Inc. (N.Y.) 10/1/71 which reincorporated in Delaware 8/3/77
(See Airco, Inc. (Del.))

OHIO CITIES WATER CORP. (DE)
Completely liquidated in October 1947
Each share 6% Preferred exchanged for first and final distribution of $158.60 cash

OHIO CTZNS BANCORP INC (OH)
Acquired by National City Corp. 09/07/1982
Each share Common $10 par exchanged for $20 principal amount of 14-1/4% Notes due 09/07/1992, $20 principal amount of 11-1/4% Convertible Subordinated Notes due 09/07/1997 and $20 cash

OHIO CTZNS TR CO (TOLEDO, OH)
Common $15 par changed to $20 par 03/06/1937
Common $20 par changed to $10 par and (1) additional share issued 12/28/1971
Stock Dividends - 66-2/3% 01/21/1949; 10% 06/01/1954; 10% 12/02/1956; 10% 12/02/1957; 10% 12/28/1973; 33-1/3% 09/03/1976; 11.111% 09/02/1977
Reorganized as Ohio Citizens Bancorp, Inc. 08/01/1980
Each share Common $10 par exchanged for (1) share Common $10 par
(See Ohio Citizens Bancorp, Inc.)

OHIO CONFECTION CO. (OH)
Each share Class A no par exchanged for (1) share Preferred $10 par and (10) shares Common $1 par 00/00/1946
Preferred liquidation completed 01/09/1958
Common liquidation completed 01/30/1959
Details not available

OHIO COPPER CO. OF UTAH
Property sold in 1951
No stockholders' equity

OHIO CRANKSHAFT CO. (OH)
Each share old Common no par exchanged for (5) shares new Common no par 6/14/48
New Common no par changed to $15 par 10/25/54
Stock Dividend - 20% 4/1/64
Merged into Park-Ohio Industries, Inc. (OH) (Old) 6/1/67
Each share Common $15 par exchanged for (1.05) shares Common no par
Park-Ohio Industries, Inc. (OH) (Old) merged into Growth International, Inc. 11/30/71 which name changed to Park-Ohio Industries, Inc. (DE) 6/1/72 which reorganized as Park-Ohio Industries, Inc. (OH) (New) 1/23/85 which name changed to Park-Ohio Holdings Corp. 6/16/98

OHIO DINNER THEATRE CORP. (OH)
Charter cancelled for non-payment of taxes 11/30/70

OHIO EDISON CO (OH)
$6.60 Preference called for redemption 1/31/44
$7 Preference called for redemption 1/31/44
$7.20 Preference called for redemption 1/31/44
$5 Preference called for redemption 10/30/44
$6 Preference called for redemption 10/30/44
Common $8 par changed to $12 par in 1952
Common $12 par changed to $15 par and (1) additional share issued 5/11/60
Common $15 par changed to $9 par and (1) additional share issued 5/12/65
Each share Conv. Adjustable Rate Class A Preferred Ser. A $25 par exchanged for (2.08) shares Common $9 par 4/20/87
$3.92 Preference no par called for redemption 11/20/87
$3.50 Class A Preferred $25 par called for redemption 4/1/88
10.48% Preferred $100 par called for redemption 7/1/88
10.76% Preferred $100 par called for redemption 7/1/88
$1.80 Conv. Preference no par called for redemption 10/1/89
Adjustable Rate Class A Preferred Ser. B $25 par called for redemption 7/1/91
8.64% Preferred $100 par called for redemption 5/3/93
9.12 Preferred $100 par called for redemption 5/3/93
Market Auction Preferred Unit 1000 $100 par called for redemption 2/22/94
7.24% Preferred $100 par called for redemption 11/6/95
7.36% Preferred $100 par called for redemption 11/6/95
8.20% Preferred $100 par called for redemption 11/6/95
Under plan of merger name changed to FirstEnergy Corp. 11/8/97
7.75% Class A Preferred called for redemption at $25 on 7/1/2002
3.90% Preferred $100 par called for redemption at $103.625 plus $0.075833 accrued dividends on 7/7/2006
4.40% Preferred $100 par called for redemption at $108 plus $0.085556 accrued dividends on 7/7/2006
4.44% Preferred $100 par called for redemption at $103.50 plus $0.086333 accrued dividends on 7/7/2006
4.56% Preferred $100 par called for redemption at $103.375 plus $0.468667 accrued dividends on 7/7/2006

OHIO EDISON FING TR (DE)
9% Trust Preferred Captial Securities Ser. A called for redemption at $25 on 8/15/2002

OHIO ELECTRIC MFG. CO. (OH)
Acquired by Howell Electric Motors Co. 03/23/1959
Each share Common $1 par exchanged for (1) share Common $1 par
Howell Electric Motors Co. name changed to Howell International, Inc. (MI) 11/01/1966 which reincorporated in Delaware as Butler Aviation International, Inc. 06/01/1968 which name changed to Butler International, Inc. (DE) 06/20/1974 which merged into North American Ventures, Inc. 02/02/1987 which recapitalized as Butler International Inc. (MD) 06/29/1992
(See Butler International Inc. (MD))

OHIO FARMERS GROWTH FUND, INC. (OH)
Name changed to Westfield Growth Fund, Inc. 02/09/1971
Westfield Growth Fund, Inc. merged into Investment Co. of America 02/21/1978

OHIO FERRO ALLOYS CORP (OH)
Name changed 03/22/1995
Each share old Common $1 par exchanged for (3) shares new Common $1 par 00/00/1946
Stock Dividends - 50% 01/15/1956; 25% 01/15/1957; 25% 01/15/1958; 10% 01/15/1960; 10% 01/15/1962;

150% 07/26/1965; 25% 05/18/1966; 10% 01/25/1967; 10% 01/29/1969; 10% 01/27/1970; 10% 06/25/1974; 10% 03/31/1975; 10% 01/28/1976
Under plan of reorganization name changed to Simetco Inc. 11/22/1988
Simetco Inc. name changed back to Ohio Ferro-Alloys Corp. 03/22/1995
Charter cancelled for failure to file reports or pay taxes 12/22/1998

OHIO FINANCE CO.
Acquired by American Investment Co. of Illinois in 1949
Each share 5% Preference $100 par exchanged for (4) shares $1.25 Preference $25 par
Each share 4-1/2% Preferred $100 par exchanged for (4) shares 4-1/2% Preference $25 par
Each share Common no par exchanged for (0.8) share $1.25 Preference $25 par
American Investment Co. of Illinois name changed to American Investment Co. 11/30/63
(See American Investment Co.)

OHIO FIRST FARM LOAN CO. (OH)
Charter cancelled for non-payment of taxes 2/25/27

OHIO FORGE & MACHINE CORP. (OH)
Each share Common no par exchanged for (2) shares Common $5 par in 1940
Common $5 par changed to no par 5/31/62
Common no par split (2) for (1) by issuance of (1) additional share 12/14/62
Under plan of merger name changed to Curtis Noll Corp. 12/31/64
(See Curtis Noll Corp.)

OHIO GRAVEL CO. (OH)
Name changed to Aggregates, Inc. 10/1/63 which completed liquidation 12/16/66

OHIO HERITAGE BANCORP INC (OH)
Merged into Peoples Bancorp Inc. 08/22/2014
Each share Common no par exchanged for (3.9855) shares Common no par and $16.50 cash

OHIO-INDIANA MUTUAL INVESTMENTS, INC. (OH)
Merged into Koehler Management Corp. 06/29/1970
Each share Common $1 par exchanged for (2.76) shares Common no par
(See Koehler Management Corp.)

OHIO IRON & STEEL CO.
Dissolved in 1941

OHIO KENTUCKY GAS CO.
Acquired by Kentucky Ohio Gas Co. 00/00/1933
Details not available

OHIO LEGACY CORP (OH)
Each share old Common no par exchanged for (0.1) share new Common no par 09/18/2012
Acquired by United Community Financial Corp. 01/31/2017
Each share new Common no par exchanged for $18 cash

OHIO MATCH CO. (DE)
Each share Common no par exchanged for (5) shares Common $5 par 00/00/1951
Name changed to Hunt Foods & Industries, Inc. 04/03/1957
Hunt Foods & Industries, Inc. merged into Simon (Norton), Inc. 07/17/1968 which merged into Esmark, Inc. (Inc. 03/14/1969) 09/09/1983
(See Esmark, Inc. (Inc. 03/14/1969))

OHIO MATTRESS CO (DE)
Common $1 par split (3) for (2) by issuance of (0.5) additional share 7/29/88
Merged into GGvA Holding Corp. 8/9/89
Each share Common $1 par exchanged for (7.0515) Ohio Mattress Holding Co. Common Stock Purchase Warrants expiring 8/9/94

OHIO MATTRESS CO (OH)
Common $1 par split (5) for (4) by issuance of (0.25) additional share 1/31/84
Reorganized under the laws of Delaware as Ohio Mattress Co. 7/11/84
Each share Common $1 par exchanged for (1) share Common $1 par
(See Ohio Mattress Co. (DE))

OHIO MATTRESS HLDG CO (DE)
Name changed to Sealy Holdings Inc. 03/07/1990
Sealy Holdings Inc. name changed to Sealy Corp. 11/06/1991
(See Sealy Corp.)

OHIO MID-CITIES CORP.
Assets sold in 1934

OHIO MINES DEVELOPMENT CO. LTD.
Liquidated in 1953

OHIO NATIONAL LIFE INSURANCE CO. (OH)
Mutualization completed 2/5/59

OHIO OIL & GAS CO. (DE)
Business discontinued 12/31/57
Declared inoperative and void for non- payment of taxes 4/1/60

OHIO OIL CO. (OH)
Each share Common $25 par exchanged for (2) shares Common no par in 1930
Common no par split (2) for (1) through the issuance of (1) additional share 6/8/55
Name changed to Marathon Oil Co. 4/31/62
(See Marathon Oil Co.)

OHIO PWR CO (OH)
$3.75 Preferred $25 par called for redemption 06/01/1987
14% Preferred $100 par called for redemption 06/01/1987
14% Preferred Ser. A $100 par called for redemption 07/01/1987
$2.27 Preferred $25 par called for redemption 04/25/1993
7.72% Preferred $100 par called for redemption 10/23/1993
8.48% Preferred $100 par called for redemption 10/23/1993
7.76% Preferred $100 par called for redemption 11/14/1993
7.60% Preferred $100 par called for redemption 11/18/1995
7 6/10% Preferred $100 par called for redemption 11/18/1995
8.04% Preferred $100 par called for redemption 11/18/1995
6.35% Preferred called for redemption at $100 on 06/01/2003
6.02% Preferred called for redemption at $100 on 12/01/2003
5.90% Preferred $100 par called for redemption at $100 on 01/01/2005
4.08% Preferred $100 par called for redemption at $103 on 12/01/2011
4.20% Preferred $100 par called for redemption at $103.20 on 12/01/2011
4.40% Preferred $100 par called for redemption at $104 on 12/01/2011
4.50% Preferred $100 par called for redemption at $110 on 12/01/2011

OHIO PUBLIC SERVICE CO.
Merged into Ohio Edison Co. 5/1/50
Preferred exchanged share for share
Common exchanged (0.548) for (1)
(See Ohio Edison Co.)

OHIO RADIO, INC. (OH)
Voluntarily dissolved 5/29/80
Details not available

OHIO REAL ESTATE EQUITIES CO. (OH)
Merged into United Western Corp. 5/31/78
Each Trust Unit of Bene. Int. no par exchanged for (2.16) shares Common no par
(See United Western Corp.)

OHIO REAL ESTATE INVT CO (OH)
Merged into United Western Corp. 05/31/1978
Each Trust Unit of Bene. Int. no par exchanged for (1) share Common no par
(See United Western Corp.)

OHIO RESORTS INC. (OH)
Common $10 par changed to no par and (9) additional shares issued 11/13/68
Completely liquidated 7/1/75
Each share Common no par exchanged for first and final distribution of $3.4962 cash

OHIO RES CORP (AB)
Reincorporated 07/09/1997
Place of incorporation changed from (BC) to (ALTA) 07/09/1997
Name changed to Causeway Energy Corp. 11/16/1998
Causeway Energy Corp. merged into Bushmills Energy Corp. 08/29/2001 which merged into Brooklyn Energy Corp. 02/03/2003
(See Brooklyn Energy Corp.)

OHIO RIV BK (IRONTON, OH)
Merged into Premier Financial Bancorp, Inc. 3/20/98
Each share Common $8 par exchanged for (1.2) shares Common no par

OHIO RIVER COLLIERIES CO. (OH)
6% Conv. Preferred $100 par retired 12/1/59

OHIO RIVER EDISON CO.
Absorbed by Ohio Edison Co. 7/5/30
Details not available

OHIO RIVER RAILWAY & POWER CO.
Dissolved in 1937

OHIO RIVER SAND & GRAVEL CO.
Reorganized as Iron City-Ohio River Corp. 00/00/1935
Details not available

OHIO RIVER SAND CO.
Recapitalized as Ohio River Sand Co., Inc. in 1949
Each share 7% 1st Preferred $100 par exchanged for (7.5) shares 6% Preferred $20 par and 58-1/3¢ in cash
Each share 6% 2nd Preferred $50 par exchanged for (2) shares Common $10 par
Each share Common $1 par exchanged for (0.1) share Common $10 par
Ohio River Sand Co., Inc. completely liquidated 4/30/71

OHIO RIVER SAND CO., INC. (KY)
Each share Common $10 par exchanged for (4) shares Common $2.50 par in 1954
Completely liquidated 4/30/71
Each share Common $2.50 par exchanged for $12 cash

OHIO RUBBER CO. (DE)
Liquidation approved in 1953

OHIO SAVINGS & LOAN CO. (OH)
Recapitalized as Ohio Savings Association on an (10) for (1) basis 01/16/1956
Ohio Savings Association merged into Ohio Savings Financial Corp. 12/30/1977 which name changed to AmTrust Financial Corp. 06/28/2007

OHIO SVGS ASSN (OH)
Merged into Ohio Savings Financial Corp. 12/30/1977
Each share Capital Stock $5 par exchanged for (1) share Capital Stock no par
Ohio Savings Financial Corp. name changed to AmTrust Financial Corp. 06/28/2007

OHIO SVGS FINL CORP (OH)
7.50% Preferred Ser. A no par called for redemption at $650 on 07/01/1999
Name changed to AmTrust Financial Corp. 06/28/2007

OHIO SEALY MATTRESS MFG CO (OH)
Common $1 par split (3) for (2) by issuance of (0.5) additional share 7/24/72
Common $1 par split (3) for (2) by issuance of (0.5) additional share 7/31/79
Common $1 par split (2) for (1) by issuance of (1) additional share 7/31/81
Common $1 par split (5) for (4) by issuance of (0.25) additional share 4/29/83
Common $1 par split (3) for (2) by issuance of (0.5) additional share 7/29/83
Under plan of merger name changed to Ohio Mattress Co. (OH) 12/22/83
Ohio Mattress Co. (OH) reorganized in Delaware 7/11/84
(See Ohio Mattress Co. (DE))

OHIO SEAMLESS TUBE CO. (OH)
Common no par changed to $5 par in 1940
Each share Common $5 par exchanged for (2) shares Common no par in 1947
Acquired by Copperweld Steel Co. and dissolved in 1953
(See Copperweld Steel Co.)

OHIO SERVICE HOLDING CORP. (DE)
Each share Common $1 par exchanged for (9.0) shares Class A Common $1 par and (4.0) shares Class B Common $1 par 05/19/1955
Name changed to Telephone Service Co. of Ohio 05/21/1956
Telephone Service Co. of Ohio acquired by United Utilities, Inc. 01/25/1967 which name changed to United Telecommunications, Inc. 06/02/1972 which name changed to Sprint Corp. (KS) 02/26/1992 which name changed to Sprint Nextel Corp. 08/12/2005 which merged into Sprint Corp. (DE) 07/10/2013

OHIO SHEET & TIN PLATE CORP.
Sold under foreclosure in 1940

OHIO ST FINL SVCS INC (OH)
Merged into Advance Financial Bancorp 9/7/2001
Each share Common no par exchanged for $16 cash

OHIO ST LIFE INS CO (OH)
Each share Capital Stock $100 par exchanged for (10) shares Capital Stock $10 par 00/00/1937
Capital Stock $10 par changed to $2 par and (4) additional shares issued 02/11/1960
Capital Stock $2 par changed to $1 par and (1) additional shares issued 04/25/1968
Stock Dividends - 100% 03/01/1940; 100% 03/01/1963
Acquired by Farmers New World Life Insurance Co. 12/29/1972
Each share Capital Stock $1 par exchanged for (0.5) share Capital Stock $1 par
Farmers New World Life Insurance Co. merged into Farmers Group, Inc. 12/21/1977
(See Farmers Group, Inc.)

OHIO STATE MORTGAGE CO. (OH)
Charter revoked for failure to file reports and pay fees 11/15/37

OHIO TERMINAL CO.
Reorganized as Railway Warehouses, Inc. in 1934 which was completely liquidated 4/7/58

OHIO UTILITIES CO.
Acquired by Southern Ohio Electric Co. 00/00/1929
Details not available

OHIO VALLEY AIRWAYS, INC. (OH)
Merged into Polar Vac Industries, Inc. 7/31/69
Each share Class A Common $1 par or Class B Common $1 par exchanged for (1.1) shares Common no par
Polar Vac Industries, Inc. charter cancelled 12/15/80

OHIO VY ALUM INC (IN)
Acquired by Interlock Industries, Inc. 00/00/1985
Each share Class A Common $2.50 par exchanged for approximately $23.92 cash

OHIO VY BANCORP (IN)
Merged into Merchants National Corp. 08/31/1987
Each share Common no par exchanged for (1.8) shares Common no par
Merchants National Corp. merged into National City Corp. 05/02/1992 which was acquired by PNC Financial Services Group, Inc. 12/31/2008

OHIO VALLEY BK CO GALLIPOLIS (OH)
Reorganized as Ohio Valley Banc Corp. 10/23/92
Each share Common $10 par exchanged for (1) share Common $10 par

OHIO VALLEY GAS CORP.
Merged into West Virginia Gas Corp. 00/00/1938
Details not available

OHIO WAX PAPER CO.
Liquidation completed in 1946

OHIO WTR SVC CO (OH)
Each share 5.5% Preferred $100 par exchanged for (1) share Class A Common no par 00/00/1935
Each share 6% Preferred $100 par exchanged for (1) share Class A Common no par and $0.83 cash 00/00/1935
Each share Class A Common no par exchanged for (3) shares Common $10 par 00/00/1945
Acquired by Consumers Water Co. 03/23/1973
Each share Common $10 par exchanged for (1.333333) shares Common $1 par
Consumers Water Co. merged into Philadelphia Surburban Corp. 03/10/1999 which name changed to Aqua America, Inc. 01/16/2004

OHLEN-BISHOP CO.
Name changed to Ohlen-Bishop Manufacturing Co. in 1941
Ohlen-Bishop Manufacturing Co. name changed to Rockwell Tools, Inc. in 1951
(See Rockwell Tools, Inc.)

OHLEN-BISHOP MANUFACTURING CO.
Name changed to Rockwell Tools, Inc. in 1951
(See Rockwell Tools, Inc.)

OHM CORP (OH)
Reincorporated 05/20/1994
State of incorporation changed from (DE) to (OH) 05/20/1994
Each share Common 10¢ par received distribution of (0.141774) share NSC Corp. Common 1¢ par payable 03/06/1998 to holders of record 02/24/1998
Merged into International Technology Corp. 06/11/1998
Each share Common 10¢ par exchanged for (1.081) shares Common 10¢ par and $2.58 cash
International Technology Corp. name changed to IT Group, Inc. 12/24/1998
(See IT Group, Inc.)

OHMART CORP (OH)
Common $1 par changed to no par and (2) additional shares issued 5/26/61
Stock Dividend - 20% 8/15/60
Merged into OM Acquisition Corp. 4/29/93
Each share Common no par exchanged for $48 cash

OHMER CORP.
Acquired by Rockwell Manufacturing Co. in 1946
Details not available

OHMER FARE REGISTER CO.
Reorganized as Ohmer Corp. 00/00/1945
Each share Preferred $100 par received $87 cash
Common no par cancelled and are valueless

OHS CAP CORP (AB)
Name changed to Pay Linx Financial Corp. 04/18/2007
(See Pay Linx Financial Corp.)

OHSL FINL CORP (DE)
Common 1¢ par split (2) for (1) by issuance of (1) additional share payable 04/06/1998 to holders of record 03/16/1998
Merged into Provident Financial Group, Inc. 12/03/1999
Each share Common 1¢ par exchanged for (0.5458) share Common no par
Provident Financial Group, Inc. merged into National City Corp. 07/01/2004 which was acquired by PNC Financial Services Group, Inc. 12/31/2008

OIA INC (DE)
Each share Common $0.0001 par exchanged for (0.01) share Common 1¢ par 04/08/1991
Name changed to Biorelease Corp. 11/02/1992
Biorelease Corp. recapitalized as BRL Holdings, Inc. 07/02/2001 which name changed to Element 21 Golf Co. (DE) 10/18/2004 which reincorporated in Nevada as American Rare Earths & Materials, Corp. 07/20/2010

OICCO ACQUISITION I INC (DE)
Name changed to Champion Pain Care Corp. 10/31/2014

OIL & GAS OFFSETS (ON)
Acquired by Acme Gas & Oil Co. Ltd. 00/00/1952
Each share Capital Stock $1 par exchanged for (0.5) share Capital Stock no par
(See Acme Gas & Oil Co. Ltd.)

OIL & GAS PROPERTY MANAGEMENT, INC. (NY)
Completely liquidated 5/28/59
Each share Common $1 par exchanged for first and final distribution of (1) share Dorchester Corp. Common no par and $10 cash 5/28/59
Dorchester Corp. name changed to Dorchester Gas Producing Co. 1/2/62 which merged into Panoil Co. 11/26/68 which name changed to Dorchester Gas Corp. 2/1/72
(See Dorchester Gas Corp.)

OIL & GAS SEEKERS INC (NV)
Name changed to Bacterin International, Inc. 4/9/2004

OIL & MINERALS QUEST N L (AUSTRALIA)
Name changed to Bass Strait Oil & Gas Holdings N.L. 12/21/1981
Bass Strait Oil & Gas Holdings N.L. name changed to Federation Resources N.L. 10/20/1988
(See Federation Resources N.L.)

OIL & NATURAL GAS SHARES, INC.
Dissolved in 1931

OIL & PPTYS INC (MO)
Completely liquidated 03/25/1970
Each share Common $1 par exchanged for first and final distribution of (2) shares Clark Manufacturing Co. Common 1¢ par
(See Clark Manufacturing Co.)

OIL BALTIJA GROUP LTD (NJ)
Merged into Baltic Oil Holdings Ltd. of Delaware 9/19/2002
Each share Common no par exchanged for $5 cash

OIL BASE INC (DE)
Merged into Hughes Tool Co. 10/23/1979
Each share Common $1 par exchanged for $36.50 cash

OIL CITY LUBRICANTS LTD (BC)
Recapitalized as Thunder Sword Resources Inc. 05/03/1996
Each share Common no par exchanged for (0.2) share Common no par
Thunder Sword Resources Inc. recapitalized as Rainmaker Mining Corp. 11/23/2009 which name changed to Rainmaker Resources Ltd. (BC) 05/08/2014 which reorganized in Ontario as Indiva Ltd. 12/19/2017

OIL CITY NATIONAL BANK (OIL CITY, PA)
Merged into Northwest Pennsylvania Bank & Trust Co. (Oil City, PA) 04/30/1962
Each share Capital Stock $20 par exchanged for (1.1) shares Common $20 par
Northwest Pennsylvania Bank & Trust Co. (Oil City, PA) reorganized as Northwest Pennsylvania Corp. 07/01/1981 which merged into Mellon National Corp. 04/12/1984 which name changed to Mellon Bank Corp. 09/30/1984 which name changed to Mellon Financial Corp. 10/17/1999 which merged into Bank of New York Mellon Corp. 07/01/2007

OIL CITY PETE INC (TX)
SEC revoked common stock registration 11/07/2008
Stockholders' equity unlikely

OIL CITY TRUST CO. (OIL CITY, PA)
Name changed to First Seneca Bank & Trust Co. (Oil City, PA) 07/01/1954
First Seneca Bank & Trust Co. (Oil City, PA) reorganized as First Seneca Corp. 06/01/1982 which merged into Pennbancorp 12/31/1983 which merged into Integra Financial Corp. 01/26/1989 which merged into National City Corp. 05/03/1996 which was acquired by PNC Financial Services Group, Inc. 12/31/2008

OIL CO LUKOIL (RUSSIA)
Each Sponsored ADR for Preferred exchanged for (0.5) Sponsored ADR for Ordinary 12/26/2001
Sponsored ADR's for Ordinary split (4) for (1) by issuance of (3) additional ADR's payable 05/04/2005 to holders of record 05/03/2005 Ex date - 05/05/2005
Sponsored 144A ADR's for Ordinary split (4) for (1) by issuance of (3) additional ADR's payable 05/04/2005 to holders of record 05/03/2005
Basis changed from (1:4) to (1:1) 05/05/2005
Name changed to PJSC Lukoil 10/20/2015

OIL EXPLORATION CO.
Merged into Wichita River Oil Corp. (VA) (Old) 00/00/1952
Each share Common $1 par exchanged for (1) share Common $1 par
Wichita River Oil Corp. name changed to Wichita Industries, Inc. 01/08/1969 which merged into Wichita River Oil Corp. (VA) (New) 11/04/1987 which reincorporated in Delaware 03/30/1990
(See Wichita River Oil Corp. (DE))

OIL EXPLORATION INTERNATIONAL, INC. (DE)
Charter cancelled and declared inoperative and void for non-payment of taxes 04/15/1972

OIL EXTRACTORS OF AMERICA (UT)
Name changed to R.W. Technology, Inc. (UT) 3/11/87
R.W. Technology, Inc. (UT) reincorporated in Delaware 10/22/87
(See R.W. Technology, Inc.)

OIL FINANCE CORP. (DE)
Declared inoperative and void for non- payment of Delaware taxes in January, 1961

OIL HUNTERS, INC. (OK)
Charter cancelled for failure to pay franchise tax 4/18/60

OIL INC (NV)
Merged into Oil Resources, Inc. 10/13/1971
Each share Common $1 par exchanged for (1) share Common no par
Oil Resources, Inc. liquidated for Capital Energy Corp. 12/31/1979 which name changed to Life Chemistry Inc. 11/28/1983
(See Life Chemistry Inc.)

OIL INDUSTRIES FACTORS, INC. (TX)
Charter revoked for failure to file reports and pay fees 3/4/63

OIL INTL LTD (CO)
Declared defunct and inoperative for failure to pay taxes and file annual reports 3/1/2001

OIL LEASE DEVELOPMENT CO.
Reorganized as Middle States Petroleum Corp. 00/00/1929
Details not available

OIL MOP INC (LA)
Name changed to Enertech, Inc. 06/01/1982
(See Enertech, Inc.)

OIL PATCH EQUIPMENT SALES & RENTAL LTD. (AB)
Name changed to Oil Patch Industries Ltd. 06/11/1973
Oil Patch Industries Ltd. name changed to OPI Ltd. (ALTA) 04/21/1975 which reincorporated in Canada 00/00/1982 which name changed to Oil Patch Group Inc. 09/22/1986
(See Oil Patch Group Inc.)

OIL PATCH GROUP INC (CANADA)
Delisted from Toronto Stock Exchange 08/09/1989

OIL PATCH INDS LTD (AB)
Name changed to OPI Ltd. (ALTA) 04/21/1975
OPI Ltd. (ALTA) reincorporated in Canada 00/00/1982 which name changed to Oil Patch Group Inc. 09/22/1986
(See Oil Patch Group Inc.)

OIL PRODUCERS, INC. (DE)
Merged into Gulf Coast Western Oil Co. 12/04/1956
Each share Common 10¢ par

OIL-OIL FINANCIAL INFORMATION, INC.

exchanged for (0.1) share Common $1 par
Gulf Coast Western Oil Co. recapitalized as General Energy Corp. (AZ) 01/08/1968
(See General Energy Corp. (AZ))

OIL PRODUCERS & REFNG INC (NV)
Merged into Transcontinental Energy Corp. 1/22/73
Each share Common 50¢ par exchanged for (0.2) share Common 50¢ par
(See Transcontinental Energy Corp.)

OIL PRODUCERS EQUIP CORP (TX)
Company reported in bankruptcy in 1988
Details not available

OIL PRODUCTIONS, INC. (VA)
Charter cancelled and proclaimed dissolved for failure to file reports 12/31/1991

OIL PROSPECTORS, INC. (NV)
Charter cancelled for failure to file reports and pay fees 3/2/53

OIL RECOVERY CORP. (NY)
Each share Common 10¢ par exchanged for (80) shares Common 1¢ par to effect a (10) for (1) split and a 700% stock dividend 11/18/1959
Each share Common 1¢ par exchanged for (0.25) share Common 2¢ par 09/09/1966
Name changed to Basin Petroleum Corp. 11/14/1967
(See Basin Petroleum Corp.)

OIL REFINERIES LTD (ISRAEL)
ADR agreement terminated 08/06/2018
No ADR's remain outstanding

OIL RES INC (NV)
Liquidation completed
Each share Common no par exchanged for initial distribution of (0.4255) share Capital Energy Corp. Common no par 12/14/1977
Each share Common no par received second distribution of (0.0284) share Capital Energy Corp. Common no par 12/14/1978
Each share Common no par received third and final distribution of (0.0113) share Capital Energy Corp. Common no par 12/31/1979
Capital Energy Corp. name changed to Life Chemistry Inc. 11/28/1983
(See Life Chemistry Inc.)

OIL RETRIEVAL SYS INC (AZ)
SEC revoked common stock registration 11/07/2008
Stockholders' equity unlikely

OIL SANDS & ENERGY MEGA PROJS TR (ON)
Merged into Sentry Energy Growth & Income Fund 02/04/2011
Each Trust Unit no par received (0.988) Ser. A Unit no par

OIL SANDS LTD. (AB)
Liquidation completed 08/18/1967
Each share Capital Stock no par exchanged for (0.020833) share Great Canadian Oil Sands Ltd. Common no par and (1) share Oil Sands (1967) Ltd. Capital Stock no par
(See each company's listing)

OIL SANDS 1967 LTD (AB)
Completely liquidated 04/26/1976
Each share Capital Stock no par exchanged for $0.007 cash

OIL SANDS SECTOR FD (ON)
Trust terminated 06/29/2018
Each Unit received $4.613778 cash

OIL SANDS SPLIT TR (ON)
Preferred Securities no par called for redemption at $17 plus $0.36125 accrued dividends on 09/15/2010
Trust terminated 09/15/2010

Each Capital Unit no par received first and final distribution of $108.304 cash

OIL SECS & METALS CORP (UT)
Name changed to Oil Securities, Inc. (UT) and Common no par changed to 5¢ par 12/10/1969
Oil Securities, Inc. (UT) reincorporated in Nevada 05/27/1982 which recapitalized as Digital Technologies Media Group Inc. 07/26/1996 which reorganized as Central Capital Venture Corp. 05/08/2000
(See Central Capital Venture Corp.)

OIL SECS INC (NV)
Reincorporated 05/27/1982
Stock Dividend - 10% 01/30/1981
State of incorporation changed from (UT) to (NV) 05/27/1982
Recapitalized as Digital Technologies Media Group Inc. 07/26/1996
Each share Common 5¢ par exchanged for (0.01) share Common 5¢ par
Digital Technologies Media Group Inc. reorganized as Central Capital Venture Corp. 05/08/2000
(See Central Capital Venture Corp.)

OIL SECURITIES & GAS CORP. (UT)
Name changed to Oil Securities & Metals Corp. and Common $1 par changed to no par 02/06/1968
Oil Securities & Metals Corp. name changed to Oil Securities, Inc. (UT) 12/10/1969 which reincorporated in Nevada 05/27/1982 which recapitalized as Digital Technologies Media Group Inc. 07/26/1996 which reorganized as Central Capital Venture Corp. 05/08/2000
(See Central Capital Venture Corp.)

OIL SECURITIES & URANIUM CORP. (UT)
Name changed to Oil Securities & Gas Corp. 07/01/1956
Oil Securities & Gas Corp. name changed to Oil Securities & Metals Corp. 02/06/1968 which name changed to Oil Securities, Inc. (UT) 12/10/1969 which reincorporated in Nevada 05/27/1982 which recapitalized as Digital Technologies Media Group Inc. 07/26/1996 which reorganized as Central Capital Venture Corp. 05/08/2000
(See Central Capital Venture Corp.)

OIL SECURITIES CO., INC. (UT)
Merged into Oil Securities & Uranium Corp. 00/00/1955
Each share Common exchanged for (0.33333333) share Common
Oil Securities & Uranium Corp. name changed to Oil Securities & Gas Corp. 07/01/1956 which name changed to Oil Securities & Metals Corp. 02/06/1968 which name changed to Oil Securities, Inc. (UT) 12/10/1969 which reincorporated in Nevada 05/27/1982 which recapitalized as Digital Technologies Media Group Inc. 07/26/1996 which reorganized as Central Capital Venture Corp. 05/08/2000
(See Central Capital Venture Corp.)

OIL SELECTIONS LTD. (CANADA)
Acquired by Quonto Petroleums Ltd. 00/00/1957
Each share Capital Stock no par exchanged for (0.25) share Common $1 par
Quonto Petroleums Ltd. name changed to Quonto Explorations Ltd. 07/27/1962
(See Quonto Explorations Ltd.)

OIL SVC HLDRS TR (DE)
Trust terminated
Each Depositary Receipt received first and final distribution of $114.722447 cash payable

01/07/2013 to holders of record 12/20/2012

OIL SHALE & URANIUM RES INC (DE)
Name changed to Minerals & Industries, Inc. 06/18/1969
Minerals & Industries, Inc. name changed to Techno-Design, Ltd. 06/22/1987

OIL SHALE CORP (NV)
Name changed to Tosco Corp. 07/28/1976
Tosco Corp. merged into Phillips Petroleum Co. 09/14/2001 which name changed to ConocoPhillips 08/30/2002

OIL SHARES, INC.
Name changed to Oils & Industries, Inc. in 1934
Oils & Industries, Inc. merged into Chesapeake Industries, Inc. 2/14/55 which name changed to America Corp. (OH) 8/10/59 which recapitalized as America Corp. (DE) 12/31/63 which name changed to Pathe Industries, Inc. (DE) 11/20/64
(See Pathe Industries, Inc. (DE))

OIL SPRINGS ENERGY CORP (ON)
Recapitalized as OSE Corp. 08/07/2002
Each share Common no par exchanged for (0.25) share Common no par
OSE Corp. recapitalized as Petro Basin Energy Corp. (ON) 09/19/2011 which reincorporated in British Columbia as Peace River Capital Corp. 09/16/2016 which name changed to Liberty One Lithium Corp. 12/02/2016

OIL STATE REFINING CO. (OK)
Charter revoked for failure to file reports and pay fees 10/15/23

OIL VENTURES, INC. (CO)
Declared defunct and inoperative for non-payment of taxes 10/11/61

OIL WELL SUPPLY CO.
Name changed to Pittsburgh United Corp. 00/00/1930
(See Pittsburgh United Corp.)

OIL WELL SUPPLY INVESTMENT CO.
Name changed to Pennsylvania Industries, Inc. in 1929
Pennsylvania Industries, Inc. was liquidated 12/15/54

OILCO RES LTD (AB)
Name changed to Canadian Hydro Developers, Inc. 02/20/1991
(See Canadian Hydro Developers, Inc.)

OILEX INC (NV)
Each share old Common $0.001 par exchanged for (0.05) share new Common $0.001 par 01/26/1998
SEC revoked common stock registration 12/01/2006
Stockholders' equity unlikely

OILEX INDS LTD (AB)
Merged into L.K. Resources Ltd. 10/04/1979
Each share Capital Stock no par exchanged for (1) share Common no par
L.K. Resources Ltd. name changed to XL Food Systems Ltd. 04/21/1986 which name changed to XL Foods Ltd. 06/15/1989 which name changed to Sevenway Capital Corp. 03/09/1999 which merged into Glacier Ventures International Corp. (Canada) (New) 04/28/2000 which name changed to Glacier Media Inc. 07/01/2008

OILEX INTL INVTS INC (NV)
Name changed to Oilex, Inc. 07/08/1996
(See Oilex, Inc.)

OILEXCO INC (AB)
Recapitalized as ScotOil Petroleum Ltd. (AB) 06/09/2011
Each share Common no par exchanged for (0.1) share Common no par
ScotOil Petroleum Ltd. (AB) reincorporated in British Columbia as 0915988 B.C. Ltd. 07/27/2011
(See 0915988 B.C. Ltd.)

OILFIELD STEEL SUPPLY SHAREHOLDERS LIQUIDATING TRUST (CA)
Liquidation completed
Each Ctf. of Bene. Int. received initial distribution of $0.27 cash 6/25/82
Each Ctf. of Bene. Int. received second distribution of $0.009 cash 10/6/82
Each Ctf. of Bene. Int. received third distribution of $0.1123 cash 12/27/82
Each Ctf. of Bene. Int. received fourth distribution of $0.3145 cash 3/21/83
Each Ctf. of Bene. Int. received fifth distribution of $0.2471 cash 6/30/83
Each Ctf. of Bene. Int. received sixth distribution of $0.1438 cash 9/20/83
Each Ctf. of Bene. Int. received seventh distribution of $0.1617 cash 12/23/83
Each Ctf. of Bene. Int. received eighth distribution of $0.314505 cash 3/19/84
Each Ctf. of Bene. Int. received ninth distribution of $0.314505 cash 6/20/84
Each Ctf. of Bene. Int. received tenth distribution of $0.161746 cash 9/20/84
Each Ctf. of Bene. Int. received eleventh distribution of $0.16624 cash 12/18/84
Each Ctf. of Bene. Int. received twelfth distribution of $0.15725 cash 3/25/85
Each Ctf. of Bene. Int. received thirteenth distribution of $0.34146 cash 6/28/85
Each Ctf. of Bene. Int. received fourteenth distribution of $0.15725 cash 9/23/85
Each Ctf. of Bene. Int. received fifteenth distribution of $0.93 cash 12/23/85
Each Ctf. of Bene. Int. received sixteenth distribution of $0.91 cash 3/31/86
Each Ctf. of Bene. Int. received seventeenth distribution of $1.56 cash 6/20/86
Each Ctf. of Bene. Int. received eighteenth distribution $1.61 cash 9/30/86
Each Ctf. of Bene. Int. received nineteenth distribution of $3.71 cash 11/6/86
Each Ctf. of Bene. Int. received twentieth distibution of $1.04 cash 12/23/86
Each Ctf. of Bene. Int. received twenty-first distribution of $1 cash 3/31/87
Each Ctf. of Bene. Int. received twenty-second distribution of $1.05 cash 6/24/87
Each Ctf. of Bene. Int. received twenty-third distribution of $1 cash 9/29/87
Each Ctf. of Bene. Int. received twenty-fourth distribution of $1.59 cash 12/30/87
Each Ctf. of Bene. Int. received twenty-fifth distribution of $1.05 cash 3/31/88
Each Ctf. of Bene. Int. received twenty-sixth distribution of $1.01 cash 6/30/88
Additional cash distributions made quarterly. Final distribution 5/31/91

OILFIELD STL SUPPLY (CA)
Liquidation completed
Each share Capital Stock no par

received initial distribution of $1 cash 7/21/81
Each share Capital Stock no par exchanged for second distribution of approximately (0.2) share of Castle (A.M.) & Co. (DE) Common no par, (1) Oilfield Steel Supply Shareholders Liquidating Trust Ctf. of Bene. Int. and approximately $6 cash 3/22/82
(See each company's listing)

OILGEAR CO (WI)
Each share Common $25 par exchanged for (2) shares Common $12.50 par in 1947
Each share Common $12.50 par exchanged for (2) shares Common $6.25 par 10/20/60
Common $6.25 par split (2) for (1) by issuance of (1) additional share 11/2/64
Common $6.25 par split (2) for (1) by issuance of (1) additional share 10/10/68
Common $6.25 par changed to $1 par 4/16/69
Common $1 par split (3) for (2) by issuance of (0.5) additional share payable 1/20/98 to holders of record 12/22/97
Merged into Mason Wells Buyout Fund II, LP 12/15/2006
Each share Common $1 par exchanged for $15.25 cash

OILMONT PETROLEUMS CORP. (QC)
Merged into International Metal & Petroleum Corp. on an (1) for (2.5) basis 11/4/57
International Metal & Petroleum Corp. charter annulled 4/13/74

OILS & INDUSTRIES, INC. (MD)
Merged into Chesapeake Industries, Inc. 2/14/55
Each share Preferred $1 par exchanged for (0.2) share $4 Preferred $10 par
Each share Common $1 par exchanged for (0.125) share $4 Preferred $10 par and (3.75) shares Common $1 par
Chesapeake Industries, Inc. name changed to America Corp. (OH) 8/10/59 which recapitalized as America Corp. (DE) 12/31/63 which name changed to Pathe Industries, Inc. (DE) 11/20/64
(See Pathe Industries, Inc. (DE))

OILSANDS CDA CORP (ON)
Issue Information - 5,000,000 UNITS consisting of (1) share COM and (0.5) WT offered at $10 per Unit on 08/02/2007
Name changed to Middlefield Tactical Energy Corp. 11/11/2010
Middlefield Tactical Energy Corp. name changed to MBN Corp. 02/27/2012

OILSANDS QUEST INC (CO)
Completely liquidated
Each share Common $0.001 par received first and final distribution of CAD$0.0252269 cash payable 09/05/2014 to holders of record 08/21/2014

OILSTOCKS LTD.
Liquidation completed in 1945

OILTANKING PARTNERS L P (DE)
Common Units split (2) for (1) by issuance of (1) additional Unit payable 07/14/2014 to holders of record 07/07/2014 Ex date - 07/15/2014
Merged into Enterprise Products Partners L.P. 02/13/2015
Each Common Unit exchanged for (1.3) Common Units

OILTEC RES LTD (AB)
Merged into Forte Resources Inc. 6/23/2004
Each share Common no par exchanged for (0.2662074) share Common no par and $0.5717992 cash

OILTECH INC (NV)
Each share old Common 1¢ par exchanged for (0.1) share new Common 1¢ par 01/25/1984
Name changed to AMERECO 12/26/1991
(See AMERECO)

OILTEX INTL LTD (ON)
Merged into International Oiltex Ltd. 10/01/1989
Each share Common no par exchanged for (0.55390921) share Common no par
International Oiltex Ltd. merged into Aztec Resources Ltd. 09/02/1994 which recapitalized as Pursuit Resources Inc. (New) 02/13/1997 which merged into EnerMark Income Fund 04/11/2000 which merged into Enerplus Resources Fund 06/22/2001 which reorganized as Enerplus Corp. 01/03/2011

OIS OPTICAL IMAGING SYS INC (DE)
Completely liquidated 12/21/1999
No stockholders' equity

OJAI CMNTY BK (OJAI, CA)
Common no par split (5) for (4) by issuance of (0.25) additional share payable 04/03/2006 to holders of record 03/03/2006 Ex date - 04/04/2006
Under plan of reorganization each share Common no par automatically became (1) share OCB Bancorp Common no par 12/17/2013
OCB Bancorp merged into Sierra Bancorp 10/02/2017

OJI PAPER CO LTD OLD (JAPAN)
Name changed to New Oji Paper Co., Ltd. 08/08/1994
New Oji Paper Co., Ltd. name changed to Oji Paper Co., Ltd. (New) 10/01/1996 which name changed to Oji Holdings Corp. 10/01/2012

OJI PAPER LTD NEW (JAPAN)
Name changed to Oji Holdings Corp. 10/01/2012

OJIBWAY PRESS, INC. (DE)
Acquired by Harcourt, Brace & World, Inc. 4/23/68
Each share Common $1 par exchanged for (0.080652) share Common $1 par
Harcourt, Brace & World, Inc. name changed to Harcourt Brace Jovanovich, Inc. 6/2/70 which merged into General Cinema Corp. 11/25/91 which name changed to Harcourt General, Inc. 3/15/93
(See Harcourt General, Inc.)

OJSC CHERKIZOVO GROUP (RUSSIA)
GDR basis changed from (1:0.00666666) to (1:0.667) 07/24/2007
Name changed to Cherkizovo Group PJSC 06/08/2015

OJSC CONCERN KALINA (RUSSIA)
Acquired by Unilever PLC 06/25/2012
Each Reg. S GDR for Ordinary exchanged for $130.0891 cash
Each Sponsored ADR for Ordinary exchanged for $130.0891 cash
Each Unsponsored 144A GDR for Ordinary exchanged for $130.0891 cash

OJSC POLYUS GOLD (RUSSIA)
Sponsored ADR's for Common split (2) for (1) by issuance of (1) additional ADR payable 07/12/2006 to holders of record 12/30/2005
Sponsored ADR's for Common split (2) for (1) by issuance of (1) additional ADR payable 06/10/2008 to holders of record 06/06/2008 Ex date - 06/11/2008
Basis changed from (1:1) to (1:0.5) 06/10/2008
Name changed to Polyus Gold PJSC 03/04/2016
Polyus Gold PJSC name changed to Polyus PJSC 05/24/2016

OKA BATHURST MINING CORP. LTD. (QC)
Charter annulled for failure to file reports or pay fees 11/4/78

OKA COLUMBIUM & METALS LTD. (QC)
Thru purchases from time to time 100% acquired by St. Lawrence Columbium & Metals Corp. in 1963

OKA RARE METALS MINING CO. LTD. (ON)
Merged into Manoka Mining & Smelting Co. Ltd. on a (0.25) for (1) basis 5/4/62
Manoka Mining & Smelting Co. Ltd. recapitalized as Cat Lake Mines Ltd. 10/18/71 which merged into Fundy Chemical International Ltd. 3/16/73
(See Fundy Chemical International Ltd.)

OKA URANIUM & METALS LTD. (QC)
Name changed to Oka Columbium & Metals Ltd. 11/21/59
(See Oka Columbium & Metals Ltd.)

OKALLA CORP (AB)
Recapitalized as SportsClick Inc. 07/10/2008
Each share Common no par exchanged for (0.10309278) share Common no par

OKALTA OILS LTD (CANADA)
Common no par changed to $1 par 11/20/1948
Common $1 par changed to 90¢ par 12/29/1948
Common 90¢ par changed to no par 05/28/1962
Recapitalized as Oakwood Petroleums Ltd. 06/10/1970
Each share Common no par exchanged for (0.142857) share Common no par
Oakwood Petroleums Ltd. acquired by Sceptre Resources Ltd. 03/14/1989 which merged into Canadian Natural Resources Ltd. 08/15/1996

OKANA VENTURES INC (NV)
Name changed to Vansen Pharma Inc. 08/30/2013

OKANAGAN HELICOPTERS LTD (BC)
6% Conv. 2nd Preferred $10 par called for redemption 01/15/1976
6% 1st Preferred $10 par called for redemption 11/26/1979
Acquired by 246455 British Columbia Ltd. 06/17/1982
Each share $0.80 Conv. Preference Ser. A no par exchanged for $9 cash
Each share Ordinary Stock no par exchanged for $15 cash

OKANAGAN HLDGS LTD (BC)
Common no par split (3) for (1) by issuance of (2) additional shares 9/14/83
Merged into Okanagan Skeena Group Ltd. 7/2/86
Each share Common no par exchanged for (1) share 8% Retractable Preferred Ser. A no par and (2) shares Common no par
(See Okanagan Skeena Group Ltd.)

OKANAGAN SKEENA GROUP LTD (BC)
Each share Common no par exchanged for (1) share Class A Subordinate no par and (1) share Class B Multiple Stock no par 3/8/93
Merged into TCI Acquisition Corp. 6/4/99
Each share 5% Retractable Preferred Ser. A no par exchanged for $11.25 cash
Each share Class A Subordinate no par exchanged for $9 cash
Each share Class B Multiple no par exchanged for $9 cash

OKANAGAN TEL CO (BC)
Preferred $9 par called for redemption 12/27/1978
Public interest eliminated

OKANAGAN VALLEY TELEPHONE CO. LTD.
Merged into Okanagan Telephone Co. on a share for share basis in 1952

OKANE INTL ENTERPRISES INC (NV)
Name changed to Superwire.Com, Inc. 04/30/1999
Superwire.Com, Inc. name changed to Superwire, Inc. 07/12/2002 which recapitalized as Cannalink, Inc. 09/09/2014

OKANOGAN DEV INC (WA)
Name changed to Montana Precision Mining, Ltd. 4/30/85
Montana Precision Mining, Ltd. name changed to MPM Technologies, Inc. 8/14/95

OKANTEX OIL & GAS CO. (OK)
Charter revoked for failure to file reports and pay fees 12/15/30

OKAW LAND DEVELOPMENT CO. (IL)
Involuntarily dissolved by the Attorney General in Superior Court of Cook County 12/22/61

OKAY DRILLING & OIL CO. LTD. (MB)
Liquidated in 1956

OKC CORP. LIQUIDATING TRUST (DE)
In process of liquidation
Each Share of Bene. Int. received initial distribution of (5) OKC Limited Partnership Depositary Receipts 6/23/81
(See OKC Limited Partnership)

OKC CORP (DE)
Common 25¢ par split (2) for (1) by issuance of (1) additional share 2/14/75
In process of liquidation
Each share Common 25¢ par received initial distribution of $15 cash 7/24/80
Each share Common 25¢ par received second distribution of $10 cash 1/2/81
Each share Common 25¢ par received third distribution of $15 cash 2/23/81
Assets transferred to OKC Corp. Liquidating Trust 5/12/81
(See OKC Corp. Liquidating Trust)

OKC LTD PARTNERSHIP (TX)
Reorganized under the laws of Delaware as Box Energy Corp. 4/15/92
Each Depositary Receipt exchanged for (1) share Class B Common $1 par
Box Energy Corp. name changed to Remington Oil & Gas Corp. 12/5/97 which merged into Helix Energy Solutions Group, Inc. 7/1/2006

OKLAHOMA AMALGAMATED OIL COMPANIES LTD. (AZ)
Charter expired by time limitation 2/24/36

OKLAHOMA BAR CORP. (OK)
Involuntarily dissolved for failure to pay fees 06/29/1994

OKLAHOMA BRICK CORP (OK)
Each (1,500) shares old Common $150 par exchanged for (1) share new Common $150 par 5/15/78
Note: In effect holders received $0.70 cash per share and public interest was eliminated

OKL-OLD   FINANCIAL INFORMATION, INC.

OKLAHOMA CAREY TRUST
Acquired by Prugh Petroleum Co. 12/31/1953
Each Unit of Bene. Int. no par exchanged for (2.4) shares Common $5 par
Prugh Petroleum Co. merged into Livingston Oil Co. 09/01/1956 which name changed to LVO Corp. 09/24/1969 which merged into Utah International Inc. 10/31/1974 which merged into General Electric Co. 12/20/1976

OKLAHOMA CEMENT CO. (DE)
Name changed to OKC Corp. 01/30/1967
OKC Corp. assets transferred to OKC Corp. Liquidating Trust 05/12/1981
(See OKC Corp. Liquidating Trust)

OKLAHOMA CO.
Acquired by Oklahoma Oil Corp. 00/00/1932
Details not available

OKLAHOMA CORP. (OK)
Merged into United Founders Life Insurance Co. on a (0.605) for (1) basis 6/30/61
(See United Founders Life Insurance Co.)

OKLAHOMA COUNTY TRUST
Trust liquidated in 1947

OKLAHOMA CRUDE LTD (BC)
Recapitalized as International Telesis Industries Corp. 03/04/1986
Each share Common no par exchanged for (0.25) share Common no par
International Telesis Industries Corp. name changed to Madonna Educational Group of Canada Ltd. 02/06/1989
(See Madonna Educational Group of Canada Ltd.)

OKLAHOMA ENERGIES CORP (OK)
Charter cancelled for failure to pay taxes 2/13/84

OKLAHOMA ENERGY CORP (OK)
Charter suspended for failure to pay taxes 01/29/1999

OKLAHOMA GAS & ELEC CO (OK)
Each share Common $20 par exchanged for (2) shares Common $10 par in 1950
Each share Common $10 par exchanged for (2) shares Common $5 par 11/24/58
Common $5 par changed to $2.50 par and (1) additional share issued 3/22/63
8.56% Preferred $100 par called for redemption 7/18/86
8.74% Preferred $100 par called for redemption 7/18/86
9.45% Preferred $100 par called for redemption 7/18/86
Under plan of reorganization each share Common $2.50 par automatically became (1) share OGE Energy Corp. Common 1¢ par 12/31/96
4% Preferred $20 par called for redemption at $20 on 1/15/98
4.20% Preferred $100 par called for redemption at $102 on 1/20/98
4.24% Preferred $100 par called for redemption at $102.875 on 1/20/98
4.44% Preferred $100 par called for redemption at $102 on 1/20/98
4.80% Preferred $100 par called for redemption at $102 on 1/20/98
5.34% Preferred $100 par called for redemption at $101 on 1/20/98
Public interest eliminated

OKLAHOMA GASOHOL INC (OK)
Merged into American Syn-Fuels, Inc. 4/28/83
Each share Common 5¢ par exchanged for (0.0333) share Common 20¢ par
American Syn-Fuels, Inc. name changed to American Fuel Technologies Inc. 10/21/83
(See American Fuel Technologies Inc.)

OKLAHOMA INDL ENERGIES INC (OK)
Merged into Cambridge Oil Co. (DE) 02/24/1984
Each share Common 10¢ par exchanged for (1) share Common 3¢ par
(See Cambridge Oil Co. (DE))

OKLAHOMA INTST MNG CO (DE)
7% 1st Preferred $45 par called for redemption 1/31/60
5% 2nd Preferred $50 par called for redemption 2/1/60
Charter cancelled and declared inoperative and void for non-payment of taxes 3/1/78

OKLAHOMA LD & EXPL CO (OK)
Name changed to Leadership Properties, Inc. 11/07/1983
(See Leadership Properties, Inc.)

OKLAHOMA METROPOLITAN OIL & GAS CORP. (DE)
No longer in existence having become inoperative and void for non-payment of taxes 4/1/55

OKLAHOMA-MISSISSIPPI RIVER PRODUCTS LINE, INC. (DE)
Merged into Sunray DX Oil Co. 02/07/1967
Each share Capital Stock 1¢ par exchanged for (0.2) share Common $1 par
Sunray DX Oil Co. merged into Sun Oil Co. (NJ) 10/25/1968 which reincorporated in Pennsylvania 09/30/1971 which name changed to Sun Co., Inc. 04/27/1976
(See Sun Co., Inc.)

OKLAHOMA NAT GAS CO (DE)
Common $15 par split (4) for (3) by issuance of (0.33333333) additional share 11/29/1946
Common $15 par split (4) for (3) by issuance of (0.33333333) additional share 04/18/1949
Common $15 par changed to $7.50 par and (1) additional share 04/21/1953
Common $7.50 par split (4) for (3) by issusuance of (0.33333333) additional share 12/10/1958
4.92% Preferred Ser. A $50 par called for redemption 06/28/1963
Common $7.50 par changed to no par and (0.5) additional share issued 01/03/1966
Common no par split (3) for (2) by issuance of (0.5) additional share 01/16/1978
Stock Dividend - 10% 08/31/1962
Name changed to ONEOK Inc. (DE) 12/10/1980
ONEOK Inc. (DE) merged into ONEOK, Inc. (New) 11/26/1997

OKLAHOMA NATURAL GAS CO.
Property sold to Oklahoma Natural Gas Corp. (MD) 00/00/1927
Details not available

OKLAHOMA NATURAL GAS CORP. (MD)
Reorganized as Oklahoma Natural Gas Co. (DE) 12/01/1933
Details not available

OKLAHOMA OIL & REFINING CO. (DE)
Charter cancelled for non-payment of taxes in 1925

OKLAHOMA OIL CO. (DE)
No longer in existence having become inoperative and void for non-payment of taxes 03/19/1919

OKLAHOMA OIL CO (CO)
Each share Common 5¢ par exchanged for (0.05) share Common $1 par 12/31/1958
Reorganized under the laws of Nevada 08/31/1973
Each share Common $1 par exchanged for (1) share Common 10¢ par
Oklahoma Oil Co. (NV) acquired by Cimarron Corp. (DE) 08/05/1981
(See Cimarron Corp. (DE))

OKLAHOMA OIL CO (NV)
Stock Dividend - 100% 10/15/1980
Acquired by Cimarron Corp. (DE) 08/05/1981
Each share Common 10¢ par exchanged for (2.8) shares Common 10¢ par
(See Cimarron Corp. (DE))

OKLAHOMA SVGS INC (DE)
Acquired by Fourth Financial Corp. 1/6/95
Each share Common 1¢ par exchanged for (0.84) share Common $5 par
Fourth Financial Corp. merged into Boatmen's Bancshares, Inc. 1/31/96 which merged into NationsBank Corp. 1/7/97 which reincorporated in Delaware as BankAmerica Corp. (Old) 9/25/98 which merged into BankAmerica Corp. (New) 9/30/98 which name changed to Bank of America Corp. 4/28/99

OKLAHOMA-SOUTHWESTERN RAILWAY CO.
Dismantled in 1930

OKLAHOMA ST BK (ADA, OK)
Acquired by First United Bank (Ada, OK) 11/5/99
Each share Common exchanged for $450.15 cash

OKLAHOMA TEXAS OIL CO. (DE)
Charter cancelled and declared inoperative and void for non-payment of taxes 3/21/23

OKLAHOMA-TEXAS TRUST
Liquidation completed in 1956

OKLAHOMA UNION RAILWAY CO.
Assets sold at Receivers Sale 00/00/1930
Stockholders' equity unlikely

OKLAHOMA URANIUM CORP. (DE)
Consent to Dissolution filed in Delaware 12/14/55

OKLAHOMA WOODCHUCK ZINC LEAD CO. (DE)
Nearing bankruptcy in 1957
Became inoperative and void for non-payment of taxes 4/1/64

OKLECO MINES LTD. (ON)
Merged into Oklend Gold Mines Ltd. on a (1) for (2) basis in 1956
Oklend Gold Mines Ltd. charter revoked 11/16/67

OKLEND GOLD MINES LTD. (ON)
Charter revoked for failure to file reports and pay fees 11/16/67

OKLIANA CORP. (OK)
Charter suspended for failure to file reports and pay taxes 03/08/1974

OKMULGEE PRODUCING & REFINING CO. (DE)
Charter cancelled and declared inoperative and void for non-payment of taxes 9/26/21

OKONA URANIUM CORP. (NV)
Charter revoked for failure to file reports and pay fees 3/4/57

OKONITE CO. (NJ)
Each share 7% Preferred $100 par exchanged for (1.55) shares 6% Preferred $100 par in 1936
Each share Common $100 par exchanged for (4) shares Common $25 par plus a stock dividend of (1) additional share paid in 1950
Stock Dividend - 12-1/2% 11/15/48
Acquired by Kennecott Copper Corp. on a share for share basis 11/25/58
Kennecott Copper Corp. name changed to Kennecott Corp. 5/7/80
(See Kennecott Corp.)

OKONITE CO (DE)
Merged into Ling-Temco-Vought, Inc. 5/1/70
Each share Common 50¢ par exchanged for (0.4) share Common 50¢ par
Ling-Temco-Vought, Inc. name changed to LTV Corp. (Old) 5/5/72 which reorganized as LTV Corp. (New) 6/28/93
(See LTV Corp. (New))

OKURAYA DAVOS INTL INC (NY)
Adjudicated bankrupt 03/03/1978
No stockholders' equity

OL JATO URANIUM CO. (UT)
Each share Common 1¢ par exchanged for (0.005) share Common $2 par 5/10/66
Acquired by Sundance Oil Co. 8/8/67
Each share Common $2 par exchanged for (5) shares Common 10¢ par
(See Sundance Oil Co.)

OLAA SUGAR CO., LTD. (HI)
Name changed to Puna Sugar Co., Ltd. 04/01/1960
Puna Sugar Co., Ltd. merged into Amfac, Inc. 01/09/1969
(See Amfac, Inc.)

OLAN LABS INTL INC (NY)
Recapitalized as Mile Marker International, Inc. (NY) 12/28/1993
Each share Common 1¢ par exchanged for (0.1) share Common $0.001 par
Mile Marker International, Inc. (NY) reincorporated in Florida 11/22/2000
(See Mile Marker International, Inc.)

OLAS INC (DE)
Recapitalized as eDiets.com, Inc. 11/17/1999
Each share Class A Common 1¢ par exchanged for (0.13224347) share Common $0.001 par

OLCO PETE GROUP INC (CANADA)
Acquired by Mayfred of Canada Ltd. 08/24/2005
Each share Class A Common no par exchanged for $0.50 cash
Note: Unexchanged certificates were cancelled and became without value 08/24/2011

OLD AMER STORES INC (DE)
Reorganized under Chapter 11 Federal Bankruptcy Code in 1997
No stockholders' equity

OLD & 3RD NATL BK (UNION CITY, TN)
Stock Dividend - 100% 3/2/70
Merged into Tennessee Valley Bancorp, Inc. 5/9/74
Each share Common $10 par exchanged for (7.1111) shares Common $6.66-2/3 par
Tennessee Valley Bancorp, Inc. name changed to Commerce Union Corp. 4/20/82 which merged into Sovran Financial Corp. 11/1/87 which merged into C&S/Sovran Corp. 9/1/90 which merged into NationsBank Corp. 12/31/91 which reincorporated in Delaware as BankAmerica Corp. (Old) 9/25/98 which merged into BankAmerica Corp. (New) 9/30/98 which name changed to Bank of America Corp. 4/28/99

OLD BEN COAL CORP. (DE)
Each share 8% Preferred $100 par exchanged for (1) share Common no par in 1934
Each share Common $50 par exchanged for (1/16) share Common no par in 1934
Common no par split (5) for (1) by issuance of (4) additional shares in 1947

Common no par changed to $5 par 5/6/55
Merged into Standard Oil Co. (OH) 8/30/68
Each share Common $5 par exchanged for (1) share Common $5 par
(See Standard Oil Co. (OH))

OLD CANADA INVESTMENT CO. LTD. (CANADA)
Each share Class B Common $5 par exchanged for (4) shares Common no par 5/25/59
Acquired by Old Canada Investment Corp. Ltd. (ONT) 12/1/69
Each share Common no par received (1) share 6% 1st Preference Ser. A $2 par, (1) share 2nd Preference 75¢ par, (1) share Common no par, (1) Common Stock Purchase Warrant expiring 8/29/79 plus 40¢ cash
Certificates were not required to be surrendered and are now valueless
Old Canada Investment Corp. Ltd. (ONT) reorganized under the laws of Canada as Headline Media Group Inc. 11/21/2000 which name changed to Score Media Inc. 2/23/2005

OLD CDA INVT LTD (ON)
8% 1st Preference Ser. A $2 par called for redemption 06/02/1986
Each share 2nd Part. Preference 75¢ par exchanged for (0.2) share 8% 1st Preference Ser. A $2 par 03/17/1971
$0.76 Conv. 1st Preference Ser. B no par called for redemption 09/01/1993
Reincorporated under the laws of Canada as Headline Media Group Inc. and Common no par reclassified as Subordinate Class B Common no par 11/21/2000
Headline Media Group Inc. name changed to Score Media Inc. 02/23/2005 which reorganized as theScore, Inc. 10/19/2012

OLD COLONY INVESTMENT TRUST
Acquired by General Capital Corp. (Del.) at net value in 1943
(See General Capital Corp.)

OLD COLONY LIFE INSURANCE CO.
Out of business 00/00/1934
Details not available

OLD COLONY LIGHT & POWER ASSN.
Liquidated in 1936

OLD COLONY RAILROAD CO. (MA)
Involuntarily dissolved for failure to file reports and pay taxes 5/25/49

OLD COLONY TRUST ASSOCIATES
Trust terminated 00/00/1944
Details not available

OLD COMMONWEALTH MORTGAGE CO. (KY)
Administratively dissolved 11/1/2000

OLD COMRADES BREWERY LTD. (CANADA)
Completely liquidated in 5/11/71
Each share Common no par exchanged for first and final distribution of $0.2525 cash

OLD COUNTRY TROTTING ASSOCIATION, INC. (NY)
Each share Common no par exchanged for (4) shares Common $3 par in 1948
Stock Dividend - 10% 10/15/54
Merged into Roosevelt Raceway, Inc. share for share 11/23/54
Roosevelt Raceway, Inc. merged into Madison Square Garden Corp. (Mich.) 12/21/73
(See Madison Square Garden Corp. (Mich.))

OLD DOMINION BK (ARLINGTON, VA)
Merged into First Virginia Bankshares Corp. 9/5/69
Each share Capital Stock $10 par exchanged for (15) shares Common $1 par
First Virginia Bankshares Corp. name changed to First Virginia Banks, Inc. 9/1/78 which merged into BB&T Corp. 7/1/2003

OLD DOMINION CO.
Liquidation completed in 1942

OLD DOMINION COAL CO. (DE)
Name changed to Old Dominion Resources, Inc. 2/28/82
Each share Common 1¢ par exchanged for (1) share Common 1¢ par
Old Dominion Resources, Inc. charter forfeited 12/17/83

OLD DOMINION REAL ESTATE INVT TR (VA)
Shares of Bene. Int. no par split (3) for (2) by issuance of (0.5) additional share 07/29/1983
Merged into United Dominion Realty Trust, Inc. (VA) 12/31/1984
Each Share of Bene. Int. no par exchanged for (1) share Common $1 par
United Dominion Realty Trust, Inc. (VA) reincorporated in Maryland 06/11/2003 which name changed to UDR, Inc. 03/14/2007

OLD DOMINION RES INC (DE)
Charter forfeited for failure to maintain a registered agent 12/17/83

OLD DOMINION SYS INC (VA)
Name changed to Microlog Corp. (VA) 10/16/1989
Microlog Corp. (VA) reincorporated in Delaware as Nutroganics, Inc. 09/25/2013

OLD EMPIRE, INC. (NJ)
Adjudicated bankrupt 8/13/64
No stockholders' equity

OLD EMPIRE MINING CO. (WY)
Charter revoked 4/15/71

OLD EQUITY FINL CORP (DE)
Reincorporated 12/31/1968
Name changed 11/10/1969
State of incorporation changed from (IN) to (IL) 12/31/1968
Under plan of reorganization name changed from Old Equity Life Insurance Co. (IL) to Old Equity Financial Corp. (DE) 11/10/1969
Merged into Richmond Corp. 03/29/1973
Each share Common $1 par exchanged for (0.222222) share Common $5 par
Richmond Corp. merged into Continental Group, Inc. 06/29/1977 which merged into KMI Continental Inc. 11/02/1984
(See KMI Continental Inc.)

OLD EQUITY LIFE INS CO (IL)
Reincorporated 12/31/1968
State of incorporation changed from (IN) to (IL) 12/31/1968
Under plan of reorganization each share Common $1.66-2/3 par automatically became (1) share Old Equity Financial Corp. Common $1 par 11/10/1969
Old Equity Financial Corp. merged into Richmond Corp. 03/29/1973 which merged into Continental Group, Inc. 06/29/1977 which merged into KMI Continental Inc. 11/02/1984
(See KMI Continental Inc.)

OLD FAITHFUL LIFE INS CO (WY)
Charter revoked for failure to pay taxes 07/28/2009

OLD FAITHFUL URANIUM, INC. (WY)
Charter revoked for failure to pay taxes 3/21/62

OLD FASHION FOODS INC (GA)
Merged into a private company 11/1/2005
Each share Common 1¢ par exchanged for $8.30 cash

OLD FLA BANKSHARES INC (FL)
Merged into Bank of Florida Corp. 04/24/2007
Each share Common 1¢ par exchanged for (1.39144482) shares Common 1¢ par and $8.59733428 cash
(See Bank of Florida Corp.)

OLD FLA RUM CO (FL)
Recapitalized as Corda Diversified Technologies, Inc. 10/04/1982
Each share Common 50¢ par exchanged for (0.2) share Common no par
Note: Exchange of certificates not requested until 12/11/1982
(See Corda Diversified Technologies, Inc.)

OLD FORGE BK (OLD FORGE, PA)
Acquired by Penseco Financial Services Corp. 04/01/2009
Each share Common $2.50 par exchanged for (2.9012) shares Common 1¢ par
Penseco Financial Services Corp. merged into Peoples Financial Services Corp. 12/02/2013

OLD FORT INDS INC (IN)
Common no par split (2) for (1) by issuance of (1) additional share 7/7/67
Name changed to Fort Holdings, Inc. 1/3/80
(See Fort Holdings, Inc.)

OLD FORT SUPPLY CO., INC. (IN)
Common $10 par changed to no par and (2) additional shares issued 7/2/60
5% Preferred $100 par called for redemption 8/25/61
Name changed to Old Fort Industries, Inc. 3/24/66
Old Fort Industries, Inc. name changed to Fort Holdings, Inc. 1/3/80
(See Fort Holdings, Inc.)

OLD FRONTIER URANIUM, INC. (WA)
Out of business and automatically dissolved for non-payment of State fees 7/1/62

OLD GOAT ENTERPRISES INC (NV)
Common $0.00001 par changed to $0.001 par and (9) additional shares issued payable 09/25/2003 to holders of record 09/22/2003
Ex date - 09/26/2003
Name changed to Zone 4 Play, Inc. 02/05/2004
Zone 4 Play, Inc. name changed to Win Gaming Media, Inc. 05/01/2008 which name to Win Global Markets, Inc. 11/09/2011 which name changed to EZTrader, Inc. (NV) 10/09/2014 which reincorporated in Delaware as EZTD Inc. 12/29/2015

OLD GUARD GROUP INC (PA)
Merged into Ohio Farmers Insurance Co. 10/1/2000
Each share Common no par exchanged for $12 cash

OLD GWAL, INC. (CA)
Charter suspended for failure to file reports and pay fees 04/01/1982

OLD HBR BK (CLEARWATER, FL)
Closed and FDIC appointed receiver 10/21/2011
Stockholders' equity unlikely

OLD HERITAGE CORP (IL)
Each share Class B Common no par exchanged for (1) share Class A Common 50¢ par 09/22/1970
Class A Common 50¢ par reclassified as Common 50¢ par 09/30/1970
Common 50¢ par changed to 40¢ par and (0.25) additional share issued 10/14/1970
Acquired by Central-National Financial Corp. 10/31/1978
Each share Common 40¢ par exchanged for $1.80 cash

OLD HICKORY COPPER CO (DE)
Charter forfeited for failure to maintain a registered agent 10/24/1983

OLD JUDGE FOODS CORP. (DE)
Merged into Williams (R.C.) & Co., Inc. 12/9/57
Each share 5-1/2% Preferred $25 par exchanged for (0.6) share 5-1/2% Preferred $25 par
Each share 5-1/2% Preferred $10 par exchanged for (0.24) share 5-1/2% Preferred $25 par
Each share Class A $1 par or Common $1 par exchanged for (0.112) share 5-1/2% Preferred $25 par and (1/15) share Common $1 par
(See Williams (R.C.) & Co., Inc.)

OLD KENT BK & TR CO (GRAND RAPIDS, MI)
Stock Dividends - 25% 2/28/49; 100% 3/1/65
Reorganized as Old Kent Financial Corp. (DE) 10/16/72
Each share Common $10 par exchanged for (2) shares Common $10 par
Old Kent Financial Corp. (DE) reincorporated in Michigan 4/16/84 which merged into Fifth Third Bancorp 4/2/2001

OLD KENT FINL CORP (MI)
Reincorporated 04/16/1984
Common $10 par split (4) for (3) by issuance of (1/3) additional share 12/15/1978
State of incorporation changed from (DE) to (MI) and Common $10 par changed to $1 par 04/16/1984
14% Conv. Preferred Ser. A no par called for redemption 04/01/1990
Common $1 par split (3) for (2) by issuance of (0.5) additional share 12/28/1984
Common $1 par split (3) for (2) by issuance of (0.5) additional share 12/15/1986
Common $1 par split (3) for (2) by issuance of (0.5) additional share 09/15/1992
Common $1 par split (2) for (1) by issuance of (1) additional share payable 12/15/1997 to holders of record 11/14/1997
Stock Dividends - 5% payable 07/25/1996 to holders of record 06/25/1996; 5% payable 07/28/1997 to holders of record 06/27/1997; 5% payable 07/17/1998 to holders of record 06/26/1998; 5% payable 07/19/1999 to holders of record 06/29/1999; 5% payable 07/14/2000 to holders of record 06/30/2000
Merged into Fifth Third Bancorp 04/02/2001
Each share Common $1 par exchanged for (0.74) share Common no par

OLD LINE BK (WALDORF, MD)
Reorganized as Old Line Bancshares, Inc. 9/15/2003
Each share Common $10 par exchanged for (1) share Common 1¢ par 9/15/2003

OLD LINE INVESTMENT CORP. (MD)
Charter annulled for failure to file annual reports 4/18/73

OLD LINE LIFE INS CO AMER (WI)
Capital Stock $10 par changed to $2 par and (4) additional shares issued plus a 20% stock dividend paid 03/26/1962

OLD-OLD

Capital Stock $2 par changed to $1.33-1/3 par and (0.5) additional share issued 03/20/1964
Stock Dividends - 20% 07/08/1966; 20% 06/28/1972
Acquired by USLIFE Corp. 12/20/1972
Each share Capital Stock $1.33-1/3 par exchanged for (0.808) share Common $2 par
USLIFE Corp. merged into American General Corp. 06/17/1967 which merged American International Group, Inc. 08/29/2001

OLD LINE NATL BK (ROCKVILLE, MD)
Merged into University National Bank (College Park, MD) 05/15/1969
Each share Capital Stock $10 par exchanged for (0.6) share Common $8 par
University National Bank (College Park, MD) changed location to University National Bank (Rockville, MD) 05/01/1970
(See University National Bank (Rockville, MD))

OLD LINE NATL BK (WALDORF, MD)
Recapitalized as Old Line Bank (Waldorf, MD) 6/28/2002
Each share Common $5 par exchanged for (0.5) share Common $10 par
Old Line Bank (Waldorf, MD) reorganized as Old Line Bancshares, Inc. 9/15/2003

OLD LYME HLDG CORP (DE)
Name changed to Kaye Group Inc. 10/2/95
(See Kaye Group Inc.)

OLD MILL CORP. (UT)
Recapitalized as Rocky Mountain Recreation Corp. 02/07/1972
Each share Common 1¢ par exchanged for (0.02) share Common 50¢ par
Rocky Mountain Recreation Corp. name changed to Planformation, Inc. 01/31/1973
(See Planformation, Inc.)

OLD MILL GOLD MINES, LTD. (QC)
Charter annulled for failure to file reports 8/18/73

OLD MILL ROAD CORP. (NY)
In process of liquidation
Each share Common no par received initial distribution of (0.918632) share Madison Fund, Inc. Common $1 par 8/16/67
No additional information on liquidation
Madison Fund, Inc. name changed to Madison Resources, Inc. 6/13/84 which merged into Adobe Resources Corp. 10/31/85

OLD MISSION ASSMT CORP (FL)
Recapitalized as Global Development & Enviromental Resources, Inc. 7/25/2005
Each share Common $0.001 par exchanged for (0.001) share Common no par

OLD MISSION PORTLAND CEMENT CO.
Merged into Pacific Portland Cement Co. in 1927
Details not available

OLD MUT CLAYMORE LONG-SHORT FD (MA)
Name changed to Guggenheim Enhanced Equity Income Fund (MA) 06/21/2010
Guggenheim Enhanced Equity Income Fund (MA) reincorporated in Delaware 03/20/2017

OLD MUT GLOBAL SHS TR (DE)
Completely liquidated
Each GlobalShares All-World ex US Fund received first and final distribution of $19.64124 cash payable 10/22/2010 to holders of record 10/08/2010
Each GlobalShares Developed Countries ex US Fund received first and final distribution of $26.98378 cash payable 10/22/2010 to holders of record 10/08/2010
Each GlobalShares FTSE All-Cap Asia Pacific ex Japan Fund received first and final distribution of $20.78947 cash payable 10/22/2010 to holders of record 10/08/2010
Each GlobalShares FTSE All-World Fund received first and final distribution of $19.59478 cash payable 10/22/2010 to holders of record 10/08/2010
Each GlobalShares FTSE Emerging Markets Fund received first and final distribution of $22.02702 cash payable 10/22/2010 to holders of record 10/08/2010

OLD MUT PLC (UNITED KINGDOM)
Each old ADR for Ordinary exchanged for (0.875) new ADR for Ordinary 04/23/2012
ADR agreement terminated 07/19/2018
Each new ADR for Ordinary exchanged for $21.166163 cash

OLD NATL BANCORPORATION (DE)
Reincorporated 07/01/1977
State of incorporation changed from (WA) to (DE) 07/01/1977
Stock Dividends - 10% 03/02/1976; 10% 03/06/1981; 10% 03/05/1982
Merged into U.S. Bancorp (OR) 07/01/1987
Each share Common $5 par exchanged for $46 cash

OLD NATL BK (EVANSVILLE, IN)
Each share Common $100 par exchanged for (5) shares Common $20 par 00/00/1946
Under plan of merger Common $20 par changed to $10 par and (1-2/3) additional shares issued 08/28/1950
Under plan of merger each share Common $10 par received (2/25) additional share 05/01/1951
Stock Dividends - 5% 02/11/1954; 12-1/2% 02/08/1956; 14-2/7% 01/28/1958; 20% 02/03/1960; 16-2/3% 09/05/1960; 16-2/3% 09/05/1960; 16-2/3% 01/30/1963; 14-2/7% 02/05/1965; 12-1/2% 02/07/1966; 11-1/9% 02/06/1967; 20% 02/08/1968
Under plan of reorganization each share Common $10 par automatically became (1) share Old National Bancorp Common no par 01/04/1983

OLD NATL BK (HUNTINGTON, WV)
Merged into City Holding Co. 1/24/97
Each share Common $2.50 par exchanged for (6.413) shares Common $2.50 par

OLD NATL BK WASH (SPOKANE, WA)
Stock Dividend - 10% 2/15/66
Merged into US Bancorp (OR) 7/1/87
Each share Common $10 par exchanged for $46 cash per share

OLD NATIONAL CORP. (WA)
Class A no par and Class B no par changed to $10 par in 1946
Stock Dividend - Paid in Class A to holders of Class A & B - 25% 4/10/68
Recapitalized as Washington Bancshares, Inc. 8/29/68
Each share Class A $10 par or Class B $10 par exchanged for (2) shares Common $5 par
Washington Bancshares, Inc. name changed to Old National Bancorporation (Wash.) 6/21/76 which reincorporated in Delaware 7/1/77
(See Old National Bancorporation (Del.))

OLD NATL LIFE INS CO (CO)
Merged into Pacific Western Corp. 07/01/1970
Each share Common $1.65 par exchanged for (0.5) share Common 10¢ par
(See Pacific Western Corp.)

OLD NEVADA MINING CORP. (NV)
Charter revoked for failure to file reports and pay fees 3/5/62

OLD NIGHT INC (NV)
Each share old Common $0.001 par exchanged for (11) shares new Common $0.001 par 6/2/2000
Name changed to NxGen Networks, Inc. 9/1/2000

OLD NORTH ST BK (KING, NC)
Common $5 par split (1.922) for (1) by issuance of (0.922) additional share payable 11/29/1995 to holders of record 11/03/1995
Merged into LSB Bancshares, Inc. 08/11/1997
Each share Common $5 par exchanged for (0.938) share Common $5 par
LSB Bancshares, Inc. name changed to NewBridge Bancorp 07/31/2007 which merged into Yadkin Financial Corp. 03/01/2016 which merged into F.N.B. Corp. 03/11/2017

OLD ORCHARD BK & TR CO (SKOKIE, IL)
Common Capital Stock $15 par changed to $10 par and (0.5) additional share issued plus a 10% stock dividend paid 12/31/1961
Stock Dividends - 20% 04/02/1963; 20.25% 02/02/1966; 10% 02/05/1969; 29.87% 02/27/1970; 10% 02/26/1971; 13.64% 03/01/1972; 20% 03/01/1973; 33-1/3% 02/28/1974
Merged into First of America Bank Corp. 10/31/1985
Each share Common Capital Stock $10 par exchanged for (2.12765957) shares Common $10 par
First of America Bank Corp. merged into National City Corp. 03/31/1998 which was acquired by PNC Financial Services Group, Inc. 12/31/2008

OLD PACKAGING CORP. (MI)
Charter declared inoperative and void for failure to file reports 07/15/1997

OLD PHOENIX NATL BK (MEDINA, OH)
Each share Capital Stock $100 par exchanged for (4) shares Capital Stock $25 par 01/26/1954
Capital Stock $25 par changed to $10 par and (1.5) additional shares issued plus a 25% stock dividend paid 11/20/1967
Stock Dividends - 100% 00/00/1943; 33.33333333% 00/00/1947; 25% 08/25/1960; 10% 02/20/1964; 50% 10/12/1972; 100% 03/15/1979
Reorganized as First Bancorporation of Ohio, Inc. 12/30/1981
Each share Capital Stock $10 par exchanged for (1.5) shares Common $10 par
First Bancorporation of Ohio, Inc. name changed to FirstMerit Corp. 12/26/1994 which merged into Huntington Bancshares Inc. 08/16/2016

OLD REP INS CO (PA)
Capital Stock $5 par reclassified as Common $5 par 04/00/1967
99.5% acquired by Old Republic International Corp. through exchange offer which expired 11/02/1971
Public interest eliminated

OLD REP INTL CORP (DE)
Recapitalized 12/01/1988
Each share $4 Conv. Exchangeable Preferred Ser. F no par exchanged for $50 principal amount of 8% Conv. Debentures due 06/01/2015
$1 Conv. Preferred Ser. E no par called for redemption 07/31/1995
8.75% Preferred Ser. H no par called for redemption 12/13/1996
(Additional Information in Active)

OLD REP LIFE INS CO (IL)
Capital Stock $1.50 par changed to $1 par and (0.5) additional share issued 05/11/1964
Stock Dividend - 10% 12/28/1955
Reorganized under the laws of Delaware as Old Republic International Corp. 08/08/1969
Each share Capital Stock $1 par exchanged for (1) share Common $1 par

OLD REPUBLIC CREDIT LIFE INSURANCE CO. (IL)
Common $1 par changed to $1.50 par in 1946
Name changed to Old Republic Life Insurance Co. 12/2/55
Old Republic Life Insurance Co. reorganized as Old Republic International Corp. 8/8/69

OLD 2ND NATL BK (AURORA, IL)
Each share Capital Stock $100 par exchanged for (5) shares Capital Stock $20 par in 1951
Each share Capital Stock $20 par exchanged for (2.222222) shares Capital Stock $10 par to effect a (2) for (1) split and a 11% stock dividend 5/20/62
Stock Dividends - 10% 1/30/59; 25% 7/1/65; 20% 12/2/68; 20% 3/25/71; 20% 9/25/75; 25% 9/25/78
Reorganized as Old Second Bancorp, Inc. 6/1/82
Each share Capital Stock $10 par exchanged for (2) shares Capital Stock $5 par

OLD SETTLERS' OILS LTD. (AB)
Merged into King Solomon Resources Ltd. 3/10/67
Each share Capital Stock no par exchanged for (0.166666) share Common no par
King Solomon Resources Ltd. merged into Acroll Oil & Gas Ltd. 6/29/67 which recapitalized as Acroll Petroleums Ltd. 12/30/77 which merged into Trans-Canada Resources Ltd. (New) 11/1/82 which recapitalized as Consolidated Trans-Canada Resources Ltd. 9/22/88 which merged into Ranchmen's Resources Ltd. 9/30/89

OLD SMOKY OIL & GAS LTD. (ON)
Recapitalized as Largo Oils & Mines Ltd. 5/11/67
Each share Common $1 par exchanged for (0.01) share Common $1 par
Largo Oils & Mines Ltd. name changed to Wardean Drilling Co. Ltd. 1/8/68
(See Wardean Drilling Co. Ltd.)

OLD SPAGHETTI WHSE INC (TX)
Common 1¢ par split (5) for (4) by issuance of (0.25) additional share 6/6/90
Stock Dividend - 25% 6/2/89
Name changed to Spaghetti Warehouse, Inc. 10/30/90
(See Spaghetti Warehouse, Inc.)

OLD STATE BANK CORP. (MI)
Merged into First Michigan Bank Corp. 06/20/1994
Each share Common $10 par exchanged for (2.523) shares Common $1 par
First Michigan Bank Corp. merged into Huntington Bancshares Inc. 09/30/1997

OLD STATE BANK OF FREMONT (FREMONT, MI)
Common $10 par split (3) for (2) by issuance of (0.5) additional share 05/03/1982
Under plan of reorganization each share Common $10 par automatically became (1) share Old State Bank Corp. Common $10 par 05/01/1992
Old State Bank Corp. merged into First Michigan Bank Corp. 06/20/1994 which merged into Huntington Bancshares Inc. 09/30/1997

OLD STATE CORP.
Dissolved in 1945

OLD STONE CORP (RI)
Conv. Preferred Ser. A $1 par called for redemption 12/15/1985
Common $1 par split (4) for (3) by issuance of (1/3) additional share 06/13/1986
$2.60 Conv. Preferred Ser. C $1 par called for redemption 06/15/1988
Each share $2.40 Conv. Preferred Ser. B $1 par exchanged for $54.35 cash and (0.0616) share new $2.40 Conv. Preferred Ser. B in a pro-rata partial redemption 07/31/2007
Company dissolved 07/31/2007
No Common stockholders' equity Completely liquidated
Each share new $2.40 Conv. Preferred Ser. B $1 par received first and final distribution of $8.5026847 cash payable 06/10/2013 to holders of record 06/05/2013 Ex date - 06/11/2013

OLD STONE MTG & RLTY TR (MA)
Merged into Old Stone Corp. 05/20/1977
Each share of Bene. Int. no par exchanged for (1) share Conv. Preferred Ser. A $1 par
(See Old Stone Corp.)

OLD SUN RES LTD (AB)
Name changed to Ripper Oil & Gas Inc. (AB) 06/14/2001
Ripper Oil & Gas Inc. (AB) reorganized in British Columbia 05/29/2012

OLD TEXAS MINING & OIL CO. (DE)
Reorganized 5/31/57
Common changed to Class A Common and Class B Common 10¢ par
Class A Common then exchanged for Common 10¢ par of Continental Materials Corp.
(See Continental Material Corp.)
Voluntarily dissolved 1/15/64
Details not available

OLD TEXAS MINING CO. (DE)
Name changed to Old Texas Mining & Oil Co. 8/25/56
Old Texas Mining & Oil Co. dissolved 1/15/64

OLD TOWN CORP (NY)
Common $5 par changed to $1 par and (1) share 40¢ Preferred $7 par distributed 00/00/1953
Each share 40¢ Preferred $7 par exchanged for (1) Common Stock Purchase Warrant expiring 06/06/1979 and (0.5) share Common $1 par 06/06/1969
Adjudicated bankrupt 11/07/1974
Stockholders' equity unlikely

OLD TOWN GARDENS, INC. (IL)
Proclaimed dissolved for failure to pay taxes and file reports 12/17/68

OLD TOWN RIBBON & CARBON CO., INC.
Name changed to Old Town Corp. in 1951
Old Town Corp. adjudicated bankrupt 11/7/74

OLD TUCSON CORP (DE)
Common $1 par split (2) for (1) by issuance of (1) additional share 11/10/77
Name changed to Westworld, Inc. 5/14/79
Westworld, Inc. name changed to Westworld Resources, Inc. 7/25/88 which merged into Battle Mountain Gold Co. 5/28/91 which merged into Newmont Mining Corp. 1/10/2001

OLD TUCSON DEVELOPMENT CO. (DE)
Reincorporated 9/18/73
State of incorporation changed from (AZ) to (DE) 9/18/73
Reorganized as Old Tucson Corp. 2/6/74
Each share Common $1 par exchanged for (1) share Common $1 par
Old Tucson Corp. name changed to Westworld, Inc. 5/14/79 which name changed to Westworld Resources, Inc. 7/25/88 which merged into Battle Mountain Gold Co. 5/28/91 which merged into Newmont Mining Corp. 1/10/2001

OLD TYME SOFT DRINKS INC (DE)
Merged into Bob Soda Corp. 10/18/88
Details not available

OLD WELCH CO., INC. (NY)
In liquidation in 1956

OLD YELLER INC (UT)
Involuntarily dissolved 12/31/1984

OLD YORK RD BANCORP INC (PA)
Merged into Midlantic Bank. 6/28/95
Each share Common $1 par exchanged for (0.3721) share Common $1 par and $10 cash

OLDE WINDSOR BANCORP INC (DE)
Name changed to New England Community Bancorp, Inc. 9/27/94
New England Community Bancorp, Inc. merged into Webster Financial Corp. 12/1/99

OLDETYME DISTILLERS CORP.
Name changed to Delendo Corp. in 1940 which completed liquidation for cash in 1943

OLDS INDS INC (BC)
Delisted from Vancouver Stock Exchange 03/02/1998

OLDWEBSITES COM INC (UT)
Voluntarily dissolved 12/29/2011
Company had no assets or revenue
Stockholders' equity unlikely

OLE REMEDIATION LTD (BC)
Recapitalized as Silk Road Ventures Ltd. (BC) 08/22/2013
Each share Common no par exchanged for (0.15384615) share Common no par
Silk Road Ventures Ltd. (BC) reorganized in Cayman Islands as Silk Road Finance Inc. 12/02/2014
(See Silk Road Finance Inc.)

OLEN CO., INC. (DE)
Merged into Green (H.L.) Co., Inc. 10/31/1958
Each share 5% Preferred $100 par exchanged for (2.99) shares Common $1 par
Each share Class A Common $1 par exchanged for (0.425) share Common $1 par
Each share Class B Common $1 par exchanged for (0.38) share Common $1 par
Green (H.L.) Co., Inc. merged into McCrory Corp. 06/21/1961
(See McCrory Corp.)

OLERAMMA INC (NV)
Name changed to BuckTV.com, Inc. 04/12/2000
BuckTV.com, Inc. recapitalized as Multi-Tech International Corp. 11/22/2002 which recapitalized as Australian Forest Industries 10/21/2004 which recapitalized as Lone Pine Holdings, Inc. 02/11/2009 which name changed to Flux Power Holdings, Inc. 06/11/2012

OLGA CO (CA)
Common $1 par changed to 50¢ par and (1) additional share issued 05/15/1969
Acquired by Warnaco Inc. 06/04/1984
Each share Common 50¢ par exchanged for $36 cash

OLGA GAS, LTD. (ON)
Charter cancelled and dissolved 11/15/60
No stockholders' equity

OLGA GAS & OIL CO., LTD. (ON)
Name changed to Olga Gas, Ltd. in 1936
(See Olga Gas, Ltd.)

OLICOM A S (DENMARK)
Company went into liquidation 06/18/2010
Stockholders' equity unlikely

OLICROM OPERATING CORP. (NY)
Liquidation completed
Each share Capital Stock $1 par received initial distribution of $30 cash 01/00/1954
Each share Capital Stock $1 par received second distribution of $10 cash 10/00/1956
Each share Capital Stock $1 par received third distribution of $2 cash 08/00/1957
Each share Capital Stock $1 par received fourth distribution of $14 cash 01/26/1959
Each share Capital Stock $1 par received fifth distribution of $3.50 cash 12/18/1959
Each share Capital Stock $1 par received sixth distribution of $2 cash 01/20/1961
Each share Capital Stock $1 par received seventh distribution of $2.50 cash 12/20/1961
Each share Capital Stock $1 par exchanged for eighth and final distribution of $51 cash 11/27/1962

OLIDAN ENERGY CORP (UT)
Recapitalized as Columbine Capital Corp. 7/15/88
Each share Common 1¢ par exchanged for (0.5) share Common 1¢ par
(See Columbine Capital Corp.)

OLIN CORP (VA)
Each share Conversion Preferred Ser. A $1 par exchanged for (1) share Common $1 par 03/01/1995
(Additional Information in Active)

OLIN INDUSTRIES, INC. (DE)
Stock Dividend - 200% 12/26/1951
Merged into Olin Mathieson Chemical Corp. 00/00/1954
Each share Preferred $100 par exchanged for (1) share 4.25% Preferred $100 par
Each share Common $1 par exchanged for (1) share Common $5 par
Olin Mathieson Chemical Corp. name changed to Olin Corp. 09/01/1969

OLIN MATHIESON CHEM CORP (VA)
4-1/4% Preferred 1951 Ser. called for redemption 04/14/1958
Common $5 par split (3) for (2) by issuance of (0.5) additional share 03/03/1969
Name changed to Olin Corp. 09/01/1969

OLIN OIL & GAS CORP. (DE)
Acquired by Standard Oil Co. (NJ) 06/13/1962
Each share Common $1 par exchanged for (0.490667) share Capital Stock $7 par
Preferred Ser. A $50 par called for redemption 07/13/1962
Standard Oil Co. (NJ) name changed to Exxon Corp. 11/01/1972 which name changed to Exxon Mobil Corp. 11/30/1999

OLINDA LAND CO.
Liquidated in 1938

OLINKRAFT INC (DE)
Merged into Johns-Manville Corp. 1/19/79
Each share Common $1 par exchanged for (1) share $5.40 Preferred $1 par
Johns-Manville Corp. reincorporated in Delaware as Manville Corp. 10/30/81
Manville Corp. name changed to Schuller Corp. 3/29/96 which name changed to Johns-Manville Corp. (New) 5/5/97
(See Johns-Manville Corp. (New))

OLIPHANT JAMES H & CO INC (DE)
Liquidation completed
Each share Common 1¢ par received initial distribution of $0.50 cash 03/15/1976
Each share Common 1¢ par received second distribution of $0.90 cash 06/14/1976
Each share Common 1¢ par received third distribution of $0.10 cash 08/09/1976
Each share Common 1¢ par exchanged for fourth and final distribution of $0.0625 cash 09/30/1977

OLIVE & MYERS MANUFACTURING CO. (TX)
Capital Stock $100 par changed to $10 par in 1951
Merged into Olive-Myers-Spalti Manufacturing Co. 5/2/55
Each share Capital Stock $10 par exchanged for (1.4) shares Common $10 par
Olive-Myers-Spalti Manufacturing Co. name changed to Mathes Manufacturing Co. 4/22/58 which name changed to Curtis Mathes Manufacturing Co. 8/28/59 which merged into Curtis Mathes Corp. 1/19/70
(See Curtis Mathes Corp.)

OLIVE GOLD MINES, LTD. (ON)
Charter cancelled by Province of Ontario 3/12/56

OLIVE-MYERS-SPALTI MANUFACTURING CO. (TX)
Common $10 par changed to $5 par in 1956
Name changed to Mathes Manufacturing Co. 4/22/58
Mathes Manufacturing Co. name changed to Curtis Mathes Manufacturing Co. 8/28/59 which merged into Curtis Mathes Corp. 1/19/70
(See Curtis Mathes Corp.)

OLIVER BUILDING TRUST (MA)
Liquidation completed 11/2/60

OLIVER CORP. (DE)
Common no par changed to $1 par in 1950
Stock Dividend - 100% 7/9/52
Name changed to Cletrac Corp. 10/31/60
Cletrac Corp. merged into Hess Oil & Chemical Corp. 5/23/62 which merged into Amerada Hess Corp. 6/20/69 which name changed to Hess Corp. 5/3/2006

OLIVER CREEK RES INC (NV)
Name changed to Independence Energy Corp. 08/12/2008

OLIVER FARM EQUIPMENT CO. (DE)
Recapitalized as Oliver Corp. on a (2) for (1) basis in 1944
Oliver Corp. name changed to Cletrac Corp. 10/31/60 which merged into Hess Oil & Chemical Co. 5/23/62 which merged into Amerada Hess Corp. 6/20/69 which name changed to Hess Corp. 5/3/2006

OLIVER GOLD CORP (BC)
Recapitalized as Canico Resource Corp. 02/06/2002
Each (9.3) shares Common no par exchanged for (1) share Common no par
(See Canico Resource Corp.)

OLIVER IRON & STEEL CORP. (PA)
Each share Common $1 par exchanged for (1.075) shares new Common $1 par in 1951
Merged into Oliver Tyrone Corp. on a (1) for (20) basis 12/31/56
(See Oliver Tyrone Corp.)

OLIVER RES LTD (BC)
Recapitalized as Dyna Gold Resources Inc. 01/29/1986
Each share Capital Stock no par exchanged for (1/6) share Common no par
(See Dyna Gold Resources Inc.)

OLIVER-SEVERN GOLD MINES LTD. (ON)
Charter cancelled for failure to pay taxes and file returns 1/27/76

OLIVER TRANSN INC (DE)
SEC revoked common stock registration 11/07/2008
Stockholders' equity unlikely

OLIVER TYRONE CORP (PA)
Common $50 par changed to $10 par and (2) additional shares issued 6/1/57
In process of liquidation
Each share Common $10 par exchanged for initial distribution of $10 cash in December 1977
Each share Common $10 par received second distribution of $27.50 cash in April 1978
Each share Common $10 par received third distribution of $10 cash 12/27/78
Note: Details on subsequent distributions, if any, are not available

OLIVER UNITED FILTERS, INC. (NV)
Merged into Dorr-Oliver, Inc. in 1954
Each share Class A no par exchanged for (1) share Preferred $32.50 par
Each share Class B no par exchanged for (2) shares Common $7.50 par
(See Dorr-Oliver, Inc.)

OLIVERS STORES INC (NJ)
Charter declared void for non-payment of taxes 1/31/94

OLIVETTI ING C & CO S P A (ITALY)
Each old ADR for Ordinary 1000 Lira par exchanged for (0.64) new ADR for Ordinary 1000 Lira par 07/21/1997
Each old ADR for Preference 1000 Lira par exchanged for (0.64) new ADR for Preference 1000 Lira par 07/21/1997
Each new ADR for Preference 1000 Lira par exchanged for (1) ADR for Ordinary 1000 Lira par 12/07/2001
Stock Dividend - 10% 11/19/1962
Merged into Telecom Italia S.p.A. (New) 08/04/2003
Each ADR for Ordinary EUR 1000 par exchanged for (0.0471553) ADR for Ordinary

OLIVIA INC (DE)
Name changed to Bio-En Holdings Corp. 07/28/2014

OLIVIER MGMT CORP (DE)
Charter cancelled and declared inoperative and void for non-payment of taxes 03/01/1988

OLIX INDS INC (TX)
Merged into Abode Oil & Gas Corp. 7/22/81
Each share Common no par exchanged for (0.4723696) share Common 30¢ par
Adobe Oil & Gas Corp. merged into Adobe Resources Corp. 10/31/85 which merged into Santa Fe Energy Resources, Inc. 5/19/92 which name changed to Santa Fe Snyder Corp. 5/5/99 which merged into Devon Energy Corp. (New) 8/29/2000

OLLA INDS INC (NJ)
Name changed to RE Capital Corp. 7/16/86
RE Capital Corp. (NJ) reincorporated in Delaware 8/10/89
(See RE Capital Corp. (DE))

OLLY INDS INC (BC)
Name changed to Aurea Mining Inc. 06/16/2004
Aurea Mining Inc. was acquired by Newstrike Capital Inc. 06/26/2008 which merged into Timmins Gold Corp. 05/28/2015 which recapitalized as Alio Gold Inc. 05/16/2017

OLME PRECISION, INC. (OH)
Acquired by Fawick Corp. 9/15/67
Each share Common $5 par exchanged for (0.285714) share Common $2 par
Fawick Corp. merged into Eaton Yale & Towne Inc. 3/31/68 which name changed to Eaton Corp. 4/21/71

OLOKELE SUGAR LTD (HI)
Acquired by Gay & Robinson Sugar Co. 04/00/1994
Details not available

OLS ASIA HLDGS LTD (AUSTRALIA)
Each old Sponsored ADR for Class A no par exchanged for (0.25) new Sponsored ADR for Class A no par 12/16/1998
Name changed to China Prosperity International Holdings Ltd. 06/08/1999
China Prosperity International Holdings Ltd. name changed to China Broadband Corp. Ltd. 06/29/2000 which name changed to China Convergent Corp. Ltd. 12/21/2000
(See China Convergent Corp. Ltd.)

OLS ENTERPRISE LTD (SINGAPORE)
ADR agreement terminated 03/05/2018
No ADR's remain outstanding

OLSEN (C.A.) MANUFACTURING CO. (OH)
Common $7 par changed to $5 par in December 1954
Merged into Westinghouse Electric Corp. on a (1) for (3) basis 9/30/55
Westinghouse Electric Corp. name changed to CBS Corp. 12/1/97 which merged into Viacom Inc. (Old) 5/4/2000
(See Viacom Inc. (Old))

OLSEN (W.H.) MANUFACTURING CO. LTD. (ON)
Merged into Johnson Corp. 3/31/68
Details not available

OLSON AIRCRAFT CORP. (NC)
Placed in final receivership 2/24/67
Assets sold for benefit of creditors
No stockholders' equity

OLSON BROTHERS, INC. (DE)
Name changed to Olson Farms, Inc. 6/28/78
Olson Farms, Inc. name changed to Olson Industries, Inc. 9/5/85 which merged into Dolco Packaging Corp. 7/29/91
(See Dolco Packaging Corp.)

OLSON INDS INC (DE)
Name changed 9/5/85
Each share Common $1 par exchanged for (1/3) share Common $3 par 7/26/71
Name changed from Olson Farms, Inc. to Olson Industries, Inc. 9/5/85
Merged into Dolco Packaging Corp. 7/29/91
Each share Common $3 par exchanged for (0.20127) share Common 1¢ par
Note: Each share Common $3 par received an additional distribution of (0.008563) share Dolco Packaging Corp. Common 1¢ par 4/23/92
(See Dolco Packaging Corp.)

OLSON LABS INC (MN)
Merged into OLI, Inc. 03/03/1978
Each share Common 10¢ par exchanged for $0.07 cash

OLSTEN CORP (DE)
Common 10¢ par split (3) for (2) by issuance of (0.5) additional share 09/16/1977
Common 10¢ par split (3) for (2) by issuance of (0.5) additional share 11/17/1978
Common 10¢ par split (3) for (2) by issuance of (0.5) additional share 12/08/1981
Common 10¢ par split (3) for (2) by issuance of (0.5) additional share 03/15/1985
Common 10¢ par split (3) for (2) by issuance of (0.5) additional share 03/17/1986
Common 10¢ par split (3) for (2) by issuance of (0.5) additional share 06/09/1987
Common 10¢ par split (5) for (4) by issuance of (0.25) additional share 09/01/1989
Common 10¢ par split (3) for (2) by issuance of (0.5) additional share 02/23/1993
Common 10¢ par split (3) for (2) by issuance of (0.5) additional share payable 03/15/1996 to holders of record 02/28/1996 Ex date - 03/13/1996
Each share Common 10¢ par received distribution of (0.25) share Gentiva Health Services, Inc. Common 10¢ par payable 03/24/2000 to holders of record 01/18/2000
Merged into Adecco S.A. 03/15/2000
Each share Common 10¢ par exchanged for either (0.12472) Sponsored ADR for Ordinary, $8.75 cash, or a combination thereof
Adecco S.A. name changed to Adecco Group AG 06/03/2016

OLYMCO INC (DE)
Plan of reorganization under Chapter 11 Federal Bankruptcy proceedings confirmed 11/10/1986
No stockholders' equity

OLYMPIA BREWING CO (WA)
Each share Preferred $1 par or Common $1 par exchanged for (1) share Common $5 par in 1952
Common $5 par changed to $10 par and (1) additional share issued 4/30/60
Common $10 par split (2) for (1) by issuance of (1) additional share 5/2/66
Merged into Pabst Brewing Co. 3/18/83
Each share Common $10 par exchanged for (1) share new Common no par
(See Pabst Brewing Co.)

OLYMPIA BROADCASTING CORP (DE)
Charter cancelled and declared inoperative and void for non-payment of taxes 03/01/1992

OLYMPIA CAP CORP (CO)
Recapitalized as Shareholder Communication Systems Inc. 09/24/1993
Each share Common no par exchanged for (0.01) share Common no par
(See Shareholder Communication Systems Inc.)

OLYMPIA ENERGY INC (AB)
Class A Common no par reclassified as Common no par 06/19/2001
Merged into Provident Energy Trust 06/01/2004
Each share Common no par exchanged for either (0.345) Trust Unit and (0.1) share Accrete Energy Inc. Common no par or (0.345) Provident Energy Ltd. Exchangeable Share no par and (0.1) share Accrete Energy Inc. Common no par
Note: Canadian residents option to receive Exchangeable Shares expired 05/26/2004
(See each company's listing)

OLYMPIA MINES INC (DE)
Charter cancelled and declared inoperative and void for non-payment of taxes 4/15/73

OLYMPIA MINING EXPLORATION LTD. (QC)
Charter cancelled for failure to file reports and pay fees 10/19/74

OLYMPIA RECORD INDUSTRIES, INC. (NY)
Name changed to Jade Panther Corporation of America 10/27/1989
(See Jade Panther Corporation of America)

OLYMPIA ST BK (CHICAGO HEIGHTS, IL)
Capital Stock $25 par changed to $5 par and (4) additional shares issued 03/14/1973
Name changed to Heritage/Olympia Bank (Chicago Heights, IL) 11/00/1974
(See Heritage/Olympia Bank (Chicago Heights, IL))

OLYMPIAD CORP (NV)
Each share old Common $0.001 par exchanged for (0.1) share new Common $0.001 par 12/30/1993
Charter permanently revoked 03/31/2003

OLYMPIAN BANCORP (CA)
Charter suspended for failure to pay taxes 2/1/93

OLYMPIAN INTL RES LTD (BC)
Struck off register and declared dissolved for failure to file returns 6/17/83

OLYMPIC BK (EVERETT, WA)
Merged into First Interstate Bancorp 01/28/1985
Each share Capital Stock $10 par exchanged for (4.9175) shares Common $2 par
First Interstate Bancorp merged into Wells Fargo & Co. (Old) 04/01/1996 which merged into Wells Fargo & Co. (New) 11/02/1998

OLYMPIC BROADCASTING CORP (DE)
Name changed to Olympia Broadcasting Corp. 05/26/1989
(See Olympia Broadcasting Corp.)

OLYMPIC-CADILLAC GOLD MINES LTD.
Name changed to Wolfe Lake Mines Ltd. in 1939

OLYMPIC CASCADE FINL CORP (DE)
Stock Dividends - 5% payable 05/30/1997 to holders of record 05/20/1997; 5% payable 09/10/1997 to holders of record 08/29/1997; 5% payable 12/22/1997 to holders of record 12/08/1997
Name changed to National Holdings Corp. 03/20/2006

OLYMPIC CLO I LTD (CAYMAN ISLANDS)
Accredited Investors Preferred called for redemption 10/29/2013
144A 3c7 Preferred called for redemption 10/29/2013

FINANCIAL INFORMATION, INC.

OLY-OM

OLYMPIC COMPUTER SYS CORP (BC)
Name changed to OCS Technologies Corp. 05/31/1991
(See OCS Technologies Corp.)

OLYMPIC DEVELOPMENT CO. (DE)
Name changed to Barnes Engineering Co. 6/30/55
(See Barnes Engineering Co.)

OLYMPIC ENTMT GROUP INC (NV)
Each (15) shares old Common 1¢ par exchanged for (1) share new Common 1¢ par 06/14/2004
Name changed to Exam USA, Inc. 08/30/2004
Exam USA, Inc. name changed to Pachinko World, Inc. 03/31/2006
(See Pachinko World, Inc.)

OLYMPIC ENVIRONMENTAL LTD (NV)
Merged into Neoteric Group Inc. 06/17/2002
Each share Common $0.001 par exchanged for (3) shares Common $0.001 par
(See Neoteric Group Inc.)

OLYMPIC FIN CORP A (DE)
Exchangeable Auction Market Preferred no par called for redemption 02/19/1992

OLYMPIC FIN CORP B (DE)
Exchangeable Auction Market Preferred no par called for redemption 02/25/1992

OLYMPIC FINL LTD (MN)
8% Conv. Exchangeable Preferred 1¢ par called for redemption 12/2/96
Name changed to Arcadia Financial Ltd. 4/29/97
Arcadia Financial Ltd. merged into Citigroup Inc. 11/30/2000

OLYMPIC FOREST PRODUCTS CO.
Merged into Rayonier, Inc. in 1937
Each share $2 Preferred exchanged for (1) share $2 Preferred $25 par and (0.02) share Common $1 par
Each share Common exchanged for (1.02) shares Common $1 par
Rayonier, Inc. merged into International Telephone & Telegraph Corp. (DE) 4/26/68 which name changed to ITT Corp. 12/31/83 which reorganized in Indiana as ITT Industries, Inc. 12/19/95 which name changed to ITT Corp. 7/1/2006

OLYMPIC FUNDING CORP. (DE)
No longer in existence having become inoperative and void for non-payment of taxes 4/1/57

OLYMPIC GAS & OIL INC (WA)
Charter cancelled and proclaimed dissolved for failure to pay fees 10/13/86

OLYMPIC GEOPHYSICAL CO (TX)
Completely liquidated 11/12/70
Each share Common 15¢ par exchanged for first and final distribution of (0.1700579) share Dresser Industries, Inc. (New) Common 25¢ par

OLYMPIC HOLDING CORP. OF AMERICA (UT)
Proclaimed dissolved for failure to pay taxes 12/31/83

OLYMPIC INTL BK & TR CO (BOSTON, MA)
Under plan of reorganization each share Common $1 par automatically became (1) share USA Bancorp, Inc. Common $1 par 02/22/1988
(See USA Bancorp, Inc.)

OLYMPIC LIFE INS CO (TX)
Merged into National Western Life Insurance Co. (CO) 06/16/1976
Each share Common no par exchanged for (0.09090909) share Class A Common $1 par National Western Life Insurance Co.

(CO) reincorporated in Delaware as National Western Life Group, Inc. 10/02/2015

OLYMPIC NATATORIUM CORP. (NJ)
Charter cancelled for failure to file reports and pay fees in 1935

OLYMPIC NATIONAL AGENCIES, INC. (WA)
Acquired by Olympic National Life Insurance Co. 08/29/1969
Each share Preferred $5 par exchanged for (0.277778) share Class B Common $1 par
Each share Common no par exchanged for (12.048542) shares Class B Common $1 par
Olympic National Life Insurance Co. name changed to Unigard Olympic Life Insurance Co. 10/01/1972
(See Unigard Olympic Life Insurance Co.)

OLYMPIC NATL BANCORP (CA)
Closed by the Comptroller of currency and the FDIC was named receiver 4/9/93
Stockholders' equity undetermined

OLYMPIC NATL LIFE INS CO (WA)
Each share Common $10 par exchanged for (10) shares Class B Common $1 par 09/30/1965
Stock Dividend - 100% 02/01/1963
Name changed to Unigard Olympic Life Insurance Co. 10/01/1972
(See Unigard Olympic Life Insurance Co.)

OLYMPIC OIL & GAS LTD (BC)
Recapitalized as Channel Resources Ltd. (Old) 05/28/1984
Each share Common no par exchanged for (0.25) share Common no par
Channel Resources Ltd. (Old) merged into Channel Resources Ltd. (New) 10/31/1989 which merged into West African Resources Ltd. 01/17/2014

OLYMPIC PLASTICS INC (CA)
Voluntarily dissolved 04/22/1980
Details not available

OLYMPIC PRODUCTS CO., INC. (DE)
Name changed to Schaefer (J.B.) Industries, Inc. 12/31/66
Schaefer (J.B.) Industries, Inc. name changed to Furntec Industries, Inc. 5/21/71
(See Furntec Industries, Inc.)

OLYMPIC RADIO & TELEVISION, INC. (NY)
Stock Dividends - 20% 5/1/50; 10% 4/25/51
Name changed to Unitronics Corp. 8/6/56
Unitronics Corp. merged into Siegler Corp. 9/13/57 which name changed to Lear Siegler, Inc. 6/5/62
(See Lear Siegler, Inc.)

OLYMPIC RES INC (UT)
Recapitalized as Barter Resources Inc. 04/09/1984
Each share Common $0.001 par exchanged for (0.2) share Common $0.005 par
(See Barter Resources Inc.)

OLYMPIC RES LTD (BC)
Issue Information - 2,000,000 shares COM offered at $0.10 per share on 12/31/2010
Each share old Common no par exchanged for (0.5) share new Common no par 12/19/2013
Name changed to Kapuskasing Gold Corp. 02/28/2014

OLYMPIC RES LTD (WY)
Reincorporated 01/08/2003
Place of incorporation changed from (BC) to (WY) 01/08/2003
Reorganized under the laws of Nevada as Whittier Energy Corp. 01/02/2004
Each share Common no par

exchanged for (0.1) share Common no par
(See Whittier Energy Corp.)

OLYMPIC ROM WORLD INC (ON)
Recapitalized as Century Financial Capital Group Inc. 11/01/1998
Each share Common no par exchanged for (0.1) share Common no par
Century Financial Capital Group Inc. name changed to FSD Pharma Inc. 05/29/2018

OLYMPIC SVGS & LN ASSN (CA)
Merged into Coast Federal Savings & Loan Association 11/22/1982
Each share Guarantee Stock no par exchanged for $28.5487 principal amount of savings accounts

OLYMPIC SVGS BK (SEATTLE, WA)
Each share old Common $1 par exchanged for (0.25) share new Common $1 par 12/26/1990
Merged into Puget Sound Bancorp 07/31/1992
Each share new Common $1 par exchanged for $8.25 cash

OLYMPIC SECURITY LIFE INSURANCE CO. (UT)
Class A Common $4 par changed to $2 par 3/23/70
Class A Common $2 par changed to $1 par and (1) additional share issued plus a 20% stock dividend paid 9/1/71
Merged into Reserve Underwriters, Inc. 6/1/81
Each share Class A Common $1 par exchanged for (2) shares 10% Preferred 50¢ par

OLYMPIC SOLAR CORP (DE)
Each share Common 1¢ par exchanged for (0.2) share Common 5¢ par 05/29/1981
Name changed to Olymco, Inc. 07/18/1985
(See Olymco, Inc.)

OLYMPIC TRADING & SUPPLY CO. (WA)
Charter cancelled for failure to pay taxes in 1919

OLYMPIC URANIUM, INC. (UT)
Name changed to Central Minerals Co., Inc. 3/5/59
Central Minerals Co., Inc. name changed to Combined Production Associates, Ltd. 12/8/59 which was acquired by Intergeneral Industries, Inc. 5/21/69 which became bankrupt in 1970

OLYMPIC URANIUM CO., INC. (WA)
Name changed to Columbia Uranium, Inc. 6/10/54
Columbia Uranium, Inc. dissolved 7/1/61

OLYMPIC VICTOR CORP (ON)
Recapitalized as Olympic Victor Enterprises Inc. 09/19/1986
Each share Common no par exchanged for (1/7) share Common no par
Olympic Victor Enterprises Inc. name changed to TCS Energy Systems Ltd. 11/17/1992 which name changed to Advanced Pultrusion Technologies Inc. 06/29/1993
(See Advancved Pultrusion Technologies Inc.)

OLYMPIC VICTOR ENTERPRISES INC (ON)
Name changed to TCS Energy Systems Ltd. 11/17/1992
TCS Energy Systems Ltd. name changed to Advanced Pultrusion Technologies Inc. 06/29/1993
(See Advanced Pultrusion Technologies Inc.)

OLYMPIC WEDDINGS INTL INC (NV)
Name changed to CornerWorld Corp. 05/30/2007

OLYMPUS CAP CORP (UT)
Acquired by Washington Mutual, Inc. 04/28/1995
Each share Common $1 par exchanged for (0.743) share Common $1 par
(See Washington Mutual, Inc.)

OLYMPUS EDL SOFTWARE INC (DE)
Name changed to Olympus Technology Corp. 04/11/1988
Olympus Technology Corp. recapitalized as Investors First Bancorp 07/26/1989

OLYMPUS FUND (CA)
Name changed to Industrial Index Fund 12/15/76

OLYMPUS M T M CORP (UT)
Each (150) shares old Common $0.001 par exchanged for (1) share new Common $0.001 par 8/20/96
Name changed to Internet Advisory Corp. 8/20/98
Internet Advisory Corp. name changed to Scores Holding Co., Inc. 7/11/2002

OLYMPUS MINES LTD. (ON)
Charter cancelled and company declared dissolved for default in filing returns 1/20/71

OLYMPUS OPTICAL LTD (JAPAN)
Name changed to Olympus Corp. 11/14/2003

OLYMPUS PAC MINERALS INC (CANADA)
Recapitalized 11/29/1996
Reincorporated 11/17/1997
Reincorporated 07/13/2006
Recapitalized from Olympus Holdings Ltd. to Olympus Pacific Minerals Inc. 11/29/1996
Each share Common no par exchanged for (0.33333333) share Common no par
Place of incorporation changed from (BC) to (YT) 11/17/1997
Place of incorporation changed from (YT) to (Canada) 07/13/2006
Name changed to Besra Gold Inc. 11/23/2012

OLYMPUS SVC CORP (DE)
Merged into Uniservice Corp. 3/31/76
Each share Common 10¢ par exchanged for (0.178571) share Common $1 par
(See Uniservice Corp.)

OLYMPUS STONE INC (YT)
Recapitalized as Gobi Gold Inc. (YT) 10/12/2004
Each share Common no par exchanged for (0.5) share Common no par
Gobi Gold Inc. (YT) reincorporated in British Columbia 09/26/2005 which reorganized as East Energy Corp. 08/29/2006 which name changed to Rare Earth Metals Inc. 12/16/2009 which name changed to Canada Rare Earth Corp. 02/08/2013

OLYMPUS TECHNOLOGY CORP (DE)
Recapitalized as Investors First Bancorp 07/26/1989
Each share Common 1¢ par exchanged for (0.1) share Common $0.001 par

OLYMPUS VENTURES INC (WA)
Each share old Common $0.00001 par exchanged for (0.1) share new Common $0.00001 par 09/11/1995
Each share new Common $0.00001 par exchanged again for (1/30) share new Common $0.00001 par 01/22/1997
Name changed to Rocky Mountain International Ltd. 10/06/1997
(See Rocky Mountain International Ltd.)

OM ASSET MANAGEMENT PLC (ENGLAND & WALES)
Name changed to BrightSphere Investment Group PLC 03/26/2018

OM GROUP INC (DE)
Common 1¢ par split (3) for (2) by issuance of (0.5) additional share payable 12/02/1996 to holders of record 11/15/1996
Acquired by Duke Acquisition Holdings, LLC 10/28/2015
Each share Common 1¢ par exchanged for $34 cash

OMAB ENTERPRISES LTD (BC)
Recapitalized as Consolidated Omab Enterprises Ltd. 12/10/1986
Each share Common no par exchanged for (1/3) share Common no par
(See Consolidated Omab Enterprises Ltd.)

OMAHA & COUNCIL BLUFFS RAILWAY & BRIDGE CO. (IA)
Liquidation completed 12/21/55

OMAHA NATL BK (OMAHA, NE)
Each share Capital Stock $100 par exchanged for (5) shares Capital Stock $20 par 00/00/1945
Capital Stock $20 par changed to $10 par and (1) additional share issued plus a 25% stock dividend paid 11/15/1962
Stock Dividends - 20% 05/20/1940; 33-1/3% 10/10/1950; (1.5) for (1) 04/23/1953; 16-2/3% 11/16/1959; (1) for (1) 10/10/1961
Merged into Omaha National Corp. 12/12/1981
Each share Capital Stock $10 par exchanged for (2.1) shares Common $5 par
Omaha National Corp. name changed to FirsTier, Inc. 06/01/1984 which name changed to FirsTier Financial Inc. 05/18/1987 which merged into First Bank System, Inc. 02/16/1996 which name changed to U.S. Bancorp 08/01/1997

OMAHA NATL CORP (NE)
Under plan of merger name changed to FirsTier, Inc. 06/01/1984
FirsTier, Inc. name changed to FirsTier Financial Inc. 05/18/1987 which merged into First Bank System, Inc. 02/16/1996 which name changed to U.S. Bancorp 08/01/1997

OMAHA PROPERTIES CO. (WI)
Merged into Northwest Chemco, Inc. 11/26/74
Each share Preferred $100 par exchanged for $18.60 cash
Each share Common $100 par exchanged for $15 cash

OMAP HLDGS INC (NV)
Recapitalized as China Food & Beverage Co. 4/10/97
Each share Common $0.001 par exchanged for (1/3) share Common $0.001 par

OMAR, INC. (DE)
Name changed to Ramo Investment Co. 11/29/58
Ramo Investment Co. name changed to Ramo, Inc. 11/21/60 which merged into Telecom Corp. 11/23/71 which name changed to TCC Industries, Inc. 6/1/94
(See TCC Industries, Inc.)

OMAR OIL & GAS CO. (DE)
Name changed to Phoenix Oil Co. 00/00/1928
(See Phoenix Oil Co.)

OMAR TECHNOLOGIES INC (AB)
Name changed 02/21/1989
Name changed from Omar Resources Ltd. to Omar Technologies Inc. 02/21/1989
Recapitalized as Pilgrim Resource Corp. 04/14/1993
Each share Common no par exchanged for (0.2) share Common no par
Pilgrim Resource Corp. merged into International Gryphon Resources Inc. (New) 04/27/1995 which recapitalized as Wirbac Resources Inc. 12/05/2000 which recapitalized as Virtus Energy Ltd. 09/12/2001 which merged into Titan Exploration Ltd. 06/23/2005 which was acquired by Penn West Energy Trust 01/11/2008 which reorganized as Penn West Petroleum Ltd. (New) 01/03/2011 which name changed to Obsidian Energy Ltd. 06/29/2017

OMARK INDS INC (OR)
Common no par split (2) for (1) by issuance of (1) additional share 12/15/1980
Acquired by Blount, Inc. 01/31/1985
Each share Common no par exchanged for $37.50 cash

OMAX RES LTD (AB)
Reincorporated 10/20/2000
Place of incorporation changed from (Yukon) to (ALTA) 10/20/2000
Reincorporated under the laws of British Columbia as Euromax Resources Ltd. 7/19/2004

OMC CAPITAL CORP (AB)
Reorganized under the laws of British Columbia as ReMac Zinc Corp. 06/04/2007
Each share Common no par exchanged for (0.5) share Common no par
ReMac Zinc Corp. name changed to Corazon Gold Corp. 01/19/2011 which name changed to NanoSphere Health Sciences Inc. 12/05/2017

OMC CARD INC (JAPAN)
Name changed to Cedyna Financial Corp. 10/09/2009
(See Cedyna Financial Corp.)

OMEGA ADVISORS U S CAP APPRECIATION FD (ON)
Combined Units separated 03/30/2011
Name changed to Artemis U.S. Capital Appreciation Fund 01/10/2013
(See Artemis U.S. Capital Appreciation Fund)

OMEGA ALPHA INC (DE)
Common 1¢ par changed to $1 par 03/07/1972
Each share Common $1 par exchanged for (0.1) share Common $5 par 01/03/1973
Reorganized under Chapter X bankruptcy proceedings 06/29/1976
No stockholders' equity

OMEGA DEV CORP (NV)
Recapitalized as BBJ Environmental Technologies, Inc. 06/01/2000
Each share Common $0.001 par exchanged for (0.33333333) share Common $0.001 par
(See BBJ Environmental Technologies, Inc.)

OMEGA DYNAMICS INC (DE)
SEC revoked common stock registration 10/22/2008
Stockholders' equity unlikely

OMEGA ENERGY INC (UT)
Recapitalized as Olivier International Energy, Inc. 01/07/1980
Each share Common $0.0001 par exchanged for (0.25) share Common $0.0004 par

OMEGA ENVIRONMENTAL INC (DE)
Common $0.0025 par split (6) for (5) by issuance of (0.2) additional share 8/24/92
Recapitalized as O.N.E. World Distributing, Inc. 9/5/2006
Each share Common $0.0025 par exchanged for (1) share Common $0.0025 par

OMEGA EQUITIES CORP (DE)
Class A $1 par reclassified as Common 1¢ par 1/2/76
Recapitalized as Ben Wa International Inc. 6/29/81
Each share Common 1¢ par exchanged for (0.5) share Common 1¢ par
Ben Wa International Inc. name changed to CEC Properties, Inc. 3/1/96
(See CEC Properties, Inc.)

OMEGA FD INC (MA)
Name changed to Keystone America Omega Fund, Inc. (MA) 4/19/89
Keystone America Omega Fund, Inc. (MA) reincorporated in Delaware as Evergreen Omega Fund 10/31/97

OMEGA FINL CORP (PA)
Common $5 par split (3) for (1) by issuance of (2) additional shares 01/12/1990
Common $5 par split (3) for (2) by issuance of (0.5) additional share payable 04/30/1997 to holders of record 04/18/1997
Merged into F.N.B. Corp. 04/01/2008
Each share Common $5 par exchanged for (2.022) shares Common 1¢ par

OMEGA GOLD CORP (BC)
Merged into Akiko Gold Resources Ltd. (BC) 11/09/1992
Each share Common no par exchanged for (0.4) share Common no par
Akiko Gold Resources Ltd. (BC) reincorporated in Yukon as Prospex Mining Inc. 07/30/1997 which merged into Semafo Inc. 06/30/1999

OMEGA GOLD MINES LTD.
Recapitalized as Lomega Gold Mines Ltd. on a (2) for (1) basis in 1950
Lomega Gold Mines Ltd. name changed to Lomega Explorations in 1956
(See Lomega Explorations)

OMEGA HEALTH SYS INC (DE)
Name changed to VisionAmerica Inc. 8/16/99
(See VisionAmerica Inc.)

OMEGA HEALTHCARE INVS INC (MD)
Issue Information - 2,000,000 shares 9.25% PFD SER A offered at $25 per share on 04/25/1997
9.25% Preferred Ser. A $1 par called for redemption at $25 plus $0.57813 accrued dividend on 04/30/2004
8.625% Preferred Ser. B $1 par called for redemption at $25 on 05/02/2005
8.375% Preferred Ser. D $1 par called for redemption at $25 plus $0.21519 accrued dividends on 03/07/2011
(Additional Information in Active)

OMEGA HYDROCARBONS LTD (AB)
Capital Stock no par split (3) for (1) by issuance of (2) additional shares 1/20/83
Merged into Inuvialuit Energy 3/13/96
Each share Common no par exchanged for $2.90 cash

OMEGA INSURANCE CO. (WA)
Common $10 par changed to $1 par and (9) additional shares issued 1/5/87
Merged into Laurentian Capital Corp. 7/7/87
Each share Common $1 par exchanged for (0.1) share $6 Conv. Preferred Ser. A 1¢ par and $62.50 cash
(See Laurentian Capital Corp.)

OMEGA MINES LTD (BC)
Name changed to Black Owl Resources Ltd. 12/28/78
(See Black Owl Resources Ltd.)

OMEGA MINING & EXPL CORP (WA)
Reincorporated under the laws of Nevada as Cardio Infrared Technologies, Inc. and Common no par changed to $0.001 par 08/06/2007
Cardio Infrared Technologies, Inc. (NV) reorganized in Wyoming 07/15/2010 which recapitalized as Enchanted World, Inc. 12/08/2014

OMEGA MINING CORP. LTD. (QC)
Acquired by Aqua Mining Corp. Ltd. 08/00/1962
Each share Capital Stock $1 par exchanged for (0.4166666) share Capital Stock $1 par
(See Aqua Mining Corp. Ltd.)

OMEGA NATURAL GAS CO. LTD. (AB)
Name changed to Omega Hydrocarbons Ltd. 11/1/67
(See Omega Hydrocarbons Ltd.)

OMEGA NAVIGATION ENTERPRISES INC (MARSHALL ISLANDS)
Issue Information - 12,000,000 shares CL A COM offered at $17 per share on 04/12/2006
Plan of reorganization under Chapter 11 Federal Bankruptcy proceedings effective 05/22/2013
Stockholders' equity unlikely

OMEGA OPTICAL INC (TX)
Stock Dividends - 25% 4/3/78; 50% 10/2/78
Merged into Optical Radiation Corp. 8/16/84
Each share Common 5¢ par exchanged for (0.211) share Common 50¢ par and $0.25 cash
Optical Radiation Corp. acquired by Benson Eyecare Corp. 10/12/94 which merged into BEC Group, Inc. 5/3/96 which recapitalized as Lumen Technologies, Inc. 3/12/98
(See Lumen Technologies, Inc.)

OMEGA ORTHODONTICS INC (DE)
Merged into Pentegra Dental Group, Inc. 07/01/1999
Each share Common 1¢ par exchanged for (0.356) share Common $0.001 par
Pentegra Dental Group, Inc. name changed to e-dentist.com, Inc. 08/25/2000 which name changed to EDT Learning, Inc. 08/02/2001 which name changed to iLinc Communications, Inc. 02/05/2004
(See iLinc Communications, Inc.)

OMEGA PRECISION, INC. (DE)
Adjudicated bankrupt 4/15/64
No stockholders' equity

OMEGA PROJ HLDGS CO LTD (JAPAN)
Name changed 04/01/2005
Name changed from Omega Project Inc. to Omega Project Holdings Co., Ltd. 04/01/2005
ADR agreement terminated 08/27/2009
Details not available

OMEGA PROTEIN CORP (NV)
Acquired by Cooke Inc. 12/19/2017
Each share Common 1¢ par exchanged for $22 cash

OMEGA RESH INC (FL)
Issue Information - 3,700,000 shares COM offered at $11 per share on 09/30/1997
Merged into TradeStation Group, Inc. 12/29/2000
Each share Common 1¢ par exchanged for (1) share Common 1¢ par
(See TradeStation Group, Inc.)

OMEGA RES INC (DE)
Charter cancelled and declared inoperative and void for non-payment of taxes 3/1/83

OMEGA UTD INC (NV)
Common $0.001 par split (5) for (1) by issuance of (4) additional shares payable 04/14/2008 to holders of record 04/14/2008
Name changed to SkyPostal Networks, Inc. 07/28/2008
SkyPostal Networks, Inc. name changed to SkyShop Logistics, Inc. 08/16/2010

OMEGA WORLDWIDE INC (MD)
Merged into Four Seasons Health Care Ltd. 9/20/2002
Each share Common 10¢ par exchanged for $3.32 cash

OMENICA RES LTD (BC)
Recapitalized as Marilyn Resources Inc. 01/30/1984
Each share Class A no par exchanged for (0.2) share Class A no par
Each share Class B no par exchanged for (0.2) share Class B no par
(See Marilyn Resources Inc.)

OMEX (CA)
Reacquired 12/29/1986
Each share Common no par exchanged for $0.55 cash

OMG MINERAL EXPLORATION INC (ON)
Name changed to Gold Reef International, Inc. 05/08/2006
Gold Reef International, Inc. recapitalized as Montana Gold Mining Co. Inc. 01/05/2011 which name changed to Peloton Minerals Corp. 07/18/2016

OMI CORP (DE)
Recapitalized 4/3/89
Each share $1.50 Conv. Exchangeable Preferred $1 par exchanged for $20 principal amount of 7.5% Conv. Subord. Debentures due 10/1/2011
Each share Common 50¢ par received distribution of (1) share OMI Corp. (Marshall Islands) Common 50¢ par payable 6/17/98 to holders of record 6/16/98
Recapitalized as Marine Transport Corp. 6/18/98
Each share Common 50¢ par exchanged for (0.1) share Common 50¢ par
(See Marine Transport Corp.)

OMI CORP (MARSHALL ISLANDS)
Merged into Teekay Corp. 06/08/2007
Each share Common 50¢ par exchanged for $29.25 cash

OMI HLDGS LTD (AUSTRALIA)
ADR agreement terminated 02/04/2013
Each Sponsored ADR for Ordinary exchanged for (10) shares Ordinary

OMICRON INDS INC (UT)
Each share Common $0.001 par exchanged for (0.1) share Common 1¢ par 08/01/1986
Name changed to Supermail International, Inc. 07/20/1987
Supermail International, Inc. name changed to First Automated, Inc. 10/27/2003 which recapitalized as PBHG, Inc. 07/19/2004
(See PBHG, Inc.)

OMICRON TECHNOLOGIES INC (FL)
Each share old Common $0.001 par exchanged for (0.005) share new Common $0.001 par 06/17/2002
Name changed to North Star Diamonds Inc. 06/04/2003
North Star Diamonds Inc. recapitalized as Chanaral Resources, Inc. 04/23/2007 which name changed to Alkane, Inc. 04/03/2009

OMII CORP (NV)
Common $0.001 par split (3) for (1) by issuance of (2) additional shares payable 10/4/2005 to holders of record 10/3/2005
Name changed to Vemics, Inc. 11/7/2005

OMINECA MINING & MILLING CO., LTD. (BC)
Struck from British Columbia Registrar of Companies and proclaimed dissolved 7/6/39

OMNET CORP (NV)
Name changed to Performance Nutrition, Inc. 03/10/1992

OMNI ADVANTAGE INC (LA)
Reincorporated under the laws of Delaware as Go Call, Inc. 03/16/1998
Go Call, Inc. (DE) reorganized in Nevada as Medical Institutional Services Corp. 10/23/2006 which recapitalized as National Pharmaceuticals Corp. 12/04/2009 which recapitalized as Ghana Gold Corp. 07/11/2012 which name changed to BrightRock Gold Corp. 11/11/2013

OMNI ALLIANCE GROUP INC (LA)
Reorganized under the laws of Nevada as EMTA Holdings, Inc. 04/04/2006
Each (233) shares Common no par exchanged for (1) share Common $0.001 par
Note: No holder will receive fewer than (10) shares
EMTA Holdings, Inc. name changed to Green Planet Group, Inc. 07/08/2009

OMNI-ANSWERS INC (LA)
Name changed to Premier Ventures & Exploration Inc. 12/20/96
Premier Ventures & Exploration Inc. name changed to New Directions Manufacturing Inc. 3/14/97 which recapitalized as American Soil Technologies Inc. (NV) 1/18/2000

OMNI ASSETS INC (LA)
Reincorporated under the laws of Delaware as Inamco International Corp. and Common no par changed to 1¢ par 2/8/2000

OMNI BANCSHARES INC (LA)
Merged into IBERIABANK Corp. 05/31/2011
Each share Common $1 par exchanged for (0.3313) share Common $1 par

OMNI BANK N A (MONTEREY PARK, CA)
100% acquired through purchase offer which expired 04/14/1990
Public interest eliminated

OMNI CAP CORP (NV)
Charter revoked for failure to file reports and pay fees 10/1/98

OMNI CAP GROUP INC (NC)
Common $1 par split (3) for (2) by issuance of (0.5) additional share 8/28/89
Merged into Security Capital Bancorp 6/30/92
Each share Common $1 par exchanged for (2.25) shares Common no par
Security Capital Bancorp merged into CCB Financial Corp. 5/19/95 which merged into National Commerce Bancorporation 7/5/2000 which name changed to National Commerce Financial Corp. 4/25/2001 which merged into SunTrust Banks, Inc. 10/1/2004

OMNI COMPUTER SYS INC (MA)
Voluntarily dissolved 03/21/1997
Details not available

OMNI CORP (CO)
Name changed to Builders Warehouse Association, Inc. 08/18/1992
Builders Warehouse Association, Inc. merged into Osicom Technologies, Inc. 09/30/1996 which name changed to Sorrento Networks Corp. (NJ) 01/17/2001 which reincorporated in Delaware 06/04/2003 which merged into Zhone Technologies, Inc. 07/01/2004 which name changed to DASAN Zhone Solutions, Inc. 09/12/2016

OMNI DOORS INC (FL)
Each share old Common no par exchanged for (0.1) share new Common no par 10/31/2001
New Common no par split (4.369) for (1) by issuance of (3.369) additional shares payable 1/23/2002 to holders of record 1/18/2002 Ex date - 1/24/2002
Name changed to King Ball International Technology Corp. 6/25/2002
King Ball International Technology Corp. recapitalized as Kid Castle Educational Corp. 8/22/2002

OMNI ENERGY SVCS CORP (LA)
Each share old Common 1¢ par exchanged for (0.33333333) share new Common 1¢ par 07/02/2002
Acquired by Wellspring OMNI Holdings Corp. 10/27/2010
Each share new Common 1¢ par exchanged for $2.75 cash

OMNI ENTMT GROUP INC (NV)
Common $0.001 par split (1.89) for (1) by issuance of (0.89) additional share payable 03/07/2006 to holders of record 03/06/2006 Ex date - 03/13/2006
Name changed to Entertainment Financial Services, Inc. 03/29/2006
(See Entertainment Financial Services, Inc.)

OMNI EQUITIES INC (MA)
Involuntarily dissolved for failure to file reports and pay fees 08/31/1998

OMNI EXPL INC (DE)
Recapitalized as Cairn Energy USA, Inc. 09/29/1992
Each share Common 1¢ par exchanged for (0.07) share Common 1¢ par
Cairn Energy USA, Inc. merged into Meridian Resource Corp. 11/05/1997
(See Meridian Resource Corp.)

OMNI FILMS INTL INC (FL)
Acquired by Iwerks Entertainment Inc. 5/18/94
Each share Common 1¢ par exchanged for (0.424303) share Common $0.001 par and $1.42 cash
(See Iwerks Entertainment Inc.)

OMNI FINL SVCS INC (GA)
Issue Information - 3,350,000 shares COM offered at $9.50 per share on 09/28/2006
Company's sole asset placed in receivership 03/27/2009
Stockholders' equity unlikely

OMNI GLOBAL TECHNOLOGIES INC (NV)
Name changed to Blockchain Industries, Inc. 01/10/2018

OMNI HUT ENTERPRISES INC (TN)
Charter revoked for failure to file reports 12/04/1974

OMNI INDS CORP (NY)
Dissolved by proclamation 9/25/91
Stock Dividend - 100% 7/10/72

OMNI INS GROUP INC (GA)
Merged into Hartford Fire Insurance Co. 02/12/1998
Each share Common 1¢ par exchanged for $31.75 cash

OMNI INTL TRADING INC (MN)
Statutorily dissolved 9/25/2000

OMNI INVT FD (MA)
Name changed to Berger Omni Investment Trust 02/24/1997
Berger Omni Investment Trust merged into Janus Investment Fund 04/21/2003

OMNI LABS INC (MA)
Proclaimed dissolved for failure to file reports and pay fees 10/19/83

OMNI-LITE INDS CORP (AB)
Recapitalized as Omni-Lite Industries Canada Inc. 11/11/97
Each share Common no par exchanged for (1/3) share Common no par

OMNI MED HLDGS INC (UT)
Each share old Common $0.001 par exchanged for (0.25) share new Common $0.001 par 11/04/2005
SEC revoked common stock registration 09/21/2011

OMNI MULTIMEDIA GROUP INC (MA)
Chapter 11 bankruptcy proceedings converted to Chapter 7 on 6/4/98
Stockholders' equity unlikely

OMNI NUTRACEUTICALS INC (DE)
SEC revoked common stock registration 10/09/2008
Stockholders' equity unlikely

OMNI OIL & GAS INC (IL)
Name changed to American Gold Resources Corp. 10/19/2009
(See American Gold Resources Corp.)

OMNI PK PASS COM INC (NV)
Recapitalized as Invvision Capital Inc. 04/25/2001
Each share Common $0.001 par exchanged for (0.125) share Common $0.001 par
Invvision Capital Inc. name changed to RG America, Inc. (NV) 08/30/2004 which reorganized in Colorado as Sprout Tiny Homes, Inc. 04/21/2015

OMNI RESH INC (PR)
Company dissolved in 1992
No stockholders' equity

OMNI RES INC (BC)
Merged into Tagish Lake Gold Corp. 12/01/2000
Each share Common no par exchanged for (0.2257) share Common no par
(See Tagish Lake Gold Corp.)

OMNI SPECTRA INC (DE)
Reincorporated 03/05/1979
Common $1 par split (3) for (2) by issuance of (0.5) additional share 12/16/1971
Common $1 par split (3) for (2) by issuance of (0.5) additional share 10/13/1972
State of incorporation changed from (MI) to (DE) 03/05/1979
Merged into M/A-Com, Inc. 08/25/1980
Each (3.16667) shares Common $1 par exchanged for (1) share Common $1 par
M/A-Com, Inc. merged into AMP Inc. 06/30/1995 which merged into Tyco International Ltd. (Bermuda) 04/01/1999 which reincorporated in Switzerland 03/17/2009 which merged into Johnson Controls International PLC 09/06/2016

OMNI TECH INTL CORP (OR)
Involuntarily dissolved for failure to pay fees 08/15/1983

OMNI U S A INC (NV)
Each share old Common $0.000333 par exchanged for (0.06666666) share new Common $0.004995 par 12/20/1992
Each share new Common $0.004995 par exchanged again for (0.33333333) share new Common $0.004995 par 06/18/2001

OMN-ON-

Name changed to Brendan Technologies, Inc. 09/15/2006
(See Brendan Technologies, Inc.)

OMNI WAVE ELECTRS INC (DE)
Each share Common 50¢ par exchanged for (0.1) share Common 1¢ par 08/07/1975
Merged into OW Acquisition Corp. 01/12/1983
Each share Common 1¢ par exchanged for $1 cash

OMNIA HLDGS LTD (SOUTH AFRICA)
ADR agreement terminated 04/19/2018
No ADR's remain outstanding

OMNIAMERICA HOLDING CORP. (NV)
Merged into Specialty Teleconstructors, Inc. (NV) 04/23/1998
Each share Common no par exchanged for (1) share Common 1¢ par
Specialty Teleconstructors, Inc. (NV) reincorporated in Delaware as Omniamerica Inc. 09/15/1998 which merged into American Tower Corp. (Old) 02/25/1999 which reorganized as American Tower Corp. (New) 01/03/2012

OMNIAMERICA INC (DE)
Merged into American Tower Corp. (Old) 02/25/1999
Each share Common 1¢ par exchanged for (1.1) shares Class A Common 1¢ par
American Tower Corp. (Old) reorganized as American Tower Corp. (New) 01/03/2012

OMNIAMERICAN BANCORP INC (MD)
Merged into Southside Bancshares, Inc. 12/17/2014
Each share Common 1¢ par exchanged for (0.4459) share Common $1.25 par and $13.125 cash

OMNIBANK CONN INC MADISON (CT)
Acquired by NESB Corp. 06/29/1988
Each share Common 1¢ par exchanged for $21.50 cash

OMNIBANK CORP (MI)
Merged into NBD Bancorp, Inc. 12/31/86
Each share Common $5 par exchanged for $66.50 cash

OMNIBUS COMPUTER GRAPHICS INC (ON)
Ceased operations in 1987

OMNIBUS CORP. (DE)
Common no par changed to $6 par in 1939
Name changed to Hertz Corp. 11/19/54
Hertz Corp. merged into Radio Corp. of America 5/11/67 which name changed to RCA Corp. 5/9/69
(See RCA Corp.)

OMNIBUS INVESTMENT (UT)
Proclaimed dissolved for failure to pay taxes 3/31/80

OMNICARE INC (DE)
Common $1 par split (3) for (2) by issuance of (0.5) additional share 03/10/1983
Common $1 par split (2) for (1) by issuance of (1) additional share 06/21/1995
Common $1 par split (2) for (1) by issuance of (1) additional share payable 06/27/1996 to holders of record 06/05/1996 Ex date - 06/28/1996
Acquired by CVS Health Corp. 08/18/2015
Each share Common $1 par exchanged for $98 cash

OMNICITY CORP (NV)
SEC revoked common stock registration 05/22/2014

OMNICO INC (WA)
Charter cancelled and proclaimed dissolved for failure to file reports 3/31/2000

OMNICOM DATA INC (MN)
Name changed to Omnicom Ventures, Inc. 11/17/1988
Omnicom Ventures, Inc. recapitalized as Omnicom Sports & Entertainment Inc. 05/01/1997 which name changed to Double Five Financial Corp. 03/18/1998 which name changed to EXA International, Inc. (MN) 07/24/1998 which reincorporated in Florida as Exa Inc. 12/31/2002 which name changed to ATI Nationwide Holding Corp. 06/07/2017

OMNICOM SPORTS & ENTMT INC (MN)
Name changed to Double Five Financial Corp. 03/18/1998
Double Five Financial Corp. name changed to EXA International, Inc. (MN) 07/24/1998 which reincorporated in Florida as Exa Inc. 12/31/2002 which name changed to ATI Nationwide Holding Corp. 06/07/2017

OMNICOM VENTURES INC (MN)
Recapitalized as Omnicom Sports & Entertainment Inc. 05/01/1997
Each share Common no par exchanged for (0.01) share Common 1¢ par
Omnicom Sports & Entertainment Inc. name changed to Double Five Financial Corp. 03/18/1998 which name changed to EXA International, Inc. (MN) 07/24/1998 which reincorporated in Florida as Exa Inc. 12/31/2002 which name changed to ATI Nationwide Holding Corp. 06/07/2017

OMNICORDER TECHNOLOGIES INC (DE)
Name changed to Advanced BioPhotonics, Inc. 06/08/2005
(See Advanced BioPhotonics, Inc.)

OMNICORP LTD (DE)
SEC revoked common stock registration 10/22/2008
Stockholders' equity unlikely

OMNIDENTIX SYS CORP (MA)
Proclaimed dissolved for failure to file reports and pay fees 12/31/90

OMNIFUND INC (CO)
Each share old Common $0.0001 par exchanged for (0.01) share new Common $0.0001 par 5/14/87
Name changed to Two Count Holding Co. 4/12/88
(See Two Count Holding Co.)

OMNIMED INTL INC (NV)
Name changed to MedeFile International, Inc. 01/17/2006
MedeFile International, Inc. recapitalized as Tech Town Holdings Inc. 11/02/2017 which name changed to Hash Labs Inc. 03/06/2018

OMNIMEDIA PLC (UNITED KINGDOM)
ADR agreement terminated 8/31/2004
No ADR holders' equity

OMNIMEDICAL INC (CA)
Name changed 06/09/1978
Name changed from Omnimedical Services, Inc. to Omnimedical 06/09/1978
Plan of reorganization under Chapter 11 Federal Bankruptcy proceedings confirmed 02/24/1986
No stockholders' equity

OMNINET MEDIA CORP (NV)
Name changed 06/01/2001
Name changed from Omninet Media.com Inc. Omninet Media Corp. 06/01/2001
Name changed to Aquagold International, Inc. 03/28/2008

OMNIPOINT CORP (DE)
Merged into Voicestream Wireless Corp. 2/28/2000
Each share Common 1¢ par exchanged for either (0.8795) share Common no par, (0.825) share Common no par and $8 cash, or $129 cash
Note: Option to receive stock or cash only expired 3/14/2000
Holders electing cash received (0.7627745) share Common and $17.134019 cash
Voicestream Wireless Corp. merged into Deutsche Telekom AG 5/31/2001

OMNIPOWER INC (CA)
Merged out of existence 12/31/89
Details not available

OMNIQUIP INTL INC (DE)
Issue Information - 8,000,000 shares COM offered at $14 per share on 03/20/1997
Merged into Textron Inc. 9/27/99
Each share Common 1¢ par exchanged for $21 cash

OMNIRELIANT HLDGS INC (NV)
Name changed to Infusion Brands International, Inc. 01/07/2011

OMNIS TECHNOLOGY CORP (DE)
Name changed to Raining Data Corp. 12/04/2000
Raining Data Corp. name changed to TigerLogic Corp. 04/17/2008
(See TigerLogic Corp.)

OMNISKY CORP (DE)
Issue Information - 9,100,000 shares COM offered at $12 per share on 09/20/2000
Plan of reorganization under Chapter 11 Federal Bankruptcy Code effective 11/11/2002
Stockholders' equity unlikely

OMNISOURCE INC (NV)
Charter revoked for failure to file reports and pay fees 12/01/1990

OMNITEC CORP (DE)
Name changed to Bastian-Blessing Co., Inc. 09/19/1977
Bastian-Blessing Co., Inc. merged into Bastian Industries, Inc. 11/24/1980
(See Bastian Industries, Inc.)

OMNITEC INC (UT)
Assets foreclosed on 09/00/1990
No stockholders' equity

OMNITECH CAP CORP (CANADA)
Reincorporated 02/11/2004
Place of incorporation changed from (BC) to (Canada) 02/11/2004
Recapitalized as One Person Health Sciences Inc. 03/01/2004
Each share Common no par exchanged for (0.5) share Common no par
One Person Health Sciences Inc. name changed to HealthPricer Interactive Ltd. 10/17/2006 which recapitalized as Disani Capital Corp. (Canada) 03/18/2013 which reorganized in British Columbia as NeutriSci International Inc. 12/04/2014

OMNITECH CONSULTANT GROUP INC (CANADA)
Assets assigned for the benefit of creditors 09/28/2007
Stockholders equity unlikely

OMNITRANS EXPLORATION LTD. (ON)
Name changed to Majortrans Oil & Mines Ltd. 1/4/57

Majortrans Oil & Mines Ltd. charter revoked 11/9/67

OMNITRONICS RESH CORP (NV)
Charter revoked for failure to file reports and pay fees 11/01/1986

OMNITURE INC (DE)
Merged into Adobe Systems Inc. 10/23/2009
Each share Common $0.001 par exchanged for $21.50 cash

OMNIVISION TECHNOLOGIES INC (DE)
Common $0.001 par split (2) for (1) by issuance of (1) additional share payable 02/17/2004 to holders of record 01/30/2004 Ex date - 02/18/2004
Acquired by Seagull International Ltd. 01/28/2016
Each share Common $0.001 par exchanged for $29.75 cash

OMOCO HLDGS LTD (BC)
Struck off register and declared dissolved for failure to file returns 11/5/93

OMOPLATA INC (DE)
Name changed to Jet Neko, Inc. 05/27/2011
(See Jet Neko, Inc.)

OMRIX BIOPHARMACEUTICALS INC (DE)
Issue Information - 3,437,500 shares COM offered at $10 per share on 04/20/2006
Acquired by Johnson & Johnson 12/30/2008
Each share Common 1¢ par exchanged for $25 cash

OMRON TATEISI ELECTRS CO (JAPAN)
Name changed to OMRON Corp. 01/01/1990

OMSI/KIT, INC. (OR)
Name changed to Learning Resource Center, Inc. 5/24/72
Learning Resource Center, Inc. name changed to Therapeutic Medco, Inc. 7/7/86
(See Therapeutic Medco, Inc.)

OMT INC (MB)
Each share old Common no par exchanged for (0.11111111) share new Common no par 07/12/2011
Reorganized under the laws of British Columbia as AnalytixInsight Inc. 07/11/2013
Each share Common no par exchanged for (0.33333333) share Common no par

OMTHERA PHARMACEUTICALS INC (DE)
Issue Information - 8,000,000 shares COM offered at $8 per share on 04/11/2013
Acquired by Zeneca Inc. 07/18/2013
Each share Common $0.001 par exchanged for (1) Contingent Value Right and $12.70 cash

OMTOOL LTD (DE)
Each share old Common 1¢ par exchanged for (0.14285714) share new Common 1¢ par 01/14/2003
New Common 1¢ par split (2) for (1) by issuance of (1) additional share payable 04/27/2004 to holders of record 04/07/2004 Ex date - 04/28/2004
Acquired by Upland Software, Inc. 01/10/2017
Each share new Common 1¢ par exchanged for $4.16 cash

OMX CORP (CO)
Recapitalized as Wellington Financial Services Inc. 05/13/1991
Each share Common $0.0001 par exchanged for (0.004) share Common $0.025 par
Wellington Financial Services Inc. name changed to Fajita Junction,

Inc. 03/30/1993 which name changed to Tostel Corp. 03/23/1995 which merged into Polus, Inc. 06/22/1998
(See Polus, Inc.)

OMZ OJSC URALMASH-IZHORA GROUP (RUSSIA)
ADR agreement terminated 03/17/2014
Each Sponsored Reg. S ADR for Ordinary exchanged for $1.058572 cash
Each Sponsored ADR for Ordinary exchanged for $1.058572 cash

ON-AIR IMPACT INC (NV)
Name changed to Ecosciences, Inc. 06/23/2014

ON ASSIGNMENT INC (DE)
Common 1¢ par split (2) for (1) by issuance of (1) additional share payable 10/20/1997 to holders of record 10/13/1997
Common 1¢ par split (2) for (1) by issuance of (1) additional share payable 04/03/2000 to holders of record 03/27/2000
Name changed to ASGN Inc. 04/02/2018

ON COMMAND CORP (DE)
Merged into Liberty Media Corp. (New) 12/08/2003
Each share Common 1¢ par exchanged for (0.175) share Common Ser. A 1¢ par
Liberty Media Corp. (New) reorganized as Liberty Media Corp. (Incorporated 02/28/2006) 05/10/2006 which name changed to Liberty Interactive Corp. 09/26/2011 which name changed to Qurate Retail, Inc. 04/10/2018

ON DEMAND HEAVY DUTY CORP (NV)
Name changed to China Executive Education Corp. 04/12/2010
(See China Executive Education Corp.)

ON GUARD CORP AMER (NY)
Dissolved by proclamation 12/24/91

ON LINE MEDIA INC (DE)
Stock Dividend - 100% 5/15/81
Charter cancelled and declared inoperative and void for non-payment of taxes 3/1/84

ON LINE SOFTWARE INTL INC (DE)
Common 1¢ par split (3) for (2) by issuance of (0.5) additional share 5/27/87
Merged into LWB Merge, Inc. 9/28/91
Each share Common 1¢ par exchanged for $15.75 cash

ON LINE SYS INC (DE)
Common 1¢ par split (3) for (2) by issuance of (0.5) additional share 03/07/1973
Common 1¢ par split (3) for (2) by issuance of (0.5) additional share 11/14/1978
Merged into United Telecommunications, Inc. 11/01/1979
Each share Common 1¢ par exchanged for (1.26) shares Common $2.50 par
United Telecommunications, Inc. name changed to Sprint Corp. (KS) 02/26/1992 which name changed to Sprint Nextel Corp. 08/12/2005 which merged into Sprint Corp. (DE) 07/10/2013

ON-POINT TECHNOLOGY SYS INC (NV)
Each share Common 1¢ par exchanged for (0.33333333) share Common 3¢ par 11/06/2000
Name changed to Global ePoint, Inc. 06/05/2001

ON QUEUE INC (OLD) (NV)
Name changed to Mactavish International, Inc. 01/24/1992
Mactavish International, Inc. name changed to On Queue, Inc. (New) 08/10/1992 which name changed to Sunlogic, Inc. 07/01/1994 which name changed to Dawson Science Corp. (NV) 03/17/1995 which reorganized in Delaware as Integrated Transportation Network Group Inc. 06/30/1998
(See Integrated Transportation Network Group Inc.)

ON QUEUE INC NEW (NV)
Name changed to Sunlogic, Inc. 07/01/1994
Sunlogic, Inc. name changed to Dawson Science Corp. (NV) 03/17/1995 which reorganized in Delaware as Integrated Transportation Network Group Inc. 06/30/1998
(See Integrated Transportation Network Group Inc.)

ON SITE ENERGY SYS CORP (NY)
Company believed private 00/00/1989
Details not available

ON-SITE SOURCING INC (DE)
Merged into Docuforce, LLC 2/27/2004
Each share Common 1¢ par exchanged for $2.87 cash

ON-SITE TOXIC CTL INC (CO)
Each share Common $0.0001 par exchanged for (0.008) share Common $0.125 par 6/26/89
Proclaimed dissolved for failure to file reports and pay fees 4/1/2002

ON STAGE ENTMT INC (NV)
Each share old Common 1¢ par exchanged for (0.000001) share new Common 1¢ par 12/31/2003
Note: In effect holders received $0.01 cash per share and public interest was eliminated

ON TECHNOLOGY CORP (DE)
Issue Information - 2,800,000 shares COM offered at $15 per share on 08/01/1995
Merged into Symantec Corp. 2/13/2004
Each share Common 1¢ par exchanged for $4 cash

ON THE BORDER CAFES INC (TX)
Merged into Brinker International, Inc. 5/18/94
Each share Common 2¢ par exchanged for (0.328881) share Common 10¢ par

ON THE GO HEALTHCARE INC (DE)
Each (30) shares old Common $0.0001 par exchanged for (1) share new Common $0.0001 par 10/04/2004
Each share new Common $0.0001 par exchanged again for (0.02) share new Common $0.0001 par 08/10/2006
Each share new Common $0.0001 par exchanged again for (0.02) share new Common $0.0001 par 11/16/2007
Recapitalized as Metro One Development, Inc. 04/14/2008
Each share Common $0.0001 par exchanged for (0.001) share Common $0.0001 par

ON THE MOVE SYS CORP (NV)
Reorganized 03/05/2015
Reorganized from Florida to under the laws of Nevada 03/05/2015
Each share Common $0.0001 par exchanged for (0.002) share Common $0.001 par
Note: No holder will receive fewer than (5) post-split shares
Recapitalized as Artificial Intelligence Technology Solutions Inc. 08/24/2018
Each share Common $0.001 par exchanged for (0.01) share Common $0.001 par

ON TIME FILINGS INC (NV)
Common $0.001 par split (44) for (1) by issuance of (43) additional shares payable 05/19/2011 to holders of record 05/19/2011
Name changed to Empowered Products, Inc. 07/13/2011

ON-TRACK LEARNING SYS LTD (BC)
Recapitalized as Torq Media Corp. 5/18/2004
Each (12) shares Common no par exchanged for (1) share Common no par
Torq Media Corp. recapitalized as Quizam Media Corp. 5/18/2005

ON TV INC (AR)
Name changed to Auction TV Network, Inc. 6/6/97
Auction TV Network, Inc. name changed to Auction Television Network, Inc. 12/23/97 which name changed to Bidnow.com, Inc. 2/3/99

ON WAH INVTS CORP (BC)
Delisted from Canadian Venture Exchange 10/31/1991

ONA ENERGY INC (AB)
Recapitalized as Ona International Inc. 06/05/2002
Each share Common no par exchanged for (0.2) share Common no par
Ona International Inc. name changed to Ona Exploration Inc. (AB) 08/06/2004 which reincorporated in British Columbia 01/30/2006 which name changed to Ona Energy Inc. 05/25/2007 which recapitalized as Ona Power Corp. 07/16/2009 which recapitalized as AAN Ventures Inc. 04/30/2012 which recapitalized as Parana Copper Corp. 08/28/2017 which name changed to Redfund Capital Corp. 08/14/2018

ONA ENERGY INC (BC)
Recapitalized as Ona Power Corp. 07/16/2009
Each share Common no par exchanged for (0.2) share Common no par
Ona Power Corp. recapitalized as AAN Ventures Inc. 04/30/2012 which recapitalized as Parana Copper Corp. 08/28/2017

ONA EXPL INC (BC)
Reincorporated 01/30/2006
Place of incorporation changed from (AB) to (BC) 01/30/2006
Name changed to Ona Energy Inc. 05/25/2007
Ona Energy Inc. recapitalized as Ona Power Corp. 07/16/2009 which recapitalized as AAN Ventures Inc. 04/30/2012 which recapitalized as Parana Copper Corp. 08/28/2017

ONA INTL INC (AB)
Reorganized as Ona Exploration Inc. (AB) 08/06/2004
Each share Common no par exchanged for (2) shares Common no par
Ona Exploration Inc. (AB) reincorporated in British Columbia 01/30/2006 which name changed to Ona Energy Inc. 05/25/2007 which recapitalized as Ona Power Corp. 07/16/2009 which recapitalized as AAN Ventures Inc. 04/30/2012 which recapitalized as Parana Copper Corp. 08/28/2017

ONA POWER CORP (BC)
Recapitalized as AAN Ventures Inc. 04/30/2012
Each share Common no par exchanged for (0.33333333) share Common no par
AAN Ventures Inc. recapitalized as Parana Copper Corp. 08/28/2017 which name changed to Redfund Capital Corp. 08/14/2018

ONACA EXPLS LTD (BC)
Name changed to Osec Petroleum Corp. in November 1977
Osec Petroleum Corp. recapitalized as ProAm Explorations Corp. 12/6/93

ONAN CORP (DE)
Majority acquired by Hawker Siddeley Overseas Investments Ltd. through purchase offer which expired 12/22/1975
Public interest eliminated

ONAPING MINES LTD (ON)
Name changed to Onaping Resources Ltd. 10/05/1978
Onaping Resources Ltd. merged into Durham Resources Inc. 03/28/1984 which name changed to Landmark Corp. (Old) 04/21/1987 which merged into Landmark Corp. (New) 01/31/1992 which recapitalized as Landmark Global Financial Corp. 07/05/1996

ONAPING RES LTD (ON)
Merged into Durham Resources Inc. 3/28/84
Each share Capital Stock no par exchanged for (1) share Subordinate Stock no par
Durham Resources Inc. name changed to Landmark Corp. (Old) 4/21/87 which merged into Landmark Corp. (New) 1/31/92 which recapitalized as Landmark Global Financial Corp. 7/5/96

ONASCO COS INC (WA)
Each share old Common $0.001 par exchanged for (0.05) share new Common $0.001 par 09/15/1992
Reorganized under the laws of Tennessee as Tengasco, Inc. 05/05/1995
Each share new Common $0.001 par exchanged for (0.5) share new Common $0.001 par
Tengasco, Inc. (TN) reincorporated in Delaware 06/28/2011

ONB CAP TR I (DE)
9.5% Trust Preferred Securities called for redemption at $25 on 5/23/2005

ONB CAP TR II (DE)
8% Trust Preferred Securities called for redemption at $25 on 12/15/2010

ONB CORP (DE)
Merged into Community Bank System, Inc. 12/1/2006
Each share Common no par exchanged for $210 cash

ONBANCORP INC (DE)
6.750% Conv. Preferred Ser. B $1 par called for redemption 1/8/97
Merged into First Empire State Corp. 4/1/98
Each share Common $1 par exchanged for either (0.161) share Common $5 par or $69.50 cash
Note: Option to receive stock expired 3/24/98
First Empire State Corp. name changed to M&T Bank Corp. 6/1/98

ONBUS TECHNOLOGIES INC. (AB)
Reorganized under the laws of British Columbia as Royal Monashee Gold Corp. 07/07/2006
Each share Common no par exchanged for (2) shares Common no par
Royal Monashee Gold Corp. name changed to Plus8 Global Ventures, Ltd. 11/07/2012 which name changed to ParcelPal Technology Inc. 03/22/2016

ONCBIO INC (NV)
Recapitalized as Stem Cell Ventures, Inc. 12/05/2005
Each share Common $0.001 par

exchanged for (0.125) share Common $0.001 par
Stem Cell Ventures, Inc. recapitalized as Pipejoin Technologies, Inc. 09/11/2007

ONCO PETE INC (CANADA)
Placed in receivership 03/31/2010
Stockholders' equity unlikely

ONCOGENE SCIENCE INC (DE)
Name changed to OSI Pharmaceuticals, Inc. 10/01/1997
(See OSI Pharmaceuticals, Inc.)

ONCOGENEX PHARMACEUTICALS INC (DE)
Recapitalized as Achieve Life Sciences, Inc. 08/03/2017
Each share Common $0.001 par exchanged for (0.09090909) share Common $0.001 par

ONCOLIN THERAPEUTICS INC (NV)
Recapitalized as Bering Exploration, Inc. 10/14/2010
Each share Common $0.001 par exchanged for (0.05) share Common $0.001 par
Bering Exploration, Inc. name changed to Breitling Energy Corp. 01/22/2014

ONCOLOGY LABS INC (DE)
Charter cancelled and declared inoperative and void for non-payment of taxes 3/1/84

ONCOLOGY MED INC (DE)
Recapitalized as Bellatora Inc. 09/28/2016
Each share Common $0.001 par exchanged for (0.00066666) share Common $0.001 par

ONCOLOGY MED INC (TX)
Recapitalized as Haz Holdings, Inc. (TX) 2/22/2007
Each share Common $0.001 par exchanged for (0.002) share Common $0.001 par
Haz Holdings, Inc. (TX) reincorporated in Delaware 3/15/2007

ONCOR INC (MD)
SEC revoked common stock registration 07/15/2008
Stockholders' equity unlikely

ONCORMED INC (DE)
Merged into Gene Logic Inc. 09/28/1998
Each share Common 1¢ par exchanged for (0.4673) share Common 1¢ par
Gene Logic Inc. name changed to Ore Pharmaceuticals Inc. 12/14/2007 which reorganized as Ore Pharmaceutical Holdings Inc. 10/21/2009 which reorganized as Ore Holdings Inc. 06/13/2011
(See Ore Holdings Inc.)

ONCORX INC (DE)
Name changed to Vion Pharmaceuticals, Inc. 04/29/1996
(See Vion Pharmaceuticals, Inc.)

ONCOTHERM CORP (CA)
Merged out of existence 11/30/92
Details not available

ONCOTHYREON INC (DE)
Name changed to Cascadian Therapeutics, Inc. 06/09/2016
(See Cascadian Therapeutics, Inc.)

ONCOURSE TECHNOLOGIES INC (NV)
Each share old Common $0.001 par exchanged for (0.06666666) share new Common $0.001 par 01/20/2006
SEC revoked common stock registration 10/09/2008

ONCTHERA INC (DE)
Name changed to Evolve Oncology Inc. 11/26/2003
Evolve Oncology Inc. recapitalized as Reparotech, Inc. 09/26/2007 which name changed to Nextrata Energy Inc. 01/07/2010

ONCURE MED CORP (DE)
Each (3,000) shares old Common $0.001 par exchanged for (1) share new Common $0.001 par 04/06/2004
Note: In effect holders received $0.15 cash per share and public interest was eliminated

ONCURE TECHNOLOGIES CORP (FL)
Reincorporated under the laws of Delaware as Oncure Medical Corp. 4/21/2003
(See Oncure Medical Corp.)

ONDAATJE LTD (ON)
Name changed to Global Equity Corp. 06/27/1996
Global Equity Corp. merged into PICO Holdings Inc. (CA) 12/16/1998 which reincorporated in Delaware 05/31/2017

ONDINE BIOMEDICAL INC (BC)
Merged into 0902337 B.C. Ltd. 09/06/2011
Each share Common no par exchanged for $0.33 cash
Note: Unexchanged certificates were cancelled and became without value 09/06/2017

ONDINE BIOPHARMA CORP (BC)
Recapitalized as Ondine Biomedical Inc. 10/14/2010
Each (15) shares Common no par exchanged for (1) share Common no par
(See Ondine Biomedical Inc.)

ONDISPLAY INC (DE)
Merged into Vignette Corp. 07/05/2000
Each share Common $0.001 par exchanged for (1.58) shares Common 1¢ par
Vignette Corp. merged into Open Text Corp. 07/22/2009

ONE AMERN CORP (LA)
Each share old Common $2.50 par exchanged for (0.0005) share new Common $2.50 par 11/19/2002
Note: In effect holders received $34 cash per share and public interest was eliminated

ONE BANCORP (ME)
Common $1 par split (2) for (1) by issuance of (1) additional share 4/15/86
Plan of reorganization under Chapter 11 Federal Bankruptcy Code effective 5/23/94
Stockholders' equity unlikely

ONE CLEAN PLANET INC (NV)
Common $0.001 par split (526.3) for (1) by issuance of (525.3) additional shares payable 02/27/2013 to holders of record 02/27/2013
Recapitalized as Kashin, Inc. 07/27/2015
Each share Common $0.001 par exchanged for (0.02857142) share Common $0.001 par

ONE CLICK VENTURES INC (BC)
Acquired by Lund Gold Ltd. 07/29/2003
Each share Common no par exchanged for (1) share Common no par
Lund Gold Ltd. recapitalized as Lund Enterprises Corp. 12/19/2013

ONE E-COMMERCE CORP (NV)
Recapitalized as Islet Sciences, Inc. 02/23/2012
Each (45) shares Common $0.001 par exchanged for (1) share Common $0.001 par

1-800-AUTOTOW INC (DE)
Recapitalized as Home Shopping Latino, Inc. 11/6/2006
Each share Common $0.001 par exchanged for (0.01) share Common $0.001 par

1-800-CONSUMER INTL INC (DE)
Recapitalized as ISA Internationale Inc. 05/09/1998
Each share Common $0.001 par exchanged for (0.5) share Common $0.0001 par

1-800 CONTACTS INC (DE)
Issue Information - 2,200,000 shares COM offered at $12.50 per share on 02/09/1998
Common 1¢ par split (2) for (1) by issuance of (1) additional share payable 08/01/2000 to holders of record 07/24/2000
Merged into Alta Parent Corp. 09/06/2007
Each share Common 1¢ par exchanged for $24.25 cash

180 CONNECT EXCHANGECO INC (CANADA)
Merged into DIRECTV Group, Inc. 07/09/2008
Each Exchangeable Share no par exchanged for $1.80 cash

180 CONNECT INC (CANADA)
Issue Information 5,702,200 shares COM offered at US$8 per share on 04/16/2004
Merged into 180 Connect Inc. (DE) 08/24/2007
Each share Common no par exchanged for (0.6) share Common $0.0001 par
(See 180 Connect Inc. (DE))

180 CONNECT INC (DE)
Merged into DIRECTV Group, Inc. 07/09/2008
Each share Common $0.0001 par exchanged for $1.80 cash

180 E. 79TH ST. CORP. (NY)
Merged into Great American Realty Corp. 6/10/65
Each share Common 10¢ par exchanged for $10.28 in cash

188 RANDOLPH BLDG CORP (IL)
In process of liquidation
Each share Common no par received initial distribution of $150 cash 04/01/1982
Assets transferred to 188 Randolph Liquidation Trust 08/16/1982
(See 188 Randolph Liquidation Trust)

188 RANDOLPH BLDG. LIQUIDATION TRUST (IL)
Property transferred and each Trust Certificate exchanged for (1) share Common no par of 188 Randolph Building Corp. 5/20/59
188 Randolph Building Corp. assets transferred to 188 Randoplh Liquidation Trust 8/16/82
(See 188 Randolph Liquidation Trust)

188 RANDOLPH LIQUIDATION TRUST (IL)
Liquidation completed
Each share Common no par exchanged for second distribution of $110 cash 8/17/82
Each share Common no par received third and final distribution of $11.04 cash 9/24/84
(See Randolph Building Corp. for previous distribution)

111 PENN CORP. (CA)
Liquidation completed
Each share Common $1 par received initial distribution of $5.85 cash 3/15/67
Each share Common $1 par received second distribution of $6.59 cash 1/18/68
Each share Common $1 par exchanged for third and final distribution of $0.74 cash 6/12/72

111 RLTY CORP (IN)
Merged into American Fletcher Corp. 5/4/70
Each share Common $1 par exchanged for (1/3) share Common $10 par
American Fletcher Corp. merged into Banc One Corp. (DE) 1/26/87 which reincorporated in Ohio 5/1/89 which merged into Bank One Corp. 10/2/98 which into J.P. Morgan Chase & Co. 12/31/2000 which name changed to JPMorgan Chase & Co. 7/20/2004

ONE EXPL INC (AB)
Each share Class B Common no par reclassified as (10) shares Class A Common no par 02/01/2010
Recapitalized as TriOil Resources Ltd. 04/07/2010
Each share Class A Common no par exchanged for (0.05) share Class A Common no par
(See TriOil Resources Ltd.)

ONE FAMILY INVT INC (FL)
Acquired by OneFamily.com, Inc. 11/08/1999
Each share Common no par exchanged for (0.66) share Common
Note: Company is now private

ONE FD INC (MD)
Plan of liquidation effective 11/15/2002
Each Core Growth Portfolio exchanged for net asset value
Each Growth Portfolio exchanged for net asset value
Each Income & Growth Portfolio exchanged for net asset value
Each Income Portfolio exchanged for net asset value
Each Income Portfolio exchanged for net asset value
Each Money Market Portfolio exchanged for net asset value
Each S&P 500 Index Portfolio exchanged for net asset value
Each Small Capital Portfolio exchanged for net asset value

ONE FI TECHNOLOGY INC (NV)
Each share old Common $0.001 par exchanged for (0.0002) share new Common $0.001 par 07/01/2010
Recapitalized as Seesmart Technologies, Inc. 02/17/2012
Each share new Common $0.001 par exchanged for (0.0001) share Common $0.001 par
(See Seesmart Technologies, Inc.)

1 GLOBAL CITY INC (FL)
Name changed 02/18/2001
Name changed from 1 Global City.Com, Inc. to 1 Global City, Inc. 02/18/2001
Each share old Common $0.001 par exchanged for (0.33333333) share new Common $0.001 par 02/18/2002
Administratively dissolved 09/19/2003

ONE GROUP (MA)
Merged into JPMorgan Trust II 02/19/2005
Details not available

ONE HLDGS CORP (FL)
Recapitalized as ONE Bio, Corp. 11/17/2009
Each share Common 1¢ par exchanged for (0.2) share Common $0.001 par

ONE HORIZON GROUP INC (PA)
Reorganized under the laws of Delaware 08/29/2013
Each share Common $0.0001 par exchanged for (0.00166666) share Common $0.0001 par

ONE HOUR CLEANERS, INC. (MN)
Thru voluntary purchase offer 100% reacquired in 1973

ONE HOUR VALET INC (DE)
Name changed to Uniservices, Inc. 2/24/65
(See Uniservices, Inc.)

ONE HUNDRED & ONE FD INC (MD)
Name changed to Berger One Hundred & One Fund, Inc. 01/09/1996
Berger One Hundred & One Fund, Inc. name changed to Berger Growth & Income Fund, Inc. 01/31/2000 which name changed to Berger Large Cap Growth Fund, Inc. 01/29/2001 which merged into Janus Investment Fund 04/21/2003

ONE HUNDRED ASSOCIATES OF AMERICA, INC. (NV)
Charter revoked for failure to file reports and pay fees 3/4/63

ONE HUNDRED FD INC (MD)
Name changed to Berger Growth Fund, Inc. 01/28/2000
Berger Growth Fund, Inc. merged into Janus Investment Fund 04/21/2003

100 NORTH LA SALLE STR BLDG CORP (IL)
Dissolved 00/00/1968
Details not available

101 WEST JEFFERSON LIQUIDATING CORP. (MD)
Liquidation completed
Each share Class A Common 20¢ par exchanged for initial distribution of (0.018518) share Litton Industies, Inc. Common $1 par 09/15/1968
Each share Class A Common 20¢ par received second and final distribution of (0.021978) share Litton Industries, Inc. Common $1 par 09/21/1971
(See Litton Industries, Inc.)

103RD STREET & WEST END AVENUE, INC. (NY)
Dissolved by proclamation of the Secretary of State 12/16/63
Capital Stock is valueless

103 PRINCE STREET CORP. (NY)
Dissolved by Court Order 4/11/55

ONE IP VOICE INC (DE)
SEC revoked common stock registration 08/19/2011

ONE LA SALLE CO. (IL)
Voluntarily dissolved 5/29/61
Details not available

1 LANE TECHNOLOGIES CORP (DE)
Common $0.0001 par split (5) for (1) by issuance of (4) additional shares payable 08/01/2008 to holders of record 07/31/2008 Ex date - 08/04/2008
Name changed to Adama Technologies Corp. 03/20/2009

ONE LIBERTY FIRESTONE PROPERTIES, INC. (MD)
Name changed to One Liberty Properties, Inc. 10/21/85

ONE LIBERTY PPTYS INC (MD)
$1.60 Conv. Preferred $1 par called for redemption at $16.50 on 12/30/2003
(Additional Information in Active)

ONE LINK 4 TRAVEL INC (DE)
Name changed to OneLink Corp. 3/15/2006

1-900 JACKPOT INC (NV)
Each share old Common $0.001 par exchanged for (0.01351351) share new Common $0.001 par 04/04/2006
New Common $0.001 par split (10) for (1) by issuance of (9) additional shares payable 08/15/2007 to holders of record 07/31/2007 Ex date - 08/16/2007
Name changed to Exmocare, Inc. 03/07/2008
Exmocare, Inc. name changed to Second Solar, Inc. 07/01/2009
(See Second Solar, Inc.)

119 WEST AUSTIN CORP. (IL)
Liquidated for cash 6/16/64

ONE PERSON HEALTH SCIENCES INC (CANADA)
Name changed to HealthPricer Interactive Ltd. 10/17/2006
HealthPricer Interactive Ltd. recapitalized as Disani Capital Corp. (Canada) 03/18/2013 which reorganized in British Columbia as NeutriSci International Inc. 12/04/2014

1 POTATO 2 INC (MN)
Reorganized under Chapter 11 Federal Bankruptcy Code
Each share old Common 1¢ par received distribution of (0.05) share new Common 1¢ par 10/28/1986
Note: Certificates were not required to be surrendered and are without value
Each share new Common 1¢ par exchanged for (0.001) share Common $500 par 11/04/1987
Note: In effect holders received $0.50 cash per share and public interest was eliminated

ONE PRICE CLOTHING STORES INC (DE)
Common 1¢ par split (3) for (2) by issuance of (0.5) additional share 10/15/87
Common 1¢ par split (3) for (2) by issuance of (0.5) additional share 4/29/94
Each (3.5) shares old Common 1¢ par exchanged for (1) share new Common 1¢ par 9/5/2001
Chapter 11 Bankruptcy proceedings converted to Chapter 7 on 3/23/2005
Stockholders' equity unlikely

ONE PUNCH PRODTNS INC (DE)
Name changed to Caltas Fitness, Inc. 08/21/2006
Caltas Fitness, Inc. name changed to Cinemaya Media Group, Inc. 02/06/2007 which recapitalized as SNM Global Holdings 11/14/2008

117-14 UNION TURNPIKE, INC.
Dissolved in 1941

117 W. 70TH STREET CORP.
Liquidated in 1950

ONE SIGNATURE FINL CORP (ON)
Delisted from CNQ 04/26/2007

165 BROADWAY BUILDING, INC. (NY)
Reorganized 5/1/60
Each share Common $1 par exchanged for (1) share Class C Common 10¢ par
Property sold and all classes of stock declared worthless 12/12/63

162 EAST OHIO ST. HOTEL CORP.
Name changed to St. Clair Hotel, Inc. in 1944 which liquidated in 1948

162 EAST ONTARIO ST. HOTEL CORP.
Name changed to Eastgate Hotel, Inc. 00/00/1945
(See Eastgate Hotel, Inc.)

ONE STOP COM INC (FL)
Name changed 09/17/1999
Name changed from One Stop Car of Florida, Inc. to One Stop.com, Inc. 09/17/1999
Reincorporated under the laws of Delaware as Metiscan, Inc. 11/18/2008
Metiscan, Inc. recapitalized as Aclor International, Inc. 01/04/2012
(See Aclor International, Inc.)

ONE STOP FOOD MARTS INC (DE)
Adjudicated bankrupt 11/17/1970
Stockholders' equity unlikely

ONE STOP INC (NV)
Charter revoked for failure to file reports and pay fees 03/04/1974

110 LIVINGSTON STREET CORP. (NY)
Completely liquidated 1/11/37

Each share Common $1 par exchanged for first and final distribution of $10 cash

110 MEDIA GROUP INC (DE)
Old Common $0.0001 par split (7) for (4) by issuance of (0.75) additional share payable 07/16/2004 to holders of record 07/09/2004 Ex date - 07/19/2004
Each (15) shares old Common $0.0001 par exchanged for (1) share new Common $0.0001 par 10/04/2005
Name changed to Web2 Corp. 07/31/2006
Web2 Corp. recapitalized as Full Motion Beverage, Inc. 12/08/2008

135 WEST MAGNOLIA BOULEVARD CORP. (CA)
Liquidation completed
Each share Common no par exchanged for initial distribution of (0.1682) share $1 Preference $2 par and (0.5045) share Common $1 par of Dynamics Corp. of America (NY) 4/26/63
Each share Common no par received second and final distribution of (0.0533) share Common $1 par of Dynamics Corp. of America (NY) 4/5/66
Dynamics Corp. of America (NY) merged into CTS Corp. 10/16/97

133 GEARY CORP.
Liquidated in 1938

ONE TOUCH TOTAL DEVELOPMENT INC (NV)
Name changed 06/10/2004
Name changed from One Touch Total Communications Inc. to One Touch Total Development Inc. 06/10/2004
Name changed to Carbon Jungle, Inc. 03/27/2006
Carbon Jungle, Inc. recapitalized as Global New Energy Industries Inc. 01/17/2013 which name changed to Coin Citadel 11/06/2014

125 EAST 63RD STREET, INC. (NY)
Dissolved 2/27/58

124 FIFTH AVENUE CORP. (NY)
Certificate of voluntary dissolution filed with State of New York 5/5/52

123 INTL SOFTWARE INC (BC)
Name changed to Environmental Earth Solutions, Ltd. 8/26/2005
Environmental Earth Solutions, Ltd. name changed to Environmental Capital, Ltd. 9/9/2005 which name changed to Mobiclear Technologies, Ltd. 1/9/2006

ONE UP CORP (FL)
Name changed to MigraTEC Inc. (FL) 3/19/98
MigraTEC Inc. (FL) reincorporated in Delaware 8/11/2000
(See MigraTEC Inc.)

ONE VY BANCORP INC (WV)
Name changed 04/30/1996
Common $10 par split (3) for (2) by issuance of (0.5) additional share 03/25/1986
Common $10 par split (3) for (2) by issuance of (0.5) additional share 11/23/1987
Common $10 par split (3) for (2) by issuance of (0.5) additional share 05/15/1992
Common $10 par split (6) for (5) by issuance of (0.2) additional share 02/15/1993
Under plan of merger name changed from One Valley Bancorp of West Virginia, Inc. to One Valley Bancorp, Inc. 04/30/1996
Common $10 par split (5) for (4) by issuance of (0.25) additional share payable 10/09/1996 to holders of record 09/30/1996
Common $10 par split (5) for (4) by issuance of (0.25) additional share payable 09/12/1997 to holders of record 08/29/1997 Ex date - 09/15/1997
Merged into BB&T Corp. 07/06/2000
Each share Common $10 par exchanged for (1.28) shares Common $5 par

ONE VOICE TECHNOLOGIES INC (NV)
Each share old Common $0.001 par exchanged for (0.05) share new Common $0.001 par 06/16/2009
SEC revoked common stock registration 06/28/2012

1 WEST 39TH STREET CORP. (NY)
Liquidation completed 11/10/60

ONE WORLD ENTMT CORP (DE)
Each share Common $0.0001 par exchanged for (0.1) share Common 1¢ par 01/02/1987
Name changed to Sun Scientific Group, Inc. 04/07/1987
(See Sun Scientific Group, Inc.)

ONE WORLD HLDGS INC (NV)
Each share old Common $0.0025 par exchanged for (0.00133333) share new Common $0.0025 par 01/13/2014
Name changed to Tonner-One World Holdings, Inc. and new Common $0.0025 par changed to $0.001 par 07/28/2016

ONE WORLD INVTS INC (BC)
Name changed to One World Minerals Inc. 02/28/2017
One World Minerals Inc. name changed to One World Lithium Inc. 01/19/2018

ONE WORLD MINERALS INC (BC)
Name changed to One World Lithium Inc. 01/19/2018

ONE WORLD ONLINE COM INC (UT)
Ceased operations 07/25/2001
Stockholders' equity unlikely

ONEAL JONES & FELDMAN INC (MO)
Common no par split (2) for (1) by issuance of (1) additional share 08/08/1973
Merged into Chromalloy American Corp. (DE) 01/13/1978
Each share Common no par exchanged for (0.0645161) share $5 Conv. Preferred $1 par
Chromalloy American Corp. (DE) merged into Sun Chemical Corp. 12/23/1986 which name changed to Sequa Corp. 05/08/1987
(See Sequa Corp.)

ONEBEACON INS GROUP LTD (BERMUDA)
Acquired by Intact Financial Corp. 09/28/2017
Each share Class A Common 1¢ par exchanged for USD$18.10 cash

ONECAP (NV)
Each share old Common $0.001 par exchanged for (1/7) share new Common $0.001 par 12/29/2003
Acquired by OneCap Holdings Inc. 02/01/2006
Each share new Common $0.001 par exchanged for $7.84 cash

ONECAP INVT CORP (CANADA)
Name changed to Origin Gold Corp. 07/23/2018

ONECARD HEALTH SYS CORP (DE)
Charter cancelled and declared inoperative and void for non-payment of taxes 3/1/99

ONECARD INTL INC (DE)
Charter cancelled and declared inoperative and void for non-payment of taxes 3/1/91

ONECENTRAL BK (GLENDALE, CA)
Merged into Glendale Federal Bank, FSB (Glendale, CA) 1/31/97

ONE-ONE

Each share Common $5 par exchanged for $9.50 cash

ONECLASS SYNERGY CORP (DE)
Recapitalized as ABCI Holdings Inc. (DE) 08/13/2001
Each share Common $0.16666666 par exchanged for (0.02) share Common $0.16666666 par
ABCI Holdings Inc. (DE) reorganized in Nevada as Metaphor Corp. 01/06/2005 which name changed to China Media Networks International, Inc. 08/25/2005 which name changed to Medical Solutions Management Inc. 08/04/2006
(See Medical Solutions Management Inc.)

ONECOMM CORP (DE)
Acquired by Nextel Communications, Inc. 07/31/1995
Each share Common $0.001 par exchanged for (1.077) shares Common $0.001 par
Nextel Communications, Inc. merged into Sprint Nextel Corp. 08/12/2005 which merged into Sprint Corp. (DE) 07/10/2013

ONEDENTIST RES INC (CO)
Each share old Common no par exchanged for (0.1) share new Common no par 01/06/2003
Recapitalized as Ashcroft Homes Corp. 03/28/2003
Each (3.5) shares new Common no par exchanged for (1) share Common no par
(See Ashcroft Homes Corp.)

ONEGO CORP (PA)
Adjudicated bankrupt 02/20/1968
No stockholders' equity

ONEIDA COMMUNITY LTD.
Name changed to Oneida Ltd. 00/00/1934
(See Oneida Ltd.)

ONEIDA ENERGY & RES CORP (ON)
Merged into Consolidated Dixie Resources Inc. 08/31/1987
Each share Common no par exchanged for (2/3) share Common no par
Consolidated Dixie Resources Inc. recapitalized as United Dixie Resources Inc. 12/15/1992 which merged into United Pacific Capital Resources Corp. 03/12/1998
(See United Pacific Capital Resources Corp.)

ONEIDA FINANCE CORP.
Liquidated in 1945

ONEIDA FINL CORP (MD)
Merged into Community Bank System, Inc. 12/04/2015
Each share Common 1¢ par exchanged for $20 cash

ONEIDA FINL CORP (USA)
Reincorporated 07/18/2001
Place of incorporation changed from (DE) to (USA) and Common 10¢ par changed to 1¢ par 07/18/2001
Common 1¢ par split (3) for (2) by issuance of (0.5) additional share payable 04/23/2002 to holders of record 04/09/2002 Ex date - 04/24/2002
Common 1¢ par split (3) for (2) by issuance of (0.5) additional share payable 02/24/2004 to holders of record 02/10/2004 Ex date - 02/25/2004
Reorganized under the laws of Maryland 07/07/2010
Each share Common 1¢ par exchanged for (0.9136) share Common 1¢ par
(See Oneida Financial Corp. (MD))

ONEIDA GEN CORP (UT)
Each share old Common no par exchanged for (1/3) share new Common 1¢ par 02/25/1985
Each share new Common 1¢ par exchanged for (0.02) share Common no par 08/31/1995
Name changed to Communitronics of America, Inc. (UT) 10/26/1998
Communitronics of America, Inc. (UT) reorganized in Nevada as RPM Advantage, Inc. 04/12/2006
(See RPM Advantage, Inc.)

ONEIDA HEATER INC (NY)
Each share Common 50¢ par exchanged for (0.01) share Common $50 par 1/12/65
Charter cancelled and proclaimed dissolved for failure to pay taxes 3/25/92

ONEIDA LTD (NY)
7% Preferred called for redemption 9/15/44
Common $12.50 par changed to $6.25 par and (1) additional share issued 7/1/64
Common $6.25 par split (5) for (4) by issuance of (0.25) additional share 8/12/77
Common $6.25 par split (5) for (4) by issuance of (0.25) additional share 6/14/78
Common $6.25 par split (2) for (1) by issuance of (1) additional share 3/13/80
Common $6.25 par split (5) for (4) by issuance of (0.25) additional share 12/12/80
Common $6.25 par split (5) for (4) by issuance of (0.25) additional share 7/15/87
Common $6.25 par split (3) for (2) by issuance of (0.5) additional share payable 12/30/97 to holders of record 12/10/97
Stock Dividends - 100% 1/1/66; 20% 12/23/66; 10% 12/15/88; 10% 12/15/89
Plan of reorganization under Chapter 11 Federal Bankruptcy Code effective 9/15/2006
No stockholders' equity

ONEIDA NATL BK & TR CO CENT N Y (UTICA, NY)
Common $10 par split (2) for (1) by issuance of (1) additional share 7/31/78
Stock Dividends - 10% 1/24/64; 40% 2/25/66; 50% 2/28/69; 10% 4/5/77
Merged into Norstar Bancorp Inc. 2/1/82
Each share Common $10 par exchanged for (2) shares Common $5 par
Norstar Bancorp Inc. merged into Fleet/Norstar Financial Group, Inc. 1/1/88 which name changed to Fleet Financial Group, Inc. (New) 4/15/92 which name changed to Fleet Boston Corp. 10/1/99 which name changed to FleetBoston Financial Corp. 4/18/2000 which merged into Bank of America Corp. 4/1/2004

ONEIDA PERLITE CORP. (UT)
Merged into Oglebay Norton Co. in December, 1986
Each share Capital Stock $1 par exchanged for cash

ONEIDA RESOURCES CORP. (BC)
Merged into New Frontier Petroleum Corp. 01/18/1982
Each share Common no par exchanged for (0.2) share Common no par
New Frontier Petroleum Corp. recapitalized as PetroMac Energy Inc. 08/30/1985
(See PetroMac Energy Inc.)

ONEIDA RES INC (BC)
Cease trade order effective 5/4/94
Stockholders' equity unlikely

ONEIDA VY BANCSHARES INC (NY)
Common $5 par changed to $2.50 par and (1) additional share issued 10/31/1988
Stock Dividends - 10% 08/01/1985; 10% 04/24/1987; 10% 10/19/1990; 10% 05/22/1992; 10% 06/01/1994
Merged into Alliance Financial Corp. 11/25/1998
Each share Common $2.50 par exchanged for (1.8) shares Common $1 par
Alliance Financial Corp. merged into NBT Bancorp Inc. 03/08/2013

ONEIDA VALLEY NATL BK (ONEIDA, NY)
Capital Stock $25 par changed to $10 par and (1.5) additional shares issued 01/22/1965
Stock Dividends - 60% 12/16/1949; 12-1/2% 07/31/1970; (1) for (9) 04/00/1972; 10% 03/01/1976; (1) for (8) 04/25/1980; (1) for (9) 07/26/1982
Reorganized as Oneida Valley Bancshares, Inc. 10/31/1984
Each share Capital Stock $10 par exchanged for (2) shares Common $5 par
Oneida Valley Bancshares, Inc. merged into Alliance Financial Corp. 11/25/1998 which merged into NBT Bancorp Inc. 03/08/2013

ONEIL FD (CA)
Merged into Selected Special Shares, Inc. 05/07/1975
Each share Common $1 par exchanged for (0.9232) share Common 25¢ par
Selected Special Shares, Inc. name changed to Selected International Fund, Inc. 05/01/2011

ONEIL INSTL FD (CA)
Name changed to OIF Fund 5/15/70
(See OIF Fund)

ONEITA INDS INC (DE)
Chapter 11 bankruptcy proceedings converted to Chapter 7 on 8/13/2000
Stockholders' equity unlikely

ONEITA KNITTING MLS (NY)
7% Preferred $100 par changed to 4-1/2% Preferred $100 par in 1946
Each share Common $100 par exchanged for (4) shares Common $25 par in 1946
Each share 4-1/2% Preferred $100 par exchanged for (1) share 6% Preferred $50 par and (1) share Part. Non-Vtg. Stock $25 par in 1956
Common $25 par changed to $1 par in 1956
Each share Part. Non-Vtg. Stock $25 par exchanged for (4) shares Common $2 par 6/26/68
Each share Common $1 par exchanged for (4) shares Common $2 par 6/26/68
6% Preferred $50 par called for redemption 9/1/68
Common $2 par split (2) for (1) by issuance of (1) additional share 3/1/73
Common $2 par split (8) for (1) by issuance of (7) additional shares 9/1/83
Acquired by Instrument Systems Corp. 10/10/84
Each share Common $2 par exchanged for $7 cash

ONELIFE HEALTH PRODS INC (NV)
Name changed to Crown Oil & Gas Inc. 01/28/2008
(See Crown Oil & Gas Inc.)

ONELINK COMMUNICATIONS INC (MN)
Recapitalized as OneLink Inc. 12/01/2003
Each share Common 1¢ par exchanged for (0.33333333) share Common 1¢ par
OneLink Inc. name changed to Spectre Gaming, Inc. 01/22/2004
(See Spectre Gaming, Inc.)

ONELINK INC (MN)
Name changed to Spectre Gaming, Inc. 01/22/2004
(See Spectre Gaming, Inc.)

ONEMAINCOM INC (DE)
Merged into EarthLink, Inc. 09/12/2000
Each share Common $0.001 par exchanged for (0.3562) share Common 1¢ par
EarthLink, Inc. name changed to EarthLink Holdings Corp. 01/02/2014 which merged into Windstream Holdings, Inc. 02/27/2017

ONEMOVE TECHNOLOGIES INC (BC)
Each share old Common no par exchanged for (0.1) share new Common no par 08/28/2012
Acquired by Plantro Ltd. 06/10/2013
Each share new Common no par exchanged for $0.425 cash
Note: Unexchanged certificates will be cancelled and become without value 06/10/2019

ONEOK INC (DE)
Common no par split (2) for (1) by issuance of (1) additional share 02/28/1990
4.75% Preferred Ser. A $50 par called for redemption at $53 plus accrued dividends on 04/30/1997
Merged into ONEOK, Inc. (New) 11/26/1997
Each share Common no par exchanged for (1) share Common 1¢ par

ONEOK INC NEW (OK)
Each 8.5% Corporate Unit received (1.2119) shares Common 1¢ par 02/16/2006
(Additional Information in Active)

ONEOK PARTNERS L P (DE)
Common Units split (2) for (1) by issuance of (1) additional Unit payable 07/12/2011 to holders of record 06/30/2011 Ex date - 07/13/2011
Merged into ONEOK, Inc. (New) 06/30/2017
Each Common Unit exchanged for (0.985) share Common 1¢ par

ONEREIT (ON)
Acquired by Smart Real Estate Investment Trust 10/05/2017
Each Trust Unit exchanged for $4.275 cash

161671 CANADA INC. (CANADA)
Proclaimed dissolved 3/22/96

ONESOURCE INFORMATION SVCS INC (DE)
Issue Information - 3,636,000 shares COM offered at $12 per share on 05/19/1999
Merged into infoUSA Inc. 06/09/2004
Each share Common 1¢ par exchanged for $8.85 cash

ONESOURCE TECHNOLOGIES INC (DE)
SEC revoked common stock registration 12/23/2015

ONESTEEL LTD (AUSTRALIA)
Name changed to Arrium Ltd. 07/17/2012

1STOPSALE COM HLDGS INC (DE)
Recapitalized as Global Energy Group, Inc. 10/12/2001
Each share Common 2¢ par exchanged for (0.05) share Common $0.001 par
(See Global Energy Group, Inc.)

ONETRAVEL HLDGS INC (DE)
Each share old Common 4¢ par exchanged for (0.1) share new Common 4¢ par 07/07/2005
Chapter 11 bankruptcy proceedings converted to Chapter 7 on 12/19/2006

No stockholders' equity

1TWOE COM INC (NV)
Recapitalized as DMT Energy Inc.
06/23/2003
Each (800) shares Common $0.001
par exchanged for (1) share
Common $0.001 par
(See DMT Energy Inc.)

ONEWAVE INC (DE)
Name changed to Primix Solutions
Inc. 9/11/98
(See Primix Solutions Inc.)

ONEWORLD SYS INC (DE)
Each share old Common $0.001 par
exchanged for (0.1) share new
Common $0.001 par 07/06/1999
Assets sold for the benefit of creditors
04/28/2000
No stockholders' equity

ONEX PACKAGING INC (ON)
Merged into Ball-Onex Packaging
Corp. 12/08/1988
Each share Subordinate no par
exchanged for $11 cash

1068877 BC LTD (BC)
Name changed to Whistler Blackcomb
Holdings Inc. (New) 10/20/2016

ONFEM HLDGS LTD (HONG KONG)
ADR agreement terminated
06/15/2007
Each Sponsored ADR for Ordinary
HK$0.10 par exchanged for
$1.83693 cash

ONGARD SYS INC (DE)
SEC revoked common stock
registration 10/22/2008
Stockholders' equity unlikely

ONHEALTH NETWORK CO (MN)
Merged into WebMD Corp.
09/12/2000
Each share Common 1¢ par
exchanged for (0.189435) share
Common $0.001 par
WebMD Corp. name changed to
Emdeon Corp. 10/17/2005 which
name changed to HLTH Corp.
05/21/2007 which merged into
WebMD Health Corp. 10/23/2009
(See WebMD Health Corp.)

ONI INTL INC (DE)
Liquidation completed
Each share Common no par
exchanged for initial distribution of
$4.75 cash 2/20/95
Each share Common no par received
second distribution of $1.25 cash
10/10/95
Each share Common no par received
third distribution of $0.50 cash
10/25/96
Each share Common no par received
fourth distribution of $0.90 cash
10/17/97
Each share Common no par received
fifth distribution of $0.2021 cash
4/29/98
Each share Common no par received
sixth distribution of $0.07 cash in
January 1999
Each share Common no par received
seventh and final distribution of
$15.32 cash payable 1/29/2002 to
holders of record 1/29/2002

ONI SYS CORP (DE)
Issue Information - 8,000,000 shares
COM offered at $25 per share on
05/31/2000
Merged into CIENA Corp. 6/21/2002
Each share Common $0.0001 par
exchanged for (0.7104) share
Common 1¢ par

ONITAP RES INC (CANADA)
Recapitalized as Red Oak Resources
Inc. 9/30/92
Each share Common no par
exchanged for (0.0655173) share
Common no par
Red Oak Resources Inc. merged into
Neutrino Resources Inc. 10/6/95
(See Neutrino Resources Inc.)

ONIX SYS INC (DE)
Issue Information - 3,300,000 shares
COM offered at $14.50 per share on
03/24/98
Merged into Thermo Instrument
Systems Inc. 4/13/2000
Each share Common 1¢ par
exchanged for $9 cash

ONLINE CONSORTIUM CORP (BC)
Each share old Common no par
exchanged for (0.33333333) share
new Common no par 02/21/2002
Name changed to Equicap Financial
Corp. 07/10/2003
Equicap Financial Corp. name
changed to Zecotek Medical
Systems, Inc. 02/10/2005 which
name changed to Zecotek Photonics
Inc. 11/26/2007

ONLINE CR INTL LTD (HONG KONG)
Sponsored ADR's for Ordinary split
(10) for (1) by issuance of (9)
additional ADR's payable
02/22/2000 to holders of record
02/18/2000
Name changed to Heng Fung
Holdings Ltd. 11/16/2001
Heng Fung Holdings Ltd. name
changed to China Credit Holdings
Ltd. 02/01/2005 which name
changed to Xpress Group Ltd.
06/13/2007 which name changed to
Heng Fai Enterprises Ltd.
10/22/2013
(See Heng Fai Enterprises Ltd.)

ONLINE DIRECT INC (CANADA)
Dissolved for non-compliance
09/19/2003

ONLINE ENERGY INC (AB)
Acquired by Madalena Ventures Inc.
11/01/2012
Each share Common no par
exchanged for $0.35 cash

ONLINE ENTMT INC (NV)
Each share old Common no par
exchanged for (0.1) share new
Common no par 07/29/1996
Name changed to Online Power
Supply Inc. 12/14/1999
(See Online Power Supply Inc.)

ONLINE GAMING SYS LTD (DE)
Name changed to Advanced
Resources Group, Ltd. 02/15/2007

ONLINE HEARING DOT COM CO (FL)
Name changed to Rompus Interactive
Corp. 07/30/1999
(See Rompus Interactive Corp.)

ONLINE HLDGS INC (NV)
Name changed to Standard Drilling,
Inc. 10/02/2006
Standard Drilling, Inc. recapitalized as
EFactor Group Corp. 11/04/2013

ONLINE INNOVATION INC (DE)
Name changed to Moventis Capital,
Inc. 02/14/2006
(See Moventis Capital, Inc.)

ONLINE INTL CORP (NV)
Name changed to Finotec Group Inc.
2/14/2002

ONLINE NETWORK INC (DE)
Charter cancelled and declared
inoperative and void for
non-payment of taxes 3/1/90

ONLINE ORIGINALS INC (NV)
Common $0.001 par split (30) for (1)
by issuance of (29) additional
shares payable 09/01/2010 to
holders of record 08/10/2010
Ex date - 09/02/2010
Name changed to Creenergy Corp.
09/08/2010
Creenergy Corp. name changed to
Peptide Technologies, Inc.
10/25/2011

ONLINE PWR SUPPLY INC (NV)
Chapter 7 bankruptcy proceedings
terminated 05/23/2011

No stockholders' equity

ONLINE PROCESSING INC (NV)
Each share Common $0.001 par
exchanged for (0.6) share Common
$0.001 par 02/22/2006
Name changed to Diguang
International Development Co., Ltd.
03/07/2006

ONLINE PRODTN SVCS INC (NV)
Recapitalized as Wavenetworx, Inc.
08/26/2004
Each share Common $0.001 par
exchanged for (0.02) share Common
no par
Wavenetworx, Inc. recapitalized as
Clear Peak Energy, Inc. 03/15/2010

ONLINE RES CORP (DE)
Name changed 09/11/2000
Name changed from Online
Resources & Communications Corp.
to Online Resources Corp.
09/11/2000
Acquired by ACI Worldwide Inc.
03/11/2013
Each share Common $0.0001 par
exchanged for $3.85 cash

ONLINE SALES STRATEGIES INC (FL)
Recapitalized as Growth Technologies
International, Inc. 12/20/2007
Each share Common $0.001 par
exchanged for (0.004) share
Common $0.001 par
Growth Technologies International,
Inc. recapitalized as Alternafuels,
Inc. 03/18/2011
(See Alternafuels, Inc.)

ONLINE SECRETARY INC (NV)
Reorganized as SharkReach, Inc.
11/05/2015
Each share Common $0.001 par
exchanged for (83) shares Common
$0.001 par

ONLINE SYS SVCS INC (CO)
Name changed to Webb Interactive
Services Inc. 09/09/1999
Webb Interactive Services, Inc. name
changed to Web Global Holdings,
Inc. 06/01/2018

ONLINE TELE-SOLUTIONS INC (NV)
Each share Common $0.001 par
exchanged for (30) shares Common
$0.0001 par 05/09/2012
Name changed to Tungsten Corp.
12/03/2012

ONLINE TRANSACTION SYS INC (NV)
Name changed to Delta Mining &
Exploration Corp. 01/28/2004
(See Delta Mining & Exploration Corp.)

ONLINE YEARBOOK (NV)
Name changed to RMR Industrials,
Inc. 12/08/2014

ONLINEOFFICE COM INC. (CO)
Adminstratively dissolved 3/1/2002

ONLINETRADING COM GROUP INC (FL)
Under plan of merger name changed
to TradeStation Group, Inc.
12/29/2000
(See TradeStation Group, Inc.)

ONLINETRADINGINC COM CORP (FL)
Issue Information - 2,250,000 shares
COM offered at $7 per share on
06/11/1999
Merged into TradeStation Group, Inc.
12/29/2000
Each share Common 1¢ par
exchanged for (1.7172) shares
Common 1¢ par

ONODA CEM LTD (JAPAN)
Name changed to Chichibu Onoda
Cement Corp. 9/6/95
Chichibu Onoda Cement Corp. name
changed to Taiheiyo Cement Corp.
10/1/98

ONOMEA SUGAR CO. (HI)
Common $20 par changed to $5 par
in 1959
Merged into Mauna Kea Sugar Co.,
Inc. 7/26/65
Each share Common $5 par
exchanged for (1) share Common
$10 par
(See Mauna Kea Sugar Co., Inc.)

ONONDAGA HOTEL CORP.
Insolvent 00/00/1944
Stockholders' equity unlikely

ONONDAGA POTTERY CO. (NY)
Name changed to Syracuse China
Corp. 1/18/66
Syracuse China Corp. name changed
to Fayette-Court Corp. 11/23/71
which completed liquidation 9/21/73

ONONDAGA SVGS BK (SYRACUSE, NY)
Reorganized under the laws of
Delaware as Onbancorp, Inc.
9/18/89
Each share Common $1 par
exchanged for (1) share Common
$1 par
Onbancorp, Inc. merged into First
Empire State Corp. 4/1/98 which
name changed to M&T Bank Corp.
6/1/98

ONSALE INC (DE)
Issue Information - 2,500,000 shares
COM offered at $6 per share on
04/17/1997
Under plan of merger name changed
to Egghead.Com, Inc. 11/22/99
(See Egghead.Com, Inc.)

ONSCREEN TECHNOLOGIES INC (CO)
Name changed to Waytronx, Inc.
01/07/2008
Waytronx, Inc. name changed to CUI
Global, Inc. 01/04/2011

ONSET CORP (DE)
Charter cancelled and declared
inoperative and void for
non-payment of taxes 04/15/1972

ONSINO CAP CORP (ON)
Recapitalized as Quia Resources Inc.
01/05/2011
Each share Common no par
exchanged for (0.66666666) share
Common no par
Quia Resources Inc. recapitalized as
Tinley Beverage Co. Inc. 10/06/2015

ONSOURCE CORP (DE)
Name changed to Ceragenix
Pharmaceuticals, Inc. 06/27/2005
(See Ceragenix Pharmaceuticals, Inc.)

ONSPAN NETWORKING INC (NV)
Each share old Common $0.001 par
exchanged for (0.08333333) share
new Common $0.001 par
10/09/2001
Recapitalized as Double Eagle
Holdings, Ltd. 04/02/2007
Each share new Common $0.001 par
exchanged for (0.09090909) share
Common $0.001 par
Double Eagle Holdings, Ltd. name
changed to Fuse Science, Inc.
11/03/2011

ONSTED ST BK (ONSTED, MI)
Stock Dividends - 10% payable
07/15/1999 to holders of record
06/30/1999; 10% payable
06/15/2001 to holders of record
05/31/2001 Ex date - 06/15/2001;
30% payable 06/15/2003 to holders
of record 05/31/2003 Ex date -
06/16/2003
Location changed from Onsted, MI to
Brooklyn, MI 10/01/2004

ONTARGET CAP INC (AB)
Name changed to Gene Screen Inc.
10/20/1994
Gene Screen Inc. recapitalized as
Gene Screen Corp. 07/09/1996

which name changed to GeneVest Inc. 06/25/1998 which merged into Pinetree Capital Corp. 06/01/2004 which recapitalized as Pinetree Capital Ltd. 06/02/2004

ONTARIO & QUE RY CO (CANADA)
Merged into Canadian Pacific Ltd. (New) 10/13/98
Each share Common $100 par exchanged for the equivalent of $2,300 in Common no par
(See Canadian Pacific Ltd. (New))

ONTARIO BEAUTY SUPPLY CO. LTD. (CANADA)
Name changed to Obsco Corp. Ltd. 3/24/64

ONTARIO BISCUIT CO.
Acquired by United Biscuit Co. of America 00/00/1929
Details not available

ONTARIO CAP OPPORTUNITIES INC (ON)
Recapitalized as Biorem Inc. 1/21/2005
Each share Common no par exchanged for (0.25) share Common no par

ONTARIO EQUITABLE LIFE & ACCIDENT INSURANCE CO.
Reorganized as Equitable Life Insurance Co. of Canada in 1936 which completed mutualization 9/9/63

ONTARIO HOSE SPECIALTIES INC (ON)
Reincorporated under the laws of British Columbia as Bordeaux Energy, Inc. 03/13/2007
Bordeaux Energy, Inc. recapitalized as Enterprise Energy Resources Ltd. 11/10/2008 which merged into LNG Energy Ltd. 08/20/2013 which recapitalized as Esrey Energy Ltd. 11/18/2013 which name changed to Esrey Resources Ltd. 10/16/2017

ONTARIO JOCKEY CLUB (ON)
Name changed to Jockey Club Ltd. 3/12/59
(See listing for Jockey Club Ltd.)

ONTARIO LOAN & DEBENTURE CO. (ON)
Each share Common $50 par exchanged for (5) shares Common $10 par in 1953
Merged into Royal Trust Co. Mortgage Corp. 2/28/69
(See Royal Trust Co. Mortgage Corp.)

ONTARIO MANUFACTURING CO. (IN)
Merged into National Silver Co. and each $15 of book value as of 12/31/54 of Common no par exchanged for (1) share 6% Preferred $15 par 9/30/55

ONTARIO NICKEL CORP. LTD.
Acquired by Ontario Nickel Mines Ltd. on a (1) for (5) basis in 1943
Ontario Nickel Mines Ltd. completed liquidation in 1958

ONTARIO NICKEL MINES LTD. (ON)
Liquidation completed 00/00/1958
Details not available

ONTARIO PHOSPHATE INDUSTRIES, LTD. (ON)
Charter cancelled in 1956

ONTARIO POWER CO.
Merged into Southern California Edison Co. 00/00/1928
Details not available

ONTARIO PYRITES CO. LTD. (ON)
Recapitalized as Consolidated Sudbury Basin Mines Ltd. 00/00/1954
Each share Capital Stock no par exchanged for (0.5) share Capital Stock no par
Consolidated Sudbury Basin Mines Ltd. merged into Giant Yellowknife Mines Ltd. 07/07/1960 which merged into Royal Oak Mines Inc. 07/23/1991 which recapitalized as Royal Oak Ventures Inc. 02/14/2000
(See Royal Oak Ventures Inc.)

ONTARIO-QUEBEC PROSPECTORS LTD. (CANADA)
Charter abandoned in 1963
No stockholders' equity

ONTARIO RARE METAL MINES LTD. (ON)
Liquidation completed 5/2/58

ONTARIO SILKNIT, LTD. (ON)
Reincorporated under the laws of Canada as Silknit Ltd. in 1945
(See Silknit Ltd.)

ONTARIO SILVER MINING CO.
Merged into Park Utah Consolidated Mines Co.
Details not available

ONTARIO SOLAR ENERGY CORP (ON)
Name changed to Blackrock Oil Corp. 08/08/2014

ONTARIO STL PRODS CO LTD (CANADA)
Each share Common $100 par exchanged for (4) shares old Common no par in 1927
Each share old Common no par exchanged for (5) shares new Common no par in 1952
Common no par split (3) for (1) by issuance of (2) additional shares 7/16/62
7% Conv. Preferred $100 par called for redemption 6/30/67
Thru voluntary purchase offer 100% acquired by North American Rockwell Corp. in 1969
Public interest eliminated

ONTARIO STORE FIXTURE CO. LTD. (ON)
Name changed to OSF Industries Ltd. 8/30/68
(See OSF Industries Ltd.)

ONTARIO TR CO (TORONTO, ON)
Common $5 par changed to no par 04/25/1974
Merged into Canada Trust Co.-La Societe Canada Trust (London, ON) 12/31/1976
Each share Common no par exchanged for (1) share Common $2 par

ONTECO CORP (NV)
Each share old Common $0.001 par exchanged for (0.001) share new Common $0.001 par 01/11/2012
Recapitalized as Inelco Corp. 05/10/2013
Each share Common $0.001 par exchanged for (0.0005) share Common $0.001 par
(See Inelco Corp.)

ONTEL CORP. (NY)
Merged into Caesars World, Inc. 2/26/79
Each share Common 25¢ par exchanged for (1.71) shares Common 10¢ par
(See Caesars World, Inc.)

ONTEX RES LTD (ON)
Recapitalized 05/04/1981
Common $1 par changed to no par 01/02/1972
Recapitalized from Ontex Mining Ltd. to Ontex Resources Ltd. 05/04/1981
Each share Common no par exchanged for (1/3) share Common no par
Recapitalized as Goldstone Resources Inc. 12/22/2009
Each share Common no par exchanged for (1/3) share Common no par
Goldstone Resources Inc. merged into Premier Gold Mines Ltd. 08/16/2011

ONTOGENY INC (DE)
Merged into Curis, Inc. 07/31/2000
Each share Conv. Preferred Ser. B exchanged for (0.2564) share Common 1¢ par
Each share Conv. Preferred Ser. E exchanged for (0.2564) share Common 1¢ par

ONTONAGON FIBRE CO.
Succeeded by Ontonagon Fibre Corp. in 1931
(See Ontonagon Fibre Corp.)

ONTONAGON FIBRE CORP.
Acquired by National Container Corp. (Del.) in 1945
(See National Container Corp. (Del.))

ONTRACK DATA INTL INC (MN)
Merged into Kroll Inc. 6/13/2002
Each share Common 1¢ par exchanged for (0.6447) share Common 1¢ par
(See Kroll Inc.)

ONTRAK SYS INC (CA)
Merged into Lam Research Corp. 8/5/97
Each share Common no par exchanged for (0.83) share Common $0.001 par

ONTRO INC (CA)
Issue Information - 3,400,000 UNITS consisting of (1) share COM and (1) WT offered at $5.50 per Unit on 05/11/1998
SEC revoked common stock registration 10/09/2008
Stockholders' equity unlikely

ONTUS TELECOMMUNICATIONS CORP (NV)
Name changed to VoIPLabs Holdings, Inc. 04/08/2005
VoIPLabs Holdings, Inc. name changed to Concorde Resources Corp. 10/04/2005 which recapitalized as Real Hip Hop Matrix Corp. 11/03/2006 which name changed to RHNMedia 01/12/2007 which name changed to Massive G Media Corp. 03/16/2007 which name changed to International Minerals Mining Group, Inc. 06/21/2007 which name changed to Advanced Content Services, Inc. 02/05/2008 which recapitalized as New Wave Holdings, Inc. 12/08/2014 which name changed to PAO Group, Inc. 06/29/2017

ONTV INC (DE)
Name changed to True Product ID, Inc. 05/22/2006

ON2 TECHNOLOGIES INC (DE)
Reincorporated 06/20/2000
Name changed 05/24/2001
State of incorporation changed from (CO) to (DE) and Common no par changed to 1¢ par 06/20/2000
Name changed from On2.com, Inc. to On2 Technologies, Inc. 05/24/2001
Merged into Google Inc. 02/19/2010
Each share Common 1¢ par exchanged for (0.001) share Class A Common $0.001 par and $0.15 cash
Google Inc. name changed to Alphabet Inc. 10/05/2015

ONTZINC CORP (ON)
Recapitalized as HudBay Minerals Inc. (ONT) 12/24/2004
Each (30) shares Common no par exchanged for (1) share Common no par
HudBay Minerals Inc. (ONT) reincorporated in Canada 10/25/2005

ONVANTAGE INC (NV)
SEC revoked common stock registration 10/09/2008
Stockholders' equity unlikely

ONVIA INC (DE)
Name changed 06/25/2004
Each share old Common $0.0001 par exchanged for (0.1) share new Common $0.0001 par 07/17/2002
Name changed from Onvia.com, Inc. to Onvia, Inc. 06/25/2004
Acquired by Project Olympus Merger Sub, Inc. 11/17/2017
Each share new Common $0.0001 par exchanged for $9 cash

ONWARD ENERGY INC (AB)
Merged into Avenir Diversified Income Trust 01/16/2003
Each share Common no par exchanged for (0.2) Trust Unit and $0.32 cash
Avenir Diversified Income Trust reorganized as AvenEx Energy Corp. 01/07/2011 which merged into Spyglass Resources Corp. 04/04/2013

ONWARD KASHIYAMA LTD (JAPAN)
Name changed to Onward Holdings Co., Inc. 09/06/2007

ONWORD LEARNING SYS INC (BC)
Recapitalized as International Onward Learning Systems Inc. 6/11/93
Each share Common no par exchanged for (0.25) share Common no par
International Onward Learning Systems Inc. recapitalized as Catalyst Ventures Corp. 4/2/96 which recapitalized as International Catalyst Ventures Inc. (BC) 2/23/2000 which reincorporated in Yukon 9/8/2000 which recapitalized as Aberdeen International Inc. 11/23/2001 which reincorporated in Ontario 7/4/2006

ONX ENTERPRISE SOLUTIONS INC (ON)
Name changed 11/22/2001
Issue Information - 3,810,000 shares COM offered at $10.50 per share on 04/06/2000
Name changed from OnX Inc. to OnX Enterprise Solutions Inc. 11/22/2001
Name changed to Momentum Advanced Solutions Inc. 12/06/2006
(See Momentum Advanced Solutions Inc.)

ONYX ACCEP CORP (DE)
Merged into Capital One Financial Corp. 1/12/2005
Each share Common 1¢ par exchanged for $28 cash

ONYX CHEMICAL CORP. (DE)
Merged into Millmaster Onyx Corp. 11/17/64
Each share Common no par exchanged for (4) shares Common $1 par
(See Millmaster Onyx Corp.)

ONYX CHINA INC (NV)
Reorganized as Lux Energy Corp. 05/22/2009
Each share Common $0.001 par exchanged for (5) shares Common $0.001 par
Lux Energy Corp. recapitalized as Sunbelt International Corp. 10/03/2011 which recapitalized as Nevcor Business Solutions Inc. 02/06/2014 which name changed to CPSM, Inc. 07/15/2014 which name changed to Astro Aerospace Ltd. 07/24/2018

ONYX-FIVE INC (MN)
Name changed to Southwest Industrial Products, Inc. 07/17/1997
Southwest Industrial Products, Inc. recapitalized as Aubryn International, Inc. 08/17/1998 which recapitalized as Pacific Sunset Investments, Inc. 01/21/2004 which name changed to Gen-ID Lab Services, Inc. 10/10/2005 which recapitalized as Adventura Corp. 11/01/2009

ONYX HLDG CORP (CO)
Each share old Common $0.001 par

exchanged for (0.5) share new Common $0.001 par 9/28/89
Recapitalized as Onyx Corp. 8/26/92
Each share new Common $0.001 par exchanged for (0.05) share Common $0.001 par

ONYX HOSIERY, INC.
Acquired by Gotham Silk Hosiery Co. 00/00/1926
Details not available

ONYX HYDROCARBON RECOVERY CORP (DE)
Name changed to Magna Diversified Inc. 3/22/84
Magna Diversified Inc. name changed to Energizer 500 Inc. 6/8/84 which name changed to Opportunity 21 on 6/16/85
(See Opportunity 21)

ONYX IMI INC (CA)
Merged into Corvus Systems, Inc. 07/30/1985
Each share Common no par exchanged for (1.3) shares Common no par
(See Corvus Systems, Inc.)

ONYX PETE EXPL LTD (AB)
Name changed to Lasmo Canada Inc. 1/14/88
Lasmo Canada Inc. name changed to Elan Energy Inc. 10/29/92 which merged into Ranger Oil Ltd. (Canada) 10/9/97 which merged into Canadian Natural Resources Ltd. 7/28/2000

ONYX PHARMACEUTICALS INC (DE)
Acquired by Amgen Inc. 10/01/2013
Each share Common $0.001 par exchanged for $125 cash

ONYX SOFTWARE CORP (WA)
Issue Information - 3,100,000 shares COM offered at $13 per share on 02/11/1999
Old Common 1¢ par split (2) for (1) by issuance of (1) additional share payable 3/1/2000 to holders of record 2/15/2001
Each share old Common 1¢ par exchanged for (0.25) share new Common 1¢ par 7/24/2003
Merged into M2M Holdings, Inc. 8/2/2006
Each share new Common 1¢ par exchanged for $4.80 cash

OOK INC (MD)
Completely liquidated
Each share Common $0.001 par received first and final distribution of $33.19239 cash payable 09/30/2010 to holders of record 09/24/2010

OOREDOO QSC (QATAR)
GDR agreement terminated 08/30/2017
Each 144A GDR for Ordinary exchanged for $9.486229 cash
Each Reg. S GDR for Ordinary exchanged for $9.486229 cash

OP-TECH ENVIRONMENTAL SVCS INC (DE)
Acquired by NRC US Holding Co., LLC 07/30/2013
Each share Common 1¢ par exchanged for $0.116 cash

OPACT ENERGY 1983 LTD (AB)
Recapitalized 2/22/84
Name changed from Opact Energy Ltd. to Opact Energy (1983) Ltd. 2/22/84
Each share Common no par exchanged for (0.25) share new Common no par
Merged into Intensity Resources Ltd. 7/21/84
Each (4.21) shares new Common no par exchanged for (1) share Common no par
Intensity Resources Ltd. merged into Renata Resources Inc. 4/25/97 which merged into Rio Alto Exploration Ltd. 6/21/2000 which merged into Canadian Natural Resources Ltd. 7/1/2002

OPACT RES LTD (BC)
Recapitalized as Blue Lighting Ventures Inc. 07/21/1999
Each share Common no par exchanged for (0.33333333) share Common no par
Blue Lighting Ventures Inc. name changed to Universal Uranium Ltd. 05/03/2005 which name changed to Expedition Mining Inc. 07/07/2010 which name changed to Imagin Medical Inc. 02/24/2016

OPAGOLD MINES, LTD. (QC)
Liquidated in 1955
Each share Common $1 par exchanged for (1) share Lingside Copper Mining Co. Ltd. Capital Stock $1 par
(See Lingside Copper Mining Co. Ltd.)

OPAL ENERGY CORP (BC)
Each share old Common no par exchanged for (0.02) share new Common no par 06/13/2011
Name changed to Versus Systems Inc. 07/13/2016

OPAL ENERGY INC (CANADA)
Acquired by Founders Energy Ltd. 01/12/1999
Each share Common no par exchanged for (0.44) share Common no par and $0.42 cash
Founders Energy Ltd. reorganized as Provident Energy Trust 03/06/2001 which reorganized as Provident Energy Ltd. (New) 01/03/2011 which merged into Pembina Pipeline Corp. 04/02/2012

OPAL INC (DE)
Merged into Applied Materials, Inc. 1/9/97
Each share Common 1¢ par exchanged for $18.50 cash

OPAL TECHNOLOGIES INC (NV)
SEC revoked common stock registration 10/09/2008
Stockholders' equity unlikely

OPAWICA EXPLS INC (ON)
Reincorporated under the laws of British Columbia 09/29/2006

OPAWICA GOLD MINES LTD. (ON)
Charter cancelled 10/17/60

OPCOA INC (DE)
Merged into AVX Corp. 08/22/1973
Each share Common 10¢ par exchanged for (0.465116) share Common $1 par
AVX Corp. acquired by Kyocera Corp. 01/18/1990

OPE HLDGS LTD (AB)
Name changed to SSP Offshore Inc. 05/21/2009
(See SSP Offshore Inc.)

OPEL INTL INC (NB)
Reincorporated 01/30/2007
Place of incorporation changed from (ON) to (NB) 01/30/2007
Reincorporated under the laws of Ontario as OPEL Solar International Inc. 12/01/2010
OPEL Solar International Inc. name changed to OPEL Technologies Inc. 08/29/2011 which name changed to POET Technologies Inc. 07/25/2013

OPEL SOLAR INTL INC (ON)
Name changed to OPEL Technologies Inc. 08/29/2011
OPEL Technologies Inc. name changed to POET Technologies Inc. 07/25/2013

OPEL TECHNOLOGIES INC (ON)
Name changed to POET Technologies Inc. 07/25/2013

OPELIKA MFG CORP (IL)
Common $5 par split (4) for (3) by issuance of (1/3) additional share 1/25/77
Each share old Common $5 par exchanged for (1/3) share new Common $5 par 6/17/83
Chapter 11 Federal Bankruptcy Code converted to Chapter 7 on 1/20/87
Stockholders' equity unlikely

OPELL INC (UT)
Each share old Common $0.001 par exchanged for (0.0002) share new Common $0.001 par 01/20/1996
Note: No holder will receive fewer than (100) shares
Name changed to Wall Street Records Inc. 01/28/1998
Wall Street Records Inc. name changed to ANTRA Holdings Group, Inc. 04/16/1998 which recapitalized as Peku Manufacturing, Inc. 11/15/2005 which name changed to GHL Technologies, Inc. 03/03/2006 which recapitalized as NXGen Holdings, Inc. 09/07/2007 which name changed to Green Bridge Industries, Inc. 08/20/2009

OPEMISCA DUFAULT MINES LTD (QC)
Reported out of business 00/00/1983
Details not available

OPEMISCA EXPLORERS LTD (QC)
Merged into Allied Mining Corp. 09/22/1969
Each share Capital Stock $1 par exchanged for (0.06666666) share Common no par
Allied Mining Corp. merged into United Asbestos Inc. 06/29/1973 which merged into Campbell Resources Inc. (New) 06/08/1983
(See Campbell Resources Inc. (New))

OPEMISKA COPPER MINES (QUEBEC) LTD. (QC)
Acquired by Opemiska Copper Mines (Quebec) Ltd. share for share in 1937

OPEMISKA COPPER MINES LTD (QC)
Merged into Falconbridge Copper Ltd. 12/16/1971
Each share Capital Stock $1 par exchanged for (1) share Capital Stock no par
Falconbridge Copper Ltd. name changed to Corporation Falconbridge Copper 07/09/1980 which name changed to Minnova Inc. 05/26/1987 which merged into Metall Mining Corp. 05/05/1993 which name changed to Inmet Mining Corp. 05/04/1995 which was acquired by First Quantum Minerals Ltd. 04/09/2013

OPEMISKA MINES LTD. (CANADA)
Deemed not to be subsisting company by the Dominion Secretary of State 2/19/39

OPEN AIR MKTS INC (VA)
Merged into Farm Fresh, Inc. 09/27/1986
Each share Common 5¢ par exchanged for (0.8) share Common 1¢ par
(See Farm Fresh, Inc.)

OPEN BK (LOS ANGELES, CA)
Under plan of reorganization each share Common no par automatically became (1) share OP Bancorp Common no par 06/29/2016

OPEN DOOR ONLINE INC (NJ)
Reorganized under the laws of Delaware as Blue Moon Group, Inc. 11/29/2002
Each (30) shares Common $0.0001 par exchanged for (1) share Common $0.0001 par
Blue Moon Group, Inc. recapitalized as One Punch Productions, Inc. 12/07/2005 which name changed to Caltas Fitness, Inc. 08/21/2006 which name changed to Cinemaya Media Group, Inc. 02/06/2007 which recapitalized as SNM Global Holdings 11/14/2008

OPEN EC TECHNOLOGIES INC (BC)
Merged into QHR Technologies Inc. 10/25/2012
Each share Common no par exchanged for $0.04 cash
Note: Unexchanged certificates were cancelled and became without value 10/25/2018

OPEN END MINES LTD (ON)
Completely liquidated 4/28/72
Each share Capital Stock no par exchanged for first and final distribution of (0.5) share New York Oils Ltd. (BC) Capital Stock no par
New York Oils Ltd. (BC) reincorporated in Alberta 7/19/82 which was acquired by Sceptre Resources Ltd. 3/14/89 which merged into Canadian Natural Resources Ltd. 8/15/96

OPEN ENERGY CORP (NV)
Name changed to Applied Solar, Inc. 01/20/2009
(See Applied Solar, Inc.)

OPEN ENVIRONMENT CORP (DE)
Merged into Borland International, Inc. 11/18/1996
Each share Common 1¢ par exchanged for (0.66) share Common 1¢ par
Borland International, Inc. name changed to Inprise Corp. 06/05/1998 which name changed to Borland Software Corp. 01/22/2001
(See Borland Software Corp.)

OPEN GOLD CORP (BC)
Recapitalized as betterU Education Corp. (BC) 03/08/2017
Each share Common no par exchanged for (0.10526315) share Common no par
betterU Education Corp. (BC) reincorporated in Canada 10/13/2017

OPEN INVTS PJSC (RUSSIA)
Name changed to Ingrad PJSC 02/08/2018

OPEN JT STK CO-VIMPEL COMMUNICATIONS (RUSSIA)
Sponsored ADR's for Common split (3) for (1) by issuance of (2) additional ADR's payable 11/22/2004 to holders of record 11/19/2004 Ex date - 11/23/2004
Sponsored Reg. S ADR's for Common split (3) for (1) by issuance of (2) additional ADR's payable 11/22/2004 to holders of record 11/19/2004
Basis changed from (1:0.75) to (1:0.25) 11/22/2004
Sponsored ADR's for Common split (5) for (1) by issuance of (4) additional ADR's payable 08/21/2007 to holders of record 08/17/2007 Ex date - 08/22/2007
Basis changed from (1:0.25) to (1:0.05) 08/22/2007
Acquired by VimpelCom Ltd. 08/09/2010
Each Sponsored ADR for Common exchanged for approximately $19.11 cash

OPEN MARKET INC (DE)
Merged into divine, inc. 10/19/2001
Each share Conv. Preferred Ser. C exchanged for (0.8326) share Class A Common $0.001 par
Each share Common $0.001 par exchanged for (0.8326) share Class A Common $0.001 par
(See divine, inc.)

OPEN PLAN SYS INC (VA)
Chapter 11 bankruptcy proceedings converted to Chapter 7 on 09/25/2002

Stockholders' equity unlikely

OPEN RANGE CAP CORP (AB)
Name changed to New Range Resources Ltd. 03/30/2006
New Range Resources Ltd. recapitalized as Relentless Resources Ltd. 06/11/2010

OPEN RANGE ENERGY CORP NEW (AB)
Acquired by Peyto Exploration & Development Corp. 08/14/2012
Each share Common no par exchanged for (0.0723) share Common no par
Note: Unexchanged certificates were cancelled and became without value 08/14/2018

OPEN RANGE ENERGY CORP OLD (AB)
Plan of arrangement effective 11/01/2011
Each share Common no par exchanged for (1) share Open Range Energy Corp. (New) Common no par and (0.8839) share Poseidon Concepts Corp. Common no par
Note: Unexchanged certificates were cancelled and became without value 11/01/2014
Open Range Energy Corp. (New) acquired by Peyto Exploration & Development Corp. 08/14/2012

OPEN RD CAMPERS INC (CA)
Name changed to Open Road Industries, Inc. 04/28/1969
Open Road Industries, Inc. name changed to Orico 10/20/1977 which name changed to Sargent Industries, Inc. (CA) 06/01/1979
(See Sargent Industries, Inc. (CA))

OPEN RD INDS INC (CA)
Name changed to ORICO 10/20/1977
ORICO name changed to Sargent Industries, Inc. (CA) 06/01/1979
(See Sargent Industries, Inc. (CA))

OPEN SOLUTIONS INC (DE)
Merged into Carlyle Group LLC 01/23/2007
Each share Common 1¢ par exchanged for $38 cash

OPEN SOURCE HEALTH INC (AB)
Recapitalized as Weekend Unlimited Inc. 10/15/2018
Each share Common no par exchanged for (0.5) share Common no par

OPEN STAIR DWELLINGS CO., INC. (NY)
Liquidated 2/5/59

OPEN TEXT CORP (ON)
Common no par split (2) for (1) by issuance of (1) additional share payable 10/28/2003 to holders of record 10/22/2003
Reincorporated under the laws of Canada 12/29/2005

OPENCELL BIOMED INC (NV)
Recapitalized as Preferred Commerce Inc. 06/20/2014
Each share Common $0.0001 par exchanged for (0.00425531) share Common $0.0001 par

OPENLANE INC (AZ)
Acquired by KAR Auction Services, Inc. 10/03/2011
Each share Preferred Ser. D no par exchanged for $7.98457223 cash
Each share Common no par exchanged for $7.73134357 cash
Each share Preferred Ser. D no par received an initial additional distribution of $0.24132109 cash from escrow payable 05/17/2013 to holders of record 10/03/2011
Each share Common no par received an initial additional distribution of $0.23366765 cash from escrow payable 05/17/2013 to holders of record 10/03/2011
Each share Preferred Ser. D no par received a second additional distribution of $0.24132109 cash from escrow payable 05/17/2013 to holders of record 10/03/2011
Each share Common no par received an second additional distribution of $0.23366765 cash from escrow payable 05/17/2013 to holders of record 10/03/2011
Each share Preferred Ser. D no par received a third additional distribution of $0.39926037 cash from escrow payable 02/07/2014 to holders of record 10/03/2011
Each share Common no par received a third additional distribution of $0.38659797 cash from escrow payable 02/07/2014 to holders of record 10/03/2011

OPENLIMIT INC (FL)
Recapitalized as SunVesta, Inc. 08/27/2007
Each share Common 1¢ par exchanged for (0.02) share Common 1¢ par

OPENROUTE NETWORKS INC (MA)
Merged into Netrix Corp. 12/22/99
Each share Common 1¢ par exchanged for (1) share Common 5¢ par
Netrix Corp. name changed to Nx Networks, Inc. 9/19/2000

OPENSKY CAP INDEX INCOME FD (ON)
Completely liquidated
Each Trust Unit no par received first and final distribution of $7.32 cash payable 06/02/2008 to holders of record 05/30/2008

OPENSKY CAP MANAGED PROTN INCOME TR FD (ON)
Name changed to OpenSky Capital Index Income Fund 02/26/2007
(See OpenSky Capital Index Income Fund)

OPENTABLE INC (DE)
Acquired by Priceline Group Inc. 07/24/2014
Each share Common $0.0001 par exchanged for $103.00 cash

OPENTV CORP (BRITISH VIRGIN ISLANDS)
Issue Information - 7,500,000 shares CL A ORD offered at $20 per share on 11/23/1999
Class A Ordinary no par called for redemption at $1.55 on 03/26/2010

OPENVISION TECHNOLOGIES INC (DE)
Merged into Veritas Software Corp. 4/25/97
Each share Common $0.001 par exchanged for (0.346) share Common no par
Veritas Software Corp. merged into Symantec Corp. 7/2/2005

OPENWAVE SYS INC (DE)
Each share old Common $0.001 par exchanged for (0.33333333) share new Common $0.001 par 10/21/2003
Name changed to Unwired Planet, Inc. 05/09/2012
Unwired Planet, Inc. name changed to Great Elm Capital Group, Inc. 06/17/2016

OPERA SOFTWARE ASA (NORWAY)
Name changed to Otello Corporation ASA 10/15/2018

OPERATION MATCH INC (NY)
Dissolved by proclamation 6/24/81

OPERATOR CONSOLIDATED MINES CO. (NV)
Completely liquidated 3/13/64
Each share Common 10¢ par exchanged for first and final distribution of (0.017) share Coast Exploration Co. Common $1 par
Coast Exploration Co. completed liquidation 12/14/66

OPES EXPL INC (NV)
Name changed to Almadaro Minerals Corp. 03/24/2008
Almadaro Minerals Corp. name changed to TapSlide, Inc. 09/04/2008

OPEXA THERAPEUTICS INC (TX)
Common 50¢ par changed to 1¢ par 11/12/2009
Each share old Common 1¢ par exchanged for (0.25) share new Common 1¢ par 12/17/2012
Each share new Common 1¢ par exchanged again for (0.125) share new Common 1¢ par 09/29/2015
Recapitalized as Acer Therapeutics Inc. (TX) 09/21/2017
Each share new Common 1¢ par exchanged for (0.09656678) share Common 1¢ par
Acer Therapeutics Inc. (TX) reincorporated in Delaware 05/15/2018

OPHIDIAN PHARMACEUTICALS INC (DE)
Reincorporated 04/26/1999
State of incorporation changed from (WI) to (DE) 04/26/1999
Each share old Common $0.0025 par exchanged for (0.125) share new Common $0.0025 par 09/20/1999
Under plan of partial liquidation each share new Common $0.0025 par received distribution of $0.83 cash payable 04/30/2001 to holders of record 04/23/2001
Stock Dividend - 3.6046% payable 08/31/2001 to holders of record 08/17/2001 Ex date - 08/23/2001
Name changed to Hemoxymed Inc. 11/14/2001
Hemoxymed Inc. name changed to Applied NeuroSolutions, Inc. 10/30/2003
(See Applied NeuroSolutions, Inc.)

OPHIR CORP. (CO)
Acquired by Silver Bell Mines Co. 8/23/54
Each share Class A $1 par exchanged for (1) share Class A $1 par
Silver Bell Mines Co. name changed to Silver Bell Industries, Inc. 1/1/70 which liquidated for Union Oil Co. of California 12/8/78 which reorganized as Unocal Corp. 4/25/83 which merged into Chevron Corp. 8/10/2005

OPHIR GOLD MINES CO (CO)
Each share Common 10¢ par exchanged for (10) shares Common 1¢ par 00/00/1951
Each share old Common 1¢ par exchanged for (0.005) share new Common 1¢ par 08/03/1993
Name changed to U N Dollars 01/29/2002
U N Dollars reincorporated in Nevada as Slateco International Group Inc. 01/29/2002 which reincorporated in Wyoming as Terrablock Development, Inc. 02/21/2006 which name changed to Linked Media Group, Inc. 12/30/2008
(See Linked Media Group, Inc.)

OPHIR GOLD MINING CO. (UT)
Charter revoked for failure to file reports and pay fees 3/30/54

OPHIR INTL INC (UT)
Involuntarily dissolved 12/31/1986

OPHIR RES CO (NV)
Charter revoked 08/13/2014

OPHIR VENTURES INC (AB)
Recapitalized as Consolidated Ophir Ventures Inc. (AB) 12/02/2005
Each share Common no par exchanged for (0.02) share Common no par
Consolidated Ophir Ventures Inc. (AB) reorganized in British Virgin Islands as CIC Energy Corp. 03/14/2006
(See CIC Energy Corp.)

OPHIRAVENCAP INC (QC)
Name changed to Exploration Knick Inc. 02/12/2009

OPHTHALIX INC (DE)
Reincorporated 04/02/2012
State of incorporation changed from (NV) to (DE) 04/02/2012
Each share old Common $0.001 par exchanged for (0.22222222) share new Common $0.001 par 08/07/2013
Name changed to Wize Pharma, Inc. 11/16/2017

OPHTHALMIC IMAGING SYS (CA)
Each share old Common no par exchanged for (0.33333333) share new Common no par 12/01/1994
Merged into Merge Healthcare Inc. 08/04/2011
Each share new Common no par exchanged for (0.1693) share Common 1¢ par
(See Merge Healthcare Inc.)

OPI LTD (CANADA)
Reincorporated 00/00/1982
Common no par reclassified as Conv. Class A Common no par 02/21/1977
Conv. Class A Common no par reclassified as Common no par 05/16/1980
Conv. Class B Common no par reclassified as Common no par 05/16/1980
Common no par split (2) for (1) by issuance of (1) additional share 05/30/1980
Common no par split (3) for (1) by issuance of (2) additional shares 05/29/1981
Place of incorporation changed from (ALTA) to (Canada) 00/00/1982
Common no par reclassified as Class A Common no par 04/11/1986
Name changed to Oil Patch Group Inc. 09/22/1986
(See Oil Patch Group Inc.)

OPIANT PHARMACEUTICALS INC (NV)
Reincorporated under the laws of Delaware 10/02/2017

OPIC CORP (NY)
Voluntarily dissolved 9/6/2000
Details not available

OPIMIAN CALIF VINEYARDS CORP (CANADA)
Charter dissolved for failure to pay fees 3/6/2000

OPINION RESH CORP (DE)
Merged into infoUSA Inc. 12/05/2006
Each share Common 1¢ par exchanged for $12 cash

OPLINK COMMUNICATIONS INC (CA)
Each share old Common $0.001 par exchanged for (0.14285714) share new Common $0.001 par 11/10/2005
Acquired by Koch Industries, Inc. 12/23/2014
Each share new Common $0.001 par exchanged for $24.25 cash

OPMEDIC GROUP INC (QC)
Acquired by Kemourmedic Group Inc. 11/08/2013
Each share Common no par exchanged for $2.90 cash

OPNET TECHNOLOGIES INC (DE)
Acquired by Riverbed Technology, Inc. 12/19/2014
Each share Common $0.001 par exchanged for (0.2774) share

Common $0.0001 par and $36.55 cash
(See Riverbed Technology, Inc.)

OPNEXT INC (DE)
Issue Information - 16,909,375 shares COM offered at $15 per share on 02/14/2007
Merged into Oclaro, Inc. 07/23/2012
Each share Common 1¢ par exchanged for (0.42) share Common 1¢ par

OPOWER INC (DE)
Acquired by Oracle Corp. 06/14/2016
Each share Common $0.000005 par exchanged for $10.30 cash

OPPENHEIM COLLINS & CO., INC. (DE)
Capital Stock no par changed to $10 par 00/00/1944
Merged into City Specialty Stores, Inc. 00/00/1953
Each share Capital Stock $10 par exchanged for (3) shares Common $1 par
City Specialty Stores, Inc. merged into City Stores Co. 01/28/1961 which name changed to CSS Industries, Inc. 09/24/1985

OPPENHEIMER (S.) & CO.
Name changed to S.O. Realization Co. in 1933 which was liquidated in 1936

OPPENHEIMER A I M FD (MD)
Reincorporated in January 1986
State of incorporation changed from (MD) to (MA) in January 1986
Name changed to Oppenheimer Global Fund 2/1/87

OPPENHEIMER ASSET ALLOCATION FD (MA)
Shares of Bene. Int. $0.001 par reclassified as Class A $0.001 par 11/01/1993
Name changed to Oppenheimer Multiple Strategies Fund 03/05/1997
Oppenheimer Multiple Strategies Fund name changed to Oppenheimer Balanced Fund 02/20/2004 which merged into Oppenheimer Equity Income Fund, Inc. (New) 08/18/2011

OPPENHEIMER BALANCED FD (MA)
Name changed 02/20/2004
Name changed from Oppenheimer Multiple Strategies Fund to Oppenheimer Balanced Fund 02/20/2004
Merged into Oppenheimer Equity Income Fund, Inc. (New) 08/18/2011
Each share Class A $0.001 par exchanged for (0.45131693) share Class A $0.001 par
Each share Class B $0.001 par exchanged for (0.50653163) share Class B $0.001 par
Each share Class C $0.001 par exchanged for (0.50819852) share Class C $0.001 par
Each share Class N $0.001 par exchanged for (0.45734541) share Class N $0.001 par

OPPENHEIMER CAP L P (DE)
Units of Ltd. Partnership Int. split (1.67) for (1) by issuance of (0.67) additional Unit payable 12/15/1997 to holders of record 12/01/1997
Ex date - 12/16/1997
Name changed to PIMCO Advisors Holdings L.P. 01/01/1998
(See PIMCO Advisors Holdings L.P.)

OPPENHEIMER DIRECTORS FD (MD)
Merged into Oppenheimer Target Fund, Inc. in 1991
Each Share of Bene. Int. $1 par exchanged for (0.950425) Share of Bene. Int. $1 par
Oppenheimer Target Fund, Inc. name changed to Oppenheimer Capital Appreciation Fund 12/18/96

OPPENHEIMER EQUITY INCOME FD (MA)
Reincorporated 11/01/1986
Name and state of incorporation changed from Oppenheimer Equity Income Fund, Inc. (Old) (MD) to Oppenheimer Equity Income Fund (MA) and Capital Stock $1 par reclassified as Shares of Bene. Int. no par 11/01/1986
Shares of Bene. Int. no par reclassified as Class A no par 08/17/1993
Class A, B, C and N no par changed to $0.001 par 08/04/1995
Name changed to Oppenheimer Capital Income Fund 03/03/1999

OPPENHEIMER FD (MA)
Name changed 11/01/1985
Common $1 par split (3) for (1) by issuance of (2) additional shares 02/15/1968
Name and state of incorporation changed from Oppenheimer Fund, Inc. (NY) to Oppenheimer Fund (MA) 11/01/1985
Capital Stock $1 par reclassified as Shares of Bene. Int. no par 11/01/1985
Trust terminated 11/05/1997
Details not available

OPPENHEIMER GLOBAL BIO TECH FD (MA)
Name changed to Oppenheimer Global Emerging Growth Fund 9/19/94

OPPENHEIMER GLOBAL GROWTH & INCOME FD (MA)
Name changed to Oppenheimer Global Opportunities Fund 6/1/2003

OPPENHEIMER GROWTH FD (MA)
Merged into Oppenheimer Capital Appreciation Fund 11/08/2007
Each share Class A no par exchanged for Class A $0.001 par on a net asset basis
Each share Class B no par exchanged for Class B $0.001 par on a net asset basis
Each share Class C no par exchanged for Class C $0.001 par on a net asset basis
Each share Class N no par exchanged for Class N $0.001 par on a net asset basis
Each share Class Y no par exchanged for Class Y $0.001 par on a net asset basis

OPPENHEIMER HLDGS INC (CANADA)
Reincorporated 05/11/2005
Place of incorporation changed from (ONT) to (Canada) 05/11/2005
Reincorporated under the laws of Delaware 05/11/2009

OPPENHEIMER INCOME FD BOSTON INC (MD)
Name changed to Eaton Vance Income Fund of Boston, Inc. 11/16/82
Eaton Vance Income Fund of Boston, Inc. name changed to Eaton Vance Series Trust II 10/3/2003

OPPENHEIMER INCOME FUND, INC. (MD)
Name changed to Oppenheimer Income Fund of Boston, Inc. 12/7/76
Oppenheimer Income Fund of Boston, Inc. name changed to Eaton Vance Income Fund of Boston, Inc. 11/16/82 which name changed to Eaton Vance Series Trust II 10/3/2003

OPPENHEIMER INDS INC (DE)
Charter cancelled and declared inoperative and void for non-payment of taxes 3/1/96

OPPENHEIMER INTL VALUE FD (DE)
Name changed 08/29/2003
Reorganized 09/14/2009
Name changed 04/12/2012
Reincorporated 10/11/2013
Name changed from Oppenheimer Quest Global Value Fund, Inc. to Oppenheimer Quest International Value Fund, Inc. (MD) 08/29/2003
Under plan of reorganization each share Class A Common 1¢ par, Class B Common 1¢ par, Class C Common 1¢ par, Class N Common 1¢ par and Class Y Common 1¢ par automatically became (1) Oppenheimer Quest International Value Fund (MA) Class A Share of Bene. Int. 1¢ par, Class B Share of Bene. Int. 1¢ par, Class C Share of Bene. Int. 1¢ par, Class N Share of Bene. Int. 1¢ par or Class Y Share of Bene. Int. 1¢ par respectively 09/14/2009
Name changed from Oppenheimer Quest International Value Fund to Oppenheimer International Value Fund (MA) 04/12/2012
State of incorporation changed from (MA) to (DE) 10/11/2013
Class N 1¢ par reclassified as Class R 1¢ par 07/01/2014
Name changed to Oppenheimer International Equity Fund 12/28/2016

OPPENHEIMER MONETARY BRDG INC (MD)
Name changed to Oppenheimer Money Market Fund Inc. 06/16/1980

OPPENHEIMER MULTI-GOVT TR (MA)
Name changed to Oppenheimer World Bond Fund 7/26/96

OPPENHEIMER MUN BD FD (MA)
Name changed to Oppenheimer AMT-Free Municipals 10/27/2003

OPPENHEIMER N Y MUN FD (MA)
Name changed 10/10/96
Name changed from Oppenheimer New York Tax-Exempt Fund to Oppenheimer New York Municipal Fund and Shares of Bene. Int. no par reclassified as Shares of Bene. Int. Class A 1¢ par 10/10/96
Name changed to Oppenheimer AMT-Free New York Municipal Fund 1/22/2003

OPPENHEIMER OPT INCOME FD INC (MD)
Name changed to Oppenheimer Premium Income Fund, Inc. (MD) 03/08/1984
Oppenheimer Premium Income Fund, Inc. (MD) reincorporated in Massachusetts as Oppenheimer Premium Income Fund 03/04/1986
(See Oppenheimer Premium Income Fund)

OPPENHEIMER PREM INCOME FD (MA)
Reincorporated 03/04/1986
Reincorporated from Oppenheimer Premium Income Fund, Inc. (MD) to under the laws of Massachusetts as Oppenheimer Premium Income Fund 03/04/1986
Trust terminated 05/24/1993
Details not available

OPPENHEIMER QUEST CAP VALUE FD INC (MD)
Name changed to Oppenheimer Equity Income Fund, Inc. 08/01/2007

OPPENHEIMER REGENCY FD (MA)
Reincorporated 05/11/1987
Reincorporated from Oppenheimer Regency Fund, Inc. (MD) to under the laws of Massachusetts as Oppenheimer Regency Fund and Common no par reclassified as Shares of Bene. Int. no par 05/11/1987
Trust terminated 05/24/1993
Details not available

OPPENHEIMER RETIREMENT FD (MA)
Blue Chips Stocks Fund $0.001 par reclassified as Selective Stocks Fund $0.001 par 08/29/1986
Name changed to Oppenheimer Asset Allocation Fund and Quality Money Market Fund $0.001 par, Selective Stocks Fund $0.001 par, and U.S. Government Securities Fund $0.001 par reclassified as Shares of Bene. Int. $0.001 par 04/24/1987
Oppenheimer Asset Allocation Fund name changed to Oppenheimer Multiple Strategies Fund 03/05/1997 which name changed to Oppenheimer Balanced Fund 02/20/2004 which merged into Oppenheimer Equity Income Fund, Inc. (New) 08/18/2011

OPPENHEIMER REV WEIGHTED ETF TR (DE)
Trust terminated 12/16/2016
Each share Navellier Overall A-100 Revenue ETF received $47.93315 cash
Trust terminated 03/16/2017
Each share ADR Revenue ETF received $34.09819 cash
Each share Global Growth Revenue ETF received $49.80771 cash

OPPENHEIMER RISING DIVIDS FD INC (MD)
Name changed 08/01/2007
Name changed from Oppenheimer Quest Value Fund, Inc. to Oppenheimer Rising Dividends Fund, Inc. 08/01/2007
Under plan of reorganization each share Class A Common $1 par, Class B Common $1 par, Class C Common $1 par, Class N Common $1 par and Class Y Common $1 par automatically became (1) Oppenheimer Rising Dividends Fund (MA) Class A Share of Bene. Int. $1 par, Class B Share of Bene. Int. $1 par, Class C Share of Bene. Int. $1 par, Class N Share of Bene. Int. $1 par or Class Y Share of Bene. Int. $1 par respectively 09/14/2009

OPPENHEIMER SPL FD (MA)
Reincorporated 11/01/1985
Reincorporated from Oppenheimer Special Fund, Inc. (MD) to under the laws of Massachusetts as Oppenheimer Special Fund and Capital Stock $1 par reclassified as Shares of Bene. Int. no par 11/01/1985
Shares of Bene. Int. no par reclassified as Class A no par 09/29/1994
Name changed to Oppenheimer Growth Fund 12/21/1994
Oppenheimer Growth Fund merged into Oppenheimer Capital Appreciation Fund 11/08/2007

OPPENHEIMER TARGET FD (MA)
Reincorporated 00/00/1987
State of incorporation changed from (MD) to (MA) 00/00/1987
Shares of Bene. Int. $1 par reclassified as Class A $1 par 11/01/1993
Name changed to Oppenheimer Capital Appreciation Fund 12/18/1996

OPPENHEIMER TAX EXEMPT BD FD (MA)
Name changed to Oppenheimer Municipal Fund 10/10/96

OPPENHEIMER TAX FREE BD FD (MA)
Name changed to Oppenheimer Municipal Bond Fund 11/22/2002
Oppenheimer Municipal Bond Fund

name changed to Oppenheimer AMT-Free Municipals 10/27/2003

OPPENHEIMER TIME FD (MA)
Reincorporated 11/01/1985
Reincorporated from Oppenheimer Time Fund, Inc. (MD) to under the laws of Massachusetts as Oppenheimer Time Fund and Capital Stock $1 par reclassified as Shares of Bene. Int. no par 11/01/1985
Reorganized as Oppenheimer Target Fund, Inc. 08/23/1995
Each Share of Bene. Int. no par exchanged for Class A $1 par on a net asset basis
Oppenheimer Target Fund, Inc. name changed to Oppenheimer Capital Appreciation Fund 12/18/1996

OPPENHEIMER TOTAL RETURN FD INC (MD)
Common reclassified as Class A 5/3/93
Name changed to Oppenheimer Equity Fund, Inc. 8/29/2003

OPPENHEIMER TRINITY GROWTH FD (MA)
Reorganized as Oppenheimer Large Capital Growth Fund 10/12/2001
Each share Class A exchanged for (0.9291109) share Class A
Each share Class B exchanged for (0.93449865) share Class B
Each share Class C exchanged for (0.93394206) share Class C
Each share Class N exchanged for (0.92220103) share Class N
Each share Class Y exchanged for (0.92769855) share Class Y

OPPORTUNISTICS INC (DE)
Name changed to North American Integrated Marketing, Inc. 07/25/1989
North American Integrated Marketing, Inc. name changed to Directcom Inc. 04/09/1997
(See Directcom Inc.)

OPPORTUNITY INVT CORP (SC)
Charter forfeited 10/28/1996

OPPORTUNITY 21 INC (MI)
Name changed to Dixie Mining & Milling Corp. 11/05/1984
Dixie Mining & Milling Corp. recapitalized as Digital Gas, Inc. 12/21/1998
(See Digital Gas, Inc.)

OPPORTUNITY 21 (DE)
Charter revoked for failure to file reports and pay fees 09/01/1987

OPSEC SEC GROUP PLC (UNITED KINGDOM)
ADR agreement terminated 08/23/2017
No ADR's remain outstanding

OPSWARE INC (DE)
Merged into Hewlett-Packard Co. 09/21/2007
Each share Common $0.001 par exchanged for $14.25 cash

OPTA CORP OLD (DE)
Each share Common $0.001 par exchanged for (1) share Opta Corp. (New) Common $0.001 par to reflect a (1) for (5,000) reverse split followed by a (5,000) for (1) forward split 8/24/2006
Note: Holders of (4,999) or fewer pre-split shares received $0.06 cash per share

OPTA FOOD INGREDIENTS INC (DE)
Merged into Stake Technology Ltd. 12/18/2002
Each share Common 1¢ par exchanged for $2.50 cash

OPTA MINERALS INC (CANADA)
Acquired by Wedge Acquisition Holdings Inc. 04/08/2016
Each share Common no par exchanged for $0.52 cash

Note: Unexchanged certificates will be cancelled and become without value 04/08/2022

OPTEK TECHNOLOGY INC (DE)
Merged into Dyson-Kissner-Moran Corp. 06/21/1999
Each share Common 1¢ par exchanged for $25.50 cash

OPTEL CORP (DE)
Each share old Common 1¢ par exchanged for (0.125) share new Common 1¢ par 11/30/1980
Name changed to Moore Medical Corp. 05/22/1985
(See Moore Medical Corp.)

OPTEL INC (DE)
Plan of reorganization under Chapter 11 Federal Bankruptcy Code effective 1/31/2002
No stockholders' equity

OPTELECOM-NKF INC (DE)
Name changed 04/13/2005
Each share Common 1¢ par exchanged for (1/3) share Common 3¢ par 06/11/1992
Stock Dividend - 5% payable 12/01/1997 to holders of record 11/17/1997
Name changed from Optelecom, Inc. to Optelecom-NKF, Inc. 04/13/2005
Acquired by TKH Group N.V. 01/27/2011
Each share Common 3¢ par exchanged for $2.45 cash

OPTEUM INC (MD)
Name changed to Bimini Capital Management, Inc. 09/28/2007

OPTEX BIOMEDICAL INC (DE)
Charter cancelled and declared inoperative and void for non-payment of taxes 3/1/97

OPTI CDA INC (CANADA)
Conv. Preferred Ser. C no par called for redemption at $29.50 plus $0.74 accrued dividends on 02/16/2006
Common no par split (2) for (1) by issuance of (1) additional share payable 06/06/2006 to holders of record 06/01/2006 Ex date - 06/01/2006
Plan of arrangement under Companies' Creditors Arrangement Act effective 11/28/2011
Each share Common no par received first and final distribution of $0.12 cash

OPTI INC (CA)
Each share Common no par received distribution of (0.1666) share Tripath Technology Inc. Common $0.001 par payable 05/30/2002 to holders of record 04/24/2002
Liquidation completed
Each share Common no par received initial distribution of $1.10 cash payable 07/03/2012 to holders of record 06/26/2012
Each share Common no par received second and final distribution of $0.6369 cash payable 12/23/2016 to holders of record 12/08/2016 Ex date - 12/27/2016

OPTI SCAN DATA APPLICATIONS INC (NY)
Charter cancelled and proclaimed dissolved for failure to pay taxes and file reports 12/16/1974

OPTICAL ACQUISITION CORP (TX)
Reincorporated 09/00/1997
State of incorporation changed from (DE) to (TX) 09/00/1997
Name changed to Hilltop Acquisition Holding Corp. 06/26/1998
Hilltop Acquisition Holding Corp. recapitalized as Alford Refrigerated Warehouses, Inc. 12/15/1998
(See Alford Refrigerated Warehouses, Inc.)

OPTICAL-AUDIO RECORDING ENTERPRISES, INC. (NV)
Charter revoked for failure to file reports and pay fees 3/2/64

OPTICAL COATING LAB INC (DE)
Reincorporated 11/1/87
Common no par split (2) for (1) by issuance of (1) additional share 5/17/68
Common no par split (2) for (1) by issuance of (1) additional share 5/16/83
State of incorporation changed from (CA) to (DE) and Common no par changed to 1¢ par 11/1/87
Common 1¢ par split (3) for (1) by issuance of (2) additional shares 7/1/88
Common 1¢ par split (2) for (1) by issuance of (1) additional share payable 11/30/99 to holders of record 11/8/99
Merged into JDS Uniphase Corp. 2/4/2000
Each share Common 1¢ par exchanged for (1.856) shares Common 1¢ par

OPTICAL COMMUNICATION PRODS INC (DE)
Merged into Oplink Communications, Inc. 10/31/2007
Each share Class A Common $0.001 par exchanged for $1.65 cash

OPTICAL CONCEPTS AMER INC (FL)
Each share old Common $0.001 par exchanged for (0.1) share new Common $0.001 par 09/14/1998
Each share new Common $0.001 par exchanged again for (0.25) share new Common $0.001 par 05/12/2003
Recapitalized as IBSG International, Inc. 11/14/2003
Each share new Common $0.001 par exchanged for (0.02) share Common $0.001 par

OPTICAL DATA CORP (ON)
Recapitalized as AVL Information Systems Inc. 03/20/1992
Each share Capital Stock no par exchanged for (0.2) share Common no par
AVL Information Systems Inc. recapitalized as AVL Information Systems Ltd. 07/31/1996 which recapitalized as AVL Ventures Inc. 02/17/2003
(See AVL Ventures Inc.)

OPTICAL DATA SYS INC (AB)
Name changed to Compression Technologies Inc. 12/19/1994
Compression Technologies Inc. recapitalized as Compression & Encryption Technologies Inc. 07/17/1996

OPTICAL DATA SYS INC (DE)
Reincorporated 10/31/95
Common no par split (2) for (1) by issuance of (1) additional share 5/5/95
State of incorporation changed from (TX) to (DE) and Common no par changed to 1¢ par 10/31/95
Name changed to ODS Networks, Inc. 4/24/97
ODS Networks, Inc. name changed to Intrusion.com, Inc. 6/1/2000 which name changed to Intrusion Inc. 11/1/2001

OPTICAL DEVELOPMENT CORP. (NY)
Charter cancelled and proclaimed dissolved for non-payment of taxes 12/15/45

OPTICAL EXPRESS INC (UT)
Reorganized under the laws of Delaware as Bassett (J.R.) Optical Inc. 09/23/1994
Each share Common $0.001 par exchanged for (10) shares Common $0.001 par
Bassett (J.R.) Optical Inc. recapitalized as Samurai Energy Corp. (DE) 11/28/2005 which reincorporated in Nevada as ECCO Energy Corp. 09/01/2006 which recapitalized as Eagle Ford Oil & Gas, Corp. 07/27/2010

OPTICAL MOLECULAR IMAGING INC (DE)
Name changed to ImmunoCellular Therapeutics, Ltd. 11/30/2006

OPTICAL RADIATION CORP (CA)
Common 50¢ par split (2) for (1) by issuance of (1) additional share 1/14/83
Common 50¢ par split (2) for (1) by issuance of (1) additional share 7/5/83
Acquired by Benson Eyecare Corp. 10/12/94
Each share Common 50¢ exchanged for (1.0476) shares Common 1¢ par and $17 cash
Benson Eyecare Corp. merged into BEC Group Inc. 5/3/96 which recapitalized as Lumen Technologies, Inc. 3/12/98
(See Lumen Technologies, Inc.)

OPTICAL RESH & DEV CO (CA)
Name changed to Schwem Instruments and Capital Stock $1 par changed to 25¢ par 03/31/1982
Schwem Instruments name changed to Schwem Technology Inc. 04/19/1984
(See Schwem Technology Inc.)

OPTICAL SCANNING CORP (PA)
Name changed to Infoton Inc. (PA) 08/30/1977
Infoton Inc. (PA) reincorporated in Delaware as General Terminal Corp. 12/31/1979
(See General Terminal Corp.)

OPTICAL SEC GROUP INC (CO)
Each share old Common $0.005 par exchanged for (0.2) share new Common $0.005 par 2/28/95
Merged into Applied Holographics PLC 2/15/2000
Each share new Common $0.005 par exchanged for $7 cash

OPTICAL SENSORS INC (DE)
Each share old Common no par exchanged for (0.16666666) share new Common no par 09/16/2002
Name changed to Vasamed, Inc. 07/13/2007

OPTICAL SPECIALTIES INC (CA)
Each share old Common no par exchanged exchanged for (0.1) share new Common no par 08/01/1992
SEC revoked common stock registration 10/09/2008
Stockholders' equity unlikely

OPTICAL SYS CORP (DE)
Charter cancelled and declared inoperative and void for non-payment of taxes 3/1/81

OPTICAL SYS HLDGS INC (FL)
Name changed to Optical Systems, Inc. (FL) 07/3/1997
Optical Systems, Inc. (FL) reincorporated in Nevada as Benchmark Energy Corp. 09/08/2011

OPTICAL SYS INC (FL)
Reincorporated under the laws of Nevada as Benchmark Energy Corp. and Common $0.0001 par changed to $0.001 par 09/08/2011

OPTICARE HEALTH SYS INC (DE)
Merged into Refac Optical Group 3/6/2006
Each share Common $0.001 par exchanged for (0.0472) share Common $0.001 par

(See Refac Optical Group)

OPTICKS INC (TX)
Common $1 par split (3) for (2) by issuance of (0.5) additional share 8/15/67
Class B Common $1 par split (3) for (2) by issuance of (0.5) additional share 8/15/67
Acquired by Will Ross, Inc. 1/23/69
Each share Common $1 par or Class B Common $1 par exchanged for (0.76923) share Common $1 par
Will Ross, Inc. merged into Searle (G.D.) & Co. (DE) 12/31/73
(See Searle (G.D.) & Co. (DE))

OPTICO CORP (UT)
Name changed to Diamondback Financial Corp. 08/13/1984
(See Diamondback Financial Corp.)

OPTICO INC (NY)
Stock Dividend - 10% 10/22/1969
Completely liquidated 12/30/1976
Each share Common 10¢ par exchanged for first and final distribution of (1) share MPO Videotronics, Inc. Common $1 par
(See MPO Videotronics, Inc.)

OPTICOMP DATA MGMT CORP (NY)
Name changed to Capital Facilities Corp. 05/06/1971
(See Capital Facilities Corp.)

OPTICON MED INC (DE)
Name changed to Nextelligence, Inc. 6/9/2004

OPTICON SYS INC (NV)
Each share old Common $0.001 par exchanged for (0.05) share new Common $0.001 par 06/12/2008
Name changed to Infrax Systems Inc. 01/07/2010

OPTICORP INC (DE)
Reincorporated 03/00/1995
Common $0.001 par split (4) for (3) by issuance of (1/3) additional share 09/08/1989
State of incorporation changed from (FL) to (DE) 03/00/1995
Recapitalized as Viking Management Group Inc. 05/19/1995
Each share Common $0.001 par exchanged for (0.01) share Common $0.0001 par
Viking Management Group Inc. name changed to Viking Resources International Inc. 10/09/1995
(See Viking Resources International Inc.)

OPTICS TECHNOLOGY INC (CA)
Common $1 par changed to 10¢ par 02/28/1974
Each share old Common 10¢ par exchanged for (0.25) share new Common 10¢ par 01/01/1975
Merged into Interim Development Corp. 12/31/1976
Each share new Common 10¢ par exchanged for $0.30 cash

OPTIFAB INC (AZ)
Name changed to Optifund Inc. 6/26/89

OPTIKA INC (DE)
Name changed 12/10/98
Name changed from Optika Imaging Systems, Inc. to Optika, Inc. 12/10/98
Merged into Stellent, Inc. 5/28/2004
Each share Common $0.001 par exchanged for (0.44) share Common 1¢ par
(See Stellent, Inc.)

OPTIKA INVT INC (NV)
Reincorporated under the laws of Delaware as USA Broadband, Inc. 7/10/2001

OPTIMA PETE CORP (BC)
Recapitalized 07/09/1992
Recapitalized from Optima Energy Corp. to Optima Petroleum Corp. 07/09/1992

Each share Common no par exchanged for (0.4) share Common no par
Reincorporated under the laws of Delaware as Petroquest Energy, Inc. and Common no par changed to $0.001 par 09/01/1998

OPTIMAL ANALYTICS COM INC (NV)
Recapitalized as Optimal Ventures Inc. 02/20/2002
Each share Common $0.001 par exchanged for (0.25) share Common $0.001 par
Optimal Ventures Inc. name changed to Greenwind Power Corp. USA 04/08/2004 which recapitalized as HD Retail Solutions Inc. 07/07/2009 which name changed to Greenscape Laboratories, Inc. 06/10/2014 which recapitalized as Ultrack Systems, Inc. 04/11/2016

OPTIMAL COMPUTER SVCS INC (DE)
Name changed to Pantique, Inc. and Common 10¢ par reclassified as Class A 10¢ par 5/15/75
Pantique, Inc. name changed to Jetline Stores, Inc. 12/13/77 which name changed to NRX Technologies Inc. 1/4/80
(See NRX Technologies Inc.)

OPTIMAL GEOMATICS INC (CANADA)
Merged into Aeroquest International Ltd. 09/30/2009
Each share Common no par exchanged for (0.04761904) share Common no par
Note: Unexchanged certificates were cancelled and became without value 09/30/2015
(See Aeroquest International Ltd.)

OPTIMAL GROUP INC (CANADA)
Name changed 04/06/2004
Issue Information - 3,000,000 shares CL A offered at US$5.50 per share on 10/24/1996
Secondary Offering - 2,000,000 shares CL A NEW offered at $39 per share on 03/28/2000
Each share old Class A Common no par exchanged for (0.2) share new Class A Common no par 10/25/1996
Name changed from Optimal Robotics Corp. to Optimal Group Inc. 04/06/2004
Each share old Class A no par exchanged for (0.2) share new Class A no par 08/26/2009
Acquired by 7293411 Canada Inc. 07/09/2010
Each share new Class A no par exchanged for USD $2.40 cash

OPTIMAL VENTURES INC (NV)
Name changed to Greenwind Power Corp. USA 04/08/2004
Greenwind Power Corp. USA recapitalized as HD Retail Solutions Inc. 07/07/2009 which name changed to Greenscape Laboratories, Inc. 06/10/2014 which recapitalized as Ultrack Systems, Inc. 04/11/2016

OPTIMARK DATA SYS INC (BC)
Delisted from Toronto Venture Stock Exchange 09/18/2002

OPTIMAX INDS INC (CO)
Common 2¢ par changed to $0.001 par 11/01/2007
Each share old Common $0.001 par exchanged for (0.00666666) share new Common $0.001 par 09/23/2008
Name changed to Electric Motors Corp. 04/09/2009

OPTIMER PHARMACEUTICALS INC (DE)
Merged into Cubist Pharmaceuticals, Inc. 10/24/2013
Each share Common $0.001 par exchanged for (1) Contingent Value Right and $10.75 cash
Each Contingent Value Right received $0.059225 cash 02/02/2015

OPTIMISTICS INC (DE)
Name changed to Resnick Worldwide, Inc. 11/13/1989
Resnick Worldwide, Inc. recapitalized as Standard Brands of America Inc. 06/19/1995 which name changed to Lionshare Group, Inc. 05/07/1998
(See Lionshare Group, Inc.)

OPTIMIZED TRANSN MGMT INC (DE)
SEC revoked common stock registration 08/14/2012

OPTIMIZER INDS INC (MN)
Recapitalized as Metropane, Inc. 11/03/1994
Each share Common 2¢ par exchanged for (0.1) share Common $0.001 par
Metropane, Inc. name changed to Intermountain Ventures Inc. 08/28/2007 which name changed to Voice One Corp. 01/11/2011

OPTIMIZERX CORP (CO)
Reincorporated under the laws of Nevada 09/04/2008

OPTIMUM ELECTRS INC (DE)
Charter forfeited for failure to maintain a registered agent 2/25/98

OPTIMUM GEN INC (CANADA)
Merged into Optimum Group Inc. 12/21/2007
Each share Class A Subordinate no par exchanged for $5.15 cash

OPTIMUM HLDG CORP (NY)
Charter cancelled and proclaimed dissolved for failure to pay taxes 06/23/1993

OPTIMUM SOURCE INTL (NV)
Reincorporated under the laws of Nevada as Optimum Source International, Ltd. 06/29/1990

OPTIMUMBANK COM (PLANTATION, FL)
Under plan of reorganization each share Common $2.50 par automatically became (1) share OptimumBank Holdings, Inc. Common 1¢ par 5/6/2004

OPTIMUMCARE CORP (DE)
Stock Dividend - 20% payable 10/18/1996 to holders of record 10/01/1996
Company terminated common stock registration and is no longer public as of 05/13/2004

OPTIMUS INVTS LTD (AB)
Merged into Veritas Energy Services Inc. 11/01/1994
Each share Common no par exchanged for (0.101262) share Common no par
Veritas Energy Services Inc. merged into Veritas DGC Inc. 08/30/1996 which merged into Compagnie Generale de Geophysique-Veritas 01/12/2007 which name changed to CGG 05/29/2013

OPTIO SOFTWARE INC (GA)
Merged into Bottomline Technologies (DE), Inc. 04/21/2008
Each share Common no par exchanged for $1.85 cash

OPTION CARE INC (DE)
Common 1¢ par split (5) for (4) by issuance of (0.25) additional share payable 05/01/2002 to holders of record 04/10/2002 Ex date - 05/02/2002
Common 1¢ par split (3) for (2) by issuance of (0.5) additional share payable 03/31/2005 to holders of record 03/17/2005 Ex date - 04/01/2005
Merged into Walgreen Co. 08/20/2007

Each share Common 1¢ par exchanged for $19.50 cash

OPTION-NFA INC (BC)
Name changed to Sandwell Mining Ltd. (BC) 09/16/2009
Sandwell Mining Ltd. (BC) reorganized in Canada as MBAC Fertilizer Corp. 12/30/2009 which reorganized in Cayman Islands 11/07/2016 which name changed to Itafos 01/06/2017

OPTION NV (BELGIUM)
Sponsored ADR's for Ordinary split (4) for (1) by issuance of (3) additional ADR's payable 04/28/2006 to holders of record 04/27/2006
ADR agreement terminated 11/30/2017
Each Sponsored ADR for Ordinary exchanged for (1) share Ordinary

OPTION SECS CORP (DE)
Charter cancelled and declared inoperative and void for non-payment of taxes 03/01/1990

OPTIONS TALENT GROUP (NV)
Each share old Common $0.001 par exchanged for (0.01) share new Common $0.001 par 09/20/2002
Name changed to Trans Continental Entertainment Group Inc. 01/16/2003
(See Trans Continental Entertainment Group Inc.)

OPTIONSXPRESS HLDGS INC (DE)
Issue Information - 12,000,000 shares COM offered at $16.50 per share on 01/26/2005
Merged into Schwab Charles Corp. 09/01/2011
Each share Common $0.0001 par exchanged for (1.02) shares Common 1¢ par

OPTISYSTEMS SOLUTIONS LTD (ISRAEL)
Merged into BMC Software, Inc. 08/08/2000
Each share Ordinary ILS 0.05 par exchanged for $10 cash

OPTIUM CORP (DE)
Issue Information - 5,200,000 shares COM offered at $17.50 per share on 10/26/2006
Merged into Finisar Corp. 08/29/2008
Each share Common $0.0001 par exchanged for (6.262) shares Common $0.001 par

OPTIVAL INTL LABS INC (BC)
Recapitalized as Triad Technologies Ltd. (BC) 03/03/1994
Each share Common no par exchanged for (0.2) share Common no par
Triad Technologies Ltd. (BC) reincorporated in Yukon 05/20/1994 which recapitalized as MPAC Industries Corp. (Yukon) 12/16/1999 which reincorporated in British Columbia 07/28/2006

OPTIVISION INC (DE)
Charter cancelled and declared inoperative and void for non-payment of taxes 03/01/1984

OPTO MECHANIK INC (DE)
Assets sold for the benefit of creditors 07/05/1995
No stockholders' equity

OPTOMEDIC MED TECHNOLOGIES LTD (ISRAEL)
Ceased trading 00/00/2003
Stockholders' equity unlikely

OPTRIX RADIATION INC (CANADA)
Reorganized as Southern Arizona Mining & Smelting Corp. 09/19/1988
Each share Common no par exchanged for (1) share Common no par
Southern Arizona Mining & Smelting

OPT-ORA

OPT-ORA (continued)
Corp. recapitalized as Unirom Technologies Inc. 03/12/1997
(See Unirom Technologies Inc.)

OPTRONICS INTL INC (MA)
Merged into Intergraph Corp. 05/08/1986
Each share Common 1¢ par exchanged for (0.078) share Common 10¢ par
(See Intergraph Corp.)

OPTRONICS SYS INC (DE)
Charter cancelled and declared inoperative and void for non-payment of taxes 04/15/1973

OPTROTECH LTD (ISRAEL)
Ordinary Stock IS1.4 par split (3) for (2) by issuance of (0.5) additional share 04/09/1985
Name changed to Orbotech Ltd. 11/09/1992

OPTUS NAT GAS DISTR INCOME FD (ON)
Name changed to Direct Energy 09/01/1999
(See Direct Energy)

OPUS COMMTYS INC (TX)
Name changed to Virtual Ed Link, Inc. 12/31/2007

OPUS COMPUTER PRODS INC (OH)
Charter cancelled for failure to pay taxes 01/31/1992

OPUS MAGNUM AMERIS INC (FL)
Administratively dissolved 09/27/2013

OPUS MINERALS INC (ON)
Name changed to Investorlinks.com, Inc. 07/28/2000
Investorlinks.com, Inc. recapitalized as API Electronics Group Inc. (ON) 09/10/2001 which reorganized in Delaware as API Electronics Group Corp. 09/15/2004 which merged into API Nanotronics Corp. 11/07/2006 which name changed to API Technologies Corp. 10/27/2009
(See API Technologies Corp.)

OPUS RES GROUP INC (CO)
Recapitalized 9/29/2003
Recapitalized from Opus Media Group, Inc. to Opus Resource Group, Inc. 09/29/2003
Each share Common $0.001 par exchanged for (0.06666666) share Common $0.001 par
Recapitalized as BlastGard International, Inc. 03/31/2004
Each share Common $0.001 par exchanged for (0.2) share Common $0.001 par
BlastGard International, Inc. name changed to HighCom Global Security, Inc. 08/03/2017

OPUS360 CORP (DE)
Issue Information - 7,700,000 shares COM offered at $10 per share on 04/07/2000
Name changed to Artemis International Solutions Corp. 11/20/2001
(See Artemis International Solutions Corp.)

ORA ELECTRONICS INC (DE)
Chapter 11 bankruptcy proceedings terminated 01/17/2003
Stockholders' equity unlikely

ORA INDS INC (DE)
Name changed to Hospitality Health Care, Inc. 09/28/1977
(See Hospitality Health Care, Inc.)

ORA MINING CORP. (NV)
Charter revoked for failure to file reports and pay fees in March 1951

ORA RES INC (SK)
Reorganized under the laws of Alberta as Calahoo Petroleum Ltd. 05/27/1993
Each share Class A Common no par exchanged for (0.33333333) share Common no par
(See Calahoo Petroleum Ltd.)

ORACLE HEALTHCARE ACQUISITION CORP (DE)
Issue Information - 15,000,000 UNITS consisting of (1) share COM and (1) WT offered at $8 per Unit on 03/02/2006
Completely liquidated 05/07/2008
Each share Common $0.0001 par exchanged for first and final distribution of $8.04 cash

ORACLE MINERALS INC (BC)
Recapitalized as Prophet Minerals Corp. 05/02/1997
Each share Common no par exchanged for (0.2) share Common no par
Prophet Minerals Corp. name changed to Meridex Network Corp. 12/21/1999 which recapitalized as Meridex Software Corp. 02/13/2003 which name changed to Cannabis Technologies Inc. 05/21/2014 which name changed to InMed Pharmaceuticals Inc. 10/21/2014

ORACLE RES LTD (AB)
Merged into American Eagle Petroleums Ltd. 11/30/89
Each share Common no par exchanged for $0.55 cash

ORACLE SYS CORP (DE)
Reincorporated 3/25/87
State of incorporation changed from (CA) to (DE) and Common no par changed to 1¢ par 3/25/87
Common 1¢ par split (2) for (1) by issuance of (1) additional share 3/25/87
Common 1¢ par split (2) for (1) by issuance of (1) additional share 12/18/87
Common 1¢ par split (2) for (1) by issuance of (1) additional share 6/30/89
Common 1¢ par split (2) for (1) by issuance of (1) additional share 11/8/93
Common 1¢ par split (3) for (2) by issuance of (0.5) additional share 2/22/95
Under plan of merger name changed to Oracle Corp. 5/30/95

ORAL VISUAL MED INC (DE)
Name changed to Florida Sunshine Plants, Inc. 12/23/76
Florida Sunshine Plants, Inc. recapitalized as General Growth Industries, Inc. 7/24/79 which name changed to Silver Reclamation Industries, Inc. 5/1/80 which recapitalized as Inter America Industries, Inc. 1/28/83 which name changed to Kendee's International Foods Inc. 11/20/85
(See Kendee's International Foods Inc.)

ORALABS HLDG CORP (CO)
Each share old Common 1¢ par exchanged for (0.5) share new Common 1¢ par 12/16/2003
Name changed to China Precision Steel, Inc. (CO) 12/28/2006
China Precision Steel, Inc. (CO) reincorporated in Delaware 11/16/2007

ORALIFE GROUP INC (ON)
Merged into Nordic Acquisitions 1/26/2000
Each share Common no par exchanged for $0.163 cash

ORAMED PHARMACEUTICALS INC (NV)
Reincorporated under the laws of Delaware 03/11/2011

ORAMERICAS CORP (BC)
Reincorporated 02/21/2014
Place of incorporation changed from (ON) to (BC) 02/21/2014
Name changed to Backstageplay Inc. 02/09/2016

ORANAMICS INC (DE)
Recapitalized as Collegiate Distributing Corp. 12/22/86
Each share Common 1¢ par exchanged for (1/7) share Common 1¢ par
(See Collegiate Distributing Corp.)

ORANGE & ROCKLAND ELECTRIC CO. (NY)
Common $100 par changed to no par in 1935
Merged into Orange & Rockland Utilities, Inc. 2/28/58
Each share 4% Preferred $100 par exchanged for (1) share 4% Preferred Series D $100 par
Each share Common no par exchanged for (3.75) shares Common $10 par
Orange & Rockland Utilities, Inc. merged into Consolidated Edison, Inc. 7/8/99

ORANGE & ROCKLAND UTILS INC (NY)
5.75% Preferred Ser. C $100 par called for redemption 05/27/1959
5% Preferred Ser. E $100 par called for redemption 05/12/1961
Common $10 par changed to $5 par and (1) additional share issued 06/19/1963
$1.52 Conv. Preference Ser. A no par called for redemption at $32.50 plus $0.2702 accrued dividends on 04/06/1999
4% Preferred Ser. D $100 par called for redemption at $100 on 04/20/1999
4.65% Preferred Ser. A $100 par called for redemption at $104.25 on 04/20/1999
4.68% Preferred Ser. F $100 par called for redemption at $102 on 04/20/1999
4.75% Preferred Ser. B $100 par called for redemption at $102 on 04/20/1999
7.10% Preferred Ser. G $100 par called for redemption at $101 on 04/20/1999
8.08% Preferred Ser. H $100 par called for redemption at $102.43 on 04/20/1999
8-1/8% Preferred Ser. I $100 par called for redemption 04/20/1999
Merged into Consolidated Edison, Inc. 07/08/1999
Each share Common $5 par exchanged for $58.02 cash

ORANGE BANCORP (CA)
Merged into Bank of Orange County (Fountain Valley, CA) 11/30/96
Each share Common no par exchanged for (0.6830601) share Common no par
(See Bank of Orange County (Fountain Valley, CA))

ORANGE BLOSSOM PRODS INC (DE)
Charter cancelled and declared inoperative and void for non-payment of taxes 6/25/87

ORANGE BOWL CORP (DE)
Each share Common 10¢ par exchanged for (0.04) share Common $2.50 par 06/04/1976
Charter cancelled and declared inoperative and void for non-payment of taxes 03/01/1997

ORANGE-CO INC (DE)
Stock Dividend - 15% 06/07/1976
Name changed to Stoneridge Resources, Inc. 04/29/1987
Stoneridge Resources, Inc. recapitalized as Acceptance Insurance Companies Inc. 12/22/1992
(See Acceptance Insurance Companies Inc.)

ORANGE-CO INC NEW (FL)
Merged into Reservoir Capital Group, L.L.C. 11/1/99
Each share Common 50¢ par exchanged for $7 cash

ORANGE COAST SAVINGS & LOAN ASSOCIATION (CA)
Common $5 par changed to $3.33-1/3 par and (0.5) additional share issued 11/15/1979
Name changed to Charter Savings Bank (Huntington Beach, CA) 01/00/1986
(See Charter Savings Bank (Huntington Beach, CA))

ORANGE CMNTY BANCORP (CA)
Common no par split (5) for (4) by issuance of (0.25) additional share payable 06/15/2007 to holders of record 05/16/2007 Ex date - 06/18/2007
Acquired by Grandpoint Capital Inc. 08/29/2011
Each share Common no par exchanged for $12.01 cash

ORANGE CMNTY BK (ORANGE, CA)
Common no par split (3) for (2) by issuance of (0.5) additional share payable 07/06/2004 to holders of record 06/07/2004 Ex date - 07/07/2004
Under plan of reorganization each share Common no par automatically became (1) share Orange Community Bancorp Common no par 12/20/2006
(See Orange Community Bancorp)

ORANGE CONCENTRATES ASSOCIATES, INC.
Liquidation completed in 1951

ORANGE CNTY BUSINESS BK N A (NEWPORT BEACH, CA)
Stock Dividend - 10% payable 04/17/2007 to holders of record 03/30/2007 Ex date - 03/28/2007
Merged into HomeStreet, Inc. 02/01/2016
Each share Common no par exchanged for (0.5206) share Common no par and $1.1641 cash

ORANGE COUNTY PUBLIC SERVICE CO.
Merged into Rockland Light & Power Co. 00/00/1926
Details not available

ORANGE CNTY TEL CO (NY)
Common $100 par changed to no par in 1950
Completely liquidated 5/16/68
Each share Common no par exchanged for first and final distribution of (3) shares General Telephone & Electronics Corp. Common $3.33-1/3 par
General Telephone & Electronics Corp. name changed to GTE Corp. 7/1/82 which merged into Verizon Communications Inc. 6/30/2000

ORANGE CNTY TR CO (MIDDLETOWN, NY)
Common $100 par split (10) for (1) by issuance of (9) additional shares payable 06/29/2001 to holders of record 06/29/2001
Stock Dividends - 100% 01/08/1952; 25% 06/24/1952
Under plan of reorganization each share Common $100 par automatically became (1) share Orange County Bancorp, Inc. Common 50¢ par 08/01/2007

ORANGE CRUSH CO. (IL)
Name changed to Crush International Inc. 1/1/60
Crush International Inc. acquired by Crush International Ltd. (Ont.) 10/29/62 which reincorporated in British Columbia 2/19/81 which name changed to Great Pacific Industries, Inc. 3/10/81

(See Great Pacific Industries, Inc.)

ORANGE CRUSH DE CUBA, S.A. (CUBA)
Merged into Orange Crush del Caribe, S.A. share for share 1/31/56

ORANGE CRUSH LTD. (ON)
Each share 1st Preference $35 par exchanged for (4) shares 70¢ Preference no par and (3) shares Common no par 00/00/1936
Each (40) shares 2nd Preference no par exchanged for (4) shares 70¢ Preference no par and (10) shares Common no par 00/00/1936
Each share Common $1 par exchanged for (0.2) share Common no par 00/00/1936
Name changed to Crush International Ltd. (ON) 10/01/1959
Crush International Ltd. (ON) reincorporated in British Columbia 02/19/1981 which name changed to Great Pacific Industires, Inc. 03/10/1981
(See Great Pacific Industries, Inc.)

ORANGE CRYSTALS, INC. (FL)
Name changed to Plant Industries, Inc. (FL) 4/24/59
Plant Industries, Inc. (FL) reincorporated in Delaware 9/27/68
(See Plant Industries, Inc. (DE))

ORANGE EMPIRE NATIONAL BANK (ANAHEIM, CA)
Merged into Standard Systems International, Inc. 5/14/71
Each share Capital Stock $6 par exchanged for (0.5) share Capital Stock 50¢ par
Standard Systems International, Inc. charter forfeited 11/30/73

ORANGE FED SVGS & LN ASSN CHAPEL HILL N C (USA)
Common 1¢ par split (3) for (2) by issuance of (0.5) additional share 04/22/1988
Common 1¢ par split (5) for (4) by issuance of (0.25) additional share 10/24/1988
Merged into Centura Banks, Inc. 12/31/1992
Each share Common 1¢ par exchanged for (1) share Common no par
Centura Banks, Inc. merged into Royal Bank of Canada (Montreal, QC) 06/05/2001

ORANGE FREE ST INVT TR LTD (SOUTH AFRICA)
Under plan of merger each ADR for Ordinary Rand-1 par automatically became (1) Anglo American Gold Investment Co., Ltd. ADR for Ordinary Rand-1 par 6/12/72
Anglo American Gold Investment Co., Ltd. merged into Anglo American plc 5/24/99

ORANGE FREE ST INVTS LTD (SOUTH AFRICA)
Plan of arrangement effective 4/19/94
Each (100) ADR's for Ordinary Rand-50 par exchanged for (261) FreeState Consolidated Gold Mines Ltd. ADR's for Ordinary Rand-50 par
FreeState Consolidated Gold Mines Ltd. merged into AngloGold Ltd. 6/29/98 which name changed to AngloGold Ashanti Ltd. 4/26/2004

ORANGE JULIUS INTL INC (DE)
Name changed to Crescott, Inc. 08/14/1987
Crescott, Inc. recapitalized as China Career Builder Corp. 11/17/2006 which recapitalized as iMing Corp. 06/08/2012

ORANGE MAIL INC (NY)
Charter cancelled and proclaimed dissolved for failure to pay taxes 09/24/1997

ORANGE NATL BANCORP (CA)
Merged into CVB Financial Corp. 10/4/99
Each share Common $1.66-2/3 par exchanged for (1.5) shares Common no par

ORANGE NATIONAL BANK (ORANGE, CT)
Merged into CBT Corp. 9/13/82
Each share Common $5 par exchanged for (0.3976) share Common $10 par and $8 cash
Note: Option to receive all stock or cash expired 9/30/82
CBT Corp. merged into Bank of New England Corp. 6/14/85
(See Bank of New England Corp.)

ORANGE PLC (ENGLAND & WALES)
ADR agreement terminated 03/13/2000
Each ADR for Ordinary 20p par exchanged for approximately $199.67 cash

ORANGE POLSKA S A (POLAND)
GDR agreement terminated 05/11/2015
Each 144A Sponsored GDR for Common exchanged for $2.689171 cash
Each Reg. S Sponsored GDR for Common exchanged for $2.689171 cash

ORANGE SVGS BK (ORANGE, MA)
Common 10¢ par split (3) for (2) by issuance of (0.5) additional share 11/16/1987
Common 10¢ par split (3) for (2) by issuance of (0.5) additional share 11/17/1988
Acquired by CFX Corp. 04/28/1995
Each share Common $1 par exchanged for (0.8075) share Common $1 par
CFX Corp. merged into Peoples Heritage Financial Group, Inc. 04/10/1998 which name changed to Banknorth Group, Inc. (ME) 05/10/2000 which merged into TD Banknorth Inc. 03/01/2005
(See TD Banknorth Inc.)

ORANGE-STATE LIFE INSURANCE CO. (FL)
Merged into Founders Financial Corp. (FL) 6/16/69
Each share Capital Stock $1 par exchanged for (1) share Common $1 par
Founders Financial Corp. (FL) merged into Laurentian Capital Corp. (FL) 12/1/86 which reincorporated in Delaware 7/24/87
(See Laurentian Capital Corp.)

ORANGE 21 INC (DE)
Issue Information - 3,480,000 shares COM offered at $8.75 per share on 12/13/2004
Name changed to Spy Inc. 02/15/2012

ORANGE VALLEY BK (ORANGE, NJ)
Merged into First National State Bancorporation 12/07/1970
Each share Common $10 par exchanged for (2) shares Common $6.25 par
First National State Bancorporation name changed to First Fidelity Bancorporation (Old) 05/01/1985 which merged into First Fidelity Bancorporation (New) 02/29/1988 which merged into First Union Corp. 01/01/1996 which name changed to Wachovia Corp. (Ctfs. dated after 09/01/2001) 09/01/2001 which merged into Wells Fargo & Co. (New) 12/31/2008

ORANGEBURG MANUFACTURING CO., INC. (NY)
Each share Common $10 par exchanged for (2) shares Common $5 par 11/16/55
Assets sold to Flintkote Co. and each share Common $5 par exchanged for (0.28) share $4.50 2nd Preferred A $100 par 12/1/58
(See Flintkote Co.)

ORANGEROOF CDA LTD (CANADA)
Under plan of merger each share Class B Common no par exchanged for $1.30 cash 12/29/1977

ORANTA JT STK CO NATL JT STK INS CO (UKRAINE)
GDR agreement terminated 11/10/2015
Each GDR for Ordinary exchanged for (1) share Ordinary
Note: Unexchanged GDR's will be sold and the proceeds, if any, held for claim

ORAPHARMA INC (DE)
Issue Information - 4,000,000 shares COM offered at $18 per share on 03/09/2000
Merged into Johnson & Johnson 2/10/2003
Each share Common $0.001 par exchanged for $7.41 cash

ORASCOM CONSTR INDS S A E (EGYPT)
Sponsored 144A GDR's for Ordinary split (2) for (1) by issuance of (1) additional GDR payable 10/25/2004 to holders of record 10/20/2004
Sponsored Reg. S GDR's for Ordinary split (2) for (1) by issuance of (1) additional GDR payable 10/25/2004 to holders of record 10/20/2004
Sponsored 144A GDR's for Ordinary split (2) for (1) by issuance of (1) additional GDR payable 05/07/2009 to holders of record 05/06/2009 Ex date - 05/07/2009
Sponsored Reg. S GDR's for Ordinary split (2) for (1) by issuance of (1) additional GDR payable 05/07/2009 to holders of record 05/06/2009 Ex date - 05/07/2009
GDR basis changed from (1:2) to (1:1) 05/07/2009
Stock Dividends - 5% payable 10/25/2002 to holders of record 10/10/2002 Ex date - 10/08/2002; in Reg. S GDR's to holders of Reg. S GDR's 10% payable 01/15/2003 to holders of record 01/09/2003
ADR agreement terminated 11/24/2014
Each Sponsored ADR for Ordinary exchanged for $20.957825 cash
GDR agreement terminated 11/24/2014
Each Sponsored 144A GDR for Ordinary exchanged for $20.957825 cash
Each Sponsored Reg. S GDR for Ordinary exchanged for $20.957825 cash

ORASCOM TELECOM HLDG S A E (EGYPT)
Basis changed from (1:0.5) to (1:1) 01/23/2006
Basis changed from (1:1) to (1:5) 03/25/2007
Each 144A GDR for Ordinary received distribution of $1.028951 cash payable 07/06/2012 to holders of record 01/20/2012
Each Reg. S GDR for Ordinary received distribution of $1.028951 cash payable 07/06/2012 to holders of record 01/20/2012
Name changed to Global Telecom Holding S.A.E. 10/01/2013
(See Global Telecom Holding S.A.E.)

ORATEC INTERVENTIONS INC (DE)
Issue Information - 4,000,000 shares COM offered at $14 per share on 04/04/2000
Merged into Smith & Nephew PLC 4/1/2002
Each share Common $0.001 par exchanged for $12.50 cash

ORATRONICS INC (NY)
Each share old Common 10¢ par exchanged for (0.1) share new Common 10¢ par 11/8/93
Merged into Oratronics Acquisition 10/28/94
Each share Common 10¢ par exchanged for $1.50 cash

ORAVAX INC (DE)
Merged into Peptide Therapeutics Group PLC 5/11/99
Each share Common 1¢ par exchanged for (0.50913) Ordinary Share 10p par
Peptide Therapeutics Group PLC name changed to Acambis PLC 12/5/2000
(See Acambis PLC)

ORAVEST INTL INC (CO)
Recapitalized as Camdon Holdings, Inc. 06/22/1990
Each share Common $0.001 par exchanged for (0.025) share Common 1¢ par
Camdon Holdings, Inc. name changed to American Temperature Control, Inc. 11/03/1993 which name changed to Connectivity & Technologies, Inc. 12/10/1993 which recapitalized as Peacock Financial Corp. (CO) 02/27/1996 which reorganized in Nevada as Broadleaf Capital Partners, Inc. 03/22/2002 which recapitalized as EnergyTek Corp. 07/23/2014 which recapitalized as TimefireVR Inc. 11/22/2016

ORBANCO FINL SVCS CORP (OR)
Name changed 5/9/80
4.2% Conv. Preference $10 par called for redemption 3/30/77
Stock Dividend - 10% 4/30/77
Name changed from Orbanco, Inc. to Orbanco Financial Services Corp. 5/9/80
Acquired by Security Pacific Corp. 4/15/87
Each share Common no par exchanged for (0.3766) share Common $10 par and $1.50 cash
Security Pacific Corp. merged into BankAmerica Corp. (Old) 4/22/92 which merged into BankAmerica Corp. (New) 9/30/98 which name changed to Bank of America Corp. 4/28/99

ORBEX INDS INC (BC)
Name changed 02/17/1986
Name changed from Orbex Minerals Ltd. to Orbex Industries Inc. 02/17/1986
Recapitalized as Silver Glance Resources Inc. 03/07/1990
Each share Common no par exchanged for (0.2) share Common no par
Silver Glance Resources Inc. name changed to Silverspar Minerals Inc. (BC) 06/17/1992 which reincorporated in Ontario 09/23/1997 which name changed to Internet Identity Presence Co. Inc. 02/02/2001 which name changed to Geophysical Prospecting, Inc. 12/06/2005 which name changed to Revolution Technologies Inc. 03/18/2008

ORBIMAGE HLDGS INC (DE)
Name changed 06/20/2005
Name changed from Orbimage Inc. to Orbimage Holdings Inc. 06/20/2005
Name changed to GeoEye, Inc. 10/05/2006
GeoEye, Inc. merged into DigitalGlobe, Inc. 02/01/2013 which merged into MacDonald, Dettwiler & Associates Ltd. 10/05/2017 which name changed to Maxar Technologies Ltd. 10/10/2017

ORBIS DEV INC (NV)
Ctfs. dated prior to 06/18/1998
Name changed to Struthers Inc. 06/18/1998
Struthers Inc. name changed to Global Marine Ltd. 08/02/2004
(See Global Marine Ltd.)

ORBIS DEV INC (NV)
Ctfs. dated after 06/18/1998
Recapitalized as Global Pari-Mutuel Services, Inc. 09/06/2005
Each share Common $0.001 par exchanged for (0.2) share Common $0.001 par
(See Global Pari-Mutel Services, Inc.)

ORBIS INC (RI)
Reorganized under the laws of Delaware as Industrial Imaging Corp. 1/7/97
Each share Common 1¢ par exchanged for (1/18) share Common 1¢ par

ORBIT BRANDS CORP (DE)
Chapter 11 bankruptcy proceedings dismissed 02/25/2008
Stockholders' equity unlikely

ORBIT E COMMR INC (NV)
SEC revoked common stock registration 06/27/2012

ORBIT GAS CO (KY)
Name changed to Orco, Inc. 4/13/92
(See Orco, Inc.)

ORBIT INDUSTRIES, INC. (PR)
Completely liquidated 8/10/68
Each share Common 10¢ par exchanged for first and final distribution of (0.18116) share Hubbell (Harvey), Inc. Class B Common $5 par
Hubbell (Harvey), Inc. name changed to Hubbell Inc. 5/12/86

ORBIT INSTRUMENT CORP (DE)
Reincorporated 12/22/86
Capital Stock 10¢ par split (6) for (1) by issuance of (5) additional shares 1/5/81
Stock Dividend - 100% 4/26/83
State of incorporation changed from (NY) to (DE) 12/22/86
Name changed to Orbit International Corp. 12/22/91

ORBIT OIL & GAS LTD (AB)
Merged into Sunoma Energy Corp. 1/23/98
Each share Common no par exchanged for $1.77 cash
7.5% Conv. Preferred Ser. 2 Class A no par called for redemption at $10 plus $0.1125 accrued dividend on 2/23/98
8.50% Conv. Preferred Ser. 3 Class A no par called for redemption at $10 plus $0.1275 accrued dividend on 2/23/98
Non-Dividend Preferred Ser. 1 Class A no par called for redemption 2/23/98
Public interest eliminated

ORBIT OILS LTD. (SK)
Struck off register for failure to file annual returns 8/8/69

ORBIT PETE INC (NV)
Chapter 11 bankruptcy proceedings converted to Chapter 7 on 01/18/2012
Stockholders' equity unlikely

ORBIT SEMICONDUCTOR INC (DE)
Merged into DII Group Inc. 08/22/1996
Each share Common $0.001 par exchanged for (0.45) share Common $0.001 par
DII Group Inc. merged into Flextronics International Ltd. 04/03/2000 which name changed to Flex Ltd. 09/28/2016

ORBIT STORES, INC. (DE)
Acquired by Stop & Shop, Inc. 1/18/65
Each share Common 10¢ par exchanged for (0.125) share Common $1 par
Stop & Shop, Inc. name changed to Stop & Shop Companies, Inc. 5/26/70
(See Stop & Shop Companies, Inc.)

ORBIT TECHNOLOGIES INC (DE)
Name changed to Technology Visions Group Inc. and Common 1¢ par changed to $0.001 par 12/26/2000
Technology Visions Group Inc. recapitalized as Sutura, Inc. 8/22/2005

ORBITAL ATK INC (DE)
Acquired by Northrop Grumman Corp. 06/06/2018
Each share Common 1¢ par exchanged for $134.50 cash

ORBITAL CORP LTD (AUSTRALIA)
Name changed 11/15/2004
Each old Sponsored ADR for Ordinary exchanged for (0.625) new Sponsored ADR for Ordinary 12/11/1991
Each new Sponsored ADR for Ordinary exchanged again for (0.2) new Sponsored ADR for Ordinary par 05/08/2003
ADR basis changed from (1:8) to (1:40) 05/08/2003
Name changed from Orbital Engine Corp. Ltd. to Orbital Corp. Ltd. 11/15/2004
Each old Sponsored ADR for Ordinary exchanged for (0.25) new Sponsored ADR for Ordinary 04/15/2010
ADR basis changed from (1:40) to (1:160) 04/15/2010
ADR basis changed from (1:160) to (1:16) 11/22/2010
ADR agreement terminated 12/09/2013
Each new Sponsored ADR for Ordinary exchanged for $2.272403 cash

ORBITAL ENTERPRISES (NV)
Each share old Common $0.001 par exchanged for (0.01) share new Common $0.001 par 06/04/2007
Charter revoked for failure to file reports and pay fees 12/31/2009

ORBITAL SCIENCES CORP (DE)
Merged into Orbital ATK, Inc. 02/09/2015
Each share Common 1¢ par exchanged for (0.449) share Common 1¢ par
(See Orbital ATK, Inc.)

ORBITE ALUMINAE INC (CANADA)
Name changed to Orbite Technologies Inc. 06/17/2015

ORBITEX INC (NV)
Recapitalized as OTX, Inc. 8/15/74
Each share Common 1¢ par exchanged for (0.25) share Common 4¢ par
OTX, Inc. name changed to Mills-Jennings Co. 6/4/81
(See Mills-Jennings Co.)

ORBITRON CAP CORP (DE)
Each share old Common $0.00001 par exchanged for (0.01) share new Common $0.00001 par 08/31/1989
Charter cancelled and declared inoperative and void for non-payment of taxes 03/01/1996

ORBITTRAVEL COM CORP (DE)
Name changed to Orbit Brands Corp. 10/12/2005
(See Orbit Brands Corp.)

ORBITZ INC (DE)
Issue Information - 12,180,000 shares CL A offered at $26 per share on 12/16/2003
Merged into Cendant Corp. 11/15/2004
Each share Class A Common $0.001 par exchanged for $27.50 cash

ORBITZ WORLDWIDE INC (DE)
Acquired by Expedia, Inc. 09/17/2015
Each share Common 1 par exchanged for $12 cash

ORBOT SYS LTD (ISRAEL)
Acquired by Optrotech Ltd. 08/17/1992
Details not available

ORCA GROUP INC (NV)
Name changed to Triton Productions, Inc. 11/09/1987

ORCA INTL LANGUAGE SCHS INC (BC)
Name changed to SGB International Holdings Inc. 03/04/2009
SGB International Holdings Inc. name changed to Grand China Energy Group Ltd. 08/19/2014

ORCA PETE INC (AB)
Reorganized under the laws of British Columbia as Nautilus Minerals Inc. 5/10/2006
Each share Common no par exchanged for (1/6) share Common no par

ORCA PWR CORP (BC)
Reorganized under the laws of Canada as AFG Flameguard Ltd. 04/11/2012
Each share Common no par exchanged for (0.25) share Common no par

ORCA TECHNOLOGIES INC (UT)
SEC revoked common stock registration 08/09/2012

ORCA TOUCHSCREEN TECHNOLOGIES LTD (BC)
Common no par split (4) for (1) by issuance of (3) additional shares payable 07/11/2014 to holders of record 07/11/2014 Ex date - 07/09/2014
Recapitalized as Biome Grow Inc. 10/09/2018
Each share Common no par exchanged for (0.02) share Common no par

ORCA WIND PWR CORP (BC)
Reorganized as Gorilla Resources Corp. 10/13/2011
Each share Common no par exchanged for (0.05) share Common no par
Gorilla Resources Corp. name changed to Winston Resources Inc. 06/25/2012

ORCAD INC (DE)
Merged into Cadence Design Systems, Inc. 07/29/1999
Each share Common 1¢ par exchanged for $13 cash

ORCAS CORP (UT)
Recapitalized as Systems For Health Care, Inc. 3/5/87
Each share Common $0.001 par exchanged for (0.02) share Common 5¢ par
(See Systems For Health Care, Inc.)

ORCAS LTD (NV)
Reincorporated under the laws of Delaware as Ezcomm Inc. 1/18/2000
Ezcomm Inc. name changed to Ezcomm Enterprises Inc. 7/19/2004 which recapitalized as Eugene Science, Inc. 1/13/2006

ORCATECH INC (CANADA)
Recapitalized as Tele-Radio Systems Ltd. 2/5/88
Each share Common no par exchanged for (0.1) share Common no par
(See Tele-Radio Systems Ltd.)

ORCATRON COMMUNICATIONS LTD (BC)
Company reported out of business 00/00/2004
Details not available

ORCHAN MINES LTD (ON)
Name changed 5/20/77
Capital Stock $1 par reclassified as Conv. Class A Capital Stock $1 par 9/10/75
Name changed from Orchan Mines Ltd. to Orchan Mines Ltd.-Mines Orchan Ltee. 5/20/77
Merged into Noranda Mines Ltd. 12/31/78
Each share Conv. Class A Capital Stock $1 par exchanged for (1/6) share Conv. Class A no par
Each share Conv. Class B Capital Stock $1 par exchanged for (1/6) share Conv. Class B no par
Noranda Mines Ltd. name changed to Noranda Inc. 5/28/84 which name changed to Falconbridge Ltd. (New) 2005 on 7/1/2005
(See Falconbridge Ltd. (New) 2005)

ORCHAN URANIUM MINES LTD. (ON)
Name changed to Orchan Mines Ltd. 7/30/57
Orchan Mines Ltd. name changed to Orchan Mines Ltd.-Mines Orchan Ltee. 5/20/77 which merged into Noranda Mines Ltd. 12/31/78 which name changed to Noranda Inc. 5/28/84 which name changed to Falconbridge Ltd. (New) 2005 on 7/1/2005
(See Falconbridge Ltd. (New) 2005)

ORCHARD ENTERPRISES INC (DE)
Merged into Dimensional Associates, L.L.C. 07/30/2010
Each share Common 1¢ par exchanged for $2.05 cash and (1) Contingent Right

ORCHARD FARM BAKING CO.
Merged into Jersey Farm Baking Co. (Del.) through a share for share exchange of Preferred and Common in 1947
Jersey Farm Baking Co. name was changed to Farm Crest Bakeries, Inc. 3/8/65 which merged into Ward Foods, Inc. 12/25/65
(See Ward Foods, Inc.)

ORCHARD FARM PIE CO.
Name changed to Orchard Farm Baking Co. in 1945 which merged into Jersey Farm Baking Co. (Del.) in 1947 which name was changed to Farm Crest Bakeries, Inc. 3/8/65 which merged into Ward Foods, Inc. 12/25/65
(See Ward Foods, Inc.)

ORCHARD SUPPLY BLDG CO (CA)
Liquidation completed
Each share Common $1 par exchanged for initial distribution of (1.61974) shares Grace (W.R.) & Co. (CT) Common $1 par and $1.2886 cash 01/31/1979
Each share Common $1 par received second and final distribution of (0.17997) share Grace (W.R.) & Co. (CT) Common $1 par 04/01/1980
Grace (W.R.) & Co. (CT) reincorporated in New York 05/19/1988
(See Grace (W.R.) & Co.)

ORCHARD SUPPLY HARDWARE STORES CORP (DE)
Merged into Sears Roebuck & Co. 09/26/1996
Each share Common 1¢ par exchanged for $35 cash
Name changed to OSH 1 Liquidating Corp. 09/27/2013

ORCHARDS WEST LTD (AB)
Reorganized under the laws of Ontario as China Clipper Gold Mines Ltd. 07/08/1996
Each share Common no par exchanged for (0.25) share Common no par
China Clipper Gold Mines Ltd. recapitalized as Kinloch Resources

Inc. (ON) 05/07/2001 which
reincorporated in Alberta 06/29/2001
which recapitalized as Stylus Energy
Inc. 03/01/2005
(See Stylus Energy Inc.)

ORCHESTRA THERAPEUTICS INC (DE)
Chapter 7 bankruptcy proceedings
terminated 08/18/2009
No stockholders' equity

ORCHESTREAM HLDGS PLC (ENGLAND)
ADR agreement terminated
11/27/2002
Each Sponsored ADR for Ordinary
10p par exchanged for $0.9165 cash

ORCHID BIOSCIENCES INC (DE)
Issue Information - 6,000,000 shares
COM offered at $8 per share on
05/04/2001
Each share old Common $0.001 par
exchanged for (0.2) share new
Common $0.001 par 03/31/2004
Name changed to Orchid Cellmark
Inc. 06/15/2005
Each share new Common $0.001 par
exchanged for (1) share Common
$0.001 par
(See Orchid Cellmark Inc.)

ORCHID CELLMARK INC (DE)
Acquired by Laboratory Corp. of
America Holdings 12/19/2011
Each share Common $0.001 par
exchanged for $2.80 cash

ORCHID CHEMICALS & PHARMACEUTICALS LTD (INDIA)
Name changed to Orchid Pharma Ltd.
04/29/2016

ORCKIT COMMUNICATIONS LTD (ISRAEL)
Each share Ordinary ILS 0.10 par
exchanged for (0.2) share Ordinary
no par 11/27/2002
Ordinary no par split (3) for (1) by
issuance of (2) additional shares
payable 04/13/2005 to holders of
record 04/04/2005 Ex date -
04/05/2005
Completely liquidated 07/29/2015
No stockholders' equity

ORCO INC (KY)
Each share old Common no par
exchanged for (0.005) share new
Common no par 3/10/94
Merged into LRM Holding Co., Inc.
11/4/96
Each share new Common no par
exchanged for $750 cash

ORCO RES INC (CANADA)
Merged into Minorca Resources Inc.
12/30/1994
Each share Common no par
exchanged for (0.383) share
Common no par
Minorca Resources Inc. merged into
McWatters Mining Inc. 10/26/1998
(See McWatters Mining Inc.)

ORCOUR GOLD MINES (1940) LTD. (ON)
Former transfer agent advised charter
was reported cancelled in May 1968

ORCOUR GOLD MINES LTD.
Acquired by Orcour Gold Mines
(1940) Ltd. on a (100) for (1) basis
in 1940
Orcour Gold Mines (1940) Ltd. charter
cancelled in May 1968

ORDALA MINES LTD. (ON)
Ceased operations 08/31/1967
Had no assets as of 12/30/1969

ORDER LOGISTICS INC (DE)
Each share old Common $0.001 par
exchanged for (0.1) share new
Common $0.001 par 07/26/2007
Name changed to World Logistics
Services, Inc. 12/21/2007

ORDERPRO LOGISTICS INC (NV)
Recapitalized as Securus Renewable
Energy Inc. 02/08/2010
Each share Common $0.0001 par
exchanged for (0.004) share
Common $0.0001 par
(See Securus Renewable Energy Inc.)

ORDNANCE ENGR ASSOC INC (IL)
Reincorporated under the laws of
Delaware as OEA, Inc. and
Common no par changed to 10¢ par
12/5/69
(See OEA, Inc.)

ORDORADO RES CORP (CANADA)
Name changed to Eagle Star
Petroleum Corp. 06/22/2006
Eagle Star Petroleum Corp. name
changed to Eagle Star Minerals
Corp. 07/06/2010 which name
changed to DuSolo Fertilizers Inc.
(Canada) 02/28/2014 which
reincorporated in British Columbia
07/19/2016 which name changed to
Fengro Industries Corp. 12/18/2017

ORDZHONIKIDZEVSKY ORE MNG & PROCESSING ENTERPRISE OPEN JT STK CO (UKRAINE)
ADR agreement terminated
05/30/2017
No ADR's remain outstanding

ORE-BEST INC (DE)
Charter cancelled and declared
inoperative and void for
non-payment of taxes 6/26/90

ORE HLDGS INC (DE)
Reorganized 06/13/2011
Reorganized from Ore
Pharmaceutical Holdings Inc. to Ore
Holdings Inc. 06/13/2011
Each share Common 1¢ par
exchanged for (1) share Common
1¢ par to reflect a (1) for (10,000)
reverse split followed by a (10,000)
for (1) forward split
Note: Holders of (9,999) or fewer
pre-split shares received $0.081398
cash per share
Acquired by Steel Partners Ltd.
08/17/2017
Each share Common 1¢ par
exchanged for $0.20 cash

ORE-IDA FOODS, INC. (OR)
Acquired by Heinz (H.J.) Co.
10/31/1965
Each share Common no par
exchanged for (0.1) share $3.50 2nd
Convertible Preferred 2nd Series
$18.50 par and (0.3667) share
Common $8.33-1/3 par
(See Heinz (H.J.) Co.)

ORE-LEAVE CAP INC (CANADA)
Name changed to Carpathian Gold
Inc. 07/02/2004
Carpathian Gold Inc. name changed
to Euro Sun Mining Inc. 08/26/2016

ORE MORE RES INC (AB)
Name changed to Cougar Oil & Gas
Canada Inc. 02/22/2010
(See Cougar Oil & Gas Canada Inc.)

ORE PHARMACEUTICALS INC (DE)
Each share old Common 1¢ par
exchanged for (0.2) share new
Common 1¢ par 05/27/2008
Reorganized as Ore Pharmaceutical
Holdings Inc. 10/21/2009
Each share new Common 1¢ par
exchanged for (1) share Common
1¢ par
Ore Pharmaceutical Holdings Inc.
reorganized as Ore Holdings Inc.
06/13/2011
(See Ore Holdings Inc.)

OREANIUM, INC. (OR)
Merged into Idaho Investment Corp.
4/12/65
Each share Common $1 par
exchanged for (1/6) share Capital
Stock no par

OREANO MINING CO.
Acquired by Sherman Lead Co.
00/00/1928
Details not available

ORECAN MINES LTD. (BC)
Adjudicated bankrupt 11/1/66
No stockholders' equity

ORECAN OIL LTD. (SK)
Name changed to American Eagle
Petroleums Ltd. (SK) 08/27/1968
American Eagle Petroleums Ltd. (SK)
reincorporated in Alberta 10/20/1982
which reincorporated in Canada
09/17/1992 which merged into CS
Resources Ltd./ Les Ressources CS
Ltee. 08/01/1993
(See CS Resources Ltd./ Les Ressources CS Ltee.)

ORECLONE CONCENTRATING CORP. (DE)
Charter revoked for non-payment of
taxes 4/1/64

ORECRAFT INC (UT)
Proclaimed dissolved for failure to
pay taxes 03/29/1979

OREFINDERS RES INC OLD (BC)
Plan of arrangement effective
06/01/2018
Each share Common no par
exchanged for (1) share Orefinders
Resources Inc. (New) Common no
par and (0.059819) share share
PowerOre Inc. Common no par

OREGON AMERICAN LUMBER CO.
Reorganized as Oregon-American
Lumber Corp. in 1935 which was
completely liquidated in 1953

OREGON-AMERICAN LUMBER CORP. (OR)
Liquidation completed in 1953

OREGON BK (PORTLAND, OR)
Acquired by Orbanco, Inc. 08/30/1969
Details not available

OREGON FIBRE PRODUCTS, INC. (OR)
Completely liquidated 1/27/66
Each share Common $1 par
exchanged for first and final
distribution of $5 cash

OREGON FREEZE DRY FOODS INC (OR)
Common $1 par split (6) for (5) by
issuance of (0.2) additional share
08/18/1967
Common $1 par split (6) for (5) by
issuance of (0.2) additional share
08/19/1968
Merged into Seven-Up Co.
02/16/1978
Each share Common $1 par
exchanged for $10.50 cash

OREGON GOLD INC (OR)
Each share old Common $0.001 par
exchanged for (0.04347826) share
new Common $0.001 par
11/12/2010
Name changed to China Ceetop.com,
Inc. 01/31/2011
China Ceetop.com, Inc. name
changed to Ceetop Inc. 09/19/2013

OREGON KING CONSOLIDATED MINES, INC. (NV)
Charter revoked for failure to file
reports and pay fees 3/7/66

OREGON KING GOLD MINING CO. (OR)
Charter revoked for failure to file
reports and pay fees 1/20/06

OREGON METALLURGICAL CORP (OR)
Common $1 par split (3) for (1) by
issuance of (2) additional shares
02/20/1981
Merged into Allegheny Teledyne Inc.
03/24/1998
Each share Common $1 par
exchanged for (1.296) shares
Common 10¢ par
Allegheny Teledyne Inc. name
changed to Allegheny Technologies
Inc. 11/29/1999

OREGON MONARCH GOLD MINING CO. (AZ)
Charter expired by time limitation
9/14/26

OREGON NATIONAL GAS RESERVES LTD. (ON)
Bankrupt 07/12/1961
No stockholders' equity

OREGON NATL LIFE INS CO (OR)
Merged into First Farwest Corp.
12/28/73
Each share Common 30¢ par
exchanged for (0.4) share Common
50¢ par
(See First Farwest Corp.)

OREGON OUTERWEAR INC (NV)
Name changed to Pacific Sports
Holdings, Inc. 06/18/1998
Pacific Sports Holdings, Inc.
recapitalized as Tahoe Pacific Corp.
08/30/1999 which name changed to
Ameri-First Financial Group, Inc.
(NV) 01/06/2000 which
reincorporated in Delaware
03/22/2000 which reincorporated in
Nevada as Eight Dragons Co.
12/07/2007 which name changed to
Rokk3r Inc. 06/18/2018

OREGON PAC BKG CO (OR)
Reorganized as Oregon Pacific
Bancorp 01/01/2003
Each share Common $0.044 par
exchanged for (1) share Common
no par

OREGON PORTLAND CEM CO (NV)
5% Conv. Preferred $100 par called
for redemption 12/15/1950
Class A Common no par reclassified
as Common no par and (3)
additional shares issued 03/16/1959
Acquired by Ash Grove Cement Co.
08/24/1983
Each share Common no par
exchanged for $61 cash

OREGON RES CORP (BC)
Recapitalized as International Oregon
Resources Corp. 01/10/1992
Each share Common no par
exchanged for (0.33333333) share
Common no par
International Oregon Resources Corp.
recapitalized as Dalphine
Enterprises Ltd. 03/16/1993 which
name changed to Inflazyme
Pharmaceuticals Ltd. 12/10/1993
which recapitalized as Eacom
Timber Corp. 08/26/2008
(See Eacom Timber Corp.)

OREGON ST BK (CORVALLIS, OR)
Merged into Umpqua Holdings Corp.
12/31/2001
Each share Class A Common
exchanged for (1.3) shares Common
83-1/3¢ par

OREGON STL MLS INC (DE)
Common 1¢ par split (2) for (1) by
issuance of (1) additional share
10/10/1990
Merged into Evraz Group S.A.
01/23/2007
Each share Common 1¢ par
exchanged for $63.25 cash

OREGON TERMINALS, INC. (OR)
Dissolved in 1957

OREGON TRAIL CO. (OR)
Name changed to Pixieland Corp.
5/17/68
Pixieland Corp. involuntarily dissolved
10/24/78

OREGON TRAIL FINL CORP (OR)
Merged into FirstBank NW Corp.
11/03/2003
Each share Common 1¢ par
exchanged for $22 cash

OREGON TRAIL SVGS & LN ASSN (OR)
Merged into First Federal Savings & Loan Association of Vancouver 04/01/1982
Each Reserve Fund Stock $2 par exchanged for $5 principal amount of 6% 10-year Mutual Capital Certificates Ser. A

OREGON-WASHINGTON BRIDGE CO.
Liquidated in 1951
No Common stockholders' equity

ORELIA MINES, LTD. (ON)
Charter cancelled by the order of the Provincial Secretary 11/27/61

ORELL COPPER MINES LTD. (BC)
Name changed to Orell Resources Ltd. 5/23/80
Orell Resources Ltd. recapitalized as Killick Gold Co. Ltd. 7/25/84
(See Killick Gold Co. Ltd.)

ORELL RES LTD (BC)
Recapitalized as Killick Gold Co. Ltd. 7/25/84
Each share Common no par exchanged for (0.2) share Common no par
(See Killick Gold Co. Ltd.)

ORELOCK EXPLS LTD (ON)
Merged into A.H.A. Automotive Technologies Corp. 4/2/84
Each share Capital Stock $1 par exchanged for (0.1) share Retractable Class A Special Share no par and (0.1) share Common no par
(See A.H.A. Automotive Technologies Corp.)

OREMEX RES INC (CANADA)
Name changed to Oremex Silver Inc. 09/09/2011
Oremex Silver Inc. name changed to Monarca Minerals Inc. 08/24/2016

OREMEX SILVER INC (CANADA)
Name changed to Monarca Minerals Inc. 08/24/2016

OREMOND GOLD MINES, LTD. (ON)
Charter cancelled and company declared dissolved by default 9/19/60

OREMONT, INC. (MT)
Dissolved 6/1/61
No stockholders' equity

OREMONT LTD. (AUSTRALIA)
Name changed to Echelon Resources Ltd. 11/25/2004
Echelon Resources Ltd. name changed to Fusion Resources Ltd. 08/27/2007 which was acquired by Paladin Energy Ltd. 02/16/2009
(See Paladin Energy Ltd.)

OREMONT MINES LTD. (BC)
Dissolved 1/31/77

ORENADA GOLD MINES LTD. (QC)
Name changed to Orenada Mines Ltd. 04/14/1956
Orenada Mines Ltd. recapitalized as First Orenada Mines Ltd. 08/03/1965 which merged into Brominco Inc. 06/01/1976 which merged into Aur Resources Inc. 05/16/1985 which was acquired by Teck Cominco Ltd. 09/28/2007 which name changed to Teck Resources Ltd. 04/27/2009

ORENADA MINES LTD. (QC)
Recapitalized as First Orenada Mines Ltd. 08/03/1965
Each share Common $1 par exchanged for (0.25) share Common $1 par
First Orenada Mines Ltd. merged into Brominco Inc. 06/01/1976 which merged into Aur Resources Inc. 05/16/1985 which was acquired by Teck Cominco Ltd. 09/28/2007 which name changed to Teck Resources Ltd. 04/27/2009

ORENDA FOREST PRODS LTD (BC)
Merged into Repap Enterprises Inc. 9/5/96
Each share Common no par exchanged for $3 cash

OREON RENT CORP (NV)
Reorganized as American Liberty Petroleum Corp. 06/25/2010
Each share Common $0.00001 par exchanged for (70) shares Common $0.00001 par
American Liberty Petroleum Corp. recapitalized as Avant Diagnostics, Inc. 03/02/2015

ORETECH INC (NV)
Involuntary Chapter 11 bankruptcy proceedings converted to Chapter 7 on 05/09/2007
Stockholders' equity unlikely

ORETEK INC (FL)
Involuntarily dissolved for failure to file annual reports 11/04/1988

OREX CORP (DE)
Name changed 11/08/1999
Name changed from Orex Gold Mines Corp. to Orex Corp. 11/08/1999
Each share old Common $0.0001 par received distribution of (0.05) share Orex Minerals Corp. Common $0.0001 par payable 01/25/2000 to holders of record 12/31/1999
Each share old Common $0.0001 par exchanged for (0.0133333) share new Common $0.0001 par 12/06/2000
Name changed to EarthNet.Tv, Inc. 12/11/2000
EarthNet.Tv, Inc. name changed to Nocera Inc. 02/08/2002

OREX MINERALS INC OLD (BC)
Each share old Common no par exchanged for (0.2) share new Common no par 10/20/2010
Reorganized as Orex Minerals Inc. (New) 09/29/2015
Each share new Common no par exchanged for (1) share Common no par and (1) share Barsele Minerals Corp. Common no par

OREX RES LTD (ON)
Name changed to Carlin Gold Co. Inc. 7/20/88
Carlin Gold Co. Inc. recapitalized as Altair International Gold Inc. 3/8/94 which name changed to Altair International Inc. (ONT) 11/6/96 which reincorporated in Canada 7/2/2002 which name changed to Altair Nanotechnologies Inc. 7/17/2002

OREX VENTURES INC (BC)
Name changed to Orex Minerals Inc. (Old) 11/01/2007
Orex Minerals Inc. (Old) reorganized as Orex Minerals Inc. (New) 09/29/2015

OREXANA CORP (FL)
Name changed to Advent Technologies, Inc. 05/14/1993
Advent Technologies, Inc. recapitalized as Newreach Communications Inc. 09/26/1996 which name changed to Henley Group, Inc. (FL) 04/02/1997 which name changed to CIS.com, Inc. 05/27/1999 which name changed to InterAmerican Resources, Inc. 08/13/2001 which name changed to Allixon Corp. 06/04/2004 which recapitalized as Simcoe Mining Resources Corp. 01/16/2008

OREZONE RES INC (CANADA)
Class A Common no par reclassified as Common no par 09/03/2004
Merged into IAMGOLD Corp. 02/25/2009
Each share Common no par exchanged for (0.08) share Common no par and (0.125) share Orezone Gold Corp. Common no par

(See each company's listing)

ORFA CORP AMER (UT)
Filed petition under Chapter 11 Federal Bankruptcy Code 3/20/90
Company subsequently dissolved

ORFE S A (POLAND)
GDR agreement terminated 07/29/2003
No GDR holders' equity

ORFORD RES LTD (ON)
Name changed to Afton Food Group Ltd. 3/29/94
(See Afton Food Group Ltd.)

ORGAN CORP. OF AMERICA (NY)
Merged into Estey Electronics, Inc. on a share for share basis 5/29/61 which was adjudicated bankrupt 2/5/65

ORGANA GARDENS INTL INC (NV)
Recapitalized as Bravo Enterprises Ltd. 06/08/2012
Each share Common $0.001 par exchanged for (0.05) share Common $0.001 par

ORGANA TECHNOLOGIES GROUP INC (DE)
Company terminated common stock registration and is no longer public as of 04/28/2009

ORGANETIX INC (DE)
Stock Dividend - 10% payable 02/06/2004 to holders of record 01/30/2004 Ex date - 01/28/2004
Name changed to Seafarer Exploration Corp. (DE) 07/18/2008
Seafarer Exploration Corp. (DE) reincorporated in Florida 07/05/2011

ORGANIC EARTH CORP (AB)
Merged into Planet Organic Health Corp. 09/05/2003
Each share Common no par exchanged for (0.1300654) share Common no par
Planet Organic Health Corp. name changed to Planet Health Corp. 05/15/2014

ORGANIC FOOD CORP (DE)
Adjudicated bankrupt 12/03/1975
No stockholders' equity

ORGANIC FOOD PRODS INC (CA)
Name changed to Spectrum Organic Products, Inc. 10/20/99
Spectrum Organic Products, Inc. merged into Hain Celestial Group, Inc. 12/19/2005

ORGANIC INC (DE)
Acquired by Seneca Investments LLC 1/15/2002
Each share Common $0.001 par exchanged for $0.33 cash

ORGANIC PETE ADDITIVE CORP (NY)
Name changed to Stanton Industries, Inc. 05/11/1982
Stanton Industries, Inc. name changed to International Monetary Funding Corp. 06/28/1982 which recapitalized as Hawaiian Sugar Technologies, Inc. 01/20/1983 which recapitalized as Entertainment Inns of America, Inc. 10/21/1983 which name changed to Tiger Marketing, Inc. 11/08/1984 which recapitalized as U.S. Health Services, Inc. 04/08/1986 which name changed to Diamond Trade Center, Inc. 10/30/1990
(See Diamond Trade Center, Inc.)

ORGANIC RECYCLING TECHNOLOGIES INC (NV)
Name changed to Global 8 Environmental Technologies, Inc. 05/15/2008

ORGANIC RESOURCE MGMT INC (CANADA)
Each share old Common no par exchanged for (0.05) share new Common no par 11/30/2007
Acquired by Walker Industries Holdings Ltd. 12/17/2012
Each share new Common no par exchanged for $3.25 cash
Note: Unexchanged certificates will be cancelled and become without value 12/17/2018

ORGANIC SOIL BUILDER, INC. (NY)
Certificate of voluntary dissolution filed 9/27/62

ORGANIC SOILS COM INC (NV)
Name changed to Inhibiton Therapeutics, Inc. 06/06/2005
Inhibiton Therapeutics, Inc. name changed to AlumiFuel Power Corp. 07/06/2009

ORGANIC SOLUTIONS INC (NV)
Reincorporated 04/28/2000
Each share Common $0.001 par received distribution of (0.25) share Nutrafeed Inc. Common $0.001 par payable 06/13/1996 to holders of record 03/11/1996
State of incorporation changed from (DE) to (NV) 04/28/2000
Recapitalized as iWorld Projects & Systems, Inc. 01/11/2005
Each share Common $0.001 par exchanged for (0.1) share Common $0.001 par
(See iWorld Projects & Systems, Inc.)

ORGANIC SPICE IMPORTS INC (DE)
Name changed to X-Factor Communications Holdings, Inc. 05/18/2012

ORGANIC TO GO FOOD CORP (DE)
Each (30,000) shares Common $0.001 par exchanged for (1) share OM Foods Ltd. Common $0.001 par 10/09/2009
Note: In effect holders received $0.07 cash per share and public interest was eliminated

ORGANIC TREEHOUSE LTD (NV)
Common $0.001 par split (20) for (1) by issuance of (19) additional shares payable 06/20/2013 to holders of record 05/31/2013 Ex date - 06/21/2013
Name changed to SunVault Energy, Inc. 06/28/2013

ORGANICS, INC. (CO)
Declared defunct and inoperative for failure to pay franchise taxes 10/11/61

ORGANIK TECHNOLOGIES INC (WA)
Each share old Common no par exchanged for (1/6) share new Common no par 3/11/94
Recapitalized as Telemax Global Communications, Inc. 2/8/2002
Each share Common no par exchanged for (0.05) share Common no par
Telemax Global Communications, Inc. name changed to ICBS, Ltd. 6/1/2006

ORGANITECH USA INC (DE)
SEC revoked common stock registration 01/21/2014

ORGANIZED INVESTORS CORP. (OK)
Acquired by Organized Investors Life Insurance Co. 01/28/1966
Each share Common 10¢ par exchanged for (1.4) shares Common 8¢ par
Organized Investors Life Insurance Co. liquidated for Organized Security Life Insurance Co. 01/01/1968 which was acquired by Western American Life Insurance Co. (NM) 06/09/1971
(See Western American Life Insurance Co. (NM))

ORGANIZED INVESTORS LIFE INSURANCE CO. (OK)
Completely liquidated 01/01/1968
Each share Common 8¢ par

exchanged for first and final distribution of (0.41579) share Organized Security Life Insurance Co. Common $0.032 par
Organized Security Life Insurance Co. acquired by Western American Life Insurance Co. (NM) 06/09/1971
(See Western American Life Insurance Co. (NM))

ORGANIZED PRODUCING ENERGY CORP (UT)
Involuntarily dissolved for failure to pay taxes 03/01/1986

ORGANIZED SECURITY LIFE INSURANCE CO. (OK)
Acquired by Western American Life Insurance Co. (NM) 06/09/1971
Each share Common $0.032 par exchanged for (0.029013) share Capital Stock 25¢ par
(See Western American Life Insurance Co.)

ORGANIZERS & UNDERWRITERS INC (IA)
Name changed to O & U, Inc. 04/20/1970
(See O & U, Inc.)

ORGANO MED PRODS LTD (DE)
Charter cancelled and declared inoperative and void for non-payment of taxes 03/01/1988

ORGANOGENESIS INC (DE)
Common 1¢ par split (2) for (1) by issuance of (1) additional share 9/11/87
Common 1¢ par split (5) for (4) by issuance of (0.25) additional share 9/8/95
Common 1¢ par split (5) for (4) by issuance of (0.25) additional share payable 5/2/97 to holders of record 4/25/97 Ex date - 5/5/97
Common 1¢ par split (5) for (4) by issuance of (0.25) additional share payable 11/28/97 to holders of record 11/21/97 Ex date - 12/1/97
Stock Dividend - 25% payable 4/29/98 to holders of record 4/22/98 Ex date - 4/30/98
Plan of reorganization under Chapter 11 Federal Bankruptcy Code effective 9/10/2003
No stockholders' equity

ORIANA CAP INC (AB)
Name changed to Strathcona Brewing Investments Inc. 04/16/1992
(See Strathcona Brewing Investments Inc.)

ORIANA DEVS LTD (BC)
Recapitalized as Ajax Resources Ltd. (Ctfs. dated after 8/5/80) 8/5/80
Each share Common no par exchanged for (0.2) share Common no par
(See Ajax Resources Ltd. (Ctfs. dated after 8/5/80))

ORIANA RES CORP (BC)
Recapitalized as Hut 8 Mining Corp. 03/06/2018
Each share Common no par exchanged for (0.01894739) share Common no par

ORICO (CA)
Name changed to Sargent Industries, Inc. (CA) 06/01/1979
(See Sargent Industries, Inc. (CA))

ORIEL RESOURCES PLC (ENGLAND & WALES)
Acquired by Mechel OAO 09/19/2008
Each share Ordinary 1p par exchanged for $2.1986 cash

ORIENS TRAVEL & HOTEL MGMT CORP (NV)
Recapitalized as Pure Hospitality Solutions, Inc. 11/12/2014
Each share Common $0.001 par exchanged (0.00166666) share Common $0.001 par

ORIENT EXPRESS ENTERPRISES LTD (AB)
Recapitalized as Priva Inc. 07/20/1993
Each share Common no par exchanged for (0.5) share Common no par
Priva Inc. name changed to AXQP Inc. (AB) 03/10/2008 which reincorporated in British Columbia as Canamex Silver Corp. 10/07/2009 which name changed to Canamex Resources Corp. 10/18/2010 which name changed to Canamex Gold Corp. 11/08/2017

ORIENT EXPRESS HOTELS INC (NY)
Merged into Sea Containers Ltd. 08/08/1994
Each share Common $0.125 par exchanged for (0.17) share Class A Common 1¢ par
(See Sea Containers Ltd.)

ORIENT EXPRESS HOTELS LTD (BERMUDA)
Name changed to Belmond Ltd. 07/01/2014

ORIENT OIL & GAS CO. (DE)
Charter cancelled and declared inoperative and void for non-payment of taxes 3/19/24

ORIENT PACKAGING HLDGS LTD (DE)
Name changed to China Gateway Holdings Inc. 12/01/1999
China Gateway Holdings Inc. name changed to Chemical Consortium Holdings Inc. 10/12/2001 which name changed to New NRG, Inc. 05/21/2007
(See New NRG, Inc.)

ORIENT PAPER INC (NV)
Each share old Common $0.001 par exchanged for (0.25) share new Common $0.001 par 11/05/2009
Name changed to IT Tech Packaging, Inc. 08/01/2018

ORIENT PETE & ENERGY INC (NV)
Recapitalized as Chun Can International Group 01/27/2017
Each share Common $0.001 par exchanged for (0.001) share Common $0.001 par
Chun Can International Group name changed to Yutudao Marine Biotechnology Inc. 03/27/2018

ORIENT VENTURE CAP INC (BC)
Name changed to Nickel North Exploration Corp. 08/09/2012

ORIENT VENTURE CAP II INC (BC)
Name changed to China Select Capital Partners Corp. 04/22/2010
China Select Capital Partners Corp. name changed to Urban Select Capital Corp. 10/19/2011

ORIENTAL BK & TR (SAN JUAN, PR)
Common $1 par split (4) for (3) by issuance of (1/3) additional share 10/05/1994
Common $1 par split (5) for (4) by issuance of (0.25) additional share 10/02/1995
Common $1 par split (6) for (5) by issuance of (0.2) additional share payable 10/16/1996 to holders of record 09/30/1996 Ex date - 10/17/1996
Under plan of reorganization each share Common $1 par automatically became (1) share Oriental Financial Group Inc. Common $1 par 01/27/1997
Oriental Financial Group Inc. name changed to OFG Bancorp 04/26/2013

ORIENTAL CONSOLIDATED MINING CO.
Dissolution completed in 1942

ORIENTAL CRYSTAL INTL LTD (AUSTRALIA)
ADR agreement terminated 09/20/2007
No ADR's remain outstanding
Note: Name changed to XState Resources Ltd. 07/11/2006

ORIENTAL FED SVGS BK (HUMACAO, PR)
Common $1 par split (8) for (7) by issuance of (0.14285714) additional share 10/15/1992
Common $1 par split (3) for (2) by issuance of (0.5) additional share 08/16/1993
Stock Dividend - 10% 12/15/1991
Name changed to Oriental Bank & Trust (San Juan, PR) 07/01/1994
Oriental Bank & Trust (San Juan, PR) reorganized as Oriental Financial Group Inc. 01/27/1997 which name changed OFG Bancorp 04/26/2013

ORIENTAL FINL GROUP INC (PR)
Common $1 par split (5) for (4) by issuance of (0.25) additional share payable 10/15/1997 to holders of record 09/30/1997 Ex date - 10/16/1997
Common $1 par split (4) for (3) by issuance of (1/3) additional share payable 10/15/1998 to holders of record 09/30/1998 Ex date - 10/16/1998
Stock Dividends - 10% payable 04/15/2002 to holders of record 04/01/2002 Ex date - 03/27/2002; 25% payable 01/15/2003 to holders of record 12/30/2002; 10% payable 01/17/2005 to holders of record 12/31/2004 Ex date - 12/29/2004
Name changed to OFG Bancorp 04/26/2013

ORIENTAL FOCUS INTL LTD (DE)
Charter cancelled and declared inoperative and void for non-payment of taxes 03/01/1996

ORIENTAL MINERALS INC (BC)
Reincorporated 11/01/2007
Place of incorporation changed from (YT) to (BC) 11/01/2007
Name changed to Woulfe Mining Corp. 02/25/2010
Woulfe Mining Corp. merged into Almonty Industries Inc. 09/14/2015

ORIFLAME COSMETICS SA (LUXEMBOURG)
Each Unsponsored ADR for Ordinary exchanged for (1) Sponsored ADR for Ordinary 02/19/2013
ADR agreement terminated 07/02/2018
Each Sponsored ADR for Ordinary exchanged for (0.5) share Ordinary
Note: Unexchanged ADR's will be sold and the proceeds, if any, held for claim after 01/02/2019

ORIGIN ENERGY LTD (AUSTRALIA)
Each Sponsored ADR for Ordinary received distribution of (1) Boral Ltd. (New) Sponsored ADR for Ordinary A$0.50 par payable 07/21/2000 to holders of record 02/17/2000
ADR agreement terminated 12/15/2000
Each Sponsored ADR for Ordinary exchanged for $5.88 cash
Note: Cash distributed 04/00/2002 (Additional Information in Active)

ORIGIN INVT GROUP INC (MD)
Recapitalized as International Wireless, Inc. 1/2/2002
Each share Common $0.001 par exchanged for (1/9) share Common $0.001 par
International Wireless, Inc. name changed to Heartland, Inc. 6/22/2004

ORIGINAL CAKE & STEAK HOUSE, INC. (WA)
Dissolved 5/19/77

ORIGINAL COMPUTER CAMP INC (CA)
Name changed to ExperTelligence, Inc. (CA) 10/11/1984
ExperTelligence, Inc. (CA) reincorporated in Nevada 06/26/2006 which reorganized as Pay Mobile, Inc. 07/07/2011 which name changed to Dephasium Corp. 04/18/2013 which recapitalized as Allied Ventures Holdings Corp. 04/05/2016 name changed to Longwen Group Corp. 01/26/2017

ORIGINAL CONEY ISLAND INC (DE)
Charter subsequently forfeited for failure to maintain a Resident Agent 03/21/1975

ORIGINAL DIET PIZZA INC (DE)
Charter cancelled and declared inoperative and void for non-payment of taxes 3/1/92

ORIGINAL ITALIAN PASTA PRODS INC (MA)
Completely liquidated 2/17/98
Each share Common 2¢ par exchanged for first and final distribution of $1.28 cash

ORIGINAL MEDIA INC (DE)
Each share Common no par received distribution of (0.1) share She's Got Network, Inc. Common $0.00001 par payable 10/19/2001 to holders of record 5/31/2000
Recapitalized as OMDA Oil & Gas Inc. 6/7/2002
Each share Common no par exchanged for (0.001) share Common no par

ORIGINAL NEW YORK SELTZER OF CDA LTD (CANADA)
Placed in receivership 08/12/1988
No stockholders' equity

ORIGINAL OILS CO. (MT)
Charter expired by time limitation 4/24/60

ORIGINAL SOURCE ENTMT INC (NV)
Reincorporated under the laws of Delaware as NeuroOne Medical Technologies Corp. 07/03/2017

ORIGINALA PETE INC (TX)
Reincorporated 01/13/1981
Common 10¢ par split (5) for (3) by issuance of (2/3) additional share 10/22/1965
Common 10¢ par split (5) for (3) by issuance of (2/3) additional share 01/31/1968
Name and state of incorporation changed from Originala Inc. (NY) to Originala Petroleum Corp. (TX) 01/13/1981
Plan of reorganization under Chapter 11 bankruptcy proceedings confirmed 08/07/1984
No stockholders' equity

ORIGINALLY NEW YORK INC (NV)
Common $0.001 par split (2) for (1) by issuance of (1) additional share payable 05/25/2005 to holders of record 05/25/2005 Ex date - 05/26/2005
Common $0.001 par split (3) for (1) by issuance of (2) additional shares payable 10/16/2006 to holders of record 10/16/2006 Ex date - 10/17/2006
Name changed to Greenbelt Resources Corp. 06/19/2007

ORIGINOIL INC (NV)
Each share old Common $0.0001 par exchanged for (0.03333333) share new Common $0.0001 par 08/11/2011
Name changed to OriginClear, Inc. 04/16/2015

ORIGO ACQUISITION CORP (CAYMAN ISLANDS)
Completely liquidated 08/15/2018
Each Unit exchanged for $11 cash

Each share Ordinary $0.0001 par exchanged for $11 cash

ORINDA PETROLEUM CO. LTD. (CA)
Merged into Buttes Gas & Oil Co. (CA) in 1954
Each share Class A Common $25 par exchanged for (98) shares Common $1 par
Each share Class B Common $25 par exchanged for (90) shares Common $1 par
Buttes Gas & Oil Co. (CA) reincorporated in Delaware 11/30/77 which reorganized in Pennsylvania 2/16/89 which reorganized in Delaware as Reunion Resources Co. 6/28/93 which name changed to Reunion Industries, Inc. 4/19/96

ORINOCO GOLD INC (BC)
Name changed to Active Assets & Associates Inc. 09/16/1999
Active Assets & Associates Inc. recapitalized as Focus Ventures Ltd. (BC) 05/16/2002 which reorganized in Yukon as CROPS Inc. 04/23/2018

ORINOCO RES INC (DE)
Recapitalized as El Alacran Gold Mine Corp. 05/23/2006
Each share Common $0.0001 par exchanged for (0.001) share Common $0.0001 par

ORIOLA-KD CORP (FINLAND)
ADR agreement terminated 12/26/2017
No ADR's remain outstanding

ORIOLE COMMUNICATIONS INC (BC)
Recapitalized as Consolidated Oriole Communications Inc. 09/10/1993
Each share Common no par exchanged for (0.1) share Common no par
Consolidated Oriole Communications Inc. name changed to Oriole Systems Inc. 03/26/1996
(See Oriole Systems Inc.)

ORIOLE HOMES CORP. (FL)
Name changed 6/5/72
Name changed from Oriole Land & Development Corp. to Oriole Homes Corp. 6/5/72
Common 10¢ par split (3) for (2) by issuance of (0.5) additional share 1/17/73
Common 10¢ par reclassified as Conv. Class A Common 10¢ par and (1) additional share issued 3/31/83
Stock Dividend - 10% 1/16/81
Merged into Levy Acquisition Co. 2/10/2003
Each share Conv. Class A Common 10¢ par exchanged for $4.90 cash
Each share Class B Common 10¢ par exchanged for $4.90 cash

ORIOLE SYS INC (BC)
Delisted from Toronto Venture Stock Exchange 06/20/2003

ORION ACQUISITION CORP II (DE)
Name changed to Medivation, Inc. 06/27/2005
(See Medivation, Inc.)

ORION BANCORP INC (FL)
Company's sole asset placed in receivership 11/13/2009
Stockholders' equity unlikely

ORION BROADCAST GROUP INC (CO)
Each share old Common no par exchanged for (0.0625) share new Common no par 12/31/1989
Name changed to Orion Financial Ltd. 01/11/1990
(See Orion Financial Ltd.)

ORION CAP CORP (DE)
$1.90 Conv. Exchangeable Preferred $1 par called for redemption 11/2/92
Common $1 par split (5) for (4) by issuance of (0.25) additional share 12/7/92
$2.125 Conv. Exchangeable Preferred $1 par called for redemption 1/21/93
Adjustable Rate Preferred $1 par called for redemption 4/7/93
Common $1 par split (5) for (4) by issuance of (0.25) additional share 11/15/93
Common $1 par split (2) for (1) by issuance of (1) additional share payable 7/7/97 to holders of record 6/23/97 Ex date - 7/8/97
Merged into Royal & Sun Alliance Insurance Group plc 11/16/99
Each share Common $1 par exchanged for $50 cash

ORION DIVERSIFIED TECHNOLOGIES INC (NJ)
Reorganized under Chapter 11 Federal Bankruptcy Code 10/01/1990
Each share old Common 1¢ par exchanged for (0.42857142) share new Common 1¢ par, (1) Common Stock Purchase Warrant Ser. A expiring 01/31/1992 and (1) Common Stock Purchase Warrant Ser. B expiring 04/30/1993
Note: Unexchanged certificates were cancelled and became without value 11/15/1990
Name changed to Ovale Group, Inc. 01/23/2008
Each share Common 10¢ par exchanged for (1) share Common 10¢ par
(See Ovale Group, Inc.)

ORION ENERGY INC (BC)
Acquired by American Fluorite Corp. 9/18/81
Each share Common no par exchanged for (0.25) share Common no par
American Fluorite Corp. name changed to AFC Energy Corp. 3/26/83
(See AFC Energy Corp.)

ORION ENERGY TR (AB)
Acquired by ARC Energy Trust 03/17/1999
Each Trust Unit exchanged for (0.875) Trust Unit no par and (0.175) Trust Unit Purchase Warrant expiring 06/15/2004
ARC Energy Trust reorganized as ARC Resources Ltd. 01/06/2011

ORION ENTERPRISES INC (AB)
Recapitalized as Akademia Enterprises Inc. 1/24/94
Each share Class A Common no par exchanged for (0.25) share Class A Common no par
(See Akademia Enterprises Inc.)

ORION ETHANOL INC (NV)
SEC revoked common stock registration 06/27/2012

ORION FINL GROUP INC (WY)
Recapitalized as U-Mind Space, Inc. 09/28/2017
Each share Common $0.001 par exchanged for (0.025) share Common $0.0001 par

ORION FINL LTD (CO)
Chapter 11 bankruptcy proceedings dismissed 06/20/2000
Stockholders' equity unlikely

ORION FOOD SYSTEMS, INC. (DE)
Merged into Munzig International, Inc. 09/08/1972
Each share Common 1¢ par exchanged for (0.05) share Common 5¢ par
(See Munzig International, Inc.)

ORION INDS INC (DE)
Common 10¢ par split (5) for (4) by issuance of (0.25) additional share 12/14/71
Common 10¢ par split (3) for (2) by issuance of (0.5) additional share 12/5/72
Merged into Allen Group Inc. 10/15/74
Each share Common 10¢ par exchanged for $7.647 principal amount of 11-1/2% Conv. Subord. Debentures due 7/1/94

ORION INDS LTD (CO)
Name changed to American Resources Group, Inc. 07/01/1982

ORION INTL MINERALS CORP (BC)
Recapitalized as Laurier Resources, Inc. 05/04/1998
Each share Common no par exchanged for (1/6) share Common no par
Laurier Resources, Inc. name changed to Zarcan International Resources Inc. 11/08/1999 which name changed to Bighorn Petroleum Ltd. 01/30/2006 which recapitalized as Sunset Pacific Petroleum Ltd. 05/07/2009

ORION MGMT INC (CO)
Name changed to Concierge Inc. 07/05/1988

ORION MARINE GROUP INC (DE)
Name changed to Orion Group Holdings, Inc. 06/02/2016

ORION NETWORK SOLUTIONS INC (CO)
Each share old Common no par exchanged for (0.003) share new Common no par 5/21/91
Proclaimed dissolved for failure to file an annual report 4/1/97

ORION NETWORK SYS INC (DE)
Merged into Loral Space & Communications Ltd. 3/20/98
Each share Common 1¢ par exchanged for (0.71553) share Common no par
(See Loral Space & Communications Ltd.)

ORION OIL & GAS CORP (AB)
Merged into WestFire Energy Ltd. 06/30/2011
Each share Common no par exchanged for (0.125) share Common no par
WestFire Energy Ltd. name changed to Long Run Exploration Ltd. 10/29/2012
(See Long Run Exploration Ltd.)

ORION PETE CORP (NV)
Name changed to Aquarian Gold Corp. 3/14/2005

ORION PETE LTD (SK)
Under plan of dissolution each share Common $2 par received (0.08000216) share Cambridge Royalty Co. 6% Conv. Preferred $10 par 11/2/82
Note: Certificates were not required to be surrendered and are now valueless
(See Cambridge Royalty Co.)

ORION PICTURES CORP (DE)
$2.75 Conv. Exchangeable Preferred Class E Ser. 1 no par called for redemption 08/14/1986
Conv. Preferred Ser. A $1 par called for redemption 09/22/1989
Conv. Preferred Ser. C no par called for redemption 09/22/1989
Plan of reorganization under Chapter 11 Federal Bankruptcy Code effective 11/05/1992
Each share old Common 25¢ par exchanged for (0.00710877) share new Common 25¢ par
Merged into Metromedia International Group, Inc. 11/01/1995
Each share new Common 25¢ par exchanged for (0.57143) share Common $1 par
(See Metromedia International Group, Inc.)

ORION POWER HLDGS INC (DE)
Issue Information - 27,500,000 shares COM offered at $20 per share on 11/13/2000
Merged into Reliant Resources, Inc. 2/19/2002
Each share Common 1¢ par exchanged for $26.80 cash

ORION RESH INC (MA)
Common 10¢ par split (2) for (1) by issuance of (1) additional share 9/19/85
Merged into Warburg, Pincus Capital Co., L.P. 12/29/88
Each share Common 10¢ par exchanged for $11.125 cash

ORION RES INC (NV)
Name changed to Orion Systems International, Inc. 2/23/85
Orion Systems International, Inc. name changed to Johnson Geneva (USA) Ltd. 7/8/85

ORION RES LTD (BC)
Recapitalized as Muirfield Investment Corp. 12/11/1989
Each share Common no par exchanged for (1/3) share Common no par
Muirfield Investment Corp. recapitalized as First Western Minerals Inc. 04/05/1994 which name changed to Augusta Metals Inc. 07/04/1997 which name changed to CyberCom Systems Inc. 09/14/2000
(See CyberCom Systems Inc.)

ORION SYSTEMS INTERNATIONAL, INC. (NV)
Name changed to Johnson Geneva (USA) Ltd. 7/8/85

ORION TECHNOLOGIES INC (NV)
Each share old Common $0.001 par exchanged for (0.05) share new Common $0.001 par 07/09/1999
SEC revoked common stock registration 09/05/2006

ORITANI FINL CORP (USA)
Reorganized under the laws of Delaware 06/24/2010
Each share Common 1¢ par exchanged for (1.5) shares Common 1¢ par

ORKIN EXTERMINATING CO., INC. (GA)
Completely liquidated 09/01/1964
Details not available

ORKO GOLD CORP (BC)
Name changed to Orko Silver Corp. 04/10/2006
Orko Silver Corp. acquired by Coeur d'Alene Mines Corp. (ID) 04/16/2013 which reincorporated in Delaware as Coeur Mining, Inc. 05/17/2013

ORKO SILVER CORP (BC)
Acquired by Coeur d'Alene Mines Corp. (ID) 04/16/2013
Each share Common no par exchanged for (0.0815) share Common 1¢ par, (0.01118) Common Stock Purchase Warrant expiring 04/16/2017 and CAD$0.70 cash
Note: Unexchanged certificates were cancelled and became without value 04/16/2016
Coeur d'Alene Mines Corp. (ID) reincorporated in Delaware as Coeur Mining, Inc. 05/17/2013

ORLA MNG LTD (BC)
Reorganized under the laws of Canada 12/07/2016
Each share Common no par exchanged for (1) share Common no par

ORLAC RED LAKE MINES LTD.
Recapitalized as Consolidated Orlac Mines Ltd. on a (0.5) for (1) basis in 1953
Consolidated Orlac Mines Ltd. recapitalized as Abbican Mines Ltd. 5/18/56 which charter cancelled 9/28/64

ORLANDO BK & TR CO (ORLANDO, FL)
Merged into First Florida Bancorporation 08/29/1970
Each share Common exchanged for (4) shares Common $1 par
First Florida Bancorporation name changed to United First Florida Banks, Inc. 06/30/1974 which merged into Sun Banks, Inc. 01/01/1984 which merged into SunTrust Banks, Inc. 07/01/1985

ORLANDO CORP (ON)
Acquired by Wesbar Holdings Ltd. 09/25/1978
Each share Common no par exchanged for $23.50 cash

ORLANDO HARVESTING CORP. (FL)
Name changed to Frasure Holding Corp. 06/03/1969
Frasure Hull Holding Corp. recapitalized as South Central Industries Corp. 07/26/1971
(See South Central Industries Corp.)

ORLANDO PREDATORS ENTMT INC (FL)
Issue Information - 550,000 UNITS consisting of (2) shares CL A and (1) CL A WT offered at $10 per Unit on 12/10/1997
Name changed to Football Equities, Inc. and Class A Common no par reclassified as Common no par 01/22/2004
(See Football Equities, Inc.)

ORLANDO RLTY LTD (ON)
Name changed to Orlando Corp. 08/14/1975
(See Orlando Corp.)

ORLANDO RES LTD (BC)
Recapitalized as Tornado Resources Ltd. 12/15/1994
Each share Common no par exchanged for (0.25) share Common no par
(See Tornado Resources Ltd.)

ORLEANS ENERGY LTD (AB)
Name changed to RMP Energy Inc. 05/17/2011
RMP Energy Inc. name changed to Iron Bridge Resources Inc. 11/27/2017

ORLEANS HOMEBUILDERS INC (DE)
Plan of reorganization under Chapter 11 Federal Bankruptcy Code effective 02/14/2011
No stockholders' equity

ORLEANS PRODUCING & REFINING CORP. (DE)
Charter cancelled and declared inoperative and void for non-payment of franchise taxes 3/19/24

ORLETTO CAP INC (CANADA)
Recapitalized as Devonian Health Group Inc. 05/19/2017
Each share Common no par exchanged for (0.36363636) Subordinate Share no par

ORMAND COMMUNICATIONS INC (DE)
Merged into Ormand Industries, Inc. 02/28/1977
Each share Common 10¢ par exchanged for $5 cash

ORMC LABS INC (UT)
Proclaimed dissolved for failure to file reports 12/31/86

ORMCO CORP (CA)
Name changed to Consyne Corp. (CA) 11/02/1970
Consyne Corp. (CA) reincorporated in Delaware 06/11/1974 which merged into American Hospital Supply Corp. 02/28/1977 which merged into Baxter Travenol Laboratories, Inc. 11/25/1985 which name changed to Baxter International Inc. 05/18/1988

ORMET CORP (DE)
Common 1¢ par changed to $0.001 par and (9) additional shares issued payable 02/21/2007 to holders of record 02/20/2007 Ex date - 02/22/2007
Chapter 11 bankruptcy proceedings dismissed 12/17/2014
Stockholders' equity unlikely

ORMICO EXPL LTD (CANADA)
Recapitalized as Osisko Exploration Ltee. 09/24/1998
Each share Common no par exchanged for (0.5) share Common no par
Osisko Exploration Ltee. name changed to Osisko Mining Corp. 06/13/2008
(See Osisko Mining Corp.)

ORMOND BEACH 1ST NATL BK (ORMOND BEACH, FL)
Name changed to Flagship First National Bank (Ormond Beach, FL) 11/8/74
(See Flagship First National Bank (Ormond Beach, FL))

ORMONT EXPLS LTD (BC)
Name changed to C.E.L. Industries Ltd. 02/27/1987
C.E.L. Industries Ltd. name changed to Pan Smak Pizza Inc. 07/20/1995
(See Pan Smak Pizza Inc.)

ORMSBY MINES LTD. (ON)
Merged into Discovery Mines Ltd. (ON) 04/14/1964
Each share Common $1 par exchanged for (0.25) share Capital Stock $1 par
Discovery Mines Ltd. (ON) reincorporated in Canada 01/15/1982 which merged into Discovery West Corp. 03/01/1987

ORNATE HLDGS INC (DE)
Recapitalized 9/20/2001
Ornate Solutions Inc. recapitalized as Ornate Holdings Inc. 9/20/2001
Each share Common $0.001 par exchanged for (0.002) share Common $0.001 par
Name changed to Absolute Health & Fitness, Inc. 5/14/2004

ORNDA HEALTHCORP (DE)
Merged into Tenet Healthcare Corp. 01/30/1997
Each share Common 1¢ par exchanged for (1.35) shares Common $0.075 par

ORO AMIGO CO. (NV)
Out of existence 00/00/1953
Details not available

ORO BELLE RES INC (BC)
Merged into Viceroy Resource Corp. 06/30/1998
Each share Common no par exchanged for (0.125) share Common no par
Viceroy Resource Corp. merged into Quest Capital Corp. (BC) 06/30/2003 which reincorporated in Canada 05/27/2008 which name changed to Sprott Resource Lending Corp. 09/10/2010 which merged into Sprott Inc. 07/24/2013

ORO BLANCO RES CORP (BC)
Merged into Minpro International Ltd. 3/6/98
Each share Common no par exchanged for (0.4) share Common no par

ORO BRAVO RES LTD (BC)
Reorganized under the laws of Yukon as Bravo Resource Partners Ltd. 01/21/2000
Each share Common no par exchanged for (0.33333333) share Common no par
(See Bravo Resource Partners Ltd.)

ORO BUENO INC (NV)
Name changed to Ceva International, Inc. 6/16/99

ORO CAP CORP INC (NV)
Common $0.00001 par split (30) for (1) by issuance of (29) additional shares payable 04/21/2014 to holders of record 04/17/2014 Ex date - 04/22/2014
Name changed to Synergy Strips Corp. 04/28/2014
Synergy Strips Corp. name changed to Synergy CHC Corp. 08/18/2015

ORO DONNA GOLD MINES, LTD. (ON)
Charter cancelled in 1955

ORO GOLD RES LTD (BC)
Each share Common no par received distribution of (0.25) share Oro Silver Resources Ltd. Common no par and (0.125) Common Stock Purchase Warrant expiring 06/08/2007 payable 02/08/2007 to holders of record 02/08/2007
Under plan of merger name changed to Oro Mining Ltd. 10/22/2010
Oro Mining Ltd. name changed to Marlin Gold Mining Ltd. 11/20/2012

ORO MINES LTD (BC)
Merged into Ronoco Resources Inc. 1/24/77
Each share Capital Stock 50¢ par exchanged for (0.2) share Common no par
(See Ronoco Resources Inc.)

ORO MNG LTD (BC)
Name changed to Marlin Gold Mining Ltd. (Old) 11/20/2012
(See Marlin Gold Mining Ltd. (Old))

ORO NEGRO, LTD. (UT)
Name changed to Locklin Oil Co. 03/04/1981
(See Locklin Oil Co.)

ORO NEV RES INC (AB)
Name changed to Martlet Venture Management Ltd. 9/2/99
Martlet Venture Management Ltd. merged into Knorr Capital Partner AG 9/28/2000

ORO PLATA MINING CORP. LTD.
Succeeded by Transcontinental Resources Ltd. share for share in 1940

ORO SILVER RES LTD (BC)
Merged into Oro Mining Ltd. 10/22/2010
Each share Common no par exchanged for (0.25) share Common no par
Note: Unexchanged certificates were cancelled and became without value 10/22/2016
Oro Mining Ltd. name changed to Marlin Gold Mining Ltd. 11/20/2012

ORO VOLCANICO CORP (DE)
Name changed to Nemo Motors Corp 06/11/2009

ORO YELLOWNKIFE GOLD MINES LTD. (ON)
Succeeded by Ormsby Mines Ltd. 00/00/1954
Each share Capital Stock $1 par exchanged for (0.08333333) share Common $1 par
Ormsby Mines Ltd. merged into Discovery Mines Ltd. (ON) 01/14/1964 which reincorporated in Canada 01/15/1982 which merged into Discovery West Corp. 03/01/1987
(See Discovery West Corp.)

OROAMERICA INC (DE)
Merged into Aurafin LLC 6/21/2001
Each share Common $0.001 par exchanged for $14 cash

OROANDES RES CORP (CANADA)
Name changed to Fort St. James Nickel Corp. 12/02/2011

OROCAN RESOURCE CORP (BC)
Name changed to Standard Graphite Corp. 02/03/2012
Standard Graphite Corp. name changed to Choom Holdings Inc. 11/22/2017

OROCO OIL & GAS CO. (DE)
Merged into Stekoll Petroleum Corp. on a (1) for (5) basis 05/04/1959
Stekoll Petroleum Corp. name changed to Sunac Petroleum Corp. 06/11/1962
(See Sunac Petroleum Corp.)

OROFINO GOLD CORP (NV)
Stock Dividend - 10% payable 08/25/2014 to holders of record 04/15/2014
Name changed to Bakken Energy Corp. 09/03/2014

OROFINO LIME PRODUCTS, INC. (ID)
Charter forfeited for failure to file reports 11/30/55

OROFINO MINES LTD (ON)
Recapitalized as Consolidated Orofino Resources Ltd. 01/11/1980
Each share Capital Stock $1 par exchanged for (0.25) share Capital Stock no par
Consolidated Orofino Resources Ltd. name changed to Orofino Resources Ltd. 03/08/1983 which merged into CanGold Resources Inc. (BC) 01/31/1994 which reorganized in Ontario as Amalgamated CanGold Inc. 07/31/1995 which merged into Central Asia Goldfields Corp. 01/08/1996
(See Central Asia Goldfields Corp.)

OROFINO RES LTD (ON)
Merged into CanGold Resources Inc. (BC) 01/31/1994
Each share Common no par exchanged for (0.0833) share Common no par
CanGold Resources Inc. (BC) reorganized in Ontario as Amalgamated CanGold Inc. 07/31/1995 which merged into Central Asia Goldfields Corp. 01/08/1996
(See Central Asia Goldfields Corp.)

OROGEN MINERALS LTD (AUSTRALIA)
GDR agreement terminated 05/07/2002
Each 144A GDR for Ordinary exchanged for $9.4849 cash
Each Reg. S GDR for Ordinary exchanged for $9.4849 cash

OROGRANDE RES INC (AB)
Recapitalized as Volcanic Metals Exploration Inc. (ALTA) 7/9/2001
Each share Common no par exchanged for (0.1) share Common no par
Volcanic Metals Exploration Inc. (ALTA) reincorporated in Ontario 5/17/2005 which name changed to Energy Fuels Inc. 6/27/2006

OROMAQUE MINES, LTD. (ON)
Charter cancelled 7/1/63

OROMIN EXPLORATIONS LTD NEW (BC)
Merged into Teranga Gold Corp. 10/08/2013
Each share Common no par exchanged for (0.6) share Common no par

OROMIN EXPLORATIONS LTD OLD (BC)
Merged into Oromin Explorations Ltd. (New) 02/25/2002
Each share Common no par exchanged for (1) share Common no par
Oromin Explorations Ltd. (New) merged into Teranga Gold Corp. 10/08/2013

ORO-ORW

OROMONTE RES INC (CANADA)
Recapitalized as Georox Resources Inc. 08/26/2008
Each share Common no par exchanged for (0.33333333) share Common no par
Georox Resources Inc. name changed to Prospera Energy Inc. 07/19/2018

ORONO PULP & PAPER CO.
Acquired by Eastern Manufacturing Co. (ME) 00/001930
Details not available

ORONOVA RESOURCE CORP (BC)
Each share old Common no par exchanged for (0.14285714) share new Common no par 07/26/2012
Name changed to Oronova Energy Inc. 12/16/2016

OROPERU RES INC (BC)
Recapitalized as New Oroperu Resources Inc. 06/06/2001
Each share Common no par exchanged for (0.1) share Common no par

OROPEX MINERALS INC (YT)
Reorganized under the laws of British Columbia as En-R-Tech International Inc. 11/12/1992
Each share Common no par exchanged for (0.5) share Common no par
En-R-Tech International Inc. reorganized as International En-R-Tech Inc. 11/16/1993 which recapitalized as National Telcom Solutions Inc. 10/16/2000
(See National Telcom Solutions Inc.)

OROTEK RES CORP (BC)
Recapitalized as Doucette Developments Corp. 12/29/1992
Each share Common no par exchanged for (0.21276595) share Common no par
Doucette Developments Corp. name changed to Traders International Franchise Systems Inc. 08/30/1995 which recapitalized as NewQuest Ventures Corp. 05/22/1998 which recapitalized as Aster Ventures Corp. 05/26/1999 which recapitalized as Knight Petroleum Corp. 03/22/2001 which name changed to Knight Resources Ltd. 03/07/2003 which recapitalized as Knight Metals Ltd. 05/25/2011 which name changed to Africa Hydrocarbons Inc. (BC) 02/02/2012 which reincorporated in Alberta 04/25/2013 which name changed to Blockchaink2 Corp. 05/30/2018

OROVERO RES CORP (BC)
Name changed to Standard Tolling Corp. 03/10/2014
(See Standard Tolling Corp.)

OROVISTA RES LTD (AB)
Name changed to Total Image Capital Corp. 8/24/99
(See Total Image Capital Corp.)

ORPHAN BOY RES INC (BC)
Name changed to International Bethlehem Mining Corp. 7/28/2006

ORPHAN INC (MI)
Automatically dissolved 07/15/2001

ORPHAN MED INC (DE)
Reincorporated 09/01/2000
State of incorporation changed from (MN) to (DE) 09/01/2000
Merged into Jazz Pharmaceuticals, Inc. 06/24/2005
Each share Common 1¢ par exchanged for $10.75 cash

ORPHEUM BLDG CO (DE)
Common no par changed to $4 par 00/001939
Liquidation completed
Each share Common $4 par exchanged for initial distribution of $10 cash 10/06/1980
Each share Common $4 par received second and final distribution of $2.2221 cash 04/09/1982

ORPHEUM CIRCUIT, INC.
Liquidated in 1938

ORPIT MINES LTD.
Succeeded by Piccadilly Porcupine Gold Mines Ltd. on a (1) for (3) basis in 1945
Piccadilly Porcupine Gold Mines Ltd. name changed to Piccadilly Petroleum Ltd. which merged into Redwater- Piccadilly Petroleum Ltd. in 1950 which name changed to Redpic Petroleums Ltd. in 1951 which recapitalized as Stanwell Oil & Gas Ltd. in 1952 which recapitalized as Cordwell International Developments Ltd. 12/16/66
(See Cordwell International Developments Ltd.)

ORR (J.HERBERT) ENTERPRISES, INC. (AL)
Name changed to Orrtronics, Inc. 10/1/64
Orrtronics, Inc. merged into Faraday, Inc. 12/2/69
(See Faraday, Inc.)

ORR INDUSTRIES, INC. (AL)
Merged into Ampex Corp. 10/7/59
Each (2.2) shares Common 25¢ par exchanged for (1) share Common $1 par
Ampex Corp. merged into Signal Companies, Inc. 1/15/81 which merged into Allied- Signal Inc. 9/19/85 which name changed to Allied Signal Inc. 4/26/93

ORRADIO INDUSTRIES, INC. (AL)
Name changed to Orr Industries, Inc. 10/6/59
Orr Industries, Inc. merged into Ampex Corp. 10/7/59 which merged into Signal Companies, Inc. 1/15/81 which merged into Allied-Signal Inc. 9/19/85 which name changed to AlliedSignal Inc. 4/26/93 which name changed to Honeywell International Inc. 12/1/99

ORRINGTON CO. (IL)
Completely liquidated in 1962
Each share Common no par exchanged for first and final distribution of $150 cash

ORROX CORP (AL)
Common $1 par changed to no par 04/21/1980
Name changed to CMX Corp. 01/30/1985
CMX Corp. acquired by Chyron Corp. 01/31/1989 which name changed to ChyronHego Corp. 05/23/2013
(See ChyronHego Corp.)

ORRTRONICS INC (AL)
Merged into Faraday, Inc. 12/02/1969
Each share Common $2 par exchanged for (0.430725) share Common 10¢ par
(See Faraday, Inc.)

ORRVILLE SVGS BK (ORRVILLE, OH)
Merged into Banc Services Corp. 3/31/87
Each share Common $10 par exchanged for (1) share Common $10 par
Banc Services Corp. merged into Wayne Bancorp, Inc. (OH) 5/31/2003
(See Wayne Bancorp, Inc. (OH))

ORRWELL ENERGY LTD (AB)
Name changed to Harkema Industries Ltd. 07/09/1986
Harkema Industries Ltd. name changed to Acuma International Inc. 06/14/1990
(See Acuma International Inc.)

ORS AUTOMATION INC (DE)
Reorganized as Somerset International Group, Inc. 02/23/2004
Each (21) shares Common 1¢ par exchanged for (1) share Common $0.001 par
(See Somerset International Group, Inc.)

ORS CORP (OK)
Name changed to Electromagnetic Oil Recovery, Inc. (OK) 04/22/1991
Electromagnetic Oil Recovery, Inc. (OK) reorganized in Delaware as Fountain Oil Inc. 12/16/1994 which merged into CanArgo Energy Corp. 07/15/1998
(See CanArgo Energy Corp.)

ORSA VENTURES CORP (BC)
Reincorporated 12/31/2007
Place of incorporation changed from (YT) to (BC) 12/31/2007
Acquired by Alamos Gold Inc. 09/13/2013
Each share Common no par exchanged for $0.10 cash

ORSINA RES LTD (BC)
Struck off register and declared dissolved for failure to file returns 9/4/92

ORTEC INTL INC (DE)
Each share old Common $0.001 par exchanged for (0.1) share new Common $0.001 par 06/25/2003
Each share new Common $0.001 par exchanged again for (0.06666666) share new Common $0.001 par 07/25/2006
Name changed to Forticell Bioscience, Inc. 01/10/2008
(See Forticell Bioscience, Inc.)

ORTECH INDS INC (FL)
Proclaimed dissolved for failure to file reports and pay fees 11/09/1990

ORTEGA MINERALS LTD (BC)
Struck off register and declared dissolved for failure to file returns 01/31/1977

ORTEIG (JULES), LTD. (MD)
Charter annulled for failure to file reports and pay taxes 10/31/62

ORTEL CORP (DE)
Issue Information - 3,800,000 shares COM offered at $13 per share on 10/20/1994
Merged into Lucent Technologies Inc. 4/27/2000
Each share Common $0.001 par exchanged for (3.135) shares Common $0.001 par
Lucent Technologies Inc. merged into Alcatel-Lucent S.A. 11/30/2006

ORTHALLIANCE INC (DE)
Issue Information - 2,600,000 shares CL A offered at $12 per share on 08/21/1997
Merged into Orthodontic Centers of America, Inc. 11/9/2001
Each share Class A Common $0.001 par exchanged for (0.10135) share Common 10¢ par
Each share Class B Common $0.001 par exchanged for (0.10135) share Common 10¢ par
Orthodontic Centers of America, Inc. name changed to OCA, Inc. 8/30/2004
(See OCA, Inc.)

ORTHO TRONICS MED TECHNOLOGIES LTD (BC)
Name changed to PlenTech Electronics Inc. 9/1/93
PlenTech Electronics Inc. recapitalized as Consolidated Plentech Electronics Inc. 9/21/98
(See Consolidated Plentech Electronics Inc.)

ORTHODONTIC CTRS AMER INC (DE)
Common 1¢ par split (2) for (1) by issuance of (1) additional share payable 12/29/95 to holders of record 12/15/95
Common 1¢ par split (2) for (1) by issuance of (1) additional share payable 9/5/96 to holders of record 8/28/96 Ex date - 9/6/96
Name changed to OCA, Inc. 8/30/2004
(See OCA, Inc.)

ORTHODONTISTS' RESEARCH & MANUFACTURING CORP. (CA)
Name changed to Ormco Corp. 10/31/63
Ormco Corp. name changed to Consyne Corp. (Calif.) 11/2/70 which reincorporated in Delaware 6/11/74 which merged into American Hospital Supply Corp. 2/28/77 which merged into Baxter Travenol Laboratories, Inc. 11/25/85 which name changed to Baxter International Inc. 5/18/88

ORTHODONTIX INC (FL)
Each share Common $0.0001 par exchanged for (0.1) share Common $0.001 par 01/03/2007
Name changed to Protalix BioTherapeutics, Inc. (FL) 03/01/2007
Protalix BioTherapeutics, Inc. (FL) reincorporated in Delaware 04/01/2016

ORTHOFIX INTL N V (CURACAO)
Reorganized under the laws of Delaware as Orthofix Medical Inc. 08/01/2018

ORTHOLOGIC CORP (DE)
Stock Dividend - 100% payable 06/25/1996 to holders of record 06/04/1996
Name changed to Capstone Therapeutics Corp. 05/21/2010

ORTHOMET INC (MN)
Merged into Wright Acquisition, Inc. 12/7/94
Each share Common 10¢ par exchanged for $11 cash

ORTHOMOLECULAR NUTRITION INST INC (DE)
Charter cancelled and declared inoperative and void for non-payment of taxes 6/24/91

ORTHOPEDIC SVCS INC (DE)
Acquired by NovaCare, Inc. 03/18/1992
Each share Common 1¢ par exchanged for (1.3) shares Common 1¢ par
NovaCare, Inc. name changed to NAHC, Inc. 03/28/2000 which merged into J.L. Halsey Corp. 06/18/2002 which name changed to Lyris, Inc. 11/15/2007
(See Lyris, Inc.)

ORTHOPEDIC SHOES, INC.
Assets sold in 1938

ORTHOPEDIC TECHNOLOGY INC (DE)
Merged into DePuy, Inc. 4/10/96
Each share Common 1¢ par exchanged for $10.432 cash

ORTHOSOFT INC (CANADA)
Name changed 06/02/2005
Name changed from ORTHOsoft Holdings Inc. to ORTHOsoft Inc. 06/02/2005
Merged into Zimmer Holdings, Inc. 11/08/2007
Each share Common no par exchanged for $1.10 cash

ORTHOVITA INC (PA)
Acquired by Stryker Corp. 06/28/2011
Each share Common 1¢ par exchanged for $3.85 cash

ORTON CRANE & SHOVEL CO. (IN)
Name changed to Orton Crane Co. 07/25/1967
(See Orton Crane Co.)

ORTON CRANE CO (IN)
Merged into Orton-McCullough Crane Co. 00/00/1972
Details not available

ORTONA GOLD MINES LTD. (ON)
Charter revoked for failure to file reports and pay fees in June 1963

ORTRONIX INC (FL)
Adjudicated bankrupt 12/11/1969
No stockholders' equity

ORUP CORP. (NY)
Liquidation completed
Each share Capital Stock $3 par received initial distribution of $8.40 cash 2/1/78
Each share Capital Stock $3 par received second distribution of $4.40 cash 8/24/79
Each share Capital Stock $3 par received third and final distribution of $1.24 cash 10/31/80
Certificates were not required to be surrendered and are now valueless

ORWELL RES LTD (BC)
Name changed to International Rice Bran Industries Ltd. 07/24/1986
International Rice Bran Industries Ltd. recapitalized as Blue Star Investment Ltd. 03/13/1990
(See Blue Star Investment Ltd.)

ORYON HLDGS INC (NV)
Name changed to Oryon Technologies, Inc. 05/03/2012

ORYX CAP CORP (DE)
Name changed 4/26/85
Name changed from Oryx Communications Inc. to Oryx Capital Corp. 4/26/85
Charter cancelled and declared void for failure to pay franchise taxes 3/1/94

ORYX ENERGY CO (DE)
Merged into Kerr-McGee Corp. 2/26/99
Each share Common $1 par exchanged for (0.369) share Common $1 par

ORYX FABRICS CORP. (DE)
Name changed to Lea Fabrics, Inc. in 1929
(See Lea Fabrics, Inc.)

ORYX GOLD CORP (NV)
Name changed to Mediterranean Oil Corp. 11/16/95
Mediterranean Oil Corp. recapitalized as Zmax Corp. (NV) 7/23/96 which reincorporated in Delaware 12/12/97

OS GOLD SEED CO (IA)
Common no par split (3) for (2) by issuance of (0.5) additional share 4/8/75
Common no par split (3) for (1) by issuance of (2) additional shares 3/15/76
Merged into Upjohn Co. 12/19/83
Each share Common no par exchanged for $6 cash

OSAGE BANCSHARES INC (MD)
Acquired by American Bancorporation, Inc. 12/03/2012
Each share Common 10¢ par exchanged for $11.44 cash

OSAGE ENERGY CORP (NV)
Reincorporated under the laws of Delaware as Osage Exploration & Development, Inc. 07/17/2007

OSAGE ENERGY INC (TX)
Charter forfeited for failure to pay taxes 02/20/1984

OSAGE ENTERPRISE CORP (DE)
Name changed to R'Vibrant, Inc. 03/11/2010
R'Vibrant, Inc. name changed to Markray Corp. 02/16/2011

OSAGE FED FINL INC (USA)
Merged into Osage Bancshares, Inc. 01/17/2007
Each share Common 10¢ par exchanged for (1.5739) shares Common 10¢ par
(See Osage Bancshares, Inc.)

OSAGE FOOTWEAR INC (AR)
Merged into Mac, Inc. 8/18/94
Each share Common 1¢ par exchanged for $0.125 cash

OSAGE HILLS ENERGY CO (UT)
Proclaimed dissolved for failure to pay taxes 12/01/1987

OSAGE OIL & EXPLORATION LTD. (ON)
Charter cancelled for failure to pay taxes and file returns 6/7/73

OSAGE SYS GROUP INC (DE)
Chapter 11 bankruptcy proceedings converted to Chapter 7 on 7/9/2001
Stockholders' equity unlikely

OSB FINL CORP (WI)
Merged into FCB Financial Corp. 05/01/1997
Each share Common 1¢ par exchanged for (1.46) shares Common 1¢ par
FCB Financial Corp. merged into Anchor BanCorp Wisconsin Inc. 06/07/1999
(See Anchor BanCorp Wisconsin Inc.)

OSBORN COMMUNICATIONS CORP (DE)
Each share old Common 1¢ par exchanged for (0.5) share new Common 1¢ par 7/11/94
Stock Dividend - 25% 9/15/87
Merged into Capstar Broadcasting Partners 2/20/97
Each share new Common 1¢ par exchanged for $15.375 cash

OSBORN MANUFACTURING CO. (OH)
Each share Common $50 par exchanged for (5) shares Common $10 par in 1946
Each share Common $10 par exchanged for (3) shares Common $5 par in 1953
Stock Dividends - 20% 12/28/59; 20% 12/21/62
Merged into Sherwin-Williams Co. 9/3/68
Each share Common $5 par exchanged for (0.5) share $4.40 Conv. Preferred Ser. B no par

OSBORNE & CHAPPEL GOLDFIELDS LTD (BERMUDA)
Recapitalized as South American Gold & Copper Co. Ltd. (Bermuda) 05/12/1994
Each share Common no par exchanged for (0.25) share Common no par
South American Gold & Copper Co. Ltd. (Bermuda) reincorporated in Canada 05/03/2007 which recapitalized as Cerro Grande Mining Corp. 04/14/2011

OSBORNE MILLS
Sold at foreclosure 00/00/1929
Stockholders' equity unlikely

OSCA INC (DE)
Merged into BJ Serivces Co. 05/31/2002
Each share Class A Common 1¢ par exchanged for $28 cash
Each share Class B Common 1¢ par exchanged for $28 cash

OSCAR MAYER & CO., INC. (DE)
See - Mayer (Oscar) & Co. Inc.

OSCAR NEBEL CO., INC.
See - Nebel (Oscar) Co., Inc.

OSCAR RES LTD (BC)
Recapitalized as Overture Ventures Ltd. 07/20/1989
Each share Common no par exchanged for (0.4) share Common no par
Overture Ventures Ltd. recapitalized as Xyquest Venture Corp.
01/11/1994 which name changed to Polar Bear Ventures Ltd. 11/25/1996 which recapitalized as Iciena Ventures Inc. 02/24/1999 which recapitalized as Barksdale Capital Corp. 02/08/2013

OSCEOLA LOAN & SAVINGS ASSOCIATION (FL)
Dissolved by proclamation 010/21/1974

OSCEOLA REFINING CO., INC. (MI)
Liquidation completed
Each share Common $1 par exchanged for initial distribution of $1 cash in April 1964
Each share Common $1 par received second distribution of $0.50 cash in July 1964
Each share Common $1 par received third and final distribution of $6.505 cash in October 1964

OSCIENT PHARMACEUTICALS CORP (MA)
Each share old Common 10¢ par exchanged for (0.125) share new Common 10¢ par 11/16/2006
Plan of reorganization under Chapter 11 Federal Bankruptcy proceedings effective 06/30/2010
No stockholders' equity

OSE CORP (ON)
Recapitalized as Petro Basin Energy Corp. (ON) 09/19/2011
Each share Common no par exchanged for (0.5) share Common no par
Petro Basin Energy Corp. (ON) reincorporated in British Columbia as Peace River Capital Corp. 09/16/2016 which name changed to Liberty One Lithium Corp. 12/02/2016

OSE USA INC (DE)
Merged into Orient Semiconductor Electronics, Ltd. 2/14/2006
Each share Common no par exchanged for $0.006 cash

OSEC PETE CORP (BC)
Recapitalized as ProAm Explorations Corp. 12/6/93
Each share Class A Common no par exchanged for (1/3) share Class A Common no par

OSF INC (DE)
Reincorporated 07/25/2003
State of incorporation changed from (FL) to (DE) 07/25/2003
Recapitalized as Tensas Inc. 04/01/2005
Each share Common $0.0005 par exchanged for (0.1) share Common $0.001 par
Tensas Inc. name changed to PGI Energy, Inc. 02/28/2011

OSF INC (ON)
Merged into Centre Partners Management LLC 3/21/2000
Each share Common no par exchanged for $7.25 cash

OSF INDS LTD (ON)
Common no par split (3) for (1) by issuance of (2) additional shares 9/20/68
Charter cancelled for failure to pay taxes and file returns 4/27/81

OSG AMERICA L P (DE)
Merged into Overseas Shipholding Group, Inc. 12/17/2009
Each Common Unit 1¢ par exchanged for $10.25 cash

OSGOOD CO. (OH)
Completely liquidated for cash in 1956

OSH ONE LIQUIDATING CORP (DE)
Plan of reorganization under Chapter 11 Federal Bankruptcy proceedings effective 02/24/2014
No stockholders' equity

OSHAP TECHNOLOGIES LTD (ISRAEL)
Each share Ordinary IS1 par received distribution of (0.07808) share Tecnomatix Technologies Ltd. Ordinary NIS0.01 par and $0.31235 cash payable 10/5/98 to holders of record 9/23/98
Merged into SunGard Data Systems Inc. 7/13/99
Each share Ordinary IS1 par exchanged for (0.386293) share Common 1¢ par 7/13/99
(See SunGard Data Systems Inc.)

OSHAWA BUILDINGS LTD. (ON)
Preference no par called 3/31/58

OSHAWA GROUP LTD. (ON)
Name changed 08/13/1971
Common no par and Class A no par split (2) for (1) respectively by issuance of (1) additional share 06/19/1964
Common no par and Class A no par split (2) for (1) respectively by issuance of (1) additional share 10/29/1965
Common no par and Class A no par split (2) for (1) respectively by issuance of (1) additional share 10/20/1967
Name changed from Oshawa Wholesale Ltd. to Oshawa Group Ltd. 08/13/1971
Class A no par split (2) for (1) by issuance of (1) additional share 07/13/1984
Class A no par split (2) for (1) by issuance of (1) additional share 07/03/1986
Acquired by Sobeys Canada Inc. 01/25/1999
Each share Class A Common no par exchanged for (0.451966) share Class A Common no par and $27.921041 cash
Sobeys Canada Inc. name changed to Sobeys Inc. 06/01/1999
(See Sobeys Inc.)

OSHKOSH B GOSH INC (DE)
$2 Preferred no par reclassified as $1.50 Preferred no par in 1942
$1.50 Preferred no par called for redemption 12/1/50
Common no par changed to $5 par 3/4/55
Each share Common $5 par exchanged for (15) shares Class A Common 1¢ par and (5) shares Class B Common 1¢ par 3/19/85
Class A Common 1¢ par split (2) for (1) by issuance of (1) additional share payable 9/19/98 to holders of record 9/2/98
Stock Dividends - 25% 1/14/57; 100% 2/15/60; 10% 2/1/66; 100% 6/9/72; 100% 11/3/87
Merged into Carter's Inc. 7/14/2005
Each share Class A Common 1¢ par exchanged for $26 cash
Each share Class B Common 1¢ par exchanged for $26 cash

OSHKOSH MOTOR TRUCK, INC. (WI)
Name changed to Oshkosh Truck Corp. 03/27/1967
Oshkosh Truck Corp. name changed to Oshkosh Corp. 02/05/2008

OSHKOSH OVERALL CO.
Name changed to Oshkosh B'Gosh, Inc. in 1937
(See Oshkosh B'Gosh, Inc.)

OSHKOSH TRUCK CORP (WI)
7% Preferred $10 par called for redemption 07/01/1970
Class A Common $1 par changed to 1¢ par 08/23/1985
Non-Vtg. Class B Common $1 par changed to 1¢ par 08/23/1985
Non-Vtg. Class B Common $1 par reclassified as Common 1¢ par 05/22/1997
Common 1¢ par split (3) for (2) by

issuance of (0.5) additional share payable 08/19/1999 to holders of record 08/05/1999
Class A Common 1¢ par split (2) for (1) by issuance of (1) additional share payable 08/13/2003 to holders of record 08/06/2003 Ex date - 08/14/2003
Common 1¢ par split (2) for (1) by issuance of (1) additional share payable 08/13/2003 to holders of record 08/06/2003 Ex date - 08/14/2003
Class A Common 1¢ par reclassified as Common 1¢ par 05/03/2005
Common 1¢ par split (2) for (1) by issuance of (1) additional share payable 08/26/2005 to holders of record 08/16/2005
Name changed to Oshkosh Corp. 02/05/2008

OSHMANS SPORTING GOODS INC (DE)
Conv. Preferred Ser. A $1 par called for redemption in September 1977
Stock Dividends - 50% 7/30/71; 50% 6/16/72; 50% 7/21/78; 50% 7/31/81
Merged into Gart Sports Co. 6/8/2001
Each share Common $1 par exchanged for (0.55) share Common 1¢ par and $7 cash
Gart Sports Co. name changed to Sports Authority, Inc. (New) 8/4/2003
(See Sports Authority, Inc. (New))

OSI GEOSPATIAL INC (BC)
Each share old Common no par exchanged for (0.000004) share new Common no par 07/12/2012
Note: In effect holders received $0.06 cash per share and public interest was eliminated

OSI PHARMACEUTICALS INC (DE)
Merged into Astellas Pharma Inc. 06/08/2010
Each share Common 1¢ par exchanged for $57.50 cash

OSI RESTAURANT PARTNERS INC (DE)
Merged into Kangaroo Holdings, Inc. 6/14/2007
Each share Common 1¢ par exchanged for $41.15 cash

OSI SYS INC (CA)
Issue Information - 3,700,000 shares COM offered at $13.50 per share on 10/01/1997
Reincorporated under the laws of Delaware and Common no par changed to $0.001 par 03/05/2010

OSIA VENTURES LTD (BC)
Name changed to Sunshine Agri-Tech Inc. 07/28/2010

OSIAS ORGANIZATIONS INC (FL)
Stock Dividends - 50% 9/15/69; 50% 12/15/69
Name changed to Comprehensive Communities Corp. 4/19/71
Comprehensive Communities Corp. recapitalized as University Properties Investment Corp. 8/2/79 which name changed to John Phillip Tuba Corp. 4/22/83
(See John Phillip Tuba Corp.)

OSIAS RES CDA LTD (CANADA)
Recapitalized as Troy Gold Industries Ltd. 06/12/1974
Each share Capital Stock 50¢ par exchanged for (0.33333333) share Capital Stock no par
(See Troy Gold Industries Ltd.)

OSICOM TECHNOLOGIES INC (NJ)
Each share Common 1¢ par exchanged for (0.1) share Common 10¢ par 12/28/1993
Each share old Common 10¢ par exchanged for (0.5) share new Common 10¢ par 11/07/1994
New Common 10¢ par split (2) for (1) by issuance of (1) additional share payable 02/12/1996 to holders of record 02/12/1996
Each share new Common 10¢ par exchanged for (0.33333333) share Common 30¢ par 07/24/1998
Each share Common 30¢ par received distribution of (0.25) share Entrada Networks Inc. Common $0.001 par payable 12/01/2000 to holders of record 11/15/2000
Name changed to Sorrento Networks Corp. (NJ) 01/17/2001
Sorrento Networks Corp. (NJ) reincorporated in Delaware 06/04/2003 which merged into Zhone Technologies, Inc. 07/01/2004 which name changed to DASAN Zhone Solutions, Inc. 09/12/2016

OSIM INTL LTD (SINGAPORE)
ADR agreement terminated 08/29/2016
Each ADR for Ordinary exchanged for $10.256985 cash

OSIRIS THERAPEUTICS INC (DE)
Reincorporated under the laws of Maryland 05/31/2010

OSISKO EXPL LTEE (CANADA)
Common no par split (2) for (1) by issuance of (1) additional share payable 06/26/2007 to holders of record 06/21/2007 Ex date - 06/19/2007
Name changed to Osisko Mining Corp. 06/13/2008
(See Osisko Mining Corp.)

OSISKO LAKE MINES LTD (ON)
Capital Stock $1 par changed to no par 09/21/1973
Name changed to Graph/Max Inc. 10/18/1989
Graph/Max Inc. recapitalized as GRF Technology Inc. 01/28/1996 which merged into Mustang Gold Corp. 07/15/1997 which recapitalized as Mustang Minerals Corp. 03/11/1999 which name changed to Grid Metals Corp. 06/08/2018

OSISKO MNG CORP (CANADA)
Plan of arrangement effective 06/16/2014
Each share Common no par exchanged for (0.07264) share Agnico Eagle Mines Ltd. Common no par, (0.1) share Osisko Gold Royalties Ltd. Common no par, (0.26471) share Yamana Gold Inc. Common Stock no par and $2.09 cash
(See each company's listing)
Note: Unexchanged certificates will be cancelled and become without value 06/16/2020

OSISKO ROUYN EXPLORATION CO. LTD. (QC)
Declared dissolved for failure to file reports or pay fees 5/14/77

OSITO VENTURES LTD (BC)
Name changed to Sennen Resources Ltd. 08/08/1997
Sennen Resources Ltd. name changed to Sennen Potash Corp. 04/15/2013

OSK CAP II CORP (NV)
Name changed to Teliphone Corp. 08/21/2006

OSL HLDGS INC (NV)
Each share old Common $0.001 par exchanged for (0.001) share new Common $0.001 par 01/09/2013
SEC revoked common stock registration 10/06/2017

OSLER INC (NV)
Each share old Common $0.001 par exchanged for (0.1) share new Common $0.001 par 06/23/2010
Name changed to America Greener Technologies, Inc. 04/22/2014

OSLER RES INC (BC)
Recapitalized as Arvida Exploration Ltd. 11/17/1993
Each share Common no par exchanged for (0.5) share Common no par
Arvida Exploration Ltd. name changed to Jade International Industrial Group Ltd. 03/15/1995
(See Jade International Industrial Group Ltd.)

OSLO BORS VPS HLDG ASA (NORWAY)
ADR agreement terminated 02/15/2013
No ADR's remain outstanding

OSMIC INC (DE)
Merged into Rigaku Acquisition Corp. 3/1/2000
Each share Common 1¢ par exchanged for $4.99 cash
Note: An additional $0.26 cash per share is being held in escrow to be distributed 12/17/2001

OSMONICS INC (DE)
Common 1¢ par split (3) for (2) by issuance of (0.5) additional share 3/29/85
Common 1¢ par split (3) for (2) by issuance of (0.5) additional share 6/22/90
Common 1¢ par split (3) for (2) by issuance of (0.5) additional share 5/13/91
Common 1¢ par split (3) for (2) by issuance of (0.5) additional share 3/21/94
Stock Dividends - 100% 5/20/77; 50% 9/19/80
Merged into General Electric Co. 2/28/2003
Each share Common 1¢ par exchanged for (0.7412) share Common 16¢ par

OSOYOOS MINES OF CANADA LTD.
Bankrupt in 1941

OSPREY ENERGY ACQUISITION CORP (DE)
Units separated 08/24/2018
Name changed to Falcon Minerals Corp. 08/24/2018

OSPREY ENERGY LTD (AB)
Plan of Arrangement effective 8/8/94
Each share Common no par exchanged for $1.25 cash

OSPREY ENERGY LTD (BC)
Delisted from Toronto Venture Stock Exchange 07/13/2009

OSPREY GOLD CORP (NV)
Recapitalized as Gilla Inc. 03/30/2007
Each share Common $0.0002 par exchanged for (0.02) share Common $0.0002 par

OSPREY MEDIA INCOME FD (ON)
Acquired by Quebecor Media Inc. 08/08/2007
Each Trust Unit no par received $8.45 cash

OSPREY VENTURES INC (WY)
Reorganized as All American Gold Corp. 10/15/2010
Each share Common $0.001 par exchanged for (10) shares Common $0.001 par

OSR CORP (DE)
Stock Dividend - 10% 04/15/1977
Recapitalized as Resort Connections, Inc. 05/10/1988
Each share Common 10¢ par exchanged for (0.25) share Common $0.001 par
Resort Connections, Inc. name changed to D-Lanz Development Group Inc. 01/30/1990 which name changed to eWeb21 Corp. 11/24/2000 which recapitalized as Texas Wyoming Drilling, Inc. 07/21/2008 which recapitalized as Drone USA, Inc. 05/19/2016

OSROW PRODS CORP (DE)
Charter cancelled and declared inoperative and void for non-payment of taxes 6/23/88

OSROW PRODS INC (NY)
Common 10¢ par split (4) for (1) by issuance of (3) additional shares 08/21/1969
Reincorporated under the laws of Delaware as OSR Corp. 12/01/1972
OSR Corp. recapitalized as Resort Connections, Inc. 05/10/1988 which name changed to D-Lanz Development Group Inc. 01/30/1990 which name changed to eWeb21 Corp. 11/24/2000 which recapitalized as Texas Wyoming Drilling, Inc. 07/21/2008 which recapitalized as Drone USA, Inc. 05/19/2016

OSSA RES INC (BC)
Recapitalized as Pactech Ventures Ltd. 04/13/1994
Each share Common no par exchanged for (0.125) share Common no par
Pactech Ventures Ltd. name changed to Intercontinental Mining Corp. (BC) 08/12/1996 which reincorporated in Alberta as Maple Leaf Reforestation Inc. 03/03/2005 which name changed to Maple Leaf Green World Inc. 10/05/2012

OSSIAN GOLD MINES LTD.
Acquired by Minedel Mines Ltd. on a (1) for (30) basis 00/00/1948
Minedel Mines Ltd. name changed to Havelock Energy & Resources Inc. 05/01/1980 which recapitalized as Municipal Ticket Corp. 03/04/1994 which recapitalized as I.D. Investments Inc. 11/18/1994 which recapitalized as BioLink Corp. 03/12/1997 which recapitalized as First Empire Entertainment.com Inc. 03/31/2000 which recapitalized as First Empire Corp. 08/14/2003 which reorganized as Nobel House Entertainment Inc. (ON) 11/01/2004 which reincorporated in Canada as LiveReel Media Corp. 12/01/2006

OSTARA CORP (NV)
Name changed to Rheologics Technologies, Inc. 10/18/2005
Rheologics Technologies, Inc. name changed to KKS Venture Management, Inc. 07/24/2007 which recapitalized as Codima, Inc. 06/09/2008
(See Codima, Inc.)

OSTASHKOV INDL INC (WY)
Administratively dissolved 12/09/2014

OSTECH INC (DE)
Name changed to Norland Medical Systems, Inc. 10/1/95
Norland Medical Systems, Inc. name changed to Orthometrix, Inc. 4/11/2002

OSTEO SYS INC (CO)
Recapitalized as Sattel Global Networks, Inc. 10/12/2000
Each (15) shares Common $0.001 par exchanged for (1) share Common $0.001 par
Sattel Global Networks, Inc. recapitalized as Urbani Holdings, Inc. 01/28/2002 which name changed to United Specialties, Inc. 07/28/2003 which name changed to WaterColor Holdings Corp. 04/10/2006
(See WaterColor Holdings Corp.)

OSTEOIMPLANT TECHNOLOGY INC (NJ)
Acquired by Encore Medical Corp. 02/22/2005
Details not available

OSTEOLOGIX INC (DE)
Reincorporated under the laws of

Ireland as Osteologix Holdings PLC 07/28/2011

OSTEOTECH INC (DE)
Common 1¢ par split (3) for (2) by issuance of (0.5) additional share payable 03/19/1999 to holders of record 03/05/1999
Acquired by Medtronic, Inc. 11/16/2010
Each share Common 1¢ par exchanged for $6.50 cash

OSTER MANUFACTURING CO. (OH)
Name changed to O-M Co. 5/7/62
O-M Co. completed liquidation 12/19/66

OSTERLOH & DURHAM INS BROKERS NORTH AMER INC (UT)
Company believed out of business 00/00/1989
Details not available

OSTERREICHISCHE ELEKTRIZITATSWIRTSCHAFTS AKTIENGESELLSCHAFT (AUSTRIA)
Sponsored ADR's for Ordinary ATS 100 par split (10) for (1) by issuance of (9) additional ADR's payable 05/26/2006 to holders of record 05/22/2006
Name changed to Verbund AG 06/15/2010

OSTEX INTL INC (WA)
Merged into Inverness Medical Innovations, Inc. 07/01/2003
Each share Common 1¢ par exchanged for (0.1263) share Common $0.001 par
Inverness Medical Innovations, Inc. name changed to Alere Inc. 07/14/2010
(See Alere Inc.)

OSTRANDER FIXED INCOME TR (MA)
Ceased operations 12/15/1994
Details not available

OSTRICH PRODS AMER INC (NV)
Name changed to PayPro, Inc. 07/11/2005
PayPro, Inc. name changed to Panamersa Corp. 02/16/2007 which recapitalized as Eagle Worldwide Inc. 01/12/2012

OSULAKE MINES LTD. (ON)
Recapitalized as Lake-Osu Mines Ltd. on a (1) for (2) basis in 1950
Lake-Osu Mines Ltd. charter cancelled 11/8/77

O SULLIVAN CORP (VA)
5% Preferred $50 par called for redemption 1/1/76
Merged into Geon Co. 8/23/99
Each share Common $1 par exchanged for $12.25 cash

O SULLIVAN RUBR CORP (VA)
Common no par changed to $1 par in 1946
Each share 5% Preferred $100 par exchanged for (5) shares 5% Preferred $20 par in 1947
Common $1 par split (6) for (5) by issuance of (0.2) additional share 12/15/67
Common $1 par split (3) for (2) by issuance of (0.5) additional share 12/16/68
Stock Dividends - 10% 12/23/64; 10% 11/29/66
Name changed to O'Sullivan Corp. 1/1/71
(See O'Sullivan Corp.)

OSWAY EXPLS LTD (AB)
Reorganized under the laws of Canada as Jerome Gold Mines Corp. 8/23/84
Each (2.6) shares Class A no par exchanged for (1) share Common no par
Jerome Gold Mines Corp. merged into Pacific Metals Inc. 5/7/91 which recapitalized as Crescendo Capital Corp. 6/29/95 which name changed to Tragoes Inc. 7/24/96 which name changed to Rightsmarket.com Inc. 7/30/99 which name changed to RightsMarket Inc. 6/7/2000 which reorganized as RightsMarket Ltd. 12/31/2003

OSWEGO & SYRACUSE RAILROAD CO.
Merged into Delaware, Lackawanna & Western Railroad Co. and each share Common exchanged for $50 of Bonds and $18.75 in cash in 1946

OSWEGO CITY SVGS BK (OSWEGO, NY)
Under plan of reorganization each share Common $1 par automatically became (1) share Pathfinder Bancorp, Inc. (DE) Common 10¢ par 12/30/1997
Pathfinder Bancorp, Inc. (DE) reincorporated in USA 06/19/2001 which reorganized in Maryland 10/16/2014

OSWEGO CNTY BANCORP INC (DE)
Common 1¢ par split (3) for (1) by issuance of (2) additional shares payable 03/19/2002 to holders of record 03/04/2002 Ex date - 03/20/2002
Merged into Bridge Street Financial Inc. 01/06/2003
Each share Common 1¢ par exchanged for (1.02612) shares Common 1¢ par
Bridge Street Financial Inc. merged into Alliance Financial Corp. 10/06/2006 which merged into NBT Bancorp Inc. 03/08/2013

OSWEGO FALLS CORP. (NY)
Recapitalized in 1936
Each share 2nd Preferred $100 par exchanged for (16) shares Common $5 par
Each share Common $100 par exchanged for (8) shares Common $5 par
Stock Dividend - 100% 5/15/51
Name changed to Sealright-Oswego Falls Corp. 3/26/57
Sealright-Oswego Falls Corp. was acquired by Phillips Petroleum Co. 10/15/64 which name changed to ConocoPhillips 8/30/2000

OSWEGO LIQUIDATING CORP. (OR)
Liquidation completed
Each share Capital Stock 50¢ par exchanged for initial distribution of (0.203868) share Mr. Gasket Co. Common no par plus a Non-Transferable Receipt representing beneficial rights to addition- al distributions 3/8/71
Each Non-Transferable Receipt received second and final distribution of (0.1707) share Grace (W.R.) & Co. (Conn.) Common $1 par 12/19/75
Note: Non-Transferable Receipts were not required to be surrendered and are now valueless
(See each company's listing)

OSWEGO MINING CO. (SD)
Charter expired by time limitation 6/7/22

OT COMPUTER TRAINING CORP (DE)
Recapitalized as COA Development Corp. 7/28/2000
Each share Common $0.001 par exchanged for (0.05) share Common $0.001 par
COA Development Corp. recapitalized as International Child Care Corp. 12/17/2001 which recapitalized as World Wide Child Care Corp. 5/21/2007

OT ENTERPRISES INC (UT)
Recapitalized as Covenant Environmental Technologies, Inc. 2/25/92
Each share Common $0.001 par exchanged for (0.567612) share Common $0.001 par
(See Covenant Environmental Technologies, Inc.)

OT INDS INC (BC)
Name changed to Golden Princess Mining Corp. 03/12/1987
Golden Princess Mining Corp. recapitalized as Pandora Industries Inc. 09/28/1992 which recapitalized as Georgia Ventures Inc. 03/01/2000 which name changed to Creston Moly Corp. 10/19/2007 which merged into Mercator Minerals Ltd. 06/21/2011

OTARION ELECTRS INC (NY)
Charter cancelled and proclaimed dissolved for failure to pay taxes 12/20/1977

OTARION LISTENER CORP. (NY)
Name changed to Otarion Electronics, Inc. 11/15/61
Otarion Electronics, Inc. charter cancelled 12/20/77

OTATCO INC (AB)
Each share old Common no par exchanged for (0.1) share new Common no par 8/5/99
Merged into Integrated Production Services Ltd. 3/31/2000
Each share new Common no par exchanged for (0.68517) share Common no par
(See Integrated Production Services Ltd.)

OTC AMER INC (CO)
Each share old Common $0.0001 par exchanged for (0.01) share new Common $0.0001 par 10/28/1998
New Common $0.0001 par split (4) for (1) by issuance of (3) additional shares payable 03/01/2000 to holders of record 02/29/2000
Name changed to e.Nvizion Communications Group Ltd. 06/16/2000
(See e.Nvizion Communications Group Ltd.)

OTC COMMUNICATIONS INC (UT)
Name changed to Teleworld, Inc. (UT) 11/23/87

OTC STK JOURNAL INC (MT)
Involuntarily dissolved 12/3/90

OTEC INC (UT)
Name changed to Innstar Corp. 10/29/1987
Innstar Corp. recapitalized as Guinness Telli-Phone Corp. 09/13/1993
(See Guinness Telli-Phone Corp.)

OTEEGEE INNOVATIONS INC (NV)
Name changed to Tucana Lithium Corp. 06/01/2011
Tucana Lithium Corp. recapitalized as Rimrock Gold Corp. 02/08/2013

OTELCO INC (DE)
Plan of reorganization under Chapter 11 Federal Bankruptcy proceedings effective 05/24/2013
Each Income Deposit Security exchanged for (0.2) share new Class A Common 1¢ par
No stockholders' equity for old Class A Common 1¢ par
Note: Each IDS consisted of $7.50 principal amount of Sr. Sub. Notes due 00/00/2019 and (1) share Class A Common 1¢ par
(Additional Information in Active)

OTENCO ENERGY CORP (WA)
Recapitalized as Xytec Inc. 05/19/1983
Each share Common 1¢ par exchanged for (0.1) share Common 10¢ par
Xytec Inc, name changed to Xytec International Industries, Inc. 09/16/1983
(See Xytec International Industries, Inc.)

OTF EQUITIES INC (DE)
Common Stock 1¢ par split (2) for (1) by issuance of (1) additional share 4/8/85
Charter declared inoperative and void for failure to file reports 5/15/90

OTG SOFTWARE INC (DE)
Merged into Legato Systems, Inc. 05/14/2002
Each share Common 1¢ par exchanged for (0.6876) share Common $0.0001 par and $2.50 cash
Legato Systems, Inc. merged into EMC Corp. 10/21/2003 which merged into Dell Technologies Inc. 09/07/2016

OTHER TEL CO (MN)
Name changed to Eastern Electric Inc. 03/05/1975
Eastern Electric Inc. name changed to Texergy Corp. 05/04/1981

OTHNET INC (DE)
Name changed to AVP, Inc. 03/21/2005
(See AVP, Inc.)

OTI TECHNOLOGIES INC (CANADA)
Struck off register and declared dissolved for failure to file reports 08/29/2003

OTIS, MCALLISTER & CO. (CA)
Adjudicated bankrupt 3/16/62
No stockholders' equity

OTIS CAP CORP (BC)
Name changed to Otis Gold Corp. 01/14/2009

OTIS CO.
Liquidated 00/00/1940
Details not available

OTIS ELEVATOR CO (NJ)
Each share Common $50 par exchanged for (4) shares Common no par 00/00/1929
Each share 6% Preferred $100 par exchanged for (1.6) shares $4 Preferred $62.50 par or $165 cash 00/00/1949
Common no par changed to $6.25 par and (1) additional share issued 01/27/1956
Common $6.25 par changed to $3.125 par and (1) additional share issued 02/29/1960
Merged into United Technologies Corp. 07/08/1976
Each share Common $3.125 par exchanged for (0.45) share $7.32 Conv. Preferred $1 par

OTIS J EXPL CORP (BC)
Name changed to Sedex Mining Corp. 2/29/96

OTIS OIL & GAS CORP (CO)
Each share old Common 5¢ par exchanged for (0.1) share new Common 5¢ par 07/07/1972
Administratively dissolved 01/01/1989

OTIS STEEL CO.
Acquired by Jones & Laughlin Steel Corp. in 1942
Each share Preferred exchanged for (0.25) share 5% Preferred A $100 par, (0.25) share 5% Preferred B $100 par, (1) share Common no par and $5.75 cash
Each share Common exchanged for (0.25) share Common no par
(See Jones & Laughlin Steel Corp.)

OTIS-WINSTON LTD (NV)
Name changed to Sparrowtech Multimedia Corp. 09/16/2004
Sparrowtech Multimedia Corp. name changed to Sparrowtech Resources, Inc. 03/28/2007 which merged into Converge Global, Inc. (Old)

10/26/2009 which recapitalized as Converge Global, Inc. (New) 09/03/2010 which name changed to Marijuana Co. of America, Inc. 12/01/2015

OTISCO INC (CO)
Name changed to Impact Income Investments, Inc. 03/10/1993
Impact Income Investments, Inc. name changed to Financial Freedom Enterprises Inc. 06/24/1996 which name changed to Cambridge Universal Corp. (CO) 07/15/1997 which reorganized in Florida as Whitehall Limited, Inc. 06/23/1999
(See Whitehall Limited, Inc.)

OTISH ENERGY INC (BC)
Each share old Common no par exchanged for (0.25) share new Common no par 11/10/2009
Name changed to Arrowhead Gold Corp. 08/11/2011
Arrowhead Gold Corp. recapitalized as Kontrol Energy Corp. 08/09/2016

OTISH MTN DIAMOND CO (NV)
Name changed to Gulf Coast Oil & Gas, Inc. 01/27/2005

OTISH MTN EXPL INC (BC)
Name changed to ISX Resources Inc. (BC) 07/06/2005
ISX Resources Inc. (BC) reincorporated in Canada as Potash One Inc. 12/06/2007
(See Potash One Inc.)

OTISH RES INC (DE)
Name changed to China-Biotics, Inc. 03/21/2006

OTISVILLE BIOPHARM INC (NY)
Name changed 12/11/1986
Name changed from Otisville Biotech, Inc to Otisville BioPharm, Inc. 12/11/1986
Name changed to Alliance Pharmaceutical Corp. 02/24/1989
(See Alliance Pharmaceutical Corp.)

OTIX GLOBAL INC (DE)
Each share Common $0.001 par exchanged for (0.2) share Common $0.005 par 03/29/2010
Merged into William Demant Holding A/S 11/30/2010
Each share Common $0.005 par exchanged for $11.01 cash

OTL RES LTD (BC)
Name changed to Raytec Capital Corp. 04/21/1993
Raytec Capital Corp. recapitalized as Raytec Development Corp. 06/04/2001 which name changed to Raytec Metals Corp. 11/19/2007 which name changed to Lion Energy Corp. 09/16/2009 which was acquired by Africa Oil Corp. 06/20/2011

OTM INTL DEV INC (BC)
Name changed to Epic Energy Inc. (BC) 06/14/1995
Epic Energy Inc. (BC) reincorporated in Alberta 04/15/1996
(See Epic Energy Inc.)

OTR EXPRESS INC (KS)
Company announced 05/09/2001 it would cease operations and shareholders should not expect any distributions; common stock registration subsequently terminated 06/20/2001

OTRA SECS GROUP INC (DE)
Each share old Common 1¢ par exchanged for (0.1) share new Common 1¢ par 06/30/1989
Stock Dividend - 10% 09/30/1991
Name changed to RKS Financial Group, Inc. 05/28/1992
RKS Financial Group, Inc. name changed to JB Oxford Holdings Inc. 08/23/1994 which name changed to Cambridge Capital Holdings, Inc. 04/18/2006

(See Cambridge Capital Holdings, Inc.)

OTS HLDG INC (CO)
Each share old Common no par exchanged for (0.01) share new Common no par 03/15/2000
Name changed to Thin Film Battery Inc. and (3) additional shares issued 04/14/2000
Thin Film Battery Inc. name changed to Global Acquisition, Inc. 04/17/2001 which name changed to Oak Ridge Micro-Energy, Inc. 02/21/2002 which name changed to Oak Ridge Energy Technologies, Inc. 08/28/2013 which name changed to Oakridge Global Energy Solutions, Inc. 11/07/2014

OTSEGO FOREST PRODUCTS COOPERATIVE ASSOCIATION, INC. (NY)
Dissolved by proclamation 6/15/64

OTT CHEMICAL CO. (MI)
Acquired by Corn Products Co. 09/29/1965
Each share Common $5 par exchanged for (1.5895) shares Common 50¢ par
Corn Products Co. name changed to CPC International Inc. 04/23/1969 which name changed to BestFoods 01/01/1998
(See BestFoods)

OTTAWA & HULL POWER CO., LTD.
Acquired by Gatineau Power Co. 00/00/1928
Details not available

OTTAWA CORP (DE)
Charter cancelled and declared inoperative and void for non-payment of taxes 3/1/85

OTTAWA ELECTRIC RAILWAY CO.
Liquidated in 1949

OTTAWA FINL CORP (DE)
Stock Dividends - 10% payable 9/30/97 to holders of record 9/12/97; 10% payable 8/31/98 to holders of record 8/12/98; 10% payable 6/30/99 to holders of record 6/14/99; 10% payable 6/30/2000 to holders of record 6/14/2000
Merged into Fifth Third Bancorp 12/8/2000
Each share Common 1¢ par exchanged for (0.54) share Common no par

OTTAWA LIGHT, HEAT & POWER CO. LTD.
Acquired by Interprovincial Utilities, Ltd. share for share in 1950
Interprovincial Utilities, Ltd. completed liquidation 9/30/57

OTTAWA MONTREAL POWER CO., LTD.
Acquired by Gatineau Power Co. in 1927 which name was changed to Gatineau Power Co.-Compagnie D'Electricite Gatineau 5/4/62 which was acquired by the Quebec Hydro-Electric Commission 11/25/63

OTTAWA PETE & EXPL INC (DE)
Name changed to Ottawa Corp. 07/24/1972
(See Ottawa Corp.)

OTTAWA RIVER POWER CO., LTD.
Merged into Gatineau Power Co. 00/00/1928
Details not available

OTTAWA SVGS BANCORP INC (USA)
Reorganized under the laws of Maryland as Ottawa Bancorp, Inc. 10/11/2016
Each share Common 1¢ par exchanged for (1.1921) shares Common 1¢ par

OTTAWA SILVER MINES LTD. (BC)
Recapitalized as Slocan Ottawa Mines Ltd. 05/06/1965

Each share Common 50¢ par exchanged for (0.125) share Common no par
Slocan Ottawa Mines Ltd. name changed to Slocan Development Corp. Ltd. 04/19/1972 which recapitalized as International Slocan Development Ltd. 10/07/1992 which recapitalized as Slocan Holdings Ltd. 08/15/1995 which recapitalized as Galaxy Energy Corp. 10/26/1999 which recapitalized as Galaxy Sports Inc. 08/10/2001
(See Galaxy Sports Inc.)

OTTAWA SILVER MINING & MILLING CO. (WA)
Charter revoked for failure to file reports and pay fees 7/1/60

OTTAWA STRUCTURAL SVCS LTD (ON)
Recapitalized as Forsys Corp. 11/12/96
Each share Common no par exchanged for (0.1) share Common no par
Forsys Corp. recapitalized as Forsys Technologies Inc. 4/16/2003 which name changed to Forsys Metals Corp. 7/14/2005

OTTAWA TRACTION CO.
Reorganized as Ottawa Electric Railway Co. in 1937 which liquidated in 1949

OTTAWA URANIUM MINES LTD. (BC)
Name changed to Ottawa Silver Mines Ltd. 05/00/1961
Ottawa Silver Mines Ltd. recapitalized as Slocan Ottawa Mines Ltd. 05/06/1965 which name changed to Slocan Development Corp. Ltd. 04/19/1972 which recapitalized as International Slocan Development Ltd. 10/07/1992 which recapitalized as Slocan Holdings Ltd. 08/15/1995 which recapitalized as Galaxy Energy Corp. 10/26/1999 which recapitalized as Galaxy Sports Inc. 08/10/2001
(See Galaxy Sports Inc.)

OTTAWA VY PWR CO (QC)
Acquired by Canelco Services Ltd. 12/00/1962
Each share Common no par exchanged for (0.8236) share Common no par and (2.8102) shares 1% Non-Cum. 2nd Preferred $1 par

OTTER LAKE RES INC (NV)
Each share old Common $0.001 par exchanged for (0.005) share new Common $0.001 par 11/13/2006
SEC revoked common stock registration 07/01/2010

OTTER TAIL CORP (MN)
Name changed 04/10/2001
Each share Special and Founders Common no par exchanged for (5) shares Common $10 par 00/00/1941
Each share Common $10 par exchanged for (2) shares Common $5 par 00/00/1948
Common $5 par split (2) for (1) by issuance of (1) additional share 06/01/1963
Common $5 par split (2) for (1) by issuance of (1) additional share 06/15/1988
Common $5 par split (2) for (1) by issuance of (1) additional share payable 03/15/2000 to holders of record 02/15/2000
Name changed from Otter Tail Power Co. to Otter Tail Corp. 04/10/2001
6.35% Preferred no par called for redemption at $100.635 on 12/31/2001

OTTER TAIL POWER CO. (DE)
Dissolution approved in 1936

OTTERBURN RES CORP (ON)
Recapitalized as K92 Mining Inc. 05/25/2016
Each share Common no par exchanged for (0.33333333) share Common no par

OTTERBURN VENTURES INC (BC)
Name changed to Finore Mining Inc. 09/26/2011
Finore Mining Inc. recapitalized as Micro Waste Technologies Inc. 10/26/2017

O2DIESEL CORP (DE)
Reincorporated 08/16/2004
State of incorporation changed from (WA) to (DE) 08/16/2004
Plan of reorganization under Chapter 11 Federal Bankruptcy proceedings effective 10/01/2009
No stockholders' equity

O2MICRO INTL LTD (CAYMAN ISLANDS)
Issue Information - 4,000,000 ORD shs. offered at $9 per share on 08/22/2000
Each share Ordinary $0.001 par exchanged for (1) ADR for Ordinary 11/28/2005

O2WIRELESS SOLUTIONS INC (GA)
Issue Information - 6,100,000 shares COM offered at $12 per share on 05/10/2000
Merged into Baran Group, Ltd. 11/13/2002
Each share Common $0.0001 par exchanged for (0.014919) Ordinary share NIS 1 par

OTX INC (NV)
Name changed to Mills-Jennings Co. 6/4/81
(See Mills-Jennings Co.)

OUACHITA NATL BANCSHARES INC (LA)
Common $10 par changed to $5 par and (1) additional share issued 11/29/83
Merged into Louisiana Bancshares, Inc. 1/10/85
Each share Common $10 par exchanged for (2.22756) shares Common no par
Louisiana Bancshares, Inc. name changed to Premier Bancorp, Inc. 4/15/87 which merged into Banc One Corp. 1/2/96 which merged into Bank One Corp. 10/2/98 which merged into J.P. Morgan Chase & Co. 12/31/2000 which name changed to JPMorgan Chase & Co. 7/20/2004

OUACHITA NATL BK (MONROE, LA)
Capital Stock $100 par changed to $20 par and (4) additional shares issued plus a 33-1/3% stock dividend paid 1/10/56
Capital Stock $20 par changed to $10 par and (1) additional share issued plus a 21.21% stock dividend paid 2/13/64
Stock Dividends - (4) for (11) 2/17/54; (3) for (22) 1/22/57; 13.64% 1/22/58; 20% 2/3/60; 10% 2/2/62; 25% 3/15/68; 20% 6/15/71; 20% 3/1/74; (1) for (6) 3/1/76; (1) for (9) 4/2/79; 20% 4/6/81
Under plan of reorganization each share Capital Stock $10 par automatically became (1) share Ouachita National Bancshares, Inc. Common $10 par 5/1/83
Ouachita National Bancshares, Inc. merged into Louisiana Bancshares, Inc. 1/10/85 which name changed to Premier Bancorp, Inc. 4/15/87 which merged into Banc One Corp. 1/2/96 which merged into Bank One Corp. 10/2/98 which merged into J.P. Morgan Chase & Co. 12/31/2000 which name changed to JPMorgan Chase & Co. 7/20/2004

OUR HOUSE INC (DE)
Charter cancelled and declared inoperative and void for non-payment of taxes 3/1/77

OURANOS RES INC (TX)
Each share old Common no par exchanged for (0.0005) share new Common no par 01/17/2006
SEC revoked common stock registration 10/24/2007

OURGOLD MNG LTD (ON)
Charter cancelled for failure to pay taxes and file returns 11/13/1974

OURO BRASIL LTD (YT)
Recapitalized as Consolidated Ouro Brasil Ltd. 02/18/2000
Each share Common no par exchanged for (0.1) share Common no par
Consolidated Ouro Brasil Ltd. name changed to Superior Diamonds Inc. (YT) 09/03/2002 which reincorporated in British Columbia 06/30/2004 which name changed to Northern Superior Resources Inc. 04/15/2008

OUROMINAS MINERALS INC (YT)
Recapitalized as Thistle Mining Inc. 04/27/1999
Each share Common no par exchanged for (0.1) share Common no par
(See Thistle Mining Inc.)

OUT-TAKES INC (DE)
Reorganized under the laws of Nevada as James Maritime Holdings, Inc. 02/26/2015
Each share Common 1¢ par exchanged for (0.005) share Common $0.001 par

OUT WEST ENTMT LTD (AB)
Issue Information - 3,000,000 shares COM offered at $0.10 per share on 06/27/1997
Name changed to SURE Print & Copy Centres, Inc. 7/30/99

OUT WEST URANIUM & OIL CO. (CO)
Recapitalized as General Minerals Corp. (CO) 5/23/61
Each share Common 10¢ par exchanged for (0.1) share Common $1 par
(See General Minerals Corp. (CO))

OUTBACK ENERGY CORP (NV)
Each share old Common $0.001 par exchanged for (0.5) share new Common $0.001 par 06/12/2008
Recapitalized as PetroNational Corp. 07/08/2008
Each share Common $0.001 par exchanged for (0.5) share Common $0.001 par
PetroNational Corp. name changed to Custom Restaurant & Hospitality Group, Inc. 11/20/2008

OUTBACK STEAKHOUSE INC (DE)
Common 1¢ par split (3) for (2) by issuance of (0.5) additional share 12/16/91
Common 1¢ par split (2) for (1) by issuance of (1) additional share 10/15/92
Common 1¢ par split (3) for (2) by issuance of (0.5) additional share 2/18/94
Common 1¢ par split (3) for (2) by issuance of (0.5) additional share payable 3/2/99 to holders of record 2/16/99
Name changed to OSI Restaurant Partners, Inc. 4/25/2006
(See OSI Restaurant Partners, Inc.)

OUTBOARD JET INC (IN)
Charter revoked for failure to file reports 04/02/1969

OUTBOARD MARINE CORP (DE)
Name changed 08/01/1956
Each share Common $5 par exchanged for (2) shares Common $2.50 par 00/00/1945
Common $2.50 par changed to $0.83-1/3 par and (2) additional shares issued 00/00/1954
Name changed from Outboard Marine & Manufacturing Co. to Outboard Marine Corp. 08/01/1956
Common $0.83-1/3 par changed to 30¢ par and (2) additional shares issued 06/03/1957
Common 30¢ par changed to 15¢ par and (1) additional share issued 05/25/1984
Stock Dividend - 20% 03/16/1953
Merged into Greenmarine Holdings LLC 09/30/1997
Each share Common 15¢ par exchanged for $18 cash

OUTBOARD MOTORS CORP.
Merged into Outboard Marine & Manufacturing Co. in 1936
Each share Class A Preference exchanged for (1.25) shares Common $5 par
Each (8) shares Class B Common exchanged for (1) share Common $5 par
Outboard Marine & Manufacturing Co. name changed to Outboard Marine Corp. 8/1/56
(See Outboard Marine Corp.)

OUTDOOR CHANNEL HLDGS INC (DE)
Reincorporated 09/14/2004
State of incorporation changed from (AK) to (DE) 09/14/2004
Common 2¢ par split (5) for (2) by issuance of (1.5) additional shares payable 09/15/2004 to holders of record 09/14/2004
Acquired by Kroenke Sports & Entertainment, LLC 05/17/2013
Each share new Common 2¢ par exchanged for $10.25 cash

OUTDOOR DEV INC (GA)
Acquired by Consolidated Mortgage & Investment Corp. 1/31/64
Each share Common exchanged for (0.4) share Common
Consolidated Mortgage & Investment Corp. name changed to Outdoor Development Co., Inc. (DE) 4/14/66
(See Outdoor Development Co., Inc. (DE))

OUTDOOR DEVELOPMENT CO., INC. (DE)
Voluntarily dissolved 05/17/1967
Details not available

OUTDOOR RESORTS INC (FL)
Name changed to Intelliworxx Inc. 12/01/1998
(See Intelliworxx Inc.)

OUTDOOR SPORTMAN'S TRAVEL, LTD. (NY)
Name changed to Anglo American Properties, Inc. 03/31/1978
(See Anglo American Properties, Inc.)

OUTDOOR SPORTS INDS INC (DE)
Merged into Brown Group, Inc. 07/27/1979
Each share Common 1¢ par exchanged for $15 cash

OUTDOOR SUPPLY INC (NY)
Name changed to Servinational, Inc. (NY) 10/17/1973
Servinational, Inc. (NY) reincorporated in Ohio 05/22/1991 which reincorporated in Nevada as Shikisai International, Inc. 11/25/2005 which name changed to Life Design Station International, Inc. 08/21/2007

OUTDOOR SYS INC (DE)
Common 1¢ par split (3) for (2) by issuance of (0.5) additional share payable 7/22/96 to holders of record 7/8/96
Common 1¢ par split (3) for (2) by issuance of (0.5) additional share payable 11/22/96 to holders of record 11/11/96
Common 1¢ par split (3) for (2) by issuance of (0.5) additional share payable 7/3/97 to holders of record 6/23/97
Common 1¢ par split (3) for (2) by issuance of (0.5) additional share payable 12/31/97 to holders of record 12/19/97 Ex date - 1/2/98
Common 1¢ par split (3) for (2) by issuance of (0.5) additional share payable 5/29/98 to holders of record 5/19/98 Ex date - 6/1/98
Merged into Infinity Broadcasting Corp. (New) 12/7/99
Each share Common 1¢ par exchanged for (1.25) shares Class A Common 1¢ par
Infinity Broadcasting Corp. (New) merged into Viacom Inc. (Old) 2/21/2001
(See Viacom Inc. (Old))

OUTER EDGE INTL INC (ON)
Recapitalized 07/15/1997
Recapitalized from Outer Edge Inc. to Outer Edge International Inc. 07/15/1997
Each share Common no par exchanged for (0.05) share Common no par
Recapitalized as Vision Global Solutions, Inc. (ON) 02/05/2001
Each share Common no par exchanged for (0.2) share Common no par
Vision Global Solutions, Inc. (ON) reincorporated in Nevada 01/07/2005 which recapitalized as Eco-Stim Energy Solutions, Inc. 12/11/2013

OUTERWALL INC (DE)
Acquired by Apollo Global Management, LLC 09/27/2016
Each share Common $0.001 par exchanged for $52 cash

OUTFRONT COS (NV)
Charter revoked 04/01/2013

OUTLAND RES CORP (BC)
Recapitalized as OTL Resources Ltd. 07/09/1992
Each share Common no par exchanged for (0.2) share Common no par
OTL Resources Ltd. name changed to Raytec Capital Corp. 04/21/1993 which recapitalized as Raytec Development Corp. 06/04/2001 which name changed to Raytec Metals Corp. 11/19/2007 which name changed to Lion Energy Corp. 09/16/2009 which was acquired by Africa Oil Corp. 06/20/2011

OUTLAW HOTEL CORP. (NV)
Charter revoked for failure to file reports and pay fees in March 1964

OUTLET CO (RI)
Common no par split (5) for (1) by issuance of (4) additional shares 2/9/60
Common no par split (2) for (1) by issuance of (1) additional share 8/2/65
Common no par split (3) for (2) by issuance of (0.5) additional share 5/4/77
Common no par split (3) for (2) by issuance of (0.5) additional share 5/4/83
5-1/2% Conv. Preferred $100 par called for redemption 5/4/83
Merged into Rockefeller Center Inc. 1/31/84
Each share $5 Preferred Ser. PA no par exchanged for $100 cash
Each share $5 Conv. Preferred Ser. PB no par exchanged for $370.97 cash
Each share 5.75% Conv. Preferred $100 par exchanged for $247.27 cash
Each share Common no par exchanged for $45.333 cash

OUTLET COMMUNICATIONS INC (DE)
Merged into Broadcasting Company, Inc. 2/2/96
Each share Class A Common 1¢ par exchanged for $47.25 cash

OUTLOOK EXPLORATIONS LTD. (ON)
Charter cancelled for default in filing annual returns 11/10/66

OUTLOOK GROUP CORP (WI)
Name changed 11/1/94
Name changed from Outlook Graphics Corp. to Outlook Group Corp. 11/1/94
Merged into Vista Group Holdings, LLC 7/26/2006
Each share Common 1¢ par exchanged for $13.50 cash

OUTLOOK RES INC (ON)
Filed a proposal under the Bankruptcy and Insolvency Act 01/28/2011

OUTLOOK SPORTS TECHNOLOGY INC (DE)
Name changed to Fusion Fund Inc. 03/31/2000
Fusion Fund Inc. name changed to Zenascent Inc. 01/08/2001 which name changed to Cedric Kushner Promotions Inc. 01/16/2003 which name changed to Ckrush, Inc. 12/27/2005
(See Ckrush, Inc.)

OUTPATIENT TREATMENT CENTERS, INC. (ID)
Charter forfeited for failure to file reports and pay taxes 12/01/1989

OUTRIDER ENERGY CORP (BC)
Each share old Common no par exchanged for (0.05) share new Common no par 03/26/2015
Name changed to Pinedale Energy Ltd. and new Common no par reclassified as Class A Common no par 06/02/2017

OUTRIDER RES LTD (AB)
Merged into 712919 Alberta Ltd. 12/18/96
Each share Common no par exchanged for $0.85 cash

OUTSOURCE INTL INC (FL)
Issue Information - 3,700,000 shares COM offered at $15 per share on 10/24/1997
Chapter 11 Federal Bankruptcy proceedings converted to Chapter 7 on 11/5/2002
Stockholders' equity unlikely

OUTWEST ENTMT INC (NV)
Each share old Common $0.001 par exchanged for (0.5) share new Common $0.001 par 10/08/1998
Charter revoked for failure to file reports and pay fees 02/01/2005

OUVO INC (DE)
Reorganized as Trustcash Holdings, Inc. 06/13/2007
Each share Common $0.0001 par exchanged for (3) shares Common $0.001 par

OVABLOC INC (DE)
Charter cancelled and declared inoperative and void for non-payment of taxes 03/01/1989

OVALE GROUP INC (NJ)
Company terminated common stock registration and is no longer public as of 08/04/2008

OVATION MUSIC & STUDIOS INC (FL)
Recapitalized as TLD3 Entertainment Group, Inc. 01/19/2017
Each share Common $0.001 par exchanged for (0.005) share Common $0.001 par

OVATION RESH INC (NV)
Name changed to Weed Growth Fund, Inc. 11/10/2014
(See Weed Growth Fund, Inc.)

OVER THE COUNTER SECS GROUP INC (MD)
Reincorporated 01/04/1985
Reincorporated 12/31/1988
Capital Stock $1 par changed to 50¢ par and (1) additional share issued 10/17/1983
Stock Dividend - 200% 01/31/1958
State of incorporation changed from (DE) to (PA) 01/04/1985
Reincorporated from Over-The-Counter Securities Fund, Inc. (PA) to under the laws of Maryland as Over-The-Counter Securities Group, Inc. 12/31/1988
Reorganized as Price (T. Rowe) International Trust 09/02/1992
Details not available

OVERBRIDGE CATTLE LTD (BC)
Dissolved 3/17/89
Details not available

OVERBRIDGE FARMS INTL LTD (CANADA)
Name changed to Wex Technologies Inc. 06/30/1992
Wex Technologies Inc. recapitalized as International Wex Technologies Inc. 08/28/1996 which name changed to WEX Pharmaceuticals Inc. 10/22/2004
(See WEX Pharmaceuticals Inc.)

OVERHEAD DOOR CORP (IN)
Common $1 par split (2) for (1) by issuance of (1) additional share 7/19/72
Name changed to Dallas Corp. 1/22/85
(See Dallas Corp.)

OVERHILL CORP (NV)
Each share Common no par received distribution of (0.5) share Overhill Farms, Inc. Common 1¢ par payable 10/29/2002 to holders of record 9/30/2002 Ex date - 10/30/2002
Name changed to TreeCon Resources, Inc. 10/28/2002

OVERHILL FARMS INC (NV)
Acquired by Bellisio Foods, Inc. 08/09/2013
Each share Common 1¢ par exchanged for $5 cash

OVERLAND BK (TEMECULA, CA)
Merged into FP Bancorp Inc. 03/31/1995
Each share Common no par exchanged for (0.1006) share Common no par
FP Bancorp Inc. merged into Zions Bancorporation 05/22/1998 which merged into Zions Bancorporation, N.A. (Salt Lake City, UT) 10/01/2018

OVERLAND CORP. (DE)
Under plan of merger each share Common $1 par exchanged for $22.75 in cash and (1/2,682,494th) interest in a Special Reserve 12/10/62
Completely liquidated by exchange of 1953 Receipts, 1962 Receipts and 1962
Merger Receipts for cash 4/15/65

OVERLAND DATA INC (CA)
Name changed to Overland Storage, Inc. 07/01/2002
Overland Storage, Inc. merged into Sphere 3D Corp. 12/01/2014 which reorganized as Sphere 3D Corp. (New) 03/24/2015

OVERLAND EXPRESS INC (MN)
Statutorily dissolved 06/15/1995

OVERLAND EXPRESS LTD (ON)
Name changed to Overland Western Ltd. 10/20/1971
(See Overland Western Ltd.)

OVERLAND GOLD CORP (WA)
Name changed to Winchester Gold, Corp. 10/30/1986

OVERLAND INDUSTRIES, LTD. (AB)
Struck off register and declared dissolved for failure to file reports or pay fees 6/30/56

OVERLAND OIL, INC. (CO)
Declared defunct and inoperative for non-payment of taxes 10/10/1962

OVERLAND OILS & MINERALS LTD. (ON)
Name changed to Sheba Mines Ltd. 1/18/57
Sheba Mines Ltd. charter cancelled 3/16/76

OVERLAND PRODUCING & REFINING CO. (CO)
Charter dissolved for failure to file annual reports 1/1/37

OVERLAND RLTY LTD (CANADA)
Acquired by Cominar Real Estate Investment Trust 03/16/2010
Each share Common no par exchanged for $0.82 cash

OVERLAND STORAGE INC (CA)
Each share old Common no par exchanged for (0.33333333) share new Common no par 12/09/2009
Each share new Common no par exchanged again for (0.2) share new Common no par 04/10/2014
Merged into Sphere 3D Corp. (Old) 12/01/2014
Each share new Common no par exchanged for (0.46385) share Common no par
Sphere 3D Corp. (Old) reorganized as Sphere 3D Corp. (New) 03/24/2015

OVERLAND WESTN LTD (ON)
Acquired by Alltrans Holdings (Ont.) Ltd. 01/09/1976
Each share 60¢ Conv. 1st Preference no par exchanged for $30 cash
Each share Part. 2nd Preference no par exchanged for $6 cash
Each share Common no par exchanged for $12 cash

OVERLINE CORP (DE)
Each share old Common $0.0005 par exchanged for (0.1) share new Common $0.0005 par 07/18/1988
Each share new Common $0.0005 par exchanged for (0.1) share Common $0.005 par 11/23/1994
Reincorporated under the laws of Colorado as Megalith Corp. 10/13/1995

OVERLOOK HEALTH CARE SYS INC (ID)
Recapitalized as International Digital Technologies Inc. 7/1/98
Each share old Common no par exchanged for (0.008) share new Common no par

OVERLORD CAP LTD (BC)
Name changed to Avanti Energy Inc. 05/16/2013

OVERLORD FINL INC (AB)
Name changed to Aston Hill Financial Inc. 06/05/2007
Aston Hill Financial Inc. name changed to LOGiQ Asset Management Inc. 12/16/2016

OVERLORD RES LTD (BC)
Name changed to Devran Petroleum Ltd. (BC) 03/17/1986
Devran Petroleum Ltd. (BC) reincorporated in Canada 09/24/1986 which name changed to Reserve Royalty Corp. 11/16/1995 which merged into PrimeWest Energy Trust 07/27/2000
(See PrimeWest Energy Trust)

OVERMAN CUSHION TIRE CO., INC.
Out of business in 1937
No stockholders' equity

OVERMYER CORP (IN)
Common no par split (3) for (2) by issuance of (0.5) additional share 10/11/1974
Liquidating Plan of Reorganization under Chapter 11 Federal Bankruptcy proceedings confirmed 12/27/1993
No stockholders' equity

OVERNITE CORP (VA)
Issue Information - 25,000,000 shares COM offered at $19 per share on 10/30/2003
Merged into United Parcel Service Inc. 8/8/2005
Each share Common 1¢ par exchanged for $43.25 cash

OVERNITE TRANSN CO (VA)
Common 50¢ par changed to $1 par 12/14/61
Common $1 par split (3) for (2) by issuance of (0.5) additional share 11/16/70
Common $1 par split (2) for (1) by issuance of (1) additional share 8/31/71
Common $1 par split (2) for (1) by issuance of (1) additional share 5/19/81
Common $1 par split (2) for (1) by issuance of (1) additional share 5/17/83
Common $1 par split (2) for (1) by issuance of (1) additional share 2/28/86
Stock Dividends - 100% 5/28/59; 100% 2/15/62
Merged into Union Pacific Corp. 12/16/86
Each share Common $1 par exchanged for $43.25 cash

OVERSEAS FILMGROUP INC (DE)
Name changed to First Look Media, Inc. 1/17/2001

OVERSEAS INDUSTRIES, S.A. (LUXEMBOURG)
Name changed to Overseas Inns S.A. 5/12/71
(See Overseas Inns S.A.)

OVERSEAS INNS S A (LUXEMBOURG)
Completely liquidated 10/19/1987
Each share Common $2 par exchanged for first and final distribution of $6.40 cash

OVERSEAS NATL AWYS (DE)
Liquidation completed
Each share Common $1 par exchanged for initial distribution of $8 cash 01/25/1979
Each share Common $1 par received second distribution of $0.60 cash 12/09/1980
Each share Common $1 par received third distribution of $0.16 cash 06/23/1983
Each share Common $1 par received fourth and final distribution of $0.09 cash 12/28/1984

OVERSEAS PLATINUM CORP (BC)
Recapitalized as Broadlands Resources Ltd. (Old) 05/28/1991
Each share Common no par exchanged for (0.2) share Common no par
Broadlands Resources Ltd. (Old) merged into International Broadlands Resources Ltd. 04/06/1995 which recapitalized as Broadlands Resources Ltd. (New) 03/15/1999 which recapitalized as Pinnacle Mines Ltd. (Ctfs. dated after 07/16/2003) 07/16/2003 which name changed to Jayden Resources Inc. (BC) 06/29/2010 which reincorporated in Cayman Islands 10/03/2012

OVERSEAS SECS INC (NY)
Capital Stock no par changed to $1 par 00/00/1941

Name changed to Interwest Corp. 10/01/1985
(See Interwest Corp.)

OVERSEAS SHIPHOLDING GROUP INC OLD (DE)
Common $1 par split (3) for (2) by issuance of (0.5) additional share 11/13/1973
Common $1 par split (3) for (2) by issuance of (0.5) additional share 03/17/1980
Common $1 par split (3) for (2) by issuance of (0.5) additional share 06/12/1981
Common $1 par split (7) for (5) by issuance of (0.4) additional share 03/13/1989
Under plan of reorganization each share Common $1 par automatically became (1) share Overseas Shipholding Group, Inc. (New) Class B Common $1 par 08/06/2014
Note: Non-U.S. holders received (1) Class B Common Stock Purchase Warrant expiring 08/05/2039

OVERSEAS TERMINAL LTD. (HI)
Merged into Oahu Railway & Land Co. in 1954
Oahu Railway & Land Co. merged into Dillingham Corp. 12/29/61
(See Dillingham Corp.)

OVERSEAS UN BK LTD (SINGAPORE)
Stock Dividends - 10% 06/29/1994; 10% payable 06/25/1999 to holders of record 05/13/1999; 14.2% payable 09/29/1999 to holders of record 09/15/1999
ADR agreement terminated 12/18/2001
Each ADR for Ordinary S$1 par exchanged for $5.034 cash

OVERTECH CORP (NV)
Common $0.001 par split (24) for (1) by issuance of (23) additional shares payable 08/04/2014 to holders of record 08/01/2014 Ex date - 08/05/2014
Name changed to Medicus Homecare Inc. 12/12/2014

OVERTHRUST DOME ENERGY INC. (UT)
Name changed to Data Conversion International, Inc. and Common $0.001 par changed to 1¢ par 08/11/1983
Data Conversion International, Inc. name changed to Aztec Energy Corp. (UT) 08/00/1991 which reorganized in Delaware as Blaze Energy Corp. 06/26/2007
(See Blaze Energy Corp.)

OVERTHRUST INTL CORP (UT)
Recapitalized 6/19/89
Recapitalized from Overthrust Oil & Gas Corp. to Overthrust International Corp. 6/19/89
Each share Common 1¢ par exchanged for (0.01) share Common 1¢ par
Recapitalized as KWT Ltd. 10/5/98
Each (70) shares new Common 1¢ par exchanged for (1) share Common 1¢ par

OVERTHRUST OIL RTY CORP (CO)
Each share old Common no par exchanged for (0.001666) share new Common no par 1/2/94
Note: Unexchanged certificates will become void and valueless 2/20/95
Reorganized under the laws of Nevada as KnowledgeBroker Inc. 4/28/95
Each share new Common no par exchanged for (0.5) share Common 1¢ par

OVERTHRUST RES LTD (CO)
Proclaimed dissolved for failure to file reports 10/1/2000

OVERTON BANCSHARES INC (TX)
Merged into Cullen/Frost Bankers Inc. 5/29/98
Each share Common $4 par exchanged for (3.71) shares Common $5 par

OVERTURE ACQUISITION CORP (CAYMAN ISLANDS)
Issue Information - 15,000,000 UNITS consisting of (1) share ORD and (1) WT offered at $10 per Unit on 01/30/2008
Completely liquidated 02/02/2010
Each Unit exchanged for first and final distribution of $10.0363 cash
Each share Ordinary $0.0001 par exchanged for first and final distribution of $10.0363 cash

OVERTURE SVCS INC (DE)
Acquired by Yahoo!, Inc. 10/7/2003
Each share Common $0.0001 par exchanged for (0.6108) share Common $0.001 par and $4.75 cash

OVERTURE VENTURES LTD (BC)
Recapitalized as Xyquest Venture Corp. 01/11/1994
Each share Common no par exchanged for (0.2) share Common no par
Xyquest Venture Corp. name changed to Polar Bear Ventures Ltd. 11/25/1996 which recapitalized as Iciena Ventures Inc. 02/24/1999 which recapitalized as Barksdale Capital Corp. 02/08/2013

OVEX FERTILITY CORP (DE)
Reincorporated 8/20/87
State of incorporation changed from (NY) to (DE) 8/20/87
Name changed to American Vaccine Corp. 1/13/89
American Vaccine Corp. merged into North American Vaccine, Inc. 2/28/90 which merged into Baxter International Inc. 6/26/2000

OVID CAP VENTURES INC (CANADA)
Name changed to BIOflex Technologies Inc. 08/19/2015
BIOflex Technologies Inc. name changed to Relevium Technologies Inc. 12/23/2015

OVID TECHNOLOGIES INC (DE)
Merged into Wolters Kluwer N.V. 11/9/98
Each share Common 1¢ par exchanged for $24.59 cash

OVINGTON BROTHER'S CO.
Acquired by Ovington's Gift Shop, Inc. in 1932 which became insolvent in 1950

OVINGTON'S GIFT SHOP, INC.
Insolvent 00/00/1950
Stockholders' equity unlikely

OVITRON CORP (DE)
Name changed to General Indicator Corp. 3/31/77
(See General Indicator Corp.)

OVIVO INC (QC)
Acquired by SKion GmbH 09/19/2016
Each share Class A Subordinate no par exchanged for $4 cash
Each share Class B Multiple no par exchanged for $4 cash

OVM INTL HLDG CORP (NV)
Recapitalized as Premier Holding Corp. 12/01/2008
Each share Common $0.0001 par exchanged for (0.025) share Common $0.0001 par

OVONIC IMAGING SYS INC (DE)
Name changed to OIS Optical Imaging Systems, Inc. 7/12/90
(See OIS Optical Imaging Systems, Inc.)

OVONIC SYNTHETIC MATLS INC (DE)
Name changed to Osmic, Inc. 7/26/94

OVUTRON CORP (NV)
Name changed to Colt Energy Corp. 12/4/86
(See Colt Energy Corp.)

OVVIO BETTER LIFE INC (WA)
Name changed to Animal Cloning Sciences, Inc. 11/21/2000
(See Animal Cloning Sciences, Inc.)

OW OFFICE WHSE INC (DE)
Merged into OM Acquisition Corp. 06/30/1992
Each share Common 1¢ par exchanged for $11 cash

OWASSO COTTON AND GRAIN CO. (OK)
Charter cancelled for failure to pay taxes in 1910

OWEN HEALTHCARE INC (TX)
Common no par split (5) for (2) by issuance of (1.5) additional shares 6/30/95
Merged into Cardinal Health, Inc. 3/18/97
Each share Common no par exchanged for (0.45) share Common no par

OWEN LABS INC (TX)
Acquired by Alcon Laboratories, Inc. 04/29/1972
Each share Common 50¢ par exchanged for (0.55) share Common 25¢ par
(See Alcon Laboratories, Inc.)

OWEN-OREGON LUMBER CO.
Sold at foreclosure in 1932

OWEN SOUND INDUSTRIAL DEVELOPMENTS LTD. (ON)
Preference $10 par called for redemption 1/15/70
Charter allowed to lapse in 1971
No Common stockholders' equity

OWEN VENTURES LTD (BC)
Cease trade order effective 02/03/1989
Stockholders' equity unlikely

OWENS & MINOR DRUG CO., INC. (VA)
Name changed to Owens, Minor & Bodeker, Inc. 6/10/55
Owens, Minor & Bodeker, Inc. name changed to Owens & Minor, Inc. (Old) 7/30/81 which merged into Owens & Minor, Inc. (New) 5/10/94

OWENS & MINOR INC OLD (VA)
Common $2 par split (2) for (1) by issuance of (1) additional share 10/29/82
Common $2 par split (3) for (2) by issuance of (0.5) additional share 8/30/85
Common $2 par split (3) for (2) by issuance of (0.5) additional share 5/31/88
Common $2 par split (3) for (2) by issuance of (0.5) additional share 7/16/91
Common $2 par split (3) for (2) by issuance of (0.5) additional share 3/22/93
Stock Dividend - 10% 3/31/82
Under plan of merger each share Common $2 par automatically became (1) share Owens & Minor, Inc. (New) Common $2 par 5/10/94

OWENS & MINOR TR I (DE)
144A Guaranteed Term Conv. Securities Ser. A called for redemption at $51 on 09/04/2003
Guaranteed Term Conv. Securities Ser. A called for redemption at $51 on 09/04/2003

OWENS BOTTLE CO.
Merged into Owens-Illinois Glass Co. in 1929
(See Owens-Illinois Glass Co.)

OWENS CORNING FIBERGLAS CORP NEW (DE)
Recapitalized 11/5/86
Common $5 par changed to $1 par and (1) additional share issued 5/18/56
Common $1 par split (2) for (1) by issuance of (1) additional share 7/27/70
Common $1 par split (2) for (1) by issuance of (1) additional share 5/12/78
Recapitalized from Owens-Corning Fiberglass Corp. (Old) to Owens-Corning Fiberglass Corp. (New) 11/5/86
Each share Common $1 par exchanged for $35 principal amount of 15% Jr. Subord. Discount Debentures due 12/1/2006, (1) share Common 10¢ par and $52 cash
Name changed to Owens Corning (Old) 1/2/96
(See Owens Corning (Old))

OWENS CORNING OLD (DE)
Plan of reorganization under Chapter 11 Federal Bankruptcy Code effective 10/31/2006
Each share Common 10¢ par received approximately (0.14) Owens Corning (New) Common Stock Purchase Warrants Ser. B expiring 10/31/2013
Note: Certificates were not required to be surrendered and are without value

OWENS ILL GLASS CO (OH)
Each share Common $25 par exchanged for (2) shares Common $12.50 par in 1937
Common $12.50 par changed to $6.25 par and (1) additional share issued 10/18/55
Name changed to Owens-Illinois, Inc. 4/28/65
(See Owens-Illinois, Inc.)

OWENS ILL INC (OH)
Common $6.25 par changed to $3.125 par and (1) additional share issued 05/28/1965
Common $3.125 par split (2) for (1) by issuance of (1) additional share 04/08/1977
Common $3.125 par split (2) for (1) by issuance of (1) additional share 06/16/1986
Merged into Owens-Illinois Holdings Corp. 03/24/1987
Each share Common $3.125 par exchanged for $60.50 cash
4% Preferred $100 par called for redemption 04/22/1987
$4.75 Conv. Preference no par called for redemption 04/22/1987
Each share $2.375 Conv. Preferred 1¢ par exchanged for (0.9424) share Common 1¢ par 03/31/2008
(Additional Information in Active)

OWENS METAL CO. (MO)
Under plan of merger name changed to Owens Plastics Co. 1/7/63 which was acquired by Borg-Warner Corp. for cash 9/8/66

OWENS MINOR & BODEKER INC (VA)
Common $10 par changed to $2.50 par and (3) additional shares issued 04/08/1971
5-1/2% Preferred 1952 Ser. $25 par called for redemption 08/01/1973
5-1/2% Preferred 1955 Ser. $25 par called for redemption 08/01/1973
Common $2.50 par changed to $2 par and (0.25) additional share issued 08/25/1976
Stock Dividends - 50% 06/30/1975; 10% 03/31/1981
Name changed to Owens & Minor, Inc. (Old) 07/30/1981
Owens & Minor, Inc. (Old) merged into Owens & Minor, Inc. (New) 05/10/1994

OWENS PLASTICS CO. (MO)
Common $2 par changed to 20¢ par 6/30/65
Acquired by Borg-Warner Corp. 9/8/66
Each share Common 20¢ par exchanged for $12.34 cash

OWENS-WELLS OIL CO. (IL)
Completely liquidated 12/2/68
Each share 7% Preferred $10 par exchanged for first and final distribution of $10 cash
Each share Common $1 par exchanged for first and final distribution of $3.425177 cash

OWENS YACHT CO., INC. (MD)
Acquired by Brunswick-Balke-Collender Co. on a (2) for (7) basis 4/1/60 which name was changed to Brunswick Corp. 4/18/60

OWINGS MILLS DISTILLERY, INC.
Dissolved in 1942

OWL DRUG CO.
Assets sold in 1933

OWL DRUG CO. OF COLORADO (CO)
Name changed to Cable Car Burger Inc. 3/30/68
Cable Car Burger Inc. recapitalized as Winthrop-Scott Corp. 11/3/72
(See Winthrop-Scott Corp.)

OWNER OPERATING CORP.
Dissolved in 1950

OWNERS DISC CORP (IN)
Class A $10 par reclassified as Common $10 par by share for share exchange 07/01/1954
Name changed to Valley Financial Services, Inc. 03/23/1973

OWNERTEL INC (GA)
Recapitalized as Ficaar Inc. 02/12/2008
Each share Common $0.001 par exchanged for (0.0001) share Common $0.001 par

OWOSSO CORP (PA)
Issue Information - 1,865,000 shares COM offered at $12 per share on 10/25/1994
Merged into Allied Motion Technologies, Inc. 5/10/2004
Each share Common 1¢ par exchanged for (0.068) share Common no par

OX-BOW SILVER MINING CO. LTD. (ON)
Charter cancelled for failure to pay taxes and file returns 6/23/80

OX FIBRE BRUSH CO., INC. (DE)
Each share Common $100 par exchanged for (4) shares Common $25 par 00/00/1951
Stock Dividend - 10% 06/10/1959
Name changed to OFB Corp. 05/12/1965
(See OFB Corp.)

OXBORO MED INC (MN)
Name changed 3/17/2000
Common 1¢ par split (2) for (1) by issuance of (1) additional share 4/5/91
Each share old Common 1¢ par exchanged for (0.2) share new Common 1¢ par 8/13/99
Name changed from Oxboro Medical International, Inc. to Oxboro Medical, Inc. 3/17/2000
Name changed to Sterion, Inc. 1/15/2002
Sterion, Inc. name changed to STEN Corp. 1/31/2005

OXBOW ENTERPRISES LTD (AB)
Recapitalized as Palliser Energy Inc. 8/5/91
Each share Common no par

exchanged for (0.25) share Class A Common no par
(See Palliser Energy Inc.)

OXBOW EQUITIES CORP (AB)
Reincorporated under the laws of Canada as MonoGen, Inc. 11/06/2006
(See MonoGen, Inc.)

OXBOW EXPL INC (AB)
Name changed to Volterra Resources Inc. 06/19/1998
Volterra Resources Inc. merged into Edge Energy Inc. 05/27/1999 which merged into Ventus Energy Ltd. 08/11/2000 which name changed Navigo Energy Inc. 05/24/2002
(See Navigo Energy Inc.)

OXBOW RES CORP (DE)
Common $0.001 par split (3) for (1) by issuance of (2) additional shares payable 03/03/2008 to holders of record 02/27/2008 Ex date - 03/04/2008
Recapitalized as Texas Sweet Crude Oil Corp. 12/31/2008
Each share Common $0.001 par exchanged for (0.00066666) share Common $0.001 par
(See Texas Sweet Crude Oil Corp.)

OXBOW RES LTD (BC)
Recapitalized as Pasadena Energy Corp. 7/21/81
Each share Common no par exchanged for (0.25) share Common no par
Pasadena Energy Corp. name changed to Pasadena Technology Corp. 6/3/85 which name changed to EMS Systems Ltd. 8/11/86
(See EMS Systems Ltd.)

OXBOW SILVER MINES LTD.
Name changed to Silver Arrow Mines Ltd. (Ont.) in 1946
Silver Arrow Mines Ltd. (Ont.) charter revoked 7/13/62

OXFORD BANK (OXFORD, MI)
Name changed 06/01/1985
Stock Dividend - 25% 02/15/1972
Name changed from Oxford Savings Bank (Oxford, MI) to Oxford Bank (Oxford, MI) 06/01/1985
Under plan of reorganization each share Common $25 par automatically became (1) share Oxford Bank Corp. Common $25 par 07/20/1987

OXFORD CAP CORP (CT)
Common 5¢ par changed to $0.005 par and (1) additional share issued 2/15/90
Common $0.005 par split (3) for (1) by issuance of (2) additional shares 1/20/94
Name changed to Americas Gaming International Inc. 11/22/95

OXFORD CHEMICAL CORP. (GA)
Name changed to OCC Liquidating Co. 12/16/66
(See OCC Liquidating Co.)

OXFORD CITY FOOTBALL CLUB INC (FL)
Each share old Common $0.0001 par exchanged for (0.0005) share new Common $0.0001 par 08/21/2015
Administratively dissolved 09/23/2016

OXFORD CONS INC (DE)
Each share Conv. Preferred Ser. A $10 par exchanged for (7) shares Common 1-1/3¢ par 2/28/90
Each share Common 10¢ par exchanged for (0.0499995) share Common 1-1/3¢ par 2/28/90
Each share new Common 1-1/3¢ par exchanged for (0.0001) share Common no par 3/4/94
Note: In effect holders received $6.60 cash per share and public interest was eliminated

OXFORD DEV GROUP LTD (AB)
$1.75 Class Y Preference $5 par called for redemption 6/1/79
Under plan of acquisition each share $1 Conv. First Preference Ser. A $11 par and Common no par exchanged for $26 cash respectively 6/24/80

OXFORD EDL SVCS INC (FL)
Reincorporated under the laws of Delaware as Aspen Global Corp. 01/02/2008
Aspen Global Corp. name changed to Diversified Mortgage Workout Corp. 08/08/2008 which recapitalized as Arem Pacific Corp. 07/29/2013

OXFORD ELEC CORP (DE)
Reincorporated 12/13/67
Stock Dividends - 10% 1/18/57; 10% 1/24/58; 10% 1/19/59; 10% 1/15/60
State of incorporation changed from (IL) to (DE) 12/13/67
Each share $2.80 Conv. Preferred Ser. A $20 par exchanged for (5) shares 56¢ Conv. Preferred Ser. A $4 par 5/29/69
Common $1 par changed to 50¢ par 6/30/72
Name changed to Seaport Corp. 9/15/73
(See Seaport Corp.)

OXFORD ENERGY CO (DE)
Liquidating plan of reorganization under Chapter 11 Federal Bankruptcy proceedings confirmed 08/17/1993
Stockholders' equity unlikely

OXFORD ENTERPRISES INC (UT)
Recapitalized as Photonic Security Systems, Inc. 2/20/89
Each (6) shares Common 1¢ par exchanged for (1) share Common $0.001 par
(See Photonic Security Systems, Inc.)

OXFORD EQUITY INC (AB)
Recapitalized as Schomburg Industries (Canada) Inc. 03/31/1994
Each share Class A Common no par exchanged for (0.5) share Common no par
(See Schomburg Industries (Canada) Inc.)

OXFORD EXPL CO (CO)
Merged into Oxford Consolidated, Inc. 09/18/1985
Each share Common 1¢ par exchanged for (0.0734704) share Common 10¢ par
(See Oxford Consolidated, Inc.)

OXFORD FDG CORP (WY)
Recapitalized as Emerging Healthcare Solutions, Inc. 08/12/2009
Each share Common $0.001 par exchanged for (0.002) share Common $0.001 par

OXFORD FIN INC (PA)
Preferred $19.25 par called for redemption 07/01/1966
Stock Dividend - 10% 12/20/1967
Each share Class A no par exchanged for (1) share Oxford First Corp. (DE) Common $1 par 07/01/1969
Under plan of reorganization each share Common $1 par exchanged for (1) share Oxford First Corp. (DE) Common $1 par 07/01/1969
(See Oxford First Corp. (DE))
4-1/2% Jr. Preferred Ser. B $10 par called for redemption 11/00/1986
Public interest eliminated

OXFORD FINL HLDGS LTD (CO)
Name changed to Mighty Mack USA, Ltd. 08/03/1999
Mighty Mack USA, Ltd. name changed to Sao Luis Mining, Inc. (CO) 05/26/2006 which reorganized in Nevada as Brazilian Mining Corp. 03/26/2009 which name changed to Sierra Desert Holdings Inc.

10/18/2010 which recapitalized as Telefix Communications Holdings, Inc. 03/12/2012

OXFORD FINL INC (CO)
Name changed to Clancy Systems International, Inc. 4/20/87

OXFORD 1ST CORP (PA)
Reincorporated 05/21/1970
State of incorporation changed from (DE) to (PA) 05/21/1970
Common $1 par split (3) for (2) by issuance of (0.5) additional share 02/03/1987
Stock Dividends - 10% 07/21/1981; 10% 07/21/1983
Acquired by Cawsl Corp. 09/07/1988
Each share Common $1 par exchanged for $25 cash

OXFORD FUTURES FD LTD (CO)
Voluntarily dissolved 07/19/2000
Details not available

OXFORD GLYCOSCIENCES PLC (ENGLAND & WALES)
Issue Information - 11,764,705 ADR's offered at $18.36 per ADR on 12/07/2000
Acquired by Celltech Group PLC 7/18/2003
Each Sponsored ADR for Ordinary 5p par exchanged for $2.9573 cash

OXFORD HEALTH PLANS INC (DE)
Common 1¢ par split (2) for (1) by issuance of (1) additional share 10/27/1993
Common 1¢ par split (2) for (1) by issuance of (1) additional share 03/27/1995
Common 1¢ par split (2) for (1) by issuance of (1) additional share payable 04/01/1996 to holders of record 03/25/1996
Merged into UnitedHealth Group Inc. (MN) 07/30/2004
Each share Common 1¢ par exchanged for (0.6357) share Common 1¢ par and $16.17 cash
UnitedHealth Group Inc. (MN) reincorporated in Delaware 07/01/2015

OXFORD INVT INC (NV)
Each share old Common $0.001 par exchanged for (0.1) share new Common $0.001 par 5/16/94
Name changed to Oxford Capital Corp. 11/9/95

OXFORD KNIGHT INTL INC (TX)
Reincorporated 11/20/2001
State of incorporation changed from (DE) to (TX) 11/20/2001
Each share old Common $0.00001 par exchanged for (0.02) share new Common $0.00001 par 12/1/2001
Each share new Common $0.00001 par exchanged again for (0.001) share new Common $0.00001 par 1/29/2004
Name changed to Montrose National Partners Inc. 2/23/2004
Montrose National Partners Inc. name changed to Cross Atlantic Life & Science Technology Inc. 8/19/2005 which name changed to Deep Earth Resources, Inc. 5/5/2006

OXFORD LABS (CA)
Stock Dividend - 50% 12/05/1972
Merged into Searle (G.D.) & Co. (DE) 05/31/1974
Each share Common no par exchanged for (0.85) share Common 33-1/3¢ par
(See Searle (G.D.) & Co. (DE))

OXFORD LAKE MINES LTD.
Name changed to Blouin Lake Gold Mines Ltd. 00/00/1934
(See Blouin Lake Gold Mines Ltd.)

OXFORD LANE CAP CORP (MD)
8.5% Term Preferred Ser. 2017 1¢ par called for redemption at $25 plus $0.13577 accrued dividends on 07/24/2015

8.125% Term Preferred Ser. 2024 1¢ par called for redemption at $25 plus $0.07336 accrued dividends on 07/14/2017
(Additional Information in Active)

OXFORD LIFE INSURANCE CO. (AZ)
Merged into Protective Security Life Insurance Co. on a (0.5) for (1) basis 2/9/61
Protective Security Life Insurance Co. name changed to American Pacific Life Insurance Co. of California 4/13/65
(See American Pacific Life Insurance Co. of California)

OXFORD LUMBER CO. (MI)
Name changed 02/12/1969
Name changed from Oxford Lumber & Coal Co. to Oxford Lumber Co. 02/12/1969
Charter dissolved by time limitation 07/15/2003

OXFORD MANUFACTURING CO., INC. (GA)
Class B-1 Common $1 par reclassified as Class A Common $1 par 7/31/63
Class B-2 Common $1 par reclassified as Class A Common $1 par 7/31/66
Stock Dividend - In Class A & B Common - 100% 5/10/63
Name changed to Oxford Industries, Inc. 5/31/67

OXFORD MEDIA INC (NV)
Recapitalized as SVI Media, Inc. 09/14/2007
Each (30) shares Common $0.001 par exchanged for (1) share Common $0.001 par
(See SVI Media, Inc.)

OXFORD PAPER CO. (ME)
Common no par changed to $15 par and (1) additional share issued in 1951
$5 Preferred no par called for redemption 7/1/63
Common $15 par changed to $5 par and (2) additional shares issued 5/20/66
Merged into Ethyl Corp. 8/1/67
Each share Common no par exchanged for (0.5) share $2.40 Conv. 2nd Preferred Ser. A $10 par
Ethyl Corp. reorganized as NewMarket Corp. 6/18/2004

OXFORD PENDAFLEX CORP (NY)
100% acquired by EAB Business Systems, Inc. through purchase offer which expired 07/07/1976
Public interest eliminated

OXFORD PPTYS CDA LTD (ON)
Merged into Oxford Properties Group Inc. 7/25/95
Each share 1st Preferred no par exchanged for (0.16125) share 1st Preferred no par
Each share 2nd Preferred no par exchanged for (0.56) share 2nd Preferred no par
Each share Common no par exchanged for (0.012) share Common no par
(See Oxford Properties Group Inc.)

OXFORD PPTYS GROUP INC (ON)
Common no par split (2) for (1) by issuance of (1) additional share payable 06/02/1998 to holders of record 05/24/1998
Acquired by BPC Properties Ltd. 10/17/2001
Each share Common no par exchanged for $23.75 cash

OXFORD RADIO CORP.
Name changed to Oxford Electric Corp. (IL) in 1947
Oxford Electric Corp. (IL) reincorporated in Delaware 12/13/67 which name changed to Seaport Corp. 9/15/73

FINANCIAL INFORMATION, INC.   OXF-P.

(See Seaport Corp.)

OXFORD RESOURCE PARTNERS LP (DE)
Recapitalized as Westmoreland Resource Partners, L.P. 01/02/2015
Each Common Unit of Ltd. Partnership Int. exchanged for (0.08333333) Common Unit of Ltd. Partnership Int.

OXFORD RES CORP (NY)
Merged into Barnett Banks, Inc. 4/1/97
Each share Class A Common 1¢ par exchanged for (0.9085) share Common $2 par
Barnett Banks, Inc. merged into NationsBank Corp. 1/9/98 which reincorporated in Delaware as BankAmerica Corp. (Old) 9/25/98 which merged into BankAmerica Corp. (New) 9/30/98 which name changed to Bank of America Corp. 4/28/99

OXFORD RES LTD (BC)
Struck off register and declared dissolved for failure to file returns 4/26/85

OXFORD SOFTWARE DEVELOPERS INC (ON)
Name changed to Oxford Investments Holdings Inc. 12/16/2003

OXFORD TAX EXEMPT FD II LTD PARTNERSHIP (MD)
Merged into Apartment Investment & Management Co. 3/26/2001
Each Unit of Limited Partnership Int. exchanged for (0.547) share Conv. Preferred Class P 1¢ par and (0.299) share Class A Common 1¢ par

OXFORD VENTURE CORP (NV)
Name changed to Christmas Guild Inc. 6/24/88
Christmas Guild Inc. name changed to Cypress Financial Services, Inc. 12/4/95 which name changed to RevCare, Inc. 8/9/2000
(See RevCare, Inc.)

OXFORD VENTURES INC (NV)
Common $0.001 par split (3.25) for (1) by issuance of (2.25) additional shares payable 12/19/2003 to holders of record 12/19/2003 Ex date - 12/22/2003
Common $0.001 par split (4) for (1) by issuance of (3) additional shares payable 3/1/2004 to holders of record 3/1/2004 Ex date - 3/2/2004
Recapitalized as Uluru Inc. 4/5/2006
Each share Common $0.001 par exchanged for (0.0025) share Common $0.001 par

OXI OIL CORP (ID)
Charter forfeited for failure to file reports 12/1/86

OXIANA LTD (AUSTRALIA)
Name changed to OZ Minerals Ltd. 07/29/2008
(See OZ Minerals Ltd.)

OXIDITE BATTERY CORP. (SD)
Charter expired by time limitation 11/30/1947

OXIDYNE GROUP INC (DE)
Out of business in 1990
No stockholders' equity

OXIGENE INC (DE)
Each share old Common 1¢ par exchanged for (0.05) share new Common 1¢ par 02/23/2011
Each share new Common 1¢ par exchanged again for (0.08333333) share new Common 1¢ par 12/28/2012
Name changed to Mateon Therapeutics, Inc. 06/20/2016

OXIN INDS LTD (BC)
Struck off register and declared dissolved for failure to file returns 7/6/90

OXIS INTL INC (DE)
Each share Common 50¢ par exchanged for (0.2) share old Common $0.001 par 10/21/1998
Each share old Common $0.001 par exchanged for (0.004) share new Common $0.001 par 12/15/2015
Recapitalized as GT Biopharma, Inc. 08/21/2017
Each share new Common $0.001 par exchanged for (0.00333333) share Common $0.001 par

OXITENO S A INDUSTRIA E COMERCIO (BRAZIL)
Acquired by Ultrapar Participacoes S.A. 10/30/2002
Details not available

OXOCO INC (DE)
Name changed 06/16/1983
Name changed from Oxoco (CA) to Oxoco Inc. (DE) 06/16/1983
Reorganized under Chapter 11 Federal Bankruptcy Code 01/01/1987
Each share $3 Conv. Preferred $1 par exchanged for (0.1836) share Common 1¢ par
Each share Common 10¢ par exchanged for (0.01143) share Common 1¢ par
Note: Holdings of (6) to (499) shares of Preferred exchanged for $0.0509 cash per share
Holdings of (5) shares or fewer did not participate
Holdings of (88) to (10,000) shares of Common exchanged for $0.0032 cash per share
Holdings of (87) shares of fewer did not participate
Name changed to Ironstone Group, Inc. 09/15/1988

OXTEC MEDICAL INDUSTRIES, INC. (UT)
Recapitalized as Federal Medical Industries, Inc. 5/12/86
Each share Common no par exchanged for (0.25) share Common no par
(See Federal Medical Industries, Inc.)

OXY CAP TR I (DE)
8.16% Trust Originated Preferred Securities called for redemption at $25 on 1/20/2004

OXY CATALYST INC (PA)
Each VTC for Capital Stock exchanged for (1) share Capital Stock no par 12/31/1963
Acquired by Research-Cottrell, Inc. 09/24/1971
Each share Capital Stock no par exchanged for (0.3638) share Capital Stock $1 par
(See Research-Cottrell, Inc.)

OXYGEN BIOTHERAPEUTICS INC (DE)
Each share old Common $0.0001 par exchanged for (0.06666666) share new Common $0.0001 par 11/09/2009
Each share new Common $0.0001 par exchanged again for (0.05) share new Common $0.0001 par 05/13/2013
Name changed to Tenax Therapeutics, Inc. 09/19/2014

OXYGEN ENRICHMENT LTD (NY)
Proclaimed dissolved 9/24/97

OXYSURE THERAPEUTICS INC (DE)
Name changed 02/12/2016
Name changed from OxySure Systems, Inc. to OxySure Therapeutics, Inc. 02/12/2016
Chapter 7 bankruptcy proceedings terminated 04/21/2017
No stockholders' equity

OY WARTSILA AB (FINLAND)
Merged into Lohja Oy 01/16/1991

Each ADR for Non-Restricted Ser. 2 M60 par exchanged for $55.20 cash

OYAMA INDS LTD (AB)
Issue Information - 3,000,000 shares COM offered at $0.10 per share on 03/14/1997
Name changed to Shaker Petroleum Inc. 10/30/2001
Shaker Petroleum Inc. recapitalized as Shaker Resources Inc. 06/28/2002 which merged into Caribou Resources Corp. 09/30/2004 which merged into JED Oil Inc. 07/31/2007
(See JED Oil Inc.)

OYO GEOSPACE CORP (DE)
Name changed to Geospace Technologies Corp. (DE) 10/01/2012
Geospace Technologies Corp. (DE) reincorporated in Texas 04/20/2015

OYSTERMENS BK & TR CO (SAYVILLE, NY)
Stock Dividend - 10% 02/05/1971
Merged into First Commercial Banks, Inc. 09/30/1974
Each share Common $5 par exchanged for either $45.36 cash or $32.66 principal amount of 7-1/2% Non-Assignable Promissory Installment Notes due 1975/80 and $12.70 cash
Note: Option to receive cash only expired 11/01/1974

OZ INVTS CO LTD (ISRAEL)
Acquired by Sahar Investments Ltd. 07/01/2004
Each share Ordinary ILS 1 par exchanged for USD $0.30 cash

OZ MINERALS LTD (AUSTRALIA)
ADR basis changed from (1:5) to (1:0.5) 06/10/2011
ADR agreement terminated 04/02/2013
Each Sponsored ADR for Ordinary exchanged for $1.819603 cash

OZ PUBLISHING CORP. (NY)
Assets sold for benefit of creditors 1/8/65
No stockholders' equity

OZALID CO. LTD. (ENGLAND)
ADR's for Ord. Reg. 5s par changed to 25p par per currency change 02/15/1971
Name changed to Ozalid Group Holdings Ltd. 01/01/1973
(See Ozalid Group Holdings Ltd.)

OZALID GROUP HLDGS LTD (ENGLAND)
Acquired by Oce Van Der Grinten Finance Ltd. 03/14/1978
Each ADR for Ordinary Registered 25p par exchanged for $1.582 cash

OZARK AIR LINES INC (DE)
Reincorporated 08/16/1974
Class A Common $1 par, General Common $1 par, and Class B Common 40¢ par reclassified as Common no par 04/15/1961
Common no par split (2) for (1) by issuance of (1) additional share 07/17/1967
State of incorporation changed from (MO) to (DE) and Common no par changed to 50¢ par 08/16/1974
Under plan of reorganization each share Common 50¢ par automatically became (1) share Ozark Holdings, Inc. Common 50¢ par 10/01/1984
(See Ozark Holdings, Inc.)

OZARK CAP TR (DE)
9% Guaranteed Trust Preferred Securities called for redemption at $10 on 6/18/2004

OZARK HLDGS INC (DE)
Acquired by Trans World Airlines, Inc. 09/15/1986
Each share Common 50¢ par exchanged for $19 cash

OZARK NATL LIFE INS CO (MO)
Majority acquired by I.C.H. Corp. (Old) through exchange which expired 07/01/1970
Public interest eliminated

OZARK POWER & WATER CO.
Acquired by Empire District Electric Co. 00/00/1927
Details not available

OZARK REALTY CO. (IA)
Charter cancelled for failure to file annual reports 4/14/24

OZCAPITAL VENTURES INC (AB)
Name changed to Strata-X Ltd. 09/26/2011
Strata-X Ltd. name changed to Strata-X Energy Ltd. 10/12/2012

OZEMAIL LTD (AUSTRALIA)
Merged into UUNET Holdings Australia Pty. Ltd. 03/01/1999
Each Sponsored ADR for Ordinary exchanged for $22 cash

OZFOREX GROUP LTD (AUSTRALIA)
Name changed to OFX Group Ltd. 07/31/2017

OZITE CORP (DE)
Ctfs. dated prior to 08/16/1974
Common $5 par changed to $1 par and (4) additional shares issued 12/30/1965
Voting Trust Agreement terminated 05/02/1966
Each VTC for Common $1 par exchanged for (1) share Common $1 par
Stock Dividends - 25% 01/31/1967; 20% 01/31/1968
Merged into Brunswick Corp. 08/16/1974
Each share $6 Preferred no par exchanged for (1) share $6 Preferred Ser. A no par
Each share Common $1 par exchanged for (0.823529) share Common no par

OZITE CORP (DE)
Reincorporated 8/28/90
State of incorporation changed from (TX) to (DE) 8/28/90
Merged into Pure Tech International, Inc. (New) 7/31/95
Each share old Common 25¢ par exchanged for (0.19) share Common 5¢ par
Pure Tech International, Inc. (New) name changed to Puretec Corp. 5/7/96
(See Puretec Corp.)

OZO DIVERSIFIED AUTOMATION INC (CO)
Each share Common $0.0001 par exchanged for (0.001) share Common 10¢ par 3/7/91
Name changed to Bio-Medical Automation Inc. 4/30/99
Bio-Medical Automation Inc. name changed to Ridgefield Acquisition Corp. (CO) 1/14/2003 which reincorporated in Nevada 6/26/2006

OZOLUTIONS INC (DE)
Reorganized under the laws of Nevada as International Development Corp. 12/09/2004
Each share Common $0.001 par exchanged for (1) share Common $0.001 par
International Development Corp. recapitalized as Global Wataire, Inc. 04/17/2006 which name changed to Global Earth Energy, Inc. 03/10/2008
(See Global Earth Energy, Inc.)

OZON PRODUCTS, INC. (NY)
Common 50¢ par changed to 25¢ par and (1) additional share issued 12/23/1963
Acquired by Borden Co. 02/02/1966
Each share Common 25¢ par exchanged for (0.215669) share Capital Stock $3.75 par

COPYRIGHTED MATERIAL   1995   NO UNAUTHORIZED REPRODUCTION

Borden Co. name changed to Borden, Inc. 04/17/1968 which merged into RJR Nabisco Holdings Corp. 03/14/1995 which name changed to Nabsico Group Holdings Corp. 06/15/1999
(See Nabisco Group Holdings Corp.)

OZONATOR CORP (NY)
Adjudicated bankrupt 06/27/1977
Stockholders' equity unlikely

OZONE MAN INC (FL)
Name changed to TOMI Environmental Solutions, Inc. 08/18/2009

OZONE TECHNOLOGY INC (FL)
Each share old Common $1 par exchanged for (0.02) share new Common $1 par 01/13/1999
Name changed to Enwisen.com, Inc. (FL) 05/11/1999
Enwisen.com, Inc. (FL) reincorporated in Delaware as Enwisen, Inc. 05/28/2004
(See Enwisen, Inc.)

P

P. & W. CREDITORS CORP. (NY)
Assets sold in 1934
Company filed certificates of dissolution with New York State Corporation Bureau 12/28/49

P. A. & S. SMALL CO. (PA)
See - Small (P. A. & S.) Co.

P. B. CORP.
Dissolved in 1946

P & A INDS INC (CT)
Merged into Cadence Industries Corp. 03/01/1974
Each share Capital Stock no par exchanged for $10 cash

P & C FOOD MKTS INC (NY)
Common $5 par changed to $2.50 par and (1) additional share issued 12/1/66
Acquired by Pneumo Dynamics Corp. 5/26/71
Each share Common $2.50 par exchanged for $12 principal amount of 7% Conv. Subord. Debentures due 7/1/80 and $2.40 cash
Merged into Penn Traffic Co. (New) 10/16/91
Each share 8% Conv. Preferred 1¢ par exchanged for (1.225) shares Common $1.25 par
Public interest eliminated

P & C FOODS INC (DE)
Merged into Penn Traffic Co. 8/15/88
Each share Common 1¢ par exchanged for $27 cash

P & F INDS INC (DE)
$1 Preferred $10 par called for redemption 1/30/97

P & G MFG CO (OR)
Name changed to Oswego Liquidating Corp. 03/08/1971
(See Oswego Liquidating Corp.)

P & H TUBE CORP (LA)
Merged into Southwestern Pipe, Inc. 01/01/1976
Each share Common $1 par exchanged for $18 cash

P & I PERS & INFORMATIK AG (GERMANY)
ADR agreement terminated 11/26/2014
Each ADR for Ordinary exchanged for $29.49 cash

P & L COAL HLDGS CORP (DE)
Name changed to Peabody Energy Corp. (Old) 05/01/2001
(See Peabody Energy Corp. (Old))

P & M EXPLORATION & MINING CO. CANADA, LTD. (ON)
Charter cancelled for failure to file reports and pay taxes 5/19/58

P & O PRINCESS CRUISES P L C (ENGLAND & WALES)
Reorganized as Carnival PLC 04/17/2003
Each ADR for Ordinary exchanged for (1.2016) ADR's for Ordinary

P & V ATLAS INDL CTR INC (WI)
Recapitalized as Univest Corp. 09/25/1969
Each share Common no par exchanged for (1) share Common $1 par
(See Univest Corp.)

P A C E INST (UT)
Recapitalized as Vault Industries Inc. 05/25/1995
Each share Common $0.001 par exchanged for (0.1) share Common $0.001 par
(See Vault Industries Inc.)

P-A-W GROWTH FUND, INC. (NY)
Name changed to Kaufmann Fund, Inc. (NY) 06/30/1970
Kaufmann Fund, Inc. (NY) reincorporated in Maryland 02/09/1993 which reorganized as Federated Equity Funds 04/20/2001

P B BANCORP OF CEDAR RAPIDS, INC. (IA)
Merged into Norwest Corp. 07/28/1988
Each share Common $5 par exchanged for $163.34 cash

P C CAP FD INC (MA)
Name changed to Phoenix Total Return Fund Inc. 07/09/1986
Phoenix Total Return Fund Inc. name changed to Phoenix Strategic Allocation Fund, Inc. 07/03/1992 which name changed to Phoenix-Oakhurst Strategic Allocation Fund, Inc. (MA) 10/29/1999 which reincorporated in Delaware as Phoenix-Oakhurst Strategic Allocation Fund 00/00/2001 which name changed to Phoenix Strategic Allocation Fund 01/01/2005
(See Phoenix Strategic Allocation Fund)

P C CONNECTION MIAMI INC (FL)
Each share old Common $0.001 par exchanged for (0.1) share new Common $0.001 par 7/22/97
Name changed to International Digital Holding Inc. 9/8/97

P C QUOTE INC (DE)
Reincorporated 8/12/87
Each share old Common no par exchanged for (0.05) share new Common no par 11/29/85
State of incorporation changed from (IL) to (DE) and Common no par changed to $0.001 par 8/12/87
Name changed to Hyperfeed Technologies, Inc. 6/16/99
(See Hyperfeed Technologies, Inc.)

P C R INDS LTD (BC)
Recapitalized as Consolidated P.C.R. Industries Ltd. 07/04/1986
Each share Common no par exchanged for (0.33333333) share Common no par
Consolidated P.C.R. Industries Ltd. name changed to Oregon Resources Corp. 12/02/1988 which recapitalized as International Oregon Resources Corp. 01/10/1992 which recapitalized as Dalphine Enterprises Ltd. 03/16/1993 which name changed to Inflazyme Pharmaceuticals Ltd. 12/10/1993 which recapitalized as Eacom Timber Corp. 08/26/2008
(See Eacom Timber Corp.)

P C TELEMART INC (DE)
Charter forfeited for failure to maintain a registered agent 11/19/1985

P-COM INC (DE)
Common $0.0001 par split (2) for (1) by issuance of (1) additional share 10/27/1995
Common $0.0001 par split (2) for (1) by issuance of (1) additional share payable 09/25/1997 to holders of record 09/10/1997
Each share old Common $0.0001 par exchanged for (0.2) share new Common $0.0001 par 06/27/2002
Each (30) shares new Common $0.0001 par exchanged again for (1) share new Common $0.0001 par 07/19/2004
Name changed to Wave Wireless Corp. 08/22/2005
(See Wave Wireless Corp.)

P D C INDL COATINGS INC (DE)
Recapitalized as Advanced Industrial Minerals Inc. 12/13/93
Each share Common no par exchanged for (1/3) share Common no par
Advanced Industrial Minerals Inc. merged into Aim Group, Inc. 3/31/95 which name changed to Cereus Technolgy Partners, Inc. 12/6/99 which merged into Verso Technologies, Inc. 10/2/2000

P D C INNOVATIVE INDS INC (NV)
Each share old Common $0.001 par exchanged for (0.025) share new Common $0.001 par 01/20/1999
Each share new Common $0.001 par exchanged again for (0.05) share new Common $0.001 par 01/05/2004
Each share new Common $0.001 par exchanged again for (0.25) share new Common $0.001 par 06/07/2006
Stock Dividend - 5% payable 01/22/2001 to holders of record 01/12/2001 Ex date - 01/16/2001
Name changed to Medspas of America, Inc. 08/07/2006
Medpas of America, Inc. recapitalized as i Brands Corp. 03/16/2009

P-D CORP. (AZ)
Charter revoked for failure to file reports and pay fees 5/10/77

P E C INDS INC (FL)
Completely liquidated 3/14/75
Each share Common 10¢ par exchanged for (1) share Reliance Electric Co. Common $2.50 par
(See Reliance Electric Co.)

P F CHANGS CHINA BISTRO INC (DE)
Common $0.001 par split (2) for (1) by issuance of (1) additional share payable 05/01/2002 to holders of record 04/17/2002 Ex date - 05/02/2002
Acquired by Wok Parent L.L.C. 07/02/2012
Each share Common $0.001 par exchanged for $51.50 cash

P-G PRODUCTS MFG. CO., INC. (NY)
Completely liquidated 02/27/1968
Each share Common 50¢ par exchanged for first and final distribution of (0.11843) share Allen Electric & Equipment Co. (MI) Common $1 par
Allen Electric & Equipment Co. (MI) reincorporated in Delaware 05/01/1969 which name changed to Allen Group Inc. 05/05/1972 which name changed to Allen Telecom Inc. 02/28/1997 which merged into Andrew Corp. 07/15/2003 which merged into CommScope, Inc. 12/27/2007
(See CommScope, Inc.)

P.J.R. CORP. (UT)
Name changed to Ditto Bike, Inc. 8/11/86
Ditto Bike, Inc. name changed to Breakthru Industries Group, Inc. (Utah) 11/21/88 which reorganized in Delaware 5/24/90

P K MGMT CORP (NY)
Common 1¢ par split (3) for (1) by issuance of (2) additional shares 10/25/74
Chapter 11 converted to Chapter 7 bankruptcy proceedings 9/30/82
No stockholders' equity

P M A INSURANCE FUND, INC. (DE)
Name changed to First Security Growth Fund, Inc. 02/08/1967
First Security Growth Fund, Inc. acquired by Mutual of Omaha Growth Fund, Inc. (NE) 12/11/1972 which reincorporated in Delaware as Pioneer Growth Shares 12/01/1993 which reorganized as Pioneer Independence Fund 12/07/2007

P M A RESTAURANTS INC (DE)
Name changed to Philly Mignon International, Inc. 8/8/81
(See Philly Mignon International, Inc.)

P M C TECHNOLOGIES LTD (BC)
Struck off register and declared dissolved for failure to file returns 7/13/90

P.M.G. CORP. (MA)
Liquidation completed
Each share Preferred $100 par exchanged for first and final distribution of $100 cash plus $1.75 dividend 6/1/69
Each share Common no par exchanged for initial distribution of $7 cash 7/7/69
Each share Common no par received second distribution of $7 cash 10/15/69
Each share Common no par received third and final distribution of $4.62 principal amount of Perkins Machine & Gear Co., Inc. 7% Conv. Subord. Notes due 6/1/84 and $3.65 cash 4/15/70

P P & L RES INC (PA)
Name changed to PPL Corp. 2/14/2000

P P M DEV CORP (BC)
Recapitalized as Consolidated P.P.M. Development Corp. 04/27/1999
Each share Common no par exchanged for (1/3) share Common no par
Consolidated P.P.M. Development Corp. name changed to Consolidated Global Diamond Corp. 04/23/2004 which name changed to Gem International Resources Inc. 10/30/2009

P R G GROUP INC (NV)
SEC revoked common stock registration 02/15/2012

P R INK INC (CO)
Name changed to Precision Standard Inc. (CO) 03/05/1987
Precision Standard Inc. (CO) reincorporated in Delaware as Pemco Aviation Group, Inc. 05/23/2000 which name changed to Alabama Aircraft Industries, Inc. 09/19/2007

P.R.M., INC. (DE)
Name changed to Associated Artists Productions Corp. 11/28/1956 which name changed back to P.R.M., Inc. 11/26/1958
Name changed to World-Wide Artists Inc. 05/11/1961
(See World-Wide Artists Inc.)

P R P EXPLS LTD (BC)
Merged into August Petroleums Ltd. 09/24/1973
Each share Capital Stock $1 par exchanged for (1) share Common no par
August Petroleums Ltd. recapitalized as Cheyenne Petroleum Corp. 10/13/1976
(See Cheyenne Petroleum Corp.)

P S I INDS INC (IL)
Completely liquidated 06/30/1969
Each share Common $1 par exchanged for first and final distribution of $4.894 cash

P S M TECHNOLOGIES INC (BC)
Delisted from Vancouver Stock Exchange 03/04/1991

P T C BANCORP (IN)
Merged into Indiana United Bancorp 04/30/1998
Each share Common $1 par exchanged for (1.075) shares Common $0.001 par
Indiana United Bancorp name changed to MainSource Financial Group, Inc. 05/01/2002 which merged into First Financial Bancorp 04/02/2018

P T INTI INDORAYON UTAMA (INDONESIA)
Name changed to P.T. Toba Pulp Lestari Tbk 02/06/2002
(See P.T. Toba Pulp Lestari Tbk)

P T P RESOURCE CORP (BC)
Each share Common no par received distribution of (0.5) share Transamerican Petroleum Corp. Common 1¢ par 04/25/1986
Struck from the register and dissolved 03/06/1992

P T PASIFIK SATELIT NUSANTARA (INDONESIA)
ADR agreement terminated 12/16/2013
Each Sponsored ADR for Common exchanged for (3) shares Common
Note: Unexchanged ADR's were sold and the proceeds, if any, held for claim after 12/16/2014

P T TAMBANG TIMAH (INDONESIA)
ADR agreement terminated 10/20/2006
Each 144A GDR for Ordinary exchanged for $2.600452 cash

P T TOBA PULP LESTARI (INDONESIA)
ADR agreement terminated 07/01/2009
Each Sponsored ADR for Ordinary IDR 1,000 par exchanged for $0.112674 cash

P T TRI POLYTA INDONESIA (INDONESIA)
Issue Information - 6,500,000 SPONSORED ADR's offered at $21 per ADR on 07/25/1994
Name changed to PT Chandra Asri Petrochemical Tbk 02/15/2011
(See PT Chandra Asri Petrochemical Tbk)

P.V. OBIECUNAS & CO. (WV)
Proclaimed dissolved for non-payment of taxes 5/12/31

P W & E INC (DE)
In process of liquidation
Each share Common 10¢ par exchanged for initial distribution of (0.398) share National Co., Inc. Common $1 par 1/16/68
Amount or number of subsequent distributions, if any, are unknown
(See National Co., Inc.)

P Z RESORT SYS INC (BC)
Name changed to RSI International Systems, Inc. 1/26/2005

PA TEX INC (LA)
Charter revoked for failure to file annual reports 10/21/85

PA-TEX PETROLEUM CO., INC. (DE)
Charter cancelled and declared inoperative and void for non-payment of taxes 3/17/26

PAA NAT GAS STORAGE L P (DE)
Merged into Plains All American Pipeline, L.P. 12/31/2013
Each Common Unit of Ltd. Partnership Int. exchanged for (0.445) Common Unit

PAAUHAU SUGAR LTD (HI)
Merged into Hawaiian Sugar Co. Ltd. 8/25/74
Each share Capital Stock $15 par exchanged for $55.85 cash

PAAUHAU SUGAR PLANTATION CO. (CA)
Capital Stock $20 par changed to $15 par in 1929
Reincorporated under the laws of Hawaii as Paauhau Sugar Co. Ltd. 12/31/55
(See Paauhau Sugar Co. Ltd.)

PAB BANKSHARES INC (GA)
Common no par split (2) for (1) by issuance of (1) additional share payable 03/10/1998 to holders of record 02/17/1998 Ex date - 03/11/1998
Stock Dividend - 2% payable 07/15/2008 to holders of record 06/30/2008 Ex date - 06/26/2008
Principal asset closed 04/29/2011
Stockholders' equity unlikely

PABCO PRODUCTS, INC. (DE)
Name changed to Fibreboard Paper Products Corp. 5/1/56
Fibreboard Paper Products Corp. name changed to Fibreboard Corp. 7/5/66

PABST BREWING CO (DE)
Common no par split (2) for (1) by issuance of (1) additional share 6/2/69
Under plan of merger each share old Common no par exchanged for $24 principal amount of 15% Subordinated Sinking Fund Notes due 3/15/93 effective 3/18/83
New Common no par split (4) for (1) by issuance of (3) additional shares 6/14/83
Stock Dividend - 200% 4/11/49
Merged into S&P Co. 5/8/85
Each share new Common no par exchanged for $10 cash

PAC AM INVT & LD DEV CORP (NV)
Name changed to IpTel Global, Inc. 8/21/2004
IpTel Global, Inc. name changed to Orion Petroleum Corp. 9/21/2004 which name changed to Aquarian Gold Corp. 3/14/2005

PAC ED SYS CORP (BC)
Name changed to Autobyte Systems Corp. 4/4/91
(See Autobyte Systems Corp.)

PAC FINL CORP (IN)
Involuntarily dissolved for failure to file reports and pay fees 11/14/1990

PAC-RIM CONSULTING INC (NV)
Each share old Common $0.001 par exchanged for (0.05) share new Common $0.001 par 3/9/99
Recapitalized as Telemonde, Inc. (NV) 5/6/99
Each share Common $0.001 par exchanged for (4) shares Common $0.001 par
Telemonde, Inc. (NV) reincorporated in Delaware 11/9/99
(See Telemonde, Inc. (DE))

PAC-RIM ENTERPRISES INC (NV)
Name changed to Pac-Rim Resources Ltd. 07/23/2006
(See Pac-Rim Resources Ltd.)

PAC RIM HLDG CO (DE)
Merged into SNTL Acquisition Corp. 4/11/97
Each share Common 1¢ par exchanged for $2.105 cash

PAC-RIM RES LTD (NV)
Common no par split (3) for (1) by issuance of (2) additional shares payable 07/21/2006 to holders of record 07/03/2006 Ex date - 07/24/2006
Charter revoked for failure to file reports and pay fees 06/30/2008

PAC WEST INDS LTD (AB)
Struck off register 01/01/1986

PAC-WEST TELECOMM INC (CA)
Issue Information - 12,600,000 shares COM offered at $10 per share on 11/03/1999
Plan of reorganization under Chapter 11 Federal Bankruptcy Code effective 11/30/2007
No stockholders' equity

PACAD INC (DE)
Charter cancelled and declared inoperative and void for non-payment of taxes 6/24/91

PACALTA OILS, LTD.
Succeeded by Pacalta Oils Co., Ltd. 00/00/1944
Details not available

PACALTA OILS CO., LTD.
Reorganized as New Pacalta Oils Co., Ltd. 00/00/1948
Each share Common no par exchanged for (0.25) share Common no par
New Pacalta Oils Ltd. recapitalized as Wespac Petroleums Ltd. 05/27/1955 which recapitalized as Canada Geothermal Oil Ltd. 09/07/1971
(See Canada Geothermal Oil Ltd.)

PACALTA RES LTD (CANADA)
Merged into Alberta Energy Co. Ltd. 5/28/99
Each share Common no par exchanged for (0.275) share Common no par
Alberta Energy Co. Ltd. merged into EnCana Corp. 1/3/2003

PACCOM VENTURES INC (BC)
Name changed to Vangold Resources Ltd. 08/29/2003
Vangold Resources Ltd. name changed to Vangold Mining Corp. 05/10/2017

PACE AMERN GROUP INC (DE)
SEC revoked common stock registration 03/05/1997

PACE CORP (ON)
Certificate of incorporation cancelled and dissolved for cause 12/04/1998

PACE GROUP INTL INC (CO)
Each share old Common $0.0001 par exchanged for (0.04) share new Common $0.0001 par 10/23/1989
Recapitalized as Riley Investments Inc. 01/31/1996
Each (15) shares new Common $0.0001 par exchanged for (1) share Common $0.0001 par
Riley Investments Inc. name changed to Grand Adventures Tour & Travel Publishing Corp. (OR) 10/07/1996 which reincorporated in Delaware 06/05/2000
(See Grand Adventures Tour & Travel Publishing Corp. (DE))

PACE HEALTH MGMT SYS INC (IA)
Reorganized under the laws of Delaware as Conmed Healthcare Management, Inc. 03/15/2007
Each share Common no par exchanged for (0.05) share Common $0.0001 par
(See Conmed Healthcare Management, Inc.)

PACE HLDGS CORP (CAYMAN ISLANDS)
Units separated 03/13/2017
Merged into Playa Hotels & Resorts N.V. 03/13/2017
Each share Class A Ordinary $0.0001 par exchanged for (1) share Ordinary EUR 0.10 par

PACE INDS INC (DE)
Reincorporated 5/29/69
State of incorporation changed from (CO) to (DE) 5/29/69
Each share old Common 10¢ par exchanged for (1) share new Common 10¢ par 6/22/70
Charter cancelled and declared inoperative and void for non-payment of taxes 4/15/72

PACE INDUSTRIES LTD. (BC)
Incorporated 04/07/1981
Name changed to Pace II Industries Ltd. 09/27/1983
Pace II Industries Ltd. recapitalized as Consolidated Pace II Industries Ltd. 08/27/1986 which recapitalized as Canadian Pacer Petroleum Corp. 07/11/1988 which name changed to Providence Innovations Inc. 10/30/1989 which recapitalized as Providence Industries Inc. 10/04/1991 which merged into Gold City Mining Corp. 12/07/1994 which recapitalized as Consolidated Gold City Mining Corp. 10/24/1997 which recapitalized as Gold City Industries Ltd. (BC) 08/26/1998 which reincorporated in Manitoba 06/21/2005 which merged into San Gold Corp. 07/07/2005
(See San Gold Corp.)

PACE INDS LTD (BC)
Incorporated in 1965
In process of liquidation
Each share Capital Stock no par exchanged for initial distribution of $1 cash 2/3/78
Each share Capital Stock no par received second distribution of $0.50 cash 4/10/78
Each share Capital Stock no par received third distribution of $0.50 cash 11/2/78
Each share Capital Stock no par received fourth distribution of $0.225 cash 3/8/79
Note: Details on subsequent distributions, if any, are not available

PACE MEMBERSHIP WHSE INC (CO)
Merged into K mart Corp. 12/6/89
Each share Common 1¢ par exchanged for $23 cash

PACE OIL & GAS LTD (AB)
Reorganized as Spyglass Resources Corp. 04/04/2013
Each share Common no par exchanged for (1.3) shares Common no par

PACE II INDS LTD (BC)
Recapitalized as Consolidated Pace II Industries Ltd. 08/27/1986
Each share Common no par exchanged for (0.33333333) share Common no par
Consolidated Pace II Industries Ltd. recapitalized as Canadian Pacer Petroleum Corp. 07/11/1988 which name changed to Providence Innovations Inc. 10/30/1989 which recapitalized as Providence Industries Inc. 10/04/1991 which merged into Gold City Mining Corp. 12/07/1994 which recapitalized as Consolidated Gold City Corp. 10/24/1997 which recapitalized as Gold City Industries Ltd. (BC) 08/26/1998 which reincorporated in Manitoba 06/21/2005 which merged into San Gold Corp. 07/07/2005
(See San Gold Corp.)

PACEL CORP (VA)
Reincorporated 01/19/2005
Each share old Common no par exchanged for (0.05) share new Common no par 04/24/1998
Each share new Common no par exchanged again for (0.25) share new Common no par 10/07/1999
Each share new Common no par exchanged again for (0.01) share new Common no par 04/10/2002
Each share new Common no par received distribution of (1) share Resourcing Solutions Group Inc.

Common no par payable 03/07/2003 to holders of record 12/10/2002
Ex date - 12/06/2002
Each share new Common no par exchanged again for (0.03333333) share new Common no par 03/17/2003
Each share new Common no par exchanged again for (0.01) share new Common no par 02/25/2004
Each share new Common no par exchanged again for (0.01) share new Common no par 09/13/2004
State of incorporation changed from (VA) to (NV) and Common no par changed to $0.001 par 01/19/2005
Each share old Common $0.001 par exchanged for (0.001) share new Common $0.001 par 02/25/2005
Each share new Common $0.001 par exchanged again for (0.001) share new Common $0.001 par 06/20/2005
Each share new Common $0.001 par exchanged again for (0.001) share new Common $0.001 par 10/25/2005
Each share new Common $0.001 par exchanged again for (0.001) share new Common $0.001 par 01/24/2006
Each share new Common $0.001 par exchanged again for (0.001) share new Common $0.001 par 06/15/2006
SEC revoked common stock registration 10/14/2011

PACEMAKER BOAT TRAILER CO., INC. (PA)
Name changed to Pacemaker Industries, Inc. 10/16/1961
(See Pacemaker Industries, Inc.)

PACEMAKER INDUSTRIES, INC. (PA)
Bankrupt 12/17/1962
No stockholders' equity

PACEMAKER LIFE INSURANCE CO. (AZ)
Merged into Western Empire Life Insurance Co. 5/10/65
Each share Capital Stock $1 par exchanged for (0.181818) share Common $1.35 par
Western Empire Life Insurance Co. merged into Bankers Union Life Insurance Co. 3/12/73 which merged into I.C.H. Corp. 10/14/82 which name changed to Southwestern Life Corp. (New) 6/15/94 which name changed to I.C.H. Corp. (New) 10/10/95
(See I.C.H. Corp. (New))

PACEMAKER MINES & OIL LTD (ON)
Charter cancelled for failure to file returns and pay fees 08/09/1972

PACEMAKER PETROLEUMS LTD. (ON)
Name changed to Pacemaker Mines & Oils Ltd, 00/00/1953
(See Pacemaker Mines & Oils Ltd.)

PACEMASTER INC (FL)
Merged into Farm Stores Inc. 08/10/1976
Each share Common 10¢ par exchanged for $6.09 cash

PACEPARTNERS INC (AB)
Name changed to Vivione Biosciences Inc. 07/23/2013

PACER CORP (DE)
Charter cancelled and declared inoperative and void for non-payment of taxes 3/1/82

PACER CORP (WA)
Merged into Wembley, Inc. 12/12/1988
Each share Common no par exchanged for $10.50 cash

PACER ENERGY CORP (DE)
Charter cancelled and declared inoperative and void for non-payment of taxes 6/17/93

PACER FDS TR (DE)
Trust terminated 12/23/2016
Each share Autopilot Hedged European Index ETF received $26.7488421 cash
(Additional Information in Active)

PACER INTERNATIONAL CORP. (DE)
Name changed to Bread Basket Corp. 06/26/1969
(See Bread Basket Corp.)

PACER INTL INC (TN)
Merged into XPO Logistics, Inc. 04/01/2014
Each share Common 1¢ par exchanged for (0.1017) share Common $0.001 par and $6 cash

PACER PHENIX CORP (KS)
Charter cancelled for failure to file annual report 05/15/1978

PACER TECHNOLOGY & RESOURCES, INC. (WY)
Reincorporated under the laws of California as Pacer Technology 11/15/84
(See Pacer Technology)

PACER TECHNOLOGY (CA)
Each share old Common 1¢ par exchanged for (0.2) share new Common 1¢ par 11/27/2000
Merged into Cyan Holding Co. 12/9/2003
Each share new Common 1¢ par exchanged for $6.95 cash

PACESETTER BUILDING SYSTEMS, INC. (NE)
Stock Dividends - 100% 6/30/77; 50% 8/21/78
Name changed to Pacesetter Corp. (Nebr.) 9/26/78
(See Pacesetter Corp. (Nebr.))

PACESETTER BUSINESS PPTYS (CA)
Filed a petition under Chapter 11 Federal Bankruptcy Code 03/11/1993
Stockholders' equity unlikely

PACESETTER CORP (AR)
Merged into Solomon, Inc. 3/8/73
Each share Common 10¢ par exchanged for (0.3) share Common 10¢ par
(See Solomon, Inc.)

PACESETTER CORP (NE)
Merged into Pacesetter Holding, Inc. 10/01/1985
Each share Common 25¢ par exchanged for $20 cash

PACESETTER FINL CORP (MI)
Reincorporated 3/10/80
Common $10 par split (3) for (2) by issuance of (0.5) additional share 8/15/78
Stock Dividend - 20% 8/1/77
State of incorporation changed from (DE) to (MI) 3/10/80
Merged into Old Kent Financial Corp. 3/31/83
Each share Common $10 par exchanged for $13 cash

PACESETTER INDS INC (NY)
Stock Dividend - 100% 03/10/1972
Merged into Remington Apparel Co., Inc. 12/28/1983
Each share Common 5¢ par exchanged for $0.25 cash

PACESETTER OSTRICH FARM INC (DE)
Name changed to Primelink Systems Inc. 02/14/2000
Primelink Systems Inc. recapitalized as MaxWiFi Communications, Inc. 09/04/2008 which recapitalized as Tivus, Inc. 01/27/2010

PACGEN BIOPHARMACEUTICALS CORP (BC)
Each share old Common no par exchanged for (0.5) share new Common no par 06/08/2010
Name changed to Pacgen Life Science Corp. 05/01/2012

PACHAMAMA RES LTD (BC)
Merged into Regulus Resources Inc. (Old) 05/16/2012
Each share Common no par exchanged for (0.815) share Common no par
Note: Unexchanged certificates will be cancelled and become without value 05/16/2022
Regulus Resources Inc. (Old) merged into Regulus Resources Inc. (New) 10/03/2014

PACHENA INDS LTD NEW (BC)
Merged 06/02/1997
Each share old Common no par exchanged for (1/3) share new Common no par 12/22/1995
Merged from Pachena Industries Ltd. (Old) to Pachena Industries Ltd. (New) 06/02/1997
Each share new Common no par exchanged for (1) share Common no par
Merged into AimGlobal Technologies Co., Inc. 03/31/1999
Each share Common no par exchanged for (0.622209) share Common no par and $0.91 cash
(See AimGlobal Technologies Co., Inc.)

PACHINKO INC (DE)
SEC revoked common stock registration 03/05/2009

PACHINKO WORLD INC (NV)
Merged into Kisorin USA Inc. 06/09/2009
Each share Common 1¢ par exchanged for $0.20 cash

PACHOLDER HIGH YIELD FD INC (MD)
Name changed 11/18/1999
Name changed from Pacholder Fund, Inc. to Pacholder High Yield Fund, Inc. 11/18/1999
Auction Rate Preferred Ser. W 1¢ par called for redemption at $25,000 on 12/22/2016
Liquidation completed
Each share Common 1¢ par received initial distribution of $7.8405 cash payable 07/11/2017 to holders of record 07/10/2017
Each share Common 1¢ par received second and final distribution of $0.1691 cash payable 08/29/2017 to holders of record 07/10/2017

PACIFIC & ATLANTIC TELEGRAPH CO. (PA)
Dissolved 10/28/59

PACIFIC & SOUTHN BROADCASTING INC (DE)
Merged into Combined Communications Corp. 08/27/1974
Each share Common $1 par exchanged for (0.6924) share Common no par
Combined Communications Corp. merged into Gannett Co., Inc. (Old) 06/07/1979 which name changed to TEGNA Inc. 06/26/2015

PACIFIC & WESTN BK CDA (LONDON, ON)
Name changed to VersaBank (Old) (London, ON) 05/17/2016
VersaBank (Old) (London, ON) name changed to VersaBank (New) (London, ON) 02/02/2017

PACIFIC & WESTN CR CORP NEW (CANADA)
Each share Common no par received distribution of (0.53) share Discovery Air Inc. Class A Common no par payable 03/07/2007 to holders of record 02/16/2007 Ex date - 02/14/2007
Each share Class B Preferred no par received distribution of (0.029) share Common no par payable 09/30/2009 to holders of record 09/10/2009
Ex date - 09/10/2009
Each share Class B Preferred no par received distribution of (0.099) share Common no par payable 12/31/2009 to holders of record 12/21/2009
Ex date - 12/17/2009
Each share Class B Preferred no par received distribution of (0.092) share Common no par payable 03/31/2010 to holders of record 03/19/2010
Each share Class B Preferred no par received distribution of (0.118) share Common no par payable 06/30/2010 to holders of record 06/11/2010
Each share Class B Preferred no par received distribution of (0.118) share Common no par payable 09/30/2010 to holders of record 09/10/2010
Ex date - 09/08/2010
Each share Class B Preferred no par received distribution of (0.114) share Common no par payable 12/31/2010 to holders of record 12/17/2010
Ex date - 12/15/2010
Each share Class B Preferred no par received distribution of (0.106) share Common no par payable 03/31/2011 to holders of record 03/18/2011
Ex date - 03/16/2011
Each share Class B Preferred no par received distribution of (0.175) share Common no par payable 06/30/2011 to holders of record 06/20/2011
Each share Class B Preferred no par received distribution of (0.196) share Common no par payable 09/30/2011 to holders of record 09/09/2011
Ex date - 09/07/2011
Each share Class B Preferred no par received distribution of (0.307) share Common no par payable 12/31/2011 to holders of record 12/16/2011
Ex date - 12/14/2011
Each share Class B Preferred no par received distribution of (0.183) share Common no par payable 03/31/2012 to holders of record 03/19/2012
Ex date - 03/15/2012
Each share Class B Preferred no par received distribution of (0.2) share Common no par payable 06/30/2012 to holders of record 06/18/2012
Ex date - 06/14/2012
Each share Class B Preferred no par received distribution of (0.233) share Common no par payable 09/30/2012 to holders of record 09/11/2012
Ex date - 09/07/2012
Each share Class B Preferred no par received distribution of (0.254) share Common no par payable 03/31/2013 to holders of record 03/15/2013
Ex date - 03/13/2013
Each share Class B Preferred no par received distribution of (0.272) share Common no par payable 06/30/2013 to holders of record 06/17/2013
Ex date - 06/13/2013
Each share Class B Preferred no par received distribution of (0.229) share Common no par payable 09/30/2013 to holders of record 09/10/2013
Ex date - 09/06/2013
Each share Class B Preferred no par received distribution of (0.296) share Common no par payable 12/31/2013 to holders of record 12/16/2013
Ex date - 12/12/2013
Each share Class B Preferred no par received distribution of (0.327) share Common no par payable 03/31/2014 to holders of record 03/14/2014
Ex date - 03/12/2014
Name changed to PWC Capital Inc. 04/25/2014
PWC Capital Inc. merged into VersaBank (New) (London, ON) 02/02/2017

PACIFIC & WESTN CR CORP OLD (AB)
Name changed 06/03/1994
Name changed from Pacific & Western Trustco Ltd. to Pacific &

Western Credit Corp. (Old) 06/03/1994
7.5% Conv. Preferred Class A Ser. 2 called for redemption at $2 on 09/08/2000
7.5% Conv. Preferred Class A Ser. 3 called for redemption at $3 on 09/08/2000
Merged into Pacific & Western Credit Corp. (New) 01/01/2002
Each share Common no par exchanged for (0.2) share Common no par
Pacific & Western Credit Corp. (New) name changed to PWC Capital Inc. 04/25/2014 which merged into VersaBank (New) (London, ON) 02/02/2017

PACIFIC (EASTERN) GOLD MINES, LTD. (ON)
Recapitalized as PCE Explorations Ltd. 08/07/1957
Each share Capital Stock $1 par exchanged for (1/3) share Capital Stock $1 par
PCE Explorations Ltd. recapitalized as Pan Central Explorations Ltd. 01/24/1972
(See Pan Central Explorations Ltd.)

PACIFIC ACQUISITIONS INC (CO)
Name changed to With Design In Mind International Inc. 8/30/88
With Design In Mind International Inc. name changed to Janex International, Inc. 8/16/94
(See Janex International, Inc.)

PACIFIC AD-LINK CORP (BC)
Name changed to Pacific E-Link Corp. 07/15/1999
(See Pacific E-Link Corp.)

PACIFIC ADERA FINL CORP (BC)
Merged into Adera Development Corp. 5/31/93
Each share Common no par exchanged for $0.65 cash

PACIFIC AEROSPACE & ELECTRONICS INC (WA)
Each share old Common $0.001 par exchanged for (0.005) share new Common $0.001 par 2/17/2003
Each (11,000) shares new Common $0.001 par exchanged again for (1) share new Common $0.001 par 4/12/2004
Note: In effect holders received $0.168 cash per share and public interest was eliminated

PACIFIC AGRIC HLDGS INC (CA)
Reorganized under the laws of Delaware as Cadiz Land Co. 05/26/1992
Each share Common no par exchanged for (0.2) share Common 1¢ par
Cadiz Land Co. name changed to Cadiz Inc. 09/01/1998

PACIFIC AIR FREIGHT, INC. (WA)
Merged into Airborne Freight Corp. (DE) 10/17/1968
Each share Common 25¢ par exchanged for (1) share Common $1 par
Airborne Freight Corp. (DE) reorganized as Airborne, Inc. 12/26/2000 which merged into ABX Air, Inc. 08/15/2003 which name changed to ABX Holdings, Inc. 12/31/2007 which name changed to Air Transport Services Group, Inc. 06/16/2008

PACIFIC AIR LINES, INC. (AZ)
Stock Dividend - 10% 4/15/66
Reincorporated under the laws of Delaware 7/14/66
Pacific Air Lines, Inc. (Del.) name changed to Air West, Inc. 4/17/68 which name changed to AW Liquidating Co. 4/1/70
(See AW Liquidating Co.)

PACIFIC AIR LINES, INC. (DE)
Under plan of merger name changed to Air West, Inc. and Common 50¢ par changed to $1 par 4/17/68
Air West, Inc. name changed to AW Liquidating Co. 4/1/70
(See AW Liquidating Co.)

PACIFIC AIR TRANS INC (UT)
Name changed to Pacific Air Transport International Inc. 9/28/70
Pacific Air Transport International Inc. recapitalized as Chase Hanover Corp. 9/17/83
(See Chase Hanover Corp.)

PACIFIC AIR TRANS INTL INC (UT)
Recapitalized as Chase Hanover Corp. 09/17/1983
Each share Capital Stock no par exchanged for (0.02) share Capital Stock 1¢ par
(See Chase Hanover Corp.)

PACIFIC AIR TRANSPORT CO.
Acquired by United Aircraft & Transport Corp. in 1929
Details not available

PACIFIC AIRLS INC (UT)
Proclaimed dissolved for failure to file annual reports 10/1/87

PACIFIC AIRMOTIVE CORP. (CA)
Voting Trust Agreement terminated 12/30/1949
Each VTC for Capital Stock $1 par exchanged for (1) share Capital Stock $1 par
Completely liquidated 09/15/1967
Each share Capital Stock $1 par exchanged for first and final distribution of (0.7) share Purex Corp., Ltd. Common $1 par
Purex Corp., Ltd. name changed to Purex Corp. (CA) 11/05/1973 which in Delaware as Purex Industries, Inc. 10/31/1978
(See Purex Industries, Inc.)

PACIFIC ALLIANCE CORP (DE)
Each share old Common $0.001 par exchanged for (0.05) share new Common $0.001 par 12/23/2009
SEC revoked common stock registration 02/13/2014

PACIFIC ALLIANCE VENTURES LTD (NV)
Name changed to Eurasia Energy Ltd. (NV) 01/12/2006
Eurasia Energy Ltd. (NV) reincorporated in British West Indies 12/31/2007

PACIFIC AMBER RES LTD (AB)
Reincorporated 07/25/2002
Place of incorporation changed from (BC) to (ALTA) 07/25/2002
Recapitalized as Grand Banks Energy Corp. 05/14/2003
Each share Common no par exchanged for (0.2) share Common no par
(See Grand Banks Energy Corp.)

PACIFIC AMERICAN ASSOCIATES, INC.
Merged into Goldman Sachs Trading Corp. 00/00/1929
Details not available

PACIFIC AMERICAN CO. (DE)
Name changed to Pacific American Fisheries, Inc. 00/00/1930
Pacific American Fisheries, Inc. name changed to Pacific American Corp. (DE) 06/01/1961
(See Pacific American Corp. (DE))

PACIFIC AMERICAN CORP. (DE)
Merged into VWR United Corp. 2/27/67
Each share Common $5 par exchanged for $31.25 cash

PACIFIC AMERN CORP (NV)
All directors and officers dismissed and company's wholly owned subsidiary placed in receivership 12/15/1978
No stockholders' equity

PACIFIC AMERICAN FIRE INSURANCE CO.
Liquidation completed in 1944

PACIFIC AMERICAN FISHERIES, INC. (DE)
Common no par changed to $5 par 00/00/1935
Name changed to Pacific American Corp. (DE) 06/01/1961
(See Pacific American Corp. (DE))

PACIFIC AMERN GROUP INC (DE)
Charter forfeited for failure to maintain a registered agent 6/25/85

PACIFIC AMERN INCOME SHS INC (DE)
Name changed to Western Asset Income Fund 06/30/2005
Western Asset Income Fund name changed to Western Asset Investment Grade Income Fund Inc. 03/29/2018

PACIFIC AMERN INDS INC (CA)
Name changed to Dr Pepper Bottling Co. of Southern California 06/03/1976
Dr Pepper Bottling Co. of Southern California merged into Dr Pepper Co. 02/23/1977
(See Dr Pepper Co.)

PACIFIC-AMERICAN INVESTORS, INC. (DE)
Merged into American Mutual Fund, Inc. (DE) 02/01/1956
Each share Preferred $5 par exchanged for Common $1 par on a net asset value basis
Each share Common 10¢ par exchanged for Common $1 par on a net asset value basis
American Mutual Fund, Inc. (DE) reincorporated in Maryland 09/20/1983 which reincorporated in Delaware as American Mutual Fund 01/01/2011

PACIFIC AMERN LIFE INS CO (AZ)
Each share Common 10¢ par exchanged for (0.1) share Common $1 par 6/25/68
Merged into Pacific American Corp. (NV) 5/9/69
Each share Common $1 par exchanged for (1) share Common $1 par
(See Pacific American Corp. (NV))

PACIFIC AMERN OIL CO (OK)
Merged into Universal Acceptance Corp. International Ltd. 11/22/1971
Each share Common 1¢ par exchanged for (1) share Common 1¢ par
(See Universal Acceptance Corp.)

PACIFIC ANIMATED IMAGING CORP (DE)
Common $0.0001 par split (2) for (1) by issuance of (1) additional share 02/14/1992
Each (3.5) shares old Common $0.0001 par exchanged for (1) share new Common $0.0001 par 12/08/1995
Name changed to Strategic Solutions Group Inc. 05/23/1997
Strategic Solutions Group Inc. recapitalized as Southern Software Group, Inc. 03/13/2003 which name changed to SecureD Services, Inc. 07/30/2003
(See SecureD Services, Inc.)

PACIFIC AQUA FOODS LTD (BC)
Recapitalized as International Aqua Foods Ltd. 10/8/93
Each share Common no par exchanged for (0.1) share Common no par
(See International Aqua Foods Ltd.)

PACIFIC ASBESTOS CORP (NV)
Adjudicated bankrupt 08/27/1974
Stockholders' equity unlikely

PACIFIC ASBESTOS LTD (AB)
Name changed to Woodsreef Minerals Ltd. 07/26/1972
Woodsreef Minerals Ltd. recapitalized as Transpacific Asbestos, Inc. 04/30/1981 which name changed to Transpacific Resources Inc. 09/06/1984
(See Transpacific Resources Inc.)

PACIFIC ASIA CHINA ENERGY INC (BC)
Merged into Green Dragon Gas Ltd. 07/10/2008
Each share Common no par exchanged for $0.35 cash

PACIFIC ASIA PETE INC (DE)
Name changed to CAMAC Energy Inc. 04/07/2010
CAMAC Energy Inc. recapitalized as Erin Energy Corp. 04/23/2015

PACIFIC ASIA TECHNOLOGIES INC (BC)
Recapitalized as Sunblush Technologies Corp. 12/08/1997
Each share Common no par exchanged for (1/30) share Common no par
Sunblush Technologies Corp. recapitalized as FreshXtend Technologies Corp. 12/31/2003
(See FreshXtend Technologies Corp.)

PACIFIC ASSOC INC (CA)
In process of liquidation
Each share 6% Prior Preference $25 par received initial distribution of $22.50 cash payable 04/25/1978 to holders of record 04/25/1978
Note: Details on subsequent distributions, if any, are not available
No stockholders' equity for 6.50% Preference and Common

PACIFIC ASSOCIATES, INC.
Reorganized as Pacific Associates, Ltd. 00/00/1931
Details not available

PACIFIC ASSOCIATES, LTD. (DE)
Name changed to California Associates, Inc. 03/02/1936
(See California Associates, Inc.)

PACIFIC ATLANTIC CDN INVT LTD (QC)
Liquidation completed
Each share 5% Preferred Ser. A $50 par exchanged for first and final distribution of $53.125 cash 10/15/75
Each share Common $1 par exchanged for initial distribution of $5 cash 10/15/75
Each share Common $1 par received second and final distribution of $0.3777 cash 1/5/77

PACIFIC ATLANTIC LIFE INSURANCE CO. (WY)
Merged into Pacific Western Life Insurance Co. 1/30/68
Each share Common $1 par exchanged for (0.54) share Common $1 par
Pacific Western Life Insurance Co. reorganized as Pacific Western Corp. 12/31/69
(See Pacific Western Corp.)

PACIFIC ATLANTIC OIL SERVICE CORP. (AZ)
Charter revoked for non-payment of fees 10/2/52

PACIFIC AUTOMATION PRODS INC (DE)
Reorganized 07/25/1969
Reorganized from (CA) to under the laws of Delaware 07/25/1969
Each share Capital Stock $1 par exchanged for (0.25) share Common $1 par
Name changed to Pacific International Equities, Inc. 02/15/1972
(See Pacific International Equities, Inc.)

PACIFIC AXIS VENTURES INC (BC)
Reincorporated under the laws of Yukon as Petrolex Energy Corp. and Common no par changed to 1¢ par 02/03/1997
(See Petrolex Energy Corp.)

PACIFIC BANCORPORATION (CA)
Each share old Common no par exchanged for (0.2) share new Common no par 6/2/81
Merged into ValliCorp Holdings, Inc. 11/5/93
Each share new Common no par exchanged for (0.8) share Common 1¢ par
ValliCorp Holdings, Inc. merged into Westamerica Bancorporation 4/12/97

PACIFIC BANCSHARES LTD.
Liquidated in 1935

PACIFIC BK NATL ASSN (SAN FRANCISCO, CA)
Each share Common $5 par exchanged for (0.1) share Common $3 par 10/18/93
Common $3 par changed to $1.50 par and (1) additional share issued payable 12/31/98 to holders of record 11/2/98
Merged into City National Corp. 2/29/2000
Each share Common $1.50 par exchanged for (0.9344) share Common $1 par

PACIFIC BASIN BULK SHIPPING LTD (BERMUDA)
Merged into Konsortium Perkapalan Berhad 09/17/1996
Each share Common $0.7327 par exchanged for $16.22 cash

PACIFIC BASIN DEV CORP (BC)
Recapitalized as Jersey Goldfields Corp. 7/20/94
Each share Common no par exchanged for (0.25) share Common no par
Jersey Goldfields Corp. name changed to Jersey Petroleum Inc. 3/4/98 which recapitalized as International Choice Ventures Inc. (BC) 8/17/2000 which reincorporated in Alberta as Rhodes Resources Corp. 11/20/2002 which merged into Terra Energy Corp. 1/30/2004

PACIFIC BASIN TRAVEL SYS CORP (DE)
Charter forfeited for failure to maintain a registered agent 12/30/73

PACIFIC BASIN VENTURES INC (NV)
Recapitalized as Media Development Industries, Ltd. 06/08/1990
Each share Common $0.001 par exchanged for (0.05) share Common $0.001 par

PACIFIC BAY MINERALS LTD OLD (BC)
Name changed 07/17/1995
Name changed from Pacific Bay Street Systems, Ltd. to Pacific Bay Minerals Ltd. (Old) 07/17/1995
Recapitalized as Consolidated Pacific Bay Minerals Ltd. 08/29/2000
Each share Common no par exchanged for (1/3) share Common no par
Consolidated Pacific Bay Minerals Ltd. name changed to Pacific Bay Minerals Ltd. (New) 07/22/2008

PACIFIC BIOCHEMICAL, INC. (HI)
Involuntarily dissolved 6/1/76

PACIFIC BIOMARKERS INC (DE)
Name changed to NorWesTech, Inc. 09/15/2011
NorWesTech, Inc. name changed to Grandparents.com, Inc. 03/09/2012
(See Grandparents.com, Inc.)

PACIFIC BIOMETRICS INC (DE)
Each share old Common 1¢ par exchanged for (0.33333333) share new Common 1¢ par 03/14/2003
Name changed to Pacific Biomarkers, Inc. 03/08/2010
Pacific Biomarkers, Inc. name changed to NorWesTech, Inc. 09/15/2011 which name changed to Grandparents.com, Inc. 03/09/2012
(See Grandparents.com, Inc.)

PACIFIC BIOSYSTEMS INC (NV)
Chapter 11 bankruptcy proceedings converted to Chapter 7 on 07/00/1993
No stockholders' equity

PACIFIC BRANDS LTD (AUSTRALIA)
ADR agreement terminated 08/12/2016
Each ADR for Common exchanged for $7.872217 cash

PACIFIC BURT CO., LTD.
Merged into Moore Corp. Ltd. 00/00/1928
Details not available

PACIFIC BUSINESS BK (CARSON, CA)
Acquired by East West Bancorp, Inc. 03/14/2003
Each share Common no par exchanged for $5.37 cash

PACIFIC BUTTE MINES CO. (NV)
Name changed to Pacific Uranium Co. in 1954
Pacific Uranium Co. merged into Kerr-McGee Oil Industries, Inc. 12/30/60 which name was changed to Kerr-McGee Corp. 11/1/65

PACIFIC CABINET & RADIO CO. (CA)
Name changed to Pacific Mercury Television Manufacturing Corp. in 1950
Pacific Mercury Television Manufacturing Corp. name changed to Pacific Mercury Electronics 12/8/58 which merged into Warwick Electronics Inc. 10/28/63 which name changed to Thomas International Corp. 3/1/77
(See Thomas International Corp.)

PACIFIC CAN CO. (NV)
Common no par changed to $5 par and (1) additional share distributed in 1945
Liquidation completed 6/1/55

PACIFIC CAP BANCORP NEW (DE)
Reorganized 12/29/2010
Common no par split (4) for (3) by issuance of (1/3) additional share payable 06/11/2002 to holders of record 05/21/2002 Ex date - 06/12/2002
Common no par split (4) for (3) by issuance of (1/3) additional share payable 06/08/2004 to holders of record 05/25/2004 Ex date - 06/09/2004
Reorganized from (CA) to under the laws of Delaware 12/29/2010
Each share Common no par exchanged for (0.01) share Common $0.001 par
Acquired by UnionBanCal Corp. 12/04/2012
Each share Common $0.001 par exchanged for $46 cash

PACIFIC CAP BANCORP OLD (CA)
Stock Dividend - 5% payable 12/19/1997 to holders of record 12/01/1997
Merged into Pacific Capital Bancorp (New) (CA) 12/30/1998
Each share Common no par exchanged for (1.935) shares Common no par
Pacific Capital Bancorp (New) (CA) reorganized in Delaware 12/29/2010
(See Pacific Capital Bancorp (New))

PACIFIC CAP LTD (AUSTRALIA)
ADR agreement terminated 01/29/2003
Each Sponsored ADR for Ordinary exchanged for (10) shares Ordinary

PACIFIC CAR & FDRY CO (WA)
Class B 7% Preferred $100 par changed to no par 00/00/1934
Class A Preferred $100 par exchanged for new Preferred $100 par share for share 00/00/1943
Class B Preferred no par exchanged for new Common no par share for share
Old Common no par cancelled
6% Preferred called for redemption 06/01/1948
Common no par split (10) for (1) by issuance of (9) additional shares 00/00/1945
Each share Common no par exchanged for (3) shares Common $20 par 03/16/1956
Common $20 par changed to $6-2/3 par and (2) additional shares issued 07/01/1956
Stock Dividends - 10% 12/21/1953; 10% 01/21/1955; 10% 02/05/1963; 20% 01/15/1964; 30% 09/30/1969; 10% 02/26/1971
Reincorporated under the laws of Delaware as PACCAR Inc and Common $6-2/3 par changed to $24 par 02/01/1972

PACIFIC CART SVCS LTD (NV)
Name changed to Maverick Minerals Corp. 3/22/2002

PACIFIC CASCADE RES CORP (BC)
Name changed to Pacific Sapphire Co. Ltd. 11/09/2000
Pacific Sapphire Co. Ltd. recapitalized as Radiant Resources Inc. 01/30/2003 which merged into Tiomin Resources Inc. 09/26/2008 which recapitalized as Vaaldiam Mining Inc. 03/26/2010
(See Vaaldiam Mining Inc.)

PACIFIC CASSIAR LTD (CANADA)
Reincorporated 04/26/1984
Capital Stock no par reclassified as Class A no par 04/14/1981
Place of incorporation changed from (BC) to (Canada) 04/26/1984
Merged into NCE Petrofund 12/01/2000
Each share Class A no par exchanged for $6.05 cash
Each share Non-Vtg. Common no par exchanged for $6.05 cash

PACIFIC CASSIAR MINES LTD. (BC)
Name changed to Pacific Cassiar Ltd. 11/20/78
(See Pacific Cassiar Ltd.)

PACIFIC CEMENT & AGGREGATES, INC. (CA)
Acquired by Lone Star Cement Corp. (ME) 8/31/65
Each share Common $5 par exchanged for (0.225) share $4.50 Conv. Preferred no par
Lone Star Cement Corp. (ME) reincorporated under the laws of Delaware 5/29/69 which name changed to Lone Star Industries, Inc. 5/20/71
(See Lone Star Industries, Inc.)

PACIFIC CENTERS, INC. (CA)
Name changed to Big "A" Stores 11/13/1962
Big "A" Stores name changed to Newport Western Inc. 11/05/1970 which name changed to Pride N Joy Industries, Inc. 07/18/1972
(See Pride N Joy Industries, Inc.)

PACIFIC CENTRAL CO. (NV)
Charter revoked for failure to file reports and pay fees 3/6/61

PACIFIC CENTY CYBERWORKS LTD (HONG KONG)
Name changed to PCCW Ltd. 08/09/2002

PACIFIC CENTY EXPLS LTD (BC)
Recapitalized as Goldwater Resources Ltd. 06/10/1994
Each share Common no par exchanged for (0.2) share Common no par
Goldwater Resources Ltd. name changed to First Goldwater Resources Inc. 12/24/1999 which name changed to Baja Mining Corp. 07/20/2004 which recapitalized as Camrova Resources Inc. 10/17/2016

PACIFIC CENTY FINL CORP (DE)
Reincorporated 4/24/98
Common $2 par split (2) for (1) by issuance of (1) additional share payable 12/12/97 to holders of record 11/21/97 Ex date - 12/15/97
Common $2 par split (2) for (1) by issuance of (1) additional share payable 3/13/98 to holders of record 2/20/98
State of incorporation changed from (HI) to (DE) and Common $2 par changed to 1¢ par 4/24/98
Name changed to Bank of Hawaii Corp. 4/26/2002

PACIFIC CHEM INC (DE)
Recapitalized as RegalTech, Inc. 3/15/2005
Each share Common $0.001 par exchanged for (0.001) share Common $0.001 par
RegalTech, Inc. name changed to Asante Networks, Inc. 10/17/2005

PACIFIC CITY BANK (HUNTINGTON BEACH, CA)
Common $5 par changed to $1.67 par and (2) additional shares issued in March, 1978
Merged into Sumitomo Bank of California (San Francisco, CA) 12/11/81
Each share Common $1.67 par exchanged for $19 cash

PACIFIC CITY BK (LOS ANGELES, CA)
Common no par split (2) for (1) by issuance of (1) additional share payable 03/29/2007 to holders of record 03/16/2007 Ex date - 03/30/2007
Under plan of reorganization each share Common no par automatically became (1) share Pacific City Financial Corp. Common no par 07/10/2007

PACIFIC CLAY PRODS (CA)
Capital Stock no par changed to $10 par 00/00/1948
Capital Stock $10 par split (4) for (1) by issuance of (3) additional shares 00/00/1953
Each share Capital Stock $10 par exchanged for (1.25) shares Capital Stock $8 par 00/00/1954
Stock Dividend - 25% 04/21/1959
Reorganized under the laws of Delaware as Pacific Holding Corp. 07/14/1969
Each share Capital Stock $8 par exchanged for (1) share Common $1 par
(See Pacific Holding Corp.)

PACIFIC CMA INC (CO)
Reincorporated under the laws of Delaware and Common no par changed to $0.001 par 3/31/2004

PACIFIC COAL RES LTD (BC)
Each share old Common no par exchanged for (0.14285714) share new Common no par 03/25/2013
Name changed to Caribbean Resources Corp. 02/10/2016
(See Caribbean Resources Corp.)

PACIFIC COAST AGGREGATES, INC. (CA)
Reorganized in 1934
Each share Preferred no par exchanged for (0.14) share Common $10 par

Each share Common no par exchanged for (0.025) share Common $10 par
Recapitalized in 1939
Common $10 par changed to $5 par
Name changed to Pacific Cement & Aggregates, Inc. 10/1/56
Pacific Cement & Aggregates, Inc. acquired by Lone Star Cement Corp. (ME) 8/31/65 which reincorporated in Delaware 5/29/69 which name changed to Lone Star Industries, Inc. 5/20/71
(See Lone Star Industries, Inc.)

PACIFIC COAST APPAREL INC (CA)
Recapitalized as BDW Holdings, Ltd. (CA) 07/29/2005
Each share Common no par exchanged for (0.001) share Common no par
BDW Holdings, Ltd. (CA) reorganized as International Energy Group, Inc. (FL) 03/08/2006 which name changed to International Energy Ltd., Inc. 11/06/2009 which name changed to Standard Oil Company USA, Inc. 05/13/2010 which name changed to Gold Mining USA Inc. 05/24/2012 which name changed to Vita Mobile Systems, Inc. 01/31/2018

PACIFIC COAST BANK (SAN DIEGO, CA)
Bank closed by California Superintendent of Banks 4/29/82
No stockholders' equity

PACIFIC COAST BISCUIT CO.
Acquired by National Biscuit Co. 00/00/1930
Details not available

PACIFIC COAST CEMENT CORP. (FL)
Merged into Permanente Cement Co. in 1952
Each share $7 Preferred exchanged for (6.5) shares Common $1 par
Common no par cancelled
Permanente Cement Co. name changed to Kaiser Cement & Gypsum Corp. 7/1/64 which name changed to Kaiser Cement Corp. 5/1/79 which reincorporated in Delaware 5/4/82
(See Kaiser Cement Corp. (Del.))

PACIFIC COAST CO. (DE)
Merged into EDL, Inc. 4/18/68
Each share Common $1 par exchanged for $32 cash

PACIFIC COAST CO. (NJ)
Recapitalized in 1933 1st and 2nd Preferred $100 par changed to no par
Common $100 par changed to $10 par
Recapitalized 5/12/55
Each share 5% 1st Preferred no par exchanged for (4) shares 5% Conv. Preferred $25 par
Each share 4% 2nd Preferred no par exchanged for (2) shares 5% Conv. Preferred $25 par
Each share Common $10 par exchanged for (4) shares Common $1 par
Merged into Pacific Coast Co. (DE) on a share for share basis 4/20/62
(See Pacific Coast Co. (DE))

PACIFIC COAST ELECTRONICS CORP. (CA)
Recapitalized as Pacific Coast Medical Enterprises 10/2/68
Each share Common $2 par exchanged for (0.5) share Common $1 par
(See Pacific Coast Medical Enterprises)

PACIFIC COAST FDG & RES INC (BC)
Name changed to Alliance Resources Ltd. 04/23/1987
Alliance Resources Ltd. recapitalized as Acrex Ventures Ltd. 10/19/1993 which recapitalized as Alba Minerals Ltd. 07/10/2014

PACIFIC COAST HOLDINGS, INC. (CA)
Name changed to Bell National Corp. 01/03/1983
Bell National Corp. reincorporated in Delaware as Ampersand Medical Corp. 05/26/1999 which name changed to Molecular Diagnostics, Inc. 09/17/2001 which name changed to CytoCore, Inc. 08/17/2006 which name changed to Medite Cancer Diagnostics, Inc. 12/11/2014

PACIFIC COAST INTL INC (DE)
Name changed to AMS Inc. (DE) 06/12/1989
AMS Inc. (DE) reincorporated in Oklahoma as Advantage Marketing Systems, Inc. 12/11/1995 which name changed to AMS Health Sciences, Inc. 09/10/2004 which recapitalized as SA Recovery Corp. 11/20/2008 which name changed to Truli Media Group, Inc. (OK) 08/21/2012 which reorganized in Delaware 03/17/2015

PACIFIC COAST KNITTING MLS INC (DE)
Name changed to State-O-Maine, Inc. 10/22/75
State-O-Maine, Inc. name changed to Nautica Enterprises, Inc. 7/14/93
(See Nautica Enterprises, Inc.)

PACIFIC COAST MED ENTERPRISES (CA)
Stock Dividend - 100% 5/29/69
Filed a petition under Chapter 11 Federal Bankruptcy Code in March 1982
Stockholders' equity undetermined

PACIFIC COAST MORTGAGE CO.
Liquidation completed 11/1/60

PACIFIC COAST NATL BANCORP (CA)
Chapter 7 bankruptcy proceedings terminated 02/11/2010
No stockholders' equity

PACIFIC COAST NICKEL CORP (BC)
Recapitalized as Prophecy Platinum Corp. 06/20/2011
Each share Common no par exchanged for (0.1) share Common no par
Prophecy Platinum Corp. name changed to Wellgreen Platinum Ltd. 12/19/2013 which name changed to Nickel Creek Platinum Corp. 01/11/2018

PACIFIC COAST OIL CO.
Assets sold in 1929
No stockholders' equity

PACIFIC COAST PAPER MILLS OF WASHINGTON, INC. (WA)
Merged into Puget Sound Pulp & Timber Co. on a (0.8) for (1) basis 7/1/58

PACIFIC COAST PPTYS INC (DE)
Common $1 par changed to 5¢ par 11/02/1977
Name changed to Communications & Cable Inc. 05/07/1982
Communications & Cable Inc. name changed to IMNET, Inc. 03/22/1989 which name changed to IMGE, Inc. 10/07/1992 which name changed to nStor Technologies, Inc. 11/15/1996
(See nStor Technologies, Inc.)

PACIFIC COAST SVGS & LN ASSN SAN FRANCISCO (CA)
Guarantee Stock $10 par split (15) for (1) by issuance of (14) additional shares 09/03/1986
Guarantee Stock $10 par split (2) for (1) by issuance of (1) additional share 11/06/1987
Placed in conservatorship 03/16/1990
No stockholders' equity

PACIFIC COAST TERMS LTD (BC)
Capital Stock $10 par changed to no par in 1939
Capital Stock no par split (5) for (1) by issuance of (4) additional shares 5/15/62
Capital Stock no par reclassified as Common no par 6/25/65
5-3/4% Preference $100 par called for redemption 6/30/67
Acquired by Sultran Ltd. in July 1982
Each share Common no par exchanged for $18 cash

PACIFIC COMM BANCORP (CA)
Merged into First Choice Bancorp 07/31/2018
Each share Common no par exchanged for (0.47689) share Common no par

PACIFIC COMM BK (CHULA VISTA, CA)
Stock Dividend - 5% payable 11/12/1997 to holders of record 10/28/1997
Merged into Scripps Bank (La Jolla, CA) 08/31/1998
Each share Common no par exchanged for (2.1789) shares Common no par
Scripps Bank (La Jolla, CA) reorganized as Scripps Financial Corp. 07/01/1999 which merged into U.S. Bancorp 10/13/2000

PACIFIC COMM BK (LOS ANGELES, CA)
Name changed 09/28/2007
Name changed from Pacific Commerce Bank N.A. (Los Angeles, CA) to Pacific Commerce Bank (Los Angeles, CA) 09/28/2007
Under plan of reorganization each share Common $5 par automatically became (1) share Pacific Commerce Bancorp Common no par 11/03/2015
Pacific Commerce Bancorp merged into First Choice Bancorp 07/31/2018

PACIFIC COMMERCIAL CO., INC. (PHILIPPINES)
Dissolved 00/00/1951
Details not available

PACIFIC CONCORD HOLDING (CANADA) LTD. (BC)
Name changed to Pacific Stratus Ventures Ltd. 06/12/1998
Pacific Stratus Ventures Ltd. name changed to Pacific Stratus Energy Ltd. 06/14/2005 which merged into Pacific Rubiales Energy Corp. 01/23/2008 which name changed to Pacific Exploration & Production Corp. 08/18/2015 which name changed to Frontera Energy Corp. 06/14/2017

PACIFIC CONCORD HLDG LTD (HONG KONG)
Stock Dividends - 3.3333% payable 07/27/1999 to holders of record 06/23/1999; 3.3333% payable 12/16/1999 to holders of record 11/24/1999; 3.33333% payable 07/25/2000 to holders of record 06/21/2000
Acquired by private investors 11/03/2000
Each Sponsored ADR for Ordinary HKD $0.10 par exchanged for $2.46 cash

PACIFIC CONCORD RESOURCE CORP (BC)
Name changed to Pacific Engineered Materials Inc. 01/11/1989
(See Pacific Engineered Materials Inc.)

PACIFIC CONTL BK (EUGENE, OR)
Common $1 par split (5) for (4) by issuance of (0.25) additional share payable 09/30/1997 to holders of record 09/15/1997
Common $1 par split (3) for (2) by issuance of (0.5) additional share payable 03/16/1998 to holders of record 03/01/1998
Under plan of reorganization each share Common $1 par automatically became (1) share Pacific Continental Corp. Common $1 par 06/07/1999
Pacific Continental Corp. merged into Columbia Banking System, Inc. 11/01/2017

PACIFIC CONTL CORP (OR)
Common $1 par split (4) for (3) by issuance of (0.33333333) additional share payable 10/15/2003 to holders of record 09/30/2003 Ex date - 10/16/2003
Common $1 par changed to no par 04/20/2004
Common no par split (5) for (4) by issuance of (0.25) additional share payable 10/15/2004 to holders of record 09/30/2004 Ex date - 10/18/2004
Stock Dividends - 10% payable 10/19/2001 to holders of record 10/05/2001; 10% payable 06/15/2007 to holders of record 05/31/2007 Ex date - 05/29/2007
Merged into Columbia Banking System, Inc. 11/01/2017
Each share Common no par exchanged for (0.643) share Common no par

PACIFIC COPPER CORP (DE)
SEC revoked common stock registration 11/19/2014

PACIFIC COPPER MINES LTD (AB)
Name changed to Pacific Trans-Ocean Resources Ltd. 02/22/1984
Pacific Trans-Ocean Resources Ltd. recapitalized as Northern Minerals Ltd. 08/30/1989 which merged into Capilano International Inc. 02/11/1991 which name changed to Kelman Technologies Inc. 08/14/1996
(See Kelman Technologies Inc.)

PACIFIC COPPERFIELDS INC (BC)
Name changed to Botswana Diamondfields, Inc. 12/9/93
Botswana Diamondfields, Inc. merged into Crew Development Corp. 1/14/2000 which name changed to Crew Gold Corp. 1/26/2004

PACIFIC CORP. (UT)
Proclaimed dissolved for failure to pay taxes 11/9/74

PACIFIC CREST CAP INC (DE)
Common 1¢ par split (2) for (1) by issuance of (1) additional share payable 11/12/2002 to holders of record 10/30/2002 Ex date - 11/13/2002
Merged into Pacific Capital Bancorp (New) 03/08/2004
Each share Common 1¢ par exchanged for $26 cash

PACIFIC CREST INVTS (NV)
Name changed to Pacific Peak Investments 05/16/2005
Pacific Peak Investments name changed to Global Beverage Solutions, Inc. 10/26/2005 which recapitalized as Real Brands, Inc. 10/22/2013

PACIFIC CROSS INTERNATIONAL (UT)
Recapitalized as Alpha Energy & Gold (UT) 05/26/1977
Each share Common 1¢ par exchanged for (5) shares Common 1¢ par
Alpha Energy & Gold (UT) reorganized in (DC) as Century Industries Inc. 04/30/1993 which reorganized in Nevada 02/16/2000

(See Century Industries Inc. (NV))

PACIFIC CYPRESS MINERALS LTD (BC)
Recapitalized as International Pacific Cypress Minerals Ltd. 3/4/85
Each share Common no par exchanged for (0.25) share Common no par
(See International Pacific Cypress Minerals Ltd.)

PACIFIC DAIRY PRODUCTS CO.
Merged into Golden State Milk Products Co. 00/00/1928
Details not available

PACIFIC DATAVISION INC (DE)
Name changed to pdvWireless, Inc. 11/09/2015

PACIFIC DELTA GAS INC (CA)
5% Preferred $25 par called for redemption 5/16/67
Merged into Pargas, Inc. 6/1/67
Each share Common $2.50 par exchanged for (0.25) share $2.64 Conv. Preference Ser. A no par
(See Pargas, Inc.)

PACIFIC DEV CORP (CO)
Each share old Common $0.001 par exchanged for (0.02) share new Common $0.001 par 12/20/1999
Reincorporated under the laws of Delaware as Cheshire Distributors Inc. 03/24/2000
Cheshire Distributors Inc. recapitalized as LMIC, Inc. 07/21/2003 which name changed to Z Holdings Group, Inc. 10/15/2012 which name changed to Ariel Clean Energy, Inc. 08/20/2015

PACIFIC DIAGNOSTIC TECHNOLOGIES INC (NV)
Each share Common $0.001 par exchanged for (0.04) share Common 1¢ par 01/15/1999
Reincorporated under the laws of California as Quintek Technologies Inc. 04/05/1999
(See Quintek Technologies Inc.)

PACIFIC DIESEL ENGINE CO.
Acquired by Atlas Imperial Diesel Engine Co. 00/00/1928
Details not available

PACIFIC DISTILLERS, INC.
Name changed to Lac Chemicals, Inc. 00/00/1941
(See Lac Chemicals, Inc.)

PACIFIC DIVERSIFIED HLDGS CORP (UT)
Name changed to Agora Holdings, Inc. 05/01/1998

PACIFIC DOOR & SASH CO.
Assets sold to Pacific Wood Products Corp. in 1934 which was liquidated in 1944

PACIFIC DRUG DISTRIBUTORS, INC. (DE)
100% acquired by Amfac, Inc. through purchase offer which expired 04/01/1973
Public interest eliminated

PACIFIC DUNLOP LTD (AUSTRALIA)
Stock Dividends - 10% 10/24/1986; 10% 07/07/1987; 10% 05/25/1989; 10% 10/13/1993
Recapitalized as Ansell Ltd. 04/30/2002
Each ADR for Ordinary AUD $1 par exchanged for (0.2) ADR for Ordinary AUD $1 par
(See Ansell Ltd.)

PACIFIC E-LINK CORP (BC)
Delisted from Toronto Venture Stock Exchange 03/30/2005

PACIFIC EAGLE TREASURE SALVORS INC (NV)
Name changed to Aluminum Laminating Insulation Manufacturing Co., Inc. 12/05/1990

PACIFIC EAST ADVISORS INC (DE)
Name changed to Pacific Asia Petroleum, Inc. 06/06/2007
Pacific Asia Petroleum, Inc. name changed to CAMAC Energy Inc. 04/07/2010 which recapitalized as Erin Energy Corp. 04/23/2015

PACIFIC EASTERN CORP.
Merged into Atlas Corp. 10/31/1936
Each share Capital Stock exchanged for (0.05) share 6% Preferred $50 par and (0.25) share Common $5 par
(See Atlas Corp.)

PACIFIC EASTERN GOLD LTD.
Succeeded by Pacific (Eastern) Gold Mines Ltd. 00/00/1945
Each share Capital Stock no par exchanged for (0.125) share Capital Stock $1 par
Pacific (Eastern) Gold Mines Ltd. recapitalized as PCE Explorations Ltd. 08/07/1957 which recapitalized as Pan Central Explorations Ltd. 01/24/1972
(See Pan Central Explorations Ltd.)

PACIFIC EASTN CORP (DE)
Charter cancelled and declared inoperative and void for failure to maintain a registered agent 10/29/1991

PACIFIC ELECTRICORD CO (CA)
Stock Dividend - 50% 02/28/1969
Merged into Leviton Manufacturing Co., Inc. 12/04/1972
Each share Common $1 par exchanged for $10 cash

PACIFIC ELECTRO MAGNETICS INC (CA)
Reincorporated under the laws of Delaware as Pemco, Inc. and Common no par changed to 1¢ par 8/28/69
Pemco, Inc. name changed to Dimode Industries, Inc. 1/8/70
(See Dimode Industries, Inc.)

PACIFIC EMPIRE HOLDINGS, INC. (DE)
No longer in existence having become inoperative and void for non-payment of taxes 4/1/44

PACIFIC EMPIRE LIFE INSURANCE (ID)
Capital Stock $20 par changed to $2 par and (9) additional shares issued 5/21/68
Stock Dividends - 25% 3/30/73; 25% 3/30/75
Merged into First Centennial Corp. 4/24/84
Each share Capital Stock $2 par exchanged for (1/3) share Class A Common $1 par and $5.50 cash
Note: Holdings of (50) shares or fewer received $8.25 cash per share
First Centennial Corp. acquired by Citizens, Inc. 7/31/92

PACIFIC EMPLOYERS INSURANCE CO. (CA)
Each share Capital Stock $100 par exchanged for (10) shares Capital Stock $10 par 00/00/1950
Each share Capital Stock $10 par exchanged for (2) shares Capital Stock $5 par 10/13/1955
Acquired by Insurance Co. of North America 01/00/1965
Each share Capital Stock $5 par exchanged for (0.052632) share Capital Stock $5 par
Insurance Co. of North America acquired by INA Corp. 05/29/1968 which merged into Cigna Corp. 04/01/1982

PACIFIC ENERGY CORP (NV)
Common $5 par changed to 50¢ par and (9) additional shares issued 08/00/1976
Name changed to Aimco, Inc. 09/01/1977

Aimco, Inc. recapitalized as Colt Technology, Inc. 03/31/1983

PACIFIC ENERGY PARTNERS L P (DE)
Merged into Plains All American Pipeline, L.P. 11/15/2006
Each Common Unit exchanged for (0.77) Common Unit

PACIFIC ENERGY RES LTD (DE)
Each share old Common no par exchanged for (1/3) share new Common no par 08/31/2004
Place of incorporation changed from (BC) to (DE) and Common no par changed to $0.0001 par 02/04/2005
Plan of reorganization under Chapter 11 bankruptcy proceedings effective 12/23/2010
No stockholders' equity

PACIFIC ENGINEERED MATLS INC (BC)
Struck off register and declared dissolved for failure to file returns 3/19/93

PACIFIC ENGR & PRODTN CO NEV (NV)
Merged into American Pacific Corp. 04/19/1982
Each share Common $1 par exchanged for (0.900009) share Common 10¢ par
(See American Pacific Corp.)

PACIFIC ENGR SYS INC (DE)
Common $0.001 par split (2) for (1) by issuance of (1) additional share payable 6/15/98 to holders of record 5/15/98
Recapitalized as Royal Pet Meals, Inc. 3/28/2005
Each share Common $0.001 par exchanged for (0.001) share Common $0.001 par
Royal Pet Meals, Inc. recapitalized as Kodiak Gaming, Inc. 5/10/2006 which name changed to Straight Up Brands, Inc. 8/7/2006

PACIFIC ENTERPRISES (CA)
$7.64 Preferred no par called for redemption 06/19/1995
Merged into Sempra Energy 06/26/1998
Each share Common no par exchanged for (1.5038) shares Common no par
$4.36 Preferred no par called for redemption at $101 on 06/30/2011
$4.40 Preferred no par called for redemption at $101.50 on 06/30/2011
$4.50 Preferred no par called for redemption at $100 on 06/30/2011
$4.75 Preferred no par called for redemption at $100 on 06/30/2011
$4.75 Conv. Preferred no par called for redemption at $101 on 06/30/2011
Public interest eliminated

PACIFIC ENTMT CORP (CA)
Reincorporated under the laws of Nevada as Genius Brands International, Inc. 11/28/2011

PACIFIC ENTMT GROUP INC (NV)
Name changed to International Brewing & Manufacturing Inc. 05/14/1990
International Brewing & Manufacturing Inc. name changed to Juina Mining Corp. 12/16/1997 which name changed to AC Energy, Inc. (NV) 02/23/2007
(See AC Energy, Inc. (NV))

PACIFIC ENZYME PRODUCTS, INC. (HI)
Name changed to Pacific Biochemical, Inc. 7/11/66
Pacific Biochemical, Inc. involuntarily dissolved 6/1/76

PACIFIC EQUITIES, INC.
Merged into Pacific Associates, Inc. 00/00/1929

Details not available

PACIFIC EXPL & PRODTN CORP (BC)
Each share old Common no par exchanged for (0.00001) share new Common no par 11/02/2016
Note: Holdings of (99,999) or fewer pre-split shares were cancelled and are without value
Name changed to Frontera Energy Corp. 06/14/2017

PACIFIC EXPRESS HLDG INC (CA)
Charter cancelled for failure to file reports and pay taxes 11/1/94

PACIFIC FACTORS INC.
Liquidated in 1933
No stockholders' equity

PACIFIC FALKON RES INC (BC)
Recapitalized as Pacific Consolidated Resources Corp. 6/29/98
Each share Common no par exchanged for (0.2) share Common no par

PACIFIC FAR EAST LINE INC (DE)
Each share Common $20 par exchanged for (4) shares Common $5 par 07/19/1955
Preferred $25 par called for redemption 06/01/1962
Common $5 par changed to $1 par 12/31/1976
Stock Dividends - 10% 11/08/1963; 25% 12/31/1976
Adjudicated bankrupt 08/04/1978
Stockholders' equity unlikely

PACIFIC FASHION RETAILERS CORP (BC)
Struck off register and declared dissolved for failure to file returns 2/19/93

PACIFIC FID CORP (NV)
Common $5 par changed to $1 par 3/15/66
Charter revoked for failure to file reports and pay fees 3/2/70

PACIFIC FIN CORP (DE)
5% Preferred $25 par called for redemption 09/30/1959
Name changed to Transamerica Corp. 03/29/1968
(See Transamerica Corp.)

PACIFIC FINANCE CORP. OF CALIFORNIA (DE)
Name changed to Pacific Finance Corp. 00/00/1952
Pacific Finance Corp. name changed to Transamerica Financial Corp. 03/29/1968 which was acquired by Transamerica Corp. 08/03/1961
(See Transamerica Financial Corp.)

PACIFIC FINL SOLUTIONS INC (NV)
Old Common $0.001 par split (2) for (1) by issuance of (1) additional share payable 04/01/2006 to holders of record 03/23/2006 Ex date - 04/03/2006
Each share old Common $0.001 par exchanged for (0.14285714) share new Common $0.001 par 05/09/2008
Name changed to Continental Prison Systems, Inc. 06/20/2008
Continental Prison Systems, Inc. recapitalized as General Payment Systems, Inc. 09/03/2013

PACIFIC FIRE INSURANCE CO. (NY)
Each share Capital Stock $25 par exchanged for (2.5) shares Capital Stock $10 par in 1952
Stock Dividend - 100% 6/2/55
Name changed to Pacific Insurance Co. of New York 5/20/57
Pacific Insurance Co. of New York name changed to American International Insurance Co. in August 1969

PACIFIC FIRST FED SVGS BK (TACOMA, WA)
Under plan of reorganization each

share Common $1 par automatically became (1) share Pacific First Financial Corp. Common $1 par 06/28/1985
(See Pacific First Financial Corp.)

PACIFIC FIRST FINL CORP (WA)
Acquired by Royal Trustco Ltd. 12/01/1989
Each share Common $1 par exchanged for $27 cash

PACIFIC FOAM FORM INC (BC)
Struck off register and declared dissolved for failure to file returns 09/20/1985

PACIFIC FRANCHISES INTERNATIONAL, INC. (WA)
Placed in receivership and case closed in November 1973
No stockholders' equity

PACIFIC FRUIT & PRODUCE CO.
Merged into Pacific Gamble Robinson Co. 00/00/1942
Details not available

PACIFIC FST CORP (NV)
Name changed to Green Capital Group, Inc. 04/30/1998
(See Green Capital Group, Inc.)

PACIFIC FST PRODS LTD (BC)
Acquired by Doman Industries Ltd. 12/10/97
Each share Common no par exchanged for $29 cash

PACIFIC FUEL CELL CORP (NV)
Chapter 7 bankruptcy proceedings terminated 11/18/2010
No stockholders' equity

PACIFIC GALLEON MNG CORP (BC)
Recapitalized as Prospector International Resources Inc. 05/29/1998
Each share Common no par exchanged for (0.08333333) share Common no par
Prospector International Resources Inc. recapitalized as Prospector Consolidated Resources Inc. 09/11/2001 which recapitalized as Prospector Resources Corp. (BC) 01/31/2011 which reincorporated in Ontario as Rio2 Ltd. (Old) 04/28/2017 which merged into Rio2 Ltd. (New) 07/27/2018

PACIFIC GAMBLE ROBINSON CO (DE)
Each share Common $10 par exchanged for (3) shares Common $5 par 00/00/1946
Acquired by Miller-Cascade, Inc. 05/28/1986
Each share Common $5 par exchanged for $28.25 cash

PACIFIC GAS & ELEC CO (CA)
Each share 6% Preferred $100 par exchanged for (4) shares 6% Preferred $25 par 00/00/1927
Each share Common $100 par exchanged for (4) shares Common $25 par 00/00/1927
Common $25 par changed to $10 par and (2) additional shares issued 01/19/1962
Common $10 par changed to $5 par and (1) additional share issued 07/15/1983
16.24% 1st Preferred $25 par called for redemption 07/07/1986
17.38% 1st Preferred $25 par called for redemption 02/01/1987
12.80% 1st Preferred $25 par called for redemption 07/31/1987
14.75% 1st Preferred $100 par called for redemption 08/01/1987
10.46% 1st Preferred $25 par called for redemption 07/31/1991
9.28% 1st Preferred $25 par called for redemption 08/15/1992
10.28% 1st Preferred $25 par called for redemption 08/15/1992
10.18% 1st Preferred $25 par called for redemption 09/30/1992
9.48% 1st Preferred $25 par called for redemption 02/28/1993
9% 1st Preferred $25 par called for redemption 07/31/1993
9.30% 1st Preferred $25 par called for redemption 07/31/1993
8.16% 1st Preferred $25 par called for redemption 02/18/1994
7.84% 1st Preferred $25 par called for redemption 09/01/1995
8% 1st Preferred $25 par called for redemption 09/01/1995
8.20% 1st Preferred $25 par called for redemption 09/01/1995
Under plan of reorganization each share Common $5 par automatically became (1) share PG&E Corp. Common no par 01/01/1997
7.44% 1st Preferred $25 par called for redemption at $25 plus $0.465 accrued dividends on 01/31/1998
6.875% 1st Preferred $25 par called for redemption at $25 on 07/31/1998
Plan of reorganization under Chapter 11 Federal Bankruptcy Code effective 04/12/2004
Each share 7.90% Deferrable Debenture exchanged for $25.060347 cash
6.30% 1st Preferred $25 par called for redemption at $25 plus $0.06999 accrued dividends on 05/31/2005
6.57% Preferred $25 par called for redemption at $25 plus $0.072999 accrued dividends on 05/31/2005
7.04% 1st Preferred called for redemption at $25.70 on 08/31/2005
(Additional Information in Active)

PACIFIC GAS TRANSMISSION CO (CA)
Common no par split (2) for (1) by issuance of (1) additional share 11/7/80
Acquired by Pacific Gas & Electric Co. 3/21/86
Each share Common no par exchanged for (1.5621) shares Common $5 par

PACIFIC GATEWAY EXCHANGE INC (DE)
Plan of reorganization under Chapter 11 Federal Bankruptcy Code effective 11/25/2003
No stockholders' equity

PACIFIC GATEWAY PPTYS INC (MD)
Merged into Mission Orchard Statutory Trust 8/31/2000
Each share Common $1 par exchanged for $12.60 cash
Note: Each share Common $1 par received an initial additional distribution of approximately $0.04 cash payable 11/24/2000 to holders of record 8/31/2000
Each share Common $1 par received a second and final additional distribution of approximately $0.03 cash payable 7/30/2001 to holders of record 8/31/2000

PACIFIC GATEWAY PPTYS INC (NY)
Reincorporated under the laws of Maryland 9/2/99
(See Pacific Gateway Properties Inc. (MD))

PACIFIC GEN INC (UT)
Involuntarily dissolved 12/04/2002

PACIFIC GENESIS TECHNOLOGIES INC (BC)
Reincorporated under the laws of Alberta as Ware Solutions Corp. 10/01/2001
(See Ware Solutions Corp.)

PACIFIC GIANT STL ORES LTD (BC)
Struck off register and declared dissolved for failure to file returns 07/12/1973

PACIFIC GLOBAL COMMUNICATIONS GROUP INC (NV)
Charter revoked for failure to file reports and pay fees 12/30/2011

PACIFIC GOLD, INC. (CO)
Each share Common $1 par exchanged for (10) shares Common 10¢ par 11/03/1960
Name changed to Cine Chrome Laboratories, Inc. 07/05/1973
Cine Chrome Laboratories, Inc. name changed to Medco Health Care Services, Inc. 05/21/1984 which name changed to Cine-Chrome Video Corp. 10/21/1985 which name changed to Network 4, Inc. 06/25/1986 which recapitalized as CEEE Group Corp. (CO) 05/00/1987 which reorganized in Delaware as Atlantic International Entertainment, Ltd. 11/26/1996 which name changed to Online Gaming Systems, Ltd. 10/01/1999 which name changed to Advanced Resources Group Ltd. 02/15/2007

PACIFIC GOLD & URANIUM, INC. (NV)
Name changed to Pacific Gold Corp. 9/18/86
Pacific Gold Corp. name changed to Nevada Gold & Casinos Inc. 1/24/94

PACIFIC GOLD & URANIUM MINES LTD. (BC)
Liquidated in 1956

PACIFIC GOLD CORP (NV)
Each share Common 1¢ par exchanged for (0.25) share Common 4¢ par 11/16/88
Name changed to Nevada Gold & Casinos Inc. 1/24/94

PACIFIC GOLD CORP (ON)
Reincorporated 05/12/1994
Reincorporated 06/27/1995
Place of incorporation changed from (BC) to (ALTA) 05/12/1994
Place of incorporation changed from (ALTA) to (ONT) 06/27/1995
Name changed to Worldtek (Canada) Ltd. 07/04/1996
(See Worldtek (Canada) Ltd.)

PACIFIC GOLDEN SPIKE RES LTD (BC)
Recapitalized as Island Mountain Gold Mines Ltd. 04/22/1999
Each share Common no par exchanged for (0.16666666) share Common no par
Island Mountain Gold Mines Ltd. recapitalized as Lions Gate Energy Inc. 02/01/2006 which recapitalized as Starr Peak Exploration Ltd. 07/27/2015

PACIFIC GOLDRIM RES INC (NV)
Name changed to SmartHeat Inc. 05/20/2008

PACIFIC GREYSTONE CORP (DE)
Merged into Lennar Corp. 10/31/97
Each share Common 1¢ par exchanged for (1) share Common 10¢ par
Each share Common 1¢ par received additional distribution of (0.138) share Common 10¢ par 10/31/97

PACIFIC GUARDIAN LIFE INS LTD (HI)
Merged into Meiji Mutual Life Insurance Co. 06/01/1985
Each share Capital Stock $2 par exchanged for $6 cash

PACIFIC GULF PPTYS INC (MD)
Issue Information - 3,900,000 shares COM offered at $18.25 per share on 02/10/1994
Each share Common 1¢ par received distribution of (1) Pacific Gulf Properties Inc. Liquidating Trust Share of Bene. Int. payable 8/23/2001 to holders of record 8/23/2001
Merged into FountainGlen Properties LLC 8/23/2001
Each share Common 1¢ par exchanged for $3.1251 cash

PACIFIC GULF PROPERTIES INC. LIQUIDATION TRUST (NY)
Liquidation completed
Each Share of Bene. Int. received initial distribution of $1 cash payable 12/31/2001 to holders of record 8/23/2001
Each Share of Bene. Int. received second distribution of $0.75 cash payable 9/18/2002 to holders of record 8/23/2001
Each Share of Bene. Int. received third distribution of $0.22 cash payable 5/9/2003 to holders of record 8/23/2001
Each Share of Bene. Int. received fourth and final distribution of $0.066236 cash payable 12/17/2003 to holders of record 8/23/2001

PACIFIC HARBOUR CAP LTD (BC)
Name changed to Oceanic Iron Ore Corp. 12/06/2010

PACIFIC HAWAIIAN PRODUCTS CO. (CA)
Stock Dividends - 100% 7/21/58; 200% 3/6/59; 100% 12/30/61
Name changed to PHP Co., Inc. 2/14/63
PHP Co., Inc. completed liquidation 2/1/66

PACIFIC HERITAGE BK (TORRANCE, CA)
Bank closed by California Superintendent of Banks 07/28/1995
No stockholders' equity

PACIFIC HLDG CORP (DE)
$1.20 Conv. Preferred $1 par called for redemption 07/01/1978
Merged into Murdock Holding Corp. (DE) 08/29/1978
Each share Common $1 par exchanged for $32.50 cash

PACIFIC HOME INDS (CA)
Adjudicated bankrupt 11/30/1973
Stockholders' equity unlikely

PACIFIC HORIZON FDS INC (MD)
Convertible Securities Fund $0.001 par reclassified as Capital Income Fund 09/16/1991
Corporate Bond Fund $0.001 par reclassified as Flexible Income Fund $0.001 par 04/25/1994
Aggressive Growth Portfolio Class D $0.001 par merged into Nations Fund, Inc. 05/14/1999
Details not available
Capital Income Fund $0.001 par merged into Nations Institutional Reserves 05/14/1999
Details not available
Horizon Tax Exempt Money Fund $0.001 par and Horizon Tax Exempt Money Fund Service Shares $0.001 par merged into Nations Institutional Reserves 05/14/1999
Details not available
Pacific Horizon Tax Exempt Money Market Fund $0.001 par merged into Nations Institutional Reserves 05/14/1999
Details not available
Prime Fund Horizon Shares, Horizon Service Shares and Pacific Horizon Shares $0.001 par merged into Nations Institutional Reserves 05/14/1999
Details not available
Tax Exempt Money Market Fund $0.001 par merged into Nations Institutional Reserves 05/14/1999
Details not available
Treasury Fund Horizon Shares, Horizon Service Shares and Pacific Horizon Shares $0.001 par merged into Nations Institutional Reserves 05/14/1999
Details not available
U.S. Government Securities Fund $0.001 par merged into Nations Fund, Inc. 05/14/1999
Details not available

California Tax Exempt Bond Fund $0.001 par merged into Nations Institutional Reserves 05/21/1999
Details not available
California Tax Exempt Money Market Fund $0.001 par merged into Nations Institutional Reserves 05/21/1999
Details not available

PACIFIC HORIZON TAX EXEMPT MONEY MKT PORTFOLIO INC (MD)
Under plan of reorganization each share Class A Common $0.001 par automatically became (1) Pacific Horizon Funds, Inc. Prime Fund Pacific Horizon Share or Treasury Fund Pacific Horizon Share 1/19/90

PACIFIC HOTHOUSES INC (NV)
Common $0.001 par split (7) for (1) by issuance of (6) additional shares payable 02/09/2001 to holders of record 02/02/2001 Ex date - 02/12/2001
Name changed to Zenxus, Inc. 06/08/2001
Zenxus, Inc. name changed to Stafford Ventures Inc. 10/08/2001 which name changed to Stafford Energy Inc. 08/01/2002 which recapitalized as Nucon-RF, Inc. 05/23/2006 which name changed to NNRF, Inc. 09/10/2007

PACIFIC HOUSTON RES INC (BC)
Struck off register and declared dissolved for failure to file returns 3/26/93

PACIFIC INDEMNITY CO. (CA)
Each share Capital Stock $50 par exchanged for (4) shares Capital Stock $10 par 00/00/1929
Capital Stock $10 par changed to $3.33333333 par and (2) additional shares issued 10/20/1960
Stock Dividends - 20% 04/01/1954; 33.33333333% 05/15/1955; 10% 01/30/1962; 10% 10/31/1963; 10% 10/30/1964
Over 99% held by Federal Insurance Co. as of 01/20/1975
Public interest eliminated

PACIFIC INDS INC (CA)
Each share Common $1 par exchanged for (0.1) share Common $2 par 5/6/57
Reincorporated under the laws of Delaware as Frye Industries, Inc. 12/31/70
Frye Industries, Inc. merged into Wheelabrator-Frye Inc. 11/4/71 which merged into Signal Companies, Inc. 2/1/83 which merged into AlliedSignal Inc. 9/19/85 which name changed to Honeywell International Inc. 12/1/99

PACIFIC INLAND BANCORP (CA)
Liquidated in November 1997
Details not available

PACIFIC-INLAND OIL CORP. (TX)
Merged into I.G.E., Inc. 3/2/72
Each share Capital Stock 10¢ par exchanged for (2.5) shares Common 1¢ par
I.G.E., Inc. recapitalized as Life Partners Holdings Inc. (MA) 2/9/2000 which reincorporated in Texas 2/19/2003

PACIFIC INSIGHT ELECTRS CORP (BC)
Acquired by Methode Electronics, Inc. 10/04/2017
Each share Common no par exchanged for $18.50 cash
Note: Unexchanged certificates will be cancelled and become without value 10/04/2023

PACIFIC INSURANCE CO. OF NEW YORK (NY)
Name changed to American International Insurance Co. in August 1969

(See American International Insurance Co.)

PACIFIC INTERMEDIA INC (CO)
Name changed to Raptor Networks Technology, Inc. (CO) 12/03/2003
Raptor Networks Technology, Inc. (CO) reorganized in Wyoming as Mabwe Minerals Inc. 06/28/2012 which reorganized in Delaware as Fonon Corp. 07/29/2015

PACIFIC INTERMOUNTAIN EXPRESS CO (NV)
Each share Common $10 par exchanged for (2.5) shares Common $5 par in 1948
Each share Common $5 par exchanged for (3) shares Common $2 par 5/1/56
Acquired by International Utilities Corp. 11/30/71
Each share Common $2 par exchanged for (1) share $1.25 Conv. Preferred no par
(See International Utilities Corp.)

PACIFIC INTL BANCORP (WA)
Each old share Common no par exchanged for (2) shares new Common no par 03/15/2007
Merged into BBCN Bancorp, Inc. 02/15/2013
Each share new Common no par exchanged for (0.14121) share Common $0.001 par
BBCN Bancorp, Inc. name changed to Hope Bancorp, Inc. 08/01/2016

PACIFIC INTL ENTERPRISES INC (NV)
Each share old Common $0.001 par exchanged for (0.04) share new Common $0.001 par 08/29/1994
Each share new Common $0.001 par exchanged for (0.2) share Common no par 10/17/1995
SEC revoked common stock registration 09/11/2009

PACIFIC INTL EQUITIES INC (DE)
Merged into Pacific Exchange Corp. 08/31/1980
Each share Common $1 par exchanged for $0.40 cash

PACIFIC INTL HARDWOODS INC (BC)
Recapitalized as PIH Pacific International Hardwoods Inc. 11/12/1996
Each share Common no par exchanged for (0.25) share Common no par
(See PIH Pacific International Hardwoods Inc.)

PACIFIC INTL HLDG INC (UT)
Each share old Common $0.001 par exchanged for (0.1) share new Common $0.001 par 4/6/98
Each share new Common $0.001 par exchanged again for (0.01) share new Common $0.001 par 3/22/2002
Name changed to Interactive Motorsports & Entertainment Corp. 8/5/2002

PACIFIC INTL INC (HI)
Name changed to EMB Corp. (HI) 07/05/1996
EMB Corp. (HI) reorganized in Nevada as AMT Group, Inc. 03/15/2007
(See AMT Group, Inc.)

PACIFIC INTL SVCS CORP (CA)
Assets surrendered for the benefit of creditors 11/13/1996
No stockholders' equity

PACIFIC INTERNET LTD (SINGAPORE)
Issue Information - 3,000,000 ORD shares offered at $17 per share on 02/05/1999
Acquired by Pacnet Ltd. 09/20/2008
Each share Ordinary exchanged for $11.20 cash

Note: Amendment to Companies Act abolished par value 01/30/2006

PACIFIC INVESTING CORP.
Merged into Pacific Southern Investors, Inc. 00/00/1932
Details not available

PACIFIC INVESTORS, INC.
Dissolved in 1938

PACIFIC JADE INDUSTRIES INC. (BC)
Struck off register and declared dissolved for failure to file returns 2/4/83

PACIFIC KENRIDGE VENTURES INC (BC)
Struck off register and declared dissolved for failure to file returns 3/3/95

PACIFIC LAURENTIAN CAP CORP (AB)
Recapitalized as FAS International Ltd. 02/07/1997
Each share Common no par exchanged for (0.1) share Common no par
(See FAS International Ltd.)

PACIFIC LEISURE ENTERPRISES INC (DE)
Charter cancelled and declared inoperative and void for non-payment of taxes 6/23/86

PACIFIC LIBERTY BK (HUNTINGTON BEACH, CA)
Merged into First Community Bancorp (CA) 10/07/2005
Each share Common no par exchanged for (0.812) share Common no par
First Community Bancorp (CA) reincorporated in Delaware as PacWest Bancorp 05/14/2008

PACIFIC LINK CAP INC (BC)
Recapitalized as Miza Enterprises Inc. 04/23/2015
Each share Common no par exchanged for (0.14285714) share Common no par
Miza Enterprises Inc. name changed to BQ Metals Corp. 06/21/2017 which name name changed to BeMetals Corp. 04/18/2018

PACIFIC LMBR CO (ME)
Capital Stock $100 par changed to $10 par and (9) additional shares issued 11/26/1963
Capital Stock $10 par changed to $3-1/3 par and (2) additional shares issued 07/07/1969
Capital Stock $3-1/3 par changed to $1-1/9 par and (2) additional shares issued 10/16/1975
Capital Stock $1-1/9 par changed to 50¢ par and (1) additional share issued 03/03/1981
Merged into Maxxam Group Inc. (DE) 02/26/1986
Each share Capital Stock 50¢ par exchanged for $40 cash

PACIFIC LTG CORP (CA)
$5 Preferred no par called for redemption 06/09/1949
Common no par split (2) for (1) by issuance of (1) additional share 10/23/1953
Common no par split (2) for (1) by issuance of (1) additional share 06/22/1964
Name changed to Pacific Enterprises 02/16/1988
(See Pacific Enterprises)

PACIFIC MAGTRON INTL CORP (NV)
Under plan of reorganization of Chapter 11 Federal Bankruptcy Code each share Common $0.001 par received distribution of (1) share Herborium Group, Inc. Common $0.001 par payable 12/14/2006 to holders of record 8/11/2006
Note: Certificates were not required to be surrendered and are without value

PACIFIC MAIL STEAMSHIP CO.
Dissolved in 1926

PACIFIC MARINER EXPLS LTD (BC)
Name changed to Abitibi Mining Corp. 12/14/95

PACIFIC MED GROUP INC (NV)
Recapitalized as Tandem Energy Holdings Inc. 03/07/2005
Each share Common $0.001 par exchanged for (0.002) share Common $0.001 par
(See Tandem Energy Holdings Inc.)

PACIFIC MEDIA GROUP ENTERPRISES INC (DE)
Common $0.0001 par split (54) for (1) by issuance of (53) additional shares payable 07/24/2017 to holders of record 06/23/2017 Ex date - 07/25/2017
Name changed to Extract Pharmaceuticals, Inc. 08/01/2017
Extract Pharmaceuticals, Inc. name changed to Token Communities Ltd. 03/21/2018

PACIFIC MERCANTILE BK (NEWPORT BEACH, CA)
Common no par split (5) for (4) by issuance of (0.25) additional share payable 06/16/1999 to holders of record 05/25/1999
Common no par split (2) for (1) by issuance of (1) additional share payable 04/14/2000 to holders of record 04/03/2000
Under plan of reorganization each share Common no par automatically became (1) share Pacific Mercantile Bancorp Common no par 06/14/2000

PACIFIC MERCANTILE LTD (AB)
Merged into Mercury Partners & Co. Inc. 09/28/2001
Each share Common no par exchanged for (5) shares Common no par
Mercury Partners & Co. Inc. name changed to Black Mountain Capital Corp. 05/02/2005 which recapitalized as Grand Peak Capital Corp. (YT) 11/20/2007 which reincorporated in British Columbia 04/27/2010

PACIFIC MERCURY ELECTRONICS (CA)
Merged into Warwick Electronics Inc. 10/28/63
Each share Class A Common 50¢ par exchanged for (1.1) shares Common 50¢ par
Each share Class B Common 50¢ par exchanged for (1.065) shares Common 50¢ par
Warwick Electronics Inc. name changed to Thomas International Corp. 3/1/77
(See Thomas International Corp.)

PACIFIC MERCURY TELEVISION MANUFACTURING CORP. (CA)
Each share Capital Stock $10 par exchanged for (12.5) shares Common 50¢ par in 1950
Common 50¢ par redesignated as Class A Common 50¢ par in 1952
Name changed to Pacific Mercury Electronics 12/8/58
Pacific Mercury Electronics merged into Warwick Electronics Inc. 10/28/63 which name changed to Thomas International Corp. 3/1/77
(See Thomas International Corp.)

PACIFIC METALS CORP (NV)
Each share old Common $0.001 par exchanged for (0.04) share new Common $0.001 par 01/09/2015
Name changed to GMCI Corp. 04/17/2015

PACIFIC METALS INC (CANADA)
Recapitalized as Crescendo Capital Corp. 06/29/1995
Each share Common no par exchanged for (0.1) share Common no par
Crescendo Capital Corp. name changed to Tragoes Inc. 07/24/1996 which name changed to Rightsmarket.com Inc. 07/30/1999 which name changed to RightsMarket Inc. 06/07/2000 which reorganized as RightsMarket Ltd. 12/31/2003

PACIFIC MILLS (MA)
Capital Stock $100 par changed to no par 00/00/1934
Capital Stock no par split (2) for (1) by issuance of (1) additional share 04/15/1946
Merged into Burlington Industries, Inc. (Old) on a (3) for (1) basis 11/16/1959
(See Burlington Industries, Inc. (Old))

PACIFIC MILLS LTD. (BC)
Each share Common $100 par exchanged for (4) shares Common $25 par in 1947
Each share Common $25 par exchanged for (2.5) shares Ordinary $10 par in 1951
Name changed to Crown Zellerbach Canada Ltd. in 1954
Crown Zellerbach Canada Ltd. name changed to Crown Forest Industries Ltd. 11/9/83 which was acquired by Fletcher Challenge Canada Inc. 1/1/88

PACIFIC MINERALS & CHEM INC (UT)
Recapitalized as Nevada Magic Holdings Inc. 1/7/97
Each share Common $0.001 par exchanged for (0.005) share Common $0.001 par
Nevada Magic Holdings Inc. name changed to To4c Corp. 6/29/99 which reorganized in Nevada as Aplox Corp. 4/27/2001 which name changed to Mirador Inc. 7/25/2001 which name changed to VWAY International 7/5/2004 which name changed to WorldWide Cannery & Distribution, Inc. 2/8/2006 which name changed to Global Diamond Exchange Inc. 9/22/2006

PACIFIC MINERALS INC (BC)
Name changed to Jinshan Gold Mines Inc. 03/17/2004
Jinshan Gold Mines Inc. name changed to China Gold International Resources Corp. Ltd. 07/19/2010

PACIFIC MINES, INC. (AZ)
Charter revoked for failure to file reports and pay fees 11/12/69

PACIFIC MINES & METALS, INC. (NV)
Name changed to Bagdad Chase Consolidated Mines Co. 03/22/1927
Bagdad Chase Consolidated Mines Co. name changed to Roosevelt Mines, Inc. 06/14/1929 which name changed to Bagdad Chase Mining Co. 02/23/1949 which recapitalized as Bagdad Chase, Inc. 05/04/1968
(See Bagdad Chase, Inc.)

PACIFIC MINESEARCH LTD (BC)
Delisted from Vancouver Stock Exchange 04/20/1992

PACIFIC MULTIMEDIA, INC. (WA)
Charter expired 04/30/2007

PACIFIC MULTIMEDIA CORP (NV)
Recapitalized as Qwikcap Corp. 01/04/1999
Each share Class A Common 1¢ par exchanged for (0.01) share Class A Common 1¢ par
Each share Common 1¢ par exchanged for (0.01) share Common 1¢ par
(See Qwikcap Corp.)

PACIFIC MUTUAL LIFE INSURANCE CO. OF CALIFORNIA (CA)
Liquidation completed
Each share Capital Stock $1 par or VTC for Capital Stock $1 par stamped to indicate initial distribution of $2 cash 10/30/62
Each share Stamped Capital Stock $1 par or Stamped VTC for Capital Stock $1 par stamped to indicate second distribution of $10.65 cash 6/14/65
Each share Stamped Capital Stock $1 par or Stamped VTC for Capital Stock $1 par exchanged for third and final distribution of $0.5615 cash 5/17/67

PACIFIC NATIONAL BANK (NEWPORT BEACH, CA)
Under plan of reorganization each share Common $5 par automatically became (1) share PNB Financial Group Common no par 4/29/83
PNB Financial Group merged into Western Bancorp 12/30/98 which merged into U.S. Bancorp (Old) 11/15/99 which merged into U.S. Bancorp (New) 2/27/2001

PACIFIC NATIONAL BANK (SAN FRANCISCO, CA)
Each share Common $100 par exchanged for (5) shares Common $20 par in 1953
Common $20 par changed to Common Capital Stock $10 par and (1) additional share issued 1/13/60
Stock Dividend - 100% 4/2/52
Merged into Security Pacific National Bank (Los Angeles, CA) 7/1/68
Each share Common Capital Stock $10 par exchanged for (1.24422) shares Capital Stock $10 par
Security Pacific National Bank (Los Angeles, CA) reorganized as Security Pacific Corp. 6/30/72 which merged into BankAmerica Corp. (Old) 4/22/92 which merged into BankAmerica Corp. (New) 9/30/98 which name changed to Bank of America Corp. 4/28/99

PACIFIC NATL BK (SEATTLE, WA)
Under plan of merger each share Common $100 par exchanged for (11.666666) shares Common $10 par 2/28/55
Stock Dividends - 20% 1/25/51; 10% 2/2/59; (1) for (6.5) 2/15/65; 10% 1/27/67
Merged into Pacific National Bank of Washington (Seattle, WA) 8/17/70
Each share Common $10 par exchanged for (1.35) shares Western Bancorporation Capital Stock $2 par
Pacific National Bank of Washington (Seattle, WA) merged into Western Bancorporation 1/1/81 which name changed to First Interstate Bancorp 6/1/81 which merged into Wells Fargo & Co. (Old) 4/1/96 which merged into Wells Fargo & Co. (New) 11/2/98

PACIFIC NATL BK WASH (SEATTLE, WA)
Merged into Western Bancorporation 1/1/81
Each share Common $12.50 par exchanged for (2.75) shares Capital Stock $2 par
Western Bancorporation name changed to First Interstate Bancorp 6/1/81 which merged into Wells Fargo & Co. (Old) 4/1/96 which merged into Wells Fargo & Co. (New) 11/2/98

PACIFIC NATIONAL CO. (CA)
Each share Capital Stock $100 par exchanged for (4) shares new Capital Stock $25 par 00/00/1928
Each share Capital Stock $25 par exchanged for (4) shares new Capital Stock $1 par 00/00/1935

Charter suspended for failure to file reports and pay fees 01/05/1944

PACIFIC NATL CORP (MA)
Acquired by BankBoston Corp. 10/31/1997
Each share Common $100 par exchanged for approximately (279) shares Common no par
BankBoston Corp. merged into FleetBoston Corp. 10/01/1999 which name changed to FleetBoston Financial Corp. 04/18/2000 which merged into Bank of America Corp. 04/01/2004

PACIFIC NATL FINL CORP (BC)
Declared bankrupt in July 1995
No stockholders' equity

PACIFIC NATIONAL LIFE ASSURANCE CO. (UT)
Merged into Pacific National Life Assurance Co. (Calif.) on a (0.2634) for (1) basis 11/26/57
Pacific National Life Assurance Co. (Calif.) merged into Republic National Life Insurance Co. 2/5/71
Republic National Life Insurance Co. merged into Gulf United Corp. 4/6/81
(See Gulf United Corp.)

PACIFIC NATL LIFE ASSURN CO (CA)
Capital Stock $100 par changed to $5.30 par 10/14/1959
Merged into Republic National Life Insurance Co. 02/05/1971
Each share Capital Stock $5.30 par exchanged for (2) shares Capital Stock $1 par
Republic National Life Insurance Co. merged into Gulf United Corp. 04/06/1981
(See Gulf United Corp.)

PACIFIC NATL SEAFARMS LTD (BC)
Reorganized under the laws of Delaware as Starbase Corp. 10/21/92
Each share Common no par exchanged for (0.5) share Common 1¢ par
(See Starbase Corp.)

PACIFIC NATL VENTURES INC (NV)
Recapitalized as FirstAmerica Automotive, Inc. 9/6/95
Each share Common $0.001 par exchanged for (0.01) share Common $0.001 par
(See FirstAmerica Automotive, Inc.)

PACIFIC NATURAL GAS CO. (WA)
Merged into Cascade Natural Gas Corp. share for share 08/28/1962
(See Cascade Natural Gas Corp.)

PACIFIC NICKEL MINES LTD. (BC)
Liquidation completed
Each share Capital Stock $1 par received initial distribution of $0.70 cash 11/15/1961
Each share Capital Stock $1 par received second and final distribution of $0.35 cash 03/30/1962
Note: Certificates were not required to be surrendered and are without value

PACIFIC NICKEL MINES LTD (QC)
Charter annulled for failure to file annual reports 03/22/1986

PACIFIC NORTH AMERN INC (UT)
Involuntarily dissolved 03/01/1999

PACIFIC NORTH WEST CAP CORP (BC)
Reincorporated 07/13/2004
Place of incorporation changed from (AB) to (BC) 07/13/2004
Each share old Common no par exchanged for (0.33333333) share new Common no par 01/14/2014
Recapitalized as New Age Metals Inc. 02/01/2017
Each share new Common no par exchanged for (0.33333333) share Common no par

PACIFIC NORTH WEST RES LTD (BC)
Merged into Electra North West Resources Ltd. 12/01/1981
Each share Common no par exchanged for (1) share Common no par
Electra North West Resources Ltd. recapitalized as Electra Mining Consolidated Ltd. 08/21/1992 which name changed to Electra Gold Ltd. 02/07/1997 which name changed to Electra Stone Ltd. 02/02/2015

PACIFIC NORTHERN AIRLINES, INC. (AK)
Merged into Western Air Lines, Inc. 7/1/67
Each share Common $1 par exchanged for (0.5) share Capital Stock $1 par
Western Air Lines, Inc. acquired by Delta Air Lines, Inc. 12/18/86
(See Delta Air Lines, Inc.)

PACIFIC NORTHN GAS LTD (BC)
Non-Vtg. Class A Common $5 par changed to $2.50 par and (1) additional share issued 08/24/1993
Non-Vtg. Class A Common $2.50 par reclassified as Common $2.50 par 12/18/2003
Class B Common $2.50 par reclassified as Common $2.50 par 12/18/2003
Acquired by AltaGas Ltd. 12/20/2011
Each share Common $2.50 par exchanged for $36.75 cash
Note: Unexchanged certificates were cancelled and declared without value 12/20/2017
6.75% Preferred $25 par called for redemption at $26 plus $0.26425 accrued dividends on 02/27/2012
Public interest eliminated

PACIFIC NORTHN OILS & INDS LTD (BC)
Reorganized 04/29/1970
Reorganized from Pacific Northern Oils to Pacific Northern Oils & Industries Ltd. 04/29/1970
Each share Class A no par exchanged for (1) share Common no par
Struck off register and proclaimed dissolved for failure to file returns 09/07/1976

PACIFIC NORTHN VENTURES LTD (BC)
Name changed to Pacific International Hardwoods Inc. 02/25/1994
Pacific International Hardwoods Inc. recapitalized as PIH Pacific International Hardwoods Inc. 11/12/1996
(See PIH Pacific International Hardwoods Inc.)

PACIFIC NORTHWEST BANCORP (WA)
Merged into Wells Fargo & Co. (New) 11/03/2003
Each share Common no par exchanged for (0.6965) share Common $1-2/3 par

PACIFIC NORTHWEST BK (SEATTLE, WA)
Merged into Interwest Bancorp, Inc. 06/15/1998
Each share Common $1 par exchanged for (3.95) shares Common 20¢ par
Interwest Bancorp, Inc. name changed to Pacific Northwest Bancorp 09/01/2000 which merged into Wells Fargo & Co. (New) 11/03/2003

PACIFIC NORTHWEST BELL TEL CO (WA)
Merged into American Telephone & Telegraph Co. 12/22/80

Each share Common $11 par exchanged for (0.395) share Common $16-2/3 par
American Telephone & Telegraph Co. name changed to AT&T Corp. 4/20/94 which merged into AT&T Inc. 11/18/2005

PACIFIC NORTHWEST EQUIP LEASING CORP (BC)
Name changed to Pacific National Financial Corp. 7/23/86
(See Pacific National Financial Corp.)

PACIFIC NORTHWEST GAS & OIL CORP. (WA)
Charter cancelled and declared dissolved for non-payment of fees 7/1/68

PACIFIC NORTHWEST LIFE INS CO (OR)
Certificate of authority cancelled 12/18/1995
Stockholders' equity unlikely

PACIFIC NORTHWEST PARTNERS LTD (BC)
Reincorporated under the laws of Canada as Enablence Technologies Inc. 7/24/2006

PACIFIC NORTHWEST PIPELINE CORP. (DE)
Merged into El Paso Natural Gas Co. 12/31/59
Each share Common $1 par exchanged for (1.75) shares Common $3 par
$3.30 Preferred no par called for redemption 1/30/60
$5.60 Preferred Ser. A no par called for redemption 1/30/60
El Paso Natural Gas Co. reorganized as El Paso Co. 6/13/74 which merged into Burlington Northern Inc. 12/13/83 which name changed to Burlington Northern Santa Fe Corp. 9/22/95

PACIFIC NORTHWEST PRODUCTIONS INC (NV)
Name changed to China Housing & Land Development, Inc. 5/5/2006

PACIFIC NORTHWEST PUBLIC SERVICE CO.
Name changed to Portland Electric Power Co. in 1933
Portland Electric Power Co. reorganized as Portland General Electric Co. in 1948

PACIFIC NUCLEAR SYS INC (WA)
Name changed to Vectra Technologies Inc. 01/07/1994
(See Vectra Technologies Inc.)

PACIFIC NUTRIENT & CHEM CO (WA)
Name changed to Eastern & Pacific Industries Corp. 03/15/1969
(See Eastern & Pacific Industries Corp.)

PACIFIC OIL & GAS DEV CORP (CA)
Each share Capital Stock $1 par exchanged for (3) shares Capital Stock 33-1/3¢ par 00/00/1952
Name changed to Callon Petroleum Co. 11/01/1974
(See Callon Petroleum Co.)

PACIFIC OIL & REFINERY LTD.
Recapitalized as New Pacific Coal & Oils Ltd. 00/00/1950
Each share Capital Stock no par exchanged for (0.25) share Common no par
New Pacific Coal & Oils Ltd. recapitalized as Consolidated New Pacific Ltd. 02/01/1960 which name changed to Conuco Ltd. 12/22/1969 which merged into Brinco Ltd. 12/17/1979 which merged into Consolidated Brinco Ltd. 05/30/1986 which merged into Hillsborough Resources Ltd. (ON) 02/06/1992 which reincorporated in Canada 11/05/1997
(See Hillsborough Resources Ltd. (Canada))

PACIFIC OIL CO. (DE)
Liquidated in 1930

PACIFIC OIL CO (NV)
Each share old Common $0.001 par exchanged for (0.005) share new Common $0.001 par 02/19/2015
Name changed to Financial Gravity Companies, Inc. 01/30/2017

PACIFIC OUTDOOR ADVERTISING CO (CA)
Each share Common no par exchanged for (10) shares Common $5 par 00/00/1958
Common $5 par changed to $2.50 par and (1) additional share issued 02/13/1969
Name changed to Pacific United Services Corp., Inc. (CA) 06/19/1970
Pacific United Services Corp., Inc. (CA) reincorporated in Delaware 01/30/1974 which name changed to Pacific United Services Corp. 03/21/1975 which merged into Combined Communications Corp. 09/24/1975 which merged into Gannett Co., Inc. (Old) 06/07/1979 which name changed to TEGNA Inc. 06/26/2015

PACIFIC PARTNERS REALTY INCOME FUND (WA)
Partnership term expired 07/31/2009
Details not available

PACIFIC PAY TEL INC (DE)
Each share old Common $0.0001 par exchanged for (0.05) share new Common $0.0001 par 3/1/87
Charter cancelled and declared inoperative and void for non-payment of taxes 3/1/93

PACIFIC PEAK INVTS (NV)
Name changed to Global Beverage Solutions, Inc. 10/26/2005
Global Beverage Solutions, Inc. recapitalized as Real Brands, Inc. 10/22/2013

PACIFIC PETES LTD (BC)
Common $1 par changed to no par 06/02/1977
Acquired by Petro-Canada Inc. 04/20/1979
Each share Common no par exchanged for $65.02 cash

PACIFIC PETROLEUM CO. (DE)
Incorporated 07/22/1913
No longer in existence having become inoperative and void for non-payment of taxes 03/22/1916

PACIFIC PETROLEUM CO. (DE)
Incorporated 11/10/1922
No longer in existence having become inoperative and void for non-payment of taxes 04/01/1932

PACIFIC PHARMACEUTICALS INC (DE)
Merged into Procept, Inc. 03/17/1999
Each share Common 20¢ par exchanged for (0.10865) share new Common 1¢ par
Procept, Inc. name changed to HeavenlyDoor.com, Inc. 01/31/2000 which name changed to Paligent Inc. 12/31/2000 which recapitalized as International Fight League, Inc. 11/29/2006 which recapitalized as IFLI Acquisition Corp. 07/08/2010 which name changed to SimplePons, Inc. 12/27/2011 which recapitalized as Eco-Shift Power Corp. 11/26/2013

PACIFIC PHARMACEUTICALS I INC (DE)
Recapitalized as Sunmark Industries I, Inc. 06/27/1994
Each share Common $0.001 par exchanged for (0.25) share Common $0.001 par
Sunmark Industries I, Inc. name changed to Mark I Industries, Inc. 05/14/1998 which name changed to Foodvision.com Inc. 06/00/1999
(See Foodvision.com Inc.)

PACIFIC PHYSICIAN SVCS INC (DE)
Common 1¢ par split (3) for (2) by issuance of (0.5) additional share 7/6/93
Merged into Medpartners/Mullikin Inc. 2/22/96
Each share Common 1¢ par exchanged for (0.62048) share Common 1¢ par
Medpartners/Mullikin Inc. name changed to MedPartners, Inc. (New) 9/5/96 which name changed to CareMark Rx, Inc. 9/13/99 which merged into CVS/Caremark Corp. 3/22/2007 which name changed to CVS Caremark Corp. 5/10/2007

PACIFIC PLANTRONICS INC (CA)
Each share Capital Stock $10 par exchanged for (4) shares Capital Stock $2.50 par 3/1/65
Capital Stock $2.50 par reclassified as Common $2 par 10/17/66
Common $2 par changed to $1 par and (1) additional share issued 4/18/67
Common $1 par split (3) for (2) by issuance of (0.5) additional share 11/21/71
Name changed to Plantronics, Inc. (CA) (New) 12/1/72
Plantronics, Inc. (CA) (New) reincorporated in Delaware 6/11/87
(See Plantronics, Inc. (DE))

PACIFIC PORTLAND CEMENT CO. (CA)
Common $100 par changed to $10 par in 1939
Stock Dividends - 400% 1/16/50; 25% 12/20/50
Merged into Ideal Cement Co. in 1953
Each share Common $10 par exchanged for (0.5) share Capital Stock $10 par
Ideal Cement Co. merged into Ideal Basic Industries, Inc. (CO) 12/31/67 which reincorporated in Delaware 5/15/87 which merged into Holnam Inc. 3/8/90
(See Holnam Inc.)

PACIFIC PORTLAND CEMENT CONSOLIDATED
Merged into Pacific Portland Cement Co. 00/00/1927
Details not available

PACIFIC POTASH CORP (BC)
Each share old Common no par exchanged for (0.1) share new Common no par 09/14/2015
Name changed to Pacific Silk Road Resources Group Inc. 06/08/2018

PACIFIC PWR & LT CO (ME)
Each share 7% Preferred $100 par exchanged for (1) share 5% Preferred $100 par and $5 cash 00/00/1947
Each share $6 Preferred no par exchanged for (1) share 5% Preferred $100 par 00/00/1947
Each share old Common no par exchanged for (3.5) shares new Common no par 00/00/1950
New Common no par changed to $6.50 par 00/00/1954
Common $6.50 par changed to $3.25 par and (1) additional share issued 02/26/1962
6.16% Preferred $100 par called for redemption 09/06/1963
5.64% Preferred $100 par called for redemption 03/05/1965
Name changed to PacifiCorp (ME) 06/15/1984
PacifiCorp (ME) reincorporated in Oregon 01/01/1989

PACIFIC POWER & WATER CO. LTD.
Acquired by West Canadian Hydro Electric Corp. 00/00/1942
Preferred exchanged par for par for Debentures
Common exchanged (1) for (2)
(See West Canadian Hydro Electric Corp.)

PACIFIC PWR GROUP INC (NV)
Each share old Common $0.001 par exchanged for (1/3) share new Common $0.001 par 03/14/1996
Name changed to LP Holdings, Inc. 12/20/2005
LP Holdings, Inc. name changed to Tanke, Inc. 10/17/2007

PACIFIC PUBLIC SERVICE CO. (CA)
Recapitalized in 1931
Each share Class A Common no par exchanged for (1) share 1st Preferred no par and (0.5) share Non-Voting Common no par
Each share Class B Common no par exchanged for (1) share 2nd Preferred no par and (245/300) share new Common no par
Recapitalized in 1938
Voting and Non-Voting Common no par exchanged for new Common no par
Merged into Pacific Gas & Electric Co. in 1954
Each share Preferred no par exchanged for (0.7) share Common $25 par
Each share Common no par exchanged for (0.53) share Common $25 par

PACIFIC RANGER PETE INC (AB)
Reorganized under the laws of Canada as In-Touch Survey Systems Ltd. 02/04/2002
Each share Common no par exchanged for (0.1) share Common no par
In-Touch Survey Systems Ltd. name changed to Intouch Insight Ltd. 07/15/2016

PACIFIC REALM INC (DE)
Common $0.0001 par changed to $0.00008 par and (0.25) additional share issued 07/16/1984
Each share old Common $0.00008 par exchanged for (0.05) share new Common $0.00008 par 11/04/2002
Each share new Common $0.00008 par exchanged again for (3) shares new Common $0.00008 par 01/10/2003
Common $0.00008 par split (2) for (1) by issuance of (1) additional share payable 09/19/2003 to holders of record 09/12/2003 Ex date - 09/22/2003
Name changed to aeroTelesis, Inc. 10/22/2003
(See aeroTelesis, Inc.)

PACIFIC RLTY TR (OR)
Shares of Bene. Int. $1 par reclassified as Common Shares of Bene. Int. $1 par 10/26/81
Merged into PRT Holdings Co. 2/17/83
Each Common Share of Bene. Int. $1 par exchanged for $38.50 cash

PACIFIC REFINERS LTD. (HI)
Liquidation completed 2/28/62

PACIFIC REGENCY BANCORP (CA)
Charter cancelled for failure to file reports and pay taxes 12/01/1989

PACIFIC REHABILITATION & SPORTS MEDICINE INC (DE)
Merged into Horizon/CMS Healthcare Corp. 12/30/1996
Each share Common 1¢ par exchanged for $6.50 cash

PACIFIC RESH & ENGR CORP (CA)
Merged into Harris Corp. 10/5/99
Each share Common no par exchanged for $2.35 cash

PACIFIC RES DEV LTD (BC)
Recapitalized as Nu Pacific Resources Ltd. 04/04/1984
Each share Capital Stock no par exchanged for (0.2) share Common no par
Nu Pacific Resources Ltd. recapitalized as Iron Lady Resources Inc. 03/11/1988 which recapitalized as Takepoint Ventures Ltd. (BC) 08/03/1994 which reorganized in Yukon as Consolidated Takepoint Ventures Ltd. 06/25/2002 which name changed to Lake Shore Gold Corp. (YT) 12/18/2002 which reincorporated in British Columbia 06/30/2004 which reincorporated in Canada 07/18/2008 which merged into Tahoe Resources Inc. 04/07/2016

PACIFIC RES INC (DE)
Charter cancelled and declared inoperative and void for non-payment of taxes 03/01/2002

PACIFIC RES INC (HI)
Common $6-2/3 par changed to no par and (1) additional share issued 09/15/1971
Common no par split (3) for (2) by issuance of (0.5) additional share 06/27/1980
Conv. Depositary Preferred no par called for redemption 08/15/1986
$10 Conv. Exchangeable Preferred no par called for redemption 04/24/1989
Conv. Exchangeable Depositary Preferred no par called for redemption 04/24/1989
Stock Dividends - 10% 01/16/1978; 10% 12/08/1978; 10% 10/15/1979; 10% 12/31/1981
Merged into Broken Hill Proprietary Co. Ltd. 05/11/1989
Each share Common no par exchanged for $19 cash

PACIFIC RES INC (NV)
Name changed to Comstock Gold, Silver & Copper Mines, Inc. 10/26/73
(See Comstock Gold, Silver & Copper Mines, Inc.)

PACIFIC RESTAURANT HLDGS INC (DE)
Chapter 7 bankruptcy proceedings terminated 12/22/2009
No stockholders' equity

PACIFIC RETAIL TR (MD)
Merged into Regency Realty Corp. 02/28/1999
Each share Common 1¢ par exchanged for (0.48) share Common 1¢ par
Regency Realty Corp. name changed to Regency Centers Corp. 02/12/2001

PACIFIC RIDGE RES CORP (BC)
Recapitalized as Ecos Resources Ltd. 10/04/1988
Each share Common no par exchanged for (0.29411764) share Common no par
(See Ecos Resources Ltd.)

PACIFIC RIM CONTAINER SALES LTD (BC)
Struck off register and declared dissolved for failure to file returns 4/23/93

PACIFIC RIM ENERGY CORP (BC)
Recapitalized as North Pacific Industries Corp. 2/27/87
Each share Common no par exchanged for (1/6) share Common no par
(See North Pacific Industries Corp.)

PACIFIC RIM ENTMT INC (DE)
Each share old Common 1¢ par exchanged for (0.04) share new Common 1¢ par 3/27/95

Each share new Common 1¢ par exchanged again for (0.1) share new Common 1¢ par 2/22/96
Name changed to Osage Systems Group, Inc. 3/10/98
(See Osage Systems Group, Inc.)

PACIFIC RIM MNG CORP (BC)
Each share old Common no par exchanged for (1) share new Common no par 04/10/2002
Merged into OceanaGold Corp. 12/02/2013
Each share Common no par exchanged for (0.04006) share Common no par

PACIFIC RODERA ENERGY INC (AB)
Name changed 06/22/2004
Reincorporated 06/14/2006
Name changed from Pacific Rodera Ventures Inc. to Pacific Rodera Energy Inc. 06/22/2004
Place of incorporation changed from (BC) to (AB) 06/14/2006
Name changed to PRD Energy Inc. 08/12/2010

PACIFIC ROYAL VENTURES LTD (BC)
Merged into Pacific Rodera Ventures Inc. 03/01/1999
Each share Common no par exchanged for (0.2) share Common no par
Pacific Rodera Ventures Inc. name changed to Pacific Rodera Energy Inc. (BC) 06/22/2004 which reincorporated in Alberta 06/14/2006 which name changed to PRD Energy Inc. 08/12/2010

PACIFIC RUBBER & TIRE MANUFACTURING CO.
Succeeded by Pacific Rubber Co. in 1946
Details not available

PACIFIC RUBBER CO. (CA)
Name changed to Oakland Rubber Co. in 1948, which completed dissolution 4/18/60

PACIFIC RUBIALES ENERGY CORP (BC)
Each share old Common no par exchanged for (0.16666666) share new Common no par 05/09/2008
Name changed to Pacific Exploration & Production Corp. 08/18/2015
Pacific Exploration & Production Corp. name changed to Frontera Energy Corp. 06/14/2017

PACIFIC SAFETY EQUIPMENT CO., INC.
Name changed to Sentinel of Safety, Inc. in 1952

PACIFIC SAFETY PRODS INC (BC)
Reincorporated 12/31/2010
Place of incorporation changed from (BC) to (Canada) 12/31/2010
Acquired by Med-Eng Holdings ULC 12/23/2016
Each share Common no par exchanged for $0.21 cash
Note: Unexchanged certificates will be cancelled and become without value 12/23/2021

PACIFIC SAPPHIRE CO LTD (BC)
Recapitalized as Radiant Resources Inc. 01/30/2003
Each share Common no par exchanged for (0.25) share Common no par
Radiant Resources Inc. merged into Tiomin Resources Inc. 09/26/2008 which recapitalized as Vaaldiam Mining Inc. 03/26/2010
(See Vaaldiam Mining Inc.)

PACIFIC SVGS & LN ASSN (CA)
Guarantee Stock 18¢ par split (3) for (2) by issuance of (0.5) additional share 06/08/1972
Merged into California Federal Savings & Loan Association 01/02/1975

Each share Guarantee Stock 18¢ par exchanged for a regular passbook savings account in the amount of $29.13 cash

PACIFIC SAVINGS & LOAN ASSOCIATION (HI)
Completely liquidated 12/23/77
Each share Guarantee Stock $1 par exchanged for first and final distribution of $7.72 cash

PACIFIC SCIENTIFIC CO (CA)
10% Preferred Ser. B $1 par called for redemption 03/31/1992
Merged into Danaher Corp. 03/31/1998
Each share Common $1 par exchanged for $30.25 cash

PACIFIC SEABOARD FOUNDATION
Dissolved 00/00/1935
Details not available

PACIFIC SEADRIFT RES LTD (AB)
Reincorporated 6/3/82
Place of incorporation changed from (BC) to (ALTA) 6/3/82
Recapitalized as Seadrift International Exploration Ltd. 6/1/85
Each share Common no par exchanged for (1/3) share Common no par
Seadrift International Exploration Ltd. merged into Deak International Resources Corp. 12/30/88 which name changed to Deak Resources Corp. 3/27/89 which name changed to AJ Perron Gold Corp. 10/7/94
(See AJ Perron Gold Corp.)

PACIFIC SENTINEL GOLD CORP (BC)
Common no par split (2) for (1) by issuance of (1) additional share 05/25/1988
Recapitalized as Great Basin Gold Ltd. 12/18/1997
Each share Common no par exchanged for (0.2) share Common no par
(See Great Basin Gold Ltd.)

PACIFIC SILVER CORP (HI)
Merged into Alta Gold Co. 11/24/1989
Each share Common 25¢ par exchanged for (0.667) share Common $0.001 par
(See Alta Gold Co.)

PACIFIC SILVER MINES & OILS LTD (AB)
Struck off register for failure to file annual returns 04/15/1978

PACIFIC SNAX CORP (NV)
Charter revoked for failure to file reports and pay fees 10/1/96

PACIFIC SOFTWORKS INC (CA)
Name changed to PASW, Inc. (CA) 06/09/2000
PASW, Inc. (CA) reincorporated in Delaware 05/30/2007 which recapitalized as VirnetX Holding Corp. 10/30/2007

PACIFIC SOUTHEAST CORP (NV)
Name changed to Cellular Group Inc. 11/10/92

PACIFIC SOUTHERN INVESTORS, INC. (DE)
Merged into Pacific-American Investors, Inc. (DE) 08/27/1943
Each share old Preferred exchanged for (2) shares new Preferred $5 par, (0.5) share Common 10¢ par and 90¢ in cash
Each share Class A Common exchanged for (3.5) shares Common 10¢ par
Each share Class B Common exchanged for (0.2) share Common 10¢ par
Pacific-American Investors, Inc. (DE) merged into American Mutual Fund, Inc. (DE) 02/01/1956 which reincorporated in Maryland 09/20/1983 which reincorporated in

Delaware as American Mutual Fund 01/01/2011

PACIFIC SOUTHN MTG TR (CA)
Acquired by Old Stone Corp. 06/30/1982
Each (1.8) Shares of Bene. Int. $1 par exchanged for (1) share $2.60 Conv. Preferred Ser. C $1 par
Note: An additional distribution of approximately (0.137) share $2.60 Conv. Preferred Ser. C $1 par and $0.65 cash per share issued in above acquisition was made in 07/00/1985
(See Old Stone Corp.)

PACIFIC SOUTHWEST AIRLS (CA)
Ctfs. dated prior to 02/28/1973
Common no par split (7) for (5) by issuance of (0.4) additional share 02/17/1964
Common no par split (3) for (2) by issuance of (0.5) additional share 09/01/1966
Common no par split (3) for (2) by issuance of (0.5) additional share 07/11/1967
Under plan of reorganization each share Common no par automatically became (1) share PSA, Inc. Common $1 par 02/28/1973
PSA, Inc. name changed to PS Group, Inc. 11/19/1986 which recapitalized as PS Group Holdings, Inc. 06/05/1996
(See PS Group Holdings, Inc.)

PACIFIC SOUTHWEST AIRLS NEW (CA)
Ctfs. dated after 7/24/86
Merged into USAir Group, Inc. 5/29/87
Each share Common 25¢ par exchanged for $17 cash

PACIFIC SOUTHWEST CORP (NV)
Common 2¢ par split (5) for (4) by issuance of (0.25) additional share 2/28/90
Stock Dividend - 10% 10/31/90
Charter revoked for failure to file reports and pay taxes 2/1/2002

PACIFIC SOUTHWEST LIFE INSURANCE CO. (AZ)
Reorganized as Pacific American Life Insurance Co. on a (0.25) for (1) basis 10/14/64
Pacific American Life Insurance Co. reorganized as Pacific American Corp. (NV) 5/9/69
(See Pacific American Corp. (NV))

PACIFIC SPECIAL ACQUISITION CORP (BRITISH VIRGIN ISLANDS)
Units separated 08/21/2017
Name changed to Borqs Technologies, Inc. 08/21/2017

PACIFIC SPORTS HLDGS INC (NV)
Recapitalized as Tahoe Pacific Corp. 08/30/1999
Each share Common $0.001 par exchanged for (0.2) share Common $0.001 par
Tahoe Pacific Corp. name changed to Ameri-First Financial Group, Inc. (NV) 01/06/2000 which reincorporated in Delaware 03/22/2000 which reincorporated in Nevada as Eight Dragons Co. 12/07/2007 which name changed to Rokk3r Inc. 06/18/2018

PACIFIC ST BK (REEDSPORT, OR)
Merged into Security Bank Holding Co. 11/21/97
Each share Common no par exchanged for (3.1) shares Common $5 par
Security Bank Holding Co. name changed to Independent Financial Network Inc. 5/15/2000 which merged into Umpqua Holdings Corp. 12/31/2001

PACIFIC ST BK (STOCKTON, CA)
Under plan of reorganization each

share Common no par automatically became (1) share Pacific State Bancorp Common no par 6/24/2002

PACIFIC STANDARD LIFE CO. (AZ)
Reincorporated under the laws of Delaware 05/13/1974
Pacific Standard Life Co. (DE) merged into Southmark Corp. 08/30/1983

PACIFIC STAR RES CORP (AB)
Issue Information - 2,000,000 shares COM offered at $0.10 per share on 08/21/1997
Name changed to Virtual China Travel Services Co., Ltd. (AB) 09/05/2002
Virtual China Travel Services Co., Ltd. (AB) reorganized in British Columbia as Melco China Resorts (Holding) Ltd. 05/27/2008 which name changed to Mountain China Resorts (Holding) Ltd. 10/22/2010

PACIFIC STAR TECHNOLOGY CORP (DE)
Recapitalized as C F Green Corp. 12/15/2003
Each share Common $0.001 par exchanged for (0.25) share Common $0.001 par
C F Green Corp. name changed to Eco-Safe Systems USA, Inc. 11/13/2006

PACIFIC STATE BANK (HAWTHORNE, CA)
Stock Dividends - 10% 12/14/62; 10% 1/20/65
Merged into United States National Bank (San Diego, CA) 7/30/65
Each share Capital Stock $3 par exchanged for (0.4552) share Capital Stock $10 par

PACIFIC STATES FIRE & INDEMNITY INSURANCE CO.
Merged into Western Pacific Insurance Co. and each share Capital Stock $100 par exchanged for (9) new shares Capital Stock $10 par in 1952
(See Western Pacific Insurance Co.)

PACIFIC STATES LUMBER CO.
Reorganized as Coos Bay Lumber Co. in 1928
(See Coos Bay Lumber Co.)

PACIFIC STATES REALTY IMPROVEMENT CO. LTD.
Dissolved in 1929

PACIFIC STD FD INC (MD)
Merged into Empire Fund, Inc. 04/28/1975
Each share Capital Stock $1 par exchanged for (0.793755) share Capital Stock $1 par
Empire Fund, Inc. merged into American Leaders Fund, Inc. 04/09/1979 which name changed to Federated American Leaders Fund Inc. 03/31/1996 which reorganized as Federated Equity Funds 09/18/2009

PACIFIC STD LIFE CO (DE)
Merged into Southmark Corp. 08/30/1983
Each share Common $1 par exchanged for (0.511999) share Conv. Preferred Ser. A $2 par
Note: An additional escrow distribution of (0.1089) share Common $1 par or $0.97 cash per share was made 07/30/1984
(See Southmark Corp.)

PACIFIC STD LIFE INS CO (AZ)
Under plan of reorganization each share Common $1 par automatically became (1) share Pacific Standard Life Co. (DE) Common $1 par 07/01/1969
Pacific Standard Life Co. (DE) merged into Southmark Corp. 08/30/1983
(See Southmark Corp.)

PACIFIC STD LIFE INS CO TEX (TX)
98.1% held by Pacific Standard Life Insurance Co. as of 01/01/1975
Public interest eliminated

PACIFIC STEAMSHIP CO.
Reorganized as Pacific Steamship Lines Ltd. in 1932 which became bankrupt in 1939

PACIFIC STEAMSHIP LINES LTD.
Bankrupt in 1939

PACIFIC STEEL BOILER CORP.
Acquired by United States Radiator Corp. 00/00/1928
Details not available

PACIFIC STORES INC. (DE)
Charter cancelled and declared inoperative and void for non-payment of taxes 4/1/29

PACIFIC STRATUS ENERGY LTD (BC)
Each share old Common no par exchanged for (0.1) share new Common no par 05/26/2006
Merged into Pacific Rubiales Energy Corp. 01/23/2008
Each share Common no par exchanged for (9.5) shares Common no par
Pacific Rubiales Energy Corp. name changed to Pacific Exploration & Production Corp. 08/18/2015 which name changed to Frontera Energy Corp. 06/14/2017

PACIFIC STRATUS VENTURES LTD (BC)
Name changed to Pacific Stratus Energy Ltd. 06/14/2005
Each share new Common no par exchanged for (1) share Common no par
Pacific Stratus Energy Ltd. merged into Pacific Rubiales Energy Corp. 01/23/2008 which name changed to Pacific Exploration & Production Corp. 08/18/2015 which name changed to Frontera Energy Corp. 06/14/2017

PACIFIC SUGAR MILL
Merged into Honokaa Sugar Co. in 1928
(See Honokaa Sugar Co.)

PACIFIC SULPHUR CORP. (DE)
No longer in existence having become inoperative and void for non-payment of taxes 4/1/57

PACIFIC SUMMA ENVIRONMENTAL CORP (BC)
Name changed 10/22/1991
Name changed from Pacific Summa Capital Corp. to Pacific Summa Environmental Corp. 10/22/1991
Recapitalized as Truax Ventures Corp. 08/09/2000
Each (30) shares Common no par exchanged for (1) share Common no par
Truax Ventures Corp. recapitalized as Aries Resource Corp. 09/02/2004 which recapitalized as Alderon Resource Corp. 09/24/2008 which name changed to Alderon Iron Ore Corp. 10/05/2011

PACIFIC SUN RESOURCE CORP (BC)
Name changed to Masterpiece Quality Products, Inc. 8/16/93
Masterpiece Quality Products, Inc. recapitalized as Aruma Ventures, Inc. 3/21/97 which recapitalized as Dot.Com Technologies Inc. 9/7/99 which recapitalized as BCS Collaborative Solutions Inc. 7/12/2002 which recapitalized as BCS Global Networks Inc. 9/2/2003
(See BCS Global Networks Inc.)

PACIFIC SUNSET INVTS INC (MN)
Name changed to Gen-ID Lab Services, Inc. 10/10/2005
Gen-ID Lab Services, Inc.

recapitalized as Adventura Corp. 11/01/2009

PACIFIC SUNWEAR CALIF INC (CA)
Common 1¢ par split (3) for (2) by issuance of (0.5) additional share payable 10/18/1996 to holders of record 10/09/1996
Common 1¢ par split (3) for (2) by issuance of (0.5) additional share payable 10/17/1997 to holders of record 10/09/1997
Common 1¢ par split (3) for (2) by issuance of (0.5) additional share payable 06/19/1998 to holders of record 06/08/1998
Common 1¢ par split (3) for (2) by issuance of (0.5) additional share payable 06/18/1999 to holders of record 06/08/1999
Common 1¢ par split (3) for (2) by issuance of (0.5) additional share payable 12/30/2002 to holders of record 12/18/2002 Ex date - 12/31/2002
Common 1¢ par split (3) for (2) by issuance of (0.5) additional share payable 09/05/2003 to holders of record 08/25/2003 Ex date - 09/08/2003
Plan of reorganization under Chapter 11 Federal Bankrutpcy proceedings effective 09/07/2016
No stockholders' equity

PACIFIC SYNDICATED RES INC (NV)
Name changed to Znomics, Inc. 01/04/2008
Znomics, Inc. name changed to Williston Holding Co., Inc. 11/27/2013

PACIFIC SYNDICATION INC (DE)
Recapitalized as Pacific Alliance Corp. 06/08/1997
Each share Common exchanged for (0.16666666) share Common $0.001 par
(See Pacific Alliance Corp.)

PACIFIC SYS CTL TECHNOLOGY INC (DE)
Each share Common $0.0001 par received distribution of (0.05882352) share PeopleNet International Corp. Common $0.0001 par payable 02/07/2002 to holders of record 01/16/2002
SEC revoked common stock registration 01/09/2006

PACIFIC TALC LTD (BC)
Recapitalized as Columbia Copper Co. Ltd. (BC) 11/12/1998
Each share Common no par exchanged for (0.25) share Common no par
Columbia Copper Co. Ltd. (BC) reincorporated in Yukon as Kodiak Oil & Gas Corp. 09/28/2001 which merged into Whiting Petroleum Corp. 12/08/2014

PACIFIC TEL & TELEG CO (CA)
Common $100 par changed to $14-2/7 par and (6) additional shares issued 9/1/59
Merged into American Telephone & Telegraph Co. 5/12/82
Each share Preferred $100 par exchanged for $60 cash
Each share Common $14-2/7 par exchanged for (0.35) share Common $16-2/3 par
American Telephone & Telegraph Co. name changed to AT&T Corp. 4/20/94 which merged into AT&T Inc. 11/18/2005

PACIFIC TELCOM INC (IL)
Stock Dividend - 20% payable 02/01/2001 to holders of record 12/31/2000 Ex date - 02/26/2001
Proclaimed dissolved for failure to pay taxes and file reports 10/01/2004

PACIFIC TELECOIN CORP. (DE)
Declared inoperative and void for non-payment of taxes 4/1/56

PACIFIC TELECOM INC (WA)
Common $1 par split (2) for (1) by issuance of (1) additional share 1/5/83
Merged into Pacificorp Holdings Corp. 9/27/95
Each share Preferred $25 par exchanged for $30 cash
Each share Common $1 par exchanged for $30 cash

PACIFIC TELESIS FING I (DE)
7.56% Trust Originated Preferred Securities called for redemption at $25 on 2/15/2001

PACIFIC TELESIS FING II (DE)
8.50% Trust Originated Preferred Securities called for redemption 6/18/2001 at $25 plus $0.46 accrued dividends

PACIFIC TELESIS GROUP (NV)
Common 10¢ par split (2) for (1) by issuance of (1) additional share 6/9/86
Common 10¢ par split (2) for (1) by issuance of (1) additional share 3/24/87
Merged into SBC Communications, Inc. 4/1/97
Each share Common 10¢ par exchanged for (0.73145) share Common $1 par
SBC Communications, Inc. name changed to AT&T Inc. 11/18/2005

PACIFIC THERAPEUTICS LTD (BC)
Each share old Class A Common no par exchanged for (0.03333333) share new Class A Common no par 03/11/2016
Name changed to Tower One Wireless Corp. 01/26/2017

PACIFIC TIGER ENERGY INC (QC)
Recapitalized as Tiger Petroleum Inc. 12/30/2004
Each share Common no par exchanged for (0.33333333) share Common no par
(See Tiger Petroleum Inc.)

PACIFIC TIN CONS CORP (DE)
Reincorporated 4/23/86
State of incorporation changed from (ME) to (DE) 4/23/86
Name changed to Zemex Corp. (DE) 6/13/86
Zemex Corp. (DE) reincorporated in Canada 1/21/99
(See Zemex Corp. (Canada))

PACIFIC TIN CORP.
Merged into Pacific Tin Consolidated Corp. (ME) in 1939
Each share Capital Stock $1 par exchanged for (4.6) shares Special Stock no par
Pacific Tin Consolidated Corp. (ME) reincorporated in Delaware 4/23/86 which name changed to Zemex Corp. (DE) 6/13/86 which reincorporated under the laws of Canada 1/21/99
(See Zemex Corp. (Canada))

PACIFIC TITAN RESOURCE CORP (BC)
Struck off register and declared disssolved for failure to file returns 4/8/94

PACIFIC TOPAZ RES LTD (BC)
Each share old Common no par exchanged for (0.2) share new Common no par 11/28/2012
Each share new Common no par exchanged again for (0.5) share new Common no par 02/27/2014
Recapitalized as Western Atlas Resources Inc. 06/20/2018
Each share new Common no par exchanged for (0.5) share Common no par

PACIFIC TRADING POST COM INC (NV)
Recapitalized as IDC Technologies Inc. 11/23/2001
Each share Common $0.001 par exchanged for (0.1) share Common $0.001 par
IDC Technologies Inc. name changed to Jill Kelly Productions Holding, Inc. 08/20/2003 which name changed to eWorldCompanies, Inc. 03/13/2007

PACIFIC TRANS OCEAN RES LTD (AB)
Recapitalized as Northern Minerals Ltd. 08/30/1989
Each share Common no par exchanged for (0.2) share Common no par
Northern Minerals Ltd. merged into Capilano International Inc. 02/11/1991 which name changed to Kelman Technologies Inc. 08/14/1996
(See Kelman Technologies Inc.)

PACIFIC TRUCK SERVICE, INC. (CA)
Dissolved in December 1967

PACIFIC TRUST CO. (NEW YORK, NY)
Liquidation completed
Each share Capital Stock $100 par exchanged for first and final distribution of (1/80,000) Ctf. of Bene. Int. no par and $191.50 cash 6/30/30
Each (1/80,000) Ctf. of Bene. Int. no par exchanged for initial distribution of $0.40 cash 2/27/36
Each (1/80,000) Ctf. of Bene. Int. no par received second and final distribution of $0.008129 cash 8/25/36

PACIFIC UN BK (LOS ANGELES, CA)
Stock Dividends - 10% payable 06/15/2001 to holders of record 05/21/2001; 12% payable 05/15/2002 to holders of record 04/19/2002 Ex date - 04/17/2002
Merged into Hanmi Financial Corp. 04/30/2004
Each share Common no par exchanged for (1.156) shares Common $0.001 par

PACIFIC UNICORN RES LTD (BC)
Recapitalized as Biopac Industries Inc. 08/21/1992
Each share Common no par exchanged for (1/6) share Common no par
Biopac Industries Inc. recapitalized as BPI Industries Inc. 01/18/1995 which name changed to BPI Energy Holdings, Inc. 02/09/2006
(See BPI Energy Holdings, Inc.)

PACIFIC UNION BANK & TRUST CO. (MENLO PARK, CA)
Name changed to Franklin Bank (San Mateo, CA) 11/9/87

PACIFIC UNION GAS CO. (DE)
Acquired by Texas American Oil Corp. 09/27/1967
Each share Common $1 par exchanged for (0.2) share Common 10¢ par
Texas American Oil Corp. reorganized as Texas American Energy Corp. 06/13/1980 which name changed to Kent Financial Services, Inc. (DE) 07/27/1990 which reincorporated in Nevada 12/15/2006
(See Kent Financial Services, Inc.)

PACIFIC UTD SVCS CORP (DE)
Reincorporated 01/30/1974
Name changed 03/21/1975
State of incorporation changed from (CA) to (DE) 01/30/1974
Name changed from Pacific United Services Corp., Inc. to Pacific United Services Corp. 03/21/1975
Merged into Combined Communications Corp. 09/24/1975

Each share Common $2.50 par exchanged for (2) shares Common no par and $10.42 cash
Combined Communications Corp. merged into Gannett Co., Inc. (Old) 06/07/1979 which name changed to TEGNA Inc. 06/26/2015

PACIFIC URANIUM & OIL CORP. (DE)
Charter cancelled and declared inoperative and void for non-payment of taxes 4/1/58

PACIFIC URANIUM MINES CO. (NV)
Merged into Kerr-McGee Oil Industries, Inc. on a (0.05) for (1) basis 12/30/60
Kerr-McGee Oil Industries, Inc. name changed to Kerr-McGee Corp. 11/1/65

PACIFIC VY BK (SAN JOSE, CA)
Reorganized as Pacific Western Bancshares (CA) 03/06/1981
Each share Capital Stock $6.75 par exchanged for (2) shares Common no par
Pacific Western Bancshares (CA) reincorporated in Delaware as Pacific Western Bancshares, Inc. 06/30/1989 which merged into Comerica, Inc. 03/30/1994

PACIFIC VANGOLD MINES LTD (BC)
Recapitalized as Paccom Ventures Inc. 04/18/2000
Each share Common no par exchanged for (0.1) share Common no par
Paccom Ventures Inc. name changed to Vangold Resources Ltd. 08/29/2003 which name changed to Vangold Mining Corp. 05/10/2017

PACIFIC VECTOR HLDGS INC (CANADA)
Ceased operations 07/16/2014
Stockholders' equity unlikely

PACIFIC VEGAS GLOBAL STRATEGIES INC (BC)
Reorganized under the laws of Canada as Cathay Forest Products Corp. 09/30/2004
Each share Common no par exchanged for (0.2) share Common no par
(See Cathay Forest Products Corp.)

PACIFIC VEGETABLE OIL CORP (CA)
Capital Stock $10 par changed to $5 par and (1) additional share issued 12/11/1959
Stock Dividends - 10% 11/26/1951; 10% 11/24/1952; 10% 01/25/1954; 10% 01/21/1957; 10% 04/07/1958; 10% 09/07/1959
Name changed to PVO International Inc. 04/05/1972
(See PVO International Inc.)

PACIFIC VENDING TECHNOLOGY LTD (BC)
Name changed to Nelson Vending Technology Ltd. (BC) 7/10/87
Nelson Vending Technology Ltd. (BC) reincorporated in Canada 7/23/87 which was acquired by Cinram Ltd. 7/31/93 which name changed to Cinram International Inc. 6/12/97 which reorganized as Cinram International Income Fund 5/8/2006

PACIFIC VENTURES INC (AB)
Name changed to Weda Bay Minerals Inc. 6/19/96
(See Weda Bay Minerals Inc.)

PACIFIC VIDEO CDA LTD (BC)
Reorganized as Command Post & Transfer Corp. (BC) 05/01/1999
Each share Common no par exchanged for (1) share Common no par
Command Post & Transfer Corp. (BC) reincorporated in Ontario 06/24/1999
(See Command Post & Transfer Corp. (ONT))

PACIFIC VIDEO INDS INC (NV)
Charter revoked for failure to file reports and pay fees 04/01/1983

PACIFIC VIKING RES INC (BC)
Name changed to International Viking Resources Inc. 02/18/1988
International Viking Resources Inc. recapitalized as Saxony Explorations Ltd. (BC) 11/13/1992 which reorganized in Yukon as Century Mining Corp. 09/24/2003 which reincorporated in Canada 07/22/2004 which merged into White Tiger Gold Ltd. 10/20/2011 which name changed to Mangazeya Mining Ltd. 09/23/2013

PACIFIC VISION GROUP INC (NV)
SEC revoked common stock registration 10/20/2005

PACIFIC VISTA INDS INC (YUKON)
Reincorporated 5/27/93
Place of incorporation changed from (BC) to (Yukon) 5/27/93
Delisted from Vancouver Stock Exchange 3/15/99

PACIFIC VITAMIN CORP (CA)
Liquidation completed
Each share Common 10¢ par received initial distribution of $1.19 cash 05/15/1978
Each share Common 10¢ par exchanged for second and final distribution of $0.08425 cash 08/24/1978

PACIFIC WASTE MGMT INC (NV)
Charter revoked for failure to file reports and pay fees 05/31/2002

PACIFIC WEBWORKS INC (NV)
Each share old Common $0.001 par exchanged for (0.00215517) share new Common $0.001 par 04/12/2018
Name changed to Heyu Biological Technology Corp. 06/28/2018

PACIFIC WEST FUND (WA)
Name changed to Pacific West Realty Trust 6/29/71
Pacific West Realty Trust name changed to Asiamerica Equities Ltd. 3/10/86 which name changed to Mercer International Inc. 1/1/92

PACIFIC WEST RLTY TR (WA)
Shares of Bene. Int. $10 par changed to $1 par 09/13/1973
Name changed to Asiamerica Equities Ltd. and Shares of Bene. Int. $1 par reclassified as Common $1 par 03/10/1986
Asiamerica Equities Ltd. name changed to Mercer International Inc. 01/01/1992

PACIFIC WESTERN BREWING CO. LTD. (CANADA)
Merged into International Potter Distilling Corp. 12/31/86
Each share Common no par exchanged for (2.41) shares Common no par
International Potter Distilling Corp. name changed to Cascadia Brands Inc. 3/30/95
(See Cascadia Brands Inc.)

PACIFIC WESTERN INVESTMENT CO. LTD.
Acquired by West Canadian Hydro Electric Corp. in 1942
Each share Preferred exchanged for (1) share Common
Each (10) shares Common exchanged for (1) share new Common
(See West Canadian Hydro Electric Corp.)

PACIFIC WESTERN LIFE INSURANCE CO. (WY)
Reorganized as Pacific Western Corp. 12/31/69
Each share Common $1 par

exchanged for (1) share Common 10¢ par
(See Pacific Western Corp.)

PACIFIC WESTERN OIL CORP. (DE)
Capital Stock no par changed to $10 par in 1937
Capital Stock $10 par redesignated as Common $10 par and (1) share 4% Preferred $10 par distributed as a stock dividend in 1950
Common $10 par changed to $4 par and (2) additional shares issued in 1951
Stock Dividends - 10% 3/15/51; 10% 5/12/53
Name changed to Getty Oil Co. 4/25/56
(See Getty Oil Co.)

PACIFIC WESTN AIRLS CORP (AB)
Name changed to PWA Corp. 5/14/87
PWA Corp. recapitalized as Canadian Airlines Corp. 5/11/95
(See Canadian Airlines Corp.)

PACIFIC WESTN AIRLS LTD (BC)
Common no par split (2) for (1) by issuance of (1) additional share 12/18/1972
99.9% acquired through purchase offer as of 01/06/1984
Through purchase offer 100% of 6% 1st Preferred $10 par, 6% 2nd Preferred $10 par and $2.20 Redm. Preferred Ser. A no par acquired by the Province of Alberta as of 08/05/1975
Public interest eliminated

PACIFIC WESTN BANCSHARES (DE)
Reincorporated 06/30/1989
Stock Dividend - 10% 07/22/1985
Name and state of incorporation changed from Pacific Western Bancshares (CA) to Pacific Western Bancshares, Inc. (DE) 06/30/1989
Merged into Comerica, Inc. 03/30/1994
Each share Common no par exchanged for (0.358) share Common $5 par

PACIFIC WESTN CAP CORP (BC)
Recapitalized as Telcoplus Enterprises Inc. 10/02/1996
Each share Common no par exchanged for (0.1) share Common no par
Telcoplus Enterprises Inc. name changed to Yamiri Gold & Energy Inc. 12/05/2005 which name changed to Cannon Point Resources Ltd. 04/27/2010 which merged into Northern Dynasty Minerals Ltd. 10/29/2015

PACIFIC WESTN CORP (WY)
Liquidation completed
Each share Common 10¢ par exchanged for initial distribution of $5.15 cash 12/15/1975
Each share Common 10¢ par received second and final distribution of $0.38 cash 09/07/1976

PACIFIC WESTN INDS INC (NV)
Company believed private 00/00/1995
Details not available

PACIFIC WESTN INDS INC (WA)
Stock Dividend - 10% 09/15/1975
Name changed to Timberland Industries, Inc. 05/24/1977
(See Timberland Industries, Inc.)

PACIFIC WESTN INVTS INC (BC)
Merged into Revenue Properties Co. Ltd. 01/01/1992
Each (7.5) shares Common no par exchanged for (1) Unit consisting of (1) share new Common no par and (0.5) Common Stock Purchase Warrant expiring 12/31/1992
Revenue Properties Co. Ltd. merged into Morguard Corp. 12/01/2008

PACIFIC WESTN NATL BK (PICO RIVERA, CA)
Stock Dividends - 5% payable 05/20/1996 to holders of record 04/12/1996; 5% payable 05/29/1998 to holders of record 04/30/1998; 5% payable 05/28/1999 to holders of record 04/16/1999; 5% payable 07/28/2000 to holders of record 06/30/2000; 5% payable 07/27/2001 to holders of record 6/29/2001 Ex date - 06/27/2001
Merged into First Community Bancorp 01/31/2002
Each share Common no par exchanged for $37.15 cash

PACIFIC WHITE CEDAR CO.
Name changed to Port Orford Cedar Co. in 1936
(See Port Orford Cedar Co.)

PACIFIC WIRELESS TELEGRAPH CO. (WA)
Charter cancelled and proclaimed dissolved for failure to pay fees 7/1/23

PACIFIC WOOD PRODUCTS CORP.
Liquidated in 1944

PACIFICA BANCORP INC (WA)
Merged into UCBH Holdings, Inc. 11/01/2005
Each share Common no par exchanged for approximately (0.3615) share Common 1¢ par and $4.12 cash
(See UCBH Holdings, Inc.)

PACIFICA PAPERS INC (CANADA)
Merged into Norske Skog Canada Ltd. (BC) 08/27/2001
Each share Common no par exchanged for (2.1) shares Common no par
Norske Skog Canada Ltd. (BC) reincorporated in Canada 08/27/2001 which name changed to Catalyst Paper Corp. (Old) 10/06/2005
(See Catalyst Paper Corp. (Old))

PACIFICA RES LTD (BC)
Name changed to Selwyn Resources Ltd. 06/07/2007
Selwyn Resources Ltd. name changed to ScoZinc Mining Ltd. 10/01/2015

PACIFICAMERICA EQUITIES INC (BC)
Name changed to SGI Capital Corp. (BC) 06/11/1995
SGI Capital Corp. (BC) reincorporated in (YT) 01/05/1996 which recapitalized as Lariat Property Corp. 12/10/1997 which name changed to Lariat Resources Ltd. 06/02/2003 which recapitalized as Lariat Energy Ltd. (YT) 09/23/2004 which reincorporated in British Columbia 04/01/2006 which name changed to Global Daily Fantasy Sports Inc. 07/11/2016

PACIFICAMERICA MONEY CTR INC (DE)
Common 1¢ par split (2) for (1) by issuance of (1) additional share payable 8/13/97 to holders of record 7/31/97
Recapitalized as Complete Care Medical, Inc. 5/27/2005
Each share Common 1¢ par exchanged for (0.002) share Common 1¢ par

PACIFICAP ENTMT HLDGS INC (NV)
Charter revoked for failure to file reports and pay fees 04/23/2013

PACIFICARE HEALTH SYS INC (DE)
Common 50¢ par split (2) for (1) by issuance of (1) additional share 08/31/1989
Common 50¢ par reclassified as Class A Common 1¢ par 06/05/1992
Each share Class A Common 1¢ par received distribution of (1) share Class B Common 1¢ par 06/10/1992
Under plan of merger each share Class A Common 1¢ par and Class B Common 1¢ par automatically became (1) share PacifiCare Health Systems, Inc. (New) Class A Common 1¢ par or Class B Common 1¢ par respectively 02/14/1997
PacifiCare Health Systems, Inc. (New) merged into UnitedHealth Group Inc. (MN) 12/20/2005 which reincorporated in Delaware 07/01/2015

PACIFICARE HEALTH SYS INC NEW (DE)
Conv. Preferred Ser. A $1 par called for redemption at $25.75 on 6/23/98
Class A Common 1¢ par reclassified as Common 1¢ par 6/25/99
Class B Common 1¢ par reclassified as Common 1¢ par 6/25/99
Common 1¢ par split (2) for (1) by issuance of (1) additional share payable 1/20/2004 to holders of record 1/7/2004 Ex date - 1/21/2004
Merged into UnitedHealth Group Inc. 12/20/2005
Each share Common 1¢ par exchanged for (1.1) shares Common 1¢ par and $21.50 cash

PACIFICNET INC (DE)
Name changed 04/23/2002
Name changed from PacificNet.com, Inc. to PacificNet Inc. 04/23/2002
Each share old Common $0.0001 par exchanged for (0.2) share new Common $0.0001 par 01/06/2003
SEC revoked common stock registration 08/22/2012

PACIFICORE MNG CORP (BC)
Name changed to Vanadiumcorp Resource Inc. 11/22/2013

PACIFICORP (OR)
Reincorporated 01/09/1989
$3.75 Ser. Preferred no par called for redemption 11/02/1984
$4.07 Ser. Preferred no par called for redemption 06/19/1986
$2.29 Ser. Preferred no par called for redemption 05/15/1987
$2.48 Ser. Preferred no par called for redemption 05/15/1987
State of incorporation changed from (ME) to (OR) 01/09/1989
Common $3.25 par split (2) for (1) by issuance of (1) additional share 03/01/1990
Market Auction Preferred Ser. D no par called for redemption 12/29/1992
$1.76 Preferred no par called for redemption 07/12/1996
$1.98 Preferred no par called for redemption 07/12/1996
$2.13 Preferred no par called for redemption 07/12/1996
7.96% Serial Preferred $100 par called for redemption 07/12/1996
8.92% Preferred $100 par called for redemption 07/12/1996
9.08% Preferred $100 par called for redemption 07/12/1996
Market Auction Preferred Ser. C no par called for redemption 07/29/1996
Dutch Auction Rate Preferred Ser. A-1 no par called for redemption 08/19/1996
$7.12 Serial Preferred no par called for redemption at $100 on 03/31/1997
Merged into Scottish Power PLC 11/29/1999
Each share Common $3.25 par exchanged for (0.58) Sponsored ADR for Ordinary
(See Scottish Power PLC)
$1.16 Preferred no par called for redemption at $26.11 on 12/27/1999
$1.18 Preferred no par called for redemption at $26.15 on 12/27/1999
$1.28 Preferred no par called for redemption at $26.35 on 12/27/1999
$7.70 Preferred no par called for redemption at $100 on 08/15/2001
$7.48 Preferred no par called for redemption at $100 plus $0.83 accrued dividends on 06/15/2007
5% Serial Preferred $100 par called for redemption at $100 plus $0.25 accrued dividends on 05/24/2013
4.52% Preferred $100 par called for redemption at $103.50 plus $0.03 accrued dividends on 11/08/2013
4.56% Preferred $100 par called for redemption at $102.34 plus $0.03 accrued dividends on 11/08/2013
4.72% Preferred $100 par called for redemption at $103.50 plus $0.03 accrued dividends on 11/08/2013
5% Preferred $100 par called for redemption at $110 plus $0.03 accrued dividends on 11/08/2013
5.40% Preferred $100 par called for redemption at $101 plus $0.03 accrued dividends on 11/08/2013
(Additional Information in Active)

PACIFICORP CAP I (DE)
8.25% Guaranteed Quarterly Income Preferred Securities Ser. A called for redemption at $25 on 8/29/2003

PACIFICORP CAP II (DE)
7.70% Trust Preferred Securities Ser. B called for redemption at $25 on 8/29/2003

PACIFICORP HLDGS LTD (NV)
Name changed to Cannabis Leaf Inc. 06/27/2017
Cannabis Leaf Inc. name changed to Apotheca Biosciences, Inc. 08/24/2018

PACK FUERTE INC (NV)
Name changed to Nami Corp. 12/12/2016

PACKAGE CONFECTIONERY CO.
Liquidated in 1930

PACKAGE FACTORS, INC. (NY)
Name changed to Sta-Tite Conduit Corp. 06/02/1961
Sta-Tite Conduit Corp. name changed to Cadillac Conduit Corp. 08/30/1961 which name changed to Cadillac Cable Corp. 11/27/1968 which merged into Ag-Met, Inc. 08/29/1974 which name changed to Refinemet International Co. 09/18/1980
(See Refinemet International Co.)

PACKAGE MACHY CO (DE)
Reincorporated 2/24/87
Common $50 par changed to no par in 1935
Common no par changed to $10 par in 1954
4-1/2% Preferred $100 par called for redemption 10/1/67
Common $10 par changed to $1 par 4/29/70
Common $1 par split (2) for (1) by issuance of (1) additional share 6/14/85
Common $1 par split (5) for (4) by issuance of (0.25) additional share 6/20/86
State of incorporation changed from (MA) to (DE) 2/24/87
Common $1 par split (5) for (4) by issuance of (0.25) additional share 5/1/89
Stock Dividends - 15% 2/21/49; 100% 4/9/54
In process of liquidation
Each share Common $1 par received initial distribution of $5.26 cash payable 12/30/96 to holders of record 12/5/96
Note: Details on subsequent distributions, if any, are not available

PACKAGE PRODS INC (NC)
Each share Common $5 par exchanged for (1.5) shares Common $1 par 9/25/68
Common $1 par split (3) for (2) by issuance of (0.5) additional share 8/21/69
Name changed to Engraph, Inc. 10/1/73
(See Engraph, Inc.)

PACKAGED HOME SOLUTIONS INC (FL)
Administratively dissolved 09/14/2007

PACKAGED ICE INC (TX)
Issue Information - 10,750,000 shares COM offered at $8.50 per share on 01/29/1999
Merged into CAC Holdings Corp. 8/15/2003
Each share Common 1¢ par exchanged for $3.638 cash

PACKAGING CORP AMER (DE)
6% Preferred $25 par called for redemption 12/31/1962
Acquired by Tennessee Gas Transmission Co. 06/08/1965
Each share Common $5 par exchanged for (1.2) shares Common $5 par
Tennessee Gas Transmission Co. name changed to Tenneco Inc. 04/11/1966 which merged into El Paso Natural Gas Co. 12/12/1996 which reorganized as El Paso Energy Corp. 08/01/1998 which name changed to El Paso Corp. 02/05/2001
12.375% Exchangeable Preferred Ser. B called for redemption at $112.375 on 03/03/2000
(Additional Information in Active)

PACKAGING DYNAMICS CORP (DE)
Merged into Kohlberg & Co. 6/9/2006
Each share Common 1¢ par exchanged for $14 cash

PACKAGING PLUS SVCS INC (DE)
Each share Common $0.001 par exchanged for (0.2) share old Common $0.005 par 11/14/1989
Plan of reorganization under Chapter 11 Federal Bankruptcy Code effective 03/31/1994
Each share old Common $0.005 par exchanged for (0.02) share new Common $0.005 par
Each (12) shares new Common $0.005 par exchanged again for (1) share new Common $0.005 par 11/08/1996
Reorganized under the laws of Nevada as Universal Express Inc. 06/30/1998
Each share new Common $0.005 par exchanged for (0.01428571) share Common $0.005 par

PACKAGING PRODS & DESIGN CORP (NJ)
Name changed to PPD Corp. 10/03/1974
PPD Corp. name changed to GCI, Inc. 09/20/1976
(See GCI, Inc.)

PACKAGING SYS CORP (NY)
6% 2nd Conv. Preferred $1 par called for redemption 4/7/76
Common 10¢ par split (2) for (1) by issuance of (1) additional share 9/18/86
Stock Dividends - 10% 12/30/76; 10% 5/25/79; 10% 6/23/80; 10% 1/26/82; 10% 1/28/83; 25% 9/23/83; 10% 7/8/85
Name changed to PAXAR Corp. 3/9/87
PAXAR Corp. name changed to Paxar Corp. 5/1/98

PACKARD-BELL CO. (CA)
Each share Common $1 par exchanged for (2) shares Common 50¢ par 00/00/1950
Name changed to Packard-Bell Electronics Corp. 10/23/1956
Packard-Bell Electronics Corp.

merged into Teledyne, Inc. 05/28/1968 which merged into Allegheny Teledyne Inc. 08/15/1996 which name changed to Allegheny Technologies Inc. 11/29/1999

PACKARD-BELL ELECTRONICS CORP. (CA)
Merged into Teledyne, Inc. 05/28/1968
Each share Capital Stock 50¢ par exchanged for (0.1374) share Common $1 par
Teledyne, Inc. merged into Allegheny Teledyne Inc. 08/15/1996 which name changed to Allegheny Technologies Inc. 11/29/1999

PACKARD BIOSCIENCE CO (DE)
Issue Information - 12,000,000 shares COM offered at $9 per share on 04/19/2000
Merged into PerkinElmer, Inc. 11/13/2001
Each share Common $0.002 par exchanged for (0.311) share Common $1 par

PACKARD INSTRUMENT CO., INC. (IL)
Acquired by American Bosch Arma Corp. 6/30/67
Each share Common no par exchanged for (0.25) share Common $2 par
American Bosch Arma Corp. name changed to Ambac Industries, Inc. 4/30/68 which merged into United Technologies Corp. 7/14/78

PACKARD MOTOR CAR CO. (MI)
Each share Capital Stock $10 par exchanged for (5) shares Capital Stock no par in 1929
Merged into Studebaker-Packard Corp. in 1954
Each share Capital Stock no par exchanged for (0.2) share Common $10 par
Studebaker-Packard Corp. name changed to Studebaker Corp. (Mich.) 6/29/62 which merged into Studebaker-Worthington, Inc. 11/27/67
(See Studebaker-Worthington, Inc.)

PACKARD RES LTD (BC)
Recapitalized as Conpac Resources Ltd. (BC) 09/09/1986
Each share Common no par exchanged for (0.2) share Common no par
Conpac Resources Ltd. (BC) reincorporated in Canada as ConPak Seafoods Inc. 04/10/1987
(See ConPak Seafoods Inc.)

PACKENO YUKON MINES LTD. (ON)
Charter revoked for failure to file reports and pay fees 11/9/64

PACKER C S ASSOC INC (IL)
Liquidation completed
Each share Common $1 par received initial distribution of $2 cash 10/15/1965
Each share Common $1 par received second distribution of $0.25 cash 09/30/1966
Each share Common $1 par received third and final distribution of $0.182 cash 06/29/1967
Note: Certificates were not required to be surrendered are without value

PACKER CORP. (DE)
Liquidation completed
Each share Common no par received initial distribution of $20 cash 12/15/52
Each share Common no par received second distribution of $10 cash 9/15/53
Each share Common no par received third distribution of $15 cash 8/15/54
Each share Common no par received fourth distribution of $10 cash 2/10/55
Each share Common no par received fifth distribution of $8 cash 2/10/56
Each share Common no par exchanged for sixth and final distribution of $2.22 cash 10/25/56

PACKER CORP. (NJ)
Purchased by Metromedia, Inc. 12/4/64
All stock surrendered for cancellation and company was formally dissolved 6/28/65

PACKER'S SUPER MARKETS, INC. (NY)
Merged into Bohack (H.C.) Co. Inc. 10/18/68
Each share Common $1 par exchanged for (0.455) share Common $1 par
Bohack (H.C.) Co. Inc. name changed to Bohack Corp. 6/6/69 which merged into Key International Manufacturing, Inc. 12/28/79
(See Key International Manufacturing, Inc.)

PACKERS LIQUIDATING CORP. (DE)
Liquidation completed
Each share Common $5 par exchanged for initial distribution of (0.517124) share Ogden Corp. Common 50¢ par 7/27/66
Each share Common $5 par received second and final distribution of (0.028731) share Ogden Corp. Common 50¢ par 7/31/68
Ogden Corp. name changed to Covanta Energy Corp. 3/14/2001
(See Covanta Energy Corp.)

PACKETEER INC (DE)
Issue Information - 4,000,000 shares COM offered at $15 per share on 07/27/1999
Merged into Blue Coat Systems, Inc. 06/06/2008
Each share Common $0.001 par exchanged for $7.10 cash

PACKETPORT COM INC (NV)
Each share old Common $0.003 par exchanged for (0.05) share new Common $0.003 par 02/20/2008
Name changed to Wyndstorm Corp. 05/05/2008
(See Wyndstorm Corp.)

PACMIN MNG CORP LTD (AUSTRALIA)
Acquired by Sons of Gwalia Ltd. 10/26/2001
Details not available

PACO, INC. (IL)
Liquidation completed 05/25/1962
Details not available

PACO, INC. (WV)
Liquidation completed
Each share Common $1 par received initial distribution of $11.25 cash 1/2/64
Each share Common $1 par received second and final distribution of $1.40 cash 3/30/67
Certificates were not retired and are now without value

PACO CORP CDA LTD (ON)
Company went private in August 1985
Each share Common no par exchanged for $6 cash

PACO INDS INC (NJ)
Name changed to Computer Microdata Corp. 11/24/71
(See Computer Microdata Corp.)

PACO INTEGRATED ENERGY INC (NV)
Charter revoked for failure to file reports and pay fees 04/30/2012

PACO OIL & GAS INC (NV)
Recapitalized as Paco Integrated Energy, Inc. 05/04/2009
Each share Common $0.001 par exchanged for (0.05882352) share Common $0.001 par
(See Paco Integrated Energy, Inc.)

PACO PHARMACEUTICAL SVCS INC NEW (DE)
Merged into West Co., Inc. 04/27/1995
Each share Common 1¢ par exchanged for $12.25 cash

PACO PHARMACEUTICAL SVCS INC OLD (DE)
Common 1¢ par split (3) for (2) by issuance of (0.5) additional share 4/27/83
Stock Dividend - 50% 12/8/82
Merged into Scherer (R.P.) Corp. (Old) 2/12/88
Each share Common 1¢ par exchanged for $15.25 cash

PACO PRODUCTS, INC. (SC)
Foreclosure completed rendering stock worthless 9/20/62

PACOLET INDUSTRIES, INC. (SC)
Merged into Deering Milliken, Inc. 10/01/1967
Each share Common $10 par exchanged for $35.87 cash

PACOLET MANUFACTURING CO. (SC)
Each share Common $100 par exchanged for (5) shares Common $20 par 00/00/1941
Merged into Pacolet Industries, Inc. 12/03/1962
Each share Common $20 par exchanged for (0.13793103) share Common $10 par
(See Pacolet Industries, Inc.)

PACOLUND MINES LTD. (ON)
Succeeded by Aer Nickel Corp. Ltd. 00/00/1955
Details not available

PACOTRONICS, INC. (NY)
Merged into Precision Apparatus, Inc. on a share for share basis 3/12/63
Precision Apparatus, Inc. merged into Atlantic Services, Inc. 6/30/66
(See Atlantic Services, Inc.)

PACRIM ENTMT GROUP INC (BC)
Name changed to Evergreen International Technology Inc. 1/9/91
Evergreen International Technology Inc. name changed to Jot-It! Software Corp. 2/1/97 which name changed to Sideware Systems Inc. (BC) 2/18/98 which reincorporated in Yukon 1/2/2002 which reincorporated in Delaware as Knowledgemax, Inc. 5/21/2002
(See Knowledgemax, Inc.)

PACRIM INFORMATION SYS INC (CA)
Charter suspended for failure to file reports and pay fees 04/17/1997

PACRIM RES LTD (CANADA)
Delisted from Toronto Venture Stock Exchange 06/25/2007

PACT RES N L (AUSTRALIA)
Name changed to Iron Carbide Australia Ltd. 2/12/97
Iron Carbide Australia Ltd. name changed to ION Ltd. 2/12/2001
(See ION Ltd.)

PACTECH VENTURES LTD (BC)
Name changed to Intercontinental Mining Corp. (BC) 08/12/1996
Intercontinental Mining Corp. (BC) reincorporated in Alberta as Maple Leaf Reforestation Inc. 03/03/2005 which name changed to Maple Leaf Green World Inc. 10/05/2012

PACTEL CORP (CA)
Name changed to AirTouch Communications (CA) 4/6/94
AirTouch Communications (CA) reincorporated in (DE) as AirTouch Communications, Inc. 12/21/94 which merged into Vodafone Group PLC (Old) 6/30/99 witch name change to Vodafone Group PLC (New) 6/28/2000

PACTERA TECHNOLOGY INTL LTD (CAYMAN ISLANDS)
Acquired by BCP (Singapore) VI Cayman Acquisition Co. Ltd. 03/27/2014
Each Sponsored ADR for Ordinary exchanged for $7.25 cash

PACTIV CORP (DE)
Acquired by Reynolds Group Holdings Ltd. 11/16/2010
Each share Common 1¢ par exchanged for $33.25 cash

PACVEN INC (NV)
Charter revoked for failure to file a list of officers 08/01/1991

PACVEST CAP INC (CANADA)
Merged into First Toronto Mining Corp. 01/01/1989
Each share Common no par exchanged for (0.1428571) share Common no par
(See First Toronto Mining Corp.)

PACWEST BANCORP (OR)
Merged into KeyCorp (NY) 11/07/1986
Each share Common $5 par exchanged for either $41 principal amount of Installment Promissory Notes due 11/07/1991, (1.69) shares Common $5 par, or $41 cash
Note: Holders of (99) or fewer shares will receive cash
KeyCorp (NY) merged into KeyCorp (New) (OH) 03/01/1994

PACWEST EQUITIES INC (NV)
Each share old Common $0.001 par exchanged for (3) shares new Common $0.001 par 11/05/2012
Charter revoked 06/30/2014

PACWEST VENTURES LTD (ON)
Merged into Pacific & Western Credit Corp. (New) 01/01/2002
Each share 7% Conv. Preferred Class A no par exchanged for (1) share Class A Preferred no par
Each share Common no par exchanged for (0.1) share Common no par
Pacific & Western Credit Corp. (New) name changed to PWC Capital Inc. 04/25/2014 which merged into VersaBank (New) (London, ON) 02/02/2017

PADANG RES LTD (AUSTRALIA)
Name changed to Palace Resources Ltd. (New) 05/03/2013
(See Palace Resources Ltd. (New))

PADDINGTON CORP (DE)
Reincorporated 05/19/1967
Class A Common $1 par and Class B Common $1 par changed to 50¢ par and (1) additional share issued respectively 07/24/1961
All Class B Common 50¢ par voluntarily converted to Class A Common 50¢ par by 07/00/1964
Class A Common 50¢ par reclassified as Common 25¢ par and (1) additional share issued 01/20/1966
Under plan of merger state of incorporation changed from (NY) to (DE) 05/19/1967
Under plan of merger each share Common 25¢ par exchanged for $70 cash 12/30/1971

PADDOCK BUILDING TRUST
Liquidation completed in 1947

PADDOCK OF CALIFORNIA (CA)
Stock Dividend - 10% 11/6/56
Bankrupt in 1963; no stockholders' equity

PADDY PWR PLC (IRELAND)
Each old ADR for Common exchanged for (0.9) new ADR for Common 05/29/2015
Name changed to Paddy Power Betfair PLC 07/08/2016

PADRE RES LTD (BC)
Recapitalized as Repadre Resources Ltd. (BC) 11/29/84
Each share Common no par exchanged for (0.2) share Common no par
Repadre Resources Ltd. (BC) reincorporated in Ontario as Repadre Capital Corp. 3/7/90 which was acquired by IAMGold Corp. 1/7/2003

PADUCAH BK SHS INC (KY)
Under plan of merger each share Common $25 par exchanged for $175 cash 12/20/2001

PADUCAH ELECTRIC CO.
Merged into Kentucky Utilities Co. 00/00/1926
Details not available

PADUCAH-OHIO RIVER BRIDGE CO.
Sold to Kentucky State Highway Commission in 1935
Details not available

PADUCAH WATER WORKS CO.
Sold to City of Paducah, Kentucky in 1930

PAE THAILAND PUB CO LTD (THAILAND)
ADR agreement terminated 05/26/2011
Details not available

PAEPCKE CORP.
In process of liquidation in 1942

PAETEC HLDG CORP (DE)
Merged into Windstream Corp. 12/01/2011
Each share Common 1¢ par exchanged for (0.46) share Common $0.0001 par
Windstream Corp. name changed to Windstream Holdings, Inc. 09/03/2013

PAFCO FINL HLDGS LTD (CANADA)
Name changed to Goran Capital Inc. 01/29/1991

PAGE & SHAW, INC. (MA)
Sold by Referee in bankruptcy in 1931

PAGE ACTIVE HLDGS INC (NV)
Name changed to TriVantage Group, Inc. 8/7/2001
TriVantage Group, Inc. recapitalized as Proteo Inc. 1/28/2002

PAGE AMER GROUP INC (NY)
Name changed 3/25/83
Name changed from Page America Communications, Inc. to Page America Group, Inc. 3/25/83
Each share Common 1¢ par exchanged for (0.1) share Common 10¢ par 1/25/91
Each share 10% Conv. Preferred Ser. C $1 par converted into (1) share Common 10¢ par 9/12/94
Completely liquidated 1/3/2000
Each share Common 10¢ par exchanged for first and final distribution of $0.05688 cash
Note: Holders of (90) or fewer shares did not receive any distribution

PAGE AWYS INC (NY)
Merged into Guthrie Corp. Ltd. 10/31/1981
Each share Common $1 par exchanged for $57.65 cash

PAGE BANKSHARES INC (VA)
Common $1 par split (2) for (1) by issuance of (1) additional share payable 4/1/99 to holders of record 3/1/99
Name changed to Pioneer Bankshares Inc. 7/8/99

PAGE DAIRY CO. (OH)
Ceased operations 4/30/75
No stockholders' equity

PAGE-HARLEY MINES LTD. (ON)
Charter cancelled for failure to file reports and pay taxes in 1962

PAGE HERSEY TUBES LTD (CANADA)
Each share Capital Stock no par exchanged for (4) shares Capital Stock no par 00/00/1945
Each share Capital Stock no par exchanged for (4) shares Capital Stock no par 05/12/1958
Acquired by Steel Co. of Canada Ltd. 10/15/1964
Each share Capital Stock no par exchanged for (1.15625) shares Common no par
Steel Co. of Canada Ltd. name changed to Stelco Inc. 07/09/1980
(See Stelco Inc.)

PAGE IMPERO HLDGS INC (UT)
Name changed to China Continental Inc. (UT) 01/18/1994
China Continental Inc. (UT) reincorporated in Nevada 01/11/2002
(See China Continental Inc.)

PAGE INTL INC (NV)
Reincorporated 12/31/1997
Place of incorporation changed from (KY) to (NV) 12/31/1997
Each share old Common $0.001 par exchanged for (0.03333333) share new Common $0.001 par 02/13/2007
Name changed to China TianRen Organic Food, Inc. 06/14/2007

PAGE PETE LTD (AB)
Company placed in receivership 00/00/1988
No stockholders equity

PAGECORP INC (ON)
Merged into GYR Properties Ltd. 01/07/1988
Each share Class A no par exchanged for $9.25 cash

PAGELAB NETWORK INC (MN)
Name changed to Subjex Corp. 01/03/2003
(See Subjex Corp.)

PAGEMART WIRELESS INC (DE)
Name changed to WebLink Wireless, Inc. 12/1/99
(See WebLink Wireless, Inc.)

PAGEPROMPT USA (CA)
Name changed 03/09/1994
Name changed from Pagers Plus to Pageprompt USA 03/09/1994
Chapter 7 bankruptcy proceedings terminated 12/16/2005
Stockholders' equity unlikely

PAGES INC (DE)
Declared insolvent 03/27/1972
No stockholders' equity

PAGES INC (DE)
Reincorporated 10/13/94
Common no par split (5) for (4) by issuance of (0.25) additional share 10/15/93
State of incorporation changed from (OH) to (DE) and Common no par changed to 1¢ par 10/13/94
Recapitalized as Media Source Inc. 3/9/99
Each share Common 1¢ par exchanged for (0.05) share Common 1¢ par
(See Media Source Inc.)

PAGESTAR INC (NV)
Name changed to Satellite Control Technologies Inc. 5/1/97
Satellite Control Technologies Inc. name changed to SATX, Inc. 8/19/99 which reorganized as Peninsula Holdings Group, Ltd. 12/7/2002
(See Peninsula Holdings Group, Ltd.)

PAGET MINERALS CORP (BC)
Each share old Common no par exchanged for (0.06666666) share new Common no par 01/21/2016
Recapitalized as Ascent Industries Corp. 08/10/2018
Each share new Common no par exchanged for (0.16666666) share Common no par

PAGET RES LTD (BC)
Name changed to Peltech Industries Inc. 07/24/1990
Peltech Industries Inc. recapitalized as Gold Win Ventures Inc. 04/02/1996 which recapitalized as Consolidated Gold Win Ventures, Inc. 06/17/1998 which name changed to Encore Renaissance Resources Corp. 04/09/2009

PAGING NETWORK INC (DE)
Common 1¢ par split (3) for (2) by issuance of (0.5) additional share 10/15/1993
Common 1¢ par split (2) for (1) by issuance of (1) additional share 09/29/1995
Plan of reorganization under Chapter 11 Federal Bankruptcy proceedings effective 11/10/2000
Each share Common 1¢ par exchanged for (0.04796505) share Arch Wireless, Inc. Common 1¢ par, (0.01279666) share Vast Solutions Inc. Class B1 1¢ par, (0.01279666) share Class B2 1¢ par, and (0.01279666) share Class B3 1¢ par
(See each company's listing)

PAGING PARTNERS CORP (DE)
Issue Information - 1,700,000 Units consisting of (1) share COM and (1) WT offered at $6 per Unit on 05/19/1994
Name changed to Aquis Communications Group, Inc. 3/31/99

PAGURIAN LTD (ON)
Class A Special Stock no par split (2) for (1) by issuance of (1) additional share 12/17/80
Class A Special no par reclassified as Class A no par 9/30/82
Class A no par split (2) for (1) by issuance of (1) additional share 7/2/85
Name changed to Edper Group Ltd. (Old) 5/10/95
Edper Group Ltd. (Old) merged into Edper Group Ltd. (New) 1/1/97 which name changed to EdperBrascan Corp. 8/1/97 which name changed to Brascan Corp. 4/28/2000 which name changed to Brookfield Asset Management, Inc. 11/10/2005

PAHANG RUBR LTD (HI)
Liquidation completed
Each share Common $2.50 par exchanged for initial distribution of (1.56) shares Selama-Dindings Plantation, Ltd. Capital Stock $5 par, (0.1) share Cincinnati Union Stock Yards Co. Common Capital Stock no par, (0.15) share Metropolitan Industries, Inc. (OH) Common $4 par and $2 cash 4/10/73
(See each company's listing)
Each share Common $2.50 par received second and final distribution of $0.17 cash 10/12/1973

PAICINES PROPERTIES CO. (CA)
Liquidation completed
Each share Common 10¢ par received initial distribution of $20 cash 10/23/67
Each share Common $10 par received second distribution of $5 cash 10/20/68
Each share Common $10 par exchanged for third and final distribution of $0.241742 cash 12/21/81

PAIDCARD NET INC (NV)
Name changed to Valudyne Inc. 4/25/2001
Valudyne Inc. name changed to Prosperity Software Inc. 9/21/2001 which name changed to Polarwearz Inc. 6/25/2003 which name changed to Risingtide, Inc. 6/2/2004 which name changed to Equiline Corp. 4/8/2005 which recapitalized as Chelsea Collection, Inc. 6/15/2005 which recapitalized as G-H-3 International, Inc. 10/30/2006

PAIGE-DETROIT MOTOR CAR CO. (MI)
Name changed to Graham-Paige Motors Corp. 1/5/28 which name was changed to Graham-Paige Corp. 9/18/50 which name was changed to Madison Square Garden Corp. (Mich.) 4/4/62
(See Madison Square Garden Corp. (Mich.))

PAIGE PETROLEUM LTD. (ON)
Acquired by Porcupine Prime Mines Ltd. share for share in April 1960
Porcupine Prime Mines Ltd. name changed to Prime Potash Corp. of Canada Ltd. 12/16/65
(See Prime Potash Corp. of Canada Ltd.)

PAIN CTL CTRS INC (MN)
Out of business 00/00/1980

PAIN PREVENTION INC (IL)
Reincorporated under the laws of Utah as PPI Capital Corp. 11/15/1997
PPI Capital Corp. (UT) recapitalized as PPI Capital Group, Inc. (UT) 06/01/1998 which reincorporated in Delaware as DirectPlacement Inc. 11/28/2001 which name changed to PCS Research Technology, Inc. 10/07/2002 which name changed to Sagient Research Systems, Inc. 05/20/2004
(See Sagient Research Systems, Inc.)

PAIN SUPPRESSION LABS INC (NJ)
Charter revoked for failure to file annual reports 11/4/94

PAINCARE HLDGS INC (FL)
SEC revoked common stock registration 06/27/2012

PAINE WEBBER CASHFUND INC (MD)
Name changed to UBS PaineWebber Cashfund, Inc. 04/12/2001
UBS PaineWebber Cashfund, Inc. name changed to UBS Cashfund, Inc. 06/09/2003

PAINE WEBBER GROUP INC (DE)
Name changed 05/21/1984
$1.30 Conv. Preferred Ser. A $20 par called for redemption 07/27/1981
Common $1 par split (4) for (3) by issuance of (0.33333333) additional share 11/29/1982
Name changed from Paine Webber Inc. to Paine Webber Group Inc. 05/21/1984
Common $1 par split (5) for (4) by issuance of (0.25) additional share 08/25/1986
$2.25 Conv. Exchangeable Preferred $20 par called for redemption 12/15/1986
Common $1 par split (3) for (2) by issuance of (0.5) additional share 12/09/1991
$1.375 Exchangeable Preferred $20 par called for redemption 11/03/1993
Common $1 par split (3) for (2) by issuance of (0.5) additional share 03/10/1994
Common $1 par split (3) for (2) by issuance of (0.5) additional share payable 11/17/1997 to holders of record 10/24/1997 Ex date - 11/18/1997
Merged into UBS AG 11/03/2000

Each share Common $1 par exchanged for either (0.4954) Sponsored ADR for Ordinary SFr 20 par, $73.50 cash, or a combination thereof
(See UBS AG)

PAINE WEBBER JACKSON & CURTIS INC (DE)
Under plan of reorganization each share $1.30 Conv. Preferred Ser. A $20 par and Common $1 par automatically became (1) share Paine Webber Inc. $1.30 Conv. Preferred Ser. A $20 par and Common $1 par respectively 2/1/74
Paine Webber Inc. name changed to Paine Webber Group Inc. 5/21/84 which merged into UBS AG 11/3/2000
(See UBS AG)

PAINE WEBBER MASTER GLOBAL INCOME FD (MA)
Under plan of reorganization each Share of Bene. Int. $0.001 par automatically became (1) PaineWebber Investment Series Global Income Fund Class B Share of Bene. Int. $0.001 par 07/22/1991
(See PaineWebber Investment Series)

PAINE WEBBER TAX EXEMPT INCOME FD INC (MD)
Reincorporated under the laws of Massachusetts as PaineWebber Managed Municipal Trust and Common $0.001 par reclassified as National Tax-Free Income Fund Shares of Bene. Int. Class A $0.001 par 07/22/1991

PAINEWEBBER CALIF TAX FREE INCOME FD (MD)
Reorganized as PaineWebber Mutual Fund Trust 04/30/1992
Details not available

PAINEWEBBER CLASSIC FLEXIBLE INCOME FD INC (MD)
Voluntarily dissolved 03/09/1992
Details not available

PAINEWEBBER INSD MTG PARTNERS 1 (DE)
Completely liquidated 08/31/2000
Details not available

PAINEWEBBER/KIDDER, PEABODY CALIFORNIA TAX EXEMPT MONEY MARKET FUND (MA)
Trust terminated 06/05/1997
Details not available

PAINEWEBBER PREMIER HIGH INCOME TR INC (MD)
Name changed to Managed High Yield Fund 08/14/1995
Managed High Yield Fund merged into Managed High Yield Plus Fund Inc. 06/02/2000
(See Managed High Yield Plus Fund Inc.)

PAINEWEBBER PREMIER INSD MUN INCOME FD INC (MD)
Name changed to Insured Municipal Income Fund 08/14/1995
Auction Preferred Rate Ser. C $0.001 par called for redemption at $50,000 on 10/13/2009
Auction Preferred Rate Ser. D $0.001 par called for redemption at $50,000 on 10/14/2009
Auction Preferred Rate Ser. A $0.001 par called for redemption at $50,000 on 10/16/2009
Auction Preferred Rate Ser. B $0.001 par called for redemption at $50,000 on 10/19/2009
Insured Municipal Income Fund name changed to Special Opportunities Fund, Inc. 12/22/2009

PAINEWEBBER PREMIER INTER TAX-FREE INCOME FD (MD)
Merged into PaineWebber Premier Insured Municipal Income Fund Inc. 11/28/1994
Each share Auction Preferred $0.001 par exchanged for (1) share Auction Rate Preferred Ser. D $0.001 par
Each share Common $0.001 par exchanged for (1) share Common $0.001 par
(See PaineWebber Premier Insured Municipal Income Fund Inc.)

PAINEWEBBER PREMIER TAX-FREE INCOME FD INC (MD)
Name changed to Investment Grade Municipal Income Fund 08/14/1995
(See Investment Grade Municipal Income Fund)
Auction Preferred Ser. A called for redemption at $50,000 on 04/16/2010
Auction Preferred Ser. B called for redemption at $50,000 on 04/19/2010

PAINEWEBBER R&D PARTNERS L P (DE)
Completely liquidated 00/00/2001
Details not available for Units of Ltd. Partnership
Completely liquidated 12/31/2001
Details not available for Units of Ltd. Partnership II
Completely liquidated 05/14/2007
Each Unit of Ltd. Partnership III received first and final distribution of approximately $65.76 cash

PAINEWEBBER RESIDENTIAL RLTY INC (MD)
Name changed to Columbia Real Estate Investments, Inc. 5/11/88
(See Columbia Real Estate Investments, Inc.)

PAINT A CAR INTL CORP (DE)
Charter cancelled and declared inoperative and void for non-payment of taxes 03/01/1974

PAINTED DESERT FARMS INC (NV)
Each share old Common $0.001 par exchanged for (0.04) share new Common $0.001 par 01/17/1997
Name changed to Third Millennium Software Corp. 01/05/1998
Third Millennium Software Corp. recapitalized as BidHit.com, Inc. 05/17/1999 which name changed to U.S. National Commercial Partners Inc. 09/11/2001 which recapitalized as Data-Fit, Inc. 09/10/2003 which recapitalized as Real Security Co., Inc. 12/12/2005
(See Real Security Co., Inc.)

PAINTED DESERT URANIUM & OIL INC (WA)
Each share old Common 1¢ par exchanged for (0.1) share new Common 1¢ par 09/01/1986
Reincorporated under the laws of Nevada as Royal Pacific Resources Inc. 06/13/2003
Royal Pacific Resources Inc. recapitalized as Great American Family Parks, Inc. 02/03/2004 which name changed to Parks! America, Inc. 06/25/2008

PAINTED PONY PETE LTD (AB)
Each share Class B Common no par exchanged for (0.825) share Class A Common no par 12/01/2011
Class A Common no par reclassified as Common no par 06/11/2012
Name changed to Painted Pony Energy Ltd. 05/23/2017

PAIRGAIN TECHNOLOGIES INC (DE)
Common $0.001 par split (2) for (1) by issuance of (1) additional share payable 06/17/1996 to holders of record 06/14/1996
Common $0.001 par split (2) for (1) by issuance of (1) additional share payable 12/18/1996 to holders of record 12/11/1996
Merged into ADC Telecommunications, Inc. 06/28/2000
Each share Common $0.001 par exchanged for (0.86) share Common 20¢ par
(See ADC Telecommunications, Inc.)

PAISLEY PRODS INC (DE)
Reported out of business 00/00/1980
Details not available

PAIUTE OIL & MNG CORP (UT)
Chapter 11 bankruptcy proceedings converted to Chapter 7 on 09/22/1986
Stockholders' equity unlikely

PAIVIS CORP (NV)
Each share old Common $0.0002 par exchanged for (0.005) share new Common $0.0002 par 08/04/2006
Note: Holders of (19,999) pre-split shares or fewer will receive (100) shares
SEC revoked common stock registration 07/14/2009

PAJARO VALLEY BANCORPORATION (CA)
Merged into Pacific Capital Bancorp (Old) 11/07/1990
Each share Common no par exchanged for (0.45) share Common no par
Pacific Capital Bancorp (Old) merged into Pacific Capital Bancorp (New) (CA) 12/30/1998 which reorganized in Delaware 12/29/2010
(See Pacific Capital Bancorp (New))

PAK MAIL CTRS AMER INC (CO)
Each share old Common $0.001 par exchanged for (0.02) share new Common $0.001 par 3/24/95
Merged into Pak Mail Acquisition Corp. 5/12/2003
Each share new Common $0.001 par exchanged for $0.0516 cash

PAK MAN RES INC (BC)
Struck off register and declared dissolved for failure to file returns 12/3/93

PAK VENTURES INC (DE)
Each share old Common $0.0001 par exchanged for (0.04) share new Common $0.0001 par 08/08/1986
Charter cancelled and declared inoperative and void for non-payment of taxes 03/07/1987

PAK WELL CORP (CO)
Class A no par reclassified as Common no par 5/29/69
Class B no par reclassified as Common no par 5/29/69
Common no par split (2) for (1) by issuance of (1) additional share 9/18/72
Merged into Great Northern Nekoosa Corp. 12/31/75
Each (2.735) shares Common no par exchanged for (1) share Common $10 par
(See Great Northern Nekoosa Corp.)

PAKCO COS INC (NJ)
Merged into Ockap Corp. 12/12/1977
Each share Common $1 par exchanged for $2.50 cash

PAKCO MANAGEMENT & DEVELOPMENT CO. (NJ)
Name changed to Pakco Companies, Inc. 9/25/62
(See Pakco Companies, Inc.)

PAKISTAN CEM CO LTD (PAKISTAN)
Name changed to Lafarge Pakistan Cement Ltd. 03/20/2009

PAKISTAN INVT FD INC (MD)
Completely liquidated 6/22/2001
Each share Common no par exchanged for first and final distribution of $2.92 cash

PAKO CORP (DE)
Common $5 par changed to $2.50 par 10/00/1960
Merged into Blohorn Group of France 12/10/1980
Each share Common $2.50 par exchanged for $22.50 cash

PAL KNITS INC (NJ)
Name changed to Telecom Equipment Corp. 12/18/74
Telecom Equipment Corp. name changed to Telecom Plus International, Inc. 10/1/82 which name changed to TPI Enterprises, Inc. 4/1/87 which merged into Shoney's Inc. 9/9/96
(See Shoney's Inc.)

PALABORA MNG LTD (SOUTH AFRICA)
Each ADR for Class A Ordinary exchanged for (1) ADR for Ordinary 00/00/1990
ADR agreement terminated 05/08/2000
Each ADR for Ordinary exchanged for $5.73 cash

PALACE CASINOS INC (UT)
Common $0.001 par split (2) for (1) by issuance of (1) additional share 01/31/1994
Recapitalized as Xcel Management Inc. (UT) 08/09/1999
Each share Common $0.001 par exchanged for (0.01) share Common $0.001 par
Xcel Management Inc. (UT) reincorporated in Delaware as InsynQ, Inc. 08/04/2000 which reincorporated in Nevada 12/24/2002
(See InsynQ, Inc. (NV))

PALACE CLOTHING CO (MO)
Under plan of merger each share 5% Preferred 1947 Ser. $100 par or 5% Preferred 1949 Ser. $100 par exchanged for $40 principal amount of 5% Subord. Debentures due 02/01/1982 and (1) share Common $1 par 01/31/1967
Charter forfeited for failure to file reports 01/01/1983

PALACE CLOTHING CO TOPEKA INC (DE)
Charter cancelled and declared inoperative and void for non-payment of taxes 03/01/1985

PALACE CORP (MI)
Under plan of merger each share Common $1 par exchanged for (0.1) share Common no par 8/31/68
12/24/68 was last date to exchange old stock; after that date all unexchanged ctfs. became worthless
Charter declared inoperative and void for failure to file reports 5/15/77

PALACE EXPLS INC (QC)
Recapitalized as X-Chequer Resources Inc. 12/02/1996
Each share Common no par exchanged for (0.1) share Common no par
X-Chequer Resources Inc. recapitalized as International X-Chequer Resources Inc. (QC) 09/29/2004 which reorganized in British Columbia as Passport Metals Inc. 10/18/2007 which name changed to Passport Potash Inc. 11/10/2009

PALACE REALTY CO. (OH)
Charter cancelled for failure to file reports and pay taxes 6/1/65

PALACE RES INC (BC)
Name changed to N-Tone International Ltd. 09/24/1986
(See N-Tone International)

PALACE RES LTD NEW (AUSTRALIA)
ADR agreement terminated 11/30/2015
Each Sponsored ADR for Ordinary exchanged for $0.053197 cash

PAL-PAL   FINANCIAL INFORMATION, INC.

PALACE RES LTD OLD (AUSTRALIA)
Name changed to Padang Resources Ltd. 12/20/2011
Padang Resources Ltd. name changed to Palace Resources Ltd. (New) 05/03/2013
(See Palace Resources Ltd. (New))

PALACE TRAVEL COACH CORP.
Name changed to Palace Corp. in 1943
(See listing for Palace Corp.)

PALADIN CAP CORP (AB)
Name changed to D.R.W. Environmental Technologies Inc. 02/26/1993
(See D.R.W. Environmental Technologies Inc.)

PALADIN ENERGY LTD (AUSTRALIA)
ADR agreement terminated 10/12/2018
Each ADR for Ordinary exchanged for (0.2) share Ordinary
Note: Unexchanged ADR's will be sold and the proceeds, if any, held for claim after 04/12/2019

PALADIN ENERGY LTD (AUSTRALIA)
Name changed 11/27/2007
Name changed from Paladin Resources Ltd. to Paladin Energy Ltd. 11/27/2007
Shares transferred to Australian share register 02/03/2018

PALADIN FUEL TECH INC (BC)
Recapitalized as Prima Developments Ltd. 09/21/1993
Each share Common no par exchanged for (0.125) share Common no par
Prima Developments Ltd. name changed to ECL Enviroclean Ventures Ltd. 06/28/2010

PALADIN HLDGS INC (FL)
Administratively dissolved for failure to file annual report 09/24/2010

PALADIN INTL CORP (NV)
SEC revoked common stock registration 10/20/2008

PALADIN LABS INC (CANADA)
Reincorporated 07/24/1998
Place of incorporation changed from (BC) to (Canada) 07/24/1998
Merged into Endo International PLC 03/03/2014
Each share Common no par exchanged for (1.6331) shares Ordinary USD$0.0001 par, (1) share Knight Therapeutics Inc. Common no par and $0.16 cash

PALADIN RESOURCES LTD. (BC)
Name changed to Paladin Fuel Technology, Inc. 07/31/1987
Paladin Fuel Technology, Inc. recapitalized as Prima Developments Ltd. 09/21/1993 which name changed to ECL Enviroclean Ventures Ltd. 06/28/2010

PALADYNE CORP (DE)
Recapitalized as Market Central, Inc. 02/05/2003
Each share Common $0.001 par exchanged for (0.1) share Common $0.001 par
Market Central, Inc. name changed to Scientigo, Inc. 02/17/2006 which recapitalized as Incumaker, Inc. 06/01/2011

PALAL MNG CORP (NV)
Common $0.00001 par split (5) for (1) by issuance of (4) additional shares payable 04/23/2001 to holders of record 04/20/2001
Name changed to TexEn Oil & Gas Inc. 04/30/2002
TexEn Oil & Gas Inc. name changed to SNRG Corp. 08/02/2005
(See SNRG Corp.)

PALATINE CAP CORP (BC)
Name changed to Digital Shelf Space Corp. 01/04/2011
Digital Shelf Space Corp. name changed to Movit Media Corp. (BC) 07/09/2015 which reorganized in British Columbia as Ether Capital Corp. 04/19/2018

PALATKA ATLANTIC NATL BK (PALATKA, FL)
100% acquired by Atlantic Bancorporation through exchange offer as of 10/01/1973
Public interest eliminated

PALCAN FUEL CELLS LTD (YT)
Name changed to Palcan Power Systems Inc. 08/10/2004

PALCO ACQUISITION CO (DE)
Name changed to Thermadyne Industries, Inc. 9/12/88
(See Thermadyne Industries, Inc.)

PALERMO GOLD MINES LTD. (ON)
Declared dissolved 9/17/62
No stockholders' equity

PALERMO RES INC (BC)
Name changed to Tarn Pure Technology Corp. 03/29/1985
(See Tarn Pure Technology Corp.)

PALESTINE COTTON MLS LTD (ISRAEL)
Adjudicated bankrupt 07/00/1962
No stockholders' equity

PALESTINE ECONOMIC CORP. (ME)
Each share Common $100 par exchanged for (4) shares Common $25 par 00/00/1949
Name changed to PEC Israel Economic Corp. 09/19/1962
(See PEC Israel Economic Corp.)

PALEX INC (DE)
Merged into IFCO Systems N.V. 03/08/2000
Each share Common 1¢ par exchanged for either (0.6040) share Ordinary EUR 2 par, $9 cash, or a combination thereof
Note: Option to receive stock or stock and cash expired 03/01/2000
(See IFCO Systems N.V.)

PALEY MANUFACTURING CORP. (NY)
Recapitalized as Circle Air Industries, Inc. and each share Common 25¢ par exchanged for (3) shares Common 5¢ par in March 1955

PALFED INC (SC)
Common $1 par split (5) for (4) by issuance of (0.25) additional share 12/15/88
Merged into Regions Financial Corp. (Old) 2/12/98
Each share Common $1 par exchanged for (0.7) share Common $0.625 par
Regions Financial Corp. (Old) merged into Regions Financial Corp. (New) 7/1/2004

PALI TECHNOLOGY CORP (NV)
Name changed to Audio Magnetics Inc. 3/23/89
(See Audio Magnetics Inc.)

PALIGENT INC (DE)
Recapitalized as International Fight League, Inc. 11/29/2006
Each share Common 1¢ par exchanged for (0.05) share Common 1¢ par
International Fight League, Inc. recapitalized as IFLI Acquisition Corp. 07/08/2010 which name changed to SimplePons, Inc. 12/27/2011 which recapitalized as Eco-Shift Power Corp. 11/26/2013

PALISADE AIRCRAFT CORP (NJ)
Charter cancelled for non-payment of taxes 05/31/1974

PALISADES CORP.
Liquidation completed in 1953

PALISADES NEPHELINE MINING CO, LTD. (ON)
Charter cancelled for failure to file reports and pay taxes April 1958

PALISADES TRUST CO. (ENGLEWOOD, NJ)
Each share Capital Stock $100 par exchanged for (5) shares Capital Stock $20 par 5/15/56
Stock Dividend - 25% 3/1/54
Merged into Peoples Trust Co. of Bergen County (Hackensack, NJ) 11/8/63
Each share Capital Stock $20 par exchanged for (3.375) shares Capital Stock $5 par
Peoples Trust Co. of Bergen County (Hackensack, NJ) name changed to Peoples Trust of New Jersey (Hackensack, NJ) 2/25/69 which reorganized as United Jersey Banks 10/1/70 which name changed to UJB Financial Corp. 6/30/98 which name which name changed to Summit Bancorp 3/1/96 which merged into FleetBoston Financial Corp. 3/1/2001 which merged into Bank of America Corp. 4/1/2004

PALISADES VENTURES INC (BC)
Recapitalized as Fremont Gold Ltd. 07/07/2017
Each share Common no par exchanged for (0.75) share Common no par

PALKO ENVIRONMENTAL LTD (AB)
Merged into Gibson Energy Inc. 12/08/2011
Each share Common no par exchanged for $3.05 cash

PALL CORP (NY)
Class A $1 par split (2) for (1) by issuance of (1) additional share 06/17/1959
Class B $1 par split (2) for (1) by issuance of (1) additional share 06/17/1959
Class A $1 par split (3) for (2) by issuance of (0.5) additional share 12/05/1963
Class B $1 par split (3) for (2) by issuance of (0.5) additional share 12/05/1963
Class B $1 par all converted to Class A $1 par 02/15/1972
Class A $1 par reclassified as Common $1 par 11/22/1972
Common $1 par split (2) for (1) by issuance of (1) additional share 12/04/1975
Common $1 par split (3) for (2) by issuance of (0.5) additional share 12/15/1977
Common $1 par split (3) for (2) by issuance of (0.5) additional share 12/27/1978
Common $1 par split (3) for (2) by issuance of (0.5) additional share 12/27/1979
Common $1 par changed to 50¢ par 11/20/1980
Common 50¢ par split (3) for (2) by issuance of (0.5) additional share 12/19/1980
Common 50¢ par split (4) for (3) by issuance of (0.33333333) additional share 12/17/1982
Common 50¢ par changed to 25¢ par 11/18/1983
Common 25¢ par split (3) for (2) by issuance of (0.5) additional share 12/27/1985
Common 25¢ par split (4) for (3) by issuance of (0.33333333) additional share 12/26/1986
Common 25¢ par split (3) for (2) by issuance of (0.5) additional share 02/15/1991
Common 25¢ par split (3) for (2) by issuance of (0.5) additional share 12/27/1991
Common 25¢ par split (4) for (3) by issuance of (0.33333333) additional share 12/26/1992
Common 25¢ par changed to 10¢ par 11/18/1993
Acquired by Danaher Corp. 08/31/2015
Each share Common 10¢ par exchanged for $127.20 cash

PALL-MALL COPPER MINES LTD. (ON)
Merged into Indian Mountain Metal Mines Ltd. 06/24/1971
Each share Capital Stock $1 par exchanged for (0.117647) share Capital Stock $1 par
Indian Mountain Metal Mines Ltd. merged into Initiative Explorations Inc. 02/13/1980 which merged into Canhorn Chemical Corp. 04/26/1995 which merged into Nayarit Gold Inc. 05/02/2005 which merged into Capital Gold Corp. 08/02/2010 which merged into Gammon Gold Inc. (QC) 04/08/2011 which reincorporated in Ontario as AuRico Gold Inc. 06/14/2011 which merged into Alamos Gold Inc. (New) 07/06/2015

PALLADIUM COMMUNICATIONS INC (NV)
Each share old Common $0.001 par exchanged for (0.01) share new Common $0.001 par 03/31/2003
Name changed to Peak Entertainment Holdings, Inc. 05/20/2003
Peak Entertainment Holdings, Inc. name changed to Encore Energy Systems, Inc. 08/20/2007
(See Encore Energy Systems, Inc.)

PALLADIUM RESOURCE CORP (AB)
Delisted from Alberta Stock Exchange 05/13/1998

PALLAS RES CORP (NV)
Chapter 11 bankruptcy proceedings converted to Chapter 7 on 03/07/2007
Stockholders' equity unlikely

PALLAUM MINERALS LTD (CANADA)
Recapitalized as Canoe Resources Ltd. 5/31/2005
Each share Common no par exchanged for (0.1) share Common no par
Note: Canoe Resources Ltd. is awaiting reactivation

PALLET MGMT SYS INC (FL)
Each share old Common $0.001 par exchanged for (0.25) share new Common $0.001 par 02/16/1998
Plan of reorganization under Chapter 11 Federal Bankruptcy proceedings effective 09/00/2003
No stockholders' equity

PALLISER ENERGY CORP (AB)
Acquired by Search Energy Corp. 8/9/2000
Each share Common no par exchanged for $1.50 cash

PALLISER ENERGY INC (AB)
Plan of reorganization effective 8/28/97
Each share Class A no par exchanged for (0.5) share Palliser Energy Corp. Common no par and (0.5) share Petro Well Energy Services Inc. Common no par
(See each company's listing)

PALLISER INTL ENERGY INC (BC)
Recapitalized as Elan Industries Inc. 12/19/1986
Each share Common no par exchanged for (0.2) share Common no par
Elan Industries Inc. recapitalized as Trylox Environmental Corp. (BC) 08/17/1990 which reincorporated in Wyoming 09/14/1990
(See Trylox Environmental Corp. (WY))

PALLISER OIL & GAS CORP (AB)
Discharged from receivership
01/20/2017
No stockholders' equity

PALLISER PETES INC (AB)
Name changed to Petrostar
Petroleums Inc. (Old) 6/14/89
Petrostar Petroleums Inc. (Old)
merged into Petrostar Petroleums
Inc. (New) 6/11/92 which merged
into Crestar Energy Inc. 6/7/96
which was acquired by Gulf Canada
Resources Ltd. 11/13/2000
(See Gulf Canada Resources Ltd.)

PALLISER PETES LTD (ON)
Name changed to Dundee-Palliser
Resources Inc. 05/17/1973
Dundee-Palliser Resources Inc.
recapitalized as Scorpion Minerals
Inc. 04/01/1996 which name
changed to Nextair Inc. 03/05/2001
which recapitalized as NXA Inc.
02/23/2005 which recapitalized as
Ellipsiz Communications Ltd.
11/26/2015

PALLISER RES INC (BC)
Merged into Palliser International
Energy Inc. 6/1/82
Each share Common no par
exchanged for (1) share Common
no par
Pallister International Energy Inc.
recapitalized as Elan Industries Inc.
12/19/86 which recapitalized as
Trylox Environmental Corp. (BC)
8/17/90 which reincorporated in
Wyoming 9/14/90
(See Trylox Environmental Corp.
(WY))

PALM BEACH CO (ME)
Common $1 par changed to 50¢ par
and (1) additional share issued
03/15/1968
Common 50¢ par changed to 25¢ par
and (1) additional share issued
04/03/1969
Under plan of reorganization each
share Common 25¢ par
automatically became (1) share
Palm Beach Inc. (Old) Common 25¢
par 05/19/1978
Palm Beach Inc. (Old) merged into
Palm Beach Inc. (New) 12/11/1985
(See Palm Beach Inc. (New))

PALM BEACH CNTY UTILS CORP (FL)
Voluntarily dissolved 8/22/91
Details not available

PALM BEACH-DADE CORP. (FL)
Name changed to Cape Canaveral
Corp. 05/23/1962
Cape Canaveral Corp. name changed
to Electronomic Industries, Inc. (FL)
11/17/1969 which reincorporated in
New York as Electronomic Industries
Corp. 02/23/1979 which name
changed to Quantech Electronics
Corp. (NY) 02/23/1983 which
reincorporated in Colorado
12/15/2003 which name changed to
Signal Bay, Inc. 10/24/2014 which
recapitalized as EVIO, Inc.
09/06/2017

PALM BEACH DIVERSIFIED ENTERPRISES INC (FL)
Adjudicated bankrupt 12/26/73

PALM BEACH DIVERSIFIELD FD INC (FL)
Proclaimed dissolved for failure to file
reports and pay fees 8/10/89

PALM BEACH GAS CORP (FL)
Name changed to Niagara Corp.
11/30/1989
Niagara Corp. name changed to NC
Sales Corp. 08/25/1995
(See NC Sales Corp.)

PALM BEACH INC. OLD (DE)
Common 25¢ par split (5) for (4) by
issuance of (0.25) additional share
7/6/78
Merged into Palm Beach Inc. (New)
12/11/85
Each share Common 25¢ par
exchanged for (1) share 10%
Exchangeable Preferred 1¢ par and
$32 cash
(See Palm Beach Inc. (New))

PALM BEACH INC NEW (DE)
Each share 10% Exchangeable
Preferred 1¢ par exchanged for
$8.98 principal amount of 10%
Junior Subordinate Debentures due
12/31/1995 on 12/01/1988

PALM BEACH NATL BK & TR CO (PALM BEACH, FL)
Under plan of reorganization each
share Common 1¢ par automatically
became (1) share Palm Beach
National Holding Co. Common $4.87
par 05/01/1997
Palm Beach National Holding Co.
merged into Colonial BancGroup,
Inc. 09/03/2002
(See Colonial BancGroup, Inc.)

PALM BEACH NATL HLDG CO (FL)
Merged into Colonial BancGroup, Inc.
09/03/2002
Each share Common $4.87 par
exchanged for (3.5714) shares
Common $2.50 par
(See Colonial BancGroup, Inc.)

PALM BEACH PARTNERS INC (NV)
Name changed to Datcha Holdings of
America Inc. 3/1/93
(See Datcha Holdings of America
Inc.)

PALM DESERT ART INC (DE)
Charter cancelled and declared
inoperative and void for
non-payment of taxes 3/1/2001

PALM DESERT NATL BK (PALM DESERT, CA)
Common $5 par changed to $4 par
and (0.25) additional share issued
08/07/1985
Each share old Common $4 par
exchanged for (0.00019252) share
new Common $4 par 12/17/2001
Note: Holders of (5,193) or fewer
shares received $34.45 cash per
share
Bank failed 04/27/2012
Stockholders' equity unlikely

PALM DEVELOPERS LTD (BAHAMAS)
Reorganized under the laws of
Delaware as Applied Concepts, Inc.
3/27/69
Each share Ordinary 1s par
exchanged for (1) share Common
1¢ par
Applied Concepts, Inc. (DE) name
changed to Citipostal Inc. 7/8/83
(See Citipostal Inc.)

PALM HBR HOMES INC (FL)
Issue Information - 1,055,000 shares
COM offered at $12 per share on
07/07/1995
Common 1¢ par split (5) for (4) by
issuance of (0.25) additional share
payable 08/02/1996 to holders of
record 07/26/1996
Common 1¢ par split (5) for (4) by
issuance of (0.25) additional share
payable 07/21/1997 to holders of
record 07/08/1997
Common 1¢ par split (5) for (4) by
issuance of (0.25) additional share
payable 07/28/1998 to holders of
record 07/14/1998
Plan of reorganization under Chapter
11 Federal Bankruptcy proceedings
effective 12/02/2011
No stockholders' equity

PALM INC NEW (DE)
Common $0.001 par split (2) for (1)
by issuance of (1) additional share
payable 03/14/2006 to holders of
record 02/28/2006 Ex date -
03/15/2006
Merged into Hewlett-Packard Co.
07/01/2010
Each share Common $0.001 par
exchanged for $5.70 cash

PALM INC OLD (DE)
Each share old Common 1¢ par
exchanged for (0.05) share new
Common 1¢ par 10/15/2002
Each share new Common 1¢ par
received distribution of (0.30980417)
share PalmSource, Inc. Common
$0.001 par payable 10/28/2003 to
holders of record 10/28/2003
Name changed to palmOne, Inc.
10/28/2003
palmOne, Inc. name changed to
Palm, Inc. (New) 07/14/2005
(See Palm, Inc. (New))

PALM SPRINGS AWYS CORP (NV)
Recapitalized as New Dimension
Holdings, Inc. 08/01/2013
Each share Common $0.001 par
exchanged for (0.33333333) share
Common $0.001 par

PALM SPRINGS LIFESTYLE INC (MN)
Statutorily dissolved 11/12/1991

PALM SPRINGS NATL BK (PALM SPRINGS, CA)
Merged into First National Bank &
Trust Co. (Ontario, CA) 1/1/74
Each share Capital Stock $10 par
exchanged for (0.589275) share
Common $4 par
First National Bank & Trust Co.
(Ontario, CA) name changed to First
Trust Bank (Ontario, CA) 4/2/79
(See First Trust Bank (Ontario, CA))

PALM SPRINGS SAVINGS & LOAN ASSOCIATION (CA)
Guarantee Stock $5 par changed to
$2.50 par and (1) additional share
issued 4/15/83
Name changed to Palm Springs
Savings Bank and Guarantee Stock
$2.50 par reclassified as Guarantee
Common $2.50 par 1/1/84
Palm Springs Savings Bank acquired
by HF Bancorp 9/27/96
(See HF Bancorp Inc.)

PALM SPRINGS SVGS BK (PALM SPRINGS, CA)
Acquired by HF Bancorp 9/27/96
Each share Common $2.50 par
exchanged for $14.375 cash

PALM STATE BANK (PALM HARBOR, FL)
Acquired by Landmark Union Trust
Bank of St. Petersburg, N.A. (St.
Petersburg, FL) 08/16/1985
Details not available

PALM TELEPHONE SERVICE, INC. (FL)
Proclaimed dissolved for failure to file
reports and pay fees 5/13/69

PALM WORKS INC (NV)
Name changed to Zydant Corp.
10/17/2000
(See Zydant Corp.)

PALMAREJO GOLD CORP (AB)
Name changed to Palmarejo Silver &
Gold Corp. 12/19/2005
Palmarejo Silver & Gold Corp.
merged into Coeur d'Alene Mines
Corp. (ID) 12/21/2007 which
reincorporated in Delaware as
Coeur Mining, Inc. 05/17/2013

PALMAREJO SILVER & GOLD CORP (CANADA)
Merged into Coeur d'Alene Mines
Corp. (ID) 12/21/2007
Each share Common no par
exchanged for (2.715) shares
Common $1 par and $0.004 cash
Coeur d'Alene Mines Corp. (ID)
reincorporated in Delaware as
Coeur Mining, Inc. 05/17/2013

PALMDALE EXECUTIVE HOMES CORP (NV)
Name changed to California Mines
Corp. 06/14/2013

PALMER ARNOLD GOLF CO (TN)
Merged into APGC Acquisition Corp.
9/22/99
Each share Common 50¢ par
exchanged for $1.20 cash

PALMER BANCORP INC (IL)
Reorganized 8/30/85
Under plan of reorganization each
share Palmer-American National
Bank of Danville (Danville, IL)
Common $10 par automatically
became (1) share Palmer Bancorp,
Inc. Common $10 par 8/30/85
Acquired by Old National Bancorp
12/31/92
Each share Common $10 par
exchanged for (6) shares Common
no par

PALMER BK CORP (FL)
Stock Dividend - 100% 04/02/1973
Merged into Southeast Banking Corp.
01/15/1976
Each share Common $1 par
exchanged for (0.275) share Limited
Dividend Conv. Preferred Ser. A no
par and (0.2) Common Stock
Purchase Warrant expiring
12/01/1978
(See Southeast Banking Corp.)

PALMER BLOCK CORP. (IL)
Completely liquidated 10/18/65
Each share Common no par
exchanged for first and final
distribution of $77.25 cash

PALMER CO. (DE)
Consent to Dissolution filed with
Delaware Secretary of State 7/6/64

PALMER (JOHN) CO., LTD. (NB)
Assets sold to Palmer-McLellan
(United) Ltd. 1/5/59
Each share Class A no par
exchanged for (1) share Class A $10
par and 25¢ in cash

PALMER CORP. OF LOUISIANA
Acquired by United Gas Corp.
00/00/1930
Details not available

PALMER FIRST NATL BK & TR CO (SARASOTA, FL)
Capital Stock $100 par changed to
$10 par and (9) additional shares
issued plus a 25% stock dividend
paid 02/24/1969
Capital Stock $10 par changed to $5
par and (1) additional share issued
plus a 25% stock dividend paid
03/15/1971
Stock Dividend - 100% 03/10/1961
99% held by Palmer Bank Corp. as of
12/31/1971
Public interest eliminated

PALMER (ARNOLD) GOLF CO. (OH)
Acquired by Professional Golf Co.
6/23/72
Each share Common 50¢ par
exchanged for (0.584359) share
Common 50¢ par
Professional Golf Co. name changed
to ProGroup Inc. 2/25/75 which
name changed to Palmer (Arnold)
Golf Co. (TN) 7/17/96
(See Palmer (Arnold) Golf Co. (TN))

PALMER INDS LTD (BC)
Name changed to Palmer Resources
Ltd. 09/18/1996
Palmer Resources Ltd. merged into
Lyon Lake Mines Ltd. 02/05/1999
(See Lyon Lake Mines Ltd.)

PALMER MATCH CO.
Name changed to Palmer Co. in 1950
Palmer Co. filed consent to
dissolution 7/6/64

PAL-PAL   FINANCIAL INFORMATION, INC.

PALMER-MCLELLAN (UNITED) LTD. (NB)
Class A $10 par called for redemption 6/15/80
Public interest eliminated

PALMER MED INC (CO)
Recapitalized as Edatenow.Com, Inc. 02/03/1999
Each share Common $0.001 par exchanged for (0.05) share Common $0.001 par
Edatenow.Com, Inc. name changed to Encounter.Com, Inc. 05/31/1999 which name changed to Encounter Technologies Inc. 02/18/2010

PALMER OIL DEVELOPMENT CO. LTD. (ON)
Merged into Rio Palmer Oils Ltd. 7/25/55
Each share Common no par exchanged for (0.35) share Capital Stock $1 par
Rio Palmer Oils Ltd. merged into Devon- Palmer Oils Ltd. 11/6/56 which merged into Triad Oil Manitoba Ltd. for cash 3/8/67

PALMER RES LTD (BC)
Merged into Lyon Lake Mines Ltd. 02/05/1999
Each share Common no par exchanged for (1) share Common no par
(See Lyon Lake Mines Ltd.)

PALMER STENDEL OIL CORP. (CA)
Common $1 par changed to 50¢ par 00/00/1952
Common 50¢ par changed to 10¢ par 04/07/1953
Recapitalized as Petrocarbon Chemicals, Inc. (CA) 06/03/1955
Each share Common 10¢ par exchanged for (0.1) share Common $1 par
Petrocarbon Chemicals, Inc. (CA) reincorporated in Maryland 06/27/1956
Petrocarbon Chemicals, Inc. (MD) merged into Great Western Producers, Inc. 12/30/1957 which liquidated for Taylor Wine Co., Inc. 11/30/1966 which merged into Coca-Cola Co. 01/21/1977

PALMER TUBE MLS LTD (AUSTRALIA)
Underlying shares delisted at company's request 10/26/1994
Details not available

PALMER UNION OIL CO.
Succeeded by Palmer Stendel Oil Corp. 00/00/1932
Details not available

PALMER WIRELESS INC (DE)
Acquired by Price Communications Corp. 10/06/1997
Each share Common 1¢ par exchanged for $17.50 cash

PALMERSTON STK AGY INC (DE)
Recapitalized as Magnolia Lane Income Fund 08/13/2013
Each share Common $0.0001 par exchanged for (0.125) share Common $0.0001 par
Magnolia Lane Income Fund name changed to Huntwicke Capital Group Inc. 09/23/2016

PALMETEX CORP. (DE)
No longer in existence having become inoperative and void for non-payment of taxes 4/1/54

PALMETTO BANCSHARES INC (SC)
Common $5 par split (2) for (1) by issuance of (1) additional share payable 01/14/2000 to holders of record 01/03/2000
Common $5 par changed to 1¢ par 08/06/2010
Each share old Common 1¢ par exchanged for (0.25) share new Common 1¢ par 06/30/2011
Acquired by United Community Banks, Inc. 09/01/2015
Each share new Common 1¢ par exchanged for $19.25 cash

PALMETTO BANK (LAURENS, SC)
Reorganized as Palmetto Bancshares Inc. 05/06/1983
Each share Common $5 par exchanged for (1) share Common $5 par
(See Palmetto Bancshares Inc.)

PALMETTO CORP. (TX)
Merged into Tenneco Realty Inc. 10/13/72
Each share Common $1 par exchanged for $35 cash

PALMETTO FED SVGS & LN ASSN (FL)
Merged into Goldome Bank, F.S.B (St. Petersburg, FL) 08/12/1983
Each share Common 1¢ par exchanged for $33 cash

PALMETTO FED SVGS BK S C (AIKEN, SC)
Under plan of reorganization each share Common $1 par automatically became (1) share PALFED, Inc. Common $1 par 1/27/87
PALFED, Inc. merged into Regions Financial Corp. (Old) 2/12/98 which merged into Regions Financial Corp. (New) 7/1/2004

PALMETTO HORTICULTURAL INC (SC)
Charter forfeited 10/10/86

PALMETTO INDL CORP (SC)
Reorganized as Palmetto Real Estate Trust 6/1/72
Each share Common $1 par exchanged for (1) Share of Bene. Int. $1 par
(See Palmetto Real Estate Trust)

PALMETTO PULP & PAPER CORP. (SC)
Name changed to Palmetto Industrial Corp. 5/27/68
Palmetto Industrial Corp. reorganized as Palmetto Real Estate Trust 6/1/72
(See Palmetto Real Estate Trust)

PALMETTO REAL ESTATE TR (SC)
Company went private 01/02/2007
Each Share of Bene. Int. $1 par exchanged for $5.50 cash
Note: Holders of (1,000) or more shares retained their interests

PALMETTO RES LTD (AB)
Name changed to Corlac Oilfield Leasing Ltd. 03/31/1998
Corlac Oilfield Leasing Ltd. name changed to Enhanced Energy Services Ltd. 03/31/2000 which recapitalized as EnSource Energy Services Inc. 03/12/2001 which was acquired by Enerflex Systems Ltd. (Canada) 07/24/2002 which reorganized in Alberta as Enerflex Systems Income Fund 10/02/2006 which merged into Toromont Industries Ltd. 02/26/2010

PALMETTO ST LIFE INS CO (SC)
Capital Stock $10 par changed to $2.50 par and (3) additional shares issued 09/12/1956
Stock Dividends - 33-1/3% 04/16/1951; 50% 02/27/1962; 10% 10/10/1967
Merged into Capital Holding Corp. 06/01/1971
Each share Capital Stock $2.50 par exchanged for (1.25) shares Common $1 par
Capital Holding Corp. name changed to Providian Corp. 05/12/1994 which name changed to Aegon N.V. 06/10/1997

PALMETTO SYNTHETIC CDO LTD (CAYMAN ISLANDS)
Accredited Investors Preferred Shares called for redemption 8/8/2006

PALMO REALTY CO.
Dissolved in 1947

PALMOLIVE-PEET CO. (DE)
Name changed to Colgate-Palmolive-Peet Co. 8/8/28 which name was changed to Colgate-Palmolive Co. 10/30/53

PALMONE INC (DE)
Name changed to Palm, Inc. (New) 07/14/2005
(See Palm, Inc. (New))

PALMS PASADENA HOSP CORP (FL)
Common $1 par changed to 40¢ par and (1.5) additional shares issued 10/21/1968
Stock Dividend - 10% 06/01/1968
Name changed to Medfield Corp. 12/10/1969
Medfield Corp. merged into National Medical Enterprises, Inc. 02/28/1979 which name changed to Tenet Healthcare Corp. 06/23/1995

PALMSOURCE INC (DE)
Merged into ACCESS Co., Ltd. 11/14/2005
Each share Common $0.001 par exchanged for $18.50 cash

PALMYRIA RES CORP (BC)
Common no par split (2) for (1) by issuance of (1) additional share 07/30/1986
Reorganized as Med-Tech Systems Inc. 09/24/1986
Each share Common no par exchanged for (2) shares Common no par
(See Med-Tech Systems Inc.)

PALO ALTO SALINAS SVGS & LN ASSN (CA)
Name changed to Northern California Savings & Loan Association 05/09/1972
Northern California Savings & Loan Association reorganized as Northern California Savings, A Federal Savings & Loan Association 05/14/1982 which merged into Great Western Financial Corp. 07/31/1982 which merged into Washington Mutual Inc. 07/01/1997
(See Washington Mutual, Inc.)

PALO ALTO SAVINGS & LOAN ASSOCIATION (CA)
Merged into Palo Alto-Salinas Savings & Loan Association 07/01/1969
Each share Guarantee Stock $1 par exchanged for (3) shares Guarantee Stock no par
Palo Alto-Salinas Savings & Loan Association name changed to Northern California Savings & Loan Association 05/09/1972 which reorganized as Northern California Savings, A Federal Savings & Loan Association 05/14/1982 which merged into Great Western Financial Corp. 07/31/1982 which merged into Washington Mutual Inc. 07/01/1997
(See Washington Mutual, Inc.)

PALO DURO ENERGY INC (BC)
Reincorporated 12/19/2014
Each share old Common no par exchanged for (0.2) share new Common no par 04/11/2011
Place of incorporation changed from (AB) to (BC) 12/19/2014
Recapitalized as CarbonOne Technologies Inc. 07/28/2015
Each share Common no par exchanged for (0.25) share Common no par
CarbonOne Technologies Inc. name changed to TekModo Industries Inc.
10/12/2016 which recapitalized as Lincoln Ventures Ltd. 07/16/2018

PALO VERDE MINING CORP. (DE)
Charter cancelled and declared inoperative and void for non-payment of taxes 1/1/40

PALOMA PETE LTD (AB)
Common no par split (2) for (1) by issuance of (1) additional share 6/28/79
Merged into Sunalta Acquisition 12/24/96
Each share Common no par exchanged for $2.40 cash

PALOMA VENTURES INC (BC)
Recapitalized as Paloma Resources Inc. 2/25/2004
Each share Common no par exchanged for (0.2) share Common no par

PALOMAR CAP CORP (BC)
Acquired by PCC Acquisition Corp. 08/27/1990
Each share Common no par exchanged for $0.41 cash

PALOMAR ENTERPRISES INC (NV)
Each share old Common $0.001 par exchanged for (0.01) share new Common $0.001 par 06/21/2004
Each share new Common $0.001 par exchanged for (0.001) share old Common $0.00001 par 12/08/2004
Each share old Common $0.00001 par exchanged for (0.001) share new Common $0.00001 par 07/05/2005
Each share new Common $0.00001 par received distribution of (0.0008) share Blackhawk Fund new Common $0.001 par payable 03/28/2007 to holders of record 03/08/2007 Ex date - 05/01/2007
Each share new Common $0.00001 par received distribution of (0.00082) share Blackhawk Fund new Common $0.001 par payable 07/11/2007 to holders of record 06/22/2007 Ex date - 07/16/2007
Each share new Common $0.00001 par exchanged again for (0.00333333) share new Common $0.00001 par 02/04/2008
Name changed to Angel Acquisition Corp. 04/21/2008
(See Angel Acquisition Corp.)

PALOMAR FINL (CA)
Merged into T & N Holding Co. 6/23/83
Each share Common $1 par exchanged for $6 cash

PALOMAR GOLD MINES LTD. (ON)
Completely liquidated in December 1964
Each share Capital Stock $1 par exchanged for first and final distribution of $0.00475 cash

PALOMAR MED TECHNOLOGIES INC (DE)
Each share old Common 1¢ par exchanged for (0.14285714) share new Common 1¢ par 05/10/1999
Merged into Cynosure, Inc. 06/25/2013
Each share new Common 1¢ par exchanged for (0.2819) share Class A Common $0.001 par and $6.825 cash
(See Cynosure, Inc.)

PALOMAR MTG CO (CA)
Common $1 par split (2) for (1) by issuance of (1) additional share 1/4/62
Name changed to Palomar Financial 5/28/69
Palomar Financial merged into T & N Holding Co. 6/23/83
(See Palomar Financial)

PALOMAR MTG INVS (CA)
Shares of Bene. Int. $1 par split (2)

PAL-PAN

PALOMAR SVGS & LN (CA)
for (1) by issuance of (1) additional share 05/17/1971
Name changed to Mission Investment Trust 03/10/1975
Mission Investment Trust reorganized as Mission West Properties (CA) 07/22/1982 which reorganized in Maryland as Mission West Properties, Inc. 12/28/1998 which liquidated for Mission West Liquidating Trust 12/28/2012
(See Mission West Liquidating Trust)

PALOMAR SVGS & LN (CA)
Stock Dividend - 5% payable 2/18/98 to holders of record 2/2/98
Merged into Community West Bancshares 12/14/98
Each share Common $4 par exchanged for (2.11) shares Common $2.50 par

PALOMINE MNG INC (NV)
Name changed to Universal Bioenergy, Inc. 11/13/2007

PALOMINO EXPLORATIONS LTD. (ON)
Merged into Proto Explorations & Holdings Inc. 2/24/72
Each (25) shares Capital Stock $1 par exchanged for (3) shares Common no par
Proto Explorations & Holdings Inc. name changed to Baxter Resources Corp. 6/26/81 which merged into Baxter Technologies Corp. 12/31/81 which name changed to Standard-Modern Technologies Corp. 10/8/85
(See Standard-Modern Technologies Corp.)

PALOMINO RES INC (AB)
Completely liquidated
Each share Common no par received first and final distribution of $0.1075838 cash payable 11/30/2007 to holders of record 11/30/2007
Note: Certificates were not required to be surrendered and are without value

PALOS VERDES NATL BK (ROLLING HILLS ESTATES, CA)
Bank closed by California Superintendent of Banks 05/20/1993
No stockholders' equity

PALSTON MINING & DEVELOPMENT CO. LTD. (ON)
Charter revoked for failure to file reports and pay fees 3/16/67

PALWEB CORP (DE)
Reorganized under the laws of Oklahoma 6/25/2002
Each share Common 10¢ par exchanged for (0.02) share Common 10¢ par
Palweb Corp. (OK) name changed to Greystone Logistics Inc. 3/18/2005

PALWEB CORP (OK)
Name changed to Greystone Logistics Inc. 3/18/2005

PAM HLDGS INC (CA)
Completely liquidated
Each share Class A no par received first and final distribution of $0.09 cash payable 12/15/2017 to holders of record 12/02/2017 Ex date - 12/18/2017

PAMBELLE MINING CO., LTD. (ON)
Charter cancelled for failure to file reports and pay taxes in 1953

PAMECO CORP (DE)
Reincorporated 7/21/2000
Issue Information - 3,578,644 shares COM offered at $14 per share on 06/04/1997
Reorganized from under the laws of (GA) to (DE) 7/21/2000
Each share Common 1¢ par exchanged for (1/3) share Common 1¢ par

Acquired by Littlejohn Fund II, L.P. 5/29/2001
Each share Common 1¢ par exchanged for $0.45 cash

PAMERICA CORP (CANADA)
Name changed to Wanted Technologies Corp. 10/03/2005
(See Wanted Technologies Corp.)

PAMET SYS INC (MA)
Each share old Common 1¢ par exchanged for (0.1) share new Common 1¢ par 10/18/2005
Company advised it became private 00/00/2008
Details not available

PAMEX FOODS INC (DE)
Stock Dividends - 10% 05/24/1976; 10% 04/29/1977
Name changed back to Pancho's Mexican Buffet, Inc. 06/04/1982
(See Pancho's Mexican Buffet, Inc.)

PAMIDA HLDGS CORP (DE)
Merged into ShopKo Stores Inc. 7/9/99
Each share Common 1¢ par exchanged for $11.50 cash

PAMIDA INC (NE)
Common 50¢ par split (2) for (1) by issuance of (1) additional share 5/28/71
Common 50¢ par split (2) for (1) by issuance of (1) additional share 5/16/72
Name changed to PMD Investment Co. 1/15/81
(See PMD Investment Co.)

PAMLICO RES LTD (BC)
Name changed 02/02/1998
Name changed from Pamlico Gold Corp. to Pamlico Resources Ltd. 02/02/1998
Cease trade order effective 12/07/2001
Stockholders' equity unlikely

PAMOIL LTD. (AB)
Merged into Canadian Industrial Gas & Oil Ltd. 03/08/1965
Each share Capital Stock 20¢ par exchanged for (0.06711409) share Common no par
Canadian Industrial Gas & Oil Ltd. merged into Norcen Energy Resources Ltd. 10/28/1975 which reincorporated in Canada 04/15/1977 which merged into Union Pacific Resources Group Inc. 04/17/1998 which merged into Anadarko Petroleum Corp. 07/14/2000

PAMOREX MINERALS INC (CANADA)
Merged into Royal Oak Mines Inc. 07/23/1991
Each share Common no par exchanged for (0.6) share Common no par
Royal Oak Mines Inc. recapitalized as Royal Oak Ventures Inc. 02/14/2000
(See Royal Oak Ventures Inc.)

PAMOUR INC (CANADA)
Name changed 07/11/1986
Capital Stock no par reclassified as Conv. Class A Common no par 10/01/1975
Conv. Class A Common no par reclassified as Common no par 06/19/1980
Conv. Class B Common no par reclassified as Common no par 06/19/1980
Name changed from Pamour Porcupine Mines Ltd. to Pamour Inc. 07/11/1986
Merged into Royal Oak Mines Inc. 07/23/1991
Each share Common no par exchanged for (0.75) share Common no par
Royal Oak Mines Inc. recapitalized as Royal Oak Ventures Inc. 02/14/2000

(See Royal Oak Ventures Inc.)

PAMPA OIL & REFINING CO. (TX)
Charter expired by time limitations 8/3/51

PAMRAPO BANCORP INC (NJ)
Reincorporated 03/29/2001
State of incorporation changed from (DE) to (NJ) 03/29/2001
Common 1¢ par split (2) for (1) by issuance of (1) additional share payable 05/29/2002 to holders of record 05/15/2002 Ex date - 05/30/2002
Merged into BCB Bancorp, Inc. 07/06/2010
Each share Common 1¢ par exchanged for (1) share Common no par

PAN ACHERON RES LTD (BC)
Merged into Acheron Resources Ltd. 10/01/1982
Each share Common no par exchanged for (0.25) share Common no par
Acheron Resources Ltd. recapitalized as Abaddon Resources Inc. 09/12/1994 which recapitalized as Consolidated Abaddon Resources Inc. 01/31/2001 which name changed to Aben Resources Ltd. 01/13/2011

PAN AFRICAN MNG CORP (BC)
Merged into African Queen Mines Ltd. 06/27/2008
Each share Common no par exchanged for (1) share Common no par and $4.50 cash

PAN AFRICAN OIL LTD (AB)
Reincorporated 08/05/2014
Place of incorporation changed from (ON) to (AB) 08/05/2014
Merged into Eco (Atlantic) Oil & Gas Ltd. 01/28/2015
Each share Common no par exchanged for (0.323) share Common no par

PAN AFRICAN RESOURCES CORP. (YUKON)
Merged into Golden Star Resources Ltd. 4/21/98
Each share Common no par exchanged for (0.02) share Common no par

PAN AJAX RES LTD (BC)
Recapitalized as Aleta Resource Industries Ltd. 10/10/1974
Each share Common no par exchanged for (0.2) share Common no par
Aleta Resource Industries Ltd. name changed to Mandarin Capital Corp. 09/12/1984 which reorganized as H.I.S.A. Investments Ltd. 12/29/1989
(See H.I.S.A. Investments Ltd.)

PAN-ALASKA CORP. (TX)
Merged into Australamerica Corp. (TX) on a (0.1) for (1) basis 6/5/61
(See Australamerica Corp. (TX))

PAN ALASKA FISHERIES INC (WA)
Merged into Castle & Cooke, Inc. (Old) 06/18/1975
Each share Common 50¢ par exchanged for (1/3) share Common $10 par
Castle & Cooke, Inc. (Old) name changed to Dole Food Co., Inc. (HI) 07/30/1991 which reincorporated in Delaware 07/01/2001
(See Dole Food Co., Inc. (Old) (DE))

PAN AM CORP (DE)
Plan of reorganization under Chapter 11 Federal Bankruptcy Code withdrawn 12/08/1991
No stockholders' equity

PAN AM CORP (FL)
Plan of reorganization under Chapter 11 Federal Bankruptcy proceedings confirmed 06/29/1998

No stockholders' equity

PAN AMERICAN AIRWAYS CORP. (DE)
Recapitalized as Pan American World Airways, Inc. 00/00/1949
Each share Capital Stock $2.50 par exchanged for (1) share Capital Stock $1 par
Pan American World Airways, Inc. reorganized in Delaware as Pan Am Corp. 09/14/1984
(See Pan Am Corp.)

PAN AMERICAN BANCSHARES, INC. (FL)
Name changed to Pan American Banks Inc. 5/1/81
Pan American Banks Inc. merged into NCNB Corp. 12/31/85 which name changed to NationsBank Corp. 12/31/91 which reincorporated in Delaware as BankAmerica Corp. (Old) 9/25/98 which merged into BankAmerica Corp. (New) 9/30/98 which name changed to Bank of America Corp. 4/28/99

PAN AMERN BK (LOS ANGELES, CA)
Each share old Common $5 par exchanged for (0.001) share new Common $5 par 07/31/2015
Acquired by Beneficial State Bancorp 06/17/2016
Each share new Common $5 par exchanged for $29.39 cash

PAN AMERN BK (MIAMI, FL)
Merged into Pan American Bancshares, Inc. (FL) 12/30/78
Each share Capital Stock $10 par exchanged for (3.36) shares Capital Stock $5 par
Pan American Bancshares, Inc. name changed to Pan American Banks Inc. 5/11/81 which merged into NCNB Corp. 12/13/85 which name changed to NationsBank Corp. 12/31/91 which reincorporated in Delaware as BankAmerica Corp. (Old) 9/25/98 which merged into BankAmerica Corp. (New) 9/30/98 which name changed to Bank of America Corp. 4/28/99

PAN AMERICAN BANK (MIAMI BEACH, FL)
Merged into Pan American Bancshares, Inc. 12/30/78
Each share Capital Stock $10 par exchanged for (1.13) shares Capital Stock $5 par
Pan American Bancshares, Inc. name changed to Pan American Banks Inc. 5/1/81 which merged into NCNB Corp. 12/13/85 which name changed to NationsBank Corp. 12/31/91 which reincorporated in Delaware as BankAmerica Corp. (Old) 9/25/98 which merged into BankAmerica Corp. (New) 9/30/98 which name changed to Bank of America Corp. 4/28/99

PAN AMERN BK (SARASOTA, FL)
98.75% acquired by Pan American Bancshares, Inc. through purchase offer as of 06/01/1978
Public interest eliminated

PAN AMERN BK DADE CNTY (NORTH MIAMI BEACH, FL)
Merged into Pan American Bancshares, Inc. 12/30/78
Each share Capital Stock $10 par exchanged for (2.61) shares Capital Stock $5 par
Pan American Bancshares, Inc. name changed to Pan American Banks Inc. 5/1/81 which merged into NCNB Corp. 12/13/85 which name changed to NationsBank Corp. 12/31/91 which reincorporated in Delaware as BanakAmerica Corp. (Old) 9/25/98 which merged into BankAmerica Corp. (New) 9/30/98

which name changed to Bank of America Corp. 4/28/99

PAN AMERICAN BANK OF KENDALE LAKES, N.A. (MIAMI, FL)
Under plan of merger name changed to Pan American Bancshares, Inc. and Capital Stock $10 par changed to $5 par 12/30/77
Pan American Bancshares, Inc. name changed to Pan American Banks Inc. 5/1/81 which merged into NCNB Corp. 12/13/85 which name changed to NationsBank Corp. 12/31/91 which reincorporated in Delaware as BankAmerica Corp. (Old) 9/25/98 which merged into BankAmerica Corp. (New) 9/30/98 which name changed to Bank of America Corp. 4/28/99

PAN AMERICAN BANK OF ORLANDO, N.A. (ORLANDO, FL)
98.2% held by Pan American Bancshares, Inc. as of 05/30/1972
Public interest eliminated

PAN AMERICAN BANK OF WEST DADE (MIAMI, FL)
Merged into Pan American Bancshares, Inc. 12/30/78
Each share Capital Stock $10 par exchanged for (1.41) shares Capital Stock $5 par
Pan American Bancshares, Inc. name changed to Pan American Banks Inc. 5/1/81 which merged into NCNB Corp. 12/13/85 which name changed to NationsBank Corp. 12/31/91 which reincorporated in Delaware as BankAmerica Corp. (Old) 9/25/98 which merged into BankAmerica Corp. (New) 9/30/98 which name changed to Bank of America Corp. 4/28/99

PAN AMERN BK TAMPA N A (TAMPA, FL)
99% held by Pan American Banks, Inc. as of 06/30/1981
Public interest eliminated

PAN AMERN BKS INC (FL)
Merged into NCNB Corp. 12/31/1985
Each share Common $1 par exchanged for (1) share Common $2.50 par
NCNB Corp. name changed to NationsBank Corp. 12/31/1991 which reincorporated in Delaware as BankAmerica Corp. (Old) 09/25/1998 which merged into BankAmerica Corp. (New) 09/30/1998 which name changed to Bank of America Corp. 04/28/1999

PAN AMERICAN CORP. (ID)
Charter forfeited 12/2/96

PAN AMERN DYNAMIC CORP (NY)
Name changed to Sharp International Corp. 02/23/1986
(See Sharp International Corp.)

PAN AMERN ENERGY CORP (CA)
Reorganized under the laws of Nevada as Pan American Industries, Inc. 10/11/1994
Each share Common 10¢ par exchanged for (0.01428571) share Common $0.001 par
Pan American Industries, Inc. name changed to Sunbase Asia Inc. 01/31/1995 which name changed to Centire International, Inc. (NV) 06/08/2007 which reincorporated in Florida as Jericho Energy Co., Inc. 07/18/2008

PAN AMERN ENERGY CORP (NV)
Name changed to Morgan Beaumont, Inc. 08/06/2004
Morgan Beaumont, Inc. recapitalized as nFinanSe Inc. 12/26/2006

PAN AMERN ENERGY INC (NV)
Merged into Colorado River & Eagle Co. 7/1/81
Each share Common 1¢ par exchanged for (0.1) share Class A Common 10¢ par and (0.01) share Class B Common 10¢ par
(See Colorado River & Eagle Co.)

PAN AMERN ENERGY INC (UT)
Completely liquidated 10/23/1970
Each share Common 10¢ par exchanged for first and final distribution of (1) share Pan American Energy, Inc. (NV) Common 1¢ par
Note: Pan American Energy, Inc. (UT) certificates were orginally issued as straight name change from Indian Creek Uranium & Oil Corp. but state of Utah never sanctioned the change
Therefore name legally remained Indian Creek Uranium & Oil Corp. which liquidated 10/23/1970 per same terms as indicated above
This listing for the benefit of those holders of certificates which were invalidly issued
(See Indian Creek Uranium & Oil Corp.)

PAN AMERICAN ENVELOPE CO., INC. (FL)
Name changed to Viking Lithographers, Inc. 04/06/1967
Viking Lithographers, Inc. name changed to Viking General Corp. 04/10/1969 which name changed to American Capital Corp. 05/18/1977 which name changed to America Capital Corp. 05/30/1996

PAN AMERN FERTILIZER CORP OLD (BC)
Merged into Pan American Fertilizer Corp. (New) 08/07/2013
Each share Common no par exchanged for (0.3936) share Common no par

PAN AMERICAN FOREIGN CORP.
Dissolved in 1936

PAN-AMERICAN FRUIT & FIBRE CO. (AZ)
Charter expired by time limitation 1/22/33

PAN AMERN GOLD CORP (ON)
Recapitalized as Newcastle Resources Ltd. (ON) 11/28/2008
Each (30) shares Common no par exchanged for (1) share Common no par
Newcastle Resources Ltd. (ON) reincorporated in British Columbia as RepliCel Life Sciences Inc. 07/01/2011

PAN AMERN GOLD INC (FL)
Administratively dissolved for failure to file annual reports 11/9/90

PAN AMERICAN GOLD RES CORP (NV)
Name changed to Dragon Venture 4/25/2005
Dragon Venture name changed to Dragon Capital Group Corp. 12/13/2005

PAN AMERICAN INDUSTRIAL CORP.
Assets sold in 1937

PAN AMERN INDS INC (NV)
Name changed to Sunbase Asia Inc. 01/31/1995
Sunbase Asia Inc. name changed to Centire International, Inc. (NV) 06/08/2007 which reincorporated in Florida as Jericho Energy Co., Inc. 07/18/2008

PAN AMERN INTL INC (NV)
Each share old Common 3¢ par exchanged for (0.1) share new Common 3¢ par 07/20/1982
Charter permanently revoked 04/30/2004

PAN AMERICAN INVESTMENT FUND, INC. (DE)
Name changed to Counselors Investment Fund, Inc. 00/00/1950
Counselors Investment Fund, Inc. acquired by Pegasus Fund, Inc. 07/02/1973 which name changed to Vanderbilt Growth Fund, Inc. 07/01/1975 which merged into St. Paul Capital Fund, Inc. 06/14/1977 which name changed to AMEV Capital Fund, Inc. 05/01/1985 which reorganized as Fortis Equity Portfolios Inc. 02/22/1992
(See Fortis Equity Portfolios Inc.)

PAN AMERICAN INVESTMENTS, INC. (UT)
Name changed to Oxtec Medical Industries, Inc. 11/18/83
Oxtec Medical Industries, Inc. recapitalized as Federal Medical Industries, Inc. 5/12/86
(See Federal Medical Industries, Inc.)

PAN AMERN LITHIUM CORP (BC)
Name changed to First Potash Corp. 11/26/2012
(See First Potash Corp.)

PAN AMERICAN MATCH CORP.
Name changed to Universal Match Corp. 00/00/1942
Universal Match Corp. name changed to UMC Industries, Inc. 05/17/1966 which name changed to Unidynamics Corp. 04/19/1984
(See Unidynamics Corp.)

PAN AMERN MINERALS CORP (BC)
Name changed 9/27/84
Name changed from Pan American Energy Corp. to Pan American Minerals Corp. 9/27/84
Name changed to Pan American Silver Corp. 4/21/95

PAN AMERN MINES LTD (QC)
Charter cancelled for failure to file reports 05/08/1976

PAN AMERN MTG CORP (FL)
Merged into Atico Financial Corp. 07/31/1987
Each share Common $1 par exchanged for (0.5) share Common $1 par
Atico Financial Corp. merged into Intercontinental Bank (Miami, FL) 03/30/1991 which merged into NationsBank 12/13/1995 which reincorporated in Delaware as BankAmerica Corp. (Old) 09/25/1998 which merged into BankAmerica Corp. (New) 09/30/1998 which name changed to Bank of America Corp. 04/28/1999

PAN AMERN MOTORSPORTS INC (UT)
Name changed to Queench Inc. 11/7/2002

PAN AMERN NATL BK (SAN ANTONIO, TX)
Name changed to Windsor Park Bank, N.A. (San Antonio, TX) 09/15/1976
Windsor Park Bank, N.A. (San Antonio, TX) merged into First City Bancorporation of Texas, Inc. (TX) 05/01/1981
(See First City Bancorporation of Texas, Inc. (TX))

PAN-AMERICAN PETROLEUM & SULPHUR CORP. (DE)
Name changed to Petroleum & Sulphur Development Co. 1/3/57
Petroleum & Sulphur Development Co. recapitalized as Mining Royalty Corp. 2/1/58 which name changed to First U.S. Southern Corp. 10/10/60
(See First U.S. Southern Corp.)

PAN AMERICAN PETROLEUM & TRANSPORT CO. (DE)
Common and Class B $50 par changed to $5 par in 1932
Each share Common and Class B $5 par exchanged for (1) share new Common $5 par in 1933
Merged into Standard Oil Co. (Ind.) in 1954
Each share new Common $5 par exchanged for (0.777) share Capital Stock $25 par
Standard Oil Co. (Ind.) name changed to Amoco Corp. 4/23/85

PAN AMERICAN PETROLEUM CO. OF CALIFORNIA
Reorganized as Richfield Oil Corp. in 1937
No stockholders' equity

PAN AMERN PPTYS (CA)
Merged into Pan-American Properties, Inc. 01/15/1981
Each share Common $1 par exchanged for (1) share $3 Preferred Ser. A $1 par and $30 cash
(See Pan-American Properties, Inc.)

PAN AMERN PPTYS INC (DE)
Liquidation completed
Each share $3 Preferred Ser. A $1 par exchanged for initial distribution of $3 cash 12/18/1989
Each share $3 Preferred Ser. A $1 par received second and final distribution of $0.25 cash 11/30/1990

PAN AMERN RES INC (DE)
Common 25¢ par changed to 5¢ par and (4) additional shares issued 7/13/62
Charter cancelled and declared inoperative and void for non-payment of taxes 3/1/99

PAN AMERN RES INC (ON)
Name changed to ONTZINC Corp. 08/08/2002
ONTZINC Corp. recapitalized as HudBay Minerals Corp. (ONT) 12/24/2004 which reincorporated in Canada 10/25/2005

PAN AMERICAN SHARE CORP.
Merged into Marine Union Investors, Inc. 00/00/1929
Details not available

PAN AMERICAN SOUTHERN CORP.
Acquired by Standard Oil Co. (ID) 00/00/1941
Details not available

PAN AMERN SULPHUR CO (DE)
Capital Stock 10¢ par changed to 70¢ par 00/00/1952
Capital Stock 70¢ par split (2) for (1) by issuance of (1) additional share 05/31/1965
Name changed to Pasco, Inc. 06/09/1972
(See Pasco, Inc.)

PAN AMERN SUPERMARKETS INC (NY)
Adjudicated bankrupt 10/25/1972
Stockholders' equity unlikely

PAN-AMERICAN URANIUM, INC. (DE)
Merged into Pan-American Petroleum & Sulphur Corp. share for share 05/25/1956
Pan-American Petroleum & Sulphur Corp. name changed to Petroleum & Sulphur Development Co. 01/03/1957 which recapitalized as Mining Royalty Corp. 02/01/1958 which name changed to First U.S. Southern Corp. 10/10/1960
(See First U.S. Southern Corp.)

PAN AMERICAN VAN LINES, INC. (CA)
Merged into MPS International Corp. 1/19/73
Each share Common 10¢ par exchanged for (0.05) share Common 10¢ par
MPS International Corp. adjudicated bankrupt 5/26/78

PAN AMERICAN WESTERN PETROLEUM CO.
Dissolved in 1929

PAN AMERN WORLD AWYS INC (NY)
Capital Stock $1 par changed to 50¢

par and (1) additional share issued 06/19/1964
Capital Stock 50¢ par changed to 25¢ par and (1) additional share issued 05/26/1967
Reincorporated under the laws of Delaware as Pan Am Corp. and Capital Stock 25¢ par reclassified as Common 25¢ par 09/14/1984
(See Pan Am Corp.)

PAN ARCTIC EXPLS LTD (BC)
Merged into Consolidated Strategic Metals Inc. 03/29/1982
Each share Common 50¢ par exchanged for (1) share Common no par
Consolidated Strategic Metals Inc. name changed to New Strategic Metals Inc. 05/25/1983 which name changed to P.S.M. Technologies Inc. 12/29/1986
(See P.S.M. Technologies Inc.)

PAN ASIA COMMUNICATIONS CORP (NV)
Recapitalized as Hubei Pharmaceutical Group Ltd. 04/02/2003
Each share Common $0.001 par exchanged for (0.1) share Common $0.001 par
Hubei Pharmaceutical Group Ltd. name changed to Amersin Life Sciences Corp. 01/14/2005 which recapitalized as Golden Tech Group, Ltd. 05/21/2007 which name changed to Mega Win Investments, Inc. 03/02/2018 which name changed to Invech Holdings, Inc. 08/07/2018

PAN ASIA MNG CORP (YT)
Name changed to China Diamond Corp. 01/02/2004
(See China Diamond Corp.)

PAN ATLANTIC INC (DE)
Name changed 05/25/1989
Name changed from Pan Atlantic Re. Inc. to Pan Atlantic, Inc. 05/25/1989
Recapitalized as U.S. Capital Group, Inc. 07/15/1993
Each share Common 10¢ par exchanged for (0.25) share Common 10¢ par

PAN AUSTRALIAN MNG LTD (AUSTRALIA)
Name changed to Mount Leyshon Gold Mines Ltd. 06/07/1991
Mount Leyshon Gold Mines Ltd. name changed to Normandy Mount Leyshon Ltd. 10/20/1997 which name changed to Leyshon Resources Ltd. 12/05/2001
(See Leyshon Resources Ltd.)

PAN CANA RES LTD (AB)
Merged into Geocrude Energy Inc. 02/04/1983
Each share Class A Common no par exchanged for (1.94) shares Common no par
Each share Class B Common no par exchanged for (1.94) shares Common no par
(See Geocrude Energy Inc.)

PAN-CANADIAN GOLD MINES LTD.
Acquired by West Malartic Mines Ltd. in March 1966
Each share Capital Stock $1 par exchanged for (0.1) share Capital Stock $1 par
West Malartic Mines Ltd. charter surrendered 2/28/69

PAN CENT EXPLS LTD (ON)
Charter cancelled for failure to file reports and pay taxes 04/29/1991

PAN EAST PETE INC (ON)
Recapitalized 8/11/92
Name changed from Pan East Resources Inc. to Pan East Petroleum Inc. 8/11/92
Each share Common no par exchanged for (0.25) share Common no par
Merged into Poco Petroleums Ltd. 12/4/98
Each share Common no par exchanged for either (0.1797) share Common 1¢ par, $2.65 cash, or a combination thereof
Poco Petroleums Ltd. merged into Burlington Resources Inc. 11/18/99 which merged into ConocoPhillips 3/31/2006

PAN ELEC INDS LTD (SINGAPORE)
Stock Dividend - 100% 06/25/1984
Out of business 00/00/1985
No ADR holders' equity

PAN ENERGY RES INC (MT)
Involuntarily dissolved 12/2/96

PAN ENVIRONMENTAL CORP (DE)
Name changed 02/22/1994
Name changed from P A N Environmental Services Inc. to PAN Environmental Corp. 02/22/1994
Each share old Common $0.0001 par exchanged for (1/3) share new Common $0.0001 par 06/02/1994
Name changed to Pan International Gaming Inc. 12/30/1998
Pan International Gaming Inc. name changed to SearchHound.com, Inc. 06/07/2000 which recapitalized as Coach Industries Group, Inc. 08/25/2003
(See Coach Industries Group, Inc.)

PAN FOREIGN CORP.
Merged into Standard Oil Co. (NJ) 00/00/1944
Details not available

PAN GEO ATLAS CORP. (DE)
100% held by Wester Corp. as of 07/03/1968
Public interest eliminated

PAN-GLOBAL ENERGY LTD (BC)
Merged into Pearl Exploration & Production Ltd. 05/01/2006
Each share Common no par exchanged for (1/6) share Common no par
Pearl Exploration & Production Ltd. name changed to BlackPearl Resources Inc. 05/14/2009

PAN-GLOBAL ENTERPRISES INC (BC)
Recapitalized as Pan-Global Ventures Ltd. 03/07/2002
Each share Common no par exchanged for (0.05) share Common no par
Pan-Global Ventures Ltd. name changed to Pan-Global Energy Ltd. 11/12/2003 which merged into Pearl Exploration & Production Ltd. which name changed to BlackPearl Resources Inc. 05/14/2009

PAN-GLOBAL VENTURES LTD (BC)
Name changed to Pan-Global Energy Ltd. 11/12/2003
Pan-Global Energy Ltd. merged into Pearl Exploration & Production Ltd. 05/01/2006 which name changed to BlackPearl Resources Inc. 05/14/2009

PAN HEMISPHERE TRANS INC (DE)
Charter cancelled and declared inoperative and void for non-payment of taxes 3/1/82

PAN-HOLDING, INC. (PANAMA)
Each share Common $100 par exchanged for (10) shares Common $10 par 12/01/1959
Reincorporated under the laws of Luxembourg as Pan-Holding S.A. 01/25/1965

PAN INTL GAMING INC (DE)
Name changed to SearchHound.com, Inc. 06/07/2000
SearchHound.com, Inc. recapitalized as Coach Industries Group, Inc. 08/25/2003
(See Coach Industries Group, Inc.)

PAN-INTERNATIONAL HLDGS INC (DE)
Each share old Common 1¢ par exchanged for (0.5) share new Common 1¢ par 10/19/2001
Name changed to Global Business Services Inc. 12/17/2001
Global Business Services Inc. recapitalized as Energetics Holdings, Inc. 11/09/2007 which recapitalized as Pavilion Energy Resources, Inc. 07/25/2008 which recapitalized as Matchtrade, Inc. 05/02/2012
(See Matchtrade, Inc.)

PAN-INTL HLDGS INC (FL)
Recapitalized as Curtin International Productions, Inc. (New) 09/15/1989
Each share Common $0.0001 par exchanged for (0.1) share Common $0.0001 par
Curtin International Productions, Inc. (New) name changed to First Response Medical, Inc. 11/23/1989 which recapitalized as RMS Titanic, Inc. 05/19/1993 which name changed to Premier Exhibitions, Inc. 10/18/2004

PAN IS RESOURCE CORP (BC)
Name changed to Western Harvest Seafarms Ltd. 1/5/88
(See Western Harvest Seafarms Ltd.)

PAN-ISRAEL OIL CO., INC. (PANAMA)
Merged into Magellan Petroleum Corp. (Panama) 07/02/1959
Each share Common 1¢ par exchanged for (0.2) share Common 1¢ par
Magellan Petroleum Corp. (Panama) reincorporated in Delaware 10/23/1967 which name changed to Tellurian Inc. 02/10/2017

PAN KAI DEV USA INC (NV)
Name changed to America Time East Media Group Inc. 3/7/2001
America Time East Media Group Inc. name changed to Starwin Media Holdings Inc. 7/18/2005

PAN MINERALS INC (NV)
Each share Common 10¢ par exchanged for (5) shares Common 2¢ par 05/04/1971
Charter revoked for failure to file reports and pay fees 03/01/1979

PAN MOTOR CO. (DE)
Charter proclaimed repealed and declared inoperative and void for non-payment of taxes 1/24/27

PAN-NEVADA GOLD CORP (BC)
Merged into Midway Gold Corp. 04/13/2007
Each share Common no par exchanged for (0.28000224) share Common no par
(See Midway Gold Corp.)

PAN-OCEAN ENERGY CORP LTD (CHANNEL ISLANDS)
Conv. Preferred Ser. A $1 par called for redemption at CAD$2.40 plus $0.105 accrued dividends on 06/07/2004
Plan of arrangement effective 08/31/2004
Each share Class A Common $2 par exchanged for (1) share EastCoast Energy Corp. Class A Common no par and (1) share Pan-Ocean Energy Ltd. Class A Common no par
Note: U.S. and Canadian holders received CAD$37.25 cash from the sale of shares
Each share Class B Subordinate $2 par exchanged for (1) share EastCoast Energy Corp. Class B Common no par and (1) share Pan-Ocean Energy Ltd. Class B Subordinate no par
Note: U.S. and Canadian holders received CAD$21.86 cash from the sale of shares

PAN-OCEAN ENERGY LTD. (CHANNEL ISLANDS)
Acquired by Addax Petroleum Corp. 09/07/2006
Each share Class A no par exchanged for CAD$65.80 cash
Each share Class B Subordinate no par exchanged for CAD$58.50 cash

PAN OCEAN EXPLORATIONS INC (BC)
Delisted from Toronto Venture Stock Exchange 06/05/2002

PAN OCEAN OIL CORP (DE)
Merged into Marathon Oil Co. 05/28/1976
Each share Common 1¢ par exchanged for $18 cash

PAN OCEANIC VENTURES INC (BC)
Recapitalized as Falcon Ventures International Corp. 12/03/1991
Each share Common no par exchanged for (0.125) share Common no par
Falcon Ventures International Corp. recapitalized as Falcon Ventures Inc. (BC) 12/24/2002 which reincorporated in Alberta as Falcon Ventures International Inc. 06/26/2008 which reorganized in British Columbia as Firebird Resources Inc. 11/05/2009

PAN PAC BK (FREMONT, CA)
Merged into California Bank of Commerce (Lafayette, CA) 12/31/2015
Each share Common no par exchanged for (0.339353) share Common no par
California Bank of Commerce (Lafayette, CA) reorganized as California BanCorp 07/03/2017

PAN PAC RETAIL PPTYS INC (MD)
Issue Information - 7,000,000 shares COM offered at $19.50 per share on 08/07/1997
Merged into Kimco Realty Corp. 10/31/2006
Each share Common 1¢ par exchanged for (0.2253) share Common 1¢ par and $60.24 cash

PAN PACIFIC DEV CORP (ON)
Merged into Revenue Properties Co. Ltd. 06/11/1993
Each share Common no par exchanged for (0.37037037) share new Common no par
Revenue Properties Co. Ltd. merged into Morguard Corp. 12/01/2008

PAN PACIFIC PETE INC (BC)
Delisted from Vancouver Stock Exchange 07/29/1994

PAN PETE MLP (KS)
Merged into Panaco, Inc. 9/1/92
Each Depositary Receipt exchanged for (1) share Common 1¢ par

PAN RICA MINERALS CO. (DE)
No longer in existence having become inoperative and void for non-payment of taxes 4/1/58

PAN SINO INTL HLDG LTD (CAYMAN ISLANDS)
ADR agreement terminated 07/27/2009
Each ADR for Ordinary exchanged for (10) shares Ordinary
Note: Unexchanged ADR's will be sold and the proceeds, if any, held for claim after 07/27/2010

PAN SMAK PIZZA INC (BC)
SEC revoked common stock registration 02/01/2010

PAN TERRA INDS INC (CANADA)
Each share old Common no par exchanged for (0.2) share new Common no par 09/10/2009

PAN-PAN

Name changed to Kombat Copper Inc. 04/30/2012
Kombat Copper Inc. name changed to Trigon Metals Inc. 12/28/2016

PAN WESTERN OILS LTD. (AB)
Common no par changed to 10¢ par 00/00/1949
Acquired by United Canso Oil & Gas Ltd. (Canada) 09/26/1958
Each share Common 10¢ par exchanged for (0.166666) share VTC for Capital Stock $1 par
United Canso Oil & Gas Ltd. (Canada) reincorporated in Nova Scotia 06/06/1980
(See United Canso Oil & Gas Ltd. (NS))

PAN WESTN CORP (DE)
Merged into North American National Corp. 08/30/1984
Each share Common $1 par exchanged for (1) share Common 1¢ par
(See North American National Corp.)

PAN WESTN ENERGY CORP (OK)
Reorganized under the laws of Colorado as IntelliReady, Inc. 11/08/2000
Each share Common no par exchanged for (0.1210974) share Common no par
IntelliReady, Inc. (CO) reorganized in Nevada as Unitech Water & Renewable Energy, Inc. 02/29/2008
(See Unitech Water & Renewable Energy, Inc.)

PAN WESTN LIFE INS CO (OH)
Merged into Pan-Western Corp. 08/06/1980
Each share Common $1.10 par exchanged for (2.4) shares Common $1 par
Pan-Western Corp. merged into North American National Corp. 08/30/1984
(See North American National Corp.)

PAN WORLD CORP (NV)
Each share old Common $0.001 par exchanged for (2) shares new Common $0.001 par 06/24/1999
Reincorporated under the laws of Delaware as Tribeworks, Inc. 12/23/1999
Tribeworks, Inc. name changed to Atlas Technology Group, Inc. 08/16/2007

PAN WORLD MINERALS INTL INC (NV)
Charter revoked for failure to file reports and pay fees 12/31/2004

PAN WORLD VENTURES INC (BC)
Common no par split (3) for (1) by issuance of (2) additional shares 12/14/1987
Recapitalized as Weymin Mining Corp. 02/04/1997
Each share Common no par exchanged for (0.2) share Common no par
Weymin Mining Corp. recapitalized as GCP Mining Corp. 09/10/2002 which name changed to Kodiak Exploration Ltd. 09/08/2003 which name changed to Prodigy Gold Inc. 01/04/2011

PANA-MINERALES S A (NV)
Common $0.001 par split (8) for (1) by issuance of (7) additional shares payable 09/07/2011 to holders of record 09/06/2011 Ex date - 09/08/2011
Name changed to Cortronix Biomedical Advancement Technologies Inc. 11/23/2012

PANACAN MINERALS & OILS LTD (QC)
Acquired by Sackville Oils & Minerals Ltd. 5/5/75
Each share Capital Stock no par exchanged for (1) share Common no par
Sackville Oils & Minerals Ltd. merged into Seagull Resources Ltd. 1/3/78
(See Seagull Resources Ltd.)

PANACAN RES LTD (QC)
Merged into Panacan Minerals & Oils Ltd.-Societe des Mineraux et des Petroles Panacan Ltee. 4/8/74
Each share Capital Stock $1 par exchanged for (1/3) share Capital Stock no par
Panacan Minerals & Oils Ltd.-Societe des Mineraux et des Petroles Panacan Ltee. acquired by Sackville Oils & Minerals Ltd. 5/5/75 which merged into Seagull Resources Ltd. 1/3/78
(See Seagull Resources Ltd.)

PANACEA SPRINGS CO., INC. (NC)
Charter cancelled for failure to file annual reports 3/1/28

PANACHE BEVERAGE INC (FL)
Reincorporated under the laws of Delaware 11/04/2013

PANACHE RES INC (BC)
Recapitalized as Caprice-Greystoke Enterprises Ltd. 07/16/1991
Each share Common no par exchanged for (1/3) share Common no par
(See Caprice-Greystoke Enterprises Ltd.)

PANACO INC (DE)
Plan of reorganization under Chapter 11 Federal Bankruptcy Code effective 11/16/2004
No stockholders' equity

PANACOLOR INC (DE)
Charter cancelled and declared inoperative and void for non-payment of taxes 3/1/82

PANACON CORP (MI)
Merged into Celotex Corp. 06/30/1972
Each share Common $1 par exchanged for $6 cash

PANACOS PHARMACEUTICALS INC (DE)
Company terminated common stock registration and is no longer public 03/19/2009

PANAFON HELLENIC TELECOMMUNICATIONS CO S A (GREECE)
Sponsored Reg. S GDR's for Ordinary split (2) for (1) by issuance of (1) additional GDR payable 11/05/1999 to holders of record 10/21/1999
144A Sponsored GDR's for Ordinary split (2) for (1) by issuance of (1) additional GDR payable 11/05/1999 to holders of record 10/21/1999
Name changed to Vodafone-Panafon Hellenic Telecommunications Co. S.A. 04/10/2002

PANAFRICAN ENERGY CORP LTD (CHANNEL ISLANDS)
Name changed to Pan-Ocean Energy Corporation Ltd. 08/14/2001
Pan-Ocean Energy Corporation Ltd. reorganized as Pan-Ocean Energy Ltd. 08/31/2004
(See Pan-Ocean Energy Ltd.)

PANAGRA INTL CORP (NY)
Name changed to Minghua Group International Holdings Ltd. 08/02/2001
Minghua Group International Holdings Ltd. recapitalized as China Longyi Group International Holdings Ltd. 12/12/2007

PANAMA DREAMING INC (NV)
Name changed to Asia Pacific Boiler Corp. 11/09/2012
Asia Pacific Boiler Corp. name changed to Wunong Asia Pacific Co. Ltd. 09/07/2018

PANAMA INDS LTD (DE)
Name changed to Xiom Corp. 04/21/2004
Xiom Corp. name changed to Environmental Infrastructure Holdings Corp. 01/27/2010

PANAMA MINES LTD (BC)
Recapitalized as Panama Resources Ltd. 06/04/1980
Each share Capital Stock $1 par exchanged for (1/3) share Capital Stock no par
Panama Resources Ltd. merged into Freedom Marine Ltd. 04/07/1986
(See Freedom Marine Ltd.)

PANAMA POWER & LIGHT CORP.
Dissolved in 1936

PANAMA PWR & LT CO (FL)
Liquidation completed
Each share $3 Preferred no par exchanged changed for first and final distribution of $51.07 cash 04/09/1973
Each share Common no par exchanged for initial distribution of $25 cash 05/21/1973
Each share Common no par received second and final distribution of $2.38 cash 05/31/1974

PANAMA RES LTD (BC)
Merged into Freedom Marine Ltd. 4/7/86
Each share Capital Stock no par exchanged for (0.5) share Common no par
(See Freedom Marine Ltd.)

PANAMED CORP (NV)
Name changed to Endexx Corp. 7/8/2005

PANAMERICAN AUTOMOTIVE CORP (DE)
Common $0.001 par split (5) for (1) by issuance of (4) additional shares payable 01/25/2001 to holders of record 01/13/2001 Ex date - 01/26/2001
Recapitalized as Lexor International Inc. 11/16/2001
Each share Common $0.001 par exchanged for (0.14285714) share Common $0.001 par
Lexor International Inc. recapitalized as Grayling Wireless USA, Inc. 01/16/2003
(See Grayling Wireless USA, Inc.)

PANAMERICAN BANCORP NEW (DE)
Each share old Common 1¢ par exchanged for (0.2) share new Common 1¢ par 07/15/2003
Name changed to Sun American Bancorp 01/23/2006
(See Sun American Bancorp)

PANAMERICAN BANCORP OLD (DE)
Charter cancelled and declared inoperative and void for non-payment of taxes 3/1/2001

PANAMERICAN BEVERAGES INC (PANAMA)
Common reclassified as (5) shares Non-Vtg. Class A 1¢ par and (1) share Class B Common 03/31/1993
Non-Vtg. Class A 1¢ par split (2) for (1) by issuance of (1) additional share payable 03/31/1997 to holders of record 03/14/1997 Ex date - 04/01/1997
Class B Common 1¢ par split (2) for (1) by issuance of (1) additional share payable 03/31/1997 to holders of record 03/14/1997 Ex date - 04/01/1997
Merged into Coca-Cola FEMSA, S.A. de C.V. 05/06/2003
Each share Non-Vtg. Class A 1¢ par exchanged for $22 cash
Each share Class B Common 1¢ par exchanged for $38 cash

PANAMERICAN VENTURES LTD. (CANADA)
Name changed to Westfield Minerals Ltd. 5/27/58
(See Westfield Minerals Ltd.)

PANAMERSA CORP (NV)
Each share old Common $0.001 par exchanged for (0.1) share new Common $0.001 par 05/17/2010
Recapitalized as Eagle Worldwide Inc. 01/12/2012
Each share new Common $0.001 par exchanged for (0.01) share Common $0.001 par

PANAMEX RES INC (BC)
Recapitalized as Ross River Minerals Inc. 5/31/2002
Each share Common no par exchanged for (0.2) share Common no par

PANAMINT SILVER REDUCTION INC (NV)
Name changed to Med-Index, Inc. 3/13/86
Med-Index, Inc. name changed to Venmark, Inc. 9/11/87
(See Venmark, Inc.)

PANAMSAT CORP NEW (DE)
Merged into DIRECTV Group, Inc. 8/18/2004
Each share Common 1¢ par exchanged for $23.50 cash

PANAMSAT CORP OLD (DE)
Merged into PanAmSat Corp. (New) 5/16/97
Each share Common 1¢ par exchanged for either (1) share Common 1¢ par (stock election), (0.5) share Common 1¢ par and $15 cash (standard election), or (0.45) share Common 1¢ par and $16.38 cash (cash election)
Note: Non-electors received standard election
(See PanAmSat Corp. (New))

PANAMSAT HLDG CORP (DE)
Issue Information - 50,000,000 shares COM offered at $18 per share on 03/16/2005
Merged into Intelsat, Ltd. 7/3/2006
Each share Common 1¢ par exchanged for $25.00927 cash

PANARIM RES INC (BC)
Recapitalized as Kismet Ventures Inc. 12/07/1994
Each share Common no par exchanged for (1/9) share Common no par
Kismet Ventures Inc. name changed to Mighty Beaut Minerals Inc. (BC) 12/15/1998 which reincorporated in Yukon 08/30/2000 which recapitalized as MBMI Resources Inc. (YT) 12/20/2002 which reincorporated in British Columbia 11/15/2005 which reorganized in Ontario 06/22/2012

PANASIA BK (FORT LEE, NJ)
Acquired by National Penn Bancshares, Inc. 07/11/2000
Each share Common $5 par exchanged for $29 cash

PANASONI ENERGY CORP (BC)
Dissolved 02/23/1990
Details not available

PANASONIC ELEC WKS CO LTD (JAPAN)
Merged into Panasonic Corp. 04/01/2011
Each ADR for Common JPY 50 par exchanged for $114.071787 cash

PANATECH RESH & DEV CORP (NV)
Merged into Titan Enterprises, Inc. 2/27/97
Each share Common 1¢ par exchanged for $7 cash

PANATLAS ENERGY INC (ON)
Each share old Common no par

exchanged for (0.25) share new Common no par 4/14/2000
Acquired by Velvet Exploration Ltd. 7/17/2000
Each share Common no par exchanged for either (0.70857) share Common no par or $3.72 cash
Note: Non-Canadian residents received cash only
(See Velvet Exploration Ltd.)

PANATOMICS, INC. (DE)
Charter cancelled and declared inoperative and void for non-payment of taxes 4/15/72

PANAVISION INC (DE)
Merged into PX Holding Corp. 6/4/98
Each share old Common 1¢ par exchanged for either (1) share new Common 1¢ par or (0.0475) share new Common 1¢ par and $25.72 cash
Note: Option to retain shares expired 6/3/98
Merged into MacAndrew & Forbes Holdings Inc. 7/25/2006
Each share new Common 1¢ par exchanged for $8.50 cash

PANAX CORP (DE)
Reincorporated 1/1/72
State of incorporation changed from (MI) to (DE) 1/1/72
Each share Common $1 par exchanged for (0.2) share Common $5 par 6/12/72
In process of liquidation
Each share Common $5 par exchanged for initial distribution of $5 cash 3/10/81
Each share Common $5 par received second distribution of $2 cash 6/9/81
Assets transferred to Panax Corp. Liquidating Trust 8/28/81
Each share Common $5 par received third distribution of $8 cash 9/24/81
Each share Common $5 par received fourth distribution of $0.10 cash 2/11/82
Each share Common $5 par received fifth distribution of $0.25 cash 6/4/82
Each share Common $5 par received sixth distribution of $0.30 cash 11/10/82
Each share Common $5 par received seventh distribution of $0.45 cash 5/10/83
Each share Common $5 par received eighth distribution of $0.20 cash 2/28/84
Each share Common $5 par received ninth distribution of $0.50 cash 6/12/84
Each share Common $5 par received tenth distribution of $0.75 cash 12/6/84
Each share Common $5 par received eleventh distribution of $0.30 cash 6/21/85
Each share Common $5 par received twelfth distribution of $1.15 cash 9/13/85
Each share Common $5 par received thirteenth distribution of $0.15 cash 12/16/85
Each share Common $5 par received fourteenth distribution of $2.40 cash 7/23/86
Each share Common $5 par received fifteenth distribution of $0.45 cash 12/18/86
Each share Common $5 par received sixteenth distribution of $0.20 cash 7/10/87
Each share Common $5 par received seventeenth distribution of $0.20 cash 12/30/87
Each share Common $5 par received eigtheenth distribution of $7.45385 cash 1/13/89
Each share Common $5 par received nineteenth distribution of $0.12 cash 8/31/89
Each share Common $5 par received twentieth distribution of $0.15 cash 3/20/90
Each share Common $5 par received twenty-first and final distribution of $0.2297 cash in 1996

PANAX PHARMACEUTICAL LTD (NY)
Name changed to InKine Pharmaceutical Co., Inc. 11/06/1997
InKine Pharmaceutical Co., Inc. merged into Salix Pharmaceuticals, Ltd. 10/03/2005
(See Salix Pharmaceuticals, Ltd.)

PANCAKE LAKE COPPERMINES LTD. (ON)
Charter cancelled and declared dissolved for failure to file reports 12/16/70

PANCAKE PL FOOD SYS INC (OK)
Common $1 par changed to 33-1/3¢ par and (2) additional shares issued 2/23/70
Name changed to Management Systems, Inc. 11/16/70
(See Management Systems, Inc.)

PANCAL OIL CORP. (NY)
Charter cancelled and proclaimed dissolved for failure to pay taxes and file reports 12/15/61

PANCANA INDS LTD (AB)
Each share Capital Stock no par exchanged for (0.5) share Class A Common no par and (0.5) share Class B Common no par
Name changed to Pan Cana Resources Ltd. 03/06/1980
Pan Cana Resources Ltd. merged into Geocrude Energy Inc. 02/04/1983
(See Geocrude Energy Inc.)

PANCANA MINERALS LTD (CANADA)
Merged into American Barrick Resources Corp. 01/17/1987
Each share Common no par exchanged for (0.476) share Common no par
American Barrick Resources Corp. name changed to Barrick Gold Corp. 01/18/1995

PANCANADIAN ENERGY CORP (CANADA)
Name changed to EnCana Corp. 04/05/2002

PANCANADIAN PETE LTD (AB)
Each share Capital Stock $1 par exchanged for (4) shares Common no par 04/21/1983
Common no par split (2) for (1) by issuance of (1) additional share payable 06/30/1997 to holders of record 05/08/1997
Reincorporated under the laws of Canada as PanCanadian Energy Corp. 10/01/2001
PanCanadian Energy Corp. name changed to EnCana Corp. 04/05/2002

PANCHOS MEXICAN BUFFET INC (DE)
Name changed to Pamex Foods, Inc. 5/5/72 which name changed back to Pancho's Mexican Buffet, Inc. 6/4/82
Common 10¢ par split (2) for (1) by issuance of (1) additional share 6/10/83
Each share old Common 10¢ par exchanged for (1/3) share new Common 10¢ par 1/27/99
Stock Dividend - 10% 8/29/86
Merged into Pancho's Foods, Inc. 8/1/2001
Each share new Common 10¢ par exchanged for $4.60 cash

PANCO POULTRY LTD (BC)
Acquired by Federal Grain, Ltd. 11/17/1969
Each share $2.75 Conv. Preference Ser. A $50 par exchanged for $59 cash
Each share Common no par exchanged for $29.50 cash

PANCOASTAL INC (DE)
Voting Trust Agreement expired and each VTC for Common 14¢ par automatically became (1) share Common 14¢ par 11/14/72
Charter cancelled and declared inoperative and void for non-payment of taxes 3/1/82

PANCOASTAL OIL CO., C.A.
Reorganized 8/7/51
Each share Capital Stock 1 Bolivar par exchanged for (1) share Common 1 Bolivar par of Pancoastal Oil Corp., C.A. and (0.4) share Capital Stock $1 par of Canada Southern Oils Ltd.
(See each company's listing)

PANCOASTAL OIL CORP., C.A. (VENEZUELA)
Reorganized 02/06/1953
Each share Common 1 Bolivar par exchanged for (0.5) VTC for Common 2 Bolivars par of Pancoastal Petroleum Co. (Venezuela) and (0.8) share VTC for Common 10¢ par of Coastal Caribbean Oils, Inc.
(See each company's listing)

PANCOASTAL PETROLEUM CO. (VENEZUELA)
Reincorporated under the laws of Bermuda as Pancoastal Petroleum Ltd. 8/16/63
Each VTC for Common 2 Bolivars par exchanged for (1) VTC for Common 1s par
Pancoastol Petroleum Ltd. (Bermuda) reincorporated in Delaware as Pancoastal, Inc. 10/30/67
(See Pancoastol, Inc.)

PANCOASTAL PETROLEUM LTD. (BERMUDA)
Reorganized under the laws of Delaware as Pancoastal, Inc. 10/30/1967
Each VTC for Common 1s par exchanged for (1) VTC for Common 14¢ par
(See Pancoastal, Inc.)

PANCONTINENTAL ENERGY INC (AB)
Recapitalized as Immunall Science Inc. (Old) 07/10/2007
Each share Common no par exchanged for (0.25) share Common no par
Immunall Science Inc. (Old) reorganized as Immunall Science Inc. (New) (AB) 03/31/2011 which reincorporated in British Columbia 06/30/2016 which recapitalized as AREV Nutrition Sciences Inc. 01/23/2017 which name changed to AREV Brands International Ltd. 09/12/2018

PANCONTINENTAL GOLD CORP (CANADA)
Name changed to Pancontinental Resources Corp. 07/13/2018

PANCONTINENTAL MARKETING CORP (AB)
Issue Information - 2,000,000 shares COM offered at $0.15 per share on 07/24/1997
Name changed to Onsat.net Canada Inc. 12/20/99

PANCONTINENTAL MNG LTD (AUSTRALIA)
ADR agreement terminated 04/27/1998
Each ADR for Ordinary exchanged for $0.335359 cash

PANCONTINENTAL OIL LTD (AB)
Merged into Inverness Petroleum Ltd. 8/2/91
Each share Common no par exchanged for (0.975) share Common no par
Inverness Petroleum Ltd. merged into Rigel Energy Corp. 1/10/96

PANCONTINENTAL URANIUM CORP (CANADA)
Name changed to Pancontinental Gold Corp. 07/29/2016
Pancontinental Gold Corp. name changed to Pancontinental Resources Corp. 07/13/2018

PANCRETEC INC (CA)
Acquired by Abbott Laboratories 07/31/1989
Each share Common no par exchanged for $15 cash

PANDA CAP INC (CANADA)
Each share old Common no par exchanged for (0.125) share new Common no par 09/29/2015
Name changed to ABcann Global Corp. 05/04/2017
ABcann Global Corp. name changed to VIVO Cannabis Inc. 08/07/2018

PANDA ETHANOL INC (NV)
Dissolved 07/16/2009
Stockholders' equity unlikely

PANDA PROJ INC (FL)
Reorganized under the laws of Delaware as Coda Octopus Group, Inc. 08/11/2004
Each (300) shares Common 1¢ par exchanged for (1) share Common $0.001 par

PANDEL BRADFORD INC (MA)
Merged into Compo Industries, Inc. 12/21/1977
Each (15) shares Common 10¢ par exchanged for (1) share Common $1 par
Compo Industries, Inc. merged into Ausimont Compo N.V. 11/04/1985 which name changed to Ausimont N.V. 05/08/1987
(See Ausimont N.V.)

PANDEM OIL CORP. (DE)
Charter cancelled and declared inoperative and void for non-payment of taxes 4/1/34

PANDICK INC (DE)
Reincorporated 6/19/84
Common 10¢ par split (3) for (2) by issuance of (0.5) additional share 1/16/84
State of incorporation changed from (NY) to (DE) 6/19/84
Merged into FP Acquisition Inc. 1/20/87
Each share Common 10¢ par exchanged for $25.50 cash

PANDICK PRESS INC (NY)
Common 10¢ par split (2) for (1) by issuance of (1) additional share 1/15/81
Stock Dividends - 25% 1/15/82; 25% 1/17/83
Name changed to Pandick, Inc. (NY) 12/27/83
Pandick, Inc. (NY) reincorporated in Delaware 6/19/84
(See Pandick, Inc. (DE))

PANDORA CADILLAC GOLD MINES, LTD. (ON)
Charter cancelled and proclaimed dissolved for failure to pay taxes and file annual reports 6/1/64

PANDORA GOLD LTD.
Name changed to Canadian Pandora Gold Mines Ltd. 00/00/1931
(See Canadian Pandora Gold Mines Ltd.)

PANDORA INC (NV)
Name changed to Oryx Gold Corp. 5/4/92
Oryx Gold Corp. name changed to Mediterranean Oil Corp. 11/16/95 which recapitalized as Zmax Corp. (NV) 7/23/96 which reincorporated in Delaware 12/12/97

PANDORA INDS INC (BC)
Recapitalized as Georgia Ventures Inc. 03/01/2000
Each share Common no par exchanged for (0.125) share Common no par
Georgia Ventures Inc. name changed to Creston Moly Corp. 10/19/2007 which merged into Mercator Minerals Ltd. 06/21/2011

PANDORAS GOLDEN BOX (NV)
Name changed to Cole Computer Corp. 02/02/1999
Cole Computer Corp. name changed to Wilson Holdings, Inc. (NV) 09/29/2005 which reincorporated in Texas as Green Builders, Inc. 04/08/2008
(See Green Builders, Inc.)

PANEL CONSOLIDATED URANIUM MINES LTD. (ON)
Merged into Northspan Uranium Mines Ltd. 7/5/56
Each share Capital Stock $1 par exchanged for (0.28) share Capital Stock $1 par
Northspan Uranium Mines Ltd. merged into Rio Algom Mines Ltd. 6/30/60 which name changed to Rio Algom Ltd. 4/30/75
(See Rio Algom Ltd.)

PANEL-LIFT DOOR CORP. (DE)
Completely liquidated 2/26/65
Each share Class A 1¢ par received first and final distribution of $0.03 cash
Certificates were not required to be surrendered and are now valueless

PANELFAB INC (FL)
Merged into Panelfab International Corp. 3/10/70
Each share Common 10¢ par exchanged for (1) share Common 10¢ par
(See Panelfab International Corp.)

PANELFAB INTL CORP (FL)
Each share Common 10¢ par exchanged for (0.2) share Common 50¢ par 4/28/72
Proclaimed dissolved for failure to file reports and pay fees 11/4/88

PANELGRAPHIC CORP (NJ)
Common 10¢ par split (5) for (4) by issuance of (0.25) additional share 11/4/87
Stock Dividends - 15% 11/6/86; 50% 6/27/88
Merged into Marathon Acquisition Corp. 9/29/89
Each share Common 10¢ par exchanged for $3.50 cash

PANELLIT, INC. (IL)
Liquidation completed
Each share Common $1 par exchanged for initial distribution of (0.2) share Information Systems, Inc. Common $1 par and $5 cash 3/18/60
Each share Common $1 par received second and final distribution of $2.08 cash 1/9/61
Information Systems, Inc. merged into Scam Instrument Corp. (Ill.) 4/10/63 which reincorporated under the laws of Delaware 2/17/70 which name changed to Riley Co. 10/31/71
(See Riley Co.)

PANELMASTER CORP (DE)
Recapitalized as Paramount Gold Mining Corp. 05/05/2005
Each share Common $0.001 par exchanged for (0.001) share Common $0.001 par
Paramount Gold Mining Corp. name changed to Paramount Gold & Silver Corp. 08/27/2007 which merged into Coeur Mining, Inc. 04/17/2015

PANELRAMA CORP (PA)
Name changed to Patlex Corp. 12/24/1979
Patlex Corp. acquired by AutoFinance Group Inc. 12/11/1992 which was acquired by KeyCorp (New) 09/27/1995

PANENERGY CORP (DE)
Merged into Duke Energy Corp. (NC) 6/18/97
Each share Common $1 par exchanged for (1.0444) shares Common no par
Duke Energy Corp. (NC) merged into Duke Energy Corp. (DE) 4/3/2006

PANERA BREAD CO (DE)
Class A Common $0.0001 par split (2) for (1) by issuance of (1) additional share payable 06/24/2002 to holders of record 06/10/2002 Ex date - 06/25/2002
Class B Common $0.0001 par split (2) for (1) by issuance of (1) additional share payable 06/24/2002 to holders of record 06/10/2002 Ex date - 06/25/2002
Acquired by JAB Holdings B.V. 07/18/2017
Each share Class A Common $0.0001 par exchanged for $315 cash
Each share Class B Common $0.0001 par exchanged for $315 cash

PANEX INDS INC (DE)
In process of liquidation
Each share Common 10¢ par received initial distribution of $6 cash 09/25/1984
Each share Common 10¢ par received second distribution of $16 cash 12/31/1984
Each share Common 10¢ par received third distribution of (1) share Wundies Industries, Inc. Preferred $2.40 par, (0.25) share Common 1¢ par and $23 cash 09/12/1985
(See Wundies Industries, Inc.)
Assets transferred to Panex Industries Stockholders Liquidating Trust 09/20/1985
Each share Common 10¢ par exchanged for (1) Share of Bene. Int. 10¢ par
(See Panex Industries Stockholders Liquidating Trust)

PANEX INDS INC (DE)
In process of liquidation
Details not available

PANGEA GOLDFIELDS INC (ON)
Acquired by Barrick Gold Corp. 8/2/2000
Each share Common no par exchanged for $7 cash

PANGEA NETWORKS INC (NV)
Acquired by Innovative Communications Technologies, Inc. 12/22/2009
Each share Common $0.0001 par exchanged for (20) shares Common $0.001 par
Innovative Communications Technologies, Inc. recapitalized as Baristas Coffee Co., Inc. 05/07/2010

PANGEA PETE CO (DE)
Reincorporated 05/26/1987
State of incorporation changed from (CA) to (DE) and Common no par changed to 1¢ par 05/26/1987
Name changed to Harcor Energy, Inc. 01/06/1988
(See Harcor Energy, Inc.)

PANGEA PETE CORP (CO)
Recapitalized as AvStar Aviation Group, Inc. 09/21/2009
Each share Common $0.001 par exchanged for (0.01) share Common $0.001 par
AvStar Aviation Group, Inc. recapitalized as Spotlight Capital Holdings, Inc. 11/06/2014

PANGEA PICTURES CORP (NV)
Name changed to Tintic Standard Gold Mines, Inc. 02/21/2008

PANGEA RES LTD (AUSTRALIA)
Acquired by Pegasus Gold Corp. 11/03/1989
Each Unsponsored ADR for Ordinary exchanged for $0.435 cash

PANGENEX CORP (NV)
Each share old Common $0.001 par exchanged for (0.00142857) share new Common $0.001 par 02/26/2009
Stock Dividend - 10% payable 01/30/2010 to holders of record 01/10/2010 Ex date - 01/22/2010
Recapitalized as Virtual Sourcing, Inc. 08/31/2012
Each share new Common $0.001 par exchanged for (0.00066666) share Common $0.001 par
Note: Holders of (1,499) or fewer pre-split shares will receive $0.15 cash per share

PANGEO PHARMA INC (CANADA)
Reincorporated 09/21/2000
Place of incorporation changed from (BC) to (Canada) 09/21/2000
Recapitalized as Silvio Ventures Inc. 01/09/2006
Each share Common no par exchanged for (0.04) share Common no par
Silvio Ventures Inc. name changed to Regency Gold Corp. 07/17/2008

PANGLOBEL COM INC (AB)
Name changed to Coyotenet Communications Group Inc. (AB) 01/31/2002
Coyotenet Communications Group Inc. (AB) reorganized in British Columbia as Magnate Ventures Inc. 09/01/2006 which merged into Thor Explorations Ltd. (New) 09/01/2009

PANGO GOLD MINES LTD (ON)
Merged into Canhorn Mining Corp. 01/09/1986
Each share Capital Stock no par exchanged for (0.16666666) share Common no par
Canhorn Mining Corp. merged into Canhorn Chemical Corp. 04/26/1995 which merged into Nayarit Gold Inc. 05/02/2005 which merged into Capital Gold Corp. 08/02/2010 which merged into Gammon Gold Inc. (QC) 04/08/2011 which reincorporated in Ontario as AuRico Gold Inc. 06/14/2011 which merged into Alamos Gold Inc. (New) 07/06/2015

PANHANDLE BANCORP (ID)
Common $2.50 par split (3) for (1) by issuance of (2) additional shares payable 10/29/1998 to holders of record 09/02/1998
Stock Dividend - 10% payable 02/28/2000 to holders of record 01/19/2000
Name changed to Intermountain Community Bancorp 06/05/2000
Intermountain Community Bancorp merged into Columbia Banking System, Inc. 11/01/2014

PANHANDLE COOP RTY CO (OK)
Merged into Panhandle Royalty Co. 10/01/1979
Each share Capital Stock $50 par exchanged for (50) shares Class A Common 10¢ par
Panhandle Royalty Co. name changed to Panhandle Oil & Gas Inc. 04/03/2007

PANHANDLE EASTN CORP (DE)
Name changed to Panenergy Corp. 4/26/96
Panenergy Corp. merged into Duke Energy Corp. (NC) 6/18/97 which merged into Duke Energy Corp. (DE) 4/3/2006

PANHANDLE EASTN PIPE LINE CO (DE)
Common no par split (2) for (1) by issuance of (1) additional share 04/02/1945
Common no par split (2) for (1) by issuance of (1) additional share 12/27/1949
Common no par split (2) for (1) by issuance of (1) additional share 12/27/1956
Common no par split (2) for (1) by issuance of (1) additional share 05/14/1965
4% Preferred $100 par called for redemption 07/01/1975
Common no par split (2) for (1) by issuance of (1) additional share 05/30/1980
Under plan of reorganization each share Common no par automatically became (1) share Panhandle Eastern Corp. Common $1 par 05/22/1981
4.64% Preferred $100 par called for redemption 07/01/1992
8.60% Preferred $100 par called for redemption 10/01/1993
Panhandle Eastern Corp. name changed to Panenergy Corp. 04/26/1996 which merged into Duke Energy Corp. (NC) 06/18/1997 which merged into Duke Energy Corp. (DE) 04/03/2006

PANHANDLE LUMBER CO.
Dissolved in 1942

PANHANDLE OIL CORP. (DE)
Merged into American Petrofina, Inc. 10/1/56
Each share Common $1 par exchanged for (1.3) shares Class A Common $1 par
American Petrofina, Inc. name changed to Fina, Inc. 4/18/91
(See Fina, Inc.)

PANHANDLE PRODUCING & REFINING CO.
Name changed to Panhandle Oil Corp. in 1952
Panhandle Oil Corp. merged into American Petrofina, Inc. 10/1/56 which name changed to Fina, Inc. 4/18/91
(See Fina, Inc.)

PANHANDLE RES CORP (AB)
Name changed to Abacan Resource Corp. (Old) 01/27/1993
Abacan Resource Corp. (Old) merged into Abacan Resource Corp. (New) 02/10/1995
(See Abacan Resource Corp. (New))

PANHANDLE RTY CO (OK)
Class A Common 10¢ par changed to $0.0333 par and (2) additional shares issued 06/01/1999
Class A Common $0.0333 par changed to $0.01666 par and (1) additional share issued payable 04/15/2004 to holders of record 04/01/2004
Class A Common $0.01666 par split (2) for (1) by issuance of (1) additional share payable 01/09/2006 to holders of record 12/29/2005 Ex date - 01/10/2006
Name changed to Panhandle Oil & Gas Inc. 04/03/2007

PANHANDLE ST BK (SANDPOINT, ID)
Under plan of reorganization each share Common $2.50 par automatically became (1) share Panhandle Bancorp Common $2.50 par 01/27/1998
Panhandle Bancorp name changed to International Community Bancorp 06/05/2000 which merged into Columbia Banking System, Inc. 11/01/2014

PANHELLENIC HOUSE ASSOCIATION, INC. (NY)
Liquidation for cash completed 5/14/65

PANIFLEX CORP (NY)
Dissolved by proclamation 9/27/95

PANJA INC (TX)
Name changed to AMX Corp. (New) 8/23/2001
(See AMX Co. (New))

PANNATIONAL GROUP INC (DE)
Common $10 par changed to $5 par and (1) additional share issued 3/29/73
Merged into Mercantile Texas Corp. 4/8/82
Each share Common $5 par exchanged for (1.8) shares Common $5 par
Mercantile Texas Corp. name changed to MCorp 10/11/84
(See MCorp)

PANNEX INDS INC (AB)
Struck off register for failure to file annual returns 09/01/1997

PANNILL KNITTING CO (VA)
8% Preferred $100 par called for redemption 04/01/1984
Acquired by PKC Acquisition, Inc. 04/18/1984
Each share 10% Preferred $100 par exchanged for $1,000 cash
Each share Common $1 par exchanged for $520 cash

PANNILL KNITTING INC (DE)
Merged into PKC Merger Corp. 06/26/1989
Each share Common 1¢ par exchanged for $12 cash

PANNONIA VENTURES CORP (BC)
Name changed to First Americas Gold Corp. 02/02/2012
First Americas Gold Corp. name changed to Intact Gold Corp. 02/03/2016

PANNONPLAST (HUNGARY)
ADR agreement terminated 07/23/2015
No ADR's remain outstanding

PANOIL CO (DE)
Each share old Capital Stock 10¢ par exchanged for (0.2) share Capital Stock 50¢ par 09/19/1960
Capital Stock 50¢ par changed to new Capital Stock 10¢ par 03/20/1961
Capital Stock 10¢ par reclassified as Common 10¢ par 11/26/1968
Name changed to Dorchester Gas Corp. 02/01/1972
(See Dorchester Gas Corp.)

PANOIL RES LTD (AB)
Merged into Caravan Oil & Gas Ltd. 11/19/99
Each share Common no par exchanged for (1/7) share Common no par and (0.07142857) Common Stock Purchase Warrant expiring 5/5/2001
Caravan Oil & Gas Ltd. acquired by Ketch Energy Ltd. 11/30/2000 which merged into Acclaim Energy Trust 10/1/2002
(See Acclaim Energy Trust)

PANORAMA BOWL INC. (CA)
Name changed to Transwestern Bowling Corp. 5/9/62
Transwestern Bowling Corp. charter revoked 1/2/68

PANORAMA INDS INC (NV)
90.73% acquired by Arrow Management Inc. as of 09/30/1993
Public interest eliminated

PANORAMA INVTS CORP (NV)
Reorganized as Lucas Energy, Inc. 06/13/2006
Each share Common $0.001 par exchanged for (2.4) shares Common $0.001 par
Lucas Energy, Inc. name changed to Camber Energy, Inc. 01/05/2017

PANORAMA PETE INC (BC)
Recapitalized as Stamper Oil & Gas Corp. 04/06/2017
Each share Common no par exchanged for (0.18181818) share Common no par

PANORAMA RES LTD (BC)
Incorporated 12/19/2005
Reincorporated under the laws of Ontario as Ethiopian Potash Corp. 03/09/2011
Ethiopian Potash Corp. name changed to AgriMinco Corp. 07/15/2013

PANORAMA RES LTD (BC)
Name changed 11/10/1987
Name changed from Panorama Petroleums Ltd. to Panorama Resources Ltd. 11/10/1987
Recapitalized as International Panorama Resource Corp. 04/14/1993
Each share Common no par exchanged for (0.2) share Common no par
International Panorama Resource Corp. recapitalized as Kakanda Development Corp. 09/27/2002
(See Kakanda Development Corp.)

PANORAMA RESOURCES NL (AUSTRALIA)
Acquired by Tanganyika Gold NL 04/16/1998
Each share Common exchanged for (0.75) share Ordinary
Note: A holder who is not an accredited investor will receive cash from sale of shares

PANORAMA TRADING LTD (AB)
Name changed to Perfect Fry Corp. 05/21/1993
Perfect Fry Corp. name changed to Woodrose Corp. (AB) 09/01/2010 which reincorporated in British Columbia as Woodrose Ventures Corp. 11/07/2016 which recapitalized as Novoheart Holdings Inc. 10/03/2017

PANORAMIC CARE SYS INC (DE)
Name changed to MDI Technologies Inc. 8/13/2001
(See MDI Technologies Inc.)

PANORAMIC ELECTRONICS, INC. (NY)
Acquired by Singer Manufacturing Co. 9/20/62
Each (7) shares Common $20 par exchanged for (1) share Capital Stock $20 par
(See Singer Co.)

PANORAMIC MIRRORS INC (BC)
Name changed to GLG Life Tech Ltd. 06/05/1998
GLG Life Tech Ltd. recapitalized as GLG Life Tech Corp. 03/14/2007

PANORO RES LTD (BC)
Merged into Panoro Minerals Ltd. 6/5/2003
Each share Common no par exchanged for (1) share Common no par

PANSOFT CO LTD (BRITISH VIRGIN ISLANDS)
Acquired by Timesway Group Ltd. 11/09/2012
Each share Common $0.0059 par exchanged for $4.15 cash

PANSOPHIC SYS INC (IL)
Common no par split (2) for (1) by issuance of (1) additional share 4/2/87
Merged into M5 Merge, Inc. 1/2/92
Each share Common no par exchanged for $16.15 cash

PANTAN MINES LTD. (ON)
Merged into Medallion Mines Ltd. 5/22/64
Each share Capital Stock $1 par exchanged for (1) share Common no par
Medallion Mines Ltd. charter cancelled in March, 1968

PANTAN RES LTD (CANADA)
Name changed to Greenwood Environmental Inc. 02/06/1992
(See Greenwood Environmental Inc.)

PANTASOTE CO. (DE)
Name changed to Pantasote Inc. 11/1/78
(See Pantasote Inc.)

PANTASOTE CO. (NJ)
Reincorporated under the laws of Delaware 12/31/66
Pantasote Co. (Del.) name changed to Pantasote Inc. 11/1/78
(See Pantasote Inc.)

PANTASOTE INC (DE)
Acquired by Newsote Inc. 09/15/1989
Each share Common $1 par exchanged for $13.70 cash

PANTEN & CO INC (DE)
Name changed to NFS Financial Services, Inc. 01/30/1976
NFS Financial Services, Inc. name changed to NFS Services, Inc. 10/25/1977
(See NFS Services, Inc.)

PANTEPEC INTL INC (DE)
Voting trust expired 12/31/1974
Each VTC for Common 14¢ par automatically became (1) share Common 14¢ par
Recapitalized as Levcor International, Inc. 09/08/1995
Each share Common 14¢ par exchanged for (0.25) share Common 56¢ par

PANTEPEC INTERNATIONAL PETROLEUM, LTD. (BERMUDA)
Reorganized under the laws of Delaware as Pantepec International, Inc. 10/30/1967
Each VTC for Capital Stock 1s par exchanged for (1) VTC for Capital Stock 14¢ par
Pantepec International, Inc. recapitalized as Levcor International, Inc. 09/08/1995

PANTEPEC OIL CO., C.A. (VENEZUELA)
Reorganized 08/15/1965
Each American Share 1 Bolivar par exchanged for (1) VTC for Capital Stock 1s par and (0.1) Pantepec International Petroleum, Ltd. (Bermuda) Bearer Purchase Warrant
Pantepec International Petroleum, Ltd. (Bermuda) reorganized as Pantepec International, Inc. (DE) 10/30/1967 which recapitalized as Levcor International, Inc. 09/08/1995

PANTEPEC OIL CO. OF VENEZUELA, C.A.
Reorganized 8/19/48
Each share Capital Stock 1 Bolivar par exchanged for (1) share Capital Stock 1 Bolivar par of Pantepec Oil Co., C.A. and a VTC for (2) shares Capital Stock 1 Bolivar par of Pancoastal Oil Co., C.A.
(See each company's listing)

PANTEPEC OIL CO. OF VENEZUELA (DE)
Dissolved in 1938

PANTERA DRILLING INCOME TR (AB)
Merged into Western Energy Services Corp. 12/23/2010
Each Unit no par exchanged for (21.9048) shares Common no par

PANTERA ENTERPRISES INC (AB)
Name changed to Mill City International Corp. 12/10/2002

Mill City International Corp. reorganized as Mill City Gold Corp. 09/01/2004 which name changed to FPS Pharma Inc. 09/10/2015

PANTERA PETE INC (NV)
Recapitalized as ESP Resources, Inc. 01/27/2009
Each share Common $0.001 par exchanged for (0.05) share Common $0.001 par

PANTERAS CORP (MO)
Reorganized under Chapter 11 Federal Bankruptcy Code as Pizza Inn, Inc. (MO) 09/05/1990
Each share Common 1¢ par exchanged for (0.0546448) share Common 1¢ par
Pizza Inn, Inc. (MO) name changed to Pizza Inn Holdings, Inc. 09/26/2011 which name changed to Rave Restaurant Group, Inc. 01/09/2015

PANTERRA ENERGY INC (BC)
Recapitalized as Enrich Ventures Ltd. 2/11/93
Each (4.3) shares Common no par exchanged for (1) share Common no par

PANTERRA EXPL CORP (BC)
Recapitalized as PanTerra Resource Corp. (BC) 09/03/2004
Each share Common no par exchanged for (0.5) share Common no par
PanTerra Resource Corp. (BC) reincorporated in Alberta 10/27/2005 which recapitalized as Ikkuma Resources Corp. 09/22/2014

PANTERRA MINERALS INC (BC)
Recapitalized as Neodym Technologies Inc. 05/03/2001
Each share Common no par exchanged for (0.25) share Common no par
Neodym Technologies Inc. recapitalized as Neoteck Solutions Inc. 09/06/2012 which recapitalized as Hello Pal International Inc. 05/13/2016

PANTERRA RESOURCE CORP (AB)
Reincorporated 10/27/2005
Place of incorporation changed from (BC) to (AB) 10/27/2005
Each share old Common no par exchanged for (0.1) share new Common no par 10/16/2009
Recapitalized as Ikkuma Resources Corp. 09/22/2014
Each share Common no par exchanged for (0.1) share Common no par

PANTEX MANUFACTURING CORP. (DE)
Common $1 par changed to 12-1/2¢ par and (7) additional shares issued 5/15/59
Adjudicated bankrupt 1/15/63

PANTEX PRESSING MACHINE, INC. (DE)
Reorganized as Pantex Manufacturing Corp. 11/30/45, which was adjudicated bankrupt 1/15/63

PANTHCO RES INC (ON)
Merged into ZTEST Electronics Inc. 07/01/1996
Each share Common 1¢ par exchanged for (0.125) share Common 1¢ par and (0.125) Class A Special Share no par

PANTHEON (NV)
Name changed to Medical Dispensing Systems, Inc., Northeast and Common $1 par changed to 10¢ par 07/20/1983
(See Medical Dispensing Systems, Inc., Northeast)

PANTHEON CHINA ACQUISITION CORP (DE)
Reincorporated under the laws of Cayman Islands as China Cord

PAN-PAR   FINANCIAL INFORMATION, INC.

Blood Corp. and Common $0.0001 par reclassified as Ordinary $0.0001 par 07/30/2009
China Cord Blood Corp. name changed to Global Cord Blood Corp. 03/22/2018

PANTHEON INDS INC (CO)
Each share old Common $0.0001 par exchanged for (0.2) share new Common $0.0001 par 07/17/1989
Each share new Common $0.00001 par exchanged again for (0.03333333) share new Common $0.0001 par 05/19/1993
SEC revoked common stock registration 10/20/2008

PANTHEON OIL CO.
Dissolved in 1940

PANTHEON TECHNOLOGIES INC (FL)
Name changed to Canceroption.com, Inc. 04/14/1999
Canceroption.com, Inc. name changed to BioImmune Inc. 06/22/2001
(See BioImmune Inc.)

PANTHEON VENTURES LTD (BC)
Each share old Common no par exchanged for (0.1) share new Common no par 09/08/2014
Recapitalized as Moovly Media Inc. 08/02/2016
Each share new Common no par exchanged for (0.66666666) share Common no par

PANTHER BIOTECHNOLOGY INC (NV)
Name changed to ProBility Media Corp. 02/10/2017

PANTHER CREEK OIL CORP.
Dissolved in 1950

PANTHER ENERGY INC (NV)
Name changed to Falcon Crest Energy Inc. 09/02/2014
Falcon Crest Energy Inc. recapitalized as Cherubim Interests, Inc. 06/16/2015

PANTHER INTERNATIONAL MINING CO. LTD. (ON)
Merged into Consolidated Panther Mines Ltd. on a (0.75) for (1) basis 7/12/60
Consolidated Panther Mines Ltd. recapitalized as Panthco Resources Inc. 7/3/87 which merged into Ztest Electronics, Inc. 7/1/96

PANTHER MINING CO. LTD. (ON)
Acquired by Panther International Mining Co. Ltd. on a (1) for (10) basis 6/2/58
Panther International Mining Co. Ltd. merged into Consolidated Panther Mines Ltd. 7/12/60 which recapitalized as Panthco Resources Inc. 7/3/87

PANTHER MTN WTR PK INC (DE)
Recapitalized as Electric Moto Corp. 01/25/2008
Each share Common $0.00001 par exchanged for (0.0025) share Common $0.00001 par
Electric Moto Corp. recapitalized as Empire Diversified Energy, Inc. 12/22/2014

PANTHER OIL & GAS CO. (CO)
Charter revoked for failure to file reports and pay fees 10/15/73

PANTHER RES LTD (NV)
Recapitalized as PhantomFilm.Com 06/15/1999
Each share Common $0.001 par exchanged for (0.1) share Common $0.001 par
PhantomFilm.Com recapitalized as Komodo, Inc. 10/08/2001
(See Komodo, Inc.)

PANTHERA EXPL INC (BC)
Name changed to Iron South Mining Corp. 02/28/2012
Iron South Mining Corp. name changed to Argentina Lithium & Energy Corp. 09/21/2016

PANTIQUE INC (DE)
Name changed to Jetline Stores, Inc. 12/13/77
Jetline Stores, Inc. name changed to NRX Technologies Inc. 1/4/80
(See NRX Technologies Inc.)

PANTONE INC (NY)
Merged into Herbert Group, Inc. 07/29/1977
Each share Common 1¢ par exchanged for $1 cash

PANTORAMA INDS INC (CANADA)
Acquired by 6149286 Canada Inc. 3/5/2004
Each share Common no par exchanged for $0.80 cash

PANTRY INC (DE)
Acquired by Alimentation Couche-Tard Inc. 03/16/2015
Each share Common 1¢ par exchanged for $36.75 cash

PANTRY PRIDE INC NEW (DE)
Name changed 01/20/1983
Under plan of merger name changed from Pantry Pride, Inc. (Old) to Pantry Pride, Inc. (New) 01/20/1983
Each share Liquidating Preferred Ser. A $1 par exchanged for (0.875) share Common 1¢ par and $1 cash
Each share Liquidating Preferred Ser. B $1 par exchanged for (0.5) share Common 1¢ par and $0.55 cash
Each share Liquidating Preferred Ser. C $1 par exchanged for (0.6) share Common 1¢ par $0.85 cash
Each share Class A Conv. Preferred $1 par exchanged for (1.2) shares Common 1¢ par and $1.20 cash
Each share Class B Preferred $1 par exchanged for (0.3) share Common 1¢ par and $1.10 cash
Each share $4.20 Preferred 1951 Ser. $15 par exchanged for (2) shares Common 1¢ par and $2.50 cash
Each share Common $1 par automatically became (1) share Common 1¢ par
Name changed to Revlon Group Inc. 04/07/1986
(See Revlon Group Inc.)
$14.875 Exchangeable Preferred Ser. B $1 par called for redemption at $100 on 05/07/1998

PANTS N STUFF SHED HOUSE INC (NY)
Voluntarily dissolved 05/20/1991
Details not available

PANWESTERN ENERGY INC (AB)
Name changed to Valeura Energy Inc. 07/06/2010

PAOLO NEV ENTERPRISES INC (CO)
Reorganized under the laws of Nevada as David Loren Corp. 11/13/2006
Each share Common no par exchanged for (0.005) share Common $0.001 par
David Loren Corp. recapitalized as Kibush Capital Corp. 08/23/2013

PAPA BELLO ENTERPRISES INC (FL)
Name changed to WO Group, Inc. 08/03/2017

PAPEKOTE INC (NY)
Charter cancelled and proclaimed dissolved for failure to file reports and pay taxes 12/15/1969

PAPELES NACIONALES S A (COLOMBIA)
GDR agreement terminated 11/24/2004
Each GDR for Ordinary exchanged for $2.1219 cash

PAPER COMPUTER CORP (NV)
Recapitalized as PNG Ventures Inc. (New) 07/05/2001
Each share Common no par exchanged for (0.5) share Common no par
(See PNG Ventures Inc. (New))

PAPER CORP AMER (DE)
Ser. B Preferred 1¢ par called for redemption 06/30/1991
Public interest eliminated

PAPER WHSE INC (MN)
Each share Common 1¢ par exchanged for (0.33333333) share Common 3¢ par 04/17/2001
Plan of reorganization under Chapter 11 Federal Bankruptcy Code effective 08/05/2004
No stockholders' equity

PAPERBACK SOFTWARE INTL (CA)
Each share old Common no par exchanged for (0.1) share new Common no par 10/1/87
Charter cancelled for failure to file reports and pay taxes 3/1/93

PAPERBOARD INDS CORP (ON)
Name changed 11/12/1986
Name changed from Paperboard Industries Corp. Inc. to Paperboard Industries Corp. 11/12/1986
Acquired by Kinburn Industrial Corp. 03/08/1988
Each share Common no par exchanged for $12 cash

PAPERBOARD INDS INTL INC (CANADA)
Merged into Cascades Inc. 12/31/2000
Each share Common no par exchanged for (0.24) share Common no par

PAPERCLIP SOFTWARE INC (DE)
Name changed 11/26/96
Common 1¢ par split (2) for (1) by issuance of (1) additional share payable 5/30/96 to holders of record 5/23/96
Name changed from PaperClip Imaging Software, Inc. to PaperClip Software, Inc. 11/26/96
Recapitalized as China Dongsheng International, Inc. 3/29/2007
Each (37) shares Common 1¢ par exchanged for (1) share Common 1¢ par

PAPERCRAFT CORP (PA)
Common $1 par split (2) for (1) by issuance of (1) additional share 12/11/59
Common $1 par split (2) for (1) by issuance of (1) additional share 12/18/61
Common $1 par split (5) for (4) by issuance of (0.25) additional share 12/14/81
Common $1 par split (3) for (2) by issuance of (0.5) additional share 9/17/82
Common $1 par split (3) for (2) by issuance of (0.5) additional share 6/15/83
$5 Non-Cum. Conv. Preferred $1 par called for redemption 10/24/85
Merged into Papercraft Holding Corp. 10/30/85
Each share Common $1 par exchanged for $8.24 principal amount of Jr. Subord. Debentures due 10/30/2000 and $16 cash

PAPERLINX LTD (AUSTRALIA)
Name changed to Spicers Ltd. 12/01/2015

PAPERT KOENIG LOIS INC (NY)
Class A 30¢ par split (3) for (2) by issuance of (0.5) additional share 12/10/1964
Name changed to PKL Companies, Inc. 09/25/1969
(See PKL Companies, Inc.)

PAPERWORKS INC (NV)
Name changed to VuMee Inc. 05/08/2012

PAPILLON RES LTD (AUSTRALIA)
ADR agreement terminated 02/23/2015
Each ADR for Common exchanged for $12.209666 cash

PAPNET OHIO INC (OH)
Common no par split (2) for (1) by issuance of (1) additional share 5/11/94
Name changed to Netmed, Inc. 12/16/96

PAPOOSE YELLOWKNIFE MINES, LTD. (ON)
Charter cancelled and proclaimed dissolved for failure to pay taxes and file returns 10/21/57

PAPP FOCUS FD INC (MD)
Completely liquidated
Each share Common 1¢ par received first and final distribution of $10.63 cash payable 1/28/2004 to holders of record 1/23/2004
Note: Certificates were not required to be surrendered and are without value

PAPUAN PRECIOUS METALS CORP (BC)
Each share Common no par received distribution of (0.25) share Pioneer Pacific Finance Corp. Common no par payable 10/15/2014 to holders of record 09/30/2014 Ex date - 09/26/2014
Name changed to Ironside Resources Inc. 04/21/2015

PAQUETTE MALARTIC MINES, LTD. (ON)
Charter cancelled for failure to file reports and pay taxes in 1949

PAQUIN GOLD MINES LTD. (QC)
Charter surrendered for failure to file reports and pay fees 4/11/61

PAR ADVANCE TECHNOLOGIES CORP (CO)
Name changed to ACI Global Corp. 06/20/2005

PAR BEVERAGE CORP. (NY)
Merged into Kenner Products Co. 3/14/62
Each share Capital Stock no par exchanged for (3.475) shares Common $1 par
Kenner Products Co. name changed to Rennek Co. 12/20/67 which was acquired by General Mills, Inc. 12/20/67

PAR INVT CORP (UT)
Merged into Toklan Oil Corp. 09/01/1981
Each share Common Capital Stock 1¢ par exchanged for (1) share Capital Stock $0.001 par
(See Toklan Oil Corp.)

PAR PETE CORP (DE)
Each share old Common 1¢ par exchanged for (0.1) share new Common 1¢ par 01/29/2014
Name changed to Par Pacific Holdings Inc. 10/20/2015

PAR PHARMACEUTICAL COS INC (DE)
Acquired by Sky Growth Holdings Corp. 09/28/2012
Each share Common 1¢ par exchanged for $50 cash

PAR PHARMACEUTICAL INC (NJ)
Common 1¢ par split (3) for (2) by issuance of (0.5) additional share 3/11/85
Common 1¢ par split (3) for (2) by issuance of (0.5) additional share 3/11/87
Under plan of reorganization each share Common 1¢ par automatically became (1) share Pharmaceutical

FINANCIAL INFORMATION, INC.   **PAR-PAR**

Resources, Inc. (NJ) Common 1¢ par 8/12/91
Pharmaceutical Resources, Inc. (NJ) reincorporated in Delaware 6/24/2003 which name changed to Par Pharmaceutical Companies, Inc. 5/27/2004

PAR SYS CORP (MN)
Merged into GCA Corp. 6/4/81
Each share Common 10¢ par exchanged for (0.729) share Common 60¢ par
GCA Corp. acquired by General Signal Corp. 6/7/88 which merged into SPX Corp. 10/6/98

PAR TECHNOLOGY CORP (NY)
Reincorporated under the laws of Delaware 04/23/1993

PARA DYNAMICS CORP. (AZ)
Name changed to P-D Corp. 4/23/75
P-D Corp. charter cancelled 5/10/77

PARA INDS INC (NY)
Dissolved by proclamation 12/30/81

PARA-LINK INC (TX)
Each share old Common $0.001 par exchanged for (0.2) share new Common $0.001 par 01/10/1999
Name changed to iChargeit, Inc. (TX) 03/16/1999
iChargeit, Inc. (TX) reincorporated in Delaware 11/12/1999 which reincorporated in Nevada as Freestone Resources, Inc. 08/15/2006

PARA MAS INTERNET INC (NV)
Each share old Common 1¢ par exchanged for (0.1) share new Common 1¢ par 04/12/2004
SEC revoked common stock registration 08/22/2007

PARA MED ENTERPRISES INC (FL)
Each share Common no par exchanged for (4) shares Common 25¢ par 08/01/1972
Name changed to Key Energy Enterprises, Inc. 01/29/1980
(See Key Energy Enterprises, Inc.)

PARABEL INC (DE)
SEC revoked common stock registration 10/04/2017

PARACALE GOLD MINING CO., INC. (PHILIPPINES)
Dissolved 06/30/1966
No stockholders' equity

PARACALE NATIONAL GOLD MINING CO., INC. (PHILIPPINES)
Dissolved 06/30/1966
No stockholders' equity

PARACELSIAN INC (DE)
SEC revoked common stock registration 11/16/2005
Stockholders' equity unlikely

PARACELSUS HEALTHCARE CORP (CA)
Plan of reorganization under Chapter 11 Federal Bankruptcy Code effective 07/09/2001
No stockholders' equity

PARACOMP TECHNOLOGIES INC (BC)
Struck off register and declared dissolved for failure to file returns 02/26/1993

PARACORP LTD (AB)
Struck off register and declared dissolved for failure to file returns 07/01/1992

PARADERM LABORATORIES, INC. (ME)
Charter suspended for non-payment of franchise taxes 12/1/64

PARADIGM ADVANCED TECHNOLOGIES INC (DE)
Filed a petition under Chapter 7 Federal Bankruptcy Code 11/07/2003
Stockholders' equity unlikely

PARADIGM CAP TR II (DE)
Floating Rate Trust Preferred Securities called for redemption at $10 plus $0.142361 accrued dividends on 2/28/2006

PARADIGM ENTERPRISES INC (NV)
Name changed to Paradigm Oil & Gas, Inc. 02/07/2005

PARADIGM GENETICS INC (DE)
Name changed to Icoria, Inc. 08/17/2004
Icoria, Inc. merged into Clinical Data, Inc. (New) 12/20/2005
(See Clinical Data, Inc. (New))

PARADIGM GEOPHYSICAL LTD (ISRAEL)
Issue Information - 3,350,000 ORD shares offered at $7 per share on 06/10/1998
Merged into Paradigm Geotechnology B.V. 8/13/2002
Each share Ordinary NIS0.5 par exchanged for $5.15 cash

PARADIGM HLDGS INC (NV)
Acquired by CACI International Inc. 09/01/2011
Each share Common 1¢ par exchanged for $0.2934 cash

PARADIGM HLDGS INC (WY)
Reincorporated under the laws of Nevada 12/14/2010
(See Paradigm Holdings, Inc. (NV))

PARADIGM HOTEL MORTGAGE FUND (UT)
Involuntarily dissolved 6/1/98

PARADIGM MED INDS INC (CA)
Each share old Common no par exchanged for (0.2) share new Common no par 4/5/94
Reincorporated under the laws of Delaware and Common no par changed to $0.001 par 2/8/96

PARADIGM MUSIC ENTMT CO (DE)
Merged into TCI Music, Inc. 12/31/1997
Each share Common 1¢ par exchanged for (0.61) share Class A Common 1¢ par
TCI Music, Inc. name changed to Liberty Digital Inc. 09/10/1999 which merged into Liberty Media Corp. (New) 03/14/2002 which reorganized as Liberty Media Corp. (Incorporated 02/28/2006) 05/10/2006 which name changed to Liberty Interactive Corp. 09/26/2011 which name changed to Qurate Retail, Inc. 04/10/2018

PARADIGM RESOURCE MGMT CORP (NV)
Recapitalized as Alternative Investment Corp. 02/25/2016
Each share Common $0.001 par exchanged for (0.025) share Common $0.001 par

PARADIGM TACTICAL PRODS INC (DE)
Old Common 1¢ par split (10) for (1) by issuance of (9) additional shares payable 11/27/2006 to holders of record 11/24/2006 Ex date - 11/28/2006
Each share old Common 1¢ par exchanged for (0.01333333) share new Common 1¢ par 05/29/2009
Name changed to Zenergy International, Inc. 07/31/2009

PARADIGM TECHNOLOGY INC (DE)
Each share old Common 1¢ par exchanged for (0.1) share new Common 1¢ par 05/04/1998
Acquired by IXYS Corp. 09/23/1998
Each share new Common 1¢ par exchanged for (0.057842) share Common 1¢ par
(See IXYS Corp.)

PARADISE EXPLORATIONS LTD. (BC)
Charter revoked for failure to file reports and pay fees 3/3/66

PARADISE FRUIT INC (FL)
Each share Common 10¢ par exchanged for (1/3) share Common 30¢ par 3/11/66
Name changed to Paradise Inc. 8/12/93

PARADISE HLDGS INC (DE)
Chapter 11 bankruptcy proceedings converted to Chapter 7 on 07/05/2000
Stockholders' equity unlikely

PARADISE MUSIC & ENTMT INC (DE)
Issue Information - 1,000,000 shares COM offered at $6 per share on 01/21/1997
Name changed to Suncast Solar Energy, Inc. 12/20/2011

PARADISE PETES INC (AB)
Name changed to Santa Fe Energy Group Inc. 7/19/88
Santa Fe Energy Group Inc. name changed to European Technologies International Inc. 6/2/92 which name changed to Steely Group Inc. 6/1/2001
(See Steely Group Inc.)

PARADISE RIDGE HYDROCARBONS INC (FL)
Common $0.00001 par split (3) for (1) by issuance of (2) additional shares payable 08/03/2017 to holders of record 07/31/2017 Ex date - 08/04/2017
Name changed to Grupo Resilient International, Inc. 08/10/2017

PARADISE TAN INC (TX)
Recapitalized as General Red International, Inc. 09/19/2008
Each (45) shares Common 1¢ par exchanged for (1) share Common 1¢ par
(See General Red International, Inc.)

PARADOX OIL & GAS CORP (UT)
Involuntarily dissolved 03/31/1984

PARADOX PRODTN CORP (NV)
Name changed to Production Industries Corp. 07/27/1981

PARADOX URANIUM MINING CORP. (DE)
Merged into Consolidated Uranium Mines, Inc. on a (1) for (5) basis in 1954
(See Consolidated Uranium Mines, Inc.)

PARADYM VENTURES INC (BC)
Recapitalized as Pacific Paradym Energy Inc. 10/01/2007
Each share Common no par exchanged for (0.25) share Common no par

PARADYNAMICS, INC. (DE)
Adjudicated bankrupt 12/28/64
No stockholders' equity

PARADYNE CORP (DE)
Common 10¢ par split (4) for (3) by issuance of (1/3) additional share 3/26/80
Common 10¢ par split (2) for (1) by issuance of (1) additional share 11/26/80
Common 10¢ par split (3) for (2) by issuance of (0.5) additional share 3/21/83
Merged into American Telephone & Telegraph Co. 2/7/89
Each share Common 10¢ par exchanged for $10.25 cash

PARADYNE NETWORKS INC (DE)
Merged into Zhone Technologies, Inc. 09/01/2005
Each share Common $0.001 par exchanged for (1.0972) shares Common $0.001 par
Zhone Technologies, Inc. name changed to DASAN Zhone Solutions, Inc. 09/12/2016

PARAFFINE COMPANIES, INC.
Name changed to Pabco Products, Inc. in 1950
Pabco Products, Inc. name changed to Fibre-board Paper Products Corp. 5/1/56 which name changed to Fibreboard Corp. 7/5/66
(See Fibreboard Corp.)

PARAGON ACQUISITIONS GROUP INC (CO)
Name changed to Sun Up Foods, Inc. 03/27/1990

PARAGON COML CORP (NC)
Reclassification effective 06/30/2008
Holders of (11) or more shares Common $1 par reclassified as Class A Common $1 par
Holders of (10) or fewer shares Common $1 par reclassified as Class B Common $1 par
Class A Common $1 par reclassified as Common $1 par 05/28/2014
Class B Common $1 par reclassified as Common $1 par 05/28/2014
Common $1 par changed to $0.008 par and (124) additional shares issued payable 06/23/2014 to holders of record 06/09/2014
Merged into TowneBank (Portsmouth, VA) 01/29/2018
Each share Common $0.008 par exchanged for (1.725) shares Common $1.667 par

PARAGON COMMUNICATION SYS INC (DE)
Merged into Executone, Inc. 09/23/1985
Each share Common 1¢ par exchanged for $0.75 cash

PARAGON COOLERS INC (CO)
Declared defunct and inoperative for failure to pay taxes and file annual reports 9/9/93

PARAGON ELECTRIC CO. (WI)
Common $2.50 par changed to Class A Common $2.50 par and (1) additional share Class B Common $2.50 par issued 2/11/60
Stock Dividend - 10% 2/3/60
Acquired by American Machine & Foundry Co. 2/2/61
Each (2.6623) shares Class A and/or B Common exchanged for (1) share Common $3.50 par
American Machine & Foundry Co. name changed to AMF Inc. 4/30/70
(See AMF Inc.)

PARAGON ENTMT CORP (ON)
Filed for protection under Companies' Creditors Arrangement Act 04/00/1998
Stockholders' equity unlikely

PARAGON EXPLS LTD (ON)
Recapitalized as Sagewood Resources Ltd. 10/06/1983
Each share Capital Stock no par exchanged for (1) share Class A no par or (1) share Conv. Class B no par
Note: If no election is made Conv. Class B no par will be issued
(See Sagewood Resources Ltd.)

PARAGON FINL CORP (DE)
Name changed to NewMarket Latin America, Inc. 05/04/2007
(See NewMarket Latin America, Inc.)

PARAGON GROUP INC (MD)
Issue Information - 12,000,000 shares COM offered at $21.25 per share on 07/20/1994
Merged into Camden Property Trust 4/15/97
Each share Common 1¢ par exchanged for (0.64) share Common no par

PARAGON HEALTH NETWORK INC (DE)
Common $0.001 par split (3) for (1) by issuance of (2) additional shares

payable 12/30/97 to holders of record 12/15/97 Ex date - 12/31/97
Name changed to Mariner Post-Acute Network, Inc. 7/31/98
(See Mariner Post-Acute Network, Inc.)

PARAGON MINERALS CORP (CANADA)
Merged into Canadian Zinc Corp. 09/24/2012
Each share Common no par exchanged for (0.136) share Common no par
Note: Unexchanged certificates were cancelled and became without value 09/24/2018
Canadian Zinc Corp. name changed to NorZinc Ltd. 09/11/2018

PARAGON MTG CORP (IL)
Proclaimed dissolved for failure to pay taxes and file reports 10/02/2000

PARAGON NATL CORP (DE)
Name changed to PNC Liquidating Corp. 11/30/1970
PNC Liquidating Corp. liquidated for Oxford First Corp. (PA) 11/30/1970
(See Oxford First Corp. (PA))

PARAGON OFFSHORE PLC (ENGLAND & WALES)
Plan of reorganization under Chapter 11 Federal Bankruptcy proceedings effective 07/18/2017
No stockholders' equity

PARAGON PETE CORP (AB)
Acquired by Northrock Resources Ltd. 03/27/1998
Each share Common no par exchanged for $4.10 cash

PARAGON PETE LTD (ON)
Merged into Paragon Petroleum Corp. 01/01/1991
Each share Common no par exchanged for (1) share Common no par
(See Paragon Petroleum Corp.)

PARAGON PHARMACIES LTD (AB)
Name changed to PGNX Capital Corp. 08/03/2012
(See PGNX Capital Corp.)

PARAGON POLARIS STRATEGIES COM INC (NV)
Name changed to Icoworks, Inc. 12/05/2002
Icoworks, Inc. recapitalized as Bioquest Technologies, Inc. 11/09/2006 which name changed to Texas Hill Country Barbecue Inc. 06/28/2010 which name changed to South American Properties, Inc. 04/10/2013 which name changed to USA Restaurant Funding Inc. 11/17/2014 which name changed to Chron Organization, Inc. 03/24/2016 which name changed to Zenergy Brands, Inc. 12/01/2017

PARAGON PPTYS LTD (AB)
Acquired by Daon Development Corp. 07/28/1974
Each share Common no par exchanged for $3.27 cash

PARAGON REAL ESTATE EQUITY & INVT TR (MD)
Each share old Common 1¢ par exchanged for (0.01333333) share new Common 1¢ par 07/28/2006
Name changed to Pillarstone Capital REIT 06/20/2016

PARAGON REFINING CO.
Assets sold in 1930

PARAGON RES LTD (BC)
Recapitalized as SAMEX Mining Corp. 09/11/1995
Each share Common no par exchanged for (0.2) share Common no par
(See SAMEX Mining Corp.)

PARAGON SECS CO (NJ)
Adjudicated bankrupt 08/28/1973
Stockholders' equity unlikely

PARAGON SEMITECH USA INC (DE)
Recapitalized as Master Silicon Carbide Industries, Inc. (DE) 11/12/2008
Each share Common $0.001 par exchanged for (0.1) share Common $0.001 par
Master Silicon Carbide Industries, Inc. (DE) reincorporated in Nevada 11/02/2009
(See Master Silicon Carbide Industries, Inc.)

PARAGON TECHNOLOGIES INC (PA)
Reincorporated under the laws of Delaware 12/7/2001

PARAGON TRADE BRANDS INC (DE)
Reorganized under Chapter 11 Federal Bankruptcy Code 01/28/2000
Each share old Common 1¢ par exchanged for (0.0149) share new Common 1¢ par and (0.0524) Common Stock Purchase Warrant expiring 01/28/2010
Merged into Tyco International Ltd. 01/18/2002
Each share new Common 1¢ par exchanged for $43.50 cash

PARAGUAY MINING CORP. (LIBERIA)
Became defunct 02/01/1964
No stockholders' equity

PARAHO DEV CORP (CO)
Under plan of merger name changed to New Paraho Corp. (CO) 07/22/1986
New Paraho Corp. (CO) reincorporated in Nevada as NPC Holdings Inc. 07/12/2000 which name changed to Regent Energy Corp. 03/12/2001
(See Regent Energy Corp.)

PARAISO OIL CO. (CA)
Charter suspended for failure to file reports and pay fees 3/1/19

PARALAX VIDEO ENTERPRISES INC (NJ)
Chapter 11 Federal Bankruptcy Code converted to Chapter 7 on 7/10/89
Stockholders' equity unlikely

PARALLAN COMPUTER INC (CA)
Name changed to Meridian Data Inc. (CA) 12/1/94
Meridian Data Inc. (CA) reincorporated in Delaware 5/29/97 which merged into Quantum Corp. 9/10/99

PARALLAX ENTMT INC (TX)
Old Common 1¢ par split (20) for (1) by issuance of (19) additional shares payable 11/5/2001 to holders of record 11/2/2001 Ex date - 11/6/2001
Each share old Common 1¢ par exchanged for (0.002) share new Common 1¢ par 1/27/2003
Recapitalized as Sunrise Real Estate Development Group, Inc. 12/23/2003
Each share new Common 1¢ par exchanged for (0.2) share Common 1¢ par
Sunrise Real Estate Development Group, Inc. name changed to Sunrise Real Estate Group, Inc. 5/23/2006

PARALLEL CAP CORP (BC)
Name changed to Parallel Resources Ltd. 12/17/2009
Parallel Resources Ltd. recapitalized as Parallel Mining Corp. 12/19/2011

PARALLEL DEV GROUP INC (IA)
Administratively dissolved 09/03/1992

PARALLEL PETE CORP (DE)
Acquired by PLLL Holdings, LLC 11/25/2009
Each share Common 1¢ par exchanged for $3.15 cash

PARALLEL PETE CORP (TX)
Each share Common $0.001 par exchanged for (0.1) share Common 1¢ par 08/06/1982
Reincorporated under the laws of Delaware 12/12/1984
(See Parallel Petroleum Corp. (DE))

PARALLEL RES LTD (BC)
Recapitalized as Parallel Mining Corp. 12/19/2011
Each (4.5) shares Common no par exchanged for (1) share Common no par

PARALLEL TECHNOLOGIES INC (NV)
Recapitalized as Fushi International, Inc. 01/30/2006
Each (245.27) shares Common $0.006 par exchanged for (1) share Common $0.006 par
Note: Holders of between (5,000) and (24,526) shares received (100) shares
Fushi International, Inc. name changed to Fushi Copperweld, Inc. 01/15/2008

PARAMAQUE MINES LTD (ON)
Charter cancelled for default in filing returns and paying fees 11/28/1973

PARAMARK ENTERPRISES INC (DE)
Name changed to Raptor Investments Inc. (DE) 11/01/2001
Raptor Investments Inc. (DE) reincorporated in Florida 12/04/2001 which name changed to Snap 'N' Sold Corp. 07/22/2005 which name changed to Hot Web, Inc. 09/25/2006 which name changed to Gold Coast Mining Corp. 07/02/2009 which name changed to Green Leaf Innovations, Inc. 03/10/2015

PARAMAX RES LTD (BC)
Each share old Common no par exchanged for (0.1) share new Common no par 04/26/2012
Name changed to Sabre Graphite Corp. 06/10/2013
Sabre Graphite Corp. name changed to DraftTeam Daily Fantasy Sports Corp. 03/13/2015 which name changed to Fantasy Aces Daily Fantasy Sports Corp. 10/06/2015

PARAMCO FINL GROUP INC (DE)
Reorganized 04/09/2003
Reorganized from under the laws of (NV) to (DE) 04/09/2003
Each share old Common $0.001 par exchanged for (0.1) share new Common $0.001 par
Recapitalized as TRAC Financial Group, Inc. 01/27/2006
Each share new Common $0.001 par exchanged for (0.001) share Common $0.001 par
TRAC Financial Group, Inc. name changed to FINI Group, Inc. 07/28/2006 which name changed to Avalon Capital Holdings Corp. 08/24/2007
(See Avalon Capital Holdings Corp.)

PARAMED, INC. (WA)
Adjudicated bankrupt 05/02/1967
No stockholders' equity

PARAMED INC (NY)
Name changed to Total Resources, Inc. 04/27/1971
(See Total Resources, Inc.)

PARAMETRIC SOUND CORP (NV)
Each share old Common $0.001 par exchanged for (0.2) share new Common $0.001 par 03/22/2012
Name changed to Turtle Beach Corp. 05/28/2014

PARAMETRIC TECHNOLOGY CORP (MA)
Old Common 1¢ par split (3) for (2) by issuance of (0.5) additional share 06/27/1991
Old Common 1¢ par split (2) for (1) by issuance of (1) additional share 02/25/1992
Old Common 1¢ par split (2) for (1) by issuance of (1) additional share 02/25/1993
Old Common 1¢ par split (2) for (1) by issuance of (1) additional share payable 02/29/1996 to holders of record 02/22/1996
Old Common 1¢ par split (2) for (1) by issuance of (1) additional share payable 03/06/1998 to holders of record 02/27/1998
Each share old Common 1¢ par exchanged for (0.4) share new Common 1¢ par 02/28/2006
Name changed to PTC Inc. 01/28/2013

PARAMETRIC VENTURES INC (BC)
Recapitalized as Centura Resources Inc. 11/12/1999
Each share Common no par exchanged for (0.2) share Common no par
Centura Resources Inc. recapitalized as Polar Resources Corp. 02/14/2005

PARAMOUNT ACQUISITION CORP (DE)
Name changed to Chem Rx Corp. 10/26/2007
(See Chem Rx Corp.)

PARAMOUNT AIRCRAFT PRODUCTS, INC. INC.
Assets sold in 1940

PARAMOUNT BK FSB (BAKERSFIELD, CA)
Merged into Bank of Stockdale, F.S.B. (Bakersfield, CA) 7/31/95
Each share Preferred 1¢ par exchanged for (0.29785) share Preferred 1¢ par
Each share Common 1¢ par exchanged for (0.22934) share Guarantee Stock 1¢ par
Bank of Stockdale, F.S.B. (Bakersfield, CA) merged into VIB Corp. 1/28/99
(See VIB Corp.)

PARAMOUNT CAB MANUFACTURING CORP. (DE)
Name changed to Paramount Motors Corp. 00/00/1931
Paramount Motors Corp. name changed to Paramount Communities Corp. 10/01/1974
(See Paramount Communities Corp.)

PARAMOUNT CMNTYS CORP (DE)
Voluntarily dissolved 07/06/1978
Details not available

PARAMOUNT COMMUNICATIONS INC (DE)
$5.75 S.F. Preferred $2.50 par called for redemption 12/26/1989
Merged into Viacom Inc. (Old) 07/07/1994
Each share Common $1 par exchanged for $17.50 principal amount of 8% Exchangeable Subordiated Debentures due 2006 (0.93065) share Class B Common 1¢ par, (0.93065) Contingent Value Right, (0.5) Class B Common Stock Purchase Warrant expiring 07/07/1997 and (0.3) Class B Common Stock Purchase Warrant which expired 07/07/1997
(See Viacom Inc. (Old))

PARAMOUNT COMMUNICATIONS LTD (INDIA)
Basis changed from (1:1) to (1:5) 02/09/2007
GDR agreement terminated 05/31/2016
Each Reg. S Sponsored GDR for Ordinary exchanged for $0.083942 cash

PARAMOUNT COMPUTER SYSTEMS CORP (DE)
Under plan of merger name changed to TyCodyne Industries Corp. and (0.12) additional share issued 7/26/98
(See TyCodyne Industries Inc.)

PARAMOUNT ENERGY TR (AB)
Plan of Arrangement effective 07/06/2010
Each Trust Unit no par exchanged for (1) share Perpetual Energy Inc. Common no par
Note: Unexchanged certificates were cancelled and became without value 07/06/2015

PARAMOUNT ENTERPRISES, INC. (NY)
Incorporated in 1945
Proclaimed dissolved by New York Secretary of State 12/15/54

PARAMOUNT ENTERPRISES, INC. (NY)
Incorporated in 1956
Adjudicated bankrupt 2/16/59
No stockholders' equity

PARAMOUNT FAMOUS LASKY CORP.
Succeeded by Paramount Publix Corp. 00/00/1930
Details not available

PARAMOUNT FDG CORP (ON)
Acquired by Trical Resources Inc. 08/18/1989
Each share Class A no par exchanged for (0.75) share Common no par
Trical Resources Inc. recapitalized as Voyager Energy Inc. 02/19/1990 which merged into Poco Petroleums Ltd. 06/01/1991 which merged into Burlington Resources Inc. 11/18/1999 which merged into ConocoPhillips 03/31/2006

PARAMOUNT FINL CORP (DE)
Each share old Common 4¢ par exchanged for (0.25) share new Common 4¢ par 05/20/1998
Name changed to 5B Technologies Corp. 02/14/2000
(See 5B Technologies Corp.)

PARAMOUNT FIRE INSURANCE CO. (NY)
Each share Common $100 par exchanged for (10) shares Common $10 par in 1949
Merged into Pacific National Fire Insurance Co. and each share Common $10 par received $54 cash 3/31/59

PARAMOUNT FOAM INDS (NJ)
Merged into Seagrave Corp. (DE) 10/20/69
Each share Common 10¢ par exchanged for (0.083333) share Common $2.50 par
Seagrave Corp. (DE) name changed to Vista Resources, Inc. 9/30/80 which name changed to Fuqua Enterprises, Inc. 9/8/95 which merged into Graham-Field Health Products Inc. 12/30/97
(See Graham-Field Health Products Inc.)

PARAMOUNT GOLD & SILVER CORP (DE)
Name changed 08/27/2007
Common $0.001 par split (2) for (1) by issuance of (1) additional share payable 07/22/2005 to holders of record 07/18/2005 Ex date - 07/25/2005
Name changed from Paramount Gold Mining Corp. to Paramount Gold & Silver Corp. 08/27/2007
Each share Common $0.001 par received distribution of (0.05) share Paramount Gold Nevada Corp. Common 1¢ par payable 04/17/2015 to holders of record 04/14/2015

Merged into Coeur Mining, Inc. 04/17/2015
Each share Common $0.001 par exchanged for (0.2016) share Common 1¢ par

PARAMOUNT INTL COIN CORP (OH)
Merged into Parasub, Inc. 09/03/1980
Each share Common no par exchanged for $42 cash

PARAMOUNT LEASING CORP (DE)
Common $1 par changed to 1¢ par 11/9/70
Name changed to Alcorn Food Products Co., Inc. 7/26/79
Alcorn Food Products Co., Inc. name changed to Freedom Synthetic Oil Co., Inc. 1/24/80
(See Freedom Synthetic Oil Co., Inc.)

PARAMOUNT LIFE INS CO (AB)
Company liquidated in 1995
No distributions to stockholders

PARAMOUNT LIFE INS CO (AR)
Each share Common $2 par exchanged for (0.1) share old Common no par in 1984
Each share old Common no par exchanged for (0.1) share new Common no par 6/30/86
Acquired by Jefferson National Life Insurance Co. in September 1995
Details not available

PARAMOUNT MINES CORP. (ID)
Merged into Yreka United, Inc. (ID) 06/07/1957
Each share Common exchanged for (1/3) share Common 50¢ par
Yreka United, Inc. (ID) reorganized in Nevada as Southern Home Medical Equipment, Inc. 10/23/2006 which name changed to Southern Home Medical, Inc. 07/27/2012

PARAMOUNT MINING & DEVELOPMENT CORP. (NV)
Charter revoked for failure to file reports and pay fees 03/03/1969

PARAMOUNT MINING CORP. LTD. (QC)
Completely liquidated in 1951
Each share Capital Stock received first and final distribution of (0.038865) share New Formaque Mines, Ltd. Capital Stock $1 par
Note: Certificates were not required to be surrendered and are without value
New Formaque Mines, Ltd. recapitalized as Sobiga Mines Ltd.-Les Mines Sobiga Ltee. 1/16/74
(See Sobiga Mines Ltd.-Les Mines Sobiga Ltee.)

PARAMOUNT MNG LTD (BC)
Each share Common 50¢ par exchanged for (1) share Common no par 4/16/74
Struck off register and declared dissolved for failure to file returns 2/25/83

PARAMOUNT MTRS CORP (DE)
Capital Stock no par changed to $1 par 00/00/1932
Name changed to Paramount Communities Corp. 10/01/1974
(See Paramount Communities Corp.)

PARAMOUNT MUT FD INC (DE)
Capital Stock $1 par changed to 25¢ par and (3) additional shares issued 04/20/1964
Name changed to FPA Paramount Fund, Inc. 06/01/1984

PARAMOUNT OIL CO. (UT)
Name changed to Paramount General Corp. 05/12/1965
(See Paramount General Corp.)

PARAMOUNT PACIFIC INC. (NV)
Merged into Zapata Norness Inc. 09/30/1969
Each share Common $1 par exchanged for (0.3) share Common 25¢ par

Zapata Norness Inc. name changed to Zapata Corp. (DE) 02/15/1972 which reincorporated in Nevada 04/30/1999 which reincorporated in Delaware as Harbinger Group Inc. 12/23/2009 which name changed to HRG Group, Inc. 03/11/2015 which recapitalized as Spectrum Brands Holdings, Inc. (New) 07/16/2018

PARAMOUNT PACKAGING CORP (DE)
Merged into Paramount Acquisition Corp. 05/10/1985
Each share Common 10¢ par exchanged for $9.25 cash

PARAMOUNT PETROLEUM & MINERAL CORP. LTD. (SK)
Acquired by Bison Petroleum & Minerals Ltd. 09/15/1960
Each share Common no par exchanged for (0.25) share Capital Stock $1 par
Bison Petroleum & Minerals Ltd. recapitalized as United Bison Resources Ltd. 12/22/1987 which merged into Nalcap Holdings Inc. 04/25/1991 which recapitalized as Arbatax International Inc. (Canada) 03/28/1996 which reincorporated in Yukon 08/06/1996 which name changed to MFC Bancorp Ltd. (YT) 03/03/1997 which reincorporated in British Columbia 11/03/2004 which name changed to KHD Humboldt Wedag International Ltd. 11/01/2005 which reorganized as Terra Nova Royalty Corp. 03/30/2010 which name changed to MFC Industrial Ltd. 09/30/2011 which name changed to MFC Bancorp Ltd. (BC) 02/16/2016
(See MFC Bancorp Ltd. (BC))

PARAMOUNT PICTURES, INC.
Under plan of reorganization each share Common $1 par exchanged for (0.5) share Common $1 par of Paramount Pictures Corp. and a Certificate of Interest in (0.5) share Common $1 par of United Paramount Theatres, Inc. 12/31/49
(See each company's listing)

PARAMOUNT PICTURES CORP. (NY)
Merged into Gulf & Western Industries, Inc. (MI) 10/19/1966
Each share Common $1 par exchanged for (0.21) share $5.75 Preferred $2.50 par, (0.389) share $3.50 Conv. Preferred Ser. B $2.50 par, and (1.458) shares Common $1 par
Gulf & Western Industries, Inc. (MI) reincorporated in Delaware 07/12/1967 which name changed to Gulf + Western Inc. 05/01/1986 which name changed to Paramount Communications Inc. 06/05/1989 which merged into Viacom Inc. (Old) 07/07/1994
(See Viacom Inc. (Old))

PARAMOUNT PUBLIX CORP.
Reorganized as Paramount Pictures, Inc. 00/00/1935
Details not available

PARAMOUNT RES INC (BC)
Recapitalized as Xanaro Technologies Inc. 07/08/1985
Each share Common no par exchanged for (2) shares Common no par
Xanaro Technologies Inc. name changed to Canadian Industrial Minerals Corp. (BC) 11/24/86 which reincorporated in Alberta 01/20/1995 which merged into Abacan Resource Corp. (New) 02/10/1995
(See Abacan Resource Corp. (New))

PARAMOUNT SVCS CORP (DE)
Reorganized as Wowtown.com Inc. 02/25/2000
Each share Common $0.0001 par exchanged for (2) shares Common $0.0001 par
Wowtown.com Inc. recapitalized as Phoenix Star Ventures, Inc. 04/12/2001 which name changed to WPCS International Inc. 05/29/2002 which recapitalized as DropCar, Inc. 01/31/2018

PARAMOUNT SUPPLY INC (NV)
Name changed to Nine Alliance Science & Technology Group 10/25/2017

PARAMOUNT URANIUM CORP. (UT)
Merged into Atlas Uranium Corp. on a (1) for (15) basis in 1955
Atlas Uranium Corp. name changed to Atlas Mining & Milling Corp. 7/30/57 which name changed to Coronado Corp. 7/31/61
(See Coronado Corp.)

PARAMOUNT VENTURES & FIN INC (BC)
Reincorporated 08/24/1993
Place of incorporation changed from (ON) to (BC) 08/24/1993
Plan of arrangement effective 08/24/1998
Each share Class A no par exchanged for (1) share Common no par and (0.0978) share Paramax Resources Ltd. Common no par
(See Paramax Resources Ltd.)
Delisted from Toronto Venture Stock Exchange 06/16/2004

PARAMOUNT VENTURES INC NEW (NV)
Recapitalized as Good Times Restaurants, Inc. 1/18/90
Each share Common $0.001 par exchanged for (0.01) share Common $0.001 par

PARAMOUR PRODUCTIONS INC (NV)
Name changed to Com 101 Inc. 07/16/1998
Com 101 Inc. name changed to Optimal Analytics.com Inc. 06/18/1999 which recapitalized as Optimal Ventures Inc. 02/20/2002 which name changed to Greenwind Power Corp. USA 04/08/2004 which recapitalized as HD Retail Solutions Inc. 07/07/2009 which name changed to Greenscape Laboratories, Inc. 06/10/2014 which recapitalized as Ultrack Systems, Inc. 04/11/2016

PARAMUS SUPER-MARKET, INC. (NJ)
Reorganized as Valley Fair Enterprises, Inc. 2/28/63
No stockholders' equity

PARANA BANCO S A NEW (BRAZIL)
ADR agreement terminated 02/21/2017
Each Sponsored ADR for Preferred exchanged for $20.198915 cash

PARANA BANCO S A OLD (BRAZIL)
Recapitalized as Parana Banco S.A. (New) 08/18/2009
Each Sponsored ADR for Preferred exchanged for (0.2) Sponsored ADR for Preferred
(See Parana Banco S.A. (New))

PARANA COPPER CORP (BC)
Each share old Common no par exchanged for (0.33333333) share new Common no par 12/12/2017
Name changed to Redfund Capital Corp. 08/14/2018

PARAPET PETE INC (ON)
Merged into D'Eldona Resources Ltd. 10/15/84
Each (13) shares Common no par exchanged for (1) share Common no par
D'Eldona Resources Ltd. recapitalized as Western D'Eldona Resources Ltd. 6/1/88

PAR-PAR

(See Western D'Eldona Resources Ltd.)

PARAPHERNALIA INC (NY)
Merged into Puritan Fashions Corp. 10/09/1974
Each share Common 10¢ par exchanged for (0.75) share Common $1 par
(See Puritan Fashions Corp.)

PARAVANT INC (FL)
Name changed 11/1/98
Common $0.045 par changed to $0.015 par and (2) additional shares issued payable 7/25/96 to holders of record 7/22/96
Name changed from Paravant Computer Systems Inc. to Paravant Inc. 11/1/98
Merged into DRS Technologies, Inc. 11/29/2002
Each share Common $0.015 par exchanged for $4.75 cash

PARAVOX, INC. (OH)
Charter cancelled for failure to file reports and pay taxes 11/20/64

PARBEC MALARTIC GOLD MINES LTD. (ON)
Name changed to Parbec Mines Ltd. 00/00/1953
Parbec Mines Ltd. merged into Hydra Explorations Ltd. 11/16/1959 which name changed to Hydra Capital Corp. 12/30/1992 which name changed to Waterford Capital Management Inc. 11/12/1996 which merged into CPI Plastics Group Ltd. 09/21/1998
(See CPI Plastics Group Ltd.)

PARBEC MINES LTD. (ON)
Merged into Hydra Explorations Ltd. on an (0.04) for (1) basis 11/16/1959
Hydra Explorations Ltd. name changed to Hydra Capital Corp. 12/30/1992 which name changed to Waterford Capital Management Inc. 11/12/1996 which merged into CPI Plastics Group Ltd. 09/21/1998
(See CPI Plastics Group Ltd.)

PARCPLACE-DIGITALK INC (DE)
Name changed 8/29/95
Name changed from ParcPlace Systems, Inc. to ParcPlace-Digitalk, Inc. 8/29/95
Name changed to Objectshare, Inc. 10/1/97
Objectshare, Inc. merged into Starbase Corp. 4/14/2000
(See Starbase Corp.)

PARDEE & CURTIN RLTY TR (PA)
Completely liquidated
Each share Preferred $1 par received first and final distribution of $0.109 cash payable 12/31/2002 to holders of record 1/2/2002

PARDEE AMALGAMATED MINES LTD. (ON)
Liquidation completed 11/09/1961
Each share Common $1 par exchanged for (0.02857142) share Rio Algom Mines Ltd. Capital Stock no par and $0.0025 cash
Rio Algom Mines Ltd. name changed to Rio Algom Ltd. 04/30/1975
(See Rio Algom Ltd.)

PARDEE RES CO (PA)
Ser. B Preferred called for redemption at $25 on 9/30/2004
(Additional Information in Active)

PARENT CO (CO)
Plan of reorganization under Chapter 11 Federal Bankruptcy proceedings effective 09/01/2010
No stockholders' equity

PARENT LAKE MINES LTD. (ON)
Reorganized under the laws of Quebec as Atlas Sulphur & Iron Co. Ltd. 00/00/1951
Each share Capital Stock $1 par exchanged for (0.1) share Capital Stock $1 par
Atlas Sulphur & Iron Co. Ltd. recapitalized as International Atlas Development & Exploration Ltd. 06/26/1963
(See International Atlas Development & Exploration Ltd.)

PARENTECH INC (DE)
Recapitalized as Bridgetech Holdings International, Inc. 2/11/2005
Each share Common $0.000001 par exchanged for (0.005) share Common $0.001 par

PARETO CORP (ON)
Merged into Pareto Holdings Ltd. 03/18/2011
Each share Common no par exchanged for $2.72 cash

PAREXEL INTL CORP (MA)
Common 1¢ par split (2) for (1) by issuance of (1) additional share payable 02/21/1997 to holders of record 02/07/1997 Ex date - 02/24/1997
Common 1¢ par split (2) for (1) by issuance of (1) additional share payable 03/03/2008 to holders of record 02/22/2008 Ex date - 03/04/2008
Acquired by Pamplona Capital Management, LLP 09/29/2017
Each share Common 1¢ par exchanged for $88.10 cash

PARGAS ENTERPRISES LTD (AB)
Reincorporated under the laws of Canada as Silk Road Resources Ltd. 12/29/2003
Silk Road Resources Ltd. acquired by EurOmax Resources Ltd. 06/30/2009

PARGAS INC (MD)
Common $1 par split (5) for (4) by issuance of (0.25) additional share 3/4/63
Common $1 par split (2) for (1) by issuance of (1) additional share 3/5/65
$2.64 Preference Ser. A no par called for redemption 10/12/83
Stock Dividend - 15% 3/1/82
Merged into Reliance Group Holdings, Inc. 12/22/83
Each share Common $1 par exchanged for $37.25 cash

PARI-MUTUEL EQUIPMENT CORP. (NY)
Charter revoked for failure to file reports and pay fees 12/15/66

PARIA URANIUM & OIL CORP. (NV)
Name changed to International Retail Systems, Inc. 12/6/71

PARIBAS TR FOR INSTNS (MA)
Completely liquidated 07/10/1996
Each share Major Capitalization Index Portfolio 10¢ par received net asset value
Completely liquidated 08/29/1996
Each share Quantus Equity Managed Portfolio 10¢ par received net asset value

PARIS BUSINESS FORMS INC (PA)
Name changed 1/26/96
Stock Dividends - 10% 8/3/87; 10% 1/5/88
Name changed from Paris Business Forms, Inc. to Paris Corp. 1/26/96
Reacquired 3/15/2002
Each share Common $0.004 par exchanged for $4.50 cash

PARIS ENERGY INC (AB)
Recapitalized as Mapan Energy Ltd. 09/10/2014
Each share Common no par exchanged for (0.08333333) Common no par
Mapan Energy Ltd. merged into Tourmaline Oil Corp. 08/17/2015

PARIS ENTERPRISES INC (DE)
Name changed to R.E.M. Industries, Inc. 05/14/1973
(See R.E.M. Industries, Inc.)

PARIS INDS CORP (DE)
Charter cancelled and declared inoperative and void for non-payment of taxes 3/1/88

PARISCO FOODS LTD (BC)
Delisted from Vancouver Stock Exchange 3/3/97
Stockholders' equity unlikely

PARISH NATL CORP (LA)
Acquired by Whitney Holding Corp. 11/07/2008
Each share Common 1¢ par exchanged for (8.0523) shares Common no par
Whitney Holding Corp. merged into Hancock Holding Co. 06/04/2011 which name changed to Hancock Whitney Corp. 05/25/2018

PARISIAN INC (AL)
Acquired by P.I. Acquisition Corp. 04/26/1988
Each share Common 1¢ par exchanged for $30.65 cash

PARK & 46TH STREET CORP. (NY)
Liquidation completed 3/27/62

PARK & HAGNA (NJ)
Charter revoked for failure to file reports and pay fees in 1966

PARK & SELL CORP (NV)
Reorganized as Bidfish.com Inc. 09/24/2009
Each share Common $0.00001 par exchanged for (31) shares Common $0.00001 par
Bidfish.com Inc. name changed to DYM Energy Corp. 04/23/2012 which name changed to Four G Holdings Corp. 09/09/2015

PARK & SHOP ALEXANDRIA CORP. (VA)
In process of liquidation
Each share Capital Stock $25 par exchanged for initial distribution of $50 cash in 1980
Note: Details on subsequent distributions, if any, are not available

PARK & TILFORD, INC.
Name changed to Park & Tilford Distillers Corp. in 1950
(See Park & Tilford Distillers Corp.)

PARK & TILFORD DISTILLERS CORP. (DE)
Merged into Schenley Industries, Inc. at $43 a share 3/26/58

PARK AVE CAP INC (DE)
Reorganized as Notebook Center, Inc. 8/27/93
Each share Common $0.003 par exchanged for (6) shares Common $0.0015 par
Notebook Center, Inc. name changed to Universal Biotechnologies Inc. 1/25/94 which recapitalized as Queen Sand Resources, Inc. 3/3/95 which name changed to Devx Energy Inc. 9/19/2000
(See Devx Energy Inc.)

PARK AVE INC (UT)
Recapitalized as Electrical Generation Technology Corp. 06/09/1994
Each share Common $0.001 par exchanged for (1/6) share Common $0.001 par
(See Electrical Generation Technology Corp.)

PARK AVE INDS INC (NY)
Charter cancelled and proclaimed dissolved for failure to pay taxes 03/25/1981

PARK AVE INVT CORP (ON)
Name changed to Electric-Spin Ltd. 10/10/2007

PARK AVE MARKETING INC (FL)
Recapitalized as BSD Healthcare Industries Inc. 2/19/98
Each (14.5) shares Common $0.001 par exchanged for (1) share Common $0.001 par
BSD Healthcare Industries Inc. name changed to BSD Software Inc. 12/17/2001 which merged into NeoMedia Technologies, Inc. 3/23/2006

PARK AVE RLTY TR (NY)
Liquidation completed
Each Share of Bene. Int. no par exchanged for initial distribution of $12.75 cash 2/19/74
Each Share of Bene. Int. no par received second distribution of $1.25 cash 10/1/74
Assets transferred to Park Avenue Realty Dissolution Trust
Each Share of Bene. Int. no par received third distribution of 25¢ cash 3/20/78
Charter cancelled and proclaimed dissolved 12/30/81
Not known whether any additional distributions were made

PARK AVENUE KNITTING MILLS, INC. (NY)
Name changed to Park Avenue Industries, Inc. 11/23/71
Park Avenue Industries, Inc. charter cancelled 3/25/81

PARK AWAY PARKS, INC. (PA)
Merged 12/29/72
Details not available

PARK BANCORP INC (DE)
Acquired by Royal Financial, Inc. 04/29/2016
Each share Common 1¢ par exchanged for $0.14 cash

PARK BANKSHARES INC (FL)
Merged into 1st United Bancorp 11/01/1996
Each share Common no par exchanged for (3.52) shares Common no par
1st United Bancorp merged into Wachovia Corp. (New) (Ctfs. dated between 05/20/1991 and 09/01/2001) 11/11/1997 which merged into Wachovia Corp. (Ctfs. dated after 09/01/2001) 09/01/2001 which merged into Wells Fargo & Co. (New) 12/31/2008

PARK-BINGHAM MINING CO. (UT)
Voluntarily dissolved 12/26/72
Each share Common 10¢ par received a distribution of $0.0121 cash
Certificates were not required to be surrendered and are now valueless

PARK CASTLES APARTMENTS, INC. (MO)
Liquidation completed
Each share Capital Stock no par exchanged for initial distribution of $100 cash 7/10/68
Each share Capital Stock no par received second distribution of $40 cash 8/1/68
Each share Capital Stock no par received third distribution of $8.43 cash 1/3/69
Each share Capital Stock no par received fourth and final distribution of $1.22 cash 4/1/69

PARK CENTRAL APARTMENTS
Trust terminated in 1950
Details not available

PARK CHEM CO (MI)
Each share Preferred $2 par exchanged for (1) share Common $1 par in April 1958
Common $1 par split (3) for (2) by issuance of (0.5) additional share 6/21/68
Common $1 par split (2) for (1) by

issuance of (1) additional share 3/9/84
Merged into Whittaker Corp. 8/18/86
Each share Common $1 par exchanged for $34 cash

PARK CITIES BK & TR CO (DALLAS, TX)
Merged into First International Bancshares, Inc. 08/24/1973
Each share Common $10 par exchanged for (2.1) shares Common $5 par
First International Bancshares, Inc. name changed to Interfirst Corp. 12/31/1981 which merged into First RepublicBank Corp. 06/06/1987
(See First RepublicBank Corp.)

PARK CITY CONS MINES CO (UT)
Each share old Capital Stock 10¢ par exchanged for (0.0002) new Capital Stock 10¢ par 10/19/1988
Note: In effect holders received cash and public interest was eliminated

PARK CITY DEVELOPMENT CO. (UT)
Proclaimed dissolved for failure to pay taxes 11/9/74

PARK CITY GROUP INC (NV)
Conv. Preferred Ser. A 1¢ par called for redemption at $10 on 04/15/2013
(Additional Information in Active)

PARK CO. OF HARTFORD, INC.
Merged into Connecticut Investment Management Corp. 00/00/1931
Details not available

PARK COMMUNICATIONS INC (DE)
Common 16-2/3¢ par split (3) for (2) by issuance of (0.5) additional share 8/30/85
Common 16-2/3¢ par split (3) for (2) by issuance of (0.5) additional share 9/15/89
Acquired by Park Acquisitions Inc. 5/11/95
Each share Common 16-2/3¢ par exchanged for $30.50 cash

PARK CONSOLIDATED MOTELS, INC. (MD)
Merged into Quality Courts Motels, Inc. 04/30/1968
Each share Common 10¢ par exchanged for (0.696) share Common $1 par
Quality Courts Motels, Inc. name changed to Quality Inns International, Inc. 08/31/1972 which merged into Manor Care, Inc. 12/01/1980 which merged into HCR Manor Care, Inc. 09/25/1998 which name changed to Manor Care, Inc. (New) 09/30/1999
(See Manor Care, Inc. (New))

PARK COUNTY OIL & ROYALTY CO. (CO)
Charter dissolved for failure to pay taxes and file annual reports 1/1/40

PARK CRESCENT HOTEL INC (NY)
Merged into Unit No. 3 Corp. 7/28/66
Details not available

PARK DROP FORGE CO. (OH)
Stock Dividend - 20% 1/29/65
Under plan of merger name changed to Park-Ohio Industries, Inc. (OH) (Old) 6/1/67
Park-Ohio Industries, Inc. (OH) (Old) merged into Growth International, Inc. 11/30/71 which name changed to Park-Ohio Industries, Inc. (DE) 6/1/72 which reorganized as Park-Ohio Industries, Inc. (OH) (New) 1/23/85 which name changed to Park-Ohio Holdings Corp. 6/16/98

PARK EAST TOURS INC (NY)
Name changed to A.F.M. Holding, Inc. 07/28/1971
Each share Common 1¢ par exchanged for (1) share Common 1¢ par
(See A.F.M. Holding, Inc.)

PARK ELEKTRIK URETIM MADENCILIK SANAYI VE TICARET AS (TURKEY)
Basis changed from (1:150) to (1:0.15) 11/12/2009
Stock Dividends - 142% payable 07/07/2008 to holders of record 06/30/2008; 8% payable 07/07/2008 to holders of record 06/30/2008
GDR agreement terminated 05/19/2017
Each 144A Sponsored GDR for Class B exchanged for $0.086695 cash
Each Reg. S Sponsored GDR for Class B exchanged for $0.086695 cash
Note: Unexchanged GDR's will be sold and

PARK ESTATES, LTD.
Liquidated in 1952

PARK FD INC (DE)
Completely liquidated 12/31/1974
Each share Common $1 par exchanged for first and final distribution of $5.80 cash

PARK GALENA MINING CO.
Merged into New Park Mining Co. in 1932
New Park Mining Co. name changed to Newpark Resources, Inc. 6/9/72

PARK GROUP LTD (CO)
Each (262.154216) shares old Common $0.0001 par exchanged for (1) share new Common $0.0001 par 01/29/1999
Reincorporated under the laws of Delaware as Sonus Communication Holdings, Inc. 04/16/1999
(See Sonus Communication Holdings, Inc.)

PARK HILL GARDENS CORP.
Dissolved in 1949

PARK INVT CO (IA)
Proclaimed dissolved 11/30/88

PARK LAND CO., INC. (NJ)
Charter revoked for failure to file reports and pay fees 1/23/56

PARK LANE HOTEL, INC. (IL)
Liquidation completed 2/24/59

PARK LANE-MOUNT VERNON CORP.
Property sold in 1940
Apparently no stockholders' equity

PARK LAWN CEMETERY (ON)
Recapitalized as Park Lawn Co. Ltd. 09/24/2001
Each share Common no par exchanged for (0.1) share Common no par

PARK LAWN INCOME TR (ON)
Reorganized as Park Lawn Corp. 01/04/2011
Each Unit no par exchanged for (1) share Common no par

PARK LEXINGTON CORP.
Succeeded by Park-Lexington Co., Inc. in 1937
No stockholders' equity

PARK LEXINGTON INC (NY)
Each share Common $1 par exchanged for (0.1) share Common $10 par in 1942
Merged into Algoma Corp. 11/14/97
Each share Common $10 par exchanged for $498.55 cash

PARK MEDITECH INC (ON)
SEC revoked common stock registration 11/12/2009

PARK MERIDIAN BK (CHARLOTTE, NC)
Common $4 par split (5) for (4) by issuance of (0.25) additional share payable 8/10/96 to holders of record 7/22/96
Common $4 par split (5) for (4) by issuance of (0.25) additional share payable 11/15/97 to holders of record 10/15/97
Common $4 par split (5) for (4) by issuance of (0.25) additional share payable 9/15/98 to holders of record 9/1/98
Under plan of reorganization each share Common $4 par automatically became (1) share Park Meridian Financial Corp. Common 1¢ par 8/3/2000
Park Meridian Financial Corp. merged into Regions Financial Corp. (Old) 11/14/2001 which merged into Regions Financial Corp. (New) 7/1/2004

PARK MERIDIAN FINL CORP (NC)
Merged into Regions Financial Corp. (Old) 11/14/2001
Each share Common 1¢ par exchanged for (0.5688) share Common $0.625 par
Regions Financial Corp. (Old) merged into Regions Financial Corp. (New) 7/1/2004

PARK-N-SHOP, INC. (FL)
Under plan of dissolution each share Capital Stock $100 par exchanged for first and final distribution of $109.77 cash 9/15/81

PARK N VIEW INC (DE)
Name changed to PNV Inc. 06/04/1999
(See PNV Inc.)

PARK NATL BK (CHICAGO, IL)
Bank closed and FDIC appointed receiver 10/30/2009
Stockholders' equity unlikely

PARK NATL BK (HOLYOKE, MA)
Merged into Park West Bank & Trust Co. (West Springfield, MA) 07/16/1976
Each share Common $50 par exchanged for (14) shares Common $5 par
Park West Bank & Trust Co. (West Springfield, MA) reorganized as Westbank Corp. 07/01/1984 which merged into NewAlliance Bancshares, Inc. 01/02/2007 which merged into First Niagara Financial Group, Inc. (New) 04/15/2011 which merged into KeyCorp (New) 08/01/2016

PARK NATL BK (HOUSTON, TX)
Acquired by Cullen/Frost Bankers Inc. 2/15/96
Each share Common $5 par exchanged for $117.9225833 cash

PARK NATL BK (KNOXVILLE, TN)
Each share Capital Stock $100 par exchanged for (10) shares Capital Stock $10 par in 1940
Stock Dividends - 100% 1/22/57; 33-1/3% 2/28/75
Merged into First American Corp. (TN) 11/7/83
Each share Capital Stock $10 par exchanged for (6.25) shares Common $5 par
First American Corp. (TN) merged into AmSouth Bancorporation 10/1/99 which merged into Regions Financial Corp. 11/4/2006

PARK NATL BK (NEWARK, OH)
Common $25 par changed to $10 par and (1.5) additional shares issued plus a 100% stock dividend paid 12/10/1968
Common $10 par changed to $8 par and (0.25) additional share issued 05/20/1986
Stock Dividends - 100% 01/23/1962; 50% 02/15/1973; 33-1/3% 03/10/1975; 25% 03/11/1977; 15% 03/31/1979; 10% 02/20/1981; 58.10276% 05/20/1983
Reorganized as Park National Corp. 03/01/1987
Each share Common $8 par exchanged for (1) share Common $8 par

PARK NELSON, INC. (UT)
Each share Capital Stock 50¢ par exchanged for (0.1) share Capital Stock no par 3/30/61
Merged into General Contracting Corp. on a (1) for (3) basis 3/30/61
General Contracting Corp. name changed to General International, Inc. 8/4/69
(See General International, Inc.)

PARK NELSON MINING CO. (UT)
Name changed to Park Nelson, Inc. 11/20/58
Park Nelson, Inc. merged into General Contracting Corp. 3/30/61 which name changed to General International, Inc. 8/4/69
(See General International, Inc.)

PARK OHIO INDS INC (DE)
Common $1 par split (2) for (1) by issuance of (1) additional share 4/3/81
Reorganized under the laws of Ohio as Park-Ohio Industries, Inc. (New) 1/23/85
Each share $0.75 Conv. Preferred $1 par exchanged for (1) share $0.75 Conv. Preferred $1 par
Each share Common $1 par exchanged for (1) share Common $1 par
Park-Ohio Industries, Inc. (New) name changed to Park-Ohio Holdings Corp. 6/16/98

PARK OHIO INDS INC NEW (OH)
$0.75 Conv. Preferred $1 par called for redemption 3/16/94
Name changed to Park-Ohio Holdings Corp. 6/16/98

PARK OHIO INDS INC OLD (OH)
Merged into Growth International, Inc. 11/30/71
Each share Common no par exchanged for (2) shares $0.75 Conv. Preferred $1 par and (1) share Common $1 par
Growth International, Inc. name changed to Park-Ohio Industries, Inc. (DE) 6/1/72 which reorganized as Park-Ohio Industries, Inc. (OH) (New) 1/23/85 which name changed to Park-Ohio Holdings Corp. 6/16/98

PARK PHARMACY CORP (CO)
Plan of reorganization under Chapter 11 Federal Bankruptcy Code effective 3/24/2004
No stockholders' equity

PARK PL ENERGY CORP (NV)
Old Common $0.00001 par split (8) for (1) by issuance of (7) additional shares payable 07/09/2007 to holders of record 07/06/2007
Ex date - 07/10/2007
Old Common $0.00001 par split (3) for (2) by issuance of (0.5) additional share payable 07/25/2007 to holders of record 07/23/2007
Ex date - 07/25/2007
Old Common $0.00001 par split (10) for (1) by issuance of (9) additional shares payable 09/02/2009 to holders of record 08/31/2009
Ex date - 09/03/2009
Each share old Common $0.00001 par exchanged for (0.00333333) share new Common $0.00001 par 03/26/2010
Reincorporated under the laws of Delaware as Park Place Energy Inc. 12/22/2015

PARK PL ENTMT CORP (DE)
Name changed to Caesars Entertainment, Inc. 01/05/2004
(See Caesars Entertainment, Inc.)

PARK RIDGE ASSOC INC (IL)
Completely liquidated 06/30/1968
Each share Common $1 par exchanged for first and final distribution of (0.547645) share All American Life & Financial Corp. Common $1 par

(See All American Life & Financial Corp.)

PARK ROYALE LIQUIDATION TRUST
Trust terminated in 1949
Details not available

PARK SHERATON CORP. (NY)
Merged into Sheraton Corp. of America on a (5) for (1) basis 3/1/60
Sheraton Corp. of America acquired by International Telephone & Telegraph Corp. (DE) 2/29/68 which name changed to ITT Corp. 12/31/83 which reorganized in Indiana as ITT Industries, Inc. 12/19/95 which name changed to ITT Corp. 7/1/2006

PARK STERLING BK (CHARLOTTE, NC)
Reorganized as Park Sterling Corp. 01/01/2011
Each share Common $4.65 par exchanged for (1) share Common $1 par
Park Sterling Corp. merged into South State Corp. 11/30/2017

PARK STERLING CORP (NC)
Merged into South State Corp. 11/30/2017
Each share Common $1 par exchanged for (0.14) share Common $$2.50 par

PARK TEKSTIL SANAYI VE TICARET A S (TURKEY)
Sponsored Reg. S GDR's for Class B split (2) for (1) by issuance of (1) additional GDR payable 06/06/2000 to holders of record 04/26/2000
Stock Dividend - 100% payable 12/07/1998 to holders of record 11/27/1998
Name changed to Park Elektrik Madencilik Anonim Sirketi 07/24/2000

PARK UTAH CONSOLIDATED MINES CO. (UT & DE)
Merged into United Park City Mines Co. 00/00/1953
Each share Capital Stock $1 par exchanged for (1.1) shares Capital Stock $1 par
(See United Park City Mines Co.)

PARK WEST BK & TR CO (WEST SPRINGFIELD, MA)
Stock Dividend - 10% 05/20/1983
Reorganized as Westbank Corp. 07/01/1984
Each share Common $5 par exchanged for (1) share Common $5 par
Westbank Corp. merged into NewAlliance Bancshares, Inc. 01/02/2007 which merged into First Niagara Financial Group, Inc. (New) 04/15/2011 which merged into KeyCorp (New) 08/01/2016

PARK WEST DEVELOPERS INC (FL)
Administratively dissolved 09/22/2000

PARKBRIDGE LIFESTYLE CMNTYS INC (AB)
Each Non-Vtg. Share no par exchanged for (1) share Common no par 02/26/2008
Merged into 1561609 Alberta Ltd. 01/11/2011
Each share Common no par exchanged for $7.30 cash

PARKCREST EXPLS LTD (BC)
Reincorporated under the laws of Yukon as Fossil Bay Resources Ltd. 6/13/2000
(See Fossil Bay Resources Ltd.)

PARKE BK (SEWELL, NJ)
Stock Dividends - 10% payable 12/12/2003 to holders of record 12/2/2003 Ex date - 11/28/2003; 20% payable 12/28/2004 to holders of record 12/14/2004 Ex date - 12/10/2004
Under plan of reorganization each share Common $5 par automatically became (1) share Parke Bancorp, Inc. Common 10¢ par 6/1/2005

PARKE DAVIS & CO (MI)
Each share Common $25 par exchanged for (5) shares Common no par in 1927
Common no par split (3) for (1) by issuance of (2) additional shares 11/28/58
Merged into Warner-Lambert Co. 11/13/70
Each share Common no par exchanged for (0.4428) share Common $1 par
Warner-Lambert Co. merged into Pfizer Co. 6/19/2000

PARKER & PARSLEY DEV PARTNERS L P (TX)
Merged into Parker & Parsley Petroleum Co. 2/19/91
Each Unit of Ltd. Partnership exchanged for (2) shares Common 1¢ par
Parker & Parsley Petroleum Co. merged into Pioneer Natural Resources Co. 8/7/97

PARKER & PARSLEY PETE CO (DE)
Merged into Pioneer Natural Resources Co. 08/07/1997
Each share Common 1¢ par exchanged for (1) share Common 1¢ par

PARKER (A.J.) CO. (PA)
Name changed to Hart Laboratories, Inc. 3/18/64
Hart Laboratories, Inc. completely liquidated 4/22/68
(See Hart Laboratories, Inc.)

PARKER (S.C.) & CO., INC. (NY)
Ctfs. dated prior to 10/1/64
Name changed to Carlyle Share, Ltd. 10/1/64 which completed liquidation 10/27/67

PARKER APPLIANCE CO. (OH)
Stock Dividends - 20% 3/20/53; 20% 3/22/57
Name changed to Parker-Hannifin Corp. 10/1/57

PARKER AUTOMOTIVE CORP (DE)
Majority acquired by Remington Co., Inc. 02/27/1991
Public interest eliminated

PARKER DRILLING CO. (OK)
Reincorporated under the laws of Delaware 3/26/76

PARKER DRILLING CO. OF CANADA LTD. (AB)
Merged into Nabors Drilling Ltd. 9/1/66
Each share Common no par exchanged for (1) share Common no par
(See Nabors Drilling Ltd.)

PARKER ENERGY TECHNOLOGY INC (UT)
Recapitalized as Source Energy Corp. 06/06/1997
Each share old Common $0.00025 par exchanged for (0.02) share Common $0.00025 par
Source Energy Corp. name changed to Innuity, Inc. (UT) 12/20/2005 which reincorporated in Washington 11/21/2008
(See Innuity, Inc.)

PARKER FINANCE CORP. (MD)
Name changed to Dale Factors Corp. 9/30/66

PARKER LEVITT CORP (DE)
Name changed to Commercial Property Corp. 06/23/1977
Commercial Property Corp. name changed to Shandong Ruitai Chemical Co., Ltd. 11/15/2006 which name changed to China Ruitai International Holdings Co., Ltd. 04/09/2007
(See China Ruitai International Holdings Co., Ltd.)

PARKER MILLS
Acquired by Berkshire Fine Spinning Associates, Inc. 00/00/1930
Details not available

PARKER OIL INC (CO)
Acquired by EMC Energies, Inc. (WY) 01/30/1974
Each share Capital Stock 1¢ par exchanged for (0.571428) share Common 5¢ par
EMC Energies, Inc. (WY) reorganized in Nevada as Metwood Inc. 01/28/2000

PARKER PEN CO (DE)
Reincorporated 12/27/1971
Each share Common $10 par exchanged for (2) shares Common $5 par 00/00/1946
Each share Common $5 par exchanged for (1.25) shares Class A Common $2 par and (1.25) shares Class B Common $2 par 00/00/1951
Class A Common $2 par and Class B Common $2 par reclassified as Common $1.50 par and (1/3) additional share issued 07/13/1964
Common $1.50 par split (3) for (2) by issuance of (0.5) additional share 02/09/1971
State of incorporation changed from (WI) to (DE) 12/27/1971
Common $1.50 par split (3) for (2) by issuance of (0.5) additional share 04/19/1972
Common $1.50 par split (5) for (4) by issuance of (0.25) additional share 08/15/1977
Common $1.50 par split (2) for (1) by issuance of (1) additional share 07/31/1979
Name changed to Manpower Inc. 01/31/1986
(See Manpower Inc.)

PARKER PETROLEUM CO., INC. (DE)
Acquired by Western Oil Fields Inc. (CO) 11/14/1962
Each share 6% Preferred $10 par exchanged for (6) shares Common $1.25 par
Each share Common 10¢ par exchanged for (1) share Common $1.25 par
Western Oil Fields Inc. (CO) reorganized in Nevada as Summit Energy, Inc. 08/01/1970 which name changed to Caspen Oil, Inc. 09/13/1988
(See Caspen Oil, Inc.)

PARKER RES INC (CA)
Name changed to Pacific Bancorporation 1/24/72
Pacific Bancorporation merged into ValliCorp Holdings, Inc. 11/5/93 which merged into Westamerica Bancorporation 4/12/97

PARKER RICH GROUP LTD (NY)
Recapitalized as Project 80's Holding Corp. 03/25/1983
Each share Common 1¢ par exchanged for (0.5) share Common 2¢ par
Project 80's Holding Corp. recapitalized as Titan Resources Inc. 06/27/1994 which recapitalized as Palm Works Inc. 09/28/1999 which name changed to Zydant Corp. 10/17/2000
(See Zydant Corp.)

PARKER RUST-PROOF CO. (MI)
Each share Common no par exchanged for (1) share Common $2.50 par plus a dividend of (2) additional shares in 1936
Stock Dividend - 100% 2/1/56
Merged into Hooker Chemical Corp. 3/30/62
Each share Common $2.50 par exchanged for (0.05) share $5 2nd Preferred Ser. C no par and (0.75) share Common $5 par
Hooker Chemical Corp. acquired by Occidental Petroleum Corp. (Calif.) 7/24/68
(See Occidental Petroleum Corp. (Calif.))

PARKER-WOLVERINE CO.
Merged into Udylite Corp. in 1946
Each share Common no par exchanged for (2.5) shares Common $1 par
Udylite Corp. merged into Hooker Chemical Corp. 1/2/68 which was acquired by Occidental Petroleum Corp. (CA) 7/24/68
(See Occidental Petroleum Corp. (CA))

PARKER WYLIE CARPET MANUFACTURING CO.
Name changed to General Carpet Corp. in 1936
(See General Carpet Corp.)

PARKER YOUNG CO.
Liquidated in 1947
Details not available

PARKERSBURG-AETNA CORP. (WV)
Name changed to Paco, Inc. (WV) 09/27/1963
(See Paco, Inc.)

PARKERSBURG NATL BK (PARKERSBURG, WV)
Common $20 par changed to $5 par and (3) additional shares issued 3/4/70
Common $5 par split (4) for (1) by issuance of (3) additional shares 4/8/74
Common $5 par changed to $2.50 par and (1) additional share issued 4/30/80
Under plan of reorganization each share Common $2.50 par automatically became (1) share United Bankshares, Inc. Common $2.50 par 5/1/84

PARKERSBURG RIG & REEL CO. (WV)
$4.25 Preferred no par reclassified as $5 Preferred no par 00/00/1952
Stock Dividend - 10% 11/15/1951
Merged into Parkersburg-Aetna Corp. 01/29/1954
Each share $5 Preferred no par exchanged for (1) share $5 Preferred no par
Each share Common $1 par exchanged for (2) shares Common $1 par
Parkersburg-Aetna Corp. name changed to Paco, Inc. (WV) 09/27/1963
(See Paco, Inc.)

PARKHILL GOLD MINES, LTD.
Reorganized as Parkhill Gold Mines (1937) Ltd. 00/00/1937
Details not available

PARKHILL GOLD MINES (1937) LTD.
Acquired by Ward Lake Gold Mines Ltd. in 1938
(See Ward Lake Gold Mines Ltd.)

PARKING STATIONS OF NEW YORK, INC.
Foreclosed 00/00/1931
No stockholders' equity

PARKLAND ENERGY SVCS INC (AB)
Received Notice of Intention to Enforce Security 12/03/2012
Stockholders' equity unlikely

PARKLAND INCOME FD (AB)
Trust Units split (3) for (1) by issuance of (2) additional Units payable 06/01/2007 to holders of record 05/25/2007 Ex date - 05/23/2007
Each Trust Unit received distribution of (0.02617) Trust Unit and $0.35 cash payable 01/15/2008 to holders of record 12/31/2007

FINANCIAL INFORMATION, INC.   PAR-PAR

Reorganized as Parkland Fuel Corp. 01/07/2011
Each Trust Unit exchanged for (1) share Common no par
Note: Unexchanged certificates were cancelled and became without value 01/07/2016

PARKLAND INDS LTD (AB)
Name changed 11/17/1977
Name changed from Parkland Beef Industries Ltd. to Parkland Industries Ltd. 11/17/1977
Common no par split (2) for (1) by issuance of (1) additional share 12/30/1985
Reorganized as Parkland Income Fund 06/28/2002
Each share Common no par exchanged for (2) Trust Units and $1 cash
Parkland Income Fund reorganized as Parkland Fuel Corp. 01/07/2011

PARKLANE EXPLS LTD (BC)
Name changed to Parklane Technologies Inc. (BC) 08/28/1986
Parklane Technologies Inc. (BC) reincorporated in Alberta 03/09/1988 which name changed to Parklane Mines & Minerals Inc. 06/26/1989 which recapitalized as Consolidated Parklane Resources Inc. (AB) 05/01/1990 which reincorporated in British Columbia 04/15/1991 which recapitalized as Micrologix Biotech Inc. 01/07/1993 which name changed to Migenix Inc. 09/20/2004 which reorganized as BioWest Therapeutics Inc. 03/19/2010 which name changed to Carrus Capital Corp. 08/22/2011 which name changed to Global Blockchain Technologies Corp. 10/05/2017

PARKLANE HOSIERY INC (NY)
Merged into New PLHC Corp. 10/15/74
Each share Common 50¢ par exchanged for $2 cash

PARKLANE INDUSTRIES, INC. (UT)
Proclaimed dissolved for failure to pay taxes 11/9/74

PARKLANE MINES & MINERALS INC (AB)
Recapitalized as Consolidated Parklane Resources Inc. (AB) 05/01/1990
Each share Common no par exchanged for (1/3) share Common no par
Consolidated Parklane Resources Inc. (AB) reincorporated in British Columbia 04/15/1991 which recapitalized as Micrologix Biotech Inc. 01/07/1993 which name changed to Migenix Inc. 09/20/2004 which reorganized as BioWest Therapeutics Inc. 03/19/2010 which name changed to Carrus Capital Corp. 08/22/2011 which name changed to Global Blockchain Technologies Corp. 10/05/2017

PARKLANE TECHNOLOGIES INC (AB)
Reincorporated 03/09/1988
Place of incorporation changed from (BC) to (AB) 03/09/1988
Name changed to Parklane Mines & Minerals Inc. 06/26/1989
Parklane Mines & Minerals Inc. recapitalized as Consolidated Parklane Resources Inc. (AB) 05/01/1990 which reincorporated in British Columbia 04/15/1991 which recapitalized as Micrologix Biotech Inc. 01/07/1993 which name changed to Migenix Inc. 09/20/2004 which reorganized as BioWest Therapeutics Inc. 03/19/2010 which name changed to Carrus Capital Corp. 08/22/2011 which name changed to Global Blockchain Technologies Corp. 10/05/2017

PARKS AIR COLLEGE, INC. (MO)
Dissolved in 1946

PARKS AIRCRAFT SALES & SERVICE CO., INC. (MO)
Liquidation completed 5/28/59

PARKS AMER INC (WA)
Reincorporated under the laws of Nevada as Grand Slam Treasures Inc. 06/20/2000
Grand Slam Treasures Inc. recapitalized as Asconi Corp. 04/16/2001
(See Asconi Corp.)

PARKS BROOK MINES LTD. (NB)
Charter revoked for failure to file reports and pay fees 12/7/66

PARKS H G INC (MD)
Merged into Norin Food Products, Inc. 10/14/1977
Each share Common 10¢ par exchanged for $10 cash

PARKSIDE INDS INC (UT)
Reorganized under the laws of Nevada as Labco Pharmaceuticals Corp. 4/23/96
Each share Common no par exchanged for (0.001) share Common $0.001 par
Labco Pharmaceuticals Corp. (NV) recapitalized as Checkpoint Genetics Pharmaceuticals Inc. 8/15/2000 which recapitalized as InterNatural Pharmaceuticals Inc. 7/13/2001

PARKSIDE PETE INC (BC)
Name changed to Bethlehem Resources Corp. 1/21/88
Bethlehem Resources Corp. merged into Imperial Metals Corp. (Old) 4/3/95 which reorganized as Imperial Metals Corp. (New) 4/30/2002

PARKSIDE REALTY CO.
Liquidated in 1944

PARKSIDE 2000 RES CORP (BC)
Name changed to Amador Gold Corp. 5/16/2003

PARKSIDE VENTURES INC (BC)
Recapitalized as International Parkside Products Inc. 2/3/95
Each share Common no par exchanged for (1/3) share Common no par

PARKVALE FINL CORP (PA)
Common $1 par split (5) for (4) by issuance of (0.25) additional share 10/28/1993
Common $1 par split (5) for (4) by issuance of (0.25) additional share 10/18/1994
Common $1 par split (5) for (4) by issuance of (0.25) additional share payable 10/14/1996 to holders of record 09/30/1996
Common $1 par split (5) for (4) by issuance of (0.25) additional share payable 10/14/1997 to holders of record 09/30/1997
Common $1 par split (5) for (4) by issuance of (0.25) additional share payable 10/14/1998 to holders of record 09/30/1998
Merged into F.N.B. Corp. 01/01/2012
Each share Common $1 par exchanged for (2.178) shares Common 1¢ par

PARKVALE SVGS ASSN (PA)
Under plan of reorganization each share Common $1 par automatically became (1) share Parkvale Financial Corp. Common $1 par 01/05/1989
Parkvale Financial Corp. merged into F.N.B. Corp. 01/01/2012

PARKVIEW CAPITAL CORP. (DE)
Charter cancelled and declared inoperative and void for non-payment of taxes 3/1/91

PARKVIEW DRUGS, INC. (DE)
35¢ Part. Preference $4.50 par called for redemption 08/01/1962
Name changed to Parkview-Gem, Inc. 05/31/1966
(See Parkview-Gem, Inc.)

PARKVIEW FED SVGS BK (CLEVELAND, OH)
Stock Dividend - 10% 02/18/1994
Reorganized as PVF Capital Corp. 10/31/1994
Each share Common no par exchanged for (1.5) shares Common 1¢ par
PVF Capital Corp. merged into F.N.B. Corp. 10/12/2013

PARKVIEW GEM INC (DE)
Declared worthless by Court Order 08/30/1979
No stockholders' equity

PARKVIEW GROUP INC (DE)
Each share old Common $0.001 par exchanged for (0.33333333) share new Common $0.001 par 06/01/2010
Name changed to Anhui Taiyang Poultry Co., Inc. 01/20/2011
(See Anhui Taiyang Poultry Co., Inc.)

PARKWAY BANCORP INC (DE)
Reincorporated 6/29/97
State of incorporation changed from (IL) to (DE) 6/29/97
Each share old Common 10¢ par exchanged for (0.01) share new Common 10¢ par 8/17/2000
Note: In effect holders received $650 cash per share and public interest was eliminated

PARKWAY BK (LENOIR, NC)
Stock Dividends - 10% payable 05/31/2005 to holders of record 05/15/2005 Ex date - 05/11/2005; 10% payable 08/14/2006 to holders of record 07/31/2006 Ex date - 07/27/2006
Bank closed and FDIC appointed receiver 04/26/2013
Stockholders' equity unlikely

PARKWAY BUILDING CORP. (IL)
Merged into 405 Fullerton Parkway Building Corp. and each share Capital Stock $5 par exchanged for (1.2) shares Capital Stock $5 par and $8.51 in cash 12/31/56
405 Fullerton Parkway Building Corp. completed liquidation 12/30/57

PARKWAY CAP CORP (CO)
Each share old Common no par exchanged for (0.02) share new Common no par 04/18/1994
Reincorporated under the laws of Delaware as QCS Corp. and Common no par changed to $0.001 par 05/06/1994
QCS Corp. name changed to SourcingLink.net, Inc. 07/20/1999

PARKWAY CASH FD INC (MD)
Charter foreited for failure to file annual report 10/08/1993

PARKWAY CO (TX)
Under plan of reorganization each Share of Bene. Int. $1 par exchanged for (1) share Common $1 par 01/07/1981
Common $1 par split (3) for (2) by issuance of (0.5) additional share payable 04/30/1996 to holders of record 04/15/1996
Reincorporated under the laws of Maryland as Parkway Properties, Inc. 08/02/1996
Parkway Properties, Inc. merged into Cousins Properties Inc. 10/06/2016

PARKWAY DISTRS INC (MA)
Common 50¢ par split (3) for (2) by issuance of (0.5) additional share 10/01/1969
Name changed to Levitt Industries, Inc. 08/21/1975
(See Levitt Industries, Inc.)

PARKWAY INC (MD)
Acquired by Canada Pension Plan Investment Board 10/12/2017
Each share Common $0.001 par exchanged for $19.05 cash

PARKWAY MINES LTD (ON)
Charter cancelled for failure to pay taxes and file returns 03/06/1979

PARKWAY PPTYS INC (MD)
8.75% Preferred Ser. A $0.001 par called for redemption at $25 plus $0.546875 accrued dividends on 06/30/2003
8% Preferred Ser. D $0.001 par called for redemption at $25 plus $0.13333 accrued dividends on 04/25/2013
Merged into Cousins Properties Inc. 10/06/2016
Each share Common $0.001 par exchanged for (1.63) shares Common $1 par

PARKWAY SILVER MINES LTD. (ON)
Name changed to Parkway Mines Ltd. in 1953
Parkway Mines Ltd. charter cancelled 3/6/79

PARKWAY TAX FREE RESV FD INC (MD)
Charter forfeited for failure to file annual report 10/8/93

PARKWOOD CORP (IN)
Name changed 06/04/1979
Name changed from Parkwood Homes, Inc. to Parkwood Corp. 06/04/1979
Merged into Vyquest Inc. 06/06/1983
Each share Common no par exchanged for $3.25 cash

PARLAKE RES LTD (ON)
Name changed to Concord Capital Corp. 07/23/1991
(See Concord Capital Corp.)

PARLANE RESOURCE CORP (BC)
Each share old Common no par exchanged for (0.2) share new Common no par 05/20/2015
Name changed to iMining Blockchain & Cryptocurrency Inc. 04/20/2018

PARLAR RES LTD (BC)
Name changed to Kwik Products International Corp. 10/16/1985
Kwik Products International Corp. recapitalized as Trend Vision Technologies, Inc. 05/20/1992
(See Trend Vision Technologies, Inc.)

PARLAY ENTMT INC (ON)
Recapitalized as Oramericas Corp. (ON) 12/10/2012
Each share Common no par exchanged for (0.5) share Common no par
Oramericas Corp. (ON) reincorporated in British Columbia 02/21/2014 which name changed to Backstageplay Inc. 02/09/2016

PARLAY INVESTMENT CORP. (UT)
Name changed to Parlay Racing Syndication 9/25/78
Parlay Racing Syndication name changed to Space Age Technology Inc. 2/22/80 which name changed to East Coast Water Refining Co., Inc. 2/12/87

PARLAY RACING SYNDICATION (UT)
Name changed to Space Age Technology Inc. 2/22/80
Space Age Technology Inc. name changed to East Coast Water Refining Co., Inc. 2/12/87

PARLE INTL INC (CO)
Name changed to Independent Entertainment Group, Inc. (CO) 3/31/89
Independent Entertainment Group, Inc. (CO) name changed to Independent TeleMedia Group Inc. (CO) 7/7/93 which reorganized under the laws of Delaware as

IndeNet, Inc. 6/28/95 which
recapitalized as Enterprise Software,
Inc. 7/15/98
(See Enterprise Software, Inc.)

PARLEX CORP (MA)
Common 10¢ par split (3) for (2) by
issuance of (0.5) additional share
payable 04/21/1997 to holders of
record 03/18/1997
Merged into Johnson Electric
Holdings Ltd. 11/10/2005
Each share Common 10¢ par
exchanged for $6.75 cash

PARLIAMENT HILL CORP (DE)
Charter cancelled and declared
inoperative and void for
non-payment of taxes 3/1/92

PARLUX FRAGRANCES INC (DE)
Common 1¢ par split (2) for (1) by
issuance of (1) additional share
11/10/1995
Common 1¢ par split (2) for (1) by
issuance of (1) additional share
payable 06/16/2006 to holders of
record 05/31/2006 Ex date -
06/19/2006
Merged into Perfumania Holdings,
Inc. 04/18/2012
Each share Common 1¢ par
exchanged for (0.2) share Common
1¢ par and $4 cash
(See Perfumania Holdings, Inc.)

PARMAC MINES LTD (BC)
Struck off register and declared
dissolved for failure to file returns
11/6/87

PARMALAT FINANZIARIA S P A (ITALY)
ADR agreement terminated
02/05/2010
ADR holders' equity unlikely

PARMASTERS GOLF TRAINING CTR (NV)
Name changed to Carolyn River
Projects, Ltd. 08/24/2007

PARMAX INC (UT)
Recapitalized as Nise Inc. 09/14/1993
Each share Common $0.001 par
exchanged for (0.1) share Common
$0.001 par
(See Nise Inc.)

PARMELEE TRANSN CO (DE)
Merged into Checker Motors Corp.
05/01/1969
Each share Common no par
exchanged for (2.25) shares $1.60
Conv. Preferred $40 par
(See Checker Motors Corp.)

PARMLEE MANITOBA MINING CO. LTD. (ON)
Name changed to Parmlee Mining
Co. Ltd. in 1958
Parmlee Mining Co. Ltd. merged into
Consolidated Panther Mines Ltd.
7/12/60 which recapitalized as
Panthco Resources Inc. 7/3/87
which merged into Ztest Electronics,
Inc. 7/1/96

PARMLEE MINING CO. LTD. (ON)
Merged into Consolidated Panther
Mines Ltd. on a (0.05) for (1) basis
7/12/60
Consolidated Panther Mines Ltd.
recapitalized as Panthco Resources
Inc. 7/3/87 which merged into Ztest
Electronics, Inc. 7/1/96

PAROLE MINING & MERCANTILE CO. (MO)
Liquidation completed
Each share Capital Stock $10 par
exchanged for initial distribution of
$13.45 cash 3/1/73
Each share Capital Stock $10 par
received second and final
distribution of $0.92 cash 3/17/78

PARQUE LA QUINTA ESTATES (NV)
Common $0.001 par split (3.5) for (1)
by issuance of (2.5) additional
shares payable 07/26/2006 to
holders of record 07/24/2006
Ex date - 07/27/2006
Name changed to Wealthcraft
Systems Inc. 10/19/2006
Wealthcraft Systems Inc. name
changed to Wealthcraft Capital, Inc.
02/01/2017

PARQUET RES INC (ON)
Name changed 07/14/1980
Name changed from Parquet Mines
Ltd. to Parquet Resources Inc.
07/14/1980
Preference $0.001 par called for
redemption 00/00/1991
Recapitalized as Plexmar Resources
Inc. (ON) 07/09/1993
Each share Common no par
exchanged for (0.125) share
Common no par
Plexmar Resources Inc. (ON)
reincorporated in Canada
08/25/1994
(See Plexmar Resources Inc.)

PARR MINES LTD (ON)
Charter cancelled for failure to file
reports and pay fees 11/08/1977

PARRAN CAP INC (BC)
Recapitalized as Asia Bio-Chem
Group Corp. 06/26/2008
Each share Common no par
exchanged for (0.13333333) share
Common no par
(See Asia Bio-Chem Group Corp.)

PARRENT OIL & GAS INC (CO)
Recapitalized as Qadrant Corp.
06/03/1983
Each share Common 1¢ par
exchanged for (0.1) share Common
10¢ par
(See Qadrant Corp.)

PARRY OIL CO. (DE)
Charter cancelled and declared
inoperative and void for
non-payment of taxes 4/1/31

PARS RES LTD (BC)
Recapitalized as WDF Capital Corp.
05/28/1992
Each share Common no par
exchanged for (0.5) share Common
no par
WDF Capital Corp. name changed to
Soligen Technologies, Inc. (BC)
03/29/1993 which reincorporated in
Wyoming 04/13/1993
(See Soligen Technologies, Inc.)

PARSONS & CO INC (OH)
Each share Common $2 par
exchanged for (0.02) share Common
no par 04/26/1973
Voluntarily dissolved 10/04/2002
Details not available

PARSONS CORP (DE)
(Issued in Units consisting of (1)
share Parsons Corp. Common $1
par and (1) share RMP International
Ltd. Common no par)
Units split (3) for (2) by issuance of
(0.5) additional Unit 08/21/1979
Units split (3) for (2) by issuance of
(0.5) additional Unit 09/22/1980
Units split (3) for (2) by issuance of
(0.5) additional Unit 05/06/1982
Units split (4) for (3) by issuance of
(1/3) additional Unit 08/22/1983
Units separated and company
acquired 01/14/1985
Each share Parsons Corp. Common
$1 par exchanged for $30.40 cash
(See RMP International, Ltd.)

PARSONS PAPER CO. (MA)
Common $100 par changed to $50
par in 1940
Acquired by National Vulcanized Fibre
Co. on a (5) for (1) basis 3/9/59
National Vulcanized Fibre Co. name
changed to NVF Co. 4/26/65
(See NVF Co.)

PARSONS RALPH M CO (NV)
Common no par split (3) for (2) by
issuance of (0.5) additional share
7/23/76
Common no par split (3) for (2) by
issuance of (0.5) additional share
9/1/78
Under plan of reorganization each
share Common no par exchanged
for (1) Non-Separable Unit of (1)
share Parsons Corp. Common $1
par and (1) share RMP International,
Ltd. Common no par 9/19/78
(See each company's listing)

PARSONS TECHNOLOGY INC (CO)
Charter suspended for failure to file
annual reports 04/01/1992

PARTA DIALOGUE INC (CANADA)
Recapitalized as Engagement Labs
Inc. 01/03/2014
Each share Common no par
exchanged for (0.1) share Common
no par

PARTA GROWTH CAP I INC (CANADA)
Recapitalized as Parta Sustainable
Solutions Inc. 05/12/2009
Each share Common no par
exchanged for (0.33333333) share
Common no par
Parta Sustainable Solutions Inc.
name changed to Parta Dialogue
Inc. 03/10/2011 which recapitalized
as Engagement Labs Inc.
01/03/2014

PARTA SUSTAINABLE SOLUTIONS INC (CANADA)
Name changed to Parta Dialogue Inc.
03/10/2011
Parta Dialogue Inc. recapitalized as
Engagement Labs Inc. 01/03/2014

PARTANEN MALARTIC GOLD MINE LTD. (ON)
Recapitalized as Nello Mining Ltd.
00/00/1955
Each share Capital Stock $1 par
exchanged for (0.5) share Capital
Stock no par
Nello Mining Ltd. name changed to
Nello Resources Inc. (ON)
07/06/1982 which reincorporated in
Alberta as Highridge Exploration Ltd.
08/03/1984 which merged into
Talisman Energy Inc. 08/05/1999
(See Talisman Energy Inc.)

PARTECH HLDGS CORP (DE)
Each share Common 1¢ par
exchanged for (0.2) share Common
5¢ par 03/10/1992
Each share Common 5¢ par
exchanged for (1/3) share Common
15¢ par 07/22/1994
Name changed to Tropic
Communications, Inc. 08/08/1995
Tropic Communications, Inc.
recapitalized as Tropic Air Cargo
Inc. 10/06/1997
(See Tropic Air Cargo Inc.)

PARTHUS TECHNOLOGIES PLC (IRELAND)
Issue Information - 130,000,000
SPONSORED ADR'S offered at
$12.60 per ADR on 05/19/2000
Merged into ParthusCeva, Inc.
10/21/2002
Each Sponsored ADR for Ordinary
IRO.025p par exchanged for
(0.15141) share Common $0.001
par and $0.95894 cash
ParthusCeva, Inc. name changed to
CEVA, Inc. 12/08/2003

PARTHUSCEVA INC (DE)
Name changed to CEVA, Inc.
12/8/2003

PARTICIPATING INCOME PPTYS LTD PARTNERSHIP (DE)
Company terminated registration of
Units of Limited Partnership Ser.
1986 06/29/1999
Details not available
Company terminated registration of
Units of Limited Partnership III on
06/29/1999
Details not available
Company terminated registration of
Units of Limited Partnership II on
07/14/1999
Details not available

PARTICLE DRILLING TECHNOLOGIES INC (NV)
Plan of reorganization under Chapter
11 Federal Bankrutpcy proceedings
effective 09/09/2009
No stockholders' equity

PARTNERRE CAP TR I (DE)
7.9% Guaranteed Preferred Securities
called for redemption at $25 on
12/21/2006

PARTNERRE HLDGS LTD (BERMUDA)
Name changed to PartnerRe Ltd.
05/08/1995
(See PartnerRe Ltd.)

PARTNERRE LTD (BERMUDA)
8% Preferred Ser. A $1 par called for
redemption at $25 plus $0.05
accrued dividends on 06/09/2003
6.75% Preferred Ser. C $1 par called
for redemption at $25 on 03/18/2013
Acquired by EXOR N.V. 03/18/2016
Each share Common $1 par
exchanged for $137.50 cash
6.5% Preferred Ser. D $1 par called
for redemption at $25 plus
$0.275347 accrued dividends on
11/01/2016
7.25% Preferred Ser. E $1 par called
for redemption at $25 plus
$0.307118 accrued dividends on
11/01/2016
(Additional Information in Active)

PARTNERS FINL CORP (FL)
Company's sole asset placed in
receivership 10/23/2009
Stockholders' equity unlikely

PARTNERS FINL GROUP INC NEW (NV)
Charter revoked for failure to file
reports and pay fees 12/14/2004

PARTNERS FINL GROUP INC OLD (NV)
Name changed to California Food &
Vending, Inc. 3/30/92
California Food & Vending, Inc. name
changed to Partners Financial
Group, Inc. (New) 8/21/92
(See Partners Financial Group, Inc.)

PARTNERS HEALTH SYSTEMS INC. (NV)
Charter revoked for failure to file
reports and pay fees 10/1/2000

PARTNERS NATL CORP (NY)
Proclaimed dissolved 3/25/92

PARTNERS OIL & MINERALS LTD (BC)
Struck off register and declared
dissolved for failure to file returns
8/25/95

PARTNERS OIL CO (DE)
Each share Common 1¢ par
exchanged for (0.1) share Class A
Common 10¢ par 03/03/1987
Name changed to Cedyco Corp.
02/09/1996
(See Cedyco Corp.)

PARTNERS PFD YIELD INC (CA)
Merged into Public Storage, Inc. (CA)
12/23/96
Each share Class A exchanged for
(0.716) share Common 10¢ par and
$0.74 cash
Public Storage, Inc. (CA)
reincorporated in Maryland as Public
Storage 6/4/2007

PARTNERS PFD YIELD II INC (CA)
Merged into Public Storage, Inc. (CA)
12/23/96
Each share Class A exchanged for

(0.766) share Common 10¢ par and $0.90 cash
Public Storage, Inc. (CA) reincorporated in Maryland as Public Storage 6/4/2007

PARTNERS PFD YIELD III INC (CA)
Merged into Public Storage, Inc. (CA) 12/23/96
Each share Class A exchanged for (0.771) share Common 10¢ par and $0.91 cash
Public Storage, Inc. (CA) reincorporated in Maryland as Public Storage 6/4/2007

PARTNERS SVGS BK (TAMPA, FL)
Merged into Manufacturers Bancshares, Inc. 06/25/1999
Each share Common no par held by Florida residents exchanged for (0.45957) share Common no par and $0.45 cash
Each share Common no par held by non-Florida residents exchanged for $1.12 cash
Manufacturers Bancshares, Inc. merged into Colonial BancGroup, Inc. 10/25/2001
(See Colonial BancGroup, Inc.)

PARTNERS TR FINL GROUP INC (DE)
Merged into M&T Bank Corp. 11/30/2007
Each share Common 10¢ par exchanged for either (0.13680138) share Common 50¢ par and $0.457625 cash or $12.50 cash
Note: Option to receive stock and cash expired 11/30/2007

PARTNERS TR FINL GROUP INC (USA)
Merged into Partners Trust Financial Group, Inc. (DE) 07/14/2004
Each share Common 10¢ par exchanged for (1.9502) shares Common 10¢ par
Partners Trust Financial Group, Inc. (DE) merged into M&T Bank Corp. 11/30/2007

PARTNERS VALUE FD INC (ON)
Name changed to Partners Value Investments Inc. 05/25/2015
Partners Value Investments Inc. reorganized as Partners Value Investments L.P. 07/04/2016

PARTNERS VALUE INVTS INC (ON)
Under plan of reorganization each share Common no par exchanged for (0.2719) Non-Vtg. Preferred Ltd. Partnership Unit Ser. 1 and (1) Non-Vtg. Ltd. Partnership Unit of Partners Value Investments L.P. and (1) Exchangeable Share Purchase Warrant expiring 06/30/2026 on 07/04/2016
Note: US and non-Qualifying holders will not receive Warrants
Unexchanged certificates will be cancelled and become without value 07/04/2022
(Additional Information in Active)

PARTNERS VALUE SPLIT CORP (ON)
Class AA Preferred Ser. 4 called for redemption at $25 plus $0.192086 accrued dividends on 07/09/2014
Class AA Preferred Ser. 1 called for redemption at $25 plus $0.091541 accrued dividends on 03/28/2016
Class AA Preferred Ser. 5 called for redemption at $25 plus $0.030653 accrued dividends on 12/10/2017
(Additional Information in Active)

PARTRIDGE CANADIAN EXPLORATIONS LTD. (ON)
Recapitalized as Newrich Explorations Ltd. 10/20/61
Each share Capital Stock $1 par exchanged for (0.25) share Capital Stock $1 par
Newrich Explorations Ltd. merged into Belle Aire Resource Explorations Ltd. 8/29/78 which name changed to Sprint Resources Ltd. 9/23/82 which name changed to Meacon Bay Resources Inc. 3/9/87 which recapitalized as Advantex Marketing International Inc. 9/16/91

PARTRIDGE RIV MINES LTD (ON)
Charter cancelled and declared dissolved for failure to file returns and pay fees 03/00/1976

PARTRIDGE YELLOWKNIFE MINES LTD. (ON)
Name changed to Partridge Canadian Explorations Ltd. 4/7/53
Partridge Canadian Explorations Ltd. recapitalized as Newrich Explorations Ltd. 10/20/61 which merged into Belle Aire Resource Explorations Ltd. 8/29/78 which name changed to Sprint Resources Ltd. 9/23/82 which name changed to Meacon Bay Resources Inc. 3/9/87 which recapitalized as Advantex Marketing International Inc. 9/16/91

PARTS COM INC (NV)
Each share old Common $0.001 par exchanged for (0.1) share new Common $0.001 par 06/27/2001
SEC revoked common stock registration 10/20/2008

PARTS SOURCE INC (FL)
Merged into General Parts Inc. 2/16/99
Each share Common $0.001 par exchanged for $3 cash

PARTSBASE INC (DE)
Name changed 6/20/2001
Name changed from Partsbase.com, Inc. (TX) to Partsbase Inc. (DE) 6/20/2001
Merged into Hammond Acquisition Corp. 2/21/2003
Each share Common no par exchanged for $1.50 cash

PARTY CITY CORP (DE)
Common 1¢ par split (3) for (2) by issuance of (0.5) additional share payable 1/16/98 to holders of record 1/2/98
Merged into Amscan Holdings, Inc. 12/23/2005
Each share Common 1¢ par exchanged for $17.50 cash

PARVIN DOHRMANN CO (DE)
$2.50 Conv. Preferred called for redemption 07/30/1969
Name changed to Recrion Corp. 12/14/1970
(See Recrion Corp.)

PARVUS MINES LTD (ON)
Name changed to Kyrgoil Corp. (ON) 09/05/1995
Kyrgoil Corp. (ON) reincorporated in British Virgin Islands as Kyrgoil Holding Corp. 01/04/2001 which recapitalized as Serica Energy Corp. (British Virgin Islands) 01/30/2004 which which reincorporated in United Kingdom as Serica Energy PLC 09/07/2005
(See Serica Energy PLC)

PASADENA ENERGY CORP (BC)
Name changed to Pasadena Technology Corp. 7/5/85
Pasadena Technology Corp. name changed to EMS Systems Ltd. 8/11/86
(See EMS Systems Ltd.)

PASADENA TECHNOLOGY CORP (BC)
Name changed to EMS Systems Ltd. 8/11/86
(See EMS Systems Ltd.)

PASADENA UNION LABOR TEMPLE ASSOCIATION (CA)
Voluntarily dissolved 11/20/1997
Details not available

PASCACK BANCORP INC (NJ)
Stock Dividend - 5% payable 03/25/2011 to holders of record 03/18/2011 Ex date - 03/16/2011
Merged into Lakeland Bancorp, Inc. 01/07/2016
Each share Common $5 par exchanged for (0.9576) share Common no par

PASCACK CMNTY BK (WESTWOOD, NJ)
Stock Dividend - 10% payable 02/06/2007 to holders of record 01/16/2007 Ex date - 01/11/2007
Under plan of reorganization each share Common $5 par automatically became (1) share Pascack Bancorp, Inc. Common $5 par 02/10/2010
Pascack Bancorp, Inc. merged into Lakeland Bancorp, Inc. 01/07/2016

PASCACK VALLEY BK & TR CO (HILLSDALE, NJ)
Merged into Citizens First National Bank of New Jersey (Ridgewood, NJ) 11/30/73
Each share Common $10 par exchanged for (1.8) shares Common $5 par
Citizens First National Bank of New Jersey (Ridgewood, NJ) reorganized as Citizens First Bancorp, Inc. 10/1/82 which merged into National Westminster Bank PLC 10/1/94

PASCAGOULA MOSS POINT BK (MOSS POINT, MS)
Acquired by Hancock Holding Co. 10/01/1985
Details not available

PASCALIS GOLD MINES, LTD. (CANADA)
Recapitalized as New Pascalis Mines, Ltd. 10/25/1962
Each share Capital Stock no par exchanged for (0.2) share Common no par
New Pascalis Mines, Ltd. merged into Tiomin Resources Inc. 10/09/1992 which recapitalized as Vaaldiam Mining Inc. 03/26/2010
(See Vaaldiam Mining Inc.)

PASCALL ENERGY CORP (NJ)
Each share Common $0.0001 par exchanged for (0.05) share Common $0.002 par 08/22/1986
Name changed to Pascall Group, Inc. 01/23/1989

PASCAR DEV LTD (MB)
Reorganized under the laws of Alberta as Trapper Resources Ltd. 09/13/1982
Each share Common no par exchanged for (0.1) share Common no par
(See Trapper Resources Ltd.)

PASCAR OILS LTD (MB)
Name changed to Pascar Development Corp. Ltd. (MB) 01/24/1969
Pascar Development Corp. Ltd. (MB) reorganized in Alberta as Trapper Resources Ltd. 09/13/1982
(See Trapper Resources Ltd.)

PASCO INC (DE)
Under plan of liquidation each share Capital Stock 70¢ par received initial distribution of $27.50 cash 01/20/1976
Each share Capital Stock 70¢ par received second distribution of $22 cash 08/04/1976
Each share Capital Stock 70¢ par exchanged for (1) Pasco Liquidating Trust Non-transferable Ctf. of Bene. Int. 12/21/1976
(See Pasco Liquidating Trust)

PASCO LIQUIDATING TR (DE)
Liquidation completed
Each Non-Transferable Ctf. of Bene. Int. received initial distribution of $7 cash 02/12/1982
Each Non-Transferable Ctf. of Bene. Int. received second and final distribution of $1.29 cash 09/14/1982
Note: Certificates were not required to be surrendered and are without value

PASCO MARITIMES GOLD LTD. (QC)
Name changed to Pasco Mining Corp. Ltd. in 1947

PASGIL MINES LTD. (ON)
Charter revoked for failure to file reports and pay fees 09/28/1964

PASHMINADEPOT COM INC (FL)
Common $0.0001 par split (10) for (1) by issuance of (9) additional shares payable 03/27/2009 to holders of record 03/24/2009 Ex date - 03/30/2009
Reincorporated under the laws of Delaware as SwissINSO Holding Inc. 11/20/2009

PASO ROBLES OIL TRUST (CA)
Charter forfeited for failure to file reports and pay taxes 11/30/10

PASQUALE FOOD INC (DE)
Common $1 par split (2) for (1) by issuance of (1) additional share 3/15/73
Common $1 par reclassified as Conv. Class B Common $1 par 8/8/83
Each share Conv. Class B Common $1 par received distribution of (1) share Class A Common $1 par 8/22/83
Class A Common $1 par split (3) for (2) by issuance of (0.5) additional share 1/15/86
Conv. Class B Common $1 par split (3) for (2) by issuance of (0.5) additional share 1/15/86
Class A Common $1 par split (3) for (2) by issuance of (0.5) additional share 4/7/86
Conv. Class B Common $1 par split (3) for (2) by isuance of (0.5) additional share 4/7/86
Stock Dividends - 25% 4/23/71; 50% 2/18/72; 50% 3/15/74; 50% 3/28/84
Merged into Labatt (John) Ltd. 1/2/87
Each share Class A Common $1 par exchanged for $18.50 cash
Each share Conv. Class B Common $1 par exchanged for $18.50 cash

PASQUANEY BAY LTD (DE)
Liquidation completed
Each share Common 10¢ par received initial distribution of $2 cash 06/25/1975
Each share Common 10¢ par exchanged for (1) Non-Transferable Liquidation Part. Certificate and $0.52 cash 10/15/1975
Each Non-Transferable Liquidation Part. Certificate received first and final distribution of $0.065 cash 09/15/1978

PASS LAKE RES LTD (BC)
Recapitalized as Arlington Ventures Ltd. Canada (BC) 11/13/92
Each share Common no par exchanged for (0.2) share Common no par
Arlington Ventures Ltd. Canada (BC) reincorporated in Yukon as Arlington Oil & Gas Ltd. 6/27/2001 which recapitalized as Cypress Hills Resource Corp. (Yukon) 3/12/2003 which reincorporated in Alberta 7/26/2005

PASSAGE HOME COMMUNICATIONS INC (CO)
Chapter 11 Federal Bankruptcy Code converted to Chapter 7 on 6/7/90
Stockholders' equity unlikely

PASSAGES TRAVEL SVCS INC (NV)
Reorganized as Emerson Oil & Gas Inc. 6/1/2004
Each share Common exchanged for (20) shares Common $0.0001 par
Emerson Oil & Gas Inc. recapitalized as BioLife Remedies Inc. 1/19/2007

PASSION MEDIA INC (ON)
Name changed to Lemontonic Inc. 03/05/2004
Lemontonic Inc. recapitalized as Pioneering Technology Inc. 04/05/2006 which recapitalized as Pioneering Technology Corp. 09/18/2008

PASSIONATE PET INC (NV)
Recapitalized as Firstin Wireless Technology, Inc. 01/31/2013
Each share Common $0.001 par exchanged for (0.004) share Common $0.001 par
Firstin Wireless Technology, Inc. recapitalized as BioNovelus, Inc. 05/14/2015

PASSPORT ARTS INC (NV)
Reincorporated under the laws of Delaware as Soupman, Inc. 02/01/2011

PASSPORT ENERGY LTD (BC)
Merged into Powder Mountain Energy Ltd. 06/20/2014
Each share Common no par exchanged for (0.0333) share Common no par
Note: Unexchanged certificates were cancelled and became without value 06/20/2017
Powder Mountain Energy Ltd. merged into Canamax Energy Ltd. 08/04/2015
(See Canamax Energy Ltd.)

PASSPORT METALS INC (BC)
Name changed to Passport Potash Inc. 11/10/2009

PASSPORT MINES LTD (BC)
Struck off register and declared dissolved for failure to file returns 7/15/83

PASSPORT RESTAURANTS INC (TX)
Reincorporated under the laws of Delaware as Pacific Restaurant Holdings, Inc. 03/30/2009
(See Pacific Restaurant Holdings, Inc.)

PASSPORT TRAVEL INC (KS)
Each share old Common no par exchanged for (0.001) share new Common no par 10/30/1990
Reincorporated under the laws of Kansas as CasaDeComputers.com, Inc. 01/23/2007
(See CasaDeComputers.com, Inc.)

PASSWALL CORP.
Name changed to Eastern Shares Corp. in 1933 which was liquidated in 1934

PAST & PRESENT VIDEO INC (NV)
Recapitalized as Turning Wheel Holdings, Inc. 03/28/2008
Each share Common $0.001 par exchanged for (0.2) share Common $0.001 par

PAST TELL LTD (NV)
Each share old Common $0.001 par exchanged for (0.2) share new Common $0.001 par 10/03/1995
Name changed to Chaos Group, Inc. 11/07/1996
Chaos Group, Inc. name changed to Luminart Corp. (NV) 04/23/1998 which reincorporated in Wyoming 05/27/2009
(See Luminart Corp.)

PASTA & CHEESE INC (NY)
Merged into Carnation Co. 01/07/1987
Each share Common 1¢ par exchanged for $16.50 cash

PASTA BELLA INC (FL)
Name changed to Global Assets Holdings Inc. 2/22/99
Global Assets Holdings Inc. name changed to Epixtar Corp. 11/25/2002

PASTA KING INC (DE)
Adjudicated bankrupt 03/22/1979
Stockholders' equity unlikely

PASTA VIA INTL INC (CO)
Charter dissolved 4/3/95

PASTABILITIES FOOD SVCS CORP (DE)
Charter cancelled and declared inoperative and void for non-payment of taxes 3/1/89

PASTEL FOOD CORP (BC)
Recapitalized as International Pastel Food Corp. 10/25/1990
Each share Common no par exchanged for (0.25) share Common no par
International Pastel Food Corp. was acquired by Comac Food Group Inc. 05/29/1991 which name changed to Canada's Pizza Delivery Corp. 01/22/2004
(See Canada's Pizza Delivery Corp.)

PASTEUR MEDICAL BUILDING CORP. (OK)
Name changed to Essex Corp. 11/29/65

PASTY HOUSE, INC. (MN)
Merged into Brothen, Inc. 11/02/1971
Each share Common 5¢ par exchanged for (1/3) share Common 5¢ par
(See Brothen, Inc.)

PASW INC (DE)
Reincorporated 05/30/2007
State of incorporation changed from (CA) to (DE) and Common $0.001 par changed to $0.00001 par 05/30/2007
Recapitalized as VirnetX Holding Corp. 10/30/2007
Each share Common $0.00001 par exchanged for (1/3) share Common $0.0001 par

PAT FASHIONS INDS INC (DE)
Reincorporated 5/30/80
Stock Dividend - 100% 5/6/71
State of incorporation changed from (NY) to (DE) 5/30/80
Name changed to TEP Fund, Inc. 11/18/82
(See TEP Fund, Inc.)

PATAGONIA CORP (DE)
Liquidation completed
Each share Common $1 par received first distribution of $5 cash 2/23/81
Each share Common $1 par received second distribution of $10 cash 7/29/81
Each share Common $1 par received third distribution of $4 cash 10/13/81
Assets transferred to Patagonia Liquidating Trust and Common $1 par reclassified as Units of Bene. Int. 10/15/89
(See Patagonia Liquidating Trust)

PATAGONIA GOLD LTD (BRITISH VIRGIN ISLANDS)
Reincorporated 11/29/2002
Reincorporated from Patagonia Gold Corp. (FL) to Patagonia Gold (BVI) Ltd. (British Virgin Islands) 11/29/2002
Name changed to Soil Biogenics Ltd. 3/3/2003

PATAGONIA GOLD PLC (ENGLAND & WALES)
Delisted from Toronto Stock Exchange 07/12/2013
Shares now trade on London Stock Exchange

PATAGONIA LIQUIDATING TRUST (DE)
Liquidation completed
Each Share of Bene. Int. received initial distribution of $0.01936 cash 2/22/86
Each Share of Bene. Int. received second distribution of $0.011898 cash 8/16/82
Each Share of Bene. Int. received third distribution of $0.09165 cash 2/4/83
Each Share of Bene. Int. received fourth distribution of $0.13735 cash 8/12/83
Each Share of Bene. Int. received fifth distribution of $0.05960 cash 1/27/84
Each Share of Bene. Int. received sixth distribution of $0.11195 cash 8/3/84
Each Share of Bene. Int. received seventh distribution of $0.09450 cash 2/15/85
Each Share of Bene. Int. received eighth distribution of $0.08170 cash 8/13/85
Note: Details on subsequent distributions, if any, are not available

PATAPSCO BANCORP INC (MD)
Common 1¢ par split (3) for (1) by issuance of (2) additional shares payable 08/30/2004 to holders of record 08/02/2004
Stock Dividends - 10% payable 12/07/2001 to holders of record 11/16/2001 Ex date - 11/14/2001; 10% payable 12/13/2002 to holders of record 11/15/2002 Ex date - 11/13/2002; 10% payable 12/12/2003 to holders of record 11/14/2003 Ex date - 11/12/2003
7.5% Perpetual Conv. Preferred Ser. A called for redemption at $25 on 03/31/2006
Merged into Howard Bancorp, Inc. 08/31/2015
Each share Common 1¢ par exchanged for (0.3547) share Common 1¢ par

PATAPSCO NATIONAL BANK (ELLICOTT CITY, MD)
Merged into First National Bank of Maryland (Baltimore, Md.) 1/29/71
Each share Capital Stock $10 par exchanged for (2.2) shares Common $5 par
First National Bank of Maryland (Baltimore, Md.) reorganized as First Maryland Bancorp 7/8/74
(See First Maryland Bancorp)

PATAPSCO VY BANCSHARES INC (MD)
Common 1¢ par split (2) for (1) by issuance of (1) additional share payable 10/01/1998 to holders of record 10/01/1998
Stock Dividend - 20% payable 04/01/1998 to holders of record 02/02/1998
Merged into F&M Bancorp 12/31/1999
Each share Common 1¢ par exchanged for (1.18) shares Common 1¢ par
F&M Bancorp merged into Mercantile Bankshares Corp. 08/12/2003 which merged into PNC Financial Services Group, Inc. 03/02/2007

PATCALL INC (AB)
Issue Information - 2,000,000 shares COM offered at $0.15 per share on 08/08/1997
Name changed to FaxMate.Com Inc. 02/17/1999
(See FaxMate.Com Inc.)

PATCH INTL INC (AB)
Reincorporated 08/29/2008
Each share old Common $0.001 par exchanged for (0.1) share new Common $0.001 par 07/25/2005
Each share new Common $0.001 par exchanged again for (2.5) share new Common $0.001 par 03/28/2016
Place of incorporation changed from (NV) to (AB) 08/29/2008
Merged into Stem Holdings, Inc. 01/20/2017
Each share new Common $0.001 par exchanged for (0.02438) share Common and (1) Contingent Value Right
Note: Unexchanged certificates will be cancelled and become without value 01/20/2020

PATCH SAFETY SVCS LTD (AB)
Recapitalized as HSE Integrated Ltd. 09/01/2004
Each share Common no par exchanged for (0.2) share Common no par
(See HSE Integrated Ltd.)

PATCH VENTURES INC (CANADA)
Name changed to Legacy Storage Systems International, Inc. 9/29/94
Legacy Storage Systems International, Inc. name changed to Tecmar Technologies International, Inc. 12/17/96 which name changed to Xencet Investments Inc. 3/31/98 which name changed to Games Trader Inc. 11/11/98 which name changed to GTR Group Inc. 6/29/99 which name changed to Mad Catz Interactive, Inc. 9/5/2001

PATCHGEAR COM INC (AB)
Delisted from Toronto Venture Stock Exchange 06/05/2002

PATCHOGUE-PLYMOUTH MILLS CORP. (NY)
Under plan of merger name changed to Patchogue-Plymouth Corp. 7/13/56
Each share Preferred $1 par exchanged for $1 principal amount 6% Debentures due 6/30/76
Each share Common no par exchanged for $100 principal amount 6% Debentures due 6/30/76

PATCO INDS LTD (DE)
Recapitalized as Optical Molecular Imaging, Inc. 1/27/2006
Each share Common $0.0001 par exchanged for (0.00434021) share Common $0.0001 par
Optical Molecular Imaging, Inc. name changed to Immunocellular Therapeutics, Ltd. 11/30/2006

PATCOR CAP INC (CANADA)
Name changed to Dion Entertainment Corp. 06/30/1992
(See Dion Entertainment Corp.)

PATENT CTRS INTL INC (OH)
Reincorporated under the laws of Delaware as Cable Communications Corp. of Delaware 09/10/1982
(See Cable Communications Corp.)

PATENT DEV CORP (TX)
Name changed to Chapel Mountain Industries, Inc. 5/1/82
(See Chapel Mountain Industries, Inc.)

PATENT ENFORCEMENT & ROYALTIES LTD (ON)
Name changed to Blue Pearl Mining Ltd. 04/15/2005
Blue Pearl Mining Ltd. name changed to Thompson Creek Metals Co., Inc. (ON) 05/15/2007 which reincorporated in British Columbia 07/29/2008 which merged into Centerra Gold Inc. 10/21/2016

PATENT LITIGATION TR (DE)
United States Court of Appeals rejected Trust's appeal of patent litigation 03/31/2004
Bene. Trust Ints. are without value
Note: SEC revoked Bene. Trust Int. registration 08/05/2010

PATENT MGMT INC (MD)
Name changed to PMI Holdings Corp. 01/19/1982
(See PMI Holdings Corp.)

PATENT PPTYS INC (DE)
Name changed to Walker Innovation Inc. 08/12/2015

PATENT RES INC (NY)
Charter revoked and proclaimed dissolved for failure to file reports and pay fees 12/15/1969

PATENTS INTL AFFILIATES LTD (NY)
Common 1¢ par split (3) for (1) by issuance of (2) additional shares 01/27/1970
Common 1¢ par split (2) for (1) by issuance of (1) additional share 11/30/1973
Adjudicated bankrupt 01/31/1978
Stockholders' equity unlikely

PATENTS INTL OVERSEAS CORP (NY)
Name changed to Energy International Overseas Corp. 10/26/1982
Energy International Overseas Corp. recapitalized as Nova Continental Development Corp. 09/19/1994
(See Nova Continental Development Corp.)

PATENTS PROFESSIONAL INC (NV)
Name changed to All Marketing Solutions Inc. 04/10/2013

PATENTS UNLIMITED INC (DE)
Name changed to Diversified Development Inc. 11/22/72
Diversified Development Inc. name changed to Ionicron Inc. 2/23/81
(See Ionicron Inc.)

PATER URANIUM MINES LTD. (ON)
Assets sold to Pronto Uranium Mines Ltd. on a (1) for (15) basis and $0.0375 cash 8/21/59
Pronto Uranium Mines Ltd. merged into Rio Algom Mines Ltd. 6/30/60 which name changed to Rio Algom Ltd. 4/30/75
(See Rio Algom Ltd.)

PATERSON & PASSAIC GAS & ELECTRIC CO.
Merged into Public Service Electric & Gas Co. and stock exchanged for a like amount of First and Refunding Mortgage Bonds in 1938

PATERSON BREWING CO.
Out of business 00/00/1950
Details not available

PATERSON (WILLIAM) LTD.
Acquired by Weston (George) Ltd. 00/00/1928
Details not available

PATERSON PARCHMENT PAPER CO (DE)
Reincorporated 09/30/1966
Each share Common $100 par exchanged for (5) shares Common $20 par 00/00/1944
Each share Common $20 par exchanged for (2) shares Common $10 par 04/15/1957
Stock Dividend - 20% 04/10/1957
State of incorporation changed from (PA) to (DE) 09/30/1966
Common $10 par changed to $5 par and (1) additional share issued 01/10/1969
Merged into CB Acquisitions Corp. 09/21/1987
Each share Common $5 par exchanged for $1.247241 cash

PATFIND INC (AB)
Reincorporated under the laws of Ontario as Engineering.com Inc. 10/10/2000

PATH 1 NETWORK TECHNOLOGIES INC (DE)
Each share old Common $0.001 par exchanged for (0.16666666) share new Common $0.001 par 07/23/2003
SEC revoked common stock registration 06/28/2012

PATHCOM INC (CA)
Plan of reorganization under Chapter 11 bankruptcy proceedings confirmed 03/22/1983
Only holdings of (710) or more shares participated and received an undetermined amount of cash
Note: Certificates were not required to be surrendered and are without value

PATHE COMMUNICATIONS CORP (DE)
97% of voting shares acquired by Credit Lyonnais Bank Nederland N.V. through purchase offer which expired 6/5/92
Note: Company has no operating assets or sources of income

PATHE COMPUTER CTL SYS CORP (DE)
Name changed to Pathe Technologies, Inc. 07/21/1992
Pathe Technologies, Inc. recapitalized as Mid-West Spring Manufacturing Co. 07/14/1995
(See Mid-West Spring Manufacturing Co.)

PATHE EQUIPMENT CO., INC. (NY)
Acquired by Kidde (Walter) & Co., Inc. (NY) 8/3/65
Each share Class A 75¢ par exchanged for (0.3318951) share Common $2.50 par
Kidde (Walter) & Co., Inc. (NY) reincorporated in Delaware 7/2/68 which name changed to Kidde, Inc. 4/18/80 which merged into Hanson Trust p.l.c. 12/31/87 which name changed to Hanson PLC (Old) 1/29/88 which reorganized as Hanson PLC (New) 10/15/2003

PATHE EXCHANGE, INC.
Reorganized as Pathe Film Corp. in 1935 which was liquidated in 1941

PATHE FILM CORP.
Liquidated in 1941

PATHE INDUSTRIES, INC. (OH)
Name changed to Chesapeake Industries, Inc. 4/30/52
Chesapeake Industries, Inc. name changed to America Corp (OH) 4/29/59 which recapitalized as America Corp. (DE) 12/31/63 which name changed to Pathe Industries, Inc. (DE) 11/20/64
(See Pathe Industries, Inc. (DE))

PATHE INDS INC (DE)
Charter cancelled and declared inoperative and void for non-payment of taxes 6/17/93

PATHE LABORATORIES, INC. (NJ)
Merged into Pathe Industries Inc. (OH) in 1944
Each share Common exchanged for (1.2235) shares 4% Preferred $100 par and (6.118) shares new Common $5 par
Pathe Industries Inc. name changed to Chesapeake Industries, Inc. 4/30/52 which name changed to America Corp. (OH) 4/29/59 which recapitalized as America Corp. (DE) 12/31/63 which name changed to Pathe Industries, Inc. (DE) 11/20/64
(See Pathe Industries, Inc. (DE))

PATHE LABORATORIES INC. OF CALIFORNIA
Merged into Pathe Industries, Inc. (OH) in 1944
Each share Common exchanged for (0.0378) share 4% Preferred $100 par and (0.1892) share new Common $5 par
Pathe Industries, Inc. (OH) name changed to Chesapeake Industries, Inc. 4/30/52 which name changed to America Corp. (OH) 8/10/59 which recapitalized as America Corp. (DE) 12/31/63 which name changed to Pathe Industries, Inc. (DE) 11/20/64
(See Pathe Industries, Inc. (DE))

PATHE NEWS, INC. (DE)
No longer in existence having become inoperative and void for non-payment of taxes 4/1/65

PATHE TECHNOLOGIES INC (DE)
Recapitalized as Mid-West Spring Manufacturing Co. 07/14/1995
Each share Common 1¢ par exchanged for (0.14285714) share Common 1¢ par
(See Mid-West Spring Manufacturing Co.)

PATHEON INC (BC)
Common no par reclassified as Restricted Voting Shares no par 05/02/2007
Acquired by JLL/Delta Patheon Holdings, L.P. 03/12/2014
Each Restricted Voting Share no par exchanged for $9.32 cash

PATHEON N V (NETHERLANDS)
Acquired by Thermo Fisher Scientific Inc. 09/13/2017
Each share Ordinary EUR 0.01 par exchanged for $35 cash

PATHFINDER BANCORP INC (USA)
Reincorporated 06/19/2001
Common 10¢ par split (3) for (2) by issuance of (0.5) additional share payable 02/05/1998 to holders of record 01/26/1998
Place of incorporation changed from (DE) to (USA) and Common 10¢ par changed to 1¢ par 06/19/2001
Reorganized under the laws of Maryland 10/16/2014
Each share Common 1¢ par exchanged for (1.6472) shares Common 1¢ par

PATHFINDER COMPUTER CTRS CORP (DE)
Charter cancelled and declared inoperative and void for non-payment of taxes 03/01/1987

PATHFINDER CONV DEB FD (AB)
Name changed to Pathfinder Income Fund 11/12/2014

PATHFINDER CORP (NV)
Name changed to Pegasus Industries Inc. 3/9/95

PATHFINDER DATA GROUP INC (CO)
SEC revoked common stock registration 10/20/2008

PATHFINDER EXPLORATION CO. LTD. (BC)
Dissolved in 1948

PATHFINDER FINL CORP (BC)
Name changed to Pathfinder Industries Ltd. 11/17/86
Pathfinder Industries Ltd. recapitalized as International Pathfinder Inc. 5/19/87
(See International Pathfinder Inc.)

PATHFINDER INCOME FD (ON)
Merged into YIELDPLUS Income Fund 09/27/2007
Each Unit received (1.19618902) Trust Units
YIELDPLUS Income Fund merged into MINT Income Fund 03/21/2017

PATHFINDER INDS LTD (BC)
Recapitalized as International Pathfinder Inc. 05/19/1987
Each share Common no par exchanged for (1/3) share Common no par
(See International Pathfinder Inc.)

PATHFINDER INTL RECREATIONAL CORP (AB)
Recapitalized as Vision Inc. 07/06/1993
Each share Common no par exchanged for (0.1) share Common no par
(See Vision Inc.)

PATHFINDER LIFE INSURANCE CO. OF AMERICA (AR)
Merged into Investors Preferred Life Insurance Co. (Ark.) 6/1/67
Each share Common $1 par exchanged for (1) share Common 12¢ par
(See Investors Preferred Life Insurance Co. (Ark.))

PATHFINDER MOBILEHOME INC (WI)
Name changed to Harmony, Inc. 04/25/1977
Harmony, Inc. merged into Isle Resources Inc. 04/19/1982
(See Isle Resources Inc.)

PATHFINDER PETE CORP (DE)
Charter cancelled and declared inoperative and void for non-payment of taxes 3/1/89

PATHFINDER PETROLEUMS LTD. (AB)
Merged into Medallion Petroleums Ltd. 9/11/56
Each share Common 50¢ par exchanged for (0.4) share Common $1.25 par
Medallion Petroleums Ltd. merged into Canadian Industrial Gas & Oil Ltd. 3/8/65 which merged into Norcen Energy Resources Ltd. (ALTA) 10/28/75 which reincorporated under the laws of Canada 4/15/77
(See Norcen Energy Resources Ltd.)

PATHFINDER RES INC (UT)
Recapitalized as C B Crest, Inc. 07/27/1987
Each share Common $0.001 par exchanged for (0.33333333) share Common $0.001 par
(See C B Crest, Inc.)

PATHFINDER RES LTD (BC)
Common 50¢ par changed to no par 12/4/74
Recapitalized as International Pathfinder Resources Ltd. 6/2/82
Each share Common no par exchanged for (0.2) share Common no par
International Pathfinder Resources Ltd. name changed to Pathfinder Financial Corp. 9/6/83 which name changed to Pathfinder Industries Ltd. 11/17/86 which recapitalized as International Pathfinder Inc. 5/19/87
(See International Pathfinder Inc.)

PATHFINDER RES LTD (CANADA)
Merged into Bayswater Uranium Corp. (Old) 08/15/2006
Each share Common no par exchanged for (0.588) share Common no par
Bayswater Uranium Corp. (Old) merged into Bayswater Uranium Corp. (New) 07/24/2007 which recapitalized as Green Thumb Industries Inc. 06/13/2018

PATHFINDER TRUST (MA)
Completely liquidated 05/30/2000
Each share Pathfinder Fund no par received net asset value

PATHFINDER URANIUM & NICKEL MINES LTD. (BC)
Name changed to Pathfinder Resources Ltd. 11/19/69
Pathfinder Resources Ltd. recapitalized as International Pathfinder Resources Ltd. 6/2/82 which name changed to Pathfinder Financial Corp. 9/6/83 which name changed to Pathfinder Industries Ltd. 11/17/86 which recapitalized as International Pathfinder Inc. 5/19/87
(See International Pathfinder Inc.)

PATHFINDER URANIUM CORP. (UT)
Merged into Northwest Uranium Mines, Inc. on a (1) for (5) basis in 1956

PATHMARK STORES INC (DE)
Merged into Great Atlantic & Pacific Tea Co., Inc. 12/03/2007
Each share Common 1¢ par exchanged for (0.12963) share Common $1 par and $9 cash
(See Great Atlantic & Pacific Tea Co., Inc.)

PATHOBIOTEK DIAGNOSTICS INC (TX)
Each share old Common $0.001 par exchanged for (0.025) share new Common $0.001 par 9/6/2001
Name changed to ATNG, Inc. (TX) 10/22/2001
ATNG, Inc. (TX) reincorporated in Nevada 9/6/2003 which recapitalized as Zann Corp. 12/3/2004

PATHOGENESIS CORP (DE)
Merged into Chiron Corp. 9/22/2000
Each share Common $0.001 par exchanged for $38.50 cash

PATHONIC NETWORK INC (CANADA)
Merged into Tele-Metropole Inc. 10/28/1988
Each share Class A Subordinate no par exchanged for $10 cash

PATHTECHNICS LTD (ON)
Delisted from Vancouver Stock Exchange 11/16/1990

PATHWAY FINL CORP (ON)
Name changed to Asia Media Group Corp. 9/27/94
(See Asia Media Group Corp.)

PATHWAYS GROUP INC (DE)
Recapitalized as Global Aerial Surveillance, Inc. 06/06/2005
Each share Common no par exchanged for (0.001) share Common no par
Global Aerial Surveillance, Inc. name changed to Bicoastal Communications Inc. 07/05/2006
(See Bicoastal Communications Inc.)

PATICAN CO. LTD. (CANADA)
Under plan of merger name changed to Patino of Canada Ltd. 10/6/55
Patino of Canada Ltd. merged into Patino Corp. Ltd. 6/11/62 which merged into Patino Mining Corp. 11/26/62 which reorganized as Patino N.V. 12/20/71
(See Patino N.V.)

PATIENT HOME MONITORING CORP NEW (BC)
Name changed to Protech Home Medical Corp. 05/07/2018

PATIENT HOME MONITORING CORP OLD (BC)
Reincorporated 12/30/2013
Place of incorporation changed from (AB) to (BC) 12/30/2013
Plan of arrangement effective 12/22/2017
Each share Common no par exchanged for (1) share Patient Home Monitoring Corp. (New) Common no par and (0.1) share Viemed Healthcare, Inc. Common no par
(See each company's listing)
Note: Unexchanged certificates will be cancelled and become without value 12/22/2023

PATIENT INFOSYSTEMS INC (DE)
Issue Information - 2,000,000 shares COM offered at $8 per share on 12/19/96
Each (12) shares old Common 1¢ par exchanged for (1) share new Common 1¢ par 1/9/2004
Each share Common 1¢ par received distribution of (0.5) share American Caresource Holdings, Inc. Common 1¢ par payable 12/23/2005 to holders of record 11/8/2005
Ex date - 12/19/2005
Name changed to CareGuide, Inc. 9/25/2006

PATIENT MED SYS CORP (NV)
Name changed to Integrated Generics, Inc. (NV) 01/21/1987
Integrated Generics, Inc. (NV) reincorporated in Delaware as Biopharmaceutics, Inc. 05/25/1988 which name changed to Feminique Corp. 06/28/1999 which recapitalized as Receivable Acquisition & Management Corp. 05/11/2004 which name changed to PwrCor, Inc. 03/29/2017

PATIENT SAFETY TECHNOLOGIES INC (DE)
Common 33¢ par split (3) for (1) by issuance of (2) additional shares payable 04/04/2005 to holders of record 03/21/2005
Acquired by Stryker Corp. 03/24/2014
Each share Common 33¢ par exchanged for $2.22 cash

PATIENT TECHNOLOGY INC (DE)
Common 5¢ par changed to 2-1/2¢ par and (1) additional share issued 6/17/83
Name changed to Graham-Field Health Products, Inc. 5/27/88
(See Graham-Field Health Products, Inc.)

PATIENTS & PHYSICIANS INC (DE)
Name changed to Flagship Global Health, Inc. 01/24/2007
(See Flagship Global Health, Inc.)

PATIMAS COMPUTERS BERHAD (MALAYSIA)
ADR agreement terminated 12/19/2006
Details not available

PATINA OIL & GAS CORP (DE)
7.125% Preferred 1¢ par called for redemption at $26.069 on 01/21/2000
Common 1¢ par split (5) for (4) by issuance of (0.25) additional share payable 06/20/2002 to holders of record 06/10/2002 Ex date - 06/21/2002
Common 1¢ par split (5) for (4) by issuance of (0.25) additional share payable 06/04/2003 to holders of record 05/27/2003 Ex date - 06/05/2003
Common 1¢ par split (2) for (1) by issuance of (1) additional share payable 03/03/2004 to holders of record 02/23/2004 Ex date - 03/04/2004
Merged into Noble Energy Inc. 05/16/2005
Each share Common 1¢ par exchanged for either (0.577344) share Common $3.33-1/3 par and $1.57392 cash or $39.3398 cash
Note: Option to receive stock and cash expired 05/10/2005

PATINO CORP. LTD. (ON)
Merged into Patino Mining Corp. 11/26/62
Each share Common no par exchanged for (1) share Capital Stock $6.50 par
Patino Mining Corp. reorganized as Patino N.V. 12/20/71
(See Patino N.V.)

PATINO ENTERPRISES OF CANADA LTD. (CANADA)
Merged into Patino of Canada Ltd. 10/06/1955
Each share Capital Stock $5 par exchanged for (2/3) share Common $2 par
Patino of Canada Ltd. merged into Patino Corp. Ltd. 06/11/1962 which merged into Patino Mining Corp. 11/26/1962 which reorganized as Patino N.V. 12/20/1971
(See Patino N.V.)

PATINO MINES & ENTERPRISES CONSOLIDATED, INC. (DE)
Capital Stock $20 par changed to no par in 1932
Capital Stock no par changed to $10 par in 1937
Capital Stock $10 par changed to $5 par in 1946
Capital Stock $5 par changed to $1 par 4/26/55
Merged into Southern Maryland Agricultural Association of Prince George's County, Maryland, Inc. 3/3/62
Each share Capital Stock $1 par exchanged for (0.5) share Common $1 par
Southern Maryland Agricultural Association of Prince George's County, Maryland, Inc. name changed to Gibraltar Pari-Mutuel, Inc. 6/25/73
(See Gibraltar Pari-Mutuel, Inc.)

PATINO MNG CORP (QC)
Reorganized under the laws of the Netherlands as Patino N.V. 12/20/1971
Each share Capital Stock $6.50 par exchanged for (1) share Capital Stock 5 Gldrs. par
(See Patino N.V.)

PATINO N V (NETHERLANDS)
Liquidation completed
Each share Capital Stock 5 Gldrs. par received initial distribution of $3.22 cash 11/23/84
Note: Details on subsequent distributions, if any, are not available

PATINO OF CANADA LTD. (CANADA)
Merged into Patino Corp., Ltd. on a share for share basis 6/11/62
Patino Corp. Ltd. merged into Patino Mining Corp. 11/26/62 which reorganized as Patino N.V. 12/20/71
(See Patino N.V.)

PATINOS INC (NJ)
Charter declared void for non-payment of taxes 11/17/1983

PATLEX CORP NEW (DE)
Under plan of reorganization each share Common 10¢ par automatically became (1) share DBT Online, Inc. Common 10¢ par 08/21/1996
DBT Online, Inc. merged into ChoicePoint Inc. 05/16/2000
(See ChoicePoint Inc.)

PATLEX CORP OLD (PA)
Conv. Preferred Initial Ser. 10¢ par called for redemption 07/31/1989
Stock Dividends - 10% 02/12/1981; in Common to holders of Preferred (1) for (7.95) 06/21/1982; (1) for (8.13) 06/20/1983
Acquired by AutoFinance Group Inc. 12/11/1992
Each share Common 10¢ par exchanged for (1.4) shares Common no par
AutoFinance Group Inc. acquired by KeyCorp (New) 09/27/1995

PATMAR RES CORP (BC)
Recapitalized as Draw Resource Corp. 02/10/1984
Each share Common no par exchanged for (1/3) share Common no par
Draw Resource Corp. recapitalized as Draw International Resources Corp. 11/21/1985
(See Draw International Resources Corp.)

PATMORE GROUP LTD (ON)
Name changed 11/01/1976
Name changed from Patmore Developments Ltd. to Patmore Group Ltd. 11/01/1976
Merged into Uranco Inc. 10/23/1980
Each share Capital Stock $1 par exchanged for (0.25) share Capital Stock no par

PATNI COMPUTER SYS LTD (INDIA)
Name changed to iGATE Computer Systems Ltd. 07/27/2012
(See iGATE Computer Systems Ltd.)

PATNORA GOLD MINES, LTD. (ON)
Charter cancelled for failure to file reports and pay taxes December 1954

PATO CONS GOLD DREDGING LTD (BC)
Reorganized under the laws of Bermuda 10/01/1976
Each share Capital Stock $1 par exchanged for (1) share Capital Stock $1 par
(See Pato Consolidated Gold Dredging, Ltd. (Bermuda))

PATO CONS GOLD DREDGING LTD (BERMUDA)
Merged into Pacific Holding Corp. 10/11/1979
Each share Capital Stock $1 par exchanged for $16.88 cash

PATOKA COAL CO. OF DELAWARE (DE)
Merged into Ayrshire Patoka Collieries Corp. 00/00/1939
Each share Common $1 par exchanged for (213.4) shares Common $1 par
Ayrshire Patoka Collieries Corp. name changed to Ayrshire Collieries Corp. (DE) 00/00/1944 which reincorporated in Indiana 06/30/1965 which merged into American Metal Climax, Inc. 10/31/1969 which name changed to Amax Inc. 07/01/1974
(See Amax Inc.)

PATON MANUFACTURING CO. LTD. (QC)
Recapitalized in 1946
Each share 7% Preferred $100 par exchanged for (5) shares 7% Preferred $20 par
Each share old Common no par exchanged for (5) shares new Common no par
Acquired by Cleyn & Tinker, Ltd. by offer effective October 1965
Each share 7% Preferred $20 par exchanged for $22.50 cash
Each share Common no par exchanged for $27.50 cash

PATRIARCH INC (DE)
Reorganized as KAL Energy, Inc. 12/29/2006
Each share Common $0.0001 par exchanged for (4) shares Common $0.0001 par

PATRICIA BIRCH LAKE GOLD MINES, LTD. (ON)
Dissolved 7/27/59

PATRICIA DENT GOLD MINES, LTD. (ON)
Charter cancelled for failure to file reports and pay taxes in 1955

PATRICIA MINES LTD (BC)
Recapitalized as Patricia Mining Corp. (BC) 09/13/1999
Each share Common no par exchanged for (0.2) share Common no par
Patricia Mining Corp. (BC) reincorporated in Ontario 01/15/2003 which was acquired by Richmont Mines Inc. 12/16/2008 which merged into Alamos Gold Inc. (New) 11/24/2017

PATRICIA MNG CORP (ON)
Reincorporated 01/15/2003
Place of incorporation changed from (BC) to (ON) 01/15/2003
Acquired by Richmont Mines Inc. 12/16/2008
Each share Common no par exchanged for (0.055) share Common no par and $0.15 cash
Richmont Mines Inc. merged into Alamos Gold Inc. (New) 11/24/2017

PATRICIAN DIAMONDS INC (ON)
Name changed 04/12/2002
Name changed from Patrician Consolidated Gold Mines Ltd. to Patrician Diamonds Inc. 04/12/2002
Recapitalized as Diamond Exploration Inc. (ON) 01/02/2009
Each share Common no par

exchanged for (0.1) share Common no par
Diamond Exploration Inc. (ON) reincorporated in British Columbia as Diamond International Exploration Inc. 10/29/2009 which name changed to Northaven Resources Corp. 03/14/2011

PATRICIAN GOLD MINES LTD (ON)
Recapitalized as Patrician Consolidated Gold Mines Ltd. 03/01/2000
Each share Common no par exchanged for (0.1) share Common no par
Patrician Consolidated Gold Mines Ltd. name changed to Patrician Diamonds Inc. 04/12/2002 which recapitalized as Diamond Exploration Inc. (ON) 01/02/2009 which reincorporated in British Columbia as Diamond International Exploration Inc. 10/29/2009 which name changed to Northaven Resources Corp. 03/14/2011

PATRICIAN PAPER INC (DE)
Under plan of liquidation each share Common 10¢ par received initial distribution of $2 cash 12/26/1978
Assets transferred to Patrician Paper Liquidating Trust 06/22/1979
(See Patrician Paper Liquidating Trust)

PATRICIAN PAPER LIQUIDATING TRUST (DE)
Liquidation completed
Each Unit received second distribution of $0.20 cash 4/5/80
Each Unit received third distribution of $1 cash 6/26/80
Each Unit received fourth distribution of $0.50 cash 12/17/80
Each Unit received fifth and final distribution of $0.10 cash 8/31/83
(See Patrician Paper Co., Inc. for previous distribution)

PATRICK COMPUTER SYS INC (CANADA)
Recapitalized as Optrix Radiation Inc. 03/01/1984
Each share Common no par exchanged for (0.1) share Common no par
Optrix Radiation Inc. reorganized as Southern Arizona Mining & Smelting Corp. 09/19/1988 which recapitalized as Unirom Technologies Inc. 03/12/1997
(See Unirom Technologies Inc.)

PATRICK HENRY BREWING CO., INC. (IN)
See - Henry (Patrick) Brewing Co., Inc.

PATRICK HENRY HOTEL, INC. (VA)
See - Henry (Patrick) Hotel, Inc.

PATRICK PETE CO (DE)
Common 10¢ par split (3) for (2) by issuance of (0.5) additional share 11/20/1980
Each share Common 10¢ par exchanged for (0.5) share Common 20¢ par 11/01/1985
Stock Dividends - 15% 03/03/1975; 10% 08/23/1976
Merged into Goodrich Petroleum Corp. 08/15/1995
Each share 8% Conv. Preferred Ser. B 1¢ par exchanged for (1) share Conv. Preferred Ser. A 1¢ par
Each share Common 20¢ par exchanged for (1) share Common 20¢ par
(See Goodrich Petroleum Corp.)

PATRICK PLYWOOD ENTERPRISES INC (IN)
Name changed to Patrick Industries, Inc. 07/07/1969

PATRIOT AMERN HOSPITALITY INC (DE)
(Issued and transferred only in Non-Separable Units of (1) share Patriot American Hospitality, Inc. Common 1¢ par and (1) share Wyndham International Inc. Common 1¢ par)
Secondary Offering - 9,200,000 PAIRED CTF'S offered at $24 per Ctf. on 07/28/1997
Each Paired Certificate received distribution of (0.0333333) share Interstate Hotels Corp. Class A Common no par payable 6/18/99 to holders of record 6/7/99 Ex date - 6/21/99
Stock Dividend - 0.927% payable 7/25/97 to holders of record 7/15/97 Ex date - 7/28/97
Merged into Wyndham International, Inc. 6/29/99
Each share 15% Preferred Ser. B 1¢ par exchanged for $25 cash
Each Paired Certificate exchanged for (1) share Class A Common 1¢ par
(See Wyndham International, Inc.)

PATRIOT AMERN HOSPITALITY INC (VA)
Issue Information - 12,700,000 shares COM offered at $24 per share on 09/27/1995
Common no par split (2) for (1) by issuance of (1) additional share payable 3/18/97 to holders of record 3/7/97 Ex date - 3/19/97
Merged into Patriot American Hospitality, Inc. (DE) 7/1/97
Each share Common no par exchanged for (0.51895) Paired Certificate
Patriot American Hospitality, Inc. (DE) merged into Wyndham International, Inc. 6/29/99
(See Wyndham International, Inc.)

PATRIOT BANCORPORATION (MA)
Common $10 par changed to $3.33 par and (2) additional shares issued 12/29/81
Stock Dividend - 25% 11/8/82
Acquired by Conifer Group Inc. (Old) 7/10/86
Each share $2.20 Conv. Preferred $1 par exchanged for (2.18625) shares Common $1 par
Each share Common $3.33 par exchanged for (1.749) shares Common $1 par
Conifer Group Inc. (Old) merged into Conifer/Essex Group, Inc. 2/17/83 which name changed back to Conifer Group Inc. (New) 1/1/85 which merged into Bank of New England Corp. 4/22/87
(See Bank of New England Corp.)

PATRIOT BK CORP (DE)
Common 1¢ par split (5) for (4) by issuance of (0.25) additional share payable 05/14/1998 to holders of record 05/01/1998
Stock Dividends - 20% payable 11/21/1996 to holders of record 11/07/1996; 20% payable 09/22/1997 to holders of record 09/08/1997
Under plan of merger each share Common 1¢ par automatically became (1) share Patriot Bank Corp. (PA) Common 1¢ par 01/22/1999
Patriot Bank Corp. (PA) merged into Susquehanna Bancshares, Inc. 06/10/2004 which merged into BB&T Corp. 08/01/2015

PATRIOT BK CORP (PA)
Stock Dividend - 10% payable 4/25/2003 to holders of record 4/11/2003 Ex date - 4/9/2003
Merged into Susquehanna Bancshares, Inc. 6/10/2004
Each share Common 1¢ par exchanged for (1.143) shares Common $2 par

PATRIOT BANK NA (FREDERICKSBURG, VA)
Stock Dividends - 10% payable 07/31/2000 to holders of record 06/30/2000 Ex date - 08/21/2000; 10% payable 07/31/2001 to holders of record 06/30/2001 Ex date - 07/20/2001; 10% payable 07/31/2002 to holders of record 06/28/2002 Ex date - 07/29/2002; 10% payable 10/31/2003 to holders of record 09/30/2003 Ex date - 11/03/2003
Merged into Carter Bank & Trust (Martinsville, VA) 12/29/2006
Each share Common $5 par exchanged for (5.775) shares Common

PATRIOT BERRY FARMS INC (NV)
Common $0.001 par split (16) for (1) by issuance of (15) additional shares payable 02/27/2013 to holders of record 02/27/2013
Name changed to Cyberfort Software, Inc. 11/16/2016

PATRIOT CAP CORP (BC)
Name changed to Patriot Petroleum Corp. (BC) 03/05/2002
Patriot Petroleum Corp. (BC) reorganized in Canada as as Standard Lithium Ltd. 12/02/2016

PATRIOT CAP FDG INC (DE)
Issue Information - 9,333,334 shares COM offered at $14 per share on 07/27/2006
Merged into Prospect Capital Corp. 12/02/2009
Each share Common 1¢ par exchanged for (0.36399236) share Common $0.001 par

PATRIOT COAL CORP (DE)
Common 1¢ par split (2) for (1) by issuance of (1) additional share payable 08/11/2008 to holders of record 08/04/2008 Ex date - 08/12/2008
Plan of reorganization under Chapter 11 Federal Bankruptcy proceedings effective 12/18/2013
No Common 1¢ par stockholders' equity
Plan of reorganization under Chapter 11 Federal Bankruptcy proceedings effective 10/26/2015
No Common $0.00001 par stockholders' equity

PATRIOT ENERGY CORP (DE)
Old Common $0.001 par split (5) for (1) by issuance of (4) additional shares payable 08/09/2002 to holders of record 08/01/2002 Ex date - 08/12/2002
Each share old Common $0.001 par exchanged for (0.142857142) share new Common $0.001 par 10/23/2002
Name changed to BigBrews Holdings Inc. (DE) 02/18/2003
BigBrews Holdings Inc. (DE) reincorporated in Nevada as Patriot Energy Corp. 09/09/2003 which name changed to Healing Hand Network International, Inc. 12/22/2003 which name changed to Patriot Energy Corp. (NV) 10/10/2005
(See Patriot Energy Corp.)

PATRIOT ENERGY CORP (NV)
Charter revoked 07/31/2014

PATRIOT ENERGY CORP (NV)
Name changed to Healing Hand Network International, Inc. 12/22/2003
Healing Hand Network International, Inc. name changed to Patriot Energy Corp. (NV) 10/10/2005

PATRIOT ENERGY LTD (AB)
Merged into Giant Pacific Petroleum Inc. 05/03/1991
Each share Common no par exchanged for (0.5) share Common no par and (0.5) Common Stock Purchase Warrant expiring 07/08/1992
Giant Pacific Petroleum Inc.
recapitalized as Red Rock Mining Corp. 12/05/1991 which name changed to American Pacific Minerals Ltd. 05/30/1994
(See American Pacific Minerals Ltd.)

PATRIOT EQUITIES CORP (AB)
Recapitalized 8/17/98
Recapitalized 7/30/99
Recapitalized from Patriot Equities Group Inc. to Patriot Equities Group Ltd. 8/17/98
Each share Common no par exchanged for (0.5) share Common no par
Recapitalized from Patriot Equities Group Ltd. to Patriot Equities Corp. 7/30/99
Each share Common no par exchanged for (0.1) share Common no par
Merged into FSI Acquisition 8/13/2002
Each share Common no par exchanged for $4.2375 cash

PATRIOT FED BK (CANAJOHARIE, NY)
Merged into Kinderhook Bank Corp. 11/10/2017
Each share Common $1 par exchanged for (0.3) share Common $0.83 par

PATRIOT FINL CORP (CO)
Reorganized under the laws of Delaware as Patriot Scientific Corp. 05/19/1992
Each share Common $0.00001 par exchanged for (1/3) share Common $0.00001 par

PATRIOT FUTURES FD L P (TN)
Certificate of cancellation filed 03/20/2007
Details not available

PATRIOT GEN LIFE INS CO (MA)
Acquired by North Bridge Corp. 12/27/74
Each share Common no par exchanged for $5.50 cash

PATRIOT GLOBAL DIVID FD (MA)
Name changed to Hancock (John) Patriot Global Dividend Fund 01/01/1995
Hancock (John) Patriot Global Dividend Fund merged into Hancock (John) Patriot Premium Dividend Fund II 06/04/2007 which name changed to Hancock (John) Premium Dividend Fund 10/18/2010

PATRIOT GROUP INVT TR (MA)
Trust terminated 10/31/1990
Details not available

PATRIOT INVT CORP (NV)
Name changed to China Forestry Inc. 01/17/2008
China Forestry Inc. name changed to China Senior Living Industry International Holding Corp. 09/28/2015

PATRIOT MECHANICAL HANDLING INC (DE)
Name changed to Kensington Industries, Inc. 08/01/2007

PATRIOT MINEFINDERS INC (NV)
Recapitalized as Rise Resources Inc. 02/09/2015
Each share Common $0.001 par exchanged for (0.0125) share Common $0.001 par
Rise Resources Inc. name changed to Rise Gold Corp. 04/07/2017

PATRIOT MOTORCYCLE CORP (NV)
Charter permanently revoked 08/31/2007

PATRIOT NATL BK (STAMFORD, CT)
Under plan of reorganization each share Common $2 par automatically became (1) share Patriot National Bancorp Inc. 12/1/99

PATRIOT NATL INC (DE)
Plan of reorganization under Chapter

PAT-PAU

PATRIOT (cont.)
11 Federal Bankruptcy proceedings effective 07/02/2018
No stockholders' equity

PATRIOT PETE CORP (BC)
Reorganized under the laws of Canada as Standard Lithium Ltd. 12/02/2016
Each share Common no par exchanged for (0.2) share Common no par

PATRIOT PFD DIVID FD (MA)
Name changed to Hancock (John) Patriot Preferred Dividend Fund 01/01/1995
Hancock (John) Patriot Preferred Dividend Fund merged into Hancock (John) Patriot Premium Dividend Fund II 05/29/2007 which name changed to Hancock (John) Premium Dividend Fund 10/18/2010

PATRIOT PREM DIVID FD I (MA)
Reorganized 10/01/1990
Reorganized from Patriot Premium Dividend Fund, Inc. (MD) to Patriot Premium Dividend Fund I (MA) 10/01/1990
Name changed to Hancock (John) Patriot Premium Dividend Fund I 01/01/1995
Hancock (John) Patriot Premium Dividend Fund I merged into Hancock (John) Patriot Premium Dividend Fund II 06/25/2007 which name changed to Hancock (John) Premium Dividend Fund 10/18/2010

PATRIOT PREM DIVID FD II (MA)
Name changed to Hancock (John) Patriot Premium Dividend Fund II 01/01/1995
Hancock (John) Patriot Premium Dividend Fund II name changed to Hancock (John) Premium Dividend Fund 10/18/2010

PATRIOT SELECT DIVID TR (MA)
Name changed to Hancock (John) Patriot Select Dividend Trust 01/01/1995
Hancock (John) Patriot Select Dividend Trust merged into Hancock (John) Patriot Premium Dividend Fund II 10/10/2007 which name changed to Hancock (John) Premium Dividend Fund 10/18/2010

PATRIOT ST BK (FUQUAY-VARINA, NC)
Acquired by CapStone Bank (Raleigh, NC) 01/31/2013
Each share Common $5 par exchanged for (0.3168) share Common $5 par and $3.8958 cash
CapStone Bank (Raleigh, NC) merged into NewBridge Bancorp 04/01/2014 which merged into Yadkin Financial Corp. 03/01/2016 which merged into F.N.B. Corp. 03/11/2017

PATRIOT TRANSN HLDG INC (FL)
Common 10¢ par split (3) for (1) by issuance of (2) additional shares payable 01/17/2011 to holders of record 01/03/2011 Ex date - 01/18/2011
Name changed to FRP Holdings, Inc. 12/05/2014

PATRIOTS VENTURE GROUP LTD (BC)
Recapitalized as Tearlach Resources Ltd. 5/22/97
Each share Common no par exchanged for (0.2) share Common no par

PATRON HLDGS INC (DE)
Name changed to Patron Systems Inc. 03/28/2003
(See Patron Systems Inc.)

PATRON SYS INC (DE)
Each share old Common 1¢ par exchanged for (0.03333333) share new Common 1¢ par 08/04/2006
Chapter 11 bankruptcy petition dismissed 05/20/2008
No stockholders' equity

PATRONE CAP CORP (NV)
Recapitalized as Global Capital Group 8/26/86
Each share Common $0.001 par exchanged for (0.05) share Common 2¢ par

PATRONE GOLD CORP (BC)
Each share old Common no par exchanged for (0.25) share new Common no par 09/06/2013
Name changed to Aurgent Gold Corp. 10/03/2013
Aurgent Gold Corp. name changed to Aurgent Resource Corp. 03/10/2014 which name changed to First Cobalt Corp. (BC) 09/23/2016 which reincorporated in Canada 09/04/2018

PATSEEK CAP INC (CANADA)
Name changed to Aastra Technologies Inc. 07/05/1996
Aastra Technologies Inc. recapitalized as Aastra Technologies Ltd. 05/01/1997 which merged into Mitel Networks Corp. 02/04/2014

PATSHARE CAP INC (CANADA)
Name changed to Everyware Development Canada Corp. 04/26/1996
Everyware Development Canada Corp. merged into EveryWare Development Canada Inc. 06/30/1997
(See EveryWare Development Canada Inc.)

PATTEN-BLINN LUMBER CO.
Dissolved 5/17/57

PATTEN CORP (MA)
Common 1¢ par split (2) for (1) by issuance of (1) additional share 09/12/1986
Common 1¢ par split (3) for (2) by issuance of (0.5) additional share 07/22/1987
Stock Dividend - 5% payable 03/28/1996 to holders of record 03/07/1996
Name changed to Bluegreen Corp. 03/08/1996
(See Bluegreen Corp.)

PATTERN PROCESSING TECHNOLOGIES INC (MN)
Name changed 02/29/1984
Name changed from Pattern Processing Corp. to Pattern Processing Technologies, Inc. 02/29/1984
Each share Common no par exchanged for (0.05) share Common 10¢ par 06/30/1989
Stock Dividend - 50% 07/22/1985
Name changed to PPT Vision, Inc. 03/08/1995
(See PPT Vision, Inc.)

PATTERSON (JOSEPH M.) & CO., INC. (DE)
Liquidated in 1954

PATTERSON BROOKE RES INC (NV)
Common $0.001 par split (25) for (1) by issuance of (24) additional shares payable 02/15/2008 to holders of record 02/15/2008 Ex date - 02/19/2008
Name changed to Cleantech Transit, Inc. 04/07/2010
Cleantech Transit, Inc. name changed to EQCO2, Inc. 07/30/2013
(See EQCO, Inc.)

PATTERSON C J CO (DE)
Reincorporated 10/1/69
Common $1 par split (5) for (2) by issuance of (1.5) additional shares 11/22/68
Stock Dividend - 25% 11/17/67
State of incorporation changed from (MO) to (DE) and Preferred $10 par reclassified as Preferred Ser. A $10 par and each share Common $1 par exchanged for (1.25) shares Common $1 par 10/1/69
Merged into CSM America, Inc. 3/10/88
Each share Preferred Ser. A $10 par exchanged for $10.555 cash
Each share Common $1 par exchanged for $36.408 cash
Each share Common $1 par received initial escrow payment of $0.289962 cash 1/18/89
Each share Common $1 par received second escrow payment of $0.696488 cash 12/22/89
Each share Common $1 par received third escrow payment of $0.665524 cash 1/19/90
Each share Common $1 par received fourth escrow payment of $5.234948 cash 3/12/90
Each share Common $1 par received fifth escrow payment of $0.396134 cash 1/18/91
Each share Common $1 par received sixth and final escrow payment of $2.180977 cash 11/15/91

PATTERSON DENTAL CO (MN)
Common 1¢ par split (3) for (2) by issuance of (0.5) additional share 06/17/1994
Common 1¢ par split (3) for (2) by issuance of (0.5) additional share payable 02/17/1998 to holders of record 01/30/1998
Common 1¢ par split (2) for (1) by issuance of (1) additional share payable 07/14/2000 to holders of record 06/30/2000
Name changed to Patterson Companies, Inc. 07/01/2004

PATTERSON (M.F.) DENTAL SUPPLY CO. OF DELAWARE (DE)
Merged into Ritter Corp. 4/27/65
Each share Common no par exchanged for (0.5851) share Common $2.50 par
Ritter Corp. merged into Ritter Pfaudler Corp. 11/1/65 which merged into Sybron Corp. 10/7/68
(See Sybron Corp.)

PATTERSON ENERGY INC (DE)
Common 1¢ par split (2) for (1) by issuance of (1) additional share payable 7/25/97 to holders of record 7/11/97
Common 1¢ par split (2) for (1) by issuance of (1) additional share payable 1/23/98 to holders of record 1/9/98
Under plan of merger name changed to Patterson-UTI Energy, Inc. 5/9/2001

PATTERSON GROUP INC (NV)
Name changed to American Pacific Financial Services Inc. 06/08/1998
American Pacific Financial Services Inc. recapitalized as FilmWorld, Inc. 07/19/1999 which name changed to SulphCo, Inc. 04/11/2001
(See SulphCo, Inc.)

PATTERSON SMITH INC (NJ)
Name changed to International Computer Sciences, Inc. 03/10/1969
(See International Computer Sciences, Inc.)

PATTON ENGINEERING CORP. (NH)
Dissolved by State of New Hampshire for non-compliance of corporation laws 7/2/63

PATTON OIL CO (CO)
Merged into Great Eastern Energy & Development Corp. 6/25/85
Each share Common 10¢ par exchanged for (0.45) share Common 10¢ par
(See Great Eastern Energy & Development Corp.)

PAUDAN INC (NY)
Name changed to American HealthChoice, Inc. 03/31/1995
(See American HealthChoice, Inc.)

PAUDASH LAKE URANIUM MINES LTD. (ON)
Name changed to Paudash Mines Ltd. 05/04/1959
(See Paudash Mines Ltd.)

PAUDASH MINES LTD (ON)
Charter cancelled for failure to pay taxes and file returns 03/16/1976

PAUL ENTMT INC (UT)
Proclaimed dissolved for failure to file reports and pay fees 2/1/92

PAUL HARDEMAN, INC. (DE)
See - Hardeman (Paul), Inc.

PAUL HARDEMAN, INC. (MI)
See - Hardeman (Paul), Inc.

PAUL HARRIS STORES INC (IN)
Class A Common no par and Class B Common no par reclassified as Common no par 07/01/1965
Common no par split (4) for (3) by issuance of (1/3) additional share 07/15/1983
Common no par split (3) for (2) by issuance of (0.5) additional share 07/29/1987
Plan of reorganization under Chapter 11 Federal Bankruptcy Code effective 09/15/1992
Each share Conv. Class B Common no par exchanged for (0.19284) share new Common no par
Each share old Common no par exchanged for (0.19284) share new Common no par
Stock Dividends - 50% 05/02/1966; 20% 10/01/1971; 100% 10/09/1975; 50% 04/03/1978; In Conv. Class B to holders of Common - 100% 06/20/1985
Chapter 11 bankruptcy proceedings dismissed 12/31/2007
No stockholders' equity

PAUL REVERE CORP (MA)
Merged into Provident Companies, Inc. 3/27/97
Each share Common $1 par exchanged for either (0.767) share Common $1 par, (0.177) share Common $1 par and $20 cash, or $26 cash
Note: Non-electing holders received cash only
Provident Companies, Inc. merged into UNUMProvident Corp. 6/30/99

PAUL REVERE INVESTORS INC. (MA)
See - Revere (Paul) Investors Inc.

PAUL SAMUEL ASSOC INC (NJ)
Name changed to Agritech & Energy Corp. 8/11/81
Agritech & Energy Corp. merged into Grayhound Electronics, Inc. 8/3/87
(See Grayhound Electronics, Inc.)

PAUL SVC STORES LTD (QC)
Recapitalized as Cantol Diversified Ltd. 03/10/1969
Each share Common no par exchanged for (5) shares Common 20¢ par
Cantol Diversified Ltd. name changed to Cantol Ltd.-Cantol Ltee. 10/15/1971
(See Cantol Ltd.-Cantol Ltee.)

PAUL-SON GAMING CORP (NV)
Issue Information - 1,200,000 shares COM offered at $11.25 per share on 03/29/1994
Name changed to Gaming Partners International Corp. 9/1/2004

PAUL Y - ITC CONSTR HLDGS LTD (BERMUDA)
Name changed to PYI Corp. Ltd. 01/10/2006
(See PYI Corp. Ltd.)

PAULA FINL (DE)
Liquidation completed
Each share Common 1¢ par received

initial distribution of $3.89 cash payable 03/19/2008 to holders of record 03/06/2008 Ex date - 03/20/2008
Each share Common 1¢ par received second distribution of $1.52 cash payable 09/15/2008 to holders of record 09/03/2008 Ex date - 09/16/2008
Each share Common 1¢ par received third distribution of $0.09 cash payable 12/15/2008 to holders of record 12/01/2008 Ex date - 11/26/2008
Each share Common 1¢ par received fourth distribution of $0.53 cash payable 11/24/2010 to holders of record 11/10/2010 Ex date - 11/26/2010
Each share Common 1¢ par exchanged for fifth and final distribution of $0.13 cash 06/30/2014

PAULEY PETE INC (DE)
Name changed to Hondo Oil & Gas Co. 1/18/90
(See Hondo Oil & Gas Co.)

PAULIN H & CO LTD (ON)
Common no par reclassified as Conv. Class A Common no par 12/03/1974
Conv. Class B no par reclassified as Conv. Class A no par 06/30/1998
Conv. Class A no par split (3) for (1) by issuance of (2) additional shares payable 06/22/2007 to holders of record 06/19/2007 Ex date - 06/15/2007
Acquired by Hillman Companies, Inc. 02/19/2013
Each share Conv. Class A no par exchanged for $27.60 cash
Note: Unexchanged certificates will be cancelled and become without value 02/19/2019

PAULORE GOLD MINES LTD. (ON)
Charter cancelled in August 1956

PAULPIC GOLD MINES LTD (ON)
Charter cancelled for failure to pay taxes and file returns 03/16/1976

PAULS PLACE INC (CO)
Involuntarily dissolved 09/03/2009

PAULSBORO CHEM INDS INC (NJ)
Merged into Essex Chemical Corp. 04/17/1970
Each share 6% Preferred Class A $5 par or 6% Preferred Class B $5 par exchanged for (0.16666666) share Conv. Preferred Ser. A no par
Each share Common $1 par exchanged for (0.11111111) share Common $1 par and (0.11111111) Common Stock Purchase Warrant
(See Essex Chemical Corp.)

PAULSBORO MANUFACTURING CO. (NJ)
Common no par changed to 1¢ par 00/00/1946
Merged into Sandura Co. 12/31/1956
Each share 6% Preferred $100 par exchanged for (15) shares 60¢ Conv. Preferred $7.50 par
Each share 4% Preference $10 par exchanged for (1.5) shares 60¢ Conv. Preferred $7.50 par
Each share Common 1¢ par exchanged for (0.66666666) share Common 5¢ par
Sandura Co. name changed to Del Penn Co. 04/26/1965
(See Del Penn Co.)

PAULSON CAP DEL CORP (DE)
Reincorporated 03/24/2014
Name and place of incorporation changed from Paulson Capital Corp. (OR) to Paulson Capital (Delaware) Corp. (DE) and Common no par changed to $0.0001 par 03/24/2014
Recapitalized as VBI Vaccines Inc. (DE) 07/29/2014
Each share Common $0.0001 par exchanged for (0.2) share Common $0.0001 par
VBI Vaccines Inc. (DE) merged into VBI Vaccines Inc. (BC) 05/09/2016

PAULSON MACHINE CO. LTD. (QC)
Completely liquidated 8/16/66
Each share Common $1 par exchanged for first and final distribution of (0.142857) share Sesame Machine & Tapes Ltd. Capital Stock no par
Sesame Machine & Tapes Ltd. dissolved 10/27/70

PAULSON MINES LTD (BC)
Recapitalized as Samson Energy Corp. 12/31/79
Each share Common no par exchanged for (0.2) share Common no par
Samson Energy Corp. merged into Kala Exploration Ltd. 9/10/82 which recapitalized as Kala Feedlots Ltd. 1/6/87 which name changed to Kala Canada Ltd. 3/27/89
(See Kala Canada Ltd.)

PAVELLE CORP (NY)
Adjudicated bankrupt 04/14/1975
Stockholders' equity unlikely

PAVETECH CORP (NV)
Recapitalized as Envirotire Inc. 03/28/1992
Each share new Common $0.001 par exchanged for (0.1) share Common $0.001 par
(See Envirotire Inc.)

PAVICHEVICH BREWING CO (IL)
SEC revoked common stock registration 10/20/2008

PAVILION BANCORP INC (MI)
Merged into First Defiance Financial Corp. 03/17/2008
Each share Common no par exchanged for (1.4209) shares Common 1¢ par and $37.50 cash

PAVILION ENERGY RES (DE)
Recapitalized as Matchtrade, Inc. 05/02/2012
Each share Common 1¢ par exchanged for (0.002) share Common 1¢ par
(See Matchtrade, Inc.)

PAVILION FOODS, LTD. (VA)
Name changed to Al-Fassi/Ali Consortium, Inc. 7/22/82
Al-Fassi/Ali Consortium, Inc. recapitalized as Consolidated American Industries, Inc. (VA) 10/5/83
(See Consolidated American Industries, Inc. (VA))

PAVING STONE CORP (NV)
SEC revoked common stock registration 10/04/2006

PAVONIA BUILDING CORP.
Dissolved in 1948

PAW INDS LTD (AB)
Recapitalized as Northside Group Inc. 8/24/95
Each share Common no par exchanged for (0.2) share Common no par
Northside Group Inc. name changed to Wittke Inc. 1/23/2002 which merged into Federal Signal Corp. 10/3/2002

PAW SPA INC (NV)
Common $0.00001 par split (20) for (1) by issuance of (19) additional shares payable 05/11/2009 to holders of record 05/08/2009 Ex date - 05/12/2009
Name changed to Iconic Brands, Inc. 05/26/2009

PAWFECT FOODS INC (FL)
Reorganized as Synergy Pharmaceuticals, Inc. (FL) 08/11/2008
Each share Common $0.00001 par exchanged for (75.69060773) shares Common $0.0001 par
Synergy Pharmaceuticals, Inc. (FL) reincorporated in Delaware 02/16/2012

PAW4MANCE PET PRODS INTL INC (NV)
Recapitalized as Fearless Films, Inc. 11/19/2014
Each share Common $0.001 par exchanged for (0.001) share Common $0.001 par

PAWLING SVGS BK (PAWLING, NY)
Reorganized as Progressive Bank, Inc. 10/17/86
Each share Common $1 par exchanged for (2) shares Common $1 par
Progressive Bank, Inc. merged into Premier National Bancorp, Inc. 7/17/98 which merged into M&T Bank Corp. 2/9/2001

PAWNBROKER COM INC (DE)
Each share old Common 1¢ par exchanged for (0.1) share new Common 1¢ par 08/01/2001
Recapitalized as Orinoco Resources, Inc. 08/05/2005
Each share new Common 1¢ par exchanged for (0.001) share Common $0.0001 par
Orinoco Resources, Inc. recapitalized as El Alacran Gold Mine Corp. 05/23/2006

PAWNBROKERS EXCHANGE INC (UT)
Each share old Common no par exchanged for (8) shares new Common no par 03/25/2002
Reincorporated under the laws of Nevada as Defense Industries International Inc. 07/08/2002
(See Defense Industries International Inc.)

PAWNEE CORP (MN)
Common $1 par changed to 50¢ par and (1) additional share issued 09/20/1968
Name changed to Sunstar Foods, Inc. 09/14/1973
Sunstar Foods, Inc. name changed to SUNF, Inc. 12/19/1989
(See SUNF, Inc)

PAWNEE INDS INC (DE)
Acquired by Pawnee Acquisition, Inc. 12/24/1986
Each share Common 1¢ par exchanged for $10 cash

PAWNEE KIRKLAND GOLD MINES LTD. (ON)
Charter cancelled for failure to file reports and pay taxes 6/25/62

PAWNEE OIL & GAS CO. (DE)
Acquired by Jupiter Oils Ltd. 1/30/56
Each share Common $1 par exchanged for (0.49) share Capital Stock 15¢ par
Jupiter Oils Ltd. reorganized as Jupiter Corp. 12/4/61 which merged into Jupiter Industries, Inc. 11/12/71
(See Jupiter Industries, Inc.)

PAWNEE OIL CORP (BC)
Recapitalized as Canadian Pawnee Oil Corp. 05/30/1983
Each share Common no par exchanged for (0.2) share Common no par
Canadian Pawnee Oil Corp. recapitalized as Britannia Gold Corp. 11/07/1989 which recapitalized as Britannia Minerals Corp. 06/14/1999 which name changed to Nanotek Inc. 08/07/2001 which name changed to Minterra Resource Corp. 10/25/2002
(See Minterra Resource Corp.)

PAWNMART INC (DE)
Each share old Common 1¢ par exchanged for (0.33333333) share new Common 1¢ par 10/30/2000
Plan of reorganization under Chapter 11 Federal Bankruptcy proceedings effective 05/31/2002
No Common stockholders' equity
Note: New Common issued to allowed unsecured claimants
Name changed to Xponential, Inc. 02/28/2003

PAWS PET CO INC (IL)
Name changed to Praxsyn Corp. (IL) 09/05/2014
Praxsyn Corp. (IL) reincorporated in Nevada 01/28/2015

PAWSPLUS INC (DE)
Completely dissolved 11/30/2011
No stockholders' equity

PAWTUCKET GAS CO. OF N.J.
Dissolved in 1935

PAX ATHABASCA URANIUM MINES LTD. (ON)
Merged into Pax International Mines Ltd. on a share for share basis 1/31/62
Pax International Mines Ltd. recapitalized as Geo-Pax Mines Ltd. in September 1968
(See Geo-Pax Mines Ltd.)

PAX BIOFUELS INC (DE)
Common $0.001 par split (20) for (1) by issuance of (19) additional shares payable 10/15/2008 to holders of record 09/29/2008 Ex date - 10/16/2008
Name changed to Pax Clean Energy, Inc. 10/16/2008

PAX INTL MINES LTD (ON)
Recapitalized as Geo-Pax Mines Ltd. 09/00/1968
Each share Capital Stock $1 par exchanged for (0.25) share Common $1 par
(See Geo-Pax Mines Ltd.)

PAX PETE LTD (BC)
Assets sold for the benefit of creditors in May 1993
No stockholders' equity

PAX WORLD BALANCED FD INC (DE)
Name changed 08/07/2000
Name changed from Pax World Fund, Inc. to Pax World Balanced Fund, Inc. 08/07/2000
Under plan of reorganization each share Common $1 par automatically became (1) share Pax World Funds Series Trust I Balanced Fund Individual Investors Class no par 10/26/2006

PAX WORLD FDS TR II (MA)
ESG Shares Europe Asia Pacific Sustainability Index ETF reclassified as MSCI EAFE ESG Index ETF 09/01/2010
ESG Shares North America Sustainability Index ETF reclassified as Pax MSCI North America ESG Index ETF 09/01/2010
Trust terminated 03/22/2013
Each share MSCI North America ESG Index ETF received $33.011401 cash
Merged into Pax World Funds Series Trust I 03/31/2014
Each share MSCI EAFE ESG Index ETF no par exchanged for (3.31029957) shares MSCI International ESG Index Fund Institutional Class no par

PAX WORLD GROWTH FD INC (DE)
Under plan of reorganization each Share of Bene. Int. $1 par automatically became (1) share Pax World Funds Series Trust I Growth Fund Individual Investors Class no par 10/26/2006

PAX WORLD HIGH YIELD FD INC (DE)
Under plan of reorganization each share Common $1 par automatically

became (1) share Pax World Funds Series Trust I High Yield Bond Fund Individual Investors Class no par 10/26/2006

PAXALL INC (DE)
Name changed 4/4/83
Name changed from Paxall, Inc. to Paxall Group, Inc. 4/4/83
4% Preferred 1947 Ser. $100 par called for redemption 4/8/85
Acquired by Sasib S.p.A. 9/15/86
Details not available

PAXAR CORP (NY)
Name changed 05/01/1998
Common 10¢ par split (5) for (4) by issuance of (0.25) additional share 09/10/1987
Common 10¢ par split (5) for (4) by issuance of (0.25) additional share 09/15/1989
Common 10¢ par split (5) for (4) by issuance of (0.25) additional share 04/11/1991
Common 10¢ par split (5) for (4) by issuance of (0.25) additional share 09/14/1992
Common 10¢ par split (5) for (4) by issuance of (0.25) additional share 01/20/1993
Common 10¢ par split (5) for (4) by issuance of (0.25) additional share 09/14/1993
Common 10¢ par split (5) for (4) by issuance of (0.25) additional share 09/09/1994
Common 10¢ par split (5) for (4) by issuance of (0.25) additional share 09/11/1995
Common 10¢ par split (5) for (4) by issuance of (0.25) additional share payable 09/09/1996 to holders of record 08/21/1996 Ex date - 09/10/1996
Common 10¢ par split (5) for (4) by issuance of (0.25) additional share payable 09/09/1997 to holders of record 08/21/1997 Ex date - 09/09/1997
Stock Dividends - 10% 09/15/1988; 10% 09/14/1990
Name changed from PAXAR Corp. to Paxar Corp. 05/01/1998
Merged into Avery Dennison Corp. 06/15/2007
Each share Common 10¢ par exchanged for $30.50 cash

PAXCO INC (DE)
Charter cancelled and declared inoperative and void for non-payment of taxes 3/1/74

PAXSON COMMUNICATIONS CORP (DE)
Common $0.001 par split (3) for (2) by issuance of (0.5) additional share 01/23/1995
12.5% Exchangeable Preferred $0.001 par called for redemption on 01/14/2002
Stock Dividends - in 9.75% Conv. Preferred Ser. A 144A to holders of 9.75% Preferred Ser. A 144A 2.4375% payable 09/30/1999 to holders of record 09/15/1999; 09/30/2000 to holders of record 09/15/2000; 03/31/2001 to holders of record 03/15/2001; 06/30/2001 to holders of record 06/15/2001; 09/30/2001 to holders of record 09/15/2001; 12/31/2001 to holders of record 12/15/2001; 06/30/2002 to holders of record 06/15/2002 Ex date - 06/12/2002; 09/30/2002 to holders of record 09/15/2002 Ex date - 09/30/2002; 12/30/2002 to holders of record 12/15/2002; 03/31/2003 to holders of record 03/15/2003; 06/30/2003 to holders of record 06/15/2003 Ex date - 06/25/2003; 12/30/2003 to holders of record 12/15/2003; 03/31/2004 to holders of record 3/15/2004; 06/30/2004 to holders of record 06/15/2004; 03/31/2005 holders of record 03/15/2005; 06/30/2005 to holders of record 06/15/2005; 09/30/2005 to holders of record 09/15/2005; 12/31/2005 to holders of record 12/15/2005; 03/31/2006 to holders of record 03/15/2006
In 12.50% Exchangeable Preferred to holders in kind 6.25% payable 10/31/1999 to holders of record 10/15/1999; 10/30/2000 to holders of record 10/15/2000; 10/30/2001 to holders of record 10/15/2001 Ex date - 10/31/2001
In 13.25% Jr. Exchangeable Preferred to holders of 13.25% Jr. Exchangeable Preferred 6.625% payable 11/15/1999 to holders of record 11/01/1999; 05/15/2000 to holders of record 05/01/2000; 05/15/2001 to holders of record 05/01/2001; 11/15/2001 to holders of record 11/01/2001; 05/15/2002 to holders of record 05/01/2002; 11/15/2002 to holders of record 11/01/2002; 12/30/2002 to holders of record 12/15/2002; 05/15/2003 to holders of record 05/01/2003 Ex date - 05/13/2003; 11/15/2003 to holders of record 11/01/2003 Ex date - 11/17/2003; 7.125% payable 05/15/2004 to holders of record 05/01/2004 Ex date - 05/18/2004; 11/15/2004 to holders of record 11/01/2004 Ex date - 11/02/2004; 05/15/2005 to holders of record 05/01/2005 Ex date - 05/10/2005; 11/15/2005 to holders of record 11/01/2005; 05/15/2006 to holders of record 05/01/2006 Ex date - 05/16/2006; In 9.75% Preferred Conv. Ser. A Accd. Invs. to holders in kind 2.4375% payable 06/30/2001 to holders of record 06/15/2001 Ex date - 06/28/2001; 09/30/2001 to holders of record 09/15/2001; 12/31/2001 to holders of record 12/15/2001; 06/30/2002 to holders of record 06/15/2002 Ex date - 06/12/2002; 09/30/2002 to holders of record 09/15/2002 Ex date - 09/30/2002; 12/30/2002 to holders of record 12/15/2002; 03/31/2003 to holders of record 03/15/2003; 06/30/2003 to holders of record 06/15/2003 Ex date - 06/25/2003; 03/31/2004 to holders of record 03/15/2004; 06/30/2004 to holders of record 06/15/2004; 03/31/2005 to holders of record 03/15/2005; 06/30/2005 to holders of record 06/15/2005; 09/30/2005 to holders of record holders of record 09/15/2005; 12/31/2005 to holders of record 12/15/2005; 03/31/2006 to holders of record 03/15/2006
Name changed to ION Media Networks, Inc. 06/30/2006
(See ION Media Networks, Inc.)

PAXTON & GALLAGHER CO. (NE)
Assets sold and name changed to Western Wine & Liquor Co. 11/12/58
(See Western Wine & Liquor Co.)

PAXTON ENERGY INC (NV)
Each share old Common $0.001 par exchanged for (1/3) share new Common $0.001 par 07/15/2010
Each share new Common $0.001 par exchanged again for (0.41548945) share new Common $0.001 par 08/06/2010
Name changed to Worthington Energy, Inc. 02/03/2012

PAXTON FRANK CO (DE)
Class A Common $2.50 par split (4) for (1) by issuance of (3) additional shares 10/04/1983
Class B Common $2.50 par split (4) for (1) by issuance of (3) additional shares 10/04/1983
Merged into a newly formed corporation 02/09/1990
Each share Class A Common $2.50 par exchanged for $20.90 cash
Each share Class B Common $2.50 par exchanged for $20.90 cash

PAXTON INTL RES LTD (AB)
Delisted from Toronto Venture Stock Exchange 06/27/2008

PAXTON (FRANK) LUMBER CO. (DE)
Name changed to Paxton (Frank) Co. 12/20/65
(See Paxton (Frank) Co.)

PAXTON MNG CORP (NV)
Name changed to Universe2U Inc. 05/15/2000
(See Universe2U Inc.)

PAXTON PAC RESOURCE PRODS INC (AB)
Recapitalized as Paxton International Resources, Inc. 11/04/1998
Each share Common no par exchanged for (0.33333333) share Common no par
(See Paxton International Resources, Inc.)

PAY BY THE DAY HLDGS INC (NV)
Reorganized as Oteegee Innovations, Inc. 04/08/2010
Each share Common $0.001 par exchanged for (10) shares Common $0.001 par
Oteegee Innovations, Inc. name changed to Tucana Lithium Corp. 06/01/2011 which recapitalized as Rimrock Gold Corp. 02/08/2013

PAY DIRT INC (NV)
Recapitalized as Affinity International Travel Systems Inc 07/01/1998
Each (1.75) shares Common $0.001 par exchanged for (1) share Common $0.001 par
(See Affinity International Travel Systems Inc.)

PAY FONE SYS INC (CA)
Stock Dividend - 100% 10/15/78
Acquired by Paychex Inc. 6/15/95
Each share Common 10¢ par exchanged for (0.2219) share Common 10¢ par

PAY LESS DRUG STORES (CA)
Merged into Pay Less Drug Stores Northwest, Inc. 7/18/80
Each share Common no par exchanged for $24 cash

PAY LESS DRUG STORES NORTHWEST INC (MD)
Common $1 par split (5) for (4) by issuance of (0.25) additional share 5/17/78
Common $1 par split (2) for (1) by issuance of (1) additional share 7/30/81
Common $1 par split (2) for (1) by issuance of (1) additional share 7/21/83
Stock Dividends - 50% 3/7/72; 25% 8/17/77
Merged into K mart Corp. 3/29/85
Each share Common $1 par exchanged for $27 cash

PAY LINX FINL CORP (AB)
Assets transferred to secured lender 05/08/2009
Stockholders' equity unlikely

PAY MOBILE INC (NV)
Each share old Common $0.0001 par exchanged for (0.5) share new Common $0.0001 par 10/14/2011
Name changed to Dephasium Corp. 04/18/2013
Dephasium Corp. recapitalized as Allied Ventures Holdings Corp. 04/05/2016 which name changed to Longwen Group Corp. 01/26/2017

PAY N PAK STORES INC (WA)
Common 10¢ par split (3) for (2) by issuance of (0.5) additional share 4/28/83
Stock Dividends - 10% 5/7/75; 10% 5/10/76; 50% 7/29/77; 33-1/3% 4/28/78; 20% 4/27/79; 10% 4/29/82
Merged into PNP Prime Corp. 3/22/88
Each share Common 10¢ par exchanged for (1) share 17% Preferred 1¢ par
(See PNP Prime Corp.)

PAY N SAVE CORP (WA)
Common $2.50 par changed to no par and (2) additional shares issued 4/29/68
Common no par split (2) for (1) by issuance of (1) additional share 5/17/72
Common no par split (2) for (1) by issuance of (1) additional share 5/27/83
Merged into NLAC Corp. 6/17/85
Each share Common no par exchanged for $23.50 cash

PAY N SAVE INC (DE)
Name changed to PSS, Inc. 07/25/1990
(See PSS, Inc.)

PAY-O-MATIC CORP (NY)
Common 10¢ par changed to 4¢ par and (1.5) additional shares issued 01/17/1972
Stock Dividends - 10% 01/10/1975; 10% 01/15/1976; 10% 02/28/1977; 10% 02/28/1978; 10% 03/27/1979; 10% 02/19/1980
Merged into FEF cash Inc. 02/11/2008
Each share Common 4¢ par exchanged for $101.98715 cash
Each share Common 4¢ par received initial distribution of $5.32238842 cash from escrow payable 02/19/2010 to holders of record 02/11/2008
Each share Common 4¢ par received second distribution of $14.0470568 cash from escrow payable 10/03/2011 to holders of record 02/11/2008

PAY POP INC (NV)
Each share old Common $0.001 par exchanged for (0.025) share new Common $0.001 par 03/16/1999
Charter permanently revoked 02/01/2005

PAY TELEVISION CORP (DE)
Charter forfeited for failure to maintain a registered agent 2/25/91

PAY'N SAVE DRUGS LTD. (AB)
Merged into Pay'n Save Corp. 1/10/66
Each share Capital Stock $10 par exchanged for (0.28125) share Common $2.50 par or $5.625 cash
(See Pay'n Save Corp.)

PAYBOX CORP (DE)
Each share old Common $0.0001 par exchanged for (0.005) share new Common $0.0001 par 06/08/2017
Note: Holders of (199) or fewer pre-split shares received $0.40 cash per share
Acquired by Output Services Group, Inc. 04/13/2018
Each share new Common $0.0001 par exchanged for $125.99 cash
Note: Holders may receive an additional $25.72 cash per share subject to certain conditions

PAYCO AMERN CORP (DE)
Common 10¢ par split (3) for (1) by issuance of (2) additional shares 4/11/83
Common 10¢ par split (2) for (1) by issuance of (1) additional share 10/31/84
Common 10¢ par split (2) for (1) by issuance of (1) additional share 9/30/85
Common 10¢ par split (2) for (1) by issuance of (1) additional share 7/31/90
Merged into OSI Holdings Corp. 11/6/96

Each share Common 10¢ par exchanged for $14 cash

PAYCO GOLD MINES LTD. (QC)
Acquired by Quesabe Mines Ltd. 00/00/1946
Each share Capital Stock $1 par exchanged for (0.5) share Capital Stock $1 par
Quesabe Mines Ltd. recapitalized as Brunston Mining Co. Ltd. 00/00/1953 which recapitalized as Sunburst Exploration Ltd. 00/00/1956 which recapitalized as Sunburst Resources 1991 Inc. 11/14/1991 which name changed to Sunburst M.C. Ltd. 02/16/1994 which name changed to Channel I Canada Inc. 01/10/1997 which recapitalized as Zaurak Capital Corp. 12/01/1999
(See Zaurak Capital Corp.)

PAYDAY RES INC (BC)
Name changed to Perimeter Ventures Ltd. 10/28/1986
Perimeter Ventures Ltd. recapitalized as Warner Ventures Ltd. 09/15/1993 which recapitalized as Copper Ridge Explorations Inc. 10/06/1998 which name changed to Redtail Metals Corp. 05/31/2011 which merged into Golden Predator Mining Corp. (AB) 04/22/2014 which reincorporated in British Columbia 10/21/2015

PAY88 INC (NV)
SEC revoked common stock registration 06/27/2012

PAYETTE INTL RES LTD (BC)
Recapitalized as Consolidated Payette International Resources Ltd. 10/31/75
Each share Common no par exchanged for (0.2) share Common no par
Consolidated Payette International Resources Ltd. name changed to Celico Resources Ltd. 6/14/76
(See Celico Resources Ltd.)

PAYETTE RIVER MINES LTD. (BC)
Name changed to Payette International Resources Ltd. and Common 50¢ par changed to no par 1/22/75
Payette International Resources Ltd. recapitalized as Consolidated Payette International Resources Ltd. 10/31/75 which name changed to Celico Resources Ltd. 6/14/76
(See Celico Resources Ltd.)

PAYFAIR MINES LTD. (BC)
Merged into Payfair Industries Ltd. 12/3/70
Each share Common no par exchanged for (1) share Common $1 par

PAYFORVIEW MEDIA GROUP HLDGS CORP (NV)
Recapitalized 04/24/2001
Old Common $0.0001 par split (2) for (1) by issuance of (1) additional share payable 01/20/1999 to holders of record 01/15/1999
Each share old Common $0.0001 par exchanged for (1.5) shares new Common $0.0001 par 04/20/1999
Recapitalized from PayForView.com Corp. to PayForView Media Group Holdings Corp. 04/24/2001
Each share Common $0.0001 par exchanged for (0.05) share Common $0.0001 par
Name changed to James Barclay Alan, Inc. 02/21/2002
James Barclay Alan, Inc. recapitalized as Titan Consolidated, Inc. 05/28/2003 which name changed to Titan Oil & Gas, Inc. (Ctfs. dated prior to 12/04/2008) 02/21/2005 which name changed to Green Star Energies, Inc. 12/04/2008 which recapitalized as Rock Ridge Resources, Inc. 12/08/2011

PAYLESS CASHWAYS INC (DE)
Reorganized 12/02/1997
Common $1 par changed to 50¢ par 05/10/1973
Common 50¢ par split (2) for (1) by issuance of (1) additional share 05/25/1983
Stock Dividends - 50% 08/16/1971; 100% 08/01/1977; 100% 09/15/1978
Merged into PCI Acquisition Corp. 10/07/1988
Each share Common 50¢ par exchanged for $27 cash
Reorganized from under the laws of (IA) to (DE) 12/02/1997
Each share old Common 1¢ par exchanged for (0.01) share new Common 1¢ par
Assets sold for the benefit of creditors 09/07/2001
No stockholders' equity

PAYLESS COMMUNICATION HLDGS INC (TX)
Common no par split (30) for (1) by issuance of (29) additional shares payable 05/27/2005 to holders of record 05/20/2005 Ex date - 05/31/2005
Recapitalized as Integrated Telecom, Inc. 11/10/2005
Each share Common no par exchanged for (0.04) share Common no par
Integrated Telecom, Inc. name changed to Payless Telecom Solutions, Inc. 12/01/2005 which name changed to WOW Holdings, Inc. 04/14/2008
(See WOW Holdings, Inc.)

PAYLESS SHOESOURCE INC (DE)
Reincorporated 05/29/1998
State of incorporation changed from (MO) to (DE) 05/29/1998
Common 1¢ par split (3) for (1) by issuance of (2) additional shares payable 03/27/2003 to holders of record 03/13/2003 Ex date - 03/28/2003
Name changed to Collective Brands, Inc. 08/17/2007
(See Collective Brands, Inc.)

PAYLESS TELECOM SOLUTIONS INC (TX)
Each share old Common no par exchanged for (0.1) share new Common no par 09/25/2006
Name changed to WOW Holdings, Inc. 04/14/2008
(See WOW Holdings, Inc.)

PAYLINE SYS INC (OR)
Involuntarily dissolved 07/27/1995

PAYMASTER CONSOLIDATED MINES LTD. (ON)
Recapitalized as Porcupine Paymaster Ltd. 04/10/1964
Each share Capital Stock $1 par exchanged for (0.33333333) share Capital Stock no par
Porcupine Paymaster Ltd. merged into Associated Porcupine Mines Ltd. 11/05/1968 which merged into American Reserve Mining Corp. 02/27/1989 which recapitalized as AMI Resources Inc. 12/21/1994 which name changed to Ashanti Sankofa Inc. 01/19/2017

PAYMASTER COPPER MINING CO. (WY)
Charter revoked for failure to file annual reports and pay fees 7/19/27

PAYMASTER RES INC (BC)
Name changed 08/07/1981
Name changed from Paymaster Mines Inc. to Paymaster Resources Inc. 08/07/1981
Recapitalized as Consolidated Paymaster Resources Ltd. 03/10/1983
Each share Common no par exchanged for (0.25) share Common no par
Consolidated Paymaster Resources Ltd. recapitalized as Albany Resources Inc. 07/05/1988 which recapitalized as International Albany Resources Inc. (BC) 04/07/1995 which reincorporated in Bahamas as Brazilian Goldfields Ltd. 03/21/1997 which recapitalized as Brazilian International Goldfields Ltd. 11/27/1998 which recapitalized as Aguila American Resources Ltd. (Bahamas) 03/08/2002 which reincorporated in British Columbia 01/14/2008 which name changed to Aguila American Gold Ltd. 05/26/2011

PAYMENT SVCS INTERACTIVE GATEWAY CORP (ON)
Reincorporated 08/03/2005
Each share old Common no par exchanged for (0.2) share new Common no par 09/12/2002
Place of incorporation changed from (AB) to (ON) 08/03/2005
Acquired by Home Capital Group Inc. 10/30/2007
Each share Common no par exchanged for $1.60 cash

PAYMENTECH INC (DE)
Merged into First Data Corp. (Old) 07/26/1999
Each share Common 1¢ par exchanged for $25.50 cash

PAYNE FURNACE & SUPPLY CO., INC.
Acquired by Dresser Industries, Inc. (PA) 00/00/1945
Details not available

PAYNE YELLOWKNIFE GOLD MINES, LTD. (ON)
Charter cancelled 1/27/71

PAYORE CONSOLIDATED MINES LTD.
Succeeded by Formaque Gold Mines Ltd. in 1944
Each share Capital Stock $1 par exchanged for (0.2) share Capital Stock $1 par
Formaque Gold Mines Ltd. acquired by New Formaque Mines Ltd. in 1948 which was recapitalized as Sobiga Mines Ltd.- Les Mines Sobiga Ltee. 1/16/74
(See Sobiga Mines Ltd.-Les Mines Sobiga Ltee.)

PAYORE GOLD MINES LTD.
Succeeded by Payore Consolidated Mines Ltd. on a (1) for (3) basis in 1939
Payore Consolidated Mines Ltd. succeeded by Formaque Gold Mines Ltd. in 1944 which was acquired by New Formaque Mines Ltd. in 1948 which recapitalized as Sobiga Mines Ltd.-Les Mines Sobiga Ltee. 1/16/74
(See Sobiga Mines Ltd.-Les Mines Sobiga Ltee.)

PAYOUT PERFORMERS INCOME FD (ON)
Merged into First Asset/BlackRock North American Dividend Achievers Trust 09/28/2007
Each Unit received (0.9051) Unit First Asset/BlackRock North American Dividend Achievers Trust merged into Criterion Global Dividend Fund 12/29/2009 which name changed to First Asset Global Dividend Fund 06/04/2012

PAYPAD INC (NV)
Name changed to 3Pea International, Inc. 10/27/2006

PAYPAL INC (DE)
Merged into eBay Inc. 10/03/2002
Each share Common $0.001 par exchanged for (0.39) share Common $0.001 par

PAYPHONE WIND DOWN CORP. (DE)
SEC revoked common stock registration 12/10/2010

PAYPRO INC (NV)
Common $0.001 par split (50) for (1) by issuance of (49) additional shares payable 07/11/2005 to holders of record 07/01/2005 Ex date - 07/12/2005
Name changed to Panamersa Corp. 02/16/2007
Panamersa Corp. recapitalized as Eagle Worldwide Inc. 01/12/2012

PAYQUEEN NICKLE MINES LTD. (ON)
Charter cancelled in 1968

PAYROCK MINES LTD (ON)
Dissolved 11/22/1972
Details not available

PAYSAVER CATALOG SHOWROOMS INC (DE)
Common 10¢ par changed to 3-1/3¢ par and (2) additional shares issued 12/21/1981
Assets assigned for benefit of creditors 00/00/1989
No stockholders' equity

PAYSTAR CORP (NV)
Name changed 10/04/2001
Name changed from PayStar Communications Corp. to PayStar Corp. 10/04/2001
SEC revoked common stock registration 10/20/2006

PAYTEL INDS LTD (BC)
Name changed to Rodera Diamond Corp. 04/19/1996
Rodera Diamond Corp. merged into Pacific Rodera Ventures Inc. 03/01/1999 which name changed to Pacific Rodera Energy Inc. (BC) 06/22/2004 which reincorporated in Alberta 06/14/2006 which name changed to PRD Energy Inc. 08/12/2010

PAYTON VENTURES INC (BC)
Name changed to Reimer Overhead Doors Ltd. 02/17/1989
Reimer Overhead Doors Ltd. name changed to Reimer Resources Ltd. 03/31/1993 which merged into Kensington Resources Ltd. 11/03/1993 which merged into Shore Gold Inc. 10/28/2005 which name changed to Star Diamond Corp. 02/12/2018

PAYUKA GOLD MINES, LTD. (ON)
Charter cancelled for failure to file reports and pay taxes 5/19/58

PB ACQUISITION CORP (DE)
Reorganized as TTTTickets Holding Corp. 05/19/2000
Each share Common $0.001 par exchanged for (2) shares Common $0.001 par
TTTTickets Holding Corp. name changed to Shelron Group, Inc. 12/04/2002

PB FINL SVCS CORP (GA)
Merged into Alabama National BanCorporation (DE) 10/02/2006
Each share Common $5 par exchanged for (1.054) shares Common $1 par
Alabama National BanCorporation (DE) merged into Royal Bank of Canada (Montreal, QUE) 02/22/2008

PBA INC (DE)
Stock Dividend - 100% 07/09/1981
Name changed to Profit Systems, Inc. 03/05/1984
(See Profit Systems, Inc.)

PBB GLOBAL LOGISTICS INCOME FD (ON)
Acquired by Livingston International Income Fund 01/17/2006
Each Unit automatically became (1) Unit
(See Livingston International Income Fund)

PBB VENTURE CORP (YUKON)
Reincorporated 5/26/97
Place of incorporation changed from (BC) to (Yukon) 5/26/97
Delisted from Canadian Venture Stock Exchange 5/31/2000

PBC INC (WY)
Administratively dissolved 05/28/2007

PBHG INC (UT)
Each share old Common 6¢ par exchanged for (0.04) share new Common 6¢ par 10/07/2004
SEC revoked common stock registration 09/17/2010

PBOC HLDGS INC (DE)
Issue Information - 12,666,667 shares COM offered at $13.75 per share on 05/12/1998
Merged into FBOP Corp. 4/30/2001
Each share Common 1¢ par exchanged for $10 cash

PBS COALS LTD (CANADA)
Acquired by OAO Severstal 11/14/2008
Each share Common no par exchanged for $8.30 cash

PBX RES LTD (BC)
Recapitalized as International PBX Ventures Ltd. 06/08/1995
Each share Common no par exchanged for (0.33333333) share Common no par
International PBX Ventures Ltd. recapitalized as Chilean Metals Inc. 02/28/2014

PC CHIPS CORP (ON)
Ceased operations 07/31/2002

PC DOCS GROUP INTL INC (ON)
Merged into Hummingbird Communications Ltd. 8/6/99
Each share Common no par exchanged for $11 cash

PC DYNAMICS INC (NY)
Charter cancelled and proclaimed dissolved for failure to pay taxes 3/25/92

PC-EPHONE INC (NV)
SEC revoked common stock registration 09/11/2009

PC ETCETERA INC (DE)
Each share old Common 1¢ par exchanged for (0.2) share new Common 1¢ par 04/19/1995
Name changed to Mentortech Inc. 08/04/1997
(See Mentortech Inc.)

PC GOLD INC (ON)
Merged into First Mining Finance Corp. 11/18/2015
Each share Common no par exchanged for (0.2571) share Common no par
Note: Unexchanged certificates will be cancelled and become without value 11/18/2021
First Mining Finance Corp. name changed to First Mining Gold Corp. 01/11/2018

PC GROUP INC (DE)
Company terminated common stock registration and is no longer public as of 04/05/2011

PC HLDGS S A (ARGENTINA)
Name changed to Perez Companc S.A. (New) 08/16/2000
Perez Companc S.A. (New) name changed to Petrobras Energia Participaciones S.A. 07/29/2003 which merged into Petrobras Energia S.A. 09/29/2009 which name changed to Petrobras Argentina S.A. 12/20/2010
(See Petrobras Argentina S.A.)

PC LIQUIDATING CORP. (PA)
Completely liquidated 1/2/79
Each share Common 10¢ par exchanged for first and final distribution of $4.43 cash

PC MALL INC (CA)
Each share Common $0.001 par received distribution of (1.2) shares eCOST.com, Inc. Common no par payable 04/11/2005 to holders of record 03/28/2005
Name changed to PCM, Inc. 01/02/2013

PC MOBILE MEDIA CORP (NV)
Name changed to Ando Holdings Ltd. 09/21/2017

PC SVC SOURCE INC (DE)
Issue Information - 1,100,000 shares COM offered at $9 per share on 03/29/1994
Chapter 11 bankruptcy proceedings converted to Chapter 7 on 03/22/2002
No stockholders' equity

PC UNIVERSE INC (NV)
SEC revoked common stock registration 01/29/2014

PC VENTURES LTD (AB)
Delisted from Alberta Stock Exchange 01/20/1995

PCA INDS INC (NY)
Dissolved by proclamation 12/27/2000

PCA INTL INC NEW (NC)
Plan of reorganization under Chapter 11 Federal Bankruptcy Code effective 07/17/2007
No stockholders' equity

PCA INTL INC OLD (NC)
Common 20¢ par split (3) for (2) by issuance of (0.5) additional share 04/08/1992
Merged into Jupiter Partners II L.P. 08/25/1998
Each share Common 20¢ par exchanged for either (1) share PCA International, Inc. (New) Common 20¢ par or $26.50 cash
Note: Option to retain stock expired 08/14/1998
(See PCA International, Inc. (New))

PCB HLDG CO (IN)
Merged into German Amercan Bancorp 10/1/2005
Each share Common 1¢ par exchanged for (0.7143) share Common $10 par and $9 cash

PCC CAP I (DE)
9.375% Trust Preferred Securities called for redemption at $10 on 9/15/2003

PCC GROUP INC (CA)
Recapitalized as Non-Lethal Weapons, Inc. (CA) 10/17/2005
Each share Common no par exchanged for (0.001) share Common no par
Non-Lethal Weapons, Inc. (CA) reorganized in Nevada as Advanced Growing Systems, Inc. 06/22/2006
(See Advanced Growing Systems, Inc.)

PCD INC (MA)
Plan of reorganization under Chapter 11 Federal Bankruptcy Code effective 6/5/2003
No stockholders' equity

PCE EXPLS LTD (ON)
Capital Stock $1 par changed to no par 01/18/1971
Recapitalized as Pan Central Explorations Ltd. 01/24/1972
Each share Capital Stock no par exchanged for (0.166666) share Capital Stock no par
(See Pan Central Explorations Ltd.)

PC411 INC (DE)
Name changed to CDSI Holdings, Inc. 01/12/1999
CDSI Holdings, Inc. name changed to SG Blocks, Inc. 11/09/2011

PCG MEDIA INC (NV)
Name changed to i2corp.com 02/16/2000

(See i2corp.com)

PCG VENTURES INC (YT)
Merged into International Health Partners Inc. 03/12/2003
Each share Common no par exchanged for (1) share Common no par
International Health Partners Inc. name changed to Patient Home Monitoring Corp. (AB) 06/08/2010 which reincorporated in British Columbia 12/30/2013
(See Patient Home Monitoring Corp.)

PCH POST CAREER HABITATS INC (BC)
Delisted from Vancouver Stock Exchange 5/4/91

PCI LIQUIDATION, INC. (VA)
Liquidation completed
Each share Common 50¢ par exchanged for initial distribution of $15.75 cash 12/30/1972
Each share Common 50¢ par received second distribution of $0.27 cash 12/21/1973
Each share Common 50¢ par received third and final distribution of $0.01 cash 08/30/1974

PCI-1 CAP CORP (ON)
Name changed to Curis Resources Ltd. (ON) 02/02/2011
Curis Resources Ltd. (ON) reincorporated in British Columbia 04/06/2011 which merged into Taseko Mines Ltd. 11/25/2014

PCI SVCS INC (DE)
Merged into Cardinal Health, Inc. 10/11/1996
Each share Common $0.001 par exchanged for (0.336) share Common no par

PCL INDS LTD (ON)
Common no par split (2) for (1) by issuance of (1) additional share 02/23/1979
Class A Preference Ser. 2 no par called redemption 04/01/1986
Delisted from Toronto Stock Exchange 03/05/1993

PCMT CORP (DE)
Common $0.0001 par split (10) for (1) by issuance of (9) additional shares payable 11/26/2007 to holders of record 11/23/2007 Ex date - 11/27/2007
Name changed to Suspect Detection Systems Inc. 03/06/2009

PCNET INTL INC (AB)
Merged into Uniserve Communications Corp. 11/20/2003
Each share Common no par exchanged for (0.7296) share Common no par

POCML 1 INC (ON)
Name changed to Mason Graphite Inc. (ON) 10/30/2012
Mason Graphite Inc. (ON) reincorporated in Canada 03/03/2016

PCORDER COM INC (DE)
Issue Information - 2,200,000 shares CL A offered at $21 per share on 02/25/1999
Merged into Trilogy Software, Inc. 12/21/2000
Each share Common 1¢ par exchanged for $6.375 cash

PCR INTL INC (NY)
Merged into New P.C.R. Inc. 2/10/95
Each share Common $0.001 par exchanged for $0.50 cash

PCS DATA PROCESSING INC (NY)
Merged into PCS Acquisition Corp. 06/08/1990
Each share Common 10¢ par exchanged for $1 cash

PCS ED SYS INC (ID)
Name changed to PCS Edventures!.com, Inc. 03/29/2000

PCS INC (DE)
Acquired by McKesson Corp. 04/16/1990
Each share Common 1¢ par exchanged for $20 cash

PCS RESH TECHNOLOGY INC (DE)
Name changed to Sagient Research Systems, Inc. 05/20/2004
(See Sagient Research Systems, Inc.)

PCS WIRELESS INC (ON)
Name changed to Unique Broadband Systems Inc. 06/01/1998
Unique Broadband Systems Inc. recapitalized as Kure Technologies Inc. 03/20/2017

PCSUPPORT COM INC (NV)
Recapitalized as Nova Energy, Inc. 06/06/2005
Each share Common $0.001 par exchanged for (0.00333333) share Common $0.001 par
Nova Energy, Inc. name changed to Savanna East Africa, Inc. 07/13/2010 which recapitalized as Algae International Group, Inc. (NV) 05/17/2013 which reincorporated in Wyoming as North American Cannabis Holdings, Inc. 06/10/2015

PD&E RESOURCE SVCS CORP (AB)
Recapitalized as Leader Energy Services Ltd. 09/28/2004
Each share Common no par exchanged for (0.25) share Common no par
(See Leader Energy Services Ltd.)

PDA ENGR (CA)
Common no par split (2) for (1) by issuance of (1) additional share 3/1/93
Merged into MacNeal-Schwendler Corp. 8/18/94
Each share Common no par exchanged for $6.85 principal amount of 7.875% Conv. Subordinated Debentures due 2004
Note: Holders not entitled to receive $1,000 or more of debentures in exchange will receive cash

PDC DIAGNOSTICS CORP (BC)
Name changed to PDC Biological Health Group Corp. 01/25/2014

PDC ENERGY INC (NV)
Reincorporated under the laws of Delaware 06/11/2015

PDC&J PRESERVATION FUND (OH)
Name changed to PC&J Preservation Fund 07/03/1992

PDG REMEDIATION INC (PA)
Reincorporated under the laws of Delaware as Ichor Corp. 11/13/96
Ichor Corp. name changed to Mymetics Corp. 7/31/2001

PDI INC (DE)
Name changed to Interpace Diagnostics Group, Inc. 12/23/2015

PDK LABS INC (NY)
Each share 7% Conv. Preferred 1¢ par received distribution of (0.2071) share Common 1¢ par 10/18/94
Each share old Common 1¢ par exchanged for (0.1) share new Common 1¢ par 6/27/95
Merged into PDK Acquisition Corp. 11/8/2000
Each share 7% Conv. Preferred 1¢ par exchanged for $8 cash
Each share Common 1¢ par exchanged for $5 cash

PDM ROYALTIES INCOME FD (ON)
Reorganized under the laws of Canada as Imvescor Restaurant Group Inc. 10/16/2009
Each Unit no par exchanged for (1) share Common no par

Note: Unexchanged certificates were cancelled and became without value 10/16/2015
Imvescor Restaurant Group Inc. merged into MTY Food Group Inc. 03/01/2018

PDS GAMING CORP (MN)
Name changed 05/15/2001
Name changed from PDS Financial Corp. to PDS Gaming Corp. 05/15/2001
Merged into PDS Holding Co., Inc. 10/25/2004
Each share Common 1¢ par exchanged for $1.25 cash
Each share Common 1¢ par received an initial distribution of $0.50 cash from escrow 10/22/2005
Each share Common 1¢ par received second distribution of $0.50 cash 10/24/2006
Each share Common 1¢ par received third and final distribution of $0.50 cash 01/14/2008

PDS LIQUIDATING CORP. (NY)
Liquidation completed
Each share Common 5¢ par exchanged for initial distribution of $0.94 cash 5/10/73
Each share Common 5¢ par received second distribution of $0.25 cash 4/1/74
Each share Common 5¢ par received third and final distribution of $0.0574 cash 12/3/74

PDT INC (DE)
Common 1¢ par split (3) for (2) by issuance of (0.5) additional share 08/07/1995
Name changed to Miravant Medical Technologies 09/12/1997
(See Miravant Medical Technologies)

PDX RES INC (AB)
Each share Common no par received distribution of (1) share Pelangio Exploration Inc. Common no par payable 09/08/2008 to holders of record 09/05/2008 Ex date - 09/03/2008
Merged into Detour Gold Corp. 03/27/2009
Each share Common no par exchanged for (0.2571) share Common no par

PDY COAL CO. (IL)
Liquidation completed
Each share 5% Prior Preferred $25 par exchanged for first and final distribution of $25.2014 cash 3/29/68
Each share Common $5 par stamped to indicate initial distribution of $45.21 cash 3/29/68
Each share Stamped Common $5 par exchanged for second distribution of $2.5535 cash 1/2/69
Each share Stamped Common $5 par received third and final distribution of $0.0369 cash 3/3/71

PE BEN OILFIELD SVCS LTD (AB)
Merged into Mullen Group Income Fund 01/17/2006
Each share Common no par exchanged for $18.50 cash

PE CORP (DE)
PE Biosystems Group Common 1¢ par split (2) for (1) by issuance of (1) additional share payable 07/26/1999 to holders of record 07/12/1999 Ex date - 07/27/1999
PE Biosystems Group Common 1¢ par split (2) for (1) by issuance of (1) additional share payable 02/18/2000 to holders of record 02/04/2000 Ex date - 02/22/2000
PE Celera Genomic Group 1¢ par split (2) for (1) by issuance of (1) additional share payable 02/18/2000 to holders of record 02/04/2000 Ex date - 02/22/2000

Name changed to Applera Corp. 11/30/2000
(See Applera Corp.)

PEABODY CAP PARTNERS CORP (ON)
Common no par split (20) for (1) by issuance of (19) additional shares payable 01/07/2003 to holders of record 01/07/2003
Name changed to Richview Resources Inc. (Old) 05/14/2004
Richview Resources Inc. (Old) reorganized as Richview Resources Inc. (New) 11/24/2004 which merged into Cadillac Ventures Inc. 01/15/2010

PEABODY COAL CO (IL)
Class B no par changed to $5 par 00/00/1936
Class B $5 par reclassified as Common $5 par 00/00/1947
Name changed to PDY Coal Co. 03/29/1968
(See PDY Coal Co.)

PEABODY ENERGY CORP OLD (DE)
Old Common 1¢ par split (2) for (1) by issuance of (1) additional share payable 03/30/2005 to holders of record 03/16/2005 Ex date - 03/31/2005
Old Common 1¢ par split (2) for (1) by issuance of (1) additional share payable 02/22/2006 to holders of record 02/07/2006 Ex date - 02/23/2006
Each share old Common 1¢ par received distribution of (0.1) share Patriot Coal Co. Common 1¢ par payable 10/31/2007 to holders of record 10/22/2007 Ex date - 11/01/2007
Each share old Common 1¢ par exchanged for (0.06666666) share new Common 1¢ par 10/01/2015
Plan of reorganization under Chapter 11 Federal Bankruptcy proceedings effective 04/03/2017
No stockholders' equity

PEABODY GALION CORP. (DE)
Common 10¢ par split (3) for (2) by issuance of (0.5) additional share 03/20/1972
Name changed to Peabody International Corp. 11/19/1976
Peabody International Corp. merged into Pullman-Peabody Co. 10/24/1985 which name changed back to Pullman Co. 02/12/1987
(See Pullman Co.)

PEABODY HOTEL CO. (TN)
Assets sold and each share Common no par had the option of receiving $225 in cash immediately or $300 in cash over a 10-Yr. period in 1954

PEABODY INTL CORP (DE)
Merged into Pullman-Peabody Co. 10/24/1985
Each share Common 10¢ par exchanged for (1.65) shares Common 10¢ par
Pullman-Peabody Co. name changed back to Pullman Co. 02/12/1987
(See Pullman Co.)

PEABODYS COFFEE INC (NV)
SEC revoked common stock registration 07/14/2009

PEACE ARCH ENTMT GROUP INC (ON)
Reincorporated 09/01/2004
Class A Multiple no par reclassified as Common no par 03/16/2004
Class B Subordinate no par reclassified as Common no par 03/16/2004
Place of incorporation changed from (BC) to (ON) 09/01/2004
Filed an assignment in bankruptcy 05/16/2013
Stockholders' equity unlikely

PEACE RIV CAP CORP (BC)
Name changed to Liberty One Lithium Corp. 12/02/2016

PEACE RIVER MNG & SMLT LTD (AB)
Assets sold for benefit of government claims 12/16/1972
No stockholders' equity

PEACE RIVER NATURAL GAS CO. LTD. (BC)
Capital Stock no par changed to $1 par in 1952
Merged into Westcoast Transmission Co. Ltd. on a (1) for (3) basis 9/23/57
Westcoast Transmission Co. Ltd. name changed to Westcoast Energy Inc. 6/1/88

PEACE RIVER PETES LTD (BC)
Recapitalized as PRP Explorations Ltd. 03/30/1973
Each share Capital Stock $1 par exchanged for (0.2) share Capital Stock $1 par
PRP Explorations Ltd. merged into August Petroleums Ltd. 09/24/1973 which recapitalized as Cheyenne Petroleum Corp. 10/13/1976
(See Cheyenne Petroleum Corp.)

PEACH STATE CORP. (GA)
Name changed to First American Corp. and Common 5¢ par reclassified as Class A Common 25¢ par 12/03/1969
(See First American Corp.)

PEACH URANIUM & METALS MINING LTD. (ON)
Each share Capital Stock $1 par exchanged for (5) shares Capital Stock 20¢ par in 1953
Liquidation completed 4/10/59

PEACHES ENTMT CORP (FL)
SEC revoked common stock registration 11/04/2009

PEACHFORD HOSPITAL, INC. (GA)
100% acquired by Charter Medical Corp. through purchase offer which expired 01/21/1974
Public interest eliminated

PEACHLAND COPPER MINES LTD (BC)
Struck off register and declared dissolved for failure to file returns 10/21/1974

PEACHTREE BANCSHARES INC (GA)
Merged into Trust Co. of Georgia 11/19/1983
Each share Common $2.50 par exchanged for (0.8) share Common $5 par
Trust Co. of Georgia merged into SunTrust Banks, Inc. 07/01/1985

PEACHTREE BK & TR CO (CHAMBLEE, GA)
Under plan of reorganization each share Capital Stock $2.50 par automatically became (1) share Peachtree Bancshares, Inc. 12/22/1980
Peachtree Bancshares, Inc. merged into Trust Co. of Georgia 11/19/1983 which merged into SunTrust Banks, Inc. 07/01/1985

PEACHTREE BK (DULUTH, GA)
Under plan of reorganization each share Common $5 par automatically became (1) share PB Financial Services Corp. Common $5 par 07/15/1999
PB Financial Services Corp. merged into Alabama National BanCorporation (DE) 10/02/2006 which merged into Royal Bank of Canada (Montreal, QUE) 02/22/2008

PEACHTREE DOORS INC (GA)
Common $1 par split (3) for (2) by issuance of (0.5) additional share 6/1/72

Stock Dividend - 10% 5/28/75
Merged into Indal Ltd. 3/23/78
Each share Common $1 par exchanged for $22.50 cash

PEACHTREE EQUITIES INC (CO)
Each share old Common $0.0001 par exchanged for (0.0025) share new Common $0.0001 par 11/27/1990
Voluntarily dissolved 05/23/2016
Details not available

PEACHTREE EQUITY SECS INC (GA)
Completely liquidated 05/11/1977
Each share Common $1 par exchanged for (1.54) shares Bullock Fund, Ltd. Capital Stock $1 par
Bullock Fund, Inc. name changed to Bullock Growth Shares, Inc. 04/08/1985 which merged into Chemical Fund, Inc. 03/13/1987 which name changed to Alliance Fund, Inc. 04/01/1987 which name changed to Alliance Mid-Capital Growth Fund Inc. 02/01/2002 which name changed to AllianceBernstein Mid-Capital Growth Fund, Inc. 03/31/2003

PEACHTREE FIBEROPTICS INC (DE)
Each share old Common 1¢ par exchanged for (0.025) share new Common 1¢ par 04/28/1999
Name changed to vFinance.com, Inc. 03/14/2000
vFinance.com, Inc. name changed to vFinance, Inc. 11/28/2001 which merged into National Holdings Corp. 07/01/2008

PEACHTREE NETWORK INC (CANADA)
Company announced decision to file for protection under the Bankruptcy and Insolvency Act 11/15/2001
Stockholders' equity unlikely

PEACOCK FINL CORP (CO)
Each share old Common $0.001 par exchanged for (0.02) share new Common $0.001 par 12/10/1998
Each share new Common $0.001 par received distribution of (0.01) share iNetPartners Inc. Common payable 07/10/2000 to holders of record 06/30/2000
Reorganized under the laws of Nevada as Broadleaf Capital Partners, Inc. 03/22/2002
Each share Common $0.001 par exchanged for (0.01) share Common $0.001 par
Broadleaf Capital Partners, Inc. recapitalized as EnergyTek Corp. 07/23/2014 which recapitalized as TimefireVR Inc. 11/22/2016

PEAK BREWING GROUP INC (AB)
Delisted from Toronto Venture Stock Exchange 06/25/2004

PEAK ENERGY SVCS LTD NEW (AB)
Acquired by Clean Harbors, Inc. 06/14/2011
Each share Common no par exchanged for $0.95 cash

PEAK ENERGY SVCS LTD OLD (AB)
Reorganized as Peak Energy Services Trust 05/01/2004
Each share Common no par exchanged for (1) share Trust Unit no par
Peak Energy Services Trust reorganized as Peak Energy Services Ltd. (New) 01/06/2011
(See Peak Energy Services Ltd. (New))

PEAK ENERGY SVCS TR (AB)
Each Exchangeable Share exchanged for (1.224) Trust Units no par 06/30/2006
Reorganized as Peak Energy Services Ltd. (New) 01/06/2011
Each Trust Unit no par exchanged for (1) share Common no par
Note: Unexchanged certificates were

PEAK ENTMT GROUP LTD (NV)
cancelled and became without value 01/06/2014
(See Peak Energy Services Ltd. (New))

PEAK ENTMT GROUP LTD (NV)
Name changed to PKG Entertainment, Inc. 02/06/2006
(See PKG Entertainment, Inc.)

PEAK ENTMT HLDGS INC (NV)
Name changed to Encore Energy Systems, Inc. 08/20/2007
(See Encore Energy Systems, Inc.)

PEAK GOLD LTD (BC)
Merged into New Gold Inc. 06/30/2008
Each share Common no par exchanged for (0.1) share Common no par and $0.0001 cash
Note: Unexchanged certificates were cancelled and became without value 06/30/2014

PEAK HEALTH CARE INC (CO)
Acquired by United HealthCare Corp. 11/7/86
Each share Common no par exchanged for $6 principal amount of Conv. Sr. Debentures due 11/1/2011 and $10 cash or $16 principal amount of Conv. Sr. Debentures due 11/1/2011
Note: Option to receive debentures only expired 12/8/86

PEAK INDS INC (DE)
Reorganized 10/19/1972
Reorganized from (NY) to under the laws of (DE) 10/19/1972
Each share Common 1¢ par exchanged for (0.1) share Common 1¢ par 10/19/1972
Liquidation completed
Each share Common 1¢ par exchanged for initial distribution of $0.34 cash 07/02/1974
Each share Common 1¢ par received second and final distribution of $0.34 cash 10/30/1974

PEAK INTL LTD (BERMUDA)
Merged into S&G Company, Ltd. 06/03/2008
Each share Common 1¢ par exchanged for $2 cash

PEAK OILS LTD. (ON)
Recapitalized as Consolidated Peak Oils Ltd. on a (1) for (4) basis 00/00/1953
Consolidated Peak Oils Ltd. acquired by Western Allenbee Oil & Gas Co. Ltd. 06/20/1960 which name changed to Convoy Capital Corp. 04/28/1989 which recapitalized as Hariston Corp. 09/25/1992 which recapitalized as Midland Holland Inc. (Canada) 02/10/1999 which reincorporated in Yukon 03/11/1999 which name changed to Mercury Partners & Co. Inc. 02/22/2000 which name changed to Black Mountain Capital Corp. 05/02/2005 which recapitalized as Grand Peak Capital Corp. (YT) 11/20/2007 which reincorporated in British Columbia 04/27/2010

PEAK PERFORMANCE PRODS INC (NV)
Recapitalized as Lumalure Manufacturing, Inc. 05/01/1986
Each share Common $0.001 par exchanged for (0.1) share Common 1¢ par
Lumalure Manufacturing, Inc. recapitalized as Sairam Technologies Ltd. 12/29/1989 which name changed to Balanced Environmental Services Technology Inc. 04/05/1991 which recapitalized as United States Indemity & Casualty, Inc. 07/08/1993

PEAK RES INC (NV)
Common $0.001 par split (10) for (1) by issuance of (9) additional shares payable 03/03/2008 to holders of record 02/28/2008 Ex date - 03/04/2008
Name changed to Mine Clearing Corp. 09/09/2008
Mine Clearing Corp. recapitalized as ClickStream Corp. 06/19/2014

PEAK RES LTD (AUSTRALIA)
ADR agreement terminated 07/06/2012
Each Sponsored ADR for Ordinary exchanged for $0.526156 cash

PEAK TECHNOLOGIES GROUP INC (DE)
Merged into Moore Corp. Ltd. 6/3/97
Each share Common 1¢ par exchanged for $18 cash

PEAK TECHNOLOGIES INC (AB)
Name changed to PeakSoft Corp. and Class A Common no par reclassified as Common no par 11/17/97
PeakSoft Corp. recapitalized as PeakSoft Multinet Corp. 12/15/98

PEAK TRENDS TR (DE)
Each Trust Enhanced Dividend Security exchanged for (1) share Peak International Ltd. Common 1¢ par 5/15/2001

PEAKSOFT CORP (AB)
Recapitalized as Peaksoft Multinet Corp. 12/15/98
Each share Common no par exchanged for (0.125) share Common no par

PEALE, PEACOCK & KERR, INC. (PA)
Liquidated in 1958

PEANUT SHACK AMER INC (NC)
Name changed to Specialty Retail Concepts, Inc. 06/02/1986
(See Specialty Retail Concepts, Inc.)

PEAPACK GLADSTONE BK (GLADSTONE, NJ)
Capital Stock $15 par changed to $7.50 par and (1) additional share issued 07/26/1973
Capital Stock $7.50 par changed to $20 par 04/13/1983
Capital Stock $20 par split (3) for (2) by issuance of (0.5) additional share 11/01/1985
Capital Stock $20 par changed to $6-2/3 par and (2) additional shares issued 10/10/1986
Capital Stock $6-2/3 par changed to $3.33 par and (1) additional share issued 05/22/1995
Stock Dividends - 10% 01/30/1970; 50% 12/06/71; 10% 11/02/1992; 5% payable 11/01/1996 to holders of record 10/01/1996
Reorganized as Peapack-Gladstone Financial Corp. 12/29/1997
Each share Common $3.33 par exchanged for (2) shares Common no par

PEAPOD INC (DE)
Merged into Koninklijke Ahold N.V. 08/31/2001
Each share Common 1¢ par exchanged for $2.15 cash

PEAR TECHNOLOGIES INC (DE)
Recapitalized as Sanswire Technologies Inc. 05/20/2002
Each share Common $0.0001 par exchanged for (0.1) share Common $0.0001 par
Sanswire Technologies Inc. name changed to Wireless Holdings Group, Inc. 03/30/2005 which recapitalized as Vega Promotional Systems, Inc. (DE) 12/26/2006 which reorganized in Wyoming as Vega Biofuels, Inc. 07/29/2010

PEARCE-SIMPSON, INC. (FL)
Acquired by Gladding Corp. 6/11/68
Each share Class A exchanged for (0.2) share Common 50¢ par
Each share Common 50¢ par exchanged for (0.066666) share Common 50¢ par
Gladding Corp. merged into Paris Industries Corp. 7/3/84
(See Paris Industries Corp.)

PEARCE SYS INTL INC (DE)
Chapter 7 bankruptcy proceedings terminated 04/29/1998
Stockholders' equity unlikely

PEARCE-UIBLE CO. (FL)
Name changed to Charter Mortgage & Investment Co. 1/22/62
Charter Mortgage & Investment Co. name changed to Charter Co. 7/1/63 which name changed to Spelling Entertainment Group Inc. (FL) 10/14/92 which reincorporated in Delaware 5/30/95
(See Spelling Entertainment Group Inc.)

PEARCE URSTADT MAYER & GREER INC (DE)
Common $1 par reclassified as Class A Common $1 par 06/30/1982
Merged into Urstadt Property Co. 08/16/1988
Each share Class A Common $1 par exchanged for $12.50 cash

PEARL ASIAN MNG INDS INC (PHILIPPINES)
Reincorporated 04/21/2004
Reorganized 02/14/2005
Place of incorporation changed from (ON) to (OR) 04/21/2004
Each share old Common no par exchanged for (5) shares new Common no par 04/30/2004
Each share new Common no par received distribution of (1) share Western Pacific Minerals Ltd. Common no par payable 10/30/2004 to holders of record 09/30/2004
Reorganized under the laws of Philippines 02/14/2005
Each share Common no par exchanged for (0.04) share Common no par
Reorganized under the laws of Wyoming 01/26/2006
Each share Common no par exchanged for (1,000) shares Common $0.001 par
Pearl Asian Mining Industries, Inc. (WY) reorganized in Delaware as ZNext Mining Corporation, Inc. 12/11/2007
(See ZNext Mining Corporation, Inc.)

PEARL ASIAN MNG INDS INC (WY)
Each share Common $0.001 par received distribution of (1,000) shares Preferred $0.00000001 par payable 03/31/2006 to holders of record 03/17/2006 Ex date - 03/15/2006
Each share Common $0.001 par received distribution of (0.01) share Philippines Royal Oil & Alternative Energy Co., Inc. Common $0.001 par payable 03/31/2007 to holders of record 02/26/2007
Mandatory buy back effective 07/20/2007
Each share Common $0.001 exchanged for $0.00002 cash per share
Note: 95% of total holdings received cash with remaining 5% issued in a new certificate
Unexchanged certificates will be cancelled and replaced with a check for 95% cash value and a certificate for the remaining 5% holding after 10/10/2007
Each share old Preferred $0.00000001 par exchanged for (0.00000014) share new Preferred $0.00000001 par 09/14/2007
Reorganized under the laws of Delaware as ZNext Mining Corporation, Inc. 12/11/2007
Each (75) shares Preferred $0.00000001 par exchanged for (1) share Preferred $0.00000001 par
Each share Common $0.001 par exchanged for (0.002) share Common $0.001 par
(See ZNext Mining Corporation, Inc.)

PEARL BREWING CO (TX)
Merged into Southdown, Inc. 12/30/69
Each share Common $1 par exchanged for (1) share $1.80 Conv. Preferred $10 par
(See Southdown Inc.)

PEARL EXPL & PRODTN LTD (AB)
Name changed to BlackPearl Resources Inc. 05/14/2009

PEARL FINL SVCS INC (WA)
Merged into Pacific MultiMedia, Inc. 00/00/1997
Each share Common no par exchanged for (0.2935133) share Common no par, $1 cash or a combination thereof
(See Pacific MultiMedia, Inc.)

PEARL ORIENTAL HLDGS LTD (HONG KONG)
Name changed 11/15/1999
Name changed from Pearl Oriental Holdings Ltd. to Pearl Oriental Cyberforce Ltd. 11/15/1999
Name changed back to Pearl Oriental Holdings Ltd. 07/06/2001
Name changed to Sun's Group Ltd. 06/18/2002
Sun's Group Ltd. name changed to Loudong General Nice Resources (China) Holdings Ltd. 07/15/2009
(See Loudong General Nice Resources (China) Holdings Ltd.)

PEARLE HEALTH SVCS INC (TX)
Merged into Paragon Investment Corp. 10/18/1985
Each share Common 1¢ par exchanged for $33 cash

PEARLSTAR CORP (NV)
Recapitalized as Guardians of Gold Inc. 04/27/2009
Each share Common $0.001 par exchanged for (0.001) share Common $0.001 par

PEARSALL CHEM CORP (NJ)
Recapitalized 04/25/1973
Recapitalized from Pearsall Corp. to Pearsall Chemical Corp. 04/25/1973
Each share Common 20¢ par exchanged for (0.33333333) share Common 60¢ par
Merged into Witco Chemical Corp. 02/29/1980
Each share Common 60¢ par exchanged for $12.25 cash

PEARSON CORP. (RI)
Merged into Grumman Allied Industries, Inc. 3/29/63
Each share Common 25¢ par exchanged for (0.333333) share Capital Stock $1 par
Grumman Allied Industries, Inc. merged into Grumman Corp. 4/30/74
(See Grumman Corp.)

PEARSON HOTEL INC (IL)
Liquidation completed
Each share Capital Stock $10 par exchanged for initial distribution of $450 cash 09/08/1971
Each share Capital Stock $10 par received second distribution of $135 cash 01/07/1972
Each share Capital Stock $10 par received third and final distribution of $11.88 cash 03/03/1972

PEARSON HOTEL LIQUIDATING TRUST
Trust terminated in 1950
Details not available

PEASE & ELLIMAN RLTY TR (MA)
Name changed to Plaza Realty Investors 06/10/1975
(See Plaza Realty Investors)

PEASE (C.F.) CO. (DE)
Each share Common no par exchanged for (5) shares Common $1 par in 1951
Liquidation completed 9/16/65
Each share Preferred no par exchanged for first and final distribution of $176.67 cash 7/31/61
Each share Common $1 par exchanged for initial distribution of $8 cash 1/11/62

PEASE OIL & GAS CO (NV)
Name changed 07/05/1994
Each share Common 50¢ par exchanged for (0.4) share Common 5¢ par 06/25/1990
Each share Common 5¢ par exchanged for (0.2) share Common 10¢ par 06/24/1993
Name changed from Pease (Willard) Oil & Gas Co. to Pease Oil & Gas Co. 07/05/1994
Each share old Common 10¢ par exchanged for (0.1) share new Common 10¢ par 12/01/1998
Name changed to Republic Resources, Inc. 07/12/2001
(See Republic Resources, Inc.)

PEAT RES LTD (ON)
Name changed to Cobalt Blockchain Inc. 03/23/2018

PEAT SORB INC (AB)
Name changed 10/04/1993
Name changed from Peat "T" Inc. to Peat Sorb Inc. 10/04/1993
Recapitalized as Redeco Energy Inc. 12/23/1997
Each share Common no par exchanged for (1) share Common no par
(See Redeco Energy Inc.)

PEAVEY CO (MN)
Stock Dividend - 50% 12/24/1975
Merged into ConAgra, Inc. 07/20/1982
Each share Common $2.50 par exchanged for (0.172) share $2.50 Conv. Preferred Class D Ser. 1 no par and (1.215) shares Common $5 par
ConAgra, Inc. name changed to ConAgra Foods, Inc. 09/28/2000 which name changed to Conagra Brands, Inc. 11/10/2016

PEBBLE BEACH ACQUISITIONS INC (NV)
Name changed to Grassie Ltd. 02/06/1989
(See Grassie Ltd.)

PEBBLE BEACH CORP (DE)
Merged into Twentieth Century-Fox Film Corp. 05/01/1979
Each share Common $2.50 par exchanged for $42.50 cash

PEBBLE BEACH ENTERPRISES INC (NV)
Name changed to CMG Holdings, Inc. 03/05/2008
CMG Holdings, Inc. name changed to CMG Holdings Group, Inc. 02/22/2013

PEBBLE GOLD RES LTD (BC)
Recapitalized as Drexel Enterprise Corp. 7/19/89
Each share Common no par exchanged for (1/3) share Common no par
Drexel Enterprise Corp. recapitalized as Graffoto Industries Corp. 6/28/93

PEBBLE SPRINGS DISTILLING CO.
Liquidation completed in 1950

PEBBLE URANIUM MINES LTD. (ON)
Charter cancelled for failure to file reports and pay taxes September 1959

PEBBLEBROOK HOTEL TR (MD)
7.875% Preferred Shares of Bene. Int. Ser. A 1¢ par called for redemption at $25 plus $0.30625 accrued dividends on 03/11/2016
8% Preferred Shares of Bene. Int. Ser. B 1¢ par called for redemption at $25 on 09/21/2016
(Additional Information in Active)

PEBERCAN INC (CANADA)
Liquidation completed
Each share Common no par received initial distribution of approximately $1.01 cash payable 03/05/2010 to holders of record 03/02/2010
Each share Common no par received second and final distribution of $0.07257205 cash payable 03/30/2011 to holders of record 03/02/2010
Note: Certificates were not required to be surrendered and are without value

PEC ELECTRS CORP (NY)
Liquidation completed
Each share Common 1¢ par exchanged for initial distribution of $1.41 cash 06/16/1980
Each share Common 1¢ par received second distribution of $0.25 cash 06/09/1981
Each share Common 1¢ par received third distribution of $0.12 cash 05/28/1982
Each share Common 1¢ par received fourth distribution of $0.20 cash 11/04/1982
Each share Common 1¢ par received fifth and final distribution of $0.07 cash 08/15/1984

PEC ENERGY CORP (BC)
Reorganized under the laws of Delaware as Perennial Energy, Inc. 10/18/1991
Each share Common no par exchanged for (0.2) share Common 1¢ par

PEC ISRAEL ECONOMIC CORP (ME)
Common $25 par changed to no par 3/23/65
Common no par changed to $1 par 6/13/83
Common $1 par split (3) for (1) by issuance of (2) additional shares 1/10/84
Common $1 par split (2) for (1) by issuance of (1) additional share 2/25/92
Stock Dividends - 10% 1/20/81; 20% 1/26/82; 20% 1/11/83; 10% 1/8/85
Merged into Discount Investment Corp. Ltd. 11/5/99
Each share Common $1 par exchanged for $36.50 cash

PEC SOLUTIONS INC (DE)
Merged into Nortel Networks Corp. (New) 06/07/2005
Each share Common 1¢ par exchanged for $15.50 cash

PECHINEY (FRANCE)
Name changed 9/15/83
Name changed from Pechiney Ugine Kuhlmann to Pechiney 9/15/83
ADR agreement terminated 2/6/2004
Each Sponsored ADR for Ordinary exchanged for $30.3279 cash

PECK, STOW & WILCOX CO. (CT)
Capital Stock $25 par changed to $10 par in 1933
Merged into B & S Co. 4/19/63
Each share Capital Stock $10 par exchanged for $35 cash

PECK (T.N.) & ASSOCIATES, INC. (DE)
Merged into Cumberland Corp. (KY) on a (1) for (5) basis 07/28/1955
(See Cumberland Corp. (KY))

PECK BROTHERS & CO.
Operations discontinued 00/00/1935
Details not available

PECK TELEVISION CORP.
Dissolved in 1945

PECKHAM HILL GOLD MINES INC. (NV)
Charter revoked for failure to file reports and pay fees 3/4/74

PECKHAM INDS INC (NY)
Preferred Ser. C called for redemption at $100 on 09/15/2004
Each share old Common $100 par exchanged for (0.01) share new Common $100 par 09/16/2005
Merged into PII Merger Inc. 08/28/2009
Each share new Common $100 par exchanged for $60,000 cash

PECO ENERGY CAP L P (DE)
Issue Information - 8,000,000 MONTHLY INCOME PFD SECS SER A 9% offered at $25 per share on 07/20/1994
9.0% Monthly Income Preferred Securities Ser. A no par called for redemption at $25 on 7/30/99

PECO ENERGY CAP TR II (DE)
Issue Information - $50,000,000 TR RCPT REPSTG MONTHLY INCOME PFD SECS SER C 8% offered at $25 per share on 07/13/1997
8% Trust Receipt Monthly Income Preferred Securities Ser. C called for redemption at $25 on 6/24/2003

PECO ENERGY CAP TR I (DE)
Trust Receipts for Monthly Income Preferred no par called for redemption at $25 on 5/15/98

PECO ENERGY CO (PA)
$7.80 Preferred no par called for redemption 09/01/1994
$7 Preferred no par called for redemption 09/15/1994
$7.375 Preferred no par called for redemption 09/15/1994
$7.75 Preferred no par called for redemption 09/15/1994
$7.85 Preferred no par called for redemption 09/15/1994
$9.875 Preferred no par called for redemption 09/15/1994
$7.96 Preferred no par called for redemption at $25 on 10/01/1997
$7.96 Depositary Preferred called for redemption at $25 on 10/01/1997
Under plan of merger name changed to Exelon Corp. 10/20/2000
$6.12 Preferred no par called for redemption at $100 on 08/01/2002
$7.48 Preferred no par called for redemption at $103.74 on 06/11/2003
$3.80 Preferred Ser. A no par called for redemption at $106 on 05/01/2013
$4.30 Preferred Ser. B no par called for redemption at $102 on 05/01/2013
$4.40 Preferred Ser. C no par called for redemption at $112.50 on 05/01/2013
$4.68 Preferred Ser. D no par called for redemption at $104 on 05/01/2013

PECO II INC (OH)
Issue Information - 5,000,000 shares COM offered at $15 per share on 08/17/2000
Each share old Common no par exchanged for (0.1) share new Common no par 05/07/2008
Merged into Lineage Power Holdings, Inc. 04/16/2010
Each share new Common no par exchanged for $5.86 cash

PECOM ENERGIA S A (ARGENTINA)
ADR agreement terminated 12/02/2002
Each Sponsored ADR for Class B exchanged for $3.38708 cash

PECONIC BANCSHARES INC (NY)
Acquired by LI Holding Corp. 03/09/1987
Details not available

PECONIC BANK (RIVERHEAD, NY)
Under plan of reorganization each share Common $4 par automatically became (1) share Peconic Bancshares, Inc. Common $4 par 12/30/1985
(See Peconic Bancshares, Inc.)

PECOS EXPLORATION CO. (DE)
Merged into Alco Oil & Gas Corp. 8/15/61
Each share Capital Stock 5¢ par exchanged for (0.285714) share Common 3-1/3¢ par
Alco Oil & Gas Corp. merged into Ladd Petroleum Corp. 7/1/69 which merged into Utah International Inc. 11/30/73 which merged into General Electric Co. 12/20/76

PECOS LAND & DEVELOPMENT CO., INC. (DE)
Merged into Western Energy Corp. 6/21/67
Each share Common $1 par exchanged for (0.1) share Common 50¢ par
Western Energy Corp. recapitalized as United Western Energy Corp. 11/29/78
(See United Western Energy Corp.)

PECOS RES LTD (BC)
Common no par split (2) for (1) by issuance of (1) additional share 03/16/1984
Merged into Granges Exploration Ltd. 06/28/1985
Each (2.1) shares Common no par exchanged for (1) share Common no par
Granges Exploration Ltd. reorganized as Granges Inc. (Old) 06/19/1989 which merged into Granges Inc. (New) 05/01/1995 which merged into Vista Gold Corp. (BC) 11/01/1996 which reincorporated in Yukon 12/27/1997 which reincorporated back in British Columbia 06/12/2013

PECOS VALLEY POWER & LIGHT CO.
Acquired by West Texas Utilities Co. and liquidated in 1944

PECOS WESTERN CORP. OF DELAWARE (DE)
Name changed to Pecos Western Corp. 6/20/80

PEDCO ENERGY LTD N P L (BC)
Merged into International Pedco Energy Corp. 11/26/93
Each share Common no par exchanged for (0.41425) share Common no par
International Pedco Energy Corp. merged into Lateral Vector Resources Inc. 2/29/96
(See Lateral Vector Resources Inc.)

PEDEN CO.
Name changed to Peden Iron & Steel Co. 00/00/1933
(See Peden Iron & Steel Co.)

PEDEN IRON & STL CO (TX)
Completely liquidated 01/31/1970
Each share Common no par exchanged for first and final distribution $64.20 cash

PEDIANET COM INC (GA)
Old Common $0.001 par split (4) for (1) by issuance of (3) additional shares payable 01/08/2001 to holders of record 01/03/2001
Each share old Common $0.001 par exchanged for (0.33333333) share new Common $0.001 par 02/28/2002
Recapitalized as Morgan Equities Group, Inc. 09/19/2005
Each share new Common $0.001 par exchanged for (0.01) share Common $0.001 par
Morgan Equities Group, Inc. name

changed to Deaf-Talk, Inc. 09/14/2010
(See Deaf-Talk, Inc.)

PEDIATRIC PROSTHETICS INC (ID)
Recapitalized as Marathon Group Corp. (ID) 08/03/2010
Each share Common $0.001 par exchanged for (0.1) share Common $0.001 par
Marathon Group Corp. (ID) reincorporated in Wyoming 06/02/2011

PEDIATRIC SVCS AMERICA INC (DE)
Issue Information - 1,700,000 shares COM offered at $8 per share on 06/03/1994
Merged into Portfolio Logic LLC 08/31/2007
Each share Common 1¢ par exchanged for $16.25 cash

PEDIATRIX MED GROUP (FL)
Common 1¢ par split (2) for (1) by issuance of (1) additional share payable 02/26/1999 to holders of record 02/02/1999 Ex date - 03/01/1999
Common 1¢ par split (2) for (1) by issuance of (1) additional share payable 04/27/2006 to holders of record 04/13/2006 Ex date - 04/28/2006
Name changed to Mednax, Inc. 12/31/2008

PEDIATRX INC (NV)
Name changed to Quint Media Inc. 08/07/2013
Quint Media Inc. recapitalized as OncBioMune Pharmaceuticals, Inc. 08/28/2015

PEDIGO CO.
Dissolution approved in 1937

PEDIGO LAKE SHOE CO.
Name changed to Pedigo Co. in 1935 whose dissolution was approved in 1937

PEDIMENT EXPL LTD (BC)
Name changed to Pediment Gold Corp. 02/26/2009
Pediment Gold Corp. merged into Argonaut Gold Inc. 02/01/2011

PEDIMENT GOLD CORP (BC)
Merged into Argonaut Gold Inc. 02/01/2011
Each share Common no par exchanged for (0.625) share Common no par

PEDLAR INDL INC (CANADA)
Placed in receivership in June 1981
No stockholders' equity

PEE DEE ST BK (TIMMONSVILLE, SC)
Acquired by Centura Banks, Inc. 3/27/98
Each share Common $5 par exchanged for (9.15927) shares Common no par
Centura Banks, Inc. merged into Royal Bank of Canada (Montreal, QC) 6/5/2001

PEEK N PEAK REC INC (NY)
Acquired by PNP Acquisition Corp. 12/13/1988
Each share Common 40¢ par exchanged for $5.50 cash

PEEK PLC (ENGLAND)
Acquired by Thermo Power Corp. 11/06/1997
Each share Common exchanged for 80p cash

PEEKAY BOUTIQUES INC (NV)
Each share old Common $0.0001 par exchanged for (0.16666666) share new Common $0.0001 par 10/29/2015
Plan of reorganization under Chapter 11 Federal Bankruptcy proceedings effective 11/22/2017
No stockholders' equity

PEEKSKILL FINL CORP (DE)
Merged into Sound Federal Bancorp 07/18/2000
Each share Common 1¢ par exchanged for $22 cash

PEEL ELDER LTD (ON)
Capital Stock no par split (3) for (2) by issuance of (0.5) additional share 2/12/69
Capital Stock no par split (2) for (1) by issuance of (1) additional share 7/25/73
Merged into Hambro Canada Ltd. 12/5/74
Each share Capital Stock no par exchanged for (3) shares Preference no par
Hambro Canada Ltd. name changed to Hatleigh Corp. (Old) 8/3/78 which merged into Hatleigh Corp. (New) 8/31/78 which merged into Dexleigh Corp. 6/30/84
(See Dexleigh Corp.)

PEEL RES LTD (BC)
Reorganized 10/30/58
Reorganized from Peel River Gas & Oil Co. Ltd. to Peel Resources Ltd. 10/30/58
Each share Common no par exchanged for (1) share Common no par
Recapitalized as McConnell-Peel Resources Ltd. 2/24/78
Each share Capital Stock no par exchanged for (0.2) share Capital Stock no par
McConnell-Peel Resources Ltd. merged into Coast Falcon Resources Ltd. (BC) 7/7/92 which reorganized in Yukon as Inside Holdings Inc. 10/6/2000 which name changed to SHEP Technologies Inc. 10/7/2002

PEELBROOKE CAP INC (CANADA)
Acquired by Dundee Wealth Management Inc. 12/10/1999
Each share Common no par exchanged for (0.3) share Common no par, (0.3) Common Stock Purchase Warrant expiring 12/09/2002, (0.2) share Dundee Bancorp Inc. Class A Subordinate no par and $1.50 cash
Note: U.S. holders received approximately $7.60 cash per share
(See each company's listing)

PEER OIL CORP.
Liquidated in 1930

PEER 1 NETWORK ENTERPRISES INC (BC)
Acquired by Cogeco Cable Inc. 04/01/2013
Each share Common no par exchanged for $3.85 cash

PEER REVIEW ANALYSIS INC (MA)
Name changed to Core, Inc. 8/1/95
(See Core, Inc.)

PEER REVIEW MEDITATION & ARBITRATION INC (FL)
SEC revoked common stock registration 04/22/2016

PEERLESS BOTTLERS, INC.
Merged into General Bottlers, Inc. 00/00/1945
Each share Common exchanged for (0.4) share Common
General Bottlers, Inc. name changed to Pepsi-Cola General Bottlers, Inc. (IL) 00/00/1953 which reincorporated in Delaware 04/23/1969 which merged into Illinois Central Industries, Inc. 02/02/1970 which name changed to IC Industries, Inc. 05/21/1975
(See IC Industries, Inc.)

PEERLESS BREWING CO.
Bankrupt in 1939

PEERLESS BULLFROG MINING (SD)
Charter expired by time limitation in 1926

PEERLESS CDN EXPLS LTD (ON)
Charter cancelled for failure to file reports 02/14/1973

PEERLESS CARPET CORP (CANADA)
Merged into C & M Acquisition Co. 1/15/99
Each share Common no par exchanged for $3.10 cash

PEERLESS CASUALTY CO. (NH)
Each share Common $12.50 par exchanged for (2.5) shares Common $5 par in 1936
Stock Dividend - 10% 11/23/55
Name changed to Peerless Insurance Co. 1/1/56
(See Peerless Insurance Co.)

PEERLESS CEMENT CORP. (MI)
Each share Preferred $100 par exchanged for (10) shares Common no par in 1935
Each share Common no par exchanged for (1) share new Common no par in 1935
Each share Common Vtg. Tr. no par exchanged for (1) share new Common $5 par in 1941
Stock Dividend - 200% 10/12/55
Merged into American Cement Corp. 12/31/57
Each share new Common $5 par exchanged for (1.268) shares Common $5 par
American Cement Corp. name changed to Amcord, Inc. 5/2/73
(See Amcord, Inc.)

PEERLESS CHAIN CO (MN)
Stock Dividends - 20% 03/04/1976; 25% 09/08/1978; 25% 06/08/1979
Merged into PAC Holding Corp. 06/18/1986
Each share Common 25¢ par exchanged for $23.50 cash

PEERLESS COAL CO.
Acquired by Peabody Coal Co. in 1928
Peabody Coal Co. name changed to PDY Coal Co. 3/29/68 which liquidation completed 3/31/71

PEERLESS CORP.
Name changed to Brewing Corp. of America in 1938
Brewing Corp. of America name changed to Carling Brewing Co., Inc. in 1954
(See Carling Brewing Co., Inc.)

PEERLESS DEV CORP (CO)
Name changed to Mediscience, Inc. 7/24/79
Mediscience, Inc. reincorporated in Delaware as Cardis Corp. 4/3/84
(See Cardis Corp.)

PEERLESS DEVS LTD (DE)
Name changed to Blockchain Loyalty Corp. 05/03/2018

PEERLESS EGYPTIAN CEMENT CO.
Name changed to Peerless Cement Corp. in 1929
Peerless Cement Corp. merged into American Cement Corp. 12/31/57 which name changed to Amcord, Inc. 5/2/73
(See Amcord, Inc.)

PEERLESS ENERGY INC (AB)
Merged into Petrobank Energy & Resources Ltd. (Old) 01/28/2008
Each share Class A Common no par exchanged for (0.095) share Common no par and $1 cash
Each share Class B Common no par exchanged for $10 cash
Petrobank Energy & Resources Ltd. (Old) reorganized as Petrobank Energy & Resources Ltd. (New) 01/07/2013 which recapitalized as Touchstone Exploration Inc. 05/20/2014

PEERLESS GROUP INC (DE)
Merged into Henry (Jack) & Associates, Inc. 12/16/98
Each share Common 1¢ par exchanged for (0.16145) share Common 1¢ par

PEERLESS INDL GROUP INC (MN)
Merged into R-B Capital Corp. 05/19/1997
Each share Common no par exchanged for $1.67 cash

PEERLESS INS CO (NH)
Common $5 par changed to $2.50 par 08/20/1969
$1.75 Conv. Preferred $2.50 par called for redemption 02/07/1979
Merged into Peerless Holdings, Inc. 03/31/1982
Each share Common $2.50 par exchanged for $17.50 cash

PEERLESS LAUNDRY SERVICE CORP.
Acquired by Peerless Laundry Services, Ltd. in 1928 which liquidation was completed 4/15/59

PEERLESS LAUNDRY SERVICES, LTD. (CA)
Recapitalized in 1940
Each (100) shares 7% Preferred $1 par exchanged for (55) shares 7% Prior Preferred $1 par and (10) shares Common $1 par
Each (10) shares Common $1 par exchanged for (1) share Common $1 par
Liquidation completed 4/15/59

PEERLESS MFG CO (TX)
Common $1 par split (3) for (2) by issuance of (0.5) additional share 05/30/1975
Common $1 par split (3) for (2) by issuance of (0.5) additional share 07/20/1990
Common $1 par split (2) for (1) by issuance of (1) additional share payable 10/18/2001 to holders of record 10/08/2001 Ex date - 10/19/2001
Common $1 par split (2) for (1) by issuance of (1) additional share payable 06/07/2007 to holders of record 05/18/2007 Ex date - 06/08/2007
Reincorporated under the laws of Delaware as PMFG, Inc., Common $1 par changed to 1¢ par and (1) additional share issued 08/18/2008
PMFG, Inc. merged into CECO Environmental Corp. 09/03/2015

PEERLESS MTG CO (CO)
Each share Common 20¢ par exchanged for (0.2) share Common $1 par 10/2/61
Name changed to Peerless Development Corp. 4/7/70
Peerless Development Corp. name changed to Mediscience, Inc. 7/24/79 which reincorporated in Delaware as Cardis Corp. 4/3/84
(See Cardis Corp.)

PEERLESS MOTOR CAR CORP.
Name changed to Peerless Corp. in 1933
Peerless Corp. name changed to Brewing Corp. of America in 1938 which name changed to Carling Brewing Co., Inc. in 1954
(See Carling Brewing Co., Inc.)

PEERLESS PORTLAND CEMENT CO.
Merged into Peerless Egyptian Cement Co. in 1927
Details not available

PEERLESS PRODTNS INC (FL)
Recapitalized as Hemdale Communications Inc. 8/25/92
Each (8.5) shares Common $0.001 par exchanged for (1) share Common $0.001 par
(See Hemdale Communications Inc.)

PEERLESS RUG LTD (CANADA)
Common no par split (2) for (1) by issuance of (1) additional share 12/6/83
Name changed to Peerless Carpet Corp. 12/7/83
(See Peerless Carpet Corp.)

PEERLESS SYS CORP (DE)
Acquired by Mobius Acquisition, LLC 02/12/2015
Each share Common $0.001 par exchanged for $7 cash

PEERLESS TUBE CO (NJ)
Capital Stock $2 par changed to $1.33-1/3 par and (0.5) additional share issued 12/22/1970
Stock Dividends - 10% 11/25/1963; 10% 11/22/1968; 10% 12/21/1979; 10% 12/19/1980; 10% 12/10/1981
Chapter 11 bankruptcy proceedings converted to Chapter 7 on 01/13/2003
Stockholders' equity unlikely

PEERLESS URANIUM MINING CORP. LTD. (ON)
Charter cancelled for failure to pay taxes and file returns 11/22/72

PEERLESS WEIGHING & VENDING MACH CORP (DE)
Merged into Rockola Corp. 12/26/96
Each share $3 Preferred no par exchanged for $53.13 cash
Note: An additional $3.04 per share is being held in escrow for possible future distribution
Each share Common $1 par exchanged for $114 cash
Note: An additional $35.96 per share is being held in escrow for possible future distribution

PEET BROS. CO.
Acquired by Palmolive-Peet Co. in 1926
Details not available

PEETS COFFEE & TEA INC (WA)
Issue Information - 3,300,000 shares COM offered at $8 per share on 01/24/2001
Acquired by JAB Holdings BV 10/30/2012
Each share Common no par exchanged for $73.50 cash

PEG TANTALUM MINES LTD.
Merged into Tantalum Refining & Mining Corp. of America Ltd. 00/00/1948
Each share Common exchanged for (1) share Common
Tantalum Refining & Mining Corp. of America Ltd. acquired by Nationwide Minerals Ltd. 00/00/1952
(See Nationwide Minerals Ltd.)

PEGA CAP CORP (ON)
Name changed from Pega Capital Resources Ltd. to Pega Capital Corp. 09/10/1987
Cease trade order effective 09/26/1996

PEGASUS AIRCRAFT PARTNERS L P (DE)
Completely liquidated 08/23/2004
Details not available

PEGASUS COMMUNICATIONS CORP (DE)
12.75% Exchangeable Preferred Ser. A 1¢ par split (2) for (1) by issuance of (1) additional share payable 05/30/2000 to holders of record 05/19/2000
Old Class A Common 1¢ par split (2) for (1) by issuance of (1) additional share payable 05/30/2000 to holders of record 05/19/2000
Each share 12.75% Exchangeable Preferred Ser. A 1¢ par exchanged for (1) share Pegasus Satellite Communications, Inc. 12.75% Exchangeable Preferred Ser. B 1¢ par 02/21/2001

(See Pegasus Satellite Communications, Inc.)
Each share 6.5% Conv. Preferred Ser. C 1¢ par received distribution of (0.03516679) share old Class A Common 1¢ par payable 10/31/2001 to holders of record 10/15/2001
Each share 6.5% Conv. Preferred Ser. C 1¢ par received distribution of (0.18461713) share old Class A Common 1¢ par payable 01/31/2002 to holders of record 01/15/2002
Each share old Class A Common 1¢ par exchanged for (0.1) share new Class A Common 1¢ par 12/31/2002
Each share 6.5% Conv. Preferred Ser. C 1¢ par received distribution of (0.00174476) share new Class A Common 1¢ par payable 07/31/2003 to holders of record 7/15/2003
Ex date - 07/25/2003
New Class A Common 1¢ par split (2) for (1) by issuance of (1) additional share payable 08/26/2004 to holders of record 08/19/2004
Recapitalized as Xanadoo Co. 01/10/2007
Each share new Class A Common 1¢ par exchanged for (0.01) share Class A Common 1¢ par
Preferred not affected except for change of name
Note: Holders of (99) or fewer pre-split shares received $3.25 cash per share
Xanadoo Co. name changed to Pegasus Companies, Inc. 06/09/2015

PEGASUS DEV GROUP INC (CO)
Name changed to SpaceDev, Inc. (CO) 12/30/1997
SpaceDev, Inc. (CO) reincorporated in Delaware 08/20/2007
(See SpaceDev, Inc.)

PEGASUS EXPLS LTD (BC)
Merged into Pegasus Gold Ltd. 6/2/81
Each share Common no par exchanged for (1) share Common no par
Pegasus Gold Ltd. merged into Pegasus Gold Inc. 8/20/84
(See Pegasus Gold Inc.)

PEGASUS FD INC (MD)
Name changed to Vanderbilt Growth Fund, Inc. 07/01/1975
Vanderbilt Growth Fund, Inc. merged into St. Paul Capital Fund, Inc. 06/14/1977 which name changed to AMEV Capital Fund, Inc. 05/01/1985 which reorganized as Fortis Equity Portfolios Inc. 02/22/1992
(See Fortis Equity Portfolios Inc.)

PEGASUS FINL GROUP INC (DE)
Name changed to Interactive Telephone Network, Inc. 09/26/1995
Interactive Telephone Network, Inc. recapitalized as T House & Co. Ltd. 12/30/1998 which name changed to Team Labs Systems Group Inc. 08/28/2000 which name changed to SciLabs Holdings, Inc. 07/17/2001
(See SciLabs Holdings, Inc.)

PEGASUS GOLD INC (BC)
Plan of reorganization under Chapter 11 Federal Bankruptcy Code effective 2/5/99
No stockholders' equity

PEGASUS GOLD LTD (BC)
Merged into Pegasus Gold Inc. 8/20/84
Each share Common no par exchanged for (1) share Common no par
(See Pegasus Gold Inc.)

PEGASUS GYMNASTICS EQUIP INC (UT)
Each share Common $0.001 par exchanged for (0.1) share Common 1¢ par 12/29/89
Proclaimed dissolved for failure to pay taxes 12/8/97

PEGASUS INCOME & CAP FD INC (DE)
Acquired by St. Paul Income Fund, Inc. 01/07/1981
Each Capital Share $1.25 par exchanged for (0.59419) share Common 1¢ par
Each Income Share $1.25 par exchanged for (0.59419) share Common 1¢ par
St. Paul Income Fund, Inc. name changed to AMEV U.S. Government Securities Fund, Inc. 05/01/1985 which name changed to Fortis Income Portfolios, Inc. 02/22/1992
(See Fortis Income Portfolios, Inc.)

PEGASUS OIL & GAS INC (AB)
Acquired by Harvest Energy Trust 08/17/2009
Each share Class A Common no par exchanged for (0.015) Trust Unit no par
Each share Class B Common no par exchanged for (0.15) Trust Unit no par
(See Harvest Energy Trust)

PEGASUS PETROLEUMS & MINING CORP. LTD. (ON)
Stricken from Register 1/15/58
Stock worthless

PEGASUS SATELLITE COMMUNICATIONS INC (DE)
Plan of reorganization under Chapter 11 Federal Bankruptcy Code effective 05/05/2005
No stockholders' equity

PEGASUS SOLUTIONS INC (DE)
Name changed 5/11/2000
Issue Information - 3,573,044 shares COM offered at $13 per share on 08/06/1997
Secondary Offering - 2,100,000 shares COM offered at $17.50 per share on 02/11/1998
Common 1¢ par split (3) for (2) by issuance of (0.5) additional share payable 1/7/2000 to holders of record 12/20/99
Name changed from Pegasus Systems, Inc. to Pegasus Solutions Inc. 5/11/2000
Merged into Perseus Holding Corp. 5/4/2006
Each share Common 1¢ par exchanged for $9.50 cash

PEGASUS TAX & FINL PLANNING SVCS INC (NV)
Name changed to Clinicor Inc. 02/27/1995
(See Clinicor Inc.)

PEGASUS WIRELESS CORP (CO)
Name changed to Homeskills, Inc. (New) 6/6/2005
Homeskills, Inc. (New) name changed to Curve Wireless Corp. 1/12/2006 which name changed to OTC Wireless, Inc. 8/7/2006

PEGASUS WIRELESS CORP (NV)
Old Common $0.001 par split (2) for (1) by issuance of (1) additional share payable 09/01/2005 to holders of record 08/31/2005 Ex date - 09/02/2005
Each share old Common $0.001 par exchanged for (0.2) share new Common $0.001 par 12/11/2006
Chapter 11 bankruptcy proceedings dismissed 04/17/2009
No stockholders' equity

PEGAZ ENERGY INC (CANADA)
Recapitalized as Argo Energy Ltd. 11/15/2002
Each share Class A Common no par exchanged for (0.1) share Common no par
(See Argo Energy Ltd.)

PEI INC (DE)
Charter cancelled and declared inoperative and void for non-payment of taxes 6/17/93

PEI INC (NV)
Name changed to Process Equipment, Inc. (NV) 11/19/90
Process Equipment, Inc. (NV) reincorporated in Delaware as HQ Sustainable Maritime Industries, Inc. 5/19/2004

PEKIN FMRS LIFE INS CO (IL)
Name changed to Pekin Life Insurance Co. 06/09/1972

PEKIN SVGS S B (IL)
Name changed 1/27/94
Name changed from Pekin Savings & Loan Association to Pekin Savings S.B. 1/27/94
Under plan of reorganization each share Common 1¢ par automatically became (1) share Progressive Bancorp, Inc. (DE) Common 1¢ par 11/6/97
(See Progressive Bancorp, Inc. (DE))

PEKO WALLSEND LTD (AUSTRALIA)
Stock Dividend - 25% 12/06/1976
Acquired by North Broken Hill Holdings Ltd. 07/07/1988
Each ADR for Ordinary exchanged for $6.984 cash

PEKOE TECHNOLOGY, INC. (UT)
Name changed to Boardroom Business Products, Inc. 10/7/85

PEKU MFG INC (UT)
Name changed to GHL Technologies, Inc. 03/03/2006
GHL Technologies, Inc. recapitalized as NXGen Holdings, Inc. 09/07/2007 which name changed to Green Bridge Industries, Inc. 08/20/2009

PELANGIO EXPL INC (AB)
Reincorporated under the laws of Canada 06/25/2009

PELANGIO LARDER MINES LTD (ON)
Capital Stock $1 par reclassified as Common no par 05/01/1980
Merged into Pelangio Mines Inc. 05/25/2000
Each share Common no par exchanged for (1.0516) shares Common no par
Pelangio Mines Inc. name changed to PDX Resources Inc. 09/03/2008 which merged into Detour Gold Corp. 03/27/2009

PELANGIO MINES INC (AB)
Name changed to PDX Resources Inc. 09/03/2008
PDX Resources Inc. merged into Detour Gold Corp. 03/27/2009

PELE MEDI CORP (CA)
Name changed to Century Medicorp 12/7/84
Century Medicorp merged into Foundation Health Corp. 10/15/92 which merged into Foundation Health Systems, Inc. 4/1/97 which name changed to Health Net, Inc. 11/6/2000

PELHAM CORP (AL)
Liquidation completed
Each share Common $1 par exchanged for initial distribution of (1.2627) shares Scudder, Stevens & Clark Balanced Fund, Inc. Capital Stock $1 par 01/08/1971
Each share Common $1 par received second and final distribution of (0.0664) share Scudder, Stevens & Clark Balanced Fund, Inc. Capital Stock $1 par 12/31/1973
Scudder, Stevens & Clark Balanced Fund, Inc. name changed to Scudder Income Fund, 03/02/1977 which name changed to Scudder Income Fund 12/31/1984
(See Scudder Income Fund)

PELHAM GOLD MINES LTD (ON)
Name changed to Pelham Gold & Grain Co. 4/6/88

PELHAM HALL CO. (MA)
Name changed to Pelham Hall Trust in 1954

PELICAN FD (MD)
Name changed to GMO Pelican Fund 07/01/2002
(See GMO Pelican Fund)

PELICAN FINL INC (DE)
Issue Information - 1,200,000 shares COM offered at $7 per share on 11/10/1999
Each share Common 1¢ par received distribution of (1) share Washtenaw Group, Inc. Common 1¢ par payable 12/31/2003 to holders of record 12/22/2003
Stock Dividend - 10% payable 07/02/2001 to holders of record 06/18/2001 Ex date - 06/14/2001
Merged into Stark Bank Group, Ltd. 04/21/2006
Each share Common 1¢ par exchanged for $5.7162 cash
Note: An additional distribution of $0.2183 cash per share was made from escrow 02/25/2011

PELION S A (POLAND)
ADR agreement terminated 04/19/2018
No ADR's remain outstanding

PELISSIER'S LTD.
Liquidated in 1936

PELL DE VEGH MUTUAL FUND, INC. (MD)
Name changed to De Vegh Mutual Fund, Inc. in 1952
De Vegh Mutual Fund, Inc. merged into Winthrop Focus Funds 2/28/96 which name changed to DLJ Winthrop Focus Funds 8/1/2000 which reorganized as Credit Suisse Warburg Pincus Capital Funds 1/18/2001 which name changed to Credit Suisse Capital Funds 12/12/2001

PELL PHARMACEUTICALS INC (PA)
Each share Common 5¢ par exchanged for (1/3) share Common 10¢ par 06/06/1967
Name changed to Pell Industries, Inc. 11/06/1970

PELLAIRE MINES LTD. (ON)
Acquired by Flagstone Mines Ltd. on a (0.1) for (1) basis 03/06/1964
Flagstone Mines Ltd. merged into Grand Prix Resources Ltd. (New) 10/29/1976 which recapitalized as Omenica Resources Ltd. 04/08/1980 which recapitalized as Marilyn Resources Inc. 01/30/1984
(See Marilyn Resources Inc.)

PELLET AMER CORP (NV)
Recapitalized as Sunflower Ltd. 10/05/1998
Each share Common no par exchanged for (0.1) share Common no par
Sunflower Ltd. recapitalized as Sunflower (USA) Ltd. 03/01/1999
(See Sunflower (USA) Ltd.)

PELLETIER LAKE GOLD MINES, LTD. (ON)
Liquidation completed 4/24/61

PELOREX CORP (DE)
Adjudicated bankrupt 01/24/1977
No stockholders' equity

PELORUS ENERGY CORP (AB)
Name changed 11/17/2004
Name changed from Pelorus Navigation Systems Inc. to Pelorus Energy Corp. 11/17/2004
Recapitalized as RedStar Oil & Gas Inc. 08/10/2005
Each share Common no par exchanged for (0.04) share Common no par
RedStar Oil & Gas Inc. merged into Great Plains Exploration Inc. (New) (Canada) 05/09/2008 which reincorporated in Alberta 01/01/2009 which merged into Avenir Diversified Income Trust 11/10/2010 which reorganized as AvenEx Energy Corp. 01/07/2011 which merged into Spyglass Resources Corp. 04/04/2013

PELOTON RES INC (NV)
Common $0.00001 par split (7) for (1) by issuance of (6) additional shares payable 05/09/2005 to holders of record 05/09/2005 Ex date - 05/10/2005
Name changed to Triangle Petroleum Corp. (NV) 05/26/2005
Triangle Petroleum Corp. (NV) reincorporated in Delaware 12/03/2012

PELSART RES N L (AUSTRALIA)
Each old ADR for Ordinary A$0.20 par exchanged for (0.1) new ADR for Ordinary A$0.20 par 03/14/1984
ADR agreement terminated 06/11/2009
No ADR holders' equity

PELTECH INDS INC (BC)
Recapitalized as Gold Win Ventures Inc. 04/02/1996
Each share Common no par exchanged for (0.2) share Common no par
Gold Win Ventures Inc. recapitalized as Consolidated Gold Win Ventures, Inc. 06/17/1998 which name changed to Encore Renaissance Resources Corp. 04/09/2009

PELTO OIL CO (DE)
Merged into Southdown, Inc. 7/1/74
Each share Series A Common $1 par exchanged for $35 cash
(See Southdown Inc.)

PELTON PETROLEUM CO. (AZ)
Charter revoked for failure to file reports and pay fees 10/14/38

PELZER MANUFACTURING CO. (MA)
Liquidation completed 6/29/43

PEMBERTON ENERGY LTD (BC)
Recapitalized as Brixton Energy Corp. 11/04/2010
Each share Common no par exchanged for (1/3) share Common no par

PEMBERTON EXPLS LTD (BC)
Recapitalized as Consolidated Pemberton Technologies Ltd. 01/27/1992
Each (3.5) shares Common no par exchanged for (1) share Common no par
Consolidated Pemberton Technologies Ltd. recapitalized as CPT Pemberton Technologies Ltd. 06/22/1995 which name changed to Pemberton Energy Ltd. 01/13/1999 which recapitalized as Brixton Energy Corp. 11/04/2010

PEMBERTON HOUSTON WILLOUGHBY INVT CORP (BC)
Acquired by RBC Dominion Securities (B.C.) Inc. 07/31/1989
Each share Non-Vtg. Class A no par exchanged for $9 cash

PEMBINA PIPE LINE LTD. (AB)
Each share Common $5 par exchanged for (4) shares Common $1.25 par 5/16/57
Each share old 5% 1st Preferred $50 par exchanged for (1) share new 5% 1st Preferred $50 par 4/5/71
Each share Common $1.25 par exchanged for (0.1) share 6% 2nd Preferred Ser. A $30 par, (4) shares Class A Common $4.15 par and (1) share Class B Common $4.15 par 4/5/71
New 5% Preferred $50 par called for redemption 8/15/72
6% 2nd Preferred Ser. A $30 par called for redemption 1/1/75
Class A Common $4.15 par reclassified as Common $4.15 par 12/30/76
Class B Common $4.15 par reclassified as Common $4.15 par 12/30/76
Name changed to Pembina Resources Ltd. 1/31/83
(See Pembina Resources Ltd.)

PEMBINA PIPELINE INCOME FD (AB)
Each Installment Receipt no par exchanged for (1) Trust Unit no par 10/23/1998
Under plan of reorganization each Trust Unit no par automatically became (1) share Pembina Pipeline Corp. Common no par 10/05/2010

PEMBINA RES LTD (AB)
Merged into Manoil Ltd. 02/01/1988
Each share Common $4.15 par exchanged for $22 cash

PEMBRIDGE INC (ON)
Acquired by Pemco Acquisition 4/14/98
Each share Common 1¢ par exchanged for $20 cash

PEMBROKE CAP CORP (BC)
Issue Information - 4,000,000 shares COM offered at $0.10 per share on 08/25/2010
Name changed to Minfocus Exploration Corp. 01/25/2012

PEMBROKE CAP INC NEW (NV)
Reincorporated 04/29/1993
State of incorporation changed from (CO) to (NV) 04/29/1993
Each share old Common no par exchanged for (0.004) share new Common no par 04/30/1993
New Common no par split (3.125) for (1) by issuance of (2.125) additional shares 10/07/1994
Each (750) shares new Common no par exchanged again for (1) share new Common no par 06/25/1998
SEC revoked common stock registration 11/08/2006

PEMBROKE STAR RES LTD (BC)
Name changed to Eskimo Resources Ltd. 06/25/1980
Eskimo Resources Ltd. name changed to Ft. Lauderdale Resources Inc. 01/05/1987 which recapitalized as Amcorp Industries Inc. 06/22/1990 which name changed to Molycor Gold Corp. 05/17/1996 which name changed to Nevada Clean Magnesium Inc. 04/17/2012

PEMCO, INC. (DE)
Name changed to Dimode Industries, Inc. 1/8/70
(See Dimode Industries, Inc.)

PEMCO AVIATION INC (DE)
Name changed to Alabama Aircraft Industries, Inc. 09/19/2007

PEMCO CORP. (MD)
Stock Dividends - 100% 8/1/55; 150% 12/19/58
6% Preferred $50 par called for redemption 9/28/56
Merged into Glidden Co. 11/6/61
Each share Common no par exchanged for (2) shares $2.125 Conv. Preferred no par
(See Glidden Co.)

PEMCO RES LTD (AB)
Name changed to Innovative Environmental Services Ltd. 09/23/1991
(See Innovative Environmental Services Ltd.)

PEMCOR INC (DE)
Common $1 par split (5) for (4) by issuance of (0.25) additional share 09/10/1976
Merged into Esmark, Inc. (Inc. 03/14/1969) 09/28/1978
Each share Common $1 par exchanged for (1.1) shares Common $1 par
(See Esmark, Inc. (Inc. 03/14/1969))

PEMI BANCORP INC (NH)
Merged into Northway Financial Inc. 9/30/97
Each share Common no par exchanged for (1.0419) shares Common $1 par

PEMMICAN MINES, LTD. (ON)
Charter cancelled for failure to file reports and pay taxes October 1957

PEMSTAR HOLDINGS LTD. (ON)
Dissolved 4/30/80

PEMSTAR INC (MN)
Issue Information - 8,400,000 shares COM offered at $11 per share on 08/07/2000
Merged into Benchmark Electronics, Inc. 1/8/2007
Each share Common 1¢ par exchanged for (0.16) share Common 10¢ par

PEN INTERCONNECT INC (UT)
Name changed to Amanda Co., Inc. 10/30/2001
(See Amanda Co., Inc.)

PEN INTL INC (UT)
Recapitalized as Telnet World Communications, Inc. (UT) 03/02/1998
Each (30) shares Common $0.001 par exchanged for (1) share Common $0.001 par
Telnet World Communications, Inc. (UT) reincorporated in Nevada as Givemepower Corp. 07/05/2001

PEN-REY GOLD MINES LTD.
Recapitalized as El Pen-Rey Mines Ltd. 00/00/1949
Each share Common exchanged for (0.33333333) share Common
El Pen-Rey Mines Ltd. name changed to El Pen-Rey Oil & Mines Ltd 00/00/1950
(See El Pen-Rey Oil & Mines Ltd.)

PENBERTHY INSTRUMENT CO., INC. (WA)
Merged into Heath Tecna-Plastics, Inc. 05/31/1962
Each share Class A Common $2.50 par exchanged for (0.35714285) share Common no par
Each share Class B Common $2.50 par exchanged for (0.43478260) share Common no par
Heath Tecna-Plastics, Inc. name changed to Heath Tecna Corp. 07/22/1965 which name changed to Criton Corp. 07/01/1980
(See Criton Corp.)

PENCARI MNG CORP (BC)
Recapitalized as Pencari Resource Corp. 02/02/2009
Each share Common no par exchanged for (0.2) share Common no par

PENCARI RESOURCE CORP (BC)
Recapitalized as Sheen Resources Ltd. 08/27/2009
Each share Common no par exchanged for (0.33333333) share Common no par

PENCRUDE RES INC (BC)
Dissolved 5/19/89
Details not available

PEND OREILLE LEAD & ZINC CO.
Name changed to Pend Oreille Mines & Metals Co. 00/00/1929
Pend Oreille Mines & Metals Co. merged into Gulf Resources & Chemical Corp. 03/13/1974 which name changed to Gulf USA Corp. 05/01/1992
(See Gulf USA Corp.)

PEND OREILLE MINES & METALS CO (WA)
Capital Stock no par changed to $1 par 00/00/1932
Merged into Gulf Resources & Chemical Corp. 03/13/1974
Each share Capital Stock $1 par exchanged for (0.44) share Common 10¢ par
Gulf Resources & Chemical Corp. name changed to Gulf USA Corp. 05/01/1992
(See Gulf USA Corp.)

PENDARIES PETE LTD (NB)
Acquired by Ultra Petroleum Corp. (BC) 01/16/2001
Each share Common no par exchanged for (1.58) shares Common no par
Ultra Petroleum Corp. (BC) reincorporated in Yukon 03/01/2000

PENDER (DAVID) GROCERY CO. (VA)
Merged into Colonial Stores, Inc. 12/19/40
Each share Class B exchanged for (1.5) shares Common $5 par
(See Colonial Stores, Inc.)

PENDER CAP CORP (AB)
Recapitalized as Garibaldi Granite Corp. 10/5/2001
Each share Common no par exchanged for (1/6) share Common no par
Garibaldi Granite Corp. name changed to Garibaldi Resources Corp. 1/12/2006

PENDER FINL GROUP CORP (BC)
Merged into 0850197 B.C. Ltd. 06/09/2009
Each share Common no par exchanged for $0.14 cash

PENDER INTL INC (DE)
Name changed to Vianet Technology Group Ltd. 06/30/2005
Vianet Technology Group Ltd. name changed to Tradestream Global Corp. 07/27/2005 which recapitalized as Empire Global Corp. 09/30/2005 which name changed to Newgioco Group, Inc. 02/16/2017

PENDLETON TOOL INDUSTRIES, INC. (CA)
Common $1 par split (3) for (2) by issuance of (0.5) additional share 05/29/1963
Stock Dividends - 20% 02/28/1957; 20% 02/28/1962
Acquired by Ingersoll-Rand Co. (NJ) on a (1/3) for (1) basis 02/28/1964
Ingersoll-Rand Co. (NJ) reorganized in Bermuda as Ingersoll-Rand Co. Ltd. 12/31/2001 which reincorporated in Ireland as Ingersoll-Rand PLC 07/01/2009

PENDRAGON CAP CORP (AB)
Name changed to Upland Global Corp. 08/15/1995
(See Upland Global Corp.)

PENDRAGON RES LTD (AB)
Recapitalized as Fibre-Klad Industries Ltd. 11/02/1989
Each share Common no par exchanged for (0.25) share Common no par
Fibre-Klad Industries Ltd. merged into Tanqueray Resources Ltd. 05/16/1994 which recapitalized as Tanqueray Exploration Ltd. 09/13/2011 which name changed to ImmunoPrecise Antibodies Ltd. 12/29/2016

PENDRELL CORP (DE)
Reincorporated under the laws of Washington 11/19/2012

PENDULUM CAP CORP (AB)
Recapitalized as PetroFrontier Corp. 01/13/2011
Each (12) shares Common no par exchanged for (1) share Common no par

PENEDERM INC (DE)
Reincorporated 07/30/1997
State of incorporation changed from (CA) to (DE) 07/30/1997
Merged into Mylan Laboratories Inc. 10/02/1998
Each share Common 1¢ par exchanged for (0.68) share Common 50¢ par
Mylan Laboratories Inc. name changed to Mylan Inc. 10/02/2007 which merged into Mylan N.V. 02/27/2015

PENELEC CAP L P (DE)
Issue Information - 4,200,000 MONTHLY INCOME PFD SECS SER A 8.75% offered at $25 per share on 06/27/1994
8.75% Monthly Income Preferred Securities Ser. A no par called for redemption at $25 on 7/16/99

PENELEC CAP TR (DE)
Issue Information - 4,000,000 TR ORIGINATED PFD SECS 7.34% offered at $25 per share on 06/09/1999
7.34% Trust Originated Preferred Securities called for redemption at $25 on 9/1/2004

PENELLE KIRKLAND MINES LTD.
Name changed to Kirkland Diorite Gold Mines Ltd. 00/00/1936
Kirkland Diorite Gold Mines Ltd. acquired by Gordon-Lebel Mines Ltd. 00/00/1957 which merged into Hoffman Exploration & Minerals Ltd. 06/29/1981 which merged into Consolidated Thompson-Lundmark Gold Mines Ltd. 01/16/1986 which name changed to Consolidated Thompson Iron Mines Ltd. 08/24/2006
(See Consolidated Thompson Iron Mines Ltd.)

PENELOPE EXPLORATIONS LTD. (ON)
Name changed to Initiative Explorations Ltd. 01/09/1965
Initiative Explorations Ltd. merged into Initiative Explorations Inc. 02/13/1980 which merged into Canhorn Chemical Corp. 04/26/1995 which merged into Nayarit Gold Inc. 05/02/2005 which merged into Capital Gold Corp. 08/02/2010 which merged into Gammon Gold Inc. (QC) 04/08/2011 which reincorporated in Ontario as AuRico Gold Inc. 06/14/2011 which merged into Alamos Gold Inc. (New) 07/06/2015

PENETRYN INTL INC (DE)
Merged into Carborundum Co. 12/08/1975
Each share Common 10¢ par exchanged for (0.1149) share Common $3 par
(See Carborundum Co.)

PENFED BANCORP INC (DE)
Merged into Third Federal Savings & Loan 12/29/2000
Each share Common 1¢ par exchanged for $24 cash

PENFIELD URANIUM MINES LTD. (ON)
Charter surrendered for failure to file reports and pay taxes January 1961

PENFOLD CAP ACQUISITION CORP (CANADA)
Recapitalized as PBS Coals Ltd. 09/24/2008
Each share Common no par exchanged for (0.1) share Common no par
(See PBS Coals Ltd.)

PENFOLD CAP ACQUISITION II CORP (CANADA)
Merged into Penfold Capital Acquisition III Corp. (New) 10/06/2010
Each share Common no par exchanged for (0.5) share Common no par
Penfold Capital Acquisition III Corp. (New) liquidated for Phonetime Inc. 01/18/2011

PENFOLD CAP ACQUISITION III CORP OLD (CANADA)
Merged into Penfold Capital Acquisition III Corp. (New) 10/06/2010
Each share Common no par exchanged for (1) share Common no par
Penfold Capital Acquisition III Corp. (New) liquidated for Phonetime Inc. 01/18/2011

PENFOLD CAP ACQUISITION III CORP NEW (CANADA)
Completely liquidated 01/18/2011
Each share Common no par received first and final distribution of approximately (1.48) shares Phonetime Inc. Common no par and (0.6) Common Stock Purchase Warrant expiring 01/18/2012
Note: Certificates were not required to be surrendered and are without value

PENFOLD CAP ACQUISITION IV CORP (ON)
Name changed to SEL Exchange Inc. 07/09/2014

PENFORD CORP (WA)
Each share Common $1 par received distribution of (1.5) shares Penwest Pharmaceuticals Co. Common $0.001 par payable 08/31/1998 to holders of record 08/10/1998
Acquired by Ingredion Inc. 03/11/2015
Each share Common $1 par exchanged for $19 cash

PENGE CORP (DE)
SEC revoked common stock registration 07/14/2009
Stockholders' equity unlikely

PENGELLY MINES LTD (BC)
Struck off register and declared dissolved for failure to file returns 10/30/92

PENGO INDS INC (TX)
Each share Common 25¢ par exchanged for (0.1) share old Common no par 11/14/1986
Reorganized under Chapter 11 Federal Bankruptcy Code 05/08/1990
Each share old Common no par exchanged for (0.0476) share new Common no par
Merged into PI Acquisition Corp. 03/16/1994
Each share new Common no par exchanged for $0.25 cash

PENGROWTH CORP (AB)
Each Exchangeable Share no par exchanged for (1.02308) shares Pengrowth Energy Corp. Common no par 01/03/2011
Note: Unexchanged certificates were cancelled and became without value 01/03/2014

PENGROWTH ENERGY TR (AB)
Name changed 05/29/1996
Name changed from Pengrowth Gas Income Fund to Pengrowth Energy Trust 05/29/1996
Old Trust Units no par reclassified as Class A Trust Units 07/28/2004
Note: Canadian holders had the option to receive Class B Trust Units
Class A Trust Units no par reclassified as new Trust Units no par 07/27/2006
Class B Trust Units no par reclassified as new Trust Units no par 07/27/2006
Reorganized as Pengrowth Energy Corp. 01/03/2011
Each new Trust Unit no par exchanged for (1) share Common no par
Note: Unexchanged certificates were cancelled and became without value 01/03/2014

PENGUIN GROUP INC (DE)
Each share Common $0.001 par exchanged for (1/6) share Common $0.006 par 8/27/87
Charter cancelled and declared inoperative and void for non-payment of taxes 3/1/91

PENICK & FORD LTD., INC. (DE)
Common no par changed to $3.50 par and (1) additional share issued 4/18/57
Common $3.50 par changed to $1 par and (2) additional shares issued 4/26/62
Stock Dividend - 100% 4/4/47
Completely liquidated for cash 6/9/65

PENICK (S.B.) & CO. (DE)
4-1/2% Preferred $100 par called for redemption 04/10/1964
Common $2 par split (2) for (1) by issuance of (1) additional share 05/09/1966
Acquired by Corn Products Co. 01/15/1968
Each share Common $2 par exchanged for (0.785) share Common 50¢ par
Corn Products Co. name changed to CPC International Inc. 04/23/1969 which name changed to BestFoods 01/01/1998
(See BestFoods)

PENINSULA BK (ENGLEWOOD, FL)
Name changed 01/01/1998
Name changed from Peninsula State Bank (Englewood, FL) to Peninsula Bank (Englewood, FL) 01/01/1998
Each share Common $10 par exchanged for (2) shares Common $5 par 06/30/2004
Common $5 par changed to $1 par 09/10/2009
Bank closed and FDIC appointed receiver 06/25/2010
Stockholders' equity unlikely

PENINSULA BK (ISHPEMING, MI)
Common $50 par changed to $25 par and (1) additional share issued 10/02/1978
Reorganized as Peninsula Financial Corp. 07/31/1986
Each share Common $25 par exchanged for (1) share Common $1 par

PENINSULA BK (SAN DIEGO, CA)
Capital Stock $5 par changed to $1.66 par 01/15/1980
Capital Stock $1.66 par split (3) for (1) by issuance of (2) additional shares 01/20/1980
Capital Stock $1.66 par split (2) for (1) by issuance of (1) additional share payable 03/27/1998 to holders of record 03/11/1998
Stock Dividend - 5% payable 07/26/1996 to holders of record 07/12/1996
Merged into U.S. Bancorp 01/14/2000
Each share Capital Stock $1.66 par exchanged for (1.548) shares Common $1.25 par

PENINSULA BK HLDG CO (CA)
Name changed to Avidbank Holdings, Inc. 08/02/2011

PENINSULA BANK OF COMM (MILLBRAE, CA)
Merged into Greater Bay Bancorp 12/23/1997
Each share Common no par exchanged for (0.9655) share Common no par
Greater Bay Bancorp merged into

Wells Fargo & Co. (New) 10/01/2007

PENINSULA COPPER CO.
Dissolved in 1945

PENINSULA FED SVGS & LN ASSN MIAMI FLA (USA)
Through exchange offer 99.6% acquired by Atico Financial Corp. as of 02/01/1990
Public interest eliminated

PENINSULA HLDGS GROUP LTD (NV)
SEC revoked common stock registration 04/23/2007
Stockholders' equity unlikely

PENINSULA LUMBER CO.
Dissolved in 1928

PENINSULA NATL BK (BURLINGAME, CA)
Under plan of partial liquidation Common Capital Stock $10 par changed to $4 par and $8 cash distributed 5/1/70
Acquired by Central Banking System, Inc. 4/1/77
Each share Common Capital Stock $4 par exchanged for (1) share Capital Stock $2.50 par
(See Central Banking System, Inc.)

PENINSULA NATL BK (CEDARHURST, NY)
Each share Common $25 par exchanged for (2) shares Common $12.50 par 1/25/55
Common $12.50 par changed to $6.25 par and (1) additional share issued 1/24/61
Common $6.25 par changed to $3.125 par and (1) additional share issued 5/15/72
Merged into United Bank Corp. of New York 7/31/80
Each share Common $3.125 par exchanged for (1) share Conv. Preferred Ser. E $20 par or $19 cash
United Bank Corp. of New York name changed to Norstar Bancorp Inc. 1/4/82 which merged into Fleet/Norstar Financial Group, Inc. 1/1/88 which name changed to Fleet Financial Group, Inc. (New) 4/15/92 which name changed to Fleet Boston Corp. 10/1/99 which name changed to FleetBoston Financial Corp. 4/18/2000 which merged into Bank of America Corp. 4/1/2004

PENINSULA OIL DEVELOPMENT CO. (NV)
Dissolved 11/8/61

PENINSULA PETE CORP (BC)
Merged into Consolidated International Petroleum Corp. 6/1/85
Each (5.08) shares Common no par exchanged for (1) share Common no par
Consolidated International Petroleum Corp. name changed to International Petroleum Corp. 6/30/86 which was acquired by Sands Petroleum AB 1/15/98

PENINSULA PUBLISHING & PRINTING CORP. (NY)
Name changed to Atlantic States Industries, Inc. (NY) 09/27/1963
Atlantic States Industries, Inc. (NY) reincorporated in Delaware 01/14/1970 which name changed to ASI Communications, Inc. 04/30/1970
(See ASI Communications, Inc.)

PENINSULA RES CORP (DE)
Stock Dividend - 50% 11/14/80
Chapter 11 Federal Bankruptcy Code converted to Chapter 7 on 10/2/89
Stockholders' equity unlikely

PENINSULA RES LTD (BC)
Reincorporated under the laws of Alberta as Zodiac Exploration Inc. 10/06/2010
Zodiac Exploration Inc. recapitalized as Mobius Resources Inc. 05/01/2014 which name changed to Sintana Energy Inc. 08/10/2015

PENINSULA SAVINGS & LOAN ASSOCIATION (AK)
Closed 8/8/86
Details not available

PENINSULA TR BK INC (GLOUCESTER, VA)
Under plan of reorganization each share Common $5 par automatically became (1) share Mid-Atlantic Community Bankgroup, Inc. Common $5 par 8/15/96
Mid-Atlantic Community Bankgroup, Inc. name changed Atlantic Financial Corp. 12/1/98 which merged into F & M National Corp. 2/26/2001 which merged into BB&T Corp. 8/9/2001

PENINSULAR & ORIENTAL STEAM NAV CO (ENGLAND)
Each Sponsored ADR for Ordinary received distribution of (0.5) P&O Princess Cruises PLC ADR for Ordinary 50¢ par payable 10/23/2000 to holders of record 10/20/2000
Merged into Ports, Customs and Free Zone Corp. 3/8/2006
Each Sponsored ADR for Ordinary exchanged for $18.098038 cash

PENINSULAR GRINDING WHEEL CO. (MI)
Stock Dividend - 200% 3/30/48
Merged into Abrasive & Metal Products Co. and each share Common $1 par exchanged for (1.2) shares Common $1 par in 1954
Abrasive & Metal Products Co. name changed to Wakefield Corp. 4/28/61
Wakefield Corp. name changed to 729 Meldrum Corp. 2/24/66 which completed liquidation 10/22/66

PENINSULAR LIFE INS CO NEW (FL)
Merged into McM Corp. 8/20/79
Each share Common $3 par exchanged for (1.8) shares Common $1 par
(See McM Corp.)

PENINSULAR LIFE INS CO OLD (FL)
Each share Common $1 par exchanged for (0.2) share Common $5 par 4/2/62
Common $5 par changed to $3 par and (0.666) additional share issued 5/2/69
Stock Dividends - 25% 7/2/62; 20% 4/19/65; 25% 12/2/68
Reorganized as McMillen Corp. 12/31/72
Each share Common $3 par exchanged for (1) share Common $3 par
McMillen Corp. merged into Peninsular Life Insurance Co. (New) 9/30/76 which merged into McM Corp. 8/20/79
(See McM Corp.)

PENINSULAR METAL PRODUCTS CORP. (MI)
6% Preferred called for redemption 09/28/1960
Name changed to Cox Instruments Corp. 05/03/1962
Cox Instruments Corp. merged into Lynch Corp. 06/28/1963 which name changed to LGL Group, Inc. (IN) 06/21/2006 which reincorporated in Delaware 08/31/2007

PENINSULAR OIL CO. (MI)
Charter revoked for failure to file reports and pay fees 5/15/63

PENINSULAR OIL CORP. LTD.
Recapitalized as New Peninsular Oil Ltd. 00/00/1952
Each share Capital Stock $1 par exchanged for (0.75) share Capital Stock $1 par
(See New Peninsular Oil Ltd.)

PENINSULAR TELEPHONE CO. (FL)
Each share Common $100 par exchanged for (5) shares Common no par in 1930
Common no par split (3) for (2) by issuance of (1) additional share for each (2) shares in 1953
Stock Dividend - 20% 2/27/53
Name changed to General Telephone Co. of Florida 4/9/58
General Telephone Co. of Florida name changed to GTE Florida Inc. 1/1/88
(See GTE Florida Inc.)

PENMAN MINES CORP. (OR)
Voluntarily dissolved 11/27/42
Details not available

PENMANS LTD (CANADA)
Each share Common $100 par exchanged for (3) shares old Common no par 00/00/1927
Each share old Common no par exchanged for (3) shares new Common no par 01/06/1956
Acquired by Dominion Textile Co., Ltd. 10/12/1965
Each share new Common no par exchanged for $45 cash
6% Preferred $100 par called for redemption 06/00/1973
Public interest eliminated

PENN AKRON CORP (NV)
Reincorporated 03/13/1999
Each share old Common 5¢ par exchanged for (0.1) new Common 5¢ par 06/20/1983
New Common 5¢ par changed to 1¢ par 03/07/1984
State of incorporation changed from (DE) to (NV) 03/13/1999
Each share Common 1¢ par exchanged for (1.75) shares Common $0.001 par 03/17/2000
Name changed to Heroes, Inc. 12/07/2000
(See Heroes, Inc.)

PENN-AMER GROUP INC (PA)
Merged into United America Indemnity, Ltd. (Cayman Islands) 01/25/2005
Each share Common 1¢ par exchanged for (0.7756) share Class A Common $0.0001 par and $1.50 cash
United America Indemnity, Ltd. (Cayman Islands) reorganized in Ireland as Global Indemnity PLC 07/02/2010 which reincorporated in Cayman Islands as Global Indemnity Ltd. 11/07/2016

PENN BAYLESS OIL & GAS CO. (DE)
No longer in existence having become inoperative and void for non-payment of taxes 4/1/59

PENN BIOTECH INC (BC)
Name changed to United Traffic System Inc. 01/13/2005
United Traffic System Inc. recapitalized as Corpus Resources Corp. 12/14/2007 which name changed to NeoMedyx Medical Corp. 08/04/2009 which name changed to Blue Marble Media Corp. 03/30/2010 which name changed to KBridge Energy Corp. 01/31/2012

PENN-BURKBURNETT OIL CO. (DE)
Charter cancelled for non-payment of taxes 1/23/24

PENN CENT BANCORP INC (PA)
Common $2.50 par split (2) for (1) by issuance of (1) additional share 11/14/1986
Common $2.50 par changed to $1.25 par and (1) additional share issued 08/18/1989
Merged into Omega Financial Corp. 01/28/1994
Each share Common $1.25 par exchanged for (1.63) shares Common $5 par
Omega Financial Corp. merged into F.N.B. Corp. 04/01/2008

PENN CENT CO (PA)
Under plan of reorganization Capital Stock $10 par reclassified as Common no par 10/1/69
Reorganized as Penn Central Corp. 10/24/78
Each (25) shares Common no par exchanged for (1) share Common $1 par
Penn Central Corp. name changed to American Premier Underwriters, Inc. 3/25/94 which merged into American Premier Group, Inc. which name changed to American Financial Group, Inc. 6/9/95 which merged into American Financial Group, Inc. (Holding Co.) 12/2/97

PENN CENT CORP (PA)
Conv. Preference Ser. A $20 par called for redemption 02/23/1981
Conv. Preference Ser. B $20 par called for redemption 02/23/1981
Ctfs. of Bene. Int. no par called for redemption 02/24/1981
Common $1 par split (3) for (2) by issuance of (0.5) additional share 01/22/1982
$5.27 Conv. Preference 1st Ser. no par called for redemption 01/16/1985
Common $1 par split (2) for (1) by issuance of (1) additional share 03/11/1988
Name changed to American Premier Underwriters, Inc. 03/25/1994
American Premier Underwriters, Inc. merged into American Premier Group, Inc. 04/03/1995 which name changed to American Financial Group, Inc. 06/09/1995 which merged into American Financial Group, Inc. (Holding Co.) 12/02/1997

PENN CENT NATL BK (HUNTINGDON, PA)
Common $5 par changed to $2.50 par and (1) additional share issued 02/10/1976
Under plan of reorganization each share Common $2.50 par automatically became (1) share Penn Central Bancorp, Inc. Common $2.50 par 04/30/1984
Penn Central Bancorp, Inc. merged into Omega Financial Corp. 01/28/1994 which merged into F.N.B. Corp. 04/01/2008

PENN CENTRAL LIGHT & POWER CO. (PA)
Name changed to Pennsylvania Edison Co. 6/10/37
Pennsylvania Edison Co. liquidation for cash was completed in 1949

PENN-CENTRAL OIL CO. (KS)
Reverted to private company by purchase of publicly held shares 00/00/1964
Details not available

PENN-COBALT SILVER MINES LTD.
Merged into Cobalt Consolidated Mining Corp. Ltd. 00/00/1953
Each (13) shares Capital Stock $1 par exchanged for (1) share Capital Stock $1 par
Cobalt Consolidated recapitalized as Agnico Mines Ltd. 10/25/1957 which merged into Agnico-Eagle Mines Ltd. 06/01/1972 which name changed to Agnico Eagle Mines Ltd. 04/30/2013

PENN CONTROLS, INC. (DE)
Acquired by Johnson Service Co. 10/28/1968
Each share Common $2.50 par exchanged for (1) share $2 Conv. Preferred Ser. A $1 par

Johnson Service Co. name changed to Johnson Controls, Inc. 12/02/1974 which merged into Johnson Controls International PLC 09/06/2016

PENN CONTROLS, INC. (IN)
Stock Dividend - 25% 10/15/1965
Reincorporated under the laws of Delaware 02/18/1966
Penn Controls, Inc. (DE) acquired by Johnson Service Co. 10/28/1968 which name changed to Johnson Controls, Inc. 12/02/1974 which merged into Johnson Controls International PLC 09/06/2016

PENN CORP (DE)
Merged into Nnep Corp. 04/05/1982
Each share Common $1 par exchanged for $50 cash

PENN DAIRIES INC (PA)
Common no par changed to $5 par 00/00/1941
Each share Common $5 par exchanged for (4) shares Class A Common $5 par and (1) share Class B Common $5 par 07/07/1954
6% Preferred $100 par reclassified as $6 Preferred no par 10/09/1963
Class A & B Common $5 par changed to no par 10/09/1963
Merged into Crowley Foods, Inc. 07/12/1990
Each share $6 Preferred no par exchanged for $110.22 cash
Each share Class A Common no par exchanged for $31 cash
Each share Class B Common no par exchanged for $31 cash

PENN-DIXIE CEMENT CORP. (DE)
Capital Stock $7 par changed to $1 par and (2) additional shares issued 05/06/1955
Capital Stock $1 par reclassified as Common $1 par 04/23/1969
Name changed to Penn-Dixie Industries, Inc. 04/17/1973
Penn-Dixie Industries, Inc. name changed to Continental Steel Corp. (DE) 03/18/1982
(See Continental Steel Corp. (DE))

PENN DIXIE INDS INC (DE)
Preferred Ser. C $1 par called for redemption 08/00/1981
Name changed to Continental Steel Corp. (DE) 03/18/1982
(See Continental Steel Corp. (DE))

PENN DIXIE LEASING CORP (NY)
Name changed to Castle Capital Corp. 05/20/1970
(See Castle Capital Corp.)

PENN ELECTRIC SWITCH CO.
Merged into Penn Controls, Inc. (IN) 00/00/1951
Each share Class A $10 par exchanged for (1) share Class A $10 par
Each share Common $5 par exchanged for (2) shares Common $2.50 par
Penn Controls, Inc. (IN) reincorporated in Delaware 02/18/1966 which was acquired by Johnson Service Co. 10/28/1968 which name changed to Johnson Controls, Inc. 12/02/1974 which merged into Johnson Controls International PLC 09/06/2016

PENN ENERGY CORP (BC)
Common no par split (3) for (1) by issuance of (2) additional shares 9/29/81
Recapitalized as New Penn Energy Corp. (BC) (Old) 6/11/82
Each share Common no par exchanged for (1/3) share Common no par
New Penn Energy Corp. (BC) (Old) merged into New Penn Energy Corp. (BC) (New) 11/22/82 which reincorporated in Canada 1/29/85

which merged into International Interlake Industries Inc. 12/31/86
(See International Interlake Industries Inc.)

PENN ENGR & MFG CORP (DE)
Common $1 par split (3) for (2) by issuance of (0.5) additional share 12/18/78
Common $1 par reclassified as Class A Common 1¢ par 5/23/96
Each share Class A Common 1¢ par received distribution of (3) shares Non-Vtg. Common 1¢ par 5/23/96
Class A Common 1¢ par split (2) for (1) by issuance of (1) additional share payable 5/1/2001 to holders of record 4/11/2001 Ex date - 5/2/2001
Non-Vtg. Common 1¢ par split (2) for (1) by issuance of (1) additional share payable 5/1/2001 to holders of record 4/11/2001 Ex date - 5/2/2001
Stock Dividends - 33-1/3% 3/29/68; 10% 12/17/73
Merged into PEM Holding Co. 5/25/2005
Each share Class A Common 1¢ par exchanged for $18.25 cash
Each share Non-Vtg. Common 1¢ par exchanged for $18.25 cash

PENN FED CORP (DE)
Completely liquidated 06/26/1969
No stockholders' equity

PENN FRUIT INC (PA)
Reincorporated 02/11/1960
Common $5 par exchanged (2) for (1) 00/00/1954
State of incorporation changed from (DE) to (PA) 02/11/1960
4.60% Preferred $50 par called for redemption 06/01/1974
Name changed to Penn Merchandising Corp. 06/22/1982
(See Penn Merchandising Corp.)

PENN FUEL GAS INC (PA)
$1.50 Preferred $22.40 par called for redemption 6/30/63
$1.10 Preferred Ser. G $22.40 par called for redemption 2/1/89
Acquired by PP&L Resources Inc. 8/21/98
Each share Common $1 par exchanged for approximately (7.742) shares Common no par

PENN (WILLIAM) GAS CO., INC. (DE)
Merged into Fremont Uranium Corp. (CO) 09/21/1955
Each share Common exchanged for (1/6) share Common
Fremont Uranium Corp. (CO) merged into King Oil, Inc. 09/05/1956 which recapitalized as Lane Wood, Inc. 08/10/1964
(See Lane Wood, Inc.)

PENN GEN AGYS INC (DE)
Merged into Penncorp Financial, Inc. 1/28/80
Each (7) shares Common 10¢ par exchanged for (1) share Common 50¢ par
Penncorp Financial, Inc. merged into American Can Co. 1/11/83 which name changed to Primerica Corp. (NJ) 4/28/87 which was acquired by Primerica Corp. (DE) 12/15/88 which name changed to Travelers Inc. 12/31/93 which name changed to Travelers Group Inc. 4/16/95 which name changed to Citigroup Inc. 10/8/98

PENN GENERAL CASUALTY CO.
In process of liquidation in 1936

PENN-GOLD RES INC (BC)
Recapitalized as Moreno Ventures Inc. 04/07/1998
Each share Common no par exchanged for (0.07692308) share Common no par
Moreno Ventures Inc. recapitalized as Niogold Mining Corp. 09/24/2002 which merged into Oban Mining Corp. 03/11/2016 which name

changed to Osisko Mining Inc. 06/21/2016

PENN HEAT CONTROL CO.
Dissolved in 1932

PENN HLDGS INC (ON)
Recapitalized as Raider Ventures Ltd. 09/06/1989
Each share Common no par exchanged for (0.33333333) share Common no par
Raider Ventures Ltd. name changed to IFM Food Management (Canada) Ltd. 11/30/1990 which name changed to Air Systems Plus Corp. 02/25/1992 which name changed to Sales Initiatives International Inc. 06/01/1993 which name changed to Greenlight Communications Inc. 06/14/1994
(See Greenlight Communications Inc.)

PENN INVESTMENT CO. (DE)
Common no par changed to $1 par 00/00/1935
Recapitalized 00/00/1940
$4 Cum. Preferred no par changed to $4 Non-Cum. Preferred no par
Common $1 par changed to 10¢ par
Liquidation completed 01/20/1961
Preferred holders received $49.56 per share
No consideration for Common

PENN JERSEY WATER SERVICE CO.
Merged into Northeastern Water Co. in 1947
Each share $2 Preferred exchanged for (10) shares new Common
Each share Common exchanged for (2) shares new Common
Northeastern Water Co. merged into American Water Works Co., Inc. 8/17/62
(See American Water Works Co., Inc.)

PENN LAUREL FINL CORP (PA)
Common $5 par split (3) for (1) by issuance of (2) additional shares payable 09/15/2003 to holders of record 09/02/2003 Ex date - 09/22/2003
Merged into Northwest Bancorp, Inc. 06/22/2007
Each share Common $5 par exchanged for $31 cash

PENN (WILLIAM) LIFE INSURANCE CO. (FL)
Name changed to Eagle National Life Insurance Co. 05/31/1965
Eagle National Life Insurance Co. merged into National Life Insurance Co. of Florida 07/01/1967 which reorganized as National Life of Florida Corp. 10/31/1968 which name changed to Voyager Group, Inc. 07/01/1980
(See Voyager Group, Inc.)

PENN LYNC RES LTD (ON)
Recapitalized as Penn Holdings Inc. 01/13/1988
Each share Common no par exchanged for (0.5) share Common no par
Penn Holdings Inc. recapitalized as Raider Ventures Ltd. 09/06/1989 which name changed to IFM Food Management (Canada) Ltd. 11/30/1990 which name changed to Air Systems Plus Corp. 02/25/1992 which name changed to Sales Initiatives International Inc. 06/01/1993 which name changed to Greenlight Communications Inc. 06/14/1994
(See Greenlight Communications Inc.)

PENN MERCANTILE PROPERTIES
Liquidation completed in 1949

PENN MERCHANDISING CORP (PA)
Merged into New Penn Merchandising Corp. 11/29/1983
Each share 4.68% Preferred $50 par exchanged for $23.035 cash

Each share Common $5 par exchanged for $4 cash
Note: An additional distribution of $1.94 cash per share was made to former holders of Common $5 par 11/27/1984

PENN METAL FABRICATORS INC (DE)
Merged into Merco Inc. 10/01/1985
Each share Common 10¢ par exchanged for $2.10 cash

PENN-MEX FUEL CO.
Liquidation completed in 1942

PENN MILLERS HLDG CORP (PA)
Acquired by ACE American Insurance Co. 11/30/2011
Each share Common 1¢ par exchanged for $20.50 cash

PENN-NEVADA CORP.
Ceased operations 00/00/1934
Details not available

PENN OCTANE CORP (DE)
Each share Common 1¢ par received distribution of (0.125) share Rio Vista Energy Partners L.P. Common Unit payable 09/30/2004 to holders of record 09/17/2004
SEC revoked common stock registration 03/24/2014

PENN-OHIO EDISON CO.
Acquired by Commonwealth & Southern Corp. in 1930
Details not available

PENN OHIO GAS CO. (DE)
Liquidation completed
Each share 5% Preferred $10 par exchanged for $10 cash 10/15/64
Each share Common 10¢ par stamped to indicate initial distribution of 30¢ cash 10/15/64 and a second distribution of 15¢ cash 2/17/65
Each share Stamped Common 10¢ par exchanged for third and final distribution of 11¢ cash 9/15/65

PENN OHIO OIL & GAS CO. OF DEL.
Out of existence 00/00/1937
Details not available

PENN OHIO SECURITIES CORP.
Acquired by Penn-Ohio Edison Co. in 1929
Details not available

PENN OPTICAL INC. (CA)
Name changed to 2930 Bristol Street Corp. 9/14/62 which was liquidated 10/8/62

PENN PAC CORP (NV)
Reincorporated 07/01/1971
Reincorporated 04/04/2005
State of incorporation changed from (PA) to (DE) 07/01/1971
Each share old Common 50¢ par exchanged for (1/3) share new Common 50¢ 03/31/1978
New Common 50¢ par changed to 10¢ par 09/16/1987
Each share old Common 10¢ par exchanged for (0.1) share new Common 10¢ par 03/03/1995
Each share new Common 10¢ par exchanged for (0.05) share new Common 10¢ par 12/30/1998
State of incorporation changed from (DE) to Nevada and new Common 10¢ par changed to $0.00001 par 04/04/2005
Charter revoked for failure to file reports and pay fees 04/30/2010

PENN RIVET CORP.
Liquidated in 1947

PENN SVGS BK F S B (WYOMISSING, PA)
Reorganized as Sovereign Bancorp, Inc. 12/21/1987
Each share Common $1 par exchanged for (1) share Common $1 par

Sovereign Bancorp, Inc. merged into Banco Santander, S.A. 01/30/2009

PENN SEABOARD STEEL CORP. (NY)
Assets liquidated for benefit of creditors in 1930
No stockholders' equity

PENN SEC BK & TR CO (SCRANTON, PA)
Capital Stock $10 par split (3) for (1) by issuance of (2) additional shares 06/16/1986
Recapitalized as Penseco Financial Services Corp. 12/31/1997
Each share Capital Stock $10 par exchanged for (4) shares Common 1¢ par
Penseco Financial Services Corp. merged into Peoples Financial Services Corp. 12/02/2013

PENN SECS CO (PA)
100% acquired by General Finance Services Corp. through purchase offer which expired 11/30/1972
Public interest eliminated

PENN ST INVS CORP (PA)
Name changed to Penn-Pacific Corp. (PA) 05/31/1966
Penn-Pacific Corp. (PA) reincorporated in Delaware 07/01/1971 which reincorporated in Nevada 04/04/2005
(See Penn-Pacific Corp. (NV))

PENN STEEL CASTINGS CO.
Property sold in 1928

PENN SUGAR PROPERTIES CORP.
Liquidated in 1945

PENN TECH CORP (DE)
Charter cancelled and declared inoperative and void for non-payment of taxes 4/15/75

PENN-TEXAS CORP. (PA)
Under plan of merger Capital Stock $10 par reclassified as Common $10 par 9/30/55
Common $10 par changed to $1 par 10/14/58
Name changed to Fairbanks Whitney Corp. 5/29/59
Fairbanks Whitney Corp. recapitalized as Colt Industries Inc. (Pa.) 5/15/64 which reincorporated in Delaware 10/17/68 then reincorporated in Pennsylvania 5/6/76
(See Colt Industries Inc. (Pa.))

PENN TIDE CORP (OH)
Merged into Cambridge Foods Inc. 12/31/91
Each share Common no par exchanged for $0.30 cash

PENN TRAFFIC CO NEW (DE)
Reincorporated 9/18/92
State of incorporation changed from (PA) to (DE) 9/18/92
Each share old Common $1.25 par exchanged for (0.01) share new Common $1.25 par 6/29/99
Plan of reorganization under Chapter 11 Federal Bankruptcy Code effective 4/13/2005
No stockholders' equity

PENN TRAFFIC CO OLD (PA)
Capital Stock $2.50 par changed to $1.25 par and (1) additional share issued 6/15/77
Capital Stock $1.25 par split (2) for (1) by issuance of (1) additional share 9/30/86
Stock Dividend - 15% 5/7/76
Acquired by Miller Tabak Hirsch & Co. 4/22/87
Each share Capital Stock $1.25 par exchanged for $31.60 cash

PENN-UTAH URANIUM, INC. (NV)
Merged into Montana Chemical & Milling Corp. on a (1) for (3) basis 2/10/56
(See Montana Chemical & Milling Corp.)

PENN VA CORP OLD (VA)
Common $25 par changed to $12.50 par and (1) additional share issued 09/02/1971
Common $12.50 par changed to $6.25 par and (1) additional share issued 08/15/1975
Common $6.25 par split (2) for (1) by issuance of (1) additional share 11/21/1980
Common $6.25 par split (2) for (1) by issuance of (1) additional share payable 08/15/1997 to holders of record 08/01/1997
Common $6.25 par changed to 1¢ par and (1) additional share issued payable 06/10/2004 to holders of record 06/03/2004 Ex date - 06/14/2004
Common 1¢ par split (2) for (1) by issuance of (1) additional share payable 06/19/2007 to holders of record 06/12/2007 Ex date - 06/20/2007
Plan of reorganization under Chapter 11 Federal Bankrutpcy proceedings effective 09/12/2016
No stockholders' equity

PENN VA GP HLDGS L P (DE)
Merged into Penn Virginia Resource Partners, L.P. 03/10/2011
Each Common Unit exchanged for (0.98) Common Unit
Penn Virginia Resource Partners, L.P. name changed to PVR Partners, L.P. 08/27/2012 which merged into Regency Energy Partners L.P. 03/21/2014 which merged into Energy Transfer Partners, L.P. (Old) 04/30/2015 which merged into Energy Transfer Partners, L.P. (New) 05/01/2017 which merged into Energy Transfer L.P. 10/19/2018

PENN VA RESOURCE PARTNERS L P (DE)
Common Units split (2) for (1) by issuance of (1) additional share payable 04/04/2006 to holders of record 03/28/2006 Ex date - 04/05/2006
Name changed to PVR Partners, L.P. 08/27/2012
PVR Partners, L.P. merged into Regency Energy Partners L.P. 03/21/2014 which merged into Energy Transfer Partners, L.P. (Old) 04/30/2015 which merged into Energy Transfer Partners, L.P. (New) 05/01/2017 which merged into Energy Transfer L.P. 10/19/2018

PENN VALLEY CRUDE OIL CORP. (DE)
Liquidation completed in 1955

PENN WEST ENERGY TR (AB)
Reorganized as Penn West Petroleum Ltd. (New) 01/03/2011
Each Trust Unit exchanged for (1) share Common no par
Note: Unexchanged certificates were cancelled and became without value 01/03/2014
Penn West Petroleum Ltd. (New) name changed to Obsidian Energy Ltd. 06/29/2017

PENN WEST PETE LTD NEW (AB)
Name changed to Obsidian Energy Ltd. 06/29/2017

PENN WEST PETE LTD OLD (AB)
Each share Class A no par exchanged for (1) share Common no par 11/15/1984
Each share old Common no par exchanged for (0.2) share a new Common no par 06/09/1993
Reorganized as Penn West Energy Trust 05/31/2005
Each share new Common no par exchanged for (3) Trust Units
Penn West Energy Trust reorganized as Penn West Petroleum Ltd. (New)
01/03/2011 which name changed to Obsidian Energy Ltd. 06/29/2017

PENN WESTERN GAS & ELECTRIC CO.
Dissolved in 1939

PENN YAN EXPRESS INC (NY)
Merged into Consolidated Freightways, Inc. 11/22/1983
Each share Class A $1 par exchanged for $7.50 cash

PENN-YORK OIL & GAS CORP. (DE)
No longer in existence having become inoperative and void for non-payment of taxes 7/1/40

PENNACO ENERGY INC (DE)
Merged into Marathon Oil Co. 3/27/2001
Each share Common $0.001 par exchanged for $19 cash

PENNANT DRILLING CO., INC. (CO)
Acquired by Great Basins Petroleum Co. 02/17/1954
Details not available

PENNANT ENERGY INC (BC)
Merged into Blackbird Energy Inc. 04/22/2014
Each share Common no par exchanged for (0.42857) share Common no par
Note: Unexchanged certificates were cancelled and became without value 04/22/2017

PENNANT PAC RES INC (CO)
Merged into Asia Oil & Minerals Ltd. 09/28/1983
Each share Common 1¢ par held by United States residents exchanged for $0.0053 cash
Each share Common 1¢ par held by foreign residents exchanged for (11) shares Ordinary A$0.25 par
(See Asia Oil & Minerals Ltd.)

PENNANT PUMA OILS LTD (AB)
Acquired by Algas Mineral Enterprises Ltd. 12/24/1976
Each share Common no par exchanged for $6 cash

PENNANT RES LTD (ON)
Recapitalized as PNR Food Industries Ltd. 11/23/1987
Each share Capital Stock no par exchanged for (0.05) share Conv. Class A Multiple Part. no par and (0.05) share Class B Subordinate Part. no par
(See PNR Food Industries Ltd.)

PENNAQUE MINING CORP. LTD. (ON)
Recapitalized as Lakeshore Minerals Inc. 04/30/1986
Each share Capital Stock $1 par exchanged for (0.2) share Common no par
Lakeshore Minerals Inc. recapitalized as Leggo Holdings Inc. 07/18/1990 which name changed to Transarctic Petroleum Corp. 09/29/1997 which name changed to ivyNET Corp. 03/26/1999 which recapitalized as Saratoga Capital Corp. 08/25/2000
(See Saratoga Capital Corp.)

PENNATE CORP (DE)
Name changed to Kalex Corp. 01/02/1996
(See Kalex Corp.)

PENNBANCORP (PA)
Common $5 par split (2) for (1) by issuance of (1) additional share 09/01/1985
Common $5 par split (3) for (2) by issuance of (0.5) additional share 03/01/1987
Stock Dividend - 25% 01/06/1984
Merged into Integra Financial Corp. 01/26/1989
Each share Common $5 par exchanged for (1.0146) shares Common $1 par
Integra Financial Corp. merged into National City Corp. 05/03/1996 which was acquired by PNC Financial Services Group, Inc. 12/31/2008

PENNBEC MNG CORP (QC)
Declared dissolved for failure to file reports or pay fees 10/12/1974

PENNCO ENTERPRISES INC (NY)
Under plan of merger each share Common 1¢ par automatically became (1) share Safelite Industries, Inc. Common 10¢ par 01/21/1972
(See Safelite Industries, Inc.)

PENNCORE FINL SERVICES CORP (PA)
Merged into ML Bancorp, Inc. 09/08/1997
Each share Common $5 par exchanged for either (2.5) shares Common no par, $36.56 cash, or (1.75526) shares Common no par and $5.1184 cash
ML Bancorp, Inc. merged into Sovereign Bancorp, Inc. 02/27/1998 which merged into Banco Santander, S.A. 01/30/2009

PENNCORP FINL GROUP INC (DE)
Issue Information - 2,000,000 shares PFD CONV $3.375 offered at $50 per share on 07/14/1995
Reorganized under Chapter 11 Bankruptcy Code as Southwestern Life Holdings, Inc. 6/19/2000
Each share $3.375 Conv. Preferred 1¢ par exchanged for (1) share Common 1¢ par
Each share Conv. Preferred Ser. II exchanged for (1) share Common 1¢ par
All Common 1¢ par were cancelled and are without value
(See Southwestern Life Holding, Inc.)

PENNCORP FINL INC (DE)
Merged into American Can Co. 01/11/1983
Each share Common 50¢ par exchanged for $13.75 principal amount of 13.25% Notes due 01/01/1993 or (0.5) share $3 Conv. Preferred no par or (0.1375) share $13.75 Preferred no par
American Can Co. name changed to Primerica Corp. (NJ) 04/28/1987 which was acquired by Primerica Corp. (DE) 12/15/1988 which name changed to Travelers Inc. 12/31/1993 which name changed to Travelers Group Inc. 04/16/1995 which name changed to Citigroup Inc. 10/08/1998

PENNELL URANIUM CORP (UT)
Recapitalized as Strategic Oils 03/08/1969
Each share Common 1¢ par exchanged for (0.1) share Common 10¢ par
(See Strategic Oils)

PENNEY (J.C.) CASUALTY INSURANCE CO. (OH)
Over 99.9% owned by Penney (J.C.) Co., Inc. as of 04/01/1976
Public interest eliminated

PENNEY (J.C.) CO. (DE)
Common no par changed to $1 par and (2) additional shares issued 6/20/60
Stock Dividend - 200% 1/16/46
Name changed to Penney (J.C.) Co., Inc. 10/17/68

PENNEY (JC) INC (DE)
Preferred Stock Purchase Rights declared for Common stockholders of record 02/07/1986 were redeemed at $0.10 per right 02/21/1990 for holders of record 02/14/1990
(Additional Information in Active)

PENNFED CAP TR I (DE)
8.90% Trust Preferred Securities

called for redemption at $25 plus $0.203958 accrued dividend on 6/3/2003

PENNFED FINL SVCS INC (MD)
Reincorporated 10/30/2003
Common 1¢ par split (2) for (1) by issuance of (1) additional share payable 2/10/98 to holders of record 1/27/98
State of incorporation changed from (DE) to (MD) 10/30/2003
Common 1¢ par split (2) for (1) by issuance of (1) additional share payable 10/29/2004 to holders of record 10/15/2004 Ex date - 11/1/2004
Merged into New York Community Bancorp, Inc. 4/2/2007
Each share Common 1¢ par exchanged for (1.222) shares Common 1¢ par

PENNFIRST BANCORP INC (PA)
Common 1¢ par split (6) for (5) by issuance of (0.2) additional share 01/25/1992
Common 1¢ par split (6) for (5) by issuance of (0.2) additional share 07/25/1992
Common 1¢ par split (6) for (5) by issuance of (0.2) additional share 01/25/1993
Common 1¢ par split (6) for (5) by issuance of (0.2) additional share 06/07/1993
Common 1¢ par split (6) for (5) by issuance of (0.2) additional share 01/25/1994
Common 1¢ par split (6) for (5) by issuance of (0.2) additional share 01/25/1995
Stock Dividend - 10% payable 08/25/1997 to holders of record 07/31/1997
Name changed to ESB Financial Corp. 05/01/1998
ESB Financial Corp. merged into WesBanco, Inc. 02/10/2015

PENNFIRST CAP TR I (DE)
8.625% Trust Preferred Securities called for redemption at $10 on 1/15/2004

PENNICHUCK CORP (NH)
Name changed 05/03/1985
Name changed from Pennichuck Water Works to Pennichuck Corp. 05/03/1985
Common $1 par split (3) for (2) by issuance of (0.5) additional share payable 09/01/1998 to holders of record 08/18/1998
Common $1 par split (4) for (3) by issuance of (1/3) additional share payable 12/03/2001 to holders of record 11/19/2001 Ex date - 12/04/2001
Common $1 par split (4) for (3) by issuance of (1/3) additional share payable 06/01/2005 to holders of record 05/18/2005 Ex date - 06/02/2005
Acquired by City of Nashua, New Hampshire 01/25/2012
Each share Common $1 par exchanged for $29 cash

PENNILANE DEV CORP (BC)
Recapitalized as Mandarin Industries Ltd. (BC) 03/01/1994
Each share Common no par exchanged for (0.666) share Common no par
Mandarin Industries Ltd. (BC) reincorporated in the Cayman Islands 10/08/1997 which recapitalized as Leitak Enterprises Ltd. 10/09/1997
(See Leitak Enterprises Ltd.)

PENNINGTONS STORES LTD (ON)
Preference no par called for redemption 07/03/1984
Capital Stock no par split (2) for (1) by issuance of (1) additional share 11/27/1972
Under plan of recapitalization each share Capital Stock no par reclassified as (1) share Common no par and (0.25) share Preference no par distributed 02/02/1979
Common no par split (2) for (1) by issuance of (1) additional share 02/12/1979
Assets sold for the benefit of creditors 02/00/1995
No stockholders' equity

PENNOK OIL CORP.
Acquired by Simms Petroleum Co. in 1929 which was liquidated in 1947

PENNRAM MOTOR INNS, INC. (PA)
Out of business 12/18/74
No stockholders' equity

PENNROAD CORP. (DE)
Common no par changed to $1 par in 1933
Name changed to Madison Fund, Inc. 10/15/58
Madison Fund, Inc. name changed to Madison Resources, Inc. 6/13/84 which merged into Adobe Resources Corp. 10/31/85 which merged into Santa Fe Energy Resources, Inc. 5/19/92 which name changed to Santa Fe Snyder Corp. 5/5/99 which merged into Devon Energy Corp. (New) 8/29/2000

PENNROCK FINL SVCS CORP (PA)
Common $2.50 par split (2) for (1) by issuance of (1) additional share 11/17/1987
Common $2.50 par split (3) for (2) by issuance of (0.5) additional share 05/15/1990
Common $2.50 par split (3) for (2) by issuance of (0.5) additional share 09/14/1993
Stock Dividends - 10% 02/17/1987; 10% 10/27/1992; 5% payable 08/10/2001 to holders of record 07/24/2001 Ex date - 07/20/2001; 10% payable 08/13/2002 to holders of record 07/23/2002; 10% payable 08/12/2003 to holders of record 07/22/2003 Ex date - 07/18/2003
Merged into Community Banks, Inc. 07/01/2005
Each share Common $2.50 par exchanged for (1.4) shares Common $5 par
Community Banks, Inc. merged into Susquehanna Bancshares, Inc. 11/16/2007 which merged into BB&T Corp. 08/01/2015

PENNS GROVE NATL BK & TR CO (PENN'S GROVE, NJ)
Common $100 par changed to $10 par and (12.5) additional shares issued to effect a (10) for (1) split plus a 25% stock dividend paid 11/20/62
Stock Dividend - 50% 5/1/45
Merged into Statewide Bancorp 12/31/86
Each share Common $10 par exchanged for (16) shares Common $2.50 par
(See Statewide Bancorp)

PENNSALT CHEMS CORP (PA)
Common $10 par changed to $3 par and (2) additional shares issued 07/10/1959
Under plan of merger name changed to Pennwalt Corp. and Common $3 par changed to $1 par 03/31/1969
(See Pennwalt Corp.)

PENNSAUKEN BK (PENNSAUKEN, NJ)
Common $10 par changed to $5 par and (1) additional share issued 07/18/1969
Name changed to Fidelity Bank & Trust Co. of New Jersey (Pennsauken, NJ) 08/14/1969
(See Fidelity Bank & Trust Co. of New Jersey (Pennsauken, NJ))

PENNSVILLE NATIONAL BANK (PENNSVILLE, NJ)
Reorganized as Penn Bancshares, Inc. 4/1/85
Each share Common $10 par exchanged for (1) share Common $15 par

PENNSYLVANIA & SOUTHN GAS CO (DE)
Common no par changed to $1 par in 1940
Common $1 par changed to 25¢ par in 1943
Each share Common 25¢ par exchanged for (0.2) share Common $1.25 par 9/10/56
Common $1.25 par split (3) for (1) by issuance of (2) additional shares 3/10/66
Merged into NUI Corp. (Old) 4/19/94
Each share Common $1.25 par exchanged for (2.8977) shares Common no par
NUI Corp. (Old) reorganized as NUI Corp. (New) 3/1/2001
(See NUI Corp. (New))

PENNSYLVANIA AIRLINES & TRANSPORT CO.
Acquired by Pennsylvania-Central Airlines Corp. in 1936
Details not available

PENNSYLVANIA ALUMNI REALTY CORP. (NY)
Charter cancelled and proclaimed dissolved for failure to pay taxes 12/16/40

PENNSYLVANIA-AMERICAN WTR CO (PA)
4.50% Preferred $100 par called for redemption at $103.50 plus $0.95 accrued dividends on 04/01/2013

PENNSYLVANIA BK & TR CO (TITUSVILLE, PA)
Capital Stock $10 par changed to $5 par and (1) additional share issued 03/01/1975
Stock Dividends - 10% 02/04/1966; 10% 02/10/1967
Under plan of reorganization each share Capital Stock $5 par automatically became (1) share Pennbancorp Common $5 par 12/31/1980
Pennbancorp merged into Integra Financial Corp. 01/26/1989 which merged into National City Corp. 05/03/1996 which was acquired by PNC Financial Services Group, Inc. 12/31/2008

PENNSYLVANIA BANKSHARES & SECURITIES CORP. (PA)
Each share 5% Preferred $50 par exchanged for (1) share $2.50 Preferred $10 par 00/00/1942
Recapitalized 00/00/1945
Each share $2.50 Preferred $10 par exchanged for (2) shares Common $5 par
Each (50) shares Common no par exchanged for (1) share Common $5 par
Liquidation completed 12/12/1957
Details not available

PENNSYLVANIA-BRADFORD CO.
Liquidation completed in 1943

PENNSYLVANIA BUILDING INC. (NY)
Dissolved 1/8/54

PENNSYLVANIA CAP BK (PITTSBURGH, PA)
Merged into Three Rivers Bancorp, Inc. 07/01/2001
Each share Class A Common exchanged for (4.15) shares Common 1¢ par and $4.15 cash
Each share Common 1¢ par exchanged for (4.15) shares Common 1¢ par and $4.15 cash
Three Rivers Bancorp, Inc. merged into Sky Financial Group, Inc. 10/01/2002 which merged into Huntington Bancshares Inc. 07/02/2007

PENNSYLVANIA CASH CREDIT CORP.
Merged into Franklin Plan Corp. in 1932 which became bankrupt in 1933

PENNSYLVANIA-CENTRAL AIRLINES CORP. (DE)
Name changed to Capital Airlines, Inc. in 1948
Capital Airlines, Inc. merged into United Air Lines, Inc. 6/1/61 which reorganized as UAL, Inc. 8/1/69 which name changed to Allegis Corp. 4/30/87 which name changed to UAL Corp. 5/27/88
(See UAL Corp.)

PENNSYLVANIA CITRUS GROVES, INC. (PA)
Name changed to Indian River Citrus Fruits, Inc. 12/2/59
(See Indian River Citrus Fruits, Inc.)

PENNSYLVANIA CO. FOR BANKING & TRUSTS (PHILADELPHIA, PA)
Under plan of merger name changed to First Pennsylvania Banking & Trust Co. (Philadelphia, PA) 09/30/1955
First Pennsylvania Banking & Trust Co. (Philadelphia, PA) reorganized as First Pennsylvania Corp. 01/31/1969 which merged into CoreStates Financial Corp 03/05/1990 which merged into First Union Corp. 04/28/1998 which name changed to Wachovia Corp. (Ctfs. dated after 09/01/2001) 09/01/2001 which merged into Wells Fargo & Co. (New) 12/31/2008

PENNSYLVANIA CO. FOR INSURANCE ON LIVES & GRANTING ANNUITIES (PA)
Each share Capital Stock $100 par exchanged for (10) shares Capital Stock $10 par 00/00/1929
Name changed to Pennsylvania Co. for Banking & Trusts (Philadelphia, PA) 03/29/1947
Pennsylvania Co. for Banking & Trusts (Philadelphia, PA) name changed to First Pennsylvania Banking & Trust Co. (Philadelphia, PA) 09/30/1955 which reorganized as First Pennsylvania Corp. 01/31/1969 which merged into CoreStates Financial Corp 03/05/1990 which merged into First Union Corp. 04/28/1998 which name changed to Wachovia Corp. (Ctfs. dated after 09/01/2001) 09/01/2001 which merged into Wells Fargo & Co. (New) 12/31/2008

PENNSYLVANIA CO (DE)
4-5/8% Preferred $100 par called for redemption 06/21/1983
Public interest eliminated

PENNSYLVANIA COAL & COKE CORP. (PA)
Capital Stock $50 par changed to $10 par in 1934
Stock Dividend - 10% 12/31/53
Name changed to Penn-Texas Corp. in 1954
Penn-Texas Corp. name changed to Fairbanks Whitney Corp. 5/29/59 which recapitalized as Colt Industries Inc. (Pa.) 5/15/64 which reincorporated in Delaware 10/17/68 then reincorporated in Pennsylvania 5/6/76
(See Colt Industries Inc. (Pa.))

PENNSYLVANIA COMM BANCORP INC (PA)
Common $1 par split (2) for (1) by issuance of (1) additional share payable 02/25/2005 to holders of

record 02/10/2005 Ex date - 02/28/2005
Stock Dividends - 5% payable 02/18/2000 to holders of record 02/04/2000; 5% payable 02/16/2001 to holders of record 02/02/2001; 5% payable 02/25/2002 to holders of record 02/11/2002; 5% payable 02/24/2003 to holders of record 02/07/2003 Ex date - 02/05/2003; 5% payable 02/24/2004 to holders of record 02/06/2004
Name changed to Metro Bancorp, Inc. 06/15/2009
Metro Bancorp, Inc. merged into F.N.B. Corp. 02/12/2016

PENNSYLVANIA-CONLEY TANK CAR CO.
Acquired by General American Transportation Corp. in 1936
General American Transportation Corp. name changed to GATX Corp. 6/27/75

PENNSYLVANIA-DIXIE CEMENT CORP.
Name changed to Penn-Dixie Cement Corp. 00/00/1951
Penn-Dixie Cement Corp. name changed to Penn-Dixie Industries, Inc. 04/17/1973 which name changed to Continental Steel Corp. (DE) 03/18/1982
(See Continental Steel Corp. (DE))

PENNSYLVANIA EDISON CO. (PA)
Incorporated 10/26/1915
Liquidation completed 00/00/1949
Details not available

PENNSYLVANIA EDISON CO. (PA)
Incorporated 6/22/21
Merged into Metropolitan Edison Co. in 1928

PENNSYLVANIA ELEC CO (PA)
$5.10 Preferred Ser. A no par called for redemption 11/27/43
10.88% Preferred Ser. K no par called for redemption 7/1/86
11.72% Preferred Ser. J no par called for redemption 7/1/86
9% Preferred Ser. L no par called for redemption 5/1/91
8.12% Preferred Ser I no par called for redemption 9/15/93
8.36% Preferred Ser. H no par called for redemption 9/26/94
3.70% Preferred Ser. C no par called for redemption at $105 plus $0.822 accrued interest on 2/19/99
4.05% Preferred Ser. D no par called for redemption at $104.53 plus $0.90 accrued interest on 2/19/99
4.40% Preferred Ser. B no par called for redemption at $108.25 plus $0.978 accrued interest on 2/19/99
4.50% Preferred Ser. F no par called for redemption at $104.27 plus $1 accrued interest on 2/19/99
4.60% Preferred Ser. G no par called for redemption at $104.25 plus $1.022 accrued interest on 2/19/99
4.70% Preferred Ser. E no par called for redemption at $105.25 plus $1.044 accrued interest on 2/19/99

PENNSYLVANIA ENGR CORP (DE)
Reincorporated 3/26/68
Common no par changed to $1 par 4/12/54
Common $1 par split (2) for (1) by issuance of (1) additional share 11/10/67
State of incorporation changed from (PA) to (DE) 3/26/68
Common $1 par split (5) for (2) by issuance of (1.5) additional shares 6/17/68
Common $1 par changed to 10¢ par 6/10/76
Stock Dividends - 25% 12/1/54; 10% 11/25/57; 10% 9/2/75; 10% 3/3/76; 10% 9/2/76; 10% 3/8/77; 10% 9/1/77; 10% 3/1/78; 10% 9/1/78; 10% 9/14/79; 10% 3/3/80

Filed a petition under Chapter 7 Federal Bankruptcy Code 2/4/92
Stockholders' equity unlikely

PENNSYLVANIA ENTERPRISES INC (PA)
Common no par split (2) for (1) by issuance of (1) additional share payable 04/02/1997 to holders of record 03/20/1997 Ex date - 04/03/1997
Merged into Southern Union Co. (New) 11/04/1999
Each share Common no par exchanged for (1.59006) shares Common $1 par and $3 cash
Southern Union Co. (New) merged into Energy Transfer Equity, L.P. 03/26/2012 which name changed to Energy Transfer L.P. 10/19/2018

PENNSYLVANIA FIRST NATIONAL CORP. (DE)
No longer in existence having become inoperative and void for non-payment of taxes 4/1/32

PENNSYLVANIA FORGE CORP.
Name changed to Milnor Corp. for purpose of liquidation in 1948 which was completely liquidated in 1953

PENNSYLVANIA GAS & ELECTRIC CO.
Name changed to York County Gas Co. in 1941
York County Gas Co. acquired by Columbia Gas System, Inc. 8/29/69 which name changed to Columbia Energy Group 1/16/98 which merged into NiSource Inc. 11/1/2000

PENNSYLVANIA GAS & ELECTRIC CORP. (DE)
Liquidated in 1953
Each share 7% Preferred $100 par received (15) shares Capital Stock $5 par of North Penn Gas Co., (0.5) share Common $10 par of Crystal City Gas Co. and $14.96 in cash
Each share 7 Preferred no par received (15) shares Capital Stock $5 par of North Penn Gas Co., (0.5) share Common $10 par of Crystal City Gas Co. and $14.96 in cash
Each share Class A Common no par received (0.2) share Common $10 par of Crystal City Gas Co.
Each share Class B Common no par received (0.025) share Common $10 par of Crystal City Gas Co.
(See each company's listing)

PENNSYLVANIA GAS & WTR CO (PA)
Common no par split (2) for (1) by issuance of (1) additional share 12/20/1963
Under plan of reorganization each share Common no par automatically became (1) share Pennsylvania Enterprises, Inc. Common no par 07/31/1974
9.68% Preferred $100 par called for redemption 08/22/1990
8.9% Preferred $100 par called for redemption 12/16/1994
Name changed to PG Energy Inc. 02/19/1996
(See each company's listing)

PENNSYLVANIA GAS CO. (PA)
Each share Capital Stock $25 par exchanged for (2) shares Capital Stock no par in 1926
Under S.E.C. plan each share Capital Stock no par exchanged for (1.45) shares National Fuel Gas Co. Common $10 par 4/11/62

PENNSYLVANIA GLASS SAND CORP (PA)
Each share Common no par exchanged for (2) shares Common $1 par in 1950
5% Preferred called for redemption 12/31/54
Common $1 par split (2) for (1) by

issuance of (1) additional share 11/18/59
Stock Dividends - 10% 3/6/53; 10% 12/16/55
Merged into International Telephone & Telegraph Corp. (DE) 6/27/68
Each share Common $1 par exchanged for (0.27) share $4.50 Conv. Preferred Ser. I no par and (0.628) share Common $1 par
International Telephone & Telegraph Corp. (DE) name changed to ITT Corp. 12/31/83 which reorganized in Indiana as ITT Industries, Inc. 12/19/95 which name changed to ITT Corp. 7/1/2006

PENNSYLVANIA GOLD MINING CO. (DE)
Charter cancelled and declared inoperative and void for non-payment of taxes 03/17/1920

PENNSYLVANIA GROWTH EQUITIES, INC. (PA)
Company dissolved 11/07/1988
Details not available

PENNSYLVANIA ILLUM CORP (DE)
Company believed out of business 00/00/1971
Details not available

PENNSYLVANIA INDPT OIL CO (DE)
Voluntarily dissolved 4/19/78
Details not available

PENNSYLVANIA INDL CHEM CORP (PA)
Acquired by Hercules Inc. 05/31/1973
Each share Common $10 par exchanged for (2.355909) shares Common no par
Hercules Inc. acquired by Ashland Inc. (New) (KY) 11/13/2008 which reincorporated in Delaware as Ashland Global Holdings Inc. 09/20/2016

PENNSYLVANIA INDUSTRIES, INC. (DE)
Preferred $100 par changed to $25 par in 1942
Common no par changed to $1 par in 1948
Each (25) shares Common $1 par exchanged for (1) share Common $25 par in 1949
Liquidated as of 12/15/54

PENNSYLVANIA INVESTING CO.
Liquidated in 1934

PENNSYLVANIA LIFE CO (DE)
Reincorporated 12/31/68
Common no par split (3) for (2) by issuance of (0.5) additional share 5/14/65
Common no par split (5) for (2) by issuance of (1.5) additional shares 12/17/68
State of incorporation changed from (NV) to (DE) and Common no par changed to $1 par 12/31/68
Common $1 par changed to 66-2/3¢ par and (0.5) additional share issued 9/10/70
Common 66-2/3¢ par changed to 50¢ par and (0.333) additional share issued 6/16/72
Stock Dividend - 33-1/3% 2/15/68
Name changed to Penncorp Financial, Inc. 6/5/79
Penncorp Financial, Inc. merged into American Can Co. 1/11/83 which name changed to Primerica Corp. (NJ) 4/28/87 which was acquired by Primerica Corp. (DE) 12/15/88 which name changed to Travelers Inc. 12/31/93 which name changed to Travelers Group Inc. 4/16/95 which name changed to Citigroup Inc. 10/8/98

PENNSYLVANIA MFRS CORP (PA)
Name changed to PMA Capital Corp. 12/07/1998
PMA Capital Corp. merged into Old

Republic International Corp. 10/01/2010

PENNSYLVANIA MUT FD INC (DE)
Capital Stock $1 par split (2) for (1) by issuance of (1) additional share 04/04/1969
Under plan of merger each share Common $1 par automatically became (1) share Royce Fund Pennsylvania Mutual Fund Investment Class $0.001 par 06/28/1996

PENNSYLVANIA NATL BK & TR CO (POTTSVILLE, PA)
Stock Dividend - 300% 9/30/83
Under plan of reorganization each share Common $10 par automatically became (1) share Pennsylvania National Financial Corp. Common $10 par 5/24/85
Pennsylvania National Financial Corp. merged into Keystone Financial, Inc. 12/17/86 which merged into M&T Bank Corp. 10/6/2000

PENNSYLVANIA NATL FINL CORP (PA)
Common $10 par split (3) for (1) by issuance of (2) additional shares 7/15/85
Merged into Keystone Financial, Inc. 12/17/86
Each share Common $10 par exchanged for (1.92) shares Common $2 par
Keystone Financial, Inc. merged into M&T Bank Corp. 10/6/2000

PENNSYLVANIA NATL TURF CLUB INC (PA)
Each share Class A Common 10¢ par exchanged for (0.00001) share Class C Common 10¢ par 08/15/1986
Note: In effect holders received $0.50 principal amount of 10% Promissory Notes due 08/01/1987, 00/00/1988 and 00/00/1989 respectively and $0.25 cash and public interest was eliminated

PENNSYLVANIA NEW YORK CENTRAL TRANSPORTATION CO. (PA)
Name changed to Penn Central Co. 5/8/68
Penn Central Co. reorganized as Penn Central Corp. 10/24/78 which name changed to American Premier Underwriters, Inc. 3/25/94 which merged into American Premier Group, Inc. 4/3/95 which name changed to American Financial Group, Inc. 6/9/95 which merged into American Financial Group, Inc. (Holding Co.) 12/2/97

PENNSYLVANIA OHIO ELECTRIC CO.
Dissolved in 1928

PENNSYLVANIA-OHIO POWER & LIGHT CO.
Merged into Ohio Edison Co. 7/5/30
Details not available

PENNSYLVANIA PWR & LT CO (PA)
$5 Preferred no par called for redemption 1/9/46
$6 Preferred no par called for redemption 1/9/46
$7 Preferred no par called for redemption 1/9/46
Common no par split (2) for (1) by issuance of (1) additional share 5/15/59
$13 Preference 2nd Ser. no par called for redemption 2/15/86
$15 Preference no par called for redemption 2/19/86
$3.75 Depositary Preference no par called for redemption 2/19/86
$3.42 Depositary Preference no par called redemption 4/1/86
$13.68 Preference no par called for redemption 4/1/86

$3.75 Depositary Preference no par called for redemption 6/13/86
$13 Preference no par called for redemption 12/15/86
$2.90 Depositary Preference no par called for redemption 2/18/87
$11.60 Preference no par called for redemption 2/18/87
$11 Preference no par called for redemption 8/7/87
9% Preferred $100 par called for redemption 2/1/92
9.24% Preferred $100 par called for redemption 2/1/92
Common no par split (2) for (1) by issuance of (1) additional share 5/11/92
5.95% Preferred $100 par called for redemption 7/15/93
6.05% Preferred $100 par called for redemption 7/15/93
6.15% Preferred $100 par called for redemption 7/15/93
8.60% Preferred $100 par called for redemption 7/15/93
$8 Preference no par called for redemption 9/15/93
$8.40 Preference no par called for redemption 9/15/93
$8.70 Preference no par called for redemption 9/15/93
7.375% Preferred $100 par called for redemption 11/1/93
7.82% Preferred $100 par called for redemption 11/1/93
6.875% Preferred $100 par called for redemption 5/1/94
7% Preferred $100 par called for redemption 5/1/94
Under plan of reorganization each share Common no par automatically became (1) share PP&L Resources Inc. Common no par 4/27/95
(See PP&L Resources Inc.)
Name changed to PP&L Inc. 9/16/97
PP&L Inc. name changed to PPL Electric Utilities Corp. 2/14/2000

PENNSYLVANIA PWR CO (PA)
5% Preferred no par called for redemption 12/10/45
Issue Information - 250,000 shares PFD 7.75% offered at $100 per share on 06/25/1993
8.48% Preferred $100 par called for redemption 7/16/93
9.16% Preferred $100 par called for redemption 7/16/93
11% Preferred $100 par called for redemption 1/1/94
7.64% Preferred $100 par called for redemption at $101.42 on 6/15/99
8% Preferred $100 par called for redemption at $102.07 on 7/1/99
7.75% Preferred $100 par called for redemption at $100 on 5/16/2005
4.24% Preferred $100 par called for redemption at $103.125 on 12/15/2006
4.25% Preferred $100 par called for redemption at $105 on 12/15/2006
4.64% Preferred $100 par called for redemption at $102.98 on 12/15/2006

PENNSYLVANIA PUMP & COMPRESSOR CO. (PA)
Acquired by Cooper-Bessemer Corp. 11/30/1964
Details not available

PENNSYLVANIA RAILROAD CO. (PA)
Capital Stock $50 par changed to $10 par 06/21/1957
Under plan of merger name changed to Pennsylvania New York Central Transportation Co. 02/01/1968
Pennsylvania New York Central Transportation Co. name changed to Penn Central Co. 05/08/1968 which reorganized as Penn Central Corp. 10/24/1978 which name changed to American Premier Underwriters, Inc. 03/25/1994 which merged into American Premier Group, Inc. 04/03/1995 which name changed to American Financial Group, Inc. 06/09/1995 which merged into American Financial Group, Inc. (Holding Co.) 12/02/1997

PENNSYLVANIA REAL ESTATE INVT TR (PA)
Common Share of Bene. Int. Purchase Rights declared for holders of record 05/14/1999 were redeemed at $0.001 per right 03/15/2006 for holders of record 03/01/2006
11% Sr. Preferred $1 par called for redemption at $52.50 plus $0.7486 accrued dividends on 07/31/2007
8.25% Perpetual Preferred Shares of Bene. Int. Ser. A 1¢ par called for redemption at $25 on 10/12/2017 (Additional Information in Active)

PENNSYLVANIA REFINING CO. (PA)
Capital Stock no par changed to $1 par in 1949
Capital Stock $1 par changed to $5 par 9/7/65
Merged into Pennzoil Co. (DE) 1/26/73
Each share Capital Stock $5 par exchanged for (1) share Common 83-1/3¢ par
Pennzoil Co. name changed to PennzEnergy Co. 12/30/98

PENNSYLVANIA RUBBER CO.
Acquired by General Tire & Rubber Co. 00/00/1945
Details not available

PENNSYLVANIA SALT MFG CO (PA)
Each share Capital Stock $50 par exchanged for (5) shares Capital Stock $10 par in 1944
Capital Stock $10 par reclassified as Common $10 par in 1947
Name changed to Pennsalt Chemicals Corp. 4/24/57
Pennsalt Chemicals Corp. merged into Pennwalt Corp. 3/31/69
(See Pennwalt Corp.)

PENNSYLVANIA SVGS BK (PHILADELPHIA, PA)
Reorganized as PSB Bancorp Inc. 5/14/98
Each share Common $1 par exchanged for (2.572374) shares Common $1 par
(See PSB Bancorp Inc.)

PENNSYLVANIA ST BK (CAMP HILL, PA)
Stock Dividends - 5% payable 06/01/1999 to holders of record 04/27/1999; 3% payable 06/01/2000 to holders of record 04/25/2000; 3% payable 06/25/2001 to holders of record 05/22/2001 Ex date - 05/24/2001; 5% payable 06/25/2002 to holders of record 05/28/2002 Ex date - 05/29/2002; 6% payable 05/23/2003 to holders of record 04/24/2003 Ex date - 04/22/2003
Under plan of reorganization each share Common 1¢ par automatically became (1) share Pennsylvania State Banking Co. Common $2.50 par 01/01/2004
Pennsylvania State Banking Co. merged into Sterling Financial Corp. 12/30/2004
(See Sterling Financial Corp.)

PENNSYLVANIA ST BKG CO (PA)
Stock Dividend - 6% payable 04/16/2004 to holders of record 03/05/2004 Ex date - 03/03/2004
Merged into Sterling Financial Corp. 12/30/2004
Each share Common $2.50 par exchanged for (0.125674) share Common $5 par and $18.43753 cash
(See Sterling Financial Corp.)

PENNSYLVANIA SUGAR CO.
Liquidated in 1941

PENNSYLVANIA TAX FREE INCOME TR (PA)
Completely liquidated 4/29/82
Each Share of Bene. Int. no par received first and final distribution of $10.82 cash
Note: Certificates were not required to be surrendered and are now valueless

PENNSYLVANIA TELEPHONE CORP.
Name changed to General Telephone Co. of Pennsylvania in 1952
General Telephone Co. of Pennsylvania merged into GTE MTO Inc. 3/31/87 which name changed to GTE North Inc. 1/1/88
(See GTE North Inc.)

PENNSYLVANIA TITLE INSURANCE CO.
Merged into Commonwealth Title Co. of Philadelphia in 1944
(See Commonwealth Title Co. of Philadelphia)

PENNSYLVANIA TRUST SECURITIES CORP. (DE)
No longer in existence having become inoperative and void for non-payment of taxes 4/1/55

PENNSYLVANIA UTILS INVT CORP (PA)
Capital Stock $1 par split (5) for (2) by issuance of (0.2) additional share 09/16/1957
Capital Stock $1 par split (2) for (1) by issuance of (1) additional share 08/17/1959
Stock Dividend - 100% 05/16/1955
All but (64) shares have been acquired by General Waterworks Corp. through purchase offer as of 03/04/1966
Public interest eliminated

PENNSYLVANIA WATER SERVICE CO.
Dissolved in 1946

PENNSYLVANIA WTR & PWR CO (PA)
Each share Common $100 par exchanged for (4) shares Common no par in 1927
Merged into Pennsylvania Power & Light Co. 6/1/55
Each share Common no par exchanged for (0.25) share 4.40% Preferred $100 par and (0.5) share Common no par

PENNTEX MIDSTREAM PARTNERS LP (DE)
Acquired by Energy Transfer Partners, L.P (New) 06/30/2017
Each Common Unit exchanged for $20 cash

PENNVIEW SVGS ASSN SOUDERTON (PA)
Acquired by Univest Corp. of Pennsylvania 7/31/90
Each share Common $1 par exchanged for $25.50 cash

PENNWALT CORP (PA)
$2.50 Conv. Preference $1 par called for redemption 10/17/1988
Conv. Preference 2nd Ser. $1 par called for redemption 10/17/1988
Merged into Elf Aquitaine, Inc. 10/11/1989
Each share Common $1 par exchanged for $132 cash

PENNWOOD BANCORP INC (PA)
Merged into Fidelity Bancorp, Inc. 7/14/2000
Each share Common 1¢ par exchanged for $13.10 cash

PENNWOOD SVGS BK (BELLEVUE, PA)
Under plan of reorganization each share Common 1¢ par automatically became (1) share Pennwood Bancorp, Inc. Common 1¢ par 1/27/97
(See Pennwood Bancorp, Inc.)

PENNY SPRUCE MILLS LTD. (AB)
Liquidated in July, 1961. No Preference or Common stockholders' equity

PENNY STK FD NORTH AMER INC (CO)
Name changed to Infinity Speculative Fund, Inc. 10/15/90
Infinity Speculative Fund, Inc. name changed to Redwood Microcap Fund, Inc. 7/26/91
(See Redwood Microcap Fund, Inc.)

PENNY STK INVT INC (FL)
Recapitalized as Palm Beach Diversified Equity Fund, Inc. 08/27/1986
Each share Common 1¢ par exchanged for (0.02) share Common 50¢ par
(See Palm Beach Diversified Equity Fund, Inc.)

PENNYRILE BANCSHARES, INC. (KY)
Acquired by CBT Corp. (KY) 05/14/1994
Details not available

PENNYSAVER HOME DISTR CORP (NY)
Name changed to Cal-Am Corp. 7/17/74
(See Cal-Am Corp.)

PENNZENERGY CO (DE)
Merged into Devon Energy Corp. (New) 08/17/1999
Each share 6.49% Preferred Ser. A $1 par exchanged for (1) share 6.49% Preferred Ser. A $1 par
Each share Common $0.83333333 par exchanged for (0.4475) share Common 10¢ par

PENNZOIL CO. NEW (PA)
Ctfs. dated after 7/2/63
Common $5 par changed to $2.50 par and (1) additional share issued 6/30/64
Merged into Pennzoil United, Inc. 4/1/68
Each share Common $2.50 par exchanged for (1) share Common $2.50 par
Pennzoil United, Inc. name changed to Pennzoil Co. (DE) 6/1/72 which name changed to PennzEnergy Co. 12/30/98 which merged into Devon Energy Corp. (New) 8/17/99

PENNZOIL CO. OLD (PA)
Ctfs. dated prior to 6/30/55
Each share Common $25 par exchanged for (2.5) shares Common $10 par in 1948
Merged into South Penn Oil Co. 6/30/55
Each share Preferred $100 par exchanged for (5) shares Common $12.50 par
Each share Common $10 par exchanged for (1) share Common $12.50 par
South Penn Oil Co. name changed to Pennzoil Co. (PA) (New) 7/3/63 which merged into Pennzoil United, Inc. 4/1/68 which name changed to Pennzoil Co. (DE) 6/1/72 which name changed to PennzEnergy Co. 12/30/98 which merged into Devon Energy Corp. (New) 8/17/99

PENNZOIL CO (DE)
$1.33333333 Conv. Preference Common $0.83333333 par called for redemption 12/06/1978
$8 Preferred $1 par called for redemption 11/15/1985
Common $0.83333333 par split (3) for (2) by issuance of (0.5) additional share 12/14/1979
Each share Common $0.8333333 par received distribution of (1) share Pennzoil-Quaker State Co. Common $1 par payable 12/30/1998 to

holders of record 12/10/1998
Ex date - 12/31/1998
Name changed to PennzEnergy Co. 12/30/1998
PennzEnergy Co. merged into Devon Energy Corp. (New) 08/17/1999

PENNZOIL LA & TEX OFFSHORE INC (DE)
Class A Common $1 par and Class B Common $1 par reclassified as Common $1 par 11/01/1976
Merged into Pennzoil Co. 10/01/1979
Each share Common $1 par exchanged for $4 cash
(See Pennzoil Co.)

PENNZOIL OFFSHORE GAS OPERATORS INC (DE)
Class A Common $1 par and Class B Common $1 par reclassified as Common $1 par 11/01/1976
Name changed to Pogo Producing Co. 08/02/1977
Pogo Producing Co. merged into Plains Exploration & Production Co. 11/06/2007 which merged into Freeport-McMoRan Copper & Gold Inc. 05/31/2013 which name changed to Freeport-McMoRan Inc. 07/14/2014

PENNZOIL-QUAKER ST CO (DE)
Merged into Royal Dutch Petroleum Co. 10/1/2002
Each share Common $1 par exchanged for $22 cash

PENNZOIL UTD INC (DE)
$4.75 Conv. Preference Common $2.50 par reclassified as $1.58333333 Conv. Preference Common $0.83333333 par and (2) additional shares issued 10/31/1968
$4 Conv. Preference Common $2.50 par reclassified as $1.33333333 Conv. Preference Common $0.83333333 par and (2) additional shares issued 10/31/1968
Common $2.50 par changed to $0.83333333 par and (2) additional shares issued 10/31/1968
Name changed to Pennzoil Co. (DE) 06/01/1972
Pennzoil Co. (DE) name changed to PennzEnergy Co. 12/30/1998 which merged into Devon Energy Corp. (New) 08/17/1999

PENOBSCOT CHEMICAL FIBRE CO. (ME)
Common no par changed to $2 par 6/17/58
Common $2 par changed to $1 par and (2) additional shares issued 1/15/60
Name changed to Penobscot Co. 6/16/64
Penobscot Co. merged into Diamond International Corp. 7/19/67
(See Diamond International Corp.)

PENOBSCOT CO. (ME)
Merged into Diamond International Corp. 7/19/67
Each share Vtg. Common $1 par or Non- Vtg. Common $1 par exchanged for (0.625) share Common 50¢ par
(See Diamond International Corp.)

PENOBSCOT MNG LTD (ON)
Charter cancelled for failure to file returns and pay fees 02/05/1980

PENOBSCOT SHOE CO (ME)
Common $1 par split (5) for (4) by issuance of (0.25) additional share 11/25/68
Common $1 par split (5) for (2) by issuance of (1.5) additional shares 4/28/87
Merged into Riedman Corp. 1/19/2000
Each share Common $1 par exchanged for $11.75 cash

PENOLA INC (NV)
Reorganized as Empress Mining Inc. 01/28/2015
Each share Common $0.001 par exchanged for (30) shares Common $0.001 par

PENRIL DATA COMMUNICATIONS, INC. (DE)
Name changed to Penril Corp. 04/25/1974
Penril Corp. name changed to Penril DataComm Networks Inc. 03/28/1991 which merged into Bay Networks, Inc. 11/18/1996 which merged into Northern Telecom Ltd.-Northern Telecom Ltee. 08/31/1998 which name changed to Nortel Networks Corp. (Old) 04/30/1999 which reorganized as Nortel Networks Corp. (New) 05/01/2000
(See Nortel Networks Corp. (New))

PENRIL DATACOMM NETWORKS INC (DE)
Name changed 03/28/1991
Common 1¢ par split (5) for (4) by issuance of (0.25) additional share 05/02/1990
Stock Dividend - 20% 05/19/1989
Name changed from Penril Corp. to Penril DataComm Networks, Inc. 03/28/1991
Common 1¢ par split (4) for (3) by issuance of (0.33333333) additional share 04/26/1991
Each share Common 1¢ par received distribution of (1) share Access Beyond Inc. Common 1¢ par payable 11/18/1996 to holders of record 11/14/1996
Merged into Bay Networks, Inc. 11/18/1996
Each share Common 1¢ par exchanged for (0.448) share Common 1¢ par
Bay Networks, Inc. merged into Northern Telecom Ltd.-Northern Telecom Ltee. 08/31/1998 which name changed to Nortel Networks Corp. (Old) 04/30/1999 which reorganized as Nortel Networks Corp. (New) 05/01/2000
(See Nortel Networks Corp. (New))

PENROSE INDS CORP (DE)
No longer in existence having become inoperative and void for non-payment of taxes 01/00/1970

PENROSE RESOURCE CORP (BC)
Recapitalized as Network One Holdings Corp. 05/28/1993
Each share Common no par exchanged for (1/3) share Common no par
(See Network One Holdings Corp.)

PENSACOLA ELECTRIC CO.
Merged into Gulf Power Co. 00/00/1926
Details not available

PENSEC EXPLS INC (ON)
Merged into Portfield Industries Inc. 10/22/1980
Each share Common no par exchanged for (0.25) share Common no par
Portfield Industries Inc. recapitalized as Canmine Resources Corp. 05/01/1991
(See Canmine Resources Corp.)

PENSECO FINL SVCS CORP (PA)
Merged into Peoples Financial Services Corp. 12/02/2013
Each share Common 1¢ par exchanged for (1.3636) shares Common $5 par

PENSION ARCHITECTS INC (DE)
Charter cancelled and declared inoperative and void for non-payment of taxes 3/1/91

PENSION EQUITY FD INC (DE)
Liquidation completed

Each share Capital Stock $1 par received initial distribution of $104.22 cash 09/20/1972
Each share Capital Stock $1 par received second and final distribution of $1.50 cash 04/30/1973

PENSION INS GROUP AMER INC (DE)
Merged into Academy Insurance Group, Inc. (PA) 06/18/1987
Each share Common 1¢ par exchanged for (0.316) share Common 10¢ par
Academy Insurance Group, Inc. (PA) reincorporated in Delaware 06/17/1988
(See Academy Insurance Group, Inc. (DE))

PENSION LIFE INS CO AMER (NJ)
Common $2 par changed to $1.33 par and (0.5) additional share issued 11/09/1964
Common $1.33 par changed to $1 par 10/24/1966
Acquired by Academy Life Insurance Co. 10/14/1980
Each share Common $1 par exchanged for $8 cash

PENSIVE-YELLOWKNIFE GOLD MINES LTD. (CANADA)
Succeeded by Pensive Yellowknife Mines Ltd. (ON) on a (10) for (1) basis 00/00/1944
(See Pensive Yellowknife Mines Ltd.)

PENSIVE YELLOWKNIFE MINES LTD. (ON)
Charter revoked for failure to file reports and pay fees 12/27/1967

PENSKE MOTORSPORTS INC (DE)
Merged into International Speedway Corp. 8/9/99
Each share Common 1¢ par exchanged for (1.042) shares Class A Common 1¢ par

PENSON WORLDWIDE INC (DE)
Issue Information - 7,465,761 shares COM offered at $17 per share on 05/17/2006
Plan of reorganization under Chapter 11 Federal Bankruptcy proceedings effective 08/15/2013
Stockholders' equity unlikely

PENSTAR PETE LTD (AB)
Merged into Commercial Oil & Gas Ltd. 5/31/84
Each share Common no par exchanged for (0.1) share Common no par
(See Commercial Oil & Gas Ltd.)

PENSTAR WIRECOM LTD (ON)
Recapitalized as Neuro-Biotech Corp. 12/11/1997
Each share Common no par exchanged for (0.1) share Common no par
Neuro-Biotech Corp. name changed to DPC Biosciences, Corp. 10/31/2001 which name changed to iGaming Corp. 09/05/2006 which name changed to Big Stick Media Corp. 06/29/2007
(See Big Stick Media Corp.)

PENTA COMPUTER ASSOC INC (NY)
Merged into Redcor Corp. 06/26/1970
Each share Common 1¢ par exchanged for (0.607399) share Common no par
Redcor Corp. name changed to Silicon General Inc. 06/27/1982 which name changed to Symmetricom, Inc. (CA) 11/01/1993 which reincorporated in Delaware 01/07/2002
(See Symmetricom, Inc.)

PENTA SYS INTL INC (MD)
Assets sold at public auction 10/22/92
No stockholders' equity

PENTACON INC (DE)
Issue Information - 5,200,000 shares COM offered at $10 per share on 03/09/1998
Plan of reorganization under Chapter 11 Federal Bankruptcy Code effective 9/20/2002
Each share Common 1¢ par received initial distribution of $0.14 cash payable payable 1/10/2003 to holders of record 9/20/2002
Ex date - 1/16/2003
Each share Common 1¢ par received second and final distribution of $0.05 cash 12/30/2004
Note: Certificates were not required to be surrendered and are without value

PENTAFOUR SOFTWARE & EXPTS LTD (INDIA)
Name changed to Pentamedia Graphics Ltd. 01/24/2000
(See Pentamedia Graphics Ltd.)

PENTAGON RES LTD (BC)
Recapitalized as Quintel Industries Ltd. 8/22/83
Each share Common no par exchanged for (0.2) share Common no par
(See Qunitel Industries Ltd.)

PENTAIR INC (MN)
Name changed 04/25/1978
Common 50¢ par changed to $0.16666666 par and (2) additional shares issued 06/06/1969
Name changed from Pentair Industries, Inc. to Pentair, Inc. 04/25/1978
$2.0625 Conv. Preferred $1 par called for redemption 04/02/1984
$1.50 Conv. Preferred 1987 Ser. 10¢ par called for redemption 03/15/1993
Common $0.16666666 par split (3) for (2) by issuance of (0.5) additional share 06/11/1993
Common $0.16666666 par split (2) for (1) by issuance of (1) additional share payable 02/16/1996 to holders of record 02/02/1996
Common $0.16666666 par split (2) for (1) by issuance of (1) additional share payable 06/08/2004 to holders of record 06/01/2004 Ex date - 06/09/2004
Preferred Stock Purchase Rights declared for Common stockholders of record 07/31/1995 were redeemed at $0.0025 per right 02/11/2005 to holders of record 01/28/2005
Stock Dividends - 10% 11/15/1973; 10% 11/15/1974; 10% 10/31/1975; 50% 08/11/1978; 25% 02/24/1982; 25% 11/15/1983; 25% 03/29/1985; 10% 04/04/1986; 10% 06/24/1988
Reorganized under the laws of Switzerland as Pentair Ltd. 10/01/2012
Each share Common $0.16666666 par exchanged for (1) share Common CHF 0.5 par
Pentair Ltd. (Switzerland) reorganized in Ireland as Pentair PLC 06/03/2014

PENTAIR LTD (SWITZERLAND)
Reorganized under the laws of Ireland as Pentair PLC 06/03/2014
Each share Common CHF 0.5 par exchanged for (1) share Ordinary USD$0.01 par

PENTAMEDIA GRAPHICS LTD (INDIA)
Stock Dividend - 10% payable 01/03/2003 to holders of record 09/26/2002 Ex date - 09/24/2002
GDR agreement terminated 04/08/2008
Each Reg. S GDR for Ordinary exchanged for $0.059 cash 10/08/2008

PENTANOVA ENERGY CORP (BC)
Recapitalized as CruzSur Energy Corp. 09/04/2018
Each share Common no par exchanged for (0.1) share Common no par

PENTASOFT TECHNOLOGIES LTD (INDIA)
Stock Dividend - 20% payable 06/30/2003 to holders of record 10/15/2002 Ex date - 10/10/2002
GDR agreement terminated 05/15/2009
Each Sponsored Reg. S GDR for Ordinary exchanged for (1) Ordinary share
Note: Unexchanged GDR's will be sold and the proceeds, if any, held for claim after 11/17/2009

PENTASTAR COMMUNICATIONS INC (DE)
Issue Information - 1,250,000 shares COM offered at $10 per share on 10/26/1999
Receiver appointed to collect all collateral for the benefit of creditor and company subsequently ceased operations 04/09/2002
Stockholders' equity unlikely

PENTECH INTL INC (DE)
Acquired by JAKKS Pacific, Inc. 7/31/2000
Each share Common 1¢ par exchanged for $1.60 cash

PENTECO RES LTD (BC)
Name changed to Pennant Energy Inc. 04/29/2004
Pennant Energy Inc. merged into Blackbird Energy Inc. 04/22/2014

PENTEGRA DENTAL GROUP INC (DE)
Issue Information - 2,500,000 shares COM offered at $8.50 per share on 03/24/1998
Name changed to e-dentist.com, Inc. 08/25/2000
e-dentist.com, Inc. name changed to EDT Learning, Inc. 08/02/2001 which name changed to iLinc Communications, Inc. 02/05/2004
(See iLinc Communications, Inc.)

PENTEX ENERGY PLC (UNITED KINGDOM)
ADR agreement terminated 08/28/1998
Each Sponsored ADR for Ordinary exchanged for $2.1393 cash

PENTHOUSE INTL INC (FL)
Common $0.0025 par split (3) for (1) by issuance of (2) additional shares payable 05/22/2003 to holders of record 05/12/2003 Ex date - 05/23/2003
Administratively dissolved 09/16/2005

PENTLAND FIRTH VENTURES LTD (AB)
Name changed 10/06/1994
Name changed from Pentland Firth Holdings Ltd. to Pentland Firth Ventures Ltd. 10/06/1994
Name changed to Tesoro Energy Corp. 08/23/2001
Tesoro Energy Corp. recapitalized as Peregrine Energy Ltd. 07/23/2004 which merged into Mahalo Energy Ltd. 06/05/2006
(See Mahalo Energy Ltd.)

PENTLAND INDS PLC (ENGLAND)
Acquired by Bertrams Investment Trust PLC 02/13/1990
Each Sponsored ADR for Ordinary 10p par exchanged for $11.84 cash

PENTON INC (DE)
Liquidation completed
Each share Common $2.50 par exchanged for initial distribution of $18.50 cash 07/02/1976
Each share Common $2.50 par received second and final distribution of $0.50 cash 12/01/1976

PENTON MEDIA INC (DE)
Merged into Prism Business Media Holdings, Inc. 2/1/2007
Each share Common 1¢ par exchanged for $0.8058 cash

PENTON PUBLISHING CO. (DE)
Name changed to Penton, Inc. 4/4/75

PENTON PUBLISHING CO. (OH)
Each share old Common no par exchanged for (2.5) shares new Common no par 11/30/1950
New Common no par changed to $5 par 00/00/1953
Common $5 par changed to $2.50 par and (1) additional share issued 04/23/1962
Common $2.50 par split (2) for (1) by issuance of (1) additional share 09/01/1967
Reincorporated under the laws of Delaware 12/31/1968
Penton Publishing Co. (DE) name changed to Penton, Inc. 04/04/1975
(See Penton, Inc.)

PENTOS PLC (UNITED KINGDOM)
Each Unsponsored ADR for Ordinary exchanged for (1) Sponsored ADR for Ordinary 12/08/1989
Placed in receivership 03/00/1995
No ADR holders' equity

PENTRON CORP. (DE)
Name changed to Koala Technologies Corp. 4/3/89
Koala Technologies Corp. recapitalized as Rotonics Manufacturing Inc. 12/17/92
(See Rotonics Manufacturing Inc.)

PENTRON ELECTRS CORP (IL)
Common $1 par changed to no par 6/30/61
Name changed to Pentron Industries, Inc. (IL) 11/3/70
Pentron Industries, Inc. (IL) reincorporated in Delaware 12/8/86 which name changed to Pentron Corp. 12/16/86 which name changed to Koala Technologies Corp. 4/3/89 which recapitalized as Rotonics Manufacturing Inc. 12/17/92
(See Rotonics Manufacturing Inc.)

PENTRON INDS INC (DE)
Reincorporated 12/8/86
State of incorporation changed from (IL) to (DE) 12/8/86
Name changed to Pentron Corp. 12/16/86
Pentron Corp. name changed to Koala Technologies Corp. 4/3/89 which recapitalized as Rotonics Manufacturing Inc. 12/17/92
(See Rotonics Manufacturing Inc.)

PENTRONIX, INC. (MI)
Merged into Wolverine-Pentronix, Inc. 4/30/69
Each share Capital Stock $2 par exchanged for (0.416666) share Common $1 par
Wolverine-Pentronix, Inc. name changed back to Wolverine Aluminum Corp. 5/10/76

PENULTIMATE INC (DE)
Each share old Common $0.001 par exchanged for (0.4) share new Common $0.001 par 7/13/93
Each share new Common $0.001 par exchanged again for (1/3) share new Common $0.001 par 12/20/93
Each share new Common $0.001 par exchanged again for (0.00922619) share new Common $0.001 par 5/23/96
Name changed to MobiNetix Systems, Inc. 8/26/96
MobiNetix Systems, Inc. name changed to @POS.com Inc. 6/29/99
(See @POS.com Inc.)

PENWAY EXPLORERS LTD (ON)
Delisted from Alberta Stock Exchange 02/19/1991

PENWEST LTD (WA)
Reincorporated 01/24/1995
Common $1 par split (2) for (1) by issuance of (1) additional share 07/17/1987
Common $1 par split (3) for (2) by issuance of (0.5) additional share 03/21/1990
State of incorporation changed from (DE) to (WA) 01/24/1995
Name changed to Penford Corp. 12/05/1997
(See Penford Corp.)

PENWEST PHARMACEUTICALS CO (WA)
Acquired by Endo Pharmaceuticals Holdings Inc. 11/04/2010
Each share Common $0.001 par exchanged for $5 cash

PENWOOD GOLD MINES LTD. (ON)
Charter surrendered for failure to file reports and pay taxes in 1960

PEOPLE DYNAMICS HLDGS INC (FL)
SEC revoked common stock registration 06/15/2011

PEOPLE EXPRESS AIRLS INC (DE)
Common 1¢ par split (2) for (1) by issuance of (1) additional share 07/18/1983
Under plan of reorganization each share $2.50 Conv. Preferred Ser. B 1¢ par, $2.64 Conv. Preferred Ser. A 1¢ par and Common 1¢ par automatically became (1) share People Express, Inc. $2.50 Conv. Preferred Ser. B 1¢ par, $2.64 Conv. Preferred Ser. A 1¢ par and Common 1¢ par respectively 08/28/1985
People Express, Inc. merged into Texas Air Corp. 12/29/1986 which name changed to Continental Airlines Holdings, Inc. 06/11/1990
(See Continental Airlines Holdings, Inc.)

PEOPLE EXPRESS INC (DE)
Each share Common 1¢ par received distribution of (0.1) share Class B Common 1¢ par 9/16/85
Merged into Texas Air Corp. 12/29/86
Each share $2.50 Conv. Preferred Ser. B 1¢ par exchanged for (1.4) shares 12% Depositary Preferred 10¢ par
Each share $2.64 Conv. Preferred Ser. A 1¢ par exchanged for (1.1) shares 12% Depositary Preferred 10¢ par
Each share Common 1¢ par exchanged for (0.25) share 6.50% Depositary Preferred 10¢ par and (0.05042) share Common 1¢ par
Each share Class B Common 1¢ par exchanged for (0.25) share 6.50% Depositary Preferred 10¢ par and (0.05042) share Common 1¢ par
Texas Air Corp. name changed to Continental Airlines Holdings, Inc. 6/11/90
(See Continental Airlines Holdings, Inc.)

PEOPLE RIDESHARING SYS INC (NJ)
Stock Dividends - 10% 11/4/86; 10% 7/1/87
Petition under Chapter 11 Federal Bankruptcy Code converted to Chapter 7 on 7/11/94

PEOPLE'S BANK (CHESAPEAKE, VA)
Acquired by United Virginia Bankshares, Inc. 1/21/87
Each share Capital Stock $10 par exchanged for (5) shares Common $5 par
United Virginia Bankshares, Inc. name changed to Crestar Financial Corp. 9/1/87 which merged into SunTrust Banks, Inc. 12/31/98

PEOPLE'S FINANCE CORP. (CO)
Name changed to Consumer Finance Corp. of America 10/04/1957
Consumer Finance Corp. of America acquired by General Acceptance Corp. (New) 06/09/1960 which name changed to GAC Corp. (PA) 07/01/1968 which reincorporated under the laws of Delaware 12/20/1973
(See GAC Corp. (DE))

PEOPLE'S OIL CO. (MT)
Charter expired by time limitation 5/28/57

PEOPLELINE INC (NV)
Recapitalized as Peopleline Telecom, Inc. 1/17/2007
Each share Common $0.001 par exchanged for (0.001) share Common $0.001 par

PEOPLENET INTL CORP (DE)
Name changed to hereUare, Inc. 04/17/2007
(See hereUare, Inc.)

PEOPLEPC INC (CA)
Acquired by EarthLink, Inc. 07/30/2002
Each share Common $0.0001 par exchanged for $0.0221 cash

PEOPLES ACCEPTANCE CO.
Dissolved in 1941

PEOPLES AMERN BK (ATLANTA, GA)
Name changed to First Georgia Bank (Atlanta, GA) 03/31/1972
First Georgia Bank (Atlanta, GA) acquired by First Georgia Bancshares, Inc. 08/01/1973 which merged into First Railroad & Banking Co. of Georgia 06/26/1986 which was acquired by First Union Corp. 11/01/1986 which name changed to Wachovia Corp. (Ctfs. dated after 09/01/2001) 09/01/2001 which merged into Wells Fargo & Co. (New) 12/31/2008

PEOPLES BAN CORP (WA)
Acquired by U.S. Bancorp (OR) 12/22/1987
Each share Common Capital Stock $5 par exchanged for (2.6) shares Common $5 par
U.S. Bancorp (OR) merged into U.S. Bancorp (Old) (DE) 08/01/1997 which merged into U.S. Bancorp 02/27/2001

PEOPLES BANCORP (IN)
Old Common $1 par split (2) for (1) by issuance of (1) additional share 09/15/1993
Old Common $1 par split (3) for (2) by issuance of (0.5) additional share payable 11/24/1997 to holders of record 11/07/1997
Each share old Common $1 par exchanged for (1) share new Common $1 par to reflect a (1) for (760) reverse split followed by a (760) for (1) forward split 03/28/2008
Note: Holders of (759) or fewer pre-split shares received $16.75 cash per share
Merged into Horizon Bancorp 07/01/2015
Each share new Common $1 par exchanged for (0.95) share Common no par and $9.75 cash
Note: Holders of (99) or fewer shares will receive $33.14 cash per share
Horizon Bancorp name changed to Horizon Bancorp, Inc. 05/08/2018

PEOPLES BANCORP (NJ)
Acquired by Valley National Bancorp 06/19/1993
Details not available

PEOPLES BANCORP (WA)
Merged into German American Bancorp 03/04/1997
Each share Common $1 par exchanged for (1.0372) shares Common $1 par

PEOPLES BANCORP INC (DE)
Merged into Sovereign Bancorp, Inc. 07/01/1999
Each share Common 1¢ par exchanged for (0.8) share Common no par
Sovereign Bancorp, Inc. merged into Banco Santander, S.A. 01/30/2009

PEOPLES BANCORP INC (GA)
Merged into United Community Banks, Inc. 11/08/2001
Each share Common $1 par exchanged for (0.4473684) share Common $1 par

PEOPLES BANCORP INC (NJ)
Reorganized under the laws of Delaware as Peoples Bancorp Inc. 04/08/1998
Each share Common 10¢ par exchanged for (3.8243) shares Common 1¢ par
Peoples Bancorp Inc. (DE) merged into Sovereign Bancorp, Inc. 07/01/1999 which merged into Banco Santander, S.A. 01/30/2009

PEOPLES BANCORP INC (OH)
Common $1 par split (3) for (2) by issuance of (0.5) additional share 10/15/1981
Common $1 par split (2) for (1) by issuance of (1) additional share 10/30/1987
Stock Dividends - 10% 09/16/1985; 10% 07/17/1989; 10% 04/15/1993
Reincorporated under the laws of Delaware and Common $1 par changed to no par 04/15/1993

PEOPLES BANCORP INC (PA)
Merged into Meridian Bancorp, Inc. 12/04/1992
Each share Common $1 par exchanged for (0.9278) share Common $5 par
Meridian Bancorp, Inc. merged into CoreStates Financial Corp 04/09/1996 which merged into First Union Corp. 04/28/1998 which name changed to Wachovia Corp. (Ctfs. dated after 09/01/2001) 09/01/2001 which merged into Wells Fargo & Co. (New) 12/31/2008

PEOPLES BANCORP N C INC (NC)
5% Perpetual Preferred Ser. A no par called for redemption at $1,000 plus $8.75 accrued dividends on 01/17/2014
(Additional Information in Active)

PEOPLES BANCORP WORCESTER INC (DE)
Merged into Shawmut National Corp. 05/23/1994
Each share Common 10¢ par exchanged for (2.444) shares Common 1¢ par
Shawmut National Corp. merged into Fleet Financial Group Inc. (New) 11/30/1995 which name changed to Fleet Boston Corp. 10/01/1999 which name changed to FleetBoston Financial Corp. 04/18/2000 which merged into Bank of America Corp. 04/01/2004

PEOPLES BANCORPORATION (NC)
Reorganized 1/1/83
Under plan of reorganization each share Peoples Bancorp, Inc. Common no par automatically became (1) share Peoples Bancorporation Common no par 1/1/83
Common $5 par changed to no par and (2) additional shares issued 7/16/84
Common no par split (5) for (4) by issuance of (0.25) additional share 9/2/86
Merged into Centura Banks, Inc. 11/5/90
Each share Common no par exchanged for (1) share Common no par
Centura Banks, Inc. merged into Royal Bank of Canada (Montreal, QC) 6/5/2001

PEOPLES BANCORPORATION INC (SC)
Common $1.11 par split (3) for (2) by issuance of (0.5) additional share payable 10/04/2004 to holders of record 09/20/2004 Ex date - 10/05/2004
Stock Dividends - 5% payable 12/07/1998 to holders of record 11/19/1998; 5% payable 01/14/2000 to holders of record 12/31/1999; 5% payable 01/04/2002 to holders of record 12/17/2001 Ex date - 12/13/2001; 5% payable 11/18/2002 to holders of record 11/04/2002 Ex date - 10/31/2002; 5% payable 11/17/2003 to holders of record 11/03/2003 Ex date - 10/30/2003; 5% payable 01/04/2005 to holders of record 12/14/2004 Ex date - 12/10/2004; 5% payable 12/30/2005 to holders of record 12/15/2005 Ex date - 12/13/2005; 5% payable 01/05/2007 to holders of record 12/22/2006 Ex date - 12/20/2006; 5% payable 01/04/2008 to holders of record 12/21/2007 Ex date - 12/19/2007
Acquired by SCBT Financial Corp. 04/26/2012
Each share Common $1.11 par exchanged for (0.1413) share Common $2.50 par
SCBT Financial Corp. name changed to First Financial Holdings, Inc. 07/30/2013 which name changed to South State Corp. 06/30/2014

PEOPLES BANCORPORATION NORTHN KY INC (KY)
Common no par split (2) for (1) by issuance of (1) additional share payable 05/03/1999 to holders of record 03/29/1999
Stock Dividends - 2% payable 03/20/2001 to holders of record 01/26/2001 Ex date - 03/28/2001; 2% payable 03/25/2002 to holders of record 03/01/2002 Ex date - 04/22/2002
Voluntarily dissolved 11/22/2002
Details not available

PEOPLES BANCSHARES CAP TR
Trust Preferred Securities called for redemption at $10 on 6/30/2002

PEOPLES BANCSHARES INC. (LA)
Merged into First Commerce Corp. 10/2/95
Each share Common $25 par exchanged for (39.35195) shares Common $25 par
First Commerce Corp. merged into Banc One Corp. 6/12/98 which merged into Bank One Corp. 10/2/98 which merged into J.P. Morgan Chase & Co. 12/31/2000 which name changed to JPMorgan Chase & Co. 7/20/2004

PEOPLES BANCSHARES INC (MA)
Merged into Firstfed America Bancorp, Inc. 2/28/2002
Each share Common 10¢ par exchanged for $22 cash

PEOPLES BANCSHARES INC (OH)
Liquidation completed
Each share Common $10 par received initial distribution of $35 cash 04/19/1976
Each share Common $10 par exchanged for second distribution of $7.47 cash 07/10/1976
Each share Common $10 par received third and final distribution of $0.08 cash 05/15/1979

PEOPLES BANCTRUST INC (AL)
Common $1 par split (2) for (1) by issuance of (1) additional share 12/15/1990
Common $1 par split (2) for (1) by issuance of (1) additional share 03/15/1995
Common $1 par split (2) for (1) by issuance of (1) additional share payable 06/15/1997 to holders of record 06/06/1997
Stock Dividend - 10% payable 06/15/2001 to holders of record 06/07/2001 Ex date - 06/05/2001
Merged into BancTrust Financial Group, Inc. 10/15/2007
Each share Common $1 par exchanged for (1.0614) shares Common 1¢ par and $6.375 cash
BancTrust Financial Group, Inc. merged into Trustmark Corp. 02/15/2013

PEOPLES BANK & TRUST CO. (INDIANAPOLIS, IN)
Each share Capital Stock $100 par exchanged for (13-1/3) shares Capital Stock $10 par 10/1/65
Stock Dividends - 50% 12/31/62; 50% 10/1/69; 33-1/3% 6/30/72; 25% 6/30/73; 40% 6/30/77
Under plan of reorganization each share Capital Stock $10 par automatically became (1) share Peoples Bank Corp. of Indianapolis Non-Vtg. Common no par 11/4/86
Peoples Bank Corp. of Indianapolis merged into Fifth Third Bancorp 11/19/99

PEOPLES BK & TR CO (ANCHORAGE, AK)
Acquired by Rainier Bancorporation 4/30/83
Each share Common $5 par exchanged for $56.675 cash

PEOPLES BK & TR CO (CEDAR RAPIDS, IA)
Stock Dividends - 20% 00/00/1944; 33-1/3% 00/00/1951; 25% 00/00/1954; 20% 02/17/1958
Under plan of reorganization each share Capital Stock $20 par automatically became (1) share P B Bancorp of Cedar Rapids, Inc. Common $5 par 12/06/1982
(See P B Bancorp of Cedar Rapids, Inc.)

PEOPLES BK & TR CO (GRAND HAVEN, MI)
99.9% acquired by Great Lakes Financial Corp. through exchange offer which expired 09/16/1974
Public interest eliminated

PEOPLES BK & TR CO (MONTGOMERY, AL)
100% acquired by Central & State National Corp. of Alabama through exchange offer which expired 11/15/1972
Public interest eliminated

PEOPLES BK & TR CO (ROCKY MOUNT, NC)
Stock Dividends - 20% 11/30/76; 20% 2/28/79; 25% 1/29/82
Under plan of reorganization each share Common $5 par automatically became (1) share Peoples Bancorp (NC), Inc. Common $5 par 12/20/82
Peoples Bancorp (NC), Inc. reorganized as Peoples Bancorporation 1/1/83 which merged into Centura Banks, Inc. 11/5/90 which merged into Royal Bank of Canada (Montreal, QC) 6/5/2001

PEOPLES BK & TR CO (SELMA, AL)
Reorganized as Peoples BancTrust Co., Inc. 04/30/1985
Each share Capital Stock $5 par exchanged for (1) share Common $1 par
Peoples BancTrust Co., Inc. merged into BancTrust Financial Group, Inc. 10/15/2007 which merged into Trustmark Corp. 02/15/2013

PEOPLES BK & TR CO (WATERLOO, IA)
Each share Capital Stock $100 par exchanged for (5) shares Capital Stock $20 par 02/05/1968
Acquired by Peoples Bankshares Ltd. 07/10/1979
Each share Capital Stock $20 par exchanged for $3.30 cash

PEOPLES BK & TR CO ST BERNARD (CHALMETTE, LA)
Merged into First Commerce Corp. 10/2/95
Each share Common $25 par exchanged for (38.22895) shares Common $25 par
First Commerce Corp. merged into Banc One Corp. 6/12/98 which merged into Bank One Corp. 10/2/98 which merged into J.P. Morgan Chase & Co. 12/31/2000 which name changed to JPMorgan Chase & Co. 7/20/2004

PEOPLES BK (BRIDGEPORT, CT)
8.50% Conv. Preferred Ser. A no par called for redemption 9/20/96
Common no par split (3) for (2) by issuance of (0.5) additional share payable 5/15/97 to holders of record 5/1/97
Common no par split (3) for (2) by issuance of (0.5) additional share payable 5/15/2004 to holders of record 5/1/2004 Ex date - 5/18/2004
Common no par split (3) for (2) by issuance of (0.5) additional share payable 5/15/2005 to holders of record 5/1/2005 Ex date - 5/16/2005
Reorganized as People's United Financial, Inc. 4/16/2007
Each share Common no par exchanged for (2.1) shares Common 1¢ par

PEOPLES BK (CHESTERFIELD, VA)
Merged into F & M National Corp. 4/1/98
Each share Common $10 par exchanged for (2.58) shares Common $2 par
F & M National Corp. merged into BB&T Corp. 8/9/2001

PEOPLES BK (DICKSON, TN)
Merged into First American Corp. (TN) 10/1/98
Each share Common no par exchanged for (3.7) shares Common $5 par
First American Corp. (TN) merged into AmSouth Bancorporation 10/1/99 which merged into Regions Financial Corp. 11/4/2006

PEOPLES BK (HARRINGTON, DE)
Acquired by Wilmington Trust Co. (Wilmington, DE) 12/18/1990
Each share Common $25 par exchanged for (12.04) shares Common $1 par
Wilmington Trust Co. (Wilmington, DE) reorganized as Wilmington Trust Corp. 08/23/1991 which merged into M&T Bank Corp. 05/16/2011

PEOPLES BANK (INDIANOLA, MS)
Name changed to Community Bank (Indianola, MS) 06/25/1995
(See Community Bank (Indianola, MS))

PEOPLES BK (IVA, SC)
Under plan of reorganization each share Common automatically became (1) share Peoples Financial Group Inc. Common 8/14/2000

PEOPLES BK (KENT COUNTY, MD)
Under plan of reorganization each

share Common $10 par automatically became (1) share Peoples Bancorp, Inc. Common $10 par 03/24/1997

PEOPLES BANK (LAKELAND, FL)
Stock Dividends - 100% 00/00/1951; 66.66666666% 00/00/1953; 50% 00/00/1956
Acquired by Huntington National Bank of Florida N.A. (Lakeland, FL) 08/00/1996
Details not available

PEOPLES BK (MONTVALE, NJ)
Acquired by United Jersey Banks 12/31/71
Each share Capital Stock $5 par exchanged for (0.428571) share Common $5 par
United Jersey Banks name changed to UJB Financial Corp. 6/30/89 which name changed to Summit Bancorp 3/1/96 which merged into FleetBoston Financial Corp. 3/1/2001 which merged into Bank of America Corp. 4/1/2004

PEOPLES BK (NEWTON, NC)
Common $5 par split (3) for (2) by issuance of (1) additional share payable 3/22/99 to holders of record 2/22/99
Stock Dividends - 10% 6/10/92; 10% 12/10/93; 15% 12/15/95; 10% payable 5/16/97 to holders of record 5/1/97
Under plan of reorganization each share Common $5 par automatically became (1) share Peoples Bancorp of North Carolina, Inc. Common no par 9/7/99

PEOPLES BK (OXFORD, PA)
Stock Dividend - 10% payable 02/17/1998 to holders of record 01/30/1998
Name changed to Peoples First Inc. 07/27/2000
Peoples First Inc. merged into National Penn Bancshares, Inc. 06/10/2004 which merged into BB&T Corp. 04/01/2016

PEOPLES BK (PALM HARBOR, FL)
Under plan of reorganization each share Common $5 par automatically became (3) shares Peoples Florida Banking Corp.
Common $5 par in October 1998

PEOPLES BANK (PILESGROVE TOWNSHIP, NJ)
Name changed to Peoples Bank of South Jersey (Pilesgrove Township, NJ) 01/21/1968
Peoples Bank of South Jersey (Pilesgrove, Township, NJ) location changed to Peoples Bank of South Jersey (Washington, Township, NJ) 07/24/1970 which location changed to Peoples Bank of South Jersey (Clayton, NJ) 01/01/1974 which merged into Citizens Bancorp (NJ) 08/31/1979
(See Citizens Bancorp (NJ))

PEOPLES BK (RIDGEWOOD, NJ)
Acquired by United Jersey Banks 12/31/71
Each share Capital Stock $5 par exchanged for (0.428571) share Common $5 par
United Jersey Banks name changed to UJB Financial Corp. 6/30/89 which name changed to Summit Bancorp 3/1/96 which merged into FleetBoston Financial Corp. 3/1/2001 which merged into Bank of America Corp. 4/1/2004

PEOPLES BANK (TALLAHASSEE, FL)
Acquired by United First Florida Banks, Inc. 02/28/1974
Each share Common $10 par exchanged for (2) shares Common $1 par
United First Florida Banks, Inc. name changed to Flagship Banks Inc. 06/30/1974 which merged into Sun Banks, Inc. 01/01/1984 which merged into SunTrust Banks, Inc. 07/01/1985

PEOPLES BK (VIRGINIA BEACH, VA)
Ctfs. dated prior to 1/1/69
Under plan of reorganization each share Capital Stock $5 par automatically became (1) share Peoples Corp. Capital Stock $5 par 1/1/69
(See Peoples Corp.)

PEOPLES BK CORP INDIANAPOLIS IND (IN)
Common no par split (2) for (1) by issuance of (1) additional share payable 7/18/97 to holders of record 6/30/97
Non-Vtg. Common no par split (2) for (1) by issuance of (1) additional share payable 7/18/97 to holders of record 6/30/97
Merged into Fifth Third Bancorp 11/19/99
Each share Non-Vtg. Common no par exchanged for (1.09) shares Common no par
Each share Common no par exchanged for (1.09) shares Common no par

PEOPLES BK ELKTON (ELKTON, MD)
Merged into Fulton Financial Corp. 8/31/97
Each share Common $10 par exchanged for (4.158) shares Common $2.50 par

PEOPLES BK N A (BELLEVILLE, NJ)
Reorganized as Peoples BanCorp 03/01/1982
Each share Common Capital Stock $10 par exchanged for (1) share Common no par
(See Peoples BanCorp)

PEOPLES BK NEW (VIRGINIA BEACH, VA)
Merged into Jefferson Bankshares, Inc. 02/11/1993
Each share Common $5 par exchanged for (0.1333) share Common $2.50 par
Jefferson Bankshares, Inc. merged into Wachovia Corp. (New) (Ctfs. dated between 05/20/1991 and 09/01/2001) 10/31/1997 which merged into Wachovia Corp. (Ctfs. dated after 09/01/2001) 09/01/2001 which merged into Wells Fargo & Co. (New) 12/31/2008

PEOPLES BK OF FLEMING CNTY (FLEMINGSBURG, KY)
Under plan of reorganization each share Common $25 par automatically became (1) share Peoples of Fleming County Bancorp, Inc. Common $25 par 10/31/1995

PEOPLES BANK OF FRONT ROYAL (FRONT ROYAL, VA)
Common $10 par changed to $5 par and (1) additional share issued 04/00/1981
Merged into Jefferson Bankshares, Inc. 12/17/1992
Each share Common $5 par exchanged for (3.5) shares Common $2.50 par
Jefferson Bankshares, Inc. merged into Wachovia Corp. (New) (Ctfs. dated between 05/20/1991 and 09/01/2001) 10/31/1997 which merged into Wachovia Corp. (Ctfs. dated after 09/01/2001) 09/01/2001 which merged into Wells Fargo & Co. (New) 12/31/2008

PEOPLES BANK OF SOUTH JERSEY (CLAYTON, NJ)
Merged into Citizens Bancorp (N.J.) 8/31/79
Each share Common $6.25 par exchanged for (1) share Common no par
(See Citizens Bancorp (N.J.))

PEOPLES BANK OF SOUTH JERSEY (PILESGROVE TOWNSHIP, NJ)
Common $10 par changed to $6.25 par 1/2/70
Location changed to Peoples Bank of South Jersey (Washington Township, N.J.) 7/24/70
Peoples Bank of South Jersey (Washington Township, N.J.) location changed to Peoples Bank of South Jersey (Clayton, N.J.) 1/1/74 which merged into Citizens Bancorp (N.J.) 8/31/79
(See Citizens Bancorp (N.J.))

PEOPLES BANK OF SOUTH JERSEY (WASHINGTON TOWNSHIP, NJ)
Location changed to Peoples Bank of South Jersey (Clayton, N.J.) 1/1/74
Peoples Bank of South Jersey (Clayton, N.J.) merged into Citizens Bancorp (N.J.) 8/31/79
(See Citizens Bancorp (N.J.))

PEOPLES BK SOUTH BERGEN CNTY (CARLSTADT, NJ)
Acquired by United Jersey Banks 12/31/71
Each share Capital Stock $5 par exchanged for (0.428571) share Common $5 par
United Jersey Banks name changed to UJB Financial Corp. 6/30/89 which name changed to Summit Bancorp 3/1/96 which merged into FleetBoston Financial Corp. 3/1/2001 which merged into Bank of America Corp. 4/1/2004

PEOPLES BK UNITY (PLUM BORO, PA)
Acquired by S&T Bancorp, Inc. 5/2/97
Each share Common $50 par exchanged for (26.25) shares Common $2.50 par

PEOPLES BK VA (RICHMOND, VA)
Merged into First Community Bancshares, Inc. (NV) 05/31/2012
Each share Common $5 par exchanged for (1.07) shares Common $1 par and $6.08 cash
First Community Bancshares, Inc. (NV) reincorporated in Virginia 10/09/2018

PEOPLES BK WESTERN PA (NEW CASTLE, PA)
Common $10 par split (5) for (1) by issuance of (4) additional shares 5/7/93
Acquired by First Commonwealth Financial Corp. 12/31/93
Each share Common $10 par exchanged for (2) shares Common $5 par

PEOPLES BANKCORP INC (NY)
Merged into Community Bank System, Inc. 9/5/2003
Each share Common 1¢ par exchanged for $30 cash

PEOPLES BKG & TR CO (MARIETTA, OH)
Each share Capital Stock $100 par exchanged for (6-2/3) shares Capital Stock $25 par to effect a (4) for (1) split and a 66-2/3% stock dividend 1/25/54
Capital Stock $25 par changed to $12.50 par and (1) additional share issued 1/11/67
Capital Stock $12.50 par changed to $6.25 par and (1.2) additional shares issued to effect a (2) for (1) split and a 10% stock dividend 2/15/77
Stock Dividends - 33-1/3% 6/1/40; 20% 6/25/45; 20% 2/1/61; 25% 2/1/65; 10% 2/1/70; 13.63% 2/1/71
Reorganized under the laws of Delaware as Peoples Bancorp Inc. 12/30/81
Each share Capital Stock $6.25 par exchanged for (1) share Common no par
Peoples Bancorp Inc. reincorporated in Ohio 4/15/93

PEOPLES BKG CORP (MI)
Common $10 par changed to $5 par and (1) additional share issued 4/28/75
Name changed to NewCentury Bank Corp. 7/1/84
NewCentury Bank Corp. merged into First of America Bank Corp. 12/31/86 which merged into National City Corp. 3/31/98

PEOPLES BREWING CO. (WI)
Charter dissolved for failure to file annual reports 7/1/80

PEOPLES CHOICE TV CORP (DE)
Merged into Sprint Corp. 9/24/99
Each share Common 1¢ par exchanged for $10 cash

PEOPLES CMNTY BANCORP INC (MD)
Reincorporated 05/31/2002
State of incorporation changed from (DE) to (MD) 05/31/2002
Company's sole asset placed in receivership 07/31/2009
Stockholders' equity unlikely

PEOPLES CMNTY BANCSHARES INC (FL)
Merged into Superior Bancorp 07/27/2007
Each share Common 1¢ par exchanged for (2.9036) shares Common $0.001 par
(See Superior Bancorp)

PEOPLES CMNTY BK (SARASOTA, FL)
Reorganized as People's Community Bancshares, Inc. 05/29/2002
Each share Common 1¢ par exchanged for (1) share Common 1¢ par
People's Community Bancshares, Inc. merged into Superior Bancorp 07/27/2007

PEOPLES CMNTY CAP CORP (SC)
Stock Dividends - 5% payable 01/02/2002 to holders of record 12/15/2001 Ex date - 12/12/2001; 5% payable 01/29/2003 to holders of record 01/15/2003; 5% payable 01/29/2004 to holders of record 01/15/2004
Merged into First Citizens Bancorporation, Inc. 05/02/2005
Each share Common 1¢ par exchanged for $30 cash

PEOPLES CORP (VA)
99.8% acquired by Fidelity American Bankshares, Inc. through exchange offer which expired 03/15/1973
Public interest eliminated

PEOPLES CR JEWELLERS LTD (CANADA)
6% Preferred $100 par reclassified as 6% 1st Preferred $100 par 12/10/1962
Each share Common no par received distribution of (2) Class A no par 12/10/1962
Common no par and Class A no par split (2) for (1) by issuance of (1) additional share respectively 11/30/1971
Name changed to Peoples Jewellers Ltd. 05/09/1973
(See Peoples Jewellers Ltd.)

PEOPLES CREDIT SECURITIES LTD. (ON)
Dissolved and each share Capital Stock no par exchanged for (7.5) shares of Peoples Credit Jewellers Ltd. 6% Preferred $100 par, (2) shares Common no par and $10 in cash in 1954
Peoples Credit Jewellers Ltd. name

changed to Peoples Jewellers Ltd. 5/9/73
(See Peoples Jewellers Ltd.)

PEOPLES DEPT STORES LTD (CANADA)
Common no par split (2) for (1) by issuance of (1) additional share 9/24/71
Common no par split (3) for (1) by issuance of (2) additional shares 6/29/72
Name changed to Marks & Spencer Canada Inc. 2/5/79
(See Marks & Spencer Canada Inc.)

PEOPLES DOWNTOWN NATL BK (MIAMI, FL)
Acquired by Pan American Banks Inc. 04/15/1982
Details not available

PEOPLES DRUG STORES, INC. (DE)
Succeeded by Peoples Drug Stores, Inc. (Maryland) in 1928
(See Peoples Drug Stores, Inc. (Md.))

PEOPLES DRUG STORES INC (MD)
Each share Common no par exchanged for (2) shares Common $5 par in 1940
Common $5 par split (2) for (1) by issuance of (1) additional share 4/27/65
Common $5 par split (2) for (1) by issuance of (1) additional share 5/15/72
Common $5 par split (5) for (4) by issuance of (0.25) additional share 10/6/82
Common $5 par split (3) for (2) by issuance of (0.5) additional share 7/8/83
Stock Dividend - 10% 12/31/47
Merged into Imasco Ltd.-Imasco Ltee. 5/3/84
Each share Common $5 par exchanged for $34 cash

PEOPLES ENERGY CORP (IL)
Under plan of reorganization each share Common no par received distribution of (1) share MidCon Corp. Common no par 12/18/1981
Merged into Integrys Energy Group, Inc. 02/21/2007
Each share Common no par exchanged for (0.825) share Common $1 par
Integrys Energy Group, Inc. merged into WEC Energy Group, Inc. 06/30/2015

PEOPLES FED BANCSHARES INC (MD)
Merged into Independent Bank Corp. 02/20/2015
Each share Common 1¢ par exchanged for $21 cash

PEOPLES FED SVGS & LN ASSN OF CHICAGO (IL)
Merged into Mid-City National Bank of Chicago 4/10/95
Each share Common 1¢ par exchanged for $19 cash

PEOPLES FED SVGS BK DEKALB CNTY F S B (AUBURN, IN)
Under plan of reorganization each share Common $1 par automatically became (1) share Peoples Bancorp Common $1 par 02/01/1991
Peoples Bancorp merged into Horizon Bancorp 07/01/2015

PEOPLES FINANCE CORP. (VA)
Voluntarily dissolved 2/4/81
Details not available

PEOPLES FINL CORP (OH)
Merged into National Bancshares Corp. 4/3/2002
Each share Common no par exchanged for $12.25 cash

PEOPLES FINL INC (PA)
Common 30¢ par split (2) for (1) by issuance of (1) additional share payable 2/10/99 to holders of record 1/20/99
Merged into S&T Bancorp, Inc. 9/9/2002
Each share Common 30¢ par exchanged for $52.50 cash

PEOPLES FIRST CORP (KY)
Common no par split (2) for (1) by issuance of (1) additional share 01/04/1994
Stock Dividends - 5% payable 03/18/1996 to holders of record 02/19/1996; 5% payable 03/20/1997 to holders of record 02/21/1997
Merged into Union Planters Corp. 07/01/1998
Each share Common no par exchanged for (0.6) share Common $5 par
Union Planters Corp. merged into Regions Financial Corp. (New) 07/01/2004

PEOPLES FIRST INC (PA)
Merged into National Penn Bancshares, Inc. 06/10/2004
Each share Common $1 par exchanged for (1.505) shares Common $5 par
National Penn Bancshares, Inc. merged into BB&T Corp. 04/01/2016

PEOPLES FIRST NATIONAL BANCSHARES, INC. (FL)
Voluntarily dissolved 10/28/1991
Details not available

PEOPLES 1ST NATL BK (MIAMI SHORES, FL)
98% held by Pan American Banks, Inc. as of 06/02/1982
Public interest eliminated

PEOPLES FIRST NATL BK & TR CO (PADUCAH, KY)
Reorganized as Peoples First Corp. 9/19/83
Each share Capital Stock $100 par exchanged for (1) share Common no par
Peoples First Corp. merged into Union Planters Corp. 7/1/98 which merged into Regions Financial Corp. (New) 7/1/2004

PEOPLES 1ST NATL BK & TR CO (HAZLETON, PA)
Capital Stock $10 par changed to $1.25 par and (7) additional shares issued 6/10/86
Merged into First Eastern Corp. 8/8/88
Each share Capital Stock $1.25 par exchanged for (2.07) shares Common $10 par
(See First Eastern Corp.)

PEOPLES 1ST NATL BK (NORTH MIAMI BEACH, FL)
Reorganized as Peoples First National Bancshares, Inc. 01/29/1984
Each share Capital Stock $15 par exchanged for (7) shares Capital Stock $2.50 par
(See Peoples First National Bancshares, Inc.)

PEOPLES FOOD HLDGS LTD (BERMUDA)
ADR agreement terminated 03/28/2016
No ADR's remain outstanding

PEOPLES GAS & ELECTRIC CO. OF OSWEGO
Merged into Niagara Hudson Public Service Corp. which name was changed to Central New York Power Corp. 7/31/37
Each share Preferred exchanged for (10) shares Common no par
Central New York Power Corp. merged into Niagara Mohawk Power Corp. 1/5/50

PEOPLES GAS & FUEL CO.
Reorganized in 1938
No stockholders' equity

PEOPLES GAS & FUEL CORP.
Merged into Southwest Natural Gas Co. in 1940
Each share Common exchanged for $33 principal amount of First Mortgage Bonds and (10) shares Common or $30 cash
Southwest Natural Gas Co. merged into Arkansas Louisiana Gas Co. 10/2/61 which name changed to Arkla, Inc. 11/23/81 which name changed to NorAm Energy Corp. 5/11/94 which merged into Houston Industries Inc. 8/6/97 which name changed to Reliant Energy Inc. 2/8/99 which reorganized as CenterPoint Energy, Inc. 8/31/2002

PEOPLES GAS CO (IL)
Common no par split (4) for (3) by issuance of (0.33333333) additional share 09/02/1977
Name changed to Peoples Energy Corp. 02/01/1980
Peoples Energy Corp. merged into Integrys Energy Group, Inc. 02/21/2007 which merged into WEC Energy Group, Inc. 06/30/2015

PEOPLES GAS LT & COKE CO (IL)
Capital Stock $100 par changed to $25 par and (3) additional shares issued 5/8/57
Capital Stock $25 par changed to no par and (1) additional share issued 11/17/61
Capital Stock no par split (5) for (4) by issuance of (0.25) additional share 11/6/64
Acquired by Peoples Gas Co. 9/26/68
Each share Capital Stock no par exchanged for (1) share Common no par
Note: Unexchanged certificates became valueless on 9/25/83
Peoples Gas Co. name changed to Peoples Energy Corp. 2/1/80 which merged into Integrys Energy Group, Inc. 2/21/2007

PEOPLES GAS SYS INC (FL)
Name changed 00/00/1957
Name changed from Peoples Water & Gas Co. to Peoples Gas System, Inc. 00/00/1957
Capital Stock $10 par reclassified as Class B $3.33-1/3 par and (2) additional shares issued 05/15/1961
Class A and B Voting Trust terminated 06/15/1961
Each share Class A $3.33-1/3 par exchanged for (1) share Common $3.33-1/3 par 00/00/1978
Each share Class B $3.33-1/3 par exchanged for (1) share Common $3.33-1/3 par 00/00/1978
Merged into Tampa Electric Co. 06/16/1997
Details not available

PEOPLES HERITAGE FINL GROUP INC (ME)
Reorganized 06/20/1988
Reorganized from Peoples Heritage Savings Bank (Portland, ME) to Peoples Heritage Financial Group, Inc. 06/20/1988
Each share Common $1 par exchanged for (1) share Common 1¢ par
Common 1¢ par split (2) for (1) by issuance of (1) additional share payable 05/18/1998 to holders of record 05/08/1998
Under plan of merger name changed to Banknorth Group, Inc. (ME) 05/10/2000
Banknorth Group, Inc. (ME) merged into TD Banknorth Inc. 03/01/2005
(See TD Banknorth Inc.)

PEOPLES HLDG CO (MS)
Common $5 par split (3) for (2) by issuance of (0.5) additional share payable 5/20/96 to holders of record 4/30/96
Common $5 par split (3) for (2) by issuance of (0.5) additional share payable 1/20/98 to holders of record 1/1/98 Ex date - 1/21/98
Common $5 par split (3) for (2) by issuance of (0.5) additional share payable 12/1/2003 to holders of record 11/7/2003
Name changed to Renasant Corp. 4/19/2005

PEOPLES HOME SVGS BK (BEAVER FALLS, PA)
Under plan of reorganization each share Common 10¢ par automatically became (1) share PHS Bancorp Inc. Common 10¢ par 08/20/1998
PHS Bancorp Inc. reorganized as PHSB Financial Corp. 12/20/2001 which merged into ESB Financial Corp. 02/11/2005 which merged into WesBanco, Inc. 02/10/2015

PEOPLES INDUSTRIAL BANK (NEW YORK, NY)
Acquired by Manufacturers Trust Co. (New York, NY) 9/4/53
Details not available

PEOPLES INSURANCE SERVICE, INC. (GA)
Merged into Peoples Financial Corp. 4/30/62
Each share Common $10 par exchanged for (10) shares Common $1 par

PEOPLES JEWELLERS LTD (CANADA)
Old Common no par and Class A no par split (2) for (1) by issuance of (1) additional share respectively 05/15/1973
Class A no par reclassified as Conv. Class A no par 07/28/1975
Old Common no par reclassified as Conv. Class C no par 05/11/1976
6% 1st Preferred $100 par called for redemption 12/31/1976
Conv. Class A no par reclassified as Class A no par 02/07/1979
Conv. Class B no par reclassified as Class A no par 02/07/1979
Conv. Class C no par reclassified as new Common no par 02/07/1979
Conv. Class D no par reclassified as new Common no par 02/07/1979
Declared bankrupt 07/29/1993
No stockholders' equity

PEOPLES LIBERATION INC (DE)
Name changed to Sequential Brands Group, Inc. (Old) 03/26/2012
Sequential Brands Group, Inc. (Old) reorganized as Sequential Brands Group, Inc. (New) 12/07/2015

PEOPLES LIBERTY BANCORPORATION (KY)
Acquired by First National Cincinnati Corp. 02/01/1988
Each share Common $10 par exchanged for (4.62) shares Common $5 par
First National Cincinnati Corp. name changed to Star Banc Corp. 04/13/1990 which merged into Firstar Corp. (New) 11/20/1998 which merged into U.S. Bancorp (DE) 02/27/2001

PEOPLES LIBERTY BK & TR CO (COVINGTON, KY)
Conv. Preferred Ser. A $175 par called for redemption 04/01/1980
Preferred Ser. B $175 par called for redemption 04/01/1980
Common $10 par split (3) for (2) by issuance of (0.5) additional share 07/02/1981
Stock Dividend - 10% 03/01/1976
Reorganized as Peoples Liberty Bancorporation 01/15/1983
Each share Common $10 par exchanged for (1) share Common $10 par
Peoples Liberty Bancorporation acquired by First National Cincinnati

Corp. 02/01/1988 which
recapitalized as Star Banc Corp.
04/13/1990 which merged into
Firstar Corp. (New) 11/20/1998
which merged into U.S. Bancorp
(DE) 02/27/2001

**PEOPLES LIBERTY NATL BK
(NORTH MIAMI, FL)**
Name changed to Kislak National
Bank (North Miami, FL) 11/15/1984
(See Kislak National Bank (North Miami, FL))

PEOPLES LIFE INSURANCE CO. (IN)
Control acquired by Home Insurance
Co. through purchase offer in
January 1958

PEOPLES LIFE INS CO (DC)
Stock Dividends - 16-2/3%
05/25/1959; 14-2/7% 05/26/1961; (1)
for (5.25) 05/21/1962
99.99% acquired by Capital Holding
Corp. through offer which expired
07/15/1981
Public interest eliminated

PEOPLES LIGHT & POWER CO.
Reorganized as Texas Public Service
Co. in 1946
Each share Preferred exchanged for
(3) shares new Common and $16
cash
Each share Class A or B Common
exchanged for (0.2) share new
Common
Texas Public Service Co. merged into
Southern Union Gas Co. (Del.)
(New) 7/21/49
(See Southern Union Gas Co. (Del.) (New))

PEOPLES LIGHT & POWER CORP.
Reorganized as Peoples Light &
Power Co. in 1938
Stockholders received 10-Year
Warrants which expired in 1948

PEOPLES LOAN & FINANCE CORP. (GA)
Each share Common $100 par
exchanged for (20) shares Common
$5 par 01/31/1955
Merged into Peoples Financial Corp.
04/30/1962
Each share Preferred $100 par
exchanged for (1) share 6%
Preferred $100 par
Each share Common $5 par
exchanged for (2) shares Common
$1 par

PEOPLES MERCHANTS TR CO (CANTON, OH)
Capital Stock $25 par changed to
$12.50 par and (1) additional share
issued plus a 6% stock dividend
paid 04/15/1970
Stock Dividends - 23.07%
02/17/1959; 10% 02/21/1967; 10%
03/31/1969
Merged into Peoples Bancshares Inc.
10/01/1973
Each share Capital Stock $12.50 par
exchanged for (1) share Common
$10 par
(See Peoples Bancshares Inc.)

PEOPLES NAT GAS CO S C (DE)
Common $1 par split (5) for (1) by
issuance of (4) additional shares
10/15/79
Merged into SCANA Corp. (Old)
10/25/90
Each share Common $1 par
exchanged for (1.1) shares Common
no par
SCANA Corp. (Old) merged into
SCANA Corp. (New) 2/10/2000

PEOPLES NATL BANCORP INC (PA)
Common $5 par split (3) for (1) by
issuance of (2) additional shares
08/30/1985
Under plan of merger name changed
to Omega Financial Corp.
12/31/1986

Omega Financial Corp. merged into
F.N.B. Corp. 04/01/2008

**PEOPLES NATIONAL BANK &
TRUST CO. (LYNCHBURG, VA)**
Each share Capital Stock $100 par
exchanged for (5) shares Capital
Stock $20 par 00/00/1945
Merged into First & Merchants
National Bank (Richmond, VA)
01/31/1963
Each share Capital Stock $20 par
exchanged for (2.1) shares Common
$10 par
First & Merchants National Bank
(Richmond, VA) reorganized as First
& Merchants Corp. 02/26/1969
which merged into Sovran Financial
Corp. 12/31/1983 which merged into
C&S/Sovran Corp. 09/01/1990 which
merged into NationsBank Corp.
12/31/1991 which reincorporated in
Delaware as BankAmerica Corp.
(Old) 09/25/1998 which merged into
BankAmerica Corp. (New)
09/30/1998 which name changed to
Bank of America Corp. 04/28/1999

**PEOPLES NATIONAL BANK &
TRUST CO. (NORRISTOWN, PA)**
Each share Common $25 par
exchanged for (2.5) shares Common
$10 par 09/10/1964
Merged into American Bank & Trust
Co. of Pennsylvania (Reading, PA)
09/23/1968
Each share Common $10 par
exchanged for (1.8) shares Capital
Stock $5 par
American Bank & Trust Co. of
Pennsylvania (Reading, PA)
reorganized as American Bancorp,
Inc. 09/02/1981 which merged into
Meridian Bancorp, Inc. 06/30/1983
which merged into CoreStates
Financial Corp 04/09/1996 which
merged into First Union Corp.
04/28/1998 which name changed to
Wachovia Corp. (Ctfs. dated after
09/01/2001) 09/01/2001 which
merged into Wells Fargo & Co.
(New) 12/31/2008

**PEOPLES NATIONAL BANK &
TRUST CO. (PITTSBURGH, PA)**
Merged into Pittsburgh National Bank
(Pittsburgh, PA) 09/11/1959
Each share Capital Stock $20 par
exchanged for (1) share Capital
Stock $20 par
Pittsburgh National Bank (Pittsburgh,
PA) reorganized as Pittsburgh
National Corp. 04/30/1969 which
merged into PNC Financial Corp.
01/19/1983 which name changed to
PNC Bank Corp. 02/08/1993 which
name changed to PNC Financial
Services Group, Inc. 03/15/2000

**PEOPLES NATL BK & TR CO
(BAY CITY, MI)**
Capital Stock $20 par changed to $10
par and (1) additional share issued
12/27/60
Stock Dividends - 100% 12/27/56;
20% 12/15/61; 16.65% 9/1/64;
11-1/9% 11/1/66; 25% 12/1/68; 20%
12/26/72
Reorganized as Peoples Banking
Corp. 11/19/73
Each share Capital Stock $10 par
exchanged for (1) share Common
$10 par
Peoples Banking Corp. name
changed to NewCentury Bank Corp.
7/1/84 which merged into First of
America Bank Corp. 12/31/86 which
merged into National City Corp.
3/31/98

**PEOPLES NATL BK & TR CO
(BELLEVILLE, NJ)**
Name changed to Peoples Bank N.A.
(Belleville, NJ) 05/01/1977
Peoples Bank N.A. (Belleville, NJ)
reorganized as Peoples BanCorp
03/01/1982

(See Peoples BanCorp)

**PEOPLES NATL BK
(BAY HARBOR ISLANDS, FL)**
Name changed to First National Bank
(Bay Harbor Islands, FL) 09/13/1968
(See First National Bank (Bay Harbor Islands, FL))

**PEOPLES NATIONAL BANK
(BROOKLYN, NY)**
Each share Capital Stock $50 par
exchanged for (2) shares Capital
Stock $20 par 00/00/1946
Stock Dividend - 19.05% 10/01/1942
Merged into Commercial Bank of
North America (New York, NY)
05/31/1962
Each share Capital Stock $20 par
exchanged for (0.4) share Capital
Stock $5 par
Commercial Bank of North America
(New York, NY) name changed to
Bank of North America (New York,
NY) (New) 03/15/1965
(See Bank of North America (New York, NY) (New))

**PEOPLES NATIONAL BANK
(CHARLOTTESVILLE, VA)**
Capital Stock $20 par changed to $5
par and (3) additional shares issued
2/5/60
Stock Dividends - 25% 2/5/46; 20%
1/24/50
Name changed to Peoples National
Bank of Central Virginia
(Charlottesville, VA) 6/29/62
Peoples National Bank of Central
Virginia (Charlottesville, VA) merged
into Virginia National Bank (Norfolk,
VA) 4/26/63 which reorganized as
Virginia National Bankshares, Inc.
7/10/72 which merged into Sovran
Financial Corp. 12/31/83 which
merged into C&S/Sovran Corp.
9/1/90 which merged into
NationsBank Corp. 12/31/91 which
reincorporated in Delaware as
BankAmerica Corp. (Old) 9/25/98
which merged into BankAmerica
Corp. (New) 9/30/98 which name
changed to Bank of America Corp.
4/28/99

PEOPLES NATL BK (DANVILLE, VA)
Name changed 3/14/96
Name changed from Peoples Bank of
of Danville (Danville, VA) to Peoples
National Bank (Danville, VA) 3/14/96
Stock Dividends - 10% payable
7/31/2001 to holders of record
6/30/2001 Ex date - 7/26/2001; 10%
payable 7/31/2002 to holders of
record 6/28/2002 Ex date -
7/29/2002; 10% payable 10/31/2003
to holders of record 9/30/2003
Ex date - 11/3/2003
Merged into Carter Bank & Trust
(Martinsville, VA) 12/29/2006
Each share Common $1 par
exchanged for (1.945) shares
Common

PEOPLES NATL BK (DENVILLE, NJ)
Name changed to Peoples National
Bank of North Jersey (Denville, NJ)
04/10/1975
Peoples National Bank of North
Jersey (Denville, NJ) merged into
First Jersey National Corp.
04/01/1985
(See First Jersey National Corp.)

**PEOPLES NATL BK
(EDWARDSVILLE, PA)**
Capital Stock $25 par changed to
$12.50 par and (1) additional share
issued 01/26/1971
Stock Dividend - 50% 00/00/1962
Name changed to First Peoples
National Bank (Edwardsville, PA)
03/04/1986
(See First Peoples National Bank (Edwardsville, PA))

**PEOPLES NATL BK
(GREENVILLE, SC)**
Each share Capital Stock $100 par
exchanged for (10) shares Capital
Stock $10 par 1/9/30
Each share Capital Stock $10 par
exchanged for (2) shares Capital
Stock $5 par 5/27/66
Stock Dividends - 50% 9/20/50; 25%
1/17/55; 25% 1/20/59; 33-1/3%
10/31/60; 50% 8/24/64; 10% 1/10/69
Merged into Bankers Trust of South
Carolina, N.A. (Columbia, SC)
10/15/73
Each share Capital Stock $5 par
exchanged for (1.6) shares Common
$10 par
Bankers Trust of South Carolina, N.A.
(Columbia, SC) name changed back
to Bankers Trust of South Carolina
(Columbia, SC) 12/10/74 which was
acquired by NCNB Corp. 1/1/86
which name changed to
NationsBank Corp. 12/31/98 which
reincorporated in Delaware as
BankAmerica Corp. (Old) 9/25/98
which merged into BankAmerica
Corp. (New) 9/30/98 which name
changed to Bank of America Corp.
4/28/99

**PEOPLES NATIONAL BANK
(HUNTSVILLE, AL)**
Merged into Alabama Financial
Group, Inc. 12/13/1972
Each share Capital Stock $5 par
exchanged for (0.575) share
Common $10 par
Alabama Financial Group, Inc. name
changed to Southern Bancorporation
04/17/1974 which name changed to
Southern Bancorporation of
Alabama 04/21/1975 which name
changed to SouthTrust Corp.
09/18/1981 which merged into
Wachovia Corp. (Ctfs. dated after
09/01/2001) 11/01/2004 which
merged into Wells Fargo & Co.
(New) 12/31/2008

PEOPLES NATL BK (LEBANON, PA)
Common Capital Stock $50 par
changed to $6.25 par and (1)
additional share issued 04/18/1978
Common Capital Stock $6.25 par split
(3) for (1) by issuance of (2)
additional shares 04/15/1987
Stock Dividends - 25% 02/26/1975;
10% 01/20/1982; 10% 11/15/1983;
10% 01/31/1985; 10% 01/16/1990
Under plan of reorganization each
share Common $6.25 par
automatically became (1) share
Peoples Bancorp Inc. (PA) Common
$1 par 04/01/1990
Peoples Bancorp Inc. (PA) merged
into Meridian Bancorp, Inc.
12/04/1992 which merged into
CoreStates Financial Corp
04/09/1996 which merged into First
Union Corp. 04/28/1998 which name
changed to Wachovia Corp. (Ctfs.
dated after 09/01/2001) 09/01/2001
which merged into Wells Fargo &
Co. (New) 12/31/2008

**PEOPLES NATIONAL BANK
(MIAMI SHORES, FL)**
Name changed to Peoples First
National Bank (Miami Shores, FL)
02/10/1964
(See Peoples First National Bank (Miami Shores, FL))

**PEOPLES NATIONAL BANK
(NAPLES, FL)**
Name changed to Southeast National
Bank of Naples (Naples, Fla.)
12/28/73

**PEOPLES NATL BK
(NEW BRUNSWICK, NJ)**
Each share Common $100 par
exchanged for (4) shares Common
$25 par 4/22/59
Common $25 par changed to $10 par
and (1.5) additional shares issued

plus a 20% stock dividend paid 2/15/68
Stock Dividend - 25% 3/23/59
Name changed to Peoples National Bank of Central Jersey (Piscataway, NJ) 2/3/69
(See Peoples National Bank of Central Jersey (Piscataway, NJ))

PEOPLES NATIONAL BANK (NORTH MIAMI BEACH, FL)
Name changed to Peoples First National Bank (North Miami Beach, FL) 05/16/1965
Peoples First National Bank (North Miami Beach, FL) reorganized as Peoples First National Bancshares, Inc. 01/29/1984
(See Peoples First National Bancshares, Inc.)

PEOPLES NATL BK (ROCKY MOUNT, VA)
Merged into First Virginia Bankshares Corp. 12/23/75
Each share Capital Stock $10 par exchanged for (4) shares 7% Conv. Preferred Ser. C $10 par and (9) shares Common $1 par
First Virginia Bankshares Corp. name changed to First Virginia Banks, Inc. 9/1/78 which merged into BB&T Corp. 7/1/2003

PEOPLES NATL BK (RURAL VALLEY, PA)
Merged into BT Financial Corp. 10/23/98
Each share Common no par exchanged for (12.11) shares Common $5 par
BT Financial Corp. name changed to Promistar Financial Corp. 11/15/2000 which merged into F.N.B. Corp. (FL) 1/18/2002

PEOPLES NATL BK (STATE COLLEGE, PA)
Name changed to Peoples National Bank of Central Pennsylvania (State College, PA) 09/10/1973
Peoples National Bank of Central Pennsylvania (State College, PA) reorganized as Peoples National Bancorp, Inc. 12/07/1982 which name changed to Omega Financial Corp. 12/31/1986 which merged into F.N.B. Corp. 04/01/2008

PEOPLES NATL BK (TARENTUM, PA)
Each share Capital Stock $100 par exchanged for (4) shares Capital Stock $25 par in 1947
Stock Dividend - 100% 1/21/47
Merged into Southwest National Bank of Pennsylvania (Greensburg, PA) 6/30/70
Each share Capital Stock $25 par exchanged for (4.5) shares Common $10 par
Southwest National Bank of Pennsylvania (Greensburg, PA) reorganized as Southwest National Corp. (PA) 11/6/81 which merged into First Commonwealth Financial Corp. 12/31/98

PEOPLES NATL BK (TYLER, TX)
Capital Stock $20 par changed to $10 par and (1) additional share issued 01/14/1964
Capital Stock $10 par changed to $5 par and (1) additional share issued 04/01/1973
Capital Stock $5 par changed to $2.50 par and (1.2) additional shares issued to provide for a (2) for (1) split and 10% stock dividend 04/27/1981
Stock Dividends - 33-1/3% 01/23/1959; 10% 04/01/1969; 10% 03/19/1976; 50% 03/18/1977; 10% 03/17/1980
Merged into InterFirst Corp. 05/18/1982
Each share Capital Stock $2.50 par exchanged for (1.75) shares Common $5 par
InterFirst Corp. merged into First RepublicBank Corp. 06/06/1987
(See First RepublicBank Corp.)

PEOPLES NATL BK CENT JERSEY (PISCATAWAY, NJ)
Acquired by Ultra Bancorporation 07/31/1984
Each share Capital Stock $5 par exchanged for $50 cash

PEOPLES NATL BK CENT PA (STATE COLLEGE, PA)
Common $20 par changed to $10 par and (1) additional share issued 08/05/1974
Common $10 par changed to $5 par and (1) additional share issued 01/11/1978
Under plan of reorganization each share Common $5 par automatically became (1) share Peoples National Bancorp, Inc. Common $5 par 12/07/1982
Peoples National Bancorp, Inc. name changed to Omega Financial Corp. 12/31/1986 which merged into F.N.B. Corp. 04/01/2008

PEOPLES NATL BK COMM (MIAMI, FL)
Bank failed 09/11/1999
Stockholders' equity unlikely

PEOPLES NATL BK LONG ISLAND (PATCHOGUE, NY)
Merged into Bankers Trust New York Corp. 06/20/1969
Each share Capital Stock $5 par exchanged for (0.85) share Common $10 par
Bankers Trust New York Corp. name changed to Bankers Trust Corp. 04/23/1998
(See Bankers Trust Corp.)

PEOPLES NATL BK MONMOUTH CNTY (HAZLET, NJ)
Capital Stock $25 par changed to $2.50 par and (9) additional shares issued 7/15/66
Under plan of reorganization each share Capital Stock $2.50 par exchanged for (2.1645) shares United Jersey Banks Common $5 par 10/1/70
United Jersey Banks name changed to UJB Financial Corp. 6/30/89 which name changed to Summit Bancorp 3/1/96 which merged into FleetBoston Financial Corp. 3/1/2001 which merged into Bank of America Corp. 4/1/2004

PEOPLES NATL BK N J (WESTMONT, NJ)
Common Capital Stock $7.50 par changed to $6.75 par and (1/9) additional share issued 09/12/1969
Common Capital Stock $6.75 par changed to $3.375 par and (1) additional share issued 03/05/1971
Name changed to First Peoples National Bank of New Jersey (Westmont, NJ) 06/30/1974
First Peoples National Bank of New Jersey (Westmont, NJ) name changed to First Peoples Bank of New Jersey (Westmont, NJ) 04/20/1978 which reorganized as First Peoples Financial Corp. 03/03/1987 which merged into CoreStates Financial Corp 09/03/1992 which merged into First Union Corp. 04/28/1998 which name changed to Wachovia Corp. (Ctfs. dated after 09/01/2001) 09/01/2001 which merged into Wells Fargo & Co. (New) 12/31/2008

PEOPLES NATL BK NORTH JERSEY (DENVILLE, NJ)
Stock Dividend - 50% 05/18/1982
Merged into First Jersey National Corp. 04/01/1985
Each share Common $10 par exchanged for (2.375) shares Common $5 par
(See First Jersey National Corp.)

PEOPLES NATIONAL BANK OF CAMDEN COUNTY (HADDON TOWNSHIP, NJ)
Name changed to Peoples National Bank of New Jersey (Westmont, NJ) 03/03/1969
Peoples National Bank of New Jersey (Westmont, NJ) name changed to First Peoples National Bank of New Jersey (Westmont, NJ) 06/30/1974 which name changed to First Peoples Bank of New Jersey (Westmont, NJ) 03/20/1978 which reorganized as First Peoples Financial Corp. 03/03/1987 which merged into CoreStates Financial Corp 09/03/1992 which merged into First Union Corp. 04/28/1998 which name changed to Wachovia Corp. (Ctfs. dated after 09/01/2001) 09/01/2001 which merged into Wells Fargo & Co. (New) 12/31/2008

PEOPLES NATIONAL BANK OF CENTRAL VIRGINIA (CHARLOTTESVILLE, VA)
Merged into Virginia National Bank (Norfolk, VA) 4/26/63
Each share Capital Stock $5 par exchanged for (1) share Common $5 par
Virginia National Bank (Norfolk, VA) reorganized as Virginia National Bankshares, Inc. 7/10/72 which merged into Sovran Financial Corp. 12/31/83 which merged into C&S/Sovran Corp. 9/1/90 which merged into NationsBank Corp. 12/31/91 which reincorporated in Delaware as BankAmerica Corp. (Old) 9/25/98 which merged into BankAmerica Corp. (New) 9/30/98 which name changed to Bank of America Corp. 4/28/99

PEOPLES NATL BK SUSQUEHANNA CNTY (HALLSTEAD, PA)
Reorganized as Peoples Financial Services Corp. 07/01/1986
Each share Common $25 par exchanged for (5) shares Common $5 par

PEOPLES NATL BK SUSSEX CNTY (SPARTA, NJ)
Merged into New Jersey Bank (N.A.) (Clifton, NJ) 01/09/1970
Each share Common $10 par exchanged for (1.5) shares Capital Stock $5.50 par
New Jersey Bank (N.A.) (Clifton, NJ) reorganized as Greater Jersey Bancorp. 04/13/1972 which merged into Midlantic Banks Inc. 08/12/1983 which merged into Midlantic Corp. 01/30/1987 which merged into PNC Bank Corp. 12/31/1995 which name changed to PNC Financial Services Group, Inc. 03/15/2000

PEOPLES NATL BK WASH (SEATTLE, WA)
Common Capital Stock $20 par changed to $10 par and (1) additional share issued 04/15/1977
Common Capital Stock $10 par changed to $5 par and (1) additional share issued 04/11/1979
Stock Dividends - 66-2/3% 09/22/1949; 16-2/3% 08/12/1955; 25% 02/06/1959; 20% 02/03/1961; 20% 04/01/1963; 25% 02/17/1967; 25% 02/17/1969; 25% 03/24/1976
Reorganized as Peoples Ban Corp. 06/30/1981
Each share Common Capital Stock $5 par exchanged for (1) share Common Capital Stock $5 par
Peoples Ban Corp. acquired by U.S. Bancorp (OR) 12/22/1987 which merged into U.S. Bancorp (Old) (DE) 08/01/1997 which merged into U.S. Bancorp 02/27/2001

PEOPLES NATIONAL FIRE INSURANCE CO. (NY)
Merged into Baltimore American Insurance Co. in 1931
Details not available

PEOPLES OHIO FINL CORP (OH)
Merged into MainSource Financial Group, Inc. 06/19/2006
Each share Common no par exchanged for (0.329764) share Common no par
MainSource Financial Group, Inc. merged into First Financial Bancorp 04/02/2018

PEOPLES OIL LTD (AB)
Name changed to Sterling Resources Ltd. 04/15/1997
Sterling Resources Ltd. name changed to PetroTal Corp. 06/06/2018

PEOPLES PASSENGER RAILWAY CO.
Acquired by Philadelphia Transportation Co. in 1940
Each Stock Trust Certificate exchanged for $288.16 principal amount of 3%-6% Consolidated Mortgage Bonds and (2.4135) shares $1 Part. Preferred $20 par Philadelphia Transportation Co. completed liquidation 11/20/73

PEOPLES PFD CAP CORP (MD)
9.75% Exchangeable Preferred Ser. A called for redemption at $25 plus $0.297916 accrued dividend on 5/16/2003

PEOPLES PROT CORP (TN)
Class A Common $1 par and Class B Common $1 par changed to 10¢ par and (2) additional shares issued respectively 06/15/1972
Class A Common 10¢ par and Class B Common 10¢ par split (2) for (1) by issuance of (1) additional share respectively 09/14/1973
Adjudicated bankrupt 11/11/1974
Stockholders' equity unlikely

PEOPLES PROT LIFE INS CO (TN)
Under plan of reorganization name changed to Peoples Protective Corp. 12/10/1968
(See Peoples Protective Corp.)

PEOPLES RESTAURANTS INC (TX)
Common $1 par changed to 1¢ par 06/07/1985
Plan of reorganization under Chapter 11 Federal Bankruptcy proceedings confirmed 07/09/1986
No stockholders' equity

PEOPLES SAVINGS & LOAN CO. (OH)
Each share Common $5 par exchanged for (5) shares Common $1 par 3/30/79
Name changed to Peoples Savings Bank (Ashtabula, OH) 4/6/86
Peoples Savings Bank (Ashtabula, OH) acquired by First Bancorporation of Ohio, Inc. 9/30/90 which name changed to FirstMerit Corp. 12/26/94

PEOPLES SAVINGS BANK (ASHTABULA, OH)
Acquired by First Bancorporation of Ohio, Inc. 09/30/1990
Each share Common $1 par exchanged for (0.775) share Common $3.33333333 par
First Bancorporation of Ohio, Inc. name changed to FirstMerit Corp. 12/26/1994 which merged into Huntington Bancshares Inc. 08/16/2016

PEOPLES SVGS BK (BROCKTON, MA)
Reorganized as Peoples Bancshares Inc. 2/8/96
Each share Common 10¢ par exchanged for (1) share Common 10¢ par

FINANCIAL INFORMATION, INC.   PEO-PEO

(See Peoples Bancshares Inc.)

PEOPLES SVGS BK (NEW BRITAIN, CT)
Under plan of reorganization each share Common $1 par automatically became (1) share People's Savings Financial Corp.
Common $1 par 7/31/89
People's Savings Financial Corp. merged into Webster Financial Corp. 7/31/97

PEOPLES SVGS BK (TROY, OH)
Common $1 par split (3) for (2) by issuance of (0.5) additional share payable 10/14/1996 to holders of record 09/30/1996
Common $1 par split (2) for (1) by issuance of (1) additional share payable 03/30/1998 to holders of record 03/09/1998
Common $1 par split (2) for (1) by issuance of (1) additional share payable 05/17/1999 to holders of record 05/05/1999
Reorganized as Peoples Ohio Financial Corp. 01/31/2002
Each share Common $1 par exchanged for (1) share Common no par
Peoples Ohio Financial Corp. merged into MainSource Financial Group, Inc. 06/19/2006 which merged into First Financial Bancorp 04/02/2018

PEOPLES SVGS BK (WORCESTER, MA)
Under plan of reorganization each share Common 10¢ par automatically became (1) share Peoples Bancorp of Worcester, Inc. Common 10¢ par 03/01/1988
Peoples Bancorp of Worcester, Inc. merged into Shawmut National Corp. 05/23/1994 which merged into Fleet Financial Group, Inc. (New) 11/30/1995 which name changed to Fleet Boston Corp. 10/01/1999 which name changed to FleetBoston Financial Corp. 04/18/2000 which merged into Bank of America Corp. 04/01/2004

PEOPLES SVGS BK FSB (MONROE, MI)
Acquired by Standard Federal Bank (Troy, MI) 11/17/89
Each share Common $1 par exchanged for $18.65 cash

PEOPLES SVGS FINL CORP (CT)
Merged into Webster Financial Corp. 7/31/97
Each share Common $1 par exchanged for (0.85) share Common 1¢ par

PEOPLES SVGS FINL CORP (PA)
Merged into Emclaire Financial Corp. 8/31/98
Each share Common 1¢ par exchanged for either (1.24) shares Common $1.25 par, $26 cash, or a combination thereof

PEOPLES SEC BK MD SUITLAND (LANDOVER, MD)
Stock Dividend - 10% 3/20/81
Merged into Citizens Bancorp (MD) 3/16/84
Each share Capital Stock $10 par exchanged for $45 cash

PEOPLES SECURITIES CORP. (NY)
Capital Stock $10 par changed to $1 par 12/06/1955
Capital Stock $1 par changed to 50¢ par and (1) additional share issued 05/05/1961
Name changed to McDonnell Fund Inc. 09/26/1967
McDonnell Fund Inc. name changed to Businessman's Fund, Inc. 01/14/1970 which merged into MagnaCap Fund Inc. 09/22/1972 which name changed to Pilgrim Magnacap Fund, Inc. 06/20/1985 which merged into Pilgrim Investment Funds, Inc. 07/03/1992 which name changed to Pilgrim America Investment Funds, Inc. 07/14/1995 which name changed back to Pilgrim Investment Funds, Inc. 11/16/1998 which name changed to ING Investment Funds, Inc. 03/01/2002

PEOPLES SECURITY BANK (SUITLAND, MD)
Stock Dividend - 10% 3/17/80
Location changed to Landover, Md. 11/10/80
(See Peoples Security Bank (Landover, Md.))

PEOPLES ST BK (CARO, MI)
Stock Dividend - 25% 02/01/1972
Acquired by United Michigan Corp. 01/26/1977
Holdings exchanged for 24% in cash and 76% in 9% 10-yr. Notes

PEOPLES ST BK (EAST BERLIN, PA)
Stock Dividend - 7% payable 05/10/1996 to holders of record 04/01/1996
Merged into Community Banks, Inc. 03/31/1998
Each share Common $1 par exchanged for (0.889) share Common $5 par
Community Banks, Inc. merged into Susquehanna Bancshares, Inc. 11/16/2007 which merged into BB&T Corp. 08/01/2015

PEOPLES ST BK (EAST TAWAS, MI)
Merged into Michigan National Corp. 7/2/81
Each share Common $100 par exchanged for $57.13 cash

PEOPLES ST BK (GROVELAND, FL)
Merged into Alabama National BanCorporation (DE) 01/31/2001
Each share Common exchanged for (1.164) shares Common $1 par
Alabama National BanCorporation (DE) merged into Royal Bank of Canada (Montreal, QUE) 02/22/2008

PEOPLES ST BK (HAMTRAMCK, MI)
Stock Dividend - 10% payable 05/21/2002 to holders of record 04/30/2002 Ex date - 04/30/2002
Reorganized as PSB Group, Inc. 05/31/2003
Each share Common $1 par exchanged for (3) shares Common no par
(See PSB Group, Inc.)

PEOPLES ST BK (HOLLAND, MI)
Stock Dividend - 100% 2/1/71
Acquired by Old Kent Financial Corp. (DE) 12/31/73
Each share Capital Stock $10 par exchanged for (2.392) shares Common $10 par
Old Kent Financial Corp. (DE) reincorporated in Michigan 4/16/84 which merged into Fifth Third Bancorp 4/2/2001

PEOPLES ST BK (MANITO, IL)
Stock Dividend - 8.421% payable 02/03/2000 to holders of record 02/02/2000
Reorganized under the laws of Delaware as Manito Bank Services Inc. 01/02/2002
Each share Common $10 par exchanged for (1) share Common $10 par
(See Manito Bank Services Inc.)

PEOPLES ST BK (ST. JOSEPH, MI)
Stock Dividends - 100% 12/3/76; 10% 2/26/80; 10% 4/1/83
Reorganized as Pinnacle Financial Services, Inc. 7/1/86
Each share Common $10 par exchanged for (1) share Common $10 par
Pinnacle Financial Services, Inc. merged into CNB Bancshares Inc. 4/17/98 which merged into Fifth Third Bancorp 10/29/99

PEOPLES ST BK (WILLIAMSTON, MI)
Acquired by Republic Bancorp Inc. 12/26/1986
Each share Common $5 par exchanged for $34 cash

PEOPLES ST BK WYALUSING PA (WYALUSING, PA)
Under plan of reorganization each share Capital Stock $50 par automatically became (1) share Peoples Ltd. Common 50¢ par 07/00/1987

PEOPLES TELE CO INC (NY)
Common 1¢ par split (3) for (2) by issuance of (0.5) additional share 09/27/1993
Merged into Davel Communications, Inc. 12/23/1998
Each share Common 1¢ par exchanged for (0.235) share Common 1¢ par
(See Davel Communications, Inc.)

PEOPLES TELEPHONE CO. (NY)
Merged into Peoples Telephone Co., Inc. 07/00/1987
Each share Common 1¢ par exchanged for (1) share Common 1¢ par
Peoples Telephone Co., Inc. merged into Davel Communications, Inc. 12/23/1998
(See Davel Communications, Inc.)

PEOPLES TELEPHONE CORP. (PA)
Each share Common $100 par exchanged for (0.5) shares Common $50 par 01/31/1953
Common $50 par changed to $10 par and (4) additional shares issued 05/26/1961
4-1/2% Preferred $100 par called for redemption 08/01/1966
Acquired by United Utilities, Inc. 09/27/1966
Each share Common $10 par exchanged for (0.28571428) shares Common $2.50 par
United Utilities, Inc. name changed to United Telecommunications, Inc. 06/02/1972 which name changed to Sprint Corp. (KS) 02/26/1992 which name changed to Sprint Nextel Corp. 08/12/2005 which merged into Sprint Corp. (DE) 07/10/2013

PEOPLES TRACTION CO.
Acquired by Philadelphia Transportation Co. in 1940
Philadelphia Transportation Co. completed liquidation 11/20/73

PEOPLES TR & SVGS CO (FORT WAYNE, IN)
Capital Stock $20 par changed to $10 par and (1) additional share issued 2/15/68
Stock Dividends - 66-2/3% 1/18/51; 200% 1/19/61; 33-1/3% 8/15/67
Under plan of reorganization each share Capital Stock $10 par automatically became (1) share Financial Inc. Common no par 12/31/69
Financial Inc. name changed to Summit Bancorp 12/31/83 which merged into SummCorp 4/24/84 which merged into NBD Bancorp, Inc. 7/1/92 which name changed to First Chicago NBD Corp. 12/1/95 which merged into Bank One Corp. 10/2/98 which merged into J.P. Morgan Chase & Co. 12/31/2000 which name changed to JPMorgan Chase & Co. 7/20/2004

PEOPLES TRUST CITY BANK (READING, PA)
Name changed to Bank of Pennsylvania (Reading, Pa.) 7/1/68
Bank of Pennsylvania (Reading, Pa.) reorganized as B O P Corp. 8/12/69 which name changed to Bancorp of Pennsylvania 3/25/81
(See Bancorp of Pennsylvania)

PEOPLES TRUST CO. (WYOMISSING, PA)
Under plan of merger name changed to Peoples Trust City Bank (Reading, Pa.) 8/1/60
Peoples Trust City Bank (Reading, Pa.) name changed to Bank of Pennsylvania (Reading, Pa.) 7/1/68 which reorganized as B O P Corp. 8/12/69 which name changed to Bancorp of Pennsylvania 3/25/81
(See Bancorp of Pennsylvania)

PEOPLES TR CO (ROCK HILL, SC)
Merged into Galloway Acquisition 1/20/2000
Each share Common exchanged for $11.48 cash

PEOPLES TR CO BERGEN CNTY (HACKENSACK, NJ)
Each share Capital Stock $25 par exchanged for (5) shares Capital Stock $5 par in 1953
Stock Dividend - 33-1/3% 2/1/52
Name changed to Peoples Trust of New Jersey (Hackensack, NJ) 2/25/69
Peoples Trust of New Jersey (Hackensack, NJ) reorganized as United Jersey Banks 10/1/70 which name changed to UJB Financial Corp. 6/30/89 which name changed to Summit Bancorp 3/1/96 which merged into FleetBoston Financial Corp. 3/1/2001 which merged into Bank of America Corp. 4/1/2004

PEOPLES TR N J (HACKENSACK, NJ)
Under plan of reorganization each share Capital Stock $5 par exchanged for (1) share United Jersey Banks Common $5 par 10/1/70
United Jersey Banks name changed to UJB Financial Corp. 6/30/89 which name changed to Summit Bancorp 3/1/96 which merged into FleetBoston Financial Corp. 3/1/2001 which merged into Bank of America Corp. 4/1/2004

PEOPLES UN BK & TR CO (MCKEESPORT, PA)
Name changed 11/08/1968
Each share Capital Stock $25 par exchanged for (2) shares Capital Stock $12.50 par 03/02/1959
Name changed from Peoples Union Bank & Trust Co. to Peoples Union Bank & Trust Co., N.A. 11/08/1968
Merged into Union National Bank (Pittsburgh, PA) 12/31/1969
Each share Capital Stock $12.50 par exchanged for (2.3438) shares Common $10 par
Union National Bank (Pittsburgh, PA) reorganized as Union National Corp. 02/08/1982 which merged into Integra Financial Corp. 01/26/1989 which merged into National City Corp. 05/03/1996 which was acquired by PNC Financial Services Group, Inc. 12/31/2008

PEOPLES UNION OIL CO. (SD)
Charter expired by time limitation 9/2/21

PEOPLES WAYNE COUNTY BANK (ECORSE, MI)
Name changed to Ecorse Savings Bank (Ecorse, MI) 8/2/34
Ecorse Savings Bank (Ecorse, MI) name changed to Wayne County Bank (Ecorse, MI) 6/5/44 which name changed to Ecorse-Lincoln Park Bank (Lincoln Park, MI) 6/13/44 which name changed to Security Bank (Lincoln Park, MI) 7/25/50 which name changed to Security Bank & Trust Co. (Southgate, MI) 2/4/65

(See Security Bank & Trust Co. (Southgate, MI))

PEOPLES WESTCHESTER SVGS BK (HAWTHORNE, NY)
Merged into First Fidelity Bancorporation (New) 12/30/1993
Each share Common $1 par exchanged for either (0.939) share Common $1 par or $40.86 cash
First Fidelity Bancorporation (New) merged into First Union Corp. 01/01/1996 which name changed to Wachovia Corp. (Ctfs. dated after 09/01/2001) 09/01/2001 which merged into Wells Fargo & Co. (New) 12/31/2008

PEOPLESOFT INC (DE)
Merged into Oracle Corp. 1/7/2005
Each share Common 1¢ par exchanged for $26.50 cash

PEOPLESTRING CORP (DE)
Recapitalized as Vape Holdings, Inc. 01/08/2014
Each share Common $0.00001 par exchanged for (0.025) share Common $0.00001 par

PEOPLESUPPORT INC (DE)
Issue Information - 6,818,182 shares COM offered at $7 per share on 09/30/2004
Merged into Essar Services, Mauritius 10/30/2008
Each share Common $0.001 par exchanged for $12.25 cash

PEOPLEVIEW INC (NV)
Recapitalized as Auxilio, Inc. (NV) 06/21/2004
Each share Common $0.001 par exchanged for (0.33333333) share Common $0.001 par
Auxilio, Inc. (NV) reincorporated in Delaware as CynergisTek, Inc. 09/08/2017

PEORIA & BUREAU VALLEY RR CO (IL)
Company became private 00/00/1980
Details not available

PEORIA & EASTN RY CO (IL)
Merged into Penn Central Corp. 2/19/82
Each share Capital Stock $100 par exchanged for (0.3839) share Common $1 par and $69.30 cash
Note: a) Distribution is certain only for certificates surrendered prior to 5/1/85 b) Distribution may also be made for certificates surrendered between 5/1/85 and 12/31/86 c) No distribution will be made for certificates surrendered after 12/31/86
Penn Central Corp. name changed to American Premier Underwriters, Inc. 3/25/94 which merged into American Premier Group, Inc. 4/3/95 which name changed to American Financial Group, Inc. 6/9/95 which merged into American Financial Group, Inc. (Holding Co.) 12/2/97

PEORIA SERVICE CO. (IL)
Recapitalized 00/00/1937
Each share Preferred exchanged for (4) shares Common $5 par
Old Common cancelled
Completely liquidated 04/12/1965
Each share Common $5 par exchanged for first and final distribution of (0.2) share American Consumer Industries, Inc. Common no par
(See American Consumer Industries, Inc.)

PEP BOYS MANNY MOE & JACK (PA)
Common $1 par split (2) for (1) by issuance of (1) additional share 06/14/1982
Common $1 par split (3) for (1) by issuance of (2) additional shares 04/25/1983
Common $1 par split (2) for (1) by issuance of (1) additional share 07/12/1985
Common $1 par split (3) for (1) by issuance of (2) additional shares 07/27/1987
Acquired by Icahn Enterprises L.P. 02/04/2016
Each share Common $1 par exchanged for $18.50 cash

PEPCAP VENTURES INC (AB)
Reincorporated under the laws of British Columbia as Pepcap Resources, Inc. 05/20/2015

PEPCO HLDGS INC (DE)
Acquired by Exelon Corp. 03/24/2016
Each share Common 1¢ par exchanged for $27.25 cash

PEPCOM INDS INC (DE)
Common 25¢ par split (3) for (2) by issuance of (0.5) additional share 1/26/70
Common 25¢ par split (2) for (1) by issuance of (1) additional share 12/7/77
Merged into Suntory Bottling Co. 9/30/80
Each share Common 25¢ par exchanged for $38 cash

PEPEEKEO SUGAR CO (HI)
Merged into Brewer (C.) & Co., Ltd. 04/25/1973
Each share Common $20 par exchanged for $44 cash

PEPI INC (MD)
Each share Class A Common $5 par exchanged for (1) share Common $5 par 1/5/70
Merged into North American Philips Corp. 10/31/73
Each share Common $5 par exchanged for (1.1) shares Common $5 par
(See North American Philips Corp.)

PEPKOR LTD (SOUTH AFRICA)
ADR agreement terminated 6/15/2004
Each Reg. S Sponsored ADR for Ordinary Rand-2 par exchanged for $3.5744 cash
Each 144A Sponsored ADR for Ordinary Rand-2 par exchanged for $3.5744 cash

PEPPA RES LTD (BC)
Struck off register and declared dissolved for failure to file returns 7/17/92

PEPPER ROCK RES CORP (NV)
Old Common $0.00001 par split (5) for (1) by issuance of (4) additional shares payable 10/30/2009 to holders of record 10/30/2009
Each share old Common $0.00001 par exchanged for (0.005) share new Common $0.00001 par 12/06/2010
SEC revoked common stock registration 12/18/2014

PEPPERBALL TECHNOLOGIES INC (CO)
Assets sold for the benefit of creditors 01/19/2012
No stockholders' equity

PEPPERCORN INDL CORP (NV)
Name changed to Vinex Wines, Inc. 08/11/2000
(See Vinex Wines, Inc.)

PEPPERELL MANUFACTURING CO. (MA)
Each share Capital Stock $100 par exchanged for (5) shares Capital Stock $20 par 9/17/45
Capital Stock $20 par changed to $5 par and (3) additional shares issued 9/28/64
Merged into West Point-Pepperell, Inc. on a (0.9) for (1) basis 3/29/65
(See West Point-Pepperell, Inc.)

PEPPERESS MINES LTD. (ON)
Name changed to Dupel Mines Ltd. in July 1954
Dupel Mines Ltd. acquired by Goldale Ltd. 6/18/64 which recapitalized as Canadian Goldale Corp. Ltd. 6/16/65 which name changed to Hambro Canada (1972) Ltd. 1/9/73 which name changed to Hambro Canada Ltd. 5/28/74 which name changed to Hatleigh Corp. (Old) 8/3/78 which merged into Hatleigh Corp. (New) 8/31/78 which merged into Dexleigh Corp. 6/30/84
(See Dexleigh Corp.)

PEPPERMILL CAP CORP (NV)
Name changed to Varner Technologies Inc. 08/22/2001
(See Varner Technologies Inc.)

PEPPERMINT PK PRODUCTIONS INC (NV)
Recapitalized as Axxess Inc. 02/14/1997
Each share Common $0.001 par exchanged for (0.04) share Common $0.001 par
Axxess Inc. name changed to Financialweb.Com, Inc. 01/01/1999
(See Financialweb.Com, Inc.)

PEPPY HAMBURGERS INC (DE)
Name changed to Peppy's/Biff's, Inc. 5/22/70
Peppy's/Biff's, Inc. name changed to Biff's, Inc. 7/24/72
(See Biff's, Inc.)

PEPPYS BIFFS INC (DE)
Common 10¢ par split (2) for (1) by issuance of (1) additional share 12/31/70
Name changed to Biff's, Inc. 7/24/72
(See Biff's, Inc.)

PEPSI BOTTLING GROUP INC (DE)
Issue Information - 100,000,000 shares COM offered at $23 per share on 03/30/1999
Common 1¢ par split (2) for (1) by issuance of (1) additional share payable 12/04/2001 to holders of record 11/27/2001
Merged into PepsiCo, Inc. 02/26/2010
Each share Common 1¢ par exchanged for (0.3251514) share Common 1-2/3¢ and $18.048467 cash

PEPSI-COLA BOTTLING CO. OF LONG ISLAND, INC. (DE)
Name changed to PepCom Industries, Inc. 6/1/68
(See PepCom Industries, Inc.)

PEPSI COLA BOTTLING CO WASHINGTON D C (DE)
Merged into General Cinema Corp. 05/19/1977
Each share Common 10¢ par exchanged for $20 cash

PEPSI-COLA CO. (DE)
Under plan of merger each Capital Stock $5 par exchanged for (8.43) shares Capital Stock $1 par in 1941
Each share Capital Stock $1 par exchanged for (3) shares Capital Stock 33-1/3¢ par in 1944
Under plan of merger name changed to PepsiCo, Inc. (Del.) 6/10/65
PepsiCo, Inc. (Del.) reincorporated in North Carolina 12/4/86

PEPSI COLA GEN BOTTLERS INC (DE)
Reincorporated 04/23/1969
Common $1 par split (2) for (1) by issuance of (1) additional share 05/17/1955
State of incorporation changed from (IL) to (DE) 04/23/1969
Merged into Illinois Central Industries, Inc. 02/02/1970
Each share Common $1 par exchanged for (0.4) share $3.50 Conv. 2nd Preferred Ser. 1 no par
Illinois Central Industries, Inc. name changed to IC Industries, Inc. 05/21/1975
(See IC Industries, Inc.)

PEPSI-COLA PUERTO RICO BOTTLING CO (PR)
Issue Information - 7,000,000 shares CL B offered at $14 per share on 09/19/1995
Each share Class B Common 1¢ par received distribution of (0.2681828) Buenos Aires Embotelladora S.A. Sponsored ADR for Class B 0.01 Peso par payable 06/17/1998 to holders of record 05/28/1998
Name changed to PepsiAmericas, Inc. (PR) 10/15/1999
PepsiAmericas, Inc. (PR) merged into Whitman Corp. (New) 11/30/2000 which name changed to PepsiAmericas, Inc. (DE) 01/24/2001 which merged into PepsiCo, Inc. 02/26/2010

PEPSI-COLA UNITED BOTTLERS, INC. (NY)
Name changed to PUB United Corp. 5/29/64
PUB United Corp. name changed to Rheingold Corp. 4/27/65 which merged into PepsiCo, Inc. 12/31/73

PEPSI-GEMEX S A DE C V (MEXICO)
GDR agreement terminated 12/26/2002
Each GDR for Ordinary no par exchanged for $10.3691 cash

PEPSIAMERICAS INC (DE)
Merged 11/30/2000
PepsiAmericas, Inc. (PR) merged into Whitman Corp. (New) 11/30/2000
Each share Class B Common 1¢ par exchanged for either (0.2773) share Common 1¢ par, (0.2043) share Common 1¢ par plus the right to receive up to (0.1092) additional share subject to performance levels reached between 2000-2002, or $3.80 cash
Note: Option to receive cash expired 12/14/2000
Whitman Corp. (New) name changed to PepsiAmericas, Inc. (DE) 01/24/2001
Merged into PepsiCo, Inc. 02/26/2010
Each share Common 1¢ par exchanged for (0.2595378) share Common 1-2/3¢ par and $13.77115212 cash

PEPSICO INC (DE)
Capital Stock 33-1/3¢ par changed to 16-2/3¢ par and (1) additional share issued 7/7/67
Capital Stock 16-2/3¢ par changed to 5¢ par and (2) additional shares issued 5/27/77
Capital Stock 5¢ par changed to 1-2/3¢ par and (2) additional shares issued 5/28/86
Reincorporated under the laws of North Carolina 12/4/86

PEPTIDE THERAPEUTICS GROUP PLC (ENGLAND & WALES)
Name changed to Acambis PLC 12/5/2000
(See Acambis PLC)

PEQUANOC RUBBER CO.
Merged into American Hard Rubber Co. 00/00/1941
Details not available

PEQUOT RES INC (NV)
Name changed to Resolute Oncology Inc. 01/09/2013
Resolute Oncology Inc. name changed to BestnPet, Inc. 04/17/2018

PER-SE TECHNOLOGIES INC (DE)
Each share old Common 1¢ par exchanged for (1/3) share new Common 1¢ par 11/24/99
Merged into McKesson Corp. 1/26/2007

Each share new Common 1¢ par exchanged for $28 cash

PERAGIS INC (ON)
Delisted from Toronto Venture Stock Exchange 06/05/2002

PERALTO RES CORP (BC)
Struck off register and declared dissolved for failure to file returns 9/4/92

PERATHON INC (NY)
Name changed to Pope, Evans & Robbins Inc. 11/16/1971
(See Pope, Evans & Robbins Inc.)

PERCEPTION TECHNOLOGY CORP (MA)
Merged into Brite Voice Systems, Inc. 7/30/93
Each share Common 10¢ par exchanged for (1) share Common no par
Brite Voice Systems, Inc. merged into InterVoice-Brite, Inc. 8/12/99 which name changed to InterVoice, Inc. (New) 8/30/2002

PERCEPTION VENTURES INC (MA)
Adjudicated bankrupt 06/13/1974
Stockholders' equity unlikely

PERCEPTRONICS INC (DE)
Reincorporated 09/09/1987
Common 1¢ par split (3) for (2) by issuance of (0.5) additional share 11/13/1985
State of incorporation changed from (CA) to (DE) and Common 1¢ par changed to $0.001 par 09/09/1987
Name changed to Alpha Virtual, Inc. 10/23/2001
Alpha Virtual, Inc. name changed to Veridicom International, Inc. 02/23/2004

PERCIPIO BIOTHERAPEUTICS INC (NV)
SEC revoked common stock registration 06/22/2012

PERCIVAL CORP. (SC)
Completely liquidated 1/30/79
Each (22.29) shares Common 50¢ par exchanged for first and final distribution of (1) share Recognition Equipment Inc. Common 25¢ par
Recognition Equipment Inc. name changed to Recognition International Inc. 3/12/93

PERCLOSE INC (DE)
Merged into Abbott Laboratories 11/19/99
Each share Common no par exchanged for (1.35) shares Common no par

PERCO INDUSTRIES LTD. (BC)
Reorganized as Mercuria Industries Ltd. 12/10/1970
Each share Class A no par exchanged for (2) shares Common no par
Each share Class B no par exchanged for (0.4) share Common no par
(See Mercuria Industries Ltd.)

PERCON INC (WA)
Merged into PSC Inc. 1/20/2000
Each share Common no par exchanged for $15 cash

PERCY STR CAP CORP (CANADA)
Recapitalized as LiveWell Canada Inc. 06/21/2018
Each share Common no par exchanged for (0.33333333) share Common no par

PERDIGAO S A (BRAZIL)
Name changed 07/18/1997
Name changed from Perdigao S A Comercio E Industria to Perdigao S.A. 07/18/1997
Each old Sponsored ADR for Preferred no par exchanged for (0.5) new Sponsored ADR for Preferred no par 06/26/2000

New Sponsored ADR's for Preferred no par reclassified as Sponsored ADR's for Common no par 04/12/2006
New Sponsored ADR's for Common no par split (3) for (1) by issuance of (2) additional ADR's payable 04/19/2006 to holders of record 04/18/2006 Ex date - 04/20/2006
Name changed to BRF-Brasil Foods S.A. 07/09/2009
BRF-Brasil Foods S.A. name changed to BRF S.A. 05/01/2013

PERDUE HSG INDS INC (OK)
Charter cancelled for failure to pay taxes 04/06/1981

PERE MARQUETTE PETES LTD (AB)
Struck off register for failure to file returns 06/30/1977

PERE MARQUETTE RAILWAY CO.
Merged into Chesapeake & Ohio Railway Co. 00/00/1947
Each share Prior Preference exchanged for (1) share 3-1/2% Conv. Preferred $100 par and (1/3) share Common $25 par
Each share 5% Preferred exchanged for (0.8) share 3-1/2% Conv. Preferred $100 par and (0.4) share Common $25 par
Each share Common exchanged for (0.5) share Common $25 par
Chesapeake & Ohio Railway Co. reorganized as Chessie System, Inc. 06/15/1973 which merged into CSX Corp. 11/01/1980

PEREGRINE DIAMONDS LTD (CANADA)
Acquired by De Beers Canada Inc. 09/14/2018
Each share Common no par exchanged for $0.24 cash
Note: Unexchanged certificates will be cancelled and become without value 09/14/2024

PEREGRINE ENERGY LTD (AB)
Merged into Mahalo Energy Ltd. 06/05/2016
Each share Common no par exchanged for (0.48) share Common no par
(See Mahalo Energy Ltd.)

PEREGRINE ENTMT LTD (UT)
Each share old Common no par exchanged for (0.25) share new Common no par 10/07/1985
New Common no par split (4) for (3) by issuance of (1/3) additional share 07/31/1986
Filed a petition under Chapter 11 Federal Bankruptcy Code 01/31/1989
Stockholders' equity unlikely

PEREGRINE INC (NV)
Name changed to Nighthawk Systems, Inc. 07/01/2002
Nighthawk Systems, Inc. name changed to Video River Networks, Inc. 03/03/2011

PEREGRINE INSTS & MONITORING INC (ON)
Name changed to Justice Electronic Monitoring Systems Inc. 04/05/1990
Justice Electronic Monitoring Systems Inc. recapitalized as Jemtec Inc. 04/28/1994

PEREGRINE INVTS HLDGS LTD (BERMUDA)
ADR agreement terminated 6/30/2003
No ADR holders' equity

PEREGRINE METALS LTD (CANADA)
Merged into Stillwater Mining Co. 10/04/2011
Each share Common no par exchanged for (0.08136) share Common 1¢ par and USD$1.35 cash
Note: Unexchanged certificates were cancelled and became without value 10/04/2017

(See Stillwater Mining Co.)

PEREGRINE OIL & GAS LTD (AB)
Recapitalized 09/15/1994
Recapitalized from Peregrine Petroleum Ltd. to Peregrine Oil & Gas Ltd. 09/15/1994
Each share Common no par exchanged for (0.25) share new Common no par
Merged into Surge Petroleum Inc. 07/07/2000
Each share new Common no par exchanged for (0.2741679) share Common no par
Surge Petroleum Inc. merged into Innova Exploration Ltd. 04/16/2004
(See Innova Exploration Ltd.)

PEREGRINE PHARMACEUTICALS INC (DE)
Each share old Common $0.001 par exchanged for (0.2) share new Common $0.001 par 10/19/2009
Each share new Common $0.001 par exchanged again for (0.14285714) share new Common $0.001 par 07/10/2017
Name changed to Avid Bioservices, Inc. 01/08/2018

PEREGRINE REAL ESTATE TR (CA)
Merged into WinShip Properties 3/19/2001
Each Share of Bene Int. $1 par exchanged for $0.59 cash
Note: Each Share of Bene. Int. $1 par received an additional distribution of approximately $0.26 cash from escrow payable 2/2/2007 to holders of record 3/19/2007

PEREGRINE SEMICONDUCTOR CORP (DE)
Acquired by Murata Manufacturing Co., Ltd. 12/12/2014
Each share Common $0.001 par exchanged for $12.50 cash

PEREGRINE SYS INC (DE)
Common $0.001 par split (2) for (1) by issuance of (1) additional share payable 02/12/1999 to holders of record 01/29/1999
Common $0.001 par split (2) for (1) by issuance of (1) additional share payable 02/18/2000 to holders of record 02/04/2000
Plan of reorganization under Chapter 11 Bankruptcy Code effective 08/07/2003
Each share old Common $0.001 par received (0.0205108) share new Common $0.001 par
Note: Certificates were not required to be surrendered and are without value
Merged into Hewlett-Packard Co. 12/21/2005
Each share new Common $0.001 par exchanged for $26.08 cash

PERENNIAL DEV CORP (CO)
Name changed to In-House Rehab Corp. 12/17/1996
In-House Rehab Corp. name changed to Perennial Health Systems, Inc. 11/16/1998
(See Perennial Health Systems, Inc.)

PERENNIAL HEALTH SYS INC (CO)
Placed in receivership 03/10/2000
Stockholders' equity unlikely

PEREZ COMPANC S A NEW (ARGENTINA)
Name changed to Petrobras Energia Participaciones S.A. 07/29/2003
Petrobras Energia Participaciones S.A. merged into Petrobras Energia S.A. 09/29/2009 which name changed to Petrobras Argentina S.A. 12/20/2010
(See Petrobras Argentina S.A.)

PEREZ COMPANC S A OLD (ARGENTINA)
Name changed to Pecom Energia S.A. 07/24/2000

(See Pecom Energia S.A.)

PERFECT CIRCLE CO.
Reorganized as Perfect Circle Corp. on a (4) for (1) basis 00/00/1947
Perfect Circle Corp. was acquired by Dana Corp. 07/01/1963
(See Dana Corp.)

PERFECT CIRCLE CORP. (IN)
Stock Dividends - 10% 12/15/1954; 20% 01/03/1956; 20% 12/15/1956; 10% 12/15/1959
Acquired by Dana Corp. on a share for share basis 07/01/1963
(See Dana Corp.)

PERFECT FILM & CHEM CORP (DE)
$3.50 Conv. Preferred $100 par reclassified as $3.50 Conv. Preferred Ser. A $50 par 05/28/1968
Name changed to Cadence Industries Corp. 10/22/1970
(See Cadence Industries Corp.)

PERFECT FIT INC (DE)
Merged into Home Furnishings Enterprises, Inc. 11/07/1985
Each share Common 1¢ par exchanged for $12.25 cash

PERFECT FIT INDS INC (DE)
Reincorporated 04/00/1965
State of incorporation changed from (PA) to (DE) 04/00/1965
Name changed to PRF Corp. 07/15/1969
PRF Corp. name changed to XYZ Liquidating Corp. 05/14/1981
(See XYZ Liquidating Corp.)

PERFECT FRY CORP (AB)
Name changed to Woodrose Corp. (AB) 09/01/2010
Woodrose Corp. (AB) reincorporated in British Columbia as Woodrose Ventures Corp. 11/07/2016 which recapitalized as Novoheart Holdings Inc. 10/03/2017

PERFECT GOLF INC (UT)
Name changed to Golf Star, Inc. 7/14/95
Golf Star, Inc. name changed to Star Entertainment Group, Inc. 8/3/98
(See Star Entertainment Group, Inc.)

PERFECT HEALTH CARE CORP (NV)
Charter permanently revoked 03/31/2009

PERFECT LINE MFG CORP (NY)
Merged into Midland-Ross Corp. 02/04/1982
Each share Common 10¢ par exchanged for $18 cash

PERFECT PHOTO INC (PA)
Common 20¢ par changed to no par and (2) additional shares issued 7/18/61
Acquired by United Whelan Corp. 6/30/66
Each share Common no par exchanged for (0.2125) share Common $1.20 par
United Whelan Corp. name changed to Perfect Film & Chemical Corp. 5/31/67 which name changed to Cadence Industries Corp. 10/22/70
(See Cadence Industries Corp.)

PERFECT PLUS HOSIERY INC (IL)
Merged into Illinois Perfect Plus, Inc. 09/17/1973
Each share Common $1 par exchanged for $6.875 cash

PERFECT WEB TECHNOLOGIES INC (FL)
Each share Common $0.001 par received distribution of (0.0133689) share Willing Holding, Inc. Restricted Common $0.0001 par payable 08/08/2008 to holders of record 07/31/2008
Each share Common $0.001 par received distribution of (0.1) share Fierce Fit, Inc. Restricted Common payable 12/08/2014 to holders of record 12/01/2014

Name changed to Ovation Music & Studios, Inc. 02/03/2015
Ovation Music & Studios, Inc. recapitalized as TLD3 Entertainment Group, Inc. 01/19/2017

PERFECT WORLD CO LTD (CAYMAN ISLANDS)
Acquired by Perfect Peony Holding Co. Ltd. 07/28/2015
Each Sponsored ADR for Class B exchanged for $20.20 cash

PERFECTDATA CORP (DE)
Reincorporated 11/29/2004
Each share Common no par received distribution of (0.05) share Starnet Universe Internet, Inc. Common 25¢ par payable 7/18/96 to holders of record 7/2/96
Each share Common no par received distribution of (1/30) share Vision Aerospace, Inc. Common no par payable 6/27/97 to holders of record 5/30/97
Each share Common no par received distribution of (0.25) share Staruni Corp. Common 25¢ par payable 8/14/97 to holders of record 7/17/97
Each share Common no par received distribution of (0.005) share Flamemaster Corp. Common 25¢ par payable 1/27/2000 to holders of record 1/11/2000
State of incorporation changed from (CA) to (DE) and Common no par changed to 1¢ par 11/29/2004
Name changed to Sona Mobile Holdings Corp. 12/1/2005

PERFECTING SERVICE CO. (NC)
Each share Common $10 par exchanged for (2) shares Common $5 par 09/30/1963
Acquired by Reed International, Inc. 07/01/1966
Each share Common $5 par exchanged for $17 cash

PERFECTION DEV CORP (CO)
Name changed to Vertica Software, Inc. 1/21/99
Vertica Software, Inc. name changed to New Century Energy Corp. 11/1/2004

PERFECTION ENTERPRISES INC (IL)
Each share old Common no par exchanged for (0.25) share new Common no par 12/23/1968
Proclaimed dissolved for failure to pay taxes and file reports 12/01/1982

PERFECTION INDUSTRIES, INC. (OH)
Merged into Hupp Corp. 9/30/55
Each share Common $25 par exchanged for (0.4) share 5% Preferred Ser. A $50 par and (2) shares Common $1 par
(See Hupp Corp.)

PERFECTION STOVE CO. (OH)
Name changed to Perfection Industries, Inc. 4/1/55
Perfection Industries, Inc. merged into Hupp Corp. 9/30/55
(See Hupp Corp.)

PERFECTION TIRE & RUBBER CO. (DE)
Assets sold at foreclosure in 1928
No stockholders' equity

PERFECTO MFG INC (FL)
Merged into Dade Engineering Corp. 04/22/1977
Each share Common 10¢ par exchanged for (1/3) share Common 1¢ par

PERFEX CORP (WI)
Each share Common no par exchanged for (10) shares Common $4 par 00/00/1940
4-1/2% Preferred called for redemption 11/30/1964
Stock Dividends - 25% 09/30/1959; 100% 12/20/1965; 10% 01/25/1967

Merged into McQuay-Perfex Inc. 06/23/1971
Each share Common $4 par exchanged for (1) share Common $1 par
McQuay-Perfex Inc. name changed to McQuay Inc. 05/31/1983
(See McQuay Inc.)

PERFEX LTD. (BC)
Name changed to Perco Industries Ltd. 8/1/56
Perco Industries Ltd. reorganized as Mercuria Industries Ltd. 12/10/70 which was struck off register 5/28/79

PERFEX RADIATOR CO.
Name changed to Perfex Corp. in 1937
Perfex Corp. merged into McQuay-Perfex Inc. 6/23/71 which name changed to McQuay Inc. 5/31/83
(See McQuay Inc.)

PERFISANS HLDGS INC (MD)
Each share old Common $0.001 par exchanged for (0.04) share new Common $0.001 par 11/14/2007
Name changed to Aspire International Inc. 12/18/2007

PERFORATING GUNS ATLAS CORP. (DE)
Name changed to Pan Geo Atlas Corp. 8/3/59
(See Pan Geo Atlas Corp.)

PERFORMANCE FOOD GROUP CO (TN)
Common 1¢ par split (3) for (2) by issuance of (0.5) additional share payable 07/15/1996 to holders of record 07/01/1996
Common 1¢ par split (2) for (1) by issuance of (1) additional share payable 04/30/2001 to holders of record 04/23/2001 Ex date - 05/01/2001
Merged into Vistar Corp. 05/23/2008
Each share Common 1¢ par exchanged for $34.50 cash

PERFORMANCE HEALTH TECHNOLOGIES INC (DE)
SEC revoked common stock registration 07/11/2012

PERFORMANCE INDS INC (OH)
Each share old Common no par exchanged for (0.25) share new Common no par 7/1/96
Each (1,500) shares new Common no par exchanged again for (1) share new Common no par 4/30/2003
Note: In effect holders received $1 cash per share and public interest was eliminated

PERFORMANCE INTERCONNECT CORP
Filed plan of liquidation under Chapter 7 Federal Bankruptcy Code 10/20/2006
Stockholders' equity unlikely

PERFORMANCE MINERALS CDA LTD (BC)
Delisted from Vancouver Stock Exchange 4/4/92

PERFORMANCE PPTY CAP INC (CANADA)
Name changed to Innovative Properties Inc. 11/8/2002

PERFORMANCE SPORTS GROUP LTD (BC)
Name changed to Old PSG Wind-down Ltd. 03/20/2017

PERFORMANCE SYS INC (TN)
Common 10¢ par changed to 3-1/3¢ par and (2) additional shares issued 03/14/1969
Recapitalized as DSI Corp. 09/29/1978
Each share Common 3-1/3¢ par exchanged for (0.2) share Common 16-2/3¢ par
(See DSI Corp.)

PERFORMANCE SYS INTL INC (NY)
Name changed to PSINet Inc. 11/13/95
(See PSINet Inc.)

PERFORMANCE TECHNOLOGIES INC (DE)
Common 1¢ par split (3) for (2) by issuance of (0.5) additional share payable 09/15/1997 to holders of record 08/29/1997
Common 1¢ par split (3) for (2) by issuance of (0.5) additional share payable 09/01/1999 to holders of record 08/26/1999
Acquired by Sonus Networks, Inc. (Old) 02/19/2014
Each share Common 1¢ par exchanged for $3.75 cash

PERFORMAX, INC. (MN)
Name changed to Eastern Industries Corp. and Common 10¢ par changed to 1¢ par 6/22/71
Eastern Industries Corp. merged into Graphic Service, Inc. 8/31/73 which was adjudicated bankrupt 4/13/77

PERFORMER BOAT CORP. (DE)
No longer in existence having become inoperative and void for non-payment of taxes 4/1/65

PERFORMING BRANDS INC (DE)
Chapter 7 bankruptcy proceedings terminated 06/15/2012
No stockholders' equity

PERFUMANIA COM INC (FL)
Issue Information - 3,500,000 shares COM offered at $7 per share on 09/29/1999
Reincorporated under the laws of Delaware as Envision Development Corp. 02/14/2000
(See Envision Development Corp.)

PERFUMANIA HLDGS INC (FL)
Plan of reorganization under Chapter 11 Federal Bankruptcy proceedings effective 10/11/2017
Holders who provide a Stockholder Release Form in a timely manner will receive $2 cash per share

PERFUMANIA INC (FL)
Name changed to E Com Ventures Inc. 02/01/2000
E Com Ventures Inc. name changed to Perfumania Holdings, Inc. 08/11/2008
(See Perfumania Holdings, Inc.)

PERGAMON PRESS INC (NY)
Merged into PPI Holding Corp. 07/25/1974
Each share Common $1 par exchanged for $7 cash
Each share Class A Capital Stock $1 par exchanged for $7 cash

PERI ASSOC INC (NY)
Acquired by Rivers & Horton Industries, Inc. 03/31/1972
Each share Common no par exchanged for (2) shares Common 5¢ par
Rivers & Horton Industries, Inc. name changed to Rivers Industries, Inc. 07/01/1973
(See Rivers Industries, Inc.)

PERICOM SEMICONDUCTOR CORP (CA)
Common no par split (2) for (1) by issuance of (1) additional share payable 09/08/2000 to holders of record 08/24/2000 Ex date - 09/11/2000
Acquired by Diodes Inc. 11/24/2015
Each share Common no par exchanged for $17.75 cash

PERIGEE INC (ON)
Merged into Legg Mason, Inc. 05/26/2000
Each share Common no par exchanged for (0.387) Legg Mason Canada Holdings Ltd. Exchangeable Share

Legg Mason Canada Holdings Ltd. exchanged for Legg Mason, Inc. 05/26/2010

PERIHELION GLOBAL INC (NV)
Reincorporated 04/01/2008
State of incorporation changed from (DE) to (NV) 04/01/2008
Each share old Common $0.001 par exchanged for (0.00188679) share new Common $0.001 par 06/17/2008
Recapitalized as Nymet Holdings Inc. 04/21/2009
Each share Common $0.001 par exchanged for (0.1) share Common $0.001 par

PERIMETER VENTURES LTD (BC)
Recapitalized as Warner Ventures Ltd. 09/15/1993
Each share Common no par exchanged for (0.25) share Common no par
Warner Ventures Ltd. recapitalized as Copper Ridge Explorations Inc. 10/06/1998 which name changed to Redtail Metals Corp. 05/31/2011 which merged into Golden Predator Mining Corp. (AB) 04/22/2014 which reincorporated in British Columbia 10/21/2015

PERINI CORP (MA)
$2.125 Conv. Exchangeable Depositary Preferred $1 par called for redemption at $25 plus $22.6793 accrued dividends on 05/17/2006
Name changed to Tutor Perini Corp. 05/29/2009

PERINI ELECTRONIC CORP. (CA)
Name changed to Dasa Corp. (CA) 09/29/1964
Dasa Corp. (CA) reincorporated in Massachusetts 04/01/1966
(See Dasa Corp. (MA))

PERINI INVT PPTYS INC (NY)
$1.10 Conv. Preferred $1 par called for redemption 4/15/88
Name changed to Pacific Gateway Properties Inc. 6/1/92
Pacific Gateway Properties Inc.(NY) reincorporated in Maryland 9/2/99
(See Pacific Gateway Properties Inc. (MD))

PERIOTEC INC (FL)
Recapitalized as Aurora Medical Technology, Inc. 02/10/2006
Each share Common no par exchanged for (0.2) share Common no par
(See Aurora Medical Technology, Inc.)

PERIPHERAL CONNECTIONS INC (NV)
Name changed to Skynet Telematics Inc. 01/21/1999
Skynet Telematics Inc. recapitalized as Brisam Corp. 08/10/2007

PERIPHERAL SYS INC (OR)
Plan of reorganization under Chapter 11 Federal Bankruptcy proceedings confirmed 04/18/1994
No stockholders' equity

PERIPHONICS CORP (DE)
Common 1¢ par split (2) for (1) by issuance of (1) additional share payable 10/31/1996 to holders of record 10/15/1996
Merged into Nortel Networks Corp. (Old) 11/12/1999
Each share Common 1¢ par exchanged for (0.62) share Common no par
Nortel Networks Corp. (Old) reorganized as Nortel Networks Corp. (New) 05/01/2000
(See Nortel Networks Corp. (New))

PERITRONICS MED INC (BC)
Recapitalized as Consolidated Peritronics Medical Inc. 11/06/1989
Each share Common no par exchanged for (1/3) share Common no par

Consolidated Peritronics Medical Inc. recapitalized as Peritronics Medical Inc. (New) 11/15/1996
(See Peritronics Medical Inc. (New))

PERITRONICS MED LTD (BC)
Delisted from Vancouver Stock Exchange 03/01/1999

PERITUS SOFTWARE SVCS INC (MA)
Issue Information - 3,500,000 shares COM offered at $16 per share on 07/02/1997
Merged into Rocket Software, Inc. 6/29/2001
Each share Common 1¢ par exchanged for $0.19 cash

PERK INC (ON)
Name changed 06/28/2016
Name changed from Perk.com Inc. to Perk Inc. 06/28/2016
Merged into RhythmOne PLC 01/20/2017
Each share Common no par exchanged for (4.5116) shareS Ordinary £0.01 par
Note: Unexchanged certificates will be cancelled and become without value 01/20/2023

PERK PAK INC (DE)
Voluntarily dissolved 1/3/73
Details not available

PERKIN ELMER CORP (NY)
Each share Common no par exchanged for (10) shares Common $1 par 01/25/1950
Common $1 par split (2) for (1) by issuance of (1) additional share 09/01/1959
Common $1 par split (2) for (1) by issuance of (1) additional share 01/26/1966
Common $1 par split (2) for (1) by issuance of (1) additional share 01/02/1968
Common $1 par split (2) for (1) by issuance of (1) additional share 05/02/1972
Common $1 par split (2) for (1) by issuance of (1) additional share 01/05/1981
Stock Dividend - 100% 03/04/1952
Under plan of recapitalization each share Common $1 par automatically became (1) share PE Corp. (DE) PE Biosystems Group Common 1¢ par and received distribution of (0.5) share PE Celera Genomics Group Common 1¢ par 05/05/1999
PE Corp. name changed to Applera Corp. 11/30/2000
(See Applera Corp.)

PERKINS DOROTHY COSMETICS INC (DE)
Charter cancelled and declared inoperative and void for non-payment of taxes 04/15/1971

PERKINS FAMILY RESTAURANTS L P (DE)
Merged into Restaurant Co. 12/22/97
Each Depositary Unit exchanged for $14 cash

PERKINS FOODS INC (TN)
Common $1 par changed to 10¢ par 05/29/1976
Merged into Perkins 'Cake & Steak Inc. 05/01/1978
Each share Common 10¢ par exchanged for $3.51 cash
Note: Each share Common 10¢ par received an additional and final distribution of $0.15 cash 09/01/1978

PERKINS GLUE CO. (DE)
Acquired by Spencer Chemical Co. on a (17) for (1) basis 12/1/61
(See Spencer Chemical Co.)

PERKINS MACH & GEAR CO (MA)
Each share Common no par exchanged for (2) shares Common $10 par 00/00/1952

Common $10 par changed to no par 10/18/1962
Stock Dividend - 100% 10/01/1957
Name changed to P.M.G. Corp. 05/01/1969
(See P.M.G. Corp.)

PERKINS OIL LTD (BC)
Struck off register and declared dissolved for failure to file returns 11/28/88

PERKINS PAPERS LTD (CANADA)
Merged into Cascades Inc. 12/31/2000
Each share Common no par exchanged for (0.64) share Common no par

PERKIOMEN TOWNSHIP GAS CO.
Merged into Philadelphia Electric Co. 00/00/1929
Details not available

PERLE SYS LTD (ON)
Common no par split (2) for (1) by issuance of (1) additional share 11/7/94
Each (2,000,000) shares old Common no par exchanged for (1) share new Common no par 12/2/2003
Note: In effect holders received $0.04 cash per share and public interest was eliminated

PERLIS PLANTATIONS BERHAD (MALAYSIA)
Stock Dividends - 33-1/3% 12/18/1989; 20% 12/02/1992
Name changed to PPB Group Berhad 06/09/2000

PERLITE MINING CORP. LTD. (ON)
Charter cancelled for failure to pay taxes and file returns 3/11/76

PERMA BILT INDS (CA)
Common 10¢ par split (2) for (1) by issuance of (1) additional share 8/25/75
Stock Dividends - 10% 8/22/77; 10% 8/31/78
Merged into Perma-Bilt of California, Inc. 3/9/81
Each share Common 10¢ par exchanged for $3 cash

PERMA GLASS FIBRE FABRICS, INC. (DE)
Charter cancelled and declared inoperative and void for non-payment of taxes 4/1/61

PERMA GOLD MINES, LTD. (ON)
Charter revoked for failure to file reports and pay fees 8/3/64

PERMA GRASS INC (DE)
Charter cancelled and declared inoperative and void for non-payment of taxes 4/15/72

PERMA SHARP MFG CORP (NY)
Name changed to UF Industries Inc. 8/1/72
UF Industries Inc. name changed to RDA Industries, Inc. 5/3/76
(See RDA Industries, Inc.)

PERMA-TECHNOLOGICAL INDS INC (UT)
Each share old Capital Stock 1¢ par exchanged for (0.05) share new Capital Stock 1¢ par 06/01/1990
Reorganized as China Basic Industries, Inc. 10/30/1995
Each share new Capital Stock 1¢ par exchanged for (0.005) share Common $0.001 par
(See China Basic Industries, Inc.)

PERMA-TUNE ELECTRONICS INC (TX)
Reincorporated under the laws of Nevada as Trans Max Technologies, Inc. and (1) additional share issued 12/01/2003
Trans Max Technologies, Inc. name changed to Recovery Enterprises, Inc. 09/30/2008 which name changed to KMT Global Holdings

Inc. 05/03/2011 which recapitalized as StarPower ON Systems, Inc. 03/23/2017

PERMA VINYL CORP. (FL)
Name changed to Dade Plastics Co. 12/15/64
Dade Plastics Co. acquired by United States Pipe & Foundry Co. 4/22/65 which merged into Walter (Jim) Corp. 8/30/69
(See Walter (Jim) Corp.)

PERMACHEM CORP. (FL)
Reincorporated 00/00/1955
State of incorporation changed from (DE) to (FL) 00/00/1955 Bankrupt 07/31/1961
No stockholders' equity

PERMAGLASS INC (OH)
Merged into Guardian Industries Corp. 12/02/1969
Each share Common no par exchanged for (0.25911) share Common $1 par
(See Guardian Industries Corp.)

PERMALOY CORP (UT)
Each share Common $0.005 par exchanged for (5) shares Common $0.001 par 05/26/1972
Involuntarily dissolved for failure to file annual reports 12/31/1985

PERMANEER CORP (DE)
Stock Dividend - 100% 11/22/1968
Under plan of reorganization each share Common 50¢ par exchanged for (0.05714285) share Spartan Manufacturing Corp. Common 50¢ par 01/04/1978
Spartan Manufacturing Corp. name changed to Spartech Corp. 05/16/1983 which merged into PolyOne Corp. 03/13/2013

PERMANENT BANCORP INC (DE)
Common 1¢ par split (2) for (1) by issuance of (1) additional share payable 4/14/98 to holders of record 3/31/98
Merged into Old National Bancorp, Inc. 7/27/2000
Each share Common 1¢ par exchanged for (0.7719) share Common 1¢ par

PERMANENT FILTER CORP. (CA)
Name changed to Commercial Filters Corp. of California 1/12/66
(See Commercial Filters Corp. of California)

PERMANENT MORTGAGE CORP. (DE)
Charter cancelled and declared inoperative and void for non-payment of taxes 7/1/36

PERMANENTE CEMENT CO. (CA)
Common $1 par split (2) for (1) by issuance of (1) additional share in 1954
Common $1 par split (2) for (1) by issuance of (1) additional share 8/15/56
Stock Dividend - 100% 4/29/50
Name changed to Kaiser Cement & Gypsum Corp. 7/1/64
Kaiser Cement & Gypsum Corp. name changed to Kaiser Cement Corp. (CA) 5/1/79 which reincorporated in Delaware 5/4/82
(See Kaiser Cement Corp. (DE))

PERMANENTE METALS CORP.
Name changed to Kaiser Aluminum & Chemical Corp. in 1949
(See Kaiser Aluminum & Chemical Corp.)

PERMASPRAY MFG CORP (DE)
Reincorporated 5/1/70
State of incorporation changed from (TX) to (DE) and each share Common 10¢ par exchanged for (1) share Common 10¢ par 5/1/70
Name changed to Browning Enterprises, Inc. 4/26/82

Browning Enterprises, Inc. recapitalized as Cabec Energy Corp. 4/1/93 which name changed to Palweb Corp. (DE) 4/19/99 which reorganized in Oklahoma 6/25/2002 which name changed to Greystone Logistics Inc. 3/18/2005

PERMATTACH DIAMOND TOOL CO (NH)
Merged into Asper Inc. 02/28/1991
Each share Common 40¢ par exchanged for $11 cash

PERMCO LTD (NV)
Common $0.001 par split (4) for (1) by issuance of (1) additional share payable 06/04/1999 to holders of record 05/24/1999 Ex date - 06/07/1999
Name changed to Computer Mortgages of America Holdings Co. 06/07/1999
Computer Mortgages of America Holdings Co. recapitalized as Kensington Energy Corp. 07/01/2005 which name changed to Emerald Organic Products Inc. 08/28/2012

PERMEATOR CORP (DE)
Charter cancelled and declared inoperative and void for non-payment of taxes 03/01/1984

PERMIAN BASIN PETROLEUM CO. (NV)
Charter revoked for failure to file reports and pay fees 3/4/72

PERMIAN BASIN PIPELINE CO. (DE)
Merged into Northern Natural Gas Co. 12/30/60
Each share Common $1 par exchanged for (0.45) share Common $10 par
Northern Natural Gas Co. name changed to InterNorth, Inc. 3/28/80 which name changed to Enron Corp. (DE) 5/12/86 which reincorporated in Oregon 7/1/97
(See Enron Corp. (OR))

PERMIAN BASIN URANIUM CORP. (NM)
Charter revoked for failure to file reports and pay fees 8/29/61

PERMIAN CORP. (DE)
Merged into Occidental Petroleum Corp. (Calif.) 10/31/66
Each share Common 10¢ par exchanged for (0.75) share Capital Stock 20¢ par
Occidental Petroleum Corp. (Calif.) reincorporated in Delaware 5/21/86

PERMIAN CORP. (TX)
Common no par changed to 10¢ par and (2) additional shares issued 6/1/61
Reincorporated under the laws of Delaware 11/17/61
Permian Corp. (Del.) merged into Occidental Petroleum Corp. (Calif.) 10/31/66 which reincorporated in Delaware 5/21/86

PERMIAN OIL CO. (TX)
Name changed to Permian Corp. (Tex.) 8/12/60
Permian Corp. (Tex.) reincorporated under the laws of Delaware 11/17/61
Permian Corp. (Del.) merged into Occidental Petroleum Corp. (Calif.) 10/31/66 which reincorporated in Delaware 5/21/86

PERMIAN PARTNERS LP (DE)
Conv. Preference Units exchanged for $3.5625 cash 11/13/90

PERMIAN RES LTD (BC)
Recapitalized as Cass (M.L.) Petroleum Corp. (BC) 12/23/1988
Each share Common no par exchanged for (0.25) share Common no par
Cass (M.L.) Petroleum Corp. (BC) reincorporated in Alberta 09/22/1994

(See Cass (M.L.) Petroleum Corp.)

PERMISSION MARKETING SOLUTIONS INC (BC)
Name changed to Pacific Asia China Energy Inc. 01/04/2006
(See Pacific Asia China Energy Inc.)

PERMO, INC. (IL)
Name changed to Fidelitone, Inc. 2/28/58
Fidelitone, Inc. name changed to Fidelitone Microwave, Inc. 3/13/61 which name changed back to Fidelitone, Inc. 10/17/63
(See Fidelitone, Inc.)

PERMO GAS & OIL LTD (ON)
4-1/2% Preference $2 par reclassified as Common no par on a (1.2) for (1) basis 09/01/1961
Completely liquidated 01/01/1972
Each share Common no par exchanged for first and final distribution of (0.036) share Pan Ocean Oil Corp. Common 1¢ par
(See Pan Ocean Oil Corp.)

PERMO PRODUCTS CORP. (IL)
Name changed to Permo, Inc. in 1946
Permo, Inc. name changed to Fidelitone, Inc. 2/28/58 which name to Fidelitone Microwave, Inc. 3/13/61 which name changed back to Fidelitone, Inc. 10/17/63
(See Fidelitone, Inc.)

PERMUTIT CO. (DE)
Merged into Pfaudler Permutit, Inc. 10/1/57
Each share Capital Stock $1 par exchanged for (1) share Common $10 par
Pfaudler Permutit, Inc. merged into Ritter Pfaudler Corp. 11/1/65 which merged into Sybron Corp. 10/7/68
(See Sybron Corp.)

PERNOD RICARD S A (FRANCE)
Stock Dividend - 25% payable 02/19/2003 to holders of record 02/13/2003 Ex date - 02/11/2003
ADR agreement terminated 03/30/2006
Each Sponsored ADR for Ordinary exchanged for $47.37003 cash
(Additional Information in Active)

PERO DEV GROUP INC (AB)
Merged into Canadiana Genetics Inc. 04/30/1996
Each share Common no par exchanged for (0.1) share Common no par
(See Canadiana Genetics Inc.)

PEROT SYS CORP (DE)
Merged into Dell Inc. 11/03/2009
Each share Class A Common 1¢ par exchanged for $30 cash

PERPETUAL AMERN BK F S B (ALEXANDRIA, VA)
Name changed to Perpetual Savings Bank, F.S.B. (Alexandria, VA) 06/02/1986
Perpetual Savings Bank, F.S.B. (Alexandria, VA) reorganized in Delaware as Perpetual Financial Corp. 10/01/1988
(See Perpetual Financial Corp.)

PERPETUAL BK F S B (ANDERSON, SC)
Reorganized under the laws of Delaware as SouthBanc Shares, Inc. 4/14/98
Each share Common $1 par exchanged for (2.85164) shares Common 1¢ par
SouthBanc Shares, Inc. merged into National Commerce Financial Corp. 11/19/2001 which merged into SunTrust Banks, Inc. 10/1/2004

PERPETUAL ENERGY PRODS INC (DE)
Charter cancelled and declared inoperative and void for non-payment of taxes 3/1/80

PERPETUAL FINL CORP (DE)
Reorganized 10/01/1988
Common 1¢ par split (2) for (1) by issuance of (1) additional share 10/17/1986
Under plan of reorganization each share Perpetual Savings, F.S.B. (Alexandria, VA) Common 1¢ par automatically became (1) share Perpetual Financial Corp. (DE) Common 1¢ par 10/01/1988
Taken over by RTC 01/19/1992
Stockholders' equity unlikely

PERPETUAL INVESTMENT CORP. (UT)
Merged into Government Concepts, Inc. 02/10/1978
Each share Common 1¢ par exchanged for (0.4) share Common 1¢ par
Government Concepts, Inc. name changed to Kemgas International Inc. (UT) 03/09/1984 which reorganized in British Columbia as Kemgas Holdings Ltd. 06/15/1988 which name changed to Envirochem Inc. 11/10/1993

PERPETUAL LIFE INSURANCE CO. (CO)
Founders Shares 50¢ par changed to 25¢ par 00/00/1959
Name changed to Denver National Life Insurance Co. 03/17/1961
Denver National Life Insurance Co. name changed to Denver National Financial, Inc. 05/20/1965 which was acquired by National Western Life Insurance Co. (CO) 08/14/1967 which reincorporated in Delaware as National Western Life Group, Inc. 10/02/2015

PERPETUAL MIDWEST FINL INC (DE)
Merged into Commercial Federal Corp. 5/29/98
Each share Common 1¢ par exchanged for (0.8636) share Common 1¢ par
(See Commercial Federal Corp.)

PERPETUAL SAVINGS & LOAN ASSOCIATION (IN)
Acquired by Mid-West Federal Savings Bank 7/1/87
Details not available

PERPETUAL SECURITY LIFE INSURANCE CO. (ID)
Merged into Pacific Standard Life Insurance Co. 09/30/1968
Each share Capital Stock 50¢ par exchanged for (0.285714) share Common $1 par
Pacific Standard Life Insurance Co. reorganized as Pacific Standard Life Co. (DE) 07/01/1969 which merged into Southmark Corp. 08/30/1983
(See Southmark Corp.)

PERPETUAL ST BK (LEXINGTON, NC)
Merged into Fidelity Bank (Lexington, NC) 9/1/96
Each share Common $5 par exchanged for $17.85 cash

PERPETUALISTICS INC (DE)
Name changed to Fujacorp Industries Inc. 10/20/89
Fujacorp Industries Inc. recapitalized as Interactive Multimedia Publishers Inc. 4/12/95
(See Interactive Multimedia Publishers Inc.)

PERREX RES INC (ON)
Delisted from Alberta Stock Exchange 10/16/1995

PERRIGO CO (MI)
Common no par split (2) for (1) by issuance of (1) additional share 08/25/1993
Merged into Perrigo Co. PLC 12/18/2013
Each share Common no par exchanged for (1) share Ordinary EUR 0.001 par and $0.01 cash

PERRINE INDUSTRIES, INC. (FL)
Adjudicated bankrupt 9/3/66
No stockholders' equity

PERRITT CAP GROWTH FD INC (MD)
Name changed to Perritt MicroCap Opportunities Fund, Inc. 02/02/1998

PERRON ENTERPRISES INC.-LES ENTERPRISES PERRON INC. (QC)
Name changed to Normick Perron Inc. 4/13/73
(See Normick Perron Inc.)

PERRON GOLD MINES LTD. (QC)
Merged into Little Long Lac Gold Mines Ltd. (The) 4/27/67
Each share Capital Stock $1 par exchanged for (0.05) share Capital Stock no par
Little Long Lac Gold Mines Ltd. (The) merged into Little Long Lac Mines Ltd. 1/8/71 which name changed to Little Long Lac Gold Mines Ltd. (New) 7/3/75 which merged into LAC Minerals Ltd. (New) 7/29/85 which was acquired by American Barrick Resources Corp. 10/17/94 which name changed to Barrick Gold Corp. 1/18/95

PERRON GOLD MINES LTD (BC)
Merged into Aurizon Mines Ltd. 08/24/1988
Each share Common no par exchanged for (0.5) share Common no par
Aurizon Mines Ltd. merged into Hecla Mining Co. 06/01/2013

PERRY CAP CORP (DE)
Name changed to FTD Corp. 5/17/95
FTD Corp. name changed to FTD, Inc. 6/28/2002
(See FTD, Inc.)

PERRY CHEM CO (NY)
Name changed to Ceramicus, Inc. 05/14/1985
(See Ceramicus, Inc.)

PERRY CNTY FINL CORP (MO)
Merged into Jefferson County Bancshares, Inc. 7/2/2001
Each share Common 1¢ par exchanged for $23.50 cash

PERRY DRUG STORES INC (MI)
Common 5¢ par split (3) for (2) by issuance of (0.5) additional share 6/30/81
Common 5¢ par split (3) for (2) by issuance of (0.5) additional share 8/12/83
Common 5¢ par split (3) for (2) by issuance of (0.5) additional share 9/10/85
Merged into Rite Aid Corp. 3/24/95
Each share Common 5¢ par exchanged for $11 cash

PERRY ELECTRONIC COMPONENTS, INC. (DE)
Adjudicated bankrupt 4/22/63
No stockholders' equity

PERRY FAY CO (OH)
Each share Common $30 par exchanged for (4) shares Common $10 par 00/00/1940
Acquired by Parker-Hannifin Corp. 06/30/1969
Each share Common $10 par exchanged for (0.5) share Common no par

PERRY OIL CO. (NV)
Charter revoked for failure to file reports and pay fees 3/6/61

PERRY RIV NICKEL MINES LTD (BC)
Merged into American Chromium Ltd. 01/01/1982
Each share Capital Stock no par exchanged for (0.1) share Conv. Class A Common no par and (0.1) share Class B Common no par
American Chromium Ltd. merged into Rhonda Mining Corp. 01/31/1992 which name changed to Rhonda Corp. 06/26/2000
(See Rhonda Corp.)

PERRY'S VICTORY MACHINE CO. (SD)
Charter expired by time limitation 5/31/22

PERRYS MAJESTIC BEER INC (DE)
Name changed to Phlo Corp. 04/20/1999
(See Phlo Corp.)

PERSEON CORP (DE)
Each share old Common $0.001 par exchanged for (0.1) share new Common $0.001 par 06/23/2015
Name changed to BSD Medical Corp. (New) 10/28/2016
(See BSD Medical Corp. (New))

PERSEPTIVE BIOSYSTEMS INC (DE)
Issue Information - 2,300,000 UNITS consisting of (1) share Perseptive Technologies II Corp. COM and (1) CL E WT offered at $22 per Unit on 12/21/1993
Merged into Perkin-Elmer Corp. 01/22/1998
Each share Common 1¢ par exchanged for (0.1926) share Common $1 par
Perkin-Elmer Corp. name changed to PE Corp. 05/05/1999 which name changed to Applera Corp. 11/30/2000
(See Applera Corp.)

PERSEPTIVE TECHNOLOGIES II CORP (DE)
Merged into Perseptive Biosystems, Inc. 03/13/1996
Each share Common 1¢ par exchanged for (1) share Common 1¢ par
Perseptive Biosystems, Inc. merged into Perkin-Elmer Corp. 01/22/1998 which name changed to PE Corp. 05/05/1999 which name changed to Applera Corp. 11/30/2000
(See Applera Corp.)

PERSEUS ART GROUP INC (CO)
Recapitalized as Medgrup Corp. 6/10/99
Each share Common $0.001 par exchanged for (0.5) share Common $0.001 par
(See Medgrup Corp.)

PERSHCOURT GOLDFIELDS LTD. (QC)
Recapitalized as Consolidated Pershcourt Mining Ltd. 9/8/55
Each share Capital Stock $1 par exchanged for (1/3) share Capital Stock $1 par
Consolidated Pershcourt Mining Ltd. merged into Abcourt Metals Inc. 2/23/71 which name changed to Les Mines d'Argent Abcourt Inc. 3/18/80 which name changed to Abcourt Mines Inc.-Mines Abcourt Inc. 4/23/85

PERSHIMCO RES INC (CANADA)
Merged into Orla Mining Ltd. (Canada) 12/07/2016
Each share Common no par exchanged for (0.19) share Common no par and (0.04) share Class A no par
Note: Unexchanged certificates will be cancelled and become without value 12/07/2022

PERSHING GOLD (NV)
Recapitalized as Pershing Products Inc. 05/31/1996
Each share Common no par exchanged for (1/7) share Common no par
Pershing Products Inc. recapitalized as Royal American Mining Properties Ltd. 07/25/1997 which recapitalized as Capita Research Group, Inc. 01/30/1998

(See Capita Research Group, Inc.)

PERSHING PRODS INC (NV)
Recapitalized as Royal American Mining Properties Ltd. 07/25/1997
Each share Common no par exchanged for (1/3) share Common no par
Royal American Mining Properties Ltd. recapitalized as Capita Research Group, Inc. 01/30/1998
(See Capita Research Group, Inc.)

PERSHON GOLD MINES LTD (ON)
Recapitalized as Golden Shadow Resources, Inc. 11/05/1982
Each share Capital Stock $1 par exchanged for (1) share Capital Stock no par
Golden Shadow Resources, Inc. recapitalized as Denroy Manufacturing Ltd. 01/21/1991 which recapitalized as Denroy Resources Corp. (ON) 06/28/2005 which reincorporated in Canada as Nevoro Inc. 05/17/2007 which was acquired by Starfield Resources Inc. 10/08/2009

PERSIAN PETROLEUM CORP. (BC)
Merged into Equus Petroleum Corp. 11/09/1982
Each share Common no par exchanged for (0.37097492) share Common no par
Equus Petroleum Corp. recapitalized as Nuequus Petroleum Corp. 09/30/1997 which name changed to Equus Energy Corp. 11/28/2002 which recapitalized as Habibi Resources Corp. 08/27/2008 which recapitalized as One World Investments Inc. 10/07/2009 which name changed to One World Minerals Inc. 02/28/2017 which name changed to One World Lithium Inc. 01/19/2018

PERSIMMON CORP (UT)
Reorganized under the laws of Delaware as Amalgamated Entertainment Inc. 01/29/1992
Each share Common $0.015 par exchanged for (0.5) share Common 1¢ par
Amalgamated Entertainment Inc. name changed to MegaMedia Networks, Inc. 11/15/1999
(See MegaMedia Networks, Inc.)

PERSISTENCE SOFTWARE INC (DE)
Each share old Common $0.001 par exchanged for (0.1) share new Common $0.001 par 06/12/2003
Merged into Progress Software Corp. 11/08/2004
Each share new Common $0.001 par exchanged for $5.70 cash

PERSON TO PERSON HEALTH SYS INC (BC)
Acquired by Technology & Resource Capital Corp. 10/10/2003
Each share Common no par exchanged for (1) share Common no par
Technology & Resource Capital Corp. name changed to P2P Health Systems Inc. 10/10/2003 which recapitalized as Salares Lithium Inc. 11/26/2009 which merged into Talison Lithium Ltd. 09/22/2010
(See Talison Lithium Ltd.)

PERSONA INC (CANADA)
Merged into Canadian Cable Acquisition Co., Inc. 7/30/2004
Each share Common no par exchanged for $6.80 cash

PERSONA RECORDS INC (CO)
Each share old Common no par exchanged for (0.02) share new Common no par 03/08/1999
Reincorporated under the laws of Nevada as HIV-VAC Inc. and Common no par changed to $0.001 par 03/08/1999

HIV-VAC Inc. name changed to Grupo International, Inc. 10/28/2010

PERSONAL COMPUTER LEARNING CTRS AMER INC (DE)
Proclaimed dissolved 07/21/1983

PERSONAL COMPUTER PRODS INC (DE)
Common 1¢ par changed to $0.005 par and (1) additional share issued 1/13/88
Each share old Common $0.005 par exchanged for (0.2) share new Common $0.005 par 2/25/97
Name changed to Imaging Technologies Corp. 5/28/97
Imaging Technologies Corp. name changed to Dalrada Financial Corp. 3/26/2004

PERSONAL DIAGNOSTICS INC (NJ)
Terminated registration and is no longer public as of 12/17/2002

PERSONAL INDUSTRIAL BANKERS, INC. (DE)
Stock Dividend - 200% 4/29/55
Merged into Kentucky Finance Co., Inc. 5/2/66
Each share $1.40 Prior Preferred no par exchanged for (1) share $1.40 Preferred $20 par
Each share Common 10¢ par exchanged for (0.4) share Common $1 par
(See Kentucky Finance Co., Inc.)

PERSONAL PORTALS ONLINE INC (NV)
Recapitalized as E Trade Systems, Inc. 09/15/2005
Each share Common $0.001 par exchanged for (0.001) share Common no par
E Trade Systems, Inc. name changed to Enterprise Traders, Inc. 11/23/2005 which name changed to Micromint, Inc. 01/16/2007
(See Micromint, Inc.)

PERSONAL PROPERTY LEASING CO. (CA)
Liquidation completed
Each (7.39003) shares Capital Stock $1 par received initial distribution of (1) share Transamerica Corp. Common $2 par 02/05/1964
Each share Capital Stock $1 par exchanged for second and final distribution of (0.03525) share Transamerica Corp. Common $2 par 06/30/1965
Transamerica Corp. merged into Aegon N.V. 07/21/1999

PERSONAL PUZZLE INC (UT)
Involuntarily dissolved 04/01/1990

PERSONNEL CONSULTANTS INC (UT)
Name changed to Westbank Development Corp. 3/18/74
Each share Common 5¢ par exchanged for (1) share Common 5¢ par
Westbank Development Corp. name changed to Valley Airlines, Inc. 2/7/75 which name changed to Pacific Airlines, Inc. (UT) 6/9/75
(See Pacific Airlines, Inc. (UT))

PERSONNEL CONTRACTORS INC (MN)
Name changed to Humate Resources, Inc. 11/12/92

PERSONNEL GROUP AMER INC (DE)
Issue Information - 8,000,000 shares COM offered at $14 per share on 09/25/1995
Common 1¢ par split (2) for (1) by issuance of (1) additional share payable 03/30/1998 to holders of record 03/16/1998 Ex date - 03/31/1998
Recapitalized as Venturi Partners, Inc. 08/05/2003
Each share Common 1¢ par exchanged for (0.04) share Common 1¢ par
Venturi Partners, Inc. name changed to COMSYS IT Partners, Inc. 09/30/2004 which merged into Manpower Inc. 04/05/2010 which name changed to ManpowerGroup 04/18/2011

PERSONNEL MANAGEMENT INC (IN)
Merged into DHI Holdings 8/28/98
Each share Common no par exchanged for $16 cash

PERSONNEL SYS INTL INC (MA)
Involuntarily dissolved 05/31/2007

PERSPECTIVE INC (WA)
Name changed to Perspective Systems, Inc. 04/07/1969
(See Perspective Systems, Inc.)

PERSPECTIVE SYS INC (WA)
Charter cancelled and proclaimed dissolved for failure to pay fees 02/30/1983

PERTEC COMPUTER CORP (DE)
Merged into Triumph Adler Inc. 01/30/1980
Each share Common 10¢ par exchanged for $16.50 cash

PERTEC CORP. (CA)
Reincorporated under the laws of Delaware as Pertec Computer Corp. 9/24/76
(See Pertec Computer Corp.)

PERTH AMBOY GAS LIGHT CO.
Merged into Elizabethtown Consolidated Gas Co. on a (0.3) for (1) basis in 1950
Elizabethtown Consolidated Gas Co. name changed to Elizabethtown Gas Co. 3/8/66 which was acquired by National Utilities & Industries Corp. 7/17/69 which name changed to NUI Corp. (Old) 4/4/83 which reorganized as NUI Corp. (New) 3/1/2001
(See NUI Corp. (New))

PERTH AMBOY NATL BK (PERTH AMBOY, NJ)
Capital Stock $20 par changed to $10 par and (1) additional share issued 07/12/1960
Merged into First Jersey National Corp. 07/14/1981
Each share Capital Stock $10 par exchanged for (6.891) shares Common $5 par
(See First Jersey National Corp.)

PERTH VENTURE CAP CORP (QC)
Name changed to Biolix Corp. 4/30/2001

PERU COPPER INC (CANADA)
Merged into Aluminum Corp. of China Ltd. 08/22/2007
Eash share Common no par exchanged for $6.60 cash

PERU PARTNERS LTD (NV)
Common $0.001 par split (10) for (1) by issuance of (9) additional shares payable 01/08/2002 to holders of record 12/21/2001
Name changed to Agra-Tech, Inc. and (9) additional shares issued 03/03/2002
(See Agra-Tech, Inc.)

PERU REAL ESTATE S A (PERU)
ADR agreement terminated 04/17/2009
No ADR's remain outstanding

PERUSAHAAN PERSEROAN PERSERO INDONESIAN SATELLITE CORP (INDONESIA)
ADR basis changed from (1:10) to (1:50) 03/18/2004
Name changed to PT Indosat Tbk 01/31/2005
(See PT Indosat Tbk)

PERUVIAN GOLD LTD (BC)
Merged into Quest Investment Corp. 07/04/2002
Each share Common no par exchanged for (0.58288645) share Common no par
Quest Investment Corp. merged into Quest Capital Corp. (BC) 06/30/2003 which reincorporated in Canada 05/27/2008 which name changed to Sprott Resource Lending Corp. 09/10/2010 which merged into Sprott Inc. 07/24/2013

PERUVIAN INVT & FIN LTD (CANADA)
Name changed 06/02/1958
Name changed from Peruvian Transport Corp. Ltd. to Peruvian Investment & Finance Ltd. 06/02/1958
Assets sold at auction 11/30/1971
No stockholders' equity

PERUVIAN OIL CONCESSIONS CO., INC. (DE)
No longer in existence having become inoperative and void for non-payment of taxes 4/1/58

PERUVIAN OILS & MINERALS LTD (ON)
Capital Stock $1 par changed to no par 06/09/1971
Name changed to Pominex Ltd. 07/11/1973
Pominex Ltd. recapitalized as Canarchon Holdings Ltd. 12/16/1985
(See Canarchon Holdings Ltd.)

PERUVIAN PRECIOUS METALS CORP (BC)
Name changed to PPX Mining Corp. 08/05/2016

PERVASIVE SOFTWARE INC (DE)
Issue Information - 4,000,000 shares COM offered at $10 per share on 09/25/1997
Acquired by Actian Corp. 04/12/2013
Each share Common $0.001 par exchanged for $9.20 cash

PERVASYS INC (NV)
Name changed to Film & Music Entertainment, Inc. 05/28/2003
(See Film & Music Entertainment, Inc.)

PERVEL CORP. (DE)
Common $1 par changed to 25¢ par in February 1941
Each (10) shares Common 25¢ par exchanged for (1) share Common $2.50 par in December 1941
Liquidation completed 2/9/62

PERWAL PETROLEUMS, LTD.
Charter cancelled in 1960

PESO SILVER MINES LTD (BC)
Recapitalized as Rex Silver Mines Ltd. 03/30/1979
Each share Common $1 par exchanged for (0.2) share Common no par
(See Rex Silver Mines Ltd.)

PESTOLITE INC (NY)
Reincorporated under the laws of Delaware as Cyton Industries Inc. 12/30/1974

PET-A-RAMA MANAGEMENT, INC. (SC)
Merged into Petcoa Industries, Inc. 7/1/72
Each share Common 10¢ par exchanged for (0.131578) share Common $1 par
Petcoa Industries, Inc. name changed to Pet Bazaar, Inc. 2/28/76

PET AWYS INC (IL)
Name changed to PAWS Pet Co., Inc. 08/18/2011
PAWS Pet Co., Inc. name changed to Praxsyn Corp. (IL) 09/05/2014 which reincorporated in Nevada 01/28/2015

PET BAZAAR INC (DE)
Charter cancelled and declared inoperative and void for non-payment of taxes 6/30/81

PET CHEM INC (FL)
Merged into Riviana Foods, Inc. (Old) 2/26/76
Each share Common $1 par exchanged for (0.2947) share Common $3.50 par
Riviana Foods, Inc. (Old) acquired by Colgate-Palmolive Co. 6/14/76

PET-CON INDS INC (DE)
Recapitalized as Premier Classic Art Inc. 9/1/99
Each share Common $0.002 par exchanged for (0.02) share Common $0.002 par
Premier Classic Art Inc. name changed to Parentech, Inc. 1/17/2003 which recapitalized as Bridgetech Holdings International, Inc. 2/11/2005

PET DRX CORP (DE)
Units separated 03/17/2010
Merged into VCA Antech, Inc. 11/01/2010
Each share Common $0.0001 par exchanged for $0.33523 cash

PET ECOLOGY BRANDS INC (TX)
Each share old Common $0.001 par exchanged for (4) shares new Common $0.001 par 11/08/2004
Each share new Common $0.001 par exchanged again for (0.08333333) share new Common $0.001 par 10/04/2007
Chapter 7 bankruptcy proceedings terminated 12/12/2014
No stockholders' equity

PET EXPRESS SUPPLY INC (NV)
Common $0.001 par split (6) for (1) by issuance of (5) additional share payable 09/26/2008 to holders of record 09/25/2008 Ex date - 09/29/2008
Name changed to Woozyfly Inc. 09/30/2008
(See Woozyfly Inc.)

PET FOOD WHSE INC (MN)
Each (3.5) shares old Common 1¢ par exchanged for (1) share new Common 1¢ par 11/23/93
Merged into Petco Animal Supplies, Inc. 12/31/96
Each share new Common 1¢ par exchanged for (0.2173913) share Common $0.0001 par
(See Petco Animal Supplies, Inc.)

PET GROUP INC (IL)
Assets assigned for benefit of creditors 12/02/1974
No stockholders' equity

PET INC NEW (DE)
Preferred Stock Purchase Rights redeemed at $0.01 per right 02/17/1995 for holders of record 02/08/1995
Acquired by Grand Metropolitan PLC 05/12/1995
Each share Common no par exchanged for $26 cash

PET INC OLD (DE)
$1 Conv. 2nd Preferred no par called for redemption 10/13/1978
80¢ Conv. Preference no par called for redemption 10/13/1978
Merged into IC Industries, Inc. 11/20/1978
Each share Common no par exchanged for $55 cash

PET MILK CO (DE)
4-1/4% Preferred $100 par called for redemption 4/10/48
4-1/4% 2nd Preferred $100 par called for redemption 4/10/48
Common no par split (2) for (1) by issuance of (1) additional share 1/16/59
Common no par split (3) for (2) by issuance of (0.5) additional share 6/30/60
Common no par split (2) for (1) by issuance of (1) additional share 9/30/65
4-1/2% Preferred $100 par called for redemption 3/31/66
Name changed to Pet Inc. 9/1/66
(See Pet Inc.)

PET PRACTICE INC (DE)
Merged into Veterinary Centers of America, Inc. 7/19/96
Each share Common 1¢ par exchanged for (0.4077) share Common 1¢ par
(See Veterinary Centers of America Inc.)

PET PRODS INC (NY)
Acquired by Hartz Mountain Corp. 2/28/95
Each share Common $0.001 par exchanged for $5.25 cash

PET VALU CDA INC (ON)
Acquired by Roark Capital Group 08/31/2009
Each Exchangeable Share no par exchanged for $13.68 cash

PET VALU INC (ON)
Name changed to Pet Valu Canada Inc. 04/23/1996
(See Pet Valu Canada Inc.)

PETACA MINING CORP. (DE)
No longer in existence having become inoperative and void for non-payment of taxes 4/1/60

PETALS DECORATIVE ACCENTS INC (DE)
SEC revoked common stock registration 07/11/2012

PETAPEER HLDGS INC (FL)
Name changed to Studio Bromont Inc. 02/14/2002
Studio Bromont Inc. name changed to United American Corp. 03/01/2004

PETAQUILLA COPPER LTD (BC)
Acquired by Inmet Mining Corp. 11/28/2008
Each share Common no par exchanged for $2.20 cash

PETCAN RES LTD (AB)
Merged into Backer Resources Ltd. 3/28/83
Each share Common no par exchanged for (0.5) share Common no par
Backer Resources Ltd. merged into Backer Petroleum Corp. 12/30/88
(See Backer Petroleum Corp.)

PETCARE TELEVISION NETWORK INC (FL)
Recapitalized as Medical Media Television, Inc. 5/4/2005
Each (30) shares Common $0.0005 par exchanged for (1) share Common $0.0005 par

PETCO ANIMAL SUPPLIES INC (DE)
Issue Information - 3,000,000 shares COM offered at $15.50 per share on 03/17/1994
Merged into Texas Pacific Group 10/2/2000
Each share old Common $0.0001 par exchanged for $22 cash
Issue Information - 14,500,000 shares NEW COM offered at $19 per share on 02/21/2002
Merged into Rover Holdings Corp. 10/26/2006
Each share new Common $0.001 par exchanged for $29 cash

PETCOA INDS INC (DE)
Name changed to Pet Bazaar, Inc. 02/28/1976
(See Pet Bazaar, Inc.)

PETEL INC (DE)
Each share old Common $0.0001 par exchanged for (0.1) share new Common $0.0001 par 09/17/2007
Stock Dividend - 25% payable 07/20/2007 to holders of record 07/16/2007 Ex date - 07/23/2007
Recapitalized as Gleeworks, Inc. 12/14/2009
Each share new Common $0.0001 par exchanged for (0.002) share Common $0.0001 par
Gleeworks, Inc. name changed to Capital Art, Inc. 05/09/2011 which name changed to Globe Photos, Inc. 06/25/2018

PETER ECKRICH & SONS, INC. (IN)
See - Eckrich (Peter) & Sons, Inc.

PETER FOX BREWING CO. (IL)
See - Fox (Peter) Brewing Co.

PETER HAMBRO MNG PLC (UNITED KINGDOM)
Name changed to Petropavlovsk PLC 09/23/2009
(See Petropavlovsk PLC)

PETER HAND BREWERY CO. (DE)
Name changed to Meister Brau, Inc. 06/01/1967
(See Meister Brau, Inc.)

PETER ISLAND RES INC (ON)
Recapitalized as Tri-Vision International Ltd. 03/19/1993
Each share Common no par exchanged for (0.1) share Common no par
Tri-Vision International Ltd. merged into Wi-LAN Inc. (AB) 06/29/2007 which reincorporated in Canada 08/02/2007 which name changed to Quarterhill Inc. 06/05/2017

PETER MILLER APPAREL GROUP INC. (ON)
See - Miller (Peter) Apparel Group Inc.

PETER PAUL INC (DE)
Common no par split (2) for (1) by issuance of (1) additional share 11/16/1962
Common no par split (3) for (2) by issuance of (0.5) additional share 11/20/1967
Stock Dividend - 300% 07/00/1946
Merged into Cadbury Schweppes Ltd. 04/28/1978
Each share Common no par exchanged for $27.50 cash

PETER RABBIT ENERGY CORP (BC)
Name changed to PBB Venture Corp. (BC) 1/24/94
PBB Venture Corp. (BC) reincorporated in Yukon 5/26/97
(See PBB Venture Corp.)

PETER-ROCK MINING CO. LTD. (ON)
Charter cancelled for failure to pay taxes and file returns 5/15/74

PETERBOROUGH CAP CORP (AB)
Recapitalized as Bowmore Exploration Ltd. 08/28/2008
Each share Common no par exchanged for (0.25) share Common no par
Bowmore Exploration Ltd. recapitalized as Osisko Metals Inc. 06/26/2017

PETERBOROUGH RAILROAD
Acquired by Boston & Maine Railroad (Me., N.H., Mass., N.Y.) in 1944
(See Boston & Maine Railroad)

PETERBOROUGH SVGS BK (PETERBOROUGH, NH)
Name changed to Primary Bank 4/17/95

PETERS CARTRIDGE CO.
Acquired by Remington Arms Co., Inc. 00/00/1935
Details not available

PETERS J M INC (DE)
Reincorporated 6/24/93
State of incorporation changed from (NV) to (DE) 6/24/93
Name changed to Capital Pacific Holdings Inc. 8/1/95
(See Capital Pacific Holdings Inc.)

PETERS PETROLEUM CORP.
Liquidated in 1950

PETERSBURG & HOPEWELL GAS CO (VA)
Merged into Commonwealth Natural Gas Corp. 12/31/68
Each share Common $10 par exchanged for (1) share $2 Conv. Preferred Ser. A $10 par
Commonwealth Natural Gas Corp. name changed to Commonwealth Natural Resources Inc. 2/28/77
(See Commonwealth Natural Resources Inc.)

PETERSBURG LONG DISTANCE INC (ON)
Name changed to PLD Telekom, Inc. (ON) 08/01/1996
PLD Telekom, Inc. (ON) reincorporated in Delaware 02/28/1997 which merged into Metromedia International Group, Inc. 09/30/1999
(See Metromedia International Group, Inc.)

PETERSBURG TEL NETWORK OPEN JT STK (RUSSIA)
Name changed to North-West Telecom OJSC 03/05/2002
(See North-West Telecom OJSC)

PETERSBURG TELEVISION CORP. (VA)
Liquidated and voluntarily dissolved 12/31/68
Details not available

PETERSEN COS INC (DE)
Merged into EMAP PLC 01/21/1999
Each share Class A Common 1¢ par exchanged for $34 cash

PETERSEN TOOL INC (UT)
Proclaimed dissolved for failure to file reports and pay taxes 09/30/1976

PETERSFIELD OIL & MINERALS LTD (BC)
Name changed to Hovik Medical Corp. 05/26/1988
Hovik Medical Corp. recapitalized as Globetel Communications Ltd. 07/14/1993
(See Globetel Communications Ltd.)

PETERSON COBALT MINES LTD. (ON)
Acquired by Trinova Cobalt Silver Mines Ltd. 11/3/62
Each share Preference $1 par exchanged for (7.4) shares Capital Stock $1 par
Each share Common $1 par exchanged for (0.0588235) share Capital Stock $1 par
Trinova Cobalt Silver Mines Ltd. name changed to Trinova Resource Exploration Ltd. 9/5/78 which merged into Flying Cross Resources Ltd. 12/4/85 which merged into International Larder Minerals Inc. 5/1/86 which merged into Explorers Alliance Corp. 10/13/2000

PETERSON (FRED J.) CO., INC. (CA)
Name changed to Phone-A-Gram System, Inc. (CA) 6/22/74
Phone-A-Gram System, Inc. (CA) reincorporated in Delaware 9/29/83 which name changed to Amserv, Inc. 10/26/87 which name changed to Amserv Healthcare Inc. 8/4/92 which merged into Star Multi Care Services, Inc. 8/23/96
(See Multi Care Services, Inc.)

PETERSON ELECTR DIE INC (NY)
Reincorporated 03/31/1969
State of incorporation changed from (NJ) to (NY) 03/31/1969
Charter cancelled and proclaimed dissolved for failure to pay taxes 06/30/2004

PETERSON HOWELL & HEATHER INC (MD)
Class A Common no par and Class B Common no par split (2) for (1) by issuance of (1) additional share respectively 02/13/1962
Class A Common no par and Class B Common no par split (5) for (4) by issuance of (0.25) additional share respectively 03/25/1966
VTC's for Class A Common no par and VTC's for Class B Common no par split (5) for (4) by issuance of (0.25) additional share respectively 03/25/1966
Class A Common no par and Class B Common no par split (2) for (1) by issuance of (1) additional share respectively 01/31/1968
VTC's for Class A Common no par and VTC's for Class B Common no par split (2) for (1) by issuance of (1) additional share respectively 01/31/1968
Voting Trust Agreement terminated 08/26/1968
Each VTC for Class A Common no par exchanged for (1) share Class A Common no par
Each VTC for Class B Common no par exchanged for (1) share Class B Common no par
Each share Class B Common no par exchanged for (1) share Class A Common no par 01/01/1969
Class A Common no par reclassified as Common no par 07/29/1969
Common no par split (2) for (1) by issuance of (1) additional share 03/31/1970
Common no par split (2) for (1) by issuance of (1) additional share 09/24/1971
Name changed to PHH Group, Inc. 12/13/1978
PHH Group, Inc. name changed to PHH Corp. 08/24/1988 which merged into HFS Inc. 04/30/1997 which merged into Cendant Corp. 12/17/1997 which reorganized as Avis Budget Group, Inc. 09/01/2006

PETERSON LAKE SILVER COBALT MINING CO.
Acquired by Peterson Cobalt Mines Ltd. on a (1) for (2) basis in 1928
Peterson Cobalt Mines Ltd. acquired by Trinova Cobalt Silver Mines Ltd. 11/3/62 which name changed to Trinova Resource Exploration Ltd. 9/5/78 which merged into Flying Cross Resources Ltd. 12/4/85 which merged into International Larder Minerals Inc. 5/1/86 which merged into Explorers Alliance Corp. 10/13/2000

PETERSON-VOGEL, INC. (NV)
Charter revoked for failure to file reports and pay fees 3/7/60

PETERSONS INC (DE)
Charter cancelled and declared inoperative and void for non-payment of taxes 4/15/72

PETES BREWING CO (CA)
Merged into PBC Holding Corp. 7/22/98
Each share Common no par exchanged for $6.375 cash

PETHEALTH INC (CANADA)
Each share old Common no par exchanged for (0.1) share new Common no par 05/28/2007
Acquired by Fairfax Financial Holdings Ltd. 11/18/2014
Each share Common no par exchanged for $2.79 cash
Note: Unexchanged certificates were cancelled and became without value 11/18/2017

PETHEALTH SYS INC (CO)
Each share old Common no par exchanged for (0.01) share new Common no par 10/25/1999
Name changed to Incubate This!, Inc. (CO) 03/01/2000
Incubate This!, Inc. (CO) reincorporated in Delaware 01/16/2001 which name changed to OrganiTECH USA Inc. 03/20/2001
(See OrganiTECH USA Inc.)

PETLIFE PHARMACEUTICALS INC OLD (NV)
Reorganized as Petlife Pharmaceuticals, Inc. (New) 09/12/2016
Each share Common $0.001 par exchanged for (0.2) share Common $0.001 par

PETMEDEXPRESS COM INC (FL)
Reorganized 2/24/99
Reorganized from Petmed Express, Inc. to Petmedexpress.Com, Inc. 2/24/99
Each share Common $0.001 par exchanged for (3) shares Common $0.001 par
Name changed to PetMed Express, Inc. 7/15/2003

PETOSKEY PORTLAND CEMENT CO. (DE)
Acquired by Penn-Dixie Cement Corp. 00/00/1954
Details not available

PETOSKEY TRANSPORTATION CO. (DE)
Acquired by Penn-Dixie Cement Corp. 00/00/1954
Details not available

PETPLANET COM INC (DE)
Name changed to eMemberDirect, Inc. 10/02/2000
(See eMemberDirect, Inc.)

PETRA PETE INC (BC)
Recapitalized as Mitra Energy Inc. 04/23/2015
Each share Common no par exchanged for (0.25) share Common no par
Mitra Energy Inc. name changed to Jadestone Energy Inc. 12/07/2016

PETRA RESOURCE CORP (BC)
Recapitalized as Olly Industries Inc. 01/20/2004
Each share Common no par exchanged for (0.04) share Common no par
Olly Industries Inc. name changed to Aurea Mining Inc. 06/16/2004 which was acquired by Newstrike Capital Inc. 06/26/2008 which merged into Timmins Gold Corp. 05/28/2015 which recapitalized as Alio Gold Inc. 05/16/2017

PETRA RES INC (OK)
Each share Common 1¢ par exchanged for (0.05) share Common 20¢ par 10/11/83
Merged into Zim Energy Corp. 6/9/86
Each share Common 20¢ par exchanged for (1) share Common 10¢ par
Zim Energy Corp. recapitalized as Mustang Resources Corp. 6/30/87
(See Mustang Resources Corp.)

PETRAMERICA OIL INC (CO)
Each share Common $0.00001 par exchanged for (0.001) share Common 5¢ par 01/20/1993
Common 5¢ par changed to no par 00/00/2002
Name changed to Triton Distribution Systems, Inc. 08/18/2006
Triton Distribution Systems, Inc. name changed to Green Cures & Botanical Distribution Inc. 05/27/2014

PETREX CORP NEW (NV)
Recapitalized as Force 10 Trading, Inc. 12/30/2001
Each share Common $0.001 par exchanged for (0.05) share Common $0.001 par
Force 10 Trading, Inc. recapitalized as F10 Oil & Gas Properties, Inc. 12/03/2002 which name changed to GFY Foods, Inc. 01/12/2004 which recapitalized as Upturn, Inc. 03/20/2009 which recapitalized as Cityside Tickets Inc. 12/10/2009 which name changed to Causeway Entertainment Co. 10/11/2010 which recapitalized as United Bullion Exchange Inc. 05/10/2011

PETREX CORP OLD (NV)
Recapitalized as Institute of Cosmetic Surgery Inc. 11/20/1998
Each share Common $0.001 par exchanged for (0.5) share Common $0.001 par
Institute of Cosmetic Surgery Inc. name changed to Petrex Corp. (New) 11/06/2000 which recapitalized as Force 10 Trading, Inc. 12/30/2001 which recapitalized as F10 Oil & Gas Properties, Inc. 12/03/2002 which name changed to GFY Foods, Inc. 01/12/2004 which recapitalized as Upturn, Inc. 03/20/2009 which recapitalized as Cityside Tickets Inc. 12/10/2009 which name changed to Causeway Entertainment Co. 10/11/2010 which recapitalized as United Bullion Exchange Inc. 05/10/2011

PETRICHOR CORP (NV)
Each share old Common $0.001 par exchanged for (0.0125) share new Common $0.001 par 02/02/2016
New Common $0.001 par split (200) for (1) by issuance of (199) additional shares payable 04/24/2017 to holders of record 04/07/2017 Ex date - 04/25/2017
Name changed to Wei Pai Electronic Commerce Co., Ltd. 05/02/2017

PETRIE CORP (DE)
Name changed to Rocking Horse Child Care Centers of America, Inc. 10/29/1985
Rocking Horse Child Care Centers of America, Inc. name changed to Nobel Education Dynamics, Inc. 06/15/1993 which name changed to Nobel Learning Communities, Inc. 11/19/1998
(See Nobel Learning Communities, Inc.)

PETRIE STORES CORP (NY)
Common $1 par split (2) for (1) by issuance of (1) additional share 1/21/70
Common $1 par split (3) for (2) by issuance of (0.5) additional share 3/29/71
Common $1 par split (2) for (1) by issuance of (1) additional share 11/22/77
Common $1 par split (3) for (2) by issuance of (0.5) additional share 10/22/81
Common $1 par split (2) for (1) by issuance of (1) additional share 2/14/86
Assets transferred to Petrie Stores Liquidating Trust and Common $1 par reclassified as Shares of Bene. Int. $1 par 1/22/96
(See Petrie Stores Liquidating Trust)

PETRIE STORES LIQUIDATING TR (NY)
Liquidation completed
Each Share of Bene. Int. $1 par received initial distribution of (0.3225536) share Toys "R" Us, Inc. Common 10¢ par and $1.50 cash payable 2/11/2000 to holders of record 1/31/2000
Each Share of Bene. Int. $1 par received second distribution of $0.75 cash payable 12/21/2000 to holders of record 12/11/2000
Each Share of Bene. Int. $1 par received third distribution of $0.50 cash payable 1/31/2003 to holders of record 1/21/2003 Ex date - 2/3/2003
Each Share of Bene. Int. $1 par received fourth distributon of $0.40 cash payable 1/30/2004 to holders of record 1/20/2004 Ex date - 2/2/2004
Each Share of Bene. Int. $1 par received fifth distributon of $0.30 cash payable 4/21/2005 to holders of record 4/11/2005 Ex date - 4/22/2005
Each Share of Bene. Int. $1 par received sixth and final distribution of $0.4725 cash payable 3/24/2006 to holders of record 3/13/2006 Ex date - 3/27/2006
Note: Certificates were not required to be surrendered and are without value

PETRO AMERN ENERGY INC (BC)
Struck off register and declared dissolved for failure to file returns 07/11/1986

PETRO ANDINA RES INC (AB)
Merged into Parex Resources Inc. 11/06/2009
Each share Class A Common no par exchanged for (1) share Common no par, (0.1) Common Stock Purchase Warrant expiring 12/06/2009 and $7.65 cash

PETRO ART INC (DE)
Each share old Common 1¢ par exchanged for (0.1) share new Common 1¢ par 5/21/93
Name changed to Class, Inc. 6/7/93
Class, Inc. recapitalized as Avery Communications, Inc. 12/12/94
(See Avery Communications, Inc.)

PETRO BASIN ENERGY CORP (ON)
Each share old Common no par exchanged for (0.25) share new Common no par 02/21/2012
Reincorporated under the laws of British Columbia as Peace River Capital Corp. 09/16/2016
Peace River Capital Corp. name changed to Liberty One Lithium Corp. 12/02/2016

PETRO CDA ENTERPRISES INC (CANADA)
$1.875 Conv. Preferred no par called for redemption 08/05/1983
Plan of dissolution approved 08/11/1983
Each share Common $10 par exchanged for $120.14 cash

PETRO CDA PRODS INC (CANADA)
Class B no par called for redemption 05/27/1985
Public interest eliminated

PETRO-CDA (CANADA)
Common no par reclassified as Variable Shares no par 04/30/1996
Variable Shares no par reclassified as Common no par 06/14/2001
Common no par split (2) for (1) by issuance of (1) additional share payable 09/14/2005 to holders of record 09/03/2005 Ex date - 09/15/2005
Merged into Suncor Energy Inc. (New) 08/01/2009
Each share Common no par exchanged for (1.28) shares Common no par
Note: Unexchanged certificates were cancelled and became without value 08/01/2015

PETRO-CHEMSOL CHEMICALS LTD. (ON)
Charter surrendered for failure to file reports and pay taxes in 1958

PETRO DEV INC (UT)
Reincorporated under the laws of Nevada as Odyssey 2000 NA, Inc. 07/21/1994
Odyssey 2000 NA, Inc. name changed to Celebrity Entertainment

Group, Inc. (NV) 01/09/1996 which reincorporated in Wyoming 01/11/1996 which reincorporated in Delaware as Sharp Holding Corp. 04/19/2001 which recapitalized as Cooper Holding Corp. 10/28/2010 which recapitalized as Crednology Holding Corp. 05/03/2013

PETRO ENERGY LTD (AUSTRALIA)
Acquired by Bond Corporation Pty, Ltd. 03/20/1989
Each ADR for Ordinary A$0.25 par exchanged for $0.14 cash

PETRO FIELD INDS INC (AB)
Name changed to Tornado Technologies Inc. 05/02/2007
Tornado Technologies Inc. merged into Empire Industries Ltd. (Old) 12/03/2007 which reorganized as Empire Industries Ltd. (New) 06/30/2016

PETRO GLOBAL INC (CO)
Recapitalized as MRI Medical Diagnostics Inc. 2/12/92
Each share Common 10¢ par exchanged for (0.1) share Common no par
MRI Medical Diagnostics Inc. recapitalized as HomeZipR Corp. (CO) 9/6/2000 which reorganized in Delaware as Advansys Companies, Inc. 12/28/2006

PETRO-GLOBE, INC. (UT)
Recapitalized as International Dynergy, Inc. (Utah) 12/12/83
Each (1-1/3) shares Common $0.001 par exchanged for (1) share Common $0.001 par
International Dynergy, Inc. (Utah) reincorporated in Delaware 4/16/84 which name changed to Unisil Inc. 11/6/91

PETRO HORIZON ENERGY CORP (BC)
Name changed to Greenlight Resources Inc. 08/13/2010
Greenlight Resources Inc. name changed to Great Atlantic Resources Corp. 06/19/2012

PETRO LEWIS CORP (CO)
44¢ Conv. Preferred Ser. A no par called for redemption 04/25/1977
Common $1 par changed to 1¢ par 04/15/1986
Stock Dividends - 100% 10/21/1977; 10% 03/01/1978; 50% 09/11/1978; 10% 03/27/1979; 50% 10/25/1979; 10% 03/14/1980; 100% 10/20/1980; 10% 06/23/1981; 10% 08/05/1983
Merged into FPCO Inc. 05/01/1987
Each share $1.65 Preferred no par exchanged for $1.58 cash
Each share $2.28 Preferred no par exchanged for $1.50 cash
Each share $3.33 Conv. Preferred no par exchanged for $2.54 cash
Each share Common 1¢ par exchanged for $0.73 cash

PETRO MED INC (NV)
Charter revoked for failure to file reports and pay fees 1/1/94

PETRO MINERAL EXPL INC (CO)
Declared defunct and inoperative for failure to pay taxes and file annual reports 03/30/1983

PETRO-MINERALS, INC. (DE)
Merged into Texas National Petroleum Co. on a (0.25) for (1) basis 5/2/60
(See Texas National Petroleum Co.)

PETRO NICHOLAS INC (DE)
Name changed to Mariah Oil & Gas Corp. 01/01/1981
Each share Common 1¢ par exchanged for (1) share Common 1¢ par
(See Mariah Oil & Gas Corp.)

PETRO-NUCLEAR, LTD. (CO)
Merged into Silver Bell Industries, Inc. 11/9/72
Each share Common 10¢ par exchanged for (0.6357) share Common 25¢ par
Silver Bell Industries, Inc. liquidated for Union Oil Co. of California 12/8/78 which reorganized as Unocal Corp. 4/25/83 which merged into Chevron Corp. 8/10/2005

PETRO OCCIDENTE CAP CORP (AB)
Name changed to North Sur Resources Inc. 08/14/2013

PETRO OIL & GAS INC (DE)
Common 20¢ par changed to 5¢ par 3/7/79
Name changed to American Plastics & Chemicals Inc. 12/2/89
(See American Plastics & Chemicals Inc.)

PETRO ONE ENERGY CORP (BC)
Merged into Goldstrike Resources Ltd. 02/29/2016
Each share Common no par exchanged for (0.25) share Common no par
Note: Unexchanged certificates were cancelled and became without value 03/01/2018

PETRO PAK RES LTD (BC)
Struck off register and declared dissolved for failure to file returns 11/29/1985

PETRO PENN INC (NJ)
Common no par split (2) for (1) by issuance of (1) additional share 7/5/83
Name changed to Teksat Corp., Inc. 2/21/85

PETRO-PLEX INC (NV)
Name changed to Drug Detection Systems Inc. 12/30/1990
Drug Detection Systems Inc. name changed to Eye Dynamics Inc. 07/14/1993 which name changed to AcuNetx, Inc. 01/03/2006
(See AcuNetx, Inc.)

PETRO PLUS INC (AB)
Recapitalized as Northern Star Resources Inc. 1/15/99
Each share Class A Common no par exchanged for (0.2) share Class A Common no par
Northern Star Resources Inc. recapitalized as Odaat Inc. 3/9/2000 which recapitalized as Explor Resources Inc. 1/29/2004

PETRO PLUS USA INC (NV)
Name changed to Petroleum Consolidators of America, Inc. 09/08/2006
Petroleum Consolidators of America, Inc. (NV) reincorporated in Delaware as CTX Virtual Technologies, Inc. 04/19/2010

PETRO QUEST INC (CO)
Declared defunct and inoperative for failure to pay taxes and file annual reports 01/01/1989

PETRO-REEF RES LTD (AB)
Name changed to Alexander Energy Ltd. 09/17/2012
Alexander Energy Ltd. recapitalized as Spartan Energy Corp. 02/28/2014 which merged into Vermilion Energy Inc. 05/31/2018

PETRO RES CORP (DE)
Name changed to Magnum Hunter Resources Corp. 07/14/2009
(See Magnum Hunter Resources Corp.)

PETRO RIO S A (BRAZIL)
Each old Sponsored GDR for Common exchanged for (0.2) new Sponsored GDR for Common 06/13/2016
GDR agreement terminated 01/27/2017
Each new Sponsored GDR for Common exchanged for $9.593723 cash

PETRO RUBIALES ENERGY CORP (BC)
Under plan of merger name changed to Pacific Rubiales Energy Corp. 01/23/2008
Pacific Rubiales Energy Corp. name changed to Pacific Exploration & Production Corp. 08/18/2015

PETRO-SERS CORP. (NV)
Name changed to Mid-Atlantic Home Health Network Inc. 12/9/94

PETRO SILVER INC (UT)
Proclaimed dissolved for failure to pay taxes 6/3/88

PETRO SUN INTL INC (ON)
Name changed 09/02/1982
Name changed from Petro-Sun, Inc. /Petro-Soleil, Inc. to Petro-Sun International Inc. 09/02/1982
Assignment in Bankruptcy under the laws of the Province of Quebec filed 01/12/1988
No stockholders' equity

PETRO UN INC (CO)
Each (220) shares Common $0.125 par exchanged for (1) share Common no par 9/9/97
Name changed to Horizontal Ventures, Inc. 7/13/98
Horizontal Ventures, Inc. name changed to GREKA Energy Corp. 3/24/99
(See GREKA Energy Corp.)

PETRO UNO RES LTD (AB)
Merged into Renegade Petroleum Ltd. 04/14/2011
Each share Common no par exchanged for (0.2) share Common no par
Renegade Petroleum Ltd. merged into Spartan Energy Corp. 04/01/2014 which merged into Vermilion Energy Inc. 05/31/2018

PETRO-URANIUM OF CANADA LTD. (AB)
Completely liquidated 10/12/1965
Each share Class A no par exchanged for first and final distribution of $0.1213 cash
Class B no par did not participate and is now without value

PETRO WELL ENERGY SVCS INC (AB)
Recapitalized as Cenalta Energy Services Inc. 11/29/1999
Each share Common no par exchanged for (0.2) share Common no par
Cenalta Energy Services Inc. acquired by Precision Drilling Corp. 10/18/2000
(See Precision Drilling Corp.)

PETROALGAE INC (DE)
Name changed to Parabel Inc. 04/03/2012
(See Parabel Inc.)

PETROAMERICA OIL CORP (AB)
Reincorporated 12/10/2010
Place of incorporation changed from (BC) to (AB) 12/10/2010
Each share old Common no par exchanged for (0.1) share new Common no par 07/30/2015
Acquired by Gran Tierra Energy Inc. 01/15/2016
Each share new Common no par exchanged for $1.33 cash
Note: Unexchanged certificates will be cancelled and become without value 01/15/2019

PETROBAKKEN ENERGY LTD NEW (AB)
Name changed to Lightstream Resources Ltd. 05/28/2013

PETROBAKKEN ENERGY LTD OLD (AB)
Under plan of reorganization each share Class A Common no par automatically became (1) share PetroBakken Energy Ltd. (New) Common no par 01/07/2013
PetroBakken Energy Ltd. (New) name changed to Lightstream Resources Ltd. 05/28/2013

PETROBANK ENERGY & RES LTD NEW (AB)
Each share Common no par received distribution of (1.1051) shares PetroBakken Energy Ltd. (New) Common no par payable 01/07/2013 to holders of record 12/31/2012 Ex date - 01/02/2013
Recapitalized as Touchstone Exploration Inc. 05/20/2014
Each share Common no par exchanged for (0.5) share Common no par

PETROBANK ENERGY & RES LTD OLD (AB)
Each share Common no par received distribution of (0.6142) share Petrominerales Ltd. Common no par payable 01/07/2011 to holders of record 12/31/2010 Ex date - 12/29/2010
Under plan of reorganization each share Common no par automatically became (1) share Petrobank Energy & Resources Ltd. (New) Common no par 01/07/2013
Petrobank Energy & Resources Ltd. (New) recapitalized as Touchstone Exploration Inc. 05/20/2014

PETROBAR EXPLS INC (ON)
Merged into Parapet Petroleum Inc. 12/29/1982
Each share Common no par exchanged for (1.5) shares Common no par
Parapet Petroleum Inc. merged into D'Eldona Resources Ltd. 10/15/1984 which recapitalized as Western D'Eldona Resources Ltd. 06/01/1988
(See Western D'Eldona Resources Ltd.)

PETROBOTICS VENTURES LTD (BC)
Common no par split (3) for (1) by issuance of (2) additional shares 4/30/85
Name changed to North American Metals Corp. 6/10/86
North American Metals Corp. merged into Wheaton River Minerals Ltd. 3/26/2004 which merged into Goldcorp Inc. 4/15/2005

PETROBRAS DISTRIBUIDORA (BRAZIL)
Sponsored ADR's for Preferred no par split (3) for (2) by issuance of (0.5) additional ADR payable 4/18/96 to holders of record 3/22/96
ADR agreement terminated 4/28/2003
Each Sponsored ADR for Ordinary no par exchanged for $13.1776 cash

PETROBRAS ENERGIA PARTICIPACIONES S A (ARGENTINA)
Merged into Petrobras Energia S.A. 09/29/2009
Each Sponsored ADR for Class B exchanged for (0.359015) Sponsored ADR for Class B
Petrobras Energia S.A. name changed to Petrobras Argentina S.A. 12/20/2010
(See Petrobras Argentina S.A.)

PETROBRAS ENERGIA S A (ARGENTINA)
Name changed from Petrobras Energia S.A. to Petrobras Argentina S.A. 12/20/2010
Sponsored ADR's for Class B Ordinary split (2) for (1) by issuance of (1) additional ADR payable 10/02/2012 to holders of record 09/25/2012 Ex date - 10/03/2012
Merged into Pampa Energia S.A. 05/16/2018
Each Sponsored ADR for Class B

Ordinary exchanged for (0.2101) Sponsored ADR for Common
Note: Unexchanged ADR's will be sold and the proceeds held for claim after 12/17/2018

PETROCAN DRILLERS LTD. (AB)
Stricken from the Register and deemed to have been dissolved for default in filing returns 10/30/54

PETROCARBON CHEMICALS, INC. (CA)
Reincorporated under the laws of Maryland 6/27/56
Petrocarbon Chemicals, Inc. (Md.) merged into Great Western Producers, Inc. 12/30/57 which liquidated for Taylor Wine Co., Inc. 11/30/66 which merged into Coca-Cola Co. 1/21/77

PETROCARBON CHEMICALS, INC. (MD)
Merged into Great Western Producers, Inc. on a (1/6) for (1) basis 12/30/57
Great Western Producers, Inc. liquidated for Taylor Wine Co., Inc. 11/30/66 which merged into Coca-Cola Co. 1/21/77

PETROCEL INDS INC (BC)
Struck off register and declared dissolved for failure to file returns 7/5/91

PETROCK VENTURES INC (BC)
Recapitalized as Croydon Mercantile Corp. 12/31/2002
Each share Common no par exchanged for (0.1) share Common no par
Croydon Mercantile Corp. name changed to World Mahjong Ltd. 12/01/2015

PETROCORP INC (TX)
Merged into Unit Corp. 2/2/2004
Each share Common 1¢ par exchanged for $13.45 cash
Note: An escrow account has been established for possible future distribution(s)

PETRODYNAMICS INC (TX)
Merged into Weco Development Corp. 4/30/73
Each share Common $1 par exchanged for (0.5) share Common 20¢ par and (0.5) Common Stock Purchase Warrant expiring 5/3/78
Weco Development Corp. name changed to Worldwide Energy Corp. 6/14/77 which merged into Triton Energy Corp. (TX) 11/18/86 which reincorporated in Delaware 5/12/95

PETRODYNE INDS INC (TX)
Name changed to Petrodynamics, Inc. 11/19/68
Petrodynamics, Inc. merged into Weco Development Corp. 4/30/73 which name changed to Worldwide Energy Corp. 6/14/77 which merged into Triton Energy Corp. (TX) 11/18/86 which reincorporated in Delaware 5/12/95

PETROFALCON CORP (AB)
Reincorporated under the laws of British Columbia as Etrion Corp. 09/16/2009

PETROFINA CDA INC (CANADA)
Name changed 09/26/1979
Name changed from Petrofina Canada Ltd. to Petrofina Canada Inc. 09/26/1979
Name changed to Petro-Canada Enterprises Inc./Entreprises Petro-Canada Inc. 11/16/1981
(See Petro-Canada Enterprises Inc./Entreprises Petro-Canada Inc.)

PETROFINA INC (DE)
Name changed to Petro Oil & Gas, Inc. 4/20/78
Petro Oil & Gas, Inc. name changed to American Plastics & Chemicals Inc. 12/2/89
(See American Plastics & Chemicals Inc.)

PETROFINA S A (BELGIUM)
ADR agreement terminated 9/1/2001
Each Sponsored ADR for Ordinary no par exchanged for $53.5571 cash

PETROFLAME INTL RES LTD (BC)
Recapitalized as Crystallex International Corp. (BC) 5/8/91
Each share Common no par exchanged for (0.2) share Common no par
Crystallex International Corp. (BC) reincorporated in Canada 1/23/98

PETROFLO PETE CORP (ON)
Merged into Flying Cross Resources Ltd. 12/04/1985
Each share Capital Stock no par exchanged for (0.25) share Common no par
Flying Cross Resources Ltd. merged into International Larder Minerals Inc. 05/01/1986 which merged into Explorers Alliance Corp. 10/13/2000
(See Explorers Alliance Corp.)

PETROFLOW ENERGY LTD (CANADA)
Class B Multiple Shares reclassified as old Class A Subordinate no par 05/31/2004
Each share old Class A Subordinate no par exchanged for (0.1) share new Class A Subordinate no par 12/07/2005
Each share new Class A Subordinate no par exchanged for (1) share Common no par 08/11/2006
Plan of reorganization under Chapter 11 Federal Bankruptcy proceedings effective 09/30/2011
For holdings of (1,000) shares or more:
Each share Common no par exchanged for (1) share North American Petroleum Corp. USA (a privately held company)
For holdings of (999) shares or fewer:
Each share Common no par exchanged for $0.34 cash
Note: Unexchanged certificates were cancelled and became without value 09/28/2012

PETROFORTE INTL LTD (AB)
Recapitalized as Canamax Energy Ltd. 02/21/2014
Each share Common no par exchanged for (0.16666666) share Common no par
(See Canamax Energy Ltd.)

PETROFUND ENERGY TR (ON)
Merged into Penn West Energy Trust 07/04/2006
Each Trust Unit exchanged for (0.6) Trust Unit and $1.10 cash
Penn West Energy Trust reorganized as Penn West Petroleum Ltd. (New) 01/03/2011 which name changed to Obsidian Energy Ltd. 06/29/2017

PETROGEN CORP (NV)
Recapitalized as Pluris Energy Group Inc. 09/12/2006
Each share Common $0.001 par exchanged for (0.2) share Common $0.001 par
Pluris Energy Group Inc. name changed to Nationwide Utilities Corp. 12/02/2009

PETROGENETICS INC (CO)
Recapitalized as FSC Holdings Inc. 06/02/1997
Each share Common $0.001 par exchanged for (0.002) share Common $0.001 par
FSC Holdings Inc. name changed to Hyperion Technologies, Inc. 01/27/1998 which name changed to Nextpath Technologies Inc. 07/22/1999
(See Nextpath Technologies Inc.)

PETROGLOBE INC (AB)
Filed a voluntary assignment in bankruptcy 11/26/2013
Stockholders' equity unlikely

PETROGLYPH ENERGY INC (DE)
Issue Information - 2,500,000 shares COM offered at $12.50 per share on 10/20/1997
Merged into Intermountain Industries, Inc. 12/31/2000
Each share Common 1¢ par exchanged for $2.85 cash

PETROGOLD FINL CORP (BC)
Name changed to Columbia Leisure Corp. 10/11/88
(See Columbia Leisure Corp.)

PETROGOLD RESOURCES CORP. (BC)
Name changed to Petrogold Financial Corp. 02/14/1986
Petrogold Financial Corp. name changed to Columbia Leisure Corp. 10/11/1988
(See Columbia Leisure Corp.)

PETROGRESS INC (FL)
Reincorporated under the laws of Delaware 11/30/2016

PETROGULF INC (NV)
Common 1¢ par changed to $0.001 par 07/27/2012
Name changed to Novagant Corp. 01/02/2014

PETROGULF RES LTD (AUSTRALIA)
ADR agreement terminated 01/28/2009
No ADR's remain outstanding

PETROHAWK ENERGY CORP (AB)
Name changed to Petrohawk Energy Ltd. 01/22/1996
Petrohawk Energy Ltd. recapitalized as Fox Energy Corp. 11/23/1999
(See Fox Energy Corp.)

PETROHAWK ENERGY CORP (DE)
Acquired by BHP Billiton Ltd. 08/25/2011
Each share Common $0.001 par exchanged for $38.75 cash

PETROHAWK ENERGY LTD (AB)
Recapitalized as Fox Energy Corp. 11/23/1999
Each share Common no par exchanged for (0.25) share Common no par
(See Fox Energy Corp.)

PETROHUNTER ENERGY CORP (MD)
SEC revoked common stock registration 08/08/2016

PETROHUNTER ENERGY LTD (AB)
Recapitalized as KT Capital Corp. 10/01/1986
Each (5.25) shares Common no par exchanged for (3) shares Common no par
(See KT Capital Corp.)

PETROINC RES LTD (ON)
Merged into Barrick Resources Corp. 5/2/83
Each share Capital Stock $1 par exchanged for (0.25) share Common no par
Barrick Resources Corp. recapitalized as American Barrick Resources Corp. 12/6/85 which name changed to Barrick Gold Corp. 1/18/95

PETROJARL ASA (NORWAY)
Name changed to Teekay Petrojarl ASA 01/29/2007
(See Teekay Petrojarl ASA)

PETROKAMCHATKA PLC (JERSEY)
Recapitalized as EastSiberian PLC 10/02/2012
Each share Common no par exchanged for (0.01) share Common no par

PETROKAZAKHSTAN INC (AB)
Merged into CNPC International Ltd. 10/26/2005
Each share Common no par exchanged for $55 cash

PETROKAZAKHSTAN OIL PRODS OJSC (KAZAKHSTAN)
ADR agreement terminated 11/12/2004
Each 144A Sponsored ADR for Common exchanged for $4.5698 cash
Each Reg. S Sponsored GDR for Common exchanged for $4.5698 cash

PETROL INDS INC (NV)
Recapitalized as Caddo International, Inc. 10/16/2007
Each (30) shares Common 10¢ par exchanged for (1) share Common 10¢ par
(See Caddo International, Inc.)

PETROL OIL & GAS INC (NV)
SEC revoked common stock registration 02/06/2014

PETROL OIL & GAS LTD (ON)
Merged into Universal Explorations (83) Ltd. 11/01/1983
Each share Common no par exchanged for (1) share Common no par
Universal Explorations (83) Ltd. name changed to Universal Explorations Ltd. (New) 12/08/1986 which merged into Canadian Conquest Exploration Inc. 04/17/1989 which merged into Cypress Energy Inc. 05/10/1999 which merged into PrimeWest Energy Trust 05/29/2001
(See PrimeWest Energy Trust)

PETROLANE GAS CO., INC. (LA)
Reorganized in 1958
No stockholders' equity

PETROLANE GAS SVC INC (CA)
Common $2 par changed to $1 par and (1) additional share issued 11/21/60
Common $1 par split (3) for (2) by issuance of (0.5) additional share 5/1/61
Name changed to Petrolane, Inc. 2/7/69
(See Petrolane, Inc.)

PETROLANE INC NEW (CA)
Merged into AmeriGas Inc. 4/19/95
Each share Class A Common 1¢ par exchanged for $16 cash
Each share Class B Common 1¢ par exchanged for $16 cash

PETROLANE INC OLD (CA)
Common $1 par split (3) for (2) by issuance of (0.5) additional share 2/24/71
Common $1 par split (2) for (1) by issuance of (1) additional share 3/1/72
$1.375 Conv. Preferred Ser. A $1 par called for redemption 9/30/77
Common $1 par split (2) for (1) by issuance of (1) additional share 9/28/79
Common $1 par split (2) for (1) by issuance of (1) additional share 3/27/81
Merged into Texas Eastern Corp. 9/25/84
Each share Common $1 par exchanged for $20 cash

PETROLANE PARTNERS L P (DE)
Merged into QFB Partners 8/1/89
Each Depositary Unit exchanged for $30 cash

PETROLANTIC LTD (ON)
Name changed 10/5/87
Name changed from Petrolantic Resources Inc. to Petrolantic Ltd. 10/5/87
Name changed to Cirque Energy Ltd. 4/1/94
Cirque Energy Ltd. recapitalized as

Cirque Energy Corp. 5/11/98 which merged into Tikal Resources Corp. 5/31/99 which was acquired by BelAir Energy Corp. 12/14/2001 which merged into Purcell Energy Ltd. (New) 9/4/2003
(See Purcell Energy Ltd. (New))

PETROLEO BRASILEIRO SA PETROBRAS (BRAZIL)
Each Reg. S Sponsored ADR for Preferred exchanged for (1) Sponsored ADR for Ordinary 9/22/97
ADR agreement terminated 03/30/2001
Each 144A Sponsored ADR for Preferred exchanged for $23.6809 cash
(Additional Information in Active)

PETROLERO CORP (TX)
Voluntarily dissolved 7/1/98
Details not available

PETROLEUM & RES CORP (MD)
$1.75 Conv. Preferred $25 par called for redemption 11/05/1982
$1.575 Conv. Preferred no par called for redemption 05/19/1993
Common $1 par split (3) for (2) by issuance of (0.5) additional share payable 10/19/2000 to holders of record 09/28/2000 Ex date - 10/20/2000
Common $1 par changed to $0.001 par 11/08/2006
Name changed to Adams Natural Resources Fund, Inc. 03/31/2015

PETROLEUM & SULPHUR DEVELOPMENT CO. (DE)
Recapitalized as Mining Royalty Corp. 02/01/1958
Each share Capital Stock 1¢ par exchanged for (0.02) share Capital Stock 50¢ par
Mining Royalty Corp. name changed to First U.S. Southern Corp. 10/10/1960
(See First U.S. Southern Corp.)

PETROLEUM ACREAGE CORP TEX (TX)
Company filed petition under Chapter 11 Federal Bankruptcy Code 04/17/1985
Stockholders' equity unlikely

PETROLEUM ASSOCIATES FUND, INC. (KS)
Voluntarily dissolved 7/7/82
Details not available

PETROLEUM CAP ENERGY INC (AB)
Cease trade order effective 07/28/1993
Stockholders' equity unlikely

PETROLEUM CONS AMER INC (NV)
Each share old Common $0.001 par exchanged for (0.008) share new Common $0.001 par 03/25/2010
Reincorporated under the laws of Delaware as CTX Virtual Technologies, Inc. 04/19/2010

PETROLEUM CONVERSION CORP.
Adjudicated bankrupt 7/19/48

PETROLEUM CORP AMER (DE)
Capital Stock no par changed to $5 par 00/00/1933
Capital Stock $5 par changed to Common $1 par and (1) additional share issued 03/12/1956
Reincorporated under the laws of Maryland as Petroleum & Resources Corp. 04/13/1977
Petroleum & Resources Corp. name changed to Adams Natural Resources Fund, Inc. 03/31/2015

PETROLEUM DERIVATIVES, INC. OF MAINE (ME)
Suspended for non-payment of franchise tax 00/00/1941

PETROLEUM DEV CORP (NV)
Name changed to PDC Energy, Inc. (NV) 06/13/2012

PDC Energy, Inc. (NV) reincorporated in Delaware 06/11/2015

PETROLEUM DEVELOPMENT CORP. (TX)
Merged into Presidio Oil Co. 03/17/1987
Each share Common exchanged for (0.5242) share Class A Common 10¢ par
Note: An additional distribution of approximately (0.1505) share may be made if certain contingencies are met

PETROLEUM ENHANCEMENT TECHNOLOGY CORP (MN)
Proclaimed dissolved for failure to file reports and pay fees 10/4/91

PETROLEUM EQUIP TOOLS CO (TX)
Stock Dividend - 100% 06/22/1981
Merged into Weatherford International Inc. (Old) 11/19/1991
Each share Common 50¢ par exchanged for (0.8) share Common 10¢ par
Weatherford International Inc. (Old) recapitalized as Weatherford Enterra, Inc. 10/05/1995 which merged into EVI Weatherford, Inc. 05/27/1998 which name changed to Weatherford International Inc. (New) (DE) 09/21/1998 which reincorporated in Bermuda as Weatherford International Ltd. 06/26/2002 which reincorporated in Switzerland 02/25/2009 which reincorporated in Ireland as Weatherford International PLC 06/18/2014

PETROLEUM EXPL INC (ME)
Stock Dividend - 100% 04/01/1965
Merged into Wiser Oil Co. (DE) 12/31/1970
Each share Capital Stock $10 par exchanged for (2) shares Common $10 par
(See Wiser Oil Co. (DE))

PETROLEUM FDG CORP (CO)
Recapitalized as Nova Resources Inc. (CO) 02/28/1986
Each share Common no par exchanged for (0.05555555) share Common no par
Nova Resources Inc. (CO) reincorporated in Nevada 11/07/2007 which name changed to Fox Petroleum, Inc. 02/05/2007
(See Fox Petroleum, Inc.)

PETROLEUM FINANCE CORP. (OK)
Out of business 00/00/1944
Details not available

PETROLEUM FINANCE CORP. OF TEXAS
Out of existence 00/00/1944
Details not available

PETROLEUM GEO-SVCS ASA OLD (NORWAY)
Issue information - 5,200,000 SPONSORED ADR's offered at $13 per ADR on 04/14/1994
Sponsored ADR's for Ordinary NOK 10 par changed to NOK 5 par and (1) additional ADR issued 3/25/94
Sponsored ADR's for Ordinary NOK 5 par split (2) for (1) by issuance of (1) additional ADR payable 6/24/98 to holders of record 6/23/98 Ex date - 6/25/98
Plan of reorganization under Chapter 11 Federal Bankruptcy Code effective 11/5/2003
Each Sponsored ADR for Ordinary NOK 5 par exchanged for (0.00774113) Petroleum-Geo Services ASA Ordinary share

PETROLEUM HEAT & POWER CO.
Name changed to Taylor Oil & Gas Co. in 1952
Taylor Oil & Gas Co. merged into Delhi-Taylor Oil Corp. in 1955
(See Delhi-Taylor Oil Corp.)

PETROLEUM HEAT & PWR INC (MN)
Each share 12.875% Exchangeable Preferred Ser. B 10¢ par exchanged for (1) share 12.875% Exchangeable Preferred Ser. C 10¢ par 9/24/98
Merged into Star Gas Partners, L.P. 3/16/99
Each share Class C Common 10¢ par exchanged for (0.11758) Sr. Subordinated Unit of Ltd. Partnership Int. no par
Merged into Star Gas Partners, L.P. 3/26/99
Each share 12.875% Exchangeable Preferred Ser. C 10¢ par exchanged for $23 cash
Each share Conv. Jr. Preferred 1¢ par exchanged for (0.13064) Sr. Subordinated Unit of Ltd. Partnership Int. no par
Each share Class A Common 10¢ par exchanged for (0.11758) Sr. Subordinated Unit of Ltd. Partnership Int. no par
Each share Class B Common 10¢ par exchanged for (0.11758) Sr. Subordinated Unit of Ltd. Partnership Int. no par
Each share Common 10¢ par exchanged for (0.11758) Sr. Subordinated Unit of Ltd. Partnership Int. no par

PETROLEUM HELICOPTERS INC (LA)
Reincorporated 10/27/1994
Common 50¢ par changed to 25¢ par and (1) additional share issued 03/12/1969
Common 25¢ par changed to 8-1/3¢ par and (2) additional shares issued 03/17/1981
State of incorporation changed from (DE) to (LA), Common 8-1/3¢ par and Non-Vtg. Common 8-1/3¢ par changed to 10¢ par 10/27/1994
Stock Dividend - 10% 09/15/1972
Name changed to PHI, Inc. 01/01/2006

PETROLEUM INCOMES (CLIFTON C. CROSS), LTD.
Name changed to British Empire Oil Co. Ltd. in 1952
British Empire Oil Co. Ltd. recapitalized as Canadian British Empire Oil Co. Ltd. in 1954 which merged into Canadian Western Oil Co., Inc. 3/12/58 which merged into Westates Petroleum Co. 12/24/59 which assets were transferred to Westates Petroleum Co. Liquidating Trust 5/2/77
(See Westates Petroleum Co. Liquidating Trust)

PETROLEUM INVESTMENT CO. (DE)
Merged into Galaxy Oil Co. 1/31/73
Each share Common no par exchanged for $79.98 cash

PETROLEUM INVESTMENTS, LTD.- 1982A (OK)
Acquired by Bradmar Petroleum Corp. 08/03/1990
Each $5 in exchange value of Units of Ltd. Partnership exchanged for (1) share Common 10¢ par
Bradmar Petroleum Corp. merged into Alexander Energy Corp. 03/19/1992 which merged into National Energy Group, Inc. 08/30/1996
(See National Energy Group, Inc.)

PETROLEUM INVTS LTD (OK)
Acquired by Bradmar Petroleum Corp. 08/03/1990
Each Depositary Unit no par exchanged for (0.1) share Common 10¢ par
Bradmar Petroleum Corp. merged into Alexander Energy Corp. 03/19/1992 which merged into National Energy Group, Inc. 08/30/1996
(See National Energy Group, Inc.)

PETROLEUM LD CORP (UT)
Each share Common $0.001 par exchanged for (0.02) share Common 1¢ par 03/26/1986
Reorganized under the laws of California as Crosswind Venture Corp. 09/15/1986
Each share Common 1¢ par exchanged for (1) share Common 1¢ par
(See Crosswind Venture Corp.)

PETROLEUM PRODUCERS CO. (DE)
Acquired by Jupiter Oils Ltd. on a (0.4) for (1) basis 9/30/58
Jupiter Oils Ltd. reorganized as Jupiter Corp. 12/4/61 which merged into Jupiter Industries, Inc. 11/12/71
(See Jupiter Industries, Inc.)

PETROLEUM PRODUCTION CO. OF AMERICA (DE)
Charter cancelled and declared inoperative and void for non-payment of taxes 03/19/1924

PETROLEUM RECOVERY CORP. (UT)
Merged into Pacific Fidelity Corp. 4/16/62
Each share Capital Stock 10¢ par exchanged for (0.333333) share Common $5 par

PETROLEUM RECTIFYING CORP.
Reorganized as Petrolite Corp. Ltd. 00/00/1931
Details not available

PETROLEUM RESERVES, INC. (DE)
Completely liquidated for cash 6/4/65

PETROLEUM RES CORP (DE)
Name changed to PRC Corp. (New) 01/21/1986
(See PRC Corp. (New))

PETROLEUM RES CORP (DE)
Name changed to PRC Corp. (Old) 11/09/1970
PRC Corp. (Old) name changed to CorTerra Corp. 11/28/1972 which assets were transferred to CorTerra Corp. Liquidating Corp. 10/08/1980
(See CorTerra Corp. Liquidating Corp.)

PETROLEUM RES CORP (UT)
Name changed to Borexco, Inc. 02/25/1985
Borexco, Inc. name changed to True Health, Inc. (UT) 02/23/1986 which reorganized in Nevada as MediQuip Holdings, Inc. 05/01/2006 which name changed to Deep Down, Inc. 12/18/2006

PETROLEUM RTYS LTD (CANADA)
Merged into East Coast Energy Ltd. 11/18/1983
Each share Class A Common no par exchanged for (0.7167) share Common no par
(See East Coast Energy Ltd.)

PETROLEUM SECS AUSTRALIA LTD (AUSTRALIA)
Name changed to Petsec Energy Ltd. 03/11/1997

PETROLEUM ST INS CO (TX)
Merged into Guaranty Corp. 11/09/1978
Each share Common no par exchanged for (0.015384) share Class A Common no par

PETROLEUM TELEPHONE CO.
Merged into Pennsylvania Telephone Corp. 00/00/1930
Details not available

PETROLEUM TOOL RESEARCH, INC. (TX)
Charter forfeited for failure to pay taxes 5/8/72

PETROLEX ENERGY CORP (YT)
Cease trade order effective 09/13/2002
Stockholders' equity unlikely

PETROLIA CORP. (CA)
Liquidation completed
Each share Common $1 par received initial distribution of $1 cash 8/16/65
Each share Common $1 par exchanged for second and final distribution of 2¢ cash 11/30/65

PETROLIA INC (QC)
Recapitalized as Pieridae Energy Ltd. 11/02/2017
Each share Common no par exchanged for (0.08333333) share Common no par

PETROLIA OIL & GAS LTD (BC)
Merged into Fortune Energy Inc. 9/1/93
Each share Common no par exchanged for (1) share Common no par
(See Fortune Energy Inc.)

PETROLIAN RES CORP (AB)
Merged into Startech Energy Ltd. 8/19/91
Each share Common no par exchanged for (0.148) share Common no par

PETROLIFERA PETE LTD (CANADA)
Merged into Gran Tierra Energy Inc. (NV) 03/23/2011
Each share Common no par exchanged for (0.1241) share Common $0.001 par
Gran Tierra Energy Inc. (NV) reincorporated in Delaware 10/31/2016

PETROLIFT CORP (CO)
Each share Common $0.001 par exchanged for (1/6) share Common $0.006 par 12/14/1987
Declared defunct and inoperative for failure to pay taxes and file annual reports 01/01/1996

PETROLITE CORP., LTD. (DE)
Name changed to Petrolite Corp. 04/21/1952
Petrolite Corp. merged into Baker Hughes Inc. 07/02/1997 which merged into Baker Hughes, a GE company 07/05/2017

PETROLITE CORP (DE)
Common no par split (5) for (1) by issuance of (4) additional shares 05/08/1961
Common no par split (2) for (1) by issuance of (1) additional share 03/22/1974
Common no par split (2) for (1) by issuance of (1) additional share 10/01/1976
Common no par split (2) for (1) by issuance of (1) additional share 04/13/1981
Merged into Baker Hughes Inc. 07/02/1997
Each share Common no par exchanged for (1.6135) shares Common $1 par
Baker Hughes Inc. merged into Baker Hughes, a GE company 07/05/2017

PETROLOGIC PETE LTD (BC)
Recapitalized as P.T.P. Resource Corp. 05/01/1985
Each share Common no par exchanged for (0.25) share Common no par
(See P.T.P. Resource Corp.)

PETROLOGISTICS LP (DE)
Issue Information - 35,000,000 UNITS LTD PARTNERSHIP INT offered at $17 per Unit on 05/09/2012
Acquired by Koch Industries, Inc. 07/16/2014
Each Unit of Ltd. Partnership Interest exchanged for $14 cash

PETROMAC ENERGY INC (BC)
Placed in receivership 11/21/85
No stockholders' equity

PETROMAGDALENA ENERGY LTD (BC)
Merged into Pacific Rubiales Energy Corp. 07/27/2012
Each share Common no par exchanged for $1.60 cash

PETROMANAS ENERGY INC (BC)
Recapitalized as PMI Resources Ltd. 06/14/2016
Each share Common no par exchanged for (0.01428571) share Common no par
PMI Resources Ltd. name changed to PentaNova Energy Corp. 06/05/2017 which recapitalized as CruzSur Energy Corp. 09/04/2018

PETROMARK RES CO (TX)
Each share old Common 1¢ par exchanged for (0.1) share new Common 1¢ par 06/30/1987
Merged into Petromark Acquisitions, Inc. 12/01/1988
Each share new Common 1¢ par exchanged for $0.01 cash

PETROMAX ENERGY CORP (CO)
Charter suspended for failure to file annual reports 03/16/1987

PETROMEK NEV INC (WY)
Recapitalized as Clarity Resources, Inc. 10/13/97
Each share Common $0.001 par exchanged for (0.1) share Common $0.001 par

PETROMET RES LTD (ON)
Acquired by Talisman Energy Inc. 05/29/2001
Each share Common no par exchanged for $13.20 cash

PETROMINE EXPLORATION & FINANCE CO. LTD. (ON)
Acquired by Nationwide Minerals Ltd. on a (1) for (2) basis in 1952
Nationwide Minerals Ltd. charter cancelled 4/15/65

PETROMINERALES LTD (AB)
Merged into Alvopetro Energy Ltd. 12/04/2013
Each share Common no par exchanged for (1) share Common no par and $11 cash
Note: Unexchanged certificates were cancelled and became without value 12/03/2016

PETROMINERALES LTD (BERMUDA)
Reincorporated 11/15/2010
Place of incorporation changed from (Bahamas) to (Bermuda) 11/15/2010
Reincorporated under the laws of Alberta and Common $1 par changed to no par 12/31/2010

PETROMINES LTD (MB)
Merged into Renaissance Energy Ltd. 5/29/92
Each share Common no par exchanged for either (0.0462) share Common no par or $0.60 cash
Note: Option to elect to receive stock expired 12/30/92
Renaissance Energy Ltd. merged into Husky Energy Inc. 8/25/2000

PETROMONT OIL & GAS LTD (AB)
Name changed to Pillar Petroleums Ltd. 2/9/82
Pillar Petroleums Ltd. merged into Renaissance Energy Ltd. 1/31/83 which merged into Husky Energy Inc. 8/25/2000

PETRON CORP. (OK)
Charter cancelled for failure to file reports and pay fees 05/27/1966

PETRON CORP (PHILIPPINES)
Stock Dividends - 25% payable 08/14/1996 to holders of record 05/14/1996; 20% payable 08/19/1997 to holders of record 05/20/1997
GDR agreement terminated 08/14/2002
Each 144A GDR for Ordinary exchanged for $4.16636 cash

PETRONATIONAL CORP (NV)
Name changed to Custom Restaurant & Hospitality Group Inc. 11/20/2008

PETRONICS OF CANADA LTD. (AB)
Struck off register and deemed to be dissolved 10/31/62

PETRONOVA INC (AB)
Merged into Petroamerica Oil Corp. 07/30/2015
Each share Common no par exchanged for (0.085) share Common no par
Note: Unexchanged certificates will be cancelled and become without value 07/30/2020

PETROPAVLOVSK PLC (UNITED KINGDOM)
Stock Dividend - 5.20548% payable 07/30/2013 to holders of record 06/28/2013 Ex date - 06/26/2013
ADR agreement terminated 04/16/2018
Each Sponsored ADR for Ordinary exchanged for $0.202862 cash

PETROPLUS HLDGS AG (SWITZERLAND)
ADR agreement terminated 11/23/2015
Each ADR for Ordinary exchanged for (0.5) share Ordinary
Note: Unexchanged ADR's will be sold and the proceeds, if any, held for claim after 02/24/2016

PETROPOWER ENERGY INC (AB)
Recapitalized as Justinian Explorations Ltd. 06/30/1997
Each share Common no par exchanged for (0.14285714) share Common no par
Justinian Explorations Ltd. recapitalized as Connacher Oil & Gas Ltd. (AB) 03/23/2001 which reincorporated in Canada 03/30/2015

PETROQUEST LTD (AB)
Acquired by Decca Resources Ltd. 12/10/1977
Each share Common no par exchanged for $8 cash

PETROQUIN RES LTD (BC)
Recapitalized as Consolidated Petroquin Resources Ltd. 10/14/88
Each share Common no par exchanged for (0.4) share Common no par
Consolidated Petroquin Resources Ltd. name changed to Xemplar Energy Corp.

PETROREAL OIL CORP (BC)
Recapitalized as International PetroReal Oil Corp. (BC) 09/13/2002
Each share Common no par exchanged for (1/3) share Common no par
International PetroReal Oil Corp. (BC) reorganized in Alberta 06/28/2007 which name changed to PetroReal Energy Inc. 09/15/2008

PETROREP RES LTD (BC)
Merged into Trans Asia Resources Inc. 5/8/2000
Each share Common no par exchanged for $2.62 cash

PETROSANDS RES CDA INC (AB)
Name changed to CanRock Energy Corp. 01/03/2012
CanRock Energy Corp. merged into Alston Energy Inc. 07/24/2012
(See Alston Energy Inc.)

PETROSEARCH CORP (DE)
Reorganized under the laws of Nevada as Petrosearch Energy Corp. 12/31/2004
Each (6.5) shares Common $0.001 par exchanged for (1) share Common $0.001 par
Petrosearch Energy Corp. merged into Double Eagle Petroleum Co. 08/06/2009

PETROSEARCH ENERGY CORP (NV)
Merged into Double Eagle Petroleum Co. 08/06/2009
Each share Common $0.001 par exchanged for (0.0433) share Common 10¢ par

PETROSOUTH ENERGY CORP (NV)
Common $0.001 par split (10) for (1) by issuance of (9) additional shares payable 05/01/2007 to holders of record 05/01/2007
Name changed to West Canyon Energy Corp. 04/11/2008

PETROSOUTHERN INC (FL)
Reincorporated 7/25/86
State of incorporation changed from (DE) to (FL) 7/25/86
Recapitalized as Craft World International, Inc. 11/11/86
Each share Common no par exchanged for (0.1) share Common 1¢ par
(See Craft World International, Inc.)

PETROSTAR PETE CORP (BC)
Each share old Common no par exchanged for (0.25) share new Common no par 06/01/2011
Name changed to Cerus Energy Group Ltd. 09/01/2015

PETROSTAR PETES INC NEW (AB)
Each share old Common no par exchanged for (0.5) share new Common no par 06/11/1993
Merged into Crestar Energy Inc. 06/07/1996
Each share new Common no par exchanged for (0.06755675) share Common no par
Crestar Energy Inc. acquired by Gulf Canada Resources Ltd. 11/13/2000
(See Gulf Canada Resources Ltd.)

PETROSTAR PETES INC OLD (AB)
Merged into Petrostar Petroleums Inc. (New) 06/11/1992
Each share Class A Common no par exchanged for (1) share Common no par
Petrostar Petroleums Inc. (New) merged into Crestar Energy Inc. 06/07/1996 which was acquired by Gulf Canada Resources Ltd. 11/13/2000
(See Gulf Canada Resources Ltd.)

PETROSTATES RES CORP (BC)
Struck off register and declared dissolved for failure to file returns 7/3/92

PETROSUN DRILLING INC (NV)
Name changed to PetroSun, Inc. 9/29/2006

PETROSUR OIL CORP (DE)
Merged into Techtro-Matic Corp. 08/24/1961
Each share Common 10¢ par exchanged for (0.166666) share Common 10¢ par
(See Techtro-Matic Corp.)

PETROSURANCE INC (OH)
Charter cancelled for non-payment of taxes 12/29/1995

PETROSYSTEMS INTL INC (TN)
Recapitalized as International Transtech Corp. 06/22/1984
Each share Common 5¢ par exchanged for (0.5) share Common 10¢ par
International Transtech Corp. name changed to Automotive Franchise Corp. 02/26/1986
(See Automotive Franchise Corp.)

PETROTECH INC (DE)
Reorganized under the laws of Colorado as Great Northern Gas Co. 9/15/89
Each share Common 1¢ par exchanged for (0.1) share Common 1¢ par

(See Great Northern Gas Co.)

PETROTERRA CORP (NV)
Old Common $0.001 par split (32) for (1) by issuance of (31) additional shares payable 01/30/2012 to holders of record 01/30/2012
Each share old Common $0.001 par exchanged for (0.5) share new Common $0.001 par 12/20/2013
Each share new Common $0.001 par exchanged again for (0.4) share new Common $0.001 par 07/01/2015
Recapitalized as Transportation & Logistics Systems, Inc. 07/18/2018
Each share new Common $0.001 par exchanged for (0.004) share Common $0.001 par

PETROTEX RES LTD (BC)
Recapitalized as Fulcrum Developments Ltd. 01/28/1987
Each share Common no par exchanged for (0.2) share Common no par
Fulcrum Developments Ltd. recapitalized as Wespac Mining Corp. 07/02/1996 which name changed to Genesis II Enterprises Ltd. 11/19/1998
(See Genesis II Enterprises Ltd.)

PETROVEST INC (FL)
Stock Dividend - 100% 9/25/89
Reorganized as National Sweepstakes, Inc. 9/17/91
Each share Common $0.001 par exchanged for (1) share Common $0.001 par
National Sweepstakes, Inc. name changed to Natural Fuels Inc. 1/1/94 which name changed to CBR Brewing Co., Inc. (FL) 3/15/95 which reincorporated in British Virgin Islands as High Worth Holdings Ltd. 3/3/2003

PETROWEST ENERGY SVCS TR (AB)
Reorganized as Petrowest Corp. 07/06/2011
Each Trust Unit exchanged for (1) share Class A Common no par
Note: Unexchanged certificates were cancelled and became without value 07/06/2014

PETROWEST RES LTD (BC)
Struck off register and declared dissolved for failure to file returns 09/20/1982

PETROWORLD CORP (CAYMAN ISLANDS)
Name changed to Coastal Energy Co. 10/04/2006
(See Coastal Energy Co.)

PETROWORTH RES INC (ON)
Recapitalized as First Sahara Energy Inc. (ON) 07/04/2013
Each share Common no par exchanged for (0.1) share Common no par
First Sahara Energy Inc. (ON) reincorporated in Alberta 11/26/2014 which name changed to M Pharmaceutical Inc. 01/28/2015 which recapitalized as Callitas Health Inc. 09/20/2017

PETROX CAP CORP (AB)
Name changed to Petrox Resources Corp. 08/15/2012

PETROX ENERGY & MINERALS CORP (CANADA)
Reincorporated 08/12/1985
Place of incorporation changed from (BC) to (Canada) 08/12/1985
Name changed to HuMedaTech International Inc. 02/04/1997
HuMedaTech International Inc. recapitalized as Feathertouch E-Comm Inc. 11/10/1999
(See Feathertouch E-Comm Inc.)

PETROX INDS INC (DE)
Stock Dividend - 100% 03/10/1981
Merged into American Pacific Corp. 09/19/1983
Each share Common $1 par exchanged for $4.75 cash
Note: Unexchanged certificates were cancelled and became without value 05/31/1990

PETROX PETE CORP (BC)
Name changed to Petrox Energy & Minerals Corp. (BC) 12/24/1982
Petrox Energy & Minerals Corp. (BC) reincorporated in Canada 08/12/1985 which name changed to HuMedaTech International Inc. 02/04/1997 which recapitalized as Feathertouch E-Comm Inc. 11/10/1999
(See Feathertouch E-Comm Inc.)

PETROZ N L (AUSTRALIA)
ADR agreement terminated 06/02/1989
Each ADR for Ordinary exchanged for $0.01 cash

PETS COM INC (DE)
Issue Information - 7,500,000 shares COM offered at $11 per share on 02/10/2000
Name changed to IPET Holdings, Inc. 1/18/2001
(See IPET Holdings, Inc.)

PETSHEALTH, INC. (UT)
Proclaimed dissolved for failure to pay taxes 09/01/1999

PETSHEALTH INC (FL)
Reorganized under the laws of Nevada as Berkshire Asset Management Inc. 12/28/2001
Each share Common $0.001 par exchanged for (0.005) share Common $0.001 par
Berkshire Asset Management Inc. recapitalized as Greater Sooner Holdings, Inc. 10/11/2005 which recapitalized as Dovarri Inc. 01/07/2008
(See Dovarri Inc.)

PETSMARKETING INC (DE)
Common $0.0001 split (2) for (1) by issuance of (1) additional share payable 3/28/2002 to holders of record 3/7/2002 Ex date - 4/1/2002
Name changed to PS Management Holdings Inc. 5/15/2002
(See PS Management Holdings Inc.)

PETSMART INC (DE)
Common $0.0001 par split (3) for (2) by issuance of (0.5) additional share 05/01/1995
Common $0.0001 par split (2) for (1) by issuance of (1) additional share payable 07/19/1996 to holders of record 07/08/1996
Acquired by Argos Holdings Inc. 03/11/2015
Each share Common $0.0001 par exchanged for $83 cash

PETSTUFF INC (DE)
Acquired by PetSmart, Inc. 06/01/1995
Each share Common 1¢ par exchanged for (0.278) share Common 1¢ par
(See PetSmart, Inc.)

PETTIBONE CORP (DE)
Capital Stock $10 par split (5) for (4) by issuance of (0.25) additional share 8/2/76
Capital Stock $10 par split (5) for (4) by issuance of (0.25) additional share 8/21/78
Common $10 par changed to $1 par 7/21/83
Plan of reorganization under Chapter 11 Federal Bankruptcy Code effective 12/27/88
Each (9) shares Common $1 par exchanged for (1) share Common 1¢ par
Stock Dividend - 20% 1/2/75
Acquired by private investors 3/22/94
Each share Class A Preferred Ser. 1 1¢ par exchanged for $5.65 cash
Each share Class A Preferred Ser. 2 1¢ par exchanged for $7.18 cash
Each share Class B Preferred 1¢ par exchanged for $3.50 cash
Each share Common 1¢ par exchanged for $3.50 cash

PETTIBONE MULLIKEN CO.
Reorganized as Pettibone Mulliken Corp. in 1937
Each (4.5) shares Preferred exchanged for (1) Trust Unit
Each (61.5) shares Common exchanged for (1) Trust Unit
Pettibone Mulliken Corp. name changed to Pettibone Corp. 8/1/69
(See Pettibone Corp.)

PETTIBONE MULLIKEN CORP (DE)
Capital Stock no par changed to $25 par 00/00/1945
Capital Stock $25 par changed to $20 par 07/03/1946
Capital Stock $20 par changed to $10 par and (1) additional share issued 07/09/1965
Capital Stock $10 par split (6) for (5) by issuance of (0.2) additional share 05/10/1967
Stock Dividends - 100% 03/20/1953; 25% 03/08/1956; 20% 09/18/1959; 20% 03/20/1964
Name changed to Pettibone Corp. 08/01/1969
(See Pettibone Corp.)

PETX PETE CORP (CO)
Each (25,000) shares Common 1¢ par exchanged for (1) share Common 1¢ par 03/10/1987
Note: In effect holders received $0.05 cash per share and public interest was eliminated

PEUGEOT CITROEN S A (FRANCE)
Each ADR for Bearer exchanged for (2) ADR's for Bearer 08/03/1989
Each Unsponsored ADR for Bearer exchanged for (1) Sponsored ADR for Bearer 12/01/1993
Sponsored ADR's for Bearer split (3) for (2) by issuance of (0.5) additional ADR payable 07/09/2001 to holders of record 06/29/2001 Ex date - 07/02/2001
ADR basis changed from (1:0.25) to (1:1) 06/29/2001
Stock Dividend - 20% 08/28/1987
ADR agreement terminated 02/18/2014
Each Sponsored ADR for Bearer exchanged for $17.709882 cash

PEUGEOT S.A. OLD (FRANCE)
Stock Dividend - 25% 06/07/1976
Name changed to Peugeot-Citroen S.A. 09/30/1976
(See Peugeot-Citroen S.A.)

PEXCON INC (DE)
Name changed to Tekoil & Gas Corp. 07/18/2005
(See Tekoil & Gas Corp.)

PEXTILE CORP (NC)
Name changed 08/31/1966
Name changed from Pextile Corp. of America to Pextile Corp. and Common $1 par changed to 10¢ par 08/31/1966
Assets sold for benefit of creditors 11/17/1970
No stockholders' equity

PEYTO ENERGY TR (AB)
Trust Units no par split (2) for (1) by issuance of (1) additional Unit payable 06/07/2005 to holders of record 05/31/2005 Ex date - 05/27/2005
Reorganized as Peyto Exploration & Development Corp. (New) 01/07/2011
Each Trust Unit no par exchanged for (1) share Common no par
Note: Unexchanged certificates were cancelled and became without value 01/07/2014

PEYTO EXPL & DEV CORP OLD (AB)
Name changed to Peyto Energy Trust and Common no par reclassified as Trust Units no par 07/01/2003
Peyto Energy Trust reorganized as Peyto Exploration & Development Corp. (New) 01/07/2011

PEYTO OILS LTD (AB)
Merged into Westburne International Industries Ltd. (Canada) 12/04/1980
Each share Capital Stock no par exchanged for (0.8) share Common no par
(See Westburne International Industries Ltd. (Canada))

PEZAMERICA RES CORP (BC)
Recapitalized 8/30/82
Common no par split (3) for (1) by issuance of (2) additional shares 7/9/81
Recapitalized from Pez Resources Ltd. to Pezamerica Resources Corp. 8/30/82
Each share Common no par exchanged for (0.25) share Common no par
Merged into Royex Gold Mining Corp. 3/8/85
Each share Common no par exchanged for (0.75) share Common no par
Royex Gold Mining Corp. merged into Corona Corp. 7/1/88 which recapitalized as International Corona Corp. 6/11/91
(See International Corona Corp.)

PEZGOLD RESOURCE CORP NEW (BC)
Recapitalized as Braiden Resources Ltd. 6/15/90
Each share Common no par exchanged for (1/7) share Common no par
Braiden Resources Ltd. recapitalized as Pure Pioneer Ventures Ltd. 6/14/2002

PEZGOLD RESOURCE CORP OLD (BC)
Merged into Pezgold Resource Corp. (New) 9/1/88
Each share Common no par exchanged for (1) share Common no par
Pezgold Resource Corp. (New) recapitalized as Braiden Resources Ltd. 6/15/90 which recapitalized as Pure Pioneer Ventures Ltd. 6/14/2002

PF HOSPITALITY GROUP INC (NV)
Name changed to EXOlifestyle, Inc. 09/27/2016
EXOlifestyle, Inc. recapitalized as Sun Pacific Holding Corp. 10/13/2017

PFAUDLER CO. (NY)
Each share Common $100 par exchanged for (5) shares Common $20 par in 1943
Each share Preferred $100 par exchanged for (7) shares Common $20 par in 1946
Stock Dividends - 25% 11/1/50; 33-1/3% 2/1/57
Merged into Pfaudler Permutit, Inc. 10/1/57
Each share Common $20 par exchanged for (1.429) shares Common $10 par
Pfaudler Permutit, Inc. merged into Ritter Pfaudler Corp. 11/1/65 which merged into Sybron Corp. 10/7/68
(See Sybron Corp.)

PFAUDLER PERMUTIT, INC. (NY)
Common $10 par changed to $5 par and (1) additional share issued 5/3/61
Common $5 par split (3) for (2) by issuance of (0.5) additional share 10/1/64

Merged into Ritter Pfaudler Corp. 11/1/65
Each share Common $5 par exchanged for (1) share Common $5 par
Ritter Pfaudler Corp. merged into Sybron Corp. 10/7/68
(See Sybron Corp.)

PFBI CAP TR (DE)
Issue Information - 25,000,000 PFD SECS 9.75% offered at $25 per share on 06/05/1997
9.75% Preferred Securities called for redemption at $25 on 11/10/2006

PFEIFFER BREWING CO. (MI)
Each share Common no par exchanged for (2) shares Common $5 par 00/00/1950
Stock Dividend - 25% 09/26/1949
Under plan of merger name changed to Associated Brewing Co. and Common $5 par changed to $1 par 11/15/1962
Associated Brewing Co. name changed to Armada Corp. 03/02/1973

PFEIFFER VACUUM TECHNOLOGY AG (GERMANY)
Sponsored ADR's for Ordinary DM50 par changed to no par 07/21/1998
ADR agreement terminated 10/04/2007
Each Sponsored ADR for no par exchanged for $56.0549 cash

PFF BANCORP INC (DE)
Common 1¢ par split (3) for (2) by issuance of (0.5) additional share payable 03/03/2005 to holders of record 02/15/2005 Ex date - 03/04/2005
Stock Dividend - 40% payable 09/05/2003 to holders of record 08/15/2003 Ex date - 09/08/2003
Plan of reorganization under Chapter 11 Federal Bankruptcy proceedings effective 08/28/2013
No stockholders' equity

PFGI CAP CORP (MD)
Ser. A Preferred 1¢ par called for redemption at $25 plus $0.468229 accrued dividends on 08/13/2010

PFISTER & VOGEL LEATHER CO. (WI)
Name changed to P & V-Atlas Industrial Center, Inc. in 1942
P & V-Atlas Industrial Center, Inc. recapitalized as Univest Corp. 9/25/69
(See Univest Corp.)

PFIZER CHAS & CO INC (DE)
Merged 06/02/1951
Merged from Pfizer (Chas.) & Co., Inc. (NJ) to Pfizer (Chas.) & Co., Inc. (DE) 06/02/1951
Each share 3-1/2% Preferred $100 par exchanged for (1) share 3-1/2% Preferred $100 par
Each share Common $1 par exchanged for (3) shares Common $1 par
Common $1 par changed to 33-1/3¢ par and (2) additional shares issued 05/15/1959
3-1/2% Preferred $100 par called for redemption 03/31/1961
4% Preferred called for redemption 03/31/1961
Name changed to Pfizer Inc. 04/27/1970

PFS BANCORP INC (IN)
Merged into Peoples Community Bancorp, Inc. 12/16/2005
Each share Common 1¢ par exchanged for $23 cash

PFSB BANCORP INC (MO)
Merged into First Federal Bancshares, Inc. 11/22/2002
Each share Common 1¢ par exchanged for $21 cash

PG ENERGY INC (PA)
9% Depositary Preferred called for redemption at $26 on 12/1/98
4.10% Preferred $100 par called for redemption at $105.50 on 10/29/99
Public interest eliminated

PG&E CAP I (CA)
Plan of reorganization under Chapter 11 Federal Bankruptcy Code effective 04/12/2004
Each 7.90% Guaranteed Quarterly Income Preferred Securities Ser. A automatically became (1) Pacific Gas & Electric Co. 7.9% Quarterly Income Debt Security

PGM VENTURES CORP (CANADA)
Reincorporated 10/05/2005
Place of incorporation changed from (NB) to (Canada) 10/05/2005
Name changed to Iberian Minerals Corp. (Canada) 07/25/2006
Iberian Minerals Corp. (Canada) reincorporated in Switzerland 06/15/2009
(See Iberian Minerals Corp. (Switzerland))

PGMI INC (UT)
Each (30) shares old Common no par exchanged for (1) share new Common no par 10/12/2007
Note: Holders of between (100) and (2,999) pre-split shares received (100) shares
Holders of (99) or fewer shares were not affected
SEC revoked common stock registration 12/30/2011

PGNX CAP CORP (AB)
Completely liquidated
Each share Common no par received first and final distribution of $0.040282 cash payable 12/01/2014 to holders of record 11/28/2014

PGS TR I (DE)
Issue Information - 5,000,000 GTD TR PFD SECS 9.625% offered at $25 per share on 06/15/1999
Plan of Reorganization under Chapter 11 Federal Bankruptcy Code effective 11/5/2003
Each 9.625% Guaranteed Trust Preferred Security will receive an undetermined amount of Petroleum-Geo Services ASA (New) Ordinary shares

PGT INC (DE)
Name changed to PGT Innovations, Inc. 12/28/2016

PH ENVIRONMENTAL INC (FL)
Name changed to TNI BioTech, Inc. 05/14/2012
TNI BioTech, Inc. name changed to Immune Therapeutics, Inc. 12/11/2014

PH GROUP INC (OH)
Common no par split (5) for (4) by issuance of (0.25) additional share payable 01/02/1998 to holders of record 12/15/1997
SEC revoked common stock registration 11/12/2009
Stockholders' equity unlikely

PHAGE GENOMICS INC (NV)
Name changed to Searchlight Minerals Corp. 6/24/2005

PHAGE THERAPEUTICS INTL INC (FL)
Each share old Common $0.001 par exchanged for (0.25) share new Common $0.001 par 03/25/1999
Recapitalized as S S G I, Inc. 02/22/2008
Each shares Common $0.001 par exchanged for (0.02857142) share Common $0.001 par
S S G I, Inc. recapitalized as Vicapsys Life Sciences, Inc. 11/02/2017

PHAMIS INC (WA)
Issue Information - 2,568,000 shares COM offered at $12 per share on 12/16/1994
Merged into IDX Systems Corp. 7/9/97
Each share Common 1¢ par exchanged for (0.73) share Common 1¢ par
(See IDX Systems Corp.)

PHANARE INC (UT)
Merged into Harrison Ross Group, Inc. 3/4/93
Details not available

PHANTOM ENTMT INC (DE)
SEC revoked common stock registration 07/14/2009
Stockholders' equity unlikely

PHANTOM FIBER CORP (DE)
Each share old Common $0.001 par exchanged for (0.05) share new Common $0.001 par 05/05/2005
Recapitalized as Accelerated Technologies Holding Corp. 09/18/2017
Each share new Common $0.001 par exchanged for (0.03448275) share Common $0.001 par

PHANTOM INDUSTRIES LTD. (ON)
Recapitalized as Consolidated Phantom Industries Ltd. 10/21/66
Each share Common no par exchanged for (0.1) share Common no par
Consolidated Phantom Industries Ltd. name changed to In. Mark Corp. Ltd. 7/30/71 which name changed to Gemini Food Corp. 3/30/84
(See Gemini Food Corp.)

PHANTOMFILM COM (NV)
Recapitalized as Komodo, Inc. 10/08/2001
Each share Common $0.001 par exchanged for (0.033333333) new Common $0.001 par
(See Komodo, Inc.)

PHAOSTRON CO. (CA)
Name changed to Phaostron Instrument & Electronic Co. in 1955

PHAR-MOR INC (PA)
Plan of reorganization under Chapter 11 Federal Bankruptcy proceedings effective 09/11/1995
No 144A Common stockholders' equity
Plan of reorganization under Chapter 11 Federal Bankruptcy proceedings effective 03/28/2003
No new Common stockholders' equity

PHARAOH CAP INC (AB)
Acquired by Fairmount Energy Inc. 05/03/2005
Each share Common no par exchanged for (1/7) share Common no par
Fairmount Energy Inc. merged into Delphi Energy Corp. 11/30/2009

PHARAOH MINES LTD. (BC)
Name changed to Tannax Resources Ltd. 11/2/71
Each share Capital Stock 50¢ par exchanged for (1) share Capital Stock 50¢ par

PHARIS TIRE & RUBBER CO.
Liquidation completed in 1951

PHARM CTL LTD (DE)
SEC revoked common stock registration 04/08/2009
Stockholders' equity unlikely

PHARMA INVESTING NEWS INC (NV)
Name changed to Immunoclin Corp. 01/29/2014

PHARMA PATCH PLC (IRELAND)
Reorganized under the laws of Bermuda as Atlantic Central Enerprises Ltd. 03/31/1997
Each Sponsored ADR for Ordinary received (0.1) share Common 1¢ par

PHARMACAL INC (NV)
Each share Common 3¢ par exchanged for (3) shares Common 1¢ par 4/29/74
Name changed to Bonneville Raceway Park, Inc. 6/6/74
Bonneville Raceway Park, Inc. merged into International Teledata II Corp. 3/1/81 which name changed to International Teledata Corp. 6/12/84
(See International Teledata Corp.)

PHARMACAN CAP CORP (ON)
Name changed to Cronos Group Inc. 03/01/2017

PHARMACAPS INC (NJ)
Acquired by Iroquois Brands, Ltd. 6/30/81
Each share Common 10¢ par exchanged for $4 cash

PHARMACARE INC (DE)
Common 25¢ par changed to 1¢ par 2/4/76
Charter cancelled and declared inoperative and void for non-payment of taxes 3/1/80

PHARMACEUTICAL FORMULATIONS INC (DE)
Plan of reorganization under Chapter 11 Federal Bankruptcy proceedings effective 03/07/2006
No stockholders' equity

PHARMACEUTICAL HOLDRS TR (DE)
Trust terminated
Each Depositary Receipt received first and final distribution of $79.712145 cash payable 01/07/2013 to holders of record 12/20/2012

PHARMACEUTICAL LABS INC (NV)
Reorganized under the laws of Delaware as Annapolis Capital Holdings Inc. 07/14/2006
Each share Common $0.001 par exchanged for (0.001) share Common $0.001 par
Annapolis Capital Holdings Inc. name changed to Podium Venture Group, Inc. 08/30/2006 which name changed to Capital Oil & Gas, Inc. 08/07/2008 which recapitalized as Southcorp Capital, Inc. 01/28/2009

PHARMACEUTICAL MARKETING SVCS INC (DE)
Merged into Quintiles Transnational Corp. 3/29/99
Each share Common no par exchanged for (0.397741) share Common 1¢ par
(See Quintiles Transnational Corp.)

PHARMACEUTICAL ORGANICS, INC.
Out of existence 00/00/1950
Details not available

PHARMACEUTICAL PROD DEV INC (NC)
Common 10¢ par split (2) for (1) by issuance of (1) additional share payable 05/11/2001 to holders of record 04/27/2001 Ex date - 05/14/2001
Common 10¢ par changed to 5¢ par and (1) additional share issued payable 02/28/2006 to holders of record 02/17/2006 Ex date - 03/01/2006
Each share Common 5¢ par received distribution of (0.08333333) share Furiex Pharmaceuticals, Inc. Common $0.001 par payable 06/14/2010 to holders of record 06/01/2010
Acquired by Jaguar Holdings, L.L.C. 12/05/2011
Each share Common 5¢ par exchanged for $33.25 cash

PHARMACEUTICAL PRODUCTS CO. (FL)
Proclaimed dissolved for failure to file reports and pay fees 9/17/36

PHARMACEUTICAL RES INC (DE)
Reincorporated 06/24/2003
Each share Class A Conv. Preferred 1¢ par exchanged for (1.1) shares Common 1¢ par 07/31/1995
State of incorporation changed from (NJ) to (DE) 06/24/2003
Name changed to Par Pharmaceutical Companies, Inc. 05/27/2004
(See Par Pharmaceutical Companies, Inc.)

PHARMACEUTICAL SVGS PLAN INC (DE)
Stock Dividends - 10% 11/14/69; 10% 11/16/70
Name changed to PSP Inc. 4/7/71
PSP Inc. merged into Allied Artists Industries, Inc. 1/20/76
(See Allied Artists Industries, Inc.)

PHARMACEUTICAL VENDING CORP. (DE)
Adjudicated bankrupt 07/11/1963
No stockholders' equity

PHARMACEUTICS INTL INC (DE)
Name changed to Norvex, Inc. 07/19/1993
Norvex, Inc. recapitalized as Capital Title Group Inc. 05/23/1996 which merged into LandAmerica Financial Group, Inc. 09/08/2006
(See LandAmerica Financial Group, Inc.)

PHARMACIA & UPJOHN INC (DE)
Merged into Pharmacia Corp. 3/31/2000
Each share Common 1¢ par exchanged for (1.19) shares Common 1¢ par
Pharmacia Corp. merged into Pfizer Inc. 4/16/2003

PHARMACIA AB (SWEDEN)
Each old ADR for Non-Restricted B Shares SKr. 10 par exchanged for (2) new ADR's for Non-Restricted B Shares SKr. 10 par 9/14/83
New ADR's for Non-Restricted B Shares SKr. 10 par split (5) for (3) by issuance of (2/3) additional share 9/14/83
Each new ADR for Non-Restricted B Shares SKr. 10 par exchanged for $33.84 cash 1/13/92
Merged into Pharmacia & Upjohn Inc. 11/2/95
Each Sponsored ADR for Ser. A Skr. 25 par exchanged for (1) share Common 1¢ par
Pharmacia & Upjohn Inc. merged into Pharmacia Corp. 3/31/2000 which merged into Pfizer Inc. 4/16/2003

PHARMACIA CORP (DE)
Each share Common $2 par received distribution of (0.170593) share Monsanto Co. (New) Common 1¢ par payable 8/13/2002 to holders of record 7/29/2002 Ex date - 8/14/2002
Merged into Pfizer Inc. 4/16/2003
Each share Common $2 par exchanged for (1.4) shares Common $5 par

PHARMACITY CORP (NV)
Reorganized as WellTek Inc. (Ctfs. dated after 11/05/2009) 11/05/2009
Each share Common $0.00001 par exchanged for (40) shares Common $0.00001 par

PHARMACO MEDICO SYS CORP (CO)
Reorganized under the laws of Delaware as Myriad Industries Inc. 07/22/1992
Each share Common $0.001 par exchanged for (0.02) share Common $0.001 par
Myriad Industries Inc. name changed to Myriad International, Inc. 12/29/1995
(See Myriad International, Inc.)

PHARMACONNECT INC (NY)
Charter cancelled and proclaimed dissolved for failure to pay taxes 06/26/2002

PHARMACONTROL CORP (DE)
Each share Common 1¢ par exchanged for (0.125) share Common 8¢ par 11/16/90
Name changed to Pharmaceutical Formulations, Inc. 7/27/93
(See Pharmaceutical Formulations, Inc.)

PHARMACOPEIA INC NEW (DE)
Name changed 05/31/2007
Name changed from Pharmacopeia Drug Discovery, Inc. to Pharmacopeia, Inc. (New) 05/31/2007
Merged into Ligand Pharmaceuticals Inc. 12/23/2008
Each share Common 1¢ par exchanged for (0.5985) share Common $0.001 par, (1) Non-Transferable Contingent Value Right and $0.31 cash

PHARMACOPEIA INC OLD (DE)
Each share Common $0.0001 par received distribution of (0.5) share Pharmacopeia Drug Discovery, Inc. Common 1¢ par payable 04/30/2004 to holders of record 04/16/2004
Name changed to Accelrys, Inc. 05/12/2004
(See Accelrys, Inc.)

PHARMACY CHAIN 36.6 PJSC (RUSSIA)
Name changed 04/08/2016
Name changed from Pharmacy Chain 36.6 OAO to Pharmacy Chain 36.6 PJSC 04/08/2016
ADR agreement terminated 08/24/2018
No ADR's remain outstanding

PHARMACY CORP AMER INC (MN)
Merged into Beverly Enterprises (CA) 5/22/86
Each share Common 1¢ par exchanged for (0.1662) share Common 10¢ par
Beverly Enterprises (CA) reorganized in Delaware as Beverly Enterprises, Inc. 7/31/87
(See Beverly Enterprises, Inc.)

PHARMACY MGMT SVCS INC (FL)
Acquired by Beverly Enterprises, Inc. 6/27/95
Each share Common 1¢ par exchanged for (1.3469) shares old Common 10¢ par
(See Beverly Enterprises, Inc.)

PHARMACYCLICS INC (DE)
Merged into AbbVie Inc. 05/26/2015
Each share Common $0.0001 par exchanged for (1.6639) shares Common 1¢ par and $152.25 cash

PHARMAFRONTIERS CORP (TX)
Recapitalized as Opexa Therapeutics, Inc. 06/19/2006
Each share Common 5¢ par exchanged for (0.1) share Common 50¢ par
Opexa Therapeutics, Inc. recapitalized as Acer Therapeutics Inc. (TX) 09/21/2017 which reincorporated in Delaware 05/15/2018

PHARMAGAP INC (CANADA)
Ceased operations 02/04/2013
No stockholders' equity

PHARMAGENERIC INC (ON)
Recapitalized as GemStone X.change Corp. 7/20/2000
Each share Common no par exchanged for (0.05) share Common no par

PHARMAGLOBE INC (DE)
Reincorporated 3/1/2001
Place of incorporation changed from (ONT) to (DE) 3/1/2001
Name changed to Pharmaglobe America Group, Inc. 5/12/2004

PHARMAKINETICS LABS INC (MD)
Each share old Common $0.001 par exchanged for (0.2) share new Common $0.001 par 4/17/98
Merged into Bioanalytical Systems, Inc. 7/1/2003
Each (12) shares new Common $0.001 par exchanged for (1) share Common no par

PHARMANET DEV GROUP INC (DE)
Acquired by JLL PharmaNet Holdings, LLC 03/30/2009
Each share Common $0.001 par exchanged for $5 cash

PHARMANETICS INC (NC)
Voluntarily dissolved 10/31/2008
Details not available

PHARMAPRINT INC (CA)
SEC revoked common stock registration 12/09/2005
Stockholders' equity unlikely

PHARMASCIENCES INC (FL)
Proclaimed dissolved for failure to file reports and pay fees 8/26/91

PHARMASSET INC (DE)
Issue Information - 5,000,000 shares COM offered at $9 per share on 04/26/2007
Common $0.001 par split (2) for (1) by issuance of (1) additional share payable 08/31/2011 to holders of record 08/22/2011 Ex date - 09/01/2011
Acquired by Gilead Sciences, Inc. 01/17/2012
Each share Common $0.001 par exchanged for $137 cash

PHARMATEC INC (NV)
Name changed to Pharmos Corp. 10/29/92

PHARMATHENE INC (DE)
Recapitalized as Altimmune, Inc. 05/05/2017
Each share Common $0.0001 par exchanged for (0.1) share Common $0.0001 par 05/05/2017

PHARMCHEM LABS INC (CA)
Name changed to PharmChem, Inc. 06/14/2000

PHARMED INC (UT)
Name changed to Lunsco, Inc. and Common 50¢ par changed to $1 par 09/26/1984

PHARMENG INTL INC (ON)
Filed a petition under Bankruptcy and Insolvency Act 04/14/2009
No stockholders' equity

PHARMERICA CORP (DE)
Acquired by Phoenix Parent Holdings Inc. 12/07/2017
Each share Common 1¢ par exchanged for $29.25 cash

PHARMERICA INC (DE)
Merged into Bergen Brunswig Corp. 4/26/99
Each share Common 1¢ par exchanged for (0.275) share Class A Common $1.50 par
Bergen Brunswig Corp. merged into AmeriSourceBergen Corp. 8/29/2001

PHARMETICS INC (NY)
Merged into On-Gard Systems, Inc. 10/3/94
Each share Common $0.001 par exchanged for (1/12) share Common $0.001 par
(See On-Gard Systems, Inc.)

PHARMEX INDS INC (BC)
Name changed to PanGeo Pharma Inc. (BC) 08/21/2000
PanGeo Pharma Inc. (BC) reincorporated in Canada 09/21/2000 which recapitalized as Silvio Ventures Inc. 01/09/2006 which name changed to Regency Gold Corp. 07/17/2008

PHARMEXA A S (DENMARK)
Name changed to Affitech A.S. 07/10/2009
(See Affitech A.S.)

PHARMHOUSE CORP (NY)
Merged into Phar-Mor, Inc. 3/15/99
Each share Common 1¢ par exchanged for $2.88 cash

PHARMIATRICS INC (NY)
Name changed to Atlantic Telephone Equipment Co., Inc. 12/28/1973
(See Atlantic Telephone Equipment Co., Inc.)

PHARMION CORP (DE)
Issue Information - 6,000,000 shares COM offered at $14 per share on 11/05/2003
Merged into Celgene Corp. 03/10/2008
Each share Common $0.001 par exchanged for (0.8367) share Common 1¢ par and $25 cash

PHARMSTANDARD PJSC (RUSSIA)
Name changed 10/23/2015
Each Sponsored Reg. S GDR for Ordinary received distribution of $2.582123 cash payable 07/06/2016 to holders of record 03/27/2014
Each 144A Sponsored GDR for Ordinary received distribution of $2.582123 cash payable 07/06/2016 to holders of record 03/27/2014
Name changed from Pharmstandard to PJSC Pharmstandard 10/23/2015
ADR agreement terminated 12/22/2016
Each Sponsored Reg. S GDR for Ordinary exchanged for $4.143025 cash
Each 144A Sponsored GDR for Ordinary exchanged for $4.143025 cash

PHARMSTAR PHARMACEUTICALS INC (DE)
Reorganized under the laws of Nevada as Nexus Energy Services, Inc. 10/15/2013
Each share Common $0.025 par exchanged for (0.001) share Common $0.001 par
Note: No holder will receive fewer than (100) post-split shares
Nexus Energy Services, Inc. name changed to Illegal Restaurant Group, Inc. 06/02/2015 which name changed back to Nexus Energy Services, Inc. 08/13/2015

PHAROAH ENTERPRISES INC (NV)
Name changed to Hybrit International Inc. 06/02/1987
Hybrit International Inc. recapitalized as First Fitness Inc. 03/21/1991

PHARSIGHT CORP (DE)
Each share old Common $0.001 par exchanged for (1/3) share new Common $0.001 par 11/14/2007
Merged into Tripos (DE), Inc. 11/03/2008
Each share Common $0.001 par exchanged for $5.50 cash

PHASE FORWARD INC (DE)
Issue Information - 5,250,000 shares COM offered at $7.50 per share on 07/14/2004
Merged into Oracle Corp. 08/11/2010
Each share Common 1¢ par exchanged for $17 cash

PHASE-OUT AMER INC (DE)
Name changed to Quest Products Corp. 09/24/1997
Quest Products Corp. name changed to Quest Patent Research Corp. 03/01/2016

PHASE III MED INC (DE)
Each share $0.07 Preferred Ser. A 10¢ par exchanged for (8) shares Common $0.001 par 04/07/2006
Recapitalized as NeoStem, Inc. 08/31/2006
Each share Common $0.001 par exchanged for (0.1) share Common $0.001 par
NeoStem, Inc. name changed to Caladrius Biosciences, Inc. 06/08/2015

PHASER ENTERPRISES INC (UT)
Each share old Common $0.001 par exchanged for (0.05) share new Common $0.001 par 5/23/96
Merged into Webquest Inc. 4/28/97
Each share new Common $0.001 par exchanged for $27.50 cash

PHASER SYS INC (CA)
Reorganized under Chapter 11 Federal Bankruptcy Code as P-Corp. 04/04/1989
Each share Common 1¢ par exchanged for (0.04173622) share Common 1¢ par

PHASERTEK MED INC (NV)
Reincorporated under the laws of Delaware as Union Equity, Inc. and Common $0.001 changed to $0.0000001 par 11/23/2004
Union Equity, Inc. recapitalized as Kona Gold Solutions, Inc. 08/13/2015

PHASERX INC (DE)
Chapter 11 bankruptcy proceedings dismissed 03/23/2018
No stockholders' equity

PHAZAR CORP (TX)
Acquired by QAR Industries, Inc. 07/31/2013
Each share Common $2 par exchanged for $1.25 cash

PHC HLDGS (NV)
Recapitalized as Rudy 45 on 09/26/2005
Each (1,450) shares Common $0.001 par exchanged for (1) share Common $0.001 par
Rudy 45 name changed to NMI Group, Inc. 07/13/2007

PHC INC (MA)
Secondary Offering - 1,250,000 UNITS consisting of (1) share COM and (1) WT offered at $5 per Unit on 03/03/1994
Merged into Acadia Healthcare Co., Inc. 11/01/2011
Each share Class A Common 1¢ par exchanged for (0.25) share Common 1¢ par

PHC INC (MN)
SEC revoked common stock registration 11/12/2009
Stockholders' equity unlikely

PHD SKIN RESH LABS LTD (DE)
Recapitalized as Medipak Corp. 10/15/1990
Each share Common $0.001 par exchanged for (0.08333333) share Common $0.001 par
Medipak Corp. recapitalized as Advanced Laser Products Inc. 02/10/1995 which recapitalized as Digs Inc. 10/16/1998 which name changed to iVideoNow, Inc. (DE) 06/15/2000 which reorganized in Florida as 99 Cent Stuff, Inc. 09/15/2003
(See 99 Cent Stuff, Inc.)

PHEASANTBACK RES INC (AB)
Name changed to Multi-Glass International Inc. 08/31/1999
Multi-Glass International Inc. recapitalized as Multi-Glass International Corp. 10/28/2002
(See Multi-Glass International Corp.)

PHELAN SULPHUR CO (TX)
Name changed to International Shelters, Inc. 05/26/1970
(See International Shelters, Inc.)

PHELPS DODGE CORP (NY)
Each share Capital Stock $100 par exchanged for (4) shares Capital Stock $25 par 00/00/1929
Each share Capital Stock $25 par exchanged for (2) shares Capital Stock $12.50 par 00/00/1952
Capital Stock $12.50 par changed to $6.25 par and (1) additional share issued 11/14/1968
$5 Conv. Exchangeable Preference $1 par called for redemption 05/01/1987
Depositary Shares called for redemption 04/01/1989
$12 Conv. Exchangeable Preference $1 par called for redemption 04/01/1989
Common Stock Purchase Rights declared for Common stockholders of record 08/08/1988 were redeemed at $0.005 per right 03/10/1998 for holders of record 02/24/1998
Each share 6.75% Mandatory Conv. Preferred Ser. A exchanged for (2.083) shares Common $6.25 par 08/15/2005
Common $6.25 par split (2) for (1) by issuance of (1) additional share 06/08/1992
Common $6.25 par split (2) for (1) by issuance of (1) additional share payable 03/10/2006 to holders of record 02/17/2006 Ex date - 03/13/2006
Merged into Freeport-McMoRan Copper & Gold Inc. 03/19/2007
Each share Common $6.25 par exchanged for (0.67) share Common 10¢ par and $88 cash
Freeport-McMoRan Copper & Gold Inc. name changed to Freeport-McMoRan Inc. 07/14/2014

PHELPS ENGINEERED PLASTICS CORP (NV)
Name changed to Clayton, Dunning Group Inc. 07/29/2005
Clayton, Dunning Group Inc. recapitalized as Carlton Companies, Inc. 07/09/2008

PHELPS GOLD MINES, LTD. (ON)
Charter cancelled for failure to file reports and pay taxes in 1957

PHELPS PUBLISHING CO.
Liquidated in 1952

PHENIX CHEESE CO.
Acquired by Kraft-Phenix Cheese Co. which was reorganized as Kraft-Phenix Cheese Corp. in 1928 which was acquired by National Dairy Products Corp. in 1930

PHEOLL MANUFACTURING CO. (IL)
Name changed to Voi-Shan Industries, Inc. 4/17/59
Voi-Shan Industries, Inc. name changed to VSI Corp. (Ill.) 10/22/62 which was reincorporated under the laws of Delaware 11/1/67
(See VSI Corp. (Del.))

PHEROMONE SCIENCES CORP (CANADA)
Reincorporated 5/29/2001
Place of incorporation changed from (BC) to (Canada) 5/29/2006
Name changed to Sernova Corp. 9/20/2006

PHH CORP (MD)
Name changed 08/24/1988
Old Common no par split (2) for (1) by issuance of (1) additional share 07/31/1981
Name changed from PHH Group, Inc. to PHH Corp. 08/24/1988
Old Common no par split (2) for (1) by issuance of (1) additional share payable 07/31/1996 to holders of record 07/05/1996 Ex date - 08/01/1996
Merged into HFS Inc. 04/30/1997
Each share old Common no par exchanged for (0.825) share Common 1¢ par
HFS Inc. merged into Cendant Corp. 12/17/1997 which reorganized as Avis Budget Group, Inc. 09/01/2006
Acquired by Ocwen Financial Corp. 10/04/2018
Each share new Common 1¢ par exchanged for $11 cash

PHI ENTERPRISES INC (CA)
Charter suspended for failure to pay franchise taxes 03/02/1992

PHI GOLD CORP (NV)
Name changed 01/28/2011
Name changed from PHI Mining Group, Inc. to PHI Gold Corp. 01/28/2011
SEC revoked common stock registration 02/22/2012

PHIBRO CORP. (DE)
Name changed to Phibro-Salomon Inc. 5/20/82
Philbro-Salomon Inc. name changed to Salomon Inc. 5/7/86 which merged into Travelers Group Inc. 11/28/97 which name changed to Citigroup Inc. 10/8/98

PHIBRO SALOMON INC (DE)
Common $1 par split (2) for (1) by issuance of (1) additional share 6/30/83
Name changed to Salomon Inc. 5/7/86
Salomon Inc. merged into Travelers Group Inc. 11/28/97 which name changed to Citigroup Inc. 10/8/98

PHILADELPHIA, GERMANTOWN & NORRISTOWN RAILROAD CO. LIQUIDATING TRUST (PA)
In process of liquidation
Details on subsequent distributions, if any are not available
(See Philadelphia Germantown & Norristown Railroad Co. for previous distributions)

PHILADELPHIA, NEWTOWN & NEW YORK RAILROAD CO.
Merged into Reading Co. 12/31/45
Each share Preferred or Common $50 par exchanged for (0.04) share Common $50 par
Reading Co. merged into Reading Entertainment Inc. (DE) 10/15/96 which reincorporated in Nevada 12/29/99 which merged into Reading International, Inc. 12/31/2001

PHILADELPHIA & CHESTER VALLEY RAILROAD CO.
Merged into Reading Co. 12/31/45
Each share Preferred or Common $50 par exchanged for (0.32) share Common $50 par
Reading Co. merged into Reading Entertainment Inc. (DE) 10/15/96 which reincorporated in Nevada 12/29/99 which merged into Reading International, Inc. 12/31/2001

PHILADELPHIA & DARBY RAILWAY CO.
Acquired by Philadelphia Transportation Co. in 1940
Each share Common exchanged for $11.96 principal amount of 3%-6% Consolidated Mortgage Bonds and (0.1) share $1 Part. Preferred $20 par
Philadelphia Transportation Co. completed liquidation 11/20/73

PHILADELPHIA & GRAYS FERRY PASSENGER RAILWAY CO.
Acquired by Philadelphia Transportation Co. in 1940
Each share Common exchanged for $28.82 principal amount of 3%-6% Consolidated Mortgage Bonds and (0.241) share $1 Part. Preferred $20 par
Philadelphia Transportation Co. completed liquidation 11/20/73

PHILADELPHIA & READING COAL & IRON CO. (PA)
Reorganized 1/1/45
No stockholders' equity
Only bondholders participated under plan of reorganization

PHILADELPHIA & READING COAL & IRON CORP. (DE)
No longer in existence having become inoperative and void for non-payment of taxes 5/1/41

PHILADELPHIA & READING CORP (DE)
Reincorporated 07/01/1960
Reincorporated 10/27/1982
Common $1 par changed to 50¢ par and (1) additional share issued 05/28/1959
State of incorporation changed from (PA) to (NY) 07/01/1960
5% Class A Preferred $100 par reclassified as 6% Class A Preferred $100 par 06/10/1968
Under plan of merger each share Common 50¢ par exchanged for $250.24 cash 08/20/1980
State of incorporation changed from (NY) to (DE) 10/27/1982
6% Class A Preferred $100 par called for redemption 07/19/1985
Public interest eliminated

PHILADELPHIA & TRENTON RR CO (PA)
Merged into Penn Central Corp. 10/24/78
Each share Capital Stock $100 par exchanged for (2.63) shares Conv. Preference Ser. B $20 par, (1.18) shares Common $1 par, $28.16 principal amount of 7% General Mortgage Bonds Ser. A due 12/31/87, $24.34 principal amount of 7% General Mortgage Bonds Ser. B due 12/31/87 and $18.50 cash
Note: a) Distribution is certain only for certificates surrendered prior to 5/1/85 b) Distribution may also be made for certificates surrendered between 5/1/85 and 12/31/86 c) No distribution will be made for certificates surrendered after 12/31/86
Penn Central Corp. name changed to American Premier Underwriters, Inc. 3/25/94 which merged into American Premier Group, Inc. 4/3/95 which name changed to American Financial Group, Inc. 6/9/95 which merged into American Financial Group, Inc. (Holding Co.) 12/2/97

PHILADELPHIA & WESTERN RAILROAD CO. (PA)
Merged into Philadelphia & Western Street Railway Co. in 1952
Each share Capital Stock no par exchanged for (1) share Common no par
Philadelphia & Western Street Railway Co. merged into Philadelphia Suburban Transportation Co. in 1953 which name changed to Bryn Mawr Group, Inc. 5/15/70 which name changed to Bryn Mawr Camp Resorts, Inc. 5/10/73 which name changed to Bryn Mawr Corp. 10/31/79 which name changed to Dixon Ticonderoga Co. 9/21/83

PHILADELPHIA & WESTERN RAILWAY CO.
Reorganized as Philadelphia & Western Railroad Co. in 1946
No stockholders' equity

PHILADELPHIA & WESTERN STREET RAILWAY CO. (PA)
Merged into Philadelphia Suburban Transportation Co. in 1953
Each share Common no par exchanged for (4) shares Common $5 par
Philadelphia Suburban Transportation Co. name changed to Bryn Mawr Group, Inc. 5/15/70 which name changed to Bryn Mawr Camp Resorts, Inc. 5/10/73 which reincorporated in Delaware as Bryn Mawr Corp. 10/31/79 which name changed to Dixon Ticonderoga Co. 9/21/83

PHILADELPHIA ACCEPTANCE CORP.
Bankrupt in 1950

PHILADELPHIA AIR TERMINAL, INC.
Out of business 00/00/1929
Details not available

PHILADELPHIA AQUARIUM INC (PA)
Completely liquidated 8/9/71
Each share Capital Stock 50¢ par exchanged for $0.15 cash
Note: last date to surrender certificates was 11/1/71 after which certificates became worthless

PHILADELPHIA BOURSE INC (PA)
Common $50 par reclassified as Preference $1 par 01/01/1970
Preference $1 par called for redemption 6/30/72
Public interest eliminated

PHILADELPHIA CITY PASSENGER RAILWAY CO.
Acquired by Philadelphia Transportation Co. in 1940
Each share Common exchanged for $54.03 principal amount of 3%-6% Consolidated Mortgage Bonds and (0.452) share $1 Part. Preferred $20 par
Philadelphia Transportation Co. completed liquidation 11/20/73

PHILADELPHIA CO. (PA)
Recapitalized 00/00/1930
Each share 5% Preferred $50 par exchanged for (5) shares 5% Preferred $10 par
Each share Common $50 par exchanged for (5) shares Common no par
Under plan of liquidation 00/00/1952
Each share 5% Preferred $10 par received $12 in cash plus accrued dividends
Each share 6% Preferred $50 par received (1) share Duquesne Light Co. 4% Preferred $50 par and $13 in cash plus accrued dividends
Under plan of liquidation 00/00/1953
Each share $5 Preference no par received (3.6) shares Duquesne Light Co. Common $10 par
Each share Common no par received (177/200) share Duquesne Light Co. Common $10 par

PHILADELPHIA CONS HLDG CORP (PA)
Common no par split (2) for (1) by issuance of (1) additional share payable 11/05/1997 to holders of record 10/27/1997
Issue Information - 8,000,000 INCOME PRIDES and 1,000,000 GROWTH PRIDES offered at $10 per INCOME PRIDES and $8.501 per GROWTH PRIDES on 04/28/1998
Each Growth Preferred Redeemable Increased Dividend Equity Security received (0.3858) share Common 1¢ par 05/16/2001
Each Income Preferred Redeemable Increased Dividend Equity Security received (0.3858) share Common 1¢ par 05/16/2001
Common no par split (3) for (1) by issuance of (2) additional shares payable 03/01/2006 to holders of record 02/20/2006 Ex date - 03/02/2006
Acquired by Tokio Marine Holdings, Inc. 12/01/2008
Each share Common no par exchanged for $61.50 cash

PHILADELPHIA DAIRY PRODUCTS CO., INC. (PA)
Common no par changed to 25¢ par 00/00/1939
$6 Preferred called for redemption 01/01/1945
$4.50 Preferred called for redemption 10/01/1955
Stock Dividend - 25% 01/02/1947
Merged into Foremost Dairies, Inc. (NY) 06/30/1956
Each share Common 25¢ par exchanged for (5) shares Common $2 par plus $1.25 cash $4 2nd Preferred called for redemption 07/01/1956
Foremost Dairies, Inc. (NY) merged into Foremost-McKesson, Inc. 07/19/1967 which name changed to McKesson Corp. (MD) 07/27/1983 which reincorporated in Delaware 07/31/1987
(See McKesson Corp. (Old) (DE))

PHILADELPHIA EAGLES, INC. (NY)
Liquidation completed
Each VTC unit for (2) shares Common no par exchanged for initial distribution of $58,000 cash 2/3/64
Each VTC unit for (2) shares Common no par received second and final distribution of $2,550 cash 2/10/65

PHILADELPHIA ELEC CO (PA)
Each share old Common no par exchanged for (0.225) share $1 Div. Preference Common no par and (0.775) share new Common no par 00/00/1943
$1 Div. Preference Common no par reclassified as new Common no par 04/25/1961
New Common no par split (2) for (1) by issuance of (1) additional share 05/10/1961
17.125% Preferred $100 par called for redemption 05/01/1987
12.80% Depositary Preferred called for redemption 12/21/1990
13.35% Depositary Preferred called for redemption 12/21/1990
13.35% Preferred no par called for redemption 12/21/1990
14.15% Depositary Preferred called for redemption 12/21/1990
3.8% Preferred $100 par reclassified as $3.80 Preferred no par 10/15/1991
4.3% Preferred $100 par reclassified as $4.30 Preferred no par 10/15/1991
4.4% Preferred $100 par reclassified as $4.40 Preferred no par 10/15/1991
4.68% Preferred $100 par reclassified as $4.68 Preferred no par 10/15/1991
7% Preferred $100 par reclassified as $7 Preferred no par 10/15/1991
7.75% Preferred $100 par reclassified as $7.75 Preferred no par 10/15/1991
7.80% Preferred $100 par reclassified as $7.80 Preferred no par 10/15/1991
7.85% Preferred $100 par reclassified as $7.85 Preferred no par 10/15/1991
8.75% Preferred $100 par reclassified as $8.75 Preferred no par 10/15/1991
9.50% Preferred $100 par reclassified as $9.50 Preferred no par 10/15/1991
9.50% Preferred 1986 Ser. $100 par reclassified as $9.50 Preferred 1986 Ser. no par 10/15/1991
9.52% Preferred $100 par reclassified as $9.52 Preferred no par 10/15/1991
9.875% Preferred $100 par reclassified as $9.875 Preferred no par 10/15/1991
14.625% Preferred $100 par reclassified as $14.625 Preferred no par 10/15/1991
15.25% Preferred $100 par reclassified as $15.25 Preferred no par 10/15/1991
$14.625 Preferred no par called for redemption 07/01/1992
$15.25 Preferred no par called for redemption 12/01/1992
$9.50 Preferred no par called for redemption 12/01/1992
$8.75 Preferred no par called for redemption 08/01/1993
$9.52 Preferred no par called for redemption 08/01/1993
$9.50 Preferred 1986 Ser. no par called for redemption 11/01/1993
Name changed to PECO Energy Co. 01/01/1994

PHILADELPHIA FD INC (MD)
Reincorporated 11/30/1984
Common $1 par split (2) for (1) by issuance of (1) additional share 09/26/1972
Stock Dividends - 100% 12/30/1953; 100% 04/30/1957
State of incorporation changed from (DE) to (MD) 11/30/1984
Merged into Advisors' Inner Circle Fund 11/13/2009
Each share Common $1 par exchanged for (0.56863187) WHG LargeCap Value Fund Institutional Share

PHILADELPHIA GERMANTOWN & NORRISTOWN RR CO (PA)
In process of liquidation
Each share Capital Stock $50 par received initial distribution of $91 cash 2/26/82
Each share Capital Stock $50 par exchanged for second distribution of (1) Non-Transferable Unit of Bene. Int. of Philadelphia, Germantown & Norristown Railroad Co. Liquidating Trust plus $27 cash 9/17/82
Note: Details on subsequent distributions, if any, are not available
(See Philadelphia, Germantown & Norristown Railroad Co. Liquidating Trust)

PHILADELPHIA GRAIN ELEVATOR CO.
Dissolved in 1944

PHILADELPHIA LABORATORIES, INC. (PA)
Merged into Philadelphia Pharmaceuticals & Cosmetics, Inc. 12/5/67
Each share Common no par exchanged for (1) share Common 1¢ par
Philadelphia Pharmaceuticals & Cosmetics, Inc. name changed to PP & C Companies, Inc. 4/17/69 which merged into Keystone Centers, Inc. 4/18/75
(See Keystone Centers, Inc.)

PHILADELPHIA LIFE INS CO (PA)
Capital Stock $10 par changed to $5 par and (1) additional share issued 3/15/57
Capital Stock $5 par changed to $2 par and (1.5) additional shares issued 10/5/64
Capital Stock $2 par changed to $1 par 8/24/67
Stock Dividends - 15% 3/10/55; 20% 3/15/56; 25% 3/15/57; 20% 3/10/58; 20% 3/9/59; 20% 3/18/60; 10% 3/21/61; 10% 3/28/62; 10% 3/29/63; 20% 3/25/64; 10% 3/25/65; 10% 3/31/66; 10% 3/31/67; 10% 6/3/77
Merged into Tenneco Inc. 3/1/78
Each share Capital Stock $1 par exchanged for (0.25) share $7.40 Preference no par
Tenneco Inc. merged into El Paso Natural Gas Co. 12/12/96 which reorganized as El Paso Energy Corp. 8/1/98 which name changed to El Paso Corp. 2/5/2001

PHILADELPHIA MTG CORP (NV)
Reincorporated 6/11/2001
Shares of Bene. Int. no par reclassified as Common no par 12/22/99
Reincorporated from Philadelphia Mortgage Trust (MA) to Philadelphia Mortgage Corp. (NV) and Common no par changed to $0.001 par 6/11/2001
Each share old Common no par exchanged for (1/3) share new Common no par 8/2/2004
Name changed to Thunderball Entertainment, Inc. 6/22/2005
Thunderball Entertainment, Inc. name changed to Ready Credit Corp. 8/26/2005

PHILADELPHIA NATL BK (PHILADELPHIA, PA)
Capital Stock $20 par changed to $10 par and (2) additional shares issued 02/01/1957
Reorganized as PNB Corp. 11/01/1969
Each share Capital Stock $10 par exchanged for (1) share Common $1 par
PNB Corp. name changed to Philadelphia National Corp. 04/23/1973 which merged into CoreStates Financial Corp 05/02/1983 which merged into First Union Corp. 04/28/1998 which name changed to Wachovia Corp. (Ctfs. dated after 09/01/2001) 09/01/2001 which merged into Wells Fargo & Co. (New) 12/31/2008

PHILADELPHIA NATL CORP (PA)
Merged into CoreStates Financial Corp 05/02/1983
Each share Common $1 par exchanged for (1) share Common $1 par
CoreStates Financial Corp merged into First Union Corp. 04/28/1998 which name changed to Wachovia Corp. (Ctfs. dated after 09/01/2001) 09/01/2001 which merged into Wells Fargo & Co. (New) 12/31/2008

PHILADELPHIA NATIONAL INSURANCE CO.
Merged into Fire Association of Philadelphia on a (0.353) for (1) basis in 1950
Fire Association of Philadelphia name was changed to Reliance Insurance Co. 1/1/58
(See Reliance Insurance Co.)

PHILADELPHIA PARK AMUSEMENT CO. (DE)
Liquidation completed 4/27/59
Details not available

PHILADELPHIA PHARMACEUTICALS & COSMETICS INC (PA)
Name changed to PP & C Companies, Inc. 04/17/1969
PP & C Companies, Inc. merged into Keystone Centers, Inc. 04/18/1975
(See Keystone Centers, Inc.)

PHILADELPHIA RAILWAYS CO.
Property sold 00/00/1932
Details not available

PHILADELPHIA RAPID TRANSIT CO.
Reorganized as Philadelphia Transportation Co. in 1940
Each share Preferred exchanged for (0.5) share $1 Part. Preferred $20 par, (0.5) share Common no par and $1 cash
Each share Common exchanged for (1) share Common no par

Philadelphia Transportation Co. completed liquidation 11/20/73

PHILADELPHIA REALTY INVESTMENT CO.
Merged into 1528 Walnut Street Building Corp. (New) in 1948
Each share Common $1 par exchanged for (4.568) shares Common no par
1528 Walnut Street Building Corp. (New) was dissolved in 1950

PHILADELPHIA RECORD CO.
Name changed to W C A U, Inc. in 1948

PHILADELPHIA STORAGE BATTERY CO.
Name changed to Philco Corp. 00/00/1940
Philco Corp. acquired by Ford Motor Co. 12/11/1961

PHILADELPHIA SUBN CORP (PA)
Common $1 par split (2) for (1) by issuance of (1) additional share 06/01/1975
$4.20 Prior Preferred $1 par called for redemption 06/01/1981
$4.55 Prior Preferred $1 par called for redemption 06/01/1981
$5.70 Prior Preferred $1 par called for redemption 06/01/1981
$5.75 Prior Preferred $1 par called for redemption 06/01/1981
Each share Common $1 par exchanged for (0.5) share Common 50¢ par 07/01/1981
Common 50¢ par split (3) for (2) by issuance of (0.5) additional share 09/01/1986
Common 50¢ par split (3) for (2) by issuance of (0.5) additional share payable 07/10/1996 to holders of record 06/18/1996 Ex date - 07/11/1996
Common 50¢ par split (4) for (3) by issuance of (0.33333333) additional share payable 01/28/1998 to holders of record 12/15/1997 Ex date - 01/13/1998
Common 50¢ par split (5) for (4) by issuance of (0.25) additional share payable 12/01/2000 to holders of record 11/15/2000 Ex date - 12/04/2000
Common 50¢ par split (5) for (4) by issuance of (0.25) additional share payable 11/30/2001 to holders of record 11/16/2001 Ex date - 12/03/2001
Common 50¢ par split (5) for (4) by issuance of (0.25) additional share payable 12/01/2003 to holders of record 11/14/2003 Ex date - 12/02/2003
Name changed to Aqua America, Inc. 01/16/2004

PHILADELPHIA SUBN TRANSN CO (PA)
Each share Common no par exchanged for (4) shares Common $10 par 00/00/1945
Under plan of merger each share Common $10 par exchanged for (2) shares Common $5 par 00/00/1963
Common $5 par changed to $2.50 par and (1) additional share issued 05/23/1957
Common $2.50 par changed to $1 par and (1.5) additional shares issued 02/05/1964
Name changed to Bryn Mawr Group, Inc. 05/15/1970
Bryn Mawr Group, Inc. name changed to Bryn Mawr Camp Resorts, Inc. (PA) 05/10/1973 which reincorporated in Delaware as Bryn Mawr Corp. 10/31/1979 which name changed to Dixon Ticonderoga Co. 09/21/1983
(See Dixon Ticonderoga Co.)

PHILADELPHIA SUBN WTR CO (PA)
Each share Common no par exchanged for (2) shares Common $7.50 par in 1954
Common $7.50 par changed to $3.75 par and (1) additional share issued 5/24/61
Common $3.75 par split (5) for (4) by issuance of (0.25) additional share 3/1/65
Reorganized as Philadelphia Suburban Corp. 5/1/69
Each share 5% Preferred $100 par exchanged for (1) share $5.75 Prior Preferred $1 par
Each share 4.95% Preferred $100 par exchanged for (1) share $5.70 Prior Preferred $1 par
Each share $3.95 Preferred $100 par exchanged for (1) share $4.55 Prior Preferred $1 par
Each share $3.65 Preferred $100 par exchanged for (1) share $4.20 Prior Preferred $1 par
Each share Common $3.75 par exchanged for (1) share Common $1 par
Philadelphia Suburban Corp. name changed to Aqua America, Inc. 1/16/2004

PHILADELPHIA SUBURBAN-COUNTIES GAS & ELECTRIC CO.
Merged into Philadelphia Electric Co. 00/00/1929
Details not available

PHILADELPHIA SVG FD SOC (PHILADELPHIA, PA)
Name changed to Meritor Savings Bank (Philadelphia, PA) 6/2/86

PHILADELPHIA TERMS AUCTION CO (NJ)
Each share Common $100 par exchanged for (4) shares Common $25 par 00/00/1946
Stock Dividend - 33-1/3% 04/01/1951
Dissolved 11/30/1964
Details not available

PHILADELPHIA TITLE INS CO (PA)
Each share Common $100 par exchanged for (5) shares Common $20 par 07/00/1956
Merged into Industrial Valley Bank & Trust Co. (Jenkintown, PA) 12/31/1973
Each share Common $20 par exchanged for (1.754) shares Common $5 par
Industrial Valley Bank & Trust Co. (Jenkintown, PA) reorganized as IVB Financial Corp. 01/01/1984
(See IVB Financial Corp.)

PHILADELPHIA TRACTION CO.
Acquired by Philadelphia Transportation Co. in 1940
Each share Common exchanged for $16.82 principal amount of 3%-6% Consolidated Mortgage Bonds and (0.415) share $1 Part. Preferred $20 par
Philadelphia Transportation Co. completed liquidation 11/20/73

PHILADELPHIA TRANSN CO (PA)
Common no par changed to $10 par 00/00/1951
Each share $1 Part. Preferred $20 par exchanged for (1.33333333) shares Common $10 par 11/14/1955
Liquidation completed
Each share Common $10 par received initial distribution of $14 cash 11/01/1968
Corporate existence was terminated and each share Common $10 par was reclassified as Ctfs. of Bene. Int. no par 12/31/1969
Each Ctf. of Bene. Int. no par received initial distribution of $2.25 cash 01/19/1972
Each Ctf. of Bene. Int. no par received second and final distribution of $0.835 cash 11/20/1973
Note: Certificates were not required to be surrendered and are without value

PHILADELPHIA WAREHOUSE CO.
Dissolved in 1928

PHILADELPHIA-WARWICK CO. (PA)
Name changed to Kirkeby Hotels, Inc. in 1953
Kirkeby Hotels, Inc. name changed to Kirkeby Corp. in 1957 which merged into Natus Co. 5/26/61 which name changed to Kirkeby-Natus Corp. 6/30/61 which name changed to United Ventures, Inc. 6/24/66 which merged into Federated Development Co. 7/31/70
(See Federated Development Co.)

PHILBRICK (GEORGE A.) RESEARCHES, INC. (MA)
Completely liquidated 03/13/1967
Each share Common $1 par exchanged for first and final distribution of (0.072) share Teledyne, Inc. $3.50 Conv. Preferred $1 par and (0.056) share Common $1 par
(See Teledyne, Inc.)

PHILCO CORP. (PA)
Acquired by Ford Motor Co. 12/11/1961
Each share 3.75% Preferred $100 par exchanged for (0.8773636) share Common $5 par and $0.75 in cash
Each share Common $3 par exchanged for (0.22222222) share Common $5 par

PHILCO RES LTD (BC)
Stock Dividend - 10% 03/11/1977
Struck off register and declared dissolved for failure to file returns 08/28/1992

PHILEO MGMT INC (NV)
Name changed to NewCom International Inc. 4/28/2000
NewCom International Inc. name changed to Skogan Foods, Inc. 10/28/2003 which name changed to Sino Express Travel, Ltd. 11/1/2005

PHILEX GOLD INC (CANADA)
Acquired by Philex Mining Corp. 04/27/2010
Each share Common no par exchanged for USD $0.75 cash

PHILIP A. HUNT CHEMICAL CORP. (DE)
See - Hunt (Philip A.) Chemical Corp.

PHILIP BLUM & CO., INC.
See - Blum (Philip) & Co., Inc.

PHILIP CROSBY ASSOCIATES, INC. (FL)
See - Crosby (Philip) Associates, Inc.

PHILIP ENVIRONMENTAL INC (ON)
Name changed to Philip Services Corp. (ON) 05/22/1997
Philip Services Corp. (ON) reorganized in Delaware as Philip Services Corporation 04/07/2000
(See Philip Services Corporation)

PHILIP ENVIRONMENTAL SVCS CORP (BC)
Recapitalized as Devco Enterprises Inc. 05/17/1993
Each share Common no par exchanged for (0.5) share Common no par
Devco Enterprises Inc. recapitalized as SBI Skin Biology Inc. (BC) 11/03/1995 which reincorporated in Yukon 08/22/1996 which reorganized in British Columbia as Realm Energy International Corp. 10/26/2009 which merged into San Leon Energy PLC 11/10/2011

PHILIP MORRIS AUSTRALIA LTD (AUSTRALIA)
Stock Dividend - 33-1/3% 02/26/1976
ADR agreement terminated 03/12/1986
Details not available

PHILIP MORRIS CONSOLIDATED, INC.
See - Morris (Philip) Consolidated, Inc.

PHILIP MORRIS COS INC (VA)
Common $1 par split (2) for (1) by issuance of (1) additional share 04/10/1986
Common $1 par split (4) for (1) by issuance of (3) additional share 10/10/1989
Preferred Stock Purchase Rights declared for Common stockholders of record 11/08/1989 were redeemed at $0.01 per right 04/10/1995 for holders of record 03/15/1995
Common $1 par split (3) for (1) by issuance of (2) additional shares payable 04/10/1997 to holders of record 03/17/1997 Ex date - 04/11/1997
Name changed to Altria Group, Inc. 01/27/2003

PHILIP MORRIS INC (VA)
Name changed 6/1/55
Each share Common $10 par exchanged for (2) shares Common $5 par in 1945
Name changed from Philip Morris & Co. Ltd., Inc. to Philip Morris, Inc. 6/1/55
Common $5 par changed to $2 par and (2) additional shares issued 5/18/66
Common $2 par changed to $1 par and (1) additional share issued 5/21/69
Common $1 par split (2) for (1) by issuance of (1) additional share 5/31/74
3.90% Preferred $100 par called for redemption 4/11/79
4% Preferred $100 par called for redemption 4/11/79
Common no par split (2) for (1) by issuance of (1) additional share 5/31/79
Under plan of reorganization each share Common $1 par automatically became (1) share Morris (Philip) Companies Inc. Common $1 par 7/1/85
Morris (Philip) Companies Inc. name changed to Altria Group, Inc. 1/27/2003

PHILIP SVCS CORP (DE)
Plan of reorganization under Chapter 11 Federal Bankruptcy Code effective 12/31/2001
No stockholders' equity

PHILIP SVCS CORP (ON)
Reorganized under the laws of Delaware as Phillip Services Corporation 04/07/2000
Each share Common no par received (0.003663) share Common 1¢ par
Note: Certificates were not required to be surrendered and are without value
(See Phillip Services Corporation)

PHILIPPINE AIR LINES, INC. (PHILIPPINES)
Capital Stock PHP 10 par exchanged (10) for (1) 00/00/1947
Each (125) shares Capital Stock PHP 10 par exchanged for (80) shares Capital Stock PHP 10 par and $4.6036 distributed for each cancelled share 00/00/1954
Stock Dividend - 100% 11/08/1962
Acquired by PR Holdings 01/00/1992
Details not available

PHILIPPINE IRON MINES INC (PHILIPPINES)
Each share Common £1 par exchanged for (10) shares Common £0.10 par 10/21/1955
Each share Common £0.10 par held by Philippine Nationals exchanged

for (1) share Class A £0.10 par 04/05/1972
Each share Common £0.10 par held by Non-Philippine Nationals exchanged for (1) share Class B £0.10 par 04/05/1972
Each share Class A £0.10 par exchanged for (100) shares Class A £0.01 par 02/11/1973
Each share Class B £0.10 par exchanged for (100) shares Class B £0.01 par 02/11/1973 Declared insolvent 04/08/1976
No stockholders' equity

PHILIPPINE LONG DISTANCE TEL CO (PHILIPPINES)
Each share Common Capital Stock PHP100 par exchanged for (15) shares Common Capital Stock PHP10 par to effect a (10) for (1) split and a 50% stock dividend 00/00/1953
Old 8% Conv. Preferred P20 par called for redemption 12/29/1965
New 8% Conv. Preferred P20 called for redemption 01/31/1978
Common Capital Stock PHP10 par changed to PHP5 par and (1) additional share issued 10/20/1987
Each share Common Capital Stock PHP5 par exchanged for (1) Sponsored ADR for Common 10/19/1994
Sponsored ADR's for Ordinary split (2) for (1) by issuance of (1) additional ADR payable 07/11/1997 to holders of record 05/15/1997 Ex date - 07/14/1997
Each Global Depositary Conv. Preferred Ser. II exchanged for (1.1527) Sponsored ADR's for Common 10/27/1997
Each Sponsored GDR for Preferred Ser. III exchanged for (1.7129) Sponsored ADR for Common 12/28/2005
Stock Dividends - 10% 08/20/1959; 10% 07/15/1965; 10% 07/15/1974; 10% 07/15/1975; 10% 07/15/1977; 10% 07/14/1978; 20% 07/13/1979; 20% 07/15/1980; 20% 11/21/1987; 15% 07/15/1992
Name changed to PLDT, Inc. 09/02/2016

PHILIPPINE METALS INC (AB)
Each share old Common no par exchanged for (0.125) share new Common no par 08/21/2013
Reincorporated under the laws of British Columbia 04/17/2018

PHILIPPINE OIL DEV INC (PHILIPPINES)
Each share Capital Stock P0.03 par exchanged for (3) shares Capital Stock P0.01 par 12/31/58
Each share Capital Stock P0.01 par (Philippine Nationals) exchanged for (1) share Class A P0.01 par 4/3/70
Each share Capital Stock P0.01 par (Foreign Nationals) exchanged for (1) share Class B P0.01 par 4/3/70
Charter expired by time limitation 9/14/85

PHILIPPINES GOLD MNG CORP (NV)
Reorganized under the laws of Wyoming as Philippines Royal Oil & Alternative Energy Co., Inc. 03/16/2007
Each share Common $0.001 par exchanged for (100) shares Common $0.001 par
Philippines Royal Oil & Alternative Energy Co., Inc. recapitalized as Bio-Genex Laboratories, Inc. 05/19/2009
(See Bio-Genex Laboratories, Inc.)

PHILIPPINES ROYAL OIL & ALTERNATIVE ENERGY CO INC (WY)
Recapitalized as Bio-Genex Laboratories, Inc. 05/19/2009
Each share Common $0.001 par exchanged for (0.002) share Common $0.001 par
Note: No holder will receive fewer than (25) shares
(See Bio-Genex Laboratories, Inc.)

PHILIPS APPEL & WALDEN INC (NY)
Under plan of reorganization each share Class A Voting Common 10¢ par automatically became (1) share P.A.W. Management Corp. Common 10¢ par 10/27/1977

PHILIPS ELECTRONICS, INC. (DE)
Reincorporated under the laws of Maryland as Philips Electronics & Pharmaceutical Industries Corp. 10/19/59
Philips Electronics & Pharmaceutical Industries Corp. name changed to Pepi, Inc. 2/17/69 which merged into North American Philips Corp. 10/31/73
(See North American Philips Corp.)

PHILIPS ELECTRS & PHARMACEUTICAL INDS CORP (MD)
Name changed to Pepi, Inc. 2/17/69
Pepi, Inc. merged into North American Philips Corp. 10/31/73
(See North American Philips Corp.)

PHILIPS ELECTRS N V (NETHERLANDS)
Name changed 04/01/1998
N Y Shares 25 Gldrs. par changed to to 10 Gldrs. par and (1.5) additional shares issued plus a 10% stock dividend paid 06/01/1969
Stock Dividends - 25% 11/01/1973; 10% 05/09/1984
Name changed from Philips N.V. to Philips Electronics N.V. 05/19/1991
Name changed to Koninklijke Philips Electronics N.V. 04/01/1998
Koninklijke Philips Electronics N.V. name changed to Koninklijke Philips N.V. 05/15/2013

PHILIPS INDS INC (OH)
Common no par split (4) for (1) by issuance of (3) additional shares 7/15/65
Common no par split (2) for (1) by issuance of (1) additional share 6/5/68
Common no par split (2) for (1) by issuance of (1) additional share 6/9/69
Common no par split (2) for (1) by issuance of (1) additional share 8/4/83
Common no par split (2) for (1) by issuance of (1) additional share 8/29/86
$1 Conv. Special Preferred no par called for redemption 12/6/89
$3 Conv. Special Preferred no par called for redemption 12/6/89
Merged into Tomkins PLC 8/22/90
Each share Common no par exchanged for $18.50 cash

PHILIPS INTL RLTY CORP (MD)
Issue Information - 7,200,000 shares COM offered at $17.50 per share on 05/07/1998
Liquidation completed
Each share Common 1¢ par received initial distribution of $13 cash payable 12/22/2000 to holders of record 12/15/2000
Each share Common 1¢ par received second distribution of $1 cash payable 7/9/2001 to holders of record 7/2/2001
Each share Common 1¢ par received third distribution of $0.75 cash payable 9/24/2001 to holders of record 9/17/2001 Ex date - 9/25/2001
Each share Common 1¢ par received fourth distribution of $0.50 cash payable 11/19/2001 to holders of record 11/12/2001 Ex date - 11/20/2001
Each share Common 1¢ par received fifth distribution of $0.50 cash payable 10/22/2002 to holders of record 10/15/2002 Ex date - 10/24/2002
Each share Common 1¢ par received sixth distribution of $0.50 cash payable 3/18/2003 to holders of record 3/11/2003 Ex date - 3/19/2003
Each share Common 1¢ par received seventh distribution of $1 cash payable 9/16/2003 to holders of record 9/9/2003 Ex date - 9/17/2003
Each share Common 1¢ par received eighth distribution of $0.50 cash payable 1/6/2004 to holders of record 12/29/2003 Ex date - 1/7/2004
Each share Common 1¢ par received ninth distribution of $0.25 cash payable 8/27/2004 to holders of record 8/20/2004 Ex date - 8/30/2004
Each share Common 1¢ par received tenth distribution of $0.10 cash payable 12/30/2004 to holders of record 12/22/2004 Ex date - 12/31/2004
Each share Common 1¢ par received eleventh and final distribution of $0.05 cash payable 6/29/2005 to holders of record 6/23/2005 Ex date - 6/30/2005
Note: Certificates were not required to be surrendered and are without value

PHILIPS LTG N V (NETHERLANDS)
Name changed to Signify N.V. 06/04/2018

PHILIPSBORN INC (DE)
Merged into Outlet Co. 07/01/1975
Each share Common no par exchanged for $1.50 cash

PHILIPSBURG MINING CO. (MO)
Dissolved 9/27/44

PHILLIP RES INC (BC)
Recapitalized as Austin Mines Inc. (BC) 12/15/1989
Each (3.5) shares Common no par exchanged for (1) share Common no par
Austin Mines Inc. (BC) reincorporated in Alberta as Nighthawk Resources Inc. 03/13/1995
(See Nighthawk Resources Inc.)

PHILLIPS & JACOBS INC (PA)
Merged into Momentum Corp. 9/1/94
Each share Common 1¢ par exchanged for (1) share Common 1¢ par

PHILLIPS ALOGNA ASSOC INC (NY)
Merged into Marcon Communications, Inc. 08/29/1980
Each share Common 1¢ par exchanged for $1.72 cash

PHILLIPS CABLES LTD (CANADA)
Capital Stock no par split (5) for (1) by issuance of (4) additional shares 11/13/1967
Name changed to Phillips Cables Ltd.- Les Cables Phillips Ltee. 05/13/1975
Phillips Cables Ltd.- Les Cables Phillips Ltee. name changed to BICC Phillips, Inc. 05/25/1995
(See BICC Phillips, Inc.)

PHILLIPS (WENDELL) CO.
Liquidated in 1945

PHILLIPS CTL CORP (CO)
Charter suspended for failure to file reports and pay fees 09/30/1983

PHILLIPS-ECKARDT ELECTRONIC CORP. (IL)
Name changed to Eckmar Corp. (IL) 9/16/66
Eckmar Corp. (IL) reincorporated in Delaware 6/19/67 which name changed to Medallion Group, Inc. 11/6/75 which merged into Health-Chem Corp. 12/31/79
(See Health-Chem Corp.)

PHILLIPS ELECTRICAL CO. LTD. (CANADA)
Name changed to Phillips Cables Ltd. 11/12/1964
Phillips Cables Ltd. name changed to Phillips Cables Ltd.-Les Cables Phillips Ltee. 05/13/1975 which name changed to BICC Phillips, Inc. 05/25/1995
(See BICC Phillips, Inc.)

PHILLIPS ELECTRICAL CO. (1953) LTD. (CANADA)
Name changed to Phillips Electrical Co. Ltd. 05/02/1955
Phillips Electrical Co. Ltd. name changed to Phillips Cables Ltd. 11/12/1964 which name changed to Phillips Cables Ltd.-Les Cables Phillips Ltee. 05/13/1975 which name changed to BICC Phillips, Inc. 05/25/1995
(See BICC Phillips, Inc.)

PHILLIPS EQUITY CORP (BC)
Recapitalized as Corvette Petroleum Corp. 08/24/1979
Each share Common 50¢ par exchanged for (0.2) share Common no par
Corvette Petroleum Corp. recapitalized as Armor Development Corp. 05/17/1985
(See Armor Development Corp.)

PHILLIPS FOSCUE CORP (NC)
Merged into Leggett & Platt Acquisition Co. 06/22/1977
Each share Capital Stock 33-1/3¢ par exchanged for $7.40 cash

PHILLIPS 44 INC (WY)
Name changed to Genus International Corp. 06/22/2000
(See Genus International Corp.)

PHILLIPS GAS CO (DE)
9.32% Perpetual Preferred Ser. A no par called for redemption at $25 on 12/15/97
Public interest eliminated

PHILLIPS-JONES CORP. (NY)
Each share 7% Preferred $100 par exchanged for (1.4) shares 5% Preferred $100 par 00/00/1946
Common no par changed to $1 par and (2) additional shares issued 01/04/1956
Stock Dividend - 200% 09/10/1948
Name changed to Phillips-Van Heusen Corp. (NY) 07/31/1957
Phillips-Van Heusen Corp. (NY) reincorporated in Delaware 06/10/1976 which name changed to PVH Corp. 07/14/2011

PHILLIPS MANUFACTURING CO., INC. (MN)
Merged into Phillips-Puratronics, Inc. 11/29/67
Each share Common no par exchanged for (160.43) shares Common 5¢ par
Phillips-Puratronics, Inc. name changed to Puratronics Industries, Inc. 8/15/68 which name changed to Cambridge Corp. 5/8/70

PHILLIPS OIL CO. LTD. (AB)
Acquired by Plains Petroleums Ltd. 6/15/63
Each share Capital Stock $1 par exchanged for (1.8) shares Common no par
(See Plains Petroleums Ltd.)

PHILLIPS PACKING CO., INC. (MD)
Merged into Consolidated Foods Corp. 08/13/1957
Each share Common no par exchanged for (0.4395) share Common $1.33333333 par
Consolidated Foods Corp. name changed to Sara Lee Corp.

04/02/1985 which recapitalized as Hillshire Brands Co. 06/29/2012
(See Hillshire Brands Co.)

PHILLIPS PETE CO (DE)
Common no par split (2) for (1) by issuance of (1) additional share 07/21/1951
Common no par changed to $10 par 04/24/1956
Common $10 par changed to $5 par and (1) additional share issued 07/13/1956
Common $5 par changed to $2.50 par and (1) additional share issued 06/13/1969
Common $2.50 par changed to $1.25 par and (1) additional share issued 06/10/1977
Common $1.25 par split (3) for (1) by issuance of (2) additional shares 07/03/1985
Adjustable Rate Preferred Ser. A $1 par called for redemption 08/15/1988
Under plan of merger name changed to ConocoPhillips 08/30/2002

PHILLIPS PUMP & TANK CO.
Merged into Steel Materials Corp. in 1945 which was in process of liquidation in 1948

PHILLIPS-PURATRONICS, INC. (MN)
Name changed to Puratronics Industries, Inc. 8/15/68
Puratronics Industries, Inc. name changed to Cambridge Corp. 5/8/70
(See Cambridge Corp.)

PHILLIPS SCREW CO (DE)
Each share Capital Stock no par exchanged for (12) shares Capital Stock 10¢ par in 1941
Merged into Rule Industries, Inc. 6/2/78
Each share Capital Stock 10¢ par exchanged for (0.55) share Common 1¢ par and (0.5) Non-Transferable Unit of Residual Int.
(See Rule Industries, Inc.)

PHILLIPS 66 CAP I
8.24% Trust Originated Preferred Securities called for redemption at $25 on 5/31/2002

PHILLIPS TUTCH LATCH CO (DE)
Each share old Common 1¢ par exchanged for (0.5) share new Common 1¢ par 10/15/1973
Name changed to Viva Associates, Inc. 02/05/1974
(See Viva Associates, Inc.)

PHILLIPS VAN HEUSEN CORP (DE)
Reincorporated 06/10/1976
5% Preferred $100 par called for redemption 02/01/1963
State of incorporation changed from (NY) to (DE) 06/10/1976
Common $1 par split (2) for (1) by issuance of (1) additional share 01/03/1984
Common $1 par split (5) for (2) by issuance of (1.5) additional shares 06/16/1987
Common $1 par split (2) for (1) by issuance of (1) additional share 10/09/1991
Name changed to PVH Corp. 07/14/2011

PHILLY MIGNON INTL INC (DE)
Charter cancelled and declared inoperative and void for non-payment of taxes 3/1/84

PHILMON & HART LABORATORIES, INC. (MN)
Name changed to Spearhead Industries, Inc. 10/07/1980
(See Spearhead Industries, Inc.)

PHILMORE YELLOWKNIFE GOLD MINES LTD. (ON)
Charter cancelled for failure to file reports and pay taxes May 1957

PHILODRILL CORP (PHILIPPINES)
ADR agreement terminated 10/22/2007
No ADR's remain outstanding
(Additional Information in Active)

PHILOM BIOS INC (SK)
Acquired by Novozymes A/S 12/11/2007
Each share Common no par exchanged for $6.50 cash

PHILTREAD HOLDINGS CORP (PHILIPPINES)
Name changed to ATR KimEng Financial Corp. 07/07/2003

PHINDER TECHNOLOGIES INC (FL)
Reincorporated 01/19/2007
Place of incorporation changed from (ON) to (FL) 01/19/2007
Name changed to Zupintra Corp., Inc. 06/21/2007
(See Zupintra Corp., Inc.)

PHL PINNACLE HLDGS LTD (BC)
Recapitalized as Citrine Holdings Ltd. 01/09/1997
Each share Common no par exchanged for (0.2) share Common no par

PHLCORP INC (DE)
Merged into PHLCorp, Inc. (PA) 04/22/1987
Each share Common $1 par exchanged for (1) share Common $1 par
PHLCorp, Inc. (PA) merged into Leucadia National Corp. 12/31/1992 which name changed to Jefferies Financial Group Inc. 05/24/2018

PHLCORP INC (PA)
Merged into Leucadia National Corp. 12/31/1992
Each share Common $1 par exchanged for (0.406) share Common $1 par
Leucadia National Corp. name changed to Jefferies Financial Group Inc. 05/24/2018

PHLO CORP (DE)
Each share old Common $0.0001 par exchanged for (0.01) share new Common $0.0001 par 03/19/2008
SEC revoked common stock registration 08/27/2010
Stockholders' equity unlikely

PHM CORP (MI)
Name changed to Pulte Corp. 07/01/1993
Pulte Corp. name changed to Pulte Homes, Inc. 05/17/2001 which name changed to PulteGroup, Inc. 03/22/2010

PHOENICIAN HLDGS CORP (ON)
Name changed to Asia Now Resources Corp. 02/16/2006
(See Asia Now Resources Corp.)

PHOENICIAN OLIVE OIL INC (NV)
Charter revoked for failure to file reports and pay taxes 3/1/2001

PHOENIX-ABERDEEN WORLDWIDE OPPORTUNITIES FD (DE)
Reincorporated 10/00/2000
State of incorporation changed from (MA) to (DE) 10/00/2000
Merged into Phoenix Equity Trust 10/22/2004
Details not available

PHOENIX ADVANCED TECHNOLOGY INC (FL)
Each share Common $0.0001 par exchanged for (0.025) share Common $0.004 par 9/24/90
Name changed to Global TeleMedia International, Inc. 2/13/95
Global TeleMedia International, Inc. recapitalized as Seacoast Holding Corp. 1/26/2004

PHOENIX AMERN INC (CA)
Common no par split (2) for (1) by issuance of (1) additional share 9/19/83
Merged into Phoenix Affiliates International, Inc. 11/14/90
Each share Common no par exchanged for $5 cash

PHOENIX ASSET RESV FD (MA)
Name changed to Phoenix Multi-Sector Short Term Bond Fund 03/14/1996
(See Phoenix Multi-Sector Short Term Bond Fund)

PHOENIX ASSOCS LD SYND (NV)
Chapter 7 bankruptcy proceedings terminated 07/03/2018
No stockholders' equity

PHOENIX BANCORP INC (PA)
Common $10 par changed to $1 par and (9) additional shares issued payable 05/23/2012 to holders of record 05/09/2012
Merged into Mid Penn Bancorp, Inc. 03/01/2015
Each share Common $1 par exchanged for (0.82342) share Common $1 par and $38.184 cash

PHOENIX CALIF TAX EXEMPT BDS INC (MD)
Name changed to Phoenix-Goodwin California Tax Exempt Bonds, Inc. (MD) 08/27/1999
Phoenix-Goodwin California Tax Exempt Bonds, Inc. (MD) reincorporated in Delaware as Phoenix-Goodwin California Tax Exempt Bond Fund 08/28/2000
(See Phoenix-Goodwin California Tax Exempt Bond Fund)

PHOENIX-CAMPBELL CORP. (DE)
Dissolution approved 9/14/56

PHOENIX CANDY INC (DE)
Stock Dividend - 25% 12/01/1976
Merged into Beatrice Foods Co. 05/02/1978
Each share Common 1¢ par exchanged for (0.54417) share Common no par
Beatrice Foods Co. name changed to Beatrice Companies, Inc. 06/05/1984
(See Beatrice Companies, Inc.)

PHOENIX CAP CORP (NV)
Name changed to 21st Century Holdings, Inc. 3/12/90
21st Century Holdings, Inc. recapitalized as AFGL International, Inc. (NV) 8/24/93 which reincorporated in Delaware as Headway Corporate Resources, Inc. 11/14/96
(See Headway Corporate Resources, Inc.)

PHOENIX CAP FD INC (MD)
Acquired by Phoenix-Chase Series Fund 12/11/1980
Each share Common $1 par exchanged for (1.0905) Growth Fund Series Shares of Bene. Int. $1 par
Phoenix-Chase Series Fund name changed to Phoenix Series Fund 10/12/1982
(See Phoenix Series Fund)

PHOENIX CAP INC (NB)
Reorganized as Phoenix Capital Income Trust 06/10/2005
Each share Common no par exchanged for (0.174) Trust Unit no par
(See Phoenix Capital Income Trust)

PHOENIX CAP INCOME TR (NB)
Delisted from Toronto Venture Stock Exchange 06/24/2007

PHOENIX CARE SYS INC (OH)
Voluntarily dissolved 01/27/2000
Details not available

PHOENIX COAL INC (ON)
Reincorporated 07/11/2008
Place of incorporation changed from (AB) to (ON) 07/11/2008
Recapitalized as Elgin Mining Inc. 05/10/2010
Each share Common no par exchanged for (0.33333333) share Common no par
Elgin Mining Inc. merged into Mandalay Resources Corp. 09/11/2014

PHOENIX COMPANIES, INC. (UT)
Name changed to Tropical Development International, Inc. 00/00/1987
Tropical Development International, Inc. recapitalized as Impulse Energy Systems, Inc. 04/02/1990
(See Impulse Energy Systems, Inc.)

PHOENIX COPPER CORP (BC)
Recapitalized as Phoenix Metals Corp. 12/04/2013
Each share Common no par exchanged for (0.5) share Common no par
Phoenix Metals Corp. name changed to Envirotek Remediation Inc. 04/27/2018

PHOENIX COS INC (DE)
Charter cancelled and declared inoperative and void for non-payment of taxes 03/01/1987

PHOENIX COS INC NEW (DE)
Each Corporate Unit received (2.8343) shares Common 1¢ par 02/16/2006
Each share old Common 1¢ par received distribution of (0.05) share Virtus Investment Partners, Inc. Common 1¢ par payable 12/31/2008 to holders of record 12/22/2008 Ex date - 01/02/2009
Each share old Common 1¢ par exchanged for (0.05) share new Common 1¢ par 08/13/2012
Acquired by Nassau Reinsurance Group Holdings L.P. 06/20/2016
Each share new Common 1¢ par exchanged for $37.50 cash

PHOENIX DOWNTOWN PARKING ASSOCIATION, INC. (AZ)
Dissolved 12/16/66
Each share Capital Stock $10 par exchanged for first and final distribution of $12.72 cash

PHOENIX DUFF & PHELPS CORP (DE)
Each share Conv. Exchangeable Preferred Ser. A 1¢ par exchanged for $25 principal amount of 6% Conv. Subordinated Debentures due 11/01/2015 on 04/03/1998
Name changed to Phoenix Investment Partners, Ltd. 05/11/1998
(See Phoenix Investment Partners Ltd.)

PHOENIX ELEC OIL REFINERS CDA LTD (BC)
Name changed to Phoenix International Energy Corp. 01/28/1981
Phoenix International Energy Corp. recapitalized as International Phoenix Energy Corp. 12/01/1983 which merged into Aegis Resources Ltd. 08/01/1990 which recapitalized as New Aegis Resources Ltd. 03/17/1993 which was acquired by Norcan Resources Ltd. 08/19/1994 which recapitalized as Odyssey Exploration Inc. 06/07/2000 which recapitalized as Consolidated Odyssey Exploration Inc. 12/08/2000 which reorganized as Odyssey Petroleum Corp. 08/25/2005 which recapitalized as Petrichor Energy Inc. 03/03/2011

PHOENIX ENERGY CORP (FL)
Administratively dissolved 08/25/1995

PHOENIX ENERGY RESOURCE CORP (NV)
Old Common $0.001 par split (50) for (1) by issuance of (49) additional shares payable 07/18/2008 to holders of record 07/18/2008
Each share old Common $0.001 par exchanged for (0.03333333) share new Common $0.001 par 06/11/2010
Name changed to China Forestry Industry Group, Inc. 02/02/2011
China Forestry Industry Group, Inc. name changed to Silvan Industries, Inc. 12/20/2011
(See Silvan Industries, Inc.)

PHOENIX ENTERPRISES, INC. (AZ)
Name changed to Data World Corp. 5/6/69
Data World Corp. charter revoked 12/26/72

PHOENIX EQUITY OPPORTUNITIES FD (MA)
Name changed to Phoenix Strategic Equity Series Fund (MA) and Class A $0.001 par reclassified as Seneca Equity Opportunities Fund Class A $0.001 par 07/28/1999
Phoenix Strategic Equity Series Fund (MA) reincorporated in Delaware 08/00/2000
(See Phoenix Strategic Equity Series Fund)

PHOENIX FD INC (MD)
Acquired by Phoenix-Chase Series Fund 01/29/1981
Each share Common $1 par exchanged for (1.0489) Balanced Fund Series Shares of Bene. Int. $1 par
Phoenix-Chase Series Fund name changed to Phoenix Series Fund 10/12/1982
(See Phoenix Series Fund)

PHOENIX FILM STUDIOS (AZ)
Reincorporated under the laws of Colorado as Galaxie Industries, Inc. and Capital Stock $1 par changed to Common 25¢ par 09/16/1968
Galaxie Industries, Inc. merged into Galaxie National Corp. 12/24/1969 which reorganized as Marathon Office Supply, Inc. 05/12/1982
(See Marathon Office Supply, Inc.)

PHOENIX FINL CORP (PA)
Filed for Chapter 7 Federal Bankruptcy proceedings 7/15/87
Stockholders' equity unlikely

PHOENIX FINL HLDGS LTD (ON)
Each share Common no par exchanged for (0.5) share Class A Subordinate no par and (0.5) share Class B Multiple no par 08/11/1993
Name changed to Cornerstone Industrial Minerals Corp. 09/03/1996
(See Cornerstone Industrial Minerals Corp.)

PHOENIX FINL REPORTING GROUP INC (FL)
Recapitalized as First Reserve, Inc. 05/01/1998
Each share Common no par exchanged for (0.5) share Common no par
(See First Reserve, Inc.)

PHOENIX GEMS INC (AZ)
Each share old Class A Common $1 par exchanged for (0.1) share new Class A Common $1 par 10/20/1972
Name changed to Bower Industries, Inc. 04/21/1973
Bower Industries, Inc. name changed to Metalclad Corp. (AZ) 05/29/1987 which reincorporated in Delaware 11/24/1993 which name changed to Entrx Corp. 06/24/2002 which name changed to Entrprize Corp. (DE) 06/04/2012 which reincorporated in Indiana as Tprize, Inc. 08/18/2016

PHOENIX GLASS CO (WV)
Each share Common $1 par exchanged for (2) shares Common 50¢ par 00/00/1948
Each share Common 50¢ par exchanged for (0.05) share Common no par 03/11/1954
Acquired by Anchor Hocking Corp. 05/01/1970
Details not available

PHOENIX GLOBAL CAP INC (BC)
Struck off register and declared dissolved for failure to file returns 07/12/1991

PHOENIX GOLD INTL INC (OR)
Issue Information - 1,100,000 shares COM offered at $6.75 per share on 05/04/1995
Acquired by a private company 07/20/2006
Details not available

PHOENIX GOLD MINES LTD (ON)
Voluntarily dissolved 08/08/1990
Each (39) shares Common no par received first and final distribution of (2) shares St Andrew Goldfields Ltd. Common no par
Note: Shares held by U.S. residents were sold and cash distributed on a pro rata basis
Note: Certificates were not required to be surrendered and are without value
St Andrew Goldfields Ltd. merged into Kirkland Lake Gold Inc. 01/29/2016 which merged into Kirkland Lake Gold Ltd. 12/06/2016

PHOENIX GOLD RES LTD (BC)
Recapitalized as Terrastar Resources Corp. 06/09/1999
Each share Common no par exchanged for (0.2) share Common no par
Terrastar Resources Corp. name changed to Pine Point Mines Inc. 03/07/2002 which name changed to Mineworks Resources Corp. 01/23/2004 which name changed to Tower Energy Ltd. 07/25/2005 which recapitalized as Tower Resources Ltd. 09/20/2011

PHOENIX GOODWIN CALIF TAX EXEMPT BD FD (DE)
Reincorporated 08/28/2000
Reincorporated from Phoenix-Goodwin California Tax Exempt Bonds, Inc. (MD) to under the laws of Delaware as Phoenix-Goodwin California Tax Exempt Bond Fund 08/28/2000
Class B reclassified as Class A 10/04/2006
Merged into Phoenix Opportunities Trust 06/27/2007
Details not available

PHOENIX GROUP CORP (DE)
Each share old Common $0.001 par exchanged for (0.0625) share new Common $0.001 par 9/1/2004
Name changed to Lighting Science Group Corp. 12/23/2004

PHOENIX GROUP INTL INC (DE)
Each share old Common 10¢ par exchanged for (2) shares new Common 10¢ par 10/30/1989
Recapitalized as Canam Energy Inc. 09/27/2006
Each share new Common 10¢ par exchanged for (0.05) share Common 10¢ par
Canam Energy Inc. recapitalized as Registered Express Corp. 06/29/2009 which name changed to Proactive Pet Products, Inc. 02/20/2015 which recapitalized as GVCL Ventures, Inc. 11/02/2016 which recapitalized as Rain Forest International, Inc. 05/22/2018

PHOENIX HEALTH GROUP INC (ON)
Struck off register and declared dissolved for failure to pay taxes and file returns 10/29/2001

PHOENIX HEALTHCARE CORP (DE)
Name changed to Phoenix Group Corp. 10/10/2000
Phoenix Group Corp. name changed to Lighting Science Group Corp. 12/23/2004

PHOENIX HEDGE FD LTD PARTNERSHIP (ON)
In process of liquidation
Each Unit of Ltd. Partnership received initial distribution of $11 cash payable 05/12/2000 to holders of record 05/10/2000
Note: An additional amount of approximately $1.35 cash in residual net asset value will be distributed upon the liquidation of Phoenix Fixed Income Arbitrage Limited Partnership

PHOENIX HIGH TECH HIGH YIELD FD L P (CA)
Terminated Limited Partnership Interest registration and is no longer public as of 01/27/2000

PHOENIX HOSIERY CO. (WI)
Acquired by Kayser-Roth Corp. for cash 6/29/62

PHOENIX INCOME & GROWTH FUND (MA)
Name changed to Phoenix-Oakhurst Income & Growth Fund (MA) 10/08/1999
Phoenix-Oakhurst Income & Growth Fund (MA) reincorporated in Delaware 08/00/2000 which name changed to Phoenix Investment Series Fund 12/30/2004
(See Phoenix Investment Series Fund)

PHOENIX INDIA ACQUISITION CORP (DE)
Trust account liquidated
Each Unit received $8.03 cash payable 04/21/2008 to holders of record 04/20/2008 Ex date - 04/22/2008
Each share Common $0.0001 par received $8.03 cash payable 04/21/2008 to holders of record 04/20/2008 Ex date - 04/22/2008
Company terminated securities registration and is no longer public as of 12/09/2008

PHOENIX INDS CORP (DE)
Charter cancelled and declared inoperative and void for non-payment of taxes 03/01/1988

PHOENIX INFORMATION SYS CORP (DE)
Plan of Liquidation under Chapter 11 Federal Bankruptcy proceedings confirmed 11/02/1998
Holders received Settlement Certificates entitling the holder to a cash settlement, if any
Note: Certificates were cancelled 01/21/2000 and are without value

PHOENIX INSIGHT FDS TR (MD)
Merged into Virtus Insight Trust 10/20/2008
Details not available

PHOENIX INSURANCE CO. (CT)
Each share Capital Stock $100 par exchanged for (10) shares Capital Stock $10 par in 1929
Capital Stock $10 par changed to $5 par and (1) additional share issued 3/10/65
Stock Dividends - 25% 4/10/53; 33-1/3% 10/15/54
Acquired by Travelers Corp. 8/1/66
Each share Capital Stock $5 par received (1) share $2 Conv. Preferred no par
Each share Capital Stock $5 par then exchanged for (1) share Common $2.50 par
Travelers Corp. merged into Travelers Inc. 12/31/93 which name changed to Travelers Group Inc. 4/16/95 which name changed to Citigroup Inc. 10/8/98

PHOENIX INTL ENERGY CORP (BC)
Recapitalized as International Phoenix Energy Corp. 12/01/1983
Each share Common no par exchanged for (0.2) share Common no par
International Phoenix Energy Corp. merged into Aegis Resources Ltd. 08/01/1990 which recapitalized as New Aegis Resources Ltd. 03/17/1993 which was acquired by Norcan Resources Ltd. 08/19/1994 which recapitalized as Odyssey Exploration Inc. 06/07/2000 which recapitalized as Consolidated Odyssey Exploration Inc. 12/08/2000 which reorganized as Odyssey Petroleum Corp. 08/25/2005 which recapitalized as Petrichor Energy Inc. 03/03/2011

PHOENIX INTL INC (DE)
Issue Information - 1,633,333 shares COM offered at $0.15 per share on 07/31/2002
Reincorporated under the laws of Alberta as PICorp.Capital Ltd. 04/30/2004
PICorp.Capital Ltd. (AB) reorganized in Ontario as Aeroquest International Ltd. 11/04/2004
(See Aeroquest International Ltd.)

PHOENIX INTL INC (FL)
Common 1¢ par split (3) for (2) by issuance of (0.5) additional share payable 5/18/98 to holders of record 5/11/98
Name changed to Sphinx International, Inc. 2/23/2001
(See Sphinx International, Inc.)

PHOENIX INTL INDS INC (FL)
Name changed to Epicus Communications Group Inc. 05/07/2003
(See Epicus Communications Group Inc.)

PHOENIX INTL LIFE SCIENCES INC (CANADA)
Merged into MDS Inc. 05/15/2000
Each share Common no par exchanged for $16 cash

PHOENIX INTS INC (NV)
Each share old Common $0.001 par exchanged for (0.02) share new Common $0.001 par 01/25/2006
Each share new Common $0.001 par exchanged again for (0.00625) share new Common $0.001 par 06/01/2009
Name changed to NuMobile, Inc. 07/15/2009
NuMobile, Inc. recapitalized as Priority Aviation, Inc. 01/06/2014

PHOENIX INVT CO (GA)
Liquidation completed
Each share Common $1 par exchanged for initial distribution of $8 cash 09/20/1973
Each share Common $1 par received second distribution of $0.24 cash 07/17/1974
Each share Common $1 par received third and final distribution of $0.286 cash 08/02/1976

PHOENIX INVT PARTNERS LTD (DE)
Merged into Phoenix Home Life Mutual Insurance Co. 01/11/2001
Each share Common 1¢ par exchanged for $15.75 cash

PHOENIX INVT SER FD (DE)
Reincorporated 08/00/2000
Name changed 12/30/2004
State of incorporation changed from (MA) to (DE) 08/00/2000
Name changed from Phoenix-Oakhurst Income & Growth

Fund to Phoenix Investment Series Fund 12/30/2004
Reorganized as Phoenix Equity Trust 03/03/2008
Details not available

PHOENIX LASER SYS INC (DE)
Each share Conv. Preferred $0.001 par exchanged for (4) shares Common $0.0001 par and (1) Class B Common Stock Purchase Warrant which expires 06/22/1995 on 02/19/1991
Each share Common $0.0001 par exchanged for (0.1) share Common $0.000001 par 01/17/1992
SEC revoked common stock registration 09/11/2009
Stockholders' equity unlikely

PHOENIX LEASING CAP ASSURN FD L P (CA)
Units of Limited Partnership Int. registration terminated and Partnership no longer public as of 12/31/1996

PHOENIX LEASING CASH DISTR FD L P (CA)
Units of Ltd. Partnership Int. I completely liquidated 12/31/1995
Details not available
Units of Ltd. Partnership Int. II completely liquidated 12/31/1997
Details not available
Units of Ltd. Partnership Int. III completely liquidated 12/31/1999
Details not available
Units of Ltd. Partnership Int. IV completely liquidated 12/31/2001
Details not available
Units of Ltd. Partnership Int. V completely liquidated 12/31/2003
Details not available

PHOENIX LEISURE CORP (BC)
Delisted from Toronto Venture Stock Exchange 06/16/2004

PHOENIX MANUFACTURING CO. (IL)
Each share Capital Stock $100 par exchanged for (10) shares Capital Stock $10 par 00/00/1952
Merged into Union Tank Car Co. (NJ) on a (2.1) for (1) basis 09/09/1957
Union Tank Car Co. (NJ) reincorporated in Delaware 04/30/1968 which reorganized as Trans Union Corp. 06/01/1969
(See Trans Union Corp.)

PHOENIX MATACHEWAN MINES INC (ON)
Recapitalized as Galahad Metals Inc. (ON) 01/02/2009
Each share Common no par exchanged for (0.1) share Common no par
Galahad Metals Inc. (ON) reorganized in British Columbia as Rosehearty Energy Inc. 07/31/2014

PHOENIX MED TECHNOLOGY INC (DE)
SEC revoked common stock registration 07/14/2009
Stockholders' equity unlikely

PHOENIX MEDIA GROUP LTD (NV)
Recapitalized as TecScan International, Inc. 06/23/2003
Each share Common $0.001 par exchanged for (0.01) share Common $0.001 par
TecScan International, Inc. name changed to Bio-Life Labs, Inc. 05/19/2004
(See Bio-Life Labs, Inc.)

PHOENIX METALS CORP (BC)
Each share old Common no par exchanged for (0.25) share new Common no par 03/21/2016
Name changed to Envirotek Remediation Inc. 04/27/2018

PHOENIX METALS INC (NV)
Reincorporated 03/01/2000
State of incorporation changed from (CO) to (NV) 03/01/2000
Reorganized as TM Media Group, Inc. 09/22/2006
Each share Common $0.0001 par exchanged for (0.0002) share Common $0.0001 par
(See TM Media Group, Inc.)

PHOENIX MOLYBDENITE CORP. LTD.
Acquired by Zenith Molybdenite Corp. Ltd. share for share in 1938
(See Zenith Molybdenite Corp. Ltd.)

PHOENIX MULTI-PORTFOLIO FD (MA)
Merged into Phoenix Insight Funds Trust 10/20/2006
Details not available

PHOENIX MULTI-SECTOR FIXED INCOME FD INC (MD)
Reincorporated under the laws of Delaware as Phoenix-Goodwin Multi-Sector Fixed Income Fund, Inc. 08/27/1999
Phoenix-Goodwin Multi-Sector Fixed Income Fund, Inc. name changed to Phoenix Multi-Series Trust 10/30/2000
(See Phoenix Multi-Series Trust)

PHOENIX MULTI-SECTOR SHORT TERM BD FD (MA)
Reorganized as Phoenix Goodwin Multi-Sector Short Term Bond Fund 10/08/1999
Details not available

PHOENIX MULTI-SERIES TR (DE)
Name changed 10/30/2000
Name changed from Phoenix-Goodwin Multi-Sector Fixed Income Fund, Inc. to Phoenix Multi-Series Trust 10/30/2000
Merged into Phoenix Opportunities Trust 06/27/2007
Details not available

PHOENIX NETWORK INC (CO)
Merged into Qwest Communications International Inc. 03/30/1998
Each share Common $0.001 par exchanged for (0.0218) share Common 1¢ par
Note: An additional distribution of $0.1213 cash per share was made 08/16/1999
Qwest Communications International Inc. merged into CenturyLink, Inc. 04/01/2011

PHOENIX OIL CO., LTD. (AB)
Struck off the register and deemed dissolved for failure to file reports or pay fees 12/14/1920

PHOENIX OIL CO. (DE)
Placed in receivership 00/00/1940
Stockholders' equity unlikely

PHOENIX OIL CO. (GA)
Administratively dissolved 07/11/1990

PHOENIX OILFIELD HAULING INC (AB)
Each share old Common no par exchanged for (0.03333333) share new Common no par 11/28/2011
Name changed to Aveda Transportation & Energy Services Inc. 06/25/2012
Aveda Transportation & Energy Services Inc. merged into Daseke, Inc. 05/28/2018

PHOENIX RE CORP (CT)
Name changed to PXRE Corp. (CT) 05/19/1994
PXRE Corp. (CT) reorganized in Bermuda as PXRE Group Ltd. 10/05/1999 which merged into Argo Group International Holdings, Ltd. 08/07/2007

PHOENIX RESOURCE COS INC (DE)
Each share Common $0.001 par exchanged for (0.1) share Common 1¢ par 05/13/1992
Common 1¢ par split (2) for (1) by issuance of (1) additional share 01/31/1995
Common 1¢ par split (2) for (1) by issuance of (1) additional share 09/29/1995
Merged into Apache Corp. 05/20/1996
Each share Common 1¢ par exchanged for (0.75) share Common 1¢ par and $4 cash

PHOENIX RES CO (ME)
Conv. Class A $1 par conversion privilege expired 10/07/1979
Class A $1 par called for redemption at $20 on 04/23/1981
Class B $1 par reclassified as Common $1 par 07/16/1981
Stock Dividend - 100% 07/31/1981
Merged into Texas International Co. 06/18/1982
Each share Common $1 par exchanged for (1.1) shares Common 10¢ par
Texas International Co. reorganized as Phoenix Resource Companies, Inc. 04/09/1990 which merged into Apache Corp. 05/20/1996

PHOENIX RES TECHNOLOGIES INC (NV)
Each share Common $0.001 par received distribution of (1/3) share MVP Holdings, Inc. new Common $0.001 par payable 10/15/1997 to holders of record 10/01/1997
Each share old Common $0.001 par exchanged for (0.01) share new Common $0.001 par 10/14/1999
SEC revoked common stock registration 09/11/2009
Stockholders' equity unlikely

PHOENIX RESTAURANT GROUP INC (GA)
Name changed to Hiru Corp. 11/18/2008

PHOENIX SAVINGS & LOAN ASSOCIATION INC. (MD)
Reorganized 5/12/62
Each share Class A Common $1 par plus $1 cash exchanged for (1) share Phoenix Savings & Loan, Inc. Class A Guaranty Common $1 par
Stock not exchanged prior to 7/12/62 became null and void

PHOENIX SVGS & LN INC (MD)
Each share Class A Guaranty Common $1 par exchanged for (0.5) share Guaranty Common $1 par 03/31/1970
Receivership proceedings closed 12/00/1976
No stockholders' equity

PHOENIX SECURITIES CORP.
Dissolved in 1944

PHOENIX SER FD (MA)
Name changed 10/12/1982
Name changed from Phoenix-Chase Series Fund to Phoenix Series Fund 10/12/1982
High Quality Bond Fund merged into National Multi-Sector Fixed Income Fund Inc. 11/12/1993
Each share $1 par exchanged for (0.745103917) share Class A Common $1 par
Convertible Fund Series Shares of Bene. Int. reorganized as Phoenix Income & Growth Fund 05/27/1998
Details not available
Core Bond Fund Class A, High Yield Fund Class A and Money Market Fund Class A reorganized as Phoenix Opportunities Trust 06/27/2007
Details not available
Balanced Fund Class A, Capital Growth Fund Class A and Midcap Growth Fund Class A reorganized as Phoenix Equity Trust 03/03/2008
Details not available

PHOENIX SILK MANUFACTURING CO., INC.
Reorganized as Phoenix Silk Corp. in 1938
No stockholders' equity

PHOENIX STAR VENTURES INC (DE)
Each share old Common $0.0001 par exchanged for (0.11111111) share new Common $0.0001 par 12/07/2001
Name changed to WPCS International Inc. 05/29/2002
WPCS International Inc. recapitalized as DropCar, Inc. 01/31/2018

PHOENIX STATE BANK & TRUST CO. (HARTFORD, CT)
Each share Capital Stock $100 par exchanged for (4) shares Capital Stock $25 par in 1946
Merged into Connecticut Bank & Trust Co. Co. (Hartford, CT) 7/1/54
Each share Capital Stock $25 par exchanged for (1.05) shares Capital Stock $25 par
Connecticut Bank & Trust Co. (Hartford, CT) reorganized as CBT Corp. 2/27/70 which merged into Bank of New England Corp. 6/14/85
(See Bank of New England Corp.)

PHOENIX STL CORP (DE)
Stock Dividend - 10% 01/20/1966
Common $4 par changed to 10¢ par 03/30/1977
Plan of reorganization under Chapter 11 Federal Bankruptcy proceedings confirmed 07/31/1985
Each share Conv. Preferred Ser. A 10¢ par exchanged for (0.369) share Preferred Ser. EE 10¢ par
Each share Common 10¢ par exchanged for (0.1) share Preferred Ser. EE 10¢ par
Plan of reorganization under Chapter 11 Federal Bankruptcy proceedings confirmed 12/13/1988
No stockholders' equity

PHOENIX STRATEGIC ALLOCATION FD (DE)
Name changed 10/29/1999
Reincorporated 00/00/2001
Name changed 01/01/2005
Name changed from Phoenix Strategic Allocation Fund, Inc. to Phoenix-Oakhurst Strategic Allocation Fund, Inc. (MA) 10/29/1999
Reincorporated from Phoenix-Oakhurst Strategic Allocation Fund, Inc. (MA) to under the laws of Delaware as Phoenix-Oakhurst Strategic Allocation Fund 00/00/2001
Name changed from Phoenix-Oakhurst Strategic Allocation Fund to Phoenix Strategic Allocation Fund 01/01/2005
Merged into Phoenix Series Fund 04/29/2005
Details not available

PHOENIX STRATEGIC EQUITY SER FD (DE)
Reincorporated 08/00/2000
Seneca Equity Opportunities Fund Class A $0.001 par reclassified as Seneca Growth Fund Class A $0.001 par 05/15/2000
State of incorporation changed from (MA) to (DE) 08/00/2000
Reorganized as Virtus Strategic Equity Series Fund 07/01/2005
Details not available

PHOENIX SUMMUS CORP (NJ)
Reincorporated 01/00/1999
Each (110) shares old Common 1¢ par exchanged for (1) share new Common 1¢ par 09/26/1997
State of incorporation changed from (NV) to (NJ) 01/00/1999
Each share new Common 1¢ par exchanged for (0.005) share Common $0.001 par 04/01/1999
Note: Holders entitled to (49) or fewer post split shares received (50) shares
Name changed to I-Transaction.net, Inc. 11/11/1999
I-Transaction.net, Inc. name changed

to Global Alliance Networks Inc. 10/11/2005
(See Global Alliance Networks Inc.)

PHOENIX TECHNOLOGIES LTD (DE)
Acquired by Pharaoh Acquisition L.L.C. 11/23/2010
Each share Common $0.001 par exchanged for $4.20 cash

PHOENIX TECHNOLOGY INCOME FD (AB)
Reorganized as PHX Energy Services Corp. 01/06/2011
Each Trust Unit exchanged for (1) share Common no par
Note: Unexchanged certificates were cancelled and became without value 01/06/2016

PHOENIX TECHNOLOGY SVCS INC (AB)
Recapitalized as Phoenix Technology Income Fund 07/01/2004
Each share Common no par exchanged for (1) Trust Unit no par
Phoenix Technology Income Fund reorganized as PHX Energy Services Corp. 01/06/2011

PHOENIX TOTAL RETURN FD INC (MA)
Name changed to Phoenix Strategic Allocation Fund, Inc. 07/03/1992
Phoenix Strategic Allocation Fund, Inc. name changed to Phoenix-Oakhurst Strategic Allocation Fund, Inc. (MA) 10/29/1999 which reincorporated in Delaware as Phoenix-Oakhurst Strategic Allocation Fund 00/00/2001 which name changed to Phoenix Strategic Allocation Fund 01/01/2005
(See Phoenix Strategic Allocation Fund)

PHOENIX TR (DE)
Name changed 9/30/2002
Completely liquidated
Each share Foreign Equity Fund Class A received net asset value
Each share Foreign Equity Fund Class B received net asset value
Each share Foreign Equity Fund Class C received net asset value
Each share Foreign Equity Fund Class I received net asset value
Completely liquidated 7/31/2002
Each share Government Fund Class I received net asset value
Each share Growth & Income Fund Class A received net asset value
Each share Growth & Income Fund Class B received net asset value
Each share Growth & Income Fund Class C received net asset value
Each share Growth & Income Fund Class I received net asset value
Name changed from Phoenix-Zweig Trust to Phoenix Trust 9/30/2002
Completely liquidated 4/24/2003
Each share Phoenix-Goodwin Government Cash Fund Class A received net asset value
Each share Phoenix-Goodwin Government Cash Fund Class B received net asset value
Each share Phoenix-Goodwin Government Cash Fund Class C received net asset value
Each share Phoenix-Goodwin Government Cash Fund Class I received net asset value
Merged into Phoenix Investment Trust 97 on 4/16/2004
Each share Phoenix Appreciation Fund Class A received Small Cap Value Fund Class A shares on a net asset basis
Each share Phoenix Appreciation Fund Class B received Small Cap Value Fund Class B shares on a net asset basis
Each share Phoenix Appreciation Fund Class C received Small Cap Value Fund Class C shares on a net asset basis
Merged into Phoenix-Oakhurst Strategic Allocation Fund 4/16/2004
Each share Phoenix-Oakhurst Managed Assets Class A received Class A shares on a net asset basis
Each share Phoenix-Oakhurst Managed Assets Class B received Class B shares on a net asset basis
Each share Phoenix-Oakhurst Managed Assets Class C received Class A shares on a net asset basis
Merged into Phoenix-Oakhurst Growth & Income Fund 4/16/2004
Each share Phoenix-Oakhurst Strategy Fund Class A received Class A shares on a net asset basis
Each share Phoenix-Oakhurst Strategy Fund Class B received Class B shares on a net asset basis
Each share Phoenix-Oakhurst Strategy Fund Class C received Class C shares on a net asset basis

PHOENIX VENTURES INC (DE)
Each share old Class A Common 1¢ par exchanged for (0.0002) share new Class A Common 1¢ par 8/16/90
Note: In effect holders received $1.60 cash per share and public interest was eliminated

PHOENIX WASTE SVCS INC (DE)
Chapter 7 bankruptcy proceedings terminated 09/13/2007
No stockholders' equity

PHOENIX WORLDWIDE OPPORTUNITIES FD INC (MA)
Name changed to Phoenix-Aberdeen Worldwide Opportunities Fund (MA) 12/16/1998
Phoenix-Aberdeen Worldwide Opportunites Fund (MA) reincorporated in Delaware 10/00/2000
(See Phoenix-Aberdeen Worldwide Opportunities Fund)

PHON-NET COM INC (FL)
Name changed 6/4/99
Name changed from Phon-Net Corp. to Phon-Net.com, Inc. 6/4/99
Each share old Common $0.001 par exchanged for (0.2) share new Common $0.001 par 3/30/2001
New Common $0.001 par split (2) for (1) by issuance of (1) additional share payable 12/17/2001 to holders of record 12/13/2001 Ex date - 12/18/2001
Name changed to Environmental Strategies & Technologies International, Inc. 4/14/2002
Environmental Strategies & Technologies International, Inc. recapitalized as Tango Inc. 2/10/2003 which recapitalized as AutoBidXL Inc. 10/24/2005 which name changed to Trophy Resources, Inc. 2/28/2006

PHONE A GRAM SYS INC (DE)
Reincorporated 9/29/83
State of incorporation changed from (CA) to (DE) 9/29/83
Each share Common no par exchanged for (0.5) share Common 1¢ par 11/21/83
Name changed to Amserv, Inc. 10/26/87
Amserv, Inc. name changed to Amserv Healthcare Inc. 8/4/92 which merged into Star Multi Care Services, Inc. 8/23/96
(See Multi Care Services, Inc.)

PHONE COM INC (DE)
Common $0.001 par split (2) for (1) by issuance of (1) additional share payable 11/12/1999 to holders of record 10/29/1999
Name changed to Openwave Systems Inc. 11/20/2000
Openwave Systems Inc. name changed to Unwired Planet, Inc. 05/09/2012 which name changed to Great Elm Capital Group, Inc. 06/17/2016

PHONE MATE INC (CA)
Merged into Asahi Corp. 09/11/1989
Each share Common 10¢ par exchanged for $7.50 cash

PHONE ONE INTL INC (FL)
Name changed to Call Now Inc. 12/8/94

PHONE TIME RES INC (UT)
Recapitalized as Global Access Pagers Inc. 4/21/98
Each share Common $0.001 par exchanged for (0.025) share Common $0.001 par
Global Access Pagers Inc. name changed Integrated Communication Networks Inc. 1/29/99
(See Integrated Communication Networks Inc.)

PHONE1GLOBALWIDE CORP (DE)
Name changed to Celexpress Inc. 12/10/2007

PHONETEL TECHNOLOGIES INC (OH)
Each share old Common 1¢ par exchanged for (0.16666666) share new Common 1¢ par 12/26/1995
Plan of reorganization under Chapter 11 Federal Bankruptcy Code effective 11/17/1999
Each share new Common 1¢ par exchanged again for (0.00851483) share new Common 1¢ par and (0.01892238) Common Stock Purchase Warrant expiring 11/02/2002
Merged into Davel Communications, Inc. 07/24/2002
Each share new Common 1¢ par exchanged for (1.8233) shares Common 1¢ par
(See Davel Communications, Inc.)

PHONETICS INC (DE)
Each share Common $0.001 par exchanged for (0.04) share Common 2-1/2¢ par 03/06/1990
Acquired by Phonetics Acquisition, Inc. 12/11/1991
Each share Common 2-1/2¢ par exchanged for $0.55 cash

PHONETIME INC (ON)
Name changed to Tellza Communications Inc. 11/15/2013
Tellza Communications Inc. name changed to Tellza Inc. 12/13/2017

PHONETTIX INTELLECOM LTD (AB)
Name changed to Minacs Worldwide Inc. 07/21/1999
(See Minacs Worldwide Inc.)

PHONEX INC (DE)
Charter cancelled and declared inoperative and void for non-payment of taxes 3/1/89

PHONEXCHANGE INC (NV)
Reincorporated 07/27/1999
Each share old Common no par exchanged for (0.04) share new Common no par 02/22/1999
State of incorporation changed from (DE) to (NV) and new Common no par changed to $0.001 par 07/27/1999
Recapitalized as NetSky Holdings, Inc. 01/30/2006
Each share new Common $0.001 par exchanged for (0.02) share Common $0.0001 par
NetSky Holdings, Inc. recapitalized as Social Media Ventures, Inc. 05/28/2008

PHONOGRAPH CONTROL CORP. (DE)
Charter cancelled and declared inoperative and void for non-payment of taxes 1/23/24

PHORUM RE INVESTMENT CORP. (DE)
Charter cancelled and declared inoperative and void for non-payment of taxes 3/1/93

PHOSAGRO OJSC (RUSSIA)
Name changed to PhosAgro PJSC 09/30/2016

PHOSCAN CHEM CORP (CANADA)
Reincorporated 10/19/2006
Place of incorporation changed from (ON) to (Canada) 10/19/2006
Plan of arrangement effective 02/05/2016
Each share Common no par exchanged for (0.25) share Fox River Resources Corp. Common no par and (0.0452672) share Petrus Resources Ltd. Common no par
Note: Unexchanged certificates will be cancelled and become without value 02/05/2019

PHOSPHATE RESOURCE PARTNERS LTD PARTNERSHIP (DE)
Merged into IMC Global Inc. 10/19/2004
Each Depositary Unit exchanged for (0.2) share Common $1 par
IMC Global Inc. merged into Mosaic Co. (Old) 10/22/2004 which merged into Mosaic Co. (New) 05/25/2011

PHOTEES INC (FL)
Name changed to Tuscan Industries, Inc. 11/15/93
Tuscan Industries, Inc. recapitalized as Apache Group Inc. 12/31/95

PHOTO ACOUSTIC TECHNOLOGY INC (NV)
Each share old Common $0.001 par exchanged for (0.05) share new Common $0.001 par 09/03/1985
Name changed to SLS Industries, Inc. 01/08/1996
(See SLS Industries, Inc.)

PHOTO AMERICA INC (DE)
Name changed to Concept Digital, Inc. 07/19/2001
(See Concept Digital, Inc.)

PHOTO-ANIMATION, INC. (NY)
Dissolved 1963; stock worthless

PHOTO CTL CORP (MN)
Class A Common $1 par reclassified as Common 8¢ par 04/00/1962
Common 8¢ par split (5) for (4) by issuance of (0.25) additional share 04/02/1993
Stock Dividend - 25% 03/18/1985
Recapitalized as Nature Vision, Inc. 09/01/2004
Each share Common 8¢ par exchanged for (0.5) share Common 16¢ par
Nature Vision, Inc. name changed to Swordfish Financial, Inc. 10/13/2009 which recapitalized as SoOum, Corp. 10/01/2015

PHOTO DATA INC (DE)
Name changed to Printing Dimensions, Inc. 02/21/1990
(See Printing Dimensions, Inc.)

PHOTO DEVICES, INC. (NY)
Name changed to Reprotechnics Inc. 6/8/67
Reprotechnics Inc. completely liquidated for cash 1/22/71

PHOTO ENGRAVERS & ELECTRO TYPERS LTD (CANADA)
Common no par split (5) for (1) by issuance of (4) additional shares 12/05/1958
Common no par split (4) for (1) by issuance of (3) additional shares 04/15/1981
Acquired by Quebecor Printing Inc. 07/30/1993
Each share Common no par exchanged for $37.875 cash

PHOTO-FABRICS CORP.
Bankrupt in 1927

PHOTO GRAPHICS INC (MA)
Proclaimed dissolved for failure to file reports and pay taxes 1/10/79

PHOTO IMAGES INC (KS)
Charter forfeited for failure to file annual reports 7/15/88

PHOTO MAGIC INC (NV)
Name changed to P M Industries, Inc. 3/15/82
(See P M Industries, Inc.)

PHOTO MAGNETIC SYS INC (MD)
Out of business as of 10/00/1973
No stockholders' equity

PHOTO MED INC (DE)
Name changed to Real Med Industries, Inc. 04/12/1974
(See Real Med Industries, Inc.)

PHOTO MOTION CORP (PA)
Common 10¢ par split (2) for (1) by issuance of (1) additional share 4/11/69
Name changed to Multicom Corp. 10/30/72
Multicom Corp. name changed to Great Western Systems, Inc. 1/31/83
(See Great Western Systems, Inc.)

PHOTO SCAN CORP (DE)
Name changed to Petrofina, Inc. 2/13/78
Petrofina, Inc. name changed to Petro Oil & Gas, Inc. 4/20/78 which name changed to American Plastics & Chemicals Inc. 12/2/89
(See American Plastics & Chemicals Inc.)

PHOTO SERVICE, INC. (IL)
Merged into Crown-Bremson Industries, Inc. 9/29/61
Each (2.75) shares Common $1 par exchanged for (1) share Common $1 par
Crown-Bremson Industries, Inc. acquired by Berkey Photo, Inc. 1/28/65 which name changed to Berkey, Inc. 9/20/85
(See Berkey, Inc.)

PHOTOAMIGO INC (NV)
Name changed to Hartford Great Health Corp. 09/14/2018

PHOTOCHANNEL NETWORKS INC (BC)
Each share old Common no par exchanged for (0.1) share new Common no par 11/02/2006
Name changed to PNI Digital Media Inc. 06/09/2009
(See PNI Digital Media Inc.)

PHOTOCIRCUITS CORP. (NY)
Merged into Kollmorgen Corp. 01/30/1970
Each share Common 10¢ par exchanged for (0.402827) share Common $2.50 par
(See Kollmorgen Corp.)

PHOTOCOMM INC (AZ)
Reincorporated under the laws of Delaware as Golden Genesis Co. 6/25/98
(See Golden Genesis Co.)

PHOTOELECTRON CORP (MA)
Chapter 7 bankruptcy proceedings terminated 05/16/2007
Stockholders' equity unlikely

PHOTOGEN TECHNOLOGIES INC (NV)
Each share old Common $0.001 par exchanged for (0.25) share new Common $0.001 par 11/22/2002
Stock Dividend - 7% payable 5/21/2000 to holders of record 5/21/2000
Name changed to IMCOR Pharmaceutical Co. 2/5/2004

PHOTOGRAMMETRY INC (DE)
Completely liquidated 03/24/1969
Each share Common $1 par exchanged for first and final distribution of (0.08) share Mead Corp. Common no par
Mead Corp. merged into MeadWestvaco Corp. 01/29/2002 which merged into WestRock Co. 07/01/2015

PHOTOGRAPHIC ASSISTANCE CORP (GA)
Administratively dissolved 07/05/1998

PHOTOGRAPHIC SCIENCES CORP (NY)
Name changed to PSC Inc. 05/28/1992
(See PSC Inc.)

PHOTOLOFT COM GROUP INC (NV)
Name changed to Brightcube Inc. 12/06/2000

PHOTOMATICA INC (NV)
Name changed to Secure Runway Systems Corp. 09/15/2008
Secure Runway Systems Corp. name changed to Diversified Secure Ventures Corp. 09/24/2010 which recapitalized as Go Greeen Global Technologies Corp. 03/15/2012

PHOTOMATON, INC.
Assets sold in 1931

PHOTOMATRIX INC (CA)
Name changed to National Manufacturing Technologies Inc. 10/01/1999
(See National Manufacturing Technologies Inc.)

PHOTOMEDEX INC (NV)
Reincorporated 12/29/2010
Each share old Common 1¢ par exchanged for (0.14285714) share new Common 1¢ par 01/27/2009
Each share new Common 1¢ par exchanged again for (0.16666666) share new Common 1¢ par 02/04/2010
State of incorporation changed from (DE) to (NV) 12/29/2010
Each share old Common 1¢ par exchanged for (0.2) share new Common 1¢ par 09/23/2016
Name changed to FC Global Realty Inc. 11/01/2017

PHOTOMETRIC DATA SYS CORP (NY)
Name changed to PDS Liquidating Corp. 05/09/1973
(See PDS Liquidating Corp.)

PHOTON DYNAMICS INC (CA)
Merged into Orbotech Ltd. 10/03/2008
Each share Common no par exchanged for $15.60 cash

PHOTON INC (MA)
Common $1 par split (4) for (1) by issuance of (3) additional shares 8/19/68
Adjudicated bankrupt 2/14/75
No stockholders' equity

PHOTON SOURCES INC (MI)
Common no par split (2) for (1) by issuance of (1) additional share 10/23/81
Acquired by Lumonics Inc. 1/2/86
Each share Common no par exchanged for $3.875 cash

PHOTONIC PRODS GROUP INC (NJ)
Name changed to Inrad Optics, Inc. 04/09/2012

PHOTONIC SEC SYS INC (UT)
Recapitalized as Unified Ventures, Inc. 4/12/91
Each share Common $0.001 par exchanged for (0.3205128) share Common $0.001 par
(See Unified Ventures, Inc.)

PHOTONICS CORP (CA)
Issue Information - 1,875,000 shares COM offered at $9 per share on 11/23/1993
Each share old Common $0.001 par exchanged for (0.2) share new Common $0.001 par 03/05/1996
Reincorporated under the laws of Nevada as Small Cap Strategies, Inc. 10/02/2006
Small Cap Strategies, Inc. recapitalized as Bay Street Capital, Inc. 08/31/2010 which name changed to Los Angeles Syndicate of Technology, Inc. 10/14/2010 which name changed to Invent Ventures, Inc. 09/19/2012

PHOTOPHYSICS INC (CA)
Charter suspended for failure to file reports and pay taxes 04/01/1977

PHOTOSYSTEMS CORP (NY)
Adjudicated bankrupt 02/08/1975
Stockholders' equity unlikely

PHOTOTEX, INC. (NY)
Recapitalized as Universal Mineral Resources, Inc. 3/6/58
Each share Class A $2.45 par or Common 5¢ par exchanged for (0.2) share Common 25¢ par
Universal Mineral Resources, Inc. charter cancelled 12/15/70

PHOTOTHERM INC (DE)
Charter cancelled and declared inoperative and void for non-payment of taxes 3/1/88

PHOTOTRON CORP (DE)
Reincorporated 06/17/1976
State of incorporation changed from (AZ) to (DE) 06/17/1976
Merged into Steblay Corp. 12/24/1977
Each share Common 10¢ par exchanged for $6.16 cash

PHOTOTRON HLDGS INC (DE)
Common $0.001 par split (2) for (1) by issuance of (1) additional share payable 03/11/2011 to holders of record 02/28/2011 Ex date - 03/14/2011
Name changed to Growlife, Inc. 08/08/2012

PHOTOVOLTAIC SOLAR CELLS INC (NV)
Each share old Common $0.0001 par exchanged for (0.1) share new Common $0.0001 par 01/20/2011
Name changed to MetaStat, Inc. 04/20/2012

PHOTOVOLTAICS COM INC (DE)
Name changed to Pan-International Holdings, Inc. 06/06/2000
Pan-International Holdings, Inc. name changed to Global Business Services Inc. 12/17/2001 which recapitalized as Energetics Holdings, Inc. 11/09/2007 which recapitalized as Pavilion Energy Resources, Inc. 07/25/2008 which recapitalized as Matchtrade, Inc. 05/02/2012
(See Matchtrade, Inc.)

PHOTOVOLTAICS INC (FL)
Name changed to Billboards, Inc. 1/18/85
Billboards, Inc. name changed back to Photovoltaics, Inc. 6/3/85 which name changed to Tri-Texas, Inc. 3/17/86 which name changed to Enviromint International Inc. 6/30/92
(See Enviromint International Inc.)

PHOTOWAY CORP (WA)
Merged into Trans Film, Inc. 12/07/1979
Each share Common no par exchanged for $1.95 cash

PHOTOWORKS INC (WA)
Each share old Common 1¢ par exchanged for (0.2) share new Common 1¢ par 07/19/2005
Merged into American Greetings Corp. 01/24/2008

Each share Common 1¢ par exchanged for $0.595 cash

PHOTRAN CORP (MN)
SEC revoked common stock registration 8/28/2006
Stockholders' equity unlikely

PHOTRONIC LABS INC (CT)
Name changed to Photronics, Inc. 3/19/90

PHOTRONICS CORP (NY)
Merged into Diagnostic/Retrieval Systems, Inc. 8/12/88
Each share Common 10¢ par exchanged for $6.75 cash

PHP CO, INC. (CA)
Liquidation completed
Each share Common $1 par exchanged for initial distribution of (0.555555) share Reynolds (R.J.) Tobacco Co. Common $5 par 2/14/63
Each share Common $1 par received second distribution of $0.18 cash 1/30/64
Each share Common $1 par received third and final distribution of $0.14445 cash 2/1/66

PHP HEALTHCARE CORP (DE)
Common 1¢ par split (2) for (1) by issuance of (1) additional share 11/20/1995
Stock Dividend - 25% 02/25/1991
Plan of reorganization under Chapter 11 Federal Bankruptcy proceedings confirmed 10/12/1999
No stockholders' equity

PHREADZ INC (NV)
Name changed to Bizzingo, Inc. 05/02/2011
(See Bizzingo, Inc.)

PHRYGIAN MNG CORP (BC)
Recapitalized as Crowflight Minerals Inc. (ON) 10/12/1998
Each share Common no par exchanged for (0.66666666) share Common no par
Crowflight Minerals Inc. (ON) reincorporated in British Columbia as CaNickel Mining Ltd. 06/23/2011

PHS BANCORP INC (PA)
Reorganized as PHSB Financial Corp. 12/20/2001
Each share Common 10¢ par exchanged for (1.28123) shares Common 10¢ par
PHSB Financial Corp. merged into ESB Financial Corp. 2/11/2005

PHSB FINL CORP (PA)
Merged into ESB Financial Corp. 02/11/2005
Each share Common 10¢ par exchanged for (1.966) shares Common 1¢ par
ESB Financial Corp. merged into WesBanco, Inc. 02/10/2015

PHYAMERICA PHYSICIAN GROUP INC (DE)
Merged into Scott Group, Inc. 3/11/2002
Each share Common 1¢ par exchanged for $0.15 cash

PHYCOR INC (TN)
Common no par split (3) for (2) by issuance of (0.5) additional share 12/15/94
Common no par split (3) for (2) by issuance of (0.5) additional share payable 6/14/96 to holders of record 5/31/96
Stock Dividend - 50% 9/15/95
Plan of reorganization under Chapter 11 Federal Bankruptcy Code effective 7/22/2002
No stockholders' equity

PHYHEALTH CORP (DE)
Each share old Common $0.0001 par exchanged for (0.08333333) share new Common $0.0001 par 05/10/2012

Name changed to Osceola Gold, Inc. 07/11/2017

PHYMATRIX CORP (DE)
Name changed to Innovative Clinical Solutions, Ltd. 06/23/1999
(See Innovative Clinical Solutions, Ltd.)

PHYMED INC (OK)
SEC revoked common stock registration 07/14/2009
Stockholders' equity unlikely

PHYNOVA GROUP PLC (UNITED KINGDOM)
ADR agreement terminated 02/14/2011
Each ADR for Ordinary exchanged for (10) shares Ordinary
Note: Unexchanged ADR's will be sold and the proceeds, if any, held for claim after 06/14/2011

PHYSICAL CHEMISTRY RESEARCH CO. (DE)
Proclaimed inoperative and void for non-payment of taxes by Governor of Delaware 4/1/48

PHYSICAL SPA & FITNESS INC (DE)
Each share old Common $0.001 par exchanged for (0.7495689) share new Common $0.001 par 10/15/97
Each share new Common $0.001 par exchanged for (1.75) share new Common II 5/28/98
Name changed to Physical Property Holdings, Inc. 3/13/2007

PHYSICIAN COMPUTER NETWORK INC (NJ)
Plan of reorganization under Chapter 11 Federal Bankruptcy Code effective 04/04/2000
Each share Common 1¢ par received (1) NCP Litigation Trust Non-transferable Int. and $0.080501 cash payable 05/02/2002 to holders of record 10/13/2000

PHYSICIAN CORP AMER (DE)
Common 1¢ par split (2) for (1) by issuance of (1) additional share 9/15/93
Merged into Humana Inc. 9/8/97
Each share Common 1¢ par exchanged for $7 cash

PHYSICIAN DISPENSING SYS INC (DE)
Merged into Allscripts, LLC 12/31/2002
Details not available

PHYSICIAN RELIANCE NETWORK INC (TX)
Issue Information - 3,300,000 shares COM offered at $14 per share on 11/23/1994
Stock Dividend - 100% payable 6/10/96 to holders of record 5/31/96
Merged into U.S. Oncology, Inc. 6/15/99
Each share Common no par exchanged for (0.94) share Common no par
(See U.S. Oncology, Inc.)

PHYSICIAN SALES & SVC INC (FL)
Under plan of merger name changed to PSS World Medical, Inc. 03/27/1998
(See PSS World Medical, Inc.)

PHYSICIAN SUPPORT SYS INC (DE)
Merged into National Data Corp. 12/19/97
Each share Common $0.001 par exchanged for (0.435) share Common $0.125 par
National Data Corp. name changed to NDCHealth Corp. 10/25/2001 which merged into Per-Se Technologies, Inc. 1/6/2006
(See Per-Se Technologies, Inc.)

PHYSICIANS & SURGEONS UNDERWRITERS INSURANCE CO. (MN)
Merged into Countryside General, Inc. 05/01/1970
Each share Capital Stock $2 par exchanged for (1) share Common 10¢ par
(See Countryside General, Inc.)

PHYSICIANS ADULT DAYCARE INC (NV)
SEC revoked common stock registration 08/31/2009
Stockholders' equity unlikely

PHYSICIANS CLINICAL LAB INC (DE)
Second amended plan of reorganization under Chapter 11 bankruptcy proceedings effective 4/18/97
Each share Common 1¢ par exchanged for (1) Common Stock Purchase Warrant expiring 9/1/2002

PHYSICIANS CYBERNETIC SYS INC (NV)
Each share old Common $0.001 par exchanged for (0.5) share new Common $0.001 par 10/15/93
Name changed to Videocom International Inc. 7/20/94
Videocom International Inc. name changed to Canadian Tasty Fries, Inc. 2/1/95 which name changed to International Tasty Fries Inc. 4/13/95 which recapitalized as Filtered Souls Entertainment Inc. 11/25/98 which name changed to Skyline Entertainment, Inc. 3/31/99 which name changed to Quotemedia.Com Inc. 8/19/99 which name changed to Quotemedia, Inc. 3/11/2003

PHYSICIANS DISPENSING RX INC (CO)
Each share old Common $0.0001 par exchanged for (0.01) share new Common 1¢ par 1/1/90
Name changed to PD-RX Pharmaceuticals, Inc. 1/15/91

PHYSICIANS FORMULA HLDGS INC (DE)
Issue Information - 7,500,000 shares COM offered at $17 per share on 11/08/2006
Acquired by Markwins International Corp. 12/13/2012
Each share Common 1¢ par exchanged for $4.90 cash

PHYSICIANS HEALTH SVCS INC (DE)
Acquired by Foundation Health Systems Inc. 01/02/1998
Each share Class A Common 1¢ par exchanged for $28.25 cash

PHYSICIANS INS CO MICH (MI)
Common $1 par split (2) for (1) by issuance of (1) additional share 12/29/83
Stock Dividend - 10% 12/1/93
Name changed to PICOM Insurance Co. 8/18/94
PICOM Insurance Co. recapitalized as Professionals Insurance Company Management Group 9/3/96 which name changed to Professionals Group, Inc. 7/1/98 which merged into ProAssurance Corp. 6/27/2001

PHYSICIANS INS CO OHIO (OH)
Class A Common $8 par split (2) for (1) by issuance of (1) additional share 12/04/1980
Class A Common $8 par changed to $4 par and (1) additional share issued 01/08/1981
Class A Common $4 par changed to $2.67 par and (0.5) additional share issued 07/02/1982
Class A Common $2.67 par split (2) for (1) by issuance of (1) additional share 02/28/1983
Class A Common $2.67 par changed to $1 par 05/16/1983
Class A Common $1 par split (6) for (5) by issuance of (0.2) additional share 08/29/1986
Merged into PICO Holdings Inc. (CA) 11/20/1996
Each share Class A Common $1 par exchanged for (5.0099) shares Common $0.001 par
PICO Holdings Inc. (CA) reincorporated in Delaware 05/31/2017

PHYSICIANS INS SVCS LTD (MN)
Reincorporated under the laws of Nevada as PI Services, Inc. and Common no par changed to $0.001 par 01/12/2009
PI Services, Inc. recapitalized as China Lithium Technologies, Inc. 07/23/2010
(See China Lithium Technologies, Inc.)

PHYSICIANS PHARMACEUTICAL SVCS INC (CO)
Each share Common $0.001 par exchanged for (0.2) share Common $0.005 par 7/17/87
Proclaimed dissolved for failure to file reports and pay fees 4/1/95

PHYSICIANS REIMBURSEMENT SVCS INC (TX)
Charter forfeited for failure to maintain a registered agent 12/19/88

PHYSICIANS REMOTE SOLUTIONS INC (FL)
Name changed to HIPSO Multimedia, Inc. 08/08/2008
HIPSO Multimedia, Inc. recapitalized as Buildablock Corp. 03/07/2012

PHYSICIANS RESOURCE GROUP INC (DE)
Plan of reorganization under Chapter 11 Federal Bankruptcy Code effective 12/1/2000
Stockholders' equity unlikely

PHYSICIANS SPECIALTY CORP (DE)
Issue Information - 2,200,000 shares COM offered at $8 per share on 03/21/1997
Secondary Offering - 2,050,263 shares COM offered at $8.50 per share on 05/12/1998
Merged into TA Associates 11/1/99
Each share Common $0.001 par exchanged for $10.50 cash

PHYSICS INTL CO (CA)
Merged into Rocket Research Corp. 08/08/1975
Each share Common no par exchanged for (0.474) share Common no par
Rocket Research Corp. name changed to Rockcor Inc. 04/15/1977
(See Rockcor Inc.)

PHYSIO-CONTROL INTL CORP (DE)
Merged into Medtronic Inc. (MN) 09/30/1998
Each share Common 1¢ par exchanged for (0.48043) share Common 10¢ par
Medtronic Inc. (MN) reincorporated in Ireland as Medtronic PLC 01/27/2015

PHYSIO CTL CORP (DE)
Common $2 par changed to $1 par and (1) additional share issued 5/15/72
Common $1 par changed to 33-1/3¢ par and (2) additional shares issued 11/16/72
Common 33-1/3¢ par changed to 24¢ par and (0.5) additional share issued 7/20/78
Common 24¢ par split (2) for (1) by issuance of (1) additional share 11/16/79
Merged into Lilly (Eli) & Co. 5/7/80
Each share Common 24¢ par exchanged for (0.7) share Common 62-1/2¢ par

PHYSIO TECHNOLOGY INC (KS)
Merged into Castel Holdings Inc. 12/31/97
Each share Common no par exchanged for $0.01 cash

PHYSIODATA INC (DE)
Recapitalized as Petro Nicholas, Inc. 06/30/1980
Each share Common 1¢ par exchanged for (0.1) share Common 1¢ par
Petro Nicholas, Inc. name changed to Mariah Oil & Gas Corp. 01/01/1981
(See Mariah Oil & Gas Corp.)

PHYSIOGNOMY INTERFACE TECHNOLOGIES INC (NV)
Name changed to Ynot Education, Inc. (New) 01/10/2007
Ynot Education, Inc. (New) name changed to King Media Holdings Inc. 10/04/2007 which recapitalized as Extreme Fitness, Inc. 10/09/2007
(See Extreme Fitness, Inc.)

PHYSIOMETRIX INC (DE)
Merged into Hospira, Inc. 07/29/2005
Each share Common $0.001 par exchanged for $1.59 cash

PHYSIOTECH MED SCIENCE INC (DE)
Charter cancelled and declared inoperative and void for non-payment of taxes 3/1/90

PHYTOLABS INC (MN)
Recapitalized as LifeQuest World Corp. 08/20/2007
Each share Common no par exchanged for (0.333333333) share Common $0.001 par

PHYTOMEDICAL TECHNOLOGIES INC (NV)
Recapitalized as Ceres Ventures, Inc. 12/12/2011
Each share Common $0.00001 par exchanged for (0.02) share Common $0.00001 par

PHYTOPHARM PLC (ENGLAND & WALES)
ADR agreement terminated 11/15/2013
Each Sponsored ADR for Ordinary exchanged for $0.045821 cash

PI GRAPHIX INC (CA)
Name changed to 3DShopping.Com 3/10/99

PI SVCS INC (NV)
Each share old Common $0.001 par exchanged for (0.2) share new Common $0.001 par 03/20/2009
Recapitalized as China Lithium Technologies, Inc. 07/23/2010
Each (2.2) shares new Common $0.001 par exchanged for (1) share Common $0.001 par
(See China Lithium Technologies, Inc.)

PIA ASSET CASH TR (MA)
Voluntarily dissolved 06/25/1982
Details not available

PIA MERCHANDISING SVCS INC (DE)
Name changed to Spar Group Inc. 7/8/99

PIASECKI AIRCRAFT CORP (PA)
Common $1 par changed to 25¢ par 10/18/68
Merged into Piasecki Acquisition Corp. 9/29/92
Each share Common 25¢ par exchanged for $0.05 cash

PIASECKI HELICOPTER CORP. (PA)
Stock Dividends - 100% 5/16/51; 10% 11/17/53; 10% 11/22/54; 10% 11/21/55
Name changed to Vertol Aircraft Corp. 3/12/56 which was acquired by Boeing Airplane Co. 4/1/60 which

name was changed to Boeing Co. 5/4/61

PIC A PET INC (DE)
Name changed to Winona Mines, Inc. 12/10/75
(See Winona Mines, Inc.)

PIC CAP INC (CANADA)
Name changed to Pioneer Geophysical Services Inc. 10/11/1994
Pioneer Geophysical Services Inc. recapitalized as Xplore Technologies Corp. (Canada) 03/24/1997 which reincorporated in Delaware 06/20/2007
(See Xplore Technologies Corp.)

PIC N PAY STORES INC (DE)
Common 10¢ par split (2) for (1) by issuance of (1) additional share 6/6/72
Merged into CHB Corp. 12/16/80
Each share Common 10¢ par exchanged for $19.50 cash

PIC N SAVE CORP (DE)
Common $1 par changed to 50¢ par and (1) additional share issued 10/29/76
Common 50¢ par chaned to 25¢ par and (1) additional share issued 10/31/78
Common 25¢ par changed to $0.08333 par and (2) additional shares issued 6/29/81
Common $0.0833 par changed to $0.04167 par and (1) additional share issued 11/22/83
Common $0.04167 par changed to $0.02778 par and (0.5) additional share issued 6/10/86
Name changed to Mac Frugal's Bargain Close-Outs Inc. 6/10/92
Mac Frugal's Bargain Close-Outs Inc. merged into Consolidated Stores Corp. (DE) 1/16/98 which reincorporated in Ohio as Big Lots, Inc. 5/16/2001

PIC PRODTNS CORP (DE)
Charter cancelled and declared inoperative and void for non-payment of taxes 04/15/1973

PIC PROSPECTORS INTL CORP (BC)
Recapitalized as Starx Resource Corp. (BC) 08/22/1994
Each share Common no par exchanged for (0.25) share Common no par
Starx Resource Corp. (BC) reincorporated in Yukon as Gabriel Resources Ltd. 04/16/1997

PICADILLY RES LTD (BC)
Name changed to Allied Pacific Properties & Hotels Ltd. 09/12/1997
(See Allied Pacific Properties & Hotels Ltd.)

PICADILLY TECHNOLOGY INC (UT)
Name changed to Horizon Financial Corp. 04/20/1987
Horizon Financial Corp. name changed to Assurance Network, Inc. 06/06/1991 which recapitalized as Ult-I-Med Health Centers, Inc. (UT) 12/22/1993 which reincorporated in Delaware as Youthline USA, Inc. 08/17/1999
(See Youthline USA, Inc.)

PICARIUM GOLD MINES LTD. (ON)
Name changed to Draper Lake Frontenac Lead-Zinc Mines Ltd. in 1951
Draper Lake Frontenac Lead-Zinc Mines recapitalized as Lake Kingston Mines Ltd. in 1957
(See Lake Kingston Mines Ltd.)

PICASSO INC (AB)
Name changed to Blackline GPS Corp. 02/25/2009
Blackline GPS Corp. name changed to Blackline Safety Corp. 07/09/2015

PICCADILLY CAFETERIAS INC (LA)
Common no par split (5) for (4) by issuance of (0.25) additional share 1/2/86
Common no par split (5) for (4) by issuance of (0.25) additional share 7/1/86
Stock Dividend - 20% 7/1/81
Plan of reorganization under Chapter 11 Federal Bankruptcy Code effective 11/5/2004
No stockholders' equity

PICCADILLY PETROLEUM LTD.
Merged into Redwater-Piccadilly Petroleum Ltd. on a (1) for (2) basis in 1950
Redwater-Piccadilly Petroleum Ltd. name changed to Redpic Petroleums Ltd. in 1951 which recapitalized as Stanwell Oil & Gas Ltd. in 1952 which recapitalized as Cordwell International Developments Ltd. 12/16/66
(See Cordwell International Developments Ltd.)

PICCADILLY PORCUPINE GOLD MINES, LTD.
Name changed to Piccadilly Petroleum Ltd. in 1950
Piccadilly Petroleum Ltd. merged into Redwater-Piccadilly Petroleum Ltd. in 1950 which name changed to Redpic Petroleums Ltd. in 1951 which recapitalized as Stanwell Oil & Gas Ltd. in 1952 which recapitalized as Cordwell International Developments Ltd. 12/16/66
(See International Developments Ltd.)

PICCARD MED CORP (DE)
SEC revoked common stock registration 10/12/2007
Stockholders' equity unlikely

PICHE GOLD MINES, INC. (ON)
Merged into Branly Enterprises Inc. 12/09/1976
Each (50) shares Capital Stock no par exchanged for (11) shares Capital Stock no par
Branly Enterprises Inc. recapitalized as Consolidated Branly Resources Inc. 02/27/1984 which name changed to CBR Holdings Inc. 06/20/1985

PICK (ALBERT) & CO.
Assets transferred to Pick (Albert) Corp. in 1932
Pick (Albert) Corp. name changed to Pick (Albert) Co., Inc. in 1936 which name changed to Alpico, Inc. in October, 1953 which completed liquidation 5/13/58

PICK (ALBERT) BARTH CO., INC.
Reorganized in 1932
No stockholders' equity

PICK-BARTH HOLDING CORP.
Bankrupt in 1933

PICK COMMUNICATIONS CORP (NV)
Each share old Common $0.001 par exchanged for (0.1) share new Common $0.001 par 07/26/1999
SEC revoked common stock registration 11/04/2009
Stockholders' equity unlikely

PICK (ALBERT) CO., INC. (DE)
Name changed to Alpico, Inc. in October, 1953, which completed liquidation 5/13/58

PICK (ALBERT) CORP. (DE)
Name changed to Pick (Albert) Co., Inc. in 1936
Pick (Albert) Co., Inc. name changed to Alpico, Inc. in October, 1953 which completed liquidation 5/13/58

PICK MINES LTD. (ON)
Recapitalized as Picktex Mining & Investments Ltd. 12/30/1970
Each share Capital Stock $1 par exchanged for (1) share Capital Stock no par
(See Picktex Mining & Investments Ltd.)

PICK SZEGED RT (HUNGARY)
Each 144A Temporary 1997 Sponsored GDR for Shares exchanged for (1) 144A Sponsored GDR for Shares 03/23/1998
Sponsored GDR's for Ordinary split (5) for (1) by issuance of (4) additional GDR's payable 01/02/1998 to holders of record 12/26/1997
GDR agreement terminated 04/15/2005
Each 144A Sponsored GDR for Shares exchanged for $2.41762 cash

PICKANDS MATHER & CO. (DE)
Merged into Diamond Shamrock Corp. 1/3/69
Each share $1.15 Conv. Preferred Ser. A $25 par or $1.15 Conv. Preferred Ser. B $25 par exchanged for (1) share $1.15 Conv. Preferred Ser. E no par
Each share Common 50¢ par exchanged for (0.25) share Conv. Special Common no par and (0.8) share Common no par
Diamond Shamrock Corp. name changed to Maxus Energy Corp. 4/30/87
(See Maxus Energy Corp.)

PICKARD & BURNS CORP. (MA)
Merged into Gorham Manufacturing Co. on a (1) for (2.4) basis 3/3/60
Gorham Manufacturing Co. name changed to to Gorham Corp. 5/4/61 which liquidated for Textron Inc. (RI) 11/8/67 which reincorporated in Delaware 1/2/68

PICKERING LUMBER CO.
Reorganized as Pickering Lumber Corp. on a (1) for (2) basis in 1937
Pickering Lumber Corp. name changed to PLC Liquidating Corp. 7/26/65 which completed liquidation 6/17/66

PICKERING LUMBER CORP. (DE)
Each share Common $15 par exchanged for (2) shares Common $7.50 par 00/00/1950
Each share Common $7.50 par exchanged for (2) shares Common $3.75 par 06/03/1955
Name changed to PLC Liquidating Corp. 07/26/1965
(See PLC Liquidating Corp.)

PICKERING METAL MINES LTD (ON)
Charter cancelled for failure to pay taxes and file returns 03/16/1976

PICKERING URANIUM MINES LTD. (ON)
Name changed to Pickering Metal Mines Ltd. 00/00/1954
(See Pickering Metal Mines Ltd.)

PICKERING VALLEY RAILROAD CO.
Merged into Reading Co. on a (0.04) for (1) basis 12/31/45
Reading Co. merged into Reading Entertainment Inc. (DE) 10/15/96 which reincorporated in Nevada 12/29/99 which merged into Reading International, Inc. 12/31/2001

PICKERINGTON BK (PICKERINGTON, OH)
Merged into Huntington Bancshares, Inc. 05/01/1976
Each share Common $10 par exchanged for (0.5) share Common $10 par

PICKETT SUITE HOTEL MASTER L P 1 (DE)
Name changed to PSH Master L.P. I 11/19/90
(See PSH Master L.P. I)

PICKFORD MINERALS INC (NV)
Name changed to Novagen Solar, Inc. 07/02/2009
Novagen Solar, Inc. name changed to Novagen Ingenium Inc. 04/30/2012

PICKLE CROW EXPL LTD (ON)
Common $1 par changed to no par 10/12/1973
Merged into Highland-Crow Resources Ltd. 09/25/1978
Each share Common no par exchanged for (0.2) share Capital Stock no par
Highland-Crow Resources Ltd. merged into Noramco Mining Corp. 01/01/1988 which name changed to Quest Capital Corp. 01/03/1995 which name changed to Quest Oil & Gas Inc. 11/15/1996 which merged into EnerMark Income Fund 04/18/1997 which merged into Enerplus Resources Fund 06/22/2001 which reorganized as Enerplus Corp. 01/03/2011

PICKLE CROW GOLD MINES LTD (ON)
Merged into Silverfields Mining Corp. Ltd. 9/2/68
Each share Capital Stock $1 par exchanged for (0.005) share Silverfields Mining Corp. Ltd. Conv. Class A $4 par and (1) Pickle Crow Explorations Ltd. Common $1 par
(See each company's listing)

PICKLE CROW RES INC (AB)
Name changed to NeTrue Communications Inc. (ALTA) 3/16/2000
NeTrue Communications Inc. (ALTA) reincorporated in Delaware 4/19/2000

PICKREL WALNUT CO.
Liquidation completed in 1946

PICKTEX MNG & INVTS LTD (ON)
Charter cancelled for failure to pay taxes and file returns 08/00/1973

PICKWICK GOLD MINES, LTD. (ON)
Charter cancelled for failure to file reports and pay taxes in 1958

PICKWICK INTL INC (DE)
Reincorporated 10/27/75
Common 1¢ par changed to 50¢ par 8/21/63
Common 50¢ par changed to 40¢ par and (0.25) additional share issued 10/7/66
Common 40¢ par changed to 25¢ par and (0.5) additional share issued 9/15/67
Common 25¢ par split (3) for (2) by issuance of (0.5) additional share 7/9/71
Stock Dividend - 25% 8/5/69
State of incorporation changed from (NY) to (DE) 10/27/75
Merged into American Can Co. 6/7/77
Each share Common 25¢ par exchanged for $23 cash

PICKWICK NITECOACH CORP. LTD. (DE)
Charter cancelled and declared inoperative and void for non-payment of taxes 5/1/40

PICKWICK ORGANIZATION INC (NY)
Charter cancelled and proclaimed dissolved for failure to pay taxes 12/07/1976

PICO HLDGS INC (CA)
Each share old Common $0.001 par exchanged for (0.2) share new Common $0.001 par 12/16/1998
Reincorporated under the laws of Delaware 05/31/2017

PICO-LABORATORIES, INC. (TX)
Charter forfeited for non-payment of taxes 6/26/70

PICO PRODS INC (NY)
SEC revoked common stock registration 07/14/2009
Stockholders' equity unlikely

PICO RES LTD (BC)
Name changed to Tampico Capital Corp. 07/31/1992
(See Tampico Capital Corp.)

PICOLO VENTURES INC (NY)
Charter cancelled and declared inoperative and void for non-payment of taxes 3/24/93

PICOM INS CO (MI)
Stock Dividend - 10% 12/1/94
Recapitalized as Professionals Insurance Company Management Group 9/3/96
Each share Common $1 par exchanged for (1) share Common no par
Professionals Insurance Company Management Group name changed to Professionals Group, Inc. 7/1/98 which merged into ProAssurance Corp. 6/27/2001

PICOMETRIX INC (DE)
Name changed to Interjet Net Corp. 8/18/97
Interjet Net Corp. name changed to IJNT.net, Inc. 10/1/98 which name changed to Universal Broadband Networks Inc. 7/25/2000
(See Universal Broadband Networks Inc.)

PICORP CAP LTD (AB)
Reorganized under the laws of Ontario as Aeroquest International Ltd. 11/04/2004
Each share Common no par exchanged for (0.33333333) share Common no par
(See Aeroquest International Ltd.)

PICOSEC TECHNOLOGY LTD (BC)
Delisted from Alberta Stock Exchange 01/14/1991

PICTEL CORP (DE)
Name changed to Picturetel Corp. 04/10/1987
Picturetel Corp. merged into Polycom, Inc. 10/18/2001
(See Polycom, Inc.)

PICTOGRAPH MINING & URANIUM CO., INC. (DE)
Merged into Montana Chemical & Milling Corp. on a (0.5) for (1) basis 1/19/56
Montana Chemical & Milling Corp. charter revoked 4/1/61

PICTON URANIUM MINES LTD. (ON)
Recapitalized as New Picton Uranium Mines Ltd. 4/16/68
Each share Capital Stock $1 par exchanged for (0.25) share Capital Stock $1 par
New Picton Uranium Mines Ltd. charter cancelled 3/16/76

PICTORIAL PAPER PACKAGE CORP (IL)
Merged into American Recreation Group, Inc. 11/17/1969
Each share Common $5 par exchanged for (1) share Common $1 par
American Recreation Group, Inc. name changed to Exarg Corp. 12/09/1975
(See Exarg Corp.)

PICTORIAL PRODTNS INC (NY)
Name changed to Commercial Decal, Inc. 1/31/75
(See Commercial Decal, Inc.)

PICTURE IS COMPUTER CORP (NY)
Dissolved by proclamation 12/15/1973

PICTURE TRANSMISSION CORP.
Dissolved in 1930

PICTURETEL CORP (DE)
Each share Common $0.001 par exchanged for (0.1) share new Common 1¢ par 11/15/1989
Merged into Polycom, Inc. 10/18/2001
Each share new Common 1¢ par exchanged for (0.1177) share Common $0.0005 par and $3.11 cash
(See Polycom, Inc.)

PIE BAKERIES, INC.
Name changed to Wagner Baking Corp. in 1937
Wagner Baking Corp. adjudicated bankrupt 7/22/66

PIE BAKERIES OF AMERICA, INC.
Recapitalized as Pie Bakeries, Inc. in 1931 which name changed to Wagner Baking Corp. in 1937
Wagner Baking Corp. adjudicated bankrupt 7/22/66

PIECE GOODS SHOPS INC (NC)
Each (2,000) shares Common $1 par exchanged for (1) share Common $1 par 04/23/1979
Note: In effect holders received $7 cash per share and public interest was eliminated

PIED PIPER YACHT CHARTERS CORP (DE)
Charter cancelled and declared inoperative and void for non-payment of taxes 04/15/1973

PIEDMONT & NORTHN RY (SC)
Each share Common $100 par exchanged for (3) shares Common no par 03/15/1965
Merged into Seaboard Coast Line Railroad Co. 07/01/1969
Each share Common no par exchanged for (1.5) shares Common $20 par
Seaboard Coast Line Railroad Co. merged into Seaboard Coast Line Industries, Inc. (DE) 05/14/1971 which merged into CSX Corp. 11/01/1980

PIEDMONT AVIATION INC (NC)
$2.375 Conv. Preferred First Ser. no par called for redemption 6/6/81
Stock Dividends - 10% 5/25/61; 10% 5/27/63; 10% 6/2/69; 10% 6/5/73; 20% 3/16/81; 20% 3/1/85
Merged into USAir Group, Inc. 11/5/87
Each share Common $1 par exchanged for $71.24 cash
$3.25 Conv. Exchangeable Preferred no par called for redemption 6/15/89
Public interest eliminated

PIEDMONT BANCORP INC (NC)
Merged into National Commerce Bancorporation 4/12/2000
Each share Common no par exchanged for (0.60499) share Common no par
National Commerce Bancorporation name changed to National Commerce Financial Corp. 4/25/2001 which merged into SunTrust Banks, Inc. 10/1/2004

PIEDMONT BANCSHARES CORP (NC)
Merged into Old North State Bank (King, NC) 12/28/1995
Each share Common $1 par exchanged for (1) share Common $5 par
Old North State Bank (King, NC) merged into LSB Bancshares, Inc. 08/11/1997 which name changed to NewBridge Bancorp 07/31/2007 which merged into Yadkin Financial Corp. 03/01/2016 which merged into F.N.B. Corp. 03/11/2017

PIEDMONT BK & TR CO (DAVIDSON, NC)
Stock Dividends - 10% 01/13/1970; 100% 01/19/1971
Under plan of reorganization each share Common $5 par automatically became (1) share Piedmont Corp. Common $5 par 01/01/1974
Piedmont Corp. merged into First Union Corp. 12/31/1983 which name changed to Wachovia Corp. (Ctfs. dated after 09/01/2001) 09/01/2001 which merged into Wells Fargo & Co. (New) 12/31/2008

PIEDMONT BK (STATESVILLE, NC)
Stock Dividends - 5% payable 11/01/1999 to holders of record 10/01/1999; 10% payable 12/31/2001 to holders of record 12/17/2001
Under plan of reorganization each share Common $5 par automatically became (1) share Main Street Bankshares, Inc. Common $5 par 01/02/2002
Main Street Bankshares, Inc. merged into Yadkin Valley Bank & Trust Co. (Elkin, NC) 08/02/2002 which reorganized as Yadkin Valley Financial Corp. 07/01/2006 which recapitalized as Yadkin Financial Corp. 05/28/2013 which merged into F.N.B. Corp. 03/11/2017

PIEDMONT BANKGROUP INC (VA)
Common $5 par split (5) for (4) by issuance of (0.25) additional share 11/14/83
Common $5 par split (2) for (1) by issuance of (1) additional share 8/8/86
Common $5 par split (5) for (4) by issuance of (0.25) additional share 7/30/93
Name changed to MainStreet BankGroup Inc. 1/3/96
MainStreet BankGroup Inc. name changed to MainStreet Financial Corp. 6/1/98 which merged into BB&T Corp. 3/8/99

PIEDMONT COMMERCIAL CENTER LTD. (CA)
In process of liquidation
Each share Capital Stock $1 par exchanged for initial distribution of $4 cash 12/7/62
Note: Details on subsequent distributions, if any, are not available

PIEDMONT CORP (NC)
Stock Dividend - 100% 06/08/1976
Merged into First Union Corp. 12/31/1983
Each share Common $5 par exchanged for (1.45) shares Common $3.33-1/3 par
First Union Corp. name changed to Wachovia Corp. (Ctfs. dated after 09/01/2001) 09/01/2001 which merged into Wells Fargo & Co. (New) 12/31/2008

PIEDMONT ENERGY, INC. (UT)
Reincorporated under the laws of Texas as Standard Gypsum Corp. 5/1/86
(See Standard Gypsum Corp.)

PIEDMONT FED CORP (DE)
Reorganized 12/1/88
Reorganized from Piedmont Federal Savings Bank (Manassas, VA) to under the laws of Delaware as Piedmont Federal Corp. and Common $1 par changed to 1¢ par 12/1/88
Taken over by Resolution Trust Corp. 10/9/92
No stockholders' equity

PIEDMONT INC (UT)
Recapitalized as U.S. Biodefense, Inc. 06/20/2003
Each share Common $0.001 par exchanged for (0.01) share Common $0.001 par
U.S. Biodefense, Inc. name changed to Elysium Internet, Inc. 07/28/2008 which name changed to TheDirectory.com, Inc. 08/17/2011

PIEDMONT INDS INC (DE)
Merged into Kaywin, Inc. 03/10/1983
Each share Common 10¢ par exchanged for $1.40 cash

PIEDMONT IRON & METAL CO (MT)
Recapitalized as Macomb Biotechnology, Inc. 1/30/84
Each share Common 1¢ par exchanged for (2) shares Common 1¢ par
(See Macomb Biotechnology, Inc.)

PIEDMONT LABEL INC (VA)
Common $10 par changed to $2.50 par and (3) additional shares issued 4/3/72
Stock Dividends - 10% 3/1/61; 10% 8/20/64; 10% 8/25/66
Merged into Smyth Acquisition Corp. 9/30/98
Each share Common $2.50 par exchanged for $40.60 cash

PIEDMONT LIFE INS CO (GA)
Merged into Piedmont Southern Life Insurance Co. 07/11/1960
Each share Common exchanged for (1) share Capital Stock $10 par
Piedmont Southern Life Insurance Co. acquired by Piedmont Management Co. Inc. 07/11/1968 which merged into Chartwell RE Corp. 12/13/1995 which merged into Trenwick Group Inc. which merged into Trenwick Group Ltd. 09/27/2000
(See Trenwick Group Ltd.)

PIEDMONT MGMT INC (DE)
Common $1 par changed to 50¢ par and (1) additional share issued 10/16/1972
Merged into Chartwell RE Corp. 12/13/1995
Each share Conv. Preferred Ser. A $1 par exchanged for (2) shares Common 50¢ par
Each share Common 50¢ par exchanged for (0.5656) share Common 50¢ par and $0.182219 principal amount of Contingent Value Notes
Chartwell RE Corp. merged into Trenwick Group Inc. 10/27/1999 which merged into Trenwick Group Ltd. 09/27/2000
(See Trenwick Group Ltd.)

PIEDMONT MANUFACTURING CO.
Merged into Stevens (J.P.) & Co., Inc. in 1946
Each share Capital Stock $20 par exchanged for (2.15407) shares new Capital Stock $15 par
(See Stevens (J.P.) & Co., Inc.)

PIEDMONT MNG CO (NC)
Company terminated common stock registration and is no longer public as of 10/20/1998

PIEDMONT-MT. AIRY GUANO CO. OF BALTIMORE CITY (MD)
Charter forfeited 2/16/34
Stock is worthless

PIEDMONT NAT GAS INC (NC)
Reincorporated 03/01/1994
Common $1 par changed to 50¢ par and (1) additional share issued 10/01/1959
$5.50 Preferred no par called for redemption 09/30/1983
$6 Conv. Preferred no par called for redemption 09/30/1983
$5 Preferred no par called for redemption 02/28/1985
Common 50¢ par changed to 25¢ par and (1) additional share issued 03/31/1986
Common 25¢ par split (2) for (1) by issuance of (1) additional share 03/31/1993
Stock Dividend - 10% 01/15/1980
State of incorporation changed from (NY) to (NC) and Common 25¢ par changed to no par 03/01/1994
Common no par split (2) for (1) by issuance of (1) additional share payable 10/29/2004 to holders of record 10/11/2004 Ex date - 11/01/2004
Merged into Duke Energy Corp. 10/03/2016
Each share Common no par exchanged for $60 cash

FINANCIAL INFORMATION, INC.   PIE-PIG

PIEDMONT PETROLEUM PRODUCTS CO., LTD. (AB)
Struck off register for failure to file annual returns 09/14/1918

PIEDMONT PLUSH MILLS, INC. (SC)
Name changed to 200 Easley Bridge Road Corp., Inc. 12/14/1981

PIEDMONT PRINT WORKS
Acquired by Southern Bleachery & Print Works, Inc. 00/00/1930
Details not available

PIEDMONT REAL ESTATE INVT TR (SC)
Completely liquidated
Each Share of Bene. Int. no par received first and final distribution of $21 cash 01/31/1984
Note: Certificates were not required to be surrendered and are without value

PIEDMONT SOUTHN LIFE INS CO (GA)
Capital Stock $10 par changed to $6.66-2/3 par and (0.5) additional share issued 04/15/1964
Acquired by Piedmont Management Co. Inc. 07/11/1968
Each share Capital Stock $6.66-2/3 par exchanged for (2) shares Common $1 par
Piedmont Management Co. Inc. merged into Chartwell RE Corp. 12/13/1995 which merged into Trenwick Group Inc. 10/27/1999 which merged into Trenwick Group Ltd. 09/27/2000
(See Trenwick Group Ltd.)

PIEDMONT TRUST BANK (COLLINSVILLE, VA)
Stock Dividends - 10% 2/20/70; 10% 2/15/71; 10% 2/18/72; 25% 4/29/74
Reorganized as Piedmont Bankgroup Inc. 10/31/77
Each share Common $5 par exchanged for (1) share Common $5 par
Piedmont Bankgroup Inc. name changed to MainStreet BankGroup Inc. 1/3/96 which name changed to MainStreet Financial Corp. 6/1/98 which merged into BB&T Corp. 3/8/99

PIEMONTE FOODS INC (SC)
Common no par split (3) for (2) by issuance of (0.5) additional share 09/30/1987
SEC revoked common stock registration 07/14/2009

PIER 1 IMPORTS INC (DE)
Incorporated 00/00/1969
Common 20¢ par split (3) for (2) by issuance of (0.5) additional share 03/12/1971
Common 20¢ par split (2) for (1) by issuance of (1) additional share 04/24/1972
Name changed to Pirvest Inc. 12/19/1979

PIER 1 IMPORTS INC (DE)
Incorporated 05/31/1978
Name changed 07/13/1984
Name changed 09/18/1986
Name changed from Pier 1 Imports, Inc. to Pier 1 Inc. 07/13/1984
Common $1 par split (3) for (2) by issuance of (0.5) additional share 07/18/1986
Stock Dividend - 10% 02/28/1986
Name changed from Pier 1 Inc. to Pier 1 Imports, Inc. 09/19/1986
$0.25 Preferred $1 par reclassified as Formula Rate Preferred $1 par 10/30/1987
Formula Rate Preferred $1 par called for redemption 09/18/1991

PIER MAC ENVIRONMENT MGMT INC (BC)
Recapitalized as Ebony Gold & Gas Inc. 04/07/1995
Each share Common no par exchanged for (0.33333333) share Common no par
Ebony Gold & Gas Inc. recapitalized as Running Foxes Petroleum Corp. 12/09/1998 which recapitalized as Running Fox Resource Corp. 10/17/2000

PIER 39 INC (CA)
Completely liquidated 01/15/1982
Each share Common 10¢ par exchanged for $17.45 principal amount of Pier 39 Limited Partnership Secured Installment Notes due 06/01/2012 and $4.54 cash

PIERBANK (NARRAGANSETT, RI)
Merged into Washington Trust Bancorp, Inc. 8/25/99
Each share Common $1 par exchanged for (0.468) share Common $0.0625 par

PIERCE & STEVENS CHEMICAL CORP. (NY)
Each share Class A Capital Stock $3.33-1/3 par or Class B Capital Stock $3.33-1/3 par exchanged for (2) shares Common $2 par 8/12/59
Completely liquidated 1/12/68
Each share Common $2 par exchanged for first and final distribution of (0.18844) share Pratt & Lambert, Inc. $2.25 Conv. Preferred Ser. A $10 par and (0.19035) share Common $10 par
Pratt & Lambert, Inc. name changed to Pratt & Lambert United, Inc. 8/4/94

PIERCE-ARROW MOTOR CO.
Reorganized as Pierce-Arrow Motor Corp. in 1935 which liquidated with no stockholders' equity in 1938

PIERCE-ARROW MOTOR CORP.
Liquidated in 1938
No stockholders' equity

PIERCE BUTLER & PIERCE MANUFACTURING CORP. (NY)
Reorganized as Pierce Butler Radiator Corp. 00/00/1935
Details not available

PIERCE BUTLER RADIATOR CORP. (NY)
Name changed to Ames Iron Works, Inc. 00/00/1952
(See Ames Iron Works, Inc.)

PIERCE CO., INC. (MA)
Preferred $100 par called for redemption 8/1/69
Proclaimed dissolved for failure to file reports and pay taxes 2/12/81

PIERCE FLORIDA RAMIE, INC. (FL)
Charter revoked for failure to file reports and pay fees 5/24/63

PIERCE GOVERNOR INC (IN)
Name changed to Pierce Industries, Inc. 6/5/57 which name changed back to Pierce Governor Co., Inc. 5/27/64
Common no par changed to $1 par in 1949
Common $1 par split (5) for (4) by issuance of (0.25) additional share 9/10/67
Stock Dividends - 10% 12/28/51; 10% 12/31/53
Merged into International General Industries, Inc. 4/6/71
Each share Common $1 par exchanged for (0.3636) share Common 50¢ par
International General Industries, Inc. merged into International Bank (Washington, DC) 12/31/79 which merged into USLICO Corp. 12/31/85 which merged into NWNL Companies, Inc. 1/17/95 which name changed to ReliaStar Financial Corp. 2/13/95
(See ReliaStar Financial Corp.)

PIERCE INDUSTRIES, INC. (IN)
Name changed to Pierce Governor Co., Inc. 5/27/64
Pierce Governor Co., Inc. merged into International General Industries, Inc. 4/6/71 which merged into International Bank (Washington, DC) 12/31/79 which merged into USLICO Corp. 12/31/85 which name changed to ReliaStar Financial Corp. 2/13/95
(See ReliaStar Financial Corp.)

PIERCE INTL DISCOVERY INC NEW (NV)
Name changed to Emergisoft Holding, Inc. 05/14/2001
(See Emergisoft Holding, Inc.)

PIERCE INTL DISCOVERY INC OLD (NV)
Reincorporated 04/30/1999
State of incorporation changed from (CO) to (NV) and Common no par changed to $0.001 par 04/30/1999
Recapitalized as Inshape International Inc. 05/10/1999
Each (750) shares Common $0.001 par exchanged for (1) share Common $0.001 par
Inshape International Inc. name changed to Pierce International Discovery Inc. (New) 01/31/2000 which name changed to Emergisoft Holding, Inc. 05/14/2001
(See Emergisoft Holding, Inc.)

PIERCE INTL INC (CO)
Each share old Common no par exchanged for (0.25) share new Common no par 03/13/1996
Reincorporated under the laws of Delaware as North American DataCom, Inc. 04/06/2000
(See North American DataCom, Inc.)

PIERCE LEAHY CORP (PA)
Issue Information - 5,312,614 shares COM offered at $18 per share on 06/30/1997
Stock Dividend - 10% payable 1/14/2000 to holders of record 1/7/2000
Under plan of merger name changed to Iron Mountain Inc. (PA) 2/1/2000
Iron Mountain Inc. (PA) reincorporated back in Delaware 5/27/2005

PIERCE MTN RES LTD (BC)
Recapitalized as Portal Resources Ltd. 12/03/1991
Each share Common no par exchanged for (1/3) share Common no par
Portal Resources Ltd. recapitalized as Capella Resources Ltd. (Incorporated 02/27/1987) 12/07/1994 which recapitalized as Cerro Mining Corp. 05/16/2012

PIERCE OIL CORP.
Dissolved in 1940

PIERCE PETROLEUM CORP. (DE)
Dissolved in 1939

PIERCE S S CO (MA)
Each share Common $100 par exchanged for (5) shares Common $20 par 00/00/1942
Name changed to Pierce Co., Inc. 07/07/1967
(See Pierce Co., Inc.)

PIERCE S S INC (NY)
Each share old Common $1 par exchanged for (0.5) share new Common $1 par 03/11/1978
$1 Conv. Preferred no par called for redemption 01/02/1986
Recapitalized back as Seneca Foods Corp. 11/24/1986
Each share 6% Preferred $1 par exchanged for (4) shares 6% Preferred 25¢ par
Each share new Common $1 par exchanged for (4) shares Common $1 par

PIERCING PAGODA INC (DE)
Merged into Zale Corp. 09/29/2000
Each share Common 1¢ par exchanged for $21.50 cash

PIERPONT BD FD (MA)
Reorganized as JPM Pierpont Funds 10/31/1996
Details not available

PIERPONT CAP APPRECIATION FD (MA)
Reorganized as JPM Pierpont Funds 10/31/1996
Details not available

PIERPONT EQUITY FD (MA)
Reorganized as JPM Pierpont Funds 10/31/1996
Details not available

PIERPONT FD (MA)
Reorganized as JPM Pierpont Funds 10/31/1996
Details not available

PIERPONT GOLD MINES, LTD. (ON)
Charter cancelled for failure to file reports and pay taxes August 1957

PIERPONT INTL EQUITY FD INC (MD)
Reorganized as JPM Pierpont Funds 10/31/1996
Details not available

PIERPONT TAX EXEMPT BD FD (MA)
Reorganized as JPM Pierpont Funds 10/31/1996
Details not available

PIERPONT TAX EXEMPT MONEY MKT FD (MA)
Reorganized as JPM Pierpont Funds 10/31/1996
Details not available

PIERRE ENTERPRISES LTD (BC)
Recapitalized as Leeta Gold Corp. 02/01/2011
Each share Common no par exchanged for (0.5) share Common no par
Leeta Gold Corp. name changed to HIVE Blockchain Technologies Ltd. 09/18/2017

PIERRE FOODS INC (NC)
Acquired by PF Management, Inc. 7/26/2002
Each share Common $1 par exchanged for $2.50 cash

PIEZO ELEC PRODS INC (DE)
Class A Common 1¢ par reclassified as old Common 1¢ par 2/16/83
Each share old Common 1¢ par exchanged for (0.04) share new Common 1¢ par 12/3/90
Charter cancelled and declared inoperative and void for non-payment of taxes 2/18/94

PIEZO INSTRS INC (UT)
Each share old Common $0.001 par exchanged for (0.06896551) share new Common $0.001 par 08/25/2003
Name changed to Omni Medical Holdings Inc. 09/05/2003
(See Omni Medical Holdings Inc.)

PIFHER RES INC (ON)
Name changed to Echo Energy Canada Inc. and (2) additional shares issued 10/18/2004
(See Echo Energy Canada Inc.)

PIG N WHISTLE CORP (DE)
Participating Preferred no par reclassified as Conv. Prior Preferred $7.50 par 00/00/1946
Common no par changed to 50¢ par 00/00/1946
Each share Conv. Prior Preferred $7.50 par exchanged for (3) shares Common 50¢ par 05/08/1968
Each share Special Preferred $8 par exchanged for (3) shares Common 50¢ par
Charter cancelled and declared inoperative and void for non-payment of taxes 04/15/1970

PIGALLE (MARIE), INC. (NY)
Name changed to Time-Off, Inc. 2/26/70

PIGEON HOLE PARKING OF TEXAS, INC. (TX)
Merged into Southwest Realty & Development Co., Inc. (DE) (Old) on a (0.2) for (1) basis 8/31/61
Southwest Realty & Development Co., Inc. (DE) (Old) merged into Southwest Realty & Development Co., Inc. (DE) (New) 6/24/77 which liquidated for Southwest Stockholders Liquidating Trust 6/5/78

PIGEON HOLE PKG (WA)
Each share old Common $1 par exchanged for (1) share Preferred no par and (1) share Common 10¢ par in 1953
Each share Preferred no par and Common 10¢ par exchanged for (1) share new Common $1 par in 1954
Charter cancelled for failure to pay fees 5/2/76

PIGEON LAKE PETROLEUMS LTD. (AB)
Recapitalized as Supreme Oil & Gas Ltd. 6/24/63
Each share Capital Stock no par exchanged for (0.1) share Capital Stock no par
Supreme Oil & Gas Ltd. recapitalized as Supreme Gas & Oil Ltd. 11/5/68
(See Supreme Gas & Oil Ltd.)

PIGGLY WIGGLY CALIFORNIA CO. (CA)
Name changed to Continental Food Markets of California, Inc. 9/12/65
(See Continental Food Markets of California, Inc.)

PIGGLY WIGGLY COLORADO CO. (CO)
Charter suspended for failure to file corporate reports 12/26/28

PIGGLY WIGGLY CORP (DE)
Each (300) shares Common no par exchanged for (1) share Common no par 10/08/1979
Note: In effect holders received $86.50 cash per share and public interest was eliminated

PIGGLY WIGGLY MONTANA CO. (CO)
Charter suspended for failure to file corporate reports 8/17/31

PIGGLY-WIGGLY STORES, INC.
Acquired by Kroger Grocery & Baking Co. 00/00/1929
Details not available

PIGGLY WIGGLY WESTERN STATES CO.
Merged into Safeway Stores, Inc. 00/00/1929
Details not available

PIH PAC INTL HARDWOODS INC (BC)
Cease trade order effective 02/01/2002
Stockholders' equity unlikely

PII PHOTOVISION INTL INC (BC)
Struck off register and declared dissolved for failure to file returns 03/03/1995

PIK-QUIK, INC. (MN)
Name changed to Li'l General Stores, Inc. 01/15/1962
Li'l General Stores, Inc. merged into General Host Corp. 07/19/1968
(See General Host Corp.)

PIKE CORP. OF AMERICA (CA)
Capital Stock $10 par reclassified as Common $10 par 04/15/1966
Common $10 par split (3) for (2) by issuance of (0.5) additional share 05/20/1966
Common $10 par changed to $1 par and (1) additional share issued 06/07/1967
$1 Conv. Preferred no par changed to $1 par 07/09/1968
Stock Dividend - 20% 01/28/1966
Merged into Fluor Corp. Ltd. 01/02/1969
Each share $1 Conv. Preferred $1 par exchanged for (0.24) share $3 Conv. Preferred Ser. B no par and (1.41) shares Common $0.625 par
Each share Common $1 par exchanged for (0.08) share $3 Conv. Preferred Ser. B no par and (0.47) share Common $0.625 par
Fluor Corp. Ltd. name changed to Fluor Corp. (CA) 05/22/1969 which reincorporated in Delaware 07/14/1978 which name changed to Massey Energy Co. 11/30/2000 which merged into Alpha Natural Resources, Inc. 06/01/2011
(See Alpha Natural Resources, Inc.)

PIKE CORP (NC)
Reincorporated 11/06/2013
State of incorporation and name changed from Pike Electric Corp. (DE) to Pike Corp. (NC) 11/06/2013
Acquired by Pioneer Parent, Inc. 12/22/2014
Each share Common $0.001 par exchanged for $12 cash

PIKE CNTY NATL BK (MCCOMB, MS)
Name changed to Pike National Bank (McComb, MS) 02/01/2007

PIKE COUNTY OIL CO. (MS)
Charter forfeited 04/05/1933

PIKES PEAK ACQUISITIONS COM INC (NV)
Reorganized as U.S. Mobile Dental Corp. 07/23/2004
Each share Common $0.001 par exchanged for (200) shares Common $0.001 par
U.S. Mobile Dental Corp. name changed to Ingenex Corp. 07/29/2005
(See Ingenex Corp.)

PIKES PEAK AMERN CORP (CO)
Recapitalized as Transmedia Network, Inc. (CO) 09/01/1984
Each (3.42857) shares Common 1¢ par exchanged for (1) share Common $0.001 par
Transmedia Network, Inc. (CO) reincorporated in Delaware 07/20/1987 which name changed to iDine Rewards Networks Inc. 02/01/2002 which name changed to Rewards Network Inc. 12/09/2003
(See Rewards Network Inc.)

PIKES PEAK TURF CLUB INC (CO)
Name changed to Pike's Peak American Corp. 06/28/1974
Pike's Peak American Corp. recapitalized as Transmedia Network, Inc. (CO) 09/01/1984 which reincorporated in Delaware 07/20/1987 which name changed to iDine Rewards Network Inc. 02/01/2002 which name changed to Rewards Network Inc. 12/09/2003
(See Rewards Network Inc.)

PIKES PEAK URANIUM CORP. (CO)
Name changed to AGCO Industries, Inc. and Common 10¢ par changed to $0.003 par 4/27/81
AGCO Industries, Inc. declared defunct 9/30/83

PIKEVILLE NATL CORP (KY)
Common $5 par split (3) for (2) by issuance of (0.5) additional share 5/1/92
Common $5 par split (3) for (2) by issuance of (0.5) additional share 2/1/94
Name changed to Community Trust Bancorp, Inc. 7/1/97

PILAGOLD INC (BC)
Merged into Radius Gold Inc. 7/2/2004
Each (2.25) shares Common no par exchanged for (1) share Common no par

PILGRIM ACQUISITION CORP (NV)
Name changed to Zeron Acquisition I, Inc. 8/5/91
Zeron Acquisition I, Inc. name changed to Advanced Orthopedic Technologies Inc. 5/6/92
(See Advanced Orthopedic Technologies Inc.)

PILGRIM AMER BK & THRIFT FD INC (MD)
Name changed to Pilgrim Bank & Thrift Fund 11/16/98
Pilgrim Bank & Thrift Fund name changed to Pilgrim Financial Services Fund 5/22/2001 which name changed to ING Financial Services Fund, Inc. 3/1/2002

PILGRIM AMER CAP CORP (DE)
Common 1¢ par split (3) for (2) by issuance of (0.5) additional share payable 04/30/1998 to holders of record 04/20/1998
Name changed to Pilgrim Capital Corp. 06/21/1999
Pilgrim Capital Corp. merged into ReliaStar Financial Corp. 10/29/1999
(See ReliaStar Financial Corp.)

PILGRIM AMER INVT FD INC (MD)
Name changed back to Pilgrim Investment Funds, Inc. 11/16/1998
Pilgrim Investment Funds, Inc. name changed to ING Investment Funds, Inc. 03/01/2002

PILGRIM AMER PRIME RATE TR (MA)
Name changed to Pilgrim Prime Rate Trust (New) 11/16/1998
Pilgrim Prime Rate Trust (New) name changed to ING Prime Rate Trust 03/1/2002 which name changed to Voya Prime Rate Trust 05/01/2014

PILGRIM BK & THRIFT FD INC (MD)
Name changed to Pilgrim Financial Services Fund 5/22/2001
Pilgrim Financial Services Fund name changed to ING Financial Services Fund, Inc. 3/1/2002

PILGRIM CAP CORP (DE)
Merged into ReliaStar Financial Corp. 10/29/1999
Each share Common no par exchanged for (0.5) share Common no par and $12.50 cash
(See ReliaStar Financial Corp.)

PILGRIM CO.
Merged into Connecticut Investment Management Corp. 00/00/1931
Details not available

PILGRIM CO (DE)
Charter cancelled and declared inoperative and void for non-payment of taxes 3/1/75

PILGRIM COAL CORP (BC)
Name changed to Pilgrim Holdings Ltd. 09/23/1985
(See Pilgrim Holdings Ltd.)

PILGRIM CORP (IN)
Filed a petition under Chapter 11 Federal Bankruptcy Code 07/30/1980
Stockholders' equity unlikely

PILGRIM CORPORATE LEADERS TR FD (NY)
Name changed to ING Corporate Leaders Trust Fund 03/01/2002

PILGRIM EQUITY TR (MA)
Name changed to ING Equity Trust 3/1/2002

PILGRIM EXPLORATION CO.
Liquidation completed in 1948

PILGRIM FD INC (MD)
Merged into Pilgrim Magnacap Fund, Inc. 06/20/1985
Each share Common $1 par exchanged for (1.977747) shares Capital Stock 10¢ par
Pilgrim Magnacap Fund, Inc. name changed to Pilgrim America Investment Funds, Inc. 07/14/1995 which name changed back to Pilgrim Investment Funds, Inc. 11/16/1998 which name changed to ING Investment Funds, Inc. 03/01/2002

PILGRIM FINANCIAL & GROWTH FUND, INC. (MD)
Name changed to Pilgrim Fund, Inc. 7/28/66
Pilgrim Fund, Inc. merged into Pilgrim Magnacap Fund, Inc. 6/20/85

PILGRIM FINL SVCS FD (MD)
Name changed to ING Financial Services Fund, Inc. 3/1/2002

PILGRIM FORMULA SHS INC (MD)
Completely liquidated 10/31/1978
Each share Common 10¢ par exchanged for first and final distribution of (1.1094) Pilgrim Fund, Inc. $1 par
Pilgrim Fund, Inc. merged into Pilgrim MagnaCap Fund, Inc. 06/20/1985 which merged into Pilgrim Investment Funds, Inc. 07/03/1992 which name changed to Pilgrim America Investment Funds, Inc. 07/14/1995 which name changed back to Pilgrim Investment Funds, Inc. 11/16/1998 which name changed to ING Investment Funds, Inc. 03/01/2002

PILGRIM GNMA INCOME FD INC (MD)
Name changed to ING GNMA Income Fund, Inc. 03/01/2002

PILGRIM GOVT SECS FD (CA)
Merged into Pilgrim GNMA Income Fund, Inc. 02/22/2001
Each Share of Bene. Int. exchanged for Class A shares on a net asset basis
Each share of Class A exchanged for Class A shares on a net asset basis
Each share of Class B exchanged for Class B shares on a net asset basis
Each share of Class C exchanged for Class C shares on a net asset basis
Each share of Class T exchanged for Class T shares on a net asset basis
Pilgrim GNMA Income Fund, Inc. name changed to ING GNMA Income Fund, Inc. 03/01/2002

PILGRIM GROWTH & INCOME FD INC (MD)
Name changed to ING Large Company Value Fund, Inc. 3/1/2002
(See ING Large Company Value Fund, Inc.)

PILGRIM GROWTH OPPORTUNITIES FD (MA)
Name changed to ING Growth Opportunities Fund 3/1/2002

PILGRIM HELICOPTER SERVICES, INC. (DC)
Charter revoked for failure to file reports 9/13/65

PILGRIM HLDGS LTD (BC)
Struck off register and declared dissolved for failure to file returns 02/26/1993

PILGRIM INTERGROUP INVT CORP (PA)
Each share Common 20¢ par exchanged for (0.25) share Common 80¢ par 07/10/1971
Merged out of existence 09/28/1993
Details not available

PILGRIM INTL FD INC (MD)
Name changed to ING International Fund, Inc. 3/1/2002

PILGRIM INVT FDS INC (MD)
Name changed to Pilgrim America Investment Funds, Inc. 07/14/1995 which name changed back to Pilgrim Investment Funds, Inc. 11/16/1998 which name changed to ING Investment Funds, Inc. 03/01/2002

PILGRIM LIFE INS CO (IN)
Each share Common 60¢ par exchanged for (1/3) share Common $1 par 09/18/1968
Name changed to Pilgrim Corp. 07/01/1973
(See Pilgrim Corp.)

PILGRIM MAGNACAP FD INC (MD)
Under plan of merger each share Common 10¢ par automatically became (1) share Pilgrim Investment Funds, Inc. MagnaCap Fund Class A 10¢ par 07/03/1992
Pilgrim Investment Funds, Inc. name changed to Pilgrim America Investment Funds, Inc. 07/14/1995 which name changed back to Pilgrim Investment Funds, Inc. 11/16/1998 which name changed to ING Investment Funds, Inc. 03/01/2002

PILGRIM MAYFLOWER TR (MA)
Name changed to ING Mayflower Trust 3/1/2002

PILGRIM MLS INC (DE)
Name changed to MHI Telecommunications, Inc. 02/17/1983
(See MHI Telecommunications, Inc.)

PILGRIM NATIONAL BANK (BOSTON, MA)
Liquidation completed
Each share Capital Stock $10 par

stamped to indicate initial distribution of $25 cash 06/04/1958
Each share Stamped Capital Stock $10 par received second distribution of $5.50 cash 04/21/1959
Each share Stamped Capital Stock $10 par received third distribution of $1.50 cash 04/01/1960
Each share Stamped Capital Stock $10 par received fourth and final distribution of $0.20 cash 01/15/1962
Note: Certificates were not required to be surrendered and are without value

PILGRIM PETROLEUM INC. (BC)
Name changed to Pilgrim Coal Corp. 05/13/1981
Pilgrim Coal Corp. name changed to Pilgrim Holdings Ltd. 09/23/1985
(See Pilgrim Holdings Ltd.)

PILGRIM PREFERRED FUND (MA)
Name changed to Pilgrim Short-Term Multi-Market Income Fund 7/1/90

PILGRIM PRIME RATE TR NEW (MA)
Name changed to ING Prime Rate Trust 03/01/2002
ING Prime Rate Trust name changed to Voya Prime Rate Trust 05/01/2014

PILGRIM PRIME RATE TR OLD (MA)
Name changed to Pilgrim America Prime Rate Trust 04/12/1996
Pilgrim America Prime Rate Trust name changed to Pilgrim Prime Rate Trust (New) 11/16/1998 which name changed to ING Prime Rate Trust 03/01/2002 which name changed to Voya Prime Rate Trust 05/01/2014

PILGRIM REGL BK SHS INC (MD)
Name changed to Pilgrim America Bank & Thrift Fund, Inc. 4/8/96
Pilgrim America Bank & Thrift Fund, Inc. name changed to Pilgrim Bank & Thrift Fund 11/16/98 which name changed to Pilgrim Financial Services Fund 5/22/2001 which name changed to ING Financial Services Fund, Inc. 3/1/2002

PILGRIM RESOURCE CORP (AB)
Merged into International Gryphon Resources Inc. (New) 04/27/1995
Each share Common no par exchanged for (1) share Common no par
International Gryphon Resources Inc. (New) recapitalized as Wirbac Resources Inc. 12/05/2000 which recapitalized as Virtus Energy Ltd. 09/12/2001 which merged into Titan Exploration Ltd. 06/23/2005 which was acquired by Penn West Energy Trust 01/11/2008 which reorganized as Penn West Petroleum Ltd. (New) 01/03/2011 which name changed to Obsidian Energy Ltd. 06/29/2017

PILGRIM RUSSIA FD INC (MD)
Name changed to ING Russia Fund, Inc. 3/1/2002

PILGRIM SMALLCAP OPPORTUNITIES FD (MA)
Name changed to ING SmallCap Opportunities Fund 3/1/2002

PILGRIM SR INCOME FD (DE)
Under plan of reorganization each Class A Share of Bene. Int., Class B Share of Bene. Int., Class C Share of Bene. Int., and Class Q Share of Bene. Int. automatically became (1) share ING Senior Income Fund Class A, Class B, Class C, or Class Q respectively 3/1/2002

PILGRIM TROIKA DIALOG RUSSIA FD INC (MD)
Name changed to Pilgrim Russia Fund, Inc. 3/1/2001
Pilgrim Russia Fund, Inc. name changed to ING Russia Fund, Inc. 3/1/2002

PILGRIM TRUST CO. (BOSTON, MA)
Each share Capital Stock $100 par exchanged for (4) shares Capital Stock $25 par 00/00/1946
Each share Capital Stock $25 par exchanged for (2.5) shares Capital Stock $10 par 02/01/1956
Stock Dividend - 25% 03/01/1948
Name changed to Pilgrim National Bank (Boston, MA) 04/18/1958
(See Pilgrim National Bank (Boston, MA))

PILGRIM VENTURE CORP (FL)
Involuntarily dissolved for failure to maintain a resident agent 06/07/1988

PILGRIMS PRIDE CORP (DE)
Common 1¢ par reclassified as Class B Common 1¢ par 06/30/1998
Class A Common 1¢ par reclassified as Common 1¢ par 11/21/2003
Class B Common 1¢ par reclassified as Common 1¢ par 11/21/2003
Plan of reorganization under Chapter 11 Federal Bankruptcy proceedings effective 12/28/2009
Each share Common 1¢ par exchanged for (1) share Pilgrim's Pride Corp. (New) Common 1¢ par

PILL & PUFF INC (WI)
Merged into Midwest Health & Beauty Aids Inc. 11/01/1976
Each share Common 10¢ par exchanged for $7 cash

PILLAR ENTMT GROUP INC (FL)
Name changed to Chrysalis Hotels & Resorts Corp. 11/17/97

PILLAR PETES LTD (AB)
Merged into Renaissance Energy Ltd. 1/31/83
Each (4.7574) shares Common no par exchanged for (1) share Common no par
Renaissance Energy Ltd. merged into Husky Energy Inc. 8/25/2000

PILLAR RES INC (BC)
Name changed to PilaGold Inc. 10/21/2003
PilaGold Inc. merged into Radius Gold Inc. 7/2/2004

PILLEYS ISLAND COPPER PYRITE LTD. (ON)
Charter revoked for failure to file reports and pay fees 11/30/64

PILLOWTEX CORP (TX)
Plan of reorganization under Chapter 11 Federal Bankruptcy proceedings effective 05/24/2000
No stockholders' equity

PILLOWTEX CORP NEW (DE)
Plan of reorganization under Chapter 11 Federal Bankruptcy Code effective 06/29/2007
No stockholders' equity

PILLSBURY CO (DE)
Common $25 par changed to no par and (1) additional share issued 04/21/1959
$4 Preferred no par called for redemption 10/31/1963
Common no par split (2) for (1) by issuance of (1) additional share 02/26/1965
Common no par split (2) for (1) by issuance of (1) additional share 11/01/1975
Common no par split (2) for (1) by issuance of (1) additional share 11/30/1983
Common no par split (2) for (1) by issuance of (1) additional share 11/28/1986
Merged into Grand Metropolitan PLC 01/10/1989
Each share Common no par exchanged for $66 cash

PILLSBURY FLOUR MILLS, INC.
Merged into Pillsbury Flour Mills Co. (DE) 00/00/1935

Details not available

PILLSBURY FLOUR MILLS CO. (DE)
Name changed to Pillsbury Mills, Inc. 00/00/1944
Pillsbury Mills, Inc. name changed to Pillsbury Co. 09/15/1958
(See Pillsbury Co.)

PILLSBURY FLOUR MILLS CO. (MN)
Assets transferred to Pillsbury Flour Mills Co. (DE) 00/00/1935
Details not available

PILLSBURY MLS INC (DE)
Name changed to Pillsbury Co. 09/15/1958
(See Pillsbury Co.)

PILOT ENERGY LTD (AB)
Merged into Crescent Point Energy Trust 01/16/2008
Each share Common no par exchanged for (0.1284) Trust Unit no par
Crescent Point Energy Trust reorganized as Crescent Point Energy Corp. 07/07/2009

PILOT ENVIRONMENTAL INDS INC (MA)
Involuntarily dissolved 8/31/98

PILOT FD INC (TX)
Name changed to Transamerica Technology Fund and Common $1 par reclassified as Shares of Bene. Int. $1 par 06/23/1989
Transamerica Technology Fund name changed to Transamerica Capital Appreciation Fund 04/19/1991 which merged into Hancock (John) Capital Growth Fund 12/22/1994
(See Hancock (John) Capital Growth Fund)

PILOT FULL FASHION MILLS, INC. (DE)
Common $1 par changed to $5 par 00/00/1947
Stock Dividends - 10% 06/14/1946; 10% 06/01/1948
Name changed to Alba Hosiery Mills, Inc. 04/01/1955
Alba Hosiery Mills, Inc. name changed to Alba-Waldensian, Inc. 01/01/1962
(See Alba-Waldensian, Inc.)

PILOT GOLD INC (CANADA)
Name changed to Liberty Gold Corp. 05/12/2017

PILOT GOLD MINES LTD. (BC)
Dissolved in 1950

PILOT LABS CORP (BC)
Reorganized as Murex Clinical Technologies Corp. 2/20/89
Each share Common no par exchanged for (1) share Common no par
Murex Clinical Technologies Corp. recapitalized as International Murex Technologies Corp. 12/12/90
(See International Murex Technologies Corp.)

PILOT MOLYBDENITE MINES LTD.
Succeeded by Aunite Mining Corp. Ltd. share for share in 1943

PILOT NETWORK SVCS INC (DE)
Issue Information - 3,250,000 shares COM offered at $14 per share on 08/10/1998
Filed a petition under Chapter 7 Federal Bankruptcy Code 5/1/2001
No stockholders' equity

PILOT PEAK GOLD INC (BC)
Struck off register and declared dissolved for failure to file returns 03/04/1994

PILOT RADIO & TUBE CORP.
Bankrupt in 1933

PILOT RADIO CORP (NY)
Name changed 11/01/1973
Name changed from Pilot Radio-Television Corp. to Pilot Radio Corp. 11/01/1973

Completely liquidated 12/31/1974
Each share Capital Stock 10¢ par received first and final distribution of $0.18 cash

PILOT REINSURANCE CO. OF NEW YORK
Dissolved in 1942
Details not available

PILOT THERAPEUTICS HLDGS INC (DE)
Company terminated registration of common stock and is no longer public as of 03/22/2007
Details not available

PILOT TITANIUM CORP (UT)
Involuntarily dissolved 12/31/1976

PILSENER BREWING CO.
Liquidation completed in 1938

PIMA SVGS & LN ASSN (AZ)
Stock Dividends - 20% 01/07/1965; 20% 01/20/1966
Merged into Patagonia Corp. 06/11/1970
Each share Guarantee Stock $1 par exchanged for (0.739) share Common $1 par
(See Patagonia Corp.)

PIMCO ADVISORS HLDGS L P (DE)
Merged into Allianz of America 5/5/2000
Each Unit of Limited Partnership Int. exchanged for $38.75 cash

PIMCO ADVISORS L P (DE)
Each Class A Unit of Ltd. Partnership Int. exchanged for (1) Oppenheimer Capital, L.P. Unit of Ltd. Partnership Int. 12/31/97
Oppenheimer Capital, L.P. name changed to PIMCO Advisors Holdings L.P. 1/1/98
(See PIMCO Advisors Holdings L.P.)

PIMCO COML MTG SECS TR INC (MD)
Name changed to PCM Fund, Inc. 6/1/2007

PIMCO CORPORATE INCOME FD (MA)
Issue Information - 31,750,000 shares COM offered at $15 on 12/18/2001
Name changed to PIMCO Corporate & Income Strategy Fund 02/01/2012

PIMCO CORPORATE OPPORTUNITY FD (DE)
Name changed to PIMCO Corporate & Income Opportunity Fund 02/01/2012

PIMCO DYNAMIC CR INCOME FD (MA)
Name changed to PIMCO Dynamic Credit & Mortgage Income Fund 08/01/2016

PIMCO ETF TR (DE)
Australia Bond Index Fund $0.001 par reclassified as Australia Bond Index ETF $0.001 par 10/31/2012
Broad U.S. Treasury Index Fund $0.001 par reclassified as Broad U.S. Treasury Index ETF $0.001 par 10/31/2012
Build America Bond Strategy Fund $0.001 par reclassified as Build America Bond ETF $0.001 par 10/31/2012
Canada Bond Index Fund $0.001 par reclassified as Canada Bond Index ETF $0.001 par 10/31/2012
Germany Bond Index Fund $0.001 par reclassified as Germany Bond Index ETF $0.001 par 10/31/2012
Global Advantage Inflation Linked Bond Strategy Fund $0.001 par reclassified as Global Advantage Inflation Linked Bond ETF $0.001 par 10/31/2012
7-15 Year U.S. Treasury Index Fund $0.001 par reclassified as 7-15 Year U.S. Treasury Index ETF $0.001 par 10/31/2012
3-7 Year U.S. Treasury Index Fund

$0.001 par reclassified as 3-7 Year U.S. Treasury Index ETF $0.001 par 10/31/2012
Trust terminated 03/17/2014
Each share Broad U.S. Treasury Index ETF $0.001 par received $100.783666 cash
Trust terminated 10/01/2014
Each share Australia Bond Index ETF $0.001 par received $92.913519 cash
Each share Build America Bond ETF $0.001 par received $51.908992 cash
Each share Canada Bond Index ETF $0.001 par received $95.473475 cash
Each share Germany Bond Index ETF $0.001 par received $100.343241 cash
Diversified Income Exchange-Traded Fund $0.001 par reclassified as Diversified Income Active Exchange-Traded Fund $0.001 par 10/31/2014
Foreign Currency Strategy ETF $0.001 par reclassified as Foreign Currency Strategy Active ETF $0.001 par 10/31/2014
Global Advantage Inflation-Linked Bond ETF $0.001 par reclassified as Global Advantage Inflation-Linked Bond Active ETF $0.001 par 10/31/2014
Trust terminated 09/30/2015
Each share Foreign Currency Strategy Active ETF $0.001 par received $42.854479 cash
Each share 7-15 Year U.S. Treasury Index ETF $0.001 par received $86.939834 cash
Each share 3-7 Year U.S. Treasury Index ETF $0.001 par received $80.857618 cash
Trust terminated 04/07/2017
Each share Diversified Income Active ETF $0.001 par received $50.13957 cash
Each share Global Advantage Inflation-Linked Bond Active ETF $0.001 par received $43.99359 cash
(Additional Information in Active)

PIMCO FLOATING RATE INCOME FD
Issue Information - 16,250,000 shares COM offered at $20 per share on 08/26/2003
Name changed to PIMCO Income Strategy Fund 03/01/2010

PIMCO FLOATING RATE STRATEGY FD (MA)
Name changed to PIMCO Income Strategy Fund II 03/01/2010

PIMCO MUN ADVANTAGE FD INC (MD)
Auction Rate Preferred Ser. M $0.001 par called for redemption at $50,000 on 04/24/2009
Liquidation completed
Each share Common $0.001 par received initial distribution of $6.20 cash payable 06/30/2009 to holders of record 06/26/2009
Each share Common $0.001 par received second and final distribution of $3.30 cash payable 08/31/2009 to holders of record 08/28/2009
Note: Certificates were not required to be surrendered and are without value

PIMCO STRATEGIC GLOBAL GOVT FD INC (MD)
Name changed to PIMCO Strategic Income Fund, Inc. 03/03/2014

PIMI AGRO CLEANTECH INC (DE)
Name changed to Save Foods, Inc. 06/16/2016

PINACLE ENTERPRISE INC (NV)
Common $0.001 par split (100) for (1) by issuance of (99) additional shares payable 03/28/2013 to holders of record 03/28/2013
Recapitalized as Alkame Holdings, Inc. 01/08/2014
Each share Common $0.001 par exchanged for (0.33333333) share Common $0.001 par

PINCH OR POUND INC (FL)
Chapter 11 bankruptcy proceedings converted to Chapter 7 on 12/18/87
Stockholders' equity unlikely

PINCO, INC. (IA)
Charter cancelled for failure to file annual reports 11/21/72

PINCORTEZ MINES LTD. (ON)
Name changed to Porcupine Prime Mines Ltd. in September 1949
Porcupine Prime Mines Ltd. name changed to Prime Potash Corp. of Canada Ltd. 12/16/65
(See Prime Potash Corp. of Canada Ltd.)

PINDYCK CHARLES INC (NY)
Voluntarily dissolved 3/19/90
Details not available

PINE & 48TH STREET CORP.
Stock sold by Voting Trustees and distribution made in 1952

PINE BELL MINES LTD (BC)
Reincorporated 07/23/1981
Place of incorporation changed from (ON) to (BC) 07/23/1981
Recapitalized as Bell Coast Capital Corp. 11/12/1992
Each share Capital Stock $1 par exchanged for (0.25) share Common no par
Bell Coast Capital Corp. name changed to Uranium Power Corp. 03/22/2005 which merged into Titan Uranium Inc. 07/31/2009 which merged into Energy Fuels Inc. 02/24/2012

PINE BLUFF CO.
Merged into Arkansas Power & Light Co. 00/00/1926
Details not available

PINE BLUFF NATL BK (PINE BLUFF, AR)
Under plan of reorganization each share Common no par automatically became (1) share Jefferson Bancshares Inc. Common no par 6/1/95

PINE BROOK CAP INC (DE)
Completely liquidated 10/31/2012
Each share Class A exchanged for $0.18 cash

PINE BUFFALO MINES LTD (BC)
Struck off register and declared dissolved for failure to file returns 11/12/1974

PINE CHANNEL GOLD CORP (BC)
Recapitalized as Consolidated Pine Channel Gold Corp. 02/07/1991
Each share Common no par exchanged for (0.2) share Common no par
Consolidated Pine Channel Gold Corp. name changed to Star Uranium Corp. 05/11/2006 which name changed to Star Minerals Group Ltd. 10/11/2013 which name changed to Navis Resources Corp. 04/11/2016

PINE CREEK LEAD-ZINC MINING CO. (ID)
Merged into Mascot Mines, Inc. 10/18/60
Each share Common 10¢ par exchanged for (1) share Capital Stock 17-1/2¢ par
Mascot Mines, Inc. name changed to Mascot Silver-Lead Mines, Inc. 3/25/65

PINE CREST RES LTD (BC)
Name changed to Datinvest International Ltd. 06/24/1992

PINE GROVE, INC.
Dissolved in 1946

PINE HILL COAL CO.
Liquidated in 1943

PINE HILL COLLIERIES CO.
Liquidated in 1943

PINE LAKE MNG LTD (BC)
Recapitalized as Marge Enterprises Ltd. 06/28/1976
Each share Common no par exchanged for (0.2) share Common no par
Marge Enterprises Ltd. name changed to Thunderbird Projects Ltd. 09/27/1996 which recapitalized as Consolidated Thunderbird Projects Ltd. 12/17/1998 which name changed to Jenosys Enterprises, Inc. 08/16/1999 which recapitalized as Fintry Enterprises Inc. 12/10/2004 which recapitalized as Mesa Uranium Corp. 12/23/2005 which name changed to Mesa Exploration Corp. 03/30/2011

PINE MIAMI INC (FL)
Voluntarily dissolved 6/28/71
Details not available

PINE PAC MINES LTD (BC)
Struck off register and declared dissolved for failure to file returns 01/10/1977

PINE POINT MINES LTD (CANADA)
100% acquired by Nunachiaq Inc. at $50 per share through purchase offer which expired 05/23/1990
Public interest eliminated

PINE PRODUCTS CORP.
Dissolved in 1927

PINE PT MINES INC (BC)
Name changed to Mineworks Resources Corp. 01/23/2004
Mineworks Resources Corp. name changed to Tower Energy Ltd. 07/25/2005 which recapitalized as Tower Resources Ltd. 09/20/2011

PINE PT MNG LTD (ON)
Plan of arrangement effective 03/01/2018
Each share Common no par exchanged for (0.271) share Osisko Metals Inc. Common no par, (0.0677) Common Stock Purchase Warrant expiring 02/23/2019 and (1) share Generation Mining Ltd. Common no par
Note: Unexchanged certificates will be cancelled and become without value 03/01/2024

PINE RES CORP (BC)
Reincorporated under the laws of Canada as Trimble Resources Corp. 1/17/2002
(See Trimble Resources Corp. (Canada))

PINE RIDGE DEVELOPMENT CORP. (UT)
Name changed to Inter-Face International, Inc. 5/24/82
Inter-Face International, Inc. name changed to Whitepine Resources, Inc. 12/23/83 which charter was dissolved 4/30/87

PINE RIDGE EXPL LTD (ON)
Capital Stock $1 par changed to no par 7/28/71
Name changed to Eden Industries International Ltd. 4/7/72
Each share Capital Stock no par exchanged for (1) share Capital Stock no par
(See Eden Industries International Ltd.)

PINE RIDGE HLDGS INC (NV)
Name changed to Mike the Pike Productions, Inc. (NV) 08/05/2009
Mike the Pike Productions, Inc. (NV) reorganized in Wyoming 03/03/2011

PINE RIVER MINES LTD. (ON)
Merged into Trimar Holdings & Explorations Ltd. 12/10/67
Each share Capital Stock $1 par exchanged for (0.2) share Capital Stock no par
(See Trimar Holdings & Explorations Ltd.)

PINE STR FD INC (NY)
Common $1 par changed to 50¢ par and (1) additional share issued 11/6/59
Name changed to Winthrop Focus Funds Growth & Income Fund 7/10/92
Winthrop Focus Funds Growth & Income Fund name changed to DLJ Winthrop Opportunity Funds Growth & Income Fund 1/29/99 which name changed to DLJ Opportunity Funds Growth & Income Funds 8/1/2000 which name changed to Credit Suisse Warburg Pincus Capital Funds 2/6/2001 which name changed to Credit Suisse Capital Funds 12/12/2001

PINE TERRACE BUILDING CORP. (IL)
Completely liquidated 6/27/38
Each Capital Stock Trust Ctf. no par exchanged for first and final distribution of $40.34 cash

PINE TR FD INC (DE)
Ceased operations 00/00/1978
Stockholders' equity unlikely

PINE VY EXPL LTD (BC)
Name changed to V.I.P. Dynasty International Marketing Corp. 11/5/84
(See V.I.P. Dynasty International Marketing Corp.)

PINE VIEW TECHNOLOGIES CORP (NV)
Recapitalized as Videolocity International Inc. 12/5/2000
Each share Common $0.001 par exchanged for (0.61) share Common $0.001 par

PINEAPPLE HOLDING CO.
Dissolved in 1935

PINEBRAYLE GOLD MINES, LTD. (BC)
Charter cancelled for failure to file reports and pay taxes in 1952

PINECO INC (UT)
Charter suspended for failure to file report 12/31/1975

PINECO OIL & MNG CORP (UT)
Reorganized as Pineco, Inc. 1/11/71
Each share Common 10¢ par exchanged for (0.125) share Common 10¢ par
(See Pineco, Inc.)

PINECO URANIUM CORP. (UT)
Name changed to Pineco Oil & Mining Corp. 8/21/57
Pineco Oil & Mining Corp. reorganized as Pineco, Inc. 1/11/71
(See Pineco, Inc.)

PINECREST ENERGY INC (AB)
Reorganized as Virginia Hills Oil Corp. 04/17/2015
Each share Common no par exchanged for (0.01) share Common no par and (0.08) Common Stock Purchase Right expiring 05/15/2015
(See Virginia Hills Oil Corp.)

PINECREST GOLD MINES LTD.
Name changed to Craigmont Mines Ltd. in 1951
(See Craigmont Mines Ltd.)

PINECREST INVT GROUP INC (FL)
Common $0.001 par split (5) for (4) by issuance of (0.25) additional share payable 01/31/2000 to holders of record 12/31/1999
Recapitalized as Acology Inc. 02/14/2014

Each share Common $0.001 par exchanged for (0.001) share Common $0.001 par
Acology Inc. name changed to Medtainer, Inc. 10/05/2018

PINECREST SVCS INC (NV)
Name changed to Silvergraph International, Inc. 06/23/2006

PINEGROVE RES LTD (AB)
Recapitalized as Pacific Ventures Inc. 11/18/94
Each share Common no par exchanged for (0.25) share Common no par
Pacific Ventures Inc. name changed to Weda Bay Minerals Inc. 6/19/96
(See Weda Bay Minerals Inc.)

PINEHAVEN SHOPPING CENTER (SC)
Liquidation completed
Each share Common $5 par received initial distribution of $28.50 cash 1/29/74
Each share Common $5 par exchanged for second distribution of $2.39 cash 4/19/74
Each share Common $5 par received third and final distribution of $0.367 cash 12/30/75

PINEHURST CORP (CA)
Name changed to Emett & Chandler Companies, Inc. 5/24/82
(See Emett & Chandler Companies, Inc.)

PINEHURST INC (NC)
Acquired by Diamondhead Corp. 12/30/70
Each share Preferred $100 par exchanged for $100 cash
Each share Common $100 par exchanged for $6.60 cash

PINELAND ST BK (BRICKTOWN, NJ)
Common $5 par changed to $2.50 par and (1) additional share issued 10/4/72
Merged into Heritage Bancorporation 12/30/77
Each share Common $2.50 par exchanged for $20 cash

PINELAND ST BK (PINELAND, TX)
Merged into Diboll State Bancshares Inc. 03/17/1998
Each share Common $1 par exchanged for (0.62) share Common $1 par
Diboll State Bancshares Inc. merged into Southside Bancshares, Inc. 11/30/2017

PINELANDS INC (DE)
Acquired by BHC Communications, Inc. 8/24/92
Each share Common 1¢ par exchanged for $18 cash

PINELLAS CENTRAL BANK & TRUST CO. (LARGO, FL)
Stock Dividends - 10% 4/1/66; 10% 4/1/71
Name changed to Southeast First Bank of Largo (Largo, FL) 9/3/74
(See Southeast First Bank of Largo (Largo, FL))

PINELLAS COUNTY POWER CO.
Merged into Florida Power Corp. 00/00/1927
Details not available

PINELLAS INDS INC (FL)
Merged into Ewell Industries, Inc. 12/31/1984
Details not available

PINEMONT BK (HOUSTON, TX)
Merged into Southwest Bancorporation of Texas, Inc. 08/01/1997
Each share Common $1 par exchanged for (0.625) share Common $1 par
Southwest Bancorporation of Texas, Inc. name changed to Amegy Bancorporation, Inc. 05/05/2005

which merged into Zions Bancorporation 12/03/2005 which merged into Zions Bancorporation, N.A (Salt Lake City, UT) 10/01/2018

PINERIDGE CAP CORP (BC)
Recapitalized 01/14/1991
Recapitalized from Pineridge Capital Corp. to Pineridge Capital Group Inc. 01/14/1991
Each share Common no par exchanged for (0.25) share Common no par
Delisted from Vancouver Stock Exchange 03/06/1995

PINERIDGE RESOURCES LTD. (BC)
Name changed to Pineridge Capital Corp. 12/19/1988
Pineridge Capital Corp. recapitalized as Pineridge Capital Group Inc. 01/14/1991
(See Pineridge Capital Group Inc.)

PINES WINTERFRONT CO.
Assets sold in 1940

PINETREE CAP CORP (ON)
Recapitalized 01/28/1992
Recapitalized 07/08/1996
Recapitalized from Pinetree Explorations Ltd. to Pinetree Capital Inc. 01/28/1992
Each share old Common $1 par exchanged for (0.1) share new Common no par
Recapitalized from Pinetree Capital Inc. to Pinetree Capital Corp. 07/08/1996
Each share new Common no par exchanged for (1/3) share Common no par
Recapitalized as Pinetree Capital Ltd. 06/02/2004
Each (1.75) shares Common no par exchanged for (1) share Common no par

PINETREE COMPUTER SYS INC (DE)
Charter cancelled and declared inoperative and void for non-payment of taxes 3/1/89

PINETREE SOFTWARE CDA LTD (BC)
Struck off register and declared dissolved for failure to file returns 12/11/1992

PINEWEST RES INC (ON)
Recapitalized as Arcamatrix Corp. 11/16/2000
Each share Common no par exchanged for (0.5) share Common no par

PINEWOOD IMPORTS LTD (NV)
Name changed to Mill Basin Technologies, Ltd. 09/06/2006
Mill Basin Technologies, Ltd. name changed to Huiheng Medical, Inc. 10/02/2007
(See Huiheng Medical, Inc.)

PINEX MINES LTD (BC)
Completely liquidated 05/10/1972
Each share Common 50¢ par exchanged for first and final distribution of (0.144425) share Greenland Exploration Co. Ltd. Common no par
Greenland Exploration Co. Ltd. recapitalized as Pac-West Industries Ltd. 02/18/1980
(See Pac-West Industries Ltd.)

PINGCHUAN PHARMACEUTICAL INC (NC)
Each share old Common $0.001 par exchanged for (1/6) share new Common $0.001 par 1/4/2007
Reincorporated under the laws of Delaware as Shandong Zhouyuan Seed & Nursery Co., Ltd. 4/5/2007

PINGRO CORP. (DE)
Dissolved 3/9/64

PINK OTC MARKETS INC (DE)
Name changed to OTC Markets Group Inc. 01/19/2011

PINK PAGES PUBNS INC (BC)
Struck off register and declared dissolved for failure to file returns 07/10/1992

PINKERTONS INC NEW (DE)
Common $0.001 par split (3) for (2) by issuance of (0.5) additional share payable 8/27/97 to holders of record 8/7/97 Ex date - 8/28/97
Merged into Securitas AB 3/31/99
Each share Common $0.001 par exchanged for $29 cash

PINKERTONS INC OLD (DE)
Class B Common no par split (2) for (1) by issuance of (1) additional share 7/25/68
Merged into American Brands, Inc. 1/6/83
Each share Class B Common no par exchanged for $77.50 cash

PINKMONKEY COM INC (NV)
Charter revoked for failure to file reports and pay fees 10/01/2006

PINNACLE AIRL CORP (DE)
Issue Information - 19,400,000 shares COM offered at $14.00 per share on 11/24/2003
Plan of reorganization under Chapter 11 bankruptcy proceedings effective 05/01/2013
No stockholders' equity

PINNACLE BANC GROUP INC (IL)
Common $6.25 par split (5) for (4) by issuance of (0.25) additional share 01/31/1990
Common $6.25 par changed to $4.69 par and (1/3) additional share issued 02/04/1991
Common $4.69 par changed to $3.125 par and (0.5) additional share issued payable 02/10/1997 to holders of record 02/03/1997
Merged into Old Kent Financial Corp. 09/03/1999
Each share Common $3.125 par exchanged for (0.75285) share Common $1 par
Old Kent Financial Corp. merged into Fifth Third Bancorp 04/02/2001

PINNACLE BANCORP INC (OH)
Merged into Fifth Third Bancorp 3/27/92
Each share Common 1¢ par exchanged for (0.188143) share Common no par
Note: An additional and final payment of $0.94 cash per share was made under terms of merger agreement

PINNACLE BK (BEAVERTON, OR)
Placed in receivership with FDIC 02/13/2009
Stockholders' equity unlikely

PINNACLE BK (JASPER, AL)
Under plan of reorganization each share Common 1¢ par automatically became (1) share Pinnacle Bancshares, Inc. (DE) Common 1¢ par 01/31/1997

PINNACLE BUSINESS MGMT INC (NV)
Each share Common $0.001 par received distribution of (0.01) share Summit Property Group Inc. Common $0.001 par payable 03/16/2001 to holders of record 03/02/2001
Name changed to Serac Holdings Inc. 04/01/2004
(See Serac Holdings Inc.)

PINNACLE CAP INC (DE)
Recapitalized as Asset Management, International Financing Settlement, Ltd. 5/27/88
Each share Common $0.0001 par exchanged for (0.25) share Common $0.0001 par
(See Asset Management, International Financing Settlement, Ltd.)

PINNACLE DATA SYS INC (OH)
Common no par split (2) for (1) by issuance of (1) additional share payable 03/31/2000 to holders of record 03/14/2000
Common no par split (2) for (1) by issuance of (1) additional share payable 10/31/2000 to holders of record 10/16/2000 Ex date - 11/01/2000
Acquired by Avnet, Inc. 01/30/2012
Each share Common no par exchanged for $2.40 cash

PINNACLE DEVS INC (NV)
Recapitalized as Prime Petroleum Group, Inc. 08/14/2007
Each share Common $0.001 par exchanged for (0.05) share Common $0.001 par
(See Prime Petroleum Group, Inc.)

PINNACLE ENERGY CORP (NV)
Name changed to Trans-Pacific Aerospace Co., Inc. (NV) 03/05/2010
Trans-Pacific Aerospace Co., Inc. (NV) reincorporated in Wyoming 01/27/2017

PINNACLE ENTMT INC NEW (DE)
Merged into Penn National Gaming, Inc. 10/15/2018
Each share Common 1¢ par exchanged for (0.42) share Common 1¢ par and $20 cash

PINNACLE ENTMT INC OLD (DE)
Each share Common 10¢ par received distribution of (1) share Pinnacle Entertainment, Inc. (New) Common 1¢ par payable 04/28/2016 to holders of record 04/18/2016 Ex date - 04/29/2016
Merged into Gaming & Leisure Properties, Inc. 04/28/2016
Each share Common 10¢ par exchanged for (0.85) share Common 1¢ par

PINNACLE ENVIRONMENTAL INC (DE)
Name changed to Surgical Technologies, Inc. (DE) 02/18/1992
Surgical Technologies, Inc. (DE) reincorporated in (UT) 01/24/1994 which merged into 4Health Inc. 07/16/1996 which name changed to Irwin Naturals/4Health, Inc. 07/01/1998 which name changed to Omni Nutraceuticals, Inc. 08/23/1999
(See Omni Nutraceuticals, Inc.)

PINNACLE FD (IN)
Merged into Fountain Square Funds 03/06/1998
Details not available

PINNACLE FINL CORP (GA)
Reorganized 01/02/2003
Each share Common $10 par exchanged for $95.20 cash
Note: Option for holders of (2,000) or more shares to retain their stock expired 12/02/2002

PINNACLE FINL SVCS INC (MI)
Common $10 par split (5) for (4) by issuance of (0.25) additional share 3/15/90
Common $10 par split (2) for (1) by issuance of (1) additional share 8/17/92
Common $10 par changed to no par and (1) additional share issued 9/15/93
Merged into CNB Bancshares Inc. 4/17/98
Each share Common no par exchanged for (1.0365) shares Common no par
CNB Bancshares Inc. merged into Fifth Third Bancorp 10/29/99

PINNACLE FOODS INC (PA)
Name changed to Pennexx Foods Inc. 02/11/2002

PINNACLE GAS RES INC (DE)
Issue Information - 3,750,000 shares COM offered at $9 per share on 05/14/2007
Acquired by Powder Holdings, L.L.C. 01/25/2011
Each share Common 1¢ par exchanged for $0.34 cash

PINNACLE GLOBAL GROUP INC (TX)
Name changed to Sanders Morris Harris Group Inc. 05/23/2001
Sanders Morris Harris Group Inc. name changed to Edelman Financial Group Inc. 05/27/2011
(See Edelman Financial Group Inc.)

PINNACLE GOLD MINES, LTD. (ON)
Dissolved 12/1/58

PINNACLE GOVT FD INC (FL)
Reincorporated under the laws of Massachusetts as Trinity Liquid Assets Trust 01/31/1990
Trinity Liquid Assets Trust name changed to Trinity Assets Trust 11/16/1990
(See Trinity Assets Trust)

PINNACLE GROUP UNLIMITED INC (NV)
Name changed to Maverick Energy Group, Ltd. 10/3/2006

PINNACLE HLDGS INC (DE)
Issue Information - 20,000,000 shares COM offered at $14 per share on 02/19/1999
Plan of reorganization under Chapter 11 Federal Bankruptcy Code effective 11/1/2002
Each share Common $0.001 par exchanged for approximately (0.002) Common Stock Purchase Warrant expring in 2007
Each share Common $0.001 par received a second and final distribution of approximately (0.004) Common Stock Purchase Warrant expiring in 2007 on 5/27/2003
Note: Unexchanged certificates were cancelled and became without value 11/1/2003

PINNACLE HLDGS LTD (SOUTH AFRICA)
Name changed to Alviva Holdings Ltd. 03/29/2017

PINNACLE INDUSTRIES INC. (NC)
Dissolved 9/30/64

PINNACLE INTL CORP (UT)
Involuntarily dissolved 01/30/1990

PINNACLE INVESTMENT (DE)
Merged into Syntellect Inc. 3/14/96
Each share Common 1¢ par exchanged for (1.15) shares Common 1¢ par
(See Syntellect Inc.)

PINNACLE MICRO INC (DE)
Common $0.001 par split (3) for (2) by issuance of (0.5) additional share 12/15/95
Assets sold for the benefit of creditors 5/31/2002
No stockholders' equity

PINNACLE MINES LTD (BC)
Ctfs. dated after 07/16/2003
Name changed to Jayden Resources Inc. (BC) 06/29/2010
Jayden Resources Inc. (BC) reincorporated in Cayman Islands 10/03/2012

PINNACLE MINES LTD (BC)
Ctfs. dated prior to 02/24/1975
Recapitalized as Redford Mines Inc. 02/24/1975
Each share Capital Stock no par exchanged for (0.2) share Capital Stock no par
Redford Mines Inc. name changed to Redford Resources, Inc. which recapitalized as United Redford Resources, Inc. 12/07/1984
(See United Redford Resources, Inc.)

PINNACLE OIL INTL INC (NV)
Name changed to Energy Exploration Technologies (NV) 06/15/2000
Energy Exploration Technologies (NV) reincorporated in Alberta 10/24/2003 which name changed to NXT Energy Solutions Inc. 09/22/2008

PINNACLE PETE INC (CO)
Reorganized under the laws of Delaware 07/31/1984
Each share Common $0.001 par exchanged for (0.00666666) share Common 1¢ par
Pinnacle Petroleum, Inc. (DE) name changed to Golden Oil Co. (DE) 02/15/1990
(See Golden Oil Co. (DE))

PINNACLE PETE INC (DE)
Name changed to Golden Oil Co. (DE) 02/15/1990
(See Golden Oil Co. (DE))

PINNACLE PETES LTD (AB)
Merged into Paloma Petroleum Ltd. 10/1/74
Each share Common no par exchanged for (0.153846) share Common no par
(See Paloma Petroleum Ltd.)

PINNACLE RES INC (WY)
Reincorporated under the laws of Delaware as Iron Eagle Group, Inc. 04/28/2010
(See Iron Eagle Group, Inc.)

PINNACLE RES LTD NEW (AB)
Each share Class A Preferred no par exchanged for (20) shares Common no par 10/24/1990
Merged into Renaissance Energy Ltd. 07/16/1998
Each share Common no par exchanged for (0.66) share Common no par
Renaissance Energy Ltd. merged into Husky Energy Inc. 08/25/2000

PINNACLE RES LTD OLD (AB)
Merged into Pinnacle Resources Ltd. (New) 11/17/1988
Each share Preferred no par exchanged for (1) share Class A Preferred no par
Each share Common no par exchanged for (1) share Common no par
Pinnacle Resources Ltd. (New) merged into Renaissance Energy Ltd. 07/16/1998 which merged into Husky Energy Inc. 08/25/2000

PINNACLE SKI CENTRE LTD. (QC)
Adjudicated bankrupt 12/21/67
No stockholders' equity

PINNACLE SYS INC (CA)
Secondary Offering - 1,736,000 shares COM offered at $25.75 per share on 07/27/1995
Common no par split (2) for (1) by issuance of (1) additional share payable 6/4/99 to holders of record 5/14/99
Common no par split (2) for (1) by issuance of (1) additional share payable 3/24/2000 to holders of record 3/2/2000
Merged into Avid Technology, Inc. 8/9/2005
Each share Common no par exchanged for (0.0869) share Common no par and $1 cash

PINNACLE TECHNOLOGY HLDGS LTD (SOUTH AFRICA)
Name changed to Pinnacle Holdings Ltd. 05/30/2014
Pinnacle Holdings Ltd. name changed to Alviva Holdings Ltd. 03/29/2017

PINNACLE TRANSN INC (DE)
Name changed to ZYTO Corp. 09/19/2006
ZYTO Corp. name changed to Global Unicorn Holdings, Inc. 05/02/2018

PINNACOR (DE)
Merged into MarketWatch.com, Inc. (New) 1/16/2004
Each share Common 1¢ par exchanged for (0.14) share Common 1¢ par and $1.07 cash
MarketWatch.com, Inc. (New) name changed to MarketWatch, Inc. 8/11/2004

PINON URANIUM CO., INC. (DE)
Merged into Sabre-Pinon Corp. share for share 6/1/56
Sabre-Pinon Corp. merged into United Nuclear Corp. (DE) 4/4/62 which reorganized in Virginia as UNC Resources, Inc. 8/31/78 which name changed to UNC Inc. (VA) 6/3/86 which reincorporated in Delaware 4/30/87
(See UNC Inc.)

PINPOINT ADVANCE CORP (DE)
Issue Information - 2,875,000 UNITS consisting of (1) share COM and (1) WT offered at $10 per Unit on 04/19/2007
Each Unit exchanged for (0.125) share new Common $0.0001 par, (1) Common Stock Purchase Warrant expiring 04/19/2011 and $9.91 cash 05/19/2009
Each share old Common $0.0001 par exchanged for (0.125) share new Common $0.0001 par and $9.91 cash 05/19/2009
Company terminated common stock registration and is no longer public as of 11/21/2012

PINPOINT RETAIL SOLUTIONS INC (AB)
Delisted from Alberta Stock Exchange 3/12/96

PINTA LARDER GOLD MINES LTD. (ON)
Charter cancelled for failure to file reports and pay taxes in 1960

PINTO MALARTIC GOLD MINES LTD (ON)
Name changed to Continental Caretech Corp. 04/20/1987
Continental Caretech Corp. name changed to Corona Gold Corp. (Old) 05/17/1996 which reorganized as Corona Gold Corp. (New) 06/13/2002 which merged into Oban Mining Corp. 08/27/2015 which name changed to Osisko Mining Inc. 06/21/2016

PINTO TOTTA INTL FIN LTD (CAYMAN ISLANDS)
144A 7.77% Guaranteed Preference Ser. A called for redemption at $1,000 on 08/01/2007

PIOCHE BRISTOL MINING CO.
Name changed to Williston Basin Oil & Exploration Co. in 1952
Williston Basin Oil & Exploration Co. recapitalized as Whittington Oil Co., Inc. 9/5/67 which name changed to Louisiana- Pacific Resources, Inc. 10/4/71

PIONEER AERODYNAMIC SYSTEMS, INC. (DE)
Name changed to Pioneer Systems, Inc. (DE) 5/8/68
(See Pioneer Systems, Inc. (DE))

PIONEER AERONAUTICAL SERVICES, INC. (DE)
Name changed to Pioneer Hydrotex Industries, Inc. 01/28/1959
Pioneer Hydrotex Industries, Inc. name changed to Pioneer Texas Corp. 03/26/1962 which merged into DPA, Inc. 08/01/1968 which reorganized as Pioneer Texas Corp. 03/30/1973
(See Pioneer Texas Corp.)

PIONEER AIR LINES, INC. (TX)
Liquidation completed
Each share Common $1 par stamped to indicate initial distribution of (0.4) share Continental Air Lines, Inc. Common $1.25 par and $1 cash 5/9/58
Each share Stamped Common $1 par received second distribution of $0.35 cash 7/21/58
Each share Stamped Common $1 par received third distribution of $0.55 cash 8/20/58
Each share Stamped Common $1 par received fourth distribution of $0.30 cash 10/20/58
Each share Stamped Common $1 par received fifth distribution of $0.50 cash 1/2/59
Each share Stamped Common $1 par received sixth distribution of $1.825 cash 3/23/59
Each share Stamped Common $1 par exchanged for seventh and final distribution of $0.203 cash 3/1/61
Continental Air Lines, Inc. merged into Texas Air Corp. 10/28/82 which name changed to Continental Airlines Holdings, Inc. 6/11/90
(See Continental Airlines Holdings, Inc.)

PIONEER AIRLS INC (DC)
Common 10¢ par reclassified as Class A Common 10¢ par 11/23/1971
Name changed to Pioneer Industries, Inc. 11/08/1972
(See Pioneer Industries, Inc.)

PIONEER AMER FD INC (NE)
Merged into Pioneer American Income Trust 7/5/94
Each share Common 1¢ par exchanged for (1) share Class A Common no par

PIONEER AMER INCOME TR (MA)
Merged into Pioneer Series Trust IV 11/10/2006
Each share Class A no par exchanged for (1.002097977) shares Government Income Fund Class A
Each share Class B no par exchanged for (0.997132196) share Government Income Fund Class B
Each share Class C no par exchanged for (0.999531416) share Government Income Fund Class C
Each share Class R no par exchanged for (1.007582535) shares Government Income Fund Class R

PIONEER AMERN HLDG CORP (PA)
Common $10 par split (2) for (1) by issuance of (1) additional share 02/07/1994
Common $10 par split (2) for (1) by issuance of (1) additional share payable 07/15/1996 to holders of record 06/05/1996
Merged into NBT Bancorp Inc. 07/01/2000
Each share Common $10 par exchanged for (1.805) shares Common 1¢ par

PIONEER AMERN INS CO (TX)
Each share Capital Stock $10 par exchanged for (13.333333) shares Capital Stock $1 par to effect a (10) for (1) split and 33-1/3% stock dividend 06/15/1959
Stock Dividends - 100% 12/20/1949; 25% 05/13/1957; 20% 04/09/1958; 25% 08/15/1960; 14-2/7% 05/22/1968; 25% 01/10/1978
Merged into American-Amicable Life Insurance Co. 09/12/1979
Each share Capital Stock $1 par exchanged for $35 cash

PIONEER AMERICAN LIFE INSURANCE CO. (TX)
Acquired by Pioneer American Insurance Co. for cash 5/1/46

PIONEER ASTRO INDS INC (IL)
Merged into Astro Controls, Inc. 05/06/1969

Each share Common no par exchanged for (1) share Common no par
Astro Controls, Inc. merged into Golconda Corp. 09/15/1970 which reincorporated in Delaware as Rego Co. 06/17/1977 which name changed to Rego Group, Inc. 02/07/1978
(See Rego Group, Inc.)

PIONEER AUTOMATIC MERCHANDISING CORP.
Bankrupt in 1933

PIONEER BALANCED FD (DE)
Merged into Pioneer Series Trust IV 11/10/2006
Each share Class A no par exchanged for (0.985891841) share Classic Balanced Fund Class A no par
Each share Class B no par exchanged for (0.977759771) share Classic Balanced Fund Class B no par
Each share Class C no par exchanged for (0.982182163) share Classic Balanced Fund Class C no par

PIONEER BANCORP (CA)
Closed by the State Banking Commission 7/8/94
Stockholders' equity undetermined

PIONEER BANCORP INC (MA)
Merged into T.N.B. Financial Corp. 7/9/79
Each share Common $1 par exchanged for (1.2) shares Common $1 par
T.N.B. Financial Corp. merged into New England Merchants Co., Inc. 9/30/81 which name changed to Bank of New England Corp. 5/1/82
(See Bank of New England Corp.)

PIONEER BANCORP INC (NC)
Acquired by First Citizens BancShares, Inc. 9/23/93
Each share Common 1¢ par exchanged for $2.18 cash

PIONEER BANCORP INC (WA)
Merged into Interwest Bancorp, Inc. 06/16/1998
Each share Common no par exchanged for (1.3405) shares Common 20¢ par
Interwest Bancorp, Inc. name changed to Pacific Northwest Bancorp 09/01/2000 which merged into Wells Fargo & Co. (New) 11/03/2003

PIONEER BANCORPORATION (NV)
Common 1¢ par split (3) for (2) by issuance of (0.5) additional share payable 07/29/1998 to holders of record 07/27/1998
Stock Dividends - 10% payable 02/05/1997 to holders of record 01/31/1997; 10% payable 04/05/1999 to holders of record 03/29/1999
Merged into Zions Bancorporation 10/15/1999
Each share Common 1¢ par exchanged for (0.5667) share Common no par
Zions Bancorporation merged into Zions Bancorporation, N.A. (Salt Lake City, UT) 10/01/2018

PIONEER BANCSHARES INC (DE)
Common 1¢ par split (2) for (1) by issuance of (1) additional share payable 6/4/96 to holders of record 5/28/96
Merged into First American Corp. (TN) 11/20/98
Each share Common 1¢ par exchanged for (1.65) shares Common $5 par
First American Corp. (TN) merged into AmSouth Bancorporation 10/1/99 which merged into Regions Financial Corp. 11/4/2006

PIONEER BK & TR CO (CHICAGO, IL)
Through merger 100% acquired by Pioneer Bank & Trust Co. (River Grove, IL) 8/1/90

PIONEER BK & TR CO (SHREVEPORT, LA)
Each share Capital Stock $100 par exchanged for (4) shares Capital Stock $25 par 1/14/48
Capital Stock $25 par changed to Common $10 par and (1.5) additional shares issued 3/17/56
Merged into Hibernia Corp. 12/31/94
Details not available

PIONEER BK & TR CO (ST LOUIS, MO)
Each share Capital Stock $40 par exchanged for (4) shares Capital Stock $10 par 9/14/70
Acquired by Forbes Bancorp of St. Louis, Inc. (MO) 8/27/91
Details not available

PIONEER BK (CHATTANOOGA, TN)
Capital Stock $25 par changed to $27.50 par in 1956
Capital Stock $27.50 par changed to $30 par 3/27/57
Capital Stock $30 par changed to $32.50 par 1/22/58
Capital Stock $32.50 par changed to $35 par 1/27/59
Capital Stock $35 par changed to $37.50 par 1/26/60
Capital Stock $37.50 par changed to $40 par 1/24/61
Capital Stock $40 par changed to $42.50 par 3/16/61
Capital Stock $42.50 par changed to $45 par 2/19/62
Capital Stock $45 par changed to $47.50 par 2/7/63
Capital Stock $47.50 par changed to $50 par 2/19/64
Capital Stock $50 par changed to $62.50 par 1/27/70
Capital Stock $62.50 par changed to $75 par 1/23/73
Each share Capital Stock $75 par exchanged for (30) shares Capital Stock $2.50 par 2/20/76
Stock Dividends - 33-1/3% 3/15/76; 25% 1977; 20% 1978; 16.6% 1979
Reorganized under the laws of Delaware as Pioneer Bancshares, Inc. 9/30/92
Each share Common $2.50 par exchanged for (1) share Common 1¢ par
Pioneer Bancshares, Inc. merged into First American Corp. (TN) 11/20/98 which merged into AmSouth Bancorporation 10/1/99 which merged into Regions Financial Corp. 11/4/2006

PIONEER BK ARIZ (PHOENIX, AZ)
Reorganized as Westen American Industries 06/19/1969
Each share Common $10 par exchanged for (1) share Common $10 par
Western American Industries merged into Great Western Corp. (DE) 12/31/1969 which name changed to Patagonia Corp. 06/09/1970
(See Patagonia Corp.)

PIONEER BD FD INC (MA)
Common $1 par reclassified as Class A $1 par 04/04/1994
Reincorporated under the laws of Delaware and Class A, B, C, R, Y and Z $1 par changed to no par 05/17/1999

PIONEER CAP GROWTH FD (DE)
Name changed to Pioneer Mid Cap Value Fund 02/28/2000

PIONEER CARISSA GOLD MINES, INC. (UT)
Charter revoked for failure to file reports and pay fees 9/30/67

PIONEER CTZNS BK NEV (RENO, NV)
Under plan of reorganization each share Common $1 par automatically became (2) shares Pioneer Bancorporation Common 1¢ par 11/02/1993
Pioneer Bancorporation merged into Zions Bancorporation 10/15/1999 which merged into Zions Bancorporation, N.A. (Salt Lake City, UT) 10/01/2018

PIONEER COML FDG CORP (NY)
Each share old Common 1¢ par exchanged for (0.5) share new Common 1¢ par 07/19/1999
Reported out of business 00/00/2005
Stockholders' equity unlikely

PIONEER COMMUNICATIONS NETWORK INC (DE)
Charter cancelled and declared inoperative and void for non-payment of taxes 3/1/89

PIONEER CONCRETE SVCS LTD (AUSTRALIA)
Stock Dividend - 20% 01/09/1987
Name changed to Pioneer International Ltd. 01/05/1989
(See Pioneer International Ltd.)

PIONEER CORP (AR)
Liquidation completed
Each share Common 50¢ par exchanged for initial distribution of $4 cash 09/12/1979
Each share Common 50¢ par received second distribution of $1.35 cash 01/15/1981
Each share Common 50¢ par received third distribution of $1 cash 08/03/1981
Each share Common 50¢ par received fourth distribution of $0.45 cash 02/01/1982
Each share Common 50¢ par received fifth distribution of $1 cash 01/10/1983
Each share Common 50¢ par received sixth distribution of $1 cash 02/18/1983
Each share Common 50¢ par received seventh and final distribution of $2.40 cash 07/01/1983

PIONEER CORP (JAPAN)
ADR agreement terminated 03/10/2006
Each Sponsored ADR for Common 50 Yen par exchanged for $18.0284 cash
(Additional Information in Active)

PIONEER CORP (TX)
Common $1.875 par changed to $1 par and (1) additional share issued 10/15/1979
Common $1 par changed to 50¢ par and (1) additional share issued 01/20/1981
Stock Dividend - 20% 03/15/1976
Completely liquidated 07/01/1986
Each share Common 50¢ par exchanged for first and final distribution of (1.84) Mesa Limited Partnership (DE) Preference A Units and $0.31 cash
Mesa Limited Partnership (DE) reorganized in Texas as Mesa Inc. 12/31/1991 which merged into Pioneer Natural Resources Co. 08/07/1997

PIONEER COS INC (DE)
Stock Dividends - 7% payable 01/07/1997 to holders of record 12/16/1996; 7% payable 12/18/1997 to holders of record 12/01/1997; 7% payable 12/28/1998 to holders of record 12/07/1998; 7% payable 12/26/1999 to holders of record 12/06/1999
Plan of reorganization under Chapter 11 Federal Bankruptcy Code effective 12/31/2001

No old Common stockholders' equity
Merged into Olin Corp. 08/31/2007
Each share new Common 1¢ par exchanged for $35 cash

PIONEER CR CORP (MA)
Common $100 par changed to $25 par and (3) additional shares issued 11/16/1959
Stock Dividend - 10% 09/29/1962
Name changed to Taconic Investment Corp. 11/01/1972
(See Taconic Investment Corp.)

PIONEER DEVELOPMENT CORP. (NV)
Charter revoked for failure to pay fees and file reports 3/1/71

PIONEER DEVELOPMENT CORP. (WA)
Proclaimed dissolved for failure to pay taxes 7/1/72

PIONEER DRILLING CO (TX)
Name changed to Pioneer Energy Services Corp. 07/30/2012

PIONEER ELECTR CORP (JAPAN)
Each old ADR for Ordinary 50 Yen par exchanged for (5) new ADR's for Ordinary 50 Yen par 8/27/76
New ADR's for Ordinary 50 Yen par split (5) for (4) by issuance of (0.25) additional ADR 12/10/81
Each new ADR for Ordinary 50 Yen par exchanged for (2) Sponsored ADR's for Ordinary 50 Yen par 3/15/91
Stock Dividends - 10% 12/21/72; 10% 12/27/73; 10% 12/23/74; 10% 12/26/75; 25% 12/30/76; 10% 12/5/84; 10% 12/1/87; 10% 6/6/90
Name changed to Pioneer Corp. 7/2/99
(See Pioneer Corp.)

PIONEER ELECTRONICS CORP. (CA)
Common $1 par changed to no par and (1) additional share issued 5/4/60
Name changed to Pioneer World Corp. 1/10/64
Pioneer World Corp. charter revoked 12/1/64

PIONEER ENERGY SYSTEMS, INC. (IA)
Completely liquidated
Each share Common no par exchanged for first and final distribution of $0.96 cash

PIONEER ENTERPRISE FD INC (DE)
Acquired by Pioneer II, Inc. 6/28/74
Each share Capital Stock $1 par exchanged for (0.6876) share Common $1 par
Pioneer II, Inc. name changed to Pioneer Value Fund 4/2/2001

PIONEER EUROPE FD (MA)
Shares of Bene. Int. no par reclassified as Class A no par 04/04/1994
Name changed to Pioneer Europe Select Equity Fund (MA) 06/27/2005
Pioneer Europe Select Equity Fund (MA) reincorporated in Delaware 06/30/2008 which merged into Pioneer Series Trust V 06/12/2009

PIONEER EUROPE SELECT EQUITY FD (DE)
Reincorporated 06/30/2008
State of incorporation changed from (MA) to (DE) 06/30/2008
Merged into Pioneer Series Trust V 06/12/2009
Each share Class A no par received (2.46793147) shares Global Equity Fund Class A no par
Each share Class B no par received (2.23901408) shares Global Equity Fund Class B no par
Each share Class C no par received (2.20726342) shares Global Equity Fund Class C no par
Each share Class Y no par received

(2.53255696) shares Global Equity Fund Class Y no par

PIONEER EXPL INC (NV)
SEC revoked common stock registration 07/25/2016

PIONEER FD INC (MA)
Reincorporated 04/01/1967
Stock Dividends - 100% 01/05/1955; 100% 07/01/1959
State of incorporation changed from (DE) to (MA) and Capital Stock $2.50 par changed to Common $1 par 04/01/1967
Name changed to Pioneer Fund and Common $1 par changed to no par 07/03/1992

PIONEER FED BANCORP INC (DE)
Acquired by First Hawaiian, Inc. 7/26/93
Each share Common 1¢ par exchanged for $34 cash

PIONEER FED SVGS & LN ASSN HOPEWELL VA (USA)
Common $1 par split (3) for (2) by issuance of (0.5) additional share 08/01/1985
Common $1 par split (2) for (1) by issuance of (1) additional share 04/15/1986
Under plan of reorganization each share $1.88 Conv. Preferred Ser. A $1 par and Common $1 par automatically became (1) share Pioneer Financial Corp. (VA) $1.88 Conv. Preferred Ser. A $1 par and Common $1 par respectively 05/02/1988
Pioneer Financial Corp. (VA) merged into Signet Banking Corp. 08/31/1994 which merged into First Union Corp. 11/28/1997 which name changed to Wachovia Corp. (Ctfs. dated after 09/01/2001) 09/01/2001 which merged into Wells Fargo & Co. (New) 12/31/2008

PIONEER FED SVGS BK (LYNNWOOD, WA)
Common $1 par split (2) for (1) by issuance of (1) additional share 02/20/1990
Under plan of reorganization name changed to Pioneer Savings Bank (Lynnwood, WA) 08/10/1990
Pioneer Savings Bank (Lynnwood, WA) merged into Washington Mutual Savings Bank (Seattle, WA) 03/01/1993 which reorganized as Washington Mutual Inc. 11/29/1994
(See Washington Mutual, Inc.)

PIONEER FED SVGS BK (WINCHESTER, KY)
Under plan of reorganization each share Common $1 par automatically became (1) share Pioneer Financial Corp. (KY) Common $1 par 12/30/94
(See Pioneer Financial Corp. (KY))

PIONEER FINANCE CO. (MI)
5-1/2% Conv. Preferred called for redemption 2/3/58
6% Preferred $10 par called for redemption in August 1961
Acquired by General Acceptance Corp. (New) 2/28/67
Each share 6-1/4% Preferred $100 par exchanged for (4.5) shares 60¢ Preference Ser. B no par
Each share 6-1/2% Preferred $10 par exchanged for (0.4) share 60¢ Preference Ser. B no par
Each share $1.25 Preferred $20 par exchanged for (0.7) share 60¢ Preference Ser. B no par
Each share $1.60 Preferred $25 par exchanged for (0.75) share 60¢ Preference Ser. B no par
Each share Common $1 par exchanged for (0.1) share 60¢ Preference Ser. B no par
General Acceptance Corp. (New) name changed to GAC Corp. (PA) 7/1/68 which reincorporated in Delaware 12/20/73
(See GAC Corp. (DE))

PIONEER FINL CORP (KY)
Acquired by Central Bancshares 8/3/98
Each share Common $1 par exchanged for $98.50 cash

PIONEER FINL CORP (VA)
$1.88 Conv. Preferred Ser. A $1 par called for redemption 09/25/1989
Merged into Signet Banking Corp. 08/31/1994
Each share Common $1 par exchanged for (0.6232) share Common $5 par
Signet Banking Corp. merged into First Union Corp. 11/28/1997 which name changed to Wachovia Corp. (Ctfs. dated after 09/01/2001) 09/01/2001 which merged into Wells Fargo & Co. (New) 12/31/2008

PIONEER FINL SVCS INC (DE)
$2.125 Conv. Exchangeable Preferred $2.12 par called for redemption 5/15/96
Merged into Conseco, Inc. 5/30/97
Each share Common $1 par exchanged for (0.7077) share Common no par
(See Conseco, Inc.)

PIONEER FLA FDG CORP (DE)
Dutch Auction Rate Preferred called for redemption at $100,000 plus $1,116.78 accrued dividends on 12/15/89

PIONEER FLOATING RATE TR (DE)
Auction Market Preferred Ser. M7 called for redemption at $25,000 on 12/03/2013
Auction Market Preferred Ser. W7 called for redemption at $25,000 on 12/05/2013
Auction Market Preferred Ser. TH7 called for redemption at $25,000 on 12/06/2013
(Additional Information in Active)

PIONEER FOOD INDS INC (AR)
Merged into Pillsbury Co. 06/22/1979
Each share Common $1 par exchanged for (0.47387) share Common no par
(See Pillsbury Co.)

PIONEER GEOPHYSICAL SVCS INC (CANADA)
Recapitalized as Xplore Technologies Corp. 03/24/1997
Each share Common no par exchanged for (0.125) share Common no par
Xplore Technologies Corp. (Canada) reincorporated in Delaware 06/20/2007
(See Xplore Technologies Corp.)

PIONEER GOLD MINES OF BRITISH COLUMBIA LTD. (BC)
Merged into Bralorne Pioneer Mines Ltd. 03/19/1959
Each share Capital Stock $1 par exchanged for (0.2) share Captial Stock no par
Bralorne Pioneer Mines Ltd. name changed to Bralorne Can-Fer Resources Ltd. 12/03/1969 which name changed to Bralorne Resources Ltd. 05/29/1972 which recapitalized as BRL Enterprises Inc. 11/27/1990
(See BRL Enterprises Inc.)

PIONEER GOLD SHS (DE)
Completely liquidated 10/29/1999
Details not available

PIONEER GROUP INC (DE)
Common $1 par split (3) for (1) by issuance of (2) additional shares 6/15/84
Common $1 par split (2) for (1) by issuance of (1) additional share 9/1/93
Common $1 par split (2) for (1) by issuance of (1) additional share 12/9/94
Each share Common 1¢ par received distribution of (0.2) share Harbor Global Co. Ltd. Common 1¢ par payable 10/24/2000 to holders of record 8/9/2000
Merged into UniCredito Italiano S.p.A. 10/24/2000
Each share Common $1 par exchanged for $43.50 cash

PIONEER GROWTH SHS INC (DE)
Common 1¢ par reclassified as Class A no par 04/29/1995
Reorganized as Pioneer Independence Fund 12/07/2007
Each share Class A no par exchanged for (1) share Class A no par
Each share Class B no par exchanged for (1) share Class B no par
Each share Class C no par exchanged for (1) share Class C no par
Each share Class Y no par exchanged for (1) share Class Y no par

PIONEER GROWTH TR (MA)
Capital Growth Fund no par reclassified as Capital Growth Fund Class A no par 04/04/1994
Equity Income Fund no par reclassified as Equity Income Fund Class A no par 04/04/1994
Gold Shares no par reclassified as Gold Shares Class A no par 04/04/1994
Reorganized under the laws of Delaware as Pioneer Capital Growth Fund 06/30/1998
Each share Capital Growth Fund Class A no par exchanged for Class A no par on a net asset basis
Each share Capital Growth Fund Class B no par exchanged for Class B no par on a net asset basis
Reorganized under the laws of Delaware as Pioneer Equity Income Fund 06/30/1998
Each Equity Income Fund Class A no par exchanged for Class A no par on a net asset basis
Each Equity Income Fund Class B no par exchanged for Class B no par on a net asset basis
Reorganized under the laws of Delaware as Pioneer Gold Shares 06/30/1998
Each Gold Share Class A no par exchanged for Class A on a net asset basis
Each Gold Share Class B no par exchanged for Class B on a net asset basis
(See each company's listing)

PIONEER HI BRED INTL INC (IA)
Common $1 par split (3) for (1) by issuance of (2) additional shares payable 04/23/1998 to holders of record 03/27/1998 Ex date - 04/24/1998
Stock Dividends - 50% 05/24/1976; 100% 03/19/1982; 200% 07/17/1992
Merged into Du Pont (E.I.) De Nemours & Co. 10/01/1999
Each share Common $1 par exchanged for either (0.6561) share Common 30¢ par or $40 cash
Note: Option to receive stock expired 10/02/1999
Du Pont (E.I.) De Nemours & Co. merged into DowDuPont Inc. 09/01/2017

PIONEER HIGH INCOME TR (DE)
Auction Market Preferred Ser. W $0.0001 par called for redemption at $25,000 on 03/13/2014
Auction Market Preferred Ser. TH $0.0001 par called for redemption at $25,000 on 03/14/2014
Auction Market Preferred Ser. M $0.0001 par called for redemption at $25,000 on 03/18/2014
(Additional Information in Active)

PIONEER HOME OWNERS LIFE INSURANCE CO. (AL)
Merged into American Life Insurance Co. on a (0.4) for (1) basis 12/31/63
American Life Insurance Co. name changed to American-Amicable Life Insurance Co. 3/1/65
(See American-Amicable Life Insurance Co.)

PIONEER HYDROTEX INDUSTRIES, INC. (DE)
Name changed to Pioneer Texas Corp. 03/26/1962
Pioneer Texas Corp. merged into DPA, Inc. 08/01/1968 which reorganized as Pioneer Texas Corp. 03/30/1973
(See Pioneer Texas Corp.)

PIONEER INCOME FD (DE)
Reincorporated 06/30/1994
Reincorporated from Pioneer Income Fund, Inc. (NE) to under the laws of Delaware as Pioneer Income Fund and Common 1¢ par changed to no par 06/30/1994
Common no par reclassified as Class A no par 04/29/1995
Name changed to Pioneer Balanced Fund 02/01/1997
Pioneer Balanced Fund merged into Pioneer Series Trust IV 11/10/2006

PIONEER INDO-ASIA FD (DE)
Name changed 10/01/1998
Name changed from Pioneer India Fund to Pioneer Indo-Asia Fund 10/01/1998
Merged into Pioneer Emerging Markets Fund 09/28/2001
Each share Class A no par exchanged for (0.805180) share Class A no par
Each share Class B no par exchanged for (0.808863) share Class B no par
Each share Class C no par exchanged for (0.804263) share Class Y no par

PIONEER INDUSTRIES, INC. (DE)
Acquired by Soss Manufacturing Co. (NV) 09/00/1968
Details not available

PIONEER INDS INC (DC)
Company believed out of business 00/00/1981
Details not available

PIONEER INS CO (NE)
Each share old Common $1 par exchanged for (0.5) share new Common $1 par 02/29/1972
Out of business 00/00/1972
No stockholders' equity

PIONEER INT SHS (DE)
Reincorporated 08/02/1996
Name changed and state of incorporation changed from Pioneer Interest Shares, Inc. (NE) to Pioneer Interest Shares (DE) 08/02/1996
Merged into Pioneer Bond Fund 10/19/2007
Each share Common 1¢ par exchanged for (1.34413451) shares Class Y Common $1 par

PIONEER INTER TAX FREE FD (MA)
Merged into Pioneer Tax-Free Income Fund 03/31/1999
Each share Class A no par exchanged for (0.85598) share Class A
Each share Class B no par exchanged for (0.86581) share Class B
Each share Class C no par exchanged for (0.85941) share Class C

PIONEER INTL CORP (DE)
Merged into Pioneer Systems, Inc. (DE) 2/25/85
Each share Common 10¢ par exchanged for (1.7) shares Common 10¢ par
(See Pioneer Systems, Inc. (DE))

PIONEER INTL EQUITY FD (DE)
Merged into Pioneer International Value Fund 06/12/2009
Each share Class A no par exchanged for (0.87994044) share Class A no par
Each share Class B no par exchanged for (0.8564281) share Class B no par
Each share Class C no par exchanged for (0.85229595) share Class C no par
Each share Class Y no par exchanged for (0.8930339) share Class Y no par

PIONEER INTL LTD (AUSTRALIA)
Each Unsponsored ADR for Ordinary exchanged for (1) Sponsored ADR for Ordinary 06/04/1990
ADR agreement terminated 08/14/2000
Each Sponsored ADR for Ordinary exchanged for $2.6341 cash

PIONEER INTL VALUE FD (MA)
Name changed 07/30/2001
Shares of Bene. Int. no par reclassified as Class A no par 04/04/1994
Name changed from Pioneer International Growth Fund to Pioneer International Value Fund 07/30/2001
Reincorporated under the laws of Delaware 06/30/2008

PIONEER LIFE & CASUALTY CO., INC. (AL)
Each share Preferred and Common $10 par exchanged for (10) shares Preferred and Common $1 par 11/09/1954
Under plan of merger name changed to Pioneer Home Owners Life Insurance Co. 01/01/1962
Pioneer Home Owners Life Insurance Co. merged into American Life Insurance Co. 12/31/1963 which name changed to American-Amicable Life Insurance Co. 03/01/1965
(See American-Amicable Life Insurance Co.)

PIONEER LIFECO INC (CANADA)
Name changed to Wokingham Capital Corp. 7/27/92
Wokingham Capital Corp. name changed to Coniston Capital Corp. 7/18/94 which name changed to CPL Ventures Ltd. 8/8/96 which recapitalized as Manfrey Capital Corp. 11/11/96
(See Manfrey Capital Corp.)

PIONEER LTD MAT BD FD (MA)
Merged into Pioneer Bond Fund 09/28/2001
Each share Class A no par exchanged for (0.420845) share Class A no par
Each share Class B no par exchanged for (0.419417) share Class B no par
Each share Class Y no par exchanged for (0.422076) share Class Y no par

PIONEER METALS CORP NEW (BC)
Merged into Barrick Gold Corp. 3/6/2007
Each share Common no par exchanged for $1 cash

PIONEER METALS CORP OLD (BC)
Plan of arrangement effective 10/2/95
Each share Common no par exchanged for (1) share Pioneer Metals Corp. (New) Common no par and (0.0041466) share Scaffold Connection Corp. Common no par
(See each company's listing)

PIONEER METALS INC (FL)
Merged into Goodman Distributing 3/2/2000
Each share Common 10¢ par exchanged for $615.43 cash

PIONEER MICRO-CAP FD (DE)
Name changed to Pioneer Small-Cap Value Fund 09/06/2001

PIONEER MID CAP FD (DE)
Name changed to Pioneer Mid Cap Growth Fund 09/06/2001

PIONEER MILL CO. LTD. (HI)
Merged into American Factors Ltd. 1/6/61
Each share Capital Stock $10 par exchanged for (1.1) shares Capital Stock $20 par
American Factors Ltd. name changed to Amfac, Inc. 4/30/66
(See Amfac, Inc.)

PIONEER MINING & DITCH CO. (NV)
Charter revoked for failure to file reports and pay fees 3/3/24

PIONEER MINING CORP., LTD.
Merged into Huronian Mining & Finance Co., Ltd. in 1929
Details not available

PIONEER MONEY MKT ACCT INC (NE)
Under plan of merger each share Common 1¢ par automatically became (1) share Pioneer Money Market Trust (MA) Cash Reserves Fund no par on a net asset basis 06/30/1994
Pioneer Money Market Trust (MA) reincorporated in Delaware 03/31/1995

PIONEER MONEY MKT TR (DE)
Reincorporated 03/31/1995
Shares of Bene. Int. no par reclassified as Cash Reserves Fund no par 04/11/1988
State of incorporation changed from (MA) to (DE) and Cash Reserves Fund no par, Tax-Free Money Fund no par and U.S. Government Money Fund no par reclassified as Cash Reserves Fund Class A no par, Tax-Free Money Fund Class A no par and U.S. Government Money Fund Class A no par respectively 03/31/1995
Each share U.S. Government Money Fund Class A no par exchanged for (1) share Cash Reserves Fund Class A no par 07/01/1996

PIONEER MUN & EQUITY INCOME TR (DE)
Auction Market Preferred Ser. F7 called for redemption at $25,000 on 10/06/2008
Auction Market Preferred Ser. T7 called for redemption at $25,000 on 10/15/2008
Auction Market Preferred Ser. TH28 called for redemption at $25,000 on 10/24/2008
Merged into Pioneer Tax Free Income Fund 10/24/2008
Each share Common no par exchanged for (1.15225555) shares Class A Common

PIONEER MUN BD FD (MA)
Name changed to Pioneer Intermediate Tax Free Fund and Shares of Bene. Int. no par reclassified as Class A Common no par 01/01/1994
Pioneer Intermediate Tax Free Fund merged into Pioneer Tax-Free Income Fund 03/31/1999

PIONEER NAT GAS CO (TX)
Common $7.50 par changed to no par 04/20/1955
Common no par changed to $7.50 par 04/17/1956
Common $7.50 par changed to $3.75 par and (1) additional share issued 05/06/1960
Common $3.75 par changed to $1.875 par and (1) additional share issued 11/06/1964
Name changed to Pioneer Corp. (TX) 04/18/1975
Pioneer Corp. (TX) liquidated for Mesa Limited Partnership (DE) 06/30/1986 which reorganized in Texas as Mesa Inc. 12/31/1991 which merged into Pioneer Natural Resources Co. 08/07/1997

PIONEER NAT RES CDA INC (AB)
Merged into Pioneer Natural Resources Co. 12/18/2002
Each Exchangable Share no par exchanged for (1) share Common 1¢ par

PIONEER NATIONAL BANK (LOS ANGELES, CA)
Completely liquidated 1/23/67
Each share Capital Stock $10 par exchanged for first and final distribution of $26.10 cash

PIONEER NURSING CTRS INC (KS)
Stock Dividend - 20% 6/9/71
Name changed to Pacer Phenix Corp. 4/30/74
(See Pacer Phenix Corp.)

PIONEER OIL & DRILLING CO. (UT)
Name changed to Wyoming Southern Oil Corp. 10/01/1958
Wyoming Southern Oil Corp. recapitalized as Delcor Inc. 08/04/1969
(See Delcor Inc.)

PIONEER PETE & MNG INC (ID)
Charter forfeited for failure to file reports 12/1/93

PIONEER PLASTICS CORP (NJ)
Common $1 par split (2) for (1) by issuance of (1) additional share 12/10/70
Merged into Libbey-Owens-Ford Co. 11/19/75
Each share Common $1 par exchanged for $7 cash
Note: Holders of (143) shares or more had the option to receive $7 principal amount of 9% 15-year Non-Transferable Note or $7 cash Option expired 11/19/75

PIONEER PROSPECTORS CONSOLIDATED MINES LTD. (ON)
Charter cancelled for default in filing reports 4/1/58

PIONEER RAILCORP (IA)
Acquired by Pioneer Merger Corp. 8/25/2005
Each share Common $0.001 par exchanged for $2.85 cash
Note: Holders of (2,000) shares or more will retain their interests

PIONEER REALTY CO. (SD)
Proclaimed dissolved for failure to file reports and pay fees 5/11/42

PIONEER RR INC (IA)
Name changed to Pioneer Railcorp 10/13/91
(See Pioneer Railcorp)

PIONEER RUBR CO (OH)
Merged into Sherwood Medical Industries Inc. 01/01/1971
Each share Common no par exchanged for $52.92 cash

PIONEER SVGS BK (LYNNWOOD, WA)
Merged into Washington Mutual Savings Bank (Seattle, WA) 03/01/1993
Each share Common $1 par exchanged for (0.824) share Common $1 par
Washington Mutual Savings Bank (Seattle, WA) reorganized as Washington Mutual Inc. 11/29/1994
(See Washington Mutual, Inc.)

PIONEER SVGS BK F S B (CLEARWATER, FL)
Name changed 5/20/85
Name changed 7/21/89
Name changed from Pioneer Savings Bank, F.S.B. (Clearwater, FL) to Pioneer Savings Bank (Clearwater, FL) 5/20/85
Each share Common $1 par exchanged for (1) share Common $1 par
Under plan of reorganization name changed from Pioneer Savings Bank back to Pioneer Savings Bank, F.S.B. 7/21/89
Declared insolvent and closed by the office of Thrift Supervision 3/1/91

PIONEER SVGS BK INC ROCKY MT (NC)
Reorganized as Pioneer Bancorp, Inc. 12/28/1988
Each share Common $1 par exchanged for (1) share Common 1¢ par
(See Pioneer Bancorp, Inc.)

PIONEER SECURITIES CORP. (NY)
Bankrupt in 1945

PIONEER SVCS INTL LTD (NV)
Name changed to Jacobson Resonance Enterprises, Inc. 7/30/98
(See Jacobson Resonance Enterprises, Inc.)

PIONEER SHORT TERM INCOME TR (MA)
Shares of Bene. Int. no par reclassified as Class A no par 04/04/1994
Name changed to Pioneer Limited Maturity Bond Fund 09/17/1999
Pioneer Limited Maturity Bond Fund merged into Pioneer Bond Fund 09/28/2001

PIONEER SOUTHWEST ENERGY PARTNERS L P (DE)
Issue Information - 8,250,000 UNITS LTD PARTNERSHIP INT offered at $19 per Unit on 04/30/2008
Merged into Pioneer Natural Resources Co. 12/17/2013
Each Unit of Ltd. Partnership Int. exchanged for (0.2325) share Common 1¢ par

PIONEER SPIRIT 2000 INC (NV)
Name changed to Mighty Star Ltd. 05/02/2000
Mighty Star Ltd. name changed to Shao Tong Chuan Health Vegetarian Foods (USA) Holdings Ltd. (NV) 06/13/2003 which reorganized in Delaware as Standard Commerce, Inc. 01/29/2007 which recapitalized as China Jianye Fuel, Inc. 01/18/2008
(See China Jianye Fuel, Inc.)

PIONEER ST BK (GLOUCESTER TOWNSHIP, NJ)
Recapitalized as Continental Bank of New Jersey (Gloucester Township, NJ) 3/1/79
Each share Common $5 par exchanged for (1) share Common $2 par
Continental Bank of New Jersey (Gloucester Township, NJ) reorganized as Continental Bancorporation 7/1/89
(See Continental Bancorporation (NJ))

PIONEER STD ELECTRS INC (OH)
Common no par split (3) for (2) by issuance of (0.5) additional share 12/01/1972
Common no par split (3) for (2) by issuance of (0.5) additional share 05/01/1977
Common no par split (3) for (2) by

issuance of (0.5) additional share 09/01/1978
Common no par split (3) for (2) by issuance of (0.5) additional share 06/02/1980
Common no par split (2) for (1) by issuance of (1) additional share 08/01/1984
Common no par split (3) for (2) by issuance of (0.5) additional share 03/15/1993
Common no par split (3) for (2) by issuance of (0.5) additional share 08/01/1994
Common no par split (3) for (2) by issuance of (0.5) additional share 09/06/1995
Name changed to Agilysys Inc. 09/16/2003

PIONEER STD FINL TR (DE)
Each share 6.75% 144A Conv. Securities Preferred Trust exchanged for (1) share 6.75% Conv. Securities Preferred Trust 09/17/1998
6.75% Conv. Trust Preferred Securities called for redemption at $51.0125 plus $0.703125 accrued dividends on 06/15/2005

PIONEER STEAMSHIP CO. (DE)
Common no par split (5) for (1) by issuance of (4) additional shares 5/15/57
Liquidation completed
Each share Common no par stamped to indicate initial distribution of $60 cash 7/5/62
Each share Stamped Common no par exchanged for second distribution of $20.28 cash 4/8/63
Each share Stamped Common no par received third distribution of $1 cash 12/15/64
Each share Stamped Common no par received fourth and final distribution of $0.377 cash 4/22/66

PIONEER SYS INC (DE)
Common 10¢ par split (2) for (1) by issuance of (1) additional share 8/23/68
Charter forfeited for failure to maintain a registered agent 6/7/98

PIONEER SYSTEMS, INC. (CA)
Name changed to Pioneer Take Out Corp. 7/17/70
(See Pioneer Take Out Corp.)

PIONEER TAKE OUT CORP. (CA)
Charter suspended for failure to file reports and pay fees 11/9/89

PIONEER TAX ADVANTAGED BALANCED TR (DE)
Issue Information - 25,600,000 shares COM offered at $15 per share on 01/27/2004
Name changed to Pioneer Municipal & Equity Income Trust 11/07/2007
Pioneer Municipal & Equity Income Trust merged into Pioneer Tax Free Income Fund 10/24/2008

PIONEER TAX-FREE INCOME FD INC (DE)
Common 1¢ par reclassified as Class A 04/29/1995
Name changed to Pioneer Tax Free Income Fund 06/30/1994

PIONEER TAX-FREE ST SER TR (MA)
Completely liquidated 04/10/1996
Details not available

PIONEER TELEPHONE CO. (MN)
Reincorporated 12/31/1964
Each share Common $10 par exchanged for (2) shares Common no par 00/00/1954
Each share Common no par exchanged for (2) shares Common $1 par 00/00/1957
Common $1 par changed to $0.33333333 par and (2) additional shares issued 07/28/1962

State of incorporation changed from (DE) to (MN) 12/31/1964
4.5% Preferred Ser. A $100 par called for redemption 07/01/1967
5% Preferred Ser. B $100 par called for redemption 07/01/1967
5% Preferred Ser. D $100 par called for redemption 07/01/1967
5% Preferred Ser. E $100 par called for redemption 07/01/1967
5.5% Ser. C $100 par called for redemption 07/01/1967
5.25% Ser. F $100 par called for redemption 07/01/1967
Merged into United Utilities, Inc. 04/30/1968
Each share Common $0.33333333 par exchanged for (1.2) shares Common $2.50 par
United Utilities, Inc. name changed to United Telecommunications, Inc. 06/02/1972 which name changed to Sprint Corp. (KS) 02/26/1992 which name changed to Sprint Nextel Corp. 08/12/2005 which merged into Sprint Corp. (DE) 07/10/2013

PIONEER TEX CORP (DE)
Ctfs. dated after 03/30/1973
Plan of reorganization under Chapter 11 Federal Bankruptcy proceedings confirmed 11/26/1984
No stockholders' equity

PIONEER TEXAS CORP. (DE)
Ctfs. dated prior to 08/01/1968
Merged into DPA, Inc. 08/01/1968
Each share Common $1 par exchanged for (0.4) share $1.60 Conv. Preferred Ser. B $10 par
DPA, Inc. reorganized as Pioneer Texas Corp. 03/30/1973
(See Pioneer Texas Corp.)

PIONEER THREE INC (MA)
Reincorporated under the laws of Delaware as Pioneer Mid Cap Fund 01/31/1996
Pioneer Mid Cap Fund name changed to Pioneer Mid Cap Growth Fund 09/06/2001

PIONEER TR & SVGS BK (CHICAGO, IL)
Capital Stock $100 par changed to $25 par and a 25% stock dividend paid 2/2/59
Stock Dividends - 33-1/3% 2/14/44; 50% 1/15/51; 33-1/3% 1/15/55; 20% 1/12/63
Name changed to Pioneer Bank & Trust Co. (Chicago, IL) 8/10/75
(See Pioneer Bank & Trust Co. (Chicago, IL))

PIONEER II INC (DE)
Reincorporated 5/1/96
Stock Dividend - 100% 10/19/78
State of incorporation changed from (MA) to (DE) and Common Stock reclassified as Cl A shares 5/1/96
Name changed to Pioneer Value Fund 4/2/2001

PIONEER U S GOVT TR (MA)
Shares of Bene. Int. no par reclassified as Class A no par 04/29/1994
Name changed to Pioneer America Income Trust 07/07/1994
Pioneer America Income Trust merged into Pioneer Series Trust IV 11/10/2006

PIONEER WESTN CORP (DE)
Acquired by Kansas City Southern Industries Inc. 6/28/79
Each share Common $1 par exchanged for $17 cash

PIONEER WINTHROP REAL ESTATE INVT FD (MA)
Reincorporated under the laws of Delaware as Pioneer Real Estate Shares 09/01/1995

PIONEER WORLD CORP (CA)
Charter revoked for failure to file reports and pay fees 12/01/1964

PIONEERING TECHNOLOGY INC (ON)
Recapitalized as Pioneering Technology Corp. 09/18/2008
Each share Common no par exchanged for (0.1) share Common no par

PIONEERS OIL CO.
Dissolved in 1951

PIPE NT CORP (ON)
Preferred no par called for redemption at $25 on 3/3/2003
Capital Shares no par called for redemption at $25 on 3/3/2003

PIPECOTE SERVICE CO. INC. (DE)
Name changed to Pipelife Corp. and Common $1 par changed to 10¢ par 04/28/1955
Pipelife Corp. merged into Financial South Corp. 05/01/1969
(See Financial South Corp.)

PIPEDREAMS MFG INC (AB)
Recapitalized as Inter-Link Communications Inc. 2/14/90
Each share Common no par exchanged for (1/3) share Common no par
Inter-Link Communications Inc. recapitalized as International Inter-Link Inc. 8/3/93 which name changed to Parton Capital Inc. 11/10/97

PIPELIFE CORP (DE)
Merged into Financial South Corp. 05/01/1969
Each share Common 10¢ par exchanged for (0.1) share Common 1¢ par
(See Financial South Corp.)

PIPELINE DATA INC (DE)
Each share Common $0.001 par received distribution of (0.3116) Common Stock Purchase Warrant, Class B expiring 04/23/2005 payable 01/29/2001 to holders of record 12/29/2000 Ex date - 01/30/2001
Plan of reorganization under Chapter 11 Federal Bankruptcy proceedings effective 10/28/2013
Stockholders' equity unlikely

PIPELINE TECHNOLOGIES INC (CO)
SEC revoked common stock registration 11/04/2009
Stockholders' equity unlikely

PIPER AIRCRAFT CORP (PA)
Common $1 par exchanged (4) for (1) in 1944
Common $1 par split (3) for (2) by issuance of (0.5) additional share 11/27/64
Merged into Bangor Punta Corp. 5/9/78
Each share Common $1 par exchanged for (3) shares Common $1 par and $7.8625 cash
(See Bangor Punta Corp.)

PIPER CAP INC (AB)
Merged into Garson Gold Corp. 07/04/2007
Each share Common no par exchanged for (1) share Common no par
Garson Gold Corp. merged into Alexis Minerals Corp. 04/29/2010 which recapitalized as QMX Gold Corp. 07/05/2012

PIPER INDS INC (TN)
Reacquired 00/00/1982
Each share Common $1.35-1/10 par exchanged for $18 cash

PIPER JAFFRAY & HOPWOOD INC (DE)
Under plan of reorganization each share Common $1 par automatically became (1) share Piper Jaffray, Inc. Common $1 par 5/31/74
Piper Jaffray, Inc. name changed to Piper Jaffray Companies, Inc. 4/13/92

(See Piper Jaffray Companies, Inc.)

PIPER JAFFRAY COS INC (DE)
Name changed 4/13/92
Common $1 par split (3) for (1) by issuance of (2) additional shares 10/3/83
Common $1 par split (2) for (1) by issuance of (1) additional share 12/10/91
Name changed from Piper Jaffray, Inc. to Piper Jaffray Companies, Inc. 4/13/92
Acquired by Cub Acquisition Corp. 5/1/98
Each share Common $1 par exchanged for $37.25 cash

PIPER JAFFRAY INVT TR INC (MN)
Merged into First American Investment Funds Inc. 7/31/98
Each share Balanced Fund 1¢ par exchanged for (0.9579837) share Balanced Fund Class A $0.0001 par
Each share Equity Strategy Fund 1¢ par exchanged for (0.5499189) share Small Capital Growth Fund Class A $0.0001 par
Each share Government Income Fund 1¢ par exchanged for (0.8217646) share Fixed Income Fund $0.0001 par
Each share Growth Fund 1¢ par exchanged for (0.563622510) share Large Cap Growth Fund Class A 1¢ par
Merged into First American Investment Funds Inc. 8/7/98
Each share Emerging Growth Fund 1¢ par exchanged for (1) share Midcap Growth Fund 1¢ par

PIPER PETES LTD (BC)
Merged into Giant Piper Exploration Inc. 11/17/1981
Each share Common no par exchanged for (1) share Common no par
Giant Piper Exploration Inc. name changed to Giant Pacific Petroleum Inc. 05/12/1988 which recapitalized as Red Rock Mining Corp. 12/05/1991 which name changed to American Pacific Minerals Ltd. 05/30/1994
(See American Pacific Minerals Ltd.)

PIPER PETROLEUMS LTD (AB)
Merged into Dalton Resources Ltd. (New) 12/31/1995
Each share Class A Common no par exchanged for (0.28571428) share Common no par
Dalton Resources Ltd. (New) merged into Tiverton Petroleums Ltd. 10/01/2000 which merged into Arsenal Energy Inc. (New) 03/13/2006 which merged into Prairie Provident Resources Inc. 09/16/2016

PIPESTONE NARROWS GOLD MINES LTD. (ON)
Charter cancelled for failure to file reports and pay taxes August 1957

PIPESTONE PETES INC (BC)
Merged into Blue Range Resource Corp. 07/11/1995
Each share Common no par exchanged for (0.07692307) share Class A Common no par
Blue Range Resource Corp. merged into Big Bear Exploration Ltd. 02/12/1999 which merged into Avid Oil & Gas Ltd. 02/02/2000
(See Avid Oil & Gas Ltd.)

PIPEX PHARMACEUTICALS INC (DE)
Each share old Common $0.001 par exchanged for (1/3) share new Common $0.001 par 04/25/2007
Name changed to Adeona Pharmaceuticals, Inc. (DE) 10/16/2008
Adeona Pharmaceuticals, Inc. (DE) reincorporated in Nevada 10/16/2009

PIPPIN ATHABASCA URANIUM MINES LTD. (ON)
Name changed to Pippin Mining & Uranium Corp. Ltd. 1/26/56
Pippin Mining & Uranium Corp. Ltd. charter cancelled 6/26/79

PIPPIN MINING & URANIUM CORP. LTD. (ON)
Charter cancelled for failure to pay taxes and file returns 6/26/79

PIQUA HOSIERY CO.
Acquired by B.V.D., Inc. 00/00/1930
Details not available

PIQUA NATL BK & TR CO (PIQUA, OH)
Stock Dividends - 50% 02/00/1957; 20% 02/29/1968; 16-2/3% 02/26/1971; 14.3% 03/31/1975; 12-1/2% 03/31/1978; 11.11% 04/15/1980; 10% 04/15/1982
Reorganized as Comp One Corp. 05/31/1985
Each share Capital Stock $10 par exchanged for (1) share Common $10 par
Comp One Corp. merged into C&H Bancorp 12/31/1986 which was acquired by Fifth Third Bancorp 04/01/1988

PIR-O-WOOD INDUSTRIES, INC. (NY)
Adjudicated bankrupt 5/12/65

PIRAEUS PORT AUTH S A (GREECE)
ADR agreement terminated 08/06/2018
No ADR's remain outstanding

PIRANHA INC (DE)
SEC revoked common stock registration 10/13/2004

PIRANHA INTERACTIVE PUBG INC (NV)
Name changed to Piranha Ventures, Inc. 12/02/2009
Piranha Ventures, Inc. name changed to Realgold International, Inc. 12/14/2011 which name changed to Asia Travel Corp. 06/05/2013 which name changed to Square Chain Corp. 04/11/2018

PIRANHA VENTURES INC (NV)
Each share old Common $0.001 par exchanged for (0.1) share new Common $0.001 par 06/13/2011
Note: No holder will receive fewer than (100) shares
Name changed to Realgold International, Inc. 12/14/2011
Realgold International, Inc. name changed to Asia Travel Corp. 06/05/2013 which name changed to Square Chain Corp. 04/11/2018

PIRATES GOLD CORP (BC)
Delisted from Vancouver Stock Exchange 11/02/1988

PIRELLI & C SPA (ITALY)
Each Unsponsored ADR for Common exchanged for (1) Sponsored ADR for Common 11/02/2011
ADR agreement terminated 11/12/2015
Each Sponsored ADR for Common exchanged for $16.1245 cash

PIRELLI S P A (ITALY)
ADR agreement with First National City Bank, New York terminated 00/00/1949
Each American Share for Ordinary Class A 500 Lire par exchanged for (4.8) shares Ordinary Class A 500 Lire par
Note: All foreign shares were sold and each (1) American Share became exchangeable for $89.34 cash plus accrued dividends 05/11/1962
Stock Dividends - 50% 09/07/1962; 10% 05/13/1988
ADR agreement terminated 09/12/2003
Each ADR for Ordinary EUR 1000 par exchanged for $0.883 cash

Note: Due to ADR's being unsponsored exchange rate may vary dependent upon depositary agent

PIRRANA CORP (ON)
Merged into Laser Friendly Inc. 04/27/1987
Details not available

PISCES CAP CORP (ON)
Name changed to Petrolympic Ltd. 01/03/2008

PISTOL PETE INC (BC)
Delisted from Vancouver Stock Exchange 01/09/1989

PIT BOSS ENTMT INC (NV)
Name changed to US Energy Holdings, Inc. 03/08/2006
US Energy Holdings, Inc. name changed to Lonestar Group Holdings, Co. 01/10/2007 which recapitalized as Guardian Angel Group, Inc. 12/14/2007 which recapitalized as Ree International, Inc. 06/29/2011

PIT STOP AUTO CTRS INC (NV)
Recapitalized as Resources of the Pacific Corp. 08/04/1995
Each share Common 5¢ par exchanged for (0.05) share Common $0.001 par
Resources of the Pacific Corp. name changed to Semper Resources Corp. (NV) 06/21/1996 which reincorporated in Oklahoma 00/00/2005 which name changed to Cyberfund, Inc. (OK) 09/01/2006 which reincorporated in Delaware as ROK Entertainment Group Inc. 12/31/2007
(See ROK Entertainment Group Inc.)

PITCH ORE URANIUM MINES LTD. (ON)
Recapitalized as Allied Pitch-Ore Mines Ltd. on a (1) for (5) basis 4/18/63
Allied Pitch-Ore Mines Ltd. charter cancelled 5/24/72

PITCHBLACK RES LTD (ON)
Each share old Common no par exchanged for (0.1) share new Common no par 11/02/2015
Recapitalized as Troilus Gold Corp. 01/03/2018
Each share new Common no par exchanged for (0.25) share Common no par

PITCHGOMA MINES LTD. (ON)
Merged into Consolidated Frederick Mines Ltd. on a (1) for (29) basis 9/9/57
Consolidated Frederick Mines Ltd. liquidation was completed 10/23/61

PITCHSTONE EXPLORATION LTD (BC)
Merged into Fission Energy Corp. 07/05/2012
Each share Common no par exchanged for (0.2145) share Common no par

PITCHVEIN MINES LTD (ON)
Charter cancelled 05/06/1980

PITMAN NATIONAL BANK & TRUST CO. (PITMAN, NJ)
Merged into National Bank & Trust Co. of Gloucester County (Woodbury, NJ) 07/17/1970
Each share Capital Stock $25 par exchanged for (5) shares Capital Stock $10 par
National Bank & Trust Co. of Gloucester County (Woodbury, NJ) reorganized as Community Bancshares Corp. 10/01/1975 which merged into First Fidelity Bancorporation (Old) 09/28/1985 which merged into First Fidelity Bancorporation (New) 02/29/1988 which merged into First Union Corp. 01/01/1996 which name changed to

Wachovia Corp. (Ctfs. dated after 09/01/2001) 09/01/2001 which merged into Wells Fargo & Co. (New) 12/31/2008

PITMEL INC (PA)
Acquired by Fundamental Investors, Inc. (DE) 03/06/1969
Each share Capital Stock $2 par exchanged for (1.9512) shares Capital Stock $1 par
Fundamental Investors, Inc. (DE) reincorporated in Maryland 02/01/1990 which reorganized in Delaware as Fundamental Investors 09/01/2010

PITNEY-BOWES POSTAGE METER CO.
Name changed to Pitney Bowes Inc. and Common no par changed to $2 par 00/00/1945

PITOOEY INC (NV)
Name changed to Raadr, Inc. 10/13/2015

PITT AIRLINES, INC. (DE)
Charter cancelled and declared inoperative and void for non-payment of taxes 3/1/76

PITT DESMOINES INC (PA)
Common no par split (3) for (2) by issuance of (0.5) additional share payable 3/28/97 to holders of record 3/14/97 Ex date - 3/31/97
Common no par split (2) for (1) by issuance of (1) additional share payable 6/26/98 to holders of record 6/12/98 Ex date - 6/29/98
Merged into Ironbridge Holding LLC 3/13/2002
Each share Common no par exchanged for $33.90 cash

PITT GOLD MNG LTD (ON)
Charter cancelled and proclaimed dissolved for failure to pay taxes and file returns 06/30/1980

PITTENCRIEFF COMMUNICATIONS INC (DE)
Reincorporated 01/16/1996
State of incorporation changed from (TX) to (DE) 01/16/1996
Merged into Nextel Communications, Inc. 11/12/1997
Each share Common 1¢ par exchanged for (0.2237136) share Common $0.001 par
Nextel Communications, Inc. merged into Sprint Nextel Corp. 08/12/2005 which merged into Sprint Corp. (DE) 07/10/2013

PITTENCRIEFF PLC (UNITED KINGDOM)
Completely liquidated 06/14/1994
Details not available

PITTOCK FINL SVCS INC (CO)
Stock Dividend - 10% 12/28/1983
Completely liquidated 04/15/1986
Each share Common 1¢ par exchanged for first and final distribution of $0.90 principal amount of Rafco, Ltd. 12% Sr. Subord. Notes due 03/04/1994

PITTS & SPITTS INC (NV)
Name changed to PSPP Holdings, Inc. 06/17/2004
PSPP Holdings, Inc. recapitalized as Mod Hospitality, Inc. 09/22/2008 which recapitalized as Stakool, Inc. 12/16/2009 which name changed to Fresh Promise Foods, Inc. 11/12/2013

PITTS & SPITTS TEX INC (NV)
Name changed to Energy Drilling Industries, Inc. 12/22/97
Energy Drilling Industries, Inc. name changed to American International Industries Inc. 6/30/98

PITTS ENGR CONSTR LTD (ON)
Name changed 10/4/74
Common no par split (2) for (1) by issuance of (1) additional share 1/16/70
Each share Common no par exchanged for (2) shares Class C no par 9/15/72
Name changed from Pitts (C.A.) Engineering Construction Ltd. to Pitts Engineering Construction Ltd. 10/4/74
Merged into Banister Continental Construction Ltd. 8/31/78
Each share Class B no par exchanged for $9.75 cash
Each share Class C no par exchanged for $9.75 cash

PITTSBURG, BESSEMER & LAKE ERIE RAILROAD CO.
Merged into Bessemer & Lake Erie Railroad Co. in 1949
Each share 6% Preferred exchanged for (1) share $3 Preferred
Each share Common exchanged for (1) share $1.50 Preferred

PITTSBURG, SHAWMUT & NORTHERN RAILROAD CO.
Property sold in 1947
No stockholders' equity Receivers' certificates liquidated in 1950

PITTSBURG & SHAWMUT RAILROAD CO. (PA)
Capital Stock $100 par reclassified as Common $1 par 1/1/57
Acquired by Genesee & Wyoming Inc. in 1996
Details not available

PITTSBURG SILVER MNG CO (MT)
Involuntarily dissolved 12/04/2007

PITTSBURGH, CINCINNATI, CHICAGO & ST. LOUIS RAILROAD CO. (IL, IN, OH, PA & WV)
Merged into Philadelphia, Baltimore & Washington Railroad Co. at $125 per share 4/2/56

PITTSBURGH & BIRMINGHAM PASSENGER RAILROAD CO.
Merged into Pittsburgh Railways Co. for cash 9/30/50

PITTSBURGH & BIRMINGHAM TRACTION CO.
Merged into Pittsburgh Railways Co. for cash 9/30/50

PITTSBURGH & LAKE ERIE RAILROAD CO. (PA & OH)
Merged into Pittsburgh & Lake Erie Railroad Co. (DE) share for share 01/31/1965
(See Pittsburgh & Lake Erie Railroad Co. (DE))

PITTSBURGH & LAKE ERIE RR CO (DE)
Merged into Pittsburgh & Lake Erie Co. 09/17/1979
Each share Capital Stock $50 par exchanged for $115 cash

PITTSBURGH & SUSQUEHANNA RAILROAD CO.
Road abandoned in 1936

PITTSBURGH & W VA RR (PA)
Reincorporated under the laws of Maryland as Power REIT and Common Shares of Bene. Int. no par changed to $0.001 par 12/05/2011

PITTSBURGH & W VA RY CO (PA & WV)
Common $100 par changed to $20 par and (4) additional shares issued 5/18/65
Each (15,100) shares Common $20 par exchanged for (1) share Common no par 12/28/67
In effect public interest was eliminated

PITTSBURGH AVIATION INDUSTRIES CORP.
Dissolution approved in 1934

PITTSBURGH BOND & SHARE CO.
Acquired by State Street Investment Corp. 00/00/1932
Details not available

PITTSBURGH BREWING CO (PA)
Preferred $50 par and Common $50 par changed to no par 00/00/1934
Each share $3.50 Preferred no par exchanged for (1) share $2.50 Preferred $25 par and (9) shares Common $2.50 par 00/00/1950
Each share Common no par exchanged for (1) share Common $2.50 par 00/00/1950
Common $2.50 par changed to $1 par 01/15/1957
$2.50 Preferred $25 par called for redemption 02/20/1986
Merged into Swan Acquisition Corp. 04/29/1986
Each share Common $1 par exchanged for $22.50 cash

PITTSBURGH COAL CO.
Merged into Pittsburgh Consolidation Coal Co. in 1945
Each share Preferred exchanged for $26.327 principal amount of 3-1/2% Debentures and (3.226) shares Common $1 par
Each share Common exchanged for (0.25) share Common $1 par
Pittsburgh Consolidation Coal Co. name changed to Consolidation Coal Co. 5/1/58
(See Consolidation Coal Co.)

PITTSBURGH COKE & CHEM CO (DE)
Reincorporated 08/19/1970
Common no par changed to $10 par 04/06/1956
$4.80 Preferred no par called for redemption 07/10/1970
$5 Preferred no par called for redemption 07/10/1970
State of incorporation changed from (PA) to (DE) 08/19/1970
Merged into Pittsburgh-Wilmington, Inc. 06/30/1972
Each share Common $10 par exchanged for $151.90 cash

PITTSBURGH COKE & IRON CO.
Name changed to Pittsburgh Coke & Chemical Co. (PA) 00/00/1944
Pittsburgh Coke & Chemical Co. (PA) reincorporated in Delaware 08/19/1970
(See Pittsburgh Coke & Chemical Co. (DE))

PITTSBURGH CONSOLIDATION COAL CO. (PA)
Common $1 par split (3) for (1) by issuance of (2) additional shares 2/24/56
Name changed to Consolidation Coal Co. 5/1/58
(See Consolidation Coal Co.)

PITTSBURGH DES MOINES CORP (PA)
Under plan of reorganization each share Common no par automatically became (1) share Pitt-Des Moines, Inc. Common no par 9/1/85
(See Pitt-Des Moines, Inc.)

PITTSBURGH-DES MOINES STEEL CO. (PA)
Common no par split (2) for (1) by issuance of (1) additional share 1/14/74
Stock Dividend - 100% 1/1/81
Name changed to Pittsburgh-Des Moines Corp. 1/1/81
Pittsburgh-Des Moines Corp. reorganized as Pitt-Des Moines, Inc. 9/1/85
(See Pitt-Des Moines, Inc.)

PITTSBURGH EQUITABLE METER CO. (PA)
Recapitalized as Rockwell Manufacturing Co. 12/1/45
Each share Common no par exchanged for (4) shares Common $2.50 par
Rockwell Manufacturing Co. merged into Rockwell International Corp. (Old) 2/16/73 which merged into Boeing Co. 12/6/96

PITTSBURGH ERIE SAW CORP (DE)
Voting Trust Agreement terminated 10/01/1963
Each VTC for Common no par exchanged for (1) share Common no par
Through 1967 purchase offer of $19.25 cash for each share Common no par, Keene Corp. has acquired 100% as of 11/05/1970
Public interest eliminated

PITTSBURGH FAIRFAX CORP (PA)
Voting Trust Agreement terminated 6/30/55
Each VTC for Capital Stock no par exchanged for (1) share Capital Stock 5¢ par
In process of liquidation
Each share Capital Stock 5¢ par exchanged for initial distribution of $55 cash 7/10/75
Each share Capital Stock 5¢ par received second distribution of $15.25 cash 10/31/75
Each share Capital Stock 5¢ par received third distribution of $1.50 cash 12/30/76
Note: Details on subsequent distributions, if any, are not available

PITTSBURGH FIN BLDG CORP (PA)
Voting Trust Agreement terminated 06/30/1955
Each VTC for Capital Stock no par exchanged for (1) share Capital Stock 5¢ par
Liquidation completed
Each share Capital Stock 5¢ par exchanged for initial distribution of $34 cash 06/10/1974
Each share Capital Stock 5¢ par received second distribution of $12.50 cash 12/04/1974
Each share Capital Stock 5¢ par received third and final distribution of $0.87 cash 01/20/1978

PITTSBURGH FINL CORP (PA)
Merged into First Commonwealth Financial Corp. 12/8/2003
Each share Common 1¢ par exchanged for $20 cash

PITTSBURGH FORGINGS CO (DE)
Capital Stock no par changed to $1 par 00/00/1933
Capital Stock $1 par split (2) for (1) by issuance of (1) additional share 12/29/1966
Capital Stock $1 par reclassified as Common $1 par 03/29/1967
Stock Dividends - 50% 12/30/1947; 40% 12/20/1950; 15% 12/19/1951; 20% 01/20/1966; 10% 01/24/1975; 15% 01/23/1976; 10% 01/21/1977
Merged into Ampco-Pittsburgh Corp. 10/31/1979
Each share Common $1 par exchanged for $38 cash

PITTSBURGH FORT WAYNE & CHICAGO RY CO (IL, IN & PA)
Merged into Penn Central Corp. 10/24/78
Each share 7% Preferred $100 par exchanged for (1.04) shares Common $1 par, $37.98 principal amount of 7% General Mortgage Bonds Ser. A due 12/31/87, $46.27 principal amount of 8% Secured Notes Ser. C-2 due 12/31/87 and $25.08 cash
Each share 7% Original Guaranteed Stock exchanged for (1.04) shares Common $1 par, $37.98 principal amount of 7% General Mortgage Bonds Ser. A due 12/31/87, $46.27 principal amount of 8% Secured Notes Ser. C-2 due 12/31/87 and $25.08 cash
Each share 7% Guaranteed Special Stock exchanged for (1.84) shares Conv. Preference Ser. B $20 par, (0.83) share Common $1 par, $36.75 principal amount of 7% General Mortgage Bonds Ser. B due 12/31/87 and $12.95 cash
Each share Common $100 par exchanged for (1.84) shares Conv. Preference Ser. B $20 par, (0.83) share Common $1 par, $36.75 principal amount of 7% General Mortgage Bonds Ser. B due 12/31/87 and $12.95 cash
Note: a) Distribution is certain only for certificates surrendered prior to 5/1/85 b) Distribution may also be made for certificates surrendered between 5/1/85 and 12/31/86 c) No distribution will be made for certificates surrendered after 12/31/86
Penn Central Corp. name changed to American Premier Underwriters, Inc. 3/25/94 which merged into American Premier Group, Inc. 4/3/95 which name changed to American Financial Group, Inc. 6/9/95 which merged into American Financial Group, Inc. (Holding Co.) 12/2/97

PITTSBURGH GAGE & SUPPLY CO (PA)
Each share Capital Stock $100 par exchanged for (1) share Capital Stock $10 par 00/00/1937
Merged into IUS Corp. 10/11/1973
Each share Capital Stock $10 par exchanged for $52.59 cash

PITTSBURGH HOME CAP TR I (DE)
Issue Information - 1,100,000 TR PFD SECS 8.56% offered at $10 per share on 01/27/1998
8.56% Trust Preferred Securities called for redemption at $10 on 1/26/2004

PITTSBURGH HOME FINL CORP (PA)
Name changed to Pittsburgh Financial Corp. 4/3/2000
(See Pittsburgh Financial Corp.)

PITTSBURGH HOTELS, INC. (PA)
Liquidation completed 12/31/56

PITTSBURGH HOTELS CO.
Succeeded by Pittsburgh Hotels Corp. in 1928 which was reorganized as Pittsburgh Hotels, Inc. in 1937 for which liquidation was approved 12/31/56

PITTSBURGH ICE CO.
Acquired by City Ice & Fuel Co. 00/00/1929
Details not available

PITTSBURGH INCLINE PLANE CO.
Merged into Pittsburgh Railways Co. for cash 9/30/50

PITTSBURGH KNIFE & FORGE CO. (PA)
Out of business 11/01/1956
Details not available

PITTSBURGH LIFE INS CO (PA)
Capital Stock $2.50 par changed to $1.50 par 11/26/1966
Name changed to Allnation Life Insurance Co. of Pennsylvania 04/04/1979
(See Allnation Life Insurance Co. of Pennsylvania)

PITTSBURGH MALLEABLE IRON CO.
Property acquired by Bondholders' Committee 00/00/1933
No stockholders' equity

PITTSBURGH MELTING CO. (PA)
Each share Capital Stock $10 par exchanged for (5) shares Capital Stock $2 par 00/00/1947
Name changed to Pitmel, Inc. 00/00/1957
Pitmel, Inc. acquired by Fundamental Investors, Inc. (DE) 03/06/1969 which reincorporated in Maryland 02/01/1990 which reorganized in Delaware as Fundamental Investors 09/01/2010

PITTSBURGH METALLURGICAL CO., INC. (DE)
Each share Common $10 par exchanged for (2) shares Common $5 par 00/00/1946
Each share Common $5 par exchanged for (2) shares Common $2.50 par 00/00/1954
Common $2.50 par changed to $1.25 par and (1) additional share issued 07/10/1957
Acquired by Air Reduction Co., Inc. 10/31/1962
Each share Common $1.25 par exchanged for (0.043478) share Common $1 par
Air Reduction Co., Inc. name changed to Airco, Inc. (NY) 10/01/1971 which reincorporated in Delaware 08/03/1977
(See Airco, Inc. (DE))

PITTSBURGH NATL BK PA (PITTSBURGH, PA)
Capital Stock $20 par changed to $10 par and (1) additional share issued 07/30/1960
Reorganized as Pittsburgh National Corp. 04/30/1969
Each share Capital Stock $10 par exchanged for (1) share Common $10 par
Pittsburgh National Corp. merged into PNC Financial Corp. 01/19/1983 which name changed to PNC Bank Corp. 02/08/1993 which name changed to PNC Financial Services Group, Inc. 03/15/2000

PITTSBURGH NATL CORP (PA)
Common $10 par changed to $5 par and (1) additional share issued 06/14/1971
Common $5 par split (2) for (1) by issuance of (1) additional share 10/01/1981
Merged into PNC Financial Corp. 01/19/1983
Each share Common $5 par exchanged for (1) share Common $5 par
PNC Financial Corp. name changed to PNC Bank Corp. 02/08/1993 which name changed to PNC Financial Services Group, Inc. 03/15/2000

PITTSBURGH OUTDOOR ADVERTISING CO. (PA)
Liquidated 10/9/64

PITTSBURGH PARKING GARAGES, INC. (PA)
Reorganized 00/00/1935
Each share Preferred $100 par exchanged for (1) share Common no par Old Common no par had no equity
Liquidation completed 12/6/57
Details not available

PITTSBURGH PLATE GLASS CO (PA)
Each share Common $100 par exchanged for (4) shares Common $25 par 00/00/1928
Each share Common $25 par exchanged for (4) shares Common $10 par 00/00/1945
Name changed to PPG Industries, Inc. 04/01/1968

PITTSBURGH RAILWAYS CO. (PA)
Common no par changed to $10 par 5/4/64
Common $10 par changed to $1 par 6/22/65
Name changed to Pittway Corp. and Common $1 par changed to 50¢ par 11/28/67
Pittway Corp. (PA) merged into Pittway Corp. (DE) 12/28/89
(See Pittway Corp. (DE))

PITTSBURGH REFLECTOR CO (NJ)
Recapitalized 6/30/64
Each share Class A Common $5 par exchanged for (1.25) shares Common $5 par
Each share Class B Common $5 par exchanged for (1) share Common $5 par
Merged into Calculator-Computer Leasing Corp. 1/29/69
Each share Common $5 par exchanged for (16.82) shares Common 10¢ par
Calculator-Computer Leasing Corp. recapitalized as Electric M & R Inc. 3/28/80
(See Electric M & R Inc.)

PITTSBURGH ROLLS CORP.
Acquired by Blaw-Knox Co. (NJ) 00/00/1929
Details not available

PITTSBURGH SCREW & BOLT CORP. (PA)
Capital Stock no par changed to $1 par 6/1/55
Name changed to Screw & Bolt Corp. of America 4/16/59
Screw & Bolt Corp. of America name changed to Ampco-Pittsburgh Corp. 12/31/70

PITTSBURGH SILVER PEAK GOLD MINING CO.
Liquidated in 1939

PITTSBURGH SPORTS CORP. (PA)
Insolvent in 1962
No stockholders' equity

PITTSBURGH STANDARD CONDUIT CO. (PA)
Name changed to Robroy Industries, Inc. 5/1/67
(See Robroy Industries, Inc.)

PITTSBURGH STEEL CO. (PA)
Common $100 par changed to no par 00/00/1936
7% Preferred $100 par reclassified as 7% Class B Preferred $100 par 00/00/1937
Common no par changed to $10 par 05/01/1955
Common $10 par changed to no par 09/29/1961
Merged into Wheeling-Pittsburgh Steel Corp. 12/05/1968
Each share 5-1/2% Prior Preferred 1st Ser. $100 par exchanged for (1) share 6% Prior Preferred $100 par
Each share 5% Class A Preferred $100 par exchanged for (0.91) share 6% Prior Preferred $100 par
Each share Common no par exchanged for (0.59) share Common $10 par
Wheeling-Pittsburgh Steel Corp. reorganized as Wheeling-Pittsburgh Corp. 01/03/1991 which reorganized as WHX Corp. 07/26/1994
(See WHX Corp.)

PITTSBURGH STEEL FOUNDRY CORP. (PA)
Each share Common no par exchanged for (3) shares Common $5 par in 1953
Stock Dividends - 10% 12/21/53; 100% 11/26/57
Acquired by Textron, Inc. (New) for cash 5/29/59

PITTSBURGH TERMINAL COAL CORP.
Reorganized as Pittsburgh Terminal Realization Corp. in 1945
Each share Preferred exchanged for (1) share Capital Stock $1 par and $50 cash
(See Pittsburgh Terminal Realization Corp.)

PITTSBURGH TERMINAL REALIZATION CORP. (PA)
Reorganized 5/23/55
Each share Capital Stock exchanged for $40 cash

PITTSBURGH TERMINAL WAREHOUSE & TRANSFER CO.
Reorganized as Pittsburgh Terminal Warehouses, Inc. in 1946. No stockholders' equity

PITTSBURGH TERMINAL WAREHOUSES, INC. (PA)
Common $10 par changed to $5 par in 1947
Name changed to Grant Fourth Corp. 1/15/64
Grant Fourth Corp. merged into Nichols Wire & Aluminum Co. (Del.) 8/17/64

PITTSBURGH TESTING LAB (PA)
Each share Capital Stock $20 par exchanged for (3) shares Capital Stock $10 par to effect a (2) for (1) split and a 50% stock dividend 01/21/1966
Merged into Inspectorate International S.A. 03/27/1986
Each share Capital Stock $10 par exchanged for $63.50 cash

PITTSBURGH TIN PLATE & STEEL CORP. (DE)
Charter cancelled and declared inoperative and void for non-payment of taxes 4/1/28

PITTSBURGH TRACTION CO.
Merged into Pittsburgh Railways Co. 9/30/50
Each share Common $50 par exchanged for (3.2) shares Common no par and $3.80 cash
Pittsburgh Railways Co. name changed to Pittway Corp. (PA) 11/28/67 which merged into Pittway Corp. (DE) 12/28/89
(See Pittway Corp. (DE))

PITTSBURGH TRANSFORMER CO.
Acquired by Allis-Chalmers Manufacturing Co. in 1928
Details not available

PITTSBURGH TUBE CO (DE)
Preferred no par called for redemption 07/02/1962
Plan of reorganization under Chapter 11 Federal Bankruptcy Code effective 07/25/2006
Note: Stockholders' did not receive a distribution under the plan but did receive approximately $0.37 cash per share from an unidentified third party

PITTSBURGH UNITED CORP.
Liquidated in 1939
No Common stockholders' equity

PITTSBURGH YOUNGSTOWN & ASHTABULA RY CO (OH & PA)
Merged into Penn Central Corp. 10/24/78
Each share Preferred $100 par exchanged for (2.16) shares Conv. Preference Ser. B $20 par, (0.97) share Common $1 par, $43.24 principal amount of 7% General Mortgage Bonds Ser. A due 12/31/87 and $15.24 cash
Note: a) Distribution is certain only for certificates surrendered prior to 5/1/85 b) Distribution may also be made for certificates surrendered between 5/1/85 and 12/31/86 c) No distribution will be made for certificates surrendered after 12/31/86
Penn Central Corp. name changed to American Premier Underwriters, Inc. 3/25/94 which merged into American Premier Group, Inc. 4/3/95 which name changed to American Financial Group, Inc. 6/9/95 which merged into American Financial Group, Inc. (Holding Co.) 12/2/97

PITTSFIELD & NORTH ADAMS RAILROAD CORP. (MA)
Merged into New York Central Railroad Co. (DE) 4/3/61
Each share Capital Stock $100 par exchanged for $100 principal amount of 5-1/4% Coll. Trust Bonds due 1/1/80

PITTSFIELD COAL GAS CO. (MA)
Each share Capital Stock $100 par exchanged for (10) shares Capital Stock $10 par 06/00/1954
Name changed to Berkshire Gas Co. 09/00/1954
Berkshire Gas Co. reorganized as Berkshire Energy Resources 01/04/1999
(See Berkshire Energy Resources)

PITTSFIELD ELECTRIC CO.
Acquired by Western Massachusetts Companies 00/00/1927
Details not available

PITTSFIELD NATL BK (PITTSFIELD, MA)
Merged into First National Boston Corp. 03/17/1980
Each share Common Capital Stock $10 par exchanged for (2) shares Common $6.25 par
First National Boston Corp. name changed to Bank of Boston Corp. 04/01/1983 which name changed to BankBoston Corp. 04/25/1997 which merged into Fleet Boston Corp. 10/01/1999 which name changed to FleetBoston Financial Corp. 04/18/2000 which merged into Bank of America Corp. 04/01/2004

PITTSONTO MINING CO. LTD. (ON)
Charter cancelled for failure to pay taxes and file returns 12/4/77

PITTSTON CO (VA)
Under plan of merger each share Common no par exchanged for (1/17) share Class B Preference $100 par and (0.5) share Common $1 par 00/00/1943
Class A Preference called for redemption 04/29/1944
5-1/2% Preferred $100 par called for redemption 09/30/1956
Common $1 par split (2) for (1) by issuance of (1) additional share 05/28/1965
$3.50 Conv. Preferred $75 par called for redemption 01/31/1966
Common $1 par split (3) for (1) by issuance of (2) additional shares 06/08/1970
Common $1 par split (2) for (1) by issuance of (1) additional share 10/29/1975
Delaware incorporation rescinded 05/14/1986
Note: Formerly incorporated in both Delaware and Virginia
Common $1 par reclassified as Services Group Common $1 par 07/26/1993
Each share Services Group Common $1 par received distribution of (0.2) share Minerals Group Common $1 par 08/05/1993
Each share Services Group Common $1 par received distribution of (0.5) share Burlington Group Common $1 par payable 01/30/1996 to holders of record 01/19/1996
Services Group Common $1 par reclassified as Brinks Group Common $1 par 01/19/1996
Burlington Group Common $1 par reclassified as BAX Group Common $1 par 05/04/1998
Each share BAX Group Common $1 par exchanged for (0.4848) share Brinks Group Common $1 par 01/14/2000
Each share Minerals Group Common $1 par exchanged for (0.0817) share Brinks Group Common $1 par 01/14/2000
Name changed to Brink's Co. and Brinks Group Common $1 par reclassified as Common $1 par 05/05/2003

PITTWAY CORP (DE)
Common $1 par split (3) for (2) by issuance of (0.5) additional share payable 3/1/96 to holders of record 2/14/96
Class A Common $1 par split (3) for (2) by issuance of (0.5) additional share payable 3/1/96 to holders of record 2/14/96
Each share Common $1 par received distribution of (1) share Penton Media Inc. Common 1¢ par payable 8/7/98 to holders of record 7/31/98 Ex date - 8/11/98
Each share Class A Common 1¢ par received distribution of (1) share Penton Media Inc. Common 1¢ par payable 8/7/98 to holders of record 7/31/98 Ex date - 8/11/98
Common 1¢ par split (2) for (1) by issuance of (1) additional share payable 9/11/98 to holders of record 9/1/98 Ex date - 9/14/98
Class A Common 1¢ par split (2) for (1) by issuance of (1) additional share payable 9/11/98 to holders of record 9/1/98 Ex date - 9/14/98
Merged into Honeywell International Inc. 2/14/2000
Each share Common $1 par exchanged for $45.50 cash
Each share Class A Common $1 par exchanged for $45.50 cash

PITTWAY CORP (PA)
Common 50¢ par split (2) for (1) by issuance of (1) additional share 1/2/68
Common 50¢ par split (3) for (2) by issuance of (0.5) additional share 12/26/75
Merged into Pittway Corp. (DE) 12/28/89
Each share Common 50¢ par exchanged for (3) shares Class A $1 par
(See Pittway Corp. (DE))

PIUTE URANIUM CORP. (UT)
Recapitalized as Mobilcraft Industries, Inc. 9/5/59
Each share Common 5¢ par exchanged for (0.1) share Common 5¢ par
Mobilcraft Industries, Inc. bankrupt and involuntarily dissolved 7/22/66

PIVOT RULES INC (NY)
Issue Information - 1,500,000 UNITS consisting of (1) share COM and (1) WT offered at $5 per Unit on 05/15/1997
Name changed to Bluefly Inc. (NY) 10/29/1998
Bluefly Inc. (NY) reincorporated in Delaware 02/02/2001

PIVOTAL CORP (BC)
Acquired by chinadotcom corp. 2/25/2004
Each share Common no par exchanged for $2 cash

PIVOTAL ENERGY LTD (AB)
Merged into Fairborne Energy Ltd. (Old) 07/08/2003
Each share Common no par exchanged for (0.485) share Common no par
(See Fairborne Energy Ltd. (Old))

PIVOTAL SELF-SERVICE TECHNOLOGIES INC (DE)
Name changed to Phantom Fiber Corp. 07/21/2004
Phantom Fiber Corp. recapitalized as Accelerated Technologies Holding Corp. 09/18/2017

PIVOTAL TECHNOLOGY INC (NV)
Name changed to Somatic Systems, Inc. 8/28/2006

PIVX SOLUTIONS INC (NV)
Name changed to Adia Nutrition, Inc. 12/20/2011

PIXAR (CA)
Common no par split (2) for (1) by

issuance of (1) additional share payable 4/18/2005 to holders of record 4/4/2005 Ex date - 4/19/2005
Merged into Disney (Walt) Co. 5/5/2006
Each share Common no par exchanged for (2.3) shares Common 1¢ par

PIXELPLUS CO LTD (KOREA)
Each old Unsponsored ADR for Common exchanged for (0.25) new Sponsored ADR for Common 04/14/2008
ADR basis changed from (1:0.5) to (1:2) 04/14/2008
Stock Dividend - 1% payable 01/22/2008 to holders of record 01/02/2008
ADR agreement terminated 02/29/2012
Each new Sponsored ADR for Common exchanged for $57.815289 cash

PIXIELAND CORP (NV)
Name changed to Integrated Food Resources, Inc. 07/29/1997
(See Integrated Food Resources, Inc.)

PIXIELAND CORP (OR)
Involuntarily dissolved for failure to file reports and pay fees 10/24/1978

PIXTECH INC (DE)
Chapter 7 bankruptcy proceedings terminated 06/18/2007
Stockholders' equity unlikely

PIZZA CORP AMER (DE)
Merged into Pizza Hut, Inc. (DE) 09/27/1974
Each share Common 1¢ par exchanged for (0.55) share Common 1¢ par
Pizza Hut, Inc. (DE) merged into PepsiCo, Inc. (DE) 11/07/1977 which reincorporated in North Carolina 12/04/1986

PIZZA ENTMT CTRS INC (NC)
Administratively dissolved 10/13/93

PIZZA HUT, INC. (KS)
Reincorporated under the laws of Delaware 1/22/70
Pizza Hut, Inc. (Del.) merged into PepsiCo, Inc. (Del.) 11/7/77 which reincorporated in North Carolina 12/4/86

PIZZA HUT INC (DE)
Common 1¢ par split (3) for (2) by issuance of (0.5) additional share 8/11/75
Merged into PepsiCo, Inc. (DE) 11/7/77
Each share Common 1¢ par exchanged for (1.55) shares Capital Stock 5¢ par
PepsiCo, Inc. (DE) reincorporated in North Carolina 12/4/86

PIZZA INN HLDGS INC (MO)
Name changed to Rave Restaurant Group, Inc. 01/09/2015

PIZZA INN INC (MO)
Name changed to Pizza Inn Holdings, Inc. 09/26/2011
Pizza Inn Holdings, Inc. name changed to Rave Restaurant Group, Inc. 01/09/2015

PIZZA INN INC (TX)
Common no par changed to $1 par 08/17/1970
Common $1 par split (5) for (4) by issuance of (0.25) additional share 09/02/1977
Stock Dividends - 20% 06/23/1975; 10% 08/04/1983
Merged into Pantera's Corp. 07/29/1987
Each share Common $1 par exchanged for (0.828456) share Common 1¢ par and $3 cash or (1) share Common 1¢ par, (1) non-transferable right to receive approximately (0.55) share Common 1¢ par under certain circumstances and $4 cash
Note: Option to receive combination of stock, non-transferable right and cash expired 10/27/1987
Note: Unexchanged certificates were cancelled and became worthless 09/01/1993
Pantera's Corp. reorganized as Pizza Inn, Inc. (MO) 09/05/1990 which name changed to Pizza Inn Holdings, Inc. 09/26/2011 which name changed to Rave Restaurant Group, Inc. 01/09/2015

PIZZA INTL INC (NV)
Name changed to Look Entertainment, Inc. 05/23/2007
Look Entertainment, Inc. recapitalized as VTEC, Inc. 07/05/2007 which name changed to United Consortium, Ltd. (Old) 03/10/2008 which reorganized as United Consortium, Ltd. (New) 05/05/2010

PIZZA PAPA INC (DE)
Name changed to Colonial Services Co. 7/24/70
(See Colonial Services Co.)

PIZZA PATIO MGMT LTD (BC)
Name changed to San Andreas Resources Corp. 08/29/1991
San Andreas Resources Corp. name changed to Canadian Zinc Corp. 05/25/1999 which name changed to NorZinc Ltd. 09/11/2018

PIZZA PIZZA RTY INCOME FD (ON)
Under plan of reorganization each Trust Unit automatically became (1) share Pizza Pizza Royalty Corp. Common no par 12/31/2012

PIZZA TIME THEATRE INC (CA)
Plan of reorganization under Chapter 11 Federal Bankruptcy Code effective 9/11/86
Each share Common no par exchanged for approximately $0.32 cash
Note: Unexchanged certificates were cancelled and became valueless 9/30/96

PIZZA TRAN AUTH INC (NC)
Administratively dissolved 09/24/1993

PIZZA VENTURES INC (MN)
Merged into Godfather's Pizza, Inc. 09/02/1983
Each share Common no par exchanged for (1.5) shares Common 1¢ par
Godfather's Pizza, Inc. name changed to Diversifoods Inc. 12/28/1983
(See Diversifoods Inc.)

PJ AMER INC (DE)
Merged into PJ Acquisition Corp. 08/31/2001
Each share Common 1¢ par exchanged for $8.75 cash

PKG ENTMT INC (NV)
Each share old Common $0.001 par exchanged for (0.00033333) share new Common $0.001 par 02/21/2006
Charter permanently revoked 08/31/2007

PKI INNOVATIONS CDA INC (BC)
Recapitalized as Newton Ventures, Inc. 6/7/2005
Each share Common no par exchanged for (1/7) share Common no par
Newton Ventures, Inc. recapitalized as Rusoro Mining Ltd. 11/9/2006

PKL COS INC (NY)
Under plan of liquidation each share Class A 30¢ par received initial distribution of $1.88 cash 09/15/1978
Assets transferred to PKL Liquidating Trust and Class A 30¢ par reclassified as Units of the Trust 00/00/1983
(See PKL Liquidating Trust)

PKL LIQUIDATING TRUST (NY)
Liquidation completed
Each Unit of the Trust received second distribution of $3 cash 2/28/89
Each Unit of the Trust received third and final distribution of $19.85 cash 5/30/89
Note: Certificates were not required to be surrendered and are now valueless

PKS COMMUNICATIONS INC (CT)
Chapter 11 bankruptcy proceedings dismissed 05/31/1988
No stockholders' equity

PL BRANDS INC (DE)
Each share old Common $0.001 par exchanged for (0.01) share new Common $0.001 par 09/15/1995
Each share new Common $0.001 par exchanged for (0.01) share Common $0.001 par 04/07/1997
Name changed to Othnet, Inc. 03/22/2001
Othnet, Inc. name changed to AVP, Inc. 03/21/2005
(See AVP, Inc.)

PL INTERNET INC (ON)
Reorganized under the laws of New Brunswick as Global Alumina Products Corp. 05/19/2004
Each share Common no par exchanged for (0.63694267) share Common no par
Global Alumina Products Corp. name changed to Global Alumina Corp. 06/24/2005
(See Global Alumina Corp.)

PLA STANDARD CORP. (DE)
Liquidation completed
Each share Common 1¢ par exchanged for initial distribution of $0.446 cash 12/1/78
Each share Common 1¢ par received second distribution of $0.53 cash 4/16/79
Each share Common 1¢ par received third distribution of $0.433 cash 7/16/79
Each share Common 1¢ par received fourth and final distribution of $0.1148 cash 4/10/80

PLACE RESOURCES CORP (ON)
Name changed 7/26/86
Name changed from Place Gas & Oil Co. Ltd. to Place Resources Corp. and Capital Stock $1 par reclassified as Common no par 7/26/86
Common no par reclassified as Class A Common no par 6/27/95
Acquired by Star Oil & Gas Ltd. 1/23/2001
Each share Class A Common no par exchanged for $3 cash

PLACENTIA LINDA SAVINGS & LOAN ASSOCIATION (CA)
Name changed to Western Empire Savings & Loan Association 6/20/83
(See Western Empire Savings & Loan Association)

PLACER DEL MAR LTD (NV)
Common $0.001 par split (20) for (1) by issuance of (19) additional shares payable 06/19/2014 to holders of record 06/19/2014 Ex date - 06/20/2014
Name changed to Urban Hydroponics, Inc. 07/10/2014

PLACER DEV LTD (BC)
Each share Capital Stock $5 par exchanged for (5) shares Capital Stock $1 par 00/00/1935
Each share Capital Stock $1 par exchanged for (3) shares Capital Stock no par 02/15/1956
Capital Stock no par split (2) for (1) by issuance of (1) additional share 01/08/1965
Under plan of merger each share Capital Stock no par exchanged for (1) share Common no par 04/26/1966
Common no par split (2) for (1) by issuance of (1) additional share 05/25/1973
Common no par split (3) for (1) by issuance of (2) additional shares 06/10/1980
Common no par split (2) for (1) by issuance of (1) additional share 06/10/1987
Merged into Placer Dome Inc. 08/13/1987
Each share Common no par exchanged for (1) share Common no par
Placer Dome Inc. merged into Barrick Gold Corp. 03/08/2006

PLACER DOME INC (CANADA)
Canadian Originated Preferred Securities called for redemption at USD $25 plus $0.143750 accrued dividends on 04/24/2003
Acquired by Barrick Gold Corp. 03/08/2006
Each share Common no par exchanged for (0.8269) share Common no par and $0.05 cash

PLACER ENGINEERS LTD.
Bankrupt in 1948

PLACER GOLD CORP (NV)
Charter revoked for failure to file reports and pay fees 08/31/2010

PLACER PAC LTD (AUSTRALIA)
ADR agreement terminated 09/08/1997
Each Sponsored ADR for Ordinary AUD $0.30 par exchanged for $10.80 cash

PLACER SVGS BK (AUBURN, CA)
Merged into PC Merger Co. 8/11/99
Each share Common no par exchanged for $22.05 cash

PLACER SIERRA BANCSHARES (CA)
Issue Information - 5,730,000 shares COM offered at $20 per share on 08/10/2004
Merged into Wells Fargo & Co. (New) 06/04/2007
Each share Common no par exchanged for (0.7788) share Common $1-2/3 par

PLACER TECHNOLOGIES INC (FL)
Name changed to Xin Net Corp. 07/24/1998
Xin Net Corp. recapitalized as China Mobility Solutions, Inc. 06/24/2004 which recapitalized as Global Peopleline Telecom Inc. 08/06/2008
(See Global Peopleline Telecom Inc.)

PLAD INC (UT)
Name changed to Elev8 Brands, Inc. 12/28/2016

PLADEO CORP (NV)
Name changed to MaryJane Group, Inc. 04/21/2014

PLAIN N FANCY DONUTS AMER INC (DC)
Charter revoked for failure to file reports and pay fees 09/08/1975

PLAINDOR MINES, LTD. (QC)
Charter annulled for failure to file reports and pay fees in 1949

PLAINFIELD LMBR & SUPPLY CO (NJ)
Liquidation completed
Each share 1st Preferred $100 par exchanged for initial distribution of $12 cash 08/17/1977
Each share 1st Preferred $100 par received second distribution of $10 cash 12/07/1977
Each share 1st Preferred $100 par

received third distribution of $8 cash 03/01/1978
Each share 1st Preferred $100 par received fourth distribution of $6 cash 02/23/1979
Each share 1st Preferred $100 par received fifth distribution of $4 cash 02/12/1980
Each share 1st Preferred $100 par received sixth and final distribution of $26 cash 11/28/1980
Note: No equity for 2nd Preferred $100 par and Common no par holders

PLAINFIELD TR ST NATL BK (PLAINFIELD, NJ)
Common $25 par changed to $5 par and (4) additional shares issued 12/1/60
Stock Dividend - 20% 12/3/62
Name changed to United National Bank of Central Jersey (Plainfield, NJ) 2/24/70
United National Bank of Central Jersey (Plainfield, NJ) name changed to United National Bank (Plainfield, NJ) 1/1/73 which reorganized as United National Bancorp 8/1/88
(See United National Bancorp)

PLAINFIELD-UNION WATER CO. (NJ)
Common no par split (3) for (1) by issuance of (2) additional shares 2/16/60
Merged into Elizabethtown Water Co. 6/30/61
Each share Common no par exchanged for (1) share Common no par
Elizabethtown Water Co. reorganized as E'town Corp. 9/1/85
(See E'town Corp.)

PLAINS CREEK PHOSPHATE CORP (BC)
Recapitalized as GB Minerals Ltd. 03/28/2013
Each share Common no par exchanged for (0.05) share Common no par
GB Minerals Ltd. merged into Itafos 02/28/2018

PLAINS ENERGY SVCS LTD (AB)
Acquired by Precision Drilling Corp. 7/10/2000
Each share Common no par exchanged for either (0.18676) share Common no par and (0.0885) Common Stock Purchase Warrant expiring 12/31/2001 or $10.75 cash
Note: Option to receive cash only expired 8/10/2000
(See Precision Drilling Corp.)

PLAINS EXPL & PRODTN CO (DE)
Merged into Freeport-McMoRan Copper & Gold Inc. 05/31/2013
Each share Common 1¢ par exchanged for (0.00748776) share Common 10¢ par and $45.768916 cash
Freeport-McMoRan Copper & Gold Inc. name changed to Freeport-McMoRan Inc. 07/14/2014

PLAINS PETE CO (DE)
Merged into Barrett Resources Corp. 7/18/95
Each share Common 1¢ par exchanged for (1.3) shares Common 1¢ par
Barrett Resources Corp. merged into Williams Companies, Inc. 8/2/2001

PLAINS PETES LTD (AB)
Merged into Scurry-Rainbow Oil Ltd. 7/24/85
Each share Common no par exchanged for $1 cash

PLAINS REFRIGERANT RECLAIM CORP (TX)
EPA revoked company's certification 03/07/1997
Stockholders' equity unlikely

PLAINS RES INC (DE)
Each share Common 2¢ par exchanged for (0.2) share Common 10¢ par 02/16/1990
$1.30 Conv. Preferred $1 par called for redemption 10/31/1995
Each share Common 10¢ par received distribution of (1) share Plains Exploration & Production Co. Common 1¢ par payable 12/18/2002 to holders of record 12/11/2002
Ex date - 12/19/2002
Merged into Vulcan Energy Corp. 07/23/2004
Each share Common 10¢ par exchanged for $17.25 cash

PLAINS SPIRIT FINL CORP (DE)
Merged into Mercantile Bancorporation Inc. 07/07/1995
Each share Common 1¢ par exchanged for $31.25 cash

PLAINSCAPITAL CORP (TX)
Merged into Hilltop Holdings Inc. 12/03/2012
Each share Common $0.001 par exchanged for (0.776) share Common 1¢ par and $9 cash

PLAINVIEW MNG CO (ID)
Merged into New Jersey Mining Co. 1/27/98
Each share Common 10¢ par exchanged for (2) shares Common no par

PLAINVIEW SILVER MINES, INC. (NV)
Recapitalized as Gulf Resources Inc. 12/24/80
Each share Capital Stock 1¢ par exchanged for (0.1) share Capital Stock 10¢ par
Gulf Resources Inc. charter revoked 7/1/85

PLAINVILLE WTR CO (CT)
Merged into New England Service Co. 5/14/97
Each share Common no par exchanged for (3) shares Common no par

PLAMETRON CORP (FL)
Recapitalized as Diversified Operations Inc. 5/25/71
Each share Common 2¢ par exchanged for (0.1) share Common 20¢ par
(See Diversified Operations Inc.)

PLAN A PROMOTIONS INC (UT)
Reincorporated under the laws of Delaware as GulfSlope Energy, Inc. and Common 1¢ par changed to $0.001 par 04/30/2012

PLANAR SYS INC (OR)
Acquired by Leyard (Hong Kong) Co., Ltd. 11/27/2015
Each share Common no par exchanged for $6.58 cash

PLANCAPITAL U S A INC (CO)
Recapitalized as Continental Capital Corp. 01/31/1995
Each share Common $0.001 par exchanged for (0.25) share Common $0.001 par
Continental Capital Corp. recapitalized as RFID Ltd. 06/21/2005 which name changed to OptimizeRx Corp. (CO) 04/30/2008 which reincorporated in Nevada 09/04/2008

PLANDEL RES INC (NV)
Name changed to Sports Asylum, Inc. 03/24/2014
Sports Asylum, Inc. name changed to Cell MedX Corp. 10/09/2014

PLANET BIOPHARMACEUTICALS INC (DE)
Acquired by Ares Allergy Holdings, Inc. 07/01/2013
Each share Common no par exchanged for $0.0251 cash

PLANET CITY (NV)
Each share old Common $0.001 par exchanged for (0.1) share new Common $0.001 par 02/13/1998
Recapitalized as Lignin Industries, Inc. 02/09/2004
Each share new Common $0.001 par exchanged for (0.06666666) share Common $0.001 par
Lignin Industries, Inc. name changed to Heritage Media Corp. 06/05/2006 which recapitalized as Oliveda International, Inc. 03/24/2017

PLANET CORP (MI)
Stock Dividends - 20% 12/01/1966; 20% 12/30/1967; 20% 03/14/1969
Merged into Maxco, Inc. 03/31/1977
Each share Common $1 par exchanged for (1) share Common $1 par
(See Maxco, Inc.)

PLANET EARTH RECYCLING INC (NV)
SEC revoked common stock registration 04/21/2010
Stockholders' equity unlikely

PLANET ENTMT CORP (FL)
Chapter 7 bankruptcy proceedings terminated 03/15/2004
No stockholders' equity

PLANET EXPL INC (AB)
Name changed to Planet Mining Exploration Inc. 04/12/2012
Planet Mining Exploration Inc. name changed to Planet Ventures Inc. 06/28/2017

PLANET 411 COM INC (DE)
Reincorporated 10/07/1999
Name and state of incorporation changed from Planet 411.com Corp. (NV) to Planet411.com Inc. (DE) 10/07/1999
Each share old Common $0.001 par exchanged for (0.002) share new Common $0.001 par 04/16/2007
Name changed to Ivany Mining, Inc. 07/27/2007
Ivany Mining, Inc. name changed to Ivany Nguyen, Inc. 02/16/2010 which name changed to Myriad Interactive Media, Inc. 07/25/2011

PLANET HOLLYWOOD INTL INC NEW (DE)
Company terminated registration of common stock and is no longer public as of 03/28/2003
Stockholders' equity unlikely

PLANET HOLLYWOOD INTL INC OLD (DE)
Plan of reorganization under Chapter 11 Federal Bankruptcy Code effective 05/09/2000
Each (5,450) shares Class A Common 1¢ par received (10) Class A Common Stock Purchase Warrants expiring 05/10/2003
Note: Holdings of (5,449) or fewer shares received (10) Class A Common Stock Purchase Warrants expiring 05/10/2003 regardless of number of shares held
Note: Certificates were not required to be surrendered and are without value

PLANET JR CORP (OR)
Common $1 par changed to $0.001 par 05/30/1975
Name changed to Riverside Metal Products Co. (OR) 07/07/1975
Riverside Metal Products Co. (OR) reorganized in Michigan 02/25/1977
(See Riverside Metal Products Co. (MI))

PLANET MNG EXPL INC (AB)
Name changed to Planet Ventures Inc. 06/28/2017

PLANET NUTRITION HLDGS INC (NV)
Each share old Common $0.0001 par exchanged for (0.01) share new Common $0.0001 par 11/07/2007
Recapitalized as GT Legend Automotive Holdings, Inc. 11/26/2008
Each share Common $0.0001 par exchanged for (0.0005) share Common $0.0001 par

PLANET OIL & MINERAL CORP (DE)
Merged into Sabine Royalty Corp. (TX) 12/31/1975
Each (6.3585) shares Common 10¢ par exchanged for (1) share Common no par
Sabine Royalty Corp. (TX) reincorporated in Louisiana as Sabine Corp. 01/03/1977
(See Sabine Corp.)

PLANET ORGANIC HEALTH CORP (AB)
Each share old Common no par exchanged for (0.1) share new Common no par 04/16/2012
Name changed to Planet Health Corp. 05/15/2014

PLANET PAYMENT INC (DE)
Name changed 06/18/2007
Name changed from Planet Group, Inc. to Planet Payment, Inc. 06/18/2007
Acquired by Fintrax Group 12/20/2017
Each share Common 1¢ par exchanged for $4.50 cash (Fintrax Group not in FSG)

PLANET RES CORP (NV)
Reorganized as Bakhu Holdings, Corp. 05/22/2009
Each share Common $0.001 par exchanged for (15) shares Common $0.001 par

PLANET RES INC NEW (DE)
Each share old Common $0.001 par exchanged for (0.19120458) share new Common $0.001 par 09/05/2002
Name changed to CeriStar Inc. 10/15/2002
CeriStar Inc. recapitalized as Endavo Media & Communications, Inc. 09/24/2004 which name changed to Integrated Media Holdings, Inc. (DE) 04/21/2006 which reorganized in Nevada as Arrayit Corp. 03/19/2009

PLANET RES INC OLD (DE)
Each share old Common 2¢ par exchanged for (0.5) share Common $0.001 par 03/30/1999
Name changed to Internet Law Library, Inc. 07/15/1999
Internet Law Library, Inc. name changed to ITIS Inc. (DE) 10/24/2001 which reorganized in Nevada as ITIS Holdings Inc. 09/18/2002
(See ITIS Holdings Inc.)

PLANET SIGNAL INC (FL)
Administratively dissolved 09/26/2008

PLANET STEAMSHIP CORP.
Assets sold 00/00/1930
Details not available

PLANET TECHNOLOGIES INC (CA)
Recapitalized 12/06/2004
Recapitalized from Planet Polymer Technologies, Inc. to Planet Technologies, Inc. 12/06/2004
Each share Common no par exchanged for (0.02) share Common no par
Reincorporated under the laws of Delaware as Planet Biopharmaceuticals, Inc. 04/22/2008
(See Planet Biopharmaceuticals, Inc.)

PLANET VENTURES INC (BC)
Reincorporated under the laws of Alberta as Antares Minerals Inc. 11/25/2004
Antares Minerals Inc. merged into First Quantum Minerals Ltd. 12/20/2010

PLANET ZANETT INC (DE)
Name changed to Zanett, Inc. 10/16/2002
(See Zanett, Inc.)

PLANETCAD INC (DE)
Each share old Common 1¢ par exchanged for (0.05) share new Common 1¢ par 10/24/2002
Name changed to Avatech Solutions, Inc. 11/19/2002
Avatech Solutions, Inc. name changed to Rand Worldwide, Inc. 12/30/2010

PLANETGOOD TECHNOLOGIES INC (NV)
Name changed to American Diamond Corp. 06/02/2004
American Diamond Corp. recapitalized as All American Coffee & Beverage, Inc. 03/21/2006
(See All American Coffee & Beverage, Inc.)

PLANETLINK COMMUNICATIONS INC (GA)
Recapitalized as DnC Multimedia Corp. 01/14/2008
Each (150) shares Common $0.001 par exchanged for (1) share Common $0.001 par
(See DnC Multimedia Corp.)

PLANETOUT INC (DE)
Issue Information - 4,650,000 shares COM offered at $9 per share on 10/13/2004
Each share old Common $0.001 par exchanged for (0.1) share new Common $0.001 par 10/02/2007
Merged into Here Media Inc. 06/11/2009
Each share Common $0.001 par exchanged for (1) share Common 1¢ par and (1) Special Share 1¢ par

PLANETRONICS, INC. (NY)
Out of business 7/23/62
Common Stock is worthless

PLANETRX COM INC (DE)
Issue Information - 6,000,000 shares COM offered at $16 per share on 10/06/1999
Each share old Common $0.0001 par exchanged for (0.125) share new Common $0.0001 par 12/04/2000
Name changed to Paragon Financial Corp. 12/20/2002
Paragon Financial Corp. name changed to NewMarket Latin America, Inc. 05/04/2007
(See NewMarket Latin America, Inc.)

PLANETSAFE ENVIRO CORP (ON)
Delisted from Canadian Dealer Network 10/13/2000

PLANEX VENTURES LTD (BC)
Name changed to Tumi Resources Ltd. 05/27/2002
Tumi Resources Ltd. name changed to Kingsmen Resources Ltd. 07/07/2015

PLANFORMATION INC (UT)
Charter cancelled for failure to file reports 12/31/1973

PLANGRAPHICS INC (CO)
Reorganized under the laws of Florida as Integrated Freight Corp. 09/07/2010
Each share Common no par exchanged for (0.00408397) share Common $0.001 par
Note: Holders of (244) or fewer pre-split shares received $0.0035 cash per share

PLANISOL INC (NV)
Recapitalized as China Good Electric, Inc. 11/14/2007
Each share Common 4¢ par exchanged for (0.00480007) share Common $0.001 par
China Good Electric, Inc. name changed to Victory Marine Holdings Corp. 05/07/2018

PLANKTOS MERGER CO (NV)
Reincorporated 05/06/2014
Name and place of incorporation changed from Planktos Corp. (NV) to Planktos Merger Co. (DE) 05/06/2014
Name changed to Solar Gold Ltd. 06/24/2014

PLANNED CMNTYS INC (NY)
Each share Class A Common 10¢ par exchanged for (21) shares Common $5 par 12/30/1966
Each share Common 10¢ par exchanged for (0.4) share Common $5 par 12/30/1966
Completely liquidated 12/15/1972
Each share Common $5 par exchanged for first and final distribution of $3.01 cash

PLANNED CR INC (OK)
Name changed to Gulf South Corp. 10/12/1972
(See Gulf South Corp.)

PLANNED DEVELOPMENT ENTERPRISES, INC. (PA)
Completely liquidated 7/15/81
Each share Class A Common 1¢ par exchanged for $0.29 cash

PLANNED FUTURE LIFE INSURANCE CO. (MN)
Completely liquidated 2/15/75
Each share Common $1 par exchanged for first and final distribution of $2.195 cash

PLANNED INVT FD INC (MA)
Name changed to Meeschaert Capital Accumulation Fund, Inc. 04/24/1984
Meeschaert Capital Accumulation Fund, Inc. reorganized as Meeschaert Capital Accumulation Trust 01/00/1986 which name changed to Anchor Capital Accumulation Trust 12/05/1990 which name changed to Progressive Capital Accumulation Trust 01/21/1999
(See Progressive Capital Accumulation Trust)

PLANNED MARKETING ASSOC INC (TX)
Merged into Kresge (S.S.) Co. 1/23/74
Each share Common $1 par exchanged for (0.9) share Common $1 par
Kresge (S.S.) Co. name changed to K mart Corp. 5/17/77
(See K mart Corp.)

PLANNING & SVC CORP (IA)
Common no par split (3) for (1) by issuance of (2) additional shares 10/23/72
Common no par split (2) for (1) by issuance of (1) additional share 5/5/73
Proclaimed dissolved 11/25/87

PLANNING FORCE INC (NV)
Each share old Common $0.001 par exchanged for (4) shares new Common $0.001 par 04/25/2006
Name changed to QPC Lasers, Inc. 05/19/2006
(See QPC Lasers, Inc.)

PLANNING RESH CORP (DE)
Reincorporated 1/4/74
Voting Trust Agreement terminated 6/30/66
Each VTC for Common $1 par exchanged for (1) share Common $1 par
Common $1 par split (2) for (1) by issuance of (1) additional share 1/10/69
Stock Dividend - 100% 12/8/67
State of incorporation changed from (CA) to (DE) 1/4/74
Merged into Emhart Corp. 12/2/86
Each share Common $1 par exchanged for $31.50 cash

PLANNING SCIENCES INTL PLC (ENGLAND)
Name changed to Gentia Software PLC 07/02/1997
(See Gentia Software PLC)

PLANO BANCSHARES INC (TX)
Merged into PBI Inc. 12/30/97
Each share Common no par exchanged for $22.55 cash

PLANO BK & TR (TX)
Merged into Plano Bancshares Inc. 10/1/95
Each share 10% Conv. Preferred Ser. A no par exchanged for (1) share Common no par

PLANO PETE CORP (CO)
Recapitalized as Search Exploration, Inc. 12/13/89
Each (49) shares Common $0.001 par exchanged for (1) share Common $0.001 par
Search Exploration, Inc. merged into Harken Energy Corp. 5/22/95 which recapitalized as HKN, Inc. 6/6/2007

PLANT (THOMAS G.)
Reorganized as Plant (Thomas G.) Corp. (MA) 00/00/1927
Details not available

PLANT GENETICS INC (CA)
Acquired by Calgene, Inc. (DE) 6/30/89
Each share Common 1¢ par exchanged for (0.4187495) share Common $0.001 par
(See Calgene, Inc.)

PLANT INDS INC (DE)
Reincorporated 9/27/68
6% Preferred $50 par called for redemption 6/1/61
Class A Common 50¢ par reclassified as Common 50¢ par 2/28/62
State of incorporation changed from (FL) to (DE) 9/27/68
Charter cancelled and declared inoperative and void for non-payment of taxes 3/1/86

PLANT THOMAS G CORP (DE)
Merged 09/03/1968
Merged from Plant (Thomas G.) Corp. (MA) to Plant (Thomas G.) Corp. (DE) 09/03/1968
Each share 1st Preferred $100 par exchanged for either (1) share Common no par or $143.22 cash
Note: Option to received stock expired 10/02/1968
2nd Preferred no par and Common no par were cancelled and are without value
Completely liquidated 11/30/1969
Each share Common no par exchanged for first and final distribution of $176.03 cash

PLANTATION CAP CORP (CO)
Recapitalized as Rehabnet Inc. 03/15/1991
Each share Common $0.0001 par exchanged for (0.01) share Common 1¢ par
Rehabnet Inc. recapitalized as Forestry International, Inc. 12/31/1992 which name changed to Infynia.com Corp. 11/06/2000
(See Infynia.com Corp.)

PLANTATION CHOCOLATE CO. (PA)
Name changed to Conel Corp. 09/15/1967
Conel Corp. name changed to Plantation Corp. 04/24/1972
(See Plantation Corp.)

PLANTATION CORP (PA)
Company reported out of business 00/00/1974
Details not available

PLANTATION DEV CORP (NV)
Name changed to Baroma Inc. 10/10/2012
Baroma Inc. recapitalized as GoooGreen, Inc. 01/20/2016

PLANTATION FINL CORP (SC)
Stock Dividends - 40% payable 12/01/1999 to holders of record 10/01/1999; 10% payable 01/15/2004 to holders of record 12/31/2003 Ex date - 01/07/2004; 40% payable 01/15/2008 to holders of record 12/31/2007 Ex date - 01/07/2004
Company's principal asset placed in receivership 04/27/2012
Stockholders' equity unlikely

PLANTERS BK & TR CO (HOPKINSVILLE, KY)
Common $100 par changed to $4 par and (24) additional shares issued 11/20/78
Stock Dividend - Common 100% 12/19/74
Reorganized as Planters Financial Corp. 6/20/84
Each share Common $4 par exchanged for (1-1/3) shares Common $4 par
Each share Common B $100 par exchanged for $100 principal amount of 6% 20-yr. Debentures due 6/20/2004
Planters Financial Corp. merged into Central South Bancorp, Inc. 1/31/86 which merged into Commerce Union Corp. 9/22/86 which merged into Sovran Financial Corp. 11/1/87 which merged into C&S/Sovran Corp. 9/1/90 which merged into NationsBank Corp. 12/31/91 which reincorporated in Delaware as BankAmerica Corp. (Old) 9/25/98 which merged into BankAmerica Corp. (New) 9/30/98 which name changed to Bank of America Corp. 4/28/99

PLANTERS BK & TR CO (STAUNTON, VA)
Under plan of reorganization each share Common $10 par automatically became (1) share Virginia Financial Corp. Common $5 par 01/02/1997
Virginia Financial Corp. name changed to Virginia Financial Group, Inc. 01/22/2002 which name changed to StellarOne Corp. 02/28/2008 which merged into Union First Market Bankshares Corp. 01/02/2014 which name changed to Union Bankshares Corp. 04/28/2014

PLANTERS CORP (NC)
Common $5 par split (2) for (1) by issuance of (1) additional share 4/29/83
Common $5 par split (3) for (2) by issuance of (0.5) additional share 3/16/87
Stock Dividend - 50% 7/15/85
Merged into Centura Banks, Inc. 11/5/90
Each share Common $5 par exchanged for (1) share Common no par
Centura Banks, Inc. merged into Royal Bank of Canada (Montreal, QC) 6/5/2001

PLANTERS FINANCIAL CORP. (KY)
Merged into Central South Bancorp, Inc. 1/31/86
Each share Common $4 par exchanged for (1.8378) shares Common $5 par
Central South Bancorp, Inc. merged into Commerce Union Corp. 9/22/86 which merged into Sovran Financial Corp. 11/1/87 which merged into C&S/Sovran Corp. 9/1/90 which merged into NationsBank Corp. 12/31/91 which reincorporated in Delaware as BankAmerica Corp. (Old) 9/25/98 which merged into BankAmerica Corp. (New) 9/30/98 which name changed to Bank of America Corp. 4/28/99

PLANTERS INDS INC (DE)
4% Conv. Preferred called for redemption at $100 plus $2 accrued dividends on 12/15/2014

PLANTERS NATL BK & TR CO (ROCKY MOUNT, NC)
Each share Capital Stock $25 par exchanged for (5.5) shares Capital Stock $5 par to effect a (5) for (1) split and a 10% stock dividend 1/20/59
Stock Dividends - 10% 6/15/60; 10% 7/30/71; 100% 4/24/73; 10% 2/4/80
Under plan of reorganization each share Capital Stock $5 par automatically became (1) share Planters Corp. Common $5 par 3/8/83
Planters Corp. merged into Centura Banks, Inc. 11/5/90 which merged into Royal Bank of Canada (Montreal, QC) 6/5/2001

PLANTERS NUT & CHOCOLATE CO. (PA)
Each share Common $100 par exchanged for (10) shares Common $10 par in 1947
Stock Dividends - 10% 1/2/51; 10% 1/2/57
Merged into Standard Brands, Inc. for cash 2/1/61

PLANTERS PEAT CO. (FL)
Proclaimed dissolved for non-payment of taxes 4/25/58

PLANTERS REALTY CO.
Dissolution approved in 1941

PLANTRONICS, INC. OLD (CA)
Name changed to Pacific Plantronics, Inc. (CA) 7/12/62
Pacific Plantronics, Inc. (CA) name changed to Plantronics, Inc. (CA) (New) 12/1/72 which reincorporated in Delaware 6/11/87
(See Plantronics, Inc. (DE))

PLANTRONICS INC OLD (DE)
Reincorporated 6/11/87
Common $1 par split (2) for (1) by issuance of (1) additional share 10/31/75
Common $1 par changed to no par 1/27/77
Common no par split (2) for (1) by issuance of (1) additional share 1/31/77
State of incorporation changed from (CA) to (DE) and Common no par changed to 1¢ par 6/11/87
Merged into PI Holdings Inc. 3/1/89
Each share Common 1¢ par exchanged for $24.74 principal amount of 18.5% Jr. Subordinated Pay-In-Kind Debentures due 3/1/2004 and $0.26 cash

PLANTS FOR TOMORROW INC (CO)
Each share Common no par exchanged for (0.05) share Common 2¢ par 08/23/1994
Name changed to Optimax Industries Inc. 01/11/1995
Optimax Industries Inc. name changed to Electric Motors Corp. 04/09/2009

PLANUM TECHNOLOGY CORP (DE)
Charter cancelled and declared inoperative and void for non-payment of taxes 06/27/1989

PLANVEST CAP CORP (BC)
Name changed to C.M. Oliver Inc. 4/10/97
C.M. Oliver Inc. recapitalized as Datawest Solutions Inc. 2/22/2000
(See Datawest Solutions Inc.)

PLANVISTA CORP (DE)
Merged into ProxyMed, Inc. 03/02/2004
Each share Common 1¢ par exchanged for (0.08271) share Common $0.001 par
(See ProxyMed, Inc.)

PLAS-TECH, INC. (MN)
Under plan of merger name changed to Magna-Tek, Inc. 03/29/1962
Magna-Tek, Inc. name changed to Moulded Products, Inc. 06/21/1966
(See Moulded Products, Inc.)

PLASER LIGHT CORP (BC)
Struck off register and declared dissolved for failure to file returns 12/24/93

PLASMA & MATLS TECHNOLOGIES INC (CA)
Issue Information - 2,750,000 shares COM offered at $14 per share on 08/23/1995
Name changed to Trikon Technologies, Inc. (CA) 03/31/1997
Trikon Technologies, Inc. (CA) reincorporated in Delaware 05/17/2002 which merged into Aviza Technology, Inc. 12/01/2005
(See Aviza Technology, Inc.)

PLASMA ENVIRONMENTAL TECHNOLOGIES INC (ON)
Each share old Common no par exchanged for (0.2) share new Common no par 08/16/1997
Each share new Common no par exchanged again for (0.1) share new Common no par 05/28/2001
Recapitalized as Blue Vista Technologies Inc. 08/17/2007
Each share new Common no par exchanged for (0.1) share Common no par
Blue Vista Technologies Inc. recapitalized as Arbitrage Exploration Inc. 01/16/2015 which name changed to Argo Gold Inc. 09/22/2016

PLASMA THERM INC (NJ)
Merged into Oerlikon Buhrle Holding AG 3/13/2000
Each share Common 1¢ par exchanged for $12.50 cash

PLASMACHEM INC (CA)
Completely liquidated 08/28/1979
Each share Common 10¢ par exchanged for first and final distribution of $0.19 cash

PLASMATECH BIOPHARMACEUTICALS INC (DE)
Name changed to Abeona Therapeutics Inc. 06/22/2015

PLASMATRONIC TECHNOLOGIES INC (DE)
Name changed to Ecological Services, Inc. and (2.75) additional shares issued 05/28/1998
Ecological Services, Inc. name changed to Stanford Capital Corp. 01/02/2003 which recapitalized as Skreem Entertainment Corp. (DE) 03/16/2004 which name changed to SKRM Interactive, Inc. 02/05/2007 which name changed to Sector 10, Inc. 04/14/2008

PLASMEDICS INC (CO)
Recapitalized as American Education Corp. (CO) 08/26/1991
Each share Common $0.001 par exchanged for (0.04) share Common $0.025 par
American Education Corp. (CO) reincorporated in Nevada 01/01/2004
(See American Education Corp.)

PLASMINE CORP (DE)
Merged into Reichhold Chemicals, Inc. 05/10/1985
Each share Common 10¢ par exchanged for $7.041 cash

PLASTEEL INTL INC (DE)
Name changed to Trans-World Pharmaceuticals, Inc. 3/9/89

PLASTI FAB LTD (AB)
Name changed to PFB Corp. 1/1/96

PLASTI LINE INC (TN)
Merged into PL Holding Corp. 1/30/98
Each share Common $0.001 par exchanged for $14.50 cash

PLASTIBEC LTD (CANADA)
Acquired by Royal Plastics Group Ltd. 12/09/1994
Each share Common no par exchanged for $7 cash

PLASTIC APPLICATORS, INC. (TX)
Stock Dividend - 10% 10/22/65
Completely liquidated 6/21/67
Each share Common $1 par exchanged for first and final distribution of (0.018181) share Schlumberger Ltd. Common $1 par

PLASTIC ASSOC INC (NY)
Merged into P.A. Industries, Inc. 06/14/1979
Each share Common 1¢ par exchanged for $4.80 cash

PLASTIC CAN CORP. (CT)
Charter cancelled for failure to pay fees 11/14/75

PLASTIC CARTON CORP AMER (DE)
Each share Common 1¢ par exchanged for (0.2) share Common 5¢ par 10/13/1971
Charter cancelled and declared inoperative and void for non-payment of taxes 04/15/1973

PLASTIC DYNAMICS CORP (FL)
Name changed to Jerry's Inc. (FL) and Common 10¢ par changed to 1¢ par 08/18/1969
Jerry's, Inc. (FL) reincorporated in Nevada 03/16/2004 which recapitalized as Diamond Ranch Foods, Ltd. 05/10/2004 which name changed to Plandai Biotechnology, Inc. 01/05/2012

PLASTIC ENGINE TECHNOLOGY CORP (ON)
Placed in receivership 05/02/1989
No stockholders' equity

PLASTIC FILM PRODUCTS CORP. (OH)
Name changed to General Fabrics Corp. 2/21/80
(See General Fabrics Corp.)

PLASTIC MATERIALS & POLYMERS, INC. (NY)
Acquired by Cities Service Co. 6/1/64
Each (16.419) shares Common 10¢ par exchanged for (1) share Common $10 par
Cities Service Co. merged into Occidental Petroleum Corp. (Calif.) 12/3/82 which reincorporated in Delaware 5/21/86

PLASTIC MOLDED ARTS CORP. (NY)
Proclaimed dissolved for failure to comply with New York corporation laws 12/15/64

PLASTIC RECYCLING INC (NY)
Charter cancelled and proclaimed dissolved for failure to pay taxes 03/28/2001

PLASTIC SPECIALTIES & TECHNOLOGIES INC (DE)
Acquired by PST Holding Inc. 3/3/98
Each share Common 1¢ par exchanged for $3.50 cash

PLASTIC SURGERY CO (GA)
Chapter 11 Federal Bankruptcy proceedings converted to Chapter 7 on 2/25/2003
Stockholders' equity unlikely

PLASTIC UNVL INC (FL)
Name changed to Lumidor Industries, Inc. 06/16/1969
(See Lumidor Industries, Inc.)

PLASTIC WIRE & CABLE CORP. (CT)
Common no par changed to $5 par in 1954
Stock Dividends - 10% 4/15/54; 10% 12/30/59; 120% 11/8/63; 10% 9/30/64
Name changed to PWC Inc. 10/29/65

PWC Inc. acquired by Triangle Conduit & Cable Co. Inc. 11/5/65 which name changed to Triangle Industries, Inc. (Old) 5/31/68
(See Triangle Industries, Inc. (Old))

PLASTICON INTL INC (WY)
Common 5¢ par changed to $0.001 par 10/10/2005
Chapter 11 bankruptcy proceedings converted to Chapter 7 on 04/11/2008
No stockholders' equity

PLASTICRETE CORP (CT)
Name changed to New England Corp. and Common $1 par changed to 10¢ par 10/02/1981
(See New England Corp.)

PLASTICS, INC. (PR)
Acquired by Drackett Co. 1/3/61
Each share Class A Common $1 par exchanged for (0.5) share new Common $1 par
Drackett Co. was acquired by Bristol-Myers Co. 8/2/65 which name changed to Bristol-Myers Squibb Co. 10/4/89

PLASTICS & FIBRES, INC. (NJ)
Reincorporated under the laws of Delaware as P & F Industries, Inc. 6/30/63

PLASTICS CORP AMER INC (MN)
Common $1 par changed to 50¢ par 6/21/62
Each share Common 50¢ par exchanged for (0.2) share Common $1 par 2/9/66
Merged into Versa/Technologies, Inc. 11/17/70
Each share Common $1 par exchanged for (1) share Conv. Preferred no par and (1) share Common 10¢ par
(See Versa/Technologies, Inc.)

PLASTICS DEV CORP AMER (PA)
Name changed to Durawood Industries, Inc. 01/02/1980

PLASTICS MATERIALS CORP. (NH)
Charter cancelled and declared dissolved for failure to pay fees in 1961

PLASTIGONE TECHNOLOGIES INC (FL)
Recapitalized as Amitelo Communications, Inc. 12/4/2003
Each (325) shares Common 1¢ par exchanged for (1) share Common 1¢ par
(See Amitelo Communications, Inc.)

PLASTIKOS CORP. (WA)
Proclaimed dissolved for non-payment of fees 7/1/76

PLASTILINE INC (DE)
Reincorporated 6/4/81
Common 10¢ par split (5) for (3) by issuance of (2/3) additional share 7/5/72
Stock Dividend - 10% 5/14/65
State of incorporation changed from (NY) to (DE) 6/4/81
Plan of reorganization under Chapter 11 confirmed in May 1984
No stockholders' equity

PLASTIMET CORP. (OR)
Charter cancelled and declared dissolved for failure to file reports and pay fees 12/19/73

PLASTINEERS, INC. (MN)
Name changed to Federated Industries, Inc. 04/23/1970
(See Federated Industries, Inc.)

PLASTINUM POLYMER TECHNOLOGIES CORP (DE)
Name changed 06/26/2007
Name changed from Plastinum Corp. to Plastinum Polymer Technologies Corp. 06/26/2007
SEC revoked common stock registration 06/11/2014

PLA-PLA

PLASTOID CABLE CORP AMER (DE)
Name changed 06/18/1964
Name changed from Plastoid Corp. of America to Plastoid Cable Corp. of America 06/18/1964
Name changed to Cable Liquidation Corp. 02/10/1969
Cable Liquidation Corp. liquidated for Babbitt (B.T.), Inc. 03/04/1969 which name changed to B.T.B. Corp. 12/05/1969 which name changed to International Banknote Co., Inc. 01/02/1973 which merged into United States Banknote Corp. (NY) 07/25/1990 which reincorporated in Delaware 09/21/1993 which name changed to American Banknote Corp. 07/03/1995
(See American Banknote Corp.)

PLASTOMEDICAL SCIENCES INC (NY)
Reincorporated under the laws of Delaware as J.R.M. Holdings, Inc. 07/30/1987
J.R.M. Holdings, Inc. name changed to Harmony Group Ltd. 03/22/1991
(See Harmony Group Ltd.)

PLASTRONICS CORP (UT)
Each share old Common no par exchanged for (0.2) share new Common no par 02/20/1976
Name changed to Continental Benefit Corp. 04/13/1987
(See Continental Benefit Corp.)

PLATA MINERALS CORP (BC)
Name changed to Briyante Software Corp. 10/5/2001
Briyante Software Corp. merged into Imagis Technologies Inc. (BC) 11/25/2003 which reincorporated in Canada as Visiphor Corp. 7/7/2005

PLATA MNG LTD (BERMUDA)
Delisted from Canadian Venture Stock Exchange 05/30/2000

PLATA-PERU RES INC (ON)
Delisted from Toronto Venture Stock Exchange 10/15/2002

PLATA RES INC (NV)
Common $0.001 par split (20) for (1) by issuance of (19) additional shares payable 02/10/2009 to holders of record 02/09/2009 Ex date - 02/11/2009
Common $0.001 par split (3) for (1) by issuance of (2) additional shares payable 03/06/2012 to holders of record 03/06/2012 Ex date - 03/07/2012
Name changed to Nexus Biopharma, Inc. 05/19/2016

PLATCOM INC (FL)
Administratively dissolved 09/23/2011

PLATE RES INC (BC)
Each share old Common no par exchanged for (0.33333333) share new Common no par 12/18/2015
Recapitalized as ArcPacific Resources Corp. 12/22/2016
Each share new Common no par exchanged for (0.5) share Common no par

PLATEAU CONSOLIDATED, INC. (NV)
Charter revoked for failure to file reports and pay taxes 3/6/61

PLATEAU METALS & INDUSTRIES LTD. (BC)
Recapitalized as Wharf Resources Ltd. 11/1/72
Each share Capital Stock no par exchanged for (0.25) share Common no par
Wharf Resources Ltd. merged into Goldcorp Inc. 12/11/96

PLATEAU METALS LTD. (BC)
Name changed to Plateau Metals & Industries Ltd. and 50¢ par changed to no par 4/21/72
Each share Capital Stock 50¢ par exchanged for (1) share Capital Stock no par
Plateau Metals & Industries Ltd. recapitalized as Wharf Resources Ltd. 11/1/72 which merged into Goldcorp Inc. 12/11/96

PLATEAU URANIUM INC (ON)
Name changed to Plateau Energy Metals Inc. 03/16/2018

PLATEAU URANIUM MINING CORP. (DE)
Dissolved in January 1955
Each (20) shares Capital Stock 1¢ par (founders shares) exchanged for (1) share Sabre Uranium Corp. Common 10¢ par
Each (10) shares Capital Stock 1¢ par (other than founders shares) exchanged for (1) share Sabre Uranium Corp. Common 10¢ par
Sabre Uranium Corp. merged into Sabre-Pinon Corp. 6/1/56 which was merged into United Nuclear Corp. (DE) 4/4/62 which reorganized in Virginia as UNC Resources, Inc. 8/31/78 which name changed to UNC Inc. (VA) 6/3/86 which reincorporated in Delaware 4/30/87
(See UNC Inc.)

PLATEAU WEST EXPL INC (UT)
Each share old Common $0.001 par exchanged for (0.05) share new Common $0.001 par 09/24/1991
Recapitalized as Kendall Management Corp. (UT) 02/07/1995
Each share new Common $0.001 par exchanged for (0.25) share Common $0.001 par
Kendall Management Corp. (UT) reincorporated in Nevada as Medical Resources Management Inc. 08/20/1996 which merged into Emergent Group Inc. 07/06/2001
(See Emergent Group Inc.)

PLATED WIRES & ELECTRONICS, INC. (DE)
Name changed to P W & E, Inc. 12/15/67
(See P W & E, Inc.)

PLATEXCO INC (YT)
Reincorporated 5/7/97
Place of incorporation changed from (ONT) to (Yukon) 5/7/97
Merged into Impala Platinum Holdings Ltd. 12/19/2000
Each share Common no par exchanged for $9.50 cash

PLATFORM RES INC (AB)
Name changed to Alberta Oilsands Inc. 06/28/2007
Alberta Oilsands Inc. name changed to Marquee Energy Ltd. (New) 12/08/2016

PLATFORMS INTL CORP (OK)
Name changed to Platforms Wireless International Corp. 2/9/2001

PLATINA ENERGY GROUP INC (DE)
Chapter 11 bankruptcy proceedings converted to Chapter 7 on 08/11/2009
No stockholders' equity

PLATINO ENERGY CORP (AB)
Acquired by 1901558 Alberta Ltd. 07/21/2015
Each share Common no par exchanged for $0.25 cash

PLATINOVA A/S (DENMARK)
Delisted from Toronto Stock Exchange 06/25/2004

PLATINOVA RES LTD (ON)
Plan of Arrangement effective 11/21/91
Each share Common no par exchanged for (1) Special Share no par and (0.25) share PVA Minerals Inc. Common no par
PVA Minerals Inc. name changed to Marmora Mineral Products Inc. 6/23/92 which merged into Gitennes Exploration Inc. 5/13/93
Each Special Share no par exchanged for (1) share Platinova A/S Common no par

PLATINUM & GOLD INC (NV)
SEC revoked common stock registration 04/08/2010
Stockholders' equity unlikely

PLATINUM CAP INC (ON)
Recapitalized 1/3/92
Recapitalized from Platinum & Gold Resources Inc. to Platinum Capital Inc. 1/3/92
Each share Common no par exchanged for (1/6) share Common no par
Merged into Softcop Corp. 6/17/94
Each share Common no par exchanged for (1) share Class B no par

PLATINUM COMMUNICATIONS CORP (AB)
Acquired by Xplornet Communications Inc. 12/16/2015
Each share Common no par exchanged for $0.16 cash
Note: Unexchanged certificates will be cancelled and become without value 12/16/2021

PLATINUM COMMUNICATIONS INC (NV)
Charter revoked for failure to file reports and pay fees 8/1/2002

PLATINUM COMMUNICATIONS SYS INC (BC)
Recapitalized as PPZ Platinum Products Inc. 12/12/90
Each share Common no par exchanged for (0.25) share Common no par
PPZ Platinum Products Inc. recapitalized as Consolidated Platinum Industries Inc. 1/20/92 which name changed to Allied Strategies Inc. 5/25/93 which recapitalized as Sleeman Breweries Ltd. 5/30/96
(See Sleeman Breweries Ltd.)

PLATINUM ENERGY RES INC (DE)
Issue Information - 14,400,000 UNITS consisting of (1) share COM and (1) WT offered at $8 per Unit on 10/24/2005
Units separated 10/23/2009
Merged into Pacific International Group Holdings L.L.C. 07/11/2011
Each share Common $0.0001 par exchanged for $1.50 cash

PLATINUM ENTMT INC (DE)
Plan of reorganization under Chapter 11 Federal Bankruptcy Code effective 10/10/2001
No stockholders' equity

PLATINUM PARI-MUTUEL HLDGS INC (NV)
Each share old Common $0.001 par exchanged for (0.01) share new Common $0.001 par 02/06/2015
Name changed to Point to Point Methodics, Inc. 04/27/2017

PLATINUM RESH ORGANIZATION INC (DE)
Reincorporated 04/13/2007
State of incorporation changed from (NV) to (DE) 04/13/2007
Filed a petition under Chapter 7 Federal Bankruptcy Code 02/17/2009
No stockholders' equity

PLATINUM RES CDA INC (ON)
Recapitalized as Portrait Impressions of Canada Ltd. 07/01/1991
Each share Common no par exchanged for (0.2) share Common no par
Portrait Impressions of Canada Ltd. name changed to Carriage Automotive Group Inc. 09/25/1998 which name changed to Cars4u.com Ltd. 02/14/2000 which name changed to Cars4u Ltd. 01/30/2003 which recapitalized as Chesswood Income Fund 05/10/2006 which reorganized as Chesswood Group Ltd. 01/04/2011

PLATINUM SOFTWARE CORP (DE)
Common $0.001 par split (3) for (2) by issuance of (0.5) additional share 09/02/1993
Name changed to Epicor Software Corp. 05/04/1999
(See Epicor Software Corp.)

PLATINUM SUPER YACHTS INC (NV)
Name changed to Royal Quantum Group, Inc. 02/01/2006
Royal Quantum Group, Inc. recapitalized as MineralRite Corp. 10/18/2012

PLATINUM TECHNOLOGY INTL INC (DE)
Name changed 01/04/1999
Common $0.001 par split (2) for (1) by issuance of (1) additional share 09/27/1991
Name changed from Platinum Technology, Inc. to Platinum Technology International Inc. 01/04/1999
Merged into Computer Associates International, Inc. 06/29/1999
Each share Common $0.001 par exchanged for $29.25 cash

PLATINUM UNDERWRITERS HLDGS LTD (BERMUDA)
Each 7% Adjustable Rate Equity Unit automatically became (0.9107) share Common 1¢ par 11/16/2005
Each share 6% Conv Preferred Ser. A automatically became (1) share Common 1¢ par 02/17/2009
Merged into RenaissanceRe Holdings Ltd. 03/02/2015
Each share Common 1¢ par exchanged for (0.296) share Common $1 par and $35.96 cash

PLATMIN LTD (BC)
Reincorporated 04/01/2009
Place of incorporation changed from (Canada) to (BC) 04/01/2009
Reincorporated under the laws of Guernsey and Common no par reclassified as Ordinary no par 12/09/2011
(See Platmin Ltd. (Guernsey))

PLATMIN LTD (GUERNSEY)
Shares transferred to Guernsey register 06/30/2012

PLATO LEARNING INC (DE)
Common 1¢ par split (4) for (3) by issuance of (1/3) additional share payable 10/26/2001 to holders of record 10/12/2001 Ex date - 10/29/2001
Acquired by Project Porsche Holdings Corp. 05/26/2010
Each share Common 1¢ par exchanged for $5.60 cash

PLATONIA DEVS INC (NY)
Name changed to Sun Gold Developments International Corp. 08/18/1988
Sun Gold Developments International Corp. recapitalized as Gridiron Resources Ltd. 01/20/1994
(See Gridiron Resources Ltd.)

PLATORO WEST HLDGS INC (BC)
Plan of Arrangement effective 12/16/2009
Each share old Common no par exchanged for (1) share new Common no par and (0.132) share Copper Ridge Explorations Inc. Common no par
Recapitalized as Silver Predator Corp. 06/24/2010
Each (12) shares new Common no par exchanged for (1) share Common no par

PLATRONICS INC (NJ)
Stock Dividend - 100% 03/01/1981
SEC revoked common stock
registration 11/17/2009
Stockholders' equity unlikely

PLATT CORP. (DE)
Merged into Adson Industries, Inc.
6/5/63
Each (6-2/3) shares Class A Common
50¢ par exchanged for (1) share
Common 10¢ par
Adson Industries, Inc. name changed
to Gaynor Industries, Inc. 1/24/69
which name changed to
Gaynor-Stafford Industries, Inc.
11/20/70
(See Gaynor-Stafford Industries, Inc.)

PLATT IRON WORKS
Dissolved in 1931

PLATT TSCHUDY NORTON FD INC (MN)
Name changed to North Star Fund,
Inc. 09/11/1973
North Star Fund, Inc. name changed
to North Star Stock Fund, Inc.
04/27/1977 which name changed to
IAI Stock Fund, Inc. 08/03/1987
(See IAI Stock Fund, Inc.)

PLAUNT MINING CO. LTD.
Name changed to Culver Gold Mines
Ltd. in 1944
(See Culver Gold Mines Ltd.)

PLAVA LAGUNA D D (CROATIA)
GDR agreement terminated
09/18/2017
Each 144A GDR for Ordinary
exchanged for (0.04) share Ordinary
Each Reg. S GDR for Ordinary
exchanged for (0.04) share Ordinary
Note: Unexchanged GDR's will be
sold and the proceeds, if any, held
for claim after 03/18/2018

PLAY BY PLAY TOYS & NOVELTIES INC (TX)
Issue Information - 2,000,000 shares
COM offered at $12.25 per share on
07/19/1995
Chapter 7 bankruptcy proceedings
terminated 03/23/2006
Stockholders' equity unlikely

PLAY CO TOYS & ENTMT CORP (DE)
Name changed 5/9/96
Name changed from Play Co. Toys to
Play Co. Toys & Entertainment Corp.
5/9/96
Each share old Common 1¢ par
exchanged for (1/3) share new
Common 1¢ par 7/2/97
Chapter 11 bankruptcy proceedings
converted to Chapter 7 on 8/29/2001
Stockholders' equity unlikely

PLAYANDWIN INC (NV)
Common $0.001 par split (4) for (1)
by issuance of (3) additional shares
payable 10/06/2000 to holders of
record 09/26/2000 Ex date -
10/10/2000
Each share old Common $0.001 par
exchanged for (0.05) share new
Common $0.001 par 10/01/2001
Each share new Common $0.001 par
received distribution of (1) share
Playandwin Canada Inc. Common
no par payable 11/20/2001 to
holders of record 10/29/2001
Name changed to D'Angelo Brands
Inc. 11/19/2001

PLAYBOX US INC (NV)
Each share old Common $0.001 par
exchanged for (0.005) share new
Common $0.001 par 06/18/2010
Reorganized under the laws of
Wyoming 12/19/2011
Each share new Common $0.001 par
exchanged for (0.0005) share
Common $0.001 par

PLAYBOY ENTERPRISES INC (DE)
4% Preferred $1 par called for
redemption 12/15/1972
Each share Common $1 par
exchanged for (0.5) share old Class
A Common 1¢ par 06/08/1990
Each share old Class A Common 1¢
par received distribution of (3)
shares old Class B Common 1¢ par
06/08/1990
Under plan of reorganization each
share old Class A Common 1¢ par
and old Class B Common 1¢ par
automatically became (1) share new
Class A Common 1¢ par and new
Class B Common 1¢ par
respectively 03/15/1999
Acquired by Icon Acquisition
Holdings, L.P. 03/04/2011
Each share new Class A Common 1¢
par exchanged for $6.15 cash
Each share new Class B Common 1¢
par exchanged for $6.15 cash

PLAYCORE INC (DE)
Merged into Playcore Holdings, L.L.C.
5/19/2000
Each share Common 1¢ par
exchanged for $10.10 cash

PLAYDIUM ENTMT CORP (BC)
Assets transferred to a privately held
company 12/03/2001
No stockholders' equity

PLAYER GARY DIRECT INC (NY)
SEC revoked common stock
registration 4/13/2006
Stockholders' equity unlikely

PLAYER PETE CORP (AB)
Reincorporated 4/29/98
Place of incorporation changed from
(BC) to (Alta) 4/29/98
Acquired by National Fuel Exploration
Corp. 8/13/2001
Each share Common no par
exchanged for $16.25 cash

PLAYER RES INC (BC)
Name changed 07/10/1984
Name changed from Player
Petroleum Inc. to Player Resources
Inc. 07/10/1984
Recapitalized as Consolidated Player
Resources Inc. 01/26/1987
Each share Common no par
exchanged for (0.5) share Common
no par
Consolidated Player Resources Inc.
recapitalized as Epping Realty Corp.
12/23/1988
(See Epping Realty Corp.)

PLAYERS CLUB INTL INC (UT)
Reorganized under the laws of
Nevada as Players International,
Inc. 9/18/86
Each share Common $0.001 par
exchanged for (0.2) share Common
$0.005 par
(See Players International Inc.)

PLAYERS GROUP COS INC (NY)
Dissolved by proclamation 9/25/91

PLAYERS INTL INC (NV)
Merged into Harrah's Entertainment,
Inc. 3/22/2000
Each share Common $0.005 par
exchanged for $8.50 cash

PLAYGROUND CORP AMER (NY)
Common 10¢ par split (3) for (1) by
issuance of (2) additional shares
4/21/69
Name changed to PCA Industries,
Inc. 10/10/75
(See PCA Industries, Inc.)

PLAYMATES PPTYS HLDGS LTD (BERMUDA)
Reorganized 01/06/1994
Reorganized from Playmates
International Holdings Ltd. to
Playmates Properties Holdings Ltd.
01/06/1994
Each old Sponsored ADR for Ordinary
10¢ par exchanged for (1) new
Sponsored ADR for Ordinary 10¢
par and approximately $1.31 cash
ADR agreement terminated
01/31/1995
Each New Sponsored ADR 10¢ par
exchanged for $0.6235486 cash

PLAYNET TECHNOLOGIES INC (DE)
Filed a petition under Chapter 7
Federal Bankruptcy Code 6/4/98
No stockholders' equity

PLAYORENA INC (NY)
Each share old Common $0.001 par
exchanged for (0.05) share new
Common $0.001 par 07/24/1998
Recapitalized as Etravnet.com, Inc.
09/29/1999
Each share new Common $0.001 par
exchanged for (0.027533) share
Common $0.001 par
Etravnet.com, Inc. name changed to
REZconnect Technologies, Inc. (NY)
08/29/2001 which reincorporated in
Delaware as YTB International, Inc.
01/04/2005
(See YTB International, Inc.)

PLAYSKOOL MANUFACTURING CO. (IL)
Completely liquidated 08/06/1968
Each share Common $1 par
exchanged for first and final
distribution of (0.7875) share
Bradley (Milton) Co. Common $1 par
Bradley (Milton) Co. merged into
Hasbro Bradley, Inc. 09/10/1984
which name changed to Hasbro Inc.
06/06/1985

PLAYSTAR CORP. NEW (ANTIGUA)
Each share Ordinary $0.0001 par
received distribution of (1) share
New Wave Media, Inc. Common
$0.001 par payable 02/08/2008 to
holders of record 12/17/2007
Ex date - 02/25/2008
SEC revoked Ordinary stock
registration 06/03/2008

PLAYSTAR CORP (DE)
Reincorporated under the laws of
Antigua as PlayStar Wyoming
Holding Corp. 09/09/1998
PlayStar Wyoming Holding Corp.
name changed to PlayStar Corp.
01/11/2001 which name changed to
V-Loan Financial Services, Inc.
10/27/2004 which recapitalized as
Biotelemetric Signaling Inc.
01/07/2005 which name changed to
Flirty Girl International Inc.
12/27/2005 which name changed to
PlayStar Corp. (Antigua) (New)
07/27/2006
(See PlayStar Corp. (Antigua) (New))

PLAYSTAR CORP OLD (ANITGUA)
Each share old Ordinary $0.0001 par
exchanged for (0.001) share new
Ordinary $0.0001 par 07/14/2004
Name changed to V-Loan Financial
Services, Inc. 10/27/2004
V-Loan Financial Services, Inc.
recapitalized as Biotelemetric
Signaling Inc. 01/07/2005 which
name changed to Flirty Girl
International Inc. 12/27/2005 which
name changed to PlayStar Corp.
(Antigua) (New) 07/27/2006
(See PlayStar Corp. (Antigua) (New))

PLAYSTAR WYOMING HLDG CORP (ANTIGUA)
Name changed to PlayStar Corp.
(Old) 01/11/2001
PlayStar Corp. (Old) name changed
to V-Loan Financial Services, Inc.
10/27/2004 which recapitalized as
Biotelemetric Signaling Inc.
01/07/2005 which name changed to
Flirty Girl International Inc.
12/27/2005 which name changed to
PlayStar Corp. (Antigua) (New)
07/27/2006
(See PlayStar Corp. (Antigua) (New))

PLAYTEX PRODS INC (DE)
Merged into Energizer Holdings, Inc.
(Old) 10/01/2007
Each share Common 1¢ par
exchanged for $18.30 cash

PLAYTIME TOYS INC (NV)
Each share old Common $0.00025
par exchanged for (0.02) share new
Common $0.00025 par 02/08/1992
New Common $0.00025 par split (2)
for (1) by issuance of (1) additional
share 08/17/1992
Merged into Quality Products, Inc.
10/02/1992
Each share new Common $0.00025
par exchanged for (1) share new
Common $0.00001 par
(See Quality Products, Inc.)

PLAYTRONICS CORP (MN)
Merged into Winland Electronics, Inc.
03/05/1990
Each share Common 1¢ par
exchanged for (0.3) share Common
1¢ par
Winland Electronics, Inc. name
changed to Winland Holdings Corp.
02/06/2018

PLAYWORLD INTERACTIVE HLDG CORP (FL)
Each share old Common $0.001 par
exchanged for (0.01) share new
Common $0.001 par 08/22/2013
Name changed to Smart Technologies
Holding Corp. 01/16/2015
Smart Technologies Holding Corp.
name changed to EM Quantum
Technologies Inc. 07/07/2016

PLAZA BANCORP (DE)
Merged into Pacific Premier Bancorp,
Inc. 11/01/2017
Each share Common 1¢ par
exchanged for (0.2) share Common
1¢ par

PLAZA BANCSHARES INC (MO)
Merged into Commerce Bancshares,
Inc. 09/01/1982
Each share Capital Stock $10 par
exchanged for (5.5) shares Common
$5 par

PLAZA BK (IRVINE, CA)
Under plan of merger each share
Common 1¢ par automatically
became (1) share Plaza Bancorp
(DE) Common 1¢ par 06/29/2015
Plaza Bancorp merged into Pacific
Premier Bancorp, Inc. 11/01/2017

PLAZA BK COMM (KANSAS CITY, MO)
Stock Dividend - 50% 02/05/1965
Reorganized as Plaza Bancshares,
Inc. 04/03/1972
Each share Common $20 par
exchanged for (2) shares Common
$10 par
Plaza Bancshares, Inc. merged into
Commerce Bancshares, Inc.
09/01/1982

PLAZA BANK OF COMMERCE (SAN JOSE, CA)
Under plan of reorganization each
share Common no par automatically
became (1) share Plaza Commerce
Bancorp Common no par 1/1/82
Plaza Commerce Bancorp merged
into Comerica Inc. 1/1/91

PLAZA COMM BANCORP (CA)
Stock Dividends - 10% 12/15/1987;
20% 08/10/1988
Merged into Comerica Inc.
01/01/1991
Each share Common no par
exchanged for (0.28571) share
Common $5 par

PLAZA COMMUNICATIONS INC (CA)
Merged into Intertec Publishing Corp.
9/16/97
Each share Common no par
exchanged for $4.225661 cash
Note: An additional payment of
$0.28991703 cash per share was
made in October 1998

PLAZA GROUP INC (DE)
Name changed to Union 69, Ltd.
04/02/1996
Union 69, Ltd. name changed to Save

on Meds.Com, Inc. 03/02/2000 which name changed to My Meds Express.Com, Inc. 07/26/2000
(See My Meds Express.Com, Inc.)

PLAZA GROUP INC (NY)
Adjudicated bankrupt 01/15/1975
Stockholders' equity unlikely

PLAZA HOME MTG CORP (DE)
Acquired by Fleet Financial Group, Inc. (New) 03/03/1995
Each share Common 1¢ par exchanged for $7.625 cash

PLAZA INVESTING CORP.
Dissolved in 1932

PLAZA NATIONAL BANK (ORLANDO, FL)
Acquired by First at Orlando Corp. 6/15/67
Each share Common $10 par exchanged for (1.9) shares Common $5 par
First at Orlando Corp. name changed to Sun Banks of Florida, Inc. 4/12/74 which name changed to Sun Banks, Inc. 5/2/83 which merged into SunTrust Banks, 7/1/85

PLAZA NATL BK (SECAUCUS, NJ)
Acquired by Greater Jersey Bancorp. 08/30/1974
Each share Capital Stock $12.50 par exchanged for $24 cash

PLAZA PETE INC (CO)
Merged into Brock Exploration Corp. 10/1/73
Each share Common 10¢ par exchanged for (0.120748) share Common 10¢ par and (0.120748) Common Stock Purchase Warrant expiring 10/1/77
Brock Exploration Corp. merged into Key Production Co., Inc. 3/28/96 which merged into Cimarex Energy Co. 9/30/2002

PLAZA RLTY INVS (MA)
Acquired by Plaza Mass Corp. 07/16/1984
Each Share of Bene. Int. $1 par exchanged for $2 cash

PLAZABANK (SEATTLE, WA)
Merged into BayCom Corp 11/06/2017
Each share Common exchanged for (0.084795) share Common no par

PLAZACORP RETAIL PPTYS LTD (NB)
Reorganized under the laws of Ontario as Plaza Retail REIT 01/08/2014
Each share Common no par exchanged for (1) Trust Unit

PLC CAP L L C (DE)
Issue Information - 2,200,000 MONTHLY INCOME PFD SECS SER A 9% offered at $25 per share on 06/02/1994
9% Monthly Income Preferred Securities Ser. A called for redemption at $25 on 6/30/99

PLC CAP TR I (DE)
8.25% Trust Originated Preferred Securities called for redemption at $25 on 10/25/2002

PLC CAP TR III (DE)
7.50% Trust Originated Preferred Securities called for redemption at $25 on 06/19/2012

PLC CAP TR IV (DE)
7.25% Trust Originated Preferred Securities called for redemption at $25 on 06/19/2012

PLC CAP TR V (DE)
6.125% Trust Originated Preferred Securities called for redemption at $25 plus $0.361545 accrued dividends on 03/25/2015

PLC LIQUIDATING CORP. (DE)
Liquidation completed
Each share Common $3.75 par exchanged for initial distribution of $7 cash 8/4/65
Each share Common $3.75 par received second and final distribution of $0.91 cash 6/17/66

PLC SYS INC (YUKON)
Recapitalized as Viveve Medical, Inc. (YT) 09/25/2014
Each share Common no par exchanged for (0.01) share Common no par
Viveve Medical, Inc. (YT) reincorporated in Delaware 05/10/2016

PLC VENTURES CORP (FL)
Recapitalized as Access Healthmax Holdings, Inc. 09/10/1998
Each (175) shares Common $0.001 par exchanged for (1) share Common $0.001 par
Access Healthmax Holdings, Inc. recapitalized as Access Health Alternatives, Inc. 03/15/1999 which name changed to IPMC Holdings Corp. (FL) 01/07/2003 which reincorporated in Nevada as Coil Tubing Technology, Inc. 12/22/2005

PLD TELEKOM INC (DE)
Reincorporated 02/28/1997
Place of incorporation changed from (ON) to (DE) and Common no par changed to 1¢ par 02/28/1997
Merged into Metromedia International Group, Inc. 09/30/1999
Each share Common 1¢ par exchanged for (0.6353) share Common $1 par
(See Metromedia International Group, Inc.)

PLEASANT KIDS INC (FL)
Each share old Common $0.001 par exchanged for (0.002) share new Common $0.001 par 07/06/2015
Name changed to Next Group Holdings, Inc. 12/30/2015
Next Group Holdings, Inc. recapitalized as Cuentas Inc. 08/13/2018

PLEASANT RLTY & FINL CORP (ON)
Delisted from Canadian Dealer Network 1/3/95

PLEASANT STREET CO., INC. (MA)
Liquidation completed
Each share Common $5 par exchanged for initial distribution of $38 cash 02/10/1964
Each share Common $5 par received second distribution of $3 cash 11/20/1964
Each share Common $5 par received third and final distribution of $1.05 cash 07/22/1970

PLEASANT VALLEY BERYLLIUM CO. (UT)
Recapitalized as Best Western Properties, Inc. 3/8/71
Each share Common 10¢ par exchanged for (2) shares Common 10¢ par
Best Western Properties, Inc. reincorporated in Colorado as Western Royalty Corp. 9/1/83

PLEASANT VALLEY OIL & MINING CORP. (UT)
Recapitalized as Pleasant Valley Beryllium Co. 12/29/1961
Each share Common 5¢ par exchanged for (0.5) share Common 10¢ par
Pleasant Valley Beryllium Co. recapitalized as Best Western Properties, Inc. (UT) 03/08/1971 which reincorporated in Colorado as Western Royalty Corp. 09/01/1983

PLEASANT VALLEY URANIUM CORP. (UT)
Recapitalized as Pleasant Valley Oil & Mining Corp. 12/14/1956
Each share Common 1¢ par exchanged for (0.2) share Common 5¢ par
Pleasant Valley Oil & Mining Corp. recapitalized as Pleasant Valley Beryllium Co. 12/29/1961 which recapitalized as Best Western Properties, Inc. (UT) 03/08/1971 which reincorporated in Colorado as Western Royalty Corp. 09/01/1983

PLEASANT VALLEY WINE CO. (NY)
Merged into Great Western Producers, Inc. 12/30/57
Each share Capital Stock $1 par exchanged for (0.22) share 6% Preferred Ser. A $30 par and (1.1) shares Common 60¢ par
Great Western Producers, Inc. liquidated for Taylor Wine Co., Inc. 11/30/66 which merged into Coca-Cola Co. 1/21/77

PLENTECH ELECTRS INC (BC)
Recapitalized as Consolidated Plentech Electronics Inc. 09/21/1998
Each share Common no par exchanged for (0.16666666) share Common no par
(See Consolidated Plentech Electronics Inc.)

PLENUM COMMUNICATIONS INC (MN)
Name changed to LION, Inc. (MN) 08/20/1999
LION, Inc. (MN) reincorporated in Washington 12/15/2000
(See LION, Inc.)

PLENUM PUBG CORP (DE)
Reincorporated 03/23/1987
Common 10¢ par split (3) for (2) by issuance of (0.5) additional share 04/14/1980
Common 10¢ par split (3) for (2) by issuance of (0.5) additional share 03/27/1984
Stock Dividends - 50% 05/06/1966; 200% 04/14/1977
State of incorporation changed from (NY) to (DE) 03/23/1987
Common 10¢ par split (5) for (2) by issuance of (1.5) additional shares 03/24/1987
Each share Common 10¢ par received distribution of (0.25) share Gradco Systems Inc. Common no par payable 03/20/1998 to holders of record 03/18/1998
Merged into Kluwer Boston, Inc. 07/21/1998
Each share Common 10¢ par exchanged for $73.50 cash

PLESK CORP (DE)
Common $0.0001 par split (15) for (1) by issuance of (14) additional shares payable 03/28/2013 to holders of record 03/25/2013
Ex date - 04/01/2013
Name changed to Yappn Corp. 04/08/2013

PLESSEY INC (DE)
Acquired by Plessey Co. PLC 06/30/1971
Each share Common 20¢ par exchanged for (6.5) ADR's for Dollar Shares 50p
(See Plessey Co. PLC)

PLESSEY PLC (ENGLAND)
ADR's for Ordinary Reg. 10s par and ADR's for Dollar Shares 10s par changed to 50p par per currency change 02/15/1971
Each old ADR for Dollar Share 50p par exchanged for (0.1) new ADR for Dollar Share 50p par 05/07/1973
ADR's for Ordinary Reg. 50p par changed to 25p par and (2) additional shares issued 08/22/1983
New ADR's for Dollar Shares 50p par changed to 25p par and (2) additional shares issued 08/22/1983
Each New ADR for Dollar Shares 25p par exchanged for (1) Sponsored ADR for Ordinary Reg. 25p par 08/20/1986
Stock Dividends - On ADR's for Ord. Reg.- 33-1/3% 09/28/1961; 100% 07/07/1964; 50% 01/05/1968
Note: Common Market regulation required all publicly held British companies to replace LTD with PLC in 1982
Acquired by GEC Siemens PLC 12/08/1989
Each Sponsored ADR for Ordinary Reg. 25p par exchanged for $44.94563 cash

PLETHORA RES INC (NV)
Name changed to Sync2 Networks Corp. 05/14/2009
Sync2 Networks Corp. recapitalized as Trex Acquisition Corp. 03/20/2014

PLEXMAR RES INC (CANADA)
Reincorporated 08/25/1994
Place of incorporation changed from (ON) to (Canada) 08/25/1994
Acquired by Dia Bras Exploration Inc. 11/19/2012
Each share Common no par exchanged for $0.01 cash

PLEXORE ROUYN GOLD MINES, LTD. (ON)
Dissolved in 1958

PLEXTERRE MINING CORP. LTD. (ON)
Merged into Medallion Mines Ltd. 5/22/64
Each share Capital Stock $1 par exchanged for (1) share Common no par
Medallion Mines Ltd. charter cancelled in March, 1968

PLEXUS ENERGY LTD (AB)
Merged into Surge Petroleum Inc. 07/07/2000
Each share Common no par exchanged for (0.35429583) share Common no par
Surge Petroleum Inc. merged into Innova Exploration Ltd. 04/16/2004
(See Innova Exploration Ltd.)

PLEXUS RES CORP (BC)
Merged into Kinross Gold Corp. 5/31/93
Each share Common no par exchanged for (1.8) shares Common no par

PLIANT CORP (DE)
Plan of reorganization under Chapter 11 Federal Bankruptcy proceedings effective 12/03/2009
No stockholders' equity

PLIANT SYS INC (DE)
Plan of reorganization under Chapter 11 Federal Bankruptcy Code effective 07/22/2002
No stockholders' equity

PLIGROWTH FD INC (DE)
Merged into Plitrend Fund, Inc. 07/23/1982
Each share Capital Stock $1 par exchanged for (1.100850865) shares Common 1¢ par
Plitrend Fund, Inc. name changed to U.S. Trend Fund, Inc. (PA) 02/00/1986 which reincorporated in Maryland as Capstone U.S. Trend Fund, Inc. 05/11/1992 which name changed to Capstone Growth Fund, Inc. 08/26/1994 which name changed to Capstone Series Fund, Inc. 01/22/2002

PLIMONEY FD INC (PA)
Name changed to Investors Cash Reserve Fund, Inc. 02/28/1986
(See Investors Cash Reserve Fund, Inc.)

PLIMPTON MANUFACTURING CO.
Liquidated in 1935

PLITREND FD INC (PA)
Name changed to U.S. Trend Fund, Inc. (PA) 02/00/1986
U.S. Trend Fund, Inc. (PA) reincorporated in Maryland as Capstone U.S. Trend Fund, Inc. 05/11/1992 which name changed to Capstone Growth Fund, Inc. 08/26/1994 which name changed to Capstone Series Fund, Inc. 01/22/2002

PLIVA D D (CROATIA)
GDR agreement terminated 06/19/2008
Each Reg. S GDR for Ordinary exchanged for $31.30 cash
Each 144A GDR for Ordinary exchanged for $31.30 cash

PLM COS INC (DE)
Name changed 12/31/85
Name changed from PLM Financial Services, Inc. (CA) to PLM Companies, Inc. (DE) and Common no par reclassified as Class B Common 1¢ par 12/31/85
Stock Dividends - In Class A Common to holders of Class B Common 100% 3/10/86
Class A Common 10% 9/30/87; Class B Common 10% 9/30/87
Name changed to Transcisco Industries, Inc. (Old) 2/1/88
Transcisco Industries, Inc. (Old) reorganized as Transcisco Industries, Inc. (New) 11/3/93 which merged into Trinity Industries, Inc. 9/3/96

PLM EQUIP GROWTH FD (CA)
Completely liquidated
Each Unit of Ltd. Partnership Int. III received first and final distribution of $0.25 cash 08/20/2004
Each Unit of Ltd. Partnership Int. II received first and final distribution of approximately $1.056 cash 12/06/2004
Each Unit of Ltd. Partnership Int. IV received first and final distribution of approximately $0.658 cash 12/20/2004
Each Unit of Ltd. Partnership Int. V received initial distribution of $0.50 cash payable 05/19/2005 to holders of record 05/01/2005 Ex date - 05/20/2005
Each Unit of Ltd. Partnership Int. V received second distribution of $2.04 cash payable 11/11/2005 to holders of record 11/01/2005 Ex date - 11/14/2005
Each Unit of Ltd. Partnership Int. V received third and final distribution of $0.73 cash payable 05/31/2007 to holders of record 05/18/2007 Ex date - 06/01/2007
Each Unit of Ltd. Partnership Int. VI received initial distribution of $0.20 cash payable 05/19/2005 to holders of record 05/01/2005 Ex date - 05/20/2007
Each Unit of Ltd. Partnership Int. VI received second distribution of $1.70 cash payable 05/30/2006 to holders of record 15/16/2006 Ex date - 05/18/2006
Each Unit of Ltd. Partnership Int. VI received third and final distribution of $1.09 cash payable 05/31/2007 to holders of record 05/18/2007 Ex date - 06/01/2007
Note: Certificates were not required to be surrendered and are without value

PLM EQUIP GROWTH FD LIQUIDATING TR (CA)
Name changed 09/30/2003
Assets transferred from PLM Equipment Growth Fund to PLM Equipment Growth Fund Liquidating Trust 09/30/2003
Completely liquidated
Each Unit of Bene. Int. received first and final distribution of approximately $1.799 cash 12/20/2004
Note: Certificates were not required to be surrendered and are without value

PLM EQUIP GROWTH FD II (CA)
Completely liquidated
Each Unit of Ltd. Partnership Int. received first and final distribution of approximately $1.056 cash 12/06/2004
Note: Certificates were not required to be surrendered and are without value

PLM GROUP LTD (AB)
Acquired by Transcontinental Inc. 11/20/2007
Each share Common no par exchanged for $3.50 cash

PLM INTL INC (DE)
Each share old Common no par exchanged for (0.005) share new Common no par to reflect a (1) for (200) reverse split followed by a (200) for (1) forward split 11/26/97
Note: Holders of (199) or fewer shares received $5.58 cash per share
Under plan of partial liquidation each share new Common no par received distribution of $5 cash payable 11/3/2000 to holders of record 10/22/2000 Ex date - 11/6/2000
Merged into MILPI Holdings, LLC 2/6/2002
Each share new Common no par exchanged for $3.46 cash

PLM TRANSPORTATION EQUIPMENT PARTNERS VII (CA)
Unit of Ltd. Partnership Int. registration terminated and Partnership no longer public as of 00/00/1998

PLOMB TOOL CO. (CA)
Stock Dividend - 20% 02/28/1956
Name changed to Pendleton Tool Industries, Inc. 01/08/1957
Pendleton Tool Industries, Inc. acquired by Ingersoll-Rand Co. (NJ) 02/28/1964 which reorganized in Bermuda as Ingersoll-Rand Co. Ltd. 12/31/2001 which reincorporated in Ireland as Ingersoll-Rand PLC 07/01/2009

PLOUGH INC (DE)
Common no par changed to $7.50 par 00/00/1939
Common $7.50 par changed to $5 par and (0.5) additional share issued 00/00/1946
Common $5 par changed to $2.50 par and (1) additional share issued 05/25/1956
Common $2.50 par changed to $1.25 par and (1) additional share issued 08/03/1962
Common $1.25 par split (2) for (1) by issuance of (1) additional share 04/26/1968
Merged into Schering-Plough Corp. 01/16/1971
Each share $2.20 Conv. Preferred $1.25 par exchanged for (1) share $2.20 Conv. Preferred Ser. A $1 par
Each share Common $1.25 par exchanged for (1.3) shares Common $1 par
Schering-Plough Corp. merged into Merck & Co., Inc. (New) 11/03/2009

PLP HLDGS INC (DE)
Each share Common $0.0001 par received distribution of (0.25) share Napuda Technologies, Inc. Common $0.001 par payable 2/2/2003 to holders of record 1/29/2003 Ex date - 1/27/2003
Each share Common $0.0001 par received distribution of (0.01) share Global Premier Investment Group Inc. Common $0.001 par payable 5/19/2003 to holders of record 5/19/2003 Ex date - 5/15/2003
Name changed to Tonogold Resources, Inc. 9/13/2004
Each share Common $0.001 par exchanged for (1) share Common $0.001 par

PLR INC (DE)
Reorganized under the laws of Nevada as Integrated Carbonics Corp. 12/08/1997
Each share Common $0.001 par exchanged for (0.01) share Common $0.001 par
Integrated Carbonics Corp. name changed to Urbana.CA, Inc. 08/11/1999 which recapitalized as Pitts & Spitts, Inc. 07/17/2002 which name changed to PSPP Holdings, Inc. 06/17/2004 which recapitalized as Mod Hospitality, Inc. 09/22/2008 which recapitalized as Stakool, Inc. 12/16/2009 which name changed to Fresh Promise Foods, Inc. 11/12/2013

PLS CORP (DE)
Charter cancelled and declared inoperative and void for non-payment of taxes 3/1/75

PLUM CREEK TIMBER CO INC (DE)
Merged into Weyerhaeuser Co. 02/22/2016
Each share Common 1¢ par exchanged for (1.6) shares Common $1.25 par

PLUM CREEK TIMBER CO L P (DE)
Depositary Units split (3) for (1) by issuance of (2) additional Units 12/06/1993
Reorganized as Plum Creek Timber Co., Inc. 07/01/1999
Each Depositary Unit exchanged for (1) share Common 1¢ par
Plum Creek Timber Co., Inc. merged into Weyerhaeuser Co. 02/22/2016

PLUM URANIUM & METAL MINING LTD. (ON)
Each share Capital Stock $1 par exchanged for (5) shares Capital Stock 20¢ par 5/4/55
Merged into Consolidated Frederick Mines Ltd. on a (5) for (8) basis 9/9/57 which completed liquidation 10/23/61

PLUMA INC (NC)
Issue Information - 3,100,000 shares COM offered at $12 per share on 03/10/1997
Plan of Liquidation under Chapter 11 Federal Bankruptcy Code effective 11/20/99
Stockholders' equity unlikely

PLUMAS BK (QUINCY, CA)
Common no par split (3) for (2) by issuance of (0.5) additional share payable 06/15/1999 to holders of record 06/01/1999
Under plan of reorganization each share Common no par automatically became (1) share Plumas Bancorp Common no par 06/21/2002

PLUMB OIL INC (TX)
Merged into Harbert Energy Corp. 08/30/1983
Each share Common 1¢ par exchanged for $1.21 cash

PLUMBIC MINES CO. (UT)
Recapitalized as Piute Uranium Corp. on a (1) for (4) basis in 1954
Piute Uranium Corp. name changed to Mobilcraft Industries, Inc. 9/5/59
(See Mobilcraft Industries, Inc.)

PLUMBING MART AMER INC (NY)
Cease trade order effective 6/28/82
Stockholders' equity unlikely

PLUMBING MART CORP (ON)
Recapitalized as PMC Corp. 3/1/88
Each share Common no par exchanged for (0.1) share Common no par
PMC Corp. name changed to Floorco Ltd. 7/6/94
(See Floorco Ltd.)

PLUME & ATWOOD BRASS & COPPER CORP. (CT)
Name changed to Plume & Atwood Industries, Inc. 5/24/68
Plume & Atwood Industries, Inc. name changed to P & A Industries, Inc. 7/21/70
(See P & A Industries, Inc.)

PLUME & ATWOOD INDS INC (CT)
Name changed to P & A Industries, Inc. 07/21/1970
(See P & A Industries, Inc.)

PLUME & ATWOOD MANUFACTURING CO. (CT)
Each share Capital Stock $25 par exchanged for (4) shares Capital Stock no par 11/7/58
Name changed to Plume & Atwood Brass & Copper Corp. 6/18/64
Plume & Atwood Brass & Copper Corp. name changed to Plume & Atwood Industries, Inc. 5/24/68 which name changed to P & A Industries, Inc. 7/21/70
(See P & A Industries, Inc.)

PLUMTREE SOFTWARE INC (DE)
Each share Preferred Ser. A $0.001 par exchanged for (1) share Common $0.001 par 01/07/2003
Merged into BEA Systems, Inc. 10/20/2005
Each share Common $0.001 par exchanged for $5.50 cash

PLURES TECHNOLOGIES INC (DE)
Assets sold for the benefit of creditors 02/27/2014
Stockholders' equity unlikely

PLURIS ENERGY GROUP INC (NV)
Name changed to Nationwide Utilities Corp. 12/02/2009

PLURISTEM LIFE SYS INC (NV)
Recapitalized as Pluristem Therapeutics Inc. 11/26/2007
Each share Common $0.00001 par exchanged for (0.005) share Common $0.00001 par

PLUS8 GLOBAL VENTURES LTD (BC)
Name changed to ParcelPal Technology Inc. 03/22/2016

PLUS INTL CORP (CANADA)
Dissolved for failure to file annual reports 06/20/2006

PLUS PRODS (CA)
Merged into MacDonald Group, Ltd. 04/25/1977
Each share Common 10¢ par exchanged for $4.20 cash

PLUS SOLUTIONS INC (NV)
SEC revoked common stock registration 11/17/2009
Stockholders' equity unlikely

PLUSH CORP (NV)
Reorganized as TRON Group Inc. 12/28/2016
Each share Common $0.001 par exchanged for (20) shares Common $0.001 par

PLUSH MALL INC (NV)
Common $0.001 par split (10) for (1) by issuance of (9) additional shares payable 10/05/2007 to holders of record 10/05/2007
Name changed to Strongbow Resources Inc. 02/11/2008
Strongbow Resources Inc. name changed to Fortem Resources Inc. 03/30/2017

PLUTON INDS LTD (BC)
Name changed 07/03/1986
Name changed from Pluton Resource Corp. to Pluton Industries Ltd. 07/03/1986

PLU-PMI

PLUTON URANIUM MINES LTD. (ON)
Recapitalized as Clarion Environmental Technologies, Inc. 12/18/1992
Each share Common no par exchanged for (0.25) share Common no par
Clarion Environmental Technologies, Inc. name changed to Clarion Resources Ltd. 12/05/1997
(See Clarion Resources Ltd.)

PLUTON URANIUM MINES LTD. (ON)
Charter revoked for failure to file reports and pay fees in September 1964

PLUTONIC CAP CORP (BC)
Recapitalized as Plutonic Capital Inc. 08/08/2003
Each share Common no par exchanged for (0.5) share Common no par
Plutonic Capital Inc. name changed to Plutonic Power Corp. 05/18/2004 which merged into Alterra Power Corp. 05/17/2011 which merged into Innergex Renewable Energy Inc. 02/07/2018

PLUTONIC PWR CORP (BC)
Name changed 05/18/2004
Name changed from Plutonic Capital Inc. to Plutonic Power Corp. 05/18/2004
Merged into Alterra Power Corp. 05/17/2011
Each share Common no par exchanged for (2.38) shares Common no par and $0.0001 cash
Note: Unexchanged certificates were cancelled and became without value 05/17/2017
Alterra Power Corp. merged into Innergex Renewable Energy Inc. 02/07/2018

PLUTONIC RESOURCES LTD. (AUSTRALIA)
Acquired by Homestake Mining Co. 04/30/1998
Each share Ordinary exchanged for (0.34) share Common $1 par
HomeStake Mining Co. merged into Barrick Gold Corp. 12/14/2001

PLUTUS CORP. (DE)
Name changed to Consolidated Mortgage & Investment Corp. 4/16/62
Consolidated Mortgage & Investment Corp. name changed to Outdoor Development Co., Inc. (DE) 4/14/66
(See Outdoor Development Co., Inc. (DE))

PLUTUS MINING CO. (UT)
Merged into Plutus Corp. on a (0.1) for (1) basis 2/6/61
Plutus Corp. name changed to Consolidated Mortgage & Investment Corp. 4/16/62 which name changed to Outdoor Development Co., Inc. (DE)
(See Outdoor Development Co., Inc.)

PLX TECHNOLOGY INC (DE)
Acquired by Avago Technologies Ltd. 08/12/2014
Each share Common $0.001 par exchanged for $6.50 cash

PLY GEM HLDGS INC (DE)
Acquired by Pisces Midco, Inc. 04/12/2018
Each share Common 1¢ par exchanged for $21.64 cash

PLY GEM INDS INC (DE)
Reincorporated 06/02/1987
6% Preferred $10 par called for redemption 01/31/1972
Common 25¢ par split (2) for (1) by issuance of (1) additional share 01/18/1983
Common 25¢ par split (3) for (2) by issuance of (0.5) additional share 12/14/1984
Common 25¢ par split (3) for (2) by issuance of (0.5) additional share 03/12/1986
Stock Dividend - 10% 01/19/1979
State of incorporation changed from (NY) to (DE) 06/02/1987
Merged into Nortek, Inc. 09/04/1997
Each share Common 25¢ par exchanged for $19.50 cash

PLYDOM LTD (ON)
Charter cancelled for failure to pay taxes and file returns 03/16/1976

PLYMOUTH BOX & PANEL CO.
Acquired by Atlas Plywood Corp. 00/00/1946
Details not available

PLYMOUTH COOPERAGE CORP.
Dissolved in 1939

PLYMOUTH CORDAGE CO. (MA)
Each share Common $100 par exchanged for (4) shares Common $25 par in 1945
Merged into Emhart Corp. (Conn.) 1/31/66
Each share Common $25 par exchanged for (2.5) shares Common $6.25 par
Emhart Corp. (Conn.) reincorporated in Virginia 5/4/76
(See Emhart Corp. (Va.))

PLYMOUTH FINL CORP (BC)
Recapitalized as New Plymouth Ventures Inc. 8/16/85
Each share Class A Common no par exchanged for (0.2) share Common no par
Each share Class B Common no par exchanged for (0.2) share Common no par
(See New Plymounth Ventures Inc.)

PLYMOUTH FINL CORP (MI)
Filed Certificate of Dissolution 08/16/2010
Details not available

PLYMOUTH FIVE CENTS SVGS BK (PLYMOUTH, MA)
Bank closed and FDIC appointed receiver 9/18/92
No stockholders' equity

PLYMOUTH FUND, INC. (FL)
Charter revoked for failure to pay taxes 8/28/64

PLYMOUTH HOME NATL BK (BROCKTON, MA)
Stock Dividend - 50% 03/01/1971
Charterbank, Inc. held 99.56% as of 09/12/1974
Public interest eliminated

PLYMOUTH NATL BK (PLYMOUTH, PA)
Merged into Northeastern Bank of Pennsylvania (Scranton, PA) 09/30/1974
Each share Common $25 par exchanged for (18) shares Capital Stock $10 par
Northeastern Bank of Pennsylvania (Scranton, PA) reorganized as Northeastern Bancorp, Inc. 08/12/1981 which merged into PNC Financial Corp. 01/30/1985 which name changed to PNC Bank Corp. 02/08/1993 which name changed to PNC Financial Services Group, Inc. 03/15/2000

PLYMOUTH OIL & GAS LTD (BC)
Recapitalized as Plymouth Financial Corp. 12/20/83
Each share Common no par exchanged for (1) share Class A Common no par and (1) share Class B Common no par
Plymouth Financial Corp. recapitalized as New Plymouth Ventures Inc. 8/16/85
(See New Plymouth Ventures Inc.)

PLYMOUTH OIL CO. (DE)
Stock Dividend - 100% 7/30/51
Liquidation completed
Each share Common $5 par stamped to indicate initial distribution of $30 cash 4/12/62
Each share Common $5 par stamped to indicate second distribution of $3 cash 8/23/62
Each share Common $5 par stamped to indicate third distribution of $0.40 cash 2/14/63
Each share Common $5 par exchanged for fourth and final distribution of $0.545 cash 5/18/66

PLYMOUTH RUBR INC (MA)
Class A Common $2 par changed to $5 par 2/24/55
Class A Common $5 par changed to $1 par in April 1987
Class B Common $5 par changed to $1 par in April 1987
Class A Common $1 par changed to 1¢ par 4/29/2003
Class B Common $1 par changed to 1¢ par 4/29/2003
Stock Dividends - (1) share Class B Common for each share Class A Common or VTC for Class A Common 8/15/63; 10% 5/23/95; 5% payable 8/19/96 to holders of record 6/24/96
Plan of reorganization under Chapter 11 Federal Bankruptcy Code effective 8/31/2006
No stockholders' equity

PLYMOUTH SECS TR (MA)
Reorganized as Fidelity Securities Trust 01/29/1992
Details not available

PLYMPTON URANIUM & METAL MINES LTD. (ON)
Merged into Consolidated Frederick Mines Ltd. on an (2) for (3) basis 9/9/57 which completed liquidation 10/23/61

PM AGRI-NUTRITION GROUP LTD (DE)
Issue Information - 2,185,000 shares COM offered at $6 per share on 07/12/1994
Name changed to Agri-Nutrition Group Ltd. 3/13/95
Agri-Nutrition Group Ltd. name changed to Virbac Corp. 3/5/99
(See Virbac Corp.)

PM INDS INC (NV)
Charter revoked for failure to file reports and pay fees 6/1/87

PM&E INC. (NY)
Dissolved 10/29/2009
Details not available

PMA CAP CORP (PA)
Common $5 par reclassified as Class A Common $5 par 04/24/2000
Merged into Old Republic International Corp. 10/01/2010
Each share Class A Common $5 par exchanged for (0.55) share Common $1 par

PMA RES INC (BC)
Recapitalized as Cassidy Gold Corp. 9/13/96
Each share Common no par exchanged for (0.25) share Common no par

PMC BETA CORP (MA)
Voluntarily dissolved 06/16/1989
Details not available

PMC CAP INC (FL)
Merged into PMC Commercial Trust (TX) 02/29/2004
Each share Common 1¢ par exchanged for (0.37) Share of Bene. Int. 1¢ par
PMC Commercial Trust (TX) reorganized in Maryland as CIM Commerical Trust Corp. 04/29/2014

PMC COML TR (TX)
Reorganized under the laws of Maryland as CIM Commerical Trust Corp. 04/29/2014
Each Share of Bene. Int. 1¢ par exchanged for (0.2) share Common $0.001 par

PMC CORP (ON)
Name changed to Floorco Ltd. 7/6/94
(See Floorco Ltd.)

PMC INTL INC (CO)
Each share old Common 1¢ par exchanged for (0.2) share new Common 1¢ par 11/15/1993
Each share new Common 1¢ par exchanged again for (0.25) share new Common 1¢ par 12/30/1997
Merged into ZACQ Corp. 12/31/1998
Each $0.325 Conv. Preferred Ser. A no par exchanged for $2.50 cash
Each share Common 1¢ par exchanged for $0.60 cash

PMC POWDERED METALS CORP (AZ)
Charter revoked for failure to file reports or pay fees 2/10/93

PMC-SIERRA INC (DE)
Reincorporated 07/10/1997
State of incorporation changed from (CA) to (DE) and Common no par changed to $0.001 par 07/10/1997
Common $0.001 par split (2) for (1) by issuance of (1) additional share payable 05/14/1999 to holders of record 04/30/1999
Common $0.001 par split (2) for (1) by issuance of (1) additional share payable 02/11/2000 to holders of record 01/31/2000
Merged into Microsemi Corp. 01/14/2016
Each share Common $0.001 par exchanged for (0.0771) share Common 20¢ par and $9.22 cash
(See Microsemi Corp.)

PMCC FINL CORP (DE)
Issue Information - 1,250,000 shares COM offered at $9 per share on 02/17/1998
Name changed to Geneva Financial Corp. 04/14/2003
(See Geneva Financial Corp.)

PMD INVT CO (NE)
Completely liquidated 11/3/2000
Each share Common 50¢ par exchanged for first and final distribution of $4.1031338 cash

PMFG INC (DE)
Merged into CECO Environmental Corp. 09/03/2015
Each share Common 1¢ par exchanged for (0.6456) share Common 1¢ par

PMG FINL INC (ON)
Stock Dividend - 10% 12/23/1993
Name changed to Printera Corp. 05/08/1996
(See Printera Corp.)

PMI CONSTR GROUP (NV)
Recapitalized as Kung Fu Dragon Group Ltd. 06/11/2015
Each share Common $0.001 par exchanged for (0.02) share Common $0.001 par

PMI FD INC (NY)
Completely liquidated 04/06/1992
Each share Common 1¢ par exchanged for first and final distribution of $5.0819 cash

PMI GOLD CORP (BC)
Each share old Common no par exchanged for (0.5) share new Common no par 10/22/2014
Merged into Asanko Gold Inc. 02/10/2014
Each share new Common no par exchanged for (0.21) share Common no par
Note: Unexchanged certificates will be cancelled and become without value 02/10/2020

PMI GROUP INC (DE)
Each 5.875% Corporate Unit

automatically became (0.578) share Common 1¢ par 11/15/2006
Common 1¢ par split (3) for (2) by issuance of (0.5) additional share payable 08/16/1999 to holders of record 07/30/1999 Ex date - 08/17/1999
Common 1¢ par split (2) for (1) by issuance of (1) additional share payable 06/17/2002 to holders of record 05/31/2002 Ex date - 06/18/2002
Plan of reorganization under Chapter 11 Federal Bankruptcy proceedings effective 10/01/2013
No stockholders' equity

PMI HLDGS CORP (MD)
Charter forfeited for failure to file annual reports 10/05/1992

PMI INC (NY)
Each share old Common $0.0001 par exchanged for (0.1) share new Common $0.0001 par 3/31/89
Charter cancelled and proclaimed dissolved for failure to pay taxes 9/29/93

PMI RES LTD (BC)
Name changed to PentaNova Energy Corp. 06/05/2017
PentaNova Energy Corp. recapitalized as CruzSur Energy Corp. 09/04/2018

PMI VENTURES LTD (BC)
Name changed to PMI Gold Corp. 05/23/2006
PMI Gold Corp. merged into Asanko Gold Inc. 02/10/2014

PML INC (DE)
Each share old Common 1¢ par exchanged for (1) share new Common 1¢ par to reflect a (1) for (150) reverse split followed by a (150) for (1) forward split 8/6/2003
Note: Holders of (149) or fewer pre-split shares received $1.50 cash per share
Merged into a private company in December 2005
Each share new Common 1¢ par exchanged for approximately $5.05 cash
Note: Each share Common 1¢ par received an additional distribution from escrow of approximately $0.53 cash 5/23/2007

PMR CORP (DE)
Each share Common 1¢ par received distribution of (1) Contingent Value Right payable 08/09/2002 to holders of record 08/02/2002
Recapitalized as Psychiatric Solutions, Inc. 08/05/2002
Each share Common 1¢ par exchanged for (1/3) share Common 1¢ par
Note: Each Contingent Value Right received distribution of $0.10160112 cash payable 11/04/2002 to holders of record 11/04/2002
(See Psychiatric Solutions, Inc.)

PMS INDS INC (NY)
Name changed to Kessler Graphics Corp. 12/27/74
(See Kessler Graphics Corp.)

PMT SVCS INC (TN)
Common 1¢ par split (2) for (1) by issuance of (1) additional share payable 1/15/96 to holders of record 12/29/95
Common 1¢ par split (3) for (2) by issuance of (0.5) additional share payable 6/12/96 to holders of record 5/28/96
Merged into Nova Corp. (GA) 9/24/98
Each share Common 1¢ par exchanged for (0.715) share Common 1¢ par
(See Nova Corp. (GA))

PMT TAX-EXEMPT BOND FUND (NY)
Name changed to PBT Tax-Exempt Bond Fund 7/1/73

PN MED GROUP INC (NV)
Common $0.001 par split (3.462) for (1) by issuance of (2.462) additional shares payable 12/16/2013 to holders of record 12/06/2013 Ex date - 12/17/2013
Name changed to Ekso Bionics Holdings, Inc. 12/23/2013

PNB CORP (PA)
Common $1 par split (2) for (1) by issuance of (1) additional share 01/02/1970
Name changed to Philadelphia National Corp. 04/23/1973
Philadelphia National Corp. merged into CoreStates Financial Corp 05/02/1983 which merged into First Union Corp. 04/28/1998 which name changed to Wachovia Corp. (Ctfs. dated after 09/01/2001) 09/01/2001 which merged into Wells Fargo & Co. (New) 12/31/2008

PNB FINL GROUP (CA)
Stock Dividend - 15% payable 4/15/98 to holders of record 3/31/98
Merged into Western Bancorp 12/30/98
Each share Common $2 par exchanged for (1) share Common no par
Western Bancorp merged into U.S Bancorp (Old) 11/15/99 which merged into U.S. Bancorp (New) 2/27/2001

PNB MTG & RLTY INVS (MD)
Shares of Bene. Int. $1 par reclassified as Common $1 par 04/22/1981
Name changed to Mortgage & Realty Trust 12/17/1984
Mortgage & Realty Trust name changed to Value Property Trust 10/27/1995 which merged into Wellsford Real Properties, Inc. 02/23/1998 which name changed to Reis, Inc. 06/01/2007
(See Reis, Inc.)

PNC CAP TR D (DE)
6.125% Capital Securities called for redemption at $25 on 04/25/2012

PNC CAP TR E (DE)
7.75% Guaranteed Trust Preferred Securities called for redemption at $25 on 07/30/2012

PNC FINL SVCS GROUP CORP (PA)
Name changed 02/08/1993
Name changed 03/15/2000
Common $5 par split (2) for (1) by issuance of (1) additional share 07/01/1985
Common $5 par split (2) for (1) by issuance of (1) additional share 11/13/1992
$2.60 Preferred Ser. E $1 par called for redemption 01/15/1993
Name changed from PNC Financial Corp. to PNC Bank Corp. 02/08/1993
Name changed from PNC Bank Corp. to PNC Financial Services Group, Inc. 03/15/2000
Adjustable Fixed Rate Preferred Ser. F $1 called for redemption at $50 plus $0.0455 accrued dividends on 10/04/2001
$1.60 Conv. Preferred Ser. C $1 par called for redemption at $20 on 10/01/2010
$1.80 Conv. Preferred Ser. D $1 par called for redemption at $20 on 10/01/2010
$1.80 Conv. Preferred Ser. A $1 par called for redemption at $40 on 04/05/2011
9.875% Depositary Preferred Ser. L $1 par called for redemption at $25 plus $0.354441 accrued dividends on 04/19/2013

(Additional Information in Active)

PNC LIQUIDATING CORP. (DE)
Completely liquidated 11/30/70
Each share Common 10¢ par exchanged for first and final distribution of (0.095) share Oxford First Corp. (Pa.) Common $1 par
(See Oxford First Corp. (Pa.))

PNEUCYCLIC SCIENCES INC (DE)
Charter cancelled and declared inoperative and void for non-payment of taxes 6/27/74

PNEUMATIC SCALE CORP. LTD. (MA)
Common $10 par changed to $5 par and (1) additional share issued 6/19/64
Name changed to Pneumatic Scale Corp. 8/12/65
(See Pneumatic Scale Corp.)

PNEUMATIC SCALE CORP (MA)
Common $5 par changed to $2.50 par and (1) additional share issued 08/27/1965
Common $2.50 par changed to $2 par and (0.25) additional share issued 06/26/1973
Merged into Value Investments Inc. 12/19/1989
Each share Common $2 par exchanged for $29 cash

PNEUMATIC TRANSN SYS INC (WY)
Charter revoked for failure to pay taxes 03/04/1987

PNEUMO CORP (DE)
Common $1 par split (3) for (2) by issuance of (0.5) additional share 11/24/1980
Common $1 par split (3) for (2) by issuance of (0.5) additional share 10/25/1982
Common $1 par split (2) for (1) by issuance of (1) additional share 05/02/1983
Merged into IC Industries, Inc. 10/18/1984
Each share Common $1 par exchanged for (1.49) shares Common no par
IC Industries, Inc. name changed to Whitman Corp. (Old) 12/01/1988 which name changed to Whitman Corp. (New) 11/30/2000 which name changed to PepsiAmericas, Inc. (DE) 01/24/2001 which merged into PepsiCo, Inc. 02/26/2010

PNEUMO DYNAMICS CORP. (DE)
Common $1 par split (2) for (1) by issuance of (1) additional share 04/19/1966
Name changed to Pneumo Corp. 04/05/1974
Pneumo Corp. merged into IC Industries, Inc. 10/18/1984 which name changed to Whitman Corp. (Old) 12/01/1988 which name changed to Whitman Corp. (New) 11/30/2000 which name changed to PepsiAmericas, Inc. (DE) 01/24/2001 which merged into PepsiCo, Inc. 02/26/2010

PNF INDS INC (DE)
Reorganized as No Fire Technologies, Inc. 08/11/1995
Each share Common $0.0001 par exchanged for (0.67) share Common $0.0001 par

PNG GOLD CORP (BC)
Each share old Common no par exchanged for (0.2) share new Common no par 11/11/2016
Name changed to Gen III Oil Corp. 05/16/2017

PNG VENTURES INC NEW (NV)
Each share old Common no par exchanged for (0.004) share new Common no par 10/25/2004
Plan of reorganization under Chapter 11 Federal Bankruptcy Code effective 03/24/2010

No stockholders' equity

PNG VENTURES INC OLD (NV)
Common no par split (3) for (1) by issuance of (2) additional shares payable 03/10/2000 to holders of record 03/06/2000
Name changed to Paper Computer Corp. 05/01/2000
Paper Computer Corp. recapitalized as PNG Ventures Inc. (New) 07/05/2001
(See PNG Ventures Inc. (New))

PNI DIGITAL MEDIA INC (BC)
Acquired by Staples, Inc. 07/16/2014
Each share Common no par exchanged for $1.70 cash

PNI TECHNOLOGIES INC (GA)
Petition filed under Chapter 11 Federal Bankruptcy Code dismissed 10/01/2004
No stockholders' equity

PNM RES INC (NM)
Each 6.75% Equity Unit received (1.9016) shares Common $5 par 05/16/2008
(Additional Information in Active)

PNO RES LTD (BC)
Each share old Common no par exchanged for (0.1) share new Common no par 01/17/2014
Merged into Sandspring Resources Ltd. 09/15/2015
Each share new Common no par exchanged for (1) share new Common no par
Note: Unexchanged certificates will be cancelled and become without value 09/15/2021

PNP PRIME CORP (DE)
Liquidation under Chapter 7 Federal Bankruptcy Code approved 7/30/92
Stockholders' equity unlikely

PNR FOOD INDS LTD (ON)
Assignment in Bankruptcy filed 05/11/1988
No stockholders' equity

PNV INC (DE)
Assets sold for the benefit of creditors 02/14/2001
No stockholders' equity

PNW CAP INC (DE)
Each share old Common $0.0001 par exchanged for (0.01) share new Common $0.0001 par 01/07/2002
Name changed to Industrial Minerals, Inc. 05/01/2002
Industrial Minerals, Inc. recapitalized as Mindesta Inc. 07/26/2011 which recapitalized as CTT Pharmaceutical Holdings, Inc. 08/28/2015

PNX INDS INC (DE)
Charter forfeited for failure to maintain a registered agent 02/25/1991

PO FOLKS INC (DE)
Reorganized under Chapter 11 Federal Bankruptcy Code 01/31/1989
No old Common stockholders' equity
Company believed out of business 00/00/2005
Details not available

POCAHONTAS BANCORP INC (DE)
Merged into IBERIABANK Corp. 2/1/2007
Each share Common 1¢ par exchanged for (0.2781) share Common $1 par

POCAHONTAS BANKSHARES CORP (WV)
Common $6.25 par changed to $2.50 par and (1.5) additional shares issued 12/01/1986
Common $2.50 par changed to $1.25 par and (1) additional share issued 05/20/1994
Name changed to First Century Bankshares Inc. 07/08/1999
(See First Century Bankshares Inc.)

POCAHONTAS FED SVGS & LN ASSN (USA)
Reorganized under the laws of Delaware as Pocahontas Bancorp, Inc. 3/31/98
Each share Common no par exchanged for (4.0245) shares Common 1¢ par
Pocahontas Bancorp, Inc. merged into IBERIABANK Corp. 2/1/2007

POCATERRA ENERGY INC (AB)
Acquired by Buffalo Oil Corp. 01/01/2007
Each share Common no par exchanged for (0.2) share Common no par and $0.575 cash
Buffalo Oil Corp. name changed to Buffalo Resources Corp. 08/03/2007 which merged into Twin Butte Energy Ltd. 10/15/2009

POCCO INC (OR)
Involuntarily dissolved for failure to pay fees 04/22/1982

POCI INC (DE)
Assets transferred 12/31/1992
In process of liquidation
Each share Common 20¢ par received initial distribution of $0.25 cash 12/15/1992
Assets transferred to POCI Inc. Liquidating Trust and Common 20¢ par reclassified as Shares of Bene. Int. 20¢ par 12/31/1992
Charter cancelled and declared inoperative and void for non-payment of taxes 09/18/1993

POCKET BOOKS, INC. (NY)
Name changed to Simon & Schuster, Inc. 6/30/66
Simon & Schuster, Inc. merged into Gulf & Western Industries, Inc. (DE) 6/12/75 which name changed to Gulf + Western Inc. 5/1/86 which name changed to Paramount Communications Inc. 6/5/89 which merged Viacom Inc. (Old) 7/7/94
(See Viacom Inc. (Old))

POCKET-SPEC TECHNOLOGIES INC (CO)
Reincorporated under the laws of Nevada as Falcon Ridge Development, Inc. 07/18/2005
(See Falcon Ridge Development, Inc.)

POCKETS HLDG CORP (AZ)
Name changed to Inworlds.Com, Inc. 5/13/99
Inworlds.Com, Inc. name changed to Avaterra.Com, Inc. 6/22/99 which recapitalized as Xtreme Motorsports of California, Inc. 2/17/2006 which name changed to Extreme Motorsports of California, Inc. 5/21/2007

POCML 4 INC (ON)
Recapitalized as MediPharm Labs Corp. 10/04/2018
Each share Common no par exchanged for (0.5) share Common no par

POCML 3 INC (ON)
Recapitalized as Neo Lithium Corp. 07/20/2016
Each share Common no par exchanged for (0.91) share Common no par

POCML 2 INC (ON)
Recapitalized as Bedrocan Cannabis Corp. 08/25/2014
Each share Common no par exchanged for (0.5) share Common no par
Bedrocan Cannabis Corp. merged into Tweed Marijuana Inc. 08/31/2015 which name changed to Canopy Growth Corp. 09/22/2015

POCO PETES LTD (AB)
Conv. 2nd Preferred Ser. A no par called for redemption 03/31/1992
Conv. 2nd Preferred Ser. D no par called for redemption 09/14/1993
Merged into Burlington Resources Inc. 11/18/1999
Each share Common no par exchanged for (0.25) share Common no par
Burlington Resources Inc. merged into ConocoPhillips 03/31/2006

POCON INC (UT)
Proclaimed dissolved for failure to pay taxes 12/31/86

POCONO CMNTY BK (STROUDSBURG, PA)
Merged into First Keystone Corp. 11/01/2007
Each share Common $2.50 par exchanged for (0.813904) share Common $2 par and $1.449 cash or $16.10 cash
Note: Holders electing stock and cash received approximately 91% of their consideration in stock and the balance in cash

POCONO HOTELS CORP (DE)
Reincorporated under the laws of Pennsylvania as Skytop Lodge Corp. 2/7/2000

POCONO MANOR ASSN (PA)
Class A Preferred no par called for redemption 07/11/1967
Class B Prefered no par called for redemption 07/11/1967
Class A Common no par called for redemption 03/01/1970
Liquidation completed
Each share Class B Common no par exchanged for initial distribution of $128 cash 06/00/1978
Each share Class B Common no par received second and final distribution of $7.45 cash 06/00/1979

PODIUM CAP CORP (CANADA)
Name changed to CRS Electronics Inc. 09/01/2009
(See CRS Electronics Inc.)

PODIUM VENTURE GROUP INC (DE)
Each share old Common $0.001 par exchanged for (0.00333333) share new Common $0.001 par 01/07/2008
Stock Dividend - 25% payable 01/15/2007 to holders of record 12/29/2006 Ex date - 01/16/2007
Name changed to Capital Oil & Gas, Inc. 08/07/2008
Capital Oil & Gas, Inc. recapitalized as Southcorp Capital, Inc. 01/28/2009

POE & BROWN INC (FL)
Name changed 04/28/1993
Common 10¢ par split (6) for (5) by issuance of (0.2) additional share 02/20/1980
Common 10¢ par split (3) for (2) by issuance of (0.5) additional share 03/23/1983
Common 10¢ par split (3) for (2) by issuance of (0.5) additional share 05/09/1986
Common 10¢ par split (5) for (4) by issuance of (0.25) additional share 05/29/1991
Name changed from Poe & Associates, Inc. to Poe & Brown, Inc. 04/28/1993
Common 10¢ par split (3) for (2) by issuance of (0.5) additional share payable 02/27/1998 to holders of record 01/30/1998 Ex date - 03/02/1998
Name changed to Brown & Brown, Inc. 04/28/1999

POET HLDGS INC (DE)
Merged into Versant Corp. 3/18/2004
Each share Ser. A Common $0.001 par exchanged for (1.4) shares Common no par

POGO PRODS LTD (NV)
Company terminated common stock registration and is no longer public as of 07/07/2005

POGO PRODUCING CO (DE)
Merged into Plains Exploration & Production Co. 11/06/2007
Each share Common $1 par exchanged for (1.187) shares Common 1¢ par
Plains Exploration & Production Co. merged into Freeport-McMoRan Copper & Gold Inc. 05/31/2013 which name changed to Freeport-McMoRan Inc. 07/14/2014

POGO TR I (DE)
6.5% Guaranteed Quarterly Income Preferred Ser. A called for redemption at $52.275 on 06/04/2002

POGUE (H. & S.) CO. (OH)
Each share Common $100 par exchanged for (5) shares Common $20 par in 1947
Each share Common $20 par exchanged for (3) shares Common $10 par in 1956
Merged into Associated Dry Goods Corp. 4/3/61
Each share Common $10 par exchanged for (0.25) share new Common $1 par
Associated Dry Goods Corp. merged into May Department Stores Co. 10/4/86 which merged into Federated Department Stores, Inc. 8/30/2005 which name changed to Macy's, Inc. 6/1/2007

POHANG IRON & STL LTD (KOREA)
Name changed to POSCO 03/15/2002

POHJOLA BANK PLC (FINLAND)
ADR agreement terminated 03/28/2016
No ADR's remain outstanding

POINSETT FINL CORP (SC)
Merged into Carolina First Corp. 06/26/1998
Each share Common 1¢ par exchanged for (3.8379) shares Common $1 par
Carolina First Corp. name changed to South Financial Group, Inc. 04/24/2000 which merged into Toronto-Dominion Bank (Toronto, ON) 09/30/2010

POINT ACQUISITION CORP (NV)
Each share old Common $0.001 par exchanged for (0.02) share new Common $0.001 par 12/11/2006
Note: No holder will receive fewer than (100) post-split shares
Name changed to China Minerals Technologies, Inc. 06/13/2007
China Minerals Technologies, Inc. name changed to China GengSheng Minerals, Inc. 07/30/2007

POINT BANCORP INC (DE)
Merged into One Valley Bancorp of West Virginia, Inc. 03/15/1995
Each share Common 1¢ par exchanged for (0.6) share Common $10 par and $7.10 cash
One Valley Bancorp of West Virginia, Inc. name changed to One Valley Bancorp, Inc. 04/30/1996 which merged into BB&T Corp. 07/06/2000

POINT BLANK SOLUTIONS INC (DE)
Plan of reorganization under Chapter 11 Federal Bankruptcy proceedings effective 11/23/2015
Holders may receive an undetermined amount of cash

POINT BUILDING, INC.
Liquidation completed in 1949

POINT GROUP HLDGS INC (NV)
Name changed to GameZnFlix, Inc. 02/05/2004
GameZnFlix, Inc. name changed to TBC Global News Network, Inc. 07/30/2009 which name changed to InCapta, Inc. 11/10/2015

POINT LOMA SAVINGS & LOAN ASSOCIATION (CA)
Common $8 par changed to $4 par 6/15/82
Name changed to Bank of Southern California, N.A. (San Diego, CA) 1/3/83
Bank of Southern California, N.A. (San Diego, CA) name changed to Bank of Southern California (San Diego, CA) 7/19/90 which merged into First National Bank (San Diego, CA) 9/30/96
(See First National Bank (San Diego, CA))

POINT NORTH ENERGY LTD (AB)
Plan of Arrangement under Companies' Creditors Arrangement Act effective 10/05/2007
No stockholders' equity

POINT OF CARE TECHNOLOGIES INC (NV)
Each share Common $0.001 par received distribution of (0.2173913) share Novolytic Corp. Common 1¢ par and (0.1) Common Stock Purchase Warrant expiring 10/5/2002 payable 8/28/2001 to holders of record 4/16/2001
Merged into La Mina Equities Corp. 9/9/2002
Each share Common $0.001 par exchanged for $0.02 cash

POINT OF SALE, INC.
Bankrupt in 1950

POINT OF SALE LTD (ISRAEL)
Issue Information - 2,750,000 shs. ORD offered at $7 per share on 07/10/1998
Name changed to Retalix Ltd. 11/20/2000
(See Retalix Ltd.)

POINT OF SALES INC. (MN)
Name changed to 324, Inc. 4/30/81
(See 324, Inc.)

POINT RES LTD (BC)
Struck off register and declared dissolved for failure to file returns 2/25/94

POINT THERAPEUTICS INC (DE)
Recapitalized as DARA BioSciences, Inc. 02/13/2008
Each share Common 1¢ par exchanged for (0.025) share Common 1¢ par
DARA BioSciences, Inc. merged into Midatech Pharma PLC 12/04/2015

POINT 360 OLD (CA)
Each share Common no par received distribution of (1) share New 360 Common no par payable 08/10/2007 to holders of record 08/07/2007
Merged into DG FastChannel, Inc. 08/14/2007
Each share Common no par exchanged for (0.1895) share Common $0.001 par
DG FastChannel, Inc. name changed to Digital Generation, Inc. 11/07/2011 which merged into Sizmek Inc. 02/07/2014
(See Sizmek Inc.)

POINT WEST CAP CORP (DE)
Filed a petition under Chapter 7 Federal Bankruptcy Code 09/24/2004
Stockholders' equity unlikely

POINTE COMMUNICATIONS CORP (NV)
Merged into Telscape International Inc. (New) 6/2/2000
Each share Common $0.00001 par exchanged for (0.223514) share Common $0.001 par
(See Telscape International Inc. (New))

POINTE FEDERAL SAVINGS BANK (BOCA RATON, FL)
Acquired by Pointe Financial Corp. 04/14/1997
Details not available

POINTER BREWING CO.
Property sold 00/00/1939
Details not available

POINTER EXPL CORP (AB)
Merged into Panatlas Energy Inc. 11/27/97
Each share Common no par exchanged for (1.4) shares Common no par
Panatlas Energy Inc. acquired by Velvet Exploration Ltd. 7/17/2000
(See Velvet Exploration Ltd.)

POINTER MINING & MILLING CO. (CO)
Charter dissolved for failure to file annual reports 01/01/1919

POINTS INTL LTD (ON)
Reincorporated under the laws of Canada 11/10/2004

POINTS NORTH DIGITAL TECHNOLOGIES INC (ON)
Name changed Peragis Inc. 01/01/2001
(See Peragis Inc.)

POINTS OF CALL AIRLS LTD (AB)
Struck off register for failure to file annual returns 04/01/1991

POINTSTAR ENTMT CORP (NV)
Each share old Common $0.001 par exchanged for (60) shares new Common $0.001 par 07/31/2007
Name changed to Bioshaft Water Technology, Inc. 09/28/2007

POKER BOOK GAMING CORP (FL)
Recapitalized as Silver Star Capital Holdings, Inc. 05/02/2007
Each share Common $0.001 par exchanged for (0.02) share Common $0.001 par
(See Silver Star Capital Holdings, Inc.)

POKER COM INC (FL)
Common $0.001 par split (3) for (1) by issuance of (2) additional shares payable 08/16/2000 to holders of record 08/04/2000 Ex date - 08/16/2000
Name changed to LegalPlay Entertainment Inc. 09/15/2003
LegalPlay Entertainment Inc. recapitalized as Synthenol Inc. (FL) 12/18/2006 which reincorporated in Nevada as SinoCubate, Inc. 11/25/2008 which name changed to Viking Investments Group, Inc. 07/16/2012 which name changed to Viking Energy Group, Inc. 05/08/2017

POKER MAGIC INC (MN)
Each (11) shares old Common $0.001 par exchanged for (1) share new Common $0.001 par 10/10/2012
Name changed to Mill City Ventures III, Ltd. 01/22/2013

POKER TV NETWORK INC (NV)
Recapitalized as PC Universe, Inc. 07/05/2006
Each share Common $0.001 par exchanged for (0.33333333) share Common $0.001 par
(See PC Universe, Inc.)

POKERTEK INC (NC)
Each share old Common no par exchanged for (0.4) share new Common no par 02/25/2011
Acquired by Multimedia Games, Inc. 10/01/2014
Each share Common no par exchanged for $1.35 cash

POL-INVEST HLDGS LTD (BC)
Name changed to Net Soft Systems Inc. 03/19/2003
Net Soft Systems Inc. recapitalized as Rhys Resources Ltd. 02/24/2011 which recapitalized as Pacific Rim Cobalt Corp. 10/24/2017

POLA RES LTD (BC)
Struck off register and declared dissolved for failure to file returns 6/11/93

POLAMET MINES LTD. (ON)
Charter revoked for failure to file reports and pay fees 9/28/64

POLAR BEAR DEV CORP (BC)
Struck off register and declared dissolved for failure to file returns 6/14/96

POLAR BEAR VENTURES LTD (BC)
Recapitalized as Iciena Ventures Inc. 02/24/1999
Each share Common no par exchanged for (0.125) share Common no par
Iciena Ventures Inc. recapitalized as Barksdale Capital Corp. 02/08/2013

POLAR CARGO SYS INC (DE)
Name changed to Coldwall, Inc. 6/2/2004
(See Coldwall, Inc.)

POLAR EXPLORATION & MINING CO. LTD. (ON)
Charter cancelled for failure to file reports and pay taxes May 1957

POLAR EXPRESS CORP (DE)
Merged into Aasche Transportation Services Inc. 12/21/95
Each share Common 1¢ par exchanged for (0.411) share Common $0.0001 par
Note: An additional distribution of (0.0105514) share per share was made 8/9/96
Aasche Transportation Services, Inc. name changed to Asche Transportation Services, Inc. 5/20/99
(See Asche Transporation Services, Inc.)

POLAR FROSTED FOODS, INC.
Dissolved 00/00/1951
Details not available

POLAR INNOVATIVE CAP INC (ON)
Recapitalized as Simplex Solutions Inc. 12/20/2004
Each share Common no par exchanged for (1/7) share Common no par

POLAR MOLECULAR CORP (UT)
Plan of reorganization under Chapter 11 Federal Bankruptcy proceedings confirmed 12/05/1994
No stockholders' equity

POLAR MOLECULAR HLDG CORP (DE)
SEC revoked common stock registration 11/25/2009
Stockholders' equity unlikely

POLAR STAR MNG CORP (CANADA)
Merged into Revelo Resources Corp. 12/17/2014
Each share Common no par exchanged for (0.26) share Common no par
Note: Unexchanged certificates will be cancelled and become without value 12/17/2020

POLAR VAC INDS INC (OH)
Charter cancelled for non-payment of taxes 12/15/1980

POLAR WAVE ICE & FUEL CO.
Acquired by City Ice & Fuel Co. 00/00/1928
Details not available

POLARAD ELECTRS CORP (NY)
Common $1 par changed to 50¢ par and (1) additional share issued 07/12/1960
Each share Common 50¢ par exchanged for (1/6) share Common 1¢ par 05/05/1971
Name changed to P.E.C. Electronics Corp. 02/07/1979
(See P.E.C. Electronics Corp.)

POLARIS ACQUISITION CORP (DE)
Issue Information - 18,000,000 UNITS consisting of (1) share COM and (1) WT offered at $10 per Unit on 01/11/2008
Name changed to HUGHES Telematics, Inc. 04/02/2009
(See HUGHES Telematics, Inc.)

POLARIS CORP. (WI)
Common $0.001 par changed to $1 par 05/01/1963
Merged into Natco Corp. 09/30/1966
Each share Common $1 par exchanged for (0.04) share $5 Conv. Preferred Ser. A $100 par
Natco Corp. name changed to Fuqua Industries, Inc. (PA) 02/13/1967 which reincorporated in Delaware 05/06/1968 which name changed to Actava Group Inc. 07/21/1993 which name changed to Metromedia International Group, Inc. 11/01/1995
(See Metromedia International Group, Inc.)

POLARIS DEVELOPMENT & MINING CO.
Assets acquired by Polaris Mining Co. in 1927
Polaris Mining Co. merged into Hecla Mining Co. (Wash.) 10/31/58 which was reincorporated in Delaware 6/6/83

POLARIS ENERGY CORP (BC)
Name changed to International Polaris Energy Corp. 03/12/1985
(See International Polaris Energy Corp.)

POLARIS FD INC (MA)
Common $1 par split (3) for (1) by issuance of (2) additional shares 8/15/68
Name changed back to Keystone International Fund Inc. 9/21/79

POLARIS FINL CORP (KS)
Common $10 par split (7) for (5) by issuance of (0.4) additional shares 4/1/76
Stock Dividend - 15% 4/1/80
Completely liquidated 9/29/83
Each share Common $10 par exchanged for first and final distribution of $37.40 cash

POLARIS GEOTHERMAL INC (YT)
Non-Vtg. Class B Common no par called for redemption at $1 on 03/31/2009
Merged into Ram Power, Corp. 10/20/2009
Each share Class A no par exchanged for (0.2467) share Common no par
Ram Power, Corp. recapitalized as Polaris Infrastructure Inc. 05/19/2015

POLARIS GOLD MINES (CANADA), LTD. (ON)
Acquired by Apollo Porcupine Mines Ltd. on a (1) for (3) basis in 1946
(See Apollo Porcupine Mines Ltd.)

POLARIS GOLD MINES OF CANADA LTD.
Succeeded by Polaris Gold Mines (Canada) Ltd. on a (1) for (5) basis in 1935
Polaris Gold Mines (Canada) Ltd. acquired by Apollo Porcupine Mines Ltd. in 1946
(See Apollo Porcupine Mines Ltd.)

POLARIS INDS PARTNERS L P (DE)
Class A Beneficial Assignment Limited Partnership Units split (2) for (1) by issuance of (1) additional Unit 08/18/1993
Merged into Polaris Industries Inc. 12/22/1994
Each Class A Beneficial Assignment Limited Partnership Unit exchanged for (1) share Common 1¢ par

POLARIS INTL METALS CORP (NV)
Reincorporated 12/30/1978
Common 10¢ par changed to 1¢ par 01/25/1974
State of incorporation changed from (AZ) to (NV) 12/30/1978
Charter revoked for failure to file reports and pay fees 09/01/1984

POLARIS MATLS CORP (BC)
Name changed 01/08/2015
Name changed from Polaris Materials Corp. to Polaris Materials Corp. 01/08/2015
Acquired by U.S. Concrete, Inc. 11/20/2017
Each share Common no par exchanged for $3.40 cash
Note: Unexchanged certificates will be cancelled and become without value 11/20/2023

POLARIS MINES LTD (BC)
Recapitalized as Titan-Polaris Mines Ltd. 5/28/73
Each share Capital Stock no par exchanged for (0.4) share Capital Stock no par
Titan-Polaris Mines Ltd. recapitalized as Saxton Industries Ltd. 7/28/75 which name changed to Delbancor Industries Inc. 10/6/87
(See Delbancor Industries Inc.)

POLARIS MINING CO. (DE)
Merged into Hecla Mining Co. (Wash.) on a (1/6) for (1) basis 10/31/58
Hecla Mining Co. (Wash.) reincorporated in Delaware 6/6/83

POLARIS MNG CO (UT)
Charter suspended for failure to file reports 12/31/1975

POLARIS OIL & GAS INC (CO)
Reorganized under the laws of Delaware as WEPCo Energy Co. 07/13/1984
Each share Common 1¢ par exchanged for (0.025) share Common 1¢ par
WEPCo Energy Co. recapitalized as American Atlas Resources Corp. 08/09/1993
(See American Atlas Resources Corp.)

POLARIS OIL CO. LTD.
Merged into Calvan Consolidated Oil & Gas Co. Ltd. and each share Common no par exchanged for (1) share new Capital Stock $1 par in 1951
Calvan Consolidated Oil & Gas Co. Ltd. completed liquidation 11/30/61

POLARIS RES INC (CO)
Proclaimed dissolved for failure to file reports 3/1/2000

POLAROID CORP (DE)
Each share assenting Class A $100 par exchanged for (2.4) shares 5% 1st Preferred $50 par and (0.2) share new Common $1 par in 1945
Each share non-assenting Class A $100 par exchanged for (2) shares 5% 1st Preferred $50 par and $20 cash in 1945
Each share assenting Class B $5 par exchanged for (2.8) shares $2.50 2nd Preferred $5 par and (0.4) share new Common $1 par in 1945
Each share non-assenting Class B $5 par exchanged for (2) shares $2.50 2nd Preferred $5 par and $40 cash in 1945
Each share old Common $1 par exchanged for (3) shares new Common $1 par in 1945
5% 1st Preferred $50 par called for redemption 9/24/63
$2.50 2nd Preferred $5 par called for redemption 9/24/63
New Common $1 par split (4) for (1) by issuance of (3) additional shares 1/28/65
New Common $1 par split (2) for (1)

by issuance of (1) additional share 3/15/68
Common $1 par split (2) for (1) by issuance of (1) additional share 6/26/87
Stock Dividends - 50% 2/26/54; 50% 2/10/56; 300% 10/10/57
Plan of reorganization under Chapter 11 Federal Bankruptcy Code effective 12/17/2003
No stockholders' equity

POLAROID HLDG CO (DE)
8% Preferred Ser. A $0.001 par called for redemption at $100 plus $5.6887 accrued dividends on 12/27/2004
Merged into Petters Group Worldwide, LLC 4/27/2005
Each share Common 1¢ par exchanged for $12.08 cash

POLARWEARZ INC (NV)
Name changed to Risingtide, Inc. 6/2/2004
Risingtide, Inc. name changed to Equiline Corp. 4/8/2005 which recapitalized as Chelsea Collection, Inc. 6/15/2005 which recapitalized as G-H-3 International Inc. 10/30/2006

POLCON CORP (QC)
Company wound up 01/13/1983
No stockholders' equity

POLE PERFECT STUDIOS INC (NV)
Common $0.001 par split (4) for (1) by issuance of (3) additional shares payable 12/14/2010 to holders of record 12/10/2010 Ex date - 12/15/2010
Name changed to Torchlight Energy Resources, Inc. 02/10/2011

POLE STAR COPPER CO. (DE)
Charter cancelled and declared inoperative and void for non-payment of taxes 03/17/1920

POLE STAR MINES LTD. (ON)
Merged into Newkirk Mining Corp. Ltd. 6/2/55
Each (12) shares Capital Stock $1 par changed for (1) share Capital Stock $1 par
Newkirk Mining Corp. Ltd. name changed to Continental Mining Exploration Ltd. 12/11/56 which merged into Augustus Exploration Ltd. 11/26/56 which merged into Consolidated Canadian Faraday Ltd. 5/4/67 which name changed to Faraday Resources Inc. 8/2/83 which merged into Conquest Exploration Co. Ltd. (New) (ALTA) 9/1/93 which merged into Alberta Energy Co. Ltd. 1/31/96 which merged into EnCana Corp. 1/3/2002

POLE TECH INTL INC (FL)
Name changed to International Construction Products Inc. 08/07/1998
International Construction Products Inc. recapitalized as Construction Products International, Inc. 03/30/1999 which recapitalized as Sports Pouch Beverage Co., Inc. 10/06/2014

POLEQUITY CORP (NY)
Reincorporated under the laws of Delaware as Total Education Corp. 6/6/69
(See Total Education Corp.)

POLICY MGMT SYS CORP (SC)
Common 1¢ par split (2) for (1) by issuance of (1) additional share 10/01/1983
Common 1¢ par split (2) for (1) by issuance of (1) additional share payable 06/15/1998 to holders of record 06/01/1998 Ex date - 06/16/1998
Name changed to MYND Corp. 09/28/2000
(See MYND Corp.)

POLICY MATIC CORP AMER (GA)
Proclaimed dissolved for failure to file annual reports 05/16/1978

POLICY VENDING CORP. (TX)
Charter revoked for failure to file reports and pay fees 5/19/50

POLICYHOLDERS' NATIONAL LIFE INSURANCE CO. (SD)
Under plan of merger name changed to National Reserve Life Insurance Co. (S.D.) 10/11/51
(See National Reserve Life Insurance Co. (S.D.))

POLIFLY FINL CORP (NJ)
SEC revoked common stock registration 01/20/2010
Stockholders' equity unlikely

POLISH AMERICAN NAVIGATION CORP. (DE)
No longer in existence having become inoperative and void for non-payment of taxes 4/1/30

POLISH TELS & MICROWAVE CORP (TX)
Issue Information - 525,000 Units consisting of (2) shares COM and (1) WT offered at $13.50 per Unit on 08/10/1994
Name changed to Telscape International Inc.(Old) 11/15/96
Telscape International Inc. (Old) merged into Telscape International Inc. (New) 6/2/2000
(See Telscape International Inc. (New))

POLITICAL CALLS INC (NV)
Each share old Common $0.001 par exchanged for (0.1) share new Common $0.001 par 01/31/2008
Name changed to Northern Empire Energy Corp. 12/01/2008
Northern Empire Energy Corp. name changed to SmartChase Corp. 12/03/2014

POLITICS COM INC (DE)
Each share Common 1¢ par received distribution of (1) share New Politics.Com, Inc. Common 1¢ par payable 01/31/2001 to holders of record 01/05/2001
Recapitalized as English Language Learning & Instruction Systems, Inc. 02/01/2001
Each share Common 1¢ par exchanged for (0.1) share Common 1¢ par
(See English Language Learning & Instruction Systems, Inc.)

POLK AUDIO INC (MD)
Merged into Polk Holding Corp. 6/23/2000
Each share Common 1¢ par exchanged for $12 cash

POLLAK MANUFACTURING CO.
Acquired by Noma Electric Corp. in 1946
Each share Common no par exchanged for (2/3) share Common $1 par
Noma Electric Corp. name changed to Northeast Capital Corp. in 1953 which merged into Mack Trucks, Inc. 10/1/59 which merged into Signal Oil & Gas Co. 9/1/67 which name changed to Signal Companies, Inc. 5/1/68 which merged into Allied-Signal Inc. 9/19/85 which name changed to AlliedSignal Inc. 4/26/93 which name changed to Honeywell International Inc. 12/1/99

POLLARD BANKNOTE INCOME FD (ON)
Reorganized under the laws of Canada as Pollard Banknote Ltd. 05/18/2010
Each Unit no par exchanged for (1) share Common no par

POLLED CATTLE LTD (AB)
Name changed to Ontarget Capital Inc. 02/22/1993
Ontarget Capital Inc. name changed to Gene Screen Inc. 10/20/1994 which recapitalized as Gene Screen Corp. 07/09/1996 which name changed to GeneVest Inc. 06/25/1998 which merged into Pinetree Capital Corp. 06/01/2004 which recapitalized as Pinetree Capital Ltd. 06/02/2004

POLLEX INC (NV)
Each share old Common $0.001 par exchanged for (0.00333333) share new Common $0.001 par 07/12/2017
Name changed to eMARINE Global Inc. 09/12/2017

POLLO TROPICAL INC (FL)
Merged into Carrols Corp. 7/20/98
Each share Common 1¢ par exchanged for $11 cash

POLLOCK PETE INC (CA)
Name changed to Pangea Petroleum Co. (CA) 5/29/84
Pangea Petroleum Co. (CA) reincorporated in Delaware 5/26/87 which name changed to Harcor Energy, Inc. 1/6/88
(See Harcor Energy, Inc.)

POLLUTION CTL & ENGR CORP (UT)
Name changed to Fremont Energy Corp. (UT) 09/22/1976
Fremont Energy Corp. reorganized in Delaware as Fremont Corp. 06/23/1993 which name changed to Wireless Frontier Internet Inc. 09/29/2003
(See Wireless Frontier Internet Inc.)

POLLUTION CTL CONSULTANTS INC (FL)
Proclaimed dissolved for failure to file reports and pay fees 09/03/1976

POLLUTION CTL INC (VT)
Charter revoked for failure to file annual reports 10/31/76

POLLUTION CTL INDS INC (DE)
Merged into Advanced Horizons Inc. 07/31/1983
Each share Common 1¢ par exchanged for $2.65 cash

POLLUTION CTL WALTHER INC (AL)
Name changed to 200 Office Park Drive, Inc. 04/18/1977
(See 200 Office Park Drive, Inc.)

POLLUTION CTLS INC (MN)
Name changed to Ensco, Inc. and Common 20¢ par changed to 1¢ par 08/13/1982
Ensco, Inc. reorganized as Environmental Systems Co. 08/18/1983
(See Environmental Systems Co.)

POLLUTION DYNAMICS CORP (NY)
Reorganized under the laws of Delaware as Environmental Dynamics, Inc. 2/9/71
Each share Common 5¢ par exchanged for (1) share Common 5¢ par
(See Environmental Dynamics, Inc.)

POLLUTION RESH & CTL CORP (CA)
Ctfs. dated prior to 6/23/88
Stock Dividend - 200% 4/30/71
Name changed to McMartin Inc. 6/23/88
(See McMartin Inc.)

POLLUTION RESH & CTL CORP (CA)
Ctfs. dated after 12/29/1989
Each share old Common no par exchanged for (0.25) share new Common no par 05/15/1998
Name changed to Universal Detection Technology 08/13/2003

POLLUTION SOLUTIONS INDS (NV)
Name changed to Amerecen Industries 3/1/72

Amerecen Industries name changed to Amrec Industries, Inc. 2/23/73
(See Amerec Industries, Inc.)

POLLY PECK INTL PLC (ENGLAND)
Each Unsponsored ADR for Ordinary 5p par exchanged for (1) Sponsored ADR for Ordinary 5p par 04/28/1987
Stock Dividends - 20% 02/13/1987; 20% 02/09/1988; 10% 06/06/1990
Placed in bankruptcy 10/25/1990
No ADR holders' equity

POLLY POND MINING CO. LTD. (ON)
Acquired by Polpond Mining Co. Ltd. on a (25) for (1) basis 8/8/58
Polpond Mining Co. Ltd. merged into Consolidated Panther Mines Ltd. 7/2/60 which recapitalized as Panthco Resources Inc. 7/3/87 which merged into Ztest Electronics, Inc. 7/1/96

POLO BIOLOGY GLOBAL GROUP CORP (BC)
Recapitalized as P&P Ventures Inc. 11/23/2012
Each share Common no par exchanged for (0.1) share Common no par

POLO EQUITIES INC (FL)
Reincorporated under the laws of Nevada as Hybrid Fuels, Inc. 06/01/1998
Hybrid Fuels, Inc. name changed to Nouveau Life Pharmaceuticals, Inc. 05/22/2012

POLO INVT CORP MO (FL)
Name changed 05/30/1984
Name changed from Polo Investment Corp. to Polo Investment Corp. of Missouri 05/30/1984
Name changed to Polo Equities Inc. (FL) 03/03/1997
Polo Equities Inc. (FL) reincorporated in Nevada as Hybrid Fuels, Inc. 06/01/1998 which name changed to Nouveau Life Pharmaceuticals, Inc. 05/22/2012

POLO PETE LTD (AB)
Merged into Attock Oil Corp. 02/04/1991
Each share Common no par exchanged for (0.54644808) share Class A Common no par
Attock Oil Corp. recapitalized as Attock Energy Corp. 08/02/1995
(See Attock Energy Corp.)

POLO RALPH LAUREN CORP (DE)
Issue Information - 29,500,000 shares CL A offered at $26 per share on 06/11/1997
Name changed to Ralph Lauren Corp. 08/16/2011

POLO RES LTD (BRITISH VIRGIN ISLANDS)
Each share old Ordinary no par exchanged for (0.1) share new Ordinary no par 02/07/2013
Shares transferred to Jersey register 04/30/2013

POLONIA BANCORP (USA)
Reorganized under the laws of Maryland as Polonia Bancorp, Inc. 11/09/2012
Each share Common 1¢ par exchanged for (1.1136) shares Common 1¢ par
(See Polonia Bancorp, Inc.)

POLONIA BANCORP INC (MD)
Acquired by Prudential Bancorp, Inc. 01/01/2017
Each share Common 1¢ par exchanged for $11.09 cash

POLORON PRODS INC (NY)
Proclaimed dissolved 6/26/96

POLPOND MINING CO. LTD. (ON)
Merged into Consolidated Panther Mines Ltd. on a (0.05) for (1) basis 7/12/60
Consolidated Panther Mines Ltd. recapitalized as Panthco Resources

Inc. 7/3/87 which merged into Ztest Electronics, Inc. 7/1/96

POLSKA GRUPA FARMACEUTYCZNA SA (POLAND)
Name changed to Pelion S.A. 02/18/2015
(See Pelion S.A.)

POLSKI KONCERN NAFTOWY ORLEN S A (POLAND)
Name changed 05/08/2000
Name changed from Polski Koncern Naftowy S.A. to Polski Koncern Naftowy Orlen S.A. 05/08/2000
GDR agreement terminated 02/27/2013
Each 144A GDR for Ordinary exchanged for $34.312413 cash
Each Reg. S GDR for Ordinary exchanged for $34.312413 cash
ADR agreement terminated 03/04/2013
Each Sponsored ADR for Ordinary exchanged for $26.869534 cash

POLTAVA GOK OPEN JT STK CO (UKRAINE)
Reg. S GDR's for Ordinary split (50) for (1) by issuance of (49) additional GDR's payable 10/11/2005 to holders of record 10/07/2005
Basis changed from (1:50) to (1:1) 10/11/2005
GDR agreement terminated 08/10/2018
Each Reg. S GDR for Ordinary exchanged for (1) share Ordinary
Note: Unexchanged GDR's will be sold and the proceeds, if any, held for claim after 02/11/2019

POLUMBUS CORP (CO)
Merged into Grace (W.R.) & Co. 12/20/76
Details not available

POLUS INC (CO)
Administratively dissolved 02/01/2001

POLUS SHOE MANUFACTURING CO., INC.
Dissolved 00/00/1929
Details not available

POLY CO AMER INC (ND)
Acquired by Energy Resources of North Dakota Inc. 04/01/1981
Each share Common 1¢ par exchanged for (1) share Common 1¢ par
Energy Resources of North Dakota Inc. name changed to Centrum Industries Inc. 09/16/1988
(See Centrum Industries Inc.)

POLY-EKO SYS INC (NY)
Recapitalized as Laidlaw Energy Group Inc. 9/30/2002
Each share Common $0.001 par exchanged for (0.2) share Common $0.001 par

POLY INDS INC (CA)
Each share old Common $1 par exchanged for (0.4) new Common $1 par 07/18/1962
Each share new Common $1 par exchanged for (0.2) share Common no par 08/00/1967
Conv. Preferred Ser. A no par called for redemption 00/00/1976
Conv. Preferred Ser. B no par called for redemption 00/00/1976
Note: New Common $1 par certificates (07/18/1962) were held in escrow and holders received Non-Transferable Escrow Receipts which were not required to be surrendered for 08/00/1967 reverse split are now without value
Name changed to Acro Energy Corp. 07/16/1980
(See Acro Energy Corp.)

POLY-PACIFIC INTL INC (AB)
Recapitalized as Global Green Matrix Corp. 02/25/2010
Each share Common no par exchanged for (0.06666666) share Common no par
Global Green Matrix Corp. name changed to Intercept Energy Services Inc. 09/23/2013

POLY PHOS MARKETING INC (MN)
Statutorily dissolved 12/9/91

POLY PPTY GROUP CO LTD (HONG KONG)
ADR agreement terminated 08/06/2014
No ADR's remain outstanding

POLY REPRO INTL LTD (NY)
Adjudicated bankrupt 05/17/1965
No stockholders' equity

POLY SEAL CORP (NY)
Each share Capital Stock $1 par exchanged for (10) shares Capital Stock 10¢ par 00/00/1954
Adjudicated bankrupt 04/01/1969
No stockholders' equity

POLY SHIELD TECHNOLOGIES INC (DE)
Name changed to Triton Emission Solutions Inc. 08/25/2014

POLY SOUTHFIELD CORP (DE)
Name changed to U.S. Playing Card Corp. 08/25/1982
U.S. Playing Card Corp. merged into Jesup Group, Inc. 12/24/1987
(See Jesup Group, Inc.)

POLY TECH INC (MN)
Merged into Carlisle Plastics, Inc. 04/07/1989
Each share Common no par exchanged for $8.50 cash

POLYAIR INTER PACK INC (ON)
Each share old Common no par exchanged for (0.0000002) share new Common no par 07/17/2009
Note: In effect holders received $0.05 cash per share and public interest was eliminated

POLYAIR TIRES INC (AB)
Recapitalized as Bartizan Capital Corp. 06/12/1998
Each share Common no par exchanged for (0.2) share Common no par
(See Bartizan Capital Corp.)

POLYANALYT INC (NY)
Recapitalized as Thor Energy Corp. (NY) 03/18/1980
Each share Common 1¢ par exchanged for (3) shares Common 1¢ par
Thor Energy Corp. (NY) reincorporated in Oklahoma 12/28/1981 which merged into Burton-Hawks, Inc. 06/27/1983 which reincorporated in Delaware as Hawks Industries, Inc. 12/29/1988 which reorganized in Wyoming 02/02/1998 which reincorporated in Nevada 02/18/2000 which name changed to Emex Corp. 02/20/2001
(See Emex Corp.)

POLYASTICS CORP (UT)
Proclaimed dissolved for failure to pay taxes 03/29/1975

POLYCAST CORP. (CT)
Reorganized as Polycast Technology Corp. 5/9/68
No stockholders' equity

POLYCAST TECHNOLOGY CORP (DE)
Incorporated 8/5/69
Reincorporated 9/11/69
State of incorporation changed from (CT) to (DE) and Common no par changed to 10¢ par 9/11/69
Name changed to Poly-Southfield Corp. 4/30/81
Poly-Southfield Corp. name changed to U.S. Playing Card Corp. 8/25/82 which merged into Jesup Group, Inc. 12/24/87
(See Jesup Group, Inc.)

POLYCAST TECHNOLOGY CORP NEW (DE)
Incorporated 11/25/80
Common 1¢ par split (3) for (2) by issuance of (0.5) additional share 6/24/83
Name changed to Jesup Group, Inc. 12/24/87
(See Jesup Group, Inc.)

POLYCHEMICAL INDUSTRIES LTD. (AB)
Acquired by Dart Industries, Inc. 00/00/1970
Details not available

POLYCHROME CORP (NY)
Stock Dividend - 25% 03/07/1963
Each share Common $1 par exchanged for (0.001) share Common $1,000 par 08/21/1979
Note: In effect holders received $26 cash per share and public interest was eliminated

POLYCLON INC (MA)
Merged into Hytek International Corp. 4/30/73
Each share Common 10¢ par exchanged for (1/3) share Common 20¢ par
(See Hytek International Corp.)

POLYCOM INC (DE)
Common $0.0005 par split (2) for (1) by issuance of (1) additional share payable 08/31/2000 to holders of record 08/15/2000
Common $0.0005 par split (2) for (1) by issuance of (1) additional share payable 07/01/2011 to holders of record 06/15/2011 Ex date - 07/05/2011
Acquired by Triangle Private Holdings I, LLC 09/27/2016
Each share Common $0.0005 par exchanged for $12.50 cash

POLYCOMPUTERS INC (CA)
Chapter 11 Federal Bankruptcy Code converted to Chapter 7 on 4/23/86
Stockholders' equity unlikely

POLYCORP INC (AB)
Reincorporated under the laws of Ontario as Atlas Cromwell Ltd. 12/27/2001
Atlas Cromwell Ltd. (ON) reincorporated in British Columbia 05/02/2006 which name changed to Terrane Metals Corp. 07/27/2006 which merged into Thompson Creek Metals Co., Inc. 10/20/2010

POLYDEX CHEMS CDA LTD (CANADA)
Reorganized 03/31/1980
Common no par split (4) for (1) by issuance of (3) additional shares 10/09/1972
Reorganized from Polydex Chemicals Ltd. (Canada) to Polydex Chemicals (Canada) Ltd. 03/31/1980
Each share Common no par exchanged for (1) Non-Separable Unit consisting of (1) share 8% Non-Cum. Class A Preference no par and (1) share Polydex Chemicals Ltd. (Bahamas) Common 1¢ par
Units split (3) for (1) by issuance of (2) additional Units 08/24/1981
Stock Dividend - 100% 09/15/1980
Paired certificates separated 04/01/1984
(See Polydex Chemicals Ltd. (Bahamas))
8% Non-Cum. Class A Preference no par called for redemption 01/25/1988
Public interest eliminated

POLYDEX CHEMS LTD (BAHAMAS)
Units split (3) for (1) by issuance of (2) additional Units 08/24/1981
Stock Dividend - 100% 09/15/1980
Paired certificates separated 04/01/1984
Each Non-Separable Unit consisting of (1) share Polydex Chemicals (Canada) Ltd. 8% Non-Cum. Class A Preference no par and (1) share Polydex Chemicals Ltd. Common 1¢ par received (1) share Polydex Chemicals (Canada) Ltd. 8% Non-Cum. Class A Preference no par and (1) share Polydex Chemicals Ltd. Common 1¢ par
(See Polydex Chemicals (Canada) Ltd.)
Name changed to Polydex Pharmaceuticals Ltd. 04/01/1984

POLYDYNE INDS INC (CO)
Each share old Common $0.00001 par exchanged for (0.05) share new Common $0.00001 par 05/30/1991
Each share new Common $0.00001 par exchanged again for (0.002) share new Common $0.00001 par 08/01/2007
Name changed to Visicom International, Inc. 07/09/2008

POLYGRAM N V (NETHERLANDS)
Acquired by Seagram Co. 12/10/98
Each share Common 50 Gldrs. par exchanged for 115 Guilders

POLYMEDICA CORP (MA)
Name changed 09/19/1997
Name changed from PolyMedica Industries, Inc. to PolyMedica Corp. 09/19/1997
Common 1¢ par split (2) for (1) by issuance of (1) additional share payable 09/29/2003 to holders of record 09/19/2003 Ex date - 09/30/2003
Merged into Medco Health Solutions, Inc. 10/31/2007
Each share Common 1¢ par exchanged for $53 cash

POLYMER CORP (PA)
Class A Common $1 par and Class B Common $1 par reclassified as Common 35¢ par and (2) additional shares issued 04/18/1969
Merged into ACF Industries, Inc. 05/17/1974
Each share Common 35¢ par exchanged for (0.232558) share Common no par
(See ACF Industries, Inc.)

POLYMER GROUP INC (DE)
Plan of reorganization under Chapter 11 Federal Bankruptcy proceedings effective 03/05/2003
Each share Common 1¢ par exchanged for (0.0125) share Class B Common 1¢ par, (0.01558399) Common Stock Purchase Warrant Ser. A and (0.01636117) Common Stock Purchase Warrant Ser. B expiring 03/04/2010
Note: Unexchanged certificates were cancelled and became without value 02/21/2004
Each share 16% Preferred Ser. A exchanged for (37.26397) shares Class A Common 1¢ par 09/15/2005
Merged into Scorpio Acquisition Corp. 01/28/2011
Each share Class A Common 1¢ par exchanged for $15.32 cash
Each share received an additional initial distribution of $0.91308211 cash 11/01/2011
Each share received an additional second and final distribution of $1.97521037 cash 12/05/2011
Each share Class B Common 1¢ par exchanged for $15.32 cash
Each share received an additional initial distribution of $0.91308211 cash 11/01/2011
Each share received an additional second and final distribution of $1.97521037 cash 12/05/2011
Each share Class C Common 1¢ par exchanged for $15.32 cash
Each share received an additional

initial distribution of $0.91308211 cash 11/01/2011
Each share received an additional second and final distribution of $1.97521037 cash 12/05/2011

POLYMER INDUSTRIES, INC. (DE)
Acquired by Morris (Philip), Inc. 04/00/1958
Details not available

POLYMER INTL CORP (DE)
Incorporated 00/00/1963
Each share 5% Non-Vtg. Conv. Preferred $3 par automatically became (1) share Common 1¢ par 06/29/1967
Merged into Picas Inc. 05/26/1978
Each share Common 1¢ par exchanged for $3 cash

POLYMER INTL CORP NEW (DE)
Incorporated in 1978
Common 1¢ par split (5) for (4) by issuance of (0.25) additional share 11/1/88
Stock Dividend - 15% 10/1/87
Merged into PIC Acquisition Inc. 6/16/89
Each share Common 1¢ par exchanged for $8.90 cash

POLYMER MATLS INC (NY)
Stock Dividend - 200% 8/28/72
Merged into Georgia-Pacific Corp. 7/25/79
Each share Common 10¢ par exchanged for (0.4042618) share Conv. Preferred Ser. B no par
(See Georgia-Pacific Corp.)

POLYMER RESH CORP AMER (NY)
Common 1¢ par split (5) for (4) by issuance of (0.25) additional share 06/27/1995
Stock Dividends - 10% 02/22/1994; 10% 03/20/1995; 10% payable 03/29/1996 to holders of record 03/15/1996; 5% payable 04/09/1997 to holders of record 04/01/1997; 5% payable 04/02/1998 to holders of record 03/23/1998; 5% payable 04/02/1999 to holders of record 03/19/1999
Chapter 11 bankruptcy proceedings converted to Chapter 7 on 02/25/2005
No stockholders' equity

POLYMER SOLUTIONS INC (NV)
Liquidation completed
Each share Common no par exchanged for initial distribution of $0.645 cash 02/03/2004
Each share Common no par received second and final distribution of $0.062 cash payable 06/03/2004 to holders of record 02/03/2004

POLYMERIC CORP (NV)
Name changed to Lew Corp. 08/27/2001
Lew Corp. name changed to Vintage Energy & Exploration, Inc. 10/02/2007
(See Vintage Energy & Exploration, Inc.)

POLYMERIX INC (DE)
Plan of reorganization under Chapter 11 Federal Bankruptcy Code effective 02/27/2002
Stockholders' equity unlikely

POLYMERS SYS INC (NY)
Recapitalized as Olan Laboratories International, Inc. 11/05/1981
Each share Common 1¢ par exchanged for (0.25) share Common 1¢ par
Olan Laboratories International, Inc. recapitalized as Mile Marker International, Inc. (NY) 12/28/1993 which reincorporated in Florida 11/22/2000
(See Mile Marker International, Inc.)

POLYMET MANUFACTURING CORP. (DE)
Charter cancelled and declared inoperative and void for non-payment of taxes 4/1/39

POLYMETAL JT STK CO (RUSSIA)
GDR agreement terminated 07/06/2012
Each Reg. S Sponsored GDR for Ordinary exchanged for $16.178 cash
Each 144A Sponsored GDR for Ordinary exchanged for $16.178 cash

POLYMETRIC DEVICES CO. (PA)
Acquired by Badger Meter Manufacturing Co. on a (1) for (10.7) basis 04/23/1965
Note: Holders of (268) or more shares of received stock
Holders of (267) shares or fewer received $4.40 cash per share
Badger Meter Manufacturing Co. name changed to Badger Meter, Inc. 04/13/1971

POLYPANE PACKAGING CO., INC. (PR)
Acquired by Polymer International Corp. 2/4/64
Each share Common $1 par exchanged for (1/3) share 5% Non-Voting Conv. Preferred $3 par
(See Polymer International Corp.)

POLYPHALT INC (ON)
Assets sold for the benefit of creditors 12/15/2003
Stockholders' equity unlikely

POLYPHASE CORP (NV)
Reincorporated 6/29/94
State of incorporation changed from (PA) to (NV) 6/29/94
Name changed to Overhill Corp. 3/22/2001
Overhill Corp. name changed to TreeCon Resources, Inc. 10/28/2002

POLYPORE INTL INC (DE)
Acquired by Asahi Kasei Corp. 08/26/2015
Each share Common 1¢ par exchanged for $60.50 cash

POLYSAR ENERGY & CHEM CORP (CANADA)
7.60% Conv. Preferred 1980 Ser. $20 par called for redemption 03/14/1988
Under plan of recapitalization each share Common no par received distribution of $1.20 cash 04/29/1988
Under plan of recapitalization each (2.574) shares Common no par received distribution of (1) share Retractable Preferred 1988 Ser. no par 05/20/1988
Acquired by Nova Corp. of Alberta 09/07/1988
Each share Common no par exchanged for (0.5) share Common no par and $14.50 cash
Retractable Sr. Preferred 1983 Ser. $25 par called for redemption 10/12/1988
Retractable Preferred 1988 Ser. no par called for redemption 10/12/1988
Nova Corp. of Alberta name changed to Nova Gas Transmission Ltd. 05/11/1994
(See Nova Gas Transmission Ltd.)

POLYSAR LTD (CANADA)
8.40% 1st Preferred Ser. A $25 par dividend rate changed to 15.5% 04/08/1982
15.5% 1st Preferred Ser. A $25 par called for redemption 07/02/1986
Public interest eliminated

POLYSONICS INC. (NY)
Merged into Atlantic Marine Industries, Inc. 03/20/1967
Each share Common 1¢ par exchanged for (1) share Common 1¢ par
(See Atlantic Marine Industries, Inc.)

POLYSOURCE HOLDINGS PLC (ENGLAND)
Delisted from Alberta Stock Exchange 06/02/1991

POLYSOURCE INDS LTD (BERMUDA)
Merged into Polysource Holdings PLC 02/06/1990
Each share Common 1¢ par exchanged for (1) share Ordinary 5p par
(See Polysource Holdings PLC)

POLYSTEEL BLDG SYS LTD (CANADA)
Name changed to Medical Pathways International Inc. 04/16/1999
(See Medical Pathways International Inc.)

POLYSYSTEMS INC (NJ)
Merged into Environmental Subsidiary Corp. 06/24/1976
Each share Common 1¢ par exchanged for $2 cash

POLYTECHNIC DATA CORP (DE)
Merged into Polytechnic Acquisition Corp. 08/31/1984
Each share Common $1 par exchanged for $3.084064 cash
Each share Common $1 par received an initial additional distribution of $0.35 cash 09/06/1985
Each share Common $1 par received a second additional distribution of $0.2454 cash 02/28/1986
Each share Common $1 par received a third and final additional distribution of $0.25 cash 09/03/1986

POLYTECHNIC INDUSTRIES, INC. (CO)
Declared defunct and inoperative for failure to pay taxes and file annual reports 1/31/77

POLYTHENE METRO INC (DE)
Name changed to Gold River Productions, Inc. 2/12/2007

POLYTRONIC RESEARCH, INC. (MD)
Charter revoked for failure to file reports and pay fees 8/30/62

POLYTRONICS LABORATORIES, INC. (NJ)
Assets sold for benefit of creditors 5/31/67
No stockholders' equity

POLYUS GOLD INTL LTD (JERSEY)
GDR agreement terminated 08/17/2011
Details not available
Acquired by Wandle Holdings Ltd. 01/19/2016
Each GDR for Ordinary exchanged for $2.92 cash

POLYUS GOLD PJSC (RUSSIA)
Name changed to Polyus PJSC 05/24/2016

POLYVISION CORP (NY)
Merged into Steelcase Inc. 11/14/2001
Each share Common $0.001 par exchanged for $2.25 cash

POM CORP (MI)
Proclaimed dissolved for failure to file reports 05/15/1975

POMAC MINES LTD (ON)
Common $1 par changed to no par 09/28/1973
Merged into Richmond Gulf Resources Ltd. 01/27/1989
Each share Common no par exchanged for (0.084327) share Subordinate no par
Richmond Gulf Resources Ltd. recapitalized as Richwest Holdings Inc. 09/01/1992
(See Richwest Holdings Inc.)

POMEL, INC. (NY)
Liquidation completed
Each share Common 10¢ par stamped to indicate initial distribution of $3 cash 7/12/63
Each share Stamped Common 10¢ par exchanged for second distribution of $0.63 cash 6/1/64
Each share Stamped Common 10¢ par received third and final distribution of $0.155 cash 12/2/65

POMEROY IT SOLUTIONS INC (DE)
Name changed 07/01/2003
Stock Dividend - 10% 06/15/1995
Common 1¢ par split (3) for (2) by issuance of (0.5) additional share payable 10/04/1996 to holders of record 09/19/1996
Common 1¢ par split (3) for (2) by issuance of (0.5) additional share payable 10/06/1997 to holders of record 09/22/1997
Name changed from Pomeroy Computer Resources, Inc. to Pomeroy IT Solutions, Inc. 07/01/2003
Acquired by Platinum Equity, LLC 11/12/2009
Each share Common 1¢ par exchanged for $6.50 cash

POMINEX LTD (ON)
Recapitalized as Canarchon Holdings Ltd. 12/16/1985
Each share Capital Stock no par exchanged for (1/15) share Common no par
(See Canarchon Holdings Ltd.)

POMONA TILE MANUFACTURING CO. (CA)
Merged into American Olean Tile Co. 12/31/68
Each share Common $1 par exchanged for $4.75 cash

POMPEIAN CORP.
Acquired by Van Camp Packing Co., Inc. in 1930 which became bankrupt in 1932

POMSTA GROUP INC (WY)
Name changed to Oidon Co., Ltd. 12/31/2010

PONCE DE LEON TROTTING ASSOCIATION, INC. (FL)
Company declared dissolved for non-payment of taxes 06/28/1965

PONCE FED BK FSB (PONCE, PR)
Common $1 par split (2) for (1) by issuance of (1) additional share 2/18/86
Stock Dividend - 11% 1/10/94
Under plan of reorganization each share Common $1 par automatically became (1) share Poncebank (Ponce, PR) Common $1 par 10/31/94
(See Poncebank (Ponce, PR))

PONCEBANK (PONCE, PR)
Merged into Banco Bilbao Vizcaya, S.A. 6/30/98
Each share Common $1 par exchanged for $26.10 cash

PONCHATOULA HOMESTEAD SVGS F A (LA)
Recapitalized as Homestead Bancorp Inc. 07/20/1998
Each share Common 10¢ par exchanged for (0.42587624) share Common 1¢ par
(See Homestead Bancorp Inc.)

POND CREEK POCAHONTAS CO. (ME)
Merged into Island Creek Coal Co. (Me.) 8/31/55
Each share Capital Stock $1 par exchanged for (2) shares Common 50¢ par
Island Creek Coal Co. (Me.) merged into Island Creek Coal Co. (Del.) 12/31/64 which merged into Occidental Petroleum Corp. (Calif.) 1/29/68

FINANCIAL INFORMATION, INC.

PON-POP

(See Occidental Petroleum Corp. (Calif.))

POND'S EXTRACT CO. (DE)
Merged into Chesebrough-Pond's, Inc. 6/30/55
Each share Common no par exchanged for (9) shares Common $10 par
(See Chesebrough-Pond's, Inc.)

PONDER INDS INC (DE)
Each share old Common 1¢ par exchanged for (0.2) share new Common 1¢ par 11/13/1998
Reorganized as N-Vision Technology, Inc. (DE) 01/02/2001
Each share new Common 1¢ par exchanged for (0.05) share Common 1¢ par
N-Vision Technology, Inc. (DE) reorganized in Nevada as Rapid Fire Marketing, Inc. 07/05/2007

PONDER OILS LTD (AB)
Capital Stock no par changed to 50¢ par 00/00/1953
Capital Stock 50¢ par changed to no par 09/19/1974
Delisted from Canadian Dealer Network 01/03/1995

PONDERAY EXPL LTD (AB)
Recapitalized as Canadian Ponderay Energy Ltd. 7/2/80
Each share Capital Stock no par exchanged for (0.2) share Class A Common no par

PONDEROSA HOMES INC (MT)
Each share old Common 10¢ par exchanged for (0.1) share new Common 10¢ par 8/15/73
Recapitalized as Washington Minerals, Inc. 7/8/82
Each share new Common 10¢ par exchanged for (0.1) share Common $0.001 par
(See Washington Minerals, Inc.)

PONDEROSA INC (DE)
Name changed 6/21/82
Common 10¢ par split (2) for (1) by issuance of (1) additional share 5/7/71
Common 10¢ par split (2) for (1) by issuance of (1) additional share 3/27/72
Name changed from Ponderosa System, Inc. to Ponderosa, Inc. 6/21/82
Common 10¢ par split (3) for (2) by issuance of (0.5) additional share 1/6/83
Merged into PON Acquisition Corp. 9/9/87
Each share Common 10¢ par exchanged for $29.25 cash

PONDEROSA INDL S A DE C V (MEXICO)
Each old Sponsored ADR for Ordinary no par exchanged for (0.1) new Sponsored ADR for Ordinary no par 4/27/92
Merged into Empaques Ponderosa, S.A. de C.V. 4/4/97
Each new Sponsored ADR for Ordinary no par exchanged for (0.04) Sponsored ADR for Ordinary no par
(See Empaques Ponderosa, S.A. de C.V.)

PONDEROSA INDS INC (DE)
Each share Common 1¢ par exchanged for (1/3) share Common 3¢ par 7/19/73
Charter cancelled and declared inoperative and void for non-payment of taxes 3/1/78

PONDEROSA LUMBER INC (DE)
Reincorporated under the laws of Nevada as National Automation Services, Inc. 10/11/2007
National Automation Services, Inc. name changed to National Energy Services, Inc. 07/15/2015

PONDEROSA VENTURES INC (BC)
Delisted from Vancouver Stock Exchange 07/07/1989

PONEMAH MILLS (CT)
Acquired by Sayles Finishing Plants, Inc. for cash in 1962

PONEY EXPLS LTD (BC)
Recapitalized as Steed Ventures Corp. 11/14/1985
Each share Capital Stock no par exchanged for (0.2) share Common no par
(See Steed Ventures Corp.)

PONINGOE LAND CO. INC. (NY)
Voluntarily dissolved 12/30/70
Details not available

PONTE NOSSA ACQUISITION CORP (DE)
Each share old Common $0.001 par exchanged for (26) shares new Common $0.001 par 07/26/2001
Name changed to VisiJet Inc. 02/12/2003
VisiJet Inc. name changed to Advanced Refractive Technologies, Inc. 07/28/2005
(See Advanced Refractive Technologies, Inc.)

PONTE VEDRA BKG CORP (FL)
Merged into SunTrust Banks Inc. 1/19/96
Each share Common $1 par exchanged for either (0.2645503) share Common $1 par or $17.50 cash
Note: Option to elect to receive cash expired 1/9/96, but the company reserves the right to issue cash or stock to any holder in order to maintain a 22% cash and 78% stock proration for the total number of shares exchanged

PONTIAC CASTLE INVTS CORP (CANADA)
Name changed to Prosys Tech Corp. 05/16/2007

PONTIAC PETROLEUMS LTD. (AB)
Struck off register for failure to file reports or pay fees 8/3/59

PONTIAC-ROUYN MINES (1939) LTD.
Recapitalized as Anglo-Rouyn Mines Ltd. 00/00/1951
Each share Capital Stock $1 par exchanged for (0.5) share Capital Stock $1 par
Anglo-Rouyn Mines Ltd. merged into Canadian Memorial Services Ltd. 09/28/1973 which name changed to Arbor Capital Resources Inc./Arbor Ressources Financieres Inc. 05/01/1975 which name changed to Arbor Capital Inc. 05/15/1986 which name changed to Arbor Memorial Services Inc. 03/31/1994

PONTIAC-ROUYN MINES LTD.
Succeeded by Pontiac-Rouyn Mines (1939) Ltd. share for share in 1939
Pontiac-Rouyn Mines (1939) Ltd. recapitalized as Anglo-Rouyn Mines Ltd. in 1951 which merged into Canadian Memorial Services Ltd. 9/28/73 which name changed to Arbor Capital Resources Inc./Arbor Ressources Financieres Inc. 5/1/75 which name changed to Arbor Capital Inc. 5/15/86 which name changed to Arbor Memorial Services Inc. 3/31/94

PONTIAC ST BK (PONTIAC, MI)
Common $10 par changed to $5 par and (1) additional share issued 5/2/75
Stock Dividends - 50% 9/30/60; 20% 2/1/64; 25% 10/19/66; 25% 10/22/68; 25% 3/30/70; 25% 4/28/72; 33-1/3% 4/1/74
Merged into NBD Bancorp, Inc. 8/27/84
Each share Common $5 par exchanged for (0.645) share Common $2.50 par
NBD Bancorp, Inc. name changed to First Chicago NBD Corp. 12/1/95 which merged into Bank One Corp. 10/2/98 which merged into J.P. Morgan Chase & Co. 12/31/2000 which name changed to JPMorgan Chase & Co. 7/20/2004

PONTIFF MNG LTD (ON)
Charter cancelled for failure to pay taxes and file returns 03/16/1976

PONTOTOC PRODTN INC (NV)
Merged into Ascent Energy Inc. 8/14/2001
Each share Common $0.0001 par exchanged for (1) share 8% Conv. Preferred Ser. B $0.001 par and $9 cash

PONTUS INDS INC (CO)
Recapitalized as Continental Orinoco Co., Inc. 5/14/96
Each share Common no par exchanged for (0.2) share Common no par

PONY EXPRESS U S A INC (NV)
SEC revoked common stock registration 09/22/2008
Stockholders' equity unlikely

PONY MEADOWS MNG CO (NV)
Recapitalized as Envirodyne, Inc. 9/3/70
Each share Capital Stock 1¢ par exchanged for (0.025) share Capital Stock 10¢ par
Envirodyne, Inc. name changed to Envirodyne Industries, Inc. 2/13/78 which name changed to Viskase Companies, Inc. 9/8/98
(See Viskase Companies, Inc.)

PONY SPORTING GOODS LTD (CANADA)
Reincorporated from under the laws of (ONT) to under the laws of Canada 7/19/82
Name changed to 161671 Canada Inc. 6/1/87
(See 161671 Canada Inc.)

POOL ENERGY SVCS CO (TX)
Merged into Nabors Industries, Inc. (DE) 11/26/99
Each share Common no par exchanged for (1.025) shares Common 10¢ par
Nabors Industries, Inc. (DE) reincorporated in Bermuda as Nabors Industries Ltd. 6/24/2002

POOLE ENGINEERING & MACHINE CO.
Bankrupt in 1932

POOLED PROTN GROUPS INC (CO)
Name changed to Global Entertainment, Inc. 10/05/1987

POOR & CO. (DE)
Recapitalized 4/26/55
$1.50 Class A Preferred no par changed to $25 par
Class B Common no par changed to $10 par
Class B Common $10 par reclassified as Common $10 par 9/7/56
$1.50 Class A Preferred $25 par called for redemption 12/1/56
Common $10 par split (3) for (2) by issuance of (0.5) additional share 3/15/67
Name changed to Portec, Inc. 7/1/68
(See Portec, Inc.)

POORE BROS INC (DE)
Name changed to Inventure Group, Inc. 05/24/2006
Inventure Group, Inc. name changed to Inventure Foods, Inc. 05/20/2010
(See Inventure Foods, Inc.)

POP ARTS INC (NY)
Charter cancelled and proclaimed dissolved for failure to pay taxes 06/24/1981

POP N GO INC (DE)
SEC revoked common stock registration 06/28/2012

POP RADIO CORP (NY)
Merged into Heritage Media Corp. 11/16/90
Each share Common 1¢ par exchanged for $21.10 cash

POP SHOPPES INTL INC (ON)
Charter cancelled for failure to file reports and pay taxes 3/17/86

POP SHOPS INC (NY)
Each share Common 2¢ par exchanged for (0.5) share Common 1¢ par 6/1/73
Charter cancelled and proclaimed dissolved for failure to pay taxes and file reports 12/15/75

POP STARZ INC (FL)
Each share Common $0.001 par received distribution of (0.1) share Pop Starz Records, Inc. Common 1¢ par payable 06/29/2007 to holders of record 06/29/2007 Ex date - 06/27/2007
Name changed to Global Entertainment Acquisition Corp. 08/01/2008
Global Entertainment Acquisition Corp. recapitalized as HydroGenetics, Inc. 10/03/2008

POP STARZ RECORDS INC (FL)
Each share Common 1¢ par received distribution of (1/3) share Apollo Entertainment Group, Inc. Common $0.001 par payable 10/17/2008 to holders of record 09/30/2008 Ex date - 10/20/2008
Each share Common 1¢ par received distribution of (0.125) share Beta Music Group, Inc. Common 1¢ par payable 03/09/2009 to holders of record 12/08/2008 Ex date - 03/06/2009
Name changed to World Mortgage Exchange Group, Inc. 11/23/2009

POP STOP INC (NV)
Recapitalized as Liquid Motion Industries 03/31/1990
Each share Common $0.001 par exchanged for (0.25) share Common $0.001 par
Liquid Motion Industries reorganized as Pacific Global Communications Group, Inc. 03/25/1996
(See Pacific Global Communications Group, Inc.)

POP WINES INC (DE)
Name changed to Montcalm Vintners, Inc. 12/18/1972
Montcalm Vintners, Inc. name changed to Filice Winery, Inc. 06/18/1975 which name changed to Crown Companies, Inc. 03/04/1986 which name changed to Crown Gold Companies Group, Ltd. 09/25/1987 which recapitalized as Tigershark Enterprises Inc. 10/28/1997 which name changed to Great White Marine & Recreation, Inc. 05/14/1998
(See Great White Marine & Recreation, Inc.)

POPBIG INC (DE)
Name changed to EMAV Holdings, Inc. 01/03/2014

POPE & TALBOT INC (DE)
Reincorporated 05/07/1979
Each share Capital Stock $10 par exchanged for (1) share 6% Preferred $5 par and (1) share Common $5 par 00/00/1953
6% Preferred $5 par called for redemption 05/15/1968
Common $5 par changed to $2 par and (2) additional shares issued 04/14/1969
Common $2 par split (3) for (2) by issuance of (0.5) additional share 05/05/1972

POP-POR

State of incorporation changed from (CA) to (DE) 05/07/1979
Common $2 par split (2) for (1) by issuance of (1) additional share 02/29/1980
Common $2 par changed to $1 par 12/12/1985
Common $1 par split (2) for (1) by issuance of (1) additional share 05/29/1987
Chapter 11 bankruptcy proceedings converted to Chapter 7 on 05/09/2008
Stockholders' equity unlikely

POPE EVANS & ROBBINS INC (NY)

Common 10¢ par split (2) for (1) by issuance of (1) additional share 07/30/1981
Common 10¢ par split (3) for (2) by issuance of (0.5) additional share 01/31/1983
Stock Dividend - 100% 10/10/1980
Assets sold for the benefit of creditors 00/00/1997
No stockholders' equity

POPE VALLEY HLDGS LTD (BC)

Recapitalized as Consolidated Pope Valley Holdings Ltd. 02/28/1994
Each share Common no par exchanged for (0.2) share Common no par
Consolidated Pope Valley Holdings Ltd. name changed to Da Capo Resources Ltd. 05/05/1994 which merged into Vista Gold Corp. (BC) 11/01/1996 which reincorporated in Yukon 12/27/1997 which reincorporated back in British Columbia 06/12/2013

POPEIL BROS INC (DE)

Merged into TSP Corp. 07/27/1979
Each share Common 40¢ par exchanged for $2 cash

POPELL (L.F.) CO. INC. (FL)

Common 10¢ par split (3) for (1) by issuance of (2) additional shares 12/11/62
Under plan of merger name changed to Concrete Maintenance Products, Inc. and Common 10¢ par reclassified as Class B Common 10¢ par 2/15/65
(See Concrete Maintenance Products, Inc.)

POPEYES LA KITCHEN INC (MN)

Acquired by Restaurant Brands International Inc. 03/27/2017
Each share Common 1¢ par exchanged for $79 cash

POPI GROUP INC (AB)

Recapitalized as Damian Capital Corp. (AB) 09/17/2003
Each share Common no par exchanged for (0.2) share Common no par
Damian Capital Corp. (AB) reincorporated in Canada as CPVC Financial Inc. 05/15/2006 which merged into CPVC Financial Corp. 11/06/2006
(See CPVC Financial Corp.)

POPLAR CREEK COAL & IRON CO (TN)

Each share Capital Stock $100 par exchanged for (1) share Capital Stock no par 3/25/71
Merged into Coal Creek Mining & Manufacturing Co. 3/28/83
Each share Capital Stock no par exchanged for (1) share Capital Stock no par
Coal Creek Mining & Manufacturing Co. name changed to Coal Creek Co. 3/16/2006

POPLAR OILS LTD. (AB)

Merged into New Gas Exploration Co. of Alberta Ltd. in 1957
Each (5) shares Capital Stock no par exchanged for (1) share Capital Stock $1 par
New Gas Exploration Co. of Alberta Ltd. merged into Medallion Petroleums Ltd. 6/18/58 which merged into Canadian Industrial Gas & Oil Ltd. 3/8/65 which merged into Norcen Energy Resources Ltd. (ALTA) 10/28/77 which reincorporated under the laws of Canada 4/15/77
(See Norcen Energy Resources Ltd.)

POPLAR RES LTD (BC)

Merged into Nordic Diamonds Ltd. 11/24/2003
Each share Common no par exchanged for (0.1) share Common no par
Nordic Diamonds Ltd. recapitalized as Western Standard Metals Ltd. 06/12/2009 which merged into Terraco Gold Corp. (AB) 01/25/2011 which reincorporated in British Columbia 06/08/2011

POPMAIL COM INC (DE)

Each share old Common 1¢ par exchanged for (0.1) share new Common 1¢ par 10/12/2000
Company terminated registration of common stock and is no longer public as of 03/13/2007
Details not available

POPSTAR COMMUNICATIONS INC (NV)

Each share old Common $0.001 par exchanged for (0.01) share new Common $0.001 par 7/5/2005
Recapitalized as Peopleline, Inc. 1/25/2006
Each share new Common $0.001 par exchanged for (0.002) share Common $0.001 par
Peopleline, Inc. recapitalized as Peopleline Telecom, Inc. 1/17/2007

POP3 MEDIA CORP (NV)

Charter revoked 02/01/2010

POPULAR BANCSHARES CORP (FL)

Merged into Southeast Banking Corp. 3/31/87
Each share Common $1 par exchanged for (0.216) share Common $5 par
(See Southeast Banking Corp.)

POPULAR BANK OF SARASOTA, N.A. (SARASOTA, FL)

Name changed to First Independent Bank, N.A. (Sarasota, Fla.) 10/13/77
(See First Independent Bank, N.A. (Sarasota, Fla.))

POPULAR INC (PR)

8.35% Monthly Income Preferred Ser. A no par called for redemption at $25.6218 plus $0.0058 accrued dividends on 01/21/2002
Each Contingent Conv. Perpetual Non-Cumulative Depositary Preferred Ser. D no par exchanged for (8.3333) shares Common 1¢ par 05/11/2010
(Additional Information in Active)

POPULAR INDS LTD (QC)

Company went private in June 1989
Details not available

POPULAR PLASTIC PRODUCTS CORP. (NY)

Proclaimed dissolved by the Secretary of State of New York 12/16/63

PORCE ALUME INC (OH)

Completely liquidated 01/28/1985
No stockholders' equity

PORCE COTE RESH & DEV CORP (NY)

Completely liquidated 7/8/71
Each share Class A 10¢ par exchanged for (0.2) share Transbanc Depository Receipt & Funding Co. Class A Common 1¢ par
(See Transbanc Depository Receipt & Funding Co.)

PORCELAIN ENAMEL & MANUFACTURING CO. (MD)

Name changed to Pemco Corp. in October 1943
Pemco Corp. merged into Glidden Co. 11/6/61
(See Glidden Co.)

PORCHER IS GOLD CORP (BC)

Recapitalized as Tetra Metals Ltd. 01/08/1999
Each share Common no par exchanged for (0.2) share Common no par
Tetra Metals Ltd. recapitalized as Palladon Ventures Ltd. 11/02/2000

PORCUPINE BALMORAL RES LTD (ON)

Name changed to Marlin Capital Foods Ltd. 06/11/1990
Marlin Capital Foods Ltd. recapitalized as Meranto Technology Ltd. 10/04/1994 which recapitalized as World Sports Merchandising Inc. 02/01/1998 which name changed to World Sales & Merchandising Inc. 02/22/2000
(See World Sales & Merchandising Inc.)

PORCUPINE CREEK SYNDICATE

Liquidated in 1941

PORCUPINE DAVIDSON GOLD MINES LTD. (ON)

Completely liquidated
Each share Preference 5s par exchanged for first and final distribution of £0.045 cash 4/30/81
Holders of Common 5s par did not participate and shares are now valueless

PORCUPINE GOLD MINES CO. (DE)

No longer in existence having become inoperative and void for non-payment of taxes 3/16/21

PORCUPINE GOLD REEF MINING CO.

Property sold in 1935

PORCUPINE GOLDOR MINES LTD.

Name changed to Porcupine Goldtop Mines Ltd. in 1944
Porcupine Goldtop Mines Ltd. charter cancelled 3/14/78

PORCUPINE GOLDTOP MINES LTD. (ON)

Charter cancelled for failure to pay taxes and file returns 3/14/78

PORCUPINE KEORA MINING CO., LTD.

Reorganized as Keora Mines, Ltd. 00/00/1926
(See Keora Mines, Ltd.)

PORCUPINE LAKE GOLD MINING CO., LTD. (ON)

Acquired by Gold City Porcupine Mines Ltd. on a (1-1/8) for (2) basis in 1957
Gold City Porcupine Mines Ltd. charter cancelled 2/14/73

PORCUPINE LD ASSN (MI)

Term expired 11/06/1999

PORCUPINE PAYMASTER LTD (ON)

Merged into Associated Porcupine Mines Ltd. 11/05/1968
Each share Capital Stock no par exchanged for (0.279958) share Capital Stock no par
Associated Porcupine Mines Ltd. merged into American Reserve Mining Corp. 02/27/1989 which recapitalized as AMI Resources Inc. 12/21/1994 which name changed to Ashanti Sankofa Inc. 01/19/2017

PORCUPINE PENINSULAR GOLD MINES, LTD. (ON)

Recapitalized as Brunhurst Mines Ltd. on a (1) for (2) basis 00/00/1953
Brunhurst Mines Ltd. merged into Hydra Explorations Ltd. 11/16/1959 which name changed to Hydra Capital Corp. 12/30/1992 which name changed to Waterford Capital Management Inc. 11/12/1996 which merged into CPI Plastics Group Ltd. 09/21/1998
(See CPI Plastics Group Ltd.)

PORCUPINE PRIME MINES LTD. (ON)

Name changed to Prime Potash Corp. of Canada Ltd. 12/16/65
Prime Potash Corp. of Canada Ltd. charter cancelled 3/5/75

PORCUPINE REEF GOLD MINES LTD. (ON)

Merged into Broulan Reef Mines Ltd. 06/00/1951
Each share Capital Stock exchanged for (1) share Capital Stock $1 par
Broulan Reef Mines Ltd. merged into Broulan Resources Inc. 04/26/1983 which merged into Cabre Exploration Ltd. 11/24/1989 which was acquired by EnerMark Income Fund 01/10/2001 which merged into Enerplus Resources Fund 06/22/2001 which reorganized as Enerplus Corp. 01/03/2011

PORCUPINE SOUTHGATE MINES LTD. (ON)

Merged into Associated Porcupine Mines Ltd. 11/05/1968
Each share Capital Stock $1 par exchanged for (0.03465411) share Capital Stock no par
Associated Porcupine Mines Ltd. merged into American Reserve Mining Corp. 02/27/1989 which recapitalized as AMI Resources Inc. 12/21/1994 which name changed to Ashanti Sankofa Inc. 01/19/2017

PORCUPINE UNITED GOLD MINES, INC. (DE)

No longer in existence having become inoperative and void for non-payment of taxes 4/1/60

POREX TECHNOLOGIES CORP (GA)

Merged into Medco Containment Services, Inc. 09/10/1987
Each share Common 1¢ par exchanged for (0.8129) share Common 1¢ par
(See Medco Containment Services, Inc.)

PORFAVOR CORP (NV)

Name changed to Explore Anywhere Holding Corp. 11/10/2010
Explore Anywhere Holding Corp. recapitalized as Multimedia Platforms, Inc. 01/16/2015

POROSITY PETROLEUMS LTD. (AB)

Acquired by Nuco Petroleums Ltd. 00/00/1954
Each share Capital Stock no par exchanged for (0.166666) share Capital Stock no par
Nuco Petroleums Ltd. acquired by Kodiak Petroleums Ltd. 02/13/1963 which was acquired by Manhattan Continental Development Corp. 10/02/1969
(See Manhattan Continental Development Corp.)

PORT ALFRED PULP & PAPER CORP.

Merged into Consolidated Paper Corp. Ltd. 00/00/1932
Details not available

PORT ARTHUR IRON ORE CORP. (DE)

No longer in existence having become inoperative and void for non-payment of taxes 10/1/67

PORT CITY CAP BK (WILMINGTON, NC)

Merged into Crescent Financial Corp. (NC) 08/31/2006
Each share Common $5 par exchanged for (2.262) shares Common $1 par and $3.30 cash Crescent Financial Corp. (NC)

FINANCIAL INFORMATION, INC. POR-POR

reincorporated in Delaware as Crescent Financial Bancshares, Inc. which name changed to VantageSouth Bancshares, Inc. 07/22/2013 which merged into Yadkin Financial Corp. 07/04/2014 which merged into F.N.B. Corp. 03/11/2017

PORT CITY CORP (UT)
Recapitalized as Interline Resources Corp. 10/22/1990
Each share Common $0.001 par exchanged for (0.1) share Common $0.005 par
Interline Resources Corp. name changed to Automated-X, Inc. 12/03/2014 which name changed to Saddle Ranch Media, Inc. 10/07/2015

PORT COLDWELL MINES & METALS LTD. (ON)
Dissolved in 1957

PORT DOVER GAS & OIL LTD (ON)
Charter cancelled for failure to pay taxes and file returns 01/01/1980

PORT FINL CORP (MA)
Merged into Citizens Financial Group, Inc. 7/31/2003
Each share Common 1¢ par exchanged for $54 cash

PORT HENRY LIGHT, HEAT & POWER CO.
Merged into New York Power & Light Corp. 00/00/1928
Details not available

PORT HURON PAPER CO (MI)
Stock Dividends - 200% 07/20/1964; 20% 06/29/1973; 25% 04/01/1974
Merged into Pentair, Inc. 10/17/1983
Each share Common $1 par exchanged for $16.25 cash

PORT HURON SULPHITE & PAPER CO. (MI)
Each share 7% Preferred $100 par exchanged for (1) share 4% Preferred $100 par and (2) shares Common no par in 1935
Common no par changed to $1 par in 1940
4% Preferred $100 par called for redemption 4/1/57
Name changed to Port Huron Paper Co. 6/30/64
(See Port Huron Paper Co.)

PORT O SAN INTL INC (DE)
Adjudicated bankrupt 10/21/1976
Stockholders' equity unlikely

PORT OF CALL ONLINE INC (NV)
Common $0.001 par split (8) for (1) by issuance of (7) additional shares payable 11/12/2014 to holders of record 11/07/2014 Ex date - 11/13/2014
Name changed to PureBase Corp. 01/12/2015

PORT ORFORD CEDAR CO.
Acquired by Coos Bay Lumber Co. in 1945
Each share Capital Stock exchanged for (1) share Preferred no par and (2) shares Common $10 par
(See Coos Bay Lumber Co.)

PORT ORFORD CEDAR PRODUCTS CO.
Reorganized as Pacific White Cedar Co. 00/00/1932
Details not available

PORT RADIUM MINES LTD. (ON)
Name changed to Silver Strike Mines Ltd. 1/19/62
Silver Strike Mines Ltd. was acquired by Fontana Mines (1945) Ltd. 2/8/62

PORT ST LUCIE NATL BK HLDG CORP (FL)
Merged into Seacoast Banking Corp. of Florida 05/30/1997
Each share Common 1¢ par exchanged for (1.00337) shares Common 1¢ par

PORT STAR INDS INC (NC)
Name changed back to Riverside Homes, Inc. 3/8/83
(See Riverside Homes, Inc.)

PORT TOWNSEND & PUGET SOUND RAILWAY CO.
Ceased operations 00/00/1929
Details not available

PORT WENTWORTH CO.
Liquidated in 1935

PORT WENTWORTH TERMINAL CORP.
Reorganized as Port Wentworth Co. in 1928 which was liquidated in 1935

PORTA BELLO INC (UT)
Name changed to Deep Gas Exploration, Inc. 02/24/1981
Deep Gas Exploration, Inc. name changed to Ratex Resources Inc. 06/07/1985
(See Ratex Resources Inc.)

PORTA-CAN INC. (DE)
Charter cancelled and declared inoperative and void for non-payment of taxes 3/1/77

PORTA LUBE AUTOMOTIVES INC (AB)
Name changed to Cottonballs Corp. 11/20/90
Cottonballs Corp. recapitalized as Consolidated Cottonballs Corp. 2/7/92 which recapitalized as CTB Industries Inc. 5/12/94
(See CTB Industries Inc.)

PORTA PRO INC (DE)
Charter cancelled and declared inoperative and void for non-payment of taxes 3/1/82

PORTA SYS CORP (DE)
Old Common 1¢ par split (2) for (1) by issuance of (1) additional share 05/08/1981
Old Common 1¢ par split (3) for (2) by issuance of (0.5) additional share 02/19/1982
Old Common 1¢ par split (2) for (1) by issuance of (1) additional share 06/30/1983
Each share old Common 1¢ par exchanged for (0.2) share new Common 1¢ par 08/02/1996
Each share new Common 1¢ par exchanged for (0.090009) share new Common 1¢ par 08/08/2008
Each share new Common 1¢ par exchanged again for (0.002) share new Common 1¢ par 02/11/2010
Name changed to North Hills Signal Processing Corp. 06/29/2010

PORTABLE ELECTRIC TOOLS, INC. (IL)
6% Preferred $100 par called for redemption 11/16/1967
Stock Dividends - 25% 11/01/1958; 20% 11/02/1959; 10% 11/01/1960; 10% 11/01/1961
Merged into Murphy (G.W.) Industries, Inc. 10/17/1967
Each share Common $1 par exchanged for (0.08333) share $2 Conv. Preferred 3rd Ser. $5 par and (0.275) share Common $5 par
Murphy (G.W.) Industries, Inc. name changed to Reed Tool Co. 09/15/1972 which merged into Baker Oil Tools, Inc. 11/26/1975 which name changed to Baker International Corp. (CA) 01/28/1976 which reincorporated in Delaware 01/27/1983 which merged into Baker Hughes Inc.04/03/1987 which merged into Baker Hughes, a GE company 07/05/2017

PORTABLE MACHINERY CO. OF NEW JERSEY
In process of liquidation in 1940

Details not available

PORTACOM WIRELESS INC (BC)
Reincorporated under the laws of Delaware 12/23/96
(See Portacom Wireless, Inc. (DE))

PORTACOM WIRELESS INC (DE)
Plan of reorganization under Chapter 11 Federal Bankruptcy Code effective 10/22/1998
Each share Common no par received initial distribution of (0.029168) share VDC Communications, Inc. Common $0.0001 par payable 12/29/1999 to holders of record 12/10/1998
Each share Common no par received second and final distribution of (0.24815) share VDC Communications, Inc. Common $0.0001 par payable 07/21/2000 to holders of record 06/12/2000
Note: Certificates were not required to be surrendered are without value
(See VDC Communications, Inc.)

PORTAFONE CORP (AZ)
Charter revoked for failure to file reports and pay fees 07/31/1975

PORTAFONE INTL CELLULAR COMMUNICATIONS INC (DE)
Each share old Common $0.0001 par exchanged for (0.02) share new Common $0.0001 par 01/25/1991
Name changed to PNF Industries, Inc. 10/10/1991
PNF Industries, Inc. reorganized as No Fire Technologies, Inc. 08/11/1995

PORTAGE AVE GOLD MINES LTD (MB)
Merged into Canadian Gold Mines Ltd. 3/24/86
Each share Capital Stock no par exchanged for (1) share Common no par
Canadian Gold Mines Ltd. merged into Consolidated Canadian Fortune Resources Inc. 12/7/90 which name changed to Canadian Fortune Resources Inc. (New) 3/15/93 which merged into Fortune Energy Inc. 9/1/93
(See Fortune Energy Inc.)

PORTAGE FDS (MA)
Name changed to Newpoint Funds and Government Money Market Fund Investment Shares and Government Money Market Fund Trust Shares reclassified as Government Money Market Fund 01/31/1995
Newpoint Funds name changed to FirstMerit Funds 01/31/2000
(See FirstMerit Funds)

PORTAGE INDS CORP (DE)
Merged into Spartech Corp. 05/09/1996
Each share Common 1¢ par exchanged for $6.60 cash

PORTAGE INDS CORP (OH)
Name changed to Sweitzer Holdings, Inc. 03/18/1976
(See Sweitzer Holdings, Inc.)

PORTAGE ISLAND (CHIBOUGAMAU) MINES LTD. (QC)
Acquired by Copper Rand Chibougamau Mines Ltd. on a (1) for (3.5) basis 08/29/1969
Copper Rand Chibougama Mines Ltd. merged into Patino Mining Corp. 12/26/1962 which reorganized as Patino N.V. 12/20/1971
(See Patino N.V.)

PORTAGE LIQUIDATING CO.
In process of liquidation in 1945

PORTAGE LONGLAC MINES LTD. (ON)
Charter dissolved for default in filing annual returns 9/24/56

PORTAGE MINERALS INC (CANADA)
Each share old Common no par exchanged for (0.2) share new Common no par 11/17/2009
Plan of reorganization effective 10/04/2013
Each share new Common no par exchanged for (7.15984912) shares Tri-Star Resources PLC Ordinary 0.005p par
Note: U.S. Securityholders will receive cash from the sale of Tri-Star shares

PORTAGE NATL BK (PORTAGE, IN)
Merged into Northern Indiana Bank & Trust Co. (Portage, IN) 01/17/1984
Each share Common $12.50 par exchanged for $152.28 cash

PORTAL RES LTD (BC)
Name changed 12/21/2004
Name changed from Portal de Oro Resources Ltd. to Portal Resources Ltd. 12/21/2004
Recapitalized as Galileo Petroleum Ltd. 04/02/2012
Each share Common no par exchanged for (0.2) share Common no par
Galileo Petroleum Ltd. name changed to Galileo Exploration Ltd. 12/21/2016

PORTAL RES LTD (BC)
Recapitalized as Capella Resources Ltd. (Incorporated 02/27/1987) 12/07/1994
Each (3.7) shares Common no par exchanged for (1) share Common no par
Capella Resources Ltd. (Incorporated 02/27/1987) recapitalized as Cerro Mining Corp. 05/16/2012

PORTAL SOFTWARE INC (DE)
Issue Information - 4,000,000 shares COM offered at $14 per share on 05/05/1999
Old Common $0.001 par split (2) for (1) by issuance of (1) additional share payable 1/19/2000 to holders of record 12/31/99
Each share old Common $0.001 par exchanged for (0.2) share new Common $0.001 par 9/26/2003
Merged into Oracle Corp. 7/3/2006
Each share new Common $0.001 par exchanged for $4.90 cash

PORTALPLAYER INC (CA)
Issue Information - 6,250,000 shares COM offered at $17 per share on 11/18/2004
Merged into NVIDIA Corp. 1/5/2007
Each share Common $0.0001 par exchanged for $13.50 cash

PORTALTOCHINA COM INC (NV)
Recapitalized as Northridge Ventures Inc. 07/09/2010
Each share Common $0.0001 par exchanged for (0.1) share Common $0.0001 par
Northridge Ventures Inc. name changed to UCP Holdings, Inc. 06/25/2013

PORTALZONE COM INC (NV)
Name changed to Status Wines of Tuscany, Inc. 07/12/2000
Status Wines of Tuscany, Inc. recapitalized as Mariner's Choice International Inc. (NV) 06/04/2007 which reorganized in Wyoming 09/02/2014 which name changed to Han Tang Technology, Inc. 09/28/2015

PORTAVIDEO MAGIC MOVIE MACH LTD (CANADA)
Reorganized as Shannock Corp. 5/8/85
Each share Class A no par exchanged for (1) share Class A no par
Shannock Corp. recapitalized as TSC Shannock Corp. 4/4/88
(See TSC Shannock Corp.)

PORTCOMM COMMUNICATIONS LTD (BC)
Name changed to Roach (Hal) Studios Corp. 11/01/1977
Roach (Hal) Studios Corp. merged into H.R.S. Industries, Inc. 05/21/1982 which merged into International H.R.S. Industries Inc. 05/15/1984 which name changed to Glenex Industries Inc. 05/25/1987 which merged into Quest Investment Corp. 07/04/2002 which merged into Quest Capital Corp. (BC) 06/30/2003 which reincorporated in Canada 05/27/2008 which name changed to Sprott Resource Lending Corp. 09/10/2010 which merged into Sprott Inc. 07/24/2013

PORTEC INC (DE)
Common $10 par changed to $1 par 1/1/76
Common $1 par split (3) for (2) by issuance of (0.5) additional share 6/15/76
Stock Dividends - 10% 3/11/74; 20% 12/16/74; 10% 12/15/75; 10% 6/15/77; 10% 12/1/92; 10% 12/14/93; 10% 12/15/94
Merged into MHD Acquisition Corp. 6/4/98
Each share Common $1 par exchanged for $16 cash

PORTEC RAIL PRODS INC (WV)
Issue Information - 2,000,000 shares COM offered at $10 per share on 01/23/2004
Merged into Foster (L.B.) Co. 12/27/2010
Each share Common $1 par exchanged for $11.80 cash

PORTEOUS GROWTH FD INC (MD)
Acquired by Channing Securities, Inc, (MD) 06/28/1974
Each share Capital Stock $1 par exchanged for (3.992) American Fund Shares 1¢ par
Channing Securities, Inc. merged into American General Shares, Inc. 09/02/1975 which merged into American General Enterprise Fund, Inc. 08/31/1979 which name changed to American Capital Enterprise Fund, Inc. (MD) 09/09/1983 which reincorporated in Delaware as Van Kampen American Capital Enterprise Fund 08/03/1995 which name changed to Van Kampen Enterprise Fund 08/31/1998

PORTER BANCORP INC (KY)
Each share old Common no par exchanged for (0.2) share new Common no par 12/19/2016
Stock Dividends - 5% payable 11/10/2008 to holders of record 11/03/2008 Ex date - 10/30/2008; 5% payable 11/19/2009 to holders of record 11/12/2009 Ex date - 11/09/2009; 5% payable 12/14/2010 to holders of record 12/05/2010 Ex date - 12/01/2010
Name changed to Limestone Bancorp, Inc. 06/19/2018

PORTER-CABLE MACHINE CO. (NY)
Each share Common no par exchanged for (2) shares Common $10 par in January 1955
Stock Dividend - 10% 12/21/56
Acquired by Rockwell Maufacturing Co. 12/29/60
Each share Common $10 par exchanged for (0.7) share Common $2.50 par
Rockwell Manufacturing Co. merged into Rockwell International Corp. (Old) 2/16/73 which merged into Boeing Co. 12/6/96

PORTER H K INC (DE)
Reincorporated 12/11/1958
State of incorporation changed from (PA) to (DE) 12/11/1958
4-1/4% Preferred $100 par called for redemption 07/31/1967
Common $5 par split (6) for (5) by issuance of (0.2) additional share 12/09/1969
5-1/2% Preference $100 par called for redemption 04/15/1987
Company went private through a tender offer 00/00/1988
Details not available

PORTER H K INC (MA)
Stock Dividends - 10% 06/10/1957; 20% 06/11/1962; 10% 06/23/1964; 10% 12/30/1968
Merged into Cooper Industries, Inc. 03/31/1987
Each share Common $1 par exchanged for $45 cash
Note: $4 cash per share was placed in escrow for possible future distribution

PORTER MCLEOD NATL RETAIL INC (DE)
Name changed to Rascals International, Inc. 08/16/1999
Rascals International, Inc. name changed to Headliners Entertainment Group, Inc. 06/02/2004
(See Headliners Entertainment Group, Inc.)

PORTER PAINT CO. (KY)
Merged into Courtaulds PLC 11/20/1987
Each share Common no par exchanged for $434.36 cash

PORTERFIELD AIRCRAFT CORP.
Property acquired by Columbia Aircraft Co. in 1941
No stockholders' equity

PORTFIELD INDS INC (ON)
Recapitalized as Canmine Resources Corp. 05/01/1991
Each share Common no par exchanged for (0.1) share Common no par
(See Canmine Resources Corp.)

PORTFIELD PETES LTD (ON)
Merged into Portfield Industries Inc. 10/22/1980
Each (8) shares Common no par exchanged for (3) shares Common no par
Portfield Industries Inc. recapitalized as Canmine Resources Corp. 05/01/1991
(See Canmine Resources Corp.)

PORTFOLIO PUBG INC (DE)
Recapitalized as Aviato International Inc. 05/13/1993
Each share Common $0.001 par exchanged for (0.2) share Common $0.001 par
Aviato International Inc. name changed to Navigato International Inc. 03/03/1994 which name changed to Businessnet International Inc. 06/10/1996 which recapitalized as Businessnet Holdings Corp. 08/28/1998 which name changed to Invicta Corp. 06/30/2000 which name changed to Executive Hospitality Corp. 05/02/2005 which recapitalized as Forest Resources Management Corp. 08/09/2006
(See Forest Resources Management Corp.)

PORTFOLIO RECOVERY ASSOCS INC (DE)
Common 1¢ par split (3) for (1) by issuance of (2) additional shares payable 08/01/2013 to holders of record 07/01/2013 Ex date - 08/02/2013
Name changed to PRA Group, Inc. 11/04/2014

PORTFOLIO VENTURES INC (DE)
Charter cancelled and declared inoperative and void for non-payment of taxes 3/1/97

PORTIS STYLE INDUSTRIES, INC. (IL)
Name changed to P.S.I. Industries, Inc. 1/2/58
P.S.I. Industries, Inc. completely liquidated 6/30/69

PORTIVITY INC (DE)
Charter cancelled and declared inoperative and void for non-payment of taxes 03/01/2000

PORTLAND & OGDENSBURG RWY. CO.
Acquired by Maine Central Railroad Co. for $18.75 per share in 1943

PORTLAND BASEBALL CLUB, INC. (OR)
Dissolved for failure to file reports and pay fees 4/16/71

PORTLAND BREWING CO (OR)
Each (600,000) shares old Common no par exchanged for (1) share new Common no par 8/2/2004
Note: In effect holders received $0.10 cash per share and public interest was eliminated

PORTLAND CANNING INC (OR)
Name changed to Pocco, Inc. 02/22/1977
(See Pocco, Inc.)

PORTLAND ELECTRIC POWER CO.
Reorganized as Portland General Electric Co. in 1948
Each share Prior Preference exchanged for (6-1/3) shares new Common
Each share 1st Preferred exchanged for (2/3) share new Common
2nd Preferred and Common had no equity

PORTLAND GAS & COKE CO (OR)
Recapitalized 00/00/1951
Each share 6% Preferred $100 par exchanged for (7) shares Common no par
Each share 7% Preferred $100 par exchanged for (8) shares Common no par
Recapitalized 00/00/1954
Common no par changed to $19 par
Recapitalized 05/31/1957
Common $19 par changed to $9.50 par and (1) additional share issued
Name changed to Northwest Natural Gas Co. 07/01/1958
Northwest Natural Gas Co. reorganized as Northwest Natural Holding Co. 10/01/2018

PORTLAND GAS LIGHT CO. (ME)
Each share 6% Preferred $100 par exchanged for (1.1) shares $5 Preferred no par and $7.75 cash in 1943
Common no par split (3) for (1) by issuance of (2) additional shares 1/15/62
Stock Dividend - 10% 1/15/60
Merged into Northern Utilities, Inc. (ME) 8/11/66
Each share $5 Preferred no par exchanged for (1) share 5% Preferred $100 par
Each share Common no par exchanged for (1) share Common $5 par
Northern Utilities, Inc. (ME) merged into Northern Utilities, Inc. (NH) 6/30/69 which merged into Bay State Gas Co. (New) 10/30/79 which merged into Nipsco Industries, Inc. 2/12/99 which name changed to NiSource Inc. (IN) 4/14/99 which reincorporated in Delaware 11/1/2000

PORTLAND GEN CORP (OR)
Merged into Enron Corp. 7/1/97
Each share Common $3.75 par exchanged for (0.9825) share Common no par
(See Enron Corp.)

PORTLAND GEN ELEC CO (OR)
Common no par changed to $15 par 00/00/1952
Common $15 par changed to $7.50 par and (1) additional share issued 00/00/1954
Common $7.50 par changed to $3.75 par and (1) additional share issued 05/09/1962
11.50% Preferred $100 par called for redemption 12/02/1985
Under plan of reorganization each share Common $3.75 par automatically became (1) share Portland General Corp. Common $3.75 par 03/28/1986
(See Portland General Corp.)
9.76% Preferred $100 par called for redemption 12/01/1986
$4.40 Preferred $25 par called for redemption 04/15/1987
$4.32 Preferred $25 par called for called for redemption 07/01/1987
$2.60 Preferred $25 par called for redemption 07/06/1992
7.88% Preferred $100 par called for redemption 11/08/1995
7.95% Preferred $100 par called for redemption 11/08/1995
8.20% Preferred $100 par called for redemption 11/08/1995
8.10% Preferred $100 par called for redemption 04/15/1996
7.75% Preferred no par called for redemption at $100 plus $1.60 accrued dividends on 06/15/2007
(Additional Information in Active)

PORTLAND GOLD MINING CO.
Acquired by United Gold Mines Co. 00/00/1934
Details not available

PORTLAND NEWSPAPER PUBLISHING CO., INC. (OR)
Charter revoked for failure to file reports and pay fees 09/20/1966

PORTLAND RAILROAD CO.
Liquidated in 1945

PORTLAND REPORTER PUBLISHING CO., INC. (OR)
Merged into Portland Newspaper Publishing Co., Inc. 04/27/1964
Details not available

PORTLAND TRAN CO (DE)
5% Conv. Preferred $25 par called for redemption 12/31/59
In process of liquidation
Each share Common $1 par received initial distribution of $3 cash 8/16/76
Each share Common $1 par received second distribution of $3 cash 12/30/77
Details on subsequent distributions, if any, are not available

PORTLAND TRUST & SAVINGS BANK (PORTLAND, OR)
Each share Common $100 par exchanged for (5) shares Common $20 par 00/00/1945
Name changed to Portland Trust Bank (Portland, OR) 12/01/1951 which name changed to Oregon Bank (Portland, OR) 06/21/1960

PORTLAND TRUST BANK (PORTLAND, OR)
Name changed to Oregon Bank (Portland, Ore.) 6/21/60
(See Oregon Bank (Portland, Ore.))

PORTLAND VEGETABLE OIL MILLS CO.
Acquired by Glidden Co. 00/00/1929
Details not available

PORTMAN EXPLS LTD (BC)
Reorganized under the laws of Yukon as Daytona Energy Corp. 01/18/1999
Each share Common no par exchanged for (0.33333333) share Common no par
Daytona Energy Corp. (YT)

reincorporated in British Columbia 01/29/2005 which reincorporated in Alberta 02/02/2007 which recapitalized as Riata Resources Corp. 09/01/2010 which name changed to Petroforte International Ltd. 11/02/2011 which recapitalized as Canamax Energy Ltd. 02/21/2014
(See Canamax Energy Ltd.)

PORTNEUF MINERAL CORP. (QC)
Charter cancelled in April 1974

PORTO ENERGY CORP (BC)
All officers and directors resigned and operations ceased 05/30/2014

PORTO RICAN AMERICAN TOBACCO CO.
Reorganized as Rican Corp. in 1940 which was liquidated in 1943

PORTO RICO POWER CO. LTD. (QC)
Liquidated in 1944

PORTO RICO RAILWAY CO. LTD.
Name changed to Porto Rico Power Co. Ltd. in 1930 which was liquidated in 1944

PORTO RICO TELEPHONE CO. (DE)
Each share Common $100 par exchanged for (5) shares Common $20 par 11/23/55
Name changed to Puerto Rico Telephone Co. (Del.) (Old) 10/1/58 which merged into Puerto Rico Telephone Co. (Del.) (New) 10/2/67
(See Puerto Rico Telephone Co. (Del.) (New))

PORTOFINO INVT INC (UT)
Name changed to Fashion Tech International, Inc. (UT) 01/31/1984
Fashion Tech International, Inc. (UT) reorganized in Nevada 04/28/1999 which name changed to China Nutrifruit Group Ltd. 08/25/2008

PORTOLA RES INC (BC)
Name changed to Lithium Energi Exploration Inc. 03/24/2017

PORTRAIT IMPRESSIONS CDA LTD (ON)
Each share old Class A Common no par exchanged for (0.66666666) share new Class A Common no par 12/28/1993
Name changed to Carriage Automotive Group Inc. 09/25/1998
Carriage Automotive Group Inc. name changed to Cars4u.com Ltd. 02/14/2000 which name changed to Cars4u Ltd. 01/30/2003 which recapitalized as Chesswood Income Fund 05/10/2006 which reorganized as Chesswood Group Ltd. 01/04/2011

PORTRUSH PETE CORP (BC)
Recapitalized as Westbridge Energy Corp. 12/11/2009
Each share Common no par exchanged for (0.1) share Common no par

PORTS OF CALL INC (DE)
Name changed to POCI, Inc. 5/10/90
POCI, Inc. assets transferred to POCI Inc. Liquidating Trust 12/31/92

PORTSMOUTH BK SHS INC (NH)
Common 10¢ par split (3) for (2) by issuance of (0.5) additional share 03/15/1994
Stock Dividends - 2% payable 03/15/1996 to holders of record 03/01/1996; 2% payable 03/15/1997 to holders of record 03/01/1997
Merged into CFX Corp. 08/29/1997
Each share Common 10¢ par exchanged for (0.9314) share Common $0.66-2/3 par
CFX Corp. merged into Peoples Heritage Financial Group, Inc. 04/10/1998 which name changed to Banknorth Group, Inc. (ME) 05/10/2000 which merged into TD Banknorth Inc. 03/01/2005
(See TD Banknorth Inc.)

PORTSMOUTH BKG CO (OH)
Merged into First National Cincinnati Corp. 08/01/1980
Each share Common $8.33 par exchanged for $160 cash

PORTSMOUTH CORP. (OH)
Liquidation completed 12/15/61

PORTSMOUTH INVT CO (CA)
Merged into International Construction Systems, Inc. 01/02/1973
Each share Common 50¢ par exchanged for (1.25) shares Common 10¢ par
International Construction Systems, Inc. name changed to X-Zel Inc. 05/10/1985
(See X-Zel Inc.)

PORTSMOUTH STEEL CORP. (OH)
Name changed to Portsmouth Corp. 4/22/59 which completed liquidation 12/15/61

PORTUCEL INDL EMPRESA PRODUTORA CELULOSE S A (PORTUGAL)
Name changed to Portucel-Empresa Produtora de Pasta e Papel, S.A. 01/05/2001

PORTUGAL FD INC (MD)
Name changed to Progressive Return Fund, Inc. 12/18/2000
Progressive Return Fund, Inc. merged into Cornerstone Strategic Value Fund, Inc. 6/28/2004

PORTUGAL TELECOM SGPS S A (PORTUGAL)
Name changed 12/26/2000
Sponsored ADR's for Ordinary split (5) for (1) by issuance of (4) additional ADR's payable 12/01/1999 to holders of record 11/29/1999 Ex date - 12/02/1999
Name changed from Portugal Telecom S.A. to Portugal Telecom, SGPS, S.A. 12/26/2000
Stock Dividend - 2% payable 07/30/2001 to holders of record 06/19/2001
Each Sponsored ADR for Ordinary received distribution of (0.176067) P.T. Multimedia Servicos de Telecomunicacoes e Multimedia Sponsored ADR for Ordinary payable 11/13/2007 to holders of record 11/01/2007 Ex date - 10/30/2007
Name changed to PHAROL, SGPS S.A. 06/26/2015

PORTUGUESE-AMERICAN TIN CO. (DE)
Merged into Yuba Consolidated Industries, Inc. on a (23) for (1) basis 08/01/1957
Yuba Consolidated Industries, Inc. reorganized as Yuba Industries, Inc. (DE) 12/06/1965
(See Yuba Industries, Inc. (DE))

PORTUGUESE RLTY INVT CORP (DE)
Name changed to Phorum Re Investment Corp. 05/22/1987
(See Phorum Re Investment Corp.)

PORTX OPERACOES PORTUARIAS S A (BRAZIL)
GDR agreement terminated 09/21/2012
Each GDR for Common exchanged for $1.269632 cash

POSEIDIS INC (FL)
Each share old Common $0.0001 par exchanged for (8) shares new Common $0.0001 par 03/31/2004
SEC revoked common stock registration 05/11/2009
Stockholders' equity unlikely

POSEIDON CAP CORP (AB)
Name changed to Acceleware Corp. 06/14/2006

Acceleware Corp. name changed to Acceleware Ltd. 05/03/2011

POSEIDON EXPLS LTD (BC)
Delisted from Vancouver Stock Exchange 11/28/1986

POSEIDON GOLD LTD (AUSTRALIA)
Name changed to Posgold Ltd. 06/29/1995
Posgold Ltd. merged into Normandy Mining Ltd. 09/11/1996 which was acquired by Newmont Mining Corp. 06/26/2002

POSEIDON LTD (AUSTRALIA)
Each Unsponsored ADR for Ordinary A$0.20 par exchanged for (0.2) Sponsored ADR for Ordinary A$0.20 par 08/29/1988
Stock Dividend - 200% 06/10/1987
Merged into Normandy Poseidon Ltd. 06/05/1991
Each Sponsored ADR for Ordinary A$0.20 par exchanged for (1.3) ADR's for Ordinary A$0.20 par
Normandy Poseidon Ltd. name changed to Normandy Mining Ltd. 06/20/1995 which was acquired by Newmont Mining Corp. 06/26/2002

POSEIDON MINERALS LTD (BC)
Reorganized under the laws of Canada as Stingray Resources Inc. 07/22/2003
Each share Common no par exchanged for (0.5) share Common no par
Stingray Resources Inc. name changed to Stingray Copper Inc. 07/18/2007 which merged into Mercator Minerals Ltd. 12/21/2009

POSEIDON POOLS AMER INC (DE)
Common 1¢ par split (3) for (1) by issuance of (2) additional shares 6/15/89
Charter cancelled and declared inoperative and void for non-payment of taxes 6/24/92

POSERA HDX INC (ON)
Reincorporated under the laws of Alberta as Posera-HDX Ltd. and Class A Common no par reclassified as Common no par 10/12/2011
Posera-HDX Ltd. name changed to Posera Ltd. 04/14/2016

POSERA HDX LTD (AB)
Name changed to Posera Ltd. 04/14/2016

POSEY IRON WKS INC (PA)
Dissolved 5/8/85
Details not available

POSGOLD LTD (AUSTRALIA)
Merged into Normandy Mining Ltd. 09/11/1996
Each Sponsored ADR for Ordinary A$0.10 par exchanged for (1.57) Sponsored ADR for Ordinary A$0.20 par
Normandy Mining Ltd. acquired by Newmont Mining Corp. 06/26/2002

POSH INTL INC (TX)
Common $0.001 par split (2) for (1) by issuance of (1) additional share payable 01/20/1997 to holders of record 01/13/1997
Recapitalized as Great Lakes Acquisition, Inc. (TX) 04/14/2003
Each share Common $0.001 par exchanged for (0.2) share Common $0.001 par
Great Lakes Acquisition, Inc. (TX) reincorporated in Nevada 12/31/2003 which recapitalized as Integrated Parking Solutions, Inc. 03/31/2006 which name changed to Integrated Cannabis Solutions, Inc. 04/21/2014

POSI SEAL INTL INC (DE)
Each share old Common 1¢ par exchanged for (0.1) share new Common 1¢ par 08/18/1971

Merged into Monsanto Co. 01/31/1985
Each share new Common 1¢ par exchanged for $8 cash

POSI TRAC RAIL INC (TX)
Completely liquidated 5/15/72
Each share Common 10¢ par exchanged for first and final distribution of (0.293) share Whitaker Oil Co. Common 10¢ par
(See Whitaker Oil Co.)

POSITECH CORP (IA)
Merged into Columbus McKinnon Corp. 05/30/1989
Each share Common 1¢ par exchanged for $0.28964 cash

POSITION INC (AB)
Issue Information - 3,600,000 shares COM offered at $1 per share on 04/07/1997
Delisted from Alberta Stock Exchange 10/04/1999

POSITIVE ENERGY PRODS INC (BC)
Recapitalized as Dimensions West Marketing Inc. 6/27/95
Each share Common no par exchanged for (0.2) share Common no par
Dimensions West Marketing Inc. name changed to Dimensions West Energy Inc. 11/14/97

POSITIVE FLIGHT CONTROL, INC. (WA)
Charter dissolved for failure to file reports and pay fees 7/7/72

POSITIVE RESPONSE TELEVISION INC (CA)
Merged into National Media Corp. 05/17/1996
Each share Common 1¢ par exchanged for (0.4512) share Common 10¢ par
National Media Corp. name changed to e4L, Inc. 02/25/1999 which recapitalized as Holographic Storage Ltd. 11/25/2005
(See Holographic Storage Ltd.)

POSITRON FIBER SYS CORP (CANADA)
Merged into Reltec Corp. 10/06/1998
Each share Common no par exchanged for $13.625 cash

POSSIS MED INC (MN)
Name changed 12/08/1971
Name changed 12/08/1993
Common 25¢ par changed to 12-1/2¢ par and (1) additional share issued 10/15/1963
Common 12-1/2¢ par changed to 40¢ par and (1) additional share issued 01/05/1970
Name changed from Possis Machine Corp. to Possis Corp. 12/08/1971
Common 40¢ par split (2) for (1) by issuance of (1) additional share 01/29/1983
Common 40¢ par split (2) for (1) by issuance of (1) additional share 01/30/1986
Common 40¢ par split (2) for (1) by issuance of (1) additional share 05/01/1987
Name changed from Possis Corp. to Possis Medical, Inc. 12/08/1993
Stock Dividend - 10% 12/14/1984
Merged into Bayer AG 04/03/2008
Each share Common 40¢ par exchanged for $19.50 cash

POST AMERN CORP (DE)
Each (300) shares old Common $1 par exchanged for (1) share new Common $1 par 03/21/1983
Merged into Fidelity National Corp. 01/31/1988
Each share 6% Preferred $10 par exchanged for $10 cash
Each share new Common $1 par exchanged for $1,232 cash

POST COACH INC (PA)
Assets taken over and out of business 05/05/1975
Stockholders' equity unlikely

POST CORP (WI)
Stock Dividends - 20% 12/31/1969; 100% 11/30/1978
Merged into Gillett Communications, Inc. 08/01/1984
Each share Common $1 par exchanged for $65 cash

POST DATA INC (NV)
Name changed to Polar Petroleum Corp. 11/06/2012

POST DATA SVCS CORP (UT)
Involuntarily dissolved 06/01/1990

POST ENERGY CORP NEW (AB)
Merged into Ketch Energy Ltd. 7/9/2001
Each share Common no par exchanged for (1.3) shares Common no par and $2.1474 principal amount of Kick Energy Partnership 6% Promissory Notes due 6/27/2011
Ketch Energy Ltd. merged into Acclaim Energy Trust 10/1/2002
(See Acclaim Energy Trust)

POST ENERGY CORP OLD (AB)
Issue Information - 3,000,000 shares COM offered at $1 per share on 10/13/1993
Merged into Post Energy Corp. (New) 12/31/94
Each share Common no par exchanged for (1) share Common no par
Post Energy Corp. (New) merged into Ketch Energy Ltd. 7/9/2001 which merged into Acclaim Energy Ltd. 10/1/2002

POST HLDGS INC (MO)
Each 5.25% Tangible Equity Unit automatically became (1.7114) shares Common 1¢ par 06/01/2017
(Additional Information in Active)

POST OAK BK (HOUSTON, TX)
Merged into Compass Bank (Houston, TX) 04/19/1996
Each share Common $12 par exchanged for $66.71 cash

POST OFFICE SQUARE CO. (MA)
Name changed to Sheraton Buildings, Inc. 00/00/1951
(See Sheraton Buildings, Inc.)

POST PETES LTD (AB)
Recapitalized as Rockford Technology Corp. 08/05/1987
Each share Common no par exchanged for (1) share Common no par
(See Rockford Technology Corp.)

POST PPTYS INC (GA)
7.625% Preferred Ser. C called for redemption at $25 plus $0.344184 accrued dividends on 03/05/2004
7.625% Preferred Ser. B 1¢ par called for redemption at $25 plus $0.386543 accrued dividends on 03/14/2011
Merged into Mid-America Apartment Communities, Inc. 12/01/2016
Each share 8.5% Preferred 1¢ par exchanged for (1) share 8.5% Preferred Ser. I 1¢ par
Each share Common 1¢ par exchanged for (0.71) share Common 1¢ par

POST PUBLISHING CO. (WI)
Name changed to Post Corp. 3/24/64
(See Post Corp.)

POST STR INVT CO (CA)
Voting Trust Agreement terminated 11/22/44
Each VTC for 4% Non-Cum. 1st Preferred $1 par exchanged for (1) share 4% Non-Cum. 1st Preferred $1 par
4% Non-Cum. 1st Preferred $1 par called for redemption 11/01/1968
5% 2nd Preferred $1 par called for redemption 11/01/1968

POSTAL INSTANT PRESS (DE)
Reincorporated 10/29/87
Common no par split (5) for (4) by issuance of (0.25) additional share 1/2/79
Common no par split (5) for (4) by issuance of (0.25) additional share 7/25/80
Common no par split (3) for (2) by issuance of (0.5) additional share 8/10/81
Common no par split (3) for (2) by issuance of (0.5) additional share 7/25/83
Stock Dividend - 25% 11/11/77
State of incorporation changed from (CA) to (DE) and Common no par changed to 1¢ par 10/29/87
Merged into PIP Holdings Corp. 2/22/89
Each share Common 1¢ par exchanged for $15.50 cash

POSTAL LIFE INSURANCE CO. (NY)
Each share Common $10 par exchanged for (5) shares Common $2 par 8/17/55
Merged into Bankers Security Life insurance Society 12/31/62
Each share Common $2 par exchanged for (2) shares Common $25 par
Bankers Security Life Insurance Society merged into United Services Life Insurance Co. 12/20/79 which reorganized in Virginia as USLICO Corp. 8/15/84 which merged into NWNL Companies, Inc. 1/17/95 which name changed to ReliaStar Financial Corp. 2/13/95
(See ReliaStar Financial Corp.)

POSTAL TELEGRAPH, INC.
Acquired by Western Union Telegraph Co. in 1943
Each share Preferred exchanged for (1) share Class B no par
Each share Common exchanged for (0.05) share Class B no par
Western Union Telegraph Co. reorganized as Western Union Corp. (Old) 1/30/70 which merged into Western Union Corp. (New) 12/31/87 which name changed to New Valley Corp. 4/22/91

POSTAL TELEGRAPH & CABLE CORP.
Reorganized as Postal Telegraph, Inc. in 1940
No stockholders' equity

POSTECH CORP (CANADA)
Assets sold for the benefit of creditors 06/00/1991
No stockholders' equity

POSTERALLEY COM INC (CO)
Common $0.0001 par split (10) for (1) by issuance of (9) additional shares payable 4/23/2002 to holders of record 4/19/2002 Ex date - 4/24/2002
Name changed to Medical International Technology Inc. 6/24/2002

POSTMARK STORES AMER INC (CO)
Recapitalized as Ryan-Murphy Inc. 01/19/1989
Each share Common $0.00067 par exchanged for (0.005) share Common $0.00067 par

POSTMASTERS INC (FL)
Name changed to Same Day Express, Inc. 01/31/1989
Same Day Express, Inc. name changed to Innovative Shipping Systems, Inc. 09/04/1992 which recapitalized as Velocity Aerospace, Inc. 11/04/2005 which name changed to Critical Power Solutions International, Inc. (FL) 08/08/2007 which reincorporated in Delaware as Critical Solutions, Inc. 03/03/2008

POSTNL N V (NETHERLANDS)
Stock Dividends - 5.5555% payable 05/15/2012 to holders of record 04/25/2012 Ex date - 04/23/2012; 6.25% payable 08/23/2012 to holders of record 08/16/2012 Ex date - 08/14/2012
ADR agreement terminated 12/22/2017
Each Sponsored ADR for Ordinary exchanged for $3.862101 cash

POSTUM CEREAL CO., INC. (DE)
Name changed to Postum Co., Inc. 3/23/27
Postum Co., Inc. name changed to General Foods Corp. 7/24/29
(See General Foods Corp.)

POSTUM CO., INC. (DE)
Name changed to General Foods Corp. 07/24/1929
(See General Foods Corp.)

POTASH CO. OF AMERICA (CO)
Each share Capital Stock no par exchanged for (2) shares Capital Stock $5 par in 1938
Merged into Ideal Basic Industries, Inc. (CO) 12/31/67
Each share Capital Stock $5 par exchanged for (0.27) share 4-3/4% Conv. Preferred $100 par and (2) shares Common $5 par
Ideal Basic Industries, Inc. (CO) reincorporated in Delaware 5/15/87 which merged into Holnam Inc. 3/8/90
(See Holnam Inc.)

POTASH CO AMER INC (CANADA)
Merged into Rio Algom Ltd. 12/31/87
Each share $2.50 Conv. Preferred Ser. 1 no par exchanged for $18 cash
Note: Option to exchange for Common expired 2/15/88

POTASH CORP SASK INC (CANADA)
Reincorporated 05/08/2002
Place of incorporation changed from (SK) to (Canada) 05/08/2002
Common no par split (2) for (1) by issuance of (1) additional share payable 08/17/2004 to holders of record 08/11/2004 Ex date - 08/18/2004
Common no par split (3) for (1) by issuance of (2) additional shares payable 05/29/2007 to holders of record 05/22/2007 Ex date - 05/30/2007
Common no par split (3) for (1) by issuance of (2) additional shares payable 02/24/2011 to holders of record 02/16/2011 Ex date - 02/25/2011
Merged into Nutrien Ltd. 01/02/2018
Each share Common no par exchanged for (0.4) share Common no par
Note: Unexchanged certificates will be cancelled and become without value 01/02/2018

POTASH NORTH RESOURCE CORP (BC)
Common no par split (2) for (1) by issuance of (1) additional share payable 06/05/2008 to holders of record 05/30/2008 Ex date - 05/30/2008
Merged into Potash One Inc. 04/17/2009
Each share Common no par exchanged for (0.3125) share Common no par
(See Potash One Inc.)

POTASH ONE INC (CANADA)
Acquired by K+S Aktiengesellschaft 03/17/2011
Each share Common no par exchanged for $4.50 cash

POTASH RIDGE CORP (ON)
Name changed to SOPerior Fertilizer Corp. 08/08/2018

POTASH WEST NL (AUSTRALIA)
Each Sponsored ADR for Ordinary received distribution of $0.020377 cash payable 05/22/2017 to holders of record 05/15/2017 Ex date - 05/11/2017
ADR agreement terminated 02/08/2018
Each Sponsored ADR for Ordinary exchanged for (40) shares Ordinary
Note: Unexchanged ADR's will be sold and the proceeds, if any, held for claim after 02/11/2019

POTENCO INC (NV)
Recapitalized as MovieO Network Inc. 3/30/2000
Each (275) shares Common $0.001 par exchanged for (1) share Common $0.001 par

POTENTIAL HLDGS INC (NV)
Name changed to RightSmile, Inc. 08/28/2009

POTENTIAL RES LTD (BC)
Name changed to Skybridge International Inc. 04/07/1986
Skybridge International Inc. name changed to International Potential Explorations Inc. 04/30/1987 which name changed to Banyan Industries International Inc. 04/12/1991 which name changed to Incentive Design Group Ltd. 11/19/1991 which recapitalized as Envoy Communications Group Inc. 01/22/1996 which name changed to Envoy Capital Group Inc. 04/05/2007 which merged into Merus Labs International Inc. (New) 12/22/2011
(See Merus Labs International Inc. (New))

POTENTIAL TECHNOLOGIES INC (AB)
Issue Information - 3,000,000 shares COM offered at $0.10 per share on 10/21/1997
Recapitalized as Delaney Energy Services Corp. 12/30/1988
Each share Common no par exchanged for (1/3) share Common no par
(See Delaney Energy Services Corp.)

POTENTIALISTICS INC (DE)
Recapitalized as Goung Hei Investment Co. Ltd. 06/17/1996
Each (15) shares Common $0.00001 par exchanged for (1) share Common $0.00001 par
Goung Hei Investment Co. Ltd. name changed to Morgan Cooper Inc. 01/28/2000
(See Morgan Cooper Inc.)

POTGIETERSRUST PLATINUMS LTD (SOUTH AFRICA)
ADR's for Ordinary ZAR 7-1/2 par changed to ZAR 2-1/2 par and (2) additional shares issued 03/29/1968
Merged into Rustenburg Platinum Holdings Ltd. 09/13/1976
Each ADR for Ordinary ZAR 2-1/2 par exchanged for (3.225) ADR's for Ordinary ZAR 10 par
Rustenburg Platinum Holdings Ltd. name changed to Anglo American Platinum Corp. Ltd. (New) 09/02/1997 which name changed to Anglo Platinum Ltd. 05/30/2005 which name changed to Anglo American Platinum Ltd. 05/25/2011

POTLATCH CORP NEW (DE)
Each share Common $1 par received distribution of (0.28571428) share Clearwater Paper Corp. Common $0.0001 par payable 12/16/2008 to holders of record 12/09/2008 Ex date - 12/17/2008
Name changed to PotlatchDeltic Corp. 02/23/2018

POTLATCH CORP OLD (DE)
Reincorporated 09/19/1955
Name changed 04/27/1973
State of incorporation changed from (ME) to (DE) and Common $25 par changed to $1 par 09/19/1955
Stock Dividends - 10% 12/27/1967; 10% 12/27/1968; 40% 09/26/1969
Name changed from Potlatch Forests, Inc. to Potlatch Corp. 04/27/1973
Common $1 par split (2) for (1) by issuance of (1) additional share 01/07/1977
$12.375 Preferred Ser. A no par called for redemption 05/16/1986
Common $1 par split (2) for (1) by issuance of (1) additional share 05/01/1987
$3.75 Conv. Exchangeable Preferred Ser. B no par called for redemption 04/15/1989
Reorganized as Potlatch Corp. (New) 02/03/2006
Each share Common $1 par exchanged for (1) share Common $1 par
Potlatch Corp. (New) name changed to PotlatchDeltic Corp. 02/23/2018

POTLATCH PETES INC (AB)
Merged into Templar Energy Ltd. 05/14/1990
Each share Common no par exchanged for (1) share Common no par
(See Templar Energy Ltd.)

POTLATCH YARDS, INC. (DE)
Merged into Boise Cascade Corp. 07/01/1957
Each share Common $5 par exchanged for (0.5) share Common $5 par
Boise Cascade Corp. name changed to OfficeMax Inc. 11/01/2004 which merged into Office Depot, Inc. 11/05/2013

POTNETWORK HLDGS INC (WY)
Each share old Common $0.00001 par exchanged for (0.001) share new Common $0.00001 par 03/21/2016
Reincorporated under the laws of Colorado 03/03/2017

POTOMAC BANCORP INC (WV)
Merged into WM Bancorp 10/1/90
Each share Common $1 par exchanged for (1.4701) shares Common $2.50 par
WM Bancorp acquired by Keystone Financial, Inc. 1/7/94 which merged into M&T Bank Corp. 10/6/2000

POTOMAC BK & TR CO (FAIRFAX, VA)
Merged into Dominion Bankshares Corp. 03/04/1977
Each share Common $3.75 par exchanged for (2.274) shares Common $5 par
Dominion Bankshares Corp. merged into First Union Corp. 03/01/1993 which name changed to Wachovia Corp. (Ctfs. dated after 09/01/2001) 09/01/2001 which merged into Wells Fargo & Co. (New) 12/31/2008

POTOMAC BK VA (FAIRFAX VA)
Stock Dividends - 20% payable 12/31/2002 to holders of record 12/31/2001; 20% payable 01/31/2004 to holders of record 01/02/2004; 20% payable 03/01/2006 to holders of record 2/15/2006 Ex date - 02/13/2006
Merged into Sandy Spring Bancorp, Inc. 02/15/2007
Each share Common $5 par exchanged for $21.75 cash

POTOMAC EDISON CO (MD & VA)
Became incorporated in Virginia also, 05/31/1974
$15.64 Preferred Ser. I $100 par called for redemption 07/11/1986
$9.40 Preferred Ser. E $100 par called for redemption 11/20/1992
$9.64 Preferred Ser. H $100 par called for redemption 11/20/1992
$4.70 Preferred Ser. B $100 par called for redemption 08/01/1993
$7 Preferred $100 par called for redemption 07/28/1995
$8.32 Preferred Ser. F $100 par called for redemption 07/28/1995
$8.00 Preferred Ser. G $100 par called for redemption 07/28/1995
$7.16 Preferred Ser. J $100 par called for redemption 07/28/1995
$3.60 Preferred $100 par called for redemption at $103.75 on 09/30/1999
$5.88 Preferred Ser. C $100 par called for redemption at $102.85 on 09/30/1999
Public interest eliminated

POTOMAC ELEC PWR CO (DC & VA)
3.6% Preferred $50 par called for redemption 03/21/1957
$5.46 Preferred 1975 Ser. $50 par called for redemption 12/22/1977
$5.50 Preferred 1974 Ser. $50 par called for redemption 12/22/1977
$4.50 Preferred 1970 Ser. $50 par called for redemption 07/18/1986
$4.04 Preferred 1971 Ser. $50 par called for redemption 05/01/1987
$4.23 Preferred 1979 Ser. $50 par called for redemption 05/01/1987
$4.375 Serial Preferred 1980 Ser. $50 par called for redemption 09/10/1990
$2.44 Conv. Preferred Ser. 66 $50 par called for redemption at $50 on 03/01/1998
$3.37 Preferred 1987 Ser. $50 par called for redemption at $51.13 on 06/01/1998
$3.82 Preferred Ser. 69 $50 par called for redemption at $51 on 06/01/1998
$3.89 Preferred $50 par called for redemption at $53.89 on 06/01/1998
Stock Auction Preferred Ser. A called for redemption at $50 on 12/01/1999
Common $10 par split (2) for (1) by issuance of (1) additional share 05/15/1963
Common $10 par changed to $1 par and (1) additional share issued 05/18/1987
Merged into Pepco Holdings, Inc. 08/01/2002
Each share Common $10 par exchanged for (1) share Common 1¢ par
$3.40 Preferred 1992 Ser. $50 par called for redemption at $50 plus $0.85 accrued dividends on 12/01/2004
$2.28 Preferred Ser. 65 called for redemption at $51 plus $0.57 accrued dividends on 03/01/2006
$2.44 Preferred Ser. 57 called for redemption at $51 plus $0.61 accrued dividends on 03/01/2006
$2.46 Preferred Ser. 58 called for redemption at $51 plus $0.615 accrued dividends on 03/01/2006
(See Pepco Holdings, Inc.)

POTOMAC ELEC PWR CO TR I (DE)
7.375% Trust Originated Preferred Securities called for redemption at $25 plus $0.143403 accrued dividend on 12/29/2003

POTOMAC ENERGY CORP (OK)
Each share old Common $0.001 par exchanged for (0.2) share new Common $0.001 par 03/31/2000
SEC revoked common stock registration 04/21/2010
Stockholders' equity unlikely

POTOMAC FINL EQUITIES INC (UT)
Involuntarily dissolved 03/01/1990

POTOMAC NATL BK MD (POTOMAC, MD)
Common $25 par changed to $12.50 par and (1) additional share issued 3/30/73
Merged into Mercantile Bankshares Corp. 10/3/77
Each share Common $12.50 par exchanged for $165 cash

POTOMAC OIL CO. (AZ)
Company assets sold at sheriff's sale and charter cancelled in 1916

POTOMSKA MILLS CORP.
Liquidated in 1935

POTOSI INVESTMENT CO. (MO)
Merged into Griesedieck Co. share for share 9/15/55
(See Griesedieck Co.)

POTRERO SUGAR CO., INC.
Dissolved in 1944

POTT INDS INC (MO)
Stock Dividends - 25% 01/31/1974; 33-1/3% 07/31/1975
Merged into Houston Natural Gas Corp. (TX) 07/25/1977
Each share Common $1 par exchanged for (1.35) shares Common $1 par
(See Houston Natural Gas Corp. (TX))

POTTER CO. (DE)
Each share Common $100 par exchanged for (5) shares Common no par 00/00/1933
Common no par changed to $1 par 00/00/1937
Common $1 par split (5) for (1) by issuance of (4) additional shares 09/07/1965
Name changed to Potter-Englewood Corp. 07/26/1968
Potter-Englewood Corp. name changed to Pemcor, Inc. 07/01/1971 which merged into Esmark, Inc. (Inc. 03/14/1969) 09/28/1978
(See Esmark, Inc. (Inc. 03/14/1969))

POTTER DISTILLERIES LTD (CANADA)
Reincorporated 1/30/78
Place of incorporation changed from (BC) to (Canada) 1/30/78
Each share Common no par exchanged for (1) share Class A Common no par and (1) share Class B Common no par 6/16/78
Stock Dividends - Class A - 10% 2/28/79; 10% 12/28/79; 10% 2/20/81; 11% 3/31/82
Merged into International Potter Distilling Corp. 12/31/86
Each share Class A Common no par exchanged for (1/3) share Common no par
Each share Class B Common no par exchanged for (1/3) share Common no par
Name changed to Cascadia Brands Inc. 3/30/95
(See Cascadia Brands Inc.)

POTTER ENGLEWOOD CORP (DE)
Under plan of merger name changed to Pemcor, Inc. 07/01/1971
Pemcor, Inc. merged into Esmark, Inc. (Inc. 03/14/1969) 09/28/1978
(See Esmark, Inc. (Inc. 03/14/1969))

POTTER INSTR INC (NY)
Chapter 11 bankruptcy proceedings dismissed 03/17/1987
No stockholders' equity

POTTER SHOE CO.
Liquidation completed in 1951

POTTERDOAL MINES LTD. (ON)
Recapitalized as New Potterdoal Mines Ltd. on a (1) for (10) basis in 1955

POTTERS BK & TR CO (EAST LIVERPOOL, OH)
Each share Capital Stock $100 par exchanged for (8) shares Capital Stock $12.80 par 03/31/1964
Merged into Ohio Bancorp 01/01/1985
Each share Capital Stock $12.50 par exchanged for (0.90426) share Common $10 par or cash
Note: Option to receive cash expired 01/02/1985
(See Ohio Bancorp)

POTTERS FINL CORP (OH)
Common $1 par split (2) for (1) by issuance of (1) additional share payable 12/1/97 to holders of record 11/17/97
Stock Dividends - 10% payable 3/29/99 to holders of record 3/10/99, 5% payable 7/24/2000 to holders of record 7/6/2000
Merged into United Community Financial Corp. 4/1/2002
Each share Common $1 par exchanged for $22 cash

POTTERS SVGS & LN CO (OH)
Recapitalized as Potters Financial Corp. 3/11/96
Each share Common $1 par exchanged for (1) share Common $1 par
(See Potters Financial Corp.)

POTTSTOWN GAS & WATER CO.
Sold to Borough of Pottstown in 1947

POTTSVILLE CMNTY HOTEL CO (DE)
Each share Preferred $100 par exchanged for liquidating distribution of $50 cash 10/22/70
Preferred and Class A and B Common were issued as units; Class A and B Common will receive nothing in the liquidation, however holders have been asked to surrender certificates along with Preferred Stock
Note: Amount or number of subsequent distributions, if any, are unavailable

POUCH TERM INC (NY)
Capital Stock no par changed to $25 par 00/00/1945
Capital Stock $25 par changed to $12.50 par and (1) additional share issued 04/00/1958
Plan of reorganization under Chapter 11 Federal Bankruptcy proceedings confirmed 03/14/1994
No stockholders' equity

POUGHKEEPSIE FINL CORP (DE)
Merged into HUBCO, Inc. 04/24/1998
Each share Common 1¢ par exchanged for (0.3) share Common no par
HUBCO, Inc. name changed to Hudson United Bancorp 04/21/1999 which merged into TD Banknorth Inc. 01/31/2006
(See TD Banknorth Inc.)

POUGHKEEPSIE SVGS BK FSB (POUGHKEEPSIE, NY)
Under plan of reorganization each share Common 1¢ par automatically became (1) share Poughkeepsie Financial Corp. (DE) Common 1¢ par 05/30/1997
Poughkeepsie Financial Corp. merged into HUBCO, Inc. 04/24/1998 which name changed to Hudson United Bancorp 04/21/1999 which merged into TD Banknorth Inc. 01/31/2006
(See TD Banknorth Inc.)

POULMAQUE GOLD MINES LTD. (ON)
Name changed to Goldmaque Mines Ltd. in 1948
(See Goldmaque Mines Ltd)

POULSEN INSURANCE CO. OF AMERICA (IL)
Common $1 par split (3) for (2) by issuance of (0.5) additional share 12/28/64
Name changed to Standard of America Life Insurance Co. 4/7/66
Standard of America Life Insurance

Co. reorganized under the laws of Delaware as Standard of America Financial Corp. 1/8/69 which merged into Sundstrand Corp. (DE) 8/5/77 which merged into United Technologies Corp 6/10/99

POUNDER VENTURE CAP CORP (CANADA)
Recapitalized as Pool Safe Inc. 04/24/2017
Each share Common no par exchanged for (0.25) share Common no par

POUNDLAND GROUP PLC (UNITED KINGDOM)
ADR agreement terminated 10/03/2016
No ADR 's remain outstanding

POUNDMAKER GOLD MINES LTD. (CANADA)
Deemed not to be a subsisting Company by the Dominion Secretary of State 1/21/43

POUR THROUGH FILTER INC (DE)
Recapitalized as DW Filters, Inc. 09/06/1995
Each share Common $0.001 par exchanged for (0.66666666) share Common $0.001 par
(See DW Filters, Inc.)

POWAY MUFFLER & BRAKE INC (CO)
Name changed to Stratex Oil & Gas Holdings, Inc. 06/13/2012

POWDER MTN ENERGY LTD (AB)
Merged into Canamax Energy Ltd. 08/04/2015
Each share Common no par exchanged for (0.954667) share Common no par
(See Canamax Energy Ltd.)

POWDER RIV BASIN GAS CORP (CO)
Reincorporated under the laws of Oklahoma as Powder River Petroleum International, Inc. 12/13/2007
(See Powder River Petroleum International, Inc.)

POWDER RIV PETE INTL INC (OK)
Chapter 7 bankruptcy proceedings terminated 07/10/2015
No stockholders' equity

POWDER RIVER OIL CO. (CO)
Name changed to Thunderbird Park Development Co. and Common 10¢ par changed to 2¢ par 6/5/64
Thunderbird Park Development Co. involuntarily dissolved 1/1/80

POWDRELL & ALEXANDER, INC. (DE)
Completely liquidated 05/31/1966
Each share Common $2.50 par exchanged for first and final distribution of $19.65 cash

POWDRELL & ALEXANDER, INC. (MA)
Each share Common no par exchanged for (4) shares Common $5 par 00/00/1936
Each share Common $5 par exchanged for (2) shares Common $2.50 par 00/00/1946
Reincorporated under the laws of Delaware 05/05/1969
(See Powdrell & Alexander, Inc. (DE))

POWELL CAP CORP (CO)
Name changed to Imagenet Systems, Inc. 06/30/1987
Imagenet Systems, Inc. recapitalized as Phoenix Metals U.S.A. II, Inc. (CO) 07/12/1993 which reincorporated in Nevada 03/01/2000 which reorganized as TM Media Group, Inc. 09/22/2006
(See TM Media Group, Inc.)

POWELL ELECTRICAL MFG CO (TX)
Merged into Process Systems, Inc. 8/9/77
Each share Common $1 par exchanged for (26.650165) shares Common no par
Process Systems, Inc. name changed to Powell Industries, Inc. (NV) 10/26/77 which reincorporated in Delaware 10/31/2004

POWELL INDS INC (NV)
Reincorporated under the laws of Delaware 10/31/2004

POWELL RIVER CO. LTD. (BC)
Recapitalized 02/05/1945
Each share 7% Preferred $100 par exchanged for (7) shares new Ordinary no par
Each share old Ordinary no par exchanged for (3) shares new Ordinary no par
Recapitalized 10/01/1951
Each share new Ordinary no par (issued after 02/05/1945) exchanged for (3) shares new Ordinary no par
New Ordinary no par (issued after 10/01/1951) split (2) for (1) by issuance of (1) additional share 10/05/1959
Name changed to MacMillan, Bloedel & Powell River Ltd. 01/04/1960
MacMillan, Bloedel & Powell River Ltd. name changed to MacMillan Bloedel Ltd. 05/10/1966 which merged into Weyerhaeuser Co. 11/03/1999

POWELL ROUYN GOLD MINES LTD (QC)
Completely liquidated 01/08/1971
Each share Capital Stock $1 par exchanged for first and final distribution of (0.1) share Lake Shore Mines, Ltd. Capital Stock $1 par
Lake Shore Mines, Ltd. merged into LAC Minerals Ltd. (New) 07/29/1985 which was acquired by American Barrick Resources Corp. 10/17/1994 which name changed to Barrick Gold Corp. 01/18/1995

POWELTON VILLAGE DEVELOPMENT ASSOCIATES, INC. (PA)
Class A Common $1 par reclassified as Common $1 par in 1963
Liquidation completed
Each share Preferred $10 par exchanged for first and final distribution of $10 cash 10/10/73
Each share Common $1 par exchanged for initial distribution of $1 cash 8/31/77
Each share Common $1 par received second distribution of $1.50 cash 3/1/79
Each share Common $1 par received third and final distribution of $0.92 cash 9/22/81

POWEO (FRANCE)
Name changed to Direct Energie 09/03/2013

POWER & LIGHT SECURITIES TRUST
Acquired by Atlas Utilities Corp. 00/00/1931
Details not available

POWER & RAIL TRUSTEED SHARES
Trust terminated 00/00/1932
Details not available

POWER AIR CORP (NV)
Each share old Common $0.001 par exchanged for (0.1) share new Common $0.001 par 09/30/2009
Chapter 7 bankruptcy proceedings terminated 11/06/2013
No stockholders' equity

POWER ALTERNATIVES INC. (NV)
Name changed to New World Minerals, Inc. 4/15/82

POWER AMERS MINERALS CORP (BC)
Each share old Common no par exchanged for (0.25) share new Common no par 09/27/2017
Name changed to Edison Cobalt Corp. 09/05/2018

POWER BATTERY HLDGS CORP (WA)
Reincorporated 12/14/1992
State of incorporation changed from (WY) to (WA) 12/14/1992
Recapitalized as Consolidated Power Battery Corp. 07/09/1998
Each share Common no par exchanged for (0.25) share Common no par
(See Consolidated Power Battery Corp.)

POWER CAN RES LTD (BC)
Name changed to P.C.R. Industries Ltd. 07/08/1982
P.C.R. Industries Ltd. recapitalized as Consolidated P.C.R. Industries Ltd. 07/04/1986 which name changed to Oregon Resources Corp. 12/02/1988 which recapitalized as International Oregon Resources Corp. 01/10/1992 which recapitalized as Dalphine Enterprises Ltd. 03/16/1993 which name changed to Inflazyme Pharmaceuticals Ltd. 12/10/1993 which recapitalized as Eacom Timber Corp. 08/26/2008
(See Eacom Timber Corp.)

POWER CAP CORP (NV)
Each share Common $2 par exchanged for (0.1) share Common 2¢ par 2/28/90
Recapitalized as Huayang International Holdings, Inc. 1/18/96
Each (23) shares Common 2¢ par exchanged for (1) share Common 2¢ par
Huayang International Holdings, Inc. recapitalized as China Energy & Carbon Black Holdings, Inc. 10/25/2004 which recapitalized as CO2 Tech Ltd. 1/9/2007

POWER CAP INC (CO)
Name changed to 1st National Film Corp. 01/14/1991 1st National Film Corp. name changed to First National Entertainment Corp. 10/28/1994
(See First National Entertainment Corp.)

POWER CAP PARTNERSHIP INC (FL)
Proclaimed dissolved for failure to file reports and pay fees 9/22/2000

POWER CAT BOAT CORP (CA)
Charter suspended for failure to file reports and pay fees 02/01/1971

POWER-CELL INC (CO)
Each share old Common $0.00001 par exchanged for (0.01) share new Common $0.00001 par 11/21/94
Name changed to Park Pharmacy Corp. 10/20/99
(See Park Pharmacy Corp.)

POWER COMPUTER SYS INC (DE)
Assets assigned for benefit of creditors 12/02/1974
No stockholders' equity

POWER CONDENSER & ELECTRS CORP (MA)
Involuntarily dissolved for failure to file reports and pay taxes 09/11/1969

POWER CONSV CORP (NV)
Name changed to Power Capital Corp. 10/29/82
Power Capital Corp. recapitalized as Huayang International Holdings, Inc. 1/18/96 which reorganized as China Energy & Carbon Black Holdings, Inc. 10/25/2004 which recapitalized as CO2 Tech Ltd. 1/9/2007

POWER CONVERSION INC (NY)
Common 1¢ par split (3) for (1) by issuance of (2) additional shares 2/28/73
Acquired by Hawker Siddeley Group PLC 7/25/86
Each share Common 1¢ par exchanged for $14.9171 cash
Note: Stockholders will be entitled to an additional amount to the extent that an escrow fund is determined to be payable to holders of Common

POWER CORP. OF NEW YORK
Merged into Niagara Hudson Power Corp. in 1935
Details not available

POWER CORP CDA LTD (CANADA)
Each share 6% Part. 2nd Preferred $50 par exchanged for (10) shares 6% Part. 2nd Preferred $5 par 01/23/1963
Common no par split (10) for (1) by issuance of (9) additional shares 01/31/1963
4-1/2% 1st Preferred $50 par called for redemption 07/05/1965
Common no par reclassified as Conv. Class A Common no par 06/01/1976
Conv. Class A Common no par reclassified as Common no par 02/05/1979
Conv. Class B Common no par reclassified as Common no par 02/05/1979
5% Conv. 2nd Preferred Ser. A $12 par called for redemption 03/30/1979
6% Part. 2nd Preferred $5 par reclassified as Class PP $13 par 12/23/1978
Class PP $13 par reclassified as 15¢ Part. Preferred $6.50 par 06/15/1979
15¢ Part. Preferred $6.50 par split (2) for (1) by issuance of (1) additional share 06/20/1979
Common no par split (2) for (1) by issuance of (1) additional share 06/20/1979
Name changed to Power Corp. of Canada-Power Corp. Du Canada and 4-3/4% 1st Preferred 1965 Ser. $50 par reclassified as $2.375 1st Preferred 1965
Ser. no par, and 15¢ Part. Preferred $6.50 par changed to no par 06/25/1980
$2.375 1st Preferred 1965 Ser. no par called for redemption 05/01/1995
(Additional Information in Active)

POWER CTL TECHNOLOGIES INC (DE)
Name changed to M & F Worldwide Corp. 05/15/1997
(See M & F Worldwide Corp.)

POWER DESIGNS INC (DE)
Reincorporated 08/08/1997
State of incorporation changed from (NY) to (DE) 08/08/1997
Plan of reorganization under Chapter 11 Federal Bankruptcy Code effective 04/06/2001
No stockholders' equity

POWER DIRECT INC (DE)
Name changed to 2U Online.com, Inc. 02/04/2000
2U Online.com, Inc. name changed to Golden Spirit Minerals Ltd. 10/08/2003 which name changed to Golden Spirit Mining Ltd. 10/18/2004 which name changed to Golden Spirit Gaming Ltd. 07/18/2005 which recapitalized as Golden Spirit Enterprises Ltd. 06/30/2006 which name changed to Terralene Fuels Corp. 11/29/2011 which recapitalized as Golden Star Enterprises Ltd. 07/16/2013

POWER DYNE VEHS INC (DE)
Charter cancelled and declared

FINANCIAL INFORMATION, INC.   POW-POW

inoperative and void for non-payment of taxes 3/1/76

POWER EXPL INC (NV)
Each share old Common 2¢ par exchanged for (0.01) share new Common 2¢ par 10/19/1999
Each share new Common 2¢ par exchanged again for (0.01) share new Common 2¢ par 10/22/2001
Name changed to Matrix Energy Services Corp. 05/25/2002
Matrix Energy Services Corp. name changed to Shi Corp. 04/09/2009

POWER EXPLORATIONS & HOLDINGS LTD. (ON)
Recapitalized as Power Explorations Inc. 7/25/85
Each share Common no par exchanged for (0.5) share Common no par
Power Explorations Inc. merged into Moss-Power Resources Inc. 2/28/90 which recapitalized as WisCan Resources Ltd. 2/14/91
(See WisCan Resources Ltd.)

POWER EXPLS INC (ON)
Merged into Moss-Power Resources Inc. 2/28/90
Each share Common no par exchanged for (1) share Common no par
Moss-Power Resources Inc. recapitalized as WisCan Resources Ltd. 2/14/91 (WisCan Resources Ltd.)

POWER FINL CORP (CANADA)
Name changed 12/04/1986
Common no par split (2) for (1) by issuance of (1) additional share 06/02/1986
Under plan of merger name changed from Power Financial Corp. to Power Financial Corp.-Corporation Financiere Power 12/04/1986
5% Preferred 1969 Ser. $25 par called for redemption at $25 on 02/02/1998
7% 1st Preferred Ser. B no par called for redemption at $25 plus $0.4375 accrued dividend on 05/30/2003
4.7% 1st Preferred Ser. J no par called for redemption at $25.50 on 07/30/2010
5.20% 1st Preferred Ser. C no par called for redemption at $25.40 plus $0.325 accrued dividends on 10/31/2010
6% 5-Yr. Rate Reset 1st Preferred Ser. M no par called for redemption at $25 plus $0.375 accrued dividends on 01/31/2014
(Additional Information in Active)

POWER FLUIDS INC (FL)
Each share old Common $0.001 par exchanged for (0.25) share new Common $0.001 par 02/10/1999
Each share new Common $0.001 par exchanged for (4) shares new Common $0.001 par 06/29/2000
Name changed to Marketing Systems USA Inc. 05/01/2001
Marketing Systems USA Inc. name changed to Icon International Holdings, Inc. 04/11/2006
(See Icon International Holdings, Inc.)

POWER GALA CORP (DE)
Name changed to Fortune Capital Financial Holding Corp. 03/18/2016

POWER GAS & WATER SECURITIES CORP.
Dissolved in 1936

POWER GOLD MINING CO. LTD.
Liquidated in 1936

POWER HYBRIDS, INC. (CA)
Merged into M/A-Com, Inc. 07/16/1981
Each share Capital Stock $0.03333333 par exchanged for (0.4095) share Common $1 par
M/A-Com, Inc. merged into AMP Inc.

06/30/1995 which merged into Tyco International Ltd. (Bermuda) 04/01/1999 which reincorporated in Switzerland 03/17/2009 which merged into Johnson Controls International PLC 09/06/2016

POWER INDL PRODS CO (DE)
Name changed to Power Computer Systems, Inc. 03/28/1969
(See Power Computer Systems, Inc.)

POWER KIOSKS INC (FL)
Name changed to Power Interactive Media, Inc. 3/6/2001

POWER MATE CORP (NJ)
Merged into General American Industries, Inc. 6/27/75
Each share Common 10¢ par exchanged for $3.15 cash

POWER MED INTERVENTIONS INC (DE)
Acquired by United States Surgical Corp. 09/08/2009
Each share Common $0.001 par exchanged for $2.08 cash

POWER MINES LTD (ON)
Merged into Power Explorations & Holdings Ltd. 12/10/72
Each share Capital Stock no par exchanged for (1/6) share Common no par
Power Explorations & Holdings Ltd. recapitalized as Power Explorations Inc. 7/25/85 which merged into Moss-Power Resources Inc. 2/28/90 which recapitalized as WisCan Resources Ltd. 2/14/91
(See WisCan Resources Ltd.)

POWER MINING CORP. (QC)
Charter annulled for failure to file annual reports 5/28/77

POWER OIL & GAS INC (CANADA)
Recapitalized as Power Resource Exploration Inc. 01/03/2012
Each share Common no par exchanged for (0.01) share Common no par

POWER OIL CO (DE)
Reincorporated 05/20/1992
State of incorporation changed from (NV) to (DE) and Common 25¢ par changed to $0.001 par 05/20/1992
Each share old Common $0.001 par exchanged for (0.1) share Common $0.001 par 10/20/1993
Recapitalized as ESCO Transportation Co. 10/11/1994
Each share new Common $0.001 par exchanged for (0.25) share Common $0.001 par
(See ESCO Transportation Co.)

POWER ONE INC NEW (DE)
Acquired by ABB Ltd. 07/25/2013
Each share Common $0.001 par exchanged for $6.35 cash

POWER-ONE INC OLD (DE)
Common $0.001 par split (3) for (2) by issuance of (0.5) additional share payable 06/02/2000 to holders of record 05/24/2000 Ex date - 06/05/2000
Common $0.001 par split (2) for (1) by issuance of (1) additional share payable 09/11/2000 to holders of record 08/31/2000 Ex date - 09/12/2000
Under plan of reorganization each share Common $0.001 par automatically became (1) share Power-One, Inc. (New) Common $0.001 par 06/15/2010
Each share Conv. Preferred Ser. A $0.001 par automatically became (740.7407407) shares Power-One, Inc. (New) Common $0.001 par 11/08/2011
(See Power-One, Inc. (New))

POWER PHONE INC (DE)
Stock Dividend - 5% payable

07/12/1996 to holders of record 06/14/1996
Name changed to TMC Agroworld Corp. 08/09/1996
TMC Agroworld Corp. name changed to Dominican Cigar Corp. 08/22/1997 which name changed to DCGR International Holdings, Inc. 06/01/1998 which recapitalized as American Way Home Based Business Systems, Inc. 04/12/2004 which name changed to American Way Business Development Corp. (DE) 09/30/2004 which reincorporated in Florida as Harvard Learning Centers, Inc. 10/30/2006 which name changed to Americas Learning Centers, Inc. 09/25/2007 which recapitalized as Hackett's Stores, Inc. 01/26/2009 which recapitalized as WiseBuys, Inc. 06/17/2010 which name changed to Empire Pizza Holdings, Inc. 04/20/2011 which recapitalized as Vestiage, Inc. 03/22/2013

POWER PHYSICS CORP (PA)
Adjudicated bankrupt 10/20/1976
Stockholders' equity unlikely

POWER PLAY DEV CORP (NV)
Recapitalized as Wikisoft Corp. 04/24/2018
Each share Common $0.001 par exchanged for (0.00666666) share Common $0.001 par

POWER PLUS CORP (AB)
Name changed to PPC Capital Corp. 08/03/1999
(See PPC Capital Corp.)

POWER RECOVERY SYS INC (DE)
Charter cancelled and declared inoperative and void for non-payment of taxes 3/1/88

POWER RESOURCES CORP. (NV)
Charter revoked for failure to file reports and pay fees 3/1/71

POWER RES CORP (WY)
Common 2¢ par split (7) for (1) by issuance of (6) additional shares 06/06/1978
Merged into Nova Natural Resources Corp. 09/29/1986
Each shares Common 2¢ par exchanged for (0.24038461) share Common 10¢ par
Nova Natural Resources Corp. name changed to Greenestone Healthcare Corp. 05/21/2012 which name changed to Ethema Health Corp. 07/12/2017

POWER RESOURCES INC. (UT)
Reorganized under the laws of Delaware as Kruger Organization, Inc. 6/3/86
Each share Common $0.001 par exchanged for (0.5) share Common $0.002 par

POWER-SAVE ENERGY CO (UT)
Each share old Common $0.001 par exchanged for (0.02857142) share new Common $0.001 par 12/29/2011
Name changed to Lustros, Inc. 04/25/2012
(See Lustros, Inc.)

POWER-SAVE ENERGY CORP (CO)
Each share old Common $0.001 par exchanged for (5) shares new Common $0.001 par 11/30/2005
Name changed to Tabatha V, Inc. (New) 01/06/2006
(See Tabatha V, Inc. (New))

POWER-SAVE ENERGY CORP (DE)
Name changed to Disability Access Corp. (DE) 11/01/2006
Disability Access Corp. (DE) reorganized in Nevada 11/30/2006
(See Disability Access Corp. (NV))

POWER-SAVE INTL INC (NV)
Name changed to Interactive Music Inc. 08/25/1999
Interactive Music Inc. name changed to Zebramart.com Inc. 01/04/2000 which name changed to Cottage Investments, Inc. 11/15/2000 which recapitalized as Paving Stone Corp. 12/19/2001
(See Paving Stone Corp.)

POWER SAVE INTL INC (NV)
Reincorporated under the laws of Maryland as Beere Financial Equity Corp. 11/14/2005
(See Beere Financial Equity Corp.)

POWER SECURITIES CORP.
Acquired by Electric Power & Light Corp. in 1930 which was liquidated in 1949

POWER SKI CORP (IL)
Proclaimed dissolved for failure to pay taxes and file reports 12/01/1977

POWER SOLUTIONS INTL INC (NV)
Reorganized under the laws of Delaware 09/01/2011
Each share Common $0.001 par exchanged for (0.03125) share Common $0.001 par

POWER SPECTRA INC (CA)
SEC revoked common stock registration 02/23/2010
Stockholders' equity unlikely

POWER SPORTS FACTORY INC (DE)
Name changed to Heringrat 478, Inc. 07/14/2006
Heringrat 478, Inc. name changed to United Music & Media Group, Inc. 06/23/2010 which recapitalized as New Generation Consumer Group, Inc. 10/07/2014

POWER SPORTS FACTORY INC (MN)
SEC revoked common stock registration 06/06/2013

POWER TECH CORP INC (QC)
Ceased operations 08/13/2010
Stockholders' equity unlikely

POWER TECH SYS INC (DE)
Charter cancelled and declared inoperative and void for non-payment of taxes 3/1/2000

POWER TECHNOLOGY INC (NV)
Common $0.001 par changed to $0.0001 par 07/18/2011
Common $0.0001 par changed to $0.00001 par 05/11/2012
Recapitalized as 1st Prestige Wealth Management 07/31/2014
Each share Common $0.00001 par exchanged for (0.0001) share Common $0.00001 par

POWER TEST CORP (DE)
Common 10¢ par split (5) for (4) by issuance of (0.25) additional share 4/17/72
Common 10¢ par split (4) for (3) by issuance of (1/3) additional share 4/24/85
Stock Dividends - 50% 7/31/79; 50% 3/31/80
Name changed to Getty Petroleum Corp. 7/11/85
Getty Petroleum Corp. name changed to Getty Realty Corp. (DE) 3/31/97 which merged into Getty Realty Corp. (MD) 1/30/98

POWER TEST INVS LTD PARTNERSHIP (NY)
Merged into Getty Realty Corp. (MD) 1/30/98
Each Unit of Ltd. Partnership exchanged for (0.44) share Conv. Participating Preferred Ser. A 1¢ par

POWER TRAIN INC (UT)
Name changed to Scanner Energy Exploration Corp. 8/28/80
(See Scanner Energy Exploration Corp.)

COPYRIGHTED MATERIAL   NO UNAUTHORIZED REPRODUCTION

POWER URANIUM CO. LTD. (QC)
Name changed to Power Mining Corp. 08/22/1956
(See Power Mining Corp.)

POWER VENTURES INC (CO)
Merged into Tatum Petroleum Corp. (DE) 6/30/86
Each share Common no par exchanged for (0.1) share Common 1¢ par
(See Tatum Petroleum Corp. (DE))

POWERBALL INTL INC (UT)
Each share old Common $0.001 par exchanged for (0.5) share new Common $0.001 par 10/28/2004
Name changed to Apollo Resources International, Inc. 02/03/2005
(See Apollo Resources International, Inc.)

POWERBRIEF INC (NV)
Plan of reorganization under Chapter 11 Federal Bankruptcy Code effective 10/04/2002
No stockholders' equity

POWERCERV CORP (FL)
Each share old Common $0.001 par exchanged for (0.11111111) share new Common $0.001 par 06/01/2001
Name changed to ioWorldMedia, Inc. (FL) 02/21/2006 ioWorldMedia, Inc. (FL) reorganized in Nevada as Radioio, Inc. 12/11/2013

POWERCHANNEL INC (DE)
Recapitalized as Qualibou Energy Inc. 02/05/2008
Each (300) shares Common 1¢ par exchanged for (1) share Common 1¢ par

POWERCHIP SEMICONDUCTOR CORP (TAIWAN)
Each Temporary 2002 Reg. S GDR for Ordinary exchanged for (1) Reg. S GDR for Ordinary 08/15/2002
Each Temporary 2002 144A Reg. S GDR for Ordinary exchanged for (1) 144A GDR for Ordinary 08/15/2002
Stock Dividends - 11.3713% payable 08/21/2000 to holders of record 06/23/2000; 18.81% payable 06/26/2001 to holders of record 05/23/2001 Ex date - 05/21/2001; 19.74% payable 07/05/2005 to holders of record 05/23/2005; 5.205% payable 09/18/2006 to holders of record 08/03/2006; 9.854% payable 09/17/2007 to holders of record 08/06/2007 Ex date - 08/02/2007
Name changed to Powerchip Technology Corp. 06/16/2010

POWERCOLD CORP (NV)
SEC revoked common stock registration 06/28/2012

POWERCOMM INC (AB)
Issue Information - 16,514,000 UNITS consisting of (1) share COM and (0.5) WT offered at $0.65 per Unit on 04/30/2007
Name changed to PetroCorp Group Inc. 12/23/2009

POWERDSINE LTD (ISRAEL)
Merged into Microsemi Corp. 01/09/2007
Each share Ordinary ILS 0.01 par exchanged for (0.1498) share Common 20¢ par and $8.25 cash
(See Microsemi Corp.)

POWEREC INTL INC (CA)
Name changed to Sensotron, Inc. 7/1/93
(See Sensotron, Inc.)

POWERGAE INC (NV)
Name changed to Spartan Gold Ltd. 08/27/2010

POWERGEM RESOURCE CORP (BC)
Recapitalized as Consolidated Powergem Resource Corp. 5/18/89
Each share Common no par exchanged for (0.28571428) share Common no par
Consolidated Powergem Resource Corp. merged into Eurus Resource Corp. 5/1/90 which merged into Crystallex International Corp. (BC) 9/29/95 which reincorporated in Canada 1/23/98

POWERGEN PLC (UNITED KINGDOM)
Stock Dividend - 150% 03/03/1995
Merged into E.ON AG 07/01/2002
Each Sponsored ADR for Final Instalment 50p par exchanged for $47.6166 cash

POWERHOUSE ENERGY CORP (BC)
Recapitalized as International Powerhouse Energy Corp. 09/18/2001
Each share Common no par exchanged for (0.1) share Common no par
International Powerhouse Energy Corp. name changed to Sea Breeze Power Corp. 07/30/2003

POWERHOUSE INTL CORP (NV)
Each share old Common $0.001 par exchanged for (0.2) share new Common $0.001 par 09/13/1999
Name changed to iLive, Inc. 10/21/1999
(See iLive, Inc.)

POWERHOUSE RES INC (CO)
SEC revoked common stock registration 03/06/2009
Stockholders' equity unlikely

POWERHOUSE TECHNOLOGIES GROUP INC (DE)
Name changed to Migo Software, Inc. 08/14/2006
(See Migo Software, Inc.)

POWERHOUSE TECHNOLOGIES INC (DE)
Merged into Anchor Gaming 06/29/1999
Each share Common 1¢ par exchanged for $19.50 cash

POWERIZE COM INC (DE)
Merged into Hoover's, Inc. 8/1/2000
Each share Common $0.0001 par exchanged for (0.2084) share Common 1¢ par and $0.335606 cash
(See Hoover's, Inc.)

POWERMAX ENERGY INC (AB)
Merged into High Plains Energy Inc. 10/18/2005
Each share Common no par exchanged for (0.33333333) share Common no par and $0.5067 cash
High Plains Energy Inc. recapitalized as Action Energy Inc. 11/27/2006
(See Action Energy Inc.)

POWERMEDCHAIRS (NV)
Name changed to Holly Brothers Pictures, Inc. 06/06/2017

POWERRAISE INC (NV)
Common $0.001 par split (10) for (1) by issuance of (9) additional shares payable 08/20/2007 to holders of record 08/20/2007 Ex date - 08/21/2007
SEC revoked common stock registration 08/02/2011

POWERS MANUFACTURING CO. (DE)
No longer in existence having become inoperative and void for non-payment of taxes 4/1/56

POWERS (JOHN ROBERT) PRODUCTS CO., INC. (DE)
Acquired by Borden Co. 10/01/1964
Details not available

POWERS REGULATOR CO (DE)
Reincorporated 7/19/68
State of incorporation changed from (IL) to (DE) 7/19/68
Common $10 par changed to $5 par and (1) additional share issued 7/31/68
Common $5 par split (3) for (2) by issuance of (0.5) additional share 9/2/71
Merged into Mark Controls Corp. 10/3/77
Each share Common $5 par exchanged for (1) share $1.20 Conv. Preferred $1 par or $20 cash
Note: Option to receive $1.20 Conv. Preferred $1 par stock expired 10/3/77 after which holders received cash only
(See Mark Controls Corp.)

POWERSECURE INTL INC (DE)
Acquired by Southern Co. 05/09/2016
Each share Common 1¢ par exchanged for $18.75 cash

POWERSHARES 1-5 YR LADDERED INVT GRADE CORPORATE BD INDEX ETF (ON)
Name changed to Invesco 1-5 Year Laddered Investment Grade Corporate Bond Index ETF 07/31/2018

POWERSHARES ACTIVELY MANAGED EXCHANGE-TRADED COMMODITY FD TR (DE)
DB Optimum Yield Diversified Commodity Strategy Portfolio reclassified as Optimum Yield Diversified Commodity Strategy No K-1 Portfolio 11/18/2016
Name changed to Invesco Actively Managed Exchange-Traded Commodity Fund Trust 06/04/2018

POWERSHARES ACTIVELY MANAGED EXCHANGE TRADED FD TR (DE)
Trust terminated 10/06/2011
Each share PowerShares Active AlphaQ Fund 1¢ par received $25.21407 cash
Each share PowerShares Active Alpha Multi-Cap Fund 1¢ par received $13.99887 cash
Trust terminated 03/07/2013
Each share PowerShares Active Low Duration Fund 1¢ par received $25.3845 cash
Each share PowerShares Active Mega Cap Fund 1¢ par received $30.35558 cash
Trust terminated 03/28/2016
Each share PowerShares China A-Share Portfolio 1¢ par received $25.80042 cash
Name changed to Invesco Actively Managed Exchange-Traded Fund Trust 06/04/2018

POWERSHARES CDN DIVID INDEX ETF (ON)
Name changed to Invesco Canadian Dividend Index ETF 07/31/2018

POWERSHARES CDN PFD SH INDEX ETF (ON)
Name changed to Invesco Canadian Preferred Share Index ETF 07/31/2018

POWERSHARES EXCHANGE-TRADED FD TR (MA)
Dynamic Market Portfolio 1¢ par split (4) for (1) by issuance of (3) additional shares payable 07/18/2003 to holders of record 07/15/2003 Ex date - 07/21/2003
Dynamic OTC Portfolio 1¢ par split (4) for (1) by issuance of (3) additional shares payable 07/18/2003 to holders of record 07/15/2003 Ex date - 07/21/2003
Trust terminated 05/22/2009
Each share Dynamic Aggressive Growth Portfolio 1¢ par received $15.69999 cash
Each share Dynamic Deep Value Portfolio 1¢ par received $17.02567 cash
Each share Dynamic Hardware & Consumer Electronics Portfolio 1¢ par received $9.25196 cash
Each share FTSE RAFI Basic Materials Sector Portfolio 1¢ par received $40.31583 cash
Each share FTSE RAFI Consumer Goods Sector Portfolio 1¢ par received $34.2704 cash
Each share FTSE RAFI Consumer Services Sector Portfolio 1¢ par received $39.06288 cash
Each share FTSE RAFI Energy Sector Portfolio 1¢ par received $50.63954 cash
Each share FTSE RAFI Financials Sector Portfolio 1¢ par received $19.30325 cash
Each share FTSE RAFI Health Care Sector Portfolio 1¢ par received $40.19824 cash
Each share FTSE RAFI Industrials Sector Portfolio 1¢ par received $35.27592 cash
Each share FTSE RAFI Telecommunications & Technology Sector Portfolio 1¢ par received $38.86898 cash
Each share FTSE RAFI Utilities Sector Portfolio 1¢ par received $39.25142 cash
Each share High Growth Rate Dividend Achievers Portfolio 1¢ par received $9.08561 cash
Value Line Industry Rotation Portfolio 1¢ par reclassified as Morningstar StockInvestor Core Portfolio 1¢ par 06/30/2010
Value Line Timeliness Select Portfolio 1¢ par reclassified as S&P 500 High Quality Portfolio 1¢ par 06/30/2010
Trust terminated 12/21/2010
Each share Dynamic Healthcare Services Sector Portfolio 1¢ par received $22.6768 cash
Each share Dynamic Telecommunications & Wireless Portfolio 1¢ par received $16.41837 cash
Each share Zacks Small Cap Portfolio 1¢ par received $22.29695 cash
Each share FTSE NASDAQ Small Cap 1¢ par received $27.43296 cash
Each share NXQ Portfolio 1¢ par received $31.01746 cash
Dynamic Large Cap Portfolio 1¢ par reclassified as Fundamental Pure Large Core Portfolio 1¢ par 06/16/2011
Dynamic Mid Cap Growth Portfolio 1¢ par reclassified as Fundamental Pure Mid Growth Portfolio 1¢ par 06/16/2011
Dynamic Mid Cap Portfolio 1¢ par reclassified as Fundamental Pure Mid Core Portfolio 1¢ par 06/16/2011
Dynamic Mid Cap Value Portfolio 1¢ par reclassified as Fundamental Pure Mid Value Portfolio 1¢ par 06/16/2011
Dynamic Small Cap Growth Portfolio 1¢ par reclassified as Fundamental Pure Small Growth Portfolio 1¢ par 06/16/2011
Dynamic Small Cap Portfolio 1¢ par reclassified as Fundamental Pure Small Core Portfolio 1¢ par 06/16/2011
Dynamic Small Cap Value Portfolio 1¢ par reclassified as Fundamental Pure Small Value Portfolio 1¢ par 06/16/2011
Golden Dragon Halter USX China Portfolio 1¢ par reclassified as Golden Dragon China Portfolio 1¢ par 04/30/2012
Trust terminated 03/07/2013
Each share Dynamic Banking Portfolio 1¢ par received $13.82661 cash
Each share Dynamic Insurance Portfolio 1¢ par received $18.99254 cash

Each share Morningstar StockInvestor Core Portfolio 1¢ par received $24.34098 cash
Trust terminated 02/18/2014
Each share Dynamic MagniQuant Portfolio 1¢ par received $37.85437 cash
Each share Lux Nanotech Portfolio 1¢ par received $8.35499 cash
DWA Technical Leaders Portfolio 1¢ par reclassified as DWA Momentum Portfolio 1¢ par 10/04/2013
Dynamic Basic Materials Sector Portfolio 1¢ par reclassified as DWA Basic Materials Momentum Portfolio 1¢ par 02/19/2014
Dynamic Consumer Discretionary Sector Portfolio 1¢ par reclassified as DWA Consumer Cyclicals Momentum Portfolio 1¢ par 02/19/2014
Dynamic Consumer Staples Sector Portfolio 1¢ par reclassified as DWA Consumer Staples Momentum Portfolio 1¢ par 02/19/2014
Dynamic Energy Sector Portfolio 1¢ par reclassified as DWA Energy Momentum Portfolio 1¢ par 02/19/2014
Dynamic Financial Sector Portfolio 1¢ par reclassified as DWA Financial Momentum Portfolio 1¢ par 02/19/2014
Dynamic Healthcare Sector Portfolio 1¢ par reclassified as DWA Healthcare Momentum Portfolio 1¢ par 02/19/2014
Dynamic Industrials Sector Portfolio 1¢ par reclassified as DWA Industrials Momentum Portfolio 1¢ par 02/19/2014
Dynamic OTC Portfolio 1¢ par reclassified as DWA NASDAQ Momentum Portfolio 1¢ par 02/19/2014
Dynamic Technology Sector Portfolio 1¢ par reclassified as DWA Technology Momentum Portfolio 1¢ par 02/19/2014
Dynamic Utilities Portfolio 1¢ par reclassified as DWA Utilities Momentum Portfolio 1¢ par 02/19/2014
Fundamental Pure Large Core Portfolio 1¢ par reclassified as Russell Top 200 Equal Weight Portfolio 1¢ par 05/26/2015
Fundamental Pure Large Growth Portfolio 1¢ par reclassified as Russell Top 200 Pure Growth Portfolio 1¢ par 05/26/2015
Fundamental Pure Large Value Portfolio 1¢ par reclassified as Russell Top 200 Pure Value Portfolio 1¢ par 05/26/2015
Fundamental Pure Mid Core Portfolio 1¢ par reclassified as Russell Midcap Equal Weight Portfolio 1¢ par 05/26/2015
Fundamental Pure Mid Growth Portfolio 1¢ par reclassified as Russell Midcap Pure Growth Portfolio 1¢ par 05/26/2015
Fundamental Pure Mid Value Portfolio 1¢ par reclassified as Russell Midcap Pure Value Portfolio 1¢ par 05/26/2015
Fundamental Pure Small Core Portfolio 1¢ par reclassified as Russell 200 Equal Weight Portfolio 1¢ par 05/26/2015
Fundamental Pure Small Growth Portfolio 1¢ par reclassified as Russell 2000 Pure Growth Portfolio 1¢ par 05/26/2015
Fundamental Pure Small Value Portfolio 1¢ par reclassified as Russell 2000 Pure Value Portfolio 1¢ par 05/26/2015
S&P 500 High Quality Portfolio 1¢ par reclassified as S&P 500 Quality Portfolio 1¢ par 03/18/2016
Each share old WilderHill Clean Energy Portfolio 1¢ par automatically became (0.2) share new WilderHill Clean Energy Portfolio 1¢ par 10/23/2017
Name changed to Invesco Exchange-Traded Fund Trust 06/04/2018

POWERSHARES EXCHANGE-TRADED FD TR II (MA)
Trust terminated 05/22/2009
Each share Dynamic Asia Pacific Portfolio 1¢ par received $15.82199 cash
Each share Dynamic Europe Portfolio 1¢ par received $11.44433 cash
Each share FTSE RAFI Asia Pacific ex-Japan Small-Mid Portfolio 1¢ par received $13.06084 cash
Each share FTSE RAFI Europe Small-Mid Portfolio 1¢ par received $12.91839 cash
Each share FTSE RAFI International Real Estate Portfolio 1¢ par received $12.03307 cash
Each share International Listed Private Equity Portfolio 1¢ par received $9.60129 cash
Trust terminated 12/21/2010
Each share FTSE RAFI Europe Portfolio 1¢ par received $36.51569 cash
Each share FTSE RAFI Japan Portfolio 1¢ par received $40.4299 cash
Each share Global Biotech Portfolio 1¢ par received $25.58383 cash
Each share Global Progressive Transportation Portfolio 1¢ par received $30.18466 cash
Each share NASDAQ-100 BuyWrite Portfolio 1¢ par received $23.1634 cash
Dynamic Developed International Opportunities Portfolio 1¢ par reclassified as S&P International Developed High Quality Portfolio 1¢ par 03/01/2012
Trust terminated 03/07/2013
Each share Convertible Securities Portfolio 1¢ par received $24.8358 cash
Each share Global Coal Portfolio 1¢ par received $18.6977 cash
Each share Global Nuclear Energy Portfolio 1¢ par received $16.32817 cash
Each share Global Steel Portfolio 1¢ par received $14.2683 cash
Each share Global Wind Energy Portfolio 1¢ par received $6.22733 cash
Each share Ibbotson Alternative Completion Portfolio 1¢ par received $11.56643 cash
Each share RiverFront Tactical Balanced Growth Portfolio 1¢ par received $12.92513 cash
Each share RiverFront Tactical Growth & Income Portfolio 1¢ par received $13.51882 cash
DWA Developed Markets Technical Leaders Portfolio 1¢ par reclassified as DWA Developed Markets Momentum Portfolio 1¢ par 10/04/2013
DWA Emerging Markets Technical Leaders Portfolio 1¢ par reclassified as DWA Emerging Markets Momentum Portfolio 1¢ par 10/04/2013
DWA SmallCap Technical Leaders Portfolio 1¢ par reclassified as DWA SmallCap Momentum Portfolio 1¢ par 10/04/2013
Trust terminated 02/18/2014
Each share KBW International Financial Portfolio 1¢ par received $24.97404 cash
Each share MENA Frontier Countries Portfolio 1¢ par received $13.60184 cash
Insured California Municipal Bond Portfolio 1¢ par reclassified as California AMT-Free Municipal Bond Portfolio 1¢ par 07/08/2014
Insured National Municipal Bond Portfolio 1¢ par reclassified as National AMT-Free Municipal Bond Portfolio 1¢ par 07/08/2014
Insured New York Municipal Bond Portfolio 1¢ par reclassified as New York AMT-Free Municipal Bond Portfolio 1¢ par 07/08/2014
NYSE Century Portfolio 1¢ par reclassified as Contrarian Opportunities Portfolio 1¢ par 05/26/2015
PowerShares S&P 500 High Dividend Portfolio 1¢ par reclassified as PowerShares S&P 500 High Dividend Low Volatility Portfolio 1¢ par 09/25/2015
S&P Emerging Markets High Beta Portfolio 1¢ par reclassified as S&P Emerging Markets Momentum Portfolio 1¢ par 03/21/2016
S&P International Developed High Beta Portfolio 1¢ par reclassified as S&P International Developed Momentum Portfolio 1¢ par 03/21/2016
S&P International Developed High Quality Portfolio 1¢ par reclassified as S&P International Developed Quality Portfolio 1¢ par 03/21/2016
Trust terminated 03/28/2016
Each share Fundamental Emerging Markets Local Debt Portfolio 1¢ par received $17.012594 cash
Each share KBW Insurance Portfolio 1¢ par received $68.392586 cash
Each share KBW Capital Markets Portfolio 1¢ par received $49.590831 cash
Build America Bond Portfolio 1¢ par reclassified as Taxable Municipal Bond Portfolio 1¢ par 05/31/2017
S&P 500 Value Portfolio 1¢ par reclassified as S&P 500 Enhanced Value Portfolio 1¢ par 06/30/2017
Trust terminated 12/29/2017
Each share Contrarian Opportunities Portfolio 1¢ par received $33.52717 cash
Each share Developed EuroPacific Currency Hedged Low Volatility Portfolio 1¢ par received $27.95008 cash
Each share Europe Currency Hedged Low Volatility Portfolio 1¢ par received $13.55086 cash
Each share Japan Currency Hedged Low Volatility Portfolio 1¢ par received $30.10584 cash
Name changed to Invesco Exchange-Traded Fund Trust II 06/04/2018

POWERSHARES EXCHANGE TRADED SELF INDEXED FD TR (DE)
Name changed to Invesco Exchange-Traded Self-Indexed Fund Trust 06/04/2018

POWERSHARES FTSE RAFI CDN FUNDAMENTAL INDEX ETF (ON)
Name changed to Invesco FTSE RAFI Canadian Index ETF 07/31/2018

POWERSHARES FTSE RAFI CDN SMALL-MID FUNDAMENTAL INDEX ETF (ON)
Name changed to Invesco FTSE RAFI Canadian Small-Mid Index ETF 07/31/2018

POWERSHARES FTSE RAFI GLOBAL + FUNDAMENTAL INDEX ETF (ON)
Name changed to Invesco FTSE RAFI Global+ Index ETF 07/31/2018

POWERSHARES FTSE RAFI GLOBAL SMALL-MID FUNDAMENTAL ETF (ON)
Name changed to Invesco FTSE RAFI Global Small-Mid ETF 07/31/2018

POWERSHARES FTSE RAFI U S FUNDAMENTAL INDEX ETF II (ON)
Name changed 01/16/2017
Name changed from PowerShares FTSE RAFI U.S. Fundamental Index ETF to PowerShares FTSE RAFI U.S. Fundamental Index ETF II 01/16/2017
Name changed to Invesco FTSE RAFI U.S. Index ETF II 07/31/2018

POWERSHARES FTSE RAFI US FUNDAMENTAL INDEX ETF (ON)
Name changed 01/16/2017
Name changed from PowerShares FTSE RAFI U.S. Fundamental (CAD Hedged) Index ETF to PowerShares FTSE RAFI U.S. Fundamental Index ETF 01/16/2017
Name changed to Invesco FTSE RAFI U.S. Index ETF 07/31/2018

POWERSHARES FUNDAMENTAL HIGH YIELD CORPORATE BD INDEX ETF (ON)
Name changed 01/16/2017
Name changed from PowerShares Fundamental High Yield Corporate Bond (CAD Hedged) Index ETF to PowerShares Fundamental High Yield Corporate Bond Index ETF 01/16/2017
Name changed to Invesco Fundamental High Yield Corporate Bond Index ETF 07/31/2018

POWERSHARES GLOBAL SHAREHOLDER YIELD ETF (ON)
Name changed to Invesco Global Shareholder Yield ETF 07/31/2018

POWERSHARES INDIA EXCHANGE TRADED FD TR (MA)
Name changed to Invesco India Exchange-Traded Fund Trust 06/04/2018

POWERSHARES LADDERRITE U S 0-5 YR CORPORATE BD INDEX ETF (ON)
Name changed to Invesco LadderRite U.S. 0-5 Year Corporate Bond Index ETF 07/31/2018

POWERSHARES LOW VOLATILITY PORTFOLIO ETF (ON)
Name changed to Invesco Low Volatility Portfolio ETF 07/31/2018

POWERSHARES 1-3 YR LADDERED FLTG RATE NT INDEX ETF (ON)
Name changed to Invesco 1-3 Year Laddered Floating Rate Note Index ETF 07/31/2018

POWERSHARES QQQ INDEX ETF (ON)
Name changed 01/16/2017
Name changed from PowerShares QQQ (CAD Hedged) Index ETF to PowerShares QQQ Index ETF 01/16/2017
Name changed to Invesco QQQ Index ETF 07/31/2018

POWERSHARES QQQ TR (NY)
Name changed to Invesco QQQ Trust 06/04/2018

POWERSHARES S&P / TSX COMPOSITE HIGH BETA INDEX ETF (ON)
Trust terminated 04/06/2015
Each Trust Unit received $10.42827 cash

POWERSHARES S&P / TSX COMPOSITE LOW VOLATILITY INDEX ETF (ON)
Name changed to Invesco S&P/TSX Composite Low Volatility Index ETF 07/31/2018

POWERSHARES S&P / TSX REIT INCOME INDEX ETF (ON)
Name changed to Invesco S&P/TSX REIT Income Index ETF 07/31/2018

POW-PPZ

POWERSHARES S&P 500 HIGH BETA CAD HEDGED INDEX ETF (ON)
Trust terminated 04/06/2015
Each Trust Unit received $32.4565 cash

POWERSHARES S&P EMERGING MKTS LOW VOLATILITY INDEX ETF (ON)
Name changed to Invesco S&P Emerging Markets Low Volatility Index ETF 07/31/2018

POWERSHARES S&P INTL DEVELOPED LOW VOLATILITY INDEX ETF (ON)
Name changed to Invesco S&P International Developed Low Volatility Index ETF 07/31/2018

POWERSHARES S&P 500 LOW VOLATILITY INDEX ETF (ON)
Name changed 01/16/2017
Name changed from PowerShares S&P 500 Low Volatility (CAD Hedged) Index ETF to PowerShares S&P 500 Low Volatility Index ETF 01/16/2017
Name changed to Invesco S&P 500 Low Volatility Index ETF 07/31/2018

POWERSHARES SR LN INDEX ETF (ON)
Name changed 01/16/2017
Name changed from PowerShares Senior Loan (CAD Hedged) Index ETF to PowerShares Senior Loan Index ETF 01/16/2017
Name changed to Invesco Senior Loan Index ETF 07/31/2018

POWERSHARES TACTICAL BD ETF (ON)
Name changed to Invesco Tactical Bond ETF 07/31/2018

POWERSHARES ULTRA DLUX LONG TERM GOVT BD INDEX ETF (ON)
Name changed to PowerShares Ultra Liquid Long Term Government Bond Index ETF 04/17/2014

POWERSOFT CORP (MA)
Acquired by Sybase, Inc. 02/13/1995
Each share Common $0.00167 par exchanged for (1.6) shares Common $0.001 par
(See Sybase, Inc.)

POWERSOFT TECHNOLOGIES INC (DE)
Reorganized under the laws of Colorado as Asia Supernet Corp. 12/22/1999
Each (30) shares Common 1¢ par exchanged for (1) share Common 5¢ par
(See Asia Supernet Corp.)

POWERSTAR INC (CO)
Company believed out of business 00/00/1988
Details not available

POWERSTORM CAP CORP (DE)
Name changed to Powerstorm Holdings, Inc. 03/12/2015

POWERTEC INC (CA)
Common no par split (5) for (4) by issuance of (0.25) additional share 5/15/85
Merged into Low & Bonar PLC 12/12/86
Each share Common no par exchanged for $15.90 cash

POWERTECH INC (NV)
Name changed to Netmeasure Technology, Inc. 03/09/2000
Netmeasure Technology, Inc. name changed to Sorell, Inc. 12/02/2005 which name changed to Emporia, Inc. 02/27/2008

POWERTECH INDS INC (BC)
Name changed to Powertech Uranium Corp. 06/05/2006
Powertech Uranium Corp. recapitalized as Azarga Uranium Corp. 10/31/2014

POWERTECH URANIUM CORP (BC)
Combined Units separated 03/15/2011
Recapitalized as Azarga Uranium Corp. 10/31/2014
Each share Common no par exchanged for (0.1) share Common no par

POWERTEL COMMUNICATIONS INC. (AB)
Name changed to Equess Communications Inc. 08/10/1998
(See Equess Communications Inc.)

POWERTEL INC (DE)
Stock Dividend - 0.75% payable 4/6/2001 to holders of record 3/23/2001 Ex date - 3/21/2001
Merged into Deutsche Telekom AG 5/31/2001
Each share Common no par exchanged for (2.6353) ADR's for Ordinary no par

POWERTEL USA INC (DE)
Name changed to Worldcall Corp. 11/25/1998
(See Worldcall Corp.)

POWERTRADER INC (DE)
Company terminated registration of common stock and is no longer public as of 08/23/2002
Details not available

POWERTRON ULTRASONICS CORP. (DE)
Acquired by Giannini Controls Corp. 11/16/62
Each share Common no par exchanged for (1/12) share Common 50¢ par, (1/12) share 5% Conv. Preferred B $20 par of Giannini Controls Corp. and (0.2) share U.S. Servicator Corp. Common 10¢ par
Giannini Controls Corp. name changed to Conrac Corp. 4/14/67
(See Conrac Corp.)

POWER2SHIP INC (NV)
Name changed to Fittipaldi Logistics, Inc. 10/23/2006
Fittipaldi Logistics, Inc. name changed to NuState Energy Holdings, Inc. (NV) 01/08/2008 which reincorporated in Florida 10/28/2015 which recapitalized as Visium Technologies, Inc. 04/25/2018

POWIN CORP (NV)
Each share old Common $0.001 par exchanged for (0.1) share new Common $0.001 par 10/17/2013
Name changed to Powin Energy Corp. 02/10/2017

POWR-PAK INDUSTRIES, INC. (DE)
Each share Common 10¢ par exchanged for (0.25) share Common 40¢ par 05/17/1965
Name changed to National Home Products, Inc. 11/09/1965
National Home Products, Inc. name changed to Damson Oil Corp. 02/04/1969
(See Damson Oil Corp.)

POWSZECHNY BK KREDYTOWY SA W WARSZAWIE (POLAND)
Reorganized as Bank Przemyslowo-Handlowy S.A. 01/02/2002
Each 144A GDR for Ordinary exchanged for (1) 144A GDR for Ordinary
Each Reg. S GDR for Ordinary exchanged for (1) Reg. S GDR for Ordinary
Bank Przemyslowo-Handlowy S.A. name changed to Bank BPH S.A. 07/15/2004
(See Bank BPH S.A.)

POYDRAS GAMING FIN CORP (BC)
Reincorporated 11/12/2015
Place of incorporation changed from (ON) to (BC) 11/12/2015
Each share old Common no par exchanged for (0.1) share new Common no par 05/02/2016
Name changed to Integrity Gaming Corp. 01/02/2018

POYNT CORP (AB)
Discharged from receivership 04/30/2013
No stockholders' equity

POZEN INC (DE)
Reorganized under the laws of British Columbia as Aralez Pharmaceuticals Inc. 02/09/2016
Each share Common $0.001 par exchanged for (1) share Common no par

PP & C COS INC (PA)
Each share Common 1¢ par exchanged for (0.2) share Common 5¢ par 01/31/1973
$2 Conv. Preferred Ser. A $1 par called for redemption 04/22/1974
Merged into Keystone Centers, Inc. 04/18/1975
Each share Common 5¢ par exchanged for (1.2) shares Common 1¢ par
(See Keystone Centers, Inc.)

PP&L CAP TR
8.20% Trust Originated Preferred Securities called for redemption at $25 on 5/10/2002

PP&L INC (PA)
Name changed to PPL Electric Utilities Corp. 2/14/2000

PP&L CAP TR II (DE)
8.10% Trust Originated Preferred Securities called for redemption at $25 plus $0.43 accrued dividend on 9/18/2002

PPC CAP CORP (AB)
Delisted from Canadian Dealer Network 05/31/2000

PPC OIL & GAS CORP (ON)
Merged into Paragon Petroleum Corp. 01/01/1991
Each share Common no par exchanged for (0.5) share Common no par
(See Paragon Petroleum Corp.)

PPD CORP (NJ)
Name changed to GCI, Inc. 09/20/1976
(See GCI, Inc.)

PPF INTL CORP (AB)
Company wound up 01/09/2003
No stockholders' equity

PPI CAP GROUP INC (UT)
Recapitalized 06/01/1998
Each share Common $0.001 par received additional distribution of (0.14285714) share payable 12/31/1997 to holders of record 11/15/1997
Recapitalized from PPI Capital Corp. to PPI Capital Group, Inc. 06/01/1998
Each share Common $0.001 par exchanged for (0.1) share old Common $0.001 par
Each share old Common $0.001 par exchanged for (0.1) share new Common $0.001 par 05/15/2001
Reincorporated under the laws of Delaware as DirectPlacement Inc. 11/28/2001
DirectPlacement Inc. name changed to PCS Research Technology, Inc. 10/07/2002 which name changed to Sagient Research Systems, Inc. 05/20/2004
(See Sagient Research Systems, Inc.)

PPJ ENTERPRISE (NV)
Each share old Common $0.001 par exchanged for (0.01) share new Common $0.001 par 10/26/2011
Reorganized under the laws of Florida as PPJ Healthcare Enterprises, Inc. 12/01/2014
Each share new Common $0.001 par exchanged for (0.01) share Common $0.001 par

PPL CAP FDG TR I (DE)
Issue Information - 20,000,000 PREMIUM EQUITY PART SECS UNITS 7.75% offered at $25 per unit on 05/03/2001
Trust terminated 5/18/2004
Each 7.75% Premium Equity Participating Security Unit received (0.4813) share PPL Corp. Common no par

PPL CORP (PA)
Each 7.75% Premium Equity Participating Security Unit received (0.4813) share Common 1¢ par 05/18/2004
Each 2010 Corporate Unit received (1.7405) share Common 1¢ par 07/01/2013
Each 2011 Corporate Unit received (1.6204) share Common 1¢ par 05/01/2014
(Additional Information in Active)

PPL ELEC UTILS CORP (PA)
5.95% Preferred $100 par called for redemption at $100 on 05/25/2001
6.15% Preferred $100 par called for redemption at $100 on 04/01/2003
6.33% Preferred $100 par called for redemption at $100 on 07/01/2003
6.125% Preferred $100 par called for redemption at $100 on 10/01/2003
3.35% Preferred $100 par called for redemption at 103.50 on 04/15/2010
4.40% Preferred $100 par called for redemption at $102 plus $0.1711 accrued dividends on 04/15/2010
4.50% Preferred $100 par called for redemption at $110 plus $0.175 accrued dividends on 04/15/2010
4.60% Preferred $100 par called for redemption at $103 on 04/15/2010
6.75% Preferred $100 par called for redemption at $101.35 on 04/15/2010
6.25% Depositary Preferred 1¢ par called for redemption at $25 on 06/18/2012

PPOL INC (CA)
Each share old Common $0.001 par exchanged for (0.01) share new Common $0.001 par 05/29/2007
Completely liquidated 12/23/2009
Each share new Common $0.001 par exchanged for first and final distribution of $11.12 cash
Note: Unclaimed funds will be escheated to the State of California 06/23/2010

PPR SA (FRANCE)
Name changed to Kering 06/24/2013

PPT VISION INC (MN)
Common 10¢ par split (3) for (2) by issuance of (0.5) additional share payable 04/05/1996 to holders of record 03/25/1996
Each share old Common 10¢ par exchanged for (0.25) share new Common 10¢ par 04/01/2005
Acquired by Datalogic S.p.A. 12/20/2011
Each share new Common 10¢ par exchanged for $0.13 cash

PPZ PLATINUM PRODS INC (BC)
Recapitalized as Consolidated Platinum Industries Inc. 1/20/92
Each share Common no par exchanged for (0.5) share Common no par
Consolidated Platinum Industries Inc. name changed to Allied Strategies Inc. 5/25/93 which recapitalized as Sleeman Breweries Ltd. 5/30/96
(See Sleeman Breweries Ltd.)

FINANCIAL INFORMATION, INC.

PR COMPLETE HLDGS INC (NV)
Name changed to YesDTC Holdings, Inc. 01/13/2010
(See YesDTC Holdings, Inc.)

PRA INTL INC (DE)
Issue Information - 3,600,000 shares COM offered at $19 per share on 11/17/2004
Merged into GG Holdings I, Inc. 12/13/2007
Each share Common 1¢ par exchanged for $30.50 cash

PRAB INC (MI)
Name changed 3/29/94
Name changed from Prab Robots, Inc. to Prab Inc. 3/29/94
Merged into Kalamazoo Acquisition Corp. 7/14/2004
Each share Common 10¢ par exchanged for $2.40 cash

PRACO CORP (NV)
Each share old Common $0.0001 par exchanged for (0.07575757) share new Common $0.0001 par 10/13/2017
Name changed to Arista Financial Corp. 02/09/2018

PRACTICAR INDS CORP (BC)
Reorganized under the laws of Canada as Practicar Systems Inc. 03/18/1991
Details not available

PRACTICAR SYSTEMS INC. (CANADA)
Acquired by Rent-A-Wreck Capital Inc. 06/17/1999
Each share Common no par exchanged for $0.50 cash

PRACTICE TENNIS CTRS INC (DE)
Name changed to Energy Control Systems of America, Inc. 4/6/79
Energy Control Systems of America, Inc. recapitalized as National Tax Accounting Inc. 2/28/97

PRACTICEWORKS INC (DE)
Merged into Eastman Kodak Co. 10/07/2003
Each share 6% Conv. Preferred Ser. B exchanged for $7.33 cash
Each share Common 1¢ par exchanged for $21.50 cash

PRACTICEXPERT INC (NV)
SEC revoked common stock registration 09/14/2011

PRADA HLDGS LTD (YT)
Reincorporated 07/26/1996
Place of incorporation changed from (BC) to (Yukon) 07/26/1996
Merged into MFC Bancorp Ltd. 10/23/2001
Each share Common no par exchanged for $0.05 cash

PRADO EXPLS LTD (ON)
Merged into Canhorn Mining Corp. 01/09/1986
Each share Capital Stock $1 par exchanged for (0.06662225) share Common no par
Canhorn Mining Corp. merged into Canhorn Chemical Corp. 04/26/1995 which merged into Nayarit Gold Inc. 05/02/2005 which merged into Capital Gold Corp. 08/02/2010 which merged into Gammon Gold Inc. (QC) 04/08/2011 which reincorporated in Ontario as AuRico Gold Inc. 06/14/2011 which merged into Alamos Gold Inc. (New) 07/06/2015

PRADO OIL & GAS CO. LTD. (ON)
Merged into Rio-Prado Consolidated Oils Ltd. 00/00/1953
Each share Capital Stock $1 par exchanged for (0.75) share new Capital Stock $1 par
Rio-Prado Consolidated Oils Ltd. merged into Rio Palmer Oils Ltd. 07/25/1955 which merged into Devon-Palmer Oils Ltd. 11/06/1956

(See Devon-Palmer Oils Ltd.)

PRAEBIUS COMMUNICATIONS INC (NV)
Recapitalized as Adaptive Ad Systems, Inc. 07/18/2014
Each share Common $0.001 par exchanged for (0.002) share Common $0.001 par

PRAECIS PHARMACEUTICALS INC (DE)
Each share old Common 1¢ par exchanged for (0.2) share new Common 1¢ par 11/02/2005
Merged into GlaxoSmithKline PLC 02/16/2007
Each share new Common 1¢ par exchanged for $5 cash

PRAEGITZER INDS INC (OR)
Merged into Tyco International Ltd. 12/07/1999
Each share Common no par exchanged for $5.50 cash

PRAETORIAN PROPERTY INC (DE)
Reincorporated under the laws of Nevada 12/30/2015

PRAGMA BIO TECH INC (NJ)
Chapter 11 bankruptcy proceedings converted to Chapter 7 on 5/14/90
No stockholders' equity

PRAIRIE CACHE RES LTD (AB)
Name changed to NEBEX Resources Ltd. 09/21/1990
(See NEBEX Resources Ltd.)

PRAIRIE CAP INC (ON)
Reorganized under the laws of Canada as Continental (CBOC) Corp. 08/30/2002
Each share Common no par exchanged for (0.5) share Subordinate no par
Continental (CBOC) Corp. name changed to Stonington Capital Corp. 06/22/2004 which merged into Pyxis Capital Inc. 02/27/2006
(See Pyxis Capital Inc.)

PRAIRIE CITIES OIL CO. LTD.
Assets sold in 1938

PRAIRIE ENERGY INC (NV)
Charter permanently revoked 02/28/2012

PRAIRIE ENERGY MINERALS (MT)
Proclaimed dissolved 12/02/1991

PRAIRIE FIRE OIL & GAS LTD (AB)
Recapitalized as Verenex Energy Inc. 07/13/2004
Each share Common no par exchanged for (0.04) share Common no par
(See Verenex Energy Inc.)

PRAIRIE GAS LTD. (SK)
Acquired by 100% acceptance of exchange offer by Canadian Industrial Gas & Oil Ltd. in 1961

PRAIRIE OIL & GAS CO.
Merged into Consolidated Oil Corp. 00/00/1932
Details not available

PRAIRIE OIL & GAS INC (NV)
Recapitalized as Prairie Energy Inc. 07/10/2007
Each share Common $0.001 par exchanged for (0.01) share Common $0.001 par
(See Prairie Energy Inc.)

PRAIRIE OIL RTYS LTD (SK)
Capital Stock $1 par changed to no par 5/8/78
Capital Stock no par split (4) for (1) by issuance of (3) additional shares 1/9/85
Plan of reorganization effective 4/28/95
Each share Common no par exchanged for $15 cash

PRAIRIE PAC ENERGY CORP (BC)
Acquired by Northrock Resources Ltd. 3/8/2006

Each share Common no par exchanged for $2.69 cash

PRAIRIE PETE INC (CO)
Declared defunct and inoperative for failure to pay taxes and file annual reports 10/19/1974

PRAIRIE PIPE LINE CO.
Merged into Consolidated Oil Corp. 00/00/1932
Details not available

PRAIRIE PIPE MANUFACTURING CO. LTD. (SK)
Under plan of merger name changed to Interprovincial Steel & Pipe Corp. Ltd. (SK) 08/31/1960
Interprovincial Steel & Pipe Corp. Ltd. (SK) reincorporated in Canada 01/28/1977 which name changed to IPSCO Inc. 04/06/1984
(See IPSCO Inc.)

PRAIRIE PRODUCING CO (TX)
Merged into Placer Development Ltd. 02/18/1985
Each share Common 1¢ par exchanged for $17.68 cash

PRAIRIE ROYALTIES, LTD.
Merged into Amalgamated Oils, Ltd. in 1941 which completed liquidation 10/15/58

PRAIRIE SCHOONER PETE LTD (AB)
Issue Information - 1,924,000 shares COM offered at $13 per share on 03/07/2005
Merged into True Energy Trust 09/26/2006
Each share Common no par exchanged for (1.22) Trust Units no par
True Energy Trust reorganized as Bellatrix Exploration Ltd. 11/02/2009

PRAIRIE STS ENERGY CO (TX)
Recapitalized as Spindletop Oil & Gas Co. 7/13/90
Each share Common $0.001 par exchanged for (0.5) share Common $0.001 par

PRAIRIE STATES LIFE INSURANCE CO. (SD)
Merged into Laurentian Capital Corp. (FL) 02/14/1986
Each share Common $1 par exchanged for (1.3) shares Common 5¢ par
Laurentian Capital Corp. (FL) reincorporated in Delaware 07/24/1987
(See Laurentian Capital Corp.)

PRAIRIE STS EXPL INC (CO)
Reorganized under Chapter 11 Federal Bankruptcy Code 9/9/85
Each share Common 1¢ par exchanged for (0.01) share Prairie States Energy Co. Common $0.001 par
Prairie States Energy Co. recapitalized as Spindletop Oil & Gas Co. 7/13/90

PRAIRIE WEST OIL & GAS LTD (NV)
Recapitalized as Pacific Oil Co. 09/16/2013
Each share Common $0.001 par exchanged for (0.01) share Common $0.001 par
Pacific Oil Co. name changed to Financial Gravity Companies, Inc. 01/30/2017

PRANDIUM INC (DE)
Plan of reorganization under Chapter 11 Federal Bankruptcy Code effective 07/02/2002
No old Common stockholders' equity Completely liquidated
Each share new Common 1¢ par exchanged for first and final distribution of $0.022297 cash 10/13/2011

PRASARA TECHNOLOGIES INC (FL)
Merged into PowerTV, Inc. 7/12/2000
Details not available

PRATECS TECHNOLOGIES INC (AB)
Recapitalized as YBM Magnex International, Inc. 10/31/95
Each share Common no par exchanged for (0.2) share Common no par
(See YBM Magnex International, Inc.)

PRATT, READ & CO., INC. (CT)
Stock Dividends - 10% 7/10/50; 10% 10/19/53; 10% 7/10/56; 10% 10/30/59; 50% 10/31/62; 10% 10/29/65
Merged into Vocaline Co. of America, Inc. 6/30/68
Each share Common $10 par exchanged for (1) share 66¢ Conv. Preferred Ser. A no par and (2.55) shares Common $1.50 par
Vocaline Co. of America, Inc. name changed to Pratt-Read Corp. 10/22/70
(See Pratt-Read Corp.)

PRATT & LAMBERT UTD INC (NY)
Name changed 08/04/1994
Common no par split (2) for (1) by issuance of (1) additional share 04/18/1962
Common no par changed to $10 par 06/23/1965
Common $10 par changed to $5 par and (1) additional share issued 05/21/1969
Common $5 par split (3) for (2) by issuance of (0.5) additional share 10/03/1983
Common $5 par changed to $1 par 05/03/1984
$2.25 Conv. Preferred Ser. A $10 par for redemption 06/29/1984
Common $1 par split (3) for (2) by issuance of (0.5) additional share 10/01/1985
Common $1 par split (2) for (1) by issuance of (1) additional share 10/01/1987
Name changed from Pratt & Lambert Inc. to Pratt & Lambert United, Inc. and Common $1 par changed to 1¢ par 08/04/1994
Merged into Sherwin-Williams Co. 01/10/1996
Each share Common 1¢ par exchanged for $35 cash

PRATT FOOD CO. (PA)
Name changed to Pratt Laboratories, Inc. 8/16/57 and then to Wesson Metal Corp. 6/1/59

PRATT HENRY CO (DE)
Reincorporated 01/06/1969
State of incorporation changed from (IL) to (DE) 01/06/1969
Capital Stock $5 par changed to no par 02/14/1970
Capital Stock no par split (3) for (2) by issuance of (0.5) additional share 03/01/1971
Capital Stock no par split (2) for (1) by issuance of (1) additional share 03/01/1972
Capital Stock no par split (3) for (2) by issuance of (0.5) additional share 08/30/1976
Capital Stock no par split (4) for (3) by issuance of (1/3) additional share 11/15/1977
Merged into Amsted Industries Inc. 07/30/1978
Each share Capital Stock no par exchanged for $20 cash
Note: Unexchanged certificates were cancelled and became without value 07/01/1985

PRATT-HEWITT OIL CORP. (DE)
Acquired by Cosden Petroleum Corp. 12/5/58
Each share Common $1 par exchanged for (3/80) share Common $1 par and $0.01 cash
(See Cosden Petroleum Corp.)

PRATT HOTEL CORP (DE)
Each share Common 1¢ par

PRATT LABORATORIES, INC. (PA)
exchanged for (0.1) share Common 10¢ par 11/16/1992
Name changed to Greate Bay Casino Corp. 12/31/1996
(See Greate Bay Casino Corp.)

PRATT LABORATORIES, INC. (PA)
Capital Stock $100 par changed to $1 par in 1958
Name changed to Wesson Metal Corp. 6/1/59 which became a division of Fansteel Metallurgical Corp. in 1961

PRATT-READ CORP (CT)
Merged into Crescent & Co. 10/15/1986
Each share 66¢ Conv. Preferred Ser. A no par exchanged for $8 cash
Each share Common $1.50 par exchanged for $9 cash

PRATT WYLCE & LORDS LTD (NV)
Name changed to Bionet Technologies, Inc. 11/2/98
(See Bionet Technologies, Inc.)

PRATT'S FRESH FROZEN FOODS, INC.
Bankrupt in 1949

PRATTVILLE FINL SVCS CORP (DE)
Merged into Whitney Holding Corp. 01/30/2001
Each share Common $10 par exchanged for (1.071) shares Common no par
Whitney Holding Corp. merged into Hancock Holding Co. 06/04/2011 which name changed to Hancock Whitney Corp. 05/25/2018

PRAXAIR INC (DE)
7.48% Preferred Ser. A 1¢ par called for redemption at $100 on 4/1/2000
6.75% Preferred Ser. B 1¢ par called for redemption at $100 on 9/5/2002
(Additional Information in Active)

PRAXIS BIOLOGICS INC (NY)
Merged into American Cyanamid Co. 11/14/1989
Each share Common 1¢ par exchanged for (0.2707) share Common $5 par
(See American Cyanamid Co.)

PRAXIS PHARMACEUTICALS INC (CA)
Name changed to Ethigen Corp. 5/22/87
(See Ethigen Corp.)

PRAXIS PHARMACEUTICALS INC (UT)
Reincorporated under the laws of Nevada as Patch International Inc. 06/15/2004
Patch International Inc. (NV) reincorporated in Alberta 08/29/2008
(See Patch International Inc.)

PRAXIS RES LTD (BC)
Recapitalized as International Praxis Resource Corp. 10/19/87
Each share Common no par exchanged for (0.5) share Common no par
(See International Praxis Resource Corp.)

PRAXIS TECHNOLOGIES CORP (ON)
Merged into Cinram Ltd. 7/1/88
Each share Common no par exchanged for $0.40 cash

PRAXSYN CORP (IL)
Reincorporated under the laws of Nevada 01/28/2015

PRB ENERGY, INC. (NV)
Name changed 06/15/2006
Issue Information - 2,000,000 shares COM offered at $5.50 per share on 04/12/2005
Name changed from PRB Gas Transportation, Inc. to PRB Energy, Inc. 06/15/2006
Plan of reorganization under Chapter 11 Federal Bankruptcy Code effective 02/02/2009

No stockholders' equity

PRC CORP NEW (DE)
Charter cancelled and declared inoperative and void for non-payment of taxes 03/01/1989

PRC CORP OLD (DE)
Name changed to CorTerra Corp. 11/28/1972
CorTerra Corp. assets transferred to CorTerra Corp. Liquidating Corp. 10/08/1980
(See CorTerra Corp. Liquidating Corp.)

PRE CAST CONCRETE INC (NJ)
Charter declared void for non-payment of taxes 01/16/1980

PRE-CELL SOLUTIONS INC (CO)
SEC revoked common stock registration 03/23/2010
Stockholders' equity unlikely

PRE PAID LEGAL SVCS INC (OK)
Common 1¢ par split (5) for (4) by issuance of (0.25) additional share 01/19/1987
Each share $2.40 Conv. Preferred $1 par exchanged for (14) shares Common 1¢ par 02/27/1995
$1 Conv. Preferred $1 par called for redemption at $13.34 on 06/30/2000
$3 Conv. Preferred $1 par called for redemption at $25 plus $0.75 accrued dividends on 06/30/2000
Each share Common 1¢ par held by holders of (99) shares or fewer exchanged for $35.87 cash 03/17/2006
Stock Dividends - 50% 01/04/1980; 500% 11/20/1980
Acquired by MidOcean Partners 06/30/2011
Each share Common 1¢ par exchanged for $66.50 cash

PRE-SETTLEMENT FDG CORP (DE)
Name changed to Seawright Holdings. Inc. 10/15/2003

PRE-STRESS CONCRETE CO., INC. (SC)
Merged into PS Charleston, Inc. 06/03/1985
Details not available

PREACHERS COFFEE INC (CO)
Name changed to Marijuana, Inc. 07/21/2010
Marijuana, Inc. name changed to Hemp, Inc. 08/30/2012

PREACHERS COFFEE INC (DE)
Each share Preferred $0.000001 par exchanged for (1) share Preachers Coffee Inc. (CO) Common $0.001 par 06/29/2009
(See Preachers Coffee Inc. (CO))
Name changed to Protein Reactor Combined Fuels Inc. 02/23/2011

PREAKNESS PROPERTIES, INC. (UT)
Name changed to Allied Energy Corp. 07/18/1977
(See Allied Energy Corp.)

PRECAMBRIAN SHIELD RES LTD (BC)
Merged into Mark Resources Inc. 7/1/93
Each share Common no par exchanged for $3.25 cash

PRECEPT BUSINESS SVCS INC (TX)
Each share old Class A Common 1¢ par exchanged for (1/7) share new Common 1¢ par 12/04/1998
Chapter 11 bankruptcy proceedings converted to Chapter 7 Federal Bankruptcy 06/28/2001
Stockholders' equity unlikely

PRECIDIAN ETFS TR (DE)
Trust terminated 03/18/2016
Each share MAXIS Nikkei 225 Index Fund received $17.90663 cash

PRECIOUS GEM INVESTMENT CO. (UT)
Name changed to Sigma Minerals & Energy Corp. 3/8/82

PRECIOUS METAL MINES INC (NV)
Each share old Common 1¢ par exchanged for (3) shares new Common 1¢ par 8/23/94
Name changed to Interactive Motorsports, Inc. 5/5/2000
Interactive Motorsports, Inc. name changed to Black Sea Oil, Inc. (Old) 12/11/2000
(See Black Sea Oil, Inc. (Old))

PRECIOUS METALS & MINERALS INC (DE)
Name changed to Symetrix, Inc. 12/28/1968
(See Symetrix, Inc.)

PRECIOUS METALS BULLION TR (ON)
Trust terminated 10/12/2017
Each Trust Unit received $9.43 cash

PRECIOUS METALS EXCHANGE CORP (NV)
Name changed to Legends Food Corp. 07/19/2011
Legends Food Corp. name changed to Republic of Texas Brands, Inc. 11/07/2011 which name changed to Totally Hemp Crazy Inc. 08/05/2014 which name changed to Rocky Mountain High Brands Inc. 10/16/2015

PRECIOUS METALS HLDGS INC (DE)
Name changed to Keystone Precious Metals Holdings, Inc. 11/20/1984
Keystone Precious Metals Holdings, Inc. name changed to Evergreen International Trust 01/00/1998

PRECIOUS METALS LTD (DE)
Charter cancelled and declared inoperative and void for non-payment of taxes 04/15/1972

PRECIOUS METALS MINING & MILLING CO. (SD)
Charter expired by time limitation 10/14/25

PRECIS INC (OK)
Name changed 07/02/2001
Name changed from Precis Smart Card Systems Inc. to Precis, Inc. 07/02/2001
Name changed to Access Plans USA, Inc. 01/31/2007
Access Plans USA, Inc. acquired by Alliance HealthCard, Inc. (GA) 04/01/2009 which reincorporated in Oklahoma as Access Plans, Inc. 01/19/2010
(See Access Plans, Inc.)

PRECISE LIFE SCIENCES LTD (NV)
Each share old Common $0.001 par exchanged for (0.1) share new Common $0.001 par 12/16/2002
Name changed to Iceberg Brands Corp. 03/03/2003
Iceberg Brands Corp. recapitalized as Avalon Gold Corp. 09/08/2003 which name changed to Avalon Energy Corp. 03/22/2005 which recapitalized as Shotgun Energy Corp. 09/25/2007 which name changed to Organa Gardens International 04/07/2009 which recapitalized as Bravo Enterprises Ltd. 06/08/2012

PRECISE POSITIONING PRODS INC (TN)
Common $0.001 par split (2) for (1) by issuance of (1) additional share payable 08/02/2002 to holders of record 08/01/2002 Ex date - 08/02/2002
Recapitalized as Free DA Connection Services, Inc. 02/14/2005
Each (380) shares Common $0.001 par exchanged for (1) share Common $0.001 par
Free DA Connection Services, Inc.

recapitalized as Earthshine International Ltd. 09/11/2007

PRECISE SOFTWARE SOLUTIONS LTD. (ISRAEL)
Issue Information - 4,250,000 ORD shs. offered at $16 per share on 06/29/2000
Merged into Veritas Software Corp. 06/30/2003
Each share Ordinary ILS 0.30 par exchanged for USD $16.50 cash

PRECISION AEROSPACE COMPONENTS INC (DE)
Each share old Common $0.001 par exchanged for (0.002) share new Common $0.001 par 12/24/2009
Each share new Common $0.001 par exchanged again for (0.0004) share new Common $0.001 par 10/18/2016
Note: Holders of (2,499) or fewer pre-split shares received $0.02 cash per share
Name changed to Amerinac Holding Corp. 06/28/2017

PRECISION AEROTECH INC (DE)
Each share Common 10¢ par exchanged for (0.01) share Common 1¢ par 4/28/94
Merged into PA Acquisition Corp. 4/25/96
Each share Common 1¢ par exchanged for $5 cash

PRECISION APPARATUS, INC. (DE)
Merged into Atlantic Services, Inc. 6/30/66
Each share Common $1 par exchanged for (1) share Common $1 par
Atlantic Services, Inc. charter cancelled 3/1/71

PRECISION ASSMT TECHNOLOGY CORP (AB)
Filed a petition under the Companies' Creditors Arrangement Act 06/25/2009
Stockholders' equity unlikely

PRECISION AUTOMOTIVE & INDUSTRIAL REBUILDERS, INC. (FL)
Name changed to Precision Rebuilders, Inc. 12/21/64
Precision Rebuilders, Inc. name changed to Needham Engineering, Inc. 2/13/68
(See Needham Engineering, Inc.)

PRECISION AUTOMOTIVE COMPONENTS CO. (MO)
Completely liquidated 8/22/66
Each share Common $1 par exchanged for first and final distribution of (0.013333) share Borg-Warner Corp. (Ill.) Common $5 par
Borg-Warner Corp. (Ill.) reincorporated under the laws of Delaware 10/31/67
(See Borg-Warner Corp. (Del.))

PRECISION CASTPARTS CORP (OR)
Common no par split (2) for (1) by issuance of (1) additional share 09/29/1978
Common no par split (3) for (2) by issuance of (0.5) additional share 03/29/1985
Common no par split (2) for (1) by issuance of (1) additional share 02/27/1987
Common no par split (3) for (2) by issuance of (0.5) additional share 08/26/1994
Common no par split (2) for (1) by issuance of (1) additional share payable 09/21/2000 to holders of record 09/01/2000 Ex date - 09/22/2000
Common no par split (2) for (1) by issuance of (1) additional share payable 09/08/2005 to holders of

record 08/29/2005 Ex date - 09/09/2005
Stock Dividends - 10% 01/12/1976; 10% 01/10/1977; 100% 03/31/1983; 25% 03/28/1986
Acquired by Berkshire Hathaway Inc. 01/29/2016
Each share Common no par exchanged for $235 cash

PRECISION CIRCUITS INC (NY)
Merged into Tenney Engineering, Inc. 6/17/83
Each share Common 20¢ par exchanged for $4.90 cash

PRECISION DRILLING CORP (AB)
Name changed 09/10/1992
Name changed from Precision Drilling (1987) Ltd. to Precision Drilling Corp. 09/10/1992
Class A Common no par reclassified as Common no par 09/24/1996
Common no par split (2) for (1) by issuance of (1) additional share payable 10/14/1997 to holders of record 09/30/1997 Ex date - 10/15/1997
Common no par split (2) for (1) by issuance of (1) additional share payable 05/31/2005 to holders of record 05/20/2005 Ex date - 06/01/2005
Plan of arrangement effective 11/07/2005
Each share Common no par exchanged for (1) Precision Drilling Trust, Trust Unit no par, (0.2089) share Weatherford International, Ltd. Common $1 par and $6.83 cash
(See Weatherford International, Ltd.)
(Additional Information in Active)

PRECISION DRILLING TR (AB)
Reorganized as Precision Drilling Corp. 06/03/2010
Each Trust Unit no par exchanged for (1) share Common no par
Note: Unexchanged certificates were cancelled and became without value 06/03/2015

PRECISION ELECTRICAL MFG CO (MN)
Stock Dividend - 50% 12/15/1969
Name changed to Iroquois Corp. 06/23/1970
Iroquois Corp. name changed to EmCom, Inc. 02/06/1973
(See EmCom, Inc.)

PRECISION ENTERPRISES INC (BC)
Recapitalized as Allante Resources Ltd. 12/18/2013
Each share Common no par exchanged for (0.33333333) share Common no par

PRECISION FILM & VIDEO CORP (NY)
Name changed 12/16/82
Name changed from Precision Film Corp. to Precision Film & Video Corp. 12/16/82
Dissolved by proclamation 6/23/93

PRECISION GRINDING WHEEL INC (MD)
Acquired by Electronic Assistance Corp. 09/10/1968
Each share Prior Preferred no par exchanged for (4.015) shares Common 10¢ par
Each share Class B no par exchanged for (6.159) shares Common 10¢ par
Electronic Assistance Corp. name changed to EAC Industries, Inc. 05/26/1976
(See EAC Industries, Inc.)

PRECISION INC (NV)
Recapitalized as Night Flight Entertainment, Inc. 05/24/1990
Each share Common $0.001 par exchanged for (0.1) share Common $0.002 par
Night Flight Entertainment, Inc. name changed to Ally Media Group, Inc. 04/19/1991 which reorganized as Success Financial Services Group, Inc. 01/31/2001 which name changed to Consolidated American Industries Corp. 03/01/2005

PRECISION INDUSTRIES, INC. (MN)
Acquired by Research, Inc. (Old) on a (1) for (7) basis 08/02/1960
(See Research, Inc. (Old))

PRECISION INDS INC (FL)
Common 12-1/2¢ par split (4) for (1) by issuance of (3) additional shares 01/05/1982
Stock Dividends - 10% 04/14/1987; 10% 04/15/1988
Name changed to American Imaging, Inc. 04/27/1998
American Imaging, Inc. name changed to Seaescape Entertainment, Inc. 06/12/2000

PRECISION INSTR CO (CA)
Each share Capital Stock no par exchanged for (0.1) share Common no par 03/10/1976
Name changed to Omex 02/21/1978
(See Omex)

PRECISION INTL RESOURCE CORP (BC)
Recapitalized as Range Petroleum Corp. 05/07/1996
Each share Common no par exchanged for (0.5) share Common no par
Range Petroleum Corp. recapitalized as Range Energy Inc. 05/15/2002
(See Range Energy Inc.)

PRECISION METAL PRODS INC (FL)
Merged into Precision Industries, Inc. (FL) 03/26/1968
Each share Common 10¢ par exchanged for (1) share Common 12-1/2¢ par
Precision Industries, Inc. name changed to American Imaging, Inc. 04/27/1998 which name changed to Seaescape Entertainment, Inc. 06/12/2000

PRECISION MICROWAVE CORP. (MA)
Adjudicated bankrupt in 1964
No stockholders' equity

PRECISION PARTS CO.
Name changed to Economy Baler Co. in 1949
Economy Baler Co. merged into American Hoist & Derrick Co. 9/27/67 which name changed to Amdura Corp. 2/13/89
(See Amdura Corp.)

PRECISION PETE SVCS INC (BC)
Name changed to American Wellhead Services Inc. 01/23/1991
American Wellhead Services Inc. recapitalized as Coronado Resources Inc. 05/13/1994 which recapitalized as Habanero Resources Inc. 10/27/1997 which recapitalized as Sienna Resources Inc. 01/24/2014

PRECISION PLASTICS CORP (CO)
Merged into American Agronomics Corp. 03/20/1981
Each share Common 3¢ par exchanged for $2.625 cash

PRECISION POLYMERS INC (DE)
Reincorporated 9/30/68
State of incorporation changed from (NJ) to (DE) 9/30/68
Name changed to Recon Pipe & Coupling Corp. in March 1994

PRECISION RADIATION INSTRUMENTS, INC. (CA)
Declared bankrupt 3/15/63

PRECISION REBUILDERS, INC. (FL)
Name changed to Needham Engineering, Inc. 2/13/68
Needham Engineering, Inc. proclaimed dissolved 6/28/71

PRECISION RES INC (NJ)
Reincorporated under the laws of Delaware as Kemp Industries Inc. 07/01/1991
(See Kemp Industries Inc.)

PRECISION RESPONSE CORP (FL)
Merged into USA Networks, Inc. 4/5/2000
Each share Common 1¢ par exchanged for (1.08) shares Common 1¢ par
USA Networks, Inc. name changed to USA Interactive 5/9/2002 which name changed to InterActiveCorp 6/23/2003 which name changed to IAC/InterActiveCorp 7/14/2004

PRECISION SHEET METAL, INC. (CA)
Merged into Fansteel Inc. 1/30/70
Each share Common $1 par exchanged for $4.65 cash

PRECISION SOUND CTRS INC (FL)
Charter cancelled and proclaimed dissolved for non-payment of taxes 07/02/1973

PRECISION SPECIALTIES INC (MO)
Merged into Warner Electric Brake & Clutch Co. 11/30/1970
Each share Common 10¢ par exchanged for $6 cash

PRECISION STABILIZERS, INC. (OR)
Involuntarily dissolved for failure to file reports and pay fees 5/22/73

PRECISION STD INC (CO)
Each share old Common $0.0001 par exchanged for (0.25) share new Common $0.0001 par 04/15/1998
Reincorporated under the laws of Delaware as Pemco Aviation Group, Inc. 05/23/2000
Pemco Aviation Group, Inc. name changed to Alabama Aircraft Industries, Inc. 09/19/2007

PRECISION SYS INC (DE)
Merged into Anschutz Digital Media 7/12/99
Each share Common 1¢ par exchanged for $1 cash

PRECISION TARGET MARKETING INC (DE)
Plan of reorganization under Chapter 11 Federal Bankruptcy proceedings confirmed 01/30/1990
No stockholders' equity

PRECISION TECHNOLOGIES (NV)
Reported out of business 00/00/1990
Details not available

PRECISION TRANSFORMER CORP (IL)
Adjudicated bankrupt 07/13/1964
Stockholders' equity unlikely

PRECISIONCRAFT ELECTRONICS, INC. (CA)
Name changed to Westamerica Automotive Corp. and Common no par changed to $1 par 6/10/76
(See Westamerica Automotive Corp.)

PRECISIONWARE, INC. (DE)
Merged into Triangle-Pacific Forest Products Corp. 9/30/65
Each share Common $1 par exchanged for (1) share Common 50¢ par
Triangle-Pacific Forest Products Corp. name changed to Triangle Pacific Corp. 6/15/73
(See Triangle Pacific Corp.)

PRECO INC (NJ)
Charter declared void for non-payment of taxes 9/13/91

PRECOM TECHNOLOGY INC (FL)
Each share old Common $0.001 par exchanged for (0.01) share new Common $0.001 par 02/05/2001
Each share new Common $0.001 par exchanged again for (10) shares new Common $0.001 par 03/19/2001
Each share new Common $0.001 par exchanged again for (0.5) share new Common $0.001 par 09/10/2002
Name changed to International Trust & Financial Systems, Inc. (FL) 10/15/2002
International Trust & Financial Systems, Inc. (FL) reincorporated in Nevada as Marmion Industries Corp. 07/14/2004

PREDATOR EXPL LTD (AB)
Reincorporated 07/02/2003
Reincorporated from Predator Capital Inc. (BC) to under the laws to Alberta as Predator Exploration Ltd. 07/02/2003
Merged into SignalEnergy Inc. 02/23/2005
Each share Common no par exchanged for (0.3846) share Common no par
SignalEnergy Inc. reorganized as Fortress Energy Inc. 02/20/2007 which name changed to Alvopetro Inc. 03/11/2013 which name changed to Fortaleza Energy Inc. 11/19/2013

PREDATOR VENTURES LTD (WY)
Reincorporated 07/14/1999
Place of incorporation changed from (BC) to (WY) 07/14/1999
Recapitalized as wwbroadcast.net Inc. 11/18/1999
Each share Common no par exchanged for (0.5) share Common no par
wwbroadcast.net Inc. name changed to Luna Gold Corp. (WY) 08/12/2003 which reincorporated in Canada 12/01/2005 which merged into Trek Mining Inc. 03/31/2017 which name changed to Equinox Gold Corp. 12/22/2017

PREDICT IT INC (DE)
Adversary proceeding case closed 02/26/2002
Stockholders' equity unlikely

PREDICTIVE SYS INC (DE)
Merged into International Network Services, Inc. 06/19/2003
Each share Common $0.001 par exchanged for $0.4645417 cash

PREFAC CONCRETE CO. LTD. (CANADA)
Capital Stock no par reclassified as Conv. Class A Capital Stock no par 9/15/75
Conv. Class A Capital Stock no par reclassified as Common no par 2/4/86
Conv. Class B Capital Stock no par reclassified as Common no par 2/4/86
Name changed to Prefac Enterprises Inc. 9/4/86
Prefac Enterprises Inc. name changed to Armbro Enterprises Inc. 9/7/88 which name changed to Aecon Group Inc. 6/18/2001

PREFAC ENTERPRISES INC (CANADA)
Name changed to Armbro Enterprises Inc. 9/7/88
Armbro Enterprises Inc. name changed to Aecon Group Inc. 6/18/2001

PREFCO CORP. (NY)
Dissolved by proclamation 06/26/2002

PREFCO ENTERPRISES INC (AB)
Placed in receivership 00/00/2006
Stockholders' equity unlikely

PREFERENCE TECHNOLOGIES INC (NV)
Charter revoked for failure to file reports and pay fees 03/01/2002

PREFERRED & CORPORATE INCOME STRATEGIES FD INC (MD)
Name changed to BlackRock Preferred & Corporate Income Strategies Fund, Inc. 10/02/2006

BlackRock Preferred & Corporate Income Strategies Fund, Inc. name changed to BlackRock Credit Allocation Income Trust I, Inc. 11/13/2009 which merged into BlackRock Credit Allocation Income Trust IV 12/10/2012 which name changed to BlackRock Credit Allocation Income Trust 02/11/2013

PREFERRED ACCIDENT INSURANCE CO. OF NEW YORK
Liquidated in 1951
No stockholders' equity

PREFERRED-AMERICAN INVESTORS CO. (CO)
Liquidation completed 10/7/60

PREFERRED BK FSB (PALMETTO, FL)
Merged into SouthTrust Corp. 11/22/96
Each share Common no par exchanged for $9.50 cash

PREFERRED DEVELOPERS CORP (MN)
Liquidation completed
Each share Common 10¢ par received initial distribution of $0.37 cash in 1978
Each share Common 10¢ par received second distribution of $0.38 cash in January 1979
Each share Common 10¢ par exchanged for third and final distribution of $0.7879 cash 9/14/79

PREFERRED EMPLOYERS HLDGS INC (DE)
Merged into International Insurance GP 06/28/2000
Each share Common 1¢ par exchanged for $5 cash

PREFERRED ENTERPRISES LTD (AB)
Name changed to Prefco Enterprises Inc. 11/15/2000
(See Prefco Enterprises Inc.)

PREFERRED ENTMT INC (DE)
Merged into People's Choice TV Corp. 9/8/95
Each share Common 1¢ par exchanged for (0.7548) share Common 1¢ par
(See People's Choice TV Corp.)

PREFERRED FINL CORP (CO)
Merged into Lincoln National Corp. (IN) 12/23/1986
Each share Common 1¢ par exchanged for $7.25 cash

PREFERRED FOODS LTD (BC)
Recapitalized as Diversified Preferred Foods Ltd. 08/24/1988
Each share Class A Common no par exchanged for (0.2) share Class A Common no par
Diversified Preferred Foods Ltd. name changed to Diversified Publishing Ltd. 01/18/1990
(See Diversified Publishing Ltd.)

PREFERRED HEALTH CARE LTD (DE)
Name changed 9/13/85
Common 1¢ par split (2) for (1) by issuance of (1) additional share 2/25/85
Name changed from Preferred Health Care Corp. to Preferred Health Care Ltd. 9/13/85
Common 1¢ par split (3) for (2) by issuance of (0.5) additional share 10/5/87
Stock Dividends - 50% 4/15/86; 10% 12/1/89
Merged into Value Health, Inc. 12/14/93
Each share Common 1¢ par exchanged for (0.88) share Common no par
(See Value Health, Inc.)

PREFERRED HOMECARE AMER INC (FL)
Acquired by Home Intensive Care, Inc. 10/14/92
Each share Common 1¢ par received approximately (0.07251631) share Common 1¢ par
Note: Certificates were not required to be surrendered and are without value
(See Home Intensive Care, Inc.)

PREFERRED INCOME FD INC (MD)
Name changed to Flaherty & Crumrine Preferred Income Fund Inc. 11/15/2003

PREFERRED INCOME MGMT FD INC (MD)
Name changed to Boulder Total Return Fund, Inc. 08/27/1999
Boulder Total Return Fund, Inc. merged into Boulder Growth & Income Fund, Inc. 03/20/2015

PREFERRED INCOME OPPORTUNITY FD INC (MD)
Name changed to Flaherty & Crumrine Preferred Income Opportunity Fund Inc. 11/15/2003

PREFERRED INCOME STRATEGIES FD INC (MD)
Issue Information - 36,000,000 shares COM offered at $25 per share on 03/25/2003
Name changed to BlackRock Preferred Income Strategies Fund Inc. 10/02/2006
BlackRock Preferred Income Strategies Fund Inc. name changed to BlackRock Credit Allocation Income Trust II, Inc. 11/13/2009 which merged into BlackRock Credit Allocation Income Trust IV 12/10/2012 which name changed to BlackRock Credit Allocation Income Trust 02/11/2013

PREFERRED INSURANCE CO. (MI)
Each share Common $10 par exchanged for (2) shares Common $5 par 8/11/56
Placed in receivership and ordered liquidated 1/31/64
Assets were sold for benefit of general claimants only and estate closed by Court Order 6/30/72
No stockholders' equity

PREFERRED INTERNET TECHNOLOGIES INC (FL)
Name changed 08/12/1996
Name changed from Preferred Trucking Corp. to Preferred Internet Technologies, Inc. 08/12/1996
Name changed to Vision Real Estate Management & Development, Inc. 08/08/2003
Vision Real Estate Management & Development, Inc. name changed to MEM Financial Solutions, Inc. 11/23/2004 which recapitalized as Sebastian River Holdings, Inc. 04/05/2006 which recapitalized as Novacab International Inc. 11/12/2013 which name changed to Global Pole Trusion Group Corp. 07/24/2017

PREFERRED LIFE INSURANCE CO. (WA)
Recapitalized as Washington Preferred Life Insurance Co. 8/16/65
Each share Common $10 par exchanged for (10) shares Common $1 par
Washington Preferred Life Insurance Co. merged into Northern National Life Insurance Co. 9/7/71 which name changed to Manhattan National Life Insurance Co. 1/1/82
(See Manhattan National Life Insurance Co.)

PREFERRED NETWORKS INC (GA)
Reincorporated 6/16/97
State of incorporation changed from (DE) to (GA) 6/16/97
Name changed to PNI Technologies Inc. 8/16/2000
(See PNI Technologies Inc.)

PREFERRED RES INC (BC)
Name changed to Shallow Resources Inc. 02/04/1985
(See Shallow Resources Inc.)

PREFERRED RISK INSURANCE CO. (AR)
Name changed to North American Guaranty Insurance Co. 12/31/64
North American Guaranty Insurance Co. in receivership 10/2/67

PREFERRED RISK LIFE ASSURANCE CO. (AR)
Merged into Life Insurance Co. of Florida 8/4/65
Each share Common no par exchanged for (0.3257329) shares Common $1 par
Life Insurance Co. of Florida reorganized as Life of Florida Corp. 12/31/68 which name changed to Context Industries, Inc. 5/28/70
(See Context Industries, Inc.)

PREFERRED RISK LIFE INS CO (CO)
Common $1 par split (3) for (2) by issuance of (0.5) additional share 4/26/72
Common $1 par split (3) for (2) by issuance of (0.5) additional share 8/25/83
Stock Dividend - 10% 5/10/66
Merged into P.R. Acquisition Co. 9/18/89
Each share Common $1 par exchanged for $35 cash

PREFERRED SVGS BK INC HIGH POINT (NC)
Name changed 2/6/86
Common $10 par changed to $2.50 par and (3) additional shares issued 3/31/84
Each share Non-Cum. Non-Vtg. Preferred $10 par reclassified as (1) share Common $2.50 par 11/6/85
Name changed from Preferred Savings & Loan Association, Inc. to Preferred Savings Bank, Inc. 2/6/86
Administratively dissolved 6/14/95

PREFERRED SECS INCOME FD (ON)
Merged into First Asset Yield Opportunity Trust 12/17/2007
Each Unit automatically became (0.7465) Ser. A Unit
First Asset Yield Opportunity Trust name changed to First Asset Active Credit Fund 12/22/2014 which merged into First Asset Active Credit ETF 01/19/2015

PREFERRED SECS LTD DURATION FD (ON)
Merged into First Asset Yield Opportunity Trust 12/17/2007
Each Ser. A Unit automatically became (0.7541) Ser. A Unit
Each Ser. B Unit automatically became (1) Ser. B Unit
First Asset Yield Opportunity Trust name changed to First Asset Active Credit Fund 12/22/2014 which merged into First Asset Active Credit ETF 01/19/2015

PREFERRED SH INVT TR (ON)
Under plan of merger each Unit automatically became (0.29955) First Asset Preferred Share ETF Unit 11/01/2016

PREFERRED/TELECOM INC (DE)
Recapitalized as Preferred Voice Inc. 03/07/1997
Each share Common $0.001 par exchanged for (0.5) share Common $0.001 par
Preferred Voice Inc. name changed to Aly Energy Services, Inc. 05/23/2013

PREFERRED UTILS MFG CORP (DE)
5-1/2% Conv. 1st Preferred $10 par called for redemption 12/17/1968
Merged into PUMC Acquisition Corp. 07/08/1986
Each share Common 10¢ par exchanged for $17 cash

PREFERRED VOICE INC (DE)
Each share old Common $0.001 par exchanged for (0.2) share new Common $0.001 par 11/27/2006
Name changed to Aly Energy Services, Inc. 05/23/2013

PREFERREDPLUS TR (DE)
7.30% Trust Certificates Ser. BLS-1 called for redemption at $25 on 03/01/2007
Trust Certificates Ser. NAI-1 called for redemption at $25 on 01/11/2007
Trust Certificates Ser. GRC-1 called for redemption at $25 on 04/15/2008
Trust Certificates Ser. FMC-1 called for redemption 12/13/2010
Class A Trust Certificates Ser. ELP-1 called for redemption at $25 plus $0.876563 accrued dividends on 12/30/2010
Class A Trust Certificates Ser. ALL-1 called for redemption at $25 on 02/15/2011
Class B Trust Certificates Ser. ALL-1 called for redemption 02/15/2011
Class B Trust Certificates Ser. GEC-1 called for redemption 09/15/2011
Trust Certificates Ser. FRD-1 called for redemption at $25 on 11/01/2012
Trust Certificates Ser. UPC-1 called for redemption at $25 on 06/15/2012
Trust Certificates Ser. LMG-1 called for redemption at $25 plus $0.249131 accrued dividends on 03/14/2013
Trust Certificates Ser. LMG-1 called for redemption at $25 plus $0.336458 accrued dividends on 03/14/2013

PREFORM BUILDING COMPONENTS, INC. (DE)
Name changed to Preform Industries, Inc. 6/24/71
Preform Industries, Inc. adjudicated bankrupt 3/20/73

PREFORM INDS INC (DE)
Adjudicated bankrupt 03/20/1973
No stockholders' equity

PREISS BYRON MULTIMEDIA INC (NY)
Issue Information - 525,000 Units consisting of (2) shares COM and (2) WTS offered at $10 per Unit on 05/11/1994
Name changed to Vmailer.com Inc. 10/6/99
(See Vmailer.com Inc.)

PREL CORP (DE)
Name changed to Landall Corp. 11/03/1976
Landall Corp. name changed to Shongum Corp. 06/26/1984 which name changed to American Water Resources, Inc. 07/19/1989
(See American Water Resources, Inc.)

PRELIM CAP INC (CANADA)
Name changed to Hudson River Minerals Ltd. 05/17/2010

PRELUDE CORP (MA)
Class A Common 50¢ par reclassified as Common 50¢ par 04/08/1971
Class B Common 50¢ par reclassified as Common 50¢ par 04/08/1971
Adjudicated bankrupt 03/14/1979
Stockholders' equity unlikely

PRELUDE LAKE MINES LTD. (ON)
Charter revoked for failure to file reports and pay fees 8/19/65

PRELUDE VENTURES INC (NV)
Each share old Common $0.001 par

exchanged for (6) shares new
Common $0.001 par 12/30/2002
Name changed to American Capital
Alliance, Inc. 02/23/2004
American Capital Alliance, Inc.
recapitalized as American Petroleum
Group, Inc. 11/01/2004 which name
changed to High Velocity Alternative
Energy Corp. 09/14/2007 which
name changed to Reflectkote, Inc.
07/31/2009

PREMA FACEMASTER SYS INC (NY)
Charter cancelled and proclaimed
dissolved for failure to pay taxes
03/26/1980

PREMA SYS INC (NV)
Recapitalized as Urban Community
Enhancement Corp. 05/12/2005
Each share Common 1¢ par
exchanged for (0.005) share
Common $0.001 par
Urban Community Enhancement
Corp. name changed to Vision
Digital Multimedia Corp. 12/22/2005
which name changed to Clinicares,
Inc. 03/08/2007 which recapitalized
as Catch By Gene, Inc. 04/09/2010
(See Catch By Gene, Inc.)

PREMARA FINL INC (NC)
Stock Dividend - 15% payable
05/22/2013 to holders of record
05/06/2013 Ex date - 05/02/2013
Merged into Select Bancorp, Inc.
(New) 12/15/2017
Each share Common 1¢ par
exchanged for either (1.043) shares
Common $1 par or $12.65 cash

PREMARK INTL INC (DE)
Common $1 par split (2) for (1) by
issuance of (1) additional share
7/5/94
Each share Common $1 par received
distribution of (1) share Tupperware
Corp. Common 1¢ par payable
5/31/96 to holders of record 5/24/96
Merged into Illinois Tool Works Inc.
11/23/99
Each share Common $1 par
exchanged for (0.8081) share
Common no par

PREMCOR INC (DE)
Issue Information - 18,000,000 shares
COM offered at $24 per share on
04/29/2002
Merged into Valero Energy Corp.
9/1/2005
Each share Common 1¢ par
exchanged for $72.76 cash

PREMDOR INC (ON)
Subordinate no par split (2) for (1) by
issuance of (1) additional share
5/25/87
Subordinate no par reclassified as
Common no par 6/18/91
Name changed to Masonite
International Corp. 1/1/2002
(See Masonite International Corp.)

PREMENOS TECHNOLOGY CORP (DE)
Merged into Harbinger Corp. 12/19/97
Each share Common 1¢ par
exchanged for (0.45) share Common
$0.0001 par
Harbinger Corp. merged into
Peregrine Systems, Inc. 6/19/2000
(See Peregrine Systems, Inc.)

PREMERE RES CORP (NV)
Charter revoked for failure to file
reports and pay fees 05/31/2011

PREMIER ALLIANCE GROUP INC (DE)
Reincorporated 09/01/2011
State of incorporation changed from
(NV) to (DE) 09/01/2011
Name changed to root9B
Technologies, Inc. 12/01/2014
root9B Technologies, Inc.
recapitalized as root9B Holdings,
Inc. 12/05/2016

PREMIER ANESTHESIA INC (DE)
Name changed to Allegiant Physician
Services, Inc. 11/15/94
(See Allegiant Physician Services, Inc.)

PREMIER ATHLETIC PRODS CORP (NJ)
Each share Common 10¢ par
exchanged for (0.1) share Common
1¢ par 01/14/1974
Merged into Equilink Premier, Inc.
09/30/1977
Each share Common 1¢ par
exchanged for $0.65 cash

PREMIER AXIOM ASP INC (NV)
Each share old Common $0.001 par
exchanged for (0.0001) share new
Common $0.001 par 7/15/2002
Name changed to Core Solutions Inc.
7/19/2002
Core Solutions Inc. recapitalized as
Sunshine Ventures Inc. 5/12/2003
which name changed to Christine's
Precious Petals Inc. 7/14/2003
which name changed to Global
Business Markets, Inc. 9/5/2003
which name changed to GREM USA
3/3/2005

PREMIER BANCORP INC (LA)
Stock Dividend - 10% 06/07/1993
Merged into Banc One Corp.
01/02/1996
Each share Common no par
exchanged for (0.617761) share
Common no par
Banc One Corp. merged into Bank
One Corp. 10/02/1998 which
merged into J.P. Morgan Chase &
Co. 07/01/2004 which name
changed to JPMorgan Chase & Co.
07/20/2004

PREMIER BANCORP INC (PA)
Stock Dividend - 5% payable
3/10/2000 to holders of record
2/29/2000
9.25% Preferred Ser. A called for
redemption at $25.50 on 8/1/2003
Merged into Fulton Financial Corp.
8/1/2003
Each share Common 33¢ par
exchanged for (1.407) shares
Common $2.50 par

PREMIER BANCSHARES INC (GA)
Common $5 par split (1.8055) for (1)
by issuance of (0.8055) additional
share payable 3/20/97 to holders of
record 3/6/97 Ex date - 3/21/97
Common $5 par changed to $1 par
and (0.5) additional share issued
payable 2/6/98 to holders of record
1/23/98
Merged into BB&T Corp. 1/13/2000
Each share Non-Voting Preferred
exchanged for (2.2945) shares
Common $5 par
Each share Common $1 par
exchanged for (0.5155) share
Common $5 par

PREMIER BANCSHARES INC (GA)
Name changed 4/28/95
Name changed from Premier Lending
Corp. to Premier Bancshares, Inc.
4/28/95
Merged into First Alliance/Premier
Bancshares, Inc. 8/31/96
Each share Common no par
exchanged for (1) share Common
$5 par
First Alliance/Premier Bancshares,
Inc. name changed to Premier
Bancshares, Inc. (New) 2/4/97 which
merged into BB&T Corp. 1/13/2000

PREMIER BK (NORTHRIDGE, CA)
Placed in receivership and assets
subsequently sold 4/9/93
No stockholders' equity

PREMIER BANKSHARES CORP (VA)
Common $2 par split (6) for (5) by
issuance of (0.2) additional share
2/1/93
Common $2 par split (4) for (3) by
issuance of (1/3) additional share
payable 1/3/96 to holders of record
12/14/95
Stock Dividend - 100% 12/31/88
Merged into First Virginia Banks, Inc.
5/23/97
Each share Common $2 par
exchanged for (0.545) share
Common $1 par
First Virginia Banks, Inc. merged into
BB&T Corp. 7/1/2003

PREMIER BORDER GOLD MINING CO., LTD. (CANADA)
Recapitalized as Calvert Gas & Oils
Ltd. 12/31/1958
Each (5) shares Capital Stock no par
exchanged for (1) share Capital
Stock no par
Calvert Gas & Oils Ltd. recapitalized
as Heenan Petroleum Ltd.
08/08/1985 which merged into
Heenan Senlac Resources Ltd.
08/07/1986 which merged into
Mining & Allied Supplies (Canada)
Ltd. 08/25/1992 which name
changed to Bearing Power (Canada)
Ltd. 03/28/1994
(See Bearing Power (Canada) Ltd.)

PREMIER BRANDS INC (UT)
Each share old Common $0.001 par
exchanged for (0.025) share new
Common $0.001 par 08/27/1996
Each share new Common $0.001 par
exchanged again for (0.01666666)
new Common $0.001 par
08/26/1998
Reincorporated under laws of
Delaware as CathayOne, Inc.
08/28/2000
(See CathayOne, Inc.)

PREMIER BRANDS INC (WY)
Common $0.001 par split (70) for (1)
by issuance of (69) additional
shares payable 06/08/2012 to
holders of record 06/08/2012
SEC revoked common stock
registration 07/25/2016

PREMIER BUSINESS BK (LOS ANGELES, CA)
Under plan of reorganization each
share Common no par automatically
became (1) share PBB Bancorp
Common no par 11/14/2014

PREMIER CABLEVISION LTD. (BC)
Name changed to Premier
Communications Ltd. 2/20/80
Premier Communications Ltd.
acquired by Canadian Cablesystems
Ltd. 12/19/80 which name changed
to Rogers Cablesystems Inc.
2/13/81 which name changed to
Rogers Communications Inc.
4/24/86

PREMIER CDN ENTERPRISES LTD (CANADA)
Reorganized as Premier Tech Inc.
12/22/99
Each share Class A Common no par
exchanged for (1.1) shares Class A
Subordinate no par or (1) share
Class B Multiple no par
Note: Option to receive Class A
Subordinate expired 12/22/99
(See Premier Tech Inc.)

PREMIER CDN INCOME FD (ON)
Trust terminated 12/31/2014
Each Trust Unit received $2.80 cash

PREMIER CAP TR I (DE)
9% Preferred Securities called for
redemption at $25 on 05/02/2012

PREMIER CLASSIC ART INC (DE)
Name changed to Parentech, Inc. and
Common $0.002 par changed to
$0.000001 par 1/17/2003
Parentech, Inc. recapitalized as
Bridgetech Holdings International,
Inc. 2/11/2005

PREMIER COML BANCORP (CA)
Common no par split (5) for (4) by
issuance of (0.25) additional share
payable 02/15/2005 to holders of
record 01/19/2005 Ex date -
02/16/2005
Common no par split (5) for (4) by
issuance of (0.25) additional share
payable 02/01/2006 to holders of
record 02/01/2006 Ex date -
02/16/2006
Common no par split (5) for (4) by
issuance of (0.25) additional share
payable 06/08/2007 to holders of
record 06/01/2007 Ex date -
06/11/2007
Stock Dividend - 1.7407% payable
01/17/2012 to holders of record
12/31/2011 Ex date - 12/28/2011
Merged into CU Bancorp 08/01/2012
Each share Common no par
exchanged for (0.9923) share
Common no par
CU Bancorp merged into PacWest
Bancorp 10/20/2017

PREMIER COML BANCORP (OR)
Merged into Heritage Financial Corp.
07/02/2018
Each share Common no par
exchanged for (0.4863) share
Common no par

PREMIER COML BK (GREENSBORO, NC)
Merged into NewBridge Bancorp
03/02/2015
Each share Common $5 par
exchanged for (0.9014) share Class
A Common no par and $2.50 cash
NewBridge Bancorp merged into
Yadkin Financial Corp. 03/01/2016

PREMIER COML BK N A (ANAHEIM, CA)
Common no par split (5) for (4) by
issuance of (0.25) additional share
payable 01/15/2003 to holders of
record 12/18/2002 Ex date -
01/16/2003
Under plan of reorganization each
share Common no par automatically
became (1) share Premier
Commercial Bancorp Common no
par 09/03/2004
Premier Commercial Bancorp merged
into CU Bancorp 08/01/2012 which
merged into PacWest Bancorp
10/20/2017

PREMIER COMMUNICATIONS LTD (BC)
Acquired by Canadian Cablesystems
Ltd. 12/19/1980
Each share Common no par
exchanged for (3) shares Class B
Non-Vtg. no par
Canadian Cablesystems Ltd. name
changed to Rogers Cablesystems
Inc. 02/13/1981 which name
changed to Rogers Communications
Inc. 04/24/1986

PREMIER CMNTY BANKSHARES INC (VA)
Merged into United Bankshares, Inc.
07/16/2007
Each share Common $1 par
exchanged for (0.6622) share
Common $2.50 par and $9.79 cash

PREMIER CONCEPTS INC (CO)
Each share Common $0.0004 par
exchanged for (0.2) share Common
$0.002 par 12/20/1996
Each share old Common $0.002 par
exchanged again for (0.5) share new
Common $0.002 par 04/22/1999
Plan of reorganization under Chapter
11 Federal Bankruptcy Code
effective 12/13/2004
Each share Common $0.002 par
received (0.09090909) share USN
Corp. (CO) Class A Common $0.002
par
Note: Certificates were not required to
be exchanged and are without value
USN Corp. (CO) reorganized in
Delaware as Holdings US, Inc.
03/30/2012 which name changed to

California Style Palms, Inc. 09/25/2013

PREMIER CONS OILFIELDS LTD (UNITED KINGDOM)
Ordinary Reg. 1s par and ADR's 1s par changed to 5p par per currency change 2/15/71
Each Unsponsored ADR for Ordinary Reg. 5p par exchanged for (0.1) Sponsored ADR for Ordinary Reg. 5p par 12/11/90
Stock Dividends for Ordinary - 10% 7/27/79; 10% 7/25/80; 10% 7/23/81; 10% 7/23/82; 10% 8/17/84; 10% 7/24/85; 10% 8/11/86; 10%8/9/89; 10%8/7/90
Stock Dividends for ADRs - 10% 8/17/79; 10% 9/4/80; 10% 8/21/81; 10% 8/27/82; 10% 10/31/83; 10% 8/31/84; 10% 9/6/85; 10% 9/14/86; 10% 9/2/87; 10% 9/14/88; 10% 8/24/89; 10% 8/22/90
Name changed to Premier Oil PLC 5/15/95

PREMIER CORP AMER (NY)
Out of business and assets sold to pay taxes 08/01/1969
No stockholders' equity

PREMIER DIAGNOSTIC HEALTH SVCS INC (BC)
Name changed to Premier Diversified Holdings Inc. 04/22/2015

PREMIER DIAMOND CORP (BC)
Reincorporated under the laws of Alberta as Mexican Silver Mines Ltd. 05/07/2007
Mexican Silver Mines Ltd. name changed to Rio Alto Mining Ltd. 07/24/2009 which merged into Tahoe Resources Inc. 04/01/2015

PREMIER DISTRIBUTING CORP. (MI)
Completely liquidated 09/07/1967
Each share Common $1 par exchanged for first and final distribution of (0.022513) share Consolidated Foods Corp. Common $1.33333333 par
Consolidated Foods Corp. name changed to Sara Lee Corp. 04/02/1985 which recapitalized as Hillshire Brands Co. 06/29/2012
(See Hillshire Brands Co.)

PREMIER DOCUMENT SVCS INC (NV)
Reorganized as Navstar Media Holdings, Inc. 12/16/2005
Each share Common $0.001 par exchanged for (2.333598463) shares Common $0.001 par
Navstar Media Holdings, Inc. recapitalized as Rodobo International, Inc. 11/12/2008

PREMIER ENERGY CORP (DE)
Reincorporated 5/31/83
State of incorporation changed from (NV) to (DE) and Common 1¢ par changed to $0.001 par 5/31/83
Charter cancelled and declared inoperative and void for non-payment of taxes 3/1/93

PREMIER ENTERPRISES HLDGS INC (DE)
Name changed to Hawaiilove.com, Inc. 1/20/2000
Hawaiilove.com, Inc. name changed to Ornate Solutions Inc. 8/2/2001 which recapitalized as Ornate Holdings Inc. 9/20/2001 which name changed to Absolute Health & Fitness, Inc. 5/14/2004

PREMIER FARNELL PLC (UNITED KINGDOM)
ADR agreement terminated 02/07/2005
Each Sponsored ADR for Preference exchanged for $23.3442 cash
Each Sponsored ADR for Preference exchanged for $5.9655 cash
ADR agreement terminated 11/15/2016

Each ADR for Ordinary exchanged for $8.991379 cash

PREMIER FINL SVCS INC (DE)
Common $5 par split (3) for (1) by issuance of (2) additional shares 10/1/84
Common $5 par split (3) for (1) by issuance of (2) additional shares 7/1/94
Stock Dividend - 10% 3/31/92
Merged into Grand Premier Financial, Inc. 8/22/96
Each share Common $5 par exchanged for (1.116) shares Common no par

PREMIER GASPE MINES LTD (ON)
Name changed to Python Resources & Investment Corp. 11/12/74
Python Resources & Investment Corp. recapitalized as Python Corp. 4/29/87

PREMIER GNMA FD (MD)
Name changed to Dreyfus Premier GNMA Fund 03/04/1997
(See Dreyfus Premier GNMA Fund)

PREMIER GOLD MINING CO., LTD.
Liquidation completed
Each share Capital Stock $1 par received initial distribution of (0.3) share Toburn Gold Mines Ltd. Capital Stock $1 par, (0.25) share Silbak Premier Mines, Ltd. Capital Stock $1 par and $0.20 cash 11/5/47
Each share Capital Stock $1 par received second and final distribution of (0.07) share Saudi Arabian Mining Syndicate Ltd. Capital Stock 5s par, (0.3) share Big Bell Mines Ltd. Capital Stock £1 par and $0.043 cash 5/17/48
Certificates were not surrendered and are now without value
(See each company's listing)

PREMIER GOLD RES INC (BC)
Recapitalized as Cryptic Ventures Inc. (BC) 4/8/92
Each share Common no par exchanged for (1/3) share Common no par
Cryptic Ventures Inc. (BC) reorganized in Yukon as Zen International Resources Ltd. 11/21/96 which reorganized in Alberta as Orca Petroleum Inc. 4/1/2002 which reorganized in British Columbia as Nautilus Minerals Inc. 5/10/2006

PREMIER GROUP LTD (SOUTH AFRICA)
ADR agreement terminated 7/23/98
Each Sponsored ADR for Ordinary exchanged for (5) Ordinary Shares

PREMIER HLDGS GROUP INC (DE)
Old Common 1¢ par split (2) for (1) by issuance of (1) additional share payable 11/09/2000 to holders of record 11/01/2000 Ex date - 11/10/2000
Each share old Common 1¢ par exchanged for (0.1) share new Common 1¢ par 05/16/2005
Each (13) shares new Common 1¢ par exchanged again for (1) new Common 1¢ par 08/28/2006
Recapitalized as Internet Song of the Year, Inc. 06/25/2007
Each share Common 1¢ par exchanged for (0.5) share Common 1¢ par
Internet Song of the Year, Inc. name changed to National Maintenance Group, Inc. 06/11/2008

PREMIER IMAGE TECHNOLOGY CORP (TAIWAN)
Stock Dividends - In GDR's for 144A payable to holders of GDR's for 144A 19.2636% payable 7/27/2001 to holders of record 6/8/2001 Ex date - 6/6/2001; 20% payable 9/17/2002 to holders of record 7/31/2002 Ex date - 7/29/2002; 10% payable 9/25/2003 to holders of record 10/27/2004 to holders of record 7/21/2004; 3% payable 10/21/2005 to holders of record 8/4/2005; 3% payable 10/5/2006 to holders of record 8/10/2006; In Reg. S GDR's for 144A payable to holders of Reg. S GDR's for 144A 3% payable 10/21/2005 to holders of record 8/4/2005
ADR agreement terminated 12/1/2006
Each 144A GDR for Common exchanged for $10.51599 cash
Each Reg. S GDR for Common exchanged for $10.51599 cash

PREMIER INDL CORP (OH)
Common $1 par split (3) for (2) by issuance of (0.5) additional share 01/10/1966
Common $1 par split (3) for (2) by issuance of (0.5) additional share 07/11/1969
Common $1 par split (2) for (1) by issuance of (1) additional share 05/12/1972
90¢ Conv. Preferred Ser. A no par called for redemption 08/01/1977
Common $1 par split (3) for (2) by issuance of (0.5) additional share 11/08/1979
Common $1 par split (2) for (1) by issuance of (1) additional share 08/20/1981
Common $1 par split (3) for (2) by issuance of (0.5) additional share 01/10/1985
Common $1 par split (3) for (2) by issuance of (0.5) additional share 01/08/1988
Each share Common $1 par exchanged for (0.91) share Common no par and $2.70 cash 11/18/1988
Common no par split (3) for (2) by issuance of (0.5) additional share 01/10/1990
Common no par split (3) for (2) by issuance of (0.5) additional share 01/08/1993
Stock Dividend - 50% 09/28/1962
Merged into Farnell Electronics PLC 04/11/1996
Each share Common no par exchanged for (0.34) Sponsored ADR for $1.35 Conv. Preference (0.422005) Sponsored ADR for Ordinary and $17 cash
Farnell Electronics PLC name changed to Premier Farnell PLC 04/11/1996
(See Premier Farnell PLC)

PREMIER INFORMATION MGMT INC (NV)
Charter permanently revoked 06/30/2011

PREMIER INVTS INC (MN)
Statutorily dissolved 8/1/97

PREMIER LAKE RES INC (ON)
Merged into Castlestar Capital Developments Corp. 03/30/1990
Each share Common no par exchanged for (0.95) share Common no par
Castlestar Capital Developments Corp. recapitalized as Southern Frontier Resources Inc. 11/11/1993
(See Southern Frontier Resources Inc.)

PREMIER LASER SYS INC (CA)
Issue Information - 2,400,000 UNITS consisting of (1) share CL A, (1) WT CL A, and (1) WT CL B offered at $5 per Unit on 11/30/1994
Plan of reorganization under Chapter 11 Federal Bankruptcy proceedings terminated 03/13/2006
Stockholders' equity unlikely

PREMIER MICROWAVE CORP (NY)
Merged into Comtech Telecommunications Corp. 1/28/83

Each share Common $1 par exchanged for $15 cash

PREMIER MINERALS LTD (BC)
Recapitalized as Premier Diamond Corp. (BC) 03/05/2001
Each share Common no par exchanged for (0.5) share Common no par
Premier Diamond Corp. (BC) reincorporated in Alberta as Mexican Silver Mines Ltd. 05/07/2007 which name changed to Rio Alto Mining Ltd. 07/24/2009 which merged into Tahoe Resources Inc. 04/01/2015

PREMIER MINING CORP. LTD. (BC)
Name changed to Premier Resources Ltd. 8/16/71
Premier Resources Ltd. recapitalized as Tyrona Resources Ltd. 2/22/82 which merged into Signal Hill Energy Corp. 12/20/82 which recapitalized as Texas Petroleum Corp. (BC) 6/13/85 which recapitalized as North American Equity Corp. 3/7/89
(See North American Equity Corp.)

PREMIER MTG RES INC (NV)
Each share old Common $0.001 par exchanged for (0.16666666) share new Common $0.001 par 04/14/1999
Each share new Common $0.001 par exchanged again for (0.1) share new Common $0.001 par 02/01/2001
Name changed to Alternaturals, Inc. 05/01/2014

PREMIER NATL BANCORP INC (NY)
Stock Dividends - 10% payable 1/15/99 to holders of record 1/6/99; 10% payable 1/14/2000 to holders of record 1/5/2000
Merged into M&T Bank Corp. 2/9/2001
Each share Common 80¢ par exchanged for (0.3091) share Common $5 par and $21 cash

PREMIER NURSING PRODS CORP (FL)
Common $0.001 par changed to $0.0001 par and (17) additional shares issued payable 08/08/2008 to holders of record 08/07/2008 Ex date - 08/11/2008
Name changed to Premier Energy Corp. 10/07/2008

PREMIER OIL FIELD SVCS INC (NV)
Name changed to American Metals Recovery & Recycling Inc. 05/02/2014

PREMIER ORGANIC FARMS GROUP INC (NV)
Recapitalized as Amstar Financial Holdings, Inc. 12/19/2006
Each share Common $0.001 par exchanged for (0.0125) share Common $0.001 par
Amstar Financial Holdings, Inc. recapitalized as China Du Kang Co. Ltd. 03/19/2008

PREMIER-PABST CORP. (DE)
Name changed to Pabst Brewing Co. in 1939
(See Pabst Brewing Co.)

PREMIER PAC INC (CA)
Common 10¢ par changed to no par 09/11/1978
Reported out of business 00/00/1979
Details not available

PREMIER PAYMASTER MINES CO. (NV)
Charter revoked for failure to file reports and pay fees 3/4/29

PREMIER PAYMASTER MINES LTD.
Merged into Paymaster Consolidated Mines Ltd. 00/00/1930
Details not available

PREMIER PHOTO SVC INC (OH)
Stock Dividend - 10% 03/01/1971

FINANCIAL INFORMATION, INC.

Name changed to Best Photo Service, Inc. 05/17/1971
Best Photo Service, Inc. acquired by Nashua Corp. (DE) 10/15/1971 which reincorporated in Massachusetts 06/12/2002 which was acquired by Cenveo, Inc. 09/15/2009
(See Cenveo, Inc.)

PREMIER PKS INC (DE)
Secondary Offering - 16,000,000 shares COM offered at $54 per share on 03/26/1998
Each share Common 1¢ par exchanged for (0.2) share Common 5¢ par 05/06/1996
Common 5¢ par changed to 2-1/2¢ par and (1) additional share issued payable 08/07/1998 to holders of record 07/24/1998 Ex date - 08/10/1998
Name changed to Six Flags, Inc. 06/30/2000
(See Six Flags, Inc.)

PREMIER PLATFORMS HLDG INC (CO)
Each share old Common no par exchanged for (0.05) share new Common no par 12/06/2004
Name changed to Paolo Nevada Enterprises, Inc. (CO) 02/17/2005
Paolo Nevada Enterprises, Inc. (CO) reorganized in Nevada as David Loren Corp. 11/13/2006 which recapitalized as Kibush Capital Corp. 08/23/2013

PREMIER RESH WORLDWIDE LTD (DE)
Issue Information - 2,750,000 shares COM offered at $17 per share on 02/03/1997
Name changed to PRWW, Ltd. 04/24/2000
PRWW, Ltd. name changed to eResearchTechnology, Inc. 04/27/2001
(See eResearchTechnology, Inc.)

PREMIER RES LTD (BC)
Recapitalized as Tyrona Resources Ltd. 2/22/82
Each share Capital Stock no par exchanged for (0.2) share Common no par
Tyrona Resources Ltd. merged into Signal Hill Energy Corp. 12/20/82 which recapitalized as Texas Petroleum Corp. (BC) 6/13/85 which recapitalized as North American Equity Corp. 3/7/89
(See North American Equity Corp.)

PREMIER RES LTD (CO)
Stock Dividend - 10% 03/31/1980
Merged into Oxford Consolidated, Inc. 01/02/1991
Each share Common no par exchanged for (0.03125) share Common 1-1/3¢ par
(See Oxford Consolidated, Inc.)

PREMIER RTY INC (ON)
Merged into Sandstorm Gold Ltd. 10/09/2013
Each share Common no par exchanged for (0.145) share Common no par
Note: Unexchanged certificates will be cancelled and become without value 10/09/2019

PREMIER SVC BK (RIVERSIDE, CA)
Merged into INDY Merger Corp. 1 on 01/31/2014
Each share Common no par exchanged for (0.1603278) share Independence Bank (Newport Beach, CA) Common and $5.392668 cash
Independence Bank (Newport Beach, CA) merged into Pacific Premier Bancorp, Inc. 01/26/2015

PREMIER SHARES, INC.
Liquidated in 1940

PREMIER STAR MINING CO. (DE)
Charter cancelled and declared inoperative and void for non-payment of taxes 3/1/58

PREMIER STEEL MILLS LTD. (CANADA)
Each share Common no par redeemed for $16 cash 3/30/63

PREMIER STEEL PRODUCTS (AB)
Acquired by Premier Steel Mills Ltd. on a (0.05) for (1) basis 1/9/62

PREMIER SUPPLEMENTS CORP (FL)
Each share old Common $0.0001 par exchanged for (0.04) share new Common $0.0001 par 11/17/1997
Name changed to CentraCan Inc. 05/15/1998
CentraCan Inc. name changed to EcoReady Corp. 12/23/2010

PREMIER TECH INC (CANADA)
Merged into 4385977 Canada Inc. 2/26/2007
Each share Class A Subordinate no par exchanged for $3 cash
Each share Class B Multiple no par exchanged for $3 cash

PREMIER TECHNOLOGY HLDG INC (DE)
Charter forfeited for failure to maintain a registered agent 9/18/86

PREMIER TECHNOLOGY INC (DE)
Under plan of merger name changed to Premier Technology Holdings, Inc. 5/5/86
(See Premier Technology Holdings, Inc.)

PREMIER TIRE & RUBBER CO. (MO)
Charter forfeited for failure to file reports 01/01/1922

PREMIER TR CO (TORONTO, ON)
Each share Capital Stock $100 par exchanged for (10) shares Capital Stock $10 par 01/31/1972
Acquired by Victoria & Grey Trustco Ltd. 08/00/1983
Each share Capital Stock $10 par exchanged for $96.50 cash

PREMIER UTD KINGDOM NT CDN LTD (ON)
Senior Dividend Shares no par called for redemption at $25 on 6/30/97
Public interest eliminated

PREMIER UTD KINGDOM NT US LTD (ON)
Senior Dividend Shares no par called for redemption 6/30/97
Public interest eliminated

PREMIER VY BK (FRESNO, CA)
Common no par split (5) for (4) by issuance of (0.25) additional share payable 07/31/2002 to holders of record 07/03/2002
Common no par split (5) for (4) by issuance of (0.25) additional share payable 10/31/2003 to holders of record 09/30/2003 Ex date - 11/03/2003
Common no par split (5) for (4) by issuance of (0.25) additional share payable 10/31/2004 to holders of record 09/30/2004 Ex date - 11/01/2004
Common no par split (2) for (1) by issuance of (1) additional share payable 10/31/2005 to holders of record 09/30/2005 Ex date - 11/01/2005
Stock Dividends - 5% payable 10/31/2006 to holders of record 10/01/2006 Ex date - 09/27/2006; 1% payable 04/15/2009 to holders of record 03/31/2009 Ex date - 03/27/2009; 1% payable 07/15/2009 to holders of record 06/30/2009 Ex date - 06/26/2009; 1% payable 10/15/2009 to holders of record 09/30/2009 Ex date - 09/28/2009; 1% payable 01/15/2010 to holders of record 12/31/2009 Ex date - 12/29/2009; 1% payable 04/15/2010 to holders of record 03/31/2010 Ex date - 03/29/2010; 1% payable 07/15/2010 to holders of record 06/30/2010 Ex date - 06/28/2010
Merged into Heartland Financial USA, Inc. 12/01/2015
Each share Common no par exchanged for (0.2042) share Common $1 par

PREMIER VALUE INCOME TR (ON)
Merged into Sentry Canadian Income Fund 02/04/2011
Each Trust Unit no par received (0.567) Ser. A Unit no par

PREMIER VENTURES & EXPL INC (LA)
Each (450) shares old Common no par exchanged for (1) share new Common no par 1/16/97
Name changed to New Directions Manufacturing Inc. 3/14/97
New Directions Manufacturing Inc. recapitalized as American Soil Technologies Inc. (NV) 1/18/2000

PREMIER WEALTH MGMT INC (DE)
SEC revoked common stock registration 07/20/2011

PREMIERE AG (GERMANY)
Name changed to Sky Deutschland AG 09/03/2009
(See Sky Deutschland AG)

PREMIERE GLOBAL SVCS INC (GA)
Acquired by Pangea Private Holdings II, LLC 12/08/2015
Each share Common 1¢ par exchanged for $14 cash

PREMIERE MNG VENTURES INC (FL)
Name changed to Pure Air Technology Inc. 02/16/1998
Pure Air Technology Inc. name changed to Startek.Com Inc. 03/06/1999 which name changed to Bentley Communications Corp. 11/29/1999 which name changed to Bentley Commerce Corp. 01/12/2004
(See Bentley Commerce Corp.)

PREMIERE OPPORTUNITIES GROUP INC (NV)
Recapitalized as Global Fashion Technologies, Inc. 09/10/2014
Each share Common $0.001 par exchanged for (0.00285714) share Common $0.001 par
Global Fashion Technologies, Inc. name changed to Eco Tek 360, Inc. 02/14/2017

PREMIERE PAGE INC (DE)
Merged into USA Mobile Communications Holdings, Inc. 12/28/1994
Each share Common 1¢ par exchanged for (0.966) share Common 1¢ par and $1.76 cash
Note: An additional distribution of (0.035) share Common per share was made 07/06/1995
USA Mobile Communications Holdings, Inc. name changed to Arch Communications Group, Inc. 09/07/1995 which name changed to Arch Wireless, Inc. 09/25/2000
(See Arch Wireless, Inc.)

PREMIERE PUBG GROUP INC (NV)
Name changed to Premiere Opportunities Group, Inc. 06/29/2011
Premiere Opportunities Group, Inc. recapitalized as Global Fashion Technologies, Inc. 09/10/2014 which name changed to Eco Tek 360, Inc. 02/14/2017

PREMIERE RADIO NETWORKS INC (DE)
Reincorporated 07/28/1995
State of incorporation changed from (CA) to (DE) 07/28/1995
Merged into Jacor Communications, Inc. 06/12/1997
Each share Common no par exchanged for (0.138) share Common no par and $13.50 cash
Jacor Communications, Inc. merged into Clear Channel Communications, Inc. 05/04/1999
(See Clear Channel Communications, Inc.)

PREMIERE TECHNOLOGIES INC (GA)
Under plan of reorganization each share Common 1¢ par automatically became (1) share PTEK Holdings, Inc. Common 1¢ par 02/17/2000
PTEK Holdings, Inc. name changed to Premiere Global Services, Inc. 01/03/2005
(See Premiere Global Services, Inc.)

PREMIERWEST BANCORP (OR)
Each share old Common no par exchanged for (0.1) share new Common no par 02/11/2011
Stock Dividends - 5% payable 06/22/2001 to holders of record 06/01/2001 Ex date - 05/30/2001; 5% payable 06/21/2002 to holders of record 06/01/2002; 5% payable 06/20/2003 to holders of record 05/30/2003 Ex date - 05/28/2003; 5% payable 06/21/2004 to holders of record 05/28/2004 Ex date - 05/26/2004; 5% payable 06/27/2005 to holders of record 06/01/2005 Ex date - 05/27/2005; 5% payable 06/29/2006 to holders of record 06/01/2006 Ex date - 05/30/2006; 5% payable 06/29/2007 to holders of record 06/01/2007 Ex date - 05/30/2007; 5% payable 04/15/2009 to holders of record 03/31/2009 Ex date - 03/27/2009
Acquired by Starbuck Bancshares, Inc. 04/09/2013
Each share new Common no par exchanged for $2 cash

PREMIS CORP (MN)
Recapitalized as NVE Corp. 12/4/2000
Each share Common 1¢ par exchanged for (0.2) share Common 1¢ par

PREMISYS COMMUNICATIONS INC (DE)
Issue Information - 2,000,000 shares COM offered at $16 per share on 04/05/1995
Common 1¢ par split (2) for (1) by issuance of (1) additional share 12/12/95
Merged into Zhone Technologies, Inc. 12/22/99
Each share Common 1¢ par exchanged for $10 cash

PREMIUM ACCEP CORP (NJ)
Merged into Dialysis Corp. of America 08/19/1977
Each share Common 1¢ par exchanged for (0.25) share Class A Common 1¢ par
(See Dialysis Corp. of America)

PREMIUM ACCEPTANCE CORP. (IN)
Name changed to PAC Financial Corp. 2/2/78

PREMIUM BRANDS INC (CANADA)
Reorganized as Premium Brands Income Fund 07/27/2005
Each share Common no par exchanged for (1) Trust Unit no par
Premium Brands Income Fund merged into Premium Brands Holdings Corp. 07/27/2009

PREMIUM BRANDS INCOME FD (CANADA)
Merged into Premium Brands Holdings Corp. 07/27/2009
Each Unit no par exchanged for (1) share Common no par

PREMIUM CIGARS INTL LTD (AZ)
Issue Information - 1,900,000 shares COM offered at $5.25 per share on 08/21/1997
Name changed to Product Express.com eBusiness Services Inc. 04/19/2000
Product Express.com eBusiness Services Inc. name changed to Emerging Enterprise Solutions Inc. 01/20/2004
(See Emerging Enterprise Solutions Inc.)

PREMIUM ENTERPRISES INC (CO)
Name changed to eTotalSource, Inc. 07/28/2003

PREMIUM EQUITY CORP (ON)
Reincorporated under the laws of British Columbia and Common 20¢ par changed to Common no par 05/01/1985

PREMIUM FDG CORP (MD)
Acquired by Southwestern Investment Co. 05/25/1972
Each share Common 20¢ par exchanged for (0.1) share Common $2.50 par
Southwestern Investment Co. acquired by Beatrice Foods Co. 07/24/1973 which name changed to Beatrice Companies, Inc. 06/05/1984
(See Beatrice Companies, Inc.)

PREMIUM IRON ORES LTD (ON)
Name changed to Premium Equity Corp. (ON) 03/09/1984
Premium Equity Corp. (ON) reincorporated in British Columbia 05/01/1985

PREMIUM LETNEY CDA INC (ON)
Delisted from Canadian Dealer Network 01/03/1995

PREMIUM PETE CORP (WY)
Each share old Common $0.0001 par exchanged for (43) shares new Common $0.0001 par 02/15/2005
Recapitalized as Premium Energy Corp. 02/12/2013
Each share new Common $0.0001 par exchanged for (0.001) share Common $0.0001 par

PREMIUM PETROLEUMS LTD. (BC)
Charter revoked for failure to file reports and pay fees 2/12/59

PREMIUM RESTAURANT CO (MN)
Company terminated registration of common stock and is no longer public as of 8/6/99

PREMIUM STD FARMS INC (DE)
Issue Information - 9,842,460 shares COM offered at $12.50 per share on 06/13/2005
Merged into Smithfield Foods, Inc. 05/07/2007
Each share Common 1¢ par exchanged for (0.678) share Common 50¢ par and $1.25 cash
(See Smithfield Foods, Inc.)

PREMIUMWEAR INC (DE)
Merged into New England Business Service, Inc. 7/14/2000
Each share Common 1¢ par exchanged for $13.50 cash

PREMIX CORP (DE)
Merged into Imperial Industries, Inc. 07/15/1971
Each share Common 10¢ par exchanged for (0.444) share Common 10¢ par
(See Imperial Industries, Inc.)

PREMIX PRODS INC (FL)
Reincorporated under the laws of Delaware as Premix Corp. 09/10/1970
Premix Corp. (DE) merged into Imperial Industries, Inc. 07/15/1971
(See Imperial Industries, Inc.)

PRENOR FINL LTD (CANADA)
Struck off register and declared dissolved for failure to file reports 2/9/2006

PRENOR GROUP LTD (QC)
Delisted from Montreal Stock Exchange 7/20/95

PRENTICE CAP INC (DE)
Each share old Common $0.0001 par exchanged for (0.04) share new Common $0.0001 par 08/05/1994
Each share new Common $0.0001 par exchanged again for (1/3) share new Common $0.0001 par 06/24/1996
Each share new Common $0.0001 par exchanged again for (1/30) share new Common $0.0001 par 11/24/1997
SEC revoked common stock registration 08/22/2007
Stockholders' equity unlikely

PRENTICE HALL INC (DE)
Common no par changed to $2.50 par and (9) additional shares issued 00/00/1947
5% Preferred $50 par called for redemption 05/29/1958
Common $2.50 par changed to $1 par and (2) additional shares issued 12/10/1958
Common $1 par changed to 66-2/3¢ par and (0.5) additional share issued 04/18/1960
Common 66-2/3¢ par changed to 33-1/3¢ par and (1) additional share issued 10/24/1967
Merged into Gulf & Western Industries, Inc. 12/21/1984
Each share Common 33-1/3¢ par exchanged for $71 cash

PRENTICE (G.E.) MANUFACTURING CO. (CT)
Each share Capital Stock $25 par exchanged for (3) shares Capital Stock $10 par to effect a (2.5) for (1) split and a 50% stock dividend in 1946
Merged into Rowland Products, Inc. 10/1/57
Each share Capital Stock $10 par exchanged for (0.5) share Common $12.50 par
Rowland Products, Inc. name changed to Rowland, Inc. 8/1/73 which name changed to Rowland Liquidating Corp. 8/22/75
(See Rowland Liquidating Corp.)

PRENTISS PPTYS TR (MD)
Issue Information - 16,000,000 COM SH BEN INT offered at $20 per share on 10/17/1996
Merged into Brandywine Realty Trust 1/5/2006
Each Share of Bene. Int. 1¢ par exchanged for (0.69) new Share of Bene. Int. 1¢ par and $21.50 cash

PRENTISS WABERS PRODUCTS CO. (WI)
Each share Common $10 par exchanged for (2) shares Common $5 par and 25% stock dividend paid in 1947
Stock Dividend - 150% 6/15/45
Name changed to Preway, Inc. (WI) in May 1953
Preway, Inc. (WI) reincorporated in (DE) 6/1/87
(See Preway, Inc. (DE))

PREO SOFTWARE INC NEW (AB)
Ceased operations 09/14/2012
No stockholders' equity

PREO SOFTWARE INC OLD (AB)
Merged into Preo Software Inc. (New) 08/03/2010
Each share Common no par exchanged for (0.5) share Common no par
(See Preo Software Inc. (New))

PREP PRODUCTS, INC. (MT)
Charter suspended by State Board of Equalization for failure to file returns and pay taxes 09/12/1963

PREPAID CARD HLDGS INC (NV)
Name changed to PrepaYd, Inc. 05/12/2011

PREPAID DEPOT INC (NV)
Recapitalized as Reed Holdings Corp. 07/30/2002
Each share Common 2¢ par exchanged for (0.00222222) share Common 2¢ par
Reed Holdings Corp. name changed to Ostara Corp., Inc. 03/12/2004 which name changed to Rheologics Technologies, Inc. 10/18/2005 which name changed to KKS Venture Management, Inc. 07/24/2007 which recapitalized as Codima, Inc. 06/09/2008
(See Codima, Inc.)

PRESCIENT APPLIED INTELLIGENCE INC (DE)
Merged into Park City Group, Inc. 01/13/2009
Each share Common $0.001 par exchanged for $0.055 cash

PRESCIENT MNG CORP (BC)
Name changed to Aurora Cannabis Inc. 12/16/2014

PRESCIENT NEUROPHARMA INC (BC)
Reincorporated 12/21/2007
Place of incorporation changed from (Canada) to (BC) 12/21/2007
Each share old Common no par exchanged for (0.33333333) share new Common no par 03/25/2003
Name changed to PNO Resources Ltd. 02/09/2012
PNO Resources Ltd. merged into Sandspring Resources Ltd. 09/15/2015

PRESCOTECH INC (PA)
Merged into Tannetics, Inc. 07/31/1975
Each share Common 33-1/3¢ par exchanged for (0.0675) share $5 Conv. Preferred $100 par
Tannetics, Inc. name changed to TNT Liquidating Co. 11/18/1983
(See TNT Liquidating Co.)

PRESCOTT DEV CORP (BC)
Name changed to U.S. Ammunition Co. Ltd. 03/22/1988
U.S. Ammunition Co. Ltd. recapitalized as Keynote Resources Inc. 11/21/1990
(See Keynote Resources Inc.)

PRESCOTT PORCUPINE GOLD MINES LTD. (ON)
Charter revoked for failure to file reports and pay fees 2/17/64

PRESCOTT RES INC (BC)
Reincorporated under the laws of Yukon as Asia Sapphires Ltd. 06/29/1998
(See Asia Sapphires Ltd.)

PRESCOTT RES LTD (BC)
Recapitalized as Prescott Development Corp. 09/25/1986
Each share Class A Common no par exchanged for (2) shares Common no par
Prescott Development Corp. name changed to U.S. Ammunition Co. Ltd. 03/22/1988 which recapitalized as Keynote Resources Inc. 11/21/1990
(See Keynote Resources Inc.)

PRESCRIPTION CORP AMER (DE)
Reincorporated 1/5/87
State of incorporation changed from (UT) to (DE) and each share Common $0.0001 par exchanged for (0.2) share Common $0.025 par 1/5/87
Name changed to CCG Capital Corp. 4/30/92
CCG Capital Corp. recapitalized as Interaxx Technologies Inc. 10/16/97
(See Interaxx Technoloies Inc.)

PRESCRIPTION LABORATORIES, INC. (MI)
Incorporated in 1933
Charter declared inoperative and void for failure to file reports 1/6/41

PRESCRIPTION LABORATORIES, INC. (MI)
Incorporated in 1946
Dissolved in 1955

PRESCRIPTION LIFE INSURANCE CO. (IN)
Recapitalized as Kennedy National Life Insurance Co. of America 5/10/67
Each share Common $1 par exchanged for (1) share Common Capital Stock $2 par
(See Kennedy National Life Insurance Co. of America)

PRESCRIPTION PEOPLE INC (FL)
Proclaimed dissolved for failure to file reports and pay fees 10/13/89

PRESDOR PORCUPINE GOLD MINES LTD. (ON)
Succeeded by Presdore Porcupine Mines (1941) Ltd. on a (1) for (3.5) basis in 1941
(See Presdore Porcupine Mines (1941) . Ltd.)

PRESDOR PORCUPINE MINES (1941) LTD. (ON)
Charter revoked for failure to file reports and pay fees 11/10/66

PRESENT INC (NY)
Each share old Common 10¢ par exchanged for (0.2) share new Common 10¢ par 01/12/1981
New Common 10¢ par split (21) for (1) by issuance of (20) additional shares 07/19/1985
Reacquired 10/00/1987
Each share new Common 10¢ par exchanged for $10 cash

PRESERVATION SCIENCES INC (FL)
Each share old Common $0.001 par exchanged for (0.2) share new Common $0.001 par 03/08/2005
Name changed to eFUEL EFN, Corp. 02/08/2008

PRESERVER GROUP INC (NJ)
Merged into Preserver Group Acquisition Corp. 4/18/2002
Each share Common 50¢ par exchanged for $7.75 cash

PRESIDENT BRAND GOLD MNG LTD (SOUTH AFRICA)
Under plan of merger each ADR for Ordinary Reg. Rand-50¢ par exchanged for ADR's for Ordinary Reg. Rand-50¢ par of Free State Consolidated Gold Mines Ltd. and Orange Free State Investments Ltd. 3/4/86
(See each company's listing)

PRESIDENT CASINOS INC (DE)
Each share Common 1¢ par exchanged for (1/6) share Common 6¢ par 08/08/1997
Under plan of reorganization each share Common 6¢ par received $1.75 cash payable 07/25/2011 to holders of record 12/08/2008

PRESIDENT ELECTRIC LTD. (ON)
Name changed to Vector Electric Ltd. 11/28/61
(See Vector Electric Ltd.)

PRESIDENT ENTERPRISES CORP (TAIWAN)
Stock Dividends - 30% 9/25/95; 20% payable 10/31/96 to holders of record 8/2/96; 20% payable 11/5/97 to holders of record 8/8/97; 20%

payable 10/19/98 to holders of record 7/22/98
Name changed to UNI-President Enterprises Corp. 5/6/99
(See UNI-President Enterprises Corp.)

PRESIDENT MINES LTD (BC)
Recapitalized as Otish Mountain Exploration Inc. 04/25/2002
Each (12) shares Class A Common no par exchanged for (1) share Common no par
Otish Mountain Exploration Inc. name changed to ISX Resources Inc. (BC) 07/06/2005 which reincorporated in Canada as Potash One Inc. 12/06/2007
(See Potash One Inc.)

PRESIDENT RIVERBOAT CASINOS INC (DE)
Common 1¢ par split (2) for (1) by issuance of (1) additional share 4/19/93
Common 1¢ par split (3) for (2) by issuance of (0.5) additional share 11/19/93
Name changed to President Casinos, Inc. 1/10/95
(See President Casinos, Inc.)

PRESIDENT SERVICE CO. (CA)
Name changed to First Builders Bancorp 8/17/70
First Builders Bancorp name changed to American Magnetics Corp. 1/30/80 which name changed to Damon Group Inc. 4/5/90 which liquidated for Damon Corp. (New) 8/29/91

PRESIDENT STEYN GOLD MNG LTD (SOUTH AFRICA)
Under plan of merger each ADR for Ordinary Reg. Rand-50¢ par exchanged for ADR's for Ordinary Reg. Rand-50¢ par of Free State Consolidated Gold Mines Ltd. and Orange Free State Investments Ltd. 3/4/86
(See each company's listing)

PRESIDENTIAL AIR CORP (NV)
Each share old Common $0.001 par exchanged for (0.01) share new Common $0.001 par 09/09/2002
Recapitalized as Safe Travel Care, Inc. 05/02/2003
Each share new Common $0.001 par exchanged for (0.005) share Common $0.001 par
Safe Travel Care, Inc. recapitalized as Titan Energy Worldwide, Inc. 12/28/2006
(See Titan Energy Worldwide, Inc.)

PRESIDENTIAL AWYS INC (DE)
Chapter 11 bankruptcy proceedings converted to Chapter 7 on 3/5/90
No stockholders' equity

PRESIDENTIAL FIRE & MARINE INSURANCE CO.
Merged into Chicago Fire & Marine Insurance Co. 00/00/1931
(See Chicago Fire & Marine Insurance Co.)

PRESIDENTIAL FST PRODS CORP (BC)
Delisted from Vancouver Stock Exchange 3/4/91
Stockholders' equity unlikely

PRESIDENTIAL FUND I LIMITED PARTNERSHIP (IL)
Voluntarily dissolved 12/31/2008
Details not available

PRESIDENTIAL HLDGS INC (NV)
Name changed to Kewl International, Inc. 11/14/2003
Kewl International, Inc. recapitalized as Meg Athletic Corp. 11/15/2004 which recapitalized as Pure H2O Inc. 05/10/2006 which recapitalized as Newron Sport 10/03/2008

PRESIDENTIAL INSURANCE CO. (FL)
Each share Capital Stock $1 par exchanged for (0.5) share Capital Stock $1 par 10/5/57
Each share old Capital Stock $1 par exchanged for (0.1) share new Capital Stock $1 par 5/16/59
Name changed to Financial Fire & Casualty Co. 9/14/59
Financial Fire & Casualty Co. proclaimed dissolved 9/3/76

PRESIDENTIAL LIFE CORP (DE)
Reincorporated 07/27/1993
Common 1¢ par split (4) for (1) by issuance of (3) additional shares 01/10/1984
Common 1¢ par split (3) for (1) by issuance of (2) additional shares 01/10/1985
Common 1¢ par split (2) for (1) by issuance of (1) additional share 01/10/1986
Common 1¢ par split (2) for (1) by issuance of (1) additional share 01/09/1987
Common 1¢ par split (4) for (3) by issuance of (1/3) additional share 01/10/1990
Stock Dividends - 25% 01/03/1972; 25% 01/02/1973
State of incorporation changed from (NY) to (DE) 07/27/1993
Acquired by Athene Annuity & Life Assurance Co. 12/31/2012
Each share Common 1¢ par exchanged for $14 cash

PRESIDENTIAL LIFE INS CO (NY)
95% acquired by Presidential Life Corp. through voluntary exchange offer which expired 02/11/1970
Public interest eliminated

PRESIDENTIAL MORTGAGE CO. (CA)
Unit of Ltd. Partnership Int. registration terminated and Partnership no longer public as of 07/25/1996

PRESIDENTIAL RLTY CORP OLD (DE)
Each share Common 10¢ par exchanged for (2/3) share Class A Common 10¢ par and (1/3) share Class B Common 10¢ par 04/06/1962
Reorganized as Presidential Realty Corp. (New) 07/06/1983
Each share Class A Common 10¢ par exchanged for (1) share Class A Common 10¢ par
Each share Class B Common 10¢ par exchanged for (1) share Class B Common 10¢ par

PRESIDENTS FINL CORP (NV)
Each share old Common $0.001 par exchanged for (0.2) share new Common $0.001 par 6/6/2005
Name changed to Humet-PBC North America, Inc. 3/12/2007

PRESIDENTS 1ST LADY SPA INC (DE)
Liquidation completed
Each share Common $1 par received initial distribution of $1.50 cash 6/2/75
Each share Common $1 par received second distribution of $1 cash 3/15/76
Each share Common $1 par received third distribution of $1 cash 9/14/76
Note: Details on subsequent distributions, if any, are not available

PRESIDENTS TELECOM INC (NV)
Name changed to VoIP Telecom Inc. 04/19/2000
VoIP Telecom Inc. name changed to Diversified Thermal Solutions Inc. 07/01/2002
(See Diversified Thermal Solutions Inc.)

PRESIDIO OIL CO (DE)
9.5% Conv. Preferred no par changed to 1¢ par 3/17/87
9.5% Conv. Preferred 1¢ par called for redemption 6/1/90
Common 10¢ par reclassified as Class B Common 10¢ par 3/17/87
Class B Common 10¢ par conversion privilege expired 9/1/87
Stock Dividends - 25% 12/29/80; In Class A Common to holders of Class B Common - 10% 3/24/87
Plan of reorganization under Chapter 11 bankruptcy proceedings effective 12/23/96
Each share Class A Common 10¢ par exchanged for (0.00265491) share of Brown (Tom), Inc. Common 10¢ par and $0.00876127 cash
(See Brown (Tom), Inc.)
Details not available for Class B Common

PRESIDIO SAVINGS & LOAN ASSOCIATION (CA)
100% acquired by Imperial Corp. of America through exchange offer which expired 06/25/1970
Public interest eliminated

PRESIDION CORP (FL)
Administratively dissolved 09/26/2008

PRESLEY COS (CA)
Common 25¢ par changed to $0.1875 par and (1/3) additional share issued 08/22/1979
Common $0.1875 par split (3) for (2) by issuance of (0.5) additional share 07/15/1983
Merged into Pacific Lighting Corp. 12/11/1984
Each share Common $0.1875 par exchanged for (0.491) share Common no par
Pacific Lightning Corp. name changed to Pacific Enterprises 02/16/1988
(See Pacific Enterprises)

PRESLEY COS NEW (DE)
Name changed to Lyon (William) Homes 12/31/99
(See Lyon (William) Homes)

PRESLEY COS OLD (DE)
Common 1¢ par reclassified as Ser. A Common 1¢ par 5/20/94
Merged into Presley Companies (New) 11/11/99
Each share Class A Common 1¢ par exchanged for (0.2) share Common 1¢ par
Presley Companies (New) name changed to Lyon (William) Homes 12/31/99
(See Lyon (William) Homes)

PRESLEY DEVELOPMENT CO. (CA)
Common $1 par changed to 50¢ par and (1) additional share issued 12/16/1969
Common 50¢ par changed to 25¢ par and (1) additional share issued 01/14/1972
Name changed to Presley Companies 02/01/1973
Presley Companies merged into Pacific Lighting Corp. 12/11/1984 which name changed to Pacific Enterprises 02/16/1988
(See Pacific Enterprises)

PRESLEY LABS INC (CANADA)
Name changed to Voice-It Technologies Inc. 09/22/1992
Voice-It Technologies Inc. recapitalized as Voice-It Solutions Inc. 04/11/1996
(See Voice-It Solutions Inc.)

PRESMAC COPPER MINES LTD. (ON)
Charter cancelled for failure to pay taxes and file returns 6/21/82

PRESMARK, INC. (IL)
Completely liquidated 12/07/1973
Each share Class B 40¢ par exchanged for first and final distribution of (0.1893) share McGraw-Edison Co. Common $1 par
(See McGraw-Edison Co.)

PRESQUE ISLE BK (ROGERS CITY, MI)
Each share Common $100 par exchanged for (20) shares Common $10 par to effect a (10) for (1) split plus a 100% stock dividend 06/08/1970
Acquired by Farmers & Merchants State Bank of Hale (Hale, MI) 09/28/1991
Details not available

PRESQUE ISLE PAPER PRODS INC (PA)
Name changed to Prescotech, Inc. 05/30/1972
Prescotech, Inc. merged into Tannetics, Inc. 07/31/1975 which name changed to TNT Liquidating Co. 11/18/1983
(See TNT Liquidating Co.)

PRESS GANEY HLDGS INC (DE)
Acquired by Emerald TopCo, Inc. 10/21/2016
Each share Common 1¢ par exchanged for $40.50 cash

PRESS INC. (VIRGIN ISLANDS)
Ceased operations 02/28/1975
Stockholders' equity unlikely

PRESSED METALS OF AMERICA, INC. (DE)
Each share Common $100 par exchanged for (4) shares Common no par 00/00/1928
Each share Common no par exchanged for (2) shares Common $1 par 00/00/1938
Name changed to P.R.M., Inc. 12/15/1955
P.R.M., Inc. name changed to Associated Artist Productions Corp. 11/28/1956 which name changed back to P.R.M., Inc. 11/26/1958 which name changed to World-Wide Artist Inc. 05/11/1961
(See World-Wide Artist Inc.)

PRESSED METALS OF AMERICA, INC. (PA)
Common 10¢ par changed to 5¢ par 04/22/1957
Recapitalized as Klion (H.L.), Inc. (PA) 10/17/1960
Each share Common 5¢ par exchanged for (0.05) share Common 25¢ par
Klion (H.L.), Inc. (PA) reincorporated in New York 10/31/1963 which was acquired by Korvette (E.J.), Inc. 08/23/1965 which merged into Spartans Industries, Inc. (NY) 09/25/1966 which merged into Arlen Realty & Development Corp. 02/26/1971 which name changed to Arlen Corp. 10/16/1985
(See Arlen Corp.)

PRESSED STEEL CAR CO.
Reorganized as Pressed Steel Car Co., Inc. (PA) 00/00/1936
Each share 7% Preferred $100 par exchanged for (0.6) share 5% 2nd Preferred $50 par and (1) share Common $1 par
Each share Common no par exchanged for (0.25) share new Common $1 par
Pressed Steel Car Co., Inc. (PA) reincorporated in Delaware 00/00/1953 which name changed to U.S. Industries, Inc. 00/00/1954
(See U.S. Industries, Inc.)

PRESSED STEEL CAR CO., INC. (DE)
Reincorporated 00/00/1953
State of incorporation changed from (PA) to (DE) 00/00/1953
Name changed to U.S. Industries, Inc. 00/00/1954

(See U.S. Industries, Inc.)

PRESSED STEEL TANK CO. (WI)
5% Preferred $20 par called 6/30/67
Public interest eliminated

PRESSTEK INC (DE)
Common 1¢ par split (5) for (4) by issuance of (0.25) additional share 09/09/1994
Common 1¢ par split (2) for (1) by issuance of (1) additional share 05/22/1995
Common 1¢ par split (2) for (1) by issuance of (1) additional share payable 07/07/1997 to holders of record 06/12/1997
Acquired by MAI Holdings, Inc. 10/31/2012
Each share Common 1¢ par exchanged for $0.50 cash

PRESSURE PIPING COMPONENTS INC (DE)
Company liquidated 12/10/96
Details not available

PRESSURELUBE, INC.
Bankrupt in 1947

PRESTIGE BANCORP INC (PA)
Stock Dividends - 15% payable 6/19/98 to holders of record 6/2/98; 5% payable 3/19/99 to holders of record 3/2/99; 12% payable 6/15/2001 to holders of record 6/1/2001 Ex date - 5/30/2001
Merged into Northwest Bancorp, Inc. (USA) 9/13/2002
Each share Common $1 par exchanged for $13.75 cash

PRESTIGE ELECTRS INC (MN)
Name changed to Multaplex Corp. 03/26/1984
(See Multaplex Corp.)

PRESTIGE FINL CORP (NJ)
Common no par split (5) for (4) by issuance of (0.25) additional share payble 04/19/1996 to holders of record 04/10/1996
Common no par split (6) for (5) by issuance of (0.2) additional share payable 04/18/1997 to holders of record 04/09/1997
Common no par split (5) for (4) by issuance of (0.25) additional share payable 04/17/1998 to holders of record 04/08/1998
Stock Dividend - 10% 03/31/1995
Merged into Commerce Bancorp, Inc. 01/15/1999
Each share Common no par exchanged for (0.4069) share Common $1.5625 par
Commerce Bancorp, Inc. merged into Toronto-Dominion Bank (Toronto, ONT) 03/31/2008

PRESTIGE GROUP NET INC (NV)
Recapitalized 03/21/2002
Recapitalized from Prestige Jewelry, Inc. to Prestige Group.net Inc. 03/21/2002
Each share Common $0.001 par exchanged for (0.2) share Common $0.001 par
Name changed to Paramco Financial Group, Inc. (NV) 10/18/2002
Paramco Financial Group, Inc. (NV) reorganized in Delaware 04/09/2003 which recapitalized as TRAC Financial Group, Inc. 01/27/2006 which name changed to FINI Group, INC. 07/28/2006 which name changed to Avalon Capital Holdings Corp. 08/24/2007
(See Avalon Capital Holdings Corp.)

PRESTIGE INDUSTRIES, INC. (NV)
Name changed to Prestige Pictures Industries, Inc. 05/02/1984
(See Prestige Pictures Industries, Inc.)

PRESTIGE PICTURES INDUSTRIES, INC. (DE)
Reincorporated under the laws of Nevada as Diversified Capital Resources Corp. 12/12/1981
Diversified Capital Resources Corp. name changed to Prestige Industries, Inc. 01/28/1984 which name changed to Prestige Pictures Industries, Inc. (NV) 05/02/1984
(See Prestige Pictures Industries, Inc.)

PRESTIGE PICTURES INDS INC (NV)
Company believed out of business 09/00/1988
Details not available

PRESTIGE PRODUCTS, INC. (IL)
Name changed to Presmark, Inc. 11/14/73
Presmark, Inc. liquidated for McGraw-Edison Co. 12/7/73
(See McGraw-Edison Co.)

PRESTIGE TELECOM INC (AB)
Proposal under Bankruptcy and Insolvency Act effective 03/06/2012
No stockholders' equity

PRESTO DYECHEM CO., INC. (NY)
Name changed to Mastro Industries, Inc. 5/18/62
(See Mastro Industries, Inc.)

PRESTO PRODS INC (WI)
Common 10¢ par split (2) for (1) by issuance of (1) additional share 6/4/76
Merged into Coca-Cola Co. 5/31/78
Each share Common 10¢ par exchanged for (0.385) share Common no par

PRESTO TEK CORP (CA)
Charter suspended for failure to file reports and pay fees 6/15/90

PRESTOLE CORP. (MI)
Merged into Bishop & Babcock Corp. 4/30/62
5% Conv. Preferred $10 par exchanged share for share
Each share Common $1 par exchanged for (1.5) shares Common no par
Bishop & Babcock Corp. acquired by Valley Mould & Iron Corp. 3/26/65 which name changed to Vare Corp. 12/4/67 which merged into Microdot Inc. (Calif.) 1/31/69 which reincorporated under the laws of Delaware 7/2/71
(See Microdot Inc. (Del.))

PRESTON CORP (MD)
Merged into Yellow Freight System, Inc. of Delaware 08/10/1993
Each share Common $1 par exchanged for $4.125 cash

PRESTON EAST DOME MINES LTD. (ON)
Capital Stock $1 par exchanged (1) for (5) in 1936
Merged into Preston Mines Ltd. share for share 8/31/60
Preston Mines Ltd. merged into Rio Algom Ltd. 1/30/80
(See Rio Algom Ltd.)

PRESTON INDUSTRIES, INC. (TX)
Charter revoked for failure to file reports and pay fees 2/18/66

PRESTON MINES LTD (ON)
4% Preference 50¢ par called for redemption 2/1/63
Merged into Rio Algom Ltd. 1/30/80
Each share Common no par exchanged for (1) share 8.5% 2nd Preference Ser. A $5 par and (0.75) share Common no par
(See Rio Algom Ltd.)

PRESTON MOSS FD INC (MA)
Name changed to GPM Balanced Fund, Inc. 12/16/1971
GPM Balanced Fund, Inc. name changed to GPM Fund, Inc. 05/19/1978
(See GPM Fund, Inc.)

PRESTON MOTORS CORP. (DE)
Charter cancelled and declared inoperative and void for non-payment of taxes 3/18/25

PRESTON OIL CO (WY)
Each share Capital Stock 1¢ par exchanged for (0.01) share Capital Stock 10¢ par 05/15/1941
Each share old Capital Stock 10¢ par exchanged for (10) shares new Capital Stock 1¢ par 00/00/1953
Completely liquidated 09/06/1968
Each share new Capital Stock 1¢ par exchanged for first and final distribution of (0.5) share International Nuclear Corp. Common 2¢ par
International Nuclear Corp. name changed to Inexco Oil Co. 04/06/1970 which merged into Louisiana Land & Exploration Co. 07/22/1986 which merged into Burlington Resources Inc. 10/22/1997 which merged into ConocoPhillips 03/31/2006

PRESTON RESOURCE CORP (BC)
Recapitalized as Golden Treasure Explorations Ltd. 5/4/93
Each share Common no par exchanged for (0.5) share Common no par
Golden Treasure Explorations Ltd. recapitalized as Foundry Holdings Corp. 6/21/2001 which name changed to Yangtze Telecom Corp. 9/8/2003

PRESTON ST BK (DALLAS, TX)
Each share Capital Stock $20 par exchanged for (2) shares Capital Stock $10 par 01/14/1958
Capital Stock $10 par changed to $5 par and (1) additional share issued plus a 33-1/3% stock dividend paid 04/12/1974
Capital Stock $5 par changed to $2.50 par and (1) additional share issued plus a 22.22223% stock dividend paid 06/28/1978
Stock Dividends - 15% 07/11/1960; 16% 01/26/1965; 10% 03/11/1968; 16% 10/27/1969; 10.0982% 03/24/1971; 12-1/2% 04/09/1976; 13.636364% 04/17/1979; 20% 04/15/1980
Merged into Southwest Bancshares, Inc. 04/15/1982
Each share Capital Stock $2.50 par exchanged for (0.75) share Common $5 par
Southwest Bancshares, Inc. merged into MCorp 10/11/1984
(See MCorp)

PRESTON TRUCKING INC (MD)
Common $1 par split (3) for (2) by issuance of (0.5) additional share 10/15/68
Common $1 par split (4) for (3) by issuance of (1/3) additional share 1/15/71
Common $1 par split (3) for (2) by issuance of (0.5) additional share 12/15/71
Common $1 par split (3) for (2) by issuance of (0.5) additional share 9/12/83
Stock Dividend - 25% 10/16/67
Under plan of reorganization each share Common $1 par automatically became (1) share Preston Corp. Common $1 par 12/31/83
(See Preston Corp.)

PRESTRESSED SYS INC (FL)
Merged into GAI Corp. 01/26/1973
Each share Common 10¢ par exchanged for $7.25 cash

PRETIUM CAP CORP (CANADA)
Name changed to Sitebrand Inc. 09/04/2008
Sitebrand Inc. recapitalized as Marchwell Ventures Ltd. 10/26/2011 which recapitalized as Sante Vertias Holdings Inc. 04/11/2018

PRETIUM INDS INC (AB)
Name changed to PetroFalcon Corp. (AB) 06/24/2003
PetroFalcon Corp. (AB) reincorporated in British Columbia as Etrion Corp. 09/16/2009

PRETORIA FINL & INVT INC (PANAMA)
Name changed to Dataforce International, Inc. 10/23/1980
(See Dataforce International, Inc.)

PRETORIA PORTLAND CEM CO LTD (SOUTH AFRICA)
Each old ADR for Ordinary exchanged for (0.92658) new ADR for Ordinary and $0.44645 cash 12/15/2008
Name changed to PPC Ltd. 10/15/2012

PRETORIA TECHNOLOGY INC (NV)
Name changed to Ion Technologies, Inc. 03/20/1984
Ion Technologies, Inc. merged into Noise Cancellation Technologies Inc. (FL) 04/04/1985 which reincorporated in Delaware 01/00/1987 which name changed to NCT Group, Inc. 10/21/1998
(See NCT Group, Inc.)

PRETORY USA INC (NV)
Name changed to Mach Five Marketing Corp. (NV) 08/07/2006
Mach Five Marketing Corp. (NV) reorganized in Washington as Sunrise Petroleum Resources, Inc. 09/05/2006
(See Sunrise Petroleum Resources, Inc.)

PREVENTION PRODUCTIONS LTD (NV)
Each share old Common $0.001 par exchanged for (0.05) share new Common $0.001 par 01/21/1997
Recapitalized as Pro Net Link Corp. 10/07/1997
Each (30) shares Common $0.001 par exchanged for (1) share Common $0.0001 par
(See Pro Net Link Corp.)

PREVENTIVE TECHNOLOGIES CORP (FL)
Recapitalized as Synergy Software Development, Inc. 2/20/2004
Each share Common no par exchanged for (0.005) share Common no par
Synergy Software Development, Inc. name changed to Universal Media Holdings, Inc. 11/15/2004 which name changed to Lyric Jeans, Inc. 3/8/2006

PREVEST MUTUAL FUND LTD. (CANADA)
Completely liquidated 10/31/1977
Each share Common received first and final distribution of (0.5953) Bolton Tremblay Income Fund Unit
Each Special Share received first and final distribution of (0.5953) Bolton Tremblay Income Fund Unit

PREVIA RES LTD (BC)
Recapitalized as Rose Marie Resources Ltd. 10/18/2006
Each share Common no par exchanged for (0.125) share Common no par
Rose Marie Resources Ltd. recapitalized as Cheetah Ventures Ltd. 07/17/2008 which name changed to Emperor Minerals Ltd. 10/21/2010 which name changed to Emperor Oil Ltd. 08/24/2012

PREVIEW PUBLISHING CO., INC. (MA)
Name changed to Hill Publishing Co., Inc. 05/29/1967
(See Hill Publishing Co., Inc.)

PREVIEW TRAVEL INC (DE)
Issue Information - 2,500,000 shares COM offered at $11 per share on 11/19/1997
Merged into Travelocity.com Inc. 3/8/2000
Each share Common $0.001 par exchanged for (1) share Common $0.001 par
(See Travelocity.com Inc.)

PREVIEWS, INC. (NY)
Common no par changed to $1 par 7/11/57
Acquired by American Land Co. (Del.) per 100% acceptance of exchange offer which expired 6/30/60
Each share Common $1 par exchanged for (10) shares Common 10¢ par
American Land Co. (Del.) charter cancelled 3/1/84

PREVIO INC (CA)
Liquidation completed
Each share Common no par received initial distribution of $2.31 cash payable 12/27/2002 to holders of record 9/25/2002 Ex date - 1/2/2003
Each share Common no par received second distribution of $0.10 cash payable 9/25/2004 to holders of record 9/25/2002 Ex date - 9/3/2004
Each share Common no par received third and final distribution of $0.07636 cash payable 8/18/2006 to holders of record 9/25/2002 Ex date - 8/31/2006
Note: Certificates were not required to be exchanged and are without value

PREVOR MAYRSOHN INTL INC (NY)
Each share old Common 10¢ par exchanged for (0.01) share new Common 10¢ par plus a stock dividend of (1.6) shares Class B Common 1¢ par 06/08/1970
Class B Common 1¢ par reclassified as Class A Common 1¢ par 12/15/1972
New Common 10¢ par reclassified as Conv. Class B Common 10¢ par 12/15/1972
Merged into PMI Fund, Inc. 01/25/1982
Each share Class A Common 1¢ par exchanged for (1) share Common 1¢ par
Each share Conv. Class B Common 10¢ par exchanged for (1) share Common 1¢ par
(See PMI Fund, Inc.)

PREVU INC (MN)
Filed a petition under Chapter 7 Federal Bankruptcy Code 09/12/2008
No stockholders' equity

PREWAY INC (DE)
Reincorporated 6/1/87
Common $5 par changed to $2.50 par and (1) additional share issued 5/24/72
Common $2.50 par split (3) for (2) by issuance of (0.5) additional share 10/15/79
Common $2.50 par changed to 50¢ par 5/5/80
Common 50¢ par split (4) for (3) by issuance of (1/3) additional share 12/15/80
Stock Dividends - 25% 5/1/59; 25% 12/15/77; 10% 12/15/78; 10% 12/28/79
State of incorporation changed from (WI) to (DE) 6/1/87
Charter cancelled and declared inoperative and void for non-payment of taxes 6/24/91

PRF CORP (DE)
Each share Class A 10¢ par exchanged for (20) shares Common 10¢ par 06/26/1975
Name changed to XYZ Liquidating Corp. 05/14/1981
(See XYZ Liquidating Corp.)

PRF LIQUIDATING TRUST (DE)
Liquidation completed
Each share Common 10¢ par exchanged for second distribution of $0.50 cash 5/17/82
Each share Common 10¢ par received third distribution of $0.15 cash 3/22/83
Each share Common 10¢ par received fourth distribution of $0.30 cash 9/30/83
Each share Common 10¢ par received fifth distribution of $0.20 cash 4/3/84
Each share Common 10¢ par received sixth and final distribution of $0.199 cash 8/15/85
(See XYZ Liquidating Corp. for previous distribution)

PRG INC (DE)
Name changed to General Rest Homes, Inc. 03/10/1970
General Rest Homes, Inc. name changed to General Residential Corp. 01/13/1971
(See General Residential Corp.)

PRG-SCHULTZ INTL INC (GA)
9% Sr. Conv. Participating Preferred Ser. A called for redemption at $136.874413 on 10/19/2007
Each share old Common no par exchanged for (0.1) share new Common no par 08/14/2008
Name changed to PRGX Global, Inc. 01/21/2010

PRI AUTOMATION CDA INC (CANADA)
Merged into Brooks-PRI Automation Canada Inc. 5/14/2002
Each Exchangeable Share no par exchanged for (1) Exchangeable Share no par
Brooks-PRI Automation Canada Inc. exchanged for Brooks Automation, Inc. (New) 7/23/2004

PRI AUTOMATION INC (MA)
Secondary Offering - 1,705,000 shares COM offered at $64 per share on 05/12/2000
Common no par split (2) for (1) by issuance of (1) additional share payable 5/3/97 to holders of record 4/22/97
Merged into Brooks-PRI Automation, Inc. 5/14/2002
Each share Common no par exchanged for (0.52) share Common 1¢ par
Brooks-PRI Automation, Inc. name changed to Brooks Automation, Inc. (New) 2/27/2003

PRI-OR LTD (ISRAEL)
99.86% owned by Mehadrin Ltd. through purchase offer which expired 04/16/1997
Public interest eliminated

PRIAM CORP (CA)
Plan of reoganization under Chapter 11 Federal Bankruptcy proceedings confirmed 06/25/1990
No stockholders' equity

PRICAM EXPLS INC (BC)
Struck off register and declared dissolved for failure to file returns 06/17/1994

PRICE BROS & CO LTD (QC)
Each share 6-1/2% Preferred $100 par exchanged for (1) share 5-1/2% Preferred $100 par and (1.75) shares old Common no par in 1937
Each share Common $100 par exchanged for (1) share old Common no par in 1937
Each share old Common no par exchanged for (4) shares new Common no par in 1951
Name changed to Price Co. Ltd. 4/21/66
(See Price Co. Ltd.)

PRICE CAP CORP (DE)
Name changed to Highland Capital Corp. 06/01/1973
(See Highland Capital Corp.)

PRICE CEREAL PRODUCTS CO. (DE)
Charter cancelled and declared inoperative and void for non-payment of taxes 1/27/23

PRICE CO (CA)
Common no par split (2) for (1) by issuance of (1) additional share 6/12/84
Common no par changed to 10¢ par 1/14/86
Common 10¢ par split (2) for (1) by issuance of (1) additional share 2/3/86
Merged into Price/Costco, Inc. 10/21/93
Each share Common 10¢ par exchanged for (2.13) shares Common 1¢ par
Price/Costco, Inc. name changed to Costco Companies, Inc. (DE) 2/6/97 which name changed to Costco Wholesale Corp. (New) 8/30/99

PRICE COMMUNICATIONS CORP (NY)
Assets transferred 08/07/2007
Common 1¢ par split (5) for (4) by issuance of (0.25) additional share 01/12/1984
Common 1¢ par split (5) for (4) by issuance of (0.25) additional share 01/26/1987
Common 1¢ par split (5) for (4) by issuance of (0.25) additional share 08/18/1987
Common 1¢ par split (5) for (4) by issuance of (0.25) additional share 01/19/1988
Common 1¢ par split (5) for (4) by issuance of (0.25) additional share 06/26/1989
Plan of reorganization under Chapter 11 Federal Bankruptcy proceedings confirmed 07/20/1992
Each share old Common 1¢ par exchanged for (0.05) share new Common 1¢ par
New Common 1¢ par split (5) for (4) by issuance of (0.25) additional share 04/08/1995
New Common 1¢ par split (5) for (4) by issuance of (0.25) additional share payable 04/01/1998 to holders of record 03/19/1998 Ex date - 04/02/1998
New Common 1¢ par split (5) for (4) by issuance of (0.25) additional share payable 04/30/1998 to holders of record 04/19/1998 Ex date - 05/01/1998
New Common 1¢ par split (2) for (1) by issuance of (1) additional share payable 08/31/1998 to holders of record 08/17/1998 Ex date - 09/01/1998
New Common 1¢ par split (5) for (4) by issuance of (0.25) additional share payable 01/25/1999 to holders of record 01/12/1999 Ex date - 01/26/1999
New Common 1¢ par split (5) for (4) by issuance of (0.25) additional share payable 05/04/1999 to holders of record 04/21/1999
Stock Dividends - 25% 04/29/1983; 25% 01/12/1985; 25% 02/18/1986; 25% payable 12/22/1997 to holders of record 12/10/1997; 5% payable 08/25/1999 to holders of record 08/12/1999; 5% payable 05/24/2004 to holders of record 05/17/2004
Liquidation completed
Each share new Common 1¢ par exchanged for initial distribution of (0.522) share Verizon Communications Inc. Common 10¢ par and $0.96 cash 08/07/2007
Assets transferred to Price Communications Corp. Liquidating Trust and new Common 1¢ par reclassified as Units of Bene. Int. 08/07/2007
Each Unit of Bene. Int. received second distribution of $0.4473 cash payable 09/24/2010 to holders of record 08/07/2007
Each Unit of Bene. Int. received third and final distribution of $0.00825818 cash payable 08/29/2012 to holders of record 08/07/2007

PRICE/COSTCO INC (DE)
Name changed to Costco Companies, Inc. (DE) 2/6/97
Costco Companies, Inc. (DE) name changed to Costco Wholesale Corp. (New) 8/30/99

PRICE ENTERPRISES INC (MD)
Reincorporated 1/2/98
Each share Common $0.0001 par received distribution of (1) share PriceSmart Inc. Common $0.0001 par payable 8/29/97 to holders of record 8/15/97
State of incorporation changed from (DE) to (MD) 1/2/98
Each share new Common $0.0001 par received distribution of (1) share 8-3/4% Cumulative Preferred Ser. A $0.0001 par payable 8/17/98 to holders of record 7/30/98 Ex date - 8/18/98
Name changed to Price Legacy Corp. 9/18/2001

PRICE LEGACY CORP (MD)
Each share Interim Dividend Preferred exchanged for (1) share 8.75% Preferred Ser. A $0.0001 par 9/19/2001
Each share old Common $0.0001 par exchanged for (0.25) share new Common $0.0001 par 3/12/2004
Merged into PL Retail LLC 12/21/2004
Each share new Common $0.0001 par exchanged for $19.097 cash
8.75% Ser. A Preferred $0.0001 par called for redemption at $16 plus $0.272 accrued dividends on 4/11/2005
6.82% Ser. 1 Preferred $0.0001 par called for redemption at $17 plus $0.25 accrued dividends on 04/26/2010
Public interest eliminated

PRICE LTD (QC)
Ordinary $5 par reclassified as First Preference no par 10/30/81
First Preference no par called for redemption 11/15/81
4% Preferred $100 par called for redemption 12/31/81
Acquired by Abitibi-Price Inc. 6/12/81
Each share Common no par exchanged for $23 cash

PRICE MFG INC (AB)
Issue Information - 666,667 Units minimum; 1,000,000 Units maximum offered at $1.50 per Unit on 10/25/1996
Recapitalized as Remworks Inc. 7/25/2000
Each share Common no par exchanged for (0.2) share Common no par

PRICE MEYERS CORP (IN)
Adjudicated bankrupt 01/12/1977
Stockholders' equity unlikely

PRICE NATIONAL CORP. (DE)
Name changed to S & P National Corp. in 1954
S & P National Corp. completed liquidation 3/4/74

PRICE OF HIS TOYS INC (UT)
Recapitalized as Buccaneer Casino & Hotel Corp. 01/22/1994
Each share Common $0.001 par exchanged for (0.02) share Common $0.001 par
Buccaneer Casino & Hotel Corp. name changed to Worthington

Venture Fund Inc. (UT) 02/06/1995 which reincorporated in Delaware 06/03/1998 which name changed to Admax Technology Inc. 08/16/1998 which name changed to Aamaxan Transport Group, Inc. 08/28/1998

PRICE PFISTER INC (DE)
Acquired by Emhart Corp. 05/23/1988
Each share Common 1¢ par exchanged for $18.50 cash

PRICE T ROWE RLTY INCOME FD (DE & MD)
Liquidation completed
Each Unit of Ltd. Partnership Int. I received initial distribution of $240 cash payable 09/19/1997 to holders of record 09/12/1997
Each Unit of Ltd. Partnership Int. I received second and final distribution of approximately $83.08 cash payable 11/18/1997 to holders of record 11/18/1997
Each Unit of Ltd. Partnership Int. II received initial distribution of $210 cash payable 09/19/1997 to holders of record 09/12/1997
Each Unit of Ltd. Partnership Int. II received second and final distribution of approximately $182 cash payable 12/05/1997 to holders of record 12/05/1997
Each Unit of Ltd. Partnership Int. III received initial distribution of $25 cash payable 09/19/1997 to holders of record 09/12/1997
Each Unit of Ltd. Partnership Int. III received second and final distribution of approximately $47 cash payable 12/05/1997 to holders of record 12/05/1997
Note: Certificates were not required to be surrendered and are without value
Partnership I is incorporated in Maryland Partnership II and III are incorporated in Delaware

PRICE REIT INC (MD)
Common 1¢ par split (40) for (1) by issuance of (39) additional shares 05/29/1992
Merged into Kimco Realty Corp. 06/19/1998
Each share Common 1¢ par exchanged for (0.36) share 7.50% Depositary Preferred Ser. D and (1) share Common 1¢ par

PRICE (T. ROWE) RENAISSANCE FUND, LTD., A SALES-COMMISSION-FREE REAL ESTATE INVESTMENT (MD)
Liquidation completed
Each share Common $0.001 par received initial distribution of $13 cash payable 09/19/1997 to holders of record 09/12/1997
Each share Common $0.001 par received second and final distribution of approximately $2.39 cash payable 11/03/1997 to holders of record 11/03/1997
Note: Certificates were not required to be surrendered and are without value

PRICE STERN SLOAN INC (DE)
Reincorporated 07/30/1979
State of incorporation changed from (NY) to (CA) and Common 10¢ par changed to no par 07/30/1979
Common no par split (2) for (1) by issuance of (1) additional share 11/15/1983
Stock Dividend - 100% 10/31/1980
Name changed from Price/Stern/Sloan Publishers, Inc. (CA) to Price/Stern/Sloan, Inc. (DE) and Common no par changed to 10¢ par 08/28/1987
Merged into PSS Acquisition Corp. 06/23/1993
Each share Common 10¢ par exchanged for $9.625 cash

PRICE T ROWE ASSOC INC (MD)
Common $1 par changed to 20¢ par and (4) additional shares issued 04/13/1983
Common 20¢ par split (2) for (1) by issuance of (1) additional share 12/29/1989
Common 20¢ par split (2) for (1) by issuance of (1) additional share 11/30/1993
Common 20¢ par split (2) for (1) by issuance of (1) additional share payable 04/30/1996 to holders of record 04/12/1996
Common 20¢ par split (2) for (1) by issuance of (1) additional share payable 04/30/98 to holders of record 04/16/1998
Name changed to Price (T. Rowe) Group Inc. 12/29/2000

PRICED IN CORP (NV)
Common $0.0001 par split (1.23) for (1) by issuance of (0.23) additional share payable 10/03/2014 to holders of record 10/01/2014
Name changed to Legacy Education Alliance, Inc. 11/21/2014

PRICELESS PIRANHA CAP CORP (BC)
Recapitalized as Mission Ready Services Inc. 12/16/2013
Each share Common no par exchanged for (0.5) share Common no par
Mission Ready Services Inc. name changed to Mission Ready Solutions Inc. 06/05/2018

PRICELINE GRP INC (DE)
Name changed 04/02/2014
Each share old Common $0.008 par exchanged for (0.16666666) share new Common $0.008 par 06/16/2003
Name changed from priceline.com Inc. to Priceline Group Inc. 04/02/2014
Name changed to Booking Holdings Inc. 02/27/2018

PRICELLULAR CORP (DE)
Class A Common 1¢ par split (5) for (4) by issuance of (0.25) additional share payable 3/28/96 to holders of record 3/13/96
Class A Common 1¢ par split (5) for (4) by issuance of (0.25) additional share payable 10/18/96 to holders of record 10/7/96 Ex date - 10/21/96
Acquired by American Cellular Corp. 6/25/98
Each share Class A Common 1¢ par exchanged for $14 cash

PRICEMORE RES INC (BC)
Name changed to First China Investment Corp. 12/14/1984
First China Investment Corp. recapitalized as China First Capital Corp. 09/08/1987 which merged into Black Hawk Mining Inc.-Compagnie Miniere Black Hawk Inc. 07/16/1990 which merged into Glencairn Gold Corp. 10/20/2003 which recapitalized as Central Sun Mining Inc. 12/05/2007 which was acquired by B2Gold Corp. 03/31/2009

PRICESTER COM INC (NV)
Name changed to Genesis Electronics Group, Inc. 12/15/2009

PRICOR INC (TN)
Name changed to Childrens Comprehensive Services Inc. 2/15/94
(See Childrens Comprehensive Services Inc.)

PRIDE AUTOMOTIVE GROUP INC (DE)
Name changed to DME Interactive Holdings, Inc. (Old) 06/24/1999
DME Interactive Holdings Inc. (Old) name changed to VidShadow.com, Inc. 06/28/2007 which name changed to DME Interactive Holdings, Inc. (New) 05/13/2008
(See DME Interactive Holdings, Inc. (New))

PRIDE BUSINESS DEV HLDGS INC (NV)
SEC revoked common stock registration 04/08/2010
Stockholders' equity unlikely

PRIDE COS L P (DE)
Each (21) old Common Units exchanged for (1) new Common Unit 12/31/1996
$2.60 Conv. Preferred Units reclassified as new Common Units 12/31/1996
Each new Common Unit exchanged again for (0.01) new Common Unit 05/05/2003
Under plan of merger each Common Unit exchanged for $90 cash 12/15/2003

PRIDE INC (DE)
Each share old Common $0.002 par exchanged for (0.1) share new Common $0.002 par 09/28/1994
Recapitalized as Mason Hill Holdings Inc. 10/01/1999
Each share new Common $0.002 par exchanged for (0.5) share Common $0.002 par
Mason Hill Holdings Inc. name changed to Attitude Drinks Inc. 06/18/2008

PRIDE INTL INC (DE)
Each share Common 1¢ par received distribution of (0.06666666) share Seahawk Drilling, Inc. Common 1¢ par payable 08/24/2009 to holders of record 08/14/2009 Ex date - 08/25/2009
Merged into Ensco PLC 06/01/2011
Each share Common 1¢ par exchanged for (0.4778) Sponsored ADR for Class A Ordinary and $15.60 cash

PRIDE INTL INC (LA)
Merged into Pride International, Inc. (DE) 09/13/2001
Each share Common no par exchanged for (1) share Common 1¢ par
Pride International, Inc. (DE) merged into Ensco PLC 06/01/2011

PRIDE MINING CO, LTD. (ON)
Charter cancelled for failure to file reports and pay taxes in 1968

PRIDE N JOY INDS INC (CA)
Charter suspended for failure to file reports and pay taxes 08/01/1973

PRIDE PETE SVCS INC (LA)
Name changed to Pride International, Inc. (LA) 06/27/1997
Pride International, Inc. (LA) merged into Pride International, Inc. (DE) 09/13/2001 which merged into Ensco PLC 06/01/2011

PRIDE RES INC (NV)
Name changed to Pressel & Co., Inc. 8/28/87

PRIDE RES LTD (BC)
Delisted from Vancouver Stock Exchange 1/10/90

PRIMA BIOMED LTD (AUSTRALIA)
Each old Sponsored ADR for Common exchanged for (0.30000003) new Sponsored ADR for Common 12/28/2016
Basis changed from (1:30) to (1:100) 12/28/2016
Name changed to Immutep Ltd. 12/01/2017

PRIMA CO. (IL)
Proclaimed dissolved for failure to file reports and pay taxes 3/13/39

PRIMA COLOMBIA HARDWOOD INC (BC)
Recapitalized as Bravern Ventures Ltd. 01/12/2015
Each share Common no par exchanged for (0.01666666) share Common no par

PRIMA DEVS LTD (BC)
Name changed to ECL Enviroclean Ventures Ltd. 06/28/2010

PRIMA DIAMOND CORP (BC)
Recapitalized as Voltaic Minerals Corp. 04/14/2016
Each share Common no par exchanged for (0.2) share Common no par

PRIMA ENERGY CORP (DE)
Reincorporated 10/1/88
Each (15) shares Common $0.001 par exchanged for (1) share Common $0.015 par 12/31/86
State of incorporation changed from (CO) to (DE) 10/1/88
Common $0.015 par split (2) for (1) by issuance of (1) additional share 8/2/93
Common $0.015 par split (3) for (2) by issuance of (0.5) additional share payable 3/4/97 to holders of record 2/20/97
Common $0.015 par split (3) for (2) by issuance of (0.5) additional share payable 2/24/2000 to holders of record 2/10/2000
Common $0.015 par split (3) for (2) by issuance of (0.5) additional share payable 12/11/2000 to holders of record 11/27/2000 Ex date - 12/12/2000
Merged into Petro-Canada 7/28/2004
Each share Common $0.015 par exchanged for $39.50 cash

PRIMA FLOURSPAR CORP (BC)
Name changed to Prima Diamond Corp. 07/03/2014
Prima Diamond Corp. recapitalized as Voltaic Minerals Corp. 04/14/2016

PRIMACOM AG (GERMANY)
ADR agreement terminated 03/27/2007
Each Sponsored ADR for Ordinary exchanged for $5.88983 cash

PRIMADONNA RESORTS INC (NV)
Merged into MGM Grand, Inc. 3/1/99
Each share Common 1¢ par exchanged for (0.33) share Common 1¢ par
MGM Grand, Inc. name changed to MGM Mirage 8/1/2000

PRIMAGES INC (DE)
Common 1¢ par reclassified as Class A Common 1¢ par 1/3/89
Charter cancelled and declared inoperative and void for non-payment of taxes 3/1/2001

PRIMARIS RETAIL REAL ESTATE INVT TR (ON)
Each Subscription Receipt automatically became (1) Unit 06/23/2011
Merged into H&R Real Estate Investment Trust/H&R Finance Trust 04/04/2013
Each Unit exchanged for (1.166) Stapled Units
(See H&R Real Estate Investment Trust/H&R Finance Trust)

PRIMARK CORP (MI)
Merged into Thomson Corp. 9/13/2000
Each share Common no par exchanged for $38 cash

PRIMARY ACCESS CORP. (CA)
Acquired by 3Com Corp. (CA) 06/09/1995
Each share Common no par exchanged for (0.2302) share Common no par 3Com Corp. (CA) reincorporated in Delaware 06/11/1997

FINANCIAL INFORMATION, INC.   PRI-PRI

(See 3Com Corp.)

PRIMARY BK (PETERBOROUGH, NH)
Stock Dividend - 5% payable 01/20/1997 to holders of record 01/06/1997
Merged into Granite State Bankshares, Inc. 10/31/1997
Each share Common 1¢ par exchanged for (1.1483) shares Common $1 par
Granite State Bankshares, Inc. merged into Chittenden Corp. 02/28/2003
(See Chittenden Corp.)

PRIMARY BUSINESS SYS INC (NV)
Recapitalized as PBS Holding, Inc. 10/3/2005
Each share Common $0.001 par exchanged for (0.125) share Common $0.001 par

PRIMARY COBALT CORP (BC)
Name changed to Primary Energy Metals Inc. 09/04/2018

PRIMARY CORP (ON)
Each share old Common no par exchanged for (0.2) share new Common no par 04/25/2011
Name changed to Marret Resource Corp. 07/06/2012

PRIMARY DEV CORP (OK)
Name changed to Bingo & Gaming International, Inc. 08/28/1995
Bingo & Gaming International, Inc. name changed to BGI Inc. 10/19/1999

PRIMARY ENERGY RECYCLING CORP (BC)
Each share old Common no par exchanged for (0.05882352) share new Common no par 08/24/2009
Each share new Common no par exchanged again for (0.33333333) share new Common no par 05/19/2011
Acquired by PERC Holdings 1 LLC 12/18/2014
Each share new Common no par exchanged for USD$5.40 cash
Note: Unexchanged certificates will be cancelled and become without value 12/18/2020

PRIMARY GOLD MINES LTD (ON)
Charter cancelled for failure to pay taxes and file returns 04/09/1975

PRIMARY HEALTH PPTYS PLC (UNITED KINGDOM)
ADR agreement terminated 03/09/2015
No ADR's remain outstanding

PRIMARY MED COMMUNICATIONS INC (DE)
Merged into Rapoca Energy Corp. 12/23/1974
Each share Common 1¢ par exchanged for (0.01) share 10% Conv. Preferred Ser. B $100 par and (0.2) share Common no par
(See Rapoca Energy Corp.)

PRIMARY METALS INC CDA (BC)
Acquired by Sojitz Corp. 10/12/2007
Each share Common no par exchanged for $3.65 cash

PRIMARY NETWORK HLDGS INC (DE)
Merged into Mpower Communications Corp. (NV) 6/23/2000
Each share Common exchanged for (0.02022) share Common $0.001 par
Mpower Communications Corp. (NV) reincorporated in Delaware as Mpower Holding Corp. 6/28/2001
(See Mpower Holding Corp.)

PRIMARY PETE CORP (AB)
Name changed to Keek Inc. 03/10/2014
Keek Inc. name changed to Peeks Social Ltd. 03/03/2017

PRIMAVERA LABS INC (DE)
Merged out of existence in 1995
Details not available

PRIMCO MGMT INC (DE)
Old Common $0.001 par split (20) for (1) by issuance of (19) additional shares payable 11/16/2012 to holders of record 11/16/2012
Each share old Common $0.001 par exchanged for (0.001) share new Common $0.001 par 03/24/2015
SEC revoked common stock registration 10/19/2017

PRIME AIR INC (NV)
Reincorporated 11/10/1996
Reincorporated 11/26/1997
State of incorporation changed from (UT) to (DE) 11/10/1996
State of incorporation changed from (DE) to (NV) 11/26/1997
Common $0.001 par split (2) for (1) by issuance of (1) additional share payable 05/15/1998 to holders of record 05/05/1998
Charter permanently revoked 11/30/2005

PRIME BANCORP INC (DE)
Common $1 par split (2) for (1) by issuance of (1) additional share 9/16/91
Common $1 par split (2) for (1) by issuance of (1) additional share payable 6/19/98 to holders of record 5/29/98
Stock Dividends - 10% 5/1/93; 10% 11/1/94; 10% payable 2/1/96 to holders of record 1/2/96
Merged into Summit Bancorp 8/1/99
Each share Common no par exchanged for (0.675) share Common 80¢ par
Summit Bancorp merged into FleetBoston Financial Corp. 3/1/2001 which merged into Bank of America Corp. 4/1/2004

PRIME BANCSHARES INC (GA)
Acquired by SouthTrust Corp. 02/17/1993
Each share Common 1¢ par exchanged for (0.89) share Common $2.50 par and $0.50 cash
SouthTrust Corp. merged into Wachovia Corp. (Ctfs. dated after 09/01/2001) 11/01/2004 which merged into Wells Fargo & Co. (New) 12/31/2008

PRIME BANCSHARES INC (TX)
Issue Information - 2,169,310 shares COM offered at $17.50 per share on 09/25/1997
Merged into Wells Fargo & Co. (New) 1/28/2000
Each share Common 25¢ par exchanged for (0.5931) share Common 25¢ par

PRIME BK (ORANGE, CT)
Acquired by Patriot National Bancorp, Inc. 05/10/2018
Each share Common no par exchanged for $18 cash

PRIME CABLE LTD PARTNERSHIP (DE)
Each Class A Unit of Ltd. Partnership Int. received distribution of (0.0791334) share General Communication, Inc. Class A Common no par payable 2/16/98 to holders of record 1/26/98
Ceased good standing for non-payment of taxes 6/26/98

PRIME CAP CORP (DE)
Assets assigned for the benefit of creditors 07/17/2000
No stockholders' equity

PRIME CAP RES INC (FL)
Reorganized under the laws of Nevada as ViaDux Health, Inc. 9/26/2005
Each share Common $0.001 par exchanged for (0.0002) share Common $0.001 par
ViaDux Health, Inc. name changed to Solos Endoscopy, Inc. 3/14/2006

PRIME CELLULAR INC (DE)
Name changed to Sentigen Holding Corp. 6/23/2000
(See Sentigen Holding Corp.)

PRIME COLL INC (UT)
Proclaimed dissolved for failure to file annual report 10/1/92

PRIME COMPUTER INC (DE)
Common $0.025 par changed to $0.0125 par and (1) additional share issued 06/09/1978
Common $0.0125 par split (2) for (1) by issuance of (1) additional share 06/11/1979
Common $0.0125 par split (3) for (2) by issuance of (0.5) additional share 04/04/1980
Common $0.0125 par split (3) for (2) by issuance of (0.5) additional share 12/19/1980
Common $0.0125 par split (3) for (2) by issuance of (0.5) additional share 06/10/1983
Merged into DR Holdings, Inc. 01/30/1990
Each share Common $0.0125 par exchanged for $22 principal amount of 15-1/2% Sr. Subordinated Debentures due 01/31/2002

PRIME EQUITIES INC (DE)
Common 10¢ par changed to 5¢ par and (1) additional share issued 7/27/72
Name changed to Prime Motor Inns Inc. 10/26/73
Prime Motor Inns Inc. reorganized as Prime Hospitality Corp. 7/31/92
(See Prime Hospitality Corp.)

PRIME EQUITIES INTL CORP (CANADA)
Recapitalized 10/28/1991
Recapitalized from Prime Equities Inc. to Prime Equities International Corp. 10/28/1991
Each share Common no par exchanged for (0.1) share Common no par
Name changed to Medera Life Science Corp. 08/11/1998
Medera Life Science Corp. name changed to Medbroadcast Corp. (Canada) 01/04/2000 which reorganized in Alberta as Rock Energy Inc. 02/18/2004 which merged into Raging River Exploration Inc. 07/26/2016 which merged into Baytex Energy Corp. 08/27/2018

PRIME ESTATES & DEVS INC (NV)
Name changed to Cosmos Holdings Inc. 12/13/2013

PRIME FED BK FSB (DE PERE, WI)
Merged into First Northern Savings Bank, S.A. (Green Bay, WI) 04/29/1994
Each share Common $1 par exchanged for (2.8275) shares Common $1 par
First Northern Savings Bank, S.A. (Green Bay, WI) reorganized as First Northern Capital Corp. 12/20/1995 which merged into Bank Mutual Corp. (USA) 11/01/2000 which reorganized in Wisconsin 10/29/2003 which merged into Associated Banc-Corp 02/01/2018

PRIME FINL PARTNERS L P (DE)
Stock Dividend - in Class A Units 12.5% 1/31/90
Company filed a petition under Chapter 11 Federal Bankruptcy Code 11/29/91
Stockholders' equity unlikely

PRIME FLA REAL ESTATE INVT TR (FL)
Assets foreclosed on 00/00/1978
No stockholders' equity

PRIME GROUP RLTY TR (MD)
Merged into Lighthouse Group LLC 07/01/2005
Each Share of Bene. Int. 1¢ par exchanged for $7.25 cash
Merged into Five Mile Capital Partners LLC 12/27/2012
Each share 9% Preferred Ser. B 1¢ par exchanged for $5.25 cash

PRIME HLDGS & INVTS INC (NV)
Each share old Common $0.001 par exchanged for (0.15384615) share new Common $0.001 par 03/28/2003
SEC revoked common stock registration 11/17/2009

PRIME HOSPITALITY CORP (DE)
Merged into BREP IV Hotels Holding L.L.C. 10/8/2004
Each share Common 1¢ par exchanged for $12.25 cash

PRIME INCOME TR (MA)
Name changed to Morgan Stanley Dean Witter Prime Income Trust 6/22/98
Morgan Stanley Dean Witter Prime Income Trust name changed to Morgan Stanley Prime Income Trust 6/18/2001

PRIME INTL PRODS INC (UT)
Each share old Common $0.001 par exchanged for (0.00534759) share new Common $0.001 par 07/20/1995
Reincorporated under the laws of Nevada as Pick Communications Corp. 08/01/1996
(See Pick Communications Corp.)

PRIME LINE CAP CORP (AB)
Recapitalized as Kirriemuir Oil & Gas Ltd. 04/02/1991
Each share Common no par exchanged for (1/3) share Common no par
Kirriemuir Oil & Gas Ltd. name changed to WWB Oil & Gas Ltd. 12/06/1994 which recapitalized as Cigar Oil & Gas Ltd. 10/22/1997 which merged into Pivotal Energy Ltd. 01/10/2003 which merged into Fairborne Energy Ltd. (Old) 07/08/2003
(See Fairborne Energy Ltd. (Old))

PRIME LINK GROUP LTD (AB)
Recapitalized 01/29/1996
Recapitalized from Prime Link Corp. to Prime-Link Group Ltd. 01/29/1996
Each share Class A Common no par exchanged for (0.5) share Class A Common no par
Class A Common no par reclassified as Common no par 09/19/1997
Name changed to TCT Logistics Inc. 07/06/1998
(See TCT Logistics Inc.)

PRIME MGMT GROUP INC (FL)
Merged into FirstService Corp. (Old) 04/15/1996
Each share Common $0.0001 par exchanged for (0.8) share Common $0.0001 par
FirstService Corp. (Old) name changed to Colliers International Group Inc. 06/01/2015

PRIME MARKETING INC (LA)
Each share old Common no par exchanged for (0.01) share new Common no par 05/19/2003
Name changed to Omni Alliance Group, Inc. (LA) 06/30/2004
Omni Alliance Group, Inc. (LA) reorganized in Nevada as EMTA Holdings, Inc. 04/04/2006 which name changed to Green Planet Group, Inc. 07/08/2009

PRIME MED SVCS INC NEW (DE)
Merged into HealthTronics, Inc. 11/10/2004
Each share Common 1¢ par

PRIME MED SVCS INC OLD (DE)
Merged into Prime Medical Services, Inc. (New) 10/18/1993
Each share Common 5¢ par exchanged for (1) share Common 1¢ par
Prime Medical Services, Inc. merged into HealthTronics, Inc. 11/10/2004
(See HealthTronics, Inc.)

PRIME MERIDIAN BK (TALLAHASSEE, FL)
Under plan of reorganization each share Common $5 par automatically became (1) share Prime Meridian Holding Co. Common 1¢ par 09/16/2010

PRIME MINERALS LTD (AUSTRALIA)
Each old Sponsored ADR for Ordinary exchanged for (0.1) new Sponsored ADR for Ordinary 10/20/2014
Name changed to Covata Ltd. 01/26/2015
(See Covata Ltd.)

PRIME MTR INNS INC (DE)
Common 5¢ par split (3) for (2) by issuance of (0.5) additional share 10/2/79
Common 5¢ par split (3) for (2) by issuance of (0.5) additional share 7/26/82
Common 5¢ par split (3) for (2) by issuance of (0.5) additional share 6/23/83
Common 5¢ par split (4) for (3) by issuance of (1/3) additional share 3/8/85
Common 5¢ par split (4) for (3) by issuance of (1/3) additional share 3/28/86
Stock Dividends - 20% 3/13/81; 10% 11/3/87
Plan of reorganization under Chapter 11 Federal Bankruptcy Code effective 7/31/92
Each share Common 5¢ par exchanged for (0.01998317) share Prime Hospitality Corp. Common 1¢ par and (0.06377606) Common Stock Purchase Warrant expiring 7/31/98
(See Prime Hospitality Corp.)

PRIME MTR INNS LTD PARTNERSHIP (DE)
Liquidation completed
Each Unit of Limited Partnership Int. received initial distribution of $2 cash payable 08/14/1998 to holders of record 08/07/1998
Each Unit of Limited Partnership Int. received second distribution of $0.55 cash payable 12/18/1998 to holders of record 08/07/1998
Each Unit of Limited Partnership Int. received third and final distribution of $0.02 cash payable 12/31/1999 to holders of record 08/07/1998
Note: Certificates were not required to be surrendered and are without value

PRIME MULTIMEDIA INC (UT)
Recapitalized as Eagle Rock Enterprises Inc. 07/01/2008
Each share Common $0.001 par exchanged for (0.1) share Common $0.001 par
Eagle Rock Enterprises Inc. name changed to Worldwide Food Services, Inc. 08/19/2009 which name changed to Global Holdings, Inc. 10/29/2013 which name changed to Element Global, Inc. 08/06/2015

PRIME PAC FINL SVCS INC (WA)
Merged into Cascade Bancorp 08/02/2016
Each share Common no par exchanged for (0.305) share new Common no par and $0.0406 cash

Cascade Bancorp merged into First Interstate BancSystem, Inc. 05/30/2017

PRIME PETE CORP (AB)
Merged into Senex Petroleum Corp. 12/31/1989
Each share Common no par exchanged for (1) share Common no par
Senex Petroleum Corp. merged into Devran Petroleum Ltd. 03/01/1993 which name changed to Reserve Royalty Corp. 11/16/1995 which merged into PrimeWest Energy Trust 07/27/2000
(See PrimeWest Energy Trust)

PRIME PETE GROUP INC (NV)
Each share old Common $0.001 par exchanged for (0.05) share new Common $0.001 par 09/17/2007
Charter permanently revoked 07/31/2009

PRIME POTASH CORP CDA LTD (ON)
Charter cancelled for failure to pay taxes and file returns 03/05/1975

PRIME PPTYS INC (NV)
Name changed to Dynavex, Inc. 10/05/1985
(See Dynavex, Inc.)

PRIME RATE INCOME & DIVID ENTERPRISES INC (CO)
Name changed to U.S. MedSys Corp. (CO) 03/29/2004
U.S. MedSys Corp. (CO) reincorporated in Delaware as InternetArray Inc. 09/12/2008

PRIME RATE INVS INC (DE)
Reincorporated 10/22/2004
Each share old Common $0.001 par exchanged for (0.002) share new Common $0.001 par 12/31/2003
Stock Dividend - 10% payable 09/08/2004 to holders of record 09/01/2004 Ex date - 08/30/2004
State of incorporation changed from (NV) to (DE) and new Common $0.001 par changed to $0.000001 par 10/22/2004
Name changed to Summus Works, Inc. 02/28/2006
Summus Works, Inc. recapitalized as XTend Medical Corp. 09/26/2007 which name changed to MultiCorp International Inc. 08/28/2012

PRIME RATE PLUS CORP (ON)
Name changed to Canadian Banc Recovery Corp. 05/07/2009
Canadian Banc Recovery Corp. name changed to Canadian Banc Corp. 01/27/2012

PRIME RESIDENTIAL INC (MD)
Name changed to Ambassador Apartments, Inc. 5/29/96
Ambassador Apartments, Inc. merged into Apartment Investment & Management Co. 5/8/98

PRIME RESOURCE INC (UT)
Name changed to BBM Holdings, Inc. (UT) 05/11/2007
BBM Holdings, Inc. (UT) reincorporated in Delaware as Ohr Pharmaceutical, Inc. 09/24/2009

PRIME RESOURCES, INC. (UT)
Name changed to IPCOR, Ltd. 09/11/1990
IPCOR, Ltd. name changed to Luxury Seaside Resorts, Inc. (UT) 12/20/1991 which reincorporated in Nevada as RE/COMM Corp. 03/22/1992 which name changed to Metro Wireless Interactive Corp. 12/27/1993 which name changed to Red Rock International Corp. (NV) 04/01/1996 which reorganized in Kentucky as Page International Inc. 11/05/1997 which reincorporated in Nevada 12/31/1997 which name changed to China TianRen Organic Food, Inc. 06/14/2007

PRIME RES CORP (BC)
Recapitalized as Prime Resources Group Inc. 01/26/1990
Each share Common no par exchanged for (0.44444444) share Common no par
Prime Resources Group Inc. merged into HomeStake Mining Co. 12/03/1998 which merged into Barrick Gold Corp. 12/14/2001

PRIME RES CORP (UT)
Each share Common $0.001 par exchanged for (0.1) share Common 1¢ par 03/26/1984
Each share Common 1¢ par exchanged for (0.2) share Common 5¢ par 05/12/1989
Name changed to Prime Telecommunications Corp. 10/19/1990
Prime Telecommunications Corp. merged into LDDS Communications, Inc. (DE) 03/24/1992 which merged into Resurgens Communications Group, Inc. 09/15/1993 which name changed to LDDS Communications, Inc. (GA) 09/15/1993 which name changed to WorldCom, Inc. 05/26/1995 which name changed to MCI WorldCom, Inc. 09/14/1998 which name changed to WorldCom Inc. (New) 05/01/2000
(See WorldCom Inc. (New))

PRIME RES GROUP INC (BC)
Merged into HomeStake Mining Co. 12/03/1998
Each share Common no par exchanged for (0.74) share Common $1 par
HomeStake Mining Co. merged into Barrick Gold Corp. 12/14/2001

PRIME RESPONSE INC (DE)
Issue Information - 3,500,000 shares COM offered at $18 per share on 03/02/2000
Merged into Chordiant Software, Inc. 03/27/2001
Each share Common 1¢ par exchanged for (0.6) share Common $0.001 par
(See Chordiant Software, Inc.)

PRIME RESTAURANTS INC (NV)
Common $0.001 par split (4) for (1) by issuance of (3) additional shares payable 09/28/2007 to holders of record 07/19/2007 Ex date - 10/01/2007
Name changed to BIH Corp. 03/19/2008
(See BIH Corp.)

PRIME RESTAURANTS INC (ON)
Merged into Fairfax Financial Holdings Ltd. 01/10/2012
Each share Class A no par exchanged for $7.50 cash
Note: Unexchanged certificates were cancelled and became without value 01/10/2018

PRIME RESTAURANTS RTY INCOME FD (ON)
Under plan of reorganization each Unit no par automatically became (1) share Prime Restaurants Inc. Class A no par 04/07/2010
(See Prime Restaurants Inc.)

PRIME RETAIL INC (MD)
Each share 8.50% Conv. Preferred Ser. B 1¢ par received distribution of (0.0598) share Horizon Group Properties, Inc. Common 1¢ par payable 6/18/98 to holders of record 6/15/98
Each share Common 1¢ par received distribution of (0.05) share Horizon Group Properties, Inc. Common 1¢ par payable 6/18/98 to holders of record 6/15/98
Merged into Prime Outlets Acquisition Co., LLC 12/12/2003
Each share 8.5% Conv. Preferred Ser. B 1¢ par exchanged for $8.169 cash
Each share 10.5% Sr. Senior Preferred Ser. A 1¢ par exchanged for $18.40 cash
Each share Common 1¢ par exchanged for $0.17 cash

PRIME SPOT MEDIA INC (BC)
Recapitalized as New Media Systems Inc. (BC) 08/11/2000
Each share Common no par exchanged for (0.1) share Common no par
New Media Systems Inc. (BC) reorganized in Canada as Wavefront Energy & Environmental Services Inc. 10/01/2003 which name changed to Wavefront Technology Solutions Inc. 03/27/2009

PRIME STAR GROUP INC (NV)
SEC revoked common stock registration 05/29/2012

PRIME SUN PWR INC (NV)
Name changed to 3Power Energy Group Inc. 03/31/2011

PRIME TECHNOLOGY INC. (DE)
Name changed to Prime Technology, Ltd. 11/18/85

PRIME TELECOMMUNICATIONS CORP (UT)
Merged into LDDS Communications, Inc. (DE) 03/24/1992
Each share Common 5¢ par exchanged for (0.07274) share Class A Common 1¢ par
LDDS Communications, Inc. (DE) merged into Resurgens Communications Group, Inc. 09/15/1993 which name changed to LDDS Communications, Inc. (GA) 09/15/1993 which name changed to WorldCom, Inc. 05/26/1995 which name changed to MCI WorldCom, Inc. 09/14/1998 which name changed to WorldCom Inc. (New) 05/01/2000
(See WorldCom Inc. (New))

PRIME TIME GROUP INC (FL)
Common $0.0001 par split (5) for (1) by issuance of (4) additional shares payable 10/06/2005 to holders of record 10/06/2005 Ex date - 10/07/2005
Recapitalized as Hunt Gold Corp. 11/30/2007
Each share Common $0.0001 par exchanged for (0.00033333) share Common $0.0001 par
(See Hunt Gold Corp.)

PRIME TIME TRAVEL INC (DE)
Common $0.000001 par split (15) for (1) by issuance of (14) additional shares payable 09/05/2012 to holders of record 09/04/2012 Ex date - 09/06/2012
Name changed to LifeApps Digital Media Inc. and Common $0.000001 par changed to $0.001 par 09/13/2012
LifeApps Digital Media Inc. recapitalized as LifeApps Brands Inc. 01/07/2016

PRIME VIEW INTL CO LTD (TAIWAN)
Name changed to E Ink Holdings Inc. 08/19/2010

PRIMEBANK FED SVGS BK (GRAND RAPIDS, MI)
Stock Dividend - 10% 4/15/87
Acquired by First of America Bank Corp. 7/31/90
Each share Common $1 par exchanged for $30 cash

PRIMEBUY INTL INC (DE)
Name changed to Russian Resources Group Inc. 05/08/2003
Russian Resources Group Inc. name changed to Petro Resources Corp. 06/20/2005 which name changed to Magnum Hunter Resources Corp. 07/14/2009

(See Magnum Hunter Resources Corp.)

PRIMEDEX HEALTH SYS INC (NY)
Each share Common 1¢ par received distribution of (1) share CareAdvantage, Inc. Common 1¢ par payable 06/28/1995
Recapitalized as RadNet, Inc. (NY) 11/28/2006
Each share Common 1¢ par exchanged for (0.5) share Common $0.0001 par
RadNet, Inc. (NY) reincorporated in Delaware 09/03/2008

PRIMEDGE INC (NV)
Each share old Common $0.001 par exchanged for (0.01) share new Common $0.001 par 01/22/2007
Each (600) shares new Common $0.001 par exchanged again for (1) share new Common $0.001 par 08/15/2007
SEC revoked common stock registration 11/08/2011

PRIMEDIA INC (DE)
Each share 144A Exchangeable Preferred Ser. E exchanged for (1) $9.20 Exchangeable Preferred Ser. F 02/17/1998
Each share Accredited Investors Exchangeable Preferred Ser. E exchanged for (1) $9.20 Exchangeable Preferred Ser. F 02/17/1998
$11.625 Exchangeable Preferred Ser. B 1¢ par called for redemption at $105.80 on 03/20/1998
$10 Exchangeable Preferred Ser. D called for redemption at $101 on 05/11/2005
$9.20 Exchangeable Preferred Ser. F called for redemption at $100 on 05/11/2005
$8.625 Exchangeable Preferred Ser. H called for redemption at $101.438 plus $1.078125 accrued dividends on 10/31/2005
Each share old Common 1¢ par exchanged for (1/6) share new Common 1¢ par 08/02/2007
Acquired by TPG Capital, L.P. 07/13/2011
Each share new Common 1¢ par exchanged for $7.10 cash

PRIMEFAX INC (TX)
Each share old Common exchanged for (0.1) share new Common 1¢ par 01/26/1990
Name changed to Maxserv Inc. (TX) 12/06/1991
Maxserv Inc. (TX) reincorporated in Delaware 05/04/1994
(See Maxserv Inc.)

PRIMEHOLDINGS COM INC (NV)
Reincorporated 02/27/2004
State of incorporation changed from (DE) to (NV) 02/27/2004
Each share Common $0.0666 par exchanged for (0.01) share old Common $0.001 par 09/08/2004
Each (1,500) shares old Common $0.001 par exchanged for (1) share new Common $0.001 par 10/25/2006
Stock Dividends - 10% payable 03/10/2003 to holders of record 03/01/2003 Ex date - 02/26/2003; 10% payable 10/21/2005 to holders of record 10/14/2005 Ex date - 10/12/2005
Name changed to Mindpix Corp. 10/16/2007

PRIMELINK SYS INC (DE)
Recapitalized as MaxWiFi Communications, Inc. 09/04/2008
Each share Common $0.001 par exchanged for (0.004) share Common $0.001 par
MaxWiFi Communications, Inc. recapitalized as Tivus, Inc. 01/27/2010

PRIMEPLAYER INC (NV)
SEC revoked common stock registration 03/19/2013

PRIMER GROUP MINERALS LTD (BC)
Recapitalized as Lada Development Ltd. 10/09/1975
Each share Capital Stock no par exchanged for (0.2) share Capital Stock no par
(See Lada Development Ltd.)

PRIMERA ENERGY RES LTD (AB)
Merged into Touchstone Exploration Inc. (BC) 12/05/2012
Each share Common no par exchanged for (0.9) share Common no par
Note: Unexchanged certificates will be cancelled and become without value 11/30/2018
Touchstone Exploration Inc. (BC) merged into Touchstone Exploration Inc. (AB) 05/20/2014

PRIMERICA CORP (NJ)
Common $1 par split (2) for (1) by issuance of (1) additional share 03/13/1987
$13.75 Preferred no par called for redemption 05/31/1988
$3 Conv. Preferred no par called for redemption 11/08/1988
Acquired by Primerica Corp. (DE) 12/15/1988
Each share Common $1 par exchanged for (1) share Common 1¢ par and $7.05 cash
Primerica Corp. (DE) name changed to Travelers Inc. 12/31/1993 which name changed to Travelers Group Inc. 04/16/1995 which name changed to Citigroup Inc. 10/08/1998

PRIMERICA CORP NEW (DE)
Common 1¢ par split (3) for (2) by issuance of (0.5) additional share 02/26/1993
Common 1¢ par split (4) for (3) by issuance of (1/3) additional share 08/27/1993
Under plan of merger name changed to Travelers Inc. 12/31/1993
Travelers Inc. name changed to Travelers Group Inc. 04/26/1995 which name changed to Citigroup Inc. 10/08/1998

PRIMERO INDS LTD (BC)
Recapitalized as PMI Ventures Ltd. 03/27/2001
Each share Common no par exchanged for (0.2) share Common no par
PMI Ventures Ltd. name changed to PMI Gold Corp. 05/23/2006 which merged into Asanko Gold Inc. 02/10/2014

PRIMERO MNG CORP (BC)
Merged into First Majestic Silver Corp. 05/11/2018
Each share Common no par exchanged for (0.03325) share Common no par
Note: Unexchanged certificates will be cancelled and become without value 05/11/2021

PRIMESOURCE COMMUNICATIONS HLDGS INC (DE)
Name changed to Primeholdings.com Inc. (DE) 07/20/1999
Primeholdings.com Inc. (DE) reincorporated in Nevada 02/27/2004 which name changed to Mindpix Corp. 10/16/2007

PRIMESOURCE CORP (DE)
Merged into Fuji Photo Film Co., Ltd. 10/15/2001
Each share Common 1¢ par exchanged for $10 cash

PRIMESOURCE HEALTHCARE INC (MA)
Name changed to LXU Healthcare, Inc. 12/10/2004
(See LXU Healthcare, Inc.)

PRIMETECH ELECTRONICS INC (CANADA)
Acquired by Celestica Inc. 8/3/2001
Each share Common no par exchanged for (0.22) share Subordinate no par

PRIMEVENTURE CORP (UT)
Proclaimed dissolved for failure to pay taxes 3/1/90

PRIMEWEST ENERGY INC (AB)
Each Class B Exchangeable Share no par exchanged for (1.09427) Class A Exchangeable Shares no par 06/14/2002
Merged into Abu Dhabi National Energy Co. 01/16/2008
Each Class A Exchangeable Share no par exchanged for $19.552378 cash

PRIMEWEST ENERGY TR (AB)
Each old Trust Unit no par exchanged for (0.25) new Trust Unit no par 08/16/2002
Merged into Abu Dhabi National Energy Co. PJSC 01/16/2008
Each Trust Unit no par exchanged for $26.75 cash

PRIMEWEST EXPL INC (AB)
Name changed to Antler Hill Oil & Gas Ltd. 03/05/2013
Antler Hill Oil & Gas Ltd. name changed to Antler Hill Mining Ltd. 06/29/2017

PRIMEWEST OIL & GAS CORP (AB)
Name changed to PrimeWest Energy Inc. and Exchangeable Shares no par reclassified as Class A Exchangeable Shares no par 01/01/2002
(See PrimeWest Energy Inc.)

PRIMEWEST RES LTD (AB)
Name changed to PrimeWest Energy Inc. and Exchangeable Shares no par reclassified as Class A Exchangeable Shares no par 1/1/2002

PRIMEX EQUITIES CORP. (DE)
No longer in existence having become inoperative and void for non-payment of taxes 4/1/65

PRIMEX FOREST PRODS LTD (BC)
Common no par split (2) for (1) by issuance of (1) additional share 05/25/1992
Common no par split (2) for (1) by issuance of (1) additional share payable 10/07/1999 to holders of record 10/1/99 10/01/1999 Ex date - 09/29/1999
Acquired by International Forest Products Ltd. 05/15/2001
Each share Common no par exchanged for $6.65 cash

PRIMEX FST INDS LTD (BC)
Name changed to Primex Forest Products, Ltd. 01/12/1990
(See Primex Forest Products, Ltd.)

PRIMEX TECHNOLOGIES INC (VA)
Common $1 par split (2) for (1) by issuance of (1) additional share payable 03/22/1999 to holders of record 02/22/1999
Merged into General Dynamics Corp. 01/26/2001
Each share Common $1 par exchanged for $32.10 cash

PRIMIX SOLUTIONS INC (DE)
Company terminated registration of securities and is no longer public 2/27/2002
Details not available

PRIMO INC (UT)
Each share Common $1 par exchanged for (0.25) share Common 25¢ par 6/20/88
Name changed to Sterling Resources Corp. (UT) 12/17/93
Sterling Resources Corp. (UT) reorganized in Delaware as Saratoga Resources Inc. 1/21/94 which recapitalized as OptiCare Health Systems, Inc. 8/13/99 which merged into Refac Optical Group 3/6/2006
(See Refac Optical Group)

PRIMO RES INTL INC (BC)
Recapitalized as Vega Gold Ltd. 05/02/2003
Each share Common no par exchanged for (0.5) share Common no par
Vega Gold Ltd. recapitalized as Vega Resources Inc. 09/10/2010 which recapitalized as Pacific Coal Resources Ltd. 03/14/2011 which name changed to Caribbean Resources Corp. 02/10/2016
(See Caribbean Resources Corp.)

PRIMO RES LTD (BC)
Name changed 04/26/1994
Name changed from Primo Gold Ltd. to Primo Resources Inc. 04/26/1994
Recapitalized as Primo Resources International Inc. 10/15/1999
Each share Common no par exchanged for (0.25) share Common no par
Primo Resources International Inc. recapitalized as Vega Gold Ltd. 05/02/2003 which recapitalized as Vega Resources Inc. 09/10/2010 which recapitalized as Pacific Coal Resources Ltd. 03/14/2011 which name changed to Caribbean Resources Corp. 02/10/2016
(See Caribbean Resources Corp.)

PRIMONT RES LTD (BC)
Common no par split (5) for (2) by issuance of (1.5) additional shares 08/16/1984
Recapitalized as Picosec Technology Ltd. 12/18/1986
Each share Common no par exchanged for (0.25) share Common no par
(See Picosec Technology Ltd.)

PRIMORSKY SHIPPING AO (RUSSIA)
Basis changed from (1:10) to (1:50) 08/22/2006
Stock Dividend - 620% payable 08/22/2006 to holders of record 08/18/2006 Ex date - 08/23/2006
Name changed to Primorsk Shipping Corp., JSC 04/03/2007

PRIMROCK MINING & EXPLORATION LTD. (ON)
Charter cancelled for failure to pay taxes and file returns 3/16/76

PRIMROSE TECHNOLOGY CORP (BC)
Reorganized 1/19/84
Reorganized from Primrose Resources Ltd. to Primrose Technology Corp. 1/19/84
Each share Common no par exchanged for (2) shares Common no par
Struck off register and declared dissolved for failure to file returns 2/8/91

PRIMUS DEV GROUP I LTD (MN)
Name changed to Classic Medical Group, Inc. 9/20/90
(See Classic Medical Group, Inc.)

PRIMUS DEV GROUP II LTD (MN)
Name changed to Celex Group Inc. 1/14/92
Celex Group Inc. name changed to Successories Inc. 8/2/96
(See Successories Inc.)

PRIMUS KNOWLEDGE SOLUTIONS INC (WA)
Issue Information - 4,150,000 shares

COM offered at $11 per share on 06/30/1999
Merged into Art Technology Group, Inc. 11/02/2004
Each share Common $0.025 par exchanged for (1.3567) shares Common 1¢ par
(See Art Technology Group, Inc.)

PRIMUS TELECOMMUNICATIONS GROUP INC (DE)
Plan of reorganization under Chapter 11 Federal Bankruptcy proceedings effective 07/07/2009
Each share Common $0.001 par received (1) Contingent Value Right expiring 07/01/2019
Name changed to PTGi Holding, Inc. 10/29/2013
PTGi Holding, Inc. name changed to HC2 Holdings, Inc. 04/14/2014

PRIMUS YELLOWKNIFE GOLD MINES, LTD. (ON)
Charter cancelled in August 1957

PRINCE & LAFAYETTE STREETS CORP. (NY)
Dissolved in 1951

PRINCE & WHITELY TRADING CORP.
Name changed to Phoenix Securities Corp. in 1931 which was dissolved in 1944

PRINCE ALBERT GOLD MINES LTD.
Acquired by Pamon Gold Mines Ltd. in 1938

PRINCE CONS MNG CO (UT)
Reorganized under the laws of Nevada as FilmWorld International Inc. 07/24/2000
Each share Common 10¢ par exchanged for (0.33333333) share Common 10¢ par
FilmWorld International Inc. name changed to Karting International Inc. 10/29/2003
(See Karting International Inc.)

PRINCE EDWARD HOTEL (WINDSOR) LTD.
Acquired by Cardy Corp. Ltd. and each share Common exchanged for $2.50 in Debentures, (0.2) share Class A and $0.99 in cash in 1947
Cardy Corp. Ltd. name was changed to Sheraton Ltd. in 1950
(See Sheraton Ltd.)

PRINCE GARDNER CO., INC. (PA)
Name changed to Settlement Corp. 10/28/1966
(See Settlement Corp.)

PRINCE GEORGES FED SVGS & LN ASSN (UPPER MARLBORO, MA)
Common $1 par split (2) for (1) by issuance of (1) additional share payable 12/26/2000 to holders of record 12/08/2000 Ex date - 01/02/2001
Common $1 par split (3) for (2) by issuance of (0.5) additional share payable 12/22/2005 to holders of record 12/09/2005 Ex date - 12/23/2005
Merged into Southern National Bancorp of Virginia, Inc. 08/01/2014
Each share Common $1 par exchanged for (1.03180200) share Common 1¢ par and $1.47323323 cash

PRINCE MARINE DRILLING & EXPL CO (DE)
Common 50¢ par changed to no par 5/27/66
Common no par changed to 1¢ par 3/16/67
Recapitalized as Prince Medical-Dental, Inc. 6/9/69
Each share Common 1¢ par exchanged for (1/3) share Common 1¢ par
Prince Medical-Dental, Inc. name changed to Medenco, Inc. 4/30/71 which name changed to Lifemark Corp. 4/26/79 which merged into American Medical International, Inc. 1/20/84 which merged into American Medical Holdings, Inc. Inc. 4/12/90 which merged into National Medical Enterprises, Inc. 2/28/95 which name changed to Tenet Healthcare Corp. 6/23/95

PRINCE MED DENTAL INC (DE)
Each share old Common 1¢ par exchanged for (1) share new Common 1¢ par 03/20/1970
Name changed to Medenco, Inc. 04/30/1971
Medenco, Inc. name changed to Lifemark Corp. 04/26/1979 which merged into American Medical International, Inc. 01/20/1984 which merged into American Medical Holdings, Inc. 04/12/1990 which merged into National Medical Enterprises, Inc. 02/28/1995 which name changed to Tenet Healthcare Corp. 06/23/1995

PRINCE MEXICO S A INC (NV)
Common $0.00001 par split (7) for (1) by issuance of (6) additional shares payable 01/22/2013 to holders of record 01/22/2013
Name changed to Luve Sports Inc. 09/20/2013
(See Luve Sports Inc.)

PRINCE STEWART MINES LTD (BC)
Recapitalized as Arodien Resources Ltd. 8/9/74
Each share Capital Stock 50¢ par exchanged for (0.2) share Capital Stock $1 par
Arodien Resources Ltd. recapitalized as Manchester Oil Corp. 3/27/78 which name changed to Manchester Resources Corp. 3/7/84 which recapitalized as Danoil Energy Ltd. 9/1/95 which merged into Acclaim Energy Trust 4/20/2001
(See Acclaim Energy Trust)

PRINCESS ANNE BK (VIRGINIA BEACH, VA)
Plan of reorganization effective 08/01/1995
Each share Common $3 par exchanged for (0.3364) share Cenit Bancorp, Inc. Common 1¢ par
Cenit Bancorp, Inc. merged into SouthTrust Corp. 08/03/2001 which merged into Wachovia Corp. (Ctfs. dated after 09/01/2001) 11/01/2004 which merged into Wells Fargo & Co. (New) 12/31/2008

PRINCESS HOMES, INC. (OH)
Common no par split (2) for (1) by issuance of (1) additional share 3/18/66
Name changed to Zimmer Homes Corp. (OH) 8/23/68
Zimmer Homes Corp. (OH) reorganized in Delaware as Zimmer Corp. 5/10/82
(See Zimmer Corp.)

PRINCESS PETROLEUMS (1950) LTD.
Merged into Canadian Atlantic Oil Co. Ltd. 10/00/1951
Each share Capital Stock no par exchanged for (0.25) share Common $2 par
Canadian Atlantic Oil Co. Ltd. was acquired by Pacific Petroluems Ltd. 12/25/1958
(See Pacific Petroluems Ltd.)

PRINCESS PETROLEUMS LTD.
Recapitalized as Princess Petroleums (1950) Ltd. 00/00/1950
Each share Capital Stock $1 par exchanged for (0.3) share Capital Stock $1 par
Princess Petroleums (1950) Ltd. merged into Canadian Atlantic Oil Co. Ltd. 10/00/1951 which was acquired by Pacific Petroluems Ltd. 12/25/1958
(See Pacific Petroluems Ltd.)

PRINCESS RES LTD (BC)
Cease trade order effective 12/07/2001
Stockholders' equity unlikely

PRINCESS ROYAL GOLD MINES LTD.
Recapitalized as Surf Inlet Consolidated Gold Mines Ltd. on a (1) for (3) basis 00/00/1935
Surf Inlet Consolidated Gold Mines Ltd. name changed to Surf Inlet Consolidated Mines Ltd. 11/02/1954 which was recapitalized as Western Surf Inlet Mines Ltd. 06/15/1959 which was acquired by Matachewan Consolidated Mines, Ltd. 04/26/1966

PRINCESS SHOPS, INC.
Name changed to Princess Vogue Shops, Inc. 00/00/1946
(See Princess Vogue Shops, Inc.)

PRINCESS VENTURES LTD (BC)
Struck off register and declared dissolved for failure to file returns 05/01/1992

PRINCESS VOGUE SHOPS, INC. (DE)
Out of business 07/00/1959
No stockholders' equity

PRINCETON ACQUISITIONS INC (CO)
Each share old Common $0.001 par exchanged for (0.01) share new Common $0.001 par 02/06/2008
Name changed to Standard Gold, Inc. (CO) 01/12/2010
Standard Gold, Inc. (CO) reincorporated in Nevada as Standard Gold Holdings, Inc. 03/06/2013 which name changed to Standard Metals Processing, Inc. 12/06/2013

PRINCETON AMERN BANCORP (NJ)
Name changed to Horizon Bancorp 12/31/1973
(See Horizon Bancorp)

PRINCETON AMERN CORP (NV)
Each share old Common no par exchanged for (0.1) share new Common no par 12/04/1995
Each share new Preferred no par exchanged for (1) share new Common no par 11/19/1997
Each share new Common no par exchanged for (1) share Common $0.001 par 09/15/2000
Note: Holdings of (10,001) or more shares were reduced to (10,000) shares
Completely liquidated
Each share Common $0.001 par received first and final distribution of $0.33 cash payable 06/19/2007 to holders of record 06/19/2007
Note: Certificates were not required to be surrendered and are without value

PRINCETON APPLIED RESH CORP (NJ)
Common no par split (1.5) for (1) by issuance of (0.5) additional share 10/17/72
Merged into EG&G, Inc. 7/29/77
Each share Common no par exchanged for (0.587) share Common $1 par
EG&G, Inc. name changed to PerkinElmer, Inc. 10/25/99

PRINCETON ASSOC HUMAN RES INC (DE)
Common 1¢ par split (2) for (1) by issuance of (1) additional share 03/01/1972
Filed for bankruptcy 04/03/1975
No stockholders' equity

PRINCETON BANC HLDG CO (DE)
Name changed to First Community Bancshares, Inc. 07/26/1983
First Community Bancshares, Inc. merged into FCFT, Inc. 05/09/1990 which reorganized as First Community Bancshares Inc. (NV) 09/30/1997 which reincorporated in Virginia 10/09/2018

PRINCETON BK & TR CO (PRINCETON, NJ)
Stock Dividend - 100% 12/29/1969
Reorganized as Princeton American Bancorp 01/01/1972
Each share Capital Stock $10 par exchanged for (1) share $3 Conv. Preferred no par
Princeton American Bancorp name changed to Horizon Bancorp 12/31/1973
(See Horizon Bancorp)

PRINCETON BK & TR CO (PRINCETON, WV)
Under plan of reorganization each share Common $5 par automatically became (1) share Princeton Banc Holding Co. Common $5 par 01/01/1983
Princeton Banc Holding Co. name changed to First Community Bancshares, Inc. 07/26/1983 which merged into FCFT, Inc. 05/09/1990 which reorganized as First Community Bancshares Inc. (NV) 09/30/1997 which reincorporated in Virginia 10/09/2018

PRINCETON CAP INC (NJ)
Name changed to Axxexs Capital, Inc. 01/27/1997
Axxexs Capital, Inc. name changed to U.S. Shanghai Chemical Corp. 10/14/2004 which name changed to AmeriWorks Financial Services, Inc. 12/16/2010 which recapitalized as AmeriWorks, Inc. 01/29/2014

PRINCETON CHEM RESH INC (NJ)
Charter void by proclamation 7/30/93

PRINCETON COML HLDGS INC (NY)
Name changed to EuroWind Energy, Inc. 04/28/2004
EuroWind Energy, Inc. name changed to First Petroleum & Pipeline Inc. 03/31/2005 which recapitalized as Luke Entertainment, Inc. 11/15/2007 which name changed to Greene Concepts, Inc. 01/14/2011

PRINCETON CONSULTING & SVCS CORP (DE)
Recapitalized as Andes Gold Corp. 09/22/2009
Each share Common $0.001 par exchanged for (0.05) share Common $0.001 par

PRINCETON DENTAL MGMT CORP (DE)
Common $0.0001 par split (3) for (1) by issuance of (2) additional shares 01/15/1993
Each share old Common $0.0001 par exchanged for (0.2) share new Common $0.0001 par 08/15/1997
Reorganized as Nix Co. Ltd. 02/27/2001
Each share new Common $0.0001 par exchanged for (0.09) share Common $0.0001 par
Nix Co. Ltd. name changed to Eco Hybrid Energy, Inc. 11/11/2003 which name changed to Global Energy Resources, Inc. 06/08/2004
(See Global Energy Resources, Inc.)

PRINCETON DIAGNOSTIC LABS AMER INC (DE)
Merged into Editek, Inc. (CA) 02/11/1994
Each share Common 1¢ par exchanged for (0.273) share Common 15¢ par
Editek, Inc. (CA) reincorporated in Delaware 09/26/1996 which name changed to Medtox Scientific, Inc. 05/16/1997
(See Medtox Scientific, Inc.)

PRINCETON ELECTR PRODS INC (NJ)
Each share old Common no par

exchanged for (0.2) share new Common no par 07/31/1991
Reincorporated under the laws of Nevada as Princeton American Corp. 09/14/1995
(See Princeton American Corp.)

PRINCETON EXPLORATION LTD. (BC)
Name changed to Samson Mines Ltd. 4/12/66
Samson Mines Ltd. recapitalized as Anglo Pacific Explorations Ltd. 4/27/73
(See Anglo Pacific Explorations Ltd.)

PRINCETON FINE ART INC (NV)
Recapitalized as Princeton-Tarryall, Inc. 12/09/1991
Each share Common 1¢ par exchanged for (1/3) share Common 1¢ par

PRINCETON GOLD MINES, LTD. (ON)
Charter cancelled for failure to pay taxes and file returns 11/12/93

PRINCETON HLDGS INC (PA)
Name changed to Axiom Management, Inc. 07/24/2007
(See Axiom Management, Inc.)

PRINCETON MEDIA GROUP INC (ON)
SEC revoked common stock registration 01/16/2014

PRINCETON MNG CO (NV)
Reincorporated 05/06/2002
State of incorporation changed from (ID) to (NV) 05/06/2002
Recapitalized as Lifestyle Innovations, Inc. 07/16/2002
Each share Common 10¢ par exchanged for (0.14285714) share Common $0.001 par
Lifestyle Innovations, Inc. recapitalized as Vought Defense Systems Corp. 02/16/2010 which name changed to Alas Defense Systems, Inc. 06/29/2010 which name changed to ALAS International Holdings, Inc. 07/11/2011 which name changed to PV Enterprises International, Inc. 08/19/2013 which recapitalized as Drone Services USA, Inc. 04/29/2015

PRINCETON MNG CORP (BC)
Reorganized under the laws of Canada as Madison Pacific Properties Inc. 5/1/98
Each share Common no par exchanged for (0.025) share Class B Common no par and (0.073) share Imperial Metals Corp. (Old) Common no par
(See each company's listing)

PRINCETON NATL BANCORP INC (DE)
Common $5 par split (3) for (2) by issuance of (0.5) additional share 05/26/1994
Common $5 par split (3) for (2) by issuance of (0.5) additional share payable 05/15/1998 to holders of record 04/24/1998
Principal asset placed in receivership 11/02/2012
Stockholders' equity unlikely

PRINCETON PLANNING CORP AMER (DE)
Acquired by American Funding Corp. (CA) 03/19/1970
Each share Common 1¢ par exchanged for (1) share Common $1 par
American Funding Corp. (CA) merged into Zenith Funding Corp. 05/13/1971 which name changed to Zenith American Corp. 05/30/1973
(See Zenith American Corp.)

PRINCETON PWR CORP (NV)
Name changed to NVS Entertainment, Inc. 11/30/2005
NVS Entertainment, Inc. name changed to Pure Vanilla eXchange, Inc. 06/06/2006
(See Pure Vanilla eXchange, Inc.)

PRINCETON RESEARCH PARK, INC. (DE)
Dissolved 5/6/64

PRINCETON RES CORP (BC)
Common no par split (2) for (1) by issuance of (1) additional share 11/8/85
Recapitalized as Canadian Graphite Ltd. 7/28/88
Each share Common no par exchanged for (0.25) share Common no par
Canadian Graphite Ltd. name changed to BFD Industries, Inc. (BC) 7/6/89 which reincorporated in (DE) as Alpha Pro Tech, Ltd. 6/24/94

PRINCETON REVIEW INC (DE)
Issue Information - 5,400,000 shares COM offered at $11 per share on 06/18/2001
Name changed to Education Holdings 1, Inc. 08/14/2012
(See Education Holdings 1, Inc.)

PRINCETON SEC TECHNOLOGIES INC (NV)
Acquired by Thermo Fisher Scientific Inc. 07/24/2012
Each share Common $0.001 par exchanged for $0.89 cash

PRINCETON TIME SHARING SVCS INC (DE)
Name changed to Octo Ltd. 1/30/73
Octo Ltd. name changed to Informedia Corp. 8/21/87 which name changed to Strategic Information, Inc. 12/15/88 which name changed to Strategic Distribution, Inc. 11/9/90
(See Strategic Distribution, Inc.)

PRINCETON VENTURES INC (NV)
Reorganized as Aero Marine Engine Inc. 07/10/2003
Each share Common $0.001 par exchanged for (3.1126202) shares Common $0.001 par
Aero Marine Engine Inc. name changed to Axial Vector Engine Corp. 06/09/2005 which recapitalized as AVEC Corp. 03/07/2011
(See AVEC Corp.)

PRINCETON VIDEO IMAGE INC (DE)
Reincorporated 09/13/2001
State of incorporation changed from (NJ) to (DE) and Common no par changed to $0.001 par 09/13/2001
Reorganized as Gabriel Technologies Corp. 07/20/2004
Each share Common $0.001 par exchanged for (0.00333333) share Common $0.001 par 07/20/2004
Note: Holders entitled to fewer than (10) post-split shares will receive $0.05 cash per share
(See Gabriel Technologies Corp.)

PRINCETON WTR CO (NJ)
All but (46) shares Capital Stock no par held by parent company Elizabethtown Water Co. as of 07/17/1967
Public interest eliminated

PRINCEVILLE CORP (CO)
Ctfs. dated prior to 07/05/1977
Merged into Consolidated Oil & Gas, Inc. (CO) 07/05/1977
Each share Common 20¢ par exchanged for $5.25 cash

PRINCEVILLE CORP (CO)
Ctfs. dated after 4/21/88
Name changed 4/21/88
Name changed from Princeville Development Corp. to Princeville Corp. 4/21/88
Merged into Princeville Acquisition Corp. 4/13/89
Each share Common 20¢ par exchanged for $15.50 cash

PRINCIPAL AGGRESSIVE GROWTH FD INC (MD)
Reorganized as Principal Variable Contracts Fund, Inc. 01/01/1998
Details not available

PRINCIPAL BALANCED FD INC (MD)
Merged into Principal Investors Fund, Inc. 06/30/2005
Details not available

PRINCIPAL BD FD INC (MD)
Merged into Principal Investors Fund, Inc. 06/30/2005
Details not available

PRINCIPAL CAP ACCUMULATION FD INC (MD)
Reincorporated 05/26/1989
State of incorporation changed from (DE) to (MD) 05/26/1989
Reorganized as Principal Variable Contracts Fund, Inc. 01/01/1998
Details not available

PRINCIPAL CAP GROUP INC NEW (NV)
Name changed to Gazoo Energy Group, Inc. 09/11/2009
(See Gazoo Energy Group, Inc.)

PRINCIPAL CAP GROUP INC OLD (NV)
Voluntarily dissolved 09/30/2008
Stockholders' equity unlikely

PRINCIPAL CAP VALUE FD INC (MD)
Merged into Principal Investors Fund, Inc. 06/30/2005
Details not available

PRINCIPAL CASH MGMT FD INC (MD)
Merged into Principal Investors Fund, Inc. 06/30/2005
Details not available

PRINCIPAL EQUITY FD INC (MD)
Proclaimed dissolved 11/14/88

PRINCIPAL EXPLORATION & MINING LTD. (BC)
Charter cancelled for failure to file returns in 1969

PRINCIPAL FINL GROUP INC (DE)
5.563% Non-Cum. Preferred Ser. A 1¢ par called for redemption at $100 on 06/30/2015
6.518% Non-Cum. Perpetual Preferred Ser. B 1¢ par called for redemption at $25 on 06/30/2015
(Additional Information in Active)

PRINCIPAL GOVT SECS INCOME FD INC (MD)
Merged into Principal Investors Fund, Inc. 06/30/2005
Details not available

PRINCIPAL GROWTH FD INC (MD)
Merged into Principal Investors Fund, Inc. 06/30/2005
Details not available

PRINCIPAL GROWTH MTG INVESTORS FD L P (DE)
Partnership terminated 01/30/1997
Partners' equity unlikely

PRINCIPAL GUARDIAN FUTURES FUND (IL)
Voluntarily dissolved 12/31/2001
Details not available

PRINCIPAL HIGH YIELD FD INC (MD)
Merged into Principal Bond Fund, Inc. 07/31/2002
Details not available

PRINCIPAL INTL FD INC (MD)
Name changed 08/01/1988
Name changed 01/01/1998
Name changed from Principal World Fund, Inc. to Princor World Fund, Inc. 08/01/1988
Common 10¢ par reclassified as Class A 10¢ par 12/05/1994
Name changed from Princor World Fund, Inc. to Principal International Fund, Inc. 01/01/1998
Merged into Principal Investors Fund, Inc. 06/30/2005

Details not available

PRINCIPAL MONEY MKT FD INC (MD)
Reorganized as Principal Variable Contracts Fund, Inc. 01/01/1998
Details not available

PRINCIPAL NEO TECH INC (CANADA)
Common no par split (3) for (1) by issuance of (2) additional shares 05/12/1984
60¢ Class A no par split (3) for (1) by issuance of (2) additional shares 05/12/1984
Common no par split (3) for (1) by issuance of (2) additional shares 05/16/1986
60¢ Class A no par split (3) for (1) by issuance of (2) additional shares 05/16/1986
Name changed to Laird Group Inc. 07/15/1988
Laird Group Inc. merged into Printera Corp. 11/22/1996
(See Printera Corp.)

PRINCIPAL PROTN GOVT INVT FD INC (MD)
Reincorporated under the laws of Massachusetts as First Trust Money Market Fund 01/01/1983
First Trust Money Market Fund name changed to Venture Trust Money Market Fund (MA) 02/01/1988 which reorganized in Maryland as Retirement Planning Funds of America, Inc. 12/31/1989 which name changed to Davis Series, Inc. 10/01/1995

PRINCIPAL SOLAR INC (NY)
Reincorporated under the laws of Delaware 10/24/2012

PRINCIPAL TAX-EXEMPT BD FD INC (MD)
Merged into Principal Investors Fund, Inc. 06/30/2005
Details not available

PRINCIPAL TAX-EXEMPT CASH MGMT FD INC (MD)
Completely liquidated 04/07/1999
Details not available

PRINCIPAL VENTURE FD LTD (CANADA)
Dissolved 04/11/1997
Details not available

PRINCIPLE SEC INTL INC (NV)
Common $0.00001 par split (5) for (2) by issuance of (1.5) additional shares payable 10/05/2009 to holders of record 10/05/2009
Name changed to Leeward Group Holdings Inc. 09/10/2010

PRINCIPLED EQUITY MKT FD (MA)
Liquidation completed
Each Share of Bene. Int. no par representing 95% of total shares received distribution of $23.37 cash payable 06/25/2015 to holders of record 06/15/2015
Each Share of Bene. Int. no par representing remaining 5% of total shares received distribution of $23.50 cash payable 08/06/2015 to holders of record 06/15/2015

PRINCOR AGGRESSIVE GROWTH FD INC (MD)
Name changed to Principal Aggressive Growth Fund, Inc. 05/01/1994
(See Principal Aggressive Growth Fund, Inc.)

PRINCOR BALANCED FD INC (MD)
Name changed 12/09/1994
Name changed from Princor Managed Fund, Inc. to Princor Balanced Fund, Inc. 12/09/1994
Name changed to Principal Balanced Fund, Inc. and Common 1¢ par reclassified as Class A 1¢ par 01/01/1998

(See Principal Balanced Fund, Inc.)

PRINCOR BD FD INC (MD)
Common 1¢ par reclassified as Class A 1¢ par 12/05/1994
Name changed to Principal Bond Fund, Inc. 01/01/1998
(See Principal Bond Fund, Inc.)

PRINCOR CAP ACCUMULATION FD INC (MD)
Reincorporated 11/01/1989
State of incorporation changed from (DE) to (MD) 11/01/1989
Common 1¢ par reclassified as Class A 1¢ par 12/05/1994
Name changed to Principal Capital Value Fund, Inc. 01/01/1998
(See Principal Capital Value Fund, Inc.)

PRINCOR CASH MGMT FD INC (MD)
Common 1¢ par reclassified as Class A 1¢ par 12/05/1994
Name changed to Principal Cash Management Fund, Inc. 01/01/1998
(See Principal Cash Management Fund, Inc.)

PRINCOR FD INC (DE)
Name changed to Princor Investment Fund, Inc. 11/01/1987
Princor Investment Fund, Inc. name changed to Principal Capital Accumulation Fund, Inc. (DE) 11/01/1988 which reincorporated in Maryland 05/26/1989
(See Principal Capital Accumulation Fund, Inc.)

PRINCOR FED GOVT SECS FD (MD)
Name changed to Princor Government Securities Income Fund, Inc. 11/01/1987
Princor Government Securities Income Fund, Inc. name changed to Principal Government Securities Income Fund, Inc. 01/01/1998
(See Principal Government Securities Income Fund, Inc.)

PRINCOR GOVT SECS INCOME FD INC (MD)
Common 1¢ par reclassified as Class A 1¢ par 12/05/1994
Name changed to Principal Government Securities Income Fund, Inc. 01/01/1998
(See Principal Government Securities Income Fund, Inc.)

PRINCOR GROWTH FD INC (MD)
Reincorporated 11/01/1989
Common 1¢ par reclassified as Class A 1¢ par 12/05/1994
State of incorporation changed from (DE) to (MD) 11/01/1989
Name changed to Principal Growth Fund, Inc. 01/01/1998
(See Principal Growth Fund, Inc.)

PRINCOR HIGH YIELD FD INC (MD)
Common 1¢ par reclassified as Class A 1¢ par 12/05/1994
Name changed to Principal High Yield Fund, Inc. 01/01/1998
(See Principal High Yield Fund, Inc.)

PRINCOR INVT FD INC (DE)
Name changed to Principal Capital Accumulation Fund, Inc. (DE) 11/01/1988
Principal Capital Accumulation Fund, Inc. (DE) reincorporated in Maryland 11/01/1989
(See Principal Capital Accumulation Fund, Inc.)

PRINCOR MONEY MKT INVT FD INC (MD)
Name changed to Principal Money Market Fund, Inc. 11/01/1988
(See Principal Money Market Fund, Inc.)

PRINCOR TAX EXEMPT BD FD INC (MD)
Common 1¢ par reclassified as Class A 1¢ par 12/05/1994
Name changed to Principal Tax-Exempt Bond Fund, Inc. 01/01/1998
(See Principal Tax-Exempt Bond Fund, Inc.)

PRINCOR TAX EXEMPT CASH MGMT FD INC (MD)
Common 1¢ par reclassified as Class A 1¢ par 12/05/1994
Name changed to Principal Tax-Exempt Cash Management Fund, Inc. 01/01/1998
(See Principal Tax-Exempt Cash Management Fund, Inc.)

PRINEVILLE BK (PRINEVILLE, OR)
Under plan of reorganization each share Common $4 par automatically became (1) share Prineville Bancorporation Common $4 par 07/17/1997

PRINGLE FURNITURE CO.
Liquidation completed in 1946

PRINT DATA CORP (DE)
Reorganized 10/11/2002
Reorganized from (NV) to under the laws of Delaware 10/11/2002
Each share old Conv. Preferred Ser. A $0.001 par exchanged for (0.002) share new Conv. Preferred Ser. A $0.001 par
Each share Common $0.001 par exchanged for (0.05) share Common $0.001 par
Each share new Conv. Preferred Ser. A $0.001 par exchanged for (5) shares new Common $0.001 par 10/11/2002
Name changed to ACL Semiconductors Inc. 12/16/2003
ACL Semiconductors Inc. name changed to USmart Mobile Device Inc. 04/17/2013 which name changed to Eagle Mountain Corp. 05/06/2015

PRINT-LOCK CORP (NV)
Charter revoked 04/30/2009

PRINT THREE EXPRESS INTL INC (ON)
Recapitalized as Le Print Express International Inc. 12/15/93
Each share Common no par exchanged for (1/3) share Common no par
(See Le Print Express International Inc.)

PRINTCAFE SOFTWARE INC (DE)
Issue Information - 3,750,000 shares COM offered at $10 per share on 06/17/2002
Merged into Electronics For Imaging, Inc. 10/21/2003
Each share Common $0.0001 par exchanged for $2.60 cash

PRINTED CIRCUITS INC (MN)
Acquired by Control Data Corp. (DE) 05/06/1969
Each share Common 10¢ par exchanged for (0.03215) share Common $5 par
Control Data Corp. (DE) name changed to Ceridian Corp. (Old) 06/03/1992
(See Ceridian Corp. (Old))

PRINTERA CORP (ON)
Company announced it been served with Notice of Intention to Enforce Security and Notice of Intention to Dispose of Collateral 07/24/2006
No stockholders' equity

PRINTING COMPONENTS INC (NV)
Common $0.00001 par split (3) for (1) by issuance of (2) additional shares payable 02/27/2008 to holders of record 02/25/2008 Ex date - 02/28/2008
Name changed to Diamond Technologies Inc. 05/27/2010
Diamond Technologies Inc. name changed to Kallo Inc. 03/10/2011

PRINTING CORP. OF AMERICA (NY)
Acquired by American Can Co. 1/26/68
Each share Common $1 par exchanged for (0.3125) share Common $12.50 par
American Can Co. name changed to Primerica Corp. (NJ) 4/28/87 which was acquired by Primerica Corp. (DE) 12/15/88 which name changed to Travelers Inc. 12/31/93 which name changed to Travelers Group Inc. 4/16/95 which name changed to Citigroup Inc. 10/8/98

PRINTING DIMENSIONS INC (DE)
Charter cancelled and declared inoperative and void for non-payment of taxes 03/01/1992

PRINTING INVESTMENTS CO. (OH)
Merged into Multi-Colortype Co. 7/1/63
Each share Capital Stock no par exchanged for (11) shares Common no par
Multi-Colortype Co. merged into Georgia-Pacific Corp. 1/8/69
(See Georgia-Pacific Corp.)

PRINTING MACHINERY CO. OLD (OH)
Operating assets sold and name changed to Printing Investments Co. 7/1/58
Printing Investments Co. merged into Multi-Colortype Co. 7/1/63 which merged into Georgia-Pacific Corp. 1/8/69
(See Georgia-Pacific Corp.)

PRINTLUX COM INC (AB)
Reincorporated under the laws of Ontario as Allana Resources Inc. 12/10/2007
Allana Resources Inc. name changed to Allana Potash Corp. 01/22/2010
(See Allana Potash Corp.)

PRINTOGS LTD (DE)
Charter cancelled and declared inoperative and void for non-payment of taxes 3/1/80

PRINTONTHENET COM INC (PA)
Name changed to NexPub, Inc. 12/19/2000
(See NexPub, Inc.)

PRINTRAK INTL INC (DE)
Merged into Motorola, Inc. 11/13/2000
Each share Common $0.0001 par exchanged for $12.1406 cash

PRINTRONIX INC (DE)
Reincorporated 12/00/1986
State of incorporation changed from (CA) to (DE) 12/00/1986
Common no par changed to 1¢ par and (0.5) additional share issued 12/21/1994
Stock Dividend - 50% payable 06/10/1996 to holders of record 05/20/1996
Merged into Pioneer Holding Corp. 01/08/2008
Each share Common 1¢ par exchanged for $16 cash

PRINTWARE INC (MN)
Completely liquidated
Each share Common no par received initial distribution of $2 cash payable 06/03/2002 to holders of record 04/16/2002 Ex date - 06/04/2002
Each share Common no par received second distribution of $1 cash payable 10/22/2002 to holders of record 04/16/2002 Ex date - 10/24/2002
Each share Common no par received third distribution of $2 cash payable 04/29/2003 to holders of record 04/16/2002 Ex date - 05/02/2003
Each share Common no par received fourth distribution of $0.80 cash payable 8/29/2003 to holders of record 04/16/2002 Ex date - 09/17/2003
Each share Common no par received fifth and final distribution of $0.062765 cash payable 09/01/2004 to holders of record 04/16/2002
Note: Certificates were not required to be surrendered and are without value

PRINTZ BIEDERMAN CO (OH)
Common no par changed to $2 par 02/05/1955
Charter cancelled for failure to pay taxes 12/24/1981

PRIOR COATED METALS INC (NY)
Merged out of existence 11/12/1981
Details not available

PRIOR RES LTD (BC)
Reincorporated 04/04/1997
Place of incorporation changed from (AB) to (BC) 04/04/1997
Recapitalized as Rondal Gold Corp. 07/14/1997
Each (17) shares Common no par exchanged for (1) share Common no par
Rondal Gold Corp. recapitalized as Cantech Ventures Inc. 02/28/2000 which recapitalized as New Cantech Ventures Inc. 08/22/2003 which name changed to Nanika Resources Inc. 06/20/2008 which recapitalized as Goldbar Resources Inc. 07/06/2012

PRIOR W F INC (MD)
Each share Common $100 par exchanged for (10) shares Common $10 par 00/00/1942
Name changed to W.F.P. Co., Inc. 01/31/1967
(See W.F.P. Co., Inc.)

PRIORITY AIR ENTERPRISES INC (ID)
Charter forfeited for failure to file reports 11/30/1977

PRIORITY HEALTHCARE CORP (IN)
Issue Information - 2,000,000 shares CL B offered at $14.50 per share on 10/24/1997
Class A Common 1¢ par split (3) for (2) by issuance of (0.5) additional share payable 5/4/99 to holders of record 4/20/99
Class B Common 1¢ par split (3) for (2) by issuance of (0.5) additional share payable 5/4/99 to holders of record 4/20/99
Class A Common 1¢ par split (2) for (1) by issuance of (1) additional share payable 11/22/2000 to holders of record 11/8/2000 Ex date - 11/24/2000
Merged into Express Scripts, Inc. 10/14/2005
Each share Class A Common 1¢ par exchanged for $28 cash
Each share Class B Common 1¢ par exchanged for $28 cash

PRIORITY ONE INC (DE)
Name changed to Executive Systems, Inc. 11/27/1989
(See Executive Systems, Inc.)

PRIORITY VENTURES LTD (BC)
Delisted from Toronto Venture Stock Exchange 10/07/2004

PRISM CAP CORP (CO)
Reorganized under the laws of Nevada as Angell Foods, Inc. 8/28/90
Each share Common no par exchanged for (0.01) share Common $0.001 par
(See Angell Foods, Inc.)

PRISM ENTMT CORP (DE)
Merged into Video City, Inc. 01/08/1997
Each (3.19) shares Common 1¢ par exchanged for (1) share Common 1¢ par
(See Video City, Inc.)

FINANCIAL INFORMATION, INC. PRI-PRO

PRISM EQUITIES INC (ON)
Name changed to Prism Medical Ltd. 06/09/2004
(See Prism Medical Ltd.)

PRISM FINL CORP (DE)
Issue Information - 2,500,000 shares COM offered at $14 per share on 05/25/1999
Merged into Royal Bank of Canada (Montreal, Que.) 04/25/2000
Each share Common 1¢ par exchanged for $7.50 cash

PRISM GROUP INC (FL)
Each share old Common 1¢ par exchanged for (0.125) share new Common 1¢ par 04/15/1996
Assets sold for the benefit of creditors 08/29/1996
Stockholders' equity unlikely

PRISM MED LTD (ON)
Acquired by Handicare Group AB 09/06/2016
Each share Common no par exchanged for $14 cash
Note: Unexchanged certificates were cancelled and became without value 09/06/2018

PRISM PETE INC (AB)
Acquired by Real Resources Inc. 09/11/2000
Each share Common no par exchanged for either (0.39609) share Common no par and $1.117 cash or (0.5) share Common no par
Note: Option to receive stock expired 10/05/2000
Real Resources Inc. merged into TriStar Oil & Gas Ltd. (New) 08/16/2007 which merged into PetroBakken Energy Ltd. (Old) 10/05/2009 which reorganized as PetroBakken Energy Ltd. (New) 01/07/2013 which name changed to Lightstream Resources Ltd. 05/28/2013

PRISM PETE LTD NEW (AB)
Recapitalized as Prism Petroleum Inc. 06/08/2000
Each share Common no par exchanged for (0.2) share Common no par
Prism Petroleum Inc. acquired by Real Resources Inc. 09/11/2000 which merged into TriStar Oil & Gas Ltd. (New) 08/16/2007 which merged into PetroBakken Energy Ltd. (Old) 10/05/2009 which reorganized as PetroBakken Energy Ltd. (New) 01/07/2013 which name changed to Lightstream Resources Ltd. 05/28/2013

PRISM PETE LTD OLD (AB)
Recapitalized as Prism Petroleum Ltd. (New) 09/01/1996
Each share Common no par exchanged for (1.47) shares Common no par
Prism Petroleum Ltd. (New) recapitalized as Prism Petroleum Inc. 06/08/2000 which was acquired by Real Resources Inc. 09/11/2000 which merged into TriStar Oil & Gas Ltd. (New) 08/16/2007 which merged into PetroBakken Energy Ltd. (Old) 10/05/2009 which reorganized as PetroBakken Energy Ltd. (New) 01/07/2013 which name changed to Lightstream Resources Ltd. 05/28/2013

PRISM RES LTD (BC)
Recapitalized as International Prism Exploration Ltd. 3/8/85
Each share Capital Stock no par exchanged for (0.5) share Common no par
International Prism Exploration Ltd. recapitalized as Prism Resources Inc. 3/15/95

PRISM SOLUTIONS INC (DE)
Merged into ARDENT Software, Inc. 4/26/99
Each share Common no par exchanged for (0.13124) share Common 1¢ par
ARDENT Software, Inc. merged into Informix Corp. 3/1/2000 which name changed to Ascential Software Corp. 7/3/2001

PRISON RLTY TR INC (MD)
Name changed 05/11/1999
Name changed from Prison Realty Corp. to Prison Realty Trust Inc. 05/11/1999
Each share Common 1¢ par received distribution of (0.05) share Conv. Preferred Ser. B 1¢ par payable 09/22/2000 to holders of record 09/14/2000 Ex date - 09/25/2000
Name changed to Corrections Corp. of America 10/01/2000
Corrections Corp. of America name changed to CoreCivic, Inc. 11/09/2016

PRISTINE INTL SEAFOOD INC (DE)
Name changed 11/08/2001
Reincorporated 08/14/2007
Name changed from Pristine Oyster.com, Inc. to Pristine International Seafood, Inc. 11/08/2001
State of incorporation changed from (FL) to (DE) 08/14/2007
Recapitalized as Strike Axe, Inc. 04/16/2008
Each share Common $0.0001 par exchanged for (0.00333333) share Common $0.0001 par
(See Strike Axe, Inc.)

PRISTINE PWR INC (CANADA)
Acquired by Fort Chicago Energy Partners L.P. 11/25/2010
Each share Common no par exchanged for (0.2703) Class A Unit of Ltd. Partnership Int. no par
Fort Chicago Energy Partners L.P. reorganized as Veresen Inc. 01/06/2011 which merged into Pembina Pipeline Corp. 10/02/2017

PRISTINE SOLUTIONS INC (NV)
Each share old Common $0.0001 par exchanged for (6) shares new Common $0.0001 par 04/02/2012
Name changed to Eaton Scientific Solutions, Inc. 01/03/2013
Eaton Scientific Solutions, Inc. recapitalized as Eco Science Solutions, Inc. 02/25/2014

PRISZM CDN INCOME FD (ON)
Name changed to Priszm Income Fund 03/08/2007
(See Priszm Income Fund)

PRISZM INCOME FD (ON)
Discharged from receivership 09/14/2011

PRIVA INC (AB)
Name changed to AXQP Inc. (AB) 03/10/2008
AXQP Inc. (AB) reincorporated in British Columbia as Canamex Silver Corp. 10/07/2009 which name changed to Canamex Resources Corp. 10/18/2010 which name changed to Canamex Gold Corp. 11/08/2017

PRIVATE & COMPUTER SCHS INC (NJ)
Common 10¢ par changed to 3-1/3¢ par and (2) additional shares issued 01/20/1969
Each share Common 3-1/3¢ par exchanged for (0.2) share Common 16-2/3¢ par 05/31/1977
Reincorporated under the laws of New York as RSK Enterprises, Inc. 11/05/1980
(See RSK Enterprises, Inc.)

PRIVATE BK CALIF (LOS ANGELES, CA)
Merged into First PacTrust Bancorp, Inc. 07/01/2013
Each share Common no par exchanged for (0.5416) share Common 1¢ par and $6.47 cash
First PacTrust Bancorp, Inc. name changed to Banc of California, Inc. 07/16/2013

PRIVATE BK PENINSULA (PALO ALTO, CA)
Under plan of reorganization each share Common no par automatically became (1) share Peninsula Bank Holding Co. Common no par 07/08/2008
Peninsula Bank Holding Co. name changed to Avidbank Holdings, Inc. 08/02/2011

PRIVATE BRAND DRUG LTD. (ON)
Charter cancelled for failure to pay taxes and file returns 1/5/67

PRIVATE BRANDS INC (DE)
Charter cancelled and declared inoperative and void for non-payment of taxes 03/01/1995

PRIVATE BUSINESS INC (TN)
Issue Information - 4,350,000 shares COM offered at $8 per share on 05/26/1999
Each share old Common no par exchanged for (0.33333333) share new Common no par 08/09/2001
Name changed to Goldleaf Financial Solutions, Inc. 05/05/2006
(See Goldleaf Financial Solutions, Inc.)

PRIVATE MEDIA GROUP INC (NV)
Old Common $0.001 par split (3) for (1) by issuance of (2) additional shares payable 06/09/2000 to holders of record 05/30/2000
Each share old Common $0.001 par exchanged for (0.33333333) share new Common $0.001 par 03/12/2010
SEC revoked common stock registration 07/25/2016

PRIVATE PAY PHONES INC (NJ)
Charter revoked for failure to file reports and pay fees 5/6/95

PRIVATE SCREENINGS INC (NJ)
Charter void by proclamation 7/30/93

PRIVATE SECRETARY INC (NV)
Common $0.001 par split (150) for (1) by issuance of (149) additional shares payable 08/23/2011 to holders of record 08/08/2011 Ex date - 08/24/2011
Name changed to Terra Tech Corp. 02/13/2012

PRIVATE TRADING SYS INC (NV)
Each share old Common $0.001 par exchanged for (0.1) share new Common $0.001 par 01/17/2006
Charter permanently revoked 07/31/2008

PRIVATEBANCORP CAP TR I (DE)
Guaranteed Trust Preferred Securities called for redemption at $10 on 12/31/2005

PRIVATEBANCORP INC (DE)
Common no par split (3) for (2) by issuance of (0.5) additional share payable 01/17/2003 to holders of record 01/13/2003 Ex date - 01/21/2003
Common no par split (2) for (1) by issuance of (1) additional share payable 05/31/2004 to holders of record 05/17/2004 Ex date - 06/01/2004
Merged into Canadian Imperial Bank of Commerce (Toronto, ON) 06/23/2017
Each share Common no par exchanged for (0.4176) share Common no par and $27.20 cash

PRIVATEER MINE LTD. (BC)
Recapitalized as New Privateer Mine Ltd. on a (1) for (5) basis 02/20/1959
New Privateer Mine Ltd. recapitalized as Phrygian Mining Corp. 06/06/1995 which recapitalized as Crowflight Minerals Inc. (BC) 10/12/1998 which reincorporated in Ontario 07/31/2003 which reincorporated in British Columbia as CaNickel Mining Ltd. 06/23/2011

PRIVATEER MINING CO. (UT)
Merged into Ultrasciences, Inc. (PA) 2/24/69
Each share Capital Stock 1¢ par exchanged for (1/3) share Capital Stock 1¢ par
Ultrasciences, Inc. (PA) reincorporated in Florida as Florida Medical Plan, Inc. 11/15/71
(See Florida Medical Plan, Inc.)

PRIVATEL INC (ON)
Charter cancelled 6/10/91

PRIVILEGED WORLD TRAVEL CLUB INC (DE)
Name changed to Formosa Liberty Corp. (DE) 10/08/2014
Formosa Liberty Corp. (DE) reorganized in Wyoming as NanoSave Technologies Inc. 03/28/2016

PRIZE ENERGY CORP (DE)
Merged into Magnum Hunter Resources, Inc. 3/15/2002
Each share Common 1¢ par exchanged for (2.5) shares Common $0.002 par and $5.20 cash
Magnum Hunter Resources, Inc. merged into Cimarex Energy Co. 6/7/2005

PRIZE ENERGY INC (AB)
Recapitalized as Canadian Superior Energy Inc. 08/28/2000
Each share Common no par exchanged for (0.5) share Common no par
Canadian Superior Energy Inc. recapitalized as Sonde Resources Corp. 06/08/2010
(See Sonde Resources Corp.)

PRO-ACTIVE SOLUTIONS INC (NV)
Name changed to General Components, Inc. 07/07/2004
General Components, Inc. name changed to Hi-Tech Wealth, Inc. 05/02/2007 which name changed to China Mobile Media Technology Inc. 12/27/2007
(See China Mobile Media Technology Inc.)

PRO AIR SYS 1972 INC (ON)
Charter cancelled for failure to pay taxes and file returns 05/25/1981

PRO AMS TR (ON)
Name changed to Government Strip Bond Trust 05/29/2006
(See Government Strip Bond Trust)

PRO-AMS U S TR (ON)
Trust terminated 01/04/2011
Each Unit received $25 cash

PRO ATHLETES GOLF LEAGUE INC (CA)
Merged into Clickese.com, Inc. 02/24/2000
Each share Common no par exchanged for (0.05) share Common $0.001 par
Clickese.com, Inc. name changed to Solutions Technology Inc. 05/08/2001 which merged into International Mercantile Corp. (MO) 01/12/2002 which reincorporated in Nevada as T & G2 03/01/2002 which name changed to Softnet Technology Corp. 08/04/2004

PRO C I R INDS INC (BC)
Name changed 05/01/1995
Name changed from Pro C.I.R. Properties Improvements Ltd. to Pro C.I.R. Industries Inc. 05/01/1995
Recapitalized as Extant Investments Inc. 09/09/1998
Each share Common no par

exchanged for (0.06666666) share Common no par
Extant Investments Inc. name changed to Sydney Resource Corp. 11/14/2001 which merged into West Timmins Gold Corp. 09/18/2006 which merged into Lake Shore Gold Corp. 11/05/2009 which merged into Tahoe Resources Inc. 04/07/2016

PRO CEL INTL INC (DE)
Reorganized under the laws of Nevada 10/04/2007
Each share Common $0.0001 par exchanged for (0.1) share Common $0.0001 par

PRO DEX INC (CA)
Reincorporated under the laws of Colorado 05/27/1994

PRO DYN INC (IL)
Involuntarily dissolved 12/1/77

PRO ELITE INC (NJ)
Name changed 05/03/2007
Each share old Common $0.0001 par exchanged for (0.16666666) share new Common $0.0001 par 01/09/2001
Each share new Common $0.0001 par exchanged again for (0.002) share new Common $0.0001 par 11/01/2006
Name changed from Pro Elite, Inc. to ProElite, Inc. 05/03/2007
SEC revoked common stock registration 08/28/2012

PRO-FAC COOP INC (NY)
Class A Preferred $1 par called for redemption at $25 plus $0.91 accrued dividends on 03/15/2010
Public interest eliminated

PRO FORMA INC (DE)
Name changed to Azkan Technology, Inc. 6/28/82
(See Azkan Technology, Inc.)

PRO GLASS TECHNOLOGIES INC (NV)
Each share old Common $0.001 par exchanged for (0.05) share new Common $0.001 par 04/17/2002
Name changed to MicroSignal Corp. 09/12/2002
MicroSignal Corp. name changed to NanoSignal Corp. 11/10/2003 which recapitalized as Nano Global Inc. 04/03/2008
(See Nano Global Inc.)

PRO GROUP, INC. (PA)
Merged into PNC Bancorp Inc. 1/13/92
Details not available

PRO-MARKET GLOBAL PLC (UNITED KINGDOM)
ADR agreement terminated 06/07/2006
No ADR holders' equity

PRO MED CAP INC (FL)
Name changed to PMC Capital, Inc. 04/04/1991
PMC Capital, Inc. merged into PMC Commercial Trust (TX) 02/29/2004 which reorganized in Maryland as CIM Commerical Trust Corp. 04/29/2014

PRO MONEY FD INC (MD)
Name changed to AMA Money Fund, Inc. 7/31/86
(See AMA Money Fund, Inc.)

PRO MTRS GROUP CORP (NV)
Recapitalized as Hydrogen Hybrid Corp. 11/25/2008
Each share Common $0.001 par exchanged for (0.0025) share Common $0.001 par
Hydrogen Hybrid Corp. name changed to Get Real USA Inc. 01/12/2011

PRO NET LINK CORP (NV)
Chapter 7 bankruptcy proceedings terminated 01/30/2009

Stockholders' equity unlikely

PRO OIL INC (DE)
Recapitalized as Electrogesic Corp. 12/18/92
Each share Common 1¢ par exchanged for (0.05) share Common 1¢ par
Electrogesic Corp. recapitalized as Midrange Marketing Solutions Inc. 10/26/98 which recapitalized as Millennium Broadcast Corp. 9/20/99 which recapitalized as Diversified Media Holdings Inc. 3/13/2003 which recapitalized as TPI International, Inc. 1/3/2006

PRO OPTIC INC (QC)
Merged into Actidev Inc. 5/1/88
Each share Common no par exchanged for (1) share Common no par
Actidev Inc. name changed to Alimentation Couche-Tard Inc. 12/15/94

PRO-PHARMACEUTICALS INC (NV)
Name changed to Galectin Therapeutics Inc. 06/16/2011

PRO-PHY-LAC-TIC BRUSH CO.
Acquired by Lambert Co. in 1930
(See Lambert Co.)

PRO-POINTER INC (NV)
Recapitalized as Coenzyme A, Inc. 02/06/2012
Each share Common $0.001 par exchanged for (0.002) share Common $0.001 par

PRO QUEST INC (CO)
Reorganized under the laws of Nevada as ProQuest Capital Corp. 9/19/97
Each share Common $0.0001 par exchanged for (0.01) share Common $0.0001 par
ProQuest Capital Corp. name changed to Hot Brands, Inc. 10/16/2003 which name changed to G&S Minerals, Inc. 10/9/2006

PRO RDS SYS INC (FL)
Each share old Common $0.001 par exchanged for (0.01) share new Common $0.001 par 08/16/2001
Reincorporated under the laws of Nevada as International Pit Boss Gaming, Inc. 01/13/2003
International Pit Boss Gaming, Inc. name changed to Logo Industries Corp. 03/23/2006 which reorganized as Malwin Ventures, Inc. 01/22/2009

PRO SCAN INC (CO)
Declared defunct and inoperative for failure to pay taxes and file annual reports 9/1/92

PRO-SPECTOR RES INC (CANADA)
Name changed to Uranium Bay Resources Inc. 07/12/2007
Uranium Bay Resources Inc. name changed to Uragold Bay Resources Inc. 07/15/2009 which name changed to HPQ-Silicon Resources Inc. 07/25/2016

PRO SYS INC (MI)
Common $1 par changed to no par 09/03/1971
Common no par changed to 20¢ par 10/31/1974
Name changed to Michigan Rivet Corp. 12/15/1975
(See Michigan Rivet Corp.)

PRO-TEC SPORTS INTL INC (DE)
Charter forfeited for failure to maintain a registered agent 8/31/92

PRO TECH COMMUNICATIONS INC (FL)
Name changed to Four Crystal Funding, Inc. 07/14/2008
(See Four Crystal Funding, Inc.)

PRO-TECH HLDGS LTD (NV)
Name changed to Cascade Energy, Inc. 05/06/2005

Cascade Energy, Inc. name changed to Cannabis Strategic Ventures 12/01/2017

PRO-TECH INVESTMENT CORP. (UT)
Name changed to Petroleum Resources Corp. 4/20/81
Petroleum Resources Corp. name changed to Borexco, Inc. 2/25/85 which name changed to True Health, Inc. (UT) 2/23/86 which reorganized in Nevada as MediQuip Holdings, Inc. 5/1/2006 which name changed to Deep Down, Inc. 12/18/2006

PRO TECH PROGRAMS INC (NY)
Recapitalized as Safeguard Protective Systems, Inc. in 01/00/1976
Each share Class A 1¢ par exchanged for (0.1) share Common 1¢ par
(See Safeguard Protective Systems, Inc.)

PRO-TECH VENTURE CORP (BC)
Cease trade order effective 09/19/2001
Stockholders' equity unlikely

PRO TRANS VENTURES INC (AB)
Assets assigned for the benefit of creditors and operations ceased 06/10/2014

PRO-VEINOR RES INC (AB)
Recapitalized as Ressources Affinor Inc. 03/14/2006
Each share Common no par exchanged for (0.16666666) share Common no par
Ressources Affinor Inc. name changed to Affinor Growers Inc. 05/30/2014

PRO-VEST GROWTH INCOME FD (ON)
Merged into Sentry Select Canadian Income Fund 06/12/2009
Each Trust Unit no par received (0.6162) Ser. A Unit no par

PRO'S PIZZA, INC. (DE)
Name changed to Pro's Inc. 6/10/71
Pro's Inc. charter cancelled 3/1/74

PROACTIVE COMPUTER SVCS INC (NV)
Name changed to CortDev, Inc. 04/05/2004
CortDev, Inc. recapitalized as Botaniex, Inc. 04/15/2005 which name changed to HE-5 Resources Corp. 03/16/2006 which recapitalized as Fansfrenzy Corp. 12/05/2017

PROACTIVE PET PRODS INC (DE)
Recapitalized as GVCL Ventures, Inc. 11/02/2016
Each share Common $0.001 par exchanged for (0.0001) share Common $0.001 par
GVCL Ventures, Inc. recapitalized as Rain Forest International, Inc. 05/22/2018

PROACTIVE TECHNOLOGIES INC (DE)
Each share old Common 1¢ par exchanged for (0.1) share new Common 1¢ par 12/28/1995
Each share new Common 1¢ par exchanged again for (0.25) share Common 4¢ par 02/01/1996
Name changed to Flightserv.com 06/21/1999
Flightserv.com name changed to eResource Capital Group, Inc. 10/06/2000 which name changed to RCG Companies Inc. 11/14/2003 which name changed to OneTravel Holdings, Inc. 06/08/2005
(See OneTravel Holdings, Inc.)

PROBAC INTL CORP (FL)
Reorganized as Trident Environmental Systems Inc. 09/14/1994
Each share Common $0.001 par

exchanged for (0.1) share Common $0.001 par
Trident Environmental Systems Inc. recapitalized as Phoenix International Industries Inc. 09/18/1996 which name changed to Epicus Communications Group Inc. 05/07/2003
(See Epicus Communications Group Inc.)

PROBE EXPL INC (AB)
Name changed from Probe Exploration & Development Ltd. to Probe Exploration, Inc. 07/22/1987
Placed in receivership 03/00/2000
Stockholders' equity unlikely

PROBE INC (UT)
Common Capital Stock 10¢ par changed to 1¢ par 11/24/1972
Name changed to Lehman Bartel, Inc. 11/23/1973
Lehman Bartel, Inc. name changed to Integrated Marketing Management, Inc. 09/19/1978
(See Integrated Marketing Management, Inc.)

PROBE MFG INC (NV)
Old Common $0.001 par split (3) for (1) by issuance of (2) additional shares payable 09/15/2008 to holders of record 09/15/2008
Ex date - 09/16/2008
Each share old Common $0.001 par exchanged for (0.1) share new Common $0.001 par 01/22/2013
Name changed to Clean Energy Technologies, Inc. 02/09/2016

PROBE MINES LTD (ON)
Capital Stock $1 par changed to old Common no par 08/23/1971
Each share old Common no par exchanged for (1) share new Common no par to reflect a (1) for (100) reverse split followed by a (100) for (1) forward split 11/08/2012
Note: Holders of (99) or fewer pre-split shares received $1.65 cash per share
Merged into Goldcorp Inc. 03/17/2015
Each share Common no par exchanged for (0.1755) share Common no par, (0.3333) share Probe Metals Inc. Common no par and $0.001 cash
Note: Unexchanged certificates will be cancelled and become without value 03/17/2021

PROBE RES LTD (BC)
Recapitalized as Rooster Energy Ltd. 05/04/2012
Each share Common no par exchanged for (0.004) share Common no par

PROBEX CORP (DE)
Reincorporated 09/01/2000
Each share old Common no par exchanged for (0.3125) share new Common no par 01/17/1994
Each share new Common no par exchanged again for (0.5) share new Common no par 12/30/1997
State of incorporation changed from (CO) to (DE) 09/01/2000
Filed a petition under Chapter 7 Federal Bankruptcy Code 05/13/2003
Stockholders' equity unlikely

PROBIOMICS LTD (AUSTRALIA)
ADR agreement terminated 11/25/2014
No ADR's remain outstanding

PROBLEMS' COOPERATIVE ASSOCIATION, INC. (NY)
Proclaimed dissolved for failure to file reports and pay taxes 6/15/48

PROBUILD PROCEEDS LTD. (CANADA)
Liquidation completed
Each share Capital Stock no par

received initial distribution of $37 cash 10/1/64
Each share Capital Stock no par exchanged for second and final distribution of $1.738 cash 1/12/66

PROBUS CORP (CO)
Recapitalized as Euroblock America, Inc. 11/30/1990
Each share Common no par exchanged for (0.1) share Common no par

PROBUSINESS SVCS INC (DE)
Issue Information - 2,500,000 shares COM offered at $11 per share on 09/09/1997
Common $0.001 par split (3) for (2) by issuance of (0.5) additional share payable 8/7/98 to holders of record 7/31/98
Merged into Automatic Data Processing, Inc. 6/20/2003
Each share 6.9% Conv. Preferred exchanged for $26.50 cash
Each share Common $0.001 par exchanged for $17 cash

PROCARE AMER INC (NV)
Name changed to Indigo-Energy, Inc. 01/20/2006
Indigo-Energy, Inc. name changed to HDIMAX MEDIA, Inc. 12/19/2014 which name changed to Zonzia Media, Inc. 03/09/2015

PROCARE INDS LTD (CO)
Each share old Common no par exchanged for (0.01) share new Common no par 07/14/1999
Name changed to Duct Utility Construction & Technologies Inc. 06/19/2001
(See Duct Utility Construction & Technologies Inc.)

PROCENTURY CORP (OH)
Merged into Meadowbrook Insurance Group, Inc. 07/31/2008
Each share Common no par exchanged for (2.5) shares Common 1¢ par
(See Meadowbrook Insurance Group, Inc.)

PROCEPT INC (DE)
Each share old Common 1¢ par exchanged for (0.14285714) share new Common 1¢ par 10/14/1997
Each share new Common 1¢ par exchanged again for (0.1) share new Common 1¢ par 06/01/1998
Name changed to HeavenlyDoor.com, Inc. 01/31/2000
HeavenlyDoor.com, Inc. name changed to Paligent Inc. 12/31/2000 which recapitalized as International Fight League, Inc. 11/29/2006 which recapitalized as IFLI Acquisition Corp. 07/08/2010 which name changed to SimplePons, Inc. 12/27/2011 which recapitalized as Eco-Shift Power Corp. 11/26/2013

PROCERA NETWORKS INC (DE)
Reincorporated 06/18/2013
Each share old Common $0.001 par exchanged for (0.1) share new Common $0.001 par 02/07/2011
State of incorporation changed from (NV) to (DE) 06/18/2013
Acquired by KDR Holding, Inc. 06/05/2015
Each share Common $0.001 par exchanged for $11.50 cash

PROCESS CORP (IL)
Merged into Masterpiece Studios, Inc. 12/31/1968
Each share Common no par exchanged for either (1) share Common no par or $25 cash
Note: Option to receive stock expired 06/29/1969

PROCESS ENERGY INC. (UT)
Name changed to Auta-Tronics International, Inc. 6/1/84

PROCESS EQUIP INC (NV)
Reincorporated under the laws of Delaware as HQ Sustainable Maritime Industries, Inc. 5/19/2004

PROCESS LITHOGRAPHERS, INC. (NY)
Adjudicated bankrupt in 1963
No stockholders' equity

PROCESS PLTS CORP (NY)
Name changed to Millcrest Products Corp. 12/14/81
Millcrest Products Corp. reincorporated under the laws of Delaware as Vestro Foods Inc. 7/14/87 which name changed to Vestro Natural Foods Inc. 7/12/94 which name changed to Westbrea Natural Inc. 7/7/97
(See Westbrae Natural Inc.)

PROCESS SYS INC (NJ)
Common 10¢ par split (3) for (1) by issuance of (2) additional shares 08/20/1973
Merged into Process Systems of New Jersey, Inc. 01/24/1984
Each share Common 10¢ par exchanged for $0.40 cash

PROCESS SYS INC (NV)
Common no par changed to 1¢ par 00/00/1974
Name changed to Powell Industries, Inc. (NV) 10/26/1977
Powell Industries, Inc. (NV) reincorporated in Delaware 10/31/2004

PROCESS SYSTEMS INSTRUMENTATION, INC. (NV)
Recapitalized as Process Systems, Inc. 2/25/70
Each share Common no par exchanged for (10) shares Common no par
Process Systems, Inc. name changed to Powell Industries, Inc. (NV) 10/26/77 which reincorporated in Delaware 10/31/2004

PROCESS TECHNOLOGIES INC (NV)
Name changed to Process Technology Systems Inc. 11/6/98
Process Technology Systems Inc. name changed to Forster Drilling Corp. 7/12/2006

PROCESS TECHNOLOGY INDS INC (CO)
Name changed to Dynaflex, Inc. 08/28/1987

PROCESS TECHNOLOGY SYS INC (NV)
Each share old Common no par exchanged for (0.02) share new Common no par 05/21/2001
Name changed to Forster Drilling Corp. 07/12/2006
(See Forster Drilling Corp.)

PROCESSING RESH INC (NV)
Proclaimed dissolved 08/17/2001

PROCHEMCO, INC. (TX)
Name changed to Procor, Inc. 2/23/78
(See Procor, Inc.)

PROCODE INC (UT)
Proclaimed dissolved for failure to file reports 4/1/89

PROCOLORO RES INC (CANADA)
Name changed to Allican Resources Inc. 08/21/1998
(See Allican Resources Inc.)

PROCOM EMERALD INC (BC)
Struck off register and declared dissolved for failure to file returns 10/22/1993

PROCOM GROUP INC (FL)
Each share old Common $0.0001 par exchanged for (0.000002) share new Common $0.0001 par 9/5/95
Note: In effect holders received $0.07 cash per share and public interest was eliminated

PROCOM TECHNOLOGY INC (CA)
Merged into Candle Acquisition Corp. 12/14/2006
Each share Common 1¢ par exchanged for $1.35 cash

PROCONCEPT MARKETING GROUP INC (FL)
Each share old Common $0.001 par exchanged for (0.0005) share new Common $0.001 par 02/26/2009
Administratively dissolved 09/27/2013

PROCOR INC (TX)
Liquidation completed
Each share Common $2 par exchanged for initial distribution of (1.79) shares AZL Resources, Inc. Common no par and $2.42 cash 04/14/1980
Each share Common $2 par received second distribution of $1 cash 05/15/1981
Each share Common $2 par received third distribution of $0.90 cash 06/19/1981
Each share Common $2 par received fourth distribution of $0.07171 cash 08/03/1983
Each share Common $2 par received fifth and final distribution of $0.0356 cash 10/08/1984

PROCORDIA EXPL LTD (BC)
Recapitalized as Earthworks Industries Inc. 9/15/93
Each share Common no par exchanged for (0.2) share Common no par

PROCOREGROUP INC (CA)
Reorganized under the laws of Nevada as Universal Property Development & Acquisition Corp. 07/11/2005
Each share Common $0.001 par exchanged for (0.01) share Common $0.001 par
(See Universal Property Development & Acquisition Corp.)

PROCORP DEVS INC (AB)
Name changed to Roadking Travel Centres Inc. 10/01/1998
(See Roadking Travel Centres Inc.)

PROCTER & GAMBLE CO (OH)
5% Preferred $100 par called for redemption 06/15/1944
(Additional Information in Active)

PROCTOR-SILEX CORP. (CT)
Merged into SCM Corp. 6/30/66
Each share Common $1 par exchanged for (1/3) share Common $5 par
(See SCM Corp.)

PROCURENET HLDGS INC (DE)
Name changed 6/10/2003
Name changed from Procurenet Inc. to Procurenet Holdings Inc. 6/10/2003
Merged into Palisades Merger Corp. 11/22/2004
Each share Common 1¢ par exchanged for $0.24943962 cash
Note: A final escrow distribution of $0.04352014 cash per share was made 4/12/2005

PROCYON BIOPHARMA INC (CANADA)
Reincorporated 4/2/2001
Place of incorporation changed from (ONT) to (Canada) 4/2/2001
Name changed to Ambrilia Biopharma, Inc. 3/3/2006

PROCYTE CORP (WA)
Merged into PhotoMedex, Inc. (DE) 03/22/2005
Each share Common 1¢ par exchanged for (0.6622) share Common 1¢ par
PhotoMedex, Inc. (DE) reincorporated in Nevada 12/29/2010 which name changed to FC Global Realty Inc. 11/01/2017

PRODEC INC. (QC)
Petitioned into bankruptcy 11/5/70
No stockholders' equity

PRODECO OIL & GAS LTD (AB)
Merged into Bow Valley Industries Ltd. 7/25/85
Each share Class A Common no par exchanged for (1/7) share $0.56 Conv. Class Z Preferred Ser. 4 no par, (0.5) Common Stock Purchase Warrant expiring 6/30/88 and (1) share Common no par
Bow Valley Industries Ltd. name changed to Bow Valley Energy Inc. 6/7/93 which was acquired by Talisman Energy Inc. 8/11/94

PRODEL INC (CO)
Name changed to American Tele Advertising Holdings Inc. 10/20/86
(See American Tele Advertising Holdings Inc.)

PRODELIN INC (NJ)
Merged into M/A-Com, Inc. 11/06/1980
Each share Common no par exchanged for (0.54606017) share Common $1 par
M/A-Com, Inc. merged into AMP Inc. 06/30/1995 which merged into Tyco International Ltd. (Bermuda) 04/01/1999 which reincorporated in Switzerland 03/17/2009 which merged into Johnson Controls International PLC 09/06/2016

PRODENT PHARMACEUTICALS INC (DE)
Charter cancelled and declared inoperative and void for non-payment of taxes 3/1/73

PRODEO TECHNOLOGIES INC (DE)
Reorganized under Chapter 11 Federal Bankruptcy Code as Findem, Inc. 10/31/2005
Each share Common $0.005 par exchanged for (0.0764805) share Common $0.005 par

PRODIGITAL FILM STUDIOS INC (NV)
Name changed 07/13/2004
Name changed from Prodigital Film Labs, Inc. to Prodigital Film Studios, Inc. 07/13/2004
Common $0.0001 par split (4) for (1) by issuance of (3) additional shares payable 08/13/2004 to holders of record 08/05/2004 Ex date - 08/16/2004
Charter permanently revoked 06/01/2009

PRODIGY ADVANCED REPAIR TECHNOLOGY CORP (NV)
Each share old Common $0.013 par exchanged for (1/13) share new Common $0.013 par 4/1/96
Name changed to Collision King Inc. 7/21/97
Collision King Inc. recapitalized as Great Outdoors, Inc. 2/10/2004 which name changed to Pivotal Technology, Inc. 8/21/2006 which name changed to Somatic Systems, Inc. 8/28/2006

PRODIGY COMMUNICATIONS CORP (DE)
Common 1¢ par reclassified as Class A Common 1¢ par 06/01/2000
Merged into SBC Communications, Inc. 11/06/2001
Each share Class A Common 1¢ par exchanged for $6.60 cash

PRODIGY GOLD INC (BC)
Merged into Argonaut Gold Inc. 12/11/2012
Each share Common no par exchanged for (0.1042) share Common no par and $0.0001 cash
Note: Unexchanged certificates will be cancelled and become without value 12/11/2018

PRODIGY SYS INC (NJ)
Acquired by MBI Business Centers, Inc. 11/03/1986
Each share Common 1¢ par exchanged for $1.08 cash

PRODUCE EXCHANGE RLTY TR (NY)
Liquidation completed
Each Share of Bene. Int. $1 par received initial distribution of $6.50 cash 12/28/1983
Each Share of Bene. Int. $1 par received second distribution of $43.50 cash 01/04/1984
Each Share of Bene. Int. $1 par received third distribution of $4 cash 02/17/1984
Assets transferred to Produce Exchange Realty Trust Liquidating Trust 12/11/1984
(See Produce Exchange Realty Trust Liquidating Trust)

PRODUCE EXCHANGE REALTY TRUST LIQUIDATING TRUST (NY)
Liquidation completed
Each Share of Bene. Int. $1 par received initial distribution of $0.35 cash 1/30/86
Each Share of Bene. Int. $1 par received second distribution of $5.85 cash 1/23/87
Each Share of Bene. Int. $1 par received third and final distribution of $0.195 cash 2/19/88
Note: Certificates were not required to be surrendered and are now valueless

PRODUCE SAFETY & SEC INTL INC (CO)
Each share old Common no par exchanged for (0.001) share new Common no par 06/27/2005
Each share new Common no par exchanged again for (0.001) share new Common no par 05/24/2007
Each share new Common no par exchanged again for (0.001) share new Common no par 10/17/2007
Each share new Common no par exchanged again for (0.002) share new Common no par 01/09/2008
Each share new Common no par exchanged again for (0.00004) share new Common no par 09/15/2008
Reincorporated under the laws of Nevada as Eco Green Team Inc. and new Common no par changed to $0.001 par 01/29/2009
Eco Green Team Inc. name changed to Champion Investments, Inc. 06/28/2012

PRODUCE TERMINAL COLD STORAGE CO. (IL)
Common no par exchanged (1) for (3) in 1935
Common no par changed to $3 par in 1943
Merged into Beatrice Foods Co. 3/13/64
Each share Common $3 par exchanged for (0.6123678) share Common $25 par
Beatrice Foods Co. name changed to Beatrice Companies, Inc. 6/5/84
(See Beatrice Companies, Inc.)

PRODUCERS & REFINERS CORP. (WY)
Assets sold 00/00/1934
No stockholders' equity

PRODUCERS CHEMICAL CO. (TX)
Name changed to Prochemco, Inc. 5/12/69
Prochemco, Inc. name changed to Procor, Inc. 2/23/78
(See Procor, Inc.)

PRODUCERS CORP.
Recapitalized as Producers Corp. of Nevada 00/00/1940
Each share Common 25¢ par exchanged for (0.25) share Common $1 par
Producers Corp. of Nevada name changed to Texam Oil Corp. 06/14/1956 which name changed to Energy Resources Corp. 10/23/1967 which merged into ENERTEC Corp. 05/04/1984
(See ENERTEC Corp.)

PRODUCERS CORP. OF NEVADA (NV)
Name changed to Texam Oil Corp. 06/14/1956
Texam Oil Corp. name changed to Energy Resources Corp. 10/23/1967 which merged into ENERTEC Corp. 05/04/1984
(See ENERTEC Corp.)

PRODUCERS COTTON OIL CO (CA)
Merged into PCO, Inc. 09/30/1975
Each share Common $1 par exchanged for $43 cash

PRODUCERS ENTMT GROUP LTD (DE)
Each share old Common $0.001 par exchanged for (0.25) share new Common $0.001 par 06/03/1996
Each share new Common $0.001 par exchanged for (1/3) share new Common $0.001 par 05/01/1998
Name changed to IAT Resources Corp. 05/26/1999
IAT Resources Corp. name changed to NetCurrents, Inc. 01/04/2000 which reorganized as NetCurrents Information Services, Inc. 08/30/2001
(See NetCurrents Information Services, Inc.)

PRODUCERS FIN CO ARIZ (AZ)
Merged into ISC Industries Inc. 12/10/70
Each share 6-1/4% Conv. Preferred Ser. B $5 par exchanged for $5 principal amount of 8% 30-day Notes
Each share Common $1 par exchanged for (0.142857) share Common $5 par
ISC Industries Inc. name changed to ISC Financial Corp. 9/26/74
(See ISC Financial Corp.)

PRODUCERS GAS CO (NY)
Common $50 par changed to $10 par and (7) additional shares issued 05/01/1963
100% acquired by National Fuel Gas Co. through exchange offer which expired

PRODUCERS LIFE INSURANCE CO. (AZ)
Merged into National Producers Life Insurance Co. 12/31/1964
Each share Common $1 par exchanged for (1.2) shares Common 50¢ par
National Producers Life Insurance Co. name changed to NPL Corp. 03/27/1981
(See NPL Corp.)

PRODUCERS OIL CORP. OF AMERICA (NV)
Capital Stock $1 par changed to 75¢ par in 1949
Liquidation completed 1/16/63
Each share Capital Stock 75¢ par exchanged for (1/3) share Petrolia Corp. Common $1 par plus cash
Petrolia Corp. liquidation for cash completed 11/30/65

PRODUCERS OILFIELD SVCS INC (AB)
Plan of arrangement effective 06/01/2006
Each share Common no par exchanged for (0.4444) share Mullen Group Income Fund Trust Unit no par, (0.1279) share Horizon North Logistics Inc. Common no par and (0.09) Common Stock Purchase Warrant

(See each company's listing)

PRODUCERS RELEASING CORP (NV)
Charter revoked for failure to file reports and pay fees 06/01/1988

PRODUCERS ROYALTY CORP.
Name changed to Producers Corp. 00/00/1936
Producers Corp. recapitalized as Producers Corp. of Nevada 00/00/1940 which name changed to Texam Oil Corp. 06/14/1956 which name changed to Energy Resources Corp. 10/23/1967 which merged into ENERTEC Corp. 05/04/1984
(See ENERTEC Corp.)

PRODUCERS URANIUM CORP. (NV)
Merged into Texota Oil Co. on a (1) for (31.25) basis 06/16/1958
Texota Oil Co. name changed to North America Resources Corp. 12/15/1968

PRODUCING PROPERTIES, INC. (DE)
Liquidation completed
Each share 6% Preferred $25 par exchanged for first and final distribution $31.625 cash 9/30/63
Each share Common 10¢ par exchanged for initial distribution of $5.25 cash 9/30/63
Each share Common 10¢ par received second distribution of $1.45 cash 8/5/64
Each share Common 10¢ par received third distribution of $0.27 cash 1/25/65
Each share Common 10¢ par received fourth distribution of $0.14 cash 9/5/69
Each share Common 10¢ par received fifth and final distribution of $0.48 cash 10/4/73

PRODUCT APPLICATIONS INC (DE)
Name changed to Globa, Inc. 08/21/1972
(See Globa, Inc.)

PRODUCT DESIGN & ENGR INC (MN)
Common 10¢ par split (2) for (1) by issuance of (1) additional share 2/14/86
Merged into Specialty Packaging Products, Inc. 12/26/86
Each share Common 10¢ par exchanged for $12 cash

PRODUCTEXPRESS COM E BUSINESS SVCS INC (AZ)
Name changed to Emerging Enterprise Solutions Inc. 01/20/2004
(See Emerging Enterprise Solutions Inc.)

PRODUCTION AIDS INC (CA)
Charter suspended for failure to file reports and pay fees 1/2/91

PRODUCTION ASSISTANT TECHNOLOGIES INC (DE)
Charter cancelled and declared inoperative and void for non-payment of taxes 03/01/2000

PRODUCTION ENHANCEMENT GROUP INC (AB)
Lender announced foreclosure proceedings and all directors resigned 10/13/2009
Stockholders' equity unlikely

PRODUCTION NATIONAL CORP. (TX)
Recapitalized as PNC Corp. and each share Common no par exchanged for (0.2) share Common no par 4/29/65

PRODUCTION OPERATORS CORP (DE)
Stock Dividend - 100% 07/01/1981
Merged into Camco International Inc. 06/13/1997
Each share Common $1 par exchanged for (1.3) shares Common 1¢ par

Camco International Inc. merged into Schlumberger Ltd. 08/31/1998

PRODUCTION OPERATORS INC (FL)
Merged into Prodop, Inc. 10/14/1977
Each share Common 1¢ par exchanged for $20 cash

PRODUCTION RESEARCH CORP. (NY)
Adjudicated bankrupt in 1958
No stockholders' equity

PRODUCTION SYS ACQUISITION CORP (DE)
Issue Information - 1,700,000 Units consisting of (1) share COM and (2) WTS offered at $6 per Unit on 06/24/1994
Name changed to Productivity Technologies Corp. 5/23/96

PRODUCTOL CHEM INC (CA)
Capital Stock $1 par split (2) for (1) by issuance of (1) additional share plus a 10% stock dividend paid 03/17/1967
Capital Stock $1 par split (2) for (1) by issuance of (1) additional share 10/07/1974
Acquired by Ferro Corp. 12/23/1975
Each share Capital Stock $1 par exchanged for (0.65) share Common $1 par

PRODUCTS & PATENTS LTD (DE)
Charter cancelled and declared inoperative and void for non-payment of taxes 3/1/89

PRODUCTS RESEARCH CO. (CA)
Common $2 par split (5) for (4) by issuance of (0.25) additional share 4/30/62
Name changed to Products Research & Chemical Corp. 2/4/66
(See Products Research & Chemical Corp.)

PRODUCTS RESH & CHEM CORP (CA)
Capital Stock $2 par reclassified as Common $2 par 02/06/1967
Common $2 par split (5) for (4) by issuance of (0.25) additional share 06/06/1977
Common $2 par split (5) for (4) by issuance of (0.25) additional share 03/23/1979
Common $2 par split (3) for (2) by issuance of (0.5) additional share 11/02/1979
Common $2 par split (3) for (2) by issuance of (0.5) additional share 03/21/1980
Common $2 par split (3) for (2) by issuance of (0.5) additional share 03/23/1983
Common $2 par split (5) for (4) by issuance of (0.25) additional share 08/23/1985
Stock Dividends - 25% 02/28/1967; 25% 02/28/1968
Merged into Courtaulds PLC 10/02/1989
Each share Common $2 par exchanged for $32 cash

PRODUCTS SVCS & TECHNOLOGY CORP (OR)
Reorganized under the laws of Utah as Wireless Data Solutions, Inc. 06/02/1997
Each share $0.001 par exchanged for (1) share Common $0.001 par
Wireless Data Solutions, Inc. (UT) reorganized in Nevada 08/09/2007

PROEX ENERGY LTD (AB)
Under plan of merger name changed to Progress Energy Resources Corp. 01/15/2009
(See Progress Energy Resources Corp.)

PROFCO RES LTD (AB)
Reincorporated 06/10/1997
Place of incorporation changed from (BC) to (AB) 06/10/1997
Under plan of merger name changed

FINANCIAL INFORMATION, INC.   PRO-PRO

to TransAtlantic Petroleum Corp. (AB) 12/02/1998
TransAtlantic Petroleum Corp. (AB) reincorporated in Bermuda as TransAtlantic Petroleum Ltd. 10/01/2009

PROFESSIONAL & BUSINESS MEN'S INSURANCE CO. (TX)
Stock Dividend - 10% 07/31/1962
Acquired by Kentucky Central Life Insurance Co. 08/28/1963
Each (2.5) shares Capital Stock no par exchanged for (1) share Class A Common $1 par
(See Kentucky Central Life Insurance Co.)

PROFESSIONAL ACCEPTANCE CORP. (CO)
Charter revoked for failure to file reports and pay fees 10/17/63

PROFESSIONAL ADJUSTING SYS AMER INC (MN)
Involuntarily dissolved 10/4/91

PROFESSIONAL AGRIC MGMT INC (DE)
Reincorporated 2/10/86
State of incorporation changed from (CA) to (DE) 2/10/86
Charter cancelled and declared inoperative and void for non-payment of taxes 3/1/91

PROFESSIONAL ASSOCS INC (DE)
Charter cancelled and declared inoperative and void for non-payment of taxes 03/01/1981

PROFESSIONAL BANCORP (PA)
Common no par changed to $0.008 par and (0.25) share issued 03/09/1990
Stock Dividend - 5% payable 06/21/1996 to holders of record 05/31/1996 Ex date - 05/29/1996
Merged into First Community Bancorp (CA) 01/16/2001
Each share Common $0.008 par exchanged for (0.55) share Common no par
First Community Bancorp (CA) reincorporated in Delaware as PacWest Bancorp 05/14/2008

PROFESSIONAL BUILDING, INC.
Liquidated in 1947

PROFESSIONAL BUSINESS BK (PASADENA, CA)
Merged into Belvedere SoCal 12/03/2007
Each share Common no par exchanged for (0.87) share Common no par
(See Belvedere SoCal)

PROFESSIONAL CAPITAL CORP. (CA)
Completely liquidated 7/21/75
Each share Capital Stock $10 par exchanged for first and final distribution of $0.095 cash

PROFESSIONAL CARE INC (NY)
Reorganized under the laws of Delaware as Health Professionals, Inc. 11/26/91
Each share Common 2¢ par exchanged for (1) share Common 2¢ par
(See Health Professionals, Inc.)

PROFESSIONAL CARE SVCS INC (DE)
Common 5¢ par split (5) for (2) by issuance of (1.5) additional shares 05/27/1982
Stock Dividend - 33% 01/14/1983
Merged into SP Corp. 09/06/1984
Each share Common 5¢ par exchanged for $11 cash

PROFESSIONAL CHEM CORP (NY)
Name changed to Advanco Industries Inc. 7/27/70
(See Advanco Industries Inc.)

PROFESSIONAL DATA SVCS INC (NY)
Common 10¢ par split (3) for (1) by issuance of (2) additional shares 5/19/71
Common 10¢ par split (2) for (1) by issuance of (1) additional share 3/3/75
Merged into PDS Acquisition Corp. 12/31/90
Each share Common 10¢ par exchanged for $2.50 cash

PROFESSIONAL DENTAL TECHNOLOGIES INC (NV)
Each share old Common 1¢ par exchanged for (0.0001) share new Common 1¢ par 9/21/99
Note: In effect holders received $0.65 cash per share and public interest was eliminated

PROFESSIONAL DETAILING INC (DE)
Name changed to PDI, Inc. 10/01/2001
PDI, Inc. name changed to Interpace Diagnostics Group, Inc. 12/23/2015

PROFESSIONAL DISCOUNT CORP. (SC)
Common $1 par changed to 75¢ par 10/20/65
Completely liquidated 4/10/69
Each share Common 75¢ par received first and final distribution of (0.25) share Security Finance Corp. of Spartanburg Common 20¢ par
Certificates were not retired and are now without value

PROFESSIONAL EDUCATORS INSURANCE AGENCY, INC. (OK)
Charter suspended for failure to pay taxes 3/8/74

PROFESSIONAL GOLF CO (TN)
Common 50¢ par split (3) for (2) by issuance of (0.5) additional share 1/24/69
Stock Dividends - 10% 4/9/62; 10% 5/17/63
Name changed to ProGroup, Inc. 2/25/75
ProGroup, Inc. name changed to Palmer (Arnold) Golf Co. (TN) 7/17/96
(See Palmer (Arnold) Golf Co. (TN))

PROFESSIONAL HEALTH CARE AMER INC (CO)
Charter suspended for failure to file annual reports 09/30/1990

PROFESSIONAL HEALTH SVCS INC (DE)
Adjudicated bankrupt 08/14/1972
Stockholders' equity unlikely

PROFESSIONAL HEALTH SYS INC (MI)
Name changed to International Dasa Corp. 12/11/1981
International Dasa Corp. name changed to Johnson International Corp. 06/18/1984
(See Johnson International Corp.)

PROFESSIONAL INS CO NEW YORK (NY)
Common $10 par changed to $6-2/3 par and (0.5) additional share issued 1/18/65
Common $6-2/3 par changed to $3 par 2/24/72
Liquidated by foreclosure 4/12/74
No stockholders' equity

PROFESSIONAL INVS INS GROUP INC (DE)
Name changed 03/11/1985
Common 10¢ par changed to $1 par 12/27/1972
Name changed from Professional Investors Insurance to Professional Investors Insurance Group, Inc. 03/11/1985
Plan of reorganization under Chapter 11 Federal Bankruptcy proceedings confirmed 01/00/1998
Stockholders' equity unlikely

PROFESSIONAL INVS LIFE INS CO (OK)
Merged into Thurston Financial Corp. 12/31/72
Each share Common 25¢ par exchanged for (1) share Common 10¢ par
Thurston Financial Corp. name changed to Professional Investors Corp. 3/5/73 which name changed to Professional Investors Insurance Group, Inc. 3/11/85
(See Professional Investors Insurance Group, Inc.)

PROFESSIONAL LEASING INC. (UT)
Proclaimed dissolved for failure to pay taxes 3/31/78

PROFESSIONAL MEN'S ASSOCIATION OF COLORADO, INC. (CO)
Advertised defunct and inoperative for failure to pay taxes 10/15/69

PROFESSIONAL MNG CONSULTANTS INC (NV)
Common $0.001 par split (2) for (1) by issuance of (1) additional share payable 05/15/2000 to holders of record 05/02/2000 Ex date - 05/16/2000
Name changed to AudioMonster Online, Inc. 05/17/2000
AudioMonster Online, Inc. name changed to Lockwave Technologies, Inc. 03/15/2001 which recapitalized as Edison Renewables, Inc. 05/19/2003 which name changed to NextPhase Wireless, Inc. 01/26/2005 which name changed to MetroConnect Inc. 02/02/2009
(See MetroConnect Inc.)

PROFESSIONAL OFFICES LTD.
Liquidation completed in 1953

PROFESSIONAL PERCEPTIONS INC (NV)
Name changed to JagNotes.com Inc. 03/16/1999
JagNotes.com Inc. recapitalized as JAG Media Holdings, Inc. 04/08/2002 which name changed to CardioGenics Holdings Inc. 10/27/2009

PROFESSIONAL PORTOFOLIO FD INC (HI)
Acquired by Pegasus Fund, Inc. 05/11/1973
Each share Common $1 par exchanged for (1.2973) shares Capital Stock $1 par
Pegasus Fund, Inc. name changed to Vanderbilt Growth Fund, Inc. 07/01/1975 which merged into St. Paul Capital Fund, Inc. 06/14/1977 which name changed to AMEV Capital Fund, Inc. 05/01/1985 which reorganized as Fortis Equity Portfolios Inc. 02/22/1992
(See Fortis Equity Portfolios Inc.)

PROFESSIONAL RECOVERY SYS LTD (NV)
Reorganized as Netbanx.com Corp. 08/02/1999
Each share Common $0.001 par exchanged for (5) shares Common $0.001 par
Netbanx.com Corp. name changed to NetJ.com Corp. 11/05/1999 which name changed to ZooLink Corp. 11/20/2002 which recapitalized as Action Energy Corp. 04/02/2009 which name changed to SMC Recordings Inc. 09/03/2009 which recapitalized as SMC Entertainment, Inc. 05/06/2011

PROFESSIONAL RESEARCH FUND, INC.
Liquidation completed 5/25/61

PROFESSIONAL SVCS NETWORK CORP (NV)
Charter revoked for failure to file reports and pay fees 10/30/2009

PROFESSIONAL SOFTWARE APPLICATIONS INC (CA)
Stock Dividend - 200% 01/18/1983
Charter suspended for failure to file reports and pay fees 05/01/1987

PROFESSIONAL SOFTWARE ASSOC INC (WA)
Name changed to Wismer-Martin, Inc. 8/1/85
Wismer-Martin, Inc. merged into Physician Computer Network, Inc. 9/10/96
(See Physician Computer Network, Inc.)

PROFESSIONAL SPORTS CARE MGMT INC (DE)
Merged into HealthSouth Corp. 08/20/1996
Each share Common 1¢ par exchanged for (0.233) share Common 1¢ par
HealthSouth Corp. name changed to Encompass Health Corp. 01/02/2018

PROFESSIONAL SPORTS HLDGS INC (FL)
Recapitalized as Sports Gaming Inc. 03/13/1998
Each share Common $0.0001 par exchanged for (0.01) share Common $0.0001 par
Sports Gaming Inc. name changed to CyberGames, Inc. 04/29/1998 which recapitalized as River Creek Holdings, Inc. 07/23/2004 which name changed to EQ Labs, Inc. 02/05/2009

PROFESSIONAL STAFF PLC (ENGLAND & WALES)
Acquired by Ohsea Holdings Ltd. 7/14/2003
Each Sponsored ADR for Ordinary exchanged for $2.07 cash

PROFESSIONAL TRANSN GROUP INC (GA)
Issue Information - 1,250,000 shares COM offered at $6 per share on 06/19/1997
SEC revoked common stock registration 12/01/2003
Stockholders' equity unlikely

PROFESSIONAL VENTURES INC (DE)
Each share old Common $0.0001 par exchanged for (0.005) share new Common $0.0001 par 8/25/93
Recapitalized as International Ventures Group, Inc. 6/10/94
Each share new Common $0.0001 par exchanged for (0.1) share Common 1¢ par
(See International Ventures Group, Inc.)

PROFESSIONAL WRESTLING ALLIANCE CORP (DE)
Recapitalized as TRSG Corp. 11/16/2000
Each share Common $0.001 par exchanged for (0.05) share Common $0.001 par
TRSG Corp. recapitalized as Worldwide Holdings Corp. 5/21/2003

PROFESSIONALISTICS INC (DE)
Recapitalized as Pacific Great China Co. Ltd. 5/31/96
Each share Common $0.00001 par exchanged for (0.5) share Common $0.00001 par

PROFESSIONALS DIRECT INC (MI)
Merged into Hanover Insurance Group, Inc. 09/14/2007
Each share Common no par exchanged for $69.61 cash

PROFESSIONALS GROUP INC (MI)
Name changed 7/1/98
Stock Dividend - 10% payable 12/16/96 to holders of record 12/4/96
Name changed from Professionals Insurance Company Management Group to Professionals Group, Inc. 7/1/98
Stock Dividends - 10% payable 12/23/98 to holders of record 12/7/98; 10% payable 12/13/99 to holders of record 11/29/99
Merged into ProAssurance Corp. 6/27/2001
Each share Common no par exchanged for (0.897) share Common 1¢ par and $13.47 cash

PROFESSOR SILVER MINES LTD. (ON)
Merged into Consolidated Professor Mines Ltd. on a (0.2) for (1) basis 3/9/64
(See Consolidated Professor Mines Ltd.)

PROFFITTS INC (TN)
Common 10¢ par split (2) for (1) by issuance of (1) additional share payable 10/27/1997 to holders of record 10/15/1997 Ex date - 10/28/1997
Under plan of merger name changed to Saks Inc. 09/17/1998
(See Saks Inc.)

PROFILE BANKSHARES INC (NH)
Name changed to Heritage Banks Inc. 04/10/1979
Heritage Banks Inc. merged into BankEast Corp. 03/01/1982
(See BankEast Corp.)

PROFILE CAP CORP (AB)
Merged into Abacan Resource Corp. (New) 2/10/95
Each share Common no par exchanged for (0.23) share Common no par
(See Abacan Resource Corp. (New))

PROFILE DIAGNOSTIC SCIENCES INC (DE)
Reincorporated 05/20/1987
State of incorporation changed from (NV) to (DE) 05/20/1987
Each share old Common $0.001 par exchanged for (0.04) share new Common $0.001 par 06/27/2005
Name changed to Penge Corp. 07/19/2005
(See Penge Corp.)

PROFILE EXTRUSIONS INC (MN)
Common 25¢ par changed to 10¢ par 6/12/67
Name changed to P.H.C., Inc. 3/18/68
(See P.H.C., Inc.)

PROFILE RES INC (AB)
Each share old Common no par exchanged for (0.1) share new Common no par 01/23/2002
Recapitalized as Teras Resources Inc. 09/27/2006
Each share new Common no par exchanged for (0.2) share Common no par

PROFILE SPORTS CORP (MD)
Out of business 12/17/1982
No stockholders' equity

PROFILE TECHNOLOGIES INC (DE)
Reorganized as WaveTrue, Inc. 11/29/2013
Each share Common $0.001 par exchanged for (0.01055123) share Common $0.001 par
Note: WaveTrue, Inc. shares are not registered and will be restricted for a minimum of one year from being traded

PROFILE VENTURES LTD (BC)
Name changed to Multivision Communications Corp. (BC) 12/21/1995
Multivison Communications Corp. (BC) reincorporated in Yukon 10/02/2000 which reorganized in British Columbia 01/24/2011 which name changed to ZoomAway Travel Inc. 10/05/2016

PROFIT BOOKING BLUE CHIP TR (ON)
Name changed to Crown Hill Dividend Fund 06/24/2005
Crown Hill Dividend Fund merged into Crown Hill Fund 12/31/2008 which merged into Citadel Income Fund 12/02/2009

PROFIT BY AIR INC (NY)
Under plan of reorganization each share Common 1¢ par automatically became (1) share PBA, Inc. Common 1¢ par 07/01/1974
PBA, Inc. name changed to Profit Systems, Inc. 03/05/1984
(See Profit Systems, Inc.)

PROFIT FINL CORP (UT)
Each share old Common 1¢ par exchanged for (2) shares new Common 1¢ par 9/10/96
New Common 1¢ par split (3) for (1) by issuance of (2) additional shares payable 9/12/97 to holders of record 9/1/97
Reincorporated under the laws of Nevada as Wade Cook Financial Corp. 9/15/97
(See Wade Cook Financial Corp.)

PROFIT RECOVERY GROUP INTL INC (GA)
Common no par split (3) for (2) by issuance of (0.5) additional share payable 08/17/1999 to holders of record 08/02/1999
Name changed to PRG-Schultz International, Inc. 01/24/2002
PRG-Schultz International, Inc. name changed to PRGX Global, Inc. 01/21/2010

PROFIT SYS INC (DE)
Merged into Lep Group plc 07/17/1990
Each share Common 1¢ par exchanged for $11.88 cash

PROFIT TECHNOLOGY INC (DE)
Charter cancelled and declared inoperative and void for non-payment of taxes 3/1/94

PROFITEER CORP (UT)
Each share Common $0.001 par exchanged for (0.02) share Common 1¢ par 5/17/88
Recapitalized as Profit Financial Corp. 9/12/91
Each share Common 1¢ par exchanged for (0.2) share Common 1¢ par
Profit Financial Corp. reincorporated in Nevada as Wade Cook Financial Corp. 9/15/97
(See Wade Cook Financial Corp.)

PROFORMIX SYS INC (DE)
Name changed to Magnitude Information Systems, Inc. 12/03/1998
Magnitude Information Systems, Inc. name changed to Kiwibox.Com, Inc. 03/02/2010

PROFOUND ENERGY INC (AB)
Merged into Paramount Energy Trust 08/19/2009
Each share Common no par exchanged for (0.2778) Trust Unit no par and $0.3951 cash
Paramount Energy Trust reorganized as Perpetual Energy Inc. 07/06/2010

PROFUTURES DIVERSIFIED FUND, L.P. (DE)
Partnership terminated 12/31/2012
Details not available

PROGAMING PLATFORMS CORP (DE)
Common $0.0001 par split (10) for (1) by issuance of (9) additional shares payable 03/01/2012 to holders of record 03/01/2012 Ex date - 03/02/2011
Name changed to BreedIT Corp. 12/24/2013
BreedIT Corp. recapitalized as TechCare Corp. 10/21/2016

PROGAS OF CANADA, INC. (DE)
Liquidation completed 6/30/61
Each share Common 25¢ par exchanged for first and final distribution of $0.022 cash

PROGEN PHARMACEUTICALS LTD (AUSTRALIA)
Name changed 03/29/2007
Name changed from Progen Industries Ltd. to Progen Pharmaceuticals Ltd. 03/29/2007
Name changed to TBG Diagnostics Ltd. 11/03/2014

PROGENITOR INC (DE)
Issue Information - 2,750,000 UNITS consisting of (1) share COM and (1) WT offered at $7 per Unit on 08/06/1997
Voluntarily dissolved 08/19/1999
Details not available

PROGINET CORP (DE)
Acquired by TIBCO Software Inc. 09/15/2010
Each share Common $0.001 par exchanged for $1.15 cash

PROGOLD RES LTD (BC)
Recapitalized as Snowcap Waters Ltd. 7/28/93
Each share Common no par exchanged for (0.1) share Common no par
Snowcap Waters Ltd. recapitalized as Seacrest Development Corp. 4/30/98 which recapitalized as Norzan Enterprises Ltd. 3/18/2004

PROGRAM ENTMT GROUP INC (NV)
Recapitalized as Santa Maria Resources Inc. 8/5/97
Each share Common $0.001 par exchanged for (0.1) share Common $0.001 par
Santa Maria Resources Inc. recapitalized as FantastiCon, Inc. 10/17/2000 which recapitalized as USCorp 3/6/2002

PROGRAMMED & REMOTE SYS CORP (MN)
Common 50¢ par changed to 10¢ par and (1) additional share issued 1/30/76
Name changed to PaR Systems Corp. 10/21/77
PaR Systems Corp. merged into GCA Corp. 6/4/81 which was acquired by General Signal Corp. 6/7/88 which merged into SPX Corp. 10/6/98

PROGRAMMED BOOKKEEPING SYS INC (NY)
Name changed to Island Resources, Inc. 5/8/80
Island Resources, Inc. merged into Future Educational Systems, Inc. 11/20/2000
(See Future Educational Systems, Inc.)

PROGRAMMED PROPRIETARY SYS INC (NY)
Common 1¢ par changed to $0.005 par and (1) additional share issued 06/27/1969
Stock Dividend - 50% 04/15/1970
Name changed back to Programmed Tax Systems, Inc. 01/28/1975
Programmed Tax Systems, Inc. merged into Automatic Data Processing, Inc. 01/22/1980

PROGRAMMED TAX SOUTH INC (NY)
Merged into Programmed Proprietary Systems, Inc. 07/16/1971
Each share Common 10¢ par exchanged for (0.166666) share Common 1¢ par
Programmed Proprietary Systems, Inc. name changed to Programmed Tax Systems, Inc. 01/28/1975 which merged into Automatic Data Processing, Inc. 01/22/1980

PROGRAMMED TAX SYS INC (NY)
Name changed to Programmed Proprietary Systems, Inc. 6/13/69 which name changed back to Programmed Tax Systems, Inc. 1/28/75
Each share Common 50¢ par exchanged for (0.4) share Common $0.0125 par 11/22/76
Merged into Automatic Data Processing, Inc. 1/22/80
Each share Common $0.0125 par exchanged for (0.1445) share Common 10¢ par

PROGRAMMERS PARADISE INC (DE)
Name changed to Wayside Technology Group, Inc. 8/23/2006

PROGRAMMING & SYS INC (NY)
Common 10¢ par changed to 5¢ par and (1) additional share issued 06/16/1966
Common 5¢ par changed to 2-1/2¢ par and (1) additional share issued 06/16/1967
Common 2-1/2¢ par changed to 8¢ par and (3) additional shares issued 03/29/1968
Common 8¢ par changed to 4¢ par and (1) additional share issued 11/09/1990
Charter cancelled and proclaimed dissolved for failure to pay taxes 06/27/2001

PROGRAMMING METHODS INC (DE)
Reincorporated 11/5/69
State of incorporation changed from (NY) to (DE) 11/5/69
Merged into General Telephone & Electronics Corp. 7/14/72
Each share Common 10¢ par exchanged for (0.8) share Common $3.33-1/3 par
General Telephone & Electronics Corp. name changed to GTE Corp. 7/1/82 which merged into Verizon Communications Inc. 6/30/2000

PROGRAMMING PRODS INC (CA)
Charter cancelled for failure to file reports and pay taxes 1/3/77

PROGRAMMING SCIENCES CORP (NY)
Common 20¢ par changed to 10¢ par and (1) additional share issued 05/18/1970
Adjudicated bankrupt 05/17/1978
Stockholders' equity unlikely

PROGRAMMING TECHNIQUES INC (NY)
Name changed to Bisi, Inc. 02/16/1970
(See Bisi, Inc.)

PROGRAMS & ANALYSIS INC (NY)
Merged into P & A Newco, Inc. 11/24/1986
Each share Common 10¢ par exchanged for $2 cash

PROGRAMS FOR TELEVISION, INC. (NY)
Charter revoked for failure to file reports and pay fees 12/15/64

PROGRAMS UNLIMITED INC (NY)
Dissolved by proclamation 9/28/94

PROGREEN PPTYS INC (NY)
Name changed to ProGreen US, Inc. 07/22/2016

PROGRESS CO. OF DELAWARE (DE)
Charter cancelled for failure to pay taxes 02/05/1913

PROGRESS CORP (UT)
Proclaimed dissolved for failure to pay taxes 12/31/1980

PROGRESS DIVERSIFIED MINERALS LTD.
Name changed to Indigo Consolidated Gold Mines Ltd. 00/00/1949
Indigo Consolidated Gold Mines Ltd. acquired by Nationwide Minerals Ltd. 00/00/1952
(See Nationwide Minerals Ltd.)

PROGRESS ENERGY INC (NC)
Merged into Duke Energy Corp. 07/02/2012
Each share Common no par exchanged for (0.87083) share Common $0.001 par

PROGRESS ENERGY LTD (AB)
Issue Information - 15,000 UNITS maximum; 10,000 UNITS minimum consisting of (200) shares COM and (90) shares CL B offered $1,000 per Unit on 12/16/1997
Each share Class B Common no par exchanged for (2.58) shares Common no par 07/06/2001
Merged into Progress Energy Trust 07/02/2004
Each share Common no par exchanged for (1) Trust Unit no par, (0.2) share ProEx Energy Ltd. Common no par and (0.2) share Cyries Energy Inc. Common no par
(See each company's listing)
Each Ser. A Exchangeable Share no par exchanged for (1.3169975) shares Progress Energy Resources Corp. Common no par 01/15/2009
(See Progress Energy Resources Corp.)

PROGRESS ENERGY RES CORP (AB)
Acquired by PETRONAS Carigali Canada Ltd. 12/17/2012
Each share Common no par exchanged for $22 cash
Note: Unexchanged certificates were cancelled and became without value 12/17/2015

PROGRESS ENERGY TR (AB)
Merged into Progress Energy Resources Corp. 01/15/2009
Each Trust Unit no par exchanged for (0.8125) share Common no par
Note: Unexchanged certificates were cancelled and became without value 01/15/2015
(See Progress Energy Resources Corp.)

PROGRESS FD INC (MD)
Name changed to State Bond Progress Fund, Inc. 12/01/1982
(See State Bond Progress Fund, Inc.)

PROGRESS FD INC (UKRAINE)
Name changed to Millennium Progress Fund Inc. 08/30/2007
(See Millennium Progress Fund Inc.)

PROGRESS FED SVGS BK (NORRISTOWN, PA)
Stock Dividend - 10% 5/30/86
Reorganized under the laws of Delaware as Progress Financial Corp. and Common no par changed to $1 par 7/18/86
Progress Financial Corp. merged into FleetBoston Financial Corp. 2/2/2004 which merged into Bank of America Corp. 4/1/2004

PROGRESS FINL CORP (DE)
Stock Dividends - 5% payable 9/15/97 to holders of record 8/29/97; 5% payable 8/31/98 to holders of record 8/10/98; 5% payable 8/31/99 to holders of record 8/6/99; 5% payable 8/11/2000 to holders of record 7/31/2000; 5% payable 5/16/2003 to holders of record 5/1/2003 Ex date - 4/29/2003
Merged into FleetBoston Financial Corp. 2/2/2004
Each share Common $1 par exchanged for (0.7105) share Common 1¢ par
FleetBoston Financial Corp. merged into Bank of America Corp. 4/1/2004

PROGRESS LAUNDRY CO (IN)
Liquidation completed
Each share Capital Stock no par exchanged for initial distribution of $6.75 cash 12/21/1970
Each share Capital Stock no par received second and final distribution of $0.406209 cash 12/10/1971

PROGRESS LIFE & ACC INS CO (OK)
Reported out of business 02/12/1993
Stockholders' equity unlikely

PROGRESS LIFE & ACCIDENT INSURANCE CO. OF ARIZONA (AZ)
Dissolved by statute 12/28/72
Each share Common 50¢ par exchanged for $1 cash

PROGRESS MANUFACTURING CO., INC. (PA)
$1.25 Conv. Preferred $20 par called for redemption 03/10/1964
Common $1 par split (4) for (3) by issuance of (0.33333333) additional share 07/01/1965
Name changed to Lighting Corp. of America 05/04/1966
Lighting Corp. of America acquired by Kidde (Walter) & Co., Inc. (NY) 06/19/1967 which reincorporated in Delaware 07/02/1968 which name changed to Kidde, Inc. 04/18/1980 which merged into Hanson Trust PLC 12/31/1987 which name changed to Hanson PLC (Old) 01/29/1988 which reorganized as Hanson PLC 10/15/2003

PROGRESS SOFTWARE CORP (MA)
Common 1¢ par split (2) for (1) by issuance of (1) additional share 11/27/1995
Common 1¢ par split (3) for (2) by issuance of (0.5) additional share payable 07/13/1998 to holders of record 06/29/1998 Ex date - 07/14/1998
Common 1¢ par split (2) for (1) by issuance of (1) additional share payable 01/21/2000 to holders of record 01/07/2000
Common 1¢ par split (3) for (2) by issuance of (0.5) additional share payable 01/28/2011 to holders of record 01/12/2011 Ex date - 01/31/2011
Reincorporated under the laws of Delaware 07/13/2015

PROGRESS VACUUM CORP.
Acquired by Eureka Vacuum Cleaner Co. in 1940
(See Eureka Vacuum Cleaner Co.)

PROGRESS WATCH CORP (NV)
Name changed to Mobile Broadcasting Holding, Inc. 11/26/2014
Mobile Broadcasting Holding, Inc. name changed to Medically Minded, Inc. 03/02/2016 which name changed to Sixty Six Oilfield Services, Inc. 05/08/2017

PROGRESS WEBSTER ELECTRONICS CORP. (PA)
Liquidation completed
Each share Common $1 par exchanged for initial distribution of $2.20 cash 9/24/65
Each share Common $1 par received second and final distribution of $0.52982 cash 10/19/66

PROGRESSIONS HEALTH SYS INC (DE)
Merged into Eugenia Hospital 12/24/96
Each share Common $0.012 par exchanged for $0.0803 cash

PROGRESSITRON CORP. (NY)
Completely liquidated for cash 3/5/65

PROGRESSIVE AMERICAN LIFE INSURANCE CO. (WV)
Completely liquidated 01/02/1969
Each share Common 50¢ par exchanged for first and final distribution of (0.0646) share Mid-America Great Plains Financial Corp. Common no par
Mid-America Great Plains Financial Corp. name changed to Mid-America/Great Plains Corp. 12/16/1981
(See Mid-America/Great Plains Corp.)

PROGRESSIVE APPLIED TECHNOLOGIES INC (BC)
Recapitalized as Pacific Vegas Global Strategies Inc. (BC) 07/23/2002
Each share Common no par exchanged for (0.5) share Common no par
Pacific Vegas Global Strategies Inc. (BC) reorganized in Canada as Cathay Forest Products Corp. 09/30/2004
(See Cathay Forest Products Corp.)

PROGRESSIVE ASSET MGMT INC (CA)
Name changed to PAM Holdings Inc. 07/09/2012
(See PAM Holdings Inc.)

PROGRESSIVE BANCORP INC (DE)
Merged into Hometown Community Bancorp, Inc. 12/8/2005
Each share Common 1¢ par exchanged for $82 cash

PROGRESSIVE BANK & TRUST CO. (NEW ORLEANS, LA)
Capital Stock $50 par changed to $12.50 par and (3) additional shares issued 1/12/59
Name changed to Bank of New Orleans & Trust Co. (New Orleans, LA) 7/5/60
Bank of New Orleans & Trust Co. (New Orleans, LA) reorganized as New Orleans Bancshares, Inc. 5/12/70 which merged into First Commerce Corp. 5/23/83 which merged into Banc One Corp. 6/12/98 which merged into Bank One Corp. 10/2/98 which merged into J.P. Morgan Chase & Co. 12/31/2000 which name changed to JPMorgan Chase & Co. 7/20/2004

PROGRESSIVE BK INC (NY)
Common $1 par split (3) for (2) by issuance of (0.5) additional share payable 12/10/96 to holders of record 11/15/96
Merged into Premier National Bancorp, Inc. 7/17/98
Each share Common $1 par exchanged for (1.82) shares Common 80¢ par
Premier National Bancorp, Inc. merged into M&T Bank Corp. 2/9/2001

PROGRESSIVE CAP ACCUMULATION TR (MA)
Minority shares called for redemption 01/20/2006
Public interest eliminated

PROGRESSIVE CORP (PA)
Stock Dividends - 10% 09/01/1974; 15% 09/12/1975; 10% 09/17/1976
Name changed to PC Liquidating Corp. 05/17/1978
(See PC Liquidating Corp.)

PROGRESSIVE DISTRIBUTING, INC. (MN)
Name changed to Progressive Companies, Inc. 11/12/73

PROGRESSIVE DYNAMICS INC (IL)
Name changed to Pro Dyn, Inc. 4/25/73
(See Pro Dyn, Inc.)

PROGRESSIVE ENVIRONMENTAL RECOVERY CORP (NV)
Name changed to Advanced Encryption Technology of America Inc. 10/01/1997
(See Advanced Encryption Technology of America Inc.)

PROGRESSIVE FIRE INSURANCE CO. (GA)
Merged into Southern General Insurance Co. on a (4) for (1) basis 8/6/58

PROGRESSIVE GAMING INTL CORP (NV)
Each share old Common 10¢ par exchanged for (0.125) share new Common 10¢ par 09/16/2008
Filed a petition under Chapter 7 Federal Bankruptcy Code 03/16/2009
No stockholders' equity

PROGRESSIVE GEN CORP (FL)
Reorganized as Crys*Tel Telecommunications.com, Inc. 12/22/1998
Each share Common $0.001 par exchanged for (6) shares Common $0.001 par
Crys*Tel Telecommunications.com, Inc. recapitalized as Juma Technology, Inc. 04/17/2006 which name changed to Silverton Mining Corp. Ltd. 07/05/2006 which recapitalized as Fleet Management Solutions Inc. 02/13/2009

PROGRESSIVE GEN LMBR CORP (FL)
Name changed to Bingo.com, Inc. (FL) 01/22/1999
Bingo.com, Inc. (FL) reincorporated in British West Indies as Bingo.com Ltd. 04/06/2005 which name changed to Shoal Games Ltd. 01/27/2015

PROGRESSIVE HEALTH MGMT INC (FL)
Proclaimed dissolved for failure to file reports and pay fees 8/26/94

PROGRESSIVE INCOME EQUITY FD INC (MD)
Name changed to Liberty Utility Fund Inc. 1/18/90
Liberty Utility Fund Inc. name changed to Federated Utility Fund Inc. 3/31/96 which reorganized in Massachusetts as Federated Capital Income Fund, Inc. 12/20/2002

PROGRESSIVE INDS CORP (OH)
Each share old Common no par exchanged for (0.002) share new Common no par 09/03/1981
Acquired by PIC Acquisition Corp. 12/29/1986
Each share new Common no par exchanged for $1,850 cash

PROGRESSIVE INVT CORP (AZ)
Common $1 par changed to no par and (4) additional shares issued 3/21/69
Charter revoked for failure to file reports or pay fees 8/10/84

PROGRESSIVE MAILER CORP (FL)
Reincorporated under the laws of Colorado as New Millennium Media International Inc. 04/30/1998
New Millennium Media International Inc. name changed to OnScreen Technologies, Inc. 07/14/2004 which name changed to Waytronx, Inc. 01/07/2008 which name changed to CUI Global, Inc. 01/04/2011

PROGRESSIVE METAL EQUIP INC (PA)
Name changed to Progressive Corp. (PA) 10/03/1969
Progressive Corp. (PA) name changed to PC Liquidating Corp. 05/17/1978
(See PC Liquidating Corp.)

PROGRESSIVE MINERALS LTD (BC)
Recapitalized as Northern Crown Mines Ltd. 02/10/1989

PROGRESSIVE MOTOR DEVICES CORP. (IL)
Each share Common no par exchanged for (0.4) share Common no par
Northern Crown Mines Ltd. name changed to Canadian Empire Exploration Corp. 08/15/2002 which recapitalized as X-Terra Resources Corp. (BC) 02/23/2007 which reincorporated in Canada 09/04/2008 which name changed to Norvista Capital Corp. 07/03/2014

PROGRESSIVE MOTOR DEVICES CORP. (IL)
Proclaimed dissolved for failure to pay taxes and file reports 1/25/49

PROGRESSIVE NATL CORP (IL)
Merged into I.C.H. Corp. 11/14/79
Each (3.9) shares Common no par exchanged for (1) share 45¢ Preferred Ser. A no par
I.C.H. Corp. name changed to Southwestern Life Corp. (New) 6/15/94 which name changed to I.C.H. Corp. (New) 10/10/95
(See I.C.H. Corp. (New))

PROGRESSIVE NATL INDS INC (UT)
Charter suspended for failure to pay taxes 09/28/1973

PROGRESSIVE NATL LIFE INS CO (MO)
Merged into I.C.H. Corp. 11/4/82
Each share Common $1 par exchanged for (0.1309) share Common $1 par
I.C.H. Corp. name changed to Southwestern Life Corp. (New) 6/15/94 which name changed to I.C.H. Corp. (New) 10/10/95
(See I.C.H. Corp. (New))

PROGRESSIVE POLYMERICS INTL INC (NV)
Each share old Common $0.001 par exchanged for (0.05) share new Common $0.001 par 04/18/1997
Name changed to Investamerica, Inc. 05/14/1997
(See Investamerica, Inc.)

PROGRESSIVE RETURN FD INC (MD)
Each share old Common $0.001 par exchanged for (0.25) share new Common $0.001 par 5/3/2002
Merged into Cornerstone Strategic Value Fund, Inc. 6/28/2004
Each share Common $0.001 par exchanged for (3.2378) shares Common $0.001 par

PROGRESSIVE SVGS BK (ALHAMBRA, CA)
Name changed 9/27/88
Guarantee Stock $3.33-1/3 par changed to $2.50 par and (1/3) additional share issued 5/4/73
Guarantee Stock $2.50 par changed to $1.25 par and (1) additional share issued 12/15/78
Guarantee Stock $1.25 par changed to $0.625 par and (1) additional share issued 4/15/80
Guarantee Stock $0.625 par reclassified as Common no par 4/30/80
Stock Dividends - 10% 10/15/76; 10% 12/15/77
Name changed from Progressive Savings & Loan Association to Progressive Savings Bank 9/27/88
Declared insolvent and taken over by FDIC 5/24/91
No stockholders' equity

PROGRESSIVE SEC LIFE INS CO (MO)
Merged into Progressive National Life Insurance Co. 12/31/70
Each share Common $1 par exchanged for (1) share Common $1 par
Progressive National Life Insurance Co. merged into I.C.H. Corp. 11/4/82 which name changed to Southwestern Life Corp. (New) 6/15/94 which name changed to I.C.H. Corp. (New) 10/10/95
(See I.C.H. Corp. (New))

PROGRESSIVE SECURITY LIFE INSURANCE CO. (IL)
Merged into Progressive Security Life Insurance Co. (MO) 12/31/68
Each share Common $1 par exchanged for (1/3) share Common $1 par
Progressive Security Life Insurance Co. (MO) merged into Progressive National Life Insurance Co. 12/31/70 which merged into I.C.H. Corp. 11/4/82 which name changed to Southwestern Life Corp. (New) 6/15/94 which name changed to I.C.H. Corp. (New) 10/10/95
(See I.C.H. Corp. (New))

PROGRESSIVE SOFTWARE HLDG INC (DE)
SEC revoked common stock registration 04/15/2005
Stockholders' equity unlikely

PROGRESSIVE TECHNOLOGIES INC (BC)
Recapitalized as Progressive Applied Technologies Inc. 08/12/1999
Each share Common no par exchanged for (0.1) share Common no par
Progressive Applied Technologies Inc. recapitalized as Pacific Vegas Global Strategies Inc. (BC) 07/23/2002 which reorganized in Canada as Cathay Forest Products Corp. 09/30/2004
(See Cathay Forest Products Corp.)

PROGRESSIVE TELECOMMUNICATIONS CORP (NV)
Name changed to Businessmall.com Inc. 3/24/2000
(See Businessmall.com Inc.)

PROGRESSIVE TRAINING INC (DE)
Name changed to Progressive Care Inc. 03/23/2011

PROGRESSIVE VENTURES INC (DE)
Merged into Schield Management Co. 11/28/1990
Each share Common $0.001 par exchanged for (1.6) shares new Common 1¢ par
Schield Management Co. name changed to PMC International Inc. 09/30/1993
(See PMC International Inc.)

PROGRESSIVE WASTE SOLUTIONS LTD (ON)
Recapitalized as Waste Connections, Inc. 06/01/2016
Each share Common no par exchanged for (0.4815) share Common no par

PROGROUP INC (TN)
Name changed to Palmer (Arnold) Golf Co. (TN) 7/17/96
(See Palmer (Arnold) Golf Co. (TN))

PROHEALTH MED TECHNOLOGIES INC (NV)
Name changed to Applied DNA Sciences, Inc. (NV) 11/18/2002
Applied DNA Sciences, Inc. (NV) reincorporated in Delaware 12/17/2008

PROINDIA INTL INC (DE)
Name changed to Electrum International, Inc. 11/19/2010
Electrum International, Inc. name changed to Consolidated Gems, Inc. 10/01/2012

PROJECT DEV PAC INC (NV)
Name changed to Trilliant Exploration Corp. 12/12/2007

PROJECT 80S HLDG CORP (NY)
Recapitalized as Titan Resources Inc. 06/27/1994
Each share Common 2¢ par exchanged for (0.04) share Common 2¢ par
Titan Resources Inc. recapitalized as Palm Works Inc. 09/28/1999 which name changed to Zydant Corp. 10/17/2000
(See Zydant Corp.)

PROJECT FIN CORP (BC)
Name changed to Alaska Hydro Corp. 09/08/2010

PROJECT GROUP INC (NV)
Common $0.001 par split (3) for (1) by issuance of (2) additional shares payable 6/17/2003 to holders of record 6/15/2003 Ex date - 6/18/2003
Common $0.001 par split (2) for (1) by issuance of (1) additional share payable 10/2/2003 to holders of record 9/22/2003 Ex date - 10/3/2003
Chapter 11 bankruptcy proceedings converted to Chapter 7 on 10/27/2006
Stockholders' equity unlikely

PROJECT ROMANIA INC (NV)
Common $0.001 par split (5) for (1) by issuance of (4) additional shares payable 06/09/2006 to holders of record 06/05/2006 Ex date - 06/12/2006
Name changed to Asian Dragon Group, Inc. (New) 08/18/2006
(See Asian Dragon Group, Inc. (New))

PROJECT 7 FILMS, INC. (DE)
Name changed to Project 7, Inc. 12/14/70
Project 7, Inc. name changed to Gloria Group, Ltd. 10/26/73
(See Gloria Group, Ltd.)

PROJECT 7 INC (DE)
Name changed to Gloria Group, Ltd. 10/26/73
(See Gloria Group, Ltd.)

PROJECT SOFTWARE & DEV INC (MA)
Issue Information - 1,950,000 shares COM offered at $8.50 per share on 04/21/1994
Common 1¢ par split (3) for (2) by issuance of (0.5) additional share 7/6/95
Common 1¢ par split (2) for (1) by issuance of (1) additional share payable 12/22/99 to holders of record 12/15/99
Name changed to MRO Software, Inc. 3/8/2001
(See MRO Software, Inc.)

PROJECTAVISION INC (DE)
Common $0.0001 par split (2) for (1) by issuance of (1) additional share 03/23/1992
Each share 8% Conv. Preferred 1¢ par received distribution of (0.205) additional share payable 03/27/1998 to holders of record 03/06/1998
Recapitalized as Vidikron Technologies Group, Inc. 03/02/1999
Each share 8% Conv. Preferred 1¢ par exchanged for (0.025) share 8% Conv. Preferred 1¢ par
Each share Common $0.0001 par exchanged for (0.025) share Common $0.0001 par
(See Vidikron Technologies Group, Inc.)

PROKOM SOFTWARE S A (POLAND)
Merged into Asseco Poland S.A. 04/01/2008
Each 144A Sponsored GDR for Ordinary exchanged for $26.22423 cash
Each Reg. S Sponsored GDR for Ordinary exchanged for $26.22423 cash

PROLAB TECHNOLOGIES INC (QC)
Each share old Class A Subordinate no par exchanged for (0.05) share new Class A Subordinate no par 09/10/2009
Each share new Class A Subordinate no par exchanged again for (0.00001) share new Class A Subordinate no par 12/06/2010
Note: In effect holders received $0.20 cash per share and public interest was eliminated

PROLER INTL CORP (DE)
Common $1 par split (3) for (1) by issuance of (2) additional shares 07/17/1989
Stock Dividend - 10% 01/10/1974
Merged into Schnitzer Steel Industries, Inc. 12/06/1996
Each share Common $1 par exchanged for $9 cash

PROLER STEEL CORP. (DE)
Name changed to Proler International Corp. 6/26/73
(See Proler International Corp.)

PROLIANCE INTL INC (DE)
Chapter 11 bankruptcy proceedings converted to Chapter 7 on 07/22/2010
Stockholders' equity unlikely

PROLIFIC PETROLEUM LTD. (BC)
Name changed to Prolific Resources Ltd. 8/26/87
Prolific Resources Ltd. recapitalized as Skeena Resources Ltd. 6/5/90

PROLIFIC RES LTD (BC)
Recapitalized as Skeena Resources Ltd. 06/05/1990
Each share Common no par exchanged for (1/3) share Common no par

PROLIFIC TECHNOLOGY INC (AB)
Recapitalized as Klad Enterprises Ltd. 3/18/2002
Each share Common no par exchanged for (0.5) share Common no par
Klad Enterprises Ltd. merged into Diamond Hawk Mining Corp. (ALTA) 2/9/2005 which reincorporated in British Columbia 7/4/2005

PROLINK HLDGS CORP (DE)
SEC revoked common stock registration 10/07/2013

PROLOGICA INTL INC (PA)
Reorganized under the laws of Delaware as Elite Pharmaceuticals, Inc. (DE) 10/25/1997
Each share Common no par exchanged for (1/3) share Common 1¢ par
Elite Pharmaceuticals, Inc. (DE) reincorporated in Nevada 01/05/2012

PROLOGIS (MD)
Name changed 05/23/2002
Conv. Preferred Shares of Bene. Int. Ser. B 1¢ par called for redemption at $25 plus $0.442 accrued dividends on 03/20/2001
Preferred Shares of Bene. Int. Ser. A 1¢ par called for redemption at $25 plus $0.2481 accrued dividends on 05/08/2001
Name changed from ProLogis Trust to ProLogis 05/23/2002
Preferred Shares of Bene. Int. Ser. E 1¢ par called for redemption at $25 plus $0.3685 accrued dividend on 07/01/2003
Preferred Shares of Bene. Int. Ser. D 1¢ par called for redemption at $25 plus $0.066 accrued dividend on 01/12/2004
Merged into Prologis, Inc. 06/03/2011
Each Preferred Share of Bene. Int. Ser. C 1¢ par exchanged for (1) share Preferred Ser. Q 1¢ par
Each Preferred Share of Bene. Int. Ser. F 1¢ par exchanged for (1) share Preferred Ser. R 1¢ par
Each Preferred Share of Bene. Int.

Ser. G 1¢ par exchanged for (1) share Preferred Ser. S 1¢ par
Each Share of Bene. Int. 1¢ par exchanged for (0.4464) share Common 1¢ par

PROLOGIS INC (MD)
Preferred Ser. R 1¢ par called for redemption at $25 plus $0.089063 accrued dividends on 04/19/2013
Preferred Ser. S 1¢ par called for redemption at $25 plus $0.089063 accrued dividends on 04/19/2013
6.50% Preferred Ser. L 1¢ par called for redemption at $25 plus $0.013542 accrued dividends on 04/19/2013
6.75% Preferred Ser. M 1¢ par called for redemption at $25 plus $0.014063 accrued dividends on 04/19/2005
6.85% Preferred Ser. P 1¢ par called for redemption at $25 plus $0.014271 accrued dividends on 04/19/2013
7.00% Preferred Ser. O 1¢ par called for redemption at $25 plus $0.014583 accrued dividends on 04/19/2013
(Additional Information in Active)

PROLOGUE (UT)
Each share old Common $0.001 par exchanged for (0.005) share new Common $0.001 par 11/19/2003
Name changed to uWink, Inc. (UT) 02/02/2004
uWink, Inc. (UT) reorganized in Delaware 07/26/2007

PROLONG INTL CORP (NV)
Company entered into an Agreement for Turn Over of Collateral 12/20/2005
Stockholders' equity unlikely

PROLOR BIOTECH INC (NV)
Merged into OPKO Health, Inc. 08/29/2013
Each share Common $0.00001 par exchanged for (0.9951) share Common 1¢ par

PROM MTR HOTEL INC (MO)
Each share Class A Common no par exchanged for (0.0004) share Class A Common no par 07/00/1995
Note: In effect holders received $22 cash per share and public interest was eliminated

PROMANA SOLUTIONS INC (NV)
Recapitalized as Crownbutte Wind Power, Inc. 07/31/2008
Each share Common $0.001 par exchanged for (0.01521537) share Common $0.001 par
Crownbutte Wind Power, Inc. name changed to Canna Brands, Inc. 09/30/2014 which name changed to Canna Consumer Goods, Inc. 06/24/2015

PROMAP CORP (CO)
Name changed to Advanced Cannabis Solutions, Inc. 10/22/2013
Advanced Cannabis Solutions, Inc. name changed to General Cannabis Corp. 06/25/2015

PROMARK SOFTWARE INC (BC)
Name changed to clipclop.com Enterprises Inc. 08/30/1999
clipclop.com Enterprises Inc. recapitalized as Worldwide Technologies Inc. 09/10/2001
(See Worldwide Technologies Inc.)

PROMATEK INDS LTD (CANADA)
Acquired by 6809618 Canada Inc. 11/08/2007
Each share Common no par exchanged for $2 cash

PROMAX COMMUNICATIONS INC (NV)
Reincorporated 00/00/1998
Reincorporated 04/19/2007
Place of incorporation changed from (BC) to (Yukon) 00/00/1998
Place of incorporation changed from (Yukon) to (NV) 04/19/2007
Recapitalized as Sipp Industries, Inc. 08/24/2007
Each share Class A Common no par exchanged for (0.001) share Class A Common no par

PROMAX ENERGY INC (AB)
Reincorporated 6/8/2000
Place of incorporation changed from (BC) to (ALTA) 6/8/2000
Placed in receivership 4/28/2004
Stockholders' equity unlikely

PROMECH CORP (NY)
Charter cancelled and proclaimed dissolved for failure to pay taxes 12/15/75

PROMED ALLIANCE INTL INC (FL)
Name changed to Biomedtex, Inc. 10/09/2007
(See Biomedtex, Inc.)

PROMED TECHNOLOGY INC (AB)
Name changed to Zavitz Technology Inc. 06/21/1983
Zavitz Technology Inc. recapitalized as Zavitz Petroleum Inc. 08/31/1993 which name changed to Jaguar Petroleum Corp. 11/21/1994 which merged into Probe Exploration Inc. 05/09/1997
(See Probe Exploration Inc.)

PROMEDCO MGMT CO (DE)
Plan of reorganization under Chapter 11 Federal Bankruptcy Code effective 05/31/2002
No stockholders' equity

PROMEDICA INC (DE)
Name changed to Zhou Lin International Inc. 11/28/1994
Zhou Lin International Inc. name changed to Renu-U-International Inc. 12/24/1996 which name changed to Colormax Technologies, Inc. 09/07/1999
(See Colormax Technologies, Inc.)

PROMETHEAN TECHNOLOGIES INC (BC)
Delisted from Vancouver Stock Exchange 03/02/1990

PROMETHES INC (CO)
Recapitalized as Triumph Oil & Gas Corp. 11/18/1986
Each share Common no par exchanged for (0.01) share Common no par

PROMETHEUS INCOME PARTNERS (CA)
Merged into PIP Acquisition, LLC 07/24/2002
Each Unit of Ltd. Partnership exchanged for $1,736 cash

PROMINENT RES CORP (BC)
Cease trade order effective 05/02/1991
Stockholders' equity unlikely

PROMIS SYS LTD (CANADA)
Merged into PRI Automation, Inc. 3/2/99
Each share Common no par exchanged for either (0.1691) share Common no par or (0.1353) PRI Automation Canada Inc. Exchangeable Share no par
PRI Automation, Inc. merged into Brooks-PRI Automation, Inc. 5/14/2002 which name changed to Brooks Automation, Inc. (New) 2/27/2003

PROMISE CO LTD (JAPAN)
Merged into Sumitomo Mitsui Financial Group, Inc. 04/01/2012
Each ADR for Common exchanged for $6.04687 cash

PROMISTAR FINL CORP (PA)
Merged into F.N.B. Corp. (FL) 1/18/2002
Each share Common $5 par exchanged for (0.926) share Common $2 par

PROMISTORA GOLD MINES LTD. (ON)
Charter revoked for failure to file reports and pay fees 3/16/67

PROMODOESWORK COM INC (NV)
Name changed to Changda International Holdings Inc. 02/19/2009

PROMOS INC (CO)
Reincorporated under the laws of Delaware as OmniCorder Technologies, Inc. 02/27/2004
OmniCorder Technologies, Inc. name changed to Advanced BioPhotonics, Inc. 06/08/2005
(See Advanced BioPhotonics, Inc.)

PROMOS TECHNOLOGIES INC (TAIWAN)
Each old 144A GDR for Ordinary exchanged for (0.35) new 144A GDR for Ordinary 10/26/2010
Each old Reg. S GDR for Ordinary exchanged for (0.35) new Reg. S GDR for Ordinary 10/26/2010
Stock Dividend - in Reg. S GDR's for Ordinary to holders of Reg. S GDR's for Ordinary 9.28% payable 08/31/2005 to holders of record 07/17/2005
GDR agreement terminated 10/31/2017
Each new 144A GDR for Ordinary exchanged for (10) shares Ordinary
Each new Reg. S GDR for Ordinary exchanged for (10) shares Ordinary
Note: Unexchanged GDR's will be sold and the proceeds, if any, held for claim after 11/05/2018

PROMOTEL INC (NV)
Recapitalized as DigiTEC 2000, Inc. 10/18/1996
Each share Common 2¢ par exchanged for (0.16666666) share Common $0.001 par
(See DigiTEC 2000, Inc.)

PROMOTIONAL PRODS INTL LTD (AB)
Reorganized under the laws of British Columbia as Ava Resources Corp. 11/20/2009
Each share Common no par exchanged for (0.1) share Common no par
(See Ava Resources Corp.)

PROMOTIONS COM INC (DE)
Merged into iVillage Inc. 5/24/2002
Each share Common 1¢ par exchanged for (0.1041) share Common 1¢ par and $0.64 cash
(See iVillage Inc.)

PROMOTIONS ON WHEELS HLDGS INC (NV)
Name changed to Blindspot Alert, Inc. 01/16/2009
Blindspot Alert, Inc. name changed to WebSafety, Inc. 09/25/2009

PROMOTORA VALLE HERMOSO INC (CO)
Each (30) shares old Common $0.001 par exchanged for (1) share new Common $0.001 par 08/10/2007
Name changed to UNR Holdings, Inc. 10/15/2009

PROMOVISION VIDEO DISPLAYS CORP (DE)
Charter cancelled and declared inoperative and void for non-payment of taxes 3/1/88

PROMUS COS INC (DE)
Name changed to Harrah's Entertainment, Inc. 06/30/1995
(See Harrah's Entertainment, Inc.)

PROMUS HOTEL CORP NEW (DE)
Merged into Hilton Hotels Corp. 11/30/1999
Each share Common 1¢ par exchanged for (3.2158) shares Common $2.50 par
(See Hilton Hotels Corp.)

PROMUS HOTEL CORP OLD (DE)
Merged into Promus Hotel Corp. (New) 12/19/1997
Each share Common 10¢ par exchanged for (0.925) share Common 1¢ par
Promus Hotel Corp. (New) merged into Hilton Hotels Corp. 11/30/1999
(See Hilton Hotels Corp.)

PRONAI THERAPEUTICS INC (DE)
Name changed to Sierra Oncology, Inc. 01/10/2017

PRONET INC (DE)
Merged into Metrocall, Inc. 12/30/97
Each share Common 1¢ par exchanged for (0.9) share Common 1¢ par
(See Metrocall, Inc.)

PRONG INDS LTD (BERMUDA)
Reincorporated 09/03/1996
Place of incorporation changed from (BC) to (Bermuda) and Common no par changed to USD$0.001 par 09/03/1996
Name changed to C&C Industries Corp. Ltd. 11/02/1998
C&C Industries Corp. Ltd. name changed to Xenex Minerals Ltd. 01/11/2008
(See Xenex Minerals Ltd.)

PRONGHORN PETE LTD (ON)
Completely liquidated 9/15/71
Each share Common no par exchanged for (1.16) shares Norco Oil Corp. Common 25¢ par
(See Norco Oil Corp.)

PRONTO CORP (NV)
Name changed to Joey New York, Inc. (Old) 09/13/2013
Joey New York, Inc. (Old) reorganized as Joey New York, Inc. (New) 08/01/2016

PRONTO EXPLS LTD (ON)
Delisted from Toronto Stock Exchange 08/10/1992

PRONTO URANIUM MINES LTD. (ON)
Merged into Rio Algom Mines Ltd. 6/30/60
Each share Common $1 par exchanged for (0.35) share Capital Stock no par
Rio Algom Mines Ltd. name changed to Rio Algom Ltd. 4/30/75
(See Rio Algom Ltd.)

PROOF LOCK INTL INC (DE)
Charter cancelled and declared inoperative and void for non-payment of taxes 3/1/74

PROPAINT SYS INC (NV)
Name changed to APC Telecommunications, Inc. 06/18/1998
APC Telecommunications, Inc. name changed to Innofone.com, Inc. 03/30/1999
(See Innofone.com, Inc.)

PROPALMS INC (NV)
Name changed 06/21/2007
Name changed from Propalms USA, Inc. to Propalms, Inc. 06/21/2007
Each share Common $0.0001 par received distribution of (0.03333333) share Infrared Systems International Restricted Common $0.001 par payable 08/16/2010 to holders of record 07/16/2010
Name changed to ProTek Capital Inc. 10/27/2010

PROPANC HEALTH GROUP CORP (DE)
Recapitalized as Propanc Biopharma, Inc. 04/20/2017
Each share Common $0.001 par exchanged for (0.004) share Common $0.001 par

PROPANE CR LTD (AB)
Name changed to Polled Cattle Corp. Ltd. 01/13/1976
Polled Cattle Corp. Ltd. name changed to Ontarget Capital Inc. 02/22/1993 which name changed to Gene Screen Inc. 10/20/1994 which recapitalized as Gene Screen Corp. 07/09/1996 which name changed to GeneVest Inc. 06/25/1998 which merged into Pinetree Capital Corp. 06/01/2004 which recapitalized as Pinetree Capital Ltd. 06/02/2004

PROPEL MULTI STRATEGY FD (ON)
Combined Units separated 01/07/2011
Trust terminated 04/30/2014
Each Unit received $7.39 cash

PROPELL CORP (DE)
Recapitalized as Propell Technologies Group, Inc. 08/31/2012
Each share Common $0.001 par exchanged for (0.02) share Common $0.001 par
Propell Technologies Group, Inc. name changed to Pledge Petroleum Corp. 03/15/2017

PROPELL TECHNOLOGIES GROUP INC (DE)
Name changed to Pledge Petroleum Corp. 03/15/2017

PROPELLEX CHEMICAL CORP. (DE)
Merged into Chromalloy Corp. 08/05/1958
Each share Common no par exchanged for (0.2) share Common 10¢ par
Chromalloy Corp. name changed to Chromalloy American Corp. (NY) 03/01/1966 which reincorporated in Delaware 10/31/1968 which merged into Sun Chemical Corp. 12/23/1986 which name changed to Sequa Corp. 05/08/1987
(See Sequa Corp.)

PROPER PWR & ENERGY INC (DE)
SEC revoked common stock registration 05/15/2014

PROPERTIES CO.
Dissolved in 1944

PROPERTIES OF AMER INC (MA)
Filed a petition under Chapter 7 Federal Bankruptcy Code 10/6/89
Stockholders' equity unlikely

PROPERTIES REALIZATION CORP.
Dissolved in 1936

PROPERTY CAP TR (MA)
Shares of Bene. Int. no par split (2) for (1) by issuance of (1) additional share 12/14/84
In process of liquidation
Each Share of Bene. Int. no par received initial distribution of $0.70 cash 12/21/88
Each Share of Bene. Int. no par received second distribution of $0.36 cash 3/15/89
Each Share of Bene. Int. no par received third distribution of $0.34 cash 6/15/89
Each Share of Bene. Int. no par received fourth distribution of $0.37 cash 9/15/89
Merged into Property Capital Trust Inc. 5/28/99
Each (60) shares Common no par exchanged for (1) share Common no par
(See Property Capital Trust Inc.)

PROPERTY CAP TR INC (MD)
Completely dissolved 8/14/2001
No stockholders' equity

PROPERTY INVS COLO (MA)
Shares of Bene. Int. $1 par split (3) for (1) by issuance of (2) additional shares 1/13/84
Name changed to JFB Realty Trust 10/3/96

PROPERTY INVS VENTURES INC (NV)
Name changed to Entertainment Arts Research, Inc. 02/05/2009

PROPERTY MGMT CORP AMER (DE)
Recapitalized as FingerMotion, Inc. 06/23/2017
Each share Common $0.0001 par exchanged for (0.25) share Common $0.0001 par

PROPERTY RES EQUITY TR (CA)
Common $10 par called for redemption 06/17/1999

PROPERTY SECD INVTS INC (CA)
Each share old Common no par exchanged for (0.25) share new Common no par 07/07/1995
Company terminated common stock registration and is no longer public as of 02/28/1997

PROPERTY SOLUTIONS USA INC (IL)
Each (60) shares old Common $0.0001 par exchanged for (1) share new Common $0.0001 par 11/12/1989
Name changed to Bright Star Corp. 11/09/1991
(See Bright Star Corp.)

PROPERTY TR AMER (MD)
State of incorporation changed from (TX) to (MD) 06/29/1982
Stock Purchase Rights declared for Bene. Int. shareholders were redeemed at $0.01 per right 08/12/1994 for holders of record 07/15/1994
Merged into Security Capital Pacific Trust 03/23/1995
Each Share of Bene. Int. $1 par exchanged for (0.611) Share of Bene. Int. $1 par
Security Capital Pacific Trust name changed to Archstone Communities Trust 07/07/1998 which name changed to Archstone-Smith Trust 10/29/2001
(See Archstone-Smith Trust)

PROPHASE LABS INC (NV)
Reincorporated under the laws of Delaware 06/19/2015

PROPHECY COAL CORP (BC)
Name changed to Prophecy Development Corp. 01/07/2015

PROPHECY ENTMT INC (BC)
Cease trade order effective 11/27/2002
Stockholders' equity unlikely

PROPHECY PLATINUM CORP (BC)
Name changed to Wellgreen Platinum Ltd. 12/19/2013
Wellgreen Platinum Ltd. name changed to Nickel Creek Platinum Corp. 01/11/2018

PROPHECY RESOURCE CORP NEW (BC)
Reorganized as Prophecy Coal Corp. 06/13/2011
Each share Common no par exchanged for (1) share Common no par and (0.94758) share Pacific Coast Nickel Corp. Common no par
Note: Unexchanged certificates were cancelled and became without value 06/13/2017
(See each company's listing)

PROPHECY RESOURCE CORP OLD (BC)
Merged into Prophecy Resource Corp. (New) 04/16/2010
Each share Common no par exchanged for (1) share Common no par
Note: Unexchanged certificates were cancelled and became without value 04/16/2016
(See Prophecy Resource Corp. (New))

PROPHESY DEVS LTD (BC)
Dissolved 09/22/1989
Details not available

PROPHET (FRED B.) CO. (MI)
Stock Dividends - 50% 12/31/47; 100% 9/22/50
Name changed to Prophet Co. 4/26/55
Prophet Co. name changed to Prophet Foods Inc. 4/25/67
(See Prophet Foods Inc.)

PROPHET CO (MI)
Common $1 par split (3) for (2) by issuance of (0.5) additional share 1/20/64
Name changed to Prophet Foods Inc. 4/25/67
(See Prophet Foods Inc.)

PROPHET FOODS INC. (MI)
Merged into Greyhound Corp. 12/31/78
Each share Common $1 par exchanged for $20 cash

PROPHET MINERALS CORP (BC)
Name changed to Meridex Network Corp. 12/21/1999
Meridex Network Corp. recapitalized as Meridex Software Corp. 02/13/2003 which name changed to Cannabis Technologies Inc. 05/21/2014 which name changed to InMed Pharmaceuticals Inc. 10/21/2014

PROPHET 21 INC (DE)
Merged into XXI Merger Corp. 1/21/2003
Each share Common 1¢ par exchanged for $16.30 cash

PROPOSITION GOLD MINING CO. (CO)
Declared defunct and inoperative for failure to pay taxes and file annual reports 09/16/1913

PROPPER-MCCALLUM HOSIERY CO., INC. (DE)
Merged into Claussner Hosiery Co. in 1952
Each share $5 2nd Preferred no par exchanged for (1) share 5% Preferred $100 par
Each share Common no par exchanged for (1/35) share 5% Preferred $100 par and (5/7) share Common $5 par
Claussner Hosiery Co. name changed to Avondale Corp. 4/29/63 which completed liquidation 8/24/68

PROPPER SILK HOSIERY MILLS, INC. (DE)
Merged into Propper-McCallum Hosiery Co., Inc. in 1930
Propper-McCallum Hosiery Co., Inc. merged into Claussner Hosiery Co. in 1952 which name changed to Avondale Corp. 4/29/63 which completed liquidation 8/24/68

PROPRIETARY INDS INC (CANADA)
Name changed 7/27/2000
Reincorporated 6/3/2002
Name changed from Proprietary Energy Industries Inc. to Proprietary Industries Inc. 7/27/2000
Stock Dividend - 3% payable 2/12/2001 to holders of record 2/2/2001
Place of incorporation changed from (ALTA) to (Canada) 6/3/2002
Name changed to Jura Energy Corp. 6/28/2006

PROPRIETARY MINES HOLDINGS LTD. (ON)
Recapitalized as Consolidated Proprietary Mines Holdings Ltd. on a (0.2) for (1) basis 10/13/64
(See Consolidated Proprietary Mines Holdings Ltd.)

PROPRIETARY MINES LTD.
Each share Capital Stock exchanged for (1) share Proprietary Mines Holdings Ltd. and (1.16) shares of Kerr Addison Gold Mines Ltd. in 1951
(See each company's listing)

PROPRIETORS CORP (OH)
Common no par split (2) for (1) by issuance of (1) additional share 6/2/78
Common no par split (4) for (3) by issuance of (1/3) additional share 4/20/80
Placed in liquidation in July 1981
No stockholders' equity

PROPRIETORS OF BOSTON PIER OR THE LONG WHARF (MA)
Completely liquidated 10/15/63
Each share Capital Stock $50 par exchanged for first and final distribution of $2 cash

PROPULSION DEVELOPMENT LABORATORIES, INC. (NV)
Merged into Auto-Control Laboratories, Inc. on a share for share basis 11/1/62
Auto-Control Laboratories, Inc. liquidated for Rucker Co. 9/26/67 which into N L Industries, Inc. 1/21/77

PROPULSION RESEARCH, INC. (MN)
Adjudicated bankrupt 10/20/67

PROQUEST CAP CORP (NV)
Name changed to Hot Brands, Inc. 10/16/2003
Hot Brands, Inc. name changed to G&S Minerals, Inc. 10/9/2006

PROQUEST CO (DE)
Name changed to Voyager Learning Co. 07/02/2007
Voyager Learning Co. merged into Cambium Learning Group, Inc. 12/09/2009

PROS INC (DE)
Charter cancelled and declared inoperative and void for non-payment of taxes 3/1/74

PROS'T BREWING CO.
Merged into Voigt-Pros't Brewing Co. in 1936 whose assets were sold in 1937

PROSACA INC (UT)
Involuntarily dissolved 12/01/1987

PROSENSA HLDG N V (NETHERLANDS)
Name changed 07/10/2013
Name changed from Prosensa Holding B.V. Prosensa Holding N.V. 07/10/2013
Completely liquidated 02/12/2015
Each share Ordinary EUR 0.01 par exchanged for first and final distribution of $17.75 cash and (1) Contingent Value Right

PROSERPINE MINES, LTD. (BC)
Succeeded Proserpine Gold Mines Ltd.
Charter surrendered for failure to file returns in 1957

PROSHARES TR (DE)
Each share old UltraShort Russell MidCap Growth no par automatically became (0.25) share new UltraShort Russell MidCap Growth no par 02/25/2011
Each share old UltraShort Russell MidCap Value no par automatically became (0.25) share new UltraShort Russell MidCap Value no par 02/25/2011
Each share old UltraShort Russell2000 Growth no par automatically became (0.2) no par 02/25/2011
Each share old UltraShort Russell2000 Value no par automatically became (0.25) share new UltraShort Russell2000 Value no par 02/25/2011
Each share old UltraShort Telecommunications no par

automatically became (0.2) share new UltraShort Telecommunications no par 02/25/2011
Each share old UltraShort Russell1000 Growth no par automatically became (0.25) share new UltraShort Russell1000 Growth no par 05/11/2012
Each share old UltraShort Russell3000 no no par automatically became (0.2) share new UltraShort Russell3000 no par 05/11/2012
New UltraShort MSCI Mexico Investable Market no par reclassified as UltraShort MSCI Mexico Capped IMI no par 02/11/2013
Ultra MSCI Mexico Investable Market no par reclassified as Ultra MSCI Mexico Capped IMI no par 02/11/2013
Ultra Russell3000 no par split (2) for (1) by issuance of (1) additional share payable 06/07/2013 to holders of record 06/05/2013 Ex date - 06/10/2013
Each share old UltraShort Russell1000 Value no par automatically became (0.25) share new UltraShort Russell1000 Value no par 06/10/2013
Each share new UltraShort Russell2000 Growth no par automatically became (0.25) share new UltraShort Russell2000 Growth no par 01/24/2014
Each share new UltraShort Russell2000 Value no par automatically became (0.25) share new UltraShort Russell2000 Value no par 01/24/2014
Each share new UltraShort Russell MidCap Growth no par automatically became (0.2) share new UltraShort Russell MidCap Growth no par 11/06/2014
Each share new UltraShort Russell MidCap Value no par automatically became (0.2) share new UltraShort Russell MidCap Value no par 11/06/2014
Each share new UltraShort Telecommunications no par automatically became (0.25) share new UltraShort Telecommunications no par 11/06/2014
Trust terminated 01/22/2015
Each share Short 30 Year TIPS/TSY Spread no par received $43.3481 cash
Each share Ultra Russell MidCap Value no par received $93.4761 cash
Each share Ultra Russell MidCap Growth no par received $113.3217 cash
Each share Ultra Russell1000 Value no par received $78.8509 cash
Each share Ultra Russell1000 Growth no par received $133.1598 cash
Each share Ultra Russell2000 Value no par received $57.6263 cash
Each share Ultra Russell2000 Growth no par received $102.7157 cash
Each share Ultra Russell3000 no par received $98.4832 cash
Each share UltraPro Short 10 Year TIPS/TSY Spread no par received $49.7964 cash
Each share UltraPro 10 Year TIPS/TSY Spread no par received $27.1345 cash
Each share UltraShort Russell MidCap Growth no par received $62.5658 cash
Each share UltraShort Russell MidCap Value no par received $62.0394 cash
Each share UltraShort Russell1000 Growth no par received $21.227 cash
Each share UltraShort Russell1000 Value no par received $31.4933 cash
Each share UltraShort Russell2000

Growth no par received $34.151 cash
Each share UltraShort Russell2000 Value no par received $51.3816 cash
Each share UltraShort Russell3000 no par received $18.7114 cash
Short KBW Regional Banking no par reclassified as Short S&P Regional Banking no par 04/16/2015
Ultra KBW Regional Banking no par reclassified as Ultra S&P Regional Banking 04/16/2015
Trust terminated 09/30/2015
Each share new UltraShort Telecommunications no par received $58.6295 cash
Trust terminated 05/27/2016
Each share CDS North American HY Credit ETF no par received $39.0617 cash
Trust terminated 09/01/2016
Each share Short Investment Grade Corporate no par received $25.3472 cash
Each share Ultra Homebuilders & Supplies no par received $20.8397 cash
Each share Ultra Investment Grade Corporate no par received $68.8478 cash
Each share Ultra MSCI Pacific Ex-Japan no par received $33.5733 cash
Each share UltraShort Homebuilders & Supplies no par received $14.4132 cash
Each share UltraShort Junior Miners no par received $1.8976 cash
Each share UltraShort MSCI Pacific Ex-Japan no par received $18.6415 cash
Ultra S&P Regional Banking no par split (2) for (1) by issuance of (1) additional share payable 01/11/2017 to holders of record 01/09/2017 Ex date - 01/12/2017
Trust terminated 09/14/2017
Each share German Sovereign/Sub-Sovereign ETF no par received $39.5203 cash
Each share Hedged FTSE Europe ETF no par received $40.8437 cash
Each share Hedged FTSE Japan ETF no par received $29.8654 cash
Short S&P Regional Banking no par received $17.3334 cash
Each share Ultra Junior Miners no par received $63.0887 cash
Each share Ultra MSCI Mexico Capped IMI no par received $28.0642 cash
Each share Ultra Oil & Gas Exploration & Production no par received $18.8295 cash
Each share Ultra S&P Regional Banking no par received $65.9004 cash
Each share UltraShort MSCI Mexico Capped IMI no par received $15.6008 cash
Each share UltraShort Oil & Gas Exploration & Production no par received $16.0546 cash
Each share UltraShort 3-7 Year Treasury no par received $26.0334 cash
Each share UltraShort TIPS no par received $24.3202 cash
Each share USD Covered Bond no par received $101.3896 cash
(Additional Information in Active)

PROSHARES TR II (DE)
UltraShort DJ-UBS Commodity no par reclassified as UltraShort Bloomberg Commodity no par 07/01/2014
Each share old Ultra Bloomberg Commodity no par automatically became (0.25) share new Ultra Bloomberg Commodity no par 05/20/2015
Trust terminated 06/29/2015
Each share Ultra Australian Dollar no par received $25.233 cash

Trust terminated 03/30/2016
Each share Managed Futures Strategy no par received $20.0492 cash
UltraShort Bloomberg Commodity no par split (3) for (1) by issuance of (2) additional shares payable 07/22/2016 to holders of record 07/20/2016 Ex date - 07/25/2016
Trust terminated 09/01/2016
Each share new Ultra Bloomberg Commodity no par received $32.4766 cash
Each share UltraShort Bloomberg Commodity no par received $38.0379 cash
(Additional Information in Active)

PROSHER CORP (DE)
Name changed to Mediacom Industries, Inc. 07/27/1983
Mediacom Industries, Inc. reorganized as Applause Networks Inc. 07/08/1998 which recapitalized as Internet Broadcast Networks Inc. 06/10/1999 which name changed to Mediacom Entertainment Inc. 08/10/2001
(See Mediacom Entertainment Inc.)

PROSHER INVT CORP (DE)
Name changed to Prosher Corp. 06/19/1970
Prosher Corp. name changed to Mediacom Industries, Inc. 07/27/1983 which reorganized as Applause Networks Inc. 07/08/1998 which recapitalized as Internet Broadcast Networks Inc. 06/10/1999 which name changed to Mediacom Entertainment Inc. 08/10/2004
(See Mediacom Entertainment Inc.)

PROSIEBEN MEDIA AKTIENGESELLSCHAFT (GERMANY)
Name changed to ProSiebenSat.1 Media AG 10/02/2000
ProSiebenSat.1 Media AG name changed to ProSiebensat.1 Media S.E. 07/22/2015

PROSIEBENSAT.1 MEDIA AG (GERMANY)
ADR agreement terminated 03/21/2005
Each ADR for Preferred Bearer shares exchanged for $34.1368 cash
ADR's for Ordinary split (8) for (1) by issuance of (7) additional ADR's payable 05/05/2014 to holders of record 05/02/2014 Ex date - 05/06/2014
Basis changed from (1:2) to (1:0.25) 05/06/2014
Name changed to ProSiebenSat.1 Media S.E. 07/22/2015

PROSOFT LEARNING CORP (NV)
Plan of reorganization under Chapter 11 Federal Bankruptcy Code effective 6/12/2006
No stockholders' equity

PROSOFTTRAINING (NV)
Name changed 10/18/96
Name changed 12/23/98
Name changed 1/17/2002
Name changed from Prosoft Development, Inc. to Prosoft I-Net Solutions, Inc. 10/18/96
Name changed from Prosoft I-Net Solutions, Inc. to ProsoftTraining.com 12/23/98
Name changed from ProsoftTraining.com to ProsoftTraining 1/17/2002
Recapitalized as Prosoft Learning Corp. 1/20/2005
Each share Common $0.001 par exchanged for (1/6) share Common $0.001 par
(See Prosoft Learning Corp.)

PROSOURCE INC (DE)
Issue Information - 3,400,000 shares

CL A offered at $14 per share on 11/11/1996
Merged into AmeriServe Food Distribution, Inc. 5/21/98
Each share Class A Common 1¢ par exchanged for $15 cash
Each share Class B Common 1¢ par exchanged for $15 cash

PROSPECT ACQUISITION CORP (DE)
Issue Information - 25,000,000 UNITS consisting of (1) share COM and (1) WT offered at $10 per Unit on 11/14/2007
Under plan of merger name changed to Kennedy-Wilson Holdings, Inc. 11/13/2009

PROSPECT DEV CO (UT)
Name changed to National Enterprises Inc. 07/07/1981

PROSPECT ENERGY CORP. (BC)
Merged into New Penn Energy Corp. (B.C.) (New) 11/22/82
Each (4.65) shares Common no par exchanged for (1) share Common no par
New Penn Energy Corp. (B.C.) (New) reincorporated under the laws of Canada 1/29/82 which merged into International Interlake Industries Inc. 12/31/86
(See International Interlake Industries Inc.)

PROSPECT ENERGY CORP (MD)
Issue Information - 7,000,000 shares COM offered at $15 per share on 07/27/2004
Name changed to Prospect Capital Corp. 06/18/2007

PROSPECT EXPLORATION, LTD. (AB)
Name changed to Canadian Prospect, Ltd. in 1951
Canadian Prospect, Ltd. name changed to Canadian Export Gas & Oil Ltd. 6/12/58
(See Canadian Export Gas & Oil Ltd.)

PROSPECT GROUP INC (DE)
Each share Common 25¢ par exchanged for (0.5) share Common 50¢ par 04/14/1986
Liquidation completed
Each share Common 50¢ par received initial distribution of (0.096868) share Forschner Group, Inc. Common 10¢ par, (0.14988) share Illinois Central Corp. Ser. A Common $0.001 par, (0.117276) share Sylvan Foods Holdings Inc. Common $0.001 par and $0.50 cash 08/20/1990
Each share Common 50¢ par received second distribution of (1) Valutron Distribution Trust Unit of Bene. Int. 12/31/1990
Each share Common 50¢ par received third distribution of $0.75 cash 06/17/1991
Each share Common 50¢ par received fourth distribution of (0.061546) share Recognition Equipment Inc. Common 25¢ par 07/31/1991
Each share Common 50¢ par received fifth distribution of (0.074177) share Recognition Equipment Inc. Common 25¢ par 05/11/1992
* Each share new Common 50¢ par exchanged for (0.1) share Common 1¢ par 06/01/1993
Each share Common 1¢ par received sixth distribution of (1) Non-Transferable Trust Unit representing approximately (0.02) share Children's Discovery Centers of America, Inc. Class A Common 1¢ par for holders of record 11/23/1992 on 12/21/1993
Each Trust Unit holder received first

and final distribution of $0.152834 cash 12/21/1993
Note: Trust Units were book entry only
Each share Common 1¢ par received seventh distribution of $11.90 cash payable 04/18/1997 to holders of record 03/31/1997
Each share Common 1¢ par received eighth distribution of $0.435 cash payable 08/25/1998 to holders of record 03/31/1997
Each share Common 1¢ par received ninth and final distribution of $0.02 cash payable 10/00/2000 to holders of record 03/31/1997
Note: Certificates were not required to be surrendered and are without value

PROSPECT HILL APARTMENTS INC. (NY)
Preferred $100 par changed to $1 par in 1946
Merged into French (Fred F.) Investing Co., Inc. 9/30/66
Each share Preferred $1 par exchanged for (7) shares Common no par and $8 cash
Each share Common no par exchanged for $2 cash
Each Unit consisting of (1) share Preferred $1 par and (1) share Common no par exchanged for (7.5) shares Common no par
(See French (Fred F.) Investing Co., Inc.)

PROSPECT INDS CORP (DE)
Acquired by Prospect Purchasing Co., Inc. 12/10/1991
Each share Common 10¢ par exchanged for $0.50 cash

PROSPECT MED HLDGS INC (DE)
Acquired by Ivy Holdings Inc. 12/15/2010
Each share Common 1¢ par exchanged for $8.50 cash

PROSPECT NATL BK (PEORIA, IL)
Merged into Commercial National Corp. (DE) 04/20/1982
Each share Common Capital Stock $20 par exchanged for (1.82) shares Common $10 par
Commercial National Corp. (DE) merged into Midwest Financial Group, Inc. 02/08/1983 which merged into First of America Bank Corp. 11/01/1989 which merged into National City Corp. 03/31/1998 which was acquired by PNC Financial Services Group, Inc. 12/31/2008

PROSPECT PARK FINL CORP (DE)
Stock Dividends - 10% 06/29/1988; 10% 06/29/1989
Chapter 7 bankruptcy proceedings terminated 10/28/1994
Stockholders' equity unlikely

PROSPECT PARK NATL BK (WAYNE, NJ)
Common $50 par changed to $25 par and (1) additional share issued plus a 400% stock dividend paid 1/30/52
Common $25 par changed to $10 par and (1.5) additional shares issued plus a 100% stock dividend paid 2/1/66
Stock Dividend - 100% 3/10/70
Merged into Bancshares of New Jersey 8/1/74
Each share Common $10 par exchanged for (1.73) shares Common $5 par
Bancshares of New Jersey name changed to Northern National Corp. 5/28/81 which merged into Horizon Bancorp 10/1/83
(See Horizon Bancorp)

PROSPECT PK SVGS BK (WEST PATERSON, NJ)
Name changed 11/16/87
Name changed from Prospect Park Savings & Loan Association to Prospect Park Savings Bank (West Paterson, NJ) 11/16/87
Reorganized under the laws of Delaware as Prospect Park Financial Corp. 6/9/88
(See Prospect Park Financial Corp.)

PROSPECT STR HIGH INCOME PORTFOLIO INC (MD)
Each share old Common 1¢ par exchanged for (1/3) share new Common 3¢ par 04/01/1998
Custody Receipt Taxable Auction Insured Preferred no par called for redemption at $100,000 on 05/15/1998
Taxable Auction Rate Preferred no par called for redemption at $100,000 on 05/15/1998
Auction Rate Preferred Ser. W 1¢ par called for redemption at $25,000 on 07/17/2008
Merged into Highland Credit Strategies Fund 07/18/2008
Each share Common 3¢ par exchanged for (0.18805) share Common $0.001 par
Highland Credit Strategies Fund name changed to Pyxis Credit Strategies Fund 01/11/2012 which name changed to NexPoint Credit Strategies Fund 06/25/2012 which name changed to NexPoint Strategic Opportunities Fund 03/19/2018

PROSPECT STR INCOME SHS INC (MD)
Auction Rate Preferred Ser. T called for redemption at $25,000 on 07/16/2008
Merged into Highland Credit Strategies Fund 07/18/2008
Each share Common $1 par exchanged for (0.36852) share Common $0.001 par
Highland Credit Strategies Fund name changed to Pyxis Credit Strategies Fund 01/11/2012 which name changed to NexPoint Credit Strategies Fund 06/25/2012 which name changed to NexPoint Strategic Opportunities Fund 03/19/2018

PROSPECTOR CONS RES INC (BC)
Recapitalized as Prospector Resources Corp. (BC) 01/31/2011
Each share Common no par exchanged for (0.03333333) share Common no par
Prospector Resources Corp. (BC) reincorporated in Ontario as Rio2 Ltd. (Old) 04/28/2017 which merged into Rio2 Ltd. (New) 07/27/2018

PROSPECTOR ENERGY INC (UT)
Reorganized under the laws of Nevada as Peoplesway.Com, Inc. 10/01/1999
Each share Common 1¢ par exchanged for (0.0025) share Common $0.001 par

PROSPECTOR INTL RES INC (BC)
Recapitalized as Prospector Consolidated Resources Inc. 09/11/2001
Each share Common no par exchanged for (0.11111111) share Common no par
Prospector Consolidated Resources Inc. recapitalized as Prospector Resources Corp. (BC) 01/31/2011 which reincorporated in Ontario as Rio2 Ltd. (Old) 04/28/2017 which merged into Rio2 Ltd. (New) 07/27/2018

PROSPECTOR RES CORP (BC)
Reincorporated under the laws of Ontario as Rio2 Ltd. (Old) 04/28/2017
Rio2 Ltd. (Old) merged into Rio2 Ltd. (New) 07/27/2018

PROSPECTORS AIRWAYS, LTD.
Acquired by Prospectors Airways Co., Ltd. 00/00/1931
Details not available

PROSPECTORS AIRWAYS CO., LTD. (CANADA)
Merged into Kerr Addison Mines Ltd. on a (0.1) for (1) basis 11/18/1963
Kerr Addison Mines Ltd. merged into Noranda Inc. 04/11/1996 which name changed to Falconbridge Ltd. (New) 2005 on 07/01/2005
(See Falconbridge Ltd. (New) 2005)

PROSPECTORS ALLIANCE CORP (ON)
Recapitalized as Explorers Alliance Corp. 10/13/2000
Each share Common no par exchanged for (0.25) share Common no par
(See Explorers Alliance Corp.)

PROSPECTORS AWYS LTD (BC)
Delisted from Vancouver Stock Exchange 03/04/1992

PROSPECTUS GROUP INC (AB)
Reincorporated under the laws of Ontario as Route1 Inc. 10/21/2004

PROSPECTUS PRESS, INC. (NY)
Name changed to FSI Corp. 10/22/69

PROSPER COLONY MANUFACTURING CO. (FL)
Proclaimed dissolved for failure to file reports and pay fees 9/16/36

PROSPER OIL & MINING CO. (UT)
Each share old Common 10¢ par exchanged for (0.05) share new Common 10¢ par 01/19/1962
Recapitalized as Anellux Systems Corp. 11/01/1969
Each share new Common 10¢ par exchanged for (0.33333333) share Common 10¢ par
(See Anellux Systems Corp.)

PROSPER OILS & MINES LTD. (BC)
Name changed to Southern Pacific Petroleum Ltd. 8/11/69
Southern Pacific Petroleum Ltd. recapitalized as Sonic-Ray Resources Ltd. 5/1/72 which recapitalized as Stryker Resources Ltd. 9/25/79 which recapitalized as Stryker Ventures Corp. 8/25/97

PROSPER OILS LTD. (BC)
Name changed to Prosper Oils & Mines Ltd. 11/29/1965
Prosper Oils & Mines Ltd. name changed to Southern Pacific Petroleum Ltd. 08/11/1969 which recapitalized as Sonic-Ray Resources Ltd. 05/01/1972 which recapitalized as Stryker Resources Ltd. 09/25/1979 which recapitalized as Stryker Ventures Corp. 08/25/1997
(See Stryker Ventures Corp.)

PROSPER-WAY, INC. (NV)
Name changed to World Mint, Inc. 9/3/69
World Mint, Inc. recapitalized as NCP Industries, Inc. 5/28/74
(See NCP Industries, Inc.)

PROSPEREX MINERALS CORP (BC)
Name changed to NAV Master Technologies Inc. 08/06/1991
NAV Master Technologies Inc. recapitalized as Starpoint Systems Inc. 02/23/1994 which name changed to Starpoint Goldfields Inc. 05/27/1996
(See Starpoint Goldfields Inc.)

PROSPERITY BK & TR CO (SPRINGFIELD, VA)
Stock Dividends - 2% payable 6/25/99 to holders of record 5/11/99; 2% payable 7/15/2000 to holders of record 5/16/2000; 5% payable 11/15/2001 to holders of record 10/16/2001; 5% payable 3/30/2004 to holders of record 2/17/2004
Ex date - 5/19/2004
Merged into Union Bancshares Corp. 4/1/2006
Each share Common $5 par exchanged for $90 cash

PROSPERITY BKG CO (FL)
Merged into Ameris Bancorp 12/23/2013
Each share Common 1¢ par exchanged for (3.125) shares Common $1 par

PROSPERITY CAP TR I (DE)
9.60% Trust Preferred Securities called for redemption at $10 on 12/31/2004

PROSPERITY CO., INC. (NY)
Class A Common no par and Class B Common no par respectively and (2) additional shares issued 10/13/55
Merged into Ward Industries Corp. 3/15/56
Each share Preferred $100 par exchanged for (4) shares $1.25 Preferred Ser. A $25 par and (0.5) share Common $1 par
Each share Class A Common no par or Class B Common $1 par exchanged for (0.16) share $1.25 Preferred Ser. A $25 par and (0.62) share Common $1 par
Ward Industries Corp. name changed to Dragor Shipping Corp. 8/14/64 which merged into American Export Industries, Inc. 10/17/67 which name changed to Aeicor, Inc. 3/31/78 which name changed to Doskocil Companies Inc. 9/30/83 which name changed to Foodbrands America Inc. 5/15/95 which merged into IBP, Inc. 5/7/97 which merged into Tyson Foods, Inc. 9/28/2001

PROSPERITY GOLDFIELDS CORP (BC)
Each share old Common no par exchanged for (0.25) share new Common no par 10/17/2013
Recapitalized as Northern Empire Resources Corp. 12/12/2014
Each share Common no par exchanged for (0.2) share Common no par
Northern Empire Resources Corp. merged into Coeur Mining, Inc. 10/01/2018

PROSPERITY GOLDFIELDS CORP (CANADA)
Merged into Prosperity Goldfields Corp. (BC) 04/24/2012
Each share Common no par exchanged for (1) share Common no par
Prosperity Goldfields Corp. (BC) recapitalized as Northern Empire Resources Corp. 12/12/2014 which merged into Coeur Mining, Inc. 10/01/2018

PROSPERITY SOFTWARE INC (NV)
Each share old Common $0.001 par exchanged for (0.25) share new Common $0.001 par 10/23/2002
Name changed to Polarwearz Inc. 6/25/2003
Polarwearz Inc. name changed to Risingtide, Inc. 6/2/2004 which name changed to Equiline Corp. 4/8/2005 which recapitalized as Chelsea Collection, Inc. 6/15/2005 which recapitalized as G-H-3 International, Inc. 10/30/2006

PROSPERO GROUP (NV)
SEC revoked common stock registration 10/13/2010

PROSPERO MINERALS CORP (NV)
Recapitalized as Prospero Group 01/05/2009
Each share Common $0.001 par exchanged for (1/7) share Common $0.001 par
(See Prospero Group)

PROSPEX MNG INC (YT)
Merged into Semafo Inc. 06/30/1999
Each share Common no par

exchanged for (0.1) share Common no par

PROSPEX RES LTD (AB)
Merged into Paramount Resources Ltd. 06/03/2011
Each share Common no par exchanged for (0.0322528) share Class A Common no par and $1.30997459 cash

PROSPORTSBOOK NET INC (NV)
Recapitalized as Ibises International Inc. 3/27/2003
Each share Common $0.001 par exchanged for (0.05) share Common $0.001 par
Ibises International Inc. recapitalized as Biomag Corp. 3/28/2006 which name changed to Biomagnetics Diagnostics Corp. 12/18/2006

PROSTAR HLDGS INC (DE)
Charter cancelled and declared inoperative and void for non-payment of taxes 3/1/99

PROTAAL RES LTD (AB)
Recapitalized as Newalta Oil & Gas Ltd. 06/14/1984
Each share Common no par exchanged for (0.2) share Common no par
Newalta Oil & Gas Ltd. name changed to Newalta Corp. 07/07/1986 which recapitalized as Newalta Income Fund 03/10/2003 which reorganized as Newalta Inc. 12/31/2008 which name changed to Newalta Corp. (New) 01/22/2010 which reorganized as Tervita Corp. 07/24/2018

PROTALEX INC (NM)
Reincorporated under the laws of Delaware and Common no par changed to $0.00001 par 12/01/2004

PROTALIX BIOTHERAPEUTICS INC (FL)
Reincorporated under the laws of Delaware 04/01/2016

PROTEC INDS INC (AZ)
Reincorporated under the laws of Washington 3/2/2004

PROTECH INC (NV)
Each share old Common $0.001 par exchanged for (1/9) share new Common $0.001 par 12/21/1989
SEC revoked common stock registration 04/08/2010
Stockholders' equity unlikely

PROTECTAIRE SYS CO (DE)
Charter cancelled and declared inoperative and void for non-payment of taxes 03/01/1990

PROTECTION DEVICES INTL INC (AB)
Name changed to Inlet Devices Corp. (ALTA) 2/6/96
Inlet Devices Corp. (ALTA) reorganized in Ontario as Sangoma.com, Inc. 5/1/2000 which name changed to Sangoma Technologies Corp. 9/17/2001

PROTECTION GOLD MINING CO. (CO)
Declared defunct and inoperative for failure to pay taxes and file annual reports 09/16/1913

PROTECTION ONE INC (DE)
Each share old Common 1¢ par exchanged for (0.02) share new Common 1¢ par 02/09/2005
Merged into Protection Holdings, LLC 06/04/2010
Each share new Common 1¢ par exchanged for $15.50 cash

PROTECTION TECHNOLOGY INC (BC)
Delisted from Vancouver Stock Exchange 03/05/1996

PROTECTIVE CORP (DE)
Common $1 par changed to 50¢ par and (1) additional share issued 01/25/1985
Name changed to Protective Life Corp. 05/08/1985
(See Protective Life Corp.)

PROTECTIVE ENERGY PROGRAMS INC (DE)
Common $0.001 par split (10) for (1) by issuance of (9) additional shares 07/02/1984
Ceased operations 06/07/1988
No stockholders' equity

PROTECTIVE INDEMNITY CO.
Merged into Preferred Accident Insurance Co. of New York in 1947
Details not available

PROTECTIVE LIFE CORP (DE)
Common 50¢ par split (2) for (1) by issuance of (1) additional share 06/01/1995
Issue Information - 2,000,000 INCOME PRIDES consisting of a stock purchase contract and (1) share PLC Capital Trust II 6.50% Trust Originated Preferred offered at $50 per Income Pride on 11/20/1997
Common 50¢ par split (2) for (1) by issuance of (1) additional share payable 04/01/1998 to holders of record 03/13/1998 Ex date - 04/02/1998
Trust terminated 02/16/2003
Details not available
Acquired by Dai-ichi Life Insurance Co., Ltd. 02/01/2015
Each share Common 50¢ par exchanged for $70 cash

PROTECTIVE LIFE INSURANCE CO. (AL)
Each share Capital Stock $100 par exchanged for (10) shares Capital Stock $10 par 05/31/1937
Capital Stock $10 par changed to $5 par and (1) additional share issued plus a 16.66666666% stock dividend paid 11/14/1958
Capital Stock $5 par changed to $2 par and (1.5) additional shares issued plus a 10% stock dividend paid 12/04/1964
Capital Stock $2 par changed to $1 par and (1) additional share issued 05/31/1979
Stock Dividends - 50% 07/10/1951; 0.33333333% 04/01/1955; 50% 11/15/1956; 14.286% 03/07/1960; 25% 03/10/1961; 20% 03/22/1963
Under plan of reorganization each share Capital Stock $1 par automatically became (1) share Protective Corp. Common $1 par 07/02/1981
Protective Corp. name changed to Protective Life Corp. 05/08/1985
(See Protective Life Corp.)

PROTECTIVE PRODS AMER INC (DE)
Plan of reorganization under Chapter 11 Federal Bankruptcy proceedings effective 10/05/2011
No stockholders' equity

PROTECTIVE SECURITY CO. (CA)
Completely liquidated 06/19/1967
Each share Common $1 par exchanged for first and final distribution of (0.375) share of American Pacific Group, Inc. Common $1 par
American Pacific Group, Inc. liquidated for Hawaii Corp. 03/03/1972
(See Hawaii Corp.)

PROTECTIVE SECURITY LIFE INSURANCE CO. (CA)
Each share Capital Stock $10 par exchanged for (10) shares Capital Stock 60¢ par 10/17/58
Capital Stock 60¢ par changed to 40¢ par 12/28/62
Name changed to American Pacific Life Insurance Co. of California 4/13/65
(See American Pacific Life Insurance Co. of California)

PROTECTIVE TECHNOLOGIES INTL MARKETING INC (NV)
Recapitalized as Armed Alert Security Inc. 6/4/99
Each share Common $0.001 par exchanged for (0.2) share Common $0.001 par
Armed Alert Security Inc. recapitalized as Acquired Sales Corp. 3/1/2006

PROTECTOR INDS INC (AB)
Recapitalized as Life Medical Corp. 04/14/2000
Each share Common no par exchanged for (0.25) share Common no par
(See Life Medical Corp.)

PROTECTUS MED DEVICES INC (DE)
SEC revoked common stock registration 01/21/2014

PROTECWERX INC (NV)
Name changed to China Media, Inc. 10/26/2009

PROTEIN DATABASES INC (DE)
Each share Common $0.0001 par exchanged for (0.0083843) share Common 1¢ par 10/16/92
Name changed to IDP Liquidating Corp. 10/30/97
(See IDP Liquidating Corp.)

PROTEIN DESIGN LABS INC (DE)
Common 1¢ par split (2) for (1) by issuance of (1) additional share payable 8/22/2000 to holders of record 8/1/2000
Common 1¢ par split (2) for (1) by issuance of (1) additional share payable 10/9/2001 to holders of record 9/18/2001 Ex date - 10/10/2001
Name changed to PDL BioPharma, Inc. 1/9/2006

PROTEIN POLYMER TECHNOLOGIES INC (DE)
Chapter 7 bankruptcy proceedings terminated 09/06/2017
Stockholders' equity unlikely

PROTEON INC (MA)
Name changed to Openroute Networks Inc. 6/10/98
Openroute Networks Inc. merged into Netrix Corp. 12/22/99 which name changed to Nx Networks, Inc. 9/19/2000

PROTERION CORP (DE)
Reported out of business 08/00/2004
Details not available

PROTEUS FOODS & INDS INC (DE)
Adjudicated bankrupt 02/04/1971
Stockholders' equity unlikely

PROTEUS GROUP INC (UT)
Proclaimed dissolved for failure to pay taxes 09/30/1985

PROTEUS MINERALS LTD. (ON)
Charter cancelled for failure to file reports and pay taxes in 1971

PROTEUS RES INC (BC)
Merged into Silverside Resources Inc. 07/20/1989
Each share Common no par exchanged for (0.4) share Common no par
Silverside Resources Inc. recapitalized as Starmin Mining Inc. 06/12/1991 which recapitalized as First Dynasty Mines Ltd. 08/16/1994 which name changed to Sterlite Gold Ltd. 05/21/2002
(See Sterlite Gold Ltd.)

PROTHERICS PLC (UNITED KINGDOM)
Name changed 09/15/1999
Under plan of merger name changed from Proteus International PLC to Protherics PLC 09/15/1999
Merged into BTG PLC 12/04/2008
Each Sponsored ADR for Ordinary exchanged for $6.673877 cash

PROTIDE PHARMACEUTICALS INC (MN)
Company terminated common stock registration and is no longer public as of 03/08/2004

PROTO EXPLORATIONS LTD. (ON)
Merged into Proto Explorations & Holdings Inc. 02/24/1978
Each share Capital Stock $1 par exchanged for (0.13333333) share Common no par
Proto Explorations & Holdings Inc. name changed to Baxter Resources Corp. 06/26/1981 which merged into Baxter Technologies Corp. 12/31/1981 which name changed to Standard-Modern Technologies Corp. 10/08/1985
(See Standard-Modern Technologies Corp.)

PROTO EXPLS & HLDGS INC (ON)
Name changed to Baxter Resources Corp. 6/26/81
Baxter Resources Corp. merged into Baxter Technologies Corp. 12/31/81 which name changed to Standard-Modern Technologies Corp. 10/8/85
(See Standard-Modern Technologies Corp.)

PROTO RES & INVTS LTD (AUSTRALIA)
Each old Sponsored ADR for Ordinary exchanged for (0.025) new Sponsored ADR for Ordinary 05/19/2014
Basis changed from (1:50) to (1:200) 05/19/2014
ADR agreement terminated 04/27/2015
Each new Sponsored ADR for Ordinary exchanged for (200) shares Ordinary
Note: Unexchanged ADR's will be sold and the proceeds, if any, held for claim after 04/29/2016

PROTOCOL COMPUTERS INC (CA)
Acquired by Telematics International Inc. 07/31/1986
Each share Common $0.001 par exchanged for $1.40 cash

PROTOCOL SYS INC (OR)
Merged into Welch Allyn, Inc. 8/25/2004
Each share Common 1¢ par exchanged for $16 cash

PROTOCOM DEVICES INC (DE)
Charter cancelled and declared inoperative and void for non-payment of taxes 3/1/90

PROTON ENERGY SYS INC (DE)
Issue Information - 7,000,000 shares COM offered at $17 per share on 09/28/2000
Under plan of merger each share Common 1¢ par automatically became (1) share Distributed Energy Systems Corp. Common 1¢ par 12/10/2003
(See Distributed Energy Systems Corp.)

PROTON LABS INC (WA)
Recapitalized as Good Water Co., Inc. 05/23/2013
Each share Common $0.0001 par exchanged for (0.00142857) share Common $0.0001 par

PROTOX THERAPEUTICS INC (BC)
Name changed to Sophiris Bio Inc. 04/05/2012

PROTRONICS INC (DE)
Name changed to U.S. West Investments, Inc. 06/12/1973
(See U.S. West Investments, Inc.)

PROTYLE PRESS, INC. (DE)
Recapitalized as Protyle Services, Inc. 8/30/74
Each share Common 1¢ par exchanged for (0.5) share Common 1¢ par
(See Protyle Services, Inc.)

PROTYLE SVCS INC (DE)
Charter cancelled and declared inoperative and void for non-payment of taxes 3/1/78

PROVADIR FINL CORP (UT)
Name changed to Phaser Enterprises, Inc. 2/20/87
(See Phaser Enterprises, Inc.)

PROVALIS PLC (UNITED KINGDOM)
Each old Sponsored ADR for Ordinary 1p par exchanged for (1/6) new Sponsored ADR for Ordinary 1p par 08/05/2002
ADR agreement terminated 08/27/2005
Each new Sponsored ADR for Ordinary 1p par exchanged for $1.14765 cash

PROVALL MINES LTD. (ON)
Dissolved by default and charter cancelled 8/18/58

PROVANT INC (DE)
Completely liquidated
Each share Common 1¢ par received first and final distribution of $0.027 cash payable 12/31/2007 to holders of record 04/04/2007
Note: Certificates were not required to be surrendered and are without value

PROVANTAGE HEALTH SVCS INC (DE)
Merged into Merck & Co., Inc. (Old) 06/21/2000
Each share Common 1¢ par exchanged for $12.25 cash

PROVECTUS PHARMACEUTICALS INC (NV)
Reincorporated under the laws of Delaware as Provectus Biopharmaceuticals, Inc. 01/23/2014

PROVELL INC (MN)
Plan of reorganization under Chapter 11 Federal Bankruptcy Code effective 02/19/2003
No stockholders' equity

PROVEN RES LTD (BC)
Name changed to Shayna International Industries Ltd. 05/28/1987

PROVENA FOODS INC (CA)
Merged into Hormel Foods Corp. 12/18/2006
Each share Common no par exchanged for (0.08) share Common $0.0586 par

PROVENOR INC (AB)
Recapitalized as Pro-Veinor Resources Inc. 10/29/2003
Each share Common no par exchanged for (0.25) share Common no par
Pro-Veinor Resources Inc. recapitalized as Ressources Affinor Inc. 03/14/2006 which name changed to Affinor Growers Inc. 05/30/2014

PROVENTURE INCOME FD (AB)
Name changed to Summit Industrial Income REIT 10/05/2012

PROVEST GLOBAL INC (NV)
Common $0.001 par split (10) for (1) by issuance of (9) additional shares payable 12/19/2014 to holders of record 12/19/2014
Name changed to Imperial Plantation Corp. 05/04/2015

PROVIDE COMM INC (DE)
Merged into Liberty Media Corp. (New) 02/09/2006
Each share Common $0.001 par exchanged for $33.75 cash

PROVIDENCE, WARREN & BRISTOL RAILROAD CO.
Merged into New York, New Haven & Hartford Railroad Co. under plan of reorganization on basis of (1) share Common no par for each $100 of allowed claims 05/26/1948
(See New York, New Haven & Hartford Railroad Co.)

PROVIDENCE, WEBSTER & SPRINGFIELD RAILROAD CO. (MA)
Liquidation completed 3/3/61

PROVIDENCE & WORCESTER CO (DE)
Under plan of reorganization each share Common $100 par exchanged for (20) shares Common $1 par 10/02/1980
Reincorporated under the laws of Rhode Island 04/27/1983
Providence & Worcester Co. (RI) name changed to Capital Properties, Inc. 07/31/1984

PROVIDENCE & WORCESTER CO (RI)
Name changed to Capital Properties, Inc. 07/31/1984

PROVIDENCE & WORCESTER RR (RI & MA)
Reincorporated under the laws of Delaware as Providence & Worcester Co. and Capital Stock $100 par reclassified as Common $100 par 07/31/1969
Providence & Worcester Co. (DE) reincorporated in Rhode Island 04/27/1983 which name changed to Capital Properties, Inc. 07/31/1984

PROVIDENCE & WORCESTER RR CO (RI)
Each share $0.05 Conv. Preferred 50¢ par exchanged for (1) share Common 50¢ par 07/06/1994
Acquired by Genesee & Wyoming Inc. 11/01/2016
Each share 10% Preferred $50 par exchanged for $2,500 cash
Each share Common 50¢ par exchanged for $25 cash

PROVIDENCE BILTMORE HOTEL, INC.
Dissolved in 1948

PROVIDENCE BILTMORE HOTEL CO.
Reorganized as Providence Biltmore Hotel, Inc. in 1936 which was dissolved in 1948

PROVIDENCE CAP CORP (BC)
Name changed to Providence Resources Corp. 01/24/2011
Providence Resources Corp. merged into Desert Star Resources Ltd. (New) 04/15/2015 which name changed to Kutcho Copper Corp. 12/21/2017

PROVIDENCE DIAMOND CORP (CANADA)
Name changed to CIC Mining Resources Ltd. 07/25/2005
CIC Mining Resources Ltd. name changed to CIC Capital Ltd. (Canada) 05/31/2013 which reincorporated in British Columbia 11/23/2013
(See CIC Capital Ltd.)

PROVIDENCE ENERGY CORP (RI)
Merged into Southern Union Co. (New) 09/28/2000
Each share Common $1 par exchanged for $42.50 cash

PROVIDENCE GAS CO (RI)
Each share Common $50 par exchanged for (5) shares Common no par in 1929
Common no par changed to $1 par 4/5/76
Stock Dividend - 10% 11/25/67
Under plan of reorganization each share Common $1 par automatically became (1) share Providence Energy Corp. Common $1 par 2/1/81
(See Providence Energy Corp.)

PROVIDENCE HEALTH CARE INC (DE)
Merged into Multicare Companies, Inc. 3/18/94
Each share Common 1¢ par exchanged for $7.50 cash

PROVIDENCE HOCKEY CLUB INC (RI)
Voluntarily dissolved 12/21/77
Details not available

PROVIDENCE ICE CO.
Acquired by Rhode Island Ice Co. 00/00/1928
Details not available

PROVIDENCE INDS INC (BC)
Recapitalized 10/04/1991
Recapitalized from Providence Innovations Inc. to Providence Industries Inc. 10/04/1991
Each share Common no par exchanged for (0.25) share Common no par
Merged into Gold City Mining Corp. 12/07/1994
Each share Common no par exchanged for (1.25) share Common no par
Gold City Mining Corp. recapitalized as Consolidated Gold City Mining Corp. 10/24/1997 which recapitalized as Gold City Industries Ltd. (BC) 08/26/1998 which reincorporated in Manitoba 06/21/2005 which merged into San Gold Corp. 07/07/2005
(See San Gold Corp.)

PROVIDENCE INVS CO (RI)
Common $2.50 par changed to $1.25 par and (1) additional share issued 05/10/1972
Acquired by Massachusetts Financial Total Return Trust 12/16/1991
Each share Common $1.25 par exchanged for approximately (4.4) shares Common $1 par
Massachusetts Financial Total Return Trust name changed to MFS Total Return Fund 08/03/1992

PROVIDENCE JOURNAL CO (DE)
Merged into Belo (A.H.) Co. 02/28/1997
Each share Class A Common $1 par exchanged for either (0.8652) share Common Ser. A $1.67 par, $37.15 cash, or a combination thereof
Each share Class B Common $1 par exchanged for either (0.8652) share Common Ser. A $1.67 par, $37.15 cash, or a combination thereof
Note: Option to elect cash, or a combination of stock and cash expired 02/18/1997
Belo (A.H.) Corp. name changed to Belo Corp. 01/01/2001
(See Belo Corp.)

PROVIDENCE RES CORP (BC)
Merged into Desert Star Resources Ltd. (New) 04/15/2015
Each share Common no par exchanged for (0.4) share Common no par and (0.4) Common Stock Purchase Warrant expiring 00/00/2017
Note: Unexchanged certificates will be cancelled and become without value 04/15/2021
Desert Star Resources Ltd. (New) name changed to Kutcho Copper Corp. 12/21/2017

PROVIDENCE SVGS & LN ASSN VIENNA (VA)
Common $100 par changed to $10 par 07/08/1964
Common $10 par changed to $5 par and (1) additional share issued 05/31/1974
Stock Dividends - 10% 09/06/1966; 100% 06/30/1970; 50% 09/29/1972; 50% 12/31/1973; 10% 10/14/1977; 10% 10/13/1978; 10% 11/19/1979
Merged into Miller & Smith Holding Inc. 07/22/1987
Each share Common $5 par exchanged for $74.40 cash

PROVIDENCE UNION NATIONAL BANK (PROVIDENCE, RI)
Merged into Industrial National Bank (Providence, RI) 2/1/54
Each share Common $25 par exchanged for (1.5) shares Common $20 par
Industrial National Bank (Providence, RI) name changed to Industrial National Bank of Rhode Island (Providence, RI) 10/3/61 which merged into Industrial Bancorp, Inc. 9/18/68 which reincorporated under the laws of Rhode Island as Industrial National Corp. 4/29/70 which name changed to Fleet Financial Group, Inc. (Old) 4/14/82 which merged into Fleet/Norstar Financial Group, Inc. 1/1/88 which name changed to Fleet Financial Group, Inc. (New) 4/15/92 which name changed to Fleet Boston Corp. 10/1/99 which name changed to FleetBoston Financial Corp. 4/18/2000 which merged into Bank of America Corp. 4/1/2004

PROVIDENCE WASH INS CO (RI)
Each share Capital Stock $100 par exchanged for (10) shares Capital Stock $10 par 00/00/1930
Capital Stock $10 par reclassified as Common $10 par 00/00/1950
$2 Conv. Preferred $10 par called for redemption 11/10/1969
Acquired by Associates First Capital Corp. 12/01/1975
Each share Common $10 par exchanged for $39 cash

PROVIDENCE WHOLESALE DRUG CO. (RI)
Merged into Harris Wholesale Co. 7/18/85
Each share Capital Stock $50 par exchanged for $400 cash

PROVIDENCIA BANK (BURBANK, CA)
Merged into Valley National Bank (Glendale, Calif.) 5/1/67
Each share Common $10 par or VTC for Common $10 par exchanged for $3 principal amount of 6% Ser. A Conv. Capital Notes due 5/1/70; $2.50 principal amount of 6% Ser. B Conv. Capital Notes due 5/1/70; $2.50 principal amount of 6% Ser. C Conv. Capital Notes due 5/1/70 and $7 cash

PROVIDENT AMERN CORP (PA)
Stock Dividend - 10% 05/28/1993
Name changed to HealthAxis Inc. 02/01/2000
HealthAxis Inc. name changed to BPO Management Services, Inc. 12/30/2008
(See BPO Management Services, Inc.)

PROVIDENT BANCORP INC (DE)
Name changed to Provident New York Bancorp 06/30/2005
Provident New York Bancorp name changed to Sterling Bancorp 11/01/2013

PROVIDENT BANCORP INC (OH)
Each share old Common no par exchanged for (0.5) share new Common no par 05/19/1982
New Common no par split (4) for (1) by issuance of (3) additional shares 11/03/1986
New Common no par split (3) for (2)

by issuance of (0.5) additional share 11/23/1988
New Common no par split (3) for (2) by issuance of (0.5) additional share 01/20/1993
New Common no par split (3) for (2) by issuance of (0.5) additional share payable 05/24/1996 to holders of record 05/07/1996
New Common no par split (3) for (2) by issuance of (0.5) additional share payable 12/19/1996 to holders of record 12/12/1996
Name changed to Provident Financial Group, Inc. 06/02/1997
Provident Financial Group, Inc. merged into National City Corp. 07/01/2004 which was acquired by PNC Financial Services Group, Inc. 12/31/2008

PROVIDENT BANCORP INC (USA)
Reorganized under the laws of Delaware as Provident Bancorp, Inc. 01/14/2004
Each share Common 10¢ par exchanged for (4.4323) shares Common 1¢ par
Provident Bancorp, Inc. name changed to Provident New York Bancorp 06/30/2005 which name changed to Sterling Bancorp 11/01/2013

PROVIDENT BANKSHARES CORP (MD)
Common $1 par split (2) for (1) by issuance of (1) additional share payable 02/13/1998 to holders of record 02/02/1998
Stock Dividends - 5% payable 05/10/1996 to holders of record 04/29/1996; 5% payable 05/09/1997 to holders of record 04/28/1997; 5% payable 05/08/1998 to holders of record 04/27/1998; 5% payable 05/14/1999 to holders of record 05/03/1999; 5% payable 05/12/2000 to holders of record 05/01/2000; 5% payable 05/11/2001 to holders of record 04/30/2001 Ex date - 04/26/2001
Acquired by M&T Bank Corp. 05/26/2009
Each share Common $1 par exchanged for (0.171625) share Common $5 par

PROVIDENT CAP TR II (DE)
8.75% Subordinated Capital Income Securities called for redemption at $25 on 9/30/2004

PROVIDENT CAP TR III (DE)
10.25% Guaranteed Trust Preferred Securities called for redemption at $25 on 12/30/2005

PROVIDENT CAP TR IV (DE)
9.45% Trust Preferred Securities called for redemption at $25 on 3/30/2006

PROVIDENT CMNTY BANCSHARES INC (DE)
Acquired by Park Sterling Corp. 05/01/2014
Each share Common 1¢ par exchanged for $0.78 cash

PROVIDENT COS INC (DE)
Issue Information - 5,917,500 shares COM offered at $53 per share on 05/05/1997
Common $1 par split (2) for (1) by issuance of (1) additional share payable 9/30/97 to holders of record 8/28/97 Ex date - 10/1/97
8.10% Depositary Preferred called for redemption at $25 on 2/24/98
Merged into UNUMProvident Corp. 6/30/99
Each share Common $1 par exchanged for (0.73) share Common 10¢ par
UNUMProvident Corp. name changed to Unum Group 3/2/2007

PROVIDENT ENERGY LTD NEW (AB)
Merged into Pembina Pipeline Corp. 04/02/2012
Each share Common no par exchanged for (0.425) share Common no par

PROVIDENT ENERGY LTD OLD (AB)
Each Exchangeable Share no par exchanged for (1.30698) Provident Energy Trust, Trust Units no par 01/15/2005
Provident Energy Trust reorganized as Provident Energy Ltd. (New) 01/03/2011 which merged into Pembina Pipeline Corp. 04/02/2012

PROVIDENT ENERGY TR (AB)
Each Trust Unit no par received distribution of (0.12225) share Pace Oil & Gas Ltd. Common no par payable 07/13/2010 to holders of record 07/09/2010 Ex date - 07/14/2010
Reorganized as Provident Energy Ltd. (New) 01/03/2011
Each Trust Unit no par exchanged for (1) share Common no par
Note: Unexchanged certificates were cancelled and became without value 01/03/2016
Provident Energy Ltd. (New) merged into Pembina Pipeline Corp. 04/02/2012

PROVIDENT FD INCOME INC (DE)
Name changed to American Capital Equity Income Fund, Inc. 07/23/1990
(See American Capital Equity Income Fund, Inc.)

PROVIDENT FINL CORP (NC)
Merged into South Carolina National Corp. 08/31/1973
Each share Common $1 par exchanged for (0.5382) share Common $5 par
South Carolina National Corp. merged into Wachovia Corp. (New) (Ctfs. dated between 05/20/1991 and 09/01/2001) 12/06/1991 which merged into Wachovia Corp. (Ctfs. dated after 09/01/2001) 09/01/2001 which merged into Wells Fargo & Co. (New) 12/31/2008

PROVIDENT FINL GROUP INC / PFGI CAP CORP (MD)
Each Income Pride received (0.9764) share National City Corp. Common $4 par 8/17/2005

PROVIDENT FINL GROUP INC (OH)
Merged into National City Corp. 07/01/2004
Each share Common no par exchanged for (1.135) shares Common no par
National City Corp. acquired by PNC Financial Services Group, Inc. 12/31/2008

PROVIDENT HLDGS INC (NV)
Name changed to QMAC Energy Inc. 01/14/2004
(See QMAC Energy Inc.)

PROVIDENT HOUSE, INC. (NC)
Charter cancelled for failure to pay franchise taxes 4/13/70

PROVIDENT INSTN FOR SVGS TOWN BOSTON (BOSTON, MA)
Acquired by Hartford National Corp. 04/01/1986
Each share Common $1 par exchanged for $23.25 cash

PROVIDENT LIFE & ACC INS CO AMER (TN)
Reorganized 9/1/87
Capital Stock $25 par changed to $40 par 12/27/43
Capital Stock $40 par changed to $60 par in 1945
Capital Stock $60 par changed to $100 par in 1953
Each share Capital Stock $100 par exchanged for (14) shares Capital Stock $10 par to effect a (10) for (1) split and a 40% stock dividend 8/20/57
Each share Capital Stock $10 par exchanged for (3) shares Capital Stock $5 par to effect a (2) for (1) split and a 50% stock dividend 12/21/62
Capital Stock $5 par split (3) for (2) by issuance of (0.5) additional share 5/1/73
Capital Stock $5 par changed to $3 par and (2/3) additional share issued 5/1/74
Capital Stock $3 par changed to $1 par and (3) additional shares issued 5/10/85
Stock Dividend - 33-1/3% 11/8/68
Reorganized from Provident Life & Accident Insurance Co. to Provident Life & Accident Insurance Co. of America 9/1/87
Each share Capital Stock $1 par exchanged for (1) share Class B Common $1 par
Each share Class B Common $1 par received distribution of (0.25) share Class A Common $1 par 10/7/88
Merged into Provident Companies, Inc. 12/27/95
Each 8.10% Depositary Preferred share exchanged for (1) 8.10% Depositary Preferred share
Each share Class A Common $1 par exchanged for (1) share Common $1 par
Each share Class B Common $1 par exchanged for (1) share Common $1 par
Provident Companies, Inc. merged into UNUMProvident Corp. 6/30/99 which name changed to Unum Group 3/2/2007

PROVIDENT LIFE INS CO (ND)
Common $10 par and VTC's for Common $10 par changed to $2.50 par respectively and (3) additional shares issued 5/1/62
Stock Dividends - In Common & VTC's for Common - 100% 4/16/57; 33-1/3% 4/15/58; 10% 5/2/60; 10% 5/22/61; 10% 5/22/63; 10% 6/5/64; 10% 6/4/65; 10% 6/3/66; 10% 6/2/69; 10% 6/2/70
Merged into Equitable of Iowa Companies 11/3/78
Each share Common $2.50 par exchanged for $36 cash
Each VTC for Common $2.50 par exchanged for $36 cash

PROVIDENT MUT FD LTD (CANADA)
Special Shares $1 par reclassified as Mutual Fund Shares $1 par 03/02/1970
Name changed to Investors Dividend Fund Ltd. 02/27/1978

PROVIDENT NATL BK (PHILADELPHIA, PA)
Reorganized as Provident National Corp. 08/13/1969
Each share Capital Stock $12 par exchanged for (3) shares Common $1 par
Provident National Corp. merged into PNC Financial Corp. 01/19/1983 which name changed to PNC Bank Corp. 02/08/1993 which name changed to PNC Financial Services Group, Inc. 03/15/2000

PROVIDENT NATL CORP (PA)
Common $1 par changed to 50¢ par and (1) additional share issued 05/20/1982
Merged into PNC Financial Corp. 01/19/1983
Each share $1.80 Conv. Preferred $1 par exchanged for (1) share $1.80 Conv. Preferred Ser. A $1 par
Each share $1.80 Conv. Preferred 1971 Ser. $1 par exchanged for (1) share $1.80 Conv. Preferred Ser. B $1 par
Each share Common 50¢ par exchanged for (1) share Common $5 par
PNC Financial Corp. name changed to PNC Bank Corp. 02/08/1993 which name changed to PNC Financial Services Group, Inc. 03/15/2000

PROVIDENT NEW YORK BANCORP (DE)
Under plan of merger name changed to Sterling Bancorp 11/01/2013

PROVIDENT PHARMACEUTICAL CO. (TN)
Merged into Reid-Provident Laboratories Inc. 6/18/64
Each share Common $1 par exchanged for (1.64) shares Common $1 par
Reid-Provident Laboratories Inc. name changed to Reid-Rowell, Inc. 12/4/85
(See Reid-Rowell, Inc.)

PROVIDENT SAVINGS BANK & TRUST CO. (CINCINNATI, OH)
Name changed to Provident Bank (Cincinnati, Ohio) 3/31/59

PROVIDENT SECURITY LIFE INSURANCE CO. (AZ)
Merged into Continental Life & Accident Co. 6/14/67
Each share Common 25¢ par exchanged for (0.181818) share Common 50¢ par
(See Continental Life & Accident Co.)

PROVIDENT ST BK (PRESTON, MD)
Under plan of reorganization each share Common $10 par automatically became (1) share PSB Holding Corp. Common $10 par 10/31/96

PROVIDENT TRADESMENS BANK & TRUST CO. (PHILADELPHIA, PA)
Name changed to Provident National Bank (Philadelphia, PA) 11/12/1964
Provident National Bank (Philadelphia, PA) reorganized as Provident National Corp. 08/13/1969 which merged into PNC Financial Corp. 01/19/1983 which name changed to PNC Bank Corp. 02/08/1993 which name changed to PNC Financial Services Group, Inc. 03/15/2000

PROVIDENT TR II (DE)
10% Trust Preferred Securities called for redemption at $25 on 3/31/2005

PROVIDENT TUOLUMNE GOLD MINES, INC. (CA)
Merged into Celtor Chemical Corp. 05/14/1962
Each share Capital Stock 25¢ par exchanged for (0.005) share Common $10 par
(See Celtor Chemical Corp.)

PROVIDENT VENTURES CORP (AB)
Delisted from Alberta Stock Exchange 07/30/1999

PROVIDENTIAL CORP (DE)
Merged into WS Acquisition Corp. 11/16/94
Each share Common $0.0001 par exchanged for $4 cash

PROVIDENTIAL HLDGS INC (NV)
Name changed 02/09/2000
Name changed from Providential Securities Inc. to Providential Holdings Inc. 02/09/2000
Each share Common 4¢ par received distribution of (0.18479711) share ATC Technologies Corp. Common no par payable 07/27/2004 to holders of record 12/31/2003 Ex date - 12/29/2003
Name changed to PHI Group, Inc. and Common 4¢ par changed to $0.001 par 05/15/2009

PROVIDENTIAL INVESTMENT CORP. (TX)
Dissolved by Court Order 7/7/65

PROVIDENTMUTUAL FED MONEYFUND INC (DE)
Voluntarily dissolved 06/14/1991
Details not available

PROVIDENTMUTUAL GROWTH FD INC (DE)
Voluntarily dissolved 12/03/1993
Details not available

PROVIDENTMUTUAL INCOME SHS INC (DE)
Voluntarily dissolved 06/14/1991
Details not available

PROVIDENTMUTUAL INVT SHS INC (DE)
Voluntarily dissolved 12/03/1993
Details not available

PROVIDENTMUTUAL MONEYFUND INC (DE)
Ceased operations 01/09/1997
Details not available

PROVIDENTMUTUAL PA TAX FREE TR (PA)
Name changed to Sentinel Pennsylvania Tax-Free Trust 07/03/1992
Sentinel Pennsylvania Tax-Free Trust merged into Federated Municipal Securities Fund, Inc. 07/21/2006

PROVIDENTMUTUAL SPL FD INC (DE)
Ceased operations 10/08/1991
Details not available

PROVIDENTMUTUAL TAX FREE BD FD INC (DE)
Merged into Sentinel Group Funds, Inc. 03/01/1993
Each share Common $1 par received shares of Sentinel Common Stock Fund Class A 1¢ par on a net asset basis

PROVIDENTMUTUAL TAX FREE MONEYFUND INC (MD)
Voluntarily dissolved 09/25/1991
Details not available

PROVIDENTMUTUAL U S GOVT FD FOR INCOME INC (MD)
Ceased operations 01/09/1997
Details not available

PROVIDENTMUTUAL VALUE SHS INC (MD)
Ceased operations 01/09/1997
Details not available

PROVIDENTMUTUAL VENTURE SHS INC (DE)
Ceased operations 10/08/1991
Details not available

PROVIDENTMUTUAL WORLD FD INC (DE)
Ceased operations 01/09/1997
Details not available

PROVIDIAN BANCORP INC (DE)
Name changed to Providian Financial Corp. 05/30/1997
Providian Financial Corp. merged into Washington Mutual, Inc. 10/01/2005
(See Washington Mutual, Inc.)

PROVIDIAN CORP (DE)
Each share Common $1 par received distribution of (1) share Providian Financial Corp. Common 1¢ par payable 06/13/1997 to holders of record 06/10/1997
Merged into Aegon N.V. 06/10/1997
Each share Common $1 par exchanged for (0.434417) share Ordinary Reg. 2.50 Gldrs. par

PROVIDIAN FINL CORP (DE)
Common 1¢ par split (3) for (2) by issuance of (0.5) additional share payable 12/15/1998 to holders of record 12/01/1998 Ex date - 12/16/1998
Common 1¢ par split (2) for (1) by issuance of (1) additional share payable 11/30/2000 to holders of record 11/15/2000
Merged into Washington Mutual, Inc. 10/01/2005
Each share Common 1¢ par exchanged for (0.4005) share Common no par and $2 cash
(See Washington Mutual, Inc.)

PROVIDIAN LLC (TURKS & CAICOS ISLANDS)
Name changed to Commonwealth General LLC 11/24/1997
(See Commonwealth General LLC)

PROVIDOR GROWTH FD (DE)
Merged into Putnam Investors Fund, Inc. 02/03/1978
Each share Common $1 par exchanged for (1.0109269) shares Common $1 par

PROVIDOR INVS FD (DE)
Merged into Putnam Income Fund, Inc. 02/03/1978
Each share Common $1 par exchanged for (1.4156039) shares Common $1 par
Putnam Income Fund, Inc. name changed to Putnam Income Fund (New) 11/08/1982

PROVIGO INC NEW (QC)
1st Preferred Ser. 1 $25 par called for redemption 4/10/97
Acquired by Loblaw Companies Ltd. 12/10/98
Each share Common no par exchanged for either (0.27) share Common no par and $7.25 cash, (0.50226) share Common no par and $0.05 cash, or $15.62 cash
Note: Option to receive anything other than (0.27) share Common and $7.25 cash expired 2/5/99

PROVIGO INC OLD (QC)
Common no par split (4) for (1) by issuance of (3) additional shares 7/2/81
Common no par split (2) for (1) by issuance of (1) additional share 11/20/85
Common no par split (2) for (1) by issuance of (1) additional share 7/3/87
Name changed to Univa Inc. 5/22/92
Univa Inc. name changed to Provigo Inc. (New) 5/25/94 which was acquired by Loblaw Companies Ltd. 12/10/98

PROVIMI S A (FRANCE)
Acquired by Korofrance Capital 11/06/2009
Each Unsponsored ADR for Ordinary exchanged for $20.67 cash

PROVINCE HEALTHCARE CO (DE)
Common 1¢ par split (3) for (2) by issuance of (0.5) additional share payable 09/28/2000 to holders of record 09/15/2000 Ex date - 09/29/2000
Common 1¢ par split (3) for (2) by issuance of (0.5) additional share payable 04/30/2002 to holders of record 04/20/2002 Ex date - 05/01/2002
Merged into LifePoint Hospitals, Inc. 04/15/2005
Each share Common 1¢ par exchanged for (0.2917) share Common 1¢ par and $11.375 cash
LifePoint Hospitals, Inc. name changed to LifePoint Health, Inc. 05/12/2015

PROVINCES X EXPL LTD (CANADA)
Merged into Laduboro Oil Ltd.-Les Petroles Laduboro Ltee. 12/28/1984
Each share Capital Stock no par exchanged for (1.5) shares Capital Stock $1 par
Laduboro Oil Ltd.-Les Petroles Laduboro Ltee. name changed to Laduboro Enterprises Ltd.-Les Entreprises Laduboro Ltee. 07/04/1985 which recapitalized as Laduboro Ltd. 06/02/1987 which reorganized as Monterey Capital Inc. 11/30/1989 which merged into Nymox Pharmaceutical Corp. (Canada) 12/18/1995 which reincorporated in Bahamas 11/20/2015

PROVINCETOWN BOSTON AIRL INC (MA)
Plan of reorganization under Chapter 11 Federal Bankruptcy proceedings confirmed 05/03/1986
No stockholders' equity

PROVINCIAL BANK OF CANADA (OLD) (MONTREAL, QUE)
See - Banque Provinciale du Canada (Montreal, Que.) (Old)

PROVINCIAL BANK OF CANADA NEW (MONTREAL, QUE)
See - Banque Provinciale du Canada (Montreal, Que.) (New)

PROVINCIAL DEVELOPMENT, LTD.
Struck off register and declared dissolved for failure to file returns 11/17/32

PROVINCIAL HOUSE INC (DE)
Stock Dividend - 10% 10/11/1971
Merged into Proco Management, Inc. 12/21/1979
Each share Common no par exchanged for $3.75 cash

PROVINCIAL MNG & DEV LTD (ON)
Dissolved 01/00/1974
Each share Capital Stock no par exchanged for first and final distribution of $0.0125 cash

PROVINCIAL MOLYBDENUM CORP. LTD. (QC)
Out of business in 1960
No stockholders' equity

PROVINCIAL TRANSPORT CO. (QC)
5% Preferred $50 par called 12/31/63
Public interest eliminated

PROVINI C R FINL SVCS CORP (BC)
Recapitalized as DataWave Vending Inc. 01/24/1994
Each share Common no par exchanged for (0.2) share Common no par
DataWave Vending Inc. name changed to DataWave Systems Inc. (BC) 01/15/1997 which reincorporated in Yukon 09/19/2000 which reincorporated in Delaware 02/23/2005
(See DataWave Systems Inc.)

PROVO GAS PRODUCERS LTD. (AB)
Acquired by Dome Petroleum Ltd. 06/28/1967
Each share Capital Stock no par exchanged changed for (0.125) share Capital Stock $2.50 par
(See Dome Petroleum Ltd.)

PROVO INTL INC (DE)
Each share old Common 1¢ par exchanged for (0.16666666) share new Common 1¢ par 01/30/2004
Recapitalized as Ebenefitsdirect, Inc. 03/23/2007
Each share new Common 1¢ par exchanged for (0.005) share Common 1¢ par
Ebenefitsdirect, Inc. recapitalized as Seraph Security, Inc. 12/02/2008 which name changed to Commerce Online, Inc. 06/18/2009 which name changed to Cannabis Medical Solutions, Inc. 03/04/2010 which name changed to MediSwipe Inc. 07/08/2011 which name changed to Agritek Holdings, Inc. 05/20/2014

PROVO MINING CO.
Merged into Eureka Lilly Consolidated Mining Co. 00/00/1937
Each share exchanged for (0.426603) share Common 10¢ par
Eureka Lilly Consolidated Mining Co. merged into Eureka Standard Consolidated Mining Co. 11/25/1974 which merged into South Standard Mining Co. 07/29/1983 which merged into Chief Consolidated Mining Co. 07/01/1996
(See Chief Consolidated Mining Co.)

PROXICOM INC (DE)
Issue Information - 4,500,000 shares COM offered at $13 per share on 04/19/1999
Common 1¢ par split (2) for (1) by issuance of (1) additional share payable 2/24/2000 to holders of record 2/9/2000
Merged into Dimension Data Holdings PLC 6/20/2001
Each share Common 1¢ par exchanged for $7.50 cash

PROXIM CORP (DE)
Each share old Class A Common 1¢ par exchanged for (0.1) share new Class A Common 1¢ par 10/25/2004
Assets sold for the benefit of creditors 07/27/2005
No stockholders' equity

PROXIM INC (DE)
Issue Information - 2,000,000 shares COM offered at $9 per share on 12/15/1993
Merged into Proxim Corp. 3/26/2002
Each share Common $0.001 par exchanged for (1.8896) shares Class A Common 1¢ par
(See Proxim Corp.)

PROXIMA CORP (DE)
Merged into BD Acquisition Corp. 4/14/98
Each share Common $0.001 par exchanged for $11 cash

PROXIMITY MANUFACTURING CO.
Merged into Cone Mills Corp. in 1948
Each share Common $1 par exchanged for (3) shares Common $10 par
(See Cone Mills Corp.)

PROXITY DIGITAL NETWORKS INC (NV)
Name changed to Proxity, Inc. 01/14/2005
Proxity, Inc. recapitalized as CAVU Resources Inc. 05/06/2009

PROXITY INC (NV)
Recapitalized as CAVU Resources Inc. 05/06/2009
Each share Common $0.001 par exchanged for (0.004) share Common $0.001 par

PROXYMED INC (FL)
Name changed 07/01/1994
Name changed from Proxymed Pharmacy, Inc. to ProxyMed, Inc. 07/01/1994
Old Common $0.001 par split (3) for (2) by issuance of (0.5) additional share payable 07/08/1996 to holders of record 06/24/1996
Each share old Common $0.001 par exchanged for (0.06666666) share new Common $0.001 par 08/21/2001
Plan of reorganization under Chapter 11 Federal Bankruptcy proceedings effective 07/27/2009
No stockholders' equity

PRT FST REGENERATION INCOME FD (BC)
Reorganized under the laws of Canada as PRT Growing Services Ltd. 10/06/2011
Each Trust Unit no par exchanged for (1) share Common no par
(See PRT Growing Services Ltd.)

PRT GROUP INC (DE)
Name changed to Enherent Corp. 7/13/2000

PRT GROWING SVCS LTD (CANADA)
Acquired by Mill Road Capital, L.P. 12/19/2012

Each share Common no par exchanged for $4.45 cash
Note: Unexchanged certificates were cancelled and became without value 12/19/2017

PRUDENCE-BONDS CORP. (NY)
Advised stock valueless 3/28/56
Proclaimed dissolved by the New York Secretary of State 12/15/59

PRUDENCE CO., INC.
Reorganized for purposes of liquidation in 1939
No stockholders' equity

PRUDENT REAL ESTATE TR (NY)
Name changed 05/26/1971
Shares of Bene. Int. $1 par split (2) for (1) by issuance of (1) additional share 04/22/1969
Name changed from Prudent Resources Trust to Prudent Real Estate Trust 05/26/1971
Merged into Johncamp Realty Inc. 12/10/1979
Each Share of Bene. Int. $1 par exchanged for $7 cash

PRUDENT SPECULATOR FD (MA)
Name changed to Pathfinder Trust and Leverage Fund no par reclassified as Pathfinder Fund no par 01/29/1997
(See Pathfinder Trust)

PRUDENTIAL ALLOCATION FD (MA)
Strategy Portfolio Class A 1¢ par reclassified as Balanced Portfolio Class A 1¢ par 07/25/1997
Strategy Portfolio Class B 1¢ par reclassified as Balanced Portfolio Class B 1¢ par 07/25/1997
Strategy Portfolio Class C 1¢ par reclassified as Balanced Portfolio Class C 1¢ par 07/25/1997
Strategy Portfolio Class Z 1¢ par reclassified as Balanced Portfolio Class Z 1¢ par 07/25/1997
Name changed to Prudential Balanced Fund and Balanced Portfolio Class A 1¢ par, Class B 1¢ par, Class C 1¢ par, and Class Z 1¢ par reclassified as Class A 1¢ par, Class B 1¢ par, Class C 1¢ par, or Class Z 1¢ par respectively 07/25/1997
Prudential Balanced Fund merged into Prudential Investment Portfolios, Inc. 11/10/2000

PRUDENTIAL BACHE EQUITY FD INC (MA)
Common 1¢ par reclassified as Class B 1¢ par 01/22/1990
Name changed to Prudential Equity Fund, Inc. 12/06/1993
Prudential Equity Fund, Inc. name changed to Strategic Partners Equity Fund, Inc. 06/27/2003 which name changed to Jennison Blend Fund, Inc. 03/23/2005

PRUDENTIAL BACHE FLEXIFUND (MA)
Name changed to Prudential FlexiFund 03/15/1991
Prudential FlexiFund name changed to Prudential Allocation Fund 07/28/1994 which name changed to Prudential Balanced Fund 07/25/1997 which merged into Prudential Investment Portfolios, Inc. 11/10/2000

PRUDENTIAL BACHE GLOBAL FD INC (MD)
Common 1¢ par split (2) for (1) by issuance of (1) additional share 05/15/1986
Common 1¢ par reclassified as Class B 1¢ par 01/22/1990
Name changed to Prudential Global Fund, Inc. 12/30/1991
Prudential Global Fund, Inc. name changed to Prudential World Fund, Inc. 07/03/1992

PRUDENTIAL BACHE GLOBAL GENESIS FD INC (MD)
Common 1¢ par reclassified as Class B 1¢ par 01/22/1990
Name changed to Prudential Global Genesis Fund, Inc. 03/15/1991
Prudential Global Genesis Fund, Inc. merged into Prudential World Fund, Inc. 05/30/2001

PRUDENTIAL BACHE GLOBAL NAT RES FD INC (MD)
Common 1¢ par reclassified as Class B 1¢ par 01/22/1990
Name changed to Prudential Global Natural Resources Fund, Inc. 03/15/1991
Prudential Global Natural Resources Fund, Inc. name changed to Prudential Natural Resources Fund, Inc. 07/10/1996 which name changed to Jennison Natural Resources Fund, Inc. 07/07/2003

PRUDENTIAL BACHE GOVT PLUS FD INC (MD)
Common 1¢ par reclassified as Class B 1¢ par 01/22/1990
Name changed to Prudential Government Income Fund, Inc. 07/03/1992
Prudential Government Income Fund, Inc. name changed to Dryden Government Income Fund, Inc. 06/30/2003

PRUDENTIAL BACHE GROWTH OPPORTUNITY FD INC (MD)
Name changed to Prudential Growth Opportunity Fund Inc. 03/15/1991
Prudential Growth Opportunity Fund Inc. name changed to Prudential Small Companies Fund, Inc. 05/30/1996 which name changed to Jennison Small Company Fund, Inc. 11/25/2003

PRUDENTIAL BACHE HIGH YIELD FD INC (MD)
Common 1¢ par reclassified as Class B 1¢ par 01/22/1990
Name changed to Prudential High Yield Fund, Inc. 06/03/1992
Prudential High Yield Fund, Inc. name changed to Dryden High Yield Fund, Inc. 09/15/2003

PRUDENTIAL BACHE MUN BD FD (MA)
Name changed to Prudential Municipal Bond Fund 05/27/1991
Prudential Municipal Bond Fund name changed to Dryden Municipal Bond Fund 07/07/2003

PRUDENTIAL BACHE NEW DECADE GROWTH FD INC (MD)
Name changed to Prudential-Bache Growth Opportunity Fund, Inc. 06/00/1985
Prudential-Bache Growth Opportunity Fund, Inc. name changed to Prudential Growth Opportunity Fund Inc. 03/15/1991 which name changed to Prudential Small Companies Fund, Inc. 05/30/1996 which name changed to Jennison Small Company Fund, Inc. 11/25/2003

PRUDENTIAL BACHE OPT GROWTH FD INC (MD)
Common 1¢ par reclassifed as Class B 1¢ par 01/22/1990
Name changed to Prudential Option Growth Fund, Inc. 03/15/1991
(See Prudential Option Growth Fund, Inc.)

PRUDENTIAL BACHE RESH FD INC (MD)
Name changed 10/30/1991
Common 1¢ par reclassified as Class B 1¢ par 01/22/1990
Name changed from Prudential-Bache Research, Inc. to Prudential-Bache Research Fund, Inc. 10/30/1991

Name changed to Prudential Growth Fund, Inc. 04/30/1992
Prudential Growth Fund, Inc. name changed to Prudential Strategist Fund, Inc. 08/01/1994
(See Prudential Strategist Fund, Inc.)

PRUDENTIAL BACHE STRATEGIC INCOME FD INC (MD)
Name changed to Prudential Strategic Income Fund, Inc. (New) 03/15/1991
(See Prudential Strategic Income Fund, Inc. (New))

PRUDENTIAL-BACHE TELECOMMUNICATIONS FUND, INC. (MD)
Name changed to Prudential-Bache Government Plus Fund, Inc. 01/27/1985
Prudential-Bache Government Plus Fund, Inc. name changed to Prudential Government Income Fund, Inc. 07/03/1992 which name changed to Dryden Government Income Fund, Inc. 06/30/2003

PRUDENTIAL BALANCED FD (MA)
Merged into Prudential Investment Portfolios, Inc. 11/10/2000
Each share Class A exchanged for Active Balanced Fund Class A 1¢ par on a net asset basis
Each share Class B exchanged for Active Balanced Fund Class B 1¢ par on a net asset basis
Each share Class C exchanged for Active Balanced Fund Class C 1¢ par on a net asset basis
Each share Class Z exchanged for Active Balanced Fund Class Z 1¢ par on a net asset basis

PRUDENTIAL BANCORP INC PA (PA)
Reorganized as Prudential Bancorp, Inc. 10/10/2013
Each share Common 1¢ par exchanged for (0.9442) share Common 1¢ par

PRUDENTIAL BANCORPORATION (WA)
Common 10¢ par changed to no par 01/16/1986
Stock Dividends - 10% 05/23/1986; 10% 05/26/1987
Acquired by Pacific First Financial Corp. 04/11/1988
Each share Common no par exchanged for $32 cash

PRUDENTIAL BK F S B (SEATTLE, WA)
Reorganized as Prudential Bancorporation 04/30/1985
Each share Common $5 par exchanged for (1) share Common 10¢ par
(See Prudential Bancorporation)

PRUDENTIAL BLDG MAINTENANCE CORP (DE)
Common 10¢ par split (2) for (1) by issuance of (1) additional share 4/12/68
Common 10¢ par split (3) for (2) by issuance of (0.5) additional share 12/10/69
Name changed to ISS International Service System, Inc. 9/10/82
(See ISS International Service System, Inc.)

PRUDENTIAL CORP.
Dissolved in 1940

PRUDENTIAL CORP PLC (ENGLAND & WALES)
Sponsored ADR's for Ordinary 25p par changed to 5p par and (4) additional ADR's issued 05/26/1988
Name changed to Prudential PLC 10/01/1999

PRUDENTIAL DISCOUNT CORP. (TX)
Charter forfeited for failure to pay taxes 7/1/60

PRUDENTIAL EMERGING GROWTH FD (MD)
Name changed to Prudential U.S. Emerging Growth Fund, Inc. 06/29/2000
Prudential U.S. Emerging Growth Fund, Inc. name changed to Jennison U.S. Emerging Growth Fund, Inc. 07/07/2003 which name changed to Jennison Mid-Cap Growth Fund, Inc. 03/19/2007

PRUDENTIAL ENERGY CO (DE)
Charter cancelled and declared inoperative and void for non-payment of taxes 4/18/89

PRUDENTIAL ENERGY INCOME FUND 1983 P-3 (TX)
Merged into Parker & Parsley Acquisition Co. 12/22/1993
Details not available

PRUDENTIAL EQUITY FD INC (MA)
Name changed to Strategic Partners Equity Fund, Inc. 06/27/2003
Strategic Partners Equity Fund, Inc. name changed to Jennison Blend Fund, Inc. 03/23/2005

PRUDENTIAL EQUITY INCOME FD (MA)
Name changed 03/12/1991
Name changed from Prudential-Bache Equity Income Fund to Prudential Equity Income Fund 03/12/1991
Name changed to Prudential Value Fund 09/15/2000
Prudential Value Fund name changed to Jennison Value Fund 07/07/2003 which name changed to JennisonDryden Portfolios 10/09/2007

PRUDENTIAL FD BOSTON INC (MA)
Merged into Boston Mutual Fund, Inc. 12/31/74
Each share Capital Stock $1 par exchanged for (5.1509) shares Common $1 par
(See Boston Mutual Fund, Inc.)

PRUDENTIAL FED SVGS & LN ASSN (USA)
Under plan of acquisition each share Common $1 par automatically became (1) share Prudential Financial Services Corp. Common $1 par 03/01/1983
Prudential Financial Services Corp. name changed to Olympus Capital Corp. 08/01/1988 which was acquired by Washington Mutual Inc. 04/28/1995
(See Washington Mutual, Inc.)

PRUDENTIAL FINANCE CORP. LTD. (ON)
Adjudicated bankrupt 12/5/66
No stockholders' equity

PRUDENTIAL FINANCE CORP. OF AMERICA (DE)
Recapitalized as Prudential Enterprises, Inc. 12/24/57
Each share Class A 1¢ par exchanged for (1) share Common 1¢ par
Each share Common 10¢ par exchanged for (0.2) share Preferred $1 par

PRUDENTIAL FINL INC (NJ)
Each 6.75% Equity Security Unit received (1.47) shares Common 1¢ par 11/15/2004
(Additional Information in Active)

PRUDENTIAL FINL SVCS CORP (UT)
Name changed to Olympus Capital Corp. 08/01/1988
Olympus Capital Corp. acquired by Washington Mutual Inc. 04/28/1995
(See Washington Mutual, Inc.)

PRUDENTIAL FLEXIFUND (MA)
Name changed to Prudential Allocation Fund and Conservatively Managed Portfolio Class A 1¢ par,

Class B 1¢ par, and Class C 1¢ par reclassified as Balanced Portfolio Class A 1¢ par, Class B 1¢ par, or Class C 1¢ par respectively 07/28/1994
Prudential Allocation Fund name changed to Prudential Balanced Fund 07/25/1997 which merged into Prudential Investment Portfolios, Inc. 11/10/2000

PRUDENTIAL FUNDS, INC. (DE)
Common 10¢ par split (3) for (2) by issuance of (0.5) additional share 12/23/69
Each share Common 10¢ par exchanged for (0.3) share Common 33-1/3¢ par 3/21/73
Name changed to Prudential Group, Inc. 11/25/75

PRUDENTIAL GLOBAL FD INC (MD)
Name changed to Prudential World Fund, Inc. and Class A 1¢ par, Class B 1¢ par, Class C 1¢ par, and Class Z 1¢ par reclassified as Global Growth Fund Class A 1¢ par, Class B 1¢ par or Class C 1¢ par or Class Z 1¢ par respectively 07/03/1992

PRUDENTIAL GLOBAL GENESIS FD INC (MD)
Merged into Prudential World Fund, Inc. 05/30/2001
Each share Class A 1¢ par exchanged for Global Growth Fund Class A 1¢ par on a net asset basis
Each share Class B 1¢ par exchanged for Global Growth Fund Class B 1¢ par on a net asset basis
Each share Class C 1¢ par exchanged for Global Growth Fund Class C 1¢ par on a net asset basis
Each share Class Z 1¢ par exchanged for Global Growth Fund Class Z 1¢ par on a net asset basis

PRUDENTIAL GLOBAL NAT RES FD INC (MD)
Name changed to Prudential Natural Resources Fund, Inc. 07/10/1996
Prudential Natural Resources Fund, Inc. name changed to Jennison Natural Resources Fund, Inc. 07/07/2003

PRUDENTIAL GLOBAL SHORT DURATION HIGH YIELD FD INC (MD)
Name changed to PGIM Global Short Duration High Yield Fund, Inc. 06/11/2018

PRUDENTIAL GLOBAL TOTAL RETURN FD INC (MD)
Name changed to Dryden Global Total Return Fund, Inc. 07/07/2003

PRUDENTIAL GOLD MINING CO. (NV)
Charter revoked for failure to file reports and pay fees 3/3/24

PRUDENTIAL GOVT INCOME FD INC (MD)
Name changed 08/01/1994
Name changed from Prudential Government Plus Fund to Prudential Government Income Fund, Inc. 08/01/1994
Name changed to Dryden Government Income Fund, Inc. 06/30/2003

PRUDENTIAL GROUP INC (DE)
Name changed 11/25/1975
Each share Common 10¢ par exchanged for (0.3) share Common 33-1/3¢ par 03/21/1973
Name changed from Prudential Funds Inc. to Prudential Group, Inc. 11/25/1975
Filed a petition under Chapter 11 Federal Bankruptcy Code 04/26/1984
Stockholders' equity unlikely

PRUDENTIAL GROWTH FD INC (MD)
Name changed to Prudential Strategist Fund, Inc. 08/01/1994

(See Prudential Strategist Fund, Inc.)

PRUDENTIAL GROWTH OPPORTUNITY FD INC (MD)
Class A Common 1¢ par split (3) for (2) by issuance of (0.5) additional share 09/20/1993
Class B Common 1¢ par split (3) for (2) by issuance of (0.5) additional share 09/20/1993
Name changed to Prudential Small Companies Fund, Inc. 05/23/1996
Prudential Small Companies Fund, Inc. name changed to Jennison Small Company Fund, Inc. 11/25/2003

PRUDENTIAL HIGH YIELD FD INC (MD)
Name changed to Dryden High Yield Fund, Inc. 09/15/2003

PRUDENTIAL INCOMEVERTIBLE FD INC (MD)
Name changed 03/15/1991
Name changed 08/17/1992
Name changed from Prudential-Bache IncomeVertible Plus Fund, Inc. to Prudential IncomeVertible Plus Fund, Inc. 03/15/1991
Name changed from Prudential IncomeVertible Plus Fund, Inc. to Prudential IncomeVertible Fund, Inc. 08/17/1992
Charter forfeited 10/06/1998

PRUDENTIAL INDUSTRIES, INC. (PA)
Name changed to Atlas Chain & Precision Products Co., Inc. 12/31/63
(See Atlas Chain & Precision Products Co., Inc.)

PRUDENTIAL INDUSTRIES, INC. (TX)
Merged into Satellite Systems Corp. 2/8/71
Each share Common no par exchanged for (3) shares Common no par
Satellite Systems Corp. charter cancelled 5/8/72

PRUDENTIAL INTER GLOBAL INCOME FD INC (MD)
Name changed 10/07/1991
Under plan of reorganization name changed from Prudential Intermediate Income Fund, Inc. to Prudential Intermediate Global Income Fund, Inc. and Common 1¢ par reclassifed as Class A 1¢ par 10/07/1991
Merged into Prudential Global Total Return Fund, Inc. 10/22/1999
Each share Class A 1¢ par exchanged for Class A 1¢ par on a net asset basis
Each share Class B 1¢ par exchanged for Class B 1¢ par on a net asset basis
Each share Class C 1¢ par exchanged for Class C 1¢ par on a net asset basis
Each share Class Z 1¢ par exchanged for Class Z 1¢ par on a net asset basis
Prudential Global Total Return Fund, Inc. name changed to Dryden Global Total Return Fund, Inc. 07/07/2003

PRUDENTIAL INTL BD FD INC (MD)
Merged into Prudential Global Total Return Fund, Inc. 05/04/2001
Each share Class A 1¢ par exchanged for Class A 1¢ par on a net asset basis
Each share Class B 1¢ par exchanged for Class B 1¢ par on a net asset basis
Each share Class C 1¢ par exchanged for Class C 1¢ par on a net asset basis
Each share Class Z 1¢ par exchanged for Class Z 1¢ par on a net asset basis
Prudential Global Total Return Fund,

Inc. name changed to Dryden Global Total Return Fund, Inc. 07/07/2003

PRUDENTIAL INVESTING CORP.
Acquired by Axe-Houghton Fund, Inc. on a (0.568) for (1) basis 02/14/1947
Axe-Houghton Fund, Inc. name changed to Axe-Houghton Fund A, Inc. (DE) (New) 02/23/1961 which reincorporated in Maryland 00/00/1973 which name changed to Axe-Houghton Income Fund, Inc. 09/24/1976 which reorganized as Axe-Houghton Funds, Inc. Income Fund 10/31/1990
(See Axe-Houghton Funds, Inc.)

PRUDENTIAL INVESTORS, INC.
Liquidation completed in 1943

PRUDENTIAL JENNISON FD INC (MD)
Name changed to Prudential Investment Portfolios, Inc. 05/29/1998

PRUDENTIAL LOAN CORP. (DE)
Assets sold to Guardian Consumer Finance Corp. in 1956
Each (3.5) shares 6% Preferred $10 par exchanged for (1) share 60¢ Preferred $10 par
Each share Class A $1 par or Class B 10¢ par exchanged for (0.1) share Class A Common $1 par
Guardian Consumer Finance Corp. merged into Liberty Loan Corp. 4/4/60 which name changed to LLC Corp. 3/14/80 which name changed to Valhi, Inc. 3/10/87

PRUDENTIAL MINERALS EXPLS CO (DE)
Name changed to Del Mar Petroleum, Inc. 12/16/1971
Del Mar Petroleum, Inc. merged into Shenandoah Oil Corp. 05/31/1973
(See Shenandoah Oil Corp.)

PRUDENTIAL MINING CO. OF CANADA LTD. (ON)
Merged into Resource Exploration & Development Co. Ltd. 6/11/68
Each share Capital Stock $1 par exchanged for (0.082644) share Capital Stock no par
Resource Exploration & Development Co. Ltd. charter cancelled 5/13/80

PRUDENTIAL MUN BD FD (MA)
Modified Term Series Class A 1¢ par reclassified as Intermediate Series Class A 1¢ par 06/29/1995
Modified Term Series Class B 1¢ par reclassified as Intermediate Series Class B 1¢ par 06/29/1995
Modified Term Series Class C 1¢ par reclassified as Intermediate Series Class C 1¢ par 06/29/1995
High Yield Series Class A 1¢ par reclassified as High Income Series Class A 1¢ par 06/23/1998
High Yield Series Class B 1¢ par reclassified as High Income Series Class B 1¢ par 06/23/1998
High Yield Series Class C 1¢ par reclassified as High Income Series Class C 1¢ par 06/23/1998
Under plan of reorganization each share Intermediate Series Class A 1¢ par, Class B 1¢ par, or Class C 1¢ par automatically became (1) share Prudential National Municipals Fund, Inc. Class A 1¢ par, Class B 1¢ par, or Class C 1¢ par respectively 01/14/1999
(See Prudential National Municipals Fund, Inc.)
Name changed to Dryden Municipal Bond Fund, Inc. 07/07/2003

PRUDENTIAL NAT RES FD INC (MD)
Name changed to Jennison Natural Resources Fund, Inc. 07/07/2003

PRUDENTIAL NATL MUNS FD INC (MD)
Name changed 06/02/1992
Name changed from

Prudential-Bache National Municipals Fund, Inc. to Prudential National Municipals Fund, Inc. 06/02/1992
Name changed to Dryden National Municipals Fund, Inc. 08/27/2003

PRUDENTIAL OPT GROWTH FD INC (MD)
Dissolved 03/23/1993
Details not available

PRUDENTIAL PERSONAL FINANCE CORP.
Name changed to Prudential United Corp. in 1947

PRUDENTIAL PETROLEUM CORP. (DE)
Each share Common 10¢ par exchanged for (0.1) share Common $1 par 5/7/57
Name changed to Intercon Development Corp. 5/18/60
Intercon Development Corp. acquired by United Improvement & Investing Corp. 5/24/63 which name changed to U.I.P. Corp. 5/7/68 which merged into Eastmet Corp. 12/20/79
(See Eastmet Corp.)

PRUDENTIAL PETROLEUMS LTD. (BC)
Recapitalized as New Prudential Petroleums Ltd. 04/06/1965
Each share Capital Stock $1 par exchanged for (0.25) share Capital Stock $1 par
New Prudential Petroleums Ltd. name changed to Consolidated Prudential Mines Ltd. 12/23/1965 which merged into Davenport Oil & Mining Ltd. 02/29/1972 which name changed to Davenport Industries Ltd. 11/01/1973 which recapitalized as DVO Industries Ltd. 08/19/1991
(See DVO Industries Ltd.)

PRUDENTIAL REAL ESTATE TRUST (NY)
Ctfs. of Bene. Int. $1 par split (3) for (2) by issuance of (0.5) additional share 4/22/68
Name changed to Prudent Resources Trust 5/1/68
Prudent Resources Trust name changed to Prudent Real Estate Trust 5/26/71
(See Prudent Real Estate Trust)

PRUDENTIAL RLTY ACQUISITION FD L P (DE)
Completely liquidated 08/11/1997
Details not available

PRUDENTIAL RLTY TR (MA)
Completely liquidated
Each Income Share of Bene. Int. 1¢ par exchanged for first and final distribution of $5.30 cash 12/1/95

PRUDENTIAL REFINING CORP.
Acquired by Marland Oil Co.
(See Marland Oil Co.)

PRUDENTIAL REINS HLDGS INC (DE)
Issue Information - 44,000,000 shares COM offered at $16.75 per share on 10/02/1995
Name changed to Everest Reinsurance Holdings, Inc. 5/28/96
Everest Reinsurance Holdings, Inc. merged into Everest Re Group, Ltd. 2/23/2000

PRUDENTIAL RES INC (NV)
Name changed back to Acme International Corp. 8/13/91
Acme International Corp. name changed to Beckett Industries Inc. 10/5/94 which name changed to International Supercell Ltd. 5/11/95 which name changed to Bargaincity.com, Inc. 3/25/99
(See Bargaincity.com, Inc.)

PRUDENTIAL SHORT DURATION HIGH YIELD FD INC (MD)
Name changed to PGIM Short

Duration High Yield Fund, Inc. 06/11/2018

PRUDENTIAL SMALL COS FD INC (MD)
Name changed to Jennison Small Company Fund, Inc. 11/25/2003

PRUDENTIAL STL LTD (AB)
Common no par split (3) for (1) by issuance of (2) additional shares payable 11/28/97 to holders of record 11/25/97
Merged into Maverick Tube (Canada) Ltd. 9/22/2000
Each share Common no par exchanged for (0.52) Exchangeable Share
Maverick Tube (Canada) Ltd. exchanged for Maverick Tube Corp. 9/30/2005
(See Maverick Tube Corp.)

PRUDENTIAL STRATEGIC INCOME FD INC NEW (MD)
Merged into Prudential Intermediate Global Income Fund, Inc. 00/00/1992
Details not available

PRUDENTIAL STRATEGIC INCOME FD INC OLD (MD)
Name changed to Prudential-Bache Strategic Income Fund, Inc. and Common 1¢ par reclassified as Class A Common $0.001 par 09/04/1990
Prudential-Bache Strategic Income Fund, Inc. name changed to Prudential Strategic Income Fund, Inc. (New) 03/15/1991
(See Prudential Strategic Income Fund, Inc. (New))

PRUDENTIAL STRATEGIST FD (MD)
Charter forfeited 10/06/1998

PRUDENTIAL TRADING TRUST
Acquired by Prudential Investing Corp. 00/00/1936
Details not available

PRUDENTIAL U S EMERGING GROWTH FD INC (MD)
Name changed to Jennison U.S. Emerging Growth Fund, Inc. 07/07/2003
Jennison U.S. Emerging Growth Fund, Inc. name changed to Jennison Mid-Cap Growth Fund, Inc. 03/19/2007

PRUDENTIAL U S GOVT FD (MA)
Name changed 10/23/1989
Name changed 01/20/1992
Name changed from Prudential-Bache Government Plus Fund II to Prudential-Bache U.S. Government Fund 10/23/1989
Common 1¢ par reclassified as Class B 1¢ par 01/22/1990
Name changed from Prudential-Bache U.S. Government Fund to Prudential U.S. Government Fund 01/20/1992
Trust terminated 10/21/1996
Details not available

PRUDENTIAL VALUE FD (MA)
Name changed to Jennison Value Fund 07/07/2003
Jennison Value Fund name changed to JennisonDryden Portfolios 10/09/2007

PRUETT-SCHAEFFER CHEMICAL CO.
Merged into Hachmeister-Lind Co. in 1930 which became bankrupt in 1935

PRUFCOAT LABORATORIES, INC. (MA)
Acquired by Hooker Chemical Corp. 9/22/64
Each (2.75) shares Common $1 par exchanged for (1) share Common $5 par
Hooker Chemical Corp. acquired by Occidental Petroleum Corp. (Calif.) 7/24/68
(See Occidental Petroleum Corp. (Calif.))

PRUGH PETROLEUM CO. (OK)
Merged into Livingston Oil Co. 9/1/56
Each share Common $5 par exchanged for (1.56) shares Common 10¢ par
Livingston Oil Co. name changed to LVO Corp. 9/24/69 which merged into Utah International Inc. 10/31/74 which merged into General Electric Co. 12/20/76

PRUMO LOGISTICA S A (BRAZIL)
Each old Sponsored ADR for Ordinary exchanged for (0.1) new Sponsored ADR for Ordinary 12/21/2015
ADR agreement terminated 10/25/2018
Each new Sponsored ADR for Ordinary exchanged for $3.064372 cash

PRWW LTD (DE)
Name changed to eResearchTechnology, Inc. 04/27/2001
(See eResearchTechnology, Inc.)

PRYME ENERGY LTD (AUSTRALIA)
Each old Sponsored ADR for Ordinary exchanged for (0.1) new Sponsored ADR for Ordinary 06/24/2013
Basis changed from (1:10) to (1:100) 06/24/2013
Each new Sponsored ADR for Ordinary exchanged again for (0.33333333) new Sponsored ADR for Ordinary 06/24/2014
Basis changed from (1:100) to (1:300) 06/24/2014
Basis changed from (1:300) to (1:30) 05/24/2016
Name changed to Indago Energy Ltd. 06/10/2016

PRYME ENERGY RES LTD (BC)
Recapitalized as Newjay Resources Ltd. 08/23/1985
Each share Common no par exchanged for (0.4) share Common no par
Newjay Resources Ltd. recapitalized as Consolidated Newjay Resources Ltd. 08/25/1993 which name changed to Indo-Pacific Energy Ltd. (BC) 05/09/1995 which reincorporated in Yukon 10/15/1997 which name changed to Austral Pacific Energy Ltd. (YT) 01/02/2004 which reincorporated in British Columbia 10/16/2006
(See Austral Pacific Energy Ltd.)

PRYME OIL & GAS LTD (AUSTRALIA)
Sponsored ADR's for Ordinary split (2) for (1) by issuance of (1) additional ADR payable 06/15/2007 to holders of record 06/14/2007
Ex date - 06/18/2007
Basis changed from (1:20) to (1:10) 06/15/2007
Name changed to Pryme Energy Ltd. 07/01/2011
Pryme Energy Ltd. name changed to Indago Energy Ltd. 06/10/2016

PRYNE & CO., INC. (DE)
Merged into Emerson Electric Manufacturing Co. on a (1) for (4.225) basis 4/1/57
Emerson Electric Manufacturing Co. name changed to Emerson Electric Co. 2/6/64

PRYOR MANUFACTURING CO. (DE)
Completely liquidated 6/22/60
Each share Common $1 par exchanged for first and final distribution of $6.425 cash

PS BUSINESS PKS INC (CA)
9.25% Depositary Preferred Ser. A called for redemption at $25 plus $0.19271 accrued dividends on 04/30/2004
9.5% Depositary Preferred Ser. D called for redemption at $25 plus $0.25729 accrued dividends on 05/10/2006
8.75% Depositary Preferred Ser. F called for redemption at $25 plus $0.17014 accrued dividends on 01/29/2007
7.95% Depositary Preferred Ser. K called for redemption at $25 plus $0.36438 accrued dividends on 06/07/2010
7.6% Depositary Preferred Ser. L called for redemption at $25 plus $0.19528 accrued dividends on 11/08/2010
7.375% Depositary Preferred Ser. O called for redemption at $25 plus $0.2151 accrued dividends on 02/13/2012
7.2% Depositary Preferred Ser. M called for redemption at $25 plus $0.23 accrued dividends on 02/17/2012
6.875% Depositary Preferred Ser. I called for redemption at $25 plus $0.3533 accrued dividends on 06/15/2012
7% Depositary Preferred Ser. H called for redemption at $25 plus $0.35972 accrued dividends on 06/15/2012
6.7% Depositary Preferred Ser. P called for redemption at $25 plus $0.037222 accrued dividends on 10/09/2012
6.875% Depositary Preferred Ser. R called for redemption at $25 plus $0.06684 accrued dividends on 10/15/2015
6.45% Depositary Preferred Ser. S called for redemption at $25 plus $0.07615 accrued dividends on 01/18/2017
6% Depositary Preferred Ser. T called for redemption at $25 on 01/03/018 (Additional Information in Active)

PS BUSINESS PKS INC (CA)
Merged into Public Storage, Inc. (CA) 3/19/96
Each share Class A 1¢ par exchanged for (0.923) share Common 1¢ par
Public Storage, Inc. (CA) reincorporated in Maryland as Public Storage 6/4/2007

PS FINL INC (DE)
Merged into PNA Holding Co. 11/30/2001
Each share Common 1¢ par exchanged for $14.06 cash

PS GROUP HLDGS INC (DE)
Merged into Integration Capital Associates, Inc. 03/23/2000
Each share Common $1 par exchanged for $12 cash

PS GROUP INC (DE)
Recapitalized as PS Group Holdings, Inc. 06/05/1996
Each share Common $1 par exchanged for (1) share Common $1 par
(See PS Group Holdings, Inc.)

PS MGMT HLDGS INC (DE)
Filed a petition under Chapter 7 Federal Bankruptcy Code 10/21/2003
Stockholders' equity unlikely

PSA INC (DE)
Common $1 par split (5) for (4) by issuance of (0.25) additional share 03/24/1980
Conv. Depositary Preferred called for redemption 05/23/1986
Name changed to PS Group, Inc. 11/19/1986
PS Group, Inc. recapitalized as PS Group Holdings, Inc. 06/05/1996
(See PS Group Holdings, Inc.)

PSA INC (NV)
Each share old Common $0.001 par exchanged for (0.02) share new Common $0.001 par 09/22/1998
Each share new Common $0.001 par exchanged again for (0.05) share new Common $0.001 par 08/01/2001
Name changed to Shearson American REIT, Inc. 10/16/2009

PSB BANCORP INC (PA)
Merged into Conestoga Bancorp, Inc. 4/2/2007
Each share Common $1 par exchanged for $16.72 cash

PSB GROUP INC (MI)
Stock Dividend - 5% payable 06/14/2005 to holders of record 06/01/2005 Ex date - 05/27/2005
SEC revoked common stock registration 05/22/2014

PSB HLDGS CORP (DE)
Merged into Citfed Bancorp, Inc. 9/1/95
Each share Common 1¢ par exchanged for (0.6734) share Common 1¢ par
Citfed Bancorp, Inc. merged into Fifth Third Bancorp 6/26/98

PSB HLDGS INC (USA)
Under plan of reorganization each share Common 10¢ par automatically became (1.1907) shares PB Bancorp, Inc. Common 1¢ par 01/08/2016

PSC INC (NY)
Plan of reorganization under Chapter 11 Federal Bankruptcy Code effective 6/30/2003
No stockholders' equity

PSCO CAP TR I (DE)
Issue Information - 7,760,000 GTD TR ORIGINATED PFD SECS 7.60% offered at $25 per share on 04/03/1998
7.60% Guaranteed Trust Originated Preferred Securities called for redemption at $25 plus $0.475 accrued dividend on 6/30/2003

PSE INC (DE)
Merged into Destec Energy, Inc. 12/01/1989
Each share Common 1¢ par exchanged for $12.25 cash

PSE&G CAP TR I (DE)
8.625% Guaranteed Quarterly Income Preferred Securities called for redemption at $25 on 06/26/2001

PSE&G CAPITAL TR II (DE)
Issue Information - 3,800,000 QUARTERLY INCOME PFD SECS 8.125% offered at $25 per share on 02/04/1997
8.125% Quarterly Income Preferred Securities called for redemption at $25 on 12/31/2003

PSEG FDG TR II (DE)
8.75% Preferred Securities called for redemption at $25 on 12/17/2007

PSFS FIN INC (DE)
Completely liquidated 02/28/1990
Each share Adjustable Rate Preferred $1 par exchanged for first and final distribution of $50 cash

PSH MASTER L P I (DE)
In process of liquidation
Each Unit of Limited Partnership Int. received initial distribution of $5 cash payable 1/31/98 to holders of record 1/22/98
Note: Details on subsequent distributions, if any, are not available

PSI CORP (NV)
Name changed to Coupon Express, Inc. 01/26/2012

PSI ENERGY INC (IN)
8.38% Preferred $100 par called for redemption 12/1/93

8.52% Preferred $100 par called for redemption 12/1/93
8.96% Preferred $100 par called for redemption 12/1/93
7.15% Preferred $100 par called for redemption at $101 on 9/1/97
7.44% Preferred $25 par called for redemption at $25 on 3/1/98
6.875% Preferred $100 par called for redemption at $103.09 on 8/17/2005
3.50% Preferred $100 par called for redemption at $100 on 5/1/2006
4.16% Preferred $25 par called for redemption at $25 plus $0.1733 on 5/1/2006
4.32% Preferred $25 par called for redemption at $25 on 5/1/2006

PSI RES INC (IN)
Name changed 4/20/90
Name changed from PSI Holdings, Inc. to PSI Resources, Inc. 4/20/90
Merged into Cinergy Corp. 10/24/94
Each share Common no par exchanged for (1.023) shares Common 1¢ par
Cinergy Corp. merged into Duke Energy Corp. (DE) 4/3/2006

PSI TECHNOLOGIES HLDGS INC (PHILIPPINES)
ADR agreement terminated 02/20/2012
No ADR holders' equity

PSICOR INC (PA)
Merged into Baxter International Inc. 2/1/96
Each share Common no par exchanged for $17.50 cash

PSINET INC (NY)
Common 1¢ par split (2) for (1) by issuance of (1) additional share payable 02/11/2000 to holders of record 01/28/2000
Plan of reorganization under Chapter 11 Federal Bankruptcy Code effective 07/01/2002
No stockholders' equity

PSION CDA INC (ON)
Exchangeable Shares no par called for redemption at $1.48 on 8/22/2005

PSIRON LTD (AUSTRALIA)
Name changed to Viralytics Ltd. 01/10/2017
(See Viralytics Ltd.)

PSIVIDA CORP (DE)
Name changed to EyePoint Pharmaceuticals, Inc. 04/02/2018

PSIVIDA LTD (AUSTRALIA)
Reorganized under the laws of Delaware as pSivida Corp. 06/19/2008
Each Sponsored ADR for Ordinary no par exchanged for (0.25) share Common $0.001 par
pSivida Corp. name changed to EyePoint Pharmaceuticals, Inc. 04/02/2018

PSM CORP (NV)
Reorganized as Mentor On Call, Inc. 01/15/2000
Each share Common $0.001 par exchanged for (9) shares Common $0.001 par
Mentor On Call, Inc. recapitalized as Platinum SuperYachts, Inc. 10/08/2002 which name changed to Royal Quantum Group, Inc. 02/01/2006 which recapitalized as MineralRite Corp. 10/18/2012

PSM HLDGS INC (NV)
Reincorporated under the laws of Delaware 12/29/2011

PSN COMMUNICATIONS INC (DE)
Each share Common $0.001 par exchanged for (0.1) share Common 1¢ par 4/21/88
Charter cancelled and declared inoperative and void for non-payment of taxes 6/24/92

PSO CAP I (DE)
8% Trust Originated Preferred Securities Ser. A called for redemption at $25 plus $0.19444 accrued dividend on 5/5/2004

PSP INC (DE)
Merged into Allied Artists Industries, Inc. 1/20/76
Each share Common 10¢ par exchanged for (1.5) shares Common 10¢ par
(See Allied Artists Industries, Inc.)

PSP INDS INC (UT)
Name changed to GreenTek Corp. 09/12/2011
(See GreenTek Corp.)

PSPP HLDGS INC (NV)
Each share old Common $0.001 par exchanged for (0.01) share new Common $0.001 par 06/29/2004
Each share new Common $0.001 par exchanged again for (0.01) share new Common $0.001 par 06/02/2008
Note: No holder will receive fewer than (100) post-split shares
Recapitalized as Mod Hospitality, Inc. 09/22/2008
Each share Common $0.001 par exchanged for (0.1) share Common $0.001 par
Mod Hospitality, Inc. recapitalized as as Stakool, Inc. 12/16/2009 which name changed to Fresh Promise Foods, Inc. 11/12/2013

PSR MGMT INC (NV)
Charter revoked for failure to file reports and pay fees 6/1/2001

PSS INC (DE)
SEC revoked common stock registration 11/17/2009

PSS WORLD MED INC (FL)
Acquired by McKesson Corp. 02/25/2013
Each share Common 1¢ par exchanged for $29 cash

PST VANS INC (UT)
Merged into U.S. Xpress Enterprises, Inc. 08/28/1998
Each share Common $0.001 par exchanged for (0.2381) share Common $0.001 and $2.71 cash
(See U.S. Xpress Enterprises, Inc.)

PSW TECHNOLOGIES INC (DE)
Issue Information - 2,850,000 shares COM offered at $9 per share on 06/05/1997
Name changed to Concero, Inc. 6/12/2000
(See Concero, Inc.)

PSYCH SYS INC (MD)
Plan of reorganization under Chapter 11 Federal Bankruptcy proceedings confirmed 07/17/1986
No stockholders' equity

PSYCHIATRIC BIOSCIENCE INC (DE)
Name changed to Princeton Diagnostic Laboratories of America, Inc. 05/17/1988
Princeton Diagnostic Laboratories of America, Inc. merged into Editek, Inc. (CA) 02/11/1994 which reincorporated in Delaware 09/26/1996 which name changed to Medtox Scientific, Inc. 05/16/1997
(See Medtox Scientific, Inc.)

PSYCHIATRIC SOLUTIONS INC (DE)
Common 1¢ par split (2) for (1) by issuance of (1) additional share payable 01/09/2006 to holders of record 12/27/2005 Ex date - 01/10/2006
Acquired by Universal Health Services, Inc. 11/16/2010
Each share Common 1¢ par exchanged for $33.75 cash

PSYCHIC FRIENDS NETWORK INC (NV)
Common $0.001 par split (10) for (1) by issuance of (9) additional shares payable 02/24/2012 to holders of record 02/24/2012
Name changed to Peer to Peer Network 09/30/2014

PSYCHOLOGICAL CORP (NY)
Each share Capital Stock no par exchanged for (4) shares Common $1 par 12/31/64
Merged into Harcourt, Brace & World, Inc. 2/9/70
Each share Common $1 par exchanged for (2.48) shares Common $1 par
Harcourt, Brace & World, Inc. name changed to Harcourt Brace Jovanovich, Inc. 6/2/70 which merged into General Cinema Corp. 11/25/91 which name changed to Harcourt General, Inc. 3/15/93
(See Harcourt General, Inc.)

PSYCHOLOGICAL HEALTH CARE, INC. (UT)
Reincorporated under the laws of Illinois as Pain Prevention Inc. 02/03/1989
Pain Prevention Inc. (IL) reincorporated in Utah as PPI Capital Corp. 11/15/1997 which recapitalized as PPI Capital Group, Corp. (UT) 06/01/1998 which reincorporated in Delaware as DirectPlacement Inc. 11/28/2001 which name changed to PCS Research Technology, Inc. 10/07/2002 which name changed to Sagient Research Systems, Inc. 05/20/2004
(See Sagient Research Systems, Inc.)

PT BAKRIELAND DEV TBK (INDONESIA)
ADR agreement terminated 03/13/2018
No ADR's remain outstanding

PT BK BUANA INDONESIA TBK (INDONESIA)
ADR agreement terminated 11/16/2006
No ADR's remain outstanding

PT BK TABUNGAN NEGARA PERSERO TBK (INDONESIA)
ADR agreement terminated 09/01/2016
No ADR's remain outstanding

PT BORNEO LUMBUNG ENERGI & METAL TBK (INDONESIA)
ADR agreement terminated 09/01/2016
No ADR's remain outstanding

PT CHANDRA ASRI PETROCHEMICAL (INDONESIA)
ADR agreement terminated 03/30/2012
Each Sponsored ADR for Ordinary exchanged for $2.317997 cash
(Additional Information in Active)

PT COMPONENTS INC (DE)
Acquired by CTP Holdings Inc. 09/11/1986
Each share Common 1¢ par exchanged for $15.125 cash

PT ELANG MAHKOTA TEKNOLOGI TBK (INDONESIA)
ADR agreement terminated 08/06/2018
No ADR's remain outstanding

PT INDOSAT TBK (INDONESIA)
ADR agreement terminated 07/24/2013
Each Sponsored ADR for Ser. B exchanged for $13.739138 cash

PT INTERNATIONAL NICKEL INDONESIA TBK (INDONESIA)
Name changed to PT Vale Indonesia Tbk 02/10/2012

PT JAPFA COMFEED INDONESIA TBK (INDONESIA)
ADR agreement terminated 08/06/2018
No ADR's remain outstanding

PT MULTIMEDIA SERVICOS DE TELECOMUNICACOES E MULTIMEDIA (PORTUGAL)
Sponsored Reg. S ADR's for Ordinary EUR 0.81 par split (2) for (1) by issuance of (1) additional ADR payable 06/14/2005 to holders of record 06/13/2005
Sponsored Reg. S ADR's for Ordinary EUR 0.81 par changed to EUR 0.10 par 09/18/2006
Sponsored 144A ADR's for Ordinary EUR 0.81 par changed to EUR 0.10 par 09/18/2006
ADR agreement terminated 12/14/2007
No Sponsored 144A ADR's for Ordinary outstanding
Name changed to Zon Multimedia 02/14/2008
Zon Multimedia name changed to Zon Optimus SGPS S.A. 04/02/2014 which name changed to NOS, SGPS, S.A. 12/30/2014
(See NOS, SGPS, S.A.)

PT PLATINUM PUB LTD (UKRAINE)
GDR agreement terminated 06/07/2017
No GDR's remain outstanding

PT SEMEN GRESIK PERSERO TBK (INDONESIA)
ADR's for Ordinary split (5) for (2) by issuance of (1.5) additional ADR's payable 03/07/2012 to holders of record 03/02/2012 Ex date - 03/08/2012
ADR basis changed from (1:50) to (1:20) 03/08/2012
Name changed to PT Semen Indonesia (Persero) Tbk 01/18/2013

PTC GROUP INC (ID)
Name changed to Ocean Power Corp. 07/12/1999
(See Ocean Power Corp.)

PTC HLDGS INC (NV)
Reincorporated under the laws of Washington as Pacific Aerospace & Electronics, Inc. 11/30/96
(See Pacific Aerospace & Electronics, Inc.)

PTC INDS INC (FL)
Proclaimed dissolved for failure to file reports and pay fees 09/21/2001

PTEK HLDGS INC (GA)
Name changed to Premiere Global Services, Inc. 01/03/2005
(See Premiere Global Services, Inc.)

P10 INDS INC (DE)
Plan of reorganization under Chapter 11 bankruptcy proceedings effective 05/04/2017
Each share old Common $0.001 par exchanged for (1) share new Common $0.001 par
Name changed to P10 Holdings, Inc. 12/05/2017

PTGI HLDG INC (DE)
Name changed to HC2 Holdings, Inc. 04/14/2014

PTI HLDG INC (DE)
Each share old Common 1¢ par exchanged for (0.33333333) share new Common 1¢ par 10/10/2000
Each share new Common 1¢ par exchanged again for (0.001) share new Common 1¢ par 01/19/2001
Note: In effect holders received $0.60 cash per share and public interest was eliminated

PTM PUBLICATIONS INC (NV)
Common $0.001 par split (22) for (1) by issuance of (21) additional shares payable 05/24/2010 to

holders of record 05/23/2010
Ex date - 05/25/2010
Name changed to Magnum Oil Inc.
07/16/2010
Magnum Oil Inc. name changed to
USA Graphite Inc. 04/17/2012
(See USA Graphite Inc.)

PTN MEDIA INC (DE)
Name changed to Legend Mobile, Inc.
06/27/2002
Legend Mobile, Inc. name changed to
Cephas Holding Corp. 01/14/2009
(See Cephas Holding Corp.)

PTR RES LTD (AB)
Merged into Westlinks Resources Ltd.
06/30/1998
Each share Common no par
exchanged for (0.032) share
Common no par
Westlinks Resources Ltd. name
changed to Enterra Energy Corp.
12/18/2001 which recapitalized as
Enterra Energy Trust 11/25/2003
which reorganized as Equal Energy
Ltd. 06/03/2010
(See Equal Energy Ltd.)

PTV INC (DE)
Liquidation completed
Each share 10% Preferred 1¢ par
received initial distribution of $1.60
cash payable 01/28/2008 to holders
of record 01/18/2008 Ex date -
01/29/2008
Each share 10% Preferred 1¢ par
received second distribution of $0.77
cash payable 01/15/2009 to holders
of record 01/05/2009 Ex date -
01/16/2009
Each share 10% Preferred 1¢ par
received third and final distribution
of $0.11 cash payable 10/08/2010 to
holders of record 09/27/2010
Note: Certificates were not required to
be surrendered and are without
value

P2P HEALTH SYS INC (BC)
Recapitalized as Salares Lithium Inc.
11/26/2009
Each share Common no par
exchanged for (0.5) share Common
no par
Salares Lithium Inc. merged into
Talison Lithium Ltd. 09/22/2010
(See Talison Lithium Ltd.)

PUB CRAWL HLDGS INC (NV)
Common $0.001 par split (45) for (1)
by issuance of (44) additional
shares payable 09/17/2012 to
holders of record 09/17/2012
Name changed to Excelsis
Investments Inc. 02/24/2014
Excelsis Investments Inc. name
changed to Stealth Technologies,
Inc. 07/06/2016

PUB SINGIN INC (CO)
Recapitalized as Freerealtime.Com,
Inc. (CO) 9/11/98
Each share Common no par
exchanged for (0.2) share Common
no par
Freerealtime.Com, Inc. (CO)
reincorporated in Delaware 11/22/99
(See Freerealtime.Com, Inc. (DE))

PUB UNITED CORP. (NY)
Name changed to Rheingold Corp.
04/27/1965
(See Rheingold Corp.)

PUBBS WORLDWIDE INC (DE)
Recapitalized as Chasen's
International Inc. 05/25/1999
Each share Common 1¢ par
exchanged for (0.01) share Common
1¢ par
Chasen's International Inc. name
changed to Tril-Medianet.Com, Inc.
07/21/1999 which name changed to
Tec Factory, Inc. 11/28/2000 which
name changed to HeartSTAT
Technology, Inc. 02/26/2004 which
name changed to Verdant
Technology Corp. 03/01/2006

(See Verdant Technology Corp.)

PUBCO CORP (DE)
Reincorporated 06/07/1985
Each share Conv. Class B Common
40¢ par exchanged for (1,000)
shares Common 40¢ par 06/29/1976
Reorganized under Chapter 11
bankruptcy proceedings 11/22/1983
Each share 6% Preferred $100 par
exchanged for (100) shares
Common 1¢ par
Common 40¢ par changed to 1¢ par
11/22/1983
State of incorporation changed from
(MD) to (DE) 06/07/1985
Each share old Common 1¢ par
exchanged for (0.05) share new
Common 1¢ par 08/14/1990
Each share old Class B Common 1¢
par exchanged for (0.05) share new
Class B Common 1¢ par 08/14/1990
Each share new Common 1¢ par
exchanged again for (1) share new
Common 1¢ par to reflect a (1) for
(100) reverse split followed by a
(100) for (1) forward split 11/10/2000
Each share new Class B Common 1¢
par exchanged again for (1) share
new Class B Common 1¢ par to
reflect a (1) for (100) reverse split
followed by a (100) for (1) forward
split 11/10/2000
Acquired by Pubco Acquisition, Inc.
10/12/2007
Each share new Common 1¢ par
exchanged for $20 cash
Each share new Class B Common 1¢
par exchanged for $20 cash

PUBCO DEVELOPMENT, INC. (NM)
Name changed to Pubco Petroleum
Corp. 2/23/56
Pubco Petroleum Corp. merged into
Mesa Petroleum Co. 5/1/73
(See Mesa Petroleum Corp.)

PUBCO PETE CORP (NM)
Stock Dividends - 100% 3/15/56; 20%
6/10/63
Merged into Mesa Petroleum Co.
5/1/73
Each share Common $1 par
exchanged for (0.181818) share
Common $1 par
(See Mesa Petroleum Corp.)

PUBCOA INC (NV)
Each share old Common $0.0001 par
exchanged for (0.2) share new
Common $0.0001 par 08/05/1983
Name changed to Buffs-N-Puffs, Ltd.
08/07/1990
Buffs-N-Puffs, Ltd. name changed to
TimeOne, Inc. 07/24/1997 which
name changed to SunGlobe Fiber
Systems Corp. 07/07/2000
(See SunGlobe Fiber Systems Corp.)

PUBLIC BANK (DETROIT, MI)
Placed in receivership 10/12/66
Court approved determination of no
stockholders' equity 7/21/72

PUBLIC ELECTRIC LIGHT CO. (MA)
Merged into Central Vermont Public
Service Corp. 00/00/1953
Each share Preferred $100 par
exchanged for (1) share 4.75%
Preferred $100 par, (0.5) share
Common $6 par and $1.50 cash
Each share Common no par
exchanged for (12.5) shares
Common $6 par
(See Central Vermont Public Service
Corp.)

PUBLIC FIRE INSURANCE CO. (NJ)
Liquidated in 1938
No stockholders' equity

PUBLIC FLYERS, INC. (NY)
Proclaimed dissolved 12/15/52

PUBLIC GAS & COKE CO.
Reorganized as National Gas &
Electric Corp. 02/00/1941
Each share 7% Preferred exchanged
for $5 in cash or (1.125) shares

Common no par and dividend of 50¢
per new share
Each share Common exchanged for
(0.225) share Common no par and
dividend of 50¢ per new share
(See National Gas & Electric Corp.)

PUBLIC GAS CO (FL)
60¢ Conv. Preferred Ser. A $1 par
called for redemption 06/21/1994
$6.90 Conv. Preferred Ser. A $1 par
called for redemption 06/21/1994
Merged into National Propane Corp.
06/29/1995
Details not available

PUBLIC INDEMNITY CO. (NJ)
Merged into International
Re-Insurance Corp. (DE) 00/00/1932
Details not available

PUBLIC INDUSTRIALS CORP.
Reorganized in 1938
No stockholders' equity

PUBLIC INVESTING CO.
Liquidated in 1948

PUBLIC INVS INC (LA)
Merged into Pico Acquisition Corp.
08/11/1987
Each share Class AA no par
exchanged for $3.77 cash

PUBLIC LEASING CORP (OK)
Capital Stock 30¢ par changed to 10¢
par and (2) additional shares issued
10/04/1966
Adjudicated bankrupt 08/07/1972
Stockholders' equity unlikely

PUBLIC LIGHT & POWER CO.
Acquired by Tennessee Electric
Power Co. in 1929 which was
dissolved in 1939

PUBLIC LN CO (MI)
Merged into Multivest, Inc.
07/31/1972
Each share Common $1 par
exchanged for (0.3) share Common
1¢ par
(See Multivest, Inc.)

PUBLIC MEDIA WKS INC (DE)
Each share old Common $0.0001 par
exchanged for (0.05) share new
Common $0.0001 par 06/28/2007
Chapter 7 Federal Bankruptcy
proceedings dismissed 03/12/2014
Stockholders' equity unlikely

**PUBLIC NATIONAL BANK OF
WASHINGTON (WASHINGTON, DC)**
Common $10 par changed to $5 par
in 1971
Common $5 par changed to $4 par
12/18/74
Name changed to Bank of Columbia,
N.A. (Washington, D.C.) 2/1/75
Bank of Columbia, N.A. (Washington,
D.C.) name changed to National
Bank of Commerce (Washington,
D.C.) 10/15/81 which reorganized in
Delaware as Commerce Bancorp,
Inc. 1/31/85
(See Commerce Bancorp, Inc. (Del.))

PUBLIC NATIONAL CORP.
Dissolved in 1933

PUBLIC OIL & GAS CO. (DE)
Charter cancelled for non-payment of
taxes 1/19/25

**PUBLIC SAVINGS INSURANCE CO.
(TX)**
Merged into Public Savings Life
Insurance Co. 12/31/63
Each share Common 50¢ par
exchanged for (1) share Common
50¢ par
(See Public Savings Life Insurance
Co.)

PUBLIC SVGS LIFE INS CO (SC)
Under plan of merger each share
Common $1 par exchanged for (4)
shares Common 50¢ par 12/31/1963
Stock Dividends - 10% 11/01/1965;
20% 03/16/1981

Merged into Southlife Holding Co.
05/07/1984
Each share Common 50¢ par
exchanged for $17.50 cash

**PUBLIC SECURITY BOND &
MORTGAGE CORP. (NY)**
Charter revoked for failure to file
reports and pay fees 12/15/36

**PUBLIC SVC BK A FED SVGS BK
(ST LOUIS, MO)**
Merged into Southside Bancshares
Corp. 6/29/98
Each share Common no par
exchanged for either (2.221) shares
Common 1¢ par, $84.49 cash, or a
combination thereof
Note: Option to receive stock or stock
and cash expired 6/26/98
Southside Bancshares Corp. merged
into Allegiant Bancorp, Inc.
9/28/2001 which merged into
National City Corp. 4/9/2004

PUBLIC SERVICE CO. OF INDIANA
Merged into Public Service Co. of
Indiana, Inc. 09/06/1941
Each share $7 Prior Preferred
exchanged for (1) share 5%
Preferred $100 par, (1) share
Common no par and $30.87 cash
Each share $6 Prior Preferred
exchanged for (1) share 5%
Preferred $100 par, (1) share
Common no par and $23.08 cash
Each share $6 Preferred exchanged
for (6) shares Common no par
(See Public Service Co. of Indiana,
Inc.)

PUBLIC SVC CO COLO (CO)
7% Preferred $100 par called for
redemption 10/1/47
Each share Common $20 par
exchanged for (2) shares Common
$10 par in 1950
4.40% Preferred $100 par called for
redemption 4/24/50
Common $10 par changed to $5 par
and (2) additional shares issued
5/11/62
12.50% Preferred $100 par called for
redemption in 1986
4.25% Preferred $100 par called for
redemption at $101 on 6/10/98
8.40% Preferred $25 par called for
redemption at $25.25 on 6/10/98
4.50% Preferred $100 par called for
redemption at $101 on 6/10/98
4.90% Preferred 2nd Ser. $100 par
called for redemption at $101 on
6/10/98
4.20% Preferred $100 par called for
redemption at $101 on 6/10/98
4.64% Preferred $100 par called for
redemption at $101 on 6/10/98
4.90% Preferred $100 par called for
redemption at $101 on 6/10/98
7.15% Preferred $100 par called for
redemption at $101 on 6/10/98
Stock Dividend - 10% 11/16/56
Under plan of merger name changed
to New Century Energies, Inc.
8/1/97
New Century Energies, Inc. merged
into Xcel Energy Inc. 8/18/2000

PUBLIC SVC CO IND INC (IN)
5% Preferred $100 par called for
redemption 6/3/46
Common no par split (2) for (1) by
issuance of (1) additional share
11/4/48
4.64% Preferred $100 par called for
redemption 1/8/53
4.90% Preferred $25 par called for
redemption 8/9/54
4.20% Preferred $100 par called for
redemption 4/2/58
Common no par split (2) for (1) by
issuance of (1) additional share
4/19/62
4.80% Conv. Preferred $100 par
called for redemption 6/29/62
Common no par split (3) for (2) by

issuance of (0.5) additional share 4/26/76
9.44% Preferred $100 par called for redemption 3/16/87
9.60% Preferred $100 par called for redemption 3/16/87
Under plan of reorganization each share Common no par automatically became (1) share PSI Holding, Inc. Common no par 6/1/88
(See PSI Holding, Inc.)
Name changed to PSI Energy Inc. 4/20/90
(See PSI Energy Inc.)

PUBLIC SVC CO N C INC (NC)
Each share Common $5 par exchanged for (2) shares Common $1 par 12/31/54
5.60% Preferred $25 par called for redemption 12/8/60
4.40% Conv. Preference Ser. A $25 par called for redemption 6/30/80
8% Conv. Preference Ser. B $25 par called for redemption 6/30/80
Common $1 par split (2) for (1) by issuance of (1) additional share 4/27/87
Common $1 par split (3) for (2) by issuance of (0.5) additional share 1/4/93
Stock Dividend - 50% 4/1/93
Merged into SCANA Corp. (New) 2/10/2000
Each share Common $1 par exchanged for (1.21) shares Common no par

PUBLIC SVC CO N H (NH)
$5 Preferred no par called for redemption 06/10/1946
$6 Preferred no par called for redemption 06/10/1946
5.40% Preferred $100 par called for redemption 08/21/1954
Each share Common $10 par exchanged for (2) shares Common $5 par 00/00/1954
Reorganized under Chapter 11 Federal Bankruptcy Code 05/16/1991
Each share 3.35% Preferred $100 par, 4.50% Preferred $100 par, 5.50% Conv. Preferred $100 par, and 7.92% Preferred $100 par exchanged for $0.04403536 principal amount of 15.23% Unsecured Notes due 07/01/2000, (2.54031724) shares new Common $1 par and (1.70492569) Contingent Warrants
Each share 7.64% Preferred Stock $100 par exchanged for $44.3054 principal amount of 15.23% Unsecured Notes due 07/01/2000, (2.5403) shares new Common $1 par and (1.7049) Contingent Warrant
Each share 11% Preferred $25 par exchanged for $0.01107634 principal amount of 15.23% Unsecured Notes due 07/01/2000, (0.63507931) share new Common $1 par and (0.42623142) Contingent Warrant
Each share 11.24% Preferred $25 par exchanged for $0.01107634 principal amount of 15.23% Unsecured Notes due 07/01/2000, (0.63507931) share new Common $1 par and (0.42623142) Contingent Warrant
Each share 13% Preferred $25 par exchanged for $0.01107634 principal amount of 15.23% Unsecured Notes Notes due 07/01/2000, (0.63507931) share new Common $1 par and (0.42623142) Contingent Warrant
Each share 13.80% S.F. Preferred $25 par exchanged for $0.1107634 principal amount of 15.23% Unsecured Notes Notes due 07/01/2000, (0.63507931) share new Common $1 par and (0.42623142) Contingent Warrant

Each share 15% Preferred $25 par exchanged for $0.1107634 principal amount of 15.23% Unsecured Notes due 07/01/2000, (0.63507931) share new Common $1 par and (0.42623142) Contingent Warrant
Each share 15.444% Preferred $25 par exchanged for $11.10 principal amount of 15.23% Unsecured Notes due 07/01/2000, (0.6351) share new Common $1 par and (0.4262) Contingent Warrant
Each share 17% Preferred $25 par exchanged for $0.1107634 principal amount of 15.23% Unsecured Notes due 07/01/2000, (0.63507931) share new Common $1 par and (0.42623142) Contingent Warrant
Each share old Common $5 par exchanged for $1.4691 principal amount of 15.23% Unsecured Notes due 07/01/2000, (0.063894) share new Common $1 par and (0.06926) Contingent Warrant
Each share old Common $5 par received distribution of (0.023412220) share new Common $1 par 00/00/1991
Each share old Common $5 par received distribution of $0.012884847 cash 00/00/1992
Each share old Common $5 par received distribution of $0.1024055 cash 00/00/1993
Merged into Northeast Utilities 06/05/1992
Each share new Common $1 par exchanged for $20 cash and each Contingent Warrant exchanged for (1) Warrant expiring 06/05/1997
Ser. A Preferred called for redemption at $25 on 06/29/2001

PUBLIC SVC CO N MEX (NM)
Each share Common $7 par exchanged for (2) shares Common $5 par 00/00/1952
Common $5 par split (3) for (2) by issuance of (0.5) additional share 10/06/1961
5% Ser. A Preferred $100 par called for redemption 01/20/1965
$5.25 Preferred 1959 Ser. $100 par called for redemption 01/20/1965
9.2% Preferred 1974 Ser. $100 par changed to no par 04/23/1975
10.12% Preferred 1975 Ser. $100 par changed to no par 04/23/1975
9.16% Preferred no par called for redemption 07/28/1986
9.2% Preferred 1974 Ser. no par called for redemption 07/28/1986
10.12% Preferred 1975 Ser. no par called for redemption 07/28/1986
8.48% Preferred no par called for redemption 08/07/1995
$8.75 Preferred no par called for redemption 08/07/1995
8.8% Preferred no par called for redemption 08/07/1995
Under plan of reorganization each share Common $5 par automatically became (1) share PNM Resources Inc. Common no par 12/31/2001
(Additional Information in Active)

PUBLIC SVC CO OKLA (OK)
6% Preferred called for redemption 04/21/1941
7% Preferred called for redemption 04/21/1941
5% Preferred $100 par called for redemption 12/03/1945
4.65% Preferred $100 par called for redemption 11/01/1962
7.92% Preferred $100 par called for redemption 07/22/1987
8.88% Preferred $100 par called for redemption 07/22/1987
4% Preferred $100 par called for redemption at $105.75 on 12/01/2011
4.24% Preferred $100 par called for redemption at $103.19 on 12/01/2011

PUBLIC SVC COORDINATED TRANS (NJ)
A wholly-owned subsidiary of Public Service Electric & Gas Co.

PUBLIC SERVICE CORP. OF LONG ISLAND
Absorbed by Long Island Lighting Co. 00/00/1930
Details not available

PUBLIC SERVICE CORP. OF NEW JERSEY (NJ)
Each share old Common no par exchanged for (3) shares new Common no par in 1926
Completely liquidated 7/1/48
Each share 8% Preferred $100 par exchanged for first and final distribution of (4.7) shares Public Service Electric & Gas Co. $1.40 Dividend Preference Common no par
Each share 7% Preferred $100 par exchanged for first and final distribution of (4.15) shares Public Service Electric & Gas Co. $1.40 Dividend Preference Common no par
Each share 6% Preferred $100 par exchanged for first and final distribution of (3.7) shares Public Service Electric & Gas Co. $1.40 Dividend Preference Common no par
Each share $5 Preferred no par exchanged for first and final distribution of (3.25) shares Public Service Electric & Gas Co. $1.40 Dividend Preference Common no par
Each share new Common no par exchanged for first and final distribution of (1) share Public Service Electric & Gas Co. Common no par and (0.1) share South Jersey Gas Co. Common $5 par
(See each company's listing)
Note: Unexchanged certificates were cancelled and became without value 7/1/53

PUBLIC SERVICE CORP. OF TEXAS (DE)
Dissolved 7/3/63

PUBLIC SVC CORP (NV)
Name changed to Prodigy Advanced Repair Technology Corp. 7/15/93
Prodigy Advanced Repair Technology Corp. name changed to Collision King Inc. 7/21/97 which recapitalized as Great Outdoors, Inc. 2/10/2004 which name changed to Pivotal Technology, Inc. 8/21/2006 which name changed to Somatic Systems, Inc. 8/28/2006

PUBLIC SVC ELEC & GAS CAP L P (NJ)
9.375% Guaranteed Monthly Income Preferred Ser. A called for redemption at $25 on 3/16/2001
8% Guaranteed Monthly Income Preferred Ser. B called for redemption at $25 on 12/31/2003

PUBLIC SVC ELEC & GAS CO (NJ)
$5 Preferred no par called for redemption 06/30/1948
4.70% Preferred $100 par called for redemption 06/30/1954
Common no par split (2) for (1) by issuance of (1) additional share 05/20/1964
12.25% Preferred $100 par called for redemption 04/01/1986
13.44% Preferred $100 par called for redemption 04/01/1986
Reorganized as Public Service Enterprise Group 05/01/1986
Each share $1.40 Preference Common no par exchanged for (0.5) share Common no par
Each share Common no par automatically became (1) share Common no par

8.70% Preferred $25 par called for redemption 04/01/1987
9.62% Preferred $100 par called for redemption 04/01/1987
9.75% Preferred $25 par called for redemption 04/01/1987
12.80% Preferred $100 par called for redemption 10/01/1987
11.62% Preferred $100 par called for redemption 09/01/1988
8.08% Preferred $100 par called for redemption 03/01/1994
8.16% Preferred $100 par called for redemption 03/01/1994
7.80% Preferred $100 par called for redemption 12/16/1994
7.70% Preferred $100 par called for redemption 10/16/1995
7.40% Preferred $100 par called for redemption 06/28/1996
7.52% Preferred $100 par called for redemption 06/28/1996
6.80% Preferred $100 par called for redemption 01/31/1997
7.44% Preferred $100 par called for redemption 06/01/1997
5.97% Preferred $100 par called for redemption at $101.20 on 03/30/2001
6.75% Preferred $25 par called for redemption at $25 on 03/30/2001
4.08% Preferred $100 par called for redemption at $103 plus $0.9054 accrued dividends on 03/22/2010
4.18% Preferred $100 par called for redemption at $103 plus $0.9276 accrued dividends on 03/22/2010
4.30% Preferred $100 par called for redemption at $102.75 plus $0.9542 accrued dividends on 03/22/2010
5.05% Preferred $100 par called for redemption at $103 plus $1.1207 accrued dividends on 03/22/2010
5.28% Preferred $100 par called for redemption at $103 plus $1.1717 accrued dividends on 03/22/2010
6.92% Preferred $100 par called for redemption at $101.39 plus $1.5357 accrued dividends on 03/22/2010

PUBLIC SVC ENTERPRISE GROUP INC (NJ)
Each Corporate Unit received (1.2423) shares Common no par 11/16/2005
(Additional Information in Active)

PUBLIC SERVICE GAS CO. OF KENTUCKY
Dissolved in 1927

PUBLIC SERVICE HOLDING CORP. (DE)
Out of existence in 1954
No stockholders' equity

PUBLIC SERVICE TRUST SHARES, SERIES A
Trust terminated and liquidated 00/00/1941
Details not available

PUBLIC STEERS TR - MERRILL LYNCH DEPOSITOR INC (DE)
Public Structured Enchanced Return Trust 1998 Ser. HLT-1 called for redemption at $10.3315 on 2/16/2007
Public Structured Enchanced Return Trust 1999 Ser. REN-C1 Trust called for redemption at $25 on 3/1/2007

PUBLIC STORAGE (CA)
Reincorporated 06/04/2007
8.25% Conv. Preferred 1¢ par called for redemption at (1.6835) shares Common on 07/01/1998
8.875% Depositary Preferred Ser. G called for redemption at $25 on 09/28/2001
8.45% Depositary Preferred Ser. H called for redemption at $25 on 10/05/2001
8.625% Depositary Preferred Ser. I called for redemption at $25 on 11/13/2001

10% Preferred Ser. A 1¢ par called for redemption at $25 on 09/30/2002
8% Depositary Preferred Ser. J called for redemption at $25 on 10/07/2002
9.2% Preferred Ser. B 1¢ par called for redemption at $25 on 03/31/2003
Adjustable Rate Preferred Ser. C 1¢ par called for redemption at $25 on 06/30/2003
8.25% Depositary Preferred Ser. K called for redemption at $25 on 01/20/2004
8.25% Depositary Preferred Ser. L called for redemption at $25 on 03/10/2004
8.75% Depositary Preferred Ser. M called for redemption at $25 on 08/17/2004
9.5% Preferred Ser. D 1¢ par called for redemption at $25 on 09/30/2004
10% Preferred Ser. E 1¢ par called for redemption at $25 on 01/31/2005
9.75% Preferred Ser. F 1¢ par called for redemption at $25 on 05/02/2005
Depositary Preferred Ser. Q called for redemption at $25 on 01/19/2006
8% Depositary Preferred Ser. R called for redemption at $25 plus $0.37 accrued dividends on 09/28/2006
7.875% Depositary Preferred Ser. S called for redemption at $25 on 10/31/2006
7.625% Depositary Preferred Ser. T called for redemption at $25 on 01/18/2007
7.625% Depositary Preferred Ser. U called for redemption at $25 on 02/20/2007
Name and state of incorporation changed from Public Storage, Inc. (CA) to Public Storage (MD) 06/04/2007
Depositary Shares Ser. A called for redemption at $24.50 on 04/15/2010
7.5% Depositary Preferred Ser. V called for redemption at $25 on 05/18/2010
7.125% Depositary Preferred Ser. B called for redemption at $25 on 11/05/2010
7.25% Depositary Preferred Ser. I called for redemption at $25 on 06/20/2011
7.25% Depositary Preferred Ser. K called for redemption at $25 on 08/22/2011
7% Depositary Preferred Ser. G called for redemption at $25 on 09/30/2011
6.95% Depositary Preferred Ser. H called for redemption at $25 on 11/28/2011
6.75% Depositary Preferred Ser. L called for redemption at $25 on 02/09/2012
6.75% Depositary Preferred Ser. E called for redemption at $25 on 02/21/2012
6.85% Preferred Ser. Y 1¢ par called for redemption at $25 on 03/19/2012
6.875% Depositary Preferred Ser. M called for redemption at $25 on 04/11/2012
7% Depositary Preferred Ser. N called for redemption at $25 on 07/02/2012
6.6% Depositary Preferred Ser. C called for redemption at $25 on 07/12/2012
6.5% Depositary Preferred Ser. W called called for redemption at $25 on 08/06/2012
6.45% Depositary Preferred Ser. F called for redemption at $25 on 10/15/2012
6.45% Depositary Preferred Ser. X called for redemption at $25 on 10/15/2012
6.125% Depositary Preferred Ser. A called for redemption at $25 on 12/27/2012
6.18% Depositary Preferred Ser. D called for redemption at $25 on 12/27/2012
6.25% Depositary Preferred Ser. Z called for redemption at $25 on 12/27/2012
6.875% Depositary Preferred Ser. O called for redemption at $25 plus $0.071615 accured dividends on 04/15/2015
6.5% Depositary Preferred Ser. P called for redemption at $25 plus $0.031597 accured dividends on 10/08/2015
6.5% Depositary Preferred Ser. Q called for redemption at $25 plus $0.063194 accured dividends on 04/15/2016
6.35% Depositary Preferred Ser. R called for redemption at $25 plus $0.110243 accured dividends on 07/26/2016
5.75% Depositary Preferred Ser. T called for redemption at $25 on 09/28/2017
(Additional Information in Active)

PUBLIC STORAGE CDN PPTYS (ON)
Reorganized 12/31/1998
Each Limited Partnership I Unit of Ltd. Partnership no par exchanged for (2.2) new Units of Ltd. Partnership no par 01/31/1992
Each Limited Partnership II Unit of Ltd. Partnership no par exchanged for (2.2) new Units of Ltd. Partnership no par 01/31/1992
Each Limited Partnership III Unit of Ltd. Partnership no par exchanged for (2.2) new Units of Ltd. Partnership no par 01/31/1992
Reorganized from (AB) to under the laws of Ontario 12/31/1998
Each Limited Partnership IV Unit of Ltd. Partnership no par exchanged for (0.4) Unit of Ltd. Partnership
Note: Non-Canadian residents and holders who failed to surrender certificates prior to 12/31/1999 received $6.80 cash
Each new Unit of Ltd. Partnership no par exchanged for (1) Unit of Ltd. Partnership
Note: Non-Canadian residents and holders who failed to surrender certificates prior to 12/31/1999 received $17 cash
Merged into PS Canada Co. ULC 09/09/2010
Each Unit of Ltd. Partnership exchanged for $20 cash

PUBLIC STORAGE PPTYS VI INC (CA)
Merged into Storage Equities, Inc. 2/28/95
Each share Class A Common 1¢ par exchanged for (1.724) shares Common 10¢ par
Storage Equities, Inc. name changed to Public Storage, Inc. (CA) 11/16/95 which reincorporated in Maryland as Public Storage 6/4/2007

PUBLIC STORAGE PPTYS VII INC (CA)
Merged into Storage Equities, Inc. 6/30/95
Each share Class A 1¢ par exchanged for (1.155) shares Common 10¢ par
Storage Equities, Inc. name changed to Public Storage, Inc. (CA) 11/16/95 which reincorporated in Maryland as Public Storage 6/4/2007

PUBLIC STORAGE PPTYS VIII INC (CA)
Merged into Storage Equities, Inc. 9/30/94
Each share Class A Common 1¢ par exchanged for (1.429) shares Common 10¢ par
Storage Equities, Inc. name changed to Public Storage, Inc. (CA) 11/16/95 which reincorporated in Maryland as Public Storage 6/4/2007

PUBLIC STORAGE PPTYS IX INC (CA)
Merged into Public Storage, Inc. (CA) 3/19/96
Each share Class A 1¢ par exchanged for (0.851) share Common 1¢ par
Public Storage, Inc. (CA) reincorporated in Maryland as Public Storage 6/4/2007

PUBLIC STORAGE PPTYS X INC (CA)
Merged into Public Storage, Inc. (CA) 9/16/96
Each Class A Unit of Limited Partnership exchanged for (0.944) share Common 10¢ par and $0.71 cash
Public Storage, Inc. (CA) reincorporated in Maryland as Public Storage 6/4/2007

PUBLIC STORAGE PPTYS XI INC (CA)
Merged into PS Business Parks, Inc. 3/17/98
Each share Class A Common 1¢ par exchanged for either (1) share Common 1¢ par or $20.50 cash
Note: Non-electing holders received stock

PUBLIC STORAGE PPTYS XII INC (CA)
Merged into Public Storage, Inc. (CA) 9/16/96
Each Class A Unit of Limited Partnership exchanged for (0.993) share Common 10¢ par and $0.94 cash
Public Storage, Inc. (CA) reincorporated in Maryland as Public Storage 6/4/2007

PUBLIC STORAGE PPTYS XIV INC (CA)
Merged into Public Storage, Inc. (CA) 04/11/1997
Each share Class A Common 1¢ par exchanged for (0.729) share Common 10¢ par and $20.98 cash
Public Storage, Inc. (CA) reincorporated in Maryland as Public Storage 06/04/2007

PUBLIC STORAGE PPTYS XV (CA)
Merged into Public Storage, Inc. (CA) 04/11/1997
Each share Class A Common 1¢ par exchanged for (0.75) share Common 10¢ par and $21.58 cash
Public Storage, Inc. (CA) reincorporated in Maryland as Public Storage 06/04/2007

PUBLIC STORAGE PPTYS XVI INC (CA)
Merged into Public Storage, Inc. (CA) 06/24/1997
Each share Class A no par exchanged for (0.738) share Common 10¢ par and $0.75 cash
Public Storage, Inc. (CA) reincorporated in Maryland as Public Storage 6/4/2007

PUBLIC STORAGE PPTYS XVII INC (CA)
Merged into Public Storage, Inc. (CA) 6/24/97
Each share Class A no par exchanged for (0.698) share Common 10¢ par and $0.71 cash
Public Storage, Inc. (CA) reincorporated in Maryland as Public Storage 6/4/2007

PUBLIC STORAGE PPTYS XVIII INC (CA)
Merged into Public Storage, Inc. (CA) 6/24/97
Each share Ser. A Common no par exchanged for (0.721) share Common 10¢ par and $0.84 cash
Public Storage, Inc. (CA) reincorporated in Maryland as Public Storage 6/4/2007

PUBLIC STORAGE PPTYS XIX INC (CA)
Merged into Public Storage, Inc. (CA) 6/24/97
Each share Class A no par exchanged for (0.609) share Common 10¢ par and $0.38 cash
Public Storage, Inc. (CA) reincorporated in Maryland as Public Storage 6/4/2007

PUBLIC STORAGE PPTYS XX INC (CA)
Merged into Public Storage, Inc. (CA) 5/8/98
Each share Class A 1¢ par exchanged for either (0.687) share Common 10¢ par or $21.40 cash
Note: Non-electing holders received stock
Public Storage, Inc. (CA) reincorporated in Maryland as Public Storage 6/4/2007

PUBLIC UTILITIES CONSOLIDATED CORP.
Reorganized as Citizens Utilities Co 00/00/1935
Details not available

PUBLIC UTILITIES CORP.
Liquidated in 1936

PUBLIC UTILITIES SECURITIES CORP.
Out of business in 1941
Stock valueless

PUBLIC UTILITY HOLDING CORP. OF AMERICA
Name changed to General Investment Corp. (DE) in 1933
General Investment Corp. (DE) merged into Foundation Industrial Engineering Co., Inc. in 1942 which recapitalized as Stokely Foods, Inc. in 1943 which merged into Stokely-Van Camp, Inc. 5/29/52
(See Stokley-Van Camp, Inc.)

PUBLICARD INC (PA)
Plan of reorganization under Chapter 11 Federal Bankruptcy Code effective 01/30/2008
Each share Common 10¢ par received distribution of (0.0103154) share Chazak Value Corp. Common 1¢ par
Note: Distribution was made only to holders of (101) or more shares
Certificates were not required to be surrendered and are without value

PUBLICATION CORP (NY)
Common and Non-Vtg. Common no par changed to $5 par 04/22/1955
1st Preferred $100 par called for redemption 12/19/1963
Non-Vtg. Common $5 par reclassified as Common $5 par 04/21/1965
Common $5 par changed to $2.50 par and (1) additional share issued 05/20/1966
Merged into Crowell Collier & Macmillan, Inc. 05/31/1968
Each share Common $2.50 par exchanged for (1) share $1.20 Conv. Preferred $1 par
Crowell Collier & Macmillan, Inc. name changed to Macmillan, Inc. 01/01/1973
(See Macmillan, Inc.)

PUBLICIS-ARIELY LTD (ISRAEL)
Name changed to Oz Investments Co. Ltd. 04/11/2002
(See Oz Investments Co. Ltd.)

PUBLICKER COMMERCIAL ALCOHOL CO. (PA)
Name changed to Publicker Industries Inc. 00/00/1946
Publicker Industries Inc. name changed to PubliCARD Inc. 11/02/1998
(See PubliCARD Inc.)

PUBLICKER INDS INC (PA)
Each share Common no par

PUB-PUL   **FINANCIAL INFORMATION, INC.**

exchanged for (4) shares Common $5 par 00/00/1946
Common $5 par changed to 10¢ par 12/29/1983
Name changed to PubliCARD Inc. 11/02/1998
(See PubliCARD Inc.)

PUBLIGEST LTD (CANADA)
Adjudicated bankrupt 01/08/1976
Stockholders' equity unlikely

PUBLISHERS BROADCASTING CORP (MD)
Name changed to Camptown Industries, Inc. 11/28/1972
(See Camptown Industries, Inc.)

PUBLISHERS INC (MD)
Each share Class A Common 10¢ par exchanged for (0.25) share Common 40¢ par 02/06/1961
Each share Class B Common 10¢ par exchanged for (0.25) share Class B Common 40¢ par 02/01/1961
Class B Common 40¢ par reclassified as Conv. Class B Common 40¢ par 11/05/1970
Name changed to Pubco Corp. (MD) 07/19/1973
Pubco Corp. (MD) reincorporated in Delaware 06/07/1985
(See Pubco Corp. (DE))

PUBLISHING CO NORTH AMER INC (FL)
Name changed to Attorneys.com, Inc. 06/05/2000
Attorneys.com, Inc. name changed to 1-800-Attorney, Inc. 06/01/2001

PUBLISHING COMPUTER SVC INC (DE)
Common no par changed to 1¢ par 08/03/1972
Name changed to Great Eastern Energy Corp. 08/04/1981
Great Eastern Energy Corp. name changed to Great Eastern International Inc. 06/19/1984 which recapitalized as Cable Car Beverage Corp. 07/20/1989 which merged into Triarc Companies, Inc. 11/25/1997 which name changed to Wendy's/Arby's Group, Inc. 09/29/2008 which name changed to Wendy's Co. 07/11/2011

PUD INDS INC (NY)
Dissolved by proclamation 6/23/93

PUDA COAL INC (FL)
Each share old Common $0.001 par exchanged for (0.1) share new Common $0.001 par 09/08/2005
Reorganized under the laws of Delaware 08/06/2009
Each share new Common $0.001 par exchanged for (0.14285714) share Common $0.001 par

PUDGIES CHICKEN INC (DE)
Issue Information - 2,000,000 shares COM offered at $5 per share on 08/09/1995
Chapter 11 bankruptcy proceedings terminated 07/03/2001
No stockholders' equity

PUEBLO BK & TR CO (PUEBLO, CO)
Stock Dividends - 25% 02/25/1964; 20% 11/20/1968; 33-1/3% 02/23/1973; 25% 02/23/1976
100% acquired by private investors as of 01/00/1983
Public interest eliminated

PUEBLO INTL INC (DE)
Merged into FB Holding Corp. 06/03/1988
Each share Common $1 par exchanged for $26.15 cash

PUEBLO SAVINGS & TRUST CO. (PUEBLO, CO)
Each share Common $100 par exchanged for (10) shares Common $10 par 2/11/55
Stock Dividends - 200% 9/17/48; 66-2/3% 12/26/50
Name changed to Pueblo Bank & Trust Co. (Pueblo. Colo.) 2/4/63
(See Pueblo Bank & Trust Co. (Pueblo, Colo.))

PUEBLO SUPERMARKETS INC (PR)
Class A Common no par reclassified as Common no par 4/1/62
Common no par split (2) for (1) by issuance of (1) additional share 6/1/64
Common no par split (2) for (1) by issuance of (1) additional share 7/7/69
Reincorporated under the laws of Delaware as Pueblo International, Inc. and Common no par changed to $1 par 4/28/70
(See Pueblo International, Inc.)

PUERTO RICAN CEM INC (PR)
Common $1 par split (3) for (1) by issuance of (2) additional shares 6/30/92
Merged into Cemex, S.A. de C.V. 8/2/2002
Each share Common $1 par exchanged for $35 cash

PUERTO RICAN INVS FD INC (PR)
Completely liquidated 12/31/1974
Each share Common $1 par exchanged for first and final distribution of $5.48 cash

PUERTO RICAN LIFE INSURANCE CO. (PR)
Merged into Security National Life Insurance Co. of Puerto Rico 12/17/67
Each share Common 50¢ par exchanged for (0.227272) share Common 50¢ par

PUERTO RICO BREWING INC (PR)
Completely liquidated 07/12/1973
Each share Common no par exchanged for first and final distribution of $0.30 cash

PUERTO RICO INTL AIRLS INC (PR)
Stock Dividend - 25% 8/31/72
Ceased operations in November 1984
Details not available

PUERTO RICO INVS TAX-FREE FD III INC (PR)
S&P 500 Indexed Preferred Ser. B called for redemption at $1 on 11/3/2006

PUERTO RICO INVS TAX-FREE FD IV INC (PR)
S&P 500 Indexed Preferred Ser. A called for redemption at $1 on 8/7/2006

PUERTO RICO INVS TAX-FREE FD V INC (PR)
S&P 500 Indexed Preferred Ser. B called for redemption at $1 on 11/3/2006

PUERTO RICO TEL CO (NEW) (DE)
6-3/4% Preferred Ser. A $100 par called for redemption 9/1/74
6-1/4% Preferred Ser. B $100 par called for redemption 9/1/74
$3 Conv. Preference $10 par called for redemption 2/1/77
Public interest eliminated

PUERTO RICO TELEPHONE CO. OLD (DE)
Merged into Puerto Rico Telephone Co. (DE) (New) 10/2/67
Each share Common $20 par exchanged for (1) share $3 Conv. Preference $10 par
(See Puerto Rico Telephone Co. (DE) (New))

PUFF PAC INDS INC (DE)
Name changed to Air Packaging Technologies Inc. 09/01/1992
(See Air Packaging Technologies Inc.)

PUGET ENERGY INC NEW (WA)
Merged into Puget Holdings LLC 02/06/2009
Each share Common 1¢ par exchanged for $30 cash

PUGET SOUND BANCORP (WA)
Common $5 par split (2) for (1) by issuance of (1) additional share 08/19/1983
Common $5 par split (2) for (1) by issuance of (1) additional share 08/22/1986
Stock Dividend - 10% 08/16/1991
Merged into KeyCorp (NY) 01/15/1993
Each share Common $5 par exchanged for (1.32) shares Common $5 par
KeyCorp (NY) merged into KeyCorp (New) (OH) 03/01/1994

PUGET SOUND BANCORP INC (WA)
Merged into Heritage Financial Corp. 01/16/2018
Each share Common no par exchanged for (1.1688) shares Common no par

PUGET SOUND BANCORP INC (WA)
Merged into Interwest Bancorp, Inc. 01/15/1998
Each share Common no par exchanged for (1.66797) shares Common $2 par
Interwest Bancorp, Inc. name changed to Pacific Northwest Bancorp 09/01/2000 which merged into Wells Fargo & Co. (New) 11/03/2003

PUGET SOUND BANK (BELLEVUE, WA)
Under plan of reorganization each share Common $1 par automatically became (1) share Puget Sound Bancorp, Inc. Common no par 11/10/2015
Puget Sound Bancorp, Inc. merged into Heritage Financial Corp. 01/16/2018

PUGET SOUND DEVL CO INC (WA)
Each share old Common 1¢ par exchanged for (0.1) share new Common 1¢ par 11/24/1995
Name changed to Integrated Healthcare Inc. 09/13/1996
Integrated Healthcare Inc. name changed to Triangle Multi-Media Ltd., Inc. 09/14/1999 which recapitalized as Cinemax Pictures & Production Company International, Inc. 10/05/2007

PUGET SOUND ENERGY CAP TR II (DE)
8.40% Trust Originated Preferred Securities called for redemption at $25 plus $0.525 accrued dividends on 6/30/2006

PUGET SOUND ENERGY INC (WA)
Name changed 02/10/1997
Recapitalized 00/00/1943
Each share $5 Prior Preference no par received an additional (0.25) share
Each share $6 Preferred no par exchanged for (8) shares Common $10 par
Each (20) shares Common no par exchanged for (1) share Common $10 par
Recapitalized 11/23/1955
Common $10 par split (3) for (2) by issuance of (0.5) additional share
State of incorporation changed from (MA) to (WA) 11/16/1960
5-1/2% Preferred $100 par called for redemption 06/18/1964
7.25% Conv. Preference $50 par called for redemption 03/24/1982
$2.59 Preferred $25 par called for redemption 06/23/1986
10.90% Preferred $25 par called for redemption 06/23/1986
$4.375 Preferred $25 par called for redemption 02/02/1987
$2.34 Preferred $25 par called for redemption 06/02/1987
9.36% Preferred $25 par called for redemption 03/01/1991
Name changed from Puget Sound Power & Light Co. to Puget Sound Energy, Inc. 02/10/1997
7.875% Preferred $25 par called for redemption at $25 plus $0.329024 accrued dividend on 07/15/1997
8% Preferred $100 par called for redemption at $101 on 02/16/1998
Adjustable Rate Preferred Ser. B $25 par called for redemption at $25 on 02/02/1999
8.50% Preferred Ser. III $25 par called for redemption 09/01/1999
Under plan of reorganization each share Common no par automatically became (1) share Puget Energy, Inc. Common 1¢ par 01/01/2001
7.75% Ser. Preferred Stock called for redemption at $102.07 on 08/15/2003
7.45% Preferred Ser. II $25 par called for redemption at $25 on 11/01/2003
4.70% Preferred $100 par called for redemption at $101 on 03/13/2009
4.84% Preferred $100 par called for redemption at $102 on 03/13/2009

PUGET SOUND NATL BK (TACOMA, WA)
Par value changed from $100 to $25 00/00/1933
Each share Common $25 par exchanged for (1.25) shares Common $20 par 00/00/1944
Common $20 par changed to $10 par and (1) additional share issued plus a 33-1/3% stock dividend paid 12/18/1956
Common $10 par changed to $5 par and (1) additional share issued 04/07/1978
Stock Dividends - 25% 02/06/1961; 20% 01/21/1963; 20% 01/25/1966; 20% 01/23/1968; 11.11% 01/28/1969; 25% 01/26/1971
Under plan of reorganization each share Common $5 par automatically became (1) share Puget Sound Bancorp 10/01/1981
Puget Sound Bancorp merged into KeyCorp (NY) 01/15/1993 which merged into KeyCorp (New) (OH) 03/01/1994

PUGET SOUND NAVIGATION CO. (NV)
Liquidation completed 3/26/64

PUGET SOUND PULP & TIMBER CO. (DE)
Common no par changed to $3 par and (2) additional shares issued 7/13/56
Stock Dividend - 100% 7/25/48
Merged into Georgia-Pacific Corp. 7/2/63
Each share Common $3 par exchanged for (0.6) share Common 80¢ par
(See Georgia-Pacific Corp.)

PUGET SOUND TELEPHONE CO.
Merged into West Coast Telephone Co. in 1927
Details not available

PUGET VENTURES INC (BC)
Name changed to Global Cobalt Corp. 06/04/2013

PUGH HOLDING CO. (DE)
Dissolved in 1977

PULASKI BANCORP INC (USA)
Merged into Keary Financial Corp. 10/18/2002
Each share Common 1¢ par exchanged for $32.90 cash

PULASKI BK A SVGS BK (ST LOUIS, MO)
Under plan of reorganization each share Common $1 par automatically became (1) share Pulaski Financial Corp. (DE) Common 1¢ par 12/03/1998
Pulaski Financial Corp. (DE)

PUL-PUN

reincorporated in Missouri 02/03/2003 which merged into First Busey Corp. 05/02/2016

PULASKI FINL CORP (MO)
Reincorporated 02/02/2003
State of incorporation changed from (DE) to (MO) 02/02/2003
Common $1 par split (2) for (1) by issuance of (1) additional share payable 07/21/2003 to holders of record 07/07/2003 Ex date - 07/22/2003
Common $1 par split (3) for (2) by issuance of (0.5) additional share payable 07/18/2005 to holders of record 07/05/2005 Ex date - 07/19/2005
Fixed Rate Perpetual Preferred Ser. A 1¢ par called for redemption at $1,000 plus $19 accrued dividends on 07/31/2014
Merged into First Busey Corp. 05/02/2016
Each share Common $1 par exchanged for (0.79) share new Common $0.001 par

PULASKI FURNITURE CORP (VA)
Merged into Pine Holdings, Inc. 5/19/2000
Each share Common $1 par exchanged for $22.50 cash

PULASKI SVGS BK (SPRINGFIELD, NJ)
Under plan of reorganization each share Common 1¢ par automatically became (1) share Pulaski Bancorp, Inc. Common 1¢ par 7/12/99
(See Pulaski Bancorp, Inc.)

PULASKI VENEER & FURNITURE CORP. (VA)
Name changed to Pulaski Furniture Corp. 3/13/62
(See Pulaski Furniture Corp.)

PULAWSKI SVGS & LN ASSN SOUTH RIV (NJ)
Common $1 par split (2) for (1) by issuance of (1) additional share 12/28/87
Under plan of reorganization each share Common $1 par automatically became (1) share Pulse Bancorp, Inc. Common $1 par 6/1/90
Pulse Bancorp, Inc. merged into First Sentinel Bancorp Inc. 12/18/98 which merged into Provident Financial Services, Inc. 7/15/2004

PULITZER INC (DE)
Merged into Lee Enterprises, Inc. 06/03/2005
Each share Common 1¢ par exchanged for $64 cash

PULITZER PUBG CO (DE)
Common 1¢ par split (4) for (3) by issuance of (1/3) additional share payable 11/01/1996 to holders of record 10/10/1996 Ex date - 11/04/1996
Each share Common 1¢ par received distribution of (1) share Pulitzer Inc. Common 1¢ par payable 03/19/1999 to holders of record 03/18/1999
Stock Dividends - 10% 01/22/1993; 25% 01/24/1995
Merged into Hearst-Argyle Television, Inc. 03/18/1999
Each share Common 1¢ par exchanged for (1.63914877) shares Common 1¢ par
(See Hearst-Argyle Television, Inc.)

PULLMAN ASSOC LTD (NY)
Charter cancelled and proclaimed dissolved for failure to pay taxes 12/20/1977

PULLMAN BK & TR CO (CHICAGO, IL)
Stock Dividend - 100% 12/31/70
Name changed to Heritage/Pullman Bank & Trust Co. (Chicago, IL) 11/1/74
(See Heritage/Pullman Bank & Trust Co. (Chicago, IL))

PULLMAN CO.
Name changed to Pullman Inc. 00/00/1927
Pullman Inc. merged into Wheelabrator- Frye Inc. 11/06/1980 which merged into Signal Companies, Inc. 02/01/1983 which merged into Allied-Signal Inc. 09/19/1985 which name changed to AlliedSignal Inc. 04/26/1993 which name changed to Honeywell International Inc. 12/01/1999

PULLMAN CO NEW (DE)
Under plan of merger name changed to Pullman-Peabody Co. 10/24/85 which name changed back to Pullman Co. 2/12/87
Merged into FLPC Acquisition Corp. 9/15/88
Each share Common 10¢ par exchanged for $9.25 cash

PULLMAN INC (DE)
Capital Stock no par split (2) for (1) by issuance of (1) additional share 6/27/60
Capital Stock no par split (3) for (2) by issuance of (0.5) additional share 12/10/73
Capital Stock no par split (3) for (2) by issuance of (0.5) additional share 9/15/75
Merged into Wheelabrator-Frye Inc. 11/6/80
Each share Capital Stock no par exchanged for (1.1) shares Common 30¢ par
Wheelabrator-Frye Inc. merged into Signal Companies, Inc. 2/1/83 which merged into Allied-Signal Inc. 9/19/85 which name changed to AlliedSignal Inc. 4/26/93 which name changed to Honeywell International Inc. 12/1/99

PULLMAN PEABODY CO (DE)
Name changed back to Pullman Co. (New) 2/12/87
(See Pullman Co. (New))

PULLMAN TRANSN INC (DE)
Name changed to Pullman Co. (New) 2/21/85
Pullman Co. (New) merged into Pullman-Peabody Co. 10/24/85 which name changed back to Pullman Co. (New) 2/12/87
(See Pullman Co. (New))

PULLMAN TRUST & SAVINGS BANK (CHICAGO, IL)
Each share Capital Stock $100 par exchanged for (10) shares Capital Stock $20 par to effect a (5) for (1) split and a 100% stock dividend in 1947
Capital Stock $20 par changed to $10 par and (1) additional share issued 6/23/61
Stock Dividend - 25% 11/5/54
Name changed to Pullman Bank & Trust Co. (Chicago, IL) 11/1/62
Pullman Bank & Trust Co. (Chicago, IL) name changed to Heritage/Pullman Bank & Trust Co. (Chicago, IL) 11/1/74
(See Heritage/Pullman Bank & Trust Co. (Chicago, IL))

PULSAR ENERGY & RES INC (BC)
Recapitalized as Star One Resources Inc. 02/10/1988
Each share Common no par exchanged for (1/3) share Common no par
Star One Resources Inc. name changed to Hyder Gold Inc. 06/26/1989 which recapitalized as Gleichen Resources Ltd. (BC) 08/03/2006 which reincorporated in Ontario as Torex Gold Resources Inc. 05/04/2010

PULSAR OIL & GAS INC (UT)
Proclaimed dissolved for failure to pay taxes 03/31/1986

PULSE BANCORP INC (NJ)
Common $1 par split (2) for (1) by issuance of (1) additional share 12/28/1993
Merged into First Sentinel Bancorp Inc. 12/18/1998
Each share Common $1 par exchanged for (3.764) shares Common 1¢ par
First Sentinel Bancorp Inc. merged into Provident Financial Services, Inc. 07/15/2004

PULSE BIOSCIENCES INC (NV)
Reincorporated under the laws of Delaware 06/18/2018

PULSE CAP CORP (BC)
Name changed to ACT Aurora Control Technologies Corp. 12/07/2011
ACT Aurora Control Technologies Corp. name changed to Aurora Solar Technologies Inc. 05/28/2015

PULSE COMMUNICATIONS INC (VA)
Name changed to PCI Liquidation, Inc. 12/30/1972
(See PCI Liquidation, Inc.)

PULSE DATA INC (CANADA)
Class A Common no par reclassified as Common no par 02/15/2001
Name changed to Pulse Seismic Inc. 05/28/2009

PULSE ELECTRONICS CORP (PA)
Each share old Common $0.125 par exchanged for (0.1) share new Common $0.125 par 05/22/2013
Acquired by Oaktree Capital Management L.P. 04/13/2015
Each share new Common $0.125 par exchanged for $1.50 cash

PULSE ENGR INC (DE)
Merged into Technitrol, Inc. 09/29/1995
Each share Common 1¢ par exchanged for $8.50 cash

PULSE RES LTD (BC)
Recapitalized as Jupiter Explorations Ltd. 06/12/1992
Each share Common no par exchanged for (0.33333333) share Common no par
Jupiter Explorations Ltd. name changed to Hypaz Technology Corp. 06/29/1993 which name changed to Calibre Technologies Corp. 09/12/1994
(See Calibre Technologies Corp.)

PULSE TECHNOLOGY INC (UT)
Recapitalized as Asia Pacific Chemical Engineering Co. Ltd. 2/28/97
Each share Common $0.0015 par exchanged for (0.04) share Common no par
Asia Pacific Chemical Engineering Co. Ltd. name changed to Interactive Objects, Inc. 9/15/97 which name changed to Fullplay Media Systems, Inc. 1/7/2002
(See Fullplay Media Systems, Inc.)

PULSEPOINT COMMUNICATIONS (CA)
Merged into Unisys Corp. 8/27/99
Each share Common no par exchanged for (0.162) share Common no par

PULSOTRONICS INC (DE)
Stock Dividend - 100% 6/24/71
Recapitalized as All State Microfilm Inc. 2/23/82
Each share Common 1¢ par exchanged for (0.13605) share Common 1¢ par
All State Microfilm Inc. name changed to ECR All State Ltd. 12/18/85
(See ECR All State Ltd.)

PULTE HOME CORP (MI)
Reincorporated 04/12/1985
Common $1 par split (3) for (2) by issuance of (0.5) additional share 01/02/1979
Common $1 par split (2) for (1) by issuance of (1) additional share 09/05/1980
Common $1 par split (2) for (1) by issuance of (1) additional share 12/15/1982
Common $1 par split (2) for (1) by issuance of (1) additional share 05/27/1983
State of incorporation changed from (DE) to (MI) and Common $1 par changed to 1¢ par 04/12/1985
Under plan of reorganization each share Common 1¢ par automatically became (1) share PHM Corp. Common 1¢ par 12/07/1987
PHM Corp. name changed to Pulte Corp. 07/01/1993 which name changed to Pulte Homes, Inc. 05/17/2001

PULTE HOMES INC (MI)
Name changed 05/17/2001
Common 1¢ par split (2) for (1) by issuance of (1) additional share payable 06/01/1998 to holders of record 05/18/1998 Ex date - 06/02/1998
Name changed from Pulte Corp. to Pulte Homes, Inc. 05/17/2001
Common 1¢ par split (2) for (1) by issuance of (1) additional share payable 01/02/2004 to holders of record 12/22/2003 Ex date - 01/05/2004
Common 1¢ par split (2) for (1) by issuance of (1) additional share payable 09/01/2005 to holders of record 08/15/2005 Ex date - 09/02/2005
Name changed to PulteGroup, Inc. 03/22/2010

PULTRONEX CORP (NV)
Name changed to 1-900 Jackpot, Inc. 07/07/2005 1-900 Jackpot, Inc. name changed to Exmocare, Inc. 03/07/2008 which name changed to Second Solar, Inc. 07/01/2009
(See Second Solar, Inc.)

PUMA AG RUDOLF DASSLER SPORT (GERMANY)
ADR agreement terminated 12/31/2007
Each Sponsored ADR for Bearer shares exchanged for $318.5244 cash

PUMA ENERGY INC (FL)
Reincorporated under the laws of Nevada as Blue Diamond Ventures, Inc. 10/26/2004

PUMA MINERALS CORP (BC)
Recapitalized as Consolidated Puma Minerals Corp. 07/22/1999
Each share Common no par exchanged for (0.1) share Common no par
Consolidated Puma Minerals Corp. merged into Sage Gold Inc. 08/07/2009

PUMA PETE LTD (AB)
Merged into Pennant-Puma Oils Ltd. 07/10/1973
Each share Common no par exchanged for (1/3) share Common no par
(See Pennant-Puma Oils Ltd.)

PUMATECH INC (DE)
Name changed 12/20/2000
Name changed from Puma Technology, Inc. to Pumatech, Inc. 12/20/2000
Name changed to Intellisync Corp. 2/17/2004
(See Intellisync Corp.)

PUNA SUGAR LTD (HI)
Merged into Amfac, Inc. 01/09/1969
Each share Capital Stock $20 par

PUN-PUR   FINANCIAL INFORMATION, INC.

exchanged for (0.7) share Common no par
(See Amfac, Inc.)

PUNCH PETROLEUMS LTD. (ON)
Merged into Rio-Prado Consolidated Oils Ltd. 00/00/1953
Each share Capital Stock $1 par exchanged for (1/3) share new Capital Stock $1 par
Rio-Prado Consolidated Oils Ltd. merged into Rio Palmer Oils Ltd. 07/25/1955 which merged into Devon-Palmer Oils Ltd. 11/06/1956
(See Devon-Palmer Oils Ltd.)

PUNCH TAVERNS PLC (ENGLAND & WALES)
Each old ADR for Ordinary received distribution of $1.676111 cash payable 08/29/2011 to holders of record 08/19/2011 Ex date - 08/30/2011
Each old ADR for Ordinary exchanged for (0.05) new ADR for Ordinary 10/14/2014
ADR agreement terminated 09/25/2017
Each new ADR for Ordinary issued by Bank of New York exchanged for $4.758133 cash

PUNCHLINE ENTMT INC (NV)
Common $0.0001 par split (10) for (1) by issuance of (9) additional shares payable 07/14/2009 to holders of record 06/29/2009 Ex date - 07/15/2009
Name changed to Punchline Resources Ltd. 09/07/2012
Punchline Resources Ltd. recapitalized as Northern Minerals & Exploration Ltd. 08/13/2013

PUNCHLINE RES LTD (NV)
Recapitalized as Northern Minerals & Exploration Ltd. 08/13/2013
Each share Common $0.0001 par exchanged for (0.1) share Common $0.0001 par

PUNDATA GOLD CORP (BC)
Delisted from Alberta Stock Exchange 07/24/1991

PUNTA ALEGRE SUGAR CO.
Reorganized as Punta Alegre Sugar Corp. in 1932
(See Bangor Punta Alegre Sugar Corp.)

PUNTA ALEGRE SUGAR CORP. (DE)
Each share Capital Stock no par exchanged for (5) shares Capital Stock $1 par in 1942
Capital Stock $1 par reclassified as Common $1 par 6/19/63
Stock Dividend - 100% 7/3/47
Name changed to Bangor Punta Alegre Sugar Corp. 10/13/64 which name changed to Bangor Punta Corp. 1/20/67
(See Bangor Punta Corp.)

PUNTA GORDA ISLES INC (FL)
Common 10¢ par split (3) for (2) by issuance of (0.5) additional share 3/9/70
$1.104 Conv. Preferred $1 par called for redemption 6/9/83
Name changed to PGI Inc. 3/13/90

PUNXSUTAWNEY NATL BK (PUNXSUTAWNEY, PA)
Each share Common $100 par exchanged for (10) shares Common $25 par to effect a (4) for (1) split and 150% stock dividend 01/13/1953
Stock Dividend - 100% 03/10/1971
Name changed to Keystone National Bank (Punxsutawney, PA) 03/01/1972
(See Keystone National Bank (Punxsutawney, PA))

PUPPY ZONE ENTERPRISES INC (NV)
Common $0.001 par split (18) for (1) by issuance of (17) additional shares payable 11/09/2007 to holders of record 11/09/2007
Name changed to Actiga Corp. 01/07/2008
Actiga Corp. name changed to Avisio, Inc. 08/20/2009 which recapitalized as Deal A Day Group Corp. 11/03/2011

PURAMED BIOSCIENCE INC (MN)
Reorganized under the laws of Nevada 10/07/2014
Each share Common no par exchanged for (0.025) share Common $0.000001 par

PURATRONICS, INC. (MN)
Under plan of merger name changed to Phillips-Puratronics, Inc. 11/29/67
Phillips-Puratronics, Inc. name changed to Puratronics Industries, Inc. 8/15/68 which name changed to Cambridge Corp. 5/8/70
(See Cambridge Corp.)

PURATRONICS INC (MN)
Common 5¢ par split (3) for (2) by issuance of (0.5) additional share 9/25/68
Name changed to Cambridge Corp. 5/8/70
(See Cambridge Corp.)

PURCELL DEV LTD (BC)
Placed in receivership 00/00/1975
No stockholders' equity

PURCELL ENERGY LTD NEW (AB)
Recapitalized as Point North Energy Ltd. 11/07/2005
Each share Common no par exchanged for (0.2) share Common no par, (0.0556) share Prairie Schooner Petroleum Ltd. Common no par and (0.2) share Tenergy Ltd. Common no par
Note: Holders had the option to receive $0.61833 cash per share in lieu of stock
(See each company's listing)

PURCELL ENERGY LTD OLD (AB)
Recapitalized as Purcell Energy Ltd. (New) 03/07/1997
Each share Common no par exchanged for (0.5) share Common no par
(See Purcell Energy Ltd. (New))

PURCELL INC (DE)
Merged into McLean Industries, Inc. 03/26/1984
Each share Common $1 par exchanged for $12 principal amount of 12% Subordinated Debentures due 07/15/2003 and (1) Common Stock Purchase Warrant expiring 07/15/1990
Note: Holdings of (9) shares or fewer received cash

PURCHASE POINT MEDIA CORP (MN)
Recapitalized as Power Sports Factory, Inc. 06/10/2008
Each share Common no par exchanged for (0.05) share Common no par
(See Power Sports Factory, Inc.)

PURCHASEPRO COM INC (NV)
Issue Information - 4,000,000 shares COM offered at $12 per share on 09/13/1999
Common 1¢ par split (3) for (2) by issuance of (0.5) additional share payable 12/13/1999 to holders of record 12/01/1999
Common 1¢ par split (2) for (1) by issuance of (1) additional share payable 10/12/2000 to holders of record 09/29/2000 Ex date - 10/13/2000
Each share old Common 1¢ par exchanged for (0.2) share new Common 1¢ par 05/15/2002
Under Chapter 11 plan of reorganization each share new Common 1¢ par received approximately $0.02 cash payable 07/29/2011 to holders of record 10/21/2004
Note: Certificates were not required to be surrendered and are without value

PURCHASESOFT INC (DE)
Each share old Common 1¢ par exchanged for (0.2) share new Common 1¢ par 11/15/2005
SEC revoked common stock registration 02/17/2010
Stockholders' equity unlikely

PURDEN LAKE RESOURCE CORP (DE)
Name changed to China Baicaotang Medicine Ltd. 01/28/2010
China Baicaotang Medicine Ltd. name changed to China BCT Pharmacy Group, Inc. 07/22/2010

PURDEX MINERALS LTD (ON)
Charter cancelled and declared dissolved for failure to file returns and pay taxes 11/18/1970

PURDUE NATL BK (LAFAYETTE, IN)
Common $20 par changed to $10 par and (1) additional share issued plus a 33-1/3% stock dividend paid 02/09/1968
Stock Dividends - 25% 01/17/1962; 20% 02/01/1965; 10% 03/05/1974; 15% 04/05/1976; 20% 04/05/1978
Under plan of reorganization each share Common $10 par automatically became (1) share Purdue National Corp. Common $10 par 01/03/1983
Purdue National Corp. merged into Bank One Corp. (DE) 06/02/1986 which reincorporated in Ohio 05/01/1989 which merged into Bank One Corp. 10/02/1998 which merged into J.P. Morgan Chase & Co. 12/31/2000 which name changed to JPMorgan Chase & Co. 07/20/2004

PURDUE NATL CORP (IN)
Merged into Banc One Corp. (DE) 06/02/1986
Each share Common 10¢ par exchanged for (4.1379) shares Common no par
Banc One Corp. (DE) reincorporated in Ohio 05/01/1989 which merged into Bank One Corp. 10/02/1998 which merged into J.P. Morgan Chase & Co. 12/31/2000 which name changed to JPMorgan Chase & Co. 07/20/2004

PURDY MICA MINES LTD. (ON)
Name changed to Purdex Minerals Ltd. 6/29/56
(See Purdex Minerals Ltd.)

PURE AIR TECHNOLOGY INC (FL)
Recapitalized as Startek.Com Inc. 03/06/1999
Each share Common $0.0001 par exchanged for (0.05) share Common $0.0001 par
Startek.Com Inc. name changed to Bentley Communications Corp. 11/29/1999 which name changed to Bentley Commerce Corp. 01/12/2004
(See Bentley Commerce Corp.)

PURE ATRIA CORP (CA)
Merged into Rational Software Corp. 7/30/97
Each share Common $0.0001 par exchanged for (0.9) share Common 1¢ par
(See Rational Software Corp.)

PURE BIOFUELS CORP (NV)
Common $0.001 par split (5) for (4) by issuance of (0.25) additional share payable 08/07/2006 to holders of record 08/07/2006
Acquired by PBC Acquisition L.L.C. 04/30/2012
Each share Common $0.001 par exchanged for $0.00832 cash

PURE BIOSCIENCE (CA)
Reincorporated under the laws of Delaware as PURE Bioscience, Inc. and Common no par changed to 1¢ par 03/24/2011

PURE CAP INC (CANADA)
Each (15) shares old Common no par exchanged for (1) share new Common no par 1/17/2006
Name changed to Tombstone Exploration Corp. 2/12/2007

PURE COPPER EXPLS LTD (ON)
Acquired by Ark Explorations Ltd. 9/15/71
Each share Capital Stock no par exchanged for (1) share Common no par
Ark Explorations Ltd. merged into Ranchmen's Resources (1976) Ltd. 1/31/77 which name changed to Ranchmen's Resources Ltd. 5/31/85 which merged into Crestar Energy Inc. 10/11/95 which was acquired by Gulf Canada Resources Inc. 11/23/2000
(See Gulf Canada Resources Inc.)

PURE DIAMONDS EXPL INC (ON)
Recapitalized as Burnstone Ventures Inc. 08/14/2009
Each share Common no par exchanged for (0.1) share Common no par

PURE DRUG & CHEMICAL CORP. (NY)
Proclaimed dissolved by the Secretary of the State of New York 12/16/63

PURE ENERGY SVCS LTD (AB)
Acquired by FMC Technologies, Inc. 10/01/2012
Each share Common no par exchanged for $11 cash
Note: Unexchanged certificates were cancelled and became without value 09/30/2015

PURE FOOD STORES LTD.
Merged into Consolidated Food Products, Ltd. in 1928
Details not available

PURE GOLD MANUFACTURING CO., LTD.
Merged into Blue Ribbon Corp. Ltd. 00/00/1930
Details not available

PURE GOLD MINERALS INC (ON)
Recapitalized as Pure Diamonds Exploration Inc. 12/05/2006
Each share Common no par exchanged for (0.125) share Common no par
Pure Diamonds Exploration Inc. recapitalized as Burnstone Ventures Inc. 08/14/2009

PURE GOLD RES INC (ON)
Merged into Pure Gold Minerals Inc. 11/20/1997
Each share Common no par exchanged for (0.2) share Common no par
Pure Gold Minerals Inc. recapitalized as Pure Diamonds Exploration Inc. 12/05/2006 which recapitalized as Burnstone Ventures Inc. 08/14/2009

PURE HOSPITALITY SOLUTIONS INC (NV)
Recapitalized as Meso Numismatics, Inc. 09/26/2018
Each share Common $0.001 par exchanged for (0.001) share Common $0.001 par

PURE H2O INC (NV)
Recapitalized as Newron Sport 10/03/2008
Each (75,000) shares Common $0.001 par exchanged for (1) share Common $0.001 par

PURE INDL REAL ESTATE TR (BC)
Acquired by BPP Pristine Holdings ULC 05/24/2018
Each Class A Unit exchanged for $8.10 cash
Note: Unexchanged certificates will be cancelled and become without value 05/24/2024

PURE JUICE PRODUCERS CORP. (FL)
Charter revoked for failure to file reports and pay fees 4/30/56

PURE LIVING MEDIA INC (BC)
Each share old Common no par exchanged for (0.05) share new Common no par 02/10/2012
Name changed to Scavo Resource Corp. 08/23/2012
Scavo Resource Corp. name changed to Brabeia Inc. 08/28/2015 which name changed to Seahawk Ventures Inc. 03/01/2016

PURE NICKEL INC (YT)
Reincorporated under the laws of Canada 04/07/2009

PURE OIL CO. (OH)
Common $25 par changed to no par in 1932
Recapitalized in 1936
Each share 8% Preferred $100 par had the option of receiving in exchange either (1.34) shares 6% Preferred $100 par and $1.50 cash or (1) share new 8% Preferred $100 par, (0.24) share 6% Preferred $100 par and $1.50 cash
Each share 6% Preferred $100 par exchanged for (1.18) shares new 6% Preferred $100 par and $1.125 cash
Each share 5-1/2% Preferred $100 par exchanged for (1.16) shares new 6% Preferred $100 par and $0.875 cash
Recapitalized 4/26/55
Common no par changed to $5 par and (1) additional share issued
Merged into Union Oil Co. of California 7/16/65
Each share Common $5 par exchanged for (1) share $2.50 Convertible Preferred no par plus $0.196 cash
(See Union Oil Co. of California)

PURE PLAY MUSIC LTD (NV)
SEC revoked common stock registration 01/21/2014

PURE RES INC (DE)
Merged into Unocal Corp. 10/30/2002
Each share Common 1¢ par exchanged for (0.74) share Common $1 par
Unocal Corp. merged into Chevron Corp. 8/10/2005

PURE SILVER MINES LTD (ON)
Merged into Lacana Mining Corp. 09/29/1975
Each share Capital Stock no par exchanged for (0.6) share Common no par
Lacana Mining Corp. merged into Corona Corp. 07/01/1988 which recapitalized as International Corona Corp. 06/11/1991

PURE SOFTWARE INC (CA)
Merged into Pure Atria Corp. 8/26/96
Each share Common $0.0001 par exchanged for (1.544615) shares Common $0.0001 par
Pure Atria Corp. merged into Rational Software Corp. 7/31/97
(See Rational Software Corp.)

PURE TECH INTL INC NEW (DE)
Name changed to Puretec Corp. 5/7/96
(See Puretec Corp.)

PURE TECH INTL INC OLD (DE)
Each share Common 1¢ par exchanged for (0.2) share Common 5¢ par 11/7/91
Merged into Pure Tech International, Inc. (New) 7/31/95
Each share Common 5¢ par exchanged for (1) share Common 5¢ par
Pure Tech International, Inc. (New) name changed to Puretec Corp. 5/7/96
(See Puretec Corp.)

PURE TECHNOLOGIES LTD (AB)
Acquired by Xylem Inc. 01/31/2018
Each share Common no par exchanged for $9 cash
Note: Unexchanged certificates will be cancelled and become without value 01/29/2021

PURE VANILLA EXCHANGE INC (NV)
Charter permanently revoked 09/01/2008

PURE WORLD INC (DE)
Stock Dividend - 10% payable 01/15/1999 to holders of record 01/07/1999
Merged into Naturex S.A. 07/22/2005
Each share Common no par exchanged for $4.30 cash

PURE WTR SYS INC (NJ)
Charter declared void for non-payment of taxes 7/30/93

PURE ZINC TECHNOLOGIES INC (CANADA)
Name changed to Charityville.com International Inc. 08/27/1999
Charityville.com International Inc. name changed to eNblast productions inc. 06/14/2000
(See eNblast productions inc.)

PURECYCLE CORP (DE)
Each share old Common $0.00333-1/3 par exchanged for (0.1) share new Common $0.00333-1/3 par 04/23/2004
Reincorporated under the laws of Colorado 01/17/2008

PUREDEPTH INC (DE)
Acquired by Delphi Automotive PLC 03/23/2016
Each share Common $0.001 par exchanged for $0.03286326 cash
Note: An additional $0.011912 cash per share is being held in escrow for possible future distribution

PUREOXIA CO.
Merged into Moxie Co. in 1931
Details not available

PUREPAC CORP. (NY)
Name changed to Purepac Laboratories Corp. 4/18/68
(See Purepac Laboratories Corp.)

PUREPAC INC (DE)
Name changed to Faulding Inc. 3/1/96
(See Faulding Inc.)

PUREPAC LABS CORP (NY)
Merged into Kali-Chemie AG 09/27/1979
Each share Common 5¢ par exchanged for $15.50 cash

PURESNAX INTL INC (NV)
Each share old Common $0.001 par exchanged for (0.00005221) share new Common $0.001 par 05/09/2018
Name changed to iQSTEL Inc. 08/30/2018

PURESPECTRUM INC (NV)
Merged into PureSpectrum, Inc. (DE) 11/04/2009
Each share Common $0.001 par exchanged for (1) share Common $0.0001 par

PURETEC CORP (DE)
Merged into Tekni-Plex Inc. 3/3/98
Each share Common 5¢ par exchanged for $3.50 cash

PUREWATER SCIENCES INTL INC (DE)
Name changed to Panamerican Bancorp (Old) 2/16/99
(See Panamerican Bancorp (Old))

PUREX CORP (CA)
Name changed 11/05/1973
Each share Capital Stock $10 par exchanged for (10) shares Capital Stock $1 par 00/00/1946
Capital Stock $1 par split (2) for (1) by issuance of (1) additional share 12/29/1961
Capital Stock $1 par reclassified as Common $1 par 12/20/1963
Stock Dividends - 25% 06/14/1951; 100% 03/31/1959; 25% 09/30/1961
Name changed from Purex Corp., Ltd. to Purex Corp. 11/05/1973
Reincorporated under the laws of Delaware as Purex Industries, Inc. 10/31/1978
(See Purex Industries, Inc.)

PUREX INDS INC (DE)
Under plan of acquisition each share Common $1 par exchanged for $31.50 cash 8/11/82
Note: An additional amount of $0.105 per share will be payable at a later date
$1.35 Conv. Preferred 1, $5 par called for redemption 8/19/82

PUREZZA GROUP INC (FL)
Name changed to Puda Coal, Inc. (FL) 08/22/2005
Puda Coal, Inc. (FL) reorganized in Delaware 08/06/2009

PURICHLOR TECHNOLOGY LTD (BC)
Delisted from Vancouver Stock Exchange 07/07/1989

PURIDYNE INC (DE)
Charter cancelled and declared inoperative and void for non-payment of taxes 6/24/91

PURIFICATION SCIENCES INC (NY)
Charter cancelled and proclaimed dissolved for failure to pay taxes 3/24/93

PURIFICATION SYS INC (DE)
Charter cancelled and declared inoperative and void for non-payment of taxes 6/24/92

PURINA MLS INC NEW (DE)
Merged into Land O' Lakes Inc. 10/11/2001
Each share Common 1¢ par exchanged for $23 cash

PURINGTON BRICK & TILE CO. (IL)
Name changed to Purington Brick Co. in 1955

PURINGTON PAVING BRICK CO. (IL)
Name changed to Purington Brick & Tile Co. in 1942 which name was changed to Purington Brick Co. in 1955

PURIO INC (WY)
Reincorporated 08/14/2010
State of incorporation changed from (NV) to (WY) and Common $0.001 par changed to $0.00000001 par 08/14/2010
Each share old Common $0.00000001 par exchanged for (0.0025) share new Common $0.00000001 par 10/14/2010
Name changed to BitFrontier Capital Holdings, Inc. 02/05/2018

PURITAN BENNETT CORP (DE)
Common $1 par split (2) for (1) by issuance of (1) additional share 5/29/87
Stock Dividends - 100% 6/30/69; 100% 5/28/86
Merged into Nellcor Puritan Bennett Inc. 8/25/95
Each share Common $1 par exchanged for (0.88) share Common $1 par
(See Nellcor Puritan Bennett Inc.)

PURITAN CHEMICAL CORP. (DE)
Acquired by American Continental Industries, Inc. 12/11/67
Each share Capital Stock 10¢ par exchanged for (0.1) share Common $1 par
(See American Continental Industries, Inc.)

PURITAN CORDAGE MILLS (KY)
Completely liquidated 8/3/68
Each share Capital Stock $2 par exchanged for first and final distribution of (0.3168) share Wellington Technical Industries, Inc. 4% Conv. Preferred Ser. A $100 par and (0.396) share Common 75¢ par
Wellington Technical Industries, Inc. merged into Wellington Industries, Inc. 4/30/82

PURITAN DYE & CHEMICAL CO. (MA)
Proclaimed dissolved for failure to file reports and pay taxes 3/31/26

PURITAN FASHIONS CORP (NY)
Common $1 par split (2) for (1) by issuance of (1) additional share 8/13/71
Merged into Calvin Klein Ltd. 2/17/84
Each share Common $1 par exchanged for $17.50 cash

PURITAN FD INC (MA)
Reincorporated 10/29/54
State of incorporation changed from (DE) to (MA) and (2) additional shares issued 10/29/54
Name changed to Fidelity Puritan Fund, Inc. 11/18/80

PURITAN FINANCE CO. (MI)
Liquidation completed
Each share Common $1 par exchanged for initial distribution of $5.55 cash 12/27/67
Each share Common $1 par received second and final distribution of $0.5975 cash 11/1/68

PURITAN FINL GROUP INC (NY)
Reincorporated under the laws of Maryland as Concordis Group, Inc. 04/27/2009

PURITAN MINES LTD.
Acquired by Buckhorn Mines Ltd. share for share in 1942
(See Buckhorn Mines Ltd.)

PURITAN MORTGAGE CORP. (DE)
No longer in existence having become inoperative and void for non-payment of taxes 4/1/30

PURITAN SILK CORP.
Merged into Duplan Silk Corp. in 1929
Details not available

PURITAN SPORTSWEAR CORP. (PA)
Merged into Warner Brothers Co. 3/11/64
Each share Common no par exchanged for (0.5) share $1.22-1/2 Conv. Preferred no par
Warner Brothers Co. name changed to Warnaco Inc. 1/9/68
(See Warnaco Inc.)

PURITAN STORES, INC.
Bankrupt in 1929

PURITY BAKERIES CORP. (DE)
Merged into American Bakeries Co. (Del.) 6/15/53
Each share Common no par exchanged for (1.25) share Common no par
(See American Bakeries Co. (Del.))

PURITY DAIRIES LTD. (ON)
Each share Common $100 par exchanged for (1) share Common no par and (1) share Class A no par 00/00/1955
Through purchase offer all Class A no par and Common no par were

acquired by Dominion Dairies Ltd. as of 05/27/1967
Public interest eliminated

PURITY FLOUR MILLS, LTD. (ON)
Each share Preference $100 par exchanged for (2) shares new Preference $40 par and (2) shares Common $10 par
Common no par changed to $10 par 00/00/1945
Merged into Maple Leaf Mills Ltd. on a (1.75) for (1) basis 03/31/1961
(See Maple Leaf Mills Ltd.)

PURITY STORES INC (NV)
Name changed to Paragon Vineyard Co., Inc. 04/09/1973

PURITY STORES LTD. (NV)
Stock Dividend - 10% 12/15/56
Name changed to Purity Stores Inc. 4/29/60
Purity Stores Inc. name changed to Paragon Vineyard Co., Inc. 4/9/73

PURITY SUPREME INC (MA)
Each share Common $1 par exchanged for (0.00004) Common $25,000 par 12/23/1977
Note: In effect holders received $7.80 cash per share and public interest was eliminated

PURL CAP CORP (AB)
Name changed to MailBoxCity Corp. 1/5/2001

PURO CORP AMER (NY)
Name changed to Orup Corp. 12/29/1977
(See Orup Corp.)

PURO FILTER CORP. OF AMERICA (NY)
Name changed to Puro Corp. of America 6/10/76
Puro Corp. of America name changed to Orup Corp. 12/29/77
(See Orup Corp.)

PURO WTR GROUP INC (DE)
Merged into United States Filter Corp. (New) 12/30/1997
Each share Common $0.0063 par exchanged for (0.23) share new Common 1¢ par
(See United States Filter Corp. (New))

PUROFLOW INC (DE)
Common 10¢ par changed to $0.0666667 par and (0.5) additional share issued 03/15/1989
Common $0.0666667 par changed to 1¢ par 09/18/1995
Each share Common 1¢ par exchanged for (0.06666666) share Common 15¢ par 10/08/2001
Name changed to Argan, Inc. 10/29/2003

PUROLATOR COURIER CORP (NY)
Merged into Emery Air Freight Corp. 09/03/1987
Each share Common $1 par exchanged for $40 principal amount of 13% Jr. Subord. Debentures due 04/15/2002

PUROLATOR INC (DE)
Common $33-1/3¢ par split (2) for (1) by issuance of (1) additional share 05/05/1972
Common 33-1/3¢ par changed to 22-2/9¢ par and (0.5) additional share issued 11/18/1981
Reincorporated under the laws of New York as Purolator Courier Corp. and Common 22-2/9¢ par changed to $1 par 07/01/1984
(See Purolator Courier Corp. (NY))

PUROLATOR PRODS CO (DE)
Merged into Mark IV Industries, Inc. 11/16/1994
Each share Common 1¢ par exchanged for $25 cash

PUROLATOR PRODUCTS, INC. (DE)
Common no par changed to $1 par in 1944
Common $1 par changed to no par and (2) additional shares issued 10/1/63
Common no par changed to 33-1/3¢ par 4/19/66
Stock Dividends - 10% 12/10/51; 10% 12/31/55
Name changed to Purolator, Inc. (Del.) 4/16/68
Purolator, Inc. (Del.) reincorporated in New York as Purolator Courier Corp. 7/1/84
(See Purolator Courier Corp. (N.Y.))

PURPLE COMMUNICATIONS INC (DE)
Merged into Purple Merger Co., L.L.C. 07/19/2011
Each share Common 1¢ par exchanged for $0.16 cash

PURPLE CROSS INSURANCE CO. (WA)
Name changed to Omega Insurance Co. 1/5/87
Omega Insurance Co. merged into Laurentian Capital Corp. 7/7/87
(See Laurentian Capital Corp.)

PURSIDES GOLD MINES LTD (ON)
Recapitalized as Citadel Gold Mines Inc. 07/22/1980
Each share Common no par exchanged for (1/3) share Common no par
Citadel Gold Mines Inc. recapitalized as Anconia Resources Corp. 06/20/2011

PURSUIT RES INC NEW (AB)
Merged into EnerMark Income Fund 04/11/2000
Each share Common no par exchanged for either (0.8) Trust Unit no par, $3 cash, or a combination thereof
Note: Option to receive stock and cash or cash only expired 06/09/2000
EnerMark Income Fund merged into Enerplus Resources Fund 06/22/2001 which reorganized as Enerplus Corp. 01/03/2011

PURSUIT RES INC OLD (AB)
Recapitalized as Pursuit Resources Inc. (New) 02/13/1997
Each (2.7) shares Common no par exchanged for (1) share Common no par
Pursuit Resources Inc. (New) merged into EnerMark Income Fund 04/11/2000 which merged into Enerplus Resources Fund 06/22/2001 which reorganized as Enerplus Corp. 01/03/2011

PURSUIT VENTURE CORP (CO)
Name changed to Reliance Resources Inc. 09/08/1998
Reliance Resources Inc. name changed to SUMmedia.com, Inc. 08/20/1999
(See SUMmedia.com, Inc.)

PURUS INC (DE)
Each share old Common $0.001 par exchanged for (0.1) share new Common $0.001 par 11/21/1995
SEC revoked common stock registration 11/17/2009
Stockholders' equity unlikely

PURVIS-MARTIN OIL & GAS CO. (OH)
Voluntarily dissolved 3/27/15
Details not available

PUSH BUTTON CONTAINER CORP. (NM)
Voluntarily dissolved 05/22/1984
Details not available

PUSH ENTMT INC (DE)
Company terminated registration of common stock 04/22/2003
Shares were never publicly traded

PUSTIKAMA GOLD MINES LTD.
Name changed to Continental Lead Mines Ltd. in 1949
(See Continental Lead Mines Ltd.)

PUTNAM (J.L.) CO., INC. (ME)
Charter cancelled for non-payment of franchise taxes 12/1/62

PUTNAM CALIF INVT GRADE MUN TR (MA)
Completely liquidated
Each Share of Bene. Int. no par received first and final distribution of approximately $13.93 cash payable 4/12/2007 to holders of record 3/26/2007

PUTNAM CAP FD INC (MA)
Trust terminated 03/19/1991
Details not available

PUTNAM DAILY DIVID TR (MA)
Name changed to Putnam Money Market Fund 09/01/1994

PUTNAM DIVERSIFIED INCOME TR II (MA)
Name changed to Putnam Strategic Income Fund 2/28/98

PUTNAM DIVID INCOME FD (MA)
Auction Preferred Ser. A no par called for redemption 1/12/94
Money Market Preferred no par called for redemption 7/22/97
Completely liquidated 5/25/2001
Each Common Share of Bene. Int. no par exchanged for $10.12 cash

PUTNAM DUOFUND INC (MA)
Under plan of reorganization each share Income Share $1 par exchanged for $19.75 cash 01/03/1983
Note: Option to receive Capital Stock expired 12/19/1982
Name changed to Putnam Capital Fund 03/31/1983
(See Putnam Capital Fund)

PUTNAM DYES INC (MD)
Adjudicated bankrupt 03/04/1976
Stockholders' equity unlikely

PUTNAM EQUITIES FD INC (MA)
Name changed to Putnam International Equities Fund, Inc. 04/26/1979
Putnam International Equities Fund, Inc. name changed to Putnam Global Growth Fund 08/01/1990 which name changed to Putnam Global Equity Fund 10/01/2002

PUTNAM EQUITY INCOME FD OLD (MA)
Reorganized as Putnam Equity Income Fund (New) 09/13/1993
Details not available

PUTNAM FED INCOME TR (MA)
Name changed to Putnam High Quality Bond Fund 2/28/98

PUTNAM GELLMAN CORP (NY)
Dissolved by proclamation 9/29/93

PUTNAM GLOBAL GOVERNMENTAL INCOME TR (MA)
Under plan of reorganization each Share of Bene. Int., Class B, Class C and Class M automatically became (1) Putnam Global Income Trust Class A, Class B, Class C and Class M respectively 05/13/2002

PUTNAM GLOBAL GROWTH FD INC (MA)
Common $1 par reclassified as Class A $1 par 04/27/1992
Name changed to Putnam Global Equity Fund 10/01/2002

PUTNAM GNMA PLUS TR (MA)
Name changed to Putnam Federal Income Trust Fund 7/15/91
Putnam Federal Income Trust Fund name changed to Putnam High Quality Bond Fund 2/28/98

PUTNAM GROWTH FD (MA)
Shares of Bene. Int. $1 par changed to 50¢ par and (1) additional share issued 11/31/1961
Stock Dividend - 50% 04/29/1960
Name changed to Putnam Fund For Growth & Income 10/08/1984

PUTNAM HEALTH SCIENCES TR (MA)
Shares of Bene. Int. reclassified as Class A Shares of Bene. Int. 04/27/1992
Name changed to Putnam Global Health Care Fund 01/02/2009

PUTNAM HIGH INCOME OPPORTUNITIES TR (MA)
Name changed 8/15/2002
Name changed from Putnam Convertible Opportunities & Income Trust to Putnam High Income Opportunities Trust 8/15/2002
Merged into Putnam High Income Bond Fund 1/24/2005
Each Share of Bene. Int. no par exchanged for (2.34178251) Shares of Bene. Int. no par
Putnam High Income Bond Fund name changed to Putnam High Income Securities Fund 9/30/2005

PUTNAM HIGH INCOME SECS FD (MA)
Name changed 08/15/2002
Name changed 09/30/2005
Name changed from Putnam High Income Convertible & Bond Fund to Putnam High Income Bond Fund 08/15/2005
Name changed from Putnam High Income Bond Fund to Putnam High Income Securities Fund 09/30/2005
Name changed to High Income Securities Fund 07/23/2018

PUTNAM HIGH YIELD MUN TR (MA)
Merged into Putnam Managed Municipal Income Trust 02/15/2008
Each Share of Bene. Int. no par exchanged for (0.95972838) share Common no par

PUTNAM INCOME FD INC (MA)
Name changed to Putnam Income Fund (New) 11/08/1982

PUTNAM INCOME FUND OLD (MA)
Merged into Incorporated Income Fund 4/5/65
Each Share of Bene. Int. $1 par exchanged for (1.1106) shares Common $1 par
Incorporated Income Fund, Inc. name changed to Putnam Income Fund, Inc. 4/6/66 which name changed to Putnam Income Fund (New) 11/8/82

PUTNAM INTER GOVT INCOME TR (MA)
Under plan of reorganization each Share of Bene. Int. no par automatically became (0.95718595) Putnam Master Intermediate Income Trust Share of Bene. Int. no par 01/26/1998

PUTNAM INTL EQUITIES FD INC (MA)
Common $1 par split (4) for (1) by issuance of (3) additional shares 10/28/1989
Name changed to Putnam Global Growth Fund 08/01/1990
Putnam Global Growth Fund name changed to Putnam Global Equity Fund 10/01/2002

PUTNAM INVT GRADE MUN TR (MA)
Merged into Putnam Municipal Opportunities Trust 02/25/2008
Each share Ser. A Remarketed Preferred no par exchanged for (4) shares Ser. C Remarketed Preferred no par
Each Share of Bene. Int. no par exchanged for (0.83661019) Share of Bene. Int. no par

PUTNAM INVT GRADE MUN TR II (MA)
Name changed to Putnam Municipal Bond Fund Inc. 07/23/2001
Putnam Municipal Bond Fund Inc. merged into Putnam Municipal Opportunities Trust 02/25/2008

PUTNAM INVT GRADE MUN TR III (MA)
Merged into Putnam Municipal Bond Fund Inc. 07/23/2001
Each Share of Bene. Int. no par exchanged for (0.96952029) Share of Bene. Int. no par
Putnam Municipal Bond Fund Inc. merged into Putnam Municipal Opportunities Trust 02/25/2008

PUTNAM MANAGED HIGH YIELD TR (MA)
Merged into Putnam High Yield Trust 10/30/2006
Each Share of Bene. Int. no par exchanged for (1.14948944) shares Class A no par

PUTNAM MANAGED MUN INCOME TR (MA)
Remarketed Preferred Ser. B called for redemption at $100,000 on 12/10/2008
(Additional Information in Active)

PUTNAM MGMT INC (MA)
Merged into Marlennan Corp. 10/31/1970
Each share Common $1 par exchanged for (0.525) share Common $1 par
Non-Vtg. Common $1 par exchanged for (0.525) share Common $1 par
Marlennan Corp. name changed to Marsh & McLennan Companies, Inc. 05/21/1975

PUTNAM MASTER INCOME TR (MA)
Merged into Putnam Premier Income Trust 2/25/2005
Each Share of Bene. Int. no par exchanged for (1.01176661) Shares of Bene. Int. no par

PUTNAM MUN BD FD INC (MA)
Preferred Class A called for redemption at $50,000 on 11/01/2001
Preferred Class B called for redemption at $50,000 on 11/01/2001
Merged into Putnam Municipal Opportunities Trust 02/25/2008
Each share Ser. A Auction Rate Municipal Preferred no par exchanged for (1) share Ser. A Remarketed Preferred no par
Each share Ser. B Auction Rate Municipal Preferred no par exchanged for (1) share Ser. B Remarketed Preferred no par
Each Share of Bene. Int. no par exchanged for (1.04314418) Shares of Bene. Int. no par

PUTNAM MUN OPPORTUNITIES TR (MA)
Remarketed Preferred Ser. A no par called for redemption at $25,000 on 12/08/2008
(Additional Information in Active)

PUTNAM N Y INVT GRADE MUN TR (MA)
Remarketed Preferred called for redemption at $50,000 on 5/25/2007
Merged into Putnam New York Tax Exempt Income Fund 06/22/2007
Each Share of Bene. Int. no par exchanged for (1.58133733) Class A Shares of Bene. Int. no par

PUTNAM OPT INCOME TR (MA)
Name changed to Putnam Strategic Income Trust 03/11/1991
(See Putnam Strategic Income Trust)

PUTNAM STRATEGIC INCOME TR (MA)
Reorganized as Putnam Equity Income Fund (New) 09/13/1993
Details not available

PUTNAM TAX FREE HEALTH CARE FD (MA)
Merged into Putnam Tax Exempt Income Fund 09/17/2007
Each Share of Bene. Int. no par exchanged for (1.62514148) Class A Shares of Bene. Int. no par

PUTNAM TR CO (GREENWICH, CT)
Common $25 par changed to $10 par and (1.5) additional shares issued 12/10/58
Common $10 par changed to $5 par and (1) additional share issued 10/1/69
Common $5 par changed to no par and (2) additional shares issued 5/18/87
Stock Dividends - 42-6/7% 2/24/61; 10% 2/26/65; 12-1/2% 2/17/67; 10% 2/16/68; 11-1/9% 2/20/69; 10% 9/10/70; 10% 9/15/71; 10% 4/1/72; 10% 3/15/73; 10% 2/11/74; 10% 3/3/75; 10% 3/1/76; 10% 3/1/77; 12-1/2% 3/1/78; (1) for (7) 3/1/79; 10% 12/1/93
Acquired by Bank of New York, Inc. 9/1/95
Each share Common no par exchanged for (1.312) shares Common no par

PUTNAMS G P SONS (NY)
Merged into MCA Inc. 12/19/1975
Each share Common $1 par exchanged for (0.25) share Common no par
(See MCA Inc.)

PUYALLUP VY BK (PUYALLUP, WA)
Under plan of reorganization each share Common $10 par automatically became (1) share Valley Community Bancshares Inc. Common $1 par 07/01/1998
(See Valley Community Bancshares Inc.)

PV ENTERPRISES INTL INC (NV)
Recapitalized as Drone Services USA, Inc. 04/29/2015
Each share Common $0.001 par exchanged for (0.00384615) share Common $0.001 par

PVA MINERALS INC (ON)
Name changed to Marmora Mineral Products Inc. 6/23/92
Marmora Mineral Products Inc. merged into Gitennes Exploration Inc. 5/13/93

PVAXX CORP (CO)
Merged into PVAXX Ltd. 05/01/2003
Details not available

PVAXX LTD (BERMUDA)
Voluntarily wound up 05/24/2010
Details not available

PVC CONTAINER CORP (DE)
Each share old Common 1¢ par exchanged for (0.0005) share new Common 1¢ par 03/15/2006
Note: Holders of (1,999) shares or fewer received $2.39 cash per share
Stock Dividend - 3% payable 02/26/1996 to holders of record 02/08/1996
Acquired by Castle Harlan Inc. 02/16/2010
Each share new Common 1¢ par exchanged for $8,572.42 cash

PVF CAPITAL CORP (OH)
Common 1¢ par split (3) for (2) by issuance of (0.5) additional share payable 08/16/1996 to holders of record 07/27/1996
Common 1¢ par split (3) for (2) by issuance of (0.5) additional share payable 08/17/1998 to holders of record 07/27/1998
Stock Dividends - 10% 08/18/1995; 10% payable 09/01/1997 to holders of record 08/11/1997; 10% payable 09/07/1999 to holders of record 08/16/1999; 10% payable 09/01/2000 to holders of record 08/11/2000; 10% payable 08/31/2001 to holders of record 08/08/2001 Ex date - 08/06/2001; 10% payable 08/30/2002 to holders of record 08/16/2002; 10% payable 08/29/2003 to holders of record 08/15/2003 Ex date - 08/13/2003; 10% payable 08/31/2004 to holders of record 08/16/2004; 10% payable 08/31/2005 to holders of record 08/15/2005 Ex date - 08/11/2005
Merged into F.N.B. Corp. 10/12/2013
Each share Common 1¢ par exchanged for (0.3405) share Common 1¢ par

PVO INTL INC (CA)
Stock Dividend - 10% 4/20/77
Merged into Kay Corp. 8/29/80
Each share Capital Stock $5 par exchanged for $24 cash

PVR PARTNERS L P (DE)
Merged into Regency Energy Partners L.P. 03/21/2014
Each Common Unit exchanged for (1.02) Common Units and $0.262 cash
Regency Energy Partners L.P. merged into Energy Transfer Partners, L.P. (Old) 04/30/2015 which merged into Energy Transfer Partners, L.P. (New) 05/01/2017 which merged into Energy Transfer L.P. 10/19/2018

PW EAGLE INC (MN)
Merged into J-M Manufacturing Co., Inc. 06/22/2007
Each share Common 1¢ par exchanged for $33.50 cash

PWA CORP (AB)
Plan of arrangement effective 4/27/94
Each share $2.4375 Retractable 1st Preferred Ser. A no par exchanged for either (9.84) shares new Common no par or Non-Vtg. Common no par and (1) Common Stock Purchase Warrant expiring 4/27/99
Recapitalized as Canadian Airlines Corp. 5/11/95
Each share new Common no par exchanged for (0.05) share Common no par
Each share Non-Vtg. Common no par exchanged for (0.05) share Common no par
(See Canadian Airlines Corp.)

PWC CAP INC (CANADA)
Each share Non-Vtg. Class B Preferred received distribution of (0.372) share Common no par payable 06/30/2014 to holders of record 06/16/2014 Ex date - 06/12/2014
Each share Non-Vtg. Class B Preferred received distribution of (0.574) share Common no par payable 09/30/2014 to holders of record 09/09/2014 Ex date - 09/05/2014
Each share Non-Vtg. Class B Preferred received distribution of (0.898) share Common no par payable 12/31/2014 to holders of record 12/15/2014 Ex date - 12/11/2014
Each share Non-Vtg. Class B Preferred received distribution of (1.447) shares Common no par payable 03/31/2015 to holders of record 03/13/2015 Ex date - 03/11/2015
Non-Vtg. Non-Part. Class A Preferred called for redemption at $3 plus $0.226684 accrued dividends on 01/30/2017
Merged into VersaBank (New) (London, ON) 02/02/2017
Each share Non-Vtg. Class B Preferred exchanged for (2.793) shares Common no par
Each share Common no par exchanged for (0.01834567) share Common no par
Note: Unexchanged certificates will be cancelled and become without value 02/02/2020

PWC INC. (CT)
Completely liquidated 11/5/65
Each share Common $5 par exchanged for first and final distribution of (0.6) share Triangle Conduit & Cable Co., Inc. Capital Stock no par and $14.80 cash
Triangle Conduit & Cable Co., Inc. name changed to Triangle Industries, Inc. (Old) 5/31/68
(See Triangle Industries, Inc. (Old))

PWG CAP TR I (DE)
Issue Information - 7,000,000 shares PFD TR SECS 8.30% offered at $25 per share on 12/04/1996
8.30% Preferred Trust Securities called for redemption at $25 on 12/3/2001

PWG CAP TR II (DE)
8.08% Preferred Trust Securities called for redemption at $25 on 3/1/2002

PXRE CORP (CT)
Ser. A Depositary Preferred 1¢ par called for redemption 05/01/1995
Preferred Ser. A 1¢ par called for redemption 05/01/1995
Under plan of reorganization each share Common 1¢ par automatically became (1) share PXRE Group Ltd. (Bermuda) Common $1 par 10/05/1999
PXRE Group Ltd. merged into Argo Group International Holdings, Ltd. 08/07/2007

PXRE GROUP LTD (BERMUDA)
Reorganized as Argo Group International Holdings, Ltd. 08/07/2007
Each share Common $1 par exchanged for (0.1) share Common $1 par

PYATEROCHKA HLDG N V (RUSSIA)
Name changed to X5 Retail Group N.V. 11/10/2006
Each 144A Sponsored ADR for Ordinary exchanged for (1) 144A Sponsored ADR for Ordinary
Each Reg. S Sponsored GDR for Ordinary exchanged for (1) Reg. S Sponsored GDR for Ordinary

PYI CORP LTD (BERMUDA)
ADR agreement terminated 07/06/2015
No ADR's remain outstanding

PYKE MFG CO (UT)
Proclaimed dissolved for failure to file reports 11/7/96

PYLE NATL CO (NJ)
Common $5 par split (3) for (1) by issuance of (2) additional shares 11/2/59
Merged into Hubbell (Harvey), Inc. 11/10/70
Each share Preferred $100 par exchanged for (4.333333) shares $1.75 Conv. Preferred Ser. B no par
Each share Common $5 par exchanged for (0.6) share $1.75 Conv. Preferred Ser. B no par
(See Hubbell (Harvey), Inc.)

PYNG MED CORP (BC)
Name changed 10/14/2004
Name changed from Pyng Technologies Corp. to Pyng Medical Corp. 10/14/2004
Acquired by Teleflex Inc. 04/06/2017
Each share Common no par exchanged for USD$0.30203 cash
Note: Unexchanged certificates will be cancelled and become without value 04/06/2023

PYPO CHINA HOLDINGS LTD. (CAYMAN ISLANDS)
Name changed to Funtalk China Holdings Ltd. 12/15/2009
(See Funtalk China Holdings Ltd.)

PYPRR INC (AB)
Name changed to D.C. Corrosion Corp. 07/07/1995
D.C. Corrosion Corp. name changed to Total Telcom Inc. 06/10/1999

PYR ENERGY CORP (MD)
Reincorporated 07/30/2001
State of incorporation changed from (DE) to (MD) 07/30/2001
Merged into Samson Investment Co. 06/15/2007
Each share Common $0.001 par exchanged for $1.30 cash

PYRAMID BOND MORTGAGE & SECURITIES CORP. (DE)
No longer in existence having become inoperative and void for non-payment of taxes 4/1/34

PYRAMID BREWERIES INC (WA)
Merged into Independent Brewers United, Inc. 09/15/2008
Each share Common 1¢ par exchanged for $2.75 cash

PYRAMID COMMUNICATIONS INC (DE)
Merged into Harcourt Brace Jovanovich, Inc. 10/25/74
Each share Common 5¢ par exchanged for (0.093673) share Common $1 par
Harcourt Brace Jovanovich, Inc. merged into General Cinema Corp. 11/25/91 which name changed to Harcourt General, Inc. 3/15/93
(See Harcourt General, Inc.)

PYRAMID COMPANIES INC. (KY)
Name changed to American Pyramid Companies Inc. 7/19/66
American Pyramid Companies Inc. merged into American Consolidated Corp. 2/28/77 which merged into I.C.H. Corp. 4/18/85 which name changed to Southwestern Life Corp. (New) 6/15/94 which name changed to I.C.H. Corp. (New) 10/10/95
(See I.C.H. Corp. (New))

PYRAMID ELECTRIC CO. (NJ)
Stock Dividend - 100% 05/10/1954
Merged into General Instrument Corp. (NJ) 05/16/1961
Each share Preferred $10 par exchanged for (0.153846) share Common $1 par
Each share Common $1 par exchanged for (0.057142) share Common $1 par
General Instrument Corp. (NJ) reincorporated in Delaware 08/31/1967
(See General Instrument Corp. (Incorporated 06/12/1967))

PYRAMID ENERGY INC (AB)
Issue Information - 1,500,000 shares COM offered at $0.20 per share on 03/05/1997
Acquired by Fox Energy Corp. 4/11/2001
Each share Common no par exchanged for (0.2112) share Common no par and $0.2324 cash
(See Fox Energy Corp.)

PYRAMID GROUP, INC. (OH)
Adjudicated bankrupt 07/11/1975
No stockholders' equity

PYRAMID HOLDING CO. (NV)
Charter revoked for failure to file reports and pay fees 3/7/66

PYRAMID INVS INC (IN)
Completely liquidated 08/14/1968
Each share Common no par exchanged for first and final distribution of $11.7596 cash

PYRAMID LIFE INS CO (KS)
100% acquired by United Insurance Co. of America through purchase offer 00/00/1976
Public interest eliminated

PYRAMID LIFE INS CO (NC)
Each share Capital Stock $1 par exchanged for (0.2) share Capital Stock $5 par 2/28/63
Stock Dividends - 50% 2/10/55; 10% 2/15/56; 10% 2/21/57; 10% 2/17/61; 10% 6/28/63
Merged into All American Assurance Co. (NC) 4/28/72
Each share Capital Stock $5 par exchanged for (3) shares Common $1 par
All American Assurance Co. (NC) merged into I.C.H. Corp. 11/19/82 which name changed to Southwestern Life Corp. (New) 6/15/94 which name changed to I.C.H. Corp. (New) 10/10/95
(See I.C.H. Corp. (New))

PYRAMID MAGNETICS INC (CA)
Charter suspended for failure to file reports and pay fees 04/01/1987

PYRAMID MNG LTD (BC)
Recapitalized as New Pyramid Gold Mines Inc. 04/08/1975
Each share Common no par exchanged for (0.2) share Common no par
New Pyramid Gold Mines Inc. recapitalized as International Pyramid Mines Inc. 02/07/1977 which merged into American Pyramid Resources Inc. 07/24/1979
(See American Pyramid Resources Inc.)

PYRAMID OIL & GAS CORP. (DE)
Each share Common 10¢ par exchanged for (3) shares Common 4¢ par 11/22/1955
Acquired by Texstar Corp. 07/21/1961
Each share Common 4¢ par exchanged for (0.33333333) share Common 10¢ par
(See Texstar Corp.)

PYRAMID OIL CO. OF KENTUCKY
Liquidated 00/00/1943
Details not available

PYRAMID OIL CO (CA)
Common $1 par changed to no par 06/06/1978
Common no par split (3) for (2) by issuance of (0.5) additional share payable 05/01/2006 to holders of record 04/17/2006 Ex date - 05/02/2006
Common no par split (5) for (4) by issuance of (0.25) additional share payable 07/03/2008 to holders of record 06/24/2008 Ex date - 07/07/2008
Name changed to Yuma Energy, Inc. (CA) 09/11/2014
Yuma Energy, Inc. (CA) reorganized in Delaware 10/27/2016

PYRAMID OILS, LTD. (ON)
Charter cancelled and company declared dissolved for default in filing returns 01/06/1971

PYRAMID PORTLAND CEMENT CO.
Acquired by Pennsylvania-Dixie Cement Corp. 00/00/1928
Details not available

PYRAMID PUBNS INC (NY)
Merged into Reade (Walter) Organization, Inc. 07/31/1969
Each share Common 10¢ par exchanged for (0.9314) share Common 25¢ par
(See Reade (Walter) Organization, Inc.)

PYRAMID TECHNOLOGY CORP (DE)
Reincorporated 06/15/1987
State of incorporation changed from (CA) to (DE) and Common no par changed to 1¢ par 06/15/1987
Merged into Siemens Nixdorf Mid-Range Acquisition Corp. 03/07/1995
Each share Common 1¢ par exchanged for $16 cash 12/04/1985
(Inc. 12/02/1981) (Siemens

PYRAMIDWEST DEV CORP (DE)
Company terminated registration of common stock and is no longer public as of 04/12/2001

PYRENE C-O TWO CORP. (DE)
Recapitalized as Baker Industries, Inc. and Common $10 par changed to $1 par 06/01/1956
(See Baker Industries, Inc.)

PYRENE MANUFACTURING CO. (DE)
Name changed to Pyrene C-O Two Corp. 01/03/1956
Pyrene C-O Two Corp. recapitalized as Baker Industries, Inc. 06/01/1956
(See Baker Industries, Inc.)

PYRENEES GOLD CORP (AUSTRALIA)
Struck off register 08/25/1995
No stockholders' equity

PYRO ENERGY CORP (DE)
Merged into Costain Group PLC 08/01/1989
Each share Common 10¢ par exchanged for $12 cash

PYRO MAGNETICS CORP (MA)
Filed a petition under Chapter 7 Bankruptcy Code 04/18/1983
No stockholders' equity

PYRO TECHNOLOGY CORP (DE)
Charter cancelled and declared inoperative and void for non-payment of taxes 03/01/1989

PYROAIR TECHNOLOGY INC (BC)
Recapitalized as AMT Environmental Products Inc. (BC) 10/26/1992
Each share Common no par exchanged for (1/6) share Common no par
AMT Enviromental Products Inc. (BC) reorganized in Nevada as Polymer Solutions, Inc. 02/27/1997
(See Polymer Solutions, Inc.)

PYROCAP INTL CORP (VA)
Charter cancelled and proclaimed dissolved for failure to file reports 09/30/2009

PYROIL INC (MN)
Merged into STP Corp. 12/18/1970
Each share Common $1 par exchanged for (0.4) share Common $1 par
(See STP Corp.)

PYROIL RES INC (AB)
Name changed to Jumbo Development Corp. 12/16/1999
Jumbo Development Corp. name changed to Jumbo Petroleum Corp. 06/23/2006

PYROK GROUP PLC (CANADA)
Cease trade order effective 09/11/1990

PYROMETER CO. OF AMERICA, INC. (DE)
Each share Common 50¢ par exchanged for (0.25) share Common 10¢ par 12/20/1963
Name changed to Community Management Services, Inc. 06/02/1966
Community Management Services, Inc. merged into Texas State Network, Inc. 05/14/1969 which name changed to TSN Liquidating, Inc. 02/29/1972
(See TSN Liquidating, Inc.)

PYROTEX MINING & EXPLORATION CO. LTD. (ON)
Completely liquidated 01/09/1970
Each share Common $1 par exchanged for first and final distribution of (0.2) share Waferboard Corp. Ltd. Common $1 par
Waferboard Corp. Ltd. name changed to Malette Inc. 02/15/1989 which was acquired by Tembec Inc. (QC) 07/25/1995 which reorganized in Canada 02/29/2008 which merged into Rayonier Advanced Materials Inc. 11/21/2017

PYTHON OIL & GAS CORP (BC)
Recapitalized as Goldex Resources Corp. 7/4/2003
Each share Common no par exchanged for (0.5) share Common no par

PYTHON RES & INVT CORP (ON)
Recapitalized as Python Corp. 4/29/87
Each share Capital Stock $1 par exchanged for (0.25) share Capital Stock $1 par

PYX EXPLS LTD (ON)
Merged into Discovery Mines Ltd. (Canada) 01/15/1982
Each share Capital Stock no par exchanged for (0.6) share Capital Stock no par
(See Discovery Mines Ltd. (Canada))

PYXIS CAP INC (ON)
Merged into 1693062 Ontario Inc. 09/25/2008
Each Dividend Share no par exchanged for $11.25 cash
Each share Non-Vtg. Common no par exchanged for $0.34 cash
Each share Common no par exchanged for $0.34 cash

PYXIS CORP (DE)
Merged into Cardinal Health, Inc. 5/7/96
Each share Common 1¢ par exchanged for (0.406557) share Common 1¢ par

PYXIS CR STRATEGIES FD (DE)
Name changed to NexPoint Credit Strategies Fund 06/25/2012
NexPoint Credit Strategies Fund name changed to NexPoint Strategic Opportunities Fund 03/19/2018

PYXIS FDS I (DE)
Name changed to Highland Funds I 02/14/2013

Q

Q & A CAP INC (ON)
Recapitalized 11/05/1997
Recapitalized from Q & A Communications Inc. to Q & A Capital Inc. 11/05/1997
Each share Common no par exchanged for (0.5) share Common no par
Recapitalized as Leader Capital Corp. 08/17/1998
Each share Common no par exchanged for (0.5) share Common no par
(See Leader Capital Corp.)

Q BROADCASTING LTD (BC)
Company went private 06/00/1978
Each share Class A no par exchanged for $12 cash

Q CARS TECHNOLOGY INC (DE)
Filed a petition under Chapter 7 Federal Bankruptcy Code 10/31/1987
Stockholders' equity unlikely

Q CELLS AG (GERMANY)
Name changed to Global PVQ SE 01/22/2013

Q COMM INTL INC (UT)
Each share old Common $0.001 par exchanged for (0.06666666) share new Common $0.001 par 06/09/2003
Merged into Emida Technologies, Inc. 07/03/2007
Each share new Common $0.001 par

exchanged for (1.11566) shares Common
Note: Company is now private

Q ENERGY LTD (AB)
Merged into EOG Resources Canada Inc. 10/12/2000
Each share Common no par exchanged for $0.60 cash

Q-ENTERTAINMENT INC (NB)
Order authorizing abandonment of property, books and records issued 07/08/2008
No stockholders' equity

Q-GOLD RES LTD (AB)
Each share old Common no par exchanged for (0.06666666) share new Common no par 12/14/2009
Reincorporated under the laws of British Columbia 12/30/2011

Q-LINE INSTRUMENT CORP. (NY)
Completely liquidated 12/27/1967
Each share Common 1¢ par exchanged for first and final distribution of (0.301886) share Vernitron Corp. (Old) (NY) Common 10¢ par
Vernitron Corp. (Old) (NY) reincorporated in Delaware 06/28/1968 which reorganized as Vernitron Corp. (New) 08/28/1987 which name changed to Axsys Technologies, Inc. 12/04/1996
(See Axsys Technologies, Inc.)

Q LOTUS HLDGS INC (NV)
Common $0.0001 par split (3) for (1) by issuance of (2) additional shares payable 07/21/2010 to holders of record 06/21/2010 Ex date - 07/22/2010
SEC revoked common stock registration 01/13/2017

Q M G HLDGS INC (ON)
Charter cancelled for failure to file reports and pay taxes 02/19/1990

Q.M.I. MINERALS LTD. (CANADA)
Merged into Indusmin Ltd. 11/06/1968
Each share Capital Stock no par exchanged for (0.2) share Capital Stock no par
(See Indusmin Ltd.)

Q MED INC (DE)
Common $0.001 par split (2) for (1) by issuance of (1) additional share 05/11/1987
Name changed to QMed, Inc. 05/28/2002

Q/MEDIA SVCS CORP (BC)
Assets sold for the benefit of creditors 00/00/2003
No stockholders' equity

Q/MEDIA SOFTWARE CORP (BC)
Recapitalized as Q/Media Services Corp. 01/29/1998
Each share Common no par exchanged for (0.2) share Common no par
(See Q/Media Services Corp.)

Q-NET TECHNOLOGIES INC (DE)
SEC revoked common stock registration 04/22/2016

Q P CORP (JAPAN)
Name changed to Kewpie Corp. 02/23/2010

Q PWR INC (DE)
Name changed to Indigo Energy, Inc. 10/11/2000
Indigo Energy, Inc. recapitalized as Global Wireless Satellite Networks (USA), Inc. 09/15/2003 which name changed to Australian Agricultural & Property Development Corp. 11/29/2004 which name changed to Global Realty Development Corp. 07/11/2005

Q.R.S. CO.
Name changed to Q.R.S.-DeVry Corp. 00/00/1929
(See Q.R.S.-DeVry Corp.)

Q.R.S.-DEVRY CORP.
Declared bankrupt 00/00/1932
No stockholders' equity

Q.R.S. MUSIC CO.
Name changed to Q.R.S. Co. 00/00/1928
Q.R.S. Co. name changed to Q.R.S.-DeVry Corp. 00/00/1929
(See Q.R.S.-DeVry Corp.)

Q SEVEN SYS INC (UT)
SEC revoked common stock registration 10/24/2008

Q-STEAKS INC (FL)
Reincorporated under the laws of Minnesota as Timber Lodge Steakhouse Inc. 06/15/1995
Timber Lodge Steakhouse Inc. merged into Santa Barbara Restaurant Group, Inc. 09/01/1998 which merged into CKE Restaurants, Inc. 03/01/2002
(See CKE Restaurants, Inc.)

Q-TEL WIRELESS INC (AB)
Delisted from Toronto Venture Stock Exchange 11/14/2002

Q TRONICS INC (UT)
Involuntarily dissolved for failure to file reports and pay fees 12/31/1986

Q WEST RES INC (UT)
Reorganized under the laws of Delaware as American Consolidated Holding Corp. 6/30/88
Each share Common $0.001 par exchanged for (0.01) share Common $0.125 par

Q-ZAR INC (NB)
Name changed to Q-Entertainment, Inc. 07/31/1997
(See Q-Entertainment, Inc.)

QADRANT CORP (CO)
Charter suspended for failure to maintain a resident agent 05/18/1987

QANTAS AWYS LTD (AUSTRALIA)
ADR agreement terminated 02/19/2009
Details not available
(Additional information in Active)

QANTEL CORP (NY)
Chapter 11 bankruptcy proceedings converted to Chapter 7 on 05/04/1992
Stockholders' equity unlikely

QATAR TELECOM Q S C Q-TEL (QATAR)
Stock Dividends - In 144A GDR's payable to holders of 144A GDR's 10% payable 03/28/2008 to holders of record 03/20/2008
In Reg. S GDR's payable to holders of Reg. S GDR's 10% payable 03/28/2008 to holders of record 03/20/2008 Ex date - 03/18/2008; 30% payable 03/28/2012 to holders of record 03/22/2012 Ex date - 03/29/2012
Name changed to Ooredoo Q.S.C. 07/23/2013
(See Ooredoo Q.S.C.)

QB INTL INC (UT)
Name changed 03/07/1983
Each share old Common 1¢ par exchanged for (5) shares new Common 1¢ par 03/01/1983
Name changed from QB Manufacturing & Marketing, Inc. to QB International, Inc. 03/07/1983
Recapitalized as Quantec International Corp. 10/24/1983
Each share Common 1¢ par exchanged for (0.16666666) share Common $0.002 par
(See Quantec International Corp.)

QC OPTICS INC (DE)
Merged into KLA-Tencor Corp. 11/21/2001
Each share Common 1¢ par exchanged for $1 cash

QCC TECHNOLOGIES INC (AB)
Name changed to Cordy Oilfield Services Inc. 9/23/2005

QCF BANCORP INC (MN)
Each share old Common 1¢ par exchanged for (0.000125) share new Common 1¢ par 06/03/2003
Note: In effect holders received $33.45 cash per share and public interest was eliminated

QCI INDS LTD (ON)
Merged into Fincorp Capital Ltd. 12/13/1978
Each share Common no par exchanged for (1) share 5% Class A Preference $1 par and (0.3) share Conv. Class B Preference $0.33333333 par
Each share Part. Class A no par exchanged for (1) share 5% Class A Preference $1 par and (0.3) share Conv. Class B Preference $0.33333333 par
(See Fincorp Capital Ltd.)

QCL GROUP INC (NV)
Name changed to Compass Energy Corp. 6/28/2001
Compass Energy Corp. recapitalized as In-Systcom, Inc. 6/8/2004

QCR HLDGS CAP TR I (DE)
9.20% Capital Securities called for redemption at $10 on 6/30/2004

QCR HLDGS INC (DE)
Each share Accredited Investors Conv. Perpetual Preferred Ser. E $1 par exchanged for (82.3045) shares Common $1 par 12/23/2013
(Additional Information in Active)

QCS CORP (DE)
Name changed to SourcingLink.net, Inc. 07/20/1999

QCTV LTD (AB)
Merged into Videotron Ltee. 12/16/1986
Each share Common no par exchanged for $31 cash

QDATA SYS INC (BC)
Recapitalized as Consolidated QData Systems Inc. 09/19/1991
Each share Common no par exchanged for (1/3) share Common no par
Consolidated QData Systems Inc. name changed to Carbite Golf Inc. (BC) 01/12/1996 which reorganized in Yukon 10/12/2001
(See Carbite Golf Inc.)

QDM VENTURES LTD (YT)
Reincorporated 09/25/2001
Place of incorporation changed from (BC) to (YT) 09/25/2001
Name changed to California Exploration Ltd. 10/1/2001
California Exploration Ltd. recapitalized as Baradero Resources Ltd. (YT) 06/03/2004 which reincorporated in British Columbia 11/23/2004 which name changed to Centrasia Mining Corp. 09/16/2005 which name changed to Kola Mining Corp. 03/27/2008 which name changed to Mitchell Resources Ltd. 05/27/2015 which name changed to Hannan Metals Ltd. 01/10/2017

QE BRUSHES INC (NV)
Each share old Common $0.001 par exchanged for (0.5) share new Common $0.001 par 08/04/2010
New Common $0.001 par changed to $0.00001 par 10/19/2010
Name changed to Virtual Medical International, Inc. 12/02/2010

QELE RES INC (NV)
Common $0.001 par split (60) for (1) by issuance of (59) additional shares payable 06/18/2009 to holders of record 06/08/2009 Ex date - 06/19/2009

Name changed to Brand Neue Corp. 07/10/2009
Brand Neue Corp. name changed to Culture Medium Holdings Corp. (NV) 03/14/2011 which reincorporated in Wyoming 07/01/2014 which recapitalized as Code Navy 02/13/2015 which name changed to Universal Power Industry Corp. 06/02/2016

QEP MIDSTREAM PARTNERS LP (DE)
Merged into Tesoro Logistics L.P. 07/22/2015
Each Common Unit exchanged for (0.3088) Common Unit
Tesoro Logistics L.P. name changed to Andeavor Logistics L.P. 08/01/2017

QE2 ACQUISITION CORP (AB)
Name changed to Distinct Infrastructure Group Inc. 08/24/2015

QEVA GROUP INC (AB)
Recapitalized as Excelsior Energy Ltd. 09/06/2006
Each share Common no par exchanged for (0.33333333) share Common no par
(See Excelsior Energy Ltd.)

QEX RES INC (QC)
Delisted from Montreal Stock Exchange 12/24/97

QGX LTD (ON)
Acquired by Kerry Holdings Ltd. 10/17/2008
Each share Common no par exchanged for $5 cash

QHR CORP (CANADA)
Acquired by Loblaw Companies Ltd. 10/14/2016
Each share Common no par exchanged for $3.10 cash
Note: Unexchanged certificates will be cancelled and become without value 10/14/2022

QHR TECHNOLOGIES INC (BC)
Reincorporated under the laws of Canada as QHR Corp. 07/08/2013
(See QHR Corp.)

QI SYS INC (BC)
Reincorporated under the laws of Delaware and Common no par changed to $0.001 par 7/1/2006

QI TECHNOLOGIES CORP (BC)
Common no par split (2) for (1) by issuance of (1) additional share payable 11/3/99 to holders of record 11/1/99
Name changed to QI Systems Inc. (BC) 5/25/2001
QI Systems Inc. (BC) reincorporated in Delaware 7/1/2006

QIAO XING MOBILE COMMUNICATION CO LTD (BRITISH VIRGIN ISLANDS)
SEC revoked Ordinary share registration 08/23/2012

QIAO XING UNIV RES INC (BRITISH VIRGIN ISLANDS)
Name changed 05/26/2010
Name changed from Qiao Xing Universal Telephone, Inc. to Qiao Xing Universal Resources, Inc. 05/26/2010
SEC revoked common stock registration 08/23/2012

QIHOO 360 TECHNOLOGY CO LTD (CAYMAN ISLANDS)
Acquired by Tianjin Qixin Tongda Technology Co., Ltd. 07/15/2016
Each Sponsored ADS for Class A Ordinary exchanged for $76.93 cash

QIMONDA AG (GERMANY)
ADR agreement terminated 03/08/2010
ADR holders' equity unlikely

QIN-QUA

QINNET COM INC (DE)
Name changed to Q-Net Technologies, Inc. 08/13/2001
(See Q-Net Technologies, Inc.)

QINTEX ENTMT INC (DE)
Charter forfeited for failure to maintain a registered agent 2/25/98

QIS VENTURES INC (AB)
Name changed to Quorum Information Technologies Inc. 10/23/2001

QLIK TECHNOLOGIES INC (DE)
Acquired by Project Alpha Holding, LLC 08/22/2016
Each share Common $0.0001 par exchanged for $30.50 cash

QLOGIC CORP (DE)
Common 10¢ par split (2) for (1) by issuance of (1) additional share payable 12/31/1998 to holders of record 12/08/1998
Common 10¢ par split (2) for (1) by issuance of (1) additional share payable 02/22/1999 to holders of record 02/15/1999
Common 10¢ par split (2) for (1) by issuance of (1) additional share payable 07/30/1999 to holders of record 07/22/1999
Common 10¢ par changed to $0.001 par 01/04/2000
Common $0.001 par split (2) for (1) by issuance of (1) additional share payable 02/08/2000 to holders of record 02/02/2000
Common $0.001 par split (2) for (1) by issuance of (1) additional share payable 03/02/2006 to holders of record 02/16/2006 Ex date - 03/03/2006
Merged into Cavium, Inc. 08/16/2016
Each share Common $0.001 par exchanged for (0.098) share Common $0.001 par and $11 cash
Cavium, Inc. merged into Marvell Technology Group Ltd. 07/06/2018

QLT INC (BC)
Name changed 05/05/2000
1st Preference Ser. C no par called for redemption 06/30/1996
Name changed from QLT Phototherapeutics Inc. to QLT Inc. 05/05/2000
Name changed to Novelion Therapeutics Inc. 12/01/2016

QM VENTURE GROUP LTD (WA)
Name changed to Carancahua Resources, Inc. 01/17/1989

QMAC ENERGY INC (NV)
Old Common $0.001 par split (60) for (1) by issuance of (59) additional shares payable 01/22/2004 to holders of record 01/22/2004
Each share old Common $0.001 par exchanged for (0.03333333) share new Common $0.001 par 01/03/2005
Charter permanently revoked 06/30/2009

QMAX TECHNOLOGY GROUP INC (DE)
Common 1¢ par split (2) for (1) by issuance of (1) additional share 4/5/85
Plan of reorganization under Chapter 11 bankruptcy proceedings confirmed 9/27/90
No stockholders' equity

QMC TECHNOLOGIES INC (MN)
Each share old Common 10¢ par exchanged for (0.00000512) share new Common 10¢ par 05/31/1995
Note: In effect holders received an undetermined amount of cash per share and public interest was eliminated

QMI SEISMIC INC (BC)
Name changed to ME Resource Corp. 09/06/2011

QMS INC (DE)
Common 1¢ par split (2) for (1) by issuance of (1) additional share 9/14/84
Name changed to Minolta-QMS, Inc. 4/25/2000
(See Minolta-QMS, Inc.)

QNECTIVE INC (NV)
Common $0.001 par split (33) for (2) by issuance of (15.5) additional shares payable 03/16/2007 to holders of record 03/12/2007
Ex date - 03/19/2007
Completely liquidated 02/18/2011
Each share Common $0.001 par exchanged for first and final distribution of (1) Qnective AG Restricted Share
Note: Company is now private

QNETIX INC (AB)
Acquired by Charon Systems, Inc. 12/03/2002
Details not available

Q9 NETWORKS INC (ON)
Acquired by CDC Acquisition Corp. 10/29/2008
Each share Common no par exchanged for $17.05 cash

QOL HLDGS INC (NV)
Name changed to Global Web TV, Inc. (New) 10/05/2005
Global Web TV, Inc. (New) reorganized as Amore TV, Inc. 01/27/2006 which recapitalized as Rapid Fitness, Inc. 05/11/2007 which name changed to Tri-Star Holdings Inc. 08/27/2008 which recapitalized as Macada Holding, Inc. (NV) 08/20/2009 which reincorporated in Wyoming 02/22/2011 which recapitalized as KMA Holding, Inc. 03/17/2011
(See KMA Holding, Inc.)

QONAAR CORP (DE)
Acquired by Kroehler Mfg. Co. 10/31/1981
Each share Common $1 par exchanged for $37 cash

Q1 CORP (DE)
Charter cancelled and declared inoperative and void for non-payment of taxes 03/01/1994

QORUS COM INC (FL)
Recapitalized as DigitalFX International, Inc. 08/02/2006
Each share Common $0.001 par exchanged for (0.02) share Common $0.001 par
Note: Holders of between (100) and (4,999) shares received (100) shares
Holders of (99) shares or fewer were not affected by the reverse split
DigitalFX International, Inc. name changed to ComF5 International, Inc. 04/01/2010

QPC LASERS INC (NV)
SEC revoked common stock registration 07/16/2012

QPQ CORP (FL)
Each share old Common 1¢ par exchanged for (0.05) share new Common 1¢ par 08/18/1997
Each share new Common 1¢ par exchanged again for (1/3) share new Common 1¢ par 10/08/1997
Name changed to Regenesis Holding Inc. 11/04/1997
Regenesis Holding Inc. name changed to Fuelnation Inc. 10/19/2000
(See Fuelnation Inc.)

QPX MINERALS INC (BC)
Merged into Rea Gold Corp. 8/6/91
Each share Common no par exchanged for (0.29411764) share Common no par
(See Rea Gold Corp.)

QR CDA CAP INC (CANADA)
Recapitalized as Section Rouge Media Inc. 09/04/2003
Each share Common no par exchanged for (0.5) share Common no par
Section Rouge Media Inc. name changed to Sama Graphite Inc. 01/16/2017 which name changed to SRG Graphite Inc. 07/05/2017

QR ENERGY LP (DE)
Merged into Breitburn Energy Partners L.P. 11/19/2014
Each Unit of Ltd. Partnership Int. exchanged for (0.9856) Common Unit of Ltd. Partnership Int.
(See Breitburn Energy Partners L.P.)

QRS CAP CORP (ON)
Recapitalized as Sendero Mining Corp. 07/09/2013
Each share Common no par exchanged for (0.635516) share Common no par

QRS CORP (DE)
Common $0.001 par split (3) for (2) by issuance of (0.5) additional share payable 7/12/99 to holders of record 6/4/99
Merged into Inovis International, Inc. 11/16/2004
Each share Common $0.001 par exchanged for $7 cash

QRS MUSIC INC (DE)
Name changed to QRS Music Technologies, Inc. 01/21/1998

QRSCIENCES HLDGS LTD (AUSTRALIA)
Each old Sponsored ADR for Ordinary exchanged for (0.4) new Sponsored ADR for Ordinary 08/23/2006
ADR agreement terminated 08/15/2011
Each new Sponsored ADR for Ordinary exchanged for $0.070917 cash

QRXPHARMA LTD (AUSTRALIA)
ADR agreement terminated 05/22/2017
Each Sponsored ADR for Ordinary exchanged for (5) shares Ordinary
Notes: Unexchanged ADR's will be sold and the proceeds, if any, held for claim after 11/20/2017
Company placed in Voluntary Administration 05/22/2015

QSA TECHNOLOGY INC (DE)
Cease trade order effective 02/13/1991
Stockholders' equity unlikely

QSC AG (GERMANY)
Name changed 8/7/2001
Name changed from QS Communications AG to QSC AG 8/7/2001
ADR agreement terminated 4/2/2002
Each ADR for Ordinary exchanged for $1.4633 cash
Note: Due to ADR's being unsponsored exchange rate may vary dependent upon depositary agent

QSGI INC (DE)
SEC revoked common stock registration 02/03/2015

QSOLAR LTD (AB)
Officers resigned and company ceased operations 06/18/2015
No stockholders' equity

QSOUND LABS INC (AB)
Reincorporated 07/00/1990
Place of incorporation changed from (BC) to (AB) 07/00/1990
Each share old Common no par exchanged for (0.25) share new Common no par 07/09/2001
SEC revoked common stock registration 05/14/2015

QSP LTD (CANADA)
5% 1st Preference called for redemption 9/30/70
Assets sold for the benefit of creditors in September 1977
No stockholders' equity

QSR INC (FL)
Merged into Miami Subs Corp. 10/1/91
Each share Common 1¢ par exchanged for (1) share Common 1¢ par
Miami Subs Corp. merged into Nathan's Famous, Inc. 10/1/99

QSR LTD (ON)
Name changed to Coniagas Resources Ltd. 06/25/1999
Coniagas Resources Ltd. name changed to Lithium One Inc. 07/23/2009
(See Lithium One Inc.)

QT 5 INC (DE)
Old Common $0.001 par split (5) for (1) by issuance of (4) additional shares payable 01/08/2003 to holders of record 12/30/2002
Each share old Common $0.001 par exchanged for (0.1) share new Common $0.001 par 04/26/2004
Recapitalized as Addison-Davis Diagnostics, Inc. 11/18/2004
Each (150) shares Common $0.001 par exchanged for (1) share Common $0.001 par
(See Addison-Davis Diagnostics, Inc.)

QT&T INC (NY)
Filed a petition under Chapter 11 Federal Bankruptcy Code 02/17/1987
No stockholders' equity

Q2 GOLD RES INC (BC)
Company announced intention to cease reporting and wind up its affairs 09/02/2010. Shares are not expected to have any value once company is struck from the register. Holders should consult their financial or tax advisors.

Q2POWER TECHNOLOGIES INC (DE)
Name changed to Q2Earth, Inc. 08/31/2017

QUAD CAP CORP (DE)
Name changed to Yankee Stores, Inc. 5/1/90
Yankee Stores, Inc. name changed to Specialty Retail Ventures Inc. 8/15/90
(See Specialty Retail Ventures Inc.)

QUAD CITIES FIRST CO (DE)
Common $10 par changed to $2 par and (4) additional shares issued 05/16/1983
Merged into First of America Bank Corp. 12/31/1988
Each share Common $2 par exchanged for (1.8898) shares Common $10 par
First of America Bank Corp. merged into National City Corp. 03/31/1998 which was acquired by PNC Financial Services Group, Inc. 12/31/2008

QUAD CITY HLDGS INC (DE)
Common $1 par split (3) for (2) by issuance of (0.5) additional share payable 11/30/1998 to holders of record 11/20/1998
Name changed to QCR Holdings, Inc. 11/01/2001

QUAD ENERGY DEV CORP (AB)
Name changed to Jardin Financial Group Inc. 03/24/1992
(See Jardin Financial Group Inc.)

QUAD METALS CORP (NV)
Reorganized 12/30/2002
Common 10¢ par changed to no par 03/19/1984

FINANCIAL INFORMATION, INC. QUA-QUA

Reorganized from (WA) to under the laws of Nevada 12/30/2002
Each share Common no par exchanged for (0.02) share Common $0.001 par 12/30/2002
Name changed to DataJungle Software, Inc. 11/18/2003
DataJungle Software, Inc. name changed to Blink Logic Inc. 11/08/2007
(See Blink Logic Inc.)

QUAD PNEUMATIC LIFT CO. (NJ)
Charter declared void for non-payment of taxes 09/10/1979

QUAD SYS CORP (DE)
Plan of reorganization under Chapter 11 Federal Bankruptcy proceedings confirmed 03/18/2002
No stockholders' equity

QUAD X SPORTS COM INC (NV)
Recapitalized as Bethel Holdings Inc. 09/17/2001
Each share Common no par exchanged for (0.2) share Common $0.0001 par
Bethel Holdings Inc. reorganized as Direct Pet Health Holdings, Inc. 06/28/2006 which recapitalized as Core Resource Management, Inc. 11/13/2012

QUADEX RES LTD (BC)
Name changed to F.C. Financial Corp. 03/24/1986
F.C. Financial Corp. recapitalized as West F.C. Financial Corp. 12/13/1991
(See West F.C. Financial Corp.)

QUADRA FNX MNG LTD (BC)
Acquired by KGHM Polska Miedz S.A. 03/05/2012
Each share Common no par exchanged for $15 cash

QUADRA LEASES, LTD.
Merged into Triad Oil Co. Ltd. 10/17/51
Each share Common no par exchanged for (2.3) shares Capital Stock no par
Triad Oil Co. Ltd. name changed to BP Oil & Gas Ltd. 7/2/70 which merged into BP Canada Ltd. (Ont.) 10/18/72 which name changed to BP Canada Ltd.-BP Canada Ltee. 4/27/73 which reincorporated in Canada as BP Canada Inc. 7/6/79
(See BP Canada Inc.)

QUADRA LOGIC TECHNOLOGIES INC (BC)
Name changed to QLT Phototherapeutics Inc. 05/16/1995
QLT Phototherapeutics Inc. name changed to QLT Inc. 05/05/2000 which name changed to Novelion Therapeutics Inc. 12/01/2016

QUADRA MNG LTD (BC)
Under plan of merger name changed to Quadra FNX Mining Ltd. 05/27/2010
(See Quadra FNX Mining Ltd.)

QUADRA PPTYS CORP (BC)
Name changed to Digital Artisans Guild Inc. 12/14/2000

QUADRA PROJS INC (NV)
Old Common $0.001 par split (2) for (1) by issuance of (1) additional share payable 06/09/2009 to holders of record 06/09/2009
Each share old Common $0.001 par exchanged for (0.00333333) share new Common $0.001 par 10/14/2010
Name changed to Unwall International Inc. 02/13/2012
Unwall International Inc. name changed to 3 Shine Technologies Inc. 08/20/2015 which name changed to Rorine International Holding Corp. 10/07/2015

QUADRA RLTY TR INC (MD)
Merged into Hypo Real Estate Holding AG 03/14/2008
Each share Common $0.001 par exchanged for $10.6506 cash

QUADRA RES CORP (AB)
Acquired by Arsenal Energy Inc. (New) 08/11/2005
Each share Common no par exchanged for (0.025) share Common no par
Arsenal Energy Inc. (New) merged into Prairie Provident Resources Inc. 09/16/2016

QUADRACOMM INC (CO)
SEC revoked common stock registration 4/13/2006
Stockholders' equity unlikely

QUADRAMED CORP (DE)
Each share old Common 1¢ par exchanged for (0.2) share new Common 1¢ par 06/16/2008
Acquired by Francisco Partners 03/18/2010
Each share 144A 5.5% Conv. Preferred Ser. A 1¢ par exchanged for $13.7097 cash
Each share new Common 1¢ par exchanged for $8.50 cash

QUADRANT CAP CORP (AB)
Name changed to Bridges Energy Inc. 3/11/88
(See Bridges Energy Inc.)

QUADRANT FINL CORP (BC)
Acquired by Walker's Hook International, Ltd. 10/28/1999
Each share Common no par exchanged for (1) share Common no par
Walker's Hook International, Ltd. name changed to Quadrant Resources Corp. 11/08/1999 which recapitalized as Pinnacle Transportation Inc. 05/27/2003 which name changed to ZYTO Corp. 09/19/2006 which name changed to Global Unicorn Holdings, Inc. 05/02/2018

QUADRANT 4 SYS CORP (IL)
Reincorporated 04/25/2013
State of incorporation changed from (FL) to (IL) 04/25/2013
Plan of reorganization under Chapter 11 Federal Bankruptcy proceedings effective 09/13/2018
No stockholders' equity

QUADRANT RES CORP (DE)
Recapitalized as Pinnacle Transportation Inc. 05/27/2003
Each share Common $0.0001 par exchanged for (0.01) share Common $0.0001 par
Pinnacle Transportation Inc. name changed to ZYTO Corp. 09/19/2006 which name changed to Global Unicorn Holdings, Inc. 05/02/2018

QUADRATE EXPLS LTD (ON)
Charter cancelled for failure to pay taxes and file returns 03/16/1976

QUADRATECH INC (NV)
Reincorporated 03/19/1990
State of incorporation changed from (UT) to (NV) 03/19/1990
SEC revoked common stock registration 10/29/2004
Stockholders' equity unlikely

QUADRAX CORP NEW (DE)
Recapitalized as TTCM China, Inc. 01/18/2005
Each share Common $0.000009 par exchanged for (0.0005) share Common $0.000009 par

QUADRAX CORP OLD (DE)
Each share old Common $0.000009 par exchanged for (0.1) share new Common $0.000009 par 07/20/1994
Reorganized as Quadrax Corp. (New) 02/23/2000
Each share Common $0.000009 par exchanged for (0.025) share Common $0.000009 par
Quadrax Corp. (New) recapitalized as TTCM China, Inc. 01/18/2005

QUADREX CORP (CA)
Common no par split (3) for (2) by issuance of (0.5) additional share 05/01/1980
Common no par split (2) for (1) by issuance of (1) additional share 07/02/1981
Charter suspended for failure to file reports and pay fees 08/02/2004

QUADRON CAP CORP (BC)
Name changed to Quadron Cannatech Corp. 05/10/2017

QUADRON RES LTD (AB)
Merged into HCO Energy Ltd. 0/23/1995
Each share Preferred no par exchanged for (1) share 1st Preferred Ser B. no par
Each share Common no par exchanged for (0.625) share Common no par
HCO Energy Ltd. merged into Pinnacle Resources Ltd. (New) 10/20/1997 which merged into Renaissance Energy Ltd. 07/16/1998 which merged into Husky Energy Inc. 08/25/2000

QUADTECH INTL INC (NV)
SEC revoked common stock registration 12/18/2013

QUADTEL LTD (AUSTRALIA)
Each share old Common exchanged for (0.01) share new Common 03/15/2004
Name changed to Wytomic Ltd. 03/17/2004
Wytomic Ltd. name changed to Sultan Corp. Ltd. 12/06/2006 which name changed to Balamara Resources, Ltd. 02/07/2012

QUAIL RIDGE CAP CORP (AB)
Name changed to Performance Optician Software Corp. 11/29/2000

QUAIL RIDGE WINERY NAPA VY INC (BC)
Recapitalized as Redonda Industries Corp. 6/13/90
Each share Common no par exchanged for (1/3) share Common no par
Redonda Industries Corp. name changed to Avmin Ltd. 11/30/96
(See Avmin Ltd.)

QUAKER CASH RESVS INC (MD)
Liquidated 09/09/1983
Details not available

QUAKER CITY BANCORP INC (DE)
Common 1¢ par split (5) for (4) by issuance of (0.25) additional share payable 5/30/97 to holders of record 5/12/97
Common 1¢ par split (5) for (4) by issuance of (0.25) additional share payable 6/30/98 to holders of record 6/12/98
Common 1¢ par split (5) for (4) by issuance of (0.25) additional share payable 6/28/2002 to holders of record 6/12/2002 Ex date - 7/1/2002
Merged into Popular, Inc. 8/31/2004
Each share Common 1¢ par exchanged for $55 cash

QUAKER CITY COLD STORAGE CO.
Reorganized as Quaker City Cold Storage Co., Inc. 00/00/1948
Each share Class A no par exchanged for (1) share Common $1 par
No Class B stockholders' equity

QUAKER CITY FIRE & MARINE INSURANCE CO. (PA)
Capital Stock $10 par changed to $12.50 par 00/00/1944
Capital Stock $12.50 par changed to $20 par 00/00/1950

Each share Capital Stock $20 par exchanged for (2) shares Capital Stock $10 par 00/00/1954
Name changed to Quaker City Insurance Co. 09/20/1957
(See Quaker City Insurance Co.)

QUAKER CITY INDS INC (NY)
Filed a petition under Chapter 11 Federal Bankruptcy Code 7/6/83
Stockholders' equity unknown

QUAKER CITY INS CO (PA)
Common $10 par changed to $5 par 08/01/1967
Liquidated by Pennsylvania Insurance Commissioner 10/01/1997
No stockholders' equity

QUAKER CITY LIFE INSURANCE CO. (PA)
Capital Stock $5 par split (5) for (2) issuance of (1.5) additional shares 11/15/1963
Acquired by United Insurance Co. of America (IL) on a (5/7) for (1) basis 03/16/1964
United Insurance Co. of America (IL) reincorporated in Nevada as Unicoa Corp. 08/09/1968 which name changed to to United Insurance Co. of America (NV) 11/02/1987
(See United Insurance Co. of America (NV))

QUAKER ENERGY INC (BC)
Name changed to Quaker Resources Inc. 08/18/1983
Quaker Resources Inc. name changed to Comco Mining & Smelting Corp. 09/10/1984 which name changed to Quaker Resources Canada Ltd. 08/18/1986 which name changed to SPI Safety Packaging International Ltd. 04/25/1987
(See SPI Safety Packaging International Ltd.)

QUAKER FABRIC CORP NEW (DE)
Common 1¢ par split (3) for (2) by issuance of (0.5) additional share payable 06/19/1998 to holders of record 06/08/1998
Plan of reorganization under Chapter 11 Federal Bankruptcy Code effective 09/12/2008
No stockholders' equity

QUAKER FABRIC CORP OLD (DE)
Merged into Unione Manifatture S.p.A. 9/20/89
Each share Common 1¢ par exchanged for $10.93 cash

QUAKER INVT TR (MA)
Completely liquidated
Each share Long-Short Tactical Allocation Fund Class A received first and final distribution of $5.38 cash payable 11/07/2011 to holders of record 11/04/2011
Each share Long-Short Tactical Allocation Fund Class C received first and final distribution of $5.30 cash payable 11/07/2011 to holders of record 11/04/2011
Each share Long-Short Tactical Allocation Fund Class I received first and final distribution of $5.44 cash payable 11/07/2011 to holders of record 11/04/2011
Each share Capital Opportunities Fund Class A received first and final distribution of $8.04 cash payable 10/31/2012 to holders of record 10/09/2012
Each share Capital Opportunities Fund Class C received first and final distribution of $7.37 cash payable 10/31/2012 to holders of record 10/09/2012
Each share Capital Opportunities Fund Class I received first and final distribution of $8.07 cash payable 10/31/2012 to holders of record 10/09/2012

QUAKER OATS CO (NJ)
Each share 6% Preferred $100 par exchanged for (2) shares $3 Conv. Preferred $50 par 11/01/1968
$3 Conv. Preferred $50 par called for redemption 06/13/1977
$9.56 Preference no par called for redemption 04/20/1986
Each share Common no par exchanged for (4) shares Common $5 par 00/00/1951
Common $5 par split (2) for (1) by issuance of (1) additional share 12/04/1967
Common $5 par split (3) for (2) by issuance of (0.5) additional share 12/05/1969
Common $5 par split (3) for (2) by issuance of (0.5) additional share 10/06/1972
Common $5 par split (2) for (1) by issuance of (1) additional share 12/10/1984
Common $5 par split (2) for (1) by issuance of (1) additional share 12/10/1986
Common $5 par split (2) for (1) by issuance of (1) additional share 12/05/1994
Stock Dividend - 10% 11/20/1957
Merged into PepsiCo, Inc. 08/02/2001
Each share Common $5 par exchanged for (2.3) shares Common $0.016666666 par

QUAKER OIL CO. (DE)
Charter declared inoperative and void for non-payment of taxes 3/16/27

QUAKER RES CDA LTD (BC)
Name changed to SPI Safety Packaging International Ltd. 04/25/1987
(See SPI Safety Packaging International Ltd.)

QUAKER RES INC (BC)
Name changed to Comco Mining & Smelting Corp. 09/10/1984
Comco Mining & Smelting Corp. name changed to Quaker Resources Canada Ltd. 08/18/1986 which name changed to SPI Safety Packaging International Ltd. 04/25/1987
(See SPI Safety Packaging International Ltd.)

QUAKER ST CORP (DE)
Merged into Pennzoil-Quaker State Co. 12/30/98
Each share Common $1 par exchanged for (0.8204) share Common $1 par
(See Pennzoil-Quaker State Co.)

QUAKER ST OIL REFNG CORP (DE)
Capital Stock no par changed to $10 par in 1933
Capital Stock $10 par split (2) for (1) by issuance of (1) additional share 8/14/64
Capital Stock $10 par changed to $5 par and (1) additional share issued 11/15/67
Capital Stock $5 par changed to $2.50 par and (1) additional share issued 11/24/69
Capital Stock $2.50 par changed to $1.25 par and (1) additional share issued 6/5/72
Capital Stock $1.25 par changed to $1 par and (0.25) additional share issued 10/31/79
Name changed to Quaker State Corp. 7/1/87
Quaker State Corp. merged into Pennzoil- Quaker State Co. 12/30/98
(See Pennzoil-Quaker State Co.)

QUAKER STATE FOODS CORP. (DE)
Assets sold for benefit of creditors 1/18/67
No stockholders' equity

QUAL-MED INC (DE)
Merged into Health Systems International, Inc. 01/28/1994
Each share Common 1¢ par exchanged for (1) share Common 1¢ par
Health Systems International, Inc. name changed to Foundation Health Systems, Inc. 04/01/1997 which name changed to Health Net, Inc. 11/06/2000 which merged into Centene Corp. 03/24/2016

QUALIFIED DIVID PORTFOLIO II INC (MD)
Reincorporated under the laws of Pennsylvania as Qualified Dividend Portfolio II and Common 10¢ par reclassified as Shares of Bene. Int. no par 11/12/84

QUALIFIED DIVID PORTFOLIO INC (MD)
Reincorporated under the laws of Pennsylvania as Qualified Dividend Portfolio I and Common 10¢ par reclassified as Shares of Bene. Int. no par 11/12/84

QUALIFIED HSG PARTNERS LTD (NC)
Unit of Ltd. Partnership Int. registration terminated and Partnership no longer public as of 10/13/2007

QUALITAS MGMT CORP (ME)
Name changed to Advanced Energy Concepts, Inc. 09/23/1980
(See Advanced Energy Concepts, Inc.)

QUALITAS SPECIALTY CORP (DE)
Name changed to Duke Diversified Industries Inc. 11/12/1973
(See Duke Diversified Industries Inc.)

QUALITY CARE INC (NY)
Merged into GrandMet USA Inc. 01/02/1985
Each share Common 1¢ par exchanged for $11.75 cash

QUALITY CARE NURSING CENTERS, INC. (DE)
Name changed to Quality Care Services, Inc. 04/01/1971
Quality Care Services, Inc. name changed to Northwestern Service Corp. 01/24/1973
(See Northwestern Service Corp.)

QUALITY CARE PPTYS INC (MD)
Acquired by Welltower Inc. 07/26/2018
Each share Common 1¢ par exchanged for $20.75 cash

QUALITY CARE SVCS INC (DE)
Name changed to Northwestern Service Corp. 01/24/1973
(See Northwestern Service Corp.)

QUALITY CLOTHING CORP (NY)
Dissolved by proclamation 06/24/1992

QUALITY CORP (OH)
Liquidation completed
Each share Common no par exchanged for initial distribution of $0.50 cash 07/03/1987
Each share Common no par received second and final distribution of $0.06 cash 12/28/1987

QUALITY COURTS MOTELS INC (DE)
Class A Special Stock $1 par reclassified as Common $1 par 06/14/1966
Common $1 par split (2) for (1) by issuance of (1) additional share 07/07/1969
Name changed to Quality Inns International, Inc. 08/31/1972
Quality Inns International, Inc. merged into Manor Care, Inc. (Old) 12/01/1980 which merged into HCR Manor Care, Inc. 09/25/1998 which name changed to Manor Care, Inc. (New) 09/30/1999
(See Manor Care, Inc. (New))

QUALITY DINING INC (IN)
Merged into QDI Merger Corp. 4/13/2005
Each share Common no par exchanged for $3.20 cash

QUALITY DINO ENTMT LTD (MB)
Placed in receivership 00/00/1998
No stockholders' equity

QUALITY DISTR INC (FL)
Acquired by Gruden Acquisition, Inc. 08/18/2015
Each share Common no par exchanged for $16 cash

QUALITY EXCHANGE INC (NV)
Name changed to Protocall Technologies Inc. 7/26/2004

QUALITY FOOD CTRS INC (DE)
Common no par split (2) for (1) by issuance of (1) additional share 9/26/89
Common no par split (2) for (1) by issuance of (1) additional share 5/17/91
Merged into Meyer (Fred), Inc. (New) 3/9/98
Each share Common no par exchanged for (1.9) shares Common 1¢ par

QUALITY HOMES INC (MN)
Charter declared inoperative and void for failure to file reports 01/01/1991

QUALITY IMPORTERS, INC. (NY)
Merged into Brown-Forman Distillers Corp. 7/25/67
Each share Common $1 par exchanged for (1) share Class B Common 30¢ par
Brown-Forman Distillers Corp. name changed to Brown-Forman Inc. 7/27/84 which name changed to Brown-Forman Inc. 8/4/87

QUALITY INDUSTRIES (CA)
Name changed to Tri Financial Corp. 1/5/66
Tri Financial Corp. name changed to Crateo, Inc. 8/15/67 which was adjudicated bankrupt 8/8/73

QUALITY INNS INTL INC (DE)
Merged into Manor Care, Inc. (Old) 12/01/1980
Each share Common $1 par exchanged for (0.71) share Common 10¢ par
Manor Care, Inc. (Old) merged into HCR Manor Care, Inc. 09/25/1998 which name changed to Manor Care, Inc. (New) 09/30/1999
(See Manor Care, Inc. (New))

QUALITY LEARNING SYS INTL INC (BC)
Name changed to Carta Resources Ltd. 05/27/1996
Carta Resources Ltd. name changed to Earthramp.com Communications Inc. (BC) 12/24/1999 which reincorporated in Alberta 00/00/2001 which name changed to Champlain Resources Inc. 09/18/2007 which recapitalized as Beacon Resources Inc. 04/20/2012

QUALITY MEASUREMENT SYSTEMS, INC. (NY)
Merged into EG&G, Inc. 8/31/77
Each share Common 1¢ par exchanged for (0.18473) share Common $1 par
EG&G, Inc. name changed to PerkinElmer, Inc. 10/25/99

QUALITY MICRO SYS INC (DE)
Name changed to QMS Inc. 7/17/84
QMS Inc. name changed to Minolta-QMS, Inc. 4/25/2000
(See Minolta-QMS, Inc.)

QUALITY MLS INC (NC)
Common $2 par changed to $1 par and (1) additional share issued 12/15/83
Acquired by Russell Corp. 12/6/88

Each share 10% Preferred $1 par exchanged for $10 cash
Each share Common $1 par exchanged for $18.30 cash

QUALITY NATIONAL CORP. (DE)
Charter cancelled and declared inoperative and void for non-payment of taxes 4/15/71

QUALITY OF LIFE HEALTH CORP (NY)
Recapitalized as LifeHouse Retirement Properties, Inc. 7/14/2005
Each share Common $0.001 par exchanged for (1/3) share Common $0.0001 par

QUALITY ONE WIRELESS INC (MN)
Administratively dissolved 01/09/2008

QUALITY PACKAGING SUPPLY CORP (NY)
Dissolved by proclamation 12/28/94

QUALITY PRODS INC (DE)
Each share old Common $0.00001 par exchanged for (0.25) share new Common $0.00001 par 10/02/1992
Each share new Common $0.00001 par exchanged for (0.25) share new Common $0.00001 par 11/30/1994
Acquired by QPI Acquisition Corp. 12/22/2014
Each share new Common $0.00001 par exchanged for $21.88 cash

QUALITY PRODTN CIRCUITS INC (MN)
Merged into Advance Circuits, Inc. 1/21/82
Each share Common 10¢ par exchanged for (1) share Common 10¢ par
(See Advance Circuits, Inc.)

QUALITY PRODUCTS, INC. (WI)
Adjudicated bankrupt in 1961
No stockholders' equity

QUALITY QUEST SYS INC (BC)
Struck off register and declared dissolved for failure to file returns 07/30/1993

QUALITY RESORTS AMER INC (CA)
SEC revoked common stock registration 10/24/2008
Stockholders' equity unlikely

QUALITY RESTAURANT VENTURES INC (FL)
Each share old Common $0.001 par exchanged for (0.0005) share new Common $0.001 par 04/10/2007
Name changed to Airborne Security & Protective Services, Inc. (Ctfs. dated after 05/25/2010) 05/25/2010

QUALITY SEMICNDUCTOR INC (CA)
Issue Information - 1,500,000 shares COM offered at $9 per share on 11/17/1994
Merged into Integrated Device Technology, Inc. 4/30/99
Each share Common $0.001 par exchanged for (0.6875) share Common no par

QUALITY STEELS (CANADA) LTD. (ON)
Bankrupt 00/00/1952
Details not available

QUALITY SYS INC (CA)
Common no par changed to 1¢ par and (1) additional share issued 05/10/1983
Common 1¢ par split (2) for (1) by issuance of (1) additional share payable 03/25/2005 to holders of record 03/04/2005 Ex date - 03/28/2005
Common 1¢ par split (2) for (1) by issuance of (1) additional share payable 03/24/2006 to holders of record 03/03/2006 Ex date - 03/27/2006
Common 1¢ par split (2) for (1) by issuance of (1) additional share

payable 10/26/2011 to holders of record 10/06/2011 Ex date - 10/27/2011
Name changed to NextGen Healthcare, Inc. 09/10/2018

QUALITY WALLBEDS INC (FL)
Name changed to Sichuan Leaders Petrochemical Co. 01/17/2013
Sichuan Leaders Petrochemical Co. name changed to Horrison Resources Inc. 04/13/2018

QUALIX GROUP INC (DE)
Merged into Legato Systems, Inc. 04/19/1999
Each share Common $0.001 par exchanged for (0.1411) share Common $0.0001 par
Legato Systems, Inc. merged into EMC Corp. 10/21/2003 which merged into Dell Technologies Inc. 09/07/2016

QUALMARK CORP (CO)
Acquired by ESPEC Corp. 12/28/2015
Each share Common no par exchanged for $1.016349 cash

QUALMAX INC (DE)
Merged into New World Brands, Inc. 02/20/2009
Each share Common $0.001 par exchanged for (13.348308) shares Common $0.001 par

QUALSEC (WY)
Each share old Common no par exchanged for (0.03333333) share new Common no par 09/30/2009
Name changed to VitaminSpice 11/19/2009
(See VitaminSpice)

QUALTON INC (DE)
SEC revoked common stock registration 10/24/2008
Stockholders' equity unlikely

QUAMTEL INC (NV)
Name changed to DataJack, Inc. 12/31/2012
DataJack, Inc. name changed to Unified Signal, Inc. 11/28/2014

QUANEX CORP (DE)
Each Depositary Conv. Exchangeable Preferred no par exchanged for $25 principal amount of 9.125% Conv. Subordinated Debentures due 09/30/2008 on 12/31/1990
Each Depositary Conv. Exchangeable Preferred exchanged for $25 principal amount of 6.88% Conv. Subordinated Debentures due 06/30/2007 on 06/30/1995
Common $5 par split (3) for (2) by issuance of (0.5) additional share 01/26/1979
Common $5 par split (3) for (2) by issuance of (0.5) additional share 01/06/1981
Common $5 par split (3) for (2) by issuance of (0.5) additional share 09/21/1981
Common $5 par split (3) for (2) by issuance of (0.5) additional share payable 12/31/2004 to holders of record 12/17/2004 Ex date - 01/03/2005
Common $5 par split (3) for (2) by issuance of (0.5) additional share payable 03/31/2006 to holders of record 03/15/2006 Ex date - 04/03/2006
Each share Common $0.50 par received distribution of (1) share Quanex Building Products Corp. Common 1¢ par payable 04/24/2008 to holders of record 04/23/2008
Merged into Gerdau S.A. 04/23/2008
Each share Common $5 par exchanged for $39.20 cash

QUANTA CAP HLDGS LTD (BERMUDA)
10.25% Preferred Ser. A 1¢ par called for redemption at $22.50 on 09/25/2007
Merged into Catalina Holdings (Bermuda) Ltd. 10/10/2008
Each share Common 1¢ par exchanged for $2.80 cash

QUANTA DISPLAY INC (TAIWAN)
Merged into AU Optronics Corp. 10/1/2006
Each Reg. S Sponsored GDR for Ordinary exchanged for (0.57142857) Sponsored ADR for Ordinary NT$10 par

QUANTA INDS INC (CA)
Charter suspended for failure to file reports and pay fees 10/01/1985

QUANTA SYS CORP (CO)
Merged into Compudyne Corp. 12/26/1985
Each share Common 1¢ par exchanged for $0.10 cash

QUANTEC INTL INC (UT)
Involuntarily dissolved 03/31/1986

QUANTECH ELECTRONICS CORP (CO)
Reincorporated 12/15/2003
State of incorporation changed from (NY) to (CO) and Common 1¢ par changed to $0.0001 par 12/15/2003
Each share old Common $0.0001 par exchanged for (0.00033333) share new Common $0.0001 par 02/14/2006
Each share new Common $0.0001 par exchanged again for (0.0005) share new Common $0.0001 par 02/16/2007
Name changed to Signal Bay, Inc. 10/24/2014
Signal Bay, Inc. recapitalized as EVIO, Inc. 09/06/2017

QUANTECH LTD (MN)
Each share old Common $1 par exchanged for (0.05) share new Common $1 par 06/02/1998
Filed a petition under Chapter 7 Federal Bankruptcy Code 02/18/2003
Stockholders' equity unlikely

QUANTEX CORP (UT)
Each share old Common 1¢ par exchanged for (0.1) share new Common 1¢ par 3/31/88
Reincorporated under the laws of Delaware as Cenna Communications Group, Inc. 11/7/89
Cenna Communications Group, Inc. name changed to First Equities Corp. 9/23/96

QUANTEX DEV CORP (NV)
Charter revoked for failure to file reports and pay fees 9/1/90

QUANTITATIVE ALPHA TRADING INC (ON)
Reincorporated 12/09/2011
Place of incorporation changed from (BC) to (ON) 12/09/2011
Ceased operations 03/18/2013
Stockholders' equity unlikely

QUANTITATIVE METHODS CORP (NV)
Name changed to M45 Mining Resources, Inc. 04/23/2007
M45 Mining Resources, Inc. name changed to Neuro-Biotech Corp. 06/17/2010 which recapitalized as Institute of BioMedical Research Corp. 04/28/2014

QUANTOR CORP (DE)
Merged into NCR Corp. 12/04/1978
Each share Common 20¢ par exchanged for $3 cash

QUANTRONIX CORP (DE)
Common 1¢ par split (3) for (2) by issuance of (0.5) additional share 05/18/1984
Common 1¢ par split (3) for (2) by issuance of (0.5) additional share 12/23/1985
Acquired by Excel Technology, Inc. 10/01/1992
Each share Common 1¢ par exchanged for (0.425) share Common $0.001 par and (1) Common Stock Purchase Warrant expiring 09/30/1997
(See Excel Technology, Inc.)

QUANTSHARES ENHANCED CORE CDN EQUITY ETF (ON)
Name changed to AGFiQ Enhanced Core Canadian Equity ETF 11/02/2017

QUANTSHARES ENHANCED CORE EMERGING MKTS EQUITY ETF (ON)
Name changed to AGFiQ Enhanced Core Emerging Markets Equity ETF 11/02/2017

QUANTSHARES ENHANCED CORE INTL EQUITY ETF (ON)
Name changed to AGFiQ Enhanced Core International Equity ETF 11/02/2017

QUANTSHARES ENHANCED CORE US EQUITY ETF (ON)
Name changed to AGFiQ Enhanced Core US Equity ETF 11/02/2017

QUANTSHARES GLOBAL EQUITY ROTATION ETF (ON)
Name changed to AGFiQ Global Equity Rotation ETF 11/02/2017

QUANTSHARES MULTIASSET ALLOCATION ETF (ON)
Name changed to AGFiQ MultiAsset Allocation ETF 11/02/2017

QUANTSHARES MULTIASSET INCOME ALLOCATION ETF (ON)
Name changed to AGFiQ MultiAsset Income Allocation ETF 11/02/2017

QUANTUM BIT INDUCTION TECHNOLOGY INC (NV)
Old Common $0.001 par split (10) for (1) by issuance of (9) additional shares payable 08/29/2006 to holders of record 08/28/2006 Ex date - 08/30/2006
Each share old Common $0.001 par exchanged for (0.00005) share new Common $0.001 par 11/19/2007
Recapitalized as Quantumbit, Inc. 01/30/2012
Each share new Common $0.001 par exchanged for (0.00016666) share Common $0.001 par
Quantumbit, Inc. name changed to Sertant, Inc. 10/30/2013 which name changed to EPHS Holdings, Inc. 08/27/2018

QUANTUM CHEM CORP (VA)
Merged into Hanson PLC (Old) 10/01/1993
Each share Common $2.50 par exchanged for (1.1767) Sponsored ADR's for Ordinary 25p par
Hanson PLC (Old) reorganized as Hanson PLC (New) 10/15/2003
(See Hanson PLC (New))

QUANTUM COMMUNICATIONS GROUP INC (DE)
Recapitalized as CityMainStreet Technologies Group Holdings Inc. 11/27/2001
Each share Common 1¢ par exchanged for (0.05) share Common 1¢ par

QUANTUM CORP (DE)
Reincorporated 04/28/1987
State of incorporation changed from (CA) to (DE) and Common no par changed to 1¢ par 04/28/1987
Common 1¢ par split (3) for (2) by issuance of (0.5) additional share 05/05/1989
Common 1¢ par split (2) for (1) by issuance of (1) additional share 08/15/1989
Common 1¢ par split (3) for (2) by issuance of (0.5) additional share 04/30/1991
Common 1¢ par split (2) for (1) by issuance of (1) additional share payable 06/09/1997 to holders of record 05/27/1997
Each share Common 1¢ par exchanged for (1) share DSSG Common 1¢ par and (0.5) share HDDG Common 1¢ par 08/03/1999
Each share HDDG Common 1¢ par exchanged for (1.52) shares Maxtor Corp. Common 1¢ par 04/02/2001
(Additional Information in Active)

QUANTUM DIAGNOSTICS LTD (NY)
Dissolved by proclamation 3/24/93

QUANTUM EFFECT DEVICES INC (DE)
Merged into PMC-Sierra, Inc. 08/25/2000
Each share Common $0.001 par exchanged for (0.385) share Common $0.001 par
PMC-Sierra, Inc. merged into Microsemi Corp. 01/14/2016
(See Microsemi Corp.)

QUANTUM ENERGY CORP (BC)
Name changed to Granville Island Brewing Co. Ltd. 11/19/85
Granville Island Brewing Co. Ltd. was acquired by International Potter Distilling Corp. 8/29/89 which name changed to Cascadia Brands Inc. 3/30/95
(See Cascadia Brands Inc.)

QUANTUM ENERGY INC (UT)
Name changed to Western Bell Communications, Inc. 05/20/1985
(See Western Bell Communications, Inc.)

QUANTUM ENERGY LTD (AUSTRALIA)
ADR agreement terminated 09/25/2017
Each Sponsored ADR for Ordinary exchanged for $0.4834 cash

QUANTUM FINL HLDGS INC
Merged into United Payors & United Providers, Inc. 9/1/99
Each share Common exchanged for $22.41808 cash

QUANTUM GROUP INC. (MN)
Recapitalized as Quantum Labs, Inc. 12/11/1989
Each share Common 1¢ par exchanged for (0.1) share Common 1¢ par
(See Quantum Labs, Inc.)

QUANTUM GROUP INC (NV)
Ctfs. dtd. after 02/06/2004
Each share old Common $0.001 par exchanged for (0.04) share new Common $0.001 par 03/29/2007
Secondary Offering - 1,200,000 UNITS consisting of (3) shares COM, (2) CL A WTS and (2) CL B WTS offered at $11 per Unit on 12/12/2007
Units separated 01/17/2008
SEC revoked common stock registration 10/17/2011

QUANTUM GROUP INC (NV)
Ctfs. dtd. prior to 03/26/2001
Each share old Common $0.001 par exchanged for (0.33333333) share new Common $0.001 par 07/14/1997
Name changed to Advanced Recycling Sciences, Inc. 03/26/2001
(See Advanced Recycling Sciences, Inc.)

QUANTUM HEALTH RES INC (DE)
Merged into Olsten Corp. 06/28/1996
Each share Common 1¢ par exchanged for (0.58) share Common 10¢ par
Olsten Corp. merged into Adecco S.A. 03/15/2000 which name changed to Adecco Group AG 06/03/2016

QUANTUM INFORMATION INC (NV)
Name changed to MGMT Energy, Inc. 04/03/2009

QUA-QUE

MGMT Energy, Inc. name changed to Management Energy, Inc. 07/01/2009 which name changed to MMEX Mining Corp. 03/04/2011 which name changed to MMEX Resources Corp. 06/03/2016

QUANTUM LABS INC (MN)
Merged into Quantum Acquisition Co. 1/28/99
Each share Common 1¢ par exchanged for $2 cash

QUANTUM LEARNING SYS INC (NV)
Name changed to Costa Rica International, Inc. 08/28/1996
Costa Rica International, Inc. name changed to Rica Foods, Inc. 08/24/1998
(See Rica Foods, Inc.)

QUANTUM RARE EARTH DEVS CORP (BC)
Name changed to NioCorp Developments Ltd. 03/04/2013

QUANTUM RESOURCE CORP (BC)
Recapitalized as International Exotic Motors Corp. (BC) 04/25/1991
Each share Common no par exchanged for (0.5) share Common no par
International Exotic Motors Corp. (BC) reincorporated in Wyoming as North American Advanced Materials Corp. 10/05/1993
(See North American Advanced Materials Corp.)

QUANTUM RESTAURANT GROUP INC (DE)
Name changed to Morton's Restaurant Group Inc. 5/9/96
(See Morton's Restaurant Group Inc.)

QUANTUM SYS INDS INC (OR)
Name changed to Balboa Development Inc. 12/13/1985
(See Balboa Development Inc.)

QUANTUM TECHNOLOGY CORP (NV)
Each share old Common $0.001 par exchanged for (0.005) share new Common $0.001 par 11/17/2008
Note: No holder will receive fewer than (100) post-split shares
Name changed to One World Ventures, Inc. 02/25/2009

QUANTUM VENTURES GROUP INC (FL)
Each share old Common $0.00001 par exchanged for (0.01) share new Common $0.00001 par 12/15/89
Each share new Common $0.00001 par exchanged for (0.25) share Common 1¢ par 5/15/92
Name changed to Bernard Haldane Associates, Inc. 9/3/93
(See Bernard Haldane Associates, Inc.)

QUANTUM VENTURES INC (NV)
Name changed to QV Quantum Ventures, Inc. 02/25/2008
QV Quantum Ventures, Inc. name changed to Quantum Solar Power Corp. 06/25/2008

QUANTUMBIT INC (NV)
Name changed to Sertant, Inc. 10/30/2013
Sertant, Inc. name changed to EPHS Holdings, Inc. 08/27/2018

QUANTUS CAP INC (NV)
Recapitalized as Red Horse Entertainment Corp. 03/26/1992
Each share Common $0.001 par exchanged for (0.2) share Common $0.001 par
Red Horse Entertainment Corp. name changed to Great China International Holdings, Inc. 09/15/2005 which name changed to HH Biotechnology Holdings Co. 08/24/2016

QUANTUS DEVS LTD (BC)
Name changed to C.T.I. Technologies Corp. 05/26/1986
C.T.I. Technologies Corp. recapitalized as World Videophone Teleconferencing Technologies Ltd. 03/29/1990
(See World Videophone Teleconferencing Technologies Ltd.)

QUANTUS EXPLORATION LTD. (BC)
Recapitalized as Quantus Developments Ltd. 10/21/1981
Each share Common 50¢ par exchanged for (0.25) share Common no par
Quantus Developments Ltd. name changed to C.T.I. Technologies Corp. 05/26/1986 which recapitalized as World Videophone Teleconferencing Technologies Ltd. 03/29/1990
(See World Videophone Teleconferencing Technologies Ltd.)

QUAREX INDS INC (DE)
Common 5¢ par split (3) for (2) by issuance of (0.5) additional share 3/4/88
Stock Dividends - 25% 1/11/85; 10% 2/3/89; 10% 3/8/90; 10% 1/22/93
Name changed to Western Beef Inc. 1/13/93
(See Western Beef Inc.)

QUARRY OIL & GAS LTD (AB)
Name changed 04/24/2001
Name changed from Quarry Capital Corp. to Quarry Oil & Gas Ltd. 04/24/2001
Acquired by Assure Energy Inc. 01/12/2005
Each share Common no par exchanged for (0.36) share Common $0.001 par
Assure Energy Inc. acquired by GEOCAN Energy Inc. 09/08/2005 which merged into Arsenal Energy Inc. (New) 10/08/2008 which merged into Prairie Provident Resources Inc. 09/16/2016

QUARTERBACK EAST INC (DE)
Name changed to Unitas (Johnny) Quarterback Clubs, Inc. 12/19/69
Unitas (Johnny) Quarterback Clubs, Inc. name changed to Energy Recycling Corp. 8/11/89
(See Energy Recycling Corp.)

QUARTERBACK SPORTS FEDN INC (MN)
Common 10¢ par split (2) for (1) by issuance of (1) additional share 4/16/69
Stock Dividend - 100% 5/17/68
Adjudicated bankrupt 4/1/70
No stockholders' equity

QUARTERDECK CORP (DE)
Name changed 3/1/95
Name changed from Quarterdeck Office Systems to Quarterdeck Corp. 3/1/95
Merged into Symantec Corp. 3/29/99
Each share Common $0.001 par exchanged for $0.52 cash

QUARTERLY DISTRIBUTION SHARES, INC. (KS)
Common no par changed to $1 par and (1) additional share issued 12/15/55
Name changed to Security Investment Fund, Inc. 2/28/67
Security Investment Fund, Inc. name changed to Security Growth & Income Fund 7/6/93 which name changed to Security Large Capital Value Fund 10/1/2002

QUARTERLY INCOME SHARES, INC.
Merged into American Business Shares, Inc. on a (2.379172) for (1) basis 00/00/1944
American Business Shares, Inc. name changed to Lord Abbett Income Fund, Inc. (DE) 11/17/1975 which reincorporated in Maryland 07/09/1975 which name changed to Lord Abbett U.S. Government Securities Fund, Inc. 09/23/1985
(See Lord Abbett U.S. Government Securities Fund, Inc.)

QUARTET ENERGY RES LTD (ON)
Reincorporated 07/09/1981
Place of incorporation changed from (BC) to (ON) 07/09/1981
Name changed to Oiltex International Ltd. 04/26/1984
Oiltex International Ltd. merged into International Oiltex Ltd. 10/01/1989 which merged into Aztec Resources Ltd. 09/02/1994 which recapitalized as Pursuit Resources Inc. (New) 02/13/1997 which merged into EnerMark Income Fund 04/11/2000 which merged into Enerplus Resources Fund 06/22/2001 which reorganized as Enerplus Corp. 01/03/2011

QUARTET MERGER CORP (DE)
Each Unit separated into (1.1) shares Common $0.0001 par 10/03/2014
Reincorporated under the laws of Bermuda as Pangaea Logistics Solutions Ltd. 10/03/2014

QUARTET RES LTD (HONG KONG)
Name changed to Goldbelt Empires Ltd. 10/27/2015

QUARTEX CORP (ON)
Class A Common no par split (10) for (1) by issuance of (9) additional shares 9/30/91
Each share Non-Vtg. Class A no par exchanged for (0.25) share Common no par 4/8/94
Name changed to PC Docs Group International Inc. 6/29/94
(See PC Docs Group International Inc.)

QUARTITE CREATIVE CORP. (NY)
Acquired by Continental Can Co., Inc. 01/31/1966
Each share Common 10¢ par exchanged for (0.1371) share Common $10 par
Continental Can Co., Inc. name changed to Continental Group, Inc. 04/27/1976
(See Continental Group, Inc.)

QUARTZ CREEK GOLDMINES B C INC (BC)
Recapitalized as Pilot Peak Gold, Inc. 12/12/1989
Each share Common no par exchanged for (1/3) share Common no par
(See Pilot Peak Gold, Inc.)

QUARTZ CRYSTALS MINES LTD. (ON)
Charter cancelled for failure to pay taxes and file returns 11/00/1954

QUARTZ CRYSTALS MINING CORP. OF CANADA LTD.
Merged into Quartz Crystals Mines Ltd. 00/00/1950
Each share Capital Stock $1 par exchanged for (0.1) share Capital Stock $1 par
(See Quartz Crystals Mines Ltd.)

QUARTZ ENGR & MATLS INC (AZ)
Name changed to Amtech Systems, Inc. 06/01/1987

QUARTZ GROUP INC (CO)
Recapitalized as Tenguy World International, Inc. 09/12/2005
Each share Common no par exchanged for (0.00885739) share Common $0.0001 par
Tenguy World International, Inc. recapitalized as CMK Gaming International, Inc. 10/23/2013

QUARTZ HILL CENTRAL MINING CO.
Dissolved in 1931

QUARTZ INC (MN)
Statutorily dissolved 12/31/99

QUARTZ KING MINING CO. (AZ)
Charter expired by time limitation 8/30/29

QUARTZ MTN GOLD CORP (BC)
Recapitalized as Quartz Mountain Resources Ltd. 11/5/97
Each share Common no par exchanged for (0.1) share Common no par

QUASAR AEROSPACE INDS INC (CO)
Each share old Common $0.00001 par exchanged for (0.001) share new Common $0.00001 par 02/01/2012
Recapitalized as Green Energy Enterprises, Inc. 10/30/2015
Each share new Common $0.00001 par exchanged for (0.001) share Common $0.00001 par 10/30/2015

QUASAR ASSOC INC (DE)
Common $0.002 par split (3) for (1) by issuance of (2) additional shares 01/15/1988
Merged into Alliance Quasar Fund, Inc. 04/27/1989
Details not available

QUASAR MICROSYSTEMS INC (NY)
Name changed to QT&T Inc. 07/05/1984
(See QT&T Inc.)

QUASAR PETE LTD (AB)
Common 25¢ par split (3) for (1) by issuance of (2) additional shares 10/23/79
Merged into Oakwood Petroleums Ltd. 5/27/82
Each share Common 25¢ par exchanged for $3 cash

QUASAR SCIENCES INC (CO)
Declared defunct and inoperative for failure to file reports and pay taxes 10/16/1971

QUASAR-TECH INC (UT)
Merged into McGowen Resources Co., Inc. 8/4/92
Each share Common $0.01177 par exchanged for (0.5) share Common $0.001 par
McGowen Resources Co., Inc. name changed to Trek Resources Inc. (UT) 6/15/2000 which reincorporated in Delaware 2/7/2001

QUATECH INC (DE)
Recapitalized as Lotus Pacific, Inc. 9/23/94
Each share Common $0.001 par exchanged for (0.02) share Common $0.001 par
Lotus Pacific, Inc. name changed to Opta Corp. 9/28/2004
(See Opta Corp.)

QUATTRO G INC (DE)
Charter cancelled and declared inoperative and void for non-payment of taxes 3/1/87

QUATTRO RES LTD (BC)
Recapitalized as Aldershot Resources Ltd. 07/31/2001
Each share Common no par exchanged for (0.1) share Common no par

QUAZON CORP (NV)
Name changed to Scientific Energy, Inc. 07/16/2001
Scientific Energy, Inc. name changed to Electronic Game Card, Inc. 12/05/2003
(See Electronic Game Card, Inc.)

QUBIX GRAPHIC SYS INC (DE)
Charter forfeited for failure to maintain a registered agent 2/25/91

QUE-ON MINES, LTD. (ON)
Completely liquidated 10/10/1963
Each share Capital Stock $1 par exchanged for (0.25) free share and (0.25) escrowed share Western

Quebec Mines Co. Ltd. Capital Stock $1 par 10/10/1963 Western Quebec Mines Co. Ltd. name changed to Western Quebec Mines Inc. 06/00/1986 which merged into Wesdome Gold Mines Ltd. 07/18/2007

QUE WEST RES LTD (AB)
Merged into Channel Resources Ltd. (New) 10/31/1989
Each share Common no par exchanged for (0.15384615) share Common no par
Channel Resources Ltd. (New) merged into West African Resources Ltd. 01/17/2014

QUEBEC ASCOT COPPER LTD (QC)
Charter cancelled for failure to file reports 07/17/1972

QUEBEC AUTOBUS (1965) INC. (QC)
6.5% Preferred $20 par called for redemption 01/31/1971
Public interest eliminated

QUEBEC CHIBOUGAMAU GOLDFIELDS LTD (QC)
Merged into Allied Mining Corp. 09/22/1969
Each share Capital Stock $1 par exchanged for (0.2) share Common no par
Allied Mining Corp. merged into United Asbestos Inc. 06/29/1973 which merged into Campbell Resources Inc. (New) 06/08/1983
(See Campbell Resources Inc. (New))

QUEBEC COBALT & EXPL LTD (QC)
Merged into Consolidated Thompson-Lundmark Gold Mines Ltd. 07/01/1989
Each share Capital Stock $1 par exchanged for (0.5) share Common no par
Consolidated Thompson-Lundmark Gold Mines Ltd. name changed to Consolidated Thompson Iron Mines Ltd. 08/24/2006
(See Consolidated Thompson Iron Mines Ltd.)

QUEBEC COPPER CORP. LTD. (QC)
Recapitalizes as Sullico Mines Ltd. 10/25/60
Each share Capital Stock $1 par exchanged for (0.025) share Capital Stock $1 par
Sullico Mines Ltd. merged into Sullivan Mining Group Ltd. 9/2/69 which merged into Sullivan Mines Inc.-Mines Sullivan Inc. 7/1/83
(See Sullivan Mines Inc.-Mines Sullivan Inc.)

QUEBEC DEVELOPERS & SMELTERS LTD. (QC)
Declared dissolved for failure to file reports and pay fees 6/15/74

QUEBEC EXPLORERS LTD (QC)
Recapitalized as QEX Resources Inc. 2/15/95
Each share Common $1 par exchanged for (0.2) share Common no par
(See QEX Resources Inc.)

QUEBEC GOLD BELT LTD.
Acquired by Rubec Mines Ltd. in 1927
(See Rubec Mines Ltd.)

QUEBEC GOLD BELT MINES LTD (CANADA)
Merged into Sigma Mines (Quebec) Ltd./Les Mines Sigma (Quebec) Ltee. 11/18/1983
Each share Common no par exchanged for (0.14285714) share Capital Stock no par
Sigma Mines (Quebec) Ltd./Les Mines Sigma (Quebec) Ltee. merged into Placer Dome Inc. 06/21/1988 which merged into Barrick Gold Corp. 03/08/2006

QUEBEC GOLD MINING CORP. (QC)
Recapitalized as Consolidated Quebec Gold Mining & Metals Corp. 00/00/1951
Each share Capital Stock $1 par exchanged for (0.16) share Preferred $1 par (immediately redeemed) and (0.4) share Common $2.50 par
Consolidated Quebec Gold Mining & Metals Corp. recapitalized as Commercial Holdings & Metals Corp. 03/25/1964

QUEBEC GOLD RESEARCH CORP. LTD.
Bankrupt in 1948

QUEBEC INDL MINERALS CORP (QC)
Declared dissolved for failure to file reports and pay fees 04/14/1973

QUEBEC LABRADOR DEVELOPMENT CO., LTD. (QC)
Recapitalized as Salem Exploration Ltd. on a (1) for (7.5) basis 3/20/63
Salem Exploration Ltd. was acquired by Agena Mining Co. Ltd. 8/11/66
(See Agena Mining Co. Ltd.)

QUEBEC LITHIUM CORP (QC)
Merged into Sullivan Mining Group Ltd. 09/02/1969
Each share Common $1 par exchanged for (0.5) share Capital Stock no par
Sullivan Mining Group Ltd. merged into Sullivan Mines Inc.-Mines Sullivan Inc. 07/01/1983
(See Sullivan Mines Inc.-Mines Sullivan Inc.)

QUEBEC MANGANESE MINES LTD.
Acquired by Royran Gold Fields Ltd. on a (1) for (3) basis in 1950
Royran Gold Fields Ltd. was recapitalized as New Royran Copper Mines Ltd. 8/30/55 which merged into Copper Rand Chibougamau Mines Ltd. 9/25/56 which merged into Patino Mining Corp. 11/26/62 which reorganized as Patino N.V. 12/20/71
(See Patino N.V.)

QUEBEC MANITOU MINES LTD (ON)
Capital Stock $1 par changed to no par 7/13/71
Merged into Petro-Sun, Inc./Petro-Soleil, Inc. 2/1/80
Each share Capital Stock no par exchanged for (0.25) share Common no par
Petro-Sun, Inc./Petro-Soleil, Inc. name changed to Petro-Sun International Inc. 9/2/82
(See Petro-Sun International Inc.)

QUEBEC MATTAGAMI MINERALS LTD (ON)
Name changed to Q.M.G. Holdings Inc. and Common $1 par changed to no par 10/03/1977
(See Q.M.G. Holdings Inc.)

QUEBEC METALLURGICAL INDUSTRIES LTD. (CANADA)
Recapitalized as Q.M.I. Minerals Ltd. on a (1) for (5) basis 5/31/63
Q.M.I. Minerals Ltd. merged into Indusmin Ltd. 11/6/68
(See Indusmin Ltd.)

QUEBEC NAT GAS CORP (QC)
6% Preferred 1959 Ser. $100 par called for redemption 4/22/65
Name changed to Gaz Metropolitain, Inc. 10/4/69
Gaz Metropolitain, Inc. merged into Noverco Inc. 8/1/86
(See Noverco Inc.)

QUEBEC NICKEL CORP. LTD. (QC)
Merged into Eastern Mining & Smelting Corp. Ltd. on a (1) for (3) basis 1/3/56
Eastern Mining & Smelting Corp. recapitalized as Nickel Mining & Smelting Corp. 8/19/58 which recapitalized as Metal Mines Ltd. 12/31/63 which merged into Consolidated Canadian Faraday Ltd. 5/4/67 which name changed to Faraday Resources Inc. 8/2/83 which merged into Conwest Exploration Co. Ltd. (New) (ALTA) 9/1/93 which merged into Alberta Energy Co. Ltd. 1/31/96 which merged into EnCana Corp. 1/3/2003

QUEBEC NORTH MINES LTD (QC)
Declared dissolved for failure to file reports or pay fees 08/17/1974

QUEBEC OIL DEVELOPMENT LTD. (QC)
Acquired by New Associated Developments Ltd. 04/17/1963
Each share Capital Stock $1 par exchanged for (0.05882352) share Capital Stock $1 par
New Associated Developments Ltd. recapitalized as Consolidated Development Ltd. 05/10/1971
(See Consolidated Development Ltd.)

QUEBEC PWR CO (QC)
Each share Common $100 par exchanged for (4) shares Common no par in 1927
Acquired by Quebec Hydro-Electric Commission 9/24/63
Each share Common no par exchanged for $37 cash

QUEBEC PULP & PAPER CORP. (QC)
Completely liquidated 00/00/1949
Each share Preferred exchanged for first and final distribution of $23 cash
No Common stockholders' equity
Note: Unexchanged certificates were cancelled and became without value 04/01/1969

QUEBEC PULP & PAPER MILLS, LTD.
Assets sold to Price Bros. & Co., Ltd. and Port Alfred Pulp & Paper Corp. in 1927
(See each company's listing)

QUEBEC RAILWAY, LIGHT, HEAT & POWER, LTD.
Sold to Quebec Power Co. in 1928
Quebec Power Co. acquired by Quebec Hydro-Electric Commission for cash 9/24/63

QUEBEC SMELTING & REFINING CORP.
Acquired by Quebec Smelting & Refining Ltd. on a (60) for (1) basis in 1948
Quebec Smelting & Refining Ltd. recapitalized as Cons. Quebec Smelting & Refining Ltd. 9/13/65 which name changed to Magnetics International Ltd. 5/2/68 which name changed to Magnetics International Ltd.-Magnetique International Ltee. 11/2/70 which name changed to Mavtech Holdings Inc. 8/31/87
(See Mavtech Holdings Inc.)

QUEBEC SMELTING & REFINING LTD. (QC)
Recapitalized as Cons. Quebec Smelting & Refining Ltd. 9/13/65
Each share Capital Stock $1 par exchanged for (0.2) share Capital Stock $5 par
Cons. Quebec Smelting & Refining Ltd. name changed to Magnetics International Ltd. 5/2/68 which name changed to Magnetics International Ltd.-Magnetique International Ltee. 11/20/70 which name changed to Mavtech Holdings Inc. 8/31/87
(See Mavtech Holdings Inc.)

QUEBEC SOUTH SHORE STEEL CORP. (QC)
Acquired by Corgemines Ltd. 1/19/65
Each share Capital Stock $1 par exchanged for (1) share Common $1 par
Corgemines Ltd. charter annulled 3/22/75

QUEBEC SOUTHERN POWER CORP.
Dissolved in 1927

QUEBEC STURGEON RIV MINES LTD (ON)
Capital Stock $1 par changed to no par 06/27/1972
Merged into QSR Ltd. 09/07/1993
Each share Common no par exchanged for (0.2) share Common no par
QSR Ltd. name changed to Coniagas Resources Ltd. 06/25/1999 which name changed to Lithium One Inc. 07/23/2009
(See Lithium One Inc.)

QUEBEC TANTALUM & LITHIUM MINING CO. LTD. (QC)
Liquidation completed 10/24/58

QUEBEC TEL (QC)
Each share Common $5 par exchanged for (3) shares Common no par 4/4/55
Common no par split (2) for (1) by issuance of (1) additional share 4/24/64
5-1/2% Preferred 1958 Ser. $20 par called for redemption 4/1/65
5-1/2% Preferred 1961 Ser. $20 par called for redemption 4/1/65
5% Preferred 1950 Ser. $20 par called for redemption 9/1/71
5% Preferred 1951 Ser. $20 par called for redemption 3/31/71
6.20% Conv. Preferred Ser. A $15 par called for redemption 3/31/76
Common no par split (3) for (1) by issuance of (2) additional shares 4/25/86
$1.68 Conv. Subordinate Preferred Ser. B $15 par called for redemption 10/1/90
5% Preferred 1956 Ser. $20 par called for redemption at $21 plus accrued dividend 4/1/97
7.75% Preferred 1973 Ser. $20 par called for redemption at $20.20 plus accrued dividend 4/1/97
Under plan of reorganization each share Common no par automatically became (1) share Quebectel Group Inc. Common no par on 5/1/97
(See Quebectel Group Inc.)
5% Preferred 1955 Ser. $20 par called for redemption 12/30/97
4.75% Preferred 1965 Ser. $20 par called for redemption at $21 plus $0.2375 accrued dividend on 12/30/97
Public interest eliminated

QUEBEC TELEPHONE & POWER CORP.
Name changed to Quebec Telephone Corp. in 1947
Quebec Telephone Corp. name changed to Quebec-Telephone in 1955
(See Quebec-Telephone)

QUEBEC TELEPHONE CORP. (QC)
Recapitalized in 1950
Class A no par changed to $15 par
Class B no par changed to Common $5 par
Name changed to Quebec-Telephone in 1955

QUEBEC TUNGSTEN LTD. (QC)
Out of business 01/15/1960
Details not available

QUEBEC URANIUM MNG CORP (QC)
Merged into Cuvier Mines Ltd. 02/15/1980
Each share Capital Stock $1 par exchanged for (0.1) share Common $1 par
Cuvier Mines Ltd. merged into Kam Creed Mines Ltd. 07/13/1988
(See Kam Creed Mines Ltd.)

QUEBEC VIKING GOLD MINES LTD. (ON)
Acquired by Adnaron Copper Corp., Ltd. in 1940

QUEBEC YELLOWKNIFE GOLD MINES LTD. (QC)
Recapitalized as Consolidated Quebec Yellowknife Mines Ltd. 10/7/55
Each share Capital Stock $1 par exchanged for (0.25) share Capital Stock $1 par
Consolidated Quebec Yellowknife Mines Ltd. charter cancelled 5/4/74

QUEBECOR PRTG INC (CANADA)
Subordinate no par split (3) for (2) by issuance of (0.5) additional share 05/10/1994
Name changed to Quebecor World Inc. 04/25/2000
(See Quebecor World Inc.)

QUEBECOR WORLD INC (CANADA)
6.75% 1st Preferred Ser. 4 called for redemption at $25 plus $0.2185 accrued dividends on 04/18/2006
6.9% 1st Preferred Ser. 5 exchanged for (13.3625) shares Subordinate Common no par 09/01/2008
Plan of reorganization under Chapter 11 Federal Bankruptcy proceedings effective 07/21/2009
No stockholders' equity

QUEBECTEL GROUP INC (QC)
Merged into 9090-4002 Quebec Inc. 6/1/2000
Each share Common no par exchanged for $23 cash

QUED RES CORP (BC)
Recapitalized as Arwick International Resources Ltd. 04/23/1986
Each share Common no par exchanged for (1/3) share Common no par
Arwick International Resources Ltd. recapitalized as Gincho International Ventures Inc. 05/13/1992 which name changed to Banner Mining Corp. 08/09/1994
(See Banner Mining Corp.)

QUEEN BEE GOLD MINING CO. (CO)
Charter revoked for failure to file reports and pay fees 09/16/1913

QUEEN CASUALS INC (PA)
Stock Dividend - 20% 6/6/75
Merged into Interco Inc. (Old) 2/20/76
Each share Common 50¢ par exchanged for (0.5534) share Common no par
(See Interco Inc. (Old))

QUEEN CITY COTTON CO.
Liquidation completed in 1941

QUEEN CORP. (NV)
Charter revoked 03/00/1960

QUEEN ESTHER MINING CO. (UT)
Merged into Park City Consolidated Mines Co. 7/19/84
Each share Common 10¢ par exchanged for (1) share Common 10¢ par

QUEEN MARGARET GOLD MINES N L (AUSTRALIA)
Acquired by Spargos Mining N.L. 12/12/1988
Details not available

QUEEN OF HILLS MINING CO. (UT)
Merged into Treasure Mountain Mining Co. (UT) 04/15/1970
Each share Class A Common 5¢ par exchanged for (0.5) share Class A Common 10¢ par
Treasure Mountain Mining Co. name changed to Treasure Mountain Holdings, Inc. (UT) 02/11/1997 which reincorporated in Nevada 04/01/1997 which recapitalized as Vyteris Holdings (Nevada), Inc. 05/03/2005 which name changed to Vyteris, Inc. 07/02/2007
(See Vyteris, Inc.)

QUEEN SAND RES INC (DE)
Name changed to Devx Energy Inc. 9/19/2000
(See Devx Energy Inc.)

QUEEN STR CAMERA INC (ON)
Placed in receivership 12/05/1989
No stockholders' equity

QUEEN STR ENTMT CAP INC (ON)
Name changed to Knightscove Media Corp. 08/16/2007

QUEENCO LEISURE INTL LTD (ISRAEL)
GDR agreement terminated 01/08/2015
Each Sponsored 144A GDR for Ordinary exchanged for $0.436544 cash
Each Sponsored Reg. S GDR for Ordinary exchanged for $0.436544 cash

QUEENS BOROUGH GAS & ELECTRIC CO.
Merged into Long Island Lighting Co. 00/00/1950
Each share 6% Preferred $100 par exchanged for (5.42) shares new Common no par
Long Island Lighting Co. merged into MarketSpan Corp. 05/29/1998 which name changed to KeySpan Energy 09/10/1998 which name changed to KeySpan Corp. 05/20/1999
(See KeySpan Corp.)

QUEENS CNTY BANCORP INC (DE)
Common 1¢ par split (3) for (2) by issuance of (0.5) additional share 9/30/94
Common 1¢ par split (4) for (3) by issuance of (1/3) additional share payable 8/22/96 to holders of record 8/1/96
Common 1¢ par split (3) for (2) by issuance of (0.5) additional share payable 4/10/97 to holders of record 3/17/97
Common 1¢ par split (3) for (2) by issuance of (0.5) additional share payable 10/1/97 to holders of record 9/10/97
Common 1¢ par split (3) for (2) by issuance of (0.5) additional share payable 9/29/98 to holders of record 9/15/98
Name changed to New York Community Bancorp, Inc. 11/21/2000

QUEENS NATIONAL BANK OF NEW YORK (SPRINGFIELD GARDENS, NY)
Merged into Meadow Brook National Bank (West Hempstead, N.Y.) 11/14/60
Each share Common $25 par exchanged for (2.125) shares Capital Stock $5 par
Meadow Brook National Bank (West Hempstead, N.Y.) name changed to National Bank of North America (West Hempstead, N.Y.) 5/8/67
(See National Bank of North America (West Hempstead, N.Y.))

QUEENSBORO BRIDGE RAILWAY CO., INC. (NY)
Dissolved 06/08/2009

QUEENSLAND ACCEP LTD (ON)
Charter cancelled and proclaimed dissolved for failure to file reports 11/25/1970

QUEENSLAND EXPLORATIONS LTD. (ON)
Merged into Queensland Acceptance Corp. Ltd. 10/19/63
Each share Capital Stock $1 par exchanged for (0.1) share Capital Stock no par
Queensland Acceptance Corp. Ltd. charter cancelled 11/25/70

QUEENSLAND MINERALS LTD (BC)
Each share old Common no par exchanged for (0.33333333) share new Common no par 01/19/2010
Name changed to Dunav Resources Ltd. 05/04/2011
Dunav Resources Ltd. merged into Avala Resources Ltd. 10/02/2014 which merged into Dundee Precious Metals Inc. 04/12/2016

QUEENSRIDGE MNG RES INC (NV)
Common $0.001 par split (5.307225) for (1) by issuance of (4.307225) additional shares payable 07/10/2014 to holders of record 07/07/2014 Ex date - 07/11/2014
Name changed to iWallet Corp. 07/30/2014

QUEENSTAKE RES LTD (BC)
Reincorporated 07/19/1999
Reincorporated 07/10/2006
Place of incorporation changed from (BC) to (YT) 07/19/1999 which reincorporated back to (BC) 07/10/2006
Merged into Yukon-Nevada Gold Corp. 06/25/2007
Each share Common no par exchanged for (0.1) share Common no par
Yukon-Nevada Gold Corp. recapitalized as Veris Gold Corp. 10/11/2012

QUEENSTAKE RES LTD (YT)
Merged into Queenstake Resources Ltd. (BC) 07/19/1999
Each share Common no par exchanged for (0.4993) share Common no par
Queenstake Resources Ltd. (BC) reincorporated in Yukon 07/19/1999 which reincorporated back in British Columbia 07/10/2006 which merged into Yukon-Nevada Gold Corp. 06/25/2007 which recapitalized as Veris Gold Corp. 10/11/2012

QUEENSTON GOLD MINES LTD (CANADA)
Reincorporated 00/00/1981
Reincorporated 04/23/1985
Common $1 par changed to no par 12/20/1972
Place of incorporation changed from (ON) to (AB) 00/00/1981
Place of incorporation changed from (AB) to (Canada) 04/23/1985
Merged into Queenston Mining Inc. 01/02/1990
Each share Common no par exchanged for (1) share Common no par
Queenston Mining Inc. merged into Osisko Mining Corp. 01/02/2013
(See Osisko Mining Corp.)

QUEENSTON MNG INC (CANADA)
Merged into Osisko Mining Corp. 01/02/2013
Each share Common no par exchanged for (0.611) share Common no par
(See Osisko Mining Corp.)

QUEENSWAY MINES LTD. (ON)
Merged into Alchib Developments Ltd. 07/10/1969
Each share Capital Stock $1 par exchanged for (0.06) share Capital Stock no par
Alchib Developments Ltd. merged into Kalrock Developments Ltd. 10/23/1978 which merged into Kalrock Resources Ltd. 08/08/1990 which merged into Cercal Minerals Corp. 07/09/1993
(See Cercal Minerals Corp.)

QUEENSWEAR CDA LTD (CANADA)
Acquired by Quegroup Investments Ltd. 08/22/1979
Each share Common no par exchanged for $5.19 cash

QUEJO MINES LTD (ON)
Recapitalized as Edomar Resources Inc. 04/10/1980
Each share Common no par exchanged for (0.1) share Common no par
Edomar Resources Inc. recapitalized as Kazakstan Goldfields Corp. 10/09/1996
(See Kazakstan Goldfields Corp.)

QUEMAQUE GOLD MINES LTD.
Name changed to Quemaque Explorers Ltd. in 1952

QUEMETCO INC (CA)
Liquidation completed
Each share Common $1 par exchanged for initial distribution of $11.50 cash 12/29/1970
Each share Common $1 par received second and final distribution of $2.0748 cash 12/06/1971

QUEMONT MINING CORP., LTD. (CANADA)
Acquired by Kerr Addison Mines Ltd. 5/3/68
Each share Capital Stock no par exchanged for (0.666666) share Capital Stock no par
Kerr Addison Mines Ltd. merged into Noranda Inc. 4/11/96 which name changed to Falconbridge Ltd. (New) 2005 on 7/1/2005
(See Falconbridge Ltd. (New) 2005)

QUENNADA MINES LTD. (ON)
Charter cancelled and company declared dissolved by default 9/24/56

QUENTIN RD PRODUCTIONS INC (DE)
Name changed to Intelilabs.com, Inc. 03/23/2000
Intelilabs.com, Inc. recapitalized as Micro Capital Corp. 07/02/2004
(See Micro Capital Corp.)

QUENTIN VENTURES LTD (BC)
Name changed to Identillect Technologies Corp. 05/25/2016

QUENTRA NETWORKS INC (DE)
Plan of reorganization under Chapter 11 Federal Bankruptcy proceedings effective 09/30/2002
No stockholders' equity

QUENTRON INC (WA)
Recapitalized as Otenco Energy Corp. 09/23/1982
Each share Common no par exchanged for (0.2) share Common 1¢ par
Otenco Energy Corp. recapitalized as Xytec Inc. 05/19/1983 which name changed to Xytec International Industries, Inc. 09/16/1983
(See Xytec International Industries, Inc.)

QUEPASA CORP (DE)
Recapitalized 08/06/2003
Reincorporated 12/07/2011
Recapitalized from Quepasa.com, Inc. to Quepasa Corp. 08/06/2003
Each share Common $0.001 par exchanged for (0.05) share Common $0.001 par
State of incorporation changed from (NV) to (DE) 12/07/2011
Name changed to MeetMe, Inc. 06/01/2012
MeetMe, Inc. name changed to Meet Group, Inc. 04/10/2017

QUERYOBJECT SYS CORP (DE)
Each share Common $0.001 par exchanged for (0.33333333) share Common $0.003 par 01/28/2000
SEC revoked common stock registration 10/09/2013

QUESABE MINES LTD. (ON)
Recapitalized as Brunston Mining Co. Ltd. 00/00/1953
Each share Capital Stock $1 par exchanged for (0.5) share Capital Stock $1 par
Brunston Mining Co. Ltd. recapitalized as Sunburst Exploration Ltd. 00/00/1956 which recapitalized as

Sunburst Resources 1991 Inc. 11/14/1991 which name changed to Sunburst M.C. Ltd. 02/16/1994 which name changed to Channel I Canada Inc. 01/10/1997 which recapitalized as Zaurak Capital Corp. 12/01/1999
(See Zaurak Capital Corp.)

QUESADA RES LTD (AB)
Name changed to Advanced Material Resources Ltd. (AB) 02/11/1993
Advanced Material Resources Ltd. (AB) reincorporated in Canada 08/08/1994 which name changed to AMR Technologies, Inc. 06/10/1998 which name changed to Neo Material Technologies, Inc. 04/28/2006 which merged into Molycorp, Inc. (New) 06/14/2012
(See Molycorp, Inc. (New))

QUESNEL LAKE PLACERS LTD. (BC)
Struck off register and declared dissolved for failure to file returns 1/23/41

QUESNELLE QUARTZ MINING CO. LTD.
Liquidated in 1939
Details not available

QUEST BIOTECHNOLOGY INC (MI)
Common 1¢ par split (3) for (2) by issuance of (0.5) additional share 03/20/1987
SEC revoked common stock registration 10/15/2008
Stockholders' equity unlikely

QUEST CAP CORP (CANADA)
Reincorporated 05/27/2008
Each share Class B no par automatically became (1.25) shares Class A no par 10/11/2004
Class A no par reclassified as Common no par 05/02/2005
Place of incorporation changed from (BC) to (Canada) 05/27/2008
Name changed to Sprott Resource Lending Corp. 09/10/2010
Sprott Resource Lending Corp. merged into Sprott Inc. 07/24/2013

QUEST COMMUNICATIONS CORP (DE)
Ceased operations in 1986
No stockholders' equity

QUEST DEV INC (OK)
Charter cancelled for failure to pay taxes 1/25/91

QUEST ED CORP (DE)
Merged into Kaplan Inc. 08/01/2000
Each share Common 1¢ par exchanged for $18.35 cash

QUEST ENERGY CORP (BC)
Recapitalized as PCH Post Career Habitats Inc. 4/7/87
Each share Common no par exchanged for (0.5) share Common no par
(See PCH Post Career Habitats Inc.)

QUEST ENERGY PARTNERS L P (DE)
Issue Information - 9,100,000 COM UNITS LTD PARTNERSHIP INT offered at $18 per Unit on 11/08/2007
Merged into PostRock Energy Corp. 03/05/2010
Each Common Unit exchanged for (0.2859) share Common 1¢ par

QUEST FOR VALUE DUAL PURPOSE FD INC (MD)
Income Shares 1¢ par called for redemption 01/31/1997
Name changed to Oppenheimer Quest Capital Value Fund, Inc. and Capital Shares reclassified as Class A 03/03/1997
Oppenheimer Quest Capital Value Fund, Inc. name changed to Oppenheimer Equity Income Fund, Inc. (New) 08/01/2007

QUEST FOR VALUE FD INC (MD)
Name changed to Oppenheimer Quest Value Fund, Inc. 11/22/1995
Oppenheimer Quest Value Fund, Inc. name changed to Oppenheimer Rising Dividends Fund, Inc. 08/01/2007 which reorganized in Massachusetts as Oppenheimer Rising Dividends Fund 09/14/2009

QUEST FOR VALUE GLOBAL EQUITY FD INC (MD)
Common 1¢ par reclassified as Class A Common 1¢ par 09/01/1993
Name changed to Oppenheimer Quest Global Value Fund, Inc. 11/22/1995
Oppenheimer Quest Global Value Fund Inc. name changed to Oppenheimer Quest International Value Fund, Inc. (MD) 08/29/2003 which reorganized in Massachusetts as Oppenheimer Quest International Value Fund 09/14/2009 which name changed to Oppenheimer International Value Fund (MA) 04/12/2012 which reincorporated in Delaware 10/11/2013 which name changed to Oppenheimer International Equity Fund 12/28/2016

QUEST GROUP INTL INC (NV)
Name changed to NuRx Pharmaceuticals, Inc. 10/30/2007

QUEST INTL EQUITIES INC (DE)
Common 1¢ par reclassified as Class B Common 1¢ par 07/29/1988
Name changed to Agri-Quest Mining, Inc. (DE) 11/27/1990
Agri-Quest Mining, Inc. (DE) reorganized in Nevada as New Century Media, Ltd. 09/01/1994 which name changed to LBU, Inc. 03/24/1995
(See LBU, Inc.)

QUEST INTL RES CORP (BC)
Recapitalized as Standard Mining Corp. 06/16/1999
Each share Common no par exchanged for (0.2) share Common no par
Standard Mining Corp. merged into Doublestar Resources Ltd. (YT) 11/01/2001 which reincorporated in British Columbia 10/10/2002 which merged into Selkirk Metals Corp. 07/23/2007
(See Selkirk Metals Corp.)

QUEST INVT CORP (BC)
Merged into Quest Capital Corp. (BC) 06/30/2003
Each share Class A Subordinate no par exchanged for (1.0514) shares Class A Subordinate no par
Each share Class B Multiple no par exchanged for (1.0514) shares Class B Variable Multiple no par
Note: Non-electing holders entitled to (99) shares or fewer of Class A Subordinate received $1.10 cash per share
No payment of less than $10 cash will be made
Quest Capital Corp. (BC) reincorporated in Canada 05/27/2008 which name changed to Sprott Resource Lending Corp. 09/10/2010 which merged into Sprott Inc. 07/24/2013

QUEST MED INC (TX)
Name changed to Advanced Neuromodulation Systems, Inc. 07/01/1998
(See Advanced Neuromodulation Systems, Inc.)

QUEST MINERALS & MNG CORP. (UT)
Each share old Common $0.001 par exchanged for (0.25) share new Common $0.001 par 08/17/2007
Each share new Common $0.001 par exchanged again for (0.1) share new Common $0.001 par 12/14/2007
Each share new Common $0.001 par exchanged again for (0.1) share new Common $0.001 par 11/04/2008
Each share new Common $0.001 par exchanged again for (0.01) share new Common $0.001 par 08/04/2009
New Common $0.001 par changed to $0.0001 par 11/23/2009
Recapitalized as Kentucky Energy, Inc. 06/17/2010
Each share new Common $0.0001 par exchanged for (0.05) share Common $0.0001 par
(See Kentucky Energy, Inc.)

QUEST NATIONAL, INC. (UT)
Name changed to Castle Group Inc. 6/1/93

QUEST NET CORP (FL)
Each share old Common $0.0001 par exchanged for (0.1) share new Common $0.0001 par 10/16/1998
Recapitalized as Markland Technologies Inc. 06/21/2001
Each share new Common $0.0001 par exchanged for (0.025) share Common $0.0001 par
(See Markland Technologies Inc.)

QUEST OIL & GAS INC (BC)
Name changed 11/15/1996
Name changed from Quest Capital Corp. to Quest Oil & Gas Inc. 11/15/1996
Merged into EnerMark Income Fund 04/18/1997
Each share Common no par exchanged for (0.347) share Common no par
EnerMark Income Fund merged into Enerplus Resources Fund 06/22/2001 which reorganized as Enerplus Corp. 01/03/2011

QUEST PRODS CORP (DE)
Name changed to Quest Patent Research Corp. 03/01/2016

QUEST PUBNS INC (DE)
Recapitalized as Quest Communications Corp. 04/09/1986
Each share Common $0.0001 par exchanged for (0.04) share Common $0.0001 par
(See Quest Communications Corp.)

QUEST RARE MINERALS LTD (CANADA)
Plan of reorganization under Bankruptcy & Insolvency Act effective 04/04/2018
No stockholders' equity

QUEST RESOURCE CORP (NV)
Each share 10% Conv. Preferred Ser. A $0.001 par exchanged for (1.6) shares new Common $0.001 par 12/20/2005
Each share old Common $0.001 par exchanged for (0.4) share new Common $0.001 par 10/31/2005
Merged into PostRock Energy Corp. 03/05/2010
Each share new Common $0.001 par exchanged for (0.0575) share Common 1¢ par

QUEST RESOURCES, INC. (UT)
Recapitalized as Comanche Energy, Inc. (UT) 05/15/1995
Each share Common no par exchanged for (0.1) share Common no par
Comanche Energy, Inc. (UT) reincorporated in Oklahoma in 04/00/2001 which name changed to RoadHouse Foods Inc. (OK) 05/03/2005 which reincorporated in Delaware 07/00/2005 which name changed to Locan, Inc. 06/09/2008
(See Locan, Inc.)

QUEST SOFTWARE INC (DE)
Reincorporated 04/27/2009
Issue Information - 4,400,000 shares COM offered at $14 per share on 08/13/1999
State of incorporation changed from (CA) to (DE) and Common no par changed to $0.001 par 04/27/2009
Common $0.001 par split (2) for (1) by issuance of (1) additional share payable 03/31/2000 to holders of record 03/20/2000
Acquired by Dell Inc. 09/28/2012
Each share Common $0.001 par exchanged for $28 cash

QUEST SYS INC (DE)
Charter cancelled and declared inoperative and void for non-payment of taxes 3/1/82
Attorney opined stock is valueless

QUEST TECHNOLOGIES INC (AB)
Name changed to Quest Energy Inc. 12/1/95

QUEST TECHNOLOGIES INC (DE)
Name changed to Tri Star North America Inc. 1/5/2000

QUEST URANIUM CORP (CANADA)
Name changed to Quest Rare Minerals Ltd. 04/26/2010
(See Quest Rare Minerals Ltd.)

QUEST VENTURES INC (WY)
Recapitalized as Dorato Resources Inc. (WY) 04/24/2006
Each share Common no par exchanged for (0.5) share Common no par
Dorato Resources Inc. (WY) reincorporated in British Columbia 08/21/2006 which recapitalized as Xiana Mining Inc. 10/23/2013

QUESTA OIL & GAS CO (CO)
Each share Common $0.001 par exchanged for (0.5) share old Common 1¢ par 2/5/88
Each share old Common 1¢ par exchanged for (2) shares new Common 1¢ par to reflect a (1) for (10) reverse split and a (20) for (1) forward split 2/25/98
Merged into Unit Corp. 3/21/2000
Each share Common 1¢ par exchanged for (0.95) share Common 20¢ par

QUESTAIR TECHNOLOGIES INC (BC)
Each share old Common no par exchanged for (0.1) share new Common no par 06/27/2008
Name changed to Xebec Adsorption Inc. 06/12/2009

QUESTAR CORP (UT)
Common no par split (2) for (1) by issuance of (1) additional share 06/17/1991
Common no par split (2) for (1) by issuance of (1) additional share payable 06/15/1998 to holders of record 05/29/1998 Ex date - 06/16/1998
Common no par split (2) for (1) by issuance of (1) additional share payable 06/18/2007 to holders of record 06/04/2007 Ex date - 06/19/2007
Each share Common no par received distribution of (1) share QEP Resources, Inc. Common 1¢ par payable 06/30/2010 to holders of record 06/18/2010 Ex date - 07/01/2010
Acquired by Dominion Resources, Inc. 09/16/2016
Each share Common no par exchanged for $25 cash

QUESTAR EXPLORATION INC (AB)
Merged into Roan Resources Ltd. 12/12/1997
Each share Common no par exchanged for $1.16 cash

QUESTAR INTL INC (UT)
Name changed to DNA Medical Technologies Inc. 8/27/98

QUESTAR RES CORP (AB)
Merged into Kacee Exploration Inc. 4/3/96
Each share Common no par exchanged for (0.5) share Common no par and (0.0499) Common Stock Purchase Warrant expiring 4/2/97
Kacee Exploration Inc. name changed to Questar Exploration Inc. 4/9/96
(See Questar Exploration Inc.)

QUESTCOR PHARMACEUTICALS INC (CA)
Merged into Mallinckrodt PLC 08/14/2014
Each share Common no par exchanged for (0.897) share Ordinary 20¢ par and $30 cash

QUESTEC INC (WY)
Reincorporated 03/18/1998
Name changed 01/18/2000
Name changed 01/17/2001
Place of incorporation changed from (BC) to (WY) 03/18/1998
Common no par changed to $0.0001 par 12/16/1999
Name changed from QuesTec Imaging, Inc. to QuesTec.com, Inc. 01/18/2000
Name changed from QuesTec.com, Inc. to QuesTec, Inc. 01/17/2001
SEC revoked common stock registration 10/15/2008
Stockholders' equity unlikely

QUESTECH INC (VA)
Name changed to Caci Acquisition Corp. 11/13/98

QUESTEX GROUP LTD (CO)
Each share old Class A Common $0.00001 par exchanged for (0.25) share new Class A Common $0.00001 par 08/30/1993
Recapitalized as Ad-A-Cab America Ltd. 07/12/1994
Each share new Class A Common $0.00001 par exchanged for (0.25) share Class A Common $0.00001 par
Ad-A-Cab America Ltd. name changed to Questex Group, Ltd. (New) 09/01/1994 which recapitalized as Garcis USA, Inc. 12/28/1994
(See Garcis USA, Inc.)

QUESTEX GROUP LTD NEW (CO)
Recapitalized as Garcis USA, Inc. 12/28/1994
Each share Common $0.00001 par exchanged for (0.25) share Common $0.0001 par
(See Garcis USA, Inc.)

QUESTLINE CORP (DE)
Charter cancelled and declared inoperative and void for non-payment of taxes 6/24/91

QUESTMONT MINES LTD (BC)
Common 50¢ par changed to no par 07/25/1984
Recapitalized as Centurion Minerals Ltd. 11/04/1985
Each share Common no par exchanged for (0.5) share Common no par
Centurion Minerals Ltd. merged into Centurion Gold Ltd. 06/06/1990 which merged into Siskon Gold Corp. 08/23/1991
(See Siskon Gold Corp.)

QUESTOR CORP OLD (DE)
Merged into Q Associates 10/13/1982
Each share $2 Conv. Prior Preferred Ser. A no par exchanged for $50 cash
Each share Common $1 par exchanged for $14.25 cash

QUESTRADE FIXED INCOME CORE PLUS ETF (ON)
Under plan of merger each Unit automatically became (0.41870146) WisdomTree Yield Enhanced Canada Aggregate Bond Index ETF Non-Hedged Unit 11/30/2017

QUESTRADE GLOBAL TOTAL EQUITY ETF (ON)
Name changed to ONE Global Equity ETF 11/30/2017

QUESTRADE RUSSELL 1000 EQUAL WEIGHT US CONSUMER DISCRETIONARY INDEX ETF HEDGED TO CAD (ON)
Under plan of merger each Unit automatically became (0.82651201) WisdomTree U.S. Quality Dividend Growth Index ETF Hedged Unit 11/30/2017

QUESTRADE RUSSELL 1000 EQUAL WEIGHT US HEALTH CARE INDEX ETF HEDGED TO CAD (ON)
Under plan of merger each Unit automatically became (0.90200132) WisdomTree U.S. Quality Dividend Growth Index ETF Hedged Unit 11/30/2017

QUESTRADE RUSSELL 1000 EQUAL WEIGHT US INDUSTRIALS INDEX ETF HEDGED TO CAD (ON)
Under plan of merger each Unit automatically became (1.00944867) WisdomTree U.S. Quality Dividend Growth Index ETF Hedged Units 12/06/2017

QUESTRADE RUSSELL 1000 EQUAL WEIGHT US TECHNOLOGY INDEX ETF HEDGED TO CAD (ON)
Under plan of merger each Unit automatically became (1.19790051) WisdomTree U.S. Quality Dividend Growth Index ETF Hedged Unit 11/30/2017

QUESTRADE RUSSELL US MIDCAP GROWTH INDEX ETF HEDGED TO CAD (ON)
Under plan of merger each Unit automatically became (0.90279995) WisdomTree U.S. MidCap Dividend Index ETF Hedged Unit 11/30/2017

QUESTRADE RUSSELL US MIDCAP VALUE INDEX ETF HEDGED TO CAD (ON)
Under plan of merger each Unit automatically became (0.86522074) WisdomTree U.S. MidCap Dividend Index ETF Hedged Unit 11/30/2017

QUESTRON TECHNOLOGY INC (DE)
Each share Conv. Preferred Ser. B 1¢ par exchanged for (1.4375) shares new Common $0.001 par 07/02/1998
Each share old Common $0.001 par exchanged for (0.1) share new Common $0.001 par 01/03/1997
Plan of reorganization under Chapter 11 Federal Bankruptcy Code effective 10/24/2005
No stockholders' equity

QUESTRONICS INC (UT)
Merged into Globesat Holding Corp. 11/30/1988
Each share Common $0.005 par exchanged for (0.853574) share Common 1¢ par
(See Globesat Holding Corp.)

QUETZAL ENERGY LTD (ON)
Recapitalized as Santa Maria Petroleum Inc. (ON) 06/11/2012
Each share Common no par exchanged for (0.1) share Common no par
Santa Maria Petroleum Inc. (ON) reorganized in British Columbia as Kalytera Therapeutics, Inc. 01/11/2017

QUETZAL STUDIOS INVTS INC (CANADA)
Issue Information - 2,000,000 shares COM offered at $0.10 per share on 01/14/1998
Name changed to Fun Key Studios Inc. 11/30/1998
(See Fun Key Studios Inc.)

QUIA RES INC (ON)
Each share old Common no par exchanged for (0.1) share new Common no par 06/10/2014
Recapitalized as Tinley Beverage Co. Inc. 10/06/2015
Each share new Common no par exchanged for (0.2) share Common no par

QUICK & EASY SOFTWARE INC (NV)
Name changed to Star E Media, Corp. 10/08/2001
Star E Media, Corp. recapitalized as Demobag Brands, Inc. 01/19/2007 which recapitalized as China Gold Resource, Inc. 08/16/2007 which name changed to WiseMobi, Inc. 05/13/2008 which recapitalized as New Infinity Holdings, Ltd. 02/23/2015

QUICK & REILLY GROUP INC (DE)
Reincorporated 7/21/87
Common 10¢ par split (3) for (2) by issuance of (0.5) additional share 4/1/87
State of incorporation changed from (NY) to (DE) 7/21/87
Common 10¢ par split (3) for (2) by issuance of (0.5) additional shares 6/7/95
Common 10¢ par split (3) for (2) by issuance of (0.5) additional share 10/18/95
Common 10¢ par split (3) for (2) by issuance of (0.5) additional share payable 3/25/97 to holders of record 3/4/97 Ex date - 3/26/97
Merged into Fleet Financial Group, Inc. (New) 2/1/98
Each share Common 10¢ par exchanged for (0.578) share Common 1¢ par
Fleet Financial Group, Inc. (New) name changed to Fleet Boston Corp. 10/1/99 which name changed to FleetBoston Financial Corp. 4/18/2000 which merged into Bank of America Corp. 4/1/2004

QUICK FIRE VENTURE CAP CORP (AB)
Issue Information - 2,000,000 shares COM offered at $0.15 per share on 05/23/1997
Name changed to AM Technologies Ltd. (ALTA) 04/07/1998
AM Technologies Ltd. (ALTA) reorganized in Canada as Moncoa Corp. 07/12/2002 which recapitalized as Monument Mining Ltd. 07/09/2007

QUICK SEAL PRODS INC (DE)
Charter cancelled and declared inoperative and void for non-payment of taxes 3/1/80

QUICK TENT INC (UT)
Recapitalized as FiltaKleen Inc. 4/1/2003
Each share Common $0.001 par exchanged for (0.04) share Common $0.001 par
FiltaKleen Inc. recapitalized as IPTV Corp. 10/31/2006

QUICKEX INC (NV)
Name changed to Meshtech Wireless, Inc. 05/27/2005
Meshtech Wireless, Inc. name changed to Sleep Healers Holdings, Inc. 08/17/2006 which name changed to Sleep Holdings, Inc. 10/09/2006 which name changed to ALL-Q-TELL Corp. 11/03/2010
(See ALL-Q-TELL Corp.)

QUICKPRINT AMER INC (DE)
Reorganized as Noma Corp. (Incorporated 04/27/1981) 05/24/1985
Each share Common 1¢ par exchanged for (0.72619) share Common 1¢ par
(See Noma Corp. (Incorporated 04/27/1981))

QUICKRESPONSE SVCS INC (DE)
Reincorporated 10/21/97
Issue Information - 3,500,000 shares COM offered at $12 per share on 08/05/1993
State of incorporation changed from (CA) to (DE) and Common no par changed to $0.001 par 10/21/97
Name changed to QRS Corp. 5/11/98
(See QRS Corp.)

QUICKSILVER ENTERPRISES INC (DE)
Each share old Common 1¢ par exchanged for (8) shares new Common 1¢ par 12/20/1989
SEC revoked common stock registration 10/24/2008
Stockholders' equity unlikely

QUICKSILVER GAS SVCS LP (DE)
Name changed to Crestwood Midstream Partners L.P. (Old) 10/04/2010
Crestwood Midstream Partners L.P. (Old) merged into Crestwood Midstream Partners L.P. (New) 10/08/2013 which merged into Crestwood Equity Partners L.P. 09/30/2015

QUICKSILVER GROUP INC. (CA)
Merged into Racotek, Inc. 8/20/98
Each share Common exchanged for (1.0594) shares Common 1¢ par
Racotek, Inc. name changed to Zamba Corp. 10/7/98 which merged into Technology Solutions Co. 1/3/2005

QUICKSILVER RES INC (DE)
Common 1¢ par split (3) for (2) by issuance of (1) additional share payable 06/30/2004 to holders of record 06/15/2004
Common 1¢ par split (3) for (2) by issuance of (0.5) additional share payable 06/30/2005 to holders of record 06/15/2005 Ex date - 07/01/2005
Common 1¢ par split (3) for (2) by issuance of (1) additional share payable 01/31/2008 to holders of record 01/18/2008 Ex date - 02/01/2008
Plan of reorganization under Chapter 11 Federal Bankruptcy proceedings effective 08/31/2016
No stockholders' equity

QUICKSILVER VENTURES INC (BC)
Name changed to Keegan Resources Inc. 03/01/2005
Keegan Resources Inc. name changed to Asanko Gold Inc. 03/01/2013

QUICKTURN DESIGN SYS INC (DE)
Merged into Cadence Design Systems, Inc. 05/25/1999
Each share Common no par exchanged for (1.2712) shares Common 1¢ par

QUICKTV INC (DE)
Recapitalized as Glycology, Inc. 02/22/2005
Each share Common $0.001 par exchanged for (0.1) share Common $0.001 par
Glycology, Inc. recapitalized as Adoodle, Inc. 06/01/2007 which name changed to Olfactory Biosciences Corp. 04/20/2010

QUIET TIGER INC (NV)
Name changed to MediaMax Technology Corp. 04/01/2005
MediaMax Technology Corp. recapitalized as Exchange Media Corp. 10/01/2008 which name changed to Empire Oil Refineries Corp. 03/31/2011

QUIGLEY CORP (NV)
Each share Common $0.0001 par

exchanged for (0.1) share Common $0.001 par 12/26/1995
Common $0.001 par changed to $0.0005 par and (1) additional share issued payable 01/22/1997 to holders of record 01/15/1997 Ex date - 01/23/1997
Each share Common $0.0005 par received distribution of (0.0434) share Suncoast Naturals, Inc. Common $0.001 par payable 09/15/2004 to holders of record 09/01/2004
Name changed to ProPhase Labs, Inc. (NV) 05/10/2010
ProPhase Labs, Inc. (NV) reincorporated in Delaware 06/19/2015

QUIK-CHEK ELECTRONICS & PHOTO CORP. (DE)
Name changed to Electrocopy Corp. 2/14/66
(See Electrocopy Corp.)

QUIK PIX INC (NV)
Each share old Common $0.001 par exchanged for (1/3) share new Common $0.001 par 07/14/1997
Name changed to Solvis Group, Inc. 08/02/2005
(See Solvis Group, Inc.)

QUIKBIZ INTERNET GROUP INC (NV)
SEC revoked common stock registration 10/24/2008

QUIKBYTE SOFTWARE INC (CO)
Each share old Common $0.0001 par exchanged for (0.05) share new Common $0.0001 par 03/16/2007
Each share new Common $0.0001 par exchanged again for (0.1) share new Common $0.0001 par 10/07/2008
Reincorporated under the laws of Delaware as Sorrento Therapeutics, Inc. 12/31/2009

QUIKFLO HEALTH INC (AB)
Recapitalized as Friday Night Inc. (AB) 06/16/2017
Each share Common no par exchanged for (0.5) share Common no par
Friday Night Inc. (AB) reincorporated in British Columbia as 1933 Industries Inc. 10/01/2018

QUIKSILVER INC (DE)
Common 1¢ par split (3) for (2) by issuance of (0.5) additional share 11/19/1987
Common 1¢ par split (2) for (1) by issuance of (1) additional share payable 04/24/1998 to holders of record 04/16/1998
Common 1¢ par split (3) for (2) by issuance of (0.5) additional share payable 04/23/1999 to holders of record 04/15/1999 Ex date - 04/26/1999
Common 1¢ par split (2) for (1) by issuance of (1) additional share payable 05/08/2003 to holders of record 04/30/2003 Ex date - 05/09/2003
Common 1¢ par split (2) for (1) by issuance of (1) additional share payable 05/11/2005 to holders of record 04/27/2005 Ex date - 05/12/2005
Plan of reorganization under Chapter 11 Federal Bankruptcy proceedings effective 02/11/2016
No stockholders' equity

QUILCHENA MNG & DEV LTD (BC)
Dissolved 07/22/1974
Stockholders' equity unlikely

QUILL INDS INC (NV)
Recapitalized as Ostrich Products of America, Inc. 06/01/2005
Each share Common $0.001 par exchanged for (0.001) share Common $0.001 par
Ostrich Products of America, Inc. name changed to PayPro, Inc.

07/11/2005 which name changed to Panamersa Corp. 02/16/2007 which recapitalized as Eagle Worldwide Inc. 01/12/2012

QUILL LINE INC (UT)
Reincorporated under the laws of Delaware as Niche Business Group Inc. 11/19/1990
Niche Business Group Inc. name changed to Marbledge Group, Inc. 01/20/1993 which recapitalized as AR Growth Finance Corp. 03/13/2007
(See AR Growth Finance Corp.)

QUILLO RES INC (BC)
Name changed to Quillo Technologies Inc. 1/6/93

QUILMES INDL QUINSA SOCIETE ANONYME (LUXEMBOURG)
Sponsored ADR's for Non-Vtg. Preferred no par reclassified as Sponsored ADR's for Class B Shares no par 06/08/2001
ADR agreement terminated 05/18/2008
Each Sponsored ADR for Class B no par exchanged for $82.45056 cash

QUINALTA PETES LTD (AB)
Struck off register for failure to file annual returns 09/10/1975

QUINBY BUILDING PROPERTY (OH)
Completely liquidated 11/1/85
Each Land Trust Ctf. $500 par exchanged for first and final distribution of $246.68 cash

QUINCY COOP BK (QUINCY, MA)
Stock Dividend - 10% 6/18/86
Acquired by Co-Operative Bancorp. 5/29/87
Each share Common 10¢ par exchanged for $30 cash

QUINCY ENERGY CORP (NV)
Merged into Energy Metals Corp. 07/10/2006
Each share Common $0.001 par exchanged for (0.2) share Common no par
Energy Metals Corp. merged into Uranium One Inc. 08/10/2007
(See Uranium One Inc.)

QUINCY GOLD CORP (NV)
Name changed to Quincy Energy Corp. 05/16/2005
Quincy Energy Corp. merged into Energy Metals Corp. 07/10/2006 which merged into Uranium One Inc. 08/10/2007
(See Uranium One Inc.)

QUINCY MARKET COLD STORAGE & WAREHOUSE CO. (MA)
Each share old Common $100 par exchanged for (2) shares new Common $100 par in 1939
New Common $100 par changed to $50 par and (1) additional share issued plus a 150% stock dividend paid 12/31/57
Acquired by Beatrice Foods Co. 8/4/66
Each share Common $50 par exchanged for (2) shares Common no par
Beatrice Foods Co. name changed to Beatrice Companies, Inc. 6/5/84
(See Beatrice Companies, Inc.)

QUINCY MNG CO (MI)
Reverted to private company in 1981
Details not available

QUINCY RES INC (NV)
Name changed to Quincy Gold Corp. 07/08/2004
Quincy Gold Corp. name changed to Quincy Energy Corp. 05/16/2005 which changed to Energy Metals Corp. 07/10/2006 which merged into Uranium One Inc. 08/10/2007
(See Uranium One Inc.)

QUINCY SVGS & LN CO (OH)
Name changed to Cleveland Community Savings Co. 07/01/1979
(See Cleveland Community Savings Co.)

QUINCY SVGS BK (QUINCY, MA)
Merged into Citizens Financial Group 1/6/95
Each share Common 10¢ par exchanged for $25.75 cash

QUINCY STREET BUILDING, INC.
Liquidated in 1941

QUINCY TRUST CO. (QUINCY, MA)
Common $10 par changed to $5 par and (1) additional share issued plus a 75% stock dividend paid 12/29/67
Under plan of merger name changed to Hancock Bank & Trust Co. (Quincy, Mass.) 12/30/67
Hancock Bank & Trust Co. (Quincy, Mass.) reorganized as Hancock Group Inc. 4/19/74
(See Hancock Group Inc.)

QUINDAR ELECTR INC (DE)
Adjudicated bankrupt 07/22/1975
Stockholders' equity unlikely

QUINELLA EXPL LTD (BC)
Name changed to American Telecommunications Corp. (BC) 9/17/84
American Telecommunications Corp. (BC) reorganized in Delaware as ATC, Inc. 12/13/90 which name changed to ATC II, Inc. 7/27/93
(See ATC II, Inc.)

QUINENCO S A (CHILE)
ADR agreement terminated 1/19/2007
Each Sponsored ADR for Common no par exchanged for $16.38936 cash

QUINN RES LTD (BC)
Name changed to Allanco Iolite Monitor Corp. 06/05/1986
Allanco Iolite Monitor Corp. recapitalized as Aim Safety Co., Inc. 01/09/1989 which name changed to AimGlobal Technologies Co., Inc. 01/29/1999
(See AimGlobal Technologies Co., Inc.)

QUINNEBAUG CO.
Merged into Wauregan-Quinnebaug Mills, Inc. 00/00/1932
Details not available

QUINNIPIAC BK & TR CO (HAMDEN, CT)
Merged into Bankwell Financial Group, Inc. 10/01/2014
Each share Common 1¢ par exchanged for either (0.056) share Common no par, $12 cash or a combination thereof

QUINPARIO ACQUISITION CORP (DE)
Units separated 07/01/2014
Name changed to Jason Industries, Inc. 07/01/2014

QUINPARIO ACQUISITION CORP 2 (DE)
Name changed to Exela Technologies, Inc. 07/13/2017

QUINSAM OPPORTUNITIES I INC (ON)
Name changed to Vitalhub Corp. 12/02/2016

QUINSTAR RES CORP (BC)
Name changed 09/15/1981
Name changed from Quinstar Oil Corp. to Quinstar Resources Corp. 09/15/1981
Recapitalized as Epoch Capital Corp. 08/14/1984
Each share Common no par exchanged for (0.25) share Common no par
Epoch Capital Corp. merged into Quest Capital Corp. 10/25/1996 which name changed to Quest Oil & Gas Inc. 11/15/1996 which merged

into EnerMark Income Fund 04/18/1997 which merged into Enerplus Resources Fund 06/22/2001 which reorganized as Enerplus Corp. 01/03/2011

QUINT MEDIA INC (NV)
Common $0.0001 par split (3) for (1) by issuance of (2) additional shares payable 08/07/2013 to holders of record 08/07/2013
Recapitalized as OncBioMune Pharmaceuticals, Inc. 08/28/2015
Each share Common $0.0001 par exchanged for (0.00718222) share Common $0.0001 par

QUINTA CORP. (NM)
Acquired by United Nuclear Corp. (DE) 7/19/63
Each share Capital Stock 5¢ par exchanged for (0.1) share Common 20¢ par
United Nuclear Corp. (DE) reorganized in Virginia as UNC Resources, Inc. 8/31/78 which name changed to UNC Inc. (VA) 6/3/86 which reincorporated in Delaware 4/30/87
(See UNC Inc.)

QUINTAINE RES INC (BC)
Merged into Quinterra Resources Inc. 7/21/82
Each share Common 50¢ par exchanged for (0.65) share Class B Common no par
Quinterra Resources Inc. merged into Emtech Technology Corp. 8/16/93 which reorganized as Emtech Ltd. (Bermuda) 7/18/94

QUINTANA MARITIME LTD. (MARSHALL ISLANDS)
Issue Information - 16,700,000 shares COM offered at $11.50 on 07/14/2005
Merged into Excel Maritime Carriers Ltd. 04/15/2008
Each share Common 1¢ par exchanged for (0.3979) share Common 1¢ par and $13 cash
(See Excel Maritime Carriers Ltd.)

QUINTE & TRENT VALLEY POWER CO. LTD.
Property and assets sold 00/00/1937
No stockholders' equity

QUINTE CANLIN LTD (ON)
Name changed to QCI Industries Ltd. 07/05/1974
QCI Industries Ltd. merged into Fincorp Capital Ltd. 12/13/1978
(See Fincorp Capital Ltd.)

QUINTE IRON MINES LTD. (ON)
Charter cancelled for failure to pay taxes and file returns 08/09/1982

QUINTE MILK PRODS LTD (ON)
Recapitalized 00/00/1937
Each share Preferred exchanged for (20) shares Common no par
Each share Common exchanged for (1) share Common no par
Recapitalized 00/00/1947
Each share Common no par exchanged for (1) share Class A no par and (0.25) share Class B no par
Class A no par reclassified as participating Class A no par and Class B no par reclassified as Common no par 05/24/1956
Common no par split (5) for (1) by issuance of (4) additional shares 03/18/1970
Part. Class A no par split (3) for (1) by issuance of (2) additional shares 03/18/1970
Name changed to Quinte Canlin Ltd. 09/22/1970
Quinte Canlin Ltd. name changed to QCI Industries Ltd. 07/05/1974 which merged into Fincorp Capital Corp. 12/13/1978
(See Fincorp Capital Ltd.)

QUI-QUO   FINANCIAL INFORMATION, INC.

QUINTEC CORP (NV)
Name changed to Love International Group, Inc. 02/05/2016

QUINTEK TECHNOLOGIES INC (CA)
Common 1¢ par changed to $0.001 par 10/20/2006
SEC revoked common stock registration 06/27/2012

QUINTEKO RES LTD (ON)
Merged into McAdam Resources Inc. 12/01/1988
Each share Common no par exchanged for (0.1) share Common no par
McAdam Resources Inc. recapitalized as Boulder Mining Corp. (ON) 05/09/1995 which reincorporated in British Columbia as Opal Energy Corp. 01/09/2007 which name changed to Versus Systems Inc. 07/13/2016

QUINTEL COMMUNICATIONS INC (DE)
Name changed 08/24/1998
Name changed from Quintel Entertainment, Inc. to Quintel Communications, Inc. 08/24/1998
Name changed to Traffix Inc. 10/03/2000
Traffix Inc. merged into New Motion, Inc. 02/04/2008 which name changed to Atrinsic, Inc. 06/26/2009 which recapitalized as Protagenic Therapeutics, Inc. 07/27/2016

QUINTEL CORP (DE)
Name changed to Arizona Instrument Corp. 3/5/87

QUINTEL INDS LTD (BC)
Struck off register and declared dissolved for failure to file returns 9/18/92

QUINTERRA RES INC (BC)
Merged into Emtech Technology Corp. 8/16/93
Each share Class B Common no par exchanged for (0.75) share Common no par
Emtech Technology Corp. reorganized as Emtech Ltd. (Bermuda) 7/18/94

QUINTESSENCE HLDGS INC (DE)
Name changed to Terminus Energy, Inc. 12/04/2009

QUINTESSENCE OIL CO (WY)
Reincorporated under the laws of Delaware as Torque Engineering Corp. 10/22/1999
(See Torque Engineering Corp.)

QUINTEX ENERGY LTD (AB)
Merged into Quadron Resources Ltd. 06/01/1993
Each share Conv. Preferred no par exchanged for (1) share Conv. Preferred no par
Each share Common no par exchanged for (1) share Common no par
Quadron Resources Ltd. merged into HCO Energy Ltd. 06/23/1995 which merged into Pinnacle Resources Ltd. (New) 10/20/1997 which merged into Renaissance Energy Ltd. 07/16/1998 which merged into Husky Energy Inc. 08/25/2000

QUINTILES IMS HLDGS INC (DE)
Reincorporated 10/03/2016
Name and state of incorporation changed from Quintiles Transnational Holdings Inc. (NC) to Quintiles IMS Holdings, Inc. (DE) 10/03/2016
Name changed to IQVIA Holdings Inc. 11/15/2017

QUINTILES TRANSNATIONAL CORP (NC)
Issue Information - 2,000,000 shares COM offered at $19.50 per share on 04/20/1994
Common 1¢ par split (2) for (1) by issuance of (1) additional share 11/27/95
Common 1¢ par split (2) for (1) by issuance of (1) additional share payable 12/1/97 to holders of record 11/10/97
Merged into Pharma Services Holding, Inc. 9/25/2003
Each share Common 1¢ par exchanged for $14.50 cash

QUINTO MNG CORP NEW (BC)
Acquired by Consolidated Thompson Iron Mines Ltd. 07/08/2008
Each share Common no par exchanged for (0.2) share Common no par and approximately $0.001 cash
Note: Unexchanged certificates were cancelled and became without value 07/08/2014
(See Consolidated Thompson Iron Mines Ltd.)

QUINTO REAL CAP CORP (CANADA)
Name changed to Quinto Resources Inc. 08/18/2017

QUINTO TECHNOLOGY INC (BC)
Name changed 12/13/2000
Name changed from Quinto Mining Corp. (Old) to Quinto Technology Inc. 12/13/2000
Name changed to Quinto Mining Corp. (New) 01/10/2007
Quinto Mining Corp. (New) acquired by Consolidated Thompson Iron Mines Ltd. 07/08/2008
(See Consolidated Thompson Iron Mines Ltd.)

QUINTON CARDIOLOGY SYS INC (DE)
Reincorporated 05/21/2003
Issue Information - 4,000,000 shares COM offered at $7 per share on 05/06/2002
State of incorporation changed from (CA) to (DE) and Common no par changed to $0.001 par 05/21/2003
Merged into Cardiac Science Corp. 09/01/2005
Each share Common $0.001 par exchanged for (0.77184895) share Common $0.001 par
(See Cardiac Science Corp.)

QUINTONIX INC (NV)
Recapitalized as Icoa, Inc. 03/14/1985
Each share Common $0.001 par exchanged for (0.25) share Common $0.005 par

QUINTUS CORP (DE)
Plan of reorganization under Chapter 11 Federal Bankruptcy proceedings effective 02/28/2007
Each share Common $0.001 par exchanged for $0.42367754 cash
Each share Common $0.001 par received an additional distribution of $0.12121822 cash payable 12/02/2009 to holders of record 02/28/2007

QUIPP INC (FL)
Merged into Illinois Tool Works Inc. 06/02/2008
Each share Common 1¢ par exchanged for $5.41 cash

QUITMAN BANCORP INC (GA)
Merged into Colony Bankcorp, Inc. 3/29/2002
Each share Common 10¢ par exchanged for (0.683) share Common $10 par and $4.41 cash

QUIXIT INC (CO)
Reincorporated under the laws of Delaware as Top Group Holdings, Inc. 03/28/2003
Top Group Holdings, Inc. name changed to Soyodo Group Holdings, Inc. (DE) 09/22/2005 which reorganized in Nevada as Omphalos, Corp. 04/30/2008

QUIXOTE CORP (DE)
Common 1-2/3¢ par split (3) for (2) by issuance of (0.5) additional share 12/20/1983
Common 1-2/3¢ par split (2) for (1) by issuance of (1) additional share 04/09/1986
Stock Dividends - 200% 08/15/1980; 50% 12/15/1981
Merged into Trinity Industries, Inc. 02/05/2010
Each share Common 1-2/3¢ par exchanged for $6.38 cash

QUIZNOS CORP (CO)
Name changed 5/25/95
Name changed from Qunizo's Franchise Corp. to Quinzo's Corp. 5/25/95
Merged into Firenze Corp. 12/21/2001
Each share Common $0.001 par exchanged for $8.50 cash

QUME CORP (DE)
Name changed to DTC Data Technology Corp. 04/06/1994
DTC Data Technology Corp. merged into Photonics Corp. (CA) 03/13/2000 which reincorporated in Nevada as Small Cap Strategies, Inc. 10/02/2006 which recapitalized as Bay Street Capital, Inc. 08/31/2010 which name changed to Los Angeles Syndicate of Technology, Inc. 10/14/2010 which name changed to Invent Ventures, Inc. 09/19/2012

QUNAR CAYMAN IS LTD (CAYMAN ISLANDS)
Acquired by Ocean Management Holdings Ltd. 02/28/2017
Each Sponsored ADR for Class B Ordinary exchanged for $30.34 cash

QUNO CORP (QC)
Merged into Donohue Inc. 03/01/1996
Each share Common no par exchanged for (0.29) share Class A Subordinate no par, $2.63 principal amount of 8% Senior Notes Ser. A due 03/01/1997, $2.63 principal amount of 8% Senior Notes Ser. B due 03/01/1998 and $20.31 cash
Donohue Inc. merged into Abitibi-Consolidated Inc. 04/18/2000 which merged into AbitibiBowater Inc. 10/29/2007

QUOGUE VENTURES INC (CO)
Recapitalized as Sound City Entertainment Group, Inc. 05/09/1994
Each share Common $0.0001 par exchanged for (0.001) share Common $0.0001 par
(See Sound City Entertainment Group, Inc.)

QUOKKA SPORTS INC (DE)
Issue Information - 5,000,000 shares COM offered at $12 per share on 07/27/1999
Each share old Common $0.0001 par exchanged for (0.02) share new Common $0.0001 par 04/16/2001
Plan of reorganization under Chapter 11 Federal Bankruptcy proceedings effective 03/19/2003
No stockholders' equity

QUONTO EXPLS LTD (ON)
Charter cancelled for failure to file reports 7/26/72

QUONTO PETROLEUMS LTD. (ON)
Name changed to Quonto Explorations Ltd. 7/27/62
Quonto Explorations Ltd. charter cancelled 7/26/72

QUORUM CORP (NV)
Each share old Common $0.00001 par exchanged for (0.33333333) share new Common $0.00001 par 03/06/2015
Name changed to Ami James Brands, Inc. 09/23/2015

QUORUM GROWTH INC (CANADA)
Each share old Common no par exchanged for (1.666) Unit consisting of (1) share 1st Preference Ser. 2 no par, (1) Common Stock Purchase Warrant expiring 9/23/98 and (2.5) shares new Common no par 9/23/94
Merged into Quorum Growth Partners I, L.P. 5/23/97
Each share 1st Preference Ser. 2 no par exchanged for $8 cash
Each share new Common no par exchanged for $8 cash

QUORUM HEALTH GROUP INC (DE)
Issue Information - 6,250,000 shares COM offered at $15 per share on 05/25/1994
Common 1¢ par split (3) for (2) by issuance of (0.5) additional share payable 09/16/1997 to holders of record 09/02/1997
Merged into Triad Hospitals, Inc. 04/30/2001
Each share Common 1¢ par exchanged for (0.4107) share Common 1¢ par and $3.50 cash
Triad Hospitals, Inc. merged into Community Health Systems, Inc. 07/25/2007

QUORUM INDS INC (NY)
Merged into Looms by Andrex Inc. 12/29/1983
Each share Common 10¢ par exchanged for $0.27 cash

QUORUM RESOURCE CORP. (BC)
Recapitalized as Mirage Resource Corp. 04/16/1992
Each share Common no par exchanged for (0.33333333) share Common no par
Mirage Resource Corp. merged into Dayton Mining Corp. 04/06/2000 which merged into Pacific Rim Mining Corp. 04/11/2002 which merged into OceanaGold Corp. 12/02/2013

QUORUM VENTURES INC (NV)
Reorganized as Parmasters Golf Training Centers Inc. 06/15/2007
Each share Common $0.001 par exchanged for (7.8) shares Common $0.001 par
Parmasters Golf Training Centers Inc. name changed to Carolyn River Projects, Ltd. 08/24/2007

QUOTAMATION INC (NY)
Charter cancelled and proclaimed dissolved for failure to pay taxes 09/26/1979

QUOTE CO AMER INC (DE)
Charter cancelled and declared inoperative and void for non-payment of taxes 04/15/1973

QUOTE ME INC (DE)
Plan of reorganization under Chapter 11 Federal Bankruptcy proceedings confirmed 01/04/1985
No stockholders' equity

QUOTE RES INC (BC)
Struck off register and declared dissolved for failure to file returns 11/03/1995

QUOTEMEDIA COM INC (NV)
Name changed to QuoteMedia, Inc. 03/11/2003

QUOTESMITH COM INC (DE)
Each share Common $0.001 par exchanged for (0.33333333) share Common $0.003 par 03/07/2001
Name changed to Insure.com, Inc. 06/12/2006
Insure.com, Inc. name changed to Life Quotes, Inc. 10/28/2009
(See Life Quotes, Inc.)

QUOTEZY INC (WY)
Recapitalized as Lord Tech, Inc. 04/23/2008
Each share Common $0.001 par

exchanged for (0.0125) share
Common $0.001 par
(See Lord Tech, Inc.)

QUOTRON SYS INC (DE)
Common 10¢ par split (2) for (1) by issuance of (1) additional share 12/1/80
Common 10¢ par split (2) for (1) by issuance of (1) additional share 10/19/82
Common 10¢ par split (2) for (1) by issuance of (1) additional share 7/26/83
Merged into Citicorp 9/19/86
Each share Common 10¢ par exchanged for $19 cash

QUOVADX INC (DE)
Merged into Quartzite Holdings, Inc. 07/18/2007
Each share Common 1¢ par exchanged for $3.20 cash

QURAPPS INC (NV)
Name changed to Pulse Evolution Corp. 05/16/2014

QUSTREAM CORP (ON)
Name changed to PESA Corp. 04/10/2014

QUUIBUS TECHNOLOGY INC (NV)
Name changed to First Liberty Power Corp. 02/04/2010

QUYTA GOLD MINES LTD. (ON)
Acquired by New Athona Mines Ltd. 01/01/1955
Each share Capital Stock $1 par exchanged for (0.083333) share Capital Stock $1 par
New Athona Mines Ltd. recapitalized as Lakota Resources Inc. 11/21/1994 which recapitalized as Tembo Gold Corp. 09/26/2011

QUYTA YELLOWKNIFE MINES LTD.
Name changed to Quyta Gold Mines Ltd. 00/00/1950
Quyta Gold Mines Ltd. acquired by New Athona Mines Ltd. 01/01/1955 which recapitalized as Lakota Resources Inc. 11/21/1994 which recapitalized as Tembo Gold Corp. 09/26/2011

QV QUANTUM VENTURES INC (NV)
Common $0.001 par split (8) for (1) by issuance of (7) additional shares payable 02/25/2008 to holders of record 02/25/2008
Name changed to Quantum Solar Power Corp. 06/25/2008

QVC INC (DE)
Name changed 06/29/1994
Name changed from QVC Network, Inc. to QVC, Inc. 06/29/1994
Merged into QVC Programming 02/15/1995
Each share Common 1¢ par exchanged for $46 cash

QWEST COMMUNICATIONS INTL INC (DE)
Issue Information - 13,500,000 shares COM offered at $22 per share on 06/23/1997
Common 1¢ par split (2) for (1) by issuance of (1) additional share payable 02/24/1998 to holders of record 02/02/1998 Ex date - 02/25/1998
Common 1¢ par split (2) for (1) by issuance of (1) additional share payable 05/24/1999 to holders of record 05/03/1999
Merged into CenturyLink, Inc. 04/01/2011
Each share Common 1¢ par exchanged for (0.1664) share Common $1 par

QWIKCAP CORP (NV)
Charter revoked for failure to file reports and pay fees 02/01/2008

QWIKCAP INFORMATION SVCS INC (NV)
Recapitalized as Pacific Multimedia Corp. 09/29/1997
Each share Class A Common 1¢ par exchanged for (0.1) share Class A Common 1¢ par
Pacific Multimedia Corp. recapitalized as Qwikcap Corp. 01/04/1999
(See Qwikcap Corp.)

QWIP SYS INC (AB)
Merged into Cantronic Systems Inc. (BC) 11/30/2006
Each share Common no par exchanged for (0.9) share Common no par
Note: Unexchanged certificates were cancelled and became without value 11/30/2013
(See Cantronic Systems Inc.)

QX BIO TECH GROUP INC (NV)
Recapitalized as AcumedSpa Holdings, Inc. 09/18/2009
Each (15) shares Common $0.001 par exchanged for (1) share Common $0.001 par
AcumedSpa Holdings, Inc. recapitalized as Organic Plant Health, Inc. 02/02/2011

QXL RICARDO PLC (UNITED KINGDOM)
Name changed 11/28/2001
Sponsored ADR's for Ordinary split (3) for (1) by issuance of (2) additional ADR's payable 04/06/2000 to holders of record 04/03/2000
Name changed from QXL.com PLC to QXL Ricardo PLC 11/28/2000
Each old Sponsored ADR for Ordinary exchanged for (0.2) new Sponsored ADR for Ordinary 12/21/2000
Each new Sponsored ADR for Ordinary exchanged again for (0.1) new Sponsored ADR for Ordinary 12/31/2001
Each new Sponsored ADR for Ordinary exchanged for (0.001) new Sponsored ADR for Ordinary 03/31/2003
Sponsored ADR's for Ordinary split (20) for (1) by issuance of (19) additional ADR's payable 12/29/2006 to holders of record 12/26/2006 Ex date - 01/03/2007
Name changed to Tradus PLC 12/12/2007
(See Tradus PLC)

R

R. & S. LIQUIDATING CORP. (NY)
Out of business in 1930
No stockholders' equity

R. B. C. FUND, INC.
Liquidated in 1937

R. G. H. SECURITIES CORP.
Dissolved in 1929

R & A PRODUCTIONS INC (NV)
Name changed to American CryoStem Corp. (New) 06/15/2011

R & B FALCON CORP (DE)
Stock Dividends - in Preferred to holders of Preferred 3.468% payable 11/01/1999 to holders of record 10/15/1999; 3.46875% payable 08/01/2000 to holders of record 07/15/2000 Ex date - 07/12/2000
13.875% Sr. Preferred 1¢ par called for redemption at $1,138.75 on 12/15/2000
Merged into Transocean Sedco Forex Inc. 01/31/2001
Each share Common 1¢ par exchanged for (0.5) share Common 1¢ par
Transocean Sedco Forex Inc. name changed to Transocean Inc. (Old) 05/09/2002 which merged into Transocean Inc. (New) (Cayman Islands) 11/27/2007 which reorganized in Switzerland as Transocean Ltd. 12/18/2008

R & B INC (PA)
Common 1¢ par split (2) for (1) by issuance of (1) additional share payable 3/28/2005 to holders of record 3/15/2005 Ex date - 3/29/2005
Name changed to Dorman Products, Inc. 5/24/2006

R & D CONNECTIONS INC (NV)
Name changed to Kara International, Inc. 9/22/86
Kara International, Inc. name changed to International Heritage Inc. 3/3/98

R & M BEARINGS CDA LTD (CANADA)
Name changed to R H P Canada Ltd. 06/19/1970
(See R H P Canada Ltd.)

R & R ASSOC INC (MA)
Name changed to Medsecure Group Inc. 2/16/84
Medsecure Group Inc. charter dissolved 12/31/90

R & R RANCHING INC (NV)
Each share old Common $0.001 par exchanged for (2) shares new Common $0.001 par 03/21/2003
Name changed to GloTech Industries Inc. 03/26/2003
GloTech Industries Inc. recapitalized as Intra-Asia Entertainment Corp. 01/02/2004 which recapitalized as China TransInfo Technology Corp. 08/23/2007
(See China Transinfo Technology Corp.)

R & R RES INC (NV)
Name changed to Centenary International Corp. 12/22/1998

R & R TRAVEL INC (NV)
Reorganized as Green Star Alternative Energy, Inc. 08/08/2008
Each share Common $0.001 par exchanged for (5) shares Common $0.001 par
Green Star Alternative Energy, Inc. recapitalized as Gold Hill Resources, Inc. 11/09/2012

R & T LIQUIDATION, INC. (IA)
In process of liquidation
Each share Non-Vtg. Common $10 par exchanged for initial distribution of $200 cash 8/15/85
Each share Vtg. Common $10 par exchanged for initial distribution of $200 cash 8/15/85
Each share Non-Vtg. Common $10 par received second distribution of $45 cash 11/22/85
Each share Vtg. Common $10 par received second distribution of $45 cash 11/22/85
Each share Non-Vtg. Common $10 par received third distribution of $20 cash 8/11/86
Each share Vtg. Common $10 par received third distribution of $20 cash 8/11/86
Each share Non-Vtg. Common $10 par received fourth distribution of $16 cash 11/5/86
Each share Vtg. Common $10 par received fourth distribution of $16 cash 11/5/86
Each share Non-Vtg. Common $10 par received fifth distribution of $6 cash 1/13/88
Each share Vtg. Common $10 par received fifth distribution of $6 cash 1/13/88
Each share Non-Vtg. Common $10 par received sixth distribution of $4.50 cash 10/10/88
Each share Vtg. Common $10 par received sixth distribution of $4.50 cash 10/10/88
Note: Details on subsequent distributions, if any, are not available

R A B CAP INC (FL)
Name changed to Alma International, Inc. (FL) 06/04/1991
Alma International, Inc. (FL) reincorporated in Delaware as Dynasty Energy Resources, Inc. 12/31/2007 which recapitalized as Fifth Season International, Inc. 10/28/2010

R A N K I N TECHNOLOGIES INC (CANADA)
Name changed to Boomerang Tracking Inc. 12/04/2000
(See Boomerang Tracking Inc.)

R B CAP & EQUITIES INC (NV)
Merged into Triad Industries, Inc. 3/15/99
Details not available

R B INDS INC (DE)
Reincorporated 5/5/75
Common no par split (4) for (3) by issuance of (1/3) additional share 3/31/72
State of incorporation changed from (CA) (DE) and Common no par changed to $1 par 5/5/75
Common $1 par split (3) for (2) by issuance of (0.5) additional share 3/19/76
Common $1 par split (4) for (3) by issuance of (1/3) additional share 1/3/78
Common $1 par split (5) for (4) by issuance of (0.25) additional share 12/15/78
Acquired by RBI Acquisition Corp. 6/9/89
Each share Common $1 par exchanged for $12.5156 cash

R-B RUBR PRODS INC (OR)
Stock Dividends - 20% payable 2/17/2000 to holders of record 1/21/2000; 20% payable 6/1/2001 to holders of record 5/1/2001 Ex date - 4/27/2001
Merged into Dash Multi-Corp., Inc. 1/10/2003
Each share Common no par exchanged for $2.80 cash

R.C., INC. (PR)
Completely liquidated 12/26/1972
Each share 8% Preferred $10 par received first and final distribution of $1.73 cash
Note: Certificates were not required to be surrendered and are without value
No Common stockholders' equity

R.C. CAN CO. (MO)
Merged into Boise Cascade Corp. 07/31/1967
Each share Common $1 par exchanged for (0.825) share $1.40 Conv. Preferred no par
(See Boise Cascade Corp.)

R C J RES LTD (BC)
Name changed to Venturex Resources Ltd. 05/05/1998
Venturex Resources Ltd. recapitalized as Consolidated Venturex Holdings Ltd. 09/24/1992 which name changed to Venturex Explorations Inc. 05/24/2007 which recapitalized as Black Panther Mining Corp. 06/17/2008 which name changed to Canadian International Pharma Corp. 06/22/2015

R C L ELECTRS INC (NJ)
Merged into AMF Inc. 11/5/74
Each share Common 10¢ par exchanged for (0.88) share Common $1.75 par
(See AMF Inc.)

R C M CORP (NV)
Name changed to RCM Technologies, Inc. 8/1/81

R D G MINERALS INC (ON)
Recapitalized as Netforfun.com Inc. 8/9/2000
Each share Common no par exchanged for (0.1) share Common no par

R D I CORP (MN)
Statutorily dissolved 9/25/88

R D PRODS INC (NY)
Each share old Common 5¢ par exchanged for (0.2) share new Common 5¢ par 06/16/1977
Name changed to Griffin Technology Inc. 06/29/1982
(See Griffin Technology Inc.)

R E D M CORP (DE)
Under plan of reorganization each share Common 25¢ par automatically became (1) share REDM Industries, Inc. Common 25¢ par 12/14/1979
(See REDM Industries, Inc.)

R E M INDS INC (DE)
Charter cancelled and declared inoperative and void for non-payment of taxes 03/01/1974

R F COMMUNICATIONS ASSOCIATES (NY)
Name changed to R F Communications, Inc. 5/7/62
R F Communications, Inc. merged into Harris-Intertype Corp. 2/28/69 which name changed to Harris Corp. 5/15/74

R F COMMUNICATIONS INC (NY)
Common 5¢ par split (5) for (4) by issuance of (0.25) additional share 6/30/66
Common 5¢ par split (2) for (1) by issuance of (1) additional share 7/26/68
Merged into Harris-Intertype Corp. 2/28/69
Each share Common 5¢ par exchanged for (0.375) share Common $1 par
Harris-Intertype Corp. name changed to Harris Corp. 5/15/74

R F MGMT CORP (NY)
SEC revoked common stock registration 10/28/2009

R F OIL INDS LTD (ON)
Cease trade order effective 06/23/1986

R.G.G., INC. (CA)
Liquidation completed
Each share Capital Stock $1 par exchanged for initial distribution of $3.15 cash 08/15/1963
Each share Capital Stock $1 par received second distribution of $1.65 cash 02/07/1964
Each share Capital Stock $1 par received third distribution of $0.10 cash 12/28/1964
Each share Capital Stock $1 par received fourth and final distribution of $0.0715 cash 10/29/1965

R G S ENERGY GROUP INC (NY)
Merged into Energy East Corp. 6/28/2002
Each share Common $5 par exchanged for either (1.7626) shares Common 1¢ or $39.50 cash
Note: Option to receive stock expired 7/1/2002

R H DONNELLEY CORP (DE)
Each share old Common $1 par exchanged for (0.2) share new Common $1 par 08/24/1998
Preferred Stock Purchase Rights declared for Common stockholders of record 11/06/1998 were redeemed at $0.01 per right 05/30/2006 for holders of record 05/02/2006
Plan of reorganization under Chapter 11 Federal Bankruptcy Code effective 01/29/2010

No stockholders' equity

R H MED SVCS INC (PA)
Stock Dividends - 10% 06/30/1977; 10% 01/30/1978; 10% 06/30/1978
Liquidation completed
Each share Common $1 par exchanged for initial distribution of (1) share Mediq Inc. Common $1 par and $19.25 cash 05/01/1981
Each share Common $1 par received second distribution of $1 cash 02/10/1982
Each share Common $1 par received third distribution of $0.29 cash 02/11/1983
Each share Common $1 par received fourth distribution of $0.80 cash 06/30/1984
Each share Common $1 par received fifth and final distribution of $0.26 cash 12/29/1984

R H PHILLIPS INC (CA)
Merged into Vincor Holdings, Inc. 10/5/2000
Each share Common no par exchanged for $7 cash

R I S RES INTL CORP (BC)
Recapitalized as Ultra Holdings Inc. 12/1/99
Each share Common no par exchanged for (0.25) share Common no par
(See Ultra Holdings Inc.)

R J COMMUNICATION PRODS INC (DE)
Name changed to Inter-Comm Data Corp. 8/23/71
(See Inter-Comm Data Corp.)

R LIQUIDATING CORP. (CA)
Liquidation completed
Each share Common no par exchanged for initial distribution of (0.08007) share Whitaker Corp. Common $1 par 5/20/68
Note: Details on subsequent distributions, if any, are not available

R.N.B. CO. (CA)
Liquidation completed
Each share Capital Stock $1 par exchanged for initial distribution of (1) share Rockwell Manufacturing Co. Common $2.50 par 11/15/63
Each share Capital Stock $1 par received second and final distribution of $0.02493376 cash 5/13/68
Rockwell Manufacturing Co. merged into Rockwell International Corp. (Old) 2/16/73 which merged into Boeing Co. 12/6/96

R O C TAIWAN FD (MA)
Name changed to Taiwan Greater China Fund 12/29/2003
Taiwan Greater China Fund name changed to Shelton Greater China Fund 06/13/2011

R P INC (OK)
Charter cancelled for failure to pay taxes 8/7/70

R P INDS INC (OH)
Merged into United Shields Corp. 01/05/1998
Each share Common no par exchanged for (0.891661) share Common $0.001 par and $5.4753698 cash
(See United Shields Corp.)

R R P CORP. (NY)
Liquidation completed
Each share Class A $1 par or Class B 5¢ par exchanged for initial distribution of (0.16421124) share Talley Industries, Inc. Common $1 par 9/18/67
Each share Class A $1 par or Class B 5¢ par received second distribution of (0.021544) share Talley Industries, Inc. Common $1 par 9/9/68
Each share Class A $1 par or Class B 5¢ par received third and final distribution of (0.0144035) share Talley Industries, Inc. Common $1 par 10/8/70
(See Talley Industries, Inc.)

R R REALISATIONS LTD (ENGLAND)
Completely liquidated 07/12/1982
Each ADR for Ordinary Reg. £1 par exchanged for first and final distribution of $0.142 cash

R S IMAGING INC (NV)
Name changed to Commonwealth Associates Inc. 08/25/1993
Commonwealth Associates Inc. name changed to KCD Holdings Inc. 10/25/1994 which name changed to Sequester Holdings Inc. 04/01/1997 which recapitalized as China Biolife Enterprises Inc. 06/19/2006 which recapitalized as Asia Pacific Energy Inc. 12/07/2007

R S N PROJS INC (NJ)
Charter declared void for non-payment of taxes 07/30/1993

R SCAN CORP (DE)
Company no longer in business as of 1991
Stockholders' equity not determined

R SPLIT CORP (QC)
Preferred Shares called for redemption at $37.76 on 12/16/2004
Capital Shares called for redemption at $43.7853 on 12/16/2004

R SPLIT II CORP (ON)
Preferred Shares no par called for redemption at $30.50 plus $0.3241 accrued dividends on 05/29/2009
Capital Shares no par called for redemption at $28.6859 on 05/29/2009
Public interest eliminated

R SPLIT III CORP (ON)
Class A Preferred called for redemption at $29.22 on 05/31/2012
Trust terminated 05/31/2017
Each share Class B Preferred Ser. B received $13.60 cash
Each Capital Share received $24.2445 cash

R T & E CORP. (WI)
Stock Dividends - 100% 10/20/61; 20% 7/20/65
Name changed to RTE Corp. 6/10/66
(See RTE Corp.)

R T E CORP (WI)
Common $1 par split (2) for (1) by issuance of (1) additional share 10/25/1967
Common $1 par split (3) for (1) by issuance of (2) additional shares 08/23/1968
Stock Dividends - 100% 09/30/1961; 20% 06/30/1965
Acquired by Cooper Industries, Inc. 07/29/1988
Each share Common $1 par exchanged for $45 cash

R T NATL CORP (TN)
Charter revoked for non-payment of taxes 03/03/1975

R T SYS INC (DE)
Charter cancelled and declared inoperative and void for non-payment of taxes 6/27/89

R TEC HLDG INC (ID)
Common no par split (2) for (1) by issuance of (1) additional share payable 11/30/2000 to holders of record 10/18/2000
Ceased operations 03/16/2005
Stockholders' equity unlikely

R-TEC TECHNOLOGIES INC (NJ)
Recapitalized as ERecord Management, Inc. 01/25/2008
Each (75) shares Common $0.00001 par exchanged for (1) share Common $0.00001 par

R-TEK CORP (MB)
Name changed to Quality Dino Entertainment Ltd. 02/10/1993
(See Quality Dino Entertainment Ltd.)

R VIBRANT INC (DE)
Name changed to Markray Corp. 02/16/2011

R.W.G. CORP. (IL)
Liquidation completed 12/12/55

R W GAS GROUP INC (BC)
Recapitalized as Anglo-Canadian Gas Corp. 10/28/1996
Each share Common no par exchanged for (0.2) share Common no par
Anglo-Canadian Gas Corp. recapitalized as Jager Metal Corp. 01/20/2011 which name changed to Jagercor Energy Corp. 01/27/2014

R W TECHNOLOGY INC (DE)
Reincorporated 10/22/87
State of incorporation changed from (UT) to (DE) 10/22/87
Charter cancelled and declared inoperative and void for non-payment of taxes 3/1/89

R WIRELESS INC (GA)
Name changed to TX Holdings, Inc. 9/19/2005

RAB INDS INC (DE)
Charter cancelled and declared inoperative and void for non-payment of taxes 3/1/97

RABATCO INC (NV)
Common 25¢ par changed to $0.001 par and (4) additional shares issued 06/20/1998
Each share old Common $0.001 par exchanged for (15) shares new Common $0.001 par 01/04/2000
Name changed to MindfulEye, Inc. 05/16/2000
MindfulEye, Inc. name changed to Medbox, Inc. 10/28/2011 which name changed to Notis Global, Inc. 02/22/2016

RABBIT OIL & GAS LTD (BC)
Merged into Aurex Resources Inc. 7/11/85
Each (3.5) shares Common no par exchanged for (1) share Common no par
Aurex Resources Inc. merged into Galveston Resources Ltd. 7/29/86 which merged into Corona Corp. 7/1/88 which recapitalized as International Corona Corp. 6/11/91
(See International Corona Corp.)

RABBIT SOFTWARE CORP (PA)
Each share old Common 1¢ par exchanged for (1/6) share new Common 1¢ par 06/05/1992
Name changed to Tangram Enterprise Solutions, Inc. 07/03/1992
Tangram Enterprise Solutions, Inc. acquired by Opsware Inc. 02/20/2004
(See Opsware Inc.)

RABCO ENTERPRISES INC (PA)
Placed into receivership 10/10/1972
No stockholders' equity

RABIN CO. (CA)
Name changed to Rabin-Winters Corp. 6/7/60
Rabin-Winters Corp. acquired by Brunswig Drug Co. 4/1/66 which merged into Bergen Brunswig Corp. 3/26/69 which merged into AmeriSourceBergen Corp. 8/29/2001

RABIN-WINTERS CORP. (CA)
Common no par split (2) for (1) by issuance of (1) additional share 7/1/61
Acquired by Brunswig Drug Co. 4/1/66
Each share Common no par exchanged for (0.078463) share Common $1 par

Brunswig Drug Co. merged into Bergen Brunswig Corp. 3/26/69 which merged into AmeriSourceBergen Corp. 8/29/2001

RABULE CORP (NV)
Name changed to Combined Entertainment Organization, Inc. 8/25/90
(See Combined Entertainment Organization, Inc.)

RAC CORP (DE)
Liquidation completed
Each share Common 50¢ par received initial distribution of $10 cash 12/10/1965
Each share Common 50¢ par received second distribution of $2.443 cash 03/15/1966
Each share Common 50¢ par received third distribution of (0.5) share Fairchild Hiller Corp. Common $1 par 04/18/1966
Each share Common 50¢ par received fourth distribution of $1.25 cash 06/20/1967
Each share Common 50¢ par received fifth distribution of $1.25 cash 07/14/1969
Each share Common 50¢ par received sixth distribution of $0.50 cash 04/15/1975
Each share Common 50¢ par exchanged for seventh distribution of $0.985 cash 04/18/1978
Each share Common 50¢ par received eighth and final distribution of $0.03 cash 08/15/1979

RAC FINL GROUP INC (NV)
Common $0.001 par split (2) for (1) by issuance of (1) additional share payable 11/29/1996 to holders of record 11/15/1996
Name changed to FirstPlus Financial Group, Inc. 03/07/1997
(See FirstPlus Financial Group, Inc.)

RAC INCOME FD INC (VA)
Name changed to Mentor Income Fund, Inc. 08/27/1993
Mentor Income Fund, Inc. name changed to American Income Fund, Inc. 03/15/2001 which name changed to Nuveen Multi-Market Income Fund, Inc. (VA) 09/08/2014 which reincorporated in Massachusetts as Nuveen Multi-Market Income Fund 11/19/2014

RAC MTG INVT CORP (VA)
Name changed to Resource Mortgage Capital, Inc. 8/17/92
Resource Mortgage Capital, Inc. name changed to Dynex Capital, Inc. 4/25/97

RACAD TECHNOLOGIES LTD (ON)
Each share old Common no par exchanged for (0.025) share new Common no par 06/23/2000
Cease trade order effective 08/24/2005

RACAL ELECTRS PLC (ENGLAND)
Unsponsored ADR's for Ordinary 25p par split (2) for (1) by issuance of (1) additional share 10/13/1983
Under plan of recapitalization each Unsponsored ADR for Ordinary 25p par exchanged for (0.5) old Sponsored ADR for Ordinary 25p par 08/07/1989
ADR basis changed from (1:1) to (1:2) 08/07/1989
Each old Sponsored ADR for Ordinary 25p par received distribution of either (115.292244) shares Ordinary 5p par or (11.354392) ADR's for Ordinary 5p par of Vodafone Group PLC for every (100) ADR's owned 09/16/1991
Note: Option to elect to receive ADR's expired 10/08/1991
Each old Sponsored ADR for Ordinary 25p par exchanged for (0.2) new Sponsored ADR for Ordinary 25p par 11/15/1991
Stock Dividend - 100% 08/22/1989
ADR agreement terminated 08/31/2000
Each new Sponsored ADR for Ordinary 25p par exchanged for $12.8497 cash

RACAL TELECOM PLC (ENGLAND & WALES)
Name changed to Vodafone Group PLC (Old) 09/16/1991
Vodafone Group PLC name changed to Vodafone AirTouch PLC 06/30/1999 which name changed to Vodafone Group PLC (New) 06/28/2000

RACE CAP CORP (BC)
Issue Information - 2,000,000 shares COM offered at $0.10 per share on 05/11/2011
Name changed to Naturally Splendid Enterprises Ltd. 03/05/2013

RACE WORLD INTL INC (NV)
SEC revoked common stock registration 08/28/2015

RACELAND BK & TR CO (RACELAND, LA)
Merged into Louisiana Bancshares, Inc. 6/6/85
Each share Capital Stock $5 par exchanged for (1.1) shares Common no par and $90.55 cash
Louisiana Bancshares, Inc. name changed to Premier Bancorp, Inc. 4/15/87 which merged into Banc One Corp. 1/2/96 which merged into Bank One Corp. 10/2/98 which merged into J.P. Morgan Chase & Co. 12/31/2000 which name changed to JPMorgan Chase & Co. 7/20/2004

RACER RES LTD (BC)
Merged into Macrotrends International Ventures Inc. 08/17/1988
Each share Common no par exchanged for (1) share Common no par
Macrotrends International Ventures Inc. recapitalized as Global Election Systems Inc. 11/22/1991 which was acquired by Diebold, Inc. 01/22/2002 which name changed to Diebold Nixdorf Inc. 12/12/2016

RACHELS GOURMET SNACKS INC (MN)
Assets foreclosed upon 05/16/2003
Stockholders' equity unlikely

RACHFORD ABSTRACT & MAP CO. (TX)
Charter forfeited for failure to pay taxes 05/19/1950

RACINE HYDRAULICS & MACHY INC (WI)
6% Preferred $10 par called for redemption 8/10/56
$1.20 Conv. Preferred Ser. A $20 par called for redemption 8/31/64
Stock Dividends - 25% 7/21/64; 25% 7/7/65
Name changed to Racine Hydraulics Inc. 9/22/67
Racine Hydraulics Inc. merged into Rex Chainbelt Inc. 10/28/68 which name changed to Rexnord Inc. 1/26/73
(See Rexnord Inc.)

RACINE HYDRAULICS INC (WI)
Merged into Rex Chainbelt Inc. 10/28/1968
Each share Common $1 par exchanged for (2/3) share $2.36 Conv. Preferred Ser. B no par
Rex Chainbelt Inc. name changed to Rexnord Inc. 01/26/1973
(See Rexnord Inc.)

RACING BLOOD STABLES LTD (AB)
Recapitalized as Eagle Energy Corp. 10/15/1992
Each share Common no par exchanged for (1/6) share Common no par
Eagle Energy Corp. merged into Centurion Energy International Inc. 05/20/1997
(See Centurion Energy International Inc.)

RACING CHAMPIONS ERTL CORP (DE)
Name changed 04/03/2002
Name changed from Racing Champions Corp. to Racing Champions Ertl Corp. 04/03/2002
Name changed to RC2 Corp. 04/09/2003
(See RC2 Corp.)

RACING CORP AMER (DE)
Under plan of merger each share Common 1¢ par exchanged for $0.10 cash in January, 1992

RACING INC (PA)
Name changed to Pocono International Raceway, Inc. 03/07/1970

RACING RIVER MINES LTD. (BC)
Merged into Morrison Mines Ltd. 12/28/71
Each share Capital Stock no par exchanged for (0.1) share Capital Stock 50¢ par
Morrison Mines Ltd. merged into Ronoco Resources Inc. 1/24/77
(See Ronoco Resources Inc.)

RACINO ROYALE INC (NV)
Name changed to InterAmerican Gaming, Inc. 10/20/2008
(See InterAmerican Gaming, Inc.)

RACKABLE SYS INC (DE)
Name changed to Silicon Graphics International Corp. 05/18/2009
Silicon Graphics International Corp. merged into Hewlett Packard Enterprise Co. 11/01/2016

RACKLA RIV MINES LTD (BC)
Recapitalized as North Atlantic Resources Ltd. 07/16/1976
Each share Common 50¢ par exchanged for (1/3) share Common no par
North Atlantic Resources Ltd. recapitalized as Damascus Resources Ltd. 08/04/1978 which recapitalized as International Damascus Resources Ltd. 07/16/1982 which recapitalized as Ravenhead Recovery Corp. 07/13/1998
(See Ravenhead Recovery Corp.)

RACKSPACE HOSTING INC (DE)
Acquired by Apollo Global Management, LLC 11/03/2016
Each share Common $0.001 par exchanged for $32 cash

RACOM SYS INC (DE)
Issue Information - 1,500,000 UNITS consisting of (1) share COM and (1) WT offered at $4.75 per unit on 03/12/1997
Each (4.5) shares old Common 1¢ par exchanged for (1) share new Common 1¢ par 03/01/1999
Each (15) shares new Common 1¢ par exchanged again for (1) share new Common 1¢ par 07/12/1999
Name changed to Newstate Holdings, Inc. 09/17/1999
(See Newstate Holdings, Inc.)

RACON INC (DE)
Reincorporated 04/24/1970
State of incorporation changed from (TX) to (DE) 04/24/1970
Merged into Essex Chemical Corp. 01/26/1978
Each share Common $1 par exchanged for (0.4) share Common $1 par
(See Essex Chemical Corp.)

RACOTEK INC (DE)
Name changed to Zamba Corp. 10/7/98
Zamba Corp. merged into Technology Solutions Co. 1/3/2005

RACQUET CLUB, INC. (PR)
Name changed to R.C., Inc. 6/4/71
R.C., Inc. completely liquidated 12/26/72

RAD O LITE INC (PA)
Assets assigned for benefit of creditors 07/14/1966
No stockholders' equity

RAD SAN INC (FL)
Name changed to Phone One International Inc. 1/7/94
Phone One International Inc. name changed to Call Now Inc. 12/8/94

RAD SOURCE TECHNOLOGIES INC (FL)
Each share old Common $0.001 par exchanged for (0.33333333) share new Common $0.001 par 09/09/1999
New Common $0.001 par split (3) for (1) by issuance of (2) additional shares payable 10/05/2001 to holders of record 10/01/2001
Ex date - 10/08/2001
Acquired by Weigao Health Investment Corp. 01/31/2017
Each share new Common $0.001 par exchanged for $2.21 cash

RADAIR INC (NV)
Reorganized under the laws of Texas as Sunpoint Securities, Inc. 10/16/96
Each (4,015) shares Common $0.001 par received (1) share Common no par
Note: Certificates were not required to be surrendered and are without value
(See Sunpoint Securities, Inc.)

RADAR ACQUISITIONS CORP (AB)
Name changed to CanAm Coal Corp. 05/25/2010
(See CanAm Coal Corp.)

RADAR DESIGN CORP (NY)
Name changed to LDV Electro Science Industries, Inc. 11/20/68
(See LDV Electro Science Industries, Inc.)

RADAR-ELECTRONICS, INC. (DE)
Advised out of business in 1956
Charter cancelled for non-payment of taxes 4/1/58

RADAR MEASUREMENTS CORP. (NY)
Name changed to Ramcor Inc. 06/25/1962
(See Ramcor Inc.)

RADAR RES INC (NV)
Name changed to Vianet Technologies, Inc. 3/29/99
(See Vianet Technologies, Inc.)

RADCLIFFE RES LTD (BC)
Recapitalized as Madison Energy Corp. (BC) 11/01/1993
Each share Common no par exchanged for (1/7) share Common no par
Madison Energy Corp. (BC) reincorporated in Alberta 08/29/2003
(See Madison Energy Corp.)

RADCO BML CDA LTD (QC)
Recapitalized as Reprox Corp. 09/30/1971
Each share Common no par exchanged for (0.25) share Common no par
(See Reprox Corp.)

RADELL ACQUISITIONS INC (NV)
Name changed to Fone America, Inc. 05/12/1988
(See Fone America, Inc.)

RADEMAKER CHEMICAL CORP.
Bankrupt in 1949

RAD-RAD

RADEX MINERALS LTD (ON)
Common $1 par changed to no par 12/31/1970
Charter cancelled for failure to pay taxes and file returns 03/00/1976

RADIAL ENERGY INC (NV)
Recapitalized as iPure Labs Inc. 06/23/2014
Each share Common $0.001 par exchanged for (0.002) share Common $0.001 par

RADIAL RES 1982 LTD (AB)
Recapitalized 02/11/1982
Recapitalized from Radial Resources Ltd. to Radial Resources (1982) Ltd. 02/11/1982
Each share Common no par exchanged for (0.2) share Common no par
Name changed to Charterhall Oil Canada Ltd. 10/22/1982
(See Charterhall Oil Canada Ltd.)

RADIAN GROUP INC (DE)
$4.125 Preferred called for redemption at $54.125 on 08/15/2002
Preferred Stock Purchase Rights declared for Common stockholders were redeemed at $0.0005 per right 03/29/2004 for holders of record 03/08/2004
(Additional Information in Active)

RADIAN PETE CORP (BC)
Name changed to Jet Star Resources Ltd. 7/13/84
(See Jet Star Resources Ltd.)

RADIANCE MED SYS INC (DE)
Name changed to Endologix, Inc. 5/31/2002

RADIANT COMMUNICATIONS CORP (BC)
Each share old Common no par exchanged for (0.16666666) share new Common no par 01/12/2006
Acquired by Comwave Networks Inc. 10/18/2013
Each share new Common no par exchanged for $1.43 cash
Note: Unexchanged certificates were cancelled and became without value 10/18/2019

RADIANT CORP (DE)
Adjudicated bankrupt 10/14/1970
Stockholders' equity unlikely

RADIANT ENERGY CORP (CANADA)
Each share old Common no par exchanged for (0.04) share new Common no par 05/05/2010
Dissolved for non-compliance 12/23/2014

RADIANT INDS INC (CA)
Name changed to Caltem Liquidating, Inc. 06/30/1980
(See Caltem Liquidating, Inc.)

RADIANT LAMP CORP. (DE)
Acquired by Consolidated Electronics Industries Corp. 2/19/68
Each share Class A 10¢ par exchanged for (0.25) share Common $5 par
Consolidated Electronics Industries Corp. name changed to North American Philips Corp. 2/14/69
(See North American Philips Corp.)

RADIANT RES INC (BC)
Merged into Tiomin Resources Inc. 09/26/2008
Each share Common no par exchanged for (1) share Common no par
Note: Unexchanged certificates were cancelled and became without value 09/26/2014
Tiomin Resources Inc. recapitalized as Vaaldiam Mining Inc. 03/26/2010
(See Vaaldiam Mining Inc.)

RADIANT SYS INC (GA)
Common no par split (2) for (1) by issuance of (1) additional share payable 03/31/2000 to holders of record 03/01/2000
Acquired by NCR Corp. (New) 08/24/2011
Each share Common no par exchanged for $28 cash

RADIANT TECHNOLOGY CORP NEW (CA)
Name changed to GreenBridge Technology, Inc. 04/07/2006
(See GreenBridge Technology, Inc.)

RADIANT TECHNOLOGY CORP OLD (CA)
Each share old Common no par exchanged for (0.2) share new Common no par 02/28/1984
Reorganized as Radiant Technology Corp. (New) 08/03/1995
Each (30) shares new Common no par exchanged for (1) share Common no par and an additional distribution of (2.95) shares for each post split share received
Note: Holders entitled to (5) or fewer post split shares received $1 cash per share
Radiant Technology Corp. (New) name changed to GreenBridge Technology, Inc. 04/07/2006
(See GreenBridge Technology, Inc.)

RADIAPHONE CORP.
Bankrupt in 1948

RADIATION, INC. (FL)
Class A Common 25¢ par reclassified as Common 25¢ par in December, 1961
Merged into Harris-Intertype Corp. 7/12/67
Each share Common 25¢ par exchanged for (0.75) share Common $1 par
Harris-Intertype Corp. name changed to Harris Corp. 5/15/74

RADIATION & ENVIRONMENTAL MATLS INC (CA)
Name changed to REM Scientific, Inc. 11/13/1972
(See REM Scientific, Inc.)

RADIATION CARE INC (DE)
Acquired by Oncology Therapies Inc. 3/21/95
Each share Common 1¢ par exchanged for $2.625 cash

RADIATION DISP SYS INC (NC)
Merged into Saint James Co. (DE) 12/15/1998
Each share Common $0.001 par exchanged for (0.05) share Common $0.001 par
Saint James Co. (DE) reorganized in North Carolina 12/07/2007
(See Saint James Co. (NC))

RADIATION DYNAMICS INC (NY)
Common $1 par changed to 10¢ par 01/18/1966
Merged into Monsanto Co. 02/21/1980
Each share Common 10¢ par exchanged for $24 cash

RADIATION INSTRUMENT DEVELOPMENT LABORATORY, INC. (DE)
Common 50¢ par split (3) for (2) by issuance of (0.5) additional share 4/30/62
Merged into Nuclear-Chicago Corp. (DE) 12/31/62
Each share Common 50¢ par exchanged for (4/7) share Common $1 par
Nuclear-Chicago Corp. (DE) acquired by Searle (G.D.) & Co. (DE) 8/1/66
(See Searle (G.D.) & Co. (DE))

RADIATION INTL INC (DE)
Completely liquidated 10/11/1974
Each share Common 5¢ par exchanged for first and final distribution of $0.7375 cash

RADIATION MACHY CORP (NJ)
Completely liquidated 04/21/1971
Each share Common 5¢ par exchanged for first and final distribution of (1) share Radiation International, Inc. Common 5¢ par
(See Radiation International, Inc.)

RADIATION MATLS CORP (MA)
Name changed to Cutter, Wood & Sanderson International, Inc. 11/22/1971
(See Cutter, Wood & Sanderson International, Inc.)

RADIATION MED PRODS CORP (NY)
Merged into Sheller-Globe Corp. 05/03/1978
Each share Common 10¢ par exchanged for (0.5) share Common no par
(See Sheller-Globe Corp.)

RADIATION RESH CORP (DE)
Reincorporated 12/23/68
State of incorporation changed from (FL) to (DE) 12/23/68
Name changed to Alrac Corp. 10/14/70
(See Alrac Corp.)

RADIATION SVC ASSOC INC (DE)
Charter cancelled and declared inoperative and void for non-payment of taxes 03/01/1985

RADIATION SYS INC (NV)
Common $1 par split (3) for (2) by issuance of (0.5) additional share 5/28/81
Common $1 par split (3) for (2) by issuance of (0.5) additional share 6/18/82
Common $1 par split (3) for (2) by issuance of (0.5) additional share 8/5/83
Common $1 par split (3) for (2) by issuance of (0.5) additional share 11/22/91
Merged into Comsat Corp. 6/3/94
Each share Common $1 par exchanged for (0.78) share Common Ser. 1 no par

RADIATION TECHNOLOGY INC (NY)
Common 1¢ par split (3) for (2) by issuance of (0.5) additional share 12/15/1980
Common 1¢ par split (2) for (1) by issuance of (1) additional share 02/15/1983
Name changed to RTI Inc. 06/06/1988
(See RTI Inc.)

RADIATION THERAPY SVCS INC (FL)
Merged into Radiation Therapy Services Holdings, Inc. 02/21/2008
Each share Common $0.0001 par exchanged for $32.50 cash

RADIATRONICS INC (CA)
Name changed to R Liquidating Corp. 4/30/68
(See R Liquidating Corp.)

RADICA GAMES LTD. (BERMUDA)
Issue Information - 7,141,000 shares COM offered at $11 per share on 05/13/1994
Merged into Mattel Foreign Holdings, Ltd. 10/03/2006
Each share Common 1¢ par exchanged for $11.55 cash

RADICAL ADVANCED TECHNOLOGIES CORP (BC)
Cease trade order effective 01/21/1998
Stockholders' equity unlikely

RADICAL ELASTOMERS INC (BC)
Ceased operations 09/30/2004
Stockholders' equity unlikely

RADICE CORP (FL)
Reincorporated 02/15/1985
State of incorporation changed from (PA) to (FL), Non-Cumulative Conv. Preferred no par and Common no par changed to 20¢ par 02/15/1985
Reorganized under Chapter 11 Federal Bankruptcy Code 06/19/1989
Each share Non-Cumulative Non-Vtg. Conv. Preferred 20¢ par exchanged for (0.14064697) share new Common 20¢ par
Each share old Common 20¢ par exchanged for (0.14064697) share new Common 20¢ par
Name changed to Major Group, Inc. 05/29/1990
Major Group, Inc. merged into Stoneridge Resources, Inc. 09/25/1992 which recapitalized as Acceptance Insurance Companies Inc. 12/22/1992
(See Acceptance Insurance Companies Inc.)

RADICE REALTY & CONSTRUCTION CORP. (PA)
Name changed to Radice Corp. (PA) 11/27/1978
Radice Corp. (PA) reincorporated in Florida 02/15/1985 which name changed to Major Group, Inc. 05/29/1990 which merged into Stoneridge Resources, Inc. 09/25/1992 which recapitalized as Acceptance Insurance Companies Inc. 12/22/1992
(See Acceptance Insurance Companies Inc.)

RADIENT PHARMACEUTICALS CORP (DE)
Each share old Common $0.001 par exchanged for (0.04) share new Common $0.001 par 02/10/2012
SEC revoked common stock registration 07/03/2014

RADINSKY INVESTMENT CO. (CO)
Name changed to Commerce Investment Corp. 2/28/61
(See Commerce Investment Corp.)

RADIO & TELEVISION INC (NY)
Merged into Diversa-Graphics, Inc. 03/03/1969
Each share Capital Stock 10¢ par exchanged for (0.4) share Common 1¢ par
(See Diversa-Graphics, Inc.)

RADIO CITY PRODUCTS CO., INC. (NY)
Name changed to Planetronics, Inc. 12/21/60
(See Planetronics, Inc.)

RADIO CORP AMER (DE)
Each share 7% Preferred $5 par exchanged for (0.1) share 7% Class A Preferred $50 par 06/24/1924
Each share old Common no par exchanged for (0.2) share Class A Common no par 06/24/1924
Each share Class A Common no par exchanged for (5) shares new Common no par 03/01/1929
7% Class A Preferred no par called for redemption 04/07/1936
Each share $5 Class B Preferred no par exchanged for (1.2) shares $3.50 1st Preferred no par and (1) share new Common no par 04/07/1936
New Common no par split (3) for (1) by issuance of (2) additional shares 03/02/1964
Stock Dividend - 10% 02/01/1965
Name changed to RCA Corp. 05/09/1969
(See RCA Corp.)

RADIO DIABLO, INC. (CA)
Name changed to Television Diablo, Inc. 00/00/1954
Television Diablo, Inc. name changed to Metropolitan Broadcasting Corp. of California 04/01/1960 which name changed to KOVR Broadcasting Co. 09/09/1964
(See KOVR Broadcasting Co.)

RADIO ENGR PRODS LTD (CANADA)
Merged into Nytronics, Inc. 01/15/1972
Details not available

RADIO FREQUENCY INC (MA)
Common $1 par split (3) for (2) by issuance of (0.5) additional share 01/16/1985
Common $1 par split (2) for (1) by issuance of (1) additional share 01/17/1989
Common $1 par split (2) for (1) by issuance of (1) additional share payable 01/18/2000 to holders of record 01/04/2000
Merged into RFI Acquisition Corp. 03/31/2005
Each share Common $1 par exchanged for $3.85 cash

RADIO HILL MINES LTD (ON)
Charter cancelled and declared dissolved for failure to file returns and pay fees 03/16/1976

RADIO IWC LTD (ON)
Merged into Slaight Investments Ltd. and CFGM Broadcasting Ltd. 06/27/1979
Each share Common no par exchanged for $8.25 cash

RADIO KBUY, INC. (TX)
Completely liquidated 05/26/1967
Each share Capital Stock $1 par exchanged for first and final distribution of $1 cash

RADIO-KEITH-ORPHEUM CORP. (DE)
Reorganized 12/31/1950
Each share Common $1 par exchanged for (1) share RKO Pictures Corp. Common $1 par and (1) share RKO Theatres Corp. Common $1 par
(See each company's listing)

RADIO-KEITH-ORPHEUM CORP. (MD)
Each share Class A no par exchanged for (0.25) share Common no par in 1931
Reorganized under the laws of Delaware on a (1) for (6) basis in January 1940
(See Radio-Keith-Orpheum Corp. (Del.))

RADIO KPCN, INC. (TX)
Adjudicated bankrupt 09/10/1968
No stockholders' equity

RADIO ONE INC (DE)
Class A Common $0.001 par split (3) for (1) by issuance of (2) additional shares payable 06/06/2000 to holders of record 05/30/2000
6.5% Term Income Deferable Conv. Preferred called for redemption at $1,000 plus $6.68 accrued dividends 02/22/2005
6.5% 144A Term Income Deferable Conv. Preferred called for redemption at $1,000 plus $6.68 accrued dividends 02/22/2005
Name changed to Urban One, Inc. 05/08/2017

RADIO PACK CO.
Bankrupt 00/00/1928
Stockholders' equity unlikely

RADIO PROGRAM INFORMATION SERVICE, INC. (NY)
Charter revoked for failure to file reports and pay fees 12/15/1951

RADIO SECURITIES CORP. (DE)
Charter cancelled and declared inoperative and void for non-payment of taxes 10/01/1940

RADIO SHACK CORP. (MA)
Common $1 par changed to no par 11/15/1963
Each share Common no par exchanged for (0.1) share Common $1 par 07/08/1965
Merged into Tandy Corp. (NJ) 06/30/1967
Each share Common $1 par exchanged for (0.66666666) share Common $1 par
Tandy Corp. (NJ) reincorporated in Delaware 02/27/1968 which name changed to RadioShack Corp. 05/18/2000 which name changed to RS Legacy Corp. 09/23/2015
(See RS Legacy Corp.)

RADIO UNICA COMMUNICATIONS CORP (DE)
Plan of reorganization under Chapter 11 Federal Bankruptcy Code effective 02/04/2004
Each share Common 1¢ par expected to receive cash
Note: Certificates were not required to be surrendered and are without value

RADIO WORLD CORP (NY)
Common $0.00001 par split (10) for (1) by issuance of (9) additional shares payable 09/02/1999 to holders of record 07/27/1999
Charter cancelled and proclaimed dissolved for failure to pay taxes 06/26/2002

RADIOACTIVE PRODUCTS, INC. (MI)
Liquidation completed 12/16/1958
Details not available

RADIOFONE CORP (DE)
Merged into Metromedia, Inc. 12/01/1982
Each share Common 10¢ par exchanged for $26 cash

RADIOGRAPHIC DEV CORP (CA)
Acquired by xonics, inc. 05/15/1982
Each share Common no par exchanged for (1) share Common 10¢ par
(See xonics, inc.)

RADIOLOGIX INC (DE)
Merged into Primedex Health Systems, Inc. 11/15/2006
Each share Common $0.0001 par exchanged for (1) share Common 1¢ par and $1.79 cash
Primedex Health Systems, Inc. recapitalized as RadNet, Inc. (NY) 11/28/2006 which reincorporated in Delaware 09/03/2008

RADIOMUTUEL INC (CANADA)
Class A Subordinate no par split (2) for (1) by issuance of (1) additional share payable 02/11/1998 to holders of record 02/04/1998
Merged into Astral Communications Inc. 01/12/2000
Each share Class A Subordinate no par exchanged for $24 cash

RADIONICS INC (CA)
Merged into Expamet International PLC 04/10/1989
Each share Common no par exchanged for $20 cash

RADIOPTICS INC (NY)
Dissolved by proclamation 12/23/1992

RADIORE URANIUM MINES LTD (ON)
Merged into PYX Explorations Ltd. 07/30/1976
Each share Capital Stock $1 par exchanged for (0.4) share Capital Stock no par
PYX Explorations Ltd. merged into Discovery Mines Ltd. (Canada) 01/15/1982
(See Discovery Mines Ltd. (Canada))

RADIOSHACK CORP (DE)
Name changed to RS Legacy Corp. 09/23/2015
(See RS Legacy Corp.)

RADIOTOWER COM INC (NV)
Each share old Common $0.001 par exchanged for (1.5) shares new Common $0.001 par 06/20/2000
Name changed to Pacific Fuel Cell Corp. 08/27/2001
(See Pacific Fuel Cell Corp.)

RADIUM HILL URANIUM INC (CO)
Recapitalized under the laws of Nevada as Ventura Oil Co. 07/01/1963
Each share Common 1¢ par exchanged for (0.02) share Common 10¢ par
Ventura Oil Co. name changed to Ventura Resources, Inc. 11/30/1971
(See Ventura Resources, Inc.)

RADIUM KING MINES, INC.
Merged into Hidden Splendor Mining Co. (DE) 10/19/1959
Each share Common 1¢ par exchanged for (0.0225) share Common 50¢ par
Hidden Splendor Mining Co. (DE) merged into Atlas Corp. 08/17/1962
(See Atlas Corp.)

RADIUS EXPLORATIONS LTD (BC)
Merged into Radius Gold Inc. 7/2/2004
Each share Common no par exchanged for (1) share Common no par

RADIUS INC (CA)
Each share old Common no par exchanged for (0.5) share new Common no par 08/30/1994
Each share new Common no par exchanged again for (0.1) share new Common no par 03/09/1998
Name changed to Digital Origin Inc. 03/01/1999
Digital Origin Inc. merged into Media 100 Inc. 05/09/2000
(See Media 100 Inc.)

RADIUS RES CORP (AB)
Proposal under Bankruptcy and Insolvency Act effective 05/14/2010
No stockholders' equity

RADIX CORP (CA)
Common $1 par changed to 50¢ par and (1) additional share issued 06/01/1969
Adjudicated bankrupt 07/20/1970
No stockholders' equity

RADIX VENTURES INC (NY)
Merged into Air Express International Corp. 06/08/1995
Each share Common 1¢ par exchanged for $24.41 cash

RADLON INC (WV)
Proclaimed dissolved for non-payment of taxes 12/16/1987

RADNET INC (NY)
Reincorporated under the laws of Delaware 09/03/2008

RADO REEF RES INC (BC)
Recapitalized as National Gold & Nickel Resources Inc. 03/15/1990
Each share Common no par exchanged for (0.2) share Common no par
(See National Gold & Nickel Resources Inc.)

RADON INTL INC (UT)
Recapitalized as Separation Technology System Inc. 04/21/1992
Each share Common $0.001 par exchanged for (0.06666666) share Common $0.001 par
Separation Technology System Inc. name changed to Rochem Environmental Inc. 09/30/1993
(See Rochem Environmental Inc.)

RADON RESOURCES, INC. (NY)
Name changed to Industrial Technical Concepts, Inc. 08/25/1983
Industrial Technical Concepts, Inc. name changed to ITC Integrated Systems, Inc. 10/03/1985
(See ITC Integrated Systems, Inc.)

RADOROCK RESOURCES, INC. (NV)
Merged into Federal Resources Corp. 05/02/1960
Each share Common 10¢ par exchanged for (1) share Common 50¢ par (Federal Resources Corp.)

RADTECH INC (NM)
Charter revoked 11/08/1989

RADVISION LTD (ISRAEL)
Acquired by Avaya Inc. 06/05/2012
Each share Ordinary ILS 0.1 par exchanged for $11.85 cash

RADYNE CORP
Name changed 05/03/1999
Reincorporated 07/07/2000
Name changed 06/03/2005
Each share old Common $0.002 par exchanged for (0.125) share new Common $0.002 par 04/15/1993
Each share new Common $0.002 par exchanged again for (0.2) share new Common $0.002 par 01/23/1997
Name changed from Radyne Corp. to Radyne Comstream Inc. 05/03/1999
State of incorporation changed from (NY) to (DE) and Common $0.002 par changed to $0.001 par 07/07/2000
Name changed from Radyne Comstream Inc. to Radyne Corp. 06/03/2005
Merged into Comtech Telecommunications Corp. 08/01/2008
Each share Common $0.001 par exchanged for $11.50 cash

RAE SYS INC (DE)
Acquired by Ray Holding Corp. 06/16/2011
Each share Common $0.001 par exchanged for $2.25 cash

RAEJAC EXPLORATIONS LTD. (ON)
Merged into Boeing Holdings & Explorations Ltd. 03/26/1970
Each share Common $1 par exchanged for (0.33333333) share Common no par
Note: On 02/20/1970 the company recapitalized as Raejac Holdings & Ltd. on a (1) for (3) basis, changing the Common $1 par to no par
Certificates were not surrendered at time of recapitalization
Raejac Holdings & Explorations Ltd. merged into Boeing Holdings & Explorations Ltd. on a share for share basis
Subsequently as a result of the merger each share Raejac Explorations Ltd. Common $1 par (which actually represents (0.33333333) share Raejac Holdings & Explorations Ltd. Common no par) is exchanged for (0.33333333) share Boeing Holdings & Explorations Ltd. Common no par

RAEJAC HOLDINGS & EXPLORATIONS LTD. (ON)
Merged into Boeing Holdings & Explorations Ltd. 03/26/1970 (For complete details see Raejac Explorations Ltd.)

RAF INDS INC (DE)
Recapitalized as GSF Productions, Inc. 04/28/1971
Each share Common 10¢ par exchanged for (0.5) share Common 1¢ par
(See GSF Productions, Inc.)

RAFAEL RES LTD (BC)
Name changed to Biologix (B.C.) Ltd. 9/25/86
Biologix (B.C.) Ltd. name changed to Biologix International Ltd. 5/1/98
(See Biologix International Ltd.)

RAFALE CAP CORP (CANADA)
Name changed to Bioenvelop Technologies Corp. 12/05/2000
(See Bioenvelop Technologies Corp.)

RAG SHOPS INC (DE)
Stock Dividend - 5% payable 8/10/99 to holders of record 7/14/99
Merged into Sun Capital Partners III, LP 10/21/2004
Each share Common 1¢ par exchanged for $4.30 cash

RAG-RAI

RAGAN BRAD INC (NC)
Common $1 par split (2) for (1) by issuance of (1) additional share 7/15/71
Merged into Goodyear Tire & Rubber Co. 12/23/98
Each share Common no par exchanged for $37.25 cash

RAGAR CORP (NY)
Each share old Common $0.001 par exchanged for (0.5) share new Common $0.001 par 7/25/94
Reorganized under the laws of Delaware as Nations Flooring, Inc. 3/19/97
Each share Common $0.001 par exchanged for (0.25) share Common $0.001 par
(See Nations Flooring, Inc.)

RAGE ENERGY LTD (ON)
All officers and directors resigned 12/01/2008
Stockholders' equity unlikely

RAGEN CORP (NV)
Name changed 5/1/82
Common 25¢ par split (2) for (1) by issuance of (1) additional share 7/24/67
Common 25¢ par split (2) for (1) by issuance of (1) additional share 2/23/68
Name changed from Ragen Precision Industries, Inc. to Ragen Corp. 5/1/82
Common 25¢ par changed to 12-1/2¢ par and (1) additional share issued 11/1/83
Name changed to Pro Glass Technologies Inc. 10/28/99
Each share Common 12-1/2¢ par exchanged for (1) share Common $0.001 par
Pro Glass Technologies Inc. name changed to MicroSignal Corp. 9/12/2002 which name changed to NanoSignal Corp. Inc. 11/10/2003 which recapitalized as Nano Global Inc. 4/3/2006

RAGEN MACKENZIE GROUP INC (WA)
Issue Information - 2,350,000 shares COM offered at $14 per share on 06/22/1998
Merged into Wells Fargo & Co. 03/16/2000
Each share Common 1¢ par exchanged for (0.5208) share Common 1¢ par

RAGGED CHUTES SILVER MINES LTD. (ON)
Charter cancelled 8/20/75

RAGING RIV EXPL INC (AB)
Merged into Baytex Energy Corp. 08/27/2018
Each share Common no par exchanged for (1.36) shares Common no par
Note: Unexchanged certificates will be cancelled and become without value 08/26/2021

RAGINGMEDIAGROUP INC (NV)
Name changed to Dixon Oil & Gas Inc. 06/04/2003
Dixon Oil & Gas Inc. recapitalized as Galloway Energy Inc. 12/01/2006
(See Galloway Energy Inc.)

RAGLAN NICKEL MINES LTD. (ON)
Recapitalized as New Quebec Raglan Mines Ltd. 12/14/65
Each share Capital Stock $1 par exchanged for (0.5) share Capital Stock $1 par
New Quebec Raglan Mines Ltd. merged into Falconbridge Ltd. 6/13/89
(See Falconbridge Ltd.)

RAHALL COMMUNICATIONS CORP (DE)
Stock Dividend - 25% 01/27/1973

Merged into Gulf United Corp. 09/12/1978
Each share Common 10¢ par exchanged for (1) share $1.20 Conv. Preferred Ser. A $2.50 par
(See Gulf United Corp.)

RAHAXI INC (NV)
SEC revoked common stock registration 06/27/2012

RAHILL RED LAKE MINING CO. LTD. (ON)
Acquired by Goldray Mines Ltd. on a (1) for (3) basis 00/00/1959
Goldray Mines Ltd. merged into Canray Resources Ltd. 12/21/1976 which recapitalized as Exall Resources Ltd. 12/09/1983 which merged into Gold Eagle Mines Ltd. 12/27/2006 which was acquired by Goldcorp Inc. 09/25/2008

RAHN LAKE MINES CORP., LTD. (ON)
Dissolved 10/13/58

RAI INC (DE)
Plan of arrangement under Chapter XI Bankruptcy Act confirmed 01/11/1974
No stockholders' equity

RAI RESH CORP (NY)
Common 1¢ par split (5) for (4) by issuance of (0.25) additional share 01/02/1978
Common 1¢ par split (3) for (2) by issuance of (0.5) additional share 01/14/1980
Common 1¢ par split (2) for (1) by issuance of (1) additional share 01/16/1981
Acquired by Pall Corp. 09/30/1988
Each share Common 1¢ par exchanged for (0.36363636) share Common 25¢ par
(See Pall Corp.)

RAIDER RES INC (AB)
Recapitalized 06/24/1994
Recapitalized from Raider Resources Inc. to Raider Resources Ltd. 06/24/1994
Each share old Common no par exchanged for (0.5) share new Common no par
Each share new Common no par exchanged again for (0.125) share new Common no par 10/24/1996
Merged into Shiningbank Energy Income Fund 06/01/2000
For Canadian Residents: Each share Common no par exchanged for either (0.0831) Trust Unit no par or (0.0582) Trust Unit no par and $0.264 cash
For Non-Canadian Residents: Each share Common no par exchanged for $0.264 cash
Shiningbank Energy Income Fund merged into PrimeWest Energy Trust 07/13/2007
(See PrimeWest Energy Trust)

RAIDER VENTURES INC (NV)
Common $0.001 par split (10) for (1) by issuance of (9) additional shares payable 10/03/2012 to holders of record 10/03/2012
Name changed to Integrated Electric Systems Corp. 04/01/2013
Integrated Electric Systems Corp. name changed to KollagenX Corp. 07/30/2014

RAIDER VENTURES LTD (ON)
Name changed to IFM Food Management (Canada) Ltd. 11/30/1990
IFM Food Management (Canada) Ltd. name changed to Air Systems Plus Corp. 02/25/1992 which name changed to Sales Initiatives International Inc. 06/01/1993 which name changed to Greenlight Communications Inc. 06/14/1994
(See Greenlight Communications Inc.)

RAIFFEISEN INTL BK HLDG AG (AUSTRIA)
Name changed to Raiffeisen Bank International AG 11/12/2010

RAIFORDS INC (TN)
Merged into PRS Enterprises, Inc. 01/23/1978
Each share Common $1 par exchanged for $3 cash

RAIKE FINL GROUP INC (GA)
Name changed to Woodstock Financial Group, Inc. 10/02/2006
Woodstock Financial Group, Inc. name changed to Woodstock Holdings, Inc. 01/10/2011

RAIL ROADER FOOD CORP (CA)
Charter cancelled for failure to file reports and pay taxes 5/3/82

RAIL TRAILER CO (DE)
Name changed to R T Systems, Inc. 6/12/70
(See R T Systems, Inc.)

RAILAMERICA INC (DE)
Merged into Fortress Investment Group LLC 02/14/2007
Each share Common $0.001 par exchanged for $16.35 cash
Issue Information - 22,000,000 shares COM offered at $15 per share on 10/12/2009
Acquired by Genesee & Wyoming Inc. 10/01/2012
Each share Common 1¢ par exchanged for $27.50 cash

RAILHEAD MINES LTD. (ON)
Charter cancelled 4/29/63
No stockholders' equity

RAILHEAD RES INC (ON)
Recapitalized as Century Circuits Ltd. 09/15/1993
Each share Common no par exchanged for (1/3) share Common no par
Century Circuits Ltd. name changed to Canadian Financial Holdings Corp. 01/13/1998 which recapitalized as Calderone Corp. 07/10/1998 which name changed to Cardinal Factor Corp. 07/21/2000
(See Cardinal Factor Corp.)

RAILINK LTD (AB)
Acquired by RailAmerica, Inc. 08/20/1999
Each share Common no par exchanged for U.S.$8.75 cash

RAILPOWER TECHNOLOGIES CORP (CANADA)
Discharged from receivership 10/29/2012
No stockholders' equity

RAILROAD EMPLOYEES' CORP.
Recapitalized as Employees Credit Corp. on a (0.5) for (1) basis in 1947
(See Employees Credit Corp.)

RAILROAD FINL CORP (DE)
Common 10¢ par split (3) for (2) by issuance of (0.5) additional share 2/28/92
Common 10¢ par split (3) for (2) by issuance of (0.5) additional share 2/25/94
Merged into Commercial Federal Corp. 10/2/95
Each share Common 10¢ par exchanged for (0.6389) share Common 10¢ par
(See Commercial Federal Corp.)

RAILROAD MEN'S OIL CO. (OK)
Charter cancelled for failure to pay taxes 12/15/30

RAILROAD SHARES CORP.
Liquidated in 1943

RAILROADMENS FED SVGS & LN ASSN INDIANAPOLIS (IN)
Stock Dividends - 10% 8/31/90; 10% 7/1/92
Merged into Huntington Bancshares Inc. 12/27/93

Each share Common 1¢ par exchanged for (1.8293) shares Common no par

RAILTEX INC (TX)
Merged into RailAmerica, Inc. 2/4/2000
Each share Common 10¢ par exchanged for (1/6) share Common $0.001 par and $13.50 cash
(See RailAmerica, Inc.)

RAILTRACK GROUP PLC (ENGLAND)
Liquidation completed
Each Sponsored ADR for Ordinary 25p par received initial distribution of $31.9351 cash 01/29/2003
Each 2nd Sponsored 144A ADR for Ordinary 25p par received initial distribution of $31.9351 cash 01/29/2003
Each Sponsored ADR for Ordinary 25p par received second distribution of approximately $6.80 cash 08/27/2003
Each 2nd Sponsored 144A ADR for Ordinary 25p par received second distribution of $6.80 cash 08/27/2003
Each Sponsored ADR for Ordinary 25p par received third distribution of approximately $1.68 cash 01/25/2005
Each 2nd Sponsored 144A ADR for Ordinary 25p par received third distribution of $1.68 cash 01/25/2005
Each Sponsored ADR for Ordinary 25p par received fourth distribution of $1.49 cash 01/11/2006
Each 2nd Sponsored 144A ADR for Ordinary 25p par received fourth distribution of approximately $1.49 cash 01/11/2006
Each Sponsored ADR for Ordinary 25p par received fifth and final distribution of approximately $0.32 cash 04/01/2010
Each 2nd Sponsored 144A ADR for Ordinary 25p par received fifth and final distribution of approximately $0.32 cash 04/01/2010

RAILWAY & EXPRESS CO.
Merged into Adams Express Co. (NY) 11/00/1929
Adams Express Co. (NY) reincorporated in Maryland 05/28/1976 which name changed to Adams Diversified Equity Fund, Inc. 03/31/2015

RAILWAY & INDUSTRIAL ENGINEERING CO.
Acquired by I-T-E Circuit Breaker Co. on a (1.2) for (1) basis in 1947
I-T-E Circuit Breaker Co. merged into I-T-E Imperial Corp. 4/30/68
(See I-T-E Imperial Corp.)

RAILWAY & LIGHT SECURITIES CO. (DE)
Name changed to Colonial Fund, Inc. (DE) 00/00/1952
(See Colonial Fund, Inc. (DE))

RAILWAY & UTILITIES INVESTING CORP. (DE)
Recapitalized in 1931
Preferred $50 par changed to no par
Common $10 par changed to no par
Recapitalized in 1932
Preferred no par changed to $25 par
Common no par changed to $1 par
Liquidation completed 10/1/56

RAILWAY EQUIPMENT & REALTY CO., LTD. (DE)
Recapitalized in 1935
Each share 1st Preferred no par exchanged for (0.3) share 1st Preferred $100 par
Each share Preferred Series 1 no par exchanged for (1.562) shares 2nd Preferred no par
Each share Preferred Series 2 no par

exchanged for (1.35) shares 2nd
Preferred no par
Each share Conv. Stock no par
exchanged for (2) shares Common
no par
Each share Class A no par
exchanged for (1) share Common
no par
Each share Class B no par
exchanged for (0.5) share Common
no par
Each share Class C no par
exchanged for (0.25) share Common
no par
Recapitalized in 1936
Each share 2nd Preferred no par
exchanged for (1) share Common
no par
Each share Common no par
exchanged for (0.25) share new
Common no par
Common no par split (7) for (1) by
issuance of (6) additional shares
1/6/56
Common no par changed to $1 par
6/5/56
Liquidation completed 11/4/63
Details not available

RAILWAY EQUITIES CORP.
Dissolved in 1937

RAILWAY STORAGE BATTERY CAR CO.
Dissolved in 1926
No stockholders' equity

RAILWAY WAREHOUSES, INC. (OH)
Liquidation completed 4/7/58

RAILWAYS CORP. (DE)
Proclaimed inoperative and void for non- payment of taxes in January 1935

RAILWEIGHT INC (IN)
Merged into Mangood Corp. (DE) 11/26/1979
Each share Common $1 par exchanged for (0.04553) share Common no par
Mangood Corp. (DE) name changed to Howe Richardson Inc. 12/31/1987
(See Howe Richardson Inc.)

RAILWORKS CORP (DE)
Issue Information - 5,000,000 shares COM offered at $12 per share on 07/29/1998
Plan of reorganization under Chapter 11 Federal Bankruptcy Code effective 11/13/2002
No stockholders' equity

RAIMOUNT ENERGY INC (CANADA)
Merged into Manitok Energy Inc. 08/23/2016
Each share Common no par exchanged for (6) shares Common no par and (1.5) Common Stock Purchase Warrants expiring 00/00/2018
Note: Unexchanged certificates will be cancelled and become without value 08/23/2022

RAIN FST - MOOSE LTD (NV)
Name changed to Aarow Environmental Group, Inc. 06/13/1997
Aarow Enviromental Group, Inc. name changed to Aaro Broadband Wireless Communications, Inc. 09/25/2000
(See Aaro Broadband Wireless Communications, Inc.)

RAIN RES INC (BC)
Name changed to Octant Energy Corp. 03/09/2012

RAINBO GOLD MINES CORP. (DE)
Recapitalized as New Star Corp. 10/12/81
Each share Common no par exchanged for (5) shares Common 2¢ par

RAINBO PHOTO COLOR INC (OK)
Filed petition under Chapter 7 Federal Bankruptcy Code 03/27/1980
No stockholders' equity

RAINBOW BRDG SVCS INC (NV)
Name changed to American Custom Components Inc. 09/30/1997
(See American Custom Components Inc.)

RAINBOW CORAL CORP (FL)
Each share old Common $0.0001 par exchanged for (0.05) share new Common $0.0001 par 06/28/2012
Reorganized under the laws of Nevada 05/29/2015
Each share new Common $0.0001 par exchanged for (0.01) share Common $0.001 par

RAINBOW EQUITIES LTD (CO)
Recapitalized as Pathfinder Data Group, Inc. 10/31/86
Each share Common $0.001 par exchanged for (0.01) share Common $0.001 par

RAINBOW EXPL CORP (AB)
Recapitalized as Rainbow Petroleum Corp. 02/07/1994
Each share Common no par exchanged for (0.2) share Common no par
Rainbow Petroleum Corp. name changed to Rainbow Group of Companies Inc. 08/12/1998 which recapitalized as QWIP Systems Inc. 10/13/2005 which merged into Cantronic Systems Inc. (BC) 11/30/2006
(See Cantronic Systems Inc.)

RAINBOW FD INC (DE)
Completely liquidated 10/31/2003
Each share Common 10¢ par received net asset value
Note: Certificates were not required to be surrendered and are without value

RAINBOW GOLD LTD (ON)
Recapitalized as Jaguar Mining Inc. 10/16/2003
Each (14) shares Common no par exchanged for (1) share Common no par

RAINBOW GROUP COS INC (AB)
Recapitalized as QWIP Systems Inc. 10/13/2005
Each share Common no par exchanged for (0.2) share Common no par
QWIP Systems Inc. merged into Cantronic Systems Inc. (BC) 11/30/2006
(See Cantronic Systems Inc.)

RAINBOW LAKE RES LTD (ON)
Merged into Castlestar Capital Developments Corp. 03/30/1990
Each share Common no par exchanged for (0.915) share Common no par
Castlestar Capital Developments Corp. recapitalized as Southern Frontier Resources Inc. 11/11/1993
(See Southern Frontier Resources Inc.)

RAINBOW MED INC (FL)
Proclaimed dissolved for failure to file reports and pay fees 09/24/1999

RAINBOW MEDIA CORP (DE)
Charter cancelled and declared inoperative and void for non-payment of taxes 3/1/86

RAINBOW MINES LTD. (BC)
Recapitalized as Greenfields Development Corp. Ltd. 12/31/70
Each share Capital Stock no par exchanged for (0.2) share Capital Stock no par
(See Greenfields Development Corp. Ltd.)

RAINBOW MINES LTD (QC)
Name changed to Lederic Mines Ltd. 5/29/70
Lederic Mines Ltd. recapitalized as Lederic Group Inc. 12/1/72
(See Lederic Group Inc.)

RAINBOW MNG & MLG LTD (ID)
Merged into Coeur d'Alene Mines Corp. (ID) 06/14/1968
Each share Preferred $1 par exchanged for (1.2) shares Common $1 par
Each share Preferred 25¢ par exchanged for (1.2) shares Common $1 par
Each share Common 25¢ par exchanged for (1.2) shares Common $1 par
Coeur d'Alene Mines Corp. (ID) reincorporated in Delaware as Coeur Mining, Inc. 05/17/2013

RAINBOW OIL LTD. (AB)
Merged into Scurry-Rainbow Oil Ltd. 10/30/1954
Each share Capital Stock $5 par exchanged for (0.26315789) share Capital Stock 50¢ par
Scurry-Rainbow Oil Ltd. acquired by Home Oil Co. Ltd. (New) 11/08/1993 which merged into Anderson Exploration Ltd. 09/07/1995
(See Anderson Exploration Ltd.)

RAINBOW PAPERS LTD (INDIA)
Old Sponsored GDR's for Equity split (5) for (1) by issuance of (4) additional GDR's payable 08/13/2010 to holders of record 08/12/2010
Each old Sponsored GDR for Equity exchanged for (0.2) new Sponsored GDR for Equity 09/22/2010
Basis changed from (1:1) to (1:5) 09/22/2010
GDR agreement terminated 06/05/2015
Each new Sponsored GDR for Equity exchanged for (5) Equity Shares

RAINBOW PETE CORP (AB)
Name changed to Rainbow Group of Companies Inc. 08/12/1998
Rainbow Group of Companies Inc. recapitalized as QWIP Systems Inc. 10/13/2005 which merged into Cantronic Systems Inc. (BC) 11/30/2006
(See Cantronic Systems Inc.)

RAINBOW PHOTO INDUSTRIES, INC. (NY)
Acquired by Technicolor, Inc. on a (1) for (4.11) basis 4/24/64
(See Technicolor, Inc.)

RAINBOW PRODUCTION CORP. (OH)
Under plan of reorganization each share Common 50¢ par automatically became (1) share Alco Oil & Chemical Corp. Common 1¢ par 03/30/1956
Alco Oil & Chemical Corp. name changed to Alco Chemical Corp. 01/16/1962 which name changed to Alco Standard Corp. 01/17/1966 which name changed to IKON Office Solutions, Inc. 01/24/1997
(See IKON Office Solutions, Inc.)

RAINBOW RENTALS INC (DE)
Merged into Rent-A-Center, Inc. 05/14/2004
Each share Common no par exchanged for $16 cash

RAINBOW RES INC (ON)
Recapitalized as Braveheart Resources Inc. 11/27/2014
Each share Common no par exchanged for (0.1) share Common no par

RAINBOW RES INC (WY)
Merged into Williams Companies (NV) 8/29/78
Each share Common 10¢ par exchanged for (0.975) share Common $1 par
Williams Companies (NV) reincorporated under the laws of Delaware as Williams Companies Inc. 6/1/87

RAINBOW RES LTD (BC)
Recapitalized as Rainex Resources Ltd. 8/31/82
Each share Capital Stock no par exchanged for (0.25) share Capital Stock no par
Rainex Resources Ltd. name changed to Rainex Industries Ltd. 5/5/87
(See Rainex Industries Ltd.)

RAINBOW TECHNOLOGIES INC (DE)
Common $0.001 par split (2) for (1) by issuance of (1) additional share 07/17/1990
Common $0.001 par split (3) for (2) by issuance of (0.5) additional share payable 07/15/1998 to holders of record 07/01/1998
Common $0.001 par split (2) for (1) by issuance of (1) additional share payable 10/23/2000 to holders of record 10/09/2000 Ex date - 10/24/2000
Merged into SafeNet, Inc. 03/16/2004
Each share Common $0.001 par exchanged for (0.374) share Common 1¢ par
(See SafeNet, Inc.)

RAINCHIEF ENERGY INC (BC)
Each share old Common no par exchanged for (0.1) share new Common no par 03/22/2010
Each share new Common no par exchanged again for (0.02) share new Common no par 04/30/2013
Note: No holder will receive fewer than (100) post-split shares
Name changed to Bit-X Financial Corp. 02/19/2015
Bit-X Financial Corp. recapitalized as Digatrade Financial Corp. 06/22/2016

RAINDANCE COMMUNICATIONS INC (DE)
Merged into West Corp. 04/06/2006
Each share Common $0.0015 par exchanged for $2.70 cash

RAINDOR GOLD MINES LTD. (ON)
Recapitalized as Consolidated Raindor Mines Ltd. 04/27/1966
Each share Capital Stock $1 par exchanged for (0.1) share Capital Stock $1 par
(See Consolidated Raindor Mines Ltd.)

RAINDROP RES LTD (AB)
Issue Information - 3,000,000 shares COM offered at $0.10 per share on 11/04/1996
Recapitalized as National Health Stores Inc. 6/29/2000
Each share Common no par exchanged for (0.1) share Common no par

RAINEARTH INC (NV)
Each share old Common $0.00001 par exchanged for (0.02) share new Common $0.00001 par 05/17/2013
Name changed to CableClix (USA), Inc. 06/16/2015

RAINEX INDS LTD (BC)
Name changed 5/5/87
Name changed from Rainex Resources Ltd. to Rainex Industries Ltd. 5/5/87
Struck off register and declared dissolved for failure to file returns 8/13/93

RAINEY MTN RES INC (CANADA)
Name changed to Raimount Energy Inc. 04/23/2001
Raimount Energy Inc. merged into Manitok Energy Inc. 08/23/2016

RAI-RAL

RAINFOREST CAFE INC (MA)
Common no par split (3) for (2) by issuance of (0.5) additional share payable 07/01/1996 to holders of record 06/14/1996
Common no par split (3) for (2) by issuance of (0.5) additional share payable 01/15/1998 to holders of record 12/26/1997
Merged into Landry's Seafood Restaurants, Inc. 12/01/2000
Each share Common no par exchanged for $3.25 cash

RAINGOLD MINES, LTD. (ON)
Charter cancelled 11/5/62

RAINIER BANCORPORATION (WA)
Common $2.50 par split (2) for (1) by issuance of (1) additional share 1/14/85
Stock Dividend - 100% 3/25/77
Acquired by Security Pacific Corp. 8/31/87
Each share Common $2.50 par exchanged for (1.3) shares Common $10 par
Security Pacific Corp. merged into BankAmerica Corp. (Old) 4/22/92 which merged into BankAmerica Corp. (New) 9/30/98 which name changed to Bank of America Corp. 4/28/99

RAINIER CO., INC. (NY)
Proclaimed dissolved 12/16/68

RAINIER COS INC (WA)
Under plan of acquisition each share Capital Stock $1 par exchanged for $9.60 cash 08/11/1978

RAINIER ENERGY RES INC (BC)
Delisted from Vancouver Stock Exchange 04/03/1987

RAINIER PAC FINL GROUP INC (WA)
Company's principal asset placed in receivership 02/26/2010
Stockholders' equity unlikely

RAINIER PULP & PAPER CO.
Merged into Rayonier, Inc. in 1937
Each share Capital Stock exchanged for (0.8) share $2 Preferred $25 par and (1.2) shares Common $1 par
Rayonier, Inc. merged into International Telephone & Telegraph Corp. (DE) 4/26/68 which name changed to ITT Corp. 12/31/83 which reorganized in Indiana as ITT Industries, Inc. 12/19/95 which name changed to ITT Corp. 7/1/2006

RAINIER RLTY INVS (CA)
Liquidation completed
Each Share of Bene. Int. no par exchanged for initial distribution of $9.14 cash 07/31/1987
Each Share of Bene. Int. no par received second and final distribution of $0.1455 cash 10/28/1987

RAINIER RES LTD (BC)
Recapitalized as Prong Industries Corp. Ltd. (BC) 08/27/1996
Each share Common no par exchanged for (0.5) share Common no par
Prong Industries Corp. Ltd. (BC) reincorporated in Bermuda 09/03/1996 which name changed to C&C Industries Corp. 11/02/1998 which name changed to Xenex Minerals Ltd. 01/11/2008
(See Xenex Minerals Ltd.)

RAINING DATA CORP (DE)
Name changed to TigerLogic Corp. 04/17/2008
(See TigerLogic Corp.)

RAINMAKER ENTMT GROUP LTD. (BC)
Reincorporated 05/14/1997
Name changed 06/23/1998
Place of incorporation changed from (Canada) to (BC) 05/14/1997
Name changed from Rainmaker Digital Pictures Corp. to Rainmaker Entertainment Group Ltd. 06/23/1998
Name changed to Rainmaker Income Fund and Common no par reclassified as Units no par 05/31/2002
Rainmaker Income Fund reorganized as Rainmaker Entertainment Inc. 08/01/2008 which recapitalized as Wow! Unlimited Media Inc. 12/15/2016

RAINMAKER ENTMT INC (BC)
Recapitalized as Wow! Unlimited Media Inc. 12/15/2016
Each share Common no par exchanged for (0.1) share Common no par

RAINMAKER INCOME FD (BC)
Reorganized as Rainmaker Entertainment Inc. 08/01/2008
Each Unit no par exchanged for (1) share Common no par
Rainmaker Entertainment Inc. recapitalized as Wow! Unlimited Media Inc. 12/15/2016

RAINMAKER MNG CORP (BC)
Name changed to Rainmaker Resources Ltd. (BC) 05/08/2014
Rainmaker Resources Ltd. (BC) reorganized in Ontario as Indiva Ltd. 12/19/2017

RAINMAKER RES LTD (BC)
Each share old Common no par exchanged for (0.11764706) share new Common no par 09/04/2015
Reorganized under the laws of Ontario as Indiva Ltd. 12/19/2017
Each share new Common no par exchanged for (0.09192866) share Common no par

RAINMAKER SYS INC (DE)
Each share old Common $0.001 par exchanged for (0.2) share new Common $0.001 par 12/15/2005
Assets assigned for the benefit of creditors 07/14/2015
Stockholders' equity unlikely

RAINMAKER VENTURES LTD (AB)
Acquired by Caribou Resources Corp. 05/18/2004
Each share Common no par exchanged for (0.12996633) share Common no par
Caribou Resources Corp. merged into JED Oil Inc. 07/31/2007
(See JED Oil Inc.)

RAINSHINE CORP (DE)
Charter cancelled and declared inoperative and void for non-payment of taxes 3/1/95

RAINVILLE COPPER MINES LTD. (CANADA)
Recapitalized as Rainville Mines Ltd. 09/22/1954
Each share Capital Stock no par exchanged for (1/3) share Capital Stock
Rainville Mines Ltd. recapitalized as Dunraine Mines Ltd. 08/22/1961 which recapitalized as International Dunraine Ltd. 02/06/1990 which name changed to World Point Terminals Inc. 07/18/1996
(See World Point Terminals Inc.)

RAINVILLE INC (MN)
Preferred 1¢ par called for redemption 07/00/1978
Name changed to Universal Dynamics, Inc. 07/16/1982
(See Universal Dynamics, Inc.)

RAINVILLE MINES LTD. (CANADA)
Recapitalized as Dunraine Mines Ltd. 08/22/1961
Each share Capital Stock no par exchanged for (1/3) share Capital Stock no par
Dunraine Mines Ltd. recapitalized as International Dunraine Ltd. 02/06/1990 which name changed to World Point Terminals Inc. 07/18/1996
(See World Point Terminals Inc.)

RAINWIRE PARTNERS INC (DE)
SEC revoked common stock registration 10/30/2008
Stockholders' equity unlikely

RAINY LAKE MINING LTD. (ON)
Charter cancelled and declared dissolved for failure to file returns and pay fees 11/9/76

RAINY RIV FST PRODS INC (ON)
Merged into Stone Consolidated Corp. 11/01/1995
Each share Common no par exchanged for (1.04) shares Common no par
Stone Consolidated Corp. merged into Abitibi-Consolidated Inc. 05/30/1997 which merged into AbitibiBowater Inc. 10/29/2007
(See AbitibiBowater Inc.)

RAINY RIVER RES LTD (BC)
Merged into New Gold Inc. 10/16/2013
Each share Common no par exchanged for (0.23975175) shares Common no par and $2 cash

RAISIN MARKETS INC. (CA)
Merged into Alpha Beta Food Markets, Inc. 5/27/59
Each share Preferred $25 par exchanged for (1) share 6% Preferred $25 par which was subsequently called for redemption 11/25/60

RAIT INVT TR (MD)
Name changed to RAIT Financial Trust 12/11/2006

RAJAC INDS INC (NY)
Each share Common 10¢ par exchanged for (0.2) share Common 50¢ par 05/06/1968
Charter cancelled and proclaimed dissolved for failure to pay taxes and file reports 12/15/1971

RAJAC SELF-SERVICE, INC. (NY)
Name changed to Rajac Industries, Inc. 6/12/61
Rajac Industries, Inc. charter cancelled 12/15/71

RAJAH RED LAKE GOLD MINES LTD. (ON)
Charter cancelled by Province of Ontario by default in 1957

RAJONG RES LTD (AB)
Issue Information - 2,000,000 shares COM offered at $0.15 per share on 03/20/1997
Name changed to Deloro Minerals Ltd. 12/31/1997
Deloro Minerals Ltd. recapitalized as Deloro Resources Ltd. (ALTA) 08/23/2005 which reincorporated in British Columbia 03/10/2009

RAKO CAP CORP (NV)
Reincorporated 07/19/2001
Name changed from Rako Corp. to Rako Capital Corp. and state of incorporation changed from (ID) to (NV) 07/19/2001
SEC revoked common stock registration 10/30/2008
Stockholders' equity unlikely

RAKS ELEKTRONIK SANAYI VE TICARET A S (TURKEY)
Sponsored ADR's for Ordinary split (2) for (1) by issuance of (1) additional ADR payable 05/10/1999 to holders of record 02/22/1999
ADR agreement terminated 00/00/2000
Details not available

RAL MARKETING GROUP INC (BC)
Recapitalized as Datatracker International Inc. 04/20/1988
Each share Common no par exchanged for (1/3) share Common no par
Datatracker International Inc. name changed to California Gold Mines Inc. 02/04/1991
(See California Gold Mines Inc.)

RALCO EXPLORATION CO., LTD. (ON)
Charter cancelled for failure to file reports and pay taxes 12/21/59

RALCORP HLDGS INC NEW (MO)
Each share Common 1¢ par received distribution of (0.5) share Post Holdings, Inc. Common 1¢ par payable 02/03/2012 to holders of record 01/30/2012 Ex date - 02/06/2012
Acquired by ConAgra Foods, Inc. 01/29/2013
Each share Common 1¢ par exchanged for $90 cash

RALCORP HLDGS INC OLD (MO)
Each share Common 1¢ par received distribution of (1) share Ralcorp Holdings, Inc. (New) Common 1¢ par payable 2/13/97 to holders of record 1/31/97
Merged into General Mills Inc. 1/31/97
Each share Common 1¢ par exchanged for (0.163) share Common 10¢ par

RALEIGH APARTMENTS (IL)
Liquidated in 1950

RALEIGH BANKSHARES INC (WV)
Name changed to Horizon Bancorp, Inc. 05/01/1985
Horizon Bancorp, Inc. merged into City Holding Co. 12/31/1998

RALEIGH CNTY NATL BK (BECKLEY, WV)
Name changed 09/01/1972
Common $100 par changed to $25 par and (3) additional shares issued 01/13/1950
Common $25 par changed to $12.50 par and (1) additional share issued 02/01/1961
Stock Dividend - 100% 00/00/1961
Name changed from Raleigh County Bank (Beckley, WV) to Raleigh County National Bank (Beckley, WV) 09/01/1972
Common $12.50 par changed to $2.50 par and (6.5) additional shares issued to provide for a (5) for (1) stock split plus a 50% stock dividend 12/02/1972
Reorganized as Summit Holding Corp. 06/27/1984
Each share Common $2.50 par exchanged for (1) share Common $2.50 par
Summit Holding Corp. merged into United Bankshares, Inc. 10/21/1992

RALEIGH-DURNHAM PRODUCTS, INC. (NC)
Charter suspended for failure to file reports 12/16/1963

RALEIGH ENERGY CORP (BC)
Recapitalized as Subloo International Resource Corp. (BC) 03/09/1993
Each share Common no par exchanged for (0.2) Common no par
Subloo International Resource Corp. (BC) reincorporated in Canada 08/18/1994 which name changed to Goldminco Mining Corp. 10/07/1996 which recapitalized as Goldminco Consolidated Mining Corp. 12/22/1997 which recapitalized as Goldminco Corp. 04/06/2000
(See Goldminco Corp.)

RALEIGH FED SVGS BK (RALEIGH, NC)
Reorganized as RS Financial Corp. 03/15/1989
Each share Common $1 par exchanged for (1) share Common $1 par

RS Financial Corp. merged into First Union Corp. 01/11/1996 which name changed to Wachovia Corp. (Ctfs. dated after 09/01/2001) 09/01/2001 which merged into Wells Fargo & Co. (New) 12/31/2008

RALEIGH HOTEL CO.
Dissolved in 1946

RALLY ENERGY CORP (ON)
Merged into National Petroleum Co. S.A.E. 09/27/2007
Each share Common no par exchanged for $7.30 cash

RALLY SOFTWARE DEV CORP (DE)
Acquired by CA, Inc. 07/08/2015
Each share Common $0.0001 par exchanged for $19.50 cash

RALLYS HAMBURGERS INC (DE)
Name changed 8/27/93
Common 10¢ par split (3) for (2) by issuance of (0.5) additional share 9/10/92
Name changed from Rally's Inc. to Rally's Hamburgers, Inc. 8/27/93
Merged into Checkers Drive-In Restaurants, Inc. 8/9/99
Each share Common 10¢ par exchanged for (1.99) shares new Common $0.001 par
(See Checkers Drive-In Restaurants, Inc.)

RALPH M. PARSONS CO. (NV)
See - Parsons (Ralph M.) Co.

RALPH WILSON PLASTICS, INC. (TX)
See - Wilson (Ralph) Plastics, Inc.

RALPHS GROCERY CO NEW (DE)
Merged into Meyer (Fred), Inc. 3/9/98
Each share Common 1¢ par exchanged for (1.9) shares Common 1¢ par
Meyer (Fred), Inc. merged into Kroger Co. 5/27/99

RALSTON-CONTL BAKING GROUP (MO)
Each share Common 10¢ par exchanged for (0.0886) share Ralston Purina Co. Common 10¢ par 5/15/95
(See Ralston Purina Co.)

RALSTON PURINA CO (MO)
$1.20 Conv. Preferred Ser. A $1 par called for redemption 07/05/1973
Each Stock Appreciation Income Linked Security exchanged for $31.36 cash 08/01/2000
Common $25 par changed to $5 par and (4) additional shares issued 01/09/1957
Common $5 par changed to $2.50 par and (1) additional share issued 12/21/1961
Common $2.50 par changed to $1.25 par and (1) additional share issued 01/10/1967
Common $1.25 par changed to 41-2/3¢ par and (2) additional shares issued 02/01/1977
Common 41-2/3¢ par changed to 10¢ par and (1) additional share issued 03/08/1991
Each share Common 10¢ par reclassified as (1) share Common Ralston Purina Group 10¢ par 07/30/1993
Common Ralston Purina Group Common 10¢ par reclassified as Common 10¢ par 05/15/1995
Common Stock Purchase Rights declared for holders of record 04/10/1996
Each share Common 10¢ par received distribution of (0.1) share Agribrands International Inc.
Common 1¢ par payable 04/01/1998 to holders of record 04/01/1998 Ex date - 04/01/1998
Note: Physical certificates will be issued only upon request
Common 10¢ par split (3) for (1) by issuance of (2) additional shares payable 07/15/1998 to holders of record 06/22/1998 Ex date - 07/16/1998
Each share Common 10¢ par received distribution of (1/3) share Energizer Holdings, Inc. Common 1¢ par payable 04/03/2000 to holders of record 03/31/2000 Ex date - 04/04/2000
Stock Dividend - 50% 12/04/1950
Merged into Nestle, S.A. 12/12/2001
Each share Common 10¢ par exchanged for $33.50 cash

RAM AESTHETIC MATLS TECHNOLOGY INC (NM)
Charter revoked 07/03/2001

RAM ENERGY INC (DE)
Under plan of merger name changed to RAM Energy Resources, Inc. 05/08/2006
RAM Energy Resources, Inc. recapitalized as Halcon Resources Corp. 02/10/2012

RAM ENERGY RES INC (DE)
Recapitalized as Halcon Resources Corp. 02/10/2012
Each share Common $0.0001 par exchanged for (0.33333333) share Common $0.0001 par

RAM GOLD & EXPL INC (NV)
Name changed to DPollution International Inc. 08/31/2010
DPollution International Inc. recapitalized as Ecrid, Inc. 10/16/2017

RAM HART SYS INC (DE)
Each share Common 1¢ par exchanged for (0.0001) share Common no par 06/26/1972
Note: In effect holders received $0.50 cash per share and public interest was eliminated

RAM HOLDINGS LTD (BERMUDA)
Issue Information - 9,409,405 shares COM offered at $13 per share on 04/27/2006
Each share Common 10¢ par exchanged for (0.1) share Common $1 par 11/09/2011
Name changed to American Overseas Group Ltd. 12/19/2011

RAM INDUSTRIES (IA)
Adjudicated bankrupt 7/15/76

RAM INDS INC (NV)
Charter revoked for failure to file reports and pay fees 5/1/94

RAM KAASHYAP INVT LTD (INDIA)
Name changed to Gemmia Oiltech India Ltd. 07/29/2013
(See Gemmia Oiltech India Ltd.)

RAM OIL CO. (AZ)
Charter revoked for failure to file reports and pay fees 5/18/66

RAM PETES LTD (ON)
Common 25¢ par changed to no par 06/25/1984
Each share Common no par exchanged for (1) share Class A Common no par 12/23/1997
Each Class A Common no par received distribution of (2) shares Wollasco Minerals Inc. 12/29/1997 to holders of record 12/25/1997
Delisted from Toronto Stock Exchange 11/07/2000

RAM PWR CORP (BC)
Recapitalized as Polaris Infrastructure Inc. 05/19/2015
Each share Common no par exchanged for (0.0005) share Common no par

RAM TOOL CORP (IL)
Common 10¢ par changed to 3-1/3¢ par and (2) additional shares issued 04/09/1962
Adjudicated bankrupt 6/30/72
Stockholders' equity unlikely

RAM VENTURE HLDGS CORP (FL)
Each share old Common $0.0001 par exchanged for (0.1) share new Common $0.0001 par 04/19/2004
Company terminated registration of common stock and is no longer public as of 06/28/2005
Details not available

RAM-Z ENTERPRISES INC (DE)
Name changed to Hyperdynamics Corp. 1/9/97

RAMA FINL CORP (NV)
Each share old Common $0.001 par exchanged for (0.25) share new Common $0.001 par 09/30/1997
Name changed to Friendly Energy Corp. 06/02/1999
Friendly Energy Corp. recapitalized as Friendly Energy Exploration 03/24/2008
(See Friendly Energy Exploration)

RAMADA INC (DE)
Name changed 6/27/86
Common 10¢ par split (6) for (5) by issuance of (0.2) additional share 7/15/67
Common 10¢ par split (3) for (2) by issuance of (0.5) additional share 3/14/69
Common 10¢ par split (2) for (1) by issuance of (1) additional share 11/19/71
Stock Dividends - 10% 3/15/66; 10% 8/21/70; 10% 7/27/73
Name changed from Ramada Inns, Inc. to Ramada Inc. 6/27/86
Merged into Aztar Corp. 12/20/89
Each share Common 10¢ par exchanged for (1) share Common 1¢ par and $1.01 cash
(See Aztar Corp.)

RAMADA INN FLAME RESTAURANT INC. (AR)
Charter revoked for failure to pay taxes 2/16/73

RAMADA MINES LTD. (BC)
Name changed to Ramada Resources Ltd. 5/28/69
(See Ramada Resources Ltd.)

RAMADA RES LTD (BC)
Struck off register and declared dissolved for failure to file returns 09/23/1974

RAMAGON TOYS INC (OR)
Involuntarily dissolved for failure to file reports and pay fees 07/31/1997

RAMAPO BK (WAYNE, NJ)
Common $6 par changed to $2 par and (2) additional shares issued 10/24/69
Reorganized as Ramapo Financial Corp. 4/1/74
Each share Common $2 par exchanged for (1) share Common $2 par
Ramapo Financial Corp. merged into Valley National Bancorp 6/11/99

RAMAPO DEV INC (CO)
Name changed to Insight Environmental Corp. (CO) 06/01/1990
Insight Environmental Corp. (CO) reorganized in Maryland as American Equity Trust Inc. 07/17/1995
(See American Equity Trust Inc.)

RAMAPO FINL CORP (NJ)
Common $2 par changed to $1 par and (1) additional share issued 6/30/86
Merged into Valley National Bancorp 6/11/99
Each share Common $1 par exchanged for (0.44625) share Common no par

RAMARDO MINES LTD (ON)
Charter cancelled 6/19/80

RAMARRO RES INC (AB)
Acquired by EOG Resources Canada Co. 4/18/2002
Each share Common no par exchanged for $1.54 cash

RAMBEC EXPLORATION CORP. (NV)
Insolvent; stock worthless
Charter revoked for failure to file reports and pay fees 3/5/62

RAMBLER EXPL LTD (ON)
Charter cancelled for failure to pay taxes and file returns 03/16/1976

RAMBLER EXPLS LTD (BC)
Recapitalized as Ramcor Resources Inc. 01/14/1985
Each share Common no par exchanged for (0.2) share Common no par
Ramcor Resources Inc. recapitalized as Rampton Oil Corp. 06/01/1993 which name changed to Rampton Resource Corp. 07/17/1996 which name changed to PanTerra Exploration Corp. 08/15/2002 which recapitalized as PanTerra Resource Corp. (BC) 09/03/2004 which reincorporated in Alberta 10/27/2005 which recapitalized as Ikkuma Resources Corp. 09/22/2014

RAMBLER OIL CO (OK)
Charter expired 08/18/2009

RAMBO MED GROUP INC (NV)
Name changed to HK eBus Corp. 09/15/2015

RAMCO (SCOTLAND)
ADR agreement terminated 12/29/2000
Each Sponsored ADR for Ordinary exchanged for $4.3216 cash

RAMCO ENTERPRISES INC (NY)
Completely liquidated 12/15/71
Each share Capital Stock no par exchanged for (0.25203) share $2.80 Preferred Ser. A $1 par and (0.60684) share Common $1 par of Stetson (John B.) Co.
(See Stetson (John B.) Co.)

RAMCO-GERSHENSON PPTYS TR (MD)
Reincorporated 12/18/1997
State of incorporation changed from (MA) to (MD) and Common 10¢ par changed to Common Shares of Bene. Int. 1¢ par 12/18/1997
Issue Information - 1,755,000 PFD CONV SER C BENE INT 7.95% offered at $28.50 per share on 05/26/2004
7.95% Conv. Preferred Shares of Bene. Int. 1¢ par called for redemption at $28.50 plus $0.371346 accrued dividends on 06/01/2007
9.5% Conv. Preferred Ser. B 1¢ par called for redemption at $25 on 11/12/2007
(Additional Information in Active)

RAMCO INDS LTD (BC)
Recapitalized as Black Diamond Resources Ltd. 11/15/79
Each share Capital Stock no par exchanged for (0.25) share Capital Stock no par
Black Diamond Resources Ltd. name changed to Com-Air Containers (Canada) Inc. 1/14/87
(See Com-Air Containers (Canada) Inc.)

RAMCOR INC (NY)
Common $1 par split (3) for (2) by issuance of (0.5) additional share 01/20/1969
Out of business and assets sold by foreclosure 01/28/1970
Stockholders' equity unlikely

RAMCOR RES INC (BC)
Recapitalized as Rampton Oil Corp. 06/01/1993
Each share Common no par

exchanged for (0.2) share Common no par
Rampton Oil Corp. name changed to Rampton Resource Corp. 07/17/1996 which name changed to PanTerra Exploration Corp. 08/15/2002 which recapitalized as PanTerra Resource Corp. (BC) 09/03/2004 which reincorporated in Alberta 10/27/2005 which recapitalized as Ikkuma Resources Corp. 09/22/2014

RAMER INDS INC (DE)
Name changed to RAI, Inc. 01/26/1972
(See RAI, Inc.)

RAMEX SYNFUELS INTL INC (NV)
Each share Common $0.001 par exchanged for (0.1) share Common 1¢ par 11/16/1994
Recapitalized as Sportsend, Inc. 03/16/2001
Each (30) shares Common 1¢ par exchanged for (1) share Common 1¢ par
(See Sportsend, Inc.)

RAMID INTERNATIONAL LTD. (BC)
Recapitalized as Ramm Venture Corp. 07/08/1977
Each share Common no par exchanged for (0.2) share Common no par
(See Ramm Venture Corp.)

RAMID RESOURCES LTD. (BC)
Name changed to Ramid International Ltd. 11/12/1969
Ramid International Ltd. recapitalized as Ramm Venture Corp. 07/08/1977
(See Ramm Venture Corp.)

RAMIE CORP. (DE)
No longer in existence having become inoperative and void for non-payment of taxes 4/1/58

RAMM VENTURE CORP (BC)
Cease trade order effective 10/11/2001
Stockholders' equity unlikely

RAMO INC (DE)
Recapitalized 9/15/67
Each share Class A Common 25¢ par exchanged for (0.0125) share Common no par
Each share Common $1 par exchanged for (0.05) share Common no par
Stock Dividend - Common - 300% 2/15/62
Merged into Telecom Corp. 11/23/71
Each share Non-Cum. Conv. Preferred no par or Common no par exchanged for (0.2581) Common $1 par
Telecom Corp. name changed to TCC Industries, Inc. 6/1/94
(See TCC Industries, Inc.)

RAMO INVESTMENT CO. (DE)
Name changed to Ramo, Inc. 11/21/60
Ramo, Inc. merged into Telecom Corp. 11/23/71 which name changed to TCC Industries, Inc. 6/1/94
(See TCC Industries, Inc.)

RAMOIL MGMT LTD (WY)
Reincorporated 01/25/2011
Common $0.0001 par changed to $0.00002 par and (4) additional shares issued payable 04/13/2000 to holders of record 03/24/2000 Ex date - 04/14/2000
State of incorporation changed from (DE) to (WY) and Common $0.00002 par changed to $0.0001 par 01/25/2011
Name changed to Advantis Corp. 11/24/2015

RAMONA NATL BK (SAN DIEGO, CA)
Name changed to First Business Bank, N.A. (San Diego, CA) 08/06/2007

First Business Bank, N.A. (San Diego, CA) name changed to Bank of Southern California, N.A. (San Diego, CA) 08/12/2010

RAMP BLDGS CORP (DE)
Voluntarily dissolved 6/13/68
Details not available

RAMP CORP (DE)
Each (60) shares old Common $0.001 par exchanged for (1) share new Common $0.001 12/01/2004
Plan of reorganization under Chapter 11 Federal Bankruptcy Code effective 01/01/2008
No stockholders' equity

RAMP NETWORKS INC (DE)
Issue Information - 4,000,000 shares COM offered at $11 per share on 06/22/1999
Merged into Nokia Corp. 1/25/2001
Each share Common $0.001 par exchanged for $5.80 cash

RAMPAC (CA)
Merged into Pan-American Properties, Inc. 06/26/1984
Each Share of Bene. Int. no par exchanged for $37 cash

RAMPAGE RES INC (BC)
Recapitalized as Clyde Resources Inc. 2/21/92
Each share Common no par exchanged for (1/3) share Common no par
(See Clyde Resources Inc.)

RAMPART CAP CORP (TX)
Each share old Common 1¢ par exchanged for (0.00001) share new Common 1¢ par 11/6/2003
Note: In effect holders received $3.50 cash per share and public interest was eliminated

RAMPART EQUITIES INC (CO)
Name changed to Westar Industries International, Inc. 08/17/1989
(See Westar Industries International, Inc.)

RAMPART GEN INC (CA)
Common 2¢ par split (3) for (1) by issuance of (2) additional shares 12/19/1977
Common 2¢ par split (2) for (1) by issuance of (1) additional share 02/23/1978
Charter cancelled for failure to file reports and pay taxes 09/01/1995

RAMPART MERCANTILE INC (ON)
Reincorporated 11/24/1999
Each share old Common no par exchanged for (0.1) share new Common no par 10/15/1999
Place of incorporation changed from (BC) to (ON) 11/24/1999
Name changed to Aurquest Resources Inc. 04/14/2011
Aurquest Resources Inc. name changed to Xanthic Biopharma Inc. 04/19/2018

RAMPART RES LTD (BC)
Name changed 08/14/1984
Name changed from Rampart Mines Ltd. to Rampart Resources Ltd. 08/14/1984
Recapitalized as Trans Rampart Industries Ltd. 07/24/1987
Each share Common no par exchanged for (0.33333333) share Common no par
Trans Rampart Industries Ltd. name changed to Rampart Mercantile Inc. (BC) 05/28/1993 which reincorporated in Ontario 11/24/1999 which name changed to Aurquest Resources Inc. 04/14/2011 which name changed to Xanthic Biopharma Inc. 04/19/2018

RAMPART URANIUM CO. (CO)
Acquired by Globe Hill Mining Co. 04/11/1957
Each share Common 10¢ par exchanged for (10) shares Common 1¢ par
Globe Hill Mining Co. merged into Globe Hill Co. 09/14/1971 which name changed to Aadan Corp. 11/01/1972
(See Aadan Corp.)

RAMPART VENTURES LTD (BC)
Name changed to RPT Uranium Corp. 02/23/2007
RPT Uranium Corp. name changed to RPT Resources Ltd. (BC) 06/05/2009 which reincorporated in Alberta as ArPetrol Ltd. 04/08/2011

RAMPTON RES CORP (BC)
Name changed 07/17/1996
Name changed from Rampton Oil Corp. to Rampton Resource Corp. 07/17/1996
Each share old Common no par exchanged for (0.33333333) share new Common no par 09/01/1999
Name changed to PanTerra Exploration Corp. 08/15/2002
PanTerra Exploration Corp. recapitalized as PanTerra Resource Corp. (BC) 09/03/2004 which reincorporated in Alberta 10/27/2005 which recapitalized as Ikkuma Resources Corp. 09/22/2014

RAMROD ENERGY CORP (BC)
Recapitalized as Consolidated Ramrod Gold Corp. 08/27/1986
Each share Common no par exchanged for (0.25) share Common no par
Consolidated Ramrod Gold Corp. name changed to Quest International Resources Corp. 04/09/1996 which recapitalized as Standard Mining Corp. 06/16/1999 which merged into Doublestar Resources Ltd. (YT) 11/01/2001 which reincorporated in British Columbia 10/10/2002 which merged into Selkirk Metals Corp. 07/23/2007
(See Selkirk Metals Corp.)

RAMROD MINING CORP. (BC)
Name changed to Ramrod Resources Corp. 11/27/1981
Ramrod Resources Corp. merged into Ramrod Energy Corp. 03/01/1983 which recapitalized as Consolidated Ramrod Gold Corp. 08/27/1986 which name changed to Quest International Resources Corp. 04/09/1996 which recapitalized as Standard Mining Corp. 06/16/1999 which merged into Doublestar Resources Ltd. (YT) 11/01/2001 which reincorporated in British Columbia 10/10/2002 which merged into Selkirk Metals Corp. 07/23/2007
(See Selkirk Metals Corp.)

RAMROD RES CORP (BC)
Merged into Ramrod Energy Corp. 03/01/1983
Each share Common no par exchanged for (1) share Common no par
Ramrod Energy Corp. recapitalized as Consolidated Ramrod Gold Corp. 08/27/1986 which name changed to Quest International Resources Corp. 04/09/1996 which recapitalized as Standard Mining Corp. 06/16/1999 which merged into Doublestar Resources Ltd. (YT) 11/01/2001 which reincorporated in British Columbia 10/10/2002 which merged into Selkirk Metals Corp. 07/23/2007
(See Selkirk Metals Corp.)

RAMSAY HEALTH CARE INC (DE)
Each share Common $1 par exchanged for (1/3) share new Common $1 par 4/18/91
Name changed to Ramsay Youth Services Inc. 1/1/99
(See Ramsay Youth Services Inc.)

RAMSAY-HMO INC (DE)
Common $0.001 par split (2.4) for (1) by issuance of (1.4) additional shares 05/20/1994
Merged into United HealthCare Corp. 05/31/1994
Each share Common $0.001 par exchanged for (0.39412) share Common 1¢ par
United HealthCare Corp. name changed to UnitedHealth Group Inc. (MN) 03/01/2000 which reincorporated in Delaware 07/01/2015

RAMSAY MANAGED CARE INC (DE)
Merged into Ramsay Health Care, Inc. 6/10/97
Each share Common $1 par exchanged for (1/3) share Common $1 par
Ramsay Health Care, Inc. name changed to Ramsay Youth Services Inc. 1/1/99
(See Ramsay Youth Services Inc.)

RAMSAY YOUTH SVCS INC (DE)
Each share old Common $1 par exchanged for (1/3) share new Common $1 par 3/14/99
Merged into Psychiatric Solutions, Inc. 6/30/2003
Each share new Common $1 par exchanged for $5 cash

RAMTEK CORP (DE)
Reincorporated 00/00/1987
State of incorporation changed from (CA) to (DE) 00/00/1987
Plan of reorganization under Chapter 11 Federal Bankruptcy proceedings confirmed 11/30/1989
No old Common stockholders' equity
Each share new Common no par exchanged for (1/3) share Common 1¢ par 04/30/1993
Plan of reorganization under Chapter 11 Federal Bankruptcy proceedings confirmed 11/21/1995
Stockholders' equity unlikely

RAMTELECOM INC (AB)
Name changed to Avalite Inc. 06/11/2009
Avalite Inc. recapitalized as Innovative Wireline Solutions Inc. 07/22/2010
(See Innovative Wireline Solutions Inc.)

RAMTRON HLDGS LTD (AUSTRALIA)
Name changed 08/29/1990
Name changed from Ramtron Australia Ltd. to Ramtron Holdings Ltd. 08/29/1990
Reorganized under the laws of Delaware as Ramtron International Corp. 02/16/1993
Each Sponsored ADR for Ordinary AUS $0.20 par exchanged for (0.35) share Common 1¢ par
(See Ramtron International Corp.)

RAMTRON INTL CORP (DE)
Each share old Common 1¢ par exchanged for (0.2) share new Common 1¢ par 08/09/1999
Acquired by Cypress Semiconductor Corp. 11/21/2012
Each share new Common 1¢ par exchanged for $3.10 cash

RAMYR MANUFACTURING CO. (CA)
Voluntarily dissolved 1/19/81
Details not available

RAN COR VENTURES INC (CO)
Name changed to Special Delivery Systems Inc. 10/10/1989

RAN ENERGY INC (DE)
Charter cancelled and declared inoperative and void for non-payment of taxes 03/01/1985

RAN LUX MINES LTD (QC)
Involuntarily dissolved 12/01/1977

RANALD RES LTD (BC)
Name changed to Marlborough Productions Ltd. 10/30/1986

(See Marlborough Productions Ltd.)

RANAZ CORP (CANADA)
Each (17,000,000) shares old Common no par exchanged for (1) share new Common no par 07/15/2014
Note: In effect holders received $0.01 cash per share and public interest was eliminated
Unexchanged certificates will be cancelled and become without value 07/15/2020

RANBAXY LABORATORIES LTD (INDIA)
144A GDR's for Equity Shares INR 10 par split (2) for (1) by issuance of (1) additional GDR payable 02/25/1999 to holders of record 12/15/1998
Reg. S GDR's for Equity Shares INR 10 par changed to INR 5 par and (1) additional GDR issued payable 08/05/2005 to holders of record 08/01/2005
144A GDR's for Equity Shares INR 10 par changed to INR 5 par and (1) additional GDR issued payable 08/05/2005 to holders of record 08/01/2005
Stock Dividend - 60% payable 12/02/2002 to holders of record 10/04/2002 Ex date - 10/02/2002
GDR agreement terminated 11/14/2014
Each Reg. S GDR for Equity Shares exchanged for $5.622515 cash
Each 144A GDR for Equity Shares exchanged for $5.622515 cash

RANCH HOUSE AMER INC (FL)
Merged into Riviana Foods, Inc. (Old) 2/15/74
Each share Common 5¢ par exchanged for (0.263852) share Common $3.50 par
Riviana Foods, Inc. (Old) acquired by Colgate-Palmolive Co. 6/14/76

RANCHER ENERGY CORP (NV)
Reorganized under the laws of Colorado as T-Rex Oil, Inc. 10/29/2014
Each share Common $0.00001 par exchanged for (0.00285714) share Common $0.001 par

RANCHERO ENERGY INC (AB)
Merged into Cypress Energy Inc. 3/26/2001
Each share Class A Common no par exchanged for either (0.288022) share Class A Common no par or $1.68 cash
Note: Option to receive stock expired 5/25/2001
Cypress Energy Inc. merged into PrimeWest Energy Trust 5/29/2001

RANCHERO OIL & GAS LTD (AB)
Acquired by Newquest Energy Inc. 04/14/2000
Each share Common no par exchanged for (2.86) shares Class A Common no par
Newquest Energy Inc. recapitalized as Ranchero Energy Inc. 09/01/2000 which merged into Cypress Energy Inc. 03/26/2001 which merged into PrimeWest Energy Trust 05/29/2001

RANCHERS EXPL & DEV CORP (NM)
Each share Capital Stock 10¢ par exchanged for (0.2) share Capital Stock 50¢ par 01/31/1963
Capital Stock 50¢ par split (2) for (1) by issuance of (1) additional share 03/24/1970
Capital Stock 50¢ par split (2) for (1) by issuance of (1) additional share 03/14/1980
Capital Stock 50¢ par split (3) for (2) by issuance of (0.5) additional share 10/14/1983
Merged into Hecla Mining Co. 07/27/1984
Each share Capital Stock 50¢ par exchanged for (1.55) shares Common 25¢ par

RANCHERS PACKING CORP (DE)
Common 10¢ par changed to 5¢ par and (0.25) additional share issued 12/26/69
Name changed to Quarex Industries, Inc. 6/22/83
Quarex Industries, Inc. name changed to Western Beef Inc. 1/13/93

RANCHGATE ENERGY INC (AB)
Merged into Clear Energy Inc. 8/25/2004
Each share Common no par exchanged for (0.386) share Common no par
(See Clear Energy Inc.)

RANCHMEN'S OILS (1957) LTD. (AB)
Each share 6% Preferred $1 par exchanged for (1) share Common 10¢ par and $0.10 cash 00/00/1965
Name changed to Ranchmen's Resources Ltd. 06/02/1970
Ranchmen's Resources Ltd. merged into Ranchmen's Resources (1975) Ltd. 08/28/1975 which merged into Ranchmen's Resources (1976) Ltd. 01/31/1977 which name changed to Ranchmen's Resources Ltd. 05/31/1985 which merged into Crestar Energy Inc. 10/11/1995 which was acquired by Gulf Canada Resources Ltd. 11/13/2000
(See Gulf Canada Resources Ltd.)

RANCHMENS RES (1975) LTD (AB)
Name changed 8/28/75
Under plan of merger name changed from Ranchmen's Resources Ltd. to Ranchmen's Resources (1975) Ltd. and each share Common 10¢ par exchanged for (0.2) share Class A Common 8/28/75
Merged into Ranchmen's Resources (1976) Ltd. 1/31/77
Each share Class A Common no par exchanged for (1) share Class A Common no par
Ranchmen's Resources (1976) Ltd. name changed to Ranchmen's Resources Ltd. 5/31/85 which merged into Crestar Energy Inc. 10/11/95 which was acquired by Gulf Canada Resources Ltd. 11/13/2000
(See Gulf Canada Resources Ltd.)

RANCHMENS RES LTD (AB)
Name changed 05/31/1985
Class B Common no par reclassified as Class A Common no par 07/27/1979
Name changed from Ranchmen's Resources (1976) Ltd. to Ranchmen's Resources Ltd. 05/31/1985
Non-Vtg. Class B Common no par reclassified as Class A Common no par 06/25/1986
Class A Common no par reclassified as Common no par 06/16/1988
Class C Common no par reclassified as Common no par 06/16/1988
$2.45 1st Preferred Ser. A $25 par called for redemption 08/31/1993
Merged into Crestar Energy Inc. 10/11/1995
Each share Common no par exchanged for either (0.225) share Common no par and $2.81 cash or $6.125 cash
Note: Option to receive stock and cash expired 11/07/1995
Crestar Energy Inc. acquired by Gulf Canada Resources Ltd. 11/13/2000
(See Gulf Canada Resources Ltd.)

RANCHO BK (SAN DIMAS, CA)
Common $5 par split (2) for (1) by issuance of (1) additional share payable 06/06/2002 to holders of record 05/23/2002 Ex date - 06/07/2002
Merged into Vineyard National Bancorp 07/31/2006
Each share Common $5 par exchanged for $38.50 cash

RANCHO BERNARDO CMNTY BK (SAN DIEGO, CA)
Stock Dividend - 5% payable 06/22/2004 to holders of record 05/31/2004
Merged into Community Bancorp Inc. 08/19/2005
Each share Common no par exchanged for either (0.949) share Common $0.625 par or (0.22870235) share Common $0.625 par and $23.87836022 cash
Note: Option to receive stock and cash expired 08/24/2005
Community Bancorp Inc. merged into First Community Bancorp (CA) 10/26/2006 which reincorporated in Delaware as PacWest Bancorp 05/14/2008

RANCHO DOMINGUEZ BK N A (CARSON, CA)
Name changed to Merchants Bank of California, N.A. (Carson, CA) 10/1/96

RANCHO SANTA FE NATL BK (RANCHO SANTA FE, CA)
Under plan of reorganization each share Common $2.50 par automatically became (1) share First Community Bancorp (CA) Common no par 06/01/2000
First Community Bancorp (CA) reincorporated in Delaware as PacWest Bancorp 05/14/2008

RANCHO SANTA FE SAVINGS & LOAN ASSOCIATION (CA)
Merged into Ahmanson (H.F.) & Co. (CA) 12/29/1980
Each share Guarantee Stock $10 par exchanged for (3.3) shares Common no par
Ahmanson (H.F.) & Co. (CA) reincorporated in Delaware 05/22/1985 which merged into Washington Mutual, Inc. 10/01/1998
(See Washington Mutual, Inc.)

RANCHO VISTA NATL BK (VISTA, CA)
Merged into Bank of Commerce (San Diego, CA) 05/15/1998
Each share Common $5 par exchanged for (2) shares Common no par
Bank of Commerce (San Diego, CA) merged into U.S. Bancorp 07/15/1999

RANCO INC (OH)
Common $5 par changed to $2.50 par and (1) additional share issued 2/17/61
Common $2.50 par split (3) for (2) by issuance of (0.5) additional share 12/13/78
Merged into Siebe PLC 3/18/87
Each share Common $2.50 par exchanged for $40 cash

RANCO OIL CORP. (DE)
Charter cancelled and declared inoperative and void for non-payment of taxes 4/1/40

RANCON RLTY FD (CA)
Liquidation completed
Each Unit of Ltd. Partnership Int. V received initial distribution of $42.142 cash payable 12/17/2015 to holders of record 08/12/2015
Each Unit of Ltd. Partnership Int. V received second and final distribution 12/31/2016
Note: Trust advised all holders have been paid and will not provide details
Liquidation completed
Each Unit of Ltd. Partnership Int. IV received initial distribution of $376 cash payable 08/14/2015 to holders of record 08/01/2015
Each Unit of Ltd. Partnership Int. IV received second distribution of $5.51 cash payable 01/30/2017 to holders of record 01/01/2017
Each Unit of Ltd. Partnership Int. IV received third and final distribution of $4.32 cash payable 07/17/2017 to holders of record 01/01/2017

RAND A TECHNOLOGY CORP (ON)
Common no par split (2) for (1) by issuance of (1) additional share payable 12/17/1996 to holders of record 12/12/1996
Merged into Ampersand Ventures 11/01/2007
Each share Common no par exchanged for $2.10 cash

RAND BROADCASTING CO. (FL)
Liquidated in October, 1973

RAND DEV CORP (OH)
Adjudicated bankrupt 08/28/1972
No stockholders' equity

RAND EXTNS & EXPL LTD (SOUTH AFRICA)
Acquired by Marievale Ltd. 03/04/1989
Each ADR for Ordinary Rand-0.25 par exchanged for $0.368 cash

RAND KARDEX BUREAU, INC.
Merged into Remington Rand, Inc. in 1927
(See Remington Rand, Inc.)

RAND LOGISTICS INC (DE)
Name changed 06/19/2006
Name changed from Rand Acquisition Corp. to Rand Logistics, Inc. 06/19/2006
Plan of reorganization under Chapter 11 Federal Bankruptcy proceedings effective 03/01/2018
No stockholders' equity

RAND MCNALLY & CO (IL)
Each share old Common exchanged for (0.001) share new Common 11/6/97
Note: In effect holders received approximately $434 cash per share and public interest was eliminated

RAND MINES LTD (SOUTH AFRICA)
Ctfs. dated prior to 6/28/71
Merged into Barlow Rand Ltd. 6/28/71
Each ADR for Ordinary Rand-50¢ par exchanged for (6) shares Ordinary Rand- 10¢ par
Barlow Rand Ltd. name changed to Barlow Ltd. 1/24/94 which name changed to Barloworld Ltd. 10/2/2000

RAND MINES LTD NEW (SOUTH AFRICA)
Ctfs. dated after 11/14/85
ADR agreement terminated 05/05/2000
No ADR holders' equity

RAND MINES PPTYS LTD (SOUTH AFRICA)
Name changed to RMP Properties Ltd. 3/28/94
(See RMP Properties Ltd.)

RAND PHOENIX INC (NV)
Plan of reorganization under Chapter 11 Federal Bankruptcy proceedings confirmed 11/13/1987
No stockholders' equity

RAND REEF MINES LTD (ON)
Recapitalized as Hornby Bay Exploration Ltd. 11/01/1997
Each share Common no par exchanged for (0.5) share Common no par
Hornby Bay Exploration Ltd. name changed to Unor Inc. 05/01/2006 which recapitalized as Hornby Bay Mineral Exploration Ltd. 04/12/2010

RAND RES LTD (BC)
Capital Stock no par reclassified as Class A Capital Stock no par 04/15/1974

Struck off register and declared dissolved for failure to file returns 04/13/1982

RAND SELECTION LTD (SOUTH AFRICA)
Merged into Anglo American Corp. of South Africa Ltd. (South Africa) 05/09/1977
Each old ADR for Ordinary Reg. exchanged for (2) new ADR's for Ordinary
Anglo American Corp. of South Africa Ltd. (South Africa) reincorporated in United Kingdom as Anglo American PLC 05/24/1999

RAND SERVICE STORES (CANADA) LTD.
Acquired by Burnett Ltd. share for share in 1948
Burnett Ltd. was adjudicated bankrupt in 1955

RAND SYS INC (DE)
Charter cancelled and declared inoperative and void for non-payment of taxes 3/1/91

RAND VENTURES INC (BC)
Name changed to Formosa Resources Corp. 12/23/86
(See Formosa Resources Corp.)

RANDADO OIL & MINERALS INC (DE)
Name changed to Ran Energy Inc. 11/09/1981
(See Ran Energy Inc.)

RANDAL DATA SYS INC (CA)
Chapter 11 bankruptcy proceedings converted to Chapter 7 on 10/29/1980
No stockholders' equity

RANDALL BUILDING CORP. (IL)
Completely liquidated 5/23/42
Each Capital Participating Ctf. no par exchanged for first and final distribution of $34 cash

RANDALL CO. (OH)
Each share Class B Common no par exchanged for (2) shares Common $5 par in June 1950
Acquired by Textron, Inc. (R.I.) (New) for cash 6/18/59

RANDALL GRAPHITE BEARINGS, INC. (DE)
Stock Dividends - 10% 1/31/59; 10% 2/29/60; 10% 4/30/63
Name changed to Randall Bearings, Inc. 5/1/65

RANDALL GRAPHITE PRODUCTS CORP.
Name changed to Randall Graphite Bearings, Inc. in 1947 which name was changed to Randall Bearings, Inc. 5/1/65

RANDALL MINES CORP.
Liquidated in 1941
No stockholders' equity

RANDALL YELLOWKNIFE MINES, LTD. (ON)
Charter cancelled for failure to file reports and pay taxes 10/28/57

RANDERS KILLAM GROUP INC (UT)
Recapitalized 2/1/99
Recapitalized from Randers Group, Inc. to Randers Killam Group Inc. 2/1/99
Each share Common $0.0001 par exchanged for (0.2) share Common $0.0001 par
Merged into Thermo Electron Corp. 5/15/2000
Each share Common $0.0001 par exchanged for $4.50 cash

RANDEX CONSOLIDATED OIL CO. (DE)
Recapitalized as American-Caribbean Oil Co. 03/21/1958
Each share Common 10¢ par exchanged for (0.5) share Common 20¢ par

American-Caribbean Oil Co. merged into Elgin Gas & Oil Co. 06/30/1959
(See Elgin Gas & Oil Co.)

RANDEX LTD (SOUTH AFRICA)
ADR agreement terminated 00/00/1990
Details not available

RANDEX URANIUM MINES, INC. (DE)
Merged into Randex Consolidated Oil Co. on a (0.1) for (1) basis 00/00/1956
Randex Consolidated Oil Co. recapitalized as American-Caribbean Oil Co. 03/21/1958 which merged into Elgin Gas & Oil Co. 06/30/1959
(See Elgin Gas & Oil Co.)

RANDFONTEIN ESTATES LTD (SOUTH AFRICA)
Name changed 10/19/98
Each old ADR for Ordinary Rand-2 par exchanged for (10) new ADR's for Ordinary Rand-2 par 9/4/84
ADR's for Ordinary Rand-2 par changed to Rand-0.20 par and (9) additional ADR's issued 11/10/89
Stock Dividend - 2.39% payable 2/21/97 to holders of record 12/27/96
Name changed from Randfontein Estates Gold Mining Co. Witwatersrand Ltd. to Randfontein Estates Ltd. 10/19/98
Acquired by Harmony Gold Mining Ltd. 8/9/2000
Each ADR for Ordinary Rand-0.20 par exchanged for (0.34) Sponsored ADR for Ordinary Rand-0.50 par

R&G CAP TR III (DE)
Plan of reorganization under Chapter 11 Federal Bankruptcy proceedings effective 01/05/2012
Holders are expected to receive an undetermined amount of cash

R&G CAP TR V (DE)
Plan of reorganization under Chapter 11 Federal Bankruptcy proceedings effective 01/05/2012
Holders are expected to receive an undetermined amount of cash

R&G FINL CORP (PR)
Class B Common 1¢ par split (2) for (1) by issuance of (1) additional share payable 06/25/1998 to holders of record 06/12/1998
Class B Common 1¢ par split (3) for (2) by issuance of (0.5) additional share payable 01/29/2004 to holders of record 01/16/2004 Ex date - 01/30/2004
Stock Dividend - 80% payable 09/25/1997 to holders of record 09/15/1997
Plan of reorganization under Chapter 11 Federal Bankruptcy proceedings effective 01/05/2012
No stockholders' equity

RANDGOLD & EXPL LTD (SOUTH AFRICA)
Each Reg. S GDR for Ordinary exchanged for (1/3) Sponsored ADR for Ordinary 11/09/1998
Sponsored ADR's for Ordinary split (3) for (1) by issuance of (2) additional ADR's payable 04/30/2004 to holders of record 04/29/2004 Ex date - 05/03/2004
SEC revoked ADR registration 03/24/2008
Each Sponsored ADR for Ordinary received distribution of (0.0316193) Gold Fields Ltd. Sponsored ADR for Ordinary payable 01/21/2011 to holders of record 01/14/2011

RANDGOLD RES LTD (CHANNEL ISLANDS)
Each old 144A GDR for Ordinary exchanged for (0.5) new 144A GDR for Ordinary 06/26/2002
GDR agreement terminated 11/18/2002
Each new 144A GDR for Ordinary

exchanged for (2) 144A Ordinary shares
(Additional Information in Active)

RANDISCO, INC. (MI)
Liquidation completed
Each share Common $2.50 par exchanged for initial distribution of (0.25894) share Fedders Corp. (NY) Common $1 par 01/30/1970
Each share Common $2.50 par received second and final distribution of (0.0691355) share Fedders Corp. (NY) Common $1 par 01/01/1972
Fedders Corp. (NY) reincorporated in Delaware 01/02/1985
(See Fedders Corp.)

RANDO (JOSEPH), INC. (UT)
Name changed to Rando (Joseph) International 7/3/75
(See Rando (Joseph) International)

RANDO JOSEPH INTL (UT)
Involuntarily dissolved 12/31/1982

RANDOLPH BK & TR CO (ASHEBORO, NC)
Stock Dividends - 5% payable 12/01/1997 to holders of record 11/03/1997; 5% payable 12/01/1998 to holders of record 11/02/1998; 5% payable 12/01/1999 to holders of record 11/01/1999; 5% payable 12/01/2000 to holders of record 11/01/2000; 5% payable 12/03/2001 to holders of record 11/01/2001; 5% payable 12/02/2002 to holders of record 11/01/2002 Ex date - 10/30/2002; 5% payable 12/01/2003 to holders of record 11/03/2003 Ex date - 11/04/2003; 5% payable 12/01/2004 to holders of record 11/01/2004 Ex date - 11/01/2004; 5% payable 12/01/2005 to holders of record 11/01/2005 Ex date - 11/03/2005; 5% payable 12/01/2006 to holders of record 11/01/2006 Ex date - 11/06/2006; 5% payable 12/17/2007 to holders of record 12/03/2007 Ex date - 12/10/2007
Merged into BNC Bancorp 10/01/2013
Each share Common no par exchanged for (0.50221828) share Common no par and $4.22737605 cash
BNC Bancorp merged into Pinnacle Financial Partners, Inc. 06/16/2017

RANDOLPH COMPUTER CORP (DE)
Common $1 par split (2) for (1) by issuance of (1) additional share 5/26/67
Merged into Travelers Corp. 11/7/69
Each share Common $1 par exchanged for (1.25) shares Common $2.50 par
Travelers Corp. merged into Travelers Inc. 12/31/93 which name changed to Travelers Group Inc. 4/16/95 which name changed to Citigroup Inc. 10/8/98

RANDOLPH NATL BK (RANDOLPH, VT)
Reorganized as Central Financial Corp. 03/30/1986
Each share Common $10 par exchanged for (5) shares Common $2 par
Central Financial Corp. merged into New Hampshire Thrift Bancshares, Inc. 10/25/2013 which name changed to Lake Sunapee Bank Group 06/01/2015 which merged into Bar Harbor Bankshares 01/13/2017

RANDOLPH WELLS BLDG CORP (IL)
Voluntarily dissolved 2/21/86
No stockholders' equity

RANDOM ACCESS INC (CO)
Each share old Common $0.0001 par exchanged for (0.1) share new Common $0.0001 par 8/1/88
Each share new Common $0.0001

par exchanged again for (0.5) share new Common $0.0001 par 6/29/93
Merged into Entex Information Services, Inc. 9/20/95
Each share new Common $0.0001 par exchanged for $3.25 cash

RANDOM HOUSE, INC. (NY)
Common $1 par split (4) for (3) by issuance of (1/3) additional share 7/18/61
Merged into Radio Corp. of America 5/19/66
Each share Common $1 par exchanged for (0.62) share Common no par
Radio Corp. of America name changed to RCA Corp. 5/9/69
(See RCA Corp.)

RANDONA QUEBEC GOLD MINES LTD. (ON)
Reorganized as Larandona Mines, Ltd. in 1952
Each share Capital Stock no par exchanged for (1/3) share Capital Stock no par
Larandona Mines, Ltd. charter cancelled 4/9/75

RANDSBURG GOLD CORP (BC)
Recapitalized as Randsburg International Gold Corp. 12/30/97
Each share Common no par exchanged for (0.2) share Common no par

RANDSTAD HLDG NV (NETHERLANDS)
Name changed to Randstad N.V. 04/26/2018

RANDSTROM MFG CORP (BC)
Name changed to Francisco Gold Corp. 1/18/94
Francisco Gold Corp. merged into Glamis Gold Ltd. 7/16/2002 which merged into Goldcorp Inc. (New) 11/4/2006

RANDY GROUP LTD (DE)
Merged into International Freight Holding Corp. 12/23/85
Each share Common 2¢ par exchanged for $6 cash

RANDY INDS INC (DE)
Charter cancelled and declared inoperative and void for non-payment of taxes 4/15/71

RANDY INTERNATIONAL LTD. (DE)
Stock Dividend - 10% 4/15/75
Name changed to Randy Group Ltd. 4/26/79
(See Randy Group Ltd.)

RANES INTL HLDGS INC (NV)
Each share old Common $0.001 par exchanged for (1) share new Common $0.001 par 04/17/1998
Name changed to Whatsforfree Technologies Inc. 01/10/2000
Whatsforfree Technologies Inc. recapitalized as Krifter Holdings Inc. 04/18/2005
(See Krifter Holdings Inc.)

RANGAIRE CORP (TX)
Common 10¢ par split (3) for (2) by issuance of (0.5) additional share 2/5/87
Stock Dividends - 25% 5/25/73; 10% 3/19/76; 25% 11/29/76; 25% 7/29/77; 10% 3/17/78
Name changed to Scottish Heritable, Inc., 2/7/90
Scottish Heritable, Inc. name changed to United States Lime & Minerals Inc. 1/25/94

RANGE CAP CORP NEW (BC)
Name changed to Open Gold Corp. 11/08/2010
Open Gold Corp. recapitalized as betterU Education Corp. (BC) 03/08/2017 which reincorporated in Canada 10/13/2017

RANGE CAP CORP OLD (BC)
Merged into Range Capital Corp. (New) 08/06/2009
Each share Common no par exchanged for (0.72) share Common no par
Range Capital Corp. (New) name changed to Open Gold Corp. 11/08/2010 which recapitalized as betterU Education Corp. (BC) 03/08/2017 which reincorporated in Canada 10/13/2017

RANGE ENERGY INC (BC)
Cease trade order effective 03/07/2003
Stockholders' equity unlikely

RANGE ENERGY RES INC OLD (BC)
Name changed to Hawkstone Energy Corp. 09/01/2011
Hawkstone Energy Corp. name changed to Range Energy Resources Inc. (New) 11/17/2011

RANGE INDS LTD (BC)
Adjudicated bankrupt 02/23/1976
No stockholders' equity

RANGE METALS INC (BC)
Each share Common no par received distribution of (0.5) share Range Gold Corp. Common no par payable 04/30/2008 to holders of record 04/30/2008
Name changed to Range Energy Resources Inc. (Old) 01/13/2010
Range Energy Resources Inc. (Old) name changed to Hawkstone Energy Corp. 09/01/2011 which name changed to Range Energy Resources Inc. (New) 11/17/2011

RANGE PETE CORP (BC)
Recapitalized as Range Energy Inc. 05/15/2002
Each share Common no par exchanged for (1/6) share Common no par
(See Range Energy Inc.)

RANGE RES CORP (DE)
144A Conv. Exchangeable Preferred called for redemption on 12/20/2001 (Additional Information in Active)

RANGE RES LTD (AUSTRALIA)
Each Unsponsored ADR for Ordinary exchanged for (1) old Sponsored ADR for Ordinary 04/19/2010
Each old Sponsored ADR for Ordinary exchanged for (0.025) new Sponsored ADR for Ordinary 02/28/2012
Basis changed from (1:1) to (1:40) 02/28/2012
ADR agreement terminated 08/07/2017
Each new Sponsored ADR for Ordinary exchanged for $0.025466 cash

RANGE VENTURES INC (NV)
Reorganized under the laws of Wyoming as American Eagle Industries Inc. 07/03/1989
Each share Common $0.001 par exchanged for (0.125) share Common $0.001 par
(See American Eagle Industries, Inc.)

RANGEFORD RES CORP (NV)
Name changed to Rangeford Resources, Inc. 04/03/2014

RANGELAND RES LTD (AB)
Merged into Deena Energy Inc. 3/6/97
Each share Common no par exchanged for $1.60 cash

RANGELEY POWER CO. (ME)
Merged into Central Maine Power Co. 6/30/76
Each share 6% Preferred Ser. A $25 par exchanged for $27.8123 cash
Each share 6% Conv. Preferred Ser. B $100 par exchanged for (11.0493) shares Common $5 par
Each share Common $100 par exchanged for (11.0493) shares Common $5 par

RANGELEY SADDLEBACK CORP. (ME)
Company foreclosed by mortgagee, no stockholders' equity and charter suspended for non-payment of taxes 00/00/1966

RANGELY OIL & GAS CO. (CO)
Merged into West Toledo Mines Co. 07/00/1963
Each share Common 50¢ par exchanged for (2) shares Common 10¢ par
West Toledo Mines Co. merged into Toledo Mining Co. 09/19/1968 which name changed to Toledo Technology, Inc. 03/26/1984 which recapitalized as HIPP International Inc. 08/31/1994 which name changed to Assembly & Manufacturing Systems Corp. 04/12/1995 which recapitalized as American Ship Inc. 09/05/1997 which name changed to Petshealth, Inc. 05/20/1998
(See Petshealth, Inc.)

RANGEMORE FILM PRODUCTIONS CORP (NV)
Recapitalized as Cre8tive Works, Inc. 01/16/2014
Each share Common $0.001 par exchanged for (0.004) share Common $0.001 par
Cre8tive Works, Inc. name changed to Optium Cyber Systems, Inc. 10/03/2017

RANGER AMERS INC (DE)
Charter forfeited for failure to maintain a registered agent 8/31/90

RANGER-COMANCHE OIL CO. (DE)
Charter cancelled and declared inoperative and void for non-payment of taxes 3/18/25

RANGER ENERGY LTD (AB)
Reorganized under the laws of Ontario as North Sea Energy Inc. 10/21/2011
Each share Common no par exchanged for (0.1) share Common no par

RANGER EXTENTION OIL & GAS CO., INC. (VA)
Charter revoked and annulled 00/00/1923

RANGER INDS INC (CT)
SEC revoked common stock registration 10/30/2008
Stockholders' equity unlikely

RANGER INTL INC (FL)
Each share Class B Common 2¢ par exchanged for (0.25) share Common 2¢ par 8/10/94
Recapitalized as Imagica Entertainment, Inc. 6/1/96
Each share Common 2¢ par exchanged for (0.125) share Common 2¢ par
Imagica Entertainment, Inc. recapitalized as Broadcast Marketing Group, Inc. 5/27/2005

RANGER LAKE URANIUM CO. LTD. (DE)
Merged into Century Mining & Development Corp. on a (1) for (2) basis 07/09/1956
Century Mining & Development Corp. name changed to Century Industries, Inc. 12/17/1959 which recapitalized as 20th Century Industries, Inc. 10/11/1961
(See 20th Century Industries, Inc.)

RANGER OIL LTD (CANADA)
Name changed 06/30/1980
Common no par split (2) for (1) by issuance of (1) additional share 08/21/1978
Common no par split (2) for (1) by issuance of (1) additional share 12/28/1979
Name and place of incorporation changed from Ranger Oil (Canada) Ltd. (ON) to Ranger Oil Ltd. (Canada) 06/30/1980
9.25% Retractable Preference Ser. A no par called for redemption 04/01/1991
Common no par split (3) for (1) by issuance of (2) additional shares 11/24/1980
Merged into Canadian Natural Resources Ltd. 07/28/2000
Each share Common no par exchanged for either (0.05609) share Common no par and $5.605755 cash, or (0.175) share Common no par
Note: Option to receive stock only expired 08/21/2000

RANGER RED LAKE MINES, LTD. (ON)
Charter cancelled for failure to file reports and pay taxes in 1953

RANGER RUBBER CO., INC. (DE)
No longer in existence having become inoperative and void for non-payment of taxes 3/21/23

RANGER/USA INC (DE)
Name changed to First Capital International Inc. 08/31/1998
(See First Capital International Inc.)

RANGER WIRELESS CORP (NV)
Name changed to International Ranger Corp. 07/14/2005

RANGESTAR TELECOMMUNICATIONS LTD (BC)
Cease trade order effective 11/3/99
Stockholders' equity unlikely

RANGO ENERGY INC (NV)
Name changed to Verde Science, Inc. 05/07/2014

RANK CINTEL LTD. (ENGLAND)
Name changed to Bush & Rank Cintel Ltd. 10/06/1960
Bush & Rank Cintel Ltd. name changed to Rank Radio & Television Ltd. 12/03/1962
(See Rank Radio & Television Ltd.)

RANK GROUP PLC (UNITED KINGDOM)
ADR agreement terminated 08/31/2005
Each Sponsored ADR for Ordinary 10p par exchanged for $10.604012 cash

RANK ORGANISATION PUB LTD CO (ENGLAND)
A Ordinary Reg. 25p par (English Register) and A Ordinary Reg. 25p par (Canadian Register) reclassified as Ordinary Reg. 25p par respectively 03/17/1976
ADR's for A Ordinary Reg. reclassified as ADR's for Ordinary Reg. 03/17/1976
Stock Dividends - A Ordinary Reg. (English Register) 10% 10/06/1960 - A Ordinary Reg. (Canadian Register) - 10% 10/06/1960 - ADR's for Ordinary Reg. and ADR's for A Ordinary Reg. - 100% 05/29/1964 - A Ordinary Reg. - 100% 04/30/1973 - Ordinary Reg. - 100% 04/30/1973 - Ordinary Reg. - 100% 10/07/1973; 100% 05/02/1973 - ADR's for A Ordinary Reg. - 100% 05/02/1973
Acquired by Rank Group PLC 10/07/1996
Details not available

RANK RADIO & TELEVISION LTD. (ENGLAND)
Acquired by Rank Organisation Ltd. 12/16/1963
Each share received 35s cash
Note: Certificates were not required to be surrendered and are without value

RANKIN AUTOMOTIVE GROUP INC (LA)
Chapter 11 bankruptcy proceedings dismissed 06/05/2001
Stockholders' equity unlikely

RANKIN CENTURY CORP. (MS)
Liquidation completed
Each share Common $10 par exchanged for initial distribution of $35 cash 9/10/87
Each share Common $10 par received second distribution of $20 cash 11/11/87
Each share Common $10 par received third distribution of $2 cash 12/13/88
Each share Common $10 par received fourth and final distribution of $1.695914 cash 5/17/90

RANKIN COUNTY BANK (BRANDON, MS)
Reorganized as Rankin Century Corp. 5/24/85
Each share Common $10 par exchanged for (1) share Common $10 par
(See Rankin Century Corp.)

RANKIN INLET NICKEL MINES LTD. (ON)
Recapitalized as North Rankin Nickel Mines Ltd. on a (1) for (2) basis in 1954
North Rankin Nickel Mines Ltd. recapitalized as Tontine Mining Ltd. 2/23/70 which merged into Coldstream Mines Ltd. 1/13/72
(See Coldstream Mines Ltd.)

RANKIN RES INC (BC)
Recapitalized as Delta International Industries Corp. 03/15/1999
Each share Common no par exchanged for (0.25) share Common no par
Delta International Industries Corp. recapitalized as Delta Exploration Inc. 12/12/2003 which merged into Rockgate Capital Corp. 01/30/2009 which merged into Denison Mines Corp. 01/20/2014

RANNEY REFRIGERATOR CO (MI)
Common $2.50 par split (2) for (1) by issuance of (1) additional share 02/15/1966
Name changed to Randisco, Inc. 01/30/1970
Randisco, Inc. liquidated for Fedders Corp. (NY) 01/30/1970 which reincorporated in Delaware 01/02/1985
(See Fedders Corp.)

RANREX BERYLLIUM, INC. (NV)
Merged into Ranrex, Inc. 8/16/71
Each share Capital Stock 15¢ par exchanged for (0.05) share Common 5¢ par
Ranrex, Inc. merged into Argus Resources, Inc. (NV) 12/27/72 which reincorporated in Delaware as 1st Global Petroleum Group, Inc. 3/31/2005 which name changed to Commonwealth American Financial Group, Inc. 5/13/2005 which name changed to James Monroe Capital Corp. 5/30/2006

RANREX INC (NV)
Merged into Argus Resources, Inc. (NV) 12/27/72
Each share Common 5¢ par exchanged for (0.02) share Common 20¢ par
Argus Resources, Inc. (NV) reincorporated in Delaware as 1st Global Petroleum Group, Inc. 3/31/2005 which name changed to Commonwealth American Financial Group, Inc. 5/13/2005 which name changed to James Monroe Capital Corp. 5/30/2006

RANREX OIL & MINING CO. (NV)
Recapitalized as Ranrex Beryllium, Inc. 4/29/60

RAN-RAP

Each share Common $0.025 par exchanged for (1/6) share Capital Stock 15¢ par
Ranrex Beryllium, Inc. merged into Ranrex, Inc. 8/16/71 which merged into Argus Resources, Inc. (NV) 12/27/72 which reincorporated in Delaware as 1st Global Petroleum Group, Inc. 3/31/2005 which name changed to Commonwealth American Financial Group, Inc. 5/13/2005 which name changed to James Monroe Capital Corp. 5/30/2006

RANROUYN MINES, LTD. (ON)
Charter cancelled 9/28/64

RANSBURG CORP (IN)
Common 15¢ par split (2) for (1) by issuance of (1) additional share 12/1/80
Stock Dividend - 50% 12/3/79
Merged into Illinois Tool Works Inc. 4/3/89
Each share Common 15¢ par exchanged for $21 cash

RANSBURG ELECTRO-COATING CORP. (IN)
Name changed to Ransburg Corp. 4/20/72
(See Ransburg Corp.)

RANSOM RES LTD (BC)
Name changed to Indescor Hydrodynamics Inc. 12/04/1984
Indescor Hydrodynamics Inc. recapitalized as Consolidated Indescor Corp. 12/11/1985
(See Consolidated Indescor Corp.)

RANTEC CORP. (CA)
Merged into Emerson Electric Manufacturing Co. 8/9/63
Each (2.35) shares Common no par exchanged for (1) share $1 Conv. Preferred Ser. A $5 par
Emerson Electric Manufacturing Co. name changed to Emerson Electric Co. 2/6/64

RANWICK URANIUM MINES LTD. (ON)
Recapitalized as Consolidated Ranwick Uranium Mines Ltd. 11/00/1953
Each share Capital Stock $1 par exchanged for (0.2) share Capital Stock $1 par
Consolidated Ranwick Uranium Mines Ltd. name changed to International Ranwick Ltd. 06/29/1955 which name changed to International Molybdenum Mines Ltd. 08/00/1959 which merged into Pax International Mines Ltd. 01/31/1962 which recapitalized as Geo-Pax Mines Ltd. 09/00/1968
(See Geo-Pax Mines Ltd.)

RAO GAZPROM (RUSSIA)
Name changed to Gazprom OAO 09/14/1999
Gazprom OAO name changed to Gazprom PJSC 02/03/2016

RAP ACQUISITION CORP (CANADA)
Reincorporated 05/13/2011
Place of incorporation changed from (BC) to (Canada) 05/13/2011
Recapitalized as Ferrum Americas Mining Inc. 12/09/2011
Each share Common no par exchanged for (0.2) share Common no par
Ferrum Americas Mining Inc. recapitalized as Toachi Mining Inc. 03/14/2016

RAP-IN-WAX CO. (MN)
Name changed to Rap Industries, Inc. 08/15/1961
Rap Industries, Inc. liquidated by exchange for Champion Papers, Inc. 01/31/1965 which merged into U.S. Plywood-Champion Papers Inc. 02/28/1967 which name changed to Champion International Corp. 05/12/1972 which merged into International Paper Co. 06/20/2000

RAP INDUSTRIES, INC. (MN)
Completely liquidated 01/31/1965
Each share Common or Class A Common $1 par exchanged for (0.2) share Champion Papers, Inc. Common no par
Champion Papers merged into U.S. Plywood-Champion Papers Inc. 02/28/1967 which name changed to Champion International Corp. 05/12/1972 which merged into International Paper Co. 06/20/2000

RAPA MNG INC (NV)
Each share old Common $0.001 par exchanged for (7) shares new Common $0.001 par 02/18/2005
Name changed to Clyvia, Inc. 09/01/2005
(See Clyvia, Inc.)

RAPHAEL INDS LTD (NV)
Common $0.0001 par split (2) for (1) by issuance of (1) additional share payable 03/17/2010 to holders of record 03/12/2010 Ex date - 03/18/2010
Name changed to Sino American Oil Co. 12/14/2010

RAPHAEL WEILL & CO. (NV)
See - Weill (Raphael) & Co.

RAPHOLZ SILVER INC (FL)
Recapitalized as 8888 Acquisition Corp. (FL) 6/26/2006
Each share Common $0.0001 par exchanged for (0.1) share Common $0.0001 par
8888 Acquisition Corp. (FL) reincorporated in Nevada 7/18/2006

RAPID AMERN CORP (DE)
Class C Contingent Preference Ser. 6 no par called for redemption 02/28/1973
Class C Contingent Preference Ser. 7 no par called for redemption 02/28/1974
$2.25 Conv. Jr. Preferred $2 par called for redemption 10/31/1980
Under plan of merger each share $3 Preference no par or Common $1 par exchanged for $45 principal amount of 10% Subordinated Debentures due 08/01/2006 and $3 cash 01/31/1981
Each share Common $1 par received additional distribution of $0.25 cash 08/00/1981
$3 Class B Sr. Conv. Preferred no par called for redemption 03/02/1981
$3.15 Conv. Preferred no par called for redemption 03/02/1981

RAPID AMERN CORP (OH)
Common $1 par split (3) for (2) by issuance of (0.5) additional share 5/16/60
Each share 75¢ Conv. Preferred $1 par exchanged for (1/3) share $2.25 Conv. Preferred $2 par 11/20/67
Merged into Rapid-American Corp. (DE) 11/6/72
Each share $2.25 Conv. Preferred $2 par exchanged for (1) share $2.25 Conv. Jr. Preferred $2 par
Each share Common $1 par exchanged for (1) share Common $1 par
(See Rapid-American Corp. (DE))

RAPID BIO TESTS CORP (NV)
Name changed to Bio-Warm Corp. 12/15/2004
Each share Common $0.001 par exchanged for (1) share Common $0.001 par
Bio-Warm Corp. recapitalized as DDC Industries, Inc. 04/23/2007 which name changed to PHI Mining Group, Inc. 12/19/2008 which name changed to PHI Gold Corp. 01/28/2011

RAPID BRANDS INC (BC)
Name changed to RAP Acquisition Corp. (BC) 08/27/2010
RAP Acquisition Corp. (BC) reincorporated in Canada 05/13/2011 which recapitalized as Ferrum Americas Mining Inc. 12/09/2011 which recapitalized as Toachi Mining Inc. 03/14/2016

RAPID CDN RESOURCE CORP (BC)
Name changed to Pan-Global Enterprises Inc. 01/15/1993
Pan-Global Enterprises Inc. recapitalized as Pan-Global Ventures Ltd. 03/07/2002 which name changed to Pan-Global Energy Ltd. 11/12/2003 which merged into Pearl Exploration & Production Ltd. which name changed to BlackPearl Resources Inc. 05/14/2009

RAPID CITY BLACK HILLS & WESTERN RAILROAD CO. (SD)
Charter expired by time limitation 2/20/59

RAPID CITY NATIONAL BANK (RAPID CITY, SD)
Stock Dividends - 20% 07/23/1958; 33-1/3% 05/29/1959
Name changed to American National Bank (Rapid City, SD) 12/30/1960
American National Bank (Rapid City, SD) merged into American National Bank & Trust Co. (Rapid City, SD) 08/31/1962 which merged into First Bank System, Inc. 01/04/1968 which name changed to U.S. Bancorp 08/01/1997

RAPID DATA SYS & EQUIP LTD (CANADA)
6% Conv. Preferred $7.25 par called for redemption 5/24/72
Placed in receivership 1/31/74
No stockholders' equity

RAPID DEPLOYMENT PARACHUTE CORP (DE)
Recapitalized as Communication Technology Companies Inc. 10/19/95
Each share Common $0.001 par exchanged for (0.02) share Common $0.001 par
Communication Technology Companies Inc. recapitalized as Turquoise Development Co. 2/17/2006

RAPID ELECTROTYPE CO. (OH)
Common no par changed to $1 par and (1) additional share issued 1/31/56
Common $1 par split (2) for (1) by issuance of (1) additional share 2/1/57
Under plan of merger name changed to Rapid-American Corp. (OH) 12/31/57
Rapid-American Corp. (OH) merged into Rapid-American Corp. (DE) 11/6/72
(See Rapid-American Corp. (DE))

RAPID FILM TECHNIQUE, INC. (NY)
Completely liquidated 6/18/68
Each share Common 10¢ par exchanged for first and final distribution of (0.51066386) share Esquire, Inc. Common $1 par
(See Esquire, Inc.)

RAPID FITNESS INC (NV)
Name changed to Tri-Star Holdings Inc. 08/27/2008
Tri-Star Holdings Inc. recapitalized as Macada Holding, Inc. (NV) 08/20/2009 which reincorporated in Wyoming 02/22/2011 which recapitalized as KMA Holding, Inc. 03/17/2011
(See KMA Holding, Inc.)

RAPID GRIP & BATTEN LTD (CANADA)
Each share Common received (1) share 60¢ Class A 07/10/1961
Name changed to Bomac Batten Ltd.-Bomac Batten Ltee. 06/23/1972
Bomac Batten Ltd.-Bomac Batten Ltee. name changed to Principal Neo-Tech Inc. 05/02/1984 which name changed to Laird Group Inc. 07/15/1988 which merged into Printera Corp. 11/22/1996
(See Printera Corp.)

RAPID HLDGS INC (NV)
Name changed to IZEA Holdings, Inc. 06/01/2011
IZEA Holdings, Inc. name changed to IZEA Inc. 02/22/2012 which name changed to IZEA Worldwide, Inc. 08/23/2018

RAPID LINK INC (DE)
Name changed to Spot Mobile International Ltd. 06/10/2010
(See Spot Mobile International Ltd.)

RAPID RECOVERY HEALTH SVCS INC (NV)
Recapitalized as Tennalta Petroleum Corp. 02/02/2007
Each share Common $0.001 par exchanged for (0.01) share Common $0.001 par
Tennalta Petroleum Corp. recapitalized as GRIT International Groups Inc. 07/10/2007 which recapitalized as GRIT International Inc. 12/23/2008

RAPID RESOURCE CORP (AB)
Struck off register and declared dissolved for failure to file reports 3/1/96

RAPID RETRIEVAL SYS INC (NV)
Each share old Common $0.001 par exchanged for (0.1) share new Common $0.001 par 08/05/2000
Name changed to Eline Music.com Inc. 02/01/2001
Eline Music.com Inc. name changed to Eline Entertainment Group, Inc. (NV) 04/25/2001 which reincorporated in Wyoming 06/21/2017

RAPID RIVER RES (AB)
Recapitalized as Consolidated Rapid River Resources Ltd. 8/1/75
Each share Capital Stock no par exchanged for (1/3) share Capital Stock no par
(See Consolidated Rapid River Resources Ltd.)

RAPID SHOP CORP (MN)
Name changed to Great San Francisco Seafood Inc. 11/16/81
(See Great San Francisco Seafood Inc.)

RAPID SOLUTIONS CORP (AB)
Company's assets foreclosed upon 09/25/2009
Stockholders' equity unlikely

RAPID TRANSIT STREET RAILWAY CO. (NJ)
Acquired by Public Service Coordinated Transport through an exchange of old stock for an equal par amount of both 5-3/4% and 6% Bonds in 1940

RAPIDAIR FGHT (CA)
Recapitalized as PHI Enterprises, Inc. 07/22/1983
Each share Common 1¢ par exchanged for (0.5) share Common no par
(See PHI Enterprises, Inc.)

RAPIDAN SILVER MINES CORP (NV)
Merged into Lloyd's Acceptance Corp. 12/23/86
Each share Capital Stock 1¢ par exchanged for (0.5) share Common 10¢ par
Lloyd's Acceptance Corp.

recapitalized as Latrobe Corp. 7/21/97

RAPIDATA INC (NY)
Common 1¢ par split (2) for (1) by issuance of (1) additional share 8/1/72
Merged into National Data Corp. 12/31/81
Each share Common 1¢ par exchanged for (0.8) share Common $0.125 par
National Data Corp. name changed to NDCHealth Corp. 10/25/2001 which merged into Per-Se Technologies, Inc. 1/6/2006
(See Per-Se Technologies, Inc.)

RAPIDEK INDS INC (FL)
Proclaimed dissolved for failure to file reports and pay fees 12/11/1976

RAPIDES BK & TR CO (ALEXANDRIA, LA)
Each share Capital Stock $50 par exchanged for (5) shares Capital Stock $10 par 10/14/52
Stock Dividends - 500% 10/14/52; 33-1/3% 12/30/55
Merged into First Commerce Corp. 7/2/85
Each share Capital Stock $10 par exchanged for $60 principal amount of 12-3/4% Conv. Debentures Ser. B due 7/2/2000 and $5 cash

RAPIDFIRE RES LTD (AB)
Assets sold for the benefit of creditors 00/00/2004
No stockholders' equity

RAPIDOIL, INC. (SD)
Completely liquidated in August 1967
Each share Capital Stock 5¢ par received first and final distribution of $0.002649384 cash
Certificates were not retired and are now without value

RAPIDTRON INC (NV)
Reincorporated under the laws of Delaware 5/8/2003

RAPIER GOLD INC (BC)
Merged into GFG Resources Inc. 02/28/2018
Each share Common no par exchanged for (0.15) share Common no par
Note: Unexchanged certificates will be cancelled and become without value 02/28/2024

RAPISTAN INC (MI)
Merged into Lear Siegler, Inc. 01/04/1980
Each share Common $1 par exchanged for $145.27 cash

RAPITECH SYS INC (NY)
Dissolved by proclamation 6/23/99

RAPOCA ENERGY CORP (KY)
Merged into Field Resources, Inc. 01/26/1976
Each share Common no par exchanged for $10 cash

RAPPAHANNOCK BANKSHARES INC (VA)
Merged into Union Bankshares Corp. 07/01/1998
Each share Common $100 par exchanged for (316.418) shares Common $4 par
Union Bankshares Corp. name changed to Union First Market Bankshares Corp. 02/01/2010 which name changed to Union Bankshares Corp. 04/28/2014

RAPPAREE RES LTD (AB)
Name changed to General Fasteners Inc. 08/10/1990
(See General Fasteners Inc.)

RAPTOR CAP CORP (AB)
Recapitalized as Valparaiso Energy Inc. (AB) 02/26/2009
Each share Common no par exchanged for (0.05) share Common no par
Valparaiso Energy Inc. (AB) reincorporated in British Columbia as Catalina Gold Corp. 02/06/2017

RAPTOR INVTS INC (FL)
Reincorporated 12/04/2001
State of incorporation changed from (DE) to (FL) 12/04/2001
Name changed to Snap 'N' Sold Corp. 07/22/2005
Snap 'N' Sold Corp. name changed to Hot Web, Inc. 09/25/2006 which name changed to Gold Coast Mining Corp. 07/02/2009 which name changed to Green Leaf Innovations, Inc. 03/10/2015

RAPTOR NETWORKS TECHNOLOGY INC (CO)
Reorganized under the laws of Wyoming as Mabwe Minerals Inc. 06/28/2012
Each share Common $0.001 par exchanged for (0.1) share Common $0.001 par
Mabwe Minerals Inc. (WY) reorganized in Delaware as Fonon Corp. 07/29/2015

RAPTOR PHARMACEUTICAL CORP (DE)
Acquired by Horizon Pharma PLC 10/25/2016
Each share Common $0.001 par exchanged for $9 cash

RAPTOR PHARMACEUTICALS CORP (DE)
Merged into Raptor Pharmaceutical Corp. 09/29/2009
Each share Common $0.001 par exchanged for (0.2331234) share Common $0.001 par
(See Raptor Pharmaceutical Corp.)

RAPTOR SYS INC (DE)
Merged into Axent Technologies, Inc. 2/5/98
Each share Common 1¢ par exchanged for (0.8) share Common 2¢ par
Axent Technologies, Inc. merged into Symantec Corp. 12/18/2000

RAPTOR TECHNOLOGY GROUP INC (NV)
SEC revoked common stock registration 10/10/2014

RAQUEL INC (NV)
Recapitalized as Xynergy Corp. 02/15/2002
Each share Common $0.0001 par exchanged for (0.01) share Common $0.001 par
Xynergy Corp. name changed to Xynergy Holdings, Inc. 09/11/2008

RARA TERRA CAP CORP (BC)
Name changed to Rara Terra Minerals Corp. 05/06/2011
Rara Terra Minerals Corp. name changed to Echelon Petroleum Corp. 05/08/2013 which name changed to Trenchant Capital Corp. 05/10/2016

RARA TERRA MINERALS CORP (BC)
Name changed to Echelon Petroleum Corp. 05/08/2013
Echelon Petroleum Corp. name changed to Trenchant Capital Corp. 05/10/2016

RARE EARTH INDS LTD (CANADA)
Recapitalized as Ackroo Inc. 10/10/2012
Each share Common no par exchanged for (0.4) share Common no par

RARE EARTH METALS CORP (BC)
Each share Common no par received distribution of (0.33333333) share Harvest Gold Corp. Common no par payable 12/13/2005 to holders of record 10/14/2005
Name changed to VMS Ventures, Inc. 01/18/2007
VMS Ventures, Inc. merged into Royal Nickel Corp. 04/28/2016

RARE EARTH METALS INC (BC)
Name changed to Canada Rare Earth Corp. 02/08/2013

RARE EARTH METALS INC (FL)
Reorganized under the laws of Delaware as Americare Health Group Inc. 03/03/1993
Each share Common $0.0001 par exchanged for (0.5) share Common $0.0002 par
Americare Health Group Inc. name changed to Zagreus Inc. 03/26/1999

RARE EARTH MINERALS PLC (ENGLAND & WALES)
Name changed to Cadence Minerals PLC 10/21/2016

RARE EARTH MINING CO. LTD. (ON)
Merged into Amalgamated Rare Earth Mines Ltd. 5/27/57
Each share Capital Stock $1 par exchanged for (0.25) share Common $1 par and (0.4) share Consolidated Halo Uranium Mines Ltd. Capital Stock $1 par
(See each company's listing)

RARE EARTH MINING CORP. OF CANADA LTD. (ON)
Acquired by Rare Earth Mining Co. Ltd. share for share 3/5/56 which merged into Amalgamated Rare Earth Mines Ltd. 5/27/57
(See Amalgamated Rare Earth Mines Ltd.)

RARE EARTH RES LTD (BERMUDA)
Reincorporated in 1995
Place of incorporation changed from (BC) to (Bermuda) in 1995
Name changed to Resource Finance & Investment Ltd. 7/17/97

RARE EARTH RES LTD (ON)
Name changed to Golden Earth Resources Inc. 5/22/84
Golden Earth Resources Inc. merged into Health & Environment Technologies Inc. 5/3/89
(See Health & Environment Technologies Inc.)

RARE HOSPITALITY INTL INC (GA)
Common no par split (3) for (2) by issuance of (0.5) additional share payable 09/05/2000 to holders of record 08/15/2000
Common no par split (3) for (2) by issuance of (0.5) additional share payable 09/02/2003 to holders of record 08/12/2003 Ex date - 09/03/2003
Merged into Darden Restaurants, Inc. 10/01/2007
Each share Common no par exchanged for $38.15 cash

RARE MEDIUM GROUP INC (DE)
Each share old Common 1¢ par exchanged for (0.1) share new Common 1¢ par 07/18/2002
Name changed to SkyTerra Communications, Inc. 09/26/2003
(See SkyTerra Communications, Inc.)

RARE METALS CORP. OF AMERICA (DE)
Merged into El Paso Natural Gas Co. 07/09/1962
Details not available

RAREMETHOD CAP CORP (AB)
Name changed to Rare Method Interactive Corp. 12/12/2006

RAREMETHOD CAP INC (AB)
Name changed to RareMethod Capital Corp. 1/15/2002
RareMethod Capital Corp. name changed to Rare Method Interactive Corp. 12/12/2006

RARITAN BANCORP INC (DE)
Common 1¢ par split (3) for (2) by issuance of (0.5) additional share 12/1/93
Common 1¢ par split (3) for (2) by issuance of (0.5) additional share payable 7/1/97 to holders of record 6/10/97
Merged into United National Bancorp 3/31/99
Each share Common 1¢ par exchanged for (1.595) shares Common $2.50 par
(See United National Bancorp)

RARITAN PLASTICS CORP (NJ)
Assets sold for benefit of creditors 07/31/1972
No stockholders' equity

RARITAN VY FINL CORP (NJ)
Common 66-2/3¢ par split (2) for (1) by issuance of (1) additional share 00/00/1981
Merged into Hansen Merger Corp. 01/15/1986
Each share Common 66-2/3¢ par exchanged for $22.40 cash

RARITAN VALLEY NATL BK (EDISON, NJ)
Reorganized as Midlantic Banks Inc. 06/12/1970
Each share Common $10 par exchanged for (1.2) shares Common $10 par
Midlantic Banks Inc. merged into Midlantic Corp. 01/30/1987 which merged into PNC Bank Corp. 12/31/1995 which name changed to PNC Financial Services Group, Inc. 03/15/2000

RARITAN VY SVGS & LN ASSN EAST BRUNSWICK (NJ)
Merged into Raritan Valley Financial Corp. 08/25/1981
Each share Capital Stock 66-2/3¢ par exchanged for (2) shares Common 66-2/3¢ par
(See Raritan Valley Financial Corp.)

RARUS MINERALS INC (NV)
Name changed to Rarus Technologies Inc. 02/08/2012

RASA INVTS INC (CANADA)
Name changed to Fortune 1000 Group Inc. 08/16/2004
Fortune 1000 Group Inc. name changed to Fortsum Business Solutions Inc. 01/10/2006
(See Fortsum Business Solutions Inc.)

RASCALS INTL INC (DE)
Each share old Common $0.0001 par exchanged for (0.002) share new Common $0.0001 par 03/31/2003
Name changed to Headliners Entertainment Group, Inc. 06/02/2004
(See Headliners Entertainment Group, Inc.)

RASCALS UNLIMITED INC (DE)
Charter cancelled and declared inoperative and void for non-payment of taxes 3/1/94

RASER TECHNOLOGIES INC (DE)
Reincorporated 06/12/2007
State of incorporation changed from (UT) to (DE) 06/12/2007
Plan of reorganization under Chapter 11 Federal Bankruptcy proceedings effective 09/09/2011
No stockholders' equity

RASH-MAC EXPLORATIONS LTD. (ON)
Charter revoked for failure to file reports and pay fees 6/24/65

RASSCO PLANTATIONS LTD (ISRAEL)
Name changed to Pri-Or Ltd. 12/05/1969
(See Pri-Or Ltd.)

RASTER DEVICES CORP (MN)
Each share old Common 1¢ par

exchanged for (0.2) share new Common 1¢ par 12/04/1989
New Common 1¢ par split (3) for (2) by issuance of (0.5) additional share 06/22/1990
Name changed to Lasermaster Technologies, Inc. 06/22/1990
Lasermaster Technologies, Inc. name changed to Virtualfund.com, Inc. 04/01/1998 which recapitalized as ASFG, Inc. 08/11/2004

RASTER GRAPHICS INC (DE)
Merged into Gretag Imaging Group, Inc. 3/19/99
Each share Common $0.001 par exchanged for $1.2968 cash

RASTEROPS (CA)
Name changed to Truevision Inc. 10/30/95
Truevision Inc. merged into Pinnacle Systems, Inc. 3/12/99
Pinnacle Systems, Inc. merged into Avid Technology, Inc. 8/9/2005

RASTRA BLDG SYS INC (CO)
Each share old Common $0.00003 par exchanged for (0.1) share new Common $0.00003 par 03/26/1990
Name changed to Ener-Grid, Inc. 06/14/1995
(See Ener-Grid, Inc.)

RAT INTL MKTG LTD (BC)
Name changed 4/24/90
Name changed from Rat Resources Ltd. to Rat International (Marketing) Ltd. 4/24/90
Common no par split (2) for (1) by issuance of (1) additional share 4/30/90
Delisted from Vancouver Stock Exchange 6/20/2003

RATCHABURI ELECTRICITY GENERATING HLDG PUB CO LTD (THAILAND)
ADR agreement terminated 05/21/2018
No ADR's remain outstanding

RATEL CORP (TX)
Recapitalized as Lexxitt Life, Inc. 02/13/1991
Each share Common $0.0001 par exchanged for (0.025) share Common no par
Lexxitt Life, Inc. name changed to Replen-K Inc. 01/14/1992

RATEL GOLD LTD (BRITISH VIRGIN ISLANDS)
Each share Common no par received distribution of (0.55555555) share Ratel Group Ltd. Common no par payable 01/07/2011 to holders of record 01/06/2011 Ex date - 01/04/2011
Name changed to St. Augustine Gold & Copper Ltd. 01/21/2011

RATEL GROUP LTD (BRITISH VIRGIN ISLANDS)
Merged into RTG Mining Inc. 04/15/2013
Each share Ordinary exchanged for (1) share Ordinary

RATEX RESOURCES INC. (UT)
Each share Common 1¢ par exchanged for (0.1) share Common 10¢ par 8/10/85
Acquired by Frontier Acquisition Corp. 2/11/92
Each share Common 10¢ par exchanged for $0.1218 cash

RATEXCHANGE CORP (DE)
Name changed to MCF Corp. 07/22/2003
MCF Corp. name changed to Merriman Curhan Ford Group, Inc. 05/20/2008 which recapitalized as Merriman Holdings, Inc. 08/16/2010

RATH PACKING CO (IA)
Common $10 par changed to $1 par 07/03/1980

Stock Dividends - 40% 02/16/1942; 10% 01/16/1957
Name changed to Black Hawk Holdings, Inc. (IA) and Common $1 par changed to 1¢ par 12/30/1985
Black Hawk Holdings, Inc. (IA) reincorporated in Minnesota 10/09/1989 which name changed to Eagle Pacific Industries, Inc. 07/11/1995 which name changed to PW Eagle, Inc. 06/19/2000
(See PW Eagle, Inc.)

RATIONAL SOFTWARE CORP (DE)
Each share old Common 1¢ par exchanged for (1/3) share new Common 1¢ par 7/7/95
New Common 1¢ par split (2) for (1) by issuance of (1) additional share payable 9/10/96 to holders of record 8/27/96
New Common 1¢ par split (2) for (1) by issuance of (1) additional share payable 9/1/2000 to holders of record 8/17/2000 Ex date - 9/5/2000
Merged into IBM 2/21/2003
Each share new Common 1¢ par exchanged for $10.50 cash

RATLIFF DRILLING & EXPL CO (OK)
Assets liquidated 00/00/1990
No stockholders' equity

RATNERS GROUP PLC (UNITED KINGDOM)
Name changed to Signet Group PLC (United Kingdom) 09/10/1993
Signet Group PLC (United Kingdom) reorganized in Bermuda as Signet Jewelers Ltd. 09/11/2008

RATTLER RESOURCE LTD (BC)
Merged into Kensington Resources Ltd. 11/03/1993
Each share Common no par exchanged for (1) share Common no par
Kensington Resources Ltd. merged into Shore Gold Inc. 10/28/2005 which name changed to Star Diamond Corp. 02/12/2018

RATTLESNAKE GOLD INC (DE)
Recapitalized as Shadow Wood Corp. 09/05/1995
Each share Common $0.001 par exchanged for (0.05) share Common $0.001 par
Shadow Wood Corp. recapitalized as Magicworks Entertainment Inc. 07/24/1996 which merged into SFX Entertainment, Inc. 09/11/1998 which merged into Clear Channel Communications, Inc. 08/01/2000

RATTLESNAKE HLDG INC (DE)
Issue Information - 1,300,000 shares COM offered at $5.50 per share on 06/29/1995
Name changed to Spencer's Restaurants, Inc. 09/09/1999
Spencer's Restaurants, Inc. recapitalized as WSR Energy Resources Inc. 07/02/2001 which recapitalized as Biomass Resources Corp. 02/17/2006 which recapitalized as Eagle Resource Holdings, Inc. 05/31/2007

RATTLESNAKE VENTURES INC (ON)
Recapitalized as Minsud Resources Corp. 05/25/2011
Each share Common no par exchanged for (0.5) share Common no par

RAUCH INDS INC (NC)
Common $1 par split (3) for (2) by issuance of (0.5) additional share 6/5/92
Common $1 par split (3) for (2) by issuance of (0.5) additional share 11/5/93
Stock Dividend - 10% 6/15/84
Merged into Syratech Corp. 2/15/96
Each share Common $1 par exchanged for $13 cash

RAUMA OY (FINLAND)
Merged into Valmet Corp-Rauma Corp. 7/1/99
Each Sponsored ADR for Ordinary FIM10 par exchanged for (1.08917) Sponsored ADR's for Ordinary FIM10 par
Valmet Corp-Rauma Corp. name changed to Metso Corp. 8/24/99

RAUTARUUKKI OYJ (FINLAND)
ADR agreement terminated 04/20/2015
Each ADR for Ordinary exchanged for $2.39862 cash

RAVEN & BEACON HILL GOLD MINING CO. (WY)
Charter revoked for failure to file annual reports 7/19/27

RAVEN BIOFUELS INTL CORP (NV)
SEC revoked common stock registration 06/27/2012

RAVEN ENERGY LTD (AB)
Merged into TriStar Oil & Gas Ltd. (Old) 06/07/2006
Each share Common no par exchanged for (0.32) share Common no par
TriStar Oil & Gas Ltd. (Old) merged into TriStar Oil & Gas Ltd. (New) 08/16/2007 which merged into PetroBakken Energy Ltd. (Old) 10/05/2009 which reorganized as PetroBakken Energy Ltd. (New) 01/07/2013 which name changed to Lightstream Resources Ltd. 05/28/2013

RAVEN MOON ENTMT INC (FL)
Name changed 09/01/2001
Each share old Common $0.001 par exchanged for (0.1) share new Common $0.001 par 06/25/1999
New Common $0.001 par split (10) for (1) by issuance of (9) additional shares payable 02/15/2001 to holders of record 12/31/2000 Ex date - 02/16/2001
Name changed from Raven Moon International, Inc. to Raven Moon Entertainment, Inc. 09/01/2001
Each share old Common $0.0001 par received distribution of (0.01) share Club House Videos, Inc. Common $0.0001 par payable 04/25/2003 to holders of record 03/07/2003
Each share old Common $0.0001 par exchanged for (0.02) share new Common $0.0001 par 07/10/2003
Each share new Common $0.0001 par exchanged again for (0.001) share new Common $0.0001 par 07/15/2005
New Common $0.0001 par split (5) for (1) by issuance of (4) additional shares payable 01/30/2006 to holders of record 12/31/2005 Ex date - 01/31/2006
Each share new Common $0.0001 par exchanged again for (0.01333333) share new Common $0.0001 par 02/17/2006
Each share new Common $0.0001 par exchanged again for (0.05) share new Common $0.0001 par 07/17/2006
Each share new Common $0.0001 par exchanged again for (0.005) share new Common $0.0001 par 09/20/2006
Each share new Common $0.0001 par exchanged again for (0.0005) share new Common $0.0001 par 12/15/2006
Each share new Common $0.0001 par exchanged again for (0.00025) share new Common $0.0001 par 03/08/2007
Each share new Common $0.0001 par exchanged again for (0.00025) share new Common $0.0001 par 07/09/2007
Each share new Common $0.0001 par exchanged again for (0.00025)

share new Common $0.0001 par 10/09/2007
Each share new Common $0.0001 par exchanged again for (0.000125) share new Common $0.0001 par 01/04/2008
Each share new Common $0.0001 par exchanged again for (0.000125) share new Common $0.0001 par 05/23/2008
Stock Dividend - 100% payable 10/15/2003 to holders of record 09/19/2003
Recapitalized as Made In America Entertainment, Inc. 08/29/2008
Each share new Common $0.0001 par exchanged for (0.000125) share Common $0.0001 par
(See Made In America Entertainment, Inc.)

RAVEN ROCK STRATEGIC INCOME FD (ON)
Under plan of reorganization each Unit automatically became (0.5) Exemplar Mutual Funds Exemplar U.S. High Yield Fund Ser. A 03/16/2016

RAVENCREST RES INC (BC)
Each share Common no par received distribution of (0.5) share River Wild Exploration Inc. Common no par payable 10/01/2012 to holders of record 10/01/2012
Name changed to RavenQuest Biomed Inc. 10/04/2017

RAVENHEAD RECOVERY CORP (BC)
Cease trade order effective 03/21/2003
Stockholders' equity unlikely

RAVENROC RES LTD (BC)
Recapitalized as Rocraven Resources Ltd. 6/5/90
Each share Common no par exchanged for (0.2) share Common no par
Rocraven Resources Ltd. recapitalized as Lifetime Ventures Ltd. 10/22/2002

RAVENS METAL PRODS INC (DE)
Each share old Common 1¢ par exchanged for (0.25) share new Common 1¢ par 12/26/1995
Name changed to RVM Industries, Inc. 03/31/1997
(See RVM Industries, Inc.)

RAVENSTAR VENTURES INC (BC)
Name changed to Cancen Oil Canada Inc. (BC) 10/17/2011
Cancen Oil Canada Inc. (BC) reincorporated in Alberta 12/20/2012 which name changed to Ceiba Energy Services Inc. 07/29/2013
(See Ceiba Energy Services Inc.)

RAVENSWOOD CORP. (IL)
Liquidation completed
Each share Common no par exchanged for initial distribution of $100 cash 4/14/65
Each share Common no par received second and final distribution of $26.67 cash 9/17/65

RAVENSWOOD FINL CORP (IL)
Acquired by First Chicago Corp. 10/31/1989
Each share Common $1 par exchanged for (0.73333) share Common $5 par and $11 cash
First Chicago Corp. merged into First Chicago NBD Corp. 12/01/1995 which merged into Bank One Corp. 10/02/1998 which merged into J.P. Morgan Chase & Co. 07/01/2004 which name changed to JPMorgan Chase & Co. 07/20/2004

RAVENSWOOD MANOR CORP. (IL)
Liquidated in 1941

RAVENSWOOD-PAULINA CORP. (IL)
Liquidated in 1941

FINANCIAL INFORMATION, INC. RAV-RAY

RAVENSWOOD WINERY INC (CA)
Merged into Constellation Brands, Inc. 07/02/2001
Each share Common no par exchanged for $29.50 cash

RAVENVIEW APARTMENTS LIQUIDATION TRUST
Trust liquidated in 1951

RAVENWOOD BOURNE LTD (DE)
Name changed to PopBig, Inc. 11/07/2011
PopBig, Inc. name changed to EMAV Holdings, Inc. 01/03/2014

RAVENWOOD RES INC (AB)
Merged into Compass Petroleum Ltd. 07/23/2003
Each share Common no par exchanged for $1.05 cash

RAVINE GARDENS CORP. (FL)
Charter cancelled and company declared dissolved for non-payment of taxes 5/16/57

RAVISENT TECHNOLOGIES INC (DE)
Issue Information - 5,000,000 shares COM offered at $12 per share on 07/15/1999
Name changed to Axeda Systems Inc. 1/15/2002
Axeda Systems Inc. name changed to ITA Holdings, Inc. 12/5/2005
(See ITA Holdings, Inc.)

RAW CREEK RES INC (ON)
Recapitalized as Rally Energy Corp. 03/22/1996
Each share Common no par exchanged for (0.4) share Common no par
(See Rally Energy Corp.)

RAW DEV CORP AMER INC (MN)
Name changed to Holiday-Gulf Homes, Inc. 10/28/1977
(See Holiday-Gulf Homes, Inc.)

RAWDON RES LTD (BC)
Name changed to Advanced Ecology Systems Corp. 5/23/89
Advanced Ecology Systems Corp. recapitalized as Consolidated Advanced Ecology Corp. 1/9/90
(See Consolidated Advanced Ecology Corp.)

RAWHIDE COALITION MINES CO. (NV)
Charter revoked for failure to file reports and pay fees 3/3/24

RAWHIDE INTL INVT LTD (AB)
Name changed to STN Inc. 4/24/92
(See STN Inc.)

RAWHIDE MINING CO. (NV)
Charter revoked for failure to file reports and pay fees 3/2/31

RAWHIDE RED TOP MINING CO. (NV)
Charter revoked for failure to file reports and pay fees 3/3/24

RAWHIDE RESOURCES LTD. (ON)
Recapitalized as Restaurant Holdings of Canada Ltd. 8/13/75
Each share Common no par exchanged for (0.1) share Common no par
Restaurant Holdings of Canada Ltd. name changed to Mikes Submarines Inc. 5/15/79 which name changed to M-Corp Inc. 8/1/85 which name changed to Mikes Restaurants Inc. 12/8/98
(See Mikes Restaurants Inc.)

RAWHIDE U MINES LTD (ON)
Name changed to Rawhide Resources Ltd. and Common $1 par changed to no par 8/28/72
Rawhide Resources Ltd. recapitalized as Restaurant Holdings of Canada Ltd. 8/13/75 which name changed to Mikes Submarines Inc. 5/15/79 which name changed to M-Corp Inc. 8/1/85 which name changed to Mikes Restaurants Inc. 12/8/98

(See Mikes Restaurants Inc.)

RAWLINGS SPORTING GOODS INC (DE)
Preferred Stock Purchase Rights declared for Common stockholders of record 07/01/1994 were redeemed at $0.01 per right 01/31/2001 for holders of record 12/31/2001
Merged into K2 Inc. 03/27/2003
Each share Common 1¢ par exchanged for (1.08) shares Common $1 par
K2 Inc. merged into Jarden Corp. 08/08/2007

RAWLINS INDS INC (AB)
Name changed to Vertimac Development Inc. 6/12/89
Vertimac Development Inc. name changed to Copper States Resources Inc. 12/15/95 which recapitalized as American Coppermine Resources Inc. 8/26/96 which recapitalized as Carleton Resources Corp. 2/4/97
(See Carleton Resources Corp.)

RAWSON-KOENIG INC (TX)
Each share old Common no par exchanged for (0.01) share new Common no par 12/8/97
Merged into RKI Acquisition Inc. 1/26/98
Each share new Common no par exchanged for $215 cash

RAX RESTAURANTS INC (OH)
Plan of reorganization under Chapter 11 Federal Bankruptcy Code effective 11/08/1993
No stockholders' equity

RAY, INC. (CA)
Charter suspended for failure to file reports and pay fees 2/1/39

RAY AIR CONDITIONING CORP.
Out of business 00/00/1937
Details not available

RAY CONSOLIDATED COPPER CO.
Acquired by Nevada Consolidated Copper Co. 00/00/1927
Details not available

RAY DYNE INC (NY)
Merged into A B C Associates, Inc. 3/10/69
Each share Common 1¢ par exchanged for (0.2) share Common 1¢ par
(See A B C Associates, Inc.)

RAY HERCULES COPPER CO. (ME)
Charter revoked for failure to file reports and pay fees in 1922

RAY HERCULES MINES, INC.
Assets sold in 1927
No stockholders' equity

RAY NET COMMUNICATIONS SYS INC (BC)
Name changed to Ixora Communication Systems Inc. 12/21/88
(See Ixora Communication Systems Inc.)

RAY-O-VAC CO. (WI)
Recapitalized 00/00/1934
Each share 8% Preferred $50 par exchanged for (1) share $2 Preferred $25 par and (2) shares Common no par
Each share Common no par exchanged for (0.5) share Common no par
Recapitalized 00/00/1941
Each share Common no par exchanged for (2) shares Common $5 par
Recapitalized 00/00/1945
Each share Common $5 par exchanged for (2) shares Common $2.50 par
Stock Dividends - 100% 12/29/1950; 100% 07/06/1956
Merged into Electric Storage Battery Co. (NJ) on a (0.5) for (1) basis 11/20/1957
Electric Storage Battery Co. (NJ) reincorporated under the laws of Delaware as ESB Inc. 06/30/1967
(See ESB Inc.)

RAY PROOF CORP (DE)
Merged into Keene Corp. (DE) (Old) 8/8/73
Each share Common 50¢ par exchanged for (0.510204) share Common 10¢ par
Keene Corp. (DE) (Old) reincorporated in New York 12/31/79 which reorganized as Bairnco Corp. (NY) 4/30/81 which reincorporated in Delaware 5/1/91
(See Bairnco Corp.)

RAY RES CORP (DE)
Merged into Flying Diamond Oil Corp. 12/04/1974
Each share Common $1 par exchanged for (0.75) share Common $1 par
(See Flying Diamond Oil Corp.)

RAYBELL GOLD MINES LTD. (ON)
Charter revoked for failure to file reports and pay fees 9/24/56

RAYBESTOS CO.
Merged into Raybestos-Manhattan, Inc. in 1929
Details not available

RAYBESTOS MANHATTAN INC (CT)
Reincorporated 4/6/76
Common no par split (2) for (1) by issuance of (1) additional share 4/26/63
Common no par changed to $12.50 par 4/8/68
State of incorporation changed from (NJ) to (CT) 4/6/76
Stock Dividends - 20% 11/19/76; 10% 11/18/77; 10% 11/17/78; 10% 11/16/79
Name changed to Raymark Corp. 6/28/82
Raymark Corp. reorganized in Delaware as Raytech Corp. 10/15/86
(See Raytech Corp.)

RAYCHEM CORP (DE)
Reincorporated 04/14/1987
Common no par split (3) for (1) by issuance of (2) additional shares 11/15/1977
Common no par split (2) for (1) by issuance of (1) additional share 10/10/1979
State of incorporation changed from (CA) to (DE) and Common no par changed to $1 par 04/14/1987
Common $1 par split (3) for (1) by issuance of (2) additional shares 11/16/1987
Common $1 par split (2) for (1) by issuance of (1) additional share payable 12/03/1997 to holders of record 11/17/1997 Ex date - 12/04/1997
Merged into Tyco International Ltd. 08/12/1999
Each share Common $1 par exchanged for (0.2313) share Common $1 par and $16.06 cash

RAYCO INTL INC (OH)
Merged into FDI, Inc. 10/15/1974
Each share Conv. Preferred $100 par exchanged for (1) share Conv. Special Preferred $100 par
Each share Common no par exchanged for (0.454545) share Common $1 par
FDI, Inc. recapitalized as Interlee, Inc. 12/18/1981
(See Interlee, Inc.)

RAYCOMM INDS INC (NJ)
Each share old Common no par exchanged for (0.25) share new Common no par 04/09/1973
New Common no par split (3) for (1) by issuance of (2) additional shares 07/15/1981
Stock Dividend - 10% 12/01/1978
Merged into Raycomm Transworld Industries, Inc. 06/04/1986
Each share new Common no par exchanged for (1) share Common 1¢ par
(See Raycomm Transworld Industries, Inc.)

RAYCOMM TRANSWORLD INDS INC (DE)
SEC revoked preferred and common stock registration 10/16/2008
Stockholders' equity unlikely

RAYCON, INC. (CT)
Name changed to Windsor Nuclear, Inc. 12/8/67
Windsor Nuclear, Inc. name changed to Surgicot, Inc. 8/29/74 which merged into Squibb Corp. 6/22/79 which merged into Bristol-Myers Squibb Co. 10/4/89

RAYDON TECHNOLOGY CORP (DE)
Each share old Common 10¢ par exchanged for (0.01) share new Common 10¢ par 8/13/90
Acquired by RTC Acquisition, Inc. 10/23/92
Each share new Common 10¢ par exchanged for $40 cash

RAYETTE, INC. (MN)
Each share Common $2 par exchanged for (5) shares Common 40¢ par 9/16/59
Name changed to Rayette-Faberge, Inc. 6/15/65
Rayette-Faberge, Inc. name changed to Faberge, Inc. 6/30/69
(See Faberge, Inc.)

RAYETTE FABERGE INC (MN)
Name changed to Faberge, Inc. 06/30/1969
(See Faberge, Inc.)

RAYFIELD MNG CO (BC)
Struck off register and declared dissolved for failure to file returns 01/10/1977

RAYGO INC (MN)
Stock Dividend - 200% 03/30/1970
Merged into Foster Wheeler Corp. (NY) 05/16/1974
Each share Common 5¢ par exchanged for (0.1173) share Common $0.33333333 par
Foster Wheeler Corp. (NY) reincorporated in Bermuda as Foster Wheeler Ltd. 05/25/2001 which reorganized in Switzerland as Foster Wheeler AG 02/09/2009 which merged into Amec Foster Wheeler PLC 01/19/2015
(See Amec Foster Wheeler PLC)

RAYLLOYD MINES & EXPLORATIONS LTD. (ON)
Recapitalized as Raylloyd Resources Ltd. 4/19/83
Each share Capital Stock $1 par exchanged for (1/3) share Common no par
Raylloyd Resources Ltd. recapitalized as Consolidated Royalgroup, Inc. 1/27/89 which name changed to Aronos Multinational Inc. 11/8/91 which name changed to RDG Minerals Inc. 10/24/96 which recapitalized as Netforfun.com, Inc. 8/9/2000

RAYLLOYD RES LTD (ON)
Recapitalized as Consolidated Royalgroup, Inc. 1/27/89
Each share new Common no par exchanged for (0.14285714) share Common no par
Consolidated Royalgroup, Inc. name changed to Aronos Multinational Inc. 11/8/91 which name changed to RDG Minerals Inc. 10/24/96 which recapitalized as Netforfun.com, Inc. 8/9/2000

RAYMAC OIL CORP (BC)
Name changed to Norfolk Petroleum Ltd. 05/03/1985
Norfolk Petroleum Ltd. recapitalized as International Norfolk Industries Ltd. 03/17/1993 which merged into Ventures Resources Corp. 11/20/1996 which merged into BrazMin Corp. 04/06/2005 which name changed to Talon Metals Corp. 07/09/2007

RAYMAR BOOK CORP (CA)
Charter suspended for failure to file reports and pay fees 01/02/1987

RAYMARK CORP (CT)
Reorganized under the laws of Delaware as Raytech Corp. and Common $12.50 par changed to $1 par 10/15/86
(See Raytech Corp.)

RAYMOND-COMMERCE CORP. (IL)
Preferred called for redemption 07/25/1961
Liquidation completed 05/11/1962
Details not available

RAYMOND CONCRETE PILE CO. (NJ)
Common no par split (2) for (1) by issuance of (1) additional share in 1954
Stock Dividends - 100% 4/15/49; 10% 1/18/57; 10% 1/18/58
Name changed to Raymond International, Inc. (NJ) and Common no par changed to $10 par 4/2/58
Raymond International Inc. (NJ) reorganized in Delaware 9/12/78
(See Raymond International Inc. (DE))

RAYMOND CORP (NY)
Common $5 par changed to $2.50 par and (1) additional share issued 1/15/65
Common $2.50 par changed to $1.50 par and (2/3) additional share issued 1/11/66
Common $1.50 par split (2) for (1) by issuance of (1) additional share 6/29/84
Common $1.50 par split (3) for (2) by issuance of (0.5) additional share 9/26/86
Stock Dividend - 33% 9/13/79; 5% payable 4/12/96 to holders of record 3/29/96
Merged into Lift Acquisition Co. Inc. 8/7/97
Each share Common $1.50 par exchanged for $33 cash

RAYMOND ENGINEERING LABORATORY, INC. (CT)
Name changed to Raymond Engineering Inc. 7/12/67
Raymond Engineering Inc. name changed to Raymond Precision Industries Inc. 4/1/70 which name changed to Raymond Industries Inc. 5/12/78 which assets were transferred to Raymond Industries Liquidating Trust 2/20/85
(See Raymond Industries Liquidating Trust)

RAYMOND ENGR INC (CT)
Incorporated in 1938
Common $1 par split (3) for (2) by issuance of (0.5) additional share 4/15/68
Name changed to Raymond Precision Industries Inc. 4/1/70
Raymond Precision Industries, Inc. name changed to Raymond Industries, Inc. 5/12/78 which assets were transferred to Raymond Industries Liquidating Trust 2/20/85
(See Raymond Industries Liquidating Trust)

RAYMOND ENGR INC NEW (CT)
Incorporated in 1970
Common $1 par split (3) for (2) by issuance of (0.5) additional share 7/8/83
Merged into Kaman Corp. 12/16/86
Each share Common $1 par exchanged for $30 cash

RAYMOND INDS INC (CT)
Common $1 par split (2) for (1) by issuance of (1) additional share 5/12/81
In process of liquidation
Each share Common $1 par received initial distribution of $12 cash 5/7/84
Each share Common $1 par received second distribution of $7 cash 8/31/84
Assets transferred to Raymond Industries Liquidating Trust and Common $1 par reclassified as Non-Transferable Unit of Bene. Int. $1 par 2/20/85
(See Raymond Industries Liquidating Trust)

RAYMOND INDUSTRIES LIQUIDATING TRUST (CT)
Liquidation completed
Each Non-Transferable Unit of Bene. Int. $1 par received third distribution of $8.50 cash 3/7/85
Each Non-Transferable Unit of Bene. Int. $1 par received fourth distribution of $3 cash 11/21/90
Each Non-Transferable Unit of Bene. Int. $1 par received fifth and final distribution of $0.1717 cash 4/15/91
(See Raymond Industries Inc. for previous distributions)

RAYMOND INTL INC (DE)
Under plan of merger each share Common $3.33-1/3 par exchanged for $27.50 cash 11/10/83

RAYMOND INTL INC (NJ)
Common $10 par changed to $3.33-1/3 par and (2) additional shares issued 10/7/59
Common $3.33-1/3 par split (3) for (2) by issuance of (0.5) additional share 2/28/77
Reorganized under the laws of Delaware 9/12/78
Each share Common $3.33-1/3 par exchanged for (1) share Common $3.33-1/3 par
(See Raymond International Inc. (DE))

RAYMOND PRECISION INDS INC (CT)
Stock Dividend - 33-1/3% 6/1/77
Name changed to Raymond Industries Inc. 5/12/78
Raymond Industries Inc. assets transferred to Raymond Industries Liquidating Trust 2/20/85
(See Raymond Industries Liquidating Trust)

RAYMOND TIBLEMONT GOLD MINES LTD. (ON)
Charter cancelled for failure to pay taxes and file returns 4/9/75

RAYMOND WOOLLEN MLS LTD (INDIA)
Name changed to Raymond Ltd. 11/23/1994

RAYMOR INDS INC (BC)
Name changed 07/21/1999
Name changed from Raymor Resources Ltd. to Raymor Industries Inc. 07/21/1999
Proposal under Bankruptcy and Insolvency Act effective 02/09/2010
No stockholders' equity

RAYNE INDS INC (NY)
Dissolved by proclamation 12/24/91

RAYNO MINING CORP. LTD. (ON)
Charter cancelled for failure to file reports and pay taxes December 1960

RAYON D'OR MINES, LTD. (ON)
Charter cancelled for failure to file reports and pay taxes in 1955

RAYONIER, INC. (DE)
Common $1 par split (5) for (2) by issuance of (1.5) additional shares 7/22/55
$2 Preferred $25 par called for redemption 9/1/55
Stock Dividend - 100% 4/1/52
Merged into International Telephone & Telegraph Corp. (DE) 4/26/68
Each share Common $1 par exchanged for (0.2675) share $4.50 Conv. Preferred Ser. I no par and (0.3950) share Common $1 par
International Telephone & Telegraph Corp. (DE) name changed to ITT Corp. 12/31/83 which reorganized in Indiana as ITT Industries Inc. 12/19/95 which name changed to ITT Corp. 7/1/2006

RAYONIER TIMBERLANDS L P (DE)
Acquired by Rayonier Inc. 1/30/98
Each Class A Depositary Unit no par exchanged for $13 cash

RAYORE ENTERPRISES LTD (BC)
Name changed 1/13/72
Name changed from Rayore Mines Ltd. to Rayore Enerterprises Ltd. 1/13/72
Recapitalized as United Rayore Gas Ltd. 7/22/74
Each share Common no par exchanged for (0.2) share Common no par
United Rayore Gas Ltd. merged into StarTech Energy Inc. 8/1/97 which merged into Impact Energy Inc. (Canada) 1/31/2001 which merged into Thunder Energy Inc. 4/30/2004
(See Thunder Energy Inc.)

RAYOVAC CORP (WI)
Name changed to Spectrum Brands, Inc. 05/02/2005
(See Spectrum Brands, Inc.)

RAYPAK INC (CA)
Common 34¢ par changed to 23¢ par and (0.5) additional share issued 06/08/1977
Common 23¢ par changed to 15¢ par and (0.5) additional share issued 07/20/1979
Merged into Raypak Acquisition Inc. 04/15/1983
Each share Common 15¢ par exchanged for $4 principal amount of Variable Rate Sr. Subord. Notes due 04/15/1988 and $4 cash

RAYPATH RES LTD (BC)
Reincorporated under the laws of Alberta as Goldray Inc. 10/28/1999
(See Goldray Inc.)

RAYROCK MINES LTD. (ON)
Name changed to Rayrock Resources Ltd. and Capital Stock $1 par changed to no par 07/21/1978
Rayrock Resources Ltd. merged into Rayrock Yellowknife Resources Inc. 02/03/1986 which name changed to Rayrock Resources Inc. 11/27/1998
(See Rayrock Resources Inc.)

RAYROCK RES INC (CANADA)
Name changed 11/27/1998
Name changed from Rayrock Yellowknife Resources Inc. to Rayrock Resources Inc. 11/27/1998
Merged into Glamis Gold Ltd. 02/26/1999
Each share Subordinate no par exchanged for (2.4) shares Common no par
Note: Unexchanged certificates were cancelled and became without value 03/02/2005
Glamis Gold Ltd. merged into Goldcorp Inc. (New) 11/04/2006

RAYROCK RES LTD (ON)
Capital Stock no par reclassified as Subordinate no par 05/10/1984
Merged into Rayrock Yellowknife Resources Inc. 02/03/1986
Each share Subordinate no par exchanged for (1) share Subordinate no par
Rayrock Yellowknife Resources Inc. name changed to Rayrock Resources Inc. 11/27/1998
(See Rayrock Resources Inc.)

RAYSTAR CAP LTD (BC)
Name changed to Newmarket Gold Inc. (BC) 10/08/2013
Newmarket Gold Inc. (BC) reorganized in Ontario 07/14/2015 which recapitalized as Kirkland Lake Gold Ltd. 12/06/2016

RAYSTAR ENTERPRISES LTD (BC)
Each share old Common no par exchanged for (0.33333333) share new Common no par 10/22/2004
New Common no par split (10) for (1) by issuance of (9) additional shares payable 08/06/2007 to holders of record 08/01/2007
Recapitalized as Raystar Capital Ltd. 10/19/2007
Each share new Common no par exchanged for (0.33333333) share Common no par
Raystar Capital Ltd. name changed to Newmarket Gold Inc. (BC) 10/08/2013 which reorganized in Ontario 07/14/2015 which recapitalized as Kirkland Lake Gold Ltd. 12/06/2016

RAYTEC CAP CORP (BC)
Recapitalized as Raytec Development Corp. 06/04/2001
Each share Common no par exchanged for (0.2) share Common no par
Raytec Development Corp. name changed to Raytec Metals Corp. 11/19/2007 which name changed to Lion Energy Corp. 09/16/2009 which was acquired by Africa Oil Corp. 06/20/2011

RAYTEC DEV CORP (BC)
Name changed to Raytec Metals Corp. 11/19/2007
Raytec Metals Corp. name changed to Lion Energy Corp. 09/16/2009 which was acquired by Africa Oil Corp. 06/20/2011

RAYTEC METALS CORP (BC)
Name changed to Lion Energy Corp. 09/16/2009
Lion Energy Corp. acquired by Africa Oil Corp. 06/20/2011

RAYTECH CORP (DE)
Plan of reorganization under Chapter 11 Federal Bankruptcy Code effective 04/18/2001
Holders of (20) or more shares received $0.16 cash per share
Merged into Raytech Acquisition Corp. 01/04/2006
Each share Common $1 par exchanged for $1.32 cash

RAYTEL MED CORP (DE)
Each share old Common $0.001 par exchanged for (0.33333333) share new Common $0.001 par 05/23/2001
Merged into SHL Telemedicine Ltd. 06/04/2002
Each share new Common $0.001 par exchanged for $10.25 cash

RAYTHEON CO (DE)
5-1/2% Conv. Preferred $50 par called for redemption 2/1/66
Common $5 par changed to $2.50 par and (1) additional share issued 6/25/68
$1.12 Conv. Preferred Ser. A no par called for redemption 2/1/72
Common $2.50 par changed to $1.25 par and (1) additional share issued 6/22/77
Common $1.25 par changed to $1 par and (1) additional share issued 6/24/81
Common $1 par split (2) for (1) by issuance of (1) additional share 4/2/92
Common $1 par split (2) for (1) by

issuance of (1) additional share 10/23/95
Each share Common $1 par exchanged for (1) share Class B Common 1¢ par 12/18/97
Trust terminated 5/18/2004
Each 8.25% Equity Security Unit received (1.566) shares new Common 1¢ par
(Additional Information in Active)

RAYTHEON MANUFACTURING CO. (DE)
Common 50¢ par changed to $5 par in 1946
Stock Dividends - 200% 2/15/45; 10% 7/23/54
Name changed to Raytheon Co. 5/4/59

RAYTHERM CORP. (CA)
Name changed to Raychem Corp. (CA) 12/31/59
Raychem Corp. (CA) reincorporated in Delaware 4/14/87 which merged into Tyco International Ltd. 8/12/99

RAYTOMIC URANIUM MINES LTD. (ON)
Charter cancelled for failure to file reports and pay taxes 12/12/60

RAYTONE SCREEN CORP. (NY)
Advised of bankruptcy in 1958
Proclaimed dissolved by Secretary of State 12/15/62

RAYWHEEL INC (WA)
Each share old Common no par exchanged for (1/3) share new Common no par 11/6/89
Name changed to American Citadel, Inc. 12/19/89
American Citadel, Inc. name changed to Country Maid Foods Inc. 4/30/94 which recapitalized as Country Maid Financial, Inc. 10/9/98
(See Country Maid Financial, Inc.)

RAZOR INDS INC (DE)
Charter cancelled and declared inoperative and void for non-payment of taxes 3/1/87

RAZOR RES INC (NV)
Each share old Common $0.001 par exchanged for (15) shares new Common $0.001 par 12/26/2007
Recapitalized as You Han Data Tech Co. Ltd. 03/04/2016
Each share new Common $0.001 par exchanged for (0.002) share Common $0.001 par

RAZORE ROCK RES INC (ON)
Each share old Common no par exchanged for (0.2) share new Common no par 12/12/2017
Reincorporated under the laws of British Columbia 06/14/2018

RAZORFISH INC (DE)
Old Class A Common 1¢ par split (2) for (1) by issuance of (1) additional share share payable 01/27/2000 to holders of record 01/20/2000
Each share old Common 1¢ par exchanged for (0.03333333) share new Class A Common 1¢ par 07/16/2003
Merged into SBI & Co. 02/28/2003
Each share new Class A Common 1¢ par exchanged for $1.70 cash

RB ASSET INC (DE)
Liquidation completed
Each share 15% Preferred Ser. A $1 par received first and final distribution of $42.63 cash payable 10/01/2002 to holders of record 10/01/2002
Note: Certificates were not required to be surrendered and are without value
Merged into RB Asset Merger Corp. 08/15/2011
Each share Common 1¢ par exchanged for $4.34 cash

RB ROBOT CORP (CO)
Plan of reorganization under Chapter 11 Federal Bankruptcy Code dismissed 1/18/86
Stockholders' equity unlikely

RB&W CORP (DE)
Merged into Park-Ohio Industries, Inc. 3/31/95
Each share Common $1 par exchanged for (0.33394) share Common $1 par

RBC INC (DE)
Common $1 par split (5) for (1) by issuance of (4) additional shares payable 04/20/1999 to holders of record 03/09/1999
Company went private 11/16/2006
Each share Common $1 par exchanged for $43.50 cash
Note: Holders of (1,000) or more shares retained their interests

RBC INFORMATION SYS (RUSSIA)
ADR agreement terminated 04/01/2016
Each Sponsored ADR for Ordinary exchanged for (4) shares Ordinary
Note: Unexchanged ADR's will be sold and the proceeds, if any, held for claim after 10/03/2016

RBC TARGET 2013 CORP BD INDEX ETF (ON)
Name changed 02/29/2012
Name changed from RBC Target 2013 Corporate Bond ETF to RBC Target 2013 Corporate Bond Index ETF 02/29/2012
Trust terminated 11/22/2013
Each Trust Unit received $18.9272 cash

RBC TARGET 2014 CORP BD ETF (ON)
Name changed 02/29/2012
Name changed from RBC Target 2014 Corporate Bond ETF to RBC Target 2014 Corporate Bond Index ETF 02/29/2012
Trust terminated 11/21/2014
Each Trust Unit received $18.772 cash

RBC TARGET 2015 CORP BD INDEX ETF (ON)
Name changed 02/29/2012
Name changed from RBC Target 2015 Corporate Bond ETF to RBC Target 2015 Corporate Bond Index ETF 02/29/2012
Trust terminated 11/20/2015
Each Trust Unit received $18.9541 cash

RBC TARGET 2016 CORP BD INDEX ETF (ON)
Name changed 02/29/2012
Name changed from RBC Target 2016 Corporate Bond ETF to RBC Target 2016 Corporate Bond Index ETF 02/29/2012
Trust terminated 11/18/2016
Each Trust Unit received $18.7614 cash

RBC TARGET 2017 CORPORATE BD INDEX ETF (ON)
Name changed 02/29/2012
Name changed from RBC Target 2017 Corporate Bond ETF to RBC Target 2017 Corporate Bond Index ETF 02/29/2012
Trust terminated 11/17/2017
Each Trust Unit received $18.8164 cash

RBC TARGET 2018 CORPORATE BD ETF (ON)
Name changed to RBC Target 2018 Corporate Bond Index ETF 02/29/2012

RBC TARGET 2019 CORP BD ETF (ON)
Name changed to RBC Target 2019 Corporate Bond Index ETF 02/29/2012

RBC TARGET 2020 CORP BD ETF (ON)
Name changed to RBC Target 2020 Corporate Bond Index ETF 02/29/2012

RBD ENTERPRISES INC (BC)
Recapitalized as Texas Gas & Oil Inc. 05/11/2000
Each share Common no par exchanged for (0.5) share Common no par
Texas Gas & Oil Inc. name changed to Legend Power Systems Inc. 07/03/2008

RBI CAP TR I (DE)
9.10% Trust Preferred Securities called for redemption at $10 on 4/1/2005

RBS ACQUISITION CORP (TX)
Name changed to Microwave Transmission Systems, Inc. 09/23/1999
(See Microwave Transmission Systems, Inc.)

RBS CAP FDG TR V (DE)
5.9% Non-Cum Guaranteed Trust Preferred Securities called for redemption at $25 plus $0.295 accrued dividends on 06/13/2016

RBS CAP FDG TR VI (DE)
6.25% Non-Cum Guaranteed Trust Preerred Securities called for redemption at $25 plus $0.3125 accrued dividends on 06/13/2016

RBS CAP FDG TR VII (DE)
6.25% Non-Cum Guaranteed Trust Preferred Securities callled for redemption at $25 plus $0.304 accrued dividends on 06/13/2016

RCA CORP (DE)
$2.125 Conv. Preference no par called for redemption 08/30/1985
$4 Conv. 1st Preferred no par called for redemption 05/16/1986
Acquired by General Electric Co. 06/09/1986
Each share $3.50 1st Preferred no par exchanged for $40 cash
Each share $3.65 Preference no par exchanged for $42.50 cash
Each share Common no par exchanged for $66.50 cash

RCA TRADING CO (FL)
Name changed to Agronix, Inc. 06/18/2001
Agronix, Inc. recapitalized as China Yingxia International, Inc. 07/21/2006
(See China Yingxia International, Inc.)

RCB CORP (CA)
Stock Dividend - 10% payable 12/19/2000 to holders of record 11/21/2000 Ex date - 12/27/2000
Name changed to River City Bank (Sacramento, CA) 11/01/2010

RCC INC (MD)
Merged into Maryland Alona-Rey Homes, Inc. 01/19/1982
Each share Common no par exchanged for $10 cash

RCF COM-TRONICS, INC. (NY)
Completely liquidated 11/15/65
Each share Common 10¢ par received $0.1459 cash
Certificates were not retired and are now without value

RCG CAP INC (BC)
Issue Information - 2,000,000 shares COM offered at $0.10 per share on 04/28/2010
Recapitalized as Almonty Industries Inc. (BC) 09/28/2011
Each share Common no par exchanged for (0.14992503) share Common no par
Almonty Industries Inc. (BC) reincorporated in Canada 03/27/2012

RCG COS INC (DE)
Name changed to OneTravel Holdings, Inc. 06/08/2005
(See OneTravel Holdings, Inc.)

RCI CORP. (NETHERLANDS ANTILLES)
Name changed 9/14/94
Name changed from RCI Corp. N.V. to RCI Corp. and Common no par reclassified as Subordinate no par 9/14/94
Called for redemption 12/24/98

RCL ACQUISITION CORP (DE)
Name changed to HMG Digital Technologies Corp. 9/20/93
HMG Digital Technologies Corp. name changed to Allied Digital Technologies Corp. 1/11/95
(See Allied Digital Technologies Corp.)

RCL CAP CORP (DE)
Name changed to Disc Graphics, Inc. in October 1995
(See Disc Graphics, Inc.)

RCL CO. (NC)
Liquidation completed
Each share Common $2 par exchanged for initial distribution of $3.75 cash 7/1/74
Each share Common $2 par received second distribution of $0.50 cash 4/1/75
Each share Common $2 par received third distribution of $0.25 cash 12/1/75
Each share Common $2 par received fourth distribution of $1 cash 11/1/76
Each share Common $2 par received fifth and final distribution of $0.19 cash 12/15/77

RCM INTS INC (DE)
Name changed to Graphco Holdings Corp. 05/15/2003
(See Graphco Holdings Corp.)

RCM STRATEGIC GLOBAL GVT FD INC (MD)
Name changed to PIMCO Strategic Global Government Fund, Inc. 03/19/2002
PIMCO Strategic Global Government Fund, Inc. name changed to PIMCO Strategic Income Fund, Inc. 03/03/2014

RCN CORP (DE)
Common $1 par split (2) for (1) by issuance of (1) additional share payable 04/03/1998 to holders of record 03/20/1998
Plan of reorganization under Chapter 11 Federal Bankruptcy Code effective 12/21/2004
Each share Common $1 par exchanged for an undetermined amount of Common Stock Purchase Warrants expiring 12/21/2006
Acquired by Yankee Metro Merger Sub, Inc. 08/26/2010
Each share Common 1¢ par exchanged for $15 cash

RCO CORP. (UT)
Name changed to Sunwater Co. 1/16/76

RCOM VENTURE CORP (BC)
Name changed to Wellstar Energy Corp. 7/21/2005

RCONTEST COM INC (GA)
Recapitalized as CFI Inc. 04/30/2001
Each share Common no par exchanged for (0.2) share Common no par
CFI Inc. recapitalized as Fletcher-Flora Health Care Systems, Inc. 06/06/2005
(See Fletcher-Flora Health Care Systems, Inc.)

RCS CAP CORP (DE)
Plan of reorganization under Chapter 11 Federal Bankruptcy proceedings effective 05/23/2016

No stockholders' equity

RCS EMERGING GROWTH FD (MA)
Reorganized as Robertson Stephens Emerging Growth Fund 11/13/1990
Details not available

RCS HLDGS INC (CO)
SEC revoked common stock registration 10/30/2008
Stockholders' equity unlikely

RCS INVESTIMENTI S P A (ITALY)
ADR agreement terminated 01/31/2005
Each Sponsored ADR for Ordinary Euro 1 par exchanged for $1.09 cash

RCSB FINL INC (DE)
7% Conv. Perpetual Preferred Ser. B $1 par called for redemption 7/15/96
Merged into Charter One Financial, Inc. 10/3/97
Each share Common $1 par exchanged for (0.91) share Common 1¢ par
(See Charter One Financial, Inc.)

RC2 CORP (DE)
Acquired by TOMY Co., Ltd. 04/29/2011
Each share Common 1¢ par exchanged for $27.90 cash

RDA INDUSTRIES, INC. (NY)
Charter cancelled and proclaimed dissolved for failure to pay taxes 09/26/1977

RDA MICROELECTRONICS INC (CAYMAN ISLANDS)
Acquired by Tsinghua Unigroup Ltd. 07/18/2014
Each Sponsored ADR for Ordinary exchanged for $18.50 cash

RDI MARKETING INC (DE)
Reincorporated 06/22/1999
State of incorporation changed from (FL) to (DE) 06/22/1999
Name changed to Household Direct.com, Inc. 07/26/1999
Household Direct.com, Inc. name changed to Household Direct Inc. 01/22/2002
(See Household Direct Inc.)

RDIS CORP (DE)
Each share old Common 2¢ par exchanged for an undetermined amount of new Common 2¢ par 06/30/1993
Recapitalized as TenthGate International, Inc. 03/14/2007
Each share new Common 2¢ par exchanged for (0.01) share Common 2¢ par
TenthGate International, Inc. recapitalized as TGI Solar Power Group, Inc. 07/25/2008

RDM CORP (CANADA)
Acquired by Deluxe Corp. 04/05/2017
Each share Common no par exchanged for $5.45 cash

RDM SPORTS GROUP INC (DE)
SEC revoked common stock registration 08/31/2009
Stockholders' equity unlikely

RDO EQUIP CO (DE)
Issue Information - 4,200,000 shares CL A offered at $15.50 per share on 01/23/1997
Merged into RDO Holdings Co. 6/3/2003
Each share Class A Common 1¢ par exchanged for $6.01 cash

RDS ACQUISITION CORP (ON)
Reincorporated under the laws of British Columbia as Rapid Brands Inc. 05/31/2007
Rapid Brands Inc. name changed to RAP Acquisition Corp. (BC) 08/27/2010 which reincorporated in Canada 05/13/2011 which recapitalized as Ferrum Americas Mining Inc. 12/09/2011 which recapitalized as Toachi Mining Inc. 03/14/2016

RE CAP CORP (DE)
Reincorporated 08/10/1989
Common 10¢ par split (3) for (1) by issuance of (2) additional shares 08/25/1986
State of incorporation changed from (NJ) to (DE) 08/10/1989
Preferred Stock Purchase Rights declared for Common stockholders of record 03/06/1989 were redeemed at $0.01 per right 09/10/1991 for holders of record 08/20/1991
Acquired by Zurich Reinsurance Centre Holdings, Inc. 04/26/1995
Each share Common 10¢ par exchanged for $18.50 cash

RE-CAR, INC. (MN)
Recapitalized as McCauley Enterprises, Inc. 10/01/1971
Each share Common 5¢ par exchanged for (0.25) share Common 20¢ par
(See McCauley Enterprises, Inc.)

RE/COMM CORP. (NV)
Name changed to Metro Wireless Interactive Corp. 12/27/1993
Metro Wireless Interactive Corp. name changed to Red Rock International Corp. (NV) 04/01/1996 which reorganized in Kentucky as Page International Inc. 11/05/1997 which reincorporated in Nevada 12/31/1997 which name changed to China TianRen Organic Food, Inc. 06/14/2007

RE-CON BLDG PRODS INC (BC)
Acquired by Stone Mountain Holdings Inc. 03/15/2004
Each share Common no par exchanged for (1) share Common no par
(See Stone Mountain Holdings Inc.)

RE CON SYS CORP (DE)
Name changed to Oak Park, Inc. 01/06/1972
(See Oak Park, Inc.)

RE-INSURANCE CORP. OF AMERICA
Merged into American Reserve Insurance Co. 00/00/1930
Details not available

RE-MARK CHEMICAL CO., INC. (FL)
Adjudicated bankrupt 9/4/63
No stockholders' equity

RE-MARK CHEMICAL CO., INC. OF BELLE GLADE (FL)
Merged into Re-Mark Chemical Co., Inc. 11/23/59
Details not available

REA (J.B.) CO., INC. (CA)
Each share Common $100 par exchanged for (20) shares Common $5 par 8/1/56
Common $5 par changed to $1 par 6/9/58
Completely liquidated 8/22/63
Each share Common $1 par exchanged for (0.5) share Idaho-Maryland Industries Inc. Common 50¢ par
Idaho-Maryland Industries, Inc. was recapitalized as Allied Equities Corp. 4/1/64

REA GOLD CORP (BC)
Name changed 04/21/1983
Name changed from Rea Petro Corp. to Rea Gold Corp. 04/21/1983
Filed a petition under Bankruptcy and Insolvency Act 12/15/1997
No stockholders' equity

REACH INC (NE)
Name changed to SpanTel Corp. (NE) 06/25/1984
SpanTel Corp. (NE) reorganized under the laws of Delaware 07/30/1985
(See SpanTel Corp. (DE))

REACH VENTURES INC (BC)
Name changed to Unique Tire Recycling Inc. 11/13/1992
Unique Tire Recycling Inc. recapitalized as UKT Recycling Technologies Inc. (BC) 01/19/1998 which reorganized in Canada as Cogent Integrated Solutions Corp. 12/04/2003 which recapitalized as Cogent Integrated Healthcare Solutions Corp. 11/29/2005 which name changed to Silver Recycling Co., Inc. 01/17/2007
(See Silver Recycling Co., Inc.)

REACHLOCAL INC (DE)
Acquired by Gannett Co., Inc. (New) 08/09/2016
Each share Common $0.00001 par exchanged for $4.60 cash

REACT POSTAL SVCS INC (UT)
Involuntarily dissolved 02/01/1988

REACT SYS INC (NV)
Name changed to Infrastructure International Inc. 9/12/97
(See Infrastructure International Inc.)

REACTION MOTORS, INC. (NJ)
Each share Capital Stock no par exchanged for (2) shares Capital Stock $4 par in 1954
Merged into Thiokol Chemical Corp. 5/1/58
Each share Capital Stock $4 par exchanged for (0.8) share Capital Stock $1 par
Thiokol Chemical Corp. reincorporated in Virginia as Thiokol Corp. 11/20/73 which merged into Morton Thiokol, Inc. 9/24/82 which reorganized into Thiokol Corp. (DE) (New) 7/1/89 which name changed to Cordant Technologies Inc. 5/7/98
(See Cordant Techologies Inc.)

REACTIVE MED INC (NV)
Name changed to Artelo Biosciences, Inc. 05/02/2017

REACTOR INDS LTD (ON)
Name changed 12/16/1971
Name changed from Reactor Uranium Mines Ltd. to Reactor Industries Ltd. 12/16/1971
Recapitalized as Consolidated Reactor Uranium Mines Ltd. 02/05/1979
Each share Common no par exchanged for (0.3) share Common no par
Consolidated Reactor Uranium Mines Ltd. name changed to Canaustra Gold Explorations Ltd. 10/23/1987 which merged into Cliff Resources Corp. 01/09/1989 which name changed to Mineral Resources Corp. 09/13/1995 which name changed to Minroc Mines Inc. 06/10/1998 which name changed to Cassiar Mines & Metals, Inc. 06/10/1999 which name changed to Cassiar Magnesium Inc. 04/25/2000 which name changed to Cassiar Resources Inc. 07/25/2001 which name changed to Troutline Investments Inc. (ONT) 06/30/2003 which reorganized in Alberta as Innova Exploration Ltd. 04/16/2004
(See Innova Exploration Ltd.)

READ-AUTHIER MINE, LTD.
Charter surrendered for failure to file reports and pay taxes in 1938

READ INDS INC (UT)
Common $0.001 par split (5) for (4) by issuance of (0.25) additional share 10/31/90
Involuntarily dissolved for failure to file annual reports 6/1/92

READ-RITE CORP (DE)
Each share old Common $0.0001 par exchanged for (0.2) share new Common $0.0001 par 02/24/2003
Filed a petition under Chapter 7 Federal Bankrutpcy Code 06/17/2003

No stockholders' equity

READ STANDARD CORP. (DE)
Merged into Capitol Products Corp. share for share 11/3/56
(See Capitol Products Corp.)

READE (WALTER) ORGANIZATIONS, INC. (DE)
See - Walter Reade Organizations Inc

READERS DIGEST ASSN CDA LTD (CANADA)
Acquired by Reader's Digest Association, Inc. 12/31/82
Each share Common no par exchanged for $12.50 cash

READERS DIGEST ASSN INC (DE)
Non-Voting Class A 1¢ par reclassified as Common 1¢ par 12/13/2002
Each share Class B 1¢ par exchanged for (1.22) shares Common 1¢ par 12/13/2002
Acquired by Ripplewood Holdings LLC 3/2/2007
Each share Common 1¢ par exchanged for $17 cash

READERS DIGEST AUTOMATIC COM EXCHANGE SEC TR (DE)
Issue Information - 10,308,257 $1.93 TR AUTOMATIC COM EXCHANGE SECS TRACERS offered at $23.4375 per share on 02/10/1998
Each share Trust Automatic Common Exchange Security exchanged for (0.8696) share Reader's Digest Association, Inc. Non-Voting Class A 1¢ par 02/15/2001

READI TEMP INC (OH)
Charter cancelled for failure to file reports and pay taxes 7/13/82

READICARE INC (CA)
Merged into HealthSouth Corp. 12/02/1996
Each share Common 1¢ par exchanged for (0.2425) share Common 1¢ par
HealthSouth Corp. name changed to Encompass Health Corp. 01/02/2018

READING & BATES CORP (DE)
Name changed 02/08/1979
$1.375 Conv. 1st Preferred $1 par called for redemption 05/24/1972
$1.375 Conv. Preferred 1st Ser. $1 par called for redemption 05/24/1973
Name changed from Reading & Bates Offshore Drilling Co. to Reading & Bates Corp. 02/08/1979
Common 20¢ par split (3) for (2) by issuance of (0.5) additional share 12/31/1979
Common 20¢ par split (3) for (2) by issuance of (0.5) additional share 09/29/1980
Common 20¢ par split (3) for (2) by issuance of (0.5) additional share 10/07/1981
Each share Adjustable Rate Preferred 5th Ser. $1 par reclassified as (6.525) shares Common 20¢ par 09/01/1989
Each share $2.125 Conv. Preferred 4th Ser. $1 par reclassified as (6.525) shares Common 20¢ par 09/01/1989
Each share Conv. Class A no par reclassified as (30.60) shares Common 20¢ par 09/01/1989
Each share Common 20¢ par exchanged for (0.2) share old Common 5¢ par 09/01/1989
Each share old Common 5¢ par exchanged for (0.2) share new Common 5¢ par 10/02/1992
Merged into R&B Falcon Corp. 12/31/1997
Each share new Common 5¢ par exchanged for (1.18) shares Common 1¢ par
R&B Falcon Corp. merged into Transocean Sedco Forex Inc.

01/31/2001 which name changed to Transocean Inc. (Old) 05/09/2002 which merged into Transocean Inc. (New) (Cayman Islands) 11/27/2007 which reorganized in Switzerland as Transocean Ltd. 12/18/2008

READING & BATES PRODTN CO (DE)
Completely liquidated 09/30/1969
Each share Common 10¢ par exchanged for $2.23 cash

READING & COLUMBIA R.R. CO.
Merged into Reading Co. on a (0.04) for (1) basis 12/31/45
Reading Co. merged into Reading Entertainment Inc. (DE) 10/15/96 which reincorporated in Nevada 12/29/99 which merged into Reading International, Inc. 12/31/2001

READING AVIATION SVC INC (DE)
Name changed to Suburban Airlines Inc. 10/19/1982
(See Suburban Airlines Inc.)

READING CO (PA)
Plan of reorganization under Chapter 11 Federal Bankruptcy proceedings confirmed 12/31/1980
Each share 4% 1st Preferred $50 par exchanged for (1) share Common 1¢ par
Each share 4% 2nd Preferred $50 par exchanged for (1) share Common 1¢ par
Each share Common $50 par exchanged for (1) share Common 1¢ par
Note: Unexchanged certificates were cancelled and became without value 01/01/1986
Old Common 1¢ par split (3) for (2) by issuance of (0.5) additional share 06/01/1987
Each share old Common 1¢ par exchanged for (1) share new Common 1¢ par 10/13/1989
Merged into Reading Entertainment Inc. 10/15/1996
Each share Class A Common 1¢ par exchanged for (1) share Common $0.001 par
Each share Common 1¢ par exchanged for (1) share Common $0.001 par
Reading Entertainment Inc. (DE) reincorporated in Nevada 12/29/1999 which merged into Reading International, Inc. 12/31/2001

READING ELEC LT & PWR CO (PA)
Out of business 00/00/1972
Details not available

READING ENTMT INC (NV)
Reincorporated 12/29/99
State of incorporation changed from (DE) to (NV) 12/29/99
Merged into Reading International, Inc. 12/31/2001
Each share Common $0.001 par exchanged for (1.25) share Non-Vtg. Class A 1¢ par

READING GAS CO. (PA)
Liquidation completed 10/9/59

READING INDS INC (DE)
$1.25 1st Preferred $23.25 par reclassified as $1.25 Preferred Ser. A $23.25 par 4/5/68
Each share Class A Common $1 par exchanged for (2.5) shares Common $1 par
Common $1 par changed to 10¢ par 7/15/77
Settlement under Chapter 11 reorganization proceedings approved by the court 11/15/82
No stockholders' equity

READING RUBBER MANUFACTURING CO.
Acquired by Sanford Mills, Inc. 00/00/1936
Details not available

READING TR CO (READING, PA)
Each share Common $100 par exchanged for (10) shares Common $10 par 03/01/1930
Each share Common $10 par exchanged for (2) shares Common $5 par 02/28/1964
Merged into National Central Bank (Lancaster, PA) 12/07/1970
Each share Common $5 par exchanged for (1) share Common $10 par
National Central Bank (Lancaster, PA) reorganized as National Central Financial Corp. 12/31/1972 which merged into CoreStates Financial Corp 05/02/1983 which merged into First Union Corp. 04/28/1998 which name changed to Wachovia Corp. (Ctfs. dated after 09/01/2001) 09/01/2001 which merged into Wells Fargo & Co. (New) 12/31/2008

READING TUBE CORP. (NJ)
50¢ Class A no par changed to $6.25 par in 1948 50¢ Class A $6.25 par reclassified as $1.25 Conv. Preferred 1955 Ser. $20 par in 1954
Class B Common 10¢ par reclassified as Common 10¢ par in 1954
Common 10¢ par changed to $1 par 12/5/55
Stock Dividend - 10% 12/1/54
Merged into Progress Manufacturing Co., Inc. 7/5/60
Each share $1.25 Conv. Preferred 1955 Ser. $20 par exchanged for (1) share $1.25 Conv. Preferred $20 par
Each share Common $1 par exchanged for (0.6) share Common $1 par
Progress Manufacturing Co., Inc. name changed to Lighting Corp. of America 5/4/66 which was acquired by Kidde (Walter) & Co., Inc. (NY) 6/19/67 which reincorporated in Delaware 7/2/68 which name changed to Kidde, Inc. 4/18/80 which merged into Hanson Trust p.l.c. 12/31/87 which name changed to Hanson PLC (Old) 1/29/88 which reorganized as Hanson PLC (New) 10/15/2003

READING TUBE CORP (DE)
Name changed to Reading Industries, Inc. 12/22/1967
(See Reading Industries, Inc.)

READY BK FT WALTON BEACH HLDG CO
Merged into Synovus Financial Corp. 10/31/99
Each share Common exchanged for (3.143) shares Common $1 par

READY CAP CORP (NY)
Reorganized under the laws of Delaware as IntelliPharmaCeutics Ltd. 08/27/2004
Each share Common $0.001 par exchanged for (0.70420055) share Common $0.001 par
IntelliPharmaCeutics Ltd. merged into IntelliPharmaCeutics International Inc. 10/22/2009

READY-MADE BUILDINGS, INC. (KS)
Adjudicated as bankrupt 9/11/62
No stockholders' equity

READY MIX INC (NV)
Issue Information - 1,550,000 shares COM offered at $11 per share on 08/23/2005
Name changed to RMX Holdings, Inc. 09/08/2010
(See RMX Holdings, Inc.)

READY WHEN YOU ARE FUNWEAR INC (NV)
Recapitalized as Rhombic Corp. 02/17/1995
Each share Common $0.001 par exchanged for (0.2) share Common $0.001 par
Rhombic Corp. recapitalized as Silverado Financial Inc. 04/29/2003 which name changed to MediaTechnics Corp. 05/23/2008

REAGAN ST BK (HOUSTON, TX)
Stock Dividend - 50% 01/20/1967
Merged into Texas Commerce Bancshares, Inc. 11/20/1972
Each share Common $20 par exchanged for (4.1667) shares Common $4 par
Texas Commerce Bancshares, Inc. acquired by Chemical New York Corp. 05/01/1987 which name changed to Chemical Banking Corp. 04/29/1988 which name changed to Manhattan Corp. (New) 03/31/1996 which which name changed to J.P. Morgan Chase & Co. 12/31/2000 which name changed to JPMorgan Chase & Co. 07/20/2004

REAGIN ENGINEERING CO. (TX)
Charter forfeited for failure to pay taxes 5/19/50

REAKO EXPLS LTD (BC)
Capital Stock 50¢ par changed to no par 9/17/79
Recapitalized as Redell Mining Corp. 6/25/93
Each share Capital Stock no par exchanged for (0.2) share Common no par
Redell Mining Corp. recapitalized as FM Resources Corp. 4/16/98 which name changed to Strikewell Energy Corp. 9/1/2006

REAL AMERN BRANDS INC (DE)
Each share old Common $0.0001 par exchanged for (0.001) share new Common $0.0001 par 02/27/2008
Recapitalized as Real American Capital Corp. 06/17/2011
Each share new Common $0.0001 par exchanged for (0.05) share Common $0.0001 par

REAL DE MINAS MNG INC (BC)
Name changed to Demand Technologies Ltd. 03/04/1993
Demand Technologies Ltd. name changed to Demand Gold Ltd. 01/25/1995 which recapitalized as Demand Ventures Ltd. 03/03/1999 which name changed to Knexa.com Enterprises Inc. 08/01/2000 which name changed to Knexa Solutions Inc. 02/18/2003 which name changed to ClearFrame Solutions Inc. 02/13/2004 which recapitalized as ClearFrame Solutions Corp. 05/02/2005 which name changed to Clear Gold Resources Inc. 02/25/2013

REAL DEL MONTE MNG CORP (CANADA)
SEC revoked common stock registration 08/31/2009
Stockholders' equity unlikely

REAL EIGHT INC (FL)
Each share old Common no par exchanged for (0.1) share new Common no par 01/30/1975
Reincorporated under the laws of Nevada as Wyatt & Co. Ltd. 09/05/1984
(See Wyatt & Co. Ltd.)

REAL EQUITIES FINL INC (MN)
Statutorily dissolved 10/8/91

REAL EQUITIES LTD (UT)
Proclaimed dissolved for failure to pay taxes 03/01/1990

REAL ESTATE CONTACTS INC (FL)
Each share old Common $0.00001 par exchanged for (0.001) share new Common $0.00001 par 07/02/2014
Each share new Common $0.00001 par exchanged again for (0.1) share new Common $0.00001 par 01/27/2015
Each share new Common $0.00001 par exchanged again for (0.01) share new Common $0.00001 par 06/17/2015
Each share new Common $0.00001 par exchanged again for (0.0001) share new Common $0.00001 par 07/15/2016
Name changed to REAC Group, Inc. 02/27/2017

REAL ESTATE DATA INC (DE)
Merged into Colonial Penn Group, Inc. 09/04/1980
Each share Common 25¢ par exchanged for $7 cash

REAL ESTATE DEVELOPMENT CO. (MT)
Name changed to Jonal Corp. 8/4/69
Jonal Corp. recapitalized as General Ener-Tech, Inc. 4/6/73
(See General Ener-Tech, Inc.)

REAL ESTATE DIRECTORIES INC (FL)
Merged into Arcata National Corp. 12/19/1969
Each share Common 10¢ par exchanged for (0.572) share Common 25¢ par
Arcata National Corp. name changed to Arcata Corp. 11/30/1978 which name changed to Atacra Liquidating Corp. 06/04/1982
(See Atacra Liquidating Corp.)

REAL ESTATE FD INC (SC)
Reorganized as Real Estate Fund Investment Trust 04/01/1972
Each share Capital Stock $1 par exchanged for (1) Share of Bene. Int. $1 par
(See Real Estate Fund Investment Trust)

REAL ESTATE FD INVT TR (SC)
Completely liquidated 12/24/98
Each Share of Bene. Int. $1 par exchanged for first and final distribution of $1.78 cash

REAL ESTATE INCOME FD INC (MD)
Issue Information - 9,650,000 shares COM offered at $15 per share on 07/25/2002
Name changed to LMP Real Estate Income Fund Inc. 10/9/2006

REAL ESTATE INVT PPTYS (CA)
Shares of Bene. Int. $1 par split (2) for (1) by issuance of (1) additional share 11/10/1978
Reincorporated under the laws of Delaware as Hotel Properties, Inc. and Shares of Bene. Int. $1 par reclassified as Class A Common $1 par 12/31/1984
Hotel Properties, Inc. merged into Hotel Investors Trust 09/16/1986 which recapitalized as Starwood Lodging Trust 02/01/1995 which name changed to Starwood Hotels & Resorts Trust 01/02/1998 which name changed to Starwood Hotels & Resorts 02/24/1998 which reorganized as Starwood Hotels & Resorts Worldwide, Inc. 01/06/1999 which merged into Marriott International, Inc. (New) 09/23/2016

REAL ESTATE INVT TR AMER (MA)
Merged into REIT of America, Inc. 10/04/1983
Each Ctf. of Bene. Int. $1 par exchanged for $50 principal amount of 8% 10-yr. Conv. Sinking Fund Mortgage Bonds due 09/01/1993

REAL ESTATE INVT TR CALIF (CA)
Shares of Bene. Int. no par split (2) for (1) by issuance of (1) additional share 03/17/1977
Shares of Bene. Int. no par split (2) for (1) by issuance of (1) additional share 05/31/1985
Merged into BRE Properties, Inc. 03/15/1996
Each Share of Bene. Int. no par exchanged for (0.57) share Common 1¢ par

BRE Properties, Inc. merged into Essex Property Trust, Inc. 04/01/2014

REAL ESTATE LOAN CO. OF CANADA LTD.
Acquired by Canada Permanent Mortgage Corp. for $137.50 per share in cash in 1945

REAL ESTATE MORTGAGE & GUARANTY CORP.
Recapitalized in 1939
Each share 8% Preferred $10 par exchanged for (1) share 5% Preferred $10 par and (1) share Class A Common $5 par
Each share Common no par exchanged for (1) share Class B Common no par
Liquidation completed in 1953

REAL ESTATE OPPORTUNITIES INC (CO)
Name changed to PocketSpec Technologies Inc. (CO) 12/06/2001
PocketSpec Technologies Inc. (CO) reincorporated in Nevada as Falcon Ridge Development, Inc. 07/18/2005
(See Falcon Ridge Development, Inc.)

REAL ESTATE REFERRAL CTR INC (NV)
Common $0.00001 par split (10) for (1) by issuance of (9) additional shares payable 05/29/2009 to holders of record 05/22/2009
Ex date - 06/01/2009
Name changed to Gold Bag, Inc. 06/01/2009
Gold Bag, Inc. name changed to Focus Gold Corp. 06/06/2011

REAL ESTATE RESTORATION & RENT INC (NV)
Common $0.001 par split (10.59135) for (1) by issuance of (9.59135) additional shares payable 01/31/2012 to holders of record 01/23/2012 Ex date - 02/01/2012
Reincorporated under the laws of Delaware as Organovo Holdings, Inc. 02/14/2012

REAL ESTATE SECS INCOME FD INC (MD)
Name changed to Cohen & Steers Realty Income Fund, Inc. 5/26/93

REAL ESTATE TITLE INSURANCE CO. OF THE DISTRICT OF COLUMBIA (DC)
Under plan of merger name changed to Columbia Real Estate Title Insurance Co. 01/19/1966
(See Columbia Real Estate Title Insurance Co.)

REAL-ESTATEFORLEASE COM INC (DE)
Name changed to Uni-Pixel, Inc. 02/03/2005

REAL GOODS TRADING CORP (CA)
Merged into Gaiam, Inc. 01/30/2001
Each share Common no par exchanged for (0.1) share Class A Common $0.0001 par
Gaiam, Inc. name changed to Gaia, Inc. 07/15/2016

REAL HIP HOP MATRIX CORP (NV)
Name changed to RHNMedia 01/12/2007
RHNMedia name changed to Massive G Media Corp. 03/16/2007 which name changed to International Minerals Mining Group, Inc. 06/21/2007 which name changed to Advanced Content Services, Inc. 02/05/2008 which recapitalized as New Wave Holdings, Inc. 12/08/2014 which name changed to PAO Group, Inc. 06/29/2017

REAL IND INC (DE)
Under Chapter 11 plan of reorganization each share Common $0.001 par automatically became (0.005) share Elah Holdings, Inc. Common $0.001 par 05/09/2018
Note: Holders of (100) or fewer shares were cancelled and are without value

REAL LOGIC INC (FL)
Name changed to Andover Energy Holdings, Inc. 07/22/2008

REAL MED INDS INC (DE)
Charter cancelled and declared inoperative and void for non-payment of taxes 03/01/1975

REAL OIL CO. (CO)
Declared defunct and inoperative for failure to pay taxes and file annual reports 10/19/23

REAL PAPER DISPLAYS INC (NV)
Name changed to AquaStar Holdings, Inc. 06/16/2010
AquaStar Holdings, Inc. name changed to SUTIMCo International, Inc. 06/17/2011

REAL PAR INC (AB)
Name changed to Tundra Environmental Corp. Ltd. (ALTA) 05/11/1993
Tundra Environmental Corp. Ltd. (ALTA) reincorporated in Ontario 12/16/1994
(See Tundra Environmental Corp. Ltd.)

REAL PETE CO (DE)
Merged into Clinton Oil Co. 06/11/1971
Each share Common 1¢ par exchanged for (0.8) share Common 3-1/3¢ par
Clinton Oil Co. name changed to Energy Reserves Group, Inc. 02/10/1976
(See Energy Reserves Group, Inc.)

REAL PRIME RES INC (NV)
Charter revoked for failure to file reports and pay fees 09/01/1989

REAL PROPERTIES CORP. OF AMERICA (DE)
Name changed to Commonwealth United Corp. 02/01/1965
Commonwealth United Corp. recapitalized as Iota Industries, Inc. 12/29/1972
(See Iota Industries, Inc.)

REAL PPTY SYS INC (CA)
Charter suspended for failure to file reports and pay fees 11/01/1988

REAL RES INC (AB)
Reorganized 05/26/2000
Reorganized from Real Resources Ltd. to Real Resources Inc. 05/26/2000
Each share old Common no par exchanged for (0.25) share new Common no par
Merged into TriStar Oil & Gas Ltd. (New) 08/16/2007
Each share new Common no par exchanged for (1) share Common no par
Note: Holders of (99) shares or fewer will receive $7.535 cash per share
TriStar Oil & Gas Ltd. (New) merged into PetroBakken Energy Ltd. (Old) 10/05/2009 which reorganized as PetroBakken Energy Ltd. (New) 01/07/2013 which name changed to Lightstream Resources Ltd. 05/28/2013

REAL SEC CO INC (NV)
Charter revoked for failure to file reports and pay fees 11/01/2010

REAL SILK INVTS INC (IN)
Reincorporated 12/27/68
Name changed 5/9/89
Common $10 par changed to $5 par in 1936
State of incorporation changed from (IL) to (IN) 12/27/68
Name changed from Real Silk Hosiery Mills, Inc. to Real Silk Investments, Inc. 5/9/89
Merged into Lord Abbett Affiliated Fund, Inc. 12/14/99
Each share Common $5 par exchanged for (54.046) shares Class A

REAL TIME COMPUTER SYSTEMS, INC. (TN)
Name changed to RT National Corp. 08/17/1970
(See RT National Corp.)

REAL TIME DATAPRO LTD (ON)
Acquired by Memotec Data Inc. 12/31/85
Details not available

REAL TIME GEOPHYSICS, INC. (MA)
Name changed to Real Time Technology, Inc. 1/31/73
(See Real Time Technology, Inc.)

REAL TIME TECHNOLOGY INC (MA)
Out of business 2/1/75
Details not available

REAL VALUE ESTATES INC (NV)
Name changed to Xun Energy, Inc. 08/03/2010

REALAMERICA CO (DE)
Reorganized 12/15/82
Reorganized from under the laws of (KY) to (DE) 12/15/82
Each Share of Bene. Int. $1 par exchanged for (1) share Common $1 par
Each share Common $1 par received initial distribution of $4 cash 12/31/88
Each share Common $1 par received second distribution of $0.60 cash 8/20/89
Each share Common $1 par received third distribution of $0.15 cash 3/15/90
Each share Common $1 par received fourth distribution of $0.07 cash 11/30/90
Note: Plan of liquidation revoked 2/25/92
Previous distributions were reclassified as return of capital
Each share Common $1 par exchanged for (0.125) share Class B Common $1 par 11/15/99
Name changed to RA Global Services, Inc. and Class B Common $1 par reclassified as Common $1 par 3/6/2007

REALAMERICA INVT CORP (IA)
Completely liquidated 11/21/1981
Each share Common $1 par exchanged for first and final distribution of $20 cash

REALAX SOFTWARE A G (GERMANY)
ADR agreement terminated 5/3/2007
No ADR holders' equity

REALBIZ MEDIA GROUP INC (DE)
Each share old Common $0.061 par exchanged for (0.005) share new Common $0.001 par 01/20/2017
Each share new Common $0.001 par received distribution of (0.00111111) share Nestbuilder.com Corp. Common $0.0001 par payable 07/31/2018 to holders of record 07/02/2018
Name changed to Verus International, Inc. 10/16/2018

REALCO INC (NM)
Reincorporated under the laws of Minnesota as Oak Ridge Capital Group, Inc. 6/10/2002

REALCO INTL INC (NV)
Common $0.001 par split (4.04) for (1) by issuance of (3.04) additional shares payable 09/15/2015 to holders of record 09/11/2015
Ex date - 09/16/2015
Name changed to PeerLogix, Inc. 09/23/2015

REALD INC (DE)
Acquired by Rhombus Cinema Holdings, LLC 03/22/2016
Each share Common $0.0001 par exchanged for $11 cash

REALDATA CORP (NY)
Proclaimed dissolved 12/30/87

REALESTATE PATHWAYS INC (WY)
Common $0.001 par split (15.2) for (1) by issuance of (14.2) additional shares payable 01/22/2013 to holders of record 01/16/2013
Ex date - 01/23/2013
Name changed to NoHo, Inc. 01/31/2013

REALEX CORP (MO)
Stock Dividend - 20% 10/11/1976
Acquired by Calmar Inc. 01/11/1985
Each share Common $1 par exchanged for $48.10 cash

REALEX PPTYS CORP (AB)
Non-Vtg. Common no par reclassified as old Common no par 06/16/2010
Each share old Common no par exchanged for (0.1) share new Common no par 06/16/2010
Acquired by Dundee Real Estate Investment Trust 02/07/2011
Each share new Common no par exchanged for $8.25 cash

REALFUND (ON)
Merged into RioCan Real Estate Investment Trust 5/31/99
Each Unit exchanged for (1.45) Units

REALGOLD INTL INC (NV)
Name changed to Asia Travel Corp. 06/05/2013
Asia Travel Corp. name changed to Square Chain Corp. 04/11/2018

REALIST INC (DE)
Each share Common $1 par exchanged for (0.33333333) share Common $3 par 04/24/1962
Stock Dividends - 25% 12/28/1966; 25% 12/27/1967; 25% 12/27/1968; 10% 11/27/1978
Name changed to David White, Inc. (DE) 12/15/1989
David White, Inc. (DE) reincorporated in (WI) 05/05/1992
(See David White, Inc. (WI))

REALITY COMM CORP NEW (AB)
Recapitalized as Crossfire Holdings Inc. 11/11/2005
Each share Common no par exchanged for (0.2) share Common no par
Crossfire Holdings Inc. name changed to Crossfire Energy Services Inc. 07/01/2007
(See Crossfire Energy Services Inc.)

REALITY COMM CORP OLD (AB)
Issue Information - 3,607,200 UNITS consisting of (1) share COM and (0.5) WT offered at $0.15 per Unit on 07/08/2002
Acquired by Reality Commerce Corp. (New) 08/23/2004
Each share Common no par exchanged for (0.2) share Common no par
Reality Commerce Corp. (New) recapitalized as Crossfire Holdings Inc. 11/11/2005 which name changed to Crossfire Energy Services Inc. 07/01/2007

REALITY INTERACTIVE INC (NV)
Reincorporated 1/23/2002
State of incorporation changed from (MN) to (NV) 1/23/2002
Each share old Common $0.001 par exchanged for (0.01) share new Common $0.001 par 2/8/2002
Each share new Common $0.001 par exchanged again for (0.025) share new Common $0.001 par 2/5/2004
Note: Holders of (100) to (4,000) shares will receive (100) shares only
Holders of (99) or fewer shares were not affected by the reverse split

Name changed to Natural Gas Systems, Inc. 6/18/2004
Natural Gas Systems, Inc. name changed to Evolution Petroleum Corp. 7/17/2006

REALITY OILS LTD. (AB)
Recapitalized as Nu-Reality Oils Ltd. in 1957
Each share Capital Stock no par exchanged for (0.1) share Capital Stock no par
Nu-Reality Oils Ltd. acquired by Flag Oils Ltd. 10/11/60 which name changed to Flag Resources Ltd. 1/4/82 which recapitalized as Flag Resources (1985) Ltd. 2/18/85

REALITY RACING INC (FL)
Each share old Common $0.001 par exchanged for (4) shares new Common $0.001 par 09/19/2006
SEC revoked common stock registration 05/05/2009
Stockholders' equity unlikely

REALITY WIRELESS NETWORKS INC (NV)
Each share old Common $0.001 par exchanged for (0.5) share new Common $0.001 par 05/06/2002
Each share new Common $0.001 par exchanged again for (0.01) share new Common $0.001 par 10/04/2004
Each share new Common $0.001 par exchanged again for (0.0025) share new Common $0.001 par 05/27/2005
Recapitalized as Recab International, Inc. 05/15/2006
Each share new Common $0.001 par exchanged for (0.002) share Common $0.001 par
Recab International, Inc. recapitalized as Saudi American Holdings Corp. 06/29/2007

REALLYTHERE TECHNOLOGIES (NV)
Charter permanently revoked 10/31/2002

REALM ENERGY INTL CORP (BC) 11/10/2017
Merged into San Leon Energy PLC 11/10/2011
Each share Common no par exchanged for (3.3) shares Ordinary
Note: Unexchanged certificates will be cancelled and become without value 11/10/2017

REALM GROUP INC (AB)
Delisted from Toronto Venture Stock Exchange 06/05/2002

REALM MNG CORP LTD (MB)
Dissolved 02/15/1967
No stockholders' equity

REALM PRODTN & ENTMT INC (FL)
Each share old Common $0.005 par exchanged for (0.1) share new Common $0.005 par 09/27/1999
Name changed to TVTravel.com, Inc. 10/27/1999
TVTravel.com, Inc. name changed to Emailthatpays.com, Inc. (FL) 12/21/1999 which reorganized in Delaware as Forge, Inc. 05/13/2002 which name changed to Encore Clean Energy, Inc. (DE) 12/19/2003 which reincorporated in Necada 10/21/2005
(See Encore Clean Energy, Inc.)

REALM RESOURCES INC. (ON)
Recapitalized as New Realm Resources Inc. 08/26/1983
Each share Common no par exchanged for (0.2) share Common no par
New Realm Resources Inc. name changed to Direct Equity Corp. 05/15/1987 which merged into Envirothermic Technologies Ltd. 10/01/1993 which recapitalized as Environmental Reclamation Inc.
06/22/1998 which was acquired by Therma Freeze Inc. 02/28/2001 which name changed to Enviro-Energy Corp. 07/03/2001
(See Enviro-Energy Corp.)

REALM RES INC TEX (WY)
Reincorporated 10/30/1991
Class A Common 1¢ par reclassified as Common 1¢ par 05/12/1987
State of incorporation changed from Nevada to Wyoming 10/30/1991
Company reported out of business 00/00/1992
Details not available

REALMARK ACQUISITIONS LLC (GA)
Name changed to Realmark Acquisitions II LLC 7/12/2005

REALMARK HLDGS CORP (GA)
Each share old Common no par exchanged for (0.125) share new Common no par 05/01/1995
Acquired by Realmark Acquisitions LLC 04/13/2005
Each share new Common no par exchanged for (1) Class A Trust Unit
Realmark Acquisitions LLC name changed to Realmark Acquisitions II LLC 07/12/2005

REALMARK INC NEW (DE)
Reorganized 11/09/1989
Plan of reorganization under Chapter 11 Federal Bankruptcy proceedings effective 11/09/1989
No stockholders' equity for holders of Realmark, Inc. (Old) Common 1¢ par
Under plan of reorganization each share Realmark Inc. (New) Common no par automatically became (1) share Realmark Holdings Corp. Common no par 11/05/1990
Note: Realmark Inc. (New) Common no par issued to bondholders in Chapter 11 Reorganization
Realmark Holdings Corp. was acquired by Realmark Acquisitions LLC 04/13/2005 which name changed to Realmark Acquisitions II LLC 07/12/2005

REALMARK PPTYS INVS LTD PARTNERSHIP (DE)
Completely liquidated 12/31/2000
Each Unit of Ltd. Partnership received first and final distribution of approximately $25.76 cash

REALOGY CORP (DE)
Merged into Apollo Management, L.P. 4/10/2007
Each share Common 1¢ par exchanged for $30 cash

REALSEARCH INTL SYS CORP (BC)
Name changed to Allmed International Investments Corp. 04/11/1989
Allmed International Investments Corp. name changed to Ecoprogress Canada Holdings Inc. 02/07/1997 which recapitalized as Consolidated Ecoprogress Technology Inc. 05/06/1998

REALSEC CORP (TX)
Charter forfeited for failure to pay taxes 01/18/1988

REALSITE INC (NY)
Reorganized 03/23/1970
Each share Class A 10¢ par exchanged for (0.5) share new Common 10¢ par
Each share Common 10¢ par exchanged for (0.5) share new Common 10¢ par
Merged into First Continental Dev-Con, Inc. 05/01/1973
Each share new Common 10¢ par exchanged for (1) share Common 10¢ par
Note: Certificates not surrendered prior to 05/01/1976 were entitled only to the cash market value of the shares on that date
(See First Continental Dev-Con, Inc.)

REALTIMECARS INC (NV)
Reorganized under the laws of Florida as Siteworks, Inc. 10/25/2002
Each share Common $0.001 par exchanged for (0.005) share Common $0.001 par
Siteworks, Inc. name changed to SiteWorks Building & Development Co. (FL) 04/15/2005 which reincorporated in Nevada as SBD International, Inc. 08/03/2006 which recapitalized as Solargy Systems Inc. 10/27/2008
(See Solargy Systems Inc.)

REALTONE ELECTRONICS CORP. (NY)
Common 10¢ par changed to 5¢ par and (1) additional share issued 3/5/62
Merged into Ashkenazi Corp. 1/31/66
Each share Common 5¢ par exchanged for $2 cash

REALTY & MTG INVS PAC (CA)
Name changed to Rampac 03/20/1981
(See Rampac)

REALTY & SECURITY CO.
In liquidation in 1944

REALTY ASSOCIATES (BROOKLYN, NY)
Name changed to New York Investors, Inc. in 1929 which became bankrupt in 1938

REALTY CAP LTD (ON)
Class A no par split (2) for (1) by issuance of (1) additional share 1/24/69
Common no par split (2) for (1) by issuance of (1) additional share 1/24/69
Name changed to Federal Trustco Inc. 6/1/79
Federal Trustco Inc. name changed to Realcap Holdings Ltd. 10/2/80

REALTY CO. (OH)
Liquidated in 1952

REALTY CORP. OF NEW YORK (NY)
Charter cancelled and proclaimed dissolved for failure to pay taxes and file reports 3/17/48

REALTY EQUITIES CORP N Y (NY)
Stock Dividend - 10% 06/01/1964
Charter cancelled and proclaimed dissolved for failure to pay taxes 12/20/1977

REALTY FDS INC (MD)
Completely liquidated 07/31/2008
Each Adelante Share RE Classics ETF received net asset value
Each Adelante Share RE Composite ETF received net asset value
Each Adelante Share RE Growth ETF received net asset value
Each Adelante Share RE Kings ETF received net asset value
Each Adelante Share RE Shelter ETF received net asset value
Each Adelante Share RE Value ETF received net asset value
Each Adelante Share RE Yield Plus ETF received net asset value

REALTY FIN CORP (MD)
Name changed to CV Holdings, Inc. 11/07/2013

REALTY FINANCIAL CORP. (FL)
Merged into Roltec, Inc. 4/3/67
Each share Common $1 par exchanged for (0.3) share Common $1 par
Roltec, Inc. merged into Gould Properties, Inc. 7/24/68 which name changed to Gould Enterprises, Inc. 4/2/69 which merged into Gould Investors Trust (MA) 7/1/70 which reorganized in Delaware as Gould Investors L.P. 5/18/86

REALTY GROWTH INC (OR)
Liquidated 12/17/1980
Details not available

REALTY INCOME CORP (MD)
Reincorporated 05/28/1997
State of incorporation changed from (DE) to (MD) 05/28/1997
9.375% Class B Preferred $1 par called for redemption at $25 plus $0.429687 accrued dividends on 06/07/2004
9.5% Class C Preferred $1 par called for redemption at $25 on 07/30/2004
7.375% Monthly Income Preferred Ser. D $1 par changed to 1¢ par 08/01/2011
6.75% Monthly Income Preferred Class E $1 par changed to 1¢ par 08/01/2011
7.375% Monthly Income Preferred Ser. D 1¢ par called for redemption at $25 on 03/01/2012
6.75% Monthly Income Preferred Class E 1¢ par called for redemption at $25 plus $0.0375 accrued dividends on 10/24/2014
6.625% Monthly Income Preferred Class F 1¢ par called for redemption at $25 plus $0.101215 accrued dividends on 04/06/2017
(Additional Information in Active)

REALTY INCOME TR (MA)
Name changed to Derwood Investment Trust 9/18/85
Derwood Investment Trust name changed to Derwood Investment Corp. 7/10/86
(See Derwood Investment Corp.)

REALTY INDS INC (VA)
Merged into United Dominion Realty Trust, Inc. (VA) 12/31/1984
Each share Common $1 par exchanged for (3.125) shares Common $1 par and $4 cash
United Dominion Realty Trust, Inc. (VA) reincorporated in Maryland 06/11/2003 which name changed to UDR, Inc.

REALTY INFORMATION GROUP INC (DE)
Issue Information - 2,500,000 shares COM offered at $9 per share on 07/01/1998
Name changed to Costar Group, Inc. 8/2/99

REALTY INNS INC (OH)
Assets sold and company voluntarily dissolved 04/30/1986
No stockholders' equity

REALTY INVESTORS TRUST
Dissolved in 1939

REALTY MORTGAGE CO. (OH)
Liquidated in 1952
No Common stockholders' equity

REALTY NATL CORP (OH)
Merged into Nucorp, Inc. (OH) 7/20/76
Each share Class A no par exchanged for (1) share Common no par and $4 principal amount of 8% Subord. Debentures due 7/31/2001
Nucorp, Inc. (OH) name changed to Nucorp Energy, Inc. (Old) 5/23/80
(See Nucorp Energy, Inc. (Old))

REALTY OPERATORS, INC.
Recapitalized as Southdown Sugars, Inc. on a (2) for (1) basis 3/15/48
Southdown Sugars, Inc. name changed to Southdown, Inc. 5/12/59
(See Southdown, Inc.)

REALTY REFUND TR (OH)
Name changed to InnSuites Hospitality Trust 9/24/98

REALTY SOUTH INVS INC (MD)
Common 1¢ par split (3) for (2) by issuance of (0.5) additional share 02/23/1987

REA-REC

Reincorporated under the laws of Georgia as Equivest Inc. 06/01/1992
Equivest Inc. merged into Medical Resource Companies of America 03/24/1993 which name changed to Greenbriar Corp. 03/27/1996 which name changed to CabelTel International Corp. 02/10/2005 which name changed to New Concept Energy, Inc. 06/03/2008

REALTY TECHNOLOGIES INC (WA)
Name changed to eCourierCorps Inc. 05/16/2000
eCourierCorps Inc. name changed to Azul Studios International Inc. 09/15/2004 which name changed to Modern City Entertainment, Inc. 04/27/2007
(See Modern City Entertainment, Inc.)

REALTY TITLE INSURANCE CO., INC. (MD)
5% Preferred $50 par called for redemption 09/01/1964
Liquidation completed 05/28/1965
Each share Class B Common $1 par exchanged for cash distributions totalling $114.58 plus a Participating Certificate in Realty Title Liquidating Trust

REALTY TITLE INVESTORS CORP.
Out of business 00/00/1930
Details not available

REALTY URANIUM & MNG CO (CO)
Each share Capital Stock 25¢ par exchanged for (0.5) share Common 5¢ par 05/04/1955
Recapitalized as Empire Ventures, Inc. 11/11/1969
Each share Common 5¢ par exchanged for (0.33333333) share Common 5¢ par
(See Empire Ventures, Inc.)

REARDON CO (MO)
Name changed to Nodraer Liquidating Co. 3/1/66
(See Nodraer Liquidating Co.)

REARWIN AIRCRAFT & ENGINES, INC.
Name changed to Commonwealth Aircraft Inc. 00/00/1943
(See Commonwealth Aircraft Inc.)

REATTA RES LTD (BC)
Recapitalized as Grand Forks Mines Ltd. 10/18/1983
Each share Common no par exchanged for (0.2) share Common no par
Grand Forks Mines Ltd. recapitalized as Attwood Gold Corp. 06/16/1989 which recapitalized as Dynasty Motorcar Corp. (BC) 06/02/2000 which reincorporated in Canada 11/29/2002 which recapitalized as Comwest Capital Corp. 06/29/2004 which merged into ComWest Enterprise Corp. 12/12/2005 which name changed to Unisync Corp. 08/01/2014

REAVES UTIL INCOME FD (DE)
Auction Market Preferred Ser. F7 no par called for redemption at $25,000 on 12/09/2010
Auction Market Preferred Ser. W28 no par called for redemption at $25,000 on 12/13/2010
Auction Market Preferred Ser. M7 no par called for redemption at $25,000 on 12/14/2010
(Additional Information in Active)

REB PROJ INC (FL)
Name changed to Aspen International Holdings, Inc. 05/05/2015

REBA RES LTD (BC)
Delisted from Vancouver Stock Exchange 03/02/1988

REBAIR GOLD MINES LTD. (ON)
Charter surrendered 12/19/60
Capital Stock $1 par worthless

REBGOLD CORP (CANADA)
Each share old Common no par received distribution of (0.2) share BacTech Environmental Corp. Common no par payable 12/02/2010 to holders of record 12/01/2010
Each share old Common no par exchanged for (0.1) share new Common no par 05/30/2012
Merged into Aquila Resources Inc. 01/22/2014
Each share new Common no par exchanged for (1) share Common no par
Note: Unexchanged certificates will be cancelled and become without value 01/22/2019

REBUILDER MED INC (NV)
Name changed to Pizza International, Inc. 12/14/2006
Pizza International, Inc. name changed to Look Entertainment, Inc. 05/23/2007 which recapitalized as VTEC, Inc. 07/05/2007 which name changed to United Consortium, Ltd. (Old) 03/10/2008 which reorganized as United Consortium, Ltd. (New) 05/05/2010

REBUILDER MED TECHNOLOGIES INC (NV)
Common $0.0001 par changed to $0.001 par 01/20/2010
Each share old Common $0.001 par exchanged for (0.00666666) share new Common $0.001 par 05/31/2011
Name changed to Lion Gold Brazil, Inc. 08/23/2012
Lion Gold Brazil, Inc. recapitalized as Cannabiz Mobile, Inc. 06/24/2014

REBUS OIL LTD (AB)
Acquired by Medizone International Inc. 10/20/1992
Details not available

REC MINERALS CORP (ON)
Name changed to Reliant Gold Corp. 03/02/2011

RECAB INTL INC (NV)
Recapitalized as Saudi American Holdings Corp. 06/29/2007
Each share Common $0.001 par exchanged for (0.001) share Common $0.001 par

RECAP ENERGY INC (AB)
Recapitalized as Realex Properties Corp. 09/29/2006
Each share Common no par exchanged for (0.138075) share Common no par and (0.138075) share Non-Vtg. Common no par
(See Realex Properties Corp.)

RECCO INC (MO)
Merged into Pickwick International, Inc. (NY) 02/18/1971
Each share Class A Common 1¢ par exchanged for (0.111111) share Common 25¢ par
Pickwick International, Inc. (NY) reincorporated in Delaware 10/27/1975
(See Pickwick International, Inc. (DE))

RECCO RESH CORP (BC)
Struck off register and declared dissolved for failure to file returns 10/30/1992

RECEIVABLE ACQUISITION & MGMT CORP (DE)
Name changed to PwrCor, Inc. 03/29/2017

RECEPTAGEN LTD (CANADA)
Reorganized under the laws of Florida as Spantel Communications Inc. 10/16/2001
Each share Common no par exchanged for (0.005) share Common $0.001 par
Spantel Communications Inc. recapitalized as Systems America, Inc. 05/27/2010
(See Systems America, Inc.)

RECEPTECH CORP (DE)
Acquired by Immunex Corp. 12/22/92
Each share Common 1¢ par exchanged for $26 cash

RECEPTOS INC (DE)
Merged into Celgene Corp. 08/27/2015
Each share Common $0.001 par exchanged for $232 cash

RECFUEL HLDGS INC (NV)
Common $0.001 par split (4.33) for (1) by issuance of (3.33) additional shares payable 07/20/2007 to holders of record 07/18/2007
Ex date - 07/23/2007
Common $0.001 par split (5.38) for (1) by issuance of (4.38) additional shares payable 08/06/2007 to holders of record 07/27/2007
Ex date - 08/07/2007
Charter revoked for failure to file reports and pay fees 09/30/2008

RECKITT & COLMAN HLDGS USA INC
Exchangeable Auction Preferred called for redemption at $100,000 on 11/30/2006

RECKSON ASSOCS RLTY CORP (MD)
Issue Information - 6,120,000 shares COM offered at $24.25 per share on 03/25/1995
Common 1¢ par split (2) for (1) by issuance of (1) additional share payable 4/15/97 to holders of record 4/4/97 Ex date - 4/16/97
Each share Common 1¢ par received distribution of (0.08) share Reckson Service Industries, Inc. Common 1¢ par payable 6/11/98 to holders of record 5/26/98
Each share Class B Common 1¢ par exchanged for (1) share Common 1¢ par 11/25/2003
Conv. Preferred Ser. B 1¢ par called for redemption at $25.50 on 1/5/2004
7.625% Conv. Preferred Ser. A 1¢ par called for redemption at $25.7625 plus $0.3918 accrued dividends on 10/15/2004
Merged into SL Green Realty Corp. 1/25/2007
Each share Common 1¢ par exchanged for (0.10387) share Common 1¢ par and $31.68 cash

RECKSON SVC INDS INC (DE)
Name changed to FrontLine Capital Group 03/08/2000
(See FrontLine Capital Group)

RECLAIM INC (DE)
Each share old Common 1¢ par exchanged for (0.0125) share new Common 1¢ par 01/05/1996
SEC revoked common stock registration 10/16/2008
No stockholders' equity

RECLAMATION CONSULTING & APPLICATIONS INC (CO)
Recapitalized as Alderox, Inc. 05/20/2008
Each share Common 1¢ par exchanged for (0.5) share Common 1¢ par
(See Alderox, Inc.)

RECLAMATION MGMT LTD (ON)
Name changed to Euro-Net Investments Ltd. 8/19/99

RECLAMATION SYS INC (MA)
Proclaimed dissolved for failure to file annual reports and pay taxes 12/31/90

RECO INTL GROUP INC OLD (AB)
Reorganized as Reco International Group Inc. (New) 04/08/2015
Each share Common no par exchanged for (1) share Common no par, (1) share Reco Central Alberta Inc. Common no par, (1) share Reco Northern Alberta Inc. Common no par, and (1) share Reco Southern Alberta Inc. Common no par

RECO INTL INC (DE)
Merged into York International Corp. 07/06/1989
Each share Common 10¢ par exchanged for $7 cash

RECO MOUNTAIN BASE METALS MINES LTD. (BC)
Bankrupt in 1946

RECO SILVER MINES LTD (BC)
Name changed to Silvex Resources Corp. 05/16/1980
(See Silvex Resources Corp.)

RECOGNITION INTL INC (DE)
Name changed 3/12/93
Common $1 par changed to 25¢ par and (3) additional shares issued 3/22/68
Name changed from Recognition Equipment Inc. to Recognition International Inc. 3/12/93
Merged into Banctec, Inc. 10/13/95
Each share Common 25¢ par exchanged for (0.59) share Common 25¢ par
(See Banctec, Inc.)

RECOGNITION TECHNOLOGY INC (DE)
Charter cancelled and declared inoperative and void for non-payment of taxes 03/01/1993

RECOM MANAGED SYS INC (DE)
Each (28.74) shares old Common $0.001 par exchanged for (1) share new Common $0.001 par 11/09/2000
New Common $0.001 par split (3) for (1) by issuance of (2) additional shares payable 04/14/2003 to holders of record 04/11/2003
Ex date - 04/15/2003
Name changed to Signalife Inc. 11/15/2005
Each share new Common $0.001 par exchanged for (1) share Common $0.001 par
Signalife Inc. name changed to Heart Tronics Inc. 06/10/2009

RECOMPUTE INTL CORP (NV)
Recapitalized as Pangea Pictures Corp. 10/10/2006
Each (14) shares Common 1¢ par exchanged for (1) share Common 1¢ par
Pangea Pictures Corp. name changed to Tintic Standard Gold Mines, Inc. 02/21/2008

RECON CAP SER TR (DE)
Trust terminated 03/11/2016
Each share Recon Capital FTSE 100 ETF no par received $20.02327 cash
Name changed to Horizons ETF Trust I 02/28/2017

RECON INVT INC (UT)
Proclaimed dissolved for failure to file reports 5/16/80

RECON PIPE & COUPLING CORP (DE)
Charter cancelled and declared inoperative and void for non-payment of taxes 03/01/1995

RECONVERSION TECHNOLOGIES INC (DE)
Each share old Common $0.0001 par exchanged for (0.125) share new Common $0.0001 par 02/03/1998
Name changed to Logisoft Corp. 04/28/2000
Logisoft Corp. name changed to Team Sports Entertainment, Inc. 05/18/2001 which name changed to Idea Sports Entertainment Group, Inc. 11/09/2004 which recapitalized as HealthSport, Inc. 05/16/2006
(See HealthSport, Inc.)

REC-RED

RECOR HLDGS LTD (BERMUDA)
Name changed to Starbow Holdings Ltd. 09/27/2002
Starbow Holdings Ltd. name changed to Town Health Medical Technology Holdings Co. Ltd. 09/13/2006 which name changed to Hong Kong Health Check & Laboratory Holdings Co. Ltd. 07/20/2007 which name changed to China Gogreen Assets Investment Ltd. 09/02/2011
(See China Gogreen Assets Investment Ltd.)

RECORD OIL CO (CA)
Completely liquidated 06/01/1975
Each share Capital Stock 5¢ par exchanged for first and final distribution of $0.20 cash

RECORD RETENTION & RETRIEVAL CORP (NY)
Charter cancelled and proclaimed dissolved for failure to pay taxes 09/29/1982

RECORD ROUYN MINES, LTD. (ON)
Charter surrendered for failure to file reports and pay taxes 1955

RECORD TIRE & MFG. CO., INC. (DE)
Charter cancelled and declared inoperative and void for non-payment of taxes 3/22/22

RECORD VENDING MACHINES, INC. (CO)
Name changed to Owl Drug Co. of Colorado in July 1963
Owl Drug Co. of Colorado name changed to Cable Car Burger Inc. 3/30/68 which recapitalized as Winthrop-Scott Corp. 11/3/72
(See Winthrop-Scott Corp.)

RECORDING INDS CORP (TN)
Placed in receivership 01/09/1968
Receiver opined in 1970 that sale of assets would benefit creditors only and Common Stock should be considered worthless

RECORDLAB CORP (WA)
SEC revoked common stock registration 11/17/2008
Stockholders' equity unlikely

RECOTON CORP (NY)
Common 20¢ par split (3) for (2) by issuance of (0.5) additional share 9/19/83
Common 20¢ par split (4) for (3) by issuance of (1/3) additional share 12/11/92
Common 20¢ par split (4) for (3) by issuance of (1/3) additional share 10/14/93
Common 20¢ par split (3) for (2) by issuance of (0.5) additional share 7/11/94
Stock Dividends - 100% 10/11/78; 50% 4/28/83
Plan of reorganization under Chapter 11 Federal Bankruptcy Code effective 5/21/2004
No stockholders' equity

RECOV ENERGY CORP (DE)
Name changed to General Metals Corp. 01/26/2006
General Metals Corp. recapitalized as Cibolan Gold Corp. 05/30/2014

RECOVERY ENERGY INC (NV)
Each share old Common $0.0001 par exchanged for (0.25) share new Common $0.0001 par 10/19/2011
Name changed to Lilis Energy, Inc. 12/02/2013

RECOVERY ENGR INC (MN)
Reincorporated 5/9/96
Secondary Offering - 1,190,000 shares COM offered at $30 per share on 04/23/1998
State of incorporation changed from (DE) to (MN) 5/6/96
Merged into Procter & Gamble Co. 10/7/99

Each share Common 1¢ par exchanged for $35.25 cash

RECOVERY ENTERPRISES INC (NV)
Name changed to KMT Global Holdings Inc. 05/03/2011
KMT Global Holdings Inc. recapitalized as StarPower ON Systems, Inc. 03/23/2017

RECOVERY NETWORK INC (CO)
Issue Information - 2,100,000 UNITS consisting of (1) share COM and (1) WT offered at $5.10 per Unit on 09/29/1997
Name changed to RnetHealth.com, Inc. 06/24/1999
RnetHealth.com, Inc. name changed to RnetHealth, Inc. 01/02/2001 which recapitalized as Bryn Resources Inc. 12/26/2008

RECREAMA INC (DE)
Common 10¢ par split (2) for (1) by issuance of (1) additional share 7/10/72
Name changed to Chateau de Ville, Inc. 6/4/74
(See Chateau de Ville, Inc.)

RECREATION CORP AMER (UT)
Name changed to Engineered Construction Industries, Inc. 05/31/1974
(See Engineered Construction Industries, Inc.)

RECREATION CORP AMER INC (OH)
Bankruptcy proceedings terminated 01/27/1982
Each share Common $1 par exchanged for first and final distribution of $0.0317 cash

RECREATION ENTERPRISES, INC. (MO)
Name changed to Micom, Inc. 04/24/1962
(See Micom, Inc.)

RECREATION INC. (UT)
Name changed to Sunburst Nuclear Corp. 04/27/1978
Sunburst Nuclear Corp. name changed to Becos Industries, Inc. (UT) 08/25/1980 which reorganized in Nevada 10/31/1984 which name changed to Softpoint Inc. 09/01/1989 which recapitalized as Acquest Corp. 11/04/1996
(See Acquest Corp.)

RECREATION LEISURE LD CORP (DE)
Name changed to Acumen Trading Co., Inc. 8/20/76
(See Acumen Trading Co. Inc.)

RECREATIONAL & EDL MGMT CORP (NJ)
Name changed to Graphic Media, Inc. 6/29/82
Graphic Media, Inc. name changed to GMI Group Inc. 7/16/87
(See GMI Group Inc.)

RECREATIONAL PLANNERS INC (DE)
Charter cancelled and declared inoperative and void for non-payment of taxes 04/15/1973

RECREATIVE TECHNOLOGIES CORP (CO)
Merged into a private company 11/17/94
Details not available

RECRION CORP (DE)
Common 50¢ par changed to 25¢ par and (1) additional share issued 11/28/1972
Merged into Argent Corp. 08/31/1974
Each share Common 25¢ par exchanged for $44 cash

RECRUITS INC (NV)
Name changed to FlexWeek, Inc. 12/16/2015
FlexWeek, Inc. name changed to Holy Grail Co. 03/24/2017

RECTISEL CORP (DE)
Each share Common 1¢ par exchanged for (0.1) share Common 10¢ par 09/09/1964
Acquired by Durakool Inc. 07/18/1986
Each share Common 1¢ par exchanged for $5 cash

RECURSOS MONT S A (NV)
Name changed to Tanaris Power Holdings Inc. 03/06/2015
Tanaris Power Holdings Inc. recapitalized as Hammer Fiber Optics Holdings Corp. 05/03/2016

RECYCLE TECH INC (CO)
SEC revoked common stock registration 07/10/2012

RECYCLED NATIONAL PAPER CORP. (FL)
Merged into World Trade Enterprises, Inc. 10/18/82
Each share Common 1¢ par exchanged for (1) share Common 1¢ par
World Trade Enterprises, Inc. recapitalized as International Medical Science, Inc. 11/4/85 which recapitalized as International Investment Group, Ltd. 7/26/88 which name changed to Intermedia Net Inc. 6/1/96 which name changed to Fortune Media, Inc. 5/21/99 which name changed to Cyberedge Enterprises, Inc. 11/10/2000 which name changed to Wayne's Famous Phillies Inc. 3/10/2003

RECYCLED SOLUTIONS FOR IND INC (AB)
Name changed to Resin Systems Inc. 05/05/2000
Resin Systems Inc. name changed to RS Technologies Inc. 06/23/2010
(See RS Technologies Inc.)

RECYCLENET CORP (UT)
Each share Common 1¢ par received distribution of (0.1) share Oldwebsites.com, Inc. Common no par payable 09/08/2007 to holders of record 09/07/2007 Ex date - 09/05/2007
Recapitalized as Maydao Corp. 01/20/2010
Each share Common 1¢ par exchanged for (0.1) share Common 1¢ par
(See Maydao Corp.)

RECYCLING CTRS AMER INC (CO)
Name changed to Reclamation Consulting & Applications Inc. 02/27/2002
Reclamation Consulting & Applications Inc. recapitalized as Alderox, Inc. 05/20/2008
(See Alderox, Inc.)

RECYCLING INDS INC (CO)
Assets surrendered to creditors 12/11/2000
Stockholders' equity unlikely

RECYCLING RES INC (NY)
Dissolved 03/04/1997
Details not available

RED AREA GOLD MINES, LTD. (ON)
Charter cancelled for failure to file reports and pay taxes 8/18/58

RED ARROW GOLD CORP. (CO)
Merged into Mancos Corp. 7/10/70
Each share Capital Stock $1 par exchanged for (30) shares Capital Stock 1¢ par
Mancos Corp. acquired by Union Oil Co. of California 11/27/78 which reorganized as Unocal Corp. 4/25/83 which merged into Chevron Corp. 8/10/2005

RED BACK MNG INC (CANADA)
Merged into Kinross Gold Corp. 09/22/2010
Each share Common no par exchanged for (1.778) shares

Common no par and (0.11) Common Stock Warrant expiring 09/17/2014
Note: Unexchanged certificates were cancelled and became without value 09/17/2016

RED BANK OIL CO. (ME)
Common Capital Stock $25 par changed to no par in 1928
Common Capital Stock no par changed to $1 par in 1942
Charter revoked for failure to file reports and pay fees 12/1/67

RED BARK GOLD MINES LTD.
Name changed to Red Bark Mines Ltd. in 1953
(See Red Bark Mines Ltd.)

RED BARK MINES LTD. (ON)
Charter revoked for failure to file reports and pay fees 5/6/65

RED BELL BREWING CO (PA)
SEC revoked common stock registration 10/16/2008
Stockholders' equity unlikely

RED BRICK SYS INC (DE)
Merged into Informix Corp. 12/31/98
Each share Common no par exchanged for (0.6) share Common 1¢ par
Informix Corp. name changed to Ascential Software Corp. 7/3/2001
(See Ascential Software Corp.)

RED BUTTE ENERGY INC (NV)
Name changed to Canglobe International, Inc. 01/31/2003
Canglobe International, Inc. name changed to Globetech Environmental, Inc. 11/07/2005 which recapitalized as Global Gold Corp. 03/09/2009 which recapitalized as Fernhill Corp. 01/20/2012

RED CARPET ENTMT INC (NV)
Common $0.001 par split (8.25) for (1) by issuance of (7.25) additional shares payable 11/23/2007 to holders of record 11/22/2007 Ex date - 11/26/2007
Name changed to Purple Beverage Co., Inc. 01/07/2008

RED CARPET FINL CORP (CO)
Name changed back to Bankers National Service Corp. 07/12/1985
(See Bankers National Service Corp.)

RED CARPET INNS INTL INC (CO)
SEC revoked common stock registration 07/23/2013

RED CHIP INC (CANADA)
Reorganized under the laws of Alberta as Arrow Energy Ltd. 05/03/2004
Each share Common no par exchanged for (0.125) share Common no par
Arrow Energy Ltd. recapitalized as Kallisto Energy Corp. 11/02/2009 which name changed to Toro Oil & Gas Ltd. 11/25/2014
(See Toro Oil & Gas Ltd.)

RED CLIFF ENERGY INC (AB)
Merged into Aviva Petroleum Canada Inc. 07/10/1990
Each share Common no par exchanged for (0.18247) share Common no par
Aviva Petroleum Canada Inc. name changed to Pero Development Group Inc. 06/06/1994 which merged into Canadiana Genetics Inc. 04/30/1996
(See Canadiana Genetics Inc.)

RED CLOUD MNG & SMLT LTD (MB)
Charter cancelled for failure to file returns and pay fees 2/24/68

RED COLLEY GOLD MINES LTD. (ON)
Charter cancelled in January 1962
Stock worthless

RED CREST GOLD MINES LTD (CANADA)
Charter dissolved for failure to file annual reports 12/16/1980

RED DEER BREWING CO. LTD. (AB)
Name changed to Carling Breweries (Alberta) Ltd. 7/14/55
Carling Breweries (Alberta) Ltd. was acquired by Canadian Breweries Ltd. for cash 10/29/63

RED DIAMOND MINES LTD. (QC)
Incorporated 12/27/55
Declared dissolved for failure to file reports or pay fees 11/4/78

RED DIAMOND MINES LTD (BC)
Incorporated 06/02/1982
Recapitalized as Continental Datanet Inc. 05/08/1986
Each share Common no par exchanged for (0.5) share Common no par
(See Continental Datanet Inc.)

RED DRAGON RES CORP (BC)
Reincorporated 08/23/2007
Place of incorporation changed from (ON) to (BC) 08/23/2007
Name changed to Brazilian Gold Corp. 01/06/2010
Brazilian Gold Corp. merged into Brazil Resources Inc. (BC) 11/22/2013 which reincorporated in Canada as GoldMining Inc. 12/07/2016

RED EAGLE EXPL LTD (BC)
Merged into Red Eagle Mining Corp. 04/25/2018
Each share Common no par exchanged for (0.5) share Common no par
Note: Unexchanged certificates will be cancelled and become without value 04/25/2024

RED EAGLE RES CORP (DE)
Each share old Common 10¢ par exchanged for (0.25) share new Common 10¢ par 9/10/91
Merged into Lomak Petroleum, Inc. 2/15/95
Each share new Common 10¢ par exchanged for (0.87) share new Common 1¢ par
Lomak Petroleum, Inc. name changed to Range Resources Corp. 8/25/98

RED EARTH ENERGY LTD (SK)
Struck off register for failure to file reports and pay taxes 5/31/91

RED ELECTRICA DE ESPANA SA (SPAIN)
Name changed to Red Electrica Corporacion S.A. 07/08/2009

RED EMERALD RESOURCE CORP (BC)
Name changed to Midway Gold Corp. 07/10/2002
(See Midway Gold Corp.)

RED ENGINE EXPL LTD (BC)
Reorganized 06/09/1997
Reorganized from Red Engine Resources Corp. to Red Engine Exploration Ltd. 06/09/1997
Each share Common no par exchanged for (2) shares Common no par
Merged into Canmine Resources Corp. 11/30/1998
Each share Common no par exchanged for (0.75) share Common no par
(See Canmine Resources Corp.)

RED FAULT MINING & OIL CORP. LTD. (AB)
Acquired by Share Oils Ltd. on a (1) for (2) basis in 1957
Share Oils Ltd. name changed to Share Mines & Oils Ltd. 3/1/65 which recapitalized as Share Resources Inc. 7/4/96

RED FISH BOAT CO. (TX)
Preferred $2 par reclassified as Class A Common 10¢ par on a (2) for (1) basis 3/15/62
Adjudicated bankrupt 1/11/63 and Class A & B Common 10¢ par declared valueless 2/1/64

RED 5 LTD (AUSTRALIA)
Each old Sponsored ADS for Ordinary exchanged for (0.4) new Sponsored ADS for Ordinary 12/14/2011
Basis changed from (1:20) to (1:5) 12/14/2011
ADS agreement terminated 02/27/2017
Each new Sponsored ADS for Ordinary exchanged for $0.121688 cash

RED FOOD STORES INC (DE)
Stock Dividends - 10% 9/5/75; 33-1/3% 5/24/78
Name changed to RFS Liquidating Corp. 2/24/80
(See RFS Liquidating Corp.)

RED FORK ENERGY LTD (AUSTRALIA)
ADR agreement terminated 04/30/2015
Each Sponsored ADR for Ordinary exchanged for $0.003588 cash

RED FOX MINERALS LTD (BC)
Recapitalized as Earth King Resources Inc. (BC) 09/06/1996
Each share Common no par exchanged for (0.33333333) share Common no par
Earth King Resources Inc. (BC) reincorporated in Yukon as West African Gold Corp. 03/17/1997 which recapitalized as First AU Strategies Corp. 04/28/1999 which name changed to Cangold Ltd. (YT) 06/04/2003 which reincorporated in British Columbia 12/22/2004 which merged into Great Panther Silver Ltd. 05/27/2015

RED GIANT ENTMT INC (NV)
Common $0.0001 par split (6) for (1) by issuance of (5) additional shares payable 07/19/2012 to holders of record 07/19/2012
Reincorporated under the laws of Florida 03/06/2017

RED GOLD MINING CO. LTD.
Liquidated in 1942
No stockholders' equity

RED GORGE COAL & COKE CORP (DE)
Charter cancelled and declared inoperative and void for non-payment of taxes 6/23/86

RED HAWK GOLD MINES LTD. (BC)
Recapitalized as Mineral Mountain Mining Co. Ltd. 7/4/61
Each share Capital Stock 50¢ par exchanged for (0.1) share Capital Stock no par
Mineral Mountain Mining Co. Ltd. recapitalized as Mid Mountain Mining Ltd. 12/15/75
(See Mid Mountain Mining Ltd.)

RED HILL ENERGY INC (BC)
Merged into Prophecy Resource Corp. (New) 04/16/2010
Each share Common no par exchanged for (0.92) share Common no par and (0.25) share Elissa Resources Ltd. Common no par
Note: Unexchanged certificates were cancelled and became without value 04/16/2016
(See each company's listing)

RED HILL FLORENCE MINING CO. (NV)
Recapitalized as Red Hill Uranium Co. and Capital Stock 10¢ par changed to Common 5¢ par 5/21/55
Red Hill Uranium Co. recapitalized as Pacific Fidelity Corp. 4/16/62

RED HILL MKTG GROUP LTD (BC)
Name changed 5/16/85
Name changed from Red Hill Resources Ltd. to Red Hill Marketing Group Ltd. 5/16/85
Delisted from Vancouver Stock Exchange 3/2/90

RED HILL URANIUM CO. (NV)
Recapitalized as Pacific Fidelity Corp. 4/16/62
Each share Common 5¢ par exchanged for (0.01) share Common $5 par
(See Pacific Fidelity Corp.)

RED HORSE ENTMT CORP (NV)
Each share old Common $0.001 par exchanged for (0.03333333) share new Common $0.001 par 08/02/2003
Name changed to Great China International Holdings, Inc. 09/15/2005
Great China International Holdings, Inc. name changed to HH Biotechnology Holdings Co. 08/24/2016

RED HOT CONCEPTS INC (DE)
Each share old Common 1¢ par exchanged for (1/3) share new Common 1¢ par 11/26/1997
SEC revoked common stock registration 08/31/2009
Stockholders' equity unlikely

RED HUT METALS INC (BC)
Each share old Common no par exchanged for (0.5) share new Common no par 07/26/2016
Name changed to Providence Gold Mines Inc. 07/12/2017

RED KAP, INC. (TN)
Merged into Blue Bell, Inc. (Del.) 12/21/64
Each share Common $5 par exchanged for (0.8) share Common $5 par
(See Blue Bell, Inc. (Del.))

RED L FOODS CORP. (DE)
Merged into Gorton's of Gloucester, Inc. on a (1) for (11) basis 4/1/63
Gorton's of Gloucester, Inc. name changed to Gorton Corp. (Mass.) 6/14/65 which reincorporated under the laws of Delaware 7/1/66 which merged into General Mills, Inc. 8/16/68

RED LAKE & SUN VY RES LTD (BC)
Recapitalized as International R.S.V. Resource Corp. 12/27/1989
Each share Common no par exchanged for (0.1) share Common no par
International R.S.V. Resource Corp. recapitalized as Harambee Mining Corp. 05/05/1997 which recapitalized as Neuer Kapital Corp. 01/03/2002 which name changed to Crescent Resources Corp. 08/03/2005 which recapitalized as Coventry Resources Inc. 01/09/2013
(See Coventry Resources Inc.)

RED LAKE BUFFALO RES LTD (ON)
Name changed to Madsen Gold Corp. 03/07/1991
Madsen Gold Corp. merged into Claude Resources Inc. 06/25/1998 which merged into Silver Standard Resources Inc. 06/06/2016 which name changed to SSR Mining Inc. 08/03/2017

RED LAKE EXPL INC (NV)
Common $0.001 par split (13) for (1) by issuance of (12) additional shares payable 06/29/2007 to holders of record 06/26/2007
Ex date - 07/02/2007
Name changed to Red Metal Resources Ltd. 09/16/2008

RED LAKE GOLD SHORE MINES LTD.
Acquired by Hasaga Gold Mines Ltd. on a (1) for (18) basis in 1938
Hasaga Gold Mines Ltd. merged into Little Long Lac Gold Mines Ltd. (The) 4/27/67 which merged into Little Long Lac Mines Ltd. 1/8/71 which name changed to Little Long Lac Gold Mines Ltd. (New) 7/3/75 which merged into LAC Minerals Ltd. (New) 7/29/85 which was acquired by American Barrick Resources Corp. 10/17/94 which name changed to Barrick Gold Corp. 1/18/95

RED LAKE LABS INC (CA)
Capital Stock $2 par split (3) for (1) by issuance of (2) additional shares 11/21/1968
Name changed to Redlake Corp. 06/18/1971

RED LAKE RES INC (BC)
Name changed to Silver Fields Resources Inc. 6/19/2006

RED LANTERN CORP (AB)
Issue Information - 1,500,000 shares COM offered at $0.20 per share on 04/07/2000
Reincorporated under the laws of Ontario as TrekLogic Technologies Inc. 07/23/2002
TrekLogic Technologies Inc. name changed to Brainhunter Inc. 06/22/2004
(See Brainhunter Inc.)

RED LION HOTELS CAP TR (DE)
9.5% Trust Preferred Securities called for redemption at $25 plus $0.494791 accrued dividends on 12/15/2015

RED LION HOTELS INC (DE)
Issue Information - 8,750,000 shares COM offered at $19 per share on 07/26/1995
Merged into Doubletree Corp. 11/08/1996
Each share Common 1¢ par exchanged for (0.2314) share Common 1¢ par and $21.30 cash
Doubletree Corp. merged into Promus Hotel Corp. (New) 12/19/1997 which merged into Hilton Hotels Corp. 11/30/1999
(See Hilton Hotels Corp.)

RED LION INNS LTD PARTNERSHIP (DE)
Merged into Boykin Lodging Co. 5/22/98
Each Unit of Ltd. Partnership no par exchanged for (0.735) share Common no par and $8.34 cash
Note: An additional $0.1337 cash per share was distributed to holders of record 5/22/98
(See Boykin Lodging Co.)

RED MILE CAP CORP (AB)
Name changed to Red Mile Minerals Corp. (AB) 02/18/2010
Red Mile Minerals Corp. (AB) reincorporated in British Columbia 06/03/2010 which name changed to Orla Mining Ltd. (BC) 06/12/2015 which reorganized in Canada 12/07/2016

RED MILE MINERALS CORP (BC)
Reincorporated 06/03/2010
Place of incorporation changed from (AB) to (BC) 06/03/2010
Each share old Common no par exchanged for (0.2) share new Common no par 01/07/2015
Name changed to Orla Mining Ltd. (BC) 06/12/2015
Orla Mining Ltd. (BC) reorganized in Canada 12/07/2016

RED MOON POTASH INC (AB)
Name changed to Red Moon Resources Inc. 12/20/2016

RED MOUNTAIN CONSOLIDATED MINING CO. (MT)
Completely liquidated 12/4/68
Each share Capital Stock $10 par exchanged for first and final distribution of $0.0358 cash

RED MTN PHARMACEUTICALS INC (DE)
Name changed to Zalemark Holding Co., Inc. 12/24/2008

RED MTN RES INC (FL)
Common $0.0001 par changed to $0.00001 par and (24) additional shares issued payable 04/04/2011 to holders of record 04/04/2011
Reorganized under the laws of Texas 01/31/2014
Each share Common no par exchanged for (0.1) share Common $0.00001 par
Preferred not affected by reverse split

RED-O-LIER CORP. (NY)
Merged into Tujax Industries, Inc. 11/29/63
Each share Class A Common 10¢ par exchanged for (1) share Common no par
Tujax Industries, Inc. merged into Babbitt (B.T.), Inc. 12/4/68 which name changed to B.T.B. Corp. 12/5/69 which name changed to International Banknote Co., Inc. 1/2/73 which merged into United States Banknote Corp. (NY) 7/25/90 which reincorporated in (DE) 9/21/93 which name American Banknote Corp. 7/3/95

RED OAK BK (HANOVER TWP, NJ)
Stock Dividends - 5% payable 12/06/2002 to holders of record 11/15/2002 Ex date - 11/13/2002; 5% payable 12/08/2003 to holders of record 11/17/2003 Ex date - 11/13/2003; 5% payable 12/10/2004 to holders of record 11/19/2004 Ex date - 11/17/2004
Merged into Center Bancorp Inc. 05/21/2005
Each share Common $5 par exchanged for (0.9227) share Common no par
Center Bancorp Inc. name changed to ConnectOne Bancorp, Inc. (New) 07/01/2014

RED OAK RES INC (CANADA)
Merged into Neutrino Resources Inc. 10/06/1995
Each share Common no par exchanged for (0.1) share Common no par
(See Neutrino Resources Inc.)

RED OAK TRAIL CORP (AB)
Name changed to Innovative Water & Sewer Systems Inc. (AB) 09/05/2001
Innovative Water & Sewer Systems Inc. (AB) reincorporated in Canada as Clearford Industries Inc. 07/20/2005 which name changed to Clearford Water Systems Inc. 06/27/2014

RED OWL STORES INC (DE)
Each share Common no par exchanged for (4) shares Common $3 par in 1946 4-3/4% Ser. A Preferred $100 par called redemption 4/16/54
Common $3 par changed to no par 5/13/59
Common no par split (2) for (1) by issuance of (1) additional share 3/22/63
Merged into Gamble-Skogmo, Inc. 6/5/71
Each share Common no par exchanged for (0.875) share Common $5 par
Gamble-Skogmo, Inc. merged into Wickes Companies, Inc. 1/26/85 which name changed to Collins & Aikman Group Inc. 7/17/92

(See Collins & Aikman Group Inc.)

RED POPLAR GOLD MINES LTD. (ON)
Recapitalized as Consolidated Red Poplar Minerals Ltd. on a (1) for (3.5) basis 3/1/55
Consolidated Red Poplar Minerals Ltd. recapitalized as New Dimension Resources Ltd. 11/9/71 which recapitalized as New Dimension Industries Ltd. 9/19/89 which recapitalized as Toxic Disposal Corp. 2/15/94 which recapitalized as Global Disposal Corp. 3/29/96

RED RAVEN RES INC (AB)
Issue Information - 2,000,000 shares COM offered at $0.15 per share on 09/16/1997
Recapitalized as Rise Energy Ltd. 8/17/2001
Each share Common no par exchanged for (1/3) share Common no par
Rise Energy Ltd. merged into Delphi Energy Corp. 6/19/2003

RED REEF LABORATORIES INTL INC (FL)
Each share old Common $0.001 par exchanged for (6) shares new Common new Common $0.001 par 01/05/2007
Recapitalized as Impact Fusion International, Inc. 05/18/2009
Each share Common $0.001 par exchanged for (0.0004) share Common $0.001 par

RED RIVER EXPLORATION CO. (UT)
Each share Common $0.001 par exchanged for (0.2) share Common $0.005 par 07/03/1979
Name changed to Tuloma Energies, Inc. 01/15/1981
Tuloma Energies, Inc. name changed to Tuloma Corp. 07/28/1983

RED RIVER MINING & EXPLORATION LTD. (ON)
Acquired by Sudbay Beryllium Mines Ltd. in May 1961
Details not available

RED RIVER REFINING CO.
Name changed to Calumet Refining Co. 00/00/1950
Calumet Refining Co. acquired by Calumet Industries, Inc. 11/20/1962
(See Calumet Industries, Inc.)

RED ROBIN, INC. (MN)
Name changed to Robin Industries Inc. 5/1/69
(See Robin Industries Inc.)

RED ROCK BOTTLING CO. OF CLEVELAND (DE)
Out of business 00/00/1949
Details not available

RED ROCK BOTTLING CO. OF PITTSBURGH
Acquired by Red Rock Bottling Co. of Cleveland on a (1) for (2) basis 00/00/1947
(See Red Rock Bottling Co. of Cleveland)

RED ROCK BOTTLING CO. OF YOUNGSTOWN
Acquired by Red Rock Bottling Co. of Cleveland on a (1) for (2) basis 00/00/1947
(See Red Rock Bottling Co. of Cleveland)

RED ROCK CAP CORP (CANADA)
Recapitalized as Century Iron Mines Corp. (Canada) 05/24/2011
Each share Common no par exchanged for (0.1) share Common no par
Century Iron Mines Corp. (Canada) reincorporated in British Columbia 10/17/2014 which name changed to Century Global Commodities Corp. (BC) 11/16/2015 which

reincorporated in Cayman Islands 03/10/2016

RED ROCK CONSOLIDATED MINING CO. (AZ)
Charter revoked for failure to file reports and pay taxes 4/15/28

RED ROCK ENERGY INC (AB)
Each share old Common no par exchanged for (0.07490636) share new Common no par 04/20/2017
Name changed to New Stratus Energy Inc. 08/16/2017

RED ROCK INTL CORP (NV)
Reorganized under the laws of Kentucky as Page International Inc. 11/05/1997
Each share Common $0.001 par exchanged for (0.4641232) share Common $0.001 par
Page International Inc. (KY) reincorporated in Nevada 12/31/1997 which name changed to China TianRen Organic Food, Inc. 06/14/2007

RED ROCK MINES LTD. (BC)
Recapitalized as Alakon Metals Ltd. 04/17/1970
Each share Capital Stock no par exchanged for (0.4) share Capital Stock no par
Alakon Metals Ltd. recapitalized as Gold Valley Resources Ltd. 03/13/1974 which recapitalized as NCA Minerals Corp. 06/06/1977
(See NCA Minerals Corp.)

RED ROCK MNG CORP (BC)
Name changed to American Pacific Minerals Ltd. 05/30/1994
(See American Pacific Minerals Ltd.)

RED ROCK PICTURES HLDGS INC (NV)
Each share old Common $0.001 par exchanged for (0.01) share new Common $0.001 par 02/14/2011
Name changed to OSL Holdings Inc. 11/28/2011
(See OSL Holdings Inc.)

RED ROCKET EXPLORATIONS INC (ON)
Recapitalized as W.I.N. Gaming Corp. 12/20/1995
Each (15) shares Common no par exchanged for (1) share Common no par
W.I.N. Gaming Corp. name changed to Funtime Hospitality Corp. 02/01/2000
(See Funtime Hospitality Corp.)

RED ROOF INNS INC (OH)
Merged into Accor S.A. 8/13/99
Each share Common 1¢ par exchanged for $22.75 cash

RED ROPE INDS INC (NY)
Merged into Sheller-Globe Corp. 10/31/1973
Each share Common 10¢ par exchanged for (0.31) share Common no par
(See Sheller-Globe Corp.)

RED ROPE STATIONERY INDUSTRIES, INC. (NY)
Name changed to Red Rope Industries, Inc. 6/10/68
Red Rope Industries, Inc. merged into Sheller-Globe Corp. 10/31/73
(See Sheller-Globe Corp.)

RED SEA OIL CORP (CANADA)
Merged into Lundin Oil AB 6/6/2000
Each share Common no par exchanged for (0.47) Sponsored GDR for Class B no par
(See Lundin Oil AB)

RED SEA TECHNOLOGIES LTD (AB)
Name changed to GIE Environment Technologies Ltd. 5/1/2000

RED SHIRT LARDER GOLD MINES LTD (ON)
Charter cancelled for failure to file reports and pay taxes in 1959

RED SKY RES INC (NV)
Each share Common no par exchanged for (30) shares old Common $0.0001 par 02/17/2006
Each share old Common $0.0001 par exchanged for (1.5) shares new Common $0.0001 par 04/18/2006
Name changed to Source Petroleum Inc. 05/25/2016
(See Source Petroleum Inc.)

RED STAR CAP VENTURES INC (CANADA)
Voluntarily dissolved
Each share Common no par received first and final distribution of approximately (0.41717791) Electra Gold Ltd. Unit consisting of (1) share new Common no par and (1) Common Stock Purchase Warrant expiring 12/01/2016 payable 12/08/2014 to holders of record 10/23/2014
Electra Gold Ltd. name changed to Electra Stone Ltd. 02/02/2015

RED STAR MILLING CO.
Acquired by General Mills, Inc. in 1928
Details not available

RED STAR YEAST & PRODUCTS CO. (WI)
Common $10 par changed to $1 par and (1) additional share issued 10/12/61
Name changed to Universal Foods Corp. 1/17/62
Universal Foods Corp. name changed to Sensient Technologies Corp. 11/6/2000

RED SUN MNG INC (DE)
Reorganized as Zurvita Holdings, Inc. 09/03/2009
Each share Common $0.001 par exchanged for (4) shares Common $0.001 par

RED-TAIL INFOTECH INC (AB)
Name changed to Life Sciences Institute Inc. 03/27/2003
Life Sciences Institute Inc. recapitalized as Quattro Exploration & Production Inc. 11/23/2011

RED TOP BREWING CO. (OH)
Merged into Muskegon Motor Specialties Co. 10/1/57
Each share Class A Common $1 par exchanged for (1/18) share Class A $20 par and (0.2) share Class B $15 par
(See Muskegon Motor Specialties Co.)

RED WARRIOR MINING CO. (MN)
Charter expired by time limitation 1/27/38

REDA PUMP CO (DE)
Each share Preferred $10 par exchanged for (2) shares Common no par in 1937
Common no par changed to $1 par in 1946
Common $1 par split (5) for (4) by issuance of (0.25) additional share 12/23/64
Common $1 par split (2) for (1) by issuance of (1) additional share 7/30/65
Common $1 par split (2) for (1) by issuance of (1) additional share 12/20/67
Merged into TRW Inc. 1/24/69
Each share Common $1 par exchanged for (0.222) share $4.50 Conv. Preference II Ser. 3 no par and (0.125) share Common $1.25 par
TRW Inc. merged into Northrop Grumman Corp. 12/11/2002

REDACTRON CORP (DE)
Merged into Burroughs Corp. (MI) 1/23/76
Each share Common 10¢ par exchanged for (0.076923) share Common $5 par
Burroughs Corp. (MI) reincorporated in Delaware 5/30/84 which name changed to Unisys Corp. 11/13/86

REDAURUM LTD (ON)
Name changed 05/18/1994
Name changed from Redaurum Red Lake Mines Ltd. to Redaurum Ltd. 05/18/1994
Recapitalized as BF Minerals Ltd. 04/14/2004
Each share Common no par exchanged for (0.025) share Common no par
BF Minerals Ltd. recapitalized as Mukuba Resources Ltd. 06/27/2008 which recapitalized as FogChain Corp. 05/29/2018

REDAURUM RED LAKE GOLD MINES, LTD. (ON)
Name changed to Orelock Explorations Ltd. 7/4/77
Orelock Explorations Ltd. merged into A.H.A. Automotive Technologies Corp. 4/2/84
(See A.H.A. Automotive Technologies Corp.)

REDBACK NETWORKS INC (DE)
Issue Information - 2,500,000 shares COM offered at $23 per share on 05/17/1999
Common $0.0001 par split (2) for (1) by issuance of (1) additional share payable 08/19/1999 to holders of record 08/05/1999
Common $0.0001 par split (2) for (1) by issuance of (1) additional share payable 04/03/2000 to holders of record 03/20/2000
Plan of reorganization under Chapter 11 Federal Bankruptcy Code effective 01/02/2004
Each share old Common $0.0001 par exchanged for (0.01362536) share new Common $0.0001 par, (1) $5 Common Stock Purchase Warrant expiring 01/02/2010 and (1) $9.50 Common Stock Purchase Warrant expiring 01/02/2010
Note: Unexchanged certificates were cancelled and became without value 01/02/2005
Merged into Telefonaktiebolaget L.M. Ericsson 01/25/2007
Each share new Common $0.0001 par exchanged for $25 cash

REDBIRD GOLD CORP (ON)
Recapitalized as Metalcorp Ltd. 7/10/2002
Each share Common no par exchanged for (0.05) share Common no par

REDBUS INTERHOUSE PLC (UNITED KINGDOM)
Merged into Telecity Group PLC 5/31/2006
Each Sponsored ADR for Ordinary 5p par exchanged for $2.08364 cash

REDCELL PWR CORP (DE)
SEC revoked common stock registration 08/30/2012

REDCITY SEARCH CO INC (ON)
Recapitalized as ZipLocal Inc. 03/26/2007
Each share Common no par exchanged for (0.2) share Common no par
(See ZipLocal Inc.)

REDCLIFFE EXPL INC (AB)
Each share Class B Common no par reclassified as (10) shares Class A Common no par 05/27/2010
Acquired by Paramount Resources Ltd. 06/29/2010
Each share Class A Common no par exchanged for $0.42 cash

Note: Unexchanged certificates were cancelled and became without value 06/29/2015

REDCLIFFE EXPL LTD (AB)
Name changed to Redcliffe Exploration Inc. 03/05/2007
(See Redcliffe Exploration Inc.)

REDCON GOLD MINES LTD (ON)
Merged into Goldquest Exploration Inc. 01/01/1985
Each share Capital Stock $1 par exchanged for (0.28571428) share Common no par
Goldquest Exploration Inc. merged into Goldcorp Inc. (New) 03/31/1994

REDCOR CORP (CA)
Common no par changed to 20¢ par 09/27/1972
Each share Common 20¢ par exchanged for (0.02) share Common $1 par 07/06/1973
Common $1 par split (2) for (1) by issuance of (1) additional share 01/31/1979
Common $1 par split (2) for (1) by issuance of (1) additional share 09/24/1980
Name changed to Silicon General Inc. and Common $1 par changed to no par 06/27/1982
Silicon General Inc. name changed to Symmetricom, Inc. (CA) 11/01/1993 which reincorporated in Delaware 01/07/2002
(See Symmetricom, Inc.)

REDCORP VENTURES LTD (CANADA)
Placed in receivership 05/29/2009
Stockholders' equity unlikely

REDDI BRAKE SUPPLY CORP (NV)
Each (750) shares old Common $0.0001 par exchanged for (1) share new Common $0.0001 par 03/22/2004
New Common $0.0001 par split (2) for (1) by issuance of (1) additional share payable 05/16/2007 to holders of record 05/15/2007 Ex date - 05/17/2007
Name changed to America West Resources, Inc. 03/05/2008

REDDING BANCORP (CA)
Common no par split (3) for (1) by issuance of (2) additional shares payable 7/10/98 to holders of record 6/16/98
Stock Dividend - 10% payable 10/22/2000 to holders of record 10/1/2000 Ex date - 9/27/2000
Name changed to Bank of Commerce Holdings 5/19/2004

REDDING GOLD CORP (BC)
Recapitalized as Consolidated Redding Explorations Corp. 04/06/1993
Each share Common no par exchanged for (0.285714) share Common no par
Consolidated Redding Explorations Corp. name changed to Redex Gold Inc. 06/20/1996 which name changed to Bravo Gold Inc. 07/31/1997 which recapitalized as International Bravo Resource Corp. 09/22/1998 which recapitalized as Bravo Venture Group Inc. 03/15/2002 which name changed to Bravo Gold Corp. 02/22/2010 which recapitalized as Homestake Resource Corp. 04/16/2012 which merged into Auryn Resources Inc. 09/07/2016

REDDING SAVINGS & LOAN ASSOCIATION (CA)
99.8% acquired by First Deposit Corp. through purchase offer which expired 11/10/1982
Public interest eliminated

REDDY ICE HLDGS INC (DE)
Issue Information - 10,200,000 shares COM offered at $18.50 per share on 08/09/2005
Plan of reorganization under Chapter 11 Federal Bankruptcy proceedings effective 05/31/2012
Each share Common 1¢ par exchanged for $0.1001964 cash

REDE PAK FINE FOODS LTD (MB)
Reincorporated under the laws of Alberta as Petro Plus Inc. 10/11/90
Petro Plus Inc. recapitalized as Northern Star Resources Inc. 1/15/99 which recapitalized as Odaat Inc. 3/9/2000 which recapitalized as Explor Resources Inc. 1/29/2004

REDECARD S A (BRAZIL)
GDR agreement terminated 11/02/2012
Each Sponsored Reg. S GDR for Ordinary exchanged for $34.1285 cash
Each Sponsored 144A GDR for Ordinary exchanged for $34.1285 cash

REDECO ENERGY INC (AB)
Delisted from Toronto Venture Stock Exchange 05/16/2002

REDEKOP PPTYS INC (BC)
Name changed to RPI Properties Inc. 6/18/2001

REDELL MNG CORP (BC)
Recapitalized as FM Resources Corp. 04/16/1998
Each share Common no par exchanged for (0.05) share Common no par
FM Resources Corp. name changed to Strikewell Energy Corp. 09/01/2006

REDENVELOPE INC (DE)
Issue Information - 2,200,000 shares COM offered at $14 per share on 09/24/2003
Assets sold under Section 363 of the Bankruptcy Code 06/23/2008
No stockholders' equity

REDEX GOLD INC (BC)
Name changed to Bravo Gold Inc. 07/31/1997
Bravo Gold Inc. recapitalized as International Bravo Resource Corp. 09/22/1998 which recapitalized as Bravo Venture Group Inc. 03/15/2002 which name changed to Bravo Gold Corp. 02/22/2010 which recapitalized as Homestake Resource Corp. 04/16/2012 which merged into Auryn Resources Inc. 09/07/2016

REDEX INC (CANADA)
Reincorporated 10/21/2004
Place of incorporation changed from (AB) to Canada 10/21/2004
Dissolved for non-compliance 06/19/2011

REDFED BANCORP INC (DE)
Merged into Golden State Bancorp Inc. 7/11/98
Each share Common 1¢ par exchanged for (0.68271) share Common $1 par
(See Golden State Bancorp Inc.)

REDFERN FOODS CORP (GA)
Name changed to Byers Communications Systems, Inc. 6/10/83
Byers Communications Systems, Inc. name changed to BYCOM Systems, Inc. 3/25/85 which name changed to Superior Holding Corp. 8/22/85 which name changed to Superior TeleTec Inc. 8/21/89 which merged into Alpine Group, Inc. 11/10/93
(See Alpine Group, Inc.)

REDFERN RES LTD (BC)
Reincorporated under the laws of Canada as Redcorp Ventures Ltd. 07/10/2000

(See Redcorp Ventures Ltd.)

REDFIELD VENTURES INC (NV)
Name changed to China Energy Technology Corp., Ltd. 03/16/2015

REDFIN NETWORK INC (NV)
SEC revoked common stock registration 09/24/2013

REDFLEX HLDGS LTD (AUSTRALIA)
ADR agreement terminated 06/06/2016
Each Sponsored ADR for Ordinary exchanged for $2.127396 cash

REDFORD MINES LTD. (ON)
Charter cancelled for failure to pay taxes and file returns 7/27/76

REDFORD RES INC (BC)
Name changed 10/08/1981
Name changed from Redford Mines Inc. to Redford Resources, Inc. 10/08/1981
Recapitalized as United Redford Resources, Inc. 12/07/1984
Each share Capital Stock no par exchanged for (0.2) share Common no par
(See United Redford Resources, Inc.)

REDHAND INTL INC (NV)
Each share old Common $0.001 par exchanged for (0.1) share new Common $0.001 par 02/04/2005
Name changed to African Diamond Co., Inc. 04/17/2006
(See African Diamond Co., Inc.)

REDHAWK RES INC (BC)
Each share old Common no par exchanged for (0.33333333) share new Common no par 06/14/2018
Merged into CopperBank Resources Corp. 09/04/2018
Each share new Common no par exchanged for (0.928928) share Common no par
Note: Unexchanged certificates will be cancelled and become without value 09/04/2018

REDHEADS INC (DE)
SEC revoked common stock registration 10/28/2009
Stockholders' equity unlikely

REDHILL INVT LTD (BC)
Merged into Grosvenor International Holdings Ltd. 06/11/1973
Each share Common no par exchanged for (1) share Common no par
(See Grosvenor International Holdings Ltd.)

REDHILL RES CORP (BC)
Each share old Common no par exchanged for (0.1) share new Common no par 10/16/2013
Recapitalized as Millennial Lithium Corp. 06/24/2016
Each new share Common no par exchanged for (0.5) share Common no par

REDHOOK ALE BREWERY INC (WA)
Issue Information - 1,956,614 shares COM offered at $17 per share on 08/16/1995
Name changed to Craft Brewers Alliance, Inc. 07/01/2008
Craft Brewers Alliance, Inc. name changed to Craft Brew Alliance, Inc. 01/12/2012

REDIJET INC (CO)
Each share old Common $0.001 par exchanged for (0.02) share new Common $0.001 par 03/22/2013
Name changed to Umairco, Inc. 09/27/2013
Umairco, Inc. name changed to Digital Arts Media Network, Inc. 03/10/2015

REDKEN LABS INC (DE)
Reincorporated 12/22/80
Common 50¢ par split (2) for (1) by

issuance of (1) additional share 9/15/72
State of incorporation changed from (CA) to (DE) 12/22/80
Stock Dividends - 10% 10/23/81; 10% 10/22/82; 10% 4/21/86
Merged into RLI Acquisition Corp. 11/14/88
Each share Common 50¢ par exchanged for $35.435 cash

REDKNEE SOLUTIONS INC (CANADA)
Common no par reclassified as Subordinate Shares no par 04/28/2017
Recapitalized as Optiva Inc. 04/05/2018
Each Subordinate Share no par exchanged for (0.02) Subordinate Share no par

REDLAND LTD (ENGLAND)
ADR agreement terminated 02/06/1998
Each Sponsored ADR for Ordinary 25p par exchanged for approximately $5.60 cash

REDLAND PFD STK PLC (UNITED KINGDOM)
ADR's for Market Auction Preferred Ser. A called for redemption 4/24/95
ADR's for Market Auction Preferred Ser. B called for redemption 5/1/95
ADR's for Market Auction Preferred Ser. C called for redemption 5/8/95
ADR's for Market Auction Preferred Ser. D called for redemption 5/15/95
ADR's for Market Auction Preferred Ser. E called for redemption 5/18/95

REDLANDS CENTENNIAL BK (REDLANDS, CA)
Stock Dividends - 8% payable 8/1/96 to holders of record 7/22/96; 7% payable 12/1/97 to holders of record 11/1/97
Common no par split (5) for (4) by issuance of (0.25) additional share payable 12/2/98 to holders of record 11/1/98
Under plan of reorganization each share Common no par automatically became (1) share Centennial First Financial Services Common no par 12/23/99
Centennial First Financial Services name changed to 1st Centennial Bancorp 3/3/2003

REDLAW ENTERPRISES INC. (DE)
Name changed to Redlaw, Inc. 08/29/1977
Redlaw, Inc. merged into Redlaw Industries Inc. 07/13/1979
(See Redlaw Industries Inc.)

REDLAW INC (DE)
Merged into Redlaw Industries Inc. 07/13/1979
Each share Common 50¢ par exchanged for (2-1/3) shares Common no par
(See Redlaw Industries Inc.)

REDLAW INDS INC (ON)
Each share old Common no par exchanged for (0.2) share new Common no par 02/25/1991
Delisted from Canadian Dealer Network 10/13/2000

REDLINE PERFORMANCE PRODS INC (MN)
Issue Information - 2,222,224 shares COM offered at $4.50 per share on 05/15/2003
Filed a plan of liquidation under Chapter 7 Federal Bankruptcy Code 8/27/2004
Stockholders' equity unlikely

REDLINE RES INC (BC)
Name changed to Nickel One Resources Inc. 02/29/2016

REDM INDS INC (DE)
Merged into Pullman Transportation Co., Inc. 10/16/1984
Each share Common 25¢ par exchanged for $20.375 cash

REDMAN INDS INC (DE)
Common $1 par split (4) for (3) by issuance of (1/3) additional share 05/15/1968
Common $1 par split (2) for (1) by issuance of (1) additional share 01/31/1969
Common $1 par split (2) for (1) by issuance of (1) additional share 07/15/1971
Merged into Redman Acquisition Corp. 12/22/1988
Each share Common $1 par exchanged for $10 cash

REDMAN INDS INC NEW (DE)
Common 1¢ par split (2) for (1) by issuance of (1) additional share payable 03/08/1996 to holders of record 02/23/1996
Merged into Champion Enterprises, Inc. 10/24/1996
Each share Common 1¢ par exchanged for (1.24) shares Common $1 par

REDMAN MANUFACTURING & ENGINEERING CO. (MO)
Name changed to Redman Manufacturing Co. 12/19/66
Redman Manufacturing Co. acquired by Crown Zellerbach Corp. 7/1/68 which merged into James River Corp. of Virginia 10/30/86 which name changed to Fort James Corp. 8/13/97 which merged into Georgia-Pacific Corp. 11/27/2000
(See Georgia-Pacific Corp.)

REDMAN MANUFACTURING CO. (MO)
Completely liquidated 7/1/68
Each share Common $1 par exchanged for first and final distribution of (0.4023) share Crown Zellerbach Corp. Common $5 par
Crown Zellerbach Corp. merged into James River Corp. of Virginia 10/30/86 which name changed to Fort James Corp. 8/13/97 which merged into Georgia-Pacific Corp. 11/27/2000
(See Georgia-Pacific Corp.)

REDMAN URANIUM CO. (UT)
Merged into Sterling Uranium Corp. on a (1) for (10) basis 03/01/1955
Sterling Uranium Corp. recapitalized as Sterling Beryllium & Oil Co. 02/04/1958 which merged into Elgin Gas & Oil Co. 06/12/1959
(See Elgin Gas & Oil Co.)

REDMEX RES INC (AB)
Issue Information - 2,000,000 shares COM offered at $0.10 per share on 10/27/1993
Name changed to GOAL Energy Inc. 1/5/94
GOAL Energy Inc. merged into Tappit Resources Ltd. 8/28/98
(See Tappit Resources Ltd.)

REDMOND APARTMENTS CO. (MI)
Reverted to private company in 1960

REDMOND CAP CORP (DE)
Name changed to Dominion Capital Corp. 08/12/1985
(See Dominion Capital Corp.)

REDMOND CAP CORP (FL)
Reincorporated under the laws of Delaware as Windsor Resource Corp. and Common $0.001 par changed to $0.000001 par 02/06/2008
Windsor Resource Corp. name changed to Kleangas Energy Technologies, Inc. 02/25/2013

REDMOND GROWTH FD INC (DE)
Liquidation completed
Each share Common 25¢ par exchanged for initial distribution of $8.31 cash 06/03/1977
Each share Common 25¢ par received second and final distribution of $0.01 cash 07/05/1978

REDMOND VENTURES CORP (BC)
Recapitalized as Crown Point Ventures Ltd. (BC) 03/12/2002
Each share Common no par exchanged for (1/6) share Common no par
Crown Point Ventures Ltd. (BC) reincorporated in Alberta as Crown Point Energy Inc. 07/31/2012

REDNAL CAP CORP (NV)
Name changed to Investment Capital Associates, Ltd. 09/12/1985
(See Investment Capital Associates, Ltd.)

REDNECK FOODS INC (DE)
SEC revoked common stock registration 08/05/2004
Stockholders' equity unlikely

REDONDA INDS CORP (BC)
Name changed to Image Power, Inc. 1/23/97

REDONDO TILE CO. (DE)
Merged into Stylon Corp. (Del.) 4/29/60
Each share Common $1 par exchanged for (0.5) share Common $1 par
Stylon Corp. (Del.) name changed to DCA Development Corp. 5/25/70 which was adjudicated bankrupt 6/27/73

REDOX TECHNOLOGY CORP (DE)
Name changed to Midnight Holdings Group, Inc. 03/07/2006

REDPATH INDS LTD (CANADA)
Capital Stock no par reclassified as Conv. Class A Capital Stock no par 9/4/74
Conv. Class A Capital Stock no par and Conv. Class B Capital Stock no par split (2) for (1) by issuance of (1) additional share respectively 3/18/77
Conv. Class A Capital Stock no par reclassified as Common no par 4/3/79
Conv. Class B Capital Stock no par reclassified as Common no par 4/3/79
$1.665 Conv. Preference Ser. A no par called for redemption 2/13/84
Common no par split (3) for (1) by issuance of (2) additional shares 3/18/85
Common no par split (2) for (1) by issuance of (1) additional share 2/25/87
Acquired by SQ Acquisition Corp. 5/31/89
Each share Common no par exchanged for $20.375 cash

REDPIC PETROLEUMS LTD.
Recapitalized as Stanwell Oil & Gas Ltd. in 1952
Each share Capital Stock $1 par exchanged for (1/3) share Capital Stock $1 par
Stanwell Oil & Gas Ltd. recapitalized as Cordwell International Developments Ltd. 12/16/66
(See Cordwell International Developments Ltd.)

REDPOINT RES INC (CANADA)
Name changed to Rentown Enterprises Inc. 4/21/88
(See Rentown Enterprises Inc.)

REDPOINTE GOLD MINES, LTD. (ON)
Charter cancelled for failure to file reports and pay taxes 11/12/59

REDQUEST CAP CORP (DE)
Reorganized under the laws of Quebec as Harfang Exploration Inc. 06/30/2017
Each share Common no par exchanged for (0.25) share Common no par

REDRUTH GOLD MINES LTD (ON)
Recapitalized as Gemstar Communications Inc. 02/12/1996
Each share Common $1 par exchanged for (0.06666666) share Common no par
Gemstar Communications Inc. acquired by SIRIT Technologies Inc. 09/06/2001 which was acquired by iTech Capital Corp. 11/01/2002 which name changed to Sirit Inc. 05/05/2003
(See Sirit Inc.)

REDSTAR OIL & GAS INC (AB)
Merged into Great Plains Exploration Inc. (New) (Canada) 05/09/2008
Each share Common no par exchanged for (0.9) share Common no par
Great Plains Exploration Inc. (New) (Canada) reincorporated in Alberta 01/01/2009 which merged into Avenir Diversified Income Trust 11/10/2010 which reorganized as AvenEx Energy Corp. 01/07/2011 which merged into Spyglass Resources Corp. 04/04/2013

REDSTAR RES CORP (BC)
Recapitalized as Redstar Gold Corp. 4/26/2002
Each share Common no par exchanged for (1/6) share Common no par

REDSTONE LITERARY AGENTS INC (NV)
Name changed to Appcoin Innovations Inc. 08/17/2017
Appcoin Innovations Inc. name changed to ICOX Innovations Inc. 02/14/2018

REDSTONE MINES LTD. (ON)
Name changed to Redstone Resources Inc. 8/9/72
Redstone Resources Inc. merged into Franco-Nevada Mining Corp. Ltd. (Old) 1/30/96 which merged into Franco-Nevada Mining Corp. Ltd. (New) 9/20/99 which was acquired by Newmont Mining Corp. 2/16/2002

REDSTONE RES INC (ON)
Merged into Franco-Nevada Mining Corp. Ltd. (Old) 1/30/96
Each share Common no par exchanged for (0.05) share Common no par
Franco-Nevada Mining Corp. Ltd. (Old) name changed to Franco-Nevada Mining Corp. Ltd. (New) 9/20/99 which merged into Newmont Mining Corp. 2/16/2002

REDTAIL METALS CORP (BC)
Merged into Golden Predator Mining Corp. (AB) 04/22/2014
Each share Common no par exchanged for (0.14285714) share Class A Common no par
Note: Unexchanged certificates will be cancelled and become without value 04/22/2020
Golden Predator Mining Corp. (AB) reincorporated in British Columbia 10/21/2015

REDUX ENERGY CORP (AB)
Name changed to Thermal Control Technologies Corp. 10/01/1997
(See Thermal Control Technologies Corp.)

REDUX HLDGS INC (NV)
Each share old Common $0.001 par exchanged for (0.001) share new Common $0.001 par to reflect a (1) for (200,000) reverse split followed by a (200) for (1) forward split 10/02/2017
Note: No holder will receive fewer than (200) shares
Reincorporated under the laws of Delaware as Big Time Holdings, Inc. and new Common $0.001 par changed to $0.0001 par 02/15/2018

REDWATER LEASEHOLDS, LTD.
Acquired by Trans Empire Oils Ltd. in 1952
Each share Common no par exchanged for (0.071428) share Capital Stock no par
Trans Empire Oils Ltd. name changed to West Canadian Oil & Gas Ltd. 3/10/58 which merged into Canadian Delhi Oil Ltd. 1/1/62 which recapitalized as CanDel Oil Ltd. 1/10/72
(See CanDel Oil Ltd.)

REDWATER PETROLEUM LTD.
Merged into Redwater-Picadilly Petroleum Ltd. on a (1) for (2) basis in 1950
Redwater-Picadilly Petroleum Ltd. name changed to Redpic Petroleums Ltd. in 1951 which was recapitalized as Stanwell Oil & Gas Ltd. in 1952 which was recapitalized as Cordwell International Developments Ltd. 12/16/66
(See Cordwell International Developments Ltd.)

REDWATER-PICCADILLY PETROLEUM LTD.
Name changed to Redpic Petroleums Ltd. in 1951
Redpic Petroleums Ltd. recapitalized as Stanwell Oil & Gas Ltd. in 1952 which recapitalized as Cordwell International Developments Ltd. 12/16/66
(See Cordwell International Developments Ltd.)

REDWATER UTILITIES HOLDINGS OIL & GAS LTD. (AB)
Merged into Calvan Consolidated Oil & Gas Co. Ltd. and each (6) shares Common 50¢ par exchanged for (1) share Capital Stock $1 par in July 1954
Calvan Consolidated Oil & Gas Co. Ltd. was liquidated for cash 11/30/61

REDWING CARRIERS, INC. (FL)
Acquired by Wyle Laboratories 8/8/68
Each share Common $1.25 par exchanged for (0.5) share Common no par
Wyle Laboratories name changed to Wyle Electronics 1/26/95
(See Wyle Electronics)

REDWING RES INC (BC)
Struck off register and declared dissolved for failure to file returns 06/30/1994

REDWING VENTURES INC (DE)
Name changed to Patco Industries Ltd. 4/7/89
Patco Industries Ltd. recapitalized as Optical Molecular Imaging, Inc. 1/27/2006 which name changed to ImmunoCellular Therapeutics, Ltd. 11/30/2006

REDWOLF GOLD MINES, LTD. (ON)
Charter cancelled and declared dissolved for failure to pay taxes and file returns 12/7/77

REDWOOD ADVANTAGE MONTHLY INCOME FD (ON)
Under plan of merger each Trust Unit automatically became (0.518786) Purpose Multi-Asset Income Fund ETF Unit 05/04/2018

REDWOOD BANCORP (CA)
Merged into Empire Holdings Inc. 03/03/1980
Each share Common $3.33-1/3 par exchanged for $37.901 cash

REDWOOD BK (SAN RAFAEL, CA)
Common $5 par changed to $3.33-1/3 par and (0.5) additional share issued 12/21/1971
Under plan of reorganization each share Common $3.33-1/3 par automatically became (1) share Redwood Bancorp Common $3.33-1/3 par 07/31/1972

(See Redwood Bancorp)

REDWOOD BANK (WATERTOWN, NY)
Location changed 06/15/1988
Name changed 07/01/2003
Location changed from (Redwood, NY) to (Alexandria Bay, NY) 06/15/1988
Name and location changed from Redwood National Bank (Alexandria Bay, NY) to Redwood Bank (Watertown, NY) 07/01/2003
Name changed to WSB Municipal Bank (Watertown, NY) 06/14/2008

REDWOOD BROADCASTING INC (CO)
Name changed to FTM Media, Inc. (CO) 07/26/1999
FTM Media, Inc. (CO) reincorporated in Delaware 01/07/2000
(See FTM Media, Inc.)

REDWOOD CDN PFD SH FD (ON)
Name changed to Purpose Canadian Preferred Share Fund 06/18/2018

REDWOOD CAP BK (EUREKA, CA)
Common no par split (3) for (2) by issuance of (0.5) additional share payable 8/29/2006 to holders of record 8/15/2006 Ex date - 8/30/2006
Under plan of reorganization each share Common no par automatically became (1) share Redwood Capital Bancorp Common no par 5/29/2007

REDWOOD EMPIRE BANCORP (CA)
Perpetual Conv. Preferred Ser. A no par called for redemption at $10.39 on 4/30/98
Common no par split (3) for (2) by issuance of (0.5) additional share payable 10/19/2001 to holders of record 10/3/2001 Ex date - 10/22/2001
Common no par split (3) for (2) by issuance of (0.5) additional share payable 8/13/2003 to holders of record 7/28/2003 Ex date - 8/14/2003
Merged into Westamerica Bancorporation 3/1/2005
Each share Common no par exchanged for (0.3263) share Common no par and $11.37 cash

REDWOOD EMPIRE SAVINGS & LOAN ASSOCIATION (CA)
Acquired by Golden West Financial Corp. (CA) 12/19/1969
Each share Capital Stock $1 par exchanged for (1.21045) shares Common 50¢ par
Golden West Financial Corp. (CA) reincorporated in Delaware 10/31/1975 which merged into Wachovia Corp. (Ctfs. dated after 09/01/2001) 10/02/2006 which merged into Wells Fargo & Co. (New) 12/31/2008

REDWOOD ENERGY CR FD (ON)
Name changed to Purpose Energy Credit Fund 06/18/2018

REDWOOD ENERGY GROUP INC (NV)
Name changed to Redwood Entertainment Group Inc. 3/3/2003
Redwood Entertainment Group Inc. recapitalized as SaVi Media Group, Inc. 9/20/2004

REDWOOD ENERGY INCOME FD (ON)
Under plan of merger each Trust Unit automatically became (1.216414) Purpose Global Resource Fund Ser. F Units 05/04/2018

REDWOOD ENERGY LTD (BC)
Acquired by Compton Petroleum Corp. 04/26/2018
Each share Common no par exchanged for $0.20 cash

REDWOOD ENTMT GROUP INC (NV)
Common $0.001 par split (3) for (1) by issuance of (2) additional shares payable 03/10/2003 to holders of record 03/03/2003 Ex date - 03/11/2003
Recapitalized as SaVi Media Group, Inc. 09/20/2004
Each share Common $0.001 par exchanged for (0.04) share Common $0.001 par
Note: Holders of between (100) and (2,500) shares will receive (100) post-split shares
No holder will receive fewer than (100) shares

REDWOOD FINL INC (NV)
Name changed to Quik Pix Inc. 01/27/1988
Quik Pix Inc. name changed to Solvis Group, Inc. 08/02/2005
(See Solvis Group, Inc.)

REDWOOD FLOATING RATE BD FD (ON)
Under plan of merger each Class A and Class U Unit automatically became (0.867267) or (0.97114) Redwood Floating Rate Income Fund Class A or Class U Unit respectively 05/04/2018
Redwood Floating Rate Income Fund name changed to Purpose Floating Rate Income Fund 06/18/2018

REDWOOD FLOATING RATE INCOME FD (ON)
Name changed to Purpose Floating Rate Income Fund 06/18/2018

REDWOOD GLOBAL FINANCIALS INCOME FD (ON)
Under plan of merger each Class A or Class F Unit automatically became (0.882263) or (0.992494) Purpose U.S. Preferred Share Fund ETF Unit or Ser. F Unit respectively 05/04/2018

REDWOOD GLOBAL INFRASTRUCTURE INCOME FD (ON)
Merged into Purpose Fund Corp. 08/24/2018
Each Unit exchanged for (0.497073) share Diversified Real Asset Fund

REDWOOD GOLD MINES LTD. (ON)
Merged into New Redwood Gold Mines Ltd. in 1949
Each share Capital Stock $1 par exchanged for (1/3) share Common $1 par
(See New Redwood Gold Mines)

REDWOOD LOW VOLATILITY HIGH INCOME FD (ON)
Trust terminated 03/30/2018
Each Unit received approximately $9.31 cash

REDWOOD MICROCAP FD INC (CO)
Merged into Gibbs Holdings, LLC 7/10/2005
Each share Common $0.001 par exchanged for $1.60 cash

REDWOOD MONTHLY INCOME FD (ON)
Under plan of merger each Unit automatically became (0.490446) Purpose Multi-Asset Income Fund ETF Unit 05/04/2018

REDWOOD NATL BK (SAN RAPHAEL, CA)
Common $10 par changed to $5 par and (1) additional share issued 4/7/64
Name changed to Redwood Bank (San Rafael, CA) 5/12/69
Redwood Bank (San Rafael, CA) reorganized as Redwood Bancorp 7/31/72
(See Redwood Bancorp)

REDWOOD RES INC (BC)
Recapitalized as Trooper Explorations Ltd. 06/01/1992

Each share Common no par exchanged for (0.33333333) share Common no par
Trooper Explorations Ltd. name changed to Trooper Technologies Inc. 01/27/1995 which name changed to Stream Communications Network, Inc. 10/19/2001 which name changed to Stream Communications Network & Media Inc. 08/17/2004
(See Stream Communications Network & Media Inc.)

REDWOOD RES LTD (AB)
Reincorporated under the laws of Delaware as TRI Communication Solutions, Inc. 11/20/2000
(See TRI Communication Solutions, Inc.)

REDWOOD TR INC (MD)
Each share 9.74% Conv. Preferred Class B 1¢ par exchanged for (1) share Common 1¢ par 05/02/2003
(Additional Information in Active)

REDZONE RES LTD (AB)
Reincorporated under the laws of Ontario 03/02/2011

REEBOK INTL LTD (MA)
Common 1¢ par split (3) for (1) by issuance of (2) additional shares 06/09/1986
Common 1¢ par split (2) for (1) by issuance of (1) additional share 08/25/1987
Merged into adidas-Salomon A.G. 01/31/2006
Each share Common 1¢ par exchanged for $59 cash

REECE BUTTON HOLE MACHINE CO.
Name changed to Reece Corp. 00/00/1946
(See Reece Corp.)

REECE CORP (MA)
Under plan of merger each share Common no par exchanged for (1) share Common $1 par 00/00/1948
5% Preferred $100 par called for redemption 08/01/1961
Common $1 par split (3) for (1) by issuance of (2) additional shares 06/04/1969
Stock Dividend - 400% 05/20/1963
Acquired by TRC Acquisition Corp. 04/22/1991
Each share Common $1 par exchanged for $5.75 cash

REECE CORP (NV)
Common $0.001 par split (2) for (1) by issuance of (1) additional share payable 03/31/2006 to holders of record 03/21/2006 Ex date - 04/03/2006
Common $0.001 par split (2) for (1) by issuance of (1) additional share payable 05/03/2006 to holders of record 04/23/2006 Ex date - 05/04/2006
Common $0.001 par split (2) for (1) by issuance of (1) additional share payable 05/31/2006 to holders of record 05/30/2006 Ex date - 06/01/2006
Name changed to AmMex Gold Mining Corp. 08/18/2006
AmMex Gold Mining Corp. recapitalized as Wind Works Power Corp. 06/11/2009

REECE ENERGY EXPL CORP NEW (AB)
Merged into Penn West Energy Trust 04/30/2009
Each share Common no par exchanged for (0.125) Trust Unit
Penn West Energy Trust reorganized as Penn West Petroleum Ltd. (New) 01/03/2011 which name changed to Obsidian Energy Ltd. 06/29/2017

REECE ENERGY EXPL CORP OLD (AB)
Under plan of merger each share Common no par automatically became (1) share Reece Energy Exploration Corp. (New) Common no par 05/15/2007
Reece Energy Exploration Corp. (New) merged into Penn West Energy Trust 04/30/2009 which reorganized as Penn West Petroleum Ltd. (New) 01/03/2011 which name changed to Obsidian Energy Ltd. 06/29/2017

REECE ENERGY INC (AB)
Recapitalized as Reece Energy Exploration Corp. (Old) 05/18/2005
Each share Common no par exchanged for (0.25) share Common no par
Reece Energy Exploration Corp. (Old) merged into Reece Energy Exploration Corp. (New) 05/15/2007 which merged into Penn West Energy Trust 04/30/2009 which reorganized as Penn West Petroleum Ltd. (New) 01/03/2011 which name changed to Obsidian Energy Ltd. 06/29/2017

REECE FOLDING MACH CO (ME)
Common $10 par changed to no par 00/00/1948
Common no par changed to $2 par 00/00/1954
Acquired by Compo Industries, Inc. 04/17/1969
Each share Common $2 par exchanged for (0.41412) share Common $1 par
Compo Industries, Inc. merged into Ausimont Compo N.V. 11/04/1985 which name changed to Ausimont N.V. 05/08/1987
(See Ausimont N.V.)

REED (ALBERT E.) & CO. LTD. (ENGLAND)
Ordinary A £1 par reclassified as Ordinary £1 par 12/19/1962
Name changed to Reed Paper Group Ltd. 08/01/1963
Reed Paper Group Ltd. name changed to Reed Group Ltd. 08/11/1969 which name changed to Reed International PLC 08/03/1970 which name changed to Reed Elsevier PLC 04/22/2002 which reorganized as RELX PLC 07/01/2015

REED CO., INC.
Dissolved in 1950

REED CONTAINER CO.
Acquired by Container Corp. of America in 1941
Details not available

REED DRUG CO. (DE)
Common no par changed to $1 par in 1940
Merged into Stratford Corp. 6/1/59
Each share Class A Preferred $1 par exchanged for (0.1) share 5% Preferred $25 par
Each share Common $1 par exchanged for (1) share Common 10¢ par
Stratford Corp. name was changed to Universal Cigar Corp. 3/7/64
(See Universal Cigar Corp.)

REED ELSEVIER N V (NETHERLANDS)
Each old Sponsored ADR for Ordinary exchanged for (0.86567164) new Sponsored ADR for Ordinary and $4.3802 01/04/2008
Reorganized as RELX N.V. 07/01/2015
Each new Sponsored ADR for Ordinary exchanged for (3.076) Sponsored ADR's for Ordinary
RELX N.V. merged into RELX PLC 09/10/2018

REED ELSEVIER P L C (ENGLAND & WALES)
Each old Sponsored ADR for Ordinary exchanged for (0.86567164) new Sponsored ADR for Ordinary and $6.40896 cash 01/04/2008
Reorganized as RELX PLC 07/01/2015
Each new Sponsored ADR for Ordinary exchanged for (4) Sponsored ADR's for Ordinary

REED GROUP LTD (ENGLAND & WALES)
Name changed to Reed International PLC 08/03/1970
Reed International PLC name changed to Reed Elsevier PLC 04/22/2002 which reorganized as RELX PLC 07/01/2015

REED HLDGS CORP (NV)
Name changed to Ostara Corp., Inc. 03/12/2004
Ostara Corp., Inc. name changed to Rheologics Technologies, Inc. 10/18/2005 which name changed to KKS Venture Management, Inc. 07/24/2007 which recapitalized as Codima, Inc. 06/09/2008
(See Codima, Inc.)

REED INDUSTRIES, INC. OLD (MD)
Merged into Reed Industries, Inc. (New) 9/30/74
Each share Capital Stock $1 par exchanged for (0.224024) share Common 10¢ par
(See Reed Industries, Inc. (New))

REED INDS INC NEW (MD)
Merged into Sentry Corp. 10/28/77
Each share Capital Stock 10¢ par exchanged for $0.50 cash

REED INTERNATIONAL, INC. (TX)
Name changed to Murphy (G.W.) Industries, Inc. 04/19/1967
Murphy (G.W.) Industries, Inc. name changed to Reed Tool Co. 09/15/1972 which merged into Baker Oil Tools, Inc. 11/26/1975 which name changed to Baker International Corp. (CA) 01/28/1976 which reincorporated in Delaware 01/27/1983 which merged into Baker Hughes Inc. 04/03/1987 which merged into Baker Hughes, a GE company 07/05/2017

REED INTL PLC (ENGLAND & WALES)
Each share Ordinary 1p par exchanged for (0.25) share Ordinary 25p par 07/25/1986
Each Unsponsored ADR for Ordinary exchanged for (0.25) Unsponsored ADR for Ordinary 07/28/1986
Each Unsponsored ADR for Ordinary exchanged for (0.25) Sponsored ADR's for Ordinary 06/18/1990
Each old Sponsored ADR for Ordinary exchanged for (2) new Sponsored ADR's for Ordinary 10/04/1994
Name changed to Reed Elsevier PLC 04/22/2002
Reed Elsevier PLC reorganized as RELX PLC 07/01/2015

REED LAKE EXPL LTD (ON)
Common no par split (2) for (1) by issuance of (1) additional share 08/28/1992
Recapitalized as Westhope Capital Corp. 11/27/1996
Each share Common no par exchanged for (0.14285714) share Common no par
Westhope Capital Corp. recapitalized as EPM Mining Ventures Inc. (ON) 03/12/2010 which reincorporated in Yukon 05/20/2011 which name changed to Crystal Peak Minerals Inc. 06/26/2015

REED PAPER GROUP LTD (ENGLAND)
Name changed to Reed Group Ltd. 08/11/1969

Reed Group Ltd. name changed to Reed International PLC 08/03/1970 which name changed to Reed Elsevier PLC 04/22/2002 which reorganized as RELX PLC 07/01/2015

REED PAPER LTD (CANADA)
$2 Conv. Preferred $25 par reclassified as $1 Conv. Preferred Class A $12.50 par and (1) additional share issued 05/25/1976
Common no par reclassified as Conv. Class A Common no par and (1) additional share issued 05/25/1976
$1 Conv. Preferred Class A $12.50 par reclassified as $1 Conv. Vtg. Preferred $12.50 par 06/13/1980
$1 Conv. Vtg. Preferred $12.50 par called for redemption 10/06/1980
Merged into Reed International Ltd. 10/17/1980
Each share Conv. Class A Common no par exchanged for $12.75 cash
Each share Conv. Class B Common no par exchanged for $12.75 cash

REED-PRENTICE CORP. (MA)
Each share Common no par exchanged for (3) shares Common $5 par in 1945
Each share Common $5 par exchanged for (2) shares Common $2.50 par and (0.5) additional share issued as a stock dividend following the split in 1946
Acquired by Package Machinery Co. at $12 per share in 1954

REED PRTG & PACKAGING CORP (NY)
Name changed to Computer Tools, Inc. 12/18/1968
(See Computer Tools, Inc.)

REED RES LTD (AUSTRALIA)
Name changed to Neometals Ltd. 01/23/2015

REED ROLLER BIT CO. (TX)
Each share Common $25 par exchanged for (4) shares Common no par 00/00/1929
Each share Common no par exchanged for (3) shares new Common no par 00/00/1936
Common no par changed to $5 par 06/16/1965
Name changed to Reed International, Inc. 06/20/1966
Reed International, Inc. name changed to Murphy (G.W.) Industries, Inc. 04/19/1967 which name changed to Reed Tool Co. 09/15/1972 which merged into Baker Oil Tools, Inc. 11/26/1975 which name changed to Baker International Corp. 01/28/1976 which reincorporated in Delaware 01/27/1983 which merged into Baker Hughes Inc. 04/03/1987 which merged into Baker Hughes, a GE company 07/05/2017

REED SHAW OSLER LTD. (CANADA)
Common no par split (3) for (1) by issuance of (2) additional shares 5/31/71
Conv. Class C Common $1 par changed to $2 par 6/14/73
Common no par reclassified as Conv. Class A Common $1 par 7/11/73
Name changed to Reed Stenhouse Companies Ltd./Les Compagnies Reed Stenhouse, Ltee. 3/6/78
Reed Stenhouse Companies Ltd./ Les Compagnies Reed Stenhouse, Ltee. merged into Alexander & Alexander Services Inc. 9/9/85
(See Alexander & Alexander Services Inc.)

REED STENHOUSE COS LTD (CANADA)
Merged into Alexander & Alexander Services Inc. 09/09/1985
Each share Conv. Class A Common no par exchanged for (0.576) share

Reed Stenhouse Companies Ltd./Les Compagnies Reed Stenhouse Ltee. Class 1 Special Share no par
Each share Conv. Class C Common no par exchanged for (0.576) share Class C Common $1 par and (0.576) share Alexander & Alexander Europe PLC
Dividend Share Class 1 Special Share no par called for redemption 02/17/1997
(See each company's listing)

REED SYS INC (NV)
Common $0.001 par split (4) for (1) by issuance of (3) additional shares 03/17/1988
Name changed to Western Land & Resources Inc. 05/15/2002

REED TOOL CO (TX)
$2 Conv. Preferred 3rd Ser. $5 par called for redemption 09/15/1975
Merged into Baker Oil Tools, Inc. 11/26/1975
Each share Common $2.50 par exchanged for (0.735) share Common $1 par
Baker Oil Tools, Inc. name changed to Baker International Corp. (CA) 01/28/1976 which reincorporated in Delaware 01/27/1983 which merged into Baker Hughes Inc. 04/03/1987 which merged into Baker Hughes, a GE company 07/05/2017

REED TOYS INC (DE)
Liquidation completed
Each share Common 50¢ par exchanged for initial distribution of $1 cash 12/15/1973
Each share Common 50¢ par received second distribution of $0.60 cash 04/07/1974
Each share Common 50¢ par received third and final distribution of $0.27 cash 06/14/1976

REEDER DEV CORP (MN)
Name changed to RDI Corp. 8/8/77
(See RDI Corp.)

REEDS INC (DE)
Each share Conv. Preferred Ser. B $10 par exchanged for (8.05) shares Common $0.0001 par 02/15/2013
(Additional Information in Active)

REEDS JEWELERS INC (NC)
Common 10¢ par split (2) for (1) by issuance of (1) additional share payable 2/20/98 to holders of record 2/11/98
Stock Dividends - 10% 8/15/94; 10% 6/1/95
Merged into Sparkle, LLC 5/27/2004
Each share Common 10¢ par exchanged for $2.05 cash

REEDY CAMERA CTR INC (MN)
Stock Dividend - 10% 4/16/1970
Name changed to Sun Development Co. 01/24/1972
(See Sun Development Co.)

REEF CAP CORP (FL)
Recapitalized as Akira Corp. 11/30/1989
Each share old Common $0.0001 par exchanged for (0.02) share new Common $0.0001 par
(See Akira Corp.)

REEF ENERGY CORP (MI)
Name changed to General Energy Resources & Technology, Corp. 07/01/1987
(See General Energy Resources & Technology, Corp.)

REEF EXPLORATIONS LTD. (ON)
Recapitalized as United Reef Petroleums Ltd. 05/23/1961
Each share Common $1 par exchanged for (0.25) share Common no par
United Reef Petroleums Ltd. name changed to United Reef Ltd. 09/01/1993 which recapitalized as

New Klondike Exploration Ltd.
08/17/2012
(See New Klondike Exploration Ltd.)

REEF HYDROCARBONS LTD (AB)
Recapitalized as International Reef
Resources Ltd. 09/29/1988
Each share Common no par
exchanged for (0.2) share Common
no par
International Reef Resources Ltd.
merged into UTS Energy Corp.
06/30/1998 which merged into
SilverBirch Energy Corp. 10/01/2010
which merged into SilverWillow
Energy Corp. 04/04/2012
(See SilverWillow Energy Corp.)

REEF PETROLEUMS LTD. (ON)
Name changed to Reef Explorations
Ltd. 04/26/1956
Reef Explorations Ltd. recapitalized
as United Reef Petroleums Ltd.
05/23/1961 which name changed to
United Reef Ltd. 09/01/1993 which
recapitalized as New Klondike
Exploration Ltd. 08/17/2012
(See New Klondike Exploration Ltd.)

REEF RES CORP (BC)
Merged into United Westland
Resources Ltd. 11/25/81
Each share Capital Stock no par
exchanged for (0.5) share Common
no par
United Westland Resources Ltd.
name changed to Daleco Resources
Corp. (BC) 5/2/86 which
reincorporated in Delaware 10/1/96
which reincorporated in Nevada
4/1/2002

REEFCO MFG CORP (BC)
Delisted from Vancouver Stock
Exchange 03/06/1995

REEL ESTATE SVCS INC (NV)
Name changed to BoomJ, Inc.
01/31/2008
BoomJ, Inc. name changed to
Beyond Commerce, Inc. 02/23/2009

REEL STAFF INC (NV)
Common $0.001 par split (3.22) for
(1) by issuance of (2.22) additional
shares payable 07/30/2002 to
holders of record 07/29/2002
Ex date - 07/31/2002
Name changed to Flight Safety
Technologies, Inc. 09/01/2002
Flight Safety Technologies, Inc. name
changed to Applied Science
Products, Inc. 12/09/2009

REESE RIVER RESOURCE CORP (BC)
Recapitalized as Hurley River Gold
Corp. (BC) 03/18/1994
Each share Common no par
exchanged for (0.2) share Common
no par
Hurley River Gold Corp. (BC)
reincorporated in Yukon 12/17/1997
which recapitalized as Ouro Brasil
Ltd. 03/20/1998 which recapitalized
as Consolidated Ouro Brasil Ltd.
02/18/2000 which name changed to
Superior Diamonds Inc. (YT)
09/03/2002 which reincorporated in
British Columbia 06/30/2004 which
name changed to Northern Superior
Resources Inc. 04/15/2008

REETA EXPLORATIONS LTD. (ON)
Charter cancelled for failure to pay
taxes and file returns 1/4/72

REEVES BKG & TR CO (DOVER, OH)
Merged into Huntington Bancshares
Inc. 03/18/1982
Each share Common $10 par
exchanged for $68.50 cash

REEVES BROADCASTING CORP (DE)
Name changed 09/20/1963
Name changed from Reeves
Broadcasting & Development Corp.
to Reeves Broadcasting Corp.
09/20/1963

Name changed to Reeves Telecom
Corp. 05/09/1969
(See Reeves Telecom Corp.)

REEVES BROS INC (NY)
Common 50¢ par split (7) for (5) by
issuance of (0.4) additional share
10/4/76
Stock Dividends - 10% 9/15/65; 10%
12/23/68; 10% 9/28/73
Merged into Newreeveco, Inc. 7/2/82
Each share Common 50¢ par
exchanged for $70 cash

REEVES COMMUNICATIONS CORP (DE)
Stock Dividends - 50% 10/30/1980;
50% 07/10/1981; 50% 12/29/1982
Merged into Thames (USA) Inc.
01/17/1990
Each share Common 40¢ par
exchanged for $7 cash

REEVES-ELY LABORATORIES, INC. (NY)
Merged into Dynamics Corp. of
America (NY) 1/23/56
Each share Common 10¢ par
exchanged for (1) share $1
Preference $2 par
(See Dynamics Corp. of America (NY))

REEVES FENCES INC (FL)
Stock Dividends - 20% 04/15/1958;
40% 11/15/1958
Name changed to Reeves
Southeastern Corp. 09/27/1973
(See Reeves Southeastern Corp.)

REEVES (DANIEL), INC.
Acquired by Safeway Stores, Inc.
00/00/1941
Each share 6.50% Preferred $100 par
exchanged for (1) share 5%
Preferred $100 par
Each share Common no par
exchanged for (0.014) share new
Common no par
(See Safeway Stores, Inc.)

REEVES INDS INC (NY)
Name changed 05/03/1963
Name changed from Reeves
Soundcraft Corp. to Reeves
Industries, Inc. 05/03/1963
Name changed to RSC Industries,
Inc. 05/03/1971
RSC Industries, Inc. name changed to
Matec Corp. (NY) 04/24/1984 which
reincorporated in Delaware
07/01/1987 which reorganized in
Maryland 07/02/1998 which name
changed to Valpey-Fisher Corp.
06/03/2002
(See Valpey-Fisher Corp.)

REEVES MACDONALD MINES LTD (CANADA)
Delisted from Vancouver Stock
Exchange 07/04/1986

REEVES SOUNDCRAFT CORP. (NY)
Name changed to Reeves Industries,
Inc. 5/3/63
Reeves Industries, Inc. name
changed to RSC Industries, Inc.
5/3/71 which name changed to
Matec Corp. (NY) 4/24/87 which
reincorporated in Delaware 7/1/87
which reorganized in Maryland
7/2/98 which name changed to
Valpey-Fisher Corp. 6/3/2002

REEVES SOUTHEASTN CORP (FL)
Administratively dissolved 10/04/2002

REEVES TELECOM CORP (DE)
Liquidation completed
Each share Common $1 par received
initial distribution of $0.90 cash
02/29/1980
Each share Common $1 par received
second distribution of $2.30 cash
05/15/1980
Each share Common $1 par
exchanged for (1) Reeves Telecom
Associates Unit of Ltd. Partnership
05/17/1980

REEVES TELECOM LTD PARTNERSHIP (SC)
Each old Unit of Ltd. Partnership
received initial distribution of $0.90
cash 02/29/1980
Each old Unit of Ltd. Partnership
received second distribution of $2.30
cash 05/14/1980
Each old Unit of Ltd. Partnership
exchanged for (0.00990099) new
Unit of Ltd. Partnership 06/25/2013
Note: Holders of (100) or fewer
pre-split Units will receive $0.81
cash per Unit
Completely liquidated 01/14/2015
Each new Unit of Ltd. Partnership
received first and final distribution of
$21.975436 cash

REEVES TELETAPE CORP (DE)
Each share Common 10¢ par
exchanged for (0.25) share Common
40¢ par 01/22/1977
Name changed to Reeves
Communications Corp. 12/06/1979
(See Reeves Communications Corp.)

REFAC INC (DE)
Name changed to Refac Technology
Development Corp. 4/13/70
Refac Technology Development Corp.
name changed to Refac (Old) 6/1/99
which merged into Refac (New)
2/28/2003 which name changed to
Refac Optical Group 3/6/2006
(See Refac Optical Group)

REFAC OLD (DE)
Merged into Refac (New) 2/28/2003
Each share Common 10¢ par
exchanged for (0.2) share Common
$0.001 par and $3.60 cash

REFAC OPTICAL GROUP (DE)
Name changed 3/6/2006
Name changed from Refac (New) to
Refac Optical Group 3/6/2006
Merged into Palisade Concentrated
Equity Partnership, L.P. 4/26/2007
Each share Common $0.001 par
exchanged for $6 cash

REFAC TECHNOLOGY DEV CORP (DE)
Stock Dividends - 50% 6/9/72; 50%
12/6/77; 10% 12/29/80; 10%
12/29/81; 10% 12/22/82; 10%
12/23/83; 10% 12/27/84; 20%
12/31/85; 20% 12/31/86
Name changed to Refac (Old) 6/1/99
Refac (Old) merged into Refac (New)
2/28/2003 which name changed to
Refac Optical Group 3/6/2006
(See Refac Optical Group)

REFCO INC (DE)
Plan of reorganization under Chapter
11 Federal Bankruptcy Code
effective 12/26/2006
Stockholders who elected to become
participants in the Litigation Trust
and Private Actions Trust received
the following distributions:
Inital distribution of $0.0384117 cash
payable 06/09/2011 to holders of
record 12/26/2006
Second distribution of $0.1485256
cash payable 08/30/2011 to holders
of record 12/26/2006
Third distribution of $0.0435334 cash
payable 10/24/2012 to holders of
record 12/26/2006
Fourth distribution of $0.026888 cash
payable 08/05/2013 to holders of
record 12/26/2006
Fifth distribution of $0.0215106 cash
payable 12/18/2014 to holders of
record 12/26/2006
Sixth distribution of $0.00475623
cash payable 11/03/2015 to holders
of record 12/26/2006

REFF INC (ON)
Merged into Westinghouse Canada
Acquisition Corp. 1/17/90
Each share Common no par
exchanged for $12.75 cash

REFILL ENERGY INC (NV)
Each share old Common $0.001 par
exchanged for (0.001) share new
Common $0.001 par 02/15/2012
Name changed to Medical Cannabis
Payment Solutions 12/05/2013

REFINED SYRUPS & SUGARS, INC. (NY)
Merged into Corn Products Refining
Co. (NJ) on a (0.25807) for (1) basis
03/15/1957
Corn Products Refining Co. merged
into Corn Products Co. (NJ)
09/30/1958 which reincorporated in
Delaware 04/30/1959 which name
changed to CPC International Inc.
04/23/1969 which name changed to
BestFoods 01/01/1998
(See BestFoods)

REFINEMET INTL CO (DE)
Plan of reorganization confirmed
Stockholders had a 30-day period to
surrender their certificates for $0.20
cash per share expiring 6/18/94
Unexchanged certificates are without
value

REFINERS OIL CO.
Acquired by Standard Oil Co. (OH) in
1931
Details not available

REFINERS PETROLEUM CORP.
Liquidated in 1949

REFINITE CORP. (NE)
Involuntarily dissolved for
non-payment of taxes 04/22/1963

REFLECTION CORP. OF AMERICA (IL)
Proclaimed dissolved for failure to
pay taxes and file reports 10/6/42

REFLECTION RES LTD (AB)
Recapitalized as Corsair Petroleum
Inc. 7/14/89
Each share Common no par
exchanged for (0.1) share Common
no par
In addition holders received (0.1)
Class A warrants expiring 10/13/89
Corsair Petroleum Inc. recapitalized
as Corsair Explorations Ltd. 2/6/96
(See Corsair Explorations Ltd.)

REFLECTIX INC (IN)
Reincorporated 5/8/96
State of incorporation changed from
(UT) to (IN) 5/8/96
Merged into Sealed Air Corp.
7/14/2000
Each share Common $0.001 par
exchanged for $1.05 cash

REFLECTONE INC (FL)
Reincorporated 12/23/1985
Stock Dividend - 10% 10/15/1984
State of incorporation changed from
(DE) to (FL) 12/23/1985
Common $1 par split (5) for (4) by
issuance of (0.25) additional share
09/01/1993
Merged into British Aerospace
Holdings, Inc. 05/20/1997
Each share Common $1 par
exchanged for $24 cash

REFLECTOR CORP. OF AMERICA (DE)
Charter cancelled and declared
inoperative and void for
non-payment of taxes 3/1/76

REFLEX INC (NV)
Name changed to Landmark Energy
Enterprise, Inc. 04/19/2010
(See Landmark Energy Enterprise, Inc.)

REFLEXOR INC (DE)
Recapitalized as Advanced
Bodymetrics Corp. (DE) 07/27/1998
Each (140) shares Common $0.001
par exchanged for (1) share
Common $0.001 par
Advanced Bodymetrics Corp. (DE)
reorganized in Nevada as ICM
Telecommunications, Inc.

01/24/2002 which recapitalized as eHolding Technologies, Inc. 05/26/2006 which recapitalized as Pine Ridge Holdings, Inc. 03/10/2008 which name changed to Mike the Pike Productions, Inc. (NV) 08/05/2009 which reorganized in Wyoming 03/03/2011

REFRACTORY & INSULATION CORP. (NJ)
Stock Dividend - 10% 9/17/57
Name changed to F&H Liquidating Corp. 6/26/63
(See F&H Liquidating Corp.)

REFRACTORY MINERALS & MINING, INC. (NV)
Charter revoked for failure to file reports and pay fees 3/2/70

REFRESCO GERBER N V (NETHERLANDS)
Name changed to Refresco Group N.V. 06/10/2016

REFRESHMENT MACHY INC (PA)
Stock Dividend - 10% 01/15/1974
Merged into Gross-Given Manufacturing Co. 07/28/1983
Each share Common 10¢ par exchanged for $10 cash

REFRIGERACAO PARANA S A (BRAZIL)
Name changed to Electrolux Do Brasil S.A. 03/04/1997
(See Electrolux Do Brasil S.A.)

REFRIGERATED TRANS INC (GA)
Name changed to RTC Transportation Inc. 01/25/1982
(See RTC Transportation Inc.)

REFRIGERATION SCIENCE INC (NY)
Merged into RFS Merger Corp. 08/19/1985
Each share Common 1¢ par exchanged for $1.25 cash

REG TECHNOLOGIES INC (BC)
Name changed 02/23/1993
Name changed from Reg Resources Corp. to Reg Technologies Inc. 02/23/1993
Each share Common no par received distribution of (0.14285714) share Minewest Silver & Gold Inc. Common no par payable 12/28/2011 to holders of record 12/21/2011 Ex date - 12/19/2011
Note: Holders entitled to (99) shares or fewer received $0.20 cash per share
Each share Common no par received distribution of (1.1) shares REGI U.S., Inc. Restricted Common no par payable 04/04/2017 to holders of record 11/18/2016
Notes: Company has completed distribution of all assets and is now a shell
Certificates were not required to be surrendered and are without value

REGADO BIOSCIENCES INC (DE)
Recapitalized as Tobira Therapeutics, Inc. 05/05/2015
Each share Common $0.001 par exchanged for (0.11111111) share Common $0.001 par
(See Tobira Therapeutics, Inc.)

REGAL APPAREL LTD (NY)
100% acquired through purchase offer which expired 06/01/1981
Public interest eliminated

REGAL BANCORP INC (MD)
Merged into Old Line Bancshares, Inc. 12/23/2015
Each share Common 1¢ par exchanged for (0.7718) share Common 1¢ par

REGAL BELOIT CORP (WI)
Reincorporated 04/18/1994
Name changed 04/28/2015
Common 1¢ par split (3) for (2) by issuance of (0.5) additional share 06/15/1976
Common 1¢ par split (5) for (4) by issuance of (0.25) additional share 05/29/1980
Common 1¢ par split (3) for (2) by issuance of (0.5) additional share 11/30/1983
Common 1¢ par split (3) for (2) by issuance of (0.5) additional share 05/29/1987
Common 1¢ par split (3) for (2) by issuance of (0.5) additional share 05/16/1988
State of incorporation changed from (DE) to (WI) 04/18/1994
Common no par split (2) for (1) by issuance of (1) additional share 08/12/1994
Name changed to Regal Beloit Corp. 04/28/2015

REGAL CHEF INC (NY)
Merged into Regal Chef Inc. (DE) 09/30/1977
Each share Common 10¢ par exchanged for $1.25 cash

REGAL CINEMAS INC (TN)
Common no par split (3) for (2) by issuance of (0.5) additional share 12/8/94
Common no par split (3) for (2) by issuance of (0.5) additional share 12/13/95
Common no par split (3) for (2) by issuance of (0.5) additional share payable 9/16/96 to holders of record 9/2/96
Merged into a private company 5/27/98
Each share Common no par exchanged for $31 cash

REGAL COMMUNICATIONS CORP (NJ)
Each share old Common $0.001 par exchanged for (0.5) share new Common $0.001 par 10/26/1989
Chapter 11 bankruptcy proceedings terminated 05/06/1997
Stockholders' equity unlikely

REGAL CONS VENTURES LTD (ON)
Delisted from Toronto Venture Stock Exchange 04/29/2003

REGAL CREST INC (FL)
Proclaimed dissolved for failure to file reports and pay fees 05/23/1973

REGAL ENERGY CORP (AB)
Recapitalized as Regal Energy Ltd. 01/19/2006
Each share Common no par exchanged for (0.2) share Common no par
Regal Energy Ltd. recapitalized as Novus Energy Inc. 08/05/2009
(See Novus Energy Inc.)

REGAL ENERGY LTD (AB)
Recapitalized as Novus Energy Inc. 08/05/2009
Each share Common no par exchanged for (0.1) share Common no par
(See Novus Energy Inc.)

REGAL ENTMT GROUP (DE)
Acquired by Cineworld Group PLC 02/28/2018
Each share Class A Common $0.001 par exchanged for $23 cash

REGAL FACTORS INC (DE)
Name changed to Telstar, Inc. 12/31/68
(See Telstar, Inc.)

REGAL GOLD CORP (BC)
Name changed to International Thunderbird Gaming Corp. (BC) 06/23/1994
International Thunderbird Gaming Corp. (BC) reincorporated in Yukon 02/05/1999 which name changed to Thunderbird Resorts, Inc. (Yukon) 10/05/2005 which reorganized in British Virgin Islands 11/20/2007

REGAL GOLDFIELDS LTD (ON)
Recapitalized as Regal Consolidated Ventures Ltd. 07/27/2000
Each share Common no par exchanged for (0.1) share Preference no par and (0.1) share Common no par
(See Regal Consolidated Ventures Ltd.)

REGAL GREETINGS & GIFTS INC (CANADA)
Acquired by MDC Corp. 10/17/1994
Each share Common no par exchanged for $10.75 cash

REGAL GROUP INC (NV)
Name changed to UHF Logistics Group, Inc. 01/06/2011

REGAL INC (DE)
Completely liquidated 08/09/1968
Each share Common 25¢ par exchanged for first and final distribution of (0.166624) share Unexcelled, Inc. Common $1 par
Unexcelled, Inc. name changed to Twin Fair, Inc. 07/05/1972
(See Twin Fair, Inc.)

REGAL INDS INC (MN)
Acquired by Kayot, Inc. 09/10/1970
Each (100) shares Common 10¢ par exchanged for (3) shares Common 33-1/3¢ par and $140 principal amount of 8% 5-Year Conv. Subord. Debentures
Holders of (99) or fewer shares received $1.76 cash per share
Kayot, Inc. name changed to Harris-Kayot, Inc. 05/06/1983
(See Harris-Kayot, Inc.)

REGAL INTL HLDG INC (FL)
Name changed to Regal One Corp. (FL) 06/13/1988
Regal One Corp. (FL) reorganized in Maryland as Princeton Capital Corp. 03/23/2015

REGAL INTL INC (DE)
Each share 9% Conv. Preferred Ser. B 10¢ par converted into (7.1) shares Common 10¢ par upon surrender after 06/14/1995
Recapitalized as Asia Resources Holdings Ltd. 02/19/1999
Each (138) shares Common 10¢ par exchanged for (1) share Common 10¢ par
Asia Resources Holdings Ltd. name changed to Asia Fiber Holdings Ltd. 03/14/2000
(See Asia Fiber Holdings Ltd.)

REGAL INVESTMENT VENTURES LTD. (AB)
Officially declared defunct 8/15/70

REGAL LIFE CONCEPTS INC (NV)
Name changed to Regal Group Inc. 04/13/2010
Regal Group Inc. name changed to UHF Logistics Group, Inc. 01/06/2011

REGAL LIFESTYLE CMNTYS INC (ON)
Acquired by Welltower Inc. 10/27/2015
Each share Common no par exchanged for $12 cash
Note: Unexchanged certificates will be cancelled and become without value 10/27/2021

REGAL-MEADOWS, INC. (DE)
Name changed to Regal, Inc. 6/24/63
Regal, Inc. liquidated for Unexcelled, Inc. 8/9/68 which name changed to Twin Fair, Inc. 7/5/72
(See Twin Fair, Inc.)

REGAL MINERALS LTD. (SK)
Acquired by Westore Mines Ltd. 00/00/1959
Each share Common no par exchanged for (0.25) share Capital Stock $1 par
Westore Mines Ltd. acquired by Bison Petroleum & Minerals Ltd. 09/15/1960 which recapitalized as United Bison Resources Ltd. 12/22/1987 which merged into Nalcap Holdings Inc. 04/25/1991 which recapitalized as Arbatax International Inc. (Canada) 03/28/1996 which reincorporated in Yukon 08/06/1996 which name changed to MFC Bancorp Ltd. (YT) 03/03/1997 which reincorporated in British Columbia 11/03/2004 which name changed to KHD Humboldt Wedag International Ltd. 11/01/2005 which reorganized as Terra Nova Royalty Corp. 03/30/2010 which name changed to MFC Industrial Ltd. 09/30/2011 which name changed to MFC Bancorp Ltd. (BC) 02/16/2016
(See MFC Bancorp Ltd. (BC))

REGAL MINING & DEVELOPMENT LTD. (ON)
Merged into Resource Exploration & Development Co. Ltd. 6/11/68
Each share Capital Stock $1 par exchanged for (0.371747) share Capital Stock no par
Resource Exploration & Development Co. Ltd. charter cancelled 5/13/80

REGAL MINING CO. LTD. (BC)
Struck off register and proclaimed dissolved for failure to file returns 5/15/69

REGAL ONE CORP (FL)
Each share old Common no par exchanged for (0.125) share new Common no par 04/16/1993
Each share new Common no par received distribution of (0.03503715) share Neuralstem, Inc. Common 1¢ par payable 02/05/2007 to holders of record 02/15/2006 Ex date - 02/12/2007
Reorganized under the laws of Maryland as Princeton Capital Corp. 03/23/2015
Each share new Common no par exchanged for (0.5) share Common no par

REGAL PETE LTD (BC)
Recapitalized as Consolidated Regal Resources Ltd. 02/03/1988
Each share Common no par exchanged for (0.2) share Common no par
Consolidated Regal Resources Ltd. recapitalized as Fresco Developments Ltd. 09/18/1992 which merged into Orion Explorations Ltd. (New) 02/25/2002 which merged into Teranga Gold Corp. 10/08/2013

REGAL PETE LTD (CO)
Merged into Pinnacle Petroleum, Inc. (DE) 09/14/1989
Each share Common 1¢ par exchanged for (0.14) share Common 1¢ par
Pinnacle Petroleum, Inc. (DE) name changed to Golden Oil Co. (DE) 02/15/1990
(See Golden Oil Co. (DE))

REGAL PLASTIC CO (MO)
Merged into G.L. Williams Co. 05/29/1987
Each share Common 25¢ par exchanged for $0.50 cash

REGAL ROCK INC (NV)
Reorganized as Regal Life Concepts, Inc. 12/18/2007
Each share Common $0.001 par exchanged for (5) shares Common $0.001 par
Regal Life Concepts, Inc. name changed to Regal Group Inc. 04/13/2010 which name changed to UHF Logistics Group, Inc. 01/06/2011

REGAL SHOE CO. (MA)
Merged into Brown Shoe Co., Inc. (Old) 00/00/1954
Each share Common $1 par exchanged for (0.125) share Common $15 par
Brown Shoe Co., Inc. (Old) name changed to Brown Group, Inc. 01/14/1972 which name changed to Brown Shoe Co., Inc. (New) 05/28/1999 which name changed to Caleres, Inc. 05/29/2015

REGALITO COPPER CORP (BC)
Merged into Pan Pacific Copper Co., Ltd. 5/15/2006
Each share Common no par exchanged for $6 cash

REGALSCH INC (NV)
Name changed to Golden Opportunity Resources, Inc. 06/01/2004
Golden Opportunity Resources, Inc. recapitalized as April Energy, Inc. 06/03/2005 which name changed to AE Holding I, Inc. 01/05/2011

REGALTECH INC (DE)
Name changed to Asante Networks, Inc. 10/17/2005

REGAN HLDG CORP (CA)
Merged into The Legacy Alliance, Inc. 06/30/2010
Each share Ser. A Common no par exchanged for $0.10 cash
Each share Ser. B Common no par exchanged for $0.10 cash
Note: Holders of (4,500) or more shares will receive (1) share Common $0.001 par for each (4,500) share block and $0.10 cash for each remaining share

REGAN INDUSTRIES, INC. (CA)
Charter revoked for failure to file reports and pay fees 5/2/66

REGATTA CAP PARTNERS INC (MD)
Charter forfeited for failure to file returns 10/03/2008

REGCOURT GOLD MINES LTD. (QC)
Recapitalized as Consolidated Regcourt Mines Ltd. on a (1) for (5) basis 3/5/56
Consolidated Regcourt Mines Ltd. acquired by Kelly Lake Nickel Mines Ltd. 12/9/68 which name changed to Albany Oil & Gas Ltd. (MAN) 3/22/71 which reincorporated in Alberta 11/10/80 which name changed to Albany Corp. 5/17/88 which merged with LifeSpace Environmental Walls Inc. 8/17/93 which merged into SMED International Inc. 7/1/96
(See SMED International Inc.)

REGEENA RES INC (BC)
Name changed to Ameridian Ventures Inc. 6/9/2000

REGEN BIOLOGICS INC (DE)
Each share old Common 1¢ par exchanged for (0.05) share new Common 1¢ par 12/01/2008
Plan of reorganization under Chapter 11 Federal Bankruptcy proceedings effective 11/01/2011
Stockholders' equity unlikely

REGEN THERAPEUTICS PLC (UNITED KINGDOM)
ADR agreement terminated 03/28/2011
No ADR's remain outstanding

REGENCY BANCORP (CA)
Merged into Zions Bancorporation 10/06/1999
Each share Common no par exchanged for (0.3669) share Common no par
Zions Bancorporation merged into Zions Bancorporation, N.A. (Salt Lake City, UT) 10/01/2018

REGENCY BANCSHARES INC (NC)
Common $1 par split (5) for (4) by issuance of (0.25) additional share 7/10/92
Merged into Southern National Corp. 1/31/94
Each share Common $1 par exchanged for (1.81197) shares Common $5 par
Southern National Corp. name changed to BB&T Corp. 5/19/97

REGENCY BANK (FRESNO, CA)
Under plan of reorganization each share Common no par automatically became (1) share Regency Bancorp Common no par 03/01/1995
Regency Bancorp merged into Zions Bancorporation 10/06/1999 which merged into Zions Bancorporation, N.A. (Salt Lake City, UT) 10/01/2018

REGENCY CRUISES INC (DE)
Merged into Rainbow Cruises Inc. 5/25/93
Each share Common $0.001 par exchanged for $1.95 cash

REGENCY CTRS CORP (FL)
7.25% Depository Preferred Ser. 4 reclassified as 7.25% Preferred Ser. 4 01/01/2008
7.45% Depository Preferred Ser. 3 reclassified as 7.45% Preferred Ser. 3 01/01/2008
7.25% Preferred Ser. 4 1¢ par called for redemption at $25 plus $0.45313 accrued dividends on 03/31/2012
7.45% Preferred Ser. 3 1¢ par called for redemption at $25 plus $0.46563 accrued dividends on 03/31/2012
6.7% Preferred Ser. 5 1¢ par called for redemption at $25 plus $0.34431 accrued dividends on 09/13/2012
6.625% Preferred Ser. 6 1¢ par called for redemption at $25 plus $0.211632 accrued dividends on 02/16/2017
6% Preferred Ser. 7 1¢ par called for redemption at $25 plus $0.22083 accrued dividends on 08/23/2017
(Additional Information in Active)

REGENCY DEV CORP (NV)
Charter revoked for failure to file reports and pay fees 01/01/1984

REGENCY ELECTRS INC (IN)
Common Capital Stock no par split (2) for (1) by issuance of (1) additional share 01/26/1972
Common Capital Stock no par split (2) for (1) by issuance of (1) additional share 05/30/1975
Common Capital Stock no par split (2) for (1) by issuance of (1) additional share 02/13/1981
Common Capital Stock no par split (2) for (1) by issuance of (1) additional share 12/22/1983
Name changed to RELM Communications, Inc. 10/24/1989
RELM Communications, Inc. acquired by Adage, Inc. (PA) 01/24/1992 which reincorporated in Nevada as RELM Wireless Corp. 01/30/1998 which name changed to BK Technologies, Inc. 06/05/2018

REGENCY ENERGY PARTNERS L P (DE)
Merged into Energy Transfer Partners, L.P. (Old) 04/30/2015
Each Common Unit exchanged for (0.4124) Common Unit
Energy Transfer Partners, L.P. (Old) merged into Energy Transfer Partners, L.P. (New) 05/01/2017 which merged into Energy Transfer L.P. 10/19/2018

REGENCY EQUITIES CORP (DE)
Merged into Regency Acquisition Corp. 7/19/2004
Each share Common 1¢ par exchanged for $0.017 cash
Each share Common 1¢ par received a litigation payment of approximately $0.02 cash 3/15/2006

REGENCY FD INC (NY)
Completely liquidated 01/12/1967
Each share Common 10¢ par exchanged for first and final distribution of $2.406 cash

REGENCY FINL GROUP INC (IA)
Merged out of existence 03/16/1987
Details not available

REGENCY FINL SHS INC (VA)
Merged into Mainstreet BankGroup Inc. 3/10/98
Each share Common $2.50 par exchanged for (0.474) share Common $5 par
MainStreet BankGroup Inc. name changed to MainStreet Financial Corp. 6/1/98 which merged into BB&T Corp. 3/8/99

REGENCY FOR MEN LTD (NY)
Charter cancelled and proclaimed dissolved for failure to pay taxes 06/24/1981

REGENCY GROUP LTD (NV)
Recapitalized as Energy River Corp. 6/10/2002
Each share Common $0.001 par exchanged for (0.025) share Common $0.001 par
Energy River Corp. recapitalized as Global Freight Integrators Inc. 3/24/2003

REGENCY GROUP LTD INC (NV)
Name changed to Regency Group Ltd. 6/20/2000
Regency Group Ltd. recapitalized as Energy River Corp. 6/10/2002 which recapitalized as Global Freight Integrators Inc. 3/24/2003

REGENCY HEALTH SVCS INC (DE)
Merged into Sun Healthcare Group, Inc. (Old) 10/08/1997
Each share Common 1¢ par exchanged for $22 cash

REGENCY INVS (MA)
Reorganized under the laws of Delaware as Regency Equities Corp. and Shares of Bene. Int. $1 par reclassified as Common $5 par 7/1/84
(See Regency Equities Corp.)

REGENCY LIFE INSURANCE CO. (IL)
Thru voluntary exchange offer 100% acquired by Regency National Ltd. as of 9/18/70

REGENCY LIFE INS CO (CA)
Merged into USLIFE Holding Corp. 10/15/68
Each share Common $12.50 par exchanged for (1.68) shares Common $2 par
USLIFE Holding Corp. name changed to USLIFE Corp. 5/22/70 which merged into American General Corp. 6/17/97 which merged into American International Group, Inc. 8/29/2001

REGENCY NATL LTD (IA)
Recapitalized as Regency Financial Group, Inc. 08/23/1978
Each (2.5) shares Class A Common $1 par exchanged for (1) share Common $2.50 par
Each (25) shares Class B Common 10¢ par exchanged for (1) share Common $2.50 par
(See Regency Financial Group, Inc.)

REGENCY OILS LTD (AB)
Struck off register for failure to file annual returns 04/30/1977

REGENCY RLTY CORP (FL)
Issue Information - 5,620,779 shares COM offered at $19.25 per share on 10/29/1993
Name changed to Regency Centers Corp. 02/12/2001

REGENCY RES INC (NV)
Common $0.001 par split (30) for (1) by issuance of (29) additional shares payable 12/12/2011 to holders of record 12/12/2011
Ex date - 12/13/2011
Name changed to Digital Development Group Corp. 05/02/2012
(See Digital Development Group Corp.)

REGENCY RES LTD (BC)
Recapitalized as Raypath Resources Ltd. (BC) 09/17/1985
Each share Common 1¢ par exchanged for (0.2) share Common no par
Raypath Resources Ltd. (BC) reincorporated in Alberta as Goldray Inc. 10/28/1999
(See Goldray Inc.)

REGENCY RES LTD (DE)
Name changed to Aquatech America, Inc. 01/22/1988
(See Aquatech America, Inc.)

REGENECA INC (NV)
SEC revoked common stock registration 11/26/2014

REGENERA LTD (AUSTRALIA)
Name changed to Advanced Ocular Systems Ltd. 01/18/2006
(See Advanced Ocular Systems Ltd.)

REGENERATION TECHNOLOGIES INC (DE)
Under plan of merger name changed to RTI Biologics, Inc. 02/27/2008
RTI Biologics, Inc. name changed to RTI Surgical, Inc. 07/18/2013

REGENESIS HLDG INC (FL)
Name changed to Fuelnation Inc. 10/19/2000
(See Fuelnation Inc.)

REGENEX INC (DE)
Each share old Common $0.001 par exchanged for (0.25) share new Common $0.001 par 02/12/1992
SEC revoked common stock registration 01/20/2012

REGENT AIR CORP (DE)
Charter cancelled and declared inoperative and void for non-payment of taxes 3/1/87

REGENT ASSISTED LIVING INC (OR)
Company terminated registration of securities 1/24/2003
No stockholders' equity

REGENT BANCORP INC (FL)
Merged into Stonegate Bank (Pompano Beach, FL) 09/16/2016
Each share Common 1¢ par exchanged for for (0.2893) share Common $5 par
Stonegate Bank (Pompano Beach, FL) merged into Home BancShares, Inc. 09/26/2017

REGENT BANCSHARES CORP (NJ)
Stock Dividend - In Common to holders of Common 10% 05/26/1992
10% Conv. Preferred Ser. A 10¢ par called for redemption at $10 on 11/19/1997
Conv. Preferred Ser. B 10¢ par called for redemption at $10 on 11/19/1997
Conv. Preferred Ser. C 10¢ par called for redemption at $10 on 11/19/1997
Conv. Preferred Ser. D 10¢ par called for redemption at $10 on 11/19/1997
Conv. Preferred Ser. E 10¢ par called for redemption at $10 on 11/19/1997
Merged into JeffBanks, Inc. 07/31/1998
Each share Common 10¢ par exchanged for (0.303) share Common $1 par
JeffBanks, Inc. merged into Hudson United Bancorp 11/30/1999 which merged into TD Banknorth Inc. 01/31/2006
(See TD Banknorth Inc.)

REGENT BK (DAVIE, FL)
Under plan of reorganization each share Common 1¢ par automatically

became (1) share Regent Bancorp, Inc. Common 1¢ par 07/01/2000
Regent Bancorp, Inc. merged into Stonegate Bank (Pompano Beach, FL) 09/16/2016 which merged into Home BancShares, Inc. 09/26/2017

REGENT COMMUNICATIONS INC (DE)
Each share Conv. Preferred Ser. C. 1¢ par exchanged for (1) share Common 1¢ par 01/31/2000
Plan of reorganization under Chapter 11 Federal Bankruptcy Code effective 04/27/2010
Each share Common 1¢ par exchanged for first and final distribution of $0.13 cash

REGENT CONS CORP (NV)
Charter revoked for failure to file reports and pay fees 03/05/1973

REGENT ENERGY CORP (NV)
SEC revoked common stock registration 05/18/2006
Stockholders' equity unlikely

REGENT ENTERPRISES INC (MN)
Statutorily dissolved 12/6/88

REGENT GROUP INC (DE)
Reorganized as Millennium Biotechnologies Group, Inc. 04/01/2002
Each (12) shares Common 6-2/3¢ par exchanged for (1) share Common $0.001 par
Millennium Biotechnologies Group, Inc. name changed to Inergetics, Inc. 05/06/2010

REGENT MINES LTD. (ON)
Charter revoked for failure to file reports and pay fees 7/17/61

REGENT MNG LTD (AUSTRALIA)
ADR agreement terminated 09/12/2003
No ADR holders' equity

REGENT PETE CORP (CO)
Each share Common $0.001 par exchanged for (0.1) share Common 1¢ par 3/1/88
Name changed to Regent Technologies, Inc. 3/31/95

REGENT REFNG CDA LTD (ON)
All Capital Stock no par acquired by Texaco Canada Ltd. for cash in 1965

REGENT URANIUM LITHIUM EXPLORATIONS LTD. (AB)
Struck off register for failure to file annual returns 12/15/66

REGENT VENTURE FD LTD (CANADA)
Name changed to Eaton Venture Fund Ltd. 07/04/1974
Eaton Venture Fund Ltd. name changed to Eaton/Bay Venture Fund Ltd. 04/12/1978
(See Eaton/Bay Venture Fund Ltd.)

REGIA RES LTD (CANADA)
Reincorporated 07/07/1995
Place of incorporation changed from (BC) to (Canada) 07/07/1995
Dissolved 06/10/2004
Details not available

REGINA INC (NJ)
Common $0.0001 par split (2) for (1) by issuance of (1) additional share 08/21/1987
Plan of reorganization under Chapter 11 Federal Bankruptcy proceedings confirmed 03/30/1990
No stockholders' equity

REGINA PRODUCTS CANADA LTD. (ON)
5% Preference $3 par called for redemption 02/15/1967
Public interest eliminated

REGINA RES INC (BC)
Recapitalized as Shanell International Energy Corp. 10/02/1984
Each share Common no par exchanged for (0.5) share Common no par
Shanell International Energy Corp. recapitalized as Pacific Insight Electronics Corp. 06/14/1989
(See Pacific Insight Electronics Corp.)

REGINA YELLOWKNIFE GOLD MINES, LTD. (ON)
Charter cancelled for failure to file reports and pay taxes in 1954

REGIONAL ACCEP CORP (NC)
Common no par split (3) for (2) by issuance of (0.5) additional share 7/10/95
Merged into Southern National Corp. 9/1/96
Each share Common no par exchanged for (0.3861) share Common no par
Southern National Corp. name changed to BB&T Corp. 5/19/97

REGIONAL AIR GROUP CORP (CO)
Recapitalized as Environmental Remediation Holding Corp. 9/2/96
Each (2,095) shares Common $0.0001 par exchanged for (1) share Common $0.0001 par
Environmental Remediation Holding Corp. name changed to ERHC Energy Inc. 2/15/2005

REGIONAL BANCORP INC (DE)
Name changed to Medford Savings Bank (New) (Medford, MA) 7/22/93
Medford Savings Bank (New) (Medford, MA) recapitalized as Medford Bancorp, Inc. 11/26/97
(See Medford Bancorp, Inc.)

REGIONAL BK HOLDRS TR (DE)
Trust terminated
Each Depositary Receipt received first and final distribution of $88.240601 cash payable 01/07/2013 to holders of record 12/20/2012

REGIONAL CABLESYSTEMS INC (CANADA)
Name changed to Persona Inc. 09/10/2001
(See Persona Inc.)

REGIONAL EQUITIES CORP (CO)
Each share old Common no par exchanged for (0.0001) share new Common no par 7/12/94
Name changed to Casinos International, Inc. 9/30/94
Casinos International, Inc. name changed to Classic Restaurants International, Inc. (CO) 9/29/95 which reincorporated in Georgia 4/10/98 which recapitalized as Creative Recycling Technologies Inc. 4/30/98 which name changed to Ingen Technologies, Inc. 11/1/2004

REGIONAL FDG CORP (DE)
Charter cancelled and declared inoperative and void for non-payment of taxes 3/1/86

REGIONAL FED BANCORP INC (IN)
Merged into Indiana United Bancorp 12/31/1991
Each share Common no par exchanged for (0.5) share Common no par and $16.50 cash
Indiana United Bancorp name changed to MainSource Financial Group, Inc. 05/01/2002 which merged into First Financial Bancorp 04/02/2018

REGIONAL RES LTD (BC)
Class A Common no par reclassified as Common no par 9/22/82
Merged into Imperial Metals Corp. (Old) 11/15/96
Each share Common no par exchanged for either (0.8) share Common no par or $1 cash
Note: Option to receive cash expired 1/15/97
Imperial Metals Corp. (Old) reorganized as Imperial Metals Corp. (New) 4/30/2002

REGIONS FINL CORP NEW (DE)
Each share 10% Mandatory Conv. Preferred Ser. B $1,000 par exchanged for (235.4298) shares Common 1¢ par 06/18/2010
(Additional Information in Active)

REGIONS FINL CORP OLD (DE)
Common $0.625 par split (2) for (1) by issuance of (1) additional share payable 06/13/1997 to holders of record 05/15/1997
Merged into Regions Financial Corp. (New) 07/01/2004
Each share Common $0.625 par exchanged for (1.2346) shares Common $0.625 par

REGIONS FING TR I (DE)
8% Trust Preferred Securities called for redemption at $25 plus $0.327774 accrued dividends on 02/26/2006

REGIONS FING TR III (DE)
8.875% Trust Preferred Securities called for redemption at $25 on 12/03/2012

REGIONS OIL & GAS INC (NV)
Recapitalized as American Green Group, Inc. 02/27/2008
Each share Common $0.001 par exchanged for (0.002) share Common $0.001 par
(See American Green Group, Inc.)

REGIS CORP OLD (MN)
Common 5¢ par split (2) for (1) by issuance of (1) additional share 6/21/84
Merged into Curtis Squire, Inc. 10/13/88
Each share Common 5¢ par exchanged for $17.70 cash

REGIS DEV CORP (BC)
Recapitalized as Manus Industries Inc. 01/10/1992
Each share Capital Stock no par exchanged for (0.22222222) share Common no par
Manus Industries Inc. recapitalized as Consolidated Manus Industries Inc. 11/10/1992 which recapitalized as Westmount Resources Ltd. (New) 02/08/1996 which recapitalized as Mt. Tom Minerals Corp. 05/20/1998 which name changed to Global Net Entertainment Corp. 10/14/1999 which recapitalized as Guildhall Minerals Ltd. 02/21/2006 which name changed to Edge Resources Inc. 07/28/2009
(See Edge Resources Inc.)

REGISTER COM INC (DE)
Merged into Vector Capital Corp. 11/03/2005
Each share Common $0.0001 par exchanged for $7.81 cash

REGISTERED AGENTS SOUTHN NEV INC (NV)
Name changed to Global Boulevard International, Inc. 3/25/99
Global Boulevard International, Inc. recapitalized as Project Group, Inc. 5/7/2003
(See Project Group, Inc.)

REGISTERED EXPRESS CORP (DE)
Common $0.001 par split (4) for (1) by issuance of (3) additional shares payable 04/19/2010 to holders of record 04/09/2010 Ex date - 04/20/2010
Name changed to Proactive Pet Products, Inc. 02/20/2015
Proactive Pet Products, Inc. recapitalized as GVCL Ventures, Inc. 11/02/2016 which recapitalized as Rain Forest International, Inc. 05/22/2018

REGISTRY INC (MA)
Name changed to Renaissance Worldwide, Inc. 01/07/1998
(See Renaissance Worldwide, Inc.)

REGISTRY MAGIC INC (FL)
Under plan of merger name changed to VoiceFlash Networks, Inc. 06/26/2001
(See VoiceFlash Networks, Inc.)

REGMA BIO TECHNOLOGIES LTD (NV)
Name changed to Phage Genomics, Inc. 11/26/2003
Phage Genomics, Inc. name changed to Searchlight Minerals Corp. 6/24/2005

REGO CO. (DE)
Name changed to Rego Group, Inc. 2/7/78
(See Rego Group, Inc.)

REGO FAST FOODS INC (NY)
Charter cancelled and proclaimed dissolved for failure to pay taxes 06/27/1979

REGO GROUP INC (DE)
Merged into Marmon Group, Inc. 07/01/1985
Each share $1 Conv. Preferred $1 par exchanged for $22 cash
Each share Common no par exchanged for $13 cash

REGO INDUSTRIES, INC. (DE)
Name changed to Viking Industries, Inc. 11/19/1965
Viking Industries, Inc. name changed to Vikoa, Inc. 05/11/1967 which name changed to Acton Corp. 08/13/1976 which name changed to Sunstates Corp. (New) 01/03/1994
(See Sunstates Corp. (New))

REGO INSULATED WIRE CORP. (DE)
Name changed to Rego Industries, Inc. 04/23/1962
Rego Industries, Inc. name changed to Viking Industries, Inc. 11/19/1965 which name changed to Vikoa, Inc. 05/11/1967 which name changed to Acton Corp. 08/13/1976 which name changed to Sunstates Corp. (New) 01/03/1994
(See Sunstates Corp. (New))

REGULUS RES INC (BC)
Recapitalized as High Resources Inc. 12/18/85
Each share Common no par exchanged for (4) shares Common no par
(See High Resources Inc.)

REGULUS RES INC OLD (AB)
Merged into Regulus Resources Inc. (New) 10/03/2014
Each share Common no par exchanged for (0.33333333) share Common no par
Note: Unexchanged certificates will be cancelled and become without value 10/03/2020

REGUS PLC (ENGLAND & WALES)
ADR agreement terminated 11/03/2003
Each Sponsored ADR for Ordinary exchanged for $6.27 cash
ADR agreement terminated 01/20/2017
Each ADR for Ordinary exchanged for $29.353498 cash

REHAB CORP (PA)
Merged into American Sterilizer Co. 11/30/1973
Each share Common 1¢ par exchanged for (0.84) share Common $0.83-1/3 par
(See American Sterilizer Co.)

REHAB HOSP SVCS CORP (PA)
Merged into National Medical Enterprises, Inc. 01/28/1985
Each share Common 1¢ par exchanged for (1) share Common 2¢ par

National Medical Enterprises, Inc. name changed to Tenet Healthcare Corp. 06/23/1995

REHABCARE GROUP INC (DE)
Name changed 07/11/1995
Name changed from Rehabcare Corp. to RehabCare Group, Inc. 07/11/1995
Common 1¢ par split (3) for (2) by issuance of (0.5) additional share payable 10/01/1997 to holders of record 09/12/1997
Common 1¢ par split (2) for (1) by issuance of (1) additional share payable 06/19/2000 to holders of record 05/31/2000
Merged into Kindred Healthcare, Inc. 06/01/2011
Each share Common 1¢ par exchanged for (0.471) share Common 25¢ par and $26 cash
(See Kindred Healthcare, Inc.)

REHABCLINICS INC (DE)
Merged into NovaCare, Inc. 02/04/1994
Each share Common 1¢ par exchanged for (1.6) shares Common 1¢ par
NovaCare, Inc. name changed to NAHC, Inc. 03/28/2000 which merged into J.L. Halsey Corp. 06/18/2002 which name changed to Lyris, Inc. 11/15/2007
(See Lyris, Inc.)

REHABILICARE INC (MN)
Name changed to Compex Technologies, Inc. 12/16/2002
Compex Technologies, Inc. merged into Encore Medical Corp. 2/24/2006
(See Encore Medical Corp.)

REHABILITY CORP (TN)
Merged into Living Centers of America Inc. 6/30/95
Each share Common 1¢ par exchanged for $11.50 cash

REHABNET INC (CO)
Recapitalized as Forestry International, Inc. 12/31/1992
Each share Common 1¢ par exchanged for (0.1) share Common $0.001 par
Forestry International, Inc. name changed to Infynia.com Corp. 11/06/2000
(See Infynia.com Corp.)

REHEIS CO., INC. (NY)
Liquidation completed
Each share Class A $1 par exchanged for initial distribution of (0.3) share Armour & Co. (DE) Common $5 par 08/12/1963
Each share Class A $1 par received second and final distribution of (0.03361) share Armour & Co. (DE) Common $5 par 12/16/1963
Armour & Co. (DE) merged into Greyhound Corp. (DE) 12/28/1970 which reorganized in Arizona 10/04/1982 which name changed to Greyhound Dial Corp. 05/08/1990 which name changed to Dial Corp. (AZ) 05/14/1991 which reincorporated in Delaware 03/18/1992 which name changed to Viad Corp. 08/15/1996

REHER SIMMONS RESEARCH, INC. (CT)
Merged into Powr-Pak Industries, Inc. 10/05/1963
Each share Common exchanged for (1) share Common 10¢ par
Powr-Pak Industries, Inc. name changed to National Home Products, Inc. 11/09/1965 which name changed to Damson Oil Corp. 02/04/1969
(See Damson Oil Corp.)

REI AGRO LTD (INDIA)
144A GDR's for Ordinary split (6) for (5) by issuance of (0.2) additional GDR payable 11/28/2008 to holders of record 09/29/2008
Reg. S GDR's for Ordinary split (6) for (5) by issuance of (0.2) additional GDR payable 11/28/2008 to holders of record 09/29/2008
GDR basis changed from (1:2) to (1:1) 11/28/2008
Reg. S GDR's for Ordinary split (10) for (1) by issuance of (9) additional GDR's payable 02/19/2009 to holders of record 02/12/2009
GDR agreement terminated 04/27/2015
Each 144A GDR for Ordinary exchanged for $0.04741 cash
Each Reg. S GDR for Ordinary exchanged for $0.04741 cash

REI LIQUIDATING CORP. (NY)
Liquidation completed
Each share Common 25¢ par exchanged for initial distribution of $10.65 cash 6/18/80
Each share Common 25¢ par received second distribution of $2 cash 6/10/81
Each share Common 25¢ par received third distribution of $1 cash 5/24/82
Each share Common 25¢ par received fourth distribution of $1.70 cash 11/1/82
Each share Common 25¢ par received fifth and final distribution of $0.61 cash 8/15/84

REI TR I (DE)
7.20% Trust Originated Preferred Securities Ser. C called for redemption at $25 on 12/24/2004

REIBANC USA INC (FL)
Common $0.001 par split (2) for (1) by issuance of (1) additional share payable 3/26/2003 to holders of record 3/24/2003 Ex date - 3/27/2003
Common $0.001 par split (2) for (1) by issuance of (1) additional share payable 6/21/2005 to holders of record 6/10/2005 Ex date - 6/22/2005
Name changed to Flair Petroleum Corp. 6/30/2006

REICH & TANG L P (DE)
Name changed to New England Investment Companies, L.P. 9/15/93
New England Investment Companies, L.P. name changed to NVEST, L.P. 3/30/98
(See NVEST, L.P.)

REICHHOLD CHEMS INC (DE)
Common $1 par split (2) for (1) by issuance of (1) additional share 4/16/59
Merged into Dainippon Ink & Chemicals, Inc. 9/29/87
Each share Common $1 par exchanged for $60 cash

REICHHOLD CHEMS LTD (ENGLAND)
Stock Dividend - 12-1/2% 03/29/1960
ADR agreement terminated 01/24/1969
Each ADR for Ordinary Reg. 5s par exchanged for $4.38 cash

REICHHOLD CHEMS LTD (ON)
Name changed 7/27/73
Common $2 par changed to no par and (2) additional shares issued 12/27/68
Name changed from Reichhold Chemicals (Canada) Ltd. to Reichhold Chemicals Ltd. 7/27/73
Common no par split (3) for (1) by issuance of (2) additional shares 8/26/77
Name changed to Reichhold Ltd.-Reichhold Ltee. 11/11/77
(See Reichhold Ltd.)

REICHHOLD LTD (ON)
7-1/4% Conv. Preference Ser. A $10 par reclassified as 7-1/4% Conv. 1st Preference Ser. A $10 par 12/22/1980
Merged into Reichhold Chemicals, Inc. 04/30/1985
Each share Common no par exchanged for $15 cash
7-1/4% Conv. 1st Preference Ser. A $10 par called for redemption 01/01/1986
10-1/2% 1st Preference Ser. B $10 par called for redemption 01/01/1986
Public interest eliminated

REID (ROSE MARIE) (CA)
Out of business 8/31/65
No stockholders' equity

REID AIRCRAFT CO. LTD.
Merged into Curtiss-Reid Aircraft Co. Ltd. in 1928
Details not available

REID ASHMAN INC (CA)
Name changed to Solitec Inc. (CA) 4/21/87
Solitec Inc. (CA) reorganized in (NV) as Turn Technology, Inc. 2/14/94
(See Turn Technology Inc.)

REID BROS LTD (CA)
Adjudicated bankrupt 04/24/1967
Stockholders' equity unlikely

REID CASHON LAND & CATTLE CO.
Sold at foreclosure 00/00/1933
Stockholders' equity unlikely

REID DOMINION PACKAGING LTD (ON)
6-1/4% Preference Ser. A $50 par called for redemption 8/15/84

REID DON PRODTNS INC (DE)
Name changed to United Petroleum Corp. Common 10¢ par changed to $0.001 and (5) additional shares issued 06/18/1982
(See United Petroleum Corp.)

REID ICE CREAM CO.
Merged into Borden Co. 00/00/1927
Details not available

REID LABORATORIES INC. (GA)
Merged into Reid-Provident Laboratories Inc. 6/18/64
Each share Common $1 par exchanged for (1.25) shares Common $1 par
Reid-Provident Laboratories Inc. name changed to Reid-Rowell, Inc. 12/4/85
(See Reid-Rowell, Inc.)

REID LITHOGRAPHING LTD (ON)
Acquired by Moore Ltd. 8/1/73
Each share Common no par exchanged for $19.50 cash
Name changed to Reid Dominion Packaging Ltd. 11/7/75
(See Reid Dominion Packaging Ltd.)

REID PROVIDENT LABS INC (GA)
Stock Dividend - 10% 04/09/1974
Name changed to Reid-Rowell, Inc. 12/04/1985
(See Reid-Rowell, Inc.)

REID ROWELL INC (GA)
Merged into Solvay & Cie, S.A. 05/01/1986
Each share Common $1 par exchanged for $10.875 cash

REIGATE RES CDA LTD (AB)
Each share 12% Retractable Sr. Preferred Ser. A no par exchanged for (50) shares Class A Common no par 6/30/86
Struck off register and declared dissolved for failure to file returns 11/27/89

REIGATE RES INC (AB)
Merged into Reigate Resources (Canada) Ltd. 1/31/83
Each share Common no par exchanged for (1) share Class A Stock no par
(See Reigate Resources (Canada) Ltd.)

REII INC (DE)
Name changed to B&D Food Corp. 07/08/2005
B&D Food Corp. recapitalized as Latteno Food Corp. 10/19/2009

REILAND & BREE, INC. (IL)
Voluntarily dissolved 6/30/66
Details not available

REILLY (BRENDAN) ASSOCIATES, INC. (NY)
Adjudicated bankrupt 10/13/64

REILLY-WOLFF ASSOCIATES, INC. (NY)
Name changed to Reilly (Brendan) Associates, Inc. 8/7/61 which was adjudicated bankrupt 10/13/64

REIMER RES LTD (BC)
Name changed 03/31/1993
Name changed from Reimer Overhead Doors Ltd. to Reimer Resources Ltd. 03/31/1993
Merged into Kensington Resources Ltd. 11/03/1993
Each share Common no par exchanged for (0.5) share Common no par
Kensington Resources Ltd. merged into Shore Gold Inc. 10/28/2005 which name changed to Star Diamond Corp. 02/12/2018

REINELL INDS INC (WA)
Common no par split (2) for (1) by issuance of (1) additional share 05/12/1972
Adjudicated bankrupt 05/01/1979
Stockholders' equity unlikely

REINER PHARMACISTS INC. (NY)
Proclaimed dissolved 12/15/34

REINFORCED PLASTICS CORP. (DE)
Dissolved 5/15/59

REINHARDT BREWERY CO. LTD.
Liquidated in 1940

REINHOLD INDS INC (DE)
Stock Dividends - 10% payable 7/28/2000 to holders of record 7/11/2000; 10% payable 7/31/2001 to holders of record 7/13/2001 Ex date - 7/11/2001; 10% payable 6/21/2002 to holders of record 5/31/2002 Ex date - 5/29/2002; 10% payable 5/30/2003 to holders of record 5/16/2003 Ex date - 5/14/2003
Acquired by Jordan Co., L.P. 1/10/2007
Each share Class A Common 1¢ par exchanged for $12.50 cash

REINK CORP (DE)
Common $0.001 par split (3) for (2) by issuance of (0.5) additional share payable 09/28/2000 to holders of record 09/28/2000
Recapitalized as Adsero Corp. 03/22/2003
Each share Common $0.001 par exchanged for (0.05) share Common $0.001 par
Adsero Corp. name changed to Quantum Telecom Inc. 05/27/2008

REINSURANCE CORP. OF NEW YORK (NY)
Acquired by Piedmont Management Co. Inc. 7/11/68
Each share Capital Stock $2 par exchanged for (0.4) share $1 Conv. Preferred Ser. A $1 par and (1) share Common $1 par
Piedmont Management Co. Inc. merged into Chartwell RE Corp. 12/13/95 which merged into Trenwick Group Inc. 10/27/99 which merged into Trenwick Group Ltd. 9/27/2000
(See Trenwick Group Ltd.)

REINSURANCE GROUP AMER INC. (MO)
Issue Information - 4,300,000 shares COM NON VTG offered at $47 per share on 06/05/1998

Non-Vtg. Common 1¢ par split (3) for (2) by issuance of (0.5) additional share payable 02/26/1999 to holders of record 02/05/1999 Ex date - 03/01/1999
Non-Vtg. Common 1¢ par reclassified as (0.97) share Common 1¢ par 09/14/1999
Each Preferred Income Equity Redeemable Security separated into (1) share RGA Capital Trust I Preferred Security and (1) Reinsurance Group of America, Inc. Common Stock Purchase Warrant expiring 12/15/2050 on 02/16/2011
(See RGA Capital Trust I)
(Additional Information in Active)

REINSURANCE INVESTMENT CORP. (DE)
Name changed to RIC Group, Inc. 04/19/1963
RIC Group, Inc. name changed to RIC International Industries, Inc. 08/13/1969
(See RIC International Industries, Inc.)

REINSURANCE LIFE CO. OF AMERICA
Acquired by Security Life Insurance Co. of America (VA) 00/00/1930
Details not available

REINSURANCE TECHNOLOGIES LTD (DE)
SEC revoked common stock registration 05/28/2014

REIS INC (MD)
Acquired by Moody's Corp. 10/15/2018
Each share Common 2¢ par exchanged for $23 cash

REIS ROBERT & CO (NY)
Each share 7% 1st Preferred $100 par exchanged for (6) shares $1.25 Prior Preference $10 par and (10) shares Common $1 par 00/00/1947
Each share $7 2nd Preference no par exchanged for (13.1/3) shares 2nd Preference $1 par and (11) shares Common $1 par 00/00/1947
Each share Common no par exchanged for (1) share Common $1 par 00/00/1947
Common $1 par changed to 5¢ par 04/11/1974
Adjudicated bankrupt 10/15/1980
Stockholders' equity unlikely

REISS SS CO (DE)
Merged into American Steamship Co. 6/27/69
Each share Capital Stock no par exchanged for $128.26 principal amount of American Steamship Co. secured notes, (1) share Bethlehem Steel Corp. Common $8 par and $37.83 cash
(See Bethlehem Steel Corp.)

REISTERSTOWN FED SVGS & LN ASSN (MD)
Common $1 par split (3) for (2) by issuance of (0.5) additional share 9/30/88
Stock Dividends - 10% 9/30/87; 10% 3/31/88
Acquired by a group of investors 1/3/90
Each share Common $1 par exchanged for $21.75 cash
Each share Common $1 par received an additional payment of $2.045 cash 2/28/90

REIT AMER INC (MA)
Merged into Unicorp American Corp. (New) 12/13/1984
Each share Common $1 par exchanged for (3) shares Conv. Preferred Ser. B 1¢ par and $0.50 cash
(See Unicorp American Corp. (New))

REIT AMERICAS INC (MD)
Charter forfeited 10/03/2008

REIT INCOME FD INC (CT)
Reincorporated 3/6/74
State of incorporation changed from (DE) to (CT) 3/6/74
Name changed to RET Income Fund, Inc. (MA) 6/16/75
RET Income Fund, Inc. (MA) merged into Cyprus Corp. 12/29/80 which name changed to Astrotech International Corp. (Old) 4/6/84 which recapitalized as Astrotech International Corp. (New) 8/19/88 which merged into Iteq Inc. 10/28/97
(See Iteq Inc.)

REITER (VICTOR) CORP. (FL)
Voluntarily dissolved 7/28/82
Details not available

REITER-FOSTER OIL CORP. (DE)
Merged into Baruch-Foster Corp. 01/11/1960
Each share Common 50¢ par exchanged for (0.2) share Common 50¢ par
(See Baruch-Foster Corp.)

REK-O-KUT CO., INC. (NY)
Name changed to Koss Electronics, Inc. and Common 25¢ par changed to 1¢ par 1/3/66
Koss Electronics, Inc. reincorporated under the laws of Delaware as Koss Corp. 10/12/71

RELATIONAL TECHNOLOGY INC (DE)
Name changed to Ingres Corp. 11/06/1989
(See Ingres Corp.)

RELATIONSERVE MEDIA INC (DE)
Reincorporated 08/29/2005
State of incorporation changed from (NV) to (DE) 08/29/2005
Name changed to SendTec, Inc. 07/26/2006

RELAY CAP CORP (NV)
Charter revoked for failure to file reports and pay fees 05/30/2008

RELAY CREEK RES LTD (BC)
Name changed to AABBAX International Financial Corp. 10/20/1987
(See AABBAX International Financial Corp.)

RELAY MINES LTD (NV)
Name changed to XLR Medical Corp. 9/15/2004
Each share Common $0.00001 par exchanged for (1) share Common $0.00001 par

RELAY MOTORS CORP.
Sold to Westinghouse Electric & Manufacturing Co. 00/00/1938
Details not available

RELBARG LIQUIDATING CO. (OH)
Liquidated in 1953

RELEASE YOUR LEASE INC (NV)
Name changed to Dussault Apparel, Inc. 06/12/2007
Dussault Apparel, Inc. recapitalized as Prospect Ventures, Inc. 03/21/2014

RELEVANT LINKS INC (CO)
Name changed to Direct Response Financial Services, Inc. 06/13/2002
Direct Response Financial Services, Inc. recapitalized as Sleeping with the Enemy Inc. 08/17/2007 which name changed to Healthy Coffee International, Inc. 12/13/2007

RELIABLE (THE)
Name changed to Innes Shoe Co. 00/00/1950
(See Innes Shoe Co.)

RELIABLE ENERGY LTD (AB)
Merged into Crescent Point Energy Corp. 05/01/2012
Each share Common no par exchanged for (0.00794) share Common no par
Note: Unexchanged certificates were cancelled and became without value 05/01/2015

RELIABLE FINL CORP (DE)
Merged into First Commonwealth Financial Corp. 9/29/94
Each share Common 1¢ par exchanged for (1.6) shares Common $1 par

RELIABLE INDS INC (DE)
Charter cancelled and declared inoperative and void for non-payment of taxes 3/1/87

RELIABLE INSURANCE CO. (OH)
Assets acquired by American Heritage Life Insurance Co. on a (0.15) for (1) basis 11/5/59
American Heritage Life Insurance Co. reorganized as American Heritage Life Investment Corp. 12/31/68 which merged into Allstate Corp. 10/31/99

RELIABLE INVS CORP (NV)
Common $1 par split (5) for (4) by issuance of (0.25) additional share 8/8/75
Common $1 par split (3) for (2) by issuance of (0.5) additional share 1/25/79
Common $1 par changed to 25¢ par 6/21/79
Reorganized under Chapter 11 Bankruptcy Code 12/23/85
Each share $1.875 Conv. Preferred Ser. A $1 par exchanged for (1) share 10% Non-Cum. Conv. Non-Vtg. Preferred $1 par
Note: Unexchanged shares became valueless 7/22/90
Stock Dividend - 10% 6/28/74
Name changed to North American Group, Ltd. 5/15/86
(See North American Group, Ltd.)

RELIABLE LIFE & CASUALTY CO. (WI)
Common $3.50 par changed to $4.50 par 09/00/1967
Common $4.50 par changed to $2.25 par and (1) additional share issued 06/00/1968
96.4% held by Reliable Investors Corp. as of 12/31/1980
Public interest eliminated

RELIABLE LIFE INS CO (MO)
Common $10 par changed to $5 par and (1) additional share issued 02/01/1966
Common $5 par changed to $2 par and (1.5) additional shares issued 12/01/1972
Common $2 par reclassified as Class A Common $1 par 06/19/1986
Each share Class A Common $1 par received distribution of (10) shares Conv. Class B Common $1 par 07/01/1986
Each share Class B Common $1 par exchanged for (0.1) share Class A Common $1 par 11/04/1997
Merged into Unitrin, Inc. 05/29/1998
Each share Class A Common $1 par exchanged for (2.235) shares Common 10¢ par
Unitrin, Inc. name changed to Kemper Corp. (New) 08/25/2011

RELIABLE PWR SYS INC (CO)
SEC revoked common stock registration 11/13/2009
Stockholders' equity unlikely

RELIABLE STORES CORP (MD)
Common no par changed to $10 par and (1) additional share issued 09/14/1955
Common $10 par changed to $5 par and (1) additional share issued 06/25/1965
Common $5 par changed to $2.50 par and (1) additional share issued 02/28/1969
Name changed to RES Investment Corp. 02/02/1978
RES Investment Corp. merged into
Price (T. Rowe) Tax-Free Funds 09/22/1986

RELIABLE TRAVEL INTL INC (DE)
Name changed to Reliable Industries, Inc. 5/3/83
(See Reliable Industries, Inc.)

RELIANCE ACCEP GROUP INC (DE)
Plan of reorganization under Chapter 11 Federal Bankruptcy proceedings effective 07/31/1998
No stockholders' equity

RELIANCE BANCORP INC (DE)
Merged into North Fork Bancorporation, Inc. 2/18/2000
Each share Common 1¢ par exchanged for (2) shares Common $0.001 par
North Fork Bancorporation, Inc. merged into Capital One Financial Corp. 12/1/2006

RELIANCE BANCSHARES INC (WI)
Merged into St. Francis Capital Corp. 01/22/1999
Each share Common $1 par exchanged for (0.25) share Common 1¢ par
St. Francis Capital Corp. merged into MAF Bancorp, Inc. 12/01/2003 which merged into National City Corp. 09/01/2007 which was acquired by PNC Financial Services Group, Inc. 12/31/2008

RELIANCE BK (WHITE PLAINS, NY)
Bank failed 03/20/2004
Stockholders' equity unlikely

RELIANCE CASUALTY INSURANCE CO.
Acquired by Equitable Casualty & Surety Co. in 1929
Details not available

RELIANCE ELEC & ENGR CO (OH)
Each share Common no par exchanged for (10) shares Common $5 par in 1936
Common $5 par split (3) for (2) by issuance of (0.5) additional share 1/31/57
Common $5 par split (3) for (2) by issuance of (0.5) additional share 12/29/64
Common $5 par split (3) for (2) by issuance of (0.5) additional share 5/17/66
Stock Dividend - 100% 1/26/51
Reincorporated under the laws of Delaware as Reliance Electric Co. 2/28/69
(See Reliance Electric Co.)

RELIANCE ELEC CO NEW (DE)
$1.40 Jr. Preferred 10¢ par called for redemption 6/30/92
$1.50 Jr. Exchangeable Preferred 10¢ par called for redemption 11/28/92
Merged into ROK Acquisition Corp. 1/27/95
Each share Class A 1¢ par exchanged for $31 cash

RELIANCE ELEC CO OLD (DE)
Common $5 par changed to $2.50 par and (1) additional share issued 11/14/1969
$1.60 Conv. Preferred Ser. B no par called for redemption 03/30/1978
Merged into Exxon Corp. 12/27/1979
Each share $3 Conv. Preferred Ser. A no par exchanged for $201.97 cash
Each share Common $2.50 par exchanged for $72 cash

RELIANCE ENERGY INC (AB)
Issue Information - 3,000,000 shares COM offered at $0.10 per share on 03/17/1997
Recapitalized as Norex Exploration Services Inc. 01/21/2002
Each share Common no par exchanged for (0.1) share Common no par
Norex Exploration Services Inc. recapitalized as Tesla Exploration Ltd. 04/22/2010

RELIANCE ENERGY LTD (INDIA)
Name changed to Reliance Infrastructure Ltd. 05/12/2008

RELIANCE ENTERPRISES INC (UT)
Reorganized as Capitol Television Network Inc. 07/21/1988
Each share Common $0.0005 par exchanged for (0.2) share Common no par, (1) Common Stock Purchase Class A Warrant expiring 07/26/1990 and (1) Common Stock Purchase Class B Warrant expiring 07/26/1991
Capitol Television Network Inc. name changed to Royal Casino Group Inc. 04/19/1994 which name changed to E-Commerce West Corp. 07/31/1998 which recapitalized as Interactive Broadcasting Network Group Inc. 01/28/2002 which name changed to Baymark Technologies Inc. 08/30/2002 which name changed to Implantable Vision, Inc. 01/03/2006 which name changed to Arcland Energy Corp. 08/25/2008
(See Arcland Energy Corp.)

RELIANCE FINL GROUP INC (DE)
Name changed to Reliance Group Holdings, Inc. 3/25/82
(See Reliance Group Holdings, Inc.)

RELIANCE FINL INC (MO)
Merged into Allegiant Bancorp, Inc. 8/29/97
Each share Common 10¢ par exchanged for (1.407) shares Common 1¢ par
Allegiant Bancorp, Inc. merged into National City Corp. 4/9/2004

RELIANCE GROUP HLDGS INC (DE)
$3.12 Preferred Ser. C $1 par called for redemption 12/02/1986
$15 Preferred Ser. A $1 par called for redemption 12/16/1986
Plan of reorganization under Chapter 11 Federal Bankruptcy proceedings effective 12/01/2005
No stockholders' equity

RELIANCE GROUP INC (DE)
$2.20 Conv. Preferred Ser. B $1 par called for redemption 10/28/1981
Merged into Reliance Financial Group, Inc. 01/08/1982
Each share $2.60 Preferred Ser. C $1 par exchanged for $26 principal amount of 14% 15-yr. Debentures due 12/01/1996
Each share Common 25¢ par exchanged for $85 principal amount 17% (18% for the first year) 15-yr. Sr. Debentures due 12/15/1996 and $20 cash

RELIANCE INDS LTD II (INDIA)
GDR agreement terminated 03/21/2003
Each Reg. S GDR for exchanged for Ordinary exchanged for (15) Reg. S GDR's for Ordinary
Note: Unexchanged GDR's will be sold and proceeds held for claim after 09/21/2003

RELIANCE INSURANCE CO. OF PHILADELPHIA
Merged into Fire Association of Philadelphia on a (0.486) for (1) basis in 1950
Fire Association of Philadelphia name changed to Reliance Insurance Co. 1/1/58
(See Reliance Insurance Co.)

RELIANCE INS CO (PA)
Capital Stock $10 par changed to $5 par and (1) additional share issued 5/3/63
Capital Stock $5 par reclassified as Common $5 par 8/21/63
Common $5 par changed to $1 par and (4) additional shares issued 9/1/76
Merged into Reliance Financial Services Corp. 3/19/81
Each share Common $1 par exchanged for $20 cash
$2.68 Preferred Ser. A $1 par called for redemption 5/1/95
Public interest eliminated

RELIANCE INTERNATIONAL CORP.
Merged into Equity Corp. (New) 00/00/1935
Details not available

RELIANCE LIFE & ACC INS CO AMER (TX)
Placed in receivership 7/1/69
Opinion of attorney for receiver is that all stock is worthless

RELIANCE LIFE INSURANCE CO. (PA)
Acquired by Lincoln National Life Insurance Co. for cash in 1951

RELIANCE LIFE INSURANCE CO. OF GEORGIA (GA)
Merged into Kennesaw Life & Accident Insurance Co. 09/10/1959
Each share Common $1 par exchanged for (0.8) share Common $1 par
Kennesaw Life & Accident Insurance Co. merged into Lykes-Youngstown Financial Corp. 11/14/1969 which name changed to LifeSurance Corp. 05/10/1971 which merged into Regan Holding Corp. 10/31/1991
(See Regan Holding Corp.)

RELIANCE LIFE INSURANCE CO. OF ILLINOIS (IL)
Acquired by USLIFE Holding Corp. 11/14/68
Each share Common $1 par exchanged for (0.185185) share Common $2 par
USLIFE Holding Corp. name changed to USLIFE Corp. 5/22/70 which merged into American General Corp. 6/17/97 which merged into American International Group, Inc. 8/29/2001

RELIANCE LODGING, INC. (CO)
Charter dissolved 06/01/1998

RELIANCE MANAGEMENT CORP. (MD)
Merged into American General Corp. on a (0.25) for (1) basis 11/23/35
American General Corp. merged into Equity Corp. 10/17/50 which name changed to Wheelabrator-Frye Inc. 11/4/71 which merged into Signal Companies, Inc. 2/1/83 which merged into Allied-Signal Inc. 9/19/85 which name changed to AlliedSignal Inc. 4/26/93 which name changed to Honeywell International Inc. 12/1/99

RELIANCE MANUFACTURING CO. (IL)
Each share Common $10 par exchanged for (2) shares Common $5 par in 1948
3-1/2% Preferred $100 par called for redemption 12/31/64
Liquidation completed
Each share Common $5 par stamped to indicate initial distribution of (0.8) share Pioneer Aerodynamics Systems, Inc. Common 10¢ par and (1.05) shares Puritan Fashions Corp. Common $1 par 7/7/65
Each share Stamped Common $5 par received second and final distribution of $5 principal amount of Puritan Fashions Corp. 6% Conv. Debentures due 12/31/79 and (0.5) share Technical Tape, Inc. Common $1 par 10/27/65
Certificates were not retired and are now without value
(See each company's listing)

RELIANCE MANUFACTURING CO. (OH)
Acquired by Eaton Axle & Spring Co. 00/00/1931
Details not available

RELIANCE MINERALS CO. (NV)
Charter revoked for failure to pay franchise fees 3/5/62

RELIANCE NAT RES LTD (INDIA)
Merged into Reliance Power Ltd. 11/09/2010
Each Sponsored 144A GDR for Ordinary exchanged for $1.257 cash
Each Sponsored Reg. S GDR for Ordinary exchanged for $1.257 cash

RELIANCE NATIONAL INVESTORS CORP. (UT)
Name changed to Great West Corp. 06/18/1964
(See Great West Corp.)

RELIANCE NATIONAL LIFE INSURANCE CO. (UT)
Class A, AA & B Common $10 par changed to $12 par 00/00/1960
Each share Class A, AA & B Common $12 par exchanged for (12) shares of Class A, AA or B Common $1 par respectively 08/06/1962
Stock Dividends - Class A Common: (12/00/1963) for (1) 12/10/1962; 10% 06/24/1964
Class AA Common: (12/00/1963) for (1) 12/10/1962; 10% in Class B Common 06/24/1964
Class B Common: (12/00/1963) for (1) 12/10/1962; 10% 06/24/2+64
Merged into National Western Life Insurance Co. (CO) 09/28/1965
Each share Class A, AA or B Common $1 par exchanged for (0.6329113) share Class A Common $1 par
National Western Life Insurance Co. (CO) reincorporated in Delaware as National Western Life Group, Inc. 10/02/2015

RELIANCE OIL & GAS CO (SD)
Charter expired by time limitation 4/10/22

RELIANCE OIL & GAS CORP. (IL)
Proclaimed dissolved for failure to file reports and pay taxes 12/1/83

RELIANCE PET PRODS CORP (NY)
Merged into ILR Properties, Inc. 08/16/1977
Each share Common 10¢ par exchanged for $4 cash

RELIANCE PETE LTD (INDIA)
Merged into Reliance Industries Ltd. II 11/29/2002
Each 144A GDR for Ordinary exchanged for (0.09090909) Reg. S GDR for Ordinary
(See Reliance Industries Ltd. II)

RELIANCE PETROLEUM CORP. (NV)
Name changed to Executive Sportsman's Club, Ltd. 12/22/71
Executive Sportsman's Club, Ltd. name changed to Executive E.M.I. Corp. 3/10/75 which name changed to Nevada Silver Refinery 8/9/77
(See Nevada Silver Refinery)

RELIANCE PETROLEUM LTD. (ON)
Acquired by Supertest Petroleum Corp. Ltd. 00/00/1959
Details not available

RELIANCE PORTS & TERMS LTD (INDIA)
GDR agreement terminated 03/12/2009
No GDR's remain outstanding

RELIANCE RES INC (CO)
Each share old Common 1¢ par exchanged for (32) shares new Common 1¢ par 06/24/1999
Name changed to SUMmedia.com, Inc. 08/20/1999
(See SUMmedia.com, Inc.)

RELIANCE RES LTD (BC)
Recapitalized as Resource Capital Gold Corp. 02/29/2016
Each share Common no par exchanged for (0.2) share Common no par

RELIANCE SVCS GROUP LTD (AB)
Merged into Integrated Production Services Ltd. 03/31/2000
Each share Common no par exchanged for (0.4282325) share Common no par
(See Integrated Production Services Ltd.)

RELIANCE STD LIFE INS CO (IL)
Acquired by Dresser Standard, Inc. 12/29/1981
Each share Common $1 par exchanged for $78.709170 cash

RELIANCE STEEL CORP.
Merged into Detroit Steel Corp. 00/00/1944
Each share Common exchanged for (0.85) share Common $2 par and $3.33333333 principal amount of 6% S.F. Debentures due 00/00/1964
Detroit Steel Corp. name changed to Cliffs-St. Clair Corp. 11/16/1970 which liquidated for Cleveland-Cliffs Iron Co. 03/15/1972 which reorganized as Cleveland-Cliffs Inc. (Old) 07/01/1985 which name changed to Cliffs Natural Resources Inc. 10/15/2008 which name changed to Cleveland-Cliffs Inc. (New) 08/25/2017

RELIANCE STL & ALUM CO (CA)
Common no par split (3) for (2) by issuance of (0.5) additional share payable 06/27/1997 to holders of record 06/06/1997 Ex date - 06/30/1997
Common no par split (3) for (2) by issuance of (0.5) additional share payable 09/24/1999 to holders of record 09/02/1999 Ex date - 09/27/1999
Common no par split (2) for (1) by issuance of (1) additional share payable 07/19/2006 to holders of record 07/05/2006 Ex date - 07/20/2006
Reincorporated under the laws of Delaware and Common no par changed to $0.001 par 06/01/2015

RELIANCE UNVL INC (KY)
Common $2.50 par changed to $1.25 par and (1) additional share issued 09/10/1971
Stock Dividends - 100% 02/19/1965
Merged into Tyler Corp. (Old) 07/10/1981
Each share Common $1.25 par exchanged for $37 cash

RELIANCE URANIUM CORP. (NV)
Each share old Common 20¢ par exchanged for (0.05) share new Common 20¢ par 7/26/71
Name changed to Reliance Petroleum Corp. 8/6/71
Reliance Petroleum Corp. name changed to Executive Sportsman's Club, Ltd. 12/22/71 which name changed to Executive E.M.I. Corp. 3/10/75 which name changed to Nevada Silver Refinery 8/9/77
(See Nevada Silver Refinery)

RELIANCE UTILS & PWR LTD (INDIA)
GDR agreement terminated 03/12/2009
No GDR's remain outstanding

RELIANCE VARNISH CO. (KY)
Name changed to Reliance Universal Inc. 10/28/63
(See Reliance Universal Inc.)

RELIANT BK (BRENTWOOD, TN)
Merged into Commerce Union Bancshares, Inc. 04/01/2015
Each share Class A Common $1 par exchanged for (1.0213) shares Common $1 par
Each share Common $1 par exchanged for (1.0213) shares Common $1 par
Commerce Union Bancshares, Inc. name changed to Reliant Bancorp, Inc. 01/02/2018

RELIANT CORP (UT)
Recapitalized as Reliant Interactive Media Corp. (UT) 8/17/98
Each share Common $0.001 par exchanged for (0.2) share Common $0.001 par
Reliant Interactive Media Corp. (UT) reincorporated in Nevada 3/18/99 which merged into Thane International, Inc. 5/22/2002 which merged into Direct Marketing Holdings, Inc. 2/12/2004

RELIANT ENERGY INC (DE)
Name changed 04/26/2004
Name changed from Reliant Resources, Inc. to Reliant Energy, Inc. 04/26/2004
Name changed to RRI Energy, Inc. 05/04/2009
RRI Energy, Inc. name changed to GenOn Energy, Inc. 12/03/2010

RELIANT ENERGY INC (TX)
Under plan of reorganization each share Common no par automatically became (1) share CenterPoint Energy, Inc. Common 1¢ par 08/31/2002

RELIANT HOME WARRANTY CORP (FL)
Name changed to Reliant Financial Service Corp. 06/14/2007
Each share Common $0.001 par exchanged for (1) share Common $0.001 par

RELIANT INTERACTIVE MEDIA CORP (NV)
Reincorporated 3/18/99
State of incorporation changed from (UT) to (NV) 3/18/99
Each share old Common $0.001 par exchanged for (0.2) share new Common $0.001 par 4/15/99
Merged into Thane International, Inc. 5/22/2002
Each share new Common $0.001 par exchanged for (0.3049459) share Common $0.001 par
Thane International, Inc. merged into Direct Marketing Holdings, Inc. 2/12/2004

RELIANT RES LTD (BC)
Name changed to Soranzo International Spirits Inc. 12/09/1993
Soranzo International Spirits Inc. recapitalized as FirstLine Ventures Inc. 11/21/1997 which recapitalized as Aeon Ventures Ltd. 11/18/1999 which recapitalized as Statesman Resources Ltd. 06/28/2004

RELIANT VENTURES LTD (BC)
Name changed to Esperanza Silver Corp. 05/14/2003
Esperanza Silver Corp. name changed to Esperanza Resources Corp. 07/19/2010
(See Esperanza Resources Corp.)

RELIASTAR FINANCIAL CORP (DE)
10% Depositary Preferred called for redemption 07/01/1996
10% Preferred no par called for redemption 07/01/1996
Common no par split (2) for (1) by issuance of (1) additional share payable 09/10/1997 to holders of record 08/19/1997 Ex date - 09/11/1997
Acquired by ING Groep N.V. 09/01/2000
Each share Common no par exchanged for $54 cash

RELIASTAR FING I (DE)
8.20% Trust Originated Preferred Securities called for redemption at $25 on 03/29/2001

RELIASTAR FING II (DE)
Issue Information - 5,000,000 TR ORIGINATED PFD SECS 8.10% offered at $25 per share on 06/23/1997
8.10% Trust Originated Preferred Securities called for redemption at $25 on 07/15/2002

RELIEF ARLINGTON MINES LTD.
Liquidation completed in 1945

RELIEF HOME FUNDS CORP. (NY)
Charter cancelled and proclaimed dissolved for failure to pay taxes 12/16/40

RELIFE INC (AL)
Merged into HealthSouth Rehabilitation Corp. 12/30/94
Each share Class A Common 1¢ par exchanged for (0.7053) share Common 1¢ par
HealthSouth Rehabilitation Corp. name changed to HealthSouth Corp. 12/30/94

RELIGARE HEALTH TR (SINGAPORE)
Name changed to RHT Health Trust 12/29/2016
(See RHT Health Trust)

RELINC CORP. (HI)
Charter cancelled for failure to file annual reports 7/24/78

RELIV INTL INC (IL)
Stock Dividend - 10% payable 02/28/1997 to holders of record 02/14/1997
Reincorporated under the laws of Delaware and Common no par changed to $0.001 par 04/10/2000

RELLIM LIQUIDATING CO. (MI)
Liquidation completed
Each share Common $1 par exchanged for initial distribution of $14 cash 12/21/64
Each share Common $1 par received second and final distribution of $1 cash 11/1/65

RELM COMMUNICATIONS INC (IN)
Acquired by Adage, Inc. (PA) 01/24/1992
Each share Common Capital Stock no par exchanged for (0.19) share new Common 10¢ par
Adage, Inc. (PA) reincorporated in Nevada as RELM Wireless Corp. 01/30/1998 which name changed to BK Technologies, Inc. 06/05/2018

RELM WIRELESS CORP (NV)
Name changed to BK Technologies, Inc. 06/05/2018

RELMAR INDS (CA)
Name changed to Technology Group, Inc. 3/20/81
Technology Group, Inc. name changed to Union Reserves, Inc. 1/1/83
(See Union Reserves, Inc.)

RELTEC CORP (DE)
Merged into General Electric Co. PLC (New) 04/13/1999
Each share Common 1¢ par exchanged for $29.50 cash

RELTRON CORP (NY)
Common 1¢ par changed to $0.005 par and (1) additional share issued 1/21/83
Common $0.005 par split (3) for (2) by issuance of (0.5) additional share 8/1/83
Name changed to Voit Corp. 3/26/85
(See Voit Corp.)

RELUR CORP. (DE)
Name changed to Sly Industries, Inc. 9/2/59
(See Sly Industries, Inc.)

RELX NV (NETHERLANDS)
Merged into RELX PLC 09/10/2018
Each Sponsored ADR for Ordinary exchanged for (1) Sponsored ADR for Ordinary

RELYPSA INC (DE)
Acquired by Galenica AG 09/01/2016
Each share Common $0.001 par exchanged for $32 cash

REM METALS CORP (OR)
Involuntarily dissolved for failure to file reports and pay fees 04/24/1986

REM SCIENTIFIC, INC. (CA)
Adjudicated bankrupt 10/25/74

REMAC ZINC CORP (BC)
Each share old Common no par exchanged for (0.14285714) share new Common no par 11/26/2008
Name changed to Corazon Gold Corp. 01/19/2011
Corazon Gold Corp. name changed to NanoSphere Health Sciences Inc. 12/05/2017

REMANCO, INC. (DE)
Acquired by Canoga Electronics Corp. 7/15/65
Each share Common no par exchanged for (0.5) share Common no par
Canoga Electronics Corp. name changed to Canoga Industries 4/1/69
(See Canoga Industries)

REMAR RES LTD (BC)
Recapitalized as Golden Shamrock Resources Ltd. 07/17/1975
Each share Common no par exchanged for (0.4) share Common no par
Golden Shamrock Resources Ltd. merged into Colt Exploration Ltd. (BC) 07/08/1982 which reorganized in Alberta as Colt Exploration (Western) Ltd. 05/17/1983 which recapitalized as Colt Exploration (1988) Ltd. 06/30/1988 which reorganized as Stampede Oils Inc. 12/29/1988
(See Stampede Oils Inc.)

REMARK MEDIA INC (DE)
Name changed to Remark Holdings, Inc. 04/11/2017

REMBRANDT COSMETIC CORP (NY)
Dissolved by proclamation 12/24/91

REMBRANDT ENTERPRISES INC (MN)
$0.20 Conv. Preferred called for redemption 3/31/76
Merged out of existence 4/17/86
Details not available

REMBRANDT GOLD MINES LTD (CAYMAN ISLANDS)
Reincorporated 08/04/1992
Reincorporated 05/16/1996
Place of incorporation changed from (ON) to (Canada) 08/04/1992
Place of incorporation changed from (Canada) to Cayman Islands 05/16/1996
Delisted from Toronto Stock Venture Exchange 08/06/2002
Company is privately held

REMBRANDT GROUP LTD (SOUTH AFRICA)
Each old ADR for Ordinary Rand-0.10 par exchanged for (9) new ADR's for Ordinary Rand-0.10 par 11/2/87
Each new ADR for Ordinary Rand-0.10 par exchanged for (1) Sponsored ADR for Ordinary Rand-0.10 par 8/30/94
Name changed to Venfin Ltd. 9/26/2000
(See Venfin Ltd.)

REMBRANDT JEWELRY LTD (ON)
Merged into Sagehill Investments Ltd. 10/31/1978
Each share Common no par exchanged for $5.75 cash

REMCO ENTERPRISES INC (WA)
Merged into Sierra Oil & Gas Co. 10/13/1980
Each share Common 5¢ par exchanged for (1) share Common 1¢ par
Sierra Oil & Gas Co. recapitalized as Consolidated Lift Systems, Inc. 05/12/1987
(See Consolidated Lift Systems, Inc.)

REMCO ENVIRONMENTAL SVCS LTD (BC)
Name changed to La Plata Gold Corp. 06/30/1994
La Plata Gold Corp. name changed to Alphamin Resources Corp. (BC) 10/27/2008 which reincorporated in Mauritius 09/30/2014

REMCO INDS INC (NJ)
Common $2 par changed to 50¢ par and (3) additional shares issued 09/29/1961
Chapter XI bankruptcy proceedings closed 06/16/1972
Assets subsequently sold for benefit of creditors
No stockholders' equity

REMEC INC (CA)
Old Common 1¢ par split (3) for (2) by issuance of (0.5) additional share payable 06/27/1997 to holders of record 06/20/1997 Ex date - 06/30/1997
Old Common 1¢ par split (3) for (2) by issuance of (0.5) additional share payable 06/30/2000 to holders of record 06/19/2000 Ex date - 07/03/2000
Each share old Common 1¢ par exchanged for (0.446) share new Common 1¢ par and $2.80 cash 05/20/2005
In process of liquidation
Each share new Common 1¢ par received initial distribution of (0.3443) share Powerwave Technologies, Inc. Common no par payable 09/29/2005 to holders of record 09/02/2005
Each share new Common 1¢ par received second distribution of $1.35 cash payable 10/04/2005 to holders of record 09/13/2005
Each share new Common 1¢ par received third distribution of $0.75 cash payable 11/08/2006 to holders of record 11/01/2006 Ex date - 11/09/2006
Each share new Common 1¢ par received fourth distribution of $0.75 cash payable 12/21/2007 to holders of record 12/14/2007 Ex date - 12/24/2007
Each share new Common 1¢ par received fifth distribution of $0.50 cash payable 07/08/2008 to holders of record 06/27/2008 Ex date - 07/09/2008
Each share new Common 1¢ par received sixth distribution of $0.88 cash payable 12/10/2010 to holders of record 11/29/2010 Ex date - 12/13/2010
Assets transferred to REMEC Liquidating Trust and new Common 1¢ par reclassified as Units of Bene. Int. 01/01/2011
(See REMEC Liquidating Trust)

REMEC LIQUIDATING TR (CA)
Liquidation completed
Each Unit of Bene. Int. received first and final distribution of $0.0964 cash payable 10/01/2012 to holders of record 12/31/2010

REMEDCO INC (MN)
Administratively dissolved 06/15/1995

REMEDENT USA INC (NV)
Recapitalized as Remedent, Inc. 06/06/2005
Each share Common $0.001 par exchanged for (0.05) share Common $0.001 par

REMEDIATION SVCS INC (NV)
Name changed to LianDi Clean Technology Inc. 04/21/2010

REMEDY CORP (DE)
Common $0.00005 par split (3) for (2) by issuance of (0.5) additional share payable 3/25/96 to holders of record 3/11/96

Common $0.00005 par split (2) for (1) by issuance of (1) additional share payable 10/25/96 to holders of record 10/14/96
Acquired by Peregrine Systems, Inc. 8/27/2001
Each share Common $0.00005 par exchanged for (0.9065) share Common $0.001 par and $9 cash
(See Peregrine Systems, Inc.)

REMEDYTEMP INC (CA)
Merged into Koosharem Corp. 6/30/2006
Each share Class A Common 1¢ par exchanged for $17 cash
Each share Class B Common 1¢ par exchanged for $17 cash

REMGRO LTD (SOUTH AFRICA)
Each Sponsored ADR for Ordinary received distribution of $11.2175 cash payable 12/15/2008 to holders of record 12/04/2008
Each Sponsored ADR for Ordinary received distribution of $0.023517 cash payable 10/18/2010 to holders of record 10/06/2010 Ex date - 10/04/2010
ADR agreement terminated 10/30/2014
Each Sponsored ADR for Ordinary exchanged for $14.31573 cash

REMIDA VENTURES INC (BC)
Recapitalized as Caymus Ventures Corp. 09/16/1993
Each share Common no par exchanged for (0.4) share Common no par
Caymus Ventures Corp. name changed to West Dynamic Toll Road Ltd. (BC) 07/08/1996 which reincorporated in Bermuda 04/04/1997
(See West Dynamic Toll Road Ltd.)

REMINGTON ARMS INC (DE)
Common no par changed to $1 par 00/00/1933
6% Preferred $100 par reclassified as 4.5% Preferred $100 par 00/00/1947
Merged into Du Pont (E.I.) De Nemours & Co. 02/01/1980
Each share 4.5% Preferred $100 par exchanged for $105 cash
Each share Common $1 par exchanged for (0.574) share Common $1.66666666 par
Du Pont (E.I.) De Nemours & Co. merged into DowDuPont Inc. 09/01/2017

REMINGTON CORP. (DE)
Each share Common $5 par exchanged for (5) shares Common $1 par 00/00/1953
Stock Dividend - 10% 02/01/1954
Name changed to Helila Liquidating Corp. 06/01/1964
(See Helila Liquidating Corp.)

REMINGTON CORP. (FL)
Name changed to Nationwide Nursing Centers, Inc. 06/05/1967
(See Nationwide Nursing Centers, Inc.)

REMINGTON CREEK RES LTD (BC)
Recapitalized as Grayd Resource Corp. 02/26/1996
Each share Common no par exchanged for (1/3) share Common no par
Grayd Resource Corp. acquired by Agnico-Eagle Mines Ltd. 01/24/2012 which name changed to Agnico Eagle Mines Ltd. 04/30/2013

REMINGTON ENERGY LTD (AB)
Acquired by Dominion Resources, Inc. (Old) 04/16/1999
Each share Common no par exchanged for $1.90 cash

REMINGTON-FOX INC (NV)
Each share old Common 1¢ par exchanged for (0.25) share new Common $0.001 par 7/16/93

Each share new Common $0.001 par exchanged for (0.089529) share Common $0.001 par 3/15/2001
Plan of reorganization under Chapter 11 Federal Bankruptcy Code effective 12/7/2001
Stockholders' equity unlikely

REMINGTON GOLD CORP (UT)
Reorganized under the laws of Delaware as Remington Diversified Industries Corp. 11/16/1987
Each share Common 1¢ par exchanged for (0.04) share Common 1¢ par

REMINGTON-HALL CAP CORP (CO)
Name changed to Ault Glazer & Co., Inc. 03/12/2008
Ault Glazer & Co., Inc. name changed to Tytan Holdings Inc. 10/02/2009

REMINGTON NOISELESS TYPEWRITER CORP.
Merged into Remington Rand, Inc. 00/00/1927
Details not available

REMINGTON OIL & GAS CORP (DE)
Each share Class A Common $1 par reclassified as (1.15) shares Common $1 par 12/24/98
Each share Non-Vtg. Class B Common $1 par reclassified as (1) share Common $1 par 12/24/98
Merged into Helix Energy Solutions Group, Inc. 7/1/2006
Each share Common $1 par exchanged for (0.436) share Common no par and $27 cash

REMINGTON RAND, INC. (DE)
Common no par changed to $1 par 00/00/1932
Each share 1st Preferred $100 par exchanged for (1) share 5% Prior Preferred $25 par and (0.5) share Common $1 par 00/00/1935
Each share 2nd Preferred $100 par exchanged for (1) share $6 Preferred $25 par and (0.5) share Common $1 par 00/00/1935
Each (4) shares 5% Prior Preferred $25 par exchanged for (1) share $4.50 Preferred $25 par 00/00/1936
Each share $6 Preferred $25 par exchanged for (1) share $4.50 Preferred $25 par 00/00/1936
Each share Common $1 par exchanged for (2) shares Common 50¢ par 00/00/1947
Stock Dividend - 10% 05/01/1941
Merged into Sperry Rand Corp. 06/30/1955
Each share $4.50 Preferred $25 par exchanged for (1) share new $4.50 Preferred $25 par
Each share Common 50¢ par exchanged for (2) shares new Common 50¢ par
Sperry Rand Corp. name changed to Sperry Corp. (New) 08/01/1979 which merged into Burroughs Corp. (DE) 09/16/1986 which name changed to Unisys Corp. 11/13/1986

REMINGTON RAND CORP (MN)
Reincorporated under the laws of Georgia as Dominion Cable Corp. 7/1/88
(See Dominion Cable Corp.)

REMINGTON TYPEWRITER CO.
Merged into Remington Rand, Inc. 00/00/1927
Details not available

REMINGTON VENTURES INC (NV)
Old Common $0.001 par split (10) for (1) by issuance of (9) additional shares payable 04/17/2007 to holders of record 04/12/2007 Ex date - 04/18/2007
Each share old Common $0.001 par exchanged for (0.0001) share new Common $0.001 par 10/26/2007
Charter revoked 03/31/2010

REMITTANCE TECHNOLOGIES CORP (DE)
Charter cancelled and declared inoperative and void for non-payment of taxes 3/1/92

REMMINGTON ENTERPRISES INC (NV)
Name changed to Altovida Inc. 11/10/2014
(See Altovida Inc.)

REMO RES INC (BC)
Recapitalized as Chakana Copper Corp. 01/31/2018
Each share Common no par exchanged for (0.14565625) share Common no par

REMODEL AUCTION INC (FL)
Each share old Common $0.001 par exchanged for (0.002) share new Common $0.001 par 05/07/2010
Each share new Common $0.001 par exchanged again for (0.00033333) share new Common $0.001 par 11/10/2010
Each share new Common $0.001 par exchanged again for (0.00033333) share new Common $0.001 par 09/07/2011
Name changed to North Carolina Natural Energy, Inc. 01/11/2012
North Carolina Natural Energy, Inc. name changed to Appalachian Mountain Brewery, Inc. 01/08/2014

REMOTE KNOWLEDGE INC (DE)
Assets sold for the benefit of creditors 03/19/2009
Stockholders' equity unlikely

REMOTE MONITORING SYS INC (NY)
Recapitalized as Orange Medical Instruments, Inc. 04/20/1987
Each share Common $0.0001 par exchanged for (0.1) share Common 1¢ par

REMOTE SURVEILLANCE TECHNOLOGIES INC (NV)
Each share old Common $0.001 par exchanged for (0.1) share new Common $0.001 par 10/02/2007
Name changed to Stratera, Inc. 07/15/2008
Stratera, Inc. recapitalized as Gulf West Investment Properties, Inc. 12/16/2009

REMOTE UTILS NETWORK INC (NV)
Name changed to Runcorp, Inc. 07/16/2001
(See Runcorp, Inc.)

REMOTEMDX INC (UT)
Each share Common $0.0001 par received distribution of (0.008547) share Volu-Sol Reagents Corp. Common no par payable 02/27/2009 to holders of record 01/30/2009 Ex date - 01/28/2009
Name changed to SecureAlert, Inc. 02/22/2010
SecureAlert, Inc. name changed to Track Group, Inc. (UT) 05/26/2015 which reincorporated in Delaware 08/05/2016

REMOVE BY YOU INC (NV)
Name changed to Gain Cities Ltd, 10/28/2016

REMSCO ASSOC (NJ)
Merged into New Remsco Enterprises, Inc. 00/00/1981
Each share Common no par exchanged for $4 cash

REMSTAR RES LTD (BC)
Name changed to Avarone Metals Inc. 02/03/2014

REMY INTL INC NEW (DE)
Acquired by BorgWarner Inc. 11/10/2019
Each share Common $0.0001 par exchanged for $29.50 cash

REMY INTL INC OLD (DE)
Ser. A Preferred $0.0001 par called for redemption at $1,154.51 on 01/31/2011
Ser. B Preferred $0.0001 par called for redemption at $1,154.51 on 01/31/2011
Under plan of reorganization each share Common $0.0001 par automatically became (1) share Remy International, Inc. (New) Common $0.0001 par 01/02/2015
(See Remy International, Inc. (New))

REN CORP-USA (TN)
Merged into Gambro AB 11/30/95
Each share Common no par exchanged for $20 cash

RENABIE GOLD TR (ON)
Completely liquidated 2/17/92
Each Unit exchanged for first and final distribution of $0.05 cash
Note: Unexchanged certificates became void and without value 8/17/93

RENABIE MINES LTD (ON)
Merged into Willroy Mines Ltd. 01/08/1971
Each share Capital Stock $1 par exchanged for (0.33333333) share Capital Stock no par
Willroy Mines Ltd. merged into Lac Minerals Ltd. (Old) 12/31/1982 which merged into LAC Minerals Ltd. (New) 07/29/1985 which was acquired by American Barrick Resources Corp. 10/17/1994 which name changed to Barrick Gold Corp. 01/18/1995

RENABIE MINES LTD DOM (CANADA)
Capital Stock $1 par changed to no par 10/16/80
Name changed to Sungate Resources Ltd. 11/24/80
Sungate Resources Ltd. merged into Barrick Resources Corp. 10/14/83 which recapitalized as American Barrick Resources Corp. 12/6/85 which name changed to Barrick Gold Corp. 1/18/95

RENAIRE FOODS, INC. (PA)
Merged into Goren Foods Co. 11/27/67
Each share Common $1 par exchanged for (0.1) share 5% Preferred $1 par
(See Goren Foods Co.)

RENAISSANCE ACCEP GROUP INC (DE)
Merged into Renaissance Acquisition Corp. in 2003
Each share Common 10¢ par exchanged for $0.01 cash

RENAISSANCE ACQUISITION CORP (DE)
Issue Information - 15,600,000 UNITS consisting of (1) share COM and (2) WTS offered at $6 per Unit on 01/29/2007
Completely liquidated 02/09/2009
Each Unit exchanged for first and final distribution of $5.9318211 cash
Each share Common $0.0001 par exchanged for first and final distribution of $5.9318211 cash

RENAISSANCE BIOENERGY INC (NV)
Common $0.00001 par split (12) for (1) by issuance of (11) additional shares payable 03/09/2010 to holders of record 02/05/2010 Ex date - 03/10/2010
Name changed to ASPA Gold Corp. 12/01/2010

RENAISSANCE CAP GROWTH & INCOME FD III INC. (TX)
Name changed to RENN Global Entrepreneurs Fund, Inc. 06/04/2009
RENN Global Entrepreneurs Fund, Inc. name changed to RENN Fund, Inc. 08/18/2014

RENAISSANCE COMMUNICATIONS CORP (DE)
Common 1¢ par split (3) for (2) by issuance of (0.5) additional share 10/16/1995
Merged into Tribune Co. 03/25/1997
Each share Common 1¢ par exchanged for $36 cash

RENAISSANCE CONCEPTS INC (CO)
Recapitalized as Sourceone Environmental, Inc. 06/04/1990
Each share Common no par exchanged for (0.1) share Common no par

RENAISSANCE COSMETICS INC (DE)
Stock Dividends - In 14% Sr. Preferred Ser. B to holders of 14% Sr. Preferred Ser. B 3.5625% payable 02/17/1998 to holders of record 02/02/1998; In 14% Sr. Preferred Ser. C to holders of 14% Sr. Preferred Ser. C 3.5625% payable 02/17/1998 to holders of record 02/02/1998
Chapter 11 bankruptcy proceedings converted to Chapter 7 on 01/13/2004
Stockholders' equity unlikely

RENAISSANCE ENERGY LTD (AB)
3rd Preferred Ser. A $25 par called for redemption 03/02/1987
Each share 144A Common no par exchanged for (1) share Common no par 09/29/1999
Common no par split (2) for (1) by issuance of (1) additional share 10/14/1987
Common no par split (2) for (1) by issuance of (1) additional share 06/08/1990
Merged into Husky Energy Inc. 08/25/2000
Each share Common no par exchanged for (1) share Common no par and $2.50 cash

RENAISSANCE ENTERPRISES INC (DE)
Charter cancelled and declared inoperative and void for non-payment of taxes 3/1/86

RENAISSANCE ENTMT CORP (CO)
Each share Common $0.0001 par exchanged for (1/3) share old Common 3¢ par 9/22/94
Old Common 3¢ par split (2) for (1) by issuance of (1) additional share payable 10/21/96 to holders of record 10/17/96
Each share old Common 3¢ par exchanged for (0.2) share new Common 3¢ par 2/23/98
Merged into Ellora Entertainment, LLC 12/22/2005
Each share new Common 3¢ par exchanged for $0.03 cash

RENAISSANCE FD INC (MD)
Voluntarily dissolved 04/14/1993
Details not available

RENAISSANCE GOLF INC (CANADA)
Recapitalized as FranchiseMaster Technologies Inc. 06/20/2000
Each share Common no par exchanged for (0.05) share Common no par
(See FranchiseMaster Technologies Inc.)

RENAISSANCE GRX INC (WA)
Acquired by ZyMOS Corp. 7/30/90
Each share Common 1¢ par received (0.75) share Common no par
Note: Certificates were not required to be surrendered and are without value
ZyMOS Corp. name changed to Appian Technology Inc. (CA) 12/17/90 which reincorporated in Delaware 10/29/86
(See Appian Technology Inc.)

RENAISSANCE HOTEL GROUP N V (NETHERLANDS)
Merged into Marriott International, Inc. 03/31/1997
Each share Common NLG 1 par exchanged for $30 cash

RENAISSANCE INDL CORP (ON)
Name changed to D.A.S. Electronics Industries, Inc. 01/29/1988
D.A.S. Electronics Industries, Inc. recapitalized as Pace Corp. 09/30/1993
(See Pace Corp.)

RENAISSANCE INTL GROUP LTD (NV)
Name changed to RIGL Corp. 06/25/1998
RIGL Corp. name changed to YP.Net, Inc. 10/01/1999 which name changed to YP Corp. 07/28/2004 which recapitalized as LiveDeal, Inc. 08/27/2007 which name changed to Live Ventures Inc. 10/09/2015

RENAISSANCE LEARNING INC (WI)
Acquired by Raphael Holding Co. 10/19/2011
Each share Common 1¢ par exchanged for $16.60 cash

RENAISSANCE SOLUTIONS INC (DE)
Merged into Registry, Inc. 07/31/1997
Each share Common $0.0001 par exchanged for (0.8) share Common no par
Registry, Inc. name changed to Renaissance Worldwide, Inc. 01/07/1998
(See Renaissance Worldwide, Inc.)

RENAISSANCE WORLDWIDE INC (MA)
Merged into Aquent, Inc. 12/11/2001
Each share Common no par exchanged for $2 cash

RENAISSANCERE HLDGS LTD (BERMUDA)
8.10% Preference Ser. A $1 par called for redemption at $25 on 01/15/2007
7.30% Preference Ser. B $1 par called for redemption at $25 on 12/20/2010
6.60% Preference Ser. D $1 par called for redemption at $25 plus $0.12 accrued dividends on 06/27/2013
(Additional Information in Active)

RENAL CARE GROUP INC (DE)
Secondary Offering - 2,500,000 shares COM offered at $32 per share on 11/19/1996
Common 1¢ par split (3) for (2) by issuance of (0.5) additional shares payable 07/25/1997 to holders of record 07/07/1997
Common 1¢ par split (3) for (2) by issuance of (0.5) additional share payable 08/24/1998 to holders of record 08/07/1998
Common 1¢ par split (3) for (2) by issuance of (0.5) additional share payable 05/24/2004 to holders of record 05/07/2004 Ex date - 05/25/2004
Merged into Fresenius Medical Care AG & Co. KGAA 03/31/2006
Each share Common 1¢ par exchanged for $48 cash

RENAL DEVICES INC (NV)
Charter revoked for failure to file reports and pay fees 02/01/1982

RENAL SYS INC (MN)
Name changed to Minntech Corp. 9/15/86
Minntech Corp. merged into Cantel Medical Corp. 9/6/2001

RENAL TREATMENT CTRS INC (DE)
Common 1¢ par split (2) for (1) by issuance of (1) additional share payable 03/14/1996 to holders of record 02/29/1996 Ex date - 03/15/1996
Merged into Total Renal Care Holdings, Inc. 02/27/1998
Each share Common 1¢ par exchanged for (1.335) shares Common $0.001 par
Total Renal Care Holdings, Inc. name changed to DaVita, Inc. 10/09/2000 which name changed to DaVita HealthCare Partners Inc. 11/02/2012 which name changed back to DaVita Inc. 09/01/2016

RENARD MFG INC (FL)
Common 1¢ par split (2) for (1) by issuance of (1) additional share 09/20/1971
Name changed to Reyma, Inc. 08/31/1998
(See Reyma, Inc.)

RENASANT FINL PARTNERS LTD (ON)
Each share old Common no par exchanged for (0.00000002) share new Common no par 01/16/2009
Note: In effect holders received $1.75 cash per share and public interest was eliminated

RENATA RES INC (AB)
Merged into Rio Alto Exploration Ltd. 06/21/2000
Each share Common no par exchanged for (0.0283) share Common no par, $0.77 cash, or a combination thereof
Note: Option to receive stock or stock and cash expired 07/10/2000
Rio Alto Exploration Ltd. merged into Canadian Natural Resources Ltd. 07/01/2002

RENAULT S A (FRANCE)
ADR agreement terminated 05/06/2011
Each 144A Sponsored ADR for Ordinary exchanged for (1) share Ordinary
Note: Unexchanged ADR's will be sold and the proceeds, if any, held for claim after 05/06/2012

RENAULT WINERY INC (NJ)
Name changed back to MCC-Presidential, Inc. 05/05/1977
MCC-Presidential, Inc. merged into First Montauk Financial Corp. 11/16/1987

RENCAN RES INVTS LTD (CANADA)
Recapitalized as Norminco Developments Ltd. 06/09/1977
Each share Common no par exchanged for (0.2) share Common no par
Norminco Developments Ltd. recapitalized as Sumburgh Developments Ltd. 10/17/1983 which recapitalized as Access Banking Network Inc. 09/24/1984 which recapitalized as Access ATM Network Inc. 05/24/1985 which merged into Ancom ATM International Inc. 01/18/1988
(See Ancom ATM International Inc.)

RENCORE RES LTD (ON)
Merged into Bold Ventures Inc. 02/13/2012
Each share Common no par exchanged for (1) share Common no par

RENDEZ VOUS GOLD MNG CORP (BC)
Recapitalized as American Canadian Systems Inc. 03/04/1987
Each share Common no par exchanged for (1) share Common no par
American Canadian Systems Inc. name changed to Maxcard Systems International Inc. 04/03/1991
(See Maxcard Systems International Inc.)

RENDEZVOUS TRAILS AMER INC (OK)
Reorganized as Rain Forest-Moose Ltd. 02/23/1996
Each share Common 25¢ exchanged for (2) shares Common 25¢ par
Rain Forest-Moose Ltd. name changed to Aarow Environmental Group, Inc. 06/13/1997 which name changed to Aaro Broadband Wireless Communications, Inc. 09/25/2000
(See Aaro Broadband Wireless Communications, Inc.)

RENEAUX CAP INC (BC)
Name changed to Naturally Niagara, Inc. 6/29/93
Naturally Niagara, Inc. recapitalized as Northern Gaming Inc. 1/22/96 which recapitalized as Icon Laser Eye Centers Inc. 9/1/99

RENEGADE ENERGY CORP (WA)
Each share old Common $0.001 par exchanged for (0.001) share new Common $0.001 par 01/09/2007
Recapitalized as Carson Development Corp. 10/20/2008
Each share Common $0.001 par exchanged for (0.01) share Common $0.001 par

RENEGADE PETE LTD (AB)
Merged into Spartan Energy Corp. 04/01/2014
Each share Common no par exchanged for (0.5625) share Common no par
Note: Unexchanged certificates were cancelled and became without value 04/01/2017
Spartan Energy Corp. merged into Vermilion Energy Inc. 05/31/2018

RENEGADE VENTURE NEV CORP (NV)
Reincorporated 09/22/1997
Each share old Common $0.00001 par exchanged for (0.01) share new Common $0.00001 par 07/22/1996
Name and state of incorporation changed from Renegade Venture Corp. (CO) to Renegade Venture (Nev.) Corp. 09/22/1997
Name changed to Global Aircraft Solutions, Inc. 12/17/2004
(See Global Aircraft Solutions, Inc.)

RENEGY HLDGS INC (DE)
Each share old Common $0.001 par exchanged for (1) share new Common $0.001 par to reflect a (1) for (2,000) reverse split followed by a (2,000) for (1) forward split 03/30/2009
Note: Holders of (1,999) or fewer pre-split shares received $0.74 cash per share
Merged into Renegy Holdings, L.L.C. 01/17/2012
Each share new Common $0.001 par exchanged for (1) Membership Unit
Note: Company is now private

RENEW ENERGY RES INC (NV)
SEC revoked common stock registration 02/06/2014

RENEW ENTMT CORP (DE)
Charter cancelled and declared inoperative and void for non-payment of taxes 5/25/95

RENEWABLE ENERGY CORP ASA (NORWAY)
Name changed to REC Silicon A.S.A. 11/12/2013

RENEWABLE ENERGY DEVELOPERS INC (CANADA)
Merged into Capstone Infrastructure Corp. 10/07/2013
Each share Common no par exchanged for (0.26) share Common no par and $0.001 cash
Note: Unexchanged certificates will

be cancelled and become without value 10/07/2019
(See Capstone Infrastructure Corp.)

RENEWABLE ENERGY GROUP INC (DE)
Ser. B Preferred $0.0001 par called for redemption at $25 on 03/27/2014
(Additional Information in Active)

RENEWABLE ENERGY RES INC (FL)
Each share old Common $0.001 par exchanged for (0.03333333) share new Common $0.001 par 04/30/2008
Name changed to New Green Technologies, Inc. 07/03/2008
New Green Technologies, Inc. recapitalized as Spur Ranch, Inc. 08/25/2010 which name changed to Rounder, Inc. 01/24/2012 which name changed to Fortitude Group, Inc. 01/08/2013

RENEWABLE ENERGY TRADE BOARD CORP BRITISH VIRGIN ISLANDS
Reincorporated under the laws of Cayman Islands as New Energy Exchange Ltd. 08/12/2015

RENEX CORP (FL)
Merged into National Nephrology Associates Inc. 2/2/2000
Each share Common $0.001 par exchanged for $10 cash

RENFIELD CORP (NJ)
Company dissolved 4/24/94

RENFIELD ENTERPRISES INC (AB)
Delisted from Canadian Venture Stock Exchange 05/31/2001

RENFORT GOLD MINES, LTD. (ON)
Dissolved by default 10/17/60
No stockholders' equity

RENFREW MANUFACTURING CO.
Liquidated in 1927

RENFREW PETROLEUMS LTD. (AB)
Acquired by Western Decalta Petroleum Ltd. on a (1) for (15) basis 10/10/60
(See Western Decalta Petroleum Ltd.)

RENFREW TEXTILES LTD. (CANADA)
Bankrupt in 1954

RENGOLD MINES LTD (CANADA)
Completely liquidated 8/22/79
Each share Common no par exchanged for first and final distribution of (1/3) share Renabie Mines Ltd. (Canada) Capital Stock $1 par
Renabie Mines Ltd. (Canada) name changed to Sungate Resources Ltd. 11/24/80 which merged into Barrick Resources Corp. 10/14/83 which recapitalized as American Barrick Resources Corp. 12/6/85 which name changed to Barrick Gold Corp. 1/18/95

RENHE COML HLDGS CO LTD (CAYMAN ISLANDS)
ADR agreement terminated 01/24/2018
No ADR's remain outstanding

RENHUANG PHARMACEUTICAL INC (NV)
Name changed to China Botanic Pharmaceutical Inc. 11/22/2010

RENMAR CORP (FL)
Charter cancelled for non-payment of taxes 05/13/1969

RENMARK EXPLS LTD (ON)
Completely liquidated 06/00/1971
Each share Common no par exchanged for first and final distribution of $0.0125 cash

RENN GLOBAL ENTREPRENEURS FD INC (TX)
Name changed to RENN Fund, Inc. 08/18/2014

RENN INDS INC (BC)
Name changed to Anthes Industries Inc. 06/04/1981
Anthes Industries Inc. name changed to Patheon Inc. 05/12/1993
(See Patheon Inc.)

RENNEK CO. (DE)
Liquidation completed
Each share Common no par exchanged for initial distribution of (0.363797) share General Mills Corp. Common $1.50 par 12/20/67
Each share Common no par received second distribution of (0.0077569) share General Mills Corp. Common $1.50 par and ($0.005204186) cash 4/20/70
Note: Details on subsequent distributions, if any, are not available

RENNER, INC. (PA)
Name changed to Industrial Science Corp. 3/28/63 which was adjudicated bankrupt 7/11/63

RENNER CO (OH)
Charter cancelled for failure to file annual reports 09/30/1983

RENNIKS RES LTD (BC)
Recapitalized as Glamis Gold Ltd. 12/12/77
Each share Common no par exchanged for (1/3) share Common no par
Glamis Gold Ltd. merged into Goldcorp Inc. (New) 11/4/2006

RENO AIR INC (NV)
Merged into AMR Corp. 02/22/1999
Each share Conv. Exchangeable Preferred Ser. A 1¢ par exchanged for $27.50 cash
Each share Common 1¢ par exchanged for $7.75 cash

RENO-DEPOT INC (QC)
Acquired by Castorama Canada Inc. 4/30/97
Each share Common no par exchanged for $35 cash

RENO GOLD CORP (NV)
Each share old Common $0.001 par exchanged for (0.1) share new Common $0.001 par 09/05/2006
Company terminated registration of common stock and is no longer public as of 07/28/2005
Stockholders' equity unlikely

RENO GOLD MINES LTD. (BC)
Dissolved in 1952

RENOIR WTR INC (AB)
Name changed to Frank's Corp. 08/20/1996
Frank's Corp. recapitalized as True North Water Corp. (ALTA) 02/23/1999 which reincorporated in Canada 12/12/2003 which name changed to Watertowne International Inc. 03/19/2004 which recapitalized as Sightus Inc. 03/15/2006
(See Sightus Inc.)

RENOLD CHAINS CDA LTD (CANADA)
Completely liquidated 7/28/92
Each share $1.10 Class A no par received first and final distribution of $1.12 cash
Each share Class B no par received first and final distribution of $1.12 cash

RENOLD-COVENTRY LTD. (CANADA)
Name changed to Renold Chains Canada Ltd. 4/25/55
(See Renold Chains Canada Ltd.)

RENOVIS INC (DE)
Merged into Evotec AG 05/05/2008
Each share Common $0.001 par exchanged for (0.5271) Sponsored ADS for Bearer no par

RENOVO HLDGS (NV)
Name changed to Bebida Beverage Co. (NV) 10/14/2008
Bebida Beverage Co. (NV) reincorporated in Wyoming 12/03/2009

RENOX CREEK PETROLEUM INC. (BC)
Name changed to Renox Creek Resources Inc. 1/20/83
Renox Creek Resources Inc. name changed to Equinox Entertainment Corp. 1/30/87 which name changed to Cancorp Enterprises Inc. 8/31/88 which name changed to G.E.M. Environmental Management Inc. (B.C.) 10/2/89 which reincorporated in Delaware 7/13/90
(See G.E.M. Environmental Management Inc.)

RENOX CREEK RES INC (BC)
Name changed to Equinox Entertainment Corp. 1/30/87
Equinox Entertainment Corp. name changed to Cancorp Enterprises Inc. 8/31/88 which name changed to G.E.M. Environmental Management Inc. (BC) 10/2/89 which reincorporated in Delaware 7/13/90
(See G.E.M. Environmental Management Inc.)

RENSSELAER & SARATOGA R.R. CO.
Acquired by Delaware & Hudson Railroad Corp. through an exchange of 8% Guaranteed Stock for like amount of new bonds in 1945

RENSSELAER VALVE CO. (NY)
Assets acquired by Ludlow Valve Manufacturing Co., Inc. 12/31/1954
Details not available

RENSSELAER WATER CO.
Sold to the City of Rensselaer, NY in 1952
Details not available

RENT A CTR INC (DE)
Common $1 par split (3) for (2) by issuance of (0.5) additional share 3/31/86
Common $1 par split (3) for (2) by issuance of (0.5) additional share 4/20/87
Acquired by Thorn EMI Ltd. 9/9/87
Each share Common $1 par exchanged for $27 cash

RENT A WRECK AMER INC (DE)
Merged into MBFG, Inc. 1/26/2006
Each share Conv. Preferred Ser. A 1¢ par exchanged for $0.88 cash
Each share Common 1¢ par exchanged for $0.40 cash

RENT-A-WRECK CAP INC (CANADA)
Recapitalized as Franchise Services of North America Inc. (Canada) 12/15/2006
Each share Common no par exchanged for (0.24518236) share Common no par
Franchise Services of North America Inc. (Canada) reincorporated in Delaware 05/03/2013

RENT A WRECK INDS CORP (BC)
Recapitalized as Practicar Industries Corp. 09/07/1988
Each share Common no par exchanged for (0.2) share Common no par
(See Practicar Industries Corp.)

RENT FINDERS USA INC (NV)
Recapitalized as Church & Crawford, Inc. 3/30/2007
Each share Common no par exchanged for (0.0005) share Common $0.001 par

RENT RITE RESERVATION NETWORK INC (NM)
Name changed to Trvlsys, Inc. (NM) 10/20/1989
Trvlsys, Inc. (NM) reincorporated in Nevada 09/00/1994 which name changed to Triden Telecom, Inc. 11/23/1994 which name changed to Permanent Technologies, Inc. 12/10/2007

RENT SHIELD CORP (FL)
Common no par split (3) for (1) by issuance of (2) additional shares payable 04/29/2003 to holders of record 04/22/2003 Ex date - 04/30/2003
Name changed to RS Group of Companies, Inc. 04/23/2004
(See RS Group of Companies, Inc.)

RENT WAY INC (PA)
Common no par split (3) for (2) by issuance of (0.5) additional share 8/18/95
Merged into Rent-A-Center, Inc. 11/15/2006
Each share Common no par exchanged for $10.65 cash

RENTAL SVC CORP (DE)
Issue Information - 4,929,000 shares COM offered at $16 per share on 8/22/96
Merged into Atlas Copco North America Inc. 7/29/99
Each share Common 1¢ par exchanged for $29 cash

RENTCASH INC (ON)
Name changed to Cash Store Financial Services Inc. 04/07/2008

RENTECH INC (CO)
Each share old Common 1¢ par exchanged for (0.1) share new Common 1¢ par 08/20/2015
Plan of reorganization under Chapter 11 Federal Bankruptcy proceedings effective 04/17/2018
Holders will receive a distribution only in the event funds remain following the satisfaction of all claims and wind-down expenses

RENTECH NITROGEN PARTNERS L P (DE)
Merged into CVR Partners, L.P. 04/01/2016
Each Common Unit exchanged for (1.04) Common Units and $2.57 cash
Each Common Unit received an additional distribution of $0.1468 cash 09/23/2016

RENTERS CHOICE INC (DE)
Common 1¢ par split (3) for (2) by issuance of (0.5) additional share 06/20/1995
Common 1¢ par split (2) for (1) by issuance of (1) additional share 10/09/1995
Name changed to Rent-A-Center, Inc. 12/31/1998

RENTEX SVCS CORP (DE)
Acquired by Sketchley Public Ltd. 07/16/1982
Each share Common $1 par exchanged for $13 cash

RENTOKIL GROUP PLC (ENGLAND & WALES)
Name changed to Rentokil Initial PLC 10/2/96

RENTOWN ENTERPRISES INC (CANADA)
Assets sold for the benefit of creditors in 1991
No stockholders' equity

RENTRAK CORP (OR)
Each share Common $0.001 par received distribution of (0.11990407) share BlowOut Entertainment Inc. Common 1¢ par payable 11/26/1996 to holders of record 11/18/1996
Merged into comScore, Inc. 01/29/2016
Each share Common $0.001 par exchanged for (1.15) shares Common $0.001 par

RENU U INTL INC (DE)
Each (30) shares old Common $0.001 par exchanged for (1) share new Common $0.001 par 07/12/1999
Name changed to Colormax Technologies, Inc. 09/07/1999
(See Colormax Technologies, Inc.)

RENWELL ELECTRONICS CORP. OF DELAWARE (DE)
Under plan of merger name changed to Renwell Industries, Inc. 11/26/62
(See Renwell Industries, Inc.)

RENWELL INDUSTRIES, INC. (DE)
Common 1¢ par changed to 50¢ par and (1) additional share issued 12/10/1963
Liquidation completed
Each share Common 50¢ par exchanged for initial distribution of (0.2506) share Sunshine Mining Co. Capital Stock 5¢ par 08/07/1968
Each share Common 50¢ par received second and final distribution of (0.3278) share Sunshine Mining Co. (WA) Capital Stock 5¢ par and $0.01421 cash 12/31/1971
Sunshine Mining Co. (WA) reincorporated in Delaware 03/12/1980 which name changed Sunshine Mining & Refining Co. 06/20/1994
(See Sunshine Mining & Refining Co.)

RENWICK EXPLS LTD (BC)
Name changed to IORI. International Oil Royalties Inc. 10/11/1985
IORI. International Oil Royalties Inc. name changed to IORI. Enterprises Inc. 05/14/1986 which name changed to Golden Band Resources Inc. (BC) 03/26/1987 which reincorporated in Saskatchewan 07/04/2006
(See Golden Band Resources Inc.)

RENZY MINES LTD (QC)
Delisted from Canadian Dealer Network 01/30/1995

REO HOLDING CORP. (MI)
Capital Stock $1 par changed to no par 03/31/1955
Merged into Nuclear Corp. of America, Inc. (MI) 10/07/1955
Each share Capital Stock no par exchanged for (1) share Class A Common no par and (1) share Common no par
Nuclear Corp. of America, Inc. (MI) recapitalized as Nuclear Corp. of America (DE) 06/30/1958 which recapitalized as Nucor Corp. 12/29/1971

REO MOTOR CAR CO. (MI)
Reorganized as Reo Motors, Inc. share for share 01/02/1940
Reo Motors, Inc. name changed to Reo Holding Corp. 12/30/1954 which merged into Nuclear Corp. of America, Inc. (MI) 10/07/1955 which recapitalized as Nuclear Corp. of America (DE) 06/30/1958 which recapitalized as Nucor Corp. 12/29/1971

REO MOTORS, INC. (MI)
Stock Dividend - 10% 01/31/1953
Name changed to Reo Holding Corp. 12/30/1954
Reo Holding Corp. merged into Nuclear Corp. of America, Inc. (MI) 10/07/1955 which recapitalized as Nuclear Corp. of America (DE) 06/30/1958 which recapitalized as Nucor Corp. 12/29/1971

REO PLASTICS INC (MN)
Company went private 00/00/1975
Details not available

REO PLUS INC (TX)
Reincorporated under the laws of Delaware as Boston Omaha Corp. 03/18/2015

REON RESISTOR CORP (NY)
Each share old Common 1¢ par exchanged for (0.1) share new Common 1¢ par 02/15/1974
Liquidated and declared insolvent 06/30/1975
No stockholders' equity

REOPLATA MINES LTD. (ON)
Charter revoked for failure to file reports and pay fees 12/3/62

REORGANIZED BROKEN HILLS SILVER CORP. (NV)
Charter forfeited for non-payment of taxes 2/28/24

REORGANIZED CARRIE SILVER-LEAD MINES CORP. (NV)
Charter forfeited for non-payment of taxes 2/28/24

REORGANIZED CONSUMAT SYS INC (VA)
Name changed to Consumat Environmental Systems, Inc. 12/12/96
(See Consumat Environmental Systems, Inc.)

REORGANIZED PIONEER MINES CO. (NV)
Name changed to Pioneer Development Corp. (NV) 1/12/60
(See Pioneer Development Corp. (NV))

REORGANIZED SILVER KING DIVIDE MINING CO. (NV)
Name changed to Mt. Union Mines, Inc. in 1952
Mt. Union Mines, Inc. name changed to Mt. Union Uranium, Inc. 8/31/55 which name changed to Mt. Union Industries, Inc. 7/13/61
(See Mt. Union Industries, Inc.)

REORGANIZED TCC INC (DE)
Charter forfeited for non-payment of taxes 2/18/98

REP CORP (NV)
Merged into Little Chef Food Products, Inc. 07/01/1969
Each share Common 1¢ par exchanged for (0.4) share Common 1¢ par

REPADCO INDS INC (DE)
Charter cancelled and declared inoperative and void for non-payment of taxes 3/1/85

REPADRE CAP CORP (ON)
Name changed 3/7/90
Name changed from Repadre Resources Ltd. (BC) to Repadre Capital Corp. (ONT) 3/7/90
Acquired by IAMGold Corp. 1/7/2003
Each share Common no par exchanged for (1.6) shares Common no par

REPAIR SHOP SYS INC (NV)
Each share old Class A Common 1¢ par exchanged for (0.025) share new Class A Common 1¢ par 08/08/1991
Charter permanently revoked 09/30/1999

REPAP ENTERPRISES INC (CANADA)
Acquired by UPM-Kymmene Corp. 10/16/2000
Each share Common no par exchanged for $0.20 cash

REPAROTECH INC (DE)
Name changed to Nextrata Energy Inc. 01/07/2010

REPCO INC (DE)
Chapter 11 bankruptcy proceedings terminated 12/18/1992
Stockholders' equity unlikely

REPEATER TECHNOLOGIES INC (DE)
Issue Information - 4,750,000 shares COM offered at $9 per share on 08/08/2000
Filed a petition under Chapter 7 Federal Bankruptcy Code 10/04/2002
Stockholders' equity unlikely

REPEATSEAT LTD (AB)
Placed into receivership 09/22/2009
Stockholders' equity unlikely

REPERIO EXPL INC (NV)
Name changed to Future Now Group, Inc. 07/24/2007
(See Future Now Group, Inc.)

REPETTI, INC.
Acquired by Candy Brands, Inc. in 1930 which was liquidated in 1934

REPHEX INC (BRITISH VIRGIN ISLANDS)
SEC revoked common stock registration 12/03/2015

REPLIDYNE INC (DE)
Issue Information - 4,500,000 shares COM offered at $10 per share on 06/28/2006
Recapitalized as Cardiovascular Systems, Inc. 02/26/2009
Each share Common $0.001 par exchanged for (0.1) share Common $0.001 par

REPLOGLE STEEL CO.
Acquired by Warren Foundry & Pipe Corp. 00/00/1927
Details not available

REPOLA OY (FINLAND)
ADR agreement terminated 4/30/96
Each Sponsored ADR for Ordinary exchanged for approximately $19.60 cash

REPORTER PUBLICATIONS, INC. (DE)
Advised in 1958 out of business
Charter cancelled for non-payment of taxes 4/1/59

REPOSSESSION AUCTION INC (DE)
Name changed to Latin American Casinos, Inc. 6/20/94
Latin American Casinos, Inc. name changed to NuWay Energy, Inc. 8/15/2001 which name changed to NuWay Medical, Inc. 10/29/2002 which recapitalized as BioLargo, Inc. 3/21/2007

REPRESENTATIVE TRUST SHARES
Trust terminated in 1941
Details not available

REPROGRAPHIC MATLS INC (DE)
Merged into Ormonde Holdings, Inc. 02/28/1978
Each share Common 1¢ par exchanged for $0.01 cash

REPROS THERAPEUTICS INC (DE)
Each share old Common $0.001 par exchanged for (0.25) share new Common $0.001 par 10/15/2010
Acquired by Allergan PLC 01/31/2018
Each share new Common $0.001 par exchanged for $0.67 cash

REPROTECH INC (DE)
Recapitalized as Universal Services Group, Inc. 05/11/1990
Each share Common 1¢ par exchanged for (0.16666666) share Common 6¢ par
(See Universal Services Group, Inc.)

REPROTECHNICS INC. (NY)
Completely liquidated 1/22/71
Each share Capital Stock $10 par exchanged for first and final distribution $0.62 cash

REPROX CORP (QC)
Under bankruptcy proceedings assets assigned for benefit of creditors 11/04/1974
No stockholders' equity

REPSOL INTL CAP LTD (CAYMAN ISLANDS)
7.45% Non-Cum. Guaranteed Preference Shares Ser. A $25 par called for redemption at $25 plus $0.20 accrued dividends on 02/08/2011

REPSOL YPF S A (SPAIN)
Sponsored ADR's for Ordinary Pts. 500 par changed to EUR 1 par 04/19/1999
Name changed from Repsol S.A. to Repsol YPF S.A. 06/28/2000 which name changed back to Repsol S.A. 06/12/2012

REPTRON ELECTRS INC (FL)
Plan of reorganization under Chapter 11 Federal Bankruptcy Code effective 2/3/2004
Each share old Common 1¢ par received (0.0389578) share new Common 1¢ par
Note: Certificates were not required to be surrendered and are without value
Acquired by Kimball Electronics Manufacturing, Inc. 2/15/2007
Each share new Common 1¢ par exchanged for $0.75 cash

REPUBLIC AIRCRAFT MFG CORP (BC)
Recapitalized as International Republic Aircraft Manufacturing Corp. 6/10/92
Each share Common no par exchanged for (0.2) share Common no par
International Republic Aircraft Maunfacturing Corp. name changed to Urban Juice & Soda Co. Ltd. (BC) 5/27/93 which reincorporated in Wyoming 12/31/99 which reincorporated in Washington as Jones Soda Co. 8/3/2000

REPUBLIC AIRCRAFT PRODUCTS CORP.
Acquired by Aviation Corp. on a (1.75) for (1) basis in 1940 which name was changed to Avco Maufacturing Corp. 3/25/47 which name was changed to Avco Corp. 4/10/59

REPUBLIC AIRLS INC (WI)
Merged into NWA Inc. 08/12/1986
Each share Common 20¢ par exchanged for $17 cash

REPUBLIC ALUM CO (TX)
Each share Common 50¢ par exchanged for (0.166666) share Common $3 par 11/7/75
Ceased operations 3/18/77
No stockholders' equity

REPUBLIC AMERN CORP (DE)
Merged into Penn Central Corp. 3/31/89
Each share Common 1¢ par exchanged for $15.75 cash

REPUBLIC AUTOMOTIVE PTS INC (DE)
Common 50¢ par split (5) for (4) by issuance of (0.25) additional share 06/30/1972
Common 50¢ par split (6) for (5) by issuance of (0.2) additional share 10/24/1975
Common 50¢ par split (6) for (5) by issuance of (0.2) additional share 10/15/1976
Common 50¢ par split (6) for (5) by issuance of (0.2) additional share 10/21/1977
Merged into Keystone Automotive Industries, Inc. 06/29/1998
Each share Common 50¢ par exchanged for (0.8) share Common no par
(See Keystone Automotive Industries, Inc.)

REPUBLIC AVIATION CORP. (DE)
Conv. 2nd Preferred called for redemption 10/19/1939
Common $1 par changed to 50¢ par and (1) additional share issued 12/29/1961
Stock Dividends - 10% 12/20/1952;

10% 12/22/1953; 10% 12/17/1954; 10% 12/29/1955
Name changed to RAC Corp. 10/01/1965
(See RAC Corp.)

REPUBLIC AWYS HLDGS INC (DE)
Plan of reorganization under Chapter 11 Federal Bankruptcy proceedings effective 04/30/2017
No stockholders' equity

REPUBLIC BANCORP INC (MI)
$2.25 Conv. Preferred Ser. A no par called for redemption 08/03/1992
Common $5 par split (5) for (4) by issuance of (0.25) additional share payable 09/11/1998 to holders of record 08/14/1998
Stock Dividends - 10% 12/01/1988; 10% 12/01/1989; 10% 11/30/1990; 10% 11/29/1991; 10% 10/30/1992; 10% 10/29/1993; 10% 12/02/1994; 10% 12/01/1995; 10% payable 12/02/1996 to holders of record 11/04/1996; 10% payable 12/05/1997 to holders of record 11/07/1997; 10% payable 01/07/2000 to holders of record 12/03/1999; 10% payable 12/01/2000 to holders of record 11/10/2000 Ex date - 11/08/2000; 10% payable 12/03/2001 to holders of record 11/09/2001 Ex date - 11/07/2001; 10% payable 12/02/2002 to holders of record 11/08/2002 Ex date - 11/06/2002; 10% payable 12/01/2003 to holders of record 11/07/2003 Ex date - 11/05/2003; 10% payable 12/03/2004 to holders of record 11/05/2004; 10% payable 12/02/2005 to holders of record 11/04/2005 Ex date - 11/02/2005
Merged into Citizens Banking Corp. 12/29/2006
Each share Common $5 par exchanged for (0.5146) share Common no par
Citizens Banking Corp. name changed to Citizens Republic Bancorp, Inc. 04/26/2007 which merged into FirstMerit Corp. 04/12/2013 which merged into Huntington Bancshares Inc. 08/16/2016

REPUBLIC BANCSHARES INC (FL)
Merged into BB&T Corp. 04/14/2004
Each share Common $2 par exchanged for (0.81) share Common $5 par

REPUBLIC BANCSHARES TEX INC (TX)
Each share Common $1 par held by holders of (2,100) shares or fewer exchanged for (1) share Ser. A Preferred $1 par 2/1/2006
Merged into Trustmark Corp. 8/25/2006
Each share Ser. A Preferred $1 par exchanged for (1.3908) shares Common no par
Each share Common $1 par exchanged for (1.3908) shares Common no par

REPUBLIC BK & TR CO (CHARLOTTE, NC)
Acquired by CCB Financial Corp. 10/31/86
Each share Common $10 par exchanged for (3.62) shares Common $5 par
CCB Financial Corp. merged into National Commerce Bancorporation 7/5/2000 which name changed to National Commerce Financial Corp. 4/25/2001 which merged into SunTrust Banks, Inc. 10/1/2004

REPUBLIC BK & TR CO (TULSA, OK)
Name changed to Sunbelt Bank & Trust Co. (Tulsa, OK) 03/01/1984
Sunbelt Bank & Trust Co. (Tulsa, OK) name changed to Central Bank & Trust of Tulsa (Tulsa, OK) 11/19/1984
(See Central Bank & Trust of Tulsa (Tulsa, OK))

REPUBLIC BK (CLEARWATER, FL)
Under plan of reorganization each share Common $2 par automatically became (1) share Republic Bancshares, Inc. Common $2 par 03/22/1996
Republic Bancshares, Inc. merged into BB&T Corp. 04/14/2004

REPUBLIC BANK (GARDENA, CA)
Reorganized as American Republic Bancorp 11/2/81
Each share Common $2.50 par exchanged for (1) share Common no par
American Republic Bancorp name changed to Republic Bank (Torrance, CA) 9/9/92
(See Republic Bank (Torrance, CA))

REPUBLIC BK (PHILADELPHIA, PA)
Merged into First Republic Bancorp, Inc. 6/7/96
Each share Common $5 par exchanged for (2.02) shares Common 1¢ par
First Republic Bancorp, Inc. name changed to Republic First Bancorp, Inc. 7/15/97

REPUBLIC BK (TORRANCE, CA)
Each share old Common no par exchanged for (1/15) share new Common no par 11/27/95
Merged into First Banks, Inc. 9/15/98
Each share new Common no par exchanged for $14.73 cash

REPUBLIC BKG CORP FLA MIAMI (FL)
Common 1¢ par split (6) for (5) by issuance of (0.2) additional share payable 01/31/1996 to holders of record 12/31/1995
Acquired by Union Planters Corp. 07/16/1999
Each share Common 1¢ par exchanged for $19.25 cash

REPUBLIC BRASS CORP. (MD)
Name changed to Revere Copper & Brass Inc. 11/12/29
(See Revere Copper & Brass Inc.)

REPUBLIC CAP GROUP INC (WI)
Acquired by TCF Financial Corp. 4/21/93
Each share Common 10¢ par exchanged for (1.217) shares Common 1¢ par

REPUBLIC CAPITAL SERVICE CORP.
Liquidated in 1929
Details not available

REPUBLIC CAP TR I (DE)
8.60% Trust Preferred Securities called for redemption at $25 on 3/31/2007

REPUBLIC CARLOADING & DISTRG INC (NY)
Name changed to Republic Freight Systems, Inc. 11/08/1972
(See Republic Freight Systems, Inc.)

REPUBLIC CASUALTY CO. (PA)
Merged into Pennsylvania Surety Corp. 00/00/1928
Details not available

REPUBLIC CEMENT CORP (PHILIPPINES)
Each share Common PHP 10 par exchanged for (1) share Class A Common PHP 10 par or Class B Common PHP 10 par 04/19/1979
Note: Only Philippine Nationals may hold Class A Common
Stock Dividend - 20% 09/15/1978
Name changed to Lafarge Republic Inc. 07/13/2012

REPUBLIC COLOR INC (NY)
Adjudicated bankrupt 07/01/1975
Stockholders' equity unlikely

REPUBLIC COMMUNICATIONS CORP (DE)
Recapitalized as Republic Entertainment Corp. 04/30/1997
Each share Common $0.0001 par exchanged for (0.02) share Common $0.0001 par
Republic Entertainment Corp. name changed to Goldstar Entertainment Media Inc. 09/02/1997
(See Goldstar Entertainment Media Inc.)

REPUBLIC CORP (DE)
Reincorporated 3/21/68
$1 Conv. Preferred $10 par called for redemption 2/15/68
State of incorporation changed from (NY) to (DE) 3/21/68
Common 50¢ par split (3) for (2) by issuance of (0.5) additional share 2/28/69
Each share Common 50¢ par exchanged for (0.2) share Common $2.50 par 5/23/75
Stock Dividend - 20% 10/3/79
Merged into Triton Group Ltd. 2/15/85
Each share Common $2.50 par exchanged for (1) share $1.20 Conv. Preferred Ser. C $1 par and $33 cash
(See Triton Group Ltd.)

REPUBLIC CORP (NV)
Merged into Republic Trinidad Corp. 5/13/2005
Each share Common $1 par exchanged for $58 cash

REPUBLIC COS GROUP INC (DE)
Issue Information - 6,000,000 shares COM offered at $14 per share on 08/03/2005
Merged into Delek Group Ltd. 12/7/2006
Each share Common 1¢ par exchanged for $20.40 cash

REPUBLIC COTTON MILLS
Merged into Stevens (J.P.) & Co., Inc. in 1946
Each old share exchanged for (5.95806) shares new Capital Stock $15 par
(See Stevens (J.P.) & Co., Inc.)

REPUBLIC DRILL & TOOL CO.
Name changed to Avildsen Tools & Machines, Inc. in 1949
(See Avildsen Tools & Machines, Inc.)

REPUBLIC ELECTR INDS CORP (NY)
Each share Common 10¢ par exchanged for (0.1) share Common $1 par 02/01/1966
Acquired by Heath Tecna Corp. 04/29/1969
Each share Common $1 par exchanged for (1.7832) shares Common no par
Heath Tecna Corp. name changed to Criton Corp. 07/01/1980
(See Criton Corp.)

REPUBLIC ELECTRIC POWER CO.
Suceeded by Republic Electric Power Corp. in 1932 which was dissolved in 1940

REPUBLIC ELECTRIC POWER CORP.
Dissolved in 1940

REPUBLIC ENGINEERED STEELS INC (DE)
Merged into RES Holding Corp. 9/21/98
Each share Common 1¢ par exchanged for $7.25 cash

REPUBLIC ENTMT CORP (DE)
Name changed to Goldstar Entertainment Media Inc. 09/02/1997
(See Goldstar Entertainment Media Inc.)

REPUBLIC ENVIRONMENTAL SYS INC (DE)
Common 1¢ par split (2) for (1) by issuance of (1) additional share payable 6/30/96 to holders of record 6/14/96
Name changed to International Alliance Services, Inc. 10/21/96
International Alliance Services, Inc. name changed to Century Business Services Inc. 12/23/97 which name changed to CBIZ, Inc. 8/1/2005

REPUBLIC FINANCE & INVESTMENT CO. (IN)
Acquired by General Discount Corp. (MI) 12/01/1932
Details not available

REPUBLIC FINL (OH)
Completely liquidated 08/11/1977
Each Share of Bene. Int. no par exchanged for first and final distribution of $3.95 cash

REPUBLIC FINANCIAL CORP. (CO)
Charter revoked for failure to pay franchise taxes 10/26/64

REPUBLIC FINL SVCS INC (TX)
Common $5 par split (3) for (1) by issuance of (2) additional shares 3/20/72
Common $5 par split (2) for (1) by issuance of (1) additional share 4/27/79
Merged into Winterthur Swiss Insurance Co. 12/9/82
Each share Common $5 par exchanged for $45.50 cash

REPUBLIC FIRE INSURANCE CO. OF AMERICA
Merged into Globe & Republic Insurance Co. of America 00/00/1931
Details not available

REPUBLIC FOIL & METAL MILLS, INC. (DE)
Name changed to Republic Foil Inc. 03/06/1959
Republic Foil Inc. merged into National Steel Corp. 12/31/1968 which reorganized as National Intergroup, Inc. 09/13/1983 which name changed to FoxMeyer Health Corp. 10/12/1994 which name changed to Avatex Corp. 03/07/1997
(See Avatex Corp.)

REPUBLIC FOIL INC (DE)
Merged into National Steel Corp. 12/31/1968
Each share Common $1 par exchanged for (0.5) share Capital Stock $5 par
National Steel Corp. reorganized as National Intergroup, Inc. 09/13/1983 which name changed to FoxMeyer Health Corp. 10/12/1994 which name changed to Avatex Corp. 03/07/1997
(See Avatex Corp.)

REPUBLIC FRANKLIN INC (DE)
Name changed to Franklin Capital Corp. (DE) 06/15/1983
(See Franklin Capital Corp. (DE))

REPUBLIC FRANKLIN LIFE INS CO (OH)
Name changed to Investors Fidelity Life Assurance Corp. 04/15/1977
(See Investors Fidelity Life Assurance Corp.)

REPUBLIC FREIGHT SYSTEMS, INC. (NY)
Dissolved by proclamation 09/27/1995

REPUBLIC GAS & URANIUM CORP. (DE)
No longer in existence having become inoperative and void for non-payment of taxes 7/1/57

REPUBLIC GAS CORP.
Reorganized as Republic Natural Gas Co. 00/00/1935
Details not available

REPUBLIC GEAR INDS INC (DE)
Stock Dividend - 100% 07/10/1969

Name changed to Republic
Automotive Parts, Inc. 05/01/1972
Republic Automotive Parts, Inc.
merged into Keystone Automotive
Industries, Inc. 06/29/1998
(See Keystone Automotive Industries, Inc.)

REPUBLIC GRAPHICS INC (NY)
Charter revoked for failure to file
reports and pay fees 12/15/1967

REPUBLIC GROUP INC (DE)
Name changed 10/27/95
Name changed from Republic
Gypsum Co. to Republic Group Inc.
10/27/95
$6 Conv. Preferred $100 par called
for redemption 6/15/78
Name changed to Republic Housing
Corp. 11/3/71 which name changed
back to Republic Gypsum Co.
11/22/77
Common $1 par split (2) for (1) by
issuance of (1) additional share
8/28/79
Common $1 par split (4) for (3) by
issuance of (1/3) additional share
5/27/83
Common $1 par split (2) for (1) by
issuance of (1) additional share
3/5/84
Common $1 par split (2) for (1) by
issuance of (1) additional share
3/29/85
Stock Dividend - 10% payable
3/14/97 to holders of record 2/28/97
Merged into Premier Construction
Products Statutory Trust 11/9/2000
Each share Common $1 par
exchanged for $19 cash

REPUBLIC HEALTH CORP (DE)
Name changed to OrNda HealthCorp
4/14/92
OrNda HealthCorp merged into Tenet
Healthcare Corp. 1/30/97

REPUBLIC HEALTH CORP OLD (DE)
Merged into REPH Acquisition Co.
08/22/1986
Each share Common 5¢ par
exchanged for $19.25 cash

REPUBLIC HLDGS CORP (DE)
Recapitalized as Republic
Communications Corp. 8/15/94
Each share Common $0.0001 par
exchanged for (0.005) share
Common $0.0001 par
Republic Communications Corp.
recapitalized as Republic
Entertainment Corp. 4/30/97

REPUBLIC HOUSING CORP. (DE)
Each share Class A Common $1 par
exchanged for (1) share Common
$1 par 1/16/71
Name changed to Republic Gypsum
Co. 11/22/77

REPUBLIC INDEMNITY CO. (AZ)
Each share Common $1.40 par
exchanged for $20.11 cash
06/18/1973
Preferred $2 par called for
redemption 06/30/1973
Public interest eliminated

REPUBLIC INDTY CO AMER (AZ)
Each share Common $2 par
exchanged for (2) shares Common
85¢ par 09/01/1961
Common 85¢ par changed to $1.40
par 05/21/1968
Name changed to Republic Indemnity
Co. 02/15/1973
(See Republic Indemnity Co.)

REPUBLIC INDL CORP (DE)
Merged into Vare Corp. 12/04/1967
Each share Common $1 par
exchanged for (1.25) shares
Common $2.50 par
Vare Corp. merged into Microdot Inc.
(CA) 01/31/1969 which
reincorporated in Delaware
07/02/1971
(See Microdot Inc. (DE))

REPUBLIC INDUSTRIES, INC. (DE)
5% Preferred Ser. A $25 par called for
redemption 02/10/1957
Public interest eliminated

REPUBLIC INDS INC (DE)
Common 1¢ par split (2) for (1) by
issuance of (1) additional share
payable 6/8/96 to holders of record
5/28/96
Name changed to AutoNation, Inc.
4/6/99

REPUBLIC INTERMODAL CORP (DE)
Completely liquidated 07/01/1979
Each share Common 1¢ par
exchanged for first and final
distribution of $0.2495 cash

REPUBLIC INTL CORP (DE)
Each share old Common 1¢ par
exchanged for (0.2) share new
Common 1¢ par 05/20/1992
Each (60) shares new Common 1¢
par exchanged for (1) share
Common $0.001 par 01/04/1993
Recapitalized as Investek Corp.
03/12/1997
Each share Common $0.001 par
exchanged for (0.001) share
Common $0.001 par
(See Investek Corp.)

REPUBLIC INTL CORP (UT)
Recapitalized as Axiom Security
Solutions, Inc. 10/02/1995
Each (233.33) shares Common
$0.005 par exchanged for (1) share
Common $0.005 par
(See Axiom Security Solutions, Inc.)

REPUBLIC INVESTING CORP. (NY)
Charter cancelled and proclaimed
dissolved for non-payment of taxes
12/16/46

REPUBLIC INVESTORS FUND, INC. (DE)
Common 25¢ par changed to 5¢ par
00/00/1938
Each share Common 5¢ par
exchanged for (0.05) share Common
$1 par 00/00/1940
Name changed to Axe-Houghton
Stock Fund, Inc. (DE) 00/00/1953
Axe-Houghton Stock Fund, Inc. (DE)
reincorporated in Maryland
09/13/1974 which reorganized as
Axe-Houghton Funds, Inc. Growth
Fund 10/31/1990
(See Axe-Houghton Funds, Inc.)

REPUBLIC INVS LIFE INS CO (IL)
Acquired by United Founders Life
Insurance Co. 4/25/70
Each share Common 10¢ par
exchanged for (0.091666) share
Common $1 par
(See United Founders Life Insurance Co.)

REPUBLIC IRON & STEEL CO.
Merged into Republic Steel Corp. in
1930
(See Republic Steel Corp.)

REPUBLIC LEASING INC (DE)
Reincorporated under the laws of
Washington as Westar Financial
Services Inc. 4/1/96
(See Westar Financial Services Inc.)

REPUBLIC LEASING VI (WA)
Charter expired 01/31/2009

REPUBLIC MAINTENANCE CORP (DE)
Name changed to American Home
Shield Corp. 09/29/1972
(See American Home Shield Corp.)

REPUBLIC METAL PRODS INC (NJ)
Ctfs. dated prior to 03/02/1970
Merged into Thermo National
Industries, Inc. 03/02/1970
Each share Common 50¢ par
exchanged for (0.8) share Common
15¢ par
(See Thermo National Industries, Inc.)

REPUBLIC METAL PRODS INC NEW (NJ)
Ctfs. dated after 12/23/74
Merged into RMP Metal Corp. 2/28/78
Each share Common 10¢ par
exchanged for $2 cash
$1.30 Class A Conv. Preferred $7 par
called for redemption 3/10/78
Public interest eliminated

REPUBLIC MOBILE HOMES CORP (DE)
Charter cancelled and declared
inoperative and void for
non-payment of taxes 3/1/78

REPUBLIC MTG INVS (MA)
Under plan of reorganization each
Share of Bene. Int. no par
automatically became (1) share
Thackeray Corp. 9/25/81
(See Thackeray Corp.)

REPUBLIC MOTOR TRUCK CO., INC.
Merged into La France-Republic
Corp. 00/00/1929
Details not available

REPUBLIC N Y CORP (MD)
Common $5 par split (3) for (1) by
issuance of (2) additional shares
08/12/1980
$3.125 Preferred no par called for
redemption 01/14/1986
Common $5 par split (3) for (2) by
issuance of (0.5) additional share
02/27/1986
$2.125 Preferred no par called for
redemption 04/15/1986
Floating Rate Preferred Ser. A no par
called for redemption 05/01/1987
Common $5 par split (3) for (2) by
issuance of (0.5) additional share
10/21/1991
Floating Rate Preferred Ser. B no par
called for redemption 07/01/1994
$3.375 Convertible Preferred no par
called for redemption 07/24/1995
Remarketed Preferred Ser. B 49 Day
Book Entry called for redemption
12/26/1996
Remarketed Preferred Ser. C 49 Day
Book Entry called for redemption
01/02/1997
Remarketed Preferred Ser. D 49 Day
Book Entry called for redemption
01/09/1997
Remarketed Preferred Ser. E 49 Day
Book Entry called for redemption
01/16/1997
Remarketed Preferred Ser. F 49 Day
Book Entry called for redemption
01/23/1997
Remarketed Preferred Ser. G 49 Day
Book Entry called for redemption
01/30/1997
Remarketed Preferred Ser. A 49 Day
Book Entry called for redemption
02/06/1997
$1.9375 Preferred no par called for
redemption 02/27/1997
Money Market Preferred no par called
for redemption at $100 on
11/20/1997
Common $5 par split (2) for (1) by
issuance of (1) additional share
payable 06/01/1998 to holders of
record 05/01/1998 Ex date -
06/02/1998
Merged into HSBC Holdings plc
12/31/1999
Each share Common $5 par
exchanged for $72 cash
Name changed to HSBC USA Inc.
01/04/2000

REPUBLIC NATL BANCSHARES INC (TX)
Name changed to Charter
Bancshares, Inc. 8/25/81
Charter Bancshares, Inc. merged into
NationsBank Corp. 5/24/96 which
reincorporated in Delaware as
BankAmerica Corp. (Old) 9/25/98
which merged into BankAmerica
Corp. (New) 9/30/98 which name
changed to Bank of America Corp.
4/28/99

REPUBLIC NATIONAL BANK (AUSTIN, TX)
Acquired by National Bancshares
Corp. of Texas 08/31/1981
Each share Common $7 par
exchanged for (4.4) shares Common
$5 par
(See National Bancshares Corp. of Texas)

REPUBLIC NATL BK (DALLAS, TX)
Each share Capital Stock $20 par
exchanged for (1-2/3) shares Capital
Stock $12 par 00/00/1953
Capital Stock $12 par changed to $6
par and (1) additional share issued
11/26/1965
Stock Dividends - 25% 11/06/1959;
10% 05/01/1970
Reorganized as Republic of Texas
Corp. 05/09/1974
Each share Capital Stock $6 par
exchanged for (1) share Common
$5 par
Republic of Texas Corp. name
changed to RepublicBank Corp.
06/30/1982 which merged into First
RepublicBank Corp. 06/06/1987
(See First RepublicBank Corp.)

REPUBLIC NATL BK (MIAMI, FL)
Stock Dividends - 10% 01/15/1969;
19% 12/31/1980
93% acquired by Republic Banking
Corp. of Florida through voluntary
exchange offer which expired
11/30/1982
Public interest eliminated

REPUBLIC NATL BK (NEW YORK, NY)
Common $10 par changed to $5 par
and (1) additional share issued
02/27/1970
Stock Dividend - 50% 04/21/1971
Reorganized as Republic New York
Corp. 07/01/1974
Each share Common $5 par
exchanged for (1) share Common
$5 par
(See Republic New York Corp.)

REPUBLIC NATIONAL BANK (SAN DIEGO, CA)
Merged into Union Bank (Los
Angeles, CA) 11/12/1965
Each share Capital Stock $20 par
exchanged for (0.68) share Capital
Stock $7.50 par
(See Union Bank (Los Angeles, CA))

REPUBLIC NATL BK (TULSA, OK)
Common $10 par changed to $5 par
and (1) additional share issued
02/28/1969
Name changed to Republic Bank &
Trust Co. (Tulsa, OK) 05/10/1974
Republic Bank & Trust Co. (Tulsa,
OK) name changed to Sunbelt Bank
& Trust Co. (Tulsa, OK) 03/01/1984
which name changed to Central
Bank & Trust of Tulsa (Tulsa, OK)
11/19/1984
(See Central Bank & Trust of Tulsa (Tulsa, OK))

REPUBLIC NATIONAL BANK OF CALIFORNIA (LOS ANGELES, CA)
Recapitalized as Republic National
Bank & Trust Co. (Los Angeles)
7/15/70
Each share Common $10 par
exchanged for (4) shares Common
$2.50 par

REPUBLIC NATL LIFE INS CO (TX)
Each share Capital Stock $10 par
exchanged for (15) shares Capital
Stock $2 par to effect a (5) for (1)
split and a 200% stock dividend
10/29/56
Each share Capital Stock $2 par
exchanged for (2.5) shares Capital
Stock $1 par to effect a (2) for (1)
split and a 25% stock dividend
3/22/60

REP-RES   **FINANCIAL INFORMATION, INC.**

Stock Dividends - 20% 4/6/62; 50% 4/5/63; 10% 4/1/64; 15% 1/15/65; 25% 4/8/66; 10% 4/14/67
Merged into Gulf United Corp. 4/6/81
Each share Capital Stock $1 par exchanged for (1) share Common $1 par and $15 cash
(See Gulf United Corp.)

REPUBLIC NATURAL GAS CO. (DE)
Each share Common $1 par exchanged for (0.5) share Common $2 par in 1939
Stock Dividends - 100% 10/15/47; 100% 4/30/54
Liquidation completed
Each share Common $2 par exchanged for initial distribution of $46 cash 1/25/62
Each share Common $2 par received second distribution of $2.45 cash 11/28/62
Each share Common $2 par received third and final distribution of $0.725 cash 1/28/66

REPUBLIC OIL & MINING CORP. (UT)
Merged into Entrada Corp. on a (1/49) for (1) basis 1/17/58
Entrada Corp. recapitalized as Pacific Energy Corp. 1/14/76 which name changed to Aimco, Inc. 9/1/77 which recapitalized as Colt Technology, Inc. 3/31/83

REPUBLIC ORES & MNG LTD (ON)
Recapitalized as Sumach Resources Inc. 6/5/81
Each share Common $1 par exchanged for (2) shares Common no par
(See Sumach Resources Inc.)

REPUBLIC PETROLEUM CO.
Dissolved in 1950

REPUBLIC PICTURES CORP. (NY)
Name changed to Republic Corp. (NY) 4/6/60
Republic Corp. (NY) reincorporated under the laws of Delaware 3/21/68 which merged into Triton Group Ltd. 2/15/85
(See Triton Group Ltd.)

REPUBLIC PICTURES CORP (DE)
Class A 1¢ par reclassified as Common 1¢ par 7/27/93
Each share Class B 1¢ par exchanged for (1.2) shares Common 1¢ par 7/27/93
Merged into Spelling Entertainment Group, Inc. (FL) 4/26/94
Each share Common 1¢ par exchanged for $13 cash

REPUBLIC PORTLAND CEMENT CO.
Name changed to Longhorn Portland Cement Co. in 1937
Longhorn Portland Cement Co. merged into Kaiser Cement & Gypsum Corp. 11/10/65 which name changed to Kaiser Cement Corp. (Calif.) 5/1/79 which reincorporated in Delaware 5/4/82
(See Kaiser Cement Corp. (Del.))

REPUBLIC POWDERED METALS INC (OH)
Name changed to RPM, Inc. (OH) 11/09/1971
RPM, Inc. (OH) reincorporated in Delaware as RPM International Inc. 10/15/2002

REPUBLIC PPTY TR (MD)
Issue Information - 20,000,000 shares COM offered at $12 per share on 12/20/2005
Merged into Liberty Property Trust 10/04/2007
Each share Common 1¢ par exchanged for $14.70 cash

REPUBLIC RAILWAY & LIGHT CO.
Dissolved in 1927

REPUBLIC RLTY MTG CORP (IL)
Merged into Conill Corp. 06/16/1970
Each share Common $1 par exchanged for (0.8764) share Common $10 par
Conill Corp. name changed to Continental Illinois Corp. 03/27/1972 which reorganized as Continental Illinois Holding Corp. 09/27/1984
(See Continental Illinois Holding Corp.)

REPUBLIC RES CORP (OK)
Each share Common 1¢ par exchanged for (0.1) share Common 10¢ par 1/9/87
Name changed to Republic Waste Industries Inc. (OK) 2/14/90
Republic Waste Industries Inc. (OK) reincorporated in Delaware 5/30/91 which name changed to AutoNation, Inc. 4/6/99

REPUBLIC RES INC (NV)
SEC revoked common stock registration 08/31/2009
Stockholders' equity unlikely

REPUBLIC RES INC (TX)
Charter forfeited for non-payment of franchise tax 12/05/1988

REPUBLIC RES LTD (AB)
Merged into 100692 Holdings Ltd. 10/14/1977
Each share Common no par exchanged for $1.50 cash

REPUBLIC RUBBER CORP. (NY)
Charter revoked for failure to file reports and pay fees 11/08/1918

REPUBLIC SVGS & LN ASSN WIS MILWAUKEE (WI)
Under plan of reorganization each share Common 10¢ par automatically became (1) share Republic Capital Group, Inc. Common 10¢ par 12/23/87
Republic Capital Group, Inc. acquired by TCF Financial Corp. 4/21/93

REPUBLIC SEC FINL CORP (FL)
Name changed 11/25/1992
Name changed from Republic Savings Financial Corp. to Republic Security Financial Corp. 11/25/1992
7.50% Conv. Preferred Ser. A no par called for redemption 07/26/1996
7% Conv. Preferred Ser. C no par called for redemption at $10 on 04/30/1998
Stock Dividend - 10% 04/15/1993
Merged into Wachovia Corp. (New) (Ctfs. dated between 05/20/1991 and 09/01/2001) 03/01/2001
Each share Common 1¢ par exchanged for (0.1245) share Common $5 par
Wachovia Corp. (New) (Ctfs. dated between 05/20/1991 and 09/01/2001) merged into Wachovia Corp. (Ctfs. dated after 09/01/2001) 09/01/2001 which merged into Wells Fargo & Co. (New) 12/31/2008

REPUBLIC SERVICE CORP. (DE)
Reorganized in 1948
Each share $6 Preferred no par exchanged for (4) shares Common $10 par
Common no par had no equity and was declared to be without value
Reorganized under the laws of Pennsylvania in 1953
Each share Common $10 par exchanged for (1) share Republic Service Corp. (PA) Common $5 par and (2/7) share General Public Utilities Corp. (NY) Common $5 par
(See each company's listing)

REPUBLIC SERVICE CORP. (PA)
Liquidation completed
Each share Common $5 par exchanged for initial distribution of (0.87) share Allegheny Power System, Inc. Common $5 par 01/29/1962
Each share Common $5 par received second and final distribution of (0.03) share Allegheny Power System, Inc. Common $5 par 02/03/1964
Allegheny Power System, Inc. name changed to Allegheny Energy, Inc. 09/16/1997 which merged into FirstEnergy Corp. 02/25/2011

REPUBLIC STL CORP (NJ)
6% Preferred called for redemption 03/30/1945
6% Prior Preference Ser. A called for redemption 08/31/1954
Common no par changed to $10 par and (1) additional share issued 06/03/1955
Merged into LTV Corp. (Old) 06/29/1984
Each share $5.25 Conv. Preferred no par exchanged for (1) share $5.25 Conv. Preferred Ser. C $1 par
Each share Common $10 par exchanged for (0.3) share $1.25 Conv. Preferred Ser. D $1 par and (1.5) shares Common 50¢ par
LTV Corp. (Old) reorganized as LTV Corp. (New) 06/28/1993
(See LTV Corp. (New))

REPUBLIC SUPPLY CO. OF CALIFORNIA (CA)
Common no par changed to $10 par 00/00/1944
Stock Dividends - 10% 10/12/1956; 10% 02/08/1960
Name changed to Pike Corp. of America 09/03/1965
Pike Corp. of America merged into Fluor Corp. Ltd. 01/02/1969 which name changed to Fluor Corp. (CA) 05/22/1969 which reincorporated in Delaware 07/14/1978 which name changed to Massey Energy Co. 11/30/2000 which merged into Alpha Natural Resources, Inc. 06/01/2011
(See Alpha Natural Resources, Inc.)

REPUBLIC SYS & PROGRAMMING INC (TX)
Assets sold for benefit of creditors 10/09/1973
No stockholders' equity

REPUBLIC TECHNOLOGY FD INC (DE)
Name changed to Equity Progress Fund, Inc. 08/26/1970
Equity Progress Fund, Inc. merged into Equity Growth Fund of America Inc. 08/01/1975 which merged into American General Enterprise Fund, Inc. 12/31/1979 which name changed to American Capital Enterprise Fund, Inc. (MD) 09/09/1983 which reincorporated in Delaware as Van Kampen American Capital Enterprise Fund 08/03/1995 which name changed to Van Kampen Enterprise Fund 08/31/1998

REPUBLIC TEX BRANDS INC (NV)
Name changed to Totally Hemp Crazy Inc. 08/05/2014
Totally Hemp Crazy Inc. name changed to Rocky Mountain High Brands Inc. 10/16/2015

REPUBLIC TEX CORP (DE)
Common $5 par split (3) for (2) by issuance of (0.5) additional share 10/16/78
Stock Dividend - 20% 12/7/81
Name changed to RepublicBank Corp. 6/30/82
RepublicBank Corp. merged into First RepublicBank Corp. 6/6/87
(See First RepublicBank Corp.)

REPUBLIC-TRANSCON INDUSTRIES, INC. (MI)
Acquired by Briggs Manufacturing Co. 10/19/1965
Each share Common no par exchanged for (0.75) share Common $3.50 par
Briggs Manufacturing Co. name changed to Panacon Corp. 04/09/1970
(See Panacon Corp.)

REPUBLIC URANIUM CO. (UT)
Each (5) shares Common 1¢ par exchanged for (1) share Common 5¢ par 2/6/56
Name changed to Republic Oil & Mining Corp. in 1957
Republic Oil & Mining Corp. merged into Entrada Corp. 1/17/58 which recapitalized as Pacific Energy Corp. 1/14/76 which name changed to Aimco, Inc. 9/1/77 which recapitalized as Colt Technology, Inc. 3/31/83

REPUBLIC VAN LINES INC (MD)
Stock Dividend - 10% 09/01/1971
Ceased operations 06/21/1979
No stockholders' equity

REPUBLIC WASTE INDS INC (DE)
Reincorporated 5/30/91
Common 10¢ par changed to 1¢ par 3/23/90
State of incorporation changed from (OK) to (DE) 5/30/91
Name changed to Republic Industries Inc. 11/27/95
Republic Industries Inc. name changed to AutoNation, Inc. 4/6/99

REPUBLICBANK CORP (DE)
Under plan of merger name changed to First RepublicBank Corp. 06/06/1987
(See First RepublicBank Corp.)

REPUBLIK MEDIA & ENTMT LTD (DE)
Name changed to Global Karaoke Network, Inc. 08/03/2011
Global Karaoke Network, Inc. name changed to Anchorage International Holdings Corp. 10/22/2013

REQUEST INCOME TR (AB)
Acquired by Pulse Data Inc. 02/06/2002
For Canadian Residents: Each Trust Unit no par exchanged for (2.1) shares Common no par
For Non-Canadian Residents: Each Trust Unit no par exchanged for $2.415 cash
Pulse Data Inc. name changed to Pulse Seismic Inc. 05/28/2009

REQUEST SEISMIC SURVEYS LTD (AB)
Reorganized as Request Income Trust 03/20/2001
Each share Common no par exchanged for (0.5) share Trust Unit no par
Request Income Trust acquired by Pulse Data Inc. 02/06/2002 which name changed to Pulse Seismic Inc. 05/28/2009

RERAISE GAMING CORP (NV)
Name changed to Star Ally Inc. 09/13/2016
Star Ally Inc. name changed to DKG Capital Inc. 03/24/2017

RES-CARE INC (KY)
Common no par split (3) for (2) by issuance of (0.5) additional share payable 06/04/1996 to holders of record 05/24/1996
Common no par split (3) for (2) by issuance of (0.5) additional share payable 06/04/1998 to holders of record 05/22/1998
Acquired by Onex Rescare Acquisition, L.L.C. 12/22/2010
Each share Common no par exchanged for $13.25 cash

RES INTL INC (CANADA)
Merged into Online Direct Inc. 04/01/1999
Each share Common no par exchanged for (0.42) share Common no par
(See Online Direct Inc.)

RES INVT CORP (MD)
Merged into Price (T. Rowe) Tax-Free Funds Income Fund 09/22/1986
Each share Common $2.50 par exchanged for (1.54801) shares Capital Stock $1 par

RES-Q INTL INC (DE)
Charter cancelled and declared inoperative and void for non-payment of taxes 03/01/1990

RESALAB INC (DE)
Name changed to United Coin Services, Inc. 04/30/1973
(See United Coin Services, Inc.)

RESCO, INC. (MN)
Merged into Interplastic Corp. 5/1/62
Each share Common 10¢ par exchanged for (1) share Common 10¢ par
(See Interplastic Corp.)

RESCO INTL INC (NV)
Charter revoked for failure to file reports and pay fees 02/01/1985

RESCON TECHNOLOGY CORP (NV)
Reorganized 12/13/1999
Reorganized from (WY) to under the laws of (NV) 12/13/1999
Each share Common $0.0001 par exchanged for (0.00014285) share Common $0.0001 par
Note: No holder of (10) or more pre-split shares will receive fewer than (100) shares
Holders of (9) or fewer shares were not affected by the reverse split
Each share new Common $0.0001 par exchanged again for (0.16949152) share new Common $0.0001 par 12/17/2004
Name changed to Nayna Networks, Inc. 04/04/2005
(See Nayna Networks, Inc.)

RESDEL INDS (CA)
Name changed 05/01/1972
Name changed from Resdel Engineering Corp. to Resdel Industries 05/01/1972
Stock Dividend - 10% 02/29/1987
Charter suspended for failure to file reports and pay fees 05/19/1993

RESE ENGINEERING CO. (PA)
Name changed to Rese Industries, Inc. and Common $1 par changed to 10¢ par 4/25/63
Rese Industries, Inc. adjudicated bankrupt in September 1966

RESE INDS INC (PA)
Assets liquidated for benefit of creditors 09/00/1966
No stockholders' equity

RESEARCH CAP FD INC (CA)
Name changed to Franklin Gold Fund (CA) 10/26/83
Franklin Gold Fund (CA) reincorporated in Delaware as Franklin Gold & Precious Metals Fund 4/10/2000

RESEARCH COTTRELL INC (NJ)
Capital Stock $2 par changed to $1 par and (2) additional shares issued 09/10/1968
Merged into R-C Holding Inc. 07/13/1987
Each share Capital Stock $1 par exchanged for $43 cash

RESEARCH ENGINEERS INC (DE)
Common 1¢ par split (2) for (1) by issuance of (1) additional share payable 02/07/2000 to holders of record 01/31/2000
Name changed to netGuru, Inc. 03/03/2000
netGuru, Inc. name changed to BPO Management Services, Inc. (DE) 12/18/2006 which merged into BPO Management Services, Inc. (PA) 12/30/2008
(See BPO Management Services, Inc. (PA))

RESEARCH EQUITY FD INC (MD)
Reincorporated 09/09/1973
State of incorporation changed from (DE) to (MD) 09/09/1973
Reincorporated under the laws of California as Franklin Equity Fund 10/10/1984

RESEARCH FDG INC (NV)
Recapitalized as Goldmark Industries, Inc. 3/27/2006
Each share Common 1¢ par exchanged for (0.001) share Common 1¢ par

RESEARCH FRONTIERS INC (NY)
Reincorporated under the laws of Delaware 5/5/89

RESEARCH GAMES INC (NY)
Name changed to Athol Industries, Inc. 7/6/79
Athol Industries, Inc. name changed to A.R.C. Toys Inc. 1/1/90
(See A.R.C. Toys Inc.)

RESEARCH IN MOTION LTD (ON)
Issue Information - 6,000,000 shares COM offered at $102 per share on 10/26/2000
Common no par split (2) for (1) by issuance of (1) additional share payable 06/04/2004 to holders of record 05/27/2004 Ex date - 06/07/2004
Common no par split (3) for (1) by issuance of (2) additional shares payable 08/20/2007 to holders of record 08/17/2007 Ex date - 08/21/2007
Name changed to BlackBerry Ltd. 07/18/2013

RESEARCH INC NEW (MN)
Reorganized 10/01/1966
Each share Common 10¢ par exchanged for (0.1) share MTS Systems Corp. Common 50¢ par and (0.1) share Research, Inc. (MN) (New) Common 50¢ par
Common 50¢ par split (5) for (4) by issuance of (0.25) additional share payable 01/08/1998 to holders of record 12/31/1997
Stock Dividends - 200% 02/07/1969; 100% 06/30/1978; 100% 11/14/1980
Plan of reorganization under Chapter 11 Federal Bankruptcy Code effective 12/13/2003
No stockholders' equity

RESEARCH INDUSTRIES, INC. (MN)
Merged into RII, Inc. 12/24/86
Each share Common 20¢ par exchanged for $0.20 cash

RESEARCH INVESTING CORP (NJ)
Reorganized 06/22/1959
Reorganized from (IN) to under the laws of New Jersey 06/22/1959
Each share Preferred no par exchanged for (9) shares Capital Stock $1 par
Each share Capital Stock $1 par exchanged for (1) share new Capital Stock $1 par
Name changed to Lexington Research Investing Corp. 04/18/1967
Lexington Research Investing Corp. name changed to Lexington Research Fund, Inc. (NJ) 04/28/1969 which reincorporated in Maryland as Lexington Growth & Income Fund, Inc. 04/30/1991 which name changed to Pilgrim Growth & Income Fund, Inc. 07/26/2000 which name changed to ING Large Company Value Fund, Inc. 03/01/2002
(See ING Large Company Value Fund, Inc.)

RESEARCH INVESTMENT CORP. (DE)
Merged into Equity Corp. (Old) 05/13/1931
Each share 6% Preferred $50 par exchanged for (1) share Preferred
Each share Common no par exchanged for (1.2) shares Common
(See Equity Corp. (Old))

RESEARCH MED INC (UT)
Name changed 12/12/95
Common $1 par changed to 50¢ par and (1) additional share issued 7/20/83
Common 50¢ par split (3) for (2) by issuance of (0.5) additional share 12/15/91
Name changed from Research Industries Corp. to Research Medical Inc. 12/12/95
Merged into Baxter International Inc. 3/14/97
Each share Common 50¢ par exchanged for (0.4985) share Common $1 par

RESEARCH PARTNERS INTL INC (DE)
Name changed to Firebrand Financial Group, Inc. 07/27/2000
(See Firebrand Financial Group, Inc.)

RESEARCH RES INC (DE)
Charter cancelled and declared inoperative and void for non-payment of taxes 03/01/1985

RESEARCH SPECIALTIES CO. (CA)
Name changed to RSCO Liquidating Corp. 8/20/64 which completed liquidation 7/22/65

RESEC INC (UT)
Charter expired by time limitation 2/13/2002

RESERS FINE FOODS INC (OR)
Common $1 par changed to 25¢ par and (3) additional shares issued 10/30/1961
Common 25¢ par split (3) for (2) by issuance of (0.5) additional share 06/26/1972
Acquired by RAI Acquisition Inc. 11/06/1987
Each share Common 25¢ par exchanged for $12.50 cash

RESERVE BANCORP INC (PA)
Name changed to RSV Bancorp, Inc. 07/01/2004
(See RSV Bancorp, Inc.)

RESERVE ENERGY & CAP CORP (DE)
Charter cancelled and declared inoperative and void for non-payment of taxes 3/1/93

RESERVE EXPL CO (CO)
Each share Common 1¢ par exchanged for (0.2) share Common 5¢ par 07/30/1984
Each share old Common 5¢ par exchanged for (0.4) share new Common 5¢ par 12/01/1994
SEC revoked common stock registration 10/20/2009
Stockholders' equity unlikely

RESERVE FINANCE CORP. (CO)
Declared defunct in 1961
No stockholders' equity

RESERVE FUND
Dissolved and liquidated in 1948

RESERVE INSURANCE CO. (IL)
Each share Capital Stock $10 par exchanged for (2) shares Capital Stock $5 par in August 1947
Capital Stock $5 par changed to $4 par in December 1947
Capital Stock $4 par changed to $2.50 par in 1952
Capital Stock $2.50 par changed to $3.50 par 4/14/60
Capital Stock $3.50 par changed to $2 par and (0.5) additional share issued 5/19/67
Stock Dividends - 20% 9/9/55; 10% 12/31/55; 25% 5/24/57; 10% 12/31/65
Acquired by American Reserve Corp. 12/21/67
Each share Capital Stock $2 par exchanged for (1) share Common $2 par
(See American Reserve Corp.)

RESERVE INVESTING CORP.
Liquidation completed in 1946

RESERVE NATL INS CO (OK)
Each share Common 10¢ par exchanged for (0.1) share Common $1 par 12/2/74
Each share Common $1 par exchanged for (0.01) share Common $100 par 7/16/82
Note: In effect holders received $10 cash per share and public interest was eliminated

RESERVE OIL & GAS CO (CA)
Common $1 par split (2) for (1) by issuance of (1) additional share 02/27/1956
5.25% Conv. Preferred Ser. A $25 par called for redemption 09/07/1976
5.25% Conv. Preferred Ser. B $25 par called for redemption 09/07/1976
5.25% Conv. Preferred Ser. C $25 par called for redemption 02/28/1977
5.25% Conv. Preferred Ser. D $25 par called for redemption 02/28/1977
Stock Dividend - 100% 05/18/1961
Merged into Getty Oil Co. 01/23/1980
Each share $1.75 Conv. Preferred $1 par exchanged for $51.10 cash
Each share Common $1 par exchanged for $35 cash

RESERVE OIL & MINERALS CORP (NM)
Name changed to Reserve Industries Corp. 02/17/1987

RESERVE RESOURCES CORP.
Dissolved in 1936

RESERVE RTY CORP (CANADA)
Merged into PrimeWest Energy Trust 07/27/2000
Each share Common no par exchanged for (0.065) Trust Unit no par
(See PrimeWest Energy Trust)

RESERVENET INC (DE)
Name changed to Casino Entertainment Television, Inc. 07/26/2004
Casino Entertainment Television, Inc. reorganized as Ouvo, Inc. 05/06/2005 which reorganized as Trustcash Holdings, Inc. 06/13/2007

RESERVOIR MINERALS INC (BC)
Merged into Nevsun Resources Ltd. 06/24/2016
Each share Common no par exchanged for (2) shares Common no par and $2 cash
Note: Unexchanged certificates will be cancelled and become without value 06/24/2019

RESERVOIR PERFORMANCE INC (CO)
Administratively dissolved 11/01/2000

RESHONE INTL INVT GROUP LTD (DE)
Recapitalized as Storybook Entertainment Inc. 4/24/96
Each share Common $0.0006 par exchanged for (0.02) share Common $0.0006 par

RESHOOT & EDIT (NV)
Each share Common $0.001 par received distribution of (1) share Reshoot Production Co. Common $0.001 par payable 01/30/2008 to holders of record 01/21/2008
Ex date - 01/31/2008
Name changed to Bill The Butcher, Inc. 06/04/2010
(See Bill The Butcher, Inc.)

RESHOOT PRODTN CO (NV)
Each share old Common $0.001 par exchanged for (0.08333333) share new Common $0.001 par 09/15/2009

Note: No holder will receive fewer than (100) post-split shares
New Common $0.001 par split (2) for (1) by issuance of (1) additional share payable 06/09/2010 to holders of record 06/02/2010 Ex date - 06/10/2010
Each share new Common $0.001 par received distribution of (1.4) shares JA Energy Common $0.001 par payable 01/31/2011 to holders of record 01/27/2011 Ex date - 02/01/2011
Name changed to Smack Sportswear 07/25/2012
Smack Sportswear name changed to Almost Never Films Inc. 03/02/2016

RESIDENTIAL EQUITIES REAL ESTATE INVT TR (ON)
Each Instalment Receipt plus final payment of $4 cash received (1) Unit prior to 4/27/98
Merged into Canadian Apartment Properties Real Estate Investment Trust 6/1/2004
Each Unit exchanged for either (1.216) Trust Units or $18.60 cash
Note: Option to elect to receive cash expired 3/31/2004
Cash electors received Trust Units for 37.7% of holdings and 62.3% cash for the balance

RESIDENTIAL MTG INVTS INC (MD)
Completely liquidated 11/05/1991
Each share Common 1¢ par exchanged for first and final distribution of (0.3778) share American Southwest Mortgage Investments Corp. Common 1¢ par and $0.25 cash
American Southwest Mortgage Investments Corp. name changed to ASR Investments Corp. 06/23/1992 which merged into United Dominion Realty Trust, Inc. (VA) 03/27/1998 which reincorporated in Maryland 06/11/2003 which name changed to UDR, Inc. 03/14/2007

RESIDENTIAL RESORT DEV LTD (BAHAMAS)
Reorganized as RRD Ltd. 9/9/71
Each share Capital Stock B 10¢ par exchanged for (0.166667) share Capital Stock B 60¢ par and (0.083333) Capital Stock Purchase Warrant expiring 6/30/81
(See RRD Ltd.)

RESIDENTIAL RES MTG INVT CORP (MD)
Plan of reorganization under Chapter 11 Federal Bankruptcy proceedings confirmed 08/18/1993
Stockholders' equity unlikely

RESIDEX CORP (DE)
Merged into Sun Ventures, Inc. 09/05/1974
Each share Common 1¢ par exchanged for $2 cash

RESIDUAL COM INC (DE)
Charter cancelled and declared inoperative and void for non-payment of taxes 03/01/2001

RESIDUAL CORP (DE)
Recapitalized as Residual.com Inc. 08/30/1999
Each share Common $0.0001 par exchanged for (0.00004) share Common $0.0001 par
Note: Holders of (25,000) or fewer shares received $0.04 cash per share
(See Residual.com Inc.)

RESIDUUM RECLAMATION CORP.
Bankrupt in 1931

RESIFLEX LABORATORY, INC. (CA)
Liquidation completed 01/00/1965
Each share Capital Stock $1 par exchanged for (0.8) share Cutter Laboratories, Inc. Class A Common $1 par
(See Cutter Laboratories, Inc.)

RESILIENT RES LTD (AB)
Merged into Guardian Exploration Inc. 4/21/2006
Each share Common no par exchanged for (0.154376) share Common no par

RESIN SYS INC (AB)
Name changed to RS Technologies Inc. 06/23/2010
(See RS Technologies Inc.)

RESISTANCE WELDER CORP (MI)
Name changed to RWC, Inc. 02/22/1979

RESISTO CHEM INC (DE)
Adjudicated bankrupt 11/00/1964
No stockholders' equity

RESISTOFLEX CORP (NY)
Each share 6% Preferred $100 par exchanged for (36.25) shares Common $1 par 00/00/1944
Each share Common no par exchanged for (55) shares Common $1 par 00/00/1944
5% Preferred Ser. A $25 par called for redemption 04/11/1957
Common $1 par split (2) for (1) by issuance of (1) additional share 08/12/1977
Stock Dividend - 25% 06/25/1959
Merged into UMC Industries, Inc. 05/31/1978
Each share Common $1 par exchanged for $22 cash

RESITRON LABORATORIES, LTD. (DE)
Name changed to Beisinger Industries Corp. and Common 25¢ par changed to 1¢ par 11/28/67
(See Beisinger Industries Corp.)

RESNICK WORLDWIDE INC (DE)
Recapitalized as Standard Brands of America Inc. 06/19/1995
Each share Common $0.00001 par exchanged for (0.01) share Common $0.0001 par
Standard Brands of America Inc. name changed to Lionshare Group, Inc. 05/07/1998
(See Lionshare Group, Inc.)

RESOLUTE BAY TRADING CO., LTD. (CANADA)
Charter cancelled for failure to file reports 5/6/72

RESOLUTE CORP (ON)
Recapitalized 11/8/65
Recapitalized 7/26/88
Recapitalized from Resolute Oil & Gas Co. Ltd. to Resolute Petroleums Ltd. 11/8/65
Each share Capital Stock $1 par exchanged for (0.2) share Common no par
Recapitalized from Resolute Petroleums Ltd. to Resolute Corp. 7/26/88
Each share Common no par exchanged for (0.1) share Common no par
Trustee discharged in September 2002
No stockholders' equity

RESOLUTE ENERGY INC (AB)
Plan of arrangement effective 4/29/2005
Each share Common no par exchanged for (0.338) Esprit Energy Trust Class A Trust Unit, (0.2857143) share Cordero Energy Inc. Common no par and (0.2857143) Common Stock Purchase Warrant expiring 5/30/2005
(See each company's listing)

RESOLUTE LTD (AUSTRALIA)
ADR agreement terminated 03/11/2002
Each Sponsored ADR for Ordinary exchanged for $0.367 cash

RESOLUTE ONCOLOGY INC (NV)
Each share old Common $0.001 par exchanged for (5.5) shares new Common $0.001 par 02/01/2013
Name changed to BestnPet, Inc. 04/17/2018

RESOLUTE RES LTD (BC)
Name changed to European Garnet Ltd. 01/04/1994
European Garnet Ltd. recapitalized as Indo Metals Ltd. 12/16/1996 which recapitalized as Blue Lagoon Ventures Inc. 03/14/2001 which recapitalized as VMX Resources Inc. 12/08/2004 which name changed to Monster Uranium Corp. 09/07/2007

RESOLUTE SAMANTHA LTD (AUSTRALIA)
Name changed to Resolute Ltd. 11/29/1996
(See Resolute Ltd.)

RESOLUTION ENERGY INC (AB)
Recapitalized as Resolution Resources Ltd. 11/20/2001
Each share Common no par exchanged for (1/3) share Common no par
Resolution Resources Ltd. merged into Berens Energy Ltd. 11/19/2003
(See Berens Energy Ltd.)

RESOLUTION RES LTD (AB)
Merged into Berens Energy Ltd. 11/19/2003
Each share Common no par exchanged for (0.465) share Common no par and $0.34 cash
(See Berens Energy Ltd.)

RESOLVE BUSINESS OUTSOURCING INCOME FD (ON)
Merged into Davis + Henderson Income Fund 07/31/2009
Each Trust Unit no par automatically became (0.285) Unit
Davis + Henderson Income Fund reorganized as Davis + Henderson Corp. 01/04/2011 which name changed to DH Corp. 05/08/2014
(See DH Corp.)

RESOLVE STAFFING INC (NV)
Each share old Common $0.0001 par exchanged for (0.2) share new Common $0.0001 par 12/28/2004
New Common $0.0001 par changed to $0.001 par 01/13/2011
Recapitalized as Choose Rain, Inc. 02/06/2014
Each share Common $0.001 par exchanged for (0.01) share Common $0.001 par
Choose Rain, Inc. name changed to Rooshine Inc. 09/21/2017

RESONATE INC (DE)
Issue Information - 4,000,000 shares COM offered at $21 per share on 08/02/2000
Merged into GTG Acquisition Corp. 4/1/2003
Each share Common $0.0001 par exchanged for $1.94 cash

RESOQUEST RES CORP (AB)
Recapitalized 06/09/1992
Recapitalized from ResoQuest Energy Corp. to ResoQuest Resources Ltd. 06/09/1992
Each share Common no par exchanged for (0.125) share Common no par
Merged into Pinnacle Resources Ltd. 07/18/1994
Each share Common no par exchanged for $7.25 cash

RESORT & URBAN TIMESHARES INC (DE)
Name changed to RUTI-Sweetwater, Inc. 8/30/83
(See RUTI-Sweetwater, Inc.)

RESORT AIRLINES, INC. (NC)
Common $1 par changed to 10¢ par in 1950
Each (5) shares Common 10¢ par exchanged for (1) share Common 5¢ par 8/10/56
Recapitalized as Resort Airlines, Inc. (Del.) (New) and each share Capital Stock 5¢ par exchanged for (0.1) share Common $7.50 par 4/17/59
Resort Airlines, Inc. (Del.) (New) merged into Chatham Corp. 12/31/64

RESORT AIRLINES, INC. NEW (DE)
Merged into Chatham Corp. on a (5.47) for (1) basis 12/31/64

RESORT AIRLINES, INC. OLD (DE)
Name changed to Townsend Investment Co. 6/14/57
Townsend Investment Co. name changed to Townsend Corp. of America 4/29/59 which name changed to Chatham Corp. 12/31/64

RESORT CAR RENT SYS INC (DE)
Each share old Common 10¢ par exchanged for (0.2) share new Common 10¢ par 3/1/74
Charter cancelled and declared inoperative and void for non-payment of taxes 3/1/80

RESORT CLUBS INTL INC (FL)
Each share old Common $0.0001 par exchanged for (0.005) share new Common $0.0001 par 02/24/2005
Each share new Common $0.0001 par exchanged again for (2) shares new Common $0.0001 par 08/11/2005
Recapitalized as pH Environmental Inc. 02/27/2012
Each share new Common $0.0001 par exchanged for (0.001) share Common $0.0001 par
pH Environmental Inc. name changed to TNI BioTech, Inc. 05/14/2012 which name changed to Immune Therapeutics, Inc. 12/11/2014

RESORT CONNECTIONS INC (DE)
Name changed to D-Lanz Development Group Inc. 01/30/1990
D-Lanz Development Group Inc. name changed to eWeb21 Corp. 11/24/2000 which recapitalized as Texas Wyoming Drilling, Inc. 07/21/2008 which recapitalized as Drone USA, Inc. 05/19/2016

RESORT INCOME INVS INC (DE)
Completely liquidated 3/19/99
Each share Common 1¢ par exchanged for first and final distribution of $0.61 cash

RESORT RESOURCE GROUP INC (NY)
Name changed to Asia American Industries, Inc. 03/20/1990
(See Asia American Industries, Inc.)

RESORT WORLD ENTERPRISES INC (NV)
Name changed to Remedent USA, Inc. 10/22/1998
Remedent USA, Inc. recapitalized as Remedent, Inc. 06/06/2005

RESORT WORLD N V (NETHERLANDS ANTILLES)
Company private as of 00/00/1992
Details not available

RESORTQUEST INTL INC (DE)
Issue Information - 5,800,000 shares COM offered at $11 per share on 05/20/1998
Merged into Gaylord Entertainment Co. (New) 11/20/2003
Each share Common 1¢ par exchanged for (0.275) share Common 1¢ par
Gaylord Entertainment Co. (New) name changed to Ryman Hospitality Properties, Inc. 10/01/2012

RESORTS INTL INC (DE)
Class A Common $1 par split (3) for (1) by issuance of (1) additional share 10/3/78

Class B Common $1 par split (3) for (1) by issuance of (1) additional share 10/3/78
Acquired by Griffin Co. 11/15/88
Each share Class A Common $1 par exchanged for $36 cash
Each share Class B Common $1 par exchanged for $36 cash
Recapitalized as Griffin Gaming & Entertainment, Inc. 6/30/95
Each share new Common 1¢ par exchanged for (0.2) share Common 1¢ par
Griffin Gaming & Entertainment, Inc. merged into Sun International Hotels Ltd. 12/16/96 which name changed to Kerzner International Ltd. 7/1/2002
(See Kerzner International Ltd.)

RESORTS INTL LTD (NV)
Charter revoked for failure to file reports and pay fees 12/1/86

RESORTS UNLIMITED MGMT INC (CANADA)
Dissolved 03/06/2006
Details not available

RESORTS WORLD BHD (MALAYSIA)
Name changed to Genting Malaysia Berhad 07/22/2009

RESORTSHIPS INTL INC (DE)
Recapitalized as American Design Inc. (DE) 03/26/2007
Each share Common $0.001 par exchanged for (0.01) share Common $0.001 par
American Design Inc. (DE) reincorporated in Nevada as Ventana Biotech Inc. 11/20/2008
(See Ventana Biotech Inc.)

RESOUND CORP (CA)
Merged into GN Great Nordic Ltd. 7/7/99
Each share Common 1¢ par exchanged for $8 cash

RESOURCE ACQUISITION GROUP INC (NV)
Name changed to American Retail Group, Inc. 04/01/2011

RESOURCE AMER INC (DE)
Each share old Common 1¢ par exchanged for (0.1) share new Common 1¢ par 08/12/1992
New Common 1¢ par reclassified as Class A Common 1¢ par 10/25/1995
Class A Common 1¢ par reclassified as Common 1¢ par 11/26/1996
Common 1¢ par split (3) for (1) by issuance of (2) additional shares payable 06/05/1998 to holders of record 05/29/1998
Each share Common 1¢ par received distribution of (0.59367) share Atlas America, Inc. Common 1¢ par payable 06/30/2005 to holders of record 06/24/2005 Ex date - 07/01/2005
Stock Dividends - 6% payable 04/30/1996 to holders of record 04/16/1996; 150% payable 05/31/1996 to holders of record 05/20/1996
Acquired by C-III Capital Partners LLC 09/08/2016
Each share Common 1¢ par exchanged for $9.78 cash

RESOURCE ASSET INVT TR (MD)
Issue Information - 2,833,334 shares COM offered at $15 per share on 01/08/1998
Secondary Offering - 2,800,000 shares COM offered at $15.75 per share on 06/23/1998
Name changed to RAIT Investment Trust 2/14/2001
RAIT Investment Trust name changed to RAIT Financial Trust 12/11/2006

RESOURCE BANCSHARES MTG GROUP INC (DE)
Stock Dividends - 10% 06/30/1995; 7% payable 09/24/1996 to holders of record 09/03/1996; 5% payable 12/31/1997 to holders of record 12/18/1997
Merged into NetBank, Inc. 04/01/2002
Each share Common 1¢ par exchanged for (1.1382) shares Common 1¢ par
(See NetBank, Inc.)

RESOURCE BK (VIRGINIA BEACH, VA)
Each share old Common $1 par exchanged for (1/3) share new Common $3 par 11/15/94
New Common $3 par split (2) for (1) by issuance of (1) additional share payable 7/15/98 to holders of record 6/30/98
Under plan of reorganization each share new Common $3 par automatically became (1) share Resource Bankshares Corp. Common $1.50 par 7/1/98
Resource Bankshares Corp. merged into Fulton Financial Corp. 4/1/2004

RESOURCE BANKSHARES CORP (VA)
Common $1.50 par split (3) for (2) by issuance of (0.5) additional share payable 9/5/2003 to holders of record 8/15/2003 Ex date - 9/8/2003
Merged into Fulton Financial Corp. 4/1/2004
Each share Common $1.50 par exchanged for (1.4667) shares Common $2.50 par

RESOURCE CAP CORP (MD)
Each share old Common $0.001 par exchanged for (0.25) share new Common $0.001 par 09/01/2015
8.5% Preferred Ser. A $0.001 par called for redemption at $25 on 01/31/2018
8.25% Preferred Ser. B $0.001 par called for redemption at $25 plus $0.32083 accrued dividends on 03/26/2018
Name changed to Exantas Capital Corp. 05/29/2018

RESOURCE CAP GROUP INC (DE)
Each share old Common 1¢ par exchanged for (0.0033333) share new Common 1¢ par 03/25/2003
Note: In effect holders received $5 cash per share and public interest was eliminated

RESOURCE CAP INTL LTD (BERMUDA)
Name changed to International Equity Ltd. 08/16/1989
International Equity Ltd. name changed to Industrial & Environmental Services Ltd. 02/19/1992 which name changed to Trask Corp. 01/10/1994 which name changed to Med Net International Ltd. 01/08/1996
(See Med Net International Ltd.)

RESOURCE CAP TR I (DE)
$2.3125 Capital Securities called for redemption at $26.15625 on 05/03/2004

RESOURCE CTL INC (CT)
Charter forfeited 08/19/1988

RESOURCE ENGR INC (TX)
Name changed to ENSR Corp. 03/11/1988
(See ENSR Corp.)

RESOURCE EQUITY LTD (ON)
Reorganized under the laws of Delaware as Geovic Mining Corp. 12/04/2006
Each share Common no par exchanged for (0.42662116) share Common $0.0001 par

RESOURCE EXCHANGE AMER CORP (FL)
Each share old Common $0.0001 par exchanged for (0.01) share new Common $0.0001 par 01/31/2013
Name changed to Allerayde SAB, Inc. 04/30/2013
Allerayde SAB, Inc. name changed to Stragenics, Inc. 04/28/2014

RESOURCE EXPL & DEV LTD (ON)
Charter cancelled for failure to pay taxes and file returns 05/13/1980

RESOURCE EXPL INC (DE)
Each share Preferred $1 par exchanged for (0.4197291) share Common 1¢ par 02/24/1982
Each share Common 5¢ par exchanged for (0.16666666) share Common 1¢ par 02/24/1982
Each share Common 1¢ par exchanged for (1) share Common 1¢ par to reflect a (1) for (100) reverse split followed by a (100) for (1) forward split 01/30/1987
Note: Holders of (99) shares or fewer received $1.75 cash per share
Name changed to Resource America, Inc. 01/31/1989
(See Resource America, Inc.)

RESOURCE FIN GROUP LTD (CO)
Merged into Intelligent Decision Systems, Inc. 04/01/1996
Each share Common $0.0001 par exchanged for (0.25) share Common $0.0001 par
(See Intelligent Decision Systems, Inc.)

RESOURCE FINANCIAL CORP. (CA)
Completely liquidated 06/30/1970
Each share Common 1¢ par exchanged for first and final distribution of (0.2) share Automation Technology, Inc. Common 1¢ par
Automation Technology, Inc. name changed to Tax Corp. of America (MD) 03/11/1971
(See Tax Corp. of America (MD))

RESOURCE GEN CORP (OH)
Name changed to PH Group Inc. 04/22/1997
(See PH Group Inc.)

RESOURCE GENERATION LTD (AUSTRALIA)
ADR agreement terminated 06/10/2016
Each Sponsored ADR for Ordinary exchanged for (4) shares Ordinary

RESOURCE GROUP INC (DE)
Name changed to Ecoemissions Solutions, Inc. 07/10/2009
Ecoemissions Solutions, Inc. name changed to NuTech Energy Resources, Inc. 06/26/2015

RESOURCE HUNTER CAP CORP (BC)
Name changed to Plains Creek Phosphate Corp. 05/16/2011
Plains Creek Phosphate Corp. recapitalized as GB Minerals Ltd. 03/28/2013 which merged into Itafos 02/28/2018

RESOURCE INDS INC (NV)
Reorganized as Growth Resources, Inc. 08/19/1985
Each (400) shares Common 1¢ par exchanged for (1) share Common 1¢ par

RESOURCE MGMT CORP (DE)
Merged into Kappa Systems, Inc. (PA) 03/30/1979
Each share Common 10¢ par exchanged for $0.15 cash

RESOURCE MTG CAP INC (VA)
Name changed to Dynex Capital, Inc. 4/25/97

RESOURCE NETWORK INTL INC (DE)
Reincorporated 09/08/1987
Common $0.001 par split (2) for (1) by issuance of (1) additional share 12/28/1988
Each share old Common $0.001 par exchanged for (0.5) share new Common $0.001 par 07/12/1990
State of incorporation changed from (NY) to (DE) 09/08/1987
Name changed to International Poultry Inc. 08/13/1993
International Poultry Inc. recapitalized as Carley Enterprises, Inc. 08/15/2005
(See Carley Enterprises, Inc.)

RESOURCE PROCESSING GROUP INC (SC)
Merged into Carolina First Corp. 06/01/1998
Each share Common $1 par exchanged for (0.0439) share Common $1 par
Carolina First Corp. name changed to South Financial Group, Inc. 04/24/2000 which merged into Toronto-Dominion Bank (Toronto, ON) 09/30/2010

RESOURCE RECOVERY TECHNOLOGIES, INC. (OH)
Name changed to Resource Recycling Technologies, Inc. (OH) 11/17/1988
Resource Recycling Technologies, Inc. (OH) reincorporated in Delaware 06/29/1989
(See Resource Recycling Technologies, Inc. (DE))

RESOURCE RECYCLING TECHNOLOGIES INC (DE)
Reincorporated 06/29/1989
Stock Dividends - 10% 12/31/1988; 10% 07/31/1989
State of incorporation changed from (OH) to (DE) 06/29/1989
Common $1 par split (11.364) for (10) by issuance of (0.1364) additional share 08/15/1989
Merged into WMX Technologies Inc. 04/28/1995
Each share Common $1 par exchanged for $11.50 cash

RESOURCE RESV INC (NV)
Reincorporated under the laws of Washington as Actek, Inc. 06/02/1987

RESOURCE RESVS INC (DE)
Charter cancelled and declared inoperative and void for non-payment of taxes 6/27/89

RESOURCE SVC GROUP LTD (AB)
Common 10¢ par changed to no par 05/30/1974
Merged into 139435 Canada Inc. 05/29/1985
Each share Common no par exchanged for $3 cash

RESOURCE VENTURES CORP. (DE)
Common $1 par changed to 25¢ par 04/24/1957
Merged into Petroleum Resources Corp. 06/30/1965
Each share Common 25¢ par exchanged for (0.1) share Common 25¢ par
Petroleum Resources Corp. name changed to PRC Corp. 11/09/1970 which name changed to Corterra Corp. 11/28/1972 which assets were transferred to CorTerra Corp. Liquidating Corp. 10/08/1980
(See CorTerra Corp. Liquidating Corp.)

RESOURCE VENTURES INC (NV)
Reincorporated under the laws of British Columbia as New Dawn Mining Corp. 08/22/2006
New Dawn Mining Corp. (BC) reorganized in Canada 11/15/2007
(See New Dawn Mining Corp.)

RESOURCECAN LTD (NL)
Name changed to Stratos Global Corp. 02/26/1997
(See Stratos Global Corp.)

RES-RES

RESOURCENET COMMUNICATIONS INC (CA)
Charter suspended for failure to file reports and pay fees 08/20/1997

RESOURCEPHOENIX COM (DE)
Company terminated registration of common stock and is no longer public as of 03/07/2001

RESOURCES & FACS CORP (DE)
Name changed to Refac, Inc. 06/05/1969
Refac, Inc. name changed to Refac Technology Development Corp. 04/13/1970 which name changed to Refac (Old) 06/01/1999 which merged into Refac (New) 02/28/2003 which name changed to Refac Optical Group 03/06/2006
(See Refac Optical Group)

RESOURCES ACCRUED MTG INVS L P (DE)
Merged into Knight Fuller, Inc. 09/22/2002
Each Unit of Ltd. Partnership Int. Ser. 86 exchanged for (1) share Common $0.0001 par
Knight Fuller, Inc. name changed to CenterStaging Corp. 02/07/2006

RESOURCES ACCRUED MORTGAGE INVESTORS 2 L.P. (DE)
Name changed to Biggest Little Investments L.P. 10/08/2003

RESOURCES CORP. INTERNATIONAL (DE)
Common no par changed to $1 par in 1946
Acquired by General Timber Products, S.A. 10/31/58
Each share Common $1 par exchanged for (1) share Common $1 par

RESOURCES DEVELOPMENT CORP. (TX)
Charter revoked for failure to file reports and pay fees 12/01/1959

RESOURCES EQUIP CAP CORP (CO)
Each share old Common no par exchanged for (0.05) share new Common no par 04/11/1983
Name changed to Uniwest Financial Corp. 09/13/1983

RESOURCES GROWTH FUND (CA)
Charter suspended for failure to file reports and pay fees 02/01/1985

RESOURCES INTL LTD (DE)
Charter cancelled and declared inoperative and void for non-payment of taxes 3/1/84

RESOURCES OF THE PAC CORP (NV)
Name changed to Semper Resources Corp. (NV) 06/21/1996
Semper Resources Corp. (NV) reincorporated in Oklahoma 00/00/2005 which name changed to Cyberfund, Inc. (OK) 09/01/2006 which reincorporated in Delaware as ROK Entertainment Group Inc. 12/31/2007
(See ROK Entertainment Group Inc.)

RESOURCES PENSION SHS 1 (MA)
Shares of Bene. Int. 10¢ par split (5) for (2) by issuance of (1.5) additional shares 07/22/1985
Merged into RPS Realty Trust 12/28/1988
Each Share of Bene. Int. 10¢ par exchanged for (1.1594) Shares of Bene. Int. 10¢ par
RPS Realty Trust recapitalized as Ramco-Gershenson Properties Trust 05/10/1996

RESOURCES PENSION SHS 2 TR (MA)
Shares of Bene. Int. 10¢ par split (2) for (1) by issuance of (1) additional share 07/22/1985
Merged into RPS Realty Trust 12/28/1988
Each Share of Bene. Int. 10¢ par exchanged for (1.066) Shares of Bene. Int. 10¢ par
RPS Realty Trust recapitalized as Ramco-Gershenson Properties Trust 05/10/1996

RESOURCES PENSION SHS 3 (MA)
Shares of Bene. Int. 10¢ par split (2) for (1) by issuance of (1) additional share 7/22/85
Merged into RPS Realty Trust 12/28/1988
Each Share of Bene. Int. 10¢ par changed for (0.9932) Share of Bene. Int. 10¢ par
RPS Realty Trust recapitalized as Ramco- Gershenson Properties Trust 05/10/1996

RESOURCES PENSION SHS INC (DE)
Name changed to Resources Pension Shares 1 and Common 10¢ par reclassified as Shares of Bene. Int. 10¢ par 7/28/83
Resources Pension Shares 1 merged into RPS Realty Trust 12/28/88 which recapitalized as Ramco-Gershenson Properties Trust 5/10/96

RESOURCES PRTG & GRAPHICS INC (NV)
Name changed to Elleipsis Global Travel Solutions, Inc. 04/16/2008
Elleipsis Global Travel Solutions, Inc. recapitalized as Resource Ventures, Inc. 02/23/2010

RESOURCES UNLIMITED CORP (NV)
Name changed to Pease (Willard) Oil & Gas Co. 07/07/1972
Pease (Willard) Oil & Gas Co. recapitalized as Pease Oil & Gas Co. 07/05/1994 which name changed to Republic Resources, Inc. 07/12/2001
(See Republic Resources, Inc.)

RESOURCES WEST INC (UT)
Common $0.005 par changed to $0.001 par in 1977
Recapitalized as Magma Resources 1/27/89
Each share Common $0.001 par exchanged for (0.025) share Common no par
Magma Resources name changed to Cellura Telecommunications & Technologies Inc. 7/15/93 which recapitalized as China Biomedical Group Inc. 4/3/95 which name changed to Internet Holdings Ltd. 6/30/96 which name changed to HTTP Technology, Inc. (UT) 11/28/2000 which reincorporated in Delaware which name changed to Medicsight, Inc. 10/28/2002 which name changed to MGT Capital Investments, Inc. 1/24/2007

RESOURCEXPLORER INC (AB)
Recapitalized as Exchequer Resource Corp. (AB) 07/24/2002
Each share Common no par exchanged for (0.1) share Common no par
Exchequer Resource Corp. (AB) reincorporated in British Columbia 10/25/2004 which recapitalized as CBD MED Research Corp. 07/18/2014

RESOURCING SOLUTIONS GROUP INC (NV)
Each share old Common $0.001 par exchanged for (0.001) share new Common $0.001 par 11/19/2004
Each share new Common $0.001 par exchanged again for (0.001) share new Common $0.001 par 12/15/2006
Charter permanently revoked 12/31/2010

RESPECT YOUR UNIVERSE INC (NV)
Each share old Common $0.001 par exchanged for (0.5) share new Common $0.001 par 06/30/2014
Reincorporated under the laws of British Columbia as RYU Apparel Inc. and Common $0.001 par changed to no par 02/20/2015

RESPIRATORY CARE INC (IL)
Common no par split (2) for (1) by issuance of (1) additional share 09/29/1972
Merged into Colgate-Palmolive Co. 04/22/1977
Each share Common no par exchanged for (0.2960) share Common $1 par

RESPIRI LTD (AUSTRALIA)
ADR agreement terminated 07/20/2018
Each Sponsored ADR for Ordinary exchanged for (20) shares Ordinary
Note: Unexchanged ADR's will be sold and the proceeds, if any, held for claim after 11/23/2018

RESPIRONICS INC (DE)
Common 1¢ par split (2) for (1) by issuance of (1) additional share 06/25/1990
Common 1¢ par split (2) for (1) by issuance of (1) additional share 03/09/1992
Common 1¢ par split (2) for (1) by issuance of (1) additional share 03/17/1995
Common 1¢ par split (2) for (1) by issuance of (1) additional share payable 06/01/2005 to holders of record 05/09/2005 Ex date - 06/02/2005
Acquired by Philips Holding USA Inc. 03/17/2008
Each share Common 1¢ par exchanged for $66 cash

RESPONSE BIOMEDICAL CORP (BC)
Old Common no par split (2) for (1) by issuance of (1) additional share 05/08/1992
Each share old Common no par exchanged for (0.1) share new Common no par 05/28/2010
Each share new Common no par exchanged again for (0.05) share new Common no par 09/26/2012
Acquired by 1077801 B.C. Ltd. 12/02/2016
Each share new Common no par exchanged for $1.12 cash
Note: Unexchanged certificates will be cancelled and become without value 12/02/2019

RESPONSE GENETICS (DE)
Chapter 11 bankrutpcy proceedings dismissed 06/03/2016
Stockholders' equity unlikely

RESPONSE ONCOLOGY INC (TN)
Recapitalized 11/2/95
Response Technologies, Inc. recapitalized as Response Oncology Inc. 11/2/95
Each share Common $0.002 par exchanged for (0.2) share Common $1 par
Preferred not affected except for change of name
Each share Conv. Preferred Ser. A $1 par received distribution of (0.011) share Common $1 par payable 1/15/2002 to holders of record 12/15/2001 Ex date - 2/25/2002
Plan of reorganization under Chapter 11 Federal Bankruptcy Code effective 6/25/2002
No stockholders' equity

RESPONSE TELEVISION INC (CO)
Name changed to Paragon Coolers, Inc. 2/2/89
(See Paragon Coolers, Inc.)

RESPONSE USA INC (DE)
Each share Common $0.002 par exchanged for (0.25) share old Common $0.008 par 10/5/92
Each share old Common $0.008 par exchanged for (0.1) share new Common $0.008 par 11/20/95
Each share new Common $0.008 par exchanged again for (1/3) share new Common $0.008 par 1/8/98
Plan of reorganization under Chapter 11 Federal Bankruptcy Code effective 10/31/2002
No stockholders' equity

RESPONSIVE ENVIRONMENTS CORP (NY)
Adjudicated bankrupt 05/30/1973
Stockholders' equity unlikely

RESPONSIVE MKTS INTL INC (DE)
Name changed to No-Glug Jug Corp. 06/27/1972
Each share Common 1¢ par exchanged for (1) share Common 1¢ par
No-Glug Jug Corp. recapitalized as Jet Travel Services, Inc. 07/06/1973
(See Jet Travel Services, Inc.)

RESPONSYS INC (DE)
Issue Information - 6,619,654 shares COM offered at $12 per share on 04/20/2011
Acquired by Oracle Corp. 02/06/2014
Each share Common $0.0001 par exchanged for $27 cash

RESPRO INC. (RI)
Merged into General Tire & Rubber Co. 10/10/1955
Each (6.25) shares Common $1 par exchanged for (1) share 5% Preference $100 par
General Tire & Rubber Co. name changed to GenCorp Inc. (OH) 03/30/1984 which reincorporated in Delaware 04/14/2014
(See GenCorp Inc.)

RESSOURCES ABITEX INC (CANADA)
Recapitalized as ABE Resources Inc. 04/16/2013
Each share Common no par exchanged for (0.1) share Common no par
ABE Resources Inc. name changed to Vision Lithium Inc. 03/27/2018

RESSOURCES AFFINOR INC (AB)
Name changed to Affinor Growers Inc. 05/30/2014

RESSOURCES DIANOR INC (QC)
Placed in receivership 08/20/2015
Stockholders' equity unlikely

RESSOURCES FARBORO INC (QC)
Recapitalized as Orient Resources Inc./ Ressources Orient Inc. 04/01/1989
Each share Common no par exchanged for (0.06740861) share Common no par

RESSOURCES MAJESCOR INC (CANADA)
Each share old Common no par exchanged for (0.1) share new Common no par 12/04/2008
Each share new Common no par exchanged again for (0.1) share new Common no par 11/07/2013
Name changed to Albert Mining Inc. 08/01/2017

RESSOURCES MINIERES EIDER INC (CANADA)
Recapitalized as Noveder Inc. 6/6/88
Each share Common no par exchanged for (0.1) share Common no par
Noveder Inc. recapitalized as Atlantis Exploration Inc. 10/11/2001 which recapitalized as Noveko Echographs Inc. 2/4/2004 which name changed to Noveko International Inc. 1/11/2006

RESSOURCES MINIERES FORBEX INC (CANADA)
Recapitalized as Fieldex Exploration Inc. 2/13/95
Each share Common no par exchanged for (0.1) share Common no par

RESSOURCES MINIERES ROUYN INC (QC)
Name changed to Richmont Mines Inc. 07/30/1991
Richmont Mines Inc. merged into Alamos Gold Inc. (New) 11/24/2017

RESSOURCES ORLEANS INC (QC)
Each share old Common no par exchanged for (0.025) share new Common no par 10/01/2003
Reorganized under the laws of Alberta as Orleans Energy Ltd. 01/25/2005
Each share new Common no par exchanged for (0.25) share Common no par
Note: Unexchanged certificates were cancelled and became without value 01/26/2008
Orleans Energy Ltd. name changed to RMP Energy Inc. 05/17/2011 which name changed to Iron Bridge Resources Inc. 11/27/2017

RESSOURCES ORPHEE INC (QC)
Recapitalized as Itec-Mineral Inc. 12/5/94
Each share Common no par exchanged for (0.25) share Common no par
Itec-Mineral Inc. recapitalized as Electromed Inc. 9/25/2000 which recapitalized as Evolved Digital Systems Inc. 10/10/2003

RESSOURCES SEARCHGOLD INC (CANADA)
Each share old Common no par received distribution of (0.05) share Golden Share Mining Corp. Common no par payable 02/15/2008 to holders of record 02/08/2008 Ex date - 02/06/2008
Each share old Common no par exchanged for (0.125) share new Common no par 11/01/2011
Name changed to Gravitas Financial Inc. 07/08/2013

RESSOURCES VAL D OR INC (QC)
Recapitalized as Consolidated Val D'or Resources Inc. 05/27/1991
Each (15) shares Common no par exchanged for (1) share Common no par
(See Consolidated Val D'or Resources Inc.)

RESSOURCES WILLIAM INC (QC)
Name changed to William Multi-Tech Inc. 08/04/2000
William Multi-Tech Inc. recapitalized as Valencia Ventures Inc. (QC) 01/17/2003 which reincorporated in Ontario 06/02/2014

RESTAURANT & WALDORF ASSOCIATES, INC. (MA)
Common no par changed to $1 par 5/3/67
Name changed to Restaurant Associates Industries, Inc. (Mass.) 5/17/68
Restaurant Associates Industries, Inc. (Mass.) reincorporated under the laws of Delaware 7/15/68
(See Restaurant Associates Industries, Inc. (Del.))

RESTAURANT ACQUISITION PARTNERS INC (DE)
Issue Information - 3,333,333 UNITS consisting of (1) share COM and (2) WTS offered at $6 per Unit on 12/15/2006 Units
Completely liquidated
Each Unit exchanged for first and final distribution of $5.86050058 cash 02/04/2009
Each share Common $0.0001 par exchanged for first and final distribution of $5.86050058 cash 02/04/2009

RESTAURANT ASSOC INDS INC (DE)
Reincorporated 07/15/1968
State of incorporation changed from (MA) to (DE) 07/15/1968
Common $1 par reclassified as Conv. Class B Common $1 par 08/06/1985
Stock Dividend - In Class A Common to holders of Conv. Class B Common 40% 08/30/1985
50¢ Conv. Preferred $1 par called for redemption 06/05/1987
Merged into M Squared Corp. 03/04/1988
Each share Class A Common $1 par exchanged for $14.25 cash
Each share Conv. Class B Common $1 par exchanged for $14.25 cash

RESTAURANT ASSOCIATES, INC. (NY)
Merged into Restaurant & Waldorf Associates, Inc. 1/14/66
Each share Common 10¢ par exchanged for (1.375) shares Common no par
Restaurant & Waldorf Associates, Inc. name changed to Restaurant Associates Industries, Inc. (Mass.) 5/17/68 which reincorporated under the laws of Delaware 7/15/68
(See Restaurant Associates Industries, Inc. (Del.))

RESTAURANT CONCEPTS INC (DE)
Merged into PR Holdings Inc. 07/27/1984
Each share Common 10¢ par exchanged for $2 cash

RESTAURANT CONCEPTS OF AMER INC (NV)
Name changed to Petron Energy II, Inc. 10/17/2011

RESTAURANT ENTMT INC (CA)
Out of business 03/03/1986
No stockholders' equity

RESTAURANT GROUP PLC (UNITED KINGDOM)
ADR agreement terminated 08/06/2018
No ADR's remain outstanding

RESTAURANT HLDGS CDA LTD (ON)
Name changed to Mikes Submarines Inc. 5/15/79
Mikes Submarines Inc. name changed to M-Corp Inc. 8/1/85 which name changed to Mikes Restaurants Inc. 12/8/98
(See Mikes Restaurants Inc.)

RESTAURANT HOTLINE SYS INC (NY)
Dissolved by proclamation 9/29/93

RESTAURANT MGMT SVCS INC (GA)
Common 10¢ par split (4) for (3) by issuance of (1/3) additional share 8/12/85
Common 10¢ par split (4) for (3) by issuance of (1/3) additional share 7/29/86
Acquired by RMS Holdings, Inc. 10/31/88
Each share Common 10¢ par exchanged for $10.70 cash

RESTAURANT SYS INC (GA)
Merged into Wendy's International, Inc. 12/27/1985
Each share Common 5¢ par exchanged for (1.1867) shares Common no par
Wendy's International, Inc. merged into Wendy's/Arby's Group, Inc. 09/29/2008 which name changed to Wendy's Co. 07/11/2011

RESTAURANT TEAMS INTL INC (TX)
Each share Common 1¢ par received distribution of (0.05) share Ness Energy International Inc. Common no par payable 5/12/2000 to holders of record 3/31/2000
Recapitalized as RTIN Holdings, Inc. 12/14/2001
Each share Common 1¢ par exchanged for (0.02) share Common 1¢ par
RTIN Holdings, Inc. name changed to Safescript Pharmacies, Inc. 12/17/2003
(See Safescript Pharmacies, Inc.)

RESTEC SYS INC (OH)
Acquired by BRI Inc. 05/08/1992
Each share Common no par exchanged for $0.01 cash

RESTECH CORP (DE)
Charter cancelled and declared inoperative and void for non-payment of taxes 03/01/1986

RESTOR INDS INC (DE)
Name changed to World Access Inc. 6/25/96
(See World Access Inc.)

RESTORAGEN INC (DE)
Plan of reorganization under Chapter 11 Federal Bankruptcy Code effective 06/19/2003
No stockholders' equity

RESTORATION HARDWARE HLDGS INC (DE)
Name changed to RH 01/03/2017

RESTORATION HARDWARE INC (DE)
Issue Information - 3,300,000 shares COM offered at $19 per share on 06/18/1998
Merged into Home Holdings, LLC 06/17/2020
Each share Common $0.0001 par exchanged for $4.50 cash

RESTORE MED INC (DE)
Issue Information - 4,000,000 shares COM offered at $8 per share on 05/16/2006
Merged into Medtronic, Inc. 07/17/2008
Each share Common 1¢ par exchanged for $1.60 cash

RESTORGENEX CORP (DE)
Reincorporated 01/25/2016
State of incorporation changed from (NV) to (DE) 06/18/2015
Name changed to Diffusion Pharmaceuticals Inc. 01/25/2016

RESTOVE INDS INC (NV)
Charter permanently revoked for failure to file reports and pay fees 09/30/1999

RESTRAC INC (DE)
Issue Information - 2,500,000 shares COM offered at $11 per share on 06/25/1996
Name changed to Webhire, Inc. 06/01/1999
(See Webhire, Inc.)

RESTRUCTURING ACQUISITION CORP (DE)
Issue Information - 1,500,000 Units consisting of (1) share COM and (2) WT offered at $6 per Unit on 05/04/1994
Completely liquidated 6/24/96
Each share Common 1¢ par exchanged for first and final distribution of $5.38818827 cash

RESULT ENERGY INC (AB)
Merged into PetroBakken Energy Ltd. (Old) 04/01/2010
Each share Common no par exchanged for (0.00823231) share Class A Common no par and $0.15450794 cash
Note: Unexchanged certificates were cancelled and became without value 04/01/2014
PetroBakken Energy Ltd. (Old) reorganized as PetroBakken Energy Ltd. (New) 01/07/2013 which name changed to Lightstream Resources Ltd. 05/28/2013

RESULTS TECHNOLOGY GROUP CORP (NV)
Charter revoked for failure to file reports and pay fees 12/31/2002

RESUME IN MINUTES INC (NV)
Common $0.001 par split (37.39716) for (1) by issuance of (36.39716) additional shares payable 06/23/2011 to holders of record 06/23/2011 Ex date - 06/24/2011
Name changed to MEDL Mobile Holdings, Inc. 06/28/2011
MEDL Mobile Holdings, Inc. name changed to With, Inc. 11/04/2015

RESURGENCE PPTYS INC (MD)
Liquidation completed
Each share Common 1¢ par received initial distribution of $2.25 cash payable 10/16/97 to holders of record 10/7/97
Each share Common 1¢ par received second distribution of $1.15 cash payable 11/6/97 to holders of record 10/27/97
Each share Common 1¢ par received third distribution of $1.80 cash payable 12/4/97 to holders of record 11/24/97
Each share Common 1¢ par recieved fourth distribution of $0.60 cash payable 4/21/98 to holders of record 4/9/98
Each share Common 1¢ par received fifth distribution of $0.65 cash payable 8/14/98 to holders of record 8/6/98
Each share Common 1¢ par received sixth and final distribution of $0.07 cash payable 2/25/99 to holders of record 2/15/99
Note: Certificates were not required to be exchanged and are without value

RESURGENS COMMUNICATIONS GROUP INC (GA)
Each share old Common 1¢ par exchanged for (0.25) share new Common 1¢ par 08/12/1992
Name changed to LDDS Communications, Inc. 09/15/1993
LDDS Communications, Inc. name changed to WorldCom, Inc. 05/26/1995 which name changed to MCI WorldCom, Inc. 09/14/1998 which name changed to WorldCom Inc. (New) 05/01/2000
(See WorldCom Inc. (New))

RESURGERE MINES & MINERALS INDIA LTD (INDIA)
GDR basis changed from (1:6) to (1:180) 09/27/2010
GDR basis changed from (1:180) to (1:18) 06/18/2012
GDR agreement terminated 04/22/2014
No GDR's remain outstanding

RET INCOME FD INC (MA)
Merged into Cyprus Corp. 12/29/80
Each share $4.38 Preference 1¢ par exchanged for (3) shares $1.80 Preference 10¢ par
Each share Common 1¢ par exchanged for (8.7871) shares Common 30¢ par
Cyprus Corp. name changed to Astrotech International Corp. (Old) 4/6/84 which recapitalized as Astrotech International Corp. (New) 8/19/88 which merged into Iteq Inc. 10/28/97
(See Iteq Inc.)

RET INTERNET SVCS INC (BC)
Recapitalized as Terra Ventures Inc. 06/15/2004
Each (18) shares Common no par exchanged for (1) share Common no par
Terra Ventures Inc. merged into Hathor Exploration Ltd. 08/05/2011
(See Hathor Exploration Ltd.)

RETAIL CENTERS OF THE AMERICAS, INC. (NY)
Merged into National Industries, Inc. (KY) 07/01/1968
Each share Common 10¢ par exchanged for (0.5) share Common $1 par
National Industries, Inc. (KY) merged into Fuqua Industries, Inc. 01/03/1978 which name changed to Actava Group Inc. 07/21/1993 which name changed to Metromedia International Group, Inc. 11/01/1995
(See Metromedia International Group, Inc.)

RETAIL CR CO (GA)
Each share Common no par exchanged for (10) shares Common $2.50 par 01/26/1956
Stock Dividends - 25% 01/27/1961; 100% 05/14/1964
Name changed to Equifax Inc. 12/31/1975

RETAIL ELECTRONIC SYSTEM, INC. (NY)
Dissolved by proclamation 3/24/93

RETAIL ENTMT GROUP INC (NJ)
SEC revoked common stock registration 10/28/2009
Stockholders' equity unlikely

RETAIL HOLDRS TR (DE)
Trust terminated
Each Depositary Receipt received first and final distribution of $137.230258 cash payable 01/07/2013 to holders of record 12/20/2012

RETAIL HWY COM INC (NV)
Recapitalized as Dragon International Group Corp. 10/04/2004
Each share Common $0.001 par exchanged for (0.125) share Common $0.001 par
(See Dragon International Group Corp.)

RETAIL MERCHANTS INDS INC (OH)
Common no par split (2) for (1) by issuance of (1) additional share 6/29/72
Name changed to Buckhorn Inc. (OH) 5/1/80
Buckhorn Inc. (OH) merged into Buckhorn Inc. (DE) 12/22/81
(See Buckhorn Inc.)

RETAIL OPPORTUNITY INVTS CORP (DE)
Reincorporated under the laws of Maryland 06/02/2011

RETAIL PPTYS AMER INC (MD)
Each share Class B-1 Common $0.001 par exchanged for (1) share Class A Common $0.001 par 10/05/2012
7% Preferred Ser. A $0.001 par called for redemption at $25 plus $0.384 accrued dividends on 12/20/2017 (Additional Information in Active)

RETAIL PPTYS INC
Step Down Preferred 144A called for redemption at $963.27 on 9/30/97

RETAIL PPTYS LTD (OH)
Liquidation completed 6/10/57

RETAIL PRO INC (DE)
Chapter 11 bankruptcy proceedings converted to Chapter 7 on 12/09/2009
Stockholders' equity unlikely

RETAIL REALTY INC. (NY)
Merged into Alexander's, Inc. 1/23/69
Each share Common $1 par or VTC's for Common $1 par exchanged for (1.87265) shares Common $1 par

RETAIL SVCS INC (DE)
Charter cancelled and declared inoperative for non-payment of taxes 05/25/1995

RETAIL STORES CORP.
Liquidated in 1940

RETAIL VENTURES INC (OH)
Merged into DSW Inc. 05/26/2011
Each share Common no par exchanged for (0.435) share Class A Common no par

RETAILING CORP AMER (DE)
Charter cancelled 05/25/1995

RETAILMENOT INC (DE)
Acquired by Harland Clarke Holdings Corp. 05/23/2017
Each share Common Ser. 1 $0.001 par exchanged for $11.60 cash

RETALIX LTD (ISRAEL)
Acquired by NCR Corp. (New) 02/06/2013
Each share Ordinary ILS 1 par exchanged for $30 cash

RETECH INC (UT)
Recapitalized as Fax Broadcasting Network Corp. 10/5/95
Each share Common $0.001 par exchanged for (0.0002) share Common $0.001 par
(See Fax Broadcasting Network Corp.)

RETEK INC (DE)
Merged into Oracle Corp. 04/12/2005
Each share Common 1¢ par exchanged for $11.25 cash

RETINAPHARMA INTL INC (NV)
Each share old Common $0.001 par exchanged for (0.2) share new Common $0.001 par 07/20/2002
Name changed to Xtra-Gold Resources Corp. (NV) 12/19/2003
Xtra-Gold Resources Corp. (NV) reincorporated in British Virgin Islands 12/24/2012

RETIREMENT CARE ASSOC INC (CO)
Each share old Common $0.0001 par exchanged for (0.08) share new Common $0.0001 par 07/23/1993
Stock Dividend - 5% payable 05/15/1996 to holders of record 05/01/1996
Merged into Sun Healthcare Group, Inc. (Old) 06/30/1998
Each share Common $0.0001 par exchanged for (0.505) share Common 1¢ par
(See Sun Healthcare Group, Inc. (Old))

RETIREMENT LIVING INC (DE)
Common no par split (3) for (2) by issuance of (0.5) additional share 11/21/1980
Stock Dividend - 10% 02/15/1980
Merged into Forum Group, Inc. 09/08/1981
Each share Common no par exchanged for $4 principal amount of 10% 6-Yr. Promissory Notes due 08/31/1987, (2) Common Stock Purchase Warrants expiring 08/10/1986 and $9.50 cash

RETIREMENT LIVING TAX EXEMPT MTG FD LTD PARTNERSHIP (DE)
Name changed to Capital Senior Living Communities L.P. 3/17/93
(See Capital Senior Living Communities L.P.)

RETIREMENT PLANNING FDS AMER INC (MD)
Name changed to Davis Series, Inc. 10/01/1995

RETIREMENT RESIDENCES REAL ESTATE INVT TR (ON)
Acquired by Public Sector Pension Investment Board 02/02/2007
Each Trust Unit exchanged for $8.35 cash

RETIREMENTSOLUTION COM INC (NV)
Name changed to Global Investor Services, Inc. 10/01/2008
Global Investor Services, Inc. recapitalized as Investview, Inc. 04/09/2012

RETIX (CA)
Name changed to Vertel Corp. (CA) 04/09/1998
Vertel Corp. (CA) reorganized in Delaware as Hayden Hall, Inc. 01/05/2009

RETLAW RES INC (BC)
Name changed to Tamavack Resources Inc. 2/4/85
Tamavack Resources Inc. merged into Eurus Resource Corp. 5/1/90 which merged into Crystallex International Corp. (BC) 9/29/95 which reincorporated in Canada 1/23/98

RETREADING INTL INC (NY)
Charter cancelled and proclaimed dissolved for failure to pay taxes 06/27/1979

RETREIVER GOLD MINES CO. (CO)
Charter dissolved for failure to file annual reports 01/01/1917

RETRIEVE RES LTD (WY)
Reincorporated 01/16/1996
Place of incorporation changed from (BC) to (WY) 01/16/1996
Completely liquidated 11/01/1998
Each share Common no par received first and final distribution of (1) share Alamo Natural Resources, Inc. Common

RETROCOM REAL ESTATE INVT TR (ON)
Name changed 06/17/2013
Name changed from Retrocom Mid-Market Real Estate Investment Trust to Retrocom Real Estate Investment Trust 06/17/2013
Name changed to OneREIT 07/31/2015
(See OneREIT)

RETROSPETTIVA INC (CA)
Recapitalized as AMMO, Inc. 02/06/2017
Each share Common no par exchanged for (0.04) share Common no par

RETURN ASSUR INC (DE)
Company terminated common stock registration and is no longer public as of 01/16/2003

RETURN ON INVT CORP (DE)
Name changed to Tectonic Network, Inc. 3/10/2005

REUNION 56 OIL & GAS INC (AB)
Name changed to Call 900 Inc. 06/24/1993
Call 900 Inc. name changed to Xentel Interactive Inc. 08/03/1995 which recapitalized as Xentel DM Inc. 07/01/1998 which name changed to iMarketing Solutions Group Inc. 11/26/2010
(See iMarketing Solutions Group Inc.)

REUNION RES CO (DE)
Name changed to Reunion Industries, Inc. 4/19/96

REUNITED HLDGS INC (RI)
Charter revoked for failure to file reports or pay fees 09/22/1999

REUTER INC (MN)
Stock Dividends - 10% 6/29/79; 10% 7/2/80; 25% 12/15/81
Name changed to Green Isle Environmental Services, Inc. 7/21/92
Green Isle Environmental Services, Inc. name changed to Reuter Manufacturing, Inc. 8/25/95 which name changed to MagStar Technologies, Inc. 2/12/2001

REUTER LABS INC (MI)
Name changed to RLI, Inc. 03/14/1989
(See RLI, Inc.)

REUTER MFG INC (MN)
Name changed to MagStar Technologies, Inc. 2/12/2001

REUTERS GROUP PLC (ENGLAND)
Merged into Thomson Reuters PLC 04/17/2008
Each Sponsored ADR for Ordinary exchanged for (0.16) Sponsored ADR for Ordinary and $41.7247 cash
Thomson Reuters PLC exchanged for Thomson Reuters Corp. 09/10/2009

REUTERS HLDGS PLC (ENGLAND)
ADR's for Ordinary B 10p par reclassified as ADR's for Ordinary 10p par 04/27/1989
Stock Dividend - 100% 04/15/1994
Reorganized as Reuters Group PLC 02/18/1998
Each (15) ADR's for Ordinary 10p par exchanged for (13) Sponsored ADR's for Ordinary 25p par and $133.16712 cash
Reuters Group PLC merged into Thomson Reuters PLC 04/17/2008 which was exchanged for Thomson Reuters Corp. 09/10/2009

REVA ENTERPRISES, INC. (MA)
Name changed to Goddard Industries, Inc. 12/13/62
(See Goddard Industries, Inc.)

REVA INC (CO)
Reorganized under the laws of Delaware as Blue Wireless & Data, Inc. 11/15/2004
Each share Common 1¢ par exchanged for (1) share Common 1¢ par
Blue Wireless & Data, Inc. name changed to Big Star Media Group, Inc. 10/02/2009 which name changed to Pharmstar Pharmaceuticals, Inc. (DE) 04/08/2011 which reorganized in Nevada as Nexus Energy Services, Inc. 10/15/2013 which name changed to Illegal Restaurant Group, Inc. 06/02/2015 which name changed back to Nexus Energy Services, Inc. 08/13/2015

REVA RES CORP (BC)
Recapitalized as Grosvenor Resource Corp. 08/10/2016
Each share Common no par exchanged for (0.25) share Common no par

REVAIR CORP.
Dissolved in 1945

REVCARE INC (NV)
Each (15,000,000) shares old Common $0.001 par exchanged for (1) share new Common $0.001 par 9/19/2005
Note: In effect holders received $0.01 cash per share and public interest was eliminated

REVCO D S INC NEW (MI)
Merged into CVS Corp. 05/29/1997
Each share Common $1 par exchanged for (0.8842) share Common $1 par
CVS Corp. name changed to CVS/Caremark Corp. 03/22/2007 which name changed to CVS Caremark Corp. 05/10/2007 which name changed to CVS Health Corp. 09/04/2014

REVCO D S INC OLD (MI)
Common $1 par split (2) for (1) by issuance of (1) additional share 2/25/66
Common $1 par split (2) for (1) by issuance of (1) additional share 7/18/69
Common $1 par split (2) for (1) by issuance of (1) additional share 5/4/76
Common $1 par split (3) for (2) by issuance of (0.5) additional share 9/8/81
Common $1 par split (3) for (2) by issuance of (0.5) additional share 4/26/83

Acquired by a group of investors 12/16/86
Each share Common $1 par exchanged for $38.50 cash

REVDAY INDUSTRIES, INC. (NY)
Each Bearer Ctf. of Contingent Int. no par exchanged for $1.192 cash 08/28/1967
Completely liquidated 07/15/1968
Each share Common $1 par exchanged for first and final distribution of $47.50 cash

REVELARTIC MINES, LTD. (ON)
Charter cancelled for failure to file reports and pay taxes 11/1/52

REVELATION MIS INC (BRITISH VIRGIN ISLANDS)
Reincorporated under the laws of Florida as Jolen, Inc. and Common 1¢ par changed to $0.001 par 04/08/2015
Jolen, Inc. name changed to WOWI, Inc. 06/23/2016

REVELATION VENTURES INC (AB)
Voluntarily dissolved 03/03/2010
Each share Common no par received (0.583) ForceLogix Technologies Inc. Unit consisting of (1) share Common no par and (0.75) Common Stock Purchase Warrant expiring 12/23/2011
ForceLogix Technologies Inc. name changed to Courtland Capital Inc. (BC) 03/21/2011 which reorganized in Canada as Tree of Knowledge International Corp. 07/09/2018

REVELL INC (DE)
Reincorporated 07/06/1973
State of incorporation changed from (CA) to (DE) and Common no par changed to $1 par 07/06/1973
Stock Dividends - 10% 06/01/1973; 10% 05/01/1974; 10% 05/15/1975; 10% 05/14/1976; 10% 05/18/1977; 10% 03/17/1978
Merged into Compagnie Generale du Jouet 08/24/1979
Each share Common $1 par exchanged for $9 cash

REVELL-MONOGRAM INC (DE)
Merged into Hallmark Cards Inc. 12/21/94
Each share Common 1¢ par exchanged for $6.375 cash

REVELSTOKE COS LTD (AB)
Name changed 06/23/1972
Name changed from Revelstoke Building Materials Ltd. to Revelstoke Companies Ltd. 06/23/1972
Common no par split (3) for (1) by issuance of (2) additional shares 10/30/1972
Common no par split (2) for (1) by issuance of (1) additional share 07/13/1976
Common no par reclassified as Class A no par 07/21/1983
Each share Class A no par received distribution of (0.2) share Class B no par 07/28/1983
Merged into West Fraser Building Supplies Ltd. 09/19/1988
Each share Class A no par exchanged for $3.75 cash
Each share Class B no par exchanged for $3.75 cash
6% Preference 1961 Ser. $20 par called for redemption 10/31/1988
Public interest eliminated

REVELSTOKE INDS INC (NV)
Common $0.001 par split (4) for (1) by issuance of (3) additional shares payable 10/16/2006 to holders of record 10/13/2006 Ex date - 10/17/2006
Name changed to Geneva Gold Corp. 12/01/2006
Geneva Gold Corp. name changed to Geneva Resources, Inc. 03/05/2007 which name changed to Sono Resources, Inc. 03/11/2011 which name changed to Alaska Gold Corp. 06/27/2012
(See Alaska Gold Corp.)

REVEN HSG REIT INC (CO)
Reorganized under the laws of Maryland 11/07/2014
Each share Common $0.001 par exchanged for (0.05) share Common $0.001 par

REVENGE DESIGNS INC (NV)
Each share Common $0.001 par exchanged for (0.0000238) share Common $0.00001 par 06/24/2013
Name changed to Cartel Blue, Inc. 09/18/2015

REVENGE MARINE INC (NV)
Name changed to eTravelServe.com, Inc. 01/28/2000
(See eTravelServe.com, Inc.)

REVENUE OIL CO. (CA)
Dissolved 4/24/68

REVENUE PPTYS LTD (ON)
6% 2nd Preference $10 par called for redemption 06/30/1967
Old Common no par split (2) for (1) by issuance of (1) additional share 02/09/1968
6-1/2% Conv. 1st Preference Ser. A $20 par called for redemption 05/22/1968
6-1/2% Conv. 1st Preference Ser. B $20 par called for redemption 05/22/1968
Old Common no par split (3) for (1) by issuance of (2) additional shares 08/28/1968
Each share old Common no par exchanged for (1/3) share Class A Common no par and (2/3) share Class B Common no par 07/03/1981
Each share Class A Common no par exchanged for (1.26) shares new Common no par 12/31/1989
Each share Class B Common no par exchanged for (1) share new Common no par 12/31/1989
Each share new Common no par exchanged again for (1/7) share new Common no par 06/20/2003
Each share new Common no par exchanged again for (1) share new Common no par to reflect a (1) for (32) reverse split followed by a (32) for (1) forward split 06/22/2004
Note: Holders of (31) or fewer pre-split shares received $12.15 cash per share
Merged into Morguard Corp. 12/01/2008
Each share Common no par exchanged for (0.33) share Common no par

REVENUESHARES ETF TR (DE)
Large Cap Fund no par split (2) for (1) by issuance of (1) additional share payable 11/05/2008 to holders of record 11/03/2008 Ex date - 11/06/2008
Mid Cap Fund no par split (2) for (1) by issuance of (1) additional share payable 11/05/2008 to holders of record 11/03/2008 Ex date - 11/06/2008
Small Cap Fund no par split (2) for (1) by issuance of (1) additional share payable 11/05/2008 to holders of record 11/03/2008 Ex date - 11/06/2008
Name changed to Oppenheimer Revenue Weighted ETF Trust and ADR Fund no par, Financials Sector Fund no par, Global Growth Fund no par, Large Cap Fund no par, Mid Cap Fund no par, Navellier Overall A-100 Fund no par, Small Cap Fund no par and Ultra Dividend Fund no par reclassified as ADR Revenue ETF no par, Financials Sector Revenue ETF no par, Global Growth Revenue ETF no par, Large Cap Revenue ETF no par, Mid Cap Revenue ETF no par, Navellier Overall A-100 Revenue ETF no par, Small Cap Revenue ETF no par or Ultra Dividend Revenue ETF no par respectively 12/18/2015

REVERE AE CAP FD INC (MD)
Reincorporated 9/3/85
State of incorporation changed from (MA) to (MD) and Common $1 par changed to $0.001 par 9/3/85
Name changed to Revere Fund, Inc. 6/30/87
Revere Fund, Inc. name changed to Nature Food Centers Inc. 3/11/92
(See Nature Food Centers Inc.)

REVERE COMMUNICATIONS INC (AB)
Delisted from CDNX 01/02/2002

REVERE COPPER & BRASS INC (MD)
Class A no par changed to $10 par 00/00/1934
Common no par changed to $5 par 00/00/1934
Each share Class A $10 par exchanged for (3.5) shares Common no par 00/00/1941
Common $5 par changed to no par 00/00/1941
Common no par changed to $5 par and (1) additional share issued 05/04/1956
Common $5 par changed to $2.50 par and (1) additional share issued 05/31/1967
Merged into JOZ I Corp. 12/30/1986
Each share Common $2.50 par exchanged for $22.50 cash

REVERE (PAUL) CORP. (MA)
Merged into Avco Corp. 11/28/68
Each share Capital Stock $5 par exchanged for (1.8) shares Common $3 par and (1) share $3.20 Conv. Preferred no par
(See Avco Corp.)

REVERE FD INC (DE)
Acquired by Sigma Special Fund, Inc. 10/01/1982
Each share Capital Stock $1 par exchanged for (0.6633) share Common $1 par
Sigma Special Fund, Inc. name changed to ProvidentMutual Special Fund, Inc. 03/01/1990

REVERE FD INC NEW (MD)
Name changed to Nature Food Centers Inc. 3/11/92
(See Nature Food Centers Inc.)

REVERE (PAUL) FIRE INSURANCE CO.
Merged into Home Insurance Co. in 1948
Each share Capital Stock $10 par exchanged for (0.923) share Common $5 par
(See listing for Home Insurance Co.)

REVERE MNG LTD (ON)
Charter cancelled for failure to pay taxes and file returns 03/16/1976

REVERE OIL CO. (TX)
Charter revoked for failure to file reports and pay fees 3/15/62

REVERE PAUL COURIER FD INC (MA)
Completely liquidated 07/29/1977
Each share Capital Stock $1 par exchanged for (0.671195) share Eaton & Howard Growth Fund, Inc. Capital Stock $1 par
Eaton & Howard Growth Fund, Inc. name changed to Eaton Vance Special Equities Fund, Inc. 09/24/1982 which name changed to Eaton Vance Special Investment Trust 07/21/1992

REVERE PAUL INVS INC (MA)
Name changed to Revere AE Capital Fund, Inc. (MA) 10/1/84
Revere AE Capital Fund, Inc. (MA) reincorporated in Maryland 9/3/85 which name changed to Revere Fund, Inc. (MD) 6/30/87 which name changed to Nature Food Centers Inc. 3/11/92
(See Nature Food Centers Inc.)

REVERE RACING ASSN INC (MA)
Name changed to Westwood Group, Inc. (MA) 4/29/83
Westwood Group, Inc. (MA) reincorporated in Delaware 7/17/84
(See Westwood Group, Inc. (DE))

REVERE RES LTD (BC)
Struck off register and declared dissolved for failure to file reports 11/05/1993

REVERE TENNIS & SPORTS CORP (DE)
Merged into Garcia Corp. 05/03/1972
Each share Common 10¢ par exchanged for (1/3) share Common $1 par
Garcia Corp. name changed to TGC Inc. 12/31/1980 which recapitalized as Equion Corp. 01/31/1985
(See Equion Corp.)

REVERSIBLE COLLAR CO. (MA)
Name changed to Middlesex Products Corp. in 1935, which has been in process of liquidation since 1961

REVEST RES CORP (UT)
Name changed 06/22/1979
Name changed from Revest, Inc. to Revest Resources Corp. 06/22/1979
Involuntarily dissolved 03/31/1986

REVETT MNG CO (DE)
Name changed 02/18/2014
Each share old Common no par exchanged for (0.2) share new Common no par 11/19/2010
Name and place of incorporation changed from Revett Minerals Inc. (Canada) to Revett Mining Co., Inc. (DE) 02/18/2014
Merged into Hecla Mining Co. 06/15/2015
Each share Common no par exchanged for (0.1622) share Common 25¢ par

REVILLON, INC.
Assets acquired by Revillon Freres in 1951 which charter expired in 1959

REVILLON FRERES (NY)
Charter expired by time limitation 00/00/1959

REVISO ENERGY LTD (AB)
Name changed to Avatar Energy Ltd. 11/25/2010
(See Avatar Energy Ltd.)

REVIVE-IT CORP (NV)
Name changed to KL Energy Corp. 08/04/2008
(See KL Energy Corp.)

REVLON GROUP INC (DE)
Acquired by MacAndrews & Forbes Holdings Inc. 07/07/1987
Each share Common 1¢ par exchanged for $20.10 cash

REVLON INC (DE)
Common $1 par split (2) for (1) by issuance of (1) additional share 05/11/1961
Common $1 par split (3) for (2) by issuance of (0.5) additional share 12/01/1969
$1 Conv. Preferred $1 par called for redemption 06/01/1971
Common $1 par split (2) for (1) by issuance of (1) additional share 11/10/1976
Stock Dividend - 100% 07/03/1956
Merged into Pantry Pride, Inc. (New) 12/26/1985
Each share Conv. Preferred Ser. A $1 par exchanged for $27.15 cash
Each share $9 Conv. Exchangeable Preferred $1 par exchanged for $100 cash
Each share Common $1 par exchanged for $58 cash

Preferred Ser. A 1¢ par called for redemption at $5.21 on 10/08/2013 (Additional Information in Active)

REVNET SYS INC
Merged into Messagemedia, Inc. 8/9/99
Each share Common exchanged for (0.43) share Common $0.001 par
Messagemedia, Inc. merged into DoubleClick Inc. 1/22/2002
(See DoubleClick Inc.)

REVO VENTURES INC (NV)
Common $0.001 par split (15) for (2) by issuance of (7.5) additional shares payable 05/14/2008 to holders of record 04/23/2008
Ex date - 05/15/2008
Name changed to Vita Spirits Corp. 05/15/2008
Vita Spirits Corp. name changed to Gold Dynamics Corp. 03/05/2010

REVOLUTION COTTON MILLS
Merged into Cone Mills Corp. in 1948
Each share Common $100 par exchanged for (16.71) shares Common $10 par
(See Cone Mills Corp.)

REVOLUTION FIGHTING INC (DE)
Name changed to Legend Investment Corp. 01/24/2005
Legend Investment Corp. name changed to GiraSolar, Inc. 04/10/2006
(See GiraSolar, Inc.)

REVOLUTION RESOURCES CORP (BC)
Recapitalized as IDM Mining Ltd. 06/11/2014
Each share Common no par exchanged for (0.16666666) share Common no par

REVOLVE CAP CORP (AB)
Name changed to True North Corp. 03/14/2002
True North Corp. name changed to Empirical Inc. 11/30/2007
(See Empirical Inc.)

REVOLVER RES INC (BC)
Each share old Common no par exchanged for (0.1) share new Common no par 08/20/2014
Each share new Common no par exchanged again for (0.33333333) share new Common no par 12/08/2015
Name changed to GGX Gold Corp. 10/11/2016

REVONERGY INC (NV)
SEC revoked common stock registration 05/13/2015

REVOTEK INC (UT)
Each share old Common $0.0001 par exchanged for (0.1) share new Common $0.0001 par 6/3/91
Each (24,000) shares new Common $0.0001 par exchanged for (1) share Common no par 9/14/92
Note: In effect holders received $7.50 cash per share and public interest was eliminated

REWARD ENTERPRISES INC (NV)
Each share old Common 1¢ par exchanged for (0.1) share new Common 1¢ par 10/12/2004
Charter revoked for failure to file reports and pay fees 12/31/2010

REWARD GOLD MINING CO. (CO)
Charter dissolved for failure to file annual reports 01/01/1919

REWARD MNG CORP (BC)
Name changed to Riverdance Resources Corp. 03/11/1998
Riverdance Resources Corp. recapitalized as Luminex Ventures Inc. 05/26/1999 which recapitalized as Lateegra Resources Corp. 06/12/2002 which recapitalized as Lateegra Gold Corp. 01/12/2006 which merged into Excellon

Resources Inc. (BC) 08/05/2011 which reincorporated in Ontario 06/05/2012

REWARD RES LTD (BC)
Merged into Nexus Resource Corp. 05/05/1988
Each share Common no par exchanged for (0.33) share Common no par
Nexus Resource Corp. recapitalized as Pacific Gold Corp. (BC) 07/05/1990 which reincorporated in Alberta 05/12/1994 which reincorporated in Ontario 06/27/1995 which name changed to Worldtek (Canada) Ltd. 07/04/1996
(See Worldtek (Canada) Ltd.)

REWARDS NETWORK INC (DE)
Each share old Common 2¢ par exchanged for (1/3) share new Common 2¢ par 07/07/2009
Acquired by EGI Acquisition Parent, L.L.C. 12/14/2010
Each share new Common 2¢ par exchanged for $13.75 cash

REWARDS NEXUS INC (NV)
Recapitalized as One Step Vending, Corp. 04/06/2015
Each share Common $0.00025 par exchanged for (0.01) share Common $0.00025 par

REWORKS ENVIRONMENTAL CORP (CANADA)
Name changed to Forterra Environmental Corp. 02/22/2008

REX CHAINBELT INC (WI)
Capital Stock $10 par split (2) for (1) by issuance of (1) additional share 04/05/1966
Capital Stock $10 par reclassified as Common $10 par 05/15/1967
Common $10 par split (3) for (2) by issuance of (0.5) additional share 11/30/1972
Name changed to Rexnord Inc. 01/26/1973
(See Rexnord Inc.)

REX DIAMOND MNG CORP (YT)
Reincorporated 07/13/2000
Place of incorporation changed from (ON) to (YT) 07/13/2000
Reorganized under the laws of Ontario as Rex Opportunity Corp. 11/09/2011
Each share Common no par exchanged for (0.05) share Common no par

REX-FORGE, INC. (CT)
Name changed to Connrex Corp. (Conn.) 12/11/67
Connrex Corp. (Conn.) merged into Connrex Corp. (Del.) 10/31/68 which name changed to Chloride Connrex Corp. 8/27/73 which merged into Chloride Inc. 12/27/74

REX-HIDE, INC. (PA)
Common no par changed to $10 par and (1) additional share issued 1/10/57
Common $10 par changed to $5 par and (1) additional share issued 6/6/67
Each share Common $5 par exchanged for (4) shares Common $1.25 par 6/10/71
Reincorporated under the laws of Delaware and Common $1.25 par changed to $0.625 par 6/26/90

REX-HIDE RUBBER MANUFACTURING CO. (PA)
Name changed to Rex-Hide, Inc. in 1933

REX MNG U S A INC (NY)
Dissolved by proclamation 09/29/1993

REX MONTIS SILVER CO (UT)
Each share Common $0.001 par exchanged for (0.4) share Common $0.025 par 5/3/76

Proclaimed dissolved for failure to pay taxes 9/1/93

REX NORECO INC (NJ)
Common 10¢ par split (5) for (4) by issuance of (0.25) additional share 5/28/68
Common 10¢ par split (2) for (1) by issuance of (1) additional share 12/10/68
Common 10¢ par split (3) for (2) by issuance of (0.5) additional share 6/5/69
Merged into Itel Rail Corp. 6/29/88
Each share Common 10¢ par exchanged for $7.25 cash

REX PLASTICS INC (NC)
Each share Common $1 par exchanged for (0.01) share Common $100 par 02/23/1979
Merged into Henderson Acquisition Corp. 03/26/1984
Each share Common $100 par exchanged for $3,251.12 cash

REX PRECISION PRODS INC (CA)
Stock Dividends - 33-1/3% 02/28/1975; 50% 06/21/1976
Merged into Alco Standard Corp. 03/10/1977
Each share Common 50¢ par exchanged for (0.5125) share Common no par
Alco Standard Corp. name changed to IKON Office Solutions, Inc. 01/24/1997
(See IKON Office Solutions, Inc.)

REX PRODTNS INC (WA)
Each share old Common $0.0001 par exchanged for (0.05) share new Common $0.0001 par 11/01/1985
Company believed out of business 00/00/1989
Details not available

REX SIERRA GOLD CORP. (DE)
No longer in existence having become inoperative and void for non-payment of taxes 4/1/66

REX SILVER MINES LTD (BC)
Struck off register and declared dissolved for failure to file returns 8/3/90

REX STORES CORP (DE)
Common 1¢ par split (3) for (2) by issuance of (0.5) additional share payable 08/10/2001 to holders of record 07/31/2001 Ex date - 08/13/2001
Common 1¢ par split (3) for (2) by issuance of (0.5) additional share payable 02/11/2002 to holders of record 02/01/2002 Ex date - 02/12/2002
Name changed to REX American Resources Corp. 06/09/2010

REX URANIUM CORP. (CO)
Recapitalized as Unirex, Inc. 8/15/69
Each share Common 5¢ par exchanged for (0.2) share Common 25¢ par

REXACH CONSTR INC (PR)
Stock Dividend - 25% 1/2/69
Name changed to Rexco Industries, Inc. 5/13/70
(See Rexco Industries, Inc.)

REXALL DRUG, INC. (DE)
Merged into Rexall Drug Co. 5/6/55
Each share Common $2.50 par exchanged for (1) share Capital Stock $2.50 par
Rexall Drug Co. name changed to Rexall Drug & Chemical Co. 4/24/59 which name changed to Dart Industries, Inc. 4/22/69 which reorganized as Dart & Kraft, Inc. 9/25/80 which name changed to Kraft, Inc. (New) 11/21/86
(See Kraft, Inc. (New))

REXALL DRUG & CHEM CO (DE)
Capital Stock $2.50 par changed to

$1.25 par and (1) additional share issued 01/12/1965
Capital Stock $1.25 par reclassified as Common $1.25 par 05/03/1965
Name changed to Dart Industries, Inc. 04/22/1969
Dart Industries, Inc. reorganized as Dart & Kraft, Inc. 09/25/1980 which name changed to Kraft, Inc. (New) 11/21/1986
(See Kraft, Inc. (New))

REXALL DRUG CO. (DE)
Name changed to Rexall Drug & Chemical Co. 4/24/59
Rexall Drug & Chemical Co. name changed to Dart Industries, Inc. 4/22/69 which reorganized as Dart & Kraft, Inc. 9/25/80 which name changed to Kraft, Inc. (New) 11/21/86
(See Kraft, Inc. (New))

REXALL SUNDOWN INC (FL)
Merged into Koninklijke Numico N.V. Royal Numico N.V. 7/11/2000
Each share Common 1¢ par exchanged for $24 cash

REXAM PLC (ENGLAND & WALES)
Each old Sponsored ADR for Ordinary exchanged for (0.77777777) new Sponsored ADR for Ordinary and $0.799 cash 10/13/1998
Each new Sponsored ADR for Ordinary exchanged again for (0.2) new Sponsored ADR for Ordinary 10/23/2001
Each new Sponsored ADR for Ordinary exchanged again for (0.9) new Sponsored ADR for Ordinary 01/28/2013
Each new Sponsored ADR for Ordinary exchanged again for (0.88888888) new Sponsored ADR for Ordinary 06/02/2014
Merged into Ball Corp. 07/21/2016
Each new Sponsored ADR for Ordinary exchanged for (0.2284) share Common no par and $26.96666 cash

REXCO INDS INC (PR)
Reported in liquidation 00/00/1992
Details not available

REXCOM SYS CORP (TX)
Each share Common $0.0014 par exchanged for (0.25) share Common $0.0056 par 11/9/88
Charter forfeited for failure to pay taxes 11/18/91

REXDALE MINES LTD (ON)
Charter cancelled and declared dissolved for failure to file returns and pay fees 03/16/1976

REXEL INC (NY)
Merged into Rexel S.A. 12/30/97
Each share Common $1 par exchanged for $22.50 cash

REXENE CORP (DE)
Plan of reorganization under Chapter 11 Federal Bankruptcy Code effective 9/18/92
Each share Common 1¢ par exchanged for (0.025) share Rexene Corp. (New) Common 1¢ par
(See Rexene Corp. (New))

REXENE CORP NEW (DE)
Merged into Huntsman Corp. 8/27/97
Each share Common $1 par exchanged for $16 cash

REXFORD INC (DE)
Recapitalized as Lexon Technologies Inc. 07/21/1999
Each (70) shares Common $0.001 par exchanged for (1) share Common $0.001 par
Lexon Technologies Inc. name changed to Social Cube Inc. 03/28/2012

REXFORD MINERALS LTD (BC)
Recapitalized as Derrick Petroleum Corp. 08/22/1991

Each share Common no par exchanged for (0.25) share Common no par

Derrick Petroleum Corp. name changed to Earth Stewards, Inc. 09/29/1993 which recapitalized as Consolidated Earth Stewards Inc. 07/17/1997 which recapitalized as Royal County Minerals Corp. 08/29/2002 which was acquired by International Curator Resources Ltd. 08/01/2003 which recapitalized as Canadian Gold Hunter Corp. (BC) 12/30/2003 which reincorporated in Canada 07/29/2004 which name changed to NGEx Resources Inc. 09/22/2009

REXHALL INDS INC (CA)
Common no par split (2) for (1) by issuance of (1) additional share payable 07/19/2002 to holders of record 07/01/2002 Ex date - 07/22/2002

Stock Dividends - 5% payable 04/17/1996 to holders of record 04/03/1996; 5% payable 05/26/1997 to holders of record 05/12/1997; 5% payable 07/10/1998 to holders of record 06/19/1998; 5% payable 10/15/1999 to holders of record 09/15/1999

Plan of reorganization under Chapter 11 Federal Bankruptcy proceedings effective 10/09/2010

No stockholders' equity

REXHAM CORP (DE)
Acquired by Bowater Industries plc 11/23/87

Each share Common $1 par exchanged for $60.25 cash

REXNORD CORP (DE)
Incorporated 02/24/1987

Merged into BTR Dunlop Holdings, Inc. 01/31/1994

Each share Common 1¢ par exchanged for $22.50 cash

REXNORD INC (WI)
$2.50 Conv. Preferred Ser. A no par called for redemption 08/15/1977

$2.50 Conv. Preferred Ser. C $1 par called for redemption 08/15/1977

Common $10 par changed to $1 par and (1) additional share issued 09/30/1977

$2.36 Conv. Preferred Ser. B no par called for redemption 10/11/1983

Acquired by Banner Industries, Inc. (DE) 04/30/1987

Each share Common $1 par exchanged for $26.25 cash

REXON BUSINESS MACHS CORP (CA)
Under plan of reorganization each share Common no par automatically became (1) share Rexon, Inc. (CA) Common no par 2/28/83

Rexon, Inc. (CA) reincorporated in Delaware 3/19/91

(See Rexon, Inc.)

REXON INC (DE)
Reincorporated 3/19/91

State of incorporation changed from (CA) to (DE) 3/19/91

Assets sold for benefit of creditors 9/24/99

Stockholders' equity unlikely

REXORA MINING CORP. LTD. (ON)
Charter cancelled in 1970

REXPLORE RES INTL LTD (BC)
Name changed to Kemgas Sydney Inc. 12/29/87

Kemgas Sydney Inc. name changed to Kemgas International Ltd. (BC) 2/15/95 which reincorporated in Bermuda 6/23/95 which name changed to Kemgas Ltd. 5/28/96 which name changed to CalciTech Ltd. 7/25/2000

REXSPAR MINERALS & CHEMICALS LTD. (ON)
Recapitalized as Consolidated Rexspar Minerals & Chemicals Ltd. 6/9/67

Each share Capital Stock $1 par exchanged for (0.2) share Capital Stock $1 par

Consolidated Rexspar Minerals & Chemicals Ltd. name changed to Conrex Corp. 10/1/87 which merged into Falvo Corp. 6/30/89 which reorganized as Conrex Steel Corp. 5/28/99

(See Conrex Steel Corp.)

REXSPAR URANIUM & METALS MINING CO. LTD. (ON)
Name changed to Rexspar Minerals & Chemicals Ltd. 8/14/59

Rexpar Minerals & Chemicals Ltd. recapitalized as Consolidated Rexspar Minerals & Chemicals Ltd. 6/9/67 which name changed to Conrex Corp. 10/1/87 which merged into Falvo Corp. 6/30/89 which reorganized as Conrex Steel Corp. 5/28/99

(See Conrex Steel Corp.)

REXTERRA GOLD MINES, LTD. (ON)
Charter surrendered for failure to file reports and pay taxes 5/6/57

REXTON MINES LTD. (ON)
Charter cancelled for failure to file reports and pay taxes in 1970

REXWORKS INC (DE)
Merged into CMI Corp. 12/18/97

Each share Common 12¢ par exchanged for $1.6139 cash

REXX ENVIRONMENTAL CORP (NY)
Merged into Newtek Capital Inc. 09/19/2000

Each share Common 2¢ par exchanged for (1) share Common 2¢ par

Newtek Capital Inc. name changed to Newtek Business Services, Inc. (NY) 11/26/2002 which reincorporated in Maryland as Newtek Business Services Corp. 11/13/2014

REY-INDIN YELLOWKNIFE MINES, LTD. (ON)
Charter cancelled for failure to file reports and pay taxes in 1955

REYBARN CO., INC.
Liquidation completed in 1947

REYBOLD HOMES INC (DE)
Merged into R.I. Inc. 06/10/1976

Each share Common 5¢ par exchanged for $0.05 cash

REYMA, INC. (FL)
Proclaimed dissolved for failure to file reports and pay fees 10/04/2002

REYMER & BROTHERS, INC. (PA)
Each share Common $100 par exchanged for (8) shares Common no par 00/00/1928

Common no par changed to $6 par 00/00/1948

Acquired by Heinz (H.J.) Co. 09/30/1960

Each share Common $6 par exchanged for (0.08333333) share Common $25 par

(See Heinz (H.J.) Co.)

REYMONT GOLD MINES LTD (CANADA)
Recapitalized as Pallaum Minerals Ltd. 11/20/91

Each share Common no par exchanged for (0.1) share Common no par

(See Pallaum Minerals Ltd.)

REYNOLDS & REYNOLDS CO (OH)
Class A Common $10 par changed to $5 par and (1) additional share issued 11/15/65

Class A Common $5 par changed to $2.50 par and (1) additional share issued 4/2/68

Class A Common $2.50 par changed to $1.25 par and (1) additional share issued 3/24/72

Class A Common $1.25 par changed to 62-1/2¢ par and (1) additional share issued 4/15/86

Class A Common 62-1/2¢ par split (2) for (1) by issuance of (1) additional share 12/10/92

Class A Common 62-1/2¢ par split (2) for (1) by issuance of (1) additional share 3/15/94

Class A Common 62-1/2¢ par split (2) for (1) by issuance of (1) additional share payable 9/17/96 to holders of record 9/3/96 Ex date - 9/18/96

Class B Common 62-1/2¢ par split (2) for (1) by issuance of (1) additional share payable 9/17/96 to holders of record 9/3/96

Merged into Universal Computer Systems Holding, Inc. 10/26/2006

Each share Class A Common 62-1/2¢ par exchanged for $40 cash

Each share Class B Common 62-1/2¢ par exchanged for $40 cash

REYNOLDS ALUM CO CDA LTD (CANADA)
4-3/4% 1st Preferred $100 par called for redemption 12/30/1987

Public interest eliminated

REYNOLDS ALUMINUM SUPPLY CO. (GA)
5% Preferred called for redemption 12/31/1959

Completely liquidated 10/04/1964

Each share Common $1 par exchanged for first and final distribution of (0.212766) share Reynolds Metals Co. Common no par

Reynolds Metals Co. merged into Alcoa Inc. 05/03/2000 which name changed to Arconic Inc. (PA) 11/01/2016 which reincorporated in Delaware 12/31/2017

REYNOLDS AMERN INC (NC)
Common $0.0001 par split (2) for (1) by issuance of (1) additional share payable 08/14/2006 to holders of record 07/31/2006 Ex date - 08/15/2006

Common $0.0001 par split (2) for (1) by issuance of (1) additional share payable 11/15/2010 to holders of record 11/01/2010 Ex date - 11/16/2010

Common $0.0001 par split (2) for (1) by issuance of (1) additional share payable 08/31/2015 to holders of record 08/17/2015 Ex date - 09/01/2015

Merged into British American Tobacco PLC 07/25/2017

Each share Common $0.0001 par exchanged for (0.526) Sponsored ADR for Ordinary and $29.44 cash

REYNOLDS BROTHERS, INC.
Acquired by Reynolds Investing Co., Inc. 00/00/1930

Details not available

REYNOLDS DEBBIE HOTEL & CASINO INC (NV)
Filed a petition under Chapter 11 Federal Bankruptcy Code 07/03/1997

No stockholders' equity

REYNOLDS DIVERSIFIED CORP (NV)
Merged into Pennant Pacific Resources, Inc. 03/07/1984

For holdings registered on the transfer books of the United States transfer agent each share Common 1¢ par received $0.005295 cash

Note: Certificates were not required to be surrendered and are now valueless

For holdings registered on the transfer books of the United Kingdom transfer agent each (12.727) shares Common 1¢ par exchanged for (1) share Asia Oil & Minerals Ltd. Ordinary AUD $0.25 par and each (280) shares Common 1¢ par exchanged for (1) option to purchase (1) share Asia Oil & Minerals Ltd. Ordinary AUD $0.25 par

REYNOLDS ENGINEERING & SUPPLY, INC. (MD)
Reorganized in 1960

No stockholders' equity

REYNOLDS INVESTING CO., INC.
Reorganized as Reynolds Realization Corp. 00/00/1941

Each share Preferred exchanged for a Class A Liquidation Voting Trust Certificate for (1) share new Preferred $10 par

Each share Common exchanged for a Class B Voting Trust Certificate for (0.1) share Common 50¢ par

(See Reynolds Realization Corp.)

REYNOLDS METALS CO (DE)
Each share Class A no par exchanged for (0.75) shares Common no par 00/00/1929

Each share Class B no par exchanged for (1) share Common no par 00/00/1929

5.5% Preferred called for redemption 10/01/1953

Common no par changed to $1 par and (4) additional shares issued 09/26/1955

Common $1 par changed to no par and (0.5) additional share issued 11/04/1959

4.75% Preferred Ser. A $50 par called for redemption 02/15/1983

$2.30 Conv. Exchangeable Preferred no par called for redemption 05/14/1987

4.5% 2nd Conv. Preferred $100 par called for redemption 05/14/1987

Common no par split (2) for (1) by issuance of (1) additional share 07/01/1987

Increased Dividend Equity Securities Conv. Preferred no par called for redemption 12/31/1996

Stock Dividends - 10% 12/31/1947; 10% 12/31/1948; 10% 12/28/1950; 10% 08/08/1952

Merged into Alcoa Inc. 05/03/2000

Each share Common no par exchanged for (1.06) shares Common $1 par

Alcoa Inc. name changed to Arconic Inc. (PA) 11/01/2016 which reincorporated in Delaware 12/31/2017

REYNOLDS MINERALS CORP. (NY)
Stock Dividend - 100% 1/27/56

Charter cancelled and proclaimed dissolved for failure to pay taxes and file reports 12/15/67

REYNOLDS R J INDS INC (DE)
Common $5 par changed to no par 04/26/1978

Common no par split (2) for (1) by issuance of (1) additional share 12/10/1979

$2.25 Conv. Preferred no par called for redemption 10/01/1982

Common no par split (5) for (2) by issuance of (1.5) additional shares 06/17/1985

$4.10 Preferred Ser. A no par called for redemption 03/01/1986

Name changed to RJR Nabisco, Inc. 04/25/1986

RJR Nabisco, Inc. merged into RJR Holdings Group, Inc. 04/28/1989

(See RJR Holdings Group, Inc.)

REYNOLDS R J TOB CO (NJ)
Each share Common $25 par exchanged for (2.5) shares Common $10 par 00/00/1929

Each share Class B $25 par exchanged for (2.5) shares Class B $10 par 00/00/1929

Common $10 par reclassified as

REY-RHI

(REYNOLDS, continued)
Class B Common $10 par 03/31/1959
Class B Common $10 par changed to Common $5 par and (1) additional share issued 05/06/1959
Common $5 par split (2) for (1) by issuance of (1) additional share 10/06/1961
Each share 3.6% Preferred $100 par exchanged for $80 principal amount of 7% Subord. Debentures due 06/01/1989 and $0.425 cash 05/13/1969
Reincorporated under the laws of Delaware as Reynolds (R.J.) Industries, Inc. 06/29/1970
Reynolds (R.J.) Industries, Inc. name changed to RJR Nabisco, Inc. 04/25/1986 which merged into RJR Holdings Group, Inc. 04/28/1989
(See RJR Holdings Group, Inc.)

REYNOLDS R J TOB HLDGS INC (DE)
Merged into Reynolds American Inc. 07/30/2004
Each share Common 1¢ par exchanged for (1) share Common $0.0001 par
Reynolds American Inc. merged into British American Tobacco PLC 07/25/2017

REYNOLDS REALIZATION CORP.
Reorganized in 1946
No stockholders' equity

REYNOLDS SECS INC (DE)
Common $1 par split (3) for (2) by issuance of (0.5) additional share 5/23/75
Under plan of reorganization each share $2.50 Ser. A Conv. Preferred $1 par and Common $1 par automatically became (1) share Reynolds Securities International Inc. $2.50 Ser. A Conv. Preferred $1 par and Common $1 par respectively 1/1/76
Reynolds Securities International Inc. merged into Witter (Dean) Reynolds Organization Inc. 1/3/78 which merged into Sears, Roebuck & Co. 12/31/81 which merged into Sears Holdings Corp. 3/24/2005

REYNOLDS SECS INTL INC (DE)
Merged into Witter (Dean) Reynolds Organization Inc. 1/3/78
Each share $2.50 Ser. A Conv. Preferred $1 par exchanged for (1) share $2.50 Ser. A Conv. Preferred $1 par
Each share Common $1 par exchanged for (0.6) share Common $1 par
Witter (Dean) Reynolds Organization Inc. merged into Sears, Roebuck & Co. 12/31/81 which merged into Sears Holdings Corp. 3/24/2005

REYNOLDS SPRING CO. (DE)
Each share old Common no par exchanged for (0.2) share new Common no par in 1931
New Common no par changed to $1 par in 1934
Name changed to Consolidated Electronics Industries Corp. in 1954
Consolidated Electronics Industries Corp. name changed to North American Philips Corp. 2/14/69
(See North American Philips Corp.)

REYNOLDS URANIUM CORP. (NY)
Name changed to Reynolds Minerals Corp. 1/20/56
Reynolds Minerals Corp. charter cancelled 12/15/67

REYNOLDS VENDING CORP. (CA)
Charter suspended for failure to file reports and pay fees 4/1/64

REZ-TILE INDUSTRIES, INC. (FL)
Proclaimed dissolved for non-payment of taxes 8/28/64

REZCONNECT TECHNOLOGIES INC (NY)
Reincorporated under the laws of Delaware as YTB International, Inc. 01/04/2005
(See YTB International, Inc.)

RF MICRO DEVICES INC (NC)
Common no par split (2) for (1) by issuance of (1) additional share payable 03/31/1999 to holders of record 03/17/1999
Common no par split (2) for (1) by issuance of (1) additional share payable 08/18/1999 to holders of record 08/02/1999
Common no par split (2) for (1) by issuance of (1) additional share payable 08/25/2000 to holders of record 08/08/2000
Merged into Qorvo, Inc. 01/02/2015
Each share Common no par exchanged for (0.25) share Common $0.001 par

RF MONOLITHICS INC (DE)
Acquired by Murata Electronics North America, Inc. 07/01/2012
Each share Common $0.001 par exchanged for $1.78 cash

RF PWR PRODS INC (NJ)
Merged into Advanced Energy Industries Inc. 10/8/98
Each share Common 1¢ par exchanged for (0.329) share Common $0.001 par

RF TECHNOLOGY INC (CO)
Name changed to QuadraComm, Inc. 12/4/2000
(See QuadraComm, Inc.)

RF&P CORP (VA)
Each share 6% Guaranteed 25¢ par exchanged for (0.000008) share Common $1 par 12/23/1991
Each share 7% Guaranteed 25¢ par exchanged for (0.000008) share Common $1 par 12/23/1991
Each share Non-Vtg. Dividend Obligations 25¢ par exchanged for (0.000008) share Common $1 par 12/23/1991
Each share Common 25¢ par exchanged for (0.000008) share Common $1 par 12/23/1991
Note: In effect holders received $39 cash per share and public interest was eliminated

RFC RESOURCE FIN CORP (BC)
Acquired by Cominco Ltd. 7/12/96
Each share Common no par exchanged for U.S.$1.55 cash

RFI RLTY TR (OH)
Name changed to Discovery Realty Fund 05/06/1977
(See Discovery Realty Fund)

RFI RECYCLED FIBRE INDS INC (DE)
Name changed to Strandtek International, Inc. 10/28/1998
(See Strandtek International, Inc.)

RFID LTD (CO)
Old Common $0.001 par split (6) for (1) by issuance of (5) additional shares payable 12/15/2006 to holders of record 12/11/2006
Ex date - 12/18/2006
Each share old Common $0.001 par exchanged for (0.001) share new Common $0.001 par 04/02/2008
Name changed to OptimizeRx Corp. (CO) 04/30/2008
OptimizeRx Corp. (CO) reincorporated in Nevada 09/04/2008

RFID SYS CORP (DE)
Each (4.5) shares old Common $0.001 par exchanged for (1) share new Common $0.001 par 05/08/1998
Reincorporated under the laws of Nevada as Electronic Identification Inc. 05/03/1999
Electronic Identification Inc. name changed to Manakoa Services Corp. 03/22/2004 which recapitalized as TeslaVision Corp. 12/15/2008
(See TeslaVision Corp.)

RFM CORP (PHILIPPINES)
Sponsored ADR for Ordinary split (2) for (1) by issuance of (1) additional ADR payable 02/19/2008 to holders of record 02/15/2008 Ex date - 02/20/2008
ADR agreement terminated 08/10/2017
Each Sponsored ADR for Ordinary exchanged for (20) shares Ordinary
Note: Unexchanged ADR's will be sold and the proceeds, if any, held for claim after 08/13/2018

RFMR ACQUISITION CORP (NV)
Name changed to Great Northern Oilsands, Inc. (NV) 11/14/2006
Great Northern Oilsands, Inc. (NV) reorganized in Florida as New Asia Gold Corp. 06/05/2008 which recapitalized as New World Gold Corp. 05/08/2009

RFS BANCORP INC (MA)
Merged into Revere Federal Savings Bank (Revere, MA) 9/26/2001
Each share Common 1¢ par exchanged for $22.75 cash

RFS HOTEL INVS INC (TN)
Merged into CNL Hospitality Properties, Inc. 7/10/2003
Each share Common 1¢ par exchanged for $12.35 cash

RFS LIQUIDATING CORP. (DE)
In process of liquidation
Each share Common 10¢ par received initial distribution of $15 cash 3/28/80
Each (100) shares Common 10¢ par exchanged for second distribution of (1) Unit of Ltd. Partnership of RSR Associates L.P. plus $14 cash per share 11/17/80
(See RSR Associates L.P.)
Each share Common 10¢ par received third distribution of $1.02 cash 12/22/80
Assets transferred to RFS Trust in Dissolution and each share Common 10¢ par automatically became (1) Share of Bene. Int. 12/26/80
(See RFS Trust in Dissolution)

RFS TRUST IN DISSOLUTION (DE)
In process of liquidation
Each Share of Bene. Int. received fourth distribution of $0.40 cash 3/15/82
(See RFS Liquidating Corp. for previous distributions)
Note: Details on subsequent distributions, if any, are not available

RG AMER INC (NV)
Each share old Common $0.001 par exchanged for (0.16666667) share new Common $0.001 par 02/04/2005
Reorganized under the laws of Colorado as Sprout Tiny Homes, Inc. 04/21/2015
Each share Common $0.001 par exchanged for (0.00666666) share Common $0.001 par

RG GLOBAL LIFESTYLES INC (CA)
Common no par changed to $0.001 par 10/24/2005
Name changed to Sustainable Environmental Technologies Corp. 08/24/2010
(See Sustainable Environmental Technologies Corp.)

RG PPTYS LTD (ON)
Merged into G.A. Lee Management Ltd. 12/12/2003
Each Restricted Vtg. Share no par exchanged for $0.55 cash

RGA CAP TR I (DE)
Preferred Securities called for redemption at $50 on 06/05/2011

RGB COMPUTER & VIDEO INC (FL)
Name changed to Saf T Lok, Inc. 07/18/1996
(See Saf T Lok, Inc.)

RGV RES LTD (BC)
Struck off register and declared dissolved for failure to file returns 02/28/1992

RHAND INDS INC (AB)
Delisted from Alberta Stock Exchange 04/11/1995

RHAPSODY ACQUISITION CORP (DE)
Name changed to Primoris Services Corp. 08/18/2008

RHBT FINL CORP (SC)
Common $1 par split (5) for (4) by issuance of (0.25) additional share payable 09/10/1999 to holders of record 08/01/1999
Liquidation completed
Each share Common $1 par received initial distribution of (0.24987) share South Financial Group, Inc. Common $1 par payable 11/20/2002 to holders of record 11/11/2002
Each share Common $1 par received second and final distribution of $0.7075 cash payable 11/06/2008 to holders of record 10/31/2008
Note: Certificates were not required to be surrendered and are without value

RHEBA URANIUM MINING CORP. LTD. (ON)
Charter cancelled for failure to file reports and pay taxes in 1957

RHEEM MFG CO (CA)
4.5% Conv. Preferred $100 par called for redemption 01/02/1962
Merged into City Investing Co. (DE) 11/13/1968
Each share Common $1 par exchanged for $65 cash

RHEINGOLD CORP (NY)
Capital Stock $1 par reclassified as Common $1 par 04/24/1969
Merged into PepsiCo, Inc. 12/31/1973
Each share Common $1 par exchanged for $13 cash

RHEINGOLD EXPL CORP (BC)
Name changed to International Battery Metals Ltd. 08/29/2017

RHEOLOGICAL SYS INC (NY)
Each share old Common 1¢ par exchanged for (0.2) share new Common 1¢ par 3/2/81
Dissolved by proclamation 12/23/92

RHEOLOGICS TECHNOLOGIES INC (NV)
Name changed to KKS Venture Management, Inc. 07/24/2007
KKS Venture Management, Inc. recapitalized as Codima, Inc. 06/09/2008
(See Codima, Inc.)

RHEOMETRIC SCIENTIFIC INC (DE)
Name changed 11/30/1994
Reincorporated 11/01/2000
Name changed from Rheometrics, Inc. to Rheometric Scientific, Inc. 11/30/1994
State of incorporation changed from (NJ) to (DE) and Common no par changed to 1¢ par 11/01/2000
Name changed to Proterion Corp. 01/15/2003

RHI ENTMT INC (DE)
Issue Information - 13,500,000 shares COM offered at $14 per share on 06/17/2008
Plan of reorganization under Chapter 11 Federal Bankruptcy proceedings effective 04/01/2011
No stockholders' equity

FINANCIAL INFORMATION, INC.   RHI-RHO

RHI ENTMT INC (NY)
Merged into HC Merger Corp. 07/06/1994
Each share Common $0.001 par exchanged for $36 cash

RHINE INDS INC (NY)
Dissolved by proclamation 09/25/1991

RHINE WESTPHALIA ELEC PWR CORP (GERMANY)
Name changed to RWE AG 02/07/1990

RHINE WESTPHALIA ELECTRIC POWER CORP. (GERMANY)
See - Rheinisch-Westfalisches Elektrizitatswerk Aktien-Gesellschaft

RHINELANDER PAPER CO. (WI)
Each share Common $100 par exchanged for (5) shares Common $10 par in 1937
Each share Common $10 par exchanged for (2) shares Common $5 par in 1951
Merged into St. Regis Paper Co. share for share 12/30/58
St. Regis Paper Co. name changed to St. Regis Corp. 4/28/83 which merged into Champion International Corp. 11/20/84 which merged into International Paper Co. 6/20/2000

RHINELANDER TEL CO (WI)
Under plan of reorganization each share Common $1 par automatically became (1) share Rhinelander Telecommunications, Inc. Common $1 par 11/00/1990
Rhinelander Telecommunications, Inc. merged into Citizens Utilities Co. 11/30/1998 which name changed to Citizens Communications Co. 05/18/2000 which name changed to Frontier Communications Corp. 07/31/2008

RHINELANDER TELECOMMUNICATIONS INC (WI)
Merged into Citizens Utilities Co. 11/30/98
Each share Common $1 par exchanged for $46.62885116 cash

RHINO ECOSYSTEMS INC (FL)
SEC revoked common stock registration 06/07/2004
Stockholders' equity unlikely

RHINO ENTERPRISES GROUP INC (NV)
Recapitalized as Physicians Adult Daycare, Inc. 07/25/2006
Each share Common $0.001 par exchanged for (0.02) share Common $0.001 par
(See Physicians Adult Daycare, Inc.)

RHINO EXPL INC (BC)
Name changed to Walker River Resources Corp. 03/05/2013

RHINO HUMAN RES INC (NV)
Recapitalized as Rhino Novi, Inc. 07/23/2018
Each share Common $0.001 par exchanged for (0.01333333) share Common $0.001 par

RHINO OUTDOOR INTL INC (NV)
Recapitalized as Xtreme Motorsports International, Inc. 08/12/2008
Each share Common $0.001 par exchanged for (0.002) share Common $0.001 par
(See Xtreme Motorsports International, Inc.)

RHINO PRODUCTIONS INC (NV)
Name changed to Yakun International Investment & Holding Group 12/19/2011
Yakun International Investment & Holding Group name changed to QHY Group 09/26/2018

RHINO RES INC (BC)
Name changed to DSI Datotech Systems Inc. 04/19/1996
(See DSI Datotech Systems Inc.)

RHINO RES INC (CANADA)
Recapitalized as Immunovaccine Inc. 10/05/2009
Each share Common no par exchanged for (0.2) share Common no par
Immunovaccine Inc. recapitalized as IMV Inc. 05/10/2018

RHM PLC (UNITED KINGDOM)
Acquired by Premier Foods plc 03/16/2007
Details not available

RHN RECREATIONAL ENTERPRISES LTD (AB)
Cease trade order 08/01/2003

RHNB CORP (SC)
Common $2.50 par split (2) for (1) by issuance of (1) additional share 7/22/87
Merged into NationsBank Corp. 11/9/94
Each share Common $2.50 par exchanged for (0.35) share Common no par
NationsBank Corp. reincorporated in Delaware as BankAmerica Corp. (Old) 9/25/98 which merged into BankAmerica Corp. (New) 9/30/98 which name changed to Bank of America Corp. 4/28/99

RHNMEDIA (NV)
Name changed to Massive G Media Corp. 03/16/2007
Massive G Media Corp. name changed to International Minerals Mining Group, Inc. 06/21/2007 which name changed to Advanced Content Services, Inc. 02/05/2008 which recapitalized as New Wave Holdings, Inc. 12/08/2014 which name changed to PAO Group, Inc. 06/29/2017

RHODE ISLAND HOSP TR CO (PROVIDENCE, RI)
Each share Capital Stock $1,000 par exchanged for (20) shares Capital Stock $50 par 00/00/1945
Each share Capital Stock $50 par exchanged for (2.5) shares Capital Stock $20 par 03/01/1955
Each share Capital Stock $20 par exchanged for (2) shares Capital Stock $10 par 03/01/1962
Stock Dividends - 20% 12/31/1956; 14-2/7% 11/30/1965; 25% 11/17/1967
Reorganized as R.I.H.T. Corp. (DE) 05/29/1969
Each share Capital Stock $10 par exchanged for (1) share Common $1 par
R.I.H.T. Corp. (DE) reincorporated in Rhode Island 05/15/1970 which name changed to Hospital Trust Corp. 04/03/1973 which name changed to RIHT Financial Corp. 04/20/1983 which merged into Bank of Boston Corp. 11/14/1985 which name changed to BankBoston Corp. 04/25/1997
(See BankBoston Corp.)

RHODE ISLAND ICE CO.
Dissolved in 1951
No stockholders' equity

RHODE ISLAND INSURANCE CO. (RI)
Petitioned into receivership 7/20/50
Receivership closed and liquidation completed in December 1962
No stockholders' equity

RHODE ISLAND LIQUID AIR CO. (ME)
Charter revoked for failure to file reports and pay fees in 1901

RHODE ISLAND PUBLIC SERVICE CO.
Recapitalized in 1933
Preferred no par changed to $27.50 par
Class A no par changed to $55 par
Merged into New England Electric System 6/3/47
Each share Preferred $27.50 par exchanged for (1) share Common $20 par and $16.50 in cash
Each share Class A $55 par exchanged for (3.75) shares Common $20 par
(See New England Electric System)

RHODE ISLAND TAX FREE BD FD (MA)
Trust terminated 12/15/1989
Details not available

RHODES, INC. (GA)
Ctfs. dated prior to 10/17/1968
100% acquired by United States Finance Co., Inc. through purchase offer which expired 10/17/1968
Public interest eliminated

RHODES CHARTER HOUSE GROUP INC (UT)
Merged out of existence 1/3/94
Details not available

RHODES ENERGY CORP (AB)
Merged into Accord Capital Corp. 09/01/1989
Each share Common no par exchanged for (0.2) share Common no par
Accord Capital Corp. recapitalized as Consolidated Accord Capital Corp. 12/17/1991 which merged into Peak Energy Services Ltd. (Old) 06/14/1996 which reorganized as Peak Energy Services Trust 05/01/2004 which reorganized as Peak Energy Services Ltd. (New) 01/06/2011
(See Peak Energy Services Ltd. (New))

RHODES INC (GA)
Ctfs. dated after 7/15/79
Stock Dividends - 10% 12/15/81; 40% 4/16/84
Under plan of merger each share Common $1 par exchanged for $8.25 principal amount of 17% Jr. Subordinated Discount Debentures due 9/20/2000 and $21.50 cash 9/20/88

RHODES INC NEW (GA)
Merged into Heilig Meyers Co. 12/31/96
Each share Common no par exchanged for (0.5) share Common $2 par
(See Heilig Meyers Co.)

RHODES M H INC (DE)
Preferred $1 par called for redemption 12/15/50
Merged into Owosso Corp. 6/30/98
Each share Common $1 par exchanged for $14.51 cash

RHODES RES CORP (AB)
Merged into Terra Energy Corp. 01/30/2004
Each share Common no par exchanged for (0.2) share Common no par

RHODES RES INC (BC)
Recapitalized as International Rhodes Resources Ltd. 09/27/1982
Each share Capital Stock no par exchanged for (0.5) share Capital Stock no par
International Rhodes Resources Ltd. recapitalized as Consolidated Rhodes Resources Ltd. 02/16/1989 which recapitalized as Fairhaven Resources Ltd. 03/04/1992 which name changed to International Fairhaven Resources Ltd. 05/29/2002
(See International Fairhaven Resources Ltd.)

RHODES WESTN (CA)
Acquired by Amfac, Inc. 12/2/69
Each share Common 25¢ par exchanged for (1) share Conv. Preferred Ser. B no par
(See Amfac, Inc.)

RHODES WOLTERS & ASSOCS INC (NV)
Name changed to Skytex International, Inc. 05/29/1998
Skytex International, Inc. name changed to Majestic Companies, Ltd. 12/11/1998
(See Majestic Companies, Ltd.)

RHODESIA BROKEN HILL DEVELOPMENT CO. (ZAMBIA)
Name changed to Zambia Broken Hill Development Co. Ltd. 4/3/65
(See Zambia Broken Hill Development Co. Ltd.)

RHODESIAN ANGLO AMERICAN LTD. (ZAMBIA)
Name changed to Zambian Anglo American Ltd. (Zambia) 04/03/1965
Zambian Anglo American Ltd. (Zambia) reincorporated in Bermuda 06/26/1970 which name changed to Minerals & Resources Corp., Ltd. (Bermuda) 08/05/1974 which reincorporated in Luxembourg as Minorco 11/27/1987
(See Minorco)

RHODESIAN SELECTION TRUST LTD. (ENGLAND)
Stock Dividend - 100% 07/27/1951
Reincorporated under the laws of Northern Rhodesia 00/00/1954
Rhodesian Selection Trust Ltd. (Northern Rhodesia) reincorporated in Zambia as Roan Selection Trust Ltd. 03/31/1969 which reorganized into Botswana RST Ltd. and Roan Consolidated Mines Ltd. 08/18/1970 which name changed into Zambia Consolidated Copper Mines Ltd. 03/25/1982
(See each company's listing)

RHODESIAN SELECTION TRUST LTD. (NORTHERN RHODESIA)
Reincorporated in Zambia as Roan Selection Trust Ltd. and par value changed from Zambian 1£ to Kwacha 2 03/31/1969
(See Roan Selection Trust Ltd.)

RHODIA (FRANCE)
Each old Sponsored ADR for Ordinary exchanged for (0.0833333) new Sponsored ADR for Ordinary 06/12/2007
Acquired by Solvay S.A. 09/16/2011
Each new Sponsored ADR for Ordinary exchanged for $42.69216 cash

RHODIA-STER S A (BRAZIL)
GDR agreement terminated 4/15/2003
Each 144A GDR for Ordinary exchanged for $0.3627 cash

RHOKANA LTD (ZAMBIA)
Stock Dividend - 900% 01/25/1960
Merged into Zambia Copper Investments Ltd. 06/25/1970
Each ADR for Ordinary exchanged for either (2.407875) ADR's for Ordinary KMZ 24 par, (4.063192) Units of Loan Stock and (1) Unit of Interim Loan Stock or $2.7543 cash
Note: Option to receive stock expired 08/31/1970
Zambia Copper Investments Ltd. name changed to ZCI Ltd. 05/24/2010

RHOMBIC CORP (NV)
Recapitalized as Silverado Financial Inc. 04/29/2003
Each share Common $0.001 par exchanged for (0.2) share Common $0.001 par
Silverado Financial Inc. name changed to MediaTechnics Corp. 05/23/2008

RHONA COM ONLINE INC (BC)
Recapitalized as Winchester Minerals & Gold Exploration Ltd. 04/16/2004
Each share Common no par

exchanged for (0.5) share Common no par

RHONDA CORP (AB)
Name changed 06/26/2000
Name changed from Rhonda Mining Corp. to Rhonda Corp. 06/26/2000
Delisted from Toronto Venture Stock Exchange 10/06/2005

RHONE POULENC CAP DEV INC
Auction Rate Preferred called for redemption at $1,000,000 on 8/7/2002

RHONE POULENC EQUITY DEV INC
Auction Rate Preferred called for redemption at $500,000 on 8/28/2002

RHONE POULENC INVT CORP
Auction Rate Preferred called for redemption at $500,000 on 8/15/2002

RHONE-POULENC OVERSEAS LTD (FRANCE)
8-1/8% Guaranteed Preferred Ser. A called for redemption at US$25 plus $0.2765 accrued dividends on 11/19/2004

RHONE POULENC RORER INC (PA)
Unit Market Auction Preferred Ser. A $100 par called for redemption 09/25/1995
Depositary Shares Ser. 1 $100 par called for redemption at $100 on 08/04/1997
Merged into Rhone-Poulenc S.A. 11/25/1997
Each share Common no par exchanged for $97 cash

RHONE POULENC S A (FRANCE)
ADR agreement terminated 12/02/1994
Each ADR for Ordinary 100 Frs. par exchanged for $47.04 cash
Name changed to Aventis 12/15/1999
Aventis merged into Sanofi-Aventis 01/03/2005

RHP CDA INC (CANADA)
Through purchase offer all but (53) shares acquired by Canadian Pollard Bearings Ltd. 00/00/1971
Public interest eliminated

RHT HEALTH TR (SINGAPORE)
ADR agreement terminated 04/19/2018
No ADR's remain outstanding

RHYME INDS INC (BC)
Recapitalized as Viacorp Technologies Inc. 4/28/99
Each share Common no par exchanged for (0.25) share Common no par

RHYNUS RAMORE MINES LTD. (ON)
Charter surrendered for failure to file reports and pay taxes in 1953

RHYOLITE ROUYN MINES LTD. (ON)
Charter cancelled and declared dissolved for failure to pay taxes and file returns 12/7/77

RHYS INDS LTD (BC)
Name changed 10/6/88
Name changed from RHYS Ventures Ltd. to RHYS Industries Ltd. 10/6/88
Struck off register and declared dissolved for failure to file returns 8/30/96

RHYS RES LTD (BC)
Recapitalized as Pacific Rim Cobalt Corp. 10/24/2017
Each share Common no par exchanged for (0.25) share Common no par

RHYTHMS NETCONNECTIONS INC (DE)
Issue Information - 9,375,000 shares COM offered at $21 per share on 04/06/1999
Plan of liquidation under Chapter 11 Federal Bankruptcy Code effective 03/11/2002
No stockholders' equity

RIA RES CORP (BC)
Plan of arrangement effective 06/05/2013
Each share Common no par exchanged for (0.014) Qwest Diversified Capital Corp. Special Share Ser. 1 no par
Note: Unexchanged certificates were cancelled and became without value 06/05/2016

RIAL OIL CO (TX)
Name changed to Sage Energy Co. 06/27/1980
(See Sage Energy Co.)

RIATA RES CORP (AB)
Name changed to Petroforte International Ltd. 11/02/2011
Petroforte International Ltd. recapitalized as Canamax Energy Ltd. 02/21/2014
(See Canamax Energy Ltd.)

RIATA RES LTD (AB)
Plan of arrangement effective 07/31/1997
Each share Common no par exchanged for either (0.5) Unit of Calahoo Petroleum Ltd. consisting of (1) share Class C Preferred Ser. 1 no par, (0.5) Ser. A Warrant, and (0.5) Ser. B Warrant or $0.45 cash
Note: Option to receive Units expired 07/29/1997
(See Calahoo Petroleum Ltd.)

RIB SOFTWARE AG (GERMANY)
Name changed to RIB Software S.E. 04/10/2017

RIBAGO ROUYN MINES LTD. (ON)
Recapitalized as Consolidated Ribago Mines Ltd. 7/31/57
Each share Capital Stock $1 par exchanged for (0.25) share Capital Stock $1 par
(See Consolidated Ribago Mines Ltd.)

RIBAPHARM INC (DE)
Merged into ICN Pharmaceuticals, Inc. 08/22/2003
Each share Common 1¢ par exchanged for $6.25 cash

RIBBON CAP CORP (ON)
Name changed to SelectCore Ltd. 01/18/2007
SelectCore Ltd. name changed to Fintech Select Ltd. 08/28/2017

RIBBON COPIES CORP AMER (DE)
Charter cancelled and declared inoperative and void for non-payment of taxes 4/15/72

RIBI IMMUNOCHEM RESH INC (DE)
Common $0.001 par split (2) for (1) by issuance of (1) additional share 04/30/1985
Stock Dividend - 200% 10/25/1982
Merged into Corixa Corp. 10/06/1999
Each share Common $0.001 par exchanged for (0.1685) share Common $0.001 par
(See Corixa Corp.)

RIBLET PRODS CORP (DE)
Acquired by RPC Holding Corp. 12/22/1986
Each share Common 1¢ par exchanged for $15 cash

RIBOGENE INC (DE)
Merged into Questcor Pharmaceuticals, Inc. 11/18/1999
Each share Common $0.001 par exchanged for (1.509) shares Common no par
Questcor Pharmaceuticals, Inc. merged into Mallinckrodt PLC 08/14/2014

RIBOZYME PHARMACEUTICALS INC (DE)
Recapitalized as Sirna Therapeutics Inc. 4/17/2003
Each share Common 1¢ par exchanged for (1/6) share Common 1¢ par
(See Sirna Therapeutics Inc.)

RIBSTONE VALLEY PETROLEUMS, LTD. (ON)
Charter cancelled 2/10/58; no assets

RIC GROUP INC (DE)
Name changed to RIC International Industries, Inc. 08/13/1969
(See RIC International Industries, Inc.)

RIC INTL INDS INC (DE)
Chapter X bankruptcy proceedings filed 09/17/1970
No stockholders' equity

RICA FOODS INC (NV)
Each share old Common $0.0001 par exchanged for (1/3) share new Common $0.0001 par 12/29/1998
Acquired by Avicola Campesinos, Inc. 08/24/2011
Each share new Common $0.0001 par exchanged for $10.60 cash

RICAN CORP.
Liquidated in 1943

RICANA MINES, LTD. (ON)
Charter cancelled for failure to file reports and pay taxes 3/11/57

RICANAW MINES LTD. (QC)
Succeeded by North Sullivan Contact Mines Ltd. share for share in 1949
North Sullivan Contact Mines Ltd. charter cancelled 11/7/75

RICE, BARTON & FALES, INC. (MA)
Name changed to Rice Barton Corp. in 1941
(See Rice Barton Corp.)

RICE BARTON CORP (MA)
Preferred no par called for redemption in 1967
Name changed to Moody Holdings Ltd. 4/2/92
Note: Moody Holdings Ltd. is privately held

RICE BROADCASTING INC (GA)
Merged into Turner Communications Corp. 01/26/1970
Each share Common $1 par exchanged for (1) share Common $1 par
Turner Communications Corp. name changed to Turner Broadcasting System, Inc. 08/16/1979 which merged into Time Warner Inc. (Old) 10/10/1996 which merged into AOL Time Warner Inc. 01/11/2001 which name changed to Time Warner Inc. (New) 10/16/2003 which merged into AT&T Inc. 06/15/2018

RICE CAP MGMT PLUS INC (AB)
Reincorporated under the laws of Canada as Jovian Capital Corp. 09/29/2003
(See Jovian Capital Corp.)

RICE ENERGY INC (DE)
Merged into EQT Corp. 11/13/2017
Each share Common 1¢ par exchanged for (0.37) share Common no par and $5.30 cash

RICE LAKE GOLD MINES LTD. (CANADA)
Recapitalized as New Rice Lake Gold Mines Ltd. 7/20/67
Each share Capital Stock no par exchanged for (0.25) share Common no par
New Rice Lake Gold Mines Ltd. recapitalized as Jagor Resources Ltd. 7/24/70 which was acquired by Normandie Resource Corp. 9/12/85
(See Normandie Resource Corp.)

RICE MIDSTREAM PARTNERS LP (DE)
Merged into EQT Midstream Partners, LP 07/23/2018
Each Common Unit exchanged for (0.3319) Common Unit

RICE OIL CO. (DE)
No longer in existence having become inoperative and void for non-payment of taxes 3/22/22

RICE RANCH OIL CO. (CA)
Acquired by Reserve Oil & Gas Co. 5/25/65
Each share Common $1 par exchanged for (4/125) share 5-1/2% Conv. Preferred Series A $25 par and (43/200) share Common $1 par
(See Reserve Oil & Gas Co.)

RICE STIX, INC. (MO)
Dissolved 9/27/65

RICEX CO (DE)
Merged into NutraCea 10/04/2005
Each share Common $0.001 par exchanged for (0.7679951) share Common $0.001 par
NutraCea name changed to RiceBran Technologies 10/26/2012

RICH CAP CORP (BC)
Recapitalized as Consolidated Rich Capital Corp. 11/26/1996
Each share Common no par exchanged for (0.1) share Common no par
(See Consolidated Rich Capital Corp.)

RICH CHARTER OAK COPPER CO. (WY)
Charter forfeited for non-payment of taxes 7/19/27

RICH COAST INC (NV)
Reincorporated 07/14/1998
Each share old Common $0.001 par exchanged for (0.25) share new Common $0.001 par 06/19/1998
State of incorporation changed from (DE) to (NV) 07/14/1998
Recapitalized as Media Pal Holdings, Corp. 03/16/2010
Each share new Common $0.001 par exchanged for (0.01) share Common $0.001 par

RICH COAST RES LTD (BC)
Reincorporated under the laws of Delaware as Rich Coast Inc. 09/16/1996
Rich Coast Inc. (DE) reincorporated in Nevada 07/14/1998 which recapitalized as Media Pal Holdings, Corp. 03/16/2010

RICH COAST SULPHUR LTD (BC)
Recapitalized as Consolidated Rich Coast Sulphur Ltd. 06/19/1991
Each share Common no par exchanged for (0.2) share Common no par
Consolidated Rich Coast Sulphur Ltd. merged into Rich Coast Resources Ltd. (BC) 01/25/1993 which reincorporated in Delaware as Rich Coast Inc. 09/16/1996 which reincorporated in Nevada 07/14/1998 which recapitalized as Media Pal Holdings, Corp. 03/16/2010

RICH EARTH INC (NV)
Name changed to GlobalNet, Inc. 05/31/2000
GlobalNet, Inc. merged into Titan Corp. 03/22/2002
(See Titan Corp.)

RICH F D HSG CORP (DE)
Company advised no longer public as of 00/00/1987
Details not available

RICH GROUP YELLOWKNIFE MINES LTD (ON)
Merged into Discovery Mines Ltd. 07/01/1986
Each share Capital Stock $1 par exchanged for (0.75) share Capital Stock no par
(See Discovery Mines Ltd.)

RICH HILL MINES LTD (BC)
Recapitalized as Blackmist Resources Inc. 11/10/1980

Each share Capital Stock 50¢ par exchanged for (0.2) share Capital Stock no par
Blackmist Resources Inc. recapitalized as Stray Horse Resources Inc. 01/18/1985 which name changed to Oriole Communications Inc. 07/28/1987 which recapitalized as Consolidated Oriole Communications Inc. 09/10/1993 which name changed to Oriole Systems Inc. 03/26/1996
(See Oriole Systems Inc.)

RICH HILL RES LTD (BC)
Recapitalized as Nickolodeon Industries Corp. 06/05/1986
Each (2.75) shares Common no par exchanged for (1) share Common no par
(See Nickolodeon Industries Corp.)

RICH ICE CREAM CO., INC. (NY)
Name changed to S.B.R. Corp. 12/2/63 which completed liquidation 11/9/64

RICH INTL ENERGIES INC (NV)
Recapitalized 1/24/74
Recapitalized from Rich International, Inc. to Rich International Energies, Inc. 1/24/74
Each share Capital Stock 25¢ par exchanged for (0.1) share Capital Stock 50¢ par
Charter revoked for failure to file reports and pay fees 1/1/89

RICH LODE GOLD CORP (BC)
Stock Dividend - 10% 02/04/1985
Name changed to Mitek Industrial Corp. 10/30/1985
Mitek Industrial Corp. recapitalized as International Mitek Computer Inc. 03/27/1987
(See International Mitek Computer Inc.)

RICH MINERALS & OILS INC (NV)
Recapitalized as Rich International, Inc. 6/23/71
Each share Capital Stock 50¢ par exchanged for (0.2) share Capital Stock 25¢ par
Rich International, Inc. recapitalized as Rich International Energies, Inc. 1/24/74
(See Rich International Energies, Inc.)

RICH MINERALS CORP (AB)
Name changed to Blackhawk Resource Corp. 05/12/2009

RICH POINT MINES LTD (ON)
Name changed to Flying Cross Petroleum Corp. 05/11/1981
Flying Cross Petroleum Corp. merged into Flying Cross Resources Ltd. 12/04/1985 which merged into International Larder Minerals Inc. 05/01/1986 which merged into Explorers Alliance Corp. 10/13/2000
(See Explorers Alliance Corp.)

RICH PRODUCTS CORP.
Merged into Wilcox-Rich Corp. in 1928 which was dissolved in 1936

RICH RES LTD (BC)
Name changed to Rich Capital Corp. 03/25/1988
Rich Capital Corp. recapitalized as Consolidated Rich Capital Corp. 11/26/1996
(See Consolidated Rich Capital Corp.)

RICH S INC (DE)
Common no par split (2) for (1) by issuance of (1) additional share 5/11/55
Common no par split (3) for (2) by issuance of (0.5) additional share 5/1/64
3-3/4% Preferred $100 par called for redemption 10/1/65
Common no par split (3) for (2) by issuance of (0.5) additional share 1/12/72

Stock Dividends - 300% 11/1/48; 20% 9/29/52
Merged into Federated Department Stores, Inc. 10/29/76
Each share Common no par exchanged for (0.85) share Common $1.25 par
Federated Department Stores, Inc. name changed to Macy's, Inc. 6/1/2007

RICH STAR DEV (NV)
Name changed to China Gewan Biotechnology, Inc. 01/12/2015

RICH TOOL CO.
Merged into Wilcox-Rich Corp. in 1929 which was dissolved in 1936

RICHARD COSTAIN (CANADA) LTD. (CANADA)
See - Costain (Richard) (Canada) Ltd.

RICHARD D. IRWIN, INC. (DE)
See - Irwin (Richard D.), Inc.

RICHARD D. IRWIN, INC. (IL)
See - Irwin (Richard D.), Inc.

RICHARD PACKING CO (MN)
Statutorily dissolved 10/04/1991

RICHARD ROBERTS REAL ESTATE GROWTH TR 1 (MA)
Name changed to National Properties Investment Trust 08/20/1993
(See National Properties Investment Trust)

RICHARDS AIRCRAFT SUPPLY INC (FL)
Adjudicated bankrupt 12/22/1975
Stockholders' equity unlikely

RICHARDS MICRO TOOL INC (DE)
Merged into RM Tool Corp. 12/13/1976
Each share Common 2¢ par exchanged for $3 cash

RICHARDSON & BOYNTON CO.
Liquidated 00/00/1941
Details not available

RICHARDSON BOAT CO., INC. (NY)
Each share Common $100 par exchanged for (10) shares Common $10 par 01/00/1944
Each share Common $10 par exchanged for (10) shares Common $1 par 12/00/1944
Common $1 par changed to Common $100 par 00/00/1948
Acquired by United Marine, Inc. 12/00/1959
Details not available

RICHARDSON BOAT CO. (DE)
Adjudicated bankrupt 06/01/1962
No stockholders' equity

RICHARDSON (WILLIAM) COAL CO. (PA)
Articles of Dissolution filed 10/14/1955
Details not available

RICHARDSON ELECTRS LTD (IL)
Common 5¢ par split (3) for (2) by issuance of (0.5) additional share 6/1/85
Common 5¢ par split (3) for (2) by issuance of (0.5) additional share 5/5/86
Reorganized under the laws of Delaware 12/10/86
Each share Common 5¢ par exchanged for (0.5) share Common 5¢ par and (0.5) share Conv. Class B Common 5¢ par

RICHARDSON MERRELL INC (DE)
Common $1.25 par split (2) for (1) by issuance of (1) additional share 11/06/1968
Common $1.25 par split (2) for (1) by issuance of (1) additional share 11/02/1973
$4 Preferred Ser. A $1 par called for redemption 04/01/1974
Merged into Dow Chemical Co. 03/10/1981

Each share Common $1.25 par exchanged for (0.31158) share Common $2.50 par
Dow Chemical Co. merged into DowDuPont Inc. 09/01/2017

RICHARDSON VICKS INC (DE)
Merger into Procter & Gamble Co. 11/12/1985
Each share Common $1.25 par exchanged for $69 cash

RICHCO INVS INC (BC)
Reincorporated under the laws of Ontario 08/16/1994

RICHCOR RES LTD (CANADA)
Reincorporated 07/24/2001
Place of incorporation changed from (BC) to (Canada) 07/24/2001
Name changed to Bioxel Pharma Inc. 08/13/2001
(See Bioxel Pharma Inc.)

RICHDALE PETES LTD (BC)
Proclaimed dissolved 06/12/1978

RICHEY COMMUNICATIONS LTD (BC)
Delisted from Canadian Venture Stock Exchange 10/13/2000

RICHEY ELECTRONICS INC (DE)
Merged into Arrow Electronics, Inc. 01/07/1999
Each share Common 10¢ par exchanged for $10.50 cash

RICHEY PAC CABLEVISION LTD (BC)
Recapitalized as International Richey Pacific Cablevision, Ltd. 01/24/1992
Each share Common no par exchanged for (1/3) share Common no par
International Richey Pacific Cablevision, Ltd. name changed to Richey Communications Ltd. 02/13/1995
(See Richey Communications Ltd.)

RICHFAULT EXPLORATIONS LTD. (ON)
Completely liquidated 07/07/1971
Each share Common no par exchanged for first and final distribution of (0.25) share Avilla International Explorations Ltd. Capital Stock no par
(See Avilla International Explorations Ltd.)

RICHFIELD CARIBOO GOLD MINES LTD. (BC)
Dissolved in 1948

RICHFIELD EXPLORATIONS INC (AB)
Cease trade order effective 04/20/2001

RICHFIELD OIL & GAS CO (NV)
Each share old Common $0.001 par exchanged for (0.1) share new Common $0.001 par 10/23/2012
Merged into Stratex Oil & Gas Holdings, Inc. 12/01/2014
Each share new Common $0.001 par exchanged for (1) share Common $0.001 par

RICHFIELD OIL CO. OF CALIFORNIA
Reorganized as Richfield Oil Corp. 00/00/1937
No stockholders' equity

RICHFIELD OIL CORP (DE)
Common no par split (2) for (1) by issuance of (1) additional share 06/01/1961
Merged into Atlantic Refining Co. 01/03/1966
Each share Common no par exchanged for (1) share $3 Conv. Preference $1 par
Atlantic Refining Co. name changed to Atlantic Richfield Co. (PA) 05/03/1966 which reincorporated in Delaware 05/07/1985 which merged into BP Amoco PLC 04/18/2000

RICHFIELD PETROLEUM LTD. (CANADA)
Name changed to New Richfield Petroleum Ltd. 00/00/1952
New Richfield Petroleum Ltd. recapitalized as Twin Richfield Oils Ltd. 02/06/1969
(See Twin Richfield Oils Ltd.)

RICHFIELD UNITED OIL CO. (CA)
Charter cancelled for failure to file reports and pay taxes 00/00/1923

RICHFIELD VENTURES CORP (BC)
Each share old Common no par exchanged for (0.2) share new Common no par 05/27/2009
Merged into New Gold Inc. 06/01/2011
Each share new Common no par exchanged for (0.9217) share Common no par and $0.0001 cash
Note: Unexchanged certificates were cancelled and became without value 06/01/2017

RICHFOOD HLDGS INC (VA)
Common no par split (2) for (1) by issuance of (1) additional share 09/30/1993
Common no par split (3) for (2) by issuance of (0.5) additional share payable 09/30/1996 to holders of record 09/16/1996
Merged into Supervalu Inc. 08/31/1999
Each share Common no par exchanged for either (0.8239) share Common $1 par, $18.50 cash, or a combination thereof
(See Supervalu Inc.)

RICHFORD INDS INC (DE)
Stock Dividend - 50% 02/10/1969
Merged into Great American Industries, Inc. 03/12/1981
Each share Common 10¢ par exchanged for (0.07) share Common 50¢ par
(See Great American Industries, Inc.)

RICHLAND AVIATION, INC. (OH)
Acquired for cash 09/01/1965

RICHLAND COAL CO.
Name changed to Richland Collieries Corp. 00/00/1928
(See Richland Collieries Corp.)

RICHLAND COLLIERIES CORP.
Dissolved 00/00/1930
Details not available

RICHLAND GOLD MINES LTD.
Succeeded by Hiskerr Gold Mines Ltd. share for share 00/00/1944
(See Hiskerr Gold Mines Ltd.)

RICHLAND MINES INC (BC)
Recapitalized as Consolidated Richland Mines Inc. 01/28/1998
Each share Common no par exchanged for (0.11111111) share Common no par
Consolidated Richland Mines Inc. name changed to Apogee Minerals Ltd. (BC) 01/19/1999 which reincorporated in Ontario 01/21/2005 which name changed to Apogee Silver Ltd. 03/28/2011 which name changed to Apogee Opportunities Inc. 09/16/2016

RICHLAND OIL & GAS LTD. (AB)
Recapitalized as New Richland Oil & Gas Ltd. 04/01/1964
Each share Capital Stock no par exchanged for (0.02) share Common no par
(See New Richland Oil & Gas Ltd.)

RICHLAND OIL DEVELOPMENT CO. OF CANADA LTD. (AB)
Name changed to Richland Oil & Gas Ltd. 09/12/1955
Richland Oil & Gas Ltd. recapitalized as New Richland Oil & Gas Ltd. 04/01/1964
(See New Richland Oil & Gas Ltd.)

RICHLAND PETE CORP (AB)
Each share Class B Common no par exchanged for (0.2398) share Class A Common no par 05/12/1997
Class A Common no par reclassified as Common no par 06/05/1998
Acquired by Provident Energy Trust 01/16/2002
Each share Common no par exchanged for (0.4) Trust Unit no par and (1) share Terraquest Energy Corp. Common no par
(See each company's listing)

RICHLAND URANIUM CORP. (DE)
No longer in existence having become inoperative and void for non-payment of taxes 04/01/1965

RICHLODE INVTS CORP (BC)
Recapitalized as Thundelarra Exploration Ltd. (BC) 07/30/1998
Each share Common no par exchanged for (0.1) share Common no par
Thundelarra Exploration Ltd. (BC) reincorporated in Yukon 01/23/2001 which reincorporated in Westen Australia 09/08/2003 which name changed to Thundelarra Ltd. 03/21/2013

RICHMAC GOLD MINES (1936) LTD.
Recapitalized as Boymar Gold Mines Ltd. 00/00/1948
Each share Capital Stock $1 par exchanged for (0.33333333) share Capital Stock $1 par
Boymar Gold Mines Ltd. recapitalized as Marboy Mines Ltd. 09/20/1960
(See Marboy Mines Ltd.)

RICHMAC GOLD MINES LTD.
Reorganized as Richmac Gold Mines (1936) Ltd. 00/00/1936
Each share Capital Stock $1 par exchanged for (0.2) share Capital Stock $1 par
Richmac Gold Mines (1936) Ltd. recapitalized as Boymar Gold Mines Ltd. 00/00/1948 which recapitalized as Marboy Mines Ltd. 09/20/1960
(See Marboy Mines Ltd.)

RICHMAN BROS CO (OH)
Each share old Common no par exchanged for (3) shares new Common no par in 1929
New Common no par split (2) for (1) by issuance of (1) additional share 8/12/68
Merged into Woolworth (F.W.) Co. 3/25/69
Each share new Common no par exchanged for (1) share $2.20 Conv. Preferred Ser. A $1 par
Woolworth (F.W.) Co. reorganized as Woolworth Corp. 8/7/89 which name changed to Venator Group Inc. 6/12/98 which name changed to Foot Locker, Inc. 11/2/2001

RICHMARK RES LTD (BC)
Cease trade order effective 10/26/2001
Stockholders' equity unlikely

RICHMOND CAP CORP (CO)
Name changed to VarTech Systems Inc. 4/11/97

RICHMOND CEDAR WKS MFG CORP (VA)
Each share Capital Stock 25¢ par exchanged for (0.2) share Capital Stock $1.25 par 12/04/1962
Each share Capital Stock $1.25 par exchanged for (0.05) share Capital Stock $25 par 12/18/1968
100% owned by Company as of 00/00/1990
Public interest eliminated

RICHMOND CEDAR WORKS (VA)
Each share Capital Stock $10 par exchanged for (1) share Capital Stock $5 par, (1) share Richmond Cedar Works Manufacturing Corp. Capital Stock 25¢ par and $4.50 cash 00/00/1954
Capital Stock $5 par reclassified as Common 10¢ par 10/18/1960
(See Richmond Cedar Works Manufacturing Corp.)
Charter cancelled and proclaimed dissolved for failure to file reports 06/01/1976

RICHMOND CORP (VA)
Common $5 par split (5) for (4) by issuance of (0.25) additional share 03/02/1970
Common $5 par changed to $2.50 par and (1) additional share issued 06/11/1973
Merged into Continental Group, Inc. 06/29/1977
Each share $1.90 Conv. Preferred $5 par exchanged for (1.8) shares $2 Conv. Preference Stock Ser. A $1 par
Each share Common $2.50 par exchanged for (0.65) share $2 Conv. Preference Stock Ser. A $1 par and (0.3) share Common $1 par
Continental Group, Inc. merged into KMI Continental Inc. 11/02/1984
(See KMI Continental Inc.)

RICHMOND CNTY FINL CORP (DE)
Merged into New York Community Bancorp, Inc. 7/31/2001
Each share Common 1¢ par exchanged for (1.02) shares Common 1¢ par

RICHMOND EUREKA MNG CO (ME)
Capital Stock $10 par changed to $1 par 06/06/1960
Under plan of merger each share Capital Stock $1 par exchanged for $8.073 cash 06/20/2007

RICHMOND FREDERICKSBURG & POTOMAC RR CO (VA)
Each share 6% and 7% Guaranteed Stock, Vtg. Common and Non-Vtg. Div. Obligations $100 par exchanged for (4) shares $25 par of like classes 00/00/1949
Reorganized as RF&P Corp. 06/01/1988
Each share 6% Guaranteed Stock $25 par exchanged for (50) shares 6% Guaranteed Stock 50¢ par
Each share 7% Guaranteed Stock $25 par exchanged for (50) shares 7% Guaranteed Stock 50¢ par
Each share Non-Vtg. Div. Obligations $25 par exchanged for (50) shares Non-Vtg. Div. Obligations 50¢ par
Each share Common $25 par exchanged for (50) shares Vtg. Common 50¢ par
(See RF&P Corp.)

RICHMOND GRAPHIC SYS INC (RI)
Common $1 par changed to 50¢ par and (0.5) additional share issued 07/28/1975
Reorganized under Chapter 11 bankruptcy proceedings 03/10/1981
No stockholders' equity

RICHMOND GULF RES LTD (ON)
Recapitalized as Richwest Holdings Inc. 09/01/1992
Each share Subordinate no par exchanged for (0.1) share Subordinate no par
(See Richwest Holdings Inc.)

RICHMOND HILL SVGS BK (FLORAL PARK, NY)
Merged into North Side Savings Bank (Bronx, NY) 10/31/1988
Each share Common $1 par exchanged for $23.75 cash

RICHMOND HOMES INC (IN)
Common no par changed to $1 par 12/08/1955
Name changed to Travers, Inc. 04/24/1969

RICHMOND HOSIERY MILLS (GA)
Recapitalized 00/00/1937
Each share 8% 1st Preferred $100 par exchanged for (1) share $3.50 1st Preferred no par and (1) share Class A Preferred no par
Each share 8% Class B Preferred $100 par exchanged for (1) share Class A Preferred no par and (1) share Class B Common no par
Each share Common no par exchanged for (0.25) share Class B Common no par
Recapitalized 00/00/1947
Each share Class A Preferred no par exchanged for (4) shares Class A Preferred $7.50 par
Each share Class B Common no par exchanged for (4) shares Class B Common $7.50 par
$7.50 1st Preferred called for redemption 06/20/1964
Became insolvent and went out of business 00/00/1969-00/00/1970
Details not available

RICHMOND ICE CO., INC. (VA)
Recapitalized 00/00/1939
Each share 7% Preferred $100 par exchanged for (1) share Class B Common $10 par
Common Stock had no equity and was declared to be without value
Acquired by Richmond Cold Storage by purchase of all Class B Common shares 03/31/1962

RICHMOND INSURANCE CO. OF NEW YORK
Merged into Westchester Fire Insurance Co. 00/00/1948
Each share Capital Stock $5 par exchanged for (1.10) shares Capital Stock $2.50 par
Westchester Fire Insurance Co. acquired by Crum & Forster 11/07/1969
(See Crum & Forster)

RICHMOND LIFE INSURANCE CO., INC. (VA)
Name changed to Richmond Life Insurance Co. 04/30/1964
Richmond Life Insurance Co. merged into First Commonwealth Corp. 12/31/1972
(See First Commonwealth Corp.)

RICHMOND LIFE INS INC (VA)
Common $2.50 par changed to $1 par and (1.5) additional shares issued 05/22/1964
Voting Trust Agreement terminated 05/27/1966
Each VTC for Common $1 par exchanged for (1) share Common $1 par
Merged into First Commonwealth Corp. 12/31/1972
Each share Common $1 par exchanged for (0.444444) share Common $1 par
(See First Commonwealth Corp.)

RICHMOND NEWSPAPERS INC (VA)
Reorganized as Media General, Inc. (Old) 08/15/1969
Each share Class A Non-Vtg. Common $5 par exchanged for (1) share Class A Non-Vtg. Common $5 par
Each share Class B Common $5 par exchanged for (1) share Class B Common $5 par
Media General, Inc. (Old) merged into Media General, Inc. (New) 12/22/2014 which merged into Nexstar Media Group, Inc. 01/18/2017

RICHMOND RADIATOR CO. (DE)
Each share Preferred no par exchanged for (1.25) shares Preferred $50 par and (0.1) share Common no par 00/00/1927
Preferred $50 par changed to no par
Common no par exchanged for new Common no par 00/00/1932
Each share Preferred no par issued prior to 03/01/1935 exchanged for (4) shares Common $1 par 00/00/1935
Each share Preferred no par issued subsequent to 03/01/1935 exchanged for (3) shares Common $1 par 00/00/1935
Each share Common no par exchanged for (0.33333333) share Common $1 par 00/00/1935
Merged into Rheem Manufacturing Co. 03/30/1956
Each share Common $1 par exchanged for (0.25) share Common $1 par
(See Rheem Manufacturing Co.)

RICHMOND ROW CAP CORP (AB)
Recapitalized as Gold Royalties Corp. 08/27/2012
Each share Common no par exchanged for (0.2) share Common no par
Gold Royalties Corp. merged into Sandstorm Gold Ltd. 05/05/2015

RICHMOND SAND & GRAVEL CORP.
In process of liquidation 00/00/1945
Details not available

RICHMOND SVCS INC (DE)
Reincorporated under the laws of Nevada 04/21/1999
Richmond Services, Inc. (NV) name changed to TechNature, Inc. 08/29/1999 which name changed back to Richmond Services, Inc. 01/25/2000 which name changed to eKnowledge.com Inc. 04/28/2000 which name changed to eKnowledge Group Inc. 05/09/2000 which recapitalized as Amazon Oil & Energy Corp. 09/21/2006 which name changed to AEC Holdings, Corp. 02/20/2007
(See AEC Holdings, Corp.)

RICHMOND SVCS INC (NV)
Each share Common $0.0001 par exchanged for (0.66666666) share Common $0.0001 par 11/09/1999
Name changed to eKnowledge.com Inc. 04/28/2000
eKnowledge.com Inc. name changed to eKnowledge Group Inc. 05/09/2000 which recapitalized as Amazon Oil & Energy Corp. 09/21/2006 which name changed to AEC Holdings, Corp. 02/20/2007
(See AEC Holdings, Corp.)

RICHMOND TANK CAR & MANUFACTURING CO. (TX)
100% acquired by Business Funds, Inc. through purchase offer which expired 05/15/1969
Public interest eliminated

RICHMOND TANK CAR CO (DE)
Plan of reorganization under Chapter 11 Federal Bankruptcy proceedings confirmed 02/09/1990
No stockholders' equity

RICHMOND TELEVISION CORP.
Bankrupt 00/00/1952
No stockholders' equity

RICHMONT MINES INC (QC)
Merged into Alamos Gold Inc. (New) 11/24/2017
Each share Common no par exchanged for (1.385) share Class A Common no par
Note: Unexchanged certificates will be cancelled and become without value 11/24/2023

RICHORE GOLD MINES LTD. (ON)
Completely liquidated 07/07/1971
Each share Capital Stock $1 par exchanged for first and final distribution of (0.181818) share Avilla International Explorations Ltd. Capital Stock no par
(See Avilla International Explorations Ltd.)

RICHPINE MINES LTD. (ON)
Charter revoked for failure to file reports and pay fees 04/29/1970

RICHPORT RES LTD (BC)
Merged into Veronex Resources Ltd. 11/03/1988
Each share Common no par exchanged for (0.5) share Common no par
Veronex Resources Ltd. recapitalized as International Veronex Resources Ltd. 10/20/1992 which name changed to Veronex Technologies Inc. 12/04/1997
(See Veronex Technologies Inc.)

RICHTECH INC. (UT)
Proclaimed dissolved for failure to pay taxes 12/31/1975

RICHTON INDS LTD (NY)
Name changed to Parker Rich Group Ltd. 04/20/1981
Parker Rich Group Ltd. recapitalized as Project 80's Holding Corp. 03/25/1983 which recapitalized as Titan Resources Inc. 09/27/1994 which recapitalized as Palm Works Inc. 09/28/1999 which name changed to Zydant Corp. 10/17/2000

RICHTON INTL CORP (DE)
Common 10¢ par split (3) for (2) by issuance of (0.5) additional share 04/30/1971
Merged into Deere & Co. 10/02/2001
Each share Common 10¢ par exchanged for $36.13 cash

RICHTREE INC (ON)
Deemed to have filed an assignment under the Bankruptcy and Insolvency Act 06/14/2005
No stockholders' equity

RICHVIEW RES INC NEW (ON)
Merged into Cadillac Ventures Inc. 01/15/2010
Each share Common no par exchanged for (1/9) share Common no par

RICHVIEW RES INC OLD (ON)
Under plan of reorganization each share Common no par automatically became (1) share Richview Resources Inc. (New) Common no par 11/24/2004
Richview Resources Inc. (New) merged into Cadillac Ventures Inc. 01/15/2010

RICHWELL PETROLEUMS LTD. (ON)
Merged into North West Pacific Developments Ltd. 06/25/1962
Each share Capital Stock no par exchanged for (1) share Capital Stock no par
North West Pacific Developments Ltd. recapitalized as N.W.P. Developments Ltd. 02/28/1966 which recapitalized as N.W.P. Resources Ltd. 06/17/1981 which merged into Golden North Resource Corp. 09/11/1984 which merged into Caledonia Mining Corp. (BC) 02/04/1992 which reincorporated in Canada 03/29/1995 which reincorporated in Jersey as Caledonia Mining Corp. PLC 03/24/2016

RICHWELL RES LTD (BC)
Struck off register and declared dissolved for failure to file returns 04/15/1994

RICHWEST HLDS INC (ON)
Delisted from Canadian Dealer Network 10/13/2000

RICHWILL INCOME FUND (DE)
Name changed to Wellesley Income Fund (DE) 05/25/1970
Wellesley Income Fund (DE) reincorporated in Maryland 04/01/1973 which name changed to Vanguard/Wellesley Income Fund, Inc. (MD) 04/30/1993 which reincorporated in Delaware as Vanguard Wellesley Income Fund 05/29/1998

RICHWOOD INDS LTD (BC)
Struck off register and declared dissolved for failure to file returns 06/25/1979

RICHWOOD MUTUAL WATER CO. (CA)
Charter suspended for failure to file reports and pay fees 04/01/1992

RICHWOOD SILVER MINES LTD. (BC)
Name changed to Richwood Industries Ltd. 11/04/1969
(See Richwood Industries Ltd.)

RICKARD GOLD MINES, LTD. (ON)
Charter revoked for failure to file reports and pay fees 05/30/1960

RICKS CABARET INTL INC (TX)
Each share old Common 1¢ par exchanged for (0.5) share new Common 1¢ par 03/16/1999
Name changed to RCI Hospitality Holdings, Inc. 08/12/2014

RICKSHA INC (CO)
Charter dissolved for failure to maintain a Resident Agent 01/01/1990

RICKYS BRD SHOP INC (NV)
Common $0.001 par split (15) for (1) by issuance of (14) additional shares payable 11/18/2009 to holders of record 11/18/2009
Name changed to KlausTech, Inc. 01/29/2010

RICO ARGENTINE MNG CO (UT)
Stock Dividend - 10% 12/21/1951
Merged into Crystal Oil Co. (MD) 07/03/1974
Each share Common 50¢ par exchanged for (0.67) share Common $1 par and (1) Non-Transferable Ctf. of Contingent Int.
Note: Each Ctf. of Contingent Int. exchanged for (0.0917) share Common $1 par 07/05/1975
Crystal Oil Co. (MD) reincorporated in Louisiana 05/04/1984 which name changed to Crystal Gas Storage Inc. 06/21/1999

RICO COPPER MINES LTD. (BC)
Completely liquidated 02/20/1967
Each share Common no par exchanged for first and final distribution of (0.05) share Rico Copper (1966) Ltd. Common no par
Rico Copper (1966) Ltd. name changed to McNellen Resources Inc. 10/09/1981 which merged into Golden Goose Resources Inc. 09/30/1996 which merged into Kodiak Exploration Ltd. 12/16/2010 which name changed to Prodigy Gold Inc. 01/04/2011 which merged into Argonaut Gold Inc. 12/11/2012

RICO COPPER 1966 LTD (BC)
Name changed to McNellen Resources Inc. 10/09/1981
McNellen Resources Inc. merged into Golden Goose Resources Inc. 09/30/1996 which merged into Kodiak Exploration Ltd. 12/16/2010 which name changed to Prodigy Gold Inc. 01/04/2011 which merged into Argonaut Gold Inc. 12/11/2012

RICO DIABLO MNG INC (UT)
Reorganized under the laws of Nevada 12/27/1988
Each (15) shares Capital Stock $0.001 par exchanged for (1) share Common $0.001 par

RICOCHET INDS INC (AB)
Recapitalized as Delicious Alternative Desserts Ltd. 08/14/1997
Each share Common no par exchanged for (0.2) share Common no par
(See Delicious Alternative Desserts Ltd.)

RICOCO INC (UT)
Recapitalized as Surgimed International, Inc. 10/01/1985
Each share Common $0.001 par exchanged for (0.05) share Common 2¢ par
Surgimed International, Inc. name changed to NLB Capital Corp. 06/00/1987 which recapitalized as Integrated Masonry Systems International 11/01/1997
(See Integrated Masonry Systems International)

RICOH TIME CORP (FL)
Proclaimed dissolved for failure to file reports and pay fees 09/03/1976

RID A BUG CO (FL)
Name changed to Spectrum Group Inc. 12/15/1984
(See Spectrum Group Inc.)

RIDDELL SPORTS INC (DE)
Name changed to Varsity Brands, Inc. 9/19/2001
(See Varsity Brands, Inc.)

RIDDER BROTHERS, INC.
Reorganized as Ridder Publications, Inc. 00/00/1942
Details not available

RIDDER-JOHNS, INC. (DE)
Dissolved 2/5/63

RIDDER PUBNS INC (DE)
Common no par changed to 50¢ par and (64) additional shares issued 10/03/1969
Common 50¢ par split (4) for (3) by issuance of (1/3) additional share 04/16/1971
Merged into Knight-Ridder Newspapers, Inc. (OH) 11/30/1974
Each share $8 Conv. Preferred $1 par exchanged for (1) share Conv. Preference Ser. 1 no par
Each share Common 50¢ par exchanged for (0.6) share Common 8-1/3¢ par
Knight-Ridder Newspapers, Inc. (OH) reincorporated in Florida 08/31/1976 which name changed to Knight-Ridder, Inc. 04/30/1986 which merged into McClatchy Co. 06/27/2006

RIDDLE AIRLINES, INC. (FL)
Common $1 par changed to 5¢ par 01/30/1953
Each share Common 5¢ par exchanged for (0.25) share Common 10¢ par 08/20/1953
Name changed to Airlift International, Inc. 03/11/1964
(See Airlift International, Inc.)

RIDDLE AVIATION CO. (FL)
Name changed to Riddle Airlines, Inc. 11/17/1952
Riddle Airlines, Inc. name changed to Airlift International, Inc. 03/11/1964
(See Airlift International, Inc.)

RIDDLE URANIUM MINES, INC. (DE)
Merged into Fremont Uranium Corp. (CO) 09/21/1955
Each share Common exchanged for (1/3) share Common
Fremont Uranium Corp. (CO) merged into King Oil, Inc. 09/05/1956 which recapitalized as Lane Wood, Inc. 08/10/1964
(See Lane Wood, Inc.)

RIDE EM HARD STABLE INC (NV)
Name changed to SearchGuy.com Inc. 5/20/2004

RIDE INC (WA)
Name changed 06/30/1995
Issue Information - 500,000 UNITS consisting of (2) shares COM and (1) WT offered at $10 per Unit on 05/06/1994
Name changed from Ride Snowboard Co. to Ride Inc. 06/30/1995

Common no par split (2) for (1) by issuance of (1) additional share 07/28/1995
Merged into K2 Inc. 10/07/1999
Each share Common no par exchanged for (0.1) share Common $1 par
K2 Inc. merged into Jarden Corp. 08/08/2007

RIDE MTRS INC (NV)
Name changed to Smartdata Corp. (New) 06/15/2012
Smartdata Corp. (New) name changed to Stratean, Inc. 12/01/2014 which name changed to Cleanspark, Inc. 11/14/2016

RIDEAU CARLETON RACEWAY INVT LTD (CANADA)
Reorganized as Rideau Carleton Raceway Holdings Ltd. 10/25/71
Each share 6% Preferred $5 par exchanged for (1) share Common no par
Each share Common no par exchanged for (0.1) share Common no par

RIDEAU RES CORP (BC)
Recapitalized as Consolidated Rideau Resources Corp. 06/13/1989
Each share Common no par exchanged for (1/3) share Common no par
Consolidated Rideau Resources Corp. recapitalized as Brymore Oil & Gas Ltd. (BC) 02/01/1995 which reincorporated in Alberta 02/09/1995 which name changed to BXL Energy Ltd. 05/30/1996 which was acquired by Viking Energy Royalty Trust 06/21/2001 which merged into Harvest Energy Trust 02/07/2006
(See Harvest Energy Trust)

RIDEL RES LTD (BC)
Recapitalized as Mannix Resources Inc. 08/12/1999
Each share Common no par exchanged for (0.2) share Common no par
Mannix Resources Inc. name changed to International Tungsten Inc. 02/27/2014

RIDER EXPL INC (NV)
Common $0.001 par split (15) for (1) by issuance of (14) additional shares payable 12/01/2010 to holders of record 12/01/2010
Name changed to SSI International Ltd. 06/25/2012
(See SSI International Ltd.)

RIDER RES INC (AB)
Class A Common no par split (2) for (1) by issuance of (1) additional share payable 07/08/1998 to holders of record 07/06/1998
Class B Common no par reclassified as Class A Common no par 06/30/1999
Class A Common no par reclassified as Common no par 06/15/2000
Merged into Rider Resources Ltd. 02/21/2003
Each share Common no par exchanged for (0.9448) share Common no par
Rider Resources Ltd. merged into NuVista Energy Ltd. 03/04/2008

RIDER RES LTD (AB)
Each share old Common no par exchanged for (0.5) share new Common no par 05/28/2003
Merged into NuVista Energy Ltd. 03/04/2008
Each share Common no par exchanged for (0.354) share Common no par

RIDGE AVENUE PASSENGER RAILWAY
Acquired by Philadelphia Transportation Co. 00/00/1940
Each share Common exchanged for $86.45 principal amount of 3%-6%

Consolidated Mortgage Bonds and (0.7235) share $1 Part. Preferred $20 par
(See Philadelphia Transportation Co.)

RIDGE BIO LABS INC (UT)
Name changed to Petroleum Lift Systems Inc. 06/01/1983

RIDGE LD & DEV CO (CT)
Liquidation completed
Each share Common no par exchanged for initial distribution of $10 cash 12/20/1978
Each share Common no par received second and final distribution of $6.13 cash 01/15/1979

RIDGE REALIZATION CORP (DE)
Completely liquidated 06/01/1970
Each share Common 1¢ par exchanged for first and final distribution of $0.095 cash

RIDGE RUNNER, INC. (MN)
Out of business 12/15/72
No stockholders' equity

RIDGE TOOL CO. (OH)
Class A & B Common no par split (2) for (1) by issuance of (1) additional share respectively 2/28/66
Merged into Emerson Electric Co. 5/16/66
Each share Class A no par exchanged for (0.705) share Common $1 par
Each share Class B no par exchanged for (0.695) share Common $1 par

RIDGECREST HEALTHCARE GROUP INC (DE)
Recapitalized as Liberty Technologies, Inc. 10/20/2009
Each share Common $0.001 par exchanged for (0.005) share Common $0.001 par
Liberty Technologies, Inc. recapitalized as DomiKnow, Inc. 02/15/2013 which name changed to Gooi Global, Inc. 04/02/2015

RIDGECREST MANOR
Property sold in 1948

RIDGECREST RES LTD (BC)
Name changed to Hallicrafters Communications International Co. Ltd. 12/31/85
Hallicrafters Communications International Co. Ltd. name changed to Johnston & Frye Securities Ltd. 12/1/87
(See Johnston & Frye Securities Ltd.)

RIDGEDOME GOLD MINES LTD.
Acquired by Ridgedome Gold Mining Co. Ltd. on a (1/3) for (1) basis in 1938
Ridgedome Gold Mining Co. Ltd. name changed to Ridgegold Porcupine Mines Ltd. in 1939
(See Ridgegold Porcupine Mines Ltd.)

RIDGEDOME GOLD MINING CO. LTD.
Name changed to Ridgegold Porcupine Mines Ltd. in 1939
(See Ridgegold Porcupine Mines Ltd.)

RIDGEFIELD ACQUISITION CORP (CO)
Reincorporated under the laws of Nevada and Common 10¢ par changed to $0.001 par 6/23/2006

RIDGEFIELD EXPLORATIONS LTD. (ON)
Name changed to Pontiff Mining Ltd. 2/10/72
Pontiff Mining Ltd. charter cancelled 3/16/76

RIDGEFIELD URANIUM MINING CORP. LTD. (ON)
Name changed to Ridgefield Explorations Ltd. 3/16/64
Ridgefield Explorations Ltd. name changed to Pontiff Mining Ltd. 2/10/72

Pontiff Mining Ltd. charter cancelled 3/16/76

RIDGEGOLD PORCUPINE MINES LTD. (ON)
Charter cancelled 12/19/55

RIDGELAND MANOR BUILDING CORP. (DE)
Voluntarily dissolved 3/28/56
Details not available

RIDGELINE ENERGY SVCS INC (BC)
Name changed to RDX Technologies Corp. 08/21/2013

RIDGEMONT CAP CORP (BC)
Name changed to Ridgemont Iron Ore Corp. 11/23/2010
Ridgemont Iron Ore Corp. merged into Coastal Gold Corp. 06/28/2013 which merged into First Mining Finance Corp. 07/10/2015 which name changed to First Mining Gold Corp. 01/11/2018

RIDGEMONT IRON ORE CORP (BC)
Merged into Coastal Gold Corp. 06/28/2013
Each share Common no par exchanged for (0.593) share Common no par
Note: Unexchanged certificates will be cancelled and become without value 06/28/2019
Coastal Gold Corp. merged into First Mining Finance Corp. 07/10/2015 which name changed to First Mining Gold Corp. 01/11/2018

RIDGEPOINT MINERAL CORP (QC)
Recapitalized 10/31/97
Recapitalized from Ridgepoint Resources Ltd. to Ridgepoint Mineral Corp. 10/31/97
Each share Common no par exchanged for (1/3) share Common no par
Name changed to Jet Drill Canada Inc. 9/15/2000
(See Jet Drill Canada Inc.)

RIDGESTONE FINL SVCS INC (WI)
Stock Dividend - 5% payable 5/21/98 to holders of record 5/11/98
Merged into RAC Inc. 9/19/2006
Each share Common no par exchanged for $14 cash

RIDGESTONE RES INC (NV)
Common $0.00001 par split (7) for (1) by issuance of (6) additional shares payable 05/28/2008 to holders of record 05/28/2008
Name changed to GreenChek Technology Inc. 08/26/2008

RIDGEVIEW INC (NC)
Assets sold for the benefit of creditors in April 2001
No stockholders' equity

RIDGEVIEW OIL CO (CO)
Each share Common $0.001 par exchanged for (0.05) share Common 2¢ par 5/8/87
Reorganized under the laws of Delaware as Jaguar Corp. 10/26/98
Each share Common 2¢ par exchanged for (0.025) share Common 2¢ par
Jaguar Corp. name changed to Siberian Natural Gas Corp. 6/7/99

RIDGEWAY CORP (MI)
Capital Stock $15 par changed to $1 par 05/27/1957
Liquidation completed
Each share Capital Stock $1 par received initial distribution of $35 cash 07/01/1957
Each share Capital Stock $1 par received second distribution of $1.40 cash 02/20/1961
Each share Capital Stock $1 par received third distribution of $1.40 cash 09/15/1961
Each share Capital Stock $1 par received fourth distribution of $1.80 cash 10/01/1962

Each share Capital Stock $1 par received fifth distribution of $1 cash 06/19/1963
Each share Capital Stock $1 par received sixth distribution of $9 cash 03/12/1968
Each share Capital Stock $1 par exchanged for seventh and final distribution of $2.30 cash 12/22/1970

RIDGEWAY EXCO INC (CO)
Merged into Taurus Petroleum, Inc. 1/26/87
Each share Common $0.001 par exchanged for (0.106656) share Common no par
Taurus Petroleum, Inc. recapitalized as Taurus Entertainment Companies, Inc. 11/24/97 which name changed to Bluestar Health, Inc. 8/20/2004

RIDGEWAY OIL EXPL & DEV INC (CO)
Name changed to Ridgeway Exco Inc. 10/3/83
Ridgeway Exco Inc. merged into Taurus Petroleum, Inc. 1/26/87 which recapitalized as Taurus Entertainment Companies, Inc. 11/24/97 which name changed to Bluestar Health, Inc. 8/20/2004

RIDGEWAY PETE CORP (BC)
Name changed to Enhanced Oil Resources Inc. 06/11/2007
Enhanced Oil Resources Inc. name changed to Hunter Oil Corp. 08/16/2016

RIDGEWAY PETROLEUMS LTD. (AB)
Recapitalized as Nu-Ridgeway Petroleums Ltd. on a (0.1) for (1) basis 2/26/59
Nu-Ridgeway Petroleums name changed to Pere Marquette Petroleums Ltd. 3/20/63
(See Pere Marquette Petroleums Ltd.)

RIDGEWOOD ENERGY INDS INC (DE)
Name changed to Westridge Resources, Inc. 10/31/1990
(See Westridge Resources, Inc.)

RIDGEWOOD FINANCIAL CORP. (OH)
Dissolved 6/28/64
No stockholders' equity

RIDGEWOOD FINL INC (NJ)
Merged into Boiling Springs Bancorp 7/2/2001
Each share Common no par exchanged for $18 cash

RIDGEWOOD GAS CO.
Merged into Public Service Electric & Gas Co. in 1940
Each (2.5) shares Capital Stock exchanged for $100 principal amount of 5% Bonds

RIDGEWOOD HOTELS INC (DE)
Company terminated common stock registration and is no longer public as of 11/03/2003

RIDGEWOOD INDS INC (DE)
Adjudicated bankrupt 02/23/1979
Stockholders' equity unlikely

RIDGEWOOD MANOR
Property sold in 1948

RIDGEWOOD PPTYS INC (DE)
Each (13) shares old Common 1¢ par exchanged for (1) share new Common 1¢ par 08/28/1989
New Common 1¢ par split (2) for (1) by issuance of (1) additional share 09/20/1993
Name changed to Ridgewood Hotels, Inc. 02/19/1997
(See Ridgewood Hotels, Inc.)

RIDGTOP RES INC (NV)
Name changed to Pan World Minerals International, Inc. 12/29/1989

(See Pan World Minerals International, Inc.)

RIDGWAY L L ENTERPRISES INC (TX)
Common $1 par split (5) for (4) by issuance of (0.25) additional share 01/20/1972
Stock Dividends - 25% 04/15/1973; 10% 04/01/1974; 10% 10/15/1975
Name changed to Ridgway's Inc. 01/22/1976
(See Ridgway's Inc.)

RIDGWAYS INC (TX)
Merged into Y.R.J. Corp. 04/24/1979
Each share Common $1 par exchanged for $12.90 cash

RIDLEY INC (MB)
Name changed 02/28/2000
Name changed from Ridley Canada Ltd. to Ridley Inc. 02/28/2000
Acquired by Alltech, Inc. 06/23/2015
Each share Common no par exchanged for $40.75 cash
Note: Unexchanged certificates will be cancelled and become without value 06/23/2021

RIEDEL ENVIRONMENTAL TECHNOLOGIES INC (OR)
Reincorporated 12/29/88
State of incorporation changed from (DE) to (OR) 12/29/88
Name changed to Columbia Western Inc. 11/15/94
(See Columbia Western Inc.)

RIEGEL PAPER CORP (DE)
Reorganized 4/26/55
Each share Capital Stock $50 par exchanged for (5) shares Capital Stock $10 par in 1939
Each share Capital Stock $10 par exchanged for (2) shares Common $5 par in 1951
Reorganized from under the laws of (NJ) to (DE) and each share Common $5 par exchanged for (1.5) shares Common $10 par 4/26/55
Common $10 par changed to $5 par and (1) additional share issued 1/29/65
Acquired by Federal Paper Board Co., Inc. 1/3/72
Each share Common $5 par exchanged for (0.4) share $1.20 Conv. Preferred $1 par and (0.3) Common $5 par plus (1) (1) share Rexham Corp. Common $1 par
(See each company's listing)

RIEGEL TEXTILE CORP (DE)
Common $10 par changed to $5 par and (1) additional share issued 1/12/56
Common $5 par changed to $4 par and (0.25) additional share issued 10/22/64
Common $4 par changed to $2 par and (1) additional share issued 10/8/65
$4 Preferred Ser. A no par called for redemption 9/15/67
Common $2 par split (3) for (2) by issuance of (0.5) additional share 5/10/76
Merged into R.B. Pamplin Corp. 9/30/85
Each share Common $2 par exchanged for $23.50 cash

RIEKE CORP (IN)
99.9% acquired by Masco Industries of Indiana Inc. through purchase offer which expired 03/31/1978
Public interest eliminated

RIEKE METAL PRODUCTS CORP. (IN)
Common no par changed to $1 par and 200% stock dividend paid in 1940
Common $1 par changed to $5 par 1/29/58
Stock Dividends - 20% 9/29/50; 10% 9/29/51; 30% 6/30/59; 16% 9/30/61

Name changed to Rieke Corp.
1/28/66
(See Rieke Corp.)

RIEKES S & SONS INC (DE)
Common $1 par split (3) for (2) by issuance of (0.5) additional share 4/3/72
Merged into Alco Standard Corp. 6/2/75
Each share Common $1 par exchanged for $11.40 cash

RIES BIOLOGICALS INC (CA)
Charter cancelled for failure to file reports and pay taxes 1/2/87

RIESS MANUFACTURING CO.
Acquired by Delaware Aircraft Industries, Inc. 00/00/1942
Details not available

RIETZ INDUSTRIES INC. (NV)
Recapitalized as Modern Enterprises, Inc. 04/12/1975
Each share Common 3-1/3¢ par exchanged for (0.01) share Common 1¢ par
Holders of (99) shares or less affected only by change of name
Holders of (100) to (10,000) shares received (100) shares in exchange
Holders of (10,001) or more shares received the above ratio

RIFT BASIN RES CORP (BC)
Common no par split (2) for (1) by issuance of (1) additional share payable 10/02/2012 to holders of record 09/27/2012
Name changed to Asean Energy Corp. 08/25/2014
Asean Energy Corp. name changed to Genovation Capital Corp. 08/20/2015 which name changed to Valens Groworks Corp. 11/24/2016

RIFT RES LTD (ON)
Reincorporated 9/5/95
Place of incorporation changed from (BC) to (ONT) 9/5/95
Cease trade order effective 5/29/2001
Stockholders' equity unlikely

RIGEL ENERGY CORP (CANADA)
Merged into Talisman Energy Inc. 10/05/1999
Each share Common no par exchanged for (0.3) share Common no par and $1 cash
(See Talisman Energy Inc.)

RIGELYN SEC SYS INC (BC)
Delisted from Vancouver Stock Exchange 10/06/1989

RIGG WOOLEN MILL CO. (WV)
Dissolved 3/30/10

RIGGINS RES LTD (BC)
Recapitalized as Manhattan Minerals Corp. 06/01/1990
Each share Common no par exchanged for (0.5) share Common no par
Manhattan Minerals Corp. name changed to Mediterranean Minerals Corp. 02/23/2005 which recapitalized as Mediterranean Resources Ltd. 12/19/2005 which name changed to Blockchain Power Trust 01/04/2018

RIGGS NATL BK (WASHINGTON, DC)
Capital Stock $100 par changed to $25 par and (3) additional shares issued 01/08/1957
Capital Stock $25 par changed to $10 par and (1.5) additional shares issued plus a 10% stock dividend paid 01/15/1964
Capital Stock $10 par reclassified as Common $10 par 04/30/1968
Common $10 par changed to $5 par and (1) additional share issued 03/22/1973
$4 Conv. Preferred $10 par called for redemption 07/30/1979
Stock Dividends - 33-1/3% 01/14/1946; 20% 01/15/1954;
10.34% 01/08/1957; 10% 01/25/1966; 10% 04/08/1974
Under plan of reorganization each share Common $5 par automatically became (1) share Riggs National Corp. Common $5 par 05/31/1981
Riggs National Corp. merged into PNC Financial Services Group, Inc. 05/13/2005

RIGGS NATL CORP (DE)
Common $5 par changed to $2.50 par and (1) additional share issued 11/25/1981
Common $2.50 par split (2) for (1) by issuance of (1) additional share 03/31/1986
10.75% Restricted Perpetual Preferred Ser. B called for redemption at $27.25 on 10/01/1998
Merged into PNC Financial Services Group, Inc. 05/13/2005
Each share Common $2.50 par exchanged for (0.3008) share Common $5 par and $3.61 cash
Note: Each share Common $2.50 par received an initial litigation payment of $0.14 cash 04/04/2006
Each share Common $2.50 par received second litigation payment of $0.21 cash 05/10/2006

RIGHT MGMT CONSULTANTS INC (PA)
Common 1¢ par split (3) for (2) by issuance of (0.5) additional share 11/10/1995
Common 1¢ par split (3) for (2) by issuance of (0.5) additional share payable 07/26/1996 to holders of record 07/12/1996
Common 1¢ par split (3) for (2) by issuance of (0.5) additional share payable 04/06/2001 to holders of record 03/16/2001 Ex date - 04/09/2001
Common 1¢ par split (3) for (2) by issuance of (0.5) additional share payable 11/01/2001 to holders of record 10/26/2001 Ex date - 11/02/2001
Common 1¢ par split (3) for (2) by issuance of (0.5) additional share payable 10/15/2002 to holders of record 10/01/2002 Ex date - 10/16/2002
Merged into Manpower Inc. 01/23/2004
Each share Common 1¢ par exchanged for (0.3874) share Common 1¢ par
Manpower Inc. name changed to ManpowerGroup 04/18/2011

RIGHT START INC (CA)
Each share old Common no par exchanged for (0.5) share new Common no par 12/16/98
Reincorporated under the laws of Delaware as F.A.O., Inc. 3/26/2002
(See F.A.O., Inc.)

RIGHTCHOICE MANAGED CARE INC (DE)
Merged into WellPoint Health Networks Inc. 1/31/2002
Each share Common 1¢ par exchanged for (0.432414) share Common 1¢ par and $19.677483 cash
WellPoint Health Networks Inc. merged into WellPoint, Inc. 12/1/2004

RIGHTCHOICE MANAGED CARE INC (MO)
Issue Information - 3,250,000 shares CL A offered at $11 per share on 08/01/1994
Reincorporated under the laws of Delaware and Class A Common 1¢ par reclassified as Common 1¢ par 11/30/2000
Rightchoice Managed Care, Inc. (DE) merged into WellPoint Health Networks Inc. 1/31/2002 which merged into WellPoint, Inc. 12/1/2004

RIGHTIME FD INC (MD)
Merged into Federated Equity Funds 12/07/2001
Details not available

RIGHTNOW TECHNOLOGIES INC (DE)
Acquired by Oracle Corp. 01/25/2012
Each share Common $0.001 par exchanged for $43 cash

RIGHTSIDE GROUP LTD (DE)
Acquired by Donuts Inc. 07/28/2017
Each share Commonn $0.0001 par exchanged for $10.60 cash

RIGHTSMARKET INC (ON)
Name changed 06/07/2000
Name changed from Rightsmarket.com Inc. to Rightsmarket Inc. 06/07/2000
Plan of arrangement effective 12/31/2003
Each share Common no par exchanged for (0.025) share Grand Petroleum Inc. Common no par and (1) share RightsMarket Ltd. Common no par
(See each company's listing)

RIGHTSMARKET LTD (AB)
Acquired by Reality Commerce Corp. (New) 08/23/2004
Each share Common no par exchanged for (0.12) share Common no par
Reality Commerce Corp. (New) recapitalized as Crossfire Holdings Inc. 11/11/2005 which name changed to Crossfire Energy Services Inc. 07/01/2007
(See Crossfire Energy Services Inc.)

RIGID AIRSHIP USA INC (NV)
Each share old Common 10¢ par exchanged for (0.5) share new Common 10¢ par 08/18/2000
SEC revoked common stock registration 07/13/2007
Stockholders' equity unlikely

RIGL CORP (NV)
Name changed to YP.Net, Inc. 10/01/1999
YP.Net, Inc. name changed to YP Corp. 07/28/2004 which recapitalized as LiveDeal, Inc. 08/27/2007 which name changed to Live Ventures Inc. 10/09/2015

RIGOLETS CORP. (DE)
Voting Trust Agreement terminated and each VTC for Common $25 par automatically became (1) share Common $25 par 2/5/75
Completely liquidated 4/20/76
Each share Common $25 par received initial distribution of $803.58 cash per share 8/1/75
Each share Common $25 par received second distribution of $300 cash per share 1/15/76
Each share Common $25 par received third and final distribution of $289.39 cash per share 4/20/76
Note: Certificates were not required to be exchanged and are now valueless

RIHT CORP (RI)
Reincorporated 5/15/70
State of incorporation changed from (DE) to (RI) 5/15/70
Stock Dividend - 100% 3/23/73
Name changed to Hospital Trust Corp. 4/3/73
Hospital Trust Corp. name changed to RIHT Financial Corp. 4/20/83 which merged into Bank of Boston Corp. 11/14/85 which name changed to BankBoston Corp. 4/25/97 which merged into Fleet Boston Corp. 10/1/99 which name changed to FleetBoston Financial Corp. 4/18/2000 which merged into Bank of America Corp. 4/1/2004

RIHT FINL CORP (RI)
Merged into Bank of Boston Corp. 11/14/85
Each share Common $1 par exchanged for (0.73) share Adjustable Rate Preferred Ser. C no par
Bank of Boston Corp. name changed to BankBoston Corp. 4/25/97
(See BankBoston Corp.)

RIKE-KUMLER CO. (OH)
Common no par exchanged (4) for (1) in 1951
Common no par changed to $4 par 5/5/56
Merged into Federated Department Stores, Inc. on a (1.1) for (1) basis 10/3/59
Federated Department Stores, Inc. name changed to Macy's, Inc. 6/1/2007

RIKER CORP (DE)
Under plan of merger name changed to Riker-Maxson Corp. 03/31/1969
Riker-Maxson Corp. recapitalized as Unimax Group, Inc. 09/02/1975 which name changed to Unimax Corp. 09/11/1980
(See Unimax Corp.)

RIKER DEL CORP (DE)
Reorganized as Delstar Corp. 03/16/1972
Each share Conv. Preferred Ser. A $1 par or Conv. Preferred Ser. B $10 par exchanged for (5) shares Common 1¢ par
Each share Class A Common 10¢ par or Class B Common 10¢ par exchanged for (0.38346) share Common 1¢ par
(See Delstar Corp.)

RIKER MAXSON CORP (DE)
Recapitalized as Unimax Group, Inc. 09/02/1975
Each share Special Conv. Preference Ser. A Class A $1 par exchanged for (1/3) share Special Conv. Preference Ser. A Class A $3 par
Each share Common 25¢ par exchanged for (1/3) share Common 75¢ par
Unimax Group, Inc. name changed to Unimax Corp. 09/11/1980
(See Unimax Corp.)

RIKER PROPERTIES, INC.
Property sold and company liquidated in 1945

RIKER VIDEO INDS INC (NY)
Reincorporated under the laws of Delaware as Riker Corp. 10/28/68
Riker Corp. name changed to Riker-Maxson Corp. 3/31/69 which recapitalized as Unimax Group, Inc. 9/2/75 which name changed to Unimax Corp. 9/11/80
(See Unimax Corp.)

RIKON TECHNOLOGIES INC (AB)
Name changed to Hunter Financial Group Ltd. 03/05/1998
(See Hunter Financial Group Ltd.)

RILEY AERONAUTICS INTERNATIONAL CORP. (CO)
Name changed to Riley International Corp. 8/11/67
(See Riley International Corp.)

RILEY CO (DE)
Merged into United States Filter Corp. 12/04/1979
Each share Common $1 par exchanged for $63.153 cash

RILEY INTERNATIONAL CORP. (CO)
Declared defunct and inoperative for failure to file reports and pay taxes 10/15/69

RILEY INVTS INC (OR)
Name changed to Grand Adventures Tour & Travel Publishing Corp. (OR) 10/07/1996
Grand Adventures Tour & Travel

Publishing Corp. (OR)
reincorporated in Delaware
06/05/2000
(See Grand Adventures Tour & Travel Publishing Corp. (DE))

RILEY RES LTD (BC)
Recapitalized as International Riley Resources Ltd. 01/23/1998
Each share Common no par exchanged for (0.125) share Common no par
International Riley Resources Ltd. recapitalized as Wind River Resources Ltd. 11/22/2001 which recapitalized as Teslin River Resources Corp. 01/03/2008 which recapitalized as Siyata Mobile Inc. 07/29/2015

RILEY STOKER CORP (MA)
Common no par changed to $3 par 00/00/1940
Merged into Riley Co. 10/31/1971
Each share Common $3 par exchanged for (2.5) shares Common $1 par
(See Riley Co.)

RILEYS DATASHARE INTL LTD (AB)
Reorganized as International Datashare Corp. 1/3/97
Each share Common no par exchanged for (10) shares Common no par
International Datashare Corp. merged into Divestco Inc. 9/24/2003

RIM HLDGS INC (NV)
Name changed 07/03/2002
Name changed from Rim.Com Inc. to Rim Holdings Inc. 07/03/2002
Recapitalized as China Energy Savings Technology, Inc. 08/25/2004
Each share Common $0.001 par exchanged for (0.05) share Common $0.001 par
(See China Energy Savings Technology, Inc.)

RIM SEMICONDUCTOR CO (UT)
SEC revoked common stock registration 01/21/2014

RIMA INTL HLDGS INC (NV)
Charter revoked for failure to file reports and pay fees 08/31/2009

RIMAGE CORP (MN)
Common 1¢ par split (3) for (2) by issuance of (0.5) additional share payable 11/27/1998 to holders of record 11/13/1998
Common 1¢ par split (3) for (2) by issuance of (0.5) additional share payable 04/07/2000 to holders of record 04/01/2000
Name changed to Qumu Corp. 09/16/2013

RIMAK ELECTRONICS, INC. (CA)
Adjudicated bankrupt 1/27/65
Preferred and Common Stocks declared worthless

RIMCO FINANCIAL CORP. (TX)
Name changed to Rimco Capital Corp. 4/12/86

RIMCO INDS INC (DE)
Charter cancelled and declared inoperative and void for non-payment of taxes 03/01/1995

RIMFIRE MINERALS CORP (BC)
Merged into Kiska Metals Corp. 08/05/2009
Each share Common no par exchanged for (0.87) share Common no par
Kiska Metals Corp. merged into AuRico Metals Inc. 03/14/2017
(See AuRico Metals Inc.)

RIMOIL CORP (CANADA)
Each share old Class A Common no par exchanged for (0.2) share new Class A Common no par 12/20/1988
Merged into Barrington Petroleum Ltd. 09/22/1995
Each share new Class A Common no par exchanged for (0.190476) share Common no par
Barrington Petroleum Ltd. merged into Petrobank Energy & Resources Ltd. (Old) 07/18/2001 which reorganized as Petrobank Energy & Resources Ltd. (New) 01/07/2013 which recapitalized as Touchstone Exploration Inc. 05/20/2014

RIMPAC INDS INC (BC)
Recapitalized as Rhyme Industries Inc. 7/10/91
Each share Common no par exchanged for (1/3) share Common no par
Rhyme Industries Inc. recapitalized as Viacorp Technologies Inc. 4/28/99

RIMPAC RES LTD (NV)
SEC revoked common stock registration 10/20/2009
Stockholders' equity unlikely

RIMROCK MNG LTD (BC)
Recapitalized as Triton Resources Inc. 7/20/81
Each share Common no par exchanged for (0.2) share Common no par
(See Triton Resources Inc.)

RIMROCK TIDELANDS, INC. (DE)
Each share Capital Stock 20¢ par exchanged for (0.25) share Capital Stock 80¢ par 12/31/58
Merged into Husky Oil Co. 2/28/67
Each share Capital Stock 80¢ par exchanged for $11 cash

RIMROCK URANIUM MINES, INC. (DE)
Recapitalized as Rimrock Tidelands, Inc. on a (1) for (20) basis in 1955 which merged into Husky Oil Co. for cash 2/28/67

RIMRON RES INC (AB)
Recapitalized as Caribou Resources Corp. 01/22/2004
Each share Common no par exchanged for (0.04) share Common no par
Caribou Resources Corp. merged into JED Oil Inc. 07/31/2007
(See JED Oil Inc.)

RINCON RES INC (DE)
Name changed to Caliber Energy, Inc. 3/17/2005

RINFRET FD INC (DE)
Merged into Phoenix Capital Fund, Inc. 01/21/1974
Each share Common 50¢ par exchanged for (1.6029) shares Common $1 par
Phoenix Capital Fund, Inc. acquired by Phoenix-Chase Series Fund 12/11/1980 which name changed to Phoenix Series Fund 10/12/1982
(See Phoenix Series Fund)

RING AROUND PRODS INC (DE)
Merged into Occidental Petroleum Corp. (CA) 08/29/1978
Each share Common 20¢ par exchanged for (0.464) share Common 20¢ par
Occidental Petroleum Corp. (CA) reincorporated in Delaware 05/21/1986

RING OF FIRE RES INC (ON)
Name changed to Noble Mineral Exploration Inc. 03/07/2012

RING SIGHTS WORLDWIDE INC (ON)
Struck off register and declared dissolved for failure to file returns 12/09/1991

RINGBOLT VENTURES LTD (BC)
Name changed to North American Potash Developments Inc. 11/04/2011
North American Potash Developments Inc. recapitalized as Barolo Ventures Corp. 09/20/2018

RINGER COMMUNICATIONS INC (GA)
Administratively dissolved 07/11/1990

RINGER CORP (MN)
Name changed to Verdant Brands, Inc. 7/27/98
(See Verdant Brands, Inc.)

RINGLING BROS BARNUM & BAILEY COMBINED SHOWS INC (DE)
Merged into Mattel, Inc. 02/23/1971
Each share Common 50¢ par exchanged for (0.35971) share Common $1 par

RINGO INC (NV)
Name changed to America Asia Petroleum Corp. 03/16/2006
(See America Asia Petroleum Corp.)

RINGOR INTL LTD (CO)
Administratively dissolved 01/01/1996

RINGSIDE INTL BROADCASTING CORP (FL)
Each share Common $0.000001 par exchanged for (0.01) share Common $0.0001 par 2/2/89
Reincorporated under the laws of Delaware as Environmental Chemicals Group, Inc. 7/7/92
(See Environmental Chemicals Group, Inc.)

RINKER GROUP LTD (AUSTRALIA)
Sponsored ADR's for Ordinary split (2) for (1) by issuance of (1) additional ADR payable 04/26/2005 to holders of record 04/22/2005
Ex date - 04/27/2005
Acquired by Cemex, S.A.B. de C.V. 08/07/2007
Each Sponsored ADR for Ordinary exchanged for $79.25 cash

RINN CORP (NV)
Recapitalized as Sun Fruit, Ltd. 05/09/1974
Each share Common 50¢ par exchanged for (0.25) share Common no par
(See Sun Fruit, Ltd.)

RINOA ENTERPRISES LTD (AB)
Name changed to Paragon Pharmacies Ltd. 11/03/2006
Paragon Pharmacies Ltd. name changed to PGNX Capital Corp. 08/03/2012
(See PGNX Capital Corp.)

RIO ALGOM LTD (ON)
Conv. 2nd Preferred Ser. B called for redemption 02/15/1988
8.5% 2nd Preference Ser. A $5 par called for redemption 04/20/1990
8.5% Non-Vtg. Preference Ser. C $5 par called for redemption 01/31/1994
$5.80 1st Preference Ser. A $100 par called for redemption 04/22/1994
Common no par split (3) for (1) by issuance of (2) additional shares 10/12/1983
Merged into Billiton PLC 11/29/2000
Each share Common no par exchanged for $27 cash
9.375% Preferred Securities called for redemption at $25 plus $0.234375 accrued dividends on 08/07/2003
Public interest eliminated

RIO ALGOM MINES LTD. (ON)
Capital Stock no par reclassified as Common no par 3/14/66
Name changed to Rio Algom Ltd. 4/30/75
(See Rio Algom Ltd.)

RIO ALTO EXPL LTD (AB)
Merged into Canadian Natural Resources Ltd. 07/01/2002
Each share Common no par exchanged for (0.0652) share Common no par, (1) share Rio Alto Resources International Inc. and $14.6965 cash
(See each company's listing)

RIO ALTO MNG LTD (AB)
Merged into Tahoe Resources Inc. 04/01/2015
Each share Common no par exchanged for (0.227) share Common no par and $0.001 cash
Note: Unexchanged certificates will be cancelled and become without value 04/01/2021

RIO ALTO RES INTL INC (AB)
Acquired by West Energy Ltd. 08/28/2004
Each share Common no par exchanged for approximately (0.005) share Common no par and $1.312 cash
Note: Holders of (19,999) or fewer shares received $1.32 cash per share
West Energy Ltd. merged into Daylight Energy Ltd. 05/14/2010
(See Daylight Energy Ltd.)

RIO AMARILLO MNG LTD (BC)
Recapitalized as Globemin Resources Inc. 5/20/99
Each share Common no par exchanged for (0.1) share Common no par
Globemin Resources Inc. name changed to Sutter Gold Mining Inc. 12/29/2004

RIO BLANCO RES LTD (BC)
Name changed to Studebaker's Resource Development, Ltd. 11/28/1985
(See Studebaker's Resource Development, Ltd.)

RIO CRISTAL RES CORP (BC)
Each share old Common no par exchanged for (0.1) share new Common no par 07/31/2013
Each share new Common no par exchanged again for (0.1) share new Common no par 09/29/2014
Name changed to Armor Minerals Inc. 05/12/2015

RIO CRISTAL ZINC CORP (BC)
Name changed to Rio Cristal Resources Corp. 08/10/2009
Rio Cristal Resources Corp. name changed to Armor Minerals Inc 05/12/2015

RIO DE ORO MNG CO (NM)
Involuntarily stricken from the record 11/16/79

RIO DE ORO URANIUM MINES, INC. (DE)
Merged into Hidden Splendor Mining Co. (DE) 10/19/1959
Each share Common 1¢ par exchanged for (0.1) share 6% Preferred $11 par
Hidden Splendor Mining Co. (DE) merged into Atlas Corp. 08/17/1962
(See Atlas Corp.)

RIO FORTUNA EXPL CORP (BC)
Recapitalized as Fortune River Resource Corp. 12/21/2005
Each share Common no par exchanged for (1/3) share Common no par
Fortune River Resource Corp. merged into Bravada Gold Corp. (New) 01/07/2011

RIO GOLD MNG LTD (BC)
Delisted from Vancouver Stock Exchange 03/04/1992

RIO GRANA RES INC (NV)
Charter revoked 10/31/2014

RIO GRANDE & EAGLE PASS RWY. CO.
Abandoned 00/00/1932
Stockholders' equity unlikely

RIO GRANDE BANCSHARES INC NEW (TX)
Merged into First Security Corp. 2/2/98
Each share Common $1 par

exchanged for (37.93095) shares Common $1.25 par
First Security Corp. merged into Wells Fargo & Co. (New) 10/26/2000

RIO GRANDE COPPER CO. (NV)
Charter revoked for failure to pay fees and file reports 3/5/62

RIO GRANDE GATEWAY BRIDGE CORP. (DE)
Completely liquidated
Each share Common $1 par stamped to indicate initial distribution of $30 cash 5/1/61
Each share Common $1 par stamped to indicate second distribution of $2 cash 1/8/62
Each share Common $1 par exchanged for third and final distribution of $0.70 cash 3/2/64

RIO GRANDE INC (DE)
Reincorporated 06/01/1987
Each share Common 10¢ par exchanged for (0.02) share Common 1¢ par 12/12/1986
Name and state of incorporation changed from Rio Grande Drilling Co. (TX) to Rio Grande Inc. (DE) 06/01/1987
Plan of reorganization under Chapter 11 Federal Bankruptcy proceedings confirmed 03/05/1999
No stockholders' equity

RIO GRANDE INDS INC (DE)
80¢ Conv. Preferred Ser. A $1 par called for redemption 12/16/82
Merged into Anschutz Corp. 11/19/1984
Each share Common $1 par exchanged for $50 cash

RIO GRANDE MNG CORP (BC)
Each share old Common no par exchanged for (2) shares new Common no par 12/01/2010
Each share new Common no par exchanged again for (0.14285714) share new Common no par 05/13/2013
Recapitalized as 92 Resources Corp. 06/10/2014
Each share new Common no par exchanged for (0.2) share Common no par

RIO GRANDE NATIONAL LIFE INSURANCE CO. (TX)
Merged into Kentucky Central Life Insurance Co. 01/01/1968
Each share Common $10 par exchanged for (14.5) shares Class A Common $1 par
(See Kentucky Central Life Insurance Co.)

RIO GRANDE OIL CO. (DE)
Acquired by Consolidated Oil Corp. in 1932 which name was changed to Sinclair Oil Corp. in 1943

RIO GRANDE OIL CO. (TX)
Dissolved in 1932

RIO GRANDE VALLEY GAS CO. (DE)
Common no par changed to $1 par in 1930
Reincorporated under the laws of Texas in 1946
Rio Grande Valley Gas Co. (TX) acquired by Coastal Gas Producing Co. 7/2/68 which name changed to Coastal States Gas Corp. 1/2/73 which name changed to Coastal Corp. 1/1/80 which merged into El Paso Energy Corp. 1/29/2001 which name changed to El Paso Corp. 2/5/2001

RIO GRANDE VALLEY GAS CO. (TX)
Voting Trust Agreement terminated 1/3/65
Each VTC for Common $1 par exchanged for (1) share Common $1 par
Completely liquidated 7/2/68
Each share Common $1 par exchanged for first and final distribution of (0.302571) share Coastal States Gas Producing Co. $1.19 Conv. Preferred Ser. A no par
Coastal States Gas Producing Co. name changed to Coastal States Gas Corp. 1/2/73 which name changed to Coastal Corp. 1/1/80 which merged into El Paso Energy Corp. 1/29/2001 which name changed to El Paso Corp. 2/5/2001

RIO GRANDE VENTURES LTD (BC)
Recapitalized as RGV Resources Ltd. 03/10/1989
Each (2.4) shares Common no par exchanged for (1) share Common no par
(See RGV Resources Ltd.)

RIO GRANDE WATER POWER CO.
Sold to Maverick County Water Control & Improvement Dist. No. 1 in 1948

RIO GRANDE WESTERN URANIUM CO. (CO)
Proclaimed defunct and inoperative for failure to pay taxes 9/30/58

RIO HOTEL & CASINO INC (NV)
Secondary Offering - 3,000,000 shares COM offered at $21 per share on 11/21/1997
Merged into Harrah's Entertainment, Inc. 01/01/1999
Each share Common 1¢ par exchanged for (1) share Common 10¢ par
(See Harrah's Entertainment, Inc.)

RIO NARCEA GOLD MINES LTD (ON)
Acquired by Lundin Mining Corp. 09/28/2007
Each share Common no par exchanged for $5.50 cash

RIO NEV ENERGY INC (CANADA)
Name changed 07/03/1998
Name changed from RIO Nevada Mines Corp. to RIO Nevada Energy Inc. 07/03/1998
Dissolved 09/19/2005
No stockholders' equity

RIO NOVO GOLD INC (BRITISH VIRGIN ISLANDS)
Merged into Aura Minerals Inc. 03/06/2018
Each share Ordinary no par exchanged for (0.053) share Common no par

RIO PALMER OILS LTD. (ON)
Merged into Devon-Palmer Oils Ltd. 11/6/56
Each share Capital Stock $1 par exchanged for (1.25) shares Capital Stock 25¢ par
(See Devon-Palmer Oils Ltd.)

RIO PLATA SILVER MINES LTD. (BC)
Recapitalized as Consolidated Rio Plata Resources Ltd. 10/05/1983
Each share Capital Stock no par exchanged for (0.5) share Common no par
Consolidated Rio Plata Resources Ltd. recapitalized as New Rio Resources Ltd. 10/28/1993 which name changed to Southern Rio Resources Ltd. 08/23/1994 which recapitalized as Silver Quest Resources Ltd. 12/15/2005
(See Silver Quest Resources Ltd.)

RIO-PRADO CONSOLIDATED OILS LTD. (ON)
Merged into Rio Palmer Oils Ltd. 7/25/55
Each share Capital Stock $1 par exchanged for (1) share Capital Stock $1 par
Rio Palmer Oils Ltd. merged into Devon-Palmer Oils Ltd. 11/6/56
(See Devon-Palmer Oils Ltd.)

RIO RUPUNUNI MINES LTD (ON)
Charter cancelled for failure to pay taxes and file returns 01/10/1973

RIO SIERRA DEVS LTD (BC)
Recapitalized as River Mountain Resources Ltd. 06/30/1977
Each share Capital Stock no par exchanged for (0.33333333) share Capital Stock no par
River Mountain Resources Ltd. recapitalized as Rio Sierra Silver Corp. 02/16/1983
(See Rio Sierra Silver Corp.)

RIO SIERRA SILVER CORP (BC)
Delisted from Vancouver Stock Exchange 03/21/1989

RIO TINTO ALBERTA OILS, LTD. (ON)
Each share Capital Stock no par exchanged for (5) shares Capital Stock 25¢ par in 1952
Merged into Rio-Prado Consolidated Oils Ltd. in 1953
Each share Capital Stock 25¢ par exchanged for (1.25) shares Capital Stock $1 par
Rio-Prado Consolidated Oils Ltd. merged into Rio Palmer Oils Ltd. 7/25/55 which merged into Devon-Palmer Oils Ltd. 11/6/56 which merged into Triad Oil Manitoba Ltd. for cash 3/8/67

RIO TINTO CO. LTD. (ENGLAND)
Merged into Rio-Tinto Zinc. Corp. Ltd. on a (41) for (20) basis 07/09/1962
Rio-Tinto Zinc. Corp. PLC name changed to RTZ Corp. PLC 08/26/1987 which name changed to Rio Tinto PLC 06/02/1997

RIO TINTO LTD (AUSTRALIA)
ADR agreement terminated 04/10/2006
Each Sponsored ADR for Ordinary exchanged for $217.315766 cash

RIO TINTO MINING CO. OF CANADA LTD. (ON)
Each share Class A $100 par exchanged for (100) shares Common no par in 1957
Completely liquidated 1/27/66
Each share Common no par exchanged for first and final distribution of $0.04 cash

RIO TINTO ZINC PLC (ENGLAND)
Each ADR for Ordinary Reg. 10s par exchanged for (2) ADR's for Ordinary Reg. 5s per 05/27/1970
ADR's for Ordinary Reg. 5s par changed to 25p par per currency change 02/15/1971
Stock Dividend - 20% 04/02/1965
Name changed to RTZ Corp. PLC 08/26/1987
RTZ Corp. PLC name changed to Rio Tinto PLC 06/02/1997

RIO VERDE ENERGY CORP (DE)
Chapter 11 bankruptcy proceedings converted to Chapter 7 on 09/15/1986
Stockholders' equity unlikely

RIO VERDE MINERALS DEVELOPMENT CORP (BRITISH VIRGIN ISLANDS)
Merged into B&A Mineracao S.A. 03/13/2013
Each share Ordinary no par exchanged for CAD $0.40 cash

RIO VISTA ENERGY PARTNERS L P (DE)
Name changed to Central Energy Partners L.P. 03/31/2011

RIOCAN REAL ESTATE INVT TR (ON)
Preferred Units Ser. A called for redemption at $25 plus $0.328125 accrued dividends on 03/31/2016
Preferred Units Ser. C called for redemption at $25 on 06/30/2017 (Additional Information in Active)

RIORIDGE RES CORP (NV)
Common $0.00001 par split (8) for (1) by issuance of (7) additional shares payable 06/30/2008 to holders of record 06/30/2008
Name changed to Neohydro Technologies Corp. 08/08/2008
Neohydro Technologies Corp. name changed to Epoxy, Inc. 08/14/2014

RIOSUN RES CORP (BC)
Cease trade order effective 11/23/2001
Stockholders' equity unlikely

RIO2 LTD OLD (ON)
Merged into Rio2 Ltd. (New) 07/27/2018
Each share Common no par exchanged for (0.6667) share Common no par

RIPLEY INC (NY)
Stock Dividend - 100% 03/27/1967
Acquired by Ripley Acquisition Corp. 10/31/1990
Each share Common 50¢ par exchanged for $4.15 cash

RIPLEY INDS INC (DE)
Merged 07/31/1970
Merged from Ripley Industries, Inc. & Jomar Plastics, Inc. to Ripley Industries, Inc. 07/31/1970
Each Unit (consisting of (1) share Ripley Common $1 par and (1) share Jomar Common 1¢ par) exchanged for (1) share Common $1 par
Stock Dividend - 100% 10/01/1979
Charter cancelled and declared inoperative and void for non-payment of taxes 03/01/2002

RIPLEY INTL LTD (ON)
Shares reacquired by company in 1977
Details not available

RIPLEY SHIRT MANUFACTURING CO.
Bankrupt in 1949

RIPPED CDA ARTISTS INC (ON)
Recapitalized as Condor Gold Corp. 10/03/2002
Each share Common no par exchanged for (0.5) share Common no par
(See Condor Gold Corp.)

RIPPER OIL & GAS INC (AB)
Reorganized under the laws of British Columbia 05/29/2012
Each share Common no par exchanged for (0.125) share Common no par

RIPPLE LAKE DIAMONDS INC (BC)
Recapitalized as Devonshire Resources Ltd. 10/10/2007
Each share Common no par exchanged for (0.1) share Common no par
Devonshire Resources Ltd. recapitalized as Gold Standard Ventures Corp. 11/18/2009

RIPPLE RES LTD (BC)
Name changed to Consolidated Ripple Resources Ltd. 06/12/1987
(See Consolidated Ripple Resources Ltd.)

RIPPLE RES LTD CDA (AB)
Merged into Ramarro Resources Inc. 5/21/97
Each share Common no par exchanged for (0.142857) share Common no par
(See Ramarro Resources Inc.)

RISBY TUNGSTEN MINES LTD (BC)
Merged into Imperial Metals Corp. (Old) 12/1/81
Each share Capital Stock no par exchanged for (0.5) share Common no par
Imperial Metals Corp. (Old) reorganized as Imperial Metals Corp. (New) 4/30/2002

RISCORP INC (FL)
Merged into Griffin Acquisition Corp. 7/20/2000
Each share Class A Common 1¢ par exchanged for (1) Contingent Value Right and $3.075 cash

RISDON MFG CO (CT)
Each share Common $25 par exchanged for (3) shares Common $10 par in 1946
Common $10 par changed to no par and (1) additional share issued 12/10/71
Common no par split (5) for (4) by issuance of (0.25) additional share 3/11/77
Stock Dividends - 33-1/3% 8/15/50; 20% 1/3/66
Merged into Metal Box Ltd. 12/29/78
Each share Common no par exchanged for $20 cash

RISE ENERGY LTD (AB)
Merged into Delphi Energy Corp. 6/19/2003
Each share Common no par exchanged for (0.25) share Common no par

RISE HEALTH WARE INC (AB)
Merged into Med Access Inc. 10/27/2005
Each share Common no par exchanged for (0.095101) share Common no par
Note: Med Access Inc. is a privately held company

RISE RES INC (BC)
Common no par split (2) for (1) by issuance of (1) additional share 11/13/1984
Recapitalized as Pacific Mariner Explorations Ltd. 03/22/1993
Each share Common no par exchanged for (0.2) share Common no par
Pacific Mariner Explorations Ltd. name changed to Abitibi Mining Corp. 12/14/1995

RISE RES INC (NV)
Name changed to Rise Gold Corp. 04/07/2017

RISE TECHNOLOGY INC (MA)
Name changed to Colonial Data Technologies Corp. (MA) 8/29/89
Colonial Data Technologies Corp. (MA) reincorporated in (DE) 5/19/95 which merged into InteliData Technologies Corp. 11/7/96 which merged into Corillian Corp. 10/6/2005
(See Corillian Corp.)

RISER FOODS INC (DE)
$8 Conv. Preferred Ser. A $100 par called for redemption 7/28/95
Merged into Giant Eagle, Inc. 8/18/97
Each share Class A Common 1¢ par exchanged for $42 cash
Each share Class B Common 1¢ par exchanged for $42 cash

RISING (B.D.) PAPER CO.
Acquired by Rising Paper Co. 00/00/1928
Details not available

RISING INDIA INC (DE)
Name changed to Rising Biosciences, Inc. 05/31/2018

RISING PHOENIX DEV GROUP LTD (BC)
Acquired by Power Direct Inc. 11/15/1999
Details not available

RISING RES LTD (AB)
Merged into Gardiner Oil & Gas Ltd. 7/1/95
Each share Common no par exchanged for $3.75 cash

RISING'S ELECTRO, INC. (CA)
Charter suspended for failure to pay taxes 11/01/1965

RISINGTIDE INC (NV)
Name changed to Equiline Corp. 4/8/2005
Equiline Corp. recapitalized as Chelsea Collection, Inc. 6/15/2005 which recapitalized as G-H-3 International, Inc. 10/30/2006

RISK CAP HLDGS INC (DE)
Issue Information - 8,500,000 shares COM offered at $20 per share on 09/13/1995
Name changed to Arch Capital Group Ltd. (DE) 5/8/2000
Arch Capital Group Ltd. (DE) reincorporated in Bermuda 11/8/2000

RISKMETRICS GROUP INC (DE)
Issue Information - 14,000,000 shares COM offered at $17.50 per share on 01/24/2008
Merged into MSCI Inc. 06/01/2010
Each share Common 1¢ par exchanged for (0.1802) share Class A Common 1¢ par and $16.35 cash

RIT TECHNOLOGIES LTD (ISRAEL)
Reorganized as RiT Technologies Ltd. (New) 08/24/2019
Each share Ordinary NIS 0.1 par exchanged for (0.125) share Ordinary NIS 0.8 par

RITA CAP CORP (AB)
Name changed to Biotech Medical Sciences Inc. 06/06/2004
Biotech Medical Sciences Inc. name changed to CAPVEST Income Corp. 01/05/2005
(See CAPVEST Income Corp.)

RITA MED SYS INC (DE)
Issue Information - 3,600,000 shares COM offered at $12 per share on 07/26/2000
Merged into AngioDynamics, Inc. 1/29/2007
Each share Common $0.001 par exchanged for (0.1722) share Common 1¢ par and $0.515 cash

RITCHIE CUT STONE CO. LTD. (ON)
Common no par acquired by Canada Crushed & Cut Stone Ltd. in 1951
Details not available
Preferred no par called for redemption 11/15/63

RITCHIE GOLD MINES LTD.
Assets sold to Ritoria Mines Ltd. on a (1) for (3.5) basis in 1938

RITE AID CORP (DE)
Each share 7% Mandatory Conv. Preferred Ser. E $1 par automatically became (14.0056) shares Common $1 par 02/01/2008
Each share 5.50% Conv. Preferred Ser. I $1 par automatically became (5.6561) shares Common $1 par 11/17/2008
(Additional Information in Active)

RITE TIME MNG INC (NV)
Common $0.001 par split (2) for (1) by issuance of (1) additional share payable 05/05/2008 to holders of record 04/25/2008 Ex date - 05/06/2008
Name changed to Federal Sports & Entertainment, Inc. 05/06/2008
Federal Sports & Entertainment, Inc. name changed to Universal Gold Mining Corp. 05/12/2010

RITTENHOUSE CAP CORP (DE)
Each share old Common $0.001 par exchanged for (0.1) share new Common $0.001 par 11/14/1991
Name changed to North American Environmental Corp. 11/26/1991
North American Environmental Corp. name changed to North American Technologies Group, Inc. 08/15/1996
(See North American Technologies Group, Inc.)

RITTENHOUSE INVTS INC (DE)
Charter cancelled and declared inoperative and void for non-payment of taxes 3/1/76

RITTENHOUSE PLAZA APARTMENTS, INC.
Liquidated in 1948

RITTER CO., INC. (DE)
5% Preferred $100 par called for redemption 10/31/55
Common no par changed to $5 par and (1) additional share issued 12/15/55
Common $5 par changed to $2.50 par and (1) additional share issued 12/30/59
Under plan of merger name changed to Ritter Corp. 4/27/65
Ritter Corp. merged into Ritter Pfaudler Corp. 11/1/65 which merged into Sybron Corp. 10/7/68
(See Sybron Corp.)

RITTER CORP. (DE)
Merged into Ritter Pfaudler Corp. 11/1/65
Each share Common $2.50 par exchanged for (1) share Common $5 par
Ritter Pfaudler Corp. merged into Sybron Corp. 10/7/68
(See Sybron Corp.)

RITTER DENTAL MANUFACTURING CO., INC.
Name changed to Ritter Co., Inc. in 1941
Ritter Co., Inc. name changed to Ritter Corp. 4/27/56 which merged into Ritter Pfaudler Corp. 11/1/65 which merged into Sybron Corp. 10/7/68
(See Sybron Corp.)

RITTER FIN INC (PA)
Reorganized as Ritter Financial Corp. and Class A Common $1 par and Class B Common $1 par changed to 25¢ par 09/25/1969
Ritter Financial Corp. acquired by Manufacturers Hanover Corp. 01/03/1975 which merged into Chemical Banking Corp. 12/31/1991 which name changed to Chase Manhattan Corp. (New) 03/31/1996 which name changed to J.P. Morgan Chase & Co. 12/31/2000 which name changed to JPMorgan Chase & Co. 07/20/2004

RITTER FINL CORP (PA)
6% Preferred $50 par called for redemption 03/01/1972
Acquired by Manufacturers Hanover Corp. 01/03/1975
Each share 5.5% Conv. Preferred $50 par exchanged for (1.85) shares Common $7.50 par
Each share 5.5% Preferred Ser. B $50 par exchanged for (1) share 5.5% Preferred Ser. A no par
Each share 6% Conv. Preferred $50 par exchanged for (1.85) shares Common $7.50 par
Each Class B Common 25¢ par exchanged for (0.363636) share Common $7.50 par
Manufacturers Hanover Corp. merged into Chemical Banking Corp. 12/31/1991 which name changed to Chase Manhattan Corp. (New) 03/31/1996 which name changed to J.P. Morgan Chase & Co. 12/31/2000 which name changed to JPMorgan Chase & Co. 07/20/2004

RITTER LUMBER COMPANY (WV)
Stock Dividend - 100% 10/15/51
Merged into Georgia-Pacific Corp. on 10/3/60
Each share Common no par exchanged for (1.6) share Common 80¢ par
(See Georgia-Pacific Corp.)

RITTER P J CO (PA)
Completely liquidated 3/31/69
Each share Preferred $100 par exchanged for first and final distribution of $100 cash
Each share Common no par exchanged for an undetermined amount of cash

RITTER PFAUDLER CORP (NY)
Common $5 par changed to $2.50 par and (1) additional share issued 9/8/67
Merged into Sybron Corp. 10/7/68
Each share Common $2.50 par exchanged for (1) share Common $2.50 par
(See Sybron Corp.)

RITTER'S (TEX) CHUCKWAGON SYSTEM, INC. (DE)
Charter cancelled and declared inoperative and void for non-payment of taxes 03/01/1977

RITZ CARLTON HOTEL CO. (ATLANTIC CITY, NJ)
Liquidation completed in 1952

RITZ CARLTON HOTEL CO BOSTON (MA)
Completely liquidated 08/21/1964
Each share Preferred $100 par stamped to indicate first and final distribution $6 cash
No Common stockholders' equity

RITZ LARDER MINES LTD. (ON)
Charter cancelled for failure to file reports and pay taxes in 1957

RITZ RES LTD (BC)
Recapitalized as Trinity Control Ltd. 4/23/93
Each share Common no par exchanged for (1/3) share Common no par
Trinity Control Ltd. name changed to Sunridge Gold Corp. 5/23/2002

RITZEN GROUP INCOME PPTYS SECS LTD (TN)
Certificate of Limited Partnership cancelled 12/27/2001

RITZYS G D INC (OH)
Common no par split (3) for (2) by issuance of (0.5) additional share 7/12/83
Each share old Common no par exchanged for (0.2) share new Common no par 9/30/88
Charter cancelled by operation of law 7/20/90

RIVA GOLD CORP (BC)
Merged into Wildcat Silver Corp. 05/06/2013
Each share Common no par exchanged for (0.21276595) share Common no par
Note: Unexchanged certificates will be cancelled and become without value 05/06/2019
Wildcat Silver Corp. name changed to AZ Mining Inc. 06/05/2015 which name changed to Arizona Mining Inc. 10/28/2015
(See Arizona Mining Inc.)

RIVA PETE INC (BC)
Recapitalized as Rivera Explorations Inc. 07/28/1997
Each share Common no par exchanged for (0.2) share Common no par
Rivera Explorations Inc. recapitalized as Silverarrow Explorations, Inc. 08/06/1998 which recapitalized as Aladdin Resources Corp. 07/05/2001 which name changed to Gold Point Exploration Ltd. 01/27/2004 which name changed to Gold Point Energy Corp. 06/22/2005 which merged into San Leon Energy PLC 05/28/2009

RIVAL CO (DE)
Reincorporated 4/7/86
State of incorporation changed from (MO) to (DE) 4/7/86
Merged into Holmes Products Corp. 2/5/99

FINANCIAL INFORMATION, INC.   RIV-RIV

Each share Common 1¢ par exchanged for $13.75 cash

RIVAL ENERGY INC (AB)
Under plan of merger name changed to Rival Energy Ltd. 06/16/2003
Rival Energy Ltd. merged into Zargon Energy Trust 01/23/2008 which reorganized as Zargon Oil & Gas Ltd. (New) 01/07/2011

RIVAL ENERGY LTD (AB)
Merged into Zargon Energy Trust 01/23/2008
Each share Common no par exchanged for (0.0562) Trust Unit no par
Note: Unexchanged certificates were cancelled and became without value 01/23/2014
Zargon Energy Trust reorganized as Zargon Oil & Gas Ltd. (New) 01/07/2011

RIVAL MFG CO (MO)
Common $1 par split (3) for (2) by issuance of (0.5) additional share 1/16/83
Stock Dividends - 100% 5/15/68; 100% 7/8/74; 100% 7/3/75
Acquired by Rival Acquisitions, Inc. 4/17/86
Each share Common $1 par exchanged for $17.50 cash

RIVAL MINERALS LTD (BC)
Name changed to Europrime Capital Corp. 3/9/88
Europrime Capital Corp. recapitalized as International Europrime Capital Corp. 7/4/95
(See International Europrime Capital Corp.)

RIVAL RES INC (CO)
Merged into Trinity Oil & Gas, Inc. 6/7/84
Each share Common $0.001 par exchanged for (1) share Common $0.001 par
Trinity Oil & Gas, Inc. recapitalized as Questa Oil & Gas Co. 3/31/86 which merged into Unit Corp. 3/21/2000

RIVAL TECHNOLOGIES INC (BC)
Reincorporated under the laws of Nevada and Common no par changed to $0.001 par 10/28/2005

RIVENDELL WINERY N Y INC (NY)
Each share old Common 1¢ par exchanged for (0.5) share new Common 1¢ par 11/21/1997
Name changed to New World Wine Group, Ltd. (NY) 01/12/1998
New World Wine Group, Ltd. (NY) reincorporated in Nevada as QX Bio Tech Group, Inc. 12/04/2007 which recapitalized as AcumedSpa Holdings, Inc. 09/18/2009 which recapitalized as Organic Plant Health, Inc. 02/02/2011

RIVER BK AMER (NEW ROCHELLE, NY)
Under plan of reorganization each share 15% Preferred Ser. A $1 par and Common $1 par automatically became (1) share RB Asset, Inc. (DE) 15% Preferred Ser. A $1 par and Common $1 par respectively 05/22/1998
(See RB Asset, Inc.)

RIVER BRAND RICE MILLS, INC. (DE)
Stock Dividends - 10% 11/1/55; 50% 11/1/61; 10% 11/1/63; 10% 11/2/64
Name changed to Riviana Foods Inc. (Old) 7/19/65
Riviana Foods, Inc. (Old) acquired by Colgate-Palmolive Co. 6/14/76

RIVER CAP GROUP INC (DE)
Recapitalized as Sonterra Resources, Inc. 02/14/2008
Each share Common $0.001 par exchanged for (0.1) share Common $0.001 par
Sonterra Resources, Inc. name changed to Velocity Energy Inc. 04/14/2009

RIVER CITY BK (MECHANICSVILLE, VA)
Merged into Village Bank & Trust Financial Corp. 10/14/2008
Each share Common $5 par exchanged for (0.8) share Common $4 par and $2.20 cash

RIVER CREEK HLDGS INC (FL)
Common $0.0001 par split (15) for (1) by issuance of (14) additional shares payable 07/30/2007 to holders of record 07/25/2007
Ex date - 07/31/2007
Name changed to EQ Labs, Inc. 02/05/2009

RIVER EXPL INC (NV)
Each share old Common $0.001 par exchanged for (45) shares new Common $0.001 par 06/03/2009
Name changed to Fresh Start Private Holdings, Inc. 03/01/2010
Fresh Start Private Holdings, Inc. name changed to Tap Resources, Inc. 08/16/2012

RIVER FARMS CO. OF CALIFORNIA (CA)
Liquidation for cash completed 11/20/64
Distributions were paid to holders of record and therefore certificates are now worthless

RIVER FOREST BANCORP (MN)
Name changed 04/29/1988
Common 10¢ par split (3) for (1) by issuance of (2) additional shares 04/30/1985
Stock Dividend - 100% 06/13/1986
Name changed from River Forest Bancorp to River Forest Bancorp, Inc. 04/29/1988
Common 10¢ par split (3) for (2) by issuance of (0.5) additional share 09/01/1988
Common 10¢ par changed to 5¢ par and (1) additional share issued 09/22/1995
Name changed to Corus Bankshares, Inc. 06/10/1996
(See Corus Bankshares, Inc.)

RIVER GOLD MINES LTD (ON)
Merged into Wesdome Gold Mines Ltd. 02/01/2006
Each share Common no par exchanged for (0.65) share Common no par

RIVER HLDG CORP (DE)
Stock Dividends - 5.75% payable 4/15/2000 to holders of record 4/1/2000; 5.75% payable 10/15/2000 to holders of record 10/1/2000; 5.75% payable 4/15/2001 to holders of record 4/1/2001; 5.75% payable 10/15/2001 to holders of record 10/1/2001 Ex date - 10/16/2001; 5.75% payable 4/15/2002 to holders of record 4/1/2002 Ex date - 4/5/2002; 5.75% payable 10/15/2002 to holders of record 10/1/2002 Ex date - 10/16/2002; 5.75% payable 4/16/2003 to holders of record 4/1/2003 Ex date - 4/16/2003; 5.75% payable 10/15/2003 to holders of record 10/1/2003 Ex date - 10/8/2003; 5.75% payable 4/15/2004 to holders of record 4/1/2004 Ex date - 4/14/2004
11.5% Exchangeable Pay-In-Kind Preferred called for redemption at $104.60 on 8/5/2004

RIVER MTN RES LTD (BC)
Recapitalized as Rio Sierra Silver Corp. 02/16/1983
Each share Capital Stock no par exchanged for (0.25) share Common no par
(See Rio Sierra Silver Corp.)

RIVER OAKS BK (HOUSTON, TX)
Name changed 04/02/1984
Name changed from River Oaks Bank & Trust Co. (Houston, TX) to River Oaks Bank (Houston, TX) 04/02/1984
Stock Dividends - 10% 00/00/1970; 19-1/2% 00/00/1973
Acquired by Central Bancshares of the South, Inc. 11/19/1992
Details not available

RIVER OAKS FURNITURE INC (MS)
Assets sold for the benefit of creditors 03/00/1999
No stockholders' equity

RIVER OAKS HOSP INC (MS)
Merged into Health Management Associates Inc. (New) 01/28/1998
Each share Common 1¢ par exchanged for (3.273) shares Common 1¢ par
Health Management Associates Inc. (New) merged into Community Health Systems, Inc. 01/27/2014

RIVER OAKS INDS INC (DE)
Charter cancelled and declared inoperative and void for non-payment of taxes 03/01/1992

RIVER OAKS STATE BANK (HOUSTON, TX)
Stock Dividends - 33-1/3% 00/00/1952; 25% 00/00/1956; 53.85% 05/29/1958; 10% 01/25/1960; 10% 02/23/1961
Name changed to River Oaks Bank & Trust Co. (Houston, TX) 06/26/1962
River Oaks Bank & Trust Co. (Houston, TX) name changed to River Oaks Bank (Houston, TX) 04/02/1984
(See River Oaks Bank (Houston, TX))

RIVER RAISIN PAPER CO. (MI)
Capital Stock $10 par changed to no par in 1926 and to $5 par in 1942
Merged into Union Bag-Camp Paper Corp. on a (5) for (6) basis 5/5/60
Union Bag-Camp Paper Corp. name changed to Union Camp Corp. 4/27/66 which merged into International Paper Co. 4/30/99

RIVER VY BANCORP (IN)
Common no par split (2) for (1) by issuance of (1) additional share payable 01/09/2004 to holders of record 12/26/2003 Ex date - 01/12/2004
Merged into German American Bancorp, Inc. 03/01/2016
Each share Common no par exchanged for (0.77) share Common no par and $9.90 cash

RIVER VY CMNTY BK (YUBA CITY, CA)
Common no par split (5) for (4) by issuance of (0.25) additional share payable 08/20/2010 to holders of record 07/30/2010 Ex date - 08/23/2010
Common no par split (5) for (4) by issuance of (0.25) additional share payable 11/03/2015 to holders of record 10/30/2015 Ex date - 11/04/2015
Under plan of reorganization each share Common no par automatically became (1) share River Valley Community Bancorp Common no par 07/13/2017

RIVER VY ENERGY SVCS CORP (AB)
Recapitalized as River Valley Energy Services Ltd. 11/28/2002
Each share Common no par exchanged for (0.2) share Common no par
River Valley Energy Services Ltd. reorganized as River Valley Income Fund 10/05/2004 which name changed to Eveready Income Fund 03/31/2005 which reorganized as Eveready Inc. 01/07/2009 which was acquired by Clean Harbors, Inc. 07/31/2009

RIVER VY ENERGY SVCS LTD (AB)
Reorganized as River Valley Income Fund 10/05/2004
Each share Common no par exchanged for (1) Unit no par
River Valley Income Fund name changed to Eveready Income Fund 03/31/2005 which reorganized as Eveready Inc. 01/07/2009 which was acquired by Clean Harbors, Inc. 07/31/2009

RIVER VY INCOME FD (AB)
Name changed to Eveready Income Fund 03/31/2005
Eveready Income Fund reorganized as Eveready Inc. 01/07/2009 which was acquired by Clean Harbors, Inc. 07/31/2009

RIVER VIEW VINTNERS INC (WV)
Proclaimed dissolved for non-payment of taxes 11/02/1977

RIVERA CAP CORP (BC)
Reincorporated under the laws of Alberta as Canada Fluorspar Inc. 04/22/2009
(See Canada Fluorspar Inc. (AB))

RIVERA EXPLORATIONS INC (BC)
Recapitalized as Silverarrow Explorations, Inc. 08/06/1998
Each share Common no par exchanged for (1/6) share Common no par
Silverarrow Explorations, Inc. recapitalized as Aladdin Resources Corp. 07/05/2001 which name changed to Gold Point Exploration Ltd. 01/27/2004 which name changed to Gold Point Energy Corp. 06/22/2005 which merged into San Leon Energy PLC 05/28/2009

RIVERBANK RES INC (NV)
Name changed to Raven Gold Corp. 08/16/2006

RIVERBED TECHNOLOGY INC (DE)
Common $0.0001 par split (2) for (1) by issuance of (1) additional share payable 11/08/2010 to holders of record 11/01/2010 Ex date - 11/09/2010
Acquired by Thoma Bravo, LLC 04/24/2015
Each share Common $0.0001 par exchanged for $21 cash

RIVERBEND INTL CORP (DE)
Charter cancelled and declared inoperative and void for non-payment of taxes 5/30/96

RIVERDALE CAPITAL LTD (NV)
Each share old Common $0.001 par exchanged for (0.001) share new Common $0.001 par 04/23/2010
Each share new Common $0.001 par exchanged again for (0.0001) share new Common $0.001 par 09/09/2010
Name changed to Diversified Energy & Fuel International, Inc. 04/30/2012
Diversified Energy & Fuel International, Inc. name changed to Zyrox Mining International, Inc. 08/21/2012

RIVERDALE MNG INC (NV)
Each share old Common $0.00001 par exchanged for (0.005) share new Common $0.00001 par 06/01/2012
SEC revoked common stock registration 02/16/2016

RIVERDALE OIL & GAS CORP (DE)
Reincorporated under the laws of Nevada 07/00/2008

RIVERDANCE RES CORP (BC)
Recapitalized as Luminex Ventures Inc. 05/26/1999
Each share Common no par exchanged for (0.125) share Common no par

Luminex Ventures Inc. recapitalized as Lateegra Resources Corp. 06/12/2002 which recapitalized as Lateegra Gold Corp. 01/12/2006 which merged into Excellon Resources Inc. (BC) 08/05/2011 which reincorporated in Ontario 06/05/2012

RIVERDEEP GROUP PLC (IRELAND)
Issue Information - 36,500,000 ADR'S offered at $20 per ADR on 03/09/2000
ADR agreement terminated 11/4/2002
Each ADR for Ordinary 10¢ par exchanged for $9.06 cash

RIVERGOLD INC (NV)
Reincorporated 3/13/85
State of incorporation changed from (UT) to (NV) 3/13/85
Recapitalized as High Gold, Inc. 7/25/86
Each share Common $0.001 par exchanged for (0.2) share Common $0.001 par
(See High Gold, Inc.)

RIVERLAND BK
(FORT LAUDERDALE, FL)
Acquired by Barnett Banks of Florida, Inc. 11/15/1973
Each share Common $10 par exchanged for (1) share Common $2 par
Barnett Banks of Florida, Inc. name changed to Barnett Banks, Inc. 04/24/1987 which merged into NationsBank Corp. (NC) 01/09/1998 which reincorporated in Delaware as BankAmerica Corp. (Old) 09/25/1998 which merged into BankAmerica Corp. (New) 09/30/1998 which name changed to Bank of America Corp. 04/28/1999

RIVERRIDGE MINES LTD. (ON)
Completely liquidated 4/23/71
Each share Capital Stock $1 par exchanged for first and final distribution of $0.01158 cash

RIVERS INDS INC (GA)
Name changed 07/01/1973
Name changed from Rivers & Horton Industries, Inc. to Rivers Industries, Inc. 07/01/1973
Out of business 00/00/1975
Details not available

RIVERSIDE & DAN RIVER COTTON MILLS, INC. (VA)
Recapitalized as Dan River Mills, Inc. 8/17/46
Each share Common $25 par exchanged for (5) shares Common $5 par
Dan River Mills, Inc. name changed to Dan River Inc. 7/1/70
(See Dan River Inc.)

RIVERSIDE BANCSHARES INC (GA)
Common $1 par split (3) for (2) by issuance of (0.5) additional share payable 5/30/2001 to holders of record 5/16/2001 Ex date - 6/6/2001
Common $1 par split (3) for (2) by issuance of (0.5) additional share payable 6/15/2003 to holders of record 6/1/2003 Ex date - 6/16/2003
Plan of recapitalization effective 12/22/2004
Holders of (999) or fewer shares exchanged for $20 cash per share
Holders of (1,000) shares or more were not affected
Merged into Synovus Financial Corp. 3/24/2006
Each share Common $1 par exchanged for (1.1) shares Common $1 par
Each share Class B Common $1 par exchanged for (1.1) shares Common $1 par

RIVERSIDE BKG CO (FL)
Stock Dividend - 10% payable 03/18/1998 to holders of record 02/19/1998
Company's principal asset placed in receivership 04/16/2010
Stockholders' equity unlikely

RIVERSIDE CAP INC (CO)
Recapitalized as United National Film Corp. (CO) 3/30/92
Each share Common no par exchanged for (0.5) share Common no par
United National Film Corp. (CO) reincorporated in Nevada 10/20/2006 which name changed to Wuhan General Group (China), Inc. 3/16/2007

RIVERSIDE CEMENT CO. (DE)
$1.25 Class A no par changed to $25 par in 1951
Class B Common no par changed to $1 par in 1951
$1.25 Class A $25 par changed to $1.25 Preferred $25 par 5/15/57
Class B Common $1 par changed to Common $10 par 5/15/57
Stock Dividend - 200% 8/1/57
Merged into American Cement Corp. 12/31/57
Each share $1.25 Preferred $25 par exchanged for (1) share new $1.25 Preferred $25 par
Each share Common $10 par exchanged for (2) shares Common $5 par
American Cement Corp. name changed to Amcord, Inc. 5/2/73
(See Amcord, Inc.)

RIVERSIDE COPPER MINING CO. (ID)
Charter forfeited for non-payment of taxes 12/1/59

RIVERSIDE COUNTY OIL CO. (CA)
Charter revoked for failure to file reports and pay fees 2/27/26

RIVERSIDE DRIVE & 103RD ST. CORP.
Liquidation completed in 1951

RIVERSIDE DRIVE-82ND ST. CORP.
Reorganized in 1950
No stockholders' equity

RIVERSIDE ENTMT INC (DE)
Recapitalized as Axis Technologies Group, Inc. 10/20/2006
Each share Common $0.001 par exchanged for (0.001) share Common $0.001 par

RIVERSIDE FINL CORP (CA)
Name changed to Quanta Industries, Inc. 10/01/1983
(See Quanta Industries, Inc.)

RIVERSIDE FORGE & MACHINE CO. OF JACKSON (MI)
Acquired by Pittsburgh Forgings Co. in 1929

RIVERSIDE FST PRODS LTD (BC)
Merged into Tolko Industries Ltd. 10/26/2004
Each share Common no par exchanged for $40 cash

RIVERSIDE GROUP INC (FL)
Name changed to Western Grain International Inc. 06/16/1982 which name changed back to Riverside Group, Inc. 06/12/1984
Common 10¢ par split (3) for (2) by issuance of (0.5) additional share 07/14/1987
SEC revoked common stock registration 08/21/2009
Stockholders' equity unlikely

RIVERSIDE HOMES INC (NC)
Name changed to Port Star Industries, Inc. 12/22/1969 which name changed back to Riverside Homes, Inc. 03/08/1983
Reincorporated under the laws of Nevada as Clancy Muldoon Ice Cream Inc. 04/05/1984
(See Clancy Muldoon Ice Cream Inc.)

RIVERSIDE INFORMATION TECHNOLOGIES INC (DE)
Reincorporated under the laws of Nevada as Clean Coal Technologies, Inc. 10/12/2007

RIVERSIDE METAL CO. (NJ)
Stock Dividend - 10% 12/14/51
Acquired by Porter (H.K.) Co., Inc. (Pa.) at $21.50 a share in 1954

RIVERSIDE METAL PRODS CO (MI)
Reorganized 02/25/1977
Reorganized from (OR) to under the laws of (MI) 02/25/1977
Each share Common $0.001 par exchanged for (1/9) share Common $0.001 par
Reacquired 00/00/1984
Each share Common $0.001 par exchanged for $3 cash

RIVERSIDE MLS (GA)
Each share Common $100 par exchanged for (4) shares Common $25 par 00/00/1943
Common $25 par reclassified as Class A $25 par and (1) share Class B $25 par distributed 02/00/1949
Class A $25 par and Class B $25 par changed to $12.50 par respectively and (1) additional share issued 12/15/1966
Each share Class A $12.50 par and Class B $12.50 par exchanged for (2.5) shares Class A $5 par and Class B $5 par respectively 12/09/1968
Stock Dividend - Class A & B - 20% 08/01/1968
Adjudicated bankrupt 01/00/1978
Stockholders equity unlikely

RIVERSIDE NATL BK
(RIVERSIDE, CA)
Capital Stock $10 par changed to $5 par and (1) additional share issued 04/09/1970
Capital Stock $5 par changed to $2.50 par and (1) additional share issued 04/25/1978
Capital Stock $2.50 par changed to $1.25 par and (1) additional share issued 05/20/1983
Stock Dividends - 10% 12/29/1969; 10% 12/01/1984; 10% 12/02/1985; 10% 12/01/1986
Merged into City National Corp. 01/24/1997
Each share Common $1.25 par exchanged for (0.923) share Common $1 par
City National Corp. merged into Royal Bank of Canada (Montreal, QC) 11/02/2015

RIVERSIDE PLASTICS CORP. (NY)
Name changed to Bischoff Chemical Corp. 04/11/1960
(See Bischoff Chemical Corp.)

RIVERSIDE PORTLAND CEMENT CO.
Succeeded by Riverside Cement Co. in 1928
Riverside Cement Co. merged into American Cement Corp. 12/31/57 which name changed to Amcord, Inc. 5/2/73
(See Amcord, Inc.)

RIVERSIDE PRESS INC (TX)
Name changed to RPI Liquidation Corp. 3/7/94
(See RPI Liquidation Corp.)

RIVERSIDE PROPERTIES, INC. (CA)
Charter suspended for failure to file reports and pay fees 05/01/1979

RIVERSIDE REAL ESTATE INVESTMENT TRUST (IL)
Name changed to Riverside Properties 08/01/1975

RIVERSIDE TRACTION CO.
Acquired by Public Service Coordinated Transport through an exchange of stock for new bonds in 1940

RIVERSIDE TRUST CO.
(HARTFORD, CT)
Capital Stock $25 par changed to $10 par and (1.5) additional shares issued plus a 14-2/7% stock dividend paid 4/10/56
Stock Dividends - 20% 11/20/47; 10% 2/15/62
Merged into United Bank & Trust Co. (Hartford, CT) 6/14/65
Each share Capital Stock $10 par exchanged for (1) share Common $10 par
United Bank & Trust Co. (Hartford, CT) reorganized as First Connecticut Bancorp, Inc. 11/12/70 which merged into Fleet Financial Group, Inc. (Old) 3/17/86 which merged into Fleet/Norstar Financial Group, Inc. 1/1/88 which name changed to Fleet Financial Group, Inc. (New) 4/15/92 which name changed to Fleet Boston Corp. 10/1/99 which name changed to FleetBoston Financial Corp. 4/18/2000 which merged into Bank of America Corp. 4/1/2004

RIVERSIDE VENTURES INC (DE)
Name changed to Alpine Air Express Inc. 06/12/2000
(See Alpine Air Express Inc.)

RIVERSIDE YARNS LTD (ON)
Name changed 6/13/60
Name changed from Riverside Silk Mills, Ltd. to Riverside Yarns Ltd. 6/13/60
Each share old Conv. Class A no par exchanged for (4) shares new Conv. Class A no par and (3) shares new Common no par 1/7/70
Each share old Common no par exchanged for (2) shares new Common no par 1/7/70
Each share new Conv. Class A no par exchanged for (2) shares new Common no par 2/5/81
Completely liquidated 2/18/86
Each share new Common no par received first and final distribution of $0.86 cash
Note: Certificates were not required to be surrendered and are without value

RIVERSOURCE LASALLE INTL REAL ESTATE FD INC (MD)
Merged into Columbia Funds Series Trust I 04/08/2011
Each share Common 1¢ par exchanged for (0.79499217) share Real Estate Equity Fund Class Z 1¢ par

RIVERSTONE NETWORKS INC (DE)
Plan of reorganization and liquidation under Chapter 11 Federal Bankruptcy proceedings effective 09/25/2006
Each share Common 1¢ par received initial distribution of $1.062 cash payable 09/29/2006 to holders of record 09/25/2006
Each share Common 1¢ par received second distribution of $0.168 cash payable 12/22/2006 to holders of record 09/25/2006
Each share Common 1¢ par received third distribution of $0.052 cash payable 12/20/2007 to holders of record 09/25/2006
Each share Common 1¢ par received fourth distribution of $0.03 cash payable 03/14/2008 to holders of record 09/25/2006
Each share Common 1¢ par received fifth distribution of $0.0188 cash payable 12/00/2008 to holders of record 09/25/2006
Each share Common 1¢ par received sixth distribution of $0.045 cash payable 12/22/2010 to holders of record 09/25/2006
Each share Common 1¢ par received seventh and final distribution of

$0.012498 cash payable 11/12/2013 to holders of record 09/25/2006 Distributions of $10 or less will not be made

RIVERSTONE RES INC (BC)
Name changed to True Gold Mining Inc. 02/25/2013
True Gold Mining Inc. merged into Endeavour Mining Corp. 04/27/2016

RIVERTON LIME & STONE CO., INC. (VA)
Acquired by Chadbourn Gotham, Inc. 07/25/1956
Each share 6% 1st Preferred $50 par exchanged for (1) share 6% Preferred $50 par
Each share Common $10 par exchanged for (1) share 5% Preferred $20 par and (3) shares Common $1 par
Chadbourn Gotham, Inc. name changed to Chadbourn Inc. 01/31/1969 which reorganized as Stanwood Corp. 06/12/1975 which was acquired by Delta Woodside Industries, Inc. (DE) 09/07/1988 which merged into Delta Woodside Industries, Inc. (SC) 11/15/1989
(See Delta Woodside Industries,, Inc. (SC))

RIVERTON RES CORP (BC)
Struck off register and declared dissolved for failure to file returns 5/14/93

RIVERTON WYOMING REFINING CO. (WY)
Charter revoked for failure to file reports 7/19/27

RIVERVIEW FINL CORP OLD (PA)
Merged into Riverview Financial Corp. (New) 11/01/2013
Each share Common 50¢ par exchanged for (1) share Common no par

RIVERVIEW SVGS BK FSB (CAMAS, WA)
Stock Dividends - 10% 4/10/95; 10% payable 4/12/96 to holders of record 3/29/96; 10% payable 4/11/97 to holders of record 3/31/97
Reorganized as Riverview Bancorp, Inc. 9/30/97
Each share Common $1 par exchanged for (0.394343731) share Common 1¢ par

RIVERVIEW TERRACE, INC. (VA)
Charter revoked for failure to pay taxes 6/1/63

RIVERWAY HLDGS INC (TX)
Merged into Texas Regional Bancshares, Inc. 2/22/2002
Each share Common $1 par exchanged for (0.417425) share Class A Common $1 par
Note: Each share Common $1 par received an additional distribution of approximately (0.070976) share Class A Common $1 par from escrow in December 2004
(See Texas Regional Bancshares, Inc.)

RIVERWOOD INTL CORP (DE)
Merged into Clayton Dubilier & Rice Inc. 3/27/96
Each share Common 1¢ par exchanged for $20.25 cash

RIVETT INC. (MA)
Acquired by Applied Power Industries, Inc. for cash 1/12/66

RIVETT LATHE & GRINDER, INC. (MA)
Name changed to Rivett Inc. 3/9/65
Rivett Inc. acquired by Applied Power Industries, Inc. 1/12/66

RIVIANA FOODS INC NEW (DE)
Merged into Ebro Puleva Inc. 09/02/2004
Each share Common $1 par exchanged for $25.75 cash

RIVIANA FOODS INC OLD (DE)
Common $3.50 par split (2) for (1) by issuance of (1) additional share 11/01/1966
Common $3.50 par split (5) for (4) by issuance of (0.25) additional share 05/22/1972
Stock Dividend - 10% 11/01/1965
Acquired by Colgate-Palmolive Co. 06/14/1976
Each share Common $3.50 par exchanged for (1.1) shares Common $1 par

RIVIERA EXPLS LTD (BC)
Recapitalized as Kentucky Oil & Gas Inc. 7/20/93
Each (3.69) shares Common no par exchanged for (1) share Common no par
Kentucky Oil & Gas Inc. name changed to Integrated Card Technologies Inc. 6/6/94 which recapitalized as Rizona Ventures Ltd. 7/29/97 which name changed to Admiral Bay Resources, Inc. (BC) 8/31/98 which reincorporated in Ontario 3/10/2004 which reincorporated back in British Columbia 3/10/2006

RIVIERA HLDGS CORP (NV)
Common $0.001 par split (4) for (1) by issuance of (3) additional shares 11/16/1995
Common $0.001 par split (3) for (1) by issuance of (2) additional shares payable 03/11/2005 to holders of record 02/25/2005 Ex date - 03/14/2005
Plan of reorganization under Chapter 11 Federal Bankruptcy proceedings effective 12/01/2010
No stockholders' equity

RIVIERA INDS & RES LTD (BC)
Name changed to Leslie Oil & Gas Co. Ltd. 10/23/81
(See Leslie Oil & Gas Co. Ltd.)

RIVIERA INTL CASINOS INC (NV)
Name changed to International Casino Cruises Inc. 11/21/97
International Casino Cruises Inc. name changed to Mountain Energy Inc. 5/26/98
(See Mountain Energy Inc.)

RIVIERA MINES LTD. (BC)
Recapitalized as Riviera Industries & Resources Ltd. 5/17/71
Each share Common 50¢ par exchanged for (1) share Common no par
Riviera Industries & Resources Ltd. name changed to Leslie Oil & Gas Co. Ltd. 10/23/81
(See Leslie Oil & Gas Co. Ltd.)

RIVIERE RLTY TR (DC)
Shares of Bene. Int. no par split (100) for (1) by issuance of (99) additional Shares 01/17/1969
Name changed to EastPark Realty Trust 05/10/1983
EastPark Realty Trust liquidated for Parkway Co. (TX) 04/06/1990 which reincorporated in Maryland as Parkway Properties, Inc. 08/02/1996 which merged into Cousins Properties Inc. 10/06/2016

RIVOLI BANCORP INC (GA)
Merged into Security Bank Corp. 12/30/2005
Each share Common no par exchanged for (1.297) shares Common $1 par and $3.96 cash
(See Security Bank Corp.)

RIVOLI BK & TR (MACON, GA)
Stock Dividend - 2% payable 04/15/1999 to holders of record 03/31/1999
Under plan of reorganization each share Common no par automatically became (1) share Rivoli Bancorp, Inc. Common no par 01/01/2002

Rivoli Bancorp, Inc. merged into Security Bank Corp. 12/30/2005
(See Security Bank Corp.)

RIVTOW MARINE LTD. (BC)
Merged into Rivtow Straits Ltd. 11/16/70
Each share Common no par exchanged for (2.85083) shares Common $1 par
(See Rivtow Straits Ltd.)

RIVTOW STRAITS LTD (BC)
100% acquired through purchase offer which expired 00/00/1981
Public interest eliminated

RIVULET INTL INC (NV)
Common $0.001 par split (12.255) for (1) by issuance of (11.255) additional shares payable 04/08/2010 to holders of record 04/08/2010 Ex date - 04/09/2010
Name changed to rVue Holdings, Inc. 04/15/2010
(See rVue Holdings, Inc.)

RIVUS BD FD (DE)
Name changed to Cutwater Select Income Fund 12/09/2011
Cutwater Select Income Fund name changed to Insight Select Income Fund 12/29/2016

RIX ATHABASCA URANIUM MINES LTD (ON)
Acquired by New York Oils Ltd. (BC) 8/31/70
Each share Capital Stock $1 par exchanged for (0.25) share Capital Stock no par
New York Oils Ltd. (BC) reincorporated in Alberta 7/19/82 which was acquired by Sceptre Resources Ltd. 3/14/89 which merged into Canadian Natural Resources Ltd. 8/15/96

RIX CORP (MA)
Merged into Dunnington Super Drug Inc. 08/01/1985
Each share Common 10¢ par exchanged for $10.46 cash

RIXON ELECTRS INC (MD)
Stock Dividend - 25% 07/31/1967
Acquired by United Utilities, Inc. 07/03/1969
Each share Capital Stock 25¢ par exchanged for (0.8) share Common $2.50 par
United Utilities, Inc. name changed to United Telecommunications, Inc. 06/02/1972 which name changed to Sprint Corp. (KS) 02/26/1992 which name changed to Sprint Nextel Corp. 08/12/2005 which merged into Sprint Corp. (DE) 07/10/2013

RIXSON FIREMARK INC (DE)
Merged into Conrac Corp. 04/30/1976
Each share Common 10¢ par exchanged for (0.25) share $1.50 Conv. Preferred Ser. C $5 par
(See Conrac Corp.)

RIZONA VENTURES LTD (BC)
Name changed to Admiral Bay Resources, Inc. 8/31/98
Admiral Bay Resources, Inc. (BC) reincorporated in Ontario 3/10/2004 which reincorporated back in British Columbia 3/10/2006

RIZZEN INC (NV)
Name changed to Jialijia Group Corp. Ltd. 06/07/2018

RJ FINL CORP (FL)
Stock Dividend - 10% 01/30/1986
Name changed to Raymond James Financial, Inc. 03/01/1987

RJK MINERALS CORP (ON)
Recapitalized as RJK Explorations Ltd. 12/22/1993
Each share Class A Subordinate no par exchanged for (0.4) Class A Subordinate no par
Each share Class B Subordinate no par exchanged for (0.4) share Class A Subordinate no par

RJO BIOLOGICALS INC (CO)
Proclaimed dissolved for failure to pay taxes and file annual reports 12/1/94

RJP ELECS LTD (HONG KONG)
Delisted from Canadian Venture Stock Exchange 05/31/2001

RJR HLDGS GROUP INC (DE)
Each share Exchangeable Preferred 1¢ par exchanged for $25 principal amount of Subordinated Exchangeable Debentures due 05/01/2007 on 07/17/1989
Public interest eliminated

RJR HLDGS INC (AB)
Name changed to Sigmacor Inc. 01/15/1997
(See Sigmacor Inc.)

RJR NABISCO HLDGS CORP (DE)
11.50% Conv. Preferred 1¢ par called for redemption 12/06/1993
Each Conv. Depositary Preferred Ser. A exchanged for (1) share old Common 1¢ par 11/15/1994
Each share old Common 1¢ par exchanged for (0.2) share new Common 1¢ par 04/12/1995
Issue Information - 250,000,000 DEPOSITARY SH REPSTG 1/10 PFD C PERCS % offered at $6.50 per share on 04/29/1994
Each Depositary Preferred Ser. C exchanged for (0.2) share new Common 1¢ par 05/15/1997
Depositary Preferred Ser. B called for redemption at $25 on 10/13/1998
Each share new Common 1¢ par received distribution of (1/3) share Reynolds (R.J.) Tobacco Holdings, Inc. Common 1¢ par payable 06/14/1999 to holders of record 05/27/1999 Ex date - 06/15/1999
Name changed to Nabisco Group Holdings Corp. 06/15/1999
(See Nabisco Group Holdings Corp.)

RJR NABISCO HLDGS CAP TR I (DE)
Trust Originated Preferred Securities no par called for redemption at $25 on 06/18/1999

RJR NABISCO HLDGS CAP TR II (DE)
Name changed to Nabisco Group Holdings Capital Trust II 7/15/99
(See Nabisco Group Holdings Capital Trust II)

RJR NABISCO INC (DE)
$12.96 Preferred Ser. C no par called for redemption 12/01/1986
Merged into RJR Holdings Group, Inc. 04/28/1989
Each share $11.50 Preferred Ser. B no par exchanged for $108 cash
Each share Common no par exchanged for $31.14 principal amount of RJR Holdings Corp. Sr. Converting Debentures due 05/01/2009 and (2.803) shares RJR Holdings Group, Inc. Exchangeable Preferred 1¢ par
(See RJR Holdings Group, Inc.)

RJV NETWORK INC (NV)
Common $0.001 par split (5) for (2) by issuance of (1.5) additional shares payable 4/26/2002 to holders of record 4/24/2002 Ex date - 4/29/2002
Name changed to ProtoKinetix, Inc. 7/15/2003

RJZ MNG CORP (AB)
Issue Information - 1,000,000 shares COM offered at $0.30 per share on 04/22/1997
Name changed to Vostok Minerals Inc. 06/18/2007

RKB ENTERPRISES INC (NY)
Preferred $100 par called for redemption at $100 on 1/22/99

RKO, INC. (UT)
Name changed to Hajecate Oil Co. (UT) 11/19/1982
Hajecate Oil Co. (UT) reincorporated in Texas 02/10/1983
(See Hajecate Oil Co.)

RKO INDUSTRIES CORP. (DE)
Name changed to List Industries Corp. 6/1/56
List Industries Corp. merged into Glen Alden Corp. (Pa.) 4/21/59 which reincorporated under the laws of Delaware 5/18/67 which merged into Rapid-American Corp. (Del.) 11/6/72
(See Rapid-American Corp. (Del.))

RKO PICTURES CORP. (DE)
Merged into Atlas Corp. 05/31/1956
Each share Common $1 par exchanged for (0.76190476) share Common $1 par
(See Atlas Corp.)

RKO THEATRES CORP. (DE)
Name changed to RKO Industries Corp. 5/15/56
RKO Industries Corp. name changed to List Industries Corp. 6/1/56 which merged into Glen Alden Corp. (Pa.) 4/21/59 which reincorporated under the laws of Delaware 5/18/67 which merged into Rapid-American Corp. (Del.) 11/6/72
(See Rapid-American Corp. (Del.))

RKS FINL GROUP INC (DE)
Name changed to JB Oxford Holdings Inc. 08/23/1994
JB Oxford Holdings Inc. name changed to Cambridge Capital Holdings, Inc. 04/18/2006
(See Cambridge Capital Holdings, Inc.)

RLC CORP (DE)
Common $1 par split (3) for (2) by issuance of (0.5) additional share 12/16/77
Conv. Preferred Ser. B no par called for redemption 8/28/78
Common $1 par split (3) for (2) by issuance of (0.5) additional share 6/1/79
Common $1 par split (3) for (2) by issuance of (0.5) additional share 11/29/83
Name changed to Rollins Truck Leasing Corp. 1/25/90
(See Rollins Truck Leasing Corp.)

RLD ENTERPRISES INC (MN)
Name changed to Go-Rachels.com Corp. 1/27/99
Go-Rachels.com Corp. name changed to Rachel's Gourmet Snacks Inc. 9/17/2001
(See Rachel's Gourmet Snacks Inc.)

RLI CORP (IL)
Reincorporated 04/05/1985
Reincorporated 05/07/1993
Common $1 par split (2) for (1) by issuance of (1) additional share 05/31/1972
Common $1 par split (5) for (3) by issuance of (0.66666666) additional share 07/15/1985
Common $1 par split (3) for (2) by issuance of (0.5) additional share 07/15/1986
Stock Dividends - 20% 05/27/1977; 20% 07/15/1978; 10% 10/15/1979; 25% 01/16/1981
State of incorporation changed from (IL) to (DE) 04/05/1985
State of incorporation changed from (DE) back to (IL) 05/07/1993
Common $1 par split (5) for (4) by issuance of (0.25) additional share 06/21/1995
Common $1 par split (5) for (4) by issuance of (0.25) additional share payable 06/19/1998 to holders of record 06/05/1998 Ex date - 06/22/1998
Common $1 par split (2) for (1) by issuance of (1) additional share payable 10/15/2002 to holders of record 09/30/2002 Ex date - 10/16/2002
Common $1 par split (2) for (1) by issuance of (1) additional share payable 01/15/2014 to holders of record 12/30/2013 Ex date - 01/16/2014
Reincorporated back under the laws of Delaware and Common $1 par changed to 1¢ par 05/04/2018

RLI INC (MI)
Charter declared inoperative and void for failure to file reports 05/15/1990

RLJ ACQUISITION INC (NV)
Issue Information - 12,500,000 UNITS consisting of (1) share COM and (1) WT offered at $10 per Unit on 02/15/2011
Units separated 10/03/2012
Under plan of merger name changed to RLJ Entertainment, Inc. 10/03/2012

RLN RLTY ASSOC INC (FL)
Name changed to Netmaximizer.Com Inc. 03/01/1999
Netmaximizer.Com Inc. recapitalized as Gentech Pharma Inc. 11/14/2005 which name changed to Fintech Group, Inc. 09/20/2006 which name changed to Capital Markets Technologies, Inc. 02/20/2007
(See Capital Markets Technologies, Inc.)

RLR FINL SVCS INC (FL)
Name changed to Equitable Financial Services of America, Inc. 9/15/89
(See Equitable Financial Services of America, Inc.)

RM HEALTH INTL INC (NV)
Name changed to Blue Earth Solutions, Inc. 06/09/2008

RM INVS INC (NV)
Name changed to 20/20 Global, Inc. 05/01/2014

RMC INDS INC (NY)
Charter cancelled and proclaimed dissolved for failure to pay taxes 06/00/1979

RMD TECHNOLOGIES INC (CA)
SEC revoked common stock registration 12/01/2011

RMED INTL INC (CO)
Name changed to TenderCare International, Inc. 03/12/2004
(See TenderCare International, Inc.)

RMG CAP CORP (CA)
Common no par split (2) for (1) by issuance of (1) additional share payable 02/22/2006 to holders of record 02/08/2006 Ex date - 02/23/2006
Acquired by Opus Acquisition II, Inc. 10/31/2011
Each share Common no par exchanged for $17.4687 cash

RMG NETWORKS HLDG CORP (DE)
Units separated 04/18/2016
Each share old Common $0.0001 par exchanged for (0.25) share new Common $0.0001 par 08/15/2017
Acquired by SCG Digital, LLC 09/28/2018
Each share new Common $0.0001 par exchanged for $1.29 cash

RMH TELESERVICES INC (PA)
Merged into NCO Group, Inc. 04/02/2004
Each share Common no par exchanged for (0.215) share Common no par
(See NCO Group, Inc.)

RMI NET INC (DE)
Under plan of merger name changed to Internet Commerce & Communications, Inc. 11/29/2000
(See Internet Commerce & Communications, Inc.)

RMI TITANIUM CO (OH)
Each share old Common 1¢ par exchanged for (0.1) share new Common 1¢ par 03/31/1994
Under plan of reorganization each share new Common 1¢ par automatically became (1) share RTI International Metals, Inc. Common 1¢ par 09/30/1998
RTI International Metals, Inc. merged into Alcoa Inc. 07/23/2015 which name changed to Arconic Inc. (PA) 11/01/2016 which reincorporated in Delaware 12/31/2017

RMIC CORP (NC)
Common $1 par split (5) for (4) by issuance of (0.25) additional share 06/23/1978
Stock Dividends - 10% 03/15/1976; 30% 03/15/1977; 10% 03/22/1979
Merged into Old Republic International Corp. 02/14/1980
Each share Common $1 par exchanged for (1.225) shares Common $1 par

RMK ADVANTAGE INCOME FD INC (MD)
Name changed to Helios Advantage Income Fund, Inc. 12/29/2008
Helios Advantage Income Fund, Inc. merged into Brookfield High Income Fund Inc. 08/13/2014 which merged into Brookfield Real Assets Income Fund Inc. 12/05/2016

RMK HIGH INCOME FD INC (MD)
Name changed to Helios High Income Fund, Inc. 12/29/2008
Helios High Income Fund, Inc. merged into Brookfield High Income Fund Inc. 08/13/2014 which merged into Brookfield Real Assets Income Fund Inc. 12/05/2016

RMK MULTI-SECTOR HIGH INCOME FD INC (MD)
Name changed to Helios Multi-Sector High Income Fund, Inc. 12/29/2008
Helios Multi-Sector High Income Fund, Inc. merged into Brookfield High Income Fund Inc. 08/13/2014 which merged into Brookfield Real Assets Income Fund Inc. 12/05/2016

RMK STRATEGIC INCOME FD INC (MD)
Name changed to Helios Strategic Income Fund, Inc. 12/29/2008
Helios Strategic Income Fund, Inc. merged into Brookfield High Income Fund Inc. 08/13/2014 which merged into Brookfield Real Assets Income Fund Inc. 12/05/2016

RML MED LABS INC (ON)
Name changed to Imutec Corp. 08/25/1992
Imutec Corp. name changed to Imutec Pharma Inc. 11/27/1996 which name changed to Lorus Therapeutics Inc. (ON) 11/19/1998
(See Lorus Therapeutics Inc. (ON))

RMM VENTURES INC (ON)
Reorganized under the laws of Alberta as PowerComm Inc. 12/31/2006
Each share Common no par exchanged for (0.8333333) share Common no par
PowerComm Inc. name changed to PetroCorp Group Inc. 12/23/2009

RMN TECHNOLOGIES INC (AB)
Name changed to Global Railway Industries Ltd. (AB) 02/25/1999
Global Railway Industries Ltd. (AB) reincorporated in British Columbia 04/16/2013 which recapitalized as Chinook Tyee Industry Ltd. 08/13/2013

RMP ENERGY INC (AB)
Name changed to Iron Bridge Resources Inc. 11/27/2017

RMP INTL LTD (CAYMAN ISLANDS)
(Issued in Units consisting of (1) share Parsons Corp. Common $1 par and (1) share RMP International, Ltd. Common no par)
Units separated 1/14/85
Company liquidated 1/25/85
Each share Common no par exchanged for first and final distribution of $1.60 cash
(See Parsons Corp.)

RMP PPTYS LTD (SOUTH AFRICA)
ADR agreement terminated 03/06/2000
Each ADR for Ordinary exchanged for $0.735 cash

RMR ASIA PAC REAL ESTATE FD (MA)
Merged into RMR Asia Pacific Real Estate Fund (DE) 06/17/2009
Each share Common $0.001 par exchanged for (0.513) share Common $0.001 par
RMR Asia Pacific Real Estate Fund (DE) name changed to RMR Real Estate Income Fund (DE) (New) 01/20/2012 which reincorporated in Maryland 04/18/2017

RMR ASIA REAL ESTATE FD (MA)
Merged into RMR Asia Pacific Real Estate Fund (DE) 06/17/2009
Each Common Share of Bene. Int. $0.001 par exchanged for (0.513) share Common $0.001 par
RMR Asia Pacific Real Estate Fund (DE) name changed to RMR Real Estate Income Fund (DE) (New) 01/20/2012 which reincorporated in Maryland 04/18/2017

RMR DIVID CAPTURE FD (MA)
Merged into RMR Real Estate Income Fund (Old) 06/23/2009
Each Auction Rate Preferred Ser. F $0.001 par exchanged for (1) Auction Rate Preferred Ser. F $0.001 par
Each Common Share of Bene. Int. $0.001 par exchanged for (0.123) Common Share of Bene. Int. $0.001 par
RMR Real Estate Income Fund (Old) merged into RMR Real Estate Income Fund (DE) (New) 01/20/2012 which reincorporated in Maryland 04/18/2017

RMR F I R E FD (MA)
Merged into RMR Real Estate Income Fund (Old) 06/18/2009
Each Auction Rate Preferred Ser. W $0.001 par exchanged for (1) Auction Rate Preferred Ser. W $0.001 par
Each Common Share of Bene. Int. $0.001 par exchanged for (0.123) Common Share of Bene. Int. $0.001 par
RMR Real Estate Income Fund (Old) merged into RMR Real Estate Income Fund (DE) (New) 01/20/2012 which reincorporated in Maryland 04/18/2017

RMR HOSPITALITY & REAL ESTATE FD (MA)
Merged into RMR Real Estate Income Fund (Old) 06/22/2009
Each Auction Rate Preferred Ser. TH $0.001 par exchanged for (1) Auction Rate Preferred Ser. TH $0.001 par
Each Common Share of Bene. Int. $0.001 par exchanged for (0.174) Common Share of Bene. Int. $0.001 par
RMR Real Estate Income Fund (Old) merged into RMR Real Estate Income Fund (DE) (New) 01/20/2012 which reincorporated in Maryland 04/18/2017

RMR PREF DIV FD (MA)
Merged into RMR Real Estate Income Fund (Old) 06/24/2009
Each Auction Rate Preferred Ser. M $0.001 par exchanged for (1)

RMR REAL ESTATE FD (MA) [continued]

Auction Rate Preferred Ser. M $0.001 par
Each Common Share of Bene. Int. $0.001 par exchanged for (0.103) Common Share of Bene. Int. $0.001 par
RMR Real Estate Income Fund (Old) merged into RMR Real Estate Income Fund (DE) (New) 01/20/2012 which reincorporated in Maryland 04/18/2017

RMR REAL ESTATE FD (MA)
Merged into RMR Real Estate Income Fund (Old) 06/18/2009
Each Auction Rate Preferred Ser. T $0.001 par exchanged for (1) Auction Rate Preferred Ser. T $0.001 par
Each Common Share of Bene. Int. $0.001 par exchanged for (0.195) Common Share of Bene. Int. $0.001 par
RMR Real Estate Income Fund (Old) merged into RMR Real Estate Income Fund (DE) (New) 01/20/2012 which reincorporated in Maryland 04/18/2017

RMR REAL ESTATE INCOME FD NEW (DE)
Name changed 01/20/2012
Under plan of merger name changed from RMR Asia Pacific Real Estate Fund to RMR Real Estate Income Fund (New) 01/20/2012
Reincorporated under the laws of Maryland 04/18/2017

RMR REAL ESTATE INCOME FD OLD (DE)
Merged into RMR Real Estate Income Fund (DE) (New) 01/20/2012
Each share Common $0.001 par exchanged for (2.095) shares Common $0.001 par
Preferreds not affected except for change in name
RMR Real Estate Income Fund (DE) (New) reincorporated in Maryland 04/18/2017

RMS ELECTRONICS, INC. (DE)
Reincorporated 12/15/1971
State of incorporation changed from (NY) to (DE) 12/15/1971
Common 25¢ par changed to $0.125 par and (1) additional share issued 10/05/1977
Common $0.125 par changed to 8¢ par and (0.5) additional share issued 10/14/1980
Stock Dividends - 50% 07/15/1975; 10% 09/30/1976; 10% 10/19/1979
Name changed to RMS International, Inc. 05/27/1987
RMS International, Inc. name changed to Diversified Communications Industries Ltd. 03/31/1992
(See Diversified Communications Industries Ltd.)

RMS INTL INC (DE)
Name changed to Diversified Communications Industries Ltd. 03/31/1992
(See Diversified Communications Industries Ltd.)

RMS MED SYS INC (BC)
Recapitalized as Pacific Genesis Technologies Inc. (BC) 12/21/1999
Each share Common no par exchanged for (1/7) share Common no par
Pacific Genesis Technologies Inc. (BC) reincorporated in Alberta as Ware Solutions Corp. 10/01/2001
(See Ware Solutions Corp.)

RMS SYS INC (AB)
Merged into PHX Energy Services Corp. 12/02/2013
Each share Common no par exchanged for (0.037209) share Common no par
Note: Unexchanged certificates were cancelled and became without value 12/01/2016

RMS TITANIC INC (FL)
Name changed to Premier Exhibitions, Inc. 10/18/2004
Each share Common $0.0001 par exchanged for (1) share Common $0.0001 par

RMX HLDGS INC (NV)
Each share old Common $0.001 par exchanged for (0.00000037) share new Common $0.001 par 01/12/2011
Note: In effect holders received $0.59 cash per share and public interest was eliminated

RNC GOLD INC (CANADA)
Merged into Yamana Gold Inc. 2/28/2006
Each share Common no par exchanged for (0.12) share Common no par

RNC LIQUID ASSETS FD INC (MD)
Name changed to RNC Mutual Fund Group, Inc. in June 1996
(See RNC Mutual Fund Group, Inc.)

RNC MUT FD GROUP INC (MD)
Completely liquidated 9/24/2002
Each share Equity Fund received distribution on a pro rata basis
Each Money Market share received distribution on a pro rata basis

RNC WESTWIND FD INC (MD)
Merged into ProvidentMutual Investment Shares, Inc. 04/30/1990
Each share Common 1¢ par exchanged for (1) share Common $1 par
(See ProvidentMutual Investment Shares, Inc.)

RNETHEALTH INC (CO)
Name changed 01/02/2001
Name changed from RnetHealth.com, Inc. to RnetHealth, Inc. 01/02/2001
Each share old Common 1¢ par exchanged for (1/6) share new Common 1¢ par 06/13/2001
Recapitalized as Bryn Resources Inc. 12/26/2008
Each share Common 1¢ par exchanged for (0.05) share Common 1¢ par

RNS SOFTWARE INC (NV)
Reorganized as Hotgate Technology, Inc. 06/09/2008
Each share Common $0.0001 par exchanged for (2.5) shares Common $0.0001 par
Hotgate Technology, Inc. name changed to REDtone Asia, Inc. 03/14/2011

RO-AN HEAT RECLAIMER CORP. (NY)
Charter revoked for failure to file reports and pay fees 12/15/65

RO KO, INC. (MO)
Name changed to Columbia Toy Products, Inc. 02/21/1962
(See Columbia Toy Products, Inc.)

RO-MAC GOLD LTD (NV)
Each share Common 1¢ par exchanged for (2.5) shares Common $0.001 par 02/26/1979
Each share old Common $0.001 par exchanged for (0.05) share new Common 07/22/1996
Each share new Common $0.001 par exchanged again for (0.087299) share new Common $0.001 par 09/30/1996
Name changed to Phoenix Associates Land Syndicate 10/24/1996
(See Phoenix Associates Land Syndicate)

ROACH (W.R.) & CO.
Reorganized as Roach (W.R.) Co. 00/00/1942
No stockholders' equity

ROACH (W.R.) CO.
Merged into Stokley-Van Camp, Inc. in 1946
Each share 5% Preferred exchanged for (0.5) share 5% Prior Preference
Each share Class A Common exchanged for (2/3) share Common
Each share Class B Common exchanged for (1/15) share Common
(See Stokley-Van Camp, Inc.)

ROACH HAL STUDIOS CORP (BC)
Merged into H.R.S. Industries, Inc. 05/21/1982
Each share Class A Common no par exchanged for (1) share Class A Common no par
H.R.S. Industries, Inc. merged into International H.R.S. Industries Inc. 05/15/1984 which name changed to Glenex Industries Inc. 05/25/1987 which merged into Quest Investment Corp. 07/04/2002 which merged into Quest Capital Corp. (BC) 06/30/2003 which reincorporated in Canada 05/27/2008 which name changed to Sprott Resource Lending Corp. 09/10/2010 which merged into Sprott Inc. 07/24/2013

ROACH HAL STUDIOS INC (DE)
Merged into HRI Group, Inc. 4/8/88
Each share Common $0.001 par exchanged for (1) share Common 1¢ par
HRI Group, Inc. name changed to Qintex Entertainment Inc. 12/9/88
(See Qintex Entertainment Inc.)

ROACH HAL STUDIOS INC (NY)
Name changed to Innotek Corp. 02/10/1971
(See Innotek Corp.)

ROACH'S HOUSE CLEANING CO., INC. (NY)
Charter revoked for failure to file reports and pay fees 12/16/35

ROAD NEW MEDIA CORP (AB)
Recapitalized as Perisson Petroleum Corp. 12/19/2012
Each share Common no par exchanged for (1/7) share Common no par

ROAD WINGS INC (NV)
Recapitalized as OneFi Technology Inc. 03/02/2009
Each share Common $0.001 par exchanged for (0.0007) share Common $0.001 par
OneFi Technology Inc. recapitalized as Seesmart Technologies, Inc. 02/17/2012
(See Seesmart Technologies, Inc.)

ROADCRAFT MFG & LEASING CORP (CA)
Stock Dividend - 25% 02/23/1966
Merged into Gardena Manufacturing & Leasing Inc. 09/30/1977
Each share Common no par exchanged for $9.50 cash

ROADHOUSE FOODS INC (DE)
Reincorporated 07/00/2005
State of incorporation changed from (OK) to (DE) 07/00/2005
Each share old Common $0.0001 par exchanged for (0.01086956) share new Common $0.0001 par 07/08/2005
Name changed to Locan, Inc. 06/09/2008
(See Locan, Inc.)

ROADHOUSE GRILL INC (FL)
Issue Information - 2,500,000 shares COM offered at $6 per share on 11/26/1996
Each share Common 3¢ par received a 15% distribution payable 10/15/2002 to holders of record 09/30/2002
Chapter 11 bankruptcy proceedings converted to Chapter 7 on 05/14/2008
Stockholders' equity unlikely

ROADKING TRAVEL CTRS INC (AB)
Liquidation completed
Each share Common no par received initial distribution of $0.0395 cash payable 11/25/2014 to holders of record 11/18/2014
Each share Common no par received second and final distribution of $0.00629 cash payable 04/02/2015 to holders of record 03/30/2015

ROADMASTER INDS INC (DE)
Name changed to RDM Sports Group, Inc. 1/29/97
(See RDM Sports Group, Inc.)

ROADRUNNER ENTERPRISES INC (CO)
Merged into Circle Express, Inc. 04/30/1988
Each share Common no par exchanged for $9.75 cash

ROADRUNNER OIL & GAS INC (CANADA)
Name changed to Bowood Energy Inc. 06/21/2010
Bowood Energy Inc. recapitalized as LGX Oil + Gas Inc. (Canada) 08/22/2012 which reincorporated in Alberta 06/27/2013

ROADRUNNER VIDEO GROUP INC (DE)
Plan of reorganization under Chapter 11 Federal Bankruptcy proceedings confirmed 10/22/1998
Stockholders' equity unlikely

ROADSHIPS HLDGS INC (DE)
Common $0.001 par split (1.97576614) for (1) by issuance of (0.97576614) additional share payable 07/17/2009 to holders of record 06/15/2009 Ex date - 07/20/2009
Name changed to Tautachrome Inc. 11/05/2015

ROADWAY CORP (DE)
Name changed 5/30/2001
Name changed from Roadway Express Inc. (Ctfs. dated after 1/12/96) to Roadway Corp. 5/30/2001
Merged into Yellow Roadway Corp. 12/12/2003
Each share Common no par exchanged for approximately (0.99) share Common $1 par and $20.70 cash
Yellow Roadway Corp. name changed to YRC Worldwide Inc. 1/4/2006

ROADWAY EXPRESS INC (DE)
Ctfs. dated prior to 7/30/82
Common 25¢ par changed to no par and (1) additional share issued 5/21/63
Common no par split (2) for (1) by issuance of (1) additional share 6/11/69
Common no par split (2) for (1) by issuance of (1) additional share 10/12/71
Common no par split (2) for (1) by issuance of (1) additional share 10/19/72
Reorganized under the laws of Ohio as Roadway Services, Inc. 7/30/82
Roadway Services, Inc. name changed to Caliber System Inc. 1/2/96 which merged into FDX Corp. 1/27/98 which name changed to FedEx Corp. 1/19/2000

ROADWAY MAINTENANCE CORP (NY)
Name changed to RMC Industries, Inc. 10/01/1969
(See RMC Industries, Inc.)

ROADWAY MTR PLAZAS INC (NY)
Name changed to Travel Ports of America Inc. 11/12/91
(See Travel Ports of America Inc.)

ROADWAY SVCS INC (OH)
Common no par split (2) for (1) by

issuance of (1) additional share 5/30/84
Each share Common no par received distribution of (0.5) share Roadway Express Inc. Common no par payable 1/12/96 to holders of record 12/29/95 Ex date - 1/16/96
Name changed to Caliber System Inc. 1/2/96
Caliber System Inc. merged into FDX Corp. 1/27/98 which name changed to FedEx Corp. 1/19/2000

ROAMING MESSENGER INC (NV)
Name changed to Warp 9 Inc. 11/02/2006
Warp 9 Inc. name changed to CloudCommerce, Inc. 09/30/2015

ROAN ANTELOPE COPPER MINES LTD. (NORTHERN RHODESIA)
American Share 5s par split (9) for (5) by issuance of (0.8) share 02/12/1957
Stock Dividend - 80% 08/21/1951
Merged into Rhodesian Selection Trust Ltd. (Northern Rhodesia) 02/22/1962
Each American Share 20s par exchanged for (0.5) American Share £1 par
Rhodesian Selection Trust Ltd. (Northern Rhodesia) reincorporated in Zambia as Roan Selection Trust Ltd. 03/31/1969
(See Roan Selection Trust Ltd.)

ROAN CONS MINES LTD (ZAMBIA)
Name changed to Zambia Consolidated Copper Mines Ltd. 03/25/1982
(See Zambia Consolidated Copper Mines Ltd.)

ROAN FINL SVCS INC (DE)
Charter cancelled and declared inoperative and void for non-payment of taxes 3/1/90

ROAN SELECTION TR LTD (ZAMBIA)
American Shares ZMK 2 par split (2) for (1) by the issuance of (1) additional share 05/14/1969
Each American Share ZMK 2 par exchanged for $3 principal amount American Metal Climax Inc. 8% Subord. Debenture due 00/00/1986, $2 principal amount Zambia Industrial & Mining Corp. Ltd. 6% Gtd. Dollar Bond due 00/00/1978, (0.2) Roan Consolidated Mines Ltd. ADR for Ordinary B Shares ZMK 4 par, (0.0022002) Botswana RST Ltd. ADR for Ordinary BWP 2 par and $0.25 cash 08/18/1970
(See each company's listing)

ROANNA TOGS INC (NY)
Stock Dividend - 10% 04/15/1976
Merged into Rotog Apparel, Inc. 04/06/1978
Each share Common 10¢ par exchanged for $3 cash

ROANOKE BLDG CO (DE)
Name changed to 500-R, Inc. 01/02/1968
(See 500-R, Inc.)

ROANOKE ELEC STL CORP (VA)
Common no par split (2) for (1) by issuance of (1) additional share 1/15/81
Common no par split (3) for (2) by issuance of (0.5) additional share 4/25/86
Common no par split (3) for (2) by issuance of (0.5) additional share 9/20/88
Common no par split (3) for (2) by issuance of (0.5) additional share 5/25/95
Common no par split (3) for (2) by issuance of (0.5) additional share payable 3/25/98 to holders of record 3/6/98
Stock Dividend - 10% 11/25/74
Merged into Steel Dynamics, Inc. 4/12/2006

Each share Common no par exchanged for (0.4) share Common 1¢ par and $9.75 cash

ROANOKE EXPLS LTD (BC)
Delisted from Vancouver Stock Exchange 04/01/1985

ROANOKE GAS CO (VA)
Common $5 par split (2) for (1) by issuance of (1) additional share 7/1/94
Stock Dividends - 10% 2/23/68; 10% 2/1/76; 100% 4/20/78; 20% 12/10/82; 10% 12/14/84
Under plan of reorganization each share Common $5 par automatically became (1) share RGC Resources, Inc. Common $5 par 7/29/98

ROANOKE KNITTING MILLS, INC. (VA)
Charter revoked for failure to file reports in 1933

ROANOKE PIPE LINE CO. (VA)
Merged into Roanoke Gas Co. share for share 4/22/58
Roanoke Gas Co. reorganized as RGC Resources, Inc. 7/29/98

ROANOKE TECHNOLOGY CORP (FL)
Each share old Common $0.0001 par exchanged for (0.14285714) share new Common $0.0001 par 03/26/2001
SEC revoked common stock registration 01/15/2008

ROANOKE WATER WORKS CO.
Acquired by City of Roanoke, Va. in 1938

ROANWELL CORP (NY)
Merged into High Voltage Engineering Corp. 12/03/1979
Each share Common $1 par exchanged for (1.1) shares Common $1 par
(See High Voltage Engineering Corp.)

ROARK ENTERPRISES INC (NJ)
Name changed to First Combined Enterprises, Inc. (NJ) 12/09/1969
First Combined Enterprises, Inc. (NJ) reincorporated in Delaware 06/30/1969
(See First Combined Enterprises, Inc. (DE))

ROAST-N-ROLL (NV)
SEC revoked common stock registration 10/29/2009
Stockholders' equity unlikely

ROATAN FDG INC (DE)
Name changed to Electro Brain International Corp. and Common $0.001 par changed to $0.0001 par 03/06/1990

ROATAN MED TECHNOLOGIES INC (NV)
Reincorporated 07/00/1996
State of incorporation changed from (UT) to (NV) 07/00/1996
Name changed to Technology Acquisition Corp. 11/01/2001
Technology Acquisition Corp. name changed to Minrad International, Inc. (NV) 12/21/2004 which reincorporated in Delaware 04/25/2005
(See Minrad International, Inc.)

ROB ROY MINING CO. (ID)
Recapitalized as Royal Silver Mining Co. 7/22/69
Each share Capital Stock $1 par exchanged for (1) share Common 3¢ par

ROBB MONTBRAY MINES LTD (ON)
Recapitalized as Paragon Explorations Ltd. 11/21/1977
Each share Capital Stock $1 par exchanged for (0.1) share Capital Stock no par
Paragon Explorations Ltd.

recapitalized as Sagewood Resources Ltd. 10/06/1983
(See Sagewood Resources Ltd.)

ROBBINS & MYERS CO.
Succeeded by Robbins & Myers, Inc. 00/00/1928
Details not available

ROBBINS & MYERS INC (OH)
Preferred no par called for redemption 05/24/1965
Preferred $25 par changed to no par 00/00/1933
Common no par split (3) for (1) by issuance of (2) additional shares 06/11/1965
Common no par split (5) for (2) by issuance of (1.5) additional shares 12/01/1967
Common no par split (2) for (1) by issuance of (1) additional share 03/14/1980
Common no par split (2) for (1) by issuance of (1) additional share 01/31/1992
Common no par split (2) for (1) by issuance of (1) additional share payable 07/31/1996 to holders of record 07/12/1996
Common no par split (2) for (1) by issuance of (1) additional share payable 02/28/2008 to holders of record 02/04/2008 Ex date - 02/29/2008
Acquired by National Oilwell Varco, Inc. 02/20/2013
Each share Common no par exchanged for $60 cash

ROBBINS MILLS, INC. (NY)
Capital Stock $20 par reclassified as Common $20 par 10/00/1951
Merged into Textron American, Inc. 02/24/1955
Each share 4.50% Preferred Ser. A $50 par exchanged for (2) shares $1.25 Preferred no par and $2.0625 cash
Each share Common $20 par exchanged for (1) share Common 50¢ par
Textron American, Inc. name changed to Textron Inc. (RI) 05/15/1956 which reincorporated in Delaware 01/02/1968

ROBCOR PPTYS INC (FL)
Each share old Common no par exchanged for (0.1) share new Common no par 08/04/2006
Reincorporated under the laws of Delaware as Redpoint Bio Corp. and Common no par changed to $0.0001 par 07/02/2007

ROBEC INC (PA)
Acquired by AmeriQuest Technologies, Inc. 11/13/1995
Each share Common 1¢ par exchanged for (0.82944) share Common 1¢ par
(See AmeriQuest Technologies, Inc.)

ROBEL BEEF PACKERS INC (MN)
Name changed to Davis Covenant Corp. (MN) and Common 75¢ par changed to $0.001 par 07/25/1995
Davis Covenant Corp. (MN) reincorporated in Nevada as Boyd Energy Corp. 04/15/1998 which recapitalized as Barnett Energy Corp. 08/02/2001 which recapitalized as WorldWide Strategies Inc. 07/08/2005

ROBERDS INC (OH)
Liquidating plan of reorganization confirmed 5/4/2000
Stockholders' equity unlikely

ROBERN APPAREL INC. (DE)
Name changed to Robern Industries Inc. 10/9/92
Robern Industries, Inc. name changed to WinStar Communications Inc. 12/2/93
(See WinStar Communications Inc.)

ROBERN INDS INC (DE)
Name changed to WinStar Communications Inc. 12/2/93
(See WinStar Communications Inc.)

ROBERT MARK INC (DE)
Charter cancelled and declared inoperative and void for non-payment of taxes 03/01/1994

ROBERT MINES LTD (BC)
Recapitalized as Edinov Technologies Inc./Les Technologies Edinov Inc. 05/30/1989
Each share Common no par exchanged for (0.25) share Common no par
Edinov Technologies Inc./Les Technologies Edinov Inc. recapitalized as Edinov Corp. 04/27/1993 which reorganized into Cedar Group, Inc. 09/30/1993 which name changed to Dominion Bridge Corp. 08/01/1996
(See Dominion Bridge Corp.)

ROBERT TREAT HOTEL CO (NJ)
Assets sold 06/30/1970
No stockholders' equity

ROBERTS & MANDER CORP.
Name changed to Price National Corp. in 1952
Price National Corp. name changed to S & P National Corp. in 1954
(See S & P National Corp.)

ROBERTS & MANDER STOVE CO.
Name changed to Roberts & Mander Corp. in 1946
Roberts & Mander Corp. name changed to Price National Corp. in 1952 which name changed to S & P National Corp. in 1954
(See S & P National Corp.)

ROBERTS & PORTER INC (DE)
Reincorporated 5/12/77
Stock Dividends - 25% 4/30/63; 10% 4/25/69; 10% 4/24/70; 10% 4/23/71; 25% 4/2/75; 25% 1/26/77
State of incorporation changed from (IL) to (DE) 5/12/77
Common $1 par split (5) for (4) by issuance of (0.25) additional share 1/27/78
Common $1 par split (5) for (4) by issuance of (0.25) additional share 1/26/79
Reorganized under Chapter 11 Bankruptcy Code 8/29/84
Each share Common $1 par exchanged for $0.50 cash 9/27/84

ROBERTS BAY RES LTD (AB)
Acquired by Rider Resources Inc. 05/15/2001
Each share Common no par exchanged for (1/3) share Common no par
Rider Resources Inc. merged into Rider Resources Ltd. 02/21/2003 which merged into NuVista Energy Ltd. 03/04/2008

ROBERTS CO. NEW (NC)
Ctfs. dated after 2/27/73
Name changed to RCL Co. 5/21/74
(See RCL Co.)

ROBERTS CO. OLD (NC)
Ctfs. dated prior to 2/28/73
Stock Dividend -25% 5/6/66
Reorganized in bankruptcy 2/28/73
Common $1 par declared valueless

ROBERTS CO (CA)
Name changed to Roberts Consolidated Industries, Inc. 8/20/63
Roberts Consolidated Industries, Inc. merged into U.S. Plywood-Champion Papers Inc. 12/3/70 which name changed to Champion International Corp. 5/12/72 which merged into International Paper Co. 6/20/2000

ROBERTS (F.H.) CO.
Acquired by Daggett Chocolate Co. 00/00/1933

Details not available

ROBERTS CONS INDS INC (CA)
Merged into U.S. Plywood-Champion Papers Inc. 12/3/70
Each share Common $1 par exchanged for (0.7) share Common 50¢ par
U.S. Plywood-Champion Papers Inc. name changed to Champion International Corp. 5/12/72 which merged into International Paper Co. 6/20/2000

ROBERTS ENTERPRISES INC (WV)
Common $2.50 par changed to 83-1/3¢ par and (2) additional shares issued 7/19/69
Charter revoked 7/15/99

ROBERTS GAIL INC (NY)
Charter cancelled and proclaimed dissolved for failure to pay taxes 03/31/1982

ROBERTS-GORDON APPLIANCE CORP. (NY)
Acquired by A.J. Industries, Inc. (W. Va.) on a (1.35) for (1) basis 12/31/60
A.J. Industries, Inc. (W. Va.) reincorporated under the laws of Delaware 4/30/68
(See A.J. Industries, Inc. (Del.))

ROBERTS JOHN INC (DE)
Merged into Woods (J.R.), Inc. 07/02/1975
Each share Common 50¢ par exchanged for $4.30 cash

ROBERTS LUMBER CO. (WV)
Name changed to Roberts Enterprises, Inc. 6/12/67
(See Roberts Enterprises, Inc.)

ROBERTS OIL & GAS INC (TX)
Each (30) shares Common 1¢ par exchanged for (1) share Common 30¢ par 10/04/1989
Common 30¢ par split (2) for (1) by issuance of (1) additional share payable 05/29/1997 to holders of record 05/12/1997
Name changed to Adair International Oil & Gas Inc. and Common 30¢ par changed to no par 07/25/1997
Adair International Oil & Gas, Inc. name changed to EnDevCo, Inc. 10/09/2003
(See EnDevCo, Inc.)

ROBERTS PHARMACEUTICAL CORP (NJ)
Merged into Shire Pharmaceuticals Group plc 12/23/1999
Each share Common 1¢ par exchanged for (1.04266667) Sponsored ADR's for Ordinary 5p par
Shire Pharmaceuticals Group plc name changed to Shire plc (England & Wales) 11/25/2005 which reincorporated in Channel Islands as Shire Ltd. 05/23/2008 which name changed to Shire plc 10/01/2008

ROBERTS REALTY INVS INC (GA)
Name changed to ACRE Realty Investors Inc. 02/02/2015

ROBERTSHAW CTLS CO (DE)
Common $1 par split (2) for (1) by issuance of (1) additional share 05/15/1969
Common $1 par split (3) for (2) by issuance of (0.5) additional share 01/03/1984
Merged into Siebe PLC 10/31/1986
Each share Common $1 par exchanged for $85 cash

ROBERTSHAW-FULTON CONTROLS CO. (DE)
4.75% Preferred $25 par called for redemption 00/00/1950
5.5% Preferred $25 par called for redemption 09/08/1961
Name changed to Robertshaw Controls Co. 04/10/1963

(See Robertshaw Controls Co.)

ROBERTSON BKG CO (AL)
Reorganized under the laws of Delaware as RBC, Inc. 03/31/1997
Each share Common $1 par exchanged for (1) share Common $1 par

ROBERTSON-CATARACT ELECTRIC CO. (NY)
Name changed to Robertson Electric Co., Inc. in 1946
Robertson Electric Co. charter cancelled 12/15/69

ROBERTSON CECO CORP (DE)
Merged into Heico Companies, LLC 6/19/2000
Each share Common 1¢ par exchanged for $11.50 cash

ROBERTSON (JAMES) CO. LTD. (CANADA)
Acquired by Crane Canada Ltd. for cash in December 1962

ROBERTSON COS INC (ND)
Stock Dividend - 20% 8/12/88
Involuntarily dissolved for failure to file annual reports 8/1/93

ROBERTSON DISTR SYS INC (TX)
Merged into Pakhoed Holding N.V. 01/30/1976
Each share Common no par exchanged for $22 cash

ROBERTSON ELECTRIC CO., INC. (NY)
Charter cancelled and proclaimed dissolved for failure to pay taxes 12/15/69

ROBERTSON GROUP INC (CT)
Reincorporated under the laws of Delaware 12/14/1979

ROBERTSON H H CO (PA)
Capital Stock no par changed to $1 par 4/5/55
Capital Stock $1 par split (2) for (1) by issuance of (1) additional share 6/25/65
Capital Stock $1 par reclassified as Common $1 par 5/2/67
Common $1 par split (2) for (1) by issuance of (1) additional share 7/1/68
Common $1 par split (2) for (1) by issuance of (1) additional share 3/30/81
Stock Dividends - 10% 12/29/52; 10% 12/28/53; 10% 12/29/54; 10% 1/10/57; 10% 1/13/58
Merged into Robertson-Ceco Corp. 11/8/90
Each share Common $1 par exchanged for (1) share Common 1¢ par
(See Robertson-Ceco Corp.)

ROBERTSON P L MFG LTD (ON)
$2.50 Preference no par called for redemption 1/29/51
5% Preference $40 par called for redemption 4/20/56
6% Preference $20 par called for redemption 4/20/56
6% 1st Preference $20 par called for redemption 9/30/68
$1 Part. 2nd Preference no par reclassified as $1 Part. 3rd Preference no par 11/1/65

ROBERTSON PAPER BOX INC (CT)
Common $5 par reclassified as Class A Common $5 par and (1) share Class B Common $5 par and (1) share 6% Preferred $10 par issued 00/00/1950
Merged into Robertson Group, Inc. (DE) 11/26/1980
Each share 6% Preferred $10 par exchanged for $10 principal amount 10% Debentures due 03/31/1995
Each share Class A Common $5 par exchanged for (1) share Class A Common $5 par
Each share Class B Common $5 par exchanged for (1) share Class B Common $5 par

ROBERTSON PAPER CO.
Assets acquired by Robertson Paper Box Co., Inc. 00/00/1927
Details not available

ROBESON INDS CORP (DE)
Reincorporated 10/23/1984
Stock Dividends - 10% 6/1/83; 10% 7/6/84
State of incorporation changed from (NY) to (DE) 10/23/1984
Plan of reorganization under Chapter 11 Federal Bankruptcy Code effective 09/15/1994
Each share old Common 10¢ par exchanged for (0.0157) share new Common 10¢ par
Stock Dividend - 10% 7/8/85
Charter cancelled and declared inoperative and void for non-payment of taxes 03/01/1996

ROBIN, JONES & WHITMAN LTD. (CANADA)
Common $100 par changed to no par 00/00/1933
Recapitalized 10/30/1959
Each share 6% Preferred $100 par exchanged for (1) share 6% Preferred $25 par and $25 cash
Each share Common no par exchanged for (0.05) share 6% Preferred $25 par and $1.25 cash
6% Preferred $25 par called for redemption 1/15/65
Public interest eliminated

ROBIN INDS INC (MN)
Statutorily dissolved 6/1/2002

ROBIN INTL INC (CANADA)
Acquired by Algo Group Inc. 8/19/88
Each share Common no par exchanged for (0.0959) share Conv. 3rd Preferred Ser. I no par, (0.0599) share Class A Subordinated no par and $2.23 cash

ROBIN NODWELL MFG LTD (AB)
Name changed to Van Ness Industries Ltd. 6/17/68
Van Ness Industries Ltd. name changed to Claiborne Industries Ltd. 6/4/75
(See Claiborne Industries Ltd.)

ROBIN RED LAKE MINES LTD (ON)
Merged into Dickenson Mines Ltd. (Old) 6/30/78
Each share Capital Stock $1 par exchanged for (0.4) share Capital Stock no par
Dickenson Mines Ltd. (Old) merged into Dickenson Mines Ltd. (New) 10/31/80 which merged into Goldcorp Inc. (New) 3/31/94

ROBINA EXPLS LTD (ON)
Merged into Stand-Skat Resources Ltd. 10/16/1978
Each share Capital Stock 50¢ par exchanged for (0.12505) share Capital Stock no par
Stand-Skat Resources Ltd. merged into Ramrod Energy Corp. 03/01/1983 which recapitalized as Consolidated Ramrod Gold Corp. 08/27/1986 which name changed to Quest International Resources Corp. 04/09/1996 which recapitalized as Standard Mining Corp. 06/16/1999 which merged into Doublestar Resources Ltd. (YT) 11/01/2001 which reincorporated in British Columbia 10/10/2002 which merged into Selkirk Metals Corp. 07/23/2007
(See Selkirk Metals Corp.)

ROBINEX INTL LTD (DE)
Charter cancelled and declared inoperative and void for non-payment of taxes 3/1/81

ROBINO LADD CO (DE)
Name changed to Inproject Corp. 08/11/1978
(See Inproject Corp.)

exchanged for (1) share Class B Common $5 par

ROBINS A H INC (VA)
Common $1 par split (3) for (1) by issuance of (0.5) additional share 05/06/1966
Common $1 par split (2) for (1) by issuance of (1) additional share 05/09/1969
Common $1 par split (2) for (1) by issuance of (1) additional share 05/03/1973
Merged into American Home Products Corp. 12/15/1989
Each share Common $1 par exchanged for (0.351) share Common 33-1/3¢ par
American Home Products Corp. name changed to Wyeth 03/11/2002 which was acquired by Pfizer Inc. 10/15/2009

ROBINS CONVEYORS, INC.
Acquired by Hewitt Rubber Corp. 00/00/1945
Details not available

ROBINS INDS CORP (NY)
Merged into Rilco Equities Corp. 1/1/83
Each share Common 10¢ par exchanged for $6.95 cash

ROBINSON (DWIGHT P.) & CO., INC.
Dissolved in 1949
No stockholders' equity

ROBINSON AIRLINES CORP. (NY)
Name changed to Mohawk Airlines, Inc. in 1952
Mohawk Airlines, Inc. merged into Allegheny Airlines, Inc. 4/12/72 which name changed to U S Air, Inc. 10/29/79 which reorganized as USAir Group, Inc. 2/1/83 which name changed to US Airways Group, Inc. 2/21/97
(See US Airways Group, Inc.)

ROBINSON AVIATION, INC. (NY)
Name changed to Robinson Technical Products, Inc. 3/2/59
Robinson Technical Products, Inc. name changed to Robintech Inc. (NY) 11/4/66 which reincorporated under the laws of Delaware 12/18/72
(See Robintech Inc.)

ROBINSON CLAY PRODS CO (ME)
Acquired by Clow Corp. 06/15/1969
Each share Common $100 par exchanged for $251.50 cash

ROBINSON (J.C.) CO. (MI)
Class A called for redemption 08/31/1960 Bankrupt 10/03/1962
No stockholders' equity

ROBINSON (J.W.) CO. (CA)
Merged into Robinson Building Co. share for share 6/22/55

ROBINSON COTTON MLS LTD (ON)
3% Preference $5 par called for redemption 11/05/1960
Liquidation completed
Each share Common no par received initial distribution of $2.39 cash 09/04/1973
Each share Common no par received second distribution of $4 cash 11/19/1973
Each share Common no par received third distribution of $0.80 cash 09/27/1974
Each share Common no par exchanged for fourth and final distribution of $0.145 cash 07/10/1975

ROBINSON FURNITURE CO (DE)
Name changed to Joshua Doore, Inc. 08/20/1973
(See Joshua Doore, Inc.)

ROBINSON HALPERN CO (PA)
Stock Dividend - 10% 01/06/1984
Acquired by Teleflex Inc. 07/21/1986
Each share Common no par exchanged for (0.29253) share Common $1 par

ROBINSON LITTLE & CO LTD (CANADA)
Common no par split (10) for (1) by issuance of (9) additional shares 8/24/72
Class A no par split (10) for (1) by issuance of (9) additional shares 8/24/72
Filed for bankruptcy 3/18/85
No stockholders' equity

ROBINSON NUGENT INC (IN)
Common no par split (3) for (2) by issuance of (0.5) additional share 2/28/80
Common no par split (3) for (2) by issuance of (0.5) additional share 8/29/83
Common no par split (3) for (2) by issuance of (0.5) additional share 12/30/83
Stock Dividends - 10% 7/20/79; 10% 1/28/83
Acquired by Minnesota Mining & Manufacturing Co. 2/16/2001
Each share Common no par exchanged for (0.19) share Common 1¢ par
Minnesota Mining & Manufacturing Co. name changed to 3M Co. 4/8/2002

ROBINSON TECHNICAL PRODUCTS, INC. (NY)
Name changed to Robintech Inc. (NY) 11/4/66
Robintech Inc. (NY) reincorporated under the laws of Delaware 12/18/72
(See Robintech Inc.)

ROBINTECH INC (DE)
Reincorporated 12/18/72
Stock Dividend - 33-1/3% 10/23/74
State of incorporation changed from (NY) to (DE) 12/18/72
Proclaimed dissolved 6/5/87

ROBITECH RESEARCH CORP. (CO)
Proclaimed dissolved for failure to file reports 1/1/86

ROBIX ALTERNATIVE FUELS INC (AB)
Name changed to Robix Environmental Technologies, Inc. 03/04/2016

ROBLIN, INC. (NY)
Merged into Roblin-Seaway Industries, Inc. 04/06/1961
Each share Preferred exchanged for (1) share Preferred
Each share Common 10¢ par exchanged for (2) shares Common 10¢ par
Roblin-Seaway Industries, Inc. name changed to Roblin Steel Corp. 04/22/1964 which name changed to Roblin Industries, Inc. 04/17/1968
(See Roblin Industries, Inc.)

ROBLIN INDS INC (NY)
Class A Common 10¢ par reclassified as Common 10¢ par 5/1/70
6% Preferred no par conversion privilege expired 1/1/81
Stock Dividend - 20% 8/4/78
Chapter 11 Federal Bankruptcy Code converted to Chapter 7 on 8/12/87
Stockholders' equity unlikely

ROBLIN-SEAWAY INDUSTRIES, INC. (NY)
Common 10¢ par and Class A 10¢ par split (5) for (2) respectively by issuance of (1.5) additional shares 3/26/62
Name changed to Roblin Steel Corp. 4/22/64
Roblin Steel Corp. name changed to Roblin Industries, Inc. 4/17/68
No stockholders' equity
(See Roblin Industries, Inc.)

ROBLIN STEEL CORP. (NY)
Class A 10¢ par reclassified as Class A Common 10¢ par 06/06/1967
Name changed to Roblin Industries, Inc. 04/17/1968
(See Roblin Industries, Inc.)

ROBO WASH INC (MO)
Assets sold for benefit of creditors 09/00/1978
No stockholders' equity

ROBOCOM SYS INTL INC (NY)
Name changed 11/04/1998
Name changed from Robocom Systems, Inc. to Robocom Systems International Inc. 11/04/1998
Reorganized under the laws of Delaware as AgriVest Americas, Inc. 12/09/2011
Each share Common 1¢ par exchanged for (0.5) share Common $0.001 par
AgriVest Americas, Inc. recapitalized as NXChain Inc. 01/06/2016

ROBOMATIX TECHNOLOGIES (ISRAEL)
Acquired by Tiv Ta'am Holdings 1 Ltd. 11/29/2009
Each share Ordinary NIS 1.46 par exchanged for $0.1125 cash

ROBOP TEK CDA INC (BC)
Struck off register and declared dissolved for failure to file returns 12/14/90

ROBOSONICS, INC. (DE)
Merged into Electrospace Corp. (DE) 06/12/1967
Each share Common 25¢ par exchanged for (0.33333333) share Common 25¢ par
Electrospace Corp. (DE) reincorporated in New York 06/30/1971
(See Electrospace Corp.)

ROBOT DEFENSE SYS INC (DE)
Charter cancelled and declared void and inoperative and void for non-payment of taxes 03/01/1988

ROBOTAPE CORP. (DE)
Name changed to Horne (Lena) Beauty Products, Inc. 2/24/60
(See Horne (Lena) Beauty Products, Inc.)

ROBOTECH INC (DE)
Recapitalized as Zhen Ding Resources Inc. 07/05/2012
Each share Common $0.0001 par exchanged for (0.01) share Common $0.0001 par

ROBOTGUARD INC (DE)
Name changed to Site-Pak Industries Corp. 9/16/70
(See Site-Pak Industries Corp.)

ROBOTIC LASERS INC (NJ)
Each (55) shares old Common 1¢ par exchanged for (1) share new Common 1¢ par 07/12/1995
Recapitalized as Genisys Reservation Systems Inc. 07/29/1996
Each (55) shares old Common 1¢ par exchanged for (1) share new Common 1¢ par 07/29/1996
Genisys Reservation Systems Inc. name changed to Netcruise.com, Inc. 10/20/1999
(See Netcruise.com, Inc.)

ROBOTIC SYS & TECHNOLOGY INC (DE)
Charter cancelled and declared inoperative and void for non-payment of taxes 3/1/85

ROBOTIC VISION SYS INC (DE)
Each share old Common 1¢ par exchanged for (0.2) share new Common 1¢ par 12/01/2003
Chapter 7 bankruptcy proceedings terminated 05/25/2017
No stockholders' equity

ROBOTOOL LTD (CO)
Common 1¢ par split (2) for (1) by issuance of (1) additional share 8/6/88
Name changed to Motion Control Technology Inc. 10/7/88
(See Motion Control Technology Inc.)

ROBOTRONIX CORP (VA)
Common $0.0001 par split (3) for (2) by issuance of (0.5) additional share 05/31/1984
Proclaimed dissolved for failure to pay fees 09/01/1988

ROBROY INDS INC (PA)
Common $5 par split (2) for (1) by issuance of (1) additional share 3/31/80
Common $5 par reclassified as Class A Common no par 8/28/90
Each share Class A Common no par received distribution of (1) share Class B Common no par 9/17/90
Class A Common no par split (5) for (2) by issuance of (1.5) additional shares 12/5/94
Stock Dividend - 100% 7/25/75
Acquired by Robroy Acquisition, Inc. 1/25/2001
Each share Class A Common no par exchanged for $11.25 cash
Each share Class B no par exchanged for $11.25 cash

ROBSON PETE LTD (AB)
Completely liquidated 07/05/1991
Each share Common no par received first and final distribution of (1) share Robson Petroleum Co. Common 1¢ par 01/10/1992
Note: Certificates were not required to be surrendered and are without value

ROC COMMUNITIES INC (MD)
Merged into Chateau Properties, Inc. 2/11/97
Each share Common 1¢ par exchanged for (1.042) shares Common 1¢ par
Chateau Properties, Inc. name changed to Chateau Communities, Inc. 5/22/97
(See Chateau Communities, Inc.)

ROC PREF CORP (ON)
Preferred Shares no par called for redemption at $25 on 09/30/2009

ROC PREF II CORP (ON)
Preferred no par called for redemption at $25.32 on 12/31/2009

ROC PREF III CORP (ON)
Preferred no par called for redemption at $6.55 on 12/22/2009

ROCAMSA MINES, LTD. (ON)
Charter surrendered for failure to file reports and pay taxes in 1962

ROCAP MARKETING INC (NV)
Name changed to Spiral Toys Inc. 01/26/2015

ROCCA RES LTD (BC)
Name changed to Siegesoft Internet Solutions Inc. 3/27/2000
Siegesoft Internet Solutions Inc. name changed to Zimtu Technologies Inc. 10/26/2000 which recapitalized as International Zimtu Technologies Inc. (BC) 4/4/2003 which reincorporated in Canada as Petrol One Corp. 9/26/2006

ROCHDALE MNG CORP (NV)
Common $0.00001 par split (36) for (1) by issuance of (35) additional shares payable 02/12/2007 to holders of record 02/09/2007 Ex date - 02/13/2007
Name changed to Zoro Mining Corp. 03/19/2007
(See Zoro Mining Corp.)

ROCHE HLDG LTD (SWITZERLAND)
ADR's for Bearer no par split (2) for (1) by issuance of (1) additional ADR payable 01/24/2005 to holders of record 01/21/2005
144A ADR's for Liquid Yield Option Notes no par split (2) for (1) by issuance of (1) additional ADR payable 01/24/2005 to holders of record 01/21/2005
Sponsored 144A ADR's for Bearer no par split (2) for (1) by issuance of (1) additional ADR payable 01/24/2005 to holders of record 01/21/2005 Ex date - 01/25/2005
Sponsored ADR's Issuable Upon 144A for Non-Vtg. Equity Securities no par split (2) for (1) by issuance of (1) additional ADR payable 01/24/2005 to holders of record 01/21/2005 Ex date - 01/25/2005
ADR agreement terminated 03/23/2008
Each ADR for Bearer no par exchanged for $67.9625 cash
Each 144A ADR for Liquid Yield Option Notes no par exchanged for $67.9625 cash
Each Sponsored 144A ADR for Bearer no par exchanged for $67.9625 cash
(Additional Information in Active)

ROCHE LONG LAC GOLD MINES LTD. (ON)
Name changed to Roche Mines Ltd. 3/28/57
Roche Mines Ltd. recapitalized as North Rock Explorations Ltd. 2/28/63
(See North Rock Explorations Ltd.)

ROCHE MINES LTD. (ON)
Recapitalized as North Rock Explorations Ltd. on a (1) for (5) basis 2/28/63
North Rock Explorations Ltd. charter cancelled 3/14/78

ROCHEM ENVIRONMENTAL INC (UT)
SEC revoked common stock registration 11/13/2009
Stockholders' equity unlikely

ROCHER DE BOULE MOUNTAIN MINES LTD. (BC)
Liquidation completed 12/21/56

ROCHER DEBOULE MINERALS CORP (BC)
Name changed to American Manganese Inc. 01/20/2010

ROCHESTER, LOCKPORT & BUFFALO RAILROAD CORP.
Operations discontinued 00/00/1931
Details not available

ROCHESTER & GENESEE VALLEY RR CO (NY)
Completely liquidated 1/10/85
Each share Capital Stock $100 par exchanged for first and final distribution of $142.90 cash

ROCHESTER & PITTSBURGH COAL & IRON CO.
Merged into Rochester & Pittsburgh Coal Co. in 1928
(See Rochester & Pittsburgh Coal Co.)

ROCHESTER & PITTSBURGH COAL CO (PA)
Each share Preferred $100 par exchanged for (1) share 5% Preferred $100 par in 1939
Each share Class A Common $100 par exchanged for (1) share Common no par in 1939
Each share Class B Common $100 par exchanged for (0.05) share Common no par in 1939
Common no par split (3) for (1) by issuance of (2) additional shares 12/16/65
5% Preferred $100 par called for redemption 11/2/72
Stock Dividends - 10% 12/1/74; 10% 12/1/75; 10% 12/1/76; 10% 12/1/77; 10% 12/1/78; 10% 12/1/79; 10% 12/1/80; 10% 12/1/81; 10% 12/29/82; 10% 12/1/83; 10% 12/1/84; 10% 12/2/85; 10% 12/1/86; 10% 12/1/87; 10% 12/1/88; 10% 12/1/89; 10% 12/1/89; 10% 12/3/90
Merged into Consol Inc. 9/22/98
Each share Common no par exchanged for $43.50 cash

ROCHESTER & SYRACUSE RAILROAD CO., INC.
Sold under foreclosure in 1935
No stockholders' equity

ROCHESTER AMERICAN INSURANCE CO. (NY)
Stock Dividend - 50% 1/16/50
Merged into Great American Insurance Co. on a (1.28) for (1) basis 12/31/58
Great American Insurance Co. acquired by National General Corp. 11/16/73

ROCHESTER BUTTON CO. (NY)
Common $1 par split (1.2) for (1) by issuance of (0.2) additional share 9/21/59
Stock Dividend - 100% 12/22/59
Under plan of merger name changed to Cap-Roc Inc. 2/20/64
(See Cap-Roc Inc.)

ROCHESTER CAP LEASING CORP (NY)
Name changed to O P I C Corp. and Class A $1 par reclassified as Common $1 par 10/30/68
(See O P I C Corp.)

ROCHESTER CAPITAL CORP.
Acquired in dissolution by Chemical Fund, Inc. 00/00/1940
Details not available

ROCHESTER CENTRAL POWER CORP.
Merged into NY PA NJ Utilities Co. in 1935 which was dissolved in 1947

ROCHESTER CMNTY SVGS BK (ROCHESTER, NY)
Under plan of reorganization each share 7% Conv. Perpetual Preferred Ser. B $1 par and Common $1 par automatically became (1) share RCSB Financial Inc. 7% Conv. Perpetual Preferred Ser. B $1 par or Common $1 par respectively 9/1/95
RCSB Financial Inc. merged into Charter One Financial, Inc. 10/3/97
(See Charter One Financial, Inc.)

ROCHESTER ENERGY CORP (AB)
Merged into Southern Pacific Resource Corp. 03/04/2009
Each share Common no par exchanged for (0.1977) share Common no par

ROCHESTER ENERGY CORP (BC)
Recapitalized as International Rochester Energy Corp. (BC) 09/08/1997
Each share Common no par exchanged for (1/3) share Common no par
International Rochester Energy Corp. (BC) reorganized in Alberta as Rochester Energy Corp. 07/29/2004 which merged into Southern Pacific Resource Corp. 03/04/2009

ROCHESTER FD MUNS INC (NY)
Under plan of reorganization each share Common $1 par automatically became (1) share Rochester Fund Municipals (MA) Class A no par 02/15/1991

ROCHESTER GAS & ELEC CORP (NY)
6% Preferred Ser. D $100 par and 5% Preferred Ser. E $100 par reclassified as 4% Preferred Ser. F $100 par in 1945
4-3/4% Preferred Ser. G $100 par called for redemption 5/29/50
Common no par split (3) for (2) by issuance of (0.5) additional share 6/29/56
Common no par split (2) for (1) by issuance of (1) additional share 6/12/62
5-1/2% Preferred Ser. L $100 par called for redemption 3/1/65
Common no par changed to $5 par 5/31/72
11% Preferred Ser. O $100 par called for redemption 1/20/78
7.60% Preference Stock Ser. A $1 par called for redemption 10/1/85
10.84% Preferred Ser. Q $100 par called for redemption 4/22/87
8.60% Preferred Ser. P $100 par called for redemption 12/1/88
8.25% Preferred Ser. R $100 par called for redemption 3/1/94
7.50% Preferred Ser. N $100 par called for redemption at $102 on 4/22/97
7.45% Preferred Ser. S $100 par called for redemption at $100 on 9/2/97
7.55% Preferred Ser. T $100 par called for redemption at $100 on 9/1/98
7.65% Preferred Ser. U $100 par called for redemption at $100 on 9/1/99
Under plan of reorganization each share Common $5 par automatically became (1) share RGS Energy Group, Inc. Common $5 par 8/2/99
4% Preferred Ser. F $100 par called for redemption at $105 on 5/5/2004
4.10% Preferred Ser. H $100 par called for redemption at $101 on 5/5/2004
4.10% Preferred Ser. J $100 par called for redemption at $102.50 on 5/5/2004
4.55% Preferred Ser. M $100 par called for redemption at $101 on 5/5/2004
4.75% Preferred Ser. I $100 par called for redemption at $101 on 5/5/2004
4.95% Preferred Ser. K $100 par called for redemption at $102 on 5/5/2004
6.60% Preferred Ser. V $100 par called for redemption at $100 on 5/5/2004

ROCHESTER ICE, INC. (NY)
Common no par changed to $1 par 00/00/1936
Completely liquidated 08/04/1967
Each share $7 Preferred no par received first and final distribution of $3.4675 cash
No Common stockholders' equity
Certificates were not retired and are now without value

ROCHESTER ICE & COLD STORAGE UTILITIES, INC.
Name changed to Rochester Ice, Inc. in 1946
Rochester Ice, Inc. completely liquidated 8/4/67

ROCHESTER INSTR SYS INC (NY)
Common 5¢ par split (4) for (3) by issuance of (1/3) additional share 4/4/77
Merged into Trans Union Corp. 1/6/78
Each share Common 5¢ par exchanged for (0.45) share Common $1 par
(See Trans Union Corp.)

ROCHESTER MED CORP (MN)
Common no par split (2) for (1) by issuance of (1) additional share 12/09/1991
Common no par split (2) for (1) by issuance of (1) additional share payable 11/17/2006 to holders of record 11/14/2006 Ex date - 11/20/2006
Acquired by Bard (C.R.), Inc. 11/14/2013
Each share Common no par exchanged for $20 cash

ROCHESTER MINERALS INC (BC)
Name changed to Rochester Energy Corp. 04/28/1997
Rochester Energy Corp. recapitalized as International Rochester Energy Corp. (BC) 09/08/1997 which reorganized in Alberta as Rochester Energy Corp. 07/29/2004 which merged into Southern Pacific Resource Corp. 03/04/2009

ROCHESTER PACKING CO., INC. (NY)
Merged into Tobin Packing Co., Inc. 11/28/42
Details not available

ROCHESTER SVGS BK & TR CO (ROCHESTER, NH)
Through voluntary exchange offer all but (261) shares acquired as of 05/25/1977
Public interest eliminated

ROCHESTER SHERATON CORP. (NY)
Merged into Sheraton Corp. of America on a (11) for (1) basis 3/1/60
Sheraton Corp. of America acquired by International Telephone & Telegraph Corp. (DE) 2/29/68 which name changed to ITT Corp. 12/31/83 which reorganized in Indiana as ITT Industries Inc. 12/19/95 which name changed to ITT Corp. 7/1/2006

ROCHESTER TEL CORP (NY)
4-1/2% 1st Preferred Series A $100 par called for redemption 5/29/52
Common $10 par changed to $5 par and (1) additional share issued 5/18/65
Common $5 par changed to $2.50 par and (1) additional share issued 5/11/73
Common $2.50 par split (2) for (1) by issuance of (1) additional share 9/5/89
Common $2.50 par changed to $1 par 6/22/90
Common $1 par split (2) for (1) by issuance of (1) additional share 4/29/94
Name changed to Frontier Corp. 1/1/95
Frontier Corp. merged into Global Crossing Ltd. 9/28/99
(See Global Crossing Ltd.)

ROCHESTER TRAN CORP (NY)
In process of liquidation
Each share Common no par received first and final distribution of (1) Ctf. of Bene. Int. 1/31/69
Common Ctfs. were not retired and are now without value
Each Ctf. of Bene. Int. received initial distribution of $12 cash 5/1/69
Amount or number of subsequent distributions, if any, are unavailable

ROCHESTER TRUST & SAFE DEPOSIT CO. (ROCHESTER, NY)
Each share Capital Stock $100 par exchanged for (5) shares Capital Stock $20 par in 1929
Merged into Lincoln Rochester Trust Co. (Rochester, NY) 7/6/45
Each share Capital Stock $20 par exchanged for (1.4) shares Capital Stock $20 par plus $2 cash
Lincoln Rochester Trust Co. (Rochester, NY) merged into Lincoln First Group Inc. 5/16/67 which name changed to Lincoln First Banks Inc. 5/22/68 which merged into Chase Manhattan Corp. (Old) 7/1/84 which merged into Chase Manhattan Corp. (New) 3/31/96 which name changed to J.P. Morgan Chase & Co. 12/31/2000 which name changed to JPMorgan Chase & Co. 7/20/2004

ROCHETTE GOLD MINES LTD. (QC)
Recapitalized as Consolidated Rochette Mines Ltd. on a (0.5) for (1) basis in 1950
Consolidated Rochette Mines Ltd. recapitalized as Conro Development Corp. Ltd. 2/17/55 which charter was annulled 8/25/73

ROCK A BYE BABY INC (DE)
Recapitalized as RAB Industries Inc. 9/19/94
Each share Common 1¢ par exchanged for (0.04) share Common 1¢ par
(See RAB Industries Inc.)

ROCK BOTTOM RESTAURANTS INC (DE)
Merged into RB Capital Inc. 8/13/99
Each share Common 1¢ par exchanged for $10 cash

ROCK CAP CORP (AB)
Name changed to Terraco Energy Corp. 06/18/1999
Terraco Energy Corp. name changed to Terraco Gold Corp. (AB) 05/12/2003 which reincorporated in British Columbia 06/08/2011

ROCK CITY BOX CO. (TN)
Each share Common $10 par exchanged for (1) share Common $5 par and (1) share Non-Vtg. Common $5 par 03/31/1970
Name changed to Rock-Tenn Co. (TN) 06/01/1973
Rock-Tenn Co. (TN) reincorporated in Georgia 11/22/1985 which merged into WestRock Co. 07/01/2015

ROCK CREEK OIL & GAS CO. (KS)
Charter forfeited for failure to file annual report 07/15/1917

ROCK CREEK OIL CO.
Acquired by Mayer Oil Co. in 1929
Details not available

ROCK CREEK RES LTD (AB)
Merged into Great Plains Exploration Inc. (New) (Canada) 07/29/2005
Each share Class A Flow Thru no par exchanged for (1) share Common no par
Each share Class B Flow Thru no par exchanged for (4) shares Common no par
Great Plains Exploration Inc. (New) (Canada) reincorporated in Alberta 01/01/2009 which merged into Avenir Diversified Income Trust 11/10/2010 which reorganized as AvenEx Energy Corp. 01/07/2011 which merged into Spyglass Resources Corp. 04/04/2013

ROCK CREEK RES LTD (BC)
Recapitalized as Altra Ventures Inc. 01/06/1993
Each share Common no par exchanged for (0.5) share Common no par
Altra Ventures Inc. recapitalized as Odin Mining & Exploration Ltd. 01/23/1996 which name changed to Lumina Gold Corp. 11/01/2016

ROCK-ECHO MINES LTD. (ON)
Charter cancelled for failure to file reports and pay taxes in 1960

ROCK ENERGY CO., INC. (NV)
Name changed to Homestead Oil Co., Inc. 7/14/81
Homestead Oil Co., Inc. recapitalized as Hallmark Investment Corp. 1/13/89

ROCK ENERGY INC (AB)
Merged into Raging River Exploration Inc. 07/26/2016
Each share Common no par exchanged for (0.082) share Common no par
Note: Unexchanged certificates will be cancelled and become without value 07/26/2019
Raging River Exploration Inc. merged into Baytex Energy Corp. 08/27/2018

ROCK FINL CORP (MI)
Issue Information - 3,330,000 shares COM offered at $10 per share on 05/01/1998
Merged into Intuit, Inc. 12/9/99
Each share Common 1¢ par exchanged for (0.579832) share Common 1¢ par

ROCK FINL CORP (NJ)
Common $10 par changed to $3.333 par and (2) additional shares issued 10/20/86
Stock Dividend - 10% 10/26/87
Merged into Valley National Bancorp 11/30/94
Each share Common $3.333 par exchanged for (1.85) shares Common no par

ROCK HILL BK & TR (ROCK HILL, SC)
Under plan of reorganization each share Common $1 par automatically became (1) share RHBT Financial Corp. Common $1 par 06/04/1999
(See RHBT Financial Corp.)

ROCK HILL INDS INC (CO)
Name changed to Mid-America Petroleum, Inc. and Common 20¢ par changed to 2¢ par 08/02/1977
(See Mid-America Petroleum, Inc.)

ROCK HILL OIL CORP (CO)
Under plan of merger each share Common 20¢ par exchanged for (0.2) share Square H Industries, Inc. Common 25¢ par and (0.2) share Rock Hill Industries, Inc. Common 20¢ par 12/27/1968
(See each company's listing)

ROCK HILL URANIUM LTD. (AB)
Merged into Imperial Mines & Metals Ltd. share for share in 1955
Imperial Mines & Metals Ltd. recapitalized as New Imperial Mines Ltd. in 1957 which recapitalized as Whitehorse Copper Mines Ltd. 9/8/71
(See Whitehorse Copper Mines Ltd.)

ROCK ISLAND BK & TR CO (ROCK ISLAND, IL)
Each share Capital Stock $100 par exchanged for (10) shares Capital Stock $10 par and a 20% stock dividend paid 00/00/1950
Reorganized as Financial Services Corp. of the Midwest 01/10/1974
Each share Capital Stock $10 par exchanged for (1.3) shares Common $1 par
Financial Services Corp. of the Midwest merged into Mercantile Bancorporation, Inc. 08/03/1998 which merged into Firstar Corp. (New) 09/20/1999 which merged into U.S. Bancorp (DE) 02/27/2001

ROCK ISLAND REFINING CORP. (IN)
Merged out of existence 11/29/1989
Details not available

ROCK-LITE DEVELOPMENT CORP. LTD. (ON)
Merged into Milger Investment & Development Corp. Ltd. 7/8/71
Each share Capital Stock no par exchanged for (1/9) share Capital Stock no par
(See Milger Investment & Development Corp. Ltd.)

ROCK-LITE URANIUM MINES LTD. (ON)
Name changed to Rock-Lite Development Corp. Ltd. and Capital Stock $1 par changed to no par 6/2/69
Rock-Lite Development Corp. Ltd. merged into Milger Investment & Development Corp. Ltd. 7/8/71
(See Milger Investment & Development Corp. Ltd.)

ROCK OF AGES CORP (VT)
Reincorporated 12/07/2009
Issue Information - 3,225,000 shares CL A offered at $18.50 per share on 10/21/1997
State of incorporation changed from (DE) to (VT) and Class A Common 1¢ par changed to no par 12/07/2009
Acquired by Swenson Granite Co. L.L.C. 01/19/2011
Each share Class A Common no par exchanged for $5.25 cash

ROCK OF AGES CORP (VT)
Practically all Common no par purchased by Nortek, Inc. 05/00/1969
Public interest eliminated

ROCK ORE EXPL DEV LTD (MB)
Merged into Canhorn Mining Corp. 01/09/1986
Each share Common no par exchanged for (0.05701254) share Common no par
Canhorn Mining Corp. merged into Canhorn Chemical Corp. 04/26/1995 which merged into Nayarit Gold Inc. 05/02/2005 which merged into Capital Gold Corp. 08/02/2010 which merged into Gammon Gold Inc. (QC) 04/08/2011 which reincorporated in Ontario as AuRico Gold Inc. 06/14/2011 which merged into Alamos Gold Inc. (New) 07/06/2015

ROCK RES INC (BC)
Each share old Common no par exchanged for (0.05) share new Common no par 02/04/2002
Recapitalized as Adroit Resources Inc. 02/10/2004
Each share Common no par exchanged for (0.1) share Common no par
Adroit Resources Inc. recapitalized as iMetal Resources Inc. 11/09/2015

ROCK TECH RES INC (AB)
Reincorporated under the laws of British Columbia as Rock Tech Lithium Inc. 05/12/2010

ROCK-TENN CO (TN)
Reincorporated 11/22/1985
State of incorporation changed from (TN) to (GA) 11/22/1985
Each share Preferred $100 par, 6% Class A Preferred $100 par, 7.5% Class B Preferred $100 par, Vtg. Common $5 par and Non-Vtg. Common $5 par exchanged for (1) share Preferred $100 par, 6% Class A Preferred $100 par, 7.5% Class B Preferred $100 par, Vtg. Common $5 par and Non-Vtg. Common $5 par respectively
Each share Common $5 par and Non-Vtg. Common $5 par received distribution of (1) share Non-Vtg. Common $5 par 12/13/1993
Each share Common $5 par reclassified as (3) shares Class A Common 1¢ par 12/14/1993
Each share Non-Vtg. Common $5 par reclassified as (3) shares Class A Common 1¢ par 12/14/1993
Class B Common 1¢ par reclassified as Class A Common 1¢ par 06/30/2002
Class A Common 1¢ par split (2) for (1) by issuance of (1) additional share payable 08/27/2014 to holders of record 08/12/2014 Ex date - 08/28/2014
Stock Dividend - In Class A Common to holders of Class A Common 10% payable 11/15/1996 to holders of record 11/04/1996
Merged into WestRock Co. 07/01/2015
Each share Class A Common 1¢ par exchanged for (0.1856) share Common 1¢ par and $51.7514 cash

ROCKABEE INVTS INC (ON)
Recapitalized as Root Industries Inc. 12/31/1993
Each share Common no par exchanged for (0.33333333) share Common no par
Root Industries Inc. name changed to Armstrong Corp. 01/26/1999
(See Armstrong Corp.)

ROCKAWAY CORP (DE)
Common no par split (2) for (1) by issuance of (1) additional share 7/2/84
Common no par split (2) for (1) by issuance of (1) additional share 9/3/85
Stock Dividends - 10% 7/11/77; 10% 7/2/79; 10% 7/1/80; 10% 7/1/81
Common no par changed to 1¢ par in 1987
Acquired by Ascom Holding AG 3/16/89
Each share Common 1¢ par exchanged for $16 cash

ROCKBANDS INC (DE)
Recapitalized as American Community Development Group, Inc. 02/05/2010
Each share Common $0.0001 par exchanged for (0.005) share Common $0.0001 par
American Community Development Group, Inc. name changed to Wialan Technologies, Inc. 01/22/2014

ROCKBESTOS PRODUCTS CORP. (MA)
Acquired by Consolidated Coppermines Corp. in 1955
Each share Common $5 par exchanged for (3.3) shares Capital Stock $5 par
Consolidated Coppermines Corp. acquired by Cerro De Pasco Corp. 3/25/59 which name changed to Cerro Corp. 1/1/61 which merged Cerro-Marmon Corp. 2/4/76 which name changed to Marmon Group, Inc. 6/3/77
(See Marmon Group, Inc.)

ROCKBOUND RES INC (AB)
Name changed to Del Mar Energy Inc. 10/16/97
Del Mar Energy Inc. recapitalized as Aventura Energy Inc. 9/20/99
(See Aventura Energy Inc.)

ROCKBRIDGE ENERGY INC (BC)
Name changed to RockBridge Resources Inc. 03/31/2010

ROCKCLIFF COPPER CORP (ON)
Name changed to Rockcliff Metals Corp. 11/02/2017

ROCKCLIFF RES INC (ON)
Each share old Common no par exchanged for (0.2) share new Common no par 10/28/2013
Merged into Solvista Gold Corp. 06/19/2015
Each share new Common no par exchanged for (0.9) share Common no par
Solvista Gold Corp. name changed to Rockcliff Copper Corp. 10/21/2015 which name changed to Rockcliff Metals Corp. 11/02/2017

ROCKCOR INC (WA)
Merged into Olin Corp. 06/10/1985
Each share Common no par exchanged for $19.50 cash

ROCKCOTE PAINT CO. (IL)
Merged into Valspar Corp. 10/31/1960
Each share 7% Preferred A $10 par exchanged for (3.125) shares Common $1 par
Each share Common $1 par exchanged for (1.25) shares Common $1 par
(See Valspar Corp.)

ROCKCROFT EXPLORATIONS, LTD. (ON)
Charter revoked for failure to file reports and pay fees 2/18/65

ROCKDALE CMNTY BK (CONYERS, GA)
Merged into Regions Financial Corp. (Old) 8/15/96
Each share Common no par exchanged for (0.515116) share Common $0.625 par
Regions Financial Corp. (Old) merged into Regions Financial Corp. (New) 7/1/2004

ROCKDALE MINES LTD (ON)
Merged into PYX Explorations Ltd. 07/30/1976
Each share Capital Stock $1 par exchanged for (0.02) share Capital Stock no par
PYX Explorations Ltd. merged into Discovery Mines Ltd. (Canada) 01/15/1982
(See Discovery Mines Ltd. (Canada))

ROCKDALE RES CORP (CO)
Reincorporated under the laws of Texas as Petrolia Energy Corp. 09/02/2016

ROCKEFELLER CTR PPTYS INC (DE)
Acquired by an investor group 7/10/96
Each share Common 1¢ par exchanged for $8 cash

ROCKEFELLER HUGHES CORP (ON)
Name changed to RHC Capital Corp. 02/24/2017

ROCKEFELLER PARK HOTEL CORP. (DE)
Preferred $55 par called for redemption 7/1/56
No longer in existence having become inoperative and void for non-payment of taxes 4/1/58

ROCKEL MINES LTD (BC)
Recapitalized as Veronex Resources Ltd. 05/01/1978
Each share Common no par exchanged for (0.2) share Common no par
Veronex Resources Ltd. recapitalized as International Veronex Resources Ltd. 10/20/1992 which name changed to Veronex Technologies Inc. 12/04/1997
(See Veronex Technologies Inc.)

ROCKET/ATLAS CORP. (FL)
Recapitalized as Rocket Industries, Inc. 08/17/1966
Each share Common 10¢ par exchanged for (0.2) share Common 5¢ par
Rocket Industries, Inc. name changed to Polo Investment Corp. 04/30/1984 which name changed to Polo Investment Corp. of Missouri 05/30/1984 which name changed to Polo Equities Inc. (FL) 03/03/1997 which reincorporated in Nevada as Hybrid Fuels, Inc. 06/01/1998 which name changed to Nouveau Life Pharmaceuticals, Inc. 05/22/2012

ROCKET CITY AUTOMOTIVE GROUP INC (NV)
Stock Dividend - 20% payable 05/28/2007 to holders of record 05/25/2007 Ex date - 05/23/2007
Recapitalized as Rocket City Enterprises, Inc. 08/10/2007
Each share Common $0.001 par exchanged for (0.025) share Common $0.001 par

ROCKET ENERGY RES LTD (BC)
Name changed to MRI Medical Technologies Inc. 4/28/89
MRI Medical Technologies Inc. recapitalized as Tri-National Development Corp. 12/7/92
(See Tri-National Development Corp.)

ROCKET FUEL INC (DE)
Acquired by Sizmek Inc. 09/06/2017
Each share Common $0.001 par exchanged for $2.60 cash

ROCKET INDIN MINING CO. LTD.
Merged into Transvaal Explorations Ltd. share for share in 1949
(See Transvaal Explorations Ltd.)

ROCKET INDS INC (FL)
Name changed to Polo Investment Corp. 04/30/1984
Polo Investment Corp. name changed to Polo Investment Corp. of Missouri 05/30/1984 which name changed to Polo Equities Inc. (FL) 03/03/1997

which reincorporated in Nevada as Hybrid Fuels, Inc. 06/01/1998 which name changed to Nouveau Life Pharmaceuticals, Inc. 05/22/2012

ROCKET JET ENGINEERING CORP. (CA)
Acquired by Gulf & Western Industries, Inc. (MI) 10/1/63
Each (4.6) shares Common 75¢ par exchanged for (1) share Common $1 par
Gulf & Western Industries, Inc. (MI) reincorporated under the laws of Delaware 7/12/67 which name changed to Gulf + Western Inc. 5/1/86 which name changed to Paramount Communications Inc. 6/5/89 which merged into Viacom Inc. (Old) 7/7/94
(See Viacom Inc. (Old))

ROCKET MINES LTD (BC)
Recapitalized as Vieco Resources Ltd. 07/23/1973
Each share Capital Stock 50¢ par exchanged for (0.2) share Capital Stock no par
(See Vieco Resources Ltd.)

ROCKET MINING CORP. (UT)
Capital Stock 5¢ par reclassified as Common 1¢ par in 1956
Merged into Pioneer Carissa Gold Mines, Inc. 2/3/64
Details not available

ROCKET POWER, INC. (AZ)
Name changed to RPI Manufacturing Co. 10/7/66
RPI Manufacturing Co. completed liquidation 10/4/68

ROCKET RESH CORP (WA)
Name changed to Rockcor Inc. 04/15/1977
(See Rockcor Inc.)

ROCKET RES LTD (BC)
Name changed to Exeter Oil & Gas Ltd. (BC) 12/11/97
Exeter Oil & Gas Ltd. (BC) reincorporated in Alberta as Terradyne Energy Corp. 4/11/2000
(See Terradyne Energy Corp.)

ROCKEX MNG CORP (AB)
Reincorporated under the laws of Ontario 01/24/2011

ROCKFORD, ROCK ISLAND & ST. LOUIS RAILROAD CO. (IL)
Proclaimed dissolved for failure to pay taxes and file reports 11/1/35

ROCKFORD & INTERURBAN RWY. CO.
Sold under foreclosure 00/00/1926
Stockholders' equity unlikely

ROCKFORD BANCORP INC. (IL)
In process of Liquidation
Each share Common $100 par received initial distribution of (7) shares of AMCORE Financial, Inc. Common 50¢ par and $1,355 cash 11/18/1985
(See AMCORE Financial, Inc.)
Each share Common $100 par received second distribution of $222 cash 12/19/1985
Each share Common $100 par received third distribution of $244 cash 02/26/1986
Each share Common $100 par exchanged for fourth distribution of $17.50 cash 10/02/1986
Assets transferred to Rockford Bancorp Inc. Liquidating Trust 10/07/1986
(See Rockford Bancorp Inc. Liquidating Trust)

ROCKFORD BANCORP INC. LIQUIDATING TRUST (IL)
Liquidation completed
Each share Common $100 par received fifth distribution of $1 cash 12/31/87
Each share Common $100 par received sixth distribution of $2.64 cash 12/28/88
Each share Common $100 par received seventh and final distribution of $26.022578 cash 12/29/89
(See Rockford Bancorp Inc. for previous distributions)

ROCKFORD ELECTRIC CO.
Acquired by Central Illinois Electric & Gas Co. 00/00/1931
Details not available

ROCKFORD INDS INC (CA)
Issue Information - 1,650,000 shares COM offered at $7.75 per share on 07/19/1995
Acquired by American Express Co. 2/19/99
Each share Common no par exchanged for (0.12) share Common 60¢ par

ROCKFORD LIFE INS CO (IL)
Acquired by Liberty National Life Insurance Co. 1/1/74
Each share Common $10 par exchanged for $55 cash

ROCKFORD MACH TOOL CO (IL)
Dissolved 00/00/1963
Details not available

ROCKFORD MINERALS INC (ON)
Recapitalized as Reclamation Management Ltd. 4/30/92
Each share Common no par exchanged for (0.1) share Common no par
Reclamation Management Ltd. name changed to Euro-Net Investments Ltd. 8/19/99

ROCKFORD PRODS CORP (DE)
Name changed 10/01/1969
Name and place of incorporation changed from Rockford Screw Products Co. (IL) to Rockford Products Corp. (DE) 10/01/1969
Merged into Rexnord Inc. 10/29/1976
Each share Common $1 par exchanged for (2.2) shares Common $10 par
(See Rexnord Inc.)

ROCKFORD TECHNOLOGY CORP (AB)
Delisted from Alberta Stock Exchange 12/18/1995

ROCKGATE CAP CORP (BC)
Merged into Denison Mines Corp. 01/20/2014
Each share Common no par exchanged for (0.192) share Common no par
Note: Unexchanged certificates were cancelled and became without value 01/20/2017

ROCKHILL COAL & IRON CO.
Reorganized as Rockhill Coal Co., Inc. in 1938
No stockholders' equity

ROCKHILL COAL CO., INC. (PA)
Liquidation completed in 1958

ROCKHILL PRODUCTIONS, INC. (NY)
Assets sold for benefit of creditors 2/28/66
No stockholders' equity

ROCKIES FD INC (NV)
Stock Dividend - 10% 05/17/1985
Company terminated common stock registration and is no longer public as of 12/13/1999

ROCKIES FINL CORP (CANADA)
Name changed to Sprylogics International Corp. 10/09/2007
Sprylogics International Corp. name changed to Breaking Data Corp. 09/14/2015

ROCKING HORSE CHILD CARE CTRS AMER INC (DE)
Name changed to Nobel Education Dynamics, Inc. 06/15/1993
Nobel Education Dynamics, Inc. name changed to Nobel Learning Communities, Inc. 11/19/1998
(See Nobel Learning Communities, Inc.)

ROCKINGHAM BANCORP (NH)
Merged into Eastern Bancorp 08/31/1989
Each share Common $1 par exchanged for $17.75 cash

ROCKINGHAM HERITAGE BK (HARRISONBURG, VA)
Common $5 par split (2) for (1) by issuance of (1) additional share payable 04/30/1998 to holders of record 04/24/1998
Stock Dividends - 5% payable 03/12/1999 to holders of record 02/24/1999; 5% payable 03/11/2000 to holders of record 02/23/2000
Merged into Premier Community Bankshares, Inc. 11/20/2000
Each share Common $5 par exchanged for (1.58) shares Common $1 par
Premier Community Bankshares, Inc. merged into United Bankshares, Inc. 07/16/2007

ROCKINGHAM RES INC (BC)
Common no par split (2) for (1) by issuance of (1) additional share payable 04/30/1998 to holders of record 04/24/1998
Struck off register and declared dissolved for failure to file returns 10/30/1992

ROCKIT! INC (NV)
Charter revoked for failure to file reports and pay fees 06/30/2009

ROCKLAND & ROCKPORT LIME CORP.
Reorganized as Rockland-Rockport Lime Co., Inc. 00/00/1935
Details not available

ROCKLAND-ATLAS NATIONAL BANK (BOSTON, MA)
Each share Capital Stock $20 par exchanged for (2) shares Capital Stock $10 par in February 1955
Merged into State Street Bank & Trust Co. (Boston, MA) 4/17/61
Each share Capital Stock $10 par exchanged for (1.375) shares Capital Stock $10 par
State Street Bank & Trust Co. (Boston, MA) reorganized as State Street Boston Financial Corp. 6/15/70 which name changed to State Street Boston Corp. 5/3/77 which name changed to State Street Corp. 4/16/97

ROCKLAND GAS CO. (NY)
Merged into Rockland Light & Power Co. and each share Common no par exchanged for (4) shares Common $10 par in 1952
Rockland Light & Power Co. name changed to Orange & Rockland Utilities, Inc. 2/28/58 which merged into Consolidated Edison, Inc. 7/8/99

ROCKLAND LT & PWR CO (NY)
Each share Common $50 par exchanged for (5) shares Common $10 par in 1929
Under plan of merger name changed to Orange & Rockland Utilities, Inc. 2/28/58
Orange & Rockland Utilities, Inc. merged into Consolidated Edison, Inc. 7/8/99

ROCKLAND MINERALS CORP (BC)
Name changed to International Corona Capital Corp. 01/27/2017

ROCKLAND MNG LTD (BC)
Recapitalized as Calivada Resources Ltd. 05/13/1974
Each share Capital Stock 50¢ par exchanged for (0.25) share Capital Stock no par
Calivada Resources Ltd. recapitalized as Heritage Petroleums Inc. 06/25/1979 which merged into Heritage American Resource Corp. 07/25/1994 which recapitalized as Heritage Explorations Ltd. 09/17/2001 which merged into St Andrew Goldfields Ltd. 08/22/2005 which merged into Kirkland Lake Gold Inc. 01/29/2016 which merged into Kirkland Lake Gold Ltd. 12/06/2016

ROCKLAND NATL BK (SUFFERN, NY)
Common $10 par changed to $5 par and (1) additional share issued 10/13/1960
Stock Dividends - 10% 01/31/1966; 10% 02/08/1967; 10% 02/19/1968; 10% 12/01/1969
Merged into Empire National Bank (Middletown, NY) 03/02/1970
Each share Common $5 par exchanged for (1) share Common Capital Stock $5 par
(See Empire National Bank (Middletown, NY))

ROCKLAND ROCKPORT LIME INC (ME)
Administratively suspended for failure to file annual reports 08/26/1998

ROCKLAND TITLE & MORTGAGE GUARANTY CO. (NYACK, NY)
Liquidated in 1935

ROCKLAND TR CO (ROCKLAND, MA)
Stock Dividends - (1) for (9) 05/04/1981; 10% 04/01/1983; 10% 12/24/1984
Reorganized as Independent Bank Corp. (MA) 01/31/1986
Each share Common $3 par exchanged for (1) share Common 1¢ par

ROCKLITE INTL INC (ON)
Delisted from Toronto Stock Exchange 1/3/95

ROCKMASTER RES LTD (BC)
Name changed to Randstrom Manufacturing Corp. 10/14/87
Randstrom Manufacturing Corp. name changed to Francisco Gold Corp. 1/18/94 which merged into Glamis Gold Ltd. 7/16/2002 which merged into Goldcorp Inc. (New) 11/4/2006

ROCKMERE LAKE EXPLS LTD (ON)
Merged into Consolidated Dixie Resources Inc. 08/31/1987
Each share Common no par exchanged for (0.6) share Common no par
Consolidated Dixie Resources Inc. recapitalized as United Dixie Resources Inc. 12/15/1992 which merged into United Pacific Capital Resources Corp. 03/12/1998
(See United Pacific Capital Resources Corp.)

ROCKOWER BROS INC (PA)
Common 30¢ par changed to 15¢ par and (1) additional share issued 2/7/62
Common 15¢ par split (2) for (1) by issuance of (1) additional share 5/28/69
Common 15¢ par split (3) for (2) by issuance of (0.5) additional share 6/15/76
Liquidation completed
Each share Common 15¢ par received initial distribution of $5 cash 3/7/80
Each share Common 15¢ par received second distribution of $10 cash 8/29/80
Each share Common 15¢ par received third distribution of $5.25 cash 12/15/80
Under plan of liquidation each share Common 15¢ par automatically became (1) Rockower Brothers

Liquidating Trust Ctf. of Bene. Int. 12/17/80
(See Rockower Brothers Liquidating Trust)

ROCKOWER BROTHERS LIQUIDATING TRUST (PA)
Liquidation completed
Each Ctf. of Bene. Int. received fourth distribution of $0.05 cash 8/3/81
Each Ctf. of Bene. Int. received fifth distribution of $0.79 cash 2/26/82
Each Ctf. of Bene. Int. received sixth distribution of $0.05 cash 8/2/82
Each Ctf. of Bene. Int. received seventh distribution of $1 cash 2/25/83
Each Ctf. of Bene. Int. received eighth and final distribution of $0.263057 cash 4/30/84
Note: Certificates were not required to be surrendered and are now null and void
(See Rockower Brothers, Inc. for previous distributions)

ROCKPORT ENERGY CORP (SK)
Recapitalized as Liberty Oil & Gas (1998) Ltd. 11/30/1998
Each share Class A Common no par exchanged for (1/6) share Common no par
Liberty Oil & Gas (1998) Ltd. acquired by Lexxor Energy Inc. 07/23/2002 which reorganized as Find Energy Ltd. 09/05/2003 which was acquired by Shiningbank Energy Income Fund 09/22/2006 which merged into PrimeWest Energy Trust 07/13/2007
(See PrimeWest Energy Trust)

ROCKPORT HEALTHCARE GROUP INC (DE)
SEC revoked common stock registration 04/21/2016

ROCKPORT NATL BANCORP INC (MA)
Acquired by Institution for Savings (Newburyport, MA) 09/02/2014
Each share Common $50 par exchanged for $138.58 cash

ROCKPORT NATL BK (ROCKPORT, MA)
Under plan of reorganization each share Common $50 par automatically became (1) share Rockport National Bancorp Inc. Common $50 par 6/30/99
(See Rockport National Bancorp Inc.)

ROCKPORT RES LTD (AB)
Recapitalized as Skywest Resources Corp. 10/10/85
Each share Common no par exchanged for (0.2) share Common no par
Skywest Resources Corp. merged into Summit Resources Ltd. 6/30/87
(See Summit Resources Ltd.)

ROCKRIDGE CAP CORP (BC)
Each share old Common no par exchanged for (0.1) share new Common no par 12/16/2013
Each share new Common no par exchanged again for (0.2) share new Common no par 01/12/2015
Reorganized as Zinc One Resources Inc. 01/24/2017
Each share new Common no par exchanged for (1.5) shares Common no par

ROCKRIDGE GOLD LTD (BC)
Name changed to Rockridge Resources Ltd. 03/26/2018

ROCKRIDGE MNG CORP (BC)
Merged into Keith Resources Ltd. 07/16/1991
Each share Common no par exchanged for (0.2) share Common no par
Keith Resources Ltd. recapitalized as Avalon Ventures Ltd. 09/30/1994 which name changed to Avalon Rare Metals Inc. (BC) 02/18/2009 which reincorporated in Canada 02/09/2011 which name changed to Avalon Advanced Materials Inc. 03/03/2016

ROCKRITE PROCESSES, INC.
Merged into Tube Reducing Corp. on a (5/6) for (1) basis in 1947
Tube Reducing Corp. merged into American Metal Products Co. (MI) in 1954
(See American Metal Products Co. (MI))

ROCKSHOX INC (DE)
Merged into SRAM Corp. 3/26/2002
Each share Common 1¢ par exchanged for $0.41 cash

ROCKSPAN RES LTD (BC)
Recapitalized as Boswell International Technologies Ltd. 11/01/1989
Each share Common no par exchanged for (0.5) share Common no par
(See Boswell International Technologies Ltd.)

ROCKSTAR CAP CORP (ON)
Recapitalized as First Global Data Ltd. 11/30/2012
Each share Common no par exchanged for (0.33333333) share Common no par

ROCKSTAR INDS INC (FL)
Reincorporated under the laws of Nevada as Monster Motors, Inc. 09/22/2009
Monster Motors, Inc. name changed to Eco2 Forests, Inc. 09/08/2009 which recapitalized as International Display Advertising, Inc. 03/20/2013

ROCKVILLE FINL INC NEW (CT)
Under plan of merger name changed to United Financial Bancorp, Inc. 05/01/2014

ROCKVILLE FINL INC OLD (CT)
Reorganized as Rockville Financial, Inc. (New) 03/04/2011
Each share Common no par exchanged for (1.5167) shares Common no par
Rockville Financial, Inc. (New) name changed to United Financial Bancorp, Inc. 05/01/2014

ROCKVILLE-WILLIMANTIC LIGHTING CO.
Merged into Connecticut Light & Power Co. 00/00/1935
Details not available

ROCKWALL HLDGS INC (NV)
SEC revoked common stock registration 12/01/2011

ROCKWATER CAP CORP (ON)
Each share old Common no par exchanged for (0.1) share new Common no par 4/28/2005
Acquired by CI Financial Income Fund 5/15/2007
Each share new Common no par exchanged for $7.62 cash

ROCKWEALTH INTL RESOURCE CORP (BC)
Name changed to Strathmore Resources Ltd. 08/07/1996
Strathmore Resources Ltd. recapitalized as Strathmore Minerals Corp. 09/18/2000 which merged into Energy Fuels Inc. 08/30/2013

ROCKWELL DRILLING CO (OK)
Merged into Miramar Resources, Inc. 02/28/1990
Each share Common 1¢ par exchanged for (0.05) share Common 1¢ par
Miramar Resources, Inc. recapitalized as Franklin Credit Management Corp. (Old) 12/15/1994 which name changed to Franklin Credit Holding Corp. 04/03/2009
(See Franklin Credit Holding Corp.)

ROCKWELL INTL CORP NEW (DE)
Each share Common $1 par received distribution of (1/3) share Meritor Automotive, Inc. Common $1 par payable 9/30/97 to holders of record 9/17/97 Ex date - 10/1/97
Each share Common $1 par received distribution of (0.5) share Conexant Systems Inc. Common $1 par payable 12/31/98 to holders of record 12/11/98 Ex date - 1/4/99
Each share Common $1 par received distribution of (1) share Rockwell Collins, Inc. Common $1 par payable 6/29/2001 to holders of record 6/15/2001 Ex date - 7/2/2001
Name changed to Rockwell Automation, Inc. 2/25/2002

ROCKWELL INTL CORP OLD (DE)
Common $1 par split (2) for (1) by issuance of (1) additional share 06/13/1980
Common $1 par split (2) for (1) by issuance of (1) additional share 06/14/1983
Each share Common $1 par received distribution of (1) share Non-transferable Conv. Class A Common $1 par 04/13/1987
$4.75 Conv. Preferred Ser. A no par called for redemption 06/01/1996
$1.35 Conv. Preferred Ser. B no par called for redemption 07/01/1996
Each share Common $1 par received distribution of (1) share Rockwell International Corp. (New) Common $1 par payable 12/13/1996 to holders of record 12/06/1996
Merged into Boeing Co. 12/06/1996
Each share Common $1 par exchanged for (0.042) share Common $5 par

ROCKWELL MFG CO (PA)
Common $2.50 par split (3) for (2) by issuance of (0.5) additional share 12/20/58
Common $2.50 par split (4) for (3) by issuance of (0.333) additional share 1/5/62
Merged into Rockwell International Corp. (Old) 2/16/73
Each share Common $2.50 par exchanged for (1.1) shares Common $1 par
Rockwell International Corp. (Old) merged into Boeing Co. 12/6/96

ROCKWELL MED TECHNOLOGIES INC (MI)
Name changed to Rockwell Medical, Inc. 06/29/2012

ROCKWELL MNG CORP (BC)
Recapitalized as Kidd Resources Ltd. 7/24/84
Each share Common no par exchanged for (0.2) share Common no par
Kidd Resources Ltd. merged into Monte Carlo Resources Ltd. 12/31/87 which name changed to Provini (C.R.) Financial Services Corp. 5/17/89 which recapitalized as DataWave Vending Inc. 1/24/94 which name changed to DataWave Systems Inc. (BC) 1/15/97 which reincorporated in Yukon 9/19/2000 which reincorporated in Delaware 2/23/2005
(See DataWave Systems Inc.)

ROCKWELL SPRING & AXLE CO. (PA)
Name changed to Rockwell-Standard Corp. (PA) 4/21/58
Rockwell-Standard Corp. (PA) reincorporated in Delaware 7/31/64 which merged into North American Rockwell Corp. 9/22/67 which merged into Rockwell International Corp. (Old) 2/16/73 which merged into Boeing Co. 12/6/96

ROCKWELL-STANDARD CORP. (DE)
Reincorporated 07/31/1964
State of incorporation changed from (PA) to (DE) 07/31/1964
Common $5 par split (2) for (1) by issuance of (1) additional share 12/10/1964
Merged into North American Rockwell Corp. 09/22/1967
Each share $4.75 Conv. Preferred Ser. A $100 par exchanged for (1) share $4.75 Conv. Preferred Ser. A no par
Each share Common $5 par exchanged for (1) share Common $1 par
North American Rockwell Corp. merged into Rockwell International Corp. (Old) 02/16/1973 which merged into Boeing Co. 12/06/1996

ROCKWELL-STANDARD CORP. (PA)
Reincorporated under the laws of Delaware 7/31/64
Rockwell-Standard Corp. (DE) merged into North American Rockwell Corp. 9/22/67 which merged into Rockwell International Corp. (Old) 2/16/73 which merged into Boeing Co. 12/6/96

ROCKWELL TOOLS, INC. (OH)
Dissolved 4/30/54

ROCKWELL VENTURES INC (BC)
Each share old Common no par exchanged for (0.25) share new Common no par 1/30/2006
Name changed to Rockwell Diamonds Inc. 5/17/2007

ROCKWIN MINES LTD. (ON)
Merged into Roman Corp. Ltd. 11/21/66
Each share Capital Stock $1 par exchanged for (0.08) share Capital Stock no par
(See Roman Corp. Ltd.)

ROCKWIN OIL CORP. (DE)
Liquidation completed 9/14/61

ROCKWOOD & CO (DE)
5% Class A Preferred $100 par called for redemption 4/1/66
Completely liquidated 12/31/66
Each share Common no par exchanged for first and final distribution of $155 cash

ROCKWOOD COMPUTER CORP (NJ)
Under plan of reorganization each share Common 25¢ par automatically became (1) share Rockwood National Corp. Common 25¢ par 08/08/1973
(See Rockwood National Corp.)

ROCKWOOD CORP. (WA)
Liquidated in May 1966

ROCKWOOD FUND INC (MD)
Reorganized 02/28/1997
Reorganized from Rockwood Growth Fund, Inc. (ID) to Rockwood Fund, Inc. (MD) 02/28/1997
Name changed to Midas Magic Inc. (MD) (Old) 06/30/1999
(See Midas Magic Inc. (Old) (MD))

ROCKWOOD HLDGS INC (DE)
Merged into Albemarle Corp. 01/12/2015
Each share Common 1¢ par exchanged for (0.4803) share Common 1¢ par and $50.65 cash

ROCKWOOD NATL CORP (DE)
Charter cancelled and declared inoperative and void for non-payment of taxes 03/01/1996

ROCKWOOD SPRINKLER CO.
Acquired by Gamewell Co. 00/00/1930
Details not available

ROCKY BROOK MINES LTD. (ON)
Merged into Trimar Holdings & Explorations Ltd. 12/10/67
Each share Capital Stock $1 par

exchanged for (0.2) share Capital Stock no par
(See Trimar Holdings & Explorations Ltd.)

ROCKY HILL BK & TR CO (ROCKY HILL, CT)
Merged into New Britain Bank & Trust Co. (New Britain, CT) 12/02/1968
Each share Common $10 par exchanged for (1) share Common $10 par
New Britain Bank & Trust Co. (New Britain, CT) reorganized as Connecticut BancFederation, Inc. 12/28/1973
(See Connecticut BancFederation, Inc.)

ROCKY MOUNT MLS INC (NC)
Liquidation completed
Each share Common $50 par received initial distribution of $4 cash payable 2/23/2005 to holders of record 2/21/2005
Each share Common $50 par received second distribution of $3.85 cash payable 6/20/2005 to holders of record 6/15/2005
Each share Common $50 par exchanged for third and final distribution of $3.65 cash 12/20/2005

ROCKY MT UNDERGARMENT INC (DE)
Adversary proceeding case terminated 09/20/1993
Stockholders' equity unlikely

ROCKY MOUNTAIN BANCORPORATION (UT)
Went out of business 08/28/1987
Details not available

ROCKY MOUNTAIN FUEL CO. (WY)
Reorganized under the laws of Delaware 12/28/46
No stockholders' equity

ROCKY MOUNTAIN FUEL CO (DE)
In process of liquidation
Each share Capital Stock $1 par stamped to indicate first distribution of $0.25 cash 5/20/47
Each share Stamped Capital Stock $1 par stamped to indicate second distribution of $0.25 cash 4/12/48
Each share Stamped Capital Stock $1 par stamped to indicate third distribution of $0.125 cash 7/15/50
Each share Stamped Capital Stock $1 par stamped to indicate fourth distribution of $0.075 cash 4/15/53
Each share Stamped Capital Stock $1 par stamped to indicate fifth distribution of $0.15 cash 6/1/64
Each share Stamped Capital Stock $1 par stamped to indicate sixth distribution of $0.25 cash 2/8/74
Each share Stamped Capital Stock $1 par stamped to indicate seventh distribution of $0.20 cash 4/14/75
Each share Stamped Capital Stock $1 par stamped to indicate eighth distribution of $0.35 cash 3/19/76
Each share Stamped Capital Stock $1 par stamped to indicate ninth distribution of $0.65 cash 3/18/77
Each share Stamped Capital Stock $1 par stamped to indicate tenth distribution of $0.50 cash 10/20/77
Each share Stamped Capital Stock $1 par stamped to indicate eleventh distribution of $0.30 cash 3/20/78
Each share Stamped Capital Stock $1 par stamped to indicate twelfth distribution of $0.70 cash 10/20/78
Each share Stamped Capital Stock $1 par stamped to indicate thirteenth distribution of $0.25 cash 3/19/79
Each share Stamped Capital Stock $1 par stamped to indicate fourteenth distribution of $0.80 cash 10/19/79
Each share Stamped Capital Stock $1 par stamped to indicate fifteenth distribution of $0.25 cash 3/21/80
Each share Stamped Capital Stock $1 par stamped to indicate sixteenth distribution of $0.50 cash 10/24/80
Each share Stamped Capital Stock $1 par stamped to indicate seventeenth distribution of $0.30 cash 3/20/81
Each share Stamped Capital Stock $1 par stamped to indicate eighteenth distribution of $0.50 cash 10/23/81
Each share Stamped Capital Stock $1 par stamped to indicate nineteenth distribution of $0.40 cash 3/19/82
Each share Stamped Capital Stock $1 par stamped to indicate twentieth distribution of $0.40 cash 10/22/82
Each share Stamped Capital Stock $1 par stamped to indicate twenty-first distribution of $0.30 cash 3/18/83
Each share Stamped Capital Stock $1 par stamped to indicate twenty-second distribution of $0.35 cash 3/23/84
Each share Stamped Capital Stock $1 par stamped to indicate twenty-third distribution of $0.40 cash 3/22/85
Each share Stamped Capital Stock $1 par stamped to indicate twenty-fourth distribution of $0.25 cash 3/28/86
Each share Stamped Capital Stock $1 par stamped to indicate twenty-fifth distribution of $0.25 cash 3/27/87
Each share Stamped Capital Stock $1 par stamped to indicate twenty-sixth distribution of $0.30 cash 3/25/88
Each share Stamped Capital Stock $1 par stamped to indicate twenty-seventh distribution of $0.25 cash 3/24/89
Each share Stamped Capital Stock $1 par stamped to indicate twenty-eighth distribution of $0.30 cash 3/23/90
Each share Stamped Capital Stock $1 par stamped to indicate twenty-ninth distribution of $0.25 cash 3/22/91
Note: Details on subsequent distribution(s), if any, are not available

ROCKY MOUNTAIN HELICOPTERS INC (UT)
Liquidated under Chapter 11 Federal Bankruptcy Code
Each share Common 2¢ par exchanged for initial distribution of $0.0510825 cash 1/23/95
Each share Common 2¢ par received second distribution of $0.01131982 cash in September 1997
Each share Common 2¢ par received third and final distribution of $0.02690082 cash April 1999
All unexchanged Common Stock has been cancelled and company is now privately held

ROCKY MOUNTAIN LIFE INSURANCE CO. (NM)
Merged into National American Life Insurance Co. 02/27/1962
Each share Common exchanged for (0.48) share Common 10¢ par
(See National American Life Insurance Co.)

ROCKY MOUNTAIN NAT GAS INC (CO)
93¢ Conv. Preferred no par called for redemption 7/12/79
Merged into K N Energy, Inc. 7/1/86
Each share Common $3 par exchanged for $14 cash

ROCKY MOUNTAIN OIL CORP. (CO)
Each share Common 10¢ par exchanged for (0.2) share Common 50¢ par 2/25/58
Charter revoked for failure to file reports and pay fees 10/30/59

ROCKY MOUNTAIN QUARTER RACING ASSN INC (CO)
Each share Common $1 par exchanged for (1/70,000) share Common $1 par 6/17/82
Note: In effect holders received $1.37 cash per share and public interest was eliminated

ROCKY MOUNTAIN REC CORP (UT)
Name changed to Planformation, Inc. 01/31/1973
Each share Common 50¢ par exchanged for (1) share Common 50¢ par
(See Planformation, Inc.)

ROCKY MOUNTAIN RES INC (WY)
Recapitalized as Rocky Mountain Industries, Inc. (WY) 11/21/69
Each share Common 20¢ par exchanged for (0.1) share Common 25¢ par
Rocky Mountain Industries, Inc. (WY) reincorporated in Delaware 9/6/71
(See Rocky Mountain Industries, Inc.)

ROCKY MOUNTAIN TRENCH MINES LTD. NEW (BC)
Merged into New Copper Mountain Mines Ltd. 08/09/1974
Each share Capital Stock no par exchanged for (1) share Capital Stock no par
(See New Copper Mountain Mines Ltd.)

ROCKY MOUNTAIN TRENCH MINES LTD. OLD (BC)
Merged into Rocky Mountain Trench Mines Ltd. (New) 07/11/1973
Each share Capital Stock 50¢ par exchanged for (1) share Capital Stock no par
Rocky Mountain Trench Mines Ltd. (New) merged into New Copper Mountain Mines Ltd. 08/09/1974
(See New Copper Mountain Mines Ltd.)

ROCKY MOUNTAIN URANIUM CORP. (DE)
Name changed to Dallas Oil Co. of Texas, Inc. 11/3/58
Dallas Oil Co. of Texas, Inc. recapitalized as Dallas Oil Co., Inc. 1/18/82
(See Dallas Oil Co., Inc.)

ROCKY MTN AVIATION INC (CO)
Acquired by Texas Air Corp. 10/24/1986
Each share Common no par exchanged for $2.1427 cash

ROCKY MTN AWYS INC (CA)
Under plan of merger each share Common 1¢ par automatically became (1) share Rocky Mountain Aviation, Inc. Common no par 08/24/1984
(See Rocky Mountain Aviation, Inc.)

ROCKY MTN BK (CHANDLER, AZ)
Stock Dividends - 5% payable 4/17/98 to holders of record 4/15/98; 3% payable 7/14/2000 to holders of record 7/1/2000
Merged into First National Bank of Nevada Holding Co. 2/1/2001
Each share Common no par exchanged for $9.75 cash

ROCKY MTN BRANDS INC (NV)
Each share old Common no par exchanged for (0.06666666) share new Common no par 05/17/2005
Name changed to The Estate Vault, Inc. 01/24/2008
(See The Estate Vault, Inc.)

ROCKY MTN CHOCOLATE FACTORY INC (CO)
Each share Common 1¢ par exchanged for (0.33333333) share Common 3¢ par 08/01/1988
$1 Conv. Preferred 10¢ par called for redemption 03/17/1995
Common 3¢ par split (4) for (3) by issuance of (0.33333333) additional share payable 03/04/2002 to holders of record record 02/11/2002 Ex date - 03/05/2002
Common 3¢ par split (3) for (2) by issuance of (0.5) additional share payable 02/01/2004 to holders of record 01/20/2004 Ex date - 02/02/2004
Common 3¢ par split (4) for (3) by issuance of (0.33333333) additional share payable 06/13/2005 to holders of record 05/31/2005 Ex date - 06/14/2005
Stock Dividends - 10% payable 05/27/2004 to holders of record 05/13/2004; 5% payable 03/10/2005 to holders of record 02/28/2005; 5% payable 07/31/2007 to holders of record 07/20/2007 Ex date - 07/18/2007
Reincorporated under the laws of Delaware and Common 3¢ par changed to $0.001 par 03/02/2015

ROCKY MTN ENERGY CORP (BC)
Acquired by Enterra Energy Trust 09/29/2004
Each share Common no par exchanged for (0.35078) Trust Unit
Enterra Energy Trust reorganized as Equal Energy Ltd. 06/03/2010
(See Equal Energy Ltd.)

ROCKY MTN ENERGY CORP (NV)
Stock Dividend - 10% payable 12/06/2002 to holders of record 12/04/2002
SEC revoked common stock registration 12/23/2003
Stockholders' equity unlikely

ROCKY MTN EXPL CO (DE)
Merged into Carmel Energy, Inc. 09/07/1984
Each share Common 10¢ par exchanged for (0.5) share Common 1¢ par
(See Carmel Energy, Inc.)

ROCKY MTN FUDGE CO INC (NV)
Each share old Common $0.001 par exchanged for (0.2) share new Common $0.001 par 01/16/2008
Name changed to Bitzio, Inc. 06/14/2011

ROCKY MTN GINSENG INC (NV)
Reincorporated 04/22/2002
Each share old Common no par exchanged for (0.2) share new Common no par 06/08/2001
State of incorporation changed from (CO) to (NV) and Common no par changed to $0.001 par 04/22/2002
Name changed to Prime Rate Investors, Inc. (NV) 05/02/2002
Prime Rate Investors, Inc. (NV) reincorporated in Delaware 10/22/2004 which name changed to Summus Works, Inc. 02/28/2006 which name changed to MultiCorp International Inc. 08/28/2012

ROCKY MTN INDS INC (AB)
Delisted from Alberta Stock Exchange 08/09/1989

ROCKY MTN INDS INC (DE)
Reincorporated 09/06/1971
State of incorporation changed from (WY) to (DE) 09/06/1971
Charter cancelled and declared inoperative and void for non-payment of taxes 03/01/1978

ROCKY MTN INTL LTD (WA)
Charter expired 03/31/1999

ROCKY MTN INTERNET INC (DE)
Name changed to RMI.Net, Inc. 7/8/99
RMI.Net, Inc. name changed to Internet Commerce & Communications, Inc. 11/29/2000
(See Internet Commerce & Communications, Inc.)

ROCKY MTN LIFE INS CO (AB)
Reported out of business 01/01/1995
Details not available

ROCKY MTN MED CORP (CO)
Recapitalized as RMED International, Inc. 06/26/1989
Each share Common no par

exchanged for (0.1) share Common 1¢ par
RMED International, Inc. name changed to TenderCare International, Inc. 03/12/2004
(See TenderCare International, Inc.)

ROCKY MTN MINERALS INC (WY)
Administratively dissolved 04/12/2010

ROCKY MTN NAT RES CORP (UT)
Recapitalized as Mining Services International Corp. 10/14/1983
Each share Common $0.001 par exchanged for (0.05) share Common $0.001 par
Mining Services International Corp. name changed to Nevada Chemicals, Inc. 11/08/2001
(See Nevada Chemicals, Inc.)

ROCKY MTN NUCLEAR CORP (UT)
Proclaimed dissolved for failure to pay taxes 01/05/1982

ROCKY MTN PWR CO (CO)
Reorganized as MPEG Super Site, Inc. (CO) 10/1/99
Each share Common 5¢ par exchanged for (2) shares Common 5¢ par
MPEG Super Site, Inc. (CO) reincorporated in Nevada as Modern Manufacturing Services, Inc. 7/6/2001 which name changed to Radix Marine Inc. 5/12/2003

ROCKY MTN RES CORP (CANADA)
Name changed to American Vanadium Corp. 01/05/2011
American Vanadium Corp. recapitalized as Monitor Ventures Inc. 07/20/2017

ROCKY MTN VENTURES INC (CO)
Name changed to G/O International, Inc. and Common 1¢ par reclassified as Class A Common 1¢ par 12/11/1978
G/O International, Inc. recapitalized as G/O Business Solutions, Inc. (CO) 08/15/2006 which reorganized in Nevada as Radiant Oil & Gas Inc. 05/27/2010

ROCKY MTN WTR WKS INC (CO)
Name changed to Century Group, Ltd. 01/09/1989

ROCKY OLD MAN ENERGY INC (AB)
Ceased to be a reporting issuer 07/29/2009

ROCKY PETES LTD (ON)
Charter cancelled for failure to pay taxes and file returns 03/16/1976

ROCKY RIVER APARTMENTS, INC. (OH)
Liquidation completed 7/23/56

ROCKY SHOES & BOOTS INC (OH)
Name changed to Rocky Brands, Inc. 5/24/2006

ROCKY VY RES LTD (AB)
Struck off register for failure to file annual returns 01/01/1991

ROCKYVIEW ENERGY INC (AB)
Merged into Direct Energy Marketing Ltd. 01/30/2008
Each share Common no par exchanged for $3.16 cash

ROCKZONE MINES LTD (ON)
Charter cancelled and declared dissolved for failure to pay taxes and file returns 12/07/1977

ROCOCCO RES LTD (BC)
Struck off register and declared dissolved for failure to file returns 5/28/93

ROCOR INTL (NV)
Stock Dividend - 10% 12/31/1974
Merged into David R. Roush 11/24/1982
Each share Common no par exchanged for $5 cash

ROCRAVEN RES LTD (BC)
Recapitalized as Lifetime Ventures Ltd. 10/22/2002
Each share Common no par exchanged for (0.2) share Common no par

ROCTEST LTD (QC)
Acquired by Nova Metrix LLC 12/14/2010
Each share Common no par exchanged for $4.01 cash
Note: Unexchanged certificates were cancelled and became without value 12/14/2016

RODAC CORP (CA)
Common 10¢ par split (3) for (2) by issuance of (0.5) additional share 2/5/73
Filed for Chapter 7 bankruptcy proceedings 3/5/82
No stockholders' equity

RODALE ELECTRS INC (NY)
Common 50¢ par changed to 25¢ par and (1) additional share issued 11/17/1967
Name changed to REI Liquidating Corp. 05/29/1980
(See REI Liquidating Corp.)

RODDIS PLYWOOD CORP. (WI)
Acquired by Weyerhaeuser Co. on a (0.50627) for (1) basis 8/2/60

RODDY RECREATION PRODUCTS INC. (CA)
No longer in business having been dissolved in November 1966
No stockholders' equity

RODDY RES INC (CANADA)
Reincorporated 07/17/1989
Place of incorporation changed from (BC) to (Canada) 07/17/1989
Dissolved 06/10/2004
Details not available

RODEO CAP CORP (AB)
Reincorporated under the laws of British Columbia as Avala Resources Ltd. 08/04/2010
Avala Resources Ltd. merged into Dundee Precious Metals Inc. 04/12/2016

RODEO CAP II CORP (AB)
Reorganized under the laws of British Columbia as Shona Energy Co., Inc. 10/03/2011
Each share Common no par exchanged for (0.4) share Class A Common no par
Shona Energy Co., Inc. merged into Canacol Energy Ltd. 12/24/2012

RODEO CAP III CORP (AB)
Recapitalized as Solegear Bioplastic Technologies Inc. 03/31/2015
Each share Common no par exchanged for (0.57142857) share Common no par
Solegear Bioplastic Technologies Inc. name changed to good natured Products Inc. 10/31/2017

RODEO RES LTD (BC)
Delisted from Vancouver Stock Exchange 09/01/1988

RODERA DIAMOND CORP (BC)
Merged into Pacific Rodera Ventures Inc. 03/01/1999
Each share Common no par exchanged for (1) share Common no par
Pacific Rodera Ventures Inc. name changed to Pacific Rodera Energy Inc. (BC) 06/22/2004 which reincorporated in Alberta 06/14/2006 which name changed to PRD Energy Inc. 08/12/2010

RODIME PLC (SCOTLAND)
Name changed to Sportech PLC 9/15/2000
(See Sportech PLC)

RODINIA LITHIUM INC (ON)
Recapitalized as Routemaster Capital Inc. 09/20/2016
Each share Common no par exchanged for (0.1) share Common no par

RODINIA MINERALS INC (ON)
Reincorporated 11/03/2009
Place of incorporation changed from (BC) to (ON) 11/03/2009
Name changed to Rodinia Lithium Inc. 06/30/2010
Rodinia Lithium Inc. recapitalized as Routemaster Capital Inc. 09/20/2016

RODINIA OIL CORP (AB)
All officers and directors resigned 03/28/2014

RODMAN & RENSHAW CAP GROUP INC (DE)
Name changed to Direct Markets Holdings Corp. 06/01/2012
(See Direct Markets Holdings Corp.)

RODMAN & RENSHAW CAP GROUP INC (DE)
Preferred Stock Purchase Rights declared for Common stockholders of record 09/01/1993 were redeemed at $0.01 per right 12/31/1993 for holders of record 12/21/1993
Filed a petition under Chapter 7 Federal Bankruptcy Code 03/20/1998
Stockholders' equity unlikely

RODMAR HOSPS INC (CA)
Merged into International Funding Corp. of America 2/25/70
Each share Common no par exchanged for (1) share Common $1 par
(See International Funding Corp. of America)

RODNEY GOLD MINES LTD (ON)
Charter cancelled and declared dissolved for failure to file reports and pay taxes 11/09/1976

RODNEY METALS, INC. (NY)
Completely liquidated 02/14/1968
Each share Common $1 par exchanged for first and final distribution of (0.39266) share Teledyne, Inc. Common $1 par
Teledyne, Inc. merged into Allegheny Teledyne Inc. 08/15/1996 which name changed to Allegheny Technologies Inc. 11/29/1999

RODNEY SQUARE BENCHMARK U S TREAS FD (MA)
Name changed to Rodney Square Strategic Fixed-Income Fund and Shares of Bene. Int. no par reclassified as Municipal Income Portfolio 1¢ par 03/14/1991
(See Rodney Square Strategic Fixed-Income Fund)

RODNEY SQUARE INTL SECS FD INC (MD)
Completely liquidated 07/31/1996
Each share International Equity Fund 1¢ received first and final distribution of $13.06 cash

RODNEY SQUARE STRATEGIC FIXED- INCOME FD (MA)
Merged into WT Mutual Fund 10/31/1999
Details not available

RODNEY SQUARE TAX EXEMPT FD (MA)
Merged into WT Mutual Fund 10/31/1999
Details not available

RODOCANACHI CAP INC (QC)
Recapitalized as AlliancePharma Inc. 01/15/2015
Each share Common no par exchanged for (0.33333333) share Common no par
AlliancePharma Inc. name changed to KDA Group Inc. 02/01/2017

RODON INC (NV)
Name changed to Avicenna Global Corp. 01/10/2011

RODSTROM YELLOWKNIFE MINES LTD (BC)
Recapitalized as Imperial Modular Industries Ltd. 02/15/1972
Each share Capital Stock no par exchanged for (0.25) share Capital Stock no par
(See Imperial Modular Industries Ltd.)

ROE (A.V.) CANADA LTD. (CANADA)
Name changed to Hawker Siddeley Canada Ltd. 05/01/1962
Hawker Siddeley Canada Ltd. name changed to Hawker Siddeley Canada Inc. 07/29/1980 which was acquired by Glacier Ventures International Corp. (Canada) (New) 09/12/2001 which name changed to Glacier Media Inc. 07/01/2008

ROEBLING BUILDING, INC. (NY)
Liquidation completed 3/11/58

ROEBLING FINL CORP INC NEW (NJ)
Acquired by TF Financial Corp. 07/08/2013
Each share Common 10¢ par exchanged for $8.60 cash

ROEBLING FINL CORP INC OLD (NJ)
Merged into Roebling Financial Corp., Inc. (New) 10/01/2004
Each share Common 10¢ par exchanged for (3.9636) shares Common 10¢ par
(See Roebling Financial Corp., Inc. (New))

ROEBLING SVGS BK (ROEBLING, NJ)
Under plan of reorganization each share Common 10¢ par automatically became (1) share Roebling Financial Corp., Inc. Common 10¢ par 01/31/2000
Roebling Financial Corp., Inc. (Old) merged into Roebling Financial Corp., Inc. (New) 10/01/2004
(See Roebling Financial Corp., Inc. (New))

ROESER & PENDLETON, INC. (DE)
Liquidated in 1952

ROFFLER INDS INC (PA)
Acquired by Fuhrer (Frank B.) Holdings, Inc. 11/20/1984
Each share Common no par exchanged for $8 cash

ROFIN SINAR TECHNOLOGIES INC (DE)
Common 1¢ par split (2) for (1) by issuance of (1) additional share payable 12/05/2007 to holders of record 11/22/2007 Ex date - 12/06/2007
Acquired by Coherent, Inc. 11/07/2016
Each share Common 1¢ par exchanged for $32.50 cash

ROFORD MINES LTD. (ON)
Charter cancelled 8/20/62
Stock worthless

ROGARD RED LAKE MINES, LTD. (ON)
Charter cancelled for failure to file reports and pay taxes in 1950

ROGER LAKE MINES LTD. (ON)
Charter cancelled for failure to file reports and pay taxes 9/25/61

ROGER MILLER'S KING OF THE ROAD ENTERPRISES, INC. (TN)
See - Miller's (Roger) King of the Road Enterprises, Inc.

ROGER WILLIAMS MUSIC CORP. LTD. (ON)
See - Williams (Roger) Music Corp. Ltd.

ROGERS, KELLOGG, STILLSON, INC. (NY)
Name changed to Mortimer & Walling Securities Corp. 10/31/55
Mortimer & Walling Securities Corp. acquired by Johnston Mutual Fund Inc. in 1959 which reincorporated in Massachusetts as Johnston Capital Appreciation Fund 8/1/79 which name changed to Boston Co. Capital Appreciation Fund 5/1/81

ROGERS BROS CO (DE)
Stock Dividends - 10% 03/31/1967; 20% 08/21/1967; 50% 09/20/1972; 50% 07/24/1974
Completely liquidated 04/01/1975
Each share Common $1 par exchanged for first and final distribution of $35.50 cash

ROGERS-BROWN IRON CO.
Acquired by Hanna (M.A.) Co. 00/00/1927
Details not available

ROGERS CABLESYSTEMS INC. (CANADA)
Class A Vtg. no par conversion privilege expired 8/31/83
Name changed to Rogers Communications Inc. and Class A Vtg. no par reclassified as Conv. Class A Vtg. no par 4/24/86

ROGERS CABLESYSTEMS OF AMER INC (DE)
Merged into RCA Cablesystems Merger Co. 06/28/1988
Each share Class A Common $1 par exchanged for $22.50 cash

ROGERS CANTEL MOBILE COMMN INC (CANADA)
Class B Subordinate no par reclassified as Class B Restricted no par 5/1/97
Name changed to Rogers Wireless Communications Inc. 6/27/2000
Rogers Wireless Communications Inc. merged into Rogers Communications Inc. 12/31/2004

ROGERS COMMUNICATIONS INC (BC)
Reincorporated 10/20/1987
Place of incorporation changed from (Canada) to (BC) 10/20/1987
$1.875 Conv. Preferred Ser. VIII no par called for redemption 01/16/1989
(Additional Information in Active)

ROGERS (R.B.) COMPANIES, INC.
Merged into Indian Motocycle Co. 08/01/1947
Each share Preferred exchanged for (1) share Preferred and (0.1) share Common
Each share Common exchanged for (1.56) shares new Common
Indian Motocycle Co. recapitalized as Titeflex, Inc. 00/00/1951 which merged into Atlas Corp. 08/17/1962
(See Atlas Corp.)

ROGERS CORP (MA)
$3.60 Conv. Class A no par called for redemption 11/1/59
(Additional Information in Active)

ROGERS FIBRE CO., INC. (ME)
Merged into Colonial Board Co. 12/29/67
Each share Preferred Ser. A $100 par exchanged for (5) shares 80¢ Conv. Preferred Ser. A no par
Each share Common no par exchanged for (2.449) shares 80¢ Conv. Preferred Ser. A no par
Colonial Board Co. name changed to Lydall, Inc. (Conn.) 12/31/69 which reincorporated in Delaware 9/30/87

ROGERS INTER DESIGN INC (BC)
Name changed to Majorteck Industries Inc. 6/4/84
(See Majorteck Industries Inc.)

ROGERS JOHN CO (GA)
Completely liquidated 10/14/1968
Each share Common $1 par exchanged for first and final distribution of (0.714285) share Genuine Parts Co. Common $5 par

ROGERS (WILLIAM A.) LTD.
Acquired by Oneida Community, Ltd. in July 1929 for cash

ROGERS-MAJESTIC CORP. LTD.
Name changed to Standard Radio Ltd. in 1941
Standard Radio Ltd. name changed to Standard Broadcasting Corp. Ltd. 7/5/68
(See Standard Broadcasting Corp. Ltd.)

ROGERS PAPER MANUFACTURING CO.
Name changed to Rogers Corp. in 1945

ROGERS REFINING CO. OF LA., INC. (LA)
Charter revoked for failure to file annual reports 5/13/82

ROGERS SUGAR INCOME FD (ON)
Reorganized under the laws of Canada as Rogers Sugar Inc. 01/04/2011
Each Trust Unit exchanged for (1) share Common no par
Note: Unexchanged certificates were cancelled and became without value 01/04/2017

ROGERS WALLA WALLA, INC. (OR)
Acquired for cash by Universal Foods Corp. in June, 1986
Details not available

ROGERS WALLA WALLA CANNING CO. (OR)
Name changed to Rogers Walla Walla, Inc. 5/25/67
(See Rogers Walla Walla, Inc.)

ROGERS WIRELESS COMMUNICATIONS INC (CANADA)
Merged into Rogers Communications Inc. 12/31/2004
Each share Common no par exchanged for (1.75) shares Non-Vtg. Class B Common no par

ROGOSIN ENTERPRISES ISRAEL LTD (ISRAEL)
Reorganized 02/26/1959
Merged 03/01/1973
Reorganized from Rogosin Industries Ltd. (DE) to Rogosin Industries of Israel Ltd. (Israel) 02/26/1959
Each share Common $1 par exchanged for (20) shares Ordinary I£1 par or (20) ADR's for Ordinary I£1 par
Merged from Rogosin Industries of Israel Ltd. to Rogosin Enterprises of Israel Ltd. 03/01/1973
Each share Ordinary I£1 par exchanged for (1) share 5% Preference I£10.95 par
Each ADR for Ordinary I£1 par exchanged for (1) share 5% Preference I£10.95 par
5% Preference I£10.95 par called for redemption 01/00/1982
Public interest eliminated

ROGUE IRON ORE CORP (BC)
Name changed 01/23/2012
Name changed from Rogue Resources Inc. (Old) to Rogue Iron Ore Corp. 01/23/2012
Each share Common no par received distribution of (0.22271714) share Rapier Gold Inc. Common no par payable 03/08/2013 to holders of record 02/25/2013
Reorganized as Rogue Resources Inc. (New) 12/24/2013
Each share Common no par exchanged for (0.2) share Common no par

ROGUE WAVE SOFTWARE INC (DE)
Issue Information - 2,450,000 shares COM offered at $12 per share on 11/21/1996
Merged into Quovadx, Inc. 12/19/2003
Each share Common $0.001 par exchanged for (0.5292) share Common 1¢ par and $4.09 cash
(See Quovadx, Inc.)

ROHAT RES INC (NV)
Name changed to MY Group, Inc. 05/17/2011
MY Group, Inc. name changed to Royale Group Holding, Inc. 03/12/2013 which name changed to Royale Globe Holding Inc. 01/09/2014

ROHM & HAAS CO (DE)
Common $20 par changed to $5 par and (3) additional shares issued 05/04/1962
4% Preferred $100 par called for redemption 12/01/1964
Common $5 par changed to $2.50 par and (1) additional share issued 06/16/1972
Common $2.50 par split (2) for (1) by issuance of (1) additional share 06/06/1983
Common $2.50 par split (3) for (1) by issuance of (2) additional shares 06/12/1986
Common $2.50 par split (3) for (1) by issuance of (2) additional shares payable 09/01/1998 to holders of record 08/07/1998 Ex date - 09/02/1998
$2.75 Conv. Preferred no par called for redemption at $50.62 plus $0.57 accrued dividends on 08/16/1999
Merged into Dow Chemical Co. 04/01/2009
Each share Common $2.50 par exchanged for $78.97 cash

ROHN INDS INC (DE)
Name changed to Frankfort Tower Industries, Inc. 02/17/2004
(See Frankfort Tower Industries, Inc.)

ROHO INDS INC (NY)
Stock Dividend - 200% 06/01/1972
Charter cancelled and proclaimed dissolved for failure to pay taxes 03/31/1982

ROHR AIRCRAFT CORP. (OLD) (CA)
Acquired by International Detrola Corp. on a (1) for (1.5) basis in 1945
Name changed to Newport Steel Corp. 3/4/49
Newport Steel Corp. name changed to Newcorp, Inc. 9/18/56
(See Newcorp, Inc.)

ROHR AIRCRAFT CORP NEW (CA)
Incorporated 10/18/1949
Common $1 par split (3) for (2) by issuance of (0.5) additional share 12/16/1958
Stock Dividend - 50% 03/15/1954
Name changed to Rohr Corp. (CA) 12/14/1961
Rohr Corp. (CA) reincorporated in Delaware 08/08/1969 which name changed to Rohr Industries, Inc. 11/12/1971 which name changed to Rohr, Inc. 12/13/1991 which merged into Goodrich (B.F.) Co. 12/22/1997 which name changed to Goodrich Corp. 06/01/2001
(See Goodrich Corp.)

ROHR INC (DE)
Reincorporated 08/08/1969
Name changed 11/12/1971
Name changed 12/13/1991
Common $1 par split (3) for (2) by issuance of (0.5) additional share 09/16/1966
State of incorporation changed from (CA) to (DE) 08/08/1969
Name changed from Rohr Corp. to Rohr Industries, Inc. 11/12/1971

$3.125 Conv. Preferred Ser. B $1 par called for redemption 04/11/1983
$1.08 Conv. Preferred Ser. A $1 par called for redemption 01/12/1984
Common $1 par split (2) for (1) by issuance of (1) additional share 12/27/1985
Name changed from Rohr Industries, Inc. to Rohr, Inc. 12/13/1991
Merged into Goodrich (B.F.) Co. 12/22/1997
Each share Common $1 par exchanged for (0.7) share Common $5 par
Goodrich (B.F.) Co. name changed to Goodrich Corp. 06/01/2000
(See Goodrich Corp.)

ROHRERSTOWN, LANDISVILLE & MOUNT JOY STREET RAILWAY CO.
Merged into Conestoga Transportation Co. 00/00/1932
Details not available

ROI ACQUISITION CORP II (DE)
Completely liquidated 10/28/2015
Each Unit exchanged for first and final distribution of $10 cash
Each share Common $0.0001 par exchanged for first and final distribution of $10 cash

ROI ACQUISITION CORP (DE)
Units separated 05/22/2013
Name changed to EveryWare Global, Inc. 05/22/2013
(See EveryWare Global, Inc.)

ROI CDN HIGH INCOME MTG FD (ON)
Under plan of reorganization each Trust Unit automatically became (0.8427) Dream Hard Asset Alternatives Trust Unit and $0.9364 cash 07/08/2014

ROI CDN MTG INCOME FD (ON)
Under plan of reorganization each Trust Unit automatically became (0.8723) Dream Hard Asset Alternatives Trust Unit and $0.9693 cash 07/08/2014

ROI CDN REAL ESTATE FD (ON)
Under plan of reorganization each Trust Unit automatically became (0.8293) Dream Hard Asset Alternatives Trust Unit and $0.9215 cash 07/08/2014

ROI SCEPTRE RETIREMENT GROWTH FUND (ON)
Name changed to ROI Canadian Top 30 Small Cap Picks Fund 07/05/2010

ROIG COMMERCIAL BK (HUMACAO, PR)
Merged into Popular, Inc. 6/30/97
Each share Common exchanged for either (5.14695) shares Common $6 par, $208.12987 cash, or a combination thereof

ROJEAN ENTERPRISES INC (NY)
Each share Common 1¢ par exchanged for (0.000025) share Common no par 02/23/1978
Note: In effect holders received $1.25 cash per share and public interest was eliminated

ROJOLL EXPLS LTD (BC)
Name changed to Morrison-Grey Enterprises Ltd. 09/08/1988
Morrison-Grey Enterprises Ltd. name changed to MGP Asia Capital Inc. 05/01/1989 which recapitalized as Insular Explorations Ltd. 07/15/1991 which name changed to Masuparia Gold Corp. 09/01/1999 which name changed to MAS Gold Corp. 04/09/2018

ROK ENTMT GROUP INC (DE)
SEC revoked common stock registration 07/12/2012

ROKA BIOSCIENCE INC (DE)
Each share old Common $0.001 par

exchanged for (0.1) share new Common $0.001 par 10/12/2016
Name changed to Sorrento Tech, Inc. 11/03/2017

ROKEACH I & SONS INC (NY)
Each share Preferred $25 par exchanged for (7) shares Class B Non-Vtg. Common $5 par 00/00/1948
Each share Class A Vtg. Common $5 par or Class B Non-Vtg. Common $5 par exchanged for (2) shares Common $1 par 02/10/1956
Common $1 par changed to Class A Capital Stock 50¢ par 12/29/1958
Name changed to Exquisite Form Industries, Inc. and Class A Capital Stock 50¢ par changed to 10¢ par 10/31/1960
Exquisite Form Industries, Inc. name changed to Summit Organization, Inc. 01/05/1970
(See Summit Organization, Inc.)

ROKWADER INC (DE)
Recapitalized as True Blue Holdings, Inc. 06/28/2018
Each share Common $0.001 par exchanged for (0.525) share Common $0.001 par

ROLAC MINES, LTD. (ON)
Charter cancelled for failure to file reports and pay taxes in 1953

ROLAMITE INC (CA)
Name changed to Foothill Group, Inc. (CA) 04/12/1972
Foothill Group, Inc. (CA) reincorporated in Delaware 06/11/1987 which merged into Norwest Corp. 10/19/1995 which name changed to Wells Fargo & Co. (New) 11/02/1998

ROLAND INTL CORP (DE)
Merged into Landro Corp. 06/20/1977
Each share Common 10¢ par exchanged for $5.25 cash

ROLAND PARK CO. (MD)
Reorganized in 1939
Each share Prior Preferred $100 par exchanged for (6.666666) shares 5% Preferred $10 par, (8.25) shares new Common $1 par and (1) Participation Certificate
Each share Preferred $100 par exchanged for (6.25) shares new Common $1 par
Each share old Common $1 par exchanged for (0.5) share new Common $1 par
Dissolved 12/30/70
No record of distribution. Contact Equitable Trust Co., Baltimore who was agent when company was in liquidation in 1967

ROLAND PARK HOMELAND CO. (MD)
Merged into Roland Park Co. in 1934
(See Roland Park Co.)

ROLAND PARK MONTEBELLO CO. (MD)
Merged into Roland Park Co. in 1934
(See Roland Park Co.)

ROLFE ENTERPRISES INC (FL)
Reincorporated under the laws of Delaware as BidGive International, Inc. 04/12/2004
BidGive International, Inc. recapitalized as Med One Oak, Inc. 12/06/2012

ROLFITE CO (DE)
Charter forfeited for failure to maintain a registered agent 07/18/1989

ROLL-UP CAP CORP (AB)
Reorganized under the laws of British Columbia as VR Resources Ltd. 03/23/2017
Each share Common no par exchanged for (0.33333333) share Common no par

ROLLAND ENERGY INC (CANADA)
Recapitalized as Gale Force Petroleum Inc. 06/04/2008
Each share Common no par exchanged for (0.125) share Common no par
Gale Force Petroleum Inc. merged into Montana Exploration Corp. 09/22/2015

ROLLAND INC (CANADA)
Name changed 8/27/79
Each share Common no par exchanged for (2) shares old Class A no par and (1) share old Class B no par 12/21/55
Each share old Class A no par exchanged for (8) shares new Class A no par 3/7/61
Each share old Class B no par exchanged for (8) shares new Class B no par 3/7/61
Name changed from Rolland Paper Co. Ltd. to Rolland Inc. and 4-1/4% Preferred $100 par reclassified as $4.25 Preferred no par 8/27/79
Class B no par split (2) for (1) by issuance of (1) additional share 8/8/86
Merged into Cascades Inc. 10/21/92
Each share Class B no par exchanged for $21 cash
$4.25 Preferred no par called for redemption at $104 on 9/29/2000
Non-Vtg. Class A no par split (2) for (1) by issuance of (1) additional share 8/8/86
Each share Non-Vtg. Class A no par exchanged for (1) share Common no par 1/4/93
Common no par split (3) for (1) by issuance of (2) additional shares payable 12/22/97 to holders of record 12/12/97
Merged into Cascades Inc. 12/31/2000
Each share Common no par exchanged for (0.73) share Common no par

ROLLAND VIRTUAL BUSINESS SYS LTD (CANADA)
Name changed to Rolland Energy Inc. 02/16/2007
Rolland Energy Inc. recapitalized as Gale Force Petroleum Inc. 06/04/2008 which merged into Montana Exploration Corp. 09/22/2015

ROLLER COASTER INC (NV)
Name changed to San Diego Soccer Development Corp. 12/28/99
San Diego Soccer Development Corp. name changed to International Sports & Media Group, Inc. 1/2/2004 which name changed to US Farms, Inc. 7/17/2006

ROLLER RES INC (BC)
Reorganized as Transmedica Enterprises Inc. 01/22/1986
Each share Common no par exchanged for (3) shares Common no par
(See Transmedica Enterprises Inc.)

ROLLERBALL INTL INC (DE)
SEC revoked common stock registration 07/30/2004
Stockholders' equity unlikely

ROLLEX MINES LTD. (ON)
Charter cancelled and declared dissolved for failure to file returns and pay fees 11/9/76

ROLLFORM JAMESTOWN INC (DE)
Merged into Rollform Acquisition Corp. 10/26/1990
Each share Common 1¢ par exchanged for $10.125 cash

ROLLING HILLS COPPER MINES LTD (BC)
Recapitalized as Western Rolling Hills Mines & Oils Ltd. 12/26/73
Each share Common $1 par exchanged for (0.25) share Common no par
Western Rolling Hills Mines & Oils Ltd. merged into Invex Resources Ltd. 9/29/80 which merged into Imperial Metals Corp. (Old) 12/1/81 which reorganized as Imperial Metals Corp. (New) 4/30/2002

ROLLING PIN KITCHEN EMPORIUM INC (DE)
Charter cancelled and declared inoperative and void for non-payment of taxes 3/1/2000

ROLLING ROCK RES CORP (BC)
Merged into Mega Precious Metals Inc. 12/17/2010
Each share Common no par exchanged for (0.4) share Common no par
Note: Unexchanged certificates were cancelled and became without value 12/17/2016
Mega Precious Metals Inc. merged into Yamana Gold Inc. 06/24/2015

ROLLING TECHNOLOGIES INC (NV)
Reorganized as Solaris Power Cells, Inc. 08/12/2013
Each share Common $0.001 par exchanged for (24) shares Common $0.001 par

ROLLING THUNDER EXPL LTD NEW (AB)
Merged into Action Energy Inc. 08/30/2007
Each share Class A Common no par exchanged for (0.333) share Common no par
Each share Class B Common no par exchanged for (2.899) shares Common no par
(See Action Energy Inc.)

ROLLING THUNDER EXPL LTD OLD (AB)
Merged into Rolling Thunder Exploration Ltd. (New) 01/11/2006
Each share Class A Common no par exchanged for (1) share Class A Common no par
Each share Class B Common no par exchanged for (1) share Class B Common no par
Rolling Thunder Exploration Ltd. (New) merged into Action Energy Inc. 08/30/2007
(See Action Energy Inc.)

ROLLINOIL RES INC (AB)
Merged into Prism Petroleum Ltd. (Old) 09/01/1996
Each share Class A Common no par exchanged for (1) share Common no par
Prism Petroleum Ltd. (Old) recapitalized as Prism Petroleum Ltd. (New) 09/01/1996 which recapitalized as Prism Petroleum Inc. 06/08/2000 which was acquired by Real Resources Inc. 09/11/2000 which merged into TriStar Oil & Gas Ltd. (New) 08/16/2007 which merged into PetroBakken Energy Ltd. (Old) 10/05/2009 which reorganized as PetroBakken Energy Ltd. (New) 01/07/2013 which name changed to Lightstream Resources Ltd. 05/28/2013

ROLLINS BROADCASTING INC. (DE)
Name changed to Rollins, Inc. 1/26/65

ROLLINS BURDICK HUNTER CO (DE)
Common no par split (3) for (2) by issuance of (0.5) additional share 3/20/72
Common no par changed to 50¢ par 4/27/72
Common 50¢ par split (3) for (2) by issuance of (0.5) additional share 3/15/76
Merged into Combined International Corp. 12/3/83

Each share Common 50¢ par exchanged for $24.50 cash

ROLLINS COMMUNICATIONS INC (DE)
Merged into Heritage Communications, Inc. 12/30/1986
Each share Common 10¢ par exchanged for $40.895 cash

ROLLINS ENVIRONMENTAL SVCS INC (DE)
Common $1 par split (3) for (2) by issuance of (0.5) additional share 11/29/84
Common $1 par split (2) for (1) by issuance of (1) additional share 9/24/85
Common $1 par split (3) for (2) by issuance of (0.5) additional share 9/24/86
Common $1 par split (3) for (2) by issuance of (0.5) additional share 6/29/87
Common $1 par split (5) for (4) by issuance of (0.25) additional share 9/20/88
Name changed to Laidlaw Environmental Services, Inc. 5/15/97
Laidlaw Environmental Services, Inc. name changed to Safety-Kleen Corp. (New) 7/1/98
(See Safety-Kleen Corp. (New))

ROLLINS INTL INC (DE)
Name changed to RLC Corp. 2/7/75
RLC Corp. name changed to Rollins Truck Leasing Corp. 1/25/90
(See Rollins Truck Leasing Corp.)

ROLLINS LEASING CORP (DE)
Common $1 par split (2) for (1) by issuance of (1) additional share 2/20/69
Name changed to Rollins International, Inc. 10/23/69
Rollins International, Inc. name changed to RLC Corp. 2/7/75 which name changed to Rollins Truck Leasing Corp. 1/25/90
(See Rollins Truck Leasing Corp.)

ROLLINS RAPID REPRO FRANCHISES INC (NY)
Proclaimed dissolved for failure to file reports and pay taxes 12/15/75

ROLLINS TRUCK LEASING CORP (DE)
$1 Conv. Preferred Ser. C no par called for redemption 4/30/92
Common $1 par split (3) for (2) by issuance of (0.5) additional share 9/14/92
Common $1 par split (3) for (2) by issuance of (0.5) additional share 9/15/94
Common $1 par split (3) for (2) by issuance of (0.5) additional share payable 3/16/98 to holders of record 2/15/98 Ex date - 3/17/98
Merged into Penske Truck Leasing Co., L.P. 2/28/2001
Each share Common $1 par exchanged for $13 cash

ROLLO ENTMT INC (DE)
Name changed to Net/Guard Technologies, Inc. 11/20/1996
(See Net/Guard Technologies, Inc.)

ROLLS-ROYCE GROUP PLC (UNITED KINGDOM)
Name changed 05/24/2011
Name changed from Rolls Royce PLC to Rolls-Royce Group PLC 06/23/2003
Name changed to Rolls-Royce Holdings PLC 05/24/2011

ROLLS ROYCE LTD (ENGLAND)
Stock Dividends - 100% 08/03/1951; 50% 07/27/1954; 100% 07/29/1959; 25% 07/24/1964
Liquidation completed
Each ADR for Ordinary Reg. £1 par stamped to indicate initial distribution of $0.562 cash 03/01/1974

Each ADR for Ordinary Reg. £1 par stamped to indicate second distribution of $0.229 cash 08/05/1974
Each ADR for Ordinary Reg. £1 par stamped to indicate third distribution of $0.353 cash 03/07/1975
Each ADR for Ordinary Reg. £1 par stamped to indicate fourth distribution of $0.091 cash 03/11/1976
Name changed to R-R Realisations Ltd. 12/30/1976
(See R-R Realisations Ltd.)

ROLLS-ROYCE OF AMERICA, INC.
Name changed to Springfield Manufacturing Corp. in 1934
(See Springfield Manufacturing Corp.)

ROLLTECH INC (NV)
Recapitalized as Victoria Industries, Inc. 10/09/2003
Each share Common $0.001 par exchanged for (0.1) share Common $0.001 par
Victoria Industries, Inc. name changed to Motor Sport Country Club Holdings, Inc. 10/21/2010

ROLM CORP (CA)
Common 17¢ par changed to 8-1/2¢ par and (1) additional share issued 06/30/1978
Common 8-1/2¢ par changed to 4-1/4¢ par and (1) additional share issued 03/23/1979
Common 4-1/4¢ par changed to 2-1/8¢ par and (1) additional share issued 08/22/1980
Acquired by International Business Machines Corp. 11/21/1984
Each share Common 2-1/8¢ par exchanged for $70 principal amount of 7-7/8% Conv. Subord. Debentures due 11/21/2004

ROLTA INDIA LTD (INDIA)
144A Sponsored GDR's for Equity split (2) for (1) by issuance of (1) additional GDR payable 02/21/2008 to holders of record 01/25/2008 Ex date - 01/23/2008
Reg. S Sponsored GDR's for Equity split (2) for (1) by issuance of (1) additional GDR payable 02/21/2008 to holders of record 01/25/2008
GDR agreement terminated 10/03/2017
Each 144A Sponsored GDR for Equity Shares exchanged for (1) Equity Share
Each Reg. S Sponsored GDR for Equity Shares exchanged for (1) Equity Share
Note: Unexchanged GDR's will be sold and the proceeds, if any, held for claim after 10/03/2017

ROLTEC CORP (DE)
Name changed to Maxaxam Corp. 12/21/1983
(See Maxaxam Corp.)

ROLTEC INC (FL)
Merged into Gould Properties, Inc. 7/24/68
Each share Common $1 par exchanged for (0.5) share Class A $1 par
Gould Properties, Inc. name changed to Gould Enterprises, Inc. 4/2/69 which merged into Gould Investors Trust (MA) 7/1/70 which reorganized in Delaware as Gould Investors L.P. 5/13/86

ROLY INTL HLDGS LTD (SINGAPORE)
Sponsored ADR's for Ordinary U.S. 10¢ par split (3) for (2) by issuance of (0.5) additional ADR payable 11/3/2000 to holders of record 10/18/2000 Ex date - 10/17/2000
ADR agreement terminated 6/5/2003
Each Sponsored ADR for Ordinary U.S. 10¢ par exchanged for $2.3011 cash

ROM AMER PHARMACEUTICALS LTD (NV)
Reincorporated 11/02/1977
State of incorporation changed from (CA) to (NV) and Common no par reclassified as Class A Common 1¢ par 11/02/1977
Charter revoked for failure to file annual reports and pay fees 06/01/1988

ROM TECH INC (PA)
Name changed to Egames Inc. 03/01/1999
Egames Inc. name changed to Entertainment Games, Inc. 10/11/2011 which recapitalized as Tamino Minerals Inc. 03/25/2013

ROMA FINL CORP (USA)
Merged into Investors Bancorp, Inc. (Old) 12/06/2013
Each share Common 10¢ par exchanged for (0.8653) share Common 1¢ par
Investors Bancorp, Inc. (Old) reorganized as Investors Bancorp, Inc. (New) 05/07/2014

ROMA LAKE GOLD MINES LTD. (ON)
Charter cancelled for failure to pay taxes and file returns 3/24/81

ROMAC INTL INC (FL)
Common 1¢ par split (2) for (1) by issuance of (1) additional share payable 5/22/96 to holders of record 5/15/96
Common 1¢ par split (2) for (1) by issuance of (1) additional share payable 10/17/97 to holders of record 10/3/97
Name changed to kforce.com, Inc. 5/16/2000
kforce.com, Inc. name changed to Kforce Inc. 6/20/2001

ROMAN CAP CORP (CO)
Name changed to Recreative Technologies Corp. 9/30/89
(See Recreative Technologies Corp.)

ROMAN LTD (ON)
Old Common no par split (4) for (1) by issuance of (3) additional shares 4/20/81
Each share old Common no par exchanged for (0.2) share new Common no par 7/17/2003
Assets sold for the benefit of creditors 3/31/2006
No stockholders' equity

ROMANCE RECORDS & TAPES INC (CO)
Name changed to Chandrexx Inc. 02/17/1989

ROMANET LAKE MINES LTD (ON)
Charter cancelled and declared dissolved for failure to file returns and pay fees 07/27/1976

ROMANEX GAS CORP (NV)
Charter revoked for failure to file reports and pay fees 7/1/2003

ROMANOFF INDS INC (NY)
Name changed to Cannon Industries, Inc. 11/01/1971
Cannon Industries, Inc. name changed to Pud Industries, Inc. 05/09/1977
(See Pud Industries, Inc.)

ROMANTIQUE LTD (NY)
Name changed to Maiden Lane Jewelry, Ltd. 05/27/2014

ROMAR MINES LTD. (ON)
Charter cancelled for failure to pay taxes and file returns 2/28/73

ROMARCO MINERALS INC (BC)
Reincorporated 06/16/2006
Plan of arrangement effective 12/30/2002
Each share old Common no par exchanged for (1) share new Common no par and (1) share Tullaree Capital Inc. Common no par
(See Tullaree Capital Inc.)
Place of incorporation changed from (ON) to (BC) 06/16/2006
Note: Unexchanged certificates were cancelled and became without value 12/30/2008
Merged into OceanaGold Corp. 10/01/2015
Each share new Common no par exchanged for (0.241) share Common no par
Note: Unexchanged certificates will be cancelled and become without value 10/01/2021

ROMARCO RES INC (UT)
Recapitalized as Durasource Industries Inc. 8/29/95
Each share Common $0.005 par exchanged for (1/3) share Common $0.005 par
(See Durasource Industries Inc.)

ROME & CLINTON RAILROAD CO.
Liquidated in 1944

ROME BANCORP INC NEW (DE)
Merged into Berkshire Hills Bancorp, Inc. 04/01/2011
Each share Common 1¢ par exchanged for $11.25 cash

ROME BANCORP INC OLD (DE)
Common 1¢ par split (3) for (2) by issuance of (0.5) additional share payable 06/16/2003 to holders of record 05/29/2003 Ex date - 06/17/2003
Reorganized as Rome Bancorp, Inc. (New) 03/30/2005
Each share Common 1¢ par exchanged for (2.26784) shares Common 1¢ par
(See Rome Bancorp, Inc. (New))

ROME BRASS & COPPER CO.
Acquired by Republic Brass Corp. 00/00/1935
Details not available

ROME CABLE CORP. (NY)
Stock Dividends - 100% 06/04/1947; 10% 02/29/1956
Acquired by Aluminum Co. of America 03/31/1959
Each share Common exchanged for (0.6) share Common $1 par
Aluminum Co. of America name changed to Alcoa Inc. 01/01/1999 which name changed to Arconic Inc. (PA) 11/01/2016 which reincorporated in Delaware 12/31/2017

ROME CO., INC.
Insolvent 00/00/1935
No stockholders' equity

ROME RAILWAY & LIGHT CO.
Merged into Georgia Power Co. 00/00/1927
Details not available

ROME WIRE CO.
Acquired by General Cable Corp. 00/00/1928
Details not available

ROMEC PUMP CO.
Acquired by Lear, Inc. 7/7/48
Each share Common 50¢ par exchanged for (1.375) shares Common 50¢ par
Lear, Inc. merged into Lear Siegler, Inc. 6/5/62
(See Lear Siegler, Inc.)

ROMEX MINES & EXPL LTD (ON)
Charter cancelled and declared dissolved for failure to file returns and pay fees 05/09/1977

ROMEX RES INC (BC)
Recapitalized as DRT Resources Ltd. 08/08/1991
Each share Common no par exchanged for (0.25) share Common no par
(See DRT Resources Ltd.)

ROMFIELD BLDG LTD (ON)
Recapitalized as Dolphin Quest Inc. 9/30/96
Each share Common no par exchanged for (0.1) share Common no par
Dolphin Quest Inc. name changed to Naftex Energy Corp. (ONT) 4/10/97 which reincorporated in Yukon 9/16/98
(See Naftex Energy Corp.)

ROMLOCK INC (DE)
Recapitalized as Newlock Inc. 10/29/97
Each share Common $0.001 par exchanged for (0.00005) share Common $0.001 par
(See Newlock Inc.)

ROMPUS INTERACTIVE CORP (FL)
SEC revoked common stock registration 10/28/2009
Stockholders' equity unlikely

ROMULUS RES LTD (BC)
Incorporated 11/22/2005
Recapitalized as Osino Resources Corp. 06/28/2018
Each share Common no par exchanged for (0.1) share Common no par

ROMULUS RES LTD (BC)
Incorporated 07/09/1969
Merged into Misty Mountain Gold Ltd. 11/07/1995
Each share Common no par exchanged for (0.425) share Common no par
Misty Mountain Gold Ltd. recapitalized as Misty Mountain Gold Inc. 11/10/1995 which Recapitalized as Continental Minerals Corp. (Incorporated 02/07/1962) 10/18/2001
(See Continental Minerals Corp. (Incorporated 02/07/1962))

RON ROY URANIUM MINES LTD (ON)
Capital Stock $1 par changed to no par 12/08/1972
Merged into Exroy Resources Ltd. 07/29/1980
Each share Capital Stock no par exchanged for (0.2) share Capital Stock no par
Exroy Resources Ltd. recapitalized as Birim Goldfields Inc. 09/30/1994 which merged into Volta Resources Ltd. 03/31/2008 which merged into B2Gold Corp. 12/27/2013

RONA INC (QC)
Common no par split (2) for (1) by issuance of (1) additional share payable 04/05/2005 to holders of record 03/22/2005 Ex date - 03/18/2005
Acquired by Lowe's Companies, Inc. 05/24/2016
Each share Common no par exchanged for $24 cash
Note: Unexchanged certificates will be cancelled and become without value 05/24/2019
Acquired by Lowe's Companies, Inc. 11/21/2016
Each share Class A Floating Rate Preferred Ser. 7 no par exchanged for $24 cash
Each share 5.25% Class A 5-Yr. Rate Reset Preferred Ser. 6 no par exchanged for $24 cash
Note: Unexchanged certificates will be cancelled and become without value 11/21/2019

RONAYNE EXPLORATIONS, LTD. (ON)
Charter cancelled for failure to file reports and pay taxes 3/4/57

RONCO CORP (DE)
Chapter 11 bankruptcy proceedings converted to Chapter 7 on 08/20/2007
No stockholders' equity

RONCO INC (DE)
Name changed 01/14/1981
Name changed from Ronco Teleproducts, Inc. to Ronco Inc. 01/14/1981
Chapter 11 bankruptcy proceedings converted to Chapter 7 on 06/26/1986
Stockholders' equity unlikely

RONDAL GOLD CORP (BC)
Recapitalized as Cantech Ventures Inc. 02/28/2000
Each share Common no par exchanged for (0.2) share Common no par
Cantech Ventures Inc. recapitalized as New Cantech Ventures Inc. 08/22/2003 which name changed to Nanika Resources Inc. 06/20/2008 which recapitalized as Goldbar Resources Inc. 07/06/2012

RONDEN FOOD SYS INC (UT)
Proclaimed dissolved for failure to pay taxes 1/30/96

RONDEN VENDING CORP (FL)
Name changed to VHS Network, Inc. 1/13/97
(See VHS Network Inc.)

RONDOUT CORP (DE)
Adjudicated bankrupt 10/17/1972
Stockholders' equity unlikely

RONDOUT NATL BK (KINGSTON, NY)
Acquired by United Bank Corp. of New York 12/1/81
Each share Common $5 par exchanged for (1) share Common $5 par
United Bank Corp. of New York name changed to Norstar Bancorp Inc. 1/4/82 which merged into Fleet/Norstar Financial Group, Inc. 1/1/88 which name changed to Fleet Financial Group, Inc. (New) 4/15/92 which name changed to Fleet Boston Corp. 10/1/99 which name changed to FleetBoston Financial Corp. 4/18/2000 which merged into Bank of America Corp. 4/1/2004

RONMAR CONSULTING CORP (FL)
Recapitalized as B.D. International Inc. 3/23/99
Each share Common $0.001 par exchanged for (0.25) share Common $0.001 par

RONN MTR CO (DE)
Recapitalized as Vydrotech, Inc. 04/02/2012
Each share Common $0.001 par exchanged for (1/7) share Common $0.001 par

RONNIE SYS INC (FL)
Recapitalized as Great Wall Food & Beverage Corp. 5/22/98
Each share Common $0.0001 par exchanged for (0.1) share Common $0.0001 par
Great Wall Food & Beverage Corp. reorganized as DuraVest, Inc. 12/7/2001

RONNOCO GOLD MINES LTD. (ON)
Charter cancelled for failure to file reports and pay taxes 10/30/93

RONOCO RES INC (BC)
Struck off register and declared dissolved for failure to file returns 10/18/1982

RONRICO EXPLS LTD (BC)
Delisted from Vancouver Stock Exchange 03/05/1993

RONSON CORP (NJ)
Name changed 00/00/1954
Common $5 par changed to $2 par and (1.5) additional shares issued 00/00/1946
Name changed from Ronson Art Metal Works, Inc. to Ronson Corp. 00/00/1954
Old Common $1 par split (5) for (4) by issuance of (0.25) additional share 06/11/1964
Old Common $1 par split (4) for (3) by issuance of (1/3) additional share 06/08/1967
Each share old Common $1 par exchanged for (1/3) share new Common $1 par 03/25/1988
12% Conv. Preferred no par called for redemption at $2.25 on 06/01/2004
Stock Dividends - 25% 02/10/1956; 20% 10/27/1969; 5% payable 04/15/2002 to holders of record 04/05/2002 Ex date - 04/03/2002; 5% payable 04/15/2003 to holders of record 04/03/2003 Ex date - 04/01/2003; 5% payable 04/15/2004 to holders of record 04/01/2004 Ex date - 03/30/2004; 5% payable 04/15/2005 to holders of record 04/01/2005 Ex date - 03/30/2005; 5% payable 04/17/2006 to holders of record 03/31/2006 Ex date - 03/29/2006; 5% payable 04/16/2007 to holders of record 03/30/2007 Ex date - 03/28/2007; 5% payable 04/15/2008 to holders of record 03/28/2008 Ex date - 03/26/2008
Plan of reorganization under Chapter 11 Federal Bankruptcy proceedings effective 10/25/2011
No stockholders' equity

RONSON MINES LTD. (ON)
Acquired by Mission Financial Corp. Ltd. 00/00/1968
Each share Capital Stock $1 par exchanged for (0.1606) share Common no par
Mission Financial Corp. Ltd. merged into H.R.S. Industries, Inc. 05/21/1982 which merged into International H.R.S. Industries Inc. 05/15/1984 which name changed to Glenex Industries Inc. 05/25/1987 which merged into Quest Investment Corp. 07/04/2002 which merged into Quest Capital Corp. (BC) 06/30/2003 which reincorporated in Canada 05/27/2008 which name changed to Sprott Resource Lending Corp. 09/10/2010 which merged into Sprott Inc. 07/24/2013

RONYX LTD (ON)
Name changed to Fleet Aerospace Corp. 3/13/84
Fleet Aerospace Corp. name changed to Fleet Industries Ltd. 4/25/96 which recapitalized as Magellan Aerospace Corp. 10/22/96

ROO GROUP INC (DE)
Each share old Common $0.0001 par exchanged for (0.02) share new Common $0.0001 par 10/05/2005
Name changed to KIT digital, Inc. 05/29/2008

ROODEPOORT GOLD HLDGS LTD (SOUTH AFRICA)
Name changed to Afmin Holdings Ltd. 01/15/1990
(See Afmin Holdings Ltd.)

ROOKWOOD CORP.
Liquidation completed in 1950

ROOM PLUS INC (NY)
Voluntarily dissolved 7/1/2003
Details not available

ROOMSTORE INC (VA)
Chapter 11 bankruptcy proceedings converted to Chapter 7 on 07/24/2012
Stockholders' equity unlikely

ROOMSYSTEMS INC (NV)
Recapitalized as eRoomSystem Technologies, Inc. 3/29/2000
Each share Common $0.001 par exchanged for (0.75) share Common $0.001 par

ROONEY PACE GROUP INC (DE)
Reincorporated 2/28/83
State of incorporation changed from (NY) to (DE) 2/28/83
Charter cancelled and declared inoperative and void for non-payment of taxes 3/1/88

ROOS/ATKINS (CA)
Merged into Genesco Inc. 9/23/66
Each share Common no par exchanged for (0.5) share Common $1 par

ROOS BROS., INC. (DE)
Recapitalized in 1933
Preferred no par changed to $100 par
Common no par changed to $1 par
Merged into Roos/Atkins 2/1/65 which merged into Genesco Inc. 9/23/66

ROOSEVELT AVENUE CORP. (RI)
In process of liquidation
Each share Class A Common $1 par exchanged for initial distribution of (0.4) share Avnet, Inc. $2.50 Conv. Preferred Ser. C $1 par 3/15/68
Note: Details on subsequent distributions, if any, are not available

ROOSEVELT BK A FED SVGS BK (CHESTERFIELD, MO)
Under plan of reorganization each share Common 1¢ par automatically became (1) share Roosevelt Financial Group, Inc. Common 1¢ par 12/30/1988
Roosevelt Financial Group, Inc. merged into Mercantile Bancorporation, Inc. 07/01/1997 which merged into Firstar Corp. (New) 09/20/1999 which merged into U.S. Bancorp (DE) 02/27/2001

ROOSEVELT FED SVGS & LN ASSN CHESTERFIELD (MO)
Name changed to Roosevelt Bank, A Federal Savings Bank (Chesterfield, MO) 6/1/88
Roosevelt Bank, A Federal Savings Bank (Chesterfield, MO) reorganized in Delaware as Roosevelt Financial Group, Inc. 12/30/88 which merged into Mercantile Bancorporation, Inc. 7/1/97 which merged into Firstar Corp. (New) 9/20/99 which merged into U.S. Bancorp (New) 2/27/2001

ROOSEVELT FIELD INC (NY)
Capital Stock no par changed to $5 par 00/00/1932
Capital Stock $5 par changed to $1.50 par and (2) additional shares issued 09/09/1955
Out of business 05/07/1965
Charter subsequently cancelled and proclaimed dissolved for failure to pay taxes and file reports 12/15/1969

ROOSEVELT FINL GROUP INC (DE)
Common 1¢ par split (3) for (1) by issuance of (2) additional shares 05/18/1994
6.50% Conv. Preferred 1¢ par called for redemption at $50 plus $0.8125 accrued dividends on 05/16/1997
Merged into Mercantile Bancorporation, Inc. 07/01/1997
Each share Common 1¢ par exchanged for either (0.4211) share Common $5 par, $22 cash or combination thereof
Note: Option to receive stock expired 06/26/1997
Mercantile Bancorporation, Inc. merged into Firstar Corp. (New) 09/20/1999 which merged into U.S. Bancorp (DE) 02/27/2001

ROOSEVELT HOT SPRINGS CORP (UT)
Merged into American Geological Enterprises, Inc. (UT) 08/25/1993
Each share Common 1¢ par exchanged for either (1.6625) shares Common 1¢ par or (0.206) share Common 1¢ par and $1.50 cash
Note: Option to receive stock and cash expired 12/14/1993
American Geological Enterprises, Inc. (UT) reincorporated in Delaware as Emtec, Inc. 01/16/2001

ROOSEVELT HOTEL CO. (HOLLYWOOD, CA)
Dissolved in 1955

ROOSEVELT HOTEL CORP. (ST. LOUIS, MO)
Capital Stock $5 par changed to $1 par in 1942
Liquidation completed 6/25/58

ROOSEVELT MINES, INC. (NV)
Name changed to Bagdad Chase Mining Co. 02/23/1949
Bagdad Chase Mining Co. recapitalized as Bagdad Chase, Inc. 05/04/1968
(See Bagdad Chase, Inc.)

ROOSEVELT MINES LTD (AB)
Voluntarily dissolved 10/1/82
Details not available

ROOSEVELT NATL INVT CO (IL)
Reorganized under the laws of Delaware as Universal Guaranty Investment Co. 06/14/1990
Each share Class A Common $1 par exchanged for (1) share Class A Common $1 par
(See Universal Guaranty Investment Co.)

ROOSEVELT OIL & REFINING CORP. (DE)
Common no par changed to $1 par in 1954
Stock Dividends - 10% 12/30/52; 10% 12/31/53; 10% 12/31/54
Merged into Leonard Refineries, Inc. 11/30/55
Each (4) shares 6% Preferred $12.50 par exchanged for (1) share 6% Preferred $50 par
Each share Common $1 par exchanged for (1.5) shares Common $3 par
Leonard Refineries, Inc. merged into Total Petroleum (North America) Ltd. 10/2/70 which merged into Ultramar Diamond Shamrock Corp. 9/25/97 which merged into Valero Energy Corp. (New) 12/31/2001

ROOSEVELT RACEWAY INC (NY)
Capital Stock $3 par changed to 30¢ par and (9) additional shares issued 07/10/1957
Each share Capital Stock 30¢ par exchanged for (0.25) share Capital Stock $1.20 par 04/17/1963
Merged into Madison Square Garden Corp. (MI) 12/21/1973
Each share Capital Stock $1.20 par exchanged for $55 cash

ROOT & VAN DERVOORT ENGINEERING CO.
Dissolved in 1936

ROOT GLASS CO.
Acquired by Owens-Illinois Glass Co. 00/00/1932
Details not available

ROOT INDS INC (ON)
Name changed to Armstrong Corp. 01/26/1999
(See Armstrong Corp.)

ROOT ZINC MINING CO. (NV)
Name changed to Imperial Diversified Industries Inc. 11/04/1969
Each share Common $1 par exchanged for (1) share Common $1 par
(See Imperial Diversified Industries Inc.)

ROOT9B TECHNOLOGIES INC (DE)
Recapitalized as root9B Holdings, Inc. 12/05/2016
Each share Common $0.001 par exchanged for (0.06666666) share Common $0.001 par

ROPAK CORP (CA)
Name changed 5/17/85
Name changed from Ropak West Corp. to Ropak Corp. 5/17/85
Acquired by Linpac Mouldings Ltd. in November 1995
Each share Common no par exchanged for $11 cash

ROPAK LABS (CA)
Name changed to InVitro International 03/27/1992

ROPEC INDS INC (BC)
Struck off register and declared dissolved for failure to file returns 9/30/94

ROPER CORP (DE)
Common $1 par changed to 50¢ par and (1) additional share issued 1/5/79
Common 50¢ par split (2) for (1) by issuance of (1) additional share 7/12/83
Common 50¢ par split (2) for (1) by issuance of (1) additional share 12/30/86
Merged into General Electric Co. 4/22/88
Each share Common 50¢ par exchanged for $54 cash

ROPER (GEO. D.) CORP. (DE)
Name changed to Roper Corp. 4/22/68
(See Roper Corp.)

ROPER (GEORGE D.) CORP. (IL)
Recapitalized in 1937
Each share 7% Preferred $100 par exchanged for (1) share 5% Preferred $25 par and (1) share Common no par
Each (5) shares Common $10 par exchanged for (1) share Common no par
Recapitalized in 1940
Each share Common no par exchanged for (2-1/6) shares Common $5 par
Stock Dividend - 10% 1/7/54
Name changed to Roper Industries, Inc. 10/31/57
(See Roper Industries, Inc.)

ROPER (GEO. D.) CORP. (MA)
Merged into Roper (Geo. D.) Corp. (Del.) 6/30/64
Each share Common $1 par exchanged for (2) shares Common $1 par
Roper (Geo. D.) Corp. (Del.) name changed to Roper Corp. 4/22/68
(See Roper Corp.)

ROPER INDS INC (DE)
Common 1¢ par split (2) for (1) by issuance of (1) additional share 09/20/1993
Common 1¢ par split (2) for (1) by issuance of (1) additional share payable 08/01/1997 to holders of record 07/25/1997 Ex date - 08/04/1997
Common 1¢ par split (2) for (1) by issuance of (1) additional share payable 08/26/2005 to holders of record 08/12/2005 Ex date - 08/29/2005
Name changed to Roper Technologies, Inc. 04/29/2015

ROPER INDS INC (IL)
Merged into Dexter Corp. 06/01/1982
Details not available

ROPER REALIZATION INC (VA)
Charter cancelled and proclaimed dissolved for failure to file reports 9/1/94

ROPER RES INC (AB)
Name changed to Safe Environment Engineering Canada Ltd. 11/06/1998
(See Safe Environment Engineering Canada Ltd.)

ROPER STARCH WORLDWIDE INC (NY)
Acquired by United Business Media PLC 08/31/2001
Details not available

RORAIMA GOLD CORP (BC)
Recapitalized as International Roraima Gold Corp. 06/13/1996
Each share Common no par exchanged for (1/3) share Common no par
(See International Roraima Gold Corp.)

RORER-AMCHEM INC. (PA)
Name changed to Rorer Group Inc. 4/27/77
Rorer Group Inc. name changed to Rhone Poulenc-Rorer Inc. 7/31/90
(See Rhone Poulenc-Rorer Inc.)

RORER GROUP INC (PA)
Common no par split (3) for (2) by issuance of (0.5) additional share 02/26/1988
Common Stock Purchase Rights declared for Common stockholders of record 02/19/1985 were redeemed at $0.17 per right 05/14/1990 for holders of record 05/04/1990
Name changed to Rhone Poulenc-Rorer Inc. 07/31/1990
(See Rhone Poulenc-Rorer Inc.)

RORER WILLIAM H INC (PA)
Capital Stock $1 par changed to 33-1/3¢ par and (2) additional shares issued 4/15/59
Capital Stock 33-1/3¢ par changed to 8-1/3¢ par and (3) additional shares issued 4/14/61
Merged into Rorer-Amchem Inc. 9/30/68
Each share Capital Stock 8-1/3¢ par exchanged for (2) shares Common no par
Rorer-Amchem Inc. name changed to Rorer Group Inc. 4/27/77 which name changed to Rhone Poulenc-Rorer Inc. 7/31/90
(See Rhone Poulenc-Rorer Inc.)

ROSA CAP INC (AB)
Merged into Raimount Energy Inc. 12/18/2015
Each share Common no par exchanged for (0.1) share Common no par
Note: Unexchanged certificates will be cancelled and become without value 12/18/2020
Raimount Energy Inc. merged into Manitok Energy Inc. 08/23/2016

ROSANOVA PRODUCTIONS INC. (MI)
Charter declared inoperative and void for failure to file reports in 1983

ROSARIO RES CORP (NY)
Capital Stock $1 par split (3) for (2) by issuance of (0.5) additional share 04/10/1974
Merged into Amax Inc. 04/10/1980
Each share Capital Stock $1 par exchanged for (1.37615) shares Common $1 par
Amax Inc. merged into Cyprus Amax Minerals Co. 11/15/1993 which merged into Phelps Dodge Corp. 12/02/1999 which merged into Freeport-McMoRan Copper & Gold Inc. 03/19/2007 which name changed to Freeport-McMoRan Inc. 07/14/2014

ROSARITA MEXICAN FOODS, INC. (AZ)
Acquired by Beatrice Foods Co. on a (4.81736) for (1) basis 3/16/61
Beatrice Foods Co. name changed to Beatrice Companies, Inc. 6/5/84
(See Beatrice Companies, Inc.)

ROSAUERS SUPER MKTS INC (WA)
6% Preferred $10 par called for redemption 08/26/1977
Public interest eliminated

ROSCA INC (NV)
Name changed to Secure Path Technology Holdings Inc. 04/13/2010

ROSCAN MINERALS CORP (ON)
Name changed to Roscan Gold Corp. 10/01/2018

ROSE CORP (CANADA)
Merged into 3727955 Canada Ltd. 5/1/2000
Each share Common no par exchanged for $1.75 cash

ROSE EXPLORATIONS INC (NV)
Name changed to Silverstar Mining Corp. 03/04/2008
Silverstar Mining Corp. recapitalized as Silverstar Resources, Inc. 03/10/2015 which name changed to Creative Waste Solutions, Inc. 07/11/2016

ROSE GOLD MNG LTD (ON)
Recapitalized as AFM Hospitality Corp. 08/25/1994
Each share Common $1 par exchanged for (0.2) share Common no par
(See AFM Hospitality Corp.)

ROSE GROUP CORP NEVADA (NV)
Each share old Common $0.001 par exchanged for (0.001) share new Common $0.001 par 09/26/2005
Name changed to IDVIEWS, Inc. 01/25/2006

ROSE INTL INC (DE)
Name changed to Securities Resolution Advisors, Inc. 07/14/1998
Securities Resolution Advisors, Inc. name changed to Sales Online Direct, Inc. 03/16/1999 which name changed to Paid, Inc. 12/08/2003

ROSE INTL INC (FL)
Proclaimed dissolved for failure to file reports and pay fees 07/13/1988

ROSE-LEDUC OILS LTD. (ON)
Charter cancelled and declared dissolved for failure to file reports and pay fees 3/10/58

ROSE MARIE REID (CA)
See - Reid (Rose Marie)

ROSE MARIE RES LTD (BC)
Recapitalized as Cheetah Ventures Ltd. 07/17/2008
Each share Common no par exchanged for (0.5) share Common no par
Cheetah Ventures Ltd. name changed to Emperor Minerals Ltd. 10/21/2010 which name changed to Emperor Oil Ltd. 08/24/2012

ROSE PASS MINES LTD (BC)
Recapitalized as Range Industries Ltd. 11/8/74
Each share Common 50¢ par exchanged for (0.25) share Common no par
(See Range Industries Ltd.)

ROSE PATCH & LABEL CO. (MI)
Each share Common 50¢ par exchanged for (0.05) share Common $10 par 3/20/46
Stock Dividends - 500% 3/15/49; 100% 3/15/56; 50% 3/25/61; 25% 1/15/65; 25% 11/15/67
Name changed to Rospatch Corp. (MI) 1/25/68
Rospatch Corp. (MI) reincorporated under the laws of Delaware 5/18/70 which name changed to Ameriwood Industries International Corp. 12/31/91
(See Ameriwood Industries International Corp.)

ROSE RESOURCE CORP (BC)
Name changed to Petrostates Resource Corp. 2/13/85
(See Petrostates Resource Corp.)

ROSE ROCK MIDSTREAM L P (DE)
Merged into SemGroup Corp. 09/30/2016
Each Common Unit of Ltd. Partnership Int. exchanged for (0.8136) share Class A Common 1¢ par

ROSE SPIT RES INC (BC)
Struck off register and declared dissolved for failure to file returns 11/17/95

ROSE-WEBB LEATHERETTE CO., INC. (MA)
Involuntarily dissolved 3/31/28

ROSEBAY RES INC (AB)
Merged into Oiltec Resources Ltd. 1/31/97
Each share Common $1 par exchanged for (1/3) share Common no par
Oiltec Resources Ltd. merged into Forte Resources Inc. 6/23/2004

ROSEBON DEV CORP (UT)
Proclaimed dissolved for failure to file reports 9/1/94

ROSECAP INC (NY)
Name changed to Westbury Metals Group, Inc. 06/30/1998
(See Westbury Metals Group, Inc.)

ROSECROFT TROTTING & PACING ASSOCIATION, INC. (MD)
$6 Preferred $100 par called for redemption 06/09/1957
Charter forfeited 10/06/1998

ROSEDALE GOLD MINES LTD.
Bankrupt in 1940

ROSEFIELD PACKING CO. (CA)
Liquidation for cash completed 6/27/56

ROSEGOLD CORP (NV)
Name changed 08/03/1962
Name changed from Rosegold Beryllium Corp. to Rosegold Corp. 08/03/1962
Recapitalized as SureQuest Systems, Inc. (NV) 11/09/1996
Each share Common $0.001 par exchanged for (0.005) share Common $0.001 par
SureQuest Systems, Inc. (NV) reorganized in Delaware 04/23/2003

ROSELAND OIL & GAS INC (OK)
Reincorporated 08/16/1991
State of incorporation changed from (UT) to (OK) 08/16/1991
Each share Common no par exchanged for (0.2) share Common 1¢ par and (2) Common Stock Purchase Warrants expiring 04/29/1997 on 11/23/1991
Common 1¢ par changed to 5¢ par 00/00/1997
Reincorporated under the laws of Texas as Cubic Energy, Inc. 10/04/1999
(See Cubic Energy, Inc.)

ROSELAND RES LTD (AB)
Merged into Rival Energy Ltd. 06/16/2003
Each share Common no par exchanged for (0.2) share Common no par
Rival Energy Ltd. merged into Zargon Energy Trust 01/23/2008 which reorganized as Zargon Oil & Gas Ltd. (New) 01/07/2011

ROSELON INDS INC (PA)
Merged into Crosswicks Holdings, Inc. 3/17/82
Each share Common $1 par exchanged for $5.03 cash

ROSEMONT-PENROD CORP. (MI)
Voluntarily dissolved 10/27/1978
Details not available

ROSEMOUNT ENGINEERING CO. (MN)
Common 75¢ par changed to 37-1/2¢

par and (1) additional share issued 7/3/63
Stock Dividend - 100% 10/18/68
Name changed to Rosemount Inc. 3/9/72

ROSEMOUNT INC (MN)
Stock Dividend - 25% 10/24/1975
Acquired by Emerson Electric Co. 08/19/1976
Each share Common 37-1/2¢ par exchanged for (1.4) shares Common $1 par

ROSEN PETE CORP (DE)
Adjudicated bankrupt 06/30/1972
Stockholders' equity unlikely

ROSENAU BROS INC (PA)
Each share Class A Common $1 par exchanged for (1) share Common $1 par 01/01/1968
8% Preferred $100 par called for redemption 01/02/1968
Name changed to Cinderella Clothing Industries, Inc. and Common $1 par changed to 1¢ par 08/12/1976
(See Cinderella Clothing Industries, Inc.)

ROSENBAUM GRAIN CORP.
Reorganized as Chesapeake Trust 00/00/1937
Details not available

ROSENFELD HENRY INDS INC (FL)
Adjudicated bankrupt 08/21/1970
Stockholders' equity unlikely

ROSENTHAL A G (GERMANY)
ADR agreement terminated 09/28/2011
No ADR's remain outstanding

ROSENTHAL L M FD (DE)
Name changed to Lenox Fund 02/10/1971
Lenox Fund acquired by Bayrock Growth Fund, Inc. 04/24/1974 which was acquired by Affiliated Fund, Inc. (DE) 09/03/1975 which reincorporated in Maryland 11/26/1975 which name changed to Lord Abbett Affiliated Fund, Inc. 03/01/1996

ROSE'S 5-10-25¢ STORES, INC. (DE)
Each share Common $5 par exchanged for (5) shares Common $1 par 00/00/1937
Common $1 par changed to $10 par 00/00/1944
Name changed to Rose's Stores, Inc. 03/08/1962
Rose's Stores, Inc. name changed to Rose's Holdings, Inc. 01/31/1998 which name changed to WebFinancial Corp. 06/15/1999 which merged into WebFinancial L.P. 12/31/2008 which name changed to Steel Partners Holdings L.P. 04/08/2009

ROSES HLDGS INC (DE)
Each share Common no par exchanged for (0.5) share Common $0.001 par 11/20/1998
Note: Holders of (499) or fewer pre-split shares received $2.0375 cash per share
Name changed to WebFinancial Corp. 06/15/1999
WebFinancial Corp. merged into WebFinancial L.P. 12/31/2008 which name changed to Steel Partners Holdings L.P. 04/08/2009

ROSES STORES INC (DE)
Common $10 par changed to $1.25 par and (7) additional shares issued 10/15/1976
Class B $10 par changed to $1.25 par and (7) additional shares issued 10/15/1976
Common $1.25 par split (3) for (2) by issuance of (0.5) additional share 06/30/1983
Class B $1.25 par split (3) for (2) by issuance of (0.5) additional share 06/30/1983

Common $1.25 par changed to no par and (2) additional shares issued 11/14/1983
Class B $1.25 par changed to no par and (2) additional shares issued 11/14/1983
Common no par split (2) for (1) by issuance of (1) additional share 10/15/1986
Class B no par split (2) for (1) by issuance of (1) additional share 10/15/1986
Reorganized under Chapter 11 Federal Bankruptcy Code 12/14/1994
Each (4.377) shares old Common no par exchanged for (1) Common Stock Purchase Warrant expiring 04/28/2002
Each (4.377) share Class B no par exchanged for (1) Common Stock Purchase Warrant expiring 04/28/2002
Name changed to Rose's Holdings, Inc. 01/31/1998
Rose's Holdings, Inc. name changed to WebFinancial Corp. 06/15/1999 which merged into WebFinancial L.P. 12/31/2008 which name changed to Steel Partners Holdings L.P. 04/08/2009

ROSETO WATER CO. (PA)
Merged into Bangor Water Co. 00/00/1941
Details not available

ROSETTA EXPL INC (AB)
Recapitalized as Berkana Energy Corp. 12/11/2006
Each share Class A Common no par exchanged for (0.2) share Class A Common no par
(See Berkana Energy Corp.)

ROSETTA INPHARMATICS INC (DE)
Merged into Merck & Co., Inc. (Old) 07/19/2001
Each share Class B $0.001 par exchanged for (0.2352) share Common 1¢ par
Merck & Co., Inc. (Old) merged into Merck & Co., Inc. (New) 11/03/2009

ROSETTA RES INC (DE)
Merged into Noble Energy, Inc. 07/20/2015
Each share Common $0.001 par exchanged for (0.542) share Common 1¢ par

ROSETTA TECHNOLOGIES INC (WY)
Name changed to Tanisys Technology, Inc. 07/11/1994
(See Tanisys Technology, Inc.)

ROSEVILLE COMMUNICATIONS CO (CA)
Stock Dividend - 3% payable 12/15/1997 to holders of record 12/01/1997
Name changed to SureWest Communications 05/30/2001
SureWest Communications merged into Consolidated Communications Holdings, Inc. 07/02/2012

ROSEVILLE 1ST NATL BK (ROSEVILLE, CA)
Merged into Western Sierra Bancorp 4/30/99
Each share Common no par exchanged for (1.211) shares Common no par
Western Sierra Bancorp merged into Umpqua Holdings Corp. 6/5/2006

ROSEVILLE TEL CO (CA)
Capital Stock $10 par changed to $5 par and (1) additional share issued 09/15/1974
Capital Stock $5 par split (2) for (1) by issuance of (1) additional share 06/03/1980
Capital Stock $5 par split (2) for (1) by issuance of (1) additional share 09/15/1983
Under plan of reorganization each share Capital Stock $5 par

automatically became (1) share Roseville Communications Co. Common no par 10/01/1996
Roseville Communications Co. name changed to SureWest Communications 05/30/2001 which merged into Consolidated Communications Holdings, Inc. 07/02/2012

ROSEWIND CORP (CO)
Reorganized under the laws of Delaware as Aytu BioScience, Inc. 06/10/2015
Each share Common no par exchanged for (0.08214227) share Common $0.0001 par

ROSLYN BANCORP INC (DE)
Common 1¢ par split (3) for (2) by issuance of (0.5) additional share payable 8/22/2001 to holders of record 8/6/2001 Ex date - 8/23/2001
Merged into New York Community Bancorp, Inc. 11/3/2003
Each share Common 1¢ par exchanged for (0.75) share Common 1¢ par

ROSLYN INDUSTRIES, INC. (DE)
Name changed to Sircor Scientific, Inc. 1/3/68
Sircor Scientific, Inc. liquidated for Botar Corp. 2/15/73
(See Botar Corp.)

ROSMAC MINES LTD. (BC)
Name changed to Rosmac Resources Ltd. 08/09/1979
Rosmac Resources Ltd. merged into Golden North Resource Corp. 09/11/1984 which merged into Caledonia Mining Corp. (BC) 02/04/1992 which reincorporated in Canada 03/29/1995 which reincorporated in Jersey as Caledonia Mining Corp. PLC 03/24/2016

ROSMAC RES LTD (BC)
Merged into Golden North Resource Corp. 09/11/1984
Each share Capital Stock no par exchanged for (0.3) share Common no par
Golden North Resource Corp. merged into Caledonia Mining Corp. (BC) 02/04/1992 which reincorporated in Canada 03/29/1995 which reincorporated in Jersey as Caledonia Mining Corp. PLC 03/24/2016

ROSNEFTEGAZSTROY JSC (RUSSIA)
Each old Sponsored ADR for Ordinary exchanged for (0.01) new Sponsored ADR for Ordinary 02/05/2001
ADR agreement terminated 03/20/2009
No ADR holders' equity

ROSPATCH CORP (MI)
Reincorporated 05/18/1970
Reincorporated 06/03/1985
Common $10 par changed to $5 par and (1) additional share issued 09/15/1968
State of incorporation changed from (MI) to (DE) 05/18/1970
Common $5 par split (3) for (2) by issuance of (0.5) additional share 01/24/1973
State of incorporation changed from (DE) back to (MI) 06/03/1985
Name changed to Ameriwood Industries International Corp. 12/13/1991
(See Ameriwood Industries International Corp.)

ROSS A J LOGISTICS INC (NJ)
SEC revoked common stock registration 01/20/2012

ROSS ANDERSON GROUP INC (DE)
Recapitalized as Makaha, Inc. 06/30/1991

Each share Common $0.001 par exchanged for (0.46038396) share Common $0.001 par
Makaha, Inc. name changed to TerraCom Inc. 12/24/1993
(See TerraCom Inc.)

ROSS AVIATION INC (DE)
Merged into Sterling Oil of Oklahoma, Inc. 3/1/79
Each share Common 25¢ par exchanged for $1 cash

ROSS BUILDERS SUPPLIES, INC. (DE)
Acquired by Wickes Corp. (MI) 11/24/64
Each share Common $2 par exchanged for (0.75) share Common $2.50 par
Wickes Corp. (MI) reincorporated in Delaware 7/2/71 which merged into Wickes Companies, Inc. 8/13/80 which name changed to Collins & Aikman Group Inc. 7/17/92
(See Collins & Aikman Group Inc.)

ROSS BUILDERS SUPPLIES, INC. (SC)
Reincorporated under the laws of Delaware and Common $10 par exchanged for (5) shares Common $2 par 12/31/60
Ross Builders Supplies, Inc. (DE) merged into Wickes Corp. (MI) 11/24/64 which reincorporated in Delaware 7/2/71 which merged into Wickes Companies, Inc. 8/13/80 which name changed to Collins & Aikman Group Inc. 7/17/92
(See Collins & Aikman Group Inc.)

ROSS COSMETICS DISTR CTRS INC (NY)
Common 1¢ par split (2) for (1) by issuance of (1) additional share 2/21/92
Name changed to Tristar Corp. 3/17/93
(See Tristar Corp.)

ROSS (J.O.) ENGINEERING CORP. (NJ)
Stock Dividend - 100% 11/29/54
Merged into Midland-Ross Corp. 12/7/57
Each share Common $1 par exchanged for (0.6) share Common $5 par
(See Midland-Ross Corp.)

ROSS EXPL INC (NJ)
Each share Common $0.0001 par exchanged for (0.2) share Common $0.0005 par 12/23/83
Charter declared void for non-payment of taxes 7/30/93

ROSS (JIM) FILM PRODUCTIONS, INC. (TX)
Charter forfeited for failure to pay taxes 7/10/63

ROSS FURNITURE CORP (PA)
Common 10¢ par split (2) for (1) by issuance of (1) additional share 5/15/72
Name changed to U.G.M. Corp. 3/26/74
(See U.G.M. Corp.)

ROSS GEAR & TOOL CO., INC. (IN)
Each share Common no par exchanged for (3) shares Common $10 par 3/25/55
Common $10 par split (2) for (1) by issuance of (1) additional share 10/16/59
Acquired by Thompson Ramo Wooldridge, Inc. 6/16/64
Each share Common $1 par exchanged for (0.18) share $4.25 Conv. Preference Ser. A no par and (0.254) share Common $5 par
Thompson Ramo Wooldridge, Inc. name changed to TRW Inc. 4/30/65 which merged into Northrop Grumman Corp. 12/11/2002

ROSS INDUSTRIES CORP.
Name changed to Ross (J.O.) Engineering Corp. in 1951
Ross (J.O.) Engineering Corp. merged into Midland-Ross Corp. 12/7/57
(See Midland-Ross Corp.)

ROSS INDS INC (NY)
Merged into RI Acquisition Corp. 02/18/2005
Each share Common 10¢ par exchanged for $2.50 cash

ROSS INDS INC (VA)
Acquired by Ross Acquisition, Inc. 07/16/2018
Each share Common $1 par exchanged for $0.24 cash

ROSS ISLAND MINES LTD (BC)
Struck off register and declared dissolved for failure to file returns 4/6/92

ROSS ISLAND SAND & GRAVEL CO (OR)
100% acquired by R.B. Pamplin Corp. through purchase offer 00/00/1977
Public interest eliminated

ROSS MED CORP (CA)
Completely liquidated 06/16/1971
Each share Capital Stock $1 par exchanged for first and final distribution of (1/3) share Hospital Corp. of America Common $1 par
(See Hospital Corp. of America)

ROSS PRODUCTS, INC. (NY)
Name changed to NMS Industries, Inc. 09/01/1967
(See NMS Industries, Inc.)

ROSS-SMITH CORP. (NY)
Name changed to Phototex, Inc. in 1949
Phototex, Inc. recapitalized as Universal Mineral Resources, Inc. 3/6/58 which charter cancelled 12/15/70

ROSS STORES, INC.
Property sold 00/00/1930
Details not available

ROSS STORES INC (CA)
Reincorporated under the laws of Delaware 6/15/89

ROSS SYS INC (DE)
Reincorporated 06/29/1998
State of incorporation changed from (CA) to (DE) and Common no par changed to $0.001 par 06/29/1998
Each share old Common $0.001 par exchanged for (0.1) share new Common $0.001 par 04/27/2001
Merged into chinadotcom corp. 08/27/2004
Each share new Common $0.001 par exchanged for (1.647) shares Class A Common $0.00025 par and $11.90 cash
chinadotcom corp. name changed to CDC Corp. 04/27/2005
(See CDC Corp.)

ROSS TECHNOLOGY INC (DE)
Voluntarily dissolved 12/29/98
No stockholders' equity

ROSS VALLEY SVGS & LN ASSN SAN ANSELMO (CA)
99.94% acquired by Financial Corp. of Santa Barbara through exchange offer which expired 04/10/1972
Public interest eliminated

ROSS VIKING MERCHANDISE CORP. (DE)
Charter forfeited for failure to maintain a registered agent 11/5/97

ROSSAL RES LTD (BC)
Struck off register and declared dissolved for failure to file returns 3/26/93

ROSSCOMP CORP (CA)
Charter suspended for failure to file reports and pay fees 12/01/1986

ROSSI RESIDENCIAL S A (BRAZIL)
144A ADR's for Common reclassified as Old ADR's for Common 04/21/2000
Basis changed from (1:5) to (1:0.5) 07/21/2006
Old ADR's for Common split (2) for (1) by issuance of (1) additional ADR payable 03/18/2008 to holders of record 03/17/2008 Ex date - 03/19/2008
Each old ADR for Common exchanged for (0.2) new ADR for Common 11/14/2014
Each new ADR for Common exchanged again for (0.2) new ADR for Common 01/22/2016
Stock Dividend - 25% payable 07/21/2006 to holders of record 02/02/2006 Ex date - 07/24/2006
ADR agreement terminated 08/18/2017
Each new ADR for Common exchanged for $1.0056 cash

ROSSIA INSURANCE CO. OF AMERICA (CT)
Name changed to Northeastern Insurance Co. of Hartford in 1939
(See Northeastern Insurance Co. of Hartford)

ROSSIA INTERNATIONAL CORP.
Dissolved in 1942

ROSSLAND MINES LTD.
Recapitalized as Rossland Mining Co. Ltd. 00/00/1952
Each share Common no par exchanged for (0.5) share Common no par
Rossland Mining Co. Ltd. recapitalized as Ross Island Mining Co. Ltd. 06/29/1972
(See Ross Island Mining Co. Ltd.)

ROSSLAND MNG LTD (BC)
Recapitalized as Ross Island Mining Co. Ltd. 6/29/72
Each share Common no par exchanged for (0.2) share Common no par
(See Ross Island Mining Co. Ltd.)

ROSSMAN CORP.
Property sold 00/00/1935
Details not available

ROSSMOOR CONSTR CORP (MD)
Recapitalized as RCC, Inc. 02/12/1979
Each share Common no par exchanged for (0.1) share Common no par
(See RCC, Inc.)

ROSSMOOR CORP (CA)
In process of liquidation
Each share Common 25¢ par received initial distribution of $5.50 cash 1/15/82
Each share Common 25¢ par exchanged for second distribution of $1 cash 6/10/82
Assets transferred to Rossmoor Liquidating Trust 6/15/82
(See Rossmoor Liquidating Trust)

ROSSMOOR LIQUIDATING TRUST (CA)
In process of liquidation
Each share Common 25¢ par received third distribution of $3.25 cash 8/9/82
Each share Common 25¢ par received fourth distribution of $1 cash 4/1/83
Each share Common 25¢ par received fifth distribution of $3.25 cash 9/30/83
Each share Common 25¢ par received sixth distribution of $1.75 cash 4/2/84
Each share Common 25¢ par received seventh distribution of $1 cash 6/19/85
Each share Common 25¢ par received eighth distribution of $1 cash 6/30/86
Each share Common 25¢ par received ninth distribution of $1.30 cash 6/1/87
(See Rossmoor Corp. for previous distributions)
Note: Details on subsequent distributions, if any, are not available

ROSSVILLE ALCOHOL & CHEMICAL CORP.
Name changed to Rossville Union Distilleries, Inc. in 1933
Rossville Union Distilleries, Inc. name changed to Oldetyme Distillers Corp. in 1933 which name changed to Delendo Corp. in 1940
(See Delendo Corp.)

ROSSVILLE COMMERCIAL ALCOHOL CORP.
Merged into American Solvents & Chemical Corp. in 1930
Details not available

ROSSVILLE UNION DISTILLERIES, INC.
Name changed to Oldetyme Distillers Corp. in 1933
Oldetyme Distillers Corp. name changed to Delendo Corp. in 1940
(See Delendo Corp.)

ROSTELECOM LONG DISTANCE & INTL TELECOMMUNICATIONS OPEN JT STK CO (RUSSIA)
Name changed to Rostelecom PJSC 07/22/2015

ROSTOCK VENTURES CORP (NV)
Each share old Common $0.001 par exchanged for (7) shares new Common $0.001 par 04/24/2009
Name changed to U.S. Lithium Corp. 06/13/2016

ROSTOV ELECTROSVYAZ OPEN JT STK CO (RUSSIA)
ADR agreement terminated 2/6/2003
Each Sponsored ADR for Ordinary exchanged for (10) Ordinary Shares
Note: Unexchanged ADR's will be sold and proceeds held for claim after 8/6/2003

ROSTOVENERGO OPEN JT STK CO (RUSSIA)
Each Sponsored ADR for Preferred 1 Ruble par received distribution of $1.00712 cash payable 04/21/2006 to holders of record 01/11/2005
Each Sponsored ADR for Ordinary 1 Ruble par received distribution of $1.35264 cash payable 04/21/2006 to holders of record 01/11/2005
Merged into IDGC of South 03/31/2008
Each Sponsored ADR for Preferred 1 Ruble par exchanged for $0.231928 cash
Each Sponsored ADR for Ordinary 1 Ruble par exchanged for $0.256011 cash

ROTANELLI FOODS INC (NY)
Name changed to 2 Birch Street Corp. 3/24/86
(See 2 Birch Street Corp.)

ROTARY ELECTRIC STEEL CO. (DE)
Stock Dividends - 10% 12/29/48; 20% 12/28/51; 20% 12/29/53; 100% 4/1/55
Merged into Jones & Laughlin Steel Corp. 4/30/57
Each share Common $10 par exchanged for (0.8) share Common $10 par
(See Jones & Laughlin Steel Corp.)

ROTARY ENGR LTD (SINGAPORE)
ADR agreement terminated 02/27/2017
Each Sponsored ADR for Ordinary exchanged for $6.960585 cash

ROTARY PWR INTL INC (DE)
Charter forfeited for failure to maintain a registered agent 02/13/2004

ROTATING COMPONENTS, INC. (NY)
Completely liquidated 1/10/68
Each share Common 1¢ par exchanged for first and final distribution of (0.333333) share Instrument Systems Corp. (N.Y.) Common 25¢ par
Instrument Systems Corp. (N.Y.) reincorporated under the laws of Delaware 4/15/71

ROTECH HEALTHCARE INC (DE)
Plan of reorganization under Chapter 11 Federal Bankruptcy proceedings effective 09/27/2013
No stockholders' equity

ROTECH MED CORP (FL)
Common $0.0002 par split (2) for (1) by issuance of (1) additional share payable 5/21/96 to holders of record 4/30/96
Acquired by Integrated Health Services, Inc. 10/21/97
Each share Common $0.0002 par exchanged for (0.5806) share Common $0.001 par
(See Integrated Health Services, Inc.)

ROTEX CORP (PA)
Out of business 02/06/1976
No stockholders' equity

ROTEX INTL INC (NJ)
Charter declared void for non-payment of taxes 02/18/1977

ROTH FINL FITNESS INC (CO)
Reincorporated under the laws of Nevada as Online Entertainment, Inc. 03/15/1995
Online Entertainment, Inc. name changed to Online Power Supply, Inc. 12/14/1999
(See Online Power Supply, Inc.)

ROTH GREETING CARDS (CA)
Merged into Insilco Corp. 6/8/71
Each share Common 10¢ par exchanged for (0.5) share Common $1 par
(See Insilco Corp.)

ROTHCHILD COS INC (DE)
Reincorporated 4/8/96
State of incorporation changed from (FL) to (DE) 4/8/96
Each share old Common $0.001 par exchanged for (0.05) share new Common $0.001 par 4/30/96
Name changed to Fremont Gold Corp. 7/30/96
Fremont Gold Corp. recapitalized as JSDC Inc. 1/28/2002 which recapitalized as Housing Solutions Hawaii Inc. 11/25/2002 which name changed to Home Solutions Health, Inc. 5/14/2004

ROTHERWOOD GROUP INC (AZ)
Reorganized under the laws of Nevada as Entrada Software Inc. 09/01/1999
Holdings of (500) or more shares exchanged for (0.2) share Common $0.001 par per share
Holdings of between (499) and (101) shares exchanged for (100) shares only
Holdings of (100) or fewer shares exchanged for like number of shares
Entrada Software Inc. recapitalized as Medlink Technologies, Inc. 04/04/2006 which name changed to Cambridge Resources Corp. 06/21/2006
(See Cambridge Resources Corp.)

ROTHMANS INC (CANADA)
6.625% 2nd Preferred $20 par called for redemption 03/30/1992
6.85% Preferred Ser. A $100 par called for redemption 03/30/1992
Common no par split (6) for (1) by issuance of (5) additional shares payable 02/15/2000 to holders of record 02/10/2000 Ex date - 02/08/2000
Common no par split (2) for (1) by issuance of (1) additional share

payable 03/17/2005 to holders of record 03/04/2005
Acquired by Philip Morris International Inc. 10/09/2008
Each share Common no par exchanged for $30 cash

ROTHMANS INTL PLC (ENGLAND)
ADR's for Class B Ordinary 12-1/2p par split (2) for (1) by issuance of (1) additional ADR 09/18/1992
Acquired by British American Tobacco PLC 06/07/1999
Details not available

ROTHMANS PALL MALL CDA LTD (CANADA)
Common $10 par changed to no par 11/11/1963
Name changed to Rothmans Inc. 10/02/1985
(See Rothmans Inc.)

ROTHMOOR CORP (DE)
Each share Class A 40¢ par exchanged for (2) shares Class A 20¢ par 00/00/1947
Company went private 00/00/1973
Public interest eliminated

ROTHSAY MINES LTD. (ON)
Merged into Resource Exploration & Development Co. Ltd. 6/11/68
Each share Capital Stock $1 par exchanged for (0.3125) share Capital Stock no par
Resource Exploration & Development Co. Ltd. charter cancelled 5/13/80

ROTHSCHILD L F HLDGS INC (DE)
Name changed 05/19/1987
Name changed from Rothschild, (L.F.) Unterberg, Towbin Holdings, Inc. to Rothschild (L.F.) Holdings, Inc. 05/19/1987
Acquired by Franklin Savings Corp. 06/30/1988
Each share Common $1 par exchanged for $1.05 principal amount of 13.62% Subordinated Debentures due 02/15/1994

ROTHSCHILD L F UNTERBERG TOWBIN INVT TR (MA)
Name changed to Franklin Managed Trust (MA) and Income Portfolio 1¢ par reclassified as Investment Grade Income Portfolio 1¢ par 06/28/1988
Franklin Managed Trust (MA) reincorporated in Delaware 08/01/2007

ROTO AMERN CORP (NY)
Adjudicated bankrupt 03/31/1970
Stockholders' equity unlikely

ROTO CYLINDERS, INC. (NY)
Name changed to Armotek Industries, Inc. 03/24/1965
(See Armotek Industries, Inc.)

ROTO-ROOTER INC NEW (DE)
Name changed to Chemed Corp. 5/17/2004

ROTO ROOTER INC OLD (DE)
Merged into Chemed Corp. 9/17/96
Each share Common $1 par exchanged for $41 cash

ROTOCAST PLASTIC PRODS INC (FL)
90% reacquired through purchase offer as of 01/17/1984
Public interest eliminated

ROTODYNE INC (DE)
Name changed to CSM Systems, Inc. 12/23/1976
CSM Systems, Inc. name changed to CSM Environmental Systems, Inc. 05/31/1990 which name changed to CSM Worldwide, Inc. 12/23/1998
(See CSM Worldwide, Inc.)

ROTODYNE MFG CORP (DE)
Each share Preferred $3.50 par exchanged for (2/3) share Common 10¢ par 04/10/1969
Name changed to Rotodyne, Inc. 05/14/1970
Rotodyne, Inc. name changed to CSM Systems, Inc. 12/23/1976 which name changed to CSM Environmental Systems, Inc. 05/31/1990 which name changed to CSM Worldwide, Inc. 12/23/1998
(See CSM Worldwide, Inc.)

ROTONDO ROUYN MINES LTD. (ON)
Name changed to Cleranda Copper Mines Ltd. in 1956
Cleranda Copper Mines Ltd. charter cancelled 5/15/74

ROTONICS MFG INC (DE)
Merged into Rotonics Holding Corp. 1/29/2007
Each share Common no par exchanged for $3 cash

ROTOR-CRAFT CORP. (CA)
Charter suspended for failure to file reports and pay fees 8/1/61

ROTRON INC (NY)
Merged into EG&G, Inc. 02/25/1976
Each share Common 5¢ par received $17.22 cash
Note: Certificates were not required to be surrendered and are without value

ROTRON MFG INC (NY)
Name changed to Rotron, Inc. 11/12/68
(See Rotron, Inc.)

ROTTLUND CO (MN)
Company went private 3/22/2002
Each share Common 10¢ par exchanged for $9.15 cash

ROTUNDA OIL & MNG INC (UT)
Recapitalized as Euro Trade & Forfaiting Inc. 11/20/98
Each share Common $0.001 par exchanged for (0.01) share Common $0.001 par
(See Euro Trade & Forfaiting Inc.)

ROUANDAH GOLD & METALS LTD.
Name changed to Rouandah Oils & Mines Ltd. in 1952 which was liquidated in 1959

ROUANDAH OILS & MINES LTD. (ON)
Liquidated in 1959

ROUGE ELECTRS INC (OK)
Name changed to Rouge Industries, Inc. 06/10/1969
(See Rouge Industries, Inc.)

ROUGE INDS INC (DE)
Plan of reorganization under Chapter 11 Federal Bankruptcy proceedings effective 06/30/2009
No stockholders' equity

ROUGE INDS INC (OK)
Charter suspended for failure to pay taxes 02/28/1975

ROUGE RES LTD (BC)
Name changed to Fiore Exploration Ltd. 08/08/2016
Fiore Exploration Ltd. reorganized as Fiore Gold Ltd. 09/26/2017

ROUGE STL CO (DE)
Issue Information - 7,000,000 shares COM offered at $22 per share on 03/28/1994
Under plan of reorganization each share Class A Common 1¢ par automatically became (1) share Rouge Industries, Inc. Class A Common 1¢ par 07/30/1997
(See Rouge Industries, Inc.)

ROUGH RIV PETE CORP (BC)
Cease trade order effective 09/27/1989
Stockholders' equity unlikely

ROUGHNECK SUPPLIES INC (NV)
Common $0.001 par split (3) for (1) by issuance of (2) additional shares payable 07/01/2008 to holders of record 07/01/2008
Name changed to Omnimmune Holdings, Inc. 08/15/2008

ROULETTE GOLD MINES, LTD. (ON)
Charter cancelled for failure to file reports and pay taxes February 1957

ROUND MOUNTAIN MINES CO (NV)
Liquidation completed
Each share Capital Stock 50¢ par exchanged for initial distribution of $0.03860876 cash 3/25/70
Each share Capital Stock 50¢ par received second distribution of $0.019 3/11/71
Each share Capital Stock 50¢ par received third distribution of $0.025 cash 5/3/72
Each share Capital Stock 50¢ par received fourth distribution of $0.01 cash 5/5/73
Each share Capital Stock 50¢ par received fifth distribution of $0.02 cash 2/25/74
Each share Capital Stock 50¢ par received sixth distribution of $0.065 cash 1/20/75
Each share Capital Stock 50¢ par received seventh distribution of $0.06 cash 1/16/76
Each share Capital Stock 50¢ par exchanged for eighth and final distribution of $0.02 cash 9/7/77

ROUND OAK CORP.
Acquired by Kaiser-Frazer Corp. 00/00/1947
Details not available

ROUND ROCK OIL CO. (TX)
Incorporated 5/12/15
Charter forfeited for failure to pay taxes 5/19/50

ROUND TOP MOUNTAIN, INC. (VT)
Charter revoked for failure to file annual reports 2/28/75

ROUNDER INC (FL)
Stock Dividend - 10% payable 12/31/2012 to holders of record 12/24/2012 Ex date - 12/20/2012
Name changed to Fortitude Group, Inc. 01/08/2013

ROUNDYS INC (WI)
Acquired by Kroger Co. 12/18/2015
Each share Common 1¢ par exchanged for $3.60 cash

ROUSE CAP (DE)
9.25% Guaranteed Quarterly Income Preferred Securities called for redemption at $25 on 3/17/2004

ROUSE CO (MD)
Common 1¢ par split (2) for (1) by issuance of (1) additional share 11/15/1969
Common 1¢ par split (2) for (1) by issuance of (1) additional share 11/22/1971
Common 1¢ par split (2) for (1) by issuance of (1) additional share 06/07/1985
Common 1¢ par split (3) for (2) by issuance of (0.5) additional share 06/10/1987
Conv. Preferred Ser. A 1¢ par called for redemption 09/30/1996
Issue Information - 4,000,000 shares PFD CONV SER B 6% offered at $50 per share on 02/06/1997
6% Conv. Preferred Ser. B called for redemption at $50 on 02/10/2004
Merged into General Growth Properties, Inc. 11/12/2004
Each share Common 1¢ par exchanged for $65.20526 cash

ROUSE PPTYS INC (DE)
Acquired by BSREP II Retail Pooling LLC 07/05/2016
Each share Common 1¢ par exchanged for $18.25 cash

ROUSSEL UCLAF (FRANCE)
Acquired by Hoechst A.G. 00/00/1997
Details not available

ROUTH ROBBINS INVESTMENT CORP. (VA)
Name changed to First Investment Corp. 9/28/60
(See First Investment Corp.)

ROUVINA BROS FOOD SERVICE DISTRIBUTORS INC. (NY)
Administratively dissolved 12/27/2001

ROUYN EXPL LTD (QC)
Charter annulled for failure to file annual reports 06/18/1977

ROUYN MERGER GOLD MINES LTD.
Recapitalized as New Rouyn Merger Mines Ltd. in 1947
Each share Capital Stock $1 par exchanged for (0.5) share Capital Stock $1 par
New Rouyn Merger Mines, Ltd. recapitalized as Goldrim Mining Co. Ltd. 6/8/65
(See Goldrim Mining Co. Ltd.)

ROUYN REWARD GOLD MINES LTD. (ON)
Charter cancelled for failure to pay taxes and file returns in March, 1958

ROUYN SWAYZE GOLD MINES LTD.
Succeeded by Rouyn Reward Gold Mines Ltd. (10) for (1) in 1934
(See Rouyn Reward Gold Mines Ltd.)

ROVAC CORP (DE)
Stock Dividend - 100% 01/13/1977
SEC revoked common stock registration 12/22/2011

ROVER CREEK MINING CO. LTD.
Dissolved in 1948

ROVER GROUP PLC (ENGLAND)
Acquired by British Aerospace PLC 10/14/1988
Each ADR for Ordinary 25p par exchanged for $1.74 cash

ROVER OIL & GAS LTD (BC)
Merged into General Allied Oil & Gas Co. in 1982
Details not available

ROVER SHOE CO (FL)
Each share Common $1 par exchanged for (1) share Common 1¢ par 04/14/1969
Charter cancelled and proclaimed dissolved for non-payment of taxes 07/02/1973

ROVI CORP (DE)
Under plan of merger name changed to TiVo Corp. 09/08/2016

ROW, PETERSON & CO. (IL)
Under plan of merger name changed to Harper & Row, Publishers, Inc. (Ill.) 5/1/62
Harper & Row, Publishers, Inc. (Ill.) reincorporated under the laws of Delaware 9/5/69
(See Harper & Row, Publishers, Inc. (Del.))

ROW ENTMT INCOME FD (ON)
Name changed to Entertainment One Income Fund 07/08/2005
(See Entertainment One Income Fund)

ROWAN BANCORP INC (NC)
Merged into FNB Corp. 08/01/2002
Each share Common 1¢ par exchanged for $36 cash

ROWAN CONS MINES LTD (ON)
Recapitalized as Rowan Gold Mines Ltd. 04/01/1974
Each share Capital Stock $1 par exchanged for (0.1) share Capital Stock no par
Rowan Gold Mines Ltd. merged into Goldquest Exploration Inc. 08/09/1982 which merged into Goldcorp Inc. (New) 03/31/1994

ROWAN CONTROLLER CO (MD)
Common $10 par changed to $2.50 par and (3) additional shares issued 10/03/1960
Common $2.50 par split (5) for (4) by

issuance of (0.25) additional share 12/15/1965
Common $2.50 par split (2) for (1) by issuance of (1) additional share 11/30/1967
Stock Dividend - 25% 03/09/1964
Name changed to Rowan Industries, Inc. 05/07/1968
Rowan Industries, Inc. name changed to De Tomaso Industries, Inc. 11/02/1973 which name changed to Trident Rowan Group, Inc. 08/22/1996 which name changed to Comtech Group Inc. 08/02/2004 which name changed to Cogo Group, Inc. (MD) 05/13/2008 which reincorporated in Cayman Islands 08/03/2011 which name changed to Viewtran Group, Inc. 11/26/2013

ROWAN COS INC (DE)
Common $1 par changed to 50¢ par and (1) additional share issued 02/15/1973
Common 50¢ par changed to 25¢ par and (1) additional share issued 01/14/1977
Common 25¢ par split (2) for (1) by issuance of (1) additional share 02/23/1978
Common 25¢ par changed to $0.125 par and (1) additional share issued 05/30/1980
Common $0.125 par split (2) for (1) by issuance of (1) additional share 02/05/1981
$2.4375 Conv. Preferred Ser. A $1 par called for redemption 07/01/1983
$2.125 Conv. Exchangeable Preferred $1 par called for redemption 08/28/1987
Reorganized under the laws of England & Wales as Rowan Companies PLC 05/04/2012
Each share Common $0.125 par exchanged for (1) share Class A Ordinary USD $0.125 par

ROWAN DRILLING INC (DE)
Name changed to Rowan Companies, Inc. (DE) 10/01/1971
Rowan Companies, Inc. (DE) reorganized in England & Wales as Rowan Companies PLC 05/04/2012

ROWAN GOLD MINES LTD (ON)
Merged into Goldquest Exploration Inc. 08/09/1982
Each share Capital Stock no par exchanged for (0.20366598) share Common no par
Goldquest Exploration Inc. merged into Goldcorp Inc. (New) 03/31/1994

ROWAN INDS INC (MD)
Name changed to De Tomaso Industries, Inc. 11/02/1973
De Tomaso Industries, Inc. name changed to Trident Rowan Group Inc. 08/22/1996 which name changed to Comtech Group Inc. 08/02/2004 which name changed to Cogo Group, Inc. (MD) 05/14/2008 which reincorporated in Cayman Islands 08/03/2011 which name changed to Viewtran Group, Inc. 11/26/2013

ROWAN RED LAKE GOLD MINES LTD.
Bankrupt in 1944
No stockholders' equity

ROWAN SVGS BK SSB INC (CHINA GROVE, NC)
Under plan of reorganization each share Common 1¢ par automatically became (1) share Rowan Bancorp, Inc. Common 1¢ par 07/10/1996
(See Rowan Bancorp, Inc.)

ROWCO MFG INC (NH)
Charter dissolved for failure to file reports and pay fees 10/31/1983

ROWE CORP. (NY)
Merged into Automatic Canteen Co. of America 9/30/55
Each share Common $1 par exchanged for (0.8) share Common $5 par
Automatic Canteen Co. of America name changed to Canteen Corp. 2/16/66 which merged into International Telephone & Telegraph Corp. (DE) 4/25/69 which name changed to ITT Corp. 12/31/83 which reorganized in Indiana as ITT Industries Inc. 12/19/95 which name changed to ITT Corp. 7/1/2006

ROWE COS (NV)
Reincorporated 06/01/1985
Name changed 04/02/1999
Common $1 par split (5) for (1) by issuance of (4) additional shares 06/15/1972
State of incorporation changed from (VA) to (NV) 06/01/1985
Common $1 par split (3) for (2) by issuance of (0.5) additional share 04/13/1989
Common $1 par split (3) for (2) by issuance of (0.5) additional share 01/15/1993
Common $1 par split (3) for (2) by issuance of (0.5) additional share 10/05/1993
Common $1 par split (3) for (2) by issuance of (0.5) additional share 01/15/1994
Common $1 par split (3) for (2) by issuance of (0.5) additional share 12/05/1994
Name changed from Rowe Furniture Corp. to Rowe Companies 04/02/1999
Stock Dividends - 10% 07/15/1969; 10% 01/15/1971; 10% payable 12/07/1999 to holders of record 11/16/1999
Plan of reorganization under Chapter 11 Federal Bankruptcy proceedings effective 02/26/2010
No stockholders' equity

ROWE PRICE INTL FD INC (MD)
Reorganized as Price (T. Rowe) International Trust 05/01/1986
Details not available

ROWE PRICE PRIME RESV FD II INC (MD)
Name changed to Rowe Price Prime Reserve Fund, Inc. 08/11/1980

ROWECO REALTY CO., INC.
Dissolved in 1938

ROWECOM INC (DE)
Issue Information - 3,100,000 shares COM offered at $16 per share on 03/08/1999
Merged into divine, inc. 11/6/2001
Each share Common 1¢ par exchanged for (0.75) share Class A Common $0.001 par
(See divine, inc.)

ROWELL LABS INC (MN)
Common no par changed to $1 par and (1) additional share issued 12/00/1961
Merged into Reid-Provident Laboratories Inc. 06/04/1985
Each share Common $1 par exchanged for $6.74 cash

ROWLAND INC (CT)
Name changed to Rowland Liquidating Corp. 08/22/1975
(See Rowland Liquidating Corp.)

ROWLAND LIQUIDATING CORP. (CT)
Liquidation completed
Each share Common $5 par exchanged for initial distribution of $14 cash 9/2/75
Each share Common $5 par received second distribution of $4 cash 9/19/75
Each share Common $5 par received third distribution of $2 cash 8/2/76
Each share Common $5 par received fourth distribution of $0.50 cash 3/4/77
Each share Common $5 par received fifth and final distribution of $0.20 cash 2/15/83

ROWLAND PRODUCTS, INC. (CT)
Common $12.50 par changed to $5 par and (2) additional shares issued 10/25/60
Name changed to Rowland, Inc. 8/1/73
Rowland, Inc. name changed to Rowland Liquidating Corp. 8/22/75
(See Rowland Liquidating Corp.)

ROWLANDS LTD (AUSTRALIA)
Placed in receivership 08/07/1991
ADR holders' equity unlikely
Note: Litigation still in progress as of 00/00/2005

ROWLEY SCHER REPROGRAPHICS INC (DC)
Merged into Reprographics Acquisition Corp. 02/04/1988
Each share Common 1¢ par exchanged for $5.35 cash

ROX INDUSTRIES, INC. (VA)
Charter cancelled and proclaimed dissolved for failure to file reports 6/1/68

ROXANA OILS CO. LTD. (AB)
Recapitalized as Allied Roxana Minerals Ltd. in 1957
Each share Capital Stock no par exchanged for (0.25) share Common 10¢ par
Allied Roxana Minerals Ltd. merged into Cavalier Energy Inc. (ONT) 3/1/74 which reincorporated in Alberta as Cavalier Energy Ltd. 2/7/78
(See Cavalier Energy Ltd.)

ROXANA PETROLEUMS LTD. (AB)
Name changed to Roxana Oils Co. Ltd. in 1945
Roxana Oils Co. Ltd. recapitalized as Allied Roxana Minerals Ltd. in 1957 which merged into Cavalier Energy Inc. (ONT) 3/1/74 which reincorporated in Alberta as Cavalier Energy Ltd. 2/7/78
(See Cavalier Energy Ltd.)

ROXANA RES LTD (BC)
Recapitalized as Canadian Roxana Resources Ltd. 05/26/1993
Each share Common no par exchanged for (0.5) share Common no par
(See Canadian Roxana Resources Ltd.)

ROXBAR PORCUPINE GOLD MINES, LTD. (ON)
Charter cancelled for failure to file reports and pay taxes 3/4/57

ROXBORO OILS LTD.
Acquired by Trans Empire Oils Ltd. in 1952
Each share Common no par exchanged for (0.033333) share Capital Stock no par
Trans Empire Oils Ltd. name changed to West Canadian Oil & Gas Ltd. 3/10/58 which merged into Canadian Delhi Oil Ltd. 1/1/62 which recapitalized as CanDel Oil Ltd. 1/10/72
(See CanDel Oil Ltd.)

ROXBOROUGH KNITTING MILLS, INC.
Name changed to Roxborough Co. in 1941

ROXBOROUGH TRUST CO. (PHILADELPHIA, PA)
Dissolved 4/20/45
No stockholders' equity

ROXBURY CAP CORP (CANADA)
Merged into Optima Petroleum Corp. (BC) 9/19/95
Each share Common no par exchanged for (0.14285714) share Common no par and (0.14285714) Common Stock Purchase Warrant expiring 2/28/97
Optima Petroleum Corp. (BC) reincorporated in Delaware as Petroquest Energy Inc. 9/1/98

ROXBURY CARPET CO (MA)
Recapitalized 00/00/1941
Each share Preferred no par exchanged for (19) shares Common $1 par
Each share Common no par exchanged for (1) share Common $1 par
Merged into RCC Liquidating, Inc. 06/04/1973
Each share Common $1 par exchanged for $8 cash

ROXBURY STATE BANK (SUCCASUNNA, NJ)
Merged into Peoples National Bank of North Jersey (Denville, NJ) 05/18/1982
Each (3.795) shares Common $2.50 par exchanged for (1) share Common $10 par
Peoples National Bank of North Jersey (Denville, NJ) merged into First Jersey National Corp. 04/01/1985
(See First Jersey National Corp.)

ROXFORD MNG CORP (QC)
Declared dissolved for failure to file reports or pay fees 08/00/1973

ROXI CAP CORP (AB)
Issue Information - 1,500,000 shares COM offered at $0.20 per share on 12/08/1997
Name changed to Advantage Wallsystems, Inc. 11/1/2002
Advantage Wallsystems, Inc. acquired by PFB Corp. 5/2/2003

ROXIO INC (DE)
Name changed to Napster, Inc. 12/23/2004
(See Napster, Inc.)

ROXMARK MINES LTD (ON)
Merged into Goldstone Resources Inc. 12/22/2009
Each (3.75) shares Common no par exchanged for (1) share Common no par
Goldstone Resources Inc. merged into Premier Gold Mines Ltd. 08/16/2011

ROXTON MINING & DEVELOPMENT CO. LTD. (ON)
Charter revoked for failure to file reports and pay fees 1/5/67

ROXY GOLD MINES LTD. (MB)
Charter revoked for failure to file reports and pay fees 12/19/62

ROXY PETE LTD (AB)
Each share Common no par exchanged for (1) share Class A Common no par or Class B Common no par 03/08/1983
Note: Class B Common no par issued share for share to Canadians only
Class A Common no par issued share for share or in combination of stock and cash to non-Canadians
Improperly completed or failure to submit a declaration form by 03/13/1983 will cause the company to use its own discretion in the issuance of stock or cash
Recapitalized as Canadian Roxy Petroleum Ltd. 06/20/1985
Each share Class A Common no par exchanged for (0.33333333) share Common no par
Each share Class B Common no par exchanged for (0.33333333) share Common no par
Canadian Roxy Petroleum Ltd. merged into Numac Energy Inc. 04/01/1994
(See Numac Energy Inc.)

ROXY THEATRE, INC. (NY)
Voluntarily dissolved 5/5/59
Details not available

ROXY VENTURES INC (CO)
Each (27.7778) shares old Common no par exchanged for (1) share new Common no par 09/29/1988
Name changed to FiberOptic Medical Systems, Inc. 05/17/1989
FiberOptic Medical Systems, Inc. merged into FiberChem, Inc. (DE) 11/21/1989 which name changed to DecisionLink, Inc. 12/05/2000
(See DecisionLink, Inc.)

ROY (MILTON) CO. (PA)
See - Milton Roy Co.

ROY ASBESTOS MINES LTD. (ON)
Charter cancelled for failure to file reports and pay taxes in 1969

ROY L MERCHANT GROUP INC (ON)
Name changed to Clairvest Group Inc. 12/19/1991

ROY SILVER MINES LTD. (ON)
Recapitalized as Tiara Mines Ltd. 04/21/1955
Each share Common exchanged for (0.16666666) share Common
Tiara Mines Ltd. recapitalized as Tormont Mines Ltd. 08/04/1961
(See Tormont Mines Ltd.)

ROYAL & SUN ALLIANCE INS GROUP PLC (UNITED KINGDOM)
Each (1.1) old Sponsored ADR's for Ordinary no par exchanged for (1) new Sponsored ADR for Ordinary no par 05/14/1999
ADR agreement terminated 10/30/2006
Each new Sponsored ADR for Ordinary no par exchanged for $14.3302479 cash
Name changed to RSA Insurance Group PLC 05/17/2013

ROYAL ACCEP CORP (DE)
Each share old Common $0.001 par exchanged for (0.05) share new Common $0.001 par 02/19/1998
Recapitalized as Ganas Corp. 03/17/2008
Each share Common $0.001 par exchanged for (0.01) share Common $0.001 par
Ganas Corp. name changed to Green Automotive Company Corp. (DE) 01/28/2010 which reincorporated in Nevada as Green Automotive Co. 09/30/2011

ROYAL ACQUISITION CORP (AB)
Name changed to Invicta Energy Corp. 11/26/2010
Invicta Energy Corp. merged into Whitecap Resources Inc. 05/03/2013

ROYAL ACQUISITIONS & DEV INC (NV)
Recapitalized as Innovative Health Sciences, Inc. (NV) 06/11/2008
Each share Common $0.001 par exchanged for (0.01) share Common $0.001 par
Innovative Health Sciences, Inc. (NV) reincorporated in Delaware 02/24/2011 which name changed to Innovative Holdings Alliance, Inc. 05/27/2011

ROYAL AGASSIZ MINES LTD (MB)
Recapitalized as Agassiz Resources Ltd. 12/14/77
Each share Capital Stock no par exchanged for (0.2) share Capital Stock no par
(See Agassiz Resources Ltd.)

ROYAL ALLIANCE ENTMT INC (NV)
Name changed to Infinity Medical Group, Inc. 06/06/2007
(See Infinity Medical Group, Inc.)

ROYAL AMERICAN CORP. (DE)
Name changed to Royal American Industries, Inc. and Common 50¢ par changed to Common 10¢ par 12/22/1961
(See Royal American Industries, Inc.)

ROYAL AMERN CORP (LA)
Each share Common 20¢ par exchanged for (0.1) share Common $2 par 09/24/1970
Each share Common $2 par exchanged for (0.01) share Common $200 par 10/16/1975
Merged into Midwest Banc Holdings, Inc. 07/03/2006
Each share Common $200 par exchanged for $80 cash

ROYAL AMERN INDS INC (DE)
Each share Common 10¢ par exchanged for (0.1) share Common $1 par 3/15/71
Merged into Bankers Life & Casualty Co. 6/27/75
Each share Common $1 par exchanged for $10.30 cash

ROYAL AMERICAN LIFE INSURANCE CO. (IN)
Merged into First United Life Insurance Co. on a (0.5) for (1) basis 12/31/62
First United Life Insurance Co. reorganized as First United, Inc. 2/25/70
(See First United, Inc.)

ROYAL AMERN MNG PPTYS LTD (NV)
Recapitalized as Capita Research Group, Inc. 01/30/1998
Each share Common no par exchanged for (2) shares Common no par
(See Capita Research Group, Inc.)

ROYAL AMERICAN OIL CO. LTD. (AB)
Capital Stock no par reclassified as Class B no par 1/12/63
Recapitalized as Royal American Petroleums Ltd. on a (0.5) for (1) basis 4/1/63
Royal American Petroleums Ltd. acquired by Manhattan Continental Development Corp. 10/2/69
(See Manhattan Continental Development Corp.)

ROYAL AMERN PETES LTD (AB)
Acquired by Manhattan Continental Development Corp. 10/2/69
Each share Class B no par exchanged for (0.6468) share Common 10¢ par
(See Manhattan Continental Development Corp.)

ROYAL APEX SILVER INC (NV)
Reincorporated 06/17/1986
State of incorporation changed from (ID) to (NV) 06/17/1986
Merged into Coeur d'Alene Mines Corp. (ID) 03/08/1988
Each (5.45) shares Common 5¢ par exchanged for (1) share Common $1 par
Coeur d'Alene Mines Corp. (ID) reincorporated in Delaware as Coeur Mining, Inc. 05/17/2013

ROYAL APPLIANCE MFG CO (OH)
Merged into TechTronic Industries Co., Ltd. 4/23/2003
Each share Common no par exchanged for $7.37 cash

ROYAL ARCH OILS LTD. (AB)
Struck off register for failure to file annual returns 6/30/56

ROYAL ATLAS CORP (NY)
Dissolved by proclamation 9/30/81

ROYAL AVIATION INC (CANADA)
Acquired by Canada 3000 Inc. 5/4/2001
Each share Common no par exchanged for (0.4) share Common no par

ROYAL BAFOKENG PLATINUM LTD (SOUTH AFRICA)
ADR agreement terminated 04/19/2018
No ADR's remain outstanding

ROYAL BAKING POWDER CO.
Merged into Standard Brands, Inc. in 1937
(See Standard Brands, Inc.)

ROYAL BANCSHARES PA INC (PA)
Stock Dividends - In Class A Common to holders of Class A Common 6% payable 05/10/1996 to holders of record 04/18/1996; 4% payable 05/08/1997 to holders of record 04/28/1997; 4% payable 05/08/1998 to holders of record 05/01/1998; 4% payable 05/14/1999 to holders of record 05/03/1999; 5% payable 01/17/2000 to holders of record 01/03/2000; 5% payable 02/12/2001 to holders of record 01/29/2001 Ex date - 01/25/2001; 6% payable 02/08/2002 to holders of record 01/28/2002 Ex date - 01/24/2002; 3% payable 02/12/2003 to holders of record 01/29/2003 Ex date - 01/27/2003; 2% payable 02/18/2004 to holders of record 02/04/2004 Ex date - 02/02/2004; 2% payable 01/12/2005 to holders of record 12/29/2004 Ex date - 12/27/2004; 2% payable 01/17/2006 to holders of record 01/04/2006 Ex date - 12/30/2005; 5% payable 01/17/2007 to holders of record 01/03/2007 Ex date - 12/29/2006; In Class B common to holders of Class B Common 4% payable 05/08/1998 to holders of record 05/01/1998; 4% payable 05/14/1999 to holders of record 05/03/1999; 5% payable 01/17/2000 to holders of record 01/03/2000; 5% payable 02/12/2001 to holders of record 01/29/2001 Ex date - 01/25/2001; 6% payable 02/08/2002 to holders of record 01/28/2002 Ex date - 01/24/2002; 3% payable 02/12/2003 to holders of record 01/29/2003 Ex date - 01/27/2003; 2% payable 02/18/2004 to holders of record 02/04/2004 Ex date - 02/02/2004; 2% payable 01/12/2005 to holders of record 12/29/2004 Ex date - 12/27/2004; 2% payable 01/17/2006 to holders of record 01/04/2006 Ex date - 12/30/2005; 5% payable 01/17/2007 to holders of record 01/03/2007 Ex date - 12/29/2006
Merged into Bryn Mawr Bank Corp. 12/15/2017
Each share Class A Common $2 par exchanged for (0.1025) share Common $1 par
Each share Class B Common 10¢ par exchanged for (0.1179) share Common $1 par

ROYAL BANK & TRUST CO. (LOUISVILLE, KY)
Merged into Bank of Louisville-Royal Bank & Trust Co. 8/6/63
Each share Capital Stock $10 par exchanged for (1) share Common $10 par
Bank of Louisville-Royal Bank & Trust Co. name changed to Bank of Louisville & Trust Co. (Louisville, Ky.) 3/26/80 which reorganized as Mid-America Bancorp 3/25/83

ROYAL BK CDA (MONTREAL, QC)
$2.75 Conv. 2nd Preferred Ser. A no par called for redemption 12/12/1988
$1.88 1st Preferred Ser. A no par called for redemption 12/06/1991
$1.45 1st Preferred Ser. B no par called for redemption 07/31/1995
Floating Rate 1st Preferred Ser. C no par called for redemption 00/00/1996
Floating Rate 1st Preferred Ser. D no par called for redemption 00/00/1996
Adjustable Dividend 1st Preferred Ser. F no par called for redemption at $25 on 10/31/1999
Adjustable Dividend 1st Preferred Ser. G no par called for redemption at $25 on 10/31/1999
Adjustable Dividend 1st Preferred Ser. H no par called for redemption at $25 on 08/24/2001
1st Preferred Ser. I called for redemption at $25 plus $0.015668 accrued dividend on 11/26/2001
Floating Rate 1st Preferred Ser. E no par called for redemption at $100 on 10/11/2002
Adjustable Dividend 1st Preferred Ser. J called for redemption at $25 plus $0.014589 accrued dividend on 05/26/2003
Adjustable Dividend 1st Preferred Ser. K called for redemption at $25 plus $0.012945 accrued dividend on 05/26/2003
5.75% US$ 1st Preference Ser. P called for redemption at $25.75 plus $0.177226 accrued dividends on 10/07/2005
Non-Cum. 1st Preferred Ser. S called for redemption at $26 plus $0.183836 accrued dividends on 10/06/2006
5.5% 1st Preference Ser. O called for redemption at $25.50 plus $0.34375 accrued dividends on 11/24/2006
1st Preferred Ser. N no par called for redemption at $25 plus $0.29375 accrued dividends on 08/22/2008
Non-Cum. 1st Preferred Ser. AH no par called for redemption at $26 plus $0.150925 accrued dividends on 07/02/2013
Non-Cum. 5-Year Rate Reset Preferred 1st Preferred Ser. AN no par called for redemption at $25 plus $0.390625 accrued dividends on 02/24/2014
Non-Cum. 5-Year Rate Reset Preferred 1st Preferred Ser. AP no par called for redemption at $25 plus $0.390625 accrued dividends on 02/24/2014
Non-Cum. 5-Yr. Rate Reset Preferred 1st Preferred Ser. AR no par called for redemption at $25 plus $0.390625 accrued dividends on 02/24/2014
Non-Cum. 5-Yr. Rate Reset Preferred Ser. AT no par called for redemption at $25 on 08/24/2014
Non-Cum. 5-Yr. Rate Reset Preferred Ser. AV no par called for redemption at $25 on 08/24/2014
Non-Cum. 5-Yr. Rate Reset Preferred Ser. AX no par called for redemption at $25 plus $0.38125 accrued dividends on 11/24/2014
Non-Cum. 1st Preferred Ser. AB no par called for redemption at $25 plus $0.109452 accrued dividends on 09/27/2017
(Additional Information in Active)

ROYAL BK GROUP INC (MI)
Stock Dividends - 10% 12/10/85; 10% 12/15/86; 10% 10/1/91
Acquired by Citizens Banking Corp. 10/1/93
Each share Common $10 par exchanged for either (2.0072) shares Common $10 par or $39.14 cash

ROYAL BK PA (KING OF PRUSSIA, PA)
Common $10 par changed to $2 par and (4) additional shares issued 05/15/1982
Common $2 par reclassified as Class A Common $2 par 08/31/1984
Stock Dividends - Common 15% 03/21/1984; in Class B Common to holders of Class A Common 50% 09/28/1984; 15% 03/29/1985; in Class A Common - 60% 06/28/1985; 10% 04/04/1986; in Class B Common - 60% 06/28/1985
Under plan of reorganization each share Class A Common $2 par automatically became (1) share

Royal Bancshares of Pennsylvania, Inc. Class A Common $2 par and (1) share Class B Common 10¢ par 06/29/1995
Royal Bancshares of Pennsylvania, Inc. merged into Bryn Mawr Bank Corp. 12/15/2017

ROYAL BK SCOTLAND GROUP PLC (UNITED KINGDOM)
ADR agreement terminated 10/16/1996
Each Sponsored ADR for Preference Ser. A exchanged for $25.84 cash
Sponsored ADR's for Preference Ser. B called for redemption at $25 on 01/30/2003
Sponsored ADR's for Preference Ser. C called for redemption at $25 on 01/30/2003
Each share 5.75% Exchangeable Capital Security Ser. B exchanged for (1) Sponsored ADR for Preference Ser. L 09/30/2004
Sponsored ADR's for Preference Ser. 2 called for redemption at $1,000 on 03/31/2005
Sponsored ADR's for Ser. J Preference called for redemption at $25 on 11/28/2005
Exchangeable Capital Securities Ser. A 1¢ par called for redemption at $25 on 12/31/2005
Sponsored ADR's for Ser. D Preference called for redemption at $25 plus $0.3764 accrued dividends on 03/06/2006
Sponsored ADR's for Ser. I Preference called for redemption at $25 plus $0.3667 accrued dividends on 03/06/2006
Sponsored ADR's for Ser. K Non-Cumulative Preference called for redemption at $25 plus $0.082 accrued dividends on 12/14/2006
Sponsored ADR's for Ser. E Preference called for redemption at $25 plus $0.0844 accrued dividends on 01/16/2007
Sponsored ADR's for Ser. G Preference called for redemption at $25 plus $0.0771 accrued dividends on 01/16/2007
Sponsored ADR's for Ser. M Preference called for redemption at $25 plus $0.275556 accrued dividends on 09/01/2015
Sponsored ADR's for Ser. N Preference called for redemption at $25 plus $0.273403 accrued dividends on 09/01/2015
Sponsored ADR's for Ser. P Preference called for redemption at $25 plus $0.269097 accrued dividends on 09/01/2015
Sponsored ADR's for Ser. Q Preference called for redemption at $25 plus $0.290625 accrued dividends on 09/01/2015
ADR's for Ser. R Preference called for redemption at $25 plus $0.361545 accrued dividends on 09/23/2016
Sponsored ADR's for Ser. T Preference called for redemption at $25 plus $0.422916 accrued dividends on 09/23/2016
Sponsored ADR's for Ser. F Preference called for redemption at $25 plus $0.377778 accrued dividends on 09/04/2017
Sponsored ADR's for Ser. H Preference called for redemption at $25 plus $0.322222 accrued dividends on 09/04/2017
Sponsored ADR's for Ser. L Preference called for redemption at $25 plus $0.255556 accrued dividends on 09/04/2017
(Additional Information in Active)

ROYAL BAY GOLD CORP (BC)
Recapitalized as Featherstone Resources Ltd. 07/08/1998
Each share Common no par exchanged for (1/3) share Common no par
Featherstone Resources Ltd. recapitalized as Newcastle Minerals Ltd. 05/03/2002 which recapitalized as GoldON Resources Ltd. 03/07/2013

ROYAL BLUE EXPL INC (NV)
Name changed to CH4 Energy, Inc. 06/09/2004
CH4 Energy, Inc. recapitalized as High Sierra Acquisitions Inc. 04/17/2014 which name changed to Anasazi Energy Corp. 11/20/2014 which name changed to Solar Quartz Technologies, Inc. 12/19/2016

ROYAL BODYCARE INC (NV)
Name changed to RBC Life Sciences, Inc. 06/19/2006

ROYAL BUSINESS FORMS INC (NH)
Recapitalized 06/24/1968
Each share Class A Common $1 par exchanged for (1) share Common $1 par
Each share Class B Common $1 par exchanged for (2) shares Common $1 par
Each share Class C Common $1 par exchanged for (5) shares Common $1 par
Common $1 par split (3) for (2) by issuance of (0.5) additional share 01/25/1971
Common $1 par split (3) for (2) by issuance of (0.5) additional share 10/25/1973
Common $1 par split (3) for (2) by issuance of (0.5) additional share 10/29/1974
Name changed to Royal Business Group Inc. 10/29/1982
(See Royal Business Group Inc.)

ROYAL BUSINESS GROUP INC (NH)
Dissolved 11/3/97

ROYAL CDN MINT (CANADA)
Name changed to Royal Canadian Mint - Canadian Gold Reserves 08/13/2014

ROYAL CANADIAN OILS LTD. (AB)
Recapitalized as Royal Canadian Ventures Ltd. in 1956
Each share Capital Stock no par exchanged for (0.1) share Capital Stock no par
Royal Canadian Ventures Ltd. liquidated for Pan Ocean Oil Corp. 1/1/72
(See Pan Ocean Oil Corp.)

ROYAL CDN VENTURES LTD (AB)
Completely liquidated 01/01/1972
Each share Capital Stock no par exchanged for first and final distribution of (0.0967) share Pan Ocean Oil Corp. Common 1¢ par
(See Pan Ocean Oil Corp.)

ROYAL CAP CORP (DE)
Recapitalized as E.N. Phillips Co. 03/31/1989
Each share Common $0.0001 par exchanged for (0.01) share Common 1¢ par
E.N. Phillips Co. name changed to Nuoasis Gaming, Inc. 09/30/1994 which name changed to Group V Corp. 06/12/1997 which name changed to TotalAxcess.com, Inc. 05/17/1999
(See TotalAxcess.com, Inc.)

ROYAL CAP CORP (NY)
Name changed to Atlantech Resources Corp. 02/12/1992
Atlantech Resources Corp. name changed to Elderpower.com, Inc. 11/05/1999

ROYAL CASINO GROUP INC (UT)
Each share old Common no par exchanged for (0.05) share new Common no par 03/20/1995
Name changed to E-Commerce West Corp. 07/31/1998
E-Commerce West Corp. recapitalized as Interactive Broadcasting Network Group Inc. 01/28/2002 which name changed to Baymark Technologies Inc. 08/30/2002 which name changed to Implantable Vision, Inc. 01/03/2006 which name changed to Arcland Energy Corp. 08/25/2008
(See Arcland Energy Corp.)

ROYAL CASTLE SYS INC (FL)
In process of liquidation
Each share Common $1 par received initial distribution of $0.75 cash 8/20/75
Each share Common $1 par received second distribution of $0.75 cash 12/1/75
Each share Common $1 par received third distribution of $0.75 cash 2/27/76
Each share Common $1 par received fourth distribution of $1.25 cash 6/25/76
Each share Common $1 par received fifth distribution of $1 cash 10/1/76
Each share Common $1 par received sixth distribution of $1 cash 1/5/77
Each share Common $1 par received seventh distribution of $1 cash 10/17/77
Each share Common $1 par received eighth distribution of $0.795 cash 12/10/79
Note: Details on subsequent distributions, if any, are not available

ROYAL CHINA INC (OH)
Merged into Jeannette Glass Co. 12/28/1969
Each share Non-Cum. Preferred $2.50 par or Preferred $50 par exchanged for (2) shares Common $1 par
Each share Common $2.50 par exchanged for (0.142856) share Common $1 par
Note: Actual basis for Common was (0.178571) but (0.035715) issued directly to attorneys as legal fees
Jeannette Glass Co. name changed to Jeannette Corp. 05/14/1971
(See Jeannette Corp.)

ROYAL COACH INC (DE)
Merged into Aetna Life & Casualty Co. 2/29/72
Each share Common 10¢ par exchanged for $2.50 cash

ROYAL CONCORDE CAP INC (AB)
Recapitalized as Pacific Concorde Capital Inc. 11/28/94
Each share Common no par exchanged for (1/3) share Common no par

ROYAL CORP. (NV)
Charter revoked for failure to file reports and pay fees 3/4/63

ROYAL CNTY MINERALS CORP (BC)
Acquired by International Curator Resources Ltd. 08/01/2003
Each share Common no par exchanged for (4) shares Common no par
International Curator Resources Ltd. recapitalized as Canadian Gold Hunter Corp. (BC) 12/30/2003 which reincorporated in Canada 07/29/2004 which name changed to NGEx Resources Inc. 09/22/2009

ROYAL CR CO (FL)
Merged into Fenco Industries, Inc. 2/20/80
Each share Common 1¢ par exchanged for (2) shares Common $0.005 par
(See Fenco Industries, Inc.)

ROYAL CROWN BOTTLING CO LOUISVILLE (KY)
5% Preferred $10 par called for redemption 04/01/1963
Stock Dividend - 100% 08/11/1964
Acquired by Beatrice Foods Co. 02/23/1971
Each share Common $1 par exchanged for (1.956832) shares Common no par
Beatrice Foods Co. name changed to Beatrice Companies, Inc. 06/05/1984
(See Beatrice Companies, Inc.)

ROYAL CROWN BOTTLING CO NEWARK INC (NJ)
Name changed to Hoffman Products, Inc. 04/30/1969
(See Hoffman Products, Inc.)

ROYAL CROWN COS INC (DE)
Name changed 03/07/1978
Common $1 par split (3) for (1) by issuance of (2) additional shares 08/21/1964
Common $1 par split (3) for (2) by issuance of (0.5) additional share 03/03/1969
Name changed from Royal Crown Cola Co. to Royal Crown Companies, Inc. 03/07/1978
Merged into Chesapeake Financial Corp. 06/30/1984
Each share Common $1 par exchanged for $40 cash

ROYAL CRYSTAL RES LTD (BC)
Recapitalized as Eracon Industries Inc. 12/10/91
Each share Common no par exchanged for (0.25) share Common no par
Eracon Industries Inc. name changed to Zcomm Industries, Inc. 6/2/93 which recapitalized as Labrador International Mining Ltd. 8/25/95 which recapitalized as Royal International Venture Corp. 3/18/99 which recapitalized as RCOM Venture Corp. 7/28/2000 which name changed to Wellstar Energy Corp. 7/21/2005

ROYAL DAWN, INC. (UT)
Name changed to Osage Hills Energy Co. 11/18/82
(See Osage Hills Energy Co.)

ROYAL DEVELOPMENT CO., INC.
Liquidation completed 08/00/1949
Stockholders who filed a claim prior to 07/27/1949 received distributions totalling $1.0541 cash per share

ROYAL DUTCH CO. FOR THE WORKING OF PETROLEUM WELLS IN NETHERLANDS-INDIES
Name changed to Royal Dutch Petroleum Co. in 1949
Royal Dutch Petroleum Co. merged into Royal Dutch Shell plc 7/20/2005

ROYAL DUTCH PETE CO (NETHERLANDS)
Ordinary Shares 50 Gldrs. par changed to 20 Gldrs. par and (1.5) additional shares issued 12/14/56
Each New York Reg. for Ordinary 20 Gldrs. par exchanged for (2) New York Reg. for Ordinary 10 Gldrs. par 3/2/81
Each New York Reg. for Ordinary 10 Gldrs. par exchanged for (2) New York Reg. for Ordinary 5 Gldrs. par 1/18/89
Each (3) New York Shares for Ordinary 33-1/3 Gldrs. par exchanged for (20) New York Reg. for Ordinary 5 Gldrs. par 12/31/90
Each New York Share for Ordinary 5 Gldrs. par exchanged for (4) New York Reg. for Ordinary 1.25 Gldrs. par 6/30/97
New York Reg. for Ordinary 1.25 Gldrs. par changed to Euro 0.56 par 6/3/2002
Stock Dividends - 20% Ordinary Shares 6/30/54, New York Shares 9/3/54; 10% Ordinary Shares 5/18/61; New York Shares 6/23/61; (1/3) New York Reg. 20 Gldrs. par

for each New York Ordinary 33-1/3 Gldrs. par 4/3/64, 20% New York Reg. 20 Gldrs. par 4/3/64; (1/6) New York Reg. 20 Gldrs. par for each New York Ordinary 33-1/3 Gldrs. par 4/19/68, 10% New York Reg. 20 Gldrs. par 4/9/68, 12-1/2% New York Reg. for Ordinary 20 Gldrs. par 12/17/68; (1) New York Share for Ordinary 20 Gldrs. par for each (4.8) New York Shares for Ordinary 33-1/3 Gldrs. par 1/6/69; 11-1/9% New York Reg. for Ordinary 20 Gldrs. par 12/29/69, (1) New York Share for Ordinary 20 Gldrs. par for each (5.4) New York Shares for Ordinary 33-1/3 Gldrs. par 1/16/70
Merged into Royal Dutch Shell plc 12/21/2005
Each New York Registry Share Euro 0.56 par exchanged for $61.8585 cash

ROYAL ECOPRODUCTS LTD (ON)
Merged into Royal Group Technologies Ltd. 7/23/98
Each share Subordinate no par exchanged for (0.1) share Subordinate no par
(See Royal Group Technologies Ltd.)

ROYAL ELECTRO-TYPE CO. (PA)
Liquidation completed
Each share Capital Stock no par exchanged for initial distribution of $15 cash 01/14/1965
Each share Capital Stock no par received second and final distribution of $8.29 cash 08/31/1965

ROYAL ENERGY INC (MN)
Name changed to En/Drill America, Inc. 6/1/92
En/Drill America, Inc. merged into Jaguar Group Ltd. 12/31/94 which name changed to Tech Squared Inc. 5/9/95 which assets were transferred to Tech Squared Liquidating Trust 12/17/99
(See Tech Squared Liquidating Trust)

ROYAL EQUINE ALLIANCE CORP (NV)
Name changed to Gold Holdings Corp. 02/22/2010
Gold Holdings Corp. name changed to Ocean Electric Inc. 01/27/2012

ROYAL EQUITY EXCHANGE INC (NV)
Each share old Common $0.001 par exchanged for (0.25) share new Common $0.001 par 04/10/1996
Name changed to Procare America, Inc. 11/04/1998
Procare America, Inc. name changed to Indigo-Energy, Inc. 01/20/2006 which name changed to HDIMAX MEDIA, Inc. 12/19/2014 which name changed to Zonzia Media, Inc. 03/09/2015

ROYAL EXECUTIVE INNS AMER INC (NV)
Name changed to Rinn Corp. 03/01/1972
Rinn Corp. recapitalized as Sun Fruit, Ltd. 05/09/1974
(See Sun Fruit, Ltd.)

ROYAL FIN CORP (NJ)
Reincorporated under the laws of Delaware as Royal Acceptance Corp. 01/02/1997
Royal Acceptance Corp. recapitalized as Ganas Corp. 03/17/2008 which name changed to Green Automotive Company Corp. (DE) 01/28/2010 which reincorporated in Nevada as Green Automotive Co. 09/30/2011

ROYAL FIN INC (FL)
Recapitalized as Bio Standard Corp. 05/24/2002
Each share Common 1¢ par exchanged for (0.1) share Common 1¢ par
Bio Standard Corp. name changed to Nettel Holdings, Inc. 05/23/2003
(See Nettel Holdings, Inc.)

ROYAL FINL CORP (NV)
Recapitalized as Patriot Motorcycle Corp. 07/16/2001
Each share Common $0.001 par exchanged for (0.1) share Common $0.001 par
(See Patriot Motorcycle Corp.)

ROYAL GEN CORP (NY)
Dissolved by proclamation 9/25/91

ROYAL GOLD & SILVER CORP. (ON)
Name changed to Royal Gold Enterprises Inc. 06/16/1988
Royal Gold Enterprises Inc. name changed to Trenton Industries, Inc. 02/11/1993
(See Trenton Industries, Inc.)

ROYAL GOLD ENTERPRISES INC (ON)
Name changed to Trenton Industries, Inc. 02/11/1993
(See Trenton Industries, Inc.)

ROYAL GOLD INC (DE)
Each share 7.25% Mandatory Convertible Preferred 1¢ par exchanged for (3.4589) shares Common 1¢ par 03/10/2008
(Additional Information in Active)

ROYAL GRIP INC (NV)
Merged into Royal Precision, Inc. 8/29/97
Each share Common $0.001 par exchanged for (0.5) share Common $0.001 par
(See Royal Precision, Inc.)

ROYAL GROUP TECHNOLOGIES LTD (CANADA)
Subordinate Shares no par reclassified as Common no par 7/5/2005
Merged into Georgia Gulf Corp. 10/3/2006
Each share Common no par exchanged for $13 cash

ROYAL HAWAIIAN ORCHARDS L P (DE)
Each old Class A Depositary Unit exchanged for (1) new Class A Depositary Unit to reflect a (1) for (2,000) reverse split followed by a (2,000) for (1) forward split 06/13/2018
Note: Holders of (1,999) or fewer pre-split Units received $2.41 cash per Unit
Name changed to Hawaiian Macadamia Nut Orchards, L.P. 10/17/2018

ROYAL HOLIDAY MOBILE ESTATES INC (NV)
SEC revoked common stock registration 01/08/2008
Stockholders' equity unlikely

ROYAL HOST INC (CANADA)
Merged into Holloway Lodging Corp. 07/07/2014
Each share Common no par exchanged for (0.1) share Common no par and $1 cash
Note: Unexchanged certificates will be cancelled and become without value 07/07/2020

ROYAL HOST REAL ESTATE INVT TR (AB)
Each Installment Receipt no par exchanged for (1) Trust Unit no par 11/02/1998
Reorganized under the laws of Canada as Royal Host Inc. 01/04/2011
Each Trust Unit no par exchanged for (1) share Common no par
Note: Unexchanged certificates were cancelled and became without value 01/04/2017
Royal Host Inc. merged into Holloway Lodging Corp. 07/07/2014

ROYAL HOTELS, INC. (CA)
Completely liquidated 1/27/77

Each share Capital Stock $1 par exchanged for first and final distribution of $1.506692 cash

ROYAL INDUSTRIAL BANK (NEW YORK, NY)
Each share Capital Stock $66-2/3 par exchanged for (6-2/3) shares Capital Stock $10 par in 1945
Capital Stock $10 par changed to $5 par in 1950
Name changed to Royal State Bank of New York (New York, NY) 6/1/54
Royal State Bank of New York (New York, NY) name changed to Royal National Bank (New York, NY) 11/30/62 which merged into Security National Bank (Hempstead, NY) 5/8/72
(See Security National Bank (Hempstead, NY))

ROYAL INDS INC (DE)
Name changed 5/15/67
Reincorporated 11/25/68
Common $1 par split (2) for (1) by issuance of (1) additional share 8/22/68
Stock Dividends - 10% 3/1/68; 10% 11/11/74
Name changed from Royal Industries, Inc. to Royal Industries 5/15/67
Name changed and state of incorporation changed from Royal Industries (CA) to Royal Industries, Inc. (DE) 11/25/68
Merged into Lear Siegler, Inc. 2/18/77
Each share Common $1 par exchanged for $13.50 cash

ROYAL INNS AMER INC (CA)
Common no par split (2) for (1) by issuance of (1) additional share 12/18/67
Common no par split (2) for (1) by issuance of (1) additional share 10/31/68
Plan of reorganization under Chapter X Federal Bankruptcy Act confirmed 10/24/79
No stockholders' equity

ROYAL INTL OPTICAL CORP (TX)
Common 10¢ par split (3) for (2) by issuance of (0.5) additional share 03/07/1985
Common Stock Purchase Rights declared for Common stockholders of record 12/29/1987 were redeemed at $0.01 per right 02/15/1990 for holders of record 01/26/1990
Merged into Royal International Optical Corp. (DE) 06/28/1990
Each share Common 10¢ par exchanged for (1) share Common 1¢ par
(See Royal International Optical Corp. (DE))

ROYAL INTL OPTICAL INC (DE)
Each share old Common 1¢ par exchanged for (0.001) share new Common 1¢ par 6/1/95
Note: In effect holders received $1.25 cash per share and public interest was eliminated

ROYAL INTL VENTURE CORP (BC)
Recapitalized as RCOM Venture Corp. 7/28/2000
Each share Common no par exchanged for (0.2) share Common no par
RCOM Venture Corp. which name changed to Wellstar Energy Corp. 7/21/2005

ROYAL KPN N V (NETHERLANDS)
Name changed 07/15/1998
ADR agreement terminated 03/28/1997
Each 144A Sponsored ADR for Ordinary NLG 10 par exchanged for $34.9397 cash
Each Sponsored ADR for Ordinary NLG 10 par received distribution of (1) TNT Post Group N.V. Sponsored ADR for Ordinary NLG 1 par payable 06/29/1998 to holders of record 06/26/1998 Ex date - 06/30/1998
Name changed from Royal PTT Nederland N.V. to Royal KPN N.V. 07/15/1998
(Additional Information in Active)

ROYAL LASER CORP (AB)
Acquired by M&A Acquisition Corp. 06/16/2010
Each share Common no par exchanged for $0.47 cash

ROYAL LASER TECH CORP (ON)
Name changed to Martinrea International Inc. 6/28/2002

ROYAL LD & DEV CORP (DE)
Each share Class A Common 10¢ par exchanged for (0.2) share Class A Common 50¢ par 11/26/62
Each share Class A Common 50¢ par exchanged for (0.2) share Class A Common $2.50 par 5/20/68
Each share Class A Common $2.50 par exchanged for (0.04) share Class A Common $62.50 par 6/5/74
Each share Class A Common $62.50 par exchanged for (0.1) share Class A Common $625 par 10/7/78
Note: In effect holders received $170 cash per share and public interest was eliminated

ROYAL LEPAGE CAP PPTYS (ON)
In process of liquidation
Each Unit of Ltd. Partnership exchanged for initial distribution of $3.06 cash 11/14/1988
Each Unit of Ltd. Partnership received second distribution of $22.80 cash 11/14/1988
Note: Details on subsequent distributions, if any, are not available

ROYAL LEPAGE FRANCHISE SVCS FD (ON)
Name changed to Brookfield Real Estate Services Fund 10/31/2007
Brookfield Real Estate Services Fund reorganized as Brookfield Real Estate Services Inc. 01/04/2011

ROYAL LEPAGE LTD (ON)
Each share old Common no par exchanged for (0.33333333) share new Common no par 04/27/1998
Acquired by Trilon Financial Corp. 04/30/1999
Each share new Common no par exchanged for (0.5) Class A Common Stock Purchase Warrant expiring 02/28/2002 and $4.75 cash

ROYAL LIFESCIENCE CORP (BC)
Each share old Common no par exchanged for (0.4) share new Common no par 08/18/2016
Name changed to Rover Metals Corp. 06/29/2018

ROYAL-MCBEE CORP. (NY)
5% Preferred Ser. B $100 par called for redemption 10/31/64
5-1/2% Preferred Ser. C $100 par called for redemption 10/31/64
6% Preferred Ser. D $100 par called for redemption 10/31/64
Merged into Litton Industries, Inc. 2/28/65
Each share Common $1 par exchanged for (0.16875) share $3 Ser. A Convertible Preferred $5 par
Each share 4-1/2% A Preferred $100 par exchanged for (1) share $3 Ser. A Convertible Preferred $5 par
(See Litton Industries, Inc.)

ROYAL MILLENNIA GROUP LTD (NV)
Recapitalized as Viper International Holdings Ltd. 08/05/1998
Each share Common 1¢ par exchanged for (1/3) share Common 1¢ par
Viper International Holdings Ltd. name changed to 50on.com, Inc. 06/13/2000 which reorganized as

Design Marketing Concepts Inc. 10/31/2000 which name changed to WEB Pay-Per-View Inc. 05/30/2001 which name changed to U.S. Federal Financial Corp. 09/25/2001 which name changed to Vibe Records Inc. 04/23/2002 which name changed to Great Entertainment & Sports Inc. 03/07/2003 which name changed to Rockit!, Inc. 06/11/2007
(See Rockit!, Inc.)

ROYAL MILLING CO.
Acquired by General Mills, Inc. in 1928

ROYAL MINERALS INC (UT)
Each share Common $0.0001 par exchanged for (0.2) share Common 1¢ par 02/17/1992
Recapitalized as Consolidated Royal Mines Inc. 03/29/1994
Each share Common 1¢ par exchanged for (0.25) share Common 1¢ par
Consolidated Royal Mines Inc. name changed to Royal Silver Mines, Inc. 08/08/1995 which recapitalized as Cadence Resources Corp. 06/01/2001 which name changed to Aurora Oil & Gas Corp. 05/24/2006
(See Aurora Oil & Gas Corp.)

ROYAL MINES, CORP. (ID)
Merged into Royal Apex Silver, Inc. (ID) 05/26/1969
Each share Capital Stock 10¢ par exchanged for (0.6) share Common 5¢ par
Royal Apex Silver, Inc. (ID) reincorporated in Nevada 06/17/1986 which merged into Coeur D'Alene Mines Corp. (ID) 03/08/1988 which reincorporated in Delaware as Coeur Mining, Inc. 05/17/2013

ROYAL MINING CORP. (QC)
Charter cancelled for failure to file reports and pay fees 2/7/76

ROYAL MONASHEE GOLD CORP. (BC)
Name changed to Plus8 Global Ventures, Ltd. 11/07/2012
Plus8 Global Ventures, Ltd. name changed to ParcelPal Technology Inc. 03/22/2016

ROYAL MOTOR CAR CO (NJ)
Charter forfeited and declared void for non-payment of taxes in 1928

ROYAL NATL BK (NEW YORK, NY)
Merged into Security National Bank (Hempstead, NY) 5/8/72
Each share Capital Stock $5 par exchanged for (0.714285) share Common $5 par
(See Security National Bank (Hempstead, NY))

ROYAL NEDLLOYD N V (NETHERLANDS)
Name changed 6/7/95
ADR's for Ordinary 50 Gldrs. par split (5) for (1) by issuance of (4) additional ADR's 8/14/89
Each Unsponsored ADR for Ordinary 50 Gldrs. par exchanged for (0.4) Sponsored ADR for Ordinary 50 Gldrs. par 11/15/89
Name changed from Royal Nedlloyd Group N.V. to Royal Nedlloyd N.V. 6/7/95
Name changed to Royal P&O Nedlloyd N.V. 4/16/2004
(See Royal P&O Nedlloyd N.V.)

ROYAL NET, INC. (UT)
Reorganized under the laws of Nevada as Seychelle Environmental Technologies, Inc. 1/30/98
Each share Common $0.001 par exchanged for (0.2) share Common $0.001 par

ROYAL OAK DAIRY LTD (ON)
Each share old Class B no par exchanged for (1) share Common no par and (5) shares new Class B no par 05/11/1973
Merged into Execsil Corp. 12/27/1978
Each share Common no par exchanged for $10 cash
Each share Class A no par exchanged for $24 cash
Each share new Class B no par exchanged for $4 cash

ROYAL OAK MINES INC (ON)
Recapitalized as Royal Oak Ventures Inc. 02/14/2000
Each share Common no par exchanged for (0.01) share Common no par
(See Royal Oak Ventures Inc.)

ROYAL OAK RES CORP (UT)
Each share old Common $0.001 par exchanged for (0.5) share new Common $0.001 par 07/14/1995
Reincorporated under the laws of Delaware as Hitcom Corp. 12/01/1995
(See Hitcom Corp.)

ROYAL OAK RES LTD (AB)
Merged into Royal Oak Mines Inc. 07/23/1991
Each share Common no par exchanged for (0.83333333) share Common no par
Royal Oak Mines Inc. recapitalized as Royal Oak Ventures Inc. 02/14/2000
(See Royal Oak Ventures Inc.)

ROYAL OAK SAVINGS & LOAN ASSOCIATION (CA)
Placed in conservatorship 04/00/1989
Stockholders' equity unlikely

ROYAL OAK VENTURES INC (ON)
Acquired by Brookfield Asset Management Inc. 01/02/2014
Each share Common no par exchanged for $0.15 cash
Each Non-Vtg. Share no par exchanged for $0.15 cash
Note: Unexchanged certificates were cancelled and became without value 01/02/2016

ROYAL OIL & GAS CO. (CO)
Declared defunct and inoperative for failure to pay franchise taxes 10/26/60

ROYAL OLYMPIC CRUISE LINES INC (LIBERIA)
Issue Information - 6,100,000 shares COM offered at $15 per share on 02/04/1998
Filed for protection in the Greek Court pursuant to Article 45 on 01/27/2004
Stockholders' equity unlikely

ROYAL OPER CORP (NY)
Completely liquidated 11/12/1981
Each share Common 10¢ par exchanged for first and final distribution of $0.30 cash

ROYAL P & O NEDLLOYD N V (NETHERLANDS)
ADR agreement terminated 12/8/2004
Each Sponsored ADR for Ordinary 50 Guilders par exchanged for $34.347 cash

ROYAL PAC RES INC (NV)
Recapitalized as Great American Family Parks, Inc. 02/03/2004
Each share Common no par exchanged for (1/6) share Common no par
Great American Family Parks, Inc. name changed to Parks! America, Inc. 06/25/2008

ROYAL PAC SEA FARMS LTD (BC)
Struck from the register and dissolved 04/24/1992

ROYAL PALM BANCORP INC (FL)
Merged into Mercantile Bancorp, Inc. 11/13/2006
Each share Common $5 par exchanged for $25.32 cash
Note: An additional $0.18 cash per share is being held in escrow for possible future distribution

ROYAL PALM BK FL (NAPLES, FL)
Under plan of reorganization each share Common automatically became (1) share Royal Palm Bancorp, Inc. Common $5 par 06/02/2003
(See Royal Palm Bancorp, Inc.)

ROYAL PALM BEACH COLONY INC (FL)
Common 10¢ par split (2) for (1) by issuance of (1) additional share 11/15/69
Reorganized under the laws of Delaware and assets transferred to Royal Palm Beach Colony, Limited Partnership 7/11/85
Each share Common 10¢ par exchanged for (1) Unit of Ltd. Partnership
(See Royal Palm Beach Colony, Limited Partnership)

ROYAL PALM BEACH COLONY L P (DE)
Liquidation completed
Each Unit of Ltd. Partnership received initial distribution of $0.25 cash 04/15/1986
Each Unit of Ltd. Partnership received second distribution of $0.35 cash 08/15/1986
Each Unit of Ltd. Partnership received third distribution of $0.40 cash 12/25/1986
Each Unit of Ltd. Partnership received fourth distribution of $0.50 cash 12/15/1988
Each Unit of Ltd. Partnership received fifth distribution of $0.50 cash 07/15/1988
Each Unit of Ltd. Partnership received sixth distribution of $0.50 cash 01/15/1989
Each Unit of Ltd. Partnership received seventh distribution of $1 cash 07/17/1989
Each Unit of Ltd. Partnership received eighth distribution of $0.75 cash 09/29/1989
Each Unit of Ltd. Partnership received ninth distribution of $0.75 cash 03/30/1990
Each Unit of Ltd. Partnership received tenth distribution of $0.50 cash 07/31/1990
Each Unit of Ltd. Partnership received eleventh distribution of $0.50 cash 08/30/1991
Each Unit of Ltd. Partnership received twelfth distribution of $0.25 cash 12/15/1991
Each Unit of Ltd. Partnership received thirteenth distribution of $0.25 cash 12/16/1992
Each Unit of Ltd. Partnership received fourteenth distribution of $0.50 cash 10/27/1999
Each Unit of Ltd. Partnership received fifteenth distribution of $0.25 cash 02/17/2000
Each Unit of Ltd. Partnership received sixteenth distribution of $0.20 cash 01/18/2002
Each Unit of Ltd. Partnership received seventeenth distribution of $0.25 cash payable 02/01/2002 to holders of record 01/22/2002
Each Unit of Ltd. Partnership received eighteenth and final distribution of $0.35 cash payable 12/27/2002 to holders of record 12/16/2002 Ex date - 12/30/2002
Note: Certificates were not required to be exchanged and are without value
Each Unit of Ltd Partnership received initial contingent payment of $0.20157 cash payable 01/15/2003 to holders of record 12/30/2002 Ex date - 02/03/2003
Each Unit of Ltd Partnership received second contingent payment of $0.25197522 cash payable 01/23/2004 to holders of record 12/30/2002 Ex date - 02/19/2004
Each Unit of Ltd Partnership received third and final contingent payment of $0.0725 cash payable 10/23/2008 to holders of record 12/30/2002 Ex date - 11/04/2008

ROYAL PALM SAVINGS ASSOCIATION (FL)
Common $1.60 par split (6) for (5) by issuance of (0.2) additional share 12/02/1985
Name changed to Royal Palm Savings Bank (West Palm Beach, FL) 01/01/1988
(See Royal Palm Savings Bank (West Palm Beach, FL))

ROYAL PALM SVGS BK (WEST PALM BEACH, FL)
Declared insolvent and taken over by FDIC 7/19/89
Stockholders' equity undetermined

ROYAL PET MEALS INC (DE)
Recapitalized as Kodiak Gaming, Inc. 5/10/2006
Each (75) shares Common $0.001 par exchanged for (1) share Common $0.001 par
Kodiak Gaming, Inc. name changed to Straight Up Brands, Inc. 8/7/2006

ROYAL PHARMACEUTICAL CORP (UT)
Reincorporated under the laws of Nevada 5/1/85

ROYAL PICTURES INC (NY)
Recapitalized as Iconfidential Inc. 06/05/2001
Each share Common $0.001 par exchanged for (0.05) share Common $0.001 par
Iconfidential Inc. recapitalized as Quality of Life Health Corp. 03/04/2003 which recapitalized as LifeHouse Retirement Properties, Inc. 07/14/2005

ROYAL PLASTICS GROUP LTD (CANADA)
Name changed to Royal Group Technologies Ltd. 02/14/1997
(See Royal Group Technologies Ltd.)

ROYAL PRECISION INC (DE)
Merged into Royal Associates, Inc. 2/7/2003
Each share Common $0.001 par exchanged for $0.10 cash

ROYAL PRECISION PRODS INC (DE)
Liquidation completed
Each share Common 1¢ par exchanged for initial distribution of $1.11 cash 11/07/1984
Each share Common 1¢ par received second distribution of $0.55 cash 10/00/1985
Each share Common 1¢ par received third and final distribution of $0.4042 cash 02/12/1987

ROYAL PUBLISHERS INC (TN)
Name changed to Nelson (Thomas), Inc. 10/1/72
(See Nelson (Thomas), Inc.)

ROYAL QUANTUM GROUP INC (NV)
Recapitalized as MineralRite Corp. 10/18/2012
Each share Common $0.001 par exchanged for (0.02) share Common $0.001 par

ROYAL RDS CORP NEW (CANADA)
Reincorporated 05/30/2007
Place of incorporation changed from (AB) to Canada 05/30/2007
Name changed to Buchans Minerals Corp. 07/05/2010
(See Buchans Minerals Corp.)

ROYAL RDS CORP OLD (AB)
Under plan of reorganization each share Common no par automatically became (1) share Royal Roads Corp. (New) (AB) Common no par 04/01/2002

Royal Roads Corp. (New) (AB) reincorporated in Canada 05/30/2007 which name changed to Buchans Minerals Corp. 07/05/2010
(See Buchans Minerals Corp.)

ROYAL REGISTER CO., INC. (NH)
Name changed to Royal Business Forms, Inc. 1/27/61
Royal Business Forms, Inc. name changed to Royal Business Group Inc. 10/29/82
(See Royal Business Group Inc.)

ROYAL RES CORP (DE)
Name changed to Royal Gold, Inc. 05/12/1987

ROYAL RES LTD (CANADA)
Reincorporated 07/21/1987
Place of incorporation changed from (AB) to (Canada) 07/21/1987
Name changed to Royaledge Industries, Inc. 12/03/1987
Royaledge Industries, Inc. name changed to Royaledge Resources Inc. 12/21/1995 which recapitalized as Avalanche Networks Corp. 05/25/2000 which name changed to Avalanche Minerals Ltd. 09/14/2007 which recapitalized as OroAndes Resource Corp. 07/03/2008 which name changed to Fort St. James Nickel Corp. 12/02/2011

ROYAL ROCK VENTURES INC (BC)
Recapitalized as Bi-Optic Ventures Inc. 04/06/2001
Each share Common no par exchanged for (0.5) share Common no par
Bi-Optic Ventures Inc. name changed to Arcturus Growthstar Technologies Inc. 02/17/2016 which name changed to Future Farm Technologies Inc. 02/02/2017

ROYAL SAPPHIRE CORP (BC)
Each share old Common no par exchanged for (0.1) share new Common no par 02/11/2015
Each share new Common no par exchanged again for (4) shares new Common no par 06/15/2017
Recapitalized as Pure Global Cannabis Inc. 07/11/2018
Each share new Common no par exchanged for (0.5) share Common no par

ROYAL SCHOOL LABORATORIES, INC. (VA)
Acquired by National Industries, Inc. (KY) 11/01/1968
Each share Common 1¢ par exchanged for (0.5) share Common $1 par
National Industries, Inc. (KY) merged into Fuqua Industries, Inc. 01/03/1978 which name changed to Actava Group Inc. 07/21/1993 which name changed to Metromedia International Group, Inc. 11/01/1995
(See Metromedia International Group, Inc.)

ROYAL SCOTSMAN INNS CORP (SC)
Name changed to RSI Corp. and Common $1 par changed to 5¢ par 02/17/1978
RSI Corp. reorganized as Delta Woodside Industries, Inc. (SC) 11/15/1989
(See Delta Woodside Industries, Inc. (SC))

ROYAL SCOTT RES LTD (BC)
Merged into Tenajon Resources Corp. 08/01/1991
Each share Class A Common no par exchanged for (0.5) share Common no par
Tenajon Resources Corp. merged into Creston Moly Corp. 08/26/2009 which merged into Mercator Minerals Ltd. 06/21/2011

ROYAL SEAFOOD ENTERPRISES, INC. (DE)
Recapitalized as DataMark Holding, Inc. 01/11/1995
Each share Common $0.0001 par exchanged for (1/3) share Common $0.0001 par
DataMark Holding, Inc. name changed to Digital Courier Technologies Inc. 09/16/1998 which recapitalized as TransAxis, Inc. 05/08/2003
(See TransAxis, Inc.)

ROYAL SILVER MINES INC (UT)
Recapitalized as Cadence Resources Corp. 06/01/2001
Each share Common 1¢ par exchanged for (0.05) share Common 1¢ par
Cadence Resources Corp. name changed to Aurora Oil & Gas Corp. 05/24/2006
(See Aurora Oil & Gas Corp.)

ROYAL SOVEREIGN EXPL INC (BC)
Name changed to RSX Energy Inc. 07/11/2002
(See RSX Energy Inc.)

ROYAL SPRING WTR INC (NV)
SEC revoked common stock registration 07/21/2009
Stockholders' equity unlikely

ROYAL STATE BANK OF NEW YORK (NEW YORK, NY)
Stock Dividends - 10% 1/28/55; 10% 1/30/56; 16-2/3% 1/30/57
Name changed to Royal National Bank (New York, NY) 11/30/62
Royal National Bank (New York, NY) merged into Security National Bank (Hempstead, NY) 5/8/72
(See Security National Bank (Hempstead, NY))

ROYAL STRATUS VENTURES INC (BC)
Name changed to MPI Holdings Inc. (BC) 06/01/1994
MPI Holdings Inc. (BC) reincorporated in Wyoming 06/24/1994
(See MPI Holdings Inc.)

ROYAL STYLE DESIGN INC (FL)
Name changed to Diversified Global Holdings Group, Inc. 11/09/2010

ROYAL SUNMARK ENERGY CORP (WA)
Name changed Detex Security Systems, Inc. 10/19/2005
Detex Security Systems, Inc. name changed to Detection Security Systems, Inc. 05/15/2006 which recapitalized as Nexis International Industries, Inc. 08/30/2007
(See Nexis International Industries, Inc.)

ROYAL SVG & LN ASSN (CA)
Each share Guarantee Stock $10 par exchanged for (3) shares Guarantee Stock no par 01/28/1970
Liquidation completed
Each share Guarantee Stock no par exchanged for initial distribution of $5.35787 cash 01/06/1975
Each share Guarantee Stock no par received second and final distribution of $0.83 cash 12/31/1980

ROYAL TR CO (MONTREAL, QUE)
Capital Stock $100 par changed to $20 par and (4) additional shares issued 02/00/1930
Each share Capital Stock $20 par exchanged for (4) shares Capital Stock $5 par 02/18/1955
Capital Stock $5 par changed to $1 par and (4) additional shares issued 08/18/1967
Capital Stock $1 par changed to 50¢ par and (1) additional share issued 03/30/1973
Capital Stock 50¢ par reclassified as Conv. Class A Capital Stock 50¢ par 06/07/1974
Merged into Royal Trustco Ltd. 04/03/1979
Each share Conv. Class A Capital Stock 50¢ par exchanged for (1/3) share Common no par
Each share Conv. Class B Capital Stock 50¢ par exchanged for (1/3) share Common no par
Royal Trustco Ltd. name changed to Gentra Inc. 06/25/1993 which name changed to BPO Properties Ltd. 04/19/2001
(See BPO Properties Ltd.)

ROYAL TR CO MTG CORP (QC)
5% Preferred Ser. A $20 par called for redemption 8/26/94
Public interest eliminated

ROYAL TR ENERGY INCOME FD I (AB)
Name changed 03/22/1989
Name changed from Royal Trust Energy Income Fund to Royal Trust Energy Income Fund I 03/22/1989
Name changed to Westrock Energy Income Fund I 11/26/1993
Westrock Energy Income Fund I merged into Enerplus Resources Fund 06/08/2000 which reorganized as Enerplus Corp. 01/03/2011

ROYAL TR ENERGY INCOME FD II (AB)
Name changed to Westrock Energy Income Fund II 11/26/1993
Westrock Energy Income Fund II merged into Enerplus Resources Fund 06/08/2000 which reorganized as Enerplus Corp. 01/03/2011

ROYAL TRUSTCO LTD (CANADA)
Common no par reclassified as Conv. Class A Common no par 06/20/1979
$2.9375 Retractable Preferred Ser. C no par called for redemption 01/04/1988
$2.6875 Retractable Preferred Ser. D no par called for redemption 01/04/1988
Conv. Class A Common no par reclassified as Common no par 03/31/1989
Conv. Class B Common no par reclassified as Common no par 03/31/1989
Stock Dividends - 100% 12/20/1984; 100% 06/26/1987
Name changed to Gentra Inc. 06/25/1993
Gentra Inc. name changed to BPO Properties 04/19/2001
(See BPO Properties Ltd.)

ROYAL TYPEWRITER CO., INC. (NY)
Each share Common no par exchanged for (2) shares new Common no par in 1929
Common no par changed to $1 par and a 300% stock dividend paid in 1943
Each share 7% Preferred $100 par exchanged for (1.56) shares 4-1/2% Preferred A $100 par and (3/8) share Common $1 par in 1952
Merged into Royal-McBee Corp. in 1954
4-1/2% Preferred $100 par and Common $1 par exchanged for similar shares on a share for share basis
Royal-McBee Corp. merged into Litton Industries, Inc. 2/28/65
(See Litton Industries, Inc.)

ROYAL UN HLDG CORP (NV)
Name changed to Allied American Steel Corp. 05/16/2011

ROYAL UTD CORP (NY)
Merged into WRH Associates, Inc. 5/1/76
Each share Common 10¢ par exchanged for $1 cash

ROYAL URANIUM CORP. (NV)
Name changed to Royal Corp. 5/14/57
(See Royal Corp.)

ROYAL UTILITIES, INC. (FL)
Merged into Roltec, Inc. 4/3/67
Each share Common $1 par exchanged for (0.2) share Common $1 par
Roltec, Inc. merged into Gould Properties, Inc. 7/24/68 which name changed to Gould Enterprises, Inc. 4/2/69 which merged into Gould Investors Trust (MA) 7/1/70 which reorganized in Delaware as Gould Investors L.P. 5/13/86

ROYAL UTILS INCOME FD (AB)
Acquired by Sherritt International Corp. 05/02/2008
Each Trust Unit no par received either (0.8314754) share Common no par or (0.53898056) share Common no par and $4.46054636 cash
Note: Option to receive stock and cash expired 05/23/2008
U.S. holders received cash only

ROYAL VICTORIA MINERALS LTD (CANADA)
Acquired by St. Andrew Goldfields Ltd. 6/23/2003
Each share Common no par exchanged for (2) shares Common no par

ROYAL VOPAK N V (NETHERLANDS)
Each Sponsored ADR for Ordinary received distribution of $4.71694 cash payable 8/1/2002 to holders of record 7/31/2002
ADR agreement terminated 8/11/2003
Each Sponsored ADR for Ordinary exchanged for $18.96175 cash

ROYAL WATERLILY INC (NV)
Name changed to Royal Acquisitions & Development, Inc. 03/28/2005
Royal Acquisitions & Development, Inc. recapitalized as Innovative Health Sciences, Inc. (NV) 06/11/2008 which reincorporated in Delaware 02/24/2011 which name changed to Innovative Holdings Alliance, Inc. 05/27/2011

ROYAL WEAVING CO.
Dissolved in 1938

ROYAL ZENITH CORP (NY)
Name changed to ZR Interim Corp. 11/3/78
(See ZR Interim Corp.)

ROYALE AIRLS INC (LA)
Each share old Common no par exchanged for (0.6) share new Common no par 12/1/82
Chapter 11 Federal Bankruptcy Code converted to Chapter 7 on 2/28/89
Stockholders' equity unlikely

ROYALE ENERGY FDS INC (CA)
Recapitalized as Royale Energy Inc. 10/21/94
Each share Common no par exchanged for (0.5) share Common no par

ROYALE FURNITURE HLDGS LTD (CAYMAN ISLANDS)
ADR agreement terminated 07/23/2015
Each Sponsored ADR for Ordinary exchanged for $0.352991 cash

ROYALE GROUP HLDG INC (NV)
Name changed to Royale Globe Holding Inc. 01/09/2014

ROYALE GROUP LTD (DE)
Charter cancelled and declared inoperative and void for non-payment of taxes 3/1/92

ROYALE INVTS INC (MN)
Name changed to Corporate Office Properties Trust Inc. (MN) 1/1/98
Corporate Office Properties Trust Inc. (MN) reincorporated in Maryland as

Corporate Office Properties Trust 3/12/98

ROYALE NORI FOODS INC (BC)
Name changed to Agrotech Greenhouses Inc. 11/05/1997
Agrotech Greenhouses Inc. recapitalized as Archer Petroleum Corp. 04/30/2010 which name changed to Atlas Engineered Products Ltd. 11/09/2017

ROYALEDGE RES INC (CANADA)
Name changed 12/21/1995
Name changed from Royaledge Industries, Inc. to Royaledge Resources Inc. 12/21/1995
Recapitalized as Avalanche Networks Corp. 05/25/2000
Each share Common no par exchanged for (0.1) share Common no par
Avalanche Networks Corp. name changed to Avalanche Minerals Ltd. 09/14/2007 which recapitalized as OroAndes Resource Corp. 07/03/2008 which name changed to Fort St. James Nickel Corp. 12/02/2011

ROYALITE OIL LTD (CANADA)
Each share old Common no par exchanged for (4) shares new Common no par 00/00/1949
5-1/4% Conv. Preferred 1st Ser. $25 par called for redemption 01/01/1967
Merged into Gulf Oil Canada Ltd. 04/01/1969
Each share new Common no par exchanged for (1.2) shares Common no par
Gulf Oil Canada Ltd. name changed to Gulf Canada Ltd.-Gulf Canada Ltee. 06/02/1978 which was acquired by Gulf Canada Corp. 02/10/1986 which was reorganized as Gulf Canada Resources Ltd. 07/01/1987
(See Gulf Canada Resources Ltd.)

ROYALON, INC. (OH)
Name changed to Brookpark-Royalon, Inc. 11/9/65
Brookpark-Royalon, Inc. merged into Jeannette Glass Co. 12/28/69 which name changed to Jeannette Corp. 5/14/71
(See Jeannette Corp.)

ROYALON PETE CORP (BC)
Recapitalized as International Royalon Minerals Inc. 11/21/84
Each share Common no par exchanged for (0.2) share Common no par
International Royalon Minerals Inc. recapitalized as International Markatech Corp. 7/20/87 which recapitalized as Markatech Industries Corp. 11/3/95 which recapitalized as Ameratech Systems Corp. 2/12/2001
(See Ameratech Systems Corp.)

ROYALPAR INDS INC (NY)
Common 1¢ par split (2) for (1) by issuance of (1) additional share 09/22/1986
Common 1¢ par split (3) for (1) by issuance of (2) additional shares 06/25/1987
Merged into Raycomm Transworld Industries, Inc. 07/15/1991
Each share Common 1¢ par exchanged for (1.5) shares Preferred Ser. C 1¢ par and (0.75) share Common 1¢ par
(See Raycomm Transworld Industries, Inc.)

ROYALSTAR RES LTD (CANADA)
Recapitalized as Royal Victoria Minerals Ltd. 3/7/2000
Each share Common no par exchanged for (0.1) share Common no par
Royal Victoria Minerals Ltd. acquired by St. Andrew Goldfields Ltd. 6/23/2003

ROYALTECH CORP (DE)
Each share old Common $0.0001 par exchanged for (0.06666666) share new Common $0.0001 par 08/12/2008
Name changed to China Tractor Holdings, Inc. 10/20/2008
(See China Tractor Holdings, Inc.)

ROYALTIES MANAGEMENT CORP. (NY)
Each share Class B Common no par exchanged for (0.2) share Common no par in 1931
Common no par changed to $2 par in 1933
Common $2 par changed to $1 par in 1934
Merged into Houston Royalty Co. (NV) 7/5/66
Each share Common $1 par exchanged for (0.5) share Conv. Preferred $1 par and $5 cash
Houston Royalty Co. (NV) name changed to Houston Oil & Minerals Corp. 12/20/68
(See Houston Oil & Minerals Corp.)

ROYALTY CORP. OF AMERICA (OK)
Preferred and Common $10 par changed to $3 par in 1934
Dissolution completed 1/1/54

ROYALTY CTLS CORP (NY)
Merged into Granite Management Corp. 01/15/1979
Each share Common 1¢ par exchanged for $2.75 cash

ROYALTY DEV CORP (CO)
Completely liquidated 02/08/1984
Each share Common 1¢ par exchanged for first and final distribution of (0.08205) share Com-Tek Resources, Inc. Common 1¢ par
Com-Tek Resources, Inc. name changed to Powerhouse Resources Inc. 08/10/1995
(See Powerhouse Resources Inc.)

ROYALTY INCOME SHARES (NY)
Trust terminated and liquidated 8/19/57
Details not available

ROYALTY MTG INCOME FD (CA)
Completely liquidated 11/01/2002
Details not available

ROYALTY VENTURES CORP (DE)
Recapitalized as Seaxe Energy Corp. 03/04/1985
Each share Common 1¢ par exchanged for (0.1) share Common 10¢ par
Seaxe Energy Corp. name changed to Hadson Europe Inc. 09/28/1987 which name changed to Midwest Energy Companies, Inc. 12/20/1991

ROYALVALLEY COPPER MINES LTD. (ON)
Name changed to Systems-Air Corp. Ltd. 11/3/69
Systems-Air Corp. Ltd. charter cancelled 3/16/76

ROYBAR CHIBOUGAMAU MINES LTD.
Name changed to Roybar Uranium & Gold Mines Ltd. in 1949
Roybar Uranium & Gold Mines Ltd. recapitalized as Nubar Mines Ltd. in 1950 which was acquired by Tandem Mines Ltd. in 1954 which recapitalized as Halmon Mining & Processing Ltd. 4/3/58
(See Halmon Mining & Processing Ltd.)

ROYBAR URANIUM & GOLD MINES LTD.
Recapitalized as Nubar Mines Ltd. on a (1) for (3) basis in 1950
Nubar Mines Ltd. was acquired by Tandem Mines Ltd. in 1954 which recapitalized as Halmon Mining & Processing Ltd. 4/3/58
(See Halmon Mining & Processing Ltd.)

ROYCAM COPPER MINES LTD (ON)
Capital Stock $1 par reclassified as Common no par 2/16/77
Name changed to Bitech Energy Resources Ltd. 3/21/83
Bitech Energy Resources Ltd. name changed to Bitech Corp. (ONT) 8/11/89 which reorganized under the laws of Canada as Bitech Petroleum Corp. 11/20/96
(See Bitech Petroleum Corp.)

ROYCE BIOMEDICAL INC (NV)
Each share old Common 1¢ par exchanged for (0.2) share new Common 1¢ par 05/18/1998
Each share new Common 1¢ par exchanged for (0.2) share Common $0.001 par 05/18/1999
Name changed to Smart-Tek Solutions, Inc. 09/08/2005
Smart-Tek Solutions, Inc. name changed to Trucept, Inc. 01/03/2013

ROYCE COPPER MINES LTD. (ON)
Charter cancelled and proclaimed dissolved for failure to pay taxes and file returns 11/27/61

ROYCE FOCUS TR INC (MD)
Name changed 05/10/1999
Name changed from Royce Global Trust, Inc. to Royce Focus Trust, Inc. 05/10/1999
7.45% Preferred $0.001 par called for redemption at $25 on 10/20/2003
6% Preferred $0.001 par called for redemption at $25 plus $0.212499 accrued dividends on 11/15/2012
Name changed to Sprott Focus Trust, Inc. 03/09/2015

ROYCE INDS INC (BC)
Recapitalized as Biosource Industries Inc. 04/22/1992
Each (2.6) shares Common no par exchanged for (1) share Common no par
Biosource Industries Inc. merged into BioSource International, Inc. 05/19/1993
(See BioSource International, Inc.)

ROYCE LABS INC (FL)
Each share old Common $0.005 par exchanged for (0.33333333) share new Common $0.005 par 12/23/1993
Merged into Watson Pharmaceuticals, Inc. 04/16/1997
Each share Common $0.005 par exchanged for (0.19079) share Common $0.0033 par
Watson Pharmaceuticals, Inc. name changed to Actavis, Inc. (NV) 01/24/2013 which reorganized in Ireland as Actavis PLC 10/01/2013 which name changed to Allergan PLC 06/15/2015

ROYCE MICRO-CAP TRUST INC (MD)
Name changed 06/29/1995
Name changed from Royce OTC Micro-Cap Fund Inc. to Royce Micro-Cap Trust, Inc. 06/29/1995
6% Preferred $0.001 par called for redemption at $25 plus $0.212499 accrued dividends on 11/15/2012
(Additional Information in Active)

ROYCE RES CORP (BC)
Reincorporated 05/11/2011
Place of incorporation changed from (AB) to (BC) 05/11/2011
Each share old Common no par exchanged for (0.1) share new Common no par 11/05/2013
Name changed to Lithium X Energy Corp. 11/30/2015
(See Lithium X Energy Corp.)

ROYCE VALUE TR INC (MD)
7.30% Tax Advantaged Preferred called for redemption at $25 plus $0.09125 accrued dividends on 10/10/2003
7.8% Preferred $0.001 par called for redemption at $25 plus $0.0975 accrued dividends on 10/10/2003
5.9% Preferred $0.001 par called for redemption at $25 plus $0.208958 accrued dividends on 11/15/2012
(Additional Information in Active)

ROYCE VENTURES LTD (BC)
Merged into Bellevue Ventures Ltd. 10/3/84
Each share Common no par exchanged for (1) share Common no par
Bellevue Ventures Ltd. recapitalized as International Bellevue Ventures Ltd. 2/7/85
(See International Bellevue Ventures Ltd. Ltd.)

ROYCEFIELD RES LTD (ON)
Delisted from Toronto Stock Exchange 8/31/2001

ROYCO INSTRS INC (CA)
Merged into Hycel, Inc. 12/30/1975
Each share Common no par exchanged for (2.397437) shares Common 25¢ par
(See Hycel, Inc.)

ROYCO LTD (AUSTRALIA)
Struck off register 06/25/1992

ROYEX GOLD MNG CORP (ON)
Merged into Corona Corp. 7/1/88
Each share Conv. 1st Preference Ser. A no par exchanged for (1) share Conv. 1st Preference Ser. A no par
Each share Conv. 1st Preference Ser. B no par exchanged for (1) share Conv. 1st Preference Ser. B no par
Each share Conv. 1st Preference Ser. C no par exchanged for (1) share Conv. 1st Preference Ser. C no par
Each share Common no par exchanged for (0.61) share Class A Subordinate no par and (1/3) Class A Subordinate Share Purchase Warrant expiring 6/30/90
Corona Corp. recapitalized as International Corona Corp. 6/11/91
(See International Corona Corp.)

ROYEX MNG LTD (ON)
Merged into Royex Sturgex Mining Ltd. 7/31/74
Each share Capital Stock no par exchanged for (0.5) share Common no par
Royex Sturgex Mining Ltd. name changed to Royex Gold Mining Corp. 6/8/84 which merged into Corona Corp. 7/1/88 which recapitalized as International Corona Corp. 6/11/91
(See International Corona Corp.)

ROYEX STURGEX MNG LTD (ON)
Under plan of merger name changed to Royex Gold Mining Corp. 6/8/84
Royex Gold Mining Corp. merged into Corona Corp. 7/1/88 which recapitalized as International Corona Corp. 6/11/91
(See International Corona Corp.)

ROYFUND LTD. (CANADA)
Name changed to Royfund (Equity) Ltd. 4/5/76

ROYOP PPTYS CORP (CANADA)
Merged into H&R Real Estate Investment Trust 08/31/2000
Each share Common no par exchanged for (0.0938) Unit no par
H&R Real Estate Investment Trust reorganized as H&R Real Estate Investment Trust/H&R Finance Trust 10/03/2008

ROYRAN GOLD FIELDS LTD. (QC)
Recapitalized as New Royran Copper Mines Ltd. on a (1) for (2) basis 08/30/1955
New Royran Copper Mines Ltd. merged into Copper Rand

Chibougamau Mines Ltd. 09/25/1956 which merged into Patino Mining Corp. 11/26/1962 which reorganized as Patino N.V. 12/20/1971
(See Patino N.V.)

ROYSHEL PPTYS LTD (CANADA)
Reincorporated 12/23/1996
Place of incorporation changed from (Canada) to (BC) 12/23/1996
Recapitalized as ATC Technologies Corp. 05/30/1997
Each share Common no par exchanged for (0.05) share Common no par
(See ATC Technologies Corp.)

ROYSTER-CLARK LTD / ROYSTER-CLARK ULC (ON)
Acquired by Agrium Inc. 03/06/2006
Each Income Deposit Security received $2.70 cash and $6.0832 principal amount of 14% Subordinated Notes due 07/20/2020

ROYSTER CO (VA)
Common no par changed to 50¢ par and (119) additional shares issued 01/30/1975
7% Preferred $100 par called for redemption 06/25/1980
Merged into Universal Leaf Tobacco Co. Inc. 06/26/1980
Each share Common 50¢ par exchanged for $12.21 principal amount of 9% Restricted Notes Ser. T due 06/26/1986 plus $3.04 cash or $16 cash
Note: For holdings of (100) shares or more option to receive $16 cash per share expired 06/26/1980
Holdings of (99) shares or fewer received $16 cash per share

ROYSTER (F.S.) GUANO CO. (VA)
Name changed to Royster Co. 6/28/68
(See Royster Co.)

ROYSTON COALITION MINES LTD (NV)
Name changed to Goodell Monorail Industries, Inc. 12/20/1968
(See Goodell Monorail Industries, Inc.)

ROYWEST DEUTCHEMARK INCOME FUND (BAHAMAS)
Name changed to TrustCor Deutchemark Income Fund 9/14/88

ROYWEST U.S. DOLLAR INCOME FUND (LUXEMBOURG)
Name changed to TrustCor U.S. Dollar Income Fund 9/14/88

ROZAK PORCUPINE MINES, LTD. (ON)
Charter cancelled for failure to file reports and pay taxes October 1957

RP ENTMT INC (NV)
Name changed to LitFunding Corp. 03/03/2003
LitFunding Corp. recapitalized as Global Entertainment Holdings, Inc. 12/17/2007

RPC ENERGY SVCS INC (DE)
Name changed to RPC, Inc. 4/27/95

RPI LIQUIDATION CORP. (TX)
Charter forfeited for failure to pay taxes 2/12/99

RPI MANUFACTURING CO. (AZ)
Liquidation completed
Each share Common $1 par exchanged for initial distribution of $2.65 cash 1/31/67
Each share Common $1 par received second and final distribution of $0.35 cash 10/4/68

RPM ADVANTAGE INC (NV)
SEC revoked common stock registration 11/08/2011

RPM DENTAL INC (DE)
Common $0.000001 par split (20) for (1) by issuance of (19) additional shares payable 02/29/2012 to holders of record 02/20/2012 Ex date - 03/01/2012
Name changed to Quest Water Global, Inc. 03/09/2012

RPM INC (NV)
Acquired by North Atlantic Corp. 4/23/71
Each share Common 10¢ par exchanged for (4.5) shares Common 25¢ par
North Atlantic Corp. merged into Zemarc, Ltd. 9/15/71
(See Zemarc, Ltd.)

RPM INC (OH)
Common no par split (3) for (2) by issuance of (0.5) additional share 11/06/1987
Common no par split (5) for (4) by issuance of (0.25) additional share 12/07/1990
Common no par split (3) for (2) by issuance of (0.5) additional share 12/04/1992
Common no par split (5) for (4) by issuance of (0.25) additional share 12/08/1995
Common no par split (5) for (4) by issuance of (0.25) additional share payable 12/08/1997 to holders of record 11/17/1997
Stock Dividends - 50% 10/24/1975; 50% 10/29/1976; 50% 10/28/1977; 50% 10/30/1978; 25% 11/07/1983; 25% 11/30/1984
Reincorporated under the laws of Delaware as RPM International Inc. and Common no par changed to 1¢ par 10/15/2002

RPM TECHNOLOGIES INC (CO)
Reincorporated under the laws of Delaware 04/17/2000
(See RPM Technologies, Inc. (DE))

RPM TECHNOLOGIES INC (DE)
Each share old Common $0.001 par exchanged for (0.2) share new Common $0.001 par 12/28/2001
SEC revoked common stock registration 10/07/2013

RPS CORP (DE)
Name changed to Scherer (R.P.) Corp. (New) 8/21/91
Scherer (R.P.) Corp. (New) merged into Cardinal Health, Inc. 8/7/98

RPS ENTERPRISES INC (FL)
Administratively dissolved for failure to file annual report 10/16/98

RPS PRODS INC (MD)
Common 10¢ par split (3) for (2) by issuance of (0.5) additional share 1/2/70
Common 10¢ par split (2) for (1) by issuance of (1) additional share 3/4/71
$5 Conv. Preferred 1972 Ser. C $1 par called for redemption 7/31/72
Assets sold for benefit of creditors 3/3/88
No stockholders' equity

RPS RLTY TR (MA)
Recapitalized as Ramco-Gershenson Properties Trust 05/10/1996
Each Share of Bene. Int. 10¢ par exchanged for (0.25) Share of Bene. Int. 10¢ par

RPT RES LTD (BC)
Reincorporated under the laws of Alberta as ArPetrol Ltd. 04/08/2011

RPT URANIUM CORP (BC)
Name changed to RPT Resources Ltd. (BC) 06/05/2009
RPT Resources Ltd. (BC) reincorporated in Alberta as ArPetrol Ltd. 04/08/2011

RPV INDS CDA INC (AB)
Delisted from Alberta Stock Exchange 03/03/1994

RPX CORP (DE)
Acquired by HGGC, LLC 06/19/2018
Each share Common $0.0001 par exchanged for $10.50 cash

RR MEDIA LTD (ISRAEL)
Name changed 02/17/2015
Name changed from RRSat Global Communications Network Ltd. to RR Media Ltd. 02/17/2015
Acquired by SES Astra Services Europe S.A. 07/06/2016
Each share Ordinary ILS 0.01 par exchanged for $13.291 cash

RRD LTD (BAHAMAS)
Placed in liquidation by Court Order in September 1976
Details not available

RRI ENERGY INC (DE)
Under plan of merger name changed to GenOn Energy, Inc. 12/03/2010

RRUN VENTURES NETWORK INC (NV)
Name changed to Livestar Entertainment Group Inc. 7/10/2003
Livestar Entertainment Group Inc. name changed to Jupiter Global Holdings Corp. 12/22/2004 which merged into Paivis, Corp. 5/19/2006

RS FINL CORP (NC)
Merged into First Union Corp. 01/11/1996
Each share Common $1 par exchanged for (0.7368) share Common $1 par
First Union Corp. name changed to Wachovia Corp. (Ctfs. dated after 09/01/2001) 09/01/2001 which merged into Wells Fargo & Co. (New) 12/31/2008

RS GROUP COS INC (FL)
SEC revoked common stock registration 12/22/2011

RS LEGACY CORP (DE)
Plan of reorganization under Chapter 11 Federal Bankruptcy proceedings effective 10/07/2015
No stockholders' equity

RS TECHNOLOGIES INC (AB)
Each share old Common no par exchanged for (0.005) share new Common no par 12/02/2010
Plan of arrangement under Companies' Creditors Arrangement Act effective 09/13/2013
No stockholders' equity

RSA CORP (MI)
Common $1 par changed to 1¢ par 12/01/1975
Automatically dissolved 07/15/2001

RSA SEC INC (DE)
Common 1¢ par split (3) for (2) by issuance of (0.5) additional share payable 03/23/2001 to holders of record 03/09/2001 Ex date - 03/26/2001
Merged into EMC Corp. 09/15/2006
Each share Common 1¢ par exchanged for $28 cash

RSC HLDGS INC (DE)
Issue Information - 20,833,333 shares COM offered at $22 per share on 05/22/2007
Merged into United Rentals, Inc. 04/30/2012
Each share Common no par exchanged for (0.2783) share Common 1¢ par and $10.80 cash

RSC INDS INC (NY)
Name changed to Matec Corp. (NY) 04/24/1984
Matec Corp. (NY) reincorporated in Delaware 07/01/1987 which reorganized in Maryland 07/02/1998 which name changed to Valpey-Fisher Corp. 06/03/2002
(See Valpey-Fisher Corp.)

RSCO LIQUIDATING CORP. (CA)
Liquidation completed
Each share Common $1 par exchanged for initial distribution of $7.25 cash 9/15/64
Each share Common $1 par received second and final distribution of $0.549041 cash 7/22/65

RSI CORP (SC)
Common 5¢ par split (5) for (4) by issuance of (0.25) additional share 03/01/1987
Stock Dividends - 25% 09/01/1986; 10% 01/04/1988
Under plan of reorganization name changed to Delta Woodside Industries, Inc. (SC) and Common 5¢ par changed to 1¢ par 11/15/1989
(See Delta Woodside Industries, Inc. (SC))

RSI HLDGS INC (NC)
Each share old Common 1¢ par exchanged for (0.33333333) share new Common 1¢ par 06/13/2002
Merged into BCM Acquisition Corp. 03/17/2005
Each share new Common 1¢ par exchanged for $0.10 cash

RSI RETAIL SOLUTIONS INC (BC)
Recapitalized as Consolidated Retail Solutions Inc. 01/30/1990
Each share Common no par exchanged for (0.2) share Common no par
Consolidated Retail Solutions Inc. name changed to Ventir Challenge Enterprises Ltd. 07/18/1994 which recapitalized as Whistler Gold Corp. 02/03/2006 which name changed to Svit Gold Corp. 08/11/2008 which name changed to Catalyst Copper Corp. 02/02/2010 which merged into NewCastle Gold Ltd. 05/27/2016 which merged into Equinox Gold Corp. 12/22/2017

RSI SYS INC (MN)
Reincorporated under the laws of Nevada as Viseon, Inc. 05/29/2001
(See Viseon, Inc.)

RSK ENTERPRISES INC (NY)
Dissolved by proclamation 03/25/1992

RSL COMMUNICATIONS LTD (BERMUDA)
Commenced insolvency proceedings in the Supreme Court of Bermuda 03/19/2001
Stockholders' equity unlikely

RSP PERMIAN INC (DE)
Merged into Concho Resources Inc. 07/19/2018
Each share Common 1¢ par exchanged for (0.32) share Common $0.001 par

RSR ASSOCIATES L.P. (DE)
Completely liquidated 12/30/86
Each Unit of Ltd. Partnership received first and final distribution of $1,368.56 cash

RSR CORP (DE)
Stock Dividend - 10% 3/30/80
Acquired by RSR Holding Corp. 4/27/84
Each share Common 1¢ par exchanged for $9 cash

RSTAR CORP (DE)
Merged into Gilat Satellite Networks Ltd. 4/7/2004
Each share Common 1¢ par exchanged for $0.60 cash

RSTS CORP (CO)
Each share old Common no par exchanged for (0.5) share new Common no par 01/15/1993
Name changed to Bion Environmental Technologies, Inc. 08/30/1993

RSV BANCORP INC (PA)
Merged into Allegheny Valley Bancorp, Inc. 09/08/2006
Each share Common 10¢ par exchanged for $29 cash

RSX ENERGY INC (BC)
Acquired by Talisman Energy Inc. 03/05/2008
Each share Common no par exchanged for $1.70 cash

RT ACQUISITION ASSOC INC (NY)
Recapitalized as Information Display Technology Inc. 7/9/90
Each share Common $0.001 par exchanged for (0.5) share Common $0.001 par
Information Display Technology Inc. recapitalized as Polyvision Corp. 5/25/95
(See Polyvision Corp.)

RT ACQUISITION CORP (NY)
Name changed to BLOC Development Technologies, Inc. 5/25/88
BLOC Development Technologies, Inc. reincorporated in Delaware as BLOC Development Corp. 12/1/89 which name changed to Tiger Direct Inc. 1/3/95 which merged into Global DirectMail Corp. 11/30/95 which name changed to Systemax Inc. 5/19/99

RT INDS INC (DE)
Each share old Common $0.001 par exchanged for (0.2) share new Common $0.001 par 2/17/95
Name changed to U.S. Automotive Manufacturing Inc. 11/13/97
(See U.S. Automotive Manufacturing Inc.)

RT PETE INC (DE)
SEC revoked common stock registration 06/04/2007
Stockholders' equity unlikely

RT TECHNOLOGIES INC (NV)
Each (15) shares old Common $0.001 par exchanged for (1) share new Common $0.001 par 10/11/2011
Note: Holders of between (100) and (1,500) shares will receive (100) shares
Name changed to CAM Group, Inc. 10/09/2012

RTAI SYS INC (DE)
Recapitalized as Production Assistant Technologies, Inc. 01/19/1999
Each share Class A Common no par exchanged for (0.02) share Class A Common no par
Each share Common no par exchanged for (0.02) share Common no par
(See Production Assistant Technologies, Inc.)

RTC CORP (FL)
Charter cancelled and proclaimed dissolved for non-payment of taxes 05/22/1970

RTC TRANSN INC (GA)
Administratively dissolved 11/29/1992

RTG VENTURES INC (FL)
Each share old Common $0.001 par exchanged for (0.01) share new Common $0.001 par 02/05/2013
Name changed to Digital Brand Media & Marketing Group, Inc. 04/08/2013

R37 CAP CORP (AB)
Name changed to Rapid Solutions Corp. 10/06/2005
(See Rapid Solutions Corp.)

RTI BIOLOGICS INC (DE)
Name changed to RTI Surgical, Inc. 07/18/2013

RTI INC (NY)
Each share Common 1¢ par exchanged for (0.125) share Common 8¢ par 06/01/1995
Charter cancelled and proclaimed dissolved for failure to pay taxes 12/27/2000

RTI INTL METALS INC (OH)
Merged into Alcoa Inc. 07/23/2015
Each share Common 1¢ par exchanged for (2.8315) shares Common $1 par
Alcoa Inc. name changed to Arconic Inc. (PA) 11/01/2016 which reincorporated in Delaware 12/31/2017

RTIN HLDGS INC (TX)
Name changed to Safescript Pharmacies, Inc. 12/17/2003
(See Safescript Pharmacies, Inc.)

RTM HLDGS INC (AB)
Name changed to Sustainable Energy Technologies Ltd. 12/15/1999
Sustainable Energy Technologies Ltd. name changed to Eguana Technologies Inc. 11/18/2013

RTN STEALTH SOFTWARE INC (BC)
Common no par split (5) for (1) by issuance of (4) additional shares payable 01/11/2010 to holders of record 12/23/2009 Ex date - 12/21/2009
Name changed to Quantitative Alpha Trading Inc. (BC) 04/29/2011
Quantitative Alpha Trading Inc. (BC) reincorporated in Ontario 12/09/2011
(See Quantitative Alpha Trading Inc.)

RTO ENTERPRISES INC (ON)
Each share old Common no par exchanged for (0.1) share new Common no par 08/01/2002
Name changed to easyhome Ltd. 07/08/2003
easyhome Ltd. name changed to goeasy Ltd. 09/17/2015

RTO HLDGS INC (NV)
Name changed to Orion Ethanol, Inc. 11/7/2006

RTO INC. (DE)
Merged into Alrenco, Inc. (IN) 2/26/98
Each share Common no par exchanged for (89.795) shares Common no par
Alrenco, Inc. (IN) reincorporated in Delaware as Home Choice Holdings, Inc. 6/23/98 which merged into Rent-Way, Inc. 12/10/98
(See Rent-Way, Inc.)

RTS GOLF INC (WA)
Recapitalized as FACE Biometrics, Inc. 11/18/2004
Each share Common no par exchanged for (0.0002) share Common no par
FACE Biometrics, Inc. name changed to WIDE Entertainment, Inc. 03/10/2005 which name changed to Omega Mining & Exploration Corp. (WA) 09/12/2005 which reincorporated in Nevada as Cardio Infrared Technologies, Inc. 08/06/2007 which reorganized in Wyoming 07/15/2010 which recapitalized as Enchanted World, Inc. 12/08/2014

RTW INC (MN)
Old Common no par split (3) for (2) by issuance of (0.5) additional share 05/17/1996 to holders of record 05/06/1996
Each share old Common no par exchanged for (0.5) share new Common no par 11/25/2002
Merged into Rockhill Holding Co. 12/17/2007
Each share Common no par exchanged for $12.45 cash

R2 CORP (DE)
Recapitalized as Darox Corp. 9/10/87
Each (4.2173) shares Common 1¢ par exchanged for (1) share Common 1¢ par
(See Darox Corp.)

R2 MED SYS INC (CA)
Merged into Cardiotronics Systems, Inc. 10/19/94
Each share Common no par exchanged for $5.25 cash

RTZ PLC (ENGLAND)
Each ADR for Ordinary Reg. 25p par exchanged for (2.5) ADR's for Ordinary Reg. 10p par 11/04/1987
Each Unsponsored ADR for Ordinary Reg. 10p par exchanged for (1) Sponsored ADR for Ordinary Reg. 10p par 07/20/1988
Name changed to Rio Tinto PLC 06/02/1997

RUAL PORCUPINE MINES, LTD. (ON)
Liquidated 08/23/1960
Each share Capital Stock $1 par exchanged for (0.0208333) share Wengrace Explorations Ltd. Capital Stock no par
(See Wengrace Explorations Ltd.)

RUAN CTR CORP (IA)
Each share old Common $1 par held by holders of (99) shares or fewer exchanged for $168 cash 11/11/93
Public interest eliminated

RUB A DUB SOAP INC (NV)
Reorganized 04/17/2006
Reorganized from under the laws of (CO) to (NV) 04/17/2006
Each share Common $0.001 par exchanged for (0.1) share Common $0.001 par
Common $0.001 par split (2.12) for (1) by issuance of (1.12) additional shares payable 11/15/2007 to holders of record 11/12/2007 Ex date - 11/16/2007
Name changed to Sentaida Tire Co. Ltd. 07/11/2008

RUB MUSIC ENTERPRISES INC (NV)
Name changed to SANUWAVE Health, Inc. 11/12/2009

RUBATEX PRODUCTS, INC. (DE)
Completely liquidated 4/1/68
Each share Common $10 par received first and final distribution of $0.0077 cash
Certificates were not retired and are now without value

RUBBER & CELLULOID PRODUCTS CO.
Acquired by Bristol-Myers Co. in 1934
(See Bristol-Myers Co.)

RUBBER SERVICE LABORATORIES
Acquired by Monsanto Chemical Works (MO) 00/00/1929
Details not available

RUBBER TECHNOLOGY INTL INC (FL)
Reincorporated 05/31/2001
Each (300) shares old Common $0.0001 par exchanged for (1) share new Common $0.0001 par 02/21/1998
New Common $0.0001 par split (3) for (2) by issuance of (0.5) additional share payable 09/08/1998 to holders of record 09/01/1998
State of incorporation changed from (FL) to (NV) 05/31/2001
SEC revoked common stock registration 10/20/2006
Stockholders' equity unlikely

RUBBERMAID INC (OH)
Common $1 par split (2) for (1) by issuance of (1) additional share 11/30/1970
Common $1 par split (2) for (1) by issuance of (1) additional share 08/31/1973
Common $1 par split (2) for (1) by issuance of (1) additional share 11/30/1982
Common $1 par split (2) for (1) by issuance of (1) additional share 08/30/1985
Common $1 par split (2) for (1) by issuance of (1) additional share 07/31/1986
Common $1 par split (2) for (1) by issuance of (1) additional share 11/29/1991

Merged into Newell Rubbermaid Inc. 03/24/1999
Each share Common $1 par exchanged for (0.7883) share Common $1 par
Newell Rubbermaid Inc. name changed to Newell Brands Inc. 04/18/2016

RUBEC MINES LTD.
Bankrupt in 1949

RUBEL COAL & ICE CORP.
Name changed to Rubel Corp. in 1930

RUBEROID CO. (NJ)
Capital Stock $100 par changed to no par 07/00/1927
Each share old Capital Stock no par exchanged for (3) shares new Capital Stock no par 00/00/1937
New Capital Stock no par changed to $1 par and (1) additional share issued 05/05/1954
Capital Stock $1 par split (2) for (1) by issuance of (1) additional share 12/29/1966
Stock Dividends - 10% 12/22/1948; 10% 12/21/1949; 10% 12/20/1950
Merged into General Aniline & Film Corp. 05/26/1967
Each share Capital Stock $1 par exchanged for (1) share $1.20 Conv. Preferred $1 par
General Aniline & Film Corp. name changed to GAF Corp. 04/24/1968
(See GAF Corp.)

RUBICON CORP (TX)
Recapitalized as Osprey Holding, Inc. 12/4/92
Each share Common 1¢ par exchanged for (0.125) share Common 1¢ par

RUBICON FINL INC (DE)
Reincorporated under the laws of Nevada 08/29/2011

RUBICON MED CORP (DE)
Merged into Boston Scientific Corp. 6/14/2005
Each share Common $0.001 par exchanged for $1.50 cash
Note: An escrow account has been established for possible future distributions

RUBICON TECHNOLOGIES INC (AB)
Name changed to Burnt Sand Solutions Inc. (AB) 03/14/1996
Burnt Sand Solutions Inc. (AB) reincorporated in Canada 03/12/1998 which name changed to Burntsand Inc. 10/04/1999
(See Burntsand Inc.)

RUBIDELL REC INC (MN)
Each share old Common 1¢ par exchanged for (0.25) share new Common 1¢ par 07/14/1989
Name changed to Casino Resource Corp. 02/22/1993
Casino Resource Corp. name changed to BounceBackTechnologies.com, Inc. (MN) 01/14/2000 which reincorporated in Delaware as Name Dynamics, Inc. 11/05/2010 which name changed to UBL Interactive, Inc. 07/03/2012

RUBINCON VENTURES INC (DE)
Common $0.001 par split (4) for (1) by issuance of (3) additional shares payable 08/30/2005 to holders of record 08/26/2005 Ex date - 08/31/2005
Common $0.001 par split (4) for (1) by issuance of (3) additional shares payable 10/07/2005 to holders of record 10/06/2005 Ex date - 10/11/2005
Under plan of merger name changed to API Nanotronics Corp. 11/07/2006
API Nanotronics Corp. name changed to API Technologies Corp. 10/27/2009

RUBIOS RESTAURANTS INC (DE)
Acquired by Mill Road Capital, L.P. 08/24/2010
Each share Common $0.001 par exchanged for $8.70 cash

RUBY CREEK RES INC (BC)
Reincorporated under the laws of Nevada and Common no par changed to $0.001 par 01/29/2009

RUBY EXPL CO (NV)
Capital Stock $1 par changed to 1¢ par 12/23/71
Name changed to Scoggins Petroleum Corp. 4/19/73
Each share Capital Stock 1¢ par exchanged for (1) share Capital Stock 1¢ par
Scoggins Petroleum Corp. name changed to Fargo Energy Corp. 1/19/77 which name changed to Western Reserves, Inc. 4/29/83 which recapitalized as Great Western Equities Group, Inc. 6/10/86 which name changed to American International Marketing, Inc. 9/21/89

RUBY FOO'S ENTERPRISES LTD. (QC)
Liquidation completed
Each share Common $2 par exchanged for initial distribution of $4 cash 12/23/65
Each share Common $2 par received second and final distribution of $0.36 cash 5/25/66

RUBY METAL MNS CORP (NV)
Name changed to Biogenix, Inc. 12/19/85
(See Biogenix, Inc.)

RUBY MNG CO (CO)
Each share old Common $0.001 par exchanged for (0.05) share new Common $0.001 par 02/29/2000
Name changed to Admiralty Holding Co. 11/18/2005
(See Admiralty Holding Co.)

RUBY MTN MINES INC (BC)
Recapitalized as Syrus Capital Corp. 3/17/94
Each share Common no par exchanged for (1/3) share Common no par
Syrus Capital Corp. recapitalized as New Syrus Capital Corp. 11/19/96 which name changed to Player Petroleum Corp. (BC) 2/25/97 which reincorporated in Alberta 4/29/98
(See Player Petroleum Corp.)

RUBY RED RES INC (AB)
Recapitalized as SG Spirit Gold Inc. (AB) 10/20/2010
Each share Common no par exchanged for (0.1) share Common no par
SG Spirit Gold Inc. (AB) reincorporated in British Columbia 12/20/2011 which name changed to DOJA Cannabis Co. Ltd. 08/09/2017 which name changed to Hiku Brands Co. Ltd. 01/31/2018 which merged into Canopy Growth Corp. 09/06/2018

RUBY RES LTD (BC)
Name changed to International Domesticated Furs Ltd. 12/18/84
(See International Domesticated Furs Ltd.)

RUBY SILVER MINES INC (NV)
Name changed to Ruby Exploration Co. 10/28/1971
Ruby Exploration Co. name changed to Scoggins Petroleum Corp. 04/19/1973 which name changed to Fargo Energy Corp. 01/19/1977 which name changed to Western Reserves, Inc. 04/29/1983 which recapitalized as Great Western Equities Group, Inc. 06/10/1986 which name changed to American International Marketing, Inc. 09/21/1989

RUBY TUESDAY INC (GA)
Common 1¢ par split (2) for (1) by issuance of (1) additional share payable 05/08/1998 to holders of record 04/17/1998 Ex date - 05/11/1998
Common 1¢ par split (2) for (1) by issuance of (1) additional share payable 05/19/2000 to holders of record 04/28/2000
Acquired by RTI Holding Co. LLC 12/21/2017
Each share Common 1¢ par exchanged for $2.40 cash

RUCKER CO (CA)
Common no par split (3) for (2) by issuance of (0.5) additional share 6/15/66
Common no par split (2) for (1) by issuance of (1) additional share 3/24/67
Merged into N L Industries, Inc. 1/21/77
Each share Common no par exchanged for (1.66) shares Common $2.50 par

RUCKER PHARMACAL INC (LA)
Common no par split (3) for (2) by issuance of (0.5) additional share 02/28/1973
Stock Dividend - 10% 08/02/1974
Merged into Boots Laboratories, Inc. 07/22/1977
Each share Common no par exchanged for $17 cash

RUCKUS WIRELESS INC (DE)
Merged into Brocade Communications Systems, Inc. 05/27/2016
Each share Common $0.001 par exchanged for (0.75) share new Common $0.001 par and $6.45 cash
(See Brocade Communications Systems, Inc.)

RUDD MELIKIAN INC (PA)
Name changed to Pennstar Co. 05/05/1970

RUDDICK CORP (NC)
4% Conv. Preferred Ser. A $100 par called for redemption 07/01/1977
4% Conv. Preferred Ser. B $100 par called for redemption 07/01/1977
5% Preferred $100 par called for redemption 07/01/1977
$0.56 Conv. Preference $5 par called for redemption 05/31/1994
Common $1 par split (2) for (1) by issuance of (1) additional share 07/01/1986
Common $1 par split (2) for (1) by issuance of (1) additional share 06/28/1991
Common $1 par split (2) for (1) by issuance of (1) additional share 09/29/1995
Common $1 par changed to no par 00/00/2003
Name changed to Harris Teeter Supermarkets, Inc. (New) 04/02/2012
(See Harris Teeter Supermarkets, Inc. (New))

RUDDY MANUFACTURING CO. LTD.
Out of business 00/00/1933
Details not available

RUDOLPH GUENTHER-RUSSELL LAW, INC.
See - Guenther (Rudolph)-Russell Law, Inc.

RUDOLPH WURLITZER CO. (OH)
See - Wurlitzer (Rudolph) Co.

RUDY 45 (NV)
Name changed to NMI Group, Inc. 07/13/2007

RUDY FURNACE CO.
Name changed to Rudy Manufacturing Co. in 1948
Rudy Manufacturing Co. merged into Sundstrand Corp. (DE) 1/26/68 which name changed to United Technologies Corp. 6/10/99

RUDY MANUFACTURING CO. (MI)
Stock Dividends - 10% 4/15/55; 50% 4/22/64; 10% 10/25/66
Merged into Sundstrand Corp. (DE) 1/26/68
Each share Common $1 par exchanged for (0.4) share $3.50 Conv. Preferred no par and (0.4) share Common $1 par
Sundstrand Corp. (DE) merged into United Technologies Corp. 6/10/99

RUDY NUTRITION (NV)
Each share old Common $0.001 par exchanged for (0.25) share new Common $0.001 par 09/26/2008
SEC revoked common stock registration 10/23/2008
Stockholders' equity unlikely

RUDYS RESTAURANT GROUP INC (NV)
Merged into Benihana Inc. 12/01/1997
Each share Common 1¢ par exchanged for $5 cash
Note: an additional payment of $0.29 cash per share was made 01/28/1998

RUE DE RIVOLI PERFUMERIES AMER LTD (NV)
Each share old Common $0.001 par exchanged for (0.001) share new Common $0.001 par 9/30/94
Name changed to Enviro Solutions International Inc. in November 1994
Enviro Solutions International Inc. name changed to International Custom Pack, Inc. 11/22/95 which name changed to Global Seafood Technologies Inc. 12/15/98

RUEBRO MFG INC (NY)
Merged into Loren Industries, Inc. 08/03/1983
Each share Common 1¢ par exchanged for $0.75 cash

RUEPING FRED LEATHER CO (WI)
Each share 8% Preferred $100 par exchanged for (1-1/3) shares 6% Preferred $100 par and (1-1/3) shares Common $10 par 00/00/1935
Each share Common $100 par exchanged for (3) shares Common $10 par 00/00/1935
6% Preferred $100 par called for redemption 04/01/1948
Common $10 par changed to $7 par 08/25/1948
Filed a petition under Chapter 7 Federal Bankruptcy Code 00/00/1985
No stockholders' equity

RUE21 INC (DE)
Acquired by Rhodes Holdco, Inc. 10/10/2013
Each share Common $0.004 par exchanged for $42 cash

RUFFO LAKE MINES LTD. (ON)
Charter cancelled for failure to file reports and pay taxes in 1969

RUFFWARDS, INC. (DE)
Voluntarily dissolved 12/13/76
Details not available

RUGBY RED LAKE GOLD MINES LTD. (ON)
Dissolved 7/25/60

RUGBY RES LTD (BC)
Name changed to Euro-Ad Systems, Inc. 04/30/1993
Euro-Ad Systems, Inc. recapitalized as Sun Devil Gold Corp. 07/03/1997 which name changed to Cardero Resource Corp. 05/13/1999

RUGGED RED LAKE MINES LTD. (ON)
Charter cancelled for failure to pay taxes and file returns 5/14/75

RUGGEDCOM INC (ON)
Acquired by Siemens Canada Ltd. 04/12/2012
Each share Common no par exchanged for $33 cash

RUILI HLDGS LTD (HONG KONG)
Name changed to See Corp. Ltd. 11/07/2005
(See See Corp. Ltd.)

RUJO, INC. (UT)
Name changed to Jackson Brothers Industries, Inc. (UT) 01/14/1987
Jackson Brothers Industries, Inc. (UT) reincorporated in Nevada 05/20/1989 which recapitalized as Dynacq International Inc. (NV) 03/08/1993 which reincorporated in Delaware as Dynacq Healthcare, Inc. 11/14/2003 which reincorporated in Nevada 03/20/2007

RULE INDS INC (MA)
Each Non-Transferable Units of Residual Int. (issued per merger of Phillips Screw Co.) received distribution of 25¢ cash 6/1/79
Merged into Greenfield Industries Inc. 1/12/96
Each share Common 1¢ par exchanged for $15.30 cash

RULE RES LTD (BC)
Recapitalized as Globe Resources Inc. 03/09/1990
Each share Common no par exchanged for (0.2) share Common no par
Globe Resources Inc. recapitalized as Genco Resources Ltd. 03/30/1998 which reorganized as Silvermex Resources Inc. 11/16/2010 which merged into First Majestic Silver Corp. 07/06/2012

RUMFORD BK & TR CO (RUMFORD, ME)
Merged into Maine National Bank (Portland, ME) 8/2/68
Each share Capital Stock exchanged for (2.5) shares Capital Stock $10 par
Maine National Bank (Portland, ME) reorganized as Maine National Corp. 2/18/83 which merged into Bank of New England Corp. 12/18/85
(See Bank of New England Corp.)

RUMFORD CHEMICAL WORKS
Acquired by Heyden Chemical Corp. (DE) on a (5) for (4) basis in 1948
Heyden Chemical Corp. (DE) name changed to Heyden Newport Chemical Corp. 1/9/57 which was acquired by Tennessee Gas Transmission Co. 10/4/63 which name changed to Tenneco Inc. 4/11/66 which merged into El Paso Natural Gas Co. 12/12/96 which reorganized as El Paso Energy Corp. 8/1/98 which name changed to El Paso Corp. 2/5/2001

RUMFORD PRESS INC (NY)
Merged into Rumford National Graphics Inc. 11/10/1976
Details not available

RUMFORD PRINTING CO. (NH)
Merged into Blanchard Press, Inc. 01/00/1963
Details not available

RUMSON-FAIR HAVEN BK & TR CO (RUMSON, NJ)
Stock Dividends - 10% payable 07/23/2004 to holders of record 06/30/2004 Ex date - 06/28/2004; 10% payable 05/31/2005 to holders of record 05/06/2005 Ex date - 05/04/2005; 10% payable 06/15/2006 to holders of record 05/15/2006 Ex date - 05/11/2006; 10% payable 06/15/2007 to holders of record 05/15/2007 Ex date - 05/11/2007; 10% payable 06/11/2008 to holders of record

05/21/2008 Ex date - 05/19/2008; 10% payable 06/12/2009 to holders of record 05/22/2009 Ex date - 05/20/2009; 10% payable 08/18/2010 to holders of record 08/04/2010 Ex date - 08/02/2010; 5% payable 06/22/2011 to holders of record 05/27/2011 Ex date - 06/17/2011
Merged into 1st Constitution Bancorp 02/07/2014
Each share Common $5 par exchanged for (0.27493499) share Common no par and $4.84687022 cash

RUN OF RIV PWR INC (BC)
Reincorporated 09/13/2006
Place of incorporation changed from (AB) (BC) 09/13/2006
Acquired by Concord SCCP General Partner (I) Inc. 08/18/2014
Each share Common no par exchanged for $0.0026 cash

RUNAWAY RES LTD (BC)
Name changed to Revere Resources Ltd. 03/16/1988
(See Revere Resources Ltd.)

RUNCORP INC (NV)
Each share old Common $0.001 par exchanged for (0.1) share new Common $0.001 par 11/24/2002
Charter revoked for failure to file reports and pay fees 02/01/2007

RUNDLE OILS LTD. (AB)
Acquired by Pathfinder Petroleums Ltd. in 1954
Each share Capital Stock no par exchanged for (0.2) share Common 50¢ par
Pathfinder Petroleums Ltd. merged into Medallion Petroleums Ltd. 9/11/56 which merged into Canadian Industrial Gas & Oil Ltd. 3/8/65 which merged into Norcen Energy Resources Ltd. (ALTA) 10/28/75 which reincorporated under the laws of Canada 4/15/77
(See Norcen Energy Resources Ltd.)

RUNNING FOXES PETE CORP (BC)
Recapitalized as Running Fox Resource Corp. 10/17/2000
Each share Common no par exchanged for (0.2) share Common no par

RUPERTSLAND RES LTD (AB)
Stock Dividend - in Common to holders of 10% Conv. Retractable 1st Preference Ser. A - 12% 07/01/1983
Reorganized as Bracknell Resources Ltd. (AB) 10/18/1985
Each share 10% Conv. Retractable 1st Preference Ser. A no par reclassified as (26) shares Common no par
Each share Common no par exchanged for (0.1) share Common no par
Bracknell Resources Ltd. (AB) reincorporated in Ontario as Bracknell Corp. 06/13/1989
(See Bracknell Corp.)

RUPP INDS INC (OH)
Plan of arrangement under Chapter XI bankruptcy proceedings confirmed 08/25/1976
No stockholders' equity

RUPPERT (JACOB) (NY)
4.5% Preferred $100 par called for redemption 12/30/1965
Merged into National Equities, Inc. 02/03/1966
Each share Common $5 par exchanged for (0.33333333) share Common $10 par
National Equities, Inc. reorganized as NEI Corp. 04/01/1973 which merged into Rockwood National Corp. 07/13/1977
(See Rockwood National Corp.)

RUPUNUNI GOLD MINING CO. (CANADA) LTD. (ON)
Recapitalized as Rio Rupununi Mines Ltd. on a (1) for (3) basis 11/16/55
Rio Rupununi Mines Ltd. charter cancelled 1/10/73

RURAL CELLULAR CORP (MN)
Stock Dividends - In 11.375% Preferred to holders of 11.375% Preferred 2.84375% payable 02/16/1999 to holders of record 02/01/1999; 2.84375% payable 05/17/1999 to holders of record 05/01/1999; 2.84375% payable 08/16/1999 to holders of record 08/01/1999; 2.84375% payable 11/15/1999 to holders of record 11/01/1999; 2.84375% payable 02/15/2000 to holders of record 02/01/2000; 2.84375% payable 05/15/2000 to holders of record 05/01/2000 Ex date - 04/18/2000; 2.84375% payable 08/15/2000 to holders of record 08/01/2000 Ex date - 07/28/2000; 2.84375% payable 11/15/2000 to holders of record 11/01/2000; 2.84375% payable 02/15/2001 to holders of record 02/01/2001 Ex date - 01/30/2001; 2.84375% payable 05/15/2001 to holders of record 05/01/2001 Ex date - 04/27/2001; 2.84375% payable 08/15/2001 to holders of record 08/01/2001 Ex date - 07/30/2001; 2.84375% payable 11/15/2001 to holders of record 11/01/2001 Ex date - 10/30/2001; 2.84375% payable 02/15/2002 to holders of record 02/01/2002 Ex date - 01/30/2002; 2.84375% payable 05/15/2002 to holders of record 05/01/2002 Ex date - 04/29/2002; 2.84375% payable 08/15/2002 to holders of record 08/01/2002 Ex date - 07/30/2002; 2.84375% payable 11/15/2002 to holders of record 11/01/2002 Ex date - 10/30/2002; 2.84375% payable 02/15/2003 to holders of record 02/01/2003 Ex date - 01/29/2003; 2.84375% payable 05/15/2003 to holders of record 05/01/2003 Ex date - 04/29/2003
In 12.25% to holders of 12.25% Preferred 3.0625% payable 05/15/2000 to holders of record 05/01/2000; 3.0625% payable 08/15/2000 to holders of record 08/01/2000; 3.0625% payable 11/15/2000 to holders of record 11/01/2000; 3.0625% payable 02/15/2001 to holders of record 02/01/2001 Ex date - 01/30/2001; 3.0625% payable 05/15/2001 to holders of record 05/01/2001 Ex date - 04/27/2001; 3.0625% payable 08/15/2001 to holders of record 08/01/2001 Ex date - 07/30/2001; 3.0625% payable 11/15/2001 to holders of record 11/01/2001 Ex date - 10/30/2001; 3.0625% payable 02/15/2002 to holders of record 02/01/2002 Ex date - 01/30/2002; 3.0625% payable 05/15/2002 to holders of record 05/01/2002 Ex date - 04/29/2002; 3.0625% payable 08/15/2002 to holders of record 08/01/2002 Ex date - 07/30/2002; 3.0625% payable 11/15/2002 to holders of record 11/01/2002 Ex date - 10/30/2002; 3.0625% payable 02/15/2003 to holders of record 02/01/2003 Ex date - 01/29/2003; 3.0625% payable 05/15/2003 to holders of record 05/01/2003 Ex date - 04/29/2003; 3.0625% payable 08/15/2003 to holders of record 08/01/2003 Ex date - 07/30/2003; 3.0625% payable 11/15/2003 to holders of record 11/01/2003 Ex date - 10/29/2003; 3.0625% payable 02/15/2004 to holders of record 02/01/2004 Ex date - 01/28/2004; 3.0625% payable 05/15/2004 to holders of record 05/01/2004 Ex date - 04/28/2004; 3.0625% payable 08/15/2004 to holders of record 08/01/2004 Ex date - 07/28/2004; 3.0625% payable 11/15/2004 to holders of record 11/01/2004 Ex date - 10/28/2004; 3.0625% payable 02/15/2005 to holders of record 02/01/2005 Ex date - 01/28/2005
Each share 11.375% Sr. Exchangeable Preferred exchanged for $1,000 principal amount of 11.375% Sr. Subordinate Debentures due 05/15/2010 and $355.40 cash 05/15/2007
Merged into Cellco Partnership 08/07/2008
Each share Class A Common 1¢ par exchanged for $45 cash
12.25% Exchangeable Jr. Preferred called for redemption at $1,015.31 on 09/05/2008
Public interest eliminated

RURAL GAS SVC INC (MA)
Common no par changed to $1 par 00/00/1949
Acquired by Phillips Petroleum Co. 05/14/1965
Details not available

RURAL/METRO CORP (DE)
Acquired by WP Rocket Holdings Inc. 06/30/2011
Each share Common 1¢ par exchanged for $17.25 cash

RURBAN FINL CORP (OH)
Common no par split (2) for (1) by issuance of (1) additional share payable 06/30/1998 to holders of record 06/12/1998
Stock Dividends - 5% payable 09/29/2000 to holders of record 09/15/2000 Ex date - 09/13/2000; 5% payable 09/28/2001 to holders of record 09/14/2001
Name changed to SB Financial Group, Inc. 04/25/2013

RUSCO DEV CORP (NY)
Reincorporated under the laws of Delaware as Atlantic Medical Corp. 01/20/1972
Atlantic Medical Corp. recapitalized as I-Rock Industries, Inc. 04/05/1990 which name changed to IR Operating Corp. 04/26/1999 which name changed to Digi Link Technologies, Inc. 02/12/2001
(See Digi Link Technologies, Inc.)

RUSCO INDS INC (DE)
Reincorporated 6/3/65
State of incorporation changed from (OH) to (DE) 6/3/65
Chapter 11 Federal Bankruptcy Code converted to Chapter 7 on 2/6/89
Stockholders' equity undetermined

RUSH CREEK LD CO (VA)
Liquidation completed
Each share Capital Stock $50 par exchanged for initial distribution of $25 cash 05/17/1971
Each share Capital Stock $50 par received second distribution of $5 cash 10/01/1971
Each share Capital Stock $50 par received third and final distribution of $2.095 cash 03/28/1974

RUSH ENERGY CORP (BC)
Name changed to Rush Ventures Inc. 08/11/1986
Rush Ventures Inc. recapitalized as Rushmore Energy Corp. 08/01/1991 which name changed to Seacorp Properties Inc. 09/30/1993
(See Seacorp Properties Inc.)

RUSH EXPL INC (CANADA)
Voluntarily dissolved 12/30/2015
Details not available

RUSH FINL TECHNOLOGIES INC (TX)
Name changed to Terra Nova Financial Group, Inc. (TX) 10/27/2006
Terra Nova Financial Group, Inc. (TX) reincorporated in Illinois 06/20/2008 which name changed to TNFG Corp. 10/25/2010
(See TNFG Corp.)

RUSH INDS INC (DE)
Name changed to Post American Corp. 05/08/1973
(See Post American Corp.)

RUSH LAKE GOLD MINES LTD.
Acquired by Joburke Gold Mines Ltd. on a (1) for (2) basis 00/00/1947
Joburke Gold Mines Ltd. recapitalized as New Joburke Explorations Ltd. 08/21/1973 which name changed to Cenex Ltd. 08/16/1977
(See Cenex Ltd.)

RUSH LAKE GOLD MINES LTD. (ON)
Charter surrendered for failure to file reports and pay taxes August 1957

RUSH METALS CORP (CANADA)
Recapitalized as Rush Exploration Inc. 12/13/2011
Each share Common no par exchanged for (0.01) share Common no par
(See Rush Exploration Inc.)

RUSH VENTURES INC (BC)
Recapitalized as Rushmore Energy Corp. 08/01/1991
Each (4.5) shares Common no par exchanged for (1) share Common no par
Rushmore Energy Corp. name changed to Seacorp Properties Inc. 09/30/1993
(See Seacorp Properties Inc.)

RUSHMORE ENERGY CORP (BC)
Name changed to Seacorp Properties Inc. 09/30/1993
(See Seacorp Properties Inc.)

RUSHMORE FD INC (MD)
Over-The-Counter Index Plus Portfolio $0.001 par reorganized as CRT Funds 12/22/1995
Details not available
Stock Market Index Plus Portfolio $0.001 par reorganized as CRT Funds 12/22/1995
Details not available
Completely liquidated 08/31/1996
Each share Nova Portfolio $0.001 par received first and final distribution of $11.09 cash
Money Market Portfolio $0.001 par reorganized as Fund For Government Investors, Inc. 01/25/2002
Details not available
U.S. Government Inter-Term Securities Portfolio $0.001 par reclassified as U.S. Government Long-Term Securities Portfolio $0.001 par 04/30/2002
Name changed to FBR Rushmore Fund, Inc. and U.S. Government Long-Term Securities Portfolio $0.001 par reclassified as Total Return Bond Fund $0.001 par 02/28/2003
(See FBR Rushmore Fund, Inc.)

RUSHMORE FINL GROUP INC (TX)
Issue Information - 815,341 shares COM offered at $5.50 per share on 02/17/1998
Name changed to Rush Financial Technologies, Inc. 02/25/2004
Rush Financial Technologies, Inc. name changed to Terra Nova Financial Group, Inc. (TX) 10/27/2006 which reincorporated in Illinois 06/20/2008 which name changed to TNFG Corp. 10/25/2010
(See TNFG Corp.)

RUSHMORE URANIUM & OIL CORP. (DE)
No longer in existence having filed Consent to Dissolution 7/6/56

RUSHRIV GOLD MINES, LTD. (ON)
Charter cancelled for failure to file reports and pay taxes in 1956

RUSK PORCUPINE MINES, LTD. (ON)
Charter cancelled for failure to file reports and pay taxes July 1960

RUSKIN DEVS LTD (BC)
Recapitalized as Consolidated Ruskin Developments Ltd. (Old) 12/03/1990
Each share Common no par exchanged for (0.25) share Common no par
Consolidated Ruskin Developments Ltd. (Old) merged into Consolidated Ruskin Developments Ltd. (New) 03/31/1992 which name changed to Leisureways Marketing Ltd. (BC) 11/23/1992 which reincorporated in Yukon 11/10/1997 which name changed to LML Payment Systems Inc. (YT) 07/15/1998 which reincorporated in British Columbia 09/07/2012
(See LML Payment Systems Inc.)

RUSS BERRIE & CO INC (NJ)
Common no par split (3) for (2) by issuance of (0.5) additional share 03/31/1993
Name changed to Kid Brands, Inc. 09/22/2009
(See Kid Brands, Inc.)

RUSS BUILDING CO. (CA)
Liquidation completed 10/21/55

RUSS-RAE CHIBOUGAMAU MINES LTD. (ON)
Charter cancelled for failure to file reports and pay taxes in 1957

RUSS TOGS INC (NY)
Class A $1 par split (3) for (2) by issuance of (0.5) additional share 6/20/61
Class A $1 par split (3) for (2) by issuance of (0.5) additional share 9/20/62
Class A $1 par split (3) for (2) by issuance of (0.5) additional share 12/21/64
Class A $1 par split (3) for (2) by issuance of (0.5) additional share 12/22/66
Class A $1 par reclassified as Common $1 par 5/24/68
Common $1 par split (3) for (2) by issuance of (0.5) additional share 7/15/83
Common $1 par split (3) for (2) by issuance of (0.5) additional share 7/15/87
Filed a petition under Chapter 11 Federal Bankruptcy Code 11/6/91
Stockholders' equity unlikely

RUSSCO INC (DE)
Recapitalized as Specialized Health Products International, Inc. 07/28/1995
Each (4.875) shares Common 2¢ par exchanged for (1) share Common 2¢ par
(See Specialized Health Products International, Inc.)

RUSSCO SILVER INC (ID)
Charter forfeited for failure to file reports 12/1/92

RUSSEKS FIFTH AVENUE, INC. (NY)
Common no par changed to $5 par 00/00/1933
Each share Common $5 par exchanged for (2) shares Common $2.50 par 00/00/1937
Each share Common $2.50 par exchanged for (2) shares Common $1.25 par 00/00/1946
Common $1.25 par changed to 50¢ par 12/21/1959
Name changed to Russeks, Inc. 08/13/1963
Russeks, Inc. reincorporated in Delaware as Hemdale Enterprises Inc. 07/28/1974 which name changed to Redlaw Enterprises Inc. 12/18/1975 which name changed to Redlaw, Inc. 08/29/1977 which merged into Redlaw Industries Inc. 07/13/1979
(See Redlaw Industries Inc.)

RUSSEKS INC (NY)
Reincorporated under the laws of Delaware as Hemdale Enterprises Inc. 07/28/1974
Hemdale Enterprises Inc. name changed to Redlaw Enterprises Inc. 12/18/1975 which name changed to Redlaw, Inc. 08/29/1977 which merged into Redlaw Industries Inc. 07/13/1979
(See Redlaw Industries Inc.)

RUSSEL HUGH & SONS LTD (CANADA)
Class A no par (Old), Class B no par (Old) and Class C no par reclassified as Common no par 5/5/65
Common no par reclassified as Class A Common no par 5/1/67
Name changed to Russel (Hugh) Ltd. 7/14/71
Russel (Hugh) Ltd. name changed to Russel (Hugh) Inc. 11/8/77
(See Russel (Hugh) Inc.)

RUSSEL HUGH INC (CANADA)
Name changed 11/08/1977
9.75% 1st Preferred Ser. B no par called for redemption 12/01/1975
$1.70 Preferred Ser. C no par called for redemption 12/01/1975
Name changed from Russel (Hugh) Ltd. to to Russel (Hugh) Inc. 11/08/1977
Class A Common no par and Class B Common no par acquired by York Steel Constructions Ltd. 11/26/1980
Each share Class A Common no par exchanged for $21.50 cash
Each share Class B Common no par exchanged for $21.50 cash
Preferreds not affected will remain outstanding
Name changed to York Russel Inc. 05/19/1981
York Russel Inc. name changed to YRI-York Ltd. 03/30/1984
(See YRI-York Ltd.)

RUSSEL METALS INC (CANADA)
7.50% Conv. Preferred Class 2 Ser. C no par called for redemption at $25 plus $0.04 accrued dividends on 03/22/2004

RUSSELL ALUM CORP (FL)
Common $1 par split (3) for (2) by issuance of (0.5) additional share 09/17/1969
Completely liquidated 02/05/1973
Each share Common $1 par exchanged for first and final distribution of $10 cash

RUSSELL ARMS CORP. (MO)
Liquidation completed 9/14/56

RUSSELL BURDSALL & WARD CORP (DE)
Name changed to RB&W Corp. 4/24/86
RB&W Corp. merged into Park-Ohio Industries, Inc. 3/31/95

RUSSELL BURDSALL & WARD INC (NY)
Name changed 11/03/1973
Each share Common $100 par exchanged for (5) shares Common $20 par 00/00/1946
Name changed from Russell, Burdsall & Ward Bolt & Nut Co. to Russell, Burdsall & Ward, Inc. 11/03/1973
6% Preferred $100 par called for redemption 10/00/1974
Merged into Mangel Stores Corp. 12/31/1977
Each share Common $20 par exchanged for $290 cash

RUSSELL (F.C.) CO. (OH)
Common no par changed to $1 par in 1947
Common $1 par split (2) for (1) by issuance of (1) additional share 5/12/55
Stock Dividends - 10% 4/2/51; 10% 4/1/52
Name changed to Rusco Industries, Inc. (OH) 11/1/61
Rusco Industries, Inc. (OH) reincorporated in Delaware 6/3/65
(See Rusco Industries, Inc.)

RUSSELL CORP (DE)
Reincorporated 4/27/2005
Common $1 par split (2) for (1) by issuance of (1) additional share 5/18/76
Common $1 par split (3) for (2) by issuance of (0.5) additional share 7/17/78
Common $1 par split (2) for (1) by issuance of (1) additional share 6/15/81
Common $1 par changed to 1¢ par 5/7/82
Common 1¢ par split (8) for (5) by issuance of (0.6) additional share 6/20/83
Common 1¢ par split (2) for (1) by issuance of (1) additional share 12/1/86
10% Preferred 1988 Ser. 1¢ par called for redemption 12/31/93
State of incorporation changed from (AL) to (DE) 4/27/2005
Merged into Berkshire Hathaway Inc. 8/2/2006
Each share Common 1¢ par exchanged for $18 cash

RUSSELL EXCHANGE TRADED FDS TR (DE)
Trust terminated 10/24/2012
Each Aggressive Growth ETF received $53.77 cash
Each Consistent Growth ETF received $54.71 cash
Each Contrarian ETF received $48.87 cash
Each Developed ex-U.S. High Momentum ETF received $52.86 cash
Each Developed ex-U.S. Low Beta ETF received $52.81 cash
Each Developed ex-U.S. Low Volatility ETF received $53.65 cash
Each Equity Income ETF received $52.39 cash
Each Growth at a Reasonable Price ETF received $53.15 cash
Each High Dividend Yield ETF received $26.43 cash
Each Low P/E ETF received $50.408227 cash
Each Small Cap Aggressive Growth ETF received $63.94 cash
Each Small Cap Consistent Growth ETF received $65.19 cash
Each Small Cap Contrarian ETF received $66.65 cash
Each Small Cap High Dividend Yield ETF received $25.28 cash
Each Small Cap Low P/E ETF received $68.99 cash
Each 1000 High Beta ETF received $49.24 cash
Each 1000 High Momentum ETF received $54.28 cash
Each 1000 High Volatility ETF received $50.56 cash
Each 1000 Low Beta ETF received $55.19 cash
Each 1000 Low Volatility ETF received $53.66 cash
Each 2000 High Beta ETF received $44.85 cash
Each 2000 High Momentum ETF received $54.08 cash
Each 2000 High Volatility ETF received $41.91 cash
Each 2000 Low Beta ETF received $52.77 cash
Each 2000 Low Volatility ETF received $52.08 cash
Trust terminated 02/06/2015
Each Equity ETF received $36.259762 cash

RUSSELL FED SVGS BK (RUSSELL, KY)
Merged into Peoples Bancorp Inc. 01/01/1997
Each share Common 1¢ par exchanged for $19.41 cash

RUSSELL GRADER MANUFACTURING CO.
Acquired by Caterpillar Tractor Co. (CA) 00/00/1928
Details not available

RUSSELL HLDGS LTD (QC)
Each share old Common no par exchanged for (2) shares new Common no par 05/06/1983
Merged into Treats Inc. 04/26/1989
Each share new Common no par exchanged for (0.4) share Common no par
(See Treats Inc.)

RUSSELL INDS INC (NV)
Each share old Common $0.001 par exchanged for (5) shares new Common $0.001 par 10/06/2006
Each share new Common $0.001 par exchanged again for (0.01) share new Common $0.001 par 11/27/2006
Each share new Common $0.001 par exchanged again for (0.0002) share new Common $0.001 par 03/03/2008
Each share new Common $0.001 par exchanged for (0.0001) share old Common $0.000001 par 02/03/2009
Each share old Common $0.000001 par exchanged for (0.001) share new Common $0.000001 par 10/07/2010
Name changed to Algae Farm (USA), Inc. 01/26/2011
Algae Farm (USA), Inc. recapitalized as Diversified Energy Holdings, Inc. 07/18/2013

RUSSELL (HUGH) LTD. (CANADA)
Class A Common no par and Class B Common no par split (2) for (1) by issuance of (1) additional share respectively 7/16/71
Class A Common no par and Class B Common no par split (2) for (1) by issuance of (1) additional share respectively 11/1/72
6-1/2% Conv. 1st Preferred Ser. A $20 par called for redemption 12/1/75
Name changed to Russel (Hugh) Inc. 11/8/77
(See Russel (Hugh) Inc.)

RUSSELL MANAGEMENT LTD. (SK)
Struck off register for failure to file annual returns 9/29/78

RUSSELL MANUFACTURING CO. (CT)
Capital Stock $100 par changed to $50 par in 1936
Each share Capital Stock $50 par exchanged for (2) shares Capital Stock no par in 1940
Stock Dividends - 50% 4/47; 10% 10/10/58; 20% 12/14/60
Completely liquidated 2/1/65
Each share Capital Stock no par exchanged for first and final distribution of $25 cash

RUSSELL MLS INC (AL)
Name changed to Russell Corp. (AL) 4/26/73
Russell Corp. (AL) reincorporated in Delaware 4/27/2005
(See Russell Corp.)

**RUSSELL NATL BK
(LEWISTOWN, PA)**
Each share Common 20¢ par
exchanged for (2) shares Common
$10 par 07/16/1974
Common $10 par changed to $5 par
and (1) additional share issued
07/16/1979
Under plan of reorganization each
share Common $5 par automatically
became (1) share Heritage Financial
Services Corp. Common $5 par
01/01/1983
*(See Heritage Financial Services
Corp.)*

**RUSSELL REINFORCED PLASTICS
CORP. (NY)**
Name changed to R R P Corp.
9/18/67
Preferred $1 par called for
redemption 10/24/67
R R P Corp. liquidation completed by
exchange for Talley Industries, Inc.
Common no par 10/8/70
(See Talley Industries, Inc.)

**RUSSELL STOVER CANDIES INC
(MO)**
Stock Dividends - 100% 01/15/1965;
100% 01/10/1968; 100% 01/15/1973
Merged into Ward Paper Co.
11/02/1981
Each share Common $1 par
exchanged for $20 cash

**RUSSET RED LAKE GOLD MINES
LTD. (ON)**
Merged into Aiken-Russet Red Lake
Mines Ltd. 12/01/1965
Each share Common $1 par
exchanged for (0.33333333) share
Common no par
Aiken-Russet Red Lake Mines Ltd.
merged into Canhorn Mining Corp.
01/09/1986 which merged into
Canhorn Chemical Corp. 04/26/1995
which merged into Nayarit Gold Inc.
05/02/2005 which merged into
Capital Gold Corp. 08/02/2010
which merged into Gammon Gold
Inc. (QC) 04/08/2011 which
reincorporated in Ontario as AuRico
Gold Inc. 06/14/2011 which merged
into Alamos Gold Inc. (New)
07/06/2015

RUSSIAN CAVIAR COM INC (CA)
Common $0.001 par split (10) for (1)
by issuance of (9) additional shares
payable 12/1/2000 to holders of
record 12/1/2000
Name changed to E-Synergies Inc.
12/7/2000

RUSSIAN DEV CORP (NV)
Recapitalized as Score Medical Corp.
09/22/1997
Each share Common $0.001 par
exchanged for (0.25) share Common
$0.001 par
Score Medical Corp. name changed
to Imatters.Com, Inc. 02/10/1999
which name changed to Iweb Corp.
06/01/1999 which reorganized as
National Health Scan Inc.
05/09/2002 which name to Gaensel
Energy Group, Inc. 02/24/2015

**RUSSIAN FINANCE &
CONSTRUCTION CORP.**
In process of liquidation in 1945

RUSSIAN IMPORTS COM INC (CA)
Name changed to KIK Technology
International, Inc. 09/19/2001
*(See KIK Technology International,
Inc.)*

RUSSIAN KID MINING CO., LTD. (ON)
Recapitalized as New Russian Kid
Mining Co. Ltd. 07/00/1964
Each share Capital Stock $1 par
exchanged for (0.1) share Capital
Stock $1 par
New Russian Kid Mining Co. Ltd.
name changed to Augmitto
Explorations Ltd. 03/01/1966

(See Augmitto Explorations Ltd.)
RUSSIAN RES GROUP INC (DE)
Name changed to Petro Resources
Corp. 06/20/2005
Petro Resources Corp. name
changed to Magnum Hunter
Resources Corp. 07/14/2009
*(See Magnum Hunter Resources
Corp.)*

RUSSOIL CORP (NV)
SEC revoked common stock
registration 09/24/2012

**RUST CRAFT GREETING CARDS
INC (DE)**
Common $1 par split (3) for (2) by
issuance of (0.5) additional share
10/31/68
Common $1 par split (2) for (1) by
issuance of (1) additional share
11/16/71
Merged into Ziff Corp. 3/22/79
Each share Common $1 par
exchanged for $33.75 cash

RUST INTL INC (DE)
Acquired by WMX Technologies Inc.
7/12/95
Each share Common 1¢ par
exchanged for $16.35 cash

**RUSTENBURG PLATINUM HLDGS
LTD (SOUTH AFRICA)**
Stock Dividends - 1.137% payable
5/9/96 to holders of record 3/15/96;
2.2826% payable 10/18/96 to
holders of record 8/23/96; 0.7396%
payable 4/24/97 to holders of record
2/28/97
Name changed to Anglo American
Platinum Corp. Ltd. (New) 9/2/97
Anglo American Platinum Corp Ltd.
(New) name changed to Anglo
Platinum Ltd. 5/30/2005

RUSTEX MNG CORP (QC)
Charter annulled for failure to file
reports or pay fees 12/08/1973

RUSTLESS IRON & STEEL CORP.
Merged into American Rolling Mill Co.
share for share in 1946
American Rolling Mill Co. name
changed to Armco Steel Corp. in
1948 which name changed to Armco
Inc. 7/1/78 which merged into AK
Steel Holding Corp. 9/30/99

**RUSTY CREEK MINING CO. LTD.
(BC)**
Struck off register and declared
dissolved 9/10/68

RUSTY LAKE MNG CORP (QC)
Recapitalized as Rustex Mining Corp.
12/10/68
Each share Capital Stock $1 par
exchanged for (1/3) share Capital
Stock $1 par
(See Rustex Mining Corp.)

RUSTY LAKE RES LTD (MB)
Reorganized under the laws of British
Columbia as Seven Seas Petroleum
Inc. 06/29/1995
Each (35) shares Common no par
exchanged for (1) share Common
no par
Seven Seas Petroleum Inc. (BC)
reincorporated in Yukon 08/12/1996
which reincorporated in Cayman
Islands 03/01/2001
(See Seven Seas Petroleum Inc.)

**RUSTY PELICAN RESTAURANTS
INC (CA)**
Acquired by Vicorp Specialty
Restaurants Inc. 11/20/1987
Each share Common no par
exchanged for $9 cash

RUTEL CORP (CANADA)
Recapitalized as Rutel Networks
Corp. 11/25/2003
Each (15) shares Common no par
exchanged for (1) share Common
no par

**RUTGER STREET WAREHOUSE,
INC.**
Liquidated in 1948

**RUTH OUTDOOR ADVERTISING INC
(NY)**
Charter cancelled and proclaimed
dissolved for failure to pay taxes
09/30/1980

RUTH VERMONT MINE LTD (BC)
Struck off register and declared
dissolved for failure to file returns
04/21/1995

RUTHERFORD LABS INC (DE)
Recapitalized as Prestige Pictures
Industries, Inc. (DE) 10/20/1972
Each share Common 1¢ par
exchanged for (0.25) share Common
1¢ par
Prestige Pictures Industries, Inc. (DE)
reincorporated in Nevada as
Diversified Capital Resources Corp.
12/12/1981 which name changed to
Prestige Industries, Inc. (NV)
01/28/1984 which name changed to
Prestige Pictures Industries, Inc.
(NV) 05/02/1984
*(See Prestige Pictures Industries, Inc.
(NV))*

**RUTHERFORD-MORAN OIL CORP
(DE)**
Merged into Chevron Corp. 3/17/99
Each share Common 1¢ par
exchanged for (0.043983) share
Common $1.50 par
Chevron Corp. name changed to
ChevronTexaco Corp. 10/9/2001
which name changed back to
Chevron Corp. 5/9/2005

**RUTHERFORD VENTURES CORP
(BC)**
Name changed to Diamond Fields
Resources Inc. 04/06/1993
Diamond Fields Resources Inc.
merged into Inco Ltd. 08/21/1996
(See Inco Ltd.)

RUTHIGEN INC (DE)
Recapitalized as Pulmatrix, Inc.
06/16/2015
Each share Common $0.0001 par
exchanged for (0.4) share Common
$0.0001 par

RUTHS CHRIS STEAK HSE INC (DE)
Issue Information - 13,000,000 shares
COM offered at $18 per share on
08/08/2005
Name changed to Ruth's Hospitality
Group, Inc. 05/23/2008

RUTI SWEETWATER INC (DE)
Charter cancelled and declared
inoperative and void for
non-payment of taxes 3/1/87

**RUTLAND BK
(ST PETERSBURG, FL)**
Merged into First Florida Bank, N.A.
(Tampa, FL) 06/28/1986
Each share Common $1 par
exchanged for $30.73 cash

RUTLAND BIOTECH LTD (BC)
Dissolved and struck from the register
4/24/92

**RUTLAND CENTRAL BANK
(ST. PETERSBURG, FL)**
Merged into Rutland Bank (St.
Petersburg, FL) 5/1/81
Each share Capital Stock $10 par
exchanged for (2.0433) shares
Common $1 par
*(See Rutland Bank (St. Petersburg,
FL))*

RUTLAND CORP (VT)
Acquired by Reade (Walter)
Organization, Inc. 1/31/69
Each share 6% Preferred $65 par
exchanged for (1) share $4.55 Conv.
Preferred $1 par
Each share Common $1 par
exchanged for (6) shares Common
25¢ par

*(See Reade (Walter) Organization,
Inc.)*
**RUTLAND COUNTY BANK
(RUTLAND, VT)**
Merged into Howard National Bank &
Trust Co. (Burlington, VT)
01/31/1967
Each share Capital Stock $100 par
exchanged for (7) shares Capital
Stock $25 par
Howard National Bank & Trust Co.
(Burlington, VT) name changed to
Howard Bank (Burlington, VT)
01/01/1972 which reorganized as
Howard Bancorp 01/01/1984 which
merged into BankNorth Group, Inc.
(DE) 12/01/1989 which merged into
Banknorth Group, Inc. (ME)
05/10/2000 which merged TD
Banknorth Inc. 03/01/2005
(See TD Banknorth Inc.)

RUTLAND RAILROAD CO.
Reorganized as Rutland Railway
Corp. in 1950
No stockholders' equity

**RUTLAND RAILWAY, LIGHT &
POWER CO.**
Acquired by Central Vermont Public
Service Corp. 00/00/1929
Details not available

RUTLAND RAILWAY CORP. (VT)
Recapitalized 10/8/64
Each share Preferred $100 par
exchanged for (1) share 6%
Preferred $65 par, $50 cash and a
10-year Common Stock purchase
warrant
Common $100 par changed to $1 par
Name changed to Rutland Corp.
9/26/66
Rutland Corp. acquired by Reade
(Walter) Organization, Inc. 1/31/69
*(See Reade (Walter) Organization,
Inc.)*

RUTLAND TRANSIT CO. (VT)
Liquidation completed 11/10/61

RUTTER INC (CANADA)
Acquired by 8758875 Canada Inc.
05/02/2014
Each share Common no par
exchanged for $0.061 cash

RUTTER TECHNOLOGIES INC (QC)
Reorganized under the laws of
Canada as Rutter Inc. 03/31/2004
Each share Common no par
exchanged for (1) share Common
no par
(See Rutter Inc.)

RUUD MANUFACTURING CO. (DE)
Common no par changed to $5 par in
1933
Stock Dividend - 50% 6/13/50
Dissolved 9/30/63

RUX RES INC (ON)
Name changed to Galaxy Online Inc.
12/08/1999
(See Galaxy Online Inc.)

RV WIRELESS INC (WY)
Recapitalized as Mobicom
Communications Inc. 05/24/2006
Each share Common no par
exchanged for (0.0004) share
Common no par
Mobicom Communications Inc.
reorganized as Resource Group
International, Inc. 11/08/2007

RVA CORP (FL)
Proclaimed dissolved for failure to file
reports and pay fees 10/09/1992

RVB BANCSHARES INC (AR)
Merged into Bank of the Ozarks, Inc.
06/26/2003
Each share Common exchanged for
either (15.274) shares Common 1¢
par or $504.85 cash
Bank of the Ozarks, Inc. reorganized
as Bank of the Ozarks (Little Rock,
AR) 06/27/2017 which name

changed to Bank OZK (Little Rock, AR) 07/16/2018

RVB HOLDINGS LTD (ISRAEL)
Each share old Ordinary ILS 1 par exchanged for (0.00003282) share new Ordinary ILS 1 par 02/25/2016
Name changed to Eviation Aircraft Ltd. 03/02/2017

RVM INDS INC (DE)
Acquired by JTB Enterprises, Inc. 03/12/2003
Each share Common 1¢ par exchanged for $0.05 cash

RVUE HLDGS INC (NV)
Voluntarily dissolved 08/07/2017
No stockholders' equity

RW PACKAGING LTD (CANADA)
Reincorporated 02/17/1995
Place of incorporation changed from (BC) to (Canada) 02/17/1995
Each (69,900) shares old Common no par exchanged for (1) share new Common no par 04/18/2008
Note: In effect holders received $0.65 cash per share and public interest was eliminated

RWD TECHNOLOGIES INC (MD)
Merged into Research Park Acquisition, Inc. 9/16/2003
Each share Common 10¢ par exchanged for $2.10 cash

RWE AG (GERMANY)
ADR agreement terminated 03/01/1995
Details not available
(Additional Information in Active)

RWMC PRODUCTIONS LTD. (ON)
Name changed to International Phoenix Capital Corp. 1/18/77
International Phoenix Capital Corp. name changed to Fairway Automotive Industries Ltd. 9/25/86 which recapitalized as Fairway Industries Ltd. 2/26/88 which recapitalized as Pharmaglobe Inc. (ONT) 3/14/94 which reincorporated in Delaware 3/1/2001 which name changed to Pharmaglobe America Group, Inc. 5/12/2004

RX EXPL INC (ON)
Recapitalized 01/20/2009
Holders of (99) or fewer shares exchanged for $0.20 cash per share
Name changed to RX Gold & Silver Inc. 01/25/2012
RX Gold & Silver Inc. merged into U.S. Silver & Gold Inc. 08/13/2012 which merged into Scorpio Mining Corp. 12/31/2014 which name changed to Americas Silver Corp. 05/27/2015

RX GOLD & SILVER INC (ON)
Merged into U.S. Silver & Gold Inc. 08/13/2012
Each share Common no par exchanged for (0.109) share Common no par
Note: Unexchanged certificates were cancelled and became without value 08/13/2018
U.S. Silver & Gold Inc. merged into Scorpio Mining Corp. 12/31/2014 which name changed to Americas Silver Corp. 05/27/2015

RX MED SVCS CORP (NV)
Each share Common $0.001 par exchanged for (0.25) share Common $0.002 par 12/29/1993
Recapitalized as Super Blue Domain Technologies, Inc. 12/20/2007
Each share Common $0.002 par exchanged for (0.001) share Common $0.001 par
Super Blue Domain Technologies, Inc. name changed to Golden Energy Corp. 06/16/2009 which name changed to Golden Grail Technology Corp. 12/31/2014

RX NEUTRICEUTICALS CORP (ON)
Recapitalized as RX Exploration Inc. 05/08/2006
Each share Common no par exchanged for (0.1) share Common no par
RX Exploration Inc. name changed to RX Gold & Silver Inc. 01/25/2012 which merged into U.S. Silver & Gold Inc. 08/13/2012 which merged into Scorpio Mining Corp. 12/31/2014 which name changed to Americas Silver Corp. 05/27/2015

RX PROCESSING CORP (NV)
Stock Dividends - 3.5% payable 06/20/2006 to holders of record 06/12/2006 Ex date - 06/08/2006; 3.5% payable 03/15/2007 to holders of record 02/21/2007 Ex date - 02/16/2007; 10% payable 08/10/2007 to holders of record 07/06/2007 Ex date - 07/03/2007
Merged into RxPC Inc. 11/14/2007
Each share Common $0.001 par exchanged for (0.00941176) share Restricted Class A $0.001 par
(See RxPC Inc.)

RX SAFES INC (NV)
Each share old Common $0.001 par exchanged for (0.005) share new Common $0.001 par 11/12/2015
Name changed to GeneSYS ID, Inc. 08/01/2016

RX SCRIPTED INC (NV)
Name changed to MedCareers Group, Inc. 01/07/2010

RX STAFFING INC (NV)
Each share old Common $0.001 par exchanged for (9) shares new Common $0.001 par 09/21/2006
Each share new Common $0.001 par exchanged again for (0.33333333) share new Common $0.001 par 12/12/2006
Name changed to Jpak Group, Inc. 08/09/2007
(See Jpak Group, Inc.)

RX TECHNOLOGY HLDGS INC (NV)
Name changed to Crosspoint Group, Inc. 08/23/2005
Crosspoint Group, Inc. recapitalized as The Employer Inc. 03/08/2007 which recapitalized as Vana Blue, Inc. 02/21/2008 which name changed to Osyka Corp. 05/19/2010

RXBAZAAR INC (DE)
Chapter 7 bankruptcy case closed 12/07/2007
Stockholders' equity unlikely

RXBIDS (NV)
Recapitalized as Xsovt Brands, Inc. 02/07/2011
Each (12) shares Common 1¢ par exchanged for (1) share Common 1¢ par

RXI PHARMACEUTICALS CORP OLD (DE)
Name changed to Galena Biopharma, Inc. 09/27/2011
Galena Biopharma, Inc. recapitalized as SELLAS Life Sciences Group, Inc. 01/02/2018

RXPC INC (NV)
Merged out of existence 03/23/2009
Details not available

RXR DYNAMIC GOVT FD INC (MD)
Assets distributed to holders 7/20/90
Details not available

RXT 110 INC (ON)
Name changed to BIOSENTA Inc. 06/06/2012

RY FINL CORP (CANADA)
Part. Retractable Preferred no par called for redemption 6/30/92

RY NT FINL CORP (CANADA)
Common no par called for redemption 6/1/92

RY II FINL CORP (CANADA)
Part. Retractable Preferred no par called for redemption 06/30/1992
Public interest eliminated

RYAN AERONAUTICAL CO (CA)
Common $1 par changed to no par and (1.5) additional shares issued 06/19/1959
Common no par split (2) for (1) by issuance of (1) additional share 11/19/1965
Stock Dividends - 20% 10/30/1957; 20% 01/30/1959
Merged into Teledyne, Inc. 02/18/1969
Each share Common no par exchanged for $50 cash

RYAN BECK & CO (NJ)
Common 10¢ par split (5) for (4) by issuance of (0.25) additional share 10/19/1992
$0.60 Conv. Preferred Ser. A 10¢ par called for redemption at $6.75 on 09/11/1997
Stock Dividend - 5% payable 02/13/1996 to holders of record 02/05/1996
Merged into BankAtlantic Bancorp, Inc. 06/30/1998
Each share Common 10¢ par exchanged for (0.761) share Class A Common 1¢ par
BankAtlantic Bancorp, Inc. name changed to BBX Capital Corp. (Old) 08/06/2012
(See BBX Capital Corp. (Old))

RYAN CAR CO.
Out of business 00/00/1938
Details not available

RYAN CONSOLIDATED PETROLEUM CORP. (DE)
Capital Stock no par changed to $1 par 00/00/1954
Stock Dividend - 10% 03/20/1959
Name changed to Ormand Industries, Inc. 04/22/1968

RYAN ENERGY CORP (BC)
Name changed to Ryan Resources Ltd. 02/14/1986
Each share Common no par exchanged for (1) share Common no par
Ryan Resources Ltd. recapitalized as Canadian Crew Energy Corp. 01/21/1988 which name changed to Crew Development Corp. (BC) 03/21/1997 which reincorporated in Yukon 01/26/2000 which changed to Crew Gold Corp. 01/26/2004
(See Crew Gold Corp.)

RYAN ENERGY TECHNOLOGIES INC (AB)
Acquired by Nabors Exchangeco (Canada) Inc. 10/09/2002
Each share Common no par exchanged for $1.85 cash

RYAN-EVANS DRUG STORES, INC. (AZ)
Common $10 par changed to $2.50 par and (3) additional shares issued 7/9/62
Name changed to Ryan-Evans Liquidating Corp. 7/12/68
(See Ryan-Evans Liquidating Corp.)

RYAN-EVANS DRUG STORES (AZ)
Name changed to Ryan-Evans Drug Stores, Inc. 6/28/62
Ryan-Evans Drug Stores, Inc. name changed to Ryan-Evans Liquidating Corp. 7/12/68
(See Ryan-Evans Liquidating Corp.)

RYAN-EVANS LIQUIDATING CORP. (AZ)
Liquidation completed
Each share Common $2.50 par exchanged for initial distribution of $7.08 cash 7/12/68
Each share Common $2.50 par received second distribution of $0.80 cash 4/22/76
Each share Common $2.50 par received third and final distribution of $0.05 cash 3/3/89

RYAN GOLD CORP (ON)
Merged into Oban Mining Corp. 08/27/2015
Each share Common no par exchanged for (0.094) share new Common no par
Note: Unexchanged certificates will be cancelled and become without value 08/27/2021
Oban Mining Corp. name changed to Osisko Mining Inc. 06/21/2016

RYAN HOMES INC (PA)
Common no par split (3) for (1) by issuance of (2) additional shares 1/20/72
Acquired by NVRyan L.P. 6/23/87
Each share Common no par exchanged for (0.5772621) Unit of Ltd. Partnership and $41.78 cash
NVRyan L.P. name changed to NVR L.P. 3/22/89 which reorganized as NVR Inc. 9/30/93

RYAN HOTELS PLC (ENGLAND)
Name changed to Gresham Hotel Group PLC 04/18/2001
(See Gresham Hotel Group PLC)

RYAN INS GROUP INC (DE)
Common $1 par split (7) for (5) by issuance of (0.4) additional share 06/07/1978
Common $1 par split (3) for (2) by issuance of (0.5) additional share 04/16/1979
Stock Dividends - 33.33333333% 06/30/1980; 33.33333333% 02/27/1981
Merged into Combined International Corp. 08/27/1982
Each share Common $1 par exchanged for $34 cash

RYAN LAKE MINES LTD.
Recapitalized as New Ryan Lake Mines Ltd. on a (0.5) for (1) basis 00/00/1951
New Ryan Lake Mines Ltd. recapitalized as Min-Ore Mines Ltd. 10/01/1955
(See Min-Ore Mines Ltd.)

RYAN MTG INVS (TX)
Name changed to Arlington Realty Investors 3/6/84
(See Arlington Realty Investors)

RYAN PETROLEUM CORP.
Merged into Ryan Consolidated Petroleum Corp. 00/00/1926
Each share Capital Stock exchanged for (0.1) share Capital Stock no par
Ryan Consolidated Petroleum Corp. name changed to Ormand Industries, Inc. 04/22/1968

RYAN RES LTD (BC)
Recapitalized as Canadian Crew Energy Corp. 01/21/1988
Each share Common no par exchanged for (0.2) share Common no par
Canadian Crew Energy Corp. name changed to Crew Development Corp. (BC) 03/21/1997 which reincorporated in Yukon 01/26/2000 which name changed to Crew Gold Corp. 01/26/2004
(See Crew Gold Corp.)

RYANOR MNG LTD (ON)
Capital Stock $1 par changed to no par 12/22/1971
Dissolved 03/01/1982
Details not available

RYANS FAMILY STEAK HOUSES INC (SC)
Common $1 par split (3) for (2) by issuance of (0.5) additional share 1/19/83
Common $1 par split (2) for (1) by issuance of (1) additional share 4/19/83
Common $1 par split (3) for (2) by

issuance of (0.5) additional share 2/21/85

Common $1 par split (3) for (2) by issuance of (0.5) additional share 2/19/86

Common $1 par split (3) for (2) by issuance of (0.5) additional share 5/21/86

Common $1 par split (3) for (1) by issuance of (2) additional shares 5/20/87

Common $1 par split (3) for (2) by issuance of (0.5) additional share payable 5/29/2002 to holders of record 5/15/2002 Ex date - 5/30/2002

Name changed to Ryan's Restaurant Group, Inc. 6/7/2004

(See Ryan's Restaurant Group, Inc.)

RYANS RESTAURANT GROUP INC (SC)
Merged into Buffets, Inc. 11/1/2006
Each share Common $1 par exchanged for $16.25 cash

RYDAX INC (CA)
Merged into Johnson (E.F.) Co. 12/18/1978

Each share Common $1 par exchanged for (0.05) share Common 50¢ par

Johnson (E.F.) Co. merged into Western Union Corp. (Old) 11/30/1982 which merged into Western Union Corp. (New) 12/31/1987 which name changed to New Valley Corp. (NY) 04/22/1991 which reorganized in Delaware 07/29/1996 which was acquired by Vector Group Ltd. 12/13/2005

RYDE ENERGY INC (AB)
Name changed 06/01/1994
Name changed from Ryde Industries Inc. to Ryde Energy Inc. 06/01/1994
Recapitalized as Caswan Environmental Services Inc. 07/01/1995
Each share Common no par exchanged for (0.25) share Class A Common no par
(See Caswan Environmental Services Inc.)

RYDER SYS INC (FL)
$5 Conv. Preferred Ser. A no par called for redemption 7/31/78
Dutch Auction Rate Preferred Ser. A no par called for redemption in February, 1993
Dutch Auction Rate Preferred Ser. B no par called for redemption in February, 1993
Fixed Rate Auction Preferred Ser. A no par called for redemption in February, 1993
Fixed Rate Auction Preferred Ser. B no par called for redemption in February, 1993
Fixed Rate Auction Preferred Ser. C no par called for redemption in February, 1993
(Additional Information in Active)

RYDEX ETF TR (DE)
Completely liquidated 05/28/2010
Each share Inverse 2X Russell 2000 ETF no par received approximately $31.11 cash
Each share Inverse 2X S&P Select Sector Energy ETF no par received approximately $5.63 cash
Each share Inverse 2X S&P Select Sector Financial ETF no par received approximately $5.07 cash
Each share Inverse 2X S&P Select Sector Health Care ETF no par received approximately $37.38 cash
Each share Inverse 2X S&P Select Sector Technology ETF no par received approximately $19.20 cash
Each share 2X Russell 2000 ETF no par received approximately $35.54 cash
Each share 2X S&P MidCap 400 ETF no par received approximately $26.66 cash
Each share 2X S&P MidCap 400 Strategy no par received approximately $39.81 cash
Each share 2X S&P Select Sector Technology ETF no par received approximately $46.59 cash
Each share 2X S&P Select Sector Energy ETF no par received approximately $17.39 cash
Each share 2X S&P Select Sector Financial ETF no par received approximately $12.81 cash
Each share 2x Select Sector Health Care ETF no par received approximately $57.01 cash
Rydex Inverse S&P 500 2X Strategy ETF no par reclassified as Guggenheim Inverse 2x S&P 500 ETF no par 03/01/2012
Rydex MSCI ACWI Equal Weight ETF no par reclassified as Guggenheim MSCI ACWI Equal Weight ETF no par 03/01/2012
Rydex MSCI EAFE Equal Weight ETF no par reclassified as Guggenheim MSCI EAFE Equal Weight ETF no par 03/01/2012
Rydex MSCI Emerging Markets Equal Weight ETF no par reclassified as Guggenheim MSCI Emerging Markets Equal Weight ETF no par 03/01/2012
Rydex Russell MidCap Equal Weight ETF no par reclassified as Guggenheim Russell MidCap Equal Weight ETF no par 03/01/2012
Rydex Russell 1000 Equal Weight ETF no par reclassified as Guggenheim Russell 1000 Equal Weight ETF no par 03/01/2012
Rydex Russell Top 50 ETF no par reclassified as Guggenheim Russell Top 50 ETF no par 03/01/2012
Rydex Russell 2000 Equal Weight ETF no par reclassified as Guggenheim Russell 2000 Equal Weight ETF no par 03/01/2012
Rydex S&P 500 Equal Weight Consumer Discretionary ETF no par reclassified as Guggenheim S&P 500 Equal Weight Consumer Discretionary ETF no par 03/01/2012
Rydex S&P 500 Equal Weight Consumer Staples ETF no par reclassified as Guggenheim S&P 500 Equal Weight Consumer Staples ETF no par 03/01/2012
Rydex S&P 500 Equal Weight Energy ETF no par reclassified as Guggenheim S&P 500 Equal Weight Energy ETF no par 03/01/2012
Rydex S&P 500 Equal Weight ETF no par reclassified as Guggenheim S&P 500 Equal Weight ETF no par 03/01/2012
Rydex S&P 500 Equal Weight Financials ETF no par reclassified as Guggenheim S&P 500 Equal Weight Financials ETF no par 03/01/2012
Rydex S&P 500 Equal Weight Healthcare ETF no par reclassified as Guggenheim S&P 500 Equal Weight Healthcare ETF no par 03/01/2012
Rydex S&P 500 Equal Weight Industrials ETF no par reclassified as Guggenheim S&P 500 Equal Weight Industrials ETF no par 03/01/2012
Rydex S&P 500 Equal Weight Materials ETF no par reclassified as Guggenheim S&P 500 Equal Weight Materials ETF no par 03/01/2012
Rydex S&P 500 Equal Weight Technology ETF no par reclassified as Guggenheim S&P 500 Equal Weight Technology ETF no par 03/01/2012
Rydex S&P 500 Equal Weight Utilities ETF no par reclassified as Guggenheim S&P 500 Equal Weight Utilities ETF no par 03/01/2012
Rydex S&P 500 Pure Growth ETF no par reclassified as Guggenheim S&P 500 Pure Growth ETF no par 03/01/2012
Rydex S&P 500 Pure Value ETF no par reclassified as Guggenheim S&P 500 Pure Value ETF no par 03/01/2012
Rydex S&P MidCap 400 Equal Weight ETF no par reclassified as Guggenheim S&P MidCap 400 Equal Weight ETF no par 03/01/2012
Rydex S&P MidCap 400 Pure Growth ETF no par reclassified as Guggenheim S&P MidCap 400 Pure Growth ETF no par 03/01/2012
Rydex S&P MidCap 400 Pure Value ETF no par reclassified as Guggenheim S&P MidCap 400 Pure Value ETF no par 03/01/2012
Rydex S&P SmallCap 600 Equal Weight ETF no par reclassified as Guggenheim S&P SmallCap 600 Equal Weight ETF no par 03/01/2012
Rydex S&P SmallCap 600 Pure Growth ETF no par reclassified as Guggenheim S&P SmallCap 600 Pure Growth ETF no par 03/01/2012
Rydex S&P SmallCap 600 Pure Value ETF no par reclassified as Guggenheim S&P SmallCap 600 Pure Value ETF no par 03/01/2012
Rydex 2X S&P 500 ETF no par reclassified as Guggenheim 2X S&P 500 ETF no par 03/01/2012
Trust terminated 03/30/2012
Each share Guggenheim MSCI ACWI Equal Weight ETF no par received $37.2855 cash
Guggenheim Russell Top 50 ETF no par reclassified as Guggenheim Russell Top 50 Mega Cap ETF no par 09/10/2012
Trust terminated 03/22/2013
Each share Guggenheim Inverse 2X S&P 500 ETF no par received $18.023758 cash
Each share Guggenheim MSCI EAFE Equal Weight ETF no par received $41.384743 cash
Each share Guggenheim S&P MidCap 400 Equal Weight ETF no par received $36.682549 cash
Each share Guggenheim S&P SmallCap 600 Equal Weight ETF no par received $36.832269 cash
Each share Guggenheim 2X S&P 500 ETF no par received $62.080078 cash
Guggenheim MSCI Emerging Markets Equal Weight ETF no par reclassified as Guggenheim MSCI Emerging Markets Equal Country Weight ETF no par 01/20/2015
Guggenheim Russell MidCap Equal Weight ETF no par reclassified as Guggenheim S&P MidCap 400 Equal Weight ETF no par 01/27/2016
Under plan of reorganization each share Guggenheim Russell 1000 Equal Weight ETF no par automatically became (0.61652528) share Guggenheim S&P 500 Equal Weight ETF no par 01/27/2016
Guggenheim Russell Top 50 Mega Cap ETF no par reclassified as Guggenheim S&P 500 Top 50 ETF no par 01/27/2016
Guggenheim Russell 2000 Equal Weight ETF no par reclassified as Guggenheim S&P SmallCap 600 Equal Weight ETF no par 01/27/2016
Each share Guggenheim S&P 500 Equal Weight Financials ETF no par received distribution of (0.5) share Guggenheim S&P 500 Equal Weight Real Estate ETF no par payable 09/22/2016 to holders of record 09/21/2016 Ex date - 09/19/2016
Under plan of reorganization each share Guggenheim MSCI Emerging Markets Equal Country Weight ETF no par, Guggenheim Multi-Factor Large Cap ETF no par, Guggenheim S&P 500 Equal Weight Consumer Discretionary ETF no par, Guggenheim S&P 100 Equal Weight ETF no par, Guggenheim S&P 500 Equal Weight Consumer Staples ETF no par, Guggenheim S&P 500 Equal Weight Energy ETF no par, Guggenheim S&P 500 Equal Weight ETF no par, Guggenheim S&P 500 Equal Weight Financials ETF no par, Guggenheim S&P 500 Equal Weight Health Care ETF no par, Guggenheim S&P 500 Equal Weight Industrials ETF no par, Guggenheim S&P 500 Equal Weight Materials ETF no par, Guggenheim S&P 500 Equal Weight Real Estate ETF no par, Guggenheim S&P 500 Equal Weight Technology ETF no par, Guggenheim S&P 500 Equal Weight Utilities ETF no par, Guggenheim S&P 500 Pure Growth ETF no par, Guggenheim S&P 500 Pure Value ETF no par, Guggenheim S&P MidCap 400 Equal Weight ETF no par, Guggenheim S&P MidCap 400 Pure Growth ETF no par, Guggenheim S&P MidCap 400 Pure Value ETF no par, Guggenheim S&P 500 Top 50 ETF no par, Guggenheim S&P SmallCap 600 Equal Weight ETF no par, Guggenheim S&P SmallCap 600 Pure Growth ETF no par and Guggenheim S&P SmallCap 600 Pure Value ETF no par automatically became (1) share PowerShares Exchange-Traded Fund Trust II MSCI Emerging Markets Equal Country Weight Portfolio 1¢ par, Multi-Factor Large Cap Portfolio 1¢ par, S&P 500 Equal Weight Consumer Discretionary Portfolio 1¢ par, S&P 100 Equal Weight Portfolio 1¢ par, S&P 500 Equal Weight Consumer Staples Portfolio 1¢ par, S&P 500 Equal Weight Energy Portfolio 1¢ par, S&P 500 Equal Weight Portfolio 1¢ par, S&P 500 Equal Weight Financials Portfolio 1¢ par, S&P 500 Equal Weight Health Care Portfolio 1¢ par, S&P 500 Equal Weight Industrials Portfolio 1¢ par, S&P 500 Equal Weight Materials Portfolio 1¢ par, S&P 500 Equal Weight Real Estate Portfolio 1¢ par, S&P 500 Equal Weight Technology Portfolio 1¢ par, S&P 500 Equal Weight Utilities Portfolio 1¢ par, S&P 500 Pure Growth Portfolio 1¢ par, S&P 500 Pure Value Portfolio 1¢ par, S&P MidCap 400 Equal Weight Portfolio 1¢ par, S&P MidCap 400 Pure Growth Portfolio 1¢ par, S&P MidCap 400 Pure Value Portfolio 1¢ par, S&P 500 Top 50 Portfolio 1¢ par, S&P SmallCap 600 Equal Weight Portfolio 1¢ par, S&P SmallCap 600 Pure Growth Portfolio 1¢ par or S&P SmallCap 600 Pure Value Portfolio 1¢ par respectively 04/06/2018 (SEC filing)

RYE PATCH GOLD CORP (BC)
Each share old Common no par exchanged for (0.15384615) share new Common no par 01/12/2018
Merged into Alio Gold Inc. 05/30/2018
Each share new Common no par exchanged for (0.48) share Common no par and $0.001 cash
Note: Unexchanged certificates will be cancelled and become without value 05/30/2024

RYERSON & HAYNES INC (DE)
Reincorporated 1/30/70
Stock Dividend - 100% 9/15/50

State of incorporation changed from (MI) to (DE) 1/30/70
Charter cancelled and declared inoperative and void for non-payment of taxes 3/1/89

RYERSON (JOSEPH T.) & SON, INC.
Merged into Inland Steel Co. in 1935
(See Inland Steel Co.)

RYERSON INC (DE)
Name changed 01/01/2006
Name changed from Ryerson Tull, Inc. (New) to Ryerson, Inc. 01/01/2006
Merged into Rhombus Holding Corp. 10/19/2007
Each share $2.40 Conv. Preferred Ser. A $1 par exchanged for $34.50 cash
Each share Common $1 par exchanged for $34.50 cash

RYERSON TULL INC OLD (DE)
Merged into Ryerson Tull, Inc. (New) 02/26/1999
Each share Class A Common $1 par exchanged for (0.61) share Common $1 par
Ryerson Tull, Inc. (New) name changed to Ryerson, Inc. 01/01/2006
(See Ryerson, Inc.)

RYKA INC (DE)
Recapitalized as Global Sports, Inc. 12/15/1997
Each share Common 1¢ par exchanged for (0.05) share Common 1¢ par
Global Sports, Inc. name changed to GSI Commerce, Inc. 05/24/2002
(See GSI Commerce, Inc.)

RYKER RESOURCES LTD (BC)
Struck off register and declared dissolved for failure to file returns 02/25/1983

RYKOFF SEXTON INC (DE)
Name changed 9/14/84
Stock Dividends - 25% 6/16/75; 25% 8/2/76; 25% 8/5/77; 25% 8/4/80; 25% 8/3/81
Name changed from Rykoff (S.E.) & Co. to Rykoff Sexton Inc 9/14/84
Common 10¢ par split (5) for (4) by issuance of (0.25) additional share 1/16/89
Common 10¢ par split (5) for (4) by issuance of (0.25) additional share 1/24/95
Merged into JP Foodservice, Inc. 12/23/97
Each share Common 10¢ par exchanged for (0.775) share Common 1¢ par
JP Foodservice, Inc. name changed to U.S. Foodservice 2/27/98
(See U.S. Foodservice)

RYLAND GROUP INC (MD)
Common $1 par split (2) for (1) by issuance of (1) additional share 04/13/1973
Common $1 par split (2) for (1) by issuance of (1) additional share 07/30/1983
Common $1 par split (2) for (1) by issuance of (1) additional share 07/30/1986
Common $1 par split (2) for (1) by issuance of (1) additional share payable 05/30/2002 to holders of record 05/15/2002 Ex date - 05/31/2002
Common $1 par split (2) for (1) by issuance of (1) additional share payable 11/30/2004 to holders of record 11/15/2004 Ex date - 12/01/2004
Merged into CalAtlantic Group, Inc. 10/01/2015
Each share Common $1 par exchanged for (1.0191) shares Common 1¢ par
CalAtlantic Group, Inc. merged into Lennar Corp. 02/12/2018

RYLAND OIL CORP (ON)
Merged into Crescent Point Energy Corp. 08/23/2010
Each share Common no par exchanged for (0.0117) share Common no par
Note: Unexchanged certificates were cancelled and became without value 08/24/2016

RYMAC MTG INVT CORP (MD)
Reincorporated under the laws of Delaware as Core Materials Corp. 12/31/96
Core Materials Corp. name changed to Core Molding Technologies, Inc. 9/3/2002

RYMAX INC (DE)
Name changed to Paraplane International Inc. 07/21/1986

RYMER FOODS INC (DE)
Name changed 04/11/1989
Common $1 par split (4) for (3) by issuance of (1/3) additional share 04/27/1984
12% Conv. Preferred Ser. B $100 par called for redemption 03/24/1986
Name changed from Rymer Co. to Rymer Foods Inc. 04/11/1989
Each share $1.175 Conv. Exchangeable Preferred $10 par exchanged for (1.5) shares Common $1 par 04/07/1993
Reorganized under Chapter 11 Federal Bankruptcy Code 10/06/1997
Each share Common $1 par exchanged for (0.04) share Common 4¢ par Ceased operations 02/00/2002
Stockholders' equity unlikely

RYNCO SCIENTIFIC CORP (DE)
Charter cancelled and declared inoperative and void for non-payment of taxes 3/1/87

RYOZANPAKU INTL INC (NV)
Recapitalized as EM Energy, Inc. 01/25/2012
Each share Common $0.0001 par exchanged for (0.1) share Common $0.0001 par
EM Energy, Inc. name changed to MJ Harvest, Inc. 10/02/2018

RYSLO SILVER MINES LTD (BC)
Recapitalized as Major Resources Ltd. 05/02/1977
Each share Common 50¢ par exchanged for (0.25) share Common no par
Major Resources Ltd. recapitalized as Anvil Resources Ltd. 11/03/1982 which recapitalized as Geocore Exploration Inc. 07/24/2003 which recapitalized as Emerick Resources Corp. 12/31/2007 which name changed to Medgold Resources Corp. 12/17/2012

RYSTAR COMMUNICATIONS LTD (CANADA)
Reincorporated 03/31/1998
Name and place of incorporation changed from Rystar Development Ltd. (BC) to Rystar Communications Ltd. (Canada) 03/31/1998
Dissolved 08/15/2006
Details not available

RYTE INVESTORS CO., INC. (MA)
Liquidation completed 11/29/63

RZW VENTURES INC (DE)
Name changed to Univest Group, Inc. 2/23/90

S

S. & P. CORP. (NV)
Completely liquidated 9/2/71
Each (4.5) shares Capital Stock $1 par received first and final distribution of (1) share Paradox Production Corp. Common $1 par

Certificates were not required to be surrendered and are now valueless

S & J HLDG CORP (DE)
Charter cancelled and declared inoperative and void for non-payment of taxes 3/1/89

S & K FAMOUS BRANDS INC (VA)
Common $1 par changed to 50¢ par and (1) additional share issued 02/12/1993
Plan of reorganization under Chapter 11 Federal Bankruptcy proceedings effective 03/16/2010
No stockholders' equity

S & K PETE LTD (AB)
Completely liquidated 10/24/83
Each share Common no par exchanged for first and final distribution of (0.2) share High Plains Oil Corp. Common 10¢ par
High Plains Oil Corp. merged into Adobe Resources Corp. 5/29/87 which merged into Santa Fe Energy Resources, Inc. 5/19/92 which name changed to Santa Fe Snyder Corp. 5/5/99 which merged into Devon Energy Corp. (New) 8/29/2000

S & L DIVERSIFIED LTD (CANADA)
Common no par split (2) for (1) by issuance of (1) additional share 9/15/72
Name changed to Publigest Corp. Ltd. 9/9/75
(See Publigest Corp. Ltd.)

S & M CO (MN)
Stock Dividend - 100% 5/18/87
Acquired by private investors 9/16/94
Each share Common 1¢ par exchanged for $1.43 cash

S & M INDS INC (CO)
Declared defunct and inoperative for failure to pay taxes 10/22/1970

S & M PHOTOLABELS INC (CANADA)
Dissolved 05/06/2003
Details not available

S & M SUPPLY CO. (CO)
Name changed to S & M Industries, Inc. 3/19/69
(See S & M Industries, Inc.)

S & P NATL CORP (DE)
Liquidation completed
Each share Class A 10¢ par exchanged for initial distribution of $20.90 cash 06/04/1970
Each share Common 10¢ par exchanged for initial distribution of $4.18 cash 06/04/1970
Each share Class A 10¢ par received second and final distribution of $0.74 cash 03/04/1974
Each share Common 10¢ par received second and final distribution of $0.148 cash 03/04/1974
Note: Unexchanged certificates were cancelled and became without value 09/28/1973

S & R MANAGED PORTFOLIO (BC)
Name changed to Canadian Growth Portfolio 11/12/64
(See Canadian Growth Portfolio)

S & S CORP (VA)
Stock Dividend - 50% 08/02/1976
Merged into Ingersoll-Rand Co. (NJ) 12/15/1976
Each share Common $1 par exchanged for (0.365) share Common $2 par
Ingersoll-Rand Co. (NJ) reorganized in Bermuda as Ingersoll-Rand Co. Ltd. 12/31/2001 which reincorporated in Ireland as Ingersoll-Rand PLC 07/01/2009

S & T INDS INC (KY)
Capital Stock $25 par changed to $2.50 par and (9) additional shares issued 5/15/78
Merged into C&H Capital Inc. 4/28/83

Each share Capital Stock $2.50 par exchanged for $8.25 cash

S & T SYS INTEGRATION & TECHNOLOGY DISTR A G (AUSTRIA)
Acquired by Quanmax AG 06/14/2013
Each Sponsored ADR for Ordinary exchanged for $3.6261 cash

S A BREWING HLDGS LTD (AUSTRALIA)
Name changed to Southcorp Holdings Ltd. 11/25/1993
Southcorp Holdings Ltd. name changed to Southcorp Ltd. 01/02/1998
(See Southcorp Ltd.)

S A FABRICA DE PRODUTOS ALIMENTICIOS VIGOR (BRAZIL)
ADR agreement terminated 12/10/2010
No ADR's remain outstanding

S.A.L. CABLE COMMUNICATIONS, INC. (NY)
Name changed to S.A.L. Communications, Inc. 06/26/1984
(See S.A.L. Communications, Inc.)

S A L COMMUNICATIONS INC (NY)
Plan of liquidation under Chapter 11 Federal Bankruptcy proceedings confirmed 00/00/1986
No stockholders' equity

S A MANGANESE AMCOR LTD (SOUTH AFRICA)
Name changed to Samancor Ltd. 9/16/85
(See Samancor Ltd.)

S A Y INDS INC (MA)
Name changed to Scribe Systems, Inc. 9/4/88
(See Scribe Systems, Inc.)

S A Y PACKAGING INC (MA)
Chapter 11 bankruptcy proceedings converted to Chapter 7 on 2/11/91
Stockholders' equity unlikely

S & P 500 COVERED CALL FD INC (MD)
Issue Information - 15,600,000 shares COM offered at $20 per share on 03/28/2005
Completely liquidated
Each share Common $0.001 par received first and final distribution of $9.868001 cash payable 02/02/2010 to holders of record 01/29/2010
Note: Certificates were not required to be surrendered and are without value

S & P 500 GEARED FD INC (MD)
Completely liquidated 09/15/2009
Each share Common $0.001 par received first and final distribution of $12.111014 cash

S B & T CORP (CA)
Merged into Regions Financial Corp. (Old) 06/13/1997
Each share Common $1 par exchanged for (1) share Common $0.625 par
Regions Financial Corp. (Old) merged into Regions Financial Corp. (New) 07/01/2004

S.B.R. CORP. (NY)
Liquidation completed 11/9/64

S B VANCOUVER STUDIOS INC (BC)
Recapitalized as Algorithm Media Inc. 08/18/1999
Each share Common no par exchanged for (1/6) share Common no par
Algorithm Media Inc. recapitalized as Avere Energy Inc. 12/18/2009 which name changed to East West Petroleum Corp. 08/10/2010

S.C. LIQUIDATING CO. (CO)
Completely liquidated 8/27/73
Each share Common no par exchanged for first and final

distribution of (0.75) share Beatrice Foods Co. Common no par
Beatrice Foods Co. name changed to Beatrice Companies, Inc. 6/5/84
(See Beatrice Companies, Inc.)

S.C. PRODUCTS, INC. (MI)
Liquidation completed
Each share Common $1 par exchanged for initial distribution of $2 cash 05/31/1974
Each share Common $1 par received second distribution of $3.25 cash 04/25/1978
Each share Common $1 par received third and final distribution of $0.0051183 cash 12/15/1980

S C I FINANCIAL GROUP, INC. (IA)
Merged into Wells Fargo & Co. (New) 03/29/2001
Details not available

S C U INDS LTD (ON)
Charter cancelled for failure to pay taxes and file returns 11/07/1978

S CORP. (CT)
Completely liquidated 8/25/72
Each share Common 5¢ par exchanged for first and final distribution of $15.45 cash

S E ASIA TRADING CO INC (NV)
Name changed to Lotus Pharmaceuticals, Inc. 12/14/2006

S E C CORP (NM)
Merged into UGT Corp. 10/14/1977
Each share Common $1 par exchanged for $9.40 cash

S E INVTS LTD (INDIA)
Reg. S GDR's for Equity Shares split (2) for (1) by issuance of (1) additional GDR payable 11/12/2010 to holders of record 10/29/2010
Basis changed from (1:2) to (1:0.2) 10/24/2011
Name changed to Paisalo Digital Ltd. 02/07/2018

S E STORAGE EXPRESS INTL LTD (BC)
Struck off register and declared dissolved for failure to file returns 08/28/1992

S F O HELICOPTER AIRLS INC (CA)
Completely liquidated 5/12/77
Each share Class B Common no par exchanged for $4.6877 cash

S G METALS INDS INC (MO)
Merged into S-G Acquisition Corp. 3/29/85
Each share Class A Common $7 par exchanged for $4 cash

S G SECS INC (DE)
Name changed to Cyprus Corp. 9/7/79
Cyprus Corp. name changed to Astrotech International Corp. (Old) 4/6/84 which recapitalized as Astrotech International Corp. (New) 8/19/88 which merged into Iteq Inc. 10/28/97
(See Iteq Inc.)

S.H.E., INC. (DE)
Liquidation completed
Each share Common 10¢ par exchanged for initial distribution of (0.2) share Raymond Engineering Inc. Common $1 par 7/11/69
Each share Common 10¢ par received second and final distribution of (0.082522) share Raymond Engineering Inc. Common $1 par 12/19/70
(See Raymond Engineering Inc.)

S H S FDS INC (NY)
Over 90% reacquired by the company through purchase offer as of 09/29/1978
Public interest eliminated

S I N C L A R E GROUP INC (DE)
Each share Common $0.001 par received distribution of (1) share Cyberlinx Corp. Common 1¢ par payable 7/29/96 to holders of record 6/26/96
Charter cancelled and declared inoperative and void for non-payment of taxes 3/1/95

S I S EXPLS CORP (ON)
Recapitalized as Allegiance Equity Corp. 07/13/1987
Each share Common no par exchanged for (0.25) share Common no par
Allegiance Equity Corp. name changed to Canadian Bioceutical Corp. 12/16/2014 which name changed to MPX Bioceutical Corp. 11/06/2017

S J V CORP (IN)
Common no par split (3) for (2) by issuance of (1) additional share 3/17/72
Stock Dividends - 10% 10/20/78; 10% 11/15/79; 10% 11/26/80
Name changed to Midwest Commerce Corp. 11/1/82
(See Midwest Commerce Corp.)

S K D MFG LTD (ON)
All but (350) shares 6% 1st Preference and (1,373) shares Common were acquired by Continental Can Co. of Canada Ltd. through purchase offer which expired 01/09/1970
6-1/4% 2nd Preference $20 called for redemption 12/01/1970
Public interest eliminated

S K I LTD (DE)
Common 10¢ par split (300) for (1) by issuance of (299) additional shares 11/26/1985
Common 10¢ par split (5) for (4) by issuance of (0.25) additional share 01/17/1990
Merged into LBO Resort Enterprises 06/28/1996
Each share Common 10¢ par exchanged for $18 cash

S L RES INC (DE)
Name changed to Treats International Enterprises Inc. 01/00/1992
(See Treats International Enterprises Inc.)

S.L.S. INC. (FL)
Liquidation completed 4/28/65
Class A Common $1 par and Class B Common $1 par received initial distribution of $3 cash 7/28/64
Class A Common $1 par and Class B Common $1 par received second and final distribution of (1) Ctf. of Bene. Int. no par of S.L.S. Inc. Liquidating Trust and 95¢ cash 4/28/65
Note: Certificates were not required to be surrendered and are without value
(See S.L.S. Inc. Liquidating Trust)

S.L.S. INC. LIQUIDATING TRUST
Liquidation completed 12/13/66
Each Ctf. of Bene. Int. no par received first and final distribution of $0.33227 cash 12/13/66

S L VENTURES INC (FL)
Each share old Common $0.001 par exchanged for (0.1) share new Common $0.001 par 12/2/96
Name changed to Canadian Aerospace Group International, Inc. 2/18/99

S.M. INDUSTRIES LTD. (BC)
Struck off register and declared dissolved for failure to file returns 08/09/1976

S.M.A. CORP.
Acquired by American Home Products Corp. on a (1) for (3) basis 07/23/1938
American Home Products Corp. name changed to Wyeth 03/11/2002 which was acquired by Pfizer Inc. 10/15/2009

S M A INC (SOCIETE DE MATHEMATIQUES APPLIQUEES) (QC)
Declared dissolved for failure to file reports or pay fees 06/29/1984

S M A R T TECHNOLOGIES INC (UT)
Each share old Common 2¢ par exchanged for (0.1) share new Common 2¢ par 01/15/1998
Each (15) shares new Common 2¢ par exchanged again for (1) share new Common 2¢ par 06/30/2000
Charter expired 07/11/2001

S M A RES LTD (BC)
Name changed to Biomin Therapeutic Corp. 02/15/1994
Biomin Therapeutic Corp. name changed to Pharmex Industries Inc. 11/06/1996 which name changed to PanGeo Pharma Inc. (BC) 08/21/2000 which reincorporated in Canada 09/21/2000 which recapitalized as Silvio Ventures Inc. 01/09/2006 which name changed to Regency Gold Corp. 07/17/2008

S M B CORP (DE)
Merged into Miner, Inc. 11/24/69
Each share Common 1¢ par exchanged for (1) share Common 1¢ par
(See Miner, Inc.)

S.M.I. PROCESSES LTD. (BC)
Name changed to S.M. Industries Ltd. 3/26/69
S.M. Industries Ltd. struck off register 8/9/76

S M T R CORP (DE)
Name changed to Resource Exploration, Inc. 03/23/1970
Resource Exploration, Inc. name changed to Resource America, Inc. 01/31/1989
(See Resource America, Inc.)

S-M VACU-FREEZE CORP. (FL)
Name changed to Freeze Dry Corp. of America 11/10/70
(See Freeze Dry Corp. of America)

S.O. REALIZATION CO.
Liquidated in 1936

S.O. SYSTEMS, INC. (CA)
Completely liquidated 4/3/68
Each share Common $1 par exchanged for first and final distribution of (0.355669) share Kalvar Corp. (La.) Common 2¢ par
Kalvar Corp. (La.) reincorporated in Delaware 11/12/81
(See Kalvar Corp. (Del.))

S.O. SYSTEMS, INC. (DE)
Under plan of merger reincorporated under the laws of California 11/27/64
Each share Class A or Class B exchanged for (0.1) share Common $1 par
S.O. Systems, Inc. (Calif.) acquired by Kalvar Corp. (La.) 4/3/68
Kalvar Corp. (La.) reincorporated in Delaware 11/12/81
(See Kalvar Corp. (Del.))

S O I INDS INC (DE)
Common $0.0001 par changed to $0.000025 par and (3) additional shares issued 04/27/1988
Each share old Common $0.000025 par exchanged for (0.125) share new Common $0.000025 par 12/15/1995
Name changed to Millennia, Inc. (DE) 12/16/1996
Millennia, Inc. (DE) reincorporated in Nevada 02/23/2005 which name changed to Bonamour Pacific, Inc. 08/11/2011 which name changed to TexStar Oil Corp. 12/03/2012

S.O.R. LIQUIDATING CO. (CA)
Name changed from Social Oil & Refining Co. 5/5/65
Liquidation completed
Each share Capital Stock 50¢ par received third distribution of $0.20 cash 9/1/65
Each share Capital Stock 50¢ par received fourth and final distribution of $0.13972 cash 3/4/68

S O RES INC (BC)
Recapitalized as Crimson Tide Resources Ltd. 06/04/1985
Each share Common no par exchanged for (1) share Common no par
Crimson Tide Resources Ltd. name changed to H.E.R.O Industries Ltd. (BC) 12/22/1986 which reincorporated in Ontario as Middlefield Bancorp Ltd. 04/25/1997 which merged into Middlefield Tactical Energy Corp. 02/23/2012 which name changed to MBN Corp. 02/27/2012

S.O.S. PHOTO-CINE-OPTICS, INC. (NY)
Completely liquidated 7/12/67
Each share Common 1¢ par exchanged for (0.2) share F & B/Ceco Industries, Inc. Common 25¢ par

S P DRUG INC (NY)
Stock Dividend - 10% 08/30/1984
Merged into McKesson Corp. (MD) 10/03/1985
Each share Common 1¢ par exchanged for $18 cash

S R C LABS INC (DE)
Stock Dividends - 20% 10/15/75; 20% 4/1/76; 10% 11/15/78
Charter cancelled and declared inoperative and void for non-payment of taxes 6/26/90

S R TELECOM INC (CANADA)
Old Common no par split (3) for (1) by issuance of (2) additional shares 10/28/1993
Each share old Common no par exchanged for (0.1) share new Common no par 08/29/2003
Name changed to SRX Post Holdings Inc. 06/18/2008
(See SRX Post Holdings Inc.)

S S G I INC (FL)
Recapitalized as Vicapsys Life Sciences, Inc. 11/02/2017
Each share Common $0.001 par exchanged for (0.01) share Common $0.001 par

S T A RES CORP (BC)
Recapitalized as T.T.A. Resources Corp. 10/03/1996
Each share Common no par exchanged for (0.5) share Common no par
T.T.A. Resources Corp. name changed to Minefund Development Corp. 08/26/1999

S T I INDS INC (ON)
Cease trade order in effect 04/28/1993

S U S ENTERPRISES INC (AZ)
Name changed to Portafone Corp. of Arizona 08/12/1971
(See Portafone Corp. of Arizona)

S.W. LIQUIDATING CO. (DE)
Liquidation completed
Each (2.55) shares Common $2.50 par stamped to indicate initial distribution of (1) share Consolidated Foods Corp. Common $1.33333333 par 12/08/1960
Each (56.269) shares Common $2.50 par stamped to indicate second distribution of (1) share Consolidated Foods Corp. Common $1.33333333 par 01/14/1963
Each (53.416) shares Common $2.50 par exchanged for third and final distribution of (1) share Consolidated Foods Corp. Common $1.33333333 par 01/31/1964

S W FINL CORP (CO)
Consolidated Foods Corp. name changed to Sara Lee Corp. 04/02/1985 which recapitalized as Hillshire Brands Co. 06/29/2012
(See Hillshire Brands Co.)

S W FINL CORP (CO)
Recapitalized as Casdim International Systems, Inc. (CO) 12/11/95
Each share Common $0.00001 par exchanged for (0.02) share Common $0.00001 par
Casdim International Systems, Inc. (CO) reincorporated in Delaware 4/25/97
(See Casdim International Systems, Inc.)

S W INDS INC (MA)
Common $5 par split (3) for (2) by issuance of (0.5) additional share 04/14/1972
Common $5 par changed to $1 par 04/19/1972
Merged into BTR Ltd. 07/09/1976
Each share Common $1 par exchanged for $42 cash

S WIND-UP CORP (DE)
Liquidation completed
Each share Common $0.001 par received first and final distribution of $0.02404889 cash payable 4/16/2007 to holders of record 4/16/2007
Note: Certificates were not required to be surrendered and are without value

S Y BANCORP CAP TR I (DE)
9% Guaranteed Trust Preferred Securities called for redemption at $10 on 07/01/2006

S Y BANCORP CAP TR II (DE)
10% Trust Preferred Securities called for redemption at $10 on 12/31/2013

S Y BANCORP INC (KY)
Common no par split (2) for (1) by issuance of (1) additional share payable 09/17/1996 to holders of record 08/30/1996
Common no par split (2) for (1) by issuance of (1) additional share payable 02/26/1999 to holders of record 02/02/1999 Ex date - 03/01/1999
Common no par split (2) for (1) by issuance of (1) additional share payable 09/19/2003 to holders of record 09/03/2003 Ex date - 09/22/2003
Stock Dividends - 10% 11/01/1993; 10% 11/01/1994; 5% payable 05/26/2006 to holders of record 05/10/2006 Ex date - 05/08/2006
Name changed to Stock Yards Bancorp, Inc. 04/25/2014

S Y S ASSOC INC (NY)
Name changed to SYS Computer Corp. 11/5/70
(See SYS Computer Corp.)

S Y S INDS INC (NY)
Common 1¢ par split (10) for (1) by issuance of (9) additional shares 05/30/1975
Name changed to Rhine Industries Inc. 02/11/1977

S&W SEED CO (DE)
Issue Information - 1,400,000 UNITS consisting of (2) shares COM, (1) CL A WT and (1) CL B WT offered at $11.00 per Unit on 05/03/2010
Units separated 06/14/2010
Reincorporated under the laws of Nevada 12/13/2011

SA RECOVERY CORP (OK)
Common $0.0001 par split (2) for (1) by issuance of (1) additional share payable 08/10/2012 to holders of record 07/16/2012 Ex date - 08/13/2012
Name changed to Truli Media Group, Inc. (OK) 08/21/2012
Truli Media Group, Inc. (OK) reorganized in Delaware 03/17/2015

SA TELECOMMUNICATIONS INC (DE)
Name changed 08/03/1995
Name changed from SA Holdings, Inc. to SA Telecommunications, Inc. 08/03/1995
Chapter 11 bankruptcy proceedings converted to Chapter 7 on 08/10/2000
No stockholders' equity

SAASMAX INC (NV)
Common $0.001 par split (12) for (1) by issuance of (11) additional shares payable 04/16/2014 to holders of record 04/16/2014
Name changed to Nouveau Ventures Inc. 09/08/2014

SAATCHI & SAATCHI PLC NEW (ENGLAND)
Merged into Publicis S.A. (New) 09/08/2000
Each Sponsored ADR for Ordinary 25p par exchanged for (0.9126) Sponsored ADR for Ordinary

SAATCHI & SAATCHI PLC OLD (ENGLAND)
ADR's for Ordinary 10p par split (4) for (3) by issuance of (1/3) additional ADR 06/03/1985
ADR's for Ordinary 10p par split (4) for (3) by issuance of (1/3) additional ADR 03/27/1987
Each ADR for Ordinary 10p par exchanged for (0.1) ADR for Ordinary 25p par 06/15/1992
Name changed to Cordiant PLC 03/16/1995
Cordiant PLC name changed to Cordiant Communications Group PLC 12/12/1997 which merged into WPP Group PLC (United Kingdom) 08/01/2003 which reorganized in Jersey as WPP PLC (Old) 11/20/2008 which reorganized as WPP PLC (New) 01/02/2013

SAATY FUEL INJECTOR CORP (RI)
Each share Capital Stock $1 par exchanged for (5) shares Capital Stock 20¢ par 04/26/1956
Charter revoked for failure to file reports and pay fees 12/31/1968

SAB HARMON INDS INC (MO)
Common 25¢ par split (2) for (1) by issuance of (1) additional share 11/15/84
Stock Dividend - 100% 11/15/80
Name changed back to Harmon Industries, Inc. 5/9/86
Harmon Industries, Inc. merged into General Electric Co. 9/1/2000

SABA OIL & GAS CORP (DE)
Charter cancelled and declared inoperative and void for non-payment of taxes 3/1/84

SABA PETE CO (DE)
Reincorporated 6/10/97
Common 1¢ par split (2) for (1) by issuance of (1) additional share payable 12/16/96 to holders of record 12/9/96 Ex date - 12/17/96
State of incorporation changed from (CO) to (DE) 6/10/97
Merged into GREKA Energy Corp. 3/24/99
Each share Common 1¢ par exchanged for (1/6) share Common no par
(See GREKA Energy Corp.)

SABA SOFTWARE INC (DE)
Each share old Common $0.001 par exchanged for (0.25) share new Common $0.001 par 05/12/2003
Acquired by Vector Talent II LLC 03/30/2015
Each share new Common $0.001 par exchanged for $9 cash

SABER BOATS, INC. (MD)
Charter revoked for failure to file reports and pay fees 12/14/61

SABER CAP CORP (BC)
Reorganized under the laws of Canada as Emblem Corp. 12/05/2016
Each share Common no par exchanged for (0.25) share Common no par

SABER SOFTWARE CORP (TX)
Merged into McAfee Associates, Inc. 09/01/1995
Each share Common 1¢ par exchanged for (0.31326) share Common 1¢ par
Note: Each share Common 1¢ par received an additional distribution of (0.1450628) share Common 1¢ par 05/01/1996
McAfee Associates, Inc. name changed to Network Associates, Inc. 12/01/1997 which name changed to McAfee, Inc. 06/30/2004
(See McAfee, Inc.)

SABERDYNE, INC. (AZ)
Recapitalized as Saberdyne Systems, Inc. 9/20/71
Each share Common 25¢ par exchanged for (0.1) share Common 10¢ par
(See Saberdyne Systems, Inc.)

SABERDYNE, INC. (NV)
Under plan of merger each share Common 1¢ par automatically became (1) share Saberdyne, Inc. (AZ) Common 25¢ par 8/11/70
Saberdyne, Inc. (AZ) recapitalized as Saberdyne Systems, Inc. 9/20/71
(See Saberdyne Systems, Inc.)

SABERDYNE SYS INC (AZ)
Charter revoked for failure to file reports or pay fees 05/10/1977

SABERTOOTH HLDGS INC (BC)
Reincorporated under the laws of Canada as Harmony Integrated Solutions, Inc. 09/06/2000
(See Harmony Integrated Solutions, Inc.)

SABINA BK (SABINA, OH)
Merged into Premier Financial Bancorp Inc. 11/14/97
Each share Common no par exchanged for (4.33) shares Common no par

SABINA INDS LTD (BC)
Reorganized as New Sabina Resources Ltd. 07/20/1984
Each (10) shares Capital Stock $1 par exchanged for (5) shares Common no par, (4) shares McFinley Red Lake Mines Ltd. Common no par and (1) McFinley Red Lake Mines Ltd. Common Stock Purchase Warrant expiring 09/03/1985
(See each company's listing)

SABINA MINES LTD. (BC)
Name changed to Sabina Industries Ltd. 07/30/1971
(See Sabina Industries Ltd.)

SABINA RES LTD (BC)
Name changed to Sabina Silver Corp. 10/17/2005
Sabina Silver Corp. name changed to Sabina Gold & Silver Corp. 10/28/2009

SABINA SILVER CORP (BC)
Name changed to Sabina Gold & Silver Corp. 10/28/2009

SABINE BK (PORT ARTHUR, TX)
Reorganized as First Financial Bancorporation, Inc. 10/14/1980
Each share Common $10 par exchanged for (2.83810) shares Common no par
First Financial Bancorporation, Inc. name changed to United Bankers Inc. 09/24/1981

(See United Bankers Inc.)

SABINE CORP (LA)
Common no par split (2) for (1) by issuance of (1) additional share 01/31/1977
Common no par split (2) for (1) by issuance of (1) additional share 06/10/1980
Merged into Pacific Enterprises 05/09/1988
Each share Common no par exchanged for $24 cash

SABINE NATURAL GAS & PRODUCTS CO. (DE)
Liquidation completed 5/19/61

SABINE OIL & GAS CORP (NY)
Plan of reorganization under Chapter 11 Federal Bankruptcy proceedings effective 08/11/2016
No stockholders' equity

SABINE RTY CORP (TX)
Common no par split (2) for (1) by issuance of (1) additional share 7/1/61
Common no par split (2) for (1) by issuance of (1) additional share 5/1/64
Common no par split (3) for (1) by issuance of (2) additional shares 4/1/69
Stock Dividends - 100% 12/30/52; 25% 7/10/56; 16-2/3% 7/8/60
Reincorporated under the laws of Louisiana as Sabine Corp. 1/3/77
(See Sabine Corp.)

SABINE URANIUM MINES LTD. (ON)
Charter surrendered 6/12/61
No stockholders' equity

SABLE CORP (DE)
Recapitalized as Intercontinental Resources Group, Inc. 05/09/1991
Each share Common $0.0001 par exchanged for (0.2) share Common $0.0001 par
(See Intercontinental Resources Group, Inc.)

SABLE INC (UT)
Name changed to Big Horn Oil, Inc. 5/1/82
Big Horn Oil, Inc. recapitalized as Nova Technology Corp. 12/30/86
(See Nova Technology Corp.)

SABLE NAT RES CORP (DE)
Chapter 11 bankruptcy proceedings converted to Chapter 7 on 12/18/2017
Stockholders' equity unlikely

SABLE PALM AWYS INC (NV)
Recapitalized as Blue Grizzly Truck Inc. 08/10/1995
Each share Common $0.001 par exchanged for (0.01) share Common $0.001 par
Blue Grizzly Truck Inc. name changed to Music & Entertainment Network Inc. (NV) 12/29/1995 which reorganized in Delaware as Informatix Holdings, Inc. 06/30/1998 which recapitalized as Autologous Wound Therapy, Inc. 11/08/1999 which name changed to Cytomedix, Inc. 03/20/2000 which name changed to Nuo Therapeutics, Inc. 11/14/2014

SABLE TECHNOLOGIES LTD (AB)
Name changed to Intepac Corp. 05/15/1991
Intepac Corp. recapitalized as Intepac Inc. 01/18/1999
(See Intepac Inc.)

SABMILLER PLC (ENGLAND & WALES)
ADR agreement terminated 01/16/2014
Each Sponsored 144A ADR for Ordinary exchanged for $52.283333 cash
ADR agreement terminated 10/19/2016

FINANCIAL INFORMATION, INC.

Each Sponsored ADR for Ordinary exchanged for $54.790918 cash

SABRA HEALTH CARE REIT INC (MD)
7.125% Preferred Ser. A 1¢ par called for redemption at $25 plus $0.445313 accrued dividends on 06/01/2018
(Additional Information in Active)

SABRATEK CORP (DE)
Secondary Offering - 1,276,574 shares COM offered at $18 per share on 04/04/1997
Plan of reorganization under Chapter 11 Federal Bankruptcy Code effective 05/01/2001
No stockholders' equity

SABRE, INC. (CO)
Name changed to Beckley Industries, Inc. 11/02/1970
(See Beckley Industries, Inc.)

SABRE CRAFT BOAT CO., INC. (WA)
Name changed to American Marine Industries, Inc. 2/23/63

SABRE GRAPHITE CORP (BC)
Under plan of merger name changed to DraftTeam Daily Fantasy Sports Corp. 03/13/2015
DraftTeam Daily Fantasy Sports Corp. name changed to Fantasy Aces Daily Fantasy Sports Corp. 10/06/2015

SABRE HLDGS CORP (DE)
Name changed 7/30/99
Name changed from Sabre Group Holdings Inc. to Sabre Holdings Corp. 7/30/99
Merged into Sovereign Holdings, Inc. 3/30/2007
Each share Class A Common 1¢ par exchanged for $32.75 cash

SABRE INDL INC (DE)
Name changed to Tsingyuan Brewery Ltd. 01/19/2011
(See Tsingyuan Brewery Ltd.)

SABRE INDS INC (CO)
Charter suspended for failure to file annual reports 06/23/1989

SABRE MARKETING CORP (BC)
Recapitalized as Sabre Pacific Equities Ltd. 08/10/1994
Each share Common no par exchanged for (1/3) share Common no par
(See Sabre Pacific Equities Ltd.)

SABRE PAC EQUITIES LTD (BC)
Delisted from Vancouver Stock Exchange 03/01/1999

SABRE-PINON CORP. (DE)
Under plan of merger name changed to United Nuclear Corp. (DE) 4/4/62
United Nuclear Corp. (DE) reorganized in Virginia as UNC Resources, Inc. 8/31/78 which name changed to UNC Inc. (VA) 6/3/86 which reincorporated in Delaware 4/30/87
(See UNC Inc.)

SABRE URANIUM CORP. (DE)
Merged into Sabre-Pinon Corp. on a (0.5) for (1) basis 6/1/56
Sabre-Pinon Corp. merged into United Nuclear Corp. (DE) 4/4/62 which reorganized as UNC Resources, Inc. 8/31/78 which name changed to UNC Inc. (VA) 6/3/86 which reincorporated in Delaware 4/30/87
(See UNC Inc.)

SABRETOOTH ENERGY LTD (AB)
Name changed to Cequence Energy Ltd. 08/17/2009

SAC TECHNOLOGIES INC (MN)
Issue Information - 1,100,000 shares COM offered at $6 per share on 02/21/1997
Common $1 par split (2) for (1) by issuance of (1) additional share payable 07/24/1997 to holders of record 07/11/1997
Name changed to BIO-key International, Inc. (MN) 03/04/2002
BIO-key International, Inc. (MN) reincorporated in Delaware 01/01/2005

SACCHARUM ENERGY CORP (AB)
Name changed to SynStream Energy Corp. 06/30/201

SACHAR PROPERTIES, INC. (DE)
No longer in existence having become inoperative and void for non-payment of taxes 4/1/65

SACHEM EXPL LTD (BC)
Recapitalized as Brower Exploration Inc. (BC) 08/10/1984
Each share Capital Stock no par exchanged for (0.2) share Common no par
Brower Exploration Inc. (BC) reincorporated in Wyoming 12/29/1993 which reorganized in Massachusetts as Stocker & Yale, Inc. (New) 05/11/1994 which name changed to StockerYale, Inc. 07/03/2000 which name changed to ProPhotonix Ltd. 07/23/2010

SACHIGO RIVER EXPLORATION CO. LTD.
Liquidation completed in 1942

SACIO INC (DE)
Name changed to Freesoftwareclub.com, Inc. 03/14/2000
(See Freesoftwareclub.com, Inc.)

SACKPORT VENTURES INC (AB)
Cease trade order 09/13/2006

SACKVILLE OILS & MINERALS LTD (AB)
Merged into Seagull Resources Ltd. 1/3/78
Each share Common no par exchanged for (0.25) share Common no par
(See Seagull Resources Ltd.)

SACO INDS & RLTY LTD (AB)
Recapitalized as Royal Resources Ltd. (AB) 01/31/1986
Each share Common no par exchanged for (0.2) share Common no par
Royal Resources Ltd. (AB) reincorporated in Canada 07/21/1987 which name changed to Royaledge Industries, Inc. 12/03/1987 which name changed to Royaledge Resources Inc. 12/21/1995 which recapitalized as Avalanche Networks Corp. 05/25/2000 which name changed to Avalanche Minerals Ltd. 09/14/2007 which recapitalized as OroAndes Resource Corp. 07/03/2008 which name changed to Fort St. James Nickel Corp. 12/02/2011

SACO-LOWELL SHOPS (ME)
Each share 6% Preferred $100 par exchanged for (3) shares Class A Preferred $20 par, (3) shares Common $5 par and (6) Subscription Rights in 1937
Each share 7% 2nd Preferred $100 par exchanged for (1.5) shares Class A Preferred $20 par, (1.5) shares Common $5 par and (3) Subscription Rights in 1937
Each share Common $100 par exchanged for (0.5) share Common $5 par and (0.5) Subscription Right in 1937
Each share Common $5 par exchanged for (2) shares Common $2.50 par in 1951
Stock Dividend - 20% 8/9/48
Merged into Maremont Corp. (Ill.) 11/22/63
Each share Common $2.50 par exchanged for (0.333333) share 4-1/2% Conv. Preferred $100 par Maremont Corp. (Ill.) reincorporated in Delaware 4/30/74
(See Maremont Corp. (Del.))

SACO MNG LTD (AB)
Name changed to Saco Industries & Realty Ltd. 07/06/1977
Saco Industries & Realty Ltd. recapitalized as Royal Resources Ltd. (AB) 01/31/1986 which reincorporated in Canada 07/21/1987 which name changed to Royaledge Industries, Inc. 12/03/1987 which name changed to Royaledge Resources Inc. 12/21/1995 which recapitalized as Avalanche Networks Corp. 05/25/2000 which name changed to Avalanche Minerals Ltd. 09/14/2007 which recapitalized as OroAndes Resource Corp. 07/03/2008 which name changed to Fort St. James Nickel Corp. 12/02/2011

SACO RES LTD (AB)
Recapitalized as Manar Canada Inc. 6/24/91
Each share Common no par exchanged for (1/3) share Common no par
(See Manar Canada Inc.)

SACO SMARTVISION INC (CANADA)
Assets sold for the benefit of creditors 06/00/2004
No stockholders' equity

SACOL INC (CO)
Company went private through purchase offer which expired 12/15/1978
Public interest eliminated

SACOM (CA)
Adjudicated bankrupt 12/31/1975
Stockholders' equity unlikely

SACRAMENTO COML BK (SACRAMENTO, CA)
Merged into Sacramento Capital Co. 2/29/2000
Each share Common no par exchanged for $32.5154 cash

SACRAMENTO FIRST NATL BK (SACRAMENTO, CA)
Merged into Business & Professional Bank (Woodland, CA)
Each share Common $5 par exchanged for (0.4198) share Common no par and $6.23 cash
(See Business & Professional Bank (Woodland, CA))

SACYR VALLEHERMOSO S A (SPAIN)
Name changed to Sacry S.A. 08/21/2013

SADDLE MOUNTAIN DEVELOPMENT CORP. (AZ)
All outstanding Common $1 par stock was repurchased by principals prior to dissolution of 9/21/64

SADDLE MTN MNG CORP (AB)
Reincorporated 07/26/1994
Place of incorporation changed from (BC) to (AB) 07/26/1994
Name changed to Saddle Mountain Timber Corp. 02/09/1995
Saddle Mountain Timber Corp. name changed to Global Tree Technologies Inc. (AB) 02/25/1997 which reorganized in British Columbia as Acadia Resources Corp. 02/07/2011 which reincorporated in Jersey as Horizon Petroleum PLC 10/08/2013 which reincorporated in Alberta as Horizon Petroleum Ltd. 04/05/2016

SADDLE MTN TIMBER CORP (AB)
Name changed to Global Tree Technologies Inc. (AB) 02/25/1997
Global Tree Technologies Inc. (AB) reorganized in British Columbia as Acadia Resources Corp. 02/07/2011 which reincorporated in Jersey as Horizon Petroleum PLC 10/08/2013 which reincorporated in Alberta as Horizon Petroleum Ltd. 04/05/2016

SADDLE RES INC (AB)
Acquired by Devlan Exploration Inc. 6/28/2002
Each share Common no par exchanged for $0.52 cash

SADDLEROCK RES INC (BC)
Name changed to MDX Medical Inc. 07/07/2000
MDX Medical Inc. name changed to Urodynamix Technologies Ltd. 06/21/2006 which recapitalized as Venturi Ventures Inc. 08/29/2011
(See Venturi Ventures Inc.)

SADIA S A (BRAZIL)
Sponsored ADR's for Preferred split (3) for (1) by issuance of (2) additional ADR's payable 01/21/2005 to holders of record 01/20/2005 Ex date - 01/24/2005
ADR basis changed from (1:30) to (1:10) 01/24/2005
Sponsored ADR's for Preferred split (10) for (3) by issuance of (2.33333333) additional ADR's payable 02/05/2008 to holders of record 02/01/2008 Ex date - 02/06/2008
ADR basis changed from (1:10) to (1:3) 02/06/2008
Merged into BRF-Brasil Foods S.A. 09/21/2009
Each Sponsored ADR for Preferred exchanged for (0.199497) Sponsored ADR for Common
BRF-Brasil Foods S.A. name changed to BRF S.A. 05/01/2013

SADIE RED LAKE GOLD MINES LTD. (ON)
Charter cancelled for failure to file returns and pay taxes in 1958

SAEHAN BANCORP (CA)
Common no par split (2) for (1) by issuance of (1) additional share payable 08/21/2001 to holders of record 07/31/2001 Ex date - 08/22/2001
Common no par split (2) for (1) by issuance of (1) additional share payable 12/20/2005 to holders of record 12/05/2005 Ex date - 12/21/2005
Stock Dividends - 5% payable 05/20/1998 to holders of record 04/30/1998; 6% payable 05/15/1999 to holders of record 04/30/1999; 10% payable 05/19/2000 to holders of record 05/15/2000; 10% payable 04/20/2001 to holders of record 03/22/2001 Ex date - 03/20/2001; 10% payable 08/15/2002 to holders of record 07/01/2002 Ex date - 06/27/2002; 8% payable 05/30/2003 to holders of record 05/17/2003 Ex date - 05/14/2003; 10% payable 07/16/2004 to holders of record 06/25/2004; 5% payable 09/20/2005 to holders of record 09/01/2005 Ex date - 08/30/2005; 4% payable 07/21/2006 to holders of record 07/05/2006 Ex date - 06/30/2006; 4% payable 06/20/2007 to holders of record 06/08/2007 Ex date - 06/06/2007; 8% payable 06/26/2008 to holders of record 06/10/2008 Ex date - 06/06/2008
Merged into Wilshire Bancorp, Inc. 11/20/2013
Each share Common no par exchanged for either (0.0608) share Common no par, (0.0304) share Common no par and $0.21235 cash or $0.4247 cash
Wilshire Bancorp, Inc. merged into Hope Bancorp, Inc. 08/01/2016

SAEHAN BK (LOS ANGELES, CA)
Under plan of reorganization each share Common no par automatically became (1) share Saehan Bancorp Common no par 04/00/1998
Saehan Bancorp merged into Wilshire

Bancorp, Inc. 11/20/2013 which merged into Hope Bancorp, Inc. 08/01/2016

SAES GETTERS S P A (ITALY)
ADR agreement terminated 07/18/2003
Each Sponsored ADR for Ordinary exchanged for $8.17 cash

SAF-T-HAMMER CORP (NV)
Name changed to Smith & Wesson Holding Corp. 03/13/2002
Smith & Wesson Holding Corp. name changed to American Outdoor Brands Corp. 01/03/2017

SAF T LOK INC (FL)
Each share old Common no par exchanged for (0.1) share new Common no par 04/27/2001
Chapter 7 bankruptcy proceedings terminated 09/08/2006

SAFARI ASSOC INC (UT)
Each share old Common $0.0001 par exchanged for (0.1) share new Common $0.0001 par 04/17/2003
Recapitalized as Power-Save Energy Co. 11/28/2006
Each share new Common $0.0001 par (0.33333333) share Common $0.001 par
Power-Save Energy Co. name changed to Lustros, Inc. 04/25/2012
(See Lustros, Inc.)

SAFARI EXPLS LTD (ON)
Merged into Cavalier Energy Inc. (ONT) 3/1/74
Each share Capital Stock no par exchanged for (0.04) share Common no par
Cavalier Energy Inc. (ONT) reincorporated in Alberta as Cavalier Energy Ltd. 2/7/78
(See Cavalier Energy Ltd.)

SAFARI INTL RES LTD (BC)
Merged into Epic Oil & Gas Ltd. 06/17/1998
Each share Common no par exchanged for (0.9) share Common no par
Epic Oil & Gas Ltd. recapitalized as Blue Parrot Energy Inc. 04/11/2003 which recapitalized as RIA Resources Corp. 05/19/2009 which reorganized as Qwest Diversified Capital Corp. 06/05/2013

SAFCO INVT HLDG CORP (DE)
Recapitalized as Boly Group Holdings Corp. 01/24/2017
Each share Common $0.001 par exchanged for (0.01) share Common $0.001 par
Boly Group Holdings Corp. name changed to US VR Global.com Inc. 02/07/2018

SAFE & SECURE TV CHANNEL INC (NV)
Old Common $0.001 par split (10.85) for (1) by issuance of (9.85) additional shares payable 09/20/2010 to holders of record 08/23/2010 Ex date - 09/21/2010
Each share old Common $0.001 par exchanged for (0.00073529) share new Common $0.001 par 03/29/2012
Name changed to Cosmos Group Holdings Inc. 03/31/2016

SAFE AID PRODS INC (DE)
Recapitalized as Safe Technologies International Inc. 2/9/98
Each share Common $0.00001 par exchanged for (0.1) share Common $0.00001 par

SAFE ALTERNATIVES CORP AMER INC (FL)
Each share old Common $0.001 par exchanged for (0.004) share new Common $0.001 par 11/23/2004
Name changed to Mortgage Assistance Center Corp. 01/18/2005

(See Mortgage Assistance Center Corp.)

SAFE BULKERS INC (MARSHALL ISLANDS)
8% Perpetual Preferred Ser. B 1¢ par called for redemption at $25 plus $0.111111 accrued dividends on 02/20/2018
(Additional Information in Active)

SAFE CABINET CO.
Acquired by Remington Rand, Inc. 00/00/1927
Details not available

SAFE DEPOSIT BANK & TRUST CO. (SPRINGFIELD, MA)
Name changed to First Bank & Trust Co. of Hampden County (Springfield, MA) 05/06/1968
First Bank & Trust Co. of Hampden County (Springfield, MA) name changed to Shawmut First Bank & Trust Co. (Springfield, MA) 04/01/1975

SAFE DYNAMICS CORP (DE)
Name changed to Horizon Minerals Corp. 04/19/2013

SAFE ENVIRONMENT ENGR CDA LTD (AB)
Delisted from Toronto Stock Venture Exchange 06/20/2003

SAFE FLIGHT INSTR CORP (NY)
Merged into SF Instrument Corp. 10/02/1975
Each share Common $1 par exchanged for $6.56 cash

SAFE GUARD CHECK WRITER CORP.
Name changed to Safeguard Corp. in 1930
Safeguard Corp. name changed to Safeguard Business Systems Corp. 4/24/65 which was acquired by Safeguard Industries, Inc. 1/5/68 which name changed to Safeguard Scientifics, Inc. 5/15/81

SAFE HARBOUR CAP LTD (AB)
Issue Information - 2,000,000 shares COM offered at $0.10 per share on 01/23/1997
Name changed to Kingsmere Capital Inc. 8/12/2002
(See Kingsmere Capital Inc.)

SAFE ID CORP (NV)
Name changed to EYI Industries Inc. 12/31/2003
(See EYI Industries Inc.)

SAFE IDEA INC (NV)
Each share old Common $0.0001 par exchanged for (0.33333333) share new Common $0.0001 par 09/28/2004
Name changed to Bloodhound Search Technologies, Inc. 12/27/2005
(See Bloodhound Search Technologies, Inc.)

SAFE-T-STAT CO.
Merged into Moto Meter Gauge & Equipment Corp. in 1929
Details not available

SAFE TRANSN SYS INC (FL)
Each share old Common $0.001 par exchanged for (0.08333333) share new Common $0.001 par 11/09/2005
SEC revoked common stock registration 02/15/2006

SAFE TRAVEL CARE INC (NV)
Common $0.001 par changed to $0.0001 par 06/02/2006
Recapitalized as Titan Energy Worldwide, Inc. 12/28/2006
Each share Common $0.0001 par exchanged for (0.02) share Common $0.0001 par
(See Titan Energy Worldwide, Inc.)

SAFE-WASTE SYS INC (DE)
Charter cancelled and declared inoperative and void for non-payment of taxes 03/01/1996

SAFECARD SVCS INC (DE)
Common 1¢ par split (2) for (1) by issuance of (1) additional share 06/23/1978
Common 1¢ par split (3) for (2) by issuance of (0.5) additional share 04/15/1983
Common 1¢ par split (3) for (2) by issuance of (0.5) additional share 04/22/1985
Common 1¢ par split (3) for (2) by issuance of (0.5) additional share 03/14/1986
Common 1¢ par split (3) for (2) by issuance of (0.5) additional share 04/30/1987
Stock Dividends - 100% 10/23/1980; 100% 05/20/1981; 20% 10/31/1985
Under plan of reorganization each share Common 1¢ par automatically became (1) share Ideon Group, Inc. Common 1¢ par 04/28/1995
Ideon Group, Inc. merged into CUC International Inc. 08/07/1996 which name changed to Cendant Corp. 12/17/1997 which reorganized as Avis Budget Group, Inc. 09/01/2006

SAFECO ADVISOR SER TR (DE)
Completely liquidated 01/09/1997
Details not available

SAFECO CALIF TAX FREE INCOME FD INC (DE)
Reincorporated 09/30/1993
State of incorporation changed from (WA) to (DE) and Common 10¢ par changed to $0.001 par 09/30/1993
Merged into Pioneer Series Trust II 12/10/2004
Each share Common $0.001 par exchanged for California Tax-Free Income Fund Class A shares on a net asset basis

SAFECO COM STK TR (DE)
Small Company Stock Fund Investor Class reclassified as Small-Cap Value Fund Investor Class 10/01/2003
Each share Balanced Fund Investor Class exchanged for Pioneer Balanced Fund Investor Class shares on a net asset basis 12/10/2004
Each International Stock Fund Investor Class exchanged for Pioneer International Equity Fund Investor Class shares on a net asset basis 12/10/2004
Each share Small-Cap Value Fund Investor Class exchanged for Pioneer Small-Cap Value Fund Investor Class on a net asset basis 12/10/2004
(See each company's listing)

SAFECO CORP (WA)
4-1/2% Conv. Preferred $20 par called for redemption 03/01/1972
Common $5 par changed to no par 05/07/1986
Common no par split (2) for (1) by issuance of (1) additional share 06/05/1987
Common no par split (2) for (1) by issuance of (1) additional share 12/01/1995
Stock Dividends - 200% 06/15/1968; 100% 12/01/1971; 50% 12/15/1978; 100% 06/01/1984
Merged into Liberty Mutual Insurance Co. 09/22/2008
Each share Common no par exchanged for $68.25 cash

SAFECO EQUITY FD INC (DE)
Reincorporated 08/20/1987
Reincorporated 09/30/1993
State of incorporation changed from (DE) to (WA) 08/20/1987
State of incorporation changed from (WA) to (DE) and Common 20¢ par changed to $0.001 par 09/30/1993

Common $0.001 par reclassified as Core Equity Fund Investor Class $0.001 par 10/01/2003
Merged into Pioneer Fund 12/13/2004
Details not available

SAFECO GNMA FD (DE)
Common $0.001 par reclassified as Intermediate-Term U.S. Government Fund Investor Class 10/01/2003
Merged into Pioneer America Income Trust 12/10/2004
Each share Intermediate-Term U.S. Government Fund Investor Class exchanged for Class R on a net asset basis
Pioneer America Income Trust merged into Pioneer Series Trust IV 11/10/2006

SAFECO GROWTH FD INC (DE)
Reincorporated 09/30/1993
State of incorporation changed from (WA) to (DE) and Common 10¢ par changed to $0.001 par 09/30/1993
Ceased operations 05/10/1995
Details not available

SAFECO HIGH-YIELD BD FD INC (DE)
Reincorporated 09/30/1993
State of incorporation changed from (WA) to (DE) 09/30/1993
Merged into Pioneer High Yield Fund 12/10/2004
Each share Common $0.001 par exchanged for Class A on a net asset basis

SAFECO INCOME FD INC (DE)
Reincorporated 09/30/1993
State of incorporation changed from (WA) to (DE) and Common 10¢ par changed to $0.001 par 09/30/1993
Common $0.001 par reclassified as Large-Cap Value Fund Investor Class $0.001 par 10/01/2003
Merged into Pioneer Value Fund 12/13/2004
Details not available

SAFECO INSD MUN BD FD INC (DE)
Merged into Safeco Tax-Exempt Bond Trust 05/04/2001
Details not available

SAFECO INTER-TERM MUN BD FD (DE)
Merged into Pioneer Tax Free Income Fund 12/10/2004
Each share Common $0.001 par exchanged for Class A shares on a net asset basis

SAFECO INTER-TERM U S TREAS FD INC (DE)
Name changed 02/01/1993
Reincorporated 09/30/1993
Name changed from Safeco Intermediate-Term Bond Fund to Safeco Intermediate-Term U.S. Treasury Fund Inc. 02/01/1993
State of incorporation changed from (WA) to (DE) and Common 10¢ par changed to $0.001 par 09/30/1993
Merged into Pioneer Bond Fund 12/13/2004
Details not available

SAFECO MANAGED BD TR (DE)
Reorganized 09/30/1996
Reorganized from Safeco Institutional Series Trust to Safeco Managed Bond Trust and Fixed Income Portfolio reclassified as Managed Bond Fund Investor Class 09/30/1996
Managed Bond Fund Investor Class reclassified as Intermediate-Term Bond Fund Investor Class 10/01/2003
Merged into Pioneer Bond Fund 12/10/2004
Each Intermediate-Term Bond Fund Investor Class exchanged for Class R on a net asset basis

SAFECO MONEY MKT MUT FD INC (DE)
Reincorporated 09/30/1993
State of incorporation changed from (WA) to (DE) 09/30/1993
Merged into Pioneer Cash Reserves Fund 12/13/2004
Details not available

SAFECO MUN BD FD INC (DE)
Reincorporated 09/30/1993
State of incorporation changed from (WA) to (DE) and Common 10¢ par changed to $0.001 par 09/30/1993
Merged into Pioneer Series Trust II 12/10/2004
Each share Common $0.001 par exchanged for Municipal Bond Fund Class A shares on a net asset basis

SAFECO NORTHWEST FD INC (DE)
Merged into Safeco Managed Bond Trust 10/01/2003
Details not available

SAFECO SPL BD FD INC (DE)
Completely liquidated 02/07/1985
Each share Common 10¢ par changed for first and final distribution of $7.424 cash

SAFECO TAX FREE MONEY MKT FD INC (DE)
Reincorporated 09/30/1993
State of incorporation changed from (WA) to (DE) 09/30/1993
Merged into Pioneer Tax-Free Money Market Fund 12/13/2004
Details not available

SAFECO US GOVT SECS FD INC (DE)
Reincorporated 09/30/1993
State of incorporation changed from (WA) to (DE) 09/30/1993
Name changed to Safeco GNMA Fund 02/01/1994
Safeco GNMA Fund merged into Pioneer America Income Trust 12/10/2004 which merged into Pioneer Series Trust IV 11/10/2006

SAFECO WASH ST MUN BD FD INC (DE)
Ceased operations 05/10/1995
Details not available

SAFECO WESTERN FUND, INC. (DE)
Common $1 par changed to 10¢ par 1/29/75
Name changed to SAFECO Special Bond Fund 1/28/76
(See SAFECO Special Bond Fund)

SAFEGUARD AUTOMOTIVE CORP (DE)
Merged into Safeguard Industries, Inc. 08/02/1976
Each share Common 10¢ par exchanged for (0.5) share Conv. Preferred Ser. 10, $10 par
Safeguard Industries, Inc. name changed to Safeguard Scientifics, Inc. 05/15/1981

SAFEGUARD BIOMETRIC CORP (BC)
Reincorporated 11/30/2001
Place of incorporation changed from (WY) to (BC) 11/30/2001
Name changed to Devon Ventures Corp. 02/11/2002
Devon Ventures Corp. name changed to Pender Financial Group Corp. 06/23/2004
(See Pender Financial Group Corp.)

SAFEGUARD BUSINESS SYSTEMS CORP. (DE)
Completely liquidated 1/5/68
Each share Common 50¢ par exchanged for first and final distribution of (1/3) share Safeguard Industries, Inc. Common 10¢ par
Safeguard Industries, Inc. name changed to Safeguard Scientifics, Inc. 5/15/81

SAFEGUARD BUSINESS SYS INC (DE)
Common 10¢ par split (3) for (2) by issuance of (0.5) additional share 2/13/81
Common 10¢ par split (3) for (2) by issuance of (0.5) additional share 9/30/83
Merged into S A C Corp. 12/24/86
Each share Common 10¢ par exchanged for $20.50 cash

SAFEGUARD CORP. (DE)
Name changed to Safeguard Business Systems Corp. 4/24/65
Safeguard Business Systems Corp. acquired by Safeguard Industries, Inc. 1/5/68 which name changed to Safeguard Scientifics, Inc. 5/15/81

SAFEGUARD HEALTH ENTERPRISES INC (DE)
Reincorporated 4/27/87
Common no par split (3) for (2) by issuance of (0.5) additional share 10/15/85
State of incorporation changed from (CA) to (DE) and Common no par changed to 1¢ par 4/27/87
Each (1,500) shares old Common 1¢ par exchanged for (1) share new Common 1¢ par 7/2/2004
Note: In effect holders received $2.25 cash per share and public interest was eliminated

SAFEGUARD INDS INC (PA)
Common 10¢ par split (3) for (2) by issuance of (0.5) additional share 02/29/1968
Common 10¢ par split (4) for (3) by issuance of (0.33333333) additional share 12/17/1968
Conv. Preferred Ser. 10, $10 par called for redemption 10/30/1978
Name changed to Safeguard Scientifics, Inc. 05/15/1981

SAFEGUARD PROT SYS INC (NY)
In process of liquidation
Each share Common 1¢ par exchanged for initial distribution of $1 cash 12/29/1986
Note: Details on additional distributions, if any, are not available

SAFEGUARD SEC HLDGS INC (NV)
Each share old Common $0.001 par exchanged for (0.2) share new Common $0.001 par 05/07/2007
Chapter 7 bankruptcy proceedings terminated 08/04/2015
No stockholders' equity

SAFEGUARD VENTURES INC (BC)
Recapitalized as Amar Ventures Inc. 01/14/1994
Each share Common no par exchanged for (0.2) share Common no par
(See Amar Ventures Inc.)

SAFELITE INDS INC (DE)
Each share Common 10¢ par exchanged for (0.0005) share Common $200 par 02/10/1975
Note: In effect holders received $3 cash per share and public interest was eliminated

SAFENET INC (DE)
Merged into Vector Stealth Holdings II, LLC 04/12/2007
Each share Common 1¢ par exchanged for $28.75 cash

SAFEPACK MILLS (MA)
Merged into Ruberoid Co. in 1929
Details not available

SAFEPAY SOLUTIONS INC (DE)
Name changed to Emaji, Inc. 03/11/2008
Emaji, Inc. name changed to Broadside Enterprises, Inc. 12/01/2016

SAFER RESIDENCE CORP (NV)
Common $0.001 par split (44) for (1) by issuance of (43) additional shares payable 02/27/2006 to holders of record 02/27/2006
Ex date - 02/28/2006
Name changed to Solar Enertech Corp. (NV) 04/10/2006
Solar Enertech Corp. (NV) reincorporated in Delaware 08/13/2008

SAFER SHOT INC (NV)
Each share old Common $0.001 par exchanged for (0.01) share new Common $0.001 par 04/23/2013
Each share new Common $0.001 par exchanged for (0.001) share Common $0.00001 par 01/06/2015
Reincorporated under the laws of Florida 03/02/2015

SAFESCIENCE INC (NV)
Name changed to GlycoGenesys, Inc. 11/7/2001
(See GlycoGenesys, Inc.)

SAFESCRIPT PHARMACIES INC (TX)
Chapter 11 bankruptcy proceedings converted to Chapter 7 on 10/23/2006
No stockholders' equity

SAFESKIN CORP (FL)
Common 1¢ par split (2) for (1) by issuance of (1) additional share payable 1/2/97 to holders of record 11/29/96 Ex date - 1/3/97
Common 1¢ par split (2) for (1) by issuance of (1) additional share payable 4/1/98 to holders of record 2/27/98
Merged into Kimberly-Clark Corp. 2/8/2000
Each share Common 1¢ par exchanged for (0.1956) share Common 1¢ par

SAFESTITCH MED INC (DE)
Name changed to TransEnterix, Inc. 12/09/2013

SAFETECH INC (DE)
Name changed to Highlands Coal & Chemical Corp. 06/15/1977
Highlands Coal & Chemical Corp. name changed to Rio Verde Energy Corp. 05/07/1981
(See Rio Verde Energy Corp.)

SAFETECH INDS INC (NY)
Charter cancelled and proclaimed dissolved for failure to pay taxes 6/27/2001

SAFETEE GLASS INC (PA)
Acquired by Water Treatment Corp. 08/08/1969
Each share Common no par exchanged for (0.685) share Common 10¢ par
Water Treatment Corp. merged into Chromalloy American Corp. (DE) 06/01/1971 which merged into Sun Chemical Corp. 12/23/1986 which name changed to Sequa Corp. 05/08/1987
(See Sequa Corp.)

SAFETRAN SYS CORP (DE)
Merged into CCI Corp. 09/29/1977
Each share Class A Common 10¢ par exchanged for (2.91) shares Common 50¢ par
(See CCI Corp.)

SAFETY CABLE CO.
Merged into General Cable Corp. in 1927
(See General Cable Corp.)

SAFETY CAR HEATING & LIGHTING CO., INC. (DE)
Each share Capital Stock $50 par exchanged for (4) shares Capital Stock $12.50 par in 1948
Safety Car Heating & Lighting Co., Inc. name changed to Safety Industries, Inc. 5/1/56 which merged into American Manufacturing Co., Inc. 1/22/60 which assets were transferred to American Manufacturing Co., Inc. Liquidating Trust 5/20/80
(See American Manufacturing Co., Inc. Liquidating Trust)

SAFETY CAR HEATING & LIGHTING CO. (NJ)
Reorganized as Safety Car Heating & Lighting Co., Inc. share for share in 1939
Safety Car Heating & Lighting Co., Inc. name changed to Safety Industries Inc. 5/1/56 which merged into American Manufacturing Co., Inc. 1/22/60 which assets were transferred to American Manufacturing Co., Inc. Liquidating Trust 5/20/80
(See American Manufacturing Co., Inc. Liquidating Trust)

SAFETY COMPONENTS INTL INC (DE)
Each share old Common 1¢ par received (0.028725) share new Common 1¢ par and (0.123006) Common Stock Purchase Warrant expiring 04/10/2003 payable 10/11/2000 to holders of record 09/08/2000
Note: Certificates were not required to be surrendered and are without value
Name changed to International Textile Group, Inc. 10/26/2004
(See International Textile Group, Inc.)

SAFETY FD CORP (MA)
Common $10 par changed to $5 par and (1) additional share issued 1/23/86
Common $5 par split (2) for (1) by issuance of (1) additional share 4/28/87
Common $5 par split (3) for (2) by issuance of (0.5) additional share 11/20/95
Stock Dividends - 10% 12/31/84; 10% 12/31/85; 20% 12/31/86
Merged into CFX Corp. 7/1/96
Each share Common $5 par exchanged for (1.7) shares Common $0.66-2/3 par
CFX Corp. merged into Peoples Heritage Financial Group, Inc. 4/10/98 which name changed to Banknorth Group, Inc. (ME) 5/10/2000 which merged into TD Banknorth Inc. 3/1/2005
(See TD Banknorth Inc.)

SAFETY FD NATL BK (FITCHBURG, MA)
Each share Common $100 par exchanged for (2) shares Common $50 par 00/00/1946
Common $50 par changed to $10 par and (4) additional shares issued plus a 100% stock dividend paid 03/22/1966
Name changed to First Safety Fund National Bank (Fitchburg, MA) 11/01/1968
First Safety Fund National Bank (Fitchburg, MA) reorganized as Safety Fund Corp. 06/04/1974 which merged into CFX Corp. 07/01/1996 which merged into Peoples Heritage Financial Group, Inc. 04/10/1998 which name changed to Banknorth Group, Inc. (ME) 05/10/2000 which merged into TD Banknorth Inc. 03/01/2005
(See TD Banknorth Inc.)

SAFETY 1ST INC (MA)
Merged into Dorel Industries Inc. 7/11/2000
Each share Common 1¢ par exchanged for $13.875 cash

SAFETY INDUSTRIES, INC. (DE)
Merged into American Manufacturing Co., Inc. 1/22/60
Each share Capital Stock $12.50 par exchanged for (1) share $1.10 Class A $25 par

American Manufacturing Co., Inc. assets transferred to American Manufacturing Co., Inc. Liquidating Trust 5/20/80
(See American Manufacturing Co., Inc. Liquidating Trust)

SAFETY-JECT MED PRODS LTD (BC)
Recapitalized as International Safety-Ject Industries Inc. 09/23/1991
Each share Common no par exchanged for (0.25) share Common no par
International Safety-Ject Industries Inc. recapitalized as Specialty Medical Products Inc. 09/30/1993 which recapitalized as Fedora Industries Ltd. 10/20/1997 which name changed to Airbomb.com Marketing Inc. (BC) 02/21/2000 which reincorporated in Delaware as airbomb.com, Inc. 05/09/2000 which name changed to RT Petroleum Inc. 05/18/2005
(See RT Petroleum Inc.)

SAFETY-KLEEN CORP NEW (DE)
Each share old Common $1 par exchanged for (0.25) share new Common $1 par 11/30/98
Plan of reorganization under Chapter 11 Federal Bankruptcy Code effective 12/24/2003
No stockholders' equity

SAFETY KLEEN CORP OLD (WI)
Common 10¢ par split (2) for (1) by issuance of (1) additional share 11/25/80
Common 10¢ par split (3) for (2) by issuance of (0.5) additional share 12/6/82
Common 10¢ par split (3) for (2) by issuance of (0.5) additional share 12/10/84
Common 10¢ par split (3) for (2) by issuance of (0.5) additional share 12/9/85
Common 10¢ par split (3) for (2) by issuance of (0.5) additional share 3/5/87
Common 10¢ par split (3) for (2) by issuance of (0.5) additional share 3/7/91
Merged into Laidlaw Environmental Services Inc. 5/20/98
Each share Common 10¢ par exchanged for (2.8) shares Common $1 par and $18.30 cash
Laidlaw Environmental Services Inc. name changed to Safety-Kleen Corp. (New) 7/1/98
(See Safety-Kleen Corp. (New))

SAFETY-KLEEN INC (DE)
Acquired by Clean Harbors Inc. 12/28/2012
Each share Common 1¢ par exchanged for $17.82 cash

SAFETY QUICK LTG & FANS CORP (FL)
Name changed to SQL Technologies Corp. 08/24/2016

SAFETY RY SVC CORP (DE)
Common $5 par changed to no par and (1) additional share issued 3/31/88
Name changed to Spinnaker Industries, Inc. 10/7/94
(See Spinnaker Industries, Inc.)

SAFETY SUSPENSION SYSTEMS CORP. (DE)
Charter cancelled and declared inoperative and void for non-payment of taxes 4/15/72

SAFETY TECHNOLOGY, INC. (UT)
Recapitalized as CHS Electronics, Inc. (UT) in January 1994
Each (300) shares Common $0.001 par exchanged for (1) share Common $0.001 par
CHS Electronics, Inc. (UT) reorganized in (FL) 3/14/96
(See CHS Electronics, Inc. (FL))

SAFETYTEK CORP (DE)
Name changed to Invivo Corp. 8/12/96
(See Invivo Corp.)

SAFEWAY HEAT ELEMENTS INC (DE)
Name changed to S.H.E., Inc. 07/11/1969
S.H.E., Inc. liquidated for Raymond Engineering Inc. 07/11/1969
(See Raymond Engineering Inc.)

SAFEWAY INC (MD)
Each share old Common no par exchanged for (5) shares new Common no par 00/00/1928
Each share new Common no par exchanged for (3) shares Common $5 par 00/00/1945
5% Preferred called for redemption 04/01/1951
4.50% Conv. Preferred called for redemption 04/01/1954
Common $5 par changed to $1.66666666 par and (2) additional shares issued 11/18/1957
4.30% Conv. Preferred called for redemption 10/01/1964
Common $1.66666666 par split (2) for (1) by issuance of (1) additional share 12/28/1964
4% Preferred $100 par called for redemption 04/01/1965
Common $1.66666666 par split (2) for (1) by issuance of (1) additional share 03/31/1983
Merged into Safeway Stores Holdings Corp. 11/24/1986
Each share Common $1.66666666 par exchanged for $61.60 principal amount of Jr. Subord. Debentures due 11/21/2006 and (1) Common Stock Purchase Warrant expiring 11/24/1996
Note: Previous information is for Safeway Stores, Inc.
Common 1¢ par split (2) for (1) by issuance of (1) additional share payable 01/30/1996 to holders of record 01/16/1996
Common 1¢ par split (2) for (1) by issuance of (1) additional share payable 02/25/1998 to holders of record 02/10/1998 Ex date - 02/26/1998
Each share Common 1¢ par received distribution of (0.164291) share Blackhawk Network Holdings, Inc. Class B Common $0.001 par payable 04/14/2014 to holders or record 04/03/2014 Ex date - 04/15/2014
Merged into AB Acquisition LLC 01/30/2015
Each share Common 1¢ par exchanged for for (1) Casa Ley S.A. de C.V. Contingent Value Right, (1) Property Development Centers, LLC Contingent Value Right and $34.92 cash

SAFEWAY STORES LTD. (CANADA)
Name changed to Canada Safeway, Ltd. 6/23/47
(See Canada Safeway, Ltd.)

SAFEWAY TRAILS, INC. (MD)
Merged into Transcontinental Bus System, Inc. 9/17/66
Each share Class A Common $1 par or Class B Common $1 par exchanged for (0.36) share Common $1 par
Transcontinental Bus System, Inc. name changed to TCO Industries, Inc. 4/29/68 which merged into Holiday Inns of America, Inc. 2/27/69 which name changed to Holiday Inns, Inc. 5/22/69 which reorganized in Delaware as Holiday Corp. 5/15/85 which merged into Bass PLC 2/7/90 which name changed to Six Continents PLC 7/31/2001

SAFFELL OIL CO. (OH)
Voluntarily dissolved 1/3/11
Details not available

SAFFRON FD INC (MD)
Liquidation completed
Each share Common $0.001 par received initial distribution of $9.372 cash payable 9/2/2004 to holders of record 8/20/2004
Each share Common $0.001 par received second and final distribution of $0.2021 cash payable 11/24/2004 to holders of record 8/20/2004
Note: Certificates were not required to be surrendered and are without value

SAFLINK CORP (DE)
Each share old Common 1¢ par exchanged for (0.14285714) share new Common 1¢ par 11/19/2001
Each share Common 1¢ par received distribution of (0.0111684) share Flo Corp. Common $0.001 par payable 01/07/2008 to holders of record 12/24/2007 Ex date - 12/28/2007
Recapitalized as IdentiPHI, Inc. 02/19/2008
Each share Common 1¢ par exchanged for (0.06666666) share Common 1¢ par
(See IdentiPHI, Inc.)

SAFRAN PRTG CO (MI)
Merged into Stecher-Traung-Schmidt Corp. 4/26/76
Each share Common $1 par exchanged for $2.50 principal amount of 10% Conv. Subord. Debentures due 4/21/91, (0.5) share Common $5 par and $7.50 cash
(See Stecher-Traung-Schmidt Corp.)

SAFRON INC (UT)
Name changed to Elision International, Inc. 1/23/91
(See Elision International, Inc.)

SAFT GROUPE S A (FRANCE)
ADR agreement terminated 09/09/2016
Each ADR for Ordinary issued by Bank of New York exchanged for $82.177174 cash
Each ADR for Ordinary issued by Citibank exchanged for $81.6078 cash
Each ADR for Ordinary issued by Deutsche Bank exchanged for $82.29546 cash

SAFTICRAFT CORP. (DE)
Declared inoperative and void and charter revoked for non-payment of taxes 4/1/64

SAFWAY STEEL PRODUCTS, INC. (WI)
Stock Dividends - 100% 09/11/1950; 10% 12/30/1955; 25% 11/30/1964
Acquired by Automatic Sprinkler Corp. of America (OH) 06/09/1966
Each share Common $2 par exchanged for (0.09) share 6% 1st Preference $100 par and (0.275) share Common 10¢ par
Automatic Sprinkler Corp. of America (OH) name changed to A-T-O Inc. 10/29/1969 which name changed to Figgie International Inc. (OH) 06/01/1981 which reorganized in Delaware as Figgie International Holdings Inc. 07/18/1983 which name changed to Figgie International Inc. 12/31/1986 which name changed to Scott Technologies, Inc. 05/20/1998 which merged into Tyco International Ltd. (Bermuda) 05/03/2001 which reincorporated in Switzerland 03/17/2009 which merged into Johnson Controls International PLC 09/06/2016

SAFWAY STEEL SCAFFOLDS CO.
Name changed to Safway Steel Products, Inc. 00/00/1942

Safway Steel Products, Inc. acquired by Automatic Sprinkler Corp. of America (OH) 06/09/1966 which name changed to A-T-O Inc. 10/29/1969 which name changed to Figgie International Inc. (OH) 06/01/1981 which reorganized in Delaware as Figgie International Holdings Inc. 07/18/1983 which name changed to Figgie International Inc. 12/31/1986 which name changed to Scott Technologies, Inc. 05/20/1998 which merged into Tyco International Ltd. (Bermuda) 05/03/2001 which reincorporated in Switzerland 03/17/2009 which merged into Johnson Controls International PLC 09/06/2016

SAG HBR SVGS BK (NEW YORK, NY)
Acquired by Apple Bancorp, Inc. 11/30/89
Each share Common $1 par exchanged for $21.50 cash

SAGA ADMINISTRATIVE CORP. (NY)
Stock Dividend - 100% 7/8/71
Name changed to Saga Corp. 6/6/74
(See Saga Corp.)

SAGA CORP (NY)
Conv. Jr. Common 10¢ par reclassified as Common $1 par 06/13/1986
Stock Dividend - 100% 06/01/1983
Merged into Marriott Corp. 08/04/1986
Each share Common $1 par exchanged for $39.50 cash

SAGA PETE A S (NORWAY)
Each Sponsored ADR for Non-Voting B Shares NOK 15 par exchanged for (1) Sponsored ADR for Ordinary NOK 15 par 9/18/98
Note: Underlying shares for unexchanged ADR's will be sold and the proceeds held for claim after 3/18/99
Sponsored ADR's for Free A Shares NOK 15 par reclassified as Sponsored ADR's for Ordinary NOK 15 par 9/18/98
Acquired by Norsk Hydro A.S. 10/6/99
Each Sponsored ADR for Ordinary NOK 15 par exchanged for the U.S. equivalent of NOK 135 cash

SAGA RES LTD (BC)
Name changed to PacificAmerica Equities Inc. 07/24/1989
PacificAmerica Equities Inc. name changed to SGI Capital Corp. (BC) 06/11/1995 which reincorporated in Yukon 01/05/1996 which recapitalized as Lariat Property Corp. 12/10/1997 which name changed to Lariat Resources Ltd. 06/02/2003 which recapitalized as Lariat Energy Ltd. (YT) 09/23/2004 which reincorporated in British Columbia 04/01/2006 which name changed to Global Daily Fantasy Sports Inc. 07/11/2016

SAGA SYSTEMS INC (DE)
Merged into Software AG 2/1/2001
Each share Common 1¢ par exchanged for $11.50 cash
Note: An additional distribution of $0.08 cash per share was made 11/19/2002
A final distribution of approximately $0.058 cash per share was made in November 2003

SAGAMORE HLDGS INC (FL)
Reorganized under the laws of Nevada as Nexus Nano Electronics, Inc. 06/07/2006
Each share Common $0.001 par exchanged for (0.1) share Common $0.001 par
Nexus Nano Electronics, Inc. recapitalized as International Merchant Advisors Inc. 06/30/2008

FINANCIAL INFORMATION, INC. SAG-SAH

which name changed to DHS Holding Co. 07/15/2011

SAGE ALERTING SYS INC (DE)
Name changed to Sage Technologies, Inc. 10/28/1993
Sage Technologies, Inc. name changed to AmeriData Technologies, Inc. 09/30/1994
(See AmeriData Technologies, Inc.)

SAGE ALLEN & CO INC (DE)
Common 10¢ par split (3) for (2) by issuance of (0.5) additional share 11/25/83
Common 10¢ par split (3) for (2) by issuance of (0.5) additional share 5/30/86
Acquired by a group of investors 12/15/87
Each share Common 10¢ par exchanged for $22 cash

SAGE ANALYTICS INTL INC (DE)
Recapitalized as Advanced Business Sciences Inc. 12/17/1997
Each share Common $0.001 par exchanged for (0.05) share Common $0.001 par
Advanced Business Sciences Inc. name changed to iSecureTrac Corp. 06/19/2001 which name changed to Technology Monitoring Solutions, Inc. 04/09/2014
(See Technology Monitoring Solutions, Inc.)

SAGE BROADCASTING CORP (DE)
Name changed to SBC Technologies, Inc. 11/14/1990
SBC Technologies, Inc. merged into Sage Technologies Inc. 09/13/1994 which name changed to AmeriData Technologies, Inc. 09/30/1994
(See AmeriData Technologies, Inc.)

SAGE COURT VENTURES INC (NV)
Recapitalized as Herbalife International, Inc. 12/10/1986
Each share Common $0.001 par exchanged for (0.14285714) share Common 1¢ par
(See Herbalife International, Inc.)

SAGE DRILLING INC (KS)
Voluntarily dissolved 04/03/2013
Details not available

SAGE ENERGY CO (TX)
Common 75¢ par changed to 37-1/2¢ par and (1) additional share issued 07/17/1980
Common 37-1/2¢ par split (2) for (1) by issuance of (1) additional share 02/25/1981
Merged into Sage Acquisition Corp. 05/18/1989
Each share Common 37-1/2¢ par exchanged for $6.50 cash

SAGE GLOBAL SOLUTIONS INC (NV)
Recapitalized as Mutual Merchant Services, Inc. 08/22/2008
Each share Common $0.001 par exchanged for (0.0025) share Common $0.001 par

SAGE GROUP LTD (SOUTH AFRICA)
Under plan of merger each Sponsored ADR for Ordinary exchanged for approximately $0.64 cash 09/12/2005
Note: Holders received an initial distribution from escrow of approximately $0.02 cash 07/03/2006
Holders received a second distribution from escrow of $0.0104 cash 10/30/2006
Holders received a third distribution from escrow of $0.108 cash 06/27/2007

SAGE HIGH YIELD DEBT TR (ON)
Name changed to SAGE Income Fund 8/26/2002
SAGE Income Fund merged into MINT Income Fund 4/19/2005

SAGE INC (DE)
Merged into Genesis Microchip Inc. (DE) 2/20/2002
Each share Common 1¢ par exchanged for (0.571) share Common $0.001 par

SAGE INCOME FD (ON)
Merged into MINT Income Fund 4/19/2005
Each Trust Unit no par received (1.79391453) Trust Units no par
Note: Certificates were not required to be surrendered and are without value

SAGE INTL INC (DE)
In process of liquidation
Each share Common $1 par received initial distribution of $1 cash 04/10/1984
Each share Common $1 par exchanged for second distribution of $31 cash 12/13/1984
Assets transferred to Sage Liquidating Trust and Common $1 par reclassified as Shares of Bene. Int. 12/21/1984
(See Sage Liquidating Trust)

SAGE LABS INC (MA)
Common $1 par changed to 10¢ par and (4) additional shares issued 12/1/95
Merged into Filtronic PLC 6/25/98
Each share Common 10¢ par exchanged for $17.50 cash

SAGE LIQUIDATING TRUST (DE)
Liquidation completed
Each Share of Bene. Int. received third and final distribution of $1.172774 cash 1/31/85
(See Sage International, Inc. for previous distributions)

SAGE OIL CO. LTD. (AB)
Merged into Syracuse Oils Ltd. 10/18/66
Each share Capital Stock no par exchanged for (1) share Common no par
Syracuse Oils Ltd. merged into Bow Valley Industries Ltd. 4/30/71 which name changed to Bow Valley Energy Inc. 6/7/93 which was acquired by Talisman Energy Inc. 8/11/94

SAGE OIL INC (UT)
Liquidation completed
Each share Common no par received initial distribution of $5 cash 12/26/1975
Each share Common no par received second distribution of $5.21 cash 09/21/1976
Each share Common no par received third and final distribution of $0.0687 cash 04/16/1979
Note: Certificates were not required to be surrendered and are without value

SAGE RES LTD (BC)
Recapitalized as New Sage Resources Ltd. 08/06/1996
Each share Common no par exchanged for (0.2) share Common no par
New Sage Resources Ltd. recapitalized as Consolidated New Sage Resources Ltd. (BC) 01/30/2002 which reincorporated in Canada 10/24/2003

SAGE SOFTWARE INC (DE)
Under plan of merger name changed to Intersolv, Inc. 03/19/1991
Intersolv, Inc. merged into Micro Focus Group PLC 09/15/1998 which name changed to Merant PLC 02/16/1999 which was acquired by Serena Software, Inc. 06/30/2004
(See Serena Software, Inc.)

SAGE SYS CORP (DE)
Merged into Pitney Bowes Inc. 10/09/1970

Each share Common 25¢ par exchanged for (0.0762) share Common $2 par

SAGE TECHNOLOGIES INC (DE)
Common 1¢ par split (3) for (2) by issuance of (0.5) additional share 12/15/1993
Name changed to AmeriData Technologies, Inc. 09/30/1994
(See AmeriData Technologies, Inc.)

SAGE VENTURES INC (AB)
Name changed to Software Control Systems International Inc. 11/14/1995
(See Software Control Systems International Inc.)

SAGEBRUSH GOLD LTD (NV)
Name changed to Pershing Gold Corp. 03/26/2012

SAGEBRUSH INC (NC)
Merged into WSMP Inc. 1/28/98
Each share Common no par exchanged for (0.3822) share Common $1 par
WSMP Inc. name changed to Fresh Foods Inc. 5/7/98 which name changed to Pierre Foods Inc. 7/27/2000
(See Pierre Foods Inc.)

SAGEBRUSH RES LTD (AB)
Merged into Bralorne Resources Ltd. 3/11/82
Each share Common no par exchanged for $2 cash

SAGENT PHARMACEUTICALS INC (DE)
Acquired by Nichi-Iko Pharmaceutical Co., Ltd. 08/29/2016
Each share Common 1¢ par exchanged for $21.75 cash

SAGENT TECHNOLOGY INC (DE)
In process of liquidation
Each share Common $0.001 par received initial distribution of $0.10 cash payable 04/05/2004 to holders of record 03/31/2004 Ex date - 04/06/2004
Name changed to S Wind-up Corp. 04/15/2004
(See S Wind-up Corp.)

SAGEWOOD RES LTD (ON)
Delisted from Canadian Dealer Network 10/13/2000

SAGIENT RESH SYS INC (DE)
Each share Common $0.001 par exchanged for (1) share Common $0.001 par to reflect a (1) for (101) reverse split followed by a (101) for (1) forward split 01/10/2006
Note: Holders of (101) shares or fewer received $0.12 cash per share
Acquired by Informa Business Information, Inc. 05/31/2012
Each share Common $0.001 par exchanged for $0.415085 cash
Note: An additional initial distribution of $0.0027664 cash per share was paid from escrow 08/30/2012
A second and final additional distribution of $0.01481369 cash per share was paid from escrow 03/11/2014

SAGINAW & MANISTEE LUMBER CO. (DE)
Recapitalized 00/00/1944
Each share Preferred $100 par exchanged for (2) shares Common no par
Each (50) shares Common no par exchanged for (1) share new Common no par
Liquidation completed 00/00/1953
Details not available

SAGINAW LUMBER CO. (MI)
Charter declared inoperative and void for failure to file reports 5/15/72

SAGINAW TRANSIT CO.
Property sold in 1932
No stockholders' equity

SAGRES ENERGY INC (AB)
Enforcement of consent judgment commenced 09/11/2013
All officers and directors have resigned

SAGUARO RES INC (DE)
Reorganized as InspireMD, Inc. 04/11/2011
Each share Common $0.0001 par exchanged for (3) shares Common $0.0001 par

SAGUARO SAVINGS & LOAN ASSOCIATION (AZ)
Merged into Western Savings & Loan Association 8/27/82
Each share Permanent Reserve Guaranty Capital Stock $1 par exchanged for $2.25 cash

SAGUENAY MNG & SMLT LTD (QC)
Charter annulled for failure to file annual reports 03/05/1977

SAGUENAY PWR LTD (QC)
4.5% S.F. Preferred $100 par called for redemption 09/30/1955
Public interest eliminated

SAGUENAY PULP & POWER CO.
Succeeded by Quebec Pulp & Paper Co. 00/00/1927
Details not available

SAHA PETE LTD (AB)
Name changed to Western Plains Petroleum Ltd. 08/26/2009
(See Western Plains Petroleum Ltd.)

SAHALI RES INC (BC)
Name changed to H.T.R. Industries Inc. 10/1/84
H.T.R. Industries Inc. recapitalized as Lazer Maze Industries Inc. 6/2/89
(See Lazer Maze Industries Inc.)

SAHARA CASINO PARTNERS L P (DE)
Reorganized as Sahara Gaming Corp. 9/30/93
Each Depositary Unit exchanged for (1) share Exchangeable Preferred 1¢ par and (0.2174) share Common 1¢ par
Sahara Gaming Corp. name changed to Santa Fe Gaming Corp. 2/21/96 which name changed to Archon Corp. 5/11/2001

SAHARA GAMING CORP (NV)
Stock Dividend - 25% 2/25/94
Name changed to Santa Fe Gaming Corp. 2/21/96
Santa Fe Gaming Corp. name changed to Archon Corp. 5/11/2001

SAHARA GOLD CORP (NV)
Name changed to Inland Pacific Resources Inc. 02/08/1994
Inland Pacific Resources Inc. recapitalized as Creative Enterprises International Inc. 01/02/2002 which name changed to Skinny Nutritional Corp. 12/27/2006
(See Skinny Nutritional Corp.)

SAHARA MEDIA HLDGS INC (DE)
Name changed to YouBlast Global, Inc. 06/16/2010
(See YouBlast Global, Inc.)

SAHARA RESORTS (NV)
Merged into Sahara Gaming Corp. 9/30/93
Each share Common 20¢ par exchanged for (1) share Common 20¢ par
Sahara Gaming Corp. name changed to Santa Fe Gaming Corp. 2/21/96 which name changed to Archon Corp. 5/11/2001

SAHARA URANIUM CORP. (UT)
Acquired by United Western Minerals Co. on a (0.001449) for (1) basis 12/23/58
(See United Western Minerals Co.)

SAHELIAN GOLDFIELDS INC (ON)
Recapitalized as Sage Gold Inc. 3/3/2005

Each share Common no par exchanged for (0.04) share Common no par

SAHLEN & ASSOC INC (DE)
Plan of reorganization under Chapter 11 Federal Bankruptcy proceedings confirmed 12/02/1991
No stockholders' equity

SAHQUA MINERALS LTD (BC)
Struck off register and declared dissolved for failure to file reports and pay fees 3/29/85

SAI GROUP INC (NJ)
Merged into Proteq Verzekeringen Beheer N.V. 12/03/1990
Each share Common no par exchanged for $0.0625 cash

SAIC INC (DE)
Issue Information - 75,000,000 shares COM offered at $15 per share on 10/12/2006
Class A Preferred $0.0001 par reclassified as Common $0.0001 par 11/00/2009
Each share Common $0.0001 par received distribution of (0.14285714) share Science Applications International Corp. Common $0.0001 par payable 09/27/2013 to holders of record 09/19/2013
Recapitalized as Leidos Holdings, Inc. 09/30/2013
Each share Common $0.0001 par exchanged for (0.25) share Common $0.0001 par

SAIFUN SEMICONDUCTORS LTD. (ISRAEL)
Merged into Spansion, Inc. 03/18/2008
Each share Ordinary ILS 0.01 par exchanged for (0.7238) share Class A Common $0.001 par and $6.20 cash
(See Spansion, Inc.)

SAILTECH INTL INC (NV)
Each share old Common $0.001 par exchanged for (2) shares new Common $0.001 par 01/02/2001
Name changed to Ecoloclean Industries, Inc. and Common $0.001 par changed to $0.0001 par 12/15/2003

SAINSBURYS J PLC (ENGLAND)
Stock Dividend - 100% 07/16/1987
ADR agreement terminated 05/17/1995
Details not available

ST ANDREW GOLDFIELDS LTD (ON)
Each share Conv. Preferred no par exchanged for (1) share Common no par 06/06/1995
Each share old Common no par exchanged for (0.2) share new Common no par 06/27/1997
Each share new Common no par exchanged again for (0.05) share new Common no par 06/15/2006
Merged into Kirkland Lake Gold Inc. 01/29/2016
Each share new Common no par exchanged for (0.0906) share Common no par
Note: Unexchanged certificates will be cancelled and become without value 01/29/2022
Kirkland Lake Gold Inc. merged into Kirkland Lake Gold Ltd. 12/06/2016

SAINT ANDREWS GOLF CORP (NV)
Name changed to All-American Sportpark, Inc. 12/14/98

SAINT ANNE'S OIL PRODUCTION CO. (DE)
Merged into Tekoil Corp. on a (0.56) for (1) basis 03/15/1956
Tekoil Corp. merged into Consolidated Oil & Gas, Inc. (CO) 02/23/1962 which was acquired by Hugoton Energy Corp. 09/07/1995 which merged into Chesapeake Energy Corp. 03/10/1998

ST. ANTHONY GOLD MINES LTD.
Recapitalized as St. Anthony Mines Ltd. 00/00/1945
Each share Capital Stock $1 par exchanged for (1/3) share Capital Stock $1 par
St. Anthony Mines Ltd. merged into Can-Con Enterprises & Explorations Ltd. 11/30/1970 which name changed to Aubet Resources Inc. 09/08/1981 which recapitalized as Aubet Explorations Ltd. 09/30/1998 which name changed to Visa Gold Explorations Inc. 08/25/1999
(See Visa Gold Explorations Inc.)

ST. ANTHONY MINES LTD. (ON)
Merged into Can-Con Enterprises & Explorations Ltd. 11/30/1970
Each share Capital Stock $1 par exchanged for (0.033333) share Capital Stock no par
Can-Con Enterprises & Explorations Ltd. name changed to Aubet Resources Inc. 09/08/1981 which recapitalized as Aubet Explorations Ltd. 09/30/1998 which name changed to Visa Gold Explorations Inc. 08/25/1999
(See Visa Gold Explorations Inc.)

ST ANTHONY PRTG CO (MN)
Name changed to Northern Instruments, Inc. and Common 10¢ par changed to 2¢ par 1/15/73
Northern Instruments, Inc. name changed to Northern Instruments Corp. (MN) 4/9/76 which reincorporated in Delaware 1/30/78 which name changed to Northern Technologies International Corp. 5/3/93

ST. AUGUSTINE GAS CO.
Merged into Savannah-St. Augustine Gas Co. in 1944
Details not available

ST BARBARA MINES LTD (AUSTRALIA)
Name changed to St. Barbara Ltd. 02/27/2006

ST BERNARD BK & TR CO (ARABI, LA)
Merged into Hibernia Corp. 10/1/96
Each share Common no par exchanged for $1,241.51 cash

ST BERNARD SOFTWARE INC (DE)
Name changed to EdgeWave, Inc. 08/09/2011
(See EdgeWave, Inc.)

ST CHARLES FIN CORP (DE)
Exchangeable Auction Market Preferred no par called for redemption 07/25/1990
Public interest eliminated

ST CLAIR FIXED INCOME FD INC (MD)
Name changed to St. Clair Funds, Inc. 03/29/1993
(See St. Clair Funds, Inc.)

ST CLAIR FDS INC (MD)
Merged into Munder Series Trust 04/30/2003
Details not available

ST. CLAIR HOTEL, INC.
Liquidated in 1948

ST CLAIR MFG CORP (DE)
Common $1 par changed to 50¢ par and (1) additional share issued 06/15/1961
Acquired by Handschy Chemical Co. 03/13/1973
Each share Common 50¢ par exchanged for (0.6016) share Common $1 par
Handschy Chemical Co. name changed to Handschy Industries, Inc. 08/02/1977
(See Handschy Industries, Inc.)

ST CLAIR PAINT & WALLPAPER CORP (ON)
Each share Class A Subordinated Voting no par exchanged for (1) share Common no par 08/31/1995
Assets sold for the benefit of creditors 00/00/2002
No stockholders' equity

ST CLAIR RES LTD (BC)
Struck off register and declared dissolved for failure to file returns 09/19/1986

ST. CLAIR SAVINGS & LOAN CO. (OH)
Name changed to St. Clair Savings Association 1/11/60

ST. CLAIR SAVINGS ASSOCIATION (OH)
Thru exchange offer 98% acquired by Capital Bancorporation as of 1/3/67
Public interest eliminated

ST CLAIR SHORES NATL BK (ST CLAIR SHORES, MI)
Merged into Security Bancorp, Inc. (DE) 10/1/82
Each share Common $10 par exchanged for $86.50 cash

ST. CLAIR SPECIALTY MANUFACTURING CO., INC. (DE)
Name changed to St. Clair Mfg. Corp. 07/28/1964
St. Clair Mfg. Corp. acquired by Handschy Chemical Co. 03/13/1973 which name changed to Handschy Industries, Inc. 08/02/1977
(See Handschy Industries, Inc.)

ST CLAIR TAX FREE FD INC (MD)
Name changed 12/23/1986
Name changed from St. Clair Tax-Free Money Market Fund, Inc. to St. Clair Tax-Free Fund Inc. 12/23/1986
Name changed to Ambassador Funds and Class A $0.001 par and Class B $0.001 par reclassified as Tax Free Money Market Fund Investment Shares $0.001 par or Tax Free Intermediate Bond Fund Investment Shares $0.001 par respectively 11/24/1992
(See Ambassador Funds)

ST. CROIX MINES CORP. (UT)
Charter suspended for non-payment of taxes 00/00/1934

ST CROIX PAPER CO (ME)
Each share Common $100 par exchanged for (4) shares Common $25 par in 1949
Common $25 par changed to $12.50 par and (1) additional share issued plus a 100% stock dividend paid 8/24/55
99% acquired thru voluntary purchase offer by Georgia-Pacific Corp. in 1964
Public interest eliminated

ST. CROIX TELEPHONE CO. (WI)
Acquired by Rochester Telephone Corp. 3/26/90
Each share Capital Stock $10 par exchanged for (5.0818) shares Common $2.50 par
Rochester Telephone Corp. name changed to Frontier Corp. 1/1/95 which merged into Global Crossing Ltd. 9/28/99
(See Global Crossing Ltd.)

ST EDWARDS MINERALS LTD (BC)
Name changed to Multi-Step Industries Inc. 11/22/1988
(See Multi-Step Industries Inc.)

ST ELIAS EXPL CORP (BC)
Name changed to Bigstone Minerals Ltd. 01/19/1984
Bigstone Minerals Ltd. recapitalized as Adamas Resources Corp. 08/30/1993 which recapitalized as Britannica Resources Corp. 08/27/2002 which name changed to Trinity Valley Energy Corp. 10/08/2013 which recapitalized as Smooth Rock Ventures Corp. 11/15/2017

ST EUGENE MNG LTD (BC)
Common $1 par changed to no par 00/00/2001
Merged into Claude Resources Inc. 02/01/2012
Each share Common no par exchanged for (0.0789) share Common no par and (0.25) share Satori Resources Inc. Common no par
(See each company's listing)

ST FABIEN EXPLS INC (QC)
Name changed 02/11/1981
Name changed from St. Fabien Copper Mines Ltd. to St. Fabien Explorations Inc. 02/11/1981
Recapitalized as Fabien Explorations Inc. 07/18/1983
Each share Common $1 par exchanged for (0.25) share Common $1 par
(See Fabien Explorations Inc.)

ST FRANCIS CAP CORP (WI)
Common 1¢ par split (2) for (1) by issuance of (1) additional share payable 04/19/1999 to holders of record 04/05/1999
Merged into MAF Bancorp, Inc. 12/01/2003
Each share Common 1¢ par exchanged for (0.79) share Common 1¢ par
MAF Bancorp, Inc. merged into National City Corp. 09/01/2007 which was acquired by PNC Financial Services Group, Inc. 12/31/2008

ST FRANCIS HOTEL CORP (CA)
Name changed to Western International Hotels Co. (CA) 3/30/65
Western International Hotels Co. (CA) reincorporated under the laws of Delaware 6/13/66 which merged into UAL, Inc. 8/1/70 which name changed to Allegis Corp Corp. 4/30/87 which name changed to UAL Corp. 5/27/88
(See UAL Corp.)

ST FRANCOIS CNTY FINL CORP (DE)
Merged into New Era Bank (Fredrickburg, MO) 1/5/96
Each share Common 1¢ par exchanged for $24 cash

ST. GENEVIEVE EXPLORATIONS (1991) INC. (QC)
Merged into Exploration SEG Inc./SEG Exploration Inc. 1/1/92
Each share Common no par exchanged for (0.31545741) share Common no par
Exploration SEG Inc./SEG Exploration Inc. name changed to West Africa Mining Exploration Inc. 7/6/95

ST GENEVIEVE RES LTD (CANADA)
Each share old Common no par exchanged for (0.2) share new Common no par 01/15/2001
Acquired by Ascendant Copper Corp. 03/27/2008
Each share new Common no par exchanged for (0.1529191) share Common no par
Ascendant Copper Corp. name changed to Copper Mesa Mining Corp. 07/11/2008
(See Copper Mesa Mining Corp.)

ST GEORGE BK LTD (AUSTRALIA)
ADR agreement terminated 12/01/2008
Each Sponsored ADR for Ordinary A$1 par exchanged for $58.81 cash

ST GEORGE METALS INC (NV)
Stock Dividend - 3% payable 05/02/2003 to holders of record 04/29/2003

SEC revoked common stock
registration 09/29/2005
Stockholders' equity unlikely

ST GEORGE MINERALS INC (BC)
Completely liquidated 02/15/1991
Each share Common no par received
first and final distribution of (1) share
St. George Metals Inc. Common 1¢
par
Note: Certificates were not required to
be surrendered and are without
value
(See St. George Metals Inc.)

**SAINT GEORGES PLATINUM &
BASE METALS LTD (CANADA)**
Each share old Common no par
exchanged for (0.15384615) share
new Common par 04/22/2013
Name changed to St-Georges
Eco-Mining Corp. 12/22/2017

**ST. HELEN MINING EXPLORATION
LTD. (QC)**
Merged into Resource Exploration &
Development Co. Ltd. 6/11/68
Each share Capital Stock $1 par
exchanged for (0.404858) share
Capital Stock no par
Resource Exploration & Development
Co. Ltd. charter cancelled 5/13/80

**ST HELENA GOLD MINES LTD
(SOUTH AFRICA)**
Merged into Gold Fields Ltd. 12/20/99
Each Sponsored ADR for Ordinary
Rand-1 par exchanged for (1)
Sponsored ADR for Ordinary
Rand-50 par 12/20/99

ST IVES LABS INC (DE)
Name changed 1/1/90
Name changed from St. Ives
Laboratories, Corp. to St. Ives
Laboratories, Inc. 1/1/90
Merged into Alberto-Culver Co. 2/6/96
Each share Common 1¢ par
exchanged for $15 cash

ST JAMES CAP HLDGS INC (NV)
Charter revoked for failure to file
reports and pay taxes 09/30/2009

SAINT JAMES CO (DE)
Reorganized under the laws of North
Carolina 12/07/2007
Each share Common $0.001 par
exchanged for (1) share Common
$0.001 par
(See Saint James Co. (NC))

SAINT JAMES CO (NC)
Ceased operations 02/17/2011
Stockholders' equity unlikely

ST JAMES RES LTD (QC)
Proclaimed dissolved for failure to file
annual returns 08/07/1982

**ST. JOE CONSOLIDATED MINES
CORP. (DE)**
Charter revoked for non-payment of
taxes 10/1/63

ST JOE CORP (FL)
Under plan of partial liquidation each
share Common no par received
initial distribution of $10 cash
payable 03/25/1997 to holders of
record 03/21/1997
Under plan of partial liquidation each
share Common no par received
second distribution of $1.02 cash
payable 12/30/1997 to holders of
record 12/19/1997
Common no par split (3) for (1) by
issuance of (2) additional shares
payable 01/12/1998 to holders of
record 12/26/1997 Ex date -
01/13/1998
Name changed to St. Joe Co.
06/06/1998

ST JOE GOLD CORP (DE)
Merged into SJ Merger Corp.
01/12/1988
Each share Common 10¢ par
exchanged for $17 cash

ST JOE MINERALS CORP (NY)
Common $10 par split (2) for (1) by
issuance of (1) additional share
07/15/1975
Common $10 par changed to $1 par
05/10/1977
Common $1 par split (2) for (1) by
issuance of (1) additional share
12/19/1980
Merged into Fluor Corp. (Old)
08/03/1981
Each share Common $1 par
exchanged for (1.2) shares Common
$0.625 par
Fluor Corp. (Old) name changed to
Massey Energy Co. 11/30/2000
which merged into Alpha Natural
Resources, Inc. 06/01/2011
(See Alpha Natural Resources, Inc.)

ST JOE PAPER CO (FL)
Common $100 par changed to no par
and (349) additional shares issued
3/22/90
Name changed to St. Joe Paper Co.
5/31/96
St. Joe Corp. name changed to St.
Joe Co. 6/6/98

ST JOHN KNITS INC (CA)
Common no par split (2) for (1) by
issuance of (1) additional share
payable 05/06/1996 to holders of
record 04/08/1996 Ex date -
05/07/1996
Merged into St. John Knits
International, Inc. 07/07/1999
Each share Common no par
exchanged for either (1) share
Common 1¢ par or $30 cash
Note: Option to receive stock expired
06/25/1999

ST JOHNS PETE LTD (SK)
Merged into Westgrowth Petroleums
Ltd. (ALTA) 7/11/85
Each share Capital Stock no par
exchanged for (0.6) share Common
no par
Westgrowth Petroleums Ltd. (ALTA)
recapitalized as Canadian
Westgrowth Ltd. 10/14/86 which
merged into Ulster Petroleums Ltd.
10/27/87 which merged into
Anderson Exploration Ltd. 5/23/2000
(See Anderson Exploration Ltd.)

**ST. JOHNS RIVER BANK
(JACKSONVILLE, FL)**
Name changed to Sun Bank
(Jacksonville, FL) 03/01/1973
Sun Bank (Jacksonville, FL) name
changed to Sun Bank/North Florida,
N.A. (Jacksonville, FL) 01/01/1984
(See Sun Bank/North Florida, N.A.
(Jacksonville, FL))

**ST. JOHNSBURY & LAKE
CHAMPLAIN RAILROAD CO.**
Reorganized in 1946
No stockholders' equity

ST JOHNSBURY TRUCKING INC (VT)
Common $1 par split (3) for (2) by
issuance of (0.5) additional share
11/30/1971
Name changed to SJTC Liquidating
Co. Inc. 10/02/1975
(See SJTC Liquidating Co.)

ST JOSEPH BANCORP INC (MD)
Acquired by FSC Bancshares, Inc.
01/17/2014
Each share Common 1¢ par
exchanged for $19.13 cash

**ST JOSEPH BANCORPORATION INC
(IN)**
$2.625 Conv. Preferred Ser. A no par
called for redemption 02/28/1986
Stock Dividends - 10% 03/15/1985;
10% 01/30/1986
Merged into Trustcorp, Inc.
12/31/1986
Each share Common no par
exchanged for (1.4557) shares
Common $20 par
Trustcorp, Inc. acquired by Society
Corp. 01/05/1990 which merged into
KeyCorp (New) 03/01/1994

**ST JOSEPH BK & TR CO
(SOUTH BEND, IN)**
Each share Common $100 par
exchanged for (5) shares Common
$20 par 00/00/1942
Common $20 par changed to $10 par
and (1) additional share issued
03/11/1974
Stock Dividends - 50% 02/00/1947;
12-1/2% 03/00/1951; 10%
02/16/1970; 10% 02/11/1971; 10%
02/07/1972; 20% 01/26/1973; 20%
02/15/1974; 10% 04/01/1975; 15%
01/03/1978; 10% 04/06/1979; 15%
05/01/1980
Reorganized as St. Joseph
Bancorporation, Inc. 06/29/1982
Each share $2.625 Conv. Preferred
$10 par exchanged for (1) share
$2.625 Conv. Preferred no par and
(0.3892) share Common no par
Each share Common $10 par
exchanged for (1.2311) shares
Common no par
St. Joseph Bancorporation, Inc.
merged into Trustcorp, Inc.
12/31/1986 which was acquired by
Society Corp. 01/05/1990 which
merged into KeyCorp (New)
03/01/1994

ST JOSEPH CAP CORP (DE)
Merged into Old National Bancorp
2/1/2007
Each share Common 1¢ par
exchanged for $40 cash

ST JOSEPH LEAD CO (NY)
Capital Stock $10 par split (3) for (2)
by issuance of (0.5) additional share
09/29/1964
Capital Stock $10 par split (2) for (1)
by issuance of (1) additional share
01/15/1969
Stock Dividends - 25% 12/11/1950;
10% 06/10/1952; 10% 12/21/1962
Name changed to St. Joe Minerals
Corp. and Capital Stock $10 par
reclassified as Common $10 par
05/12/1970
St. Joe Minerals Corp. merged into
Fluor Corp. (Old) 08/03/1981 which
name changed to Massey Energy
Co. 11/30/2000 which merged into
Alpha Natural Resources, Inc.
06/01/2011
(See Alpha Natural Resources, Inc.)

ST JOSEPH LT & PWR CO (MO)
Common no par split (3) for (2) by
issuance of (0.5) additional share
00/00/1953
Common no par split (2) for (1) by
issuance of (1) additional share
05/18/1962
Common no par split (3) for (2) by
issuance of (0.5) additional share
06/15/1987
Common no par split (2) for (1) by
issuance of (1) additional share
payable 07/15/1996 to holders of
record 07/01/1996
5% Preferred Class A $100 par called
for redemption 02/23/1987
Stock Dividend - 10% 11/20/1959
Merged into UtiliCorp United Inc.
12/31/2000
Each share Common no par
exchanged for (0.7933) share
Common $1 par
UtiliCorp United Inc. name changed to
Aquila, Inc. (New) 03/15/2002 which
was acquired by Great Plains
Energy Inc. 07/14/2008 which
merged into Evergy, Inc. 06/05/2018

**ST. JOSEPH RAILWAY, LIGHT, HEAT
& POWER CO.**
Name changed to St. Joseph Light &
Power Co. 00/00/1944
St. Joseph Light & Power Co. merged
into UtiliCorp United Inc. 12/31/2000
which name changed to Aquila, Inc.
(New) 03/15/2002 which was
acquired by Great Plains Energy
Inc. 07/14/2008 which merged into
Evergy, Inc. 06/05/2018

**ST. JOSEPH, SOUTH BEND &
SOUTHERN RAILROAD CO.**
Dissolved in 1945

**ST. JOSEPH STOCK YARDS CO.
(MO)**
Capital Stock $100 changed to no par
in 1930
Merged into United Stockyards Corp.
8/1/63
Each share Capital Stock no par
exchanged for (15) shares Common
25¢ par
United Stockyards Corp. merged into
Canal-Randolph Corp. 11/1/64
(See Canal-Randolph Corp.)

**ST JOSEPH VALLEY BK
(ELKHART, IN)**
Each share Capital Stock $100 par
exchanged for (12) shares Capital
Stock $10 par to effect a (10) for (1)
split and a 20% stock dividend
12/19/1949
Stock Dividends - 16-2/3%
11/16/1951; 14-1/7% 01/18/1954;
25% 07/20/1955; 100% 10/12/1964
98.8% acquired by SJV Corp. through
exchange offer which expired
06/02/1969
Public interest eliminated

ST JUDE MED INC (MN)
Common 10¢ par split (2) for (1) by
issuance of (1) additional share
09/30/1986
Common 10¢ par split (2) for (1) by
issuance of (1) additional share
03/15/1989
Common 10¢ par split (2) for (1) by
issuance of (1) additional share
04/30/1990
Common 10¢ par split (3) for (2) by
issuance of (0.5) additional share
11/16/1995
Common 10¢ par split (2) for (1) by
issuance of (1) additional share
payable 06/28/2002 to holders of
record 06/10/2002 Ex date -
07/01/2002
Common 10¢ par split (2) for (1) by
issuance of (1) additional share
payable 11/22/2004 to holders of
record 11/01/2004 Ex date -
11/23/2004
Stock Dividends - 100% 06/15/1979;
100% 03/12/1980
Merged into Abbott Laboratories
01/04/2017
Each share Common 10¢ par
exchanged for (0.8708) share
Common 10¢ par and $46.75 cash

ST JUDE RES LTD (BC)
Merged into Golden Star Resources
Ltd. 12/21/2005
Each share Class A Common no par
exchanged for (0.72) share Common
no par

ST LANDRY FINL CORP (DE)
Merged into Teche Holding Co.
07/02/2004
Each share Common 1¢ par
exchanged for $27 cash

**ST LAURENT PAPERBOARD INC
(CANADA)**
Merged into Smurfit-Stone Container
Corp. (Old) 05/31/2000
Each share Common no par
exchanged for (0.5) share Common
1¢ par and $12.50 cash
Smurfit-Stone Container Corp. (Old)
reorganized as Smurfit-Stone
Container Corp. (New) 06/30/2010
which merged into Rock-Tenn Co.
05/27/2011 which merged into
WestRock Co. 07/01/2015

ST LAWRENCE CEM GROUP INC (QC)
Name changed 09/04/1980
Name changed 01/01/2000
Class A Subordinate no par split (3) for (1) by issuance of (2) additional shares 01/15/1974
Name changed from St. Lawrence Cement Co. to St. Lawrence Cement Inc. 09/04/1980
Class A Subordinate no par split (2) for (1) by issuance of (1) additional share 06/07/1985
Class A Subordinate no par split (2) for (1) by issuance of (1) additional share 06/06/1986
Class A Subordinate no par split (2) for (1) by issuance of (1) additional share 10/02/1987
Name changed from St. Lawrence Cement Inc. to St. Lawrence Cement Group Inc. 01/01/2000
Acquired by Holcim Ltd. 08/10/2007
Each share Class A Subordinate no par exchanged for $43.50 cash

ST LAWRENCE COLUMBIUM & METALS CORP (QC)
Proposal filed under bankruptcy act 07/02/1976 never confirmed
No stockholders' equity

ST. LAWRENCE CORP. LTD. (CANADA)
Each share 4% Preferred Ser. A $50 par exchanged for (1) share 1st Preferred $49 par, (1) share 2nd Preferred $1 par and $2 cash 00/00/1948
Each share old Common no par exchanged for (1) share Common $1 par 00/00/1948
Each share Common $1 par exchanged for (4) shares new Common no par 12/15/1956
5% Preferred Ser. A $100 par called for redemption 09/18/1978
Each share new Common no par exchanged for $0.030294 cash 10/26/1978
Public interest eliminated

ST LAWRENCE CNTY NATL BK (CANTON, NY)
Capital Stock $100 par changed to $25 par and (3) additional shares issued 00/00/1954
Capital Stock $25 par changed to $12.50 par and (1) additional share issued 02/12/1963
Capital Stock $12.50 par changed to $6.25 par and (1) additional share issued 06/15/1966
Stock Dividend - 50% 06/22/1955
Name changed to St. Lawrence National Bank (Canton, NY) 03/17/1972
St. Lawrence National Bank (Canton, NY) merged into Community Bank System, Inc. 03/15/1984

ST. LAWRENCE COUNTY UTILITIES, INC.
Merged into Niagara Hudson Public Service Corp.
(See Niagara Hudson Public Service Corp.)

ST LAWRENCE DIVERSIFIED CO (QC)
Common $1 par changed to no par 11/30/70
Recapitalized as Prenor Group Ltd.-Groupe Prenor Ltee. 6/22/73
Each share Common no par exchanged for (0.25) share Common no par
(See Prenor Group Ltd.- Groupe Prenor Ltee.)

ST LAWRENCE DIVERSIFIED LDS LTD (QC)
Name changed to St. Lawrence Diverified Co.-La Compagnie Diversifiee St-Laurent 5/20/69
St. Lawrence Diversified Co.-La Compagnie Diversifiee St-Laurent recapitalized as Prenor Group Ltd.-Groupe Prenor Ltee. 6/22/73
(See Prenor Group Ltd.-Groupe Prenor Ltee.)

ST LAWRENCE ENERGY CORP (DE)
SEC revoked common stock registration 09/13/2013

ST. LAWRENCE FLOUR MILLS CO. LTD. (CANADA)
Completely liquidated 07/31/1956
Each share 7% Preferred $100 par received first and final distribution of $101.75 cash

ST LAWRENCE NATL BK (CANTON, NY)
Capital Stock $6.25 par changed to $3.125 par and (1) additional share issued 02/14/1973
Capital Stock $3.125 par changed to $5 par 01/19/1975
Merged into Community Bank System, Inc. 03/15/1984
Each share Capital Stock $5 par exchanged for (1) share Common $5 par

ST. LAWRENCE PAPER MILLS CO. LTD.
Assets sold to St. Lawrence Corp. Ltd. and company dissolved in 1951

ST. LAWRENCE PULP & LUMBER CORP.
Property sold at foreclosure 00/00/1932
Stockholders' equity unlikely

ST LAWRENCE SEAWAY CORP (DE)
Reincorporated 08/31/2007
State of incorporation changed from (IN) to (DE) and Common $1 par changed to 1¢ par 08/31/2007
Name changed to Carbon Natural Gas Co. 05/12/2011
Carbon Natural Gas Co. name changed to Carbon Energy Corp. 06/07/2018

ST LOUIS AMUSEMENT CO (MO)
Charter forfeited for failure to file reports 01/01/1980

ST. LOUIS AVIATION CORP.
Name changed to St. Louis General Investment Corp. in 1931
(See St. Louis General Investment Corp.)

ST. LOUIS BANK BUILDING & EQUIPMENT CORP.
Name changed to Bank Building & Equipment Corp. of America in 1943
(See Bank Building & Equipment Corp. of America)

ST. LOUIS BROWNSVILLE CORP.
Name changed to Westag Corp. in 1951
Westag Corp. merged into Zapata Petroleum Corp. 12/13/56 which merged into Pennzoil, Co. (PA) (New) 7/3/63 which merged into Pennzoil United, Inc. 4/1/68 which name changed to Pennzoil Co. (DE) 6/1/72 which name changed to PennzEnergy Co. 12/30/98

ST. LOUIS CAPITAL, INC. (MO)
Completely liquidated for cash 9/17/65

ST. LOUIS CHAIN STORE PROPERTIES, INC.
Reorganized as St. Louis Properties Corp. in 1935 which was liquidated in 1948

ST LOUIS CNTY NATL BK (CLAYTON, MO)
Each share Capital Stock $20 par exchanged for (2) shares Capital Stock $10 par 08/14/1957
Stock Dividends - 20% 05/16/1955; (1) for (7.5) 08/21/1957; 10% 02/08/1965; 10% 12/17/1968
Reorganized as County National Bancorporation 08/01/1969
Each share Capital Stock $10 par exchanged for (1) share Common $10 par
County National Bancorporation name changed to County Tower Corp. 12/23/1981
(See County Tower Corp.)

ST. LOUIS GENERAL INVESTMENT CORP.
Liquidated in 1933
Details not available

ST. LOUIS INDEPENDENT PACKING CO.
Acquired by Swift & Co. (IL) 00/00/1931
Details not available

ST LOUIS INS CORP (MO)
Charter forfeited for failure to file reports 01/01/1982

ST. LOUIS MUTUAL LIFE INSURANCE CO.
Dissolved in 1949

ST LOUIS NATL STK YDS CO (DE)
Name changed to National Stock Yards Co. 06/15/1987

ST. LOUIS PROPERTIES CORP.
Liquidation completed in 1948

ST. LOUIS PUBLIC SERVICE CO. (MO)
Reorganized 00/00/1939
Each share $7 Preferred no par exchanged for either (2/3) share Class A $1 par or $2.50 cash
Each (75) shares Common no par exchanged for (1) share Class A $1 par
Recapitalized 00/00/1946
Each share Class A $1 par exchanged for (2) shares Class A 50¢ par
Recapitalized 00/00/1950
Class A 50¢ par changed to $12 par
Liquidation for cash completed 11/22/1963
Details not available

ST. LOUIS, ROCKY MOUNTAIN & PACIFIC CO. (NM)
Liquidation completed 6/10/57

ST. LOUIS-SAN FRANCISCO RAILWAY CO. OLD (MO)
Reorganized 1/1/47
Only Bondholders participated; no equity for Preferred and Common stockholders

ST LOUIS SAN FRANCISCO RY CO NEW (MO)
5% Conv. Preferred Ser. A $100 par called for redemption 10/11/1968
Merged into Burlington Northern Inc. 11/21/1980
Each share Common no par exchanged for (0.5) share $2.125 Preferred no par and (1.9) shares Common no par
Burlington Northern Inc. name changed to Burlington Northern Santa Fe Corp. 09/22/1995
(See Burlington Northern Santa Fe Corp.)

ST. LOUIS SHERATON CORP. (MO)
Liquidation completed 03/01/1956
Details not available

ST. LOUIS SHIPBUILDING-FEDERAL BARGE, INC. (MO)
6% Preferred Ser. A $100 par called for redemption in 1964
Stock Dividend - 25% 2/9/65
Name changed to Pott Industries, Inc. 1/1/68
Pott Industries, Inc. merged into Houston Natural Gas Corp. (Tex.) 7/25/77
(See Houston Natural Gas Corp. (Tex.))

ST LOUIS SOUTHWESTN RY CO (MO)
Merged into SSW Merger Corp. 09/30/1997
Details not available

ST LOUIS STL CASTING INC (MO)
Merged into Steel Holdings, Inc. 7/27/2000
Each share Common 5¢ par exchanged for $49 cash

ST. LOUIS TRAILER EXCHANGE CO. (MO)
Charter forfeited for failure to file reports 1/1/64

ST LOUIS UN TR CO (ST LOUIS, MO)
Capital Stock $20 par changed to $10 par and (1) additional share issued 1/30/60
Capital Stock $10 par split (1.5) for (1) by issuance of (0.5) additional share 1/22/65
Name changed to Centerre Trust Co. (St. Louis, MO) 1/4/82
Centerre Trust Co. (St. Louis, MO) name changed to Boatmen's Trust Co. (St. Louis, MO) 12/9/88
(See Boatmen's Trust Co. (St. Louis, MO))

ST LOUIS WHSL DRUG CO (MO)
Voluntarily dissolved in July 1977
Details not available

ST LUCIE EXPL LTD (ON)
Common $1 par changed to no par 06/07/1972
Each share old Common no par exchanged for (0.2) share new Common no par 07/15/2002
Delisted from Toronto Venture Stock Exchange 02/28/2001

ST LUCIE JUPITER DEV CORP (DE)
Adjudicated bankrupt 08/05/1975
No stockholders' equity

ST MARY LD & EXPL CO (DE)
Common 1¢ par split (2) for (1) by issuance of (1) additional share payable 09/05/2000 to holders of record 08/21/2000 Ex date - 09/06/2000
Common 1¢ par split (2) for (1) by issuance of (1) additional share payable 03/31/2005 to holders of record 03/21/2005 Ex date - 04/01/2005
Name changed to SM Energy Co. 06/01/2010

ST. MARY'S GLACIER, INC. (CO)
Name changed to Utah Coal & Chemicals Corp. (CO) 09/09/1977
Utah Coal & Chemicals Corp. (CO) reincorporated in Nevada 04/16/1979 which recapitalized as Lifestream Technologies Inc. 02/11/1994
(See Lifestream Technologies Inc.)

ST. MARY'S MINERAL LAND CO.
Acquired by Copper Range Co. 00/00/1931
Details not available

ST. MARY'S MINES LTD. (BC)
Recapitalized as Can-Base Industries, Ltd. 03/15/1971
Each share Capital Stock 50¢ par exchanged for (1) share Capital Stock no par
(See Can-Base Industries, Ltd.)

ST MAURICE CAP LTD (CANADA)
Recapitalized as Commerce Capital Corp. Ltd. 06/28/1973
Each share Common no par exchanged for (0.25) share Common no par
(See Commerce Capital Corp. Ltd.)

ST. MAURICE EXPLORATION INC.
Name changed to St. Maurice Gas Inc. 5/24/56
St. Maurice Gas Inc. liquidated for St. Maurice Capital Corp. Ltd. 2/4/71 which recapitalized as Commerce Capital Corp. Ltd. 6/28/73
(See Commerce Capital Corp. Ltd.)

ST MAURICE GAS INC (QC)
Completely liquidated 02/04/1971
Each share Common $1 par exchanged for first and final

ST. MAURICE GOLD MINES, LTD. (ON)
Charter cancelled for failure to file reports and pay taxes in 1954

ST. MAURICE POWER CO. LTD.
Merged into Shawinigan Water & Power Co. 00/00/1928
Details not available

distribution of (1) share St. Maurice Capital Corp. Ltd. Common no par
St. Maurice Capital Corp. Ltd. recapitalized as Commerce Capital Corp. Ltd. 06/28/1973
(See Commerce Capital Corp. Ltd.)

ST. MAURICE VALLEY CORP.
Merged into Consolidated Paper Corp. Ltd. 00/00/1932
Details not available

ST. MICHAEL URANIUM MINES LTD. (ON)
Merged into Cadamet Mines Ltd. on a (0.25) for (1) basis 11/17/58
Cadamet Mines Ltd. recapitalized as Terrex Mining Co. Ltd. 9/8/66
(See Terrex Mining Co. Ltd.)

ST-MORITZ CAP INC (CANADA)
Name changed to Medical Intelligence Technologies Inc. 7/18/2005

ST. PAUL ADVISERS, INC. (MN)
Name changed to AMEV Advisers, Inc. 04/01/1985
AMEV Advisers, Inc. name changed to Fortis Advisers, Inc. 02/22/1992
(See Fortis Advisers, Inc.)

ST PAUL AMMONIA PRODS INC (MN)
Voting Trust Agreement terminated 07/31/1965
Each VTC for Common 2-1/2¢ par exchanged for (1) share Common 2-1/2¢ par
Each share 5-1/2% Preferred $100 par exchanged for (56.5) shares Common 2-1/2¢ par 02/06/1970
Merged into N-Ren Corp. 10/24/1975
Each share Common 2-1/2¢ par exchanged for $2.65 cash

ST PAUL BANCORP INC (DE)
Common 1¢ par split (3) for (2) by issuance of (0.5) additional share 1/4/94
Common 1¢ par split (5) for (4) by issuance of (0.25) additional share payable 1/14/97 to holders of record 12/31/96
Common 1¢ par split (3) for (2) by issuance of (0.5) additional share payable 7/14/97 to holders of record 6/30/97
Merged into Charter One Financial, Inc. 10/1/99
Each share Common 1¢ par exchanged for (0.99225) share Common 1¢ par
(See Charter One Financial, Inc.)

ST PAUL CAP FD INC (MN)
Name changed to AMEV Capital Fund, Inc. 05/01/1985
AMEV Capital Fund, Inc. reorganized as Fortis Equity Portfolios Inc. 02/22/1992
(See Fortis Equity Portfolios Inc.)

ST PAUL CAP TR I (DE)
7.60% Trust Preferred Securities called for redemption at $25 plus $0.168888 accrued dividends on 11/17/2006

ST PAUL FIDUCIARY FD INC (MN)
Name changed to AMEV Fiduciary Fund, Inc. 05/01/1985
AMEV Fiduciary Fund, Inc. name changed to Fortis Fiduciary Fund, Inc. 02/22/1992 which merged into Fortis Equity Portfolios Inc. 10/22/1998
(See Fortis Equity Portfolios Inc.)

ST. PAUL FIRE & MARINE INSURANCE CO. (MN)
Capital Stock $25 par changed to $62.50 00/00/1939
Each share Capital Stock $62.50 par exchanged for (5) shares Capital Stock $12.50 par 00/00/1944
Each share Capital Stock $12.50 par exchanged for (4) shares Capital Stock $6.25 par to effect a (2) for (1) split and a 100% stock dividend 00/00/1951
Stock Dividends - 15% 09/16/1957; 25% 08/31/1962
Name changed to St. Paul Companies, Inc. 01/01/1968
St. Paul Companies, Inc. name changed to St. Paul Travelers Companies, Inc. 04/01/2004 which name changed to Travelers Companies, Inc. 02/27/2007

ST. PAUL GAS LIGHT CO.
Acquired by Northern States Power Co. (MN) 00/00/1926
Details not available

ST PAUL GROWTH FD INC (MN)
Name changed to AMEV Growth Fund, Inc. 05/01/1985
AMEV Growth Fund, Inc. name changed to Fortis Growth Fund, Inc. 02/22/1992
(See Fortis Growth Fund, Inc.)

ST PAUL INCOME FD INC (MN)
Name changed to AMEV U.S. Government Securities Fund, Inc. 05/01/1985
AMEV U.S. Government Securities Fund, Inc. name changed to Fortis Income Portfolios, Inc. 02/22/1992
(See Fortis Income Portfolios, Inc.)

ST. PAUL INDUSTRIES, INC.
Liquidated in 1948

ST PAUL MONEY FD INC (MN)
Name changed to AMEV Money Fund, Inc. 05/01/1985
AMEV Money Fund, Inc. name changed to Fortis Money Portfolios Inc. 02/22/1992
(See Fortis Money Portfolios Inc.)

ST PAUL SECS INC (MN)
Name changed to AMEV Securities, Inc. 12/27/1985
AMEV Securities, Inc. name changed to Fortis Securities, Inc. (MN) 01/08/1993 which reorganized in Maryland as Hartford Income Shares Fund, Inc. 07/16/2002 which merged into Rivus Bond Fund 10/22/2010 which name changed to Cutwater Select Income Fund 12/09/2011 which name changed to Insight Select Income Fund 12/29/2016

ST PAUL SPL FD INC (MN)
Name changed to AMEV Special Fund, Inc. 05/01/1985
AMEV Special Fund, Inc. name changed to Special Portfolios, Inc. 08/31/1989 which merged into Fortis Growth Fund, Inc. 03/01/1996
(See Fortis Growth Fund, Inc.)

ST PAUL TRAVELERS COS INC (MN)
Name changed 04/01/2004
Common $6.25 par changed to $3 par and (1) additional share issued 03/01/1968
Common $3 par changed to $1.50 par and (1) additional share issued 06/27/1973
Common $1.50 par changed to no par 05/05/1982
Common no par split (2) for (1) by issuance of (1) additional share 06/06/1986
Common no par split (2) for (1) by issuance of (1) additional share 06/06/1994
Common no par split (2) for (1) by issuance of (1) additional share payable 05/11/1998 to holders of record 05/06/1998 Ex date - 05/12/1998
Name changed from St. Paul Companies, Inc. to St. Paul Travelers Companies, Inc. 04/01/2004
Name changed to Travelers Companies, Inc. 02/27/2007

ST PAUL TRAVELERS COS INC (MN)
Each Equity Unit exchanged for (1.7218) shares Common no par 8/16/2005
(Additional Information in Active)

ST. PAUL UNION STOCKYARDS CO. (MN)
Each share Capital Stock $100 par exchanged for (4) shares Capital Stock no par in 1930
Merged into United Stockyards Corp. 8/1/63
Each share Capital Stock no par exchanged for (4.1) shares Common 25¢ par
United Stockyards Corp. merged into Canal-Randolph Corp. 11/1/64
(See Canal-Randolph Corp.)

ST PETERSBURG BK & TR CO (ST PETERSBURG, FL)
Merged into Rutland Bank (St. Petersburg, FL) 05/01/1981
Each share Capital Stock $10 par exchanged for (6-2/3) shares Common $1 par
(See Rutland Bank (St. Petersburg, FL)

ST PHILIPS RES INC (BC)
Merged into Royal Oak Mines Inc. 11/01/1996
Each share Common no par exchanged for $3.40 cash

ST REGIS CAP CORP (DE)
$4.30 Conv. Exchangeable Preferred 1983
Ser. $1 par called for redemption 11/5/84
Public interest eliminated

ST. REGIS CORP. (DE)
Name changed to Western Coatings & Chemical Co. 10/31/1960
Western Coatings & Chemical Co. name changed to Valley Fair Corp. 01/13/1964
(See Valley Fair Corp.)

ST REGIS CORP (NY)
Merged into Champion International Corp. 11/20/1984
Each share Common $5 par exchanged for (2.85) shares Common 50¢ par
Champion International Corp. merged into International Paper Co. 06/20/2000

ST REGIS GROWTH FD INC (RI)
Acquired by Lexington Research Fund, Inc. (NJ) 06/21/1973
Each share Common 10¢ par exchanged for (0.399) share Capital Stock $1 par
Lexington Research Fund, Inc. (NJ) reincorporated in Maryland as Lexinton Growth & Income Fund, Inc. 04/30/1991 which name changed to Pilgrim Growth & Income Fund, Inc. 07/26/2000 which name changed to ING Large Company Value Fund, Inc. 03/01/2002
(See ING Large Company Value Fund, Inc.)

ST. REGIS LEAD MINES, LTD. (ON)
Charter cancelled for failure to file returns and pay taxes in 1956

ST. REGIS PAPER CO. (NY)
Each share Common no par exchanged for (4) shares Common $10 par 00/00/1929
Common $10 par changed to $5 par 00/00/1936
4.4% 1st Preferred $100 par called for redemption 01/01/1963
Common $5 par split (3) for (2) by issuance of (0.5) additional share 12/12/1973
Name changed to St. Regis Corp. 04/28/1983
St. Regis Corp. merged into Champion International Corp. 11/20/1984 which merged into International Paper Co. 06/20/2000

ST. REGIS URANIUM CORP. (DE)
Name changed to St. Regis Corp. 08/06/1957
St. Regis Corp. name changed to Western Coatings & Chemical Co. 10/31/1960 which name changed to Valley Fair Corp. 01/13/1964
(See Valley Fair Corp.)

ST. ROBERTS METALS CORP. (QC)
Charter cancelled for failure to file reports and pay taxes 10/12/74

ST. SIMEON URANIUM CORP. (QC)
Recapitalized as Consolidated St. Simeon Mines Ltd. on a (1) for (4) basis in 1956
Consolidated St. Simeon Mines Ltd. charter annulled 5/11/74

SAINTS & SINNERS FILM DEV CO (CO)
Name changed to Saints & Sinners Entertainment Co. 3/13/89

SAIPHT CORP (NV)
Name changed 03/05/2003
Name changed from Saiph Corp. to SaiphT Corp. 03/05/2003
Name changed to Caneum, Inc. 07/30/2003
(See Caneum, Inc.)

SAIRAM TECHNOLOGIES LTD. (NV)
Name changed to Balanced Environmental Services Technology Inc. 4/5/91
Balanced Environmental Services Technology Inc. recapitalized as United States Indemnity & Casualty, Inc. 7/8/93 which name changed to Birch Financial, Inc. 1/20/2000

SAJAN INC (DE)
Each share old Common 1¢ par exchanged for (0.25) share new Common 1¢ par 06/17/2014
Acquired by Amplexor USA Inc. 07/19/2017
Each share new Common 1¢ par exchanged for $5.83 cash

SAK GROUP INC (NV)
Name changed to American Television Network, Inc. 01/28/1989

SAKAMI LAKE EXPLORATIONS LTD. (ON)
Merged into Sakfield Mines & Investments Ltd. 01/17/1968
Each share Capital Stock $1 par exchanged for (1/3) share Capital Stock no par
(See Sakfield Mines & Investments Ltd.)

SAKARI RES LTD (SINGAPORE)
ADR agreement terminated 01/28/2013
Each ADR for Common exchanged for $30.22283 cash

SAKER ONE CORP (UT)
Each share old Common 1¢ par exchanged for (10) shares Common $0.001 par 1/6/87
Each share Common $0.001 par exchanged for (0.1) share new Common 1¢ par 11/24/89
Reorganized under the laws of Nevada as Triad Compressor Inc. 1/7/99
Each (120) shares Common 1¢ par exchanged for (1) share Common $0.001 par
Triad Compressor Inc. name changed to Triad Innovations, Inc. 9/10/99

SAKFIELD MINES & INVTS LTD (ON)
Charter cancelled for failure to file reports and pay taxes 07/27/1976

SAKHA RESOURCE TECHNOLOGIES CORP (DE)
Name changed to Canary Resources Inc. 1/31/2005

SAKINAW LAKE COPPER & IRON MINING LTD. (ON)
Charter cancelled for failure to file reports and pay taxes February 1958

SAKS HLDGS INC (DE)
Merged into Saks Inc. 09/17/1998
Each share Common 1¢ par exchanged for (0.82) share Common 1¢ par
(See Saks Inc.)

SAKS INC (TN)
Acquired by Hudson's Bay Co. (New) 11/04/2013
Each share Common 10¢ par exchanged for $16 cash

SAKURA BK LTD (JAPAN)
Merged into Sumitomo Mitsui Banking Corp. 6/12/2001
Each ADR for Common 50 Yen par exchanged for (6) ADR's for Ordinary 50 Yen par
Sumitomo Mitsui Banking Corp. merged into Sumitomo Mitsui Financial Group, Inc. 1/15/2003

SAKURA FIN BERMUDA TR (JAPAN)
ADR agreement terminated 12/19/2006
Details not available

SALADA FOODS LTD (CANADA)
Acquired by Kellogg Co. 01/13/1970
Each share Common no par exchanged for $17.50 cash

SALADA-SHIRRIFF-HORSEY LTD. (CANADA)
5-1/2% Preferred Ser. A called for redemption 8/19/58
5-3/4% Preferred Ser. B called for redemption 2/17/59
Common no par split (3) for (1) by issuance of (2) additional shares 3/20/59
Name changed to Salada Foods, Ltd. 2/5/62
(See Salada Foods, Ltd.)

SALADMASTER CORP (TX)
Name changed to SMC Industries, Inc. 12/12/1969
(See SMC Industries, Inc.)

SALAMANCA SUGAR CO.
Property sold in 1931
No stockholders' equity

SALAMANCA TR CO (SALAMANCA, NY)
Merged into Financial Institutions, Inc. 03/29/1990
Each share Common $25 par exchanged for $352.67 cash

SALAMANDER ENERGY PLC (ENGLAND & WALES)
ADR agreement terminated 09/01/2016
No ADR's remain outstanding

SALANT & SALANT INC (NY)
Class A Capital Stock $5 par changed to $3.33333333 par and (0.5) additional share issued 07/15/1963
Name changed to Salant Corp. (NY) and Class A Capital Stock $3.33333333 par reclassified as Common $1 par 03/30/1971
Salant Corp. (NY) reincorporated in Delaware 06/02/1987 which name changed to Salant Corp. (New) 09/17/1993 which merged into Perry Ellis International, Inc. 06/19/2003
(See Perry Ellis International, Inc.)

SALANT CORP NEW (DE)
Plan of reorganization under Chapter 11 Federal Bankruptcy proceedings effective 05/11/1999
Each share old Common $1 par received (0.03337) share new Common 1¢ par

Note: Old Common was cancelled and is without value
Merged into Perry Ellis International, Inc. 06/19/2003
Each share new Common $1 par exchanged for (0.2056) share Common 1¢ par and $5.3538 cash
(See Perry Ellis International, Inc.)

SALANT CORP OLD (DE)
Reincorporated 06/02/1987
Common $1 par split (3) for (2) by issuance of (0.5) additional share 03/27/1973
State of incorporation changed from (NY) to (DE) 06/02/1987
Plan of Reorganization under Chapter 11 Federal Bankruptcy Code effective 09/17/1993
Each share Common $1 par received distribution of (0.68) Common Stock Purchase Warrant, Class B expiring 09/17/1996
Name changed to Salant Corp. (New) 09/17/1993
Salant Corp. (New) merged into Perry Ellis International, Inc. 06/19/2003
(See Perry Ellis International, Inc.)

SALARES LITHIUM INC (BC)
Merged into Talison Lithium Ltd. 09/22/2010
Each share Common no par exchanged for either (0.35587188) share Ordinary or (0.35587188) Talison Lithium Exchangeco Ltd. Exchangeable Share
Note: Option for Canadian residents to receive Exchangeable Shares expired 09/14/2010
Note: Unexchanged certificates were cancelled and became without value 09/22/2016
(See Talison Lithium Ltd.)

SALARY COM INC (DE)
Issue Information - 5,700,000 shares COM offered at $10.50 per share on 02/15/2006
Acquired by Kenexa Corp. 10/01/2010
Each share Common $0.0001 par exchanged for $4.07 cash

SALE KNITTING INC (VA)
Name changed to Tully Corp. of Virginia 12/3/71
Tully Corp. of Virginia name changed to Tultex Corp. 2/27/96
(See Tultex Corp.)

SALEFISH INC (UT)
Name changed to Adak Energy Corp. 12/10/1973
Adak Energy Corp. recapitalized as Post Data Services Corp. 09/22/1983
(See Post Data Services Corp.)

SALEM BK & TR CO (GOSHEN, IN)
Common $100 par changed to $25 par and (3) additional shares issued 03/31/1958
Common $25 par changed to $10 par and (1.5) additional shares issued 12/01/1972
Stock Dividends - 79.44% 06/02/1958; 33-1/3% 02/15/1967; 25% 04/15/1970; 20% 04/25/1974; 20% 06/01/1979
Under plan of reorganization each share Common $10 par automatically became (1) share Salem Financial Corp. Common no par 07/01/1982
Salem Financial Corp. merged into Trustcorp, Inc. 10/01/1986 which was acquired by Society Corp. 01/05/1990 which merged into KeyCorp (New) 03/01/1994

SALEM BK & TR NATL ASSN (SALEM, VA)
Stock Dividends - 3% payable 12/16/1996 to holders of record 11/15/1996; 4% payable 12/18/1998 to holders of record 11/13/1998; 4%

payable 12/20/1999 to holders of record 11/19/1999
Under plan of reorganization each share Common $5 par automatically became (1) share Salem Community Bankshares, Inc. Common $5 par 10/18/2000
Salem Community Bankshares, Inc. merged into FNB Corp. 12/31/2001 which merged into StellarOne Corp. 02/28/2008 which merged into Union First Market Bankshares Corp. 01/02/2014 which name changed to Union Bankshares Corp. 04/28/2014

SALEM BROSIUS INC (PA)
Each share Common 10¢ par exchanged for (0.04) share Common $2.50 par 12/22/1953
Common $2.50 par changed to 50¢ par 05/01/1967
Name changed to Salem Corp. 06/01/1970
(See Salem Corp.)

SALEM CARPET MLS INC (NC)
Stock Dividends - 100% 2/18/76; 100% 7/29/78
Merged into Shaw Industries, Inc. 5/29/92
Each share Common $1 par exchanged for (0.363) share Common no par
(See Shaw Industries, Inc.)

SALEM COMMUNICATIONS CORP (DE)
Name changed to Salem Media Group, Inc. 02/24/2015

SALEM CMNTY BANKSHARES INC (VA)
Stock Dividend - 4% payable 12/18/2000 to holders of record 11/17/2000 Ex date - 11/15/2000
Merged into FNB Corp. 12/31/2001
Each share Common $5 par exchanged for either (1.2996) shares Common $5 par or $26.49 cash
Note: Option to receive stock expired 01/04/2002
FNB Corp. merged into StellarOne Corp. 02/28/2008 which merged into Union First Market Bankshares Corp. 01/02/2014 which name changed to Union Bankshares Corp. 04/28/2014

SALEM CORP (PA)
Common 50¢ par split (3) for (2) by issuance of (0.5) additional share 01/05/1994
Merged into Tree Cities Research, Inc. 09/27/1996
Each share Common 50¢ par exchanged for $25 cash

SALEM ELECTRIC LIGHTING CO. (MA)
Under plan of merger each share Common $50 par exchanged for (3.6) shares Common $10 par of Essex County Electric Co. in 1953
Essex County Electric Co. merged into Merrimack-Essex Electric Co. 7/30/57 which Common Stock was acquired by New England Electric System 6/30/59
(See New England Electric System)

SALEM ELECTRS INC (NY)
Name changed to Salem Industries, Inc. 06/09/1970
(See Salem Industries, Inc.)

SALEM EXPLORATION LTD. (QC)
Acquired by Agena Mining Co. Ltd. 8/11/66
Each share Capital Stock $1 par exchanged for (1) share Common $1 par
Agena Mining Co. Ltd. charter cancelled 9/20/72

SALEM FD (MA)
Merged into Fidelity Magellan Fund, Inc. 6/22/81
Each share Capital Stock $1 par

exchanged for (0.375567) share Capital Stock $1 par

SALEM FDS (MA)
Name changed to First Union Funds 1/4/93

SALEM FINL CORP (IN)
Merged into Trustcorp, Inc. 10/01/1986
Each share Common no par exchanged for (3.85) shares Common $20 par
Trustcorp, Inc. acquired by Society Corp. 01/05/1990 which merged into KeyCorp (New) 03/01/1994

SALEM GAS LIGHT CO. (MA)
Capital Stock $25 par changed to $10 par in 1951
Under plan of merger each share Capital Stock $10 par exchanged for (1.5) shares Common $10 par of North Shore Gas Co. (Mass.) in 1953
North Shore Gas Co. (Mass.) completely liquidated 12/28/73

SALEM INDS INC (NY)
Charter cancelled and proclaimed dissolved for non-payment of taxes 12/15/1972

SALEM LINEN MILLS, INC. (OR)
Liquidated 11/19/56

SALEM MINES LTD (BC)
Name changed to Salem Resources Ltd. 11/19/73
(See Salem Resources Ltd.)

SALEM NATL CORP (TX)
Merged into Salem Acquisition Co. 12/23/1986
Each share Common no par exchanged for $10 cash

SALEM RES INC (NV)
Recapitalized as InterContinental Minerals & Petroleum, Inc. 4/5/84
Each share Common $0.0001 par exchanged for (0.1) share Common $0.0001 par
InterContinental Minerals & Petroleum, Inc. recapitalized as # 1 Cousin Organization, Inc. 8/30/85 which name changed to J & J Research Inc. 2/11/86

SALEM RES LTD (BC)
Charter cancelled 11/5/79

SALEM SPORTSWEAR CORP (DE)
Merged into FTL Acquisition Corp. 11/10/93
Each share Common 1¢ par exchanged for $12.75 cash

SALEM TR BK (WINSTON SALEM, NC)
Merged into CCB Financial Corp. 1/31/97
Each share Common no par exchanged for (0.36) share Common $5 par
CCB Financial Corp. merged into National Commerce Bancorporation 7/5/2000 which name changed to National Commerce Financial Corp. 4/25/2001 which merged into SunTrust Banks, Inc. 10/1/2004

SALEM WISP & CO INC (DE)
Charter cancelled and declared inoperative and void for non-payment of taxes 3/1/89

SALEOUTLET COM (NV)
Recapitalized as Gatlin Holdings Inc. 02/05/2001
Each share Common $0.001 par exchanged for (1/6) share Common $0.001 par
Gatlin Holdings Inc. recapitalized as Bio Venture Holdings Inc. 06/11/2002 which name changed to Midwest Venture Holdings, Inc. 08/16/2002 which name changed to Inspiration Products Group, Inc. 02/03/2003 which name changed to MB-Tech, Inc. 05/18/2003

(See MB-Tech, Inc.)

SALES FOLLOW UP CORP (IL)
Reincorporated under the laws of Delaware as Automated Marketing Systems, Inc. and Common no par changed to 50¢ par 07/01/1969
(See Automated Marketing Systems, Inc.)

SALES INITIATIVES INTL INC (ON)
Name changed to Greenlight Communications Inc. 06/14/1994
(See Greenlight Communications Inc.)

SALES ONLINE DIRECT INC (DE)
Name changed to Paid, Inc. 12/08/2003

SALES TRAINING INC (WA)
Adjudicated bankrupt 04/16/1974
No stockholders' equity

SALESLOGIX CORP (DE)
Issue Information - 3,325,000 shares COM offered at $9 per share on 05/27/1999
Name changed to Interact Commerce Corp. 4/25/2000
Interact Commerce Corp. merged into Sage Group plc 5/7/2001

SALESMATION COM INC
Merged into e-Synergies, Inc. 4/12/2001
Each share Common exchanged for (1.25) shares Common $0.001 par

SALESREPCENTRAL COM INC (NV)
Charter revoked for failure to file reports and pay fees 8/1/2005

SALESTACTIX INC (DE)
Name changed to Strativation, Inc. 10/14/2005
Strativation, Inc. name changed to CNS Response, Inc. 03/09/2007 which name changed to MYnd Analytics, Inc. 01/12/2016

SALEX HLDG CORP (DE)
Chapter 7 bankruptcy proceedings terminated 03/31/2004
Stockholders' equity unlikely

SALICK HEALTH CARE INC (DE)
Reincorporated 08/27/1991
Common no par split (3) for (2) by issuance of (0.5) additional share 08/30/1985
State of incorporation changed from (CA) to (DE) and Common no par changed to $0.001 par 08/27/1991
Merged into Zeneca Group PLC 04/13/1995
Each share Common $0.001 par exchanged for $18.875 cash
Callable Common $0.001 par called for redemption at $41.15 plus accrued dividend on 04/10/1997

SALIDA WEALTH PRESERVATION LISTED LTD (ON)
Trust terminated 05/03/2013
Each Trust Unit received $6.6596 cash

SALIENT CYBERTECH INC (DE)
Each share old Common $0.001 par exchanged for (0.1) share new Common $0.001 par 11/01/1999
Recapitalized as BrandAid Marketing Corp. 12/24/2001
Each share Common $0.001 par exchanged for (0.05) share Common $0.001 par
(See BrandAid Marketing Corp.)

SALIENT MLP & ENERGY INFRASTRUCTURE FD (DE)
Merged into Salient Midstream & MLP Fund 11/14/2014
Each Common Share of Bene. Int. 1¢ par exchanged for (1.14) Common Shares of Bene. Int. 1¢ par

SALIENT SYS INC (OH)
Merged into Portec Rail Products, Inc. 10/01/2004
Each share Common no par exchanged for (0.241163) share Common $1 par and $1.447 cash

Each share Common no par received first and final escrow distribution of (0.013067) share Common $1 par and $0.0784 cash 11/29/2004
(See Portec Rail Products, Inc.)

SALINE COUNTY COAL CO.
Acquired by Peabody Coal Co. in 1929
Peabody Coal Co. name changed to PDY Coal Co. 3/29/68 which liquidation completed 3/31/71

SALISBURY BK & TR CO (LAKEVILLE, CT)
Reorganized as Salisbury Bancorp, Inc. 8/24/98
Each share Common 10¢ par exchanged for (6) shares Common 10¢ par 8/24/98

SALISBURY COTTON MILLS
Merged into Proximity Manufacturing Co. 00/00/1945
Details not available

SALISH VENTURES INC (BC)
Name changed to Primary Metals Inc. 04/22/2003
(See Primary Metals Inc.)

SALIVA DIAGNOSTIC SYS INC (DE)
Each share old Common 1¢ par exchanged for (0.1) share new Common 1¢ par 08/03/1998
Each share new Common 1¢ par exchanged for (0.04) share Common $0.001 par 03/19/2002
Name changed to StatSure Diagnostic Systems, Inc. 03/22/2006

SALIX HLDGS LTD (BRITISH VIRGIN ISLANDS)
Restrictive legend removed 05/28/1998
Name changed to Salix Pharmaceuticals, Ltd. (British Virgin Islands) 08/28/1998
Salix Pharmaceuticals, Ltd. (British Virgin Islands) reincorporated in Delaware 12/31/2001
(See Salix Pharmaceuticals, Ltd. (DE))

SALIX PHARMACEUTICALS LTD (BRITISH VIRGIN ISLANDS)
Reincoporated under the laws of Delaware 12/31/2001
(See Salix Pharmaceuticals, Ltd. (DE))

SALIX PHARMACEUTICALS LTD (DE)
Common $0.001 par split (3) for (2) by issuance of (0.5) additional share payable 07/12/2004 to holders of record 06/30/2004 Ex date - 07/13/2004
Acquired by Valeant Pharmaceuticals International, Inc. 04/01/2015
Each share Common $0.001 par exchanged for $173 cash

SALKIN WELCH & CO INC (MD)
Merged into Advest Group, Inc. 6/1/81
Each share Common 10¢ par exchanged for (1/9) share Common $1 par
Advest Group, Inc. merged into MONY Group Inc. 1/31/2001
(See MONY Group Inc.)

SALLIES LTD (SOUTH AFRICA)
Acquired by Fluormin PLC 12/19/2011
Each ADR for Ordinary exchanged for $0.014766 cash

SALLY MINES LTD.
Acquired by Highland-Bell Ltd. on a (1) for (4) basis 00/00/1946
Highland-Bell Ltd. liquidated for Teck Corp. Ltd. 04/30/1971 which name changed to Teck Corp. 11/21/1978 which name changed to Teck Cominco Ltd. 09/12/2001 which name changed to Teck Resources Ltd. 04/27/2009

SALMO-MALARTIC MINES LTD. (ON)
Former transfer agent advised charter was reported cancelled in May 1969

SALMO PRINCE MINES LTD. (BC)
Struck off register and declared dissolved for failure to file reports 5/15/69

SALMON EXPRESS INC (NV)
Reorganized under the laws of Delaware as MicroMed Cardiovascular, Inc. 8/16/2005
Each (3.3528) shares Common $0.001 par exchanged for (1) share Common $0.001 par

SALMON FALLS INVESTMENT CORP. (CA)
Name changed to Morgan Equities Corp. and Capital Stock $10 par changed to no par 8/11/70
Morgan Equities Corp. name changed to California Casket Co. in June 1978
(See California Casket Co.)

SALMON FALLS MANUFACTURING CO.
Liquidated in 1930
Details not available

SALMON RIV RES LTD (BC)
All officers and directors resigned 07/13/2015

SALMONBERRY TIMBER CO.
Liquidation completed in 1942
Details not available

SALOMON BROS CAP & INCOME FD INC (MD)
Issue Information - 29,700,000 shares COM offered at $20 per share on 02/24/2004
Name changed to LMP Capital & Income Fund Inc. 10/9/2006

SALOMON BROS EMERGING MKTS DEBT FD INC (MD)
Name changed to Western Asset Emerging Markets Debt Fund Inc. 10/9/2006

SALOMON BROS EMERGING MKTS FLOATING RATE FD INC (MD)
Name changed to Western Asset Emerging Markets Floating Rate Fund Inc. 10/09/2006
Western Asset Emerging Markets Floating Rate Fund Inc. merged into Western Asset Emerging Markets Debt Fund Inc. 09/14/2009

SALOMON BROS EMERGING MKTS INCOME FD INC (MD)
Name changed to Western Asset Emerging Markets Income Fund Inc. (Old) 10/09/2006
Western Asset Emerging Markets Income Fund Inc. (Old) merged into Western Asset Emerging Markets Income Fund Inc. (New) 11/03/2008 which merged into Western Asset Emerging Markets Debt Fund Inc. 12/19/2016

SALOMON BROS FD INC (MD)
Common $1 par reclassified as Class O 12/31/1994
Name changed to Legg Mason Partners Equity Fund, Inc. 11/20/2006
Legg Mason Partners Equity Fund, Inc. name changed to Legg Mason Partners Equity Trust 04/16/2007

SALOMON BROS GLOBAL HIGH INCOME FD INC (MD)
Name changed to Western Asset Global High Income Fund Inc. 10/9/2006

SALOMON BROS GLOBAL PARTNERS INCOME FD INC (MD)
Name changed to Western Asset Global Partners Income Fund Inc. 10/09/2006
Western Asset Global Partners Income Fund Inc. merged into Western Asset Global High Income Fund Inc. 08/29/2016

SALOMON BROS HIGH INCOME FD INC (MD)
Name changed to Western Asset High Income Fund Inc. 10/09/2006
Western Asset High Income Fund Inc. merged into Western Asset High Income Opportunity Fund, Inc. 06/24/2013

SALOMON BROS INFLATION MANAGEMENT FD INC (MD)
Name changed to Western Asset Inflation Management Fund, Inc. 10/9/2006

SALOMON BROS MUN PARTNERS FD INC (MD)
Name changed to Western Asset Municipal Partners Fund, Inc. 10/09/2006

SALOMON BROS VARIABLE RATE STRATEGIC FD INC (MD)
Name changed to Western Asset Variable Rate Strategic Fund Inc. 10/9/2006

SALOMON BROS WORLDWIDE INCOME FD INC (MD)
Name changed to Western Asset Worldwide Income Fund Inc. 10/09/2006
Western Asset Worldwide Income Fund Inc. merged into Western Asset Emerging Markets Debt Fund Inc. 12/19/2016

SALOMON BROS EMERGING MKTS INCOME II FD INC (MD)
Name changed to Western Asset Emerging Markets Income Fund II, Inc. 10/09/2006
Western Asset Emerging Markets Income Fund II, Inc. name changed to Western Asset Emerging Markets Income Fund Inc. (New) 11/03/2008 which merged into Western Asset Emerging Markets Debt Fund Inc. 12/19/2016

SALOMON BROS HIGH INCOME FD II INC (MD)
Name changed to Western Asset High Income Fund II Inc. 10/9/2006

SALOMON BROS MUN PARTNERS FD II INC (MD)
Name changed to Western Asset Municipal Partners Fund II, Inc. 10/09/2006
Western Asset Municipal Partners Fund II, Inc. merged into Western Asset Municipal Partners Fund Inc. 07/23/2007

SALOMON BROS 2008 WORLDWIDE DLR GOVT TERM TR INC (MD)
Name changed to Western Asset 2008 Worldwide Dollar Government Term Trust Inc. 10/09/2006
(See Western Asset 2008 Worldwide Dollar Government Term Trust Inc.)

SALOMON INC (DE)
Depositary Shares Ser. C called for redemption 8/15/96
Preferred Ser. C no par called for redemption 8/15/96
Merged into Travelers Group Inc. 11/28/97
Each Depositary Share Ser. D exchanged for (1) Depositary Share Ser. J
Each share 8.08% Preferred Ser. D no par exchanged for (1) share 8.08% Preferred Ser. J no par
Each Depositary Share Ser. E exchanged for (1) Depositary Share Ser. K
Each share Preferred Ser. E no par exchanged for (1) share Preferred Ser. K no par
Each share Common $1 par exchanged for (1.695) shares Common 1¢ par
Travelers Group Inc. name changed to Citigroup Inc. 10/8/98

SAL-SAM

SALOMON PHIBRO OIL TR (NY)
Trust Terminated 11/1/95
Each Unit Ben Int. received $4.417026 cash

SALON COM (DE)
Name changed to Salon Media Group Inc. 5/24/2001

SALON RES CORP (BC)
Name changed 04/28/1986
Name changed from Salon Resources Corp. to Salon Resources Corp.- Corporation Miniere Salon 04/28/1986
Name changed to Corptech Industries Inc. 09/23/1987
Corptech Industries Inc. recapitalized as Forefront Ventures Ltd. 07/15/1992 which recapitalized as First Echelon Ventures, Inc. 02/16/1999 which name changed to Aumega Discoveries Ltd. 12/12/2003 which recapitalized as Fortress Base Metals Corp. 01/10/2007 which name changed to Lions Gate Metals Inc. 07/21/2008 which name changed to Block X Capital Corp. 01/25/2018

SALRO MFG CORP (NY)
Dissolved by proclamation 3/25/81

SALT CREEK CONSOLIDATED OIL CO.
Dissolved and assets sold to Argo Oil Co. which merged into Argo Oil Corp. in 1936
Argo Oil Corp. completed liquidation 5/17/68

SALT CREEK DEVELOPMENT CO., INC. (CA)
Charter suspended for failure to file reports and pay fees 07/01/1982

SALT CREEK PRODUCERS ASSN., INC.
Dissolved in 1936

SALT DOME OIL CORP.
Liquidated 00/00/1950
Details not available

SALT LAKE HARDWARE CO (DE)
Name changed to Alta Industries Corp. 06/18/1969
Alta Industries Corp. reorganized as Alta Industries Ltd. 09/13/1979

SALT LAKE TRANSPORTATION CO. (UT)
Proclaimed dissolved for failure to pay taxes in March, 1980

SALT LAKE UNION STOCK YARDS (UT)
Dissolved 8/14/68

SALTER STR FILMS LTD (NS)
Merged into Alliance Atlantis Communications Inc. 04/19/2001
Each share Common no par exchanged for (0.31) share Non-Vtg. Class B no par and $3.33 cash
(See Alliance Atlantis Communications Inc.)

SALTEX LOOMS, INC.
Dissolved in 1948
No stockholders' equity

SALTON INC (DE)
Name changed 01/13/1999
Name changed from Salton/Maxim Housewares, Inc. to Salton, Inc. 01/13/1999
Common 1¢ par split (3) for (2) by issuance of (0.5) additional share payable 07/28/1999 to holders of record 07/14/1999 Ex date - 07/29/1999
Acquired by Grill Acquisition Corp. 12/09/2008
Each share Common 1¢ par exchanged for $0.75 cash

SALTS TEXTILE MANUFACTURING CO. INC.
Property acquired by Blumenthal (Sidney) & Co. in 1928 which was merged into Burlington Industries, Inc. 11/6/61

SALTYS WHSE INC (FL)
Name changed EWorld Interactive, Inc. 01/10/2007
EWorld Interactive, Inc. recapitalized as Green Energy Renewable Solutions, Inc. 01/26/2012 which name changed to Cirque Energy, Inc. 07/01/2015

SALUDA LAND & LUMBER CO. (DE)
Merged into Greenville & Northern Railway Co. in 1952
Each share Preferred $100 par exchanged for (1) share Common $5 par
Each (100) shares Common no par exchanged for (1) share Common $5 par
(See Greenville & Northern Railway Co.)

SALUS RESOURCE CORP (BC)
Name changed to Brandon Gold Corp. 12/04/1996
Brandon Gold Corp. recapitalized as Redmond Ventures Corp. 09/16/1999 which recapitalized as Crown Point Ventures Ltd. (BC) 03/12/2002 which reincorporated in Alberta as Crown Point Energy Inc. 07/31/2012

SALVAGE & CONVERSION SYSTEMS, INC. (OK)
Completely liquidated 7/20/65
Each share Capital Stock $10 par exchanged for first and final distribution of (5) shares International Disposal Corp. Common $2 par
International Disposal Corp. charter cancelled 4/15/72

SALVAGE WORLD INC (DE)
Recapitalized as Solar Energy Ltd. 12/26/1997
Each share Common exchanged for (0.05) share Common $0.0001 par
(See Solar Energy Ltd.)

SALVATORI OPHTHALMICS INC (FL)
Common 1¢ par changed to $0.001 par and (9) additional shares issued 12/16/1988
Each share Common $0.001 par exchanged for (0.04) share Common 1¢ par 03/30/1990
Each share Common 1¢ par exchanged for (0.2) share Common 5¢ par 02/28/1992
Name changed to American Consolidated Laboratories, Inc. (FL) 09/15/1994
American Consolidated Laboratories, Inc. (FL) reorganized in Delaware as Strategic Global Investments, Inc. 06/01/2010

SALVEX RES LTD (BC)
Name changed to Brasil Gold Resources Ltd. 12/23/1988
Brasil Gold Resources Ltd. name changed to ARI Automated Recycling Inc. 10/05/1990 which recapitalized as Envipco Automated Recycling Inc. 11/01/1994 which name changed to Automated Recycling Inc. 08/20/1999 which name changed to OceanLake Commerce Inc. 03/01/2001

SAM & LIBBY INC (CA)
Name changed to Utopia Marketing Inc. (CA) 09/11/1996
Utopia Marketing Inc. (CA) reincorporated in Florida 08/03/1998 which recapitalized as Daytonabrands Inc. 09/19/2006
(See Daytonabrands Inc.)

SAM GOODY, INC. (NY)
See - Goody (Sam), Inc.

SAM HOUSTON LIFE INS CO (TX)
Merged into First Continental Life Group, Inc. 9/30/75
Each share Common no par exchanged for (0.136) share Common $1 par
(See First Continental Life Group, Inc.)

SAM P. WALLACE CO., INC. (TX)
See - Wallace (Sam P.) Co., Inc.

SAM SPORT SYS INC (AB)
Name changed to Samsports.com Inc. 12/24/99

SAMA GRAPHITE INC (CANADA)
Name changed to SRG Graphite Inc. 07/05/2017

SAMA RES INC (BC)
Reincorporated under the laws of Canada 05/21/2013

SAMANCOR LTD (SOUTH AFRICA)
ADR agreement terminated 12/21/98
Each ADR for Ordinary Rand-20 par exchanged for $7.594 cash

SAMANTHA GOLD N L (AUSTRALIA)
Name changed 01/18/1990
Name changed from Samantha Exploration N.L. to Samantha Gold N.L. 01/18/1990
Stock Dividend - 100% 09/25/1990
Name changed to Resolute Samantha Ltd. 08/15/1995
Resolute Samantha Ltd. name changed to Resolute Ltd. 11/29/1996
(See Resolute Ltd.)

SAMANTHA PETE CORP (UT)
Involuntarily dissolved 12/31/1984

SAMANTHA POLLARD INDUSTRIES, INC. (CO)
Charter cancelled for failure to file reports and pay taxes 10/19/74

SAMAR YELLOWKNIFE GOLD MINES LTD. (ON)
Succeeded by Oakridge Uranium Mines Ltd. share for share in 1950
Oakridge Uranium Mines Ltd. name changed to Oakridge Mining Corp. Ltd. in 1951
(See Oakridge Mining Corp. Ltd.)

SAMARAENERGO JSC (RUSSIA)
ADR agreement terminated 04/15/2011
Each Sponsored ADR for Preferred exchanged for $2.199492 cash
Each Sponsored ADR for Ordinary exchanged for $0.976948 cash

SAMARANTA MNG CORP (BC)
Recapitalized as Icon Exploration Inc. 10/28/2013
Each share Common no par exchanged for (0.2) share Common no par

SAMARASVYAZINFORM OPEN JT STK CO (RUSSIA)
ADR agreement terminated 7/21/2003
Each Sponsored ADR for Ordinary 130 Rubles par exchanged for $9.0243 cash

SAMARITAN PHARMACEUTICALS INC (NV)
Each share old Common $0.001 par exchanged for (1/6) share new Common $0.001 par 07/05/2007
SEC revoked common stock registration 08/15/2011

SAMARKAND RES INC (BC)
Recapitalized as Consolidated Samarkand Resources Inc. 04/05/1990
Each share Common no par exchanged for (0.5) share Common no par
Consolidated Samarkand Resources Inc. recapitalized as Soho Resources Corp. 10/15/1999 which recapitalized as Telson Resources Inc. 01/17/2013 which name changed to Telson Mining Corp. 02/21/2018

SAMARNAN INVT CORP (TX)
Liquidation completed

Each share Common $1 par exchanged for initial distribution of $10 cash 09/30/2009
Each share Common $1 par received second and final distribution of $5 cash payable 12/02/2009 to holders of record 09/30/2009

SAMBA GOLD INC (BC)
Recapitalized as Caerus Resource Corp. 02/26/2009
Each share Common no par exchanged for (1/6) share Common no par
Caerus Resource Corp. name changed to Angel Gold Corp. 10/04/2012

SAMBOS RESTAURANTS INC (CA)
Common no par split (5) for (4) by issuance of (0.25) additional share 1/30/70
Common no par split (3) for (2) by issuance of (0.5) additional share 7/15/71
Common no par split (3) for (2) by issuance of (0.5) additional share 2/3/72
Common no par split (3) for (2) by issuance of (0.5) additional share 1/15/73
Common no par split (5) for (4) by issuance of (0.25) additional share 1/16/74
Amended plan of reorganization under Chapter 11 Federal bankruptcy Code filed 6/24/85
No stockholders' equity

SAME DAY EXPRESS INC (FL)
Name changed to Innovative Shipping Systems, Inc. 09/04/1992
Innovative Shipping Systems, Inc. recapitalized as Velocity Aerospace, Inc. 11/04/2005 which name changed to Critical Power Solutions International, Inc. (FL) 08/08/2007 which reincorporated in Delaware as Critical Solutions, Inc. 03/03/2008

SAMENA RES CORP (AB)
Cease trade order 02/02/2010

SAMES CORP (DE)
Company filed a petition under Chapter 7 Federal Bankruptcy Code 8/17/2001
Stockholders' equity unlikely

SAMEX MNG CORP (BC)
Ceased operations 08/21/2013

SAMIA VENTURES INC (BC)
Delisted from Vancouver Stock Exchange 03/02/1998

SAMMY CORP (JAPAN)
Sponsored ADR's for Common split (3) for (2) by issuance of (0.5) additional ADR payable 03/05/2004 to holders of record 12/30/2003 Ex date - 12/24/2003
Merged into Sega Sammy Holdings Inc. 10/04/2004
Each Sponsored ADR for Common exchanged for (2) Sponsored ADR's for Common

SAMNA CORP (GA)
Merged into North Subsidiary Corp. 12/17/1990
Each share Common 1¢ par exchanged for $18.84 cash

SAMOS RES LTD (BC)
Name changed to Dimples Group Inc. 9/7/90
(See Dimples Group Inc.)

SAMOSET COTTON MILLS
Bankrupt in 1943

SAMOTH CAP CORP (ON)
Name changed to Sterling Financial Corp. 06/14/2000
Sterling Financial Corp. name changed to Sterling Centrecorp Inc. 06/08/2001
(See Sterling Centrecorp Inc.)

SAMOYED ENERGY CORP (NV)
Common $0.001 par split (7.3) for (1) by issuance of (6.3) additional shares payable 12/17/2007 to holders of record 12/14/2007 Ex date - 12/18/2007
Name changed to Advanced Voice Recognition Systems, Inc. 06/19/2008

SAMPLING RESH CORP (NY)
Name changed to Cable Holdings Inc. 08/19/1975
(See Cable Holdings Inc.)

SAMPSON CORP (PA)
Name changed to T.S.C. Liquidating Corp. 12/27/1977
(See T.S.C. Liquidating Corp.)

SAMPSON MILLER ASSD COS INC (PA)
Merged into Oxford First Corp. (PA) 06/28/1972
Each share Common $1 par exchanged for (0.22888) share Common $1 par
(See Oxford First Corp. (PA))

SAMRUDDHI CEM LTD (INDIA)
Merged into UltraTech Cement Ltd. 08/01/2010
Each Sponsored ADR for Equity exchanged for (0.28571428) Sponsored Reg. S GDR for Equity

SAMS (HOWARD W.) & CO., INC. (IN)
Stock Dividend - 10% 10/23/64
5% Preferred $50 par called for redemption 4/1/64
Completely liquidated 10/31/66
Each share Common $1 par exchanged for first and final distribution of (0.236) share International Telephone & Telegraph Corp. (MD) Conv. Part. Preference $10 par and (0.423) share Common no par
International Telephone & Telegraph Corp. (MD) reincorporated in Delaware 1/31/68 which name changed to ITT Corp. 12/31/83 which reorganized in Indiana as ITT Industries Inc. 12/19/95 which name changed to ITT Corp. 7/1/2006

SAMS ONLINE INC (ON)
Recapitalized as Thistletown Capital Inc. (ON) 02/14/2002
Each share Common no par exchanged for (0.14285714) share Common no par
Thistletown Capital Inc. (ON) reincorporated in Alberta as Kelso Energy Inc. 07/14/2003 which recapitalized as COSTA Energy Inc. 04/28/2006 which recapitalized as Artek Exploration Ltd. 01/20/2010 which merged into Kelt Exploration Ltd. 04/21/2015

SAMS SEAFOOD HLDGS LTD (AUSTRALIA)
ADR agreement terminated 09/19/2011
Each Sponsored ADR for Ordinary exchanged for $0.020716 cash

SAMSON CONVERTIBLE SECURITIES & CAPITAL FUND, INC. (DE)
Merged into Samson Fund, Inc. 06/28/1963
Each share Common $1 par exchanged for (6.7771) shares Common $1 par
Samson Fund, Inc. name changed to Fundamatic Investors, Inc. 02/25/1971
(See Fundamatic Investors, Inc.)

SAMSON CORDAGE WKS (MA)
Recapitalized 02/15/1967
Each VTC for Common no par exchanged for (10) VTC's for Common $1 par
Each share Common no par exchanged for (10) shares Common $1 par
Common $1 par and VTC's for Common $1 par split (10) for (1) by issuance of (9) additional shares respectively 05/12/1975
Name changed to Samson Ocean Systems, Inc. 03/15/1976
Samson Ocean Systems, Inc. liquidated for Enserch Corp. 06/05/1978 which merged into Texas Utilities Co. 08/05/1997 which reorganized as Texas Utilities Co. (Holding Co.) 08/05/1997 which name changed to TXU Corp. 05/16/2000
(See TXU Corp.)

SAMSON CORP.
Dissolved in 1939

SAMSON ENERGY CO LTD PARTNERSHIP (OK)
Merged into Samson Properties Inc. 12/9/94
Each Depositary Unit exchanged for $11.50 cash

SAMSON ENERGY CORP (BC)
Merged into Kala Exploration Ltd. 9/10/82
Each share Common no par exchanged for (0.2) share Class A Common no par
Kala Exploration Ltd. recapitalized as Kala Feedlots Ltd. 1/6/87 which name changed to Kala Canada Ltd. 3/27/89
(See Kala Canada Ltd.)

SAMSON EXPL N L (AUSTRALIA)
Each old ADR for Ordinary A$1.20 par exchanged for (0.1) new ADR for Ordinary A$1.20 par 12/17/1998
ADR agreement terminated 02/28/2005
Each new ADR for Ordinary A$1.20 par exchanged for $1.31965 cash

SAMSON FD INC (DE)
Name changed to Fundamatic Investors, Inc. 02/25/1971
(See Fundamatic Investors, Inc.)

SAMSON GOLD CORP (BC)
Name changed to Kinghorn Energy Corp. 09/20/1989
Kinghorn Energy Corp. recapitalized as Kinghorn Petroleum Corp. 04/30/1991 which recapitalized as Triple 8 Energy Corp. (BC) 11/17/1992 which reincorporated in Alberta 02/24/1994 which name changed to Oilexco Inc. 03/01/1994 which recapitalized as ScotOil Petroleum Ltd. (AB) 06/09/2011 reincorporated in British Columbia as 0915988 B.C. Ltd. 07/27/2011
(See 0915988 B.C. Ltd.)

SAMSON HEALTHCARE CORP (AB)
Recapitalized as Samena Resources Corp. 09/28/2007
Each share Common no par exchanged for (0.1) share Common no par
(See Samena Resources Corp.)

SAMSON MINES LTD (BC)
Recapitalized as Anglo Pacific Explorations Ltd. 4/27/73
Each share Capital Stock $1 par exchanged for (0.2) share Capital Stock no par
(See Anglo Pacific Explorations Ltd.)

SAMSON OCEAN SYS INC (MA)
Voting Trust Agreement terminated 07/26/1974
Each VTC for Common $1 par automatically became (1) share Common $1 par
Stock Dividend - 50% 04/05/1976
Completely liquidated 06/05/1978
Each share Common $1 par exchanged for first and final distribution of (0.658155) share Enserch Corp. Common $6.66-2/3 par
Enserch Corp. merged into Texas Utilities Co. 08/05/1997 which reorganized as Texas Utilities Co. (Holding Co.) 08/05/1997 which name changed to TXU Corp. 05/16/2000
(See TXU Corp.)

SAMSON RLTY & DEV CORP (FL)
Proclaimed dissolved for failure to file reports and pay fees 08/26/1994

SAMSON TECHNOLOGIES INC (AB)
Name changed to Samson Healthcare Corp. 02/13/1998
Samson Healthcare Corp. recapitalized as Samena Resources Corp. 09/28/2007
(See Samena Resources Corp.)

SAMSON TIRE & RUBBER CORP.
Dissolved in 1939

SAMSON UNITED CORP. (DE)
Recapitalized 00/00/1937
Each share Preferred no par exchanged for (10) shares Common $1 par
Each share Common no par exchanged for (1) share Common $1 par Declared insolvent 00/00/1953
Details not available

SAMSON URANIUM INC. (CO)
Charter revoked for failure to file reports and pay fees 10/28/59

SAMSONITE CORP (CO)
Common $1 par changed to no par and (9) additional shares issued 12/15/1969
8% Preferred $100 par called for redemption 12/31/1972
Name changed to S.C. Liquidating Co. 08/27/1973
(See S.C. Liquidating Co.)

SAMSONITE CORP NEW (DE)
Each share 13-7/8% Sr. Exchangeable Preferred exchanged for (0.240036) share Restricted Conv. Preferred and (614.29) shares Common 1¢ par 07/31/2003
Stock Dividends - in Preferred to holders of Preferred 3.46875% payable 06/15/2001 to holders of record 06/01/2001; 3.46875% payable 09/15/2001 to holders of record 09/01/2001 Ex date - 09/19/2001; 3.46875% payable 12/15/2001 to holders of record 12/01/2001 Ex date - 12/20/2001
Merged into CVC Capital Partners Ltd. 10/25/2007
Each share Common 1¢ par exchanged for $1.49 cash

SAMSUNG C&T CORP (KOREA)
Name changed 03/22/1993
Name changed 05/08/2008
Name changed from Samsung Ltd. to Samsung Corp. 03/22/1993
Name changed from Samsung Corp. to Samsung C&T Corp. 05/08/2008
GDR agreement terminated 08/21/2015
Each 144A GDR for Non-Vtg. Shares exchanged for $16.111303 cash
Each 144A GDR for Common exchanged for $23.631092 cash

SAMSUNG DISPLAY DEVICES LTD (KOREA)
Name changed to Samsung SDI Co., Ltd. 02/24/2000

SAMSUNG ENGR & CONSTR LTD (KOREA)
Merged into Samsung Corp. 12/00/1995
Details not available

SAMSYS TECHNOLOGIES INC (CANADA)
Reincorporated 03/27/2002
Place of incorporation changed from (ONT) to Canada 03/27/2002
Placed in receivership 04/07/2006
Stockholders' equity unlikely

SAMUEL (PAUL) ASSOCIATES, INC. (NJ)
See - Paul Samuel Assoc Inc

SAMUEL HAMANN GRAPHIX INC (NV)
Each share old Common $0.001 par exchanged for (0.33333333) share new Common $0.001 par 08/14/1996
Name changed to Transformation Processing, Inc. 10/03/1996
Transformation Processing, Inc. name changed to eAutoclaims.com, Inc. 06/05/2000 which name changed to eAutoclaims, Inc. 07/29/2004
(See eAutoclaims, Inc.)

SAMUEL MANU TECH INC (ON)
Common no par split (2) for (1) by issuance of (1) additional share 05/15/1995
Common no par split (2) for (1) by issuance of (1) additional share payable 05/15/1998 to holders of record 05/11/1998 Ex date - 05/07/1998
Merged into Samuel, Son & Co., Ltd. 09/09/2010
Each share Common no par exchanged for $7.50 cash

SAMUELS JEWELERS INC (DE)
Plan of reorganization under Chapter 11 Federal Bankruptcy Code effective 5/28/2004
No stockholders' equity

SAMURAI CAP CORP (BC)
Name changed to Huaxing Machinery Corp. 01/26/2011

SAMURAI ENERGY CORP (DE)
Common $0.001 par split (3) for (1) by issuance of (2) additional shares payable 07/31/2006 to holders of record 07/24/2006 Ex date - 08/01/2006
Reincorporated under the laws of Nevada as ECCO Energy Corp. 09/01/2006
ECCO Energy Corp. recapitalized as Eagle Ford Oil & Gas, Corp. 07/27/2010

SAN ANDREAS RES CORP (BC)
Common no par split (2) for (1) by issuance of (1) additional share 08/21/1992
Name changed to Canadian Zinc Corp. 05/25/1999
Canadian Zinc Corp. name changed to NorZinc Ltd. 09/11/2018

SAN ANGELO NATL BK (SAN ANGELO, TX)
Each share Capital Stock $100 par exchanged for (10) shares Capital Stock $10 par plus a 50% stock dividend paid 08/27/1957
Stock Dividends - 16-2/3% 07/25/1958; 14-2/7% 04/30/1959; 10% 01/18/1963
Merged into Texas Commerce Bancshares, Inc. 01/01/1973
Each share Capital Stock $10 par exchanged for (1.3333) shares Special Preferred Ser. A $10 par
Texas Commerce Bancshares, Inc. acquired by Chemical New York Corp. 05/01/1987 which name changed to Chemical Banking Corp. 04/29/1988 which name changed to Chase Manhattan Corp. (New) 03/31/1996 which name changed to J.P. Morgan Chase & Co. 12/31/2000 which name changed to JPMorgan Chase & Co. 07/20/2004

SAN ANGELO OIL LTD (BC)
Each share old Common no par exchanged for (0.1) share new Common no par 05/26/2016
Recapitalized as Cabral Gold Inc. 11/02/2017
Each share new Common no par exchanged for (0.2) share Common no par

SAN ANTON CAP INC (CANADA)
Recapitalized as Edleun Group, Inc. 05/27/2010
Each share Class A Common no par exchanged for (0.5) share Class A Common no par
Edleun Group, Inc. name changed to BrightPath Early Learning Inc. 08/07/2013
(See BrightPath Early Learning Inc.)

SAN ANTON RESOURCE CORP (CANADA)
Merged into Kings Minerals NL 09/29/2010
Each share Common no par exchanged for (2.5) shares Ordinary no par
Note: Unexchanged certificates were cancelled and became without value 09/29/2016
Kings Minerals NL name changed to Cerro Resources NL 12/10/2010
(See Cerro Resources NL)

SAN ANTONIO BUILDING MATERIALS CO.
Assets sold in 1934

SAN ANTONIO CORP (DE)
Voting Trust Agreement terminated 08/31/1967
Each Part. Ctf. $1 par exchanged for (1) share Common $1 par
Liquidation completed
Each share Common $1 par exchanged for initial distribution of $15 cash 07/19/1968
Each share Common $1 par received second distribution of $0.84 cash 05/29/1969
Each share Common $1 par received third and final distribution of $2.50 cash 10/08/1970

SAN ANTONIO EXPLS LTD (AB)
Reincorporated 06/04/1982
Place of incorporation changed from (BC) to (ALTA) 06/04/1982
Acquired by Wellore Resources Ltd. 00/00/1987
Details not available

SAN ANTONIO GOLD MINES LTD (MB)
Adjudicated bankrupt 07/05/1968
No stockholders' equity

SAN ANTONIO MACHINE & SUPPLY CO. (TX)
Adjudicated bankrupt 1/8/65
No stockholders' equity

SAN ANTONIO MILAM BUILDING, INC. (TX)
Out of business 00/00/1948
Details not available

SAN ANTONIO MINES LTD.
Succeeded by San Antonio Gold Mines Ltd. on a (1) for (3) basis 00/00/1931
(See San Antonio Gold Mines Ltd.)

SAN ANTONIO NATIONAL BANK (SAN ANTONIO, TX)
Name changed to First National Bank (San Antonio, Tex.) 6/12/45
First National Bank (San Antonio, Tex.) merged into First International Bancshares, Inc. 6/19/81 which name changed to InterFirst Corp. 12/31/81 which merged into First RepublicBank Corp. 6/6/87
(See First RepublicBank Corp.)

SAN ANTONIO TRANSIT CO. (DE)
Common $1 par exchanged (20) for (1) in 1947
Name changed to San Antonio Corp. 10/1/59
(See San Antonio Corp.)

SAN ANTONIO VENTURES INC (BC)
Recapitalized as Renaissance Oil Corp. 09/16/2014
Each share Common no par exchanged for (0.5) share Common no par

SAN ANTONIOS RES INC (BC)
Each share old Common no par exchanged for (0.16666666) share new Common no par 10/30/2001
Name changed to Global Precision Medical, Inc. (BC) 10/14/2002
Global Precision Medical Inc. (BC) reincorporated in Wyoming 02/05/2003
(See Global Precision Medical Inc.)

SAN BAR CORP (CA)
Common no par split (3) for (2) by issuance of (0.5) additional share 8/5/81
Stock Dividend - 50% 11/28/75
Merged into Resdel Industries 9/15/87
Each share Common no par exchanged for (1) share Common 50¢ par
(See Resdel Industries)

SAN/BAR ELECTRONICS CORP. (CA)
Name changed to San/Bar Corp. 11/5/71
San/Bar Corp. merged into Resdel Industries 9/15/87
(See Resdel Industries)

SAN BENITO BK (HOLLISTER, CA)
Common no par split (2) for (1) by issuance of (1) additional share payable 07/07/1998 to holders of record 06/17/1998
Stock Dividend - 10% payable 04/15/1998 to holders of record 03/16/1998
Merged into Pacific Capital Bancorp (New) (CA) 07/31/2000
Each share Common no par exchanged for (0.605) share Common no par
Pacific Capital Bancorp (New) (CA) reorganized in Delaware 12/29/2010
(See Pacific Capital Bancorp (New))

SAN CARLOS MILLING CO. LTD. (HI)
Capital Stock $10 par changed to $8 par in 1938
Acquired by San Carlos Milling Co., Inc. 12/31/57
Each share Capital Stock $8 par exchanged for (1) share Common P16 par

SAN CARLOS MLG INC (PHILIPPINES)
Stock Dividends - 25% 8/27/59; 25% 10/25/62; 100% 6/8/65; 50% 8/23/68; 20% 5/21/73; 38.8889% 10/3/75; 20% 5/10/76; 20% 2/28/80
Assets foreclosed upon in 2000
Stockholders' equity unlikely

SAN CLEMENTE BANCORP (CA)
Each share Common no par exchanged for (0.000005) share Common no par 10/11/1989
Note: In effect holders received $1.25 cash per share and public interest was eliminated

SAN DIEGO BANCORP (CA)
Each share old Common no par exchanged for (0.025) share new Common no par 08/10/1993
Name changed to Applied Earth Technologies Inc. 08/22/1996
Applied Earth Technologies Inc. name changed to Diatect International Corp. 06/05/1998
(See Diatect International Corp.)

SAN DIEGO CHARGERS, INC. (CA)
Liquidation completed
Each share Common no par exchanged for initial distribution of $0.96 cash 6/1/63
Each share Common no par received second distribution of $0.78 cash 4/10/64
Each share Common no par received third distribution of $0.78 cash 4/1/65
Each share Common no par received fourth and final distribution of $0.78 cash 4/1/66

SAN DIEGO CMNTY BK (CHULA VISTA, CA)
Each share Common no par exchanged for (0.2) share new Common no par 7/15/2005
Acquired by First Banks, Inc. (MO) 8/31/2006
Each share new Common no par exchanged for $9 cash

SAN DIEGO CONSOLIDATED GAS & ELECTRIC CO.
Name changed to San Diego Gas & Electric Co. in 1940
San Diego Gas & Electric Co. reorganized as Enova Corp. 1/2/96 which merged into Sempra Energy 6/26/98

SAN DIEGO CORP. (DE)
Merged into Atlas Corp. 05/31/1956
Each share Common $1 par exchanged for (2.4) shares Common $1 par
(See Atlas Corp.)

SAN DIEGO COUNTY WATER CO.
Sold to Vista Irrigation District 00/00/1946
Details not available

SAN DIEGO FINL CORP (CA)
Acquired by First Interstate Bancorp 03/18/1994
Each share Common no par exchanged for (11.26968) shares Common $2 par
First Interstate Bancorp merged into Wells Fargo & Co. (Old) 04/01/1996 which merged into Wells Fargo & Co. (New) 11/02/1998

SAN DIEGO GAS & ELEC CO (CA)
5.60% Preferred $20 par called for redemption 01/15/1963
Common 10 par changed to $5 par and (1) additional share issued 05/28/1968
$4.65 Preference no par called for redemption 11/01/1986
$2.68 Preference no par called for redemption 01/19/1987
$9.84 Preference no par called for redemption 01/19/1987
Common $5 par changed to no par 05/28/1987
$15.44 Preference no par called for redemption 06/01/1988
Common no par split (2) for (1) by issuance of (1) additional share 05/27/1992
$2.475 Preference no par called for redemption 10/05/1992
$8.25 Preferred no par called for redemption 10/05/1992
$9.125 Preference no par called for redemption 10/05/1992
$7.05 Preference no par called for redemption 10/21/1992
$7.80 Preference no par called for redemption 09/07/1993
Under plan of reorganization each share Common no par automatically became (1) share Enova Corp. Common no par 01/02/1996
$7.20 Preferred no par called for redemption 01/15/1996
Enova Corp. merged into Sempra Energy 06/26/1998
$1.7625 Preference no par called for redemption at $25 on 01/15/2008
$1.70 Preference no par called for redemption at $25 plus $0.425 accrued dividends on 10/15/2013
$1.82 Preference no par called for redemption at $25 on 10/15/2013
4.40% Preferred $20 par called for redemption at $21 on 10/15/2013
4.50% Preferred $20 par called for redemption at $21.20 on 10/15/2013
4.60% Preferred $20 par called for redemption at $20.25 plus $0.23 accrued dividends on 10/15/2013
5% Preferred $20 par called for redemption at $24 on 10/15/2013

SAN DIEGO GAS & PETROLEUM CORP. (CA)
Charter suspended for non-payment of taxes 01/06/1941

SAN DIEGO ICE & COLD STORAGE CO.
Merged into California Cold Storage & Distributing Co. in 1947
Each share Class A exchanged for (1) share Preferred
Each share Class B exchanged for (1) share Common

SAN DIEGO IMPERIAL CORP. (CA)
5-1/2% Preferred called for redemption 9/23/59
Name changed to Imperial Corp. of America (CA) 5/31/66
Imperial Corp. of America (CA) reincorporated in Delaware 9/21/87
(See Imperial Corp. of America (DE))

SAN DIEGO PRIVATE BK (CORONADO, CA)
Under plan of reorganization each share Common no par automatically became (1) share Private Bancorp of America, Inc. Common no par 12/03/2015

SAN DIEGO PROFESSIONAL ASSOCIATION (CA)
Name changed to Medical Growth Industries 12/3/68
Medical Growth Industries name changed to National Community Builders 8/26/71
(See National Community Builders)

SAN DIEGO SCIENTIFIC CORP. (CA)
Recapitalized as Electra Systems Corp. 05/10/1961
Each share Common exchanged for (0.1) share Common
(See Electra Systems Corp.)

SAN DIEGO SOCCER DEV CORP (NV)
Name changed to International Sports & Media Group, Inc. 1/2/2004
International Sports & Media Group, Inc. name changed to US Farms, Inc. 7/17/2006

SAN DIEGO TR & SVGS BK (SAN DIEGO, CA)
Capital Stock $25 par changed to $50 par 5/7/59
Capital Stock $50 par changed to $100 par 7/3/67
Capital Stock $100 par changed to $4 par and (24) additional shares issued 12/16/70
Under plan of reorganization each share Capital Stock $4 par automatically became (1) share San Diego Financial Corp. Common no par 1/7/72
San Diego Financial Corp. acquired by First Interstate Bancorp 3/18/94 which merged into Wells Fargo & Co. (Old) 4/1/96 which name changed to Wells Fargo & Co. (New) 11/2/98

SAN DIEGO TR BK (SAN DIEGO, CA)
Common no par split (3) for (2) by issuance of (0.5) additional share payable 05/13/2005 to holders of record 04/26/2005 Ex date - 05/16/2005
Stock Dividends - 3% payable 04/29/2011 to holders of record 03/31/2011 Ex date - 03/29/2011; 3% payable 04/30/2012 to holders of record 03/31/2012 Ex date - 03/28/2012
Merged into Pacific Premier Bancorp, Inc. 06/25/2013
Each share Common no par exchanged for (0.64929601) share Common 1¢ par and $5.59396809 cash

SAN DIEGO WATER SUPPLY CO.
Dissolved in 1940

SAN DOH COPPER MINES LTD (BC)
Recapitalized as Fourbar Mines Ltd. 10/16/1970
Each share Capital Stock no par exchanged for (1) share Capital Stock no par
Fourbar Mines Ltd. recapitalized as Cloverdale Resources Ltd. 03/00/1973
(See Cloverdale Resources Ltd.)

SAN DOH MINES LTD (BC)
Recapitalized as San Doh Copper Mines Ltd. 08/03/1970
Each share Capital Stock 50¢ par exchanged for (0.25) share Capital Stock no par
San Doh Copper Mines Ltd. recapitalized as Fourbar Mines Ltd. 10/16/1970 which recapitalized as Cloverdale Resources Ltd. 03/00/1973
(See Cloverdale Resources Ltd.)

SAN FERNANDO ELEC MFG CO (CA)
Stock Dividend - 50% 5/15/80
Name changed to SFE Technologies 6/18/80
(See SFE Technologies)

SAN FERNANDO MNG LTD (BC)
Reincorporated under the laws of Canada as KeyWest Energy Corp. 05/14/1998
(See KeyWest Energy Corp.)

SAN FERNANDO VALLEY BANK (PACOIMA, CA)
Stock Dividend - 10% 02/11/1963
Name changed to Trans-World Bank (Sherman Oaks, CA) 12/29/1967
Trans-World Bank (Sherman Oaks, CA) reorganized as Transworld Bancorp 10/01/1982
(See Transworld Bancorp)

SAN FRANCISCO, NAPA & CALISTOGA RAILWAY
Succeeded by San Francisco & Napa Valley Railroad in 1936 liquidation of which was completed 2/16/59

SAN FRANCISCO & MCKITTRICK OIL CO.
Acquired by Tide Water Associated Oil Co. 00/00/1926
Details not available

SAN FRANCISCO & NAPA VALLEY RAILROAD (CA)
Liquidation completed 2/16/59

SAN FRANCISCO & OAKLAND HELICOPTER AIRLS INC (CA)
Recapitalized 02/19/1965
Each share Class A $10 par exchanged for (3) shares Common Capital Stock no par
Each share Common 10¢ par exchanged for (1) share Common Capital Stock no par
Declared insolvent by bankruptcy Court 03/30/1973
Under Court arrangement reorganized as SFO Helicopter Airlines, Inc. 06/25/1973
Only debentureholders participated
No stockholders' equity

SAN FRANCISCO BANCORP (CA)
Acquired by Atlantic Financial Federal 07/12/1984
Each share Common no par exchanged for $8.50 cash

SAN FRANCISCO BANK (SAN FRANCISCO, CA)
Each share Capital Stock $1000 par exchanged for (500) shares Capital Stock $12.50 par in 1954
Name changed to First Western Bank & Trust Co. (San Francisco, CA) 11/5/54
First Western Bank & Trust Co. (San Francisco, CA) merged into United California Bank (Los Angeles, CA) 2/24/61 which merged into Western Bancorporation 1/16/78 which name changed to First Interstate Bancorp 6/1/81 which merged into Wells Fargo & Co. (Old) 4/1/96 which merged into Wells Fargo & Co. (New) 11/2/98

SAN FRANCISCO BAY TOLL BRIDGE CO. (DE)
Reorganized in 1941
No stockholders' equity
Acquired by California Toll Bridge Authority and liquidated in 1951

SAN FRANCISCO BOUTIQUES INC (CANADA)
Class A Multiple no par split (2) for (1) by issuance of (1) additional share payable 07/06/1998 to holders of record 07/06/1998
Class B Subordinate no par split (2) for (1) by issuance of (1) additional share payable 07/06/1998 to holders of record 07/06/1998
Name changed to Groupe Les Ailes de la Mode Inc. and Class A Multiple no par and Class B Subordinate no par reclassified as Common no par 08/02/2004
Groupe Les Ailes de la Mode Inc. name changed to Groupe Bikini Village Inc. 01/24/2006
(See Groupe Bikini Village Inc.)

SAN FRANCISCO BREWING CORP. (CA)
Each share Capital Stock $10 par or VTC for Capital Stock $10 par exchanged for (3) shares Capital Stock $5 par or (3) VTC's for Capital Stock $5 par respectively to effect a (2) for (1) split and 50% stock dividend 07/28/1955
Name changed to Burgermeister Brewing Corp. 01/02/1957
Burgermeister Brewing Corp. name changed to San Francisco Liquidating Co. 12/29/1961
(See San Francisco Liquidating Co.)

SAN FRANCISCO CO (DE)
Merged into First Banks, Inc. 01/02/2001
Each share 8% Conv. Preferred Ser. B 1¢ par exchanged for approximately $7 cash
Each share Class A Common 1¢ par exchanged for approximately $1.95 cash

SAN FRANCISCO FED SVGS & LN ASSN CALIF (USA)
Under plan of reorganization each share Common 1¢ par automatically became (1) share SFFed Corp. (DE) Common 1¢ par 07/01/1988
(See SFFed Corp.)

SAN FRANCISCO LIFE INSURANCE CO. (CA)
Merged into Philadelphia Life Insurance Co. 11/29/68
Each share Common $1 par exchanged for (0.4111) share Capital Stock $1 par
Philadelphia Life Insurance Co. merged into Tenneco Inc. 3/1/78 which merged into El Paso Natural Gas Co. 12/12/96 which reorganized as El Paso Energy Corp. 8/1/98 which name changed to El Paso Corp. 2/5/2001

SAN FRANCISCO LIQUIDATING CO. (CA)
Liquidation completed
Each share Capital Stock $5 par or VTC for Capital Stock $5 par exchanged for initial distribution of $17 cash 1/25/62
Each share Capital Stock $5 par or VTC for Capital Stock $5 par received second and final distribution of $0.36 cash 10/5/67

SAN FRANCISCO MINES OF MEXICO LTD. (ENGLAND)
Merged into Bay Hall Trust Ltd. 04/04/1967
Each share Capital Stock 10s par exchanged for (0.9) share Ordinary Stock 10s par
(See Bay Hall Trust Ltd.)

SAN FRANCISCO NATIONAL BANK (SAN FRANCISCO, CA)
Bank closed by the U.S. Controller of the Currency 1/22/65
Stock declared worthless 12/31/66
No Stockholders' equity

SAN FRANCISCO REAL ESTATE INVS INC (DE)
Name changed 06/30/1983
Name changed from San Francisco Real Estate Investors (CA) to San Francisco Real Estate Investors, Inc. (DE) and Shares of Bene. Int. $1 par reclassified as Common $1 par 06/30/1983
Under plan of merger each share Common $1 par automatically became (1) share REIT of America, Inc. Common $1 par 10/04/1983
REIT of America, Inc. merged into Unicorp American Corp. (New) 12/13/1984
(See Unicorp American Corp. (New))

SAN FRANCISCO REMEDIAL LOAN ASSOCIATON LTD.
Liquidation completed in 1954

SAN GABRIEL PIGMENT CO. INC. (CA)
Charter suspended for failure to file reports and pay fees 03/12/1951

SAN GABRIEL RIVER IMPT CO (CA)
Liquidation completed
Each share Common $10 par exchanged for initial distribution of $300 cash 09/10/1981
Each share Common $10 par received second and final distribution of $1.0267 cash 12/08/1982

SAN GABRIEL VY BK (EL MONTE, CA)
Merged into Pacific Business Bank (Carson, CA) 00/00/1997
Details not available

SAN GOLD CORP (MB)
Deemed to have made an assignment in bankruptcy 06/23/2015
Stockholders' equity unlikely

SAN GOLD RES CORP (MB)
Merged into San Gold Corp. 06/30/2005
Each share Common no par exchanged for (1) share Common no par
(See San Gold Corp.)

SAN GORGONIO ELECTRIC CORP.
Assets acquired by California Electric Power Co. in 1949
Each share Preferred exchanged for (16) shares Common
Each share Common exchanged for (2) shares new Common
California Electric Power Co. merged into Southern California Edison Co. 12/31/63 which reorganized as SCEcorp 7/1/88

SAN HLDGS INC (CO)
Each share old Common no par exchanged for (0.04) share new Common no par 06/29/2007
Filed a petition under Chapter 7 Bankruptcy Code 11/26/2007
No stockholders' equity

SAN JACINTO EXPLS LTD (BC)
Recapitalized as Canbec Resources Ltd. 07/14/1980
Each share Common no par exchanged for (0.2) share Common no par
(See Canbec Resources Ltd.)

SAN JACINTO NATIONAL BANK (HOUSTON, TX)
Merged into Second National Bank (Houston, TX) 00/00/1944
Each share Common exchanged for (3) shares Common $20 par
Second National Bank (Houston, TX) name changed to Bank of the Southwest N.A. (Houston, TX) 01/20/1956 which reorganized as Southwest Bancshares, Inc. 12/10/1970 which merged into MCorp 10/11/1984
(See MCorp)

SAN JACINTO PETROLEUM CORP. (DE)
Merged into Continental Oil Co. (DE) on a (1/6) for (1) basis 1/31/64
Continental Oil Co. (DE) name changed to Conoco Inc. 7/2/79 which was acquired by Du Pont (E.I.) De Nemours & Co. 9/30/81

SAN JACINTO ST BK (PASADENA, TX)
Common $5 par changed to $3 par and (0.666) additional share issued 06/19/1970
Stock Dividend - 20% 02/28/1970
Merged into First International Bancshares, Inc. 10/02/1979
Each share Common $3 par exchanged for (1.33) shares Common $5 par
First International Bancshares, Inc. name changed to InterFirst Corp. 12/31/1981 which merged into First RepublicBank Corp. 06/06/1987
(See First RepublicBank Corp.)

SAN JOAQUIN BANCORP (CA)
Stock Dividend - 10% payable 03/17/2008 to holders of record 02/28/2008 Ex date - 02/26/2008
Company's sole asset placed in receivership 10/16/2009
Stockholders' equity unlikely

SAN JOAQUIN BK (BAKERSFIELD, CA)
Under plan of reorganization each share Common no par automatically became (1) share San Joaquin Bancorp 07/31/2006
(See San Joaquin Bancorp)

SAN JOAQUIN LIGHT & POWER CORP.
Acquired by Pacific Gas & Electric Co. 00/00/1944
Details not available

SAN JOAQUIN RES INC (NV)
Name changed to Gasco Energy, Inc. 03/05/2001
(See Gasco Energy, Inc.)

SAN JOAQUIN VALLEY NATL BK (TULARE, CA)
Merged into American National Bank (Bakersfield, CA) 3/12/72
Each share Capital Stock $10 par exchanged for (1.2) share Common $3.75 par
American National Bank (Bakersfield, CA) reorganized as Central Pacific Corp. 9/15/81 which was acquired by Wells Fargo & Co. (Old) 3/31/90 which merged into Wells Fargo & Co. (New) 11/2/98

SAN JOSE INTL INC (DE)
Each share old Common $0.0001 par exchanged for (16.5) shares new Common $0.0001 par 06/08/2004
Name changed to GammaCan International Inc. 08/24/2004
(See GammaCan International Inc.)

SAN JOSE NATIONAL BANK (SAN JOSE, CA)
Under plan of reorganization each share Capital $5 automatically became (1) share SJNB Financial Corp. 02/01/1984
SJNB Financial Corp. merged into Greater Bay Bancorp 10/23/2001 which merged into Wells Fargo & Co. 10/01/2007

SAN JOSE SVGS & LN ASSN (CA)
Each share Guarantee Stock $100 par exchanged for (20) shares Guarantee Stock $5 par 04/28/1970

Charter suspended for failure to file reports and pay fees 01/03/1984

SAN JOSE WTR CO (CA)
5.25% Conv. Preferred Ser. F $25 par called for redemption 03/23/1982
Under plan of reorganization each share 4.75% Preferred Ser. A $25 par, 4.75% Conv. Preferred Ser. B $25 par, 4.7% Conv. Preferred Ser. C $25 par, 4.7% Preferred Ser. D $25 par, 5.5% Preferred Ser. E $25 par and Common $6.25 par automatically became (1) share SJW Corp. (CA) 4.75% Preferred Ser. A $25 par, 4.75% Conv. Preferred Ser. B $25 par, 4.7% Conv. Preferred Ser. C $25 par, 4.7% Preferred Ser. D $25 par, 5.5% Preferred Ser. E $25 par and Common $6.25 par respectively 07/15/1985
SJW Corp. (CA) reincorporated in Delaware as SJW Group 11/16/2016

SAN JOSE WATER WORKS (CA)
Common $25 par changed to $12.50 par and (1) additional share issued 03/18/1959
Common $12.50 par changed to $6.25 par and (1) additional share issued 04/01/1977
Name changed to San Jose Water Co. 03/16/1983
San Jose Water Co. reorganized as SJW Corp. (CA) 07/16/1985 which reincorporated in Delaware as SJW Group 11/16/2016

SAN JUAN FIBERGLASS POOLS INC (CA)
Company reported out of business 00/00/1989
Details not available

SAN JUAN FINL HLDG CO (WA)
Name changed 05/08/2002
Name changed from San Juan Bank Holding Co. to San Juan Financial Holding Co. 05/08/2002
Acquired by Banner Corp. 05/01/2007
Each share Common $1 par exchanged for (2.2503) shares Common 1¢ par and $16.48 cash

SAN JUAN INTL INC (DE)
Name changed to Adtegrity.com International, Inc. and (24.7) additional shares issued 4/24/2000

SAN JUAN MNG & DEV CO (CO)
Each share Common 1¢ par exchanged for (0.2) share Common 5¢ par 04/10/1954
Name changed to St. Mary's Glacier, Inc. 08/28/1972
St. Mary's Glacier, Inc. name changed to Utah Coal & Chemicals Corp. (CO) 09/09/1977 which reincorporated in Nevada 04/16/1979 which recapitalized as Lifestream Technologies Inc. 02/11/1994
(See Lifestream Technologies Inc.)

SAN JUAN RACING ASSOCIATION, INC. SHAREHOLDERS' LIQUIDATING TRUST (PR)
Liquidation completed
Each Trust Unit received initial distribution of $17.66 cash 2/16/90
Each Trust Unit received second distribution of $0.40 cash 1/4/91
Each Trust Unit received third distribution of $0.90 cash 12/10/91
Each Trust Unit received fourth distribution of $0.10 cash 1/12/93
Each Trust Unit received fifth distribution of $0.10 cash 1/11/94
Each Trust Unit received sixth distribution of $0.10 cash 1/20/95
Each Trust Unit received seventh and final distribution of $0.67 cash 4/11/96
Note: Distributions are subject to surrender of San Juan Racing Association, Inc. certificates

(See San Juan Racing Association, Inc. for previous distributions)

SAN JUAN RACING ASSN INC (PR)
Each VTC for Common 50¢ par exchanged for (0.2) VTC for Common $2.50 par 10/21/63
Each share Common 50¢ par exchanged for (0.2) share Common $2.50 par 10/21/63
Voting Trust Agreement terminated 9/15/65
Each VTC for Common $2.50 par exchanged for (1) share Common $2.50 par
Stock Dividends -10% 10/20/61; 10% 10/18/67; 10% 10/17/68; 10% 9/30/69 10% 10/9/70; 10% 10/18/71; 10% 12/29/72; 10% 1/9/74; 10% 11/19/74; 10% 11/17/75; 10% 12/20/76; 10% 12/23/77; 10% 12/15/78; 10% 12/7/79; 10% 12/12/80
Each share Common $2.50 par received initial distribution of $14.49 cash 11/18/81
Each share Common $2.50 par received second distribution of $1.31 cash 2/2/83
Each share Common $2.50 par received third distribution of $2 cash 12/15/86
Each share Common $2.50 par received fourth distribution of $2.25 cash 2/6/89
Assets transferred to San Juan Racing Association, Inc. Shareholders' Liquidating Trust 12/14/89
(See San Juan Racing Association, Inc. Liquidating Trust)

SAN JUAN RAMSEY CO. (NV)
Charter revoked for failure to file reports and pay fees 3/1/41

SAN JUAN URANIUM CORP. (DE)
No longer in existence having become inoperative and void for non-payment of taxes 4/1/57

SAN JUDAS MOLYBDENUM LTD (ON)
Reorganized under the laws of Canada as as Jedburgh Resources Ltd. 07/09/1982
Each share Common no par exchanged for (0.5) share Common no par
Jedburgh Resources Ltd. recapitalized as OTI Technologies Inc. 01/20/1987
(See OTI Technologies Inc.)

SAN LEON ENERGY PLC (IRELAND)
Each old Sponsored ADR for Ordinary exchanged for (0.1) new Sponsored ADR for Ordinary 07/16/2015
Basis changed from (1:50) to (1:5) 07/16/2015
ADR agreement terminated 04/12/2018
Each new Sponsored ADR for Ordinary exchanged for (5) shares Ordinary
Note: Unexchanged ADR's will be sold and the proceeds, if any, held for claim after 10/12/2018

SAN LUIS MNG CO (CA)
Liquidation completed
Each share Capital Stock $10 par received initial distribution of $823.80 cash 08/21/1979
Each share Capital Stock $10 par exchanged for second and final distribution of $194.79 cash 10/04/1979

SAN LUIS OBISPO NATL BK (SAN LUIS OBISPO, CA)
Name changed to First Central Coast Bank (San Luis Obispo, CA) 06/14/1977
(See First Central Coast Bank (San Luis Obispo, CA))

SAN LUIS RES INC (NV)
Recapitalized as Castle Holding Corp. 09/28/1990
Each share Common $0.001 par exchanged for (0.004) share Common $0.0025 par
Castle Holding Corp. name changed to Enerkon Solar International, Inc. 11/03/2017

SAN LUIS TR BK FSB (SAN LUIS OBISPO, CA)
Common $8 par split (5) for (1) by issuance of (4) additional shares payable 05/21/2004 to holders of record 05/20/2004 Ex date - 05/24/2004
Bank closed and FDIC appointed receiver 02/18/2011
Stockholders' equity unlikely

SAN-MAR ENVIRONMENTAL CORP (CANADA)
Recapitalized as Pure Zinc Technologies, Inc. 08/21/1998
Each share Common no par exchanged for (1/3) share Common no par
Pure Zinc Technologies, Inc. name changed to Charityville.com International Inc. 08/27/1999 which name changed to eNblast productions inc. 06/14/2000
(See eNblast productions inc.)

SAN MARINO MINERALS INC (FL)
Reorganized under the laws of Nevada as Centaur Technologies Inc. 7/31/98
Each share Common no par exchanged for (0.01) share Common no par
Centaur Technologies, Inc. name changed to Traderalert.Com, Inc. 5/6/99 which name changed to Equityalert.Com, Inc. 6/2/99 which recapitalized as InnoTech Corp. 7/31/2001

SAN MARINO SVGS & LN ASSN (CA)
Liquidated 12/07/1984
No stockholders' equity

SAN MATEO CNTY BANCORP (CA)
Merged into Mid Peninsula Bancorp 10/04/1994
Each share Common no par exchanged for (1) share Common no par
Mid Peninsula Bancorp merged into Greater Bay Bancorp 11/29/1996 which merged into Wells Fargo & Co. 10/01/2007

SAN MAURICIO MNG CO (PHILIPPINES)
Out of business 01/23/1984
No stockholders' equity

SAN MIGUEL BREWERY, INC. (PHILIPPINES)
Preferred PHP 1000 par changed to PHP 100 par 00/00/1949
8% Preferred called for redemption 10/25/1958
Stock Dividends - 75% 08/25/1947; 25% 04/15/1948; 100% 04/16/1949; 20% 01/26/1953; 33-1/3% 04/25/1957
Name changed to San Miguel Corp. 08/15/1963

SAN MIGUEL CORP (PHILIPPINES)
7% Preferred PHP 100 par called for redemption 12/15/1973
(Additional Information in Active)

SAN MIGUEL PURE FOODS CO INC (PHILIPPINES)
ADR agreement terminated 04/19/2018
No ADR's remain outstanding

SAN MORCOL PIPELINE, INC. (NM)
Under plan of merger name changed to Southwestern States Gas Co. 7/31/66
Southwestern States Gas Co. name changed to Midwest Energy Corp. 7/20/73 which reorganized as

Swab-Fox Companies 9/23/83 which name changed to Tribune/ Swab Fox Companies, Inc. 10/1/84 which recapitalized as T/SF Communications Corp. 5/24/95

SAN-NAP-PAK MANUFACTURING CO., INC.
Name changed to Doeskin Products, Inc. in 1949
Doeskin Products, Inc. was completely liquidated 9/29/67

SAN ORO MINES LTD. (MB)
Charter cancelled for failure to file annual reports in 1951

SAN PATRIZIO PRODUCTS, INC. (UT)
Name changed to Unison Media, Inc. in April 1986
(See Unison Media, Inc.)

SAN PAULO EXPLS LTD (ON)
Reorganized as AdvanteXCEL.com Communications Corp. 01/04/1999
Each share Common no par exchanged for (0.125) share Common no par
(See AdvanteXCEL.com Communications Corp.)

SAN RAFAEL BANCORP (CA)
Common no par split (3) for (1) by issuance of (1) additional share payable 08/29/2000 to holders of record 07/18/2000 Ex date - 08/03/2000
Common no par split (2) for (1) by issuance of (1) additional share payable 04/15/2002 to holders of record 03/25/2002 Ex date - 04/16/2002
Common no par split (3) for (2) by issuance of (0.5) additional share payable 02/14/2003 to holders of record 01/28/2003 Ex date - 02/18/2003
Name changed to Epic Bancorp 06/25/2004
Epic Bancorp name changed to Tamalpais Bancorp 06/10/2008
(See Tamalpais Bancorp)

SAN RAFAEL RES LTD (BC)
Recapitalized as Rafael Resources Ltd. 7/27/84
Each share Capital Stock no par exchanged for (0.2) share Common no par
Rafael Resources Ltd. name changed to Biologix (B.C.) Ltd. 9/25/86 which name changed to Biologix International Ltd. 5/1/98
(See Biologix International Ltd.)

SAN-RIVE MINES, LTD. (ON)
Charter cancelled for failure to file reports and pay taxes 1/1/55

SAN SABA OIL & DEVELOPMENT CO. (DE)
Charter cancelled and declared inoperative and void for non-payment of taxes 3/19/24

SAN TELMO ENERGY CORP (BC)
Common no par split (3) for (1) by issuance of (2) additional shares payable 08/21/2003 to holders of record 08/15/2003 Ex date - 08/14/2003
Merged into Rolling Thunder Exploration Ltd. (New) 01/11/2006
Each share Common no par exchanged for (0.5) share Class A Common no par
Rolling Thunder Exploration Ltd. (New) merged into Action Energy Inc. 08/30/2007
(See Action Energy Inc.)

SAN TELMO RES LTD (BC)
Common no par split (2) for (1) by issuance of (1) additional share payable 07/17/2001 to holders of record 07/13/2001
Recapitalized as San Telmo Energy Corp. 08/15/2002
Each share Common no par

exchanged for (0.14285714) share Common no par
San Telmo Energy Corp. merged into Rolling Thunder Exploration Ltd. (New) 01/11/2006 which merged into Action Energy Inc. 08/30/2007
(See Action Energy Inc.)

SAN TOY MINING CO. (ME)
Merged into Apollo Industries, Inc. (Me.) 5/31/58
Each (61.671) shares Common 10¢ par exchanged for (1) share Common $5 par
(See Apollo Industries, Inc.)

SAN VAL INC (CO)
Recapitalized as Houston A-1 Car Stereo Plus, Inc. 04/19/2000
Each share Common no par exchanged for (0.1) share Common no par
(See Houston A-1 Car Stereo Plus, Inc.)

SAN WEST INC (NV)
Reincorporated 09/13/2011
Common no par split (5) for (1) by issuance of (4) additional shares payable 11/02/2009 to holders of record 10/28/2009 Ex date - 11/03/2009
State of incorporation changed from (CA) to (NV) and Common no par changed to $0.001 par 09/13/2011
Recapitalized as AppSwarm, Inc. 09/25/2015
Each share Common $0.001 par exchanged for (0.00033333) share Common $0.001 par

SANABRIA TELEVISION CORP. (DE)
No longer in existence having become inoperative and void for non-payment of taxes 4/1/34

SANANCO ENERGY CORP (TX)
Charter forfeited for failure to pay taxes 2/13/96

SANATANA DIAMONDS INC (BC)
Name changed to Sanatana Resources Inc. 05/02/2011

SANBORN CO. (MA)
Acquired by Hewlett-Packard Co. (CA) 08/31/1961
Each share Common $1 par exchanged for (1) share 90¢ Conv. Preferred $1 par and (1.4) shares Common $1 par
Hewlett-Packard Co. (CA) reincorporated in Delaware 05/20/1998 which name changed to HP Inc. 11/02/2015

SANBORN INC (DE)
Each share Conv. Preferred Ser. A 1¢ par exchanged for (1) share Common 1¢ par 12/17/92
Filed Chapter 11 Federal Bankruptcy Code 1/21/94
No stockholders' equity

SANBORN MAP CO. (NY)
Each share Capital Stock $100 par exchanged for (5) shares Capital Stock $25 par in 1934
Name changed to First Pelham Corp. 12/31/59
(See First Pelham Corp.)

SANBORN MAP INC (NY)
98.9% acquired by Pictorial Productions Inc. through purchase offer which expired 01/21/1969
Public interest eliminated

SANBORN RES LTD (DE)
Common $0.0001 par split (100) for (1) by issuance of (99) additional shares payable 04/10/2013 to holders of record 04/05/2013 Ex date - 04/11/2013
Recapitalized as Bay Stakes Corp. 11/30/2016
Each share Common $0.0001 par exchanged for (0.06666666) share Common $0.0001 par
Bay Stakes Corp. name changed to Chill N Out Cryotherapy, Inc. 01/25/2018

SANCHEZ COMPUTER ASSOCS INC (PA)
Common no par split (2) for (1) by issuance of (1) additional share payable 6/23/99 to holders of record 6/3/99
Merged into Fidelity National Financial, Inc. 4/14/2004
Each share Common no par exchanged for (0.08365) share Common $0.0001 par and $3.25 cash
Fidelity National Financial, Inc. merged into Fidelity National Information Services, Inc. 11/9/2006

SANCHEZ PRODTN PARTNERS LLC (DE)
Reorganized as Sanchez Production Partners L.P. 03/09/2015
Each Class B Common Unit exchanged for (1) Common Unit
Sanchez Production Partners L.P. name changed to Sanchez Midstream Partners L.P. 06/05/2017

SANCHEZ PRODTN PARTNERS LP (DE)
Each old Common Unit exchanged for (0.1) new Common Unit 08/04/2015
Name changed to Sanchez Midstream Partners L.P. 06/05/2017

SANCO FINANCE CO., INC. (OK)
Name changed to Planned Credit, Inc., 12/13/1968
Planned Credit, Inc. name changed to Gulf South Corp. 10/12/1972
(See Gulf South Corp.)

SANCON RES RECOVERY INC (NV)
Recapitalized as IGS Capital Group Ltd. 06/09/2017
Each share Common $0.001 par exchanged for (0.01) share Common $0.001 par

SANCONO VENTURES INC (BC)
Name changed to Nu-Media Industries International Inc. 02/01/1989
Nu-Media Industries International Inc. recapitalized as Consolidated Nu-Media Industries Inc. (BC) 12/15/1994 which reincorporated in Yukon as Pan Asia Mining Corp. 10/08/1997 which name changed to China Diamond Corp. 01/02/2004
(See China Diamond Corp.)

SANCTION CAP CORP (AB)
Merged into Marsa Energy Inc. 09/30/2014
Each share Common no par exchanged for (0.09259259) share Common no par
Marsa Energy Inc. merged into Condor Petroleum Inc. 03/30/2016

SANCTUARY WOODS MULTIMEDIA CORP (DE)
Reorganized 04/16/1997
Reorganized from (BC) to under the laws of (DE) 04/16/1997
Each share Common no par exchanged for (0.05) share Common no par
Chapter 7 bankruptcy proceedings terminated 02/01/2006
No stockholders' equity

SANCURO CORP (NV)
Name changed to Kendall Square Research Corp. 09/08/2009

SAND HILL IT SEC ACQUISITION CORP (DE)
Issue Information - 3,600,000 UNITS consisting of (1) share COM and (2) WTS offered at $6 per Unit on 07/27/2004
Name changed to St. Bernard Software, Inc. 09/01/2006
St. Bernard Software, Inc. name changed to EdgeWave, Inc. 08/09/2011
(See EdgeWave, Inc.)

SAND LAKE GOLD MINES, LTD. (ON)
Charter surrendered for failure to file reports and pay taxes 6/23/52

SAND RIV RES LTD (BC)
Recapitalized as Rio Fortuna Exploration Corp. 11/30/1999
Each share Common no par exchanged for (1/7) share Common no par
Rio Fortuna Exploration Corp. recapitalized as Fortune River Resource Corp. 12/21/2005 which merged into Bravada Gold Corp. (New) 01/07/2011

SAND RIVER GOLD MINING CO. LTD. (ON)
Recapitalized as Sarimco Mines Ltd. on a (0.2) for (1) basis 8/18/64
Sarimco Mines Ltd. charter cancelled 3/16/76

SAND TECHNOLOGY INC (CANADA)
Recapitalized 03/24/1988
Name changed 01/27/2000
Recapitalized from Sand Technology Systems (Canada), Inc. to Sand Technology Systems International Inc. 03/24/1988
Each share old Class A Common no par exchanged for (0.04) share new Class A Common no par 07/10/1989
New Class A Common no par split (2) for (1) by issuance of (1) additional share payable 01/14/1997 to holders of record 12/31/1996
Name changed from Sand Technology Systems International Inc. to Sand Technology Inc. 01/27/2000
Acquired by Constellation Software Inc. 11/18/2013
Each share new Class A Common no par exchanged for $0.07267 cash
Note: Unexchanged certificates will be cancelled and become without value 11/15/2019

SANDALWOOD CORP (NV)
Recapitalized as SpacePlex Amusement Centers International Ltd. 11/21/1994
Each share Common $0.001 par exchanged for (0.1) share Common $0.001 par
SpacePlex Amusement Centers International Ltd. recapitalized as Air Energy Inc. 05/24/1996 which name changed to Powerhouse International Corp. 12/24/1997 which name changed to iLive, Inc. 10/21/1999
(See iLive, Inc.)

SANDALWOOD VENTURES LTD (NV)
Common $0.001 par split (28) for (1) by issuance of (27) additional shares payable 01/26/2012 to holders of record 01/26/2012
Name changed to Eco-Tek Group, Inc. 11/21/2012

SANDATA TECHNOLOGIES INC (DE)
Name changed 11/21/2001
Each share old Common $0.001 par exchanged for (1/3) share new Common $0.001 par 5/5/92
Name changed from Sandata, Inc. to Sandata Technologies, Inc. 11/21/2001
Merged into Sandata Acquisition Corp. 5/30/2003
Each share Common $0.0001 par exchanged for $2.21 cash

SANDCULTURE COM INC (NV)
Name changed to Dinozine Ventures Inc. 10/15/2001
Dinozine Ventures Inc. name changed to Zamage Digital Art Imaging, Inc. 4/5/2004

SANDENISE GOLD MINES LTD. (ON)
Charter cancelled for failure to file reports and pay taxes in 1956

SANDERS & THOMAS INC (PA)
Merged into STV, Inc. 10/01/1969
Each share Common $1 par exchanged for (1) share Common $1 par
STV, Inc. name changed to STV Engineers, Inc. 02/05/1979 which name changed to STV Group, Inc. 06/25/1991
(See STV Group, Inc.)

SANDERS ASSOC INC (DE)
Class A Common $1 par reclassified as Common $1 par 11/20/65
Common $1 par split (2) for (1) by issuance of (1) additional share 7/28/67
Common $1 par split (2) for (1) by issuance of (1) additional share 10/11/83
Stock Dividends - 100% 10/19/60; 50% 10/20/61; 20% 10/18/63
Merged into Lockheed Corp. 10/6/86
Each share Common $1 par exchanged for $60 cash

SANDERS ASSOCIATES, INC. (MA)
Reorganized under the laws of Delaware 8/1/57
Each share Class A Common $1 par exchanged for (3) shares Class A Common $1 par
(See Sanders Associates, Inc. (Del.))

SANDERS CAREER SCHS INC (NJ)
Common 1¢ par split (3) for (1) by issuance of (2) additional shares 6/15/71
Each share old Common 1¢ par exchanged for (0.5) share new Common 1¢ par 8/7/85
Charter revoked for failure to file reports and pay fees 9/9/95

SANDERS CONFECTIONERY PRODS INC (MI)
Plan of reorganization effective 04/23/1997
Old Common $0.001 par exchanged on the following basis: (84%) of total holdings exchanged for new Common $0.001 par share for share (16%) of total holdings exchanged for (1) share InMold, Inc. Common $0.001 par for each (2) shares surrendered
(See InMold, Inc.)
(Additional Information in Active)

SANDERS MORRIS HARRIS GROUP INC (TX)
Name changed to Edelman Financial Group Inc. 05/27/2011
(See Edelman Financial Group Inc.)

SANDERS MORRIS MUNDY INC (TX)
Merged into Pinnacle Global Group, Inc. 01/31/2000
Each share Common exchanged for (117.32785) shares Common no par
Pinnacle Global Group, Inc. name changed to Sanders Morris Harris Group Inc. 05/23/2001 which name changed to Edelman Financial Group Inc. 05/27/2011
(See Edelman Financial Group Inc.)

SANDERS R C TECHNOLOGY SYS INC (NH)
Name changed to Santec Corp. 04/30/1982
(See Santec Corp.)

SANDERSON TECHNOLOGIES INC (BC)
Recapitalized as Levi Developments Inc. 2/15/90
Each share Common no par exchanged for (0.25) share Common no par
Levi Developments Inc. recapitalized as R.I.S. Resources International Corp. 6/9/94 which recapitalized as Ultra Holdings Inc. 12/2/99
(See Ultra Holdings Inc.)

SANDFIELD VENTURES CORP (NV)
Name changed to Trident Brands Inc. 07/08/2013

SANDGATE CORP (DE)
Reincorporated 06/27/1969
State of incorporation changed from (NY) to (DE) 06/27/1969
Common $1 par split (2) for (1) by issuance of (1) additional share 01/23/1986
Stock Dividends - 20% 09/05/1975; 25% 10/28/1982
Charter cancelled and declared inoperative and void for non-payment of taxes 03/01/1989

SANDHURST RES LTD (BC)
Cease trade order effective 10/07/1997

SANDIA AMERN CORP (NM)
Charter revoked for failure to file reports and pay fees 10/31/2007

SANDIA AMERICAN DEVELOPMENT CORP. (NM)
Name changed to Sandia American Corp. 9/6/62

SANDIA INTL METALS CORP (FL)
Proclaimed dissolved for failure to file reports and pay fees 05/23/1973

SANDIA MINING & DEVELOPMENT CORP. (NM)
Name changed to Sandia American Development Corp. 2/2/60
Sandia American Development Corp. name changed to Sandia America Corp. 9/6/62

SANDISK CORP (DE)
Common $0.001 par split (2) for (1) by issuance of (1) additional share payable 02/22/2000 to holders of record 02/08/2000
Common $0.001 par split (2) for (1) by issuance of (1) additional share payable 02/18/2004 to holders of record 02/03/2004
Merged into Western Digital Corp. 05/12/2016
Each share Common $0.001 par exchanged for (0.2387) share Common 1¢ par and $67.50 cash

SANDOZ LTD (SWITZERLAND)
Merged into Novatis AG 12/23/96
Each Sponsored ADR for Ordinary 100 Fr par exchanged for (1) Sponsored ADR for Ordinary SFr 20 par

SANDPIPER NETWORKS INC (CA)
Merged into Digital Island, Inc. 12/29/99
Each share Common $0.001 par exchanged for (1.0727) shares Common $0.001 par
(See Digital Island, Inc.)

SANDPIPER OIL & GAS LTD (BC)
Recapitalized as Pax Petroleum Ltd. 9/11/90
Each share Common no par exchanged for (0.1) share Common no par
(See Pax Petroleum Ltd.)

SANDRIDGE ENERGY INC (DE)
Each share 6% Conv. Perpetual Preferred $0.001 par exchanged for (9.21149594) shares Common $0.001 par 12/22/2014
Each share 8.5% 144A Conv. Perpetual Preferred $0.001 par exchanged for (1) share 8.5% Conv. Perpetual Preferred $0.001 par 01/21/2010
Each share 7% 144A Conv. Perpetual Preferred $0.001 par exchanged for (1) share 7% Conv. Perpetual Preferred $0.001 par 11/10/2011
Each share 7% Conv. Perpetual Preferred $0.001 par received (1.890625) shares old Common $0.001 par payable 05/15/2015 to holders of record 05/01/2015
Ex date - 04/29/2015
Plan of reorganization under Chapter 11 Federal Bankruptcy proceedings effective 10/04/2016
No stockholders' equity

(Additional Information in Active)
SANDS MINERALS CORP (BC)
Name changed to Michele Gold Mines Ltd. 01/25/1918

SANDS PETE AB (SWEDEN)
Name changed to Lundin Oil AB 4/2/98
(See Lundin Oil AB)

SANDS REGENT (NV)
Common 10¢ par split (2) for (1) by issuance of (1) additional share 3/12/93
Merged into Herbst Gaming, Inc. 1/3/2007
Each share Common 10¢ par exchanged for $15 cash

SANDSPORT DATA SVCS INC (NY)
Recapitalized under the laws of Delaware as Sandata, Inc. 7/30/87
Each share Common $0.001 par exchanged for (1/30) share Common $0.001 par
Sandata, Inc. name changed to Sandata Technologies, Inc. 11/21/2001
(See Sandata Technologies, Inc.)

SANDSPRING RES LTD (AB)
Reincorporated under the laws of Ontario 03/31/2010

SANDSTORM EXPLORATION CO. (NV)
Capital Stock $1 par changed to 25¢ par 4/26/58
Name changed to Nevada Gold Co. and Capital Stock $1 par reclassified as Common $0.001 par 5/9/80
(See Nevada Gold Co.)

SANDSTORM METALS & ENERGY LTD (BC)
Each share old Common no par exchanged for (0.1) share new Common no par 05/15/2013
Merged into Sandstorm Gold Ltd. 05/30/2014
Each share new Common no par exchanged for (0.178) share Common no par and $0.35 cash
Note: Unexchanged certificates will be cancelled and become without value 05/30/2020

SANDSTORM RES LTD (BC)
Common no par split (2) for (1) by issuance of (1) additional share payable 04/10/2008 to holders of record 04/04/2008 Ex date - 04/02/2008
Name changed to Sandstorm Gold Ltd. 02/17/2011

SANDURA CO. (DE)
Name changed to Del Penn Co. 4/26/65
Del Penn Co. completed liquidation 12/12/69

SANDUSKY BAY BRIDGE CO.
Dissolved in 1936

SANDUSKY CEMENT CO.
Name changed to Medusa Portland Cement Co. in 1929
Medusa Portland Cement Co. name changed to Medusa Corp. 3/31/72
(See Medusa Corp.)

SANDUSKY PLASTICS INC (DE)
Name changed to Chariot Group, Inc. 5/20/87
(See Chariot Group, Inc.)

SANDVINE CORP (ON)
Acquired by PNI Canada Acquireco Corp. 09/22/2017
Each share Common no par exchanged for $4.40 cash
Note: Unexchanged certificates will be cancelled and become without value 09/22/2023

SANDWELL MNG LTD (BC)
Reorganized under the laws of Canada as MBAC Fertilizer Corp. 12/30/2009
Each share Common no par exchanged for (0.06666666) share Common no par
MBAC Fertilizer Corp. (Canada) reorganized in Cayman Islands 11/07/2016 which name changed to Itafos 01/06/2017

SANDWELL SWAN WOOSTER INC (BC)
Name changed 06/27/1986
Common no par reclassified as Class A Conv. Common no par 04/11/1975
Name changed from Sandwell & Co. Ltd. to Sandwell Swan Wooster Inc. 06/27/1986
Class A Conv. Common no par reclassified as Common no par 05/29/1989
Class B Conv. Common no par reclassified as Common no par 05/29/1989
Acquired by ElectroWatt Ltd. 12/20/1989
Each share Common no par exchanged for $40 cash

SANDWICH BANCORP INC (MA)
Merged into Seacoast Financial Services Corp. 12/04/1998
Each share Common $1 par exchanged for (6.385) shares Common 1¢ par
Seacoast Financial Services Corp. merged into Sovereign Bancorp, Inc. 07/23/2004 which merged into Banco Santander, S.A. 01/30/2009

SANDWICH CHEF INC (DE)
Reincorporated 7/31/86
Common 10¢ par changed to 7-1/2¢ par and (1/3) additional share issued 12/10/79
Common 7-1/2¢ par changed to 5¢ par and (0.5) additional share issued 8/31/81
State of incorporation changed from (AL) to (DE) 7/31/86
Common 5¢ par split (3) for (2) by issuance of (0.5) additional share 9/7/90
Stock Dividends - 10% 11/8/77; 10% 11/17/78
Name changed to Wall Street Deli, Inc. 11/10/92
(See Wall Street Deli, Inc.)

SANDWICH CO OPERATIVE BK (SANDWICH, MA)
Under plan of reorganization each share Common $1 par automatically became (1) share Sandwich Bancorp Inc. Common $1 par 09/30/1997
Sandwich Bancorp Inc. merged into Seacoast Financial Services Corp. 12/04/1998 which merged into Sovereign Bancorp, Inc. 07/23/2004 which merged into Banco Santander, S.A. 01/30/2009

SANDWICH MASTER INC (AL)
Name changed to Sandwich Chef, Inc. (AL) 9/11/74
Sandwich Chef, Inc. (AL) reincorporated in Delaware 7/31/86 which name changed to Wall Street Deli, Inc. 11/10/92
(See Wall Street Deli, Inc.)

SANDY CORP (MI)
Merged into Automatic Data Processing, Inc. 1/4/96
Each share Common 1¢ par exchanged for (0.3341542) share Common 10¢ par

SANDY CREEK CORP (FL)
Each share Common no par received distribution of (1) share Sandy Creek International Inc. Restricted Common payable 05/18/2004 to holders of record 02/02/2004
Reorganized under the laws of Nevada as Offshore Creations, Inc. 05/24/2004
Each share Common no par exchanged for (0.001) share Common $0.0001 par

Offshore Creations, Inc. name changed to Sustainable Power Corp. 02/16/2007
(See Sustainable Power Corp.)

SANDY CREEK OSTRICH RANCH INC (FL)
Name changed to Sandy Creek Corp. (FL) 10/27/1998
Sandy Creek Corp. (FL) reorganized in Nevada as Offshore Creations, Inc. 05/24/2004 which name changed to Sustainable Power Corp. 02/16/2007
(See Sustainable Power Corp.)

SANDY HILL CORP (NY)
Name changed 9/1/63
Each share Common 50¢ par exchanged for (30) shares Common $1 par 5/28/49
Name changed from Sandy Hill Iron & Brass Works to Sandy Hill Corp. 9/1/63
Name changed to Ahlstrom Kamyr Corp. 3/5/91
Ahlstrom Kamyr Corp. name changed to Ahlstrom Manufacturing Corp. 3/8/91
(See Ahlstrom Manufacturing Corp.)

SANDY SPRING CAP TR I (DE)
9.375% Trust Preferred Securities called for redemption at $25 on 11/30/2004

SANELLI POOLS LTD (ON)
Completely liquidated 08/18/1982
Each share Capital Stock no par exchanged for first and final distribution of $0.375 cash

SANFIELD CORP (MO)
Name changed to Auto-Lec Stores, Inc. 9/30/68
(See Auto-Lec Stores, Inc.)

SANFORD CORP (IL)
Common 1¢ par split (2) for (1) by issuance of (1) additional share 03/03/1987
Common 1¢ par split (3) for (2) by issuance of (0.5) additional share 05/31/1988
Common 1¢ par split (3) for (2) by issuance of (0.5) additional share 05/31/1989
Merged into Newell Co. 02/14/1992
Each share Common 1¢ par exchanged for (0.93) share Common $1 par
Newell Co. name changed to Newell Rubbermaid Inc. 03/24/1999 which name changed to Newell Brands Inc. 04/18/2016

SANFORD EXPL INC (NV)
Name changed to Angstrom Technologies Corp. 02/19/2008
Angstrom Technologies Corp. name changed to Angstrom Microsystems Corp. 05/02/2008
(See Angstrom Microsystems Corp.)

SANFORD INC (MN)
Statutorily dissolved 10/1/91

SANFORD MILLS, INC.
Merged into Goodall-Sanford, Inc. 00/00/1944
Each share Common exchanged for (1-1/4) shares new Common $10 par and $20 principal amount of Debentures
Goodall-Sanford, Inc. was acquired by Burlington Industries, Inc. (Old) 00/00/1959
(See Burlington Industries, Inc. (Old))

SANFORD TR CO (SANFORD, ME)
Capital Stock $25 par changed to $12.50 par and (1) additional share issued 08/29/1969
100% acquired by Northeast Bankshare Association through exchange offer which expired 11/30/1973
Public interest eliminated

SANFRED RES LTD (BC)
Recapitalized as Falcon Oil & Gas Ltd. 12/21/99
Each share Common no par exchanged for (0.2) share Common no par

SANGAMO BIOSCIENCES INC (DE)
Name changed to Sangamo Therapeutics, Inc. 01/09/2017

SANGAMO CO. LTD. (CANADA)
Each share old Common no par exchanged for (4) shares new Common no par 00/00/1946
100% acquired by Schlumberger Canada Ltd. through purchase offer which expired 02/25/1978
Public interest eliminated

SANGAMO ELEC CO (DE)
Reincorporated 1/2/59
Each share old Common no par exchanged for (2) shares new Common no par in 1937
Each share new Common no par exchanged for (2) shares Common $10 par in 1951
State of incorporation changed from (IL) to (DE) 1/2/59
Common $10 par changed to $5 par and (1) additional share issued 5/3/60
Common $5 par split (3) for (2) by issuance of (0.5) additional share 6/5/67
Merged into Newcorp Inc. 10/6/75
Each share Common $5 par exchanged for $23 cash

SANGER BROTHERS, INC.
Merged into Federated Department Stores, Inc. in 1951
Each (2.5) shares Common $2.50 par exchanged for (1) share Common $5 par
Federated Department Stores, Inc. name changed to Macy's, Inc. 6/1/2007

SANGER THEATRES, INC.
Acquired by Paramount Famous Lasky Corp. 00/00/1929
Details not available

SANGHI POLYESTERS LTD (INDIA)
GDR agreement terminated 03/12/2012
Each 144A GDR for Ordinary exchanged for (5) shares Ordinary

SANGOMA COM INC (ON)
Name changed to Sangoma Technologies Corp. 9/17/2001

SANGSTAT MED CORP (CA)
Merged into Genzyme Corp. 09/15/2003
Each share Common no par exchanged for $22.50 cash

SANI MED INC (FL)
Proclaimed dissolved for failure to file reports and pay fees 10/16/1998

SANI-TECH INDS INC (DE)
Charter cancelled and declared inoperative and void for non-payment of taxes 3/1/95

SANIFILL INC (DE)
Reincorporated 7/24/91
State of incorporation changed from (TX) to (DE) 7/24/91
Merged into USA Waste Services Inc. 9/3/96
Each share Common 1¢ par exchanged for (1.7) shares Common 1¢ par
USA Waste Services Inc. merged into Waste Management, Inc. 7/16/98

SANILAC CO-OPERATIVE, INC. (MI)
Voluntarily dissolved 5/12/55
Details not available

SANILOGICAL INDS LTD (BC)
Recapitalized as Encom Environmental & Communications Systems Ltd. 07/05/1988
Each share Capital Stock no par exchanged for (0.5) share Capital Stock no par
Encom Environmental & Communications Systems Ltd. recapitalized as ST Systems Corp. 11/14/1994 which recapitalized as Sky Ridge Resources Ltd. 12/24/2007 which recapitalized as Japan Gold Corp. 09/19/2016

SANIMATIC CORP (CO)
Name changed to T O R International, Inc. 11/16/1972
(See T O R International, Inc.)

SANITARY CLEANING DEVICES COMPANY OF GREAT BRITAIN (CA)
Charter forfeited for failure to pay taxes 11/30/11

SANITARY CTLS INC (NY)
Charter cancelled and proclaimed dissolved for failure to pay taxes 09/29/1982

SANITARY DISH WASHING MACHINE CO. (WI)
Involuntarily dissolved 9/17/80

SANITARY ENVIRONMENTAL MONITORING LABS, INC. (NV)
Recapitalized as Vietnam United Steel Corp. 08/28/2008
Each share Common $0.001 par exchanged for (0.01) share Common $0.001 par
Vietnam United Steel Corp. recapitalized as Vietnam Mining Corp. 07/12/2010 which name changed to Vanguard Mining Corp. 06/03/2014 which name changed to Myson Group, Inc. 06/08/2015

SANITARY GROCERY CO. LTD.
Acquired by Safeway Stores, Inc. 00/00/1928
Details not available

SANITARY PAPER MILLS, INC. (DE)
Each share Class A Common exchanged for (1) share Common no par 00/00/1936
Each share Common $1 par exchanged for (0.1) share Common no par 00/00/1936
Merged into Swanee Paper Corp. 02/20/1964
Each share Common no par exchanged for (0.56712) share Common $1 par
Swanee Paper Corp. merged into Potlatch Forests, Inc. (DE) 12/23/1968 which name changed to Potlatch Corp. (Old) 04/27/1973 which reorganized as Potlatch Corp. (New) 02/03/2006 which name changed to PotlatchDeltic Corp. 02/23/2018

SANITARY PRODUCTS CORP. (IL)
Each share Common no par exchanged for (5) shares Common $1 par 12/19/1949
Common $1 par changed to 10¢ par 07/17/1961
Dissolved 08/27/1962
Each share Common 10¢ par exchanged for (1) Sanitary Products Trust Certificate of Beneficial Interest no par
(See Sanitary Products Trust)

SANITARY PRODUCTS CORP. OF AMERICA (VA)
Class A & B Common $5 par changed to $2 par in 1939
Liquidation completed 1/20/61

SANITARY PRODUCTS TRUST (IL)
Trust terminated 9/12/72
No equity for holders of Certificates of Bene. Int. which are worthless

SANITAS INC (CT)
Name changed 01/20/1987
Each share Common $1 par exchanged for (3) shares Common no par 02/03/1969
Common no par split (3) for (2) by issuance of (0.5) additional share 03/16/1970
Each share Common no par exchanged for (0.2) share Common 10¢ par 04/06/1977
Name changed from Sanitas Service Corp. to Sanitas, Inc. 01/20/1987
Company reported insolvent 00/00/2000
No stockholders' equity

SANITEC HLDGS USA (NV)
Recapitalized as Co-Media Inc. 11/25/2000
Each share Common $0.0001 par exchanged for (0.5) share Common $0.0001 par
Co-Media Inc. reorganized as Jarvis Group Inc. 01/18/2002 which name changed to Cash 4 Homes 247 05/21/2003 which name changed to Vegas Equity International Corp. 02/01/2006
(See Vegas Equity International Corp.)

SANITECH INC (OH)
Name changed to Sorbent Technologies Corp. 01/13/1992
(See Sorbent Technologies Corp.)

SANITRON, INC. (DE)
Out of business 11/01/1955
Details not available

SANJANET APARTMENT HOTEL CO. (MO)
Liquidation completed 5/29/56

SANKO SS LTD (JAPAN)
Stock Dividends - 10% 06/15/1973; 10% 01/15/1974; 10% 06/15/1975
ADR agreement terminated 03/25/2009
No stockholders' equity

SANMARK INDS INC (DE)
Stock Dividend - 10% 01/04/1974
Merged into Sanmark-Stardust Inc. 03/12/1981
Each share Common 1¢ par exchanged for (15) shares Common 1¢ par
Sanmark-Stardust Inc. name changed to Movie Star, Inc. 01/04/1993 which recapitalized as Frederick's of Hollywood Group Inc. 01/29/2008
(See Frederick's of Hollywood Group Inc.)

SANMARK STARDUST INC (NY)
Common 1¢ par split (4) for (3) by issuance of (0.33333333) additional share 01/27/1986
Common 1¢ par split (5) for (3) by issuance of (0.66666666) additional share 01/31/1989
Common 1¢ par split (4) for (3) by issuance of (0.33333333) additional share 01/31/1990
Stock Dividends - 10% 12/28/1983; 10% 01/18/1985; 10% 01/26/1987; 10% 01/30/1988
Name changed to Movie Star, Inc. 01/04/1993
Movie Star, Inc. recapitalized as Frederick's of Hollywood Group Inc. 01/29/2008
(See Frederick's of Hollywood Group Inc.)

SANMINA-SCI CORP (DE)
Name changed 12/10/2001
Common 1¢ par split (2) for (1) by issuance of (1) additional share payable 03/11/1996 to holders of record 02/12/1996
Common 1¢ par split (2) for (1) by issuance of (1) additional share payable 06/10/1998 to holders of record 05/20/1998
Common 1¢ par split (2) for (1) by issuance of (1) additional share payable 03/22/2000 to holders of record 03/01/2000
Common 1¢ par split (2) for (1) by issuance of (1) additional share payable 01/08/2001 to holders of record 12/18/2000 Ex date - 01/09/2001
Name changed from Sanmina Corp. to Sanmina-SCI Corp. 12/10/2001
Each share Common 1¢ par exchanged for (1/6) share new Common 1¢ par 08/17/2009
Name changed back to Sanmina Corp. 11/15/2012

SANNORM MINES LTD. (ON)
Recapitalized as Consolidated Sannorm Mines Ltd. on a (1) for (2) basis 00/00/1952
(See Consolidated Sannorm Mines Ltd.)

SANO CORP (FL)
Merged into Elan Corp., PLC 02/27/1998
Each share Common 1¢ par exchanged for (0.6) Sponsored ADR for Ordinary
Elan Corp., PLC merged into Perrigo Co. PLC 12/18/2013

SANOFI-AVENTIS (FRANCE)
Name changed 08/23/2004
Name changed from Sanofi-Synthelabo S.A. to Sanofi-Aventis 08/23/2004
Name changed to Sanofi 05/09/2011

SANOMAWSOY (FINLAND)
Name changed to Sanoma Corp. 02/27/2009

SANOMEDICS INTL HLDGS INC (DE)
Each share old Common $0.001 par exchanged for (0.1) share new Common $0.001 par 12/23/2013
Recapitalized as Sanomedics, Inc. 02/09/2015
Each share new Common $0.001 par exchanged for (0.008) share Common $0.001 par

SANPAOLO-IMI S P A (ITALY)
Each Sponsored ADR for Ordinary received distribution of (2) Beni Stabili S.p.A. Ordinary Shares 200 Lira par payable 10/31/99 to holders of record 10/29/99 Ex date - 11/3/99
Merged into Intesa Sanpaolo S.p.A. 1/1/2007
Each Sponsored ADR for Ordinary exchanged for (1.03833333) Sponsored ADR's for Ordinary

SANRA MEDIA LTD (INDIA)
Name changed 11/20/2008
Name changed from Sanra Software Ltd. to Sanra Media Ltd. 11/20/2008
GDR basis changed from (1:2) to (1:20) 01/29/2009
GDR agreement terminated 06/21/2013
No GDR's remain outstanding

SANS PRIX COSMETICS, INC. (ID)
Each share Common 5¢ par exchanged for (0.1) share Common 5¢ par 5/1/88
Name changed to International Jet Engine Supply, Inc. 9/25/91

SANS SOUCI HOTEL, INC. (NV)
Bankrupt in 1959

SANSHAW MINES LTD.
Acquired by Orlac Red Lake Mines Ltd. on a (0.25) for (1) basis in 1944
Orlac Red Lake Mines Ltd. recapitalized as Consolidated Orlac Mines Ltd. in 1953 which recapitalized as Abbican Mines Ltd. 5/18/56 which charter cancelled 9/28/64

SANSIDRA CORP (NV)
Reorganized under the laws of Delaware as MW Companies Inc. 12/31/1985
Each share Common $0.001 par exchanged for (0.02) share Common 1¢ par
MW Companies Inc. name changed to Caldera, Inc. 09/14/1988 which recapitalized as Unistar Financial Service Corp. 08/17/1998

(See Unistar Financial Service Corp.)

SANSON INST HERALDRY INC (MA)
Name changed to Cardinal Industries, Inc. (MA) 04/25/1975
Cardinal Industries, Inc. (MA) reincorporated in Nevada 09/21/1999 which name changed to Maxum Development, Inc. 06/01/2000 which name changed to Tropical Leisure Resorts, Inc. 09/10/2001 which recapitalized as eWorldMedia Holdings, Inc. 10/22/2002 which name changed to Liberty Diversified Holdings, Inc. 01/09/2006 which name changed to Nutripure Beverages, Inc. 01/17/2008

SANSWIRE CORP (DE)
Name changed to World Surveillance Group Inc. 04/27/2011

SANSWIRE TECHNOLOGIES INC (DE)
Name changed to Wireless Holdings Group, Inc. 03/30/2005
Wireless Holdings Group, Inc. recapitalized as Vega Promotional Systems, Inc. (DE) 12/26/2006 which reorganized in Wyoming as Vega Biofuels, Inc. 07/29/2010

SANTA ANA SHOPPING CENTER, INC. (CA)
Name changed to California Shopping Centers, Inc. 11/24/1965
California Shopping Centers, Inc. name changed to McCombs Corp. 08/08/1978
(See McCombs Corp.)

SANTA ANA ST BK (SANTA ANA, CA)
Name changed to Pan American Bank (Los Angeles, CA) 11/02/1981
(See Pan American Bank (Los Angeles, CA))

SANTA ANITA CONS INC (CA)
Each share Capital Stock $50 par exchanged for (2) shares Capital Stock $25 par 4/12/65
Capital Stock $25 par reclassified as Common no par and (2) additional shares issued 4/10/69
Common no par split (2) for (1) by issuance of (1) additional share 9/30/71
Under plan of reorganization each share Common no par exchanged for (1) Non-Separable Unit of (1) share Santa Anita Realty Enterprises, Inc. Common 10¢ par and (1) share Santa Anita Operating Co. Common 10¢ par 12/31/79
Santa Anita Realty Enterprises Inc. merged into Meditrust Corp. 1/5/97 which name changed to La Quinta Properties, Inc. 6/20/2001 which reorganized as La Quinta Corp. 1/2/2002
(See La Quinta Corp.)

SANTA ANITA RLTY ENTERPRISES INC (DE)
Note: Issued and transferred only in Non-Separable Units of (1) share Santa Anita Realty Enterprises, Inc. Common 10¢ par and (1) share Santa Anita Operating Co. Common 10¢ par
Stock Dividend - 100% 1/30/81
Merged into Meditrust Corp. 11/5/97
Each Combined Certificate exchanged for either (1) Paired Certificate or $31 cash
Note: Non-cash electors were not required to surrender their certificates for exchange
Meditrust Corp. name changed to La Quinta Properties, Inc. 6/20/2001 which reorganized as La Quinta Corp. 1/2/2002
(See La Quinta Corp.)

SANTA BARBARA BANCORP (CA)
Common no par split (5) for (4) by issuance of (0.25) additional share 03/25/1985
Common no par split (3) for (1) by issuance of (2) additional shares 01/23/1987
Common no par split (4) for (3) by issuance of (1/3) additional share 05/15/1989
Common no par split (2) for (1) by issuance of (1) additional share payable 04/16/1998 to holders of record 03/12/1998
Stock Dividends - 10% 03/21/1983; 10% 03/28/1984; 12% 03/29/1988
Under plan of merger name changed to Pacific Capital Bancorp (New) (CA) 12/30/1998
Pacific Capital Bancorp (New) (CA) reorganized in Delaware 12/29/2010
(See Pacific Capital Bancorp (New))

SANTA BARBARA BK & TR (SANTA BARBARA, CA)
Stock Dividends - 15% 04/25/1980; 15% 03/23/1981; 10% 03/22/1982
Under plan of reorganization each share Common $5 par automatically became (1) share Santa Barbara Bancorp Common no par 07/07/1982
Santa Barbara Bancorp merged into Pacific Capital Bancorp (New) (CA) 12/30/1998 which reorganized in Delaware 12/29/2010
(See Pacific Capital Bancorp (New))

SANTA BARBARA BILTMORE CORP.
Property sold in 1936
No stockholders' equity

SANTA BARBARA NATL BK (SANTA BARBARA, CA)
Common $10 par changed to $5 par and (1) additional share issued 04/14/1972
Stock Dividends - 10% 04/23/1973; 10% 04/25/1977; 10% 04/24/1978; 12% 04/23/1979
Name changed to Santa Barbara Bank & Trust (Santa Barbara, CA) 05/01/1979
Santa Barbara Bank & Trust (Santa Barbara, CA) reorganized as Santa Barbara Bancorp 07/07/1982 which merged into Pacific Capital Bancorp (New) (CA) 12/30/1998 which reorganized in Delaware 12/29/2010
(See Pacific Capital Bancorp (New))

SANTA BARBARA RES LTD (BC)
Voluntarily dissolved
Each share Common no par received initial distribution of approximately $0.0045 cash payable 12/23/2015 to holders of record 12/17/2015
Note: Holders may receive an additional distribution from future monetization of a non-cash asset

SANTA BARBARA RESTAURANT GROUP INC (DE)
Merged into CKE Restaurants, Inc. 03/01/2002
Each share Common 10¢ par exchanged for (0.491) share Common 1¢ par
(See CKE Restaurants, Inc.)

SANTA BARBARA VENTURES LTD (BC)
Name changed to Voodoo Ventures Ltd. 06/10/1994
Voodoo Ventures Ltd. recapitalized as Pacific Royal Ventures Ltd. 03/01/1996 which merged into Pacific Rodera Ventures Inc. 03/01/1999 which name changed to Pacific Rodera Energy Inc. (BC) 06/22/2004 which reincorporated in Alberta 06/14/2006 which name changed to PRD Energy Inc. 08/12/2010

SANTA CATALINA MNG CORP (CANADA)
Recapitalized as Valkyries Petroleum Corp. 4/25/2002
Each (15) shares Common no par exchanged for (1) share Common no par
Valkyries Petroleum Corp. acquired by Lundin Petroleum AB 7/31/2006

SANTA CECELIA SUGAR CORP.
Sold under foreclosure 00/00/1930
Details not available

SANTA CLARA VY BK N A (SANTA PAULA, CA)
Acquired by Sierra Bancorp 11/14/2014
Each share Common $5 par exchanged for $6 cash

SANTA CLARITA NATIONAL BANK (NEWHALL, CA)
Acquired by Security Pacific Corp. 11/16/90
Each share Common $2.50 par exchanged for (3.309) shares Common $10 par
Security Pacific Corp. merged into BankAmerica Corp. (Old) 4/22/92 which merged into BankAmerica Corp. (New) 9/30/98 which name changed to Bank of America Corp. 4/28/99

SANTA CRUZ GOLD INC NEW (ON)
Merged into Queenstake Resources Ltd. (Yukon) 07/19/1999
Each share Common no par exchanged for (0.1035) share Common no par
Queenstake Resources Ltd. (Yukon) reincorporated in British Columbia 07/10/2006 which merged into Yukon-Nevada Gold Corp. 06/25/2007

SANTA CRUZ GOLD INC OLD (ON)
Merged into Santa Cruz Gold Inc. (New) 09/09/1997
Each share Common no par exchanged for (1) share Common no par
Santa Cruz Gold Inc. (New) merged into Queenstake Resources Ltd. (Yukon) 07/19/1999 which reincorporated in British Columbia 07/10/2006 which merged into Yukon-Nevada Gold Corp. 06/25/2007

SANTA CRUZ OPERATION INC (CA)
Name changed to Tarantella, Inc. 5/7/2001
(See Tarantella, Inc.)

SANTA CRUZ PORTLAND CEMENT CO.
In process of liquidation in 1956

SANTA CRUZ SAVINGS & LOAN ASSOCIATION (CA)
Completely liquidated 10/12/1971
Each share Guarantee Stock $1 par exchanged for first and final distribution of (4) shares Golden West Financial Corp. (CA) Common 50¢ par
Golden West Financial Corp. (CA) reincorporated in Delaware 10/31/1975 which merged into Wachovia Corp. (Ctfs. dated after 09/01/2001) 10/02/2006 which merged into Wells Fargo & Co. (New) 12/31/2008

SANTA CRUZ VENTURES INC (BC)
Name changed to Lignol Energy Corp. 01/23/2007

SANTA ELINA GOLD CORP (BRITISH VIRGIN ISLANDS)
Merged into Echo Bay Mines Ltd. 7/16/96
Each share Common no par exchanged for (0.149925) share Common no par

SANTA FE CASH RESVS INC (MD)
Recapitalized as Venture Muni Plus, Inc. 2/28/85
Each share Capital Stock $0.001 par exchanged for (0.1) share Common 1¢ par
Venture Muni Plus, Inc. name changed to Davis Tax-Free High Income Fund Inc. 10/1/95 which reorganized as Evergreen Municipal Trust 3/17/2000

SANTA FE DOWNS INC (NM)
Adjudicated bankrupt 09/10/1976
Stockholders' equity unlikely

SANTA FE DRILLING CO (CA)
Common $1 par split (3) for (2) by issuance of (0.5) additional share 3/14/68
Stock Dividends - 105% 12/15/61; 50% 12/28/62
Name changed to Santa Fe International Corp. 5/16/68
(See Santa Fe International Corp.)

SANTA FE ENERGY GROUP INC (AB)
Name changed to European Technologies International Inc. 6/2/92
European Technologies International Inc. name changed to Steely Group Inc. 6/1/2001
(See Steely Group Inc.)

SANTA FE ENERGY PARTNERS L P (DE)
Merged into Santa Fe Energy Resources Inc. 12/29/94
Details not available

SANTA FE ENERGY RES INC (DE)
Preferred Stock Purchase Rights declared for Common stockholders of record 11/30/1990 were redeemed at $0.05 per right 03/15/1991 for holders of 02/15/1991
$0.732 Dividend Enhanced Conv. Preferred Ser. A 1¢ par called for redemption 05/15/1997
Each share Common 1¢ par received distribution of (0.441074) share Monterey Resources, Inc. Common 1¢ par payable 07/25/1997 to holders of record 07/18/1997 Ex date - 07/28/1997
7% Conv. Preferred called for redemption 05/15/1997
Under plan of merger name changed to Santa Fe Snyder Corp. 05/05/1999
Santa Fe Snyder Corp. merged into Devon Energy Corp. (New) 08/29/2000

SANTA FE ENERGY TR (TX)
Completely liquidated 03/03/2008
Each Secure Prinicpal Energy Receipt exchanged for first and final distribution of $28.53617 cash

SANTA FE GAMING CORP (NV)
Stock Dividends - in Preferred to holders of Preferred 4% payable 3/29/96 to holders of record 3/8/96; 4% payable 4% payable 9/30/96 to holders of record 9/9/96 Ex date - 9/5/96
Name changed to Archon Corp. 5/11/2001

SANTA FE GOLD & COPPER MINING CO.
Adjudicated bankrupt in 1937

SANTA FE GOLD MINES, LTD. (ON)
Charter cancelled 4/17/68
No stockholders' equity

SANTA FE HLDG CO INC (NV)
Chapter 7 bankruptcy proceedings terminated 03/21/2012
Stockholders' equity unlikely

SANTA FE INDS INC (DE)
50¢ Conv. Preferred no par called for redemption 10/14/1980
Common $10 par changed to $3.33-1/3 par and (2) additional shares issued 05/29/1981
Merged into Santa Fe Southern Pacific Corp. 12/23/1983
Each share Common $3.33-1/3 par exchanged for (1.203) shares Common $1 par

Santa Fe Southern Pacific Corp. name changed to Santa Fe Pacific Corp. 04/25/1989 which merged into Burlington Northern Santa Fe Corp. 09/22/1995
(See Burlington Northern Santa Fe Corp.)

SANTA FE INTL CORP (CA)
Common $1 par split (2) for (1) by issuance of (1) additional share 11/01/1973
Common $1 par split (2) for (1) by issuance of (1) additional share 12/28/1977
Common $1 par split (2) for (1) by issuance of (1) additional share 03/24/1981
Merged into Kuwait Petroleum Corp. 12/04/1981
Each share Common $1 par exchanged for $51 cash

SANTA FE INTL CORP (CAYMAN ISLANDS)
Issue Information - 35,000,000 ORD shs. offered at $28.50 per share on 06/09/1997
Merged into GlobalSantaFe Corp. 11/20/2001
Each share Ordinary 1¢ par exchanged for (1) share Ordinary 1¢ par
GlobalSantaFe Corp. merged into Transocean Inc. (New) (Cayman Islands) 11/27/2007 which reorganized in Switzerland as Transocean Ltd. 12/18/2008

SANTA FE INTL INC (CO)
Common 1¢ par split (2) for (1) by issuance of (1) additional share payable 06/15/1998 to holders of record 05/22/1998
Voluntarily dissolved 08/01/2006
Details not available

SANTA FE NATL BK (NORWALK, CA)
Merged into Pacific Business Bank (Carson, CA) 02/23/1996
Each share Common $5 par exchanged for $19.61 cash

SANTA FE NATIONAL BANK (SANTA FE, NM)
Merged into Western Bancorporation 7/1/80
Each share Capital Stock $25 par exchanged for (3.75) shares Capital Stock $2 par
Western Bancorporation name changed to First Interstate Bancorp 6/1/81 which merged into Wells Fargo & Co. (Old) 4/1/96 which merged into Wells Fargo & Co. (New) 11/2/98

SANTA FE NATIONAL LIFE INSURANCE CO. (NM)
Merged into Guarantee Reserve Life Insurance Co. 1/1/43
Guarantee Reserve Life Insurance Co. declared insolvent 12/31/57

SANTA FE NUCLEAR INC (NM)
Name changed to Catalyst Equity Corp. 04/22/1986
(See Catalyst Equity Corp.)

SANTA FE OIL & GAS CO (NV)
Name changed 12/11/81
Name changed from Santa Fe Oil Co. (UT) to Santa Fe Oil & Gas Co. (NV) 12/11/81
Recapitalized as South Fork Oil & Gas Co. 11/30/82
Each share Common $0.001 par exchanged for (0.1) share Common $0.001 par
South Fork Oil & Gas Co. recapitalized as Tejas Oil & Gas Co. 5/28/85
(See Tejas Oil & Gas Co.)

SANTA FE PAC CORP (DE)
Name changed 04/25/1989
Name changed from Santa Fe Southern Pacific Corp. to Santa Fe Pacific Corp. 04/25/1989
Preferred Stock Purchase Rights declared for Common stockholders of record 02/13/1986 were redeemed at $0.05 per right 03/15/1991 for holders of record 02/15/1991
Merged into Burlington Northern Santa Fe Corp. 09/22/1995
Each share Common $1 par exchanged for (0.41143945) share Common 1¢ par
(See Burlington Northern Santa Fe Corp.)

SANTA FE PAC GOLD CORP (DE)
Issue Information - 18,000,000 shares COM offered at $14 per share on 06/15/1994
Merged into Newmont Mining Corp. 5/5/97
Each share Common 1¢ par exchanged for (0.43) share Common 1¢ par

SANTA FE PAC PIPELINE PARTNERS L P (DE)
Each Preference Unit exchanged for (1) Common Unit 10/24/1994
Merged into Kinder Morgan Energy Partners L.P. 03/06/1998
Each Common Unit exchanged for (1.39) Units of Ltd. Partnership Int.
Kinder Morgan Energy Partners L.P. merged into Kinder Morgan, Inc. 11/26/2014

SANTA FE PETE INC (NV)
Name changed to Partners Health Systems Inc. 05/14/1997
(See Partners Health Systems Inc.)

SANTA FE SNYDER CORP (DE)
Merged into Devon Energy Corp. 8/29/2000
Each share Common 1¢ par exchanged for (0.22) share Common 10¢ par

SANTA FE URANIUM & OIL CO., INC. (CO)
Name changed to Santa Fe International, Inc. 7/5/61

SANTA FE URANIUM CO. (UT)
Merged into Federal Uranium Corp. (NV) on a (0.025) for (1) basis 04/28/1955
Federal Uranium Corp. merged into Federal Resources Corp. 05/02/1960
(See Federal Resources Corp.)

SANTA FE WESTERN CORP. (DE)
Name changed 08/09/1954
Name changed from Santa Fe Western Gas & Oil Corp. 08/09/1954
Name changed to Beacon Steel Corp. 10/00/1958
(See Beacon Steel Corp.)

SANTA ISABEL S A (CHILE)
ADR agreement terminated 9/10/2003
Each Sponsored ADR for Ordinary exchanged for (15) Ordinary Shares
Note: Unexchanged ADR's will be sold and proceeds, if any, held for claim after 9/10/2004

SANTA LUCIA BANCORP (CA)
Stock Dividends - 2% payable 10/20/2009 to holders of record 09/30/2009 Ex date - 09/28/2009; 2% payable 04/23/2010 to holders of record 03/31/2010 Ex date - 03/29/2010
Acquired by Carpenter Fund Manager GP, L.L.C. 10/21/2011
Each share Common no par exchanged for $0.35 cash

SANTA LUCIA NATL BK (ATASCADERO, CA)
Common $5 par split (4) for (1) by issuance of (3) additional shares payable 06/30/2005 to holders of record 06/21/2005
Under plan of reorganization each share Common $5 par automatically became (1) share Santa Lucia Bancorp Common no par 04/03/2006
(See Santa Lucia Bancorp)

SANTA MARIA MINES LTD. (ON)
Name changed to Santa Maria Resources Ltd. 06/13/1980
Santa Maria Resources Ltd. recapitalized as Simax Oil & Gas Inc. 05/30/1990
(See Simax Oil & Gas Inc.)

SANTA MARIA PETE INC (ON)
Each share old Common no par exchanged for (0.08333333) share new Common no par 03/29/2016
Reorganized under the laws of British Columbia as Kalytera Therapeutics, Inc. 01/11/2017
Each share new Common no par exchanged for (0.4347826) share Common no par

SANTA MARIA RES INC (NV)
Each share old Common $0.001 par exchanged for (0.1) share new Common $0.001 par 10/31/97
Recapitalized as FantastiCon, Inc. 10/17/2000
Each share new Common $0.001 par exchanged for (0.5) share Common $0.001 par
FantastiCon, Inc. recapitalized as USCorp 3/6/2002

SANTA MARIA RES LTD (ON)
Common $1 par changed to no par 07/30/1981
Recapitalized as Simax Oil & Gas Inc. 05/30/1990
Each share Common no par exchanged for (0.1) share Common no par
(See Simax Oil & Gas Inc.)

SANTA MARINA GOLD LTD (ON)
Merged into Akiko-Lori Gold Resources Ltd. 01/16/1991
Each share Common no par exchanged for for (0.11111111) share Common no par
Akiko-Lori Gold Resources Ltd. merged into Akiko Gold Resources Ltd. (BC) 11/09/1992 which reincorporated in Yukon as Prospex Mining Inc. 07/30/1997 which merged into Semafo Inc. 06/30/1999

SANTA MONICA BK (SANTA MONICA, CA)
Name changed 7/31/58
Name changed from Santa Monica Commercial & Savings Bank (Santa Monica, CA) to Santa Monica Bank (Santa Monica, CA) 7/31/58
Capital Stock $25 par changed to $7 par and (7) additional shares issued 7/17/61
VTC's for Capital Stock $25 par changed to $3 par and (7) additional shares issued 7/17/61
Each VTC for Capital Stock $3 par exchanged for (1) share Capital Stock $3 par 1/31/92
Stock Dividends - 33-1/3% 8/28/52; 50% 2/17/65; 10% 10/31/68; 15% 1/10/78; 15% 1/9/79; 20% 4/7/80; 25% 2/9/81; 20% 2/8/82; 20% 2/7/83; 10% 2/6/84; 20% 2/4/85; 20% 2/3/86; 20% 2/2/87; 20% 2/1/88; 20% 2/1/89; 20% 2/15/90; 20% 2/1/89; 20% 2/15/90; 20% 2/15/91
Merged into Western Bancorp 1/27/98
Each share Common $3 par exchanged for (0.875) share Common no par
Western Bancorp merged into U.S. Bancorp (Old) 11/15/99 which merged into U.S. Bancorp (New) 2/27/2001

SANTA RITA CORP (NV)
Charter revoked for failure to file reports and pay fees 1/1/92

SANTA RITA EXPLORATIONS LTD. (ON)
Merged into Lumsden Building Corp. Inc. 8/15/78
Each (21) shares Common no par exchanged for (1) share Common no par

SANTA ROSA ENTERPRISES (CA)
Name changed to Codding Enterprises 09/24/1968
(See Codding Enterprises)

SANTA ROSA SHOE CO., INC. (CA)
In process of liquidation
Each share Capital Stock $10 par exchanged for initial distribution of $13.50 cash 4/24/70
Note: Details on subsequent distributions, if any, are not available

SANTA SARITA MNG LTD (BC)
Recapitalized as Solid Gold Capital Corp. 08/28/1989
Each share Capital Stock no par exchanged for (0.25) share Common no par
Solid Gold Capital Corp. merged into Consolidated Ruskin Developments Ltd. (New) 03/31/1992 which name changed to Leisureways Marketing Ltd. (BC) 11/23/1992 which reincorporated in Yukon 11/10/1997 which name changed to LML Payment Systems Inc. (YT) 07/15/1998 which reincorporated in British Columbia 09/07/2012
(See LML Payment Systems Inc.)

SANTA YNEZ VALLEY SAVINGS & LOAN ASSOCIATION (CA)
Guarantee Stock $8 par reclassified as Common $8 par 4/12/85
Common $8 par changed to $4 par and (1) additional share issued 12/19/85
Name changed to Los Padres Savings Bank (Solvang, CA) in January 1987
(See Los Padres Savings Bank (Solvang, CA))

SANTA'S WORKSHOP COLORADO CORP. (NY)
Recapitalized 00/00/1958
Class A Common $1 par reclassified as Common $1 par
Each Unit (consisting of $400 principal amount of 5% Notes and (100) shares Class B Common $1 par) exchanged for (500) shares Common $1 par
Reincorporated under the laws of Colorado 03/30/1960

SANTACK MINES LTD (ON)
Charter cancelled for failure to pay taxes and file returns 03/15/1975

SANTANA MNG INC (NV)
Charter revoked for failure to file reports and pay fees 07/31/2012

SANTANA PETE CORP (BC)
Recapitalized as International Santana Resources Inc. 12/02/1985
Each share Common no par exchanged for (0.25) share Common no par
International Santana Resources Inc. name changed to Image West Entertainment Corp. 12/19/1986

SANTANA TECHNOLOGY CORP (AB)
Name changed 3/10/88
Name changed from Santana Resources Corp. to Santana Technology Corp. 3/10/88
Each (11) shares Common no par received (1) share Caldonia Mining Corp. Common no par upon receipt of completed letter of transmittal pursuant to shareholder meeting 7/12/93
Reorganized under the laws of Ontario as Beta Brands Inc. 10/27/93
Each share Common no par

exchanged for (0.2) share Common no par

SANTANDER BANCORP (PR)
Stock Dividends - 10% payable 07/31/2002 to holders of record 07/09/2002; 10% payable 08/03/2004 to holders of record 07/20/2004
Merged into Administracion de Bancos Latinoamericanos Santander, S.L. 07/29/2010
Each share Common $2.50 par exchanged for $12.69 cash

SANTANDER FIN PFD S A UNIPERSONAL (SPAIN)
10.50% Non-Cum. Guaranteed Preferred Ser. 1 $25 par called for redemption at $25 plus $0.65625 accrued dividends on 09/29/2014
Fixed-to-Floating Non-Cum. Guaranteed Preferred Ser. 11 $1,000 par called for redemption at $1,000 on 09/29/2014
Floating Rate Guaranteed Preferred Ser. 6 $25 par registration terminated 01/19/2018
6.5% Non-Cum. Guaranteed Preferred Ser. 5 $25 par called for redemption at $25 on 04/30/2018
6.8% Non-Cum. Guaranteed Preferred Ser. 4 $25 par called for redemption at $25 on 05/21/2018
6.41% Non-Cum. Guaranteed Preferred Ser. 1 $25 par called for redemption at $25 on 06/11/2018

SANTANDER HLDGS USA INC (VA)
Depositary Preferred Ser. C called for redemption at $25 on 08/15/2018

SANTANDER OVERSEAS BK INC (PR)
$2.66 Guaranteed Preferred Ser. A $25 par called for redemption 9/30/96
8.96% Guaranteed Preferred Ser. C $25 par called for redemption at $26.12 on 3/31/98
8.70% Guaranteed Preferred Ser. B $25 par called for redemption at $25.87 on 6/18/98
8.0% Guaranteed Preferred Ser. B $25 par called for redemption at $25.80 on 8/20/99

SANTARUS INC (DE)
Issue Information - 6,000,000 shares COM offered at $9 per share on 03/31/2004
Acquired by Salix Pharmaceuticals, Ltd. 01/02/2014
Each share Common $0.0001 par exchanged for $32 cash

SANTAS VILLAGE (CA)
Adjudicated bankrupt 2/24/78

SANTAS VLG LTD (ON)
Name changed to SVL Holdings Ltd. 04/16/2004
(See SVL Holdings Ltd.)

SANTEC CORP (NH)
Charter dissolved for failure to file reports and pay fees 11/01/1989

SANTEE MILLS
Liquidation completed in 1948

SANTEK INC (FL)
Involuntarily dissolved for failure to file annual reports 10/13/1989

SANTI GROUP INC (DE)
Name changed to Earthcare Co. 9/25/98
(See Earthcare Co.)

SANTIAGO BANK (TUSTIN, CA)
Name changed to Sunwest Bank (Old) (Tustin, CA) 11/01/1980
(See Sunwest Bank (Old) (Tustin, CA))

SANTIAGO CAP CORP (BC)
Recapitalized as Fresh Ideas Food Corp. 04/04/1990
Each share Common no par exchanged for (0.5) share Common no par
Fresh Ideas Food Corp. recapitalized as Bobby Cadillac's Food Corp. 09/30/1992 which recapitalized as Immune Network Research Ltd. 04/29/1996 which name changed to Immune Network Ltd. 08/16/2000
(See Immune Network Ltd.)

SANTIAGO COMMERCIAL BANK (TUSTIN, CA)
Name changed to Santiago Bank (Old) (Tustin, CA) 04/26/1973
Santiago Bank (Tustin, CA) name changed to Sunwest Bank (Old) (Tustin, CA) 11/01/1980
(See Sunwest Bank (Old) (Tustin, CA))

SANTIAGO MINES, LTD.
Recapitalized as New Santiago Mines Ltd. in 1951
Each share Capital Stock 50¢ par exchanged for (0.25) share Capital Stock 50¢ par
New Santiago Mines Ltd. recapitalized as Santico Mining & Exploration Ltd. 8/10/70

SANTICO MNG & EXPL (BC)
Struck off register and declared dissolved for failure to file returns 12/18/1978

SANTO PITA CORP (NV)
Name changed to Santo Mining Corp. 03/26/2012

SANTONIA ENERGY INC (AB)
Merged into Tourmaline Oil Corp. 04/29/2014
Each share Common no par exchanged for (0.03012) share Common no par
Note: Unexchanged certificates were cancelled and became without value 04/29/2017

SANTOS LTD (AUSTRALIA)
Each old Unsponsored ADR for Ordinary AUD $0.25 par exchanged for (5) new Unsponsored ADR's for Ordinary AUD $0.25 par 03/01/1966
New Unsponsored ADR for Ordinary AUD $0.25 par split (3) for (1) by issuance of (2) additional shares 01/27/1978
Each new Unsponsored ADR for Ordinary AUD $0.25 par exchanged for (0.25) Sponsored ADR for Ordinary AUD $0.25 par 12/14/1987
Stock Dividends - 200% 05/09/1981; 10% 06/24/1988
ADR agreement terminated 09/30/2009
Each Sponsored ADR for Ordinary AUD $0.25 par exchanged for $54.007622 cash
(Additional Information in Active)

SANTOS RESOURCE CORP (NV)
Name changed to Discovery Energy Corp. 05/07/2012

SANTOS SILVER MINES LTD. (ON)
Acquired by Utica Mines Ltd. (New) on a (1/6) for (1) basis 9/30/64
Utica Mines Ltd. (New) recapitalized as Dankoe Mines Ltd. 9/25/71 which recapitalized as Emerald Dragon Mines Inc. 10/30/96
(See Emerald Dragon Mines Inc.)

SANTOY RES LTD NEW (AB)
Reorganized under the laws of British Columbia as Virginia Energy Resources Inc. (Old) 07/24/2009
Each share Common no par exchanged for (0.2) share Common no par and (0.25) Common Stock Purchase Warrant expiring 07/21/2010
Note: Holders of (499) or fewer shares received $0.10 cash per share in lieu of Warrants
Note: Unexchanged certificates were cancelled and became without value 07/24/2015
Virginia Energy Resources Inc. (Old) reorganized as Anthem Resources Inc. 09/28/2012 which merged into Boss Power Corp. 07/23/2015 which name changed to Eros Resources Corp. 07/29/2015

SANTOY RES LTD OLD (AB)
Merged into Santoy Resources Ltd. (AB) (New) 04/24/2003
Each share Common no par exchanged for (1) share Common no par
Santoy Resources Ltd. (AB) (New) reorganized in British Columbia as Virginia Energy Resources Ltd. (Old) 07/24/2009 which reorganized as Anthem Resources Inc. 09/28/2012 which merged into Boss Power Corp. 07/23/2015 which name changed to Eros Resources Corp. 07/29/2015

SANU RES LTD (CANADA)
Merged into Canadian Gold Hunter Corp. 08/20/2009
Each share Common no par exchanged for (0.5725) share Common no par
Canadian Gold Hunter Corp. name changed to NGEx Resources Inc. 09/22/2009

SANWA BK LTD (JAPAN)
ADR agreement terminated 6/25/2001
Each ADR for Ordinary 50 yen par exchanged for approximately $53.231 cash
Note: Due to ADR's being unsponsored exchange rate may vary dependent upon depositary agent

SANWA INTL FIN BERMUDA TR (JAPAN)
ADR agreement terminated 8/30/2004
Each Sponsored ADR for Preferred exchanged for (1) share Preferred

SANWIRE CORP (NV)
Reincorporated under the laws of Wyoming 07/07/2015

SANYO ELEC LTD (JAPAN)
Each old ADR for Common JPY 50 par exchanged for (4) new ADR's for Common JPY 50 par 06/21/1982
Stock Dividend - 10% 03/15/1985
Merged into Panasonic Corp. 04/01/2011
Each new ADR for Common JPY 50 par exchanged for $7.043762 cash

SANYO INDS INC (DE)
Each share Common $0.001 par exchanged for (0.5) share Common $0.001 par 2/17/93
Recapitalized as Brake Headquarters U.S.A., Inc. 8/8/95
Each share Common $0.001 par exchanged for (0.1) share Common $0.001 par
(See Brake Headquarters U.S.A., Inc.)

SANYO MFG CORP (DE)
Merged into New SMC, Inc. 08/31/1987
Each share Common 50¢ par exchanged for $3 cash

SANYO SEC LTD (JAPAN)
ADR agreement terminated 10/30/2007
No ADR holders' equity

SAO LUIS MNG INC (CO)
Common $0.001 par split (40) for (1) by issuance of (39) additional shares payable 06/01/2006 to holders of record 05/26/2006
Ex date - 06/02/2006
Reorganized under the laws of Nevada as Brazilian Mining Corp. 03/26/2009
Each share Common $0.001 par exchanged for (0.001) share Common $0.001 par
Brazilian Mining Corp. name changed to Sierra Desert Holdings Inc. 10/18/2010 which recapitalized as Telefix Communications Holdings, Inc. 03/12/2012

SAO PAULO ALPARGATAS S A (ARGENTINA)
ADR agreement terminated 09/30/2005
Each Sponsored ADR for Preferred no par exchanged for $22.48852 cash
Each Sponsored ADR for Common no par exchanged for $22.48852 cash

SAP AG (GERMANY)
ADR basis changed from (12:1) to (1:0.25) 06/26/2000
Sponsored ADR's for Preference reclassified as Sponsored ADR's for Ordinary 06/26/2001
ADR basis changed from (1:0.25) to (1:1) 12/21/2006
Name changed to SAP S.E. 07/08/2014

SAP'S BAKERY, INC. (IN)
Name changed to Sap's Foods, Inc. 3/27/69
Sap's Foods, Inc. merged into Beatrice Foods Co. 8/22/72 which name changed to Beatrice Companies, Inc. 6/5/84
(See Beatrice Companies, Inc.)

SAPAWE GOLD MINES LTD (ON)
Struck from the register and dissolved 10/1/94

SAPIENS INTL CORP N V (CURACAO)
Reincorporated 10/10/2010
Each share Common NLG 1 par exchanged for (0.2) share Common EUR 2.30 par 06/16/2003
Common EUR 2.30 par changed to EUR 0.01 par 08/26/2004
Place of incorporation changed from Netherlands to Curacao 10/10/2010
Reincorporated under the laws of Cayman Islands 08/22/2018

SAPIENT CORP (DE)
Common 1¢ par split (2) for (1) by issuance of (1) additional share payable 03/09/1998 to holders of record 02/20/1998
Common 1¢ par split (2) for (1) by issuance of (1) additional share payable 11/05/1999 to holders of record 11/01/1999
Common 1¢ par split (2) for (1) by issuance of (1) additional share payable 08/28/2000 to holders of record 08/14/2000
Acquired by Publicis Groupe S.A. 02/06/2015
Each share Common 1¢ par exchanged for $25 cash

SAPPHIRE INDUSTRIALS CORP (DE)
Issue Information - 80,000,000 UNITS consisting of (1) share COM and (1) WT offered at $10 per Unit on 01/17/2008
Completely liquidated 01/19/2010
Each Unit exchanged for first and final distribution of $10.0638 cash
Each share Common $0.001 par exchanged for first and final distribution of $10.0638 cash

SAPPHIRE MINES LTD (AUSTRALIA)
Name changed 02/08/2002
Name changed from Sapphire Mines N.L. to Sapphire Mines Ltd. 02/08/2002
Name changed to Central Asia Gold Ltd. 12/03/2002
ADR agreement terminated 01/08/2003
Each ADR for Ordinary exchanged for for $0.2546 cash
Central Asia Gold Ltd. name changed to CGA Mining Ltd. 12/19/2006 which merged into B2Gold Corp. 01/31/2013

FINANCIAL INFORMATION, INC.

SAPPHIRE PETROLEUMS LTD. (ON)
Common no par changed to $1 par 00/00/1952
Common $1 par changed to no par 04/06/1961
Recapitalized as Cabol Enterprises, Ltd. on a (1) for (10) basis 01/19/1962
(See Cabol Enterprises, Ltd.)

SAPS FOODS INC (IN)
Common no par split (3) for (1) by issuance of (2) additional shares 3/27/69
Merged into Beatrice Foods Co. 8/22/72
Each share Common no par exchanged for (0.1560489) share Common no par
Beatrice Foods Co. name changed to Beatrice Companies, Inc. 6/5/84
(See Beatrice Companies, Inc.)

SAPUTO GROUP INC (CANADA)
Name changed to Saputo Inc. 8/3/2000

SARA CARE INC (UT)
Involuntarily dissolved 06/01/1998

SARA CREEK GOLD CORP (NV)
Old Common $0.001 par split (15) for (1) by issuance of (14) additional shares payable 09/24/2009 to holders of record 09/24/2009
Each share old Common $0.001 par exchanged for (0.03333333) share new Common $0.001 par 02/08/2011
Name changed to Hawker Energy, Inc. 09/26/2014

SARA ENVIRONMENTAL INC (OK)
Reincorporated 01/31/1995
State of incorporation changed from (UT) to (OK) 01/31/1995
Each share Common 1¢ par exchanged for (0.1) share Common 1¢ par
Recapitalized as Sara Hallitex Corp. (OK) 06/01/1997
Each share Common 1¢ par exchanged for (0.025) share Common 1¢ par
Sara Hallitex Corp. (OK) reincorporated in Nevada as Web Capital Group, Inc. 12/08/1999 which merged into Web Capital Ventures, Inc. 03/31/2000 which recapitalized as Troy Gold & Mineral Corp. 10/09/2007

SARA HALLITEX CORP (OK)
Reincorporated under the laws of Nevada as Web Capital Group, Inc. 12/08/1999
Web Capital Group, Inc. merged into Web Capital Ventures, Inc. 03/31/2000 which recapitalized as Troy Gold & Mineral Corp. 10/09/2007

SARA LEE CORP (MD)
Common $1.33333333 par split (2) for (1) by issuance of (1) additional share 12/22/1986
Common $1.33333333 par split (2) for (1) by issuance of (1) additional share 12/22/1989
Common $1.33333333 par split (2) for (1) by issuance of (1) additional share 12/21/1992
Adjustable Rate Conv. Preferred no par called for redemption 07/26/1993
Auction Preferred Ser. F no par called for redemption at $100,000 plus $548.39 accrued dividends on 06/12/1997
Auction Preferred Ser. A no par called for redemption at $100,000 plus $556.69 accrued dividends on 06/19/1997
Auction Preferred Ser. C no par called for redemption at $100,000 on 07/17/1997
Auction Preferred Ser. E no par called for redemption at $100,000 on 07/17/1997
Auction Preferred Ser. B no par called for redemption at $100,000 on 08/21/1997
Auction Preferred Ser. D no par called for redemption at $100,000 on 08/28/1997
Common $1.33333333 changed to 1¢ par 10/00/1998
Common 1¢ par split (2) for (1) by issuance of (1) additional share payable 12/21/1998 to holders of record 12/01/1998 Ex date - 12/22/1998
Each share Common 1¢ par received distribution of (0.125) share Hanesbrands Inc. Common 1¢ par payable 09/05/2006 to holders of record 08/18/2006 Ex date - 09/06/2006
Recapitalized as Hillshire Brands Co. 06/29/2012
Each share Common 1¢ par exchanged for (0.2) share Common 1¢ par
(See Hillshire Brands Co.)

SARABAT GOLD CORP (BC)
Recapitalized as Consolidated Sarabat Gold Corp. 12/03/1996
Each share Common no par exchanged for (0.2) share Common no par
Consolidated Sarabat Gold Corp. recapitalized as CSG Resources Ltd. 11/20/1998 which name changed to Artgallerylive.com Management Ltd. 09/24/1999 which recapitalized as Adaptive Marketing Solutions Inc. 01/18/2001 which recapitalized as Permission Marketing Solutions Inc. 01/18/2002 which name changed to Pacific Asia China Energy Inc. 01/04/2006
(See Pacific Asia China Energy Inc.)

SARAFAND DEVS LTD (BC)
Recapitalized as Val D'Or Explorations Ltd. 11/15/1978
Each share Common no par exchanged for (0.25) share Common no par
Val D'Or Explorations Ltd. merged into Meridor Resources Ltd. 04/01/1985 which merged into Hughes Lang Corp. 08/01/1989 which merged into CanGold Resources Inc. (BC) 01/31/1994 which reorganized in Ontario as Amalgamated CanGold Resources Inc. 07/31/1995 which merged into Central Asia Goldfields Corp. 01/08/1996
(See Central Asia Goldfields Corp.)

SARAH ACQUISITION CORP (FL)
Reorganized under the laws of Nevada as Karts International Inc. 02/23/1996
Each share Common $0.0001 par exchanged for (0.004) share Common $0.001 par
Karts International Inc. name changed to 4D Seismic, Inc. 04/11/2006
(See 4D Seismic, Inc.)

SARAIVA S A LIVREIROS EDITORES (BRAZIL)
ADR agreement terminated 10/06/2017
No ADR's remain outstanding

SARANAC PULP & PAPER CO., INC.
Property sold in 1932
No stockholders' equity

SARANAC RIVER POWER CORP.
Out of business 00/00/1936
Details not available

SARANAC URANIUM MINES LTD. (ON)
Charter revoked for failure to file reports and pay fees 9/28/64

SARASOTA BANCORP INC (FL)
Merged into Colonial BancGroup, Inc. 10/23/2003
Each share Common 1¢ par exchanged for (4.0755) shares Common $2.50 par
(See Colonial BancGroup, Inc.)

SARATOGA & SCHENECTADY RR CO (NY)
Company advised privately held 00/00/1980
Details not available

SARATOGA BANCORP (CA)
Common no par split (3) for (2) by issuance of (0.5) additional share payable 05/01/1998 to holders of record 04/15/1998
Merged into SJNB Financial Corp. 01/05/2000
Each share Common no par exchanged for (0.7) share Common no par
SJNB Financial Corp. merged into Greater Bay Bancorp 10/23/2001 which merged into Wells Fargo & Co. (New) 10/01/2007

SARATOGA BEVERAGE GROUP INC (DE)
Merged into North Castle Partners, L.L.C. 6/21/2000
Each share Class A Common 1¢ par exchanged for $6 cash

SARATOGA BRANDS INC (NY)
Each share old Common $1 par exchanged for (0.1) share new Common $1 par 06/02/1994
Each share new Common $1 par exchanged for (0.1) share Common no par 08/28/1995
Each share Common no par exchanged for (1/3) share Common $0.001 par 11/24/1997
Name changed to Classica Group, Inc. 09/07/1999
(See Classica Group, Inc.)

SARATOGA CAP CORP (ON)
Cease trade order effective 05/16/2005

SARATOGA ELECTR SOLUTIONS INC (CANADA)
Name changed to Abba Medix Group Inc. 05/14/2015
Abba Medix Group Inc. recapitalized as Canada House Wellness Group Inc. 11/09/2016

SARATOGA EXPLORATION CO. LTD. (ON)
Merged into Landmark Mines Ltd. on a (0.1) for (1) basis in May, 1956
Landmark Mines Ltd. charter cancelled 11/1/72

SARATOGA HARNESS RACING ASSOCIATION, INC. (NY)
Name changed to Saratoga Harness Racing, Inc. 5/20/68

SARATOGA HLDGS I INC (TX)
Recapitalized as A21, Inc. (TX) 05/07/2002
Each (2.3402) shares Common no par exchanged for (1) share Common no par
A21, Inc. (TX) reincorporated in Delaware 07/31/2006
(See A21, Inc. (DE))

SARATOGA INTL HLGDS CORP (NV)
Each share old Common $0.001 par exchanged for (0.5) share new Common $0.001 par 04/10/2001
Each share new Common $0.001 par exchanged again for (0.02222222) share new Common $0.001 par 07/03/2001
Name changed to Fortune Credit & Insurance Services, Inc. and new Common $0.001 par changed to $0.0001 par 09/27/2001

SARATOGA MINES INC (CO)
Charter suspended for failure to maintain a resident agent 05/07/1988

SARATOGA PLASTICS, INC. (NY)
Name changed to Techtro-Matic Corp. 1/26/60
Techtro-Matic Corp. proclaimed dissolved 12/15/69

SARATOGA PROCESSING LTD (AB)
Merged into 172173 Canada Inc. 10/18/93
Each share Class A Common $2 par exchanged for $23 cash

SARATOGA RACING ASSOCIATION (NY)
Liquidated 10/5/55

SARATOGA RES INC (DE)
Each share Common 25¢ par received distribution of (1) share Saratoga Holdings I Inc. Common 1¢ par and (1) share Saratoga Resources Inc. (TX) Common $0.001 par payable 08/10/1999 to holders of record 08/09/1999
(See each company's listing)
Note: California residents will receive approximately $0.003 cash per share in lieu of Saratoga Holdings I Inc. stock
Recapitalized as OptiCare Health Systems, Inc. 08/13/1999
Each share Common 25¢ par exchanged for for (0.06493) share Common 25¢ par
OptiCare Health Systems, Inc. merged into Refac Optical Group 03/06/2006

SARATOGA SPRING WTR CO (DE)
Name changed to Saratoga Beverage Group Inc. 8/4/94
(See Saratoga Beverage Group Inc.)

SARATOGA STANDARDBREDS INC (NY)
Recapitalized as SSI Capital Corp. (NY) 06/16/1994
Each share Common 1¢ par exchanged for (0.1) share Common 1¢ par
SSI Capital Corp. (NY) reorganized in Colorado as OraLabs Holding Corp. 08/26/1997 which name changed to China Precision Steel, Inc. (CO) 12/28/2006 which reincorporated in Delaware 11/16/2007

SARCEE MINES LTD.
Acquired by Amalgamated Larder Mines Ltd. 00/00/1942
Each share Capital Stock $1 par exchanged for (0.48) share Capital Stock $1 par
Amalgamated Larder Mines Ltd. recapitalized as Larder Resources Inc. 09/08/1980 which merged into International Larder Minerals Inc. 05/01/1986 which merged into Explorers Alliance Corp. 10/13/2000
(See Explorers Alliance Corp.)

SARCEE PETROLEUMS LTD. (AB)
Acquired by Husky Oil Canada Ltd. for cash 12/14/64

SARDIK, INC.
Name changed to Sardik Food Products Corp. in 1946
(See Sardik Food Products Corp.)

SARDIK FOOD PRODUCTS CORP. (DE)
No longer in existence having become inoperative and void for non-payment of taxes 4/1/52
Preferred & Common stocks are without value

SARE HLDG S A DE C V (MEXICO)
ADR agreement terminated 02/08/2018
Each Sponsored ADR for Ser. B exchanged for (15) Ser. B shares
Note: Unexchanged ADR's will be sold and the proceeds, if any, held for claim after 02/11/2019

SAREPTA THERAPEUTICS INC (OR)
Reincorporated under the laws of Delaware 06/10/2013

SAR-SAT

SAREX CORP (DE)
Adjudicated bankrupt 04/14/1972
Stockholders' equity unlikely

SAREZE, INC. (FL)
Bankrupt 1958

SARGASSO CAP CORP (ON)
Name changed to C2C Industrial Properties Inc. 05/18/2011
C2C Industrial Properties Inc. merged into Dundee Industrial Real Estate Investment Trust 07/23/2013 which name changed to Dream Industrial Real Estate Investment Trust 05/08/2014

SARGENT & CO. (CT)
Common $25 par changed to $10 par in 1932
Recapitalized in 1943
Each share Preferred $100 par exchanged for (6) shares Capital Stock $15 par and $5 cash
Each share Common $10 par exchanged for (1/3) share Capital Stock $15 par
Name changed to Long Wharf Liquidating Co., Inc. 4/21/67
Long Wharf Liquidating Co., Inc. was acquired by Kidde (Walter) & Co., Inc. (NY) 4/21/67 which reincorporated in Delaware 7/2/68
(See Kidde (Walter) & Co., Inc. (DE))

SARGENT & GREENLEAF INC (NY)
Completely liquidated 2/3/81
Each share Capital Stock $1 par exchanged for first and final distribution of $30.22 cash

SARGENT ART CORP. (MD)
Name changed to Beverages, Inc. (Md.) 12/23/66
Beverages, Inc. (Md.) completely liquidated 7/20/67

SARGENT E H & CO (IL)
Merged into Sargent-Welch Scientific Co. 05/31/1968
Each share Common $20 par exchanged for (50) shares Common $1 par
(See Sargent-Welch Scientific Co.)

SARGENT INC NEW (DE)
Name changed to National Quality Care Inc. 6/18/96

SARGENT INC OLD (DE)
Reorganized as Sargent, Inc. (New) 7/25/94
Each share Common $0.001 par exchanged for (0.005) share Common 1¢ par
Sargent, Inc. (New) name changed to National Quality Care Inc. 5/28/96

SARGENT INDS INC (CA)
Acquired by Dover Corp. 09/21/1984
Each share Common no par exchanged for $8.90 cash

SARGENT INDS INC (DE)
Merged into Orico 01/10/1979
Each share 4-1/2% Conv. Preferred no par exchanged for $53 cash
Each share Common no par exchanged for $9.50 cash

SARGENT WELCH SCIENTIFIC CO (IL)
Merged into Artra Group Inc. 01/09/1987
Each share Common $1 par exchanged for $42 cash

SARGOLD RESOURCE CORP (BC)
Merged into Buffalo Gold Ltd. 10/30/2007
Each share Common no par exchanged for (0.28571428) share Common no par
(See Buffalo Gold Ltd.)

SARGON RES LTD (BC)
Recapitalized as International Sargon Resources Ltd. 07/10/1996
Each share Common no par exchanged for (0.2) share Common no par
International Sargon Resources Ltd. name changed to Canoil Exploration Corp. 07/28/1999 which name changed to AMS Homecare Inc. 03/15/2002
(See AMS Homecare Inc.)

SARICH TECHNOLOGIES LTD (AUSTRALIA)
Name changed 04/28/1989
Under plan of merger name changed from Sarich Technologies Trust to Sarich Technologies Ltd. and each Sponsored ADR for Units no par exchanged for $6.238 cash 04/28/1989
Name changed to Orbital Engine Corp. Ltd. 11/29/1990
Orbital Engine Corp. Ltd. name changed to Orbital Corp. Ltd. 11/15/2004
(See Orbital Corp. Ltd.)

SARIMCO MINES LTD (ON)
Charter cancelled for failure to pay taxes and file returns 03/16/1976

SARKIS CAP INC (DE)
Name changed to Starnet Financial Inc. 6/11/99
Starnet Financial Inc. name changed to Mobile Ready Entertainment Corp. 5/9/2006

SARLO DEVELOPMENT CORP. (UT)
Name changed to United International Gold Inc. 10/25/84
(See United International Gold Inc.)

SARMAC GOLD MINING CORP. (QC)
Charter cancelled for failure to file reports 4/27/74

SARNIA CORP (VA)
Merged into Bresler & Reiner, Inc. 01/31/2002
Each share Common 1¢ par exchanged for $1.48 cash
Note: Each share Common 1¢ par received an initial additional distribution of $0.125 cash 04/01/2003
Each share Common 1¢ par received a second and final distribution of $0.0065 cash 07/09/2003

SARNIA ST. CLAIR AIR SERVICES LTD. (ON)
Name changed to Aviation Investments Ltd. 9/13/58
Aviation Investments Ltd. charter cancelled 3/11/65

SARNOIL LTD (ON)
Charter cancelled for failure to file returns and pay taxes 08/09/1972

SARPEDON IRON MINES LTD. (ON)
Liquidated in 1952

SARS CORP (NV)
SEC revoked common stock registration 10/07/2013

SARTIGAN GRANITE CORP (CANADA)
Recapitalized as Startigan Corp. 10/29/1993
Each share Common no par exchanged for (0.2) share Common no par
Startigan Corp. reincorporated in Yukon as Ecuadorian Minerals Corp. 02/14/1994 which name changed to International Minerals Corp. 01/24/2002
(See International Minerals Corp.)

SARTIS MED SYS CDA INC (BC)
Recapitalized as United Sartis Enterprises Inc. 12/05/1995
Each share Common no par exchanged for (0.2) share Common no par
United Sartis Enterprises Inc. name changed to Wellco Energy Services Inc. (BC) 02/11/1999 which reorganized in Alberta as Wellco Energy Services Trust 08/06/2002 which merged into Peak Energy Services Trust 03/12/2008 which reorganized as Peak Energy Services Ltd. (New) 01/06/2011
(See Peak Energy Services Ltd. (New))

SASAMAT CAP CORP (BC)
Merged into KHD Humboldt Wedag International 06/01/2007
Each share Common no par exchanged for (0.1) share Common no par
KHD Humboldt Wedag International Ltd. reorganized as Terra Nova Royalty Corp. 03/30/2010 which name changed to MFC Industrial Ltd. 09/30/2011 which name changed to MFC Bancorp Ltd. (BC) 02/16/2016
(See MFC Bancorp Ltd. (BC))

SASCO COSMETICS, INC. (TX)
Name changed to Sasco Products, Inc. and Common 1¢ par changed to no par 11/12/1984
(See Sasco Products, Inc.)

SASCO PRODS INC (TX)
Ceased operations 01/00/1990
Details not available

SASHA TECHNOLOGY SYSTEMS LTD (CANADA)
Recapitalized 07/26/1988
Recapitalized from Sasha Technologies Ltd. to Sasha Technology Systems Ltd. 07/26/1988
Each share Common no par exchanged for (1/3) share Common no par
Name changed to Consolidated Sasha Technology Ltd. 09/15/1993
(See Consolidated Sasha Technology Ltd.)

SASHA VENTURES LTD (BC)
Recapitalized as eShippers.com Management Ltd. 10/24/2000
Each (2.2) shares Common no par exchanged for (1) share Common no par
eShippers.com Management Ltd. recapitalized as eShippers Management Ltd. 2/28/2003

SASKALON URANIUM & OILS LTD. (ON)
Charter cancelled by Province of Ontario for default 11/06/1961

SASKATCHEWAN CEMENT CORP. LTD. (SK)
Acquired by Inland Cement Co. Ltd. on the basis of (1) share of 6% Non-Cum. Preferred $10 par for each (6) shares of Common no par 8/13/57

SASKATCHEWAN CO-OPERATIVE CREAMERIES
Liquidated in 1926

SASKATCHEWAN OIL & GAS CORP (SK)
7.25% Conv. 2nd Preferred Ser. A no par called for redemption 3/31/90
Name changed to Wascana Energy Inc. 11/18/93
(See Wascana Energy Inc.)

SASKATCHEWAN TR CO (SASKATOON, SASK)
Liquidated 00/00/1991
No stockholders' equity

SASKATCHEWAN WHEAT POOL INC (CANADA)
Reincorporated 03/31/2005
Name and place of incorporation changed from Saskatchewan Wheat Pool (SK) to Saskatchewan Wheat Pool Inc. (Canada) 03/31/2005
Each share Non-Vtg. Class B no par received (0.05) share Common no par
Note: Certificates were not required to be surrendered and are without value
Name changed to Viterra Inc. 03/19/2008

(See Viterra Inc.)

SASKATOON PIPE LINE CO. LTD. (SK)
Acquired by Gulf Oil Canada Ltd. in October 1970
Each share Capital Stock no par exchanged for $7.17528 cash

SASKO-HOLDINGS LTD. (AB)
Struck off register for failure to file annual reports 3/15/60

SASKO OIL & GAS LTD (CANADA)
Recapitalized as Gentry Resources Ltd. 10/29/1990
Each share Class B Common no par exchanged for (0.2) share Class B Common no par
Gentry Resources Ltd. merged into Crew Energy Inc. 08/22/2008

SASKO WAINWRIGHT OIL & GAS LTD (CANADA)
Name changed to Sasko Oil & Gas Ltd. and Common no par reclassified as Class B Common no par 09/21/1981
Sasko Oil & Gas Ltd. recapitalized as Gentry Resources Ltd. 10/29/1990 which merged into Crew Energy Inc. 08/22/2008

SASKURAN EXPLS INC (ON)
Name changed to Team Energy & Minerals Inc. 11/05/1980
(See Team Energy & Minerals Inc.)

SASLOW D L INC (DE)
Common 50¢ par split (3) for (2) by issuance of (0.5) additional share 02/28/1973
Merged into Tilling (Thomas) Ltd. 01/04/1979
Each share Common 50¢ par exchanged for $12.25 cash

SASSCO FASHIONS LTD (DE)
Name changed to Kasper ASL, Ltd. 11/05/1997
(See Kasper ASL, Ltd.)

SASSOON GROUP INC (NV)
Name changed to BIB Holdings, Ltd. 12/15/2003
BIB Holdings, Ltd. name changed to Incode Technologies Corp. (NV) 02/07/2005 which reincorporated in Delaware as Inseq Corp. 07/13/2005 which name changed to GS Energy Corp. 07/19/2006 which recapitalized as EcoSystem Corp. 02/12/2008 which recapitalized as Adarna Energy Corp. 07/07/2011
(See Adarna Energy Corp.)

SASSOON INTL INC (NV)
Charter revoked for failure to file reports and pay fees 3/1/96

SASTEX OIL & GAS LTD. (AB)
Common no par changed to 1¢ par 11/8/56
Recapitalized as Sastex Petro-Minerals Ltd. 4/27/66
Each share Common 1¢ par exchanged for (1/7) share Common no par
(See Sastex Petro-Minerals Ltd.)

SASTEX PETRO MINERALS LTD (AB)
Recapitalized 4/27/66
Common no par changed to 1¢ par 11/8/56
Recapitalized from Sastex Oil & Gas Ltd. to Sastex Petro Minerals Ltd. 4/27/66
Each share Common 1¢ par exchanged for (1/7) share Common no par
Struck off register 7/1/92

SAT-TEL CORP (DE)
Merged into IROC Systems Corp. (Canada) 02/28/2003
Each share Common no par exchanged for (1/6) share Common no par
IROC Systems Corp. (Canada) name changed to IROC Energy Services

Corp. 05/22/2007 which merged into Western Energy Services Corp. 04/22/2013

SATCON TECHNOLOGY CORP (DE)
Each share old Common 1¢ par received distribution of (0.3023) share Beacon Power Corp. Common 1¢ par payable 09/28/2001 to holders of record 09/24/2001 Ex date - 10/01/2001
Each share old Common 1¢ par exchanged for (0.125) share new Common 1¢ par 07/19/2012
Chapter 7 bankruptcy proceedings terminated 01/30/2013
Stockholders' equity unlikely

SATELCO INC (TX)
Filed a petition under Chapter 11 Federal Bankruptcy Code 07/12/1985
No stockholders' equity

SATELINX INTL INC (NV)
Common 1¢ par split (15) for (1) by issuance of (14) additional shares payable 07/24/2006 to holders of record 07/21/2006 Ex date - 07/25/2006
Recapitalized as Affinity Networks, Inc. 08/13/2007
Each (35,000) shares Common 1¢ par exchanged for (1) share Common 1¢ par

SATELLINK CORP (DE)
Reincorporated 10/30/87
Common no par changed to $0.001 par 6/22/87
State of incorporation changed from (CO) to (DE) and each share Common $0.001 par exchanged for (0.1) share Common $0.001 par 10/30/87
Name changed to Anghel Laboratories, Inc. 4/29/89
(See Anghel Laboratories, Inc.)

SATELLITE AUCTION NETWORK INC (DE)
Recapitalized as Shanghai Yutong Pharmaceutical, Inc. 05/16/2005
Each share Common 1¢ par exchanged for (0.005) share Common 1¢ par
Note: Due to actions taking place by corporate identity hijacking, name changed back to Satellite Auction Network, Inc. 06/09/2005
(See Shanghai Yutong Pharmaceutical, Inc.)
SEC revoked common stock registration 07/07/2011

SATELLITE BINGO INC (UT)
Name changed to SBI Communications Inc. (UT) 05/02/1988
SBI Communications Inc. (UT) reorganized in Delaware 01/28/1993 which name changed to ValCom, Inc. 03/07/2001
(See ValCom, Inc.)

SATELLITE CMNTYS LD DEV CORP (MA)
Adjudicated bankrupt 10/26/1976
Stockholders' equity unlikely

SATELLITE COMMUNICATION CORP. (DE)
Charter cancelled and declared inoperative and void for non-payment of taxes 03/01/1996

SATELLITE CONS METALS LTD (ON)
Name changed to Phoenix Gold Mines Ltd. 06/30/1986
(See Phoenix Gold Mines Ltd.)

SATELLITE CTL TECHNOLOGIES INC (NV)
Name changed to SATX, Inc. 8/19/99
SATX, Inc. reorganized as Peninsula Holdings Group, Ltd. 12/7/2002
(See Peninsula Holdings Group, Ltd.)

SATELLITE DATA INC (CO)
Administratively dissolved 1/1/91

SATELLITE ENTERPRISES CORP (NV)
Common $0.001 par split (3) for (1) by issuance of (2) additional shares payable 03/31/2004 to holders of record 03/22/2004 Ex date - 04/01/2004
Name changed to Satellite Newspapers Corp. 11/30/2005
Satellite Newspapers Corp. recapitalized as Genmed Holding Corp. 01/28/2008
(See Genmed Holding Corp.)

SATELLITE INDS INC (DE)
Each share Common $0.001 par exchanged for (0.1) share Common 1¢ par 05/13/1983
Charter cancelled and declared inoperative and void for non-payment of taxes 03/01/1988

SATELLITE INFORMATION SYS CO (CO)
Each share old Common no par exchanged for (0.1) share new Common no par 03/07/1988
Name changed to Siscom, Inc. 02/18/1997
(See Siscom, Inc.)

SATELLITE METAL MINES LTD (ON)
Recapitalized as Satellite Consolidated Metals Ltd. 06/23/1983
Each share Capital Stock $1 par exchanged for (0.2) share Common no par
Satellite Consolidated Metals Ltd. name changed to Phoenix Gold Mines Ltd. 06/30/1986
(See Phoenix Gold Mines Ltd.)

SATELLITE MUSIC NETWORK INC (DE)
Acquired by Capital Cities/ABC, Inc. 7/31/89
Each share Common 10¢ par exchanged for $5.60 cash

SATELLITE NEWSPAPERS CORP (NV)
Recapitalized as Genmed Holding Corp. 01/28/2008
Each share Common $0.001 par exchanged for (0.0005) share Common $0.001 par
(See Genmed Holding Corp.)

SATELLITE PHONE SOURCE INC (NV)
Reincorporated under the laws of Delaware as Vision Works Media Group, Inc. 04/06/2005
Vision Works Media Group, Inc. name changed to Perihelion Global, Inc. (DE) 10/25/2006 which reincorporated in Nevada 04/01/2008 which recapitalized as Nymet Holdings Inc. 04/21/2009

SATELLITE RETAIL CORP. (CO)
Out of business 3/23/81
No stockholders' equity

SATELLITE SEC CORP (NV)
Each share old Common $0.001 par exchanged for (0.002) share new Common $0.001 par 08/20/2007
Name changed to Mobicom Corp. 05/22/2008
(See Mobicom Corp.)

SATELLITE SYNDICATED SYS INC (OK)
Name changed to Tempo Enterprises, Inc. 3/3/86
Tempo Enterprises, Inc. merged into Tele-Communications, Inc. (Old) 12/20/88 which merged into Tele-Communications, Inc. (New) 8/5/94 which merged into AT&T Corp. 3/9/99 which merged into AT&T Inc. 11/18/2005

SATELLITE SYS CORP (TX)
Charter cancelled for failure to pay taxes 05/08/1972

SATELLITE TECHNOLOGY MGMT INC (CA)
Reincorporated under the laws of Delaware as STM Wireless, Inc. 12/28/1995
(See STM Wireless, Inc.)

SATELLITE TELEVISION & ASSD RES INC (DC)
Charter revoked for failure to file reports 12/10/84

SATELLITE VIDEO TECHNOLOGY INC (NV)
Charter revoked for failure to file a list of officers 09/01/1987

SATMAX CORP (NV)
Name changed to Green Energy Solution Industries, Inc. 03/02/2012

SATO STEVIA INTL INC (BC)
Struck off register and declared dissolved for failure to file returns 07/05/1991

SATOR CAP INC (AB)
Issue Information - 3,000,000 shares COM offered at $0.10 per share on 12/09/1996
Name changed to LWT Services, Inc. 7/22/98

SATORI ENTMT CORP (NY)
Charter cancelled and proclaimed dissolved for failure to pay taxes 12/23/92

SATRA CORP (NY)
Company went out of business 00/00/1995
Details not available

SATTEL GLOBAL NETWORKS INC (CO)
Recapitalized as Urbani Holdings, Inc. 01/28/2002
Each (12) shares Common $0.001 par exchanged for (1) share Common $0.001 par
Urbani Holdings, Inc. name changed to United Specialties, Inc. 07/28/2003 which name changed to WaterColor Holdings Corp. 04/10/2006
(See WaterColor Holdings Corp.)

SATURN AWYS INC (FL)
Merged into Transamerica Corp. 11/30/1976
Each share Common $1 par exchanged for (1.2) shares Common $1 par
Transamerica Corp. merged into Aegon N.V. 07/21/1999

SATURN DISQ INC (CANADA)
Name changed to Saturn (Solutions) Inc. 08/04/1992
(See Saturn (Solutions) Inc.)

SATURN ELECTRONICS CORP. (DE)
Acquired by Saturn Industries, Inc. 1/31/66
Each share Class A Common 10¢ par exchanged for approximately (0.25) share Common 10¢ par
Saturn Industries, Inc. name changed to Tyler Corp. (Old) 2/27/90 which merged into AKZO N.V. 8/24/89 which name changed to AKZO Nobel N.V. 2/25/94

SATURN ENERGY & RES LTD (BC)
Dissolved and struck from the register 08/21/1992

SATURN INDS INC (DE)
Name changed to Tyler Corp. (Old) 2/27/70
Tyler Corp. (Old) merged into AKZO N.V. 8/24/89 which name changed to AKZO Nobel N.V. 2/25/94

SATURN MINERALS INC (BC)
Name changed to Saturn Oil & Gas Inc. 01/17/2017

SATURN SOLUTIONS INC (CANADA)
Filed an assignment in bankruptcy 04/04/2004
Stockholders' equity unlikely

SATURNS AT&T WIRELESS SVCS 2002-8 TR (DE)
Trust Units called for redemption at $25 on 02/07/2007

SATURNS BELLSOUTH CORP 2004-5 TR (DE)
Class A Trust Units called for redemption at $23.627344 on 02/07/2007

SATURNS GEN ELEC CAP CORP SER 2002-14 (DE)
Class A Trust Units called for redemption at $25 on 04/25/2011

SATURNS HERTZ CORP SER 2003-10 (DE)
Class A Units called for redemption at $25 on 12/27/2005

SATURNS JP MORGAN CHASE SER 2002-6 (DE)
Class A Trust Units called for redemption at $25 on 2/20/2007

SATURNS VERIZON GLOBAL FDG CORP SER 2002-9 (DE)
Class A Trust Units called for redemption at $25 on 08/27/2007

SATURNS WORLDCOM DEBENTURE-BKD SER 2001-5 TR (DE)
Trust Units called for redemption 08/07/2002

SATX INC (NV)
Plan of reorganization under Chapter 11 Federal Bankruptcy Code effective 12/7/2002
Each share Common $0.001 par received (1) share Peninsula Holdings Group, Ltd. Class A Common $0.001 par 12/7/2002
Note: Certificates were not required to be surrendered and are without value
(See Peninsula Holdings Group, Ltd.)

SATYAM COMPUTER SVCS LTD (INDIA)
Issue Information - 14,500,000 ADR's offered at $9.71 per ADR on 05/15/2001
ADR's for Equity Shares INR 2 par split (2) for (1) by issuance of (1) additional share payable 10/17/2006 to holders of record 10/10/2006 Ex date - 10/18/2006
ADR agreement terminated 09/12/2011
Each ADR for Equity Shares INR 2 par exchanged for $1.449785 cash

SATYAM INFOWAY LTD (INDIA)
Old Sponsored ADR's for Ordinary split (4) for (1) by issuance of (3) additional ADR's payable 01/7/2000 to holders of record 01/05/2000
ADR basis changed from (1:1) to (1:0.25) 00/00/2000
Each old Sponsored ADR for Ordinary exchanged for (0.25) new Sponsored ADR for Ordinary 09/24/2002
ADR basis changed from (1:0.25) to (1:1) 09/24/2002
Name changed to Sify Ltd. 01/13/2003
Sify Ltd. name changed to Sify Technologies Ltd. 10/26/2007

SAUCON DEVELOPMENT CORP. (QC)
Name changed to Quebec Industrial Minerals Corp. 01/10/1964
(See Quebec Industrial Minerals Corp.)

SAUCONY INC (MA)
Merged into Stride Rite Corp. 9/16/2005
Each share Class A 33-1/3¢ par exchanged for $23 cash
Each share Class B 33-1/3¢ par exchanged for $23 cash

SAUCY SUSAN PRODS INC (NY)
Merged into Briarcliff Foods, Inc. 3/10/78

Each share Common 10¢ par exchanged for $1.25 cash

SAUDI ARABIAN MINING SYNDICATE LTD. (BAHAMAS)
Completely liquidated 06/29/1955
Each share Capital Stock 5s par received first and final distribution of USD $0.939 cash
Note: Certificates were not required to be surrendered and are without value

SAUER-DANFOSS INC (DE)
Name changed 05/03/2000
Name changed from Sauer Inc. to Sauer-Danfoss Inc. 05/03/2000
Acquired by Danfoss A/S 04/12/2013
Each share Common exchanged for $58.50 cash

SAUL B F REAL ESTATE INVT TR (DC)
Shares of Bene. Int. $100 par changed to $10 par and (9) additional shares issued 07/20/1968
Shares of Bene. Int. $10 par reclassified as Common $10 par 02/10/1975
Common $10 par changed to $1 par 03/10/1977
Merged into Westminster Investing Corp. 10/24/1988
Each share Common $1 par exchanged for $28 cash

SAUL CTRS INC (MD)
9% Depository Preferred Ser. B called for redemption at $25 plus $0.4265 accrued dividends on 03/15/2013
8% Depository Preferred Ser. A called for redemption at $25 plus $0.4056 accrued dividends on 12/12/2014
(Additional Information in Active)

SAULT LEAD-ZINC MINES, LTD. (ON)
Charter cancelled for failure to file reports and pay taxes in 1958

SAULT MEADOWS ENERGY CORP (ON)
Recapitalized as International Fitness Unlimited Centres Inc. 10/20/1986
Each share Common 10¢ par exchanged for (0.2) share Common no par
(See International Fitness Unlimited Centres Inc.)

SAULT SVGS BK (SAULT STE. MARIE, MI)
Common $20 par changed to $10 par and (1) additional share issued 04/29/1977
Stock Dividends - 25% 03/01/1979; 20% 02/05/1981
Reorganized as Superior Financial Corp. 02/01/1984
Each share Common $10 par exchanged for (1) share Common $10 par
(See Superior Financial Corp.)

SAUNDERS LEASING SYSTEM, INC. (DE)
Common $1 par split (3) for (2) by issuance of (0.5) additional share 03/13/1978
Common $1 par split (4) for (3) by issuance of (1/3) additional share 08/17/1979
Common $1 par reclassified as Class B Common $1 par 01/08/1982
Each share Class B Common $1 par received distribution of (1) share Class A Common $1 par 01/29/1982
Stock Dividend - 50% 03/15/1972
Name changed to Saunders System, Inc. 01/01/1985
(See Saunders System, Inc.)

SAUNDERS (CLARENCE) STORES, INC.
Bankrupt Sold to creditors in 1931

SAUNDERS SYS INC (DE)
Merged into Ryder System, Inc. 09/30/1986
Each share Class A Common $1 par exchanged for $12.50 cash

Each share Class B Common $1 par exchanged for $12.50 cash

SAUQUOIT SPINNING CO.
Acquired by Sauquoit Spinning Mills, Inc. 00/00/1930
Details not available

SAUQUOIT SPINNING MILLS, INC.
Merged into Standard-Coosa-Thatcher Co. 00/00/1936
Details not available

SAV A STOP INC (FL)
Common 10¢ par split (3) for (2) by issuance of (0.5) additional share 09/27/1968
Common 10¢ par split (3) for (2) by issuance of (0.5) additional share 02/20/1970
Stock Dividends - 100% 05/31/1965; 10% 12/20/1965; 25% 12/19/1966
Acquired by Consolidated Foods Corp. 04/12/1982
Each share Common 10¢ par exchanged for $16 cash

SAV A STOP MIDWEST INC (AR)
Name changed to Mass Merchandisers, Inc. (AR) 11/20/1972
(See Mass Merchandisers, Inc. (AR))

SAV ON DRUGS INC (CA)
Common $1 par changed to 50¢ par and (1) additional share issued 05/10/1972
Merged into Jewel Companies, Inc. 11/06/1980
Each share Common 50¢ par exchanged for (0.72) share $2.31 Conv. Pfd. Ser. A $1 par
Jewel Companies, Inc. merged into American Stores Co. (New) 11/16/1984 which merged into Albertson's, Inc. 06/23/1999 which merged into Supervalu Inc. 06/02/2006

SAV ON INC (DE)
Common 10¢ par changed to 5¢ par and (1) additional share issued 06/17/1968
Merged into Adams Drug Co., Inc. 11/27/1979
Each share Common 5¢ par exchanged for $0.30 cash

SAV-WAY INDUSTRIES, INC.
Name changed to Vogue Recordings, Inc. 00/00/1949
(See Vogue Recordings, Inc.)

SAVA YELLOWKNIFE GOLD MINES LTD. (ON)
Charter cancelled and company declared dissolved for default in filing returns in 1953

SAVAGE ARMS CORP. NEW (DE)
Merged into American Hardware Corp. 7/26/63
Each share Common no par exchanged for (0.210526) share Common $12.50 par
American Hardware Corp. merged into Emhart Corp. (CT) 6/30/64 which reincorporated in Virginia 5/4/76
(See Emhart Corp. (VA))

SAVAGE ARMS CORP. OLD (DE)
Each share Common $100 par exchanged for (2) shares Common no par in August 1928
Each share Common no par exchanged for (4) shares Common $5 par in May 1941
Name changed to Hill Corp. 12/30/60
Hill Corp. merged into American Hardware Corp. 7/26/63 which merged into Emhart Corp. (CT) 6/30/64 which reincorporated in Virginia 5/4/76
(See Emhart Corp. (VA))

SAVAGE INDUSTRIES, INC. (AZ)
Acquired by Royal Properties, Inc. 2/11/64
Each share Common $1 par exchanged for (14) shares Common 50¢ par
Royal Properties, Inc. charter revoked 3/3/75

SAVANETTE MINES LTD. (ON)
Merged into Alchib Developments Ltd. 07/10/1969
Each share Capital Stock $1 par exchanged for (0.29) share Capital Stock no par
Alchib Developments Ltd. merged into Kalrock Developments Ltd. 10/23/1978 which merged into Kalrock Resources Ltd. 08/08/1990 which merged into Cercal Minerals Corp. 07/09/1993
(See Cercal Minerals Corp.)

SAVANNA CREEK GAS & OIL LTD (ON)
Capital Stock 50¢ par changed to no par 03/13/1969
Recapitalized as Savanna Resources Ltd. (ONT) 09/19/1973
Each share Capital Stock no par exchanged for (0.1) share Common no par
Savanna Resources Ltd. (ONT) reincorporated in Alberta 02/25/1980 which recapitalized as Hansa Corp. 02/12/2001 which name changed to Azteca Gold Corp. 12/28/2006

SAVANNA EAST AFRICA INC (NV)
Recapitalized as Algae International Group, Inc. (NV) 05/17/2013
Each share Common $0.001 par exchanged for (0.00005) share Common $0.001 par
Algae International Group, Inc. (NV) reincorporated in Wyoming as North American Cannabis Holdings, Inc. 06/10/2015

SAVANNA ENERGY SVCS CORP (AB)
Merged into Total Energy Services Inc. 06/23/2017
Each share Common no par exchanged for (0.13) share Common no par and $0.20 cash
Note: Unexchanged certificates will be cancelled and become without value 06/23/2020

SAVANNA RES LTD (AB)
Reincorporated 2/25/80
Place of incorporation changed from (ONT) to (ALTA) 2/25/80
Recapitalized as Hansa Corp. 2/12/2001
Each share Common no par exchanged for (0.04) share Common no par
Hansa Corp. name changed to Azteca Gold Corp. 12/28/2006

SAVANNAH BANCORP INC (GA)
Common $1 par split (2) for (1) by issuance of (1) additional share 07/25/1995
Common $1 par split (3) for (2) by issuance of (0.5) additional share payable 02/24/1997 to holders of record 02/07/1997
Common $1 par split (5) for (4) by issuance of (0.25) additional share payable 12/15/2006 to holders of record 12/01/2006 Ex date - 12/18/2006
Stock Dividends - 10% 05/23/1994; 10% payable 05/11/2001 to holders of record 04/27/2001; 10% payable 02/24/2003 to holders of record 02/10/2003 Ex date - 02/06/2003; 25% payable 12/17/2004 to holders of record 11/26/2004
Merged into SCBT Financial Corp. 12/14/2012
Each share Common $1 par exchanged for (0.2503) share Common $2.50 par
SCBT Financial Corp. name changed to First Financial Holdings, Inc. 07/30/2013 which name changed to South State Corp. 06/30/2014

SAVANNAH BK & TR CO (SAVANNAH, GA)
Each share Capital Stock $100 par exchanged for (10) shares Capital Stock $10 par 00/00/1950
Capital Stock $10 par changed to $5 par and (1) additional share issued 02/27/1969
Stock Dividends - 10% 02/27/1964; 10% 01/11/1968; 10% 02/23/1970; 10% 04/30/1976
Merged into SBT Corp. 04/13/1978
Each share Capital Stock $5 par exchanged for (2) shares Common $5 par
SBT Corp. merged into First Railroad & Banking Co. of Georgia 05/07/1984 which was acquired by First Union Corp. 11/01/1986 which name changed to Wachovia Corp. (Ctfs. dated after 09/01/2001) 09/01/2001 which merged into Wells Fargo & Co. (New) 12/31/2008

SAVANNAH ELEC & PWR CO (GA)
Common $10 par changed to $5 par and (1) additional share issued 03/12/1957
Common $5 par split (3) for (2) by issuance of (0.5) additional share 04/28/1964
Common $5 par split (2) for (1) by issuance of (1) additional share 08/27/1986
Each share Conv. Class A $5 par exchanged for (2.163) shares Common $5 par 10/15/1987
Acquired by Southern Co. 03/03/1988
Each share Common $5 par exchanged for (1.05) shares Common $5 par
4.36% Preferred Ser. A $100 par called for redemption 05/07/1990
5.25% Preferred Ser. B $100 par called for redemption 05/07/1990
8.92% Preferred Ser. C $100 par called for redemption 05/07/1990
$1.28 Preference $5 par called for redemption 03/15/1989
9.5% Preferred $25 par called for redemption 12/15/1993
6.64% Preferred $25 par called for redemption at $25 on 11/20/1998
Merged into Georgia Power Co. 07/01/2006
Each share 6% Non-Cum. Preferred $25 par exchanged for (1) share 6.125% Class A Preferred $25 par
(See Georgia Power Co.)

SAVANNAH ELEC CAP TR I (DE)
6.85% Guaranteed Trust Preferred Securities called for redemption at $25 on 1/16/2004

SAVANNAH FOODS & INDS INC (DE)
Common 25¢ par split (2) for (1) by issuance of (1) additional share 10/15/1985
Common 25¢ par split (2) for (1) by issuance of (1) additional share 04/01/1989
Common 25¢ par split (2) for (1) by issuance of (1) additional share 01/31/1990
Stock Dividends - 100% 01/24/1975; 100% 11/30/1981
Merged into Imperial Holly Corp. 12/22/1997
Each share Common $25 par exchanged for either (1.528302) shares Common no par or $20.25 cash
Imperial Holly Corp. name changed to Imperial Sugar Co. (New) 02/09/1999
(See Imperial Sugar Co. (New))

SAVANNAH GAS CO. (GA)
Merged into Atlanta Gas Light Co. 01/31/1966
Each share 5% Preferred $100 par exchanged for (1) share 5% Preferred $100 par
Each share Common $2.50 par

FINANCIAL INFORMATION, INC.   SAV-SAV

exchanged for (0.65) share Common $5 par
Atlanta Gas Light Co. reorganized as AGL Resources Inc. 03/06/1996
(See AGL Resources Inc.)

SAVANNAH GOLD CORP (BC)
Each share old Common no par exchanged for (0.2) share new Common no par 03/03/2017
Name changed to E3 Metals Corp. 05/19/2017

SAVANNAH NEWSPAPERS, INC. (GA)
Completely liquidated 8/1/63
Each share Common $1 par exchanged for first and final distribution of $5.70 cash

SAVANNAH RIV TECHNOLOGIES INC (SC)
Reincorporated under the laws of Nevada as RT Technologies, Inc. 10/09/2007
RT Technologies, Inc. name changed to CAM Group, Inc. 10/09/2012

SAVANNAH RIVER LUMBER CO.
Adjudicated bankrupt in 1931

SAVANNAH RIVER NAVIGATION CO. INC. (DE)
Dissolved 5/7/56

SAVANNAH-ST. AUGUSTINE GAS CO. (GA)
Reorganized as South Atlantic Gas Co. 12/21/1945
Each share Common $10 par exchanged for (2) shares Common $5 par
South Atlantic Gas Co. recapitalized as Savannah Gas Co. 10/01/1964 which merged into Atlanta Gas Light Co. 01/31/1966 which reorganized as AGL Resources Inc. 03/06/1996
(See AGL Resources Inc.)

SAVANNAH SUGAR REFNG CORP (NY)
Each share Common no par exchanged for (4) shares Common $1 par 00/00/1936
Common $1 par changed to 25¢ par and (3) additional shares issued 05/15/1959
Reincorporated under the laws of Delaware as Savannah Foods & Industries, Inc. 07/15/1970
Savannah Foods & Industries, Inc. merged into Imperial Holly Corp. 12/22/1997 which name changed to Imperial Sugar Co. (New) 02/09/1999
(See Imperial Sugar Co. (New))

SAVANNAH VENTURES LTD (BC)
Recapitalized as International Savannah Ventures Ltd. 12/01/1998
Each share Common no par exchanged for (0.16666666) share Common no par
International Savannah Ventures Ltd. name changed to Softcare EC.com, Inc. 06/10/1999 which name changed to Softcare EC Inc. 10/05/2001 which recapitalized as Open EC Technologies, Inc. 06/23/2003
(See Open EC Technologies, Inc.)

SAVANOR RES INC (QC)
Declared bankrupt 2/16/93
No stockholders' equity

SAVANT BIOTECHNOLOGY INC (DE)
Name changed to Children's Beverage Group, Inc. 5/13/97
(See Children's Beverage Group, Inc.)

SAVANT EXPLORATIONS LTD (BC)
Name changed to Blue Moon Zinc Corp. 07/05/2017

SAVANT INSTRS INC (NY)
Stock Dividend - 10% 02/10/1971
Merged into Savant Holdings, Inc. 06/04/1984

Each share Common 10¢ par exchanged for $11.90 cash

SAVARINE BUILDING CO.
Liquidated in 1944

SAVARY CAP CORP (BC)
Name changed to Savary Gold Corp. (BC) 09/17/2012
Savary Gold Corp. (BC) reincorporated in Ontario 10/18/2013

SAVARY GOLD CORP (BC)
Reincorporated under the laws of Ontario 10/18/2013

SAVE-CO. VETERANS & SERVICES DEPARTMENT STORES, INC. (CA)
Liquidation completed 1/9/63

SAVE MOR DRUGS INC (DC)
Voluntarily dissolved 3/26/84
Details not available

SAVE MOR SUPERMARKETS INC (MA)
Name changed to Purity Supreme Inc. 03/28/1969
(See Purity Supreme Inc.)

SAVE-ON AUTOMOTIVE INDS CORP (BC)
Name changed to MIS Multimedia Interactive Services Inc. (BC) 09/08/1993
MIS Multimedia Interactive Services Inc. (BC) reincorporated in Delaware as MIS International, Inc. 07/01/1997 which name changed to Cosmoz.Com, Inc. 12/07/1998 which name changed to Cosmoz Infrastructure Solutions, Inc. 04/16/2001 which recapitalized as FinancialContent, Inc. 11/13/2001
(See FinancialContent, Inc.)

SAVE ON ENERGY INC (GA)
Name changed to Hybrid Fuel Systems, Inc. 02/18/2004
Hybrid Fuel Systems, Inc. name changed to US Energy Initiatives Corp. (GA) 06/05/2006 which reincorporated in Delaware 05/26/2008 which reincorporated in Nevada as U.S. Energy Initiatives Corporation Inc. 04/03/2013

SAVE ON MEDS.COM, INC. (DE)
Name changed to My Meds Express.Com, Inc. 7/26/2000
(See My Meds Express.Com, Inc.)

SAVE ON MEDS NET (NV)
Recapitalized as Voyager Group Inc. (New) 5/31/2001
Each share Common $0.001 par exchanged for (0.01) share Common $0.001 par
Voyager Group Inc. (New) recapitalized as Neoteric Group Inc. 6/17/2002
(See Neoteric Group Inc.)

SAVE THE WORLD AIR INC (NV)
Name changed to QS Energy, Inc. 08/12/2015

SAVE THE WORLD TECHNOLOGIES INC (NV)
Company terminated common stock registration and is no longer public as of 10/18/2008

SAVE-WAY BARBER & BEAUTY SUPPLIES, INC. (FL)
Common 10¢ par split (2) for (1) by issuance of (1) additional share 4/15/77
Stock Dividend - 15% 12/15/76
Name changed to Save-Way Industries, Inc. 5/31/77
Save-Way Industries, Inc. name changed to Windmere Corp. 8/15/83 which name changed Windmere-Durable Holdings, Inc. 6/21/96 which name changed to Applica Inc. 5/10/2000
(See Applica Inc.)

SAVE WAY INDS INC (FL)
Common 10¢ par split (3) for (2) by issuance of (0.5) additional share 4/17/78
Common 10¢ par split (3) for (2) by issuance of (0.5) additional share 3/15/79
Stock Dividends - 25% 10/12/79; 33-1/3% 3/14/80
Name changed to Windmere Corp. 8/15/83
Windmere Corp. name changed to Windmere-Durable Holdings, Inc. 6/21/96 which name changed to Applica Inc. 5/10/2000
(See Applica Inc.)

SAVEALL HEALTHCARE SVCS INC (MN)
Recapitalized as Clinical Aesthetics Centre, Inc. (MN) 03/13/1997
Each share Common $0.001 par exchanged for (0.0125) share Common $0.001 par 03/13/1997
Clinical Aesthetics Centre, Inc. (MN) reincorporated in Nevada as Tricom Technology Group, Inc. 07/30/1998 which name changed to Omninet Media.com Inc. 02/18/2000 which name changed to Omninet Media Corp. 06/01/2001 which name changed to Aquagold International, Inc. 03/28/2008

SAVECO INC (WA)
Chapter 11 Federal Bankruptcy Code converted to Chapter 7 on 2/3/89
Stockholders' equity unlikely

SAVEDAILY INC (NV)
Merged into SaveDaily Holdings Corp. 12/20/2013
Each share Common $0.001 par exchanged for (1) share Common $0.001 par
Note: Company is now private

SAVERS BANCORP INC (NH)
Under plan of merger name changed to United Saver's Bancorp, Inc. 06/20/1986
United Saver's Bancorp, Inc. name changed to Dartmouth Bancorp, Inc. 04/12/1990
(See Dartmouth Bancorp, Inc.)

SAVERS FED SVGS & LN ASSN LITTLE ROCK ARK (USA)
Common 1¢ par split (2) for (1) by issuance of (1) additional share 03/31/1985
Under plan of reorganization each share Common 1¢ par automatically became (1) share Savers Inc. (DE) Common 1¢ par 02/01/1986
(See Savers Inc.)

SAVERS INC (DE)
Plan of liquidation effective 7/19/89
Details not available

SAVERS LIFE INS CO (NC)
Merged into Standard Management Corp. 03/10/1998
Each share Common no par exchanged for (1.2) shares Common no par and $1.50 cash
(See Standard Management Corp.)

SAVERS PLUS INTL INC (AB)
Name changed to Intertainment Media Inc. 4/30/2007

SAVIA S A DE C V (MEXICO)
Each Sponsored ADR for Ordinary Participation Certificates A no par received distribution of $2.1352 cash payable 10/10/2003 to holders of record 10/02/2003 Ex date - 10/14/2003
ADR agreement terminated 04/25/2005
Each Sponsored ADR for Ordinary Participation Certificates A no par exchanged for (4) Ordinary Participation Certificates A no par
Note: Unexchanged ADR's will be sold and proceeds, if any, held for claim after 04/25/2007

SAVIBANK (BURLINGTON, WA)
Under plan of reorganization each share Common no par automatically became (1) share Savi Financial Corp., Inc. Common no par 04/04/2018

SAVIENT PHARMACEUTICALS INC (DE)
Plan of reorganization under Chapter 11 Federal Bankruptcy proceedings effective 05/30/2014
No stockholders' equity

SAVILLE SYS PLC (IRELAND)
Sponsored ADR's for Ordinary 25p par split (2) for (1) by issuance of (1) additional ADR payable 11/17/1997 to holders of record 11/07/1997
Merged into ADC Telecommunications, Inc. 10/08/1999
Each Sponsored ADR for Ordinary 25p par exchanged for (0.358) share Common 20¢ par
(See ADC Telecommunications, Inc.)

SAVIN CORP (DE)
Name changed 09/20/1978
Common 10¢ par split (3) for (2) by issuance of (0.5) additional share 10/15/1968
Common 10¢ par split (2) for (1) by issuance of (1) additional share 02/18/1969
Common 10¢ par split (2) for (1) by issuance of (1) additional share 11/01/1977
Name and place of incorporation changed from Savin Business Machines Corp. (NY) to Savin Corp. (DE) 09/20/1978
Each share old Common 10¢ par exchanged for (0.01) share new Common 10¢ par 12/27/1991
Plan of reorganization under Chapter 11 Federal Bankruptcy Code effective 12/14/1993
$1.50 Conv. Preferred Ser. A $1 par, 80¢ Conv. Preferred Ser. B $0.001 par, 40¢ Conv. Preferred Ser. C $0.001 par, 10¢ Conv. Preferred Ser. D $0.001 par and new Common 10¢ par were cancelled and are without value
Merged into Ricoh Co. Ltd. 03/31/1995
Each share Common $0.001 par exchanged for $10.426 cash

SAVIN ELECTRONICS INC (NJ)
Each share Common $0.0001 par exchanged for (0.004) share Common $0.025 par 11/11/1998
Name changed to Hidenet Secure Architectures, Inc. 07/12/1999
Hidenet Secure Architectures, Inc. recapitalized as Bio Nitrogen Corp. 11/08/2011 which name changed to BioNitrogen Holdings Corp. 10/15/2013

SAVINGS & INVT CORP MUT FD CDA LTD (CANADA)
Special Shares $1 par reclassified as Mutual Fund Shares $1 par 10/31/1966
Voluntarily dissolved 02/26/1996
Details not available

SAVINGS & TR CO PA (INDIANA, PA)
Under plan of reorganization each share Common $2.50 par automatically became (1) share S & T Bancorp, Inc. Common $2.50 par 09/08/1983

SAVINGS BANK INVESTMENT FUND (MA)
Name changed to Savings Bank Investment Fund-Equity Series in September 1975

SAVINGS BANK OF PUGET SOUND (SEATTLE, WA)
Name changed to Savings Bank of Puget Sound, FSB (Seattle, WA) 6/6/85
Savings Bank of Puget Sound, FSB (Seattle, WA) merged into Puget Sound Bancorp 7/1/86 which

merged into KeyCorp (NY) 1/15/93 which merged into KeyCorp (New) (OH) 3/1/94

SAVINGS BK OF THE FINGER LAKES (GENEVA, NY)
Common 1¢ par split (2) for (1) by issuance of (1) additional share payable 3/2/98 to holders of record 2/13/98
Under plan of reorganization each share Common 1¢ par automatically became (1) share Finger Lakes Financial Corp. (USA) Common 1¢ par 8/17/98
Finger Lakes Financial Corp. (USA) reincorporated in Delaware 1/31/2000 which reorganized as Finger Lakes Bancorp, Inc. 11/22/2000
(See Finger Lakes Bancorp, Inc.)

SAVINGS BK PUGET SOUND (SEATTLE, WA)
Common $5 par split (2) for (1) by issuance of (1) additional share 07/22/1985
Merged into Puget Sound Bancorp 07/01/1986
Each share Common $5 par exchanged for (0.55) share Common $5 par
Puget Sound Bancorp merged into KeyCorp (NY) 01/15/1993 which merged into KeyCorp (New) (OH) 03/01/1994

SAVINGS BK RUSSIAN FEDN SBERBANK (RUSSIA)
Name changed to Sberbank Russia 12/06/2010

SAVINGS FINL (CA)
Liquidation completed
Each share Common $1 par exchanged for initial distribution of $14.95 cash 01/19/1970
Each share Common $1 par received second and final distribution of (0.25) share President Service Co. Common 1¢ par and $0.05 cash 05/07/1970
President Service Co. name changed to First Builders Bancorp 08/17/1970 which name changed to American Magnetics Corp. 01/30/1980 which name changed to Damon Group Inc. 04/05/1990
(See Damon Group Inc.)

SAVINGS NETWORK INC (NV)
Name changed to Woodington Group, Inc. 08/30/1989
(See Woodington Group, Inc.)

SAVOIR TECHNOLOGY GROUP INC (DE)
Secondary Offering - 3,000,000 shares COM offered at $10.50 per share on 04/29/1998
Merged into Avnet, Inc. 7/3/2000
Each share Common 1¢ par exchanged for (0.11452) share Common $1 par

SAVON COFFEE INC (NV)
Name changed to Food Concepts Inc. 3/22/96
Food Concepts Inc. name changed to Viropro Inc. 4/1/98

SAVON TEAM SPORTS INC (UT)
Reincorporated under the laws of Nevada as Small World Kids, Inc. 8/2/2004

SAVORY, INC. (NY)
Name changed to Lisk Savory Corp. 00/00/1944
(See Lisk Savory Corp.)

SAVOY CAP GROUP LTD (NV)
Name changed to Exotic Bodies, Inc. 1/5/90
Exotic Bodies, Inc. recapitalized as Eftek Corp. 8/22/94
(See Eftek Corp.)

SAVOY CAP INVTS INC (CO)
Name changed to Savoy Resources Corp. and (2) additional shares issued 3/24/2004

SAVOY INDS INC (DE)
Charter cancelled and declared inoperative and void for non-payment of taxes 6/26/90

SAVOY MINERALS LTD (CANADA)
Assets sold for the benefit of creditors 02/27/1992
No stockholders' equity

SAVOY OIL CO., INC. (DE)
Name changed to Savoy Industries, Inc. 5/13/59
(See Savoy Industries, Inc.)

SAVOY OIL CO., INC (NJ)
Reincorporated under laws of Delaware and Common $5 par changed to 25¢ par in 1947 which name was changed to Savoy Industries, Inc. 5/13/59

SAVOY PICTURES ENTMT INC (DE)
Merged into HSN, Inc. (Old) 12/20/1996
Each share Common 1¢ par exchanged for (0.14) share Common 1¢ par
HSN, Inc. (Old) name changed to USA Networks, Inc. 02/17/1998 which name changed to USA Interactive 05/09/2002 which name changed to InterActiveCorp 06/23/2003 which name changed to IAC/InterActiveCorp 07/14/2004

SAVOY-PLAZA, INC. (NY)
Merged into Hilton Hotels Corp. 12/31/1958
Each share Class A and/or Class B $1 par exchanged for (2.5) shares 5-1/2% Preferred A $25 par and (2) shares Common $2.50 par 12/31/1958
(See Hilton Hotels Corp.)

SAVOY PLAZA CORP.
Reorganized as Savoy-Plaza, Inc. 00/00/1936
No stockholders' equity

SAVOY VENTURES INC (BC)
Name changed to Hybrid Minerals Inc. 01/18/2018

SAVVIS INC (DE)
Name changed 05/18/2005
Issue Information - 17,000,000 shares COM offered at $24 per share on 02/14/2000
Name changed from SAVVIS Communications Corp. to SAVVIS, Inc. 05/18/2005
Each (15) shares old Common 1¢ par exchanged for (1) share new Common 1¢ par 06/06/2006
Merged into CenturyLink, Inc. 07/14/2011
Each share new Common 1¢ par exchanged for (0.2479) share Common $1 par and $30 cash

SAVVY BUSINESS SUPPORT INC (NV)
Name changed to Pan Global, Corp. 05/02/2013

SAWADEE VENTURES INC (NV)
Name changed to Casey Container Corp. 02/19/2010
Casey Container Corp. name changed to Snoogoo Corp. 02/24/2015

SAWAKO CORP (JAPAN)
Stock Dividends - 30% payable 10/04/1996 to holders of record 07/30/1996; 25% payable 11/15/1997 to holders of record 07/31/1997
ADR agreement terminated 12/22/2000
Each Sponsored ADR for Ordinary exchanged for $0.045235 cash
Each Sponsored ADR for Ordinary received an additional distribution of $0.054372 cash payable 03/23/2016 to holders of record 09/29/2009

SAWHILL CAP LTD (AB)
Name changed to Virtutone Networks Inc. 09/26/2008

SAWHILL TUBULAR PRODS INC (PA)
Merged into Cyclops Corp. 07/31/1968
Each share Common no par exchanged for (0.213) share $6 Conv. Preferred Ser. A $1 par
(See Cyclops Corp.)

SAWTEK INC (FL)
Common $0.0005 par split (2) for (1) by issuance of (1) additional share payable 08/23/1999 to holders of record 08/09/1999
Merged into TriQuint Semiconductor, Inc. 07/19/2001
Each share Common $0.0005 par exchanged for (1.1507) shares Common $0.001 par
TriQuint Semiconductor, Inc. merged into Qorvo, Inc. 01/02/2015

SAWTOOTH INTL RES INC (AB)
Name changed 06/06/1997
Name changed from Sawtooth Equities Inc. to Sawtooth International Resources Inc. 06/06/1997
Merged into TriStar Oil & Gas Ltd. (Old) 03/16/2006
Each share Common no par exchanged for (0.1452) share Common no par and $1.125 cash
TriStar Oil & Gas Ltd. (Old) merged into TriStar Oil & Gas Ltd. (New) 08/16/2007

SAWYER (H.M.) & SON, INC.
Liquidated in 1945

SAWYER ADECOR INTL INC (AZ)
Recapitalized as Oil Retrieval Systems, Inc. 3/14/97
Each share Common 20¢ par exchanged for (0.1) share Common 20¢ par
(See Oil Retrieval Systems, Inc.)

SAWYER-MASSEY LTD. (CANADA)
Assets acquired and each share Common no par received $5.80 in cash in 1955

SAWYER PETE CO (AZ)
Capital Stock $1 par changed to 4¢ par 00/00/1956
Recapitalized as Sawyer-Adecor International, Inc. 09/26/1969
Each share Capital Stock 4¢ par exchanged for (0.2) share Capital Stock 20¢ par
Sawyer-Adecor International, Inc. recapitalized as Oil Retrieval Systems, Inc. 03/14/1997
(See Oil Retrieval Systems, Inc.)

SAWYER RESOURCES CORP. (NV)
Name changed to Union Petrochemical Corp. of Nevada 10/9/67

SAWYER'S, INC. (OR)
Acquired by General Aniline & Film Corp. 10/31/1966
Each share Capital Stock $2.50 par exchanged for (0.9) share Common $1 par
General Aniline & Film Corp. name changed to GAF Corp. 04/24/1968
(See GAF Corp.)

SAXET CO.
Name changed to Republic Gas Corp. 00/00/1931
(See Republic Gas Corp.)

SAXON CAP INC (DE)
Name changed 10/5/2001
Name changed from Saxon Capital Acquisition Corp. to Saxon Capital, Inc. 10/5/2001
Merged into Saxon Capital, Inc. (MD) 9/24/2004
Each share 144A Common 1¢ par exchanged for (1) share Common 1¢ par and $4 cash
Each share Common 1¢ par exchanged for (1) share Common 1¢ par and $4 cash
(See Saxon Capital, Inc. (MD))

SAXON CAP INC (MD)
Merged into Morgan Stanley Mortgage Capital Inc. 12/4/2006
Each share Common 1¢ par exchanged for $14.10 cash

SAXON DIVERSIFIED VALUE TR (ON)
Name changed to Signature Diversified Value Trust 01/04/2005
(See Signature Diversified Value Trust)

SAXON ENERGY SVCS INC (AB)
Acquired by Sword Canada Acquisition Corp. 08/29/2008
Each share Common no par exchanged for $7 cash

SAXON FINL INC (ON)
Acquired by IGM Financial Inc. 10/24/2008
Each share Common no par exchanged for $21 cash

SAXON GOLD CORP (BC)
Name changed 05/16/1997
Name changed from Saxon Capital Corp. to Saxon Gold Corp. 05/16/1997
Name changed to Avatar Petroleum Inc. 12/18/2000
Avatar Petroleum Inc. merged into Quest Capital Corp. (BC) 06/30/2003 which reincorporated in Canada 05/27/2008 which name changed to Sprott Resource Lending Corp. 09/10/2010 which merged into Sprott Inc. 07/24/2013

SAXON INDS INC (DE)
Reincorporated 10/03/1975
Common 25¢ par split (3) for (1) by issuance of (2) additional shares 06/19/1970
State of incorporation changed from (NY) to (DE) 10/03/1975
Reorganized as Paper Corp. of America 04/01/1985
Holdings of (99) shares of fewer exchanged for cash
Holdings of (100) or more shares exchanged for (0.05) shares Ser. B Preferred 1¢ par
An additional distribution of (0.001996178) share Ser. B Preferred 1¢ par was made 09/22/1986
Note: Unexchanged certificates were cancelled and became without value 03/31/1986
(See Paper Corp. of America)

SAXON MINING CO. LTD. (ON)
Charter revoked for failure to file reports and pay fees 8/19/65

SAXON OIL CO (TX)
Each share Common 10¢ par exchanged for (0.1) share Common 1¢ par 11/08/1984
Stock Dividend - 100% 09/10/1981
Name changed to Hallwood Energy Corp. 08/21/1989
(See Hallwood Energy Corp.)

SAXON OIL CO LTD (BC)
Completely liquidated
Each share Common no par received first and final distribution of USD$0.0253 cash payable 04/11/2014 to holders of record 04/04/2014 Ex date - 04/02/2014

SAXON OIL DEV PARTNERS L P (DE)
Name changed to Hallwood Energy Partners, L.P. 8/21/89
Hallwood Energy Partners, L.P. reorganized as Hallwood Energy Corp. 6/8/99
(See Hallwood Energy Corp.)

SAXON PAPER CORP (NY)
6% Conv. Preferred $10 par called for redemption 07/31/1967
Name changed to Saxon Industries, Inc. 05/09/1968
Saxon Industries, Inc. (NY) reincorporated in Delaware 10/03/1975 which reorganized as Paper Corp. of America 03/22/1985
(See Paper Corp. of America)

SAXON PETE INC (AB)
Merged into Forest Oil Corp. 10/10/1998
Each share Common no par exchanged for (0.02127569) share new Common no par
Forest Oil Corp. name changed to Sabine Oil & Gas Corp. 01/13/2015
(See Sabine Oil & Gas Corp.)

SAXON URANIUM MINES LTD. (ON)
Name changed to Saxon Mining Co. Ltd. 7/30/56
(See Saxon Mining Co. Ltd.)

SAXONBURG CERAMICS INC (PA)
Assets sold for the benefit of creditors 03/12/2007
Stockholders' equity unlikely

SAXONY EXPLS LTD (BC)
Reorganized under the laws of Yukon as Century Mining Corp. 09/24/2003
Each share Common no par exchanged for (0.33333333) share Common no par
Century Mining Corp. (YT) reincorporated in Canada 07/22/2004 which merged into White Tiger Gold Ltd. 10/20/2011 which name changed to Mangazeya Mining Ltd. 09/23/2013

SAXONY INDS INC (NY)
Common 10¢ par changed to 1¢ par 09/11/1972
Name changed to Normandy Oil & Gas Co. (NY) 08/03/1984
Normandy Oil & Gas Co. (NY) reorganized in Delaware as Producers Pipeline Corp. 06/30/1994

SAXTON INDS LTD (BC)
Name changed to Delbancor Industries Inc. 10/6/87
(See Delbancor Industries Inc.)

SAY YES FOODS INC (NV)
Recapitalized as CBP Carbon Industries, Inc. (NV) 03/27/2006
Each share Common $0.001 par exchanged for (0.01) share Common $0.001 par
CBP Carbon Industries, Inc. (NV) reorganized in British Virgin Islands 02/14/2012

SAYERS & SCOVILLE CO.
Dissolved in 1942

SAYETT GROUP INC (NY)
Name changed SpatiaLight, Inc. 05/17/1996
(See SpatiaLight, Inc.)

SAYNOR VARAH INC (BC)
Merged into Anglo York Industries Ltd. 12/21/1990
Each share Common no par exchanged for $0.16 cash

SAYRE & FISHER BRICK CO. (NJ)
Reorganized in 1944
No stockholders' equity
Common $10 par changed to $5 par in 1945
Each share Common $5 par exchanged for (3) shares Common $1 par in 1946
Name changed to Sayre & Fisher Co. 5/23/57
Sayre & Fisher Co. adjudicated bankrupt 5/24/74

SAYRE & FISHER CO (NJ)
Adjudicated bankrupt 05/24/1974
No stockholders' equity

SAYVETTE LTD (CANADA)
Acquired by Loblaws Ltd. 08/11/1975
Each share Capital Stock no par exchanged for $2.50 cash

SAZTEC INTL INC (CA)
Common no par split (2) for (1) by issuance of (1) additional share 12/1/87
Each share old Common no par exchanged for (0.25) share new Common no par 11/7/97
Merged into Datamatics Technologies Ltd. 12/1/2003
Each share new Common no par exchanged for $0.10 cash

SBA BANCORP, INC. (DE)
Reincorporated under the laws of Illinois as West Central Bancshares, Inc. 01/01/2009

SBA COMMUNICATIONS CORP OLD (FL)
Merged into SBA Communications Corp. (New) 01/17/2017
Each share Class A Common 1¢ par exchanged for (1) share Class A Common 1¢ par

SBARRO INC (NY)
Common 1¢ par split (2) for (1) by issuance of (1) additional share 7/10/86
Common 1¢ par split (3) for (2) by issuance of (0.5) additional share 6/19/89
Common 1¢ par split (3) for (2) by issuance of (0.5) additional share 9/22/94
Merged into Sbarro Merger LLC 9/28/99
Each share Common 1¢ par exchanged for $28.85 cash

SBB INC (NV)
Each share old Common $0.001 par exchanged for (0.001) share new Common $0.001 par 03/03/1998
Name changed to USA Talks.Com, Inc. 08/12/1998
(See USA Talks.Com, Inc.)

SBC COMMUNICATIONS INC (DE)
Common $1 par split (2) for (1) by issuance of (1) additional share payable 3/19/98 to holders of record 2/20/98 Ex date - 3/20/98
Under plan of merger name changed to AT&T Inc. 11/18/2005

SBC FINL CORP (NY)
Merged into Oneida Financial Corp. 05/31/2002
Each share Common $15 par exchanged for $102.60 cash 06/17/1985)

SBC TECHNOLOGIES INC (DE)
Merged into Sage Technologies Inc. 09/13/1994
Each share Common 10¢ par exchanged for (0.3847) share Common 1¢ par
Sage Technologies Inc. name changed to AmeriData Technologies, Inc. 09/30/1994
(See AmeriData Technologies, Inc.)

SBC TECHNOLOGIES INC (WA)
Charter cancelled and proclaimed dissolved for failure to maintain a registered agent 8/23/88

SBD ELECTR SYS INC (DE)
Common 10¢ par split (3) for (2) by issuance of (0.5) additional share 2/25/80
Stock Dividends - 25% 12/31/80; 10% 12/31/81
Merged into BII Acquisition Corp. 11/5/84
Each share Common 10¢ par exchanged for $6.052 cash

SBD INTL INC (NV)
Each share old Common $0.001 par exchanged for (0.001) share new Common $0.001 par 09/18/2007

Recapitalized as Solargy Systems Inc. 10/27/2008
Each share Common $0.001 par exchanged for (0.0004) share Common $0.001 par
Note: No holder will receive fewer than (200) shares
(See Solargy Systems Inc.)

SBE INC (DE)
Reincorporated 12/15/1997
Common $1 par changed to no par 05/09/1980
Each share old Common no par exchanged for (0.1) share new Common no par 10/30/1990
State of incorporation changed from (CA) to (DE) and Common no par changed to $0.001 par 12/15/1997
Each share new Common $0.001 par exchanged again for (0.2) share new Common $0.001 par 04/02/2007
Name changed to Neonode, Inc. 08/10/2007

SBH, INC. (AZ)
Completely liquidated 1/30/73
Each share Common no par exchanged for first and final distribution of $6.10 cash

SBI CAP TR (DE)
9.30% Trust Preferred Securities called for redemption at $25 on 6/24/2005

SBI COMMUNICATIONS INC (DE)
Common $0.001 par split (2) for (1) by issuance of (1) additional share payable 08/14/2000 to holders of record 08/10/2000
Name changed to ValCom, Inc. 03/07/2001
(See ValCom, Inc.)

SBI COMMUNICATIONS INC (UT)
Reorganized under the laws of Delaware 01/28/1993
Each share Common $0.001 par exchanged for (0.05) share Common $0.001 par
SBI Communications Inc. (DE) name changed to ValCom, Inc. 03/07/2001
(See ValCom, Inc.)

SBI SKIN BIOLOGY INC (YT)
Reincorporated 08/22/1996
Place of incorporation changed from (BC) to (YT) 08/22/1996
Reorganized under the laws of British Columbia as Realm Energy International Corp. 10/26/2009
Each share Common no par exchanged for (0.25) share Common no par
Realm Energy International Corp. merged into San Leon Energy PLC 11/10/2011

SBK SELECT SER (MA)
Name changed to Signet Select Series 10/1/92
Signet Select Series name changed to Medalist Funds 8/15/94 which name changed to Virtus Funds 2/15/95

SBL CAPITAL BANK SHARES INC. (WI)
Merged into Associated Banc-Corp. 3/1/96
Each share Common $1 par exchanged for (222.892) shares Common 1¢ par

SBM CO (MN)
In process of liquidation
Each share Common no par received initial distribution of $2.75 cash 08/09/1995
Note: Details on subsequent distributions, if any, are not available

SBM INDS INC (DE)
Name changed Star Struck, Ltd. 05/03/1999
(See Star Struck, Ltd.)

SBN SYS INC (CANADA)
Name changed to NBS Technologies Inc. (Old) 4/14/94
NBS Technologies Inc. (Old) name changed Mist Inc. 11/1/2000 which name changed to NBS Technologies Inc. (New) 3/16/2004
(See NBS Technologies Inc. (New))

SBOR INC (NV)
Name changed to Be At TV, Inc. 12/26/2013
Be At TV, Inc. recapitalized as Epic Stores Corp. 08/18/2015

SBP LTD (CO)
Recapitalized as AMDC Group, Inc. 1/1/89
Each share Common no par exchanged for (0.1) share Common no par
(See AMDC Group, Inc.)

SBS BROADCASTING S A (LUXEMBOURG)
Completely liquidated
Each share Common EUR 2 par received first and final distribution of $55.087 cash payable 11/08/2005 to holders of record 10/18/2005
Note: Certificates were not required to be surrendered and are without value

SBS ENGR INC (NM)
Name changed to SBS Technologies, Inc. 6/30/95
(See SBS Technologies, Inc.)

SBS INDS INC (NY)
Adjudicated bankrupt 08/13/1973
Stockholders' equity unlikely

SBS INTERACTIVE CO (FL)
SEC revoked common stock registration 07/31/2013

SBS TECHNOLOGIES INC (MN)
Common no par split (2) for (1) by issuance of (1) additional share payable 09/20/2000 to holders of record 09/05/2000 Ex date - 09/21/2000
Merged into General Electric Co. 06/07/2006
Each share Common no par exchanged for $16.50 cash

SBS VENTURES CORP (FL)
Name changed to Petshealth Inc. (FL) 08/00/1998
Petshealth Inc. (FL) reorganized in Nevada as Berkshire Asset Management Inc. 12/28/2001 which recapitalized as Greater Sooner Holdings, Inc. 10/11/2005 which recapitalized as Dovarri Inc. 01/07/2008
(See Dovarri Inc.)

SBT BANCSHARES INC. (TN)
Merged into Union Planters Corp. 10/1/97
Each share Common $20 par exchanged for (45.12) shares Common $5 par
Union Planters Corp. merged into Regions Financial Corp. (New) 7/1/2004

SBT CORP (CT)
Common no par split (3) for (2) by issuance of (0.5) additional share 3/18/86
Stock Dividends - 10% 11/23/88; 10% 11/1/89
Charter forfeited 10/1/93

SBT CORP (GA)
Stock Dividend - 50% 01/01/1982
Merged into First Railroad & Banking Co. of Georgia 05/07/1984
Each share Common $5 par exchanged for (1.2427) shares Common 66-3/3¢ par
First Railroad & Banking Co. of Georgia acquired by First Union Corp. 11/01/1986 which name changed to Wachovia Corp. (Ctfs. dated after 09/01/2001) 09/01/2001

which merged into Wells Fargo & Co. (New) 12/31/2008

SBT REAL ESTATE, INC. (SC)
Merged into Southern Bancorporation, Inc. 10/31/73
Each share Common $1.25 par exchanged for (0.285714) share Common $2.50 par
(See Southern Bancorporation, Inc.)

SC BANCORP (CA)
Merged into Western Bancorp 10/10/1997
Each share Common no par exchanged for (0.4556) share Common no par
Western Bancorp merged into U.S. Bancorp (Old) 11/15/1999 which merged into U.S. Bancorp (New) 02/27/2001

SC GLOBAL DEVS LTD (SINGAPORE)
ADR agreement terminated 03/21/2014
No ADR's remain outstanding

SC&T INTL INC (AZ)
Each (18) shares old Common 1¢ par exchanged for (1) share new Common 1¢ par 04/23/1999
Name changed to Hot Products Inc.com (AZ) 12/20/1999
Hot Products Inc.com (AZ) reorganized in Washington as B-Teller, Inc. 04/03/2006 which name changed to Congo Crest Mineral Corp. 08/01/2006 which reorganized as New Wave Mobile, Inc. 11/22/2006 which name changed to New Wave Media, Inc. 03/26/2007 which name changed to CA Goldfields, Inc. 04/08/2008
(See CA Goldfields, Inc.)

SCA SVCS INC (DE)
Common $1 par split (3) for (2) by issuance of (0.5) additional share 07/24/1972
Merged into Waste Management, Inc. 09/25/1984
Each share Common $1 par exchanged for $28.50 cash

SCAFFOLD CONNECTION CORP (AB)
Assets sold for the benefit of creditors 4/10/2002
No stockholders' equity

SCAICO CTLS INC (NJ)
Charter declared void for non-payment of taxes 1/5/76

SCAILEX CORP LTD (ISRAEL)
Each share old Ordinary ILS 0.12 par exchanged for (0.004) share new Ordinary ILS 0.12 par 02/20/2015
Name changed to Suny Cellular Communication Ltd. 05/24/2017

SCAM INSTR CORP (DE)
Reincorporated 02/17/1970
Each share old Common no par exchanged for (0.2) share new Common no par 05/24/1964
New Common no par split (2) for (1) by issuance of (1) additional share 05/24/1964
State of incorporation changed from (IL) to (DE) 02/17/1970
Under plan of merger name changed to Riley Co. and Common no par changed to $1 par 10/31/1971
(See Riley Co.)

SCAN DATA CORP (PA)
Merged into BancTec, Inc. 4/2/84
Each share Common 50¢ par exchanged for (0.0783948) share Common 50¢ par
(See BancTec, Inc.)

SCAN GRAPHICS INC (PA)
Reincorporated 6/15/92
Each share old Common $0.001 par exchanged for (0.2) share new Common $0.001 par 11/1/89
State of incorporation changed from (UT) to (PA) 6/15/92
Name changed to Sedona Corp. 4/2/99

SCAN OPTICS INC (DE)
Dissolved 2/15/2006
No stockholders' equity

SCAN SYS INC (DE)
Charter cancelled and declared inoperative and void for non-payment of taxes 3/1/76

SCAN TRON CORP (CA)
Common no par split (5) for (4) by issuance of (0.25) additional share 12/16/85
Common no par split (5) for (4) by issuance of (0.25) additional share 9/30/86
Reincorporated under the laws of Delaware as Scantron Corp. 12/2/87
Scantron Corp. acquired by Harland (John H.) Co. 6/17/88
(See Harland (John H.) Co.)

SCANA CORP (OLD) (SC)
Common no par split (2) for (1) by issuance of (1) additional share 5/26/95
Merged into SCANA Corp. (New) 2/10/2000
Each share Common no par exchanged for (1) share Common no par

SCANDIA LEASING & ACCEP CORP (MN)
Statutorily dissolved 10/04/1991

SCANDINAVIA FD INC (MD)
Reorganized under the laws of Cayman Islands as Scandinavia Co., Inc. 02/22/1989
Each share Capital Stock 1¢ par exchanged for (1) share Common 1¢ par
Scandinavia Co., Inc. name changed to Xcelera.com, Inc. 10/26/1999 which name changed to Xcelera Inc. 12/06/2000
(See Xcelera Inc.)

SCANDINAVIA INC (CAYMAN ISLANDS)
Common 1¢ par split (3) for (2) by issuance of (0.5) additional share payable 09/21/1999 to holders of record 09/03/1999
Common 1¢ par split (2) for (1) by issuance of (1) additional share payable 10/22/1999 to holders of record 10/11/1999
Name changed to Xcelera.com, Inc. 10/26/1999
Xcelera.com, Inc. name changed to Xcelera Inc. 12/06/2000
(See Xcelera Inc.)

SCANDINAVIAN BROADCASTING SYSTEM S A (LUXEMBOURG)
Name changed to SBS Broadcasting S.A. 12/28/1998
(See SBS Broadcasting S.A.)

SCANDINAVIAN GOLD LTD (CANADA)
Name changed to Scandinavian Minerals Ltd. 02/10/2006
Scandinavian Minerals Ltd. acquired by First Quantum Minerals Ltd. 06/23/2008

SCANDINAVIAN MINERALS LTD (CANADA)
Acquired by First Quantum Minerals Ltd. 06/23/2008
Each share Common no par exchanged for (0.01) share Common no par and $9 cash

SCANFORMS INC (DE)
Each share Common 25¢ par exchanged for (0.2) share Common 1¢ par 12/01/1977
Stock Dividends - 100% 10/22/1979; 100% 07/21/1981
Merged into Big Flower Press Holdings, Inc. 10/04/1996
Each share Common 1¢ par exchanged for (0.4423) share Common 1¢ par
Big Flower Press Holdings, Inc. name changed to Big Flower Holdings Inc. 10/17/1997
(See Big Flower Holdings Inc.)

SCANIA AKTIEBOLAG (SWEDEN)
ADR agreement terminated 02/25/2003
Each Sponsored ADR for Ser. A exchanged for $26.0506894 cash
Each Sponsored ADR for Ser. B exchanged for $26.491668 cash
ADR agreement terminated 05/11/2015
Each ADR for Ordinary exchanged for $23.453059 cash

SCANLANS LITERARY HOUSE INC (NY)
Adjudicated bankrupt 06/01/1972
Stockholders' equity unlikely

SCANNER ENERGY EXPL CORP (UT)
Name changed to Odin-Phoenix, Ltd. 10/18/1982
Each share Class A Common 10¢ par exchanged for (1) share Class A Common 10¢ par
Note: Certificates not surrendered by 02/28/1983 became worthless unless good cause can be shown as to why they were not delivered by that date

SCANSOFT INC (DE)
Name changed to Nuance Communications, Inc. (New) 11/21/2005

SCANTEK MED INC (DE)
Plan of reorganization under Chapter 11 Federal Bankruptcy proceedings confirmed 01/25/2011
No stockholders' equity

SCANTLIN ELECTRS INC (DE)
Common no par changed to 10¢ par 04/05/1963
Name changed to Quotron Systems Inc. 03/05/1973
(See Quotron Systems Inc.)

SCANTRON CORP (DE)
Acquired by Harland (John H.) Co. 6/17/88
Each share Common no par exchanged for (0.775) share Common $1 par
(See Harland (John H.) Co.)

SCANVEC-AMIABLE, LTD (ISRAEL)
Company terminated Ordinary stock registration and is no longer public as of 12/09/2004

SCANVEC CO (1990) LTD (ISRAEL)
Name changed to Scanvec Amiable, Ltd. 02/17/1994
(See Scanvec Amiable, Ltd.)

SCARAB FISHING VENTURES LTD. (NS)
Charter revoked for non-payment of fees 12/30/71

SCARAB RESOURCE CORP (BC)
Name changed to Pilot Laboratories Corp. 6/16/86
Pilot Laboratories Corp. reorganized as Murex Clinical Technologies Corp. 2/20/89 which recapitalized as International Murex Technologies Corp. 12/12/90
(See International Murex Technologies Corp.)

SCARAB SYS INC (CO)
Each share old Common $0.001 par exchanged for (0.1) share new Common $0.001 par 12/01/2003
Name changed to Torrent Energy Corp. 07/30/2004
Torrent Energy Corp. recapitalized as 1pm Industries, Inc. 04/06/2015

SCARBORO RES LTD (AB)
Reincorporated 06/11/1980
Place of incorporation changed from (BC) to (AB) 06/11/1980
Recapitalized as Hillcrest Resources Ltd. 10/05/1987
Each share Capital Stock no par exchanged for (0.05) share Common no par
Hillcrest Resources Ltd. acquired by Mark Resources Inc. 05/09/1995 which was acquired by EnerMark Income Fund 04/09/1996 which merged into Enerplus Resources Fund 06/22/2001 which reorganized as Enerplus Corp. 01/03/2011

SCARLET ENERGY INC (BC)
Name changed to Nanotec Canada Inc. 6/5/85
Each share Common no par exchanged for (1) share Common no par
(See Nanotec Canada Inc.)

SCARLET EXPL INC (AB)
Merged into Ventus Energy Ltd. 12/31/1998
Each share Common no par exchanged for (0.125) share Common no par
Ventus Energy Ltd. name changed to Navigo Energy Inc. 05/24/2002
(See Navigo Energy Inc.)

SCARLET OILS LTD. (ON)
Acquired by Oil Selections Ltd. 00/00/1953
Each share Capital Stock $1 par exchanged for (1) share Capital Stock no par
Oil Selections Ltd. acquired by Quonto Petroleums Ltd. 00/00/1957 which name changed to Quonto Explorations Ltd. 07/27/1962
(See Quonto Explorations Ltd.)

SCARLET RES LTD (BC)
Name changed to United Mining Group, Inc. 05/10/2010
United Mining Group, Inc. name changed to United Silver Corp. 06/08/2011
(See United Silver Corp.)

SCARLETT MINERALS INC (CANADA)
Name changed to SMI Oil & Gas, Inc. 9/20/94
SMI Oil & Gas, Inc. merged into Canadian Leader Energy Inc. 11/2/95 which merged into Centurion Energy International Inc. 5/20/97
(See Centurion Energy International Inc.)

SCARSDALE FD INC (NY)
Charter cancelled and proclaimed dissolved for failure to pay taxes 09/26/1979

SCARSDALE NATL BK & TR CO (SCARSDALE, NY)
Capital Stock $20 par changed to $10 par and (1) additional share issued plus a 50% stock dividend paid 07/01/1960
Stock Dividend - 20% 04/01/1968
Merged into Charter New York Corp. 12/05/1969
Each share Capital Stock $10 par exchanged for (1.666666) shares Common $10 par
Charter New York Corp. name changed to Irving Bank Corp. 10/17/1979 which merged into Bank of New York Co., Inc. 12/30/1988 which merged into Bank of New York Mellon Corp. 07/01/2007

SCAT HOVERCRAFT INC (FL)
Each share old Common $0.001 par exchanged for (0.05) share new Common $0.001 par 03/12/1991
Plan of reorganization under Chapter 11 Federal Bankruptcy proceedings confirmed 08/29/1990
Stockholders' equity unlikely

SCATTERGOOD MANITOBA GOLD, LTD. (CANADA)
Charter cancelled for failure to file reports and pay taxes 8/8/49

SCAVO RESOURCE CORP (BC)
Name changed to Brabeia Inc. 08/28/2015
Brabeia Inc. name changed to Seahawk Ventures Inc. 03/01/2016

SCB BANCORP INC (IL)
Merged into Horizon Bancorp 04/03/2014
Each share Common no par exchanged for (0.4904) share Common no par and $5.15 cash
Note: Holders of (99) or fewer shares will receive $16.35 cash per share
Horizon Bancorp name changed to Horizon Bancorp, Inc. 05/08/2018

SCB COMPUTER TECHNOLOGY INC (TN)
Common 1¢ par split (3) for (2) by issuance of (0.5) additional share payable 09/03/1997 to holders of record 08/20/1997
Common 1¢ par split (2) for (1) by issuance of (1) additional share payable 04/27/1998 to holders of record 04/13/1998
Merged into Ciber, Inc. 03/01/2004
Each share Common 1¢ par exchanged for (0.053248) share Common 1¢ par and $1.63 cash
Ciber, Inc. name changed to CMTSU Liquidation, Inc. 12/22/2017

SCB RESTAURANT SYS INC (MI)
Involuntarily dissolved for failure to file annual reports 5/15/88

SCBT FINL CORP (SC)
Stock Dividends - 5% payable 01/01/2005 to holders of record 12/20/2004; 5% payable 03/23/2007 to holders of record 03/09/2007
Ex date - 03/07/2007
Under plan of merger name changed to First Financial Holdings, Inc. 07/30/2013
First Financial Holdings, Inc. name changed to South State Corp. 06/30/2014

SCC COMMUNICATIONS CORP (DE)
Name changed to Intrado Inc. 06/11/2001
(See Intrado Inc.)

SCC LIQUIDATING CORP. (CA)
Liquidation completed
Each share Common no par exchanged for initial distribution of (0.2523) share United Telecommunications, Inc. Common $2.50 par 11/5/76
Each (9.15) shares Common no par received second and final distribution of (1) share United Telecommunications, Inc. Common $2.50 par 5/15/81
Note: Holdings of more than (915) shares received an additional (0.7) share Common $2.50 par for each (9.15) shares in excess of (915)
United Telecommunications, Inc. name changed to Sprint Corp. 2/26/92 which name changed to Sprint Nextel Corp. 8/12/2005

SCC RESOURCE INC (AB)
Recapitalized 01/27/1992
Recapitalized from SCC Resources Corp. to SCC Resources Inc. 01/27/1992
Each share Class A Common no par exchanged for (0.2) share Class A Common no par
Name changed to Turbo Genset Inc. (AB) 12/05/1995
Turbo Genset Inc. (AB) reincorporated in Yukon as Turbo Power Systems Inc. 07/19/2006

SCE TR I (DE)
5.625% Trust Preference Securities called for redemption at $25 plus $0.13 accrued dividends on 07/19/2017

SCE&G TR I (DE)
Issue Information - 200,000 TR PFD SECS A 7.55% offered at $25 per share on 10/22/1997
7.55% Guaranteed Trust Preferred Securities Ser. A called for redemption at $25 on 6/16/2003

SCECORP (CA)
Common $4-1/6 par changed to no par and (1) additional share issued 06/21/1993
Name changed to Edison International 02/05/1996

SCENARIO SYS INTL INC (TX)
Reorganized under the laws of Wyoming as Insight ID, Inc. 09/18/2013
Each share Common $0.00001 par exchanged for (0.001) share Common $0.00001 par

SCENIC DEVELOPERS INC (DE)
Charter cancelled and declared inoperative and void for non-payment of taxes 3/1/98

SCENIC OILS LTD (AB)
Common no par changed to 20¢ par 03/29/1963
Liquidation completed
Each share Common no par exchanged for initial distribution of (1) share Canadian Scenic Oils Ltd. Common no par, (0.158393) share Ashland Canadian Oils Ltd. $2 Preferred $20 par and $1 cash 05/15/1970
Each share Common no par received second and final distribution of $0.171 cash 10/09/1970
(See each company's listing)

SCENTOVISION, INC. (NY)
Charter revoked for failure to file reports and pay fees 12/15/66

SCEPTRE INCOME & GROWTH TR (ON)
Merged into ROI Sceptre Retirement Growth Fund 09/10/2007
Each Unit no par received (1.085) Ser. C-7 Units no par
ROI Sceptre Retirement Growth Fund name changed to ROI Canadian Top 30 Small Cap Picks Fund 07/05/2010

SCEPTRE INCOME & HIGH GROWTH TR (ON)
Under plan of merger each Unit automatically became (1.174) ROI Sceptre Retirement Growth Fund Ser. C-7 Unit 09/10/2007
ROI Sceptre Retirement Growth Fund name changed to ROI Canadian Top 30 Small Cap Picks Fund 07/05/2010

SCEPTRE INVT COUNSEL LTD (ON)
Non-Vtg. Class A no par split (5) for (1) by issuance of (4) additional shares payable 06/09/1997 to holders of record 06/04/1997
Non-Vtg. Class A no par reclassified as Common no par 08/29/2003
Merged into Fiera Sceptre Inc. 09/01/2010
Each share Common no par exchanged for (1) share Class A Subordinate no par and $0.60 cash

SCEPTRE RES LTD (CANADA)
Reincorporated 10/31/1979
Place of incorporation changed from (BC) to (Canada) 10/31/1979
Each share 7% 2nd Preferred Ser. A no par exchanged for (1.6675) shares old Common no par and $5 cash 11/09/1992
Each share 8.5% 2nd Preferred Ser. B no par exchanged for (1.334) shares old Common no par and $4 cash 11/09/1992
Each share old Common no par exchanged for (0.1) share new Common no par 11/10/1992
Merged into Canadian Natural Resources Ltd. 08/15/1996
Each share new Common no par exchanged (0.38) share Common no par

SCG FINL ACQUISITION CORP (DE)
Name changed to RMG Networks Holding Corp. 07/16/2013
(See RMG Networks Holding Corp.)

SCG HLDG CORP (DE)
Issue Information - 30,000,000 shares COM offered at $16 per share on 04/27/2000
Name changed to On Semiconductor Corp. 8/9/2000

SCHAAK ELECTRS INC (MN)
Stock Dividends - 100% 10/14/77; 50% 10/13/78
Chapter 11 bankruptcy proceedings converted to Chapter 7 on 3/10/86
Stockholders' equity unlikely

SCHACHER GREENTREE & CO INC (NY)
Name changed to Greentree Software Inc. (NY) 01/22/1988
Greentree Software Inc. (NY) reincorporated in Delaware as PurchaseSoft, Inc. 11/20/1998
(See PurchaseSoft, Inc.)

SCHACHT (G.A.) MOTOR TRUCK CO.
Name changed to Le Blond-Schacht Truck Co. in 1927, and to Ahrens-Fox Fire Engine Co. in 1939
Ahrens-Fox Fire Engine Co. dissolved in 1940

SCHAEFER (F & M) BREWING CO. (NY)
5% 1st Preferred $100 par called for redemption 10/15/1967
Public interest eliminated

SCHAEFER F & M CORP (NY)
Merged into Stroh Brewery Co. 05/13/1981
Each share Common 10¢ par exchanged for $7.40 cash

SCHAEFER J B INDS INC (DE)
Each share Capital Stock 10¢ par exchanged for (0.2) share Capital Stock 50¢ par 06/09/1969
Name changed to Furntec Industries, Inc. 05/21/1971
(See Furntec Industries, Inc.)

SCHAEVITZ ENGR (NJ)
Class A Common 10¢ par and Class B Common 10¢ par reclassified as Common 10¢ par 03/28/1962
Merged into Lucas Industries Inc. 12/19/1986
Each share Common 10¢ par exchanged for $22.5910238 cash

SCHAFER VALUE TR INC (MD)
Liquidation completed
Each share Common 1¢ par received initial distribution of $10.25 cash 07/05/1990
Each share Common 1¢ par exchanged for second distribution of $0.425 cash 09/19/1990
Each share Common 1¢ par received third and final distribution of $0.0036 cash 01/25/1991

SCHAFFER FOOD SVC CORP (NY)
Dissolved by proclamation 06/23/1999

SCHAFFER S GROCERY CORP (NY)
Name changed to Schaffer Food Service Corp. 04/18/1995
(See Schaffer Food Service Corp.)

SCHAGRINS INC (FL)
Proclaimed dissolved for failure to file reports and pay fees 11/16/87

SCHAPER MFG INC (MN)
Common $4 par changed to $1 par 5/28/70
Completely liquidated 5/4/71
Each share Common $1 par exchanged for first and final distribution of (1.188575) shares Bethlehem Steel Corp. Common $8 par
(See Bethlehem Steel Corp.)

SCHARCO MANUFACTURING CORP. (NY)
Name changed to Grow-Rite Corp. 3/19/62
(See Grow-Rite Corp.)

SCHATZ FEDERAL BEARINGS CO., INC. (NY)
Dissolved by proclamation 3/25/92

SCHAWK INC (DE)
Merged into Matthews International Corp. 07/29/2014
Each share Class A Common $0.008 par exchanged for (0.20582) share Class A Common $1 par and $11.80 cash

SCHEDULED SKYWAYS INC (AR)
Merged into Air Midwest, Inc. 01/18/1985
Each (2.75) shares Common 1¢ par exchanged for (1) share Common $1 par
Air Midwest, Inc. merged into Mesa Airlines, Inc. (NM) 07/12/1991 which reincorporated in Nevada as Mesa Air Group, Inc. 09/27/1996
(See Mesa Air Group, Inc.)

SCHEELAUR MINES LTD. (ON)
Charter cancelled for failure to file reports and pay taxes in 1959

SCHEER ENERGY DEV CORP (BC)
Recapitalized as Panterra Energy Inc. 7/19/89
Each share Common no par exchanged for (1/3) share Common no par
Panterra Energy Inc. recapitalized as Enrich Ventures Ltd. 2/11/93

SCHEER FINANCIAL CORP. (DE)
Charter cancelled and declared inoperative and void for non-payment of taxes 3/1/76

SCHEFFRES INDS INC (DE)
Name changed to Link Enterprises Inc. 02/22/1971
Link Enterprises Inc. name changed to Edan Corp. 03/09/1971 which name changed to Edan Enterprise, Inc. 03/25/1971
(See Edan Enterprise, Inc.)

SCHEIB EARL INC (DE)
Capital Stock $1 par split (3) for (2) by issuance of (0.5) additional share 09/28/1970
Capital Stock $1 par split (3) for (2) by issuance of (0.5) additional share 09/28/1971
Capital Stock $1 par split (2) for (1) by issuance of (1) additional share 04/15/1986
Stock Dividend - 10% 04/15/1983
Acquired by Kelly Capital, LLC 04/30/2009
Each share Common $1 par exchanged for $2 cash

SCHEIN PHARMACEUTICAL INC (DE)
Merged into Watson Pharmaceuticals, Inc. 08/28/2000
Each share Common 1¢ par exchanged for (0.42187) share Common $0.0033 par
Watson Pharmaceuticals, Inc. name changed to Actavis, Inc. (NV) 01/24/2013 which reorganized in Ireland as Actavis PLC 10/01/2013 which name changed to Allergan PLC 06/15/2015

SCHEL INC (CO)
Name changed to Gray Publishing & Media Inc. 11/1/2004
Gray Publishing & Media Inc. recapitalized as Graystone Park Enterprises Inc. 3/14/2005

SCHELL INDUSTRIES, LTD. (ON)
Charter cancelled and declared dissolved for default in filing returns 3/31/69

SCHELLEX GOLD CORP (BC)
Recapitalized as Golden Coast Minerals Ltd. 07/23/1992
Each share Common no par exchanged for (0.25) share Common no par
Golden Coast Minerals Ltd. name changed to Golden Coast Energy Ltd. 03/16/1994 which merged into Founders Energy Ltd. 12/04/1996 which reorganized as Provident Energy Trust 03/06/2001 which reorganized as Provident Energy Ltd. (New) 01/03/2011 which merged into Pembina Pipeline Corp. 04/02/2012

SCHENECTADY DISC CORP (NY)
Merged into First Maryland Bancorp 09/30/1974
For holdings of (100) shares or more: each share Common $1 par exchanged for $8.40 principal amount of 7% Non-Transferable Notes due 00/00/1978 plus $2.10 cash
For holdings of less than (100) shares: each share Common $1 par exchanged for $10.50 cash

SCHENECTADY RAILWAY CO. (NY)
Bankrupt in 1952

SCHENECTADY TR CO (SCHENECTADY, NY)
Each share Capital Stock $100 par exchanged for (4) shares Capital Stock $25 par 00/00/1954
Capital Stock $25 par changed to $20 par and (0.25) additional share issued 10/30/1957
Capital Stock $20 par changed to $16 par and (0.25) additional share issued 06/17/1960
Capital Stock $16 par changed to $10 par and (0.6) additional share issued 06/30/1961
Capital Stock $10 par changed to $5 par and (1) additional share issued 03/31/1970
Capital Stock $5 par changed to $10 par 03/01/1973
Stock Dividends - 33-1/3% 04/11/1945; 10% 02/01/1965; 10% 03/30/1973; 10% 08/21/1980
Under plan of reorganization each share Capital Stock $10 par automatically became (1) share TrustCo Bank Corp N Y Common $10 par 07/01/1982

SCHENLEY DISTILLERS CORP.
Name changed to Schenley Industries, Inc. in 1948
(See listing for Schenley Industries, Inc.)

SCHENLEY INDS INC (DE)
Each share Common $1.75 par exchanged for (1.25) shares Common $1.40 par 00/00/1950
Common $1.40 par changed to 93-1/3¢ par and (0.5) additional share issued 04/17/1968
Acquired by Glen Alden Corp. 06/17/1971
Each share $1.40 Conv. Preferred $1 par exchanged for $27 principal amount of 7-1/2% S.F. Subord. Debentures due 05/15/1985 and $4.50 cash
Each share Common 93-1/3¢ par exchanged for $30 principal amount of 7-1/2% S.F. Subord. Debentures due 05/15/1985 and $5 cash
50¢ Conv. Preference 35¢ par called for redemption 02/13/1973

SCHENUIT INDUSTRIES, INC. (MD)
Class A Common no par and Class B Common no par split (3) for (2) by issuance of (0.5) additional share 11/21/1966
Class B Common no par all converted into Class A Common no par as of 01/00/1972
Class A Common no par reclassified as Common no par 12/21/1972
Name changed to Schenuit Investments, Inc. 12/22/1980

SCHENUIT RUBBER CO. (MD)
Name changed to Schenuit Industries, Inc. 11/1/66
Schenuit Industries, Inc. name changed to Schenuit Investments, Inc. 12/22/80

SCHERER HEALTHCARE INC (DE)
Common 1¢ par split (2) for (1) by issuance of (1) additional share 10/31/1988
Merged into Stericycle, Inc. 01/19/2003
Each share Common 1¢ par exchanged for $8.57 cash

SCHERER LEATHER CO.
Acquired by Graton & Knight Co. in 1939
Details not available

SCHERER R P CORP NEW (DE)
Each share Preferred Ser. B 1¢ par exchanged for (5/9) share new Common 1¢ par 10/11/91
Each share old Common 1¢ par exchanged for (4.35) shares new Common 1¢ par 10/11/91
17% Sr. Exchangeable Preferred 1¢ par called for redemption 11/22/91
Merged into Cardinal Health, Inc. 8/7/98
Each share Common 1¢ par exchanged for (0.95) share Common no par

SCHERER R P CORP OLD (DE)
Common $1 par changed to 33-1/3¢ par and (2) additional shares issued 10/20/72
Each share old Common 33-1/3¢ par exchanged for (0.5) share new Common 33-1/3¢ par and (0.5) share Conv. Class B Common 33-1/3¢ par 4/4/84
Merged into RPS Corp. 10/5/89
Each share $1.4375 Conv. Exchangeable Preferred Ser. A $1 par exchanged for (1.0593) shares 17% Sr. Exchangeable Preferred 1¢ par
Each share Conv. Class B Common 33-1/3¢ par exchanged for (1) share 17% Sr. Exchangeable Preferred 1¢ par
Each share new Common 33-1/3¢ par exchanged for (1) share 17% Sr. Exchangeable Preferred 1¢ par
RPS Corp. name changed to Scherer (R.P.) Corp. (New) 8/21/91 which merged into Cardinal Health, Inc. 8/7/98

SCHERING AG (GERMANY)
Acquired by Bayer Schering GmbH 09/25/2008
Each Sponsored ADR for Ordinary exchanged for $133.9343 cash
Note: Each Sponsored ADR for Ordinary received an additional distribution of $28.909054 cash 07/26/2016

SCHERING CORP (NJ)
Common 15¢ par changed to $1 par and (1) additional share issued 10/11/1957
5% Conv. Preferred $30 par called for redemption 05/15/1964
Common $1 par split (2) for (1) by issuance of (1) additional share 04/28/1966
Common $1 par split (2) for (1) by issuance of (1) additional share 05/15/1969
Merged into Schering-Plough Corp. 01/16/1971
Each share Common $1 par exchanged for (1) share Common $1 par

Schering-Plough Corp. merged into Merck & Co., Inc. (New) 11/03/2009

SCHERING PLOUGH CORP (NJ)
Common $1 par split (2) for (1) by issuance of (1) additional share 06/01/1973
$5.07 Preferred Ser. B $1 par called for redemption 04/03/1984
Common $1 par split (2) for (1) by issuance of (1) additional share 06/01/1987
Common $1 par split (2) for (1) by issuance of (1) additional share 05/29/1990
Common $1 par split (2) for (1) by issuance of (1) additional share 06/09/1995
Common $1 par split (2) for (1) by issuance of (1) additional share payable 06/03/1997 to holders of record 05/02/1997 Ex date - 06/04/1997
Preferred Stock Purchase Rights declared for Common stockholders of record 08/07/1989 were redeemed at $0.00125 per right 07/30/1997 for holders of record 07/10/1997
Common $1 par changed to 50¢ par and (1) additional share issued payable 12/02/1998 to holders of record 11/06/1998 Ex date - 12/03/1998
Issue Information - 25,000,000 shares MANDATORY PFD CONV offered at $50 per share on 08/04/2004
Issue Information - 10,000,000 shares PFD CONV MANDATORY 2007 offered at $250 per share on 08/09/2007
Each share 6% Mandatory Conv. Preferred $1 par converted into (2.2466) shares Common 50¢ par 09/14/2007
Merged into Merck & Co., Inc. (New) 11/03/2009
Each share 6% Mandatory Conv. Preferred 2007 Ser. $1 par automatically became (1) share 6% Mandatory Conv. Preferred $1 par
Each share Common 50¢ par exchanged for (0.5767) share Common 50¢ par and $10.50 cash

SCHERMACK CORP. OF AMERICA
Dissolved in 1934

SCHERR TUMICO INC (MN)
Common $2 par changed to $1 par 01/22/1974
Name changed to ST Liquidating Co. 02/28/1979
(See ST Liquidating Co.)

SCHERTLE GALLERIES INC (MD)
Incorporated 03/03/1970
Charter annulled for failure to file annual reports 12/20/1976

SCHERTLE'S GALLERIES, INC. (MD)
Merged into Lin Broadcasting Corp. 7/3/68
Each share Common $1 par exchanged for (0.6015) share Common $2 par

SCHEUTZOW HELICOPTER CORP (OH)
Charter cancelled for failure to file reports and pay fees 1/16/81

SCHICK COMPANIES INC. (DE)
Name changed to Hart Holding Co. Inc. 08/19/1988
(See Hart Holding Co. Inc.)

SCHICK ELECTRIC INC. (DE)
Name changed to Schick Inc. 01/13/1972
Schick Inc. name changed to Schick Companies Inc. 12/02/1987 which name changed to Hart Holding Co. Inc. 08/19/1988
(See Hart Holding Co. Inc.)

SCHICK INC (DE)
Common $1 par split (2) for (1) by issuance of (1) additional share 10/16/1956
Name changed to Schick Electric Inc. 04/29/1964 which name changed back to Schick Inc. 01/13/1972
Name changed to Schick Companies Inc. 12/02/1987
Schick Companies Inc. name changed to Hart Holding Co. Inc. 08/19/1988
(See Hart Holding Co. Inc.)

SCHICK INVT CO (DE)
Reincorporated 7/20/70
State of incorporation changed from (TX) to (DE) and Common $10 par changed to $1 par 7/20/70
Merged into Frawley Enterprises, Inc. 10/31/75
Each share Common $1 par exchanged for (0.5) share Common $1 par
(See Frawley Enterprises, Inc.)

SCHICK TECHNOLOGIES INC (DE)
Name changed to Sirona Dental Systems, Inc. 06/21/2006
Sirona Dental Systems, Inc. merged into DENTSPLY SIRONA Inc. 03/01/2016

SCHIELD BANTAM CO. (IA)
Acquired by Koehring Co. 8/1/63
Each share Common $5 par exchanged for (0.13) share $2.75 Conv. Preferred Ser. D no par
(See Koehring Co.)

SCHIELD MGMT CO (CO)
Each share old Common 1¢ par exchanged for (0.2) share new Common 1¢ par 09/12/1990
Name changed to PMC International Inc. 09/30/1993
(See PMC International Inc.)

SCHIELD PORTFOLIOS SER (MA)
U.S. Government Zero Bond Portfolio Shares of Bene. Int. no par reclassified as Timed Asset Allocation Fund Share of Bene. Int. no par 05/31/1988
High Yield Bond Portfolio and Timed Asset Allocation Fund were closed 12/00/1992
Details not available
Aggressive Growth Portfolio, Progressive Environmental Fund and Value Portfolio merged into Progressive Portfolios Series 11/30/1992
Details not available

SCHIFF CO.
Name changed to Shoe Corp. of America in 1947
Each share Common no par exchanged for (2) shares Class A Common no par
Shoe Corp. of America reincorporated under the laws of Delaware as SCOA Industries Inc. (Old) 5/23/69 which merged into SCOA Industries Inc. (New) 12/10/85 which name changed to Hills Stores Co. 4/9/87
(See Hills Stores Co.)

SCHIFF NUTRITION INTL INC (DE)
Acquired by Reckitt Benckiser Group PLC 12/17/2012
Each share Common 1¢ par exchanged for $42 cash

SCHIFFNER OILFIELD & TECHNOLOGY CORP (BC)
Delisted from Vancouver Stock Exchange 02/02/1989

SCHILLER CORP (DE)
Stock Dividend - 50% 11/12/1968
Name changed to Schiller Industries, Inc. 12/23/1969
(See Schiller Industries, Inc.)

SCHILLER INDS INC (DE)
Merged into Rexham Corp. 08/13/1980
Each share Common $1 par exchanged for $13.50 cash

SCHIMATIC CASH TRANSACTIONS NETWORK COM INC (FL)
Name changed 1/14/99
Name changed from Schimatic Technologies, Inc. to Schimatic Cash Transactions Network.Com Inc. 1/14/99
Common $0.001 par split (1.59) for (1) by issuance of (0.59) additional share payable 9/2/99 to holders of record 8/13/99
Merged into IC One, Inc. 9/15/99
Each share Common $0.001 par exchanged for $0.75 cash

SCHJELDAHL G T CO (MN)
Capital Stock $1 par changed to 50¢ par and (1) additional share issued in October 1960
Name changed to Sheldahl Co. and Capital Stock 50¢ par changed to 25¢ par 8/29/74
(See Sheldahl Co.)

SCHLAFLY NOLAN OIL CO., INC. (DE)
Charter cancelled and declared inoperative and void for non-payment of taxes 4/1/66

SCHLAGE LOCK CO (CA)
Common $10 par changed to $3.33-1/3 par and (2) additional shares issued plus a 10% stock dividend paid 12/01/1955
Stock Dividends - 40% 03/01/1951; 10% 11/30/1954
Merged into Ingersoll-Rand Co. (NJ) 04/16/1974
Each share Common $3.33-1/3 par exchanged for (1.23) shares Common $2 par
Ingersoll-Rand Co. (NJ) reorganized in Bermuda as Ingersoll-Rand Co. Ltd. 12/31/2001 which reincorporated in Ireland as Ingersoll-Rand PLC 07/01/2009

SCHLEE-BROCK AIRCRAFT CORP.
Bankrupt in 1930

SCHLESINGER (B.F.) & SONS, INC.
Reorganized as Schlesinger (B.F.) Co. in 1937
Each share Preferred exchanged for (2) shares Preferred and (0.666666) share Common
Each share Class A Common exchanged for (0.2) share Common
Each share Class B Common exchanged for (0.08) share Common
Schlesinger (B.F.) Co. name changed to Western Department Stores in 1941 which name changed to Rhodes Western 8/2/60 which was acquired by Amfac, Inc. 12/2/69
(See Amfac, Inc.)

SCHLESINGER (B.F.) CO.
Name changed to Western Department Stores in 1941
Western Department Stores name changed to Rhodes Western 8/2/60 which was acquired by Amfac, Inc. 12/2/69
(See Amfac, Inc.)

SCHLETTER & ZANDER, INC.
Name changed to Signature Hosiery Co., Inc. in 1931 which was liquidated in 1936

SCHLITZ JOS BREWING CO (WI)
Common $15 par changed to $7.50 par and (1) additional share issued 05/25/1966
Common $7.50 par changed to $2.50 par and (2) additional shares issued 05/25/1972
Merged into Stroh Brewing Co. 06/10/1982
Each share Common $2.50 par exchanged for $17 cash

SCHLOTZSKYS INC (TX)
Plan of reorganization under Chapter 11 Federal Bankruptcy Code effective 4/21/2006
No stockholders' equity

SCHLUDERBERG KURDLE INC (MD)
Acquired by Smithfield Foods, Inc. 10/24/1985
Each share Class A Common $2.50 par exchanged for $20 cash
Each share Class B Non-Vtg. Common $2.50 par exchanged for $18 cash

SCHLUMBERGER WELL SURVEYING CORP. (DE)
Reincorporated under the laws of Netherlands Antilles as Schlumberger Ltd. and each share Common no par exchanged for (30) shares Common $1 par 3/1/57

SCHMIDT (K.G.) BREWING CO., INC.
In receivership in 1950
No stockholders' equity

SCHMIDT BREWING CO. (MI)
Liquidation approved in 1952

SCHMIEG INDUSTRIES, INC. (MI)
Common no par changed to $1 par 7/1/55
Recapitalized as S.I. Industries, Inc. 8/2/63
Each share Common $1 par exchanged for (0.5) share Common $1 par and 55¢ cash

SCHMITT INDS INC (BC)
Reincorporated under the laws of Oregon 02/16/1996

SCHNEIDER (WALTER J.) CORP. (DE)
Name changed to Barrington Industries, Inc. 05/15/1963
Barrington Industries, Inc. merged into Wilson Brothers 09/20/1974 which name changed to Wilson Brothers USA, Inc. 08/20/1997
(See Wilson Brothers USA, Inc.)

SCHNEIDER CORP NEW (ON)
Non-Vtg. Class A no par split (2) for (1) by issuance of (1) additional share 8/18/92
Common no par split (2) for (1) by issuance of (1) additional share 8/18/92
Acquired by Smithfield Foods Inc. 12/21/98
Each share Common no par exchanged for (0.5415) share Common $1 par
Acquired by Smithfield Foods Inc. 9/28/2001
Each share Non-Vtg. Class A no par exchanged for (1.083) shares Common $1 par

SCHNEIDER ELEC SA (FRANCE)
ADR basis changed from (1:0.1) to (1:0.2) 09/09/2011
Name changed to Schneider Electric S.E. 09/26/2014

SCHNEIDER J M INC (ON)
Name changed 01/16/1976
Name changed 01/29/1979
Name changed from Schneider (J.M.) Ltd. to Schneider Corp. (Old) 01/16/1976
Name changed from Schneider Corp. (Old) to Schneider (J.M.) Inc. 01/29/1979
Name changed to Heritage Group Inc. and Class B Part. Preference no par and Class C Part. Preference no par reclassified as Class A Part. Preference no par 09/22/1980
Heritage Group Inc. name changed to Schneider Corp. (New) 06/26/1986 which merged into Smithfield Foods Inc. 12/21/1998

SCHNUR APPEL INC (DE)
Common 10¢ par changed to 1¢ par and (2) additional shares issued 09/09/1971
Completely liquidated 08/11/1977
Each share Common 1¢ par exchanged for first and final distribution of $0.1071 cash

SCHOELLKOPF, HUTTON & POMEROY, INC. (NY)
Each share 5-1/2% Preferred $100 par exchanged for (10) shares 4-3/4% Preferred $10 par in 1952
Name changed to Crescent Niagara Corp. 12/22/60
(See Crescent Niagara Corp.)

SCHOENEMAN (J.) INC. (MD)
Common no par changed to $3.50 par in 1935
Name changed to Slade, Inc. 10/3/55

SCHOENHOFEN EDELWEISS CO.
Merged into Drewry's Limited, U.S.A., Inc. and each (15) shares Common $1 par exchanged for (1) share new 5-3/4% Preferred $50 par in 1951
(See Drewry's Limited, U.S.A., Inc.)

SCHOLASTIC INC (NY)
Acquired by SI Holdings Inc. 07/16/1987
Each share Common 25¢ par exchanged for $28 principal amount of Subordinated Debentures due 06/01/2002, (0.3) share Exchangeable Preferred Ser. A 1¢ par and $20 cash

SCHOLASTIC MAGAZINES, INC. (NY)
Name changed to Scholastic Inc. 9/1/80
Scholastic Inc. acquired by SI Holdings Inc. 7/16/87

SCHOLL INC (NY)
Merged into Schering-Plough Corp. 04/03/1979
Each share Common $1 par exchanged for (0.5) share $5.07 Preferred Ser. B $1 par

SCHOLZ HOMES INC (OH)
Common $1 par changed to 50¢ par and (1) additional share issued 09/08/1969
Merged into Inland Steel Co. 02/17/1970
Each share Common 50¢ par exchanged for (0.5) share $2.40 Conv. Preferred Ser. A no par
Inland Steel Co. reorganized as Inland Steel Industries, Inc. 05/01/1986 which name changed to Ryerson Tull, Inc. (New) 02/26/1999 which name changed to Ryerson, Inc. 01/01/2006
(See Ryerson, Inc.)

SCHOMBURG INDS CDA INC (AB)
Delisted from Alberta Stock Exchange 08/04/1995

SCHOOL CORP AMER (DE)
Recapitalized as Information Dynamics Inc. 01/08/1973
Each share Common 5¢ par exchanged for (0.166666) share Common 1¢ par
(See Information Dynamics Inc.)

SCHOOL FOR COMPUTER STUDIES INC (NY)
Name changed to Kenilworth Research & Development Corp. 07/20/1972
Kenilworth Research & Development Corp. name changed to Kenilworth Systems Corp. 12/14/1979

SCHOOL PICTURES INC NEW (MS)
Stock Dividend - 10% 9/15/61
Under plan of merger name changed to Intersystems, Inc. 8/19/69 which name changed back to School Pictures, Inc. 6/30/75
Acquired by Jostens, Inc. 10/31/88
Each share Common $2 par exchanged for $11.40 cash

SCHOOL SPECIALTY INC (WI)
State of incorporation changed from (DE) to (WI) 08/31/2000
Plan of reorganization under Chapter 11 Federal Bankruptcy proceedings effective 06/11/2013
No stockholders' equity

SCHOOL SUPPLIES INC (UT)
Name changed to Hull Enterprises, Inc. 03/05/1990
(See Hull Enterprises, Inc.)

SCHOOL4CHAUFFEURS INC (DE)
Reorganized as POWRtec International Corp. 06/23/2010
Each share Common $0.001 par exchanged for (40) shares Common $0.001 par

SCHOOLEY PRINTING & STATIONERY CO. (DE)
Name changed to Schooley, Inc. 1/17/79

SCHOOLWEB SYS INC (NV)
Name changed to Alternet Systems, Inc. 05/14/2002

SCHOOLWURKS INC (DE)
SEC revoked common stock registration 05/14/2007

SCHOONER BREWERY INC (NV)
Each share Common $0.001 par exchanged for (0.2) share Common $0.005 par 07/22/1997
Name changed to GameCom, Inc. (NV) 03/03/1999
GameCom, Inc. (NV) reincorporated in Texas 02/04/2000 which name changed to VirTra Systems, Inc. (TX) 05/06/2002 which reincorporated in Nevada as VirTra, Inc. 10/07/2016

SCHORE AUTOMATIONS INC (NY)
Charter cancelled and proclaimed dissolved for failure to pay taxes 03/25/1981

SCHOTT INDS INC (OH)
Name changed to Kappa Industries, Inc. 7/3/78
Kappa Industries, Inc. name changed to Natmar, Inc. 12/31/79 which name changed to Antex Corp 4/1/85 which name changed back to Natmar, Inc. 7/5/85
(See Natmar, Inc.)

SCHRADER (H.J.) & CO. (IN)
All Class A Common no par and Class B Common no par with exception of (2) person's holdings redeemed 00/00/1969
Public interest eliminated

SCHRADER ABE CORP (DE)
Common 10¢ par split (3) for (2) by issuance of (0.5) additional share 1/29/82
Stock Dividend - 100% 8/29/75
Merged into Interco Inc. 3/15/84
Each share Common 10¢ par exchanged for $14.25 cash

SCHRAMM-JOHNSON DRUGS, INC.
Acquired by Walgreen Co. 00/00/1929
Details not available

SCHREIBER PYRAMID GOLD MINES, LTD. (ON)
Charter cancelled for failure to file reports and pay taxes in 1952

SCHREIBER RES LTD (BC)
Reincorporated 12/22/1986
Place of incorporation changed from (AB) to (BC) 12/22/1986
Recapitalized as Brier Glen Developments Corp. 12/09/1992
Each share Common no par exchanged for (0.2) share Common no par
Brier Glen Developments Corp. recapitalized as Innova Technologies Corp. 09/07/1994 which name changed to Innova Technologies Corporation 05/12/1998 which name changed to Innova LifeSciences Corp. 08/03/2000
(See Innova LifeSciences Corp.)

SCHRODER ASIAN GROWTH FD INC (MD)
Issue Information - 17,200,000 shares COM offered at $15 per share on 12/22/1993

Reincorporated under the laws of Delaware as Schroder Series Trust II and Common 1¢ par reclassified as All-Asia Fund Class A no par 03/20/1998
(See Schroder Series Trust II)

SCHRODER SER TR II (DE)
Completely liquidated 12/14/2001
Each share All-Asia Fund Class A no par received net asset value

SCHROEDER HOTEL CO. (WI)
In process of liquidation
Each share Class A Common no par or Class B Common no par exchanged for initial distribution of $200 cash 3/30/65
Each share Class A Common no par or Class B Common no par received second distribution of $15.75 cash 10/15/65
Note: Details on subsequent distributions, if any, are not available

SCHROEDER INDUSTRIES, INC. (DE)
Name changed to Gold Ribbon Foods Inc. 06/22/1966
(See Gold Ribbon Foods Inc.)

SCHUCHARDT SOFTWARE SYS INC (CA)
Reorganized under the laws of Delaware as Triumph Inc. 7/2/87
Each share new Common no par exchanged for (11.0622) shares Common 7¢ par
(See Triumph Inc.)

SCHUFF INTL INC (DE)
Name changed 07/02/2001
Name changed from Schuff Steel Co. to Schuff International, Inc. 07/02/2001
Name changed to DBM Global Inc. 10/05/2016

SCHULCO CO., INC. (NY)
Charter cancelled and proclaimed dissolved for failure to pay taxes 12/16/57

SCHULER HOMES INC (DE)
Common 1¢ par reclassified as Class A Common $0.001 par 4/2/2001
Merged into D.R. Horton, Inc. 2/21/2002
Each share Class A Common $0.001 par exchanged for (0.487) share Common 1¢ par and $4.09 cash

SCHULLER CORP (DE)
$2.70 Preferred Ser. B called for redemption at $25 on 5/5/97
Name changed to Johns-Manville Corp. (New) 5/5/97
(See Johns-Manville Corp. (New))

SCHULMAN A INC (DE)
Common $1 par split (2) for (1) by issuance of (1) additional share 11/30/1983
Common $1 par split (3) for (2) by issuance of (0.5) additional share 02/17/1987
Common $1 par split (3) for (2) by issuance of (0.5) additional share 03/22/1989
Common $1 par split (3) for (2) by issuance of (0.5) additional share 09/05/1990
Common $1 par split (3) for (2) by issuance of (0.5) additional share 01/13/1992
Common $1 par split (5) for (4) by issuance of (0.25) additional share 04/15/1994
Preferred Stock Purchase Rights declared for Common stockholders of record 02/09/2006 were redeemed at $0.01 per right 02/01/2007 for holders of record 01/19/2007
5% Preferred $100 par called for redemption at $100 on 08/14/2009
Stock Dividends - 10% 02/01/1980; 10% 02/04/1981; 10% 02/03/1982; 10% 02/02/1983; 10% 11/22/1985

Acquired by LyondellBasell Industries N.V. 08/21/2018
Each share Common $1 par exchanged for (1) Contingent Value Right and $42 cash

SCHULMAN COIN & MINT INC (NY)
Adjudicated bankrupt 02/01/1977
No stockholders' equity

SCHULT HOMES CORP (IN)
Common no par split (6) for (5) by issuance of (0.2) additional share payable 2/28/97 to holders of record 2/14/97 Ex date - 3/3/97
Merged into Oakwood Homes Corp. 4/1/98
Each share Common no par exchanged for $22.50 cash

SCHULTE (D.A.), INC. (NY)
Name changed to General Stores Corp. in 1954
General Stores Corp. reincorporated under the laws of Delaware as GSC Enterprises, Inc. 1/14/69
(See GSC Enterprises, Inc.)

SCHULTE REAL ESTATE CO., INC. (DE)
$6 Preferred completely liquidated 00/00/1953
Details not available
No Common stockholders' equity

SCHULTE RETAIL STORES CORP.
Reorganized as Schulte (D.A.), Inc. in 1940
Each share 8% Preferred exchanged for (3.25) shares Common
Each share Common exchanged for (0.04) share Common
Schulte (D.A.), Inc. name changed to General Stores Corp. in 1954 which reincorporated under the laws of Delaware as GSC Enterprises, Inc. 1/14/69
(See GSC Enterprises, Inc.)

SCHULTE-UNITED, INC.
Sold by creditors 00/00/1931
Stockholders' equity unlikely

SCHULTE-UNITED 5 CENT TO $1 STORES, INC.
Sold by creditors 00/00/1931
Stockholders' equity unlikely

SCHULTE UNITED PROPERTIES, INC.
Name changed to Retail Properties, Inc. in 1930 which was completely liquidated 6/10/57

SCHULTZ SAV O STORES INC (WI)
Common $1 par changed to 25¢ par and (3) additional shares issued 6/12/87
Common 25¢ par changed to 5¢ par and (0.5) additional shares issued 2/17/89
Common 5¢ par split (2) for (1) by issuance of (1) additional share 9/15/95
Common 5¢ par split (3) for (2) by issuance of (0.5) additional share payable 9/5/97 to holders of record 8/20/97
Stock Dividends - 10% 5/12/78; 10% 5/11/79
Name changed to Fresh Brands, Inc. 6/4/2001
(See Fresh Brands, Inc.)

SCHULZE BAKING CO.
Merged into Interstate Bakeries Corp. 00/00/1937
Each share Preferred exchanged for (1.4) shares $5 Preferred no par and (2) shares Common $1 par
Each share Common exchanged for (0.5) share Common $1 par
Interstate Bakeries Corp. name changed to Interstate Brands Corp. 07/25/1969
(See Interstate Brands Corp.)

SCHUMACHER MINING CORP. LTD.
Dissolved in 1938

SCHUMACHER WALL BOARD CORP.
Merged into Paraffine Companies, Inc. on a (1) for (1) basis in 1946
Paraffine Companies, Inc. name changed to Pabco Products, Inc. in 1950 which name changed to Fibreboard Paper Products Corp. 5/1/56 which name changed to Fibreboard Corp. 7/5/66

SCHUSTER (ED.) & CO., INC. (WI)
Each share Common no par exchanged for (8) shares Common $10 par in 1946
Acquired by Gimbel Brothers, Inc. 4/6/62
Each share 4-1/4% Preferred $100 par or 4-3/4% Preferred $100 par exchanged for (2-1/3) shares Common $5 par
Each share Common $10 par exchanged for (0.615384) share Common $5 par
Gimbel Brothers, Inc. acquired by Brown & Williamson Tobacco Co. 11/9/73

SCHUSTER EXPRESS INC (CT)
Merged into Pilot Freight Carriers of Connecticut, Inc. 03/11/1983
Each share Common $1 par exchanged for $10.56 cash

SCHUTTER CANDY CO.
Merged into Universal Match Corp. 00/00/1946
Each share Class B Common exchanged for (0.4) share Common $25 par
Universal Match Corp. name changed to UMC Industries, Inc. 05/17/1966 which name changed to Unidynamics Corp. 04/19/1984
(See Unidynamics Corp.)

SCHUTTER-JOHNSON CANDY CORP.
Name changed to Schutter Candy Co. 00/00/1937
Schutter Candy Co. merged into Universal Match Corp. 00/00/1946 which name changed to UMC Industries, Inc. 05/17/1966 which name changed to Unidynamics Corp. 04/19/1984
(See Unidynamics Corp.)

SCHUYLKILL CHEMICAL PRODUCTS CO. (DE)
Charter cancelled and declared inoperative and void for non-payment of taxes 4/1/35

SCHUYLKILL TRANSIT CO. (PA)
Liquidation completed 1/3/61

SCHUYLKILL VALLEY NAVIGATION & RAILROAD CO.
Merged into Reading Co. 2/28/50
Each share Capital Stock exchanged for (1.25) shares 1st Preferred $50 par
Reading Co. merged into Reading Entertainment Inc. (DE) 10/15/96 which reincorporated in Nevada 12/29/99 which merged into Reading International, Inc. 12/31/2001

SCHUYLKILL VALLEY TRACTION CO.
In process of liquidation in 1933

SCHWAB CHARLES CORP (DE)
6% Depository Preferred Ser. B called for redemption at $25 on 12/01/2017 (Additional Information in Active)

SCHWAB SAFE INC (IN)
Common $1 par changed to 50¢ par and (1) additional share issued 06/12/1970
Merged into NMH Corp. 04/27/1989
Each share Common 50¢ par exchanged for $19 cash

SCHWANBERG INTL INC (AB)
Name changed to Mystique Energy, Inc. 02/02/2004
Mystique Energy, Inc. recapitalized as Bella Resources Inc. 10/28/2011

which recapitalized as Angel Bioventures Inc. (AB) 08/28/2013 which reorganized in British Columbia as AbraPlata Resource Corp. 03/28/2017

SCHWARTZ (BERNARD) CIGAR CORP.
Liquidated in 1939

SCHWARTZ BROS INC (DE)
Common 10¢ par split (2) for (1) by issuance of (1) additional share 6/15/87
Each share Common 10¢ par exchanged for (0.75) share Class A Common 10¢ par and (0.25) share Class B Common 10¢ par 6/23/88
Class A Common 10¢ par split (4) for (3) by issuance of (1/3) additional share 7/5/88
Plan of reorganization under Chapter 11 Federal Bankruptcy Code effective 3/11/93
No stockholders' equity

SCHWARZ CYCLE ENGINE CORP.
Acquired by Fuel Oil Motors Corp. in 1932
Fuel Oil Motors Corp. charter revoked 6/1/33

SCHWARZ ENGINEERING CO., INC.
Name changed to Dole (James) Engineering Co. 00/00/1950
Dole (James) Engineering Co. name changed to Dole (James) Corp. 08/25/1970 which name changed to Newport Corp. 02/02/1981
(See Newport Corp.)

SCHWARZ PHARMA AG (GERMANY)
ADR basis changed from (1:0.5) to (1:1) 07/15/2002
ADR agreement terminated 07/25/2007
Each Sponsored ADR for Ordinary exchanged for $160.66282 cash

SCHWEM INSTRS (CA)
Name changed to Schwem Technology Inc. 04/19/1984
(See Schwem Technology Inc.)

SCHWEM TECHNOLOGY INC. (CA)
Voluntarily dissolved 00/00/1986
Details not available

SCHWENKSVILLE GAS CO.
Merged into Philadelphia Electric Co. in 1929
(See Philadelphia Electric Co.)

SCHWERMAN TRUCKING CO (WI)
Acquired by Tankstar USA in 1987
Details not available

SCHWITZER CORP. (IN)
Merged into Wallace (William) Corp. 11/30/64
Each share 5-1/2% Preferred $20 par exchanged for (1) share $1.10 Series A Preferred no par
Each share Common $1 par exchanged for (2.5) shares $1.10 Series A Preferred no par and (2.5) shares Common 50¢ par
Wallace (William) Corp. merged into Wallace-Murray Corp. 9/1/65 which merged into Household International, Inc. 6/29/81

SCHWITZER-CUMMINS CO. (IN)
Name changed to Schwitzer Corp. 10/31/55
Schwitzer Corp. merged into Wallace (William) Corp. 11/30/64 which merged into Wallace-Murray Corp. 9/1/65 which merged into Household International, Inc. 6/29/81

SCHWITZER INC (DE)
Preferred Stock Purchase Rights redeemed at $0.01 per right 06/07/1995 for holders of record 05/31/1995
Merged into Kuhlman Corp. 05/31/1995
Each share Common 10¢ par exchanged for (0.9615) share Common $1 par

Kuhlman Corp. merged into Borg-Warner Automotive, Inc. 03/01/1999 which name changed to BorgWarner Inc. 02/04/2000

SCI CORP (OR)
Charter cancelled for failure to file reports and pay license fees 12/10/1977

SCI EQUITY FD INC (DE)
Name changed to Stralem Technology Fund, Inc. 04/28/1972
Stralem Technology Fund, Inc. name changed to Stralem Fund, Inc. 03/28/1974 which name changed to Stralem Fund 04/30/1999
(See Stralem Fund)

SCI FIN LLC (TX)
$3.125 Conv. Term Shares Ser. A no par called for redemption at $52.50 on 6/18/97

SCI INVESTMENT FUND, INC. (DE)
Name changed to SCI Equity Fund, Inc. 12/09/1969
SCI Equity Fund, Inc. name changed to Stralem Technology Fund, Inc. 04/28/1972 which name changed to Stralem Fund, Inc. 03/28/1974 which name changed to Stralem Fund 04/30/1999
(See Stralem Fund)

SCI MED LIFE SYS INC (MN)
Common 5¢ par split (2) for (1) by issuance of (1) additional share 12/30/86
Common 5¢ par split (2) for (1) by issuance of (1) additional share 8/10/89
Merged into Boston Scientific Corp. 2/24/95
Each share Common 5¢ par exchanged for (3.4152) shares Common 1¢ par

SCI PRO INC (CO)
Each share old Common 1¢ par exchanged for (0.1) share new Common 1¢ par 11/3/81
Chapter 11 bankruptcy proceedings converted to Chapter 7 on 1/25/83
Stockholders' equity unlikely

SCI SATELLITE CONFERENCING INTL CORP (BC)
Struck off register and declared dissolved for failure to file returns 7/8/88

SCI SYS INC (DE)
Conv. Preferred Ser. B $3 par called for redemption 06/27/1977
Common 10¢ par split (7) for (5) by issuance of (0.4) additional share 08/25/1978
Common 10¢ par split (3) for (2) by issuance of (0.5) additional share 10/22/1982
Common 10¢ par split (2) for (1) by issuance of (1) additional share 07/29/1983
Common 10¢ par split (3) for (2) by issuance of (0.5) additional share 06/15/1987
Common 10¢ par split (2) for (1) by issuance of (1) additional share payable 08/22/1997 to holders of record 08/08/1997 Ex date - 08/25/1997
Common 10¢ par split (2) for (1) by issuance of (1) additional share payable 02/18/2000 to holders of record 02/04/2000
Stock Dividends - 25% 12/01/1976; 25% 11/14/1980; 50% 07/15/1981
Merged into Sanmina Corp. 12/06/2001
Each share Common 10¢ par exchanged for (1.36) shares Common 1¢ par
Sanmina Corp. name changed to Sanmina-SCI Corp. 12/10/2001 which name changed back to Sanmina Corp. 11/15/2012

SCI TEC INSTRS INC (SK)
Name changed to Kipp & Zonen Inc. 7/5/2000
(See Kipp & Zonen Inc.)

SCI-TECH VENTURES INC (FL)
Name changed to Strategic Ventures, Inc. 06/10/1991
Strategic Ventures, Inc. name changed to Internet Venture Group Inc. (FL) 10/19/1999 which reincorporated in Delaware as IVG Corp. 02/28/2001 which recapitalized as as Group Management Corp. (DE) 12/17/2001 which reincorporated in Georgia as Silver Screen Studios, Inc. 09/05/2003 which name changed to Global 1 Investment Holdings Corp. 11/13/2006
(See Global 1 Investment Holdings Corp.)

SCI TECHNICS INC (DE)
Charter cancelled and declared inoperative and void for non-payment of taxes 3/1/84

SCI TELEVISION INC (DE)
Plan of reorganization under Chapter 11 Federal Bankruptcy proceedings confirmed 05/06/1993
No stockholders' equity

SCI TEX LTD (ISRAEL)
Ordinary Stock I£3.60 par changed to I£1.80 par and (1) additional share issued 12/04/1980
Name changed to Scitex Corp. Ltd. 01/28/1981
Scitex Corp. Ltd. name changed to Scailex Corp., Ltd. 11/20/2006 which name changed to Suny Cellular Communication Ltd. 05/24/2017

SCIAX CORP (NV)
Recapitalized as RMD Entertainment Group 10/21/2005
Each (70) shares Common $0.001 par exchanged for (1) share Common $0.001 par

SCICLONE PHARMACEUTICALS INC (DE)
Reincorporated 07/22/2003
State of incorporation changed from (CA) to (DE) and Common no par changed to $0.001 par 07/22/2003
Acquired by Silver Biotech Investment Ltd. 10/13/2017
Each share Common $0.001 par exchanged for $11.18 cash

SCICOM DATA SVCS LTD (MN)
Merged into SDS Acquisitions Inc. 02/14/1989
Each share Common 10¢ par exchanged for $12 cash

SCIDEV LTD (AUSTRALIA)
ADR agreement terminated 07/21/2017
Each Sponsored ADR for Ordinary exchanged for $0.157261 cash

SCIELE PHARMA INC (DE)
Merged into Shionogi & Co., Ltd. 10/09/2008
Each share Common $0.001 par exchanged for $31 cash

SCIENCE & GOVT PUBNS INC (DE)
Acquired by ABC Industries Inc. 04/07/1972
Each share Common 10¢ par exchanged for (0.9) share Capital Stock 10¢ par
(See ABC Industries, Inc.)

SCIENCE & NUCLEAR FUND, INC. (DE)
Merged into Nucleonics, Chemistry & Electronics Shares, Inc. on an approixmate (0.8577) for (1) basis 4/16/58
Nucleonics, Chemistry & Electronics Shares, Inc. merged into Research Investing Corp. 12/31/64 which name changed to Lexington Research Investing Corp. 4/18/67 which name changed to Lexington Research Fund, Inc. 4/28/69

SCIENCE ACCESSORIES CORP (DE)
Each share Common $0.001 par exchanged for (0.25) share Common $0.004 par 11/29/93
Merged into GTCO Corp. 12/29/95
Each share Common $0.004 par exchanged for $0.09 cash

SCIENCE APPLICATIONS INTL CORP OLD (DE)
Reincorporated 10/01/1981
Name and state of incorporation changed from Science Applications, Inc. (CA) to Science Applications International Corp. (DE) 10/01/1981
Common 5¢ par split (2) for (1) by issuance of (1) additional share 10/01/1981
Merged into SAIC, Inc. 10/12/2006
Each share Class A Common 1¢ par exchanged for (2) shares Class A Preferred $0.0001 par
Each share Class B Common 5¢ par exchanged for (40) shares Class A Preferred $0.0001 par
SAIC, Inc. recapitalized as Leidos Holdings, Inc. 09/30/2013

SCIENCE CAPITAL CORP. (PA)
Name changed to Star Capital Corp. 10/01/1964
Star Capital Corp. acquired by Abacus Fund, Inc. 12/09/1969 which merged into Paine, Webber, Jackson & Curtis Inc. 04/03/1972 which reorganized as Paine Webber Inc. 02/01/1974 which name changed to Paine Webber Group Inc. 05/21/1984 which merged into UBS AG 11/03/2000
(See UBS AG)

SCIENCE DYNAMICS CORP (DE)
Recapitalized as Lattice Inc. 2/5/2007
Each share Common 1¢ par exchanged for (0.1) share Common 1¢ par

SCIENCE INDUSTRY REAL ESTATE INVESTMENT TRUST (MN)
Completely liquidated 5/8/63
Each Ctf. of Bene. Int. $100 par received (9.32) Liberty Real Estate Trust Ctfs. of Bene. Int. $1 par
Certificates were not surrendered and are now valueless

SCIENCE MGMT CORP (DE)
Common 10¢ par split (3) for (2) by issuance of (0.5) additional share 6/17/70
Plan of reorganization under Chapter 11 Federal Bankruptcy Code effective 7/15/96
For holdings of (21) shares or more each share old Common 10¢ par exchanged for (1) share new Common 10¢ par
Note: Holdings of (20) shares or fewer did not participate and are without value
Merged into Versar Inc. 10/23/97
Each share Common 10¢ par exchanged for (0.573584) share Common $0.01 par

SCIENCE RESEARCH ASSOCIATES, INC. (DE)
Acquired by International Business Machines Corp. on a (1) for (13.814) basis 2/28/64

SCIENCE RESOURCES, INC. (DE)
Class B Common 1¢ par reclassified as Common 1¢ par 3/29/63
Name changed to Cryo-Therm, Inc. 4/5/63
(See Cryo-Therm, Inc.)

SCIENCE SYS & TECHNOLOGY LTD (DE)
Charter cancelled and declared inoperative and void for non-payment of taxes 3/1/74

SCIENSCOPE INC (PA)
Reorganized under Chapter X bankruptcy proceedings 01/08/1974
Each share Common $1 par received first and final distribution of (0.5456) share Remsco Associates Common no par
Note: Certificates were not required to be surrendered and are without value

SCIENT CORP (DE)
Issue Information - 3,000,000 shares COM offered at $20 per share on 05/13/1999
Common $0.0001 par split (2) for (1) by issuance of (1) additional share payable 12/3/99 to holders of record 11/15/99
Merged into Scient, Inc. 11/8/2001
Each share Common $0.0001 par exchanged for (1.24) shares Common $0.0001 par
(See Scient, Inc.)

SCIENT INC (DE)
Each share old Common $0.0001 par exchanged for (0.05) share new Common $0.0001 par 6/13/2002
Chapter 11 bankruptcy petition dismissed 3/30/2007
No stockholders' equity

SCIENTEX CORP (NV)
Reincorporated 07/27/1979
State of incorporation changed from (CO) to (NV) 07/27/1979
Charter revoked for failure to file reports and pay fees 05/01/1989

SCIENTIFACTS CORP (NJ)
Charter declared void for non-payment of taxes 03/12/1973

SCIENTIFIC AMERICAN, INC. (DE)
Acquired by Verlagsgruppe Georg von Holtzbrinck GmbH 8/13/86
Each share Common $1 par exchanged for $258 cash

SCIENTIFIC ATLANTA INC (GA)
Common 50¢ par split (3) for (2) by issuance of (0.5) additional share 6/22/79
Common 50¢ par split (2) for (1) by issuance of (1) additional share 5/13/80
Common 50¢ par split (2) for (1) by issuance of (1) additional share 2/18/81
Common 50¢ par split (3) for (2) by issuance of (0.5) additional share 12/22/92
Common 50¢ par split (2) for (1) by issuance of (1) additional share 10/5/94
Common 50¢ par split (2) for (1) by issuance of (1) additional share payable 3/27/2000 to holders of record 3/10/2000
Stock Dividends - 10% 8/15/60; 33-1/3% 11/26/65; 33-1/3% 9/26/66; 20% 9/26/67; 33-1/3% 12/4/75
Merged into Cisco Systems, Inc. 2/24/2006
Each share Common 50¢ par exchanged for $43 cash

SCIENTIFIC BIOMEDICAL APPLICATIONS INC (NJ)
Charter declared void for non-payment of taxes 7/30/93

SCIENTIFIC CHEM TREATMENT INC (DE)
Name changed to Scientific, Inc. 03/09/1972
Scientific, Inc. name changed to Transtech Industries Inc. 06/18/1986

SCIENTIFIC COMMUNICATIONS INC (TX)
Merged into Andrew Corp. (DE) 04/17/1987
Each share Common 10¢ par exchanged for $13 cash

SCIENTIFIC COMPONENTS INC (DE)
Merged into Codi Corp. 3/31/76

Each share Common 10¢ par exchanged for $0.15 cash
Note: An additional $0.15 per share was distributed to holders who exchanged their certificates 12/15/76
(See Codi Corp.)

SCIENTIFIC COMPUTERS INC (MN)
Common 10¢ par changed to 5¢ par and (1) additional share issued 01/12/1981
Name changed to Scicom Data Services, Ltd. 11/13/1986
(See Scicom Data Services, Ltd.)

SCIENTIFIC CTL CORP (TX)
Charter forfeited for failure to pay taxes 2/26/73

SCIENTIFIC DATA SYS INC (DE)
Common 10¢ par split (3) for (2) by issuance of (0.5) additional share 6/22/67
Common 10¢ par split (3) for (2) by issuance of (0.5) additional share 6/17/68
Acquired by Xerox Corp. 5/16/69
Each share Common 10¢ par exchanged for (0.5) share Common $1 par

SCIENTIFIC DESIGN CO., INC. (DE)
Name changed to Halcon International, Inc. 04/29/1963
(See Halcon International, Inc.)

SCIENTIFIC ENERGY INC (NV)
Each share old Common $0.001 par exchanged for (0.01) share new Common $0.001 par 11/18/2003
Note: Holders of (99) or fewer shares were not affected by reverse split
Name changed to Electronic Game Card, Inc. 12/05/2003
(See Electronic Game Card, Inc.)

SCIENTIFIC ENERGY SYS CORP (MA)
Name changed to PMC/Beta Corp. 06/01/1979
(See PMC/Beta Corp.)

SCIENTIFIC ENGR INSTRS INC (UT)
Reincorporated under the laws of Delaware 10/13/87

SCIENTIFIC ENVIRONMENTAL CORP (UT)
Proclaimed dissolved for failure to pay taxes 09/30/1976

SCIENTIFIC ENVIRONMENTALS INC (DE)
Charter forfeited for failure to maintain a registered agent 2/25/91

SCIENTIFIC EXPL INC (WY)
Each share Common 1¢ par exchanged for (0.2) share Common 5¢ par 06/02/1980
Charter revoked for failure to file annual reports 03/04/1987

SCIENTIFIC GAMES CORP (DE)
Reincorporated under the laws of Nevada and Class A Common 1¢ par reclassified as Common $0.001 par 01/10/2018

SCIENTIFIC GAMES HLDGS CORP (DE)
Merged into Autotote Corp. 09/06/2000
Each share Common $0.001 par exchanged for $26 cash

SCIENTIFIC IMAGING CORP (NV)
Name changed to Liberty Communications Inc. 06/18/1990
Liberty Communications Inc. recapitalized as Big Boy Pacific Inc. 08/14/1992

SCIENTIFIC INC (DE)
Common 50¢ par split (3) for (2) by issuance of (0.5) additional share 2/14/83
Common 50¢ par split (2) for (1) by issuance of (1) additional share 10/15/84
Stock Dividend - 100% 9/30/81

Name changed to Transtech Industries, Inc. 6/18/86

SCIENTIFIC INCINERATION DEVICES INC (NJ)
Out of business 00/00/1974
No stockholders' equity

SCIENTIFIC INDUSTRIAL RESEARCH, INC. (MD)
Charter cancelled for failure to pay taxes 1/28/75

SCIENTIFIC INSTRUMENT CO. (MI)
Common $1 par exchanged (1) for (2) in 1940
Charter voided for failure to file reports and pay fees 5/15/63

SCIENTIFIC LABS INC (KS)
Each share old Common no par exchanged for (0.1) share new Common no par 6/30/83
Name changed to Cancer Diagnostic, Inc. 11/7/84
(See Cancer Diagnostic, Inc.)

SCIENTIFIC LEASING INC (DE)
Reincorporated 12/16/1982
State of incorporation changed from (CT) to (DE) and Common no par changed to 10¢ par 12/16/1982
Merged into LINC Acquisition Corp. 06/08/1988
Each share Common 10¢ par exchanged for $15.375 cash

SCIENTIFIC MEASUREMENT SYS INC (TX)
Chapter 7 bankruptcy proceedings terminated 09/12/2003
No stockholders' equity

SCIENTIFIC METALS CORP (BC)
Each share old Common no par exchanged for (0.25) share new Common no par 01/24/2017
Name changed to US Cobalt Inc. 05/25/2017
US Cobalt Inc. merged into First Cobalt Corp. (BC) 06/05/2018 which reincorporated in Canada 09/04/2018

SCIENTIFIC MICRO SYS INC (CA)
Plan of reorganization under Chapter 11 Federal Bankruptcy proceedings confirmed 01/18/1990
No stockholders' equity

SCIENTIFIC NRG INC (MN)
Each share old Common no par exchanged for (0.2) share new Common no par 10/24/1996
Reorganized under the laws of Nevada as Newbridge Capital, Inc. 01/05/2000
Each share new Common no par exchanged for (0.1) share Common $0.001 par
Newbridge Capital, Inc. name changed to SeaHAVN Corp. 06/10/2005 which recapitalized as China Travel Resort Holdings, Inc. 10/01/2009

SCIENTIFIC POLLUTION CTL CORP (NY)
Name changed to Hughes Texas Petroleum Corp. 11/6/81
(See Hughes Texas Petroleum Corp.)

SCIENTIFIC PRODTN CORP IRKUT JSC (RUSSIA)
Name changed to Irkut Corp. 12/01/2005
(See Irkut Corp.)

SCIENTIFIC RADIO SYS INC (NY)
Stock Dividend - 100% 7/31/81
Dissolved by proclamation 9/24/97

SCIENTIFIC RES CORP (PA)
Completely liquidated 5/9/75
Each share $1.65 Conv. Preferred 10¢ par received (0.5) Common Stock Purchase Warrant expiring 4/30/76 of Rocky Mountain Industries, Inc.
Each share Common 10¢ par received (0.1) Common Stock Purchase Warrant expiring 4/30/76 of Rocky Mountain Industries, Inc.
Certificates were not required to be surrendered and are now valueless

SCIENTIFIC SOFTWARE INTERCOMP INC (CO)
Name changed 05/30/1984
Common no par split (3) for (2) by issuance of (0.5) additional share 11/19/1981
Name changed from Scientific Software Corp. to Scientific Software-Intercomp, Inc. 05/30/1984
Merged into Baker Hughes Inc. 07/30/1998
Each share Common no par exchanged for $0.44 cash

SCIENTIFIC SYS INC (MA)
Non-Vtg. Class A Common 1¢ par split (3) for (2) by issuance of (0.5) additional share 03/02/1987
Proclaimed dissolved for failure to file reports and pay fees 12/31/1990

SCIENTIFIC SYS INC (PA)
Each share old Class A Common $1 par exchanged for (0.0001) share new Class A Common $1 par 03/26/2007
Each share old Class B Common $1 par exchanged for (0.0001) share new Class B Common $1 par 03/26/2007
Note: In effect holders received $17 cash per share and public interest was eliminated

SCIENTIFIC SYS SVCS INC (FL)
Acquired by Computer Task Group, Inc. 02/25/1988
Each share Common 1¢ par exchanged for $2.70 cash

SCIENTIFIC TECHNOLOGIES INC (DE)
Name changed to Northstar Electronics, Inc. in September 1999

SCIENTIFIC TECHNOLOGIES INC (OR)
Each share Common no par exchanged for (0.2) share Common $0.001 par 06/24/1998
Common $0.001 par split (2) for (1) by issuance of (1) additional share 07/27/1995
Merged into OMRON Corp. 09/12/2006
Each share Common $0.001 par exchanged for $10.67 cash

SCIENTIFIC TEXTILE SYS INC (NY)
Stock Dividend - 10% 01/05/1973
Charter cancelled and proclaimed dissolved for failure to pay taxes 09/30/1981

SCIENTIFIC TIME SHARING CORP (DE)
Name changed to STSC Inc. 10/29/1979
(See STSC Inc.)

SCIENTIGO INC (DE)
Recapitalized as Incumaker, Inc. 06/01/2011
Each (15) shares Common $0.001 par exchanged for (1) share Common $0.001 par

SCIENTIO INC (DE)
Name changed to MediCor Ltd. 02/24/2011
(See MediCor Ltd.)

SCIENTISTS POOL INC (DE)
Charter cancelled and declared inoperative and void for non-payment of taxes 04/15/1972

SCIGENICS INC (DE)
Acquired by Genetics Institute, Inc. 12/7/95
Each share Common 1¢ par exchanged for $14 cash

SCILABS HLDGS INC (DE)
Each share old Common $0.0001 par exchanged for (0.03333333) share new Common $0.0001 par 11/19/2001
SEC revoked common stock registration 05/25/2011

SCILIFE INC (UT)
Involuntarily dissolved 12/01/1989

SCILLITOE (EDGAR L.), INC. (NY)
Recapitalized as Elsin Electronics Corp. on a (1) for (2) basis 4/5/55
Elsin Electronics Corp. merged into Specialty Electronics Development Corp. 5/25/59 which name changed to Spedcor Electronics, Inc. 11/21/67 which merged into Entron, Inc. 12/31/69
(See Entron, Inc.)

SCIMINEX LTD (ON)
Charter cancelled for failure to pay taxes and file returns 03/16/1976

SCIMITAR HYDROCARBONS CORP (AB)
Acquired by Rally Energy Corp. 07/10/2002
Each share Common no par exchanged for (0.45454545) share Common no par
(See Rally Energy Corp.)

SCIMITAR RES LTD (AB)
Struck off register for failure to file annual returns 11/01/1986

SCINTILORE MINES LTD. (ON)
Name changed to Scintilore Explorations Ltd. and Common $1 par changed to no par 10/20/1975

SCINTREX LTD (ON)
Common no par split (2) for (1) by issuance of (1) additional share 8/17/70
Merged into IDS Intelligent Detection Systems Inc. 7/29/98
Each share Common no par exchanged for either (2.146) shares Common no par or (0.884) share Common no par and $8.82 cash
Note: Option to receive stock and cash expired 9/9/98

SCIONICS CORP (CA)
Merged into Acoustron Corp. 06/00/1979
Each share Capital Stock $1 par exchanged for approximately $0.08 cash

SCIOS INC (DE)
Name changed 9/4/92
Under plan of merger name changed from Scios Inc. to Scios-Nova Inc. 9/4/92 which name changed back to Scios Inc. 3/26/96
Merged into Johnson & Johnson 4/29/2003
Each share Common $0.001 par exchanged for $45 cash

SCIOTO DOWNS INC (OH)
Each Unit consisting of (1) share Class A Common $1 par and (1) share Class B Common 5¢ par exchanged for (1) share Common $1.05 par 03/07/1963
Merged into MTR Gaming Group, Inc. 07/31/2003
Each share Common $1.05 par exchanged for $32 cash
Note: Option to receive up to (10) possible contingency payments plus $17 cash expired 09/02/2003

SCIOTO INVT CO (OH)
Each share old Class A Common 33-1/3¢ par exchanged for (1/25) share new Class A Common 33-1/3¢ par 8/3/81
Each share new Class A Common 33-1/3¢ par exchanged for (50) shares Class A Common 2/3¢ par 12/14/89
Each (2,400) shares Class A Common 2/3¢ par exchanged again for (1) share new Class A Common 2/3¢ par 9/30/2003
Note: In effect holders received

$17.82 cash per share and public interest was eliminated

SCIPSCO INC (DE)
Name changed to Storer Communications 12/30/1986

SCIQUEST INC NEW (DE)
Acquired by AKKR Green Parent, LLC 07/28/2016
Each share Common $0.001 par exchanged for $17.75 cash

SCIQUEST INC OLD (DE)
Name changed 06/27/2001
Name changed from SciQuest.com, Inc. to SciQuest, Inc. (Old) 06/27/2001
Each share old Common $0.001 par exchanged for (0.13333333) share new Common $0.001 par 05/20/2003
Merged into Trinity Tarheel Acquisition LLC 07/28/2004
Each share new Common $0.001 par exchanged for $6.3346 cash

SCITEX LTD (ISRAEL)
Ordinary Stock IS 3.60 par changed to IS 1.80 par and (1) additional share issued 11/21/1980
Ordinary Stock IS 1.80 par changed to IS 1.20 par and (0.5) additional share issued 04/11/1983
Ordinary Stock IS 1.20 par changed to NIS 0.0012 par per currency change 01/01/1986
Ordinary Stock ILS 0.0012 par split (2) for (1) by issuance of (1) additional share 08/29/1990
Ordinary Stock ILS 0.0012 par changed to ILS 0.12 par 09/05/1991
Name changed to Scailex Corp., Ltd. 01/20/2006
Scailex Corp., Ltd. name changed to Suny Cellular Communication Ltd. 05/24/2017

SCITI ROCS TR (ON)
Each Unit no par received distribution of (1) Warrant expiring 08/04/2011 payable 08/04/2010 to holders of record 08/03/2010 Ex date - 07/29/2010
Trust terminated 05/15/2015
Each Unit received $5.471 cash

SCITI TOTAL RETURN TR (ON)
Trust terminated 05/16/2011
Each Trust Unit received $14.0966 cash

SCITI TR (ON)
Trust terminated 04/30/2018
Each Trust Unit received $7.6977 cash

SCITI TR II (ON)
Merged into SCITI Trust 11/03/2009
Each Trust Unit received (0.9662) Trust Unit
(See SCITI Trust)

SCIVAC THERAPEUTICS INC (BC)
Each share old Common no par exchanged for (0.025) share new Common no par 05/02/2016
Under plan of merger name changed to VBI Vaccines Inc. 05/09/2016

SCM CORP (NY)
5-1/2% Conv. Preferred $50 par called for redemption 7/8/65
Merged into Hanson Trust PLC 3/31/86
Each share Common $5 par exchanged for $75 cash

SCM MICROSYSTEMS INC (DE)
Name changed to Identive Group, Inc. 06/16/2010
Identive Group, Inc. recapitalized as Identive, Inc. 05/27/2014

SCMP GROUP LTD (BERMUDA)
Name changed to Armada Holdings Ltd. 07/06/2016
Armada Holdings Ltd. name changed to Great Wall Pan Asia Holdings Ltd. 01/20/2017

(See Great Wall Pan Asia Holdings Ltd.)

SCN LTD (NV)
Recapitalized as Health Care Centers America Inc. 1/4/94
Each share Common 2¢ par exchanged for (1/3) share Common 2¢ par
Health Care Centers America Inc. name changed to Hexagon Consolidated Companies of America Inc. 8/31/99 which name changed to NMC Inc. 9/9/2003

SCNV ACQUISITION CORP (DE)
Charter cancelled and declared inoperative and void for non-payment of taxes 03/01/2002

SCO GROUP INC (DE)
Chapter 11 bankruptcy proceedings converted to Chapter 7 on 08/24/2012
Stockholders' equity unlikely

SCOA INDS INC NEW (DE)
Name changed 12/10/85
Common $3 par changed to $1 par and (1) additional share issued 6/16/69
Common $1 par split (5) for (4) by issuance of (0.25) additional share 4/21/78
Common $1 par split (3) for (2) by issuance of (0.5) additional share 1/19/79
Common $1 par split (5) for (4) by issuance of (0.25) additional share 5/9/80
Common $1 par split (5) for (4) by issuance of (0.25) additional share 1/16/81
Common $1 par split (3) for (2) by issuance of (0.5) additional share 1/15/82
Common $1 par split (5) for (4) by issuance of (0.25) additional share 5/12/83
Under plan of merger name changed from SCOA Industries Inc. (Old) to SCOA Industries Inc. (New) and each share Common $1 par exchanged for (0.2) share Adjustable Rate Exchangeable Preferred Ser. B no par and $30 cash 12/10/85
Name changed to Hills Stores Co. (Old) 4/9/87
(See Hills Stores Co. (Old))

SCOGGINS PETE CORP (NV)
Name changed to Fargo Energy Corp. 01/19/1977
Fargo Energy Corp. name changed to Western Reserves, Inc. 04/29/1983 which recapitalized as Great Western Equities Group, Inc. 06/10/1986 which name changed to American International Marketing, Inc. 09/21/1989

SCOLLARD CAP CORP (AB)
Name changed to Label Depot Corp. 10/21/1998
Label Depot Corp. name changed to LDC Ventures Inc. 09/20/2001 which recapitalized as Mint Technology Corp. 01/22/2004 which recapitalized as Mint Corp. 08/12/2013

SCOLR INC (DE)
Name changed to SCOLR Pharma, Inc. 7/31/2004

SCOOP INC (DE)
Issue Information - 1,450,000 shares COM offered at $4.50 per share on 04/09/1997
Name changed to 24Holdings Inc. 4/2/2001

SCOOP MEDIA INC (NV)
Reincorporated under the laws of Maryland as Global Medical REIT Inc. 01/15/2014

SCOOPER DOOPER INC (DE)
Charter cancelled and declared inoperative and void for non-payment of taxes 4/15/72

SCOOT COM PLC (ENGLAND & WALES)
ADR agreement terminated 11/22/2001
Each Sponsored ADR for Ordinary 2p par exchanged for $0.0677 cash

SCOPAS TECHNOLOGY INC (DE)
Recapitalized as Patriot Mechanical Handling, Inc. 04/20/2005
Each share Common no par exchanged for (0.002) share Common no par
Patriot Mechanical Handling, Inc. name changed to Kensington Industries, Inc. 08/01/2007

SCOPE INC (NH)
Common $1 par split (3) for (1) by issuance of (2) additional shares 08/07/1967
Stock Dividend - 20% 01/06/1986
Merged into Lexicon Corp. 07/31/1987
Each share Common $1 par exchanged for (2) shares Common 10¢ par
Lexicon Corp. name changed to Florida Gaming Corp. 03/21/1994
(See Florida Gaming Corp.)

SCOPE INDS INC (ID)
Name changed to American Motorcycle Corp. 12/23/2002
(See American Motorcycle Corp.)

SCOPE RES LTD (MB)
Recapitalized as New Scope Resources Ltd. 3/1/78
Each share Common no par exchanged for (0.2) share Common no par
New Scope Resources Ltd. reincorporated in Canada as Newscope Resources Ltd. 9/13/84 which recapitalized as Canadian Newscope Resources Ltd. 12/13/90 which name changed back to Newscope Resources Ltd. 7/11/94

SCOPUS TECHNOLOGY INC (CA)
Common no par split (3) for (2) by issuance of (0.5) additional share payable 2/19/97 to holders of record 2/7/97
Merged into Siebel Systems, Inc. 5/18/98
Each share Common $0.001 par exchanged for (0.7281) share Common $0.001 par
(See Siebel Systems, Inc.)

SCOPUS VIDEO NETWORKS LTD (ISRAEL)
Issue Information - 4,500,000 shares ORD offered at $7 per share on 12/13/2005
Acquired by Harmonic Inc. 03/12/2009
Each share Ordinary ILS 1.40 par exchanged for $5.62 cash

SCOR HLDG SWITZ LTD (SWITZERLAND)
Acquired by SCOR S.E. 05/15/2008
Each Sponsored ADR for Ordinary exchanged for $8.93653 cash

SCOR U S CORP (DE)
Merged into Scor S.A. 12/21/95
Each share Common 30¢ par exchanged for $15.25 cash

SCORCORP INDS INC (BC)
Name changed to Ixtal International Technology Corp. 10/11/90
Ixtal International Technology Corp. recapitalized as Job Industries Ltd. 8/28/92

SCORE ATHLETIC PRODS INC (BC)
Delisted from Vancouver Stock Exchange 3/3/97

SCORE BRD INC (NJ)
Each share Common $0.0001 par exchanged for (0.01) share Common 1¢ par 02/21/1989

Common 1¢ par split (3) for (2) by issuance of (0.5) additional share 11/25/1991
New Common 1¢ par split (2) for (1) by issuance of (1) additional share 11/18/1993
Chapter 11 Federal Bankruptcy proceedings converted to Chapter 7 on 07/14/2003
Stockholders' equity unlikely

SCORE EXPL CORP (WY)
Recapitalized as Mystique Developments Inc. 11/11/1992
Each share Common 1¢ par exchanged for (0.01) share Common 1¢ par
Mystique Developments Inc. name changed to Colorado Wyoming Reserve Co. 10/17/1997
(See Colorado Wyoming Reserve Co.)

SCORE MED CORP (NV)
Name changed to Imatters.Com, Inc. 02/10/1999
Imatters.Com, Inc. name changed to Iweb Corp. 06/01/1999 which reorganized as National Health Scan Inc. 05/09/2002 which name changed to Gaensel Energy Group, Inc. 02/24/2015

SCORE MEDIA INC (CANADA)
Plan of arrangement effective 10/19/2012
Each share Class A Subordinate no par exchanged for (1) share theScore, Inc. Class A Subordinate no par and $1.62 cash
Note: Unexchanged certificates were cancelled and became without value 10/19/2014

SCORE ONE INC (NV)
Each share old Common $0.001 par exchanged for (1.65) shares new Common $0.001 par 03/10/1999
Each share new Common $0.001 par exchanged again for (0.0125) share new Common $0.001 par 01/11/2002
New Common $0.001 par split (18) for (1) by issuance of (17) additional shares payable 08/19/2002 to holders of record 08/17/2002 Ex date - 08/20/2002
SEC revoked common stock registration 03/08/2011

SCORE RES LTD (BC)
Struck off register and declared dissolved for failure to file returns 02/14/1992

SCORPIO CAP CORP (ON)
Name changed to Prime City One Capital Corp. 08/28/2007

SCORPIO MNG CORP (CANADA)
Name changed to Americas Silver Corp. 05/27/2015

SCORPION ENERGY CORP (AB)
Name changed to Gauntlet Energy Corp. 10/12/1999
(See Gauntlet Energy Corp.)

SCORPION MINERALS INC (ON)
Name changed to Nextair Inc. 03/05/2001
Nextair Inc. recapitalized as NXA Inc. 02/23/2005 which recapitalized as Ellipsiz Communications Ltd. 11/26/2015

SCORPION RES INC (BC)
Ctfs. dated after 09/06/2012
Each share old Common no par exchanged for (0.2) share new Common no par 05/23/2017
Name changed to Blockstrain Technologies Corp. 05/23/2018

SCORPION RES INC (BC)
Ctfs. dated prior to 07/14/1989
Name changed to Reese River Resource Corp. 07/14/1989
Reese River Resource Corp. recapitalized as Hurley River Gold

Corp. (BC) 03/18/1994 which reincorporated in Yukon 12/17/1997 which recapitalized as Ouro Brasil Ltd. 03/20/1998 which recapitalized as Consolidated Ouro Brasil Ltd. 02/18/2000 which name changed to Superior Diamonds Inc. (YT) 09/03/2002 which reincorporated in British Columbia 06/30/2004 which name changed to Northern Superior Resources Inc. 04/15/2008

SCORPION SYS INC (NY)
Dissolved by proclamation 12/24/1991

SCORPION TECHNOLOGIES INC (CO)
Each share old Class A Common $0.001 par exchanged for (1/3) share new Class A Common $0.001 par 11/25/1991
Each share new Class A Common $0.001 par exchanged again for (0.05) share new Class A Common $0.001 par 03/31/1994
SEC revoked common stock registration 07/07/2011

SCOSS CAP CORP (CANADA)
Reorganized under the laws of Ontario as InStorage Real Estate Investment Trust 08/11/2006
Each share Common no par exchanged for (1) Trust Unit no par
(See InStorage Real Estate Investment Trust)

SCOT LAD FOODS INC (DE)
Common $1 par split (5) for (4) by issuance of (0.25) additional share 11/20/1967
Common $1 par split (3) for (2) by issuance of (0.5) additional share 02/03/1969
Common $1 par split (2) for (1) by issuance of (1) additional share 07/17/1975
Stock Dividend - 10% 01/24/1984
Name changed to F/H Industries Corp. 11/15/1984
F/H Industries Corp. name changed to Diana Corp. 07/17/1985 which name changed to Coyote Network Systems, Inc. 11/20/1997 which name changed to Quentra Networks, Inc. 07/31/2000
(See Quentra Networks, Inc.)

SCOT'S DISCOUNT ENTERPRISES, INC. (DE)
Adjudicated bankrupt 2/25/63

SCOT'S INN LAND CO. (OH)
Assets sold at foreclosure in December, 1977
No stockholders' equity

SCOT'S INN MANAGEMENT CO. (OH)
Charter cancelled for non-payment of taxes 11/12/76

SCOTCH DELUXE INDS INC (MO)
Adjudicated bankrupt 03/19/1975
Stockholders' equity unlikely

SCOTCO DATA COM INC (DE)
Name changed to Telecomm Industries Corp. 12/01/1993
(See Telecomm Industries Corp.)

SCOTCO DATA LEASING INC (DE)
Name changed to Scotco Data Com, Inc. 02/25/1970
Scotco Data Com, Inc. name changed to Telecomm Industries Corp. 12/01/1993
(See Telecomm Industries Corp.)

SCOTIA PRIME MINERALS INC (NS)
Merged into Minera Andes Inc. 11/06/1995
Each share Common no par exchanged for (0.16666666) share Common no par
Minera Andes Inc. merged into McEwen Mining - Minera Andes Acquisition Corp. 01/27/2012 which exchanged for McEwen Mining Inc. 08/22/2016

SCOTIA RES LTD (BC)
Name changed to Senior Savers Guide Publishing Inc. 2/27/86
Senior Savers Guide Publishing Inc. recapitalized as Kali Venture Corp. 10/20/87
(See Kali Venture Corp.)

SCOTIA SPLIT CORP (ON)
Preferred Shares no par called for redemption at $18.85 on 5/1/2003
Capital Shares no par called for redemption at $90.5282 on 5/1/2003

SCOTLAND BANCORP INC (NC)
Merged into Centura Banks, Inc. 2/5/99
Each share Common no par exchanged for $11.75 cash

SCOTOIL PETE LTD (AB)
Reincorporated under the laws of British Columbia as 0915988 B.C. Ltd. 07/27/2011
(See 0915988 B.C. Ltd.)

SCOTSMAN INDS INC (DE)
$0.62 Conv. Preferred Ser. A $1 par called for redemption 10/25/96
Merged into Welbilt Corp. 8/18/99
Each share Common 10¢ par exchanged for $33 cash

SCOTT & FETZER CO (OH)
Each share Common no par exchanged for (3) shares Common $5 par 2/13/53
Common $5 par changed to no par and (1) additional share issued 7/15/64
Common no par split (2) for (1) by issuance of (1) additional share 12/8/67
Stock Dividend - 100% 7/1/59
Acquired by Berkshire Hathaway Inc. 1/6/86
Each share Common no par exchanged for $60.77 cash

SCOTT & STRINGFELLOW FINL INC (VA)
Common 10¢ par split (6) for (5) by issuance of (0.2) additional share 8/26/94
Common 10¢ par split (3) for (2) by issuance of (0.5) additional share payable 5/6/97 to holders of record 4/18/97
Merged into BB&T Corp. 3/26/99
Each share Common 10¢ par exchanged for (1) share Common $5 par

SCOTT & WILLIAMS, INC. (MA)
Common no par changed to $5 par in 1952
Stock Dividends - 300% 4/4/47; 25% 10/14/55; 20% 10/30/57; 25% 10/3/60
Merged into White Consolidated Industries, Inc. 8/31/66
Each share Common $5 par exchanged for (0.5) share Common $1 par
(See White Consolidated Industries, Inc.)

SCOTT AVIATION CORP. (NY)
Name changed to Scott Industries, Inc. 02/01/1966
Scott Industries, Inc. liquidated for Automatic Sprinkler Corp. of America (OH) 07/10/1967 which name changed into A-T-O Inc. 10/29/1969 which name changed to Figgie International Inc. (OH) 06/01/1981
(See Figgie International Inc. (OH))

SCOTT CABLE COMMUNICATIONS INC (TX)
Acquired by Simmons Communications Merger Corp. 1/20/88
Each share Common no par exchanged for $26.25 cash
Depositary Receipts called for redemption at $133.546914 on 2/12/99

Public interest eliminated

SCOTT CAP RES INC (CO)
Each share Common $0.001 par exchanged for (0.1) share Common 1¢ par 09/01/1988
Name changed to American Educational Products, Inc. 02/19/1990
(See American Educational Products, Inc.)

SCOTT CHIBOUGAMAU MINES LTD (QC)
Charter cancelled for failure to file reports and pay fees 11/13/1975

SCOTT CONTRACTING HLDGS INC (FL)
Name changed to Liverpool Group, Inc. 04/29/2008

SCOTT CORD LABS INC (DE)
Charter cancelled and declared inoperative and void for non-payment of taxes 3/1/75

SCOTT FORESMAN & CO (DE)
Reincorporated 09/30/1969
Common no par split (2) for (1) by issuance of (1) additional share 08/15/1966
State of incorporation changed from (IL) to (DE) and Common no par changed to $1 par 09/30/1969
Common $1 par split (2) for (1) by issuance of (1) additional share 09/22/1978
Under plan of reorganization each share $3.50 Conv. Preferred and Common $1 par automatically became (1) share SFN Companies, Inc. (Old) $3.50 Conv. Preferred $10 par or Common 50¢ par respectively 02/20/1980
(See SFN Companies, Inc. (Old))

SCOTT (EDWARD T.), INC. (NY)
Charter cancelled and proclaimed dissolved for failure to pay taxes 12/20/77

SCOTT INDUSTRIES, INC. (NY)
Completely liquidated 07/10/1967
Each share Common $1 par exchanged for first and final distribution of (0.150015) share Automatic Sprinkler Corp. of America (OH) Conv. Preference 1st Ser. $1 par
Automatic Sprinkler Corp. of America (OH) name changed to A-T-O Inc. 10/29/1969 which name changed to Figgie International Inc. (OH) 06/01/1981
(See Figgie International Inc. (OH))

SCOTT INSTRS CORP (DE)
Each (7) shares old Common 1¢ par exchanged for (1) share new Common 1¢ par 10/1/91
Recapitalized as Voice Control Systems, Inc. 8/10/94
Each share new Common 1¢ par exchanged for (0.25) share Common 1¢ par
(See Tara Voice Control Systems, Inc.)

SCOTT LA SALLE LTD (CANADA)
Common no par split (3) for (1) by issuance of (2) additional shares 3/25/68
Common no par split (3) for (1) by issuance of (2) additional shares 10/20/71
Declared bankrupt 3/14/80
No stockholders' equity

SCOTT-LEE LABORATORIES, INC. (LA)
Merged into Reid-Provident Laboratories Inc. 6/18/64
Each share Common $1 par exchanged for (1.96) shares Common $1 par
Reid-Provident Laboratories Inc. name changed to Reid-Rowell, Inc. 12/4/85
(See Reid-Rowell, Inc.)

SCOTT MATTSON FARMS INC (FL)
Acquired by Gulf & Western Industries, Inc. 11/27/1968
Each share Common $1 par exchanged for $13 cash

SCOTT MLS INC (PA)
Merged into Kleinert's, Inc. 10/10/96
Each share Common $1 par exchanged for (0.0152) share Common $2.50 and $0.03 cash
(See Kleinert's, Inc.)

SCOTT O M & SONS CO (OH)
Each share Class A Common $1 par exchanged for (6) shares Class A Common 10¢ par 12/19/58
Each share Class B Common $1 par exchanged for (6) shares Class B Common 10¢ par 12/19/58
Class A Common 10¢ par and Class B Common 10¢ par split (2) for (1) by issuance of (1) additional share respectively 1/20/70
Merged into International Telephone & Telegraph Corp. 4/8/71
Each share Class A Common 10¢ par or Class B Common 10¢ par exchanged for (0.5682) share Common $1 par
International Telephone & Telegraph Corp. name changed to ITT Corp. 12/31/83 which reorganized in Indiana as ITT Industries Inc. 12/19/95 which name changed to ITT Corp. 7/1/2006

SCOTT PAINE MARINE CORP (CT)
Almost 100% acquired by Marina America, Inc. through purchase offer which expired 07/02/1971
Public interest eliminated

SCOTT PAPER CO (PA)
Each share old Common no par exchanged for (10) shares new Common no par 00/00/1927
New Common no par split (2) for (1) by issuance of (1) additional share 00/00/1954
New Common no par split (3) for (1) by issuance of (2) additional shares 12/31/1961
Common no par split (2) for (1) by issuance of (1) additional share 03/15/1988
Common no par split (2) for (1) by issuance of (1) additional share 05/12/1995
$3.40 Sr. Preferred no par called for redemption 10/02/1995
$4 Sr. Preferred no par called for redemption 10/02/1995
Stock Dividend - 100% 07/29/1950
Merged into Kimberly-Clark Corp. 12/12/1995
Each share Common no par exchanged for (0.78) share Common $1.25 par

SCOTT PAPER LTD (BC)
Name changed 12/4/78
Name from Scott Paper Ltd. to Scott Paper Ltd./Les Papiers Scott Ltee. 12/4/78
Common no par split (3) for (1) by issuance of (2) additional shares 12/18/78
Common no par split (3) for (1) by issuance of (2) additional shares 7/5/84
Common no par split (2) for (1) by issuance of (1) additional share 7/9/86
Merged into Kruger Inc. 6/6/97
Each share Common no par exchanged for $23 cash

SCOTT RADIO LABORATORIES, INC. (IL)
Name changed 00/00/1945
Name changed from Scott (E.H.) Radio Laboratories, Inc. to Scott Radio Laboratories, Inc. 00/00/1945
Name changed to Electrovision Corp. 00/00/1959
Electrovision Corp. merged into

Monogram Precision Industries, Inc. 05/11/1962 which name changed to Monogram Industries, Inc. (CA) 12/03/1962 which reincorporated in Delaware 11/28/1969 which merged into Nortek, Inc. (RI) 08/26/1983 which reincorporated in Delaware 04/23/1987 which reorganized as Nortek Holdings, Inc. 11/20/2002
(See Nortek Holdings, Inc.)

SCOTT RED LAKE GOLD MINES LTD. (ON)
Charter revoked for failure to file reports and pay fees 5/13/65

SCOTT SCIENCE & TECHNOLOGY INC (DE)
Charter cancelled and declared inoperative and void for non-payment of taxes 3/1/87

SCOTT TECHNOLOGIES INC (DE)
Class A Common 10¢ par reclassified as Common 10¢ par 12/16/1998
Class B Common 10¢ par reclassified as Common 10¢ par 12/16/1998
Merged into Tyco International Ltd. (Bermuda) 05/03/2001
Each share Common 10¢ par exchanged for (0.4412) share Common 20¢ par
Tyco International Ltd. (Bermuda) reincorporated in Switzerland 03/17/2009 which merged into Johnson Controls International PLC 09/06/2016

SCOTTDALE BK & TR CO (SCOTTDALE, PA)
Merged into Mid Penn Bancorp, Inc. 01/08/2018
Each share Common $2.50 par exchanged for (38.88) shares Common $1 par

SCOTTDALE SVGS & TR CO (SCOTTDALE, PA)
Name changed to Scottdale Bank & Trust Co. (Scottdale, PA) 04/01/1978
Scottdale Bank & Trust Co. (Scottdale, PA) merged into Mid Penn Bancorp, Inc. 01/08/2018

SCOTTEN DILLON CO (DE)
Reincorporated 09/01/1969
State of incorporation changed from (MI) to (DE) and Common $10 par changed to $5 par 09/01/1969
Name changed to National Home Products, Inc. and Common $5 par changed to $1 par 04/02/1974
(See National Home Products, Inc.)

SCOTTEX CORP (NY)
Adjudicated bankrupt 10/21/1974
Stockholders' equity unlikely

SCOTTI COML CORP (DE)
Charter cancelled and declared inoperative and void for non-payment of taxes 3/1/77

SCOTTIE GOLD MINES LTD (BC)
Recapitalized as Royal Scot Resources Ltd. 06/02/1987
Each share Class A Common no par exchanged for (1/7) share Class A Common no par
Royal Scot Resources Ltd. merged into Tenajon Resources Corp. 08/01/1991 which merged into Creston Moly Corp. 08/26/2009 which merged into Mercator Minerals Ltd. 06/21/2011

SCOTTIES FISH & CHIPS INC (NV)
Name changed to European Day Spa & Tanning Salon Holding Co. Inc. 10/04/2000
European Day Spa & Tanning Salon Holding Co. Inc. name changed to European Diversified Holding Co. 07/18/2002 which recapitalized as NavStar Technologies, Inc. 07/30/2007 which recapitalized as Energy Revenue America, Inc. 08/01/2012

SCOTTISH & SOUTHN ENERGY PLC (UNITED KINGDOM)
Sponsored ADR's for Ordinary split (10) for (1) by issuance of (9) additional ADR's payable 03/30/2004 to holders of record 03/29/2004 Ex date - 03/31/2004
Name changed to SSE PLC 10/11/2011

SCOTTISH & UNVL INVTS LTD (UNITED KINGDOM)
Acquired by Lonrho PLC 00/00/1979
Details not available

SCOTTISH & YORK HLDGS LTD (ON)
5-1/2% Conv. 1st Preference Ser. A $50 par called for redemption 2/15/65
Common no par split (2) for (1) by issuance of (1) additional share 6/15/66
Common no par split (3) for (1) by issuance of (2) additional shares 11/20/67
Common no par split (2) for (1) by issuance of (1) additional share 11/12/71
Common no par split (2) for (1) by issuance of (1) additional share 11/15/72
Name changed to SYH Corp. 12/20/89
SYH Corp. recapitalized as Consolidated SYH Corp. 8/20/90
(See Consolidated SYH Corp.)

SCOTTISH ANNUITY & LIFE HLDGS LTD (CAYMAN ISLANDS)
Issue Information - 16,750,000 ORD shs. offered at $15 per share on 11/23/1998
Name changed to Scottish Re Group Ltd. 09/02/2003
(See Scottish Re Group Ltd.)

SCOTTISH BK (CHARLOTTE, NC)
Stock Dividends - 10% payable 01/15/2003 to holders of record 12/13/2002 Ex date - 12/11/2002; 10% payable 08/15/2004 to holders of record 08/01/2004 Ex date - 07/28/2004; 10% payable 04/10/2006 to holders of record 03/15/2006 Ex date - 03/13/2006
Reorganized as TSB Financial Corp. 09/14/2006
Each share Common 1¢ par exchanged for (1) share Common 1¢ par
TSB Financial Corp. merged into SCBT Financial Corp. 11/30/2007 which name changed to First Financial Holdings, Inc. 07/30/2013 which name changed to South State Corp. 06/30/2014

SCOTTISH HERITABLE INC (TX)
Name changed to United States Lime & Minerals Inc. 1/25/94

SCOTTISH HERITABLE TR PLC (UNITED KINGDOM)
Placed in receivership 00/00/1994
Details not available

SCOTTISH HYDRO-ELEC PLC (SCOTLAND)
Merged into Scottish & Southern Energy PLC 12/14/1998
Each Sponsored ADR for Ordinary exchanged for (1) Sponsored ADR for Ordinary
Scottish & Southern Energy PLC name changed to SSE PLC 10/11/2011

SCOTTISH INNS AMER INC (TN)
Capital Stock 33-1/3¢ par changed to 10¢ par and (2) additional shares issued 07/13/1972
Name changed to Vacation Spa Resorts Inc. 06/30/1981
Vacation Spa Resorts Inc. merged into Mego Financial Corp. 03/11/1993
(See Mego Financial Corp.)

SCOTTISH PWR PLC (SCOTLAND)
Sponsored Final Instalment ADR's for Ordinary split (5) for (2) by issuance of (1.5) additional ADR's payable 09/05/1997 to holders of record 09/04/1997
Each Sponsored Final Instalment ADR for Ordinary received distribution of $0.4544 cash 3/15/2002
Each old Sponsored Final Instalment ADR for Ordinary exchanged for (0.793651) new Sponsored Final Instalment ADR for Ordinary and $9.00048 cash 5/17/2006
Merged into Iberdrola S.A. 4/23/2007
Each new Sponsored Final Instalment ADR for Ordinary exchanged for (0.6584) Sponsored ADR for Ordinary and $31.856 cash

SCOTTISH RE GROUP LTD (CAYMAN ISLANDS)
Issue Information - 5,000,000 HYBRID CAPITAL UNITS offered at $25 per Unit on 12/11/2003
Each 5.875% Hybrid Capital Unit received (1.294) Ordinary Shares 1¢ par 02/15/2007
Merged into SRGL Acquisition, LDC 08/24/2011
Each share Ordinary 1¢ par exchanged for $0.30 cash
(Additional Information in Active)

SCOTTISH SAVINGS & LOAN ASSOCIATION, INC. OLD (NC)
Merged into Scottish Savings & Loan Association, Inc. (New) 04/01/1981
Each share Common $5 par exchanged for (1.0869) shares Common $1 par
Scottish Savings & Loan Association, Inc. (New) merged into Southeastern Savings & Loan Co. 01/17/1984 which name changed to Southeastern Savings Bank, Inc. 07/13/1988
(See Southeastern Savings Bank, Inc.)

SCOTTISH SVGS & LN ASSN INC NEW (NC)
Merged into Southeastern Savings & Loan Co. 1/17/84
Each share Common $1 par exchanged for (1.2) shares Common $6 par
Southeastern Savings & Loan Co. name changed to Southeastern Savings Bank, Inc. 7/13/88
(See Southeastern Savings Bank, Inc.)

SCOTTISH TYPE INVESTORS, INC.
Merged into Allied International Investing Corp. in 1947
Each share Class A exchanged for (0.6285) share Capital Stock $1 par
Each share Class B exchanged for (0.461) share Capital Stock $1 par
Allied International Investing Corp. name changed to Dorsey Corp. 3/26/59 which name changed to Constar International Inc. 5/1/87
(See Constar International Inc.)

SCOTTLAND INC (MN)
Statutorily dissolved 12/31/93

SCOTTS CO (OH)
Reincorporated 09/21/1994
State of incorporation changed from (DE) to (OH) and Class A Common 1¢ par reclassified as Common no par 09/21/1994
Name changed to Scotts Miracle-Gro Co. 03/18/2005

SCOTTS HOSPITALITY INC (ON)
Common no par reclassified as Subordinate no par 8/30/83
Subordinate no par split (3) for (1) by issuance of (2) additional shares 9/19/86
Conv. Class C Special no par split (3) for (1) by issuance of (2) additional shares 9/19/86
Merged into Laidlaw Inc. 8/9/96
Each share Common no par exchanged for approximately (0.3148317) share Non-Vtg. Class B Common no par and $6.25 cash
Each share Conv. Class C Special no par exchanged for approximately (0.3148317) share Non-Vtg. Class B Common no par and $6.25 cash
(See Laidlaw Inc.)

SCOTTS REAL ESTATE INVT TR (ON)
Name changed to KEYreit 07/09/2012
KEYreit acquired by Plazacorp Retail Properties Ltd. (NB) 06/28/2013 which reorganized in Ontario as Plaza Retail REIT 01/08/2014

SCOTTS RESTAURANTS INC (ON)
Merged into SR Acquisition Corp. 10/29/99
Each share Common no par exchanged for $9.25 cash

SCOTTS RESTAURANTS LTD (ON)
Old Common no par split (2) for (1) by issuance of (1) additional share 5/10/73
Each share old Common no par exchanged for (1) share Conv. Class A Common no par 5/30/77
Conv. Class A Common no par and Conv. Class B Common no par reclassified as new Common no par 2/13/80
Stock Distribution - (1) share Conv. Class C Special no par for each share new Common 2/19/80
Name changed to Scott's Hospitality Inc. 12/1/80
Scott's Hospitality Inc. merged into Laidlaw Inc. 8/9/96
(See Laidlaw Inc.)

SCOTTS SEABOARD CORP (MA)
Merged into General Host Corp. 08/02/1985
Each share Common 10¢ par exchanged for $3 cash

SCOTTSDALE CIGAR INC (NV)
Recapitalized as Niche' Resources, Inc. 06/15/1998
Each share Common 1¢ par exchanged for (0.02) share Common 1¢ par
(See Niche' Resources, Inc.)

SCOTTSDALE SCIENTIFIC INC (FL)
Name changed to Allergy Research Group, Inc. 03/08/2001
(See Allergy Research Group, Inc.)

SCOTTSDALE TECHNOLOGIES INC (DE)
SEC revoked common stock registration 8/21/2006
Stockholders' equity unlikely

SCOTTY'S HOME BUILDERS SUPPLY, INC. (FL)
Common $1 par split (2) for (1) by issuance of (1) additional share 1/31/72
Name changed to Scotty's, Inc. 10/29/73
(See Scotty's, Inc.)

SCOTTYS INC (FL)
Common $1 par split (5) for (4) by issuance of (0.5) additional share 11/1/78
Common $1 par split (5) for (4) by issuance of (0.25) additional share 7/30/82
Common $1 par split (3) for (2) by issuance of (0.5) additional share 2/1/83
Merged into GB-Inno-BM S.A. 11/2/89
Each share Common $1 par exchanged for $16.50 cash

SCOTTYS ORIG BREW INC (DE)
Each share old Common $0.001 par exchanged for (0.1) share new Common $0.001 par 12/12/97
Name changed to Themescapes, Inc. 12/16/98
Themescapes, Inc. name changed to

Cyclone Holdings, Inc. 5/17/2006 which recapitalized as digitiliti, Inc. 3/7/2007

SCOUT CAP CORP (AB)
Recapitalized as Birchcliff Energy Ltd. (Old) 1/20/2005
Each share Common no par exchanged for (0.084846) share Common no par
Birchcliff Energy Ltd. (Old) merged into Birchcliff Energy Ltd. (New) 5/31/2005

SCOVILL INC (CT)
Name changed 07/06/1979
Each share Common $10 par exchanged for (4) shares Common $25 par 00/00/1926
4.30% Preferred $100 par called for redemption 09/20/1955
Common $25 par changed to $12.50 par and (1) additional share issued 02/10/1966
Common $12.50 par changed to $6.25 par and (1) additional share issued 01/17/1992
3.65% Preferred $100 par called for redemption 02/15/1972
Name changed from Scovill Manufacturing Co. to Scovill Inc. 07/06/1979
$2.50 Conv. Preferred Ser. A no par called for redemption 03/15/1985
Merged into First City Industries Inc. 08/15/1985
Each share Common $6.25 par exchanged for $42.50 cash

SCOVILLE SOUTH BOULEVARD APARTMENTS, INC.
Liquidated in 1936

SCP POOL CORP (DE)
Common $0.001 par split (3) for (2) by issuance of (0.5) additional share payable 9/29/97 to holders of record 9/15/97
Common $0.001 par split (3) for (2) by issuance of (0.5) additional share payable 7/24/98 to holders of record 7/13/98
Common $0.001 par split (3) for (2) by issuance of (0.5) additional share payable 6/19/2000 to holders of record 5/19/2000
Common $0.001 par split (3) for (2) by issuance of (0.5) additional share payable 9/12/2003 to holders of record 8/22/2003 Ex date - 9/15/2003
Common $0.001 par split (3) for (2) by issuance of (0.5) additional share payable 9/10/2004 to holders of record 8/23/2004
Stock Dividend - 50% payable 9/7/2001 to holders of record 8/15/2001
Name changed to Pool Corp. 5/16/2006

SCPIE HLDGS INC (DE)
Issue Information - 2,000,000 shares COM offered at $18.25 per share on 01/29/1997
Merged into Doctors Co. 06/30/2008
Each share Common $0.0001 par exchanged for $28 cash

SCRANTON & WILKES-BARRE TRACTION CORP.
Dissolved in 1928

SCRANTON BOLT & NUT CO.
Acquired by Wrought Iron Co. of America in 1928
Details not available

SCRANTON CONSOLIDATED MINING CO.
Succeeded by Scranton Mines Ltd. share for share in 1952

SCRANTON ELECTRIC CO. (PA)
Merged into Pennsylvania Power & Light Co. 1/31/56
Each share 4.40% Preferred $100 par exchanged for (1) share new 4.40% Preferred $100 par

Each share 3.35% Preferred $100 par exchanged for (1) share new 3.35% Preferred $100 par
Each (2) shares Common $5 par exchanged for (1) share Common no par

SCRANTON GAS & WATER CO.
Acquired by Scranton-Spring Brook Water Service Co. 00/00/1928
Details not available

SCRANTON LACE CO. (PA)
Recapitalized as Scranton Corp. and Common $10 par changed to $1 par 5/13/58

SCRANTON LACKAWANNA TRUST CO. (SCRANTON, PA)
Merged into First National Bank & Trust Co. (Scranton, Pa.) 6/29/56
Each share Capital Stock $50 par exchanged for $155 cash

SCRANTON NATL BK (SCRANTON, PA)
Common $50 par changed to $10 par and (4) additional shares issued 02/10/1969
Common $10 par changed to $5 par and (1) additional share issued 02/28/1974
Stock Dividend - 20% 05/02/1981
Merged into First Eastern Corp. 09/15/1984
Each share Common $5 par exchanged for (2.25) shares Common $10 par
(See First Eastern Corp.)

SCRANTON SPRING BROOK WTR SVC CO (PA)
Recapitalized 00/00/1946
Each share $6 Preferred no par exchanged for (13.5) shares Common no par
Each share $5 Preferred no par exchanged for (11.995695) shares Common no par
Name changed to Pennsylvania Gas & Water Co. 10/01/1960
(See Pennsylvania Gas & Water Co.)

SCRATCH GRAVEL GOLD MINING CO. (MT)
Charter expired by time limitations 11/5/55

SCREAMINGMEDIA INC (DE)
Name changed to Pinnacor, Inc. 10/29/2002
Pinnacor, Inc. merged into MarketWatch.com, Inc. (New) 1/16/2004 which name changed to MarketWatch, Inc. 8/11/2004

SCREEN GEMS INC (DE)
Common $1 par split (5) for (4) by issuance of (0.25) additional share 10/8/64
Common $1 par split (5) for (4) by issuance of (0.25) additional share 1/14/66
Merged into Columbia Pictures Industries, Inc. (NY) 12/28/68
Each share Common $1 par exchanged for (1) share Common $2.50 par
Columbia Pictures Industries, Inc. (NY) reincorporated under the laws of Delaware 12/27/69 which merged into Coca-Cola Co. 6/21/82

SCREEN HLDGS CO LTD (JAPAN)
ADR agreement terminated 08/06/2018
No ADR's remain outstanding

SCREEN-PLAYZ COM INC (NV)
Name changed to CyberZONE, Inc. 06/04/2004

SCREEN TELEVISION & MEDIA PUBG INC (DE)
Each share Common $0.001 par exchanged for (0.005) share Common 1¢ par 04/26/1991
Charter cancelled and declared inoperative and void for non-payment of taxes 03/01/1994

SCREW & BOLT CORP AMER (PA)
Under plan of merger name changed to Ampco-Pittsburgh Corp. 12/31/1970

SCRIBE SYS INC (MA)
Involuntarily dissolved 8/31/98

SCRIP ADVANTAGE INC (NV)
Assets foreclosed on by secured creditors 05/26/2006
Stockholders' equity unlikely

SCRIPPS BK (LA JOLLA, CA)
Common no par split (3) for (2) by issuance of (0.5) additional share 02/23/1990
Common no par split (2) for (1) by issuance of (1) additional share payable 01/20/1998 to holders of record 12/26/1997
Stock Dividend - 10% payable 08/28/1997 to holders of record 08/07/1997
Under plan of reorganization each share Common no par automatically became (1) share Scripps Financial Corp. Common no par 07/01/1999
Scripps Financial Corp. merged into U.S. Bancorp 10/13/2000

SCRIPPS E W CO (DE)
Each share Class A Common 1¢ par received distribution of (1) share Scripps (E.W.) Co. (OH) Class A Common 1¢ par payable 11/29/1996 to holders of record 11/12/1996
Merged into Comcast Corp. (Old) 11/13/1996
Each share Class A Common 1¢ par exchanged for (1.15826354) shares Class A Common $1 par
Comcast Corp. (Old) merged into Comcast Corp. (New) 11/18/2002

SCRIPPS FINL CORP (CA)
Merged into U.S. Bancorp 10/13/2000
Each share Common no par exchanged for (1.067) shares Common $1.25 par

SCRIPPS HOWARD BROADCASTING CO (OH)
Common $1 par changed to 25¢ par and (3) additional shares issued 11/4/81
Merged into Scripps (E.W.) Co. 9/15/94
Each share Common 25¢ par exchanged for (3.45) shares Class A Common 1¢ par

SCRIPPS HOWARD INC (OH)
Name changed to Scripps (E.W.) Co. 11/13/1996

SCRIPPS HOWARD INVT CO (OH)
Name changed to Media Investment Co. 04/08/1976
(See Media Investment Co.)

SCRIPPS NETWORKS INTERACTIVE INC (OH)
Merged into Discovery Communications, Inc. 03/06/2018
Each share Class A Common 1¢ par exchanged for (1.0584) shares Ser. C Common 1¢ par and $65.82 cash
Each share Common 1¢ par exchanged for (1.0584) shares Ser. C Common 1¢ par and $65.82 cash
Discovery Communications, Inc. name changed to Discovery, Inc. 04/02/2018

SCRIPT SYS INC (NJ)
Each share Common $0.001 par exchanged for (0.5) share Common $0.002 par 11/14/90
Merged into InfoMed Holdings, Inc. 8/26/93
Each share Common $0.002 par exchanged for (0.3679) share Common $0.001 par
InfoMed Holdings, Inc. name changed to Simione Central Holdings, Inc. 12/19/96 which name changed to CareCentric Inc. 1/31/2001
(See CareCentric Inc.)

SCRIPTEL CORP (DE)
Recapitalized as Scriptel Holding, Inc. 06/16/1989
Each share Common 1¢ par exchanged for (0.1) share Common 10¢ par
(See Scriptel Holding, Inc.)

SCRIPTEL HLDG INC (DE)
Plan of reorganization under Chapter 11 Federal Bankruptcy Code effective 11/06/1998
No stockholders' equity

SCRIPTO INC (GA)
Each share Common $1 par exchanged for (2) shares Common 50¢ par 7/24/56
Common 50¢ par reclassified as Class A Common 50¢ par 6/30/62
Class A Common 50¢ par reclassified as Common 50¢ par 4/23/63
Merged into Allegheny International Inc. 6/17/83
Each (14.1053) shares Common 50¢ par exchanged for (1) share Common 66-2/3¢ par
Note: To holdings of (200) shares or fewer option to receive $2.437 cash per share in lieu of stock expired 9/12/83
(See Allegheny International Inc.)

SCRIPTOMATIC INC (DE)
Stock Dividend - 50% 1/18/80
Acquired by British General Electric Co. 9/19/80
Each share Common 1¢ par exchanged for $16.25 cash

SCRIVNER-BOOGAART, INC. (OK)
Common $10 par changed to $5 par and (1) additional share issued 12/15/71
Stock Dividend - 10% 3/4/71
Name changed to Scrivner, Inc. 11/1/74
(See Scrivner, Inc.)

SCRIVNER INC (OK)
Common $10 par changed to $5 par and (1) additional share issued 12/15/1971
5-1/4% Preferred $100 par called for redemption 00/00/1977
Stock Dividend - 10% 03/04/1971
Each (1,600) shares Common $5 par exchanged for (1) share Common $8,000 par 07/14/1978
Note: In effect holders received $18.50 cash per share and public interest was eliminated

SCRIVNER-STEVENS CO. (OK)
Name changed to Scrivner-Boogaart, Inc. 11/16/65
Scrivner-Boogaart, Inc. name changed to Scrivner, Inc. 11/1/74
(See Scrivner, Inc.)

SCRUBAIRE INC (NY)
Dissolved by proclamation 3/25/81

SCRUGGS (LOYD) CO. (MO)
Name changed to Lycor Co. 4/30/58 which was liquidated in 1959

SCRUGGS-VANDERVOORT-BARNEY DRY GOODS CO.
Reorganized as Scruggs-Vandervoort-Barney, Inc. in 1937
Each share 6% 1st Preferred exchanged for (1) share 6% 1st Preferred $100 par
Each share 7% 2nd Preferred exchanged for (1) share 7% 2nd Preferred $100 par
Each share Common $25 par exchanged for (1) share Common $5 par
Scruggs-Vandervoort-Barney, Inc. name changed to Sanfield Corp. 12/4/67 which name changed to Auto-Lec Stores, Inc. 9/30/68 which was adjudicated bankrupt 6/2/75

SCRUGGS VANDERVOORT BARNEY INC (MO)
Recapitalized 00/00/1947
Each share 6% 1st Preferred $100

par or 7% 2nd Preferred $100 par exchanged for (1) share $4.50 Preferred Ser. A no par
Each share 3-1/2% Preference $100 par exchanged for (0.9) share $4.50 Preferred Ser. A no par
Each share Common $5 par exchanged for (4) shares Common $1.25 par
Name changed to Sanfield Corp. 12/04/1967
Sanfield Corp. name changed to Auto-Lec Stores, Inc. 09/30/1968
(See Auto-Lec Stores, Inc.)

SCS COMPUTE INC (DE)
Merged into Thomson Corp. 2/5/96
Each share Common 10¢ par exchanged for $6.75 cash

SCS INC. (CT)
Liquidation completed
Each share Common $5 par exchanged for initial distribution of $16.50 cash 1/30/81
Each share Common $5 par received second distribution of $3.50 cash 7/31/81
Each share Common $5 par received third distribution of $0.70 cash 2/2/82
Each share Common $5 par received fourth and final distribution of $0.5876 cash 10/30/84

SCS PRODTNS CORP (FL)
Each share old Common $0.00002 par exchanged for (0.025) share new Common $0.00002 par 12/29/1989
Administratively dissolved 11/09/1990

SCS TRANSN INC (DE)
Name changed to Saia, Inc. 7/24/2006

SCUDDER, STEVENS & CLARK FUND, INC. (MA)
Capital Stock no par split (2) for (1) by issuance of (1) additional share 09/02/1947
Capital Stock no par changed to $1 par 00/00/1951
Capital Stock $1 par split (2) for (1) by issuance of (1) additional share 11/16/1959
Stock Dividend - 100% 11/23/1953
Name changed to Scudder, Stevens & Clark Balanced Fund, Inc. 03/08/1963
Scudder, Stevens & Clark Balanced Fund, Inc. name changed to Scudder Income Fund, Inc. 03/02/1977 which name changed to Scudder Income Fund 12/31/1984
(See Scudder Income Fund)

SCUDDER CAP GROWTH FD (MA)
Reincorporated 03/31/1986
Reincorporated from Scudder Capital Growth Fund, Inc. (DE) to under the laws of Massachusetts as Scudder Capital Growth Fund and Capital Shares $1 par reclassified as Shares of Bene. Int. 1¢ par 03/31/1986
Reorganized as Scudder Equity Trust 02/01/1997
Details not available

SCUDDER CASH INVT TR (MA)
Name changed to DWS Cash Investment Trust and Shares of Bene. Int. no par reclassified as Class S no par 02/06/2006

SCUDDER COM STK FD INC (MA)
Name changed to Scudder Growth & Income Fund 12/31/1984
(See Scudder Growth & Income Fund)

SCUDDER DEV FD (MA)
Reincorporated 12/31/1985
Stock Dividend - 200% 10/31/1978
State of incorporation changed from (DE) to (MA) and Capital Stock $1 par reclassified as Common 1¢ par 12/31/1985
Common 1¢ par split (3) for (1) by issuance of (2) additional shares 11/17/1986
Reorganized as Scudder Securities Trust 07/21/1995
Details not available

SCUDDER DUO VEST EXCHANGE FD INC (DE)
Income Preferred Shares $1 par and Capital Shares $1 par split (20) for (1) by issuance of (19) additional shares respectively 04/23/1969
Income Preferred Shares $1 par reclassified as (0.55812) Capital Share $1 par 01/31/1983
Merged into Scudder Common Stock Fund, Inc. 03/18/1983
Each Capital Share $1 par exchanged for (3.0517) shares Capital Stock $1 par
Scudder Common Stock Fund, Inc. name changed to Scudder Growth & Income Fund 12/31/1984
(See Scudder Growth & Income Fund)

SCUDDER DUO VEST INC (DE)
Under plan of reorganization each share 7% Income Preferred Shares $9.15 par reclassified as Capital Shares 03/31/1982
Name changed to Scudder Capital Growth Fund, Inc. (DE) 05/19/1982
Scudder Capital Growth Fund, Inc. (DE) reincorporated in Massachusetts as Scudder Capital Growth Fund 03/31/1986
(See Scudder Capital Growth Fund)

SCUDDER DYNAMIC GROWTH FD (MA)
Merged into Scudder Advisor Funds 12/20/2004
Details not available

SCUDDER FD INC (MD)
Reorganized as Lazard Funds, Inc. 08/14/1991
Details not available
Reorganized as Scudder Money Market Trust 07/14/2000
Details not available

SCUDDER FUND OF CANADA LTD. (CANADA)
Common $1 par changed to 25¢ par and (3) additional shares issued 10/17/1958
Name changed to Scudder International Investments Ltd. (Canada) 03/16/1964
Scudder International Investments Ltd. (Canada) reincorporated in Maryland as Scudder International Fund, Inc. 07/31/1975 which name changed to DWS International Fund, Inc. 02/06/2006

SCUDDER GLOBAL COMMODITIES STK FD INC (MD)
Issue Information - 24,350,000 shares COM offered at $15 per share on 09/23/2004
Name changed to DWS Global Commodities Stock Fund, Inc. 02/06/2006
DWS Global Commodities Stock Fund, Inc. name changed to DWS Enhanced Commodity Strategy Fund, Inc. 03/31/2010

SCUDDER GLOBAL FD INC (MD)
Reorganized as Global/International Fund, Inc. 05/15/1986
Details not available

SCUDDER GLOBAL HIGH INCOME FD INC (MD)
Name changed to DWS Global High Income Fund, Inc. 02/06/2006
DWS Global High Income Fund, Inc. name changed to Deutsche Global High Income Fund, Inc. 08/11/2014
(See Deutsche Global High Income Fund, Inc.)

SCUDDER GOVT MONEY FD (MA)
Name changed to Scudder U.S. Treasury Money Fund 02/28/1991
Scudder U.S. Treasury Money Fund name changed to DWS U.S. Treasury Money Fund 12/29/2005

SCUDDER GROWTH & INCOME FD (MA)
Reorganized as Scudder Investment Trust 03/06/1991
Details not available

SCUDDER GROWTH TR (MA)
Name changed 01/15/2003
Name changed from Scudder Growth Fund to Scudder Growth Trust 01/15/2003
Merged into Investment Trust 03/14/2005
Details not available

SCUDDER HIGH INCOME SER (MA)
Name changed 04/01/2003
High Yield Fund Class A reclassified as High Income Fund Class A 10/07/2002
High Yield Fund Class B reclassified as High Income Fund Class B 10/07/2002
High Yield Fund Class C reclassified as High Income Fund Class C 10/07/2002
High Yield Fund Class I reclassified as High Income Fund Class I 10/07/2002
High Yield Fund Institutional Class reclassified as High Income Fund Institutional Class 10/07/2002
Name changed from Scudder High Yield Series to Scudder High Income Series 04/01/2003
High Income Fund Class I reclassified as High Income Fund Institutional Class 08/13/2004
Name changed to DWS High Income Series 12/19/2005

SCUDDER HIGH INCOME TR (MA)
Name changed to DWS High Income Trust 02/06/2006
DWS High Income Trust name changed to Deutsche High Income Trust 08/11/2014
(See Deutsche High Income Trust)

SCUDDER INCOME FD (MA)
Name changed 12/31/1984
Name changed from Scudder Income Fund, Inc. to Scudder Income Fund and Capital Stock $1 par reclassified as Shares of Bene. Int. $1 par 12/31/1984
Reorganized as Scudder Portfolio Trust 01/13/1985
Details not available

SCUDDER INCOME TR (MA)
Name changed to DWS Income Trust 12/29/2005

SCUDDER INSTL FD INC (MD)
Reorganized as Scudder International Fund, Inc. 04/03/1998
Details not available

SCUDDER INTER GOVT TR (MA)
Name changed to Scudder Intermediate Government & Agency Trust and Shares of Bene. Int. 1¢ par reclassified as Government & Agency Trust 1¢ par 04/01/2004
(See Scudder Intermediate Government & Agency Trust)

SCUDDER INTERMEDIATE GOVERNMENT & AGENCY TRUST (MA)
Merged into Scudder U.S. Government Securities Fund 07/29/2005
Details not available

SCUDDER INTL FD INC (MD)
Reincorporated 07/31/1975
Reincorporated from Scudder International Investments Ltd. (Canada) to under the laws of Maryland as Scudder International Fund, Inc. 07/31/1975
Name changed to DWS International Fund, Inc. 02/06/2006

SCUDDER INTL RESH FD INC (MD)
Completely liquidated 05/17/2002
Each Kemper Global Blue Chip Fund Class A received net asset value
Each Kemper Global Blue Chip Fund Class B received net asset value
Each Kemper Global Blue Chip Fund Class C received net asset value
Each International Research Fund Class A received net asset value
Each International Research Fund Class B received net asset value
Each International Research Fund Class C received net asset value

SCUDDER MANAGED MUN BDS (MA)
Reorganized as Scudder Municipal Trust 03/02/1988
Details not available

SCUDDER MANAGED RESVS INC (MD)
Merged into Scudder Cash Investment Trust 12/12/1980
Each share Capital Stock $1 par exchanged for (9.96358) Shares of Bene. Int. no par
Scudder Cash Investment Trust name changed to DWS Cash Investment Trust 02/06/2006

SCUDDER MONEY FDS (MA)
Name changed to DWS Money Funds 12/19/2005

SCUDDER MULTI-MARKET INCOME TR (MA)
Name changed to DWS Multi-Market Income Trust 02/06/2006
DWS Multi-Market Income Trust name changed to Deutsche Multi-Market Income Trust 08/11/2014

SCUDDER MUN INCOME TR (MA)
Name changed to DWS Municipal Income Trust (Old) 02/06/2006
DWS Municipal Income Trust (Old) name changed to Deutsche Municipal Income Trust 08/11/2014 which name changed to DWS Municipal Income Trust (New) 07/02/2018

SCUDDER NEW ASIA FD INC (MD)
Merged into DWS International Fund, Inc. 04/17/2006
Each share Common 1¢ par exchanged for Emerging Markets Equity Fund Class S 1¢ par on a net asset basis

SCUDDER NEW EUROPE FD INC NEW (MD)
Merged into Scudder International Fund, Inc. 03/14/2005
Each share Class A exchanged for (1) share Greater Europe Fund Class A
Each share Class B exchanged for (1) share Greater Europe Fund Class B
Each share Class C exchanged for (1) share Greater Europe Fund Class C
Scudder International Fund, Inc. name changed to DWS International Fund, Inc. 02/06/2006

SCUDDER NEW EUROPE FD INC OLD (MD)
Name changed to Kemper New Europe Fund, Inc. 09/07/1999
Kemper New Europe Fund, Inc. name changed to Scudder New Europe Fund, Inc. (New) 05/25/2001 which merged into Scudder International Fund, Inc. 03/14/2005 which name changed to DWS International Fund, Inc. 02/06/2006

SCUDDER PORTFOLIOS (MA)
Merged into Scudder Cash Investment Trust 09/17/2005
Details not available

SCUDDER RREEF REAL ESTATE FD II INC (MD)
Name changed to DWS RREEF Real Estate Fund II, Inc. 02/06/2006
(See DWS RREEF Real Estate Fund II, Inc.)
Auction Preferred Ser. F 1¢ par called for redemption at $25,000 on 05/17/2010
Auction Preferred Ser. M 1¢ par called for redemption at $25,000 on 05/18/2010
Auction Preferred Ser. T 1¢ par called for redemption at $25,000 on 05/19/2010
Auction Preferred Ser. W 1¢ par called for redemption at $25,000 on 05/20/2010
Auction Preferred Ser. TH 1¢ par called for redemption at $25,000 on 05/21/2010

SCUDDER RREEF REAL ESTATE FD INC (MD)
Name changed to DWS RREEF Real Estate Fund, Inc. 02/06/2006
(See DWS RREEF Real Estate Fund, Inc.)
Auction Preferred Ser. B 1¢ par called for redemption at $25,000 on 05/17/2010
Auction Preferred Ser. A 1¢ par called for redemption at $25,000 on 05/20/2010

SCUDDER SMALL CAPITALIZATION EQUITY FD (MA)
Name changed to Scudder Dynamic Growth Fund 01/17/2002
(See Scudder Dynamic Growth Fund)

SCUDDER SPAIN & PORTUGAL FD INC (MD)
Completely liquidated 3/5/99
Each share Common 1¢ par exchanged for first and final distribution of $13.249486 cash

SCUDDER SPL FD INC (DE)
Merged into Scudder Capital Growth Fund, Inc. (DE) 09/30/1982
Each capital Capital Stock $1 par exchanged for (4.5787) Capital Shares $1 par
Scudder Capital Growth Fund, Inc. (DE) reincorporated in Massachusetts as Scudder Capital Growth Fund 03/31/1986
(See Scudder Capital Growth Fund)

SCUDDER STEVENS & CLARK BALANCED FD INC (MA)
Name changed to Scudder Income Fund, Inc. 03/02/1977
Scudder Income Fund, Inc. name changed to Scudder Income Fund 12/31/1984
(See Scudder Income Fund)

SCUDDER STEVENS & CLARK COM STK FD INC (MA)
Capital Stock no par changed to $1 par 00/00/1952
Capital Stock $1 par split (3) for (1) by issuance of (2) additional shares 11/16/1959
Name changed to Scudder Common Stock Fund, Inc. 03/07/1979
Scudder Common Stock Fund, Inc. name changed to Scudder Growth & Income Fund 12/31/1984
(See Scudder Growth & Income Fund)

SCUDDER STRATEGIC INCOME TR (MA)
Name changed to DWS Strategic Income Trust 02/06/2006
DWS Strategic Income Trust name changed to Deutsche Strategic Income Trust 08/11/2014

SCUDDER STRATEGIC MUN INCOME TR (MA)
Name changed to DWS Strategic Municipal Income Trust (Old) 02/06/2006
DWS Strategic Municipal Income Trust (Old) name changed to Deutsche Strategic Municipal Income Trust 08/11/2014 which name changed to DWS Strategic Municipal Income Trust (New) 07/02/2018

SCUDDER TAX FREE MONEY FD (MA)
Each old Share of Bene. Int. no par exchanged for (1/99) new Share of Bene. Int. no par 01/07/1983
New Shares of Bene. Int. no par reclassified as Class S 08/14/2000
Name changed to DWS Tax Free Money Fund 02/06/2006

SCUDDER TECHNOLOGY FD (MA)
Name changed to DWS Technology Fund 02/06/2006

SCUDDER TOTAL RETURN FD (MA)
Name changed to DWS Balanced Fund 02/06/2006

SCUDDER TREASRS TR (MA)
Completely liquidated 03/07/1991
Each share Auction Rate Preferred Portfolio no par received net asset value
Each share Dividend Income Portfolio no par received net asset value
Each share Liquidity Plus Portfolio no par received net asset value
Each share Money Portfolio no par received net asset value
Each share Tax Exempt Liquidity Plus Portfolio no par received net asset value
Each share Tax Exempt Money Portfolio no par received net asset value

SCUDDER U S GOVT SECS FD (MA)
Shares of Bene. Int. Class I reclassified as Shares of Bene. Int. Institutional Class 08/13/2004
Name changed to DWS U.S Government Securities Fund 02/06/2006
DWS U.S Government Securities Fund name changed to DWS Strategic Government Securities Fund 03/25/2008

SCUDDER U S TREAS MONEY FD (MA)
Common $0.001 par reclassified as Class S $0.001 par 08/14/2000
Name changed to DWS U.S. Treasury Money Fund 12/29/2005

SCUDDER VAR SER II (MA)
Scudder Growth Portfolio merged into Scudder Variable Series I Capital Growth Portfolio Class A on a net asset basis 04/20/2005
Name changed to DWS Variable Series II 01/30/2006

SCUDDER VARIABLE SERIES I (MA)
Name changed 05/01/2001
Trust terminated 00/00/1990
Details not available
Trust terminated 00/00/1995
Details not available
Name changed from Scudder Variable Life Investment Funds to Scudder Variable Series I 05/01/2001
Name changed to DWS Variable Series I and Bond Portfolio Class A, Capital Growth Portfolio Class A and International Portfolio Class A reclassified as Bond VIP Class A, Capital Growth VIP Class A and International VIP Class A respectively 01/11/2006

SCUFFY PET INC (NJ)
Adjudicated bankrupt 12/06/1977
Stockholders' equity unlikely

SCULLIN STEEL CO. (MO)
Reorganized 12/17/37
Each share $3 Part. Preference no par exchanged for (1.25) shares new Common no par
Each share old Common no par exchanged for (1/3) share new Common no par
New Common no par changed to $1 par and (1) additional share issued 6/6/56
Stock Dividend - 25% 12/27/51
Acquired by Universal Marion Corp. (D.C.) 4/28/58
Each share Common $1 par exchanged for (1.75) shares Capital Stock $14 par
Universal Marion Corp. (D.C.) reincorporated under the laws of Florida 5/29/59
(See Universal Marion Corp. (Fla.))

SCULLY RECORDING INSTRUMENTS CORP. (DE)
Completely liquidated 06/09/1967
Each share Common 10¢ par exchanged for first and final distribution of (0.150376) share Dictaphone Corp. Common $2.50 par
Dictaphone Corp. merged into Pitney Bowes Inc. 05/11/1979

SCURRY RAINBOW OIL LTD (AB)
Each share Capital Stock 50¢ par exchanged for (0.14285714) share Capital Stock $3.50 par 02/16/1959
Capital Stock $3.50 par changed to no par and (4) additional shares issued 07/27/1983
Plan of Arrangement effective 11/08/1993
Each share Common no par exchanged for (1.289) shares Home Oil Co. Ltd. (New) Common no par
Home Oil Co. Ltd. (New) merged into Anderson Exploration Ltd. 09/07/1995
(See Anderson Exploration Ltd.)

SCYTHER CORP (AB)
Name changed to Fifth Era Knowledge Inc. 07/24/2000
Fifth Era Knowledge Inc. recapitalized as Triton Capital Corp. 09/25/2003 which name changed to March Resources Corp. 09/30/2004 which recapitalized as Ranger Energy Ltd. (AB) 08/21/2009 which reorganized in Ontario as North Sea Energy Inc. 10/21/2011

SCYTHES & CO LTD (CANADA)
Common no par exchanged (2) for (1) in 1945 5% S.F. 1st Preferred $25 par called for redemption 2/28/63
Common no par split (5) for (1) by issuance of (4) additional shares 5/29/75
Reorganized 7/11/78
Each share Common no par exchanged for $4.62 cash

SCYTHIAN FUND, INC. (DE)
Company reported out of business 00/00/1977
Details not available

SDC INTL INC (DE)
Charter cancelled and declared inoperative and void for non-payment of taxes 03/01/2005

SDC SYDNEY DEV CORP (CANADA)
Filed an assignment in bankruptcy 05/23/1989
No stockholders' equity

SDI INVESTORS, INC. (NV)
Completely liquidated 12/17/84
Each share Common 60¢ par exchanged for first and final distribution of $6.81 cash

SDL INC (DE)
Common $0.001 par split (3) for (2) by issuance of (0.5) additional share payable 06/12/1996 to holders of record 05/15/1996
Common $0.001 par split (2) for (1) by issuance of (1) additional share payable 06/02/1999 to holders of record 05/14/1999
Common $0.001 par split (2) for (1) by issuance of (1) additional share payable 03/13/2000 to holders of record 02/29/2000
Merged into JDS Uniphase Corp. 02/13/2001
Each share Common $0.001 par exchanged for (3.8) shares Common $0.001 par
JDS Uniphase Corp. name changed to Viavi Solutions Inc. 08/04/2015

SDN BANCORP (DE)
Reorganized 09/27/1995
Reorganized from under the laws of (CA) to (DE) 09/27/1995
Each share Common no par exchanged for (0.04761904) share Common 1¢ par
Merged into Commerce Security Bancorp, Inc. 09/01/1996
Each share Common 1¢ par exchanged for (1) share Common 1¢ par
Commerce Security Bancorp, Inc. name changed to Eldorado Bancshares, Inc. 08/28/1998 which merged into Zions Zions Bancorporation 03/30/2001 which merged into Zions Bancorporation, N.A (Salt Lake City, UT) 10/01/2018

SDNB FINL CORP (CA)
Merged into FBOP Acquisition Corp. 2/28/97
Each share Common no par exchanged for $8.048 cash

SDW HLDGS CORP (DE)
144A Preferred called for redemption at $38.81 on 12/15/97

SE FINL CORP (PA)
Acquired by Beneficial Mutual Bancorp, Inc. 04/03/2012
Each share Common 60¢ par exchanged for $14.50 cash

SE GLOBAL EQUITIES CORP (MN)
Recapitalized as Sun New Media Inc. (MN) 09/20/2005
Each share Common 1¢ par exchanged for (0.5) share Common 1¢ par
Sun New Media Inc. (MN) reincorporated in Delaware as NextMart, Inc. 05/08/2007

SEA 1 AQUAFARMS LTD (BC)
Recapitalized as General Sea Harvest Corp. 11/26/87
Each share Common no par exchanged for (1/3) share Common no par
General Sea Harvest Corp. recapitalized as Consolidated General Sea Harvest Corp. 6/12/90
(See Consolidated General Sea Harvest Corp.)

SEA BREEZE PWR CORP (BC)
Proposal pursuant to the Bankruptcy & Insolvency Act effective 05/09/2017
No stockholders' equity

SEA CHEM INDS LTD (BC)
Recapitalized as Astra Resources Ltd. 03/10/1978
Each share Common no par exchanged for (0.25) share Common no par
(See Astra Resources Ltd.)

SEA CLIFF & GLEN COVE GAS CO.
Acquired by Long Island Lighting Co. 00/00/1928
Details not available

SEA CONTAINERS ATLANTIC LTD (BERMUDA)
Name changed to Sea Containers Ltd. 07/15/1981
(See Sea Containers Ltd.)

SEA CONTAINERS INC (NY)
Common 12-1/2¢ par reclassified as Non-Separable Unit consisting of (1) share Sea Containers Inc. Common 12-1/2¢ par and (1) share Sea Containers Atlantic Ltd. Common 1¢ par 06/18/1976
Units split (2) for (1) by issuance of (1) additional Unit 11/04/1976

Units split (2) for (1) by issuance of (1) additional Unit 10/19/1977
Name changed to SeaCo Inc. 07/15/1981
SeaCo Inc. name changed to Orient Express Hotels Inc. 10/31/1986 which merged into Sea Containers Ltd. 08/08/1994
(See Sea Containers Ltd.)

SEA CONTAINERS LTD (BERMUDA)
Paired certificates separated 03/15/1984
Each Non-Separable Unit consisting of (1) share SeaCo Inc. Common 12-1/2¢ par and (1) share Sea Containers Ltd. Common 1¢ par exchanged for (1) share SeaCo Inc. Common 12-1/2¢ par and (1) share Sea Containers Ltd. Common 1¢ par
$2.10 Preferred 1¢ par called for redemption 08/29/1991
$4.125 Conv. Preferred 1¢ par called for redemption 12/31/1996
$1.4625 Preferred 1¢ par called for redemption at $15 on 05/29/1998
$2.10 Preferred Ser. 1982 1¢ par called for redemption at $15 on 05/29/1998
$4 Conv. Preferred 1¢ par called for redemption at $51.60 plus $0.8667 accrued dividend on 07/03/1998
Common 1¢ par split (2) for (1) by issuance of (1) additional share 07/05/1991
Common 1¢ par reclassified as Conv. Class B Common 1¢ par 06/23/1992
Plan of reorganization under Chapter 11 Federal Bankruptcy Code effective 02/10/2009
No stockholders' equity

SEA DRAGON ENERGY INC (CANADA)
Recapitalized as SDX Energy Inc. 10/01/2015
Each share Common no par exchanged for (0.02857142) share Common no par 10/01/2015

SEA GALLEY STORES INC (DE)
Reincorporated 11/24/1980
State of incorporation changed from (WA) to (DE) 11/24/1980
Common 5¢ par split (3) for (2) by issuance of (0.5) additional share 06/01/1981
Chapter 11 bankruptcy proceedings converted to Chapter 7 on 12/30/1997
Stockholders' equity unlikely

SEA GOLD OIL CORP (BC)
Recapitalized as Consolidated Sea Gold Corp. 7/16/85
Each share Common no par exchanged for (0.2) share Common no par
Consolidated Sea Gold Corp. recapitalized as Sea Gold Resources Inc. 5/9/90 which recapitalized as Fairchild Investments Inc. (BC) 6/3/94 which reincorporated in Bermuda as Fairchild Investments Ltd. 6/26/95

SEA GOLD RES INC (BC)
Recapitalized as Fairchild Investments Inc. (BC) 06/03/1994
Each share Common no par exchanged for (0.33333333) share Common no par
Fairchild Investments Inc. (BC) reincorporated in Bermuda as Fairchild Investments Ltd. 06/26/1995 which name changed to Stone Resources Ltd. 11/12/2009

SEA GREEN CAP CORP (ON)
Recapitalized as Cava Resources Inc. 07/23/2012
Each share Common no par exchanged for (0.2) share Common no par
Cava Resources Inc. name changed to Gold Rush Cariboo Corp. 06/21/2018

SEA GREEN INC (FL)
Name changed to Americom Networks Corp. 06/03/1998
Americom Networks Corp. name changed to Americom Networks International Inc. (FL) 07/10/1998 which reincorporated in Delaware 02/06/2008 which recapitalized as Highland Ridge, Inc. 08/29/2008 which name changed to TEC Technology, Inc. (DE) 07/15/2010 which reincorporated in Nevada 06/30/2012

SEA HAWK ENERGY INC (ON)
Name changed to Jarl Energy Inc. 08/05/1987
Jarl Energy Inc. name changed to ALBA Petroleum Corp. 10/26/1989 which merged into Alberta Oil & Gas Ltd. 12/31/1990 which recapitalized as Alberta Oil & Gas Petroleum Corp. 11/19/1997 which recapitalized as Edge Energy Inc. 04/14/1998 which merged into Ventus Energy Ltd. 08/11/2000 which name changed to Navigo Energy Inc. 05/24/2002
(See Navigo Energy Inc.)

SEA-HIGHWAYS, INC. (DE)
No longer in existence having become inoperative and void for non-payment of taxes 4/1/63

SEA LD CORP (DE)
Merged into CSX Corp. 9/25/86
Each share Common no par exchanged for $28 cash

SEA LIFE, INC. (HI)
Under plan of merger each share Common $1 par exchanged for $2 cash 3/1/78

SEA-PAK CORP. (GA)
Stock Dividends - 10% 09/15/1964; 10% 09/15/1965
Merged into Grace (W.R.) & Co. (CT) 03/02/1967
Each share Common $1 par exchanged for (0.442) share Common $1 par
Grace (W.R.) & Co. (CT) reincorporated in New York 05/19/1988
(See Grace (W.R.) & Co.)

SEA PINES ASSOC INC (SC)
Merged into Riverstone Group, LLC 3/17/2005
Each share Common no par exchanged for $8.50 cash
Preferred called for redemption at $7.60 on 4/30/2005
Public interest eliminated

SEA PINES ASSOCS TR I (DE)
9.5% Trust Preferred Securities called for redemption at $8.50 on 4/30/2005

SEA PINES CO (GA)
Merged into Vacation Resorts Holdings, Inc. 06/10/1983
Each share Common 10¢ par exchanged for $2 cash

SEA SHELL GALLERIES INC (NV)
Name changed to Cyfit Wellness Solutions, Inc. 7/5/2001
(See Cyfit Wellness Solutions, Inc.)

SEA SUN CAP CORP (DE)
Company terminated registration of common stock and is no longer public as of 04/05/2007
Details not available

SEA 2 SKY CORP (NV)
Name changed to ecoTECH Energy Group Inc. 12/20/2010 ecoTECH Energy Group Inc. name changed to Dong Fang Hui Le Inc. 11/09/2017

SEA VENTURE CRUISES INC (DE)
Recapitalized as Internet Stock Exchange Corp. 04/14/1998
Each share Common $0.001 par exchanged for (0.001) share Common $0.001 par
Internet Stock Exchange Corp. name changed to Internet Stock Market Resources, Inc. 09/01/1998 which name changed to VentureNet, Inc. 06/26/2000 which name changed to VentureNet Capital Group, Inc. (DE) 11/06/2001 which reincorporated in Nevada 03/14/2003

SEA-WIDE INDUSTRIES, INC. (PA)
Name changed to Flying W Airways, Inc. 9/1/67
Flying W Airways, Inc. adjudicated bankrupt 7/6/72

SEA WORLD INC (CA)
Common 50¢ par split (3) for (2) by issuance of (0.5) additional share 06/11/1973
Merged into Trident Park Corp. 07/07/1977
Each share Common 5¢ par exchanged for $28.75 cash

SEABOARD & WESTERN AIRLINES, INC. (DE)
Capital Stock $1 par reclassified as Common $1 par 00/00/1952
Each share Common $1 par exchanged for (1/3) share Common $3 par 10/28/1960
Stock Dividends - 25% 04/30/1951; 20% 12/30/1955
Name changed to Seaboard World Airlines, Inc. 05/04/1961
Seaboard World Airlines, Inc. merged into Tiger International, Inc. 09/30/1980
(See Tiger International, Inc.)

SEABOARD AIR LINE RAILWAY CO.
Reorganized as Seaboard Air Line Railroad Co. in 1946
No stockholders' equity

SEABOARD AIR LINE RR CO (VA)
Each share Common no par exchanged for (2.5) shares Common $40 par in 1953
Each share Common $40 par exchanged for (2) shares Common $20 par 4/25/56
Under plan of merger name changed to Seaboard Coast Line Railroad Co. 7/1/67
Seaboard Coast Line Railroad Co. merged into Seaboard Coast Line Industries, Inc. (Del.) 5/14/71 which merged into CSX Corp. 11/1/80

SEABOARD ALLIED MLG CORP (DE)
Name changed to Seaboard Corp. (Incorporated 07/24/1946) 01/29/1982

SEABOARD AMERN CORP (DE)
Each share old Capital Stock 1¢ par exchanged for (0.08) share new Capital Stock 1¢ par 12/23/1969
Charter cancelled and declared inoperative and void for non-payment of taxes 03/01/1976

SEABOARD BANCORP INC (VA)
Merged into Life Bancorp, Inc. 1/31/96
Each share Common 1¢ par exchanged for $1.65 cash

SEABOARD CITIZENS NATIONAL BANK (NORFOLK, VA)
Each share Capital Stock $25 par exchanged for (2.5) shares Capital Stock $10 par 02/08/1957
Under plan of merger Capital Stock $10 par changed to $5 par and (1.5) additional shares issued 10/18/1963
Merged into United Virginia Bankshares, Inc. 01/01/1967
Each share Capital Stock $5 par exchanged for (0.8) share Common $10 par
United Virginia Bankshares, Inc. name changed to Crestar Financial Corp. 09/01/1987 which merged into SunTrust Banks, Inc. 12/31/1998

SEABOARD COAST LINE INDS INC (DE)
Reincorporated 06/27/1969
State of incorporation changed from (VA) to (DE) 06/27/1969
Merged into CSX Corp. 11/01/1980
Each share Common $20 par exchanged for (1.324) shares Common $1 par

SEABOARD COAST LINE RR CO (VA)
Merged into Seaboard Coast Line Industries, Inc. (DE) 5/14/71
Each share Common $20 par exchanged for (1) share Common $20 par
Seaboard Coast Line Industries, Inc. merged into CSX Corp. 11/1/80

SEABOARD COMMERCIAL CORP. (DE)
Class A and B Common $10 par exchanged for Common $10 par in 1937
Charter cancelled and declared inoperative and void for non-payment of taxes 4/1/61

SEABOARD CORP (DE)
Incorporated in 1967
Charter cancelled and declared inoperative and void for non-payment of taxes 3/1/80

SEABOARD DAIRY CREDIT CORP.
Liquidated in 1936

SEABOARD DRUG CO., INC. (DE)
Adjudicated bankrupt 4/23/58
No stockholders' equity

SEABOARD ELECTRONIC CORP. (NY)
Acquired by Stelma, Inc. 6/15/65
Each share Common 10¢ par exchanged for (0.5) share Common 10¢ par
Stelma, Inc. merged into Data Products Corp. 5/8/69 which name changed to Dataproducts Corp. 8/23/74
(See Dataproducts Corp.)

SEABOARD FIN CO (DE)
Common $1 par split (2) for (1) by issuance of (1) additional share 2/24/56
$2.75 Conv. Preferred no par called for redemption 12/8/69
Under plan of merger each share $1.275 Conv. Preferred no par exchanged for $30.60 principal amount of Avco Corp. 5-1/2% Conv. Subord. Debentures due 11/30/93 and $0.51 cash 12/12/69
Each share Common $1 par exchanged for $34 principal amount of Avco Corp. 5-1/2% Conv. Subord. Debentures due 11/30/93 and $0.44 cash 12/12/69
Name changed to Avco Financial Services, Inc. 6/1/70
Avco Financial Services, Inc. acquired by Textron Inc. in 1985

SEABOARD FINANCE CORP.
Merged into Seaboard Finance Co. 00/00/1946
Details not available

SEABOARD FRUIT CO., INC.
Out of business 00/00/1951
Details not available

SEABOARD HOMES INC (NY)
Name changed to Seaboard Industries, Inc. 08/28/1969
(See Seaboard Industries, Inc.)

SEABOARD INDS INC (NY)
Charter cancelled and proclaimed dissolved for failure to pay taxes and file reports 12/15/1975

SEABOARD INDUSTRIES LTD. (NB)
Charter forfeited for failure to file annual returns 3/2/66

SEABOARD LD CO (MD)
Class A Common $5 par and Class B

Common $5 par changed to $2.50 par respectively and (3) additional shares issued 08/15/1962
Merged into Kent Washington, Inc. 08/20/1969
Each share Class A Common $5 par exchanged for (1/3) share Common $1 par
Each share Class B Common $5 par exchanged for (1/3) share Common $1 par
Kent Washington, Inc. merged into Presidential Realty Corp. (Old) 11/12/1971 which reorganized as Presidential Realty Corp. (New) 07/06/1983

SEABOARD LEVERAGE FD (DE)
Merged into Oppenheimer A.I.M. Fund, Inc. 12/7/76
Each share Common $1 par exchanged for (0.4694490) share Capital Stock $1 par
Oppenheimer A.I.M. Fund, Inc. name changed to Oppenheimer Global Fund 2/1/87

SEABOARD LIFE INS CO (TX)
Acquired by American General Insurance Co. on a (12.5) for (1) basis in 1945
American General Insurance Co. reorganized as American General Corp. 7/1/80 which merged into American International Group, Inc. 8/29/2001

SEABOARD LIFE INS CO AMER (FL)
Recapitalized 06/30/1959
Each share Class A $1 par exchanged for (1) share old Common $1 par
Each share Class B $1 par plus $4 cash exchanged for (5) shares old Common $1 par
Each share old Common $1 par exchanged for (0.5) share new Common $1 par 06/27/1968
Ordered liquidated by Court 01/23/1976
No stockholders' equity

SEABOARD MANGANESE LTD.
Name changed to Seaboard Oil & Mines Ltd. in 1949
Seaboard Oil & Mines Ltd. merged into Landmark Mines Ltd. in May 1956
(See Landmark Mines Ltd.)

SEABOARD OIL & GAS CO. (AZ)
Charter revoked for failure to file reports and pay fees 10/13/36

SEABOARD OIL & GAS CO (CA)
Merged into McFarland Energy, Inc. 2/27/76
Each share Conv. Preferred Class B $2 par exchanged for (0.172631) share Common no par
Each share 7% Conv. Preferred Class A no par exchanged for (2.323045) shares Common no par
Each share Common 10¢ par exchanged for (0.150114) share Common no par
(See McFarland Energy, Inc.)

SEABOARD OIL & MINES, LTD. (ON)
Merged into Landmark Mines Ltd. on a (0.2) for (1) basis 05/00/1956
(See Landmark Mines Ltd.)

SEABOARD OIL CO. (DE)
Ctfs. dated prior to 5/1/59
Capital Stock no par changed to $1 par and (2) additional shares issued in 1954
Merged into Texas Co. (New) share for share 6/2/58
Texas Co. (New) name changed to Texaco Inc. 5/1/59 which merged into ChevronTexaco Corp. 10/9/2001 which name changed to Chevron Corp. 5/9/2005

SEABOARD OIL CO. (OH)
Each share 8% Preferred $100 par exchanged for (1) share Common no par in 1948
Dissolved in 1953

SEABOARD OIL CO. OF DELAWARE (DE)
Name changed to Seaboard Oil Co. in 1954
Seaboard Oil Co. merged into Texas Co. (New) 6/2/58 which name changed to Texaco Inc. 5/1/59 which merged into ChevronTexaco Corp. 10/9/2001 which name changed to Chevron Corp. 5/9/2005

SEABOARD OIL CO (DE)
Ctfs. dated after 9/15/92
Merged into Seaboard Acquisition 10/24/96
Each share Common 1¢ par exchanged for $9.75 cash

SEABOARD PLYWOOD & LMBR CORP (MA)
Merged into North American Development Corp. 10/20/1972
Each share Common $1 par exchanged for (1) share Common 10¢ par
North American Development Corp. name changed to Scotts Seaboard Corp. 07/03/1980
(See Scotts Seaboard Corp.)

SEABOARD PUBLIC SERVICE CO.
Bankrupt in 1932

SEABOARD SAND & GRAVEL CORP. (NY)
Charter cancelled and proclaimed dissolved for failure to pay taxes 12/15/49

SEABOARD SAVINGS & LOAN ASSOCIATION, INC. (NC)
Merged into Cooperative Savings & Loan Association of Wilmington 5/2/83
Each share Common $1 par exchanged for $11.76 cash

SEABOARD SVGS & LN ASSN VIRGINIA BEACH (VA)
Stock Dividends - 30% 11/18/83; 30% 10/1/84; 20% 1/15/86; 10% 7/15/87
Under plan of reorganization each share Capital Stock $5 par automatically became (1) share Seaboard Bancorp, Inc. Common 1¢ par 11/1/90
(See Seaboard Bancorp, Inc.)

SEABOARD SAVINGS BANK, INC. SSB (NC)
Merged into United Carolina Bancshares Corp. 1/25/96
Each share Common no par exchanged for (0.9104) share Common $4 par
United Carolina Bancshares Corp. merged into BB&T Corp. 7/1/97

SEABOARD SURETY CO (NY)
Capital Stock $10 par changed to $5 par and (1) additional share issued 07/27/1959
Stock Dividends - 100% 05/22/1953; 25% 06/15/1959
95.84% acquired by Home Insurance Co. as of 00/00/1968
Public interest eliminated

SEABOARD SURETY CORP. OF AMERICA
Bankrupt in 1951

SEABOARD TERMINAL & REFRIGERATION CO.
Acquired by City Ice & Fuel Co. in 1930
City Ice & Fuel Co. name changed to City Products Corp. 4/21/49
(See listing for City Products Corp.)

SEABOARD UTILITIES SHARES CORP. (DE)
Charter cancelled and declared inoperative and void for non-payment of taxes 4/1/37

SEABOARD WORLD AIRLS INC (DE)
Stock Dividend - 10% 02/28/1979
Merged into Tiger International, Inc. 09/30/1980
Each share Common $3 par exchanged for (0.25) share Common $1 par plus $10 principal amount 11-1/2% 15-Yr. Debentures due 10/01/1995
(See Tiger International, Inc.)

SEABRIDGE FGHT CORP (NV)
Name changed to University General Health System, Inc. 03/29/2011
(See University General Health System, Inc.)

SEABRIDGE GOLD INC (BC)
Name changed 06/20/2002
Name changed from Seabridge Resources Inc. to Seabridge Gold Inc. 06/20/2002
Reincorporated under the laws of Canada 10/21/2002

SEABRIGHT EXPLS INC (ON)
Recapitalized as Corner Bay Minerals, Inc. 04/22/1991
Each share Common no par exchanged for (0.2) share Common no par
Corner Bay Minerals, Inc. name changed to Corner Bay Silver, Inc. 03/01/2001 which merged into Pan American Silver Corp. 02/20/2003

SEABRIGHT HLDGS INC (DE)
Name changed 05/19/2010
Issue Information - 7,500,000 shares COM offered at $10.50 per share on 01/20/2005
Name changed from SeaBright Insurance Holdings, Inc. to SeaBright Holdings, Inc. 05/19/2010
Acquired by Enstar Group Ltd. 02/07/2013
Each share Common 1¢ par exchanged for $11.11 cash

SEABRIGHT RES INC (CANADA)
Acquired by Western Mining Corp. Holdings Ltd. 02/23/1988
Each share Class A no par exchanged for $8.50 cash

SEABROOK (C.F.) CO., INC.
Name changed to Seabrook Engineering Corp. in 1929
(See Seabrook Engineering Corp.)

SEABROOK FARMS CO. (NJ)
Merged into Seeman Brothers, Inc. 11/01/1960
Each share 4.5% Preferred $100 par exchanged for (5) shares 5% Preferred $20 par
Each share 60¢ Preference $1 par exchanged for (0.5) share 5% Preferred $20 par
Each share Common $1 par exchanged for (0.5) share 5% Preferred $20 par
Seeman Brothers, Inc. name changed to Seabrook Foods, Inc. 07/24/1970
(See Seabrook Foods, Inc.)

SEABROOK FOODS INC (NY)
Completely liquidated 03/05/1973
Each share Common $3 par exchanged for first and final distribution of $15.50 cash

SEABROOK ISLAND OCEAN CLUB INC (DE)
Chapter 7 bankruptcy proceedings terminated 09/26/1995
Stockholders' equity unlikely

SEABULK INTL INC (DE)
Merged into SEACOR Holdings Inc. 7/1/2005
Each share Common 1¢ par exchanged for (0.2694) share Common 1¢ par and $4 cash

SEACLIFF CONSTR CORP (BC)
Merged into Churchill Corp. 07/16/2010
Each share Common no par exchanged for $17.14 cash

Note: Unexchanged certificates were cancelled and became without value 07/13/2016

SEACO COMPUTER DISPLAY INC (TX)
Common no par changed to 1¢ par 03/07/1973
Each share old Common 1¢ par exchanged for (0.2) share new Common 1¢ par 02/07/1974
Charter forfeited for failure to pay taxes 03/16/1981

SEACO INC (NY)
Paired certificates separated 03/15/1984
Each Non-Separable Unit consisting of (1) share SeaCo Inc. Common 12-1/2¢ par and (1) share Sea Containers Ltd. Common 1¢ par exchanged for (1) share SeaCo Inc. Common 12-1/2¢ par and (1) share Sea Containers Ltd. Common 1¢ par
Name changed to Orient Express Hotels Inc. 10/31/1986
Orient Express Hotels Inc. merged into Sea Containers Ltd. 08/08/1994
(See Sea Containers Ltd.)

SEACO LTD (BERMUDA)
Liquidation completed
Each share Common $0.001 par received initial distribution of $0.65 cash payable 01/27/2012 to holders of record 01/19/2012
Each share Common $0.001 par received second distribution of $0.05 cash payable 04/10/2013 to holders of record 04/01/2013
Each share Common $0.001 par received third and final distribution of $0.0875 cash payable 09/30/2013 to holders of record 09/23/2013
Ex date - 10/01/2013

SEACOAST CAP TR I (DE)
8.5% Trust Preferred Securities called for redemption at $25 on 07/02/2007

SEACOAST COMM BK (CHULA VISTA, CA)
Under plan of reorganization each share Common no par automatically became (1) share Seacoast Commerce Banc Holdings Common no par 12/05/2014

SEACOAST FINL SVCS CORP (MA)
Merged into Sovereign Bancorp, Inc. 07/23/2004
Each share Common $1 par exchanged for (1.594) shares Common no par
Sovereign Bancorp, Inc. merged into Banco Santander, S.A. 01/30/2009

SEACOAST SVGS BK (DOVER, NH)
Placed in receivership with FDIC 08/29/1992
No stockholders' equity

SEACONNET MILLS
Sold under foreclosure 00/00/1927
Stockholders' equity unlikely

SEACOR SMIT INC (DE)
Name changed back to SEACOR Holdings Inc. 3/15/2004

SEACORP COMMUNICATIONS INC (BC)
Recapitalized 04/07/1995
Recapitalized from Seacorp Capital Corp. to Seacorp Communications Inc. 04/07/1995
Each share old Common no par exchanged for (0.2) share new Common no par
Cease trade order effective 10/30/1995
Stockholders' equity unlikely

SEACORP PPTYS INC (BC)
Cease trade order effective 04/17/1996
Stockholders' equity unlikely

SEACREST DEV CORP (BC)
Recapitalized as Norzan Enterprises Ltd. 3/18/2004

FINANCIAL INFORMATION, INC. SEA-SEA

Each share Common no par exchanged for (0.1) share Common no par

SEACREST INDS CORP (DE)
Recapitalized as Availent Financial, Inc. 1/14/2003
Each share Common 1¢ par exchanged for (0.1) share Common 1¢ par

SEACUBE CONTAINER LEASING LTD (BERMUDA)
Issue Information - 9,500,000 shares COM offered at $10 per share on 10/27/2010
Acquired by 2357575 Ontario Ltd. 04/24/2013
Each share Common 1¢ par exchanged for $23 cash

SEADRIFT INTL EXPL LTD (AB)
Merged into Deak International Resources Corp. 12/30/88
Each share Common no par exchanged for (0.5) share Common no par
Deak International Resources Corp. name changed to Deak Resources Corp. 3/27/89 which name changed to AJ Perron Gold Corp. 10/7/94
(See AJ Perron Gold Corp.)

SEADRIFT RES LTD (BC)
Recapitalized as Pacific Seadrift Resources Ltd. (BC) 8/13/80
Each share Common no par exchanged for (0.5) share Common no par
Pacific Seadrift Resources Ltd. (BC) reincorporated in Alberta 6/3/82 which recapitalized as Seadrift International Exploration Ltd. 6/1/85 which merged into Deak International Resources Corp. 12/30/88 which name changed to Deak Resources Corp. 3/27/89 which name changed to AJ Perron Gold Corp. 10/7/94
(See AJ Perron Gold Corp.)

SEADRILL LTD OLD (BERMUDA)
Plan of reorganization under Chapter 11 Federal Bankruptcy proceedings effective 07/02/2018
Each share Common $2 par received (0.00373455) share Seadrill Ltd. (New) Common 10¢ par

SEAENA INC (NV)
SEC revoked common stock registration 08/15/2011

SEAFARER EXPL CORP (DE)
Reincorporated under the laws of Florida 07/05/2011

SEAFERRO INC (FL)
Placed in receivership in January, 1974

SEAFIELD CAP CORP (MO)
Each share Common $1 par received distribution of (0.25) share SLH Corp. Common 1¢ par payable 03/03/1997 to holders of record 02/24/1997
Each share Common $1 par received distribution of (1.2447625) shares Response Oncology Inc. Common $1 par payable 07/25/1997 to holders record 07/11/1997
Name changed to Lab Holdings, Inc. 10/20/1997
Lab Holdings, Inc. merged into LabOne, Inc. (New) 08/10/1999
(See LabOne, Inc. (New))

SEAFIRST CORP (WA)
Each share Common $5 par received distribution of (1) additional share 07/26/1974
Common $5 par split (3) for (2) by issuance of (0.5) additional share 05/25/1978
Merged into BankAmerica Corp. (Old) 07/01/1983
Each share Common $5 par exchanged for (0.3074) share

Special Ser. Preferred no par and $7.6849 cash
BankAmerica Corp. (Old) merged into BankAmerica Corp. (New) 09/30/1998 which name changed to Bank of America Corp. 04/28/1999

SEAFOOD HARVEST GROUP INC (FL)
Name changed to Vision Media Technologies, Inc. 03/17/2004
Vision Media Technologies, Inc. recapitalized as ASF Group, Inc. (FL) 08/01/2008 which reincorporated in Georgia as American Seniors Association Holding Group, Inc. 04/28/2010

SEAFOOD HOLDING CORP. LIQUIDATING TRUST (VA)
Liquidation completed
Each share Common 20¢ par received second distribution of $0.40 cash 10/23/81
Each share Common 20¢ par exchanged for third and final distribution of $0.24628 cash 6/1/84

SEAFOOD HLDG CORP (VA)
In process of liquidation
Each share Common 20¢ par received initial distribution of $4.67 cash 08/15/1980
Assets transferred to Seafood Holding Corp. Liquidating Trust 01/02/1981
(See Seafood Holding Corp. Liquidating Trust)

SEAFOOD INC (LA)
Charter revoked for failure to file annual reports 5/15/98

SEAFOODS FROM ALASKA INC (AK)
Charter dissolved for failure to pay taxes and file reports 9/8/92

SEAFOODS PLUS LTD (DE)
Reincorporated 08/14/1998
Each share old Common $0.001 par exchanged for (0.06184291) share new Common $0.001 par 09/18/1995
Each share new Common $0.001 par exchanged again for (0.28571428) share new Common $0.001 par 06/10/1998
State of incorporation changed from (UT) to (DE) 08/14/1998
Name changed to Cadapult Graphic Systems, Inc. 09/10/1998
Cadapult Graphic Systems, Inc. name changed to Media Sciences International, Inc. 04/29/2002
(See Media Sciences International, Inc.)

SEAFORD MAR MARINA INC (NY)
Completely liquidated 09/13/1971
Each share Common 10¢ par exchanged for first and final distribution of $0.60 cash

SEAFORD RESEARCH CORP. (NY)
Charter cancelled and proclaimed dissolved for failure to pay taxes and file reports 12/13/71

SEAFORD VENTURES, INC. (DE)
Name changed to Advanced Media Inc. 08/20/1993
Advanced Media Inc. name changed to Advanced Media Training, Inc. 08/10/2004 which name changed to Dematco, Inc. 02/07/2007
(See Dematco, Inc.)

SEAFORTH MINES LTD (BC)
Merged into Quinterra Resources Inc. 7/21/82
Each share Common 50¢ par exchanged for (0.325) share Class B Common no par
Quniterra Resources Inc. merged into Emtech Technology Corp. 8/16/93 which reorganized as Emtech Ltd. (Bermuda) 7/18/94

SEAGATE TECHNOLOGY (CAYMAN ISLANDS)
Reincorporated under the laws of Ireland as Seagate Technology PLC and Common $0.00001 par reclassified as Ordinary $0.00001 par 07/06/2010

SEAGATE TECHNOLOGY (DE)
Reincorporated 02/00/1987
Common no par split (2) for (1) by issuance of (1) additional share 06/09/1983
State of incorporation changed from (CA) to (DE) and Common no par changed to 1¢ par 02/00/1987
Common 1¢ par split (2) for (1) by issuance of (1) additional share payable 11/26/1996 to holders of record 11/11/1996 Ex date - 11/27/1996
Common 144A 1¢ par reclassified as Common 1¢ par 12/16/1996
Merged into Veritas Software Corp. 11/22/2000
Each share Common 1¢ par exchanged for (0.4465) share Common 1¢ par and $8.55 cash
Each share Common 1¢ par received first distribution of $0.04291 cash from escrow 08/22/2001
Each share Common 1¢ par received second distribution of $0.206 cash from escrow 08/25/2001
Each share Common 1¢ par received third distribution of $0.13270419 cash from escrow 09/18/2001
Each share Common 1¢ par received fourth distribution of $0.07444075 cash from escrow 11/02/2001
Each share Common 1¢ par received fifth distribution of $0.06939101 cash from escrow 02/15/2002
Each share Common 1¢ par received sixth distribution of $0.00048117 cash from escrow 05/07/2002
Each share Common 1¢ par received seventh distribution of $0.02449 cash from escrow 02/10/2004
Each share Common 1¢ par received eighth distribution of $1.1717 cash from escrow 04/08/2004
Each share Common 1¢ par received ninth distribution of $0.65783 cash from escrow 10/06/2004
Each share Common 1¢ par received tenth distribution of $0.04898 cash from escrow 05/12/2005
Each share Common 1¢ par received eleventh distribution of $0.06123 cash from escrow 12/20/2005
Each share Common 1¢ par received twelfth distribution of $0.05714536 cash from escrow 05/18/2006
Each share Common 1¢ par received thirteenth distribution of $0.025 cash from escrow 11/15/2007
Each share Common 1¢ par received fourteenth and final distribution of $0.1020456 cash from escrow 09/21/2009
Veritas Software Corp. merged into Symantec Corp. 07/02/2005

SEAGO GROUP INC (DE)
Plan of reorganization under Chapter 11 Bankruptcy Code effective 12/28/1994
Each share 8% Conv. Preferred $40 par exchanged for $0.10 cash
Each share Common 10¢ par exchanged for $0.01 cash

SEAGRAM (JOSEPH E.) & SONS LTD.
Merged into Distillers Corp.-Seagrams Ltd. 00/00/1928
Details not available

SEAGRAM LTD (CANADA)
Common no par split (3) for (1) by issuance of (2) additional shares 03/28/1983
Common no par split (4) for (1) by issuance of (3) additional shares 06/10/1992
Merged into Vivendi Universal 12/08/2000
Each share Common no par exchanged for (0.8) Sponsored ADR for Ordinary
Vivendi Universal name changed to Vivendi 04/24/2006
(See Vivendi)

SEAGRAVE CORP (DE)
Reincorporated 6/30/65
6% Preferred $100 par changed to 5% Preferred $100 par in 1936
Common no par changed to $5 par in 1942
Common $5 par changed to $2.50 par and (1) additional share issued 6/21/63
State of incorporation changed from (MI) to (DE) 6/30/65
5% Conv Preferred $100 par called for redemption 6/27/66
Stock Dividend - 15% 7/15/68
Name changed to Vista Resources, Inc. 9/30/80
Vista Resources, Inc. name changed to Fuqua Enterprises, Inc. 9/8/95 which merged into Graham-Field Health Products Inc. 12/30/97
(See Graham-Field Health Products Inc.)

SEAGULL BOOK & TAPE INC (NV)
Each share old Common $0.001 par exchanged for (0.05) share new Common $0.001 par 11/11/97
Acquired by Deseret Book 12/28/2006
Each share new Common $0.001 par exchanged for approximately $2.77 cash

SEAGULL ENERGY CORP (TX)
$2.25 Conv. Exchangeable Preferred Ser. A $1 par called for redemption 03/09/1990
Common 10¢ par split (2) for (1) by issuance of (1) additional share 06/04/1993
Under plan of merger name changed to Ocean Energy, Inc. (TX) 03/30/1999
Ocean Energy, Inc. (TX) reincorporated in Delaware 05/09/2001 which merged into Devon Energy Corp. 04/25/2003

SEAGULL INDS INC (UT)
Proclaimed dissolved for failure to pay taxes 12/31/82

SEAGULL PIPELINE CORP (TX)
Name changed to Seagull Energy Corp. 05/17/1983
Seagull Energy Corp. name changed to Ocean Energy, Inc. (TX) 03/30/1999 which reincorporated in Delaware 05/09/2001 which merged into Devon Energy Corp. 04/25/2003

SEAGULL RES LTD (AB)
Under plan of merger each share old Common no par exchanged for (1) share new Common no par 10/31/80
Struck off register for failure to file annual reports 4/1/91

SEAGULL URANIUM CO (UT)
Name changed to Seagull Industries Inc. 8/20/68
(See Seagull Industries Inc.)

SEAHAVN CORP (NV)
Recapitalized as China Travel Resort Holdings, Inc. 10/01/2009
Each share Common $0.001 par exchanged for (0.0025) share Common $0.001 par

SEAHAWK CAP CORP (NJ)
Each share Common no par exchanged for (0.01) share Common $0.0001 par 03/05/1996
Name changed to Dynamicweb Enterprises Inc. 05/14/1996
Dynamicweb Enterprises Inc. name changed to eB2B Commerce, Inc. 04/18/2000 which reorganized as Mediavest, Inc. (NJ) 02/08/2005 which reincorporated in Delaware as Mandalay Media, Inc. 11/21/2007 which name changed to NeuMedia, Inc. 06/21/2010 which name

changed to Mandalay Digital Group, Inc. 02/28/2012 which name changed to Digital Turbine, Inc. 01/20/2015

SEAHAWK DEEP OCEAN TECHNOLOGY INC (CO)
Each share old Common no par exchanged for (0.02) share new Common no par 6/15/92
Administratively dissolved 7/1/2003

SEAHAWK DRILLING INC (DE)
Under Chapter 11 plan of reorganization each share Common 1¢ par exchanged for (0.0461408) share Hercules Offshore, Inc. Common 1¢ par payable 02/12/2013 to holders of record 12/28/2012
Note: Distribution was not made to holders of fewer than (21) shares
Unexchanged certificates were cancelled and became without value 02/12/2014

SEAHAWK INC (NV)
Each share old Common $0.001 par exchanged for (0.5) share new Common $0.001 par 11/25/91
Each share new Common $0.001 par exchanged for (0.25) share Common 1¢ par 1/25/94
Charter revoked for failure to file reports and pay fees 9/1/96

SEAHAWK MINERALS LTD (YT)
Delisted from Toronto Venture Stock Exchange 06/20/2003

SEAHAWK OIL & GAS LTD (BC)
Merged into Artesian Petroleum Corp. 03/31/1981
Each share Capital Stock no par exchanged for (0.33333333) share Common no par
(See Artesian Petroleum Corp.)

SEAHAWK OIL INTL INC (NJ)
Name changed to Seahawk Capital Corp. 11/28/1989
Seahawk Capital Corp. name changed to Dynamicweb Enterprises Inc. 05/14/1996 which name changed to eB2B Commerce, Inc. 04/18/2000 which reorganized as Mediavest, Inc. (NJ) 02/08/2005 which reincorporated in Delaware as Mandalay Media, Inc. 11/21/2007 which name changed to NeuMedia, Inc. 06/21/2010 which name changed to Mandalay Digital Group, Inc. 02/28/2012 which name changed to Digital Turbine, Inc. 01/20/2015

SEAHAWK OVERSEAS EXPL CORP (CA)
Reincorporated under the laws of Texas as American Energy Services Inc. 01/02/1996
(See American Energy Services Inc.)

SEAIR GROUP INC (NV)
Each share old Class A Common $0.001 par exchanged for (0.14285714) share new Class A Common $0.001 par 03/17/2000
Name changed to Gourmet Group, Inc. (NV) 09/18/2000
Gourmet Group, Inc. (NV) reorganized in Delaware as Drinks Americas Holdings, Ltd. 06/02/2005

SEAL ACCEPTANCE CORP. (DE)
Dissolved 11/28/41

SEAL BEACH OIL COMPANY (CA)
Charter suspended by order of the franchise tax board 3/8/32

SEAL COVE CORP (AB)
Struck from the register 1/1/93

SEAL FLEET INC (NV)
Reorganized under the laws of Delaware as Seal Holdings Corp. 6/30/97
Each share Class A Common 10¢ par exchanged for (0.5) share Class A Common 20¢ par to reflect a (1) for (50) reverse split and a (25) for (1) forward split
Note: Holders of (50) or fewer pre-split shares received $0.70 cash per share
Seal Holdings Corp. name changed to Le@p Technology, Inc. 7/6/2000

SEAL HLDGS CORP (DE)
Name changed to Le@p Technology, Inc. 7/6/2000

SEAL INC (DE)
Acquired by Bunzel U.S.A. 04/12/1988
Each share Common 10¢ par exchanged for $12 cash

SEAL-PEEL, INC. (NY)
Charter cancelled and proclaimed dissolved for non-payment of taxes 12/15/61

SEALANDER, INC. (MD)
Charter revoked for failure to file reports and pay fees 11/27/63

SEALANT SOLUTIONS INC (DE)
Each share old Common 1¢ par exchanged for (0.02) share new Common 1¢ par 12/26/2002
Name changed to PowerChannel, Inc. 07/28/2003
PowerChannel, Inc. recapitalized as Qualibou Energy Inc. 02/05/2008

SEALCONES, INC.
Name changed to Seco Holding Co. in 1932 which was dissolved in 1934

SEALCRAFT CORP (UT)
Recapitalized as Basic American Corp. 06/05/1973
Each share Common 25¢ par exchanged for (0.05) share Common $5 par
Basic American Corp. merged into Dynamic American Corp. 12/21/1982
(See Dynamic American Corp.)

SEALECTRO CORP (NY)
Common 25¢ par split (5) for (4) by issuance of (0.25) additional share 7/15/80
Common 25¢ par split (2) for (1) by issuance of (1) additional share 7/15/81
Stock Dividend - 10% 7/16/79
Merged into BICC Ltd. 11/24/81
Each share Common 25¢ par exchanged for $23.75 cash

SEALED AIR CORP (DE)
Reincorporated 6/24/69
State of incorporation changed from (NJ) to (DE) 6/24/69
Common 1¢ par split (2) for (1) by issuance of (1) additional share 9/16/83
Common 1¢ par split (2) for (1) by issuance of (1) additional share 9/18/92
Common 1¢ par split (2) for (1) by issuance of (1) additional share 9/29/95
Under plan of merger name changed to Sealed Air Corp. (New) 3/31/98
(See exch. of Chavannes Industrial Synthetics, Inc. 7/26/66)

SEALED AIR CORP NEW (DE)
$2 Conv. Preferred Ser. A 10¢ par called for redemption at $51 on 7/18/2003
(Additional Information in Active)

SEALED CONTAINERS CORP. OF AMERICA
Dissolved in 1946
No stockholders' equity

SEALED PWR CORP (DE)
Reincorporated 04/30/1968
Common $10 par split (3) for (2) by issuance of (0.5) additional share 12/03/1964
State of incorporation changed from (MI) to (DE) 04/30/1968
Common $10 par split (3) for (2) by issuance of (0.5) additional share 06/30/1972
Common $10 par split (5) for (4) by issuance of (0.25) additional share 09/17/1976
Common $10 par split (2) for (1) by issuance of (1) additional share 07/05/1983
Stock Dividends - 10% 12/28/1956; 10% 12/27/1957; 10% 12/28/1959; 10% 12/28/1961; 10% 12/27/1962; 10% 12/27/1963; 10% 01/04/1966; 10% 08/07/1968; 10% 08/06/1969; 10% 09/17/1973
Name changed to SPX Corp. 04/27/1988

SEALIFE CORP (DE)
Reincorporated under the laws of Nevada 10/06/2016

SEALOL, INC. (RI)
Common 5¢ par changed to $1 par 9/21/64
Merged into EG&G, Inc. 10/15/68
Each share 6% Conv. Preferred $100 par exchanged for (2) shares $4 Conv. Preferred Ser. A $1 par and (14) shares Common $1 par
Each share Common $1 par exchanged for (0.05) share $4 Conv. Preferred Ser. A $1 par and (0.35) share Common $1 par
EG&G, Inc. name changed to PerkinElmer, Inc. 10/25/99

SEALOL CORP. (RI)
Each share Common 5¢ par exchanged for (1) share 6% Conv. Preferred $100 par 11/30/55
$5 Preferred called for redemption 11/30/55
Name changed to Sealol, Inc. in 1960
Sealol, Inc. merged into EG&G, Inc. 10/15/68 which name changed to PerkinElmer, Inc. 10/25/99

SEALRIGHT INC (DE)
Common 10¢ par split (3) for (2) by issuance of (0.5) additional share 11/15/89
Each share Common 10¢ par received distribution of (0.5) share JPS Packaging Co. Common $0.001 par payable 6/30/98 to holders of record 6/10/98
Merged into Huhtamaki Oy 7/1/98
Each share Common 10¢ par exchanged for $11 cash

SEALRIGHT-OSWEGO FALLS CORP. (NY)
Common $5 par split (3) for (2) by issuance of (0.5) additional share 2/15/63
Acquired by Phillips Petroleum Co. on a (0.6) for (1) basis 10/15/64
Phillips Petroleum Co. name changed to ConocoPhillips 8/30/2002

SEALY CORP (DE)
Merged into Sandman Merger Corp. 12/18/1997
Each share Class B Common 10¢ par exchanged for $14.3027 cash offered at $16 per share on 04/06/2006
Acquired by Tempur-Pedic International Inc. 03/18/2013
Each share Common 1¢ par exchanged for $2.20 cash

SEALY HLDGS INC (DE)
Name changed to Sealy Corp. 11/06/1991
(See Sealy Corp.)

SEAMAN FURNITURE INC (DE)
Old Common 1¢ par split (2) for (1) by issuance of (1) additional share 04/10/1987
Acquired by SFC Acquisition Corp. 02/25/1988
Each share old Common 1¢ par exchanged for $26 principal amount of 15% Jr. Subordinated Debentures due 02/25/1999
Chapter 11 Federal Bankruptcy proceedings effective 10/31/1992
No old Common stockholders' equity
Merged into SFC Merger Co. 12/23/1997
Each new share Common 1¢ par exchanged for $25.05 cash

SEAMAN KENT CO. LTD.
Reorganized as Seaman Kent Co. in 1934, which company was liquidated

SEAMAN TECHNOLOGIES INC (CO)
Name changed to Demac Investments Inc. 03/02/1992
Demac Investments Inc. recapitalized as Reliance Lodging, Inc. 02/05/1993
(See Reliance Lodging, Inc.)

SEAMARK ASSET MGMT LTD (CANADA)
Merged into Matrix Asset Management Inc. 01/15/2010
Each share Common no par exchanged for (1) share Common no par
(See Matrix Asset Management Inc.)

SEAMED CORP (WA)
Issue Information - 1,850,000 shares COM offered at $11 per share on 11/18/1996
Merged into Plexus Corp. 07/23/1999
Each share Common no par exchanged for (0.4) share Common 1¢ par

SEAMENS CAP CORP (DE)
Short Term Auction Rate Preferred no par called for redemption 08/17/1988

SEAMENS CORP (DE)
Plan of liquidation and dissolution approved 9/1/90
No stockholders' equity

SEAMENS FIN INC (DE)
Dutch Auction Rate Transferable Securities Preferred no par called for redemption 07/13/1988

SEAMILES LTD (ON)
Name changed to Intellectual Capital Group Ltd. 04/03/2012

SEAMLESS CORP (NV)
Name changed 08/21/2008
Each share old Common $0.001 par received distribution of (0.00005) share 1st Global Financial Corp. Restricted Common $0.001 par payable 09/14/2007 to holders of record 09/07/2007
Note: Holders of (19,999) or fewer shares received cash equal to 10% of their holdings based upon shares closing price 09/07/2007
Each share old Common $0.001 par exchanged for (0.001) share new Common $0.001 par 02/15/2008
Name changed from Seamless Wi-Fi, Inc. to Seamless Corp. 08/21/2008
Reincorporated under the laws of Florida as GDT TEK, Inc. 11/25/2009
(See GDT TEK, Inc.)

SEAMOUNT CORP (DE)
Common $1 par changed to 33-1/3¢ par and (2) additional shares issued 08/12/1970
Charter cancelled and declared inoperative and void for non-payment of taxes 03/01/1974

SEANERGY MARITIME CORP (MARSHALL ISLANDS)
Issue Information - 22,000,000 UNITS consisting of (1) share COM and (1) WT offered at $10 per Unit on 09/24/2007
Units separated 10/15/2008
Name changed to Seanergy Maritime Holdings Corp. 01/27/2009

SEANESS CAP CORP (BC)
Name changed to Intigold Mines Ltd. 11/04/2010

SEAOSPA INC (NV)
Common $0.0001 par split (3) for (1) by issuance of (2) additional shares

payable 03/29/2010 to holders of record 03/29/2010
Name changed to Thwapr, Inc. 04/21/2010

SEAPORCEL, INC. (DE)
Name changed to Investment Property Builders, Inc. 11/16/62
Investment Property Builders, Inc. name changed to Centree Corp. 10/5/72 which name changed to Air Florida System, Inc. 12/26/73 which name changed to Jet Florida System, Inc. 8/15/85
(See Jet Florida System, Inc.)

SEAPORCEL METALS, INC. (DE)
Under plan of merger name changed to Seaporcel, Inc. 2/2/62
Seaporcel, Inc. name changed to Investment Property Builders, Inc. 11/16/62 which name changed to Centree Corp. 10/5/72 which name changed to Air Florida System, Inc. 12/26/73 which name changed to Jet Florida System, Inc. 8/15/85
(See Jet Florida System, Inc.)

SEAPORT BANCORP, INC. (ID)
Ceased operations 02/23/1986
Details not available

SEAPORT CORP (DE)
Charter cancelled and declared inoperative and void for non-payment of taxes 3/1/94

SEAQUEST ENERGY LTD (AB)
Reincorporated 07/23/1984
Place of incorporation changed from (BC) to (ALTA) 07/23/1984
Recapitalized as Alta Petroleum Ltd. 01/13/1987
Each share Common no par exchanged for (0.1) share Common no par
Alta Petroleum Ltd. merged into CanEuro Resources Ltd. 04/04/1989 which merged into Attock Oil Corp. 02/04/1991 which recapitalized as Attock Energy Corp. 08/02/1995
(See Attock Energy Corp.)

SEARAY OILS LTD (BC)
Recapitalized as Mega-Dyne Industrial Corp. 08/21/1986
Each share Common no par exchanged for (0.25) share Common no par
Mega-Dyne Industrial Corp. recapitalized as International Mega-Dyne Industrial Corp. 11/08/1989 which name changed to ESC Envirotech Systems Corp. 07/12/1991 which recapitalized as SWI Steelworks Inc. 03/29/1999
(See SWI Steelworks Inc.)

SEARCH BY HEADLINES COM CORP (NV)
Name changed to Naked Brand Group Inc. 08/30/2012
Naked Brand Group Inc. merged into Naked Brand Group Ltd. 06/20/2018

SEARCH CAP GROUP INC (MN)
Each share old Conv. Preferred 1¢ par exchanged for (0.125) share new Conv. Preferred 1¢ par 11/22/96
Each share old Common 2¢ par exchanged for (0.125) share new Common 2¢ par 11/22/96
Name changed to Search Financial Services Inc. 5/16/97
(See Search Financial Services Inc.)

SEARCH CAP INC (BC)
Name changed to Search Minerals Inc. 10/27/2008

SEARCH ENERGY CORP (AB)
Merged into Advantage Energy Income Fund 05/24/2001
Each share Common no par exchanged for (0.25) Trust Unit no par
Advantage Energy Income Fund reorganized as Advantage Oil & Gas Ltd. 07/09/2009

SEARCH ENERGY INC (NS)
Merged into Search Energy Corp. 01/09/1997
Each share Common no par exchanged for (1) share Common no par
Search Energy Corp. merged into Advantage Energy Income Fund 05/24/2001 which reorganized as Advantage Oil & Gas Ltd. 07/09/2009

SEARCH EXPL INC (CO)
Each share Common $0.001 exchanged for (1) share Common 5¢ par to reflect a (1) for (100) reverse split followed by a (100) for (1) forward split 6/13/91
Note: Holdings of (99) shares or fewer exchanged for cash
Merged into Harken Energy Corp. 5/22/95
Each share Common 5¢ par exchanged for (0.4453) share Common 1¢ par
Harken Energy Corp. recapitalized as HKN, Inc. 6/6/2007

SEARCH FINL SVCS INC (MN)
Plan of reorganization under Chapter 11 Federal Bankruptcy Code effective November 1998
No stockholders' equity

SEARCH INC (DE)
Charter forfeited for failure to maintain a resident agent 06/07/1976

SEARCH INC (UT)
Recapitalized as Western Associated Enterprises, Inc. 03/22/1972
Each share Common 5¢ par exchanged for (0.1) share Common 50¢ par
Western Associated Enterprises, Inc. name changed to WestAm Corp. 04/24/1972 which name changed to Holiday Industries 07/19/1976
(See Holiday Industries)

SEARCH INVTS CORP (DE)
Reincorporated 4/30/70
Stock Dividends - 10% 12/28/56; 10% 12/27/57; 10% 12/28/59; 10% 12/28/61; 10% 12/27/62; 10% 12/27/63; 10% 1/4/66
State of incorporation changed from (MN) to (DE) 4/30/70
Merged into MEI Corp. 2/18/77
Each share Common 10¢ par exchanged for (0.7) share Common 10¢ par
(See MEI Corp.)

SEARCH NAT RES INC (MN)
Each share old Common 2¢ par exchanged for (0.1) share new Common 2¢ par 1/5/87
Name changed to Search Capital Group Inc. 8/25/92
Search Capital Group Inc. name changed to Search Financial Services Inc. 5/16/97
(See Search Financial Services Inc.)

SEARCHCORE INC (NV)
Name changed to Wisdom Homes of America, Inc. 03/05/2015

SEARCHHELP INC (DE)
Name changed to Echo Metrix, Inc. 06/17/2009
Echo Metrix, Inc. name changed to ProText Mobility, Inc. 12/31/2010

SEARCHHOUND COM INC (DE)
Each (67) shares old Common $0.0001 par exchanged for (1) share new Common $0.0001 par 12/30/2002
Recapitalized as Coach Industries Group, Inc. 08/25/2003
Each share new Common $0.0001 par exchanged for (0.25) share Common $0.0001 par
(See Coach Industries Group, Inc.)

SEARCHLIGHT CAPITAL CORP (BC)
Issue Information - 1,500,000 shares COM offered at $0.20 per share on 08/27/2010
Name changed to LED Medical Diagnostics Inc. 11/24/2011

SEARCHLIGHT GOLD EXTRACTION CO. (AZ)
Charter forfeited 7/12/27

SEARCHMEDIA HOLDINGS LTD (CAYMAN ISLANDS)
Name changed to Tiger Media, Inc. (Cayman Islands) 12/18/2012
Tiger Media, Inc. (Cayman Islands) reorganized in Delaware 03/20/2015 which name changed to IDI, Inc. 05/04/2015 which name changed to Cogint, Inc. 09/26/2016 which name changed to Fluent, Inc. 04/16/2018

SEARCHTECH VENTURES INC (ON)
Recapitalized as PharmaCan Capital Corp. 12/17/2014
Each share Common no par exchanged for (0.14285714) share Common no par
PharmaCan Capital Corp. name changed to Cronos Group Inc. 03/01/2017

SEARDEL INVT LTD (SOUTH AFRICA)
ADR agreement terminated 03/03/2016
No ADR's remain outstanding

SEARLE G D & CO. (DE)
Reorganized 12/31/55
Common $5 par split (2) for (1) by issuance of (1) additional share 6/29/51
Reorganized from (IL) to under the laws of (DE) 12/31/55
Each share Common $5 par exchanged for (3) shares Common $2 par
Common $2 par changed to $1 par and (2) additional shares issued 12/30/63
Conv. Preferred $1 par called for redemption 3/30/73
Common $1 par changed to 33-1/3¢ par and (2) additional shares issued 6/4/73
Merged into Monsanto Co. 10/1/85
Each share Common 33-1/3¢ par exchanged for $65 cash

SEARS BK & TR CO (CHICAGO, IL)
Capital Stock $25 par changed to $10 par and (1.5) additional shares issued 1/21/64
Each share Capital Stock $10 par exchanged for (2) shares Capital Stock $5 par 12/1/72
Stock Dividends - 16-2/3% 6/30/58; 25% 4/25/66
Under plan of reorganization each share Capital Stock $5 par automatically became (1) share Midland Bancorp, Inc. Common $5 par 1/2/76
Midland Bancorp, Inc. name changed to Unibancorp, Inc. 4/25/84 which was acquired by Old Kent Financial Corp. 10/18/88 which merged into Fifth Third Bancorp 4/2/2001

SEARS-COMMUNITY STATE BANK (CHICAGO, IL)
Stock Dividends - 100% 12/31/46; 25% 6/30/52; 20% 6/29/56
Name changed to Sears Bank & Trust Co. (Chicago, IL) 1/18/57
Sears Bank & Trust Co. (Chicago, IL) reorganized as Midland Bancorp, Inc. 1/2/76 which name changed to Unibancorp, Inc. 4/25/84 which was acquired by Old Kent Financial Corp. 10/18/88 which merged into Fifth Third Bancorp 4/2/2001

SEARS EQUITY INVT TR (NY)
Trust terminated 3/1/89
Each (10,000) or more Strategic Series 1 Units of Undivided Int. had option to exchange for either distribution in kind or cash
Each (9,999) or fewer Units of Undivided Int. exchanged for cash
Each (10,000) or more Strategic Series 2 Units of Undivided Int. had option to exchange for either distribution in kind or cash
Each (9,999) or fewer Units of Undivided Int. exchanged for cash

SEARS INDS INC (MD)
Merged into Sears Holdings Ltd. 03/26/1981
Each share Common $1.66-2/3 par exchanged for $10 cash

SEARS LEATHERETTE CO., INC. (MA)
Name changed to Rose-Webb Leatherette Co., Inc. 6/24/27
(See Rose-Webb Leatherette Co., Inc.)

SEARS PLC (ENGLAND)
Name changed 08/01/1985
ADR's for A Ordinary 5s par changed to 25p par per currency change 02/15/1971
Name changed from Sears Holdings PLC to Sears PLC 08/01/1985
Each old ADR for A Ordinary 25p par exchanged for (0.1) new ADR for Ordinary 25p par 08/12/1998
ADR agreement terminated 06/07/1999
Each new ADR for Ordinary 25p par exchanged for $5.66 cash

SEARS POINT INTL RACEWAY INC (CA)
Completely liquidated 07/23/1969
Each share Common $10 par exchanged for first and final distribution of (0.714265) share Filmways, Inc. (DE) Common 25¢ par
Filmways, Inc. (DE) name changed to Orion Pictures Corp. 07/30/1982 which merged into Metromedia International Group, Inc. 11/01/1995
(See Metromedia International Group, Inc.)

SEARS (DAVID) REAL ESTATE TRUST (MA)
Completely liquidated 12/30/66
Each Share of Bene. Int. $10 par exchanged for first and final distribution of (1) Real Estate Investment Trust of America Ctf. of Bene. Int. $1 par
(See Real Estate Investment Trust of America)

SEARS ROEBUCK & CO (NY)
Each share Capital Stock $100 par exchanged for (4) shares Capital Stock no par 03/24/1926
Capital Stock no par changed to Common $3 par and (2) additional shares issued 12/16/1955
Common $3 par changed to $1.50 par and (1) additional share issued 03/22/1965
Common $1.50 par changed to 75¢ par and (1) additional share issued 07/15/1977
Adjustable Rate Preferred 1st Ser. $1 par called for redemption 05/15/1987
8.88% Depositary Preferred called for redemption at $25 on 11/12/1996
8.88% Preferred 1st Ser. $1 par called for redemption 11/12/1996
Each Mandatorily Exchangeable Depositary Preferred Ser. A exchanged for (1.240799) shares Common 75¢ par and $0.8325 cash 03/20/1995
Merged into Sears Holdings Corp. 03/24/2005
Each share Common 75¢ par exchanged for either (0.31475) share Common 1¢ par and $18.525 cash or $50 cash
Note: Option to receive stock and cash expired 03/24/2005

SEARS TAX EXEMPT INVT TR (NY)
Name changed to Dean Witter Select Municipal Trust 11/29/93

SEASHORE ORGANIC MARIJUANA CORP (BC)
Name changed to Seashore Organic Medicine Inc. 09/03/2014
Seashore Organic Medicine Inc. name changed to Veritas Pharma Inc. 12/29/2015

SEASHORE ORGANIC MEDICINE INC (BC)
Name changed to Veritas Pharma Inc. 12/29/2015

SEASIDE EXPL INC (NV)
Name changed to Sky Petroleum, Inc. 04/06/2005

SEASIDE EXPL PARTNERS CORP (BC)
Name changed to DelphX Capital Markets Inc. 04/27/2018

SEASIDE SAVINGS & LOAN ASSOCIATION (CA)
Merged into Sun Savings & Loan Association 02/09/1983
Each share Guarantee Stock $8 par exchanged for (1) share Guarantee Stock $8 par
(See Sun Savings & Loan Association)

SEASON ALL INDS INC (DE)
Reincorporated 05/11/1973
Common $1 par split (3) for (2) by issuance of (0.5) additional share 06/28/1972
State of incorporation changed from (PA) to (DE) and Common $1 par changed to 10¢ par 05/11/1973
Stock Dividends - 50% 08/23/1976; 100% 08/31/1977
Merged into Redland Ltd. 05/04/1979
Each share Common 10¢ par exchanged for $14.75 cash

SEASONAL INDUSTRIES, INC. (DE)
Charter cancelled and declared inoperative and void for non-payment of taxes 3/1/78

SEASONED INVESTMENTS, INC.
Dissolved in 1938

SEASONED SECURITIES TRUST SHARES
Trust liquidated in 1931

SEASONS SVGS BK (RICHMOND, VA)
Placed in receivership 10/31/1989
Stockholders' equity unlikely

SEASPAN CORP (MARSHALL ISLANDS)
9.5% Perpetual Preferred Ser. C 1¢ par called for redemption at $25 plus $0.336458 accrued dividends on 06/20/2016
(Additional Information in Active)

SEASTAR RESOURCE CORP (BC)
Recapitalized as National Seastar Corp. (BC) 6/30/88
Each share Common no par exchanged for (0.2) share Common no par
National Seastar Corp. (BC) recapitalized as Pacific National Seafarms Ltd. (BC) 1/16/90 which reorganized in Delaware as Starbase Corp. 10/21/92
(See Starbase Corp.)

SEATAC RES INC (BC)
Name changed to Interbev Packaging Corp. 12/09/1986
(See Interbev Packaging Corp.)

SEATEX OIL CO., INC. (CA)
Charter revoked for failure to file reports and pay fees 11/1/66

SEATING, INC. (NC)
Voluntarily dissolved 1/28/77
Details not available

SEATON GROUP INC (DE)
Each (18.65) shares old Common $0.001 par exchanged for (1) share new Common $0.001 par 11/24/97
Name changed to United Information Systems Inc. 12/5/97
(See United Information Systems Inc.)

SEATRAIN LINES INC (DE)
Each share old Class A Common no par exchanged for (20) shares new Class A Common no par in 1942
Each share new Class A Common no par exchanged for (1) share Capital Stock $4 par in 1948
Capital Stock $4 par changed to $1 par 11/10/66
Capital Stock $1 par split (3) for (1) by issuance of (2) additional shares 5/23/69
Capital Stock $1 par reclassified as Common $1 par 11/21/78
Plan of reorganization effective 4/9/87
Each share Common $1 par exchanged for (0.25) Common Stock Purchase Warrant expiring 12/31/92
Stock Dividends - 50% 12/21/49; 33-1/3% 9/8/55
Company filed a petition under Chapter 7 of the Federal Bankruptcy Code 11/17/92
No stockholders' equity

SEATTLE BREWING & MALTING CO. (WA)
Name changed to Sicks' Seattle Brewing & Malting Co. in 1945
Sicks' Seattle Brewing & Malting Co. name changed to Sicks' Rainier Brewing Co. 4/17/57 which name changed to Rainier Companies, Inc. 4/20/70
(See Rainier Companies, Inc.)

SEATTLE FILMWORKS INC (WA)
Common 1¢ par split (3) for (2) by issuance of (0.5) additional share 02/26/1993
Common 1¢ par split (2) for (1) by issuance of (1) additional share 03/16/1994
Common 1¢ par split (3) for (2) by issuance of (0.5) additional share 03/15/1995
Common 1¢ par split (3) for (2) by issuance of (0.5) additional share payable 03/15/1996 to holders of record 03/01/1996
Common 1¢ par split (3) for (2) by issuance of (0.5) additional share payable 03/17/1997 to holders of record 03/03/1997
Name changed to PhotoWorks, Inc. 02/01/2000
(See PhotoWorks, Inc.)

SEATTLE 1ST NATL BK (SEATTLE, WA)
Common $20 par changed to $10 par and (1) additional share issued 09/01/1959
Stock Dividends - 11-1/9% 06/07/1944; 14-2/7% 08/30/1954; 12-1/2% 01/17/1956; 25% 09/01/1959; 50% 02/21/1968
Under plan of reorganization each share Common $10 par automatically became (1) share Seafirst Corp. Common $5 par 07/01/1974
Seafirst Corp. merged into BankAmerica Corp. (Old) 07/01/1983 which merged into BankAmerica Corp. (New) 09/30/1998 which name changed to Bank of America Corp. 04/28/1999

SEATTLE GAS CO. (WA)
Reorganized 00/00/1935
Each share Preferred $100 par exchanged for (0.5) share Common no par
Each (20) shares Common no par exchanged for (1) share new Common no par
Recapitalized 00/00/1947
Each share 1st Preferred no par exchanged for (5.5) shares Common $10 par
Each share 2nd Preferred no par exchanged for (0.1) share Common $10 par
Common no par cancelled
Common $10 par split (2) for (1) by issuance of (1) additional share 00/00/1954
Merged into Washington Natural Gas Co. (DE) share for share 11/01/1955
Washington Natural Gas Co. (DE) reorganized in Washington as Washington Energy Co. 08/09/1978 which merged into Puget Sound Energy, Inc. 02/10/1997 which reorganized as Puget Energy, Inc. 01/01/2001

SEATTLE HARDWARE CO. (WA)
Charter cancelled and proclaimed dissolved for failure to pay taxes 01/21/2003

SEATTLE LIGHTING CO.
Name changed to Seattle Gas Co. 00/00/1930
Seattle Gas Co. merged into Washington Natural Gas Co. (DE) 11/01/1955 which reorganized in Washington as Washington Energy Co. 08/09/1978 which merged into Puget Sound Energy, Inc. 02/10/1997 which reorganized as Puget Energy, Inc. 01/01/2001

SEATTLE PACIFIC SALES CO. (WA)
Merged into Lewis (Palmer G.) Co., Inc. 5/16/84
Each share Common $20 par exchanged for (11.637) share Common $1 par
(See Lewis (Palmer G.) Co., Inc.)

SEATTLE REALTY ASSOCIATION (DE)
Dissolved 9/27/55

SEATTLE STEAM CORP (WA)
Class A & B $100 par reclassified as Common $100 par 11/21/1958
Common $100 par changed to $20 par and (4) additional shares issued 11/29/1960
Stock Dividends - 100% 01/02/1959; 15% 04/30/1960
Merged into KPK Corp. 06/14/1972
Each share Common $20 par exchanged for $46 cash

SEATTLE SUPERSONICS CORP (WA)
Name changed to First Northwest Industries of America, Inc. 8/25/69
First Northwest Industries of America, Inc. reincorporated under the laws of New York as FNI Inc. 5/30/80 which merged into New Century Productions, Ltd. 3/11/85 which name changed to New Century Entertainment Corp. 7/3/86 which name changed to New Visions Entertainment Corp. 8/8/88
(See New Visions Entertainment Corp.)

SEATTLE-TOLEDO CO. LTD. (WA)
Charter cancelled and declared dissolved for failure to pay fees 7/1/65

SEATTLE TR & SVGS BK (SEATTLE, WA)
Each share Capital Stock $50 par exchanged for (2.5) shares Capital Stock $20 par 10/4/55
Capital Stock $20 par changed to $10 par and (1) additional share issued 1/22/59
Capital Stock $10 par changed to $20 par 3/13/75
Capital Stock $20 par split (3) for (2) by issuance of (0.5) additional share 5/1/78
Capital Stock $20 par changed $14 par and (0.5) additional share issued 11/13/78
Stock Dividends -11-1/9% 12/6/51; 11-1/9% 7/27/54; 10% 2/10/61; 10% 1/16/62; 10% 2/3/64; 25% 6/15/77
Acquired by KeyCorp 7/20/87
Each share Capital Stock $14 par exchanged for $70 cash

SEATU EXPL LTD (BC)
Merged into Seagull Resources Ltd. 10/31/80
Each share Capital Stock no par exchanged for (0.2) share new Common no par
(See Seagull Resources Ltd.)

SEAVIEW, INC. (WA)
Charter cancelled and proclaimed dissolved for failure to pay fees 7/1/75

SEAVIEW ENERGY INC (AB)
Recapitalized as Charger Energy Corp. 03/08/2012
Each share Class A no par exchanged for (0.2) share Class A no par
Charger Energy Corp. merged into Spyglass Resources Corp. 04/04/2013

SEAVIEW INDUSTRIES, INC. (FL)
Reorganized as Corporation of Americas Ltd. 06/07/1965
Each share Common 10¢ par exchanged for (0.1) share Common 10¢ par
Note: Unexchanged certificates were cancelled and are without value
(See Corporation of Americas Ltd.)

SEAVIEW RES LTD (BC)
Struck off register and declared dissolved for failure to file returns 10/06/1995

SEAVIEW VIDEO TECHNOLOGY INC (NV)
Name changed 2/2/2000
Name changed from Seaview Underwater Research, Inc. to Seaview Video Technology, Inc. 2/2/2000
Name changed to Powerlinx, Inc. 12/10/2003

SEAWARD RES LTD (BC)
Recapitalized as Seaquest Energy Ltd. (BC) 9/10/82
Each share Common no par exchanged for (0.1) share Common no par
Seaquest Energy Ltd. (BC) reincorporated in Alberta 7/23/84 which recapitalized as Alta Petroleum Ltd. 1/13/87 which merged into CanEuro Resources Ltd. 4/4/89 which merged into Attock Oil Corp. 2/4/91 which recapitalized as Attock Energy Corp. 8/2/95
(See Attock Energy Corp.)

SEAWAY BASE METALS LTD (ON)
Recapitalized as Jetcom Inc. 10/31/95
Each share Common no par exchanged for (0.05) share Common no par

SEAWAY CONSTRUCTION CO., INC. (TX)
Completely liquidated 4/30/68

SEAWAY ENERGY SVCS INC (AB)
Each share old Common no par exchanged for (0.1) share new Common no par 03/21/2014
Reincorporated under the laws of British Columbia 08/15/2014

SEAWAY FINL CORP (MI)
Common $1 par split (3) for (2) by issuance of (0.5) additional share 6/1/89
Merged into Old Kent Financial Corp. 1/2/97
Each share Common $1 par exchanged for (1.1418) share Common $1 par
Old Kent Financial Corp. merged into Fifth Third Bancorp 4/2/2001

SEAWAY FOOD TOWN INC (OH)
Common no par split (4) for (3) by issuance of (0.33333333) additional share 11/27/1981
Common no par split (2) for (1) by

issuance of (1) additional share 11/04/1988
Common no par split (2) for (1) by issuance of (1) additional share payable 05/07/1997 to holders of record 04/22/1997
Common no par split (3) for (2) by issuance of (0.5) additional share payable 05/06/1998 to holders of record 04/21/1998
Stock Dividends - 50% 11/28/1975; 50% 12/01/1978
Merged into Spartan Stores Inc. 08/01/2000
Each share Common no par exchanged for (1) share Common no par and $5 cash
Spartan Stores Inc. name changed to SpartanNash Co. 05/29/2014

SEAWAY GAS & OIL LTD (QC)
Charter cancelled for failure to file annual reports 06/25/1977

SEAWAY HOTELS LTD (ON)
Name changed to Seaway Multi-Corp. Ltd. and Capital Stock no par reclassified as Common no par 12/20/68
(See Seaway Multi-Corp. Ltd.)

SEAWAY MTG CORP (CANADA)
Charter cancelled 3/29/85

SEAWAY MULTI CORP LTD (ON)
Delisted from Toronto Stock Exchange 5/19/88

SEAWAY NATIONAL BANK (WATERTOWN, NY)
Acquired by Norstar Bank of Upstate NY (Albany, NY) 12/20/1986
Details not available

SEAWAY SHOPPING CTRS INC (DE)
Each share 50¢ Conv. Preferred 1¢ par exchanged for (1.5) shares Class A Common 1¢ par 10/11/1967
Each share Class B-1 Common 1¢ par exchanged for (1) share Class A Common 1¢ par 07/17/1970
95% reacquired through purchase offer which expired 12/31/1971
Public interest eliminated

SEAWAY STEEL CORP. (NY)
Merged into Roblin-Seaway Industries, Inc. 04/06/1961
Each share Common exchanged for (1) share Common 10¢ par
Roblin-Seaway Industries, Inc. name changed to Roblin Steel Corp. 04/22/1964 which name changed to Roblin Industries, Inc. 04/17/1968
(See Roblin Industries, Inc.)

SEAWEST RES LTD (BC)
Recapitalized as Starfire Minerals Inc. 5/2/96
Each share Common no par exchanged for (0.2857412) share Common no par

SEAWIND RES INC (BC)
Delisted from Vancouver Stock Exchange 04/07/1986

SEAXE ENERGY CORP (DE)
Name changed to Hadson Europe Inc. 09/28/1987
Hadson Europe Inc. name changed to Midwest Energy Companies, Inc. 12/20/1991

SEBA EXPL LTD (AB)
Name changed to Camrex Resources Ltd. 01/22/1991
Camrex Resources Ltd. name changed to Crispin Energy Inc. 08/20/1996 which was acquired by Pengrowth Energy Trust 04/29/2005 which reorganized as Pengrowth Energy Corp. 01/03/2011

SEBASTIAN RIV HLDGS INC (FL)
Old Common $0.001 par split (4) for (1) by issuance of (3) additional shares payable 11/06/2006 to holders of record 10/31/2006 Ex date - 11/07/2006
Each share old Common $0.001 par exchanged for (0.00125) share new Common $0.001 par 04/10/2008
Recapitalized as Novacab International Inc. 11/12/2013
Each share new Common $0.001 par exchanged for (0.001) share Common $0.001 par
Novacab International Inc. name changed to Global Pole Trusion Group Corp. 07/24/2017

SEBERG TUNNEL & ROCK PLANING MACHINE CO. (AZ)
Charter expired by time limitation 5/29/34

SEBEWAING BREWING CO. (MI)
Each share old Common $1 par exchanged for (0.5) share new Common $1 par 06/15/1963
Name changed to Michigan Brewery, Inc. 05/26/1964 (Ctfs. dated prior to 05/25/1966)
(See Michigan Brewery, Inc. (Ctfs. dated prior to 05/25/1966))

SEBRING INDS INC (DE)
Charter cancelled and declared inoperative and void for non-payment of taxes 3/1/77

SEBRING RES LTD (AB)
Reincorporated under the laws of Canada as PharmaGap Inc. 04/23/2002
(See PharmaGap Inc.)

SEBRING SOFTWARE INC (NV)
Plan of reorganization under Chapter 11 Federal Bankruptcy proceedings effective 08/12/2016
Stockholders' equity unlikely

SEBRN CORP (FL)
Name changed to American Business Computers Corp. 10/3/86
American Business Computers Corp. name changed to ABC Dispensing Technologies, Inc. 5/1/96 which recapitalized as Ka Wang Holding, Inc. 3/21/2007

SECHURA INC (CANADA)
Under plan of recapitalization each share old Common no par exchanged for (1) share Class A Special Stock no par 04/25/1990
Class A Special Stock no par reclassified as new Common no par 02/09/1995
Reincorporated under the laws of Bermuda as Aaxis Ltd. 08/30/1996
Aaxis Ltd. was acquired by BHI Corp. 03/31/1998 which name changed to Carlisle Holdings Ltd. 06/02/1999 which name changed to BB Holdings Ltd. 08/18/2005
(See BB Holdings Ltd.)

SECMARK INC (UT)
Proclaimed dissolved for failure to pay taxes 01/01/1991

SECO CEMP LTD (CANADA)
7-1/4% 1st Preferred Ser. A $10 par called for redemption 05/15/1984
$2.25 Preference Ser. A no par called for redemption 07/15/1985
Variable Rate Preference Ser. B no par called for redemption 11/15/1986
$3.5625 Preference Ser. C no par called for redemption 11/16/1987
U.S. $3.22 Preference Ser. D no par called for redemption 11/18/1988
Public interest eliminated

SECO ELECTRONICS CORP. (MN)
Liquidation completed
Each share Common 10¢ par exchanged for initial distribution of (0.1) share Dana Corp. Common $1 par 08/15/1971
Each share Common 10¢ par received second distribution of (0.06) share Dana Corp. Common $1 par 07/16/1973
Each share Common 10¢ par received third distribution of (0.02) share Dana Corp. Common $1 par 06/05/1974
Each share Common 10¢ par received fourth and final distribution of (0.008) share Dana Corp. Common $1 par 09/16/1974
(See Dana Corp.)

SECO HOLDING CO.
Dissolved in 1934

SECO LIFE INSURANCE CO. (AL)
Merged into Southland Equity Corp. 12/31/74
Each share Common $1 par exchanged for (3) shares Class A Common 16-2/3¢ par
Southland Equity Corp. merged into Southland Capital Investors, Inc. 2/28/82 which recapitalized as Laurentian Capital Corp. (FL) 5/17/84 which reincorporated in Delaware 7/24/87
(See Laurentian Capital Corp.)

SECOM GEN CORP (DE)
Each share Common $0.004 par exchanged for (0.03) share old Common 10¢ par 09/04/1990
Each share old Common 10¢ par exchanged for (0.2) share new Common 10¢ par 04/14/1999
Stock Dividends - 10% 06/03/1991; 10% 06/01/1992
Liquidation completed
Each share new Common 10¢ par received initial distribution of $11.55 cash 10/31/2000
Each share new Common 10¢ par received second and final distribution of $1.69 cash payable 03/20/2007 to holders of record 02/27/2007 Ex date - 03/28/2007

SECOND & THIRD STREETS PASSENGER RAILWAY CO.
Acquired by Philadelphia Transportation Co. in 1940
Each share Common exchanged for $86.45 principal amount of 3%-6% Consolidated Mortgage Bonds and (0.7235) share $1 Part. Preferred $20 par
Philadelphia Transportation Co. completed liquidation 11/20/73

SECOND AVENUE RAILROAD CORP.
Out of business 00/00/1935
Details not available

SECOND BANCORP CAP TR I (DE)
9% Trust Preferred Securities called for redemption at $10 on 12/31/2006

SECOND BANCORP INC (OH)
$1 Conv. Preferred Ser. A no par called for redemption 06/25/1996
Common $10 par split (2) for (1) by issuance of (1) additional share 05/01/1990
Common $10 par split (3) for (2) by issuance of (0.5) additional share 05/01/1992
Common $10 par split (3) for (2) by issuance of (0.5) additional share 05/01/1995
Common $10 par split (2) for (1) by issuance of (1) additional share payable 05/01/1997 to holders of record 04/30/1997
Stock Dividend - 10% 12/09/1988
Merged into Sky Financial Group, Inc. 07/02/2004
Each share Common $10 par exchanged for (1.26) shares Common no par
Sky Financial Group, Inc. merged into Huntington Bancshares Inc. 07/02/2007

SECOND BANK-STATE STREET TRUST CO. (BOSTON, MA)
Stock Dividend - 50% 2/15/60
Name changed to State Street Bank & Trust Co. (Boston, MA) 4/15/60
State Street Bank & Trust Co. (Boston, MA) reorganized as State Street Boston Financial Corp. 6/15/70 which name changed to State Street Boston Corp. 5/3/77 which name changed to State Street Corp. 4/16/97

SECOND BAVARIAN MNG CONSULTING SVCS INC (CANADA)
Reincorporated under the laws of Wyoming as Tubac Holdings Inc. 08/20/2004
Tubac Holdings Inc. (WY) reorganized in Nevada as China Vitup Health Care Holdings, Inc. 10/13/2006 which recapitalized as Emergency Pest Services, Inc. 05/28/2015

SECOND CANADIAN GENERAL INVESTMENTS LTD.
Merged into Canadian General Investments, Ltd. 00/00/1931
Details not available

SECOND CANADIAN INTERNATIONAL INVESTMENT CO., LTD. (QC)
Recapitalized as Pacific Atlantic Canadian Investment Co. Ltd. 11/16/54
Each share Preference $5 par exchanged for (5) shares Common $1 par
Each share Common $5 par exchanged for (5) shares Common $1 par
(See Pacific Atlantic Canadian Investment Co.)

SECOND CAREY TRUST (OK)
Acquired by Prugh Petroleum Co. 12/31/53
Each Ctf. of Bene. Int. no par exchanged for (2.59) shares Common $5 par
Prugh Petroleum Co. merged into Livingston Oil Co. 9/1/56 which name changed to LVO Corp. 9/24/69 which merged into Utah International Inc. 10/31/74 which merged into General Electric Co. 12/20/76

SECOND CENTENNIAL FUND, INC. (MD)
Completely liquidated 08/30/1968
Each share Common $1 par exchanged for first and final distribution of (0.876941) share Gryphon Fund, Inc. Capital Stock $1 par
Gryphon Fund, Inc. name changed to Founders Growth Fund, Inc. 11/09/1970
(See Founders Growth Fund, Inc.)

SECOND CHANCE CORP (AB)
Delisted from Toronto Venture Stock Exchange 06/20/2003

SECOND COLONIAL MNG & ENGR SVCS INC (CANADA)
Reorganized under the laws of Florida as Homeland Integrated Security Systems, Inc. 10/18/2004
Each share Common no par exchanged for (66.113) shares Common $0.00001 par
Homeland Integrated Security Systems, Inc. recapitalized as DirectView Technology Group, Inc. 12/01/2008 which name changed to Green Bridge Technologies International, Inc. 08/25/2009 which recapitalized as Paradise Ridge Hydrocarbons, Inc. 08/20/2012 which name changed to Grupo Resilient International, Inc. 08/10/2017

SECOND CONGRESS STR FD INC (MA)
Merged into Congress Street Fund, Inc. 07/11/1975
Each share Capital Stock $1 par exchanged for (1.11717) shares Capital Stock $1 par
Congress Street Fund, Inc. name changed to Fidelity Congress Street Fund, Inc. 10/07/1980

SECOND CUP INCOME FD (ON)
Name changed 08/26/2009
Name changed from Second Cup Royalty Income Fund to Second Cup Income Fund 08/26/2009
Under plan of reorganization each Unit no par automatically became (1) share Second Cup Ltd. (Ctfs. dtd. after 01/04/2011) Common no par 01/04/2011

SECOND CUP LTD (ON)
Ctfs. dtd. prior to 02/21/2002
Subordinate no par reclassified as Common no par 05/13/1996
Acquired by Cara Operations Ltd. 02/21/2002
Each share Common no par exchanged for $8 cash

SECOND CUSTODIAN SHARES CORP.
Liquidated in 1933

2ND DEBUT COSMETICS INC (IL)
Stock Dividend - 15% 10/28/1972
Acquired by Beechem Inc. 00/00/1974
Each share Common 50¢ par exchanged for $10 cash

SECOND DIVERSIFIED STANDARD SECURITIES LTD.
Merged into Consolidated Diversified Standard Securities Ltd. 00/00/1932
Details not available

SECOND EMPIRE FD INC (MD)
Name changed to Pegasus Fund, Inc. 03/26/1971
Pegasus Fund, Inc. name changed to Vanderbilt Growth Fund, Inc. 07/01/1975 which merged into St. Paul Capital Fund, Inc. 06/14/1977 which name changed to AMEV Capital Fund, Inc. 05/01/1985 which reorganized as Fortis Equity Portfolios Inc. 02/22/1992
(See Fortis Equity Portfolios Inc.)

SECOND FED STR FD INC (MA)
Merged into Federal Street Fund, Inc. 09/25/1972
Each share Common $1 par exchanged for (1.3478) shares Common $1 par
Federal Street Fund, Inc. name changed to State Street Growth Fund, Inc. 03/11/1983
(See State Street Growth Fund, Inc.)

SECOND FINANCIAL, INC. NEW (GA)
Merged into Atlantic Services, Inc. 6/30/66
Each share Common 10¢ par exchanged for (1.666667) shares Common $1 par
(See Atlantic Services, Inc.)

SECOND FINANCIAL, INC. OLD (GA)
Each share Common 10¢ par exchanged for (0.5) share Second Financial, Inc. (New) new Common 10¢ par and (0.775) share Norco Holding Corp. Common 10¢ par 4/29/65
(See each company's listing)

SECOND GENERAL AMERICAN INVESTORS CO., INC.
Merged into General American Investors Co., Inc. 00/00/1929
Details not available

SECOND INCORPORATED EQUITIES
Merged into Incorporated Investors Equities in 1930 which name was changed to Consolidated Equities, Inc. in 1932 which was completely liquidated 8/4/55

SECOND INTER-STATE ROYALTY CORP. (CANADA)
Name changed to Woodford Royalty Corp. Ltd. 8/24/55
Woodford Royalty Corp. Ltd. name changed to Woodford Investments Ltd. 11/14/67 which name changed to Woodford Investments Ltd.-Investissements Woodford Ltee. 4/12/77
(See Woodford Investments Ltd.-Investissements Woodford Ltee. 4/12/77)

SECOND INTERNATIONAL SECURITIES CORP. (MD)
Class A Common no par changed to $1 par and Class B Common no par changed to 10¢ par 4/17/33
Merged into American General Corp. 11/23/35
Each share 6% 1st Preferred $50 par exchanged for (1.1) shares $2.50 Series Preferred $1 par
Each share Class A Common $1 par exchanged for (0.3) share Common 10¢ par
Each share Class B Common 10¢ par exchanged for (0.05) share Common 10¢ par
American General Corp. merged into Equity Corp. 10/17/50 which name changed to Wheelabrator-Frye Inc. 11/4/71 which merged into Signal Companies, Inc. 2/1/83 which merged into Allied-Signal Inc. 9/19/85 which name changed to AlliedSignal Inc. 4/26/93 which name changed to Honeywell International Inc. 12/1/99

SECOND INVESTORS CO. (RI)
Name changed to Providence Investors Co. 3/19/64
Providence Investors Co. acquired by Massachusetts Financial Total Return Trust 12/16/91 which name changed to MFS Total Return Fund 8/3/92

SECOND INVESTORS CORP.
In process of liquidation in 1941

SECOND LARKINS-WARR TRUST
Liquidation completed 12/15/55

SECOND MONGOLIAN MNG SEC SVCS INC (CANADA)
Acquired by Union First Capital Markets 12/16/2004
Details not available

SECOND MORTGAGE SECURITIES CO. (OH)
Liquidated in 1953

SECOND NATL BANCORPORATION (MD)
Assets transferred to Resolution Trust Corp. 12/4/92
No stockholders' equity

SECOND NATIONAL BANK & TRUST CO. (HEMPSTEAD, NY)
Merged into Security National Bank (Huntington, NY) 11/12/68
Each share Common $10 par exchanged for (3.25) shares Common $5 par
Security National Bank (Huntington, NY) changed location to Security National Bank (Hempstead, NY) 5/8/72

SECOND NATIONAL BANK & TRUST CO. (SAGINAW, MI)
Each share Capital Stock $100 par exchanged for (2) shares Capital Stock $50 par 01/27/1953
Each share Capital Stock $50 par exchanged for (2) shares Capital Stock $25 par 01/25/1955
Stock Dividends - 20% 12/14/1940; 33-1/3% 12/12/1944; 25% 12/14/1949; 20% 12/20/1951; 20% 11/16/1955
Name changed to Second National Bank (Saginaw, MI) 02/01/1957
Second National Bank (Saginaw, MI) merged into Century Financial Corp. of Michigan 01/22/1973 which name changed to Second National Corp. (DE) 04/13/1977 which merged into Citizens Banking Corp. 12/18/1985 which name changed to Citizens Republic Bancorp, Inc. 04/26/2007

SECOND NATL BK (ASHLAND, KY)
Each share Capital Stock $100 par exchanged for (4) shares Capital Stock $25 par 09/24/1946
Capital Stock $25 par changed to $10 par and (1.5) additional shares issued plus a 20% stock dividend paid 06/22/1956
Stock Dividend - 100% 01/21/1969
Name changed to First Bank & Trust Co. (Ashland, KY) 03/03/1980
First Bank & Trust Co. (Ashland, KY) reorganized as First Ashland Corp. 07/01/1982 which merged into First American Corp. (TN) 02/28/1986 which merged into AmSouth Bancorporation which merged into Regions Financial Corp. 11/04/2006

SECOND NATIONAL BANK (BOSTON, MA)
Capital Stock $25 par changed to $40 par in 1945
Stock Dividend - 25% 1/27/54
Merged into Second Bank-State Street Trust Co. (Boston, MA) 2/21/55
Each share Capital Stock $40 par exchanged for (1.8) shares Capital Stock $20 par
Second Bank-State Street Trust Co. (Boston, MA) name changed to State Street Bank & Trust Co. (Boston, MA) 4/15/60 which reorganized as State Street Boston Financial Corp. 6/15/70 which name changed to State Street Boston Corp. 5/3/77 which name changed to State Street Corp. 4/16/97

SECOND NATL BK (CULPEPER, VA)
Merged into Second National Financial Corp. 07/02/1990
Details not available

SECOND NATIONAL BANK (CUMBERLAND, MD)
Stock Dividend - 20% 7/21/59
Merged into First-Second National Bank & Trust Co. (Cumberland, Md.) 3/8/63
Each share Common $25 par exchanged for (1.375) shares Common $20 par
First-Second National Bank & Trust Co. (Cumberland, Md.) name changed to First National Bank & Trust Co. of Western Maryland (Cumberland, Md.) 5/1/66 which merged into First Maryland Bancorp 9/4/81
(See First Maryland Bancorp)

SECOND NATL BK (DANVILLE, IL)
Each share Common $100 par exchanged for (6) shares Common $25 par to effect a (4) for (1) split plus a 50% stock dividend 12/30/1960
Reorganized as Danville Bancshares, Inc. 05/01/1981
Each share Common $25 par exchanged for (1) share Common $5 par
(See Danville Bancshares, Inc.)

SECOND NATL BK (HAMILTON, OH)
Capital Stock $40 par changed to $10 par and (3) additional shares issued 02/18/1970
Stock Dividends - 150% 12/24/1942; 42-6/7% 01/22/1959; 25% 02/19/1965; 20% 09/25/1968; 33-1/3% 02/28/1974; 50% 03/01/1979
Acquired by First National Cincinnati Corp. 03/01/1982
Each share Capital Stock $10 par exchanged for $74 cash

SECOND NATIONAL BANK (HOUSTON, TX)
Under plan of merger each share Common $100 par exchanged for (7.5) shares Common $20 par 00/00/1944
Stock Dividends - 25% 01/02/1952; 33-1/3% 06/30/1954
Name changed to Bank of the Southwest N.A. (Houston, TX) 01/20/1956
Bank of the Southwest N.A. (Houston, TX) reorganized as Southwest Bancshares, Inc. 12/10/1970 which merged into MCorp 10/11/1984
(See MCorp)

SECOND NATL BK (JACKSON, TN)
Common $10 par changed to $5 par and (1) additional share issued 02/28/1978
Name changed to Jackson National Bank (Jackson, TN) 01/01/1980
Jackson National Bank (Jackson, TN) reorganized as Volunteer Bancshares, Inc. 05/07/1982 which was acquired by Bancorp of Mississippi 08/31/1992 which name changed to BancorpSouth, Inc. 10/06/1992 which reorganized as BancorpSouth Bank (Tupelo, MS) 11/01/2017

SECOND NATL BK (NASHUA, NH)
Merged into Bank of New Hampshire, N.A. (Manchester, NH) 11/30/69
Each share Common $10 par exchanged for (2) shares Common Capital Stock $10 par
Bank of New Hampshire, N.A. (Manchester, NH) reorganized as Bank of New Hampshire Corp. 4/30/80 which merged into Peoples Heritage Financial Group, Inc. 4/2/96 which name changed to Banknorth Group, Inc. (ME) 5/10/2000 which merged into TD Banknorth Inc. 3/1/2005
(See TD Banknorth Inc.)

SECOND NATL BK (NAZARETH, PA)
Common $10 par changed to $5 par and (1) additional share issued 04/03/1978
Under plan of reorganization each share Common $5 par automatically became (1) share First Community Bancorp, Inc. Common $5 par 08/01/1984
First Community Bancorp, Inc. merged into Fulton Financial Corp. 03/26/1990

SECOND NATL BK (NEW HAVEN, CT)
Each share Common $50 par exchanged for (4) shares Common $12.50 par 01/25/1955
Common $12.50 par changed to $10 par and (0.25) additional share issued 03/18/1969
Common $10 par changed to $5 par and (1) additional share issued 03/06/1970
Stock Dividend - 33-1/3% 01/25/1945
Name changed to Second New Haven Bank (New Haven, CT) 09/01/1972
Second New Haven Bank (New Haven, CT) acquired by Colonial Bancorp, Inc. (CT) 04/12/1975 which merged into Bank of Boston Corp. 06/20/1985 which name changed to BankBoston Corp. 04/25/1997 which merged into Fleet Boston Corp. 10/01/1999 which name changed to FleetBoston Financial Corp. 04/18/2000 which merged into Bank of America Corp. 04/01/2004

SECOND NATL BK (NORTH MIAMI, FL)
Stock Dividend - 10% 04/30/1970
Name changed to Great American Bank of Dade County (North Miami, FL) 11/26/1979
(See Great American Bank of Dade County (North Miami, FL))

SECOND NATL BK (ORANGE, NJ)
Capital Stock $10 par changed to $5 par and (1) additional share issued

plus a 50% stock dividend paid 10/06/1971
Acquired by United Jersey Banks 11/01/1972
Each share Capital Stock $5 par exchanged for (0.588235) share Common $5 par
United Jersey Banks name changed to UJB Financial Corp. 06/30/1989 which name changed to Summit Bancorp 03/01/1996 which merged into FleetBoston Financial Corp. 03/01/2001 which merged into Bank of America Corp. 04/01/2004

SECOND NATIONAL BANK (PHILADELPHIA, PA)
Merged into Provident Tradesmens Bank & Trust Co. (Philadelphia, PA) 08/17/1964
Each share Common $10 par exchanged for (0.875) share Capital Stock $12 par
Provident Tradesmens Bank & Trust Co. (Philadelphia, PA) name changed to Provident National Bank (Philadelphia, PA) 11/24/1964 which reorganized as Provident National Corp. 08/13/1969 which merged into PNC Financial Corp. 01/19/1983 which name changed to PNC Bank Corp. 02/08/1993 which name changed to PNC Financial Services Group, Inc. 03/15/2000

SECOND NATL BK (RAVENNA, OH)
Through voluntary exchange offer 97.91% acquired by Society Corp. as of 05/07/1979
Public interest eliminated

SECOND NATL BK (RICHMOND, IN)
Each share Common $100 par exchanged for (10) shares Common $10 par 00/00/1946
Stock Dividends - 25% 06/03/1947; 100% 12/31/1955; 40% 11/04/1959; 25% 02/10/1965; 42-6/7% 02/28/1969; 100% 04/28/1976
Under plan of reorganization each share Common $10 par automatically became (1) share Second National Corp. (IN) Common no par 04/01/1982
Second National Corp. (IN) merged into First National Cincinnati Corp. 09/30/1986 which name changed to Star Banc Corp. 04/13/1990 which merged into Firstar Corp. (New) 11/20/1998 which merged into U.S. Bancorp (DE) 02/27/2001

SECOND NATL BK (RICHMOND, VA)
Merged into Dominion Bankshares Corp. 03/25/1977
Each share Capital Stock $5 par exchanged for (0.8) share Common $5 par
Dominion Bankshares Corp. merged into First Union Corp. 03/01/1993 which name changed to Wachovia Corp. (Ctfs. dated after 09/01/2001) 09/01/2001 which merged into Wells Fargo & Co. (New) 12/31/2008

SECOND NATL BK (SAGINAW, MI)
Stock Dividends - 11.11111111% 01/30/1959; 12.5% 11/16/1961; 11.11111111% 03/07/1966; 20% 01/28/1969; 25% 01/03/1972
Merged into Century Financial Corp. of Michigan 01/22/1973
Each share Capital Stock $25 par exchanged for (2) shares Common $12.50 par
Century Financial Corp. of Michigan name changed to Second National Corp. (DE) 04/13/1977 which merged into Citizens Banking Corp. 12/18/1985 which name changed to Citizens Republic Bancorp, Inc. 04/26/2007 which merged into FirstMerit Corp. 04/12/2013 which merged into Huntington Bancshares Inc. 08/16/2016

SECOND NATIONAL BANK (TAMPA, FL)
Acquired by First Florida Banks, Inc. 1/14/85
Each share Common $10 par exchanged for $125 cash

SECOND NATIONAL BANK (UNIONTOWN, PA)
Name changed to Gallatin National Bank (Uniontown, PA) 01/21/1955
Gallatin National Bank (Uniontown, PA) reorganized as GNB Corp. 02/24/1970 which merged into Pennbancorp 12/31/1985 which merged into Integra Financial Corp. 01/26/1989 which merged into National City Corp. 05/03/1996 which was acquired by PNC Financial Services Group, Inc. 12/31/2008

SECOND NATL BK (WARREN, OH)
Common $50 par changed to $10 par and (4) additional shares issued 01/29/1971
Stock Dividends - 34.45378% 11/10/1950; 25% 11/18/1954; 25% 01/16/1961; 20% 01/21/1963; 33-1/3% 09/01/1965; 25% 11/15/1967; 20% 12/26/1969; 14.285714% 10/16/1972
Under plan of reorganization each share Common $10 par automatically became (1) share Second Bancorp Inc. Common $10 par 04/01/1987
Second Bancorp Inc. merged into Sky Financial Group, Inc. 07/02/2004 which merged into Huntington Bancshares Inc. 07/02/2007

SECOND NATL BLDG & LN INC (MD)
Capital Stock $1 par split (6) for (1) by issuance of (5) additional shares 07/22/1983
Capital Stock $1 par split (2) for (1) by issuance of (1) additional share 09/13/1985
Capital Stock $1 par split (2) for (1) by issuance of (1) additional share 07/21/1986
Under plan of reorganization each share Capital Stock $1 par automatically became (1) share Second National Federal Savings Bank (Annapolis, MD) Common $1 par 05/11/1987
Second National Federal Savings Bank (Annapolis, MD) reorganized as Second National Bancorporation 05/24/1991
(See Second National Bancorporation)

SECOND NATL CORP (DE)
Common $12.50 par split (3) for (2) by issuance of (0.5) additional share 11/10/1977
Common $12.50 par split (21) for (20) by issuance of (0.05) additional share payable 10/31/1978 to holders of record 10/17/1978
Stock Dividend - 20% 03/16/1984
Merged into Citizens Banking Corp. 12/18/1985
Each share Common $12.50 par exchanged for (1.375) shares Common $10 par
Citizens Banking Corp. name changed to Citizens Republic Bancorp, Inc. 04/26/2007 which merged into FirstMerit Corp. 04/12/2013 which merged into Huntington Bancshares Inc. 08/16/2016

SECOND NATL CORP (IN)
Merged into First National Cincinnati Corp. 09/30/1986
Each share Common no par exchanged for (2) shares Common $5 par
First National Cincinnati Corp. name changed to Star Banc Corp. 04/13/1990 which merged into Firstar Corp. (New) 11/20/1998 which merged into U.S. Bancorp (DE) 02/27/2001

SECOND NATL FED SVGS BK (ANNAPOLIS, MD)
Under plan of reorganization each share Common $1 par automatically became (1) share Second National Bancorporation Common $1 par 05/24/1991
(See Second National Bancorporation)

SECOND NATL FINL CORP (VA)
Name changed to Virginia Commonwealth Financial Corp. 10/08/1998
Virginia Commonwealth Financial Corp. merged into Virginia Financial Group, Inc. 01/22/2002 which name changed to StellarOne Corp. 02/28/2008 which merged into Union First Market Bankshares Corp. 01/02/2014 which name changed to Union Bankshares Corp. 04/28/2014

SECOND NATIONAL INVESTORS CORP.
Merged into National Investors Corp. (Md.) in 1937
Each share Preferred exchanged for (8.25) shares new Capital Stock $1 par and $16.60 in cash
Each share Common exchanged for (0.55) share new Capital Stock $1 par
National Investors Corp. (Md.) name changed to Seligman Growth Fund, Inc. 5/1/82

SECOND NEW HAVEN BK (NEW HAVEN, CT)
Acquired by Colonial Bancorp, Inc. (CT) 04/12/1975
Each share Common $5 par exchanged for (1) share Common $10 par
Colonial Bancorp, Inc. (CT) merged into Bank of Boston Corp. 06/20/1985 which name changed to BankBoston Corp. 04/25/1997 which merged into Fleet Boston Corp. 10/01/1999 which name changed to FleetBoston Financial Corp. 04/18/2000 which merged into Bank of America Corp. 04/01/2004

SECOND OHIO CAPITAL FUND, INC. (OH)
Merged into Ohio Capital Fund Inc. 06/30/1967
Each share Common $1 par exchanged for (1.327) shares Common $1 par
Ohio Capital Fund Inc. merged into Cardinal Fund Inc. 05/30/1975
(See Cardinal Fund Inc.)

SECOND SEATTLE REAL ESTATE ASSOCIATES (WA)
Merged into Bradley Real Estate Trust (MA) 01/20/1961
Each Trust Share $100 par exchanged for (7.9698) Trust Shares $1 par
Bradley Real Estate Trust (MA) recapitalized in Maryland as Bradley Real Estate, Inc. 10/17/1994
(See Bradley Real Estate, Inc.)

SECOND SOLAR INC (NV)
SEC revoked common stock registration 01/21/2014

SECOND SOUTHERN BANKERS SECURITIES CORP.
Assets sold to Carriers & General Corp.
Details not available

SECOND STAGE VENTURES INC (NV)
Common 1¢ par split (2) for (1) by issuance of (1) additional share payable 12/30/2003 to holders of record 12/29/2003 Ex date - 12/31/2003
Name changed to Dermisonics, Inc. 10/14/2004

which merged into U.S. Bancorp (DE) 02/27/2001

SECOND STREET LIQUIDATING CORP. (MO)
Liquidated in 1953

SECOND UN CASH MGMT FD INC (MD)
Name changed to Liberty Cash Management Fund, Inc. 09/01/1982

SECOND WAVE PETE INC (AB)
Acquired by Brookfield Bridge Lending Fund Inc. 07/03/2013
Each share Common no par exchanged for $0.30 cash
Note: Unexchanged certificates were cancelled and became without value 07/03/2018

SECOND WAVE PETE LTD (AB)
Each share Class B Common no par reclassified as (10) shares Class A Common no par 05/26/2008
Recapitalized as Second Wave Petroleum Inc. 06/27/2008
Each share Class A Common no par exchanged for (0.1) share Common no par
(See Second Wave Petroleum Inc.)

SECOND WESTN INCOME RLTY TR (CA)
Reorganized under the laws of Delaware as Western Real Estate Fund, Inc. 09/30/1987
Each Share of Bene. Int. $10 par exchanged for (0.376) share Common no par
(See Western Real Estate Fund Inc.)

SECONDARY RECOVERY OIL INC (PA)
Charter revoked for failure to file corporate tax reports 1/25/68

SECONDO MNG LTD (BC)
Struck off register and proclaimed dissolved for failure to file returns 01/31/1977

SECONN HLDG CO (CT)
Merged into Norwich Financial Corp. 1/2/96
Each share Class A Common no par exchanged for $6 cash

SECOR BK FED SVGS BK (BIRMINGHAM, AL)
Merged into First Alabama Bancshares, Inc. 12/31/93
Each share Common 1¢ par exchanged for (0.684) share Common $0.625 par
First Alabama Bancshares, Inc. name changed to Regions Financial Corp. (Old) 5/2/94 which merged into Regions Financial Corp. (New) 7/1/2004

SECORD LAURA CANDY SHOPS LTD (CANADA)
Each share old Common no par exchanged for (5) shares Common $3 par 00/00/1938
Each share Common $3 par exchanged for (2) shares new Common no par 06/06/1960
New Common no par split (2) for (1) by issuance of (1) additional share 02/07/1966
Acquired by Catelli Ltd. 10/29/1974
Each share new Common no par exchanged for $7.50 cash

SECRET PASS MINERALS CORP (BC)
Struck off register and declared dissolved for failure to file returns 02/19/1993

SECRETAIRE INDS INC (NV)
Name changed to Flint Media Group, Inc. 10/15/2007
Flint Media Group, Inc. name changed to RiverRun Resources, Inc. 08/29/2008

SECRETARIAL SVCS ORLANDO INC (FL)
Recapitalized as Sports Group International Inc. 03/08/1999
Each share Common $0.001 par

SECRETARIAT RES INC (BC)
Recapitalized as Cosmos Resources Inc. (BC) 11/27/1978
Each share Common no par exchanged for (1/3) share Common no par
(See Cosmos Resources Inc.)

SECTION ROUGE MEDIA INC (CANADA)
Each share old Common no par exchanged for (0.125) share new Common no par 05/13/2014
Name changed to Sama Graphite Inc. 01/16/2017
Sama Graphite Inc. name changed to SRG Graphite Inc. 07/05/2017

SECTOR ASSOC LTD (DE)
Each share Common $0.0001 par exchanged for (0.5) share Common $0.002 par 08/02/1993
Each share Common $0.002 par exchanged for (0.1) share Common 10¢ par 12/13/1993
Recapitalized as Viragen (Europe) Ltd. 04/24/1996
Each (14) shares Common 10¢ par exchanged for (1) share Common 1¢ par
Viragen (Europe) Ltd. name changed to Viragen International, Inc. 03/27/2002
(See Viragen International, Inc.)

SECTOR COMMUNICATIONS INC (NV)
Each share old Common $0.001 par exchanged for (0.02) share new Common $0.001 par 12/3/97
New Common $0.001 par split (5) for (1) by issuance of (4) additional shares payable 12/8/99 to holders of record 7/1/99
Name changed to Options Talent Group 1/11/2002
Options Talent Group name changed to Trans Continental Entertainment Group Inc. 1/16/2003
(See Trans Continental Entertainment Group Inc.)

SECTOR STRATEGY FD II L P (DE)
Company terminated registration of Units of Ltd. Partnership Int. and is no longer public as of 01/09/2003

SECTOR STRATEGY FD VI L P (DE)
Company terminated registration of Units of Ltd. Partnership Int. and is no longer public as of 01/09/2003

SECURA CORP (GA)
Merged into Integon Corp. (NC) 10/24/77
Each share Common $1 par exchanged for (0.6) share Common $1 par
Integon Corp. (NC) reincorporated in Delaware 5/10/79 which merged into Ashland Oil, Inc. 2/27/81 which name changed to Ashland Inc. (Old) 1/27/95
(See Ashland Inc. (Old))

SECURA LIFE INS CO (WI)
Merged into Pioneer Financial Services Inc. 12/31/96
Each share Common $1 par exchanged for $36.24 cash

SECURACOM INC (DE)
Issue Information - 1,920,000 shares COM offered at $8.50 per share on 10/01/1997
Name changed to Stratesec Inc. 12/23/1997
(See Stratesec Inc.)

exchanged for (0.5) share Common $0.001 par
Sports Group International Inc. name changed to Kahala Corp. (FL) 01/22/2001 which reincorporated in Delaware 12/31/2012
(See Kahala Corp.)

SECURE ALLIANCE HLDGS CORP (DE)
Recapitalized as aVinci Media Corp. 06/09/2008
Each share Common 1¢ par exchanged for (0.5) share Common 1¢ par
(See aVinci Media Corp.)

SECURE AMER ACQUISITION CORP (DE)
Name changed to Ultimate Escapes, Inc. 10/30/2009
(See Ultimate Escapes, Inc.)

SECURE AUTOMATED FILING ENTERPRISES INC (NV)
Common $0.00001 par split (8) for (1) by issuance of (7) additional shares payable 03/14/2005 to holders of record 03/07/2005 Ex date - 03/15/2005
Name changed to Colombia Goldfields Ltd. (NV) 05/25/2005
Colombia Goldfields Ltd. (NV) reincorporated in Delaware 07/31/2006 which merged into Medoro Resources Ltd. 11/02/2009 which merged into Gran Colombia Gold Corp. 06/14/2011

SECURE BLUE INC (NV)
Name changed to RedHand International, Inc. 10/06/2003
Redhand International, Inc. name changed to African Diamond Co., Inc. 04/17/2006
(See African Diamond Co., Inc.)

SECURE CARE TECHNOLOGIES INC (NV)
Each share old Common $0.001 par exchanged for (0.005) share new Common $0.001 par 05/21/2007
Each share new Common $0.001 par exchanged again for (0.33333333) share new Common $0.001 par 04/12/2010
Name changed to Scrypt, Inc. 03/11/2014

SECURE COMPUTING CORP (DE)
Merged into McAfee, Inc. 11/18/2008
Each share Common 1¢ par exchanged for $5.75 cash

SECURE ENTERPRISE SOLUTIONS INC (NV)
Name changed to Edgetech Services Inc. 11/20/2002
Edgetech Services Inc. name changed to Inova Technology, Inc. 05/23/2007
(See Inova Technology, Inc.)

SECURE IT CORP (DE)
Name changed to Black Stallion Oil & Gas Inc. 09/18/2013

SECURE LUGGAGE SOLUTIONS INC (DE)
Recapitalized as Kun De International Holdings Inc. 11/24/2014
Each share Common $0.001 par exchanged for (0.002) share Common $0.001 par

SECURE LUGGAGE U S A INC (FL)
Reorganized as Ambush Media, Inc. 09/16/2009
Each share Common $0.001 par exchanged for (2) shares Common $0.001 par
Ambush Media, Inc. name changed to Azia Corp. 03/19/2010 which name changed to Axxess Unlimited Inc. 03/20/2013 which name changed to Encompass Compliance Corp. 06/22/2015

SECURE NETCHECKIN INC (NV)
Name changed to Moxian China, Inc. 12/13/2013
Moxian China, Inc. name changed to Moxian, Inc. 07/29/2015

SECURE NETWERKS INC (DE)
Name changed to Start Scientific, Inc. 01/06/2012

SECURE ONE INC (AB)
Name changed to United Protection Security Group Inc. 11/28/2005
(See United Protection Security Group Inc.)

SECURE RUNWAY SYS CORP (NV)
Name changed to Diversified Secure Ventures Corp. 09/24/2010
Diversified Secure Ventures Corp. recapitalized as Go Greeen Global Technologies Corp. 03/15/2012

SECURE SIGN INC (CO)
Each share old Common no par exchanged for (0.04) share new Common no par 03/14/2003
Name changed to SVC Financial Services, Inc. 02/03/2004
(See SVC Financial Services, Inc.)

SECURE SOLUTIONS HLDGS INC (NV)
Charter revoked for failure to file reports or pay fees 08/31/2007

SECURE TECHNOLOGIES GROUP INC (DE)
SEC revoked common stock registration 05/05/2011

SECURE WINDOW BLINDS INC (NV)
Common $0.001 par split (15) for (1) by issuance of (14) additional shares payable 09/25/2012 to holders of record 09/24/2012 Ex date - 09/26/2012
Name changed to FreeButton, Inc. 10/01/2012
FreeButton, Inc. name changed to A-1 Group, Inc. 12/01/2014

SECUREALERT INC (UT)
Each share old Common $0.0001 par exchanged for (0.005) share new Common $0.0001 par 03/26/2013
Name changed to Track Group, Inc. (UT) 05/26/2015
Track Group, Inc. (UT) reincorporated in Delaware 08/05/2016

SECURECOM MOBILE INC (BC)
Old Common no par split (2) for (1) by issuance of (1) additional share payable 10/08/2014 to holders of record 10/07/2014 Ex date - 10/03/2014
Each share old Common no par exchanged for (0.25) share new Common no par 08/31/2015
Each share new Common no par exchanged again for (0.2) share new Common no par 06/03/2016
Recapitalized as Liberty Health Sciences Inc. 07/26/2017
Each share new Common no par exchanged for (0.33333333) share Common no par

SECURED-AMERICA, INC. (MD)
Recapitalized as Philpot (R.D.) Industries, Inc. 6/17/70
Each share Common 1¢ par exchanged for (0.1) share Common 1¢ par

SECURED COMMUNICATION CDA 95 INC (BC)
Delisted from Vancouver Stock Exchange 07/07/1998

SECURED DATA INC (NV)
Each (15) shares old Common $0.001 par exchanged for (1) share new Common $0.001 par 01/12/2004
Recapitalized as Huifeng Bio-Pharmaceutical Technology Inc. 10/12/2005
Each (18) shares new Common $0.001 par exchanged for (1) share Common $0.001 par

SECURED DEV INC (IN)
99% owned by company as of 00/00/1978
Public interest eliminated

SECURED DIGITAL APPLICATIONS INC (DE)
SEC revoked common stock registration 05/23/2011

SECURED DIGITAL STORAGE CORP (NM)
SEC revoked common stock registration 10/07/2013

SECURED DIVERSIFIED INVT LTD (NV)
Each share old Common $0.001 par exchanged for (0.05) share new Common $0.001 par 08/14/2006
Each share new Common $0.001 par exchanged again for (0.05) share new Common $0.001 par 10/26/2007
Plan of reorganization under Chapter 11 Federal Bankruptcy Code effective 02/06/2009
No stockholders' equity
Name changed to Galaxy Gaming, Inc. 09/01/2009

SECURED FINL NETWORK INC (NV)
Name changed to Redfin Network, Inc. 04/28/2011
(See Redfin Network, Inc.)

SECURED FIRE & MARINE INSURANCE CO. (IN)
Recapitalized as Secured Insurance Co. on a (1.3) for (1) basis 4/30/54
Secured Insurance Co. completed liquidation 12/30/64

SECURED INSURANCE CO. (IN)
Each share Common $1 par exchanged for (0.1) share Common $10 par 10/7/59
Common $10 par changed to $2 par 12/27/63
Liquidation completed
Each share Common $2 par received initial distribution of $27.50 cash 12/30/63
Each share Common $2 par received second and final distribution of $6.687 cash 12/30/64
Surrender of certificates was not required and are now valueless

SECURED INVT RES FD L P (KS)
Partnership terminated 08/20/2001
Details not available for Units of Ltd. Partnership III
Partnership terminated 01/16/2007
No Unitholders' equity for Units of Ltd. Partnership I
Each Unit of Ltd. Partnership II received distribution of (1) Everest SIR 2 Properties, L.P. Unit of Ltd. Partnership and (1) Sunwood Village Joint Venture, L.P. payable 02/29/2008 to holders of record 02/29/2008
Partnership terminated 03/12/2008
Details not available for Units of Ltd. Partnership II

SECURED SVCS INC (DE)
Assets assigned for the benefit of creditors 07/17/2006
No stockholders' equity

SECURELOGIC CORP (NV)
SEC revoked common stock registration 11/24/2014

SECUREVIEW SYS INC (BC)
Name changed to Global Immune Technologies Inc. 5/3/2005

SECUREWARE INC (NV)
Old Common $0.001 par split (3) for (2) by issuance of (0.5) additional share payable 11/16/2001 to holders of record 11/14/2001 Ex date - 11/19/2001
Each share old Common $0.001 par exchanged for (0.005) share new Common $0.001 par 02/01/2005
Reorganized as Shore Ventures Inc. 04/15/2005
Each share new Common $0.001 exchanged for (2) shares new Common $0.001 par
Shore Ventures Inc. name changed to Cosco ESP, Inc. 09/26/2005 which recapitalized as Budget Center Inc. 04/28/2009 which recapitalized as Budget Center Inc. 11/08/2017

SECUREX LTD (AB)
Delisted from Toronto Venture Stock Exchange 03/13/2003

SECURFONE AMER INC (DE)
Each share Common $0.001 par received distribution of (0.5) share Material Technologies Inc. Class A Common $0.001 par payable 9/5/97 to holders of record 7/31/97
Name changed to Ixata Group, Inc. 2/4/2000
Ixata Group, Inc. name changed to RFP Express Inc. 7/25/2001

SECURITAS EDGAR FILINGS INC (NV)
Name changed to MJ Holdings, Inc. 03/03/2014

SECURITEK INTL CORP (DE)
Charter cancelled and declared inoperative and void for non-payment of taxes 03/01/2000

SECURITEYES INTL INC (DE)
Name changed to Medify Solutions Ltd. 02/17/2005
Medify Solutions Ltd. name changed to Petel Inc. 05/08/2007 which recapitalized as Gleeworks, Inc. 12/14/2009 which name changed to Capital Art, Inc. 05/09/2011 which name changed to Globe Photos, Inc. 06/25/2018

SECURITIES ACCEPTANCE CORP. (DE)
Each share Common $4 par exchanged for (3) shares Common $2 par in 1948
Common $2 par split (4) for (3) by issuance of (1/3) additional share in 1955
Stock Dividends - 20% 3/31/44; 25% 8/20/46; 33-1/3% 9/28/51; 50% 3/31/53
Merged into Associates Investment Co. (IN) on a (1) for (6) basis 1/2/62
Associates Investment Co. (IN) reincorporated in Delaware 6/26/69
(See Associates Investment Co. (DE))

SECURITIES ACCEPTANCE CORP. (QC)
Charter cancelled for failure to file reports and pay taxes 1/31/74

SECURITIES-ALLIED CORP.
Liquidated 00/00/1933
Details not available

SECURITIES CLEARING CORP AMER (CA)
Charter suspended for failure to file reports and pay taxes 5/2/77

SECURITIES CORP. GENERAL (VA)
Recapitalized 00/00/1930
Each share 1st Preferred no par exchanged for (1) share $7 Ser. Preferred no par
Each share Common no par exchanged for (10) shares Common no par
Recapitalized 00/00/1941
$7 and $6 Ser. Preferred no par changed to $100 par
Common no par changed to $1 par
Liquidation completed
Each share $7 Ser. Preferred $100 par exchanged for first and final distribution of $101.75 cash 9/30/62
Each share $6 Ser. Preferred $100 par exchanged for first and final distribution of $101.50 cash 9/30/62
Each share Common $1 par stamped to indicate initial distribution of (0.4) share Dynamics Corp. of America (NY) Common $1 par 09/30/1962
Each share Stamped Common $1 par exchanged for second and final distribution of $0.35 cash 07/22/1963
Dynamics Corp. of America (NY) merged into CTS Corp. 10/16/1997

SECURITIES DATA CTR INC (DE)
Declared inoperative and void for non-payment of taxes 04/15/1972

SECURITIES FD INC (PA)
Reincorporated 03/01/1967
State of incorporation changed from (NJ) to (PA) and Common $1 par changed to 1¢ par 03/01/1967
Name changed to Hedberg & Gordon Fund, Inc. 02/25/1969
Hedberg & Gordon Fund, Inc. name changed to Plitrend Fund, Inc. 02/20/1974 which name changed to U.S. Trend Fund, Inc. (PA) 02/00/1986 which reincorporated in Maryland as Capstone U.S. Trend Fund, Inc. 05/11/1992 which name changed to Capstone Growth Fund, Inc. 08/26/1994 which name changed to Capstone Series Fund, Inc. 01/22/2002

SECURITIES GROUPS MONEY FD INC (MD)
Dissolved and assets liquidated
Details not available

SECURITIES HOLDING CORP. LTD.
In process of liquidation in 1944

SECURITIES HLDG CORP INC (NV)
Name changed to Nationwide Safe T Propane, Inc. 03/26/2002
Nationwide Safe T Propane, Inc. recapitalized as EMP Solutions Inc. 03/10/2015

SECURITIES INC (OH)
5% Conv. Preferred $10 par called for redemption 6/30/71
6% Preferred $10 par called for redemption 6/30/71
(Additional Information in Active)

SECURITIES INTERMOUNTAIN INC (OR)
Each share Class A 75¢ par exchanged for (0.1) share Class A $7.50 par 12/01/1962
Each share Class B 75¢ par exchanged for (0.1) share Class B $7.50 par 12/01/1962
Through voluntary exchange offer over 99% acquired by First Security Corp. as of 06/04/1979
Public interest eliminated

SECURITIES INVESTMENT CO. OF ST. LOUIS
Acquired by General Contract Corp. in 1952
Each share 5% Preferred $100 par exchanged for (1) share new 5% Preferred $100 par
Each share Common $10 par exchanged for (0.5) share new Preferred $20 par and (1.1) shares Common $2 par
General Contract Corp. name changed to General Bancshares Corp. 11/6/58 which merged into Boatmen's Bancshares, Inc. 3/29/86 which merged into NationsBank Corp. 1/7/97 which reincorporated in Delaware as BankAmerica Corp. (Old) 9/25/98 which merged into BankAmerica Corp. (New) 9/30/98 which name changed to Bank of America Corp. 4/28/99

SECURITIES INVESTMENT CORP.
Acquired by Securities Acceptance Corp. 00/00/1936
Details not available

SECURITIES RESOLUTION ADVISORS INC (DE)
Name changed to Sales Online Direct, Inc. 03/16/1999
Sales Online Direct, Inc. name changed to Paid, Inc. 12/08/2003

SECURITIES TRUST OF AMERICA
Liquidated in 1933

SECURITIES USA INC (CO)
Recapitalized as Securities PR, Inc. 04/28/1989
Each share Common $0.001 par exchanged for (0.1) share Common $0.001 par

SECURITY ACCEPTANCE CORP. LTD. (BC)
Receivership terminated 1/28/75
No stockholders' equity

SECURITY ACTION FD (KS)
Dissolved 05/15/1994
Details not available

SECURITY AMER CORP (DE)
Charter cancelled and declared inoperative and void for non-payment of taxes 03/01/1988

SECURITY AMER LIFE INS CO (PA)
Capital Stock $5 par changed to $1 par and (3) additional shares issued 12/22/1964
Capital Stock $1 par split (1.4) for (1) by issuance of (0.4) additional share 12/17/1971
Stock Dividends - 20% 03/15/1967; 33-1/3% 12/27/1972
Acquired by USLIFE Corp. 04/07/1980
Each share Capital Stock $1 par exchanged for $20 cash

SECURITY AMERN FINL ENTERPRISES INC (MN)
Common 10¢ par split (2) for (1) by issuance of (1) additional share 6/6/86
Stock Dividends - 10% 4/17/75; 10% 4/15/76; 10% 5/10/77; 10% 6/19/78; 10% 6/6/79; 10% 6/4/80; 10% 6/8/81; 10% 6/8/82; 10% 6/7/83; 10% 6/7/84; 10% 6/6/85; 10% 6/8/87; 10% 6/6/88; 10% 6/6/89
Acquired by a group of investors 11/22/89
Each share Common 10¢ par exchanged for $9.77 cash

SECURITY AMERICAN LIFE INSURANCE CO. (TN)
Merged into University National Life Insurance Co. (TN) on a share for share basis 8/16/61
University National Life Insurance Co. (TN) merged into South Coast Life Insurance Co. 9/30/63 which was acquired by USLIFE Holding Corp. 7/25/67 which name changed to USLIFE Corp. 5/22/70 which merged into American General Corp. 6/17/97 which merged into American International Group, Inc. 8/29/2001

SECURITY ASSETS CORP (DE)
Liquidation completed
Each share Capital Stock $5 par received initial distribution of $24 cash 09/16/1965
Each share Capital Stock $5 par exchanged for second distribution of (0.66) share Security Storage Co. of Washington (DE) (New) Common no par 12/01/1965
Each share Capital Stock $5 par received third distribution of $1.47 cash 03/03/1966
Each share Capital Stock $5 par received fourth and final distribution of $1.001686 cash 04/20/1971
(See Security Storage Co. of Washington (DE) (New))

SECURITY ASSOC INTL INC (DE)
Each share old Common $0.001 par exchanged for (0.1) share new Common $0.001 par 12/17/92
Merged into SAI Merger Corp. 12/30/2003
Each share new Common $0.001 par exchanged for $0.01 cash

SECURITY BANC CORP (OH)
Common $6.25 par split (2) for (1) by issuance of (1) additional share payable 06/10/1998 to holders of record 05/29/1998
Merged into Park National Corp. 03/23/2001
Each share Common $6.25 par exchanged for (0.284436) share Common no par

SECURITY BANCORP (MT)
Reorganized 11/08/1993
Under plan of reorganization each share Security Federal Savings Bank (Billings, MT) Common $1 par automatically became (1) share Security Bancorp Common $1 par 11/08/1993
Merged into WesterFed Financial Corp. 02/28/1997
Each share Common $1 par exchanged for $30 cash

SECURITY BANCORP INC (GA)
Merged into Habersham Bancorp Inc. 6/30/95
Each share Common $1 par exchanged for (1.579) shares Common $2.50 par or $17.56 cash
Note: Option to receive cash expired 7/7/95

SECURITY BANCORP INC (IN)
Common $10 par changed to $5 par and (1) additional share issued 5/1/84
Merged into Old National Bancorp 4/30/87
Each share Common $5 par exchanged for (3.675) shares Common no par

SECURITY BANCORP INC (MI)
Reincorporated 01/31/1983
State of incorporation changed from (DE) to (MI) 01/31/1983
Common 1¢ par split (3) for (2) by issuance of (0.5) additional share 10/03/1983
Common 1¢ par split (3) for (2) by issuance of (0.5) additional share 06/01/1989
Stock Dividends - 10% 11/01/1976; 15% 08/10/1977; 10% 04/02/1979; 50% 06/02/1986
Merged into First of America Bank Corp. 05/01/1992
Each share $2.64 Conv. Preferred Ser. A 1¢ par exchanged for (2.9955) shares Common $10 par
Each share Common 1¢ par exchanged for (1.3232) shares Common $10 par
First of America Bank Corp. merged into National City Corp. 03/31/1998 which was acquired by PNC Financial Services Group, Inc. 12/31/2008

SECURITY BANCSHARES INC (KS)
Acquired by One Security, Inc. 03/31/1986
Details not available

SECURITY BANK & TRUST CO. (BLOOMFIELD, CT)
Merged into Northeast Bancorp, Inc. 01/24/1983
Each share Capital Stock $10 par exchanged for (1.59) shares Common $5 par
Northeast Bancorp, Inc. merged into First Fidelity Bancorporation (New) 05/03/1993 which merged into First Union Corp. 01/01/1996 which name changed to Wachovia Corp. (Ctfs. dated after 09/01/2001) 09/01/2001 which merged into Wells Fargo & Co. (New) 12/31/2008

SECURITY BK & TR CO (SALISBURY, NC)
Common $5 par split (2) for (1) by issuance of (1) additional share 3/1/83
Stock Dividends - 25% 1/11/62; 10% 1/20/66; 10% 1/26/67; 200% 11/13/69; 10% 2/25/76; 10% 1/30/77; 10% 1/30/78; 10% 1/30/79; 10% 1/30/80; 10% 1/30/81; 10% 1/29/82
Reorganized as First Security Financial Corp. 7/13/83
Each share Common $5 par exchanged for (1) share Common $5 par
(See First Security Financial Corp.)

SECURITY BK & TR CO (SOUTHGATE, MI)
Stock Dividends - 20% 02/20/1965; 10% 05/15/1967; 10% 06/14/1969; 20% 06/05/1970
100% acquired by Security Bancorp, Inc. as of 00/00/1980
Public interest eliminated

SECURITY BK & TR CO (STROUDSBURG, PA)
Common $17 par changed to $8.50 par and (1) additional share issued 02/01/1979
Stock Dividend - 10% 02/01/1984
Merged into Continental Bancorp, Inc. 06/01/1985
Each share Common $8.50 par exchanged for (1.65) shares Common $5 par
Continental Bancorp, Inc. merged into Midlantic Corp. 01/30/1987 which merged into PNC Bank Corp. 12/31/1995 which name changed to PNC Financial Services Group, Inc. 03/15/2000

SECURITY BK & TR CO (VINCENNES, IN)
Stock Dividend - 100% 04/20/1977
Reorganized as Security Bancorp, Inc. (IN) 07/30/1982
Each share Common $10 par exchanged for (1) share Common $10 par
Security Bancorp, Inc. (IN) merged into Old National Bancorp 04/30/1987

SECURITY BK (LINCOLN PARK, MI)
Each share Capital Stock $100 par exchanged for (5) shares Capital Stock $20 par 8/28/51
Each share Capital Stock $20 par exchanged for (2.1) shares Capital Stock $1 par to effect a (2) for (1) split and a 5% stock dividend 1/17/61
Stock Dividends - 50% 1944; 20% 7/25/50; 16-2/3% 8/5/57; 10% 2/9/59; 10% 2/20/60; 10% 2/18/63; 20% 1/21/64
Name changed to Security Bank & Trust Co. (Southgate, MI) 2/4/65
(See Security Bank & Trust Co. (Southgate, MI))

SECURITY BANK (WASHINGTON, DC)
Each share Capital Stock $100 par exchanged for (5) shares Capital Stock $25 par to effect a (4) for (1) split and a 25% stock dividend in 1954
Capital Stock $25 par changed to $10 par and (1.5) additional shares issued plus a 10% stock dividend paid 2/15/65
Stock Dividends - 10% 2/6/58; 10% 1/31/61; 10% 1/31/63; 10% 2/15/67; 10% 2/14/69
Name changed to Security Bank, N.A. (Washington, D.C.) 4/1/69
Each share Capital Stock $10 par exchanged for (1) share Capital Stock $10 par
Security Bank, N.A. (Washington, D.C.) name changed to Security National Bank (Washington, D.C.) 6/1/71 which reorganized as Security National Corp. 6/1/82
(See Security National Corp. (Del.))

SECURITY BK CALIF (RIVERSIDE, CA)
Under plan of reorganization each share Common no par automatically became (1) share Security California Bancorp Common no par 10/10/2008
Security California Bancorp merged into Pacific Premier Bancorp, Inc. 01/31/2016

SECURITY BK CORP (GA)
Common $1 par split (2) for (1) by issuance of (1) additional share payable 05/27/2005 to holders of record 05/16/2005 Ex date - 05/31/2005
Chapter 7 bankruptcy proceedings terminated 06/02/2014
Stockholders' equity unlikely

SECURITY BK CORP (VA)
Merged into F & M National Corp. 03/22/1999
Each share Common $5 par exchanged for (0.653) share Common $2 par
F & M National Corp. merged into BB&T Corp. 08/09/2001

SECURITY BK HLDG CO (OR)
Common $5 par split (3) for (2) by issuance of (0.5) additional share payable 1/5/96 to holders of record 12/26/95
Stock Dividends - 5% payable 8/20/99 to holders of record 8/6/99; 5% payable 2/25/2000 to holders of record 2/11/2000
Name changed to Independent Financial Network Inc. 5/15/2000
Independent Financial Network Inc. merged into Umpqua Holdings Corp. 12/31/2001

SECURITY BK N A (WASHINGTON, DC)
Stock Dividend - 12.8% 03/02/1971
Name changed to Security National Bank (Washington, DC) 06/01/1971
Security National Bank (Washington, DC) reorganized as Security National Corp. 06/01/1982
(See Security National Corp. (DE))

SECURITY BK NEV (RENO, NV)
Acquired by Valley Capital Corp. 12/31/1987
Each share Capital Stock $2.50 par exchanged for (1) share Common $1 par
Valley Capital Corp. merged into BankAmerica Corp. (Old) 03/13/1992 which merged into BankAmerica Corp. (New) 09/30/1998 which name changed to Bank of America Corp. 04/28/1999

SECURITY BK ORE (PORTLAND, OR)
Each share Capital Stock $100 par exchanged for (5) shares Capital Stock $20 par 11/12/58
Capital Stock $20 par changed to $10 par and (1) additional share issued 1/21/69
Merged into Orbanco Inc. 7/8/75
Each share Capital Stock $10 par exchanged for (0.18182) share Common no par
Orbanco Inc. name changed to Orbanco Financial Services Corp. 5/9/80 which was acquired by Security Pacific Corp. 4/15/87 which merged into BankAmerica Corp. (Old) 4/22/92 which merged into BankAmerica Corp. (New) 9/30/98 which name changed to Bank of America Corp. 4/28/99

SECURITY BANKNOTE CO. (PA)
Recapitalized under the laws of Delaware 11/15/1947
Each share Common $5 par exchanged for (2) shares Common $2 par and (1) share Preferred $1 par
Security Banknote Co. (DE) name changed to Security-Columbian Banknote Co. 01/16/1958 which merged into United States Banknote Corp. 03/03/1965
(See United States Banknote Corp.)

SECURITY BANKNOTE CO (DE)
Name changed to Security-Columbian Banknote Co. 1/16/58 which merged into United States Banknote Corp. 3/3/65
(See United States Banknote Corp.)

SECURITY BIOMETRICS INC (NV)
Each share old Common $0.001 par exchanged for (0.05) share new Common $0.001 par 06/10/2004
Name changed to SiVault Systems, Inc. 07/29/2004
(See SiVault Systems, Inc.)

SECURITY BD FD INC (KS)
Name changed to Security Income Fund and Common $1 par reclassified as Corporate Bond Series Common $1 par 08/15/1985

SECURITY BUSINESS BANCORP (CA)
Acquired by SBB Merger Sub Corp. 07/05/2012
Each share Common no par exchanged for $14.5057 cash

SECURITY BUSINESS BK (SAN DIEGO, CA)
Under plan of reorganization each share Common no par automatically became (1) share Security Business Bancorp Common no par 07/01/2008
(See Security Business Bancorp)

SECURITY CALIF BANCORP (CA)
Merged into Pacific Premier Bancorp, Inc. 01/31/2016
Each share Common no par exchanged for (0.9629) share Common 1¢ par

SECURITY CAP ASSURANCE LTD (BERMUDA)
Issue Information - 22,447,728 shares COM offered at $20.50 per share on 08/01/2006
Name changed to Syncora Holdings Ltd. 08/04/2008

SECURITY CAP ATLANTIC INC (MD)
Each share Common 1¢ par received distribution of (0.110866) share Homestead Village Properties Inc. Common 1¢ par and (0.074378) Common Stock Purchase Warrant expiring 10/29/1997 payable 11/12/1996 to holders of record 10/29/1996 Ex date - 11/13/1996
Merged into Archstone Communities Trust 07/07/1998
Each share Ser. A Preferred 1¢ par exchanged for (1) share Ser. C Preferred 1¢ par
Each share Common 1¢ par exchanged for (1) Share of Bene. Int. 1¢ par
Archstone Communities Trust name changed to Archstone-Smith Trust 10/29/2001
(See Archstone-Smith Trust)

SECURITY CAP BANCORP (NC)
Merged into CCB Financial Corp. 5/19/95
Each share Common no par exchanged for (0.5) share Common $5 par
CCB Financial Corp. merged into National Commerce Bancorporation 7/5/2000 which name changed to National Commerce Financial Corp. 4/25/2001 which merged into SunTrust Banks, Inc. 10/1/2004

SECURITY CAP CORP (CA)
Recapitalized as Triad American Capital Corp. 06/19/1974
Each share Common no par exchanged for (0.8) share Common $1 par
(See Triad American Capital Corp.)

SECURITY CAP CORP (DE)
Under plan of recapitalization each share Common $1 par exchanged for (0.0005) share Common 1¢ par 7/6/90
Each share Common 1¢ par received distribution of (1,999) shares Class A Common 1¢ par 7/6/90
Each share old Class A Common 1¢ par exchanged for (0.125) share new Class A Common 1¢ par 3/27/96
Each share old Common 1¢ par exchanged for (0.125) share new Common 1¢ par 3/27/96
Merged into Sedgwick CMS Holdings, Inc. 9/13/2006
Each share new Class A Common 1¢ par exchanged for $16.46 cash
Each share new Common 1¢ par exchanged for $16.46 cash

SECURITY CAP CORP (WI)
Merged into Marshall & Ilsley Corp. 10/1/97
Each share Common $1 par exchanged for (1.9494) shares Common $1 par and $10.92 cash; (1.3561) shares Common $1 par and $41.40 cash; or $111.06 cash
Note: Option to receive stock and cash expired 9/26/97

SECURITY CAP EUROPEAN RLTY (LUXEMBOURG)
Name changed 09/11/1998
Name changed from Security Capital Global Realty to Security Capital European Realty 09/11/1998
ADR agreement terminated 02/07/2011
Each Sponsored 144A ADR for Ordinary exchanged for $2.5847 cash

SECURITY CAP GROUP INC (MD)
Issue Information - 22,569,710 shares CL B offered at $28 per share on 09/17/1997
Merged into ProLogis Trust 5/14/2002
Each share Class A 1¢ par exchanged for (11.5076865) Shares of Bene. Int. 1¢ par and $1,040.145 cash
Each share Class B 1¢ par exchanged for (0.23015373) share of Bene. Int. 1¢ par and $20.8029 cash
ProLogis Trust name changed to ProLogis 5/23/2002

SECURITY CAP INDL TR (MD)
Each Conv. Preferred Share of Bene. Int. 1¢ par received distribution of (0.059676) Security Capital Group Inc. Class B Common Stock Purchase Warrant expiring 09/28/1998 payable 10/07/1997 to holders of record 09/18/1997
Each Share of Bene. Int. 1¢ par received distribution of (0.059676) Security Capital Group Inc. Class B Common Stock Purchase Warrant expiring 09/28/1998 payable 10/07/1997 to holders of record 09/18/1997
Name changed to ProLogis Trust 07/01/1998
ProLogis Trust name changed to ProLogis 05/23/2002 which merged into Prologis, Inc. 06/03/2011

SECURITY CAP LTD (ON)
Each share old Common no par exchanged for (0.01) share new Common no par and (1) share Non-Cum. Part. Class B no par 2/6/64
Common no par split (2) for (1) by issuance of (1) additional share 4/13/67
Name changed to Sentinel Holdings Ltd. 10/30/75
Sentinel Holdings Ltd. merged into Unicorp Financial Corp. 12/31/79 which name changed to Unicorp Canada Corp. 7/13/82 which recapitalized as Unicorp Energy Corp. 6/25/91 which name changed to Unicorp Inc. 5/28/99 which name changed to Wilmington Capital Management Corp. 3/8/2002

SECURITY CAP PAC TR (MD)
Each Share of Bene. Int. $1 par received distribution of (0.125694) share Homestead Village Properties Inc. Common 1¢ par and (0.084326) Common Stock Purchase Warrant expiring 10/29/1997 payable

11/12/1996 to holders of record 10/29/1996 Ex date - 11/13/1996
Under plan of merger name changed to Archstone Communities Trust 07/07/1998
Archstone Communities Trust name changed to Archstone-Smith Trust 10/29/2001
(See Archstone-Smith Trust.)

SECURITY CAP U S RLTY (LUXEMBOURG)
Merged into Security Capital Group Inc. 1/16/2001
Each Sponsored ADR for Ordinary $2 par exchanged for (1.15) shares Class B Common 1¢ par
Security Capital Group Inc. merged into ProLogis Trust 5/14/2002 which name changed to ProLogis 5/23/2002

SECURITY CAPITAL LIFE INSURANCE CO. (PA)
Completely liquidated 6/12/67
Each share Capital Stock $1 par exchanged for first and final distribution of (0.36) share Hale (Nathan) Life Insurance Co. of New York Capital Stock $1.60 par
Hale (Nathan) Life Insurance Co. of New York acquired by Washington National Corp. 6/20/72

SECURITY CASH FD INC (KS)
Under plan of merger each share Common 10¢ par automatically became (1) share Rydex Series Fund U.S. Government Money Market Fund Investor Class 2 on 07/10/2009

SECURITY CENT NATL BK (PORTSMOUTH, OH)
Capital Stock $20 par changed to $10 par and (1) additional share issued in 1968
Stock Dividends - 50% 12/22/55; 10% 1964; 10% 1967
Merged into First Banc Group of Ohio, Inc. 6/1/71
Each share Capital Stock $10 par exchanged for (2.25) shares Common no par
First Banc Group of Ohio, Inc. name changed to Banc One Corp. (DE) 10/22/79 which reincorporated in Ohio 5/1/89 which merged into Bank One Corp. 10/2/98 which merged into J.P. Morgan Chase & Co. 12/31/2000 which name changed to JPMorgan Chase & Co. 7/20/2004

SECURITY CHICAGO CORP (DE)
Merged into Alpha Acquisition 11/29/96
Each share Common $5 par exchanged for $60 cash

SECURITY CO.
Under plan of merger each share Common exchanged for (7) shares American Mutual Fund, Inc. Common $1 par, (1) share Southern Realty Co. Common 50¢ par and rights to subscribe to (7) additional shares of American Mutual Fund, Inc. 00/00/1949
(See each company's listing)

SECURITY-COLUMBIAN BANKNOTE CO. (DE)
Stock Dividend - 100% 2/2/62
Merged into United States Banknote Corp. 3/3/65
Each share Common $2 par exchanged for (1) share Common $1 par
(See United States Banknote Corp.)

SECURITY-CONN CORP (DE)
Issue Information - 8,500,000 shares COM offered at $22 per share on 01/26/1994
Merged into ReliaStar Financial Corp. 07/01/1997
Each share Common 1¢ par exchanged for (0.7367) share Common 1¢ par

(See ReliaStar Financial Corp.)

SECURITY CONN LIFE INS CO (CT)
Capital Stock $1 par split (4) for (3) by issuance of (1/3) additional share 09/05/1978
Stock Dividends - 20% 06/01/1971; 50% 11/01/1972; 10% 03/24/1977; 10% 03/23/1978
Acquired by Lincoln National Corp. 10/30/1979
Each share Capital Stock $1 par exchanged for $42 cash

SECURITY CORP (CT)
Acquired by Textron Inc. 06/29/1973
Each share Common $10 par exchanged for (2) shares Common 25¢ par

SECURITY-DANVERS NATIONAL BANK (LYNN, MA)
Name changed to Security National Bank (Lynn, Mass.) 3/15/68
(See Security National Bank (Lynn, Mass.))

SECURITY DIVERSIFIED SHS INC (NC)
Name changed to Integon Growth Fund Corp. 12/31/1969
Integon Growth Fund Corp. merged into Bullock Fund, Ltd. 01/06/1977 which name changed to Bullock Growth Shares, Inc. 04/08/1985 which merged into Chemical Fund, Inc. 03/13/1987 which name changed to Alliance Fund, Inc. 04/01/1987 which name changed to Alliance Mid-Capital Growth Fund Inc. 02/01/2000 which name changed to AllianceBernstein Mid-Capital Growth Fund, Inc. 03/31/2003

SECURITY DYNAMICS TECHNOLOGIES INC (DE)
Common 1¢ par split (2) for (1) by issuance of (1) additional share 10/30/1995
Common 1¢ par split (2) for (1) by issuance of (1) additional share payable 11/15/1996 to holders of record 11/01/1996
Name changed to RSA Security Inc. 09/13/1999
(See RSA Security Inc.)

SECURITY ELECTRONICS CORP. (DE)
No longer in existence having become inoperative and void for non-payment of taxes 4/1/61

SECURITY ENERGY CORP (AB)
Merged into Clarinet Resources Ltd. 04/03/1995
Each share Common no par exchanged for (0.86) share Common no par
Clarinet Resources Ltd. recapitalized as Symmetry Resources Inc. 08/16/1996 which merged into Berkley Petroleum Corp. 01/31/2000
(See Berkley Petroleum Corp.)

SECURITY ENGINEERING, INC. (MN)
Name changed back to Silent Knight Security Systems, Inc. 7/8/74
(See Silent Knight Security Systems, Inc.)

SECURITY ENGINEERING CO.
Acquired by Dresser Industries, Inc. 10/31/1945
Each share Common no par exchanged for (0.57142857) share Common no par
(See Dresser Industries, Inc. (PA))

SECURITY ENVIRONMENTAL SYS INC (DE)
Reincorporated 04/19/1988
Place of incorporation changed from (BC) to (DE) 04/19/1988
Each share new Common no par exchanged for (1/3) share Common 3¢ par 07/30/1993
Chapter 11 bankruptcy proceedings terminated 08/09/2000

Stockholders' equity unlikely

SECURITY EQUITY FD (KS)
Name changed 12/11/1981
Common $1 par changed to 25¢ par and (3) additional shares issued 12/31/1968
Name changed from Security Equity Fund, Inc. to Security Equity Fund 12/11/1981
Completely liquidated
Each share All Capital Value Fund Class A 25¢ par received first and final distribution of $10.88 cash payable 10/18/2012 to holders of record 10/18/2012
Each share All Capital Value Fund Class C 25¢ par received first and final distribution of $10.62 cash payable 10/18/2012 to holders of record 10/18/2012
Each share All Capital Value Fund Institutional Class received first and final distribution of $10.96 cash payable 10/18/2012 to holders of record 10/18/2012

SECURITY FED BANCORP INC (DE)
Acquired by Capstone Bancshares Inc. 11/13/2008
Each share Common 1¢ par exchanged for $20.96 cash

SECURITY FED CORP (DE)
Reincorporated under the laws of South Carolina 08/17/1998

SECURITY FED SVGS & LN ASSN CLEVELAND (OH)
Common 1¢ par split (2) for (1) by issuance of (1) additional share 06/30/1992
Reorganized as Security First Corp. 02/05/1993
Each share Common 1¢ par exchanged for (1) share Common 1¢ par
Security First Corp. merged into FirstMerit Corp. 10/23/1998 which merged into Huntington Bancshares Inc. 08/16/2016

SECURITY FIN CORP SPARTANBURG (SC)
Stock Dividend - 10% 10/9/72
Acquired by a private company 7/2/81
Each share Common 20¢ par exchanged for $12.50 cash

SECURITY FINL BANCORP INC (DE)
Merged into Standard Bancshares, Inc. 06/20/2003
Each share Common 1¢ par exchanged for $24 cash

SECURITY FINANCIAL CORP. (GA)
Merged into United States Finance Co., Inc. (FL) 08/08/1967
Each share Common $1 par exchanged for (0.38389) share Common $1 par
United States Finance Co., Inc. (FL) reincorporated in Delaware as Unicapital Corp. 07/01/1969 which name changed to Production Operators Corp. 12/08/1980 which merged into Camco International Inc. 06/13/1997 which merged into Schlumberger Ltd. 08/31/1998

SECURITY FINL CORP (DE)
Stock Dividend - 3% payable 12/14/1999 to holders of record 12/08/1999
Merged into Farmers National Banc Corp. 11/30/2009
Each share Common exchanged for (9.937) shares Common no par

SECURITY FINL GROUP INC (DE)
Merged into Metropolitan Financial Corp. 9/30/92
Each share Common 10¢ par exchanged for (1.294) shares Common 1¢ par
Metropolitan Financial Corp. merged into First Bank System, Inc. 1/24/95 which name changed to U.S.

Bancorp (Old) 8/1/97 which merged into U.S. Bancorp (New) 2/27/2001

SECURITY FIN HLDG CO (DE)
Common 1¢ par split (3) for (2) by issuance of (0.5) additional share 2/14/92
Merged into BB&T Financial Corp. 2/25/93
Each share Common 1¢ par exchanged for (0.7822) share Common $2.50 par
BB&T Financial Corp. merged into Southern National Corp. 2/28/95 which name changed to BB&T Corp. 5/19/97

SECURITY FINL SVCS INC (WI)
Common $20 par changed to $10 par 04/26/1984
Stock Dividends - 100% 06/01/1973; 10% 01/15/1977; 10% 09/10/1978; 10% 07/31/1979; 10% 04/30/1980; 20% 07/29/1983; 20% 09/05/1984
Merged into First Wisconsin Corp. 12/23/1985
Each share Common $10 par exchanged for $68 cash

SECURITY FING SVCS INC (NV)
Recapitalized as Echo Satellite Communications, Inc. 02/11/2008
Each share Common $0.0001 par exchanged for (0.005) share Common $0.0001 par
Echo Satellite Communications, Inc. recapitalized as SatMAX Corp. 05/05/2009 which name changed to Green Energy Solution Industries, Inc. 03/02/2012

SECURITY FIRE INSURANCE CO.
Merged into Hawkeye-Security Insurance Co. in 1950
Each share Common exchanged for (0.2) share Preferred $10 par to nearest (0.1) share and balance of interest in Common to nearest (0.25) share with less than (0.25) share in cash
(See Hawkeye-Security Insurance Co.)

SECURITY FIRST BK (ANAHEIM, CA)
Reorganized as California Community Bancshares, Inc. 12/22/99
Each share Common 1¢ par exchanged for (0.0938) share Common 1¢ par
(See California Community Bancshares, Inc.)

SECURITY FIRST BK (MEDIA, PA)
Merged into State Bancshares, Inc. 12/22/1994
Each share Common $4 par exchanged for (0.3397) share Common $1 par
State Bancshares, Inc. name changed to JeffBanks, Inc. 05/22/1995 which merged into Hudson United Bancorp 11/30/1999 which merged into TD Banknorth Inc. 01/31/2006
(See TD Banknorth Inc.)

SECURITY 1ST BK & TR CO (GRAND HAVEN, MI)
Reorganized as Pacesetter Financial Corp. (DE) 1/2/73
Each share Common $10 par exchanged for (1.682) shares Common $10 par
Pacesetter Financial Corp. (DE) reincorporated in Michigan 3/10/80
(See Pacesetter Financial Corp. (MI))

SECURITY FIRST CORP (OH)
Common 1¢ par split (2) for (1) by issuance of (1) additional share 09/30/1993
Common 1¢ par split (3) for (2) by issuance of (1) additional share payable 07/31/1997 to holders of record 07/15/1997
Merged into FirstMerit Corp. 10/23/1998
Each share Common 1¢ par

exchanged for (0.8855) share Common 1¢ par
FirstMerit Corp. merged into Huntington Bancshares Inc. 08/16/2016

SECURITY FIRST NATIONAL BANK (LOS ANGELES, CA)
Capital Stock $20 par changed to $25 par in 1948
Capital Stock $25 par changed to $12.50 par and (1) additional share issued plus a 25% stock dividend paid in 1954
Capital Stock $12.50 par changed to $10 par and (0.2) additional share issued plus a 20% stock dividend paid 5/28/65
Stock Dividends - 33-1/3% 2/23/55; 10% 8/31/59; 10% 2/24/61; 15% 7/15/67
Under plan of merger name changed to Security Pacific National Bank (Los Angeles, CA) 7/1/68
Security Pacific National Bank (Los Angeles, CA) reorganized as Security Pacific Corp. 6/30/72 which merged into BankAmerica Corp. (Old) 4/22/92 which merged into BankAmerica Corp. (New) 9/30/98 which name changed to Bank of America Corp. 4/28/99

SECURITY 1ST NATL BK (SHEBOYGAN, WI)
99.7% acquired by Security Financial Services, Inc. through exchange offer which expired 08/01/1970
Public interest eliminated

SECURITY FIRST NETWORK BK (ATLANTA, GA)
Under plan of reorganization each share Common no par automatically became (1) share Security First Technologies Corp. Common 1¢ par 10/01/1998
Security First Technologies Corp. name changed to S1 Corp. 11/12/1999 which was acquired by ACI Worldwide, Inc. 02/13/2012

SECURITY FIRST REAL ESTATE INVT TR (CA)
Trust terminated 00/00/1994
Details not available

SECURITY FIRST TECHNOLOGIES CORP (DE)
Common 1¢ par split (2) for (1) by issuance of (1) additional share payable 05/07/1999 to holders of record 04/26/1999
Name changed to S1 Corp. 11/12/1999
S1 Corp. acquired by ACI Worldwide, Inc. 02/13/2012

SECURITY FREEHOLD PETROLEUMS LTD. (CANADA)
Acquired by Hudson's Bay Oil & Gas Co. Ltd. 12/13/1963
Each share Common no par exchanged for (0.5) share Capital Stock $2.50 par
Hudson's Bay Oil & Gas Co. Ltd. merged into Dome Petroleum Ltd. 03/10/1982
(See Dome Petroleum Ltd.)

SECURITY GEN INS CO (TX)
Merged into Eagle Insurance Co. 06/30/1968
Each share Capital Stock $1 par exchanged for (0.00517) share $1.20 Preferred $1 par and (1.75) shares Common 50¢ par
(See Eagle Insurance Co.)

SECURITY GROUP, INC. (NC)
Completely liquidated 04/20/1964
Each share Common 30¢ par exchanged for first and final distribution of (0.2) share Avemco Corp. Common 10¢ par and (0.0625) Common Stock Purchase Warrant
(See Avemco Corp.)

SECURITY GROWTH & INCOME FD (KS)
Name changed to Security Large Cap Value Fund 10/01/2002

SECURITY HOME MTG CORP (CANADA)
Name changed 11/01/1994
Name changed from Security Home Mortgage Investment Corp. to Security Home Mortgage Corp. 11/01/1994
Placed under the control of the Superintendent of Financial Institutions 06/04/1996
No stockholders' equity

SECURITY-HOME TRUST CO. (OH)
Charter cancelled for non-payment of taxes 10/16/44

SECURITY HOUSING CORP.
In process of liquidation in 1950

SECURITY INDS AMER INC (NJ)
Charter declared void for non-payment of taxes 1/14/82

SECURITY INDS INC (DE)
Reorganized as North Wave Communications Corp. 9/2/99
Each share Common $0.0001 par exchanged for (2) shares Common $0.0001 par
North Wave Communications Corp. recapitalized as Knoway Ventures Inc. 12/23/99 which recapitalized as Olympus Mountain Gold Ltd. 8/5/2004

SECURITY INSURANCE CO. OF NEW HAVEN (CT)
Each share Capital Stock $25 par exchanged for (2.5) shares Capital Stock $10 par in 1930
Stock Dividend - 33-1/3% 10/1/62
Name changed to Security Insurance Co. of Hartford 1/1/65
Security Insurance Co. of Hartford name changed to Security Corp. 6/30/68 which was acquired by Textron Inc. 6/29/73

SECURITY INS CO HARTFORD (CT)
Under plan of reorganization name changed to Security Corp. 06/30/1968
Security Corp. acquired by Textron Inc. 06/29/1973

SECURITY INTELLIGENCE TECHNOLOGIES INC (FL)
Common $0.0001 par split (3) for (1) by issuance of (2) additional shares payable 12/05/2005 to holders of record 11/28/2005 Ex date - 12/06/2005
Chapter 7 bankruptcy proceedings terminated 01/15/2009
No stockholders' equity

SECURITY INTL CORP (PR)
Liquidation completed
Each share Common 10¢ par received initial distribution of (0.04) share International Bank (Washington, DC) Class A Common $1 par 12/29/1972
Each share Common 10¢ par received second and final distribution of $0.043 cash 03/20/1976
Note: Certificates were not required to be surrendered and are without value

SECURITY INTL INC (DE)
Name changed to International Recreation Corp. 05/06/1970
International Recreation Corp. merged into Open Road Industries, Inc. 04/24/1974 which name changed to ORICO 10/20/1977 which name changed to Sargent Industries, Inc. (CA) 06/01/1979
(See Sargent Industries, Inc. (CA))

SECURITY INVT FD INC (KS)
Name changed to Security Growth & Income Fund and Common $1 par reclassified as (1) share Class A Common $1 par and (1) share Class B Common $1 par 7/6/93
Security Growth & Income Fund name changed to Security Large Capital Value Fund 10/1/2002

SECURITY INVESTMENT TRUST, INC.
Liquidated in 1945

SECURITY INVTS GROUP INC (DE)
SEC revoked common stock registration 07/26/2010
Stockholders' equity unlikely

SECURITY LEASING CO. (UT)
Name changed to SLC, Inc. 5/30/67
SLC, Inc. completed liquidation 2/17/72

SECURITY LIFE & ACC CO (CO)
Reorganized under plan of merger 01/05/1960
Each share Full Part. $10 par exchanged for (10) shares Ser. A Common $4 par
Each share Limited Part. $1 par exchanged for (1) share Ser. B Common $4 par
Each share Ser. A Common $4 par and Ser. B Common $4 par exchanged for (2.666666) shares Ser. A Common $2 par and Ser. B Common $2 par respectively to effect a (2) for (1) split plus a 33-1/3% stock dividend 03/15/1963
Stock Dividends - 25% 03/15/1961; 20% 03/15/1962; 10% 03/13/1964; 10% 06/15/1965; 10% 06/13/1969
Name changed to Security Life of Denver Insurance Co. 05/29/1981
(See Security Life of Denver Insurance Co.)

SECURITY LIFE & TRUST CO (SALEM, NC)
Common $5 par changed to $2.50 par and (1) additional share issued plus a 25% stock dividend paid 4/1/64
Reorganized as Integon Corp. (NC) 1/2/69
Each share Common $2.50 par exchanged for (1) share Common $2.50 par
Integon Corp. (NC) reincorporated in Delaware 5/10/79 which merged into Ashland Oil, Inc. 2/27/81 which name changed to Ashland Inc. (Old) 1/27/95
(See Ashland Inc. (Old))

SECURITY LIFE DENVER INS CO (CO)
Each share Ser. A Common $2 par exchanged for (0.0001) share Ser. A Common $20,000 par 04/29/1985
Each share Ser. B Common $2 par exchanged for (0.0001) Ser. B Common $20,000 par 04/29/1982
Note: In effect holders received $30 cash per share and public interest was eliminated

SECURITY LIFE INSURANCE CO. OF AMERICA (VA)
Placed in receivership and acquired by Central Life Insurance Co. of Illinois in 1932
No stockholders' equity

SECURITY LIFE INS CO AMER (MN)
98% held by Security American Financial Enterprises, Inc. through exchange offer as of 01/30/1974
Public interest eliminated

SECURITY LIFE INS CO GA (GA)
Stock Dividends - 15% 3/30/62; 20% 3/22/63; 10% 3/26/64; 12% 4/8/66; 10% 9/15/69; 15% 5/15/70; 10% 5/15/71; 25% 6/1/72; 25% 6/1/73; 25% 9/6/74
Merged into Tenneco Inc. 1/4/85
Each share Capital Stock $1 par exchanged for $28.50 cash

SECURITY LOAN & FINANCE CO. (UT)
Name changed to Security Leasing Co. in 1957
Security Leasing Co. name changed to SLC, Inc. 5/30/67 which completed liquidation 2/17/72

SECURITY MINERALS CORP. (UT)
Each share Common 10¢ par exchanged for (5) shares Common no par 05/27/1970
Name changed to Security Industries, Inc. 03/30/1971

SECURITY MTG INVS NEW (MA)
Reorganized under the laws of Delaware as Security Capital Corp. and Shares of Bene. Int. $1 par reclassified as Common $1 par 1/23/80
(See Security Capital Corp.)

SECURITY MTG INVS OLD (MA)
Liquidation completed 5/2/72
Each Share of Bene. Int. no par automatically became (1) Security Mortgage Investors (New) Share of Bene. Int. $1 par
Security Mortgage Investors (New) reorganized as Security Capital Corp. 1/23/80
(See Security Capital Corp.)

SECURITY-MUTUAL BANK & TRUST CO. (ST. LOUIS, MO)
Capital Stock $25 par changed to $10 par and (1.5) additional shares issued 1/14/60
Name changed to Security Trust Co. (St. Louis, MO) 1/17/62
(See Security Trust Co. (St. Louis, MO))

SECURITY N Y ST CORP (NY)
Merged into Norstar Bancorp Inc. 5/1/84
Each share $1.44 Conv. Preferred Ser. B $5 par exchanged for $38.50 cash
Each share $6 Conv. Preferred Ser. A $5 par exchanged for $137.50 cash
Each share Common $5 par exchanged for (1.1268) shares Common $5 par
Norstar Bancorp Inc. merged into Fleet/Norstar Financial Group, Inc. 1/1/88 which name changed to Fleet Financial Group, Inc. (New) 4/15/92 which name changed to Fleet Boston Corp. 10/1/99 which name changed to FleetBoston Financial Corp. 4/18/2000 which merged into Bank of America Corp. 4/1/2004

SECURITY NATL BK & TR CO. OF NEW JERSEY (NEWARK, NJ)
Name changed 03/27/1975
Name changed 06/15/1982
Name changed from Security National Bank (Newark, NJ) to Security National Bank of New Jersey (Newark, NJ) 03/27/1975
Name changed from Security National Bank of New Jersey (Newark, NJ) to Security National Bank & Trust Co. of New Jersey (Newark, NJ) 06/15/1982
Merged into HUBCO, Inc. 02/05/1998
Each share Common $10 par exchanged for $34 cash

SECURITY NATL BK & TR CO (WHEELING, WV)
Stock Dividend - 400% 4/25/83
Under plan of reorganization each share Capital Stock $20 par automatically became (1) share Spectrum Financial Corp. Common $20 par 6/1/84
Spectrum Financial Corp. merged into Key Centurion Bancshares, Inc. 1/31/91 which merged into Banc One Corp. 5/3/93 which merged into Bank One Corp. 10/2/98 which merged into J.P. Morgan Chase & Co. 12/31/2000 which name

changed to JPMorgan Chase & Co. 7/20/2004

SECURITY NATL BK (ANCHORAGE, AK)
Closed by the FDIC in 1986
Stockholders' equity undetermined

SECURITY NATIONAL BANK (AUSTIN, TX)
Merged into Republic of Texas Corp. 07/10/1981
Each share Common $5 par exchanged for $17.33 cash

SECURITY NATL BK (BATTLE CREEK, MI)
Stock Dividend - 100% 03/07/1966
Name changed to SNB Bank & Trust Co. (Battle Creek, MI) 03/13/1980
(See SNB Bank & Trust Co. (Battle Creek, MI))

SECURITY NATL BK (FALLS CHURCH, VA)
Name changed to Dominion National Bank (Falls Church, VA) 01/01/1971
Dominion National Bank (Falls Church, VA) changed location to (Vienna, VA) 08/05/1974 which name changed to Dominion Bank of Northern Virginia, N.A. (Vienna, VA) 05/21/1984
(See Dominion Bank of Northern Virginia, N.A. (Vienna, VA))

SECURITY NATIONAL BANK (GREENSBORO, NC)
Each share Capital Stock $10 par exchanged for (2.2222) shares Capital Stock $5 par to effect a (2) for (1) split and a 11-1/9% stock dividend 01/22/1957
Merged into North Carolina National Bank (Charlotte, NC) 06/30/1960
Each share Capital Stock $5 par exchanged for (1.1) shares Common $5 par
North Carolina National Bank (Charlotte, NC) reorganized as NCNB Corp. 11/04/1968 which name changed to NationsBank Corp. 12/31/1991 which reincorporated in Delaware as BankAmerica Corp. (Old) 09/25/1998 which merged into BankAmerica Corp. (New) 09/30/1998 which name changed to Bank of America Corp. 04/28/1999

SECURITY NATL BK (HEMPSTEAD, NY)
Liquidation completed
Each share Common $5 par received initial distribution of $7.40 cash 06/23/1975
Each share Common $5 par exchanged for second and final distribution of $0.955 cash 09/29/1980

SECURITY NATIONAL BANK (HUNTINGTON, NY)
Common $10 par changed to $5 par and (1) additional share issued 01/10/1956
Under plan of merger name changed to Security National Bank of Long Island (Huntington, NY) 05/26/1958 which name changed back to Security National Bank (Huntington, NY) 11/12/1968
Location changed to (Hempstead, NY) 05/08/1972
(See Security National Bank (Hempstead, NY))

SECURITY NATL BK (KANSAS CITY, KS)
Each share Capital Stock $100 par exchanged for (8-1/3) share Capital Stock $20 par to effect a (5) for (1) split and a 66-2/3% stock dividend 00/00/1948
Stock Dividends - 50% 01/25/1955; 60% 12/16/1958; 10% 10/28/1968
Reorganized as Security Bancshares, Inc. 03/08/1982
Each share Capital Stock $20 par exchanged for (1) share Common $20 par
(See Security Bancshares, Inc.)

SECURITY NATL BK (LYNN, MA)
Merged into Security Bancorp Inc. 12/11/80
Each share Capital Stock $10 par exchanged for $58.95 cash

SECURITY NATL BK (NACOGDOCHES, TX)
Merged into First Commercial Corp. 11/22/96
Each share Common $5 par exchanged for (1.101) shares Common $3 par
First Commercial Corp. merged into Regions Financial Corp. (Old) 7/31/98 which merged into Regions Financial Corp. (New) 7/1/2004

SECURITY NATL BK (POTTSTOWN, PA)
Merged into Harleysville National Corp. 07/01/1994
Each share Common $8 par exchanged for (0.7483) share Common $1 par
Harleysville National Corp. merged into First Niagara Financial Group, Inc. (New) 04/09/2010 which merged into KeyCorp (New) 08/01/2016

SECURITY NATIONAL BANK (RACINE, WI)
Name changed to Heritage National Bank (Racine, Wisc.) 1/1/77

SECURITY NATL BK (ROANOKE, VA)
Merged into United Virginia Bankshares, Inc. 09/01/1971
Each share Common $10 par exchanged for (1.5) shares Common $10 par
United Virginia Bankshares, Inc. name changed to Crestar Financial Corp. 09/01/1987 which merged into SunTrust Banks Inc. 12/31/1998

SECURITY NATL BK (SIOUX CITY, IA)
Stock Dividends - 20% 05/17/1951; 20% 00/00/1954; 20% 01/31/1957; 10% 03/03/1969
Through exchange offer of (10) shares Security National Corp. Capital Stock $10 par for each share Capital Stock $100 par all but (110) shares were acquired as of 10/20/1969
Public interest eliminated

SECURITY NATL BK (SPRINGFIELD, MA)
Stock Dividend - 10% 02/20/1970
99.5% acquired by Multibank Financial Corp. through exchange offer which expired 05/30/1974
Public interest eliminated

SECURITY NATL BK (TRENTON, NJ)
Capital Stock $100 par changed to $25 par and (3) additional shares issued plus a 12-1/2% stock dividend paid 04/18/1947
Capital Stock $25 par changed to $5 par and (4) additional shares issued 02/28/1966
Stock Dividend - 10% 03/14/1969
Merged into First National State Bancorporation 07/14/1972
Each share Capital Stock $5 par exchanged for (1.1875) shares Common $6.25 par
First National State Bancorporation name changed to First Fidelity Bancorporation (Old) 05/01/1985 which merged into First Fidelity Bancorporation (New) 02/29/1988 which merged into First Union Corp. 01/01/1996 which name changed to Wachovia Corp. (Ctfs. dated after 09/01/2001) 09/01/2001 which merged into Wells Fargo & Co. (New) 12/31/2008

SECURITY NATL BK (WALNUT CREEK, CA)
Location changed 06/01/1971
Merged into Security National Bank (Oakland, CA) 10/09/1967
Each share Capital Stock $10 par exchanged for (4.5) shares Common $4 par
Security National Bank (Oakland, CA) location changed to (Walnut Creek, CA) 06/01/1971
Acquired by Hibernia Bancshares Corp. 01/01/1981
Details not available

SECURITY NATL BK (WASHINGTON, DC)
Capital Stock $10 par changed to $5 par and (1) additional share issued 04/16/1973
Reorganized as Security National Corp. (DE) 06/01/1982
Each share Capital Stock $5 par exchanged for (2) shares Common $2.50 par
(See Security National Corp. (DE))

SECURITY NATL BK LONG ISLAND (HUNTINGTON, NY)
Under plan of merger name changed to Security National Bank (Huntington, NY) 11/12/68
Security National Bank (Huntington, NY) changed location to Security National Bank (Hempstead, NY) 5/8/72

SECURITY NATL BK NEV (RENO, NV)
Capital Stock $5 par changed to $2.50 par and (1) additional share issued 4/9/79
Name changed to Security Bank of Nevada (Reno, NV) 1/7/80
Security Bank of Nevada (Reno, NV) acquired by Valley National Corp. 12/31/87 which merged into BankAmerica Corp. (Old) 3/13/92 which merged into BankAmerica Corp. (New) 9/30/98 which name changed to Bank of America Corp. 4/28/99

SECURITY NATL CORP (DE)
Merged into Signet Banking Corp. 08/31/1986
Each share Common $2.50 par exchanged for $68.50 cash

SECURITY NATIONAL LIFE INSURANCE CO. (AL)
Under plan of merger name changed to First National Life Insurance Co. (AL) 12/31/67
First National Life Insurance Co. (AL) reorganized as First National Corp. (NV) 12/31/69 which recapitalized as Seal Fleet, Inc. (NV) 8/9/79 which reorganized in Delaware as Seal Holdings Corp. 6/30/97 which name changed to Le@p Technology, Inc. 7/6/2000

SECURITY NATL LIFE INS CO (UT)
Class A Common $1.50 par reclassified as Class A Common $1 par 11/13/1968
Merged into S.N.L. Financial Corp. 03/24/1980
Each share Class A Common $1 par exchanged for (2) shares Common $1 par
S.N.L. Financial Corp. name changed to Security National Financial Corp. 12/27/1990

SECURITY NATIONAL OF INDIANA CORP. (IN)
Name changed to Conseco, Inc. 1/20/84
(See Conseco, Inc.)

SECURITY OIL CO. (NV)
Charter revoked for failure to file reports and pay fees 3/5/62

SECURITY OPTS CORP (NY)
Name changed to Venture Concepts Inc. 9/1/72
(See Venture Concepts Inc.)

SECURITY PA FINL CORP (PA)
Merged into Northeast Pennsylvania Financial Corp. 11/09/2000
Each share Common 1¢ par exchanged for $17.50 cash

SECURITY PAC CORP (DE)
Stock Dividends - 20% 02/20/1979; 20% 05/20/1983; 100% 02/08/1985
Merged into BankAmerica Corp. (Old) 04/22/1992
Each share 11% Depositary Preferred Ser. I exchanged for (1) share Depositary Preferred Ser. I
Each share 11% Preferred Ser. I no par exchanged for (1) share 11% Preferred Ser. I no par
Each share 11% Depositary Preferred Ser. J exchanged for (1) share 11% Depositary Preferred Ser. J no par
Each share 11% Preferred Ser. J no par exchanged for (1) share 11% Preferred Ser. J no par
Each share Common $10 par exchanged for (0.88) share Common $1.5625 par
BankAmerica Corp. (Old) merged into BankAmerica Corp. (New) 09/30/1998 which name changed to Bank of America Corp. 04/28/1999

SECURITY PAC NATL BK (LOS ANGELES, CA)
Stock Dividends - 20% 5/29/69; 20% 6/4/71
Under plan of reorganization each share Capital Stock $10 par automatically became (1) share Security Pacific Corp. Common $10 par 6/30/72
Security Pacific Corp. merged into BankAmerica Corp. (Old) 4/22/92 which merged into BankAmerica Corp. (New) 9/30/98 which name changed to Bank of America Corp. 4/28/99

SECURITY PACIFIC BANK NEVADA, N.A. (LAS VEGAS, NV)
Acquired by BankAmerica Corp. (Old) 06/01/1992
Details not available

SECURITY PEOPLES TR CO (ERIE, PA)
Each share Capital Stock $50 par exchanged for (6) shares Capital Stock $12.50 par to effect a (4) for (1) split and a 50% stock dividend paid 00/00/1944
Capital Stock $12.50 par changed to $6.25 par and (1) additional share issued plus a 100% stock dividend paid 02/12/1969
Stock Dividends - 11% 10/18/1947; (1) for (7-1/3) 11/01/1965
Merged into Pennbancorp 12/31/1983
Each share Capital Stock $6.25 par exchanged for $15 cash

SECURITY PETROLEUM CO. (DE)
Charter cancelled for failure to pay taxes in January 1921

SECURITY PLANNERS ASSOC INC (MA)
Proclaimed dissolved for failure to file reports and pay fees 01/10/1979

SECURITY PLASTICS INC (FL)
Merged into Security Plastics Acquisitions, Inc. 10/01/1981
Each share Common 10¢ par exchanged for $23 cash

SECURITY SAVINGS & COMMERCIAL BANK (WASHINGTON, DC)
Stock Dividend - 25% 12/22/43
Name changed to Security Bank (Washington, D.C.) 1/9/51
Security Bank (Washington, D.C.) name changed to Security Bank, N.A. (Washington, D.C.) 4/1/69 which name changed to Security National Bank (Washington, D.C.)

6/1/71 which reorganized as Security National Corp. 6/1/82
(See Security National Corp. (Del.))

SECURITY SVGS & LN (MD)
Merged into Sharon-Security Inc. 3/15/80
Each share Guaranty Stock $1 par exchanged for $5 cash
Note: An additional $1 cash per share was placed in a Reserve Fund pending conclusion of certain litigation
Additional details not available

SECURITY SVGS & LN ASSN HAYES (VA)
Merged out of existence 12/31/1982
Details not available

SECURITY SVGS & LN ASSN WATERBURY CONN (USA)
Placed in conservatorship by the Office of Thrift Supervision and RTC appointed receiver 4/1/91
Stockholders' equity unlikely

SECURITY SVGS BK S L A (VINELAND, NJ)
Name changed 06/28/1988
Name changed from Security Savings & Loan Association to Security Savings Bank, SLA (Vineland, NJ) 06/28/1988
Reorganized under the laws of Delaware as Security Investments Group, Inc. and Common $1 par changed to 10¢ par 03/06/1989
(See Security Investments Group, Inc.)

SECURITY SVGS F S B (USA)
Name changed 10/30/85
Name changed From Security Savings & Loan Association to Security Savings Bank F.S.B. 10/30/1985
Acquired by First Security Savings Bank (Bloomfield Hills, MI) 06/30/1994
Each share Common $1 par exchanged for $35 cash

SECURITY SAVINGS HOLDING CO., INC. (OH)
Acquired by Enterprise Federal Bancorp, Inc. 11/20/1998
Each share Common $10 par exchanged for $832.87 cash

SECURITY SVGS LIFE INS CO (AL)
Common $1 par changed to 50¢ par 12/29/1958
Merged into United Security Life Insurance Co. (AL) 06/08/1962
Each (0.2) share Common 50¢ par exchanged for (1) share Common $1 par
United Security Life Insurance Co. (AL) reorganized as United Security Holding Co. 01/20/1970 which liquidated for National Producers Life Insurance Co. 02/22/1978 which name changed to NPL Corp. 03/27/1981
(See NPL Corp.)

SECURITY SVGS LIFE INS CO (TX)
Certificate of authority cancelled 12/23/1988
Stockholders' equity unlikely

SECURITY SHARES INC (TX)
Merged into American State Financial 2/27/98
Each share Common $2 par exchanged for $11.42 cash

SECURITY SOUTHWEST CORP (TX)
Completely liquidated 9/21/82
Each share Common no par exchanged for first and final distribution of $1.55 cash

SECURITY ST BK (PECOS, TX)
Acquired by TransPecos Financial Corp. 01/19/2005
Details not available

SECURITY STAMPS, INC. (MN)
Name changed to SYN Corp. 2/28/72

SECURITY STORAGE CO., INC. (MD)
Dissolved 5/11/54
No stockholders' equity

SECURITY STORAGE CO. (DC)
Reincorporated under the laws of Delaware as Security Storage Co. of Washington in (Old) 1954
(See Security Storage Co. of Washington (DE) (Old))

SECURITY STORAGE CO WASHINGTON NEW (DE)
Common no par split (4) for (1) by issuance of (3) additional shares 3/25/64
Acquired by a group of investors 2/4/93
Each share Common no par exchanged for $120 cash

SECURITY STORAGE CO WASHINGTON OLD (DE)
Capital Stock $25 par changed to $5 par and (4) additional shares issued 1/3/56
Under plan of merger name changed to Security Assets Corp. 9/1/63 and holders of each share Common $5 par received $135.27 amount of Security Storage Co. of Washington (Del.) (New) Common no par 9/1/63
(See each company's listing)

SECURITY TAG SYS INC (DE)
Merged into Sensormatic Electronics Corp. 6/17/93
Each share Common $0.001 par exchanged for (0.0975) share Common 1¢ par
Sensormatic Electronics Corp. merged into Tyco International Ltd. 11/13/2001

SECURITY TECHNOLOGY INC (FL)
Involuntarily dissolved 11/04/1988

SECURITY TIRE & RUBBER CO. (DE)
Charter cancelled and declared inoperative and void for non-payment of taxes 3/22/22

SECURITY TITLE & GTY CO (NY)
Common $10 par changed to $9 par 00/00/1940
Each share Common $9 par exchanged for (9) shares Common $1 par 00/00/1951
Each share Common $1 par exchanged for (0.25) share Common $5 par 02/10/1961
Merged into Investors Funding Corp. of New York 12/29/1972
Each share Common $5 par exchanged for (2) shares Class A $5 par
(See Investors Funding Corp. of New York)

SECURITY TITLE BUILDING, INC.
Dissolved in 1946

SECURITY TITLE INSURANCE & GUARANTEE CO. (CA)
Name changed to Security Title Insurance Co. 07/01/1952
Security Title Insurance Co. name changed to Financial Corp. of America 04/30/1962 which merged into General America Corp. 07/31/1964 which name changed to Safeco Corp. 04/30/1968
(See Safeco Corp.)

SECURITY TITLE INSURANCE CO. (CA)
Common 50¢ par changed to $3 par 09/24/1954
Common $3 par changed to $1 par and (2) additional shares issued 09/03/1959
Name changed to Financial Corp. of America 04/30/1962
Financial Corp. of America merged into General America Corp. 07/31/1964 which name changed to Safeco Corp. 04/30/1968
(See Safeco Corp.)

SECURITY TRUST CO. (LEXINGTON, KY)
Each share Capital Stock $100 par exchanged for (4) shares Capital Stock $25 par in 1949
Stock Dividends - 20% 12/8/54; 66-2/3% 11/12/58
Merged into First Security National Bank & Trust Co. (Lexington, KY) 5/10/61
Each share Capital Stock $25 par exchanged for (2) shares Capital Stock $12.50 par
First Security National Bank & Trust Co. (Lexington, KY) reorganized as First Security Corp. of Kentucky 10/14/75 which was acquired by Banc One Corp. 8/21/92 which merged into Bank One Corp. 10/2/98 which merged into J.P. Morgan Chase & Co. 12/31/2000 which name changed to JPMorgan Chase & Co. 7/20/2004

SECURITY TRUST CO. (LYNN, MA)
Capital Stock $100 par changed to $20 par and (4) additional shares issued in 1929
Each share Capital Stock $20 par exchanged for (2) shares Capital Stock $10 par 1/29/60
Stock Dividend - 25% in 1955
Merged into Security-Danvers National Bank (Lynn, Mass.) 2/21/64
Each share Capital Stock $10 par exchanged for (1) share Capital Stock $10 par
Security-Danvers National Bank (Lynn, Mass.) name changed to Security National Bank (Lynn, Mass.) 3/15/68
(See Security National Bank, Lynn, Mass.))

SECURITY TRUST CO. (ST. LOUIS, MO)
Acquired by Mercantile Trust Co., N.A. (St. Louis, Mo.) 7/15/65
Each share Capital Stock $10 par exchanged for $60 cash

SECURITY TRUST CO. (WHEELING, WV)
Each share Capital Stock $100 par exchanged for (4) shares Capital Stock $25 par and a 100% stock dividend paid in 1950
Merged into Security National Bank & Trust Co. (Wheeling, WV) 6/29/62
Each share Capital Stock $20 par exchanged for (1) share Capital Stock $20 par
Security National Bank & Trust Co. (Wheeling, WV) reorganized as Spectrum Financial Corp. 6/1/84 which merged into Key Centurion Bancshares, Inc. 1/31/91 which merged into Banc One Corp. 5/3/93 which merged into Bank One Corp. 10/2/98 which merged into J.P. Morgan Chase & Co. 12/31/2000 which name changed to JPMorgan Chase & Co. 7/20/2004

SECURITY TR CO (ROCHESTER, NY)
Each share Capital Stock $100 par exchanged for (8) shares Capital Stock $25 par in 1943
Capital Stock $25 par changed to $15 par and (2/3) additional share issued 1/17/64
Stock Dividends - 100% 3/17/41; 100% 12/13/45; 57-1/7% 2/2/55; 10% 2/1/61
Merged into Security New York State Corp. 4/4/66
Each share Capital Stock $15 par exchanged for (0.5) share Common $5 par
Security New York State Corp. merged into Norstar Bancorp Inc. 5/1/84 which merged into Fleet/Norstar Financial Group, Inc. 1/1/88 which name changed to Fleet Financial Group, Inc. (New) 4/15/92 which name changed to Fleet

Boston Corp. 10/1/99 which name changed to FleetBoston Financial Corp. 4/18/2000 which merged into Bank of America Corp. 4/1/2004

SECURITY ULTRA FD INC (KS)
Common $1 par changed to 50¢ par and (1) additional share issued 2/2/81
Name changed to Security Mid Cap Growth Fund 10/1/2002

SECURITY WITH ADVANCED TECHNOLOGY INC (CO)
Recapitalized as PepperBall Technologies, Inc. 09/29/2008
Each share Common no par exchanged for (0.5) share Common no par
(See PepperBall Technologies, Inc.)

SECURUS RENEWABLE ENERGY INC (NV)
SEC revoked common stock registration 04/14/2010
Stockholders' equity unlikely

SED INTL HLDGS INC (DE)
Reincorporated under the laws of Georgia 11/10/1998

SEDA SPECIALTY PACKAGING CORP (DE)
Reincorporated 08/01/1994
State of incorporation changed from (CA) to (DE) 08/01/1994
Merged into CCL Industries Inc. 07/25/1997
Each share Common no par exchanged for $29 cash

SEDALIA MARSHALL BOONVILLE STAGE LINE INC (IA)
Each share Common 10¢ par exchanged for (0.1) share Common $1 par 07/15/1972
Merged into ABF, Inc. 10/22/1976
Each share Common $1 par received $11.20 cash
Note: Certificates were not required to be surrendered and are without value

SEDCO INC (TX)
Common $1 par split (3) for (2) by issuance of (0.5) additional share 7/30/80
Common $1 par split (2) for (1) by issuance of (1) additional share 1/30/81
Stock Dividend - 100% 1/15/69
Merged into Schlumberger Ltd. 12/24/84
Each share Common $1 par exchanged for (1.0639) shares Common 1¢ par

SEDER CAP CORP (ON)
Name changed to Covalon Technologies Ltd. 12/24/2004

SEDER PLASTICS CORP. (CO)
Name changed 10/19/49
Name changed from Seder & Son Moulded Products Co., Inc. to Seder Plastics Corp. 10/19/49
Company went private in 1981
Details not available

SEDGEWICKE BUSINESS ALLIANCE INC (NV)
Name changed to American Casinos International, Inc. in December 1994
American Casinos International, Inc. name changed to Enterprise Solutions, Inc. 3/15/99 which name changed to Enterprises Solutions Inc. 9/1/99
(See Enterprises Solutions Inc.)

SEDGLEY R F INC (DE)
Charter cancelled and declared inoperative and void for non-payment of taxes 4/15/68

SEDGWICK GROUP PLC (UNITED KINGDOM)
Acquired by Marsh & McLennan Companies, Inc. 01/05/1999
Each Sponsored ADR for Ordinary 1p par exchanged for $11.25 cash

SEDITION FILMS INC (NV)
Name changed to Select-TV Solutions, Inc. 06/23/2014

SEDMET EXPL INC (NV)
Name changed to Entertainment Boulevard Inc. 1/13/99
(See Entertainment Boulevard Inc.)

SEDNA GEOTECH INC (YT)
Struck off register and declared dissolved for failure to file returns 04/17/2008

SEDONA CORP. (NV)
Incorporated 5/5/77
Charter revoked for failure to file reports and pay fees 2/1/82

SEDONA CORP (NV)
Incorporated 01/06/1927
Charter revoked for failure to file reports and pay fees 10/01/1985

SEDONA HORIZONS CORP (NV)
Name changed to Cornerstone Entertainment, Inc. 7/21/2003
Cornerstone Entertainment, Inc. name changed to Beverly Hills Film Studios, Inc. 10/28/2003 which name changed to Big Screen Entertainment Group, Inc. 4/1/2005

SEDONA INDS LTD (BC)
Acquired by Harvard International Technologies Ltd. 6/29/94
Each share Common no par held by U.S. residents exchanged for (0.189753) share Common no par and (0.0407166) 3-year Common Stock Purchase Warrant
Each share Common no par held by Non-U.S. residents exchanged for (0.2325581) share Soranzo International Spirits Inc. Common no par and (0.1474926) Harvard International Technologies Ltd. 3-year Common Stock Purchase Warrant
(See Harvard International Technologies Ltd.)

SEDONA WORLDWIDE INC (AZ)
Name changed to Greens Worldwide Inc. (AZ) 08/10/2002
Greens Worldwide Inc. (AZ) reincorporated in Florida 12/03/2008 which recapitalized as Black Castle Developments, Inc. (FL) 03/03/2011 which reincorporated in Nevada 06/01/2011 which name changed to Black Castle Developments Holdings, Inc. 08/02/2011 which recapitalized as ingXabo Corp. 01/28/2015
(See ingXabo Corp.)

SEE (A.B.) ELEVATOR CO.
Dissolved in 1937

SEE CORP LTD (HONG KONG)
ADR agreement terminated 12/01/2015
No ADR's remain outstanding

SEEBEYOND TECHNOLOGY CORP (DE)
Reincorporated 7/9/2001
State of incorporation changed from (CA) to (DE) and Common no par changed to $0.0001 par 7/9/2001
Merged into Sun Microsystems, Inc. 8/25/2005
Each share Common $0.0001 par exchanged for $4.25 cash

SEEBOARD PLC (UNITED KINGDOM)
Sponsored ADR's Final Installment for Ordinary 50p par split (2) for (1) by issuance of (1) additional ADR 01/24/1994
Acquired by Central & South West Corp. 04/15/1996
Each Sponsored ADR Final Installment for Ordinary 50p par exchanged for $81.38 cash
Each 144A ADR Final Installment for Ordinary 50p par exchanged for $81.38 cash

SEEBURG CORP (DE)
Reincorporated 03/30/1962
State of incorporation changed from (PA) to (DE) 03/30/1962
Completely liquidated
Each share Common $1 par exchanged for first and final distribution of $7.954 principal amount of Seeburg Industries, Inc. 6% Conv. Subord. Debenture due 01/01/1978 and (0.5732) share Class A Common 50¢ par 05/23/1975
Seeburg Industries, Inc. name changed to XCOR International Inc. 12/12/1977 which name changed to Biscayne Holdings, Inc. (DE) 06/30/1986 which reorganized in Florida 07/01/1990 which name changed to Biscayne Apparel, Inc. 05/31/1994 which recapitalized as El Apparel, Inc. 08/29/2005 which recapitalized as NutriOne Corp. 07/27/2006
(See NutriOne Corp.)

SEEBURG CORP NEW (IL)
Involuntarily dissolved 4/9/93
Details not available

SEEBURG INDS INC (DE)
Name changed to XCOR International Inc. 12/12/1977
XCOR International Inc. name changed to Biscayne Holdings, Inc. (DE) 06/30/1986 which reorganized in Florida 07/01/1990 which name changed to Biscayne Apparel, Inc. 05/31/1994 which recapitalized as El Apparel, Inc. 08/29/2005 which recapitalized as NutriOne Corp. 07/27/2006
(See NutriOne Corp.)

SEEBURG PHONOGRAPH CORP (IL)
Name changed to Seeburg Corp. (IL) 4/21/87
Seeburg Corp (IL) involuntarily dissolved 4/9/93

SEEC INC (DE)
Issue Information - 1,800,000 shares COM offered at $7.25 per share on 01/22/1997
Merged into Polaris Software Lab Pte Ltd. 10/30/2008
Each share Common 1¢ par exchanged for $0.03762 cash
Note: An additional initial distribution of $0.00397 cash per share was paid from escrow 12/02/2010

SEEDLING TECHNOLOGIES CORP (DE)
Name changed to Worldmodal Network Services Inc. 10/26/2001
(See Worldmodal Network Services Inc.)

SEEDTOWN PRODUCTS, INC.
Business discontinued 00/00/1931
Details not available

SEEGER REFRIGERATOR CO. (MN)
Merged into Whirlpool-Seeger Corp.
Each share Common $5 par exchanged for (0.1875) share 4-1/4% Preferred $80 par and (1.375) shares new Common $5 par 9/15/55
Whirlpool-Seeger Corp. name was changed to Whirlpool Corp. (Del.) 4/1/57

SEEGER-SUNBEAM CORP.
Name changed to Seeger Refrigerator Co. in 1946 which merged into Whirlpool- Seeger Corp. 9/15/55 which name was changed to Whirlpool Corp. (Del.) 4/1/57

SEEK-2 VENTURES INC (CO)
Name changed to Sigma-7 Products, Inc. 04/19/1989
(See Sigma-7 Products, Inc.)

SEEK VENTURES INC (CO)
Name changed to Aqua-Buoy Corp. 06/19/1989
Aqua-Buoy Corp. name changed to Chester Holdings, Ltd. 09/30/1993 which recapitalized as First Light Resources Inc. 11/09/2005 which name changed to Invercoal, Inc. 06/28/2006 which recapitalized as Core International Ltd. 04/02/2007 which recapitalized as Therma-Med, Inc. 12/31/2008

SEEKER SOFTWARE INC (DE)
Acquired by Concur Technologies, Inc. 06/09/1999
Each share Common $0.001 par exchanged for (0.167833) share Common $0.001 par
(See Concur Technologies, Inc.)

SEEL MTG INVT CORP (CANADA)
Acquired by Mutual Trust Co. 06/26/1992
Each share Common $8 par exchanged for $7 cash

SEELEY MINING CORP. LTD. (ON)
Merged into Great Eagle Explorations & Holdings Ltd. 7/7/69
Each share Capital Stock no par exchanged for (0.142857) share Common no par
Great Eagle Explorations & Holdings Ltd. merged into Belle Aire Resource Explorations Ltd. 8/29/78 which name changed to Sprint Resources Ltd. 9/23/82 which name changed to Meacon Bay Resources Inc. 3/9/87 which recapitalized as Advantex Marketing International Inc. 9/16/91

SEELITE PLASTIC ENTERPRISES LTD.
Bankrupt in 1948

SEEMAN BROS INC (NY)
Common no par changed to $3 par 06/16/1959
5% Preferred called for redemption 10/02/1961
Stock Dividend - 200% 11/19/1945
Name changed to Seabrook Foods, Inc. 07/24/1970
(See Seabrook Foods, Inc.)

SEEMAR EXPLS INC (ON)
Recapitalized 04/10/1985
Recapitalized from Seemar Mines Ltd. to Seemar Explorations Inc. 04/10/1985
Each share Common $1 par exchanged for (0.2) share Common no par
Name changed to Goldstake Explorations Inc. 08/20/1986

SEEQ TECHNOLOGY INC (CA)
Reorganized under the laws of Delaware 02/12/1987
Each share Common 1¢ par exchanged for (0.2) share Common 1¢ par
Seeq Technology Inc. (DE) merged into LSI Logic Corp. 06/22/1999 which name changed to LSI Corp. 04/06/2007
(See LSI Corp.)

SEEQ TECHNOLOGY INC (DE)
Merged into LSI Logic Corp. 06/22/1999
Each share Common 1¢ par exchanged for (0.0759) share Common no par
LSI Logic Corp. name changed to LSI Corp. 04/06/2007
(See LSI Corp.)

SEER TECHNOLOGIES INC (DE)
Merged into Level 8 Systems, Inc. 5/26/99
Each share Common 1¢ par exchanged for $0.35 cash

SEERTECH CORP (FL)
Filed a petition under Chapter 7 Federal Bankruptcy Code 7/21/2006
No stockholders' equity

SEES CANDY SHOPS INC (CA)
Merged into Blue Chip Stamps 06/06/1978
Each share Common no par exchanged for $55 cash

SEESMART TECHNOLOGIES INC (NV)
Merged into Revolution Lighting Technologies, Inc. 12/20/2012
Details not available

SEF PRIVATE ISSUERS TR (ON)
Liquidation completed
Each Unit received initial distribution of $0.20 cash payable 06/30/2010 to holders of record 06/29/2010
Each Unit received second distribution of $0.20 cash payable 01/14/2011 to holders of record 12/31/2010
Each Unit received third and final distribution of $0.47 cash payable 01/17/2012 to holders of record 01/17/2012

SEFCO INC (CO)
Name changed to Members Financial Service Bureau, Inc. 10/31/89
Members Financial Service Bureau, Inc. recapitalized as Shared Use Network Services, Inc. 8/25/95 which name changed to Evergreen Network.Com Inc. 4/7/2000

SEFTON MANUFACTURING CORP.
Assets acquired by Container Corp. of America in 1930
Details not available

SEGA CORP (JAPAN)
Name changed 11/1/2000
Name changed from Sega Enterprises Ltd. to Sega Corp. 11/1/2000
Sponsored ADR's for Common 50 Yen par changed to no par 3/31/2002
Merged into Sega Sammy Holdings Inc. 10/4/2004
Each Sponsored ADR for Common no par exchanged for (0.28) Sponsored ADR for Common

SEGA ENTERPRISES INC (CA)
Stock Dividend - 200% 6/22/79
Merged into Gulf & Western Industries, Inc. 11/4/83
Each share Common $1 par exchanged for $10.85 cash

SEGAL LOCK & HARDWARE CO., INC. (NY)
Common no par exchanged (3) for (1) in 1929
Common no par changed to $1 par in 1936
Bankrupt 5/22/57

SEGALL BRYANT & HAMILL MID CAP FD (MN)
Merged into Reserve Fund Inc. 01/00/2005
Details not available

SEGAMI IMAGES INC (BC)
Delisted from Toronto Venture Stock Exchange 06/05/2002

SEGGOS INDS INC (DE)
Name changed to Gold'N Treasures Trading Co., Ltd. 4/27/73
(See Gold'N Treasures Trading Co., Ltd.)

SEGMENTZ INC (DE)
Name changed to Express-1 Expedited Solutions, Inc. 06/06/2006
Express-1 Expedited Solutions, Inc. recapitalized as XPO Logistics, Inc. 09/02/2011

SEGUE SOFTWARE INC (DE)
Merged into Borland Software Corp. 4/19/2006
Each share Common 1¢ par exchanged for $8.67 cash

SEGURO RES LTD (BC)
Name changed to Aura Industries Inc. 2/12/90
Aura Industries Inc. name changed to Nycal (Canada) Inc. 7/25/91
(See Nycal (Canada) Inc.)

SEGUROS COMERCIAL AMER S A DE CV (MEXICO)
Acquired by ING Groep N.V. 09/09/2001
Details not available

SEI CORP (PA)
Common 1¢ par split (2) for (1) by issuance of (1) additional share 6/22/87
Common 1¢ par split (2) for (1) by issuance of (1) additional share 7/6/93
Stock Dividend - 100% 2/22/83
Name changed to SEI Investments Co. 1/2/97

SEIBERLING RUBBER CO. (DE)
Each share 8% Preferred $100 par exchanged for (1) share 5% Class B Preferred $100 par in 1939
Common no par changed to $1 par in 1946
Stock Dividend - 10% 7/23/59
Name changed to Seilon, Inc. 2/19/65
(See Seilon, Inc.)

SEIDELHUBER STEEL ROLLING MILL CORP. (WA)
Voluntarily dissolved 4/19/66
Details not available

SEILER POLLUTION CTL SYS INC (DE)
Each share old Common $0.0001 par exchanged for (0.16666666) share new Common $0.0001 par 10/01/1998
Charter cancelled and declared inoperative and void for non-payment of taxes 03/01/1999

SEILER'S, INC. (PA)
Name changed to Burk (Louis) Co. 9/18/67
(See Burk (Louis) Co.)

SEILON INC (DE)
4-1/2% Prior Preferred $100 par called for redemption 01/20/1969
5% Class A Preferred $100 par called for redemption 01/20/1969
(Additional Information in Active)

SEINE RIV RES INC (BC)
Recapitalized as Trinity Plumas Capital Corp. 4/4/2002
Each share Common no par exchanged for (0.05) share Common no par
Trinity Plumas Capital Corp. name changed to TrueStar Petroleum Corp. 5/16/2005

SEIRIOS INTL INC (NV)
Dissolved 04/30/2008
Details not available

SEIS PROS INC (DE)
Merged into Professional Geophysics, Inc. 09/29/1987
Each share Common 1¢ par exchanged for $3 cash

SEISCOM DELTA INC (TX)
Common 10¢ par split (5) for (4) by issuance of (0.25) additional share 3/14/80
Common 10¢ par split (5) for (4) by issuance of (0.25) additional share 4/14/81
Reorganized under Chapter 11 Federal Bankruptcy Code 11/30/87
Each share Common 10¢ par exchanged for (1) Liquidation Interest in Seiscom Delta Liquidation Trust
Note: No physical certificates will be issued. Liquidation Interest will be recorded in the books of the agent
(See Seiscom Delta Liquidation Trust)

SEISCOM DELTA LIQUIDATION TRUST (TX)
In process of liquidation
Details not available

SEISDATA SVCS INC (DE)
Each share old Common 1¢ par exchanged for (1/3) share new Common 1¢ par 8/8/86

Name changed to Trakit Corp. 5/31/90
(See Trakit Corp.)

SEISMIC COMPUTING CORP. (TX)
Name changed to Seiscom Delta Inc. 2/12/73
(See Seiscom Delta Inc.)

SEISMIC ENTERPRISES INC. (DE)
Name changed to Seitel, Inc. 8/24/87
(See Seitel, Inc.)

SEISMOGRAPH SERVICE CORP. (DE)
Common $1 par split (5) for (4) by issuance of (0.25) additional share 1/30/64
Common $1 par split (5) for (4) by issuance of (0.25) additional share 1/5/66
Liquidation completed
Each share Common $1 par exchanged for initial distribution of (1) share Raytheon Co. $1.12 Preferred Ser. A no par and (0.261) share Common $5 par 12/30/66
Each share Common $1 par received second and final distribution of (0.039) share Raytheon Co. Common $5 par 1/31/68

SEITEL INC (DE)
Each share old Common 1¢ par exchanged for (0.2) share new Common 1¢ par 1/26/89
New Common 1¢ par split (2) for (1) by issuance of (1) additional share payable 12/12/97 to holders of record 12/3/97 Ex date - 12/15/97
Each share new Common 1¢ par received distribution of (0.064272) share Eagle Geophysical, Inc. Common 1¢ par payable 6/18/99 to holders of record 5/18/99
Stock Dividends - 10% 5/30/89; 10% 4/6/90
Plan of reorganiztion under Chapter 11 Federal Bankruptcy Code effective 7/2/2004
Each share new Common 1¢ par exchanged for (1) share Common 1¢ par and (1) Common Stock Purchase Warrant expiring 8/2/2004
Merged into ValueAct Capital Master Fund, L.P. 2/14/2007
Each share Common 1¢ par exchanged for $3.70 cash

SEKISUI PREFAB HOMES LTD (JAPAN)
Stock Dividends - 10% 10/25/72; 10% 4/27/73; 10% 10/19/73; 10% 4/16/74; 10% 10/24/74; 20% 4/18/75; 20% 5/20/77; 10% 5/15/78; 10% 5/11/79; 10% 5/14/80
Name changed to Sekisui House, Ltd. 4/28/82

SEKOYA HLDGS LTD (NV)
Common $0.001 par split (25) for (1) by issuance of (24) additional shares payable 06/11/2007 to holders of record 05/14/2007 Ex date - 06/12/2007
Name changed to MyECheck, Inc. 12/14/2007

SEL-DRUM INTL INC (CO)
Merged into C. Cotran Holding Inc. 3/15/2001
Each share Common 1¢ par exchanged for $0.40 cash

SEL-LEB MARKETING INC (NY)
Each share old Common no par exchanged for (0.125) share new Common no par 06/19/1998
New Common no par split (2) for (1) by issuance of (1) additional share payable 12/07/1999 to holders of record 11/24/1999
Charter cancelled and proclaimed dissolved for failure to pay taxes 04/29/2009

SEL-REX CORP. (NJ)
Common $1 par split (3) for (2) by issuance of (0.5) additional share 3/22/67
Completely liquidated 7/31/68
Each share Common $1 par exchanged for first and final distribution of (0.395) share Occidental Petroleum Corp. $3.60 Conv. Preferred $1 par

SELAMA DINDINGS PLANTATION LTD (HI)
Capital Stock $10 par changed to $5 par 00/00/1934
Involuntarily dissolved for failure to file annual reports 00/00/2005

SELAS CORP AMER (PA)
50¢ Conv. 2nd Preferred $1 par called for redemption 4/15/63
Common $1 par split (3) for (2) by issuance of (0.5) additional share 10/18/65
Common $1 par split (3) for (2) by issuance of (0.5) additional share 7/12/71
Common $1 par split (2) for (1) by issuance of (1) additional share 4/2/90
Common $1 par split (3) for (2) by issuance of (0.5) additional share payable 6/27/97 to holders of record 6/10/97 Ex date - 6/30/97
Name changed to IntriCon Corp. 4/1/2005

SELBURN OIL CO. LTD.
Merged into Bailey Selburn Oil & Gas Ltd. and each (2) shares Capital Stock no par exchanged for (1) share Class A $1 par in 1952
(See Bailey Selburn Oil & Gas Ltd.)

SELBY GREEN INTL LTD (ON)
Recapitalized as Berkshire Griffin Inc. 11/02/1995
Each share Common no par exchanged for (0.1) share Common no par
Berkshire Griffin Inc. name changed to China Wind Power International Corp. 08/05/2009
(See China Wind Power International Corp.)

SELBY MINING EXPLORATION CO. LTD. (QC)
Acquired by Amalgamated Mining Development Corp. Ltd. 00/00/1960
Each share Capital Stock $1 par exchanged for (0.13333333) share Capital Stock $1 par
Amalgamated Mining Development Corp. Ltd. acquired by Amalgamated Mining Western Ltd. 12/20/1984 which name changed to Westall Resources Ltd. 07/12/1994
(See Westall Resources Ltd.)

SELBY SHOE CO. (OH)
Common no par changed to $12.50 par in 1953
Merged into Rockwood & Co. 11/30/56
Each share Common $12.50 par exchanged for (0.2) share 6% Preferred Ser. B $100 par
(See Rockwood & Co.)

SELCK WALTER E & CO (DE)
Common 1¢ par changed to $1.50 par 10/00/1958
Each share Common $1.50 par exchanged for (2) shares Common $2.50 par 07/28/1960
Over 99% acquired by Giffen Industries, Inc. 05/00/1968
Public interest eliminated

SELCO INC (OK)
Merged into Zale Corp. 3/31/80
Each share Common $1 par exchanged for (0.4) share Common $1 par
(See Zale Corp.)

SELCO INTL PPTYS INC (BC)
In process of dissolution 06/01/1998
Details not available

SELDORE MNG LTD (ON)
Merged into Branly Enterprises Inc. 12/09/1976
Each share Capital Stock $1 par exchanged for (0.28) share Capital Stock no par
Branly Enterprises Inc. recapitalized as Consolidated Branly Resources Inc. 02/27/1984 which name changed to CBR Holdings Inc. 06/20/1985

SELECT APPOINTMENTS HLDGS PLC (ENGLAND & WALES)
Acquired by Veridor Holding UK 02/08/2000
Each Sponsored ADR for Ordinary exchanged for approximately $33.82 cash

SELECT ASSET FD III (DE)
144A Auction Market Preferred Ser. A called for redemption at $100,000 on 07/24/2002
144A Auction Market Preferred Ser. B called for redemption at $100,000 on 04/28/2004

SELECT BANCORP INC OLD (NC)
Merged into Select Bancorp, Inc. (New) 07/28/2014
Each share Common $1 par exchanged for (1.8264) shares Common $1 par

SELECT COMFORT CO (MN)
Common 1¢ par split (3) for (2) by issuance of (0.5) additional share payable 06/08/2006 to holders of record 05/25/2006 Ex date - 06/09/2006
Name changed to Sleep Number Corp. 11/01/2017

SELECT 50 S-1 INCOME TR (ON)
Merged into Sentry Select Canadian Income Fund 06/12/2009
Each Unit no par received (0.6429) Ser. A Unit no par

SELECT 50 S-1 INCOME TR II (ON)
Merged into Select 50 S-1 Income Trust 07/04/2008
Each Trust Unit received (1.01233) Units
Select 50 S-1 Income Trust merged into Sentry Select Canadian Income Fund 06/12/2009

SELECT FINL INDS LTD (CANADA)
Name changed to Deltan Corp. Ltd. 08/18/1971
(See Deltan Corp. Ltd.)

SELECT HOMES INC (MN)
Name changed to Nordic Homes, Inc. 10/31/1972
(See Nordic Homes, Inc.)

SELECT INFORMATION SYS INC (CA)
Name changed to Summa Technologies, Inc. 1/15/85
(See Summa Technologies, Inc.)

SELECT LEASED PPTY FIN LTD (ON)
Name changed to Select Properties Ltd. 07/31/1969
(See Select Properties Ltd.)

SELECT MED CORP (DE)
Common 1¢ par split (2) for (1) by issuance of (1) additional share payable 12/22/2003 to holders of record 12/5/2003 Ex date - 12/23/2003
Merged into EGL Acquisition Corp. 2/24/2005
Each share Common 1¢ par exchanged for $18 cash

SELECT MEDIA COMMUNICATIONS INC (NY)
Each (300) shares old Common $0.001 par exchanged for (1) share new Common $0.001 par 12/10/1999
SEC revoked common stock registration 03/22/2005
No stockholders' equity

FINANCIAL INFORMATION, INC.

SEL-SEL

SELECT OILS LTD. (AB)
Merged into Medallion Petroleums Ltd. 04/20/1959
Each share Common no par exchanged for (0.01) share Common $1.25 par
Medallion Petroleums Ltd. merged into Canadian Industrial Gas & Oils Ltd. 03/08/1956 which merged into Norcen Energy Resources Ltd. (AB) 10/28/1975 which reincorporated in Canada 04/15/1977
(See Norcen Energy Resources Ltd.)

SELECT PPTYS LTD (ON)
100% acquired by Orlando Corp. through purchase offer as of 08/21/1975
Public interest eliminated

SELECT RES INC (DE)
Recapitalized as Visual Telephone of New Jersey Inc. 3/22/96
Each share Common $0.001 par exchanged for (1/60) share Common $0.001 par
Visual Telephone of New Jersey Inc. name changed to Visual Telephone International, Inc. 1/2/97 which name changed to Ivoice.Com Inc. 5/15/99 which name changed to iVoice, Inc. (DE) 8/18/2001 which reincorporated in New Jersey 5/5/2003

SELECT SECTOR SPDR TR (MA)
Trust terminated 11/21/2016
Each share Financial Services Select Sector SPDR Fund 1¢ par received $34.98578 cash
(Additional Information in Active)

SELECT SOFTWARE TOOLS LTD (ENGLAND & WALES)
ADR agreement terminated 7/12/2003
No ADR holders' equity

SELECT THEATRES CORP (NY)
Merged into S.T.C. Enterprises, Inc. 11/01/1976
Each share Common 10¢ par exchanged for $19.02 cash

SELECT THERAPEUTICS INC (DE)
SEC revoked common stock registration 05/18/2011

SELECT VENTURES INC (BC)
Recapitalized as Majestic Gold Corp. 12/3/96
Each share Common no par exchanged for (0.5) share Common no par

SELECT VIDEO INC (DE)
Name changed to Webdigs, Inc. 10/24/2007
Webdigs, Inc. name changed to RealBiz Media Group, Inc. 10/05/2012 which name changed to Verus International, Inc. 10/16/2018

SELECTATECH INC (NY)
Each (30) shares old Common $0.001 par exchanged for (1) share new Common $0.001 par 7/9/90
Name changed to Clinical Homecare Ltd. 7/16/90
Clinical Homecare Ltd. merged into Curaflex Health Services, Inc. 3/5/93 which merged into Coram Healthcare Corp. 7/8/94
(See Coram Healthcare Corp.)

SELECTCORE LTD (ON)
Each share old Common no par exchanged for (0.1) share new Common no par 07/07/2015
Name changed to Fintech Select Ltd. 08/28/2017

SELECTED AMERICAN SHARES (IL)
Trust terminated in 1944
Details not available

SELECTED INDUSTRIES, INC.
Merged into Tri-Continental Corp. in 1951
Each share $5.50 Prior Preferred $25 par exchanged for (2/3) share $6 Preferred no par and (2.1) shares Common $1 par
Each share $1.50 Preferred $5 par exchanged for (2.25) shares Common $1 par
Each share Common $1 par exchanged for (0.05) share new Common $1 par and (1.25) Common Stock Purchase Warrants
Each Common Stock Purchase Warrant exchanged for (0.2) new Common Stock Purchase Warrant

SELECTED INVESTMENT CORP. (PA)
Merged into Worlco, Inc. 3/19/74
Each share Common 10¢ par exchanged for (1.12) shares Class A Common 5¢ par

SELECTED MTG INVS (OH)
Completely liquidated 03/31/1969
Each Share of Bene. Int. no par exchanged for first and final distribution of (2) National Mortgage Fund 1979 Stock Purchase Warrants

SELECTED OPPORTUNITY FD INC (DE)
Acquired by Selected Special Shares, Inc. 05/03/1976
Each share Common 25¢ par exchanged for (0.6924) share Common 25¢ par
Selected Special Shares, Inc. name changed to Selected International Fund, Inc. 05/01/2011

SELECTED PROFESSIONAL AGENTS COORDINATING ENTERPRISES INC (DE)
Name changed to Space & Leisure Time, Ltd. 07/20/1972
(See Space & Leisure Time, Ltd.)

SELECTED RISKS INDEMNITY CO. (NJ)
Stock Dividends - 10% 11/1/49; 10% 11/12/53; 12-1/2% 11/10/54; (1) for (9) 11/10/55
Name changed to Selected Risks Insurance Co. 12/31/57
Selected Risks Insurance Co. merged into SRI Corp. 1/5/78 which name changed to Selective Insurance Group, Inc. 5/2/86

SELECTED RISKS INS CO (NJ)
Common $10 par split (2) for (1) by issuance of (1) additional share 07/01/1972
Common $10 par changed to $4 par and (1.5) additional shares 05/25/1977
Stock Dividends - 11-1/2% 04/06/1959; 20% 04/05/1966; 10% 06/30/1969
Merged into SRI Corp. 01/05/1978
Each share Common $4 par exchanged for (1) share Common $4 par
SRI Corp. name changed to Selective Insurance Group, Inc. 05/02/1986

SELECTED SECURITIES CORP. (DE)
Common no par changed to $1 par in 1937
Liquidation completed
Each share Common $1 par received initial distribution of (3.757) shares American Mutual Fund, Inc. (Del.) Capital Stock $1 par 10/17/58
Each share Common $1 par received second distribution of $3.8935 cash 10/27/64
Each share Common $1 par exchanged for third and final distribution of $3.66959 cash 5/6/65
American Mutual Fund, Inc. (Del.) reincorporated in Maryland 9/20/83

SELECTED SPL SHS INC (MD)
Common 25¢ par reclassified as Class S Common 05/01/2004
Name changed to Selected International Fund, Inc. 05/01/2011

SELECTED STOCKS, INC.
Liquidated in 1932

SELECTERM INC (MA)
Merged into Microscript Inc. 11/3/93
Each share Common 5¢ par exchanged for $2 cash

SELECTICA INC (DE)
Each share old Common $0.0001 par exchanged for (0.05) share new Common $0.0001 par 02/25/2010
Name changed to Determine, Inc. 10/19/2015

SELECTION TR LTD (ENGLAND)
Each share Ordinary Reg. 10s par and ADR's for Ordinary Reg. 10s par exchanged for (3.2) shares Ordinary Reg. 5s par and ADR's for Ordinary Reg. 5s par respectively to effect a (2) for (1) split and 60% stock dividend 01/06/1964
Ordinary Reg. 5s par and ADR's for Ordinary Reg. 5s par changed to 25p par per currency change 02/15/1971
Acquired by British Petroleum Co. Ltd. 02/23/1981
Each share Ordinary Reg. 5s par exchanged for $12.75 cash
Each ADR for Ordinary Reg. 25p par exchanged for $28.08 cash

SELECTIVE BRANDS HLDGS INC (DE)
Recapitalized as East Morgan Holdings Inc. 02/28/2008
Each share Common $0.001 par exchanged for (0.001) share Common $0.001 par

SELECTIVE CAPITAL FUND LTD. (BAHAMAS)
Completely liquidated 5/4/79
Each Mutual Fund Share exchanged for first and final distribution of $0.21 cash

SELECTIVE INVESTMENTS, INC. (UT)
Merged into Equities Inc. 9/22/72
Each share Common 50¢ par exchanged for (0.75) share Common 33-1/3¢ par

SELECTIVE LIFE INS CO (AZ)
Merged into Penn-Pacific Corp. (PA) 12/17/1968
Each share Common 35¢ par exchanged for (0.5) share Common 50¢ par
Penn-Pacific Corp. (PA) reincorporated in Delaware 07/01/1971 which reincorporated in Nevada 04/04/2005
(See Penn-Pacific Corp. (NV))

SELECTORS, INC. (WA)
Reorganized under Chapter 11 Federal Bankruptcy Code as Source Capital Corp. 09/00/1991
Each share Common no par exchanged for (0.0588373) share Class B Common no par
Source Capital Corp. merged into Sterling Financial Corp. 09/28/2001 which merged into Umpqua Holdings Corp. 04/18/2014

SELECTRONICS INC (DE)
Reincorporated 1/31/90
State of incorporation changed from (MN) to (DE) 1/31/90
Name changed to Microlytics, Inc. 12/18/95
Microlytics, Inc. reorganized as Santi Group Inc. 4/30/98 which name changed to Earthcare Inc. 9/25/98

SELENA RESH CORP (BC)
Recapitalized as SLN Ventures Corp. 03/01/1994
Each share Common no par exchanged for (1/9) share Common no par
SLN Ventures Corp. recapitalized as Pan Ocean Explorations Inc. 04/01/1997
(See Pan Ocean Explorations Inc.)

SELEVISION CORP. OF AMERICA (DE)
Charter revoked for non-payment of Delaware taxes 4/1/57

SELEVISION WESTERN, INC. (DE)
Declared inoperative and void for failure to comply with Delaware corporation laws 4/1/57

SELF HELP ZONE INC (NV)
Each share old Common $0.001 par exchanged for (0.00333333) share new Common $0.001 par 07/02/2001
Name changed to U.S. Petroleum Corp. 08/30/2001
U.S. Petroleum Corp. recapitalized as Emergent Energy Corp. 07/29/2008

SELF INSURERS SVCS & UNDERWRITERS INC (NV)
Charter revoked for failure to file reports and pay fees 05/01/1989

SELF SERVICE DRUG CORP. (PA)
Liquidation completed
Each share Common no par exchanged for initial distribution of $0.25 cash 10/15/65
Each share Common no par received second and final distribution of $0.098 cash 12/23/66

SELF SVC RESTAURANTS INC (LA)
Name changed to Chart House Inc. 05/28/1974
Chart House Inc. merged into Diversifoods Inc. 12/28/1983
(See Diversifoods Inc.)

SELF STORAGE GROUP INC (MD)
Name changed to Global Self Storage, Inc. 01/19/2016

SELFCARE INC (DE)
Name changed to Inverness Medical Technology Inc. 5/9/2000
Inverness Medical Technology Inc. merged into Johnson & Johnson 11/21/2001

SELFIX INC (DE)
Stock Dividend - 10% 10/16/1989
Under plan of reorganization each share Common 1¢ par automatically became (1) share Home Products International, Inc. Common 1¢ par 02/18/1997
(See Home Products International, Inc.)

SELFLOCK NUT AND BOLT CO. (DE)
Charter cancelled for non-payment of taxes in 1938

SELGA INC (NV)
Common $0.001 par split (10) for (1) by issuance of (9) additional shares payable 01/04/2013 to holders of record 01/03/2013 Ex date - 01/07/2013
Name changed to Auxillium Energy, Inc. 02/21/2013
(See Auxillium Energy, Inc.)

SELIENT INC (QC)
Merged into Canadian Premier Holdings Ltd. 12/19/2007
Each share Common no par exchanged for $0.172526 cash

SELIGMAN & ASSOC INC (DE)
Merged into S&A Acquisition Corp. 10/19/1989
Each share Common 10¢ par exchanged for $6.50 cash

SELIGMAN & LATZ INC (DE)
Common $1 par split (3) for (2) by issuance of (0.5) additional share 10/30/67
Merged into GT Acquisition Corp. 12/4/85
Each share Common $1 par exchanged for $19.50 cash

SELIGMAN CALIF TAX EXEMPT FD SER (MA)
Name changed to Seligman Tax-Exempt Series Trust 08/06/1990
Seligman Tax-Exempt Series Trust

SEL-SEL   FINANCIAL INFORMATION, INC.

name changed to Seligman Municipal Series Trust 10/01/1996

SELIGMAN INCOME FD INC (MD)
Common $1 par reclassified as Class A $1 par 05/01/1993
Name changed to Seligman Income & Growth Fund, Inc. 11/06/2002

SELIGMAN LASALLE INTL REAL ESTATE FD INC (MD)
Issue Information - 8,900,000 shares COM offered at $25 per share on 05/24/2007
Name changed to RiverSource LaSalle International Real Estate Fund, Inc. 09/25/2009
RiverSource LaSalle International Real Estate Fund, Inc. merged into Columbia Funds Series Trust I 04/08/2011

SELIGMAN N J MUN FD INC (MD)
Name changed 10/01/1996
Name changed from Seligman New Jersey Tax-Exempt Fund, Inc. to Seligman New Jersey Municipal Fund, Inc. 10/01/1996
Class D $0.001 par reclassified as Class C $0.001 par 05/16/2008
Under plan of reorganization each share Class A $0.001 par and Class C $0.001 par automatically became (1) share Seligman Municipal Fund Series, Inc. National Series Fund Class A $0.001 par and Class C $0.001 par respectively 07/13/2009

SELIGMAN NEW TECHNOLOGIES FD II INC (MD)
Completely liquidated
Each share Common 1¢ par received first and final distribution of $6.478 cash payable 02/25/2008 to holders of record 02/25/2008
Note: Certificates were not required to be surrendered and are without value

SELIGMAN NEW TECHNOLOGIES FD INC (MD)
Liquidation completed
Each share Common 1¢ par received initial distribution of $0.30 cash payable 08/04/2004 to holders of record 08/04/2004
Each share Common 1¢ par received second distribution of $0.30 cash payable 02/23/2005 to holders of record 02/23/2005
Each share Common 1¢ par received third distribution of $0.45 cash payable 08/16/2005 to holders of record 08/16/2005
Each share Common 1¢ par received fourth distribution of $0.20 cash payable 12/07/2006 to holders of record 12/07/2006
Each share Common 1¢ par received fifth distribution of $1.75 cash payable 08/10/2007 to holders of record 08/10/2007
Each share Common 1¢ par received sixth distribution of $0.352 cash payable 12/07/2007 to holders of record 12/07/2007
Each share Common 1¢ par received seventh and final distribution of $0.10 cash payable 12/10/2007 to holders of record 12/10/2007
Note: Certificates were not required to be surrendered and are without value
All rates are approximate

SELIGMAN PA MUN FD SER (PA)
Name changed 10/01/1996
Quality Series $0.001 par reclassified as Class A $0.001 par 02/01/1994
Name changed from Seligman Pennsylvania Tax-Exempt Fund Series to Seligman Pennsylvania Municipal Fund 10/01/1996
Class D $0.001 par reclassified as Class C $0.001 par 05/16/2008
Under plan of reorganization each share Class A $0.001 par and Class C $0.001 par automatically became (1) share Seligman Municipal Fund Series, Inc. National Series Fund Class A $0.001 par and Class C $0.001 par respectively 07/13/2009

SELIGMAN PREM TECHNOLOGY GROWTH FD INC (MD)
Name changed to Columbia Seligman Premium Technology Growth Fund, Inc. 09/27/2010

SELIGMAN QUALITY MUN FD INC (MD)
Municipal Auction Rate Preferred Ser. TH called for redemption at $50,000 on 02/23/2007
Liquidation completed
Each share Common 1¢ par received initial distribution of $13.50 cash payable 02/27/2007 to holders of record 02/27/2007
Each share Common 1¢ par received second and final distribution of $0.564094 cash payable 03/23/2007 to holders of record 03/23/2007

SELIGMAN SELECT MUN FD INC (MD)
Preferred Ser. A 1¢ par called for redemption at $100,000 on 03/12/2009
Preferred Ser. B 1¢ par called for redemption at $100,000 on 03/12/2009
Acquired by Seligman Municipal Fund Series, Inc. 03/20/2009
Each share Common 1¢ par exchanged for (1.40607578) shares National Series Class A $0.001 par

SELIGMAN TAX EXEMPT FD SER INC (MD)
Name changed to Seligman Municipal Fund Series, Inc. and Colorado Tax-Exempt Ser. $0.001 par, Georgia Tax-Exempt Ser. $0.001 par, Louisiana Tax-Exempt Ser. $0.001 par, Maryland Tax-Exempt Ser. $0.001 par, Massachusetts Tax-Exempt Ser. $0.001 par, Michigan Tax-Exempt Ser. $0.001 par, Minnesota Tax-Exempt Ser. $0.001 par, Missouri Tax-Exempt Ser. $0.001 par, National Tax-Exempt Ser. $0.001 par, New York Tax-Exempt Ser. $0.001 par, Ohio Tax-Exempt Ser. $0.001 par, Oregon Tax-Exempt Ser. $0.001 par, and South Carolina Tax-Exempt Ser. $0.001 par reclassified as Colorado Ser. Class A $0.001 par, Georgia Ser. Class A $0.001 par, Louisiana Ser. Class A $0.001 par, Maryland Ser. Class A $0.001 par, Massachusetts Ser. Class A $0.001 par, Michigan Ser. Class A $0.001 par, Minnesota Ser. Class A $0.001 par, Missouri Ser. Class A $0.001 par, National Ser. Class A $0.001 par, New York Ser. Class A $0.001 par, Ohio Ser. Class A $0.001 par, Oregon Ser. Class A $0.001 par, and South Carolina Ser. Class A $0.001 par respectively 10/1/96

SELIGMAN TAX EXEMPT SER TR (MA)
Money Market Series completely liquidated 12/26/1990
Details not available
Name changed to Seligman Municipal Series Trust, Florida Tax-Exempt Ser. Class A $0.001 par reclassified as Florida Ser. Class A $0.001 par and North Carolina Tax-Exempt Ser. Class A $0.001 par reclassified as North Carolina Ser. Class A $0.001 par respectively 10/01/1996

SELIGMAN TIME HORIZON/HARVESTER SER INC (MD)
Name changed to Seligman Asset Allocation Series, Inc. and Harvester Fund Class A, Harvester Fund Class B, Harvester Fund Class C, Harvester Fund Class D, Time Horizon 10 Fund Class A, Time Horizon 10 Fund Class B, Time Horizon 10 Fund Class C, Time Horizon 10 Fund Class D, Time Horizon 20 Fund Class A, Time Horizon 20 Fund Class B, Time Horizon 20 Fund Class C, Time Horizon 20 Fund Class D, Time Horizon 30 Fund Class A, Time Horizon 30 Fund Class B, Time Horizon 30 Fund Class C, Time Horizon 30 Fund Class D reclassified as Asset Allocation Aggressive Growth Fund Class A, Asset Allocation Aggressive Growth Fund Class B, Asset Allocation Aggressive Growth Fund Class C, Asset Allocation Aggressive Growth Fund Class D, Asset Allocation Balanced Fund Class A, Asset Allocation Balanced Fund Class B, Asset Allocation Balanced Fund Class C, Asset Allocation Balanced Fund Class D, Asset Allocation Growth Fund Class A, Asset Allocation Growth Fund Class B, Asset Allocation Growth Fund Class C, Asset Allocation Growth Fund Class D, Asset Allocation Moderate Growth Fund Class A, Asset Allocation Moderate Growth Fund Class B, Asset Allocation Moderate Growth Fund Class C, Asset Allocation Moderate Growth Fund Class D respectively 01/17/2008

SELIGMANN (B.F.) & CO., INC. (WI)
Name changed to First Midwest Investment Corp. 06/10/1970
(See First Midwest Investment Corp.)

SELKIRK COMMUNICATIONS LTD (AB)
Name changed 6/14/79
Class A no par split (2) for (1) by issuance of (1) additional share 11/11/1972
Class A no par reclassified as Conv. Class A no par 06/03/1975
Name changed from Selkirk Holdings Ltd. to Selkirk Communications Ltd. 06/14/1979
Conv. Class A no par reclassified as Class A no par
Conv. Class C no par reclassified as Class A no par
Class A no par split (2) for (1) by issuance of (1) additional share 09/22/1981
Merged into MH Acquisition Inc. 04/25/1989
Each share Class A no par exchanged for $49.50 cash

SELKIRK METALS CORP (BC)
Merged into Imperial Metals Corp. (New) 11/02/2009
Each share Common no par exchanged for $0.12 cash

SELKIRK (CANADIAN) MINES LTD.
Succeeded by Poundmaker Gold Mines Ltd. 00/00/1934
Each share Common exchanged for (0.2) share Common
(See Poundmaker Gold Mines Ltd.)

SELKIRK PETE LTD (AB)
Struck off register and declared dissolved for failure to file returns 12/01/1981

SELKIRK SPRINGS INTL CORP (BC)
Name changed to Canadian Glacier Beverage Corp. 10/24/1995
Canadian Glacier Beverage Corp. recapitalized as Glacier Ventures International Corp. (BC) 08/26/1997 which reincorporated in Canada 09/20/1999 which merged into Glacier Ventures International Corp. (Canada) (New) 04/28/2000 which name changed to Glacier Media Inc. 07/01/2008

SELL 'N SERV DISPENSERS, INC. (DE)
Charter revoked for non-payment of taxes 04/01/1964

SELLCELL NET (NV)
Name changed to BodyTel Scientific, Inc. 12/29/2006
(See BodyTel Scientific, Inc.)

SELLECTEK INC (CA)
Merged into Glasgal Communications Inc. 05/02/1994
Each share Common no par exchanged for (0.25) share Common no par
Glasgal Communications Inc. name changed to Datatec Systems Inc. 01/07/1998
(See Datatec Systems Inc.)

SELLECTEK INDS INC (BC)
Name changed to Global-Pacific Minerals Inc. (BC) 08/29/1989
Global-Pacific Minerals Inc. (BC) reorganized in Wyoming as UNIREX Technologies Inc. 04/23/2001 which recapitalized as UNIREX Corp. 07/19/2001
(See UNIREX Corp.)

SELLERS CORP (TN)
Ceased operations 12/31/1974
No stockholders' equity

SELLERSVILLE SVGS & LN ASSN (PA)
Merged into National Penn Bancshares, Inc. 11/30/1990
Each share Common $1 par exchanged for $21.25 cash

SELLINGER PHARMACEUTICALS INC (DE)
Name changed to Promedica Inc. 06/28/1988
Promedica Inc. name changed to Zhou Lin International Inc. 11/28/1994 which name changed to Renu-U-International Inc. 12/24/1996 which name changed to Colormax Technologies, Inc. 09/07/1999
(See Colormax Technologies, Inc.)

SELMER H & A INC (IN)
6% Pfd. $100 par called for redemption 01/15/1963
Each share Common $2 par exchanged for (2) shares Common $1 par 01/25/1963
Common $1 par changed to 50¢ par and (1) additional share issued 04/21/1965
Common 50¢ par split (3) for (2) by issuance of (0.5) additional share 09/26/1967
Merged into Magnavox Co. 02/28/1969
Each share Common 50¢ par exchanged for (0.425) share Common $1 par
(See Magnavox Co.)

SELMIX DISPENSERS, INC. (NY)
Acquired by Jacobs (F.L.) Co., Inc. 00/00/1954
Each share 5.50% Preferred $10 par received $1.25 cash
Each share Common 1¢ par received 5¢ cash

SELVAC CORP (DE)
Name changed to Mehl/Biophile International Corp. 6/4/96
Mehl/Biophile International Corp. name changed to Hamilton-Biophile Companies (DE) 5/12/2000 which reincorporated in Nevada 11/26/2001 which recapitalized as Brampton Crest International Inc. 10/4/2005

SELWAY CAP ACQUISITION CORP (DE)
Issue Information - 2,000,000 UNITS consisting of (1) share COM SER A and (1) WT offered at $10 per Unit on 11/07/2011
Units separated 04/11/2013

Each share Ser. A Common $0.0001 par exchanged for (1) share Ser. B Common $0.0001 par 04/11/2013
Ser. B Common $0.0001 par reclassified as Common $0.0001 par 08/28/2013
Name changed to Healthcare Corporation of America 09/30/2013

SELWYN RES LTD (BC)
Each share old Common no par received distribution of (0.1083829) share Savant Explorations Ltd. Common no par payable 06/12/2007 to holders of record 06/06/2007
Ex date - 06/04/2007
Each share old Common no par exchanged for (0.01) share new Common no par 01/02/2014
Name changed to ScoZinc Mining Ltd. 10/01/2015

SEMA PLC (UNITED KINGDOM)
Name changed 12/18/2000
Name changed from Sema Group PLC to Sema PLC 12/18/2000
Merged into Schlumberger Ltd. 06/04/2001
Each Sponsored ADR for Ordinary exchanged for $15.78416 cash

SEMBAWANG LTD (SINGAPORE)
Name changed 02/01/1995
Stock Dividend - 10% 05/31/1989
Name changed from Sembawang Shipyard Ltd. to Sembawang Corp. Ltd. 02/01/1995
Each Unsponsored ADR for Ordinary S$1 par exchanged for (1) Sponsored ADR for Ordinary S$1 par 09/13/1996
Acquired by Sembcorp Industries Ltd. 00/00/1998
Details not available

SEMBCORP INDS LTD (SINGAPORE)
Each old Sponsored ADR for Ordinary exchanged for (0.94) new Sponsored ADR for Ordinary and $0.683574 cash 08/26/2005
ADR agreement terminated 12/12/2012
Each new Sponsored ADR for Ordinary exchanged for (10) shares Ordinary
(Additional Information in Active)

SEMBIOSYS GENETICS INC NEW (CANADA)
Company began process of winding down 01/01/2012
Stockholders' equity unlikely

SEMBIOSYS GENETICS INC OLD (CANADA)
Under plan of reorganization each share Common no par automatically became (1) share SemBioSys Genetics Inc. (New) Common no par 12/18/2009
(See SemBioSys Genetics Inc. (New))

SEMCAN INC (CANADA)
Each share old Common no par exchanged for (0.5) share new Common no par 04/07/2011
Name changed to STT Enviro Corp. 02/20/2013
(See STT Enviro Corp.)

SEMCO CAP TR I (DE)
Guaranteed Trust Preferred Securities called for redemption at $25 on 09/14/2005

SEMCO CAP TR II (DE)
9% Guaranteed Trust Preferred Securities called for redemption at $10 on 08/16/2005

SEMCO ENERGY GAS CO (MI)
6% Preferred Ser. A $100 par called for redemption at $105 on 11/18/1999
5.50% Preferred Ser. B $100 par called for redemption at $105 on 11/18/1999
5.50% Preferred Ser. C $100 par called for redemption at $105 on 11/18/1999
5.50% Preferred Ser. D $100 par called for redemption at $105 on 11/18/1999

SEMCO ENERGY INC (MI)
$2.3125 Conv. Preferred Ser. A $1 par called for redemption at $25 plus $0.0835 accrued dividends on 11/18/1999
Stock Dividends - 5% payable 05/15/1997 to holders of record 05/05/1997; 5% payable 05/15/1998 to holders of record 05/05/1998
Merged into Cap Rock Holding Corp. 11/09/2007
Each share 5% Conv. Preferred Ser. B $1 par exchanged for $233.042 cash
Each share Common $1 par exchanged for $8.15 cash

SEMCO INSTRS INC (DE)
Class A Common 1¢ par split (2) for (1) by issuance of (1) additional share 09/17/1982
Class A Common 1¢ par split (2) for (1) by issuance of (1) additional share 12/21/1984
Class A Common 1¢ par split (3) for (2) by issuance of (0.5) additional share 09/30/1985
Class A Common 1¢ par split (3) for (2) by issuance of (0.5) additional share 07/18/1986
Stock Dividend - 25% 05/10/1982
Acquired by TransDigm Group Inc. 09/03/2010
Each share Class A Common 1¢ par exchanged for $13.8792 cash
Note: Each share Class A Common 1¢ par received an initial additional distribution of approximately $0.59 cash from escrow 12/27/2010
Each share Class A Common 1¢ par received a second additional distribution of $0.30135132 cash from escrow 11/14/2011
Each share Class A Common 1¢ par received a third additional distribution of $0.60270263 cash from escrow 10/26/2012
Each share Class A Common 1¢ par received a fourth additional distribution of $0.09984773 cash from escrow 10/08/2013

SEMCO TECHNOLOGIES INC (AB)
Reincorporated under the laws of Canada as Semcan Inc. 02/09/2007
Semcan Inc. name changed to STT Enviro Corp. 02/20/2013
(See STT Enviro Corp.)

SEMELE GROUP INC (DE)
Each share old Common 1¢ par exchanged for (1/300) share new Common 1¢ par 6/30/98
Note: Holders of (299) or fewer shares received $0.790625 cash per share
New Common 1¢ par split (3) for (1) by issuance of (2) additional share payable 6/30/98 to holders of record 6/30/98
Each (4,001) shares new Common 1¢ par exchanged for (1) share new Common 1¢ par 8/5/2004
Note: In effect holders received $1.40 cash per share and public interest was eliminated

SEMENTES AGROCERES S A (BRAZIL)
Acquired by Monsanto Co. (Old) 00/00/1997
Details not available

SEMGROUP ENERGY PARTNERS L P (DE)
Name changed to Blueknight Energy Partners L.P. 12/11/2009

SEMI DYNE ELECTRS CORP (NY)
Assets sold for benefit of creditors 08/12/1974
No stockholders' equity

SEMI-TECH CORP (ON)
Plan of reorganization under Chapter 11 Federal Bankruptcy Code effective 3/16/2001
No stockholders' equity

SEMI TECH GLOBAL LTD (HONG KONG)
Sponsored ADR's for Ordinary HKD $1 par split (4) for (1) by issuance of (3) additional ADR's payable 12/08/1997 to holders of record 11/24/1997
Name changed to Akai Holdings Ltd. 07/30/1999
(See Akai Holdings Ltd.)

SEMI TECH MICROELECTRONICS CORP (ON)
Recapitalized as International Semi-Tech Microelectronics Inc. 7/20/87
Each share Capital Stock no par exchanged for (0.1) share Common no par
International Semi-Tech Microelectronics Inc. name changed to Semi-Tech Corp. 9/14/94
(See Semi-Tech Corp.)

SEMI-TROPIC LAND & WATER CO. (CA)
Charter suspended for failure to file reports and pay fees 08/01/1986

SEMICON INC (MA)
Class A Common no par reclassified as Common $1 par 11/30/1967
Common $1 par changed to 50¢ par and (1) additional share issued 04/15/1977
Common 50¢ par changed to 25¢ par and (1) additional share issued 02/02/1981
Stock Dividend - 100% 06/04/1979
Involuntarily dissolved 05/31/2007

SEMICON TOOLS INC (NV)
Each (150) shares old Common $0.001 par exchanged for (1) share new Common $0.001 par 2/8/93
Name changed to Seto Holdings Inc. 8/18/98

SEMICONDUCTOR COMPONENT SUBSTRATES CORP (TX)
Plan of arrangement under bankruptcy proceedings confirmed 06/10/1974
No stockholders' equity

SEMICONDUCTOR COMPUTER SYSTEMS INC. (UT)
Name changed to National Research & Development, Inc. 10/29/73

SEMICONDUCTOR HOLDRS TR (DE)
Trust terminated
Each Depositary Receipt received first and final distribution of $29.859208 cash payable 01/07/2013 to holders of record 12/20/2012

SEMICONDUCTOR LASER INTL CORP (NY)
Petition filed under Chapter 11 Federal Bankruptcy Code dismissed 10/6/2003
No stockholders' equity

SEMICONDUCTOR PKG MATLS INC (DE)
Name changed to SEMX Corp. 04/30/1998
(See SEMX Corp.)

SEMINARY ST BK (FORT WORTH, TX)
Common $10 par changed to $5 par and (1) additional share issued 08/15/1977
Acquired by Interfirst Corp. 10/31/1984
Details not available

SEMINIS INC (DE)
Issue Information - 13,750,000 shares CL A offered at $15 per share on 06/29/1999
Merged into Seminis Merger Corp. 9/29/2003
Each share Class A Common 1¢ par exchanged for $3.78 cash

SEMINOLE AMERICAN LIFE INSURANCE CO. (FL)
Merged into Coastal States Life Insurance Co. 11/2/64
Each share Capital Stock $1 par exchanged for (0.2222278) share Common $1.25 par
Coastal States Life Insurance Co. reorganized as Coastal States Corp. 10/5/72

SEMINOLE BK (SEMINOLE, FL)
Merged into F.N.B. Corp. (PA) 5/29/98
Each share Common 10¢ par exchanged for (1.53) shares Common $2 par
F.N.B. Corp. (PA) reincorporated in Florida 6/13/2001

SEMINOLE BK (TAMPA, FL)
Name changed to Great American Seminole Bank (Tampa, FL) 11/26/1979
(See Great American Seminole Bank (Tampa, FL))

SEMINOLE COTTON MILLS
Merged into Textiles, Inc. 00/00/1931
Details not available

SEMINOLE FEDERAL SAVINGS BANK (SEMINOLE, FL)
Under plan of reorganization name changed to Seminole Bank (Seminole, FL) 4/1/91
Seminole Bank (Seminole, FL) merged into F.N.B. Corp. 5/29/98 which reincorporated in Florida 6/13/2001

SEMINOLE GAS CO.
Merged into Southwest Natural Gas Co. in 1940
Details not available

SEMINOLE NATL BK (SANFORD, FL)
Merged into BanPonce Corp. 4/30/97
Each share Common $5 par exchanged for $20.37 cash

SEMINOLE OIL & GAS CORP. (DE)
Each share Common 5¢ par exchanged for (0.25) share Common 20¢ par 3/13/62
No longer in existence having become inoperative and void for non-payment of taxes 4/1/67

SEMINOLE POLLUTION EQUIP CORP (NY)
Adjudicated bankrupt 12/19/1972
No stockholders' equity

SEMINOLE RES INC (BC)
Name changed to Canadian Giant Exploration Ltd. 10/28/1987
(See Canadian Giant Exploration Ltd.)

SEMITOOL INC (MT)
Issue Information - 3,000,000 shares COM offered at $13 per share on 02/02/1995
Common no par split (3) for (2) by issuance of (0.5) additional share 08/21/1995
Common no par split (2) for (1) by issuance of (1) additional share payable 03/28/2000 to holders of record 03/14/2000
Merged into Applied Materials, Inc. 12/21/2009
Each share Common no par exchanged for $11 cash

SEMITRONICS, INC. (MA)
Charter revoked for failure to file reports and pay fees 10/20/65

SEMLER (R.B.) INC.
Merged into Williams (J.B.) Co. and each share Common $1 par exchanged for (0.2) share Common $5 par and $3 principal amount of 5% Debentures in 1952
Williams (J.B.) Co. merged into Pharmaceuticals, Inc. 6/2/59

SEMONIN PAUL CO (KY)
Merged into Semonin (Paul)
Associates, Inc. 09/06/1983
Each share Common no par
exchanged for $1.20 cash

SEMOTUS SOLUTIONS INC (NV)
Each share old Common 1¢ par
exchanged for (0.05) share new
Common 1¢ par 07/23/2007
Name changed to Flint Telecom
Group, Inc. 10/21/2008

SEMPER BARRIS INC (DE)
Each share old Common $0.0001 par
exchanged for (0.2) share new
Common $0.0001 par 05/26/1989
Charter cancelled and declared
inoperative and void for
non-payment of taxes 03/01/1993

SEMPER ENERGY LTD (AB)
Acquired by Val Vista Energy Ltd.
08/21/2003
Each share Common no par
exchanged for (1) share Common
no par
Val Vista Energy Ltd. acquired by
Avenir Diversified Income Trust
04/18/2005 which reorganized as
AvenEx Energy Corp. 01/07/2011
which merged into Spyglass
Resources Corp. 04/04/2013

SEMPER FLOWERS INC (NV)
Name changed to SF Blu Vu, Inc.
08/17/2009
SF Blu Vu, Inc. name changed to
Livewire Ergogenics, Inc. 10/07/2011

SEMPER RES CORP (OK)
Reincorporated 00/00/2005
State of incorporation changed from
(NV) to (OK) 00/00/2005
Name changed to Cyberfund, Inc.
(OK) 09/01/2006
Cyberfund, Inc. (OK) reincorporated
in Delaware as ROK Entertainment
Group Inc. 12/31/2007
(See ROK Entertainment Group Inc.)

SEMPER RES INC (BC)
Merged into David Minerals Ltd.
(New) 10/01/1981
Each share Common no par
exchanged for (1) share Common
no par
(See David Minerals Ltd. (New))

SEMPRA ENERGY (CA)
Each Equity Income Unit received
distribution of (0.819) share
Common no par 5/17/2005
(Additional Information in Active)

SEMX CORP (DE)
Acquired by Coining Holding Co.
01/22/2009
Each share Common 10¢ par
exchanged for approximately $0.025
cash

SEN RAYTO CO. (OH)
Charter cancelled for non-payment of
taxes 3/21/21

SEN YU INTL HLDGS INC (DE)
SEC revoked common stock
registration 03/21/2017

SENAK CO. OF AMERICA (DE)
Name changed to Gracious Living,
Inc. 7/1/52 which dissolved 4/16/64

SENATOR MINERALS CORP (BC)
Struck off register and declared
dissolved for failure to file returns
3/28/91

SENATOR MINERALS INC (ON)
Each share old Common no par
exchanged for (0.025) share new
Common no par 06/17/2013
Reincorporated under the laws of
British Columbia 09/22/2014

SENATOR-ROUYN LTD. (QC)
Recapitalized as New Senator-Rouyn
Ltd. 00/00/1952
Each share Capital Stock $1 par
exchanged for (0.4) share Common
no par

New Senator-Rouyn Ltd. name
changed to NSR Resources Inc.
10/02/1980

SENCO SENSORS INC (BC)
Cease trade order effective
03/28/2003
Stockholders' equity unlikely

SENCON GOLD MINES, LTD. (ON)
Charter cancelled for failure to file
reports and pay taxes in 1957

SENECA COPPER MINING CO.
Sold under foreclosure in 1937
No stockholders' equity

SENECA DEVS LTD (BC)
Recapitalized as Award Resources
Ltd. 02/08/1982
Each share Common no par
exchanged for (0.25) share Common
no par
Award Resources Ltd. recapitalized
as Tomco Developments Inc.
06/16/1990

SENECA EQUITIES CORP (AB)
Acquired by MedMira Inc. 03/08/2004
Each share Common no par
exchanged for (1) Common Share
Right expiring 04/07/2004

SENECA EXPLORATIONS LTD. (QC)
Former transfer agent advised charter
was reported cancelled in May 1967

SENECA FALLS MACHINE CO. (MA)
Reincorporated under the laws of
New Jersey as SFM Corp.
06/17/1968
SFM Corp. (NJ) reincorporated in
Nevada as EXX Inc. 10/21/1994
(See EXX Inc.)

SENECA FOODS CORP (NY)
6% Non-Voting Preferred $1 par
called for redemption 7/1/71
Name changed to Pierce (S.S.) Co.,
Inc. 12/29/77
Pierce (S.S.) Co., Inc. recapitalized
as Seneca Foods Corp. (New)
11/24/86

SENECA GORHAM TEL CORP (NY)
Acquired by Rochester Telephone
Corp. 10/27/88
Each share Common no par
exchanged for (121.28) shares
Common $2.50 par
Rochester Telephone Corp. name
changed to Frontier Corp. 1/1/95
which merged into Global Crossing
Ltd. 9/28/99
(See Global Crossing Ltd.)

SENECA GRAPE JUICE CORP. (NY)
Name changed to Seneca Foods
Corp. 12/5/66
Seneca Foods Corp. name changed
to Pierce (S.S.) Co., Inc. 12/29/77
which recapitalized back as Seneca
Foods Corp. 11/24/86

SENECA HOTEL CO. (IL)
Assets sold and liquidation completed
3/21/61

SENECA MANUFACTURING CORP., INC. (KS)
Dissolved 4/23/63
No stockholders' equity

SENECA METAL PRODUCTS LTD. (AB)
Recapitalized as Cedar Corp.
05/18/1994
Each share Common no par
exchanged for (0.1) share Common
no par
(See Cedar Corp.)

SENECA OIL & GAS CO (DE)
Name changed to Prudential Energy
Corp. 6/22/79
(See Prudential Energy Corp.)

SENECA OIL CO (DE)
Each share Class A 50¢ par
exchanged for (1) share Common
50¢ par 08/05/1957
Each share Class B 10¢ par
exchanged for (0.25) share Common
50¢ par 08/05/1957
Each share 5% Conv. Preferred Class
A 50¢ par exchanged for (0.5) share
Common 50¢ par 04/16/1976
Each share 5% Conv. Preferred Class
B 50¢ par exchanged for (1/3) share
Common 50¢ par 04/16/1976
Each share 5% Conv. Preferred Class
C 50¢ par exchanged for (0.25)
share Common 50¢ par 04/16/1976
Plan of reorganization under Chapter
11 Federal Bankruptcy proceedings
confirmed 11/21/1985
No stockholders' equity

SENERCORP VENTURES INC (AB)
Merged into United Kiev Resources
Inc. 5/18/95
Each share Common no par
exchanged for (1) share Common
no par
United Kiev Resources Inc. name
changed to Carpatsky Petroleum
Inc. 7/17/97
(See Carpatsky Petroleum Inc.)

SENESCO TECHNOLOGIES INC (DE)
Reincorporated 10/25/1999
State of incorporation changed from
(ID) to (DE) 10/25/1999
Each share Common $0.0015 par
exchanged for (2) shares Common
1¢ par
Each share old Common 1¢ par
exchanged for (0.01) share new
Common 1¢ par 10/21/2013
Name changed to Sevion
Therapeutics, Inc. 10/03/2014
Sevion Therapeutics, Inc.
recapitalized as Eloxx
Pharmaceuticals, Inc. 12/20/2017

SENET COPPER MINES LTD. (ON)
Charter revoked for failure to file
reports and pay fees 4/1/65

SENETEK PLC (ENGLAND)
Each old Sponsored ADR for Ordinary
exchanged for (0.125) new
Sponsored ADR for Ordinary
12/13/2007
Name changed to Independence
Resources PLC 12/07/2011
(See Independence Resources PLC)

SENEX CORP (AB)
Merged into Senex Petroleum Corp.
12/31/1989
Each share Common no par
exchanged for (0.2) share Common
no par
Senex Petroleum Corp. merged into
Devran Petroleum Ltd. 03/01/1993
which name changed to Reserve
Royalty Corp. 11/16/1995 which
merged into PrimeWest Energy
Trust 07/27/2000
(See PrimeWest Energy Trust)

SENEX PETE CORP (AB)
Merged into Devran Petroleum Ltd.
03/01/1993
Each share Common no par
exchanged for (0.1) share Common
no par
Devran Petroleum Ltd. name changed
to Reserve Royalty Corp.
11/16/1995 which merged into
PrimeWest Energy Trust 07/27/2000
(See PrimeWest Energy Trust)

SENIOR ATHLETIC RES INC (FL)
Involuntarily dissolved 11/1/85

SENIOR CARE INDS INC (NV)
Reincorporated 08/26/1999
State of incorporation changed from
(ID) to (NV) 08/26/1999
Each share old Common $0.001 par
exchanged for (0.03333333) share
new Common $0.001 par
03/15/2001
Stock Dividend - 10% payable
08/18/2000 to holders of record
08/15/2000 Ex date - 08/11/2000
Name changed to U.S. West Homes
Inc. 09/20/2002

U.S. West Homes Inc. recapitalized
as Investco Corp. 05/30/2003
(See Investco Corp.)

SENIOR GAS & OIL LTD. (ON)
Merged into Erieshore Industries Inc.
05/10/1971
Each share Common $1 par
exchanged for (0.222222) share
Common no par
Erieshore Industries Inc. merged into
Portfield Industries Inc. 10/22/1980
which recapitalized as Canmine
Resources Corp. 05/01/1991
(See Canmine Resources Corp.)

SENIOR GOLD PRODUCERS INCOME CORP (ON)
Name changed to Aston Hill Senior
Gold Producers Income Corp.
09/16/2011
Aston Hill Senior Gold Producers
Income Corp. merged into Aston Hill
Global Resource & Infrastructure
Fund 04/05/2013 which merged into
Aston Hill Global Resource Fund
(New) 11/06/2015

SENIOR HIGH INCOME PORTFOLIO INC (MD)
Name changed to BlackRock Senior
High Income Fund, Inc. 10/02/2006
BlackRock Senior High Income Fund,
Inc. merged into BlackRock Debt
Strategies Fund Inc. 12/09/2013

SENIOR HIGH INCOME PORTFOLIO II INC (MD)
Merged into Senior High Income
Portfolio, Inc. 04/15/1996
Each share Common 10¢ par
exchanged for (1.00082) shares
Common 10¢ par
Senior High Income Portfolio, Inc.
name changed to BlackRock Senior
High Income Fund, Inc. 10/02/2006
which merged into BlackRock Debt
Strategies Fund Inc. 12/09/2013

SENIOR OPTICIAN SVC INC (NV)
Reincorporated 08/31/2007
State of incorporation changed from
(MN) to (NV) 08/31/2007
Name changed to Vantone
International Group, Inc. 08/17/2009

SENIOR SAVERS GUIDE PUBG INC (BC)
Recapitalized as Kali Venture Corp.
10/20/87
Each share Common no par
exchanged for (0.25) share Common
no par
(See Kali Venture Corp.)

SENIOR SECURITIES, INC.
Liquidated in 1936

SENIOR SVC CORP (DE)
Name changed to CareTenders
Healthcorp 12/13/1991
CareTenders Healthcorp name
changed to Almost Family Inc.
02/01/2000 which merged into LHC
Group, Inc. 04/01/2018

SENIOR STRATEGIC INCOME FD INC (MD)
Merged into Senior High Income
Portfolio, Inc. 04/15/1996
Each share Common 10¢ par
exchanged for (1.026417) shares
Common 10¢ par
Senior High Income Portfolio Inc.
name changed to BlackRock Senior
High Income Fund, Inc. 10/02/2006
which merged into BlackRock Debt
Strategies Fund Inc. 12/09/2013

SENIOR TOUR PLAYERS DEV INC (NV)
Merged into Golf Club Partners LLC
8/20/98
Each share Common $0.001
exchanged for $3.20 cash
Note: Each share Common $0.001
received an additional distribution of
$0.08828 cash per share 8/11/99

SENLAC RES INC (ON)
Merged into Heenan Senlac Resources Ltd. 8/7/86
Each share Common no par exchanged for (1) share Common no par
Heenan Senlac Resources Ltd. merged into Mining & Allied Supplies (Canada) Ltd. 8/25/92 which name changed to Bearing Power (Canada) Ltd. 3/28/94
(See Bearing Power (Canada) Ltd.)

SENMAR CAP CORP (AB)
Name changed to Toscana Energy Income Corp. 10/18/2012

SENN D OR INC (CANADA)
Recapitalized as Venoro Gold Corp. 10/19/1993
Each share Class A Common no par exchanged for (1/3) share Class A Common no par
Venoro Gold Corp. recapitalized as New Venoro Gold Corp. 10/30/1997 which name changed to Vanteck (VRB) Technology Corp. 06/20/2000 which name changed to VRB Power Systems Inc. 01/17/2003 which name changed to Nevaro Capital Corp. (Old) 08/24/2009
(See Nevaro Capital Corp. (Old))

SENNEN RES LTD (BC)
Name changed to Sennen Potash Corp. 04/15/2013

SENNEPAS GOLD MINES LTD. (ON)
Charter cancelled for failure to file reports and pay taxes in 1955

SENNO CORP (MT)
Involuntarily dissolved for failure to file annual reports 12/01/1988

SENORE GOLD MINES LTD. (QC)
Acquired by Courville Mines Ltd. prior 07/00/1945
Each share Capital Stock $1 par exchanged for (0.05) share Capital Stock $1 par
(See Courville Mines Ltd.)

SENORX INC (DE)
Acquired by Bard (C.R.), Inc. 07/06/2010
Each share Common $0.001 par exchanged for $11 cash

SENSAR CORP (NV)
Common $0.001 par split (2) for (1) by issuance of (1) additional share payable 01/20/2000 to holders of record 01/17/2000
Name changed to VitalStream Holdings, Inc. 07/26/2002
VitalStream Holdings, Inc. merged into Internap Network Services Corp. 02/20/2007 which name changed to Internap Corp. 12/04/2014

SENSAT TECHNOLOGIES LTD (BC)
Delisted from Vancouver Stock Exchange 05/21/1991

SENSATA TECHNOLOGIES HLDG N V (NETHERLANDS)
Under plan of merger each share Common EUR 0.01 par automatically became (1) share Sensata Technologies Holding PLC Common EUR 0.01 par 03/28/2018

SENSE HLDGS INC (FL)
Common 10¢ par changed to $0.001 par 07/12/2007
Name changed to China America Holdings, Inc. 11/27/2007
China America Holdings, Inc. recapitalized as Ziyang Ceramics Corp. 01/27/2012
(See Ziyang Ceramics Corp.)

SENSE TECHNOLOGIES INC (YT)
Reincorporated under the laws of Yukon 12/14/2001 which reincorporated back in British Columbia 11/15/2007

SENSIBAR TRANSPORTATION CO.
Reorganized as Midwest Vessel Corp. in 1935 which was liquidated in 1944

SENSIENT TECHNOLOGIES CORP (WI)
Common Stock Purchase Rights declared for Common stockholders of record 08/06/1998 were redeemed at $0.01 per right on 09/03/2003 for holders of record 08/25/2003
(Additional Information in Active)

SENSIO TECHNOLOGIES INC (QC)
Deemed to have made an assignment in bankruptcy 04/22/2016
No stockholders' equity

SENSITRON INC (CA)
Common $0.047619 par changed to $0.015873 par 02/13/1973
Stock Dividend - 200% 03/24/1969
Charter suspended for failure to file reports and pay fees 09/01/1977

SENSIVIDA MED TECHNOLOGIES INC (NJ)
SEC revoked common stock registration 04/16/2015

SENSOR CTL CORP (DE)
Name changed to Safetytek Corp. 10/14/91
Safetytek Corp. name changed to Invivo Corp. 8/12/96
(See Invivo Corp.)

SENSOR SYS SOLUTIONS INC (NV)
Recapitalized as Victor Mining Industry Group Inc. 04/15/2014
Each share Common $0.001 par exchanged for (0.0005) share Common $0.001 par

SENSOR TECHNOLOGIES INC (NV)
Recapitalized as Power Play Development Corp. 04/11/2006
Each share Common $0.001 par exchanged for (0.001) share Common $0.001 par Power Play Development Corp. recapitalized as Wikisoft Corp. 04/24/2018

SENSORMATIC CDA LTD (CANADA)
Name changed 7/23/79
Name changed from Sensormatic Electronics Canada Ltd. to Sensormatic Canada Ltd. 7/23/79
Common no par split (2) for (1) by issuance of (1) additional share 7/8/83
Name changed to Senvest Capital Inc. 4/5/91

SENSORMATIC ELECTRS CORP (DE)
Common 1¢ par split (2) for (1) by issuance of (1) additional share 6/30/82
Common 1¢ par split (3) for (2) by issuance of (0.5) additional share 5/31/83
Common 1¢ par split (3) for (2) by issuance of (0.5) additional share 12/17/93
Stock Dividend - 100% 9/26/80
6% Conv. Depositary Preferred called for redemption at $26.117 on 11/12/2001
6% Conv. Preferred 1¢ par called for redemption at $259.275 plus $1.896 accrued dividends on 11/12/2001
Merged into Tyco International Ltd. 11/13/2001
Each share Common 1¢ par exchanged for (0.5189) share Common 1¢ par

SENSORSTAT SYS INC (BC)
Struck off register and declared dissolved for failure to file returns 1/20/89

SENSORY SCIENCE CORP (DE)
Merged into SONICblue Inc. 06/27/2001
Each share Common $0.001 par exchanged for (0.0913) share Common $0.0001 par
(See SONICblue Inc.)

SENSORY SYS INC (NY)
Charter cancelled and proclaimed dissolved for failure to pay taxes 06/24/1981

SENSOTRON INC (CA)
Charter suspended by order of the franchise tax board 1/4/99

SENSYTECH INC (DE)
Name changed 10/07/1999
Name changed from Sensys Technologies Inc. to Sensytech Inc. 10/07/1999
Name changed to Argon ST, Inc. 10/04/2004
(See Argon ST, Inc. 08/05/2010)

SENTERNET TECHNOLOGIES INC (ON)
Common no par split (4) for (1) by issuance of (3) additional shares payable 07/03/2007 to holders of record 07/03/2007
Name changed to Senternet Phi Gamma Inc. 01/22/2014

SENTEX SENSING TECHNOLOGY INC (NJ)
SEC revoked common stock registration 05/23/2011

SENTEX SYS LTD (AB)
Name changed to Natunola Health Biosciences Inc. 07/08/2008
Natunola Health Biosciences Inc. merged into Botaneco Corp. 10/14/2011 which name changed to Natunola AgriTech Inc. 07/09/2013
(See Natunola AgriTech Inc.)

SENTICORE INC (DE)
Each share old Common $0.001 par exchanged for (3) shares new Common $0.001 par 12/1/2003
Name changed to Integrative Health Technologies, Inc. 8/1/2006

SENTIGEN HLDG CORP (DE)
Each share Common $0.001 par received distribution of (1) share SentiSearch, Inc. Common $0.0001 par payable 11/30/2006 to holders of record 11/20/2006
Merged into Invitrogen Corp. 12/1/2006
Each share Common 1¢ par exchanged for $3.37 cash

SENTINEL COMMUNITY BK (SONORA, CA)
Name changed 10/1/96
Name changed from Sentinel Savings & Loan to Sentinel Community Bank (Sonora, CA) 10/1/96
Merged into Western Sierra Bancorp 6/1/2000
Each share Common $5 par exchanged for (1.491) shares Common no par
Western Sierra Bancorp merged into Umpqua Holdings Corp. 6/5/2006

SENTINEL CORP (OR)
Under plan of reorganization each share Common $0.005 par received (1/3) share Multi-I-Inc. Common $0.005 par 5/18/92
Note: Certificates were not required to be exchanged and are without value

SENTINEL ELECTRS CORP (MN)
Merged into Trane Co. 10/12/1978
Each share Common $0.0303 par exchanged for $2.25 cash

SENTINEL FINL CORP (MO)
Merged into Roosevelt Financial Group, Inc. 10/31/1996
Each share Common 1¢ par exchanged for (1.4231) shares Common 1¢ par
Roosevelt Financial Group, Inc. merged into Mercantile Bancorporation, Inc. 07/01/1997 which merged into Firstar Corp.

(New) 09/20/1999 which merged into U.S. Bancorp (DE) 02/27/2001

SENTINEL HLDGS LTD (ON)
Merged into Unicorp Financial Corp. 12/31/79
Each share Class A Common no par exchanged for (5/24) share Class A Common no par and (5/24) share Class B Common no par
Each share Non-Cum. Participating Class B no par exchanged for (1/24) share Class A Common no par and (1/24) share Class B Common no par
Unicorp Financial Corp. name changed to Unicorp Canada Corp. 7/13/82 which recapitalized as Unicorp Energy Corp. 6/25/91 which name changed to Unicorp Inc. 5/28/99 which name changed to Wilmington Capital Management Inc. 3/8/2002

SENTINEL LEASING INC (DE)
Voluntarily dissolved 12/29/2008
Details not available

SENTINEL LIFE INS CO (CA)
Company advised privately held 00/00/1980
Details not available

SENTINEL MINES LTD. (CANADA)
Completely liquidated 02/00/1950
Each share Capital Stock no par exchanged for first and final distribution of $0.051 cash

SENTINEL PA TAX-FREE TR (PA)
Merged into Federated Municipal Securities Fund, Inc. 07/21/2006
Each Share of Bene. 1¢ par exchanged for Class A 1¢ par on a net asset basis

SENTINEL RADIO CORP. (IL)
Name changed to Dempster Investment Co. 4/6/56
(See Dempster Investment Co.)

SENTINEL RES CORP (DE)
Name changed to Red Eagle Resources Corp. 4/29/87
Red Eagle Resources Corp. merged into Lomak Petroleum, Inc. 2/15/95 which name changed to Range Resources Corp. 8/25/98

SENTINEL RES LTD (BC)
Reincorporated under the laws of Bahamas as Ulysses International Resources Ltd. 08/30/1995
Ulysses International Resources Ltd. recapitalized as Auric Resources Ltd. (Bahamas) 03/05/1999 which reorganized in Yukon as Lalo Ventures Ltd. 11/02/2001 which reincorporated in British Columbia 07/29/2005 which name changed to Sunrise Minerals Inc. 12/20/2005 which recapitalized as Cronus Resources Ltd. (BC) 03/10/2008 which reincorporated in Ontario 06/25/2009 which merged into Continental Gold Ltd. (New) (Bermuda) 03/30/2010 which reorganized in Ontario as Continental Gold Inc. 06/12/2015

SENTINEL ROCK OIL CORP (AB)
Recapitalized as Sentinel Rock Oil Inc. 11/17/2010
Each share Common no par exchanged for (0.1) share Common no par
Sentinel Rock Oil Inc. name changed to Sundance Energy Corp. 04/25/2011 which name changed to Ceno Energy Ltd. 06/23/2014 which name changed to Vital Energy Inc. 10/10/2014

SENTINEL ROCK OIL INC (AB)
Name changed to Sundance Energy Corp. 04/25/2011
Sundance Energy Corp. name changed to Ceno Energy Ltd. 06/23/2014 which name changed to Vital Energy Inc. 10/10/2014

SENTINEL SCIENTIFIC INC (NV)
Recapitalized as TC X Calibur Inc. 08/12/1993
Each share Common $0.001 par exchanged for (0.09090909) share Common $0.001 par
TC X Calibur Inc. name changed to Medican Enterprises, Inc. 09/18/2013

SENTINEL SEC LIFE INS CO (UT)
Acquired by Advantage Capital Holdings LLC 05/12/2016
Each share Common $1 par exchanged for $62 cash

SENTINEL SELF STORAGE CORP (AB)
Merged into Cambridge Shopping Centres Ltd. 6/26/90
Each share Class A no par exchanged for $3.625 cash

SENTINEL SOLUTIONS INC (NV)
Merged into Global Monitoring Systems, Inc. 04/17/2006
Each share Common $0.001 par exchanged for (1) share Common $0.001 par
Global Monitoring Systems, Inc. name changed to Planet Signal, Inc. 11/21/2007
(See Planet Signal, Inc.)

SENTO CORP (UT)
Name changed 08/11/1998
Name changed from Sento Technical Innovations Corp. to Sento Corp. 08/11/1998
Each share old Common 25¢ par exchanged for (0.25) share new Common 25¢ par 11/25/2002
Charter expired 02/10/2009

SENTRA CONSULTING CORP (NV)
Name changed to Karat Platinum, Inc. 04/17/2008
(See Karat Platinum, Inc.)

SENTRA RES CORP (AB)
Acquired by Blue Mountain Energy Ltd. 9/30/2004
Each share Class A Common no par exchanged for (0.2) share Common no par
(See Blue Mountain Energy Ltd.)

SENTRACHEM LTD (SOUTH AFRICA)
ADR agreement terminated 12/02/1997
Each 144A GDR for Ordinary Rand-1 par exchanged for $9.625 cash
Each Sponsored ADR for Ordinary Rand-1 par exchanged for $4.7975 cash

SENTRON, INC. (MA)
Adjudicated bankrupt 9/18/75

SENTRUST BEPERK (SOUTH AFRICA)
Merged into Gencor Investments Corp. Ltd. 11/4/83
Each ADR for Ordinary Rand-20¢ par exchanged for (0.72) ADR for Ordinary Rand-1 par
Gencor Investments Corp. Ltd. name changed to Genbel Investments Ltd. 8/13/84 which name changed to Genbel South Africa Ltd. 11/24/95
(See Genbel South Africa Ltd.)

SENTRY ACCOUNTING INC (FL)
Name changed to TravelNow.Com, Inc. (FL) 7/27/99
TravelNow.Com, Inc. (FL) reincorporated in Delaware 10/19/2000

SENTRY ARMORED COURIER CORP (NY)
Name changed to Grant Enterprise Ltd. 03/30/1987

SENTRY CASH MGMT FD INC (MD)
Merged into Neuberger & Berman Government Money Fund, Inc. 03/03/1986
Each share Common 10¢ par exchanged for (1) share Common 1¢ par
(See Neuberger & Berman Government Money Fund, Inc.)

SENTRY CORP. (DE)
Each share Capital Stock 10¢ par exchanged for (0.2) share Capital Stock 50¢ par 2/23/60
Name changed to Terry Industries, Inc. 9/12/60
Terry Industries, Inc. charter cancelled 4/15/68

SENTRY DATA INC (DE)
Plan of reorganization under Chapter 11 Federal Bankruptcy proceedings confirmed 09/02/1987
No stockholders' equity

SENTRY DEV & IMPT CORP (UT)
Name changed to Microwave Components Systems Corp. 02/20/1974
(See Microwave Components Systems Corp.)

SENTRY ENTMT GROUP LTD (NV)
Name changed to International Message Switching Corp. 08/07/1986

SENTRY INVESTIGATION CORP (NY)
Name changed Sentry Armored Courier Corp. 02/23/1978
Sentry Armored Courier Corp. name changed to Grant Enterprise Ltd. 03/30/1987

SENTRY PETROLEUMS LTD. (ON)
Charter cancelled for failure to pay taxes and file returns 4/19/78

SENTRY RES CORP (BC)
Name changed 3/11/87
Name changed from Sentry Oil & Gas Corp. to Sentry Resources Corp. 3/11/87
Struck off register and declared dissolved for failure to file returns 5/3/2002

SENTRY SAFETY CONTROL CORP. (DE)
Capital Stock no par changed to $1 par in 1935
Capital Stock $1 par changed to 10¢ par in 1951
Name changed to Sentry Corp. 9/13/57
Sentry Corp. name changed to Terry Industries, Inc. 9/12/60
(See Terry Industries, Inc.)

SENTRY SELECT BLUE CHIP INCOME TR (ON)
Completely liquidated 03/31/2011
Each Trust Unit received first and final distribution of $25.54 cash

SENTRY SELECT CAP CORP (ON)
Acquired by Sentry Select Holdings Inc. 01/07/2004
Each share Common no par exchanged for $1 cash

SENTRY SELECT CHINA FUND (ON)
Trust Units reclassified as Ser. X Units 05/01/2009
Completely liquidated 03/25/2011
Each share Ser. A Unit received first and final distribution of $7.268 cash
Each share Ser. X Unit received first and final distribution of $7.346 cash

SENTRY SELECT COMMODITIES INCOME TR (ON)
Merged into Sentry Energy Growth & Income Fund 02/04/2011
Each Trust Unit no par received (1.231) Ser. A Units no par

SENTRY SELECT DIVERSIFIED INCOME TR (ON)
Name changed to Sentry Select Diversified Income Fund 01/08/2009

SENTRY SELECT FIDAC U S MTG TR (ON)
Merged into Sentry Select MBS Adjustable Rate Income Fund II 03/07/2008
Each Trust Unit no par received (1.1315) Units no par

SENTRY SELECT FOCUSED GROWTH & INCOME TR (ON)
Issue Information - 4,000,000 TR UNITS offered at $20 per Trust Unit on 12/20/2001
Trust Units split (3) for (1) by issuance of (2) additional Units payable 10/29/2004 to holders of record 10/25/2004
Merged into Sentry Select Canadian Income Fund 06/12/2009
Each Trust Unit exchanged for (0.4373) Ser. A Unit no par

SENTRY SELECT 40 SPLIT INCOME (ON)
Merged into Sentry Select Canadian Income Fund 06/12/2009
Each Preferred Security no par received approximately $10 cash
Each Capital Unit no par received (0.3689) Ser. A Unit no par

SENTRY SELECT GLOBAL INDEX INCOME TR (ON)
Trust terminated 06/22/2012
Each Trust Unit received $25.06 cash

SENTRY SELECT TOTAL STRATEGY FD (ON)
Fund terminated 03/30/2009
Each Trust Unit received first and final distribution of $3.83 cash

SENTRY TECHNOLOGY CORP (DE)
Each share 5% Preferred Class A no par exchanged for (5) shares Common no par 1/8/2001
Stock Dividends - In Preferred to holders of Preferred 5% payable 2/12/98 to holders of record 1/29/98 Ex date - 1/27/98; 5% payable 2/12/99 to holders of record 1/29/99; 5% payable 1/19/2001 to holders of record 12/29/2000 Ex date - 12/27/2000; 7.5% payable 12/28/2000 to holders of record 12/8/2000
(Additional Information in Active)

SENVIL MINES, LTD. (ON)
Charter cancelled for non-compliance with corporation laws 9/23/63
Capital Stock worthless

SEP CAP CORP (QC)
Completely liquidated
Each share Common no par received first and final distribution of (0.638) Med BioGene Inc. Unit payable 12/30/2009 to holders of record 09/11/2009
Note: Each Unit consists of (1) share Common no par and (0.5) Common Stock Purchase Warrant expiring 12/24/2011

SEPARATE UNITS, INC.
Liquidated in 1930

SEPARATION TECHNOLOGY SYS INC (UT)
Name changed to Rochem Environmental Inc. 09/30/1993
(See Rochem Environmental Inc.)

SEPAREX CORP (DE)
Merged into Parker Drilling Co. 08/22/1983
Each share Common 10¢ par exchanged for (0.1667) share Common 16-2/3¢ par

SEPHA MINES LTD.
Recapitalized as New Sepha Mines, Ltd. on a (1) for (2) basis in 1950
New Sepha Mines, Ltd. charter cancelled 6/30/80

SEPIA COMMERCIAL CORP. (NY)
Name changed to Prefco Corp. 04/23/1962
(See Prefco Corp.)

SEPIK GOLD CORP (AB)
Delisted from Canadian Venture Stock Exchange 5/31/2001

SEPPS GOURMET FOODS LTD (AB)
Each share old Common no par exchanged for (0.000002) share new Common no par 09/15/2008
Note: In effect holders received $0.052 cash per share and public interest was eliminated

SEPRACOR INC (DE)
Common 10¢ par split (2) for (1) by issuance of (1) additional share payable 02/25/2000 to holders of record 02/01/2000
Merged into Dainippon Sumitomo Pharma Co., Ltd. 10/20/2009
Each share Common 10¢ par exchanged for $23 cash

SEPRAGEN CORP (CA)
SEC revoked common stock registration 04/06/2010
Stockholders' equity unlikely

SEPROTECH SYS INC (ON)
Recapitalized as BluMetric Environmental Inc. 11/07/2012
Each share Common no par exchanged for (0.1) share Common no par

SEPTEMBER GROUP INC (NV)
Recapitalized as ProSportsBook.Net Inc. 4/10/2002
Each share Common $0.001 par exchanged for (0.025) share Common $0.001 par
ProSportsBook.Net Inc. recapitalized as Ibises International Inc. 3/27/2003 which recapitalized as Biomag Corp. 3/28/2006 which name changed to Biomagnetics Diagnostics Corp. 12/18/2006

SEPTEMBER MTN COPPER MINES LTD (ON)
Charter cancelled for failure to pay taxes and file returns 03/16/1976

SEPTEMBER PROJ II CORP (FL)
Name changed to Valusales.com Inc. 04/12/2000
Valusales.com Inc. recapitalized as Video Without Boundaries Inc. 11/19/2001 which name changed to MediaREADY, Inc. 09/22/2006 which recapitalized as China Logistics Group, Inc. 03/12/2008

SEPTEMBER PROJ III CORP (FL)
Name changed to Fahrenheit Entertainment, Inc. 11/08/2000
Fahrenheit Entertainment, Inc. name changed to Firesky Media Corp. 05/05/2006 which name changed to Sky440, Inc. 02/12/2008

SEPTEMBER PROJ IV CORP (FL)
Name changed to Fashion Handbags Inc.com 05/24/2000
Fashion Handbags Inc.com name changed to Southwestern Medical Solutions Inc. 03/10/2003

SEPTEMBER RES INC (BC)
Incorporated 08/20/1984
Merged into Uranium Resources, Inc. 12/21/1987
Each share Common no par exchanged for (1) share Common $0.001 par
Uranium Resources, Inc. name changed to Westwater Resources, Inc. 08/21/2017

SEPTEMBER RES LTD (BC)
Incorporated 00/00/1987
Name changed to Aquest Minerals Corp. 02/09/1998
Aquest Minerals Corp. recapitalized as Aquest Explorations Ltd. (BC) 01/09/2002 which reincorporated in Alberta 07/22/2005 which recapitalized as Aquest Energy Ltd. 02/04/2004 which recapitalized as Anderson Energy Ltd. 09/01/2005 which name changed to Anderson Energy Inc. 01/27/2015 which name changed to InPlay Oil Corp. 11/10/2016

SEPTIMA ENTERPRISES INC (CO)
Each share old Common no par exchanged for (0.005) share new Common no par 10/23/1992
Each share new Common no par exchanged for (0.01) share Common $0.0001 par 02/05/2001
Reorganized under the laws of Nevada as Bio-Solutions International Inc. 02/12/2001
Each share Common $0.0001 par exchanged for (0.01) share Common $0.0001 par
Bio-Solutions International, Inc. name changed to Omnimed International, Inc. 11/23/2005 which name changed to Medefile International, Inc. 01/17/2006 which recapitalized as Tech Town Holdings Inc. 11/02/2017 which name changed to Hash Labs Inc. 03/06/2018

SEQUA CORP (DE)
$5 Conv. Preferred no par called for redemption at $100 plus $1.01 accrued dividends on 04/14/2006
Merged into Blue Jay Merger Corp. 12/03/2007
Each share Class A Common no par exchanged for $175 cash
Each share Class B Common no par exchanged for $175 cash

SEQUANA THERAPEUTICS INC (CA)
Merged into AxyS Pharmaceuticals, Inc. 01/08/1998
Each share Common $0.001 par exchanged for (1.35) shares Common $0.001 par
AxyS Pharmaceuticals, Inc. merged into Applera Corp. 11/19/2001
(See Applera Corp.)

SEQUE ENERGY CORP (AB)
Acquired by Duvernay Oil Corp. 08/14/2003
Each share Common no par exchanged for (0.178571) share Common no par
(See Duvernay Oil Corp.)

SEQUEL CORP (DE)
Reincorporated 04/22/1988
State of incorporation changed from (CO) to (DE) 04/22/1988
Name changed to Hanger Orthopedic Group, Inc. 08/14/1989
Hanger Orthopedic Group, Inc. name changed to Hanger, Inc. 06/11/2012

SEQUEL TECHNOLOGY CORP (DE)
Company no longer active as of 03/18/2014

SEQUENOM INC (DE)
Each share old Common $0.001 par exchanged for (0.33333333) share new Common $0.001 par 06/02/2006
Acquired by Laboratory Corp. of America Holdings 09/07/2016
Each share new Common $0.001 par exchanged for $2.40 cash

SEQUENT COMPUTER SYS INC (OR)
Reincorporated 12/2/88
State of incorporation changed from (DE) to (OR) 12/2/88
Common 1¢ par split (2) for (1) by issuance of (1) additional share 11/13/89
Merged into International Business Machines Corp. 9/24/99
Each share Common 1¢ par exchanged for $18 cash

SEQUENTIAL BRANDS GROUP INC OLD (DE)
Each share old Common $0.001 par exchanged for (0.06666666) share new Common $0.001 par 09/11/2012
Under plan of reorganization each share Common $0.001 par automatically became (1) share Sequential Brands Group, Inc. (New) Common $0.001 par 12/07/2015

SEQUENTIAL INFORMATION SYS INC (NY)
Common 10¢ par changed to 1¢ par 4/25/72
Recapitalized as Consolidated Technology Group Ltd. 8/31/93
Each (60) shares Common 1¢ par exchanged for (1) share Common 1¢ par
Consolidated Technology Group Ltd. recapitalized as Sagemark Companies Ltd. 8/9/99

SEQUESTER HLDGS INC (NV)
Each share old Common $0.002 par exchanged for (0.1) share new Common $0.002 par 02/05/1998
Each share new Common $0.002 par exchanged again for (0.1) share new Common $0.002 par 03/10/2000
Recapitalized as China Biolife Enterprises Inc. 06/19/2006
Each share new Common $0.002 par exchanged for (0.005) share Common $0.002 par
China Biolife Enterprises Inc. recapitalized as Asia Pacific Energy Inc. 12/07/2007

SEQUIAM CORP (CA)
Chapter 11 bankruptcy proceedings dismissed 01/02/2009
No stockholders' equity

SEQUOIA ASSET MGMT GROUP INC (FL)
Each share old Common $0.001 par exchanged for (0.1) share new Common $0.001 par 11/29/2006
Each share new Common $0.001 par exchanged again for (0.01894799) share new Common $0.001 par 10/25/2007
Name changed to Platcom, Inc. 11/09/2007
(See Platcom, Inc.)

SEQUOIA BANCSHARES INC (MD)
Merged into United Bankshares, Inc. 10/10/2003
Each share Common exchanged for $39.40 cash

SEQUOIA COMMUNITY BANK (SANGER, CA)
Merged into Fresno Bancorp 9/30/87
Each share Common no par exchanged for (1.12) shares Common no par
Fresno Bancorp merged into ValliCorp Holdings, Inc. 11/30/89 which merged into Westamerica Bancorporation 4/12/97

SEQUOIA FD INC (DE)
Reincorporated under the laws of Maryland 5/1/80

SEQUOIA INS CO (CA)
Capital Stock $1 par changed to 50¢ par 03/06/1964
Each share Capital Stock 50¢ par exchanged for (0.02) share Common $25 par 01/05/1970
Each share Common $25 par exchanged for (10) shares Common $2.50 par 04/03/1972
Acquired by Kemperco, Inc. 09/28/1972
Each share Common $2.50 par exchanged for (0.3222) share Common $5 par
Kemperco, Inc. name changed to Kemper Corp. (Old) 01/15/1974
(See Kemper Corp. (Old))

SEQUOIA INTS CORP (NV)
Each share old Common $0.001 par exchanged for (0.01) share new Common $0.001 par 12/29/2003
Stock Dividend - 5% payable 12/20/2004 to holders of record 12/15/2004
Name changed to Baby Bee Bright Corp. (New) 05/02/2006
Baby Bee Bright Corp. (New) name changed to Fusion Pharm, Inc. 04/08/2011

SEQUOIA MINERALS INC (QC)
Acquired by Cambior Inc. 7/5/2004
Each share Common no par exchanged for (0.15873) share Common no par
Cambior Inc. acquired by Iamgold Corp. 11/8/2006

SEQUOIA NATL BK (SAN FRANCISCO, CA)
Merged into FNB Bancorp 04/30/2005
Each share Common $1 par exchanged for $2.03 cash
Note: Holders received an additional distribution of approximately $0.21 cash from escrow 12/15/2005

SEQUOIA NATIONAL BANK OF SAN MATEO COUNTY (REDWOOD CITY, CA)
Merged into Bank of California, N.A. (San Francisco, Calif.) 10/31/68
Each share Capital Stock $15 par exchanged for (0.75) share Common Capital Stock $10 par
Bank of California, N.A. (San Francisco, Calif.) reorganized as BanCal Tri-State Corp. 5/1/72
(See BanCal Tri-State Corp.)

SEQUOIA OIL & GAS TR (AB)
Plan of arrangement effective 9/26/2006
Each Trust Unit no par exchanged for (0.825) Daylight Resources Trust, Trust Unit no par, (0.0517) share Trafalgar Energy Ltd. Common no par and (0.0144) Common Stock Purchase Warrant expiring 10/23/2006
(See each company's listing)

SEQUOIA RES LTD (BC)
Name changed to American Technology & Information, Inc. 8/7/85
(See American Technology & Information, Inc.)

SEQUOIA SOFTWARE CORP (DE)
Merged into Citrix Systems, Inc. 05/01/2001
Each share Common $0.001 par exchanged for $5.64 cash

SEQUOIA SYS INC (DE)
Name changed to Texas Micro, Inc. 4/24/97
Texas Micro, Inc. merged into RadiSys Corp. 8/13/99

SEQUOYAH INDS INC (OK)
Common 10¢ par split (2) for (1) by issuance of (1) additional share 1/30/69
Common 10¢ par split (2) for (1) by issuance of (1) additional share 8/22/69
Reorganized under Chapter X bankruptcy proceedings 12/30/74
No stockholders' equity

SEQUUS PHARMACEUTICALS INC (DE)
Merged into Alza Corp. 3/16/99
Each share Common $0.0001 par exchanged for (0.4) share Common 1¢ par
Alza Corp. merged into Johnson & Johnson 6/22/2001

SERABI MINING PLC (ENGLAND & WALES)
Name changed to Serabi Gold PLC 10/18/2011

SERAC HLDGS INC (NV)
SEC revoked common stock registration 07/06/2004
Stockholders' equity unlikely

SERAC SPORTS LTD (AB)
Merged into Silverzipper.com, Inc. 03/22/2000
Each share Common no par exchanged for either (0.056116722) share Common $0.001 par, $0.2346 cash, or a combination thereof
Note: Option to receive cash or stock and cash only expired 04/21/2000
(See Silverzipper.com, Inc.)

SERACARE INC (DE)
Each share Common $0.001 par received distribution of (0.4) share SeraCare Life Sciences, Inc. Common $0.001 par payable 9/24/2001 to holders of record 9/24/2001
Merged into Probitas Pharma, S.A. 9/24/2001
Each share Common $0.001 par exchanged for $6.8513 cash

SERACARE LIFE SCIENCES INC (CA)
Reorganized under the laws of Delaware 05/17/2007
Each share Common no par exchanged for (1) share Common $0.001 par
(See SeraCare Life Sciences, Inc. (DE))

SERACARE LIFE SCIENCES INC (DE)
Acquired by Project Plasma Holdings Corp. 04/20/2012
Each share Common $0.001 par exchanged for $4 cash

SERAGEN INC (DE)
Merged into Ligand Pharmaceuticals Inc. 8/12/98
Each share Common 1¢ par exchanged for (0.036) share Common $0.001 par
Note: An additional final payment of $0.23 cash per share was made 8/5/99

SERANOVA INC (NJ)
Merged into Silverline Technologies Ltd. 03/02/2001
Each share Common 1¢ par exchanged for (0.35) Sponsored ADR's for 2001 Dividend
(See Silverline Technologies Ltd.)

SERAPH SEC INC (DE)
Name changed to Commerce Online, Inc. 06/18/2009
Commerce Online, Inc. name changed to Cannabis Medical Solutions, Inc. 03/04/2010 name changed to MediSwipe Inc. 07/08/2011 which name changed to Agritek Holdings, Inc. 05/20/2014

SERATOSA INC (DE)
Recapitalized as Weyland Tech, Inc. 09/01/2015
Each share Common $0.00001 par exchanged for (0.001) share Common $0.00001 par

SERCO ELECTRONICS RESEARCH CORP. (WA)
Declared dissolved for non-payment of annual corporation license fees 7/1/65

SEREBRA LEARNING CORP (AB)
Each share old Common no par exchanged for (0.25) share new Common no par 11/07/2006
Reorganized under the laws of Newfoundland and Labrador as Bluedrop Performance Learning Inc. 01/27/2012
Each share new Common no par exchanged for (0.25) share Common no par

SEREFEX CORP (DE)
SEC revoked common stock registration 05/23/2011

SERENA HEALTH SVCS INC (DE)
Name changed to Tall Feathers Farms, Inc. 10/17/1990
(See Tall Feathers Farms, Inc.)

SERENA RES LTD (BC)
Recapitalized as Consolidated Serena Resources Ltd. 5/17/2001
Each share Common no par exchanged for (0.2) share Common no par
Consolidated Serena Resources Ltd. name changed to Capstone Gold

SER-SER

Corp. 3/7/2003 which name changed to Capstone Mining Corp. 2/13/2006

SERENA SOFTWARE INC (DE)
Common $0.001 par split (3) for (2) by issuance of (0.5) additional share payable 03/29/2000 to holders of record 03/21/2000
Merged into Silver Lake Partners II, LP 03/10/2006
Each share Common $0.001 par exchanged for $24 cash

SERENDIPITY INC (CA)
Stock Dividend - 25% 01/29/1970
Name changed to Sernco, Inc. and Common no par changed to 10¢ par 12/22/1972
(See Sernco, Inc.)

SERENGETI EYEWEAR INC (NY)
Merged into Worldwide Sports & Recreation, Inc. 8/17/2000
Each share Common $0.001 par exchanged for $3.95 cash

SERENGETI MINERALS LTD (BC)
Name changed 4/26/99
Name changed from Serengeti Diamonds Ltd. to Serengeti Minerals Ltd. 4/26/99
Recapitalized as Serengeti Resources Inc. 3/22/2001
Each share Common no par exchanged for (1/15) share Common no par

SERENIC CORP (AB)
Name changed to OneSoft Solutions Inc. 08/01/2014

SERENO CAP CORP (ON)
Recapitalized as Delavaco Residential Properties Corp. 01/03/2014
Each share Common no par exchanged for (0.13586956) share Common no par
Delavaco Residential Properties Corp. name changed to Firm Capital American Realty Partners Corp. 08/02/2016

SERENPET ENERGY INC (AB)
Recapitalized as Serenpet Inc. 04/07/1992
Each share Common no par exchanged for (0.33333333) share Common no par
(See Serenpet Inc.)

SERENPET INC (AB)
Merged into Pembina Resources Ltd. 12/23/96
Each share Common no par exchanged for $4.80 cash

SERIATIM VENTURES INC (AB)
Recapitalized as Forent Energy Inc. 12/30/2008
Each share Common no par exchanged for (0.37037037) share Common no par
Forent Energy Inc. name changed to Forent Energy Ltd. 03/04/2009

SERICA ENERGY CORP (BRITISH VIRGIN ISLANDS)
Reincorporated under the laws of United Kingdom as Serica Energy PLC 09/07/2005
(See Serica Energy PLC)

SERICA ENERGY PLC (UNITED KINGDOM)
ADR agreement terminated 06/14/2018
No ADR's remain outstanding

SERICA ENERGY PLC (UNITED KINGDOM)
Shares transferred to United Kingdom register 03/31/2015

SERIES S-1 INCOME FD (AB)
Merged into Blue Ribbon Income Fund 12/31/2009
Each Trust Unit no par automatically became (0.770898) Trust Unit no par

SERINUS ENERGY INC (AB)
Reincorporated under the laws of Jersey as Serinus Energy PLC and Common no par reclassified as Ordinary no par 05/15/2018
(See Serinus Energy PLC)

SERINUS ENERGY PLC (JERSEY)
Shares transferred to AIM 06/29/2018

SERNCO INC (CA)
Completely liquidated 10/23/1979
No stockholders' equity

SEROLOGICALS CORP (GA)
Issue Information - 2,400,000 shares COM offered at $11.50 per share on 06/14/1995
Common 1¢ par split (3) for (2) by issuance of (0.5) additional share payable 2/28/97 to holders of record 2/10/97
Common 1¢ par split (3) for (2) by issuance of (0.5) additional share payable 8/14/98 to holders of record 7/31/98
Merged into Millipore Corp. 7/14/2006
Each share Common 1¢ par exchanged for $31.55 cash

SERONO S A (SWITZERLAND)
Name changed to Merck Serono S.A. 01/11/2007
(See Merck Serono S.A.)

SERRANO ENERGY LTD (AB)
Each share old Common no par exchanged for (0.5) share new Common no par 07/03/2007
Merged into Baytex Energy Ltd. 05/27/2010
Each share new Common no par exchanged for $2.256 cash
Note: Unexchanged certificates were cancelled and became without value 05/27/2015

SERRICK CORP. (OH)
Name changed to Defiance Industries, Inc. 06/22/1962
Defiance Industries, Inc. merged into El-Tronics, Inc. 10/03/1969 which name changed to ELT, Inc. 01/04/1974 which name changed to Dutch Boy, Inc. 02/23/1977 which name changed to Artra Group Inc. 12/31/1980 which merged into Entrade Inc. 09/23/1999
(See Entrade Inc.)

SERTANT INC (NV)
Name changed to EPHS Holdings, Inc. 08/27/2018

SERV QUIK INC (KY)
Adjudicated bankrupt 06/06/1973
Stockholders' equity unlikely

SERV-TECH INC (TX)
Merged into Philip Services Corp. (ON) 07/31/1997
Each share Common 50¢ par exchanged for (0.403) share Common no par
Philip Services Corp. (ON) reorganized in Delaware as Philip Services Corporation 04/07/2000
(See Philip Services Corporation)

SERVAIR INC (DE)
Completely liquidated 09/28/1971
Each share Common 1¢ par exchanged for (0.32624) share Dynalectron Corp. Common 10¢ par
Dynalectron Corp. name changed to DynCorp 05/11/1987
(See DynCorp)

SERVAL INTEGRATED ENERGY SVCS (AB)
Name changed 06/15/1998
Name changed from Serval Growth Fund to Serval Integrated Energy Services 06/15/1998
Delisted from Canadian Venture Exchange 05/31/2000

SERVAL SLIDE FASTENERS INC (NY)
Name changed to Mira Holding Corp. 7/28/81

(See Mira Holding Corp.)

SERVAM CORP (DE)
Each (44.97) shares old Common 1¢ par exchanged for (1) share new Common 1¢ par 08/12/1991
Plan of reorganization under Chapter 11 Federal Bankruptcy Code effective 07/30/1993
No stockholders' equity

SERVAMATIC SYS INC (DE)
Name changed 05/01/1984
Name changed from Servamatic Solar Systems Inc. to Servamatic Systems, Inc. 05/01/1984
Plan of reorganization under Chapter 11 Federal Bankruptcy proceedings confirmed 12/12/1989
No stockholders' equity

SERVAMERICA INC (FL)
Proclaimed dissolved for failure to file reports and pay fees 11/14/1986

SERVEL, INC. (DE)
Common no par changed to $1 par in 1932 $4.50 Preferred no par reclassified as $5.25 Preferred no par 4/1/59
Merged into Clevite Corp. 7/28/67
Each share Common $1 par exchanged for (2/9) share $2.50 Conv. Preference Ser. A no par
Clevite Corp. merged into Gould Inc. 7/31/69
(See Gould Inc.)

SERVEL CORP.
Reorganized as Servel, Inc. in 1928
No Common stockholders' equity

SERVGRO INTL LTD (SOUTH AFRICA)
ADR agreement terminated 4/20/98
Each Sponsored ADR for Ordinary Rand-8 par exchanged for (1) Ordinary Share Rand-8 par 4/20/98
Note: Unclaimed Ordinary shares will be sold and proceeds held for claim after 3/20/99

SERVICE 1ST BANCORP (CA)
Common no par split (3) for (2) by issuance of (0.5) additional share payable 10/18/2005 to holders of record 09/29/2005 Ex date - 10/19/2005
Stock Dividend - 5% payable 04/12/2004 to holders of record 03/10/2004 Ex date - 03/08/2004
Merged into Central Valley Community Bancorp 11/13/2008
Each share Common no par exchanged for (0.682304) share Common no par and $1.137 cash
Note: Each share Common no par received $0.93171889 cash from escrow 06/30/2011

SERVICE APPLIANCE CO.
Liquidated in 1928

SERVICE ASSOC INC (ID)
Charter forfeited for failure to file reports 11/30/1973

SERVICE BANCORP INC (MA)
Acquired by Middlesex Bancorp, MHC 07/02/2009
Each share Common 1¢ par exchanged for $28 cash

SERVICE CORP AMER (DE)
Charter cancelled and declared inoperative and void for non-payment of taxes 3/1/77

SERVICE CORP INTL (TX)
Variable Term Preferred Ser. B $1 par called for redemption at $1000 on 5/9/90
Variable Term Preferred Ser. A $1 par called for redemption at $1000 on 6/20/90
(Additional Information in Active)

SERVICE CORP INTL CDA LTD (CANADA)
Common no par split (2) for (1) by

issuance of (1) additional share 6/14/94
Under plan of merger each share Common no par exchanged for $22.75 cash 8/31/95

SERVICE EXPERTS INC (DE)
Issue Information - 2,500,000 shares COM offered at $22 per share on 03/18/1997
Merged into Lennox International Inc. 1/21/2000
Each share Common 1¢ par exchanged for (0.67) share Common 1¢ par

SVC FINL SVCS INC (CO)
Ceased operations 05/17/2006
Stockholders' equity unlikely

SERVICE 1ST BK (STOCKTON, CA)
Under plan of reorganization each share Common no par automatically became (1) share Service 1st Bancorp Common no par 06/26/2003
Service 1st Bancorp merged into Central Valley Community Bancorp 11/13/2008

SERVICE FRACTURING CO (TX)
Stock Dividend - 50% 2/20/81
Merged into NWS Offer Corp. 10/24/94
Each share Common $1 par exchanged for $4.55 cash

SERVICE GROUP INC (DE)
Common 10¢ par split (3) for (2) by isuance of (0.5) additional share 12/08/1969
Name changed to American Protection Industries Inc. 11/01/1971
(See American Protection Industries Inc.)

SERVICE HLDG CORP (NV)
Each share old Common $0.001 par exchanged for (0.4) share new Common $0.001 par 11/15/1988
Recapitalized as Shuangyang U.S. Enterprises, Inc. 04/16/1999
Each share new Common $0.001 par exchanged for (0.4) share Common $0.001 par
Shuangyang U.S. Enterprises, Inc. recapitalized as Polymeric Corp. 01/01/2001 which name changed to Lew Corp. 08/27/2001 which name changed to Vintage Energy & Exploration, Inc. 10/02/2007
(See Vintage Energy & Exploration, Inc.)

SERVICE LIFE INSURANCE CO. (TX)
Common no par changed to $1 par 10/16/56
Merged into World Service Life Insurance Co. (TX) 4/28/67
Each share Common $1 par exchanged for (1.3666) shares Common $1 par
World Service Life Insurance Co. (TX) merged into World Service Life Insurance Co. (CO) 7/31/78 which merged into Western Preferred Corp. 2/21/79
(See Western Preferred Corp.)

SERVICE MERCHANDISE INC (TN)
Common $1 par split (3) for (2) by issuance of (0.5) additional share 5/10/78
Common $1 par changed to 50¢ par and (1) additional share issued 4/29/83
Common 50¢ par split (3) for (2) by issuance of (0.5) additional share 3/2/89
Common 50¢ par split (5) for (4) by issuance of (0.25) additional share 5/17/91
Common 50¢ par split (3) for (2) by issuance of (0.5) additional share 5/18/92
Stock Dividends - 50% 4/16/73; 20% 5/6/74; 50% 3/24/75; 50% 12/15/75; 100% 4/1/77
Plan of reorganization under Chapter

11 Federal Bankruptcy Code effective 5/27/2003
No stockholders' equity

SERVICE METRICS INC (CO)
Merged into Exodus Communications Inc. 11/23/99
Each share Common exchanged for (0.1258) share Common $0.001 par
(See Exodus Communications Inc.)

SERVICE PETE LTD (ON)
Name changed to Cape Resources Inc. 06/13/1984
Cape Resources Inc. merged into International Pagurian Corp. Ltd. 03/27/1987 which name changed to Canadian Express Ltd. (Old) 05/12/1988 which recapitalized as Consolidated Canadian Express Ltd. 12/24/1990 which name changed to Canadian Express Ltd. (New) 05/18/2001 which recapitalized as BNN Investments Ltd. 11/02/2001 which name changed to BAM Investments Corp. 07/05/2006 which name changed to Partners Value Fund Inc. 06/10/2013 name changed to Partners Value Investments Inc. 05/25/2015 which reorganized as Partners Value Investments L.P. 07/04/2016

SERVICE PHOTO INDUSTRIES, INC. (NY)
Adjudicated bankrupt 11/26/65
No stockholders' equity

SERVICE PLUS HOSPITALITY LTD (AB)
Acquired by Gamehost Income Fund 06/04/2003
Each share Common no par exchanged for (0.328) Trust Unit
Gamehost Income Fund reorganized as Gamehost Inc. 01/10/2011

SERVICE PRODUCING CO (DE)
Adjudicated bankrupt 12/27/1973
Stockholders' equity unlikely

SERVICE RES CORP (PANAMA)
Reorganized under the laws of Delaware as Ameriscribe Corp. 07/24/1990
Each share Common $5 par exchanged for (1) share Common 1¢ par
Ameriscribe Corp. merged into Pitney Bowes Inc. 10/29/1993

SVC SECOND VENTURE CAP CORP (BC)
Name changed to Masev Communications International Inc. 02/24/2003
(See Masev Communications International Inc.)

SERVICE STATION EQUIPMENT CO. LTD.
Name changed to Service Stations Ltd. in 1929
Service Station Equipment Co. Ltd. name changed to International Metal Industries Ltd. in 1934 which name changed to Wood (John) Industries Ltd. 5/15/57 which was acquired by Wood (John) Co. 12/3/62
(See Wood (John) Co.)

SERVICE STATIONS, LTD.
Name changed to International Metal Industries Ltd. in 1934 which name changed to Wood (John) Industries Ltd. 5/15/57 which was acquired by Wood (John) Co. 12/3/62
Wood (John) Co. acquired by Anthes Imperial Ltd. in March 1964

SERVICE SYS INTL LTD (NV)
Recapitalized as UltraGuard Water Systems Corp. 12/06/2002
Each share Common $0.001 par exchanged for (0.02) share Common $0.001 par
UltraGuard Water Systems Corp. recapitalized as Creative Eateries Corp. 07/08/2005 which recapitalized as Diners Acquisition Corp. 10/20/2006 which recapitalized as LaSalle Brands Corp. 07/10/2007
(See LaSalle Brands Corp.)

SERVICEMASTER CO (DE)
Common 1¢ par split (3) for (2) by issuance of (0.5) additional share payable 08/26/1998 to holders of record 08/12/1998
Merged into CDRSVM Topco, Inc. 07/24/2007
Each share Common 1¢ par exchanged for $15.625 cash

SERVICEMASTER INDS INC (DE)
Reincorporated 06/30/1969
State of incorporation changed from (IL) to (DE) and Common no par changed to $1 par 06/30/1969
Common $1 par split (3) for (1) by issuance of (2) additional shares 06/06/1972
Common $1 par split (3) for (2) by issuance of (0.5) additional share 04/05/1977
Common $1 par split (3) for (2) by issuance of (0.5) additional share 06/20/1978
Common $1 par split (3) for (2) by issuance of (0.5) additional share 01/21/1980
Common $1 par split (3) for (2) by issuance of (0.5) additional share 06/22/1981
Common $1 par split (3) for (2) by issuance of (0.5) additional share 06/07/1983
Common $1 par split (3) for (2) by issuance of (0.5) additional share 06/04/1985
Reorganized as ServiceMaster Limited Partnership 12/30/1986
Each share Common $1 par exchanged for (1) Public Partnership Share
ServiceMaster Limited Partnership name changed to ServiceMaster Co. 12/29/1997
(See ServiceMaster Co.)

SERVICEMASTER LTD PARTNERSHIP (DE)
Public Partnership Shares split (3) for (2) by issuance of (0.5) additional share 01/31/1992
Public Partnership Shares split (3) for (2) by issuance of (0.5) additional share 06/22/1993
Public Partnership Shares split (3) for (2) by issuance of (0.5) additional share payable 06/24/1996 to holders of record 06/10/1996 Ex date - 06/25/1996
Public Partnership Shares split (3) for (2) by issuance of (0.5) additional share payable 06/25/1997 to holders of record 06/11/1997 Ex date - 06/26/1997
Under plan reorganization name changed to ServiceMaster Co. and Public Partnership shares reclassified as Common 1¢ par 12/29/1997
(See ServiceMaster Co.)

SERVICEMAX AMER INC (FL)
Name changed to SMX Corp. 11/08/1999
(See SMX Corp.)

SERVICES ACQUISITION CORP INTL (DE)
Name changed to Jamba, Inc. 11/29/2006
(See Jamba, Inc.)

SERVICES INVT CO (IA)
Name changed to International Funeral Services, Inc. 8/9/68
International Funeral Services, Inc. name changed to IFS Industries Inc. 8/16/77 which merged into Service Corp. International 12/10/81

SERVICES NATIONAL BANK (ARLINGTON, VA)
Acquired by First & Merchants Corp. 11/30/79
Each share Capital Stock $12 par exchanged for $24 cash

SERVICEWARE TECHNOLOGIES INC (DE)
Issue Information - 4,500,000 shares COM offered at $7 per share on 03/31/2000
Each share old Common 1¢ par exchanged for (0.1) share new Common 1¢ par 2/4/2005
Name changed to Knova Software, Inc. 6/1/2005
(See Knova Software, Inc.)

SERVICIOS FINANCIEROS QUADRUM S A (MEXICO)
Name changed to Banca Quadrum S.A. 3/17/95
(See Banca Quadrum S.A.)

SERVICO INC (DE)
Common $1 par changed to 10¢ par 05/23/1972
Stock Dividends - 10% 08/30/1982; 10% 10/17/1983; 10% 01/31/1985; 10% 08/31/1985
Merged into FCD Hospitality Inc. 04/26/1989
Each share Common 10¢ par exchanged for $21 cash

SERVICO INC (FL)
Secondary Offering - 10,000,000 shares COM offered at $14.50 per share on 06/24/1997
Merged into Lodgian, Inc. 12/11/1998
Each share Common 1¢ par exchanged for (1) share Common 1¢ par
(See Lodgian, Inc.)

SERVIDYNE INC (GA)
Stock Dividend - 5% payable 07/01/2008 to holders of record 06/18/2008 Ex date - 06/16/2008
Acquired by Scientific Conservation, Inc. 08/29/2011
Each share Common $1 par exchanged for $3.50 cash

SERVINATIONAL INC (NY)
Reincorporated under the laws of Ohio 05/22/1991
Servinational, Inc. (OH) reincorporated in Nevada as Shikisai International, Inc. 11/25/2005 which name changed to Life Design Station International, Inc. 08/21/2007

SERVINATIONAL INC (OH)
Reincorporated under the laws of Nevada as Shikisai International, Inc. 11/25/2005
Shikisai International, Inc. name changed to Life Design Station International, Inc. 08/21/2007

SERVING SOFTWARE INC (MN)
Merged into HBO & Co. 09/13/1994
Each share Common 1¢ par exchanged for (0.29099) share Common 5¢ par
HBO & Co. merged into McKesson HBOC Inc. 01/12/1999 which name changed to McKesson Corp. 07/31/2001

SERVISCO (NJ)
Merged into ARA Services Inc. 11/21/1986
Each share Common 50¢ par exchanged for $30 cash

SERVISOFT OF CALIFORNIA (CA)
Name changed to Quality Industries 2/11/64
Quality Industries name changed to Tri Financial Corp. 1/5/66 which name changed to Crateo, Inc. 8/15/67 which was adjudicated bankrupt 8/8/73

SERVITECH INC (DE)
Charter cancelled and declared inoperative and void for non-payment of taxes 03/01/1974

SERVO CORP AMER (NY)
Merged into Servo Acquisition Inc. 03/01/1989
Each share Common $1 par exchanged for $14.10 cash

SERVO ENGINEERING CORP. (MN)
Out of business 6/22/62
Common Stock valueless

SERVO SYSTEMS, INC. (DE)
Although overstamped certificates reflecting a change of name to Servoil Industries, Inc. have been issued, no amendments have been filed making the change effective
(See Servoil Industries, Inc.)

SERVO TREND INC (NY)
Recapitalized as Momentum Software Corp. 3/17/89
Each share Common 1¢ par exchanged for (0.1) share Common $0.001 par
(See Momentum Software Corp.)

SERVOIL INDS INC (NV)
Each share Common $0.001 par exchanged for (0.1) share Class A Common $0.001 par 02/27/1981
Note: Amendments to confirm consolidation with Servo Systems, Inc. never filed with proper authorities
Charter revoked for failure to file reports and pay fees 12/01/1986

SERVOMATION CORP (DE)
Merged into GDV, Inc. 01/27/1979
Each share Common $1 par exchanged for $49 cash

SERVOMECHANISMS, INC. (NY)
Merged into Teledyne, Inc. on a (0.1) for (1) basis 11/25/64
Teledyne, Inc. merged into Allegheny Teledyne Inc. 8/15/96 which name changed to Allegheny Technologies Inc. 11/29/99

SERVONIC INSTRUMENTS, INC. (CA)
Acquired by Gulton Industries, Inc. (N.J.) 7/31/63
Each share Common no par exchanged for (0.4) share Common $1 par
Gulton Industries, Inc. (N.J.) reincorporated under the laws of Delaware 6/28/68
(See Gulton Industries, Inc. (Del.))

SERVONICS, INC. (VA)
Name changed to American Scientific Corp. 11/30/1962
(See American Scientific Corp.)

SERVONUCLEAR CORP. (NY)
Name changed to Savant Instruments, Inc. 7/18/62
(See Savant Instruments, Inc.)

SERVOTRON CORP. (MI)
Out of business in July 1963
No stockholders' equity

SERVOTRONICS INC (NY)
Common 20¢ par split (5) for (4) by issuance of (0.25) additional share 02/09/1968
Stock Dividend - 10% 02/16/1967
Reincorporated under the laws of Delaware 12/08/1972

SERVTEX INTL INC (NY)
Reorganized under the laws of Delaware as Hymedix, Inc. 02/24/1994
Each share Common $0.001 par exchanged for (0.83333333) share Common $0.001 par

SERVUS RUBR CO (IL)
Recapitalized 00/00/1936
Each share 7% Preferred $100 par exchanged for (1) share $1 Preferred no par
$1 Preferred no par called for redemption 12/10/1942
Each share Common $10 par

exchanged for (0.1) share Common no par
Each share Common no par exchanged for (4) shares Common $1 par 00/00/1946
Acquired by a subsidiary of Chromalloy American Corp. 03/00/1970
Details not available

SESA STERLITE LTD (INDIA)
Name changed 09/25/2013
Name changed from Sesa Goa Ltd. to Sesa Sterlite Ltd. 09/25/2013
Name changed to Vedanta Ltd. 05/05/2015

SESAME MACHINE & TAPES LTD. (CANADA)
Dissolved 10/27/70
No stockholders' equity

SESSIONS CLOCK CO (CT)
Common $1 par reclassified as Class A Common $1 par 3/31/58
Merged into North American Philips Corp. 8/15/69
Each share Class A Common $1 par exchanged for (0.05) share Common $5 par
Each share Class B Common $1 par exchanged for (10) shares Common $5 par
(See North American Philips Corp.)

SETANTA VENTURES INC (BC)
Cease trade order effective 02/01/2002
Stockholders' equity unlikely

SETAY CO.
Merged into Republic Pictures Corp. in 1945
Each share Common $1 par exchanged for (6.5) shares Common $1 par
Republic Pictures Corp. name changed to Republic Corp. (N.Y.) 4/6/60 which reincorporated under the laws of Delaware 3/21/68 which merged into Triton Group Ltd. 2/15/85
(See Triton Group Ltd.)

SETCO INC (CA)
Completely liquidated 02/11/1972
Each share Common 10¢ par exchanged for first and final distribution of (0.2) share Hyatt Corp. Common 50¢ par
Hyatt Corp. merged into Elsinore Corp. 02/05/1979
(See Elsinore Corp.)

SETECH INC (DE)
Each share Common 1¢ par received distribution of (1) share Glomac Inc. Common 1¢ par payable 3/1/2001 to holders of record 3/1/2001
Merged into Setech Holdings Inc. 10/16/2002
Each share Common 1¢ par exchanged for $3.50 cash

SETH THOMAS CLOCK CO.
Acquired by General Time Instruments Corp. 00/00/1930
Details not available

SETON CO (NJ)
Common no par split (2) for (1) by issuance of (1) additional share 4/1/69
Common no par split (3) for (2) by issuance of (0.5) additional share 3/14/83
Common no par split (2) for (1) by issuance of (1) additional share 9/26/83
Common no par split (2) for (1) by issuance of (1) additional share 9/24/84
Common no par split (3) for (2) by issuance of (0.5) additional share 9/9/85
Stock Dividends - 10% 12/10/79; 10% 12/14/81
Merged into S Acquisitions Corp. 11/9/87
Each share Common 50¢ par exchanged for $15.88 cash

SETON LEATHER CO (NJ)
Common no par split (5) for (1) by issuance of (4) additional shares 4/10/61
Name changed to Seton Co. 3/20/69
(See Seton Co.)

SETTLEMENT CORP. (PA)
Liquidation completed
Each share Capital Stock $10 par exchanged for first and final distribution of (1) Participation Certificate and $89.45 cash 11/14/1966
Each Participation Certificate received initial distribution of $1.50 cash 08/14/1967
Each Participation Certificate received second distribution of $1 cash 08/29/1967
Each Participation Certificate exchanged for third and final distribution of $0.655 cash 10/15/1971

SEVCON INC (DE)
Acquired by BorgWarner Inc. 09/27/2017
Each share 4% Conv. Preferred Ser. A 10¢ par exchanged for $66 cash
Each share Common 10¢ par exchanged for $22 cash

SEVEN ANGELS VENTURES INC (NV)
Name changed to Twister Networks, Inc. 3/25/2004
Twister Networks, Inc. recapitalized as Reynaldos Mexican Food Co., Inc. 3/4/2005

SEVEN ARTS PICTURES PLC (ENGLAND)
Each share Ordinary 5p par exchanged for (0.2) share old Ordinary 25p par 01/16/2009
Each share old Ordinary 25p par exchanged for (0.2) share new Ordinary 25p par 05/12/2011
Reincorporated under the laws of Nevada as Seven Arts Entertainment Inc. and Ordinary 25p par reclassified as Common 1¢ par 09/01/2011

SEVEN ARTS PRODUCTIONS LTD. (ON)
Under plan of merger name changed to Warner Bros.-Seven Arts Ltd. 07/15/1967
Warner Bros.-Seven Arts Ltd. acquired by Kinney National Service, Inc. 07/08/1969 which name changed to Kinney Services, Inc. (NY) 02/17/1971 which reincorporated in Delaware as Warner Communications Inc. 02/11/1972
(See Warner Communications Inc.)

SEVEN CLANS RES LTD (ON)
Recapitalized as Mexgold Resources Inc. 09/15/2003
Each share Common no par exchanged for (0.5) share Common no par
Mexgold Resources Inc. acquired by Gammon Lake Resources Inc. 08/08/2006 which name changed to Gammon Gold Inc. (QC) 06/19/2007 which reincorporated in Ontario as AuRico Gold Inc. 06/14/2011 which merged into Alamos Gold Inc. (New) 07/06/2015

7 CROWNS CORP (AB)
Each share old Common no par exchanged for (0.0000001) share new Common no par 3/23/2004
Note: In effect holders received $0.90 cash per share and public interest was eliminated

7 DAYS GROUP HLDGS LTD (CAYMAN ISLANDS)
Issue Information - 10,100,000 ADR's offered at $11 per ADR on 11/19/2009
Acquired by Keystone Lodging Co. Ltd. 07/05/2013
Each ADR for Ordinary $0.125 par exchanged for $13.80 cash

7-ELEVEN INC (TX)
Each share old Common $0.0001 par exchanged for (0.2) share new Common $0.0001 par 5/1/2000
Merged into Seven-Eleven Japan Co., Ltd. 11/9/2005
Each share new Comon $0.0001 par exchanged for $37.50 cash

SEVEN ELEVEN JAPAN LTD (JAPAN)
ADR's for Common 50 Yen par changed to no par 10/01/1982
ADR's for Common no par split (6) for (5) by issuance of (0.2) additional ADR 04/30/1991
ADR's for Common no par split (2) for (1) by issuance of (1) additional ADR payable 10/26/1999 to holders of record 08/30/1999
Stock Dividends - 20% 05/02/1988; 20% 05/02/1989; 20% 05/02/1990; 10% 04/30/1992; 10% 05/02/1994; 10% 05/02/1995; 10% payable 04/30/1996 to holders of record 02/28/1996
ADR agreement terminated 11/07/2005
Each ADR for Common no par exchanged for $33.46307 cash

745 PROPERTY INVESTMENTS (MA)
Merged into Prudential Insurance Co. of America 10/29/81
Each share Common no par exchanged for $42 cash

SEVEN HILLS FINL CORP (OH)
Merged into Western Ohio Financial Corp. 11/12/96
Each share Common no par exchanged for $19.69782 cash

701 COM CORP (ON)
Name changed to 701 Media Group Inc. 8/15/2001
701 Media Group Inc. name changed to YSV Ventures Inc. 10/17/2003

701 MEDIA GROUP INC (ON)
Name changed to YSV Ventures Inc. 10/17/2003

707-713 SEWARD APARTMENTS CORP. (DE)
Charter revoked for non-payment of taxes 11/16/53

706 JUDGE BUILDING CORP. (WY)
Liquidation completed
Each share Common $1 par exchanged for initial distribution of $1.85 cash 2/20/68
Each share Common $1 par received second and final distribution of $0.1115 cash 9/27/71

700 WEST END AVENUE CORP. (NY)
Liquidation completed 6/1/42

SEVEN J STK FARM INC (TX)
Each share old Common $1 par exchanged for (0.001) share new Common $1 par 09/29/2003
Note: In effect holders received $3.89 cash per share and public interest was eliminated

SEVEN METALS MINING CO. (CO)
Charter revoked for failure to file reports and pay fees 10/22/25

SEVEN MILE HIGH RES INC (BC)
Name changed 11/09/1989
Name changed from Seven Mile High Group, Inc. to Seven Mile High Resources Inc. 11/09/1989
Name changed to Sevex Energy Inc. 11/20/1992
Sevex Energy Inc. recapitalized as Colony Energy Ltd. (BC) 11/29/1995 which reincorporated in Alberta 04/11/1996 which name changed to Big Bear Exploration Ltd.

02/28/1998 which merged into Avid Oil & Gas Ltd. 02/02/2000
(See Avid Oil & Gas Ltd.)

SEVEN OAKS FARMS LTD (DE)
Recapitalized as Mighty Power USA 11/30/95
Each share Common $0.001 par exchanged for (0.5) share Common $0.001 par
Mighty Power USA recapitalized as Globenet International Inc. 4/17/97 which name changed to Royal Bodycare Inc. 10/19/99 which name changed to RBC Life Sciences, Inc. 6/19/2006

SEVEN OAKS INTL INC (TN)
Common 10¢ par split (5) for (4) by issuance of (0.25) additional share 4/15/83
Common 10¢ par split (5) for (4) by issuance of (0.25) additional share 4/15/86
Merged into JSM Merger Sub, Inc. 11/29/95
Each share Common 10¢ par exchanged for $0.31 cash

SEVEN SEAS PETE INC (CAYMAN ISLANDS)
Reincorporated 08/12/1996
Reincorporated 03/01/2001
Place of incorporation changed from (BC) to Yukon 08/12/1996
Place of incorporation changed from Yukon to Cayman Islands and Common no par changed to $0.001 par 03/01/2001
SEC revoked common stock registration 12/19/2006
Stockholders' equity unlikely

777 SPORTS ENTMT CORP (NV)
Recapitalized as NT Mining Corp. 11/04/2008
Each share Common $0.001 par exchanged for (0.0005) share Common $0.001 par
NT Mining Corp. recapitalized as Sanwire Corp. (NV) 03/07/2013 which reincorporated in Wyoming 07/07/2015

7 STAR ENTMT INC (FL)
Recapitalized as SpectralCast, Inc. 01/15/2014
Each share Common $0.001 par exchanged for (0.0066666) share Common $0.001 par

735 JR TER BLDG CORP (IL)
Acquired by Wirtz Haynie & Ehrat Realty Corp. 12/14/2016
Each share Common $1 par exchanged for $41 cash

735 JUNIOR TERRACE BUILDING LIQUIDATING TRUST
Trust Agreement terminated 07/00/1946
Each Ctf. of Bene. Int. no par exchanged for (0.1) share 735 Junior Terrace Building Corp. Common $1 par
(See 735 Junior Terrace Building Corp.)

733 HINMAN AVENUE CORP. (IL)
Completely liquidated 7/27/61
Each share Common no par exchanged for first and final distribution of $245.50 cash

7501 EXCHANGE AVENUE, INC. (IL)
Completely liquidated 12/17/47
Each Capital Stock Trust Ctf. $1 par exchanged for $48 cash

7931 SOUTH STATE STREET CORP. (IL)
Liquidated in 1944

7030 EAST END CORP. (IL)
Dissolved in 1960

7020 JEFFERY APARTMENTS CORP. (DE)
Charter cancelled and declared inoperative and void for non-payment of taxes 4/1/59

SEVEN TROUGHS GOLD MINES CO.
Name changed to Nevada State Gold Mines Co. in 1932
Nevada State Gold Mines Co. charter revoked 3/3/52

729 MELDRUM CORP. (MI)
Liquidation completed
Each share Common $1 par exchanged for initial distribution of $17 cash 3/22/66
Each share Common $1 par received second distribution of $0.75 cash 6/22/66
Each share Common $1 par received third and final distribution of $0.3031 cash 10/22/66

721 CORP. (DE)
Merged into Genesco Inc. 9/23/66
Each share Common $1 par exchanged for (0.75) share Common $1 par

SEVEN-UP / RC BOTTLING CO SOUTHN CALIF INC (DE)
Merged into Dr. Pepper Bottling Co. of Texas 5/21/97
Each share Common 1¢ par exchanged for $12 cash

SEVEN UP BOTTLING CO LOS ANGELES INC (CA)
Stock Dividend - 100% 5/2/62
Merged into Westinghouse Electric Corp. 9/30/69
Each share Common no par exchanged for (0.45106) share Common $6.25 par
Westinghouse Electric Corp. name changed to CBS Corp. 12/1/97 which merged into Viacom Inc. (Old) 5/4/2000
(See Viacom Inc. (Old))

SEVEN UP BOTTLING CO ST LOUIS (MO)
Common no par changed to $1 par 00/00/1954
Stock Dividend - 100% 07/01/1954
Name changed to Taylor Group, Inc. 05/17/1979
(See Taylor Group, Inc.)

SEVEN UP BOTTLING CORP HOUSTON SAN ANTONIO (TX)
Completely liquidated 05/26/1970
Each share Class A Common 45¢ par exchanged for first and final distribution of $9 cash
Each share Class B Common 45¢ par exchanged for first and final distribution of $2 cash

SEVEN UP CO (MO)
Common $1 par split (2) for (1) by issuance of (1) additional share 12/1/69
Common $1 par split (2) for (1) by issuance of (1) additional share 3/1/72
$5.71 Conv. Class A Preferred Ser. 1 no par called for redemption 6/13/75
Merged into Morris (Philip), Inc. 6/19/78
Each share Common $1 par exchanged for $48 cash
6% Preferred $100 par called for redemption 7/5/78

SEVEN-UP SUSSEX LTD. (NB)
Preferred $10 par called for redemption in November 1977
Public interest eliminated

SEVEN-UP TEXAS CORP.
Name changed to Seven-Up Bottling Corp. of Houston-San Antonio in 1947
Seven-Up Bottling Corp. of Houston-San Antonio completely liquidated 5/26/70

SEVEN VENTURES INC (NV)
Each share old Common $0.001 par exchanged for (0.00571428) share new Common $0.001 par 12/16/2002
Name changed to FastFunds Financial Corp. 07/08/2004

SEVEN WELLS CORP. (DE)
Charter cancelled and declared inoperative and void for non-payment of taxes 4/1/35

SEVENSON ENVIRONMENTAL SVCS INC (DE)
Common 10¢ par split (8) for (5) by issuance of (0.6) additional share payable 10/27/97 to holders of record 10/20/97
Stock Dividend - 10% payable 8/29/2000 to holders of record 8/22/2000
Merged into SCC Contracting 3/22/2002
Each share Common 10¢ par exchanged for $16 cash

1700 WALNUT STREET, INC.
Liquidated in 1946

17 PARK AVENUE, INC. (NY)
Dissolved 8/14/59

SEVENTH ENERGY LTD (AB)
Issue Information - 8,000 Units maximum; 4,000 Units minimum offered $1,000 per Unit on 10/04/1996
Merged into Seventh Energy Ltd. (NV) 8/1/97
Each share Class A Common no par exchanged for (1) share Class A Common no par
Each share Class B Common no par exchanged for (1) share Class B Common no par
(See Seventh Energy Ltd. (NV))

SEVENTH ENERGY LTD (NV)
Each share Class B Common no par exchanged for (10) shares Class A Common no par 10/30/2002
Acquired by PrimeWest Energy Trust 3/16/2004
Each share Class A Common no par exchanged for $1 cash

SEVENTH GENERATION INC (VT)
Merged into Seventh General Acquisition Inc. 1/25/2000
Each share Common $0.000333 par exchanged for $1.30 cash

7TH LEVEL INC (DE)
Issue Information - 3,475,000 shares COM offered at $10 per share on 10/19/1994
Name changed to Learn2.com Inc. 07/20/1999
Learn2.com Inc. merged into Learn2 Corp. 09/26/2001 which name changed to LTWC Corp. 09/06/2002
(See LTWC Corp.)

SEVENTH MALARTIC MINES, LTD. (ON)
Charter cancelled in February 1961

SEVENTH WAVE CAP CORP (AB)
Merged into Imaging Dynamics Co., Ltd. 11/29/2002
Each share Common no par exchanged for (0.12693844) share Common no par and (0.12693844) Common Stock Purchase Warrant expiring 5/31/2003

724 SOLUTIONS INC (ON)
Issue Information - 6,000,000 shares COM offered at $26 per share on 01/27/2000
Each share old Common no par exchanged for (0.1) share new Common no par 4/28/2003
Merged into Austin Ventures VIII, LP 8/15/2006
Each share new Common no par exchanged for $3.34 cash

70 EAST CEDAR STREET CORP.
Liquidated in 1947

79 LEAD-COPPER CO. (DE)
Each share Capital Stock 10¢ par exchanged for (0.025) share Capital Stock 2¢ par and (0.025) share Vulcan Silver-Lead Corp. Common $1 par

79 RLTY CORP (NY)
Voluntarily dissolved 4/24/81
Details not available

71 CAP CORP (CANADA)
Recapitalized as Prodigy Ventures Inc. 09/14/2015
Each share Common no par exchanged for (0.5) share Common no par

SEVENTY SEVEN ENERGY INC (DE)
Merged into Patterson-UTI Energy, Inc. 04/20/2017
Each share Common 1¢ par exchanged for for (1.7851) shares Common 1¢ par

SEVENTY SEVEN ENERGY INC (OK)
Plan of reorganization under Chapter 11 Federal Bankruptcy proceedings effective 08/01/2016
Each Common 1¢ par received distribution of (0.05004) Seventy Seven Energy Inc. (DE) Common Stock Purchase Warrant Ser. B expiring 08/01/2021 and (0.0556) Common Stock Purchase Warrant Ser. C expiring 08/01/2023 payable 08/02/2016 to holders of record 08/01/2016

77TH & PRAIRIE APARTMENTS, INC.
Liquidated in 1940

SEVENTY SIX DEV CO (NV)
Charter revoked for failure to file reports and pay fees 6/1/95

SEVENWAY CAP CORP (AB)
Merged into Glacier Ventures International Corp. (Canada) (New) 04/28/2000
Each share Common no par exchanged for (0.446) share Common no par
Glacier Ventures International Corp. (Canada) (New) name changed to Glacier Media Inc. 07/01/2008

SEVERIDE RES INC (BC)
Name changed to Severide Environmental Industries Inc. 2/1/94

SEVERN BANCORP INC (MD)
$0.85 Preferred Ser. A 1¢ par called for redemption 12/31/97
$0.85 Conv. Preferred Ser. B 1¢ par called for redemption 12/31/97
$0.85 Conv. Preferred Ser. N 1¢ par called for redemption 12/31/97
(Additional Information in Active)

SEVERSKY AIRCRAFT CORP. (DE)
Name changed to Republic Aviation Corp. 10/19/1939
Republic Aviation Corp. name changed to RAC Corp. 10/01/1965
(See RAC Corp.)

SEVERSKY ELECTRONATOM CORP (NY)
Dissolved by proclamation 01/25/2012

SEVERSKY TUBE WKS (RUSSIA)
Name changed to Seversky Tube Works, PJSC 08/05/2015

SEVERSTAL-AUTO JSC (RUSSIA)
Name changed to Sollers Joint Stock Co. 09/04/2008

SEVERSTAL JT STK CO (RUSSIA)
Name changed to PAO Severstal 03/27/2015

SEVEX ENERGY INC (BC)
Recapitalized as Colony Energy Ltd. (BC) 11/29/1995
Each share Common no par exchanged for (0.125) share Common no par
Colony Energy Ltd. (BC) reincorporated in Alberta 04/11/1996 which name changed to Big Bear Exploration Ltd. 02/28/1998 which merged into Avid Oil & Gas Ltd. 02/02/2000
(See Avid Oil & Gas Ltd.)

SEVILLE ENERGY CORP (CO)
Name changed to Seville Technologies, Inc. 12/19/1983

Seville Technologies, Inc. recapitalized as Trinidad Corp. (CO) 01/08/1991 which reorganized in Texas as Alpha Generation, Inc. 12/31/2001 which name changed to Ouranos Resources Inc. 01/07/2005
(See Ouranos Resources Inc.)

SEVILLE INVT FDS CORP (ON)
Reorganized as under the laws of Nevada as VoIP Technologies Inc. 04/23/2004
Each share Common no par exchanged for (2) shares Common $0.001 par
(See VoIP Technologies, Inc.)

SEVILLE TECHNOLOGIES INC (CO)
Recapitalized as Trinidad Corp. (CO) 01/08/1991
Each share Common 1¢ par exchanged for (0.01) share Common 1¢ par
Trinidad Corp. (CO) reorganized in Texas as Alpha Generation, Inc. 12/31/2001 which name changed to Ouranos Resources Inc. 01/07/2005
(See Ouranos Resources Inc.)

SEVILLE VENTURES CORP (NV)
Common $0.001 par split (60) for (1) by issuance of (59) additional shares payable 12/12/2013 to holders of record 12/12/2013
Common $0.001 par split (2) for (1) by issuance of (1) additional share payable 10/22/2014 to holders of record 10/22/2014
SEC revoked common stock registration 11/01/2016

SEVION THERAPEUTICS INC (DE)
Recapitalized as Eloxx Pharmaceuticals, Inc. 12/20/2017
Each share Common 1¢ par exchanged for (0.05) share Common 1¢ par

SEW CAL LOGO INC (NV)
Recapitalized as Social Life Network, Inc. 04/11/2016
Each share Common $0.001 par exchanged for (0.0002) share Common $0.001 par
Note: No holder will receive fewer than (100) post-split shares

SEW IN INC (DE)
Merged into Insew, Inc. 02/07/1975
Each share Common 1¢ par exchanged for $0.40 cash

SEW SIMPLE INC (NY)
Dissolved by proclamation 12/23/92

SEWARD & ELMWOOD, INC.
Liquidated in 1941

SEWARD ARMS BUILDING CORP. (IL)
Involuntarily dissolved 12/1/51

SEWARD MANOR BUILDING CORP. (IL)
Merged into 707-713 Seward Apartments Corp. 3/22/51
(See 707-713 Seward Apartments Corp.)

SEWELL VENTURES INC (NV)
Name changed to Truesport Alliances & Entertainment, Ltd. 03/31/2010
Truesport Alliances & Entertainment, Ltd. recapitalized as ePunk, Inc. 07/05/2011

SEWICKLEY-REPUBLIC OIL & GAS CO. (DE)
Charter cancelled and declared inoperative and void for non-payment of taxes 3/19/24

SEXTANT ENTERPRISE CORP (AB)
Name changed to Pure Technologies Ltd. 6/29/98

SEXTANT ENTMT GROUP INC (CANADA)
Filed petition under Companies' Creditors Arrangement Act 06/05/2002
Stockholders' equity unlikely

SEXTON JOHN & CO (IL)
Stock Dividend - 33-1/3% 8/19/64
Completely liquidated 12/23/68
Each share Common no par exchanged for first and final distribution of (0.375) share Beatrice Foods Co. $4 Conv. Preference 2nd Ser. no par
(See Beatrice Foods Co.)

SEYBOLD MACHINE CO.
Merged into Harris-Seybold-Potter Co. in 1926
Details not available

SEYMOUR EXPL CORP (BC)
Name changed to Independent Nickel Corp. (BC) 06/21/2006
Independent Nickel Corp. (BC) reincorporated in Ontario 09/11/2007 which merged into Victory Nickel Inc. 01/05/2009

SEYMOUR MOSS INTL LTD (BC)
Struck off register and declared dissolved for failure to file returns 11/10/88

SEYMOUR NATL BK (SEYMOUR, IN)
Stock Dividends - 100% 02/16/1971; 50% 02/25/1975; 100% 03/07/1979
Under plan of reorganization each share Capital Stock $10 par automatically became (1) share Mid-Southern Indiana Bancorp Capital Stock $10 par 05/02/1984
Mid-Southern Indiana Bancorp merged into Merchants National Corp. 12/22/1986 which merged into National City Corp. 05/02/92 05/02/1992 which was acquired by PNC Financial Services Group, Inc. 12/31/2008

SEYMOUR RES INC (BC)
Name changed to Crowder Communications Corp. 07/23/1985
Crowder Communications Corp. recapitalized as Sigmacom Systems Inc. 08/10/1988
(See Sigmacom Systems Inc.)

SEYMOUR VENTURES CORP (CANADA)
Name changed to Rare Earth Industries Ltd. 07/13/2011
Rare Earth Industries Ltd. recapitalized as Ackroo Inc. 10/10/2012

SEYMOUR WATER CO. (IN)
6% Preferred $25 par called for redemption 10/14/81
Public interest eliminated

SEYMOUR WATER CO. (KY)
5% Preferred $25 par called for redemption 10/15/81
Acquired by American Water Works Co. 11/16/81
Each share Common no par exchanged for cash and Notes

SEYMOUR WORLDWIDE INC (DE)
Name changed to Mortgage Xpress, Inc. 03/25/2005
Mortgage Xpress, Inc. recapitalized as Alternative Energy Technology Center, Inc. 01/18/2008 which recapitalized as Alternative Energy Technology Inc. 08/04/2008

SF BLU VU INC (NV)
Name changed to Livewire Ergogenics, Inc. 10/07/2011

SF HLDGS GROUP INC (DE)
Stock Dividends - 3.44% payable 12/17/2001 to holders of record 12/10/2001; 3.44% payable 3/15/2002 to holders of record 3/10/2002 Ex date - 3/14/2002; 3.44% payable 6/17/2002 to holders of record 6/10/2002 Ex date - 6/20/2002; 3.44 payable 9/16/2002 to holders of record 9/10/2002 Ex date - 9/17/2002; 3.44% payable 12/15/2002 to holders of record 12/10/2002 Ex date - 12/19/2002; 3.44% payable 3/17/2003 to holders of record 3/10/2003 Ex date - 3/19/2003; 3.44% payable 6/16/2003 to holders of record 6/10/2003 Ex date - 6/25/2003; 3.44% payable 9/15/2003 to holders of record 9/10/2003 Ex date - 9/24/2003; 3.44% payable 12/15/2003 to holders of record 12/10/2003 Ex date - 12/18/2003
Merged into Solo Cup Co. 2/27/2004
Each 13.75% Exchangeable Preferred Ser. B $0.001 par exchanged for $10,687.50 cash

SF SVCS INC (AR)
Merged into Farmland Industries, Inc. 07/01/1998
Each share Class A Preferred no par exchanged for $100 cash

SFBC INTL INC (DE)
Issue Information - 1,250,000 shares COM offered at $8 per share on 10/11/2000
Common $0.001 par split (3) for (2) by issuance of (0.5) additional share payable 05/19/2004 to holders of record 05/10/2004 Ex date - 05/20/2004
Name changed to PharmaNet Development Group, Inc. 08/28/2006
(See PharmaNet Development Group, Inc.)

SFC FINANCIAL CORP. (NY)
Name changed back to Standard Financial Corp. 4/22/64
(See Standard Financial Corp.)

SFE TECHNOLOGIES (CA)
Common $1 par split (4) for (3) by issuance of (1/3) additional share 4/18/83
Stock Dividend - 10% 4/15/81
Charter suspended for failure to file reports and pay fees 7/15/92

SFFED CORP (DE)
Acquired by First Nationwide Bank, A Federal Savings Bank (Plano, TX) 02/01/1996
Each share Common 1¢ par exchanged for $32 cash

SFG FINANCIAL CORP (DE)
Name changed 08/04/2000
Old Common $0.001 par split (3) for (1) by issuance of (2) additional shares 04/08/1993
Name changed from SFG Corp. to SFG Financial Corp. 08/04/2000
Each share old Common $0.001 par exchanged for (0.13602096) share new Common $0.001 par 03/26/2008
SEC revoked common stock registration 04/20/2011

SFK PULP FD (QC)
Under plan of reorganization each Unit no par automatically became (1) share Fibrek Inc. (Canada) Common no par 05/27/2010
Fibrek Inc. merged into Resolute Forest Products Inc. 08/01/2012

SFM CORP (NJ)
Reorganized under the laws of Nevada as EXX Inc. 10/21/1994
Each share Common $1 par exchanged for (3) shares Class A Common 1¢ par and (1) share Class B Common 1¢ par
(See EXX Inc.)

SFN COS INC NEW (DE)
Completely liquidated 12/31/86
Each share 16-1/4% Sr. Exchangeable Preferred Ser. A no par exchanged for first and final distribution of $7.63 cash

SFN COS INC OLD (DE)
$3.50 Conv. Preferred $10 par called for redemption 06/01/1982
Common 50¢ par changed to 25¢ par 09/02/1983
Acquired by a group of investors 02/01/1985
Each share Common 25¢ par exchanged for (1) share SFN Companies, Inc. (New) 16-1/4% Sr. Exchangeable Preferred Ser. A no par and $36.82 cash
(See SFN Companies, Inc. (New))

SFN GROUP INC (DE)
Acquired by Randstad North America, L.P. 09/02/2011
Each share Common 1¢ par exchanged for $14 cash

SFORZA ENTERPRISES INC (FL)
Administratively dissolved 09/15/2006

SFP COMMUNICATIONS GROUP INC (ON)
Name changed to Motivus Inc. 5/23/2001
(See Motivus Inc.)

SFP INTL LTD (ON)
Reorganized under the laws of Switzerland as Societe Financiere Privee S.A. 1/20/93
Each share Common no par exchanged for (1) Sponsored ADR for Class A no par and (1) Sponsored ADR for Class B no par
Societe Financiere Privee S.A. name changed to Societe Bancaire Privee SA 3/2/2003

SFR ENERGY LTD (AB)
Name changed to International SoftRock Oil Co. Ltd. 01/06/2015

SFS BANCORP INC (DE)
Merged into Hudson River Bancorp, Inc. 09/03/1999
Each share Common 1¢ par exchanged for $25.10 cash

SFSB HLDG CO (PA)
Merged into Laurel Capital Group Inc. 3/28/2003
Each share Common no par exchanged for $19.05 cash

SFX BROADCASTING INC (DE)
Each share 12.625% Exchangeable Preferred Ser. E 1¢ par received distribution of (0.63125) additional share payable 01/15/1998 to holders of record 12/31/1997
Each share 6.50% 144A Conv. Exchangeable Preferred Ser. D 1¢ par received distribution of (1.0987) shares of SFX Entertainment, Inc. Class A Common 1¢ par payable 04/27/1998 to holders of record 04/20/1998
Each share 6.5% Accrued Investors Conv. Exchangeable Preferred Ser. D 1¢ par received distribution of (1.0987) shares of SFX Entertainment, Inc. Class A Common 1¢ par payable 04/27/1998 to holders of record 04/20/1998
Each share 6.50% Conv. Exchangeable Preferred Ser. D 1¢ par received distribution of (1.0987) shares of SFX Entertainment, Inc. Class A Common 1¢ par payable 04/27/1998 to holders of record 04/20/1998
Each share Class A Common 1¢ par received distribution of (1) share of SFX Entertainment, Inc. Class A Common 1¢ par payable 04/27/1998 to holders of record 04/20/1998
Each share Class B Common 1¢ par received distribution of (1) share of SFX Entertainment, Inc. Class B Common 1¢ par payable 04/27/1998 to holders of record 04/20/1998
Merged into SBI Holdings Corp. 05/29/1998
Each share 6.50% 144A Conv. Exchangeable Preferred Ser. D 1¢ par exchanged for $82.4025 cash
Each share 6.5% Accrued Investors Conv. Exchangeable Preferred Ser. D 1¢ par exchanged for $82.4025 cash
Each share 6.50% Conv. Exchangeable Preferred Ser. D 1¢ par exchanged for $82.4025 cash
Each share Class A Common 1¢ par exchanged for $75 cash
Each share Class B Common 1¢ par exchanged for $97.50 cash
12.625% Exchangeable Preferred Ser. E 1¢ par called for redemption at $100 on 10/31/2006
Public interest eliminated

SFX ENTMT INC (DE)
Class A Common 1¢ par split (3) for (2) by issuance of (0.5) additional share payable 07/27/1999 to holders of record 07/20/1999 Ex date - 07/28/1999
Class B Common 1¢ par split (3) for (2) by issuance of (0.5) additional share payable 07/27/1999 to holders of record 07/20/1999 Ex date - 07/28/1999
Merged into Clear Channel Communications, Inc. 08/01/2000
Each share Class A Common 1¢ par exchanged for (0.6) share Common 10¢ par
Each share Class B Common 1¢ par exchanged for (1) share Common 10¢ par
(See Clear Channel Communications, Inc.)
Note: This company is not related to the bankrupt SFX Entertainment, Inc.

SFX ENTMT INC (DE)
Plan of reorganization under Chapter 11 Federal Bankruptcy proceedings effective 12/02/2016
No stockholders' equity
Note: This company is not related to the merged SFX Entertainment, Inc.

SG SPIRIT GOLD INC (BC)
Reincorporated 12/20/2011
Place of incorporation changed from (AB) to (BC) 12/20/2011
Each share old Common no par exchanged for (0.4) share new Common no par 11/20/2012
Each share new Common no par exchanged again for (0.1) share new Common no par 12/18/2014
Name changed to DOJA Cannabis Co. Ltd. 08/09/2017
DOJA Cannabis Co. Ltd. name changed to Hiku Brands Co. Ltd. 01/31/2018 which merged into Canopy Growth Corp. 09/06/2018

SGB INTL HLDGS INC (BC)
Common no par split (9) for (2) by issuance of (3.5) additional shares payable 03/04/2009 to holders of record 03/04/2009
Name changed to Grand China Energy Group Ltd. 08/19/2014

SGC HLDGS INC (NV)
Common $0.001 par split (30) for (1) by issuance of (29) additional shares payable 06/16/2005 to holders of record 06/16/2005
Name changed to Medistem Laboratories, Inc. 11/10/2005
Medistem Laboratories, Inc. recapitalized as Medistem Inc. 08/11/2008 which merged into Intrexon Corp. 03/07/2014

SGI CAP CORP (YT)
Reincorporated 01/05/1996
Place of incorporation changed from (BC) to (YT) 01/05/1996
Recapitalized as Lariat Property Corp. 12/10/1997
Each share Common no par exchanged for (0.5) share Common no par
Lariat Property Corp. name changed to Lariat Resources Inc. 06/02/2003 which recapitalized as Lariat Energy Ltd. (YT) 09/23/2004 which reincorporated in British Columbia 04/01/2006 which name changed to Global Daily Fantasy Sports Inc. 07/11/2016

SGI INTL (UT)
Each share old Common no par exchanged for (0.05) share new Common no par 03/22/1995
SEC revoked common stock registration 10/24/2011

SGI SUPER GRASS INC (AB)
Name changed to Canadian-Star Industries Inc. 5/24/89
(See Canadian-Star Industries Inc.)

SGL CARBON AG (GERMANY)
ADR agreement terminated 06/25/2007
Each Sponsored ADR for Ordinary no par exchanged for $16.0822 cash

SGL INDS INC (NJ)
Common 20¢ par split (3) for (2) by issuance of (0.5) additional share 06/15/1983
Common 20¢ par split (3) for (2) by issuance of (0.5) additional share 06/14/1984
Name changed to SL Industries, Inc. (NJ) 09/20/1984
SL Industries, Inc. (NJ) reincorporated in Delaware 06/20/2013
(See SL Industries, Inc.)

SGLG INC (DE)
Acquired by General Physics Corp. in 1995
Details not available

SGM CORP (QC)
Declared dissolved for failure to file annual reports 11/07/1981

SGOCO TECHNOLOGY LTD (CAYMAN ISLANDS)
Name changed to SGOCO Group, Ltd. 11/17/2010

SGS SOCIETE GENERALE DE SURVEILLANCE HLDG SA (SWITZERLAND)
Name changed to SGS SA 10/10/2008

SGS-THOMSON MICROELECTRONICS N V (NETHERLANDS)
Issue Information - 21,000,000 SHS-NY REGISTRY offered at $22.250 per share on 12/08/1994
Name changed to STMicroelectronics N.V. 6/5/98

SGT GROUP INC (NV)
Name changed to Rocket City Automotive Group, Inc. 03/06/2007
Rocket City Automotive Group, Inc. recapitalized as Rocket City Enterprises, Inc. 08/10/2007

SGT VENTURES INC (CO)
Name changed to Stronghold Industries, Inc. 07/10/2006
Stronghold Industries, Inc. recapitalized as Image Worldwide, Inc. 11/30/2007 which recapitalized as STL Marketing Group, Inc. 09/03/2009

SGV BANCORP INC (DE)
Merged into IndyMac Mortgage Holdings, Inc. 7/3/2000
Each share Common 1¢ par exchanged for $25 cash

SGX PHARMACEUTICALS INC (DE)
Issue Information - 4,000,000 shares COM offered at $6 per share on 02/06/2006
Merged into Lilly (Eli) & Co. 08/22/2008
Each share Common $0.001 par exchanged for $3 cash

SGX RES INC (CANADA)
Recapitalized as 55 North Mining Inc. 07/03/2018
Each share Common no par exchanged for (0.33333333) share Common no par

SHAAN XI DING CHENG SCIENCE HLDG CO LTD (NV)
Name changed to China Ding Cheng Science Holdings Co., Ltd. 03/22/2007
China Ding Cheng Science Holdings Co., Ltd. name changed to China Transportation International Holdings Group Ltd. 04/23/2010
(See China Transportation International Holdings Group Ltd.)

SHABU GOLD MINES LTD (CANADA)
Name changed to Canadian Eagle Exploration Inc. 04/19/1988
(See Canadian Eagle Exploration Inc.)

SHABUTE VENTURES INC (BC)
Name changed to Northern Sun Exploration Co. Inc. 08/19/2004
Northern Sun Exploration Co. Inc. recapitalized as Reparo Energy Partners Corp. 11/08/2013

SHACKLETON PETE LTD (AB)
Reincorporated 00/00/1981
Place of incorporation changed from (BC) to (AB) 00/00/1981
Recapitalized as Europa Petroleum Ltd. 10/01/1982
Each share Common no par exchanged for (0.1) share Common no par
Europa Petroleum Ltd. merged into Orbit Oil & Gas Ltd. 11/08/1984
(See Orbit Oil & Gas Ltd.)

SHACRON OIL CORP (DE)
Class A $1 par and Class B $1 par reclassified as Common $1 par 10/22/1956
Common $1 par changed to 10¢ par 07/00/1959
Name changed to Tarpon Oil Co. 10/02/1969
(See Tarpon Oil Co.)

SHADBOLT & BOYD CO. (WI)
Administratively dissolved 06/19/1992

SHADES HLDGS INC (FL)
SEC revoked common stock registration 07/25/2016

SHADOW ART COMPANY (THE) (WA)
Charter cancelled and proclaimed dissolved for failure to pay taxes 9/20/93

SHADOW CAP CORP (AB)
Name changed to Soundcache.com Inc. 08/23/2000
Soundcache.com Inc. name changed to Genoray Advanced Technologies Ltd. 05/09/2002
(See Genoray Advanced Technologies Ltd.)

SHADOW MARKETING INC (NV)
Name changed to iTokk, Inc. 10/28/2009

SHADOW RIDGE HLDGS INC (FL)
Common no par split (2) for (1) by issuance of (1) additional share payable 08/23/2002 to holders of record 08/02/2002 Ex date - 08/26/2002
Name changed to LMWW Holdings, Inc. 07/02/2007

SHADOW STK FD INC (MD)
Merged into Tamarack Funds Trust 04/16/2004
Details not available

SHADOW TECHNOLOGIES INC (CANADA)
Name changed to Sofame Technologies Inc. 07/11/1996

SHADOW WOOD CORP (DE)
Recapitalized as Magicworks Entertainment Inc. 07/24/1996
Each share Common $0.0001 par exchanged for (0.08) share Common $0.0001 par
Magicworks Entertainment Inc. merged into SFX Entertainment, Inc. 09/11/1998 which merged into Clear Channel Communications, Inc. 08/01/2000

SHADOWFAX RES LTD (CANADA)
Each share Common no par exchanged for (0.2) share Common no par 2/15/90
Name changed to Docu-Fax International Inc. 4/10/90
Docu-Fax International Inc. recapitalized as International Telepresence (Canada) Corp. 9/14/94 which name changed to Isee3d Inc. 4/30/99

SHADOWS BEND DEV INC (NV)
Old Common 10¢ par split (2) for (1) by issuance of (1) additional share payable 02/05/2002 to holders of record 01/29/2002 Ex date - 02/06/2002
Each share old Common 10¢ par exchanged for (0.1) share new Common 10¢ par 11/21/2002
Recapitalized as FBO Air, Inc. 08/24/2004
Each share new Common 10¢ par exchanged for (0.25) share Common 10¢ par
FBO Air, Inc. name changed to FirstFlight, Inc. 01/30/2007 which name changed to Saker Aviation Services Inc. 10/02/2009

SHAER SHOE CORP (NH)
Common $1 par split (2) for (1) by issuance of (1) additional share 2/15/69
Acquired by Millyard Holding Corp. 8/29/90
Each share Common $1 par exchanged for $14.08 cash

SHAFFER OIL & REFINING CO. (DE)
Name changed to Deep Rock Oil Corp. 00/00/1930
Deep Rock Oil Corp. name changed to Crescent Corp. 07/13/1955 which name changed to Crescent Petroleum Corp. 04/16/1958 which name changed to Crescent Corp. 12/16/1963 which merged into National Industries, Inc. (KY) 07/01/1968 which merged into Fuqua Industries, Inc. 01/03/1978 which name changed to Actava Group Inc. 07/21/1993 which name changed to Metromedia International Group, Inc. 11/01/1995
(See Metromedia International Group, Inc.)

SHAFT DRILLERS INC (NV)
Voluntarily dissolved 12/28/78
Details not available

SHAFT INC (NV)
Name changed to Elegant Concrete, Inc. 2/10/2003
Each share Common $0.001 exchanged for (10) shares Common $0.001 par
Elegant Concrete, Inc. name changed to Security First International Holdings, Inc. 8/1/2005

SHAFT-ORE PORCUPINE MINES LTD. (ON)
Charter revoked for failure to file reports and pay fees 8/19/65

SHAH ALLOYS LTD (INDIA)
GDR agreement terminated 04/22/2014
No GDR's remain outstanding

SHAHMOON INDS INC (DE)
Common $2.50 par changed to $1.25 par and (1) additional share issued 03/18/1966
Name changed to Shire National Corp. 01/02/1973
Shire National Corp. name changed to Stacy Industries, Inc. 06/20/1985
(See Stacy Industries, Inc.)

SHAINBERG (SAM) CO. (TN)
Thru voluntary exchange offer of (1) share Interco Inc. 5-1/4% Conv. 1st Preferred Ser. B no par for each (3.0662) shares Common Capital Stock $1 par 100% was acquired as of December 1967

SHAKA SHOES INC (FL)
Name changed to Renuen Corp. 02/09/2012

SHAKER CO. (DE)
No longer in existence having become inoperative and void for non-payment of taxes 4/1/65

SHAKER PETE INC (AB)
Recapitalized as Shaker Resources Inc. 06/28/2002
Each share Common no par exchanged for (0.2) share Common no par
Shaker Resources Inc. merged into Caribou Resources Corp. 09/30/2004 which merged into JED Oil Inc. 07/31/2007
(See JED Oil Inc.)

SHAKER PPTYS (OH)
Liquidation completed
Each Share of Bene. Int. no par received initial distribution of $10 cash 01/21/1972
Each Share of Bene. Int. no par received second distribution of $2 cash 06/30/1972
Each share of Bene. Int. no par exchanged for third and final distribution of $0.35 cash 10/27/1972

SHAKER RLTY CORP (NY)
Liquidation completed
Each share Common no par received initial distribution of $49.74 cash 5/1/95
Each share Common no par received second and final distribution of $5.53 cash 11/1/96

SHAKER RES INC (AB)
Each share Common no par received distribution of (0.69517) share Petroflow Energy Ltd. Class A Subordinate no par payable 06/25/2004 to holders of record 06/15/2004
Acquired by Caribou Resources Corp. 09/30/2004
Each share Common no par exchanged for (0.4224) share Common no par
Caribou Resources Corp. merged into JED Oil Inc. 07/31/2007
(See JED Oil Inc.)

SHAKESPEARE CO (DE)
Reincorporated 12/20/1968
Common $5 par split (2) for (1) by issuance of (1) additional share 10/11/1962
Stock Dividends - 10% 01/20/1945; 20% 10/10/1946; 25% 10/13/1958
State of incorporation changed from (MI) to (DE) 12/20/1968
Common $5 par changed to $2.50 par and (1) additional share issued 01/15/1969
Merged into Anthony Industries, Inc. 02/05/1980
Each share Common $2.50 par exchanged for $9 principal amount of 11.25% 20-Yr. Conv. Subordinated Debentures due 01/31/2000 and $7.50 cash

SHAKESPEARE URANIUM MINES LTD. (ON)
Charter revoked for failure to file reports and pay fees 11/30/64

SHAKLEE CORP (DE)
Reincorporated 2/24/87
Common no par split (3) for (2) by issuance of (0.5) additional share 1/30/78
Common no par split (2) for (1) by issuance of (1) additional share 6/15/83
State of incorporation changed from (CA) to (DE) and Common no par changed to $0.001 par 2/24/87

Merged into Yamanouchi U.S. Holding Corp. 5/18/89
Each share Common $0.001 par exchanged for $28 cash

SHAKWAK EXPL LTD (BC)
Recapitalized as Arcturus Resources Ltd. 11/10/95
Each share Common no par exchanged for (0.125) share Common no par
Arcturus Resources Ltd. recapitalized as Arcturus Ventures Inc. 12/19/2000

SHALAKO INC (NV)
Charter revoked for failure to file reports and pay fees 04/01/1985

SHALER CO (DE)
Merged into National Rivet & Manufacturing Co. 04/25/1974
Each share Class B Common no par exchanged for $21.50 cash

SHALLBETTER INDUSTRIES, INC. (MN)
Bankruptcy proceedings converted from Chapter 11 to Chapter 7 6/14/82
No stockholders' equity

SHALLBETTER INDS INC (MN)
issuance of (2) additional shares payable
SEC revoked common stock registration

SHALLOW RES INC (BC)
Delisted from Vancouver Stock Exchange 03/02/1989

SHALMAR RES LTD (BC)
Struck off register and declared dissolved for failure to file returns 05/06/1983

SHAMAN PHARMACEUTICALS INC (DE)
Each share old Common $0.001 par exchanged for (0.05) share new Common $0.001 par 06/22/1999
Each share new Common $0.001 par exchanged again for (0.02) share new Common $0.001 par 01/31/2000
Each share Conv. Preferred Ser. R exchanged for (31) shares new Common $0.001 par 02/01/2000
Chapter 11 bankruptcy proceedings converted to Chapter 7 on 04/15/2002
Stockholders' equity unlikely

SHAMIKA 2 GOLD INC (NV)
SEC revoked common stock registration 03/16/2016

SHAMIR OPTICAL IND LTD (ISRAEL)
Acquired by Essilor International S.A. 07/01/2011
Each share Ordinary ILS 0.01 par exchanged for $14.50 cash

SHAMOKIN ANTHRACITE COAL CO.
Operations discontinued 00/00/1936
Details not available

SHAMPAN LAMPORT HLDGS LTD (WA)
Each share old Common no par exchanged for (0.33333333) share new Common no par 12/20/1999
Name changed to takeoutmusic.com Holdings Corp. 02/10/2000
(See takeoutmusic.com Holdings Corp.)

SHAMROCK FD (CA)
Merged into National Technical Services, Inc. 12/01/1975
Each share Capital Stock 10¢ par exchanged for (1) share Common 5¢ par
National Technical Services, Inc. name changed to National Technical Systems (CA) 06/24/1981 which reincorporated in Delaware as National Technical Systems, Inc. 11/15/1987 which reincorporated in California 06/28/1996

(See National Technical Systems, Inc.)

SHAMROCK GOLD MINES LTD. (BC)
Dissolved in 1948

SHAMROCK LOGISTICS L P (DE)
Issue Information - 4,500,000 COM UNIT LTD PARTNERSHIP INT offered at $24.50 per UNIT on 04/09/2001
Name changed to Valero L.P. 1/1/2002
Valero L.P. name changed to NuStar Energy L.P. 4/1/2007

SHAMROCK OIL & GAS CO.
Reorganized as Shamrock Oil & Gas Corp. in 1935
(See Shamrock Oil & Gas Corp.)

SHAMROCK OIL & GAS CORP (DE)
6% Preferred called for redemption 4/30/44
Common $1 par split (3) for (2) by issuance of (0.5) additional share 10/1/57
Common $1 par split (3) for (2) by issuance of (0.5) additional share 4/7/67
Stock Dividends - 10% 1/9/53; 50% 1/10/55; 25% 5/19/61
Merged into Diamond Shamrock Corp. 12/19/67
Each share Common $1 par exchanged for (0.5) share $1.20 Conv. Preferred Ser. D no par and (0.75) share Common no par
Diamond Shamrock Corp. name changed to Maxus Energy Corp. 4/30/87
(See Maxus Energy Corp.)

SHAMROCK PETROLEUM LTD. (AB)
Name changed to Alaska-Yukon Refiners & Distributors Ltd. 11/23/56
(See Alaska-Yukon Refiners & Distributors Ltd.)

SHAMROCK RES INC (BC)
Name changed to Pacific Energy Resources Ltd. (BC) 08/22/2003
Pacific Energy Resources Ltd. (BC) reincorporated in Delaware 02/04/2005
(See Pacific Energy Resources Ltd. (DE))

SHAMROCK URANIUM INC. (UT)
Recapitalized as Western Milling Co. 9/5/57
Each share Capital Stock 1¢ par exchanged for (0.1) share Common 10¢ par
Western Milling Co. name changed to Basic Resources Corp. 9/21/59
(See Basic Resources Corp.)

SHANDA GAMES LTD (CAYMAN ISLANDS)
Acquired by Capitalhold Ltd. 11/19/2015
Each Sponsored ADR for Class A Ordinary exchanged for $7.05 cash

SHANDA INTERACTIVE ENTMT LTD (CAYMAN ISLANDS)
Acquired by Premium Lead Co. Ltd. 02/14/2012
Each Sponsored ADR for Ordinary exchanged for $41.30 cash

SHANDON RES INC (BC)
Struck off register and declared dissolved for failure to file reports 12/24/1993

SHANDONG HAUNENG PWR DEV LTD (CHINA)
Merged into Huaneng Power International, Inc. 12/31/2000
Each Sponsored ADR for Ordinary Rmb1 par exchanged for $8.09 cash

SHANDONG LUOXIN PHARMACEUTICAL GROUP STK CO LTD (CHINA)
Name changed 01/12/2015
Name changed from Shandong Luoxin Pharmacy Stock Co., Ltd. to Shandong Luoxin Pharmaceutical Group Stock Co., Ltd. 01/12/2015
ADR agreement terminated 05/21/2018
Each Sponsored ADR for H Shares exchanged for (10) H Shares
Note: Unexchanged ADR's will be sold and the proceeds, if any, held for claim after 09/21/2018

SHANDONG RUITAI CHEM CO LTD (DE)
Name changed to China Ruitai International Holdings Co., Ltd. 04/09/2007
(See China Ruitai International Holdings Co., Ltd.)

SHANE RES LTD (SK)
Voluntarily dissolved 06/20/2014
Details not available

SHANECY INC (DE)
Common $0.001 par split (2) for (1) by issuance of (1) additional share payable 12/30/1999 to holders of record 12/30/1999
Name changed to Inc.ubator Capital Inc. 06/09/2000
Inc.ubator Capital Inc. name changed to Emergent Financial Group, Inc. 07/23/2001 which recapitalized as EGX Funds Transfer, Inc. 06/14/2002
(See EGX Funds Transfer, Inc.)

SHANELL INTL ENERGY CORP (BC)
Recapitalized as Pacific Insight Electronics Corp. 06/14/1989
Each share Common no par exchanged for (0.25) share Common no par
(See Pacific Insight Electronics Corp.)

SHANGHAI CENTURY ACQUISITION CORP (CAYMAN ISLANDS)
Issue Information - 14,375,000 UNITS consisting of (1) share ORD and (1) WT offered at $8 per Unit on 04/24/2006
Completely liquidated 08/29/2008
Each share Common $0.0005 par exchanged for first and final distribution of $7.97343381 cash

SHANGHAI CHLOR-ALKALI CHEM LTD (CHINA)
Stock Dividend - 10% payable 07/02/2000 to holders of record 06/23/2000
ADR agreement terminated 08/02/2018
Each Sponsored ADR for Class B exchanged for (10) shares Class B
Note: Unexchanged ADR's will be sold and the proceeds, if any, held for claim after 08/05/2019

SHANGHAI HAI XING SHIPPING CO LTD (CHINA)
Name changed to China Shipping Development Co. Ltd. 12/09/1997
China Shipping Development Co. Ltd. name changed to COSCO SHIPPING Energy Transportation Co., Ltd. 12/23/2016
(See COSCO SHIPPING Energy Transportation Co., Ltd.)

SHANGHAI HUAYI GROUP CORP LTD (CHINA)
ADR agreement terminated 06/04/2018
Each Sponsored ADR for Class B Ordinary exchanged for (10) shares Class B Ordinary
Note: Unexchanged ADR's will be sold and the proceeds, if any, held for claim after 12/04/2018

SHANGHAI JINQIAO EXPT PROCESSING ZONE DEV LTD (CHINA)
ADR agreement terminated 12/19/2016
No ADR's remain outstanding

SHANGHAI LUJIAZUI FIN & TRADE ZONE DEV LTD (CHINA)
ADR agreement terminated 12/01/2015
No ADR's remain outstanding

SHANGHAI OUTER GAOQIAO FREE TRADE ZONE DEV LTD (CHINA)
ADR agreement terminated 12/19/2016
No ADR's remain outstanding

SHANGHAI PETROCHEMICAL LTD (CHINA)
Name changed to Sinopec Shanghai Petrochemical Co. Ltd. 11/29/2000

SHANGHAI SHIBEI HI-TECH CO LTD (CHINA)
Name changed 06/12/2013
Stock Dividends - 10% payable 06/27/1996 to holders of record 06/10/1996; 10% payable 06/27/1997 to holders of record 06/10/1997
Name changed from Shanghai Erfangji Co. Ltd. to Shanghai Shibei Hi-Tech Co., Ltd. 06/12/2013
ADR agreement terminated 02/24/2016
Each Sponsored ADR for Class B exchanged for (10) shares Class B
Note: Unexchanged ADR's will be sold and the proceeds, if any, held for claim after 02/27/2017

SHANGHAI TYRE & RUBR LTD (CHINA)
Name changed to Double Coin Holdings Ltd. 08/14/2007
Double Coin Holdings Ltd. name changed to Shanghai Huayi Group Corp. Ltd. 06/10/2016
(See Shanghai Huayi Group Corp. Ltd.)

SHANGHAI YUTONG PHARMA INC (DE)
Name changed to ANBC, Inc. 08/23/2016

SHANGHAI YUTONG PHARMACEUTICAL INC (DE)
Name changed to L International Computers Inc. 07/15/2005
(See L International Computers Inc.)

SHANGHAI ZHENHUA PORT MACHY CO LTD (CHINA)
ADR agreement terminated 07/15/2010
No ADR's were outstanding

SHANGPHARMA CORP (CAYMAN ISLANDS)
Acquired by ShangPharma Holdings Ltd. 03/27/2013
Each Sponsored ADR for Ordinary exchanged for $8.95 cash

SHANKS GROUP PLC (ENGLAND)
Name changed to Renewi PLC 03/15/2017

SHANLEY CORP (DE)
Name changed 12/29/1986
Name changed from Shanley Oil Co. to Shanley Corp. 12/29/1986
Charter cancelled and declared inoperative and void for non-payment of taxes 03/01/1989

SHANNI INTL INC (DE)
Charter cancelled and declared inoperative and void for non-payment of taxes 03/01/1987

SHANNOCK CORP (CANADA)
Recapitalized as TSC Shannock Corp. 04/04/1988
Each share Class A no par exchanged for (1/3) share Class A Common no par
(See TSC Shannock Corp.)

SHANNON-DETROIT CO. (MI)
Charter dissolved for failure to file reports 8/31/33

FINANCIAL INFORMATION, INC. SHA-SHA

SHANNON ENVIRONMENTAL LTD (AB)
Recapitalized 3/2/93
Recapitalized from Shannon Energy Ltd. to Shannon Environmental Ltd. 3/2/93
Each share Common no par exchanged for (0.2) share Common no par
Struck off register and declared dissolved for failure to file returns 4/1/96

SHANNON GROUP INC (TX)
Bank foreclosed assets 2/28/86
No stockholders' equity

SHANNON INTERNATIONAL INC. (UT)
Recapitalized as Shannon Group Inc. (UT) 9/10/79
Each share Common 1¢ par exchanged for (30) shares Common $0.0001 par

SHANNON INTL INC (NV)
Name changed 03/16/2005
Name changed from Shannon International Resources Inc. to Shannon International Inc. 03/16/2005
SEC revoked common stock registration 06/17/2013

SHANNON OIL & GAS INC (TX)
Name changed to Shannon Group Inc. (TX) 6/21/84

SHAO TONG CHUAN HEALTH VEGETARIAN FOODS USA HLDGS LTD (NV)
Reorganized under the laws of Delaware as Standard Commerce, Inc. 01/29/2007
Each share Common $0.001 par exchanged for (0.05) share Common $0.001 par
Standard Commerce, Inc. recapitalized as China Jianye Fuel, Inc. 01/18/2008
(See China Jianye Fuel, Inc.)

SHAPELL INDS INC (DE)
Merged into NDM Corp. 07/18/1984
Each share Common $1 par exchanged for $65 cash

SHAPELY INC (OH)
Merged into Leslie Fay Co. 09/30/1983
Each share Class A Common no par exchanged for $10 cash

SHAPIRO BROS. FACTOR CORP. (NY)
Acquired by Chase Manhattan Bank (N.A.) 1/2/69
Details not available

SHAPIRO J CO (MN)
Placed in liquidation and trustee appointed 04/13/1973
No stockholders' equity

SHAPIRO ROCHESTER INDS INC (NY)
Name changed to Villa Manufacturing Inc. 7/31/70
(See Villa Manufacturing Inc.)

SHAR MAR HLDGS LTD (ON)
Name changed to OmniWeb Inc. 09/26/2001

SHARBOT LAKE MINES LTD. (QC)
Charter annulled for failure to file annual reports 11/4/78

SHARE OILS LTD. (AB)
Name changed to Share Mines & Oils Ltd. (AB) 03/01/1965
Share Mines & Oils Ltd. (AB) reincorporated in Ontario 11/20/1979 which recapitalized as Share Resources Inc. 07/04/1996
(See Share Resources Inc.)

SHARE RES INC (ON)
Reincorporated 11/20/1979
Recapitalized 07/04/1996
Place of incorporation changed from (AB) to (ON) 11/20/1979
Recapitalized from Share Mines & Oils Ltd. to Share Resources Inc. 07/04/1996
Each share Common no par exchanged for (0.25) share Common no par
Delisted from CDN 01/14/2000

SHAREBASE CORP (DE)
Merged into Teradata Corp. 6/27/90
Each share Common 1¢ par exchanged for (0.02141) share Common 1¢ par
Teradata Corp. merged into American Telephone & Telegraph Co. 2/28/92 which name changed to AT&T Corp. 4/20/94 which merged into AT&T Inc. 11/18/2005

SHARECO CAP CORP (AB)
Name changed to Binoptic International Corp. (ALTA) 2/19/93
Binoptic International Corp. (ALTA) reincorporated in Delaware 3/22/94
(See Binoptic International Corp. (DE))

SHARECOM INC (NV)
Each (2,500) shares old Common $0.001 par exchanged for (1) share new Common $0.001 par 11/4/2002
Name changed to Primary Business Systems Inc. 3/28/2003
Primary Business Systems Inc. recapitalized as PBS Holding, Inc. 10/3/2005

SHARED MED SYS CORP (DE)
Merged into Siemens A.G. 07/05/2000
Each share Common 1¢ par exchanged for $73 cash

SHARED TECHNOLOGIES CELLULAR INC (DE)
Issue Information - 950,000 shares COM offered at $5.25 per share on 04/21/1995
SEC revoked common stock registration 07/26/2010
Stockholders' equity unlikely

SHARED TECHNOLOGIES FAIRCHILD INC (DE)
Merged into Intermedia Communications Inc. 3/10/98
Each share Common $0.004 par exchanged for $15 cash

SHARED TECHNOLOGIES INC (DE)
Each share Common $0.001 par exchanged for (0.25) share Common $0.004 par 09/24/1992
Under plan of merger name changed to Shared Technologies Fairchild Inc. 03/18/1996
(See Shared Technologies Fairchild Inc.)

SHARED USE NETWORK SERVICES, INC. (CO)
Name changed to Evergreen Network.Com Inc. 04/07/2000
(See Evergreen Network.Com Inc.)

SHAREDATA INC (MN)
Common 5¢ par changed to 1¢ par and (9) additional shares issued 09/01/1983
Common 1¢ par changed to no par 04/25/1985
Each share old Common no par exchanged for (0.125) share new Common no par 12/23/1985
Each share new Common no par exchanged again for (0.25) share new Common no par 06/11/1987
Plan of reorganization under Chapter 11 Federal Bankruptcy proceedings effective 12/04/1995
Each share new Common no par exchanged again for (0.025) share new Common no par
Note: Holdings of (99) or fewer post reverse split shares were cancelled and are without value
Merged into Aztore Holdings, Inc. 02/15/1996
Each share new Common no par exchanged for (1) share Common no par, (1) Common Stock Purchase Warrant, Class A expiring 06/15/1996, (1) Common Stock Purchase Warrant, Class B expiring 06/15/1998, and (1) Common Stock Purchase Warrant, Class C expiring 06/15/2000
(See Aztore Holdings, Inc.)

SHAREHOLDER COMMUNICATION SYS INC (CO)
Administratively dissolved 02/01/1999

SHAREHOLDER PROPERTIES, INC. (CA)
Class A Common $1 par and Class B Common $1 par reclassified as Common $1 par in July 1968
Name changed to Aeroceanic Corp. (Calif.) 8/6/68
Aeroceanic Corp. (Calif.) merged into Aeroceanic Corp. (Del.) 5/15/70 which merged into Evans Industries, Inc. 5/7/75
(See Evans Industries, Inc.)

SHAREHOLDERS CAP CORP (DE)
Stock Dividend - 66-2/3% 06/30/1969
Name changed to Angeles Corp. (DE) 01/22/1975
Angeles Corp. (DE) reincorporated in California 12/15/1977
(See Angeles Corp. (CA))

SHAREHOLDERS CORP.
Acquired by Equity Fund, Inc. on a (1.528868) for (1) basis 00/00/1944
Equity Fund, Inc. name changed to Safeco Equity Fund, Inc. (DE) 06/30/1973 which reincorporated in Washington 08/20/1987 which reincorporated back in Delaware 09/30/1993
(See Safeco Equity Fund, Inc.)

SHAREHOLDERS FINL SVCS AMER (CA)
Capital Stock $1 par changed to 25¢ par and (3) additional shares issued 5/28/69
Name changed to Unit Option Corp. of America 9/10/69
Unit Option Corp. of America name changed to Securities Clearing Corp. of America 7/28/72
(See Securities Clearing Corp. of America)

SHAREHOLDERS INVT CORP (UT)
Each share Common 1¢ par exchanged for (0.04) share Common no par 3/2/72
Recapitalized as World Capital Investment Corp. 12/15/72
Each share Common no par exchanged for (0.166666) share Common 1¢ par
(See World Capital Investment Corp.)

SHAREHOLDERS TR BOSTON (MA)
Shares of Bene. Int. $1 par split (3) for (1) by issuance of (2) additional shares 00/00/1954
Shares of Bene. Int. $1 par split (5) for (4) by issuance of (0.25) additional share 01/31/1972
Acquired by Phoenix-Chase Series Fund 01/30/1981
Each Share of Bene. Int. $1 par exchanged for (1) Balanced Fund Series Share of Bene. Int. $1 par
Phoenix-Chase Series Fund name changed to Phoenix Series Fund 10/12/1982
(See Phoenix Series Fund)

SHARES CORP. OF WALL STREET
Liquidated in 1934

SHARES IN AMERICAN INDUSTRY, INC. (DE)
Name changed to Steadman's Shares in American Industry, Inc. 5/19/66
Steadman's Shares in American Industry, Inc. name changed to Steadman American Industry Fund, Inc. 10/19/67 which name changed to Ameritor Industry Fund 9/23/98
(See Ameritor Industry Fund)

SHARES IN THE SOUTH, INC.
Liquidated in 1933

SHAREWELL CAP GROUP INC (NV)
Name changed to Artemis Energy Holdings Inc. 04/11/2013
Artemis Energy Holdings Inc. name changed to Findit, Inc. 02/20/2015

SHARIN O THE GREEN INC (UT)
Completely liquidated 04/08/1971
Each share Common 5¢ par exchanged for first and final distribution of (1) share Western Recreation, Inc. Common 1¢ par
Western Recreation, Inc. name changed to Charvet/Jackson & Co., Inc. 09/20/1972
(See Charvet/Jackson & Co. Inc.)

SHARON CAP CORP (NV)
Name changed to PEI, Inc. (NV) 8/1/90
PEI, Inc. (NV) name changed to Process Equipment, Inc. (NV) 11/19/90 which reincorporated in Delaware as HQ Sustainable Maritime Industries, Inc 5/19/2004

SHARON COAL & ICE CO. (PA)
Out of business 5/30/71
No stockholders' equity

SHARON COPPER MINES LTD. (BC)
Declared dissolved for failure to file reports 5/15/69

SHARON ENERGY LTD (AB)
Reincorporated 09/24/2003
Place of incorporation changed from (BC) to (AB) 09/24/2003
Merged into Tuscany Energy Ltd. (Old) 06/23/2011
Each share Common no par exchanged for (0.84) share Common no par
Note: Unexchanged certificates were cancelled and became without value 06/23/2014
Tuscany Energy Ltd. (Old) reorganized as Tuscany Energy Ltd. (New) 07/19/2013
(See Tuscany Energy Ltd. (New))

SHARON REAL ESTATE CONSULTANTS CORP (NV)
Reincorporated 12/31/96
State of incorporation changed from (FL) to (NV) 12/31/96
Name changed to Tri-Star International Ltd. 4/23/97
Tri-Star International Ltd. name changed to Internationalstores.com Inc. 10/22/99

SHARON STEEL HOOP CO. (PA)
Name changed to Sharon Steel Corp. in 1936
(See Sharon Steel Corp.)

SHARON STL CORP (PA)
Plan of reorganization under Chapter 11 Federal Bankruptcy proceedings effective 12/28/1990
No stockholders' equity

SHARON TUBE CO (PA)
Acquired by John Maneely Co. 02/27/2007
Each share Common $10 par exchanged for $3,342.76 cash
Note: Each share Common $10 par received an initial additional distribution of $132.4366 cash payable 10/05/2010 to holders of record 02/27/2007
Each share Common $10 par received a second additional distribution of $53.54442266 cash payable 05/09/2011 to holders of record 02/27/2007
Each share Common $10 par received a third additional distribution of $56.0478 cash payable 07/05/2012 to holders of record 02/27/2007
Each share Common $10 par received a fourth additional

distribution of $56.770368 cash payable 02/22/2013 to holders of record 02/27/2007
Each share Common $10 par received a fifth and final additional distribution of $1.6477 cash payable 11/13/2014 to holders of record 02/27/2007

SHAROT-MAY CO., INC.
Bankrupt in 1948

SHARP & DOHME, INC. (MD)
Merged into Merck & Co., Inc. (Old) 00/00/1953
Each share $4.25 Preference no par exchanged for (1) share $4.25 2nd Preferred no par
Each share Common no par exchanged for (2.25) shares Common 16-2/3¢ par
Merck & Co., Inc. (Old) merged into Merck & Co., Inc. (New) 11/03/2009

SHARP HLDG CORP (DE)
Recapitalized as Cooper Holding Corp. 10/28/2010
Each share Common $0.001 par exchanged for (0.04) share Common $0.001 par
Cooper Holding Corp. recapitalized as Crednology Holding Corp. 05/03/2013

SHARP INTL CORP (NY)
Merged into New Sharp Co., Inc. 08/14/1991
Each share Common 10¢ par exchanged for $0.21 cash

SHARP MANUFACTURING CO.
Properties sold in 1936

SHARPE (E.J.) INSTRUMENTS OF CANADA LTD. (ON)
Name changed to Sharpe Instruments of Canada Ltd. 6/2/64
Sharpe Instruments of Canada Ltd. recapitalized as Scintrex Ltd. 5/25/67 which merged into IDS Intelligent Detection Systems Inc. 7/29/98

SHARPE INSTRUMENTS OF CANADA LTD. (ON)
Recapitalized as Scintrex Ltd. 5/25/67
Each share Capital Stock no par exchanged for (0.25) share Capital Stock no par
Scintrex Ltd. merged into IDS Intelligent Detection Systems Inc. 7/29/98

SHARPE RES CORP (ON)
Name changed 06/30/1996
Reincorporated 05/09/2008
Name changed from Sharpe Energy & Resources Ltd. to Sharpe Resources Corp. 06/30/1996
Place of incorporation changed from (ONT) to (Canada) 05/09/2008

SHARPER IMAGE CORP (DE)
Name changed to TSIC, Inc. 07/17/2008

SHARPROCK RES INC (NV)
Recapitalized as Evergreen-Agra, Inc. (NV) 10/23/2013
Each share Common $0.001 par exchanged for (0.01) share Common $0.001 par
Evergreen-Agra, Inc. (NV) reincorporated in Delaware as Evergreen-Agra Global Investments, Inc. 11/14/2017

SHARPS ELIM TECHNOLOGIES INC (DE)
Name changed to Armagh Group Inc. 09/19/2002
Armagh Group Inc. recapitalized as SmartVideo Technologies, Inc. 01/06/2003 which name changed to uVuMobile, Inc. 06/04/2007
(See uVuMobile, Inc.)

SHARPS ELIM TECHNOLOGIES INC (WA)
Each share old Common $0.001 par exchanged for (0.00666666) share new Common $0.001 par 05/12/2005
Name changed to Quantum MRI, Inc. 09/13/2005

SHARPSTOWN ST BK (HOUSTON, TX)
Placed in receivership 01/25/1971
No stockholders' equity

SHARUS CORP (NV)
Reincorporated 05/25/1989
State of incorporation changed from (UT) to (NV) 05/25/1989
Name changed to Golden Quest Inc. 07/07/1989
Golden Quest Inc. recapitalized as T-Bay Holdings Inc. 01/23/2002 which recapitalized as TOCCA Life Holdings, Inc. 01/12/2015

SHASPER INDS LTD (QC)
Acquired by Shasper Investments Inc. 11/08/1991
Each share Common no par exchanged for $1.60 cash

SHASTA COUNTY BANK (REDDING, CA)
Location changed 07/16/1979
Location changed from (Burney, CA) to (Redding, CA) 07/16/1979
Acquired by Tri Counties Bank (Chico, CA) 03/27/1981
Each share Capital Stock $3.33333333 par exchanged for $32 cash

SHASTA FD INC (DE)
Out of business 10/07/1975
No stockholders' equity

SHASTA MINERALS & CHEMICAL CO. (NV)
Merged into Silver King Mines, Inc. 05/21/1965
Each share Common 20¢ par exchanged for (0.25) share Capital Stock $1 par
Silver King Mines, Inc. merged into Alta Gold Co. 11/24/1989
(See Alta Gold Co.)

SHASTA MINES & OILS LTD (BC)
Recapitalized as International Shasta Resources Ltd. 03/26/1975
Each share Common 50¢ par exchanged for (0.2) share Common $2.50 par
International Shasta Resources Ltd. recapitalized as Consolidated Shasta Resources Inc. 05/20/1994 which name changed to Lima Gold Corp. 11/24/1994 which recapitalized as International Lima Recources Corp. 09/20/1999 which name changed to Crosshair Exploration & Mining Corp. 03/01/2004 which name changed to Crosshair Energy Corp. 11/02/2011 which recapitalized as Jet Metal Corp. (BC) 09/23/2013 which reorganized in Canada as Canada Jetlines Ltd. 03/07/2017

SHASTA WATER CO. (DE)
Each share Class A no par exchanged for (1) share Common no par 00/00/1932
Each share Class B no par exchanged for (0.35) share Common no par 00/00/1932
Each share Common no par exchanged for (3) shares Common $2.50 par 00/00/1954
Name changed to S.W. Liquidating Co. 12/08/1960
S.W. Liquidating Co. liquidated for Consolidated Foods Corp. 12/08/1960 which name changed to Sara Lee Corp. 04/02/1985 which recapitalized as Hillshire Brands Co. 06/29/2012
(See Hillshire Brands Co.)

SHASTINA PPTYS INC (CA)
Charter cancelled for failure to file reports and pay taxes 11/03/1980

SHATHEENA CAP CORP (ON)
Name changed to Plato Gold Corp. 6/1/2005

SHATT DENN LIQUIDATING CO. (DE)
Completely liquidated 05/22/1973
Each share Capital Stock $5 par exchanged for (0.5) share Brown Co. (DE) Common $1 par and (0.625) Common Stock Purchase Warrant expiring 05/15/1980
Brown Co. (DE) merged into James River Corp. of Virginia 10/28/1980 which name changed to Fort James Corp. 08/13/1997 which merged into Georgia-Pacific Corp. 11/27/2000
(See Georgia-Pacific Corp.)

SHATTUCK (FRANK G.) CO. (MA)
Merged into Pet Inc. 01/01/1968
Each share Capital Stock no par exchanged for (0.8) share $1 Conv. 2nd Preferred no par
(See Pet Inc.)

SHATTUCK DENN MNG CORP (DE)
Capital Stock no par changed to $5 par 00/00/1932
Name changed to Shatt Denn Liquidating Co. 05/22/1973
(See Shatt Denn Liquidating Co.)

SHATTUCK PROPERTIES CORP.
Liquidated 00/00/1943
Details not available

SHATTUCK S W CHEM CO (CO)
Name changed to JPL Enterprises, Inc. 12/30/1969
(See JPL Enterprises, Inc.)

SHAVER FOOD MARTS INC (NE)
Proclaimed dissolved 09/16/1989

SHAW BARTON INC (OH)
Common $2.50 par changed to $2 par and (0.25) additional share issued 05/19/1969
Common $2 par changed to $1 par and (1) additional share issued 06/01/1972
Stock Dividend - 25% 02/25/1966
Merged into Heritage Communications, Inc. 03/24/1981
Each share Common $1 par exchanged for (1) share $1.50 Conv. Preferred Ser. B no par
(See Heritage Communications, Inc.)

SHAW COMMUNICATIONS INC (AB)
Name changed 05/26/1993
Class A Participating no par split (3) for (1) by issuance of (2) additional shares 09/28/1987
Class B Non-Voting Participating 10¢ par changed to $0.03333333 par and (2) additional shares issued 09/28/1987
Name changed from Shaw Cablesystems Ltd. to Shaw Communications Inc. 05/26/1993
8.45% US$ Canadian Originated Preferred Securities called for redemption at $25 plus $0.528125 accrued dividends on 02/01/2005
Canadian Originated Preferred Securities called for redemption at $25 on 12/16/2005
(Additional Information in Active)

SHAW GROUP INC (LA)
Common no par split (2) for (1) by issuance of (1) additional share payable 12/15/2000 to holders of record 12/01/2000 Ex date - 12/18/2000
Merged into Chicago Bridge & Iron Co. N.V. 02/13/2013
Each share Common no par exchanged for (0.12883) share Common EUR 0.01 par and $41 cash
Chicago Bridge & Iron Co. N.V. merged into McDermott International, Inc. 05/10/2018

SHAW INDS INC (GA)
Common no par split (2) for (1) by issuance of (1) additional share 05/19/1986
Common no par split (2) for (1) by issuance of (1) additional share 06/08/1989
Common no par split (2) for (1) by issuance of (1) additional share 03/09/1992
Common no par split (2) for (1) by issuance of (1) additional share 12/22/1993
Merged into Berkshire Hathaway Inc. 01/08/2001
Each share Common no par exchanged for $19 cash

SHAW INTL INC (DE)
Name changed to Everclear International Inc. 08/17/2001
(See Everclear International Inc.)

SHAW-LOOMIS-SAYLES MUTUAL FUND, INC.
Name changed to Loomis-Sayles Mutual Fund, Inc. 00/00/1930
Loomis-Sayles Mutual Fund, Inc. name changed to CGM Trust 03/01/1991

SHAW OIL & CHEMICAL CORP. (DE)
Recapitalized as Clayton Corp. 00/00/1953
Each share Common 5¢ par exchanged for (0.1) share Common 1¢ par
Clayton Corp. name changed to Clayton Corp. of Delaware 07/11/1956 which name changed back to Clayton Corp. 04/20/1967
(See Clayton Corp.)

SHAW PETROLEUMS CORP. OF CANADA LTD. (ON)
Charter cancelled and company declared dissolved for default in filing returns 05/13/1965

SHAW PIPE INDS LTD (CANADA)
Name changed to Shaw Industries Ltd./ Les Industries Shaw Ltee. 05/30/1980
Shaw Industries Ltd./Les Industries Shaw Ltee. name changed to ShawCor Ltd. (Old) 05/10/2001 which reorganized as ShawCor Ltd. (New) 03/27/2013

SHAW PORCUPINE MINES LTD.
Recapitalized as Carshaw Porcupine Gold Mines Ltd. 00/00/1945
Each share Common exchanged for (0.33333333) share Common
(See Carshaw Porcupine Gold Mines Ltd.)

SHAW RES INC (CO)
Each share old Common $0.001 par exchanged for (0.02) share new Common $0.001 par 07/25/1988
Each (150,000) shares new Common $0.001 par exchanged again for (1) share new Common $0.001 par 09/01/1990
Note: In effect holders received $0.175 cash per share and public interest was eliminated

SHAW WALKER CO (MI)
Each share $7 Preferred $100 par exchanged for (1.2) shares 5% Preferred $100 par and $6.25 cash 00/00/1937
5% Preferred called for redemption 07/05/1955
Acquired by Westinghouse Electric Corp. 00/00/1989
Details not available

SHAW-WALKER VENTURES INC. (MI)
Charter declared inoperative and void for failure to file reports 07/15/1994

SHAWANO DEVELOPMENT CORP. (FL)
Each share Common $1 par exchanged for (4) shares Common 25¢ par 05/11/1955
Proclaimed dissolved for non-payment of taxes 06/07/1966

SHAWCOR LTD OLD (CANADA)
Name changed 05/10/2001
Common no par split (2) for (1) by issuance of (1) additional share 06/14/1980
Common no par reclassified as Class A Subordinate no par 10/27/1988
Each share Class A Subordinate no par received distribution of (0.5) share Conv. Class B no par 11/14/1988
Class A Subordinate no par split (2) for (1) by issuance of (1) additional share 06/07/1991
Conv. Class B no par split (2) for (1) by issuance of (1) additional share 06/07/1991
Class A Subordinate no par split (3) for (2) by issuance of (0.5) additional share 06/08/1992
Conv. Class B no par split (3) for (2) by issuance of (0.5) additional share 06/08/1992
Class A Subordinate no par split (3) for (1) by issuance of (2) additional shares payable 06/01/1998 to holders of record 06/01/1998
Conv. Class B no par split (3) for (1) by issuance of (2) additional shares payable 06/01/1998 to holders of record 06/01/1998
Name changed from Shaw Industries Ltd./ Les Industries Shaw Ltee. to ShawCor Ltd. (Old) 05/10/2001
Reorganized as ShawCor Ltd. (New) 03/27/2013
Each share Class A Subordinate no par exchanged for (1) share Common no par
Each share Conv. Class B no par exchanged for (0.11) share Common no par and $39.087 cash

SHAWCORE DEV CORP (NV)
Name changed to White Smile Global, Inc. (NV) 08/08/2011
White Smile Global, Inc. (NV) reincorporated in Florida as Williamsville Sears Management, Inc. 04/03/2018

SHAWINIGAN INDUSTRIES LTD. (QC)
Acquired by Power Corp. of Canada, Ltd. 03/20/1964
Each share Capital Stock no par exchanged for $5.116 cash

SHAWINIGAN WTR & PWR CO (QC)
Each share Common $100 par exchanged for (4) shares Common no par 00/00/1927
Class A Common no par split (3) for (1) by issuance of (2) additional shares 10/18/1957
Common no par split (3) for (1) by issuance of (2) additional shares 10/18/1957
Acquired by Quebec Hydro-Electric Commission 11/05/1963
Each share 4% Preferred Ser. A $50 par exchanged for $50 principal amount of 4% 10-year Debentures
4.50% Preferred Ser. B $50 par exchanged for $50 principal amount of 4.50% 10-year Debentures
Each share Class A Common no par exchanged for $30.25 cash
Each share Common no par exchanged for $30 cash

SHAWKEY GOLD MINING CO. LTD.
Reorganized as Shawkey (1945) Mines Ltd. 00/00/1945
Each share Capital Stock $1 par exchanged for (0.33333333) share Capital Stock $1 par
Shawkey (1945) Mines Ltd. recapitalized as Ultra Shawkey Mines Ltd. 10/31/1956 which recapitalized as Con-Shawkey Gold Mines Ltd. 10/01/1962 which name changed to Kenn Holdings & Mining Ltd. 09/15/1969
(See Kenn Holdings & Mining Ltd.)

SHAWKEY (1945) MINES LTD. (ON)
Recapitalized as Ultra Shawkey Mines Ltd. 10/31/1956
Each share Capital Stock $1 par exchanged for (0.25) share Capital Stock $1 par
Ultra Shawkey Mines Ltd. recapitalized as Con-Shawkey Gold Mines Ltd. 10/01/1962 which name changed to Kenn Holdings & Mining Ltd. 09/15/1969
(See Kenn Holdings & Mining Ltd.)

SHAWMUT ASSOCIATION, INC. (MA)
Common no par changed to $5 par 3/31/70
Name changed to Shawmut Corp. 4/24/75
Shawmut Corp. merged into Shawmut National Corp. 2/29/88 which merged into Fleet Financial Group Inc. (New) 11/30/95 which name changed to Fleet Boston Corp. 10/1/99 which name changed to FleetBoston Financial Corp. 4/18/2000 which merged into Bank of America Corp. 4/1/2004

SHAWMUT ASSOCIATION (MA)
Name changed to Shawmut Association, Inc. 5/6/65
Each share Common no par exchanged for (1) share Common no par
Shawmut Association, Inc. name changed to Shawmut Corp. 4/24/75 which merged into Shawmut National Corp. 2/29/88 which merged into Fleet Financial Group, Inc. (New) 11/30/95 which name changed to Fleet Boston Corp. 10/1/99 which name changed to FleetBoston Financial Corp. 4/18/2000 which merged into Bank of America Corp. 4/1/2004

SHAWMUT BANK INVESTMENT TRUST
Name changed to Mayflower Investment Trust in 1952
(See Mayflower Investment Trust)

SHAWMUT COMMUNITY BANK, N.A. (FRAMINGTON, MA)
Thru exchange offer majority held by Shawmut Corp.
Public interest eliminated

SHAWMUT CORP (MA)
Common $5 par split (2) for (1) by issuance of (1) additional share 01/13/1981
Common $5 par split (3) for (2) by issuance of (0.5) additional share 10/18/1984
Merged into Shawmut National Corp. 02/29/1988
Each share Common $5 par exchanged for (1.8) shares Common 1¢ par
Shawmut National Corp. merged into Fleet Financial Group, Inc. (New) 11/30/1995 which name changed to Fleet Boston Corp. 10/01/1999 which name changed to FleetBoston Financial Corp. 04/18/2000 which merged into Bank of America Corp. 04/01/2004

SHAWMUT COUNTY BANK, N.A. (CAMBRIDGE, MA)
Acquired by Shawmut Bank, N.A. (Boston, MA) 08/28/1987
Details not available

SHAWMUT FIRST COUNTY BANK, N.A. (BROCKTON, MA)
Merged into Shawmut Bank, N.A. (Boston, MA) 11/13/1987
Details not available

SHAWMUT NATL CORP (DE)
Merged into Fleet Financial Group, Inc. (New) 11/30/95
Each share 9.30% Depositary Preferred Share exchanged for (1) 9.30% Depositary Preferred Share
Each share 9.30% Preferred no par exchanged for (1) share 9.30% Preferred no par
Each 9.35% Depositary Preferred Share exchanged for (1) 9.35% Depositary Preferred Share
Each share 9.35% Preferred no par exchanged for (1) share 9.35% Preferred no par
Each share Adjustable Dividend Preferred no par exchanged for (1) share Adjustable Dividend Preferred no par
Each share Common 1¢ par exchanged for (0.8922) share Common 1¢ par
Fleet Financial Group, Inc. (New) name changed to Fleet Boston Corp. 10/1/99 which name changed to FleetBoston Financial Corp. 4/18/2000 which merged into Bank of America Corp. 4/1/2004

SHAWMUT NEEDHAM BANK, N.A. (NEEDHAM, MA)
Acquired by Shawmut Corp. 09/18/1987
Details not available

SHAWMUT OIL CO. (ME)
Charter revoked for failure to file reports and pay fees in 1924

SHAWMUT WINCHESTER BANK, N.A. (WINCHESTER, MA)
Merged into Shawmut County Bank, N.A. (Cambridge, MA) 06/26/1975
Each share Capital Stock $10 par exchanged for (2.5) shares Common $10 par
(See Shawmut County Bank, N.A. (Cambridge, MA))

SHAWNEE BK INC (WV)
Merged into WesBanco, Inc. 6/30/97
Each share Common $10 par exchanged for (10.094) shares Common $2.0833 par

SHAWNEE FINL SVCS CORP (PA)
Merged into Keystone Financial, Inc. 10/10/95
Each share Common $10 par exchanged for (6.25) shares Common $2 par
Keystone Financial, Inc. merged into M&T Bank Corp. 10/6/2000

SHAWNEE FLASH BRICK CO. (OH)
Charter cancelled for failure to file taxes 04/04/1918

SHAWNEE OIL CORP., INC. (KS)
Charter cancelled 10/15/59

SHAWNEE PETES LTD (ON)
Name changed to Semi-Tech Microelectronics Inc. 11/26/86
Semi-Tech Microelectronics Inc. recapitalized as International Semi-Tech Microelectronics Inc. 7/20/87 which name changed to Semi-Tech Corp. 9/14/94
(See Semi-Tech Corp.)

SHAWNEE POTTERY CO. (DE)
Each (100) shares Capital Stock $1 par exchanged for (1) share Capital Stock $100 par in 1951
Liquidation completed 6/20/63

SHAWNEE STONE CO.
Bankrupt in 1949

SHAWPRINT INC (MA)
Majority shares acquired by 00/00/1971
Public interest eliminated

SHAWS INDL CORP (AB)
Issue Information - 1,000,000 shares COM offered at $0.20 per share on 02/10/1997
Each (100,000) shares old Common no par exchanged for (1) share new Common no par 3/24/2003
Note: In effect holders received $0.20 cash per share and public interest was eliminated

SHAWS SUPERMARKETS INC (MA)
Common $1 par split (2) for (1) by issuance of (1) additional share in January 1984
Common $1 par split (6) for (1) by issuance of (5) additional shares in January 1986
Acquired by J. Sainsbury PLC 7/24/87
Each share Common $1 par exchanged for $30 cash

SHAYNEE CONS METALS & HOLDINGS LTD (ON)
Name changed 12/22/1970
Name changed from Shaynee Consolidated Mines Ltd. to Shaynee Consolidated Metals & Holdings Ltd. 12/22/1970
Charter cancelled for failure to pay taxes and file returns 02/20/1980

SHC CORP (IL)
Chapter 11 bankruptcy proceedings dismissed 04/24/2008
Stockholders' equity unlikely

SHEA CHEMICAL CORP. (TN)
Merged into Hooker Chemical Corp. 5/29/58
Each share $7 Preferred no par exchanged for (6.8667) shares Common $5 par
Each share Class A no par or Class C Common no par exchanged for (0.571428) share Common $5 par
Hooker Chemical Corp. acquired by Occidental Petroleum Corp. (Calif.) 7/24/68
(See Occidental Petroleum Corp. (Calif.))

SHEA DEV CORP (NV)
Each (12.2) shares old Common $0.001 par exchanged for (1) share new Common $0.001 par 03/02/2007
Name changed to Riptide Worldwide, Inc. 01/17/2008

SHEA'S HIPPODROME THEATRE, LTD. (ON)
Completely liquidated for cash 2/19/65

SHEA'S THEATRE CO., LTD. (ON)
Completely liquidated for cash 2/19/65

SHEAFFER (W.A.) PEN CO. (DE)
Each share Common $100 par exchanged for (20) shares Common no par 00/00/1928
Each share Common no par exchanged for (5) shares Common $1 par 00/00/1947
Each share Common $1 par exchanged for (1) share Class A $1 par and (1) share Class B Common $1 par 05/27/1957
Class A & B Common $1 par reclassified as Common $1 par 06/18/1965
Completely liquidated 04/05/1966
Each share Common $1 par exchanged for first and final distribution of $11.25 cash

SHEAR MINERALS LTD (AB)
Each share Common no par received distribution of (0.2) share Kaminak Gold Corp. Common no par payable 11/09/2005 to holders of record 11/08/2005
Recapitalized as Shear Diamonds Ltd. 12/30/2010
Each share Common no par exchanged for (0.1) share Common no par

SHEAR WIND INC (CANADA)
Reincorporated 03/01/2010
Place of incorporation changed from (AB) to (Canada) 03/01/2010
Acquired by Sprott Power Corp. 11/26/2012
Each share Common no par exchanged for $0.2260407 cash
Note: Unexchanged certificates will be cancelled and become without value 11/26/2018

SHEARHART CORP (AB)
Merged into Midnorthern Appliance Inc. 5/12/2000
Each share Common no par exchanged for $1.58 cash

SHEARON PETROLEUMS LTD. (ON)
Charter revoked for failure to file reports and pay fees 8/29/60

SHEARSON CALIF MUNS INC (MD)
Name changed to SLH California Municipals Fund Inc. 12/15/88
SLH California Municipals Fund Inc. name changed to Shearson Lehman Brothers California Municipals Fund Inc. 8/10/90 which name changed to Smith Barney Shearson California Municipals Fund Inc. 8/2/93 which name changed to Smith Barney California Municipals Fund 10/14/94

SHEARSON FINL NETWORK INC (NV)
Old Common $0.001 par split (2) for (1) by issuance of (1) additional share payable 06/15/2007 to holders of record 06/15/2007 Ex date - 06/18/2007
Each share old Common $0.001 par exchanged for (0.005) share new Common $0.001 par 08/24/2007
Plan of reorganization under Chapter 11 Federal Bankruptcy Code effective 05/07/2009
No stockholders' equity

SHEARSON FUNDAMENTAL VALUE FD INC (WA)
Name changed to SLH Fundamental Value Fund, Inc. 12/15/1988
SLH Fundamental Value Fund, Inc. name changed to Shearson Lehman Brothers Fundamental Value Fund, Inc. 08/10/1990 which name changed to Smith Barney Shearson Fundamental Value Fund Inc. 08/02/1993 which name changed to Smith Barney Fundamental Value Fund Inc. (WA) 10/14/1994 which reincorporated in Maryland 05/24/1995 which name changed to Legg Mason Partners Fundamental Value Fund, Inc. 05/01/2006
(See Legg Mason Partners Fundamental Value Fund, Inc.)

SHEARSON GLOBAL OPPORTUNITIES FD (MD)
Name changed to SLH Global Opportunities Fund 12/15/1988
SLH Global Opportunities Fund name changed to Shearson Lehman Brothers Global Opportunities Fund 08/10/1990
(See Shearson Lehman Brothers Global Opportunities Fund)

SHEARSON HAYDEN STONE INC. (DE)
8% Conv. Sr. Preferred 10¢ par called for redemption 04/30/1976
Stock Dividend - 10% 08/31/1979
Name changed to Shearson Loeb Rhoades, Inc. 12/19/1979
Shearson Loeb Rhoades, Inc. merged into American Express Co. 06/29/1981

SHEARSON HIGH YIELD FD INC (MD)
Name changed to SLH High Yield Fund Inc. 12/15/1988
(See SLH High Yield Fund Inc.)

SHEARSON INCOME FD INC (DE)
Merged into Shearson High Yield Fund Inc. 05/01/1984
Details not available

SHEARSON INVESTORS FUND, INC. (DE)
Name changed to Shearson New Directions Fund, Inc. 1/12/81

SHEARSON LEHMAN BROS APPRECIATION FD (MD)
Name changed to Smith Barney Shearson Appreciation Fund Inc. 08/02/1993
Smith Barney Shearson Appreciation Fund Inc. name changed to Smith Barney Appreciation Fund Inc. 10/14/1994 which name changed to Legg Mason Partners Appreciation Fund, Inc. 05/01/2006
(See Legg Mason Partners Appreciation Fund, Inc.)

SHEARSON LEHMAN BROS CALIF MUNS FD INC (MD)
Name changed to Smith Barney Shearson California Municipals Fund Inc. 8/2/93
Smith Barney Shearson California Municipals Fund Inc. name changed to Smith Barney California Municipals Fund 10/14/94

SHEARSON LEHMAN BROS MANAGED MUNS FD (MD)
Name changed to Smith Barney Shearson Managed Municipals Fund Inc. 8/2/93
Smith Barney Shearson Managed Municipals Fund Inc. name changed to Smith Barney Managed Municipals Fund Inc. 10/14/94

SHEARSON LEHMAN BROS N Y MUNS FD (MD)
Name changed to Smith Barney Shearson New York Municipals Fund Inc. 08/02/1993
Smith Barney Shearson New York Municipals Fund Inc. name changed to Smith Barney New York Municipals Fund Inc. 10/14/1994
(See Smith Barney New York Municipals Fund Inc.)

SHEARSON LEHMAN BROS TELECOMMUNICATIONS TR (MA)
Acquired by Smith Barney Special Equities Fund 00/00/1996
Details not available
Completely liquidated 03/12/2004
Each share Common $0.001 par exchanged first and final distribution of $12.39 cash

SHEARSON LEHMAN BROTHERS HOLDINGS INC. (DE)
Name changed to Shearson Lehman Hutton Holdings Inc. 5/9/88
Shearson Lehman Hutton Holdings Inc. acquired by American Express Co. 8/10/90

SHEARSON LEHMAN HUTTON HLDGS INC (DE)
Acquired by American Express Co. 8/10/90
Each share Common 10¢ par exchanged for (0.48) share Common 60¢ par

SHEARSON LEHMAN MICH MUNS (MA)
Name changed to SLH Michigan Municipals 12/15/1988
(See SLH Michigan Municipals)

SHEARSON LEHMAN NEW YORK MUNICIPALS INC. (MD)
Name changed to SLH New York Municipals Inc. 12/15/88
SLH New York Municipals Inc. name changed to Shearson Lehman Brothers New York Municipals Inc. 8/10/90 which name changed to Smith Barney Shearson New York Municipals Fund Inc. 8/2/93 which name changed to Smith Barney New York Municipals Fund Inc. 10/14/94

SHEARSON LEHMAN OHIO MUNS (MA)
Name changed to SLH Ohio Municipals Fund 12/15/1988
(See SLH Ohio Municipals Fund)

SHEARSON LOEB RHOADES INC (DE)
Common 10¢ par split (4) for (3) by issuance of (1/3) additional share 08/28/1980
Common 10¢ par split (3) for (2) by issuance of (0.5) additional share 11/26/1980
Merged into American Express Co. 06/29/1981
Each share 5% Conv. Jr. Preferred no par exchanged for (23.7) shares Common 60¢ par
Each share Common 10¢ par exchanged for (1.3) shares Common 60¢ par

SHEARSON MANAGED MUNS INC (MD)
Name changed to SLH Managed Municipals Fund Inc. 12/15/88
SLH Managed Municipals Fund Inc. name changed to Shearson Lehman Brothers Managed Municipals Fund Inc. 8/10/90 which name changed to Smith Barney Shearson Managed Municipals Fund Inc. Fund Inc. 8/2/93 which name changed to Smith Barney Managed Municipals Fund Inc. 10/14/94

SHEARWATER EQUITY INC (GA)
Under plan of reorganization each share Common $100 par automatically became (1) INVESCO Institutional Series Trust Equity Fund Share of Bene. Int. no par 08/11/1987
INVESCO Institutional Series Trust name changed to Financial Series Trust 12/28/1990 which name changed to INVESCO Value Trust 07/01/1993
(See INVESCO Value Trust)

SHEARWATER INCOME INC (GA)
Under plan of reorganization each share Common $100 par automatically became (1) INVESCO Institutional Series Trust Income Fund Share of Bene. Int. no par 08/11/1987
INVESCO Institutional Series Trust name changed to Financial Series Trust 12/28/1990
(See Financial Series Trust)

SHEBA COPPER MINES LTD (BC)
Merged into Coast Falcon Resources Ltd. (BC) 07/07/1993
Each share Common no par exchanged for (0.1) share Common no par
Coast Falcon Resources Ltd. (BC) reorganized in Yukon as Inside Holdings Inc. 10/06/2000 which name changed to SHEP Technologies Inc. 10/07/2002
(See SHEP Technologies Inc.)

SHEBA MINES LTD (ON)
Capital Stock $1 par changed to no par 12/31/1970
Charter cancelled for failure to pay taxes and file returns 03/16/1976

SHEBA URANIUM MINING & EXPLORATION, INC. (UT)
Charter revoked for failure to file reports and pay fees 3/31/58

SHEBANDOWAN RES LTD (BC)
Name changed to Videtics International Corp. 1/28/87
(See Videtics International Corp.)

SHEBNOR MINES, LTD. (ON)
Charter cancelled for failure to pay taxes and file returns 3/12/69

SHECOM CORP (CO)
Administratively dissolved 9/23/2004

SHEDD-BARTUSH FOODS, INC. (MI)
Merged into Beatrice Foods Co. on a (0.5) for (1) basis 5/26/59
Beatrice Foods Co. name changed to Beatrice Companies, Inc. 6/5/84
(See Beatrice Companies, Inc.)

SHEEN MINERALS INC (BC)
Name changed to S.M.M. Enterprises Ltd. 02/19/1986
Each share Common no par exchanged for (1) share Common no par
S.M.M. Enterprises Ltd. name changed to Acuvision Systems Inc. (BC) 02/20/1987 which reincorporated in Delaware 09/15/1993 which recapitalized as International Acuvision Systems Inc. 08/27/1991 which name changed to AcuBid.Com, Inc. 03/18/1999 which name changed to Asia Web Holdings, Inc. 06/01/2000 which name changed to Case Financial, Inc. 05/22/2002
(See Case Financial, Inc.)

SHEEP CREEK GOLD MINES LTD.
Name changed to Sheep Creek Mines Ltd. 03/01/1956
Sheep Creek Mines Ltd. name changed to Aetna Investment Corp. Ltd. 09/01/1965 which name changed to Aetna-Goldale Investments Ltd. 08/02/1972 which reorganized as Goldale Investments Ltd. (BC) 06/30/1977 which reincorporated in Ontario 10/12/1977 which name changed to Viner (E.A.) Holdings Ltd. 11/14/1986 which name changed to Fahnestock Viner Holdings Inc. 06/28/1988 which name changed to Oppenheimer Holdings Inc. (ONT) 09/02/2003 which reincorporated in Canada 05/11/2005 which reincorporated in Delaware 05/11/2009

SHEEP CREEK MINES LTD. (BC)
Name changed to Aetna Investment Corp. Ltd. 09/01/1965
Aetna Investment Corp. Ltd. name changed to Aetna-Goldale Investments Ltd. 08/02/1972 which reorganized as Goldale Investments Ltd. 06/30/1977 which reincorporated in Ontario 10/12/1977 which name changed to Viner (E.A.) Holdings Ltd. 11/14/1986 which name changed to Fahnestock Viner Holdings Inc. 06/28/1988 which name changed to Oppenheimer Holdings Inc. (ONT) 09/02/2003 which reincorporated in Canada 05/11/2005 which reincorporated in Delaware 05/11/2009

SHEEPROCK INVESTMENTS INC. (UT)
Name changed to New Sheeprock Investments, Inc. 10/17/85
(See New Sheeprock Investments, Inc.)

SHEER ENERGY INC (AB)
Name changed to CYGAM Energy Inc. 10/25/2005
(See CYGAM Energy Inc.)

SHEFA VENTURES LTD (NV)
Reorganized under the laws of Delaware as Flyfaire International, Inc. 03/10/1987
Each share Common $0.001 par exchanged for (0.05) share Common 2¢ par
(See Flyfaire International, Inc.)

SHEFFIELD EXPL INC (CO)
Each share old Common 1¢ par exchanged for (0.1) share new Common 1¢ par 11/16/87
Reorganized under the laws of Delaware 3/6/91
Each share $0.40 Sr. Conv. Preferred Class A 1¢ par exchanged for (0.2) share Common 1¢ par
Each share $0.50 Jr. Conv. Preferred Class B 1¢ par exchanged for (0.2) share Common 1¢ par
Each share new Common 1¢ par exchanged for (0.06) share Common 1¢ par
Sheffield Exploration Co., Inc. (DE) merged into Transmontaigne Oil Co. 6/4/96 which name changed to Transmontaigne Inc. 8/26/98
(See Transmontaigne Inc.)

SHEFFIELD EXPL INC NEW (DE)
Each share old Common 1¢ par

exchanged for (0.1) share new
Common 1¢ par 1/21/92
New Common 1¢ par split (10) for (1)
by issuance of (9) additional shares
1/22/92
Merged into Transmontaigne Oil Co.
6/4/96
Each share new Common 1¢ par
exchanged for (2.432599) shares
Common 1¢ par
Transmontaigne Oil Co. name
changed to Transmontaigne Inc.
8/26/98
(See Transmontaigne Inc.)

SHEFFIELD GROUP, INC. (MN)
Merged into Compac Computer
Systems, Inc. 12/31/69
Each share Common 5¢ par
exchanged for (0.5) share Common
10¢ par
Compac Computer Systems, Inc.
merged into Comserv Corp. in
November, 1971
(See Comserv Corp.)

SHEFFIELD INDS INC (FL)
Chapter 11 bankruptcy proceedings
converted to Chapter 7 on 8/23/93
Stockholders' equity unlikely

SHEFFIELD PHARMACEUTICALS INC (DE)
Reincorporated 09/30/1992
Reincorporated 03/15/1995
Name changed 06/27/1997
Place of incorporation changed from
(Canada) to (WY) 09/30/1992
Each share old Common no par
exchanged for (0.5) share new
Common no par 02/12/1993
State of incorporation changed from
(WY) to (DE) 03/15/1995
Name changed from Sheffield Medical
Technologies Inc. to Sheffield
Pharmaceuticals, Inc. 06/27/1997
Each share Common no par
exchanged for (0.004) share
Common $0.001 par 10/03/2005
Name changed to Pipex
Pharmaceuticals, Inc. 12/18/2006
Pipex Pharmaceuticals, Inc. name
changed to Adeona
Pharmaceuticals, Inc. (DE)
10/16/2008 which reincorporated in
Nevada 10/16/2009

SHEFFIELD RES INC (BC)
Reincorporated under the laws of
Nova Scotia as Globalstore.com,
Inc. 04/27/1999
Globalstore.com, Inc. name changed
to GSO Solutions, Inc. 03/24/2000
(See GSO Solutions, Inc.)

SHEFFIELD RES LTD (BC)
Reincorporated 04/06/2006
Place of incorporation changed from
(AB) to (BC) 04/06/2006
Acquired by Nevoro Inc. 07/29/2008
Each share Common no par
exchanged for (0.8) share Common
no par
Nevoro Inc. acquired by Starfield
Resources, Inc. 10/08/2009

SHEFFIELD STEEL CORP.
Acquired by American Rolling Mills
Co. in 1931
Details not available

SHEFFIELD STL CORP (DE)
Plan of reorganization under Chapter
11 Federal Bankruptcy Code
effective 8/14/2002
No stockholders' equity

SHEFFIELD STRATEGIC METALS INC (CANADA)
Name changed to Sheffield Medical
Technologies Inc. (Canada) 4/22/92
Sheffield Medical Technologies Inc.
(Canada) reincorporated in
Wyoming 9/30/92 which
reincorporated in Delaware 3/15/95
which name changed to Sheffield
Pharmaceuticals, Inc. 6/27/97 which

name changed to Pipex
Pharmaceuticals, Inc. 12/18/2006

SHEFFIELD WATCH CORP (DE)
Charter cancelled and declared
inoperative and void for
non-payment of taxes 3/1/77

SHELBOURNE HOTEL CO. (IL)
Each share Common no par
exchanged for (5) shares Common
$1 par in 1944
Merged into East End Park Hotel, Inc.
in 1953
Each share Common $1 par, held by
owners of more than (100) shares,
exchanged for (1) share new
Common no par
Each share Common $1 par, held by
owners of (100) shares or less,
exchanged for (1) share new 4%
Preferred $90 par
East End Park Hotel, Inc. was
liquidated in 1954

SHELBOURNE PPTYS I INC (DE)
Liquidation completed
Each share Common 1¢ par received
initial distribution of $4.50 cash
payable 11/21/2002 to holders of
record 11/15/2002 Ex date -
11/13/2002
Each share Common 1¢ par received
second distribution of $3.50 cash
payable 1/31/2003 to holders of
record 1/23/2003 Ex date -
1/21/2003
Each share Common 1¢ par received
third distribution of $52 cash
payable 3/18/2003 to holders of
record 3/10/2003 Ex date -
3/19/2003
Each share Common 1¢ par received
fourth distribution of $2.82 cash
payable 7/9/2003 to holders of
record 6/30/2003 Ex date -
6/26/2003
Each share Common 1¢ par received
fifth distribution of $3 cash payable
8/21/2003 to holders of record
8/11/2003 Ex date - 8/7/2003
Each share Common 1¢ par received
sixth distribution of $1.52 cash
payable 1/8/2004 to holders of
record 12/26/2003
Assets transferred to Shelbourne I
Liquidating Trust and Common 1¢
par reclassified as Units of Bene.
Int. 1¢ par 4/30/2004
Each Unit of Bene. Int. 1¢ par
received seventh distribution of
$10.16 cash payable 11/29/2004 to
holders of record 11/29/2004
Each Unit of Bene. Int. 1¢ par
received eighth and final distribution
of $0.81 cash payable 12/20/2004 to
holders of record 12/20/2004
Note: Certificates were not required to
be surrendered and are without
value

SHELBOURNE PPTYS II INC (DE)
Liquidation completed
Each share Common 1¢ par received
initial distribution of $14 cash
payable 11/21/2002 to holders of
record 11/15/2002 Ex date -
11/13/2002
Each share Common 1¢ par received
second distribution of $14.50 cash
payable 01/31/2003 to holders of
record 01/23/2003 Ex date -
02/03/2003
Each share Common 1¢ par received
third distribution of $30 cash
payable 03/18/2003 to holders of
record 03/10/2003 Ex date -
03/19/2003
Each share Common 1¢ par received
fourth distribution of $6.75 cash
payable 07/09/2003 to holders of
record 06/30/2003 Ex date -
07/10/2003
Assets transferred to Shelbourne II
Liquidating Trust and Common 1¢

par reclassified as Units of Bene.
Int. 1¢ par 04/30/2004
Each Unit of Bene. Int. 1¢ par
received fifth distribution of $10.26
cash payable 11/29/2004 to holders
of record 11/29/2004
Each Unit of Bene. Int. 1¢ par
received sixth and final distribution
of $11.40 cash payable 01/31/2005
to holders of record 01/31/2005
Note: Certificates were not required to
be surrendered and are without
value

SHELBOURNE PPTYS III INC (DE)
Liquidation completed
Each share Common 1¢ par received
initial distribution of $8.25 cash
payable 11/21/2002 to holders of
record 11/15/2002
Each share Common 1¢ par received
second distribution of $2.50 cash
payable 1/31/2003 to holders of
record 1/23/2003 Ex date -
1/21/2003
Each share Common 1¢ par received
third distribution of $36 cash
payable 3/18/2003 to holders of
record 3/10/2003 Ex date -
3/19/2003
Each share Common 1¢ par received
fourth distribution of $1.90 cash
payable 7/9/2003 to holders of
record 6/30/2003 Ex date -
6/26/2003
Each share Common 1¢ par received
fifth distribution of $13.21 cash
payable 1/8/2004 to holders of
record 12/26/2003
Assets transferred to Shelbourne III
Liquidating Trust and Common 1¢
par reclassified as Units of Bene Int.
1¢ 4/30/2004
Each Unit of Bene. Int. 1¢ par
received sixth distribution of $5.93
cash payable 6/14/2004 to holders
of record 6/14/2004
Each Unit of Bene. Int. 1¢ par
received seventh and final
distribution of $0.32 cash payable
11/29/2004 to holders of record
11/29/2004
Note: Certificates were not required to
be surrendered and are without
value

SHELBOURNE RLTY & CONSTR CORP (DE)
Merged into Leasing Credit Corp.
(New) 1/1/84
Each share Class A Common 10¢ par
exchanged for (1.09) shares
Common 10¢ par
(See Leasing Credit Corp. (New))

SHELBURNE, INC.
Succeeded by Shelburne Hotel Corp.
in 1939
No stockholders' equity

SHELBY BUSINESS FORMS, INC. (OH)
Acquired by GAF Corp. 8/25/69
Each share Common no par
exchanged for $45 cash

SHELBY CNTY BANCORP (IN)
Merged into Blue River Bancshares,
Inc. 6/26/98
Each share Common $1 par
exchanged for $56 cash

SHELBY FED SVGS BK (INDIANAPOLIS, IN)
Merged into First of America Bank
Corp. 09/28/1990
Each share Common $1 par
exchanged for (1.2674) shares
Common $10 par
First of America Bank Corp. merged
into National City Corp. 03/31/1998
which was acquired by PNC
Financial Services Group, Inc.
12/31/2008

SHELBY LOCKER SERVICE (IL)
Involuntarily dissolved 12/7/56

SHELBY SALESBOOK CO. (OH)
Each share old Common no par
exchanged for (3) shares new
Common no par 01/25/1952
Name changed to Shelby Business
Forms, Inc. 01/25/1963
(See Shelby Business Forms, Inc.)

SHELBY UNVL CORP (DE)
Recapitalized as NA American
Technologies, Inc. 4/3/2006
Each share Common 10¢ par
exchanged for (0.01) share Common
10¢ par
NA American Technologies, Inc. name
changed to JSX Energy, Inc.
8/30/2006

SHELBY UNVL CORP (MI)
Capital Stock $1 par split (3) for (1)
by issuance of (2) additional shares
9/11/70
Merged into Shelby Universal Corp.
(DE) 12/1/83
Each share Capital Stock $1 par
exchanged for (0.48) share Common
10¢ par and $2.50 cash
Shelby Universal Corp. (DE)
recapitalized as NA American
Technologies, Inc. 4/3/2006 which
name changed to JSX Energy, Inc.
8/30/2006

SHELBY VENTURES INC (BC)
Each share old Common no par
exchanged for (0.5) share new
Common no par 12/05/2011
Recapitalized as Solution Financial
Inc. 06/27/2018
Each share new Common no par
exchanged for (0.40799673) share
Common no par

SHELBY WILLIAMS INDUSTRIES, INC. (DE)
Ctfs. dated prior to 7/15/68
Completely liquidated 7/15/68
Each share Common $1 par
exchanged for first and final
distribution of (0.666666) share
Coronet Industries, Inc. Common
10¢ par
Coronet Industries, Inc. merged into
RCA Corp. 2/24/71
(See RCA Corp.)

SHELBY WILLIAMS INDS INC (DE)
Ctfs. dated after 12/8/83
Common 10¢ par split (4) for (3) by
issuance of (1/3) additional share
2/25/85
Common 10¢ par split (4) for (3) by
issuance of (1/3) additional share
2/11/86
Common 10¢ par changed to 5¢ par
in May 1986
Merged into Falcon Products, Inc.
6/17/99
Each share Common 10¢ par
exchanged for $16.50 cash

SHELDAHL CO (MN)
Common 25¢ par split (2) for (1) by
issuance of (1) additional share
09/16/1974
Common 25¢ par split (3) for (2) by
issuance of (0.5) additional share
02/04/1985
Common 25¢ par split (3) for (2) by
issuance of (0.5) additional share
04/24/1987
Plan of reorganization under Chapter
11 Federal Bankruptcy Code
effective 02/16/2004
No stockholders' equity

SHELDON LARDER MINES LTD (ON)
Each share old Common $1 par
exchanged for (4) shares new
Common $1 par 10/26/2007
Merged into Jubilee Gold Inc.
01/01/2010
Each share new Common $1 par
exchanged for (0.269) share
Common no par
Jubilee Gold Inc. merged into Jubilee
Gold Exploration Ltd. 01/25/2013

SHELDON PETE CO (DE)
Reincorporated 05/17/1973
Each share Common $1 par exchanged for (2) shares Common 50¢ par 08/07/1969
6% Conv. Preferred Ser. A $100 par called for redemption 03/31/1971
6% Conv. Preferred Ser. B $100 par called for redemption 03/31/1971
State of incorporation changed from (TX) to (DE) 05/17/1973
Acquired by Levinson Partners Corp. 06/12/1985
Each share Common 50¢ par exchanged for $0.70 cash

SHELDRICK MANUFACTURING CO. (MI)
Liquidation completed in 1955

SHELL BEACH PPTYS INC (LA)
Liquidation completed
Each share Capital Stock $1 par exchanged for initial distribution of $86 cash 05/07/1981
Each share Capital Stock $1 par received second and final distribution of $7.01 cash 10/15/1981

SHELL CDA LTD (CANADA)
Name changed 05/16/1975
Class A Common no par and Class B Common no par split (3) for (1) by issuance of (2) additional shares respectively 05/28/1973
Name changed from Shell Canada Ltd. to Shell Canada Ltd./Shell Canada Ltee. 05/16/1975
Floating Rate Preferred Ser. A called for redemption 11/13/1987
Class A Common no par split (3) for (1) by issuance of (2) additional shares payable 07/04/1997 to holders of record 06/30/1997
Class A Common no par reclassified as Common no par 04/26/2000
Common no par split (3) for (1) by issuance of (2) additional shares payable 06/30/2005 to holders of record 06/23/2005 Ex date - 06/21/2005
Acquired by Royal Dutch Shell plc 04/25/2007
Each share Common no par exchanged for $45 cash

SHELL EASTERN PETROLEUM PRODUCTS
Acquired by Shell Union Oil Corp. 00/00/1936
Details not available

SHELL ELECTRONICS MANUFACTURING CORP. (NY)
Adjudicated bankrupt 5/3/62
Common stock is worthless

SHELL FRONTIER OIL & GAS INC
Auction Preferred Stock Ser. A called for redemption at $100,000 on 8/1/2005
Auction Preferred Stock Ser. B called for redemption at $100,000 on 8/1/2005
Auction Preferred Stock Ser. C called for redemption at $100,000 on 8/1/2005
Auction Preferred Stock Ser. D called for redemption at $100,000 on 8/1/2005

SHELL INC (NV)
Name changed to Safe Idea, Inc. 11/00/2000
Safe Idea, Inc. name changed to Bloodhound Search Technologies, Inc. 12/27/2005
(See Bloodhound Search Technologies, Inc.)

SHELL INVTS LTD (ON)
5.50% 1st Preference $20 par called for redemption 12/01/1972
Public interest eliminated

SHELL OIL CO (DE)
Each share Common $15 par exchanged for (2) shares Common $7.50 par 00/00/1954
Common $7.50 par changed to $1 par and (1) additional share issued 01/12/1960
Common $1 par split (2) for (1) by issuance of (1) additional share 05/16/1977
Common $1 par split (2) for (1) by issuance of (1) additional share 06/16/1980
Stock Dividend - 10% 10/16/1956
Merged into Testa Corp. 06/07/1985
Each share Common $1 par exchanged for $58 cash
Note: Option to receive an additional $2 cash per share by waiver of appraisal rights expired 07/01/1985

SHELL OIL CO CDA LTD (CANADA)
Name changed to Shell Canada Ltd. 7/1/63
Shell Canada Ltd. name changed to Shell Canada Ltd./Shell Canada Ltee. 5/16/75
(See Shell Canada Ltd./Shell Canada Ltee.)

SHELL TRANS & TRADING PLC (ENGLAND)
5% 1st Preference £1 par reclassified as 5-1/2% 1st Preference £1 par 04/01/1959
Ordinary £1 par changed to 5s par and (3) additional shares issued 12/19/1961
Ordinary 5s par, American Shares for Ordinary 5s par and New York Shares for Ordinary 5s par changed to 25p par per currency change 02/15/1971
Sponsored ADR's for Ordinary 25p par split (2) for (1) by issuance of (1) additional share 06/30/1979
New York Shares for Ordinary 25p par split (2) for (1) by issuance of (1) additional share 06/30/1979
Ordinary 25p par split (2) for (1) by issuance of (1) additional share 07/30/1979
Each New York Share for Ordinary 25p par exchanged for (2) Sponsored ADR's for Ordinary 25p par 12/12/1988
Ordinary 25p par split (3) for (1) by issuance of (2) additional shares 12/12/1988
Sponsored ADR's for Ordinary 25p par split (3) for (1) by issuance of (2) additional shares 12/12/1988
New York Share basis changed from (1:4) to (1:6) 12/12/1988
Ordinary 25p par split (3) for (1) by issuance of (2) additional shares payable 06/30/1997 to holders of record 06/27/1997
Sponsored ADR's for Ordinary 25p par split (3) for (1) by issuance of (2) additional shares payable 06/30/1997 to holders of record 06/27/1997
Stock Dividends - 20% Ordinary Shares 07/01/1954; 20% American Shares 08/11/1954; 25% Ordinary Shares 07/17/1956; 20% Ordinary Shares 08/04/1961; 20% American Shares 10/20/1961; 20% New York Shares 08/10/1961; 20% Ordinary Shares 02/07/1964; 20% American Shares 03/25/1964; 20% New York Shares 02/20/1964
Merged into Royal Dutch Shell PLC 07/20/2005
Each Sponsored ADR for Ordinary 25p par exchanged for (0.86199919) Sponsored ADR for Class B Shares 25p par

SHELL UNION OIL CORP.
Name changed to Shell Oil Co. in 1949
(See Shell Oil Co.)

SHELL URANIUM INC. (UT)
Recapitalized as Canada-Ute Uranium Corp. 11/15/56
Each share Capital Stock 1¢ par exchanged for (0.01) share Capital Stock $1 par
Canada-Ute Uranium Corp. merged into Globe Minerals, Inc. 3/7/69 which recapitalized as Globe Inc. 10/16/70
(See Globe Inc.)

SHELLBRIDGE OIL & GAS INC (BC)
Acquired by True Energy Trust 06/23/2006
Each share Common no par exchanged for (0.14) Trust Unit no par
True Energy Trust reorganized as Bellatrix Exploration Ltd. 11/02/2009

SHELLCASE LTD (ISRAEL)
Acquired by Tessera Technologies, Inc. 12/27/2005
Details not available

SHELLER GLOBE CORP (OH)
Merged 12/30/66
Stock Dividends - 50% 2/46; 100% 6/15/50
Merged from Sheller Manufacturing Corp. (IN) to Sheller-Globe Corp. 12/30/66
Each share Common $1 par exchanged for (0.7289) share $1.35 Conv. Preferred no par and (0.8575) share Common no par
Common no par split (3) for (2) by issuance of (0.5) additional share 9/1/72
$1.35 Conv. Preferred no par called for redemption 3/11/83
$1.40 Conv. Preferred no par called for redemption 4/7/86
$3 Conv. Preferred no par called for redemption 4/7/86
Acquired by a group of investors 6/11/86
Each share Common no par exchanged for $15 principal amount of Jr. Subord. Notes due 6/1/2001 and $39 cash

SHELLEY MFG CO (FL)
Merged into Alco Standard Corp. 09/29/1971
Each share Common 10¢ par exchanged for (1.0509) shares Common no par
Each share Common 10¢ par received second distribution of (0.021834) share Common no par 10/12/1972
Each share Common 10¢ par received third and final distribution of (0.022712) share Common no par 07/18/1975
Alco Standard Corp. name changed to IKON Office Solutions, Inc. 01/24/1997
(See IKON Office Solutions, Inc.)

SHELLEY ROBERT PRODTNS LTD (NY)
Name changed to National Cultural Industries, Inc. 07/28/1972
National Cultural Industries, Inc. name changed to Big Rock Oil & Gas Co., Inc. 09/09/1974 which name changed to Resort Resource Group, Inc. 10/03/1986 which name changed to Asia American Industries, Inc. 03/20/1990
(See Asia American Industries, Inc.)

SHELLEY URETHANE INDUSTRIES, INC. (CA)
Name changed to Urethane Industries International, Inc. 10/19/61 which name changed to American Urethane, Inc. 9/20/62
American Urethane, Inc. completely liquidated 9/23/66

SHELLMAR PRODUCTS CORP. (DE)
Common no par changed to $6 par 00/00/1949
Name changed to General Package Corp. 00/00/1953
General Package Corp. merged into Diamond Match Co. 05/31/1955 which name changed to Diamond Gardner Corp. 11/04/1957 which name changed to Diamond National Corp. 09/28/1959 which name changed to Diamond International Corp. 10/29/1964
(See Diamond International Corp.)

SHELLS CITY INC (FL)
Merged into Hill Bros., Inc. 08/27/1971
Each share Common 25¢ par exchanged for (0.666667) share Common 5¢ par
(See Hill Bros., Inc.)

SHELLS SEAFOOD RESTAURANTS INC (DE)
Chapter 11 bankruptcy proceedings converted to Chapter 7 on 09/24/2008
No stockholders' equity

SHELTER COMPONENTS CORP (IN)
Common 1¢ par split (5) for (4) by issuance of (0.25) additional share 12/28/1992
Common 1¢ par split (3) for (2) by issuance of (0.5) additional share 03/08/1994
Common 1¢ par split (5) for (4) by issuance of (0.25) additional share payable 07/08/1996 to holders of record 06/24/1996 Ex date - 07/09/1996
Merged into Kevco, Inc. 01/16/1998
Each share Common 1¢ par exchanged for $17.50 cash

SHELTER COMPONENTS INC (IN)
Merged into Shelter Components Corp. 2/5/88
Each share Common no par exchanged for (0.797) share Common 1¢ par and $3.64 cash
(See Shelter Components Corp.)

SHELTER CORP AMER INC (MN)
Common 10¢ par split (2) for (1) by issuance of (1) additional share 9/15/72
Merged into Bor-Son Construction, Inc. 9/14/88
Each share Common 10¢ par exchanged for $1.45 cash

SHELTER GOLD LTD (BC)
Name changed to Shelter Oil & Gas Ltd. (BC) 12/22/1976
Shelter Oil & Gas Ltd. (BC) reincorporated in Alberta 11/09/1984 which merged into Tesco Corp. 12/01/1993 which merged into Nabors Industries Ltd. 12/15/2017

SHELTER HYDROCARBONS LTD (AB)
Merged into Skill Resources Ltd. 8/17/83
Each share Conv. Class A $5 par exchanged for (1) share Class B Preferred $5 par
Each share Common no par exchanged for (1) share Common no par
Skill Resources Ltd. recapitalized as Unicorp Resources Ltd. 6/27/84 which merged into Asamera Inc. 5/1/86 which was acquired by Gulf Canada Resources Ltd. 8/4/88
(See Gulf Canada Resources Ltd.)

SHELTER OIL & GAS LTD (AB)
Reincorporated 11/9/84
Place of incorporation changed from (BC) to (AB) 11/09/1984
Each share 10% 1st Preferred Ser. A $20 par converted into (86.765) shares Common no par 02/07/1991
Merged into Tesco Corp. 12/1/93
Each share Common no par exchanged for (0.25) share Common no par
Tesco Corp. merged into Nabors Industries Ltd. 12/15/2017

SHELTER RES CORP (DE)
Each share Common $1 par

exchanged for (0.02) share Common
1¢ par 07/26/1985
Liquidating plan of reorganization
under Chapter 11 Federal
Bankruptcy proceedings confirmed
07/25/1985
No stockholders' equity

SHELTERED OAK RES CORP (BC)
Merged into Foundation Resources
Inc. 04/10/2013
Each share Common no par
exchanged for (0.16666667) share
Common no par
Foundation Resources Inc.
recapitalized as Birch Hill Gold
Corp. 10/28/2013 which merged into
Canoe Mining Ventures Corp.
06/04/2014

SHELTON BANCORP INC (DE)
Merged into Webster Financial Corp.
11/01/1995
Each share Common $1 par
exchanged for (0.92) share Common
1¢ par

SHELTON CANADA CORP (AB)
Merged into Petrosibir AB 12/31/2009
Each share Common no par
exchanged for (2.708) shares Series
B
Note: Unexchanged certificates were
cancelled and became without value
12/21/2016

SHELTON SVGS BK (SHELTON, CT)
Name changed 01/25/1988
Name changed from Shelton Savings
& Loan Association Inc. (CT) to
Shelton Savings Bank (Shelton, CT)
01/25/1988
Common $1 par split (3) for (2) by
issuance of (0.5) additional share
05/09/1988
Under plan of reorganization each
share Common $1 par automatically
became (1) share Shelton Bancorp
Inc. Common $1 par 02/14/1989
Shelton Bancorp Inc. merged into
Webster Financial Corp. 11/01/1995

SHELTON-WARREN OIL CO. (NM)
Charter forfeited for non-payment of
franchise taxes 8/29/61

SHENANDOAH CORP. (DE)
Merged into Atlas Corp. 10/31/1936
Each share $3 Preference exchanged
for (1) share 6% Preferred $50 par
and (0.4) share Common $5 par
Each share Common exchanged for
(0.17) share Common $5 par
(See Atlas Corp.)

SHENANDOAH CORP (WV)
Merged into Kenton Corp. 08/31/1977
Each share Common 50¢ par
exchanged for $9.25 cash

**SHENANDOAH FED SVGS BK
(MARTINSBURG, WV)**
Name changed in January 1986
Name changed from Shenandoah
Federal Savings & Loan Association
to Shenandoah Federal Savings
Bank (Martinsburg, WV) in January
1986 Bank closed 10/15/93
No stockholders' equity

SHENANDOAH GAS CO (VA)
Acquired by Washington Gas Light
Co. 09/01/1971
Each share Common $1 par
exchanged for $6.50 cash

**SHENANDOAH NATL BK
(STAUNTON, VA)**
Stock Dividends - 10% payable
07/31/2000 to holders of record
06/30/2000 Ex date - 08/21/2000;
10% payable 07/31/2001 to holders
of record 06/30/2001; 10% payable
07/31/2002 to holders of record
06/28/2002 Ex date - 07/29/2002;
10% payable 10/31/2003 to holders
of record 09/30/2003 Ex date -
11/03/2003
Merged into Carter Bank & Trust
(Martinsville, VA) 12/29/2006

Each share Common $5 par
exchanged for (3.461) shares
Common

SHENANDOAH OIL CORP (TX)
Stock Dividend - 100% 06/30/1971
Liquidation completed
Each share Common $1 par
exchanged for initial distribution of
$20 cash 06/08/1979
Each share Common $1 par received
second distribution of $15 cash
08/20/1979
Each share Common $1 par received
third distribution of $2 cash
11/05/1979
Each share Common $1 par received
fourth distribution of $0.40 cash
10/06/1980
Each share Common $1 par received
fifth distribution of $0.75 cash
01/12/1982
Each share Common $1 par received
sixth distribution of $0.50 cash
12/15/1982
Note: Liquidation reported completed
in 1984 further details unavailable

SHENANDOAH RES LTD (BC)
Delisted from Vancouver Stock
Exchange 11/03/1992

SHENANDOAH RES LTD CDA (AB)
Placed in receivership 09/17/2002
Stockholders' equity unlikely

**SHENANDOAH TELEPHONE CO.
(VA)**
Reorganized as Shenandoah
Telecommunications Co. 8/5/81
Each share Capital Stock $20 par
exchanged for (2) shares Common
$10 par

**SHENANDOAH VALLEY NATL BK
(WINCHESTER, VA)**
Stock Dividend - 50% 02/22/1972
Merged into First American Bank of
Virginia (McLean, VA) 12/31/1983
Each share Common $10 par
exchanged for (3) shares Common
$10 par
*(See First American Bank of Virginia
(McLean, VA))*

SHENANGO GOLD MINES LTD. (ON)
Acquired by Shenango Mining Co.
Ltd. on a (1) for (3) basis in 1941
(See Shenango Mining Co. Ltd.)

SHENANGO MINING CO., LTD. (ON)
Charter cancelled and company
declared dissolved for failure to file
returns 12/19/55

**SHENANGO VALLEY WATER CO
(PA)**
5% Preferred $100 par called for
redemption at $110 on 9/1/2001

SHENG YING ENTMT CORP (NV)
Reorganized as Vitalibis, Inc.
02/08/2018
Each share Common $0.001 par
exchanged for (1.5) shares Common
$0.001 par

SHENGAS CORP (VA)
6% Preferred $25 par called for
redemption 04/01/1978
Public interest eliminated

SHENGDATECH INC (NV)
Plan of reorganization under Chapter
11 Federal Bankruptcy proceedings
effective 10/17/2012
Assets transferred to ShengdaTech
Liquidating Trust which made a first
and final distribution 10/18/2016
Details not available

SHENGRUI RES CO LTD (NV)
Name changed to Richland
Resources Corp. 04/18/2011

SHENK INDUSTRIES, INC. (OH)
Adjudicated bankrupt 4/30/65
No stockholders' equity

SHENUL CAP INC (BC)
Reincorporated under the laws of
British Virgin Islands as

Underground Energy Corp. and
Common no par changed to USD
$0.01 par 08/22/2011

**SHENZHEN SPL ECONOMIC ZONE
REAL ESTATE & PPTYS GROUP
LTD (CHINA)**
ADR agreement terminated
02/24/2016
Each Sponsored ADR for Class B
Ordinary exchanged for (10) shares
Class B Ordinary
Note: Unexchanged ADR's will be
sold and the proceeds, if any, held
for claim after 02/27/2017

SHEP TECHNOLOGIES INC (YT)
Dissolved 04/17/2008
No stockholders' equity

**SHEPARD ELECTRIC CRANE &
HOIST CO.**
Reorganized as Shepard Nile Crane
& Hoist Corp. in 1929
*(See Shepard Nile Crane & Hoist
Corp.)*

SHEPARD INC (NV)
Common $0.001 par split (7) for (1)
by issuance of (6) additional shares
payable 12/27/2006 to holders of
record 12/22/2006 Ex date -
12/28/2006
Name changed to CellCyte Genetics
Corp. 02/16/2007

**SHEPARD NILES CRANE & HOIST
CORP (NY)**
Common no par changed to $25 par
00/00/1933
Each share Common $25 par
exchanged for (5) shares Common
$5 par 00/00/1947
Merged into Vulcan, Inc. 04/01/1971
Each share Common $5 par
exchanged for (2) shares $1 Conv.
Preferred Ser. AA $1 par
(See Vulcan, Inc.)

SHEPHARD INS GROUP LTD (BC)
Recapitalized as Collingwood Capital
Corp. 03/11/1999
Each share Common no par
exchanged for (0.2) share Common
no par
Collingwood Capital Corp. name
changed to Rainy River Resources
Ltd. 06/17/2005 which merged into
New Gold Inc. 10/16/2013

SHEPHERD CASTERS CDA LTD (ON)
Name changed to Shepherd Products
Ltd. 04/04/1973
(See Shepherd Products Ltd.)

SHEPHERD ELECTR INDS INC (NY)
Charter cancelled and proclaimed
dissolved for non-payment of taxes
12/16/68

SHEPHERD LAUNDRIES CO (TX)
Common $100 par changed to no par
00/00/1949
Name changed to Shepherd of
Beaumont Inc. 02/12/1991
(See Shepherd of Beaumont Inc.)

**SHEPHERD OF BEAUMONT INC.
(TX)**
Charter forfeited for failure to pay
taxes 02/02/1993

SHEPHERD PRODS LTD (ON)
Acquired by Apex Acquisition Corp.
12/20/1989
Each share Common no par
exchanged for $33 cash

**SHEPHERD SURVEILLANCE
SOLUTIONS INC (NV)**
Charter revoked for failure to file
reports and pay fees 11/01/1999

SHEPMYERS INVT CO (PA)
Merged into Smith Barney Muni Bond
Funds 04/20/2000
Each share Common 50¢ par
exchanged for (1.46827) shares
National Portfolio Class A
Smith Barney Muni Bond Funds name
changed to Smith Barney Muni

Funds 05/25/1994 which name
changed to Legg Mason Partners
Municipal Funds 04/07/2006
*(See Legg Mason Partners Municipal
Funds)*

SHEPPARD OIL CORP. (OK)
Charter revoked for failure to file
reports and pay fees 10/15/23

SHEPPARD RES INC (FL)
Involuntarily dissolved for failure to
maintain a resident agent
06/07/1988

SHERATON, INC. (MA)
Completely liquidated 5/1/61
Each share Common no par
exchanged for first and final
distribution of $43.50 cash

SHERATON BUILDINGS INC. (MA)
Liquidation completed 9/28/55

SHERATON-CADILLAC CORP. (MI)
Merged into Sheraton Corp. of
America on a (4) for (1) basis 3/1/60
Sheraton Corp. of America acquired
by International Telephone &
Telegraph Corp. (DE) 2/29/68 which
name changed to ITT Corp.
12/31/83 which reorganized in
Indiana as ITT Industries Inc.
12/19/95 which name changed to
ITT Corp. 7/1/2006

SHERATON CORP. (DE)
Under plan of merger name changed
to United States Realty-Sheraton
Corp. 5/17/46
United States Realty-Sheraton Corp.
name changed to Sheraton Corp. of
America which was acquired by
International Telephone & Telegraph
Corp. (DE) 2/29/68 which name
changed to ITT Corp. 12/31/83
which reorganized in Indiana as ITT
Industries Inc. 12/19/95 which name
changed to ITT Corp. 7/1/2006

SHERATON CORP AMER (NJ)
$1.25 Conv. Preferred called for
redemption 4/30/52
Each share Common $1 par
exchanged for (2) shares Common
50¢ par in 1954
Stock Dividends - 10% 8/1/55; 20%
3/1/57
Acquired by International Telephone &
Telegraph Corp. (DE) 2/29/68
Each share 4% Conv. Preferred $100
par exchanged for (0.14282) share
$4 Conv. Preferred Ser. K no par
and (1.48912) shares Common $1
par
Each share Common 50¢ par
exchanged for (0.05) share $4 Conv.
Preferred Ser. K no par and (0.5212)
share Common $1 par
International Telephone & Telegraph
Corp. (DE) name changed to ITT
Corp. 12/31/83 which reorganized in
Indiana as ITT Industries Inc.
12/19/95 which name changed to
ITT Corp. 7/1/2006

SHERATON GIBSON CORP. (OH)
Liquidated for cash 4/15/63

SHERATON HOTELS LTD. (CANADA)
Preferred $10 par called for
redemption 9/15/65
Public interest was eliminated

SHERATON LOUISIANA CORP. (MA)
Liquidation completed 7/27/59

SHERATON LTD. (CANADA)
7% Preferred $1 par called for
redemption 09/15/1965
Merged into South Side Development
Ltd. 00/00/1976
Each share Class A $20 par
exchanged for $235 cash

**SHERBROOK SBK SPORT CORP
(CANADA)**
Dissolved for non-compliance.
02/10/2014

SHERBROOKE STREET REALTY CORP.
Liquidation completed in 1953

SHERBURNE CORP (VT)
Common $50 par changed to $25 par 11/30/67
Reorganized under the laws of Delaware as S-K-I Ltd. 1/15/85
Each share Common $25 par exchanged for (1) share Common 10¢ par
(See S-K-I Ltd.)

SHERER GILLETT CO (IL)
Each share Common no par exchanged for (5) shares Common $1 par in 1947
Class A no par called for redemption 7/1/67
Completely liquidated 2/23/70
Each share Common $1 par exchanged for first and final distribution of (0.65122) share Kysor Industrial Corp. (MI) Common $1 par
Kysor Industrial Corp. (MI) reincorporated under the laws of Delaware 5/14/70 which incorporated again in Michigan 5/31/85
(See Kysor Industrial Corp. (MI))

SHERIDAN-ARGYLE HOTEL CO.
Liquidated in 1949

SHERIDAN BELMONT HOTEL CO (IL)
Each share Common no par exchanged for (15) shares Common $1 par 07/24/1958
Involuntarily dissolved by court order 11/14/1966
Stockholders' equity unlikely

SHERIDAN BRIAR APARTMENTS
Trust terminated 00/00/1950
Details not available

SHERIDAN-BROMPTON APARTMENTS LIQUIDATION TRUST
Property sold and liquidated in 1945

SHERIDAN BUILDING, INC. (IL)
Completely liquidated 5/13/44
Each Capital Stock Trust Ctf. no par exchanged for $9.97 cash

SHERIDAN COURT
Trust terminated in 1950

SHERIDAN-DEVON-LOYOLA INC. TRUST
Liquidated in 1950

SHERIDAN ENERGY INC (DE)
Merged into Calpine Corp. 10/04/1999
Each share Common 1¢ par exchanged for $5.50 cash

SHERIDAN FOSTER CO (IL)
Liquidation completed
Each share Common no par received initial distribution of $38 cash 02/03/1977
Each share Common no par received second and final distribution of $4.5687 cash 12/31/1980

SHERIDAN HEALTHCARE INC (DE)
Merged into Vestar/Sheridan Holdings, Inc. 5/5/99
Each share Common 1¢ par exchanged for $9.25 cash

SHERIDAN INDS INC (NV)
Reincorporated 12/01/1998
State of incorporation changed from (UT) to (NV) 12/01/1998
Recapitalized as Diabetex International Corp. 12/23/1998
Each share Common $0.002 par exchanged for (0.0025) share Common $0.002 par
Diabetex International Corp. recapitalized as Petrone Worldwide, Inc. 02/26/2014

SHERIDAN-LAWRENCE BLDG., INC. (IL)
Liquidation completed 11/5/56

SHERIDAN RESV INC (ON)
Name changed to Nevadabobs.com, Inc. 08/04/2000
Nevadabobs.com, Inc. name changed to Nevada Bob's International Inc. 08/27/2001 which name changed to Loncor Resources Inc. 12/02/2008

SHERIDAN ROSCOE APARTMENTS
Property sold in 1949

SHERIDAN SURF BLDG CORP (IL)
Recapitalized in 1965
Each VTC for 6% Preferred $10 par exchanged for (4) shares Common 10¢ par
Each share Class A Common no par or Class B Common no par exchanged for (3) shares Common 10¢ par
In process of liquidation
Each share Common 10¢ par exchanged for initial distribution of $8.07 cash 2/8/79
Details on subsequent distributions, if any, are not available

SHERIDANE DESIGNS LTD INC (NY)
Conv. Preferred Ser. A 10¢ par called for redemption 02/19/1979
Each share Common 5¢ par exchanged for (0.05) share Common 1¢ par 04/23/1981
Merged into Sheridane Designs Ltd., Inc. (DE) 05/01/1984
Each share Common $1 par exchanged for $150 cash

SHERIFF COLD STORAGE CO (OH)
Merged into Realty Corp. 12/01/1972
Each share Capital Stock no par exchanged for $130 cash

SHERIFF STREET MARKET & STORAGE CO. (OH)
Name changed to Sheriff Cold Storage Co. in 1952
(See Sheriff Cold Storage Co.)

SHERINDA INTL INC (DE)
Common 1¢ par split (3) for (1) by issuance of (2) additional shares 1/18/77
Name changed to North American Energy, Inc. 4/9/81
North American Energy, Inc. reorganized as ORA Electronics, Inc. 12/20/96

SHERITT-LEE MINES LTD. (BC)
Name changed to Vanalta Resources Ltd. 2/15/72
(See Vanalta Resources Ltd.)

SHERMAG INC (QC)
Under plan of reorganization each share Common no par exchanged for $0.03 cash 04/23/2010

SHERMAN ARMS
Trust terminated in 1950

SHERMAN CREEK MINES, INC. (WA)
Name changed 6/19/61
Name changed from Sherman Creek Uranium Mines, Inc. to Sherman Creek Mines, Inc. 7/19/61
Company advised out of business in 1976
Details not available

SHERMAN DEAN FD INC (DE)
Stock Dividend - 400% 02/28/1980
Voluntarily dissolved 03/13/2000
Details not available

SHERMAN LEAD CO.
Merged into Day Mines, Inc. on a (0.168) for (1) basis in 1947
Day Mines, Inc. merged into Hecla Mining Co. (Wash.) 10/20/81 which was reincorporated in Delaware 6/6/82

SHERMAN PRODUCTS, INC. (MI)
Liquidation completed 5/10/63

SHERMEN WSC ACQUISITION CORP (DE)
Name changed to Westway Group, Inc. 06/12/2009
(See Westway Group, Inc.)

SHERNETH CORP.
Name changed to Sherry-Netherland Hotel Corp. in 1951
(See Sherry-Netherland Hotel Corp.)

SHEROC CORP (MN)
Statutorily dissolved 10/4/91

SHEROOMAC MINING CORP. LTD. (ON)
Charter cancelled and declared dissolved for failure to file returns and pay fees 5/9/77

SHERPA HLDGS CORP (BC)
Recapitalized as Nubeva Technologies Ltd. 03/02/2018
Each share Common no par exchanged for (0.2) share Common no par

SHERRGOLD INC (ON)
Name changed to Lynngold Resources Inc. 8/2/88
(See Lynngold Resources Inc.)

SHERRITT INC (CANADA)
Name changed 06/24/1988
Name changed 07/05/1993
Capital Stock $1 par reclassified as Conv. Class A Capital Stock $1 par 05/16/1975
Conv. Class A Capital Stock $1 par reclassified as Common $1 par 05/08/1979
Conv. Class B Capital Stock $1 par reclassified as Common $1 par 05/08/1979
Name changed from Sherritt Gordon Mines Ltd. to Sherritt Gordon Ltd. 06/24/1988
Name changed from Sherritt Gordon Ltd. to Sherritt Inc. 07/05/1993
Name changed to Viridian, Inc. 04/22/1996
Viridian, Inc. merged into Agrium Inc. 12/10/1996 which merged into Nutrien Ltd. 01/02/2018

SHERRITT INTL CORP (NB)
Each Restricted Share no par received distribution of (1) Unit of Dynatec Corp. consisting of (1) share Common no par and (0.25) Common Stock Purchase Warrant expiring 02/27/1998 payable 10/16/1997 to holders of record 10/10/1997
Reincorporated under the laws of Ontario 08/01/2007

SHERRITT PWR CORP (NB)
Acquired by Sherritt International Corp. (NB) 03/28/2003
Each share Common no par exchanged for (1.45) Restricted Shares no par
Sherritt International Corp. (NB) reincorporated in Ontario 08/01/2007

SHERRY LEE GOLD MINES LTD. (ON)
Charter cancelled in 1952

SHERRY-NETHERLAND HOTEL CORP. (NY)
Completely liquidated
Each share Common 10¢ par stamped to indicate initial distribution of $14 cash 3/1/55
Each share Common 10¢ par stamped to indicate second distribution of (1) Ctf. of Part. Int. 5/26/55
Each share Common 10¢ par exchanged for third and final distribution of $2 cash 11/2/55
Each Ctf. of Part. Int. received distributions totaling $12.008 cash between 6/15/55 and 1/15/70
Each Ctf. of Part. Int. exchanged for final distribution of $10.7768 cash 1/16/70

SHERWIN WILLIAMS CDA INC (CANADA)
Name changed 12/12/1980
Each share Common $100 par exchanged for (5) shares Common no par 00/00/1929
Name changed from Sherwin-Williams Co. of Canada Ltd. to Sherwin-Williams Canada Inc. 12/12/1980
Common no par 100% acquired through purchase offer by Sherwin-Williams Co. as of 01/01/1981
$7 Preferred $100 par called for redemption 07/31/1992
Public interest eliminated

SHERWIN WILLIAMS CO (OH)
4% Preferred $100 par called for redemption 12/01/1965
$4.40 Conv. Preferred Ser. B no par called for redemption 04/15/1983
$4 Preferred Ser. A no par called for redemption 04/23/1984
Preferred Stock Purchase Rights declared for Common stockholders of record 02/06/1989 were redeemed at $0.0025 per right 06/06/1997 for holders of record 05/06/1997
(Additional Information in Active)

SHERWOOD BRANDS INC (NC)
Administratively dissolved 01/29/2013

SHERWOOD COPPER CORP (AB)
Non-Vtg. Ser. 1 Preferred no par called for redemption at $59 plus $0.13 accrued dividends on 01/03/2007
Merged into Capstone Mining Corp. 11/25/2008
Each share Common no par exchanged for (1.566) shares Common no par
Note: Unexchanged certificates were cancelled and became without value 11/25/2014

SHERWOOD CORP (DE)
Name changed 02/24/1985
Each share Common 10¢ par exchanged for (0.01) share Common 1¢ par 07/14/1976
Name changed from Sherwood Diversified Services, Inc. to Sherwood Corp. 02/24/1985
Recapitalized as Synpro Environmental Services Inc. 08/04/1994
Each share Common 1¢ par exchanged for (0.2) share Common 1¢ par

SHERWOOD FINL LTD (NV)
Recapitalized as Max Inc. 10/19/87
Each share Common $0.001 par exchanged for (1) share Common $0.001 par
(See Max, Inc.)

SHERWOOD GROUP INC (DE)
Name changed to National Discount Brokers Group, Inc. 12/12/1997
(See National Discount Brokers Group, Inc.)

SHERWOOD LEASING CORP (NY)
Common 10¢ par split (2) for (1) by issuance of (1) additional share 05/01/1969
Reincorporated under the laws of Delaware as Sherwood Diversified Services, Inc. 05/20/1970
Sherwood Diversified Services, Inc. name changed to Sherwood Corp. 02/24/1985 which recapitalized as Synpro Environmental Services Inc. 08/04/1994
(See Synpro Environmental Services Inc.)

SHERWOOD MED INDS INC (DE)
Merged into Brunswick Corp. 12/01/1976
Each share Common $1 par exchanged for (1.372213) shares Common no par

SHERWOOD MNG CORP (AB)
Reincorporated 07/20/2000
Name changed 11/09/2001
Place of incorporation changed from (BC) to (ALTA) 07/20/2000
Name changed from Sherwood Petroleum Ltd. to Sherwood Mining Corp. 11/09/2001
Recapitalized as Sherwood Copper Corp. 09/12/2005
Each share Common no par exchanged for (0.25) share Common no par
Preferred not affected except for change of name
Sherwood Copper Corp. merged into Capstone Mining Corp. 11/25/2008

SHERWOOD VENTURES INC (DE)
Each share old Common 1¢ par exchanged for (15) shares new Common 1¢ par 06/23/1998
Name changed to Sherwood Forest Ventures, Inc. 05/30/2007

SHES GOT NETWORK INC (NV)
Name changed to Green For Energy, Inc. 03/26/2010

SHESLAY MNG INC (BC)
Old Common no par split (1.1) for (1) by issuance of (0.1) additional share payable 11/05/2014 to holders of record 11/05/2014
Name changed to Alliance Growers Corp. 06/22/2015

SHEVLIN-HIXON CO.
Liquidated in 1951

SHEWAN COPPER MNG LTD (ON)
Charter cancelled for failure to pay taxes and file returns 03/16/1976

SHFL ENTMT INC (MN)
Acquired by Bally Technologies, Inc. 11/25/2013
Each share Common 1¢ par exchanged for $23.25 cash

SHIEGA RES CORP (YT)
Recapitalized as African Metals Corp. (Yukon) 1/17/2000
Each share Common no par exchanged for (0.5) share Common no par
African Metals Corp. (Yukon) reincorporated in British Columbia 1/4/2005

SHIELD CHEMICAL CORP. (NJ)
Adjudicated bankrupt 12/28/64
No stockholders' equity

SHIELD DEV LTD (CANADA)
Dissolved 11/14/1995
Details not available

SHIELD ENTERPRISES CORP (CO)
Recapitalized as Milestone Capital, Inc. (CO) 05/18/1990
Each share Common no par exchanged for (0.001) share Common no par
Milestone Capital, Inc. (CO) reorganized in Delaware as Telestone Technologies Corp. 08/26/2004
(See Telestone Technologies Corp.)

SHIELD GOLD INC (ON)
Name changed to Great Lakes Graphite Inc. 05/15/2014

SHIELD PETROLEUM CORP. (CANADA)
Merged into Signal Hill Energy Corp. 12/20/82
Each share Class A Common no par exchanged for (0.5) share Common no par
Signal Hill Energy Corp. recapitalized as Texas Petroleum Corp. (BC) 6/13/85 which recapitalized as North American Equity Corp. 3/7/89
(See North American Equity Corp.)

SHIELD RES LTD (BC)
Name changed to Precambrian Shield Resources Ltd. 3/1/74
(See Precambrian Sheild Resources Ltd.)

SHIELDTRON, INC. (DE)
Each share Common $1 par stamped to indicate distribution of (0.2) share Zimoco Petroleum Corp. Common 10¢ par 11/18/64
Recapitalized as Ocean Research Equipment, Inc. 3/8/68
Each share Stamped Common $1 par exchanged for (0.5) share Common 5¢ par
(See each company's listing)

SHIFF HEDGE FD INC (NY)
Name changed to Integrated Growth Fund, Inc. 11/28/1969
(See Integrated Growth Fund, Inc.)

SHIFRIN CORP (DE)
Name changed to Davin Computer Corp. 3/14/89
(See Davin Computer Corp.)

SHIFT NETWORKS INC (AB)
Assets sold for the benefit of creditors 11/30/2007
No stockholders' equity

SHIKISAI INTL INC (NV)
Name changed to Life Design Station International, Inc. 08/21/2007

SHILLELAGH VENTURES CHARTERED (UT)
Each share Common $0.001 par exchanged for (0.2) share Common $0.005 par 2/16/88
Merged into Micron Solutions Inc. 9/9/97
Each share Common $0.005 par exchanged for (0.2) share Common $0.001 par
Micron Solutions Inc. recapitalized as PanaMed Corp. 3/1/2002 which name changed to Endexx Corp. 7/8/2005

SHILLER CHEMS INC (DE)
Reincorporated 11/09/1970
State of incorporation changed from (NY) to (DE) 11/09/1970
Name changed to Adhesives & Chemicals, Inc. 08/05/1975

SHILLING RES INC (AB)
Struck off register for failure to file annual returns 03/01/1992

SHILOH RES INC (NV)
Charter permanently revoked 07/01/1988

SHILOH RES LTD (BC)
Struck off register and declared dissolved for failure to file returns 01/27/1995

SHIMA RES LTD (BC)
Struck off register and declared dissolved for failure to file returns 11/10/88

SHIMMER GOLD INC (NV)
Reorganized as Absolute Life Solutions, Inc. 09/03/2010
Each share Common $0.001 par exchanged for (10) shares Common $0.00001 par
Absolute Life Solutions, Inc. name changed to Infinity Augmented Reality, Inc. 03/07/2013
(See Infinity Augmented Reality, Inc.)

SHIMODA INTL SYS INC (BC)
Struck off register and declared dissolved for failure to file reports 12/17/1993

SHIMODA MARKETING INC (FL)
Common $0.001 par split (6) for (1) by issuance of (5) additional shares payable 10/24/2008 to holders of record 10/20/2008 Ex date - 10/27/2008
Voluntarily dissolved 10/08/2009
Details not available

SHIMODA RES HLDGS INC (NV)
Each share old Common $0.001 par exchanged for (0.03333333) share new Common $0.001 par 09/04/2001
SEC revoked common stock registration 07/26/2010

SHIN CORPS PLC (THAILAND)
Name changed 04/30/2001
Each old Sponsored ADR for Ordinary B10 par exchanged for (0.125) new Sponsored ADR for Ordinary B10 par 10/04/1999
New Sponsored ADR for Ordinary B10 par changed to B1 par and (9) additional ADR's issued payable 09/10/2001 to holders of record 08/31/2001
Name changed from Shin Corporations PLC to Shin Corp. PLC 04/30/2001
Name changed to Intouch Holdings PLC 04/28/2014

SHIN MITSUBISHI HEAVY INDS (JAPAN)
Name changed to Mitsubishi Heavy Industries Ltd. 06/01/1964
(See Mitsubishi Heavy Industries Ltd.)

SHIN SATELLITE PUB CO LTD (THAILAND)
Sponsored ADR's for Ordinary split (2) for (1) by issuance of (1) additional ADR payable 08/26/2004 to holders of record 08/23/2004
Ex date - 08/27/2004
Name changed to Thaicom PLC 06/27/2008
(See Thaicom PLC)

SHINAWATRA COMPUTER & COMMUNICATIONS PUB LTD (THAILAND)
Name changed 11/13/1992
Name changed from Shinawatra Computer Communications Co., Ltd. to Shinawatra Computer & Communications PLC 11/13/1992
Name changed to Shin Corporations PLC 06/11/1999
Shin Corporations PLC name changed to Shin Corp. PLC 04/30/2001 which name changed to Intouch Holdings PLC 04/28/2014

SHINAWATRA SATELLITE PUB LTD (THAILAND)
Name changed to Shin Satellite PLC 08/23/1999
Shin Satellite PLC name changed to Thaicom PLC 06/27/2008
(See Thaicom PLC)

SHINE HLDGS INC (CO)
SEC revoked common stock registration 07/14/2007
Stockholders' equity unlikely

SHINE MEDIA ACQUISITION CORP (DE)
Completely liquidated 03/10/2009
Each Unit exchanged for first and final distribution of $5.81 cash
Each share Common $0.0001 par exchanged for first and final distribution of $5.81 cash

SHINELL GOLD MINES, LTD. (ON)
Charter cancelled for failure to file reports and pay taxes 10/26/59

SHING MEI INTL INC (NV)
Name changed to Triad Pro Innovators, Inc. 01/25/2012

SHINHAN BK (KOREA)
Reorganized as Shinhan Financial Group Co., Ltd. 09/04/2001
Each Sponsored GDR for Common exchanged for (1) Sponsored ADR for Common KRW 5,000 par

SHINHAN FINL GROUP CO LTD (KOREA)
GDR agreement terminated 10/17/2003
Each Sponsored 144A GDR for Common exchanged for $38.829527 cash
(Additional Information in Active)

SHININGBANK ENERGY INCOME FD (AB)
Merged into PrimeWest Energy Trust 07/13/2007
Each Trust Unit no par exchanged for (0.62) new Trust Unit no par
(See PrimeWest Energy Trust)

SHININGTREE GOLD RES INC (ON)
Recapitalized as Shiningtree Resources Inc. 03/12/1987
Each share Common no par exchanged for (0.2) share Common no par
(See Shiningtree Resources Inc.)

SHININGTREE RES INC (ON)
Delisted from Canadian Dealer Network 12/31/1997

SHINN INDS INC (DE)
Merged into Macrodyne-Chatillon Corp. 04/01/1969
Each share Common 10¢ par exchanged for (0.4) share Conv. Preferred Ser. A $1 par and (0.6) share Common 10¢ par
Macrodyne-Chatillon Corp. merged into Macrodyne Industries, Inc. 01/01/1974
(See Macrodyne Industries, Inc.)

SHINSEGAE DEPT STORE CO LTD (KOREA)
Name changed to Shinsegae Co. Ltd. 03/16/2001

SHINTRON INC (MA)
Proclaimed dissolved for failure to file reports and pay fees 1/4/91

SHIPPERS CAR LINE CORP. (NY)
Each share 7% Preferred $100 par exchanged for (0.5) share 5% Preferred $100 par and $50 of 4% 10-Yr. Debentures in 1939
Each share Class A no par exchanged for (0.1) share 5% Preferred $100 par in 1939
Class B no par changed to Common $1 par in 1949
Merged into ACF Industries, Inc. on a (5) for (1) basis 5/31/56
(See ACF Industries, Inc.)

SHIPPERS DISPATCH INC (IN)
Class B Common $1 par reclassified as Common $1 par 2/15/69
Common $1 par split (2) for (1) by issuance of (1) additional share 8/27/69
Common $1 par split (3) for (2) by issuance of (0.5) additional share 10/20/72
Merged into Preston Trucking Co., Inc. 12/31/76
Each share Common $1 par exchanged for (0.666666) share Common $1 par
Preston Trucking Co., Inc. reorganized as Preston Corp. 12/31/83
(See Preston Corp.)

SHIPPETTE MOBILE HOMES, INC. (IA)
Charter cancelled for failure to file reports 4/30/73

SHIPPING CORP NEW ZEALAND CDA LTD (CANADA)
$2.19 Preferred Ser. A no par called for redemption 07/17/1987
Public interest eliminated

SHIPROCK INC (NV)
Name changed to Duska Therapeutics, Inc. 08/30/2004
Duska Therapeutics, Inc. name changed to Cordex Pharma, Inc. 01/28/2009
(See Cordex Pharma, Inc.)

SHIPROCK INDS INC (CO)
Under plan of merger each share Common 50¢ par exchanged for (0.1) share Common 25¢ par 12/31/64
Name changed to Quasar Sciences, Inc. 12/11/68

(See Quasar Sciences, Inc.)

SHIPROCK URANIUM CORP. (CO)
Name changed to Shiprock Industries, Inc. 5/1/56
Shiprock Industries, Inc. name changed to Quasar Sciences, Inc. 12/11/68
(See Quasar Sciences, Inc.)

SHIPS STORES INC (WA)
Charter cancelled and proclaimed dissolved for failure to pay fees 9/16/85

SHIRAZI CORP (NV)
Recapitalized as Surface Technologies Inc. 01/10/2003
Each share Common $0.001 par exchanged for (1/3) share Common $0.001 par
Surface Technologies Inc. recapitalized as BrandQuest Development Group, Inc. 10/30/2006 which name changed to Novus Acquisition & Development Corp. 07/27/2009

SHIRE ACQUISITION INC (CANADA)
Each Exchangeable Share no par exchanged for either (3) Shire plc (England & Wales) Ordinary share or (1) Sponsored ADR for Ordinary 5p par 02/12/2008
Note: Option to receive ADR's expired 02/12/2008
Shire plc (England & Wales) reincorporated in Channel Islands as Shire Ltd. 05/23/2008 which name changed to Shire plc 10/01/2008

SHIRE LTD (CHANNEL ISLANDS)
Name changed 11/25/2005
Reincorporated 05/23/2008
Name changed from Shire Pharmaceuticals Group PLC to Shire PLC 11/25/2005
Name change and place of incorporation changed from Shire PLC (England & Wales) to Shire Ltd. (Channel Islands) 05/23/2008
Name changed to Shire PLC 10/01/2008

SHIRE NATL CORP (DE)
Name changed to Stacy Industries, Inc. 06/20/1985
(See Stacy Industries, Inc.)

SHIREX ENTERPRISES LTD. (ON)
Merged into Xtra Developments Inc. 5/25/72
Each share Capital Stock no par exchanged for (0.25) share Capital Stock no par
Xtra Developments Inc. merged into Sumtra Diversified Inc. 8/30/78

SHIRKS MOTOR EXPRESS CORP. (DE)
Name changed to Norwalk Truck Lines, Inc. of Delaware 7/31/37
(See listing for Norwalk Truck Lines, Inc. of Delaware)

SHIRLEY ATLANTA INC (GA)
Name changed to Makover Investment Co., Inc. 05/02/1977
Makover Investment Co., Inc. merged into Scudder Managed Municipal Bonds 06/22/1979
(See Scudder Managed Municipal Bonds)

SHIRMAX FASHIONS LTD (CANADA)
Acquired by Reitmans (Canada) Ltd. 6/11/2002
Each share Common no par exchanged for $7 cash

SHIRREFFS WORSTED CO.
Adjudicated bankrupt in 1940
No stockholders' equity

SHIRRIFF-HORSEY CORP. LTD. (CANADA)
Name changed to Salada-Shirriff-Horsey Ltd. 6/28/57
Salada-Shirriff-Horsey Ltd. name changed to Salada Foods, Ltd.

2/5/62 which was acquired by Kellogg Co. 1/13/70

SHIRRIFF'S LTD. (CANADA)
Name changed to Shirriff-Horsey Corp. Ltd. in 1955
Shirriff-Horsey Corp. Ltd. name changed to Salada-Shirriff-Horsey Ltd. 6/28/57 which name changed to Salada Foods, Ltd. 2/5/62 which was acquired by Kellogg Co. 1/13/70

SHIRT SHED INC (DE)
Merged into Signal Apparel Co., Inc. 07/22/1991
Each share Common 1¢ par exchanged for (0.28571428) share Class A Common 1¢ par
(See Signal Apparel Co., Inc.)

SHIRTS UNLIMITED FRANCHISE INC (NY)
Name changed to TTI Industries, Inc. 04/04/1972
TTI Industries, Inc. merged into Peoples Telephone Co., Inc. 07/00/1987 which merged into Davel Communications, Inc. 12/23/1998
(See Davel Communications, Inc.)

SHIVA CORP (MA)
Issue Information - 2,400,000 shares COM offered at $15 per share on 11/17/1994
Common 1¢ par split (2) for (1) by issuance of (1) additional share payable 4/22/96 to holders of record 4/12/96
Merged into Intel Corp. 2/27/99
Each share Common 1¢ par exchanged for $6 cash

SHIVA VENTURES INC (BC)
Recapitalized as Royal Stratus Ventures Inc. 09/11/1992
Each share Common no par exchanged for (0.5) share Common no par
Royal Stratus Ventures Inc. name changed to MPI Holdings Inc. (BC) 06/01/1994 which reincorporated in Wyoming 06/24/1994
(See MPI Holdings Inc.)

SHIVASOFT INC (AB)
Name changed to Tigrsoft Inc. 03/25/1999
Tigrsoft Inc. recapitalized as Matrikon Inc. 04/17/2001
(See Matrikon Inc.)

SHL SYSTEMHOUSE INC (CANADA)
Common no par split (2) for (1) by issuance of (1) additional share 12/30/1986
Merged into MCI Communications Corp. 11/16/1995
Each share Common no par exchanged for $13 cash

SHL TELEMEDICINE LTD (ISRAEL)
ADR agreement terminated 08/07/2017
Each Sponsored ADR for Ordinary exchanged for $6.57455 cash

SHO-ME FINL CORP (DE)
Merged into Union Planters Corp. 12/31/97
Each share Common 1¢ par exchanged for (0.7694) share Common 1¢ par
Union Planters Corp. merged into Regions Financial Corp. (New) 7/1/2004

SHOAL PETE LTD (BC)
Recapitalized as Golden Dragon Resources Ltd. 02/16/1988
Each share Common no par exchanged for (0.4) share Common no par
Golden Dragon Resources Ltd. recapitalized as Canadian Golden Dragon Resources Ltd. 05/16/1994 which name changed to Trillium North Minerals Ltd. 11/05/2007 which recapitalized as White Metal Resources Corp. 06/04/2014

SHOCHET HLDG CORP (DE)
Name changed to Sutter Holding Co., Inc. 04/04/2002
Sutter Holding Co., Inc. name changed to CIC Holding Co., Inc. 12/06/2006 which recapitalized as Global Wear Ltd. 01/10/2008 which recapitalized as Sovereign Wealth Corp. 03/12/2008 which name changed to Lenco Mobile Inc. 02/25/2009
(See Lenco Mobile Inc.)

SHOE CARNIVAL INC (DE)
Common 10¢ par split (3) for (2) by issuance of (0.5) additional share 10/22/1993
Reincorporated under the laws of Indiana and Common 10¢ par changed to no par 07/16/1996

SHOE CITY CORP (DE)
Merged into Kinder Care Inc. 2/5/88
Each share Common 10¢ par exchanged for (1) share Common 50¢ par
Kinder-Care, Inc. name changed to Enstar Group, Inc. (DE) 11/6/89
(See Enstar Group, Inc. (DE))

SHOE CORP AMER (OH)
Each share Class A Common no par exchanged for (1.333333) shares Common $3 par 09/15/1956
Stock Dividends - 50% 02/17/1951; 40% 09/19/1960; 25% 07/10/1962
Reincorporated under the laws of Delaware as SCOA Industries Inc. (Old) and Common $3 par changed to $1 par 05/23/1969
SCOA Industries Inc. (Old) merged into SCOA Industries Inc. (New) 12/10/1985 which name changed to Hills Stores Co. 04/09/1987
(See Hills Stores Co.)

SHOE PAVILION INC (DE)
Issue Information - 2,000,000 shares COM offered at $7 per share on 02/23/1998
Chapter 11 bankruptcy proceedings dismissed 11/17/2009
No stockholders' equity

SHOE TOWN INC (DE)
Acquired by a management group 01/27/1988
Each share Common 1¢ par exchanged for $9.75 cash

SHOE WORLD INC (DE)
Adjudicated bankrupt 07/12/1973
Stockholders' equity unlikely

SHOGUN CAP CORP (BC)
Name changed to ICC International Cannabis Corp. (Old) 11/29/2016
ICC International Cannabis Corp. (Old) name changed to ICC Labs Inc. 12/21/2017

SHOGUN DEVS CORP (BC)
Name changed to ESTec Systems Corp. (BC) 05/11/1988
ESTec Systems Corp. (BC) reincorporated in Alberta 12/19/2005
(See ESTec Systems Corp.)

SHOGUN PPTYS CORP (BC)
Name changed to Cyberion Networking Corp. 11/21/1995
Cyberion Networking Corp. name changed to NexMedia Technologies Inc. 12/30/1998
(See NexMedia Technologies Inc.)

SHOLIA RES LTD (BC)
Merged into AXR Resources Ltd. 6/28/88
Each share Common no par exchanged for (0.2) share Common no par
AXR Resources Ltd. merged into Greater Lenora Resources Corp. 1/5/89
(See Greater Lenora Resources Corp.)

SHOLODGE INC (TN)
Common no par split (5) for (4) by issuance of (0.25) additional share 05/14/1993
Common no par split (4) for (3) by issuance of (1/3) additional share 03/28/1994
Company terminated common stock registration and is no longer public as of 01/24/2005

SHOMEE OIL CORP. (MO)
Charter forfeited for failure to file annual reports 1/1/55

SHOMEGA LTD (AUSTRALIA)
Acquired by Pacific Magazines & Printing Ltd. 06/26/1996
Details not available

SHONA ENERGY CO INC (BC)
Merged into Canacol Energy Ltd. 12/24/2012
Each share Class A Common no par exchanged for (0.10573) share new Common no par and $0.0896 cash
Note: Unexchanged certificates were cancelled and became without value 12/24/2016

SHONEYS INC (TN)
Name changed 10/21/76
Common $1 par split (3) for (2) by issuance of (0.5) additional share 10/22/71
Common $1 par split (3) for (2) by issuance of (0.5) additional share 9/18/75
Name changed from Shoney's Big Boy Enterprises, Inc. to Shoney's Inc. 10/21/76
Common $1 par split (4) for (3) by issuance of (1/3) additional share 10/14/77
Common $1 par split (3) for (2) by issuance of (0.5) additional share 10/12/78
Common $1 par split (4) for (3) by issuance of (1/3) additional share 10/14/80
Common $1 par split (4) for (3) by issuance of (1/3) additional share 10/12/81
Common $1 par split (4) for (3) by issuance of (1/3) additional share 3/10/83
Common $1 par split (4) for (3) by issuance of (1/3) additional share 1/18/85
Common $1 par split (5) for (4) by issuance of (0.25) additional share 7/25/86
Each share Common $1 par received distribution of $4 principal amount of 12% Subordinated Debentures due 7/1/2000 and $16 cash 8/3/88
Merged into Lone Star U.S. Acquisitions LLC 4/10/2002
Each share Common $1 par exchanged for $0.36 cash

SHONEYS SOUTH INC (TN)
Common 5¢ par split (5) for (4) by issuance of (0.25) additional share 10/1/84
Merged into TPI Enterprises, Inc. 9/14/88
Each share Common 5¢ par exchanged for $18.25 cash

SHONGUM CORP (DE)
Recapitalized 12/13/1988
For holdings of (199) shares or fewer each share Common 1¢ par exchanged for $0.09375 cash
For holdings of (200) shares or more each share Common 1¢ par exchanged for (0.5) share Common 2¢ par
Name changed to American Water Resources, Inc. 07/19/1989
(See American Water Resources, Inc.)

SHONI CORP. (WY)
Name changed to Allied Nuclear Corp. 4/20/68
Allied Nuclear Corp. liquidated for New Allied Development Corp.

8/1/79 which recapitalized as Consolidated Biofuels Inc. 8/1/2005

SHONI URANIUM CORP. (WY)
Recapitalized as Shoni Corp. 5/20/63
Each share Common 1¢ par exchanged for (0.05) share Common 20¢ par
Shoni Corp. name changed to Allied Nuclear Corp. 4/20/68 which liquidated for New Allied Development Corp. 8/1/79 which recapitalized as Consolidated Biofuels Inc. 8/1/2005

SHOOTING STAR TECHNOLOGIES INC (AB)
Name changed to Gimbel Vision International Inc. 07/02/1997
Gimbel Vision International Inc. name changed to Aris Canada Ltd. 10/16/2002
(See Aris Canada Ltd.)

SHOP & GO INC (FL)
Common 1¢ par split (3) for (2) by issuance of (0.5) additional share 10/02/1981
Common 1¢ par split (3) for (2) by issuance of (0.5) additional share 02/01/1982
Common 1¢ par split (3) for (2) by issuance of (0.5) additional share 10/24/1984
Stock Dividends - 10% 12/02/1974; 25% 12/09/1976; 25% 11/30/1979; 50% 03/28/1980
Merged into Circle K Corp. 09/20/1985
Each share Common 1¢ par exchanged for $16.50 cash

SHOP & SAVE 1957 LTD (CANADA)
Each share old Common no par exchanged for (2) shares new Common no par 09/25/1959
Stock Dividend - 10% 09/15/1958
Acquired by Oshawa Wholesale Ltd. 08/29/1969
Each share new Common no par exchanged for (0.5) share Class A no par and (0.25) Class A Stock Purchase Warrant
Oshawa Wholesale Ltd. name changed to Oshawa Group Ltd. 08/13/1971 which was acquired by Sobeys Canada Inc. 01/25/1999 which name changed to Sobeys Inc. 06/01/1999
(See Sobeys Inc.)

SHOP AT HOME INC (TN)
Each share Common $0.001 par exchanged for (0.04) share Common $0.0025 par 05/18/1991
Name changed to Summit America Television, Inc. 11/01/2002
(See Summit America Television, Inc.)

SHOP RITE FOODS INC (NM)
$2.04 Conv. Preferred $20.50 par called for redemption 02/17/1982
Common $5 par changed to $3.33-1/3 par and (0.5) additional share issued 07/10/1964
Common $3.33-1/3 par changed to no par 09/20/1979
Acquired by Furr's Inc. 03/31/1986
Each share Common no par exchanged for $4.75 cash

SHOP TELEVISION NETWORK INC (DE)
Liquidation completed
Each share Common no par received initial distribution of $0.60 cash 2/16/95
Each share Common no par exchanged for second and final distribution of $0.139 cash 3/9/99

SHOP TV INC (NV)
Recapitalized as Site2Shop.com, Inc. 02/23/1999
Each share Common $0.001 par exchanged for (0.1) share Common $0.001 par
Site2Shop.com, Inc. name changed to Intermedia Marketing Solutions, Inc. 04/20/2001
(See Intermedia Marketing Solutions, Inc.)

SHOPATHOMEKIDS COM INC (TX)
Name changed to Gulftex Energy Corp. 09/19/2001
Gulftex Energy Corp. name changed to Gulftex Partners, Inc. 09/09/2003
(See Gulftex Partners, Inc.)

SHOPCO, INC. (MN)
Name changed to Module Industries, Inc. 1/29/70

SHOPCO LAUREL CENTRE L P (DE)
Partnership dissolved 6/30/97
Details not available

SHOPCO REGL MALLS L P (DE)
Partnership dissolved 06/08/2000
Each Unit Limited Partnership Interest received first and final distribution of $105.66 cash
Note: Certificates were not required to be surrendered and are without value

SHOPKO STORES INC (WI)
Reincorporated 5/22/98
Secondary Offering - 6,557,280 shares COM offered at $25 per share on 06/26/1997
State of incorporation changed from (MN) to (WI) 5/22/98
Merged into SKO Group Holding Corp. 12/28/2005
Each share Common 1¢ par exchanged for $29.07 cash

SHOPNET COM INC (DE)
Stock Dividends - 10% payable 02/01/2000 to holders of record 01/20/2000; 20% payable 06/19/2000 to holders of record 05/19/2000
SEC revoked common stock registration 02/19/2010
Stockholders' equity unlikely

SHOPNOW COM INC (WA)
Issue Information - 7,250,000 shares COM offered at $12 per share on 09/28/1999
Name changed to Network Commerce Inc. 5/18/2000
(See Network Commerce Inc.)

SHOPPERS CARRIER SVCS INC (DE)
Common 1¢ par split (4) for (1) by issuance of (3) additional shares 10/03/1983
Name changed to CSI Tele-Marketing, Inc. 10/13/1983
CSI Tele-Marketing, Inc. name changed to Precision Target Marketing Inc. 11/14/1986
(See Precision Target Marketing Inc.)

SHOPPERS CITY LTD (CANADA)
Acquired by Loeb (M.) Ltd. 6/28/68
Each share Common no par exchanged for $5.50 cash

SHOPPERS DRUG MART CORP (CANADA)
Reincorporated 07/08/2002
Place of incorporation changed from (NB) to (Canada) 07/08/2002
Merged into Loblaw Companies Ltd. 03/31/2014
Each share Common no par exchanged for (0.7363) share Common no par and $26.53 cash

SHOPPERS WALLET INC (NV)
Reorganized as CBp Carbon Green, Inc. 11/29/2007
Each share Common $0.0001 par exchanged for (15) shares Common $0.001 par
CBp Carbon Green, Inc. name changed to Millennium Energy Corp. 03/26/2008
(See Millennium Energy Corp.)

SHOPPERS WORLD STORES INC (TX)
Name changed to 50-Off Stores, Inc. (TX) 09/15/1987
50-Off Stores, Inc. (TX) reincorporated in Delaware 12/22/1992 which name changed to Lot$off Corp. 06/16/1997
(See Lot$off Corp.)

SHOPPING AT HOME INC (DE)
Merged into OIA, Inc. 11/27/1987
Each share Common $0.0001 par exchanged for (0.16666666) share Common $0.0001 par
OIA, Inc. name changed to Biorelease Corp. 11/02/1992 which recapitalized as BRL Holdings, Inc. 07/02/2001 which name changed to Element 21 Golf Co. (DE) 10/18/2004 which reincorporated in Nevada as American Rare Earths & Materials, Corp. 07/20/2010

SHOPPING AT HOME TELEVISION NETWORK INC (DE)
Name changed to TVNET Inc. 09/03/1987
TVNET Inc. name changed to Vegas Chips Inc. 02/10/1989 which name changed to Skydoor Media & Entertainment Inc. 12/15/1995 which name changed to Ice Holdings, Inc. (DE) 10/09/1996 which reorganized in Nevada as Gaia Resources, Inc. 10/20/2006 which recapitalized as Ram Gold & Exploration, Inc. 02/08/2008 which name changed to DPollution International Inc. 08/31/2010 which recapitalized as Ecrid, Inc. 10/16/2017

SHOPPING BAG FOOD STORES (CA)
Merged into Von's Grocery Co. share for share 3/28/60
Von's Grocery Co. merged into Household Finance Corp. 12/15/69 which reorganized as Household International, Inc. 6/26/81

SHOPPING CENTERS CORP. (DE)
Common $2.50 par changed to $1.25 par and (1) additional share issued 4/28/61
Stock Dividend - 10% 9/9/60
No longer in existence having become inoperative and void for non-payment of taxes 10/1/65

SHOPPING COM (CA)
Merged into Compaq Computer Corp. 03/10/1999
Each share Common no par exchanged for $19 cash

SHOPPING COM LTD (ISRAEL)
Issue Information - 6,871,160 shares ORD offered at $18 per share on 10/25/2004
Merged into eBay Inc. 08/30/2005
Each share Ordinary ILS 0.001 par exchanged for $21 cash

SHOPPING SHERLOCK INC (FL)
Name changed to ASPi Europe, Inc. (FL) 05/12/2000
ASPi Europe, Inc. (FL) reincorporated in Delaware 12/19/2000 which changed to Sharps Elimination Technologies Inc. 05/06/2002 which name changed to Armagh Group Inc. 09/19/2002 which recapitalized as SmartVideo Technologies, Inc. 01/06/2003 which name changed to uVuMobile, Inc. 06/04/2007
(See uVuMobile, Inc.)

SHOPSMITH INC (OH)
Each share old Common no par exchanged for (1) share new Common no par to reflect a (1) for (500) reverse split followed by a (500) for (1) forward split 12/06/2005
Note: Holders of (499) or fewer pre-split shares received $0.27 cash per share
Stock Dividend - 50% 09/15/1989
Merged out of existence 04/13/2009

Detals not available

SHOPSS COM INC (UT)
Name changed to AccessTel, Inc. 02/15/2001
(See AccessTel, Inc.)

SHOPWELL INC (DE)
Stock Dividends - 10% 01/11/1983; 25% 11/12/1985
Merged into Great Atlantic & Pacific Tea Co., Inc. 08/22/1986
Each share Common 50¢ par exchanged for $31 cash

SHORE BANK (ONLEY, VA)
Recapitalized as Shore Financial Corp. 03/16/1998
Each share Common 33¢ par exchanged for (0.1) share Common 33¢ par
(See Shore Financial Corp.)

SHORE CALNEVAR INC (CA)
Adjudicated bankrupt 09/06/1967
Stockholders' equity unlikely

SHORE FINL CORP (VA)
Common 33¢ par changed to $0.275 par and (0.2) additional share issued payable 09/15/2006 to holders of record 08/30/2006 Ex date - 09/18/2006
Stock Dividend - 20% payable 12/31/2003 to holders of record 12/20/2003 Ex date - 12/17/2003
Acquired by Hampton Roads Bankshares, Inc. 06/02/2008
Each share Common $0.275 par exchanged for $22 cash

SHORE GOLD INC (CANADA)
Name changed 12/05/1994
Name changed from Shore Gold Fund Inc. to Shore Gold, Inc. 12/05/1994
Each share Common no par received distribution of (0.1) share Wescan Goldfields Inc. Common no par payable 09/24/2004 to holders of record 09/10/2004 Ex date - 09/08/2004
Note: Non-residents of the filing jurisdictions (QC, ON, MB, SK, AB, BC) will receive $0.10 cash per share in lieu of stock
Name changed to Star Diamond Corp. 02/12/2018

SHORE GROUP INC (DE)
Reincorporated 01/18/1994
State of incorporation changed from (NV) to (DE) 01/18/1994
Charter cancelled and declared inoperative and void non-payment of taxes 03/01/2001

SHORE LINE FINL CORP (NV)
Name changed to Access Medical Corp. 11/15/93
Access Medical Corp. name changed to Shoreline Software Solutions Inc. 5/25/94 which name changed to American Home Alliance Industries Ltd. 5/23/95 which reorganized as Alliance Industries 9/18/96
(See Alliance Industries)

SHORE LINE OIL CO. (NV)
Charter revoked for failure to file returns and pay fees 7/1/80

SHORE NATL BK (BRICKTOWN, NJ)
Completely liquidated 08/15/1977
Each share Capital Stock $4 par exchanged for first and final distribution $12 cash

SHORE RES LTD (AB)
Name changed to Pacific & Western Trustco Ltd. 04/24/1987
Pacific & Western Trustco Ltd. name changed to Pacific & Western Credit Corp. (Old) 06/03/1994 which merged into Pacific & Western Credit Corp. (New) 01/01/2002 which name changed to PWC Capital Inc. 04/25/2014 which merged into VersaBank (New) (London, ON) 02/02/2017

SHO-SHR FINANCIAL INFORMATION, INC.

SHORE SVGS BK (ONLEY, VA)
Name changed to Shore Bank (Onley, VA) 06/10/1997
Shore Bank (Onley, VA) recapitalized as Shore Financial Corp. 03/16/1998
(See Shore Financial Corp.)

SHORE TO SHORE LTD (ON)
Common no par reclassified as Conv. Class A Common no par 10/09/1975
Merged into District Trust Co. (London, ON) 12/01/1975
Each share Conv. Class A Common no par exchanged for (1) share Conv. Class A no par or (1) share Conv. Class B no par
Each share Conv. Class B Common no par exchanged for (1) share Conv. Class A no par or (1) share Conv. Class B no par
Note: Non-electors received Conv. Class A
(See District Trust Co. (London, ON))

SHORE VENTURES INC (NV)
Name changed to Cosco ESP, Inc. 09/26/2005
Cosco ESP, Inc. recapitalized as Budget Center Inc. 04/28/2009 which recapitalized as Budget Center Inc. 11/08/2017

SHOREBANK INC (MA)
Name changed to Multibank Financial Corp. 11/21/1972
Multibank Financial Corp. acquired by Bank of Boston Corp. 07/13/1993 which name changed to BankBoston Corp. 04/25/1997 which merged into Fleet Boston Corp. 10/01/1999 which name changed to FleetBoston Financial Corp. 04/18/2000 which merged into Bank of America Corp. 04/01/2004

SHOREHAM RES LTD (BC)
Name changed to Guyana Frontier Mining Corp. 01/31/2011

SHORELAND HOTEL LIQUIDATION TRUST
Property sold in 1946

SHORELINE BK & TR CO (MADISON, CT)
Merged into Webster Financial Corp. 12/16/94
Each (2) shares Common $5 par exchanged for (1) share Common 1¢ par

SHORELINE FINL CORP (MI)
Common $1 par split (3) for (2) by issuance of (0.5) additional share 6/1/94
Common $1 par split (3) for (2) by issuance of (0.5) additional share payable 4/3/98 to holders of record 3/23/98
Common $1 par split (5) for (4) by issuance of (0.25) additional share payable 7/2/99 to holders of record 6/18/99
Stock Dividends - 10% 6/30/89; 10% 6/29/90; 10% 6/14/91; 5% payable 5/28/96 to holders of record 5/15/96; 5% payable 5/30/97 to holders of record 5/16/97; 5% payable 7/17/2000 to holders of record 7/3/2000 Ex date - 6/29/2000
Merged into Chemical Financial Corp. 1/9/2001
Each share Common $1 par exchanged for (0.64) share Common $1 par

SHORELINE SVGS ASSN (SEATTLE, WA)
Acquired by Washington Mutual Savings Bank (Seattle, WA) 04/29/1988
Each share Common 50¢ par exchanged for $5 cash

SHORELINE SOFTWARE SOLUTIONS INC (NV)
Name changed to American Home Alliance Industries Ltd. 5/23/95
American Home Alliance Industries Ltd. reorganized as Alliance Industries 9/18/96
(See Alliance Industries)

SHORETEL INC (DE)
Acquired by Mitel Networks Corp. 09/25/2017
Each share Common $0.001 par exchanged for $7.50 cash

SHOREWOOD CORP (IN)
Acquired by Philadelphia Saving Fund Society (Philadelphia, PA) 01/21/1985
Each share Common $1 par exchanged for $24 cash

SHOREWOOD EXPLS LTD (BC)
Merged into International Broadlands Resources Ltd. 04/06/1995
Each share Common no par exchanged for (1) share Common no par
International Broadlands Resources Ltd. recapitalized as Broadlands Resources Ltd. (New) 03/15/1999 which recapitalized as Pinnacle Mines Ltd. (Ctfs. dated after 07/16/2003) 07/16/2003 which name changed to Jayden Resources Inc. (BC) 06/29/2010 which reincorporated in Cayman Islands 10/03/2012

SHOREWOOD PACKAGING CORP (DE)
Merged into International Paper Co. 3/31/2000
Each share Common no par exchanged for $21 cash

SHOREY INTL LTD (CO)
Ceased operations 00/00/1988
Details not available

SHORT TAKES INC (MN)
Reorganized under the laws of Delaware as American Wireless Systems, Inc. 4/27/93
Each share Common 1¢ par exchanged for (0.4) share Common 1¢ par
American Wireless Systems, Inc. merged into Heartland Wireless Communications, Inc. 2/23/96
(See Heartland Wireless Communications, Inc.)

SHORT TERM MUN TR (PA)
Name changed to Federated Short-Term Municipal Trust 2/28/95

SHORT TERM TRUST SHARES
Trust terminated 00/00/1935
Details not available

SHORTY-HOPE MINING & MILLING CO. (OR)
Charter cancelled for non-payment of taxes in 1914

SHORTY LAVENDERS INC (NY)
Name changed to PMI Inc. 10/17/86
(See PMI Inc.)

SHOSHONI GOLD INC (BC)
Recapitalized as Consolidated Shoshoni Gold Inc. 01/23/1992
Each share Common no par exchanged for (1/3) share Common no par
Consolidated Shoshoni Gold Inc. recapitalized as New Shoshoni Ventures Ltd. 01/07/2000 which recapitalized as Shoshoni Gold Ltd. 05/09/2012

SHOTGUN ENERGY CORP (NV)
Name changed to Organa Gardens International Inc. 04/07/2009
Organa Gardens International Inc. recapitalized as Bravo Enterprises Ltd. 06/08/2012

SHOTPAK INC (NV)
Name changed to Shot Spirits Corp. 01/15/2009

SHOUP VOTING MACHINE CORP. (NY)
Merged into General Battery & Ceramic Corp. (N.Y.) on a (0.85) for (1) basis 12/29/61
General Battery & Ceramic Corp. (N.Y.) name changed to General Battery Corp. 10/3/69
(See General Battery Corp.)

SHOW OFFS DISPOSABLE PRODUCTS CORP. (NY)
Merged out of existence 12/31/86
Details not available

SHOWA SANGYO LTD (JAPAN)
Stock Dividend - 10% 06/30/1992
ADR agreement terminated 10/02/2017
No ADR's remain outstanding

SHOWBIZ PIZZA TIME INC (KS)
Each share old Common 10¢ par exchanged for (0.1) share new Common 10¢ par 10/19/1988
New Common 10¢ par split (3) for (2) by issuance of (0.5) additional share 03/26/1991
New Common 10¢ par split (3) for (2) by issuance of (0.5) additional share 03/20/1992
Name changed to CEC Entertainment, Inc. 06/25/1998
(See CEC Entertainment, Inc.)

SHOWBOAT INC (NV)
Common $1 par split (3) for (2) by issuance of (0.5) additional share 10/20/81
Common $1 par split (3) for (2) by issuance of (0.5) additional share 5/31/83
Common $1 par split (2) for (1) by issuance of (1) additional share 5/29/87
Stock Dividends - 25% 11/7/69; 50% 8/1/78
Merged into Harrah's Entertainment, Inc. 6/1/98
Each share Common $1 par exchanged for $30.75 cash

SHOWCASE CORP (MN)
Issue Information - 3,000,000 shares CDT-COM offered at $9 per share on 06/29/1999
Merged into SPSS Inc. 02/26/2001
Each share Common 1¢ par exchanged for (0.333) share Common 1¢ par
(See SPSS Inc.)

SHOWCASE COSMETICS INC (DE)
Each share Class A Common 1¢ par exchanged for (0.1) share Class A Common 10¢ par 02/14/1992
Merged into Mark Solutions, Inc. 11/10/1993
Each share Class A Common 10¢ par exchanged for (1/6) share Common 1¢ par
Mark Solutions, Inc. name changed to Mark Holdings Inc. 12/26/2001
(See Mark Holdings Inc.)

SHOWERS BROTHERS CO. (IN)
Acquired by Storkline Furniture Corp. 00/00/1955
Details not available

SHOWINTEL NETWORKS INC (NV)
Name changed to Limelight Media Group, Inc. 11/05/2003
Limelight Media Group, Inc. recapitalized as Impart Media Group, Inc. 12/22/2005
(See Impart Media Group, Inc.)

SHOWPOWER INC (DE)
Issue Information - 1,200,000 shares COM offered at $11 per share on 06/16/1998
Merged into General Electric Co. 1/31/2000
Each share Common 1¢ par exchanged for $7 cash

SHOWSCAN ENTMT INC (DE)
Name changed 08/21/1990
Name changed 08/25/1994
Name changed from Showscan Film Corp. to Showscan Corp. 08/21/1990
Name changed from Showscan Corp. to Showscan Entertainment Inc. 08/25/1994
Chapter 11 bankruptcy proceedings converted to Chapter 7 on 12/28/2001
No stockholders' equity

SHOWSTAR ONLINE COM INC (WA)
Name changed 6/25/99
Reincorporated 9/15/2000
Name changed from Showstar Entertainment Corp. to Showstar Online.Com, Inc. 6/25/99
State of incorporation changed from (CO) to (WA) 9/15/2000
Recapitalized as Sonoran Energy Inc. 6/3/2002
Each share Common no par exchanged for (0.04) share Common no par

SHOWSTOPPERS INC (UT)
Involuntarily dissolved 04/01/1989

SHREDDED WHEAT CO.
Acquired by National Biscuit Co. 00/00/1929
Details not available

SHREVEPORT-EL DORADO PIPE LINE CO.
Succeeded by Spartan Refining Co. in 1931
(See Spartan Refining Co.)

SHREVEPORT GAMING HLDGS INC (DE)
Completely liquidated
Each share Common received first and final distribution of $0.33 cash payable 11/29/2011 to holders of record 11/22/2011

SHREVEPORT PRODUCING & REFINING CORP.
Merged into Shreveport-El Dorado Pipe Line Co. in 1929
(See Shreveport-El Dorado Pipe Line Co.)

SHREVEPORT RAILWAYS CO. (LA)
Each share Common $100 par exchanged for (0.1) share Common no par in 1938
Succeeded by Shreveport Transit Co., Inc. 5/24/57
(See Shreveport Transit Co., Inc.)

SHREVEPORT TRANSIT CO., INC. (LA)
Acquired by American Transit Corp. 4/1/65
(See American Transit Corp.)

SHREWSBURY BANCORP (NJ)
Stock Dividends - 5% payable 5/31/96 to holders of record 5/17/96; 4% payable 5/29/98 to holders of record 5/15/98; 4% payable 12/11/98 to holders of record 11/27/98; 4% payable 5/28/99 to holders of record 5/7/99; 4% payable 12/10/99 to holders of record 11/26/99; 4% payable 5/26/2000 to holders of record 5/5/2000 Ex date - 5/4/2000; 4% payable 12/8/2000 to holders of record 11/17/2000 Ex date - 11/15/2000; 4% payable 5/25/2001 to holders of record 5/4/2001 Ex date - 5/25/2001; 4% payable 12/7/2001 to holders of record 11/16/2001 Ex date - 11/14/2001; 4% payable 5/24/2002 to holders of record 5/3/2002 Ex date - 5/1/2002; 4% payable 12/6/2002 to holders of record 11/15/2002 Ex date - 11/13/2002; 4% payable 5/23/2003 to holders of record 5/2/2003 Ex date - 4/30/2003; 4% payable 12/5/2003 to holders of record 11/14/2003 Ex date - 11/12/2003; 4% payable 5/28/2004 to holders of record 5/7/2004 Ex date - 5/5/2004; 4% payable 12/3/2004 to holders of record 11/12/2004
Merged into Valley National Bancorp 3/31/2005
Each share Common $5 par

exchanged for (1.862) shares Common no par

SHREWSBURY ST BK (SHREWSBURY, NJ)
Under plan of reorganization each share Common $5 par automatically became (1) share Shrewsbury Bancorp. Common $5 par 10/26/95

SHREYAS SHIPPING & LOGISTICS LTD (INDIA)
GDR agreement terminated 03/20/2015
No GDR's remain outstanding

SHRINK NANOTECHNOLOGIES INC (DE)
Each share old Common $0.001 par exchanged for (5) shares new Common $0.001 par 04/15/2010
SEC revoked common stock registration 08/08/2016

SHRIRAM INDL ENTERPRISES LTD (INDIA)
Each old Sponsored 144A GDR for Ordinary exchanged for (0.25) new Sponsored 144A GDR for Ordinary and (0.75) Siel Sugar Ltd. Sponsored 144A GDR for Ordinary 03/23/2004
Each old Sponsored Reg. S GDR for Ordinary exchanged for (0.25) new Sponsored Reg. S GDR for Ordinary and (0.75) Siel Sugar Ltd. Sponsored Reg. S for Ordinary 03/23/2004
Stock Dividend - In Sponsored 144A GDR's for Ordinary to holders of Sponsored 144A GDR's for Ordinary 20% payable 08/05/1998 to holders of record 04/29/1998
Name changed to Siel Ltd. 06/17/2004
Siel Ltd. name changed to Mawana Sugars Ltd. (New) 06/30/2008
(See Mawana Sugars Ltd. (New))

SHS BANCORP INC (PA)
Merged into ESB Financial Corp. 02/10/2000
Each share Common 1¢ par exchanged for (1.3) shares Common 1¢ par
ESB Financial Corp. merged into WesBanco, Inc. 02/10/2015

SHUAIYI INTL NEW RES DEV INC (NV)
Name changed to Nutrastar International Inc. 01/20/2010

SHUANGYANG U S ENTERPRISES INC (NV)
Recapitalized as Polymeric Corp. 01/01/2001
Each share Common $0.001 par exchanged for (0.2) share Common $0.001 par
Polymeric Corp. name changed to Lew Corp. 08/27/2001 which name changed to Vintage Energy & Exploration, Inc. 10/02/2007
(See Vintage Energy & Exploration, Inc.)

SHUBERT THEATRE CORP.
Acquired by Select Theatres Corp. in 1933
(See Select Theatres Corp.)

SHUFFLE MASTER INC (MN)
Common 1¢ par split (3) for (2) by issuance of (0.5) additional share 07/11/1995
Common 1¢ par split (3) for (2) by issuance of (0.5) additional share payable 11/30/2000 to holders of record 11/17/2000 Ex date - 12/01/2000
Common 1¢ par split (3) for (2) by issuance of (0.5) additional share payable 06/18/2001 to holders of record 06/08/2001 Ex date - 06/19/2001
Common 1¢ par split (3) for (2) by issuance of (0.5) additional share payable 04/16/2004 to holders of record 04/05/2004 Ex date - 04/19/2004
Common 1¢ par split (3) for (2) by issuance of (0.5) additional share payable 01/14/2005 to holders of record 01/03/2005 Ex date - 01/18/2005
Name changed to SHFL entertainment, Inc. 10/19/2012
(See SHFL entertainment, Inc.)

SHULLYS INDS LTD (ON)
Placed in receivership 08/23/1973
No stockholders' equity

SHULMAN TRANS ENTERPRISES INC (DE)
Adjudicated bankrupt 11/17/1978
Stockholders' equity unlikely

SHULTON INC (NJ)
Class A Common $1 par and Class B Common $1 par changed to 50¢ par and (1) additional share issued respectively 07/24/1961
Class A Common $1 par and Class B Common 50¢ par reclassified as Common 50¢ par 05/02/1966
Merged into American Cyanamid Co. 04/15/1971
Each share 5% Preferred $100 par exchanged for (3) shares Common $5 par
Each share Common 50¢ par exchanged for (0.96) share Common $5 par
(See American Cyanamid Co.)

SHUMATE INDS INC (DE)
Name changed to Hemiwedge Industries, Inc. 02/19/2009
Hemiwedge Industries, Inc. name changed to HII Technologies, Inc. 01/17/2012
(See HII Technologies, Inc.)

SHUMWAY OPTICAL INSTRS CORP (NY)
Each share Common 5¢ par exchanged for (0.5) share Class A Common 10¢ par 05/10/1974
Recapitalized as Cherokee Resources Corp. 07/08/1981
Each share Class A Common 10¢ par exchanged for (0.1) share Class A Common $1 par
(See Cherokee Resources Corp.)

SHUMWAY URANIUM MINING CORP. (UT)
Capital Stock $1 par changed to 50¢ par and (1) additional share issued 10/17/55
Name changed to Western Corp. in 1959 which recapitalized as Spring Kist Corp. 1/3/62
(See Spring Kist Corp.)

SHUN TAK HLDGS LTD (HONG KONG)
ADR agreement terminated 08/09/2018
Each Sponsored ADR for Common exchanged for (10) shares Common
Note: Unexchanged ADR's will be sold and the proceeds, if any, held for claim after 08/12/2019

SHUNSBY MINES LTD. (ON)
Name changed 11/21/1955
Name changed from Shunsby Gold Mines Ltd. to Shunsby Mines Ltd. 11/21/1955
Recapitalized as Consolidated Shunsby Mines Ltd. 05/25/1965
Each share Capital Stock $1 par exchanged for (0.2) share Capital Stock $1 par
Consolidated Shunsby Mines Ltd. recapitalized as MW Resources Ltd. 07/21/1975 which recapitalized as MW Capital Resources Corp. (ON) 09/14/1990 which reorganized in Alberta as Oro Nevada Resources Inc. 08/31/1996 which name changed to Martlet Venture Management Ltd. 09/02/1999
(See Martlet Venture Management Ltd.)

SHUR DE COR INC (NV)
Old Common $0.001 par split (2) for (1) by issuance of (1) additional share payable 03/19/1999 to holders of record 03/19/1999
Name changed to Interactive Marketing Technology, Inc. 04/07/1999
Interactive Marketing Technology, Inc. recapitalized as China Artists Agency, Inc. 12/21/2004 which name changed to China Entertainment Group, Inc. 08/22/2005 which name changed to Safe & Secure TV Channel, Inc. 08/12/2010 which name changed to Cosmos Group Holdings Inc. 03/31/2016

SHUR GRO INDS INC (NM)
Recapitalized as Enrec Corp. 3/31/80
Each share Common 25¢ par exchanged for (5) shares Common 5¢ par
(See Enrec Corp.)

SHUR-ON PROPERTIES CO., INC. (NY)
Name changed to Shuron Optical Co., Inc. 00/00/1937
Shuron Optical Co., Inc. name changed to First Geneva Corp. 03/20/1958

SHUR-ON STANDARD OPTICAL CO., INC. (NY)
Reorganized as Shur-On Properties Co., Inc. 00/00/1928
Details not available

SHUR-SCAPE SYS INC (CO)
Name changed to Seaman Technologies Inc. 02/10/1992
Seaman Technologies Inc. name changed to Demac Investments Inc. 03/02/1992 which recapitalized as Reliance Lodging, Inc. 02/05/1993
(See Reliance Lodging, Inc.)

SHURGARD STORAGE CTRS INC (DE)
Issue Information - 2,000,000 shares PFD SER B REDEEMABLE 8.80% offered at $25 per share on 04/16/1997
Issue Information - 3,000,000 shares PFD SER D 8.75% offered at $25 per share on 02/22/2001
8.80% Ser. B Preferred no par called for redemption at $25 on 08/19/2002
8.70% Ser. C Preferred no par called for redemption at $25 on 08/22/2006
8.75% Ser. D Preferred no par called for redemption at $25 on 08/22/2006
Merged into Public Storage, Inc. (CA) 08/22/2006
Each share Class A Common $0.001 par exchanged for (0.82) share Common 10¢ par
Public Storage, Inc. (CA) reincorporated in Maryland as Public Storage 06/04/2007

SHURON OPTICAL CO., INC. (NY)
Common no par changed to $5 par 00/00/1951
Stock Dividends - 20% 01/16/1950; 10% 12/22/1952
Assets sold and name changed to First Geneva Corp. 03/20/1958

SHUSWAP MINES LTD. (BC)
Charter cancelled for failure to file returns May 1957

SHUTTLE MEADOW CLUB, INC. (CT)
Liquidation completed in 1953

SHWAYDER BROTHERS, INC. (CO)
Name changed to Samsonite Corp. 4/6/65
Samsonite Corp. name changed to S.C. Liquidating Co. 8/27/73
(See S.C. Liquidating Co.)

SHWAYDER CHEMICAL METALLURGY CORP. (MI)
Preferred $10 par called for redemption 12/11/69
Public interest eliminated

SHYMKENT OIL REFINERY (KAZAKHSTAN)
Name changed to Hurricane Oil Products OJSC 10/1/2002
Hurricane Oil Products OJSC name changed to PetroKazakhstan Oil Products OJSC 7/24/2003
(See PetroKazakhstan Oil Products OJSC)

SI DIAMOND TECHNOLOGY INC (TX)
Name changed to Nano-Proprietary, Inc. 07/01/2003
Nano-Proprietary, Inc. name changed to Applied Nanotech Holdings, Inc. (TX) 07/01/2008 which reincorporated in Delaware as PEN Inc. 09/03/2014

SI FINL GROUP INC (USA)
Reorganized under the laws of Maryland 01/13/2011
Each share Common 1¢ par exchanged for (0.8981) share Common 1¢ par

SI FING TR I (DE)
9.25% Guaranteed Preferred Securities called for redemption at $25 on 6/30/2001
9.50% Trust Preferred Units called for redemption at $25 on 7/2/2001

SI HANDLING SYS INC (PA)
Common $1 par split (2) for (1) by issuance of (1) additional share 1/6/62
Common $1 par split (2) for (1) by issuance of (1) additional share 4/5/65
Common $1 par split (5) for (4) by issuance of (0.25) additional share 7/14/81
Common $1 par split (5) for (4) by issuance of (0.25) additional share 5/12/82
Common $1 par split (3) for (2) by issuance of (0.5) additional share 8/11/95
Common $1 par split (3) for (2) by issuance of (0.5) additional share payable 11/10/97 to holders of record 10/27/97
Stock Dividends - 25% 12/15/66; 150% 12/30/67; 10% 9/1/76; 10% 5/16/77; 10% 11/4/91
Name changed to Paragon Technologies, Inc. (PA) 4/5/2000
Paragon Technologies, Inc. (PA) reincorporated in Delaware 12/7/2001

SI INTL INC (DE)
Issue Information - 4,350,000 shares COM offered at $14 per share on 11/11/2002
Acquired by Serco Group plc 12/29/2008
Each share Common 1¢ par exchanged for $32 cash

SI MEI TE FOOD LTD (CAYMAN ISLANDS)
Units separated 06/17/2011
SEC revoked Ordinary stock registration 11/30/2011

SI TECHNOLOGIES INC (DE)
Merged into Vishay Intertechnology, Inc. 04/28/2005
Each share Common 1¢ par exchanged for $4 cash

SIAM CITY CEM PUB CO LTD (THAILAND)
ADR agreement terminated 05/21/2018
No ADR's remain outstanding

SIAM IMPORTS INC (NV)
Reincorporated under the laws of Delaware as Apollo Drilling, Inc. 10/17/2006
Apollo Drilling, Inc. recapitalized as Southwest Resources, Inc. 10/05/2009 which reorganized in Nevada as Puration, Inc. 02/29/2012

SIAM TRADING LTD (AB)
Plan of arrangement effective 2/14/96

Each share Common no par exchanged for (1) McCarthy Corp. PLC Ordinary share 2p par

SIBANY MFG CORP (DE)
Charter cancelled and declared inoperative and void for non-payment of taxes 3/1/77

SIBANYE GOLD LTD (SOUTH AFRICA)
Stock Dividend - 2% payable 10/16/2017 to holders of record 10/06/2017 Ex date - 10/05/2017
Name changed to Sibanye Gold Ltd., trading as Sibanye-Stillwater 09/21/2017

SIBERIAN INDS LTD (NV)
Name changed to Midastrade.com Inc. 08/23/2000
(See Midastrade.com Inc.)

SIBERIAN OIL CO (RUSSIA)
Sponsored ADR's for Ordinary split (2) for (1) by issuance of (1) additional ADR payable 01/24/2005 to holders of record 01/21/2005 Ex date - 01/25/2005
Basis changed from (1:10) to (1:5) 01/25/2005
Name changed to Gazprom Neft 06/07/2006
Gazprom Neft name changed to Gazprom Neft PJSC 12/03/2015

SIBERIAN PAC RES INC (AB)
Delisted from Alberta Stock Exchange 4/4/96

SIBIA NEUROSCIENCES INC (DE)
Merged into Merck & Co., Inc. (Old) 11/12/1999
Each share Common $0.001 par exchanged for $8.50 cash

SIBIRTELECOM OPEN JT STK CO (RUSSIA)
Sponsored ADR's for Ordinary split (4) for (1) by issuance of (3) additional ADR's payable 07/31/2008 to holders of record 07/24/2008 Ex date - 08/01/2008
Merged into Rostelecom OJSC 04/13/2011
Each Sponsored ADR for Ordinary exchanged for $23.90214 cash

SIBLEY, LINDSAY & CURR CO. (NY)
Assets sold to Associated Dry Goods Corp. and liquidated 9/25/57
(See Associated Dry Goods Corp.)

SIBLEY-ENTERPRISE CO.
Merged into Graniteville Co. in 1940
(See Graniteville Co.)

SIBLEY MANUFACTURING CO.
Merged into Sibley-Enterprise Co. in 1938
(See Sibley-Enterprise Co.)

SIBLING ENTMT GROUP HLDGS INC (TX)
Recapitalized as Sibling Group Holdings, Inc. 08/21/2012
Each share Common $0.0001 par exchanged for (0.01) share Common $0.0001 par

SIBOLA MINES LTD (BC)
Delisted from Vancouver Stock Exchange 11/16/1990

SIBONEY-CARIBBEAN PETROLEUM CO. (MD)
Name changed to Siboney Corp. 04/23/1962
(See Siboney Corp.)

SIBONEY CORP (MD)
55¢ Conv. Preferred $1 par called for redemption 00/00/1978
Assets sold for the benefit of creditors 08/10/2009
Stockholders' equity unlikely

SIBONEY DEVELOPMENT & EXPLORATION CO. (MD)
Name changed to Siboney-Caribbean Petroleum Co. 04/03/1956
Siboney-Caribbean Petroleum Co. name changed to Siboney Corp. 04/23/1962
(See Siboney Corp.)

SICAMOUS RES LTD (BC)
Name changed to Ni-Cal Developments Ltd. (BC) 11/19/1976
Ni-Cal Developments Ltd. (BC) reincorporated in Delaware as Nickel Resources Development Corp. 12/29/1988 which recapitalized as Nycal Corp. 12/15/1989
(See Nycal Corp.)

SICAN VENTURES INC (BC)
Name changed to Abattis Biologix Corp. 07/06/2009
Abattis Biologix Corp. recapitalized as Abattis Bioceuticals Corp. 09/11/2012

SICANNA INDS LTD (BC)
Name changed to Decorstone Industries Inc. 3/28/88
(See Decorstone Industries Inc.)

SICARD INC (QC)
100% acquired through purchase offer by Pacific Car & Foundry Co. as of 06/31/1967
Public interest eliminated

SICHUAN LEADERS PETROCHEMICAL CO (FL)
Name changed to Horrison Resources Inc. 04/13/2018

SICINTINE MINES LTD (BC)
Recapitalized as Mi-Lo Health & Beauty Aids, Ltd. 06/05/1978
Each share Capital Stock no par exchanged for (0.2) share Capital Stock no par
(See Mi-Lo Health & Beauty Aids, Ltd.)

SICKBAY HEALTH MEDIA INC (UT)
Name changed 08/23/2000
Name changed from Sick-Bay.Com Inc. to Sickbay Health Media, Inc. 08/23/2000
Charter expired 08/19/2002

SICKS RAINIER BREWING CO (WA)
Name changed to Rainier Companies, Inc. 04/20/1970
(See Rainier Companies, Inc.)

SICKS' BREWERIES, LTD. (CANADA)
Each share old Common no par exchanged for (4) shares new Common no par 5/31/46
Acquired by Molson's Brewery Ltd. in 1958
Each share new Common no par exchanged for (1) share 5-1/2% Preferred $40 par, (2) shares Class A no par and (2) shares Class B no par
Molson's Brewery Ltd. name changed to Molson Breweries Ltd. 3/1/62 which name changed to Molson Companies Ltd. 8/17/73 which name changed to Molson Inc. 6/29/99 which merged into Molson Coors Brewing Co. 2/9/2005

SICKS' SEATTLE BREWING & MALTING CO. (WA)
Stock Dividend - 33-1/3% 10/12/50
Name changed to Sicks' Rainier Brewing Co. 4/17/57
Sicks' Rainier Brewing Co. name changed to Rainier Companies, Inc. 4/20/70
(See Rainier Companies, Inc.)

SICLONE INDS INC (DE)
Each (136) shares old Common $0.001 par exchanged for (1) share new Common $0.001 par 07/23/2007
Note: No holder will receive fewer than (100) shares
Name changed to Apollo Medical Holdings, Inc. 07/15/2008

SICO INC (QC)
Common no par split (2) for (1) by issuance of (1) additional share payable 05/30/2005 to holders of record 05/26/2005 Ex date - 05/24/2005
Acquired by Akzo Nobel N.V. 06/07/2006
Each share Common no par exchanged for $20 cash

SICOR INC (DE)
$3.75 144A Conv. Exchangeable Preferred called for redemption at $50 on 03/01/2002
Merged into Teva Pharmaceutical Industries Ltd. 01/22/2004
Each share Common 1¢ par exchanged for (0.1906) ADR for Ordinary NIS0.001 par and $16.50 cash

SID ENERGY INC (BC)
Struck off register and declared dissolved for failure to file returns 10/28/1994

SIDAR INC (UT)
Each share Common $0.001 par exchanged for (0.0005) share Common $0.001 par 12/8/95
Name changed to Preventco, Inc. 2/22/96

SIDARI CORP (DE)
Voluntarily dissolved 05/09/2001
Details not available

SIDEL SA (FRANCE)
ADR agreement terminated 6/20/2003
Each Sponsored ADR for Ordinary exchanged for $14.5325 cash

SIDERAR S A I C (ARGENTINA)
ADR agreement terminated 09/10/2007
Each 144A Sponsored ADR for Class A exchanged for (8) Class A shares
Each Reg. S Sponsored ADR for Class A exchanged for (8) Class A shares
Note: Unexchanged ADR's will be sold and the proceeds, if any, held for claim after 09/10/2008

SIDERCA S A (ARGENTINA)
Issue Information - 1,900,000 ADR'S offered at $19.10 per ADR on 05/18/2001
99.1% acquired by Tenaris S.A. through voluntary exchange offer which expired 12/13/2002
Public interest eliminated

SIDERURGICA VENEZOLANA SIVENSA S A I C A -S A C A (VENEZUELA)
Stock Dividend - 20% 3/17/93
Name changed to Siderurgica Venezolana Sivensa S.A.C.A. 7/22/96

SIDEWARE SYS INC (YT)
Reincorporated 1/2/2002
Place of incorporation changed from (BC) to (Yukon) 1/2/2002
Reincorporated under the laws of Delaware as Knowledgemax, Inc. and Common no par changed to $0.001 par 5/21/2002
(See Knowledgemax, Inc.)

SIDEWINDER CONVERSIONS INTL INC (BC)
Recapitalized as Pacific Axis Ventures, Inc. (BC) 11/28/1995
Each share Common no par exchanged for (1/6) share Common no par
Pacific Axis Ventures, Inc. (BC) reincorporated in Yukon as Petrolex Energy Corp. 02/03/1997
(See Petrolex Energy Corp.)

SIDLES CO. (NE)
5-1/4% 1st Preferred $25 par called for redemption 3/31/68
Public interest eliminated

SIDNEY BLUMENTHAL & CO., INC. (NY)
See - Blumenthal (Sidney) & Co., Inc.

SIDNEY MNG CO (ID)
Capital Stock $1 par changed to 25¢ par 06/03/1958
Capital Stock 25¢ par changed to 10¢ par 04/22/1974
Reincorporated under the laws of Nevada as Sidney Resources Corp. and Common 10¢ par changed to $0.0001 par 03/04/2003
Sidney Resources Corp. (NV) reincorporated in Idaho 08/25/2009

SIDNEY RES CORP (NV)
Reincorporated under the laws of Idaho 08/25/2009

SIDNEY ROOFING & PAPER CO., LTD. (BC)
Name changed to Burnaby Paperboard Ltd. 9/28/62
(See Burnaby Paperboard Ltd.)

SIDNEY ST BK (SIDNEY, MI)
Common no par split (2) for (1) by issuance of (1) additional share payable 07/31/1998 to holders of record 07/01/1998
Under plan of reorganization each share Common no par automatically became (1) share Sidney Bancorp Common no par 10/01/2007

SIDON INTL RES CORP (BC)
Recapitalized as Cameo Resources Corp. 02/15/2012
Each share Common no par exchanged for (0.03333333) share Common no par
Cameo Resources Corp. name changed to Cameo Cobalt Corp. 05/25/2018

SIDUS SYS INC (ON)
Merged into EMJ Data Systems Ltd. 4/1/99
Each share Common no par exchanged for (0.02) share Common no par
(See EMJ Data Systems Ltd.)

SIE COMMUNICATIONS INC (DE)
Charter cancelled and declared inoperative and void for non-payment of taxes 03/01/1990

SIEBE PLC (UNITED KINGDOM)
Stock Dividend - 300% payable 08/25/1998 to holders of record 08/14/1998
Merged into BTR Siebe PLC 02/12/1999
Each Sponsored ADR for Ordinary exchanged for (1) Sponsored ADR for Ordinary 25p par
BTR Siebe PLC name changed to Invensys PLC 04/16/1999
(See Invensys PLC)

SIEBEL JANNA ARRANGEMENT INC (ON)
Each Exchangeable Share no par exchanged for (1) share Siebel Systems, Inc. Common $0.001 par 12/7/2005
(See Siebel Systems, Inc.)

SIEBEL SYS INC (DE)
Common $0.001 par split (2) for (1) by issuance of (1) additional share payable 12/19/96 to holders of record 12/13/96
Common $0.001 par split (2) for (1) by issuance of (1) additional share payable 3/20/98 to holders of record 3/9/98
Common $0.001 par split (2) for (1) by issuance of (1) additional share payable 11/12/99 to holders of record 11/1/99
Common $0.001 par split (2) for (1) by issuance of (1) additional share payable 9/8/2000 to holders of record 8/18/2000 Ex date - 9/11/2000
Merged into Oracle Corp. 1/31/2006
Each share Common $0.001 par exchanged for $10.66 cash

FINANCIAL INFORMATION, INC.

SIEBENS OIL & GAS LTD (AB)
Merged into Canpar Oil & Gas Ltd. 01/03/1979
Each share Capital Stock no par exchanged for $38.50 cash

SIEGEL HENRY I INC (NY)
Class A $1 par reclassified as Common $1 par 02/27/1970
Stock Dividend - 50% 10/04/1963
Merged into Seco (J.G.), Inc. 03/10/1978
Each share Common $1 par exchanged for $19 cash

SIEGER CAP MGMT LTD (BC)
Reincorporated under the laws of Canada as Sherbrook SBK Sport Corp. 05/05/2010
(See Sherbrook SBK Sport Corp.)

SIEGESOFT INTERNET SOLUTIONS INC (BC)
Name changed to Zimtu Technologies Inc. 10/26/2000
Zimtu Technologies Inc. recapitalized as International Zimtu Technologies Inc. (BC) 4/4/2003 which reincorporated in Canada as Petrol One Corp. 9/26/2006

SIEGLE (G.) CORP. OF AMERICA
Merged into Ansbacher-Siegle Corp. 00/00/1929
Details not available

SIEGLER CORP. (DE)
Under plan of merger name changed to Lear Siegler, Inc. 6/5/62
(See Lear Siegler, Inc.)

SIEL LTD (INDIA)
GDR basis changed from (1:3) to (1:1) 01/07/2008
Name changed to Mawana Sugars Ltd. (New) 06/30/2008
(See Mawana Sugars Ltd. (New))

SIEL SUGAR LTD (INDIA)
Name changed to Mawana Sugars Ltd. (Old) 03/23/2004
Mawana Sugars Ltd. (Old) merged into Siel Ltd. 01/07/2008 which name changed to Mawana Sugars Ltd. (New) 06/30/2008
(See Mawana Sugars Ltd. (New))

SIELOX INC (DE)
Name changed to Costar Technologies, Inc. 03/02/2012

SIEMENS & HALSKE A.G. (GERMANY)
Stock Dividend - 10% 04/23/1965
Name changed to Siemens A.G. 09/30/1966

SIEMONT RES LTD (BC)
Recapitalized as Eskay Gold Corp. 07/24/1990
Each share Common no par exchanged for (0.25) share Common no par
Eskay Gold Corp. recapitalized as Consolidated Eskay Gold Corp. 10/05/1992 which name changed to DBA Telecom Corp. 04/08/1993 which recapitalized as Magnum Minerals Corp. 09/20/2004 which name changed to Magnum Uranium Corp. 10/03/2005 which was acquired by Energy Fuels Inc. 07/02/2009

SIENA HLDGS INC (DE)
Each share old Common 10¢ par exchanged for (0.000002) share new Common 10¢ par 11/10/2003
Note: In effect holders received $1.41 cash per share and public interest was eliminated

SIENA TECHNOLOGIES INC (NV)
Recapitalized as XnE, Inc. 07/01/2009
Each share Common $0.001 par exchanged for (0.002) share Common $0.001 par
(See XnE, Inc.)

SIENNA DEVELOPMENT CORP. (BC)
Name changed to Sienna Resources, Ltd. (BC) 5/19/81
Sienna Resources Ltd. (BC) reincorporated in Alberta 12/14/84 which merged into Orbit Oil & Gas Ltd. 6/30/89
(See Orbit Oil & Gas Ltd.)

SIENNA GOLD INC (AB)
Reincorporated under the laws of British Columbia as Peruvian Precious Metals Corp. 07/02/2013
Peruvian Precious Metals Corp. name changed to PPX Mining Corp. 08/05/2016

SIENNA RES INC (DE)
Name changed to American Energy Fields, Inc. 01/15/2010
American Energy Fields, Inc. name changed to Continental Resources Group, Inc. 07/28/2011 which merged into Pershing Gold Corp. 03/04/2013

SIENNA RES LTD (AB)
Reincorporated 12/14/84
Place of incorporation changed from (BC) to (ALTA) 12/14/84
Merged into Orbit Oil & Gas Ltd. 6/30/89
Each (2.5) shares Common no par exchanged for (1) share Common no par
(See Orbit Oil & Gas Ltd.)

SIERRA ANCHA URANIUM CORP. (UT)
Merged into Uranium Corp. of America (UT) on a (1) for (4) basis 4/5/55
Uranium Corp. of America (UT) merged into Chemical & Metallurgical Enterprises, Inc. 11/5/56
(See Chemical & Metallurgical Enterprises, Inc.)

SIERRA CAP CO (CA)
Liquidation completed
Each share Capital Stock no par received initial distribution of $5.40 cash 08/11/1966
Each share Capital Stock no par received second distribution of $1 cash 02/28/1967
Each share Capital Stock no par received third distribution of $0.60 cash 02/16/1968
Each share Capital Stock no par received fourth distribution of $0.25 cash 02/18/1969
Each share Capital Stock no par received fifth distribution of $0.25 cash 02/27/1970
Each share Capital Stock no par received sixth distribution of $0.50 cash 10/06/1970
Each share Capital Stock no par received seventh distribution of $0.25 cash 02/24/1972
Each share Capital Stock no par received eighth distribution of $0.10 cash 03/02/1973
Each share Capital Stock no par received ninth distribution of $0.25 cash 04/26/1974
Each share Capital Stock no par received tenth distribution of $0.10 cash 03/20/1975
Each share Capital Stock no par received eleventh distribution of $0.10 cash 06/03/1977
Each share Capital Stock no par received twelfth distribution of $0.10 cash 07/21/1978
Each share Capital Stock no par received thirteenth distribution of $0.10 cash 01/17/1979
Each share Capital Stock no par exchanged for fourteenth and final distribution of (1) share Unicorn Resources Inc. Common 10¢ par 03/28/1980
(See Unicorn Resources Inc.)

SIERRA CAP RLTY TR IV (CA)
Name changed to Meridian Point Realty Trust IV Co. 10/15/1991
Meridian Point Realty Trust IV Co. merged into Meridian Industrial Trust, Inc. 02/23/1996 which merged into ProLogis Trust 03/30/1999 which name changed to ProLogis 05/23/2002 which merged into Prologis, Inc. 06/03/2011

SIERRA CAP RLTY TR VI (MO)
Reincorporated 10/03/1988
State of incorporation changed from (CA) to (MO) 10/03/1988
Name changed to Meridian Point Realty Trust VI Co. 10/15/1991
Meridian Point Realty Trust VI Co. merged into Meridian Industrial Trust, Inc. 02/23/1996 which merged into ProLogis Trust 03/30/1999 which name changed to ProLogis 05/23/2002 which merged into Prologis, Inc. 06/03/2011

SIERRA CAP RLTY TR VII (MO)
Name changed to Meridian Point Realty Trust VII Co. 10/15/1991
Meridian Point Realty Trust VII Co. merged into Meridian Industrial Trust, Inc. 02/23/1996 which merged into ProLogis Trust 03/30/1999 which name changed to ProLogis 05/23/2002 which merged into Prologis, Inc. 06/03/2011

SIERRA CAP RLTY TR VIII (MO)
Name changed to Meridian Point Realty Trust VIII Co. 10/01/1993
Meridian Point Realty Trust VIII Co. merged into EastGroup Properties, Inc. 06/01/1998

SIERRA CASCADE ENTERPRISES, INC. (NV)
Merged into Associated Smelters International 04/27/1972
Each share Capital Stock 10¢ par exchanged for (1) share Common 10¢ par
Associated Smelters International name changed to ASI 09/01/1978 which recapitalized as ASI Technology Corp. 09/01/2000 which recapitalized as Robertson Global Health Solutions Corp. 08/06/2010

SIERRA CONCEPTS INC (NV)
Reincorporated under the laws of Delaware as Pioneer Power Solutions, Inc. 01/07/2010

SIERRA DESERT HLDGS INC (NV)
Recapitalized as Telefix Communications Holdings, Inc. 03/12/2012
Each share Common $0.001 par exchanged for (0.002) share Common $0.001 par

SIERRA DIAMOND INTL CORP (NV)
Recapitalized as ITOS, Inc. 04/12/2004
Each share Common $0.001 par exchanged for (0.002) share Common $0.001 par
ITOS, Inc. recapitalized as Satellite Phone Source Inc. (NV) 08/10/2004 which reincorporated in Delaware as Vision Works Media Group, Inc. 04/06/2005 which name changed to Perihelion Global, Inc. (DE) 10/25/2006 which reincorporated in Nevada 04/01/2008 which recapitalized as Nymet Holdings Inc. 04/21/2009

SIERRA ELECTRIC CORP. (CA)
Completely liquidated 3/13/68
Each share Common $1 par plus $1 cash exchanged for first and final distribution of (0.8245) share Sola Basic Industries, Inc. Common $1 par
Sola Basic Industries, Inc. merged into General Signal Corp. 9/30/77 which merged into SPX Corp. 10/6/98

SIERRA EMPIRE MINES LTD (BC)
Proclaimed dissolved for failure to file annual reports 12/18/1978

SIERRA ENGR CO (CA)
Merged into Cap Tech Inc. 08/11/1969
Each share Prior Preferred $100 par exchanged for (1) share Prior Preferred $100 par
Each share Preferred $100 par exchanged for (1) share Preferred $100 par
Each share Common $1 par exchanged for (11) shares Common $1 par
(See Cap Tech)

SIERRA EXPL CO (CO)
Each share old Common no par exchanged for (0.2) share new Common no par 04/15/1983
Merged into Wichita River Oil Corp. (VA) (New) 11/04/1987
Each share new Common no par exchanged for (0.000833) share Common no par
Wichita River Oil Corp. (VA) (New) reincorporated in Delaware 03/30/1990
(See Wichita River Oil Corp. (DE))

SIERRA EXPLORATIONS INC (NV)
Each share old Common $0.001 par exchanged for (0.001) share new Common $0.001 par 12/30/2008
Charter revoked for failure to file reports and pay fees 11/01/2010

SIERRA GEOTHERMAL PWR CORP (BC)
Merged into Ram Power, Corp. 09/02/2010
Each share Common no par exchanged for (0.08333333) share Common no par
Ram Power, Corp. recapitalized as Polaris Infrastructure Inc. 05/19/2015

SIERRA GIGANTE RES INC (NV)
Name changed to AVVAA World Health Care Products Inc. 7/12/2002

SIERRA GOLD, INC. (NV)
Charter revoked for failure to file reports and pay fees 9/1/98

SIERRA GOLD CORP OLD (NV)
Name changed to PayForView.com Corp. 12/29/1998
PayForView.com Corp. recapitalized as PayForView Media Group Holdings Corp. 04/24/2001 which name changed to James Barclay Alan, Inc. 02/21/2002 which recapitalized as Titan Consolidated, Inc. 05/28/2003 which name changed to Titan Oil & Gas, Inc. 02/21/2005 which name changed to Green Star Energies Inc. 12/04/2008

SIERRA HEALTH SVCS INC (NV)
Common 1¢ par changed to $0.005 par and (1) additional share issued 01/11/1993
Common $0.005 par split (3) for (2) by issuance of (0.5) additional share payable 06/08/1998 to holders of record 05/18/1998 Ex date - 06/09/1998
Common $0.005 par split (2) for (1) by issuance of (1) additional share payable 12/30/2005 to holders of record 12/16/2005 Ex date - 01/03/2006
Merged into UnitedHealth Group Inc. 02/25/2008
Each share Common $0.005 par exchanged for $43.50 cash

SIERRA HLDGS GROUP INC (NV)
Name changed to InsiderStreet.com Inc. 11/02/1999
InsiderStreet.com Inc. reorganized in Delaware as Neometrix Technology Group Inc. 04/14/2003
(See Neometrix Technology Group Inc.)

SIERRA HOME SVC COS INC (CA)
In process of liquidation
Each share Common no par received initial distribution of $1.27 cash 3/13/96
Note: Details on subsequent distribution(s), if any, are not available

SIERRA INTL GROUP INC (DE)
Name changed 10/06/1999
Common $0.0005 par split (5) for (1) by issuance of (4) additional shares payable 04/12/1999 to holders of record 03/31/1999
Name changed from Sierra Idea Capital Corp. to Sierra International Group Inc. 10/06/1999
SEC revoked common stock registration 07/28/2011

SIERRA IRON ORE CORP (BC)
Name changed to Crystal Lake Mining Corp. 07/14/2016

SIERRA KITCHEN GALLERIES INC (NV)
Name changed to Montana Oil & Gas, Inc. and (1) additional share issued 6/1/2004
Montana Oil & Gas, Inc. recapitalized as Falcon Energy Inc. 4/3/2006 which recapitalized as Red Truck Entertainment Inc. 2/12/2007

SIERRA LEONE DIAMOND CO LTD (BERMUDA)
Name changed to African Minerals Ltd. 08/15/2007

SIERRA LEONE DIAMOND EXPORT CO. (OK)
Charter cancelled for failure to pay taxes 1/25/91

SIERRA LIFE INS CO (ID)
Common $5 par changed to $1 par and (4) additional shares issued 04/27/1964
Each share old Common $1 par exchanged for (0.555) share new Common $1 par 04/30/1978
Stock Dividends - 10% 04/30/1971; 10% 06/30/1972
Liquidation completed 00/00/2000
No stockholders' equity

SIERRA MADRE GOLD CORP (DE)
Name changed to Capital One Ventures Corp. 02/18/2000
Capital One Ventures Corp. name changed to Cirus Telecom, Inc. 02/08/2001 which recapitalized as THC Communications Inc. 03/08/2002
(See THC Communications Inc.)

SIERRA MADRE RES INC (BC)
Recapitalized as Camphor Ventures Inc. 02/19/1993
Each share Common no par exchanged for (0.4) share Common no par
Camphor Ventures Inc. merged into Mountain Province Diamonds Inc. 04/19/2007

SIERRA MICRO SYS INC (UT)
Proclaimed dissolved for failure to pay taxes 3/31/86

SIERRA MINERALS INC (QC)
Recapitalized as Goldgroup Mining Inc. (QC) 05/07/2010
Each share Common no par exchanged for (0.3508772) share Common no par
Goldgroup Mining Inc. (QC) reincorporated in British Columbia 07/28/2011

SIERRA MONARCH GOLD MINING CO. (CA)
Bankrupt in 1953

SIERRA NATL BK (PETALUMA, CA)
Common $10 par changed to $5 par in December 1971
Common $5 par changed to $4 par 12/31/74
Stock Dividend - 20% 8/1/72
Merged into United California Bank (Los Angeles, CA) 3/26/79
Each share Common $4 par exchanged for $23.56 cash

SIERRA NATL BK (TEHACHAPI, CA)
Merged into Bank of the Sierra (Porterville, CA) 5/19/2000
Each share Common $5 par exchanged for $11.43 cash

SIERRA NEV GOLD LTD (BC)
Delisted from Toronto Venture Stock Exchange 06/05/2002

SIERRA NEVADA, LTD. (NV)
Charter revoked for failure to file reports and pay fees 3/4/57

SIERRA NEVADA CO. (UT)
Charter cancelled for failure to pay taxes 9/2/69

SIERRA OIL & GAS CO (NV)
Recapitalized as Consolidated Lift Systems, Inc. 05/12/1987
Each (26.6667) shares Common 1¢ par exchanged for (1) share Common $0.001 par
(See Consolidated Lift Systems, Inc.)

SIERRA ON-LINE INC (DE)
Common 1¢ par split (2) for (1) by issuance of (1) additional share 03/03/1995
Stock Dividend - 50% 11/20/1991
Merged into CUC International Inc. 07/24/1996
Each share Common 1¢ par exchanged for (1.225) shares Common 1¢ par
CUC International Inc. name changed to Cendant Corp. 12/17/1997 which reorganized as Avis Budget Group, Inc. 09/01/2006

SIERRA PAC DEV FD LTD PARTNERSHIP (CA)
Merged into American Spectrum Realty, Inc. 10/19/2001
Each Unit of Limited Partnership Int. exchanged for (16.072263) shares Common 1¢ par
Each Unit of Limited Partnership Int. II exchanged for (9.127879) shares Common 1¢ par
Each Unit of Limited Partnership Int. III exchanged for (0.528949) share Common 1¢ par

SIERRA PAC GYPSUM CORP (NV)
Name changed to Sanitec Holdings USA 06/16/2000
Sanitec Holdings USA recapitalized as Co-Media Inc. 11/25/2000 which reorganized as Jarvis Group Inc. 01/18/2002 which name changed to Cash 4 Homes 247 on 05/21/2003 which name changed to Vegas Equity International Corp. 02/01/2006
(See Vegas Equity International Corp.)

SIERRA PAC INDS (CA)
Merged into Sierra Pacific Holding Co. 07/11/1977
Each share Common $1 par exchanged for $18.75 cash

SIERRA PAC INSTL PPTYS (CA)
Merged into American Spectrum Realty, Inc. 10/19/2001
Each Unit of Limited Partnership Int. V exchanged for (9.673999) shares Common 1¢ par

SIERRA PAC PENSION INVS LTD PARTNERSHIP (CA)
Merged into American Spectrum Realty, Inc. 10/19/2001
Each Unit of Limited Partnership Int. 84 exchanged for (19.922088) shares Common 1¢ par

SIERRA PAC PWR CO (NV)
Reincorporated 03/31/1965
Common $15 par changed to $7.50 par and (1) additional share issued 09/15/1955
Common $7.50 par changed to $3.75 par and (1) additional share issued 04/20/1961
State of incorporation changed from (ME) to (NV) 03/31/1965
Common $3.75 par split (2) for (1) by issuance of (1) additional share 04/23/1965
Under plan of reorganization each share Common $3.75 par automatically became (1) share Sierra Pacific Resources (Old) Common $1 par 05/31/1984
$5.32 Preferred Ser. D $50 par called for redemption 04/30/1987
Sierra Pacific Resources (Old) merged into Sierra Pacific Resources (New) 07/28/1999 which name changed to NV Energy, Inc. 11/19/2008
$2.44 Preferred Ser. A $50 par called for redemption at $51 on 11/01/1999
$2.36 Preferred Ser. B $50 par called for redemption at $50.43 on 11/01/1999
$3.90 Preferred Ser. C $50 par called for redemption at $50.98 on 11/01/1999
Class A Preferred Ser. 1 no par called for redemption at $25.683 on 06/01/2006

SIERRA PAC RES NEW (NV)
Each old Premium Income Equity Security received (3.0084) shares Common $1 par 11/15/2005
Each new Premium Income Equity Security received (3.0084) shares Common $1 par 11/15/2005
Name changed to NV Energy, Inc. 11/19/2008
(See NV Energy, Inc.)

SIERRA PAC RES OLD (NV)
Merged into Sierra Pacific Resources (New) 07/28/1999
Each share Common $1 par exchanged for either (1.44) shares Common $1 par, $37.55 cash, or a combination thereof
Note: Cash electors received 80.139% of total holdings in cash and the remaining 19.861% in stock
Holdings of (99) shares or fewer received cash
Sierra Pacific Resources (New) name changed to NV Energy, Inc. 11/19/2008

SIERRA PACIFIC ELECTRIC CO.
Merged into Sierra Pacific Power Co. (ME) in 1937
Each share Preferred exchanged for (1) share Preferred
Each share Common exchanged for (2.2) shares Common
Sierra Pacific Power Co. (ME) reincorporated under the laws of Nevada 3/31/65
(See Sierra Pacific Power Co. (NV))

SIERRA PAC PWR CAP I
8.60% Trust Originated Preferred Securities called for redemption at $25 on 11/29/2001

SIERRA PETE INC (KS)
Each share Common $1 par stamped to indicate change to 50¢ par and distribution of 20¢ cash 10/23/1959
Stamped Common 50¢ par changed to 10¢ par 12/30/1966
Merged into United Investments Corp. 07/12/1976
Each share Common 10¢ par exchanged for $2 cash

SIERRA PETROLEUM, INC.
Merged into Crusader Corp. 00/00/1952
Each share Common 5¢ par exchanged for (0.8) share Capital Stock 5¢ par
Crusader Corp. merged into Crusader Oil & Uranium Co. 04/20/1955 which merged into Crusader Oil & Gas Co. 02/06/1959 which merged into Gold Empire Mining Co. 06/15/1968
(See Gold Empire Mining Co.)

SIERRA PREFABRICATORS, INC. (DE)
Charter cancelled and declared inoperative and void for non-payment of taxes 4/15/72

SIERRA QUEEN MINING CORP. (NV)
Name changed to First National Crandall Corp. 11/3/72
First National Crandall Corp. name changed to International Commodity Resources Corp. 7/21/75 which name changed to Ovutron Corp. 4/7/77 which name changed to Colt Energy Corp. 12/4/86
(See Colt Energy Corp.)

SIERRA REAL ESTATE EQUITY TR 82 (CA)
Name changed 5/26/83
Name changed from Sierra Real Estate Equity Trust to Sierra Real Estate Trust '82 on 05/26/1983
Name changed to Meridian Point Realty Trust '82 on 10/15/1991

SIERRA REAL ESTATE EQUITY TR 83 (CA)
Name changed to Meridian Point Realty Trust '83 (CA) 10/15/1991
Meridian Point Realty Trust '83 (CA) reincorporated in Maryland as Liberty Self-Stor, Inc. 12/29/1999 which name changed to John D. Oil & Gas Co. 06/21/2005

SIERRA REAL ESTATE EQUITY TR 84 CO (MO)
Completely liquidated
Each share Common received first and final distribution of $0.0724 cash payable 12/18/95 to holders of record 12/8/95
Note: Certificates were not required to be surrendered and are without value

SIERRA RESH CORP (NY)
Common 10¢ par changed to $0.06-2/3 par and (0.5) additional share issued 2/20/81
Merged into LTV Corp. (Old) 9/8/83
Each share Common $0.06-2/3¢ par exchanged for (2.34) shares Common 50¢ par
LTV Corp. (Old) reorganized as LTV Corp. (New) 6/28/93
(See LTV Corp. (New))

SIERRA RESH CORP CDA (CANADA)
Name changed to Greystone Research Corp. 05/28/2001
Greystone Research Corp. acquired by Javelin Capital Corp. 08/04/2005 which recapitalized as Javelin Energy Inc. 03/30/2006
(See Javelin Energy Inc.)

SIERRA RESOURCE GROUP INC (NV)
Common $0.001 par split (6) for (1) by issuance of (5) additional shares payable 06/25/2010 to holders of record 06/25/2010 Ex date - 06/28/2010
SEC revoked common stock registration 01/13/2017

SIERRA RES INC (CO)
Each share Common 2¢ par exchanged for (0.2) share Common 10¢ par 06/16/1986
Name changed to Petro Global, Inc. 06/15/1987
Petro Global, Inc. recapitalized as MRI Medical Diagnostics Inc. 02/12/1992 which recapitalized as HomeZipR Corp. (CO) 09/06/2000 which reorganized in Delaware as Advansys Companies, Inc. 12/28/2006

SIERRA-ROCKIES CORP (CA)
Reorganized under the laws of Nevada as Alpha Nutraceuticals Inc. 01/29/2004
Each share Common $0.001 par exchanged for (0.01) share Common $0.001 par, (0.01) Common Stock

Purchase Warrant Ser. A expiring 12/31/2004 and (0.01) Common Stock Purchase Warrant Ser. B expiring 12/31/2005
Alpha Nutraceuticals Inc. recapitalized as Alpha Nutra, Inc. 02/08/2005 which name changed to China Broadband, Inc. 05/16/2007 which name changed to YOU On Demand Holdings, Inc. 04/05/2011 which name changed to Wecast Network, Inc. 11/14/2016 which name changed to Seven Stars Cloud Group, Inc. 07/17/2017

SIERRA SEMICONDUCTOR CORP (CA)
Common no par split (2) for (1) by issuance of (1) additional share 10/04/1995
Name changed to PMC-Sierra, Inc. (CA) 06/13/1997
PMC-Sierra, Inc. (CA) reincorporated in Delaware 07/10/1997 which merged into Microsemi Corp. 01/14/2016
(See Microsemi Corp.)

SIERRA SILVER MNG CO (NV)
Recapitalized as Pacific Western Industries, Inc. 09/02/1983
Each share Common 2¢ par exchanged for (1/3) share Common 6¢ par
(See Pacific Western Industries, Inc.)

SIERRA SMELTING & REFINING CO. (CA)
Charter suspended for failure to file reports and pay fees 1/6/40

SIERRA SOLIDS INC (NV)
Each share old Common $0.001 par exchanged for (0.1) share new Common $0.001 par 06/23/1995
Name changed to Synergy Media Inc. 05/03/1996
Synergy Media Inc. recapitalized as VIPR Industries, Inc. 02/06/2008

SIERRA SPRING WTR CO (DE)
Common 1¢ par split (3) for (2) by issuance of (0.5) additional share 1/20/86
Acquired by Anjou International Co. 5/9/88
Each share Common 1¢ par exchanged for $3.75 cash

SIERRA SYS GROUP INC (BC)
Acquired by Golden Gate Capital 1/5/2007
Each share Common no par exchanged for $9.25 cash

SIERRA TAHOE BANCORP (CA)
Stock Dividend - 10% 6/15/92
Name changed to SierraWest Bancorp 7/25/96
SierraWest Bancorp merged into BancWest Corp. (New) 7/1/99
(See BancWest Corp. (New))

SIERRA TECH INC (UT)
Recapitalized as Golf Ventures Inc. 1/6/93
Each share Common $0.001 par exchanged for (0.1) share Common $0.001 par
Golf Ventures Inc. name changed to Golf Communities of America Inc. 11/19/98
(See Golf Communities of America Inc.)

SIERRA TRADING CORP (NV)
Each share Capital Stock 25¢ par exchanged for (2.5) shares Capital Stock 10¢ par 06/02/1956
Each share Capital Stock 10¢ par exchanged for (0.2) share Capital Stock 50¢ par 10/12/1956
Court declared company insolvent 05/04/1972
No stockholders' equity

SIERRA TUCSON COS INC (DE)
Name changed to NextHealth, Inc. 10/12/95
(See NextHealth, Inc.)

SIERRA VENTURES INC (WY)
Name changed to Lucky Boy Silver Corp. (WY) 03/31/2010
Lucky Boy Silver Corp. (WY) reincorporated in Nevada 03/22/2011 which name changed to National Graphite Corp. 06/06/2012

SIERRA VISTA BK (FOLSOM, CA)
Acquired by Central Valley Community Bancorp 10/03/2016
Each share Common no par exchanged for $5.20 cash

SIERRA VISTA ENERGY LTD (AB)
Reorganized as Radius Resources Corp. 05/23/2008
Each share Class A Common no par exchanged for (0.1) share Common no par
Each share Class B Common no par exchanged for (1) share Common no par

SIERRACIN CORP (DE)
Reincorporated 5/31/77
Common $1 par split (3) for (2) by issuance of (0.5) additional share 1/26/68
State of incorporation changed from (CA) to (DE) 5/31/77
Common $1 par split (2) for (1) by issuance of (1) additional share 5/1/81
Stock Dividend - 25% 12/28/61; 25% 1/27/67; 100% 3/28/80
Acquired by SCS Acquisition Corp. 3/9/90
Each share Common $1 par exchanged for $15 cash

SIERRACITIES COM INC (DE)
Merged into American Express Travel Related Services Co., Inc. 3/27/2001
Each share Common 1¢ par exchanged for $5.68 cash

SIERRAWEST BANCORP (CA)
Stock Dividend - 5% payable 8/29/97 to holders of record 8/20/97
Merged into BancWest Corp. (New) 7/1/99
Each share Common no par exchanged for (0.82) share Common $1 par
(See BancWest Corp. (New))

SIFTON PPTYS LTD (ON)
99.1% acquired through purchase offer 03/31/1978
Note: Minority shares acquired at $75 per share 06/27/1995
Public interest eliminated

SIFY LTD (INDIA)
Name changed to Sify Technologies Ltd. 10/26/2007

SIGA PHARMACEUTICALS INC (DE)
Name changed to SIGA Technologies Inc. 02/04/2000

SIGA RES INC (NV)
Recapitalized as Gold Lakes Corp. 08/24/2015
Each share Common $0.001 par exchanged for (0.005) share Common $0.001 par

SIGA RES LTD (AB)
Issue Information - 3,500,000 shares COM offered at $0.10 per share on 04/06/1995
Merged into Open Range Capital Corp. 03/30/2016
Each share Common no par exchanged for $0.20 cash

SIGCORP INC (IN)
Common no par split (3) for (2) by issuance of (0.5) additional share payable 03/27/1997 to holders of record 02/21/1997 Ex date - 03/31/1997
Merged into Vectren Corp. 03/31/2000
Each share Common no par exchanged for (1.333) shares Common no par

SIGEM INC (CANADA)
Name changed to Mobile Knowledge Inc. 3/15/2002

SIGHT & SOUND SERVICES (UT)
Name changed to Jordan Energy Corp. 11/2/82
(See Jordan Energy Corp.)

SIGHT RESOURCE CORP (DE)
Plan of reorganization under Chapter 11 Federal Bankruptcy Code effective 11/04/2005
No stockholders' equity

SIGHTMASTER CORP. (NY)
Each share Common 25¢ par exchanged for (6) shares Common 5¢ par 00/00/1949
Reincorporated under the laws of Delaware as S.M.T.R. Corp. 06/09/1964
S.M.T.R. Corp. name changed to Resource Exploration, Inc. 03/23/1970 which name changed to Resource America, Inc. 01/31/1989
(See Resource America, Inc.)

SIGHTMIRROR TELEVISION CORP. (DE)
Proclaimed inoperative and void for non-payment of taxes 04/01/1954

SIGHTUS INC (CANADA)
Placed in receivership 03/06/2007
Stockholders' equity unlikely

SIGMA ALDRICH CORP (DE)
Common $1 par split (3) for (1) by issuance of (2) additional shares 01/02/1986
Common $1 par split (2) for (1) by issuance of (1) additional share 01/02/1991
Common $1 par split (2) for (1) by issuance of (1) additional share payable 01/02/1997 to holders of records 12/16/1996
Common $1 par split (2) for (1) by issuance of (1) additional share payable 01/02/2007 to holders of record 12/15/2006 Ex date - 01/03/2007
Stock Dividend - 100% 01/04/1982
Acquired by Merck KGaA 11/18/2015
Each share Common $1 par exchanged for $140 cash

SIGMA ALPHA GROUP LTD (DE)
Name changed 9/6/95
Each share old Common $0.001 par exchanged for (1/3) share new Common $0.001 par 11/2/92
Name changed from Sigma Alpha Entertainment Group Ltd. to Sigma Alpha Group Ltd. 9/6/95
Name changed to Clariti Telecommunications International Ltd. 3/3/98
Clariti Telecommunications International Inc. reorganized as Integrated Data Corp. 11/12/2002

SIGMA CAP SHS INC (DE)
Common $1 par split (2) for (1) by issuance of (1) additional share 06/29/1981
Common $1 par split (2) for (1) by issuance of (1) additional share 08/19/1985
Name changed to ProvidentMutual Growth Fund, Inc. 03/01/1990
(See ProvidentMutual Growth Fund, Inc.)

SIGMA CIRCUITS INC (DE)
Common $0.001 par split (2) for (1) by issuance of (1) additional share payable 02/26/1996 to holders of record 02/12/1996
Merged into Tyco International Ltd. 07/02/1998
Each share Common $0.001 par exchanged for $10.50 cash

SIGMA CONS INDS INC (MA)
Recapitalized as Med-Assist, Inc. 11/02/1972
Each share Common 1¢ par exchanged for (0.5) share Common 2¢ par
(See Med-Assist, Inc.)

SIGMA FED MONEYFUND INC (DE)
Name changed to ProvidentMutual Federal Moneyfund, Inc. 03/01/1990
(See ProvidentMutual Federal Moneyfund, Inc.)

SIGMA GOVERNMENT SECURITIES FUND, INC. (DE)
Name changed to Sigma Federal Moneyfund, Inc. 10/29/1987
Sigma Federal Moneyfund, Inc. name changed to ProvidentMutual Federal Moneyfund, Inc. 03/01/1990
(See ProvidentMutual Federal Moneyfund, Inc.)

SIGMA INC (OR)
Involuntarily dissolved 02/26/1974
No stockholders' equity

SIGMA INCOME SHS INC (DE)
Name changed to ProvidentMutual Income Shares, Inc. 03/01/1990
(See ProvidentMutual Income Shares, Inc.)

SIGMA INDS INC (MA)
Name changed to Sigma Consolidated Industries, Inc. 03/10/1969
Sigma Consolidated Industries, Inc. recapitalized as Med-Assist, Inc. 11/02/1972
(See Med-Assist, Inc.)

SIGMA INSTRS INC (MA)
Merged into Wheelabrator-Frye Inc. 08/07/1980
Each share Common $1 par exchanged for $20 cash

SIGMA INTL LTD (MO)
Merged into Sigma-Aldrich Corp. 07/31/1975
Each share Common 10¢ par exchanged for (1) share Common $1 par
(See Sigma-Aldrich Corp.)

SIGMA INVT SHS INC (DE)
Common $1 par split (2) for (1) by issuance of (1) additional share 08/31/1983
Name changed to ProvidentMutual Investment Shares, Inc. 03/01/1990
(See ProvidentMutual Investment Shares, Inc.)

SIGMA MED ASSOC INC (UT)
Proclaimed dissolved for failure to pay taxes 2/1/90

SIGMA MINES (QUEBEC), LTD. (QC)
Name changed to Sigma Mines (Quebec) Ltd./Les Mines Sigma (Quebec) Ltee. 9/16/74
Sigma Mines (Quebec) Ltd./Les Mines Sigma (Quebec) Ltee. merged into Placer Dome Inc. 6/21/88 which merged into Barrick Gold Corp. 3/8/2006

SIGMA MINES QUE LTD (QC)
Capital Stock $1 par changed to no par and (1) additional share issued 05/11/1979
Capital Stock no par split (2) for (1) by issuance of (1) additional share 05/09/1980
Capital Stock no par split (2) for (1) by issuance of (1) additional share 06/01/1981
Merged into Placer Dome Inc. 06/21/1988
Each share Capital Stock no par exchanged for (0.97) share Common no par
Placer Dome Inc. merged into Barrick Gold Corp. 03/08/2006

SIGMA MONEY MARKET FUND, INC. (DE)
Name changed to Sigma Moneyfund, Inc. 10/29/87
Sigma Moneyfund, Inc. name changed to ProvidentMutual Moneyfund, Inc. 3/1/90

SIGMA MONEYFUND INC (DE)
Name changed to ProvidentMutual Moneyfund, Inc. 03/01/1990

SIGMA PA TAX-FREE TR (PA)
Name changed to ProvidentMutual Pennsylvania Tax-Free Trust 03/06/1990
ProvidentMutual Pennsylvania Tax-Free Trust name changed to Sentinel Pennsylvania Tax-Free Trust 07/03/1992 which merged into Federated Municipal Securities Fund, Inc. 07/21/2006

SIGMA RESH INC (WA)
Plan of reorganization under Chapter 11 Federal Bankruptcy proceedings confirmed 06/08/1989
No stockholders' equity

SIGMA SCIENCE LTD (BC)
Recapitalized as Guyana Gold Corp. 7/29/94
Each (2.7) shares Common no par exchanged for (1) share Common no par
Guyana Gold Corp. name changed to Beringer Gold Corp. 11/18/96 which merged into Lions Gate Entertainment Corp. 11/13/97

SIGMA SEC INC (BC)
Recapitalized as International Sigma Security Inc. 7/11/85
Each share Common no par exchanged for (0.25) share Common no par
(See International Sigma Security Inc.)

SIGMA-7 PRODS INC (CO)
Each (75,000) shares old Common no par exchanged for (100) shares new Common no par to reflect a (1) for (75,000) reverse split followed by a (100) for (1) forward split 05/22/1998
Note: No shareholder will receive fewer than (100) shares
Administratively dissolved 08/01/1999

SIGMA SOFTWARE SYS INC (MN)
Statutorily dissolved 12/31/92

SIGMA SPL FD INC (DE)
Common $1 par split (2) for (1) by issuance of (1) additional share 08/16/1983
Name changed to ProvidentMutual Special Fund, Inc. 03/01/1990

SIGMA TAX FREE BD FD INC (DE)
Name changed to ProvidentMutual Tax-Free Bond Fund, Inc. 03/01/1990
ProvidentMutual Tax-Free Bond Fund, Inc. merged into Sentinel Group Funds, Inc. 03/01/1993

SIGMA TAX-FREE MONEYFUND INC (MD)
Name changed to ProvidentMutual Tax-Free Moneyfund, Inc. 03/01/1990
(See ProvidentMutual Tax-Free Moneyfund, Inc.)

SIGMA U S GOVT FD INC NEW (MD)
Name changed to ProvidentMutual U.S. Government Fund for Income, Inc. 03/01/1990
(See ProvidentMutual U.S. Government Fund for Income, Inc.)

SIGMA VALUE SHS INC (MD)
Name changed to ProvidentMutual Value Shares, Inc. 03/01/1990
(See ProvidentMutual Value Shares, Inc.)

SIGMA VENTURE SHS INC (DE)
Common $1 par split (2) for (1) by issuance of (1) additional share 06/15/1978
Common $1 par split (2) for (1) by issuance of (1) additional share 06/29/1981
Name changed to ProvidentMutual Venture Shares, Inc. 03/01/1990
(See ProvidentMutual Venture Shares, Inc.)

SIGMA VENTURES INC (AB)
Name changed to Sigma Industries Inc. 02/21/2008

SIGMA WORLD FD INC (DE)
Name changed to ProvidentMutual World Fund, Inc. 03/01/1990
(See ProvidentMutual World Fund, Inc.)

SIGMACOM SYS INC (BC)
Struck off register and declared dissolved for failure to file reports 12/03/1993

SIGMACOR INC (AB)
Delisted from Canadian Venture Stock Exchange 10/23/2000

SIGMAFORM CORP (CA)
Common 34¢ par changed to $0.2267 par and (0.5) additional share issued 03/07/1980
Common $0.2267 par changed to $0.11335 par and (1) additional share issued 07/09/1984
Merged into Raychem Corp. 04/01/1988
Each share Common $0.11335 par exchanged for $10 cash

SIGMATEL INC (DE)
Issue Information - 10,000,000 shares COM offered at $15 per share on 09/18/2003
Merged into Freescale Semiconductor, Inc. 05/05/2008
Each share Common $0.0001 par exchanged for $3 cash

SIGMATICS (CA)
Charter cancelled for failure to file reports and pay taxes 11/1/82

SIGMATRON NOVA INC (DE)
Charter forfeited for failure to maintain a registered agent 12/8/92

SIGMOR CORP (TX)
Common $1 par reclassified as Class A Common $1 par 03/29/1974
Class A Common $1 par split (2) for (1) by issuance of (1) additional share 08/24/1979
Class A Common $1 par split (5) for (4) by issuance of (1) additional share 08/24/1979
Class A Common $1 par split (5) for (4) by issuance of (0.25) additional share 03/27/1981
Stock Dividend - 15% 01/19/1978
Merged into Diamond Shamrock Corp. 12/01/1982
Each share Class A Common $1 par exchanged for $17.50 cash

SIGN MEDIA SYS INC (FL)
Name changed to International Consolidated Companies, Inc. 11/23/2007

SIGNAL ANALYSIS INDS CORP (NY)
Completely liquidated 10/2/72
Each share Common 5¢ par exchanged for (0.01969) share Honeywell Inc. Common $1.50 par
Honeywell Inc. merged into Honeywell International Inc. 12/1/99

SIGNAL APPAREL INC (IN)
$1.60 Conv. Preferred no par called for redemption 07/30/1992
Common $3.33333333 par reclassified as Class A Common 1¢ par 02/11/1987
Class A Common 1¢ par reclassified as Common 1¢ par 06/22/1993
Class B Common 1¢ par reclassified as Common 1¢ par 06/22/1993
Stock Dividend - In Non-transferable Conv. Class B Common to holders of Class A Common 100% 04/10/1987
Petition filed under Chapter 11 bankruptcy proceedings dismissed 03/27/2002
Stockholders' equity unlikely

SIGNAL BAY INC (CO)
Recapitalized as EVIO, Inc. 09/06/2017
Each share Common $0.0001 par exchanged for (0.01) share Common $0.0001 par

SIGNAL CHIBOUGAMAU MINING CORP. (QC)
Merged into Precious Metals, Ltd. 08/19/1968
Each share Capital Stock $1 par exchanged for (1) share Capital Stock 1¢ par
(See Precious Metals, Ltd.)

SIGNAL CORP (OH)
Merged into FirstMerit Corp. 02/12/1999
Each share Conv. Preferred Ser. B no par exchanged for (1) share 6.5% Conv. Preferred Ser. B no par
Each share Common $1 par exchanged for (1.32) shares Common no par
FirstMerit Corp. merged into Huntington Bancshares Inc. 08/16/2016

SIGNAL COS INC (DE)
$2.40 Conv. Preferred no par called for redemption 01/13/1969
$2.20 Conv. Preferred no par called for redemption 05/31/1977
$1 Conv. Preferred no par called for redemption 05/31/1977
Common $2 par split (2) for (1) by issuance of (1) additional share 12/08/1978
Common $2 par split (3) for (2) by issuance of (0.5) additional share 12/19/1980
Conv. Preferred Ser. B $1 par called for redemption 04/04/1985
Merged into Allied-Signal Inc. 09/19/1985
Each share 8.25% Conv. Preferred Ser. A $1 par exchanged for (1) share 8.25% Conv. Preferred Ser. AA no par
Each share Common $2 par exchanged for (1) share Common $1 par
Allied-Signal Inc. name changed to AlliedSignal Inc. 04/26/1993 which name changed to Honeywell International Inc. 12/01/1999

SIGNAL ENERGY LTD (AB)
Each share Common no par received distribution of (0.3246) share Siga Resources Ltd. Common no par payable 05/24/1996 to holders of record 05/21/1996
Acquired by Richland Petroleum Corp. 07/08/1996
Each share Common no par exchanged for $0.73 cash

SIGNAL EXPL INC (BC)
Common no par split (2) for (1) by issuance of (1) additional share payable 10/21/2016 to holders of record 10/19/2016 Ex date - 10/17/2016
Name changed to Southern Lithium Corp. 11/02/2016
Southern Lithium Corp. name changed to Le Mare Gold Corp. 02/02/2018

SIGNAL FIN CORP (PA)
Name changed to Signet Corp. 01/09/1969
Signet Corp. merged into Philadelphia National Corp. 06/29/1973 which merged into CoreStates Financial Corp 05/02/1983 which merged into First Union Corp. 04/28/1998 which name changed to Wachovia Corp. (Ctfs. dated after 09/01/2001) 09/01/2001 which merged into Wells Fargo & Co. (New) 12/31/2008

SIGNAL GENETICS INC (DE)
Each share old Common 1¢ par exchanged for (0.06666666) share new Common 1¢ par 11/07/2016
Name changed to Miragen Therapeutics, Inc. 02/14/2017

SIGNAL HILL ENERGY CORP (BC)
Recapitalized as Texas Petroleum Corp. (BC) 6/13/85
Each share Common no par exchanged for (0.2) share Common no par
Texas Petroleum Corp. (BC) recapitalized as North American Equity Corp. 3/7/89
(See North American Equity Corp.)

SIGNAL MINES LTD. (ON)
Charter cancelled in March, 1962
Stock worthless

SIGNAL MINING CO. (ID)
Recapitalized as Signal Silver-Gold Inc. 12/10/64
Each share Capital Stock 10¢ par exchanged for (0.4) share Capital Stock 25¢ par

SIGNAL MOUNTAIN PORTLAND CEMENT CO.
Merged into General Portland Cement Co. in 1947
Each share Preferred exchanged for (8.8126) shares Common $1 par
Common received only warrants which expired in 1950
General Portland Cement Co. name changed to General Portland Inc. 5/31/72
(See General Portland Inc.)

SIGNAL OIL & GAS CO. (DE)
Each share Class A Common no par exchanged for (6) shares Class A Common $5 par 00/00/1948
Each share Class B Common no par exchanged for (6) shares Class B Common $5 par 00/00/1948
Each share Class A Common $5 par exchanged for (3) shares Class A Common $2 par 00/00/1953
Each share Class B Common $5 par exchanged for (3) shares Class B Common $2 par 00/00/1953
5% Preferred $25 par called for redemption 07/02/1959
5.25% Sr. Preferred $50 par called for redemption 01/10/1968
Stock Dividend - Payable in Class A Common Stock to holders of Class A & B Common Stock - 15% 10/22/1958
Name changed to Signal Companies, Inc. and Class A Common $2 par and Class B Common $2 par reclassified as Common $2 par 05/01/1968
Signal Companies, Inc. merged into Allied-Signal Inc. 09/19/1985 which name changed to AlliedSignal Inc. 04/26/1993 which name changed to Honeywell International Inc. 12/01/1999

SIGNAL PETROLEUM CO. OF CALIFORNIA, LTD. (CA)
Charter suspended for failure to pay taxes 1/2/62

SIGNAL ROYALTIES CO.
Dissolved in 1949

SIGNAL SILVER GOLD INC (ID)
Charter forfeited for failure to file reports 12/1/93

SIGNAL TECHNOLOGY CORP (DE)
Merged into Crane Co. 5/29/2003
Each share Common 1¢ par exchanged for $13.25 cash

SIGNALENERGY INC (QC)
Each share Common no par received distribution of (0.037537) share G2 Resources Inc. Class A Common no par payable 08/10/2005 to holders of record 08/08/2005 Ex date - 08/04/2005
Plan of arrangement effective 02/20/2007
Each share Common no par exchanged for (0.2) share Fortress Energy Inc. Common no par
Fortress Energy Inc. name changed to Alvopetro Inc. 03/11/2013 which

name changed to Fortaleza Energy Inc. 11/19/2013

SIGNALGENE INC (QC)
Recapitalized as SignalEnergy Inc. 03/11/2004
Each share Common no par exchanged for (0.1) share Common no par
SignalEnergy Inc. reorganized as Fortress Energy Inc. 02/20/2007 which name changed to Alvopetro Inc. 03/11/2013 which name changed to Fortaleza Energy Inc. 11/19/2013

SIGNALIFE INC (DE)
Each (4,500) shares old Common $0.001 par exchanged for (1) share new Common $0.001 par 09/22/2008
Name changed to Heart Tronics Inc. 06/10/2009

SIGNALS OILS & METALS CO. LTD. (QC)
Name changed to Signal Chibougamau Mining Corp. 5/2/56
Signal Chibougamau Mining Corp. merged into Precious Metals, Ltd. 8/19/68
(See Precious Metals, Ltd.)

SIGNALSOFT CORP (DE)
Merged into Openwave Systems Inc. 07/17/2002
Each share Common no par exchanged for $2.26 cash

SIGNATURE BRANDS INC (NV)
Each (150) shares old Common $0.001 par exchanged for (1) share new Common $0.001 par 10/15/1997
Charter revoked for failure to file reports and pay fees 11/30/1998

SIGNATURE BRANDS LTD (ON)
Subordinate Shares no par reclassified as Common no par 11/21/1995
Recapitalized as CD Plus.com Ltd. 08/19/1999
Each share Common no par exchanged for (0.2) share Common no par
(See CD Plus.com Ltd.)

SIGNATURE BRANDS USA INC (DE)
Merged into Sunbeam Corp. (New) 4/7/98
Each share Common 1¢ par exchanged for $8.25 cash

SIGNATURE DIVERSIFIED VALUE TR (ON)
Trust terminated 12/14/2012
Each Trust Unit received $6.0173 cash

SIGNATURE ENERGY CORP (AB)
Recapitalized as Signature Resources Ltd. (AB) 08/19/1999
Each share Common no par exchanged for (0.2) share Common no par
Signature Resources Ltd. (AB) reincorporated in Canada as 3D Visit Inc. 04/05/2001 which recapitalized as Focus Metals Inc. 12/09/2008 which name changed to Focus Graphite Inc. 05/25/2012

SIGNATURE EXPL & PRODTN CORP (DE)
Each share old Common $0.0001 par exchanged for (0.1) share new Common $0.0001 par 10/31/2013
Name changed to GrowBLOX Sciences, Inc. 04/28/2014
GrowBLOX Sciences, Inc. name changed to GB Sciences, Inc. 04/10/2017

SIGNATURE GROUP HLDGS INC (DE)
Each share old Common $0.001 par exchanged for (1) Unit consisting of (1) share new Common $0.001 par and (1) Non-transferable Right 01/29/2015
Units terminated 02/20/2015
Name changed to Real Industry, Inc. 06/03/2015
(See Real Industry, Inc.)

SIGNATURE GROUP HLDGS INC (NV)
Each share old Common 1¢ par exchanged for (0.1) share new Common 1¢ par 10/15/2013
Reincorporated under the laws of Delaware and new Common 1¢ par changed to $0.001 par 01/07/2014
Signature Group Holdings, Inc. (DE) name changed to Real Industry, Inc. 06/03/2015
(See Real Industry, Inc.)

SIGNATURE GTEE SYS INC (NV)
Name changed to Checkmate Electronics, Inc. (NV) 10/1/86
Checkmate Electronics, Inc. (NV) reorganized in Georgia 6/24/93 which merged into IVI Checkmate Corp. 6/25/98
(See IVI Checkmate Corp.)

SIGNATURE GUARDIAN SYSTEMS, INC. (NV)
Name changed to Signature Guarantee Systems, Inc. and Common 10¢ par changed to 1¢ par 4/10/78
Signature Guarantee Systems, Inc. name changed to Checkmate Electronics, Inc. (NV) 10/1/86 which reorganized in Georgia 6/24/93 which merged into IVI Checkmate Corp. 6/25/98
(See IVI Checkmate Corp.)

SIGNATURE HORIZONS GROUP INC (DE)
Recapitalized as Summit Dental Clinics, Inc. 07/21/2008
Each share Common $0.0001 par exchanged for (0.001) share Common $0.0001 par
Summit Dental Clinics, Inc. recapitalized as AyreTrade, Inc. 08/14/2012 which name changed to Rocky Mountain Ayre, Inc. 02/05/2015

SIGNATURE HOSIERY CO., INC.
Liquidated in 1936

SIGNATURE INNS INC (IN)
Each (3.7) shares old Common no par exchanged for (1) share new Common no par 01/21/1997
Merged into Jameson Inns, Inc. 05/10/1999
Each share Conv. Preferred Ser. A no par exchanged for (1) share $1.70 Conv. Preferred Ser. A no par
Each share new Common no par exchanged for (0.5) share Common 10¢ par and $1.50 cash
(See Jameson Inns, Inc.)

SIGNATURE LOAN CO., INC. (MA)
Merged into Budget Finance Plan 9/8/58
Each share 7% Preferred $11 par exchanged for (1.25) shares 6% Preferred $10 par
Each share Class A Common $1 par exchanged for (0.475) share of 6% Preferred $10 par
Budget Finance Plan name changed to Budget Capital Corp. 12/20/72
(See Budget Capital Corp.)

SIGNATURE LTD (IN)
Units of Ltd. Partnership Int. Ser. X voluntarily dissolved 01/31/1997
Units of Ltd. Partnership Inc. Ser. XIV voluntarily dissolved 01/31/1997
Details not available

SIGNATURE MOTORCARS INC (NV)
Each share Common $0.0167 par received distribution of (0.33333333) share Cumberland Continental Corp. Common $0.001 par payable 04/15/2002 to holders of record 04/15/2002
Each share Common $0.0167 par received distribution of (0.33333333) share International Royalty & Oil Corp. Common $0.001 par payable 04/15/2002 to holders of record 04/15/2002
Each share Common $0.0167 par received distribution of (0.33333333) share Signature Financial Services Inc. Common $0.001 par payable 04/15/2002 to holders of record 04/15/2002
Each share Common $0.0167 par received distribution of (0.33333333) share Signature Healthcare Inc. Common $0.001 par payable 04/15/2002 to holders of record 04/15/2002
Recapitalized as Local Telecom Systems Inc. 04/18/2002
Each share Common $0.0167 par exchanged for (0.8) share Common $0.0167 par
Local Telecom Systems Inc. recapitalized as MBI Financial Inc. 06/06/2006
(See MBI Financial Inc.)

SIGNATURE RECORDING CORP.
Assets of the Corporation seized by the Collector of Internal Revenue and sold at public auction in 1951

SIGNATURE RESORTS INC (MD)
Common no par split (3) for (2) by issuance of (0.5) additional share payable 10/27/97 to holders of record 10/10/97
Name changed to Sunterra Corp. 7/14/98
(See Sunterra Corp.)

SIGNATURE RES LTD (AB)
Reincorporated under the laws of Canada as 3D Visit Inc. 04/05/2001
3D Visit Inc. recapitalized as Focus Metals Inc. 12/09/2008 which name changed to Focus Graphite Inc. 05/25/2012

SIGNATURE RES LTD (BC)
Incorporated 03/31/1988
Name changed to UrAsia Energy Ltd. 11/07/2005
UrAsia Energy Ltd. merged into sxr Uranium One Inc. 04/20/2007 which name changed to Uranium One Inc. 06/18/2007
(See Uranium One Inc.)

SIGNET BKG CORP (VA)
$1.15 Conv. Preferred Ser. F $20 par called for redemption 12/19/1986
Auction Preferred Ser. A $20 par called for redemption 05/31/1989
Common $5 par split (2) for (1) by issuance of (1) additional share 07/27/1993
Each share Common $5 par received distribution of (1) share Capital One Financial Corp. Common 1¢ par 02/28/1995
Merged into First Union Corp. 11/28/1997
Each share Common $5 par exchanged for (1.1) shares Common $3.33-1/3 par
First Union Corp. name changed to Wachovia Corp. (Ctfs. dated after 09/01/2001) 09/01/2001 which merged into Wells Fargo & Co. (New) 12/31/2008

SIGNET CORP (PA)
Merged into Philadelphia National Corp. 06/29/1973
Each share 34¢ Conv. Preferred 1969 Ser. no par exchanged for (0.16206) share Common $1 par
Each share 85¢ Preferred $12.50 par exchanged for $13.50 cash
Each share $1 Conv. Preferred $15 par exchanged for (0.50645) share Common $1 par
Each share $1.25 Preferred 1960 Ser. no par exchanged for $21 cash
Each share $1.50 Conv. Preferred 1959 Ser. no par exchanged for (1.01290) shares Common $1 par
Each share $3 Conv. Preferred 1963 Ser. no par exchanged for (1.62064) shares Common $1 par
Each share $3 Preferred 1964 Ser. no par exchanged for $50 cash
Each share Common $1 par exchanged for (0.40516) share Common $1 par
Philadelphia National Corp. merged into CoreStates Financial Corp 05/02/1983 which merged into First Union Corp. 04/28/1998 which name changed to Wachovia Corp. (Ctfs. dated after 09/01/2001) 09/01/2001 which merged into Wells Fargo & Co. (New) 12/31/2008

SIGNET GROUP PLC (UNITED KINGDOM)
Each Variable Term Preferred Ser. A Sponsored ADR for Ordinary, Variable Term Preferred Ser. B Sponsored ADR for Ordinary, Variable Term Preferred Ser. C Sponsored ADR for Ordinary, Variable Term Preferred Ser. D Sponsored ADR for Ordinary, Variable Term Preferred Ser. E Sponsored ADR for Ordinary, Conv. Preferred Sponsored ADR's for Ordinary, and old Sponsored ADR for Ordinary exchanged for (1) New Sponsored ADR for Ordinary respectively 07/21/1997
Each new Sponsored ADR for Ordinary 10p par exchanged for (0.1) Sponsored ADR's for Ordinary 5p par 09/04/1997
Sponsored ADR's for Ordinary 5p par split (3) for (1) by issuance of (2) additional ADR's payable 10/18/2004 to holders of record 10/15/2004 Ex date - 10/19/2004
Reorganized under the laws of Bermuda as Signet Jewelers Ltd. 09/11/2008
Each Sponsored ADR for Ordinary 5p par exchanged for (0.5) share Common 18¢ par

SIGNET MINERALS INC (AB)
Merged into Cash Minerals Ltd. 08/07/2007
Each share Common no par exchanged for (0.67) share Common no par, (0.5) Common Stock Purchase Warrant expiring 08/07/2010 and (0.25) share Troymet Exploration Corp. Common no par
Cash Minerals Ltd. recapitalized as Pitchblack Resources Ltd. 06/25/2010 which recapitalized as Troilus Gold Corp. 01/03/2018

SIGNET PETROLEUMS LTD. (ON)
Acquired by Consolidated Peak Oils Ltd. 00/00/1953
Each share Capital Stock $1 par exchanged for (1/3) share Capital Stock $1 par
Consolidated Peak Oils Ltd. acquired by Western Allenbee Oil & Gas Co. Ltd. 06/20/1960 which name changed to Convoy Capital Corp. 04/28/1989 which recapitalized as Hariston Corp. 09/25/1992 which recapitalized as Midland Holland Inc. (Canada) 02/10/1999 which reincorporated in Yukon 03/11/1999 which name changed to Mercury Partners & Co. Inc. 02/22/2000 which name changed to Black Mountain Capital Corp. 05/02/2005 which recapitalized as Grand Peak Capital Corp. (YT) 11/20/2007 which reincorporated in British Columbia 04/27/2010

SIGNET RES INC (BC)
Recapitalized as New Signet Resources Inc. 3/11/87
Each share Common no par

exchanged for (0.25) share Common no par
New Signet Resources Inc. recapitalized as Amir Ventures Corp. (BC) 6/29/93 which reorganized in Yukon Territory as America Mineral Fields Inc. 8/8/95 which name changed to Adasta Minerals Inc. 5/12/2004

SIGNET SELECT FDS (MA)
Name changed to Medalist Funds 8/15/94
Medalist Funds name changed to Virtus Funds 2/15/95

SIGNETICS CORP (CA)
Merged into U.S. Philips Corp. 06/10/1975
Each share Common no par exchanged for $8 cash

SIGNODE CORP (DE)
Common $1 par split (5) for (4) by issuance of (0.25) additional share 12/01/1968
Common $1 par split (3) for (2) by issuance of (0.5) additional share 02/28/1973
Merged into String Corp. 08/30/1982
Each share Common $1 par exchanged for $53 cash

SIGNODE STEEL STRAPPING CO. (DE)
Each share Common no par exchanged for (2) shares Common $1 par 00/00/1945
Stock Dividend - 20% 12/15/1950
Common $1 par split (2) for (1) by issuance of (1) additional share 05/16/1955
Common $1 par split (2) for (1) by issuance of (1) additional share 08/31/1960
5% Preferred called for redemption 05/01/1964
Name changed to Signode Corp. 05/01/1964
(See Signode Corp.)

SIGNTECH INC (ON)
Declared bankrupt in March 1994
No stockholders' equity

SIGNUM INC (CO)
Charter suspended for failure to file annual reports 09/30/1990

SIGUIRI BASIN MNG INC (DE)
Reorganized under the laws of Nevada as Anything Brands Online Inc. 01/17/2008
Each share Common $0.001 par exchanged for (0.00004608) share Common $0.001 par
Anything Brands Online Inc. name changed to MyFreightWorld Technologies, Inc. 05/13/2010

SIKAMAN GOLD RES LTD (CANADA)
Reincorporated 4/19/88
Reincorporated 7/12/99
Place of incorporation changed from (BC) to (ONT) 4/19/88
Place of incorporation changed from (ONT) to (Canada) 7/12/99
Name changed to SKG Interactive Inc. 10/1/2000
(See SKG Interactive Inc.)

SIKANNI SVCS LTD (AB)
Merged into EnQuest Energy Services Corp. 04/29/2008
Each (30) shares Common no par exchanged for (1) share Common no par
(See EnQuest Energy Services Corp.)

SIKES CORP (FL)
Class A Common 50¢ par changed to 25¢ par and (1) additional share issued 07/07/1981
Class A Common 25¢ par changed to 10¢ par and (1) additional share issued 07/10/1984
Class A Common 10¢ par split (2) for (1) by issuance of (1) additional share 07/08/1987

Merged into Premark International, Inc. 09/10/1990
Each share Class A Common 10¢ par exchanged for $16.42 cash
Each share Class A Common 10¢ par received an additional litigation settlement payment of $0.045 cash 01/25/1993

SIKORSKY AVIATION CORP.
Acquired by United Aircraft & Transport Corp. in 1929
Details not available

SIL-VAN CONSOLIDATED MINING & MILLING CO. LTD. (BC)
Reorganized as Sil-Van Mines Ltd. 08/30/1956
Each share Capital Stock no par exchanged for (0.2) share Common no par
Sil-Van Mines Ltd. reorganized as Dorita Silver Mines Ltd. 04/30/1969 which name changed to Liberty Petroleums Inc. 11/01/1978 which was acquired by Corrida Oils Ltd. 05/06/1982
(See Corrida Oils Ltd.)

SIL-VAN MINES LTD. (BC)
Reorganized as Dorita Silver Mines Ltd. 04/30/1969
Each share 4% Preference Ser. B $1 par exchanged for (1.5) shares Common no par
Each share Common no par exchanged for (0.1) share Common no par
Dorita Silver Mines Ltd. name changed to Liberty Petroleums Inc. 11/01/1978 which was acquired by Corrida Oils Ltd. 05/06/1982
(See Corrida Oils Ltd.)

SILA INDL GROUP LTD (BC)
Name changed to West Cirque Resources Ltd. 07/08/2011
West Cirque Resources Ltd. merged into Kaizen Discovery Inc. 07/08/2014

SILANCO MINING & REFINING CO LTD
Name changed 00/00/1945
Name changed from Silanco Mining & Smelting Corp. to Silanco Mining & Refining Co. Ltd. 00/00/1945
Recapitalized as Ansil Mines Ltd. 07/10/1957
Each share Common no par exchanged for (0.1428571) share Common no par
Ansil Mines Ltd. recapitalized as Ansil Resources Ltd. which merged into Jubilee Gold Exploration Ltd. 01/25/2013

SILAS CREEK RETAIL INC (DE)
Chapter 11 bankruptcy proceedings confirmed 11/30/99
Stockholders' equity unlikely

SILBA SILVER MINES LTD.
Merged into Consolidated Silver Banner Mines Ltd. on a (1) for (6) basis in 1950
Consolidated Silver Banner Mines Ltd. merged into Trans-Canada Explorations Ltd. in September 1955 which merged into Roman Corp. Ltd. 11/27/64
(See Roman Corp. Ltd.)

SILBAK PREMIER MINES LTD NEW (BC)
Each share Class B Common no par exchanged for (1) share Class A Common no par 09/16/1987
Merged into Pioneer Metals Corp. (Old) 05/11/1988
Each share Class A Common no par exchanged for (1) share Common no par
(See Pioneer Metals Corp. (Old))

SILBAK PREMIER MINES LTD OLD (BC)
Recapitalized as British Silbak Premier Mines, Ltd. 1/26/77

Each share Capital Stock $1 par exchanged for (0.2) share Capital Stock no par
British Silbak Premier Mines Ltd. name changed to Silbak Premier Mines, Ltd. (New) 7/23/87 which merged into Pioneer Metals Corp. (Old) 5/11/88
(See Pioneer Metals Corp. (Old))

SILCO DEVELOPMENT CO. LTD. (BC)
Struck off register and proclaimed dissolved for failure to file returns 9/3/74

SILCO INC (NV)
Each share old Common $1 par exchanged for (0.2) share new Common $1 par and (0.2) share Fort Worth National Corp. Common $5 par 01/18/1974
New Common $1 par changed to 5¢ par 10/25/1976
Charter dissolved 05/27/1992

SILCO INVS CORP (FL)
Name changed to Metatec Corp. (FL) 8/1/90
Metatec Corp. (FL) reincorporated in Ohio as Metatec International Inc. 4/30/99 which name changed to Metatec, Inc. 5/30/2003
(See Metatec, Inc.)

SILCORP LTD (ON)
Class A Non-Vtg. no par split (2) for (1) by issuance of (1) additional share 05/16/1985
Class B no par split (2) for (1) by issuance of (1) additional share 05/16/1985
Reorganized under the Companies' Creditors Arrangement Act 05/17/1993
Each share Class A Non-Vtg. no par exchanged for (1) share old Common no par
Each share Class B no par exchanged for (1) share old Common no par
Each share old Common no par exchanged for (0.1) share new Common no par 06/24/1993
New Common no par split (2) for (1) by issuance of (1) additional share payable 05/26/1998 to holders of record 05/21/1998 Ex date - 05/19/1998
Acquired by Alimentation Couche-Tard Inc. 05/27/1999
Each share new Common no par exchanged for (0.21187) share Class B Subordinate no par and approximately $18.97 cash

SILCROSS COPPER MINES LTD. (ON)
Declared dissolved 12/21/59
No stockholders' equity

SILENT CANYON RES LTD (BC)
Recapitalized as Golden Adit Resources Ltd. 4/27/88
Each share Common no par exchanged for (0.5) share Common no par
Golden Adit Resources Ltd. name changed to First Northern Developments, Inc. 6/8/90 which recapitalized as Consolidated First Northern Developments Inc. 9/20/93 which recapitalized as Golden Temple Mining Corp. 3/15/96 which recapitalized as Amerigo Resources Ltd. 3/8/2002

SILENT KNIGHT SECURITY SYSTEMS, INC. (MN)
Name changed to Security Engineering, Inc. 6/17/70 which name changed back to Silent Knight Security Systems, Inc. 7/8/74
Merged into Waycrosse, Inc. 5/31/76
Each share Common 5¢ par exchanged for $1.90 cash

SILENT PARTNER BODY ARMOR INC (NY)
Dissolved by proclamation 09/29/1993

SILENT WITNESS ENTERPRISES LTD (BC)
Each share old Common no par exchanged for (0.5) share new Common no par 7/31/96
Merged into Honeywell International Inc. 2/17/2004
Each share new Common no par exchanged for $11.27 cash

SILENTRADIO INC (DE)
Name changed to Cybernetic Services, Inc. 4/24/96
(See Cybernetic Services, Inc.)

SILENUS CORP (DE)
Charter cancelled and declared inoperative and void for non-payment of taxes 3/1/76

SILESIAN-AMERICAN CORP. (DE)
Declared insolvent 08/02/1955
Details not available

SILEURIAN CHIEFTAIN MNG LTD (BC)
Recapitalized as United Chieftain Resources Ltd. 11/1/72
Each share Capital Stock $1 par exchanged for (0.1) share Capital Stock no par
(See United Chieftain Resources Ltd.)

SILEX CO. (CT)
Common no par changed to $1 par in 1953
Name changed to Proctor-Silex Corp. 3/1/60
Proctor-Silex Corp. merged into SCM Corp. 6/30/66
(See SCM Corp.)

SILEX VENTURES LTD (BC)
Name changed to Argentum Silver Corp. 02/22/2011

SILHOUETTE BRANDS INC (DE)
Acquired by Dreyer's Grand Ice Cream Holdings, Inc. 7/26/2004
Each share Common $0.0001 par exchanged for $4.76 cash

SILICA GEL CORP. (DE)
Placed in receivership 4/22/33
Charter forfeited for failure to file reports and pay taxes 2/23/39

SILICA RES CORP (NV)
Common $0.001 par split (20) for (1) by issuance of (19) additional shares payable 08/08/2007 to holders of record 08/07/2007 Ex date - 08/09/2007
SEC revoked common stock registration 12/22/2014

SILICON ACQUISITION INC (AB)
Reincorporated under the laws of Ontario as Passion Media Inc. 07/29/2002
Passion Media Inc. name changed to Lemontonic Inc. 03/05/2004 which recapitalized as Pioneering Technology Inc. 04/05/2006 which recapitalized as Pioneering Technology Corp. 09/18/2008

SILICON DEV CORP (CO)
Charter suspended for failure to file annual reports 09/30/1984

SILICON DISK CORP (CA)
Recapitalized as Canadian Piper Air Corp. 06/23/1992
Each share Common no par exchanged for (0.03333333) share Common no par

SILICON GAMING INC (CA)
Merged into International Game Technology 03/27/2001
Each share Common $0.001 par exchanged for $0.119345 cash

SILICON GEN INC (CA)
Common no par split (2) for (1) by issuance of (1) additional share 01/21/1983

Common no par split (2) for (1) by issuance of (1) additional share 06/14/1983
Name changed to Symmetricom, Inc. (CA) 11/01/1993
Symmetricom, Inc. (CA) reincorporated in Delaware 01/07/2002
(See Symmetricom, Inc.)

SILICON GRAPHICS INC (DE)
Reincorporated 01/09/1990
State of incorporation changed from (CA) to (DE) 01/09/1990
Common $0.001 par split (2) for (1) by issuance of (1) additional share 02/21/1992
Common $0.001 par split (2) for (1) by issuance of (1) additional share 12/15/1993
Each share Common $0.001 par received distribution of (0.13858) share MIPS Technologies, Inc. Class B Common $0.001 par payable 06/20/2000 to holders of record 06/06/2000 Ex date - 06/21/2000
Plan of reorganization under Chapter 11 Federal Bankruptcy Code effective 10/17/2006
No Common $0.001 par stockholders' equity
Plan of reorganization under Chapter 11 Federal Bankruptcy Code effective 12/10/2009
No Common 1¢ par stockholders' equity

SILICON GRAPHICS INTL CORP (DE)
Acquired by Hewlett Packard Enterprise Co. 11/01/2016
Each share Common $0.001 par exchanged for $7.75 cash

SILICON IMAGE INC (DE)
Common $0.001 par split (2) for (1) by issuance of (1) additional share payable 08/18/2000 to holders of record 07/28/2000
Acquired by Lattice Semiconductor Corp. 03/09/2015
Each share Common $0.001 par exchanged for $7.30 cash

SILICON MTN HLDGS INC (CO)
Declared defunct and inoperative for failure to pay taxes and file annual reports 11/01/2011

SILICON SOUTH INC (NV)
Name changed to Alpha Wastewater, Inc. 12/20/2011

SILICON STORAGE TECHNOLOGY INC (CA)
Common no par split (3) for (1) by issuance of (2) additional shares payable 08/11/2000 to holders of record 07/28/2000
Merged into Microchip Technology Inc. 04/08/2010
Each share Common no par exchanged for $3.05 cash

SILICON SYS INC (CA)
Merged into TDK U.S.A. Corp. 05/23/1989
Each share Common no par exchanged for $20 cash

SILICON TRANSISTOR CORP (NY)
Merged into BBF Group, Inc. 12/31/72
Each share Common 20¢ par exchanged for (0.1) share Common 10¢ par
(See BBF Group, Inc.)

SILICON VY BANCSHARES (DE)
Reincorporated 4/23/99
Common no par split (3) for (2) by issuance of (0.5) additional share 2/28/89
Common no par split (2) for (1) by issuance of (1) additional share 5/15/90
Common no par split (2) for (1) by issuance of (1) additional share payable 5/1/98 to holders of record 4/17/98

State of incorporation changed from (CA) to (DE) 4/23/99
Common no par split (2) for (1) by issuance of (1) additional share payable 5/15/2000 to holders of record 4/21/2000
Stock Dividend - 10% 11/18/88
Name changed to SVB Financial Group 5/31/2005

SILICON VY GROUP INC (DE)
Reincorporated 04/28/1987
Common no par split (2) for (1) by issuance of (1) additional share 02/17/1987
State of incorporation changed from (CA) to (DE) and Common no par changed to 1¢ par 04/28/1987
Merged into ASM Lithography Holding N.V. 05/22/2001
Each share Common 1¢ par exchanged for (1.286) New York Registry Shares
ASM Lithography Holding N.V. name changed to ASML Holding N.V. 06/00/2001

SILICON VY RESH INC (CA)
Each share old Common no par exchanged for (0.5) share new Common no par 01/25/1996
Name changed to Macau Capital Investments Inc. 03/18/2008

SILICON VY VENTURES INC (CO)
Recapitalized as San Val, Inc. 10/22/1989
Each share Common no par exchanged for (0.02) share Common no par
San Val, Inc. recapitalized as Houston A-1 Car Stereo Plus, Inc. 04/19/2000
(See Houston A-1 Car Stereo Plus, Inc.)

SILICON VISION INTL CORP (QC)
Name changed to S-Vision Corp. 7/29/97

SILICONIX INC (DE)
Reincorporated 3/5/87
Capital Stock $1 par changed to no par in 1977
Capital Stock $1 par split (2) for (1) by issuance of (1) additional share 8/31/83
Capital Stock $1 par split (2) for (1) by issuance of (1) additional share 3/14/86
State of incorporation changed from (CA) to Delaware and Capital Stock no par reclassified as Common 1¢ par 3/5/87
Under plan of reorganization each share old Common 1¢ par exchanged for (0.1479589) share new Common 10¢ par 12/21/90
New Common 1¢ par split (3) for (1) by issuance of (2) additional shares payable 2/28/2000 to holders of record 2/17/2000
Merged into Vishay Intertechnology, Inc. 5/16/2005
Each share new Common 1¢ par exchanged (3.075) shares Common 1¢ par

SILICONWARE PRECISION INDS LTD (TAIWAN)
Stock Dividends - 60% payable 07/15/1996 to holders of record 05/25/1996; 40% payable 07/10/1997 to holders of record 05/21/1997; 36% payable 07/07/1998 to holders of record 05/21/1998
GDR agreement terminated 08/07/2000
Each 144A GDR for Common exchanged for approximately $8.70 cash
Each GDR for Class A exchanged for (1) Sponsored ADR for Common 09/26/2000
Stock Dividends - 14% payable 10/12/2000 to holders of record

07/28/2000; 14.5% payable 09/27/2001 to holders of record 07/20/2001 Ex date - 07/20/2001; 10% payable 09/17/2004 to holders of record 08/02/2004; Ex date - 07/29/2004; 8% payable 08/31/2005 to holders of record 08/01/2005 Ex date - 07/28/2005; 9.61729% payable 09/07/2006 to holders of record 08/03/2006 Ex date - 08/01/2006; 1.973% payable 09/10/2007 to holders of record 07/31/2007 Ex date - 07/27/2007; 1% payable 07/25/2008 to holders of record 07/10/2008 Ex date - 07/24/2008
ADR agreement terminated 04/30/2018
Each Sponsored ADR for Common exchanged for $8.470658 cash

SILIWOOD ENTMT CORP (UT)
Name changed to New Visual Entertainment, Inc. 10/07/1996
New Visual Entertainment, Inc. name changed to New Visual Corp. 07/02/2001 which name changed to Rim Semiconductor Co. 09/19/2005
(See Rim Semiconductor Co.)

SILK BOTANICALS COM INC (FL)
Each share old Common $0.001 par exchanged for (0.01428571) share new Common $0.001 par 02/05/2001
Name changed to Consolidated Resources Group, Inc. 06/03/2002
(See Consolidated Resources Group, Inc.)

SILK GREENHOUSE INC (FL)
Common 1¢ par split (3) for (2) by issuance of (0.5) additional share 09/15/1989
Plan of reorganization under Chapter 11 Federal Bankruptcy proceedings confirmed 08/21/1991
No stockholders' equity

SILK PARADE INC (UT)
Name changed to Wall Street Capital Corp. (New) 4/8/94
(See Wall Street Capital Corp. (New))

SILK RD ENTMT INC OLD (NV)
Common $0.001 par split (2) for (1) by issuance of (1) additional share payable 06/27/2000 to holders of record 06/16/2000 Ex date - 06/28/2000
Name changed to Tiwenz Group 08/10/2000 which name changed back to Silk Road Entertainment Inc. 02/01/2001
Reorganized as Silk Road Entertainment Inc. (New) 09/05/2006
Each share Common $0.001 par exchanged for (0.00071428) share Common $0.001 par

SILK RD FIN INC (CAYMAN ISLANDS)
Each share old Common USD $0.0001 par exchanged for (0.0002) share new Common USD $0.0001 par 01/20/2017
Note: Holders of (4,999) or fewer pre-split shares received CAD$1.02 cash per share
Unexchanged certificates will be cancelled and become without value 01/20/2022

SILK RD VENTURES LTD (BC)
Reorganized under the laws of Cayman Islands as Silk Road Finance Inc. 12/02/2014
Each share Common no par exchanged for (0.1) share Common USD $0.0001 par
(See Silk Road Finance Inc.)

SILK ROAD RES LTD (CANADA)
Acquired by EurOmax Resources Ltd. 06/30/2009
Each share Common no par exchanged for (2.2535) shares Common no par

SILK SILK SILK INTL INC (FL)
Chapter 11 Federal Bankruptcy Code converted to Chapter 7 on 5/22/90
No stockholders' equity

SILKNET SOFTWARE INC (DE)
Issue Information - 3,000,000 shares COM offered at $15 per share on 05/05/1999
Merged into Kana Communications, Inc. 04/19/2000
Each share Common 1¢ par exchanged for (1.66) shares Common $0.001 par
Kana Communications, Inc. name changed to Kana Software, Inc. 06/29/2001 which name changed to SWK Holdings Corp. 12/23/2009

SILKNIT LTD (CANADA)
Each share Common $5 par exchanged for (3) shares Common no par 6/2/64
Each share Common no par exchanged for (2) shares Conv. Class A Common no par and (2) shares Conv. Class B Common no par 8/21/72
5% Preferred $40 par called for redemption 10/31/78
Conv. Class A Common no par reclassified as Common no par 9/13/79
Conv. Class B Common no par reclassified as Common no par 9/13/79
Stock Dividend - 100% 12/12/63
Reacquired 3/19/86
Each share Common no par exchanged for $0.15 cash

SILKRIDGE RES LTD (BC)
Name changed to Aquatech Systems Inc. 9/19/89
(See Aquatech Systems Inc.)

SILLITTI FINANCE CORP. (NY)
Charter cancelled and proclaimed dissolved for failure to pay taxes 12/16/35

SILMIL EXPLS INC (ON)
Merged into Belle Aire Resource Explorations Ltd. 8/29/78
Each share Capital Stock no par exchanged for (0.25) share Common no par
Belle Aire Resource Explorations Ltd. name changed to Sprint Resources Ltd. 9/23/82 which name changed to Meacon Bay Resources Inc. 3/9/87 which recapitalized as Advantex Marketing International Inc. 9/16/91

SILMONAC MINES LTD (BC)
Recapitalized as Silvana Mines Inc. 9/8/77
Each share Common 50¢ par exchanged for (0.25) share Common no par
Silvania Mines Inc. merged into Dickenson Mines Ltd. (New) 10/31/80 which merged into Goldcorp Inc. (New) 3/31/94

SILMONT MINING CO. LTD. (ON)
Charter cancelled for failure to file reports and pay taxes November 1961

SILO DISCOUNT CENTERS, INC. (PA)
Name changed to Silo, Inc. 11/14/66
(See Silo, Inc.)

SILO INC (PA)
Common $1 par split (4) for (3) by issuance of (1/3) additional share 7/30/71
Common $1 par split (1.25) for (1) by issuance of (0.25) additional share 4/15/74
Common $1 par split (1.25) for (1) by issuance of (0.25) additional share 7/14/78
Merged into Cyclops Corp. 2/26/80
Each share Common $1 par exchanged for $24 cash

SILRUCA GOLD MINES LTD.
Name changed to Zinc Lake Mines Ltd. in 1952
(See Zinc Lake Mines Ltd.)

SILTEC CORP (CA)
Acquired by Mitsubishi Metal Corp. 12/17/1986
Each share Common no par exchanged for $7.95 cash

SILTRONICS INC (PA)
Liquidated by Order of Court 00/00/1971
No stockholders' equity

SILVA BAY INTL INC (DE)
Common $0.0001 par split (2) for (1) by issuance of (1) additional share payable 04/08/2003 to holders of record 04/03/2003 Ex date - 04/09/2003
Name changed to Spectrum Sciences & Software Holdings Corp. 04/08/2003
Spectrum Sciences & Software Holdings Corp. name changed to Horne International, Inc. 09/12/2006
(See Horne International, Inc.)

SILVAN INDS INC (NV)
SEC revoked common stock registration 01/19/2016

SILVANA MINES INC (BC)
Merged into Dickenson Mines Ltd. (New) 10/31/80
Each (3.5) shares Common no par exchanged for (1) share Class A no par and (1) share Class B no par
Dickenson Mines Ltd. (New) merged into Goldcorp Inc. (New) 3/31/94

SILVAR LISCO (CA)
Name changed to Silicon Valley Research Inc. 09/08/1994
Silicon Valley Research Inc. name changed to Macau Capital Investments Inc. 03/18/2008

SILVATEX INC (FL)
Name changed to Grandma's Inc. 7/30/82
(See Grandma's Inc.)

SILVER (ISAAC) & BROTHERS CO., INC.
Merged into F. & W. Grand-Silver Stores, Inc. in 1929 which was sold in bankruptcy in 1934

SILVER ACORN DEVS LTD (BC)
Recapitalized as Wydmar Development Corp. 10/6/87
Each share Capital Stock no par exchanged for (0.5) share Common no par
(See Wydmar Development Corp.)

SILVER AGE MNG CO (NV)
Name changed to Standard Systems Corp. 05/10/1969

SILVER AMER INC (NV)
Common $0.00001 par split (50) for (1) by issuance of (49) additional shares payable 03/08/2010 to holders of record 03/08/2010
Name changed to Gold American Mining Corp. 06/23/2010
Gold American Mining Corp. name changed to Inception Mining Inc. 05/17/2013

SILVER ARROW EXPLS LTD (BC)
Name changed 02/08/1966
Name changed from Silver Arrow Mines Ltd. to Silver Arrow Explorations Ltd. 02/08/1966
Merged into Stampede International Resources Ltd. 05/25/1970
Each share Common 50¢ par exchanged for (0.5) share Capital Stock no par
Stampede International Resources Ltd. merged into Stampede International Resources Inc. 05/31/1982 which merged into International H.R.S. Industries Inc. 05/15/1984 which name changed to Glenex Industries Inc. 05/25/1987

which merged into Quest Investment Corp. 07/04/2002 which merged into Quest Capital Corp. (BC) 06/30/2003 which reincorporated in Canada 05/27/2008 which name changed to Sprott Resource Lending Corp. 09/10/2010 which merged into Sprott Inc. 07/24/2013

SILVER ARROW MINES LTD. (ON)
Charter revoked for failure to file reports and pay fees 7/13/62

SILVER ASSETS INC (CA)
Merged into SSR Acquisition Inc. 10/16/2000
Each share Common 10¢ par exchanged for $0.00654 cash

SILVER BANNER MINES LTD.
Merged into Consolidated Silver Banner Mines Ltd. on a (1) for (3) basis in 1950
Consolidated Silver Banner Mines Ltd. merged into Trans-Canada Explorations Ltd. in September 1955 which merged into Roman Corp. Ltd. 11/27/64
(See Roman Corp. Ltd.)

SILVER BASIN YUKON MINES LTD.
Recapitalized as Consolidated Yukeno Mines Ltd. 00/00/1949
Each share Capital Stock $1 par exchanged for (0.33333333) share Capital Stock $1 par
Consolidated Yukeno Mines Ltd. recapitalized as Yukeno Mines Ltd. 00/00/1951 which recapitalized as Gradore Mines Ltd. 03/04/1966
(See Grador Mines Ltd.)

SILVER BAY MINES LTD. (BC)
Struck off register and declared dissolved for failure to file returns 4/4/77

SILVER BAY RLTY TR CORP (MD)
Acquired by Tricon Capital Group Inc. 05/09/2017
Each share Common 1¢ par exchanged for $21.50 cash

SILVER BAY RES INC (NV)
Name changed to Takedown Entertainment Inc. 06/30/2010
Takedown Entertainment Inc. recapitalized as Green Hygienics Holdings Inc. 07/24/2012

SILVER BEAR RES INC (ON)
Plan of arrangement effective 07/05/2017
Each share Common no par exchanged for (1) share Silver Bear Resources PLC Ordinary

SILVER BEAVER MNG CO (NV)
Reorganized 06/29/1998
Reorganized from (ID) to under the laws of Nevada 06/29/1998
Each share Common 10¢ par exchanged for (0.25) share Common 10¢ par
Recapitalized as Shadows Bend Development Inc. 04/27/2000
Each share new Common 10¢ par exchanged for (0.25) share Common 10¢ par
Shadows Bend Development Inc. recapitalized as FBO Air, Inc. 08/24/2004 which name changed to FirstFlight, Inc. 01/30/2007 which name changed to Saker Aviation Services Inc. 10/02/2009

SILVER BEEHIVE TELEPHONE CO., INC. (UT)
Name changed to Telephone Co., Inc. 7/15/69
Telephone Co., Inc. name changed to Beehive Telephone Co., Inc. 11/16/77

SILVER BELL INDS INC (CO)
Completely liquidated 12/8/78
Each share Common 25¢ par exchanged for first and final distribution of (0.054556) share Union Oil Co. of California Common $4-1/6 par
Union Oil Co. of California reorganized as Unocal Corp. 4/25/83 which merged into Chevron Corp. 8/10/2005

SILVER BELL MINES CO (CO)
Common $1 par and Class A $1 par changed to 25¢ par respectively 4/6/66
Class A 25¢ par reclassified as Common 25¢ par 12/12/68
Name changed to Silver Bell Industries, Inc. 1/1/70
Silver Bell Industries, Inc. liquidated for Union Oil Co. of California 12/8/78 which reorganized as Unocal Corp. 4/25/83 which merged into Chevron Corp. 8/10/2005

SILVER BELLE MINES 1966 LTD (ON)
Merged into Alchib Developments Ltd. 07/10/1969
Each share Capital Stock no par exchanged for (0.25) share Capital Stock no par
Alchib Developments Ltd. merged into Kalrock Developments Ltd. 10/23/1978 which merged into Kalrock Resources Ltd. 08/08/1990 which merged into Cercal Minerals Corp. 07/09/1993
(See Cercal Minerals Corp.)

SILVER BELLE MINES LTD. (ON)
Merged into Silver Belle Mines (1966) Ltd. 06/27/1966
Each share Capital Stock no par exchanged for (0.5) share Capital Stock no par
Silver Belle Mines (1966) Ltd. merged into Alchib Developments Ltd. 07/10/1969 which merged into Kalrock Developments Ltd. 10/23/1978 which merged into Kalrock Resources Ltd. 08/08/1990 which merged into Cercal Minerals Corp. 07/09/1993
(See Cercal Minerals Corp.)

SILVER BOUNTY MINES LTD. (BC)
Name changed to Copper Bounty Mines Ltd. (BC) 07/07/1971
Copper Bounty Mines Ltd. (BC) reorganized as Walmont Precious Metals Ltd. (Canada) 01/23/1984 which recapitalized as IGF Metals Inc. 08/01/1986 which name changed to Independent Growth Finders Inc. 07/10/1998
(See Independent Growth Finders Inc.)

SILVER BOWL INC (ID)
Charter forfeited for failure to file reports 12/1/93

SILVER BOX RES LTD (BC)
Struck off register and declared dissolved for failure to file reports 12/02/1994

SILVER BROOK ANTHRACITE CO. (DE)
No longer in existence having become inoperative and void for non-payment of taxes 4/1/52

SILVER BUCKLE MINING CO. (ID)
Merged into West Coast Engineering, Inc. 06/10/1963
Each share Common 10¢ par exchanged for (0.2) share Common no par
(See West Coast Engineering, Inc.)

SILVER BULLION MINING CO. (UT)
Merged into Flynn Energy Corp. 1/1/74
Each share Common 10¢ par exchanged for (0.166666) share Common 10¢ par
(See Flynn Energy Corp.)

SILVER BULLION TR (ON)
Non-Currency Hedged Units reclassified as ETF Non-Currency Hedged Units 05/26/2016

Name changed to Purpose Silver Bullion Fund 06/20/2018

SILVER BURDETT CO. (NJ)
5% Preferred $100 par called for redemption 4/23/62
Public interest eliminated

SILVER BUTTE CO (NV)
Reincorporated 03/04/2004
Common 10¢ par changed to 5¢ par 09/00/1977
Reincorporated from Silver Butte Mining Co. (ID) to under the laws of Nevada as Silver Butte Co. and Common 5¢ par changed to $0.001 par 03/04/2004
Recapitalized as Gulfmark Energy, Inc. 07/01/2011
Each share Common $0.001 par exchanged for (0.025) share Common $0.001 par
Gulfmark Energy, Inc. name changed to Gambit Energy, Inc. 11/08/2011

SILVER BUTTE MINES LTD (BC)
Recapitalized as Consolidated Silver Butte Mines Ltd. 6/28/72
Each share Capital Stock $1 par exchanged for (0.25) share Capital Stock no par
Consolidated Silver Butte Mines Ltd. name changed to Silver Butte Resources Ltd. 7/31/89 which recapitalized as Uniterre Resources Ltd. 8/17/95 which name changed to NaiKun Wind Energy Group Inc. 11/3/2006

SILVER BUTTE RES LTD (BC)
Recapitalized as Uniterre Resources Ltd. 8/17/95
Each share Common no par exchanged for (1/3) share Common no par
Uniterre Resources Ltd. name changed to NaiKun Wind Energy Group Inc. 11/3/2006

SILVER CENTY EXPLS LTD (ON)
Merged into Sudbury Contact Mines Ltd. 02/04/1999
Each share Common no par exchanged for (1) share Common no par
Sudbury Contact Mines Ltd. name changed to Contact Diamond Corp. 09/30/2004 which was acquired by Stornoway Diamond Corp. (BC) 01/17/2007 which reincorporated in Canada 10/28/2011

SILVER CHAMPION INC (ID)
Name changed to Champion Gold & Silver, Inc. 05/22/1973
Champion Gold & Silver, Inc. recapitalized as Western Continental, Inc. 06/17/1993
(See Western Continental, Inc.)

SILVER CHIEF MINERALS LTD (AB)
Merged into Quinstar Resources Corp. 11/06/1981
Each (2.5) shares Common no par exchanged for (1) share Common no par
Quinstar Resources Corp. recapitalized as Epoch Capital Corp. 08/14/1984 which merged into Quest Capital Corp. 10/25/1996 which name changed to Quest Oil & Gas Inc. 11/15/1996 which merged into EnerMark Income Fund 04/18/1997 which merged into Enerplus Resources Fund 06/22/2001 which reorganized as Enerplus Corp. 01/03/2011

SILVER CHIEFTAIN CO (ID)
Each share Common 10¢ par stamped to indicate distribution of (0.06294) share Consolidated Silver Corp. Common 10¢ par 12/28/68
(See Consolidated Silver Corp.)
Completely liquidated 9/2/74
Each share Stamped Common 10¢ par exchanged for first and final distribution of $0.0006 cash
Holders who did not advise the

Liquidating Trustee prior to 9/1/74 were barred from participating in the liquidation and their shares became valueless

SILVER CHRISTAL NAT GAS & MINERALS LTD (BC)
Name changed 02/23/1970
Name changed from Silver Christal Mines Ltd. to Silver Christal Natural Gas & Minerals Ltd. 02/23/1970
Name changed to Dominion Energy Corp. 04/02/1979
(See Dominion Energy Corp.)

SILVER CITY MINES LTD (BC)
Common $1 par changed to no par 10/27/1971
Recapitalized as Galaxy City Mines Ltd. 07/07/1977
Each share Common no par exchanged for (0.2) share Common no par
Galaxy City Mines Ltd. merged into Moly Mite Resources Inc. 03/16/1982 which recapitalized as Macrotrends Ventures Inc. 07/02/1986 which merged into Macrotrends International Ventures Inc. 08/17/1988 which recapitalized as Global Election Systems Inc. 11/22/1991 which was acquired by Diebold, Inc. 01/22/2002 which name changed to Diebold Nixdorf Inc. 12/12/2016

SILVER CITY PETES LTD (AB)
Recapitalized as Barclay Resources Ltd. 8/12/69
Each share Capital Stock no par exchanged for (1) share Capital Stock no par
Barclay Resources Ltd. name changed to Ballard Oil & Gas Ltd. 5/22/81
(See Ballard Oil & Gas Ltd.)

SILVER CLOUD MINES LTD (BC)
Merged into Angle Resources Ltd. (New) 01/01/1988
Each share Common no par exchanged for (1/3) share Common no par
Angle Resources Ltd. (New) merged into Nexus Resource Corp. 05/05/1988 which recapitalized as Pacific Gold Corp. (BC) 07/05/1990 which reincorporated in Alberta 05/12/1994 which reincorporated in Ontario 06/27/1995 which name changed to Worldtek (Canada) Ltd. 07/04/1996
(See Worldteck (Canada) Ltd.)

SILVER CONSOLIDATED MINES, INC. (ID)
Charter forfeited for failure to file reports and pay corporate taxes 11/30/64

SILVER CONTACT MINES LTD. (ON)
Merged into Silvermaque Mining Ltd. 08/21/1961
Each (1.75) shares Capital Stock no par exchanged for (1) share Common no par
Silvermaque Mining Ltd. recapitalized as Geomaque Explorations Ltd./Explorations Geomaque Ltee. 09/19/1986 which merged into Defiance Mining Corp. 06/25/2003 which merged into Rio Narcea Gold Mines, Ltd. 09/03/2004
(See Rio Narcea Gold Mines, Ltd.)

SILVER CREEK MINING CO. INC. (MT)
Charter revoked for failure to file reports and pay fees 3/8/79

SILVER CREEK NATL BK (SILVER CREEK, NY)
Merged into First National City Corp. 04/11/1972
Each share Common $25 par exchanged for (3.125) shares Common $6.75 par
First National City Corp. name changed to Citicorp 03/26/1974 which merged into Citigroup Inc. 10/08/1998

SILVER CREEK PRECISION CORP (NY)
Each share Common 10¢ par exchanged for (0.05) share Common $1 par 05/31/1968
Charter cancelled and proclaimed dissolved for failure to pay taxes 03/31/1982

SILVER CREST MINES INC (ID)
Reincorporated under the laws of Nevada as Silver Crest Resources, Inc. 12/01/2003
Silver Crest Resources, Inc. name changed to Gold Crest Mines, Inc. 09/08/2006 which name changed to Amazing Energy Oil & Gas, Co. 01/21/2015

SILVER CREST RES INC (NV)
Name changed to Gold Crest Mines, Inc. 09/08/2006
Gold Crest Mines, Inc. name changed to Amazing Energy Oil & Gas, Co. 01/21/2015

SILVER CRYSTAL MINES INC (ID)
Recapitalized as Timberline Resources Corp. (ID) 02/13/2004
Each share Common 10¢ par exchanged for (0.25) share Common $0.001 par
Timberline Resources Corp. (ID) reincorporated in Delaware 08/28/2008

SILVER CUP RES LTD (BC)
Name changed to Supertech Industries Ltd. 04/23/1987
Supertech Industries Ltd. name changed to Supertech Industries Inc. 07/24/1987 which recapitalized as Encore Products Inc. 10/11/1989
(See Encore Products Inc.)

SILVER DIME OIL CO. (TX)
Charter forfeited for failure to pay taxes 5/19/50

SILVER DINER CORP.
Out of business 00/00/1949
Details not available

SILVER DINER INC (DE)
Name changed 6/25/96
Name changed from Silver Diner Development Inc. to Silver Diner, Inc. 6/25/96
Each (5,000) shares old Common $0.00074 par exchanged for (1) share new Common $0.00074 par 10/7/2002
Note: In effect holders received $0.32 cash per share and public interest was eliminated

SILVER DIVIDE MINES CO (NV)
Acquired by Recreational Vehicles, Inc. 03/05/1971
Each share Common 5¢ par exchanged for (0.1) share Common 1¢ par

SILVER DLR MNG CO (ID)
Class A Common 10¢ par reclassified as Common 10¢ par 07/08/1969
Each share 4% Class B Preferred 10¢ par exchanged for (1) share Common 10¢ par 07/08/1969
Stock Dividend - 10% 07/18/1980
Merged into Sunshine Mining Co. 12/30/1981
Each share Common 10¢ par exchanged for (1.15) shares Capital Stock 50¢ par
Sunshine Mining Co. name changed to Sunshine Mining & Refining Co. 06/20/1994
(See Sunshine Mining & Refining Co.)

SILVER DOLLAR MINES LTD. (ON)
Name changed to Gold Ridge Mines Inc. 07/16/1973
(See Gold Ridge Mines Inc.)

SILVER DOLLY RES LTD (BC)
Recapitalized as Dolly Resources Ltd. 11/10/1976
Each share Capital Stock no par exchanged for (0.2) share Capital Stock no par
Dolly Resources Ltd. name changed to Dolly Varden Resources Inc. 04/15/1977 which merged into Dolly Varden Minerals Inc. 12/21/1979 which recapitalized as New Dolly Varden Minerals Inc. 11/16/92 which recapitalized as Dolly Varden Resources Inc. 04/17/2000 which name changed to DV Resources Ltd. 01/31/2012 which name changed to DLV Resources Ltd. 11/27/2017

SILVER DRAKE RES LTD (BC)
Name changed to Bioanalogics Systems, Inc. (BC) 02/24/1992
Bioanalogics Systems, Inc. (BC) reincorporated in Wyoming 03/13/1992 which reincorporated in Oregon 11/05/1992 which reorganized as International Bioanalogics Systems, Inc. 08/16/1993 which reincorporated in Canada 09/29/2006 which recapitalized as reWORKS Environmental Corp. 05/11/2007 which name changed to Forterra Environmental Corp. 02/22/2008

SILVER DUKE MINES LTD (BC)
Recapitalized as Totem Resources Ltd. 02/03/1976
Each share Capital Stock 50¢ par exchanged for (0.25) share Common $2 par
Totem Resources Ltd. name changed to Paragon Resources Ltd. 01/09/1978 which recapitalized as SAMEX Mining Corp. 09/11/1995
(See SAMEX Mining Corp.)

SILVER EAGLE ACQUISITION CORP (DE)
Each Unit received distribution of (1) Videocon d2h Ltd. ADR for Equity and $1 cash payable 03/31/2015 to holders of record 03/30/2015 Ex date - 04/01/2015
Each share Common $0.0001 par received distribution of (1) Videocon d2h Ltd. ADR for Equity payable 03/31/2015 to holders of record 03/30/2015 Ex date - 04/01/2015
Company terminated common stock registration and is no longer public as of 04/03/2015

SILVER EAGLE MINES INC (ON)
Merged into Excellon Resources Inc. (BC) 06/04/2009
Each share Common no par exchanged for (0.2704) share Common no par
Excellon Resources Inc. (BC) reincorporated in Ontario 06/05/2012

SILVER EAGLE MNG CO (UT)
Recapitalized as Nitecap Worldwide Communications, Inc. 05/24/1976
Each share Common 5¢ par exchanged for (0.05) share Common no par
(See Nitecap Worldwide Communications, Inc.)

SILVER EAGLE RES LTD (BC)
Recapitalized as Mercator Minerals Ltd. 3/13/2001
Each share Common no par exchanged for (0.2) share Common no par

SILVER EMPIRE INC (NV)
Each share old Capital Stock 10¢ par exchanged for (0.2) share new Capital Stock 10¢ par 10/06/1972
Stock Dividend - 10% 06/10/1974
Name changed to Du Pont Energy Control Corp. 12/01/1978
(See Du Pont Energy Control Corp.)

SILVER EMPIRE MINES (UT)
Recapitalized as Northwest Silica & Gypsum Co. 02/15/1975
Each share Common 5¢ par exchanged for (0.1) share Common 1¢ par
Northwest Silica & Gypsum Co. name changed to Egbert & Backus Excavating Co. 02/23/1976
(See Egbert & Backus Excavating Co.)

SILVER EUREKA CORP (NV)
Charter revoked for failure to file reports and pay fees 4/1/2000

SILVER EXPL INC (UT)
Recapitalized as Diversified Industries Inc. 12/16/1996
Each share Common 1¢ par exchanged for (0.05) share Common 1¢ par
Diversified Industries Inc. (UT) reorganized in Nevada as EZConnect Inc. 10/19/1999 which name changed to Encore Wireless, Inc. 02/08/2001
(See Encore Wireless, Inc.)

SILVER FALLS BK (SILVERTON, OR)
Stock Dividends - 5% payable 02/14/2003 to holders of record 01/31/2003 Ex date - 01/29/2003; 5% payable 02/27/2004 to holders of record 01/31/2004 Ex date - 01/28/2004; 5% payable 03/31/2006 to holders of record 02/28/2006 Ex date - 03/03/2006; 6% payable 02/15/2007 to holders of record 01/31/2007 Ex date - 01/29/2007; 7% payable 02/15/2008 to holders of record 01/31/2008 Ex date - 01/29/2008
Placed in receivership with FDIC 02/20/2009
Stockholders' equity unlikely

SILVER FALLS MINING, INC. (NV)
Charter revoked for failure to file reports and pay fees 3/7/60

SILVER FALLS MNG CO (WA)
Name changed to Southland Energy Corp. (WA) 12/1/76
Southland Energy Corp. (WA) reincorporated in Oklahoma 6/25/80
(See Southland Energy Corp. (OK))

SILVER FALLS RES LTD (BC)
Name changed to I.M. Technologies Inc. 08/25/1994
(See I.M Technologies Inc.)

SILVER FERN FINL LTD (AB)
Merged into eMedia Networks International Corp. 05/25/2007
Each share Common no par exchanged for (1) share Common no par
(See eMedia Networks International Corp.)

SILVER FORTUNE MNG CO (UT)
Name changed to Terra Vista, Inc. 4/3/71
(See Terra Vista, Inc.)

SILVER FUTURE, INC. (ID)
Name changed to Pioneer Petroleum & Mining, Inc. and Common 10¢ par changed to 1¢ par 11/25/81
Pioneer Petroleum & Mining, Inc. charter forfeited 12/1/93

SILVER GEORGE MINES LTD. (ON)
Acquired by Consolidated Matarrow Mines Ltd. on a (0.018) for (1) basis in 1953
Consolidated Matarrow Mines Ltd. was recapitalized as Jeanette Minerals Ltd. 6/16/55

SILVER GIANT MINES LTD.
Acquired by Giant Mascot Mines Ltd. on a (1.04) for (1) basis 00/00/1951
Giant Mascot Mines Ltd. recapitalized as G M Resources Ltd. (BC) 04/11/1977 which reincorporated in Canada 09/08/1982 which merged into Campbell Resources Inc. (New) 06/08/1983
(See Campbell Resources Inc. (New))

SILVER GLANCE RES INC (BC)
Name changed to Silverspar Minerals Inc. (BC) 06/17/1992
Silverspar Minerals Inc. (BC) reincorporated in Ontario 09/19/1997 which name changed to Internet Identity Presence Co. Inc. 02/02/2001 which name changed to Geophysical Prospecting, Inc. 12/06/2005 which name changed to Revolution Technologies Inc. 03/18/2008

SILVER-GOLD RECLAMATION, LTD. (NV)
Reorganized under the laws of Delaware as Packaging Plus Services, Inc. 02/14/1986
Each share Common $0.0001 par exchanged for (0.02) share Common $0.001 par
Packaging Plus Services, Inc. (DE) reorganized in Nevada as Universal Express Inc. 06/30/1998
(See Universal Express Inc.)

SILVER GULL CORP (NV)
Recapitalized 07/15/1973
Each share Common $1 par exchanged for (0.5) share Common $2 par 12/05/1970
Recapitalized from Silver Gull Oil & Gas Corp. to Silver Gull Corp. 07/15/1973
Each share Common $2 par exchanged for (0.1) share Common 1¢ par
Name changed to TR-3 International, Inc. 11/19/1973
TR-3 International, Inc. recapitalized as TR-3 Chemical Corp. 03/25/1975 which recapitalized as TR-3 Industries Inc. 09/30/1979 which name changed to Diversified American Industries Inc. 06/14/1990 which name changed to Thunderstone Group Inc. 11/13/1995 which name changed to Cronus Corp. 03/04/1996
(See Cronus Corp.)

SILVER HEART MINES LTD. (ON)
Charter revoked for failure to file reports and pay fees 5/13/65

SILVER HILL MINES INC (WA)
Reincorporated under the laws of Nevada 09/05/2007

SILVER HILL MINES LTD. (BC)
Ctfs. dated prior to 1959
Bankrupt in 1958
No stockholders' equity

SILVER HILL MINES LTD (BC)
Incorporated 1/15/80
Recapitalized as La Rock Mining Corp. 9/30/91
Each share Common no par exchanged for (1/3) share Common no par
La Rock Mining Corp. recapitalized as Avola Industries Inc. 7/19/2001 which recapitalized as Auramex Resource Corp. 1/16/2003

SILVER HILLS CONS MNG CO (NV)
Name changed to N-Viro Recovery, Inc. 6/9/92
N-Viro Recovery, Inc. name changed to Synagro Technologies Inc. (NV) 11/3/94 which reincorporated in Delaware 5/28/96
(See Synagro Technologies Inc.)

SILVER HOARD MINES LTD. (ON)
Charter cancelled for failure to pay taxes and file returns 3/16/76

SILVER HOARDE RES INC (BC)
Name changed to American Platinum Inc. 4/21/86
(See American Platinum Inc.)

SILVER HORIZONS, INC. (UT)
Name changed to Horizon Enterprises, Inc. 2/12/87

SILVER HORN MNG LTD (DE)
Reorganized under the laws of Nevada as Great West Resources, Inc. 04/21/2014
Each share Common $0.0001 par exchanged for (0.00666666) share Common $0.0001 par
Great West Resources, Inc. name changed to Orbital Tracking Corp. 02/20/2015

SILVER JACKPOT MINES LTD. (ON)
Name changed to Jackpot Uranium Mines Ltd. 4/7/53
Jackpot Uranium Mines Ltd. name changed to Big Jackpot Mines Ltd. 12/16/54
(See Big Jackpot Mines Ltd.)

SILVER KEY MINES LTD. (ON)
Merged into Nordev Resources Ltd. 03/24/1972
Each share Common $1 par exchanged for (0.1) share Common no par
Nordev Resources Ltd. recapitalized as Vedron Ltd. 06/05/1979 which recapitalized as Vedron Gold Inc. 01/04/1995 which name changed to VG Gold Corp. 08/07/2007 which merged into Lexam VG Gold Inc. 01/04/2011 which merged into McEwen Mining Inc. 05/01/2017

SILVER KEY MNG CO INC (NV)
Reincorporated 09/10/2001
State of incorporation changed from (ID) to (NV) 09/10/2001
Each share old Common $0.001 par exchanged for (0.2) share new Common $0.001 par 10/21/2002
Name changed to Health Systems Solutions, Inc. (NV) 12/10/2002
Health Systems Solutions, Inc. (NV) reincorporated in Delaware 02/19/2009
(See Health Systems Solutions, Inc. (DE))

SILVER KING COALITION MINES CO. (NV)
Merged into United Park City Mines Co. in 1953
Each share Capital Stock $5 par exchanged for (1.25) shares Capital Stock $1 par
(See United Park City Mines Co.)

SILVER KING COMMUNICATIONS INC (DE)
Under plan of merger name changed to HSN, Inc. (Old) 12/20/1996
HSN, Inc. (Old) name changed to USA Networks, Inc. 02/17/1998 which name changed to USA Interactive 05/09/2002 which name changed to InterActiveCorp 06/23/2003 which name changed to IAC/InterActiveCorp 07/14/2004

SILVER KING CONSOLIDATED MINING CO. OF UTAH
Acquired by Silver King Coalition Mines Co. in 1928
Details not available

SILVER KING MINES INC (NV)
Merged into Alta Gold Co. 11/24/1989
Each share Capital Stock $1 par exchanged for (1) share Common $0.001 par
(See Alta Gold Co.)

SILVER KING RES INC (DE)
Recapitalized as eNexi Holdings Inc. 07/18/2000
Each share Common $0.0001 par exchanged for (0.04) share Common $0.0001 par
eNexi Holdings Inc. recapitalized as Trinity3 Corp. 03/31/2003
(See Trinity3 Corp.)

SILVER KING WESTERN MINING & MILLING CO. (DE)
Reincorporated under the laws of Utah as Silver King Mining Co. 11/1/61

SILVER LADY RES INC (BC)
Struck off the register and declared dissolved for failure to file reports 03/04/1994

SILVER LAKE MINES LTD (ON)
Charter cancelled for failure to pay taxes and file returns 03/16/1976

SILVER LAKE RES INC (BC)
Each share old Common no par exchanged for (0.5) share new Common no par 11/04/2010
Name changed to Pacific Potash Corp. 06/27/2011
Pacific Potash Corp. name changed to Pacific Silk Road Resources Group Inc. 06/08/2018

SILVER LAKE RES INC (ON)
Name changed to International Platinum Corp. 08/25/1986
International Platinum Corp. recapitalized as International Precious Metals Corp. (ON) 10/23/1995 which reorganized in Wyoming as Innotelco, Inc. 04/05/2005 which recapitalized as Green America Land Holdings, Inc. 04/24/2008 which name changed to Green Card Capital Corp. 03/10/2009 which name changed to CUBA Beverage Co. 09/27/2010

SILVER LEADER MINES LTD (ON)
Merged into Petroflo Petroleum Corp. 08/18/1980
Each share Capital Stock $1 par exchanged for (0.5) share Capital Stock no par
Petroflo Petroleum Corp. merged into Flying Cross Resources Ltd. 12/04/1985 which merged into International Larder Minerals Inc. 05/01/1986 which merged into Explorers Alliance Corp. 10/13/2000
(See Explorers Alliance Corp.)

SILVER LEAF MINING CO. LTD.
Succeeded by Lakeleaf Silver Mining Co. Ltd. on a (1) for (10) basis in 1946

SILVER LEDGE INC (MT)
Reorganized under the laws of Nevada as Net Telecommunications, Inc. 07/11/1996
Each (40.0877) shares Common 10¢ par exchanged for (1) share Common 10¢ par
(See Net Telecommunications, Inc.)

SILVER LEE MINES LTD (BC)
Name changed to Bear International Industries Ltd. 03/25/1971
Bear International Industries Ltd. recapitalized as Consolidated Bear Industries Ltd. 03/14/1972 which merged into Resource Service Group Ltd. 07/01/1977
(See Resource Service Group Ltd.)

SILVER LINE TOURS (NV)
Charter revoked 5/1/97

SILVER MARK MINES, INC. (MT)
Involuntarily dissolved for failure to file annual reports 2/28/85

SILVER MEN MINES LTD (ON)
Charter cancelled and declared dissolved for failure to file returns and pay fees 04/20/1975

SILVER METALS INC (UT)
Recapitalized as Basin Exploration & Mining Co. 8/11/78
Each share Capital Stock 1¢ par exchanged for (0.02) share Capital Stock 1¢ par
Basin Exploration & Mining Co. name changed to Bonneville-West Corp. 6/22/84 which merged into Bonneville Pacific Corp. 11/1/87
(See Bonneville Pacific Corp.)

SILVER MILLER MINES LTD (ON)
Capital Stock $1 par changed to no par 12/16/71
Stock Dividend - 10% 11/30/52
Recapitalized as Silmil Explorations Inc. 9/20/72
Each share Capital Stock no par exchanged for (0.166666) share Capital Stock no par
Silmil Explorations Inc. merged into Belle Aire Resource Explorations Ltd. 8/29/78 which merged into Sprint Resources Ltd. 9/23/82 which name changed to Meacon Bay Resources Inc. 3/9/87 which recapitalized as Advantex Marketing International Inc. 9/16/91

SILVER MONARCH MINES (UT)
Name changed to Silver Monarch Oil & Gas Co. 11/8/77
Silver Monarch Oil & Gas Co. reorganized in Nevada as Pacific Energy Resources, Inc. 9/23/87

SILVER MONARCH OIL & GAS CO (UT)
Reorganized under the laws of Nevada as Pacific Energy Resources, Inc. 09/25/1987
Each share Common 1¢ par exchanged for (0.25) share Common $0.005 par

SILVER MONUMENT MINERALS INC (TX)
Name changed to Monument Energy Corp. 03/20/1974
Monument Energy Corp. recapitalized as Monument Energy Services, Inc. 09/19/1980 which merged into Alliance Well Service, Inc. 09/28/1984 which recapitalized as Alliance Northwest Industries, Inc. 07/30/1993
(See Alliance Northwest Industries, Inc.)

SILVER MOUNTAIN LEAD MINES INC (ID)
Name changed to Silver Syndicate Mining Corp. 10/19/2004
Silver Syndicate Mining Corp. name changed to 99 Dollar Stores, Inc. 8/17/2005 which name changed to InvestSource Communications, Inc. 1/17/2006 which name changed to United Resource Holdings Group, Inc. 2/5/2007

SILVER MOUNTAIN MINING CO. (IL)
Reincorporated under the laws of Utah as Silver Mountain Industries, Inc. and Capital Stock no par changed to $0.0005 par 8/22/78

SILVER MOUNTAIN MNG CO (WA)
Each share Common 10¢ par exchanged for (2) shares Common 5¢ par 05/05/1978
Name changed to Leadpoint Consolidated Mines Co. (WA) 08/20/1979
Leadpoint Consolidated Mines Co. (WA) reincorporated in Nevada as Point Acquisition Corp. 09/01/2006 which name changed to China Minerals Technologies, Inc. 06/13/2007 which name changed to China GengSheng Minerals, Inc. 07/30/2007

SILVER ORE ZONE MINES LTD (ON)
Charter cancelled for failure to file reports and pay taxes 07/27/1976

SILVER PACK MINES LTD. (ON)
Name changed to Silver Pack Resources Ltd. 11/28/1980
(See Silver Pack Resources Ltd.)

SILVER PACK RES LTD (ON)
Company believed out of business 00/00/1986
Details not available

SILVER PEAK RES LTD (BC)
Deemed to have made an assignment in bankruptcy 11/23/1999
Stockholders' equity unlikely

SILVER PETE CORP (NV)
Recapitalized as Applied Dental Technology Inc. 6/26/90
Each share Common $0.001 par exchanged for (0.05) share Common $0.001 par

SILVER PICK EXTENSION MINING CO. (AZ)
Charter revoked for failure to file reports and pay fees 4/6/26

SILVER PICK MINES INC (NV)
Name changed to Silver Pick Resources, Inc. 8/4/69
(See Silver Pick Resources, Inc.)

SILVER PICK RESOURCES, INC. (NV)
Charter revoked for failure to file reports and pay fees 3/5/73

SILVER PRINCESS RES INC (BC)
Delisted from Vancouver Stock Exchange 03/29/1996

SILVER PURSUIT RES LTD (BC)
Each share old Common no par exchanged for (0.25) share new Common no par 11/25/2013
Name changed to Golden Pursuit Resources Ltd. 06/15/2018

SILVER QUEST RES LTD (BC)
Merged into New Gold Inc. 12/23/2011
Each share Common no par exchanged for (0.09) share Common no par, (1/3) share Independence Gold Corp. Common no par and $0.0001 cash
(See each company's listing)
Note: Unexchanged certificates were cancelled and became without value 12/23/2017

SILVER RAMONA MNG INC (DE)
Reorganized 04/26/2000
Reorganized from Silver Ramona Mining Co. (ID) to under the laws of Delaware as Silver Ramona Mining Inc. 04/26/2000
Each (3.815968) shares Common 10¢ par exchanged for (1) share Common 10¢ par
Name changed to Achievement Tec Holdings, Inc. 07/05/2001
Achievement Tec Holdings, Inc. name changed to Clickable Enterprises, Inc. 01/06/2004
(See Clickable Enterprises, Inc.)

SILVER RECLAMATION INDS INC (DE)
Each share Common $0.001 par exchanged for (0.02) share Common 1¢ par 7/30/82
Recapitalized as Inter America Industries, Inc. 1/28/83
Each share Common 1¢ par exchanged for (1) share Common 1¢ par
Inter America Industries, Inc. name changed to Kendee's International Foods, Inc. 11/20/85
(See Kendee's International Foods, Inc.)

SILVER RECYCLING CO (CANADA)
Ceased operations 08/20/2009
Stockholders' equity unlikely

SILVER REEF MINES LTD (NV)
Name changed to Neva Equities, Inc. 06/09/1976
(See Neva Equities, Inc.)

SILVER REEF MINING CO. (NV)
Charter revoked for failure to file reports and pay fees 3/2/25

SILVER REEF URANIUM CO. (NV)
Merged into Uranium-Petroleum Co. on a (0.25) for (1) basis in 1956
Uranium-Petroleum Co. merged into General Contracting Corp. 2/28/61 which name changed to General International, Inc. 8/4/69
(See General International, Inc.)

SILVER REGENT MINES LTD (ON)
Merged into Consolidated Skeena Mines Ltd. 12/9/68
Each share Capital Stock no par exchanged for (0.5) share Common no par
Consolidated Skeena Mines Ltd. merged into International Mariner Resources Ltd. 2/9/71
(See International Mariner Resources Ltd.)

SILVER RES INC (NV)
Recapitalized as South American Minerals, Inc. 07/15/1996
Each share Common 20¢ par exchanged for (0.2) share Common 10¢ par

SILVER RESV CORP (DE)
Name changed to Infrastructure Materials Corp. 01/26/2009

SILVER RIDGE MNG LTD (BC)
Recapitalized as Consolidated Silver Ridge Mines Ltd. 03/03/1978
Each share Common 50¢ par exchanged for (0.2) share Common no par
Consolidated Silver Ridge Mines Ltd. name changed to Northcal Resources Ltd. 10/22/1981 which recapitalized as Calnor Resources Ltd. 09/20/1985 which recapitalized as Norcal Resources Ltd. 08/23/1991 which recapitalized as Troon Ventures Ltd. (BC) 06/18/2002 which reorganized in Ontario as Grenville Strategic Royalty Corp. 02/21/2014 which merged into LOGiQ Asset Management Inc. (AB) 06/07/2018 which reorganized in British Columbia as Flow Capital Corp. 06/11/2018

SILVER RIDGE RES INC (BC)
Recapitalized as International Silver Ridge Resources Inc. 04/20/1993
Each share Common no par exchanged for (0.33333333) share Common no par
International Silver Ridge Resources Inc. name changed to PNG Gold Corp. 06/13/2011 which name changed to Gen III Oil Corp. 05/16/2017

SILVER RIV VENTURES INC (NV)
Common $0.001 par split (2) for (1) by issuance of (1) additional share payable 1/31/2006 to holders of record 1/30/2006 Ex date - 2/1/2006
Name changed to BioForce Nanosciences Holdings, Inc. 2/1/2006

SILVER RUN ACQUISITION CORP (DE)
Units separated 10/12/2016
Name changed to Centennial Resource Development, Inc. 10/12/2016

SILVER RUN ACQUISITION CORP II (DE)
Units separated 02/12/2018
Name changed to Alta Mesa Resources, Inc. 02/12/2018

SILVER SATELLITE MINE INC (NV)
Name changed to Crown Colony National Corp. 03/11/1971
Each share Common 10¢ par exchanged for (1) share Common 10¢ par
(See Crown Colony National Corp.)

SILVER SCEPTRE RESOURCES LTD.-RESSOURCES SILVER SCEPTRE LTEE. (BC)
Merged into HLX Resources Ltd. 9/1/89
Each share Common no par exchanged for (0.1204) share Common no par
HLX Resources Ltd. recapitalized as Emperor Gold Corp. 3/30/92 which name changed to Emgold Mining Corp. 8/1/97

SILVER SCEPTRE RES LTD (BC)
Name changed 6/30/82
Name changed from Silver Sceptre Mines Ltd. to Silver Sceptre Resources Ltd. 6/30/92
Name changed to Silver Sceptre Resources Ltd.-Ressources Silver Sceptre Ltee. 6/1/87
Silver Sceptre Resources Ltd.-Ressources Silver Sceptre Ltee. merged into HLX Resources Ltd. 9/1/89 which recapitalized as Emperor Gold Corp. 3/30/92

SILVER SCOTT MINES INC (ID)
Reincorporated under the laws of Nevada 10/11/2004

SILVER SCREEN PARTNERS L P (DE)
Units of Ltd. Partnership II completely liquidated 12/30/1996
Details not available
Units of Ltd. Partnership III completely liquidated 12/31/1997
Details not available
Units of Ltd. Partnership I completely liquidated 11/16/1998
Details not available
Units of Ltd. Partnership IV completely liquidated 12/21/1998
Details not available

SILVER SCREEN STUDIOS INC (GA)
Name changed to Global 1 Investment Holdings Corp. 11/13/2006
(See Global 1 Investment Holdings Corp.)

SILVER SECS INC (WA)
Charter cancelled and proclaimed dissolved for failure to pay fees 6/2/89

SILVER SHIELD CORP (UT)
Charter revoked for failure to pay taxes 9/15/70

SILVER SHIELD MINES INC (ON)
Charter cancelled for failure to pay taxes and file returns 10/27/1980

SILVER SHIELD MINING & MILLING CO. (UT)
Recapitalized as Silver Shield Corp. 6/29/61
Each share Common 15¢ par exchanged for (0.1) share Common 50¢ par
Silver Shield Corp. charter revoked 9/15/70

SILVER SHIELD RES CORP (ON)
Each share old Common no par exchanged for (0.1) share new Common no par 06/04/2015
Name changed to Gunpowder Capital Corp. 05/17/2016

SILVER SPRING MINES LTD (BC)
Struck off register and declared dissolved for failure to file returns 4/15/94

SILVER SPRING NETWORKS INC (DE)
Acquired by Itron, Inc. 01/05/2018
Each share Common $0.001 par exchanged for $16.25 cash

SILVER SPUR RES INC (BC)
Common no par split (5) for (1) by issuance of (4) additional shares 06/18/1990
Recapitalized as BWI Resources Ltd. 06/08/1992
Each share Common no par exchanged for (0.1) share Common no par
BWI Resources Ltd. recapitalized as Penteco Resources Ltd. 01/02/2001 which name changed to Pennant Energy Inc. 04/30/2004 which merged into Blackbird Energy Inc. 04/22/2014

SILVER ST BANCORP (NV)
Common 10¢ par split (4) for (1) by issuance of (3) additional shares payable 06/15/2004 to holders of record 05/28/2004 Ex date - 06/16/2004
Common 10¢ par split (2) for (1) by issuance of (1) additional share payable 07/29/2005 to holders of record 07/15/2005 Ex date - 08/01/2005
Chapter 7 bankruptcy proceedings terminated 04/30/2014
Stockholders' equity unlikely

SILVER ST BK (HENDERSON, NV)
Under plan of reorganization each share Common 10¢ par automatically became (1) share Silver State Bancorp Common 10¢ par 01/21/1999
(See Silver State Bancorp)

SILVER ST MNG & EXPL INC (NV)
Recapitalized as Trivest Equities Ltd. 11/24/2004
Each share Common $0.001 par exchanged for (0.2) share Common $0.001 par
Trivest Equities Ltd. name changed to MCN Multicast Networks, Inc. 2/11/2005 which name changed to Downtown America Funding Corp. 9/8/2005 which name changed to Savior Energy Corp. 12/22/2006

SILVER ST VENDING CORP (NV)
Name changed to Pony Express U.S.A., Inc. 07/31/2002
(See Pony Express U.S.A., Inc.)

SILVER STANDARD MINING CO. (UT)
Recapitalized as Utah-New Mexico Gas Co. and each share Capital Stock 5¢ par exchanged for (0.05) share Capital Stock $1 par 8/15/59
Utah-New Mexico Gas Co. merged into Diversified Minerals, Inc. in March 1961

SILVER STAR CAP HLDGS INC (FL)
SEC revoked common stock registration 09/27/2011

SILVER STAR FD INC (MD)
Name changed to Hatteras Funds Inc. 10/5/89
Hatteras Funds Inc. name changed to Nations Fund, Inc. 9/22/92

SILVER STAR FOODS INC (NY)
Common $0.0001 par split (2) for (1) by issuance of (1) additional share payable 05/15/2000 to holders of record 05/05/2000 Ex date - 05/16/2000
Company became private 11/10/2003
Details not available

SILVER STAR INTL INC (DE)
Reincorporated 01/10/2008
State of incorporation changed from (FL) to (DE) 01/10/2008
Recapitalized as Lightman Grant, Inc. 03/12/2009
Each share Common $0.001 par exchanged for (0.01) share Common $0.001 par
Lightman Grant, Inc. name changed to QMIS Finance Securities Corp. 03/01/2013

SILVER STAR MINES INC (ID)
Reincorporated under the laws of Nevada as STI Holdings, Inc. 06/20/2007
STI Holdings, Inc. name changed to Grand Perfecta, Inc. 04/22/2013

SILVER STAR MINES LTD (BC)
Out of business 12/24/1977
No stockholders' equity

SILVER STAR QUEENS MINES INC (ID)
Charter forfeited for failure to file reports 11/30/1978

SILVER STATE CONSOLIDATED MINES CO. (NV)
Merged into Royal Apex Silver, Inc. (ID) 12/28/1975
Each share Capital Stock 10¢ par exchanged for (1) share Common 5¢ par
Royal Apex Silver, Inc. (ID) reincorporated in Nevada 06/17/1986 which merged into Coeur D'Alene Mines Corp. (ID) 03/08/1988 which reincorporated in

Delaware as Coeur Mining, Inc. 05/17/2013

SILVER ST MNG CORP (CO)
Name changed to U.S. Gold Corp. 06/23/1988
U.S. Gold Corp. name changed to McEwen Mining Inc. 01/27/2012

SILVER STATES OIL & GAS CORP. (MT)
Proclaimed dissolved for failure to file annual reports 12/29/80

SILVER STD MINES LTD (BC)
Recapitalized as Consolidated Silver Standard Mines Ltd. 09/11/1984
Each share Capital Stock 50¢ par exchanged for (0.2) share Common no par
Consolidated Silver Standard Mines Ltd. name changed to Silver Standard Resources Inc. 04/09/1990 which name changed to SSR Mining Inc. 08/03/2017

SILVER STD RES INC (BC)
Name changed to SSR Mining Inc. 08/03/2017

SILVER STREAM MNG CORP (NV)
Merged into Stratabound Minerals Corp. 05/17/2016
Each share Common $0.001 par exchanged for (2) shares Common no par

SILVER STRIKE MINES LTD. (ON)
Acquired by Fontana Mines (1945) Ltd. 2/8/62
Each share Capital Stock $1 par exchanged for (0.1) free share and (0.4) escrowed share Capital Stock $1 par

SILVER STRIKE MINING SYNDICATE LTD. (BC)
Name changed to Silver Strike Resources Ltd. 2/19/81
Silver Strike Resources Ltd. merged into United Mining Corp. 1/1/85

SILVER STRIKE RES LTD (BC)
Merged into United Mining Corp. 01/01/1985
Each share Common no par exchanged for (0.33333333) share Common 1¢ par

SILVER SUMMIT MINES LTD (ON)
Recapitalized as Consolidated Summit Mines Ltd. 1/10/74
Each share Common $1 par exchanged for (0.25) share Common no par
Consolidated Summit Mines Ltd. merged into Barrick Resources Corp. 5/2/83 which recapitalized as American Barrick Resources Corp. 12/6/85 which name changed to Barrick Gold Corp. 1/18/95

SILVER SUMMIT MINING CO.
Merged into Polaris Mining Co. and each (3) shares Capital Stock 50¢ par exchanged for (1) share new Common 25¢ par in 1952
Polaris Mining Co. merged into Helca Mining Co. (Wash.) 10/31/58 which was reincorporated in Delaware 6/6/83

SILVER SUMMIT MINING CO. LTD. (BC)
Struck off register and declared dissolved for failure to file returns 9/23/74

SILVER SUN RES CORP (BC)
Name changed to Golden Sun Mining Corp. 02/01/2013

SILVER SYND INC (ID)
Merged into Sunshine Mining Co. 12/30/1981
Each share Common 10¢ par exchanged for (0.75) share Capital Stock 50¢ par
Sunshine Mining Co. name changed to Sunshine Mining & Refining Co. 06/20/1994
(See Sunshine Mining & Refining Co.)

SILVER SYND MNG CORP (ID)
Name changed to 99 Dollar Stores, Inc. 8/17/2005
99 Dollar Stores, Inc. name changed to InvestSource Communications, Inc. 1/17/2006 which name changed to United Resource Holdings Group, Inc. 2/5/2007

SILVER TALON MINES LTD (BC)
Name changed to Score Athletic Products Inc. 6/1/93
(See Score Athletic Products Inc.)

SILVER TIP GOLD MINES LTD. (BC)
Struck off register and declared dissolved for failure to file returns 6/3/74

SILVER TIP MINING DEVELOPMENT CO. LTD. (BC)
Recapitalized as Silver Tip Gold Mines Ltd. share for share 4/11/46
Silver Tip Gold Mines Ltd. struck off register and declared dissolved 6/3/74

SILVER TITAN MINES LTD. (BC)
Completely liquidated 02/06/1968
Each share Common $1 par exchanged for first and final distribution of (0.5) share Atlas Explorations Ltd. Common 50¢ par
Atlas Explorations Ltd. recapitalized as Cima Resources Ltd. 07/26/1974 which recapitalized as Consolidated Cima Resources Ltd. (BC) 08/23/1984 which reincorporated in Canada as Hankin Atlas Industries Ltd. 08/15/1989 which name changed to Hankin Water Technologies Ltd. 03/26/1999
(See Hankin Water Technologies Ltd.)

SILVER TOWER MINES LTD (ON)
Charter cancelled for failure to file returns and pay taxes 03/16/1976

SILVER TOWN MINES LTD (ON)
Merged into Glen Lake Silver Mines Ltd. 12/16/68
Each share Capital Stock $1 par exchanged for (1/3) share Capital Stock $1 par
(See Glen Lake Silver Mines Ltd.)

SILVER TREND MNG CO (MT)
Recapitalized as Trend Mining Co. (MT) 2/17/99
Each share Common 10¢ par exchanged for (0.1) share Common 10¢ par
Trend Mining Co. (MT) reincorporated in Delaware 3/28/2001

SILVER TUSK MINES LTD (BC)
Recapitalized as Consolidated Silver Tusk Mines Ltd. (BC) 03/07/1994
Each share Common no par exchanged for (0.2) share Common no par
Consolidated Silver Tusk Mines Ltd. (BC) reincorporated in Yukon 00/00/2000
(See Consolidated Silver Tusk Mines Ltd.)

SILVER VALLEY MINES LTD.
Liquidated in 1941

SILVER WEST MNG CO (UT)
Name changed to Trans Services Corp. 4/15/71
(See Trans Services Corp.)

SILVER WHEATON CORP (ON)
Name changed to Wheaton Precious Metals Corp. 05/16/2017

SILVER X INTL MINES LTD (BC)
Struck off register and declared dissolved for failure to file returns 12/23/1974

SILVERA RES INC (AB)
Delisted from Alberta Stock Exchange 04/20/1990

SILVERADO FINL INC (NV)
Name changed to MediaTechnics Corp. 05/23/2008

SILVERADO GOLD MINES LTD (BC)
Each share old Common no par exchanged for (0.1) share new Common no par 05/26/1998
SEC revoked common stock registration 08/13/2015

SILVERADO MINES LTD (BC)
Recapitalized as Silverado Gold Mines Ltd. 05/23/1997
Each share Common no par exchanged for (1.0769231) shares Common no par
(See Silverado Gold Mines Ltd.)

SILVERADO MNG INC (CO)
Merged into Bosco Resources Corp. 06/02/1970
Each share Common 20¢ par exchanged for (0.5) share Common 10¢ par
Bosco Resources Corp. recapitalized as Appraisal Group International, Inc. 12/15/1986 which name changed to International Realty Group, Inc. 08/10/1989 which name changed to Qualton Inc. 10/17/2000
(See Qualton Inc.)

SILVERADO VENTURES INC (CO)
Name changed to Latin Foods International, Inc. 1/31/90

SILVERARROW EXPLS INC (BC)
Recapitalized as Aladdin Resources Corp. 07/05/2001
Each share Common no par exchanged for (0.125) share Common no par
Aladdin Resources Corp. name changed to Gold Point Exploration Ltd. 01/27/2004 which name changed to Gold Point Energy Corp. 06/22/2005 which merged into San Leon Energy PLC 05/28/2009

SILVERBIRCH ENERGY CORP (CANADA)
Merged into SilverWillow Energy Corp. 04/04/2012
Each share Common no par exchanged for (1) share Common no par and $8.50 cash
(See SilverWillow Energy Corp.)

SILVERBIRCH INC (ON)
Ceased operations 11/27/2008
Stockholders' equity unlikely

SILVERBUCKE MINES LTD. (ON)
Charter surrendered for failure to file reports and pay taxes 00/00/1953

SILVERCOTE PRODS INC (IL)
Each share 6% Preferred $50 par exchanged for (5) shares Class A $10 par in 1936
Recapitalized in 1952
Each share Class A $10 par exchanged for (1.5) shares Class A $5 par, (2) shares Common 10¢ par and 45¢ cash
Each share Common no par exchanged for (1) share Common 10¢ par
Merged into Johns-Manville Corp. (NY) 5/15/71
Each share Class A $5 par exchanged for (0.2) share Common $2.50 par
Each share Common 10¢ par exchanged for (0.16) share Common $2.50 par
Johns-Manville Corp. (NY) reincorporated in Delaware as Manville Corp. 10/30/81 which name changed to Schuller Corp. 3/29/96 which name changed to Johns-Manville Corp. (New) 5/5/97
(See Johns-Manville Corp. (New))

SILVERCREST CORP (CA)
Reorganized 11/13/86
Stock Dividend - 25% 6/30/76
Reorganized from Silvercrest Industries, Inc. to Silvercrest Corp. and each share Common 10¢ par automatically became (1) share Silvercrest Corp. Common 10¢ par 11/13/86
Charter forfeited for failure to file reports and pay fees 12/1/92

SILVERCREST MINES INC (BC)
Merged into First Majestic Silver Corp. 10/07/2015
Each share Common no par exchanged for (0.2769) share Common no par, (0.1667) share SilverCrest Metals Inc. Common no par and $0.0001 cash
Note: Unexchanged certificates were cancelled and became without value 10/07/2018

SILVERFIELDS MNG LTD (ON)
Completely liquidated 04/30/1971
Each share Common $1 par exchanged for first and final distribution of (0.4) share Teck Corp. Ltd. Class B Common no par
Teck Corp. Ltd. name changed to Teck Corp. 11/21/1978 which name changed to Teck Cominco Ltd. 09/12/2001 which name changed to Teck Resources Ltd. 04/27/2009

SILVERGATE BANCORP (CA)
Name changed to Silvergate Capital Corp. 12/5/97

SILVERGATE FINL SVCS INC (CA)
Name changed to Ventic Corp. 9/18/75
(See Ventic Corp.)

SILVERHAWK ENTMT GROUP INC (NV)
Name changed to Acme Sports & Entertainment, Inc. 06/27/2007
Acme Sports & Entertainment, Inc. recapitalized as Casa Havana, Inc. 06/17/2008 which name changed to Design Marketing Concepts, Inc. 12/09/2009
(See Design Marketing Concepts, Inc.)

SILVERHAWK RES LTD (BC)
Name changed to Special Waste Management Inc. 12/8/89
(See Special Waste Management Inc.)

SILVERHILL MGMT SVCS INC (DE)
Name changed to Fuel Doctor Holdings, Inc. 09/26/2011

SILVERHORN MINING & DEVELOPMENT CO. (NV)
Charter cancelled for non-payment of taxes 3/2/25

SILVERKNIFE MINES LTD (BC)
Struck off register and declared dissolved for failure to file returns 11/04/1974

SILVERLAKE NATL BK (LOS ANGELES, CA)
Merged into Republic National Bank of California (Los Angeles, CA) 2/29/68
Each share Common $10 par exchanged for (1) share Common $10 par
Republic National Bank of California (Los Angeles, CA) recapitalized as Republic National Bank & Trust Co. (Los Angeles, CA) 7/15/70

SILVERLAND CAP CORP (BC)
Issue Information - 1,500,000 shares COM offered at $0.20 per share on 05/07/2010
Reincorporated under the laws of Cayman Islands as Sino Environ-Energy Tech Corp. 07/13/2011
Sino Environ-Energy Tech Corp. name changed to Ord Mountain Resources Corp. 02/15/2012

SILVERLEAF RESORTS INC (TX)
Acquired by SL Resort Holdings Inc. 05/16/2011
Each share Common 1¢ par exchanged for $2.50 cash

SILVERLEAF RES LTD (BC)
Common no par split (3) for (2) by issuance of (2) additional shares 05/17/1984
Name changed to Pacific Concord Resource Corp. 03/15/1985
Pacific Concord Resource Corp. name changed to Pacific Engineered Materials Inc. 01/11/1989
(See Pacific Engineered Materials Inc.)

SILVERLINE INC (MN)
Acquired by Arctic Enterprises, Inc. 03/08/1970
Each share Common 10¢ par exchanged for (0.05) share Common 10¢ par
Arctic Enterprises, Inc. name changed to Minstar, Inc. (MN) 12/14/1982 which reorganized in Delaware 08/31/1985
(See Minstar, Inc. (DE))

SILVERLINE TECHNOLOGIES LTD (INDIA)
Each Sponsored ADR for 2001 Dividend exchanged for (1) Sponsored ADR for Equity Shares 07/05/2001
Each old Sponsored ADR for Equity Shares exchanged for (0.2) new Sponsored ADR for Equity Shares 03/19/2003
ADR basis changed from (1:2) to (1:10) 03/19/2003
Each new Sponsored ADR for Equity Shares exchanged again for (0.1) new Sponsored ADR for Equity Shares and $0.77017 cash 12/27/2007
ADR agreement terminated 03/20/2014
Each new Sponsored ADR for Equity Shares exchanged for (10) Equity Shares
Note: Unexchanged ADR's will be sold and the proceeds, if any, held for claim after 09/22/2014

SILVERMAQUE MNG LTD (QC)
Capital Stock $1 par reclassified as Common no par 09/30/1981
Recapitalized as Geomaque Explorations Ltd./Explorations Geomaque Ltee. 09/19/1986
Each share Common no par exchanged for (0.25) share Common no par
Geomaque Explorations Ltd./Explorations Geomaque Ltee. merged into Defiance Mining Corp. 06/25/2003 which merged into Rio Narcea Gold Mines, Ltd. 09/03/2004
(See Rio Narcea Gold Mines, Ltd.)

SILVERMET INC (ON)
Recapitalized as Global Atomic Corp. 12/27/2017
Each share Common no par exchanged for (0.36363636) share Common no par

SILVERMEX RES INC (BC)
Merged into First Majestic Silver Corp. 07/06/2012
Each share Common no par exchanged for (0.0355) share Common no par and $0.0001 cash

SILVERMEX RES LTD (BC)
Merged into Silvermex Resources Inc. 11/16/2010
Each share Common no par exchanged for (1) share Common no par
Note: Unexchanged certificates were cancelled and became without value 11/15/2016
Silvermex Resources Inc. merged into First Majestic Silver Corp. 07/06/2012

SILVERNY GOLD MINES, LTD. (ON)
Charter cancelled 1/6/58

SILVERPLACE MINES LTD (ON)
Charter cancelled and declared dissolved for failure to file returns and pay fees 11/28/1973

SILVERQUEST RES LTD (BC)
Recapitalized as Cash Resources Ltd. 12/11/1991
Each share Common no par exchanged for (0.2) share Common no par
Cash Resources Ltd. recapitalized as Cash Minerals Ltd. (BC) 05/07/2001 which reincorporated in Ontario 06/07/2005 which recapitalized as Pitchblack Resources Ltd. 06/25/2010 which recapitalized as Troilus Gold Corp. 01/03/2018

SILVERSIDE RES INC (ON)
Recapitalized 08/31/1979
Recapitalized from Silverside Mines Ltd. to Silverside Resources Inc. 08/31/1979
Each share Capital Stock $1 par exchanged for (0.5) share Common no par
Recapitalized as Starmin Mining Inc. 06/12/1991
Each share Common no par exchanged for (0.25) share Common no par
Starmin Mining Inc. recapitalized as First Dynasty Mines Ltd. 08/16/1994 which name changed to Sterlite Gold Ltd. 05/21/2002
(See Sterlite Gold Ltd.)

SILVERSMITH MINES LTD. (BC)
Liquidation completed in 1953
Details not available

SILVERSPAR MINERALS INC (ON)
Reincorporated 9/19/97
State of incorporation changed from (BC) to (ONT) 9/19/97
Name changed to Internet Identity Presence Co. Inc. 2/2/2001

SILVERSTACK MINES LTD (QC)
Merged into Long Lac Minerals Ltd. 11/02/1981
Each share Common $1 par exchanged for (1) share Common $1 par
Long Lac Minerals Ltd. merged into Lac Minerals Ltd. (Old) 12/31/1982 which merged into LAC Minerals Ltd. (New) 07/29/1985 which was acquired by American Barrick Resources Corp. 10/17/1994 which name changed to Barrick Gold Corp. 01/18/1995

SILVERSTAR HLDS LTD (BERMUDA)
Company terminated registration of common stock and is no longer public as of 05/15/2009

SILVERSTAR MNG CORP (NV)
Old Common $0.001 par split (3) for (1) by issuance of (2) additional shares payable 03/04/2008 to holders of record 03/04/2008
Each share old Common $0.001 par exchanged for (0.001) share new Common $0.001 par 09/23/2011
Recapitalized as Silverstar Resources, Inc. 03/10/2015
Each share new Common $0.001 par exchanged for (0.2) share Common $0.001 par
Silverstar Resources, Inc. name changed to Creative Waste Solutions, Inc. 07/11/2016

SILVERSTAR RES INC (NV)
Name changed to Creative Waste Solutions, Inc. 07/11/2016

SILVERSTONE CORP BERHAD (MALAYSIA)
ADR agreement terminated 11/20/2008
No ADR's remain outstanding

SILVERSTONE RES CORP (BC)
Acquired by Silver Wheaton Corp. 05/25/2009
Each share Common no par exchanged for (0.185) share Common no par
Note: Unexchanged certificates were cancelled and became without value 05/25/2015
Silver Wheaton Corp. name changed to Wheaton Precious Metals Corp. 05/16/2017

SILVERSTONE RES LTD (BC)
Recapitalized as Sorel Ventures Ltd. 10/19/2001
Each share Common no par exchanged for (0.2) share Common no par

SILVERSTREAM SOFTWARE INC (DE)
Merged into Novell, Inc. 07/19/2002
Each share Common $0.001 par exchanged for $9 cash

SILVERSWORD CORP (ON)
Cease trade order effective 04/16/2002
Stockholders' equity unlikely

SILVERTHORNE PRODTN CO (CO)
Name changed to Cognigen Networks, Inc. (CO) 07/12/2000
Cognigen Networks, Inc. (CO) reorganized in Delaware as BayHill Capital Corp. 04/23/2008 which name changed to Agricon Global Corp. 06/01/2012 which recapitalized as StrategaBiz, Inc. 12/16/2014 which name changed to CryptoSign, Inc. 07/06/2015 which name changed to NABUfit Global, Inc. 12/10/2015 which name changed to NewBridge Global Ventures, Inc. 12/12/2017

SILVERTON CORP (UT)
Recapitalized as Lifechoice, Inc. (UT) 03/05/1994
Each share Common $0.001 par exchanged for (0.01) share Common $0.001 par
Lifechoice, Inc. (UT) reorganized in Delaware as Fix-Corp International, Inc. 10/30/1995
(See Fix-Corp International, Inc.)

SILVERTON INDS INC (DE)
Name changed to Consolidated Media Corp. 07/18/1988
(See Consolidated Media Corp.)

SILVERTON MINES INC (ID)
Charter expired 12/02/2004

SILVERTON MNG CORP LTD (FL)
Recapitalized as Fleet Management Solutions Inc. 02/13/2009
Each share Common $0.001 par exchanged for (0.02) share Common $0.001 par

SILVERTON RES LTD (AB)
Merged into Inverness Petroleum Ltd. 11/16/87
Each share Common no par exchanged for (0.5) share Common no par
Inverness Petroleum Ltd. merged into Rigel Energy Corp. 1/10/96

SILVERWILLOW ENERGY CORP (CANADA)
Acquired by Value Creation Inc. 08/26/2015
Each share Common no par exchanged for $0.03 cash

SILVERWING ENERGY INC (AB)
Acquired by Bonterra Oil & Gas Ltd. 11/17/2008
Each share Common no par exchanged for $0.073 cash
Note: Unexchanged certificates were cancelled and became without value 11/18/2010

SILVERWING SYS CORP (NV)
Name changed to Advertain On-Line Inc. 08/19/1999
Advertain On-Line Inc. recapitalized as RetinaPharma International Inc. 06/18/2001 which name changed to Xtra-Gold Resources Corp. (NV) 12/19/2003 which reincorporated in British Virgin Islands 12/24/2012

SILVERWOOD DAIRIES LTD (ON)
Each share Common no par exchanged for (1) share Class A no par and (1) share Class B no par in 1946
Name changed to Silverwood Industries Ltd. 7/1/70
Silverwood Industries Ltd. name changed to Silcorp Ltd. 6/4/84 which was acquired by Alimentation Couche-Tard Inc. 5/27/99

SILVERWOOD INDS LTD (ON)
Name changed to Silcorp Ltd. 6/4/84
Silcorp Ltd. acquired by Alimentation Couche-Tard Inc. 5/27/99

SILVERWOOD WESTERN DAIRIES LTD. (ON)
Acquired by Silverwood Dairies, Ltd. 00/00/1952
Details not available

SILVERWOOD'S DAIRIES LTD.
Reorganized as Silverwood Dairies, Ltd. in 1936
Each share 7% Preference $100 par exchanged for (5) shares $0.40 Part. Preference and $50 principal amount of 6% Debentures
Each share Class A no par exchanged for (1) share Common no par
Silverwood Dairies, Ltd. name changed to Silverwood Industries Ltd. 7/1/70 which name changed to Silcorp Ltd. 6/4/84 which was acquired by Alimentation Couche-Tard Inc. 5/27/99

SILVERZIPPER COM INC (NV)
Assets seized for the benefit of creditors and operations ceased 04/20/2001
No stockholders' equity

SILVEX CORP (UT)
Involuntarily dissolved 12/31/1975

SILVEX INDS INC (NV)
Reorganized under the laws of Utah as Silvex Corp. 12/09/1971
Each share Common 10¢ par exchanged for (0.1) share Common no par
(See Silvex Corp.)

SILVEX RES CORP (BC)
Struck off register and declared dissolved for failure to file returns 11/09/1990

SILVEY BUSINESS & INVESTMENT CORP. (MO)
Name changed to Silvey Corp. 4/5/66
(See Silvey Corp.)

SILVEY CORP (MO)
Merged into Royal Group, Inc. 06/01/1984
Each share Common no par exchanged for $35 cash

SILVIO VENTURES INC (CANADA)
Name changed to Regency Gold Corp. 07/17/2008

SILVOR FOXX CAP CORP (AB)
Name changed to Silvore Fox Minerals Corp. 10/03/2008
Silvore Fox Minerals Corp. merged into Golden Share Mining Corp. (New) 08/09/2013 which name changed to Golden Share Resources Corp. 06/28/2017

SILVORE FOX MINERALS CORP (AB)
Merged into Golden Share Mining Corp. (New) 08/09/2013
Each share Common no par exchanged for (0.2) share Common no par
Golden Share Mining Corp. (New) name changed to Golden Share Resources Corp. 06/28/2017

SILVRAY LIGHTING, INC. (NY)
Under plan of merger name changed to Silvray-Litecraft Corp. 11/18/63
Silvray-Litecraft Corp. name changed

SIL-SIM

to Bluebird Inc. (N.Y.) 6/30/69 which reincorporated under the laws of Pennsylvania 8/3/70
(See Bluebird Inc. (Pa.))

SILVRAY LITECRAFT CORP (NY)
Name changed to Bluebird Inc. (NY) 06/30/1969
Bluebird Inc. (NY) reincorporated in Pennsylvania 08/03/1970
(See Bluebird Inc. (PA))

SIM KAR LTG FIXTURE INC (PA)
Merged into Victaulic Co. of America 12/22/1986
Each share Common 20¢ par exchanged for $27.41 cash

SIM TEK ENTERPRISES & EXPLS INC (ON)
Name changed to Bonaventure Technologies Inc. 9/14/83
(See Bonaventure Technologies Inc.)

SIMANCO, INC. (WI)
Liquidation completed
Each share Class A Common $1 par stamped to indicate first distribution of $31 cash 10/13/65
Each share stamped Class A Common $1 par exchanged for second and final distribution of $1.02072 cash 7/15/66

SIMARD BEAUDRY INC (QC)
Acquired by 9079-6699 Quebec Inc. 9/15/99
Each share Common $10 par exchanged for $5.75 cash

SIMARD UNITED MINES, LTD.
Acquired by Metal Amalgamations, Ltd. in 1930
Details not available

SIMAX OIL & GAS INC (ON)
Delisted from Toronto Stock Exchange 02/03/1992

SIMBA ENERGY INC (BC)
Name changed to Simba Essel Energy Inc. 04/24/2017

SIMBA MINES INC (NV)
Reincorporated 08/31/2005
Place of incorporation changed from (ON) to (NV) 08/31/2005
Charter revoked for failure to file reports and pay fees 08/31/2010

SIMBA MINES LTD. (ON)
Charter cancelled for failure to pay taxes and file returns 12/12/73

SIMBA OILS LTD. (AB)
Merged into Petromines Ltd. 12/01/1989
Each share Common no par exchanged for (0.04) share Common no par
(See Petromines Ltd.)

SIMBA RES INC (BC)
Name changed to Leeward Capital Corp. (BC) 9/18/87
Leeward Capital Corp. (BC) reincorporated in Alberta 8/20/2002

SIMBERI GOLD CORP (ON)
Name changed to Simberi Mining Corp. 08/10/2006
Simberi Mining Corp. recapitalized as Greenock Resources Inc. 09/29/2009 which name changed to BeWhere Holdings Inc. 02/03/2016

SIMBERI MNG CORP (ON)
Recapitalized as Greenock Resources Inc. 09/29/2009
Each share Common no par exchanged for (0.1) share Common no par
Greenock Resources Inc. name changed to BeWhere Holdings Inc. 02/03/2016

SIMBUD CAP CORP (AB)
Name changed to CanaDream Corp. 12/17/1998
(See CanaDream Corp.)

SIMCA, S.A. (FRANCE)
Reorganized 5/5/61

Each American Share $7.14 par exchanged for (1/6) Simca Automobiles ADR for Capital Stock 100 Frcs. par and (1/12) Simca Industries ADR for Capital Stock 100 Frcs. par
(See each company's listing)

SIMCA AUTOMOBILES (FRANCE)
Name changed to Societe des Automobiles Simca 12/29/1965
(See Societe des Automobiles Simca)

SIMCA INDS (FRANCE)
Name changed to FFSA 6/16/66
FFSA name changed to Fiat France S.A. 8/27/74
(See Fiat France S.A.)

SIMCERE PHARMACEUTICAL GROUP (CAYMAN ISLANDS)
Acquired by Simcere Holding Ltd. 12/23/2013
Each Sponsored ADR for Ordinary exchanged for $9.66 cash

SIMCO AMER INC (DE)
Name changed to Leo Motors, Inc. 11/05/2007

SIMCO STORES INC (NY)
Acquired by group of investors 04/01/1986
Each share Common 50¢ par exchanged for $4 cash

SIMCOA INC (MN)
Fraud and stock manipulation suit filed 04/12/1974
Attorney opined no stockholders' equity

SIMCOE ERIE INVS LTD (ON)
Common no par split (3) for (1) by issuance of (2) additional shares 1/2/79
Merged into GAN International 3/3/94
Each share Common no par exchanged for $7.625 cash

SIME DARBY BERHAD (MALAYSIA)
Reincorporated 12/21/1979
Name changed and place of incorporation changed from Sime Darby Holdings PLC (England) to Sime Darby Berhad (Malaysia) and ADR's for Ordinary 10p par changed to MS$0.50 par 12/21/1979
ADR agreement terminated 10/05/2007
Each Unsponsored ADR for Ordinary MS$0.50 par exchanged for $1.879495 cash
Stock Dividends - 33-1/3% 06/27/1980; 25% 12/18/1981; 50% 03/13/1990; 20% 02/21/1995
ADR agreement terminated 10/05/2007
Each Sponsored ADR for Ordinary MS$0.50 par exchanged for $1.87947 cash

SIMERA CORP (DE)
Stock Dividend - 50% 07/14/1972
Merged into IMS Media, Inc. 12/07/1982
Each share Common 10¢ par exchanged for $0.65 cash

SIMETCO INC (OH)
Name changed back to Ohio Ferro-Alloys Corp. 3/22/95
(See Ohio Ferro-Alloys Corp.)

SIMEX NK TECHNOLOGY INC (NV)
Reincorporated under the laws of Delaware as Simex Technologies, Inc. 04/06/1999
Simex Technologies, Inc. recapitalized as College Tonight, Inc. 03/28/2008 which name changed to CT Holdings, Inc. 09/03/2009

SIMEX TECHNOLOGIES INC (DE)
Recapitalized as College Tonight, Inc. 03/28/2008
Each share Common $0.001 par exchanged for (0.25) share Common $0.001 par
College Tonight, Inc. name changed to CT Holdings, Inc. 09/03/2009

SIMILKAMEEN HYDRO-PWR LTD (BC)
Recapitalized as Norte Resources Ltd. (BC) 07/25/1996
Each share Common no par exchanged for (1/3) share Common no par
Norte Resources Ltd. (BC) reorganized in Yukon as Banks Ventures Ltd. 04/06/1998 which name changed to Banks Energy Inc. 07/26/2004 which merged into Arapahoe Energy Corp. (New) 10/20/2005 which name changed to Canadian Phoenix Resources Corp. 01/07/2008 which recapitalized as Knol Resources Corp. 03/11/2013

SIMIONE CENT HLDGS INC (DE)
Each share old Common $0.001 par exchanged for (0.5) share new Common $0.001 par 6/30/97
Each share new Common $0.001 par exchanged for (0.2) share new Common $0.001 par 3/8/2000
Name changed to CareCentric Inc. 1/31/2001
(See CareCentric Inc.)

SIMKINS INDS INC (CT)
Each share old Common $1 par exchanged for (0.0001) share Common $1 par 12/31/1986
Note: In effect holders of Common received $68 cash per share and public interest was eliminated

SIMMER & JACK MINES LTD (SOUTH AFRICA)
ADR agreement terminated 04/22/2005
Each ADR for Ordinary exchanged for $0.09526 cash

SIMMETECH INC (MN)
Recapitalized as Jaguar Resorts, Inc. 07/30/2004
Each share Common $0.001 par exchanged for (0.5) share Common $0.001 par
Jaguar Resorts, Inc. recapitalized as Iptimize, Inc. (MN) 12/08/2005 which which reorganized in Delaware 10/10/2017
(See Iptimize, Inc.)

SIMMONDS CAP LTD (BC)
Reorganized from Simmons Communications Ltd. to Simmonds Capital Ltd. 10/06/1995
Each share Common no par exchanged for (0.2) share Common no par
Delisted from Toronto Stock Exchange 03/07/2003

SIMMONDS PRECISION ENGINE SYSTEMS, INC. (NY)
99.56% held by Simmonds Precision Products, Inc. as of 9/13/74
Public interest eliminated

SIMMONDS PRECISION PRODS INC (NY)
Common $1 par changed to $0.33333333 par and (2) additional shares issued 04/22/1966
Common $0.33333333 par changed to 25¢ par and (0.5) additional share issued 04/28/1967
Merged into Hercules Inc. 09/20/1983
Each share Common 25¢ par exchanged for (1.5) shares Common no par
Hercules Inc. acquired by Ashland Inc. (New) (KY) 11/13/2008 which reincorporated in Delaware as Ashland Global Holdings Inc. 09/20/2016

SIMMONS AIRLS INC (MI)
Common no par split (5) for (4) by issuance of (0.25) additional share 08/23/1985
Merged into AMR Corp. 08/08/1988
Each share Common no par exchanged for $17.50 cash

SIMMONS BOARDMAN PUBG CORP (DE)
$3 Conv. Preferred no par called for redemption at $60 on 2/15/2005
Company went private in 1995
Details not available

SIMMONS CO (DE)
Common no par split (2) for (1) by issuance of (1) additional share 5/7/65
Common no par split (2) for (1) by issuance of (1) additional share 5/10/71
Merged into Gulf & Western Industries, Inc. 6/5/79
Each share Common no par exchanged for $19 cash

SIMMONS FIRST CAP TR (AR)
Each Trust Preferred Security (color green certificate) exchanged for (1) 9.12% Trust Preferred Security (color blue certificate representing twice the number of shares) 11/17/97
9.12% Trust Preferred Securities called for redemption at $12.50 on 12/31/2004

SIMMONS 1ST NATL BK (PINE BLUFF, AR)
Stock Dividend - 20% 1/17/68
Reorganized as Simmons First National Corp. 12/31/68
Each share Capital Stock $20 par exchanged for (1) share Class A Common $20 par

SIMMONS HARDWARE & PAINT CORP.
Liquidated in 1941

SIMMONS MANUFACTURING CO.
Liquidated in 1944

SIMMONS OUTDOOR CORP (DE)
Merged into Blount International, Inc. 12/19/95
Each share Common 1¢ par exchanged for $10.40 cash

SIMMS AIRPLANE APPLIANCE CO.
Merged into Sky Specialties Corp. in 1929
Sky Specialties Corp. acquired by Mueller Brass Co. in 1933 which merged into United States Smelting Refining & Mining Co. (Me.) (New) 9/24/65 which name changed to UV Industries, Inc. 6/9/72

SIMMS PETROLEUM CO.
Liquidation completed in 1947

SIMMS T S & CO LTD (NB)
Name changed in November 1949
Name changed from Simms Brushes, Ltd. to Simms (T.S.) & Co., Ltd. in November 1949
Merged into Simms Investments Ltd. 8/1/80
Details not available

SIMON & SCHUSTER INC (NY)
6% Preferred $10 par called for redemption 1/10/72
6% Class A Preferred $100 par called for redemption 1/10/72
Class B 50¢ par called for redemption 6/4/75
Merged into Gulf & Western Industries, Inc. (DE) 6/12/75
Each share Common 50¢ par exchanged for (0.1) share Common $1 par
Gulf & Western Industries Inc. (DE) name changed to Gulf + Western Inc. 5/1/86 which name changed to Paramount Communications Inc. 6/5/89 which merged into Viacom Inc. (Old) 7/7/94
(See Viacom Inc. (Old))

SIMON (H.) & SONS, LTD. (CANADA)
Acquired by Consolidated Cigar Corp. in 1958
Details not available

FINANCIAL INFORMATION, INC.

SIMON AIRPLANE APPLIANCE CO.
Merged into Sky Specialties Corp. in 1929
(See Sky Specialties Corp.)

SIMON DEBARTOLO GROUP INC (MD)
Merged into SPG Properties, Inc. 09/24/1998
Each 8.75% Preferred Ser. B $0.0001 par exchanged for (1) share 8.75% Preferred Ser. B $0.0001 par
Each 7.89% Step Up Preferred Ser. C $0.0001 par exchanged for (1) share 7.89% Step Up Preferred Ser. C $0.0001 par
Merged into Simon Property Group, Inc. (DE) 09/24/1998
Each share Common $0.0001 par exchanged for (1) Paired Certificate

SIMON EXTENSION MINING CO. (NV)
Charter revoked for failure to file reports and pay fees 3/3/24

SIMON FRASER RES LTD (BC)
Cease trade order effective 04/22/1991
Stockholders' equity unlikely

SIMON HARDWARE CO (CA)
Common no par reclassified as Common Series A no par 9/30/63
Name changed to Simon Stores, Inc. 5/27/65
(See Simon Stores, Inc.)

SIMON (NORTON), INC (DE)
See - Norton Simon Inc.

SIMON PPTY GROUP INC (DE)
Paired certificates terminated 12/31/2002
Each Unit consisting of (1) share Simon Property Group, Inc. Common $0.00001 par and (0.01) SPG Realty Consultants Inc. Share of Bene. Int. $0.00001 par automatically became (1) share Simon Property Group, Inc. Common $0.0001 par
6.50% Conv. Preferred Ser. B $0.0001 par called for redemption at $105 plus $1.34 accrued dividend on 12/15/2003
8.75% Preferred Ser. F called for redemption at $25 plus $0.01823 accrued dividends on 10/04/2006
7.89% Step Up Preferred Ser. G called for redemption at $50 plus $0.011 accrued dividends on 10/02/2007
6% Conv. Perpetual Preferred Series I $0.0001 par called for redemption at $50 plus $0.4917 accrued dividends on 04/16/2010
(Additional Infomation in Active)

SIMON PPTY GROUP INC (MD)
Issue Information - 37,750,000 shares COM offered at $22.25 per share on 12/13/1993
Under plan of merger name changed to Simon DeBartolo Group, Inc. 8/9/96
Simon DeBartolo Group, Inc. merged into Simon Property Group, Inc. (DE) 9/24/98

SIMON STORES INC (CA)
Merged into Marc Paul, Inc. 01/31/1982
Each share Common Ser. A no par exchanged for $4 cash
Each share Common Ser. B no par exchanged for $4 cash

SIMON TRANSN SVCS INC (NV)
Plan of reorganization under Chapter 11 Federal Bankruptcy Code effective 03/23/2003
No stockholders' equity

SIMON WILLIAM BREWERY (NY)
Charter cancelled and proclaimed dissolved for failure to pay taxes and file reports 12/15/1975

SIMONDS SAW & STEEL CO. (MA)
Each share old Common no par exchanged for (10) shares new Common no par in 1937
Common no par split (3) for (1) by issuance of (2) additional shares 4/6/62
Merged into Wallace-Murray Corp. 6/30/66
Each share Common no par exchanged for (2) shares $1.10 Preferred no par
(See Wallace-Murray Corp.)

SIMONDY CORP. (UT)
Name changed to Pacific General, Inc. 03/15/1989
(See Pacific General, Inc.)

SIMONE GROUP INC (DE)
Each share old Common $0.001 par exchanged for (1/6) share new Common $0.001 par 02/18/1993
Plan of reorganization under Chapter 11 Federal Bankruptcy Code effective 00/00/1996
No stockholders' equity

SIMPATICO WINES LTD (BC)
Recapitalized as Liquest International Marketing Corp. 01/06/1989
Each share Common no par exchanged for (0.2) share Common no par
Liquest International Marketing Corp. recapitalized as Massey Mercantile Ltd. 04/09/1992 which name changed to Riosun Resources Corp. 01/22/1997
(See Riosun Resources Corp.)

SIMPLAGENE USA INC (NV)
Name changed to Dinewise, Inc. 9/28/2006

SIMPLAYER COM LTD (ISRAEL)
Company reported out of business 04/30/2001
Stockholders' equity unlikely

SIMPLE TECH INC (NV)
Common $0.0001 par split (10) for (1) by issuance of (9) additional shares payable 05/03/2009 to holders of record 05/03/2009
Name changed to Sonnen Corp. 11/17/2009

SIMPLE TECHNOLOGY INC (CA)
Issue Information - 6,364,000 shares COM offered at $11 per share on 09/29/2000
Name changed to SimpleTech, Inc. 05/07/2001
SimpleTech, Inc. name changed to STEC, Inc. 03/07/2007
(See STEC, Inc.)

SIMPLEPONS INC (DE)
Recapitalized as Eco-Shift Power Corp. 11/26/2013
Each share Common 1¢ par exchanged for (0.02) share Common no par

SIMPLETECH INC (CA)
Name changed to STEC, Inc. 03/07/2007
(See STEC, Inc.)

SIMPLEX COMPUTING MEASURE CORP.
Merged into Measuregraph Co. in 1929
(See Measuregraph Co.)

SIMPLEX DEV CORP (NY)
Merged into M.K. Reynard Inc. 04/14/1978
Each share Common 10¢ par exchanged for $0.55 cash

SIMPLEX INDS INC (MI)
Common $1 par split (2) for (1) by issuance of (1) additional share 7/15/68
Common $1 par split (2) for (1) by issuance of (1) additional share 8/1/69
Merged into Anthony Industries, Inc. 6/29/78
Each share Common $1 par exchanged for $5.90 cash

SIMPLEX LOCK CORP (NY)
Name changed to Simplex Development Corp. and Common $1 par changed to 10¢ par 07/09/1969
(See Simplex Development Corp.)

SIMPLEX MED SYS INC (CO)
Name changed to SMLX Technologies, Inc. 08/21/1998
(See SMLX Technologies, Inc.)

SIMPLEX PAPER CORP. (MI)
Name changed to Simplex Industries, Inc. 7/5/68
(See Simplex Industries, Inc.)

SIMPLEX PRECAST INDUSTRIES, INC. (DE)
No longer in existence having become inoperative and void for non-payment of taxes 4/1/64

SIMPLEX RADIO CO.
Acquired by Philco Corp. on a (1) for (3) basis in 1940
Philco Corp. was acquired by Ford Motor Co. 12/11/61

SIMPLEX SOLUTIONS INC (DE)
Issue Information - 4,000,000 shares COM offered at $12 per share on 05/01/2001
Merged into Cadence Design Systems, Inc. 06/27/2002
Each share Common $0.001 par exchanged for (0.9245) share Common 1¢ par

SIMPLEX VALVE & METER CO.
Acquired by Permutit Co. 00/00/1946
Details not available

SIMPLEX WIRE & CABLE CO (MA)
Each share old Capital Stock no par exchanged for (5) shares new Capital Stock no par 03/02/1959
New Capital Stock no par reclassified as Common $5 par 04/27/1970
Merged into Tyco Laboratories, Inc. 05/13/1974
Each share Common $5 par exchanged for $24.25 cash

SIMPLICITY BANCORP INC (MD)
Merged into HomeStreet, Inc. 03/02/2015
Each share Common 1¢ par exchanged for (1) share Common no par

SIMPLICITY COMPUTER CORP (DE)
Recapitalized as Transglobal Oil Corp. (DE) 03/13/2006
Each share Common 1¢ par exchanged for (0.001) share Common 1¢ par
Transglobal Oil Corp. (DE) reincorporated in New Mexico 06/25/2007
(See Transglobal Oil Corp. (NM))

SIMPLICITY COMPUTER LEASING CORP (DE)
Name changed to Simplicity Computer Corp. 10/08/1970
Simplicity Computer Corp. recapitalized as Transglobal Oil Corp. (DE) 03/13/2006 which reincorporated in New Mexico 06/25/2007
(See Transglobal Oil Corp. (NM))

SIMPLICITY MANUFACTURING CO. (WI)
Name changed to Simanco, Inc. 9/1/65 which completed liquidation 7/15/66

SIMPLICITY PATTERN INC (NY)
5.5% Conv. Preferred $10 par called for redemption 11/15/1947
Common $1 par changed to 50¢ par and (1) additional share issued 05/21/1962
Common 50¢ par changed to 25¢ par and (1) additional share issued 09/20/1967
Common 25¢ par changed to $0.08333333 par and (2) additional shares issued 05/25/1972
Name changed to Maxxam Group Inc. (NY) 06/08/1984
Maxxam Group Inc. (NY) reincorporated in Delaware 01/16/1985 which merged into MCO Holdings, Inc. 05/20/1988 which name changed to MAXXAM Inc. 10/06/1988
(See MAXXAM Inc.)

SIMPLIFIED BUSINESS SVCS INC (NY)
Recapitalized as World Gambling Corp. 08/10/1979
Each share Common 1¢ par exchanged for (0.33333333) share Common 1¢ par

SIMPLON RES LTD (BC)
Recapitalized as Templar Resources Corp. 07/22/1993
Each share Common no par exchanged for (0.2) share Common no par
Templar Resources Corp. recapitalized as Moneta Resources Inc. 06/07/2007 which name changed to Border Petroleum Inc. (BC) 08/08/2008 which reorganized in Alberta as Border Petroleum Corp. 09/14/2010 which recapitalized as Border Petroleum Ltd. 03/24/2014

SIMPLY INNOVATIVE PRODS INC (WY)
Common $0.001 par changed to $0.0001 par 04/13/2016
Name changed to White Label Liquid, Inc. 08/10/2018

SIMPSON ELECTRS INC (FL)
Name changed to Simpson Liquidating Corp. 04/10/1975
(See Simpson Liquidating Corp.)

SIMPSON GOLD MINES, LTD. (ON)
Name changed to Elmwood Resources Ltd. 8/1/80
Elmwood Resources Ltd. name changed to Easynet Data Corp. 7/3/85 which name changed to Vertigo 3D, Inc. 4/30/96 which recapitalized as Vertigo Software Corp. 10/27/98 which name changed to Even Technologies Inc. 6/22/2004

SIMPSON INDS INC (MI)
Stock Dividends - 50% 8/26/76; 50% 8/25/77; 50% 3/2/79
Merged into Hartland Industrial Partners, LP 12/15/2000
Each share Common 1¢ par exchanged for $13 cash

SIMPSON LEE PAPER CO (WA)
Merged into Simpson Lee Holding Co. 01/07/1977
Each share Common $10 par exchanged for $20 cash

SIMPSON LIQUIDATING CORP. (FL)
Liquidation completed
Each share Class A Common 50¢ par exchanged for initial distribution of $2 cash 4/10/75
Each share Class A Common 50¢ par received second distribution of $0.50 cash 4/15/76
Each share Class A Common 50¢ par received third and final distribution of $0.65 cash 3/15/77

SIMPSON MFG INC (CA)
Issue Information - 2,150,000 shares COM offered at $11.50 per share on 05/25/1994
Reincorporated under the laws of Delaware 5/21/99

SIMPSONS LTD (CANADA)
Each share old Class A no par exchanged for (3) shares new Class A no par in 1945
Each share old Class B no par exchanged for (3) shares new Class B no par in 1945
Each share new Class A no par

exchanged for (4-1/3) shares Common no par in 1953
Each share new Class B no par exchanged for (4) shares Common no par in 1953
Common no par split (2) for (1) by issuance of (1) additional share 5/28/64
Common no par split (2) for (1) by issuance of (1) additional share 5/30/69
Common no par split (3) for (1) by issuance of (2) additional shares 5/30/73
Merged into Hudson's Bay Co. 7/31/79
Each (8) shares Common no par exchanged for (1) share Ordinary no par or $28.50 cash

SIMPSONS SEARS LTD (CANADA)
Name changed 10/02/1975
Each share old Class A no par exchanged for (3) shares new Class A no par 12/11/1964
New Class A no par split (4) for (1) by issuance of (3) additional shares 04/27/1973
Name changed from Simpsons-Sears Ltd. to Simpsons-Sears Ltd.-Simpsons Sears Ltee. 10/02/1975
Name changed to Sears Canada Inc. and Class A no par, Class B no par reclassified as Common no par 05/31/1984

SIMS AGRIC PRODS CO (OH)
Charter cancelled 01/04/2007

SIMS COMMUNICATIONS INC (DE)
Common $0.001 par split (2) for (1) by issuance of (1) additional share 06/09/1995
Each share old Common $0.001 par exchanged for (0.1) share new Common $0.001 par 03/04/1996
Each share new Common $0.001 par exchanged for (0.25) share Common $0.0001 par 02/16/1998
Name changed to MedCom USA, Inc. 10/18/1999
(See MedCom USA, Inc.)

SIMS GROUP LTD (AUSTRALIA)
Sponsored ADR's for Ordinary A$0.50 par split (4) for (1) by issuance of (3) additional ADR's payable 12/10/2007 to holders of record 12/07/2007 Ex date - 12/11/2007
Name changed to Sims Metal Management Ltd. 11/26/2008

SIMSBURY BK & TR CO NEW (SIMSBURY, CT)
Under plan of reorganization each share Common no par automatically became (1) share SBT Bancorp, Inc. Common no par 03/02/2006

SIMSBURY BK & TR CO OLD (SIMSBURY, CT)
Common $20 par changed to $5 par and (3) additional shares issued 03/01/1968
Reorganized as First Connecticut Bancorp, Inc. 11/12/1970
Each share Common $5 par exchanged for (1.8) shares Common $10 par
First Connecticut Bancorp, Inc. merged into Fleet Financial Group, Inc. (Old) 03/17/1986 which merged into Fleet/Norstar Financial Group, Inc. 01/01/1988 which name changed to Fleet Financial Group, Inc. (New) 04/15/1992 which name changed to Fleet Boston Corp. 10/01/1999 which name changed to FleetBoston Financial Corp. 04/18/2000 which merged into Bank of America Corp. 04/01/2004

SIMSMART INC (CANADA)
Ceased operations 05/19/2006
Stockholders' equity unlikely

SIMSMETAL LTD (AUSTRALIA)
Name changed to Sims Group Ltd. 03/05/2003
Sims Group Ltd. name changed to Sims Metal Management Ltd. 11/26/2008

SIMTEK CORP (DE)
Reorganized 10/05/2006
Reorganized from under the laws of (CO) to (DE) 10/05/2006
Each share Common 1¢ par exchanged for (0.1) share Common $0.0001 par
Merged into Cypress Semiconductor Corp. 09/17/2008
Each share Common $0.0001 par exchanged for $2.60 cash

SIMULA INC (AZ)
Issue Information - 1,350,000 shares COM offered at $18 per share on 03/30/1995
Common 1¢ par split (3) for (2) by issuance of (0.5) additional share 09/28/1995
Merged into Armor Holdings, Inc. 12/09/2003
Each share Common 1¢ par exchanged for $3.21 cash

SIMULATED ENVIRONMENT CONCEPTS INC (WY)
Dissolved 08/13/2007
Details not available

SIMULATED ENVIRONMENTAL CONCEPTS INC (FL)
Reincorporated under the laws of Wyoming as Simulated Environment Concepts Inc. 07/18/2007

SIMULATED MATLS INC (MA)
Involuntarily dissolved for failure to file reports 12/11/1974

SIMULATION ENG CORP (VA)
Completely liquidated 10/29/1976
Each share Common $1 par exchanged for first and final distribution of $8 cash

SIMULATION SCIENCES INC (DE)
Merged into Siebe PLC 05/28/1998
Each share Common $0.001 par exchanged for $10 cash

SIMULATOR SYS INC (NV)
Each share old Common $0.001 par exchanged for (0.02) share new Common $0.001 par 3/15/99
Name changed to Casino Pirata.Com Ltd. 5/5/99
Casino Pirata.Com Ltd. name changed to Advantage Technologies, Inc. 11/30/99 which recapitalized as Expo Holdings Inc. 5/30/2006

SIMULMATICS CORP (NY)
Adjudicated bankrupt 08/04/1970
No stockholders' equity

SIMWARE INC (CANADA)
Merged into NetManage, Inc. 12/10/99
Each share Common no par exchanged for $3.75 cash

SIN HLDGS INC (CO)
Common $0.001 par split (20) for (1) by issuance of (19) additional shares payable 11/22/2010 to holders of record 10/05/2010 Ex date - 11/23/2010
Name changed to Legend Oil & Gas, Ltd. 11/29/2010

SIN JIN TECHNOLOGY INC (DE)
Charter forfeited for failure to maintain a registered agent 2/28/97

SIN-MAC LINES LTD.
Assets sold in 1937

SINA COM (CAYMAN ISLANDS)
Issue Information - 4,000,000 ORD shs. offered at $17 per share on 04/12/2000
Name changed to Sina Corp. 02/14/2003

SINALOA GOLD CORP (DE)
Name changed to Online Innovation, Inc. 05/05/1999
Online Innovation, Inc. name changed to Moventis Capital, Inc. 02/14/2006
(See Moventis Capital, Inc.)

SINCHAO METALS CORP (BC)
Recapitalized as Southern Legacy Minerals Inc. (BC) 07/03/2012
Each share Common no par exchanged for (0.16666666) share Common no par
Southern Legacy Minerals Inc. (BC) reorganized in Alberta as Regulus Resources Inc. (New) 10/03/2014

SINCLAIR BROADCAST GROUP INC (MD)
Issue Information - 3,000,000 shares PFD CONV EXCHANGEABLE SER D $3 PERP offered at $50 per share on 09/17/1997
Each $3 Conv. Exchangeable Perpetual Preferred Ser. D 1¢ par exchanged for $50 principal amount of 6% Conv. Subordinated Debentures due 09/15/2012 on 06/15/2005
(Additional Information in Active)

SINCLAIR CAP (MD)
Stock Dividend - 2.90625% payable 3/15/2001 to holders of record 3/1/2001 Ex date - 2/27/2001
11.625% High Yield Trust Preferred Securities called for redemption at $104.65 on 7/21/2003

SINCLAIR CONSOLIDATED OIL CORP.
Name changed to Consolidated Oil Corp. in 1932
Consolidated Oil Corp. name changed to Sinclair Oil Corp. 5/19/43 which merged into Atlantic Richfield Co. (PA) 3/4/69 which reincorporated in Delaware 5/7/85 which merged into BP Amoco p.l.c. 4/18/2000

SINCLAIR-MILLER MINES LTD. (ON)
Charter cancelled and declared dissolved for failure to file returns and pay fees 5/1/74

SINCLAIR OIL CORP (NY)
Common no par changed to $5 par 5/18/55
Merged into Atlantic Richfield Co. (PA) 3/4/69
Each share Common $5 par exchanged for (1) share $2.80 Conv. Preference $1 par and (0.6) share Common $5 par
Atlantic Richfield Co. (PA) reincorporated in Delaware 5/7/85 which merged into BP Amoco p.l.c. 4/18/2000

SINCLAIR VENEZUELAN OIL CO (DE)
Completely liquidated 05/12/1987
Each share Capital Stock $1 par exchanged for first and final distribution of $2.43 cash

SINDOR RES INC (ON)
Recapitalized as ClubLink Corp. 01/19/1994
Each share Common no par exchanged for (0.2) share Common no par
ClubLink Corp. merged into ClubLink Enterprises Ltd. 07/30/2009

SINECURE FINL CORP (CO)
Each share old Common $0.0001 par exchanged for (1/3) share new Common $0.0001 par 03/20/1992
Company terminated registration of common stock and is no longer public as of 11/09/1995

SINEQUANON CORP (NJ)
Name changed to Synthetic Blood International Inc. (NJ) 11/05/1990
Synthetic Blood International Inc. (NJ) reincorporated in Delaware as Oxygen Biotherapeutics, Inc.

07/01/2008 which name changed to Tenax Therapeutics, Inc. 09/19/2014

SINETEC HLDGS CORP (AB)
Cease trade order effective 10/23/2002

SINEWIRE NETWORKS INC (NV)
Common $0.001 par split (8) for (1) by issuance of (7) additional shares payable 5/10/2004 to holders of record 4/30/2004 Ex date - 5/11/2004
Common $0.001 par split (5) for (1) by issuance of (4) additional shares payable 2/11/2005 to holders of record 2/10/2005
Name changed to Lamperd Less Lethal Inc. 3/21/2005

SINGAPORE ARPT TERM SVCS LTD (SINGAPORE)
Name changed to SATS Ltd. 04/22/2013

SINGAPORE FD INC (MD)
Name changed to Aberdeen Singapore Fund, Inc. 11/01/2013
Aberdeen Singapore Fund, Inc. reorganized as Aberdeen Emerging Markets Equity Income Fund, Inc. 04/30/2018

SINGAPORE LD LTD (SINGAPORE)
ADR's for Ordinary split (2) for (1) by by issuance of (1) additional ADR 10/31/1990
Stock Dividend - 20% 04/13/1982
ADR agreement terminated 07/31/2014
Each ADR for Ordinary exchanged for $7.317662 cash

SINGER (PHILIP A.) & BROTHERS, INC.
Bankrupt in 1940

SINGER CO (DE)
Reincorporated 00/00/1988
Capital Stock $10 par reclassified as Common $10 par 04/27/1967
State of incorporation changed from (NJ) to (DE) 00/00/1988
Each share $1.50 Class A Conv. Preferred no par exchanged for (0.9) share Common $10 par 04/15/1988
Under plan of merger each share Common $10 par exchanged for $50 cash 04/25/1988
Name changed to Bicoastal Corp. 10/16/1989
(See Bicoastal Corp.)

SINGER CO N V (NETHERLANDS ANTILLES)
Plan of reorganization under Chapter 11 Federal Bankruptcy Code effective 09/14/2000
No old Common stockholders' equity
Name changed to Retail Holdings N.V. 11/17/2005

SINGER DAVID ASSOC INC (NY)
Completely liquidated 07/05/1978
Each share Common 10¢ par received first and final distribution of $0.35 cash
Note: Certificates were not required to be surrendered and are without value

SINGER ISLAND NATIONAL BANK (RIVIERA BEACH, FL)
Name changed to Brady National Bank (Riviera Beach, FL) 6/16/80

SINGER MANUFACTURING CO. (NJ)
Each share Capital Stock $100 par exchanged for (5) shares Capital Stock $20 par 00/00/1951
Capital Stock $20 par changed to $10 par and (1) additional share issued 03/08/1963
Name changed to Singer Co. 05/16/1963
(See Singer Co.)

SINGER MFG LTD (ENGLAND)
Acquired by Singer Co. 11/17/1970
Each ADR for Ordinary Reg. £1 par exchanged for $10.165575 cash

FINANCIAL INFORMATION, INC.

SINGLE CHIP SYS INTL INC (DE)
Recapitalized as Triple Chip Systems, Inc. (DE) 07/16/1996
Each share Common $0.0001 par exchanged for (0.005) share Common $0.0001 par
Triple Chip Systems, Inc. (DE) reincorporated in Tennessee as Miller Petroleum Inc. 01/13/1997 which name changed to Miller Energy Resources, Inc. 04/12/2011
(See Miller Energy Resources, Inc.)

SINGLE SOURCE FINL SVCS CORP (NY)
Each share old Common $0.001 par exchanged for (4) shares new Common $0.001 par 10/31/2001
Each share new Common $0.001 par exchanged again for (0.01) share new Common $0.001 par 10/02/2003
Name changed to Bio Solutions Manufacturing, Inc. (NY) 05/19/2004
Bio Solutions Manufacturing, Inc. (NY) reorganized in Nevada 11/20/2008 which name changed to Todays Alternative Energy Corp. 06/21/2010

SINGLE SOURCE INVT GROUP INC (FL)
Administratively dissolved 09/26/2014

SINGLE TOUCH SYS INC (DE)
Common $0.001 par split (3) for (1) by issuance of (2) additional shares payable 06/25/2008 to holders of record 06/24/2008 Ex date - 06/26/2008
Name changed to SITO Mobile, Ltd. 10/07/2014

SINGLEPOINT SYS CORP (MN)
Name changed to Global Maintech Corp. (New) 03/07/2001
(See Global Maintech Corp. (New))

SINGULAR CHEF INC (NV)
Name changed to One Clean Planet, Inc. 02/27/2013
One Clean Planet, Inc. recapitalized as Kashin, Inc. 07/27/2015

SINMAX MINES LTD (BC)
Recapitalized as Shelter Gold Ltd. 03/26/1973
Each share Common 50¢ par exchanged for (0.5) share Common no par
Shelter Gold Ltd. name changed to Shelter Oil & Gas Ltd. (BC) 12/22/1976 which reincorporated in Alberta 11/09/1984 which merged into Tesco Corp. 12/01/1993 which merged into Nabors Industries Ltd. 12/15/2017

SINNET INDS INC (NY)
Name changed to Alpha Petroleum Exploration Corp. 12/1/80
(See Alpha Petroleum Exploration Corp.)

SINO-AMERICAN DEV CORP (NV)
Each share old Common $0.001 par exchanged for (0.05882352) share new new Common $0.001 par 01/22/2007
Recapitalized as Harvest Bio-Organic International Co., Ltd. 12/07/2010
Each share new Common $0.001 par exchanged for (0.25) share Common $0.001 par
(See Harvest Bio-Organic International Co., Ltd.)

SINO-BIOTICS INC (DE)
Each share old Common $0.001 par exchanged for (0.001) share new Common $0.001 par 12/07/2007
New Common $0.001 par split (6) for (1) by issuance of (5) additional shares payable 03/31/2008 to holders of record 03/29/2008 Ex date - 04/01/2008
Name changed to CH Lighting International Corp. 09/10/2008
(See CH Lighting International Corp.)

SINO BON ENTMT INC (NV)
Common $0.001 par split (2) for (1) by issuance of (1) additional share payable 07/22/2010 to holders of record 07/12/2010 Ex date - 07/23/2010
SEC revoked common stock registration 02/27/2013

SINO BUSINESS MACHS INC (BC)
Dissolved and struck from the register 11/26/93

SINO-CANADIAN RES LTD (DE)
Recapitalized as Central Network Communications, Inc. 01/07/1999
Each share Common $0.0001 par exchanged for (0.25) share Common $0.0001 par
Central Network Communications, Inc. name changed to JATI Technologies, Inc. 09/14/2006 which recapitalized as Merco Sud Agro-Financial Equities Corp. 03/25/2009

SINO CEM INC (NV)
Common $0.001 par split (1.3089005) for (1) by issuance of (0.3089005) additional share payable 09/20/2010 to holders of record 09/20/2010
Name changed to Nevis Capital Corp. 07/08/2013
Nevis Capital Corp. recapitalized as ASC Biosciences, Inc. 05/10/2017

SINO CHARTER INC (NV)
Each share old Common $0.00001 par exchanged for (0.01) share new Common $0.00001 par 01/16/2009
Note: No holder will receive fewer than (100) shares
Name changed to VLOV Inc. 03/20/2009
VLOV Inc. name changed to Kali, Inc. 02/23/2016

SINO-CITY GAS INC (DE)
Name changed to SpeechLink Communications Corp. 09/23/1999
Speechlink Communications Corp. recapitalized as Eros Enterprises, Inc. 12/15/2005 which name changed to IQ Webquest, Inc. 03/03/2006

SINO ENVIRON-ENERGY TECH CORP (CAYMAN ISLANDS)
Name changed to Ord Mountain Resources Corp. 02/15/2012

SINO-EXCEL ENERGY LTD (AUSTRALIA)
ADR agreement terminated 11/12/2015
No ADR's remain outstanding

SINO EXPRESS TRAVEL LTD (NV)
SEC revoked common stock registration 06/19/2009

SINO FIBRE COMMUNICATIONS INC (NV)
Name changed to Sino Bioenergy Corp. 01/04/2012

SINO FOODS CORP (YUKON)
Recapitalized as G.R. Pacific Resource Corp. (Yukon) 1/23/97
Each share Common no par exchanged for (0.25) share Common no par
G.R. Pacific Resource Corp. (Yukon) reincorporated in British Columbia as Pacific GeoInfo Corp. 2/3/2003

SINO FORTUNE HLDG CORP (NV)
Each share old Common $0.001 par exchanged for (0.2) share new Common $0.001 par 08/07/2017
Name changed to Hui Ying Financial Holdings Corp. 12/04/2017

SINO FST CORP (CANADA)
Reincorporated 06/25/2002
Place of incorporation changed from (ON) to (Canada) 06/25/2002
Subordinate Shares no par reclassified as Common no par 06/22/2004
144A Class A Subordinate Shares no par reclassified as 144A Common no par 06/22/2004
Plan of arrangement under Companies' Creditors Arrangement Act effective 01/30/2013
Stockholders' equity unlikely

SINO GAS INTL HLDGS INC (UT)
Each share Common $0.001 par received distribution of (0.08333333) share Pegasus Tel, Inc. Restricted Common $0.0001 par payable 08/18/2008 to holders of record 08/15/2008
Acquired by Prosperity Gas Holdings Ltd. 11/26/2014
Each share Common $0.001 par exchanged for $1.30 cash

SINO MERCURY ACQUISITION CORP (DE)
Reorganized under the laws of Cayman Islands as Wins Finance Holdings Inc. 10/28/2015
Each Unit exchanged for (1.1) shares Ordinary $0.0001 par
Each share Common $0.0001 par exchanged for (1) share Ordinary $0.0001 par

SINO OCEAN LD HLDGS LTD (HONG KONG)
Name changed to Sino-Ocean Group Holdings Ltd. 06/22/2016

SINO PAC DEV LTD (BC)
Name changed to Prominex Resource Corp. 11/17/2005

SINO PAC INTL INVTS INC (BC)
Recapitalized as Paron Resources Inc. 12/16/96
Each share Common no par exchanged for (0.2) share Common no par

SINO PMTS INC (NV)
Old Common $0.00001 par split (3) for (1) by issuance of (2) additional shares payable 03/25/2009 to holders of record 03/23/2009 Ex date - 03/26/2009
Each share old Common $0.00001 par exchanged for (0.16666666) share new Common $0.00001 par 03/18/2013
Name changed to Value Exchange International, Inc. 10/05/2016

SINO SHIPPING HLDGS INC (DE)
SEC revoked common stock registration 03/19/2013

SINO SILVER CORP (NV)
Completely liquidated
Each share Common $0.001 par received first and final distribution of (0.16666666) share Silver Dragon Resources Inc. Restricted Common $0.0001 par payable 06/30/2007 to holders of record 06/05/2007
Note: Certificates were not required to be surrendered and are without value

SINO VANADIUM INC (ON)
Acquired by Fit Plus Holdings Ltd. 12/07/2011
Each share Common no par exchanged for $0.27 cash

SINOBIOMED INC (DE)
Recapitalized as Sitoa Global Inc. 08/04/2011
Each share Common $0.0001 par exchanged for (0.05) share Common $0.0001 par
Sitoa Global Inc. recapitalized as Seratosa Inc. 12/17/2013 which recapitalized as Weyland Tech, Inc. 09/01/2015

SINOBIOPHARMA INC (NV)
Common $0.0001 par split (50) for (1) by issuance of (49) additional shares payable 08/04/2008 to holders of record 08/04/2008
Acquired by Sinobp, Inc. 11/23/2011
Each share Common $0.0001 par exchanged for $0.22 cash

SINOCOKING COAL & COKE CHEM INDS INC (FL)
Name changed to Hongli Clean Energy Technologies Corp. 07/28/2015

SINOCUBATE INC (NV)
Name changed to Viking Investments Group, Inc. 07/16/2012
Viking Investments Group, Inc. name changed to Viking Energy Group, Inc. 05/08/2017

SINOENERGY CORP (NV)
Each share old Common $0.001 par exchanged for (0.5) share new Common $0.001 par 06/20/2008
Merged into Skywide Capital Management Ltd. 09/27/2010
Each share new Common $0.001 par exchanged for $1.90 cash

SINOFRESH CORP (FL)
Name changed to SinoFresh Healthcare, Inc. 09/19/2003
(See SinoFresh Healthcare, Inc.)

SINOFRESH HEALTHCARE INC (FL)
SEC revoked common stock registration 05/25/2011

SINOGAS WEST INC (AB)
Name changed to Bulldog Explorations Ltd. (AB) 05/09/2012
Bulldog Explorations Ltd. (AB) reincorporated in British Columbia as Green Arrow Resources Inc. 02/13/2013

SINOMAR CAP CORP (AB)
Name changed to Hunt Mining Corp. (AB) 02/05/2010
Hunt Mining Corp. (AB) reincorporated in British Columbia 11/06/2013

SINOPEC BEIJING YANHUA PETROCHEMICAL CO LTD (CHINA)
ADR agreement terminated 06/07/2005
Each Sponsored ADR for H Shares exchanged for $24.323 cash

SINORANK PETROLEUM RES LTD (BERMUDA)
Delisted from Toronto Venture Stock Exchange 10/12/2000

SINOTEC VENTURES CORP (BC)
Name changed to Can-Chin Entertainment Group Co. Ltd. 06/05/2003
(See Can-Chin Entertainment Group Co. Ltd.)

SINOTECH ENERGY LTD (CAYMAN ISLANDS)
Issue Information - 19,736,842 SPONSORED ADR'S offered at $8.50 per ADR on 11/03/2010
ADR agreement terminated 08/31/2012
ADR holders' equity unlikely

SINOTEL TECHNOLOGIES LTD (SINGAPORE)
ADR agreement terminated 05/06/2016
Each ADR for Ordinary exchanged for $1.879723 cash

SINOTRANS LTD (CHINA)
ADR agreement terminated 01/24/2018
No ADR's remain outstanding

SINTANA ENERGY INC (ON)
Merged into Sintana Energy Inc. (AB) 08/10/2015
Each share Common no par exchanged for (0.26316) share Common no par
Note: Unexchanged certificates were cancelled and became without value 08/10/2018

SINTER METALS INC (DE)
Issue Information - 2,550,000 shares CL A offered at $10 per share on 10/26/1994
Merged into GKN Powder Metallurgy, Inc. 6/3/97

Each share Class A Common $0.001 par exchanged for $37 cash

SINTERAL CORP (NY)
Merged into Hi-Tech Industries, Inc. 11/10/72
Each share Common 1¢ par exchanged for (0.2) share Common 6¢ par
(See Hi-Tech Industries, Inc.)

SINTRA LTD (CANADA)
Acquired by 3842312 Canada Inc. 02/19/2001
Each share Common no par exchanged for $540 cash

SIOCTA VENTURES INC (AB)
Name changed to TradeRef Software Corp. (AB) 07/11/1994
TradeRef Software Corp. (AB) reincorporated in Anguilla 12/11/1996 which name changed to Hansa.net Global Commerce, Inc. 02/20/1997 which name changed to KMT-Hansa Corp. 09/27/2013

SIONIX CORP (UT)
Name changed to Automatic Control Corp. (NV) 02/14/1996
Automatic Control Corp. (NV) reincorporated under the laws of Utah as Sionix Corp. 04/22/1996 which reincorporated back under the laws of Nevada 07/03/2003

SIOUX CITY GAS & ELECTRIC CO.
Reorganized as Iowa Public Service Co. (IA) 00/00/1949
Preferred exchanged share for share Common exchanged (2.2) for (1)
(See Iowa Public Service Co. (IA))

SIOUX CITY STOCK YARDS CO. (IA)
Each share Preferred $100 par exchanged for (4) shares Preferred no par in 1931
Each share Common $100 par exchanged for (4) shares Common no par in 1931
Preferred and Common no par changed to $15 par in 1934
Merged into United Stockyards Corp. 8/1/63
Each share Preferred and/or Common $15 par exchanged for (1) share Common 25¢ par
United Stockyards merged into Canal-Randolph Corp. 11/1/64
(See Canal-Randolph Corp.)

SIOUX FALLS CMNTY HOTEL CO (SD)
Merged into Lakeland Industries, Inc. 10/08/1985
Each share Common $50 par exchanged for $323 cash

SIOUX MINES CO (UT)
Merged into Colorado Consolidated Mines Co. 12/30/1974
Each share Common 10¢ par exchanged for (1.0716) shares Common 10¢ par
Colorado Consolidated Mines Co. merged into Eureka Standard Consolidated Mining Co. 04/22/1975 which merged into South Standard Mining Co. 07/29/1983 which merged into Chief Consolidated Mining Co. 07/01/1996
(See Chief Consolidated Mining Co.)

SIOUX MTN MINES LTD (BC)
Recapitalized as Ascot Petroleum Corp. 06/20/1978
Each share Common no par exchanged for (0.5) share Common no par
Ascot Petroleum Corp. merged into Consolidated Ascot Petroleum Corp. 02/08/1982 which name changed to Ascot Investment Corp. 03/03/1987 which recapitalized as Pacific Western Investments Inc. 08/03/1990 which merged into Revenue Properties Co. Ltd. 01/01/1992 which merged into Morguard Corp. 12/01/2008

SIOUX OIL CO (CO)
6% Preferred $1 par called for redemption 09/26/1967
Each share Common 1¢ par exchanged for (0.2) share Common 5¢ par 00/00/1952
Merged into Tesoro Petroleum Corp. (CA) 02/01/1968
Each share Common 5¢ par exchanged for (0.2345) share Common $0.33333333 par
Tesoro Petroleum Corp. (CA) reincorporated in Delaware as Tesoro Petroleum Corp. 03/03/1969 which name changed to Tesoro Corp. 11/08/2004 which name changed to Andeavor 08/01/2017 which merged into Marathon Petroleum Corp. 10/01/2018

SIOUX PETROLEUMS, LTD. (ON)
Charter cancelled by the Province of Ontario for default 3/23/64

SIP'N SNACK SHOPPES, INC. (DE)
Charter revoked for non-payment of taxes 4/1/62

SIPALD RES LTD (BC)
Recapitalized as Rawdon Resources Ltd. 5/21/87
Each share Common no par exchanged for (0.5) share Common no par
Rawdon Resources Ltd. name changed to Advanced Ecology Systems Corp. 5/23/89 which recapitalized as Consolidated Advanced Ecology Corp. 1/9/90
(See Consolidated Advanced Ecology Corp.)

SIPCO INC (DE)
Exchangeable Preferred Ser. A 1¢ par called for redemption 08/08/1989
Public interest eliminated

SIPEX CORP (DE)
Reincorporated 10/28/2003
Common 1¢ par split (2) for (1) by issuance of (1) additional share payable 08/27/1997 to holders of record 08/18/1997
State of incorporation changed from (MA) to (DE) 10/28/2003
Each share old Common 1¢ par exchanged for (0.5) share new Common 1¢ par 03/01/2007
Merged into Exar Corp. 08/25/2007
Each share new Common 1¢ par exchanged for (0.6679) share Common $0.0001 par
(See Exar Corp.)

SIPP INTL INDS INC (NV)
Common 1¢ par changed to $0.001 par 03/03/2011
Reincorporated under the laws of Colorado 02/06/2017

SIPPICAN CORP (MA)
Common $1 par split (2) for (1) by issuance of (1) additional share 5/24/79
Name changed to TSC Corp. 11/9/81
(See TSC Corp.)

SIPPICAN INC (MA)
Common $1 par split (5) for (4) by issuance of (0.25) additional share 5/31/85
Acquired by Plessey Co. plc 1/20/88
Each share Common $1 par exchanged for $18.50 cash

SIPPICAN OCEAN SYSTEMS, INC. (MA)
Common $1 par split (5) for (4) by issuance of (0.25) additional share 2/14/83
Name changed to Sippican, Inc. 4/26/84
(See Sippican, Inc.)

SIR SPEEDY INC (CA)
Conv. Preferred no par called for redemption 01/07/1980
Merged into Pictograph, Inc. 05/20/1980
Each share Common 10¢ par exchanged for $1 cash

SIR SPEEDY PRTG CENTRES PLC (ENGLAND)
ADR agreement terminated 00/00/1990
Details not available

SIR SPEEDY SOUTHWEST INC (TX)
Adjudicated bankrupt 2/14/74
Stockholders' equity unlikely

SIRA INTL CORP (CA)
Name changed to WCS International 03/20/1974
WCS International recapitalized as Adams International Metals Corp. 02/10/1987
(See Adams International Metals Corp.)

SIRCO INTL CORP (NY)
Common 10¢ par split (2) for (1) by issuance of (1) additional share payable 05/16/1997 to holders of record 05/05/1997
Stock Dividend - 100% 11/11/1983
Name changed to eLEC Communications Corp. 11/16/1999
eLEC Communications name changed to Pervasip Corp. 02/21/2008

SIRCOR SCIENTIFIC INC (DE)
Completely liquidated 2/15/73
Each share Common $1 par exchanged for first and final distribution of (0.5) share Botar Corp. Common 1¢ par
(See Botar Corp.)

SIRENA APPAREL GROUP INC (DE)
Plan of reorganization under Chapter 11 Federal Bankruptcy Code effective 8/3/2000
No stockholders' equity

SIRENZA MICRODEVICES INC (DE)
Merged into RF Micro Devices, Inc. 11/13/2007
Each share Common $0.001 par exchanged for (1.7848) shares Common no par and $5.56 cash
RF Micro Devices, Inc. merged into Qorvo, Inc. 01/02/2015

SIRF TECHNOLOGY HLDGS INC (DE)
Merged into CSR PLC 06/26/2009
Each share Common $0.0001 par exchanged for (0.741) share Ordinary £0.001 par

SIRIAN LAMP CO.
Liquidated in 1948

SIRICOMM INC (DE)
Chapter 11 bankruptcy proceedings dismissed 09/29/2008
No stockholders' equity

SIRIT INC (YT)
Merged into Federal Signal Corp. 03/05/2010
Each share Common no par exchanged for $0.46 cash

SIRIT TECHNOLOGIES INC (BC)
Acquired by iTech Capital Corp. 11/01/2002
Each share Common no par exchanged for (0.11326182) share Common no par
iTech Capital Corp. name changed to Sirit Inc. 05/05/2003
(See Sirit Inc.)

SIRIUS CORP N L (AUSTRALIA)
Recapitalized as Hallmark Gold N.L. 07/01/1991
Each ADR for Ordinary AUD $1 par exchanged for (0.05) ADR for Ordinary AUD $0.20 par

SIRIUS EXPL PLC (UNITED KINGDOM)
Name changed to Sirius Minerals PLC 10/04/2010

SIRIUS RESOURCE CORP (BC)
Struck off register and declared dissolved for failure to file returns 05/28/1993

SIRIUS RES LTD (BC)
Recapitalized as Lyra Resources Ltd. 10/14/1999
Each (2.9) shares Common no par exchanged for (1) share Common no par
Lyra Resources Ltd. name changed to Cicada Ventures Ltd. 07/02/2008

SIRIUS SATELLITE RADIO INC (DE)
Each share 10-1/2% Conv. Preferred exchanged for approximately (5.556) shares Common $0.001 par
9.2% Jr. Conv. Preferred Ser. A, B and D exchanged for an undetermined amount of of Common and Common Stock Purchase Warrants 03/00/2003
Name changed to Sirius XM Radio, Inc. 08/06/2008
Sirius XM Radio, Inc. name changed to Sirius XM Holdings Inc. 11/15/2013

SIRIUS XM CDA HLDGS INC (ON)
Merged into Sirius XM Holdings Inc. 05/26/2017
Each Class A Subordinate Share exchanged for $4.50 cash

SIRIUS XM RADIO INC (DE)
Name changed to Sirius XM Holdings Inc. 11/15/2013

SIRMAC MINES LTD (ON)
Charter cancelled for failure to pay taxes and file returns 03/16/1976

SIRNA THERAPEUTICS INC (DE)
Merged into Merck & Co., Inc. (Old) 12/29/2006
Each share Common 1¢ par exchanged for $13 cash

SIROCCO MNG INC (BC)
Merged into RB Energy Inc. 02/05/2014
Each share Common no par exchanged for (0.3916) share Common no par
Note: Unexchanged certificates will be cancelled and become without value 02/05/2020

SIRONA DENTAL SYS INC (DE)
Merged into DENTSPLY SIRONA Inc. 03/01/2016
Each share Common 1¢ par exchanged for (1.8142) shares Common 1¢ par

SIRROM CAP CORP (TN)
Issue Information - 2,300,000 shares COM offered at $11 per share on 02/06/1995
Common no par split (2) for (1) by issuance of (1) additional share payable 01/30/1998 to holders of record 01/16/1998 Ex date - 02/02/1998
Merged into FINOVA Group Inc. 03/22/1999
Each share Common no par exchanged for (0.1634) share Common 1¢ par
(See FINOVA Group Inc.)

SIRTRIS PHARMACEUTICALS INC (DE)
Merged into GlaxoSmithKline PLC 06/06/2008
Each share Common $0.001 par exchanged for $22.50 cash

SIRVA INC (DE)
Plan of reorganization under Chapter 11 Federal Bankruptcy Code effective 05/12/2008
No stockholders' equity

SIS BANCORP INC (MA)
Merged into Peoples Heritage Financial Group Inc. 11/30/1998
Each share Common 1¢ par exchanged for $2.25 cash

SIS CORP (OH)
Plan of reorganization under Chapter

11 Federal Bankruptcy proceedings confirmed 10/29/1990
No stockholders' equity

SISCALTA OILS LTD. (AB)
Acquired by Siscoe Mines Ltd. for cash 9/6/63

SISCOE CALLAHAN MNG CORP (BC)
Struck off register and declared dissolved for failure to file returns 9/15/95

SISCOE MINES LTD (QC)
Name changed 00/00/1956
Name changed from Siscoe Gold Mines Ltd. to Siscoe Mines Ltd. 00/00/1956
Recapitalized as United Siscoe Mines Ltd. 06/24/1971
Each share Capital Stock $1 par exchanged for (0.5) share Capital Stock no par
United Siscoe Mines Ltd. name changed to United Siscoe Mines Inc.-Les Mines United Siscoe Inc. 02/11/1981 which recapaitalized as Horsham Corp.- Corporation Horsham (QC) 07/08/1987 which reincorporated in Ontario as Trizec Hahn Corp. 11/01/1996 which was acquired by Trizec Canada Inc. 05/08/2002
(See Trizec Canada Inc.)

SISCOM INC (CO)
Merged into Siscom Corp. 12/15/2003
Each share Common no par exchanged for $0.0425 cash

SISKON CORP. (NV)
Each share Capital Stock 1¢ par exchanged for (0.1) share Capital Stock 10¢ par 04/11/1958
Reorganized under the laws of Delaware 10/01/1969
Each share Capital Stock 10¢ par exchanged for (0.5) share Capital Stock 20¢ par
(See Siskon Corp. (DE))

SISKON CORP (DE)
Merged into Hanna Mining Co. 06/10/1981
Each share Capital Stock 20¢ par exchanged for $10 cash

SISKON GOLD CORP (DE)
Each share old Common $0.001 par exchanged for (0.1) share new Common $0.001 par 12/22/1992
SEC revoked common stock registration 05/30/2008

SISTEMA-HALS JSC (RUSSIA)
Name changed to HALS-Development JSC 08/12/2011
HALS-Development JSC name changed to HALS-Development PJSC 08/31/2015

SISTERVILLE BANCORP INC (DE)
Acquired by Peoples Bancorp Inc. 09/13/2012
Each share Common 10¢ par exchanged for $30.81 cash

SISTO FINANCIAL CORP. (NY)
Liquidation completed in 1953

SIT GROWTH & INCOME FD INC (MN)
Name changed 11/01/1993
Name changed from Sit "New Beginning" Income & Growth Fund to Sit Growth & Income Fund Inc. 11/01/1993
Name changed to Sit Large Cap Growth Fund, Inc. 10/23/1996

SIT GROWTH FD INC (MN)
Name changed 11/01/1993
Name changed from Sit New Beginning Growth Fund, Inc. to Sit Growth Fund Inc. 11/01/1993
Common 1¢ par split (4) for (1) by issuance of (3) additional shares 12/10/1993
Name changed to Sit Mid Cap Growth Fund, Inc. 10/23/1996

SIT MONEY MKT FD INC (MN)
Completely liquidated 03/27/2009
Each share Common 1¢ par received first and final distribution of $1 cash

SIT NEW BEGINNING INVT RESV FD INC (MN)
Name changed to Sit Money Market Fund 11/01/1993
(See Sit Money Market Fund)

SIT NEW BEGINNING TAX FREE INCOME FD INC (MN)
Name changed to Sit Tax-Free Income Fund 07/03/1992

SIT NEW BEGINNING U S GOVT SECS FD INC (MN)
Name changed to SIT U.S. Government Securities Fund Inc. 11/1/93

SIT NEW BEGINNING YIELD FD INC (MN)
Name changed to Sit "New Beginning" Tax-Free Income Fund Inc. 09/29/1988
Sit "New Beginning" Tax-Free Income Fund Inc. name changed to Sit Tax-Free Income Fund 07/03/1992

SITE-BASED MEDIA INC (DE)
Name changed to Site Holdings Inc. 3/8/94
(See Site Holdings Inc.)

SITE CON INDS INC (NY)
Acquired by Diversified Earth Sciences, Inc. 03/01/1972
Each share Common 10¢ par exchanged for (0.263) share Common 80¢ par
(See Diversified Earth Sciences, Inc.)

SITE HLDGS INC (DE)
Each share old Common no par exchanged for (0.01) share new Common 6/6/95
Charter cancelled and declared inoperative and void for non-payment of taxes 3/1/97

SITE-PAK INDS CORP (DE)
Charter cancelled and declared inoperative and void for non-payment of taxes 04/15/1973

SITE TECHNOLOGIES INC (CA)
Plan of reorganization under Chapter 11 Federal Bankruptcy Code effective 07/18/2000
Each share Common no par received initial distribution of $0.62 cash payable 10/01/2001 to holders of record 08/14/2000 Ex date - 10/02/2001
Each share Common no par received second and final distribution of $0.08583 cash payable 06/30/2003 to holders of record 08/14/2000 Ex date - 07/02/2003
Note: Certificates were not required to be surrendered and are without value

SITEBRAND INC (CANADA)
Recapitalized as Marchwell Ventures Ltd. 10/26/2011
Each share Common no par exchanged for (0.2) share Common par
Marchwell Ventures Ltd. recapitalized as Sante Vertias Holdings Inc. 04/11/2018

SITEC VENTURES CORP (BC)
Recapitalized as Tulox Resources Inc. (BC) 01/17/2008
Each share Common no par exchanged for (0.5) share Common no par
Tulox Resources Inc. (BC) reorganized in Canada as Argentium Resources Inc. 09/09/2011 which recapitalized as Northern Sphere Mining Corp. 08/24/2015

SITEK INC (DE)
Name changed to Prodeo Technologies, Inc. 6/5/2000
(See Prodeo Technologies, Inc.)

SITEL CORP (MN)
Common $0.001 par split (2) for (1) by issuance of (1) additional share payable 05/13/1996 to holders of record 05/03/1996
Common $0.001 par split (2) for (1) by issuance of (1) additional share payable 10/21/1996 to holders of record 10/14/1996
Merged into Onex Corp. 01/30/2007
Each share Common $0.001 par exchanged for $4.25 cash

SITESEARCH CORP (NV)
Recapitalized as Leaplab Corp. 11/09/2011
Each (450) shares Common $0.001 par exchanged for (1) share Common $0.001 par

SITESTAR CORP (NV)
Recapitalized as Enterprise Diversified, Inc. 07/23/2018
Each share Common $0.001 par exchanged for (0.008) share Common $0.125 par

SITE2SHOP COM INC (NV)
Name changed to Intermedia Marketing Solutions, Inc. 04/20/2001
(See Intermedia Marketing Solutions, Inc.)

SITEWORKS BLDG & DEV CO (FL)
Name changed 04/15/2005
Each share old Common $0.001 par exchanged for (0.005) share new Common $0.001 par 03/31/2003
Each share new Common $0.001 par exchanged again for (0.0005) share new Common $0.001 par 08/12/2004
Name changed from Siteworks, Inc. to SiteWorks Building & Development Co. 04/15/2005
Reorganized under the laws of Nevada as SBD International, Inc. 08/03/2006
Each share Common $0.001 par exchanged for (0.04) share Common $0.001 par
Note: No holder will receive fewer than (100) shares
SBD International, Inc. recapitalized as Solargy Systems Inc. 10/27/2008
(See Solargy Systems Inc.)

SITHE ENERGIES INC (DE)
Merged into IES Acquisition, Inc. 4/4/96
Each share Common 1¢ par exchanged for $15 cash

SITKA OIL & GAS EXPLORATION, INC. (UT)
Reincorporated under the laws of Texas as First Texas Financial, Inc. 9/28/70
First Texas Financial, Inc. name changed to Triland, Inc. 7/18/72
(See Triland, Inc.)

SITKIN SMLT & REFNG INC (PA)
Common 10¢ par split (5) for (4) by issuance of (0.25) additional share 04/05/1968
Adjudicated bankrupt 07/12/1978
Stockholders' equity unlikely

SITOA GLOBAL INC (DE)
Recapitalized as Seratosa Inc. 12/17/2013
Each share Common $0.0001 par exchanged for (0.0001) share Common $0.0001 par
Seratosa Inc. recapitalized as Weyland Tech, Inc. 09/01/2015

SIUSLAW FINL GROUP INC (OR)
Reclassification effective 06/10/2007
Holders of (2,499) or fewer shares Common $1 par exchanged for (1) share Ser. A Preferred $1 par
Ser. A Preferred $1 par reclassified as Common $1 par 03/06/2015
Merged into Banner Corp. 03/06/2015
Each share Common $1 par exchanged for (0.32231) share new Common $1 par and $1.41622 cash

SIUSLAW VY BK (FLORENCE, OR)
Capital Stock $1 par split (5) for (4) by issuance of (0.25) additional share payable 05/18/1997 to holders of record 04/18/1997
Capital Stock $1 par split (2) for (1) by issuance of (1) additional share payable 07/13/1998 to holders of record 06/30/1998
Under plan of reorganization each share Common $1 par automatically became (1) share Siuslaw Financial Group Inc. Common $1 par 01/04/2002
Siuslaw Financial Group Inc. merged into Banner Corp. 03/06/2015

SIV INDS LTD (INDIA)
GDR agreement terminated 07/06/2009
Each Reg. S GDR for Ordinary exchanged for (1) share Ordinary
Each 144A GDR for Ordinary exchanged for (1) share Ordinary
Note: Unexchanged GDR's will be sold and the proceeds, if any, held for claim after 08/06/2009

SIVAULT SYS INC (NV)
Chapter 7 bankruptcy proceedings terminated 04/25/2011
No stockholders' equity

SIVOO HLDGS INC (NV)
Charter permanently revoked 07/31/2009

SIVYER STL CORP (WI)
Name changed 4/21/75
Name changed from Sivyer Steel Casting Co. to Sivyer Steel Corp. 4/21/75
Each (2,134) shares old Common no par exchanged for (1) share new Common no par 12/30/98
Note: In effect holders received $142 cash per share and public interest was eliminated

SIWOOGANOCK GTY SVGS BK (LANCASTER, NH)
Reorganized as Siwooganock Holding Co., Inc. 1/1/2004
Each share Common $100 par exchanged for (1) share Common $5 par
(See Siwooganock Holding Co., Inc.)

SIWOOGANOCK HLDG CO INC (NH)
Each share old Common $5 par exchanged for (5) shares new Common $5 par 7/1/2005
Merged into Passumpsic Bancorp 10/18/2006
Each share new Common $5 par exchanged for $35.75 cash

SIX CONTINENTS PLC (ENGLAND)
Under plan of demerger each Sponsored ADR for Ordinary exchanged for (0.847457) InterContinental Hotels Group PLC Sponsored ADR for Ordinary and (0.847457) Mitchells & Butlers PLC Sponsored ADR for Ordinary 04/15/2003
(See each company's listing)

611 WEST FORTY-THIRD STREET CORP. (NY)
Charter cancelled and proclaimed dissolved for failure to pay taxes 1/12/60

6550568 CDA INC (CANADA)
Recapitalized as Alaris Royalty Corp. 07/31/2008
Each share Common no par exchanged for (0.00184418) share Common no par

SIX FLAGS INC (DE)
Each share 7.5% Manditorily Convertible Preferred automatically became (0.5) share Common 2-1/2¢ par 04/02/2001
Plan of reorganization under Chapter 11 Federal Bankruptcy proceedings effective 04/30/2010
No stockholders' equity

614 SUPERIOR CO (OH)
Liquidation completed
Each share Common no par exchanged for initial distribution of $60 cash 02/15/1967
Each share Common no par received second distribution of $37.40 cash 08/07/1967
Each share Common no par received third and final distribution of $2.998321 cash 05/06/1968

605 WEST 132ND ST. CORP. (NY)
Charter cancelled and proclaimed dissolved for failure to pay taxes 7/24/59

609 SOUTH GRAND BUILDING CO. (CA)
Liquidation for cash completed 6/15/65

600 NORMANDIE CO. (CA)
Liquidation completed
Each share Capital Stock $1 par exchanged for initial distribution of (0.410875) share Consolidated Foods Corp. Common $1.33333333 par 06/27/1967
Each share Capital Stock $1 par received second distribution of (0.034127) share Consolidated Foods Corp. Common $1.33333333 par 09/13/1968
Each share Capital Stock $1 par received third distribution of (0.579951) share Consolidated Foods Corp. Common $1.33333333 par 10/01/1969
Each share Capital Stock $1 par exchanged for fourth and final distribution of (0.099793) share Consolidated Foods Corp. Common $1.33333333 par 09/15/1970
Consolidated Foods Corp. name changed to Sara Lee Corp. 04/02/1985 which recapitalized as Hillshire Brands Co. 06/29/2012
(See Hillshire Brands Co.)

692 BROADWAY CORP. (NY)
Property sold 10/10/60
No stockholders' equity

SIX RIVS NATL BK (EUREKA, CA)
Merged into North Valley Bancorp 10/11/2000
Each share Common $5 par exchanged for (1.4) shares Common no par
North Valley Bancorp merged into TriCo Bancshares 10/03/2014

612 NORTH MICH AVE BLDG CORP (IL)
Liquidation completed
Each share Common no par received initial distribution of $3 cash 02/28/1974
Each share Common no par exchanged for second and final distribution of $5.1847 cash 01/11/1980

625 LIBERTY AVE HLDG CORP
Liquidation completed
Each share Common received initial distribution of approximately $5 cash 7/24/96
Each share Common exchanged for second and final distribution of $6.63915 cash 12/31/97

625 MADISON AVENUE CORP. (NY)
Liquidation completed 10/24/52

626-640 WAVELAND AVE. BLDG. CORP. (IL)
Liquidation completed 1/16/61

649 COM INC (TX)
Each share old Common $0.001 par exchanged for (0.01) share new Common $0.001 par 10/15/2004
Name changed to Infinite Holdings Group, Inc. 01/24/2007
(See Infinite Holdings Group, Inc.)

1644 GREENLEAF APARTMENTS LIQUIDATION TRUST (IL)
Liquidation completed 10/17/58

16 PARK AVE INC (NY)
Voluntarily dissolved 02/17/1988
Details not available

16501 WOODWARD AVENUE CORP. (MI)
Completely liquidated 1/5/67
Each share Common $1 par exchanged for first and final distribution of $79.79 cash

SIXTH & BROADWAY BUILDING CO. (DE)
Liquidated in 1954

SIXTH AVENUE & 55TH ST. CORP.
Liquidation completed in 1950

SIXTIETH & TROY APARTMENTS, INC.
Liquidated in 1940

SIXTY EIGHT THOUSAND INC (NV)
Name changed to Arrisystems Inc. 01/17/1995
(See Arrisystems Inc.)

60 MINUTE SYS INC (FL)
Common $1 par changed to 33-1/3¢ par and (2) additional shares issued 05/01/1969
Declared insolvent 08/04/1972
No stockholders' equity

69 MADISON, INC. (NY)
Charter cancelled and proclaimed dissolved for failure to pay taxes and file reports 5/11/69

61 BROADWAY CORP. (NY)
Liquidation completed in 1954

SIXTY PLUS INCOME TR (ON)
Trust terminated 01/06/2009
Each Trust Unit no par received $11.4598 cash

SIXTY REALTY TRUST (MA)
Name changed to Realty Income Trust 6/8/66
Realty Income Trust name changed to Derwood Investment Trust 9/18/85 which name changed to Derwood Investment Corp. 7/10/86
(See Derwood Investment Corp.)

6655 WOODLAWN BUILDING CORP. (IL)
Liquidated in 1953

SIXTY SPLIT CORP (ON)
Preferred Shares called for redemption at $25 on 03/15/2011
Capital Shares called for redemption at $21.4703 on 03/15/2011

62 WEST 47TH STR CORP (NY)
Completely liquidated 01/07/1972
Each share Capital Stock 10¢ par exchanged for first and final distribution of $50 cash

SIXX HLDGS INC (DE)
Each share old Common 1¢ par exchanged for (0.125) share new Common 1¢ par 3/15/96
Merged into Bailey Acquisitions, Inc. 5/19/2006
Each share new Common 1¢ par exchanged for $5.50 cash

SIZELER PPTY INVS INC (MD)
Reincorporated 05/21/2001
State of incorporation changed from (DE) to (MD) and Common 1¢ par changed to $0.0001 par 05/21/2001
Merged into Revenue Properties Co. Ltd. 11/10/2006
Each share 9.75% Preferred Ser. B $0.0001 par exchanged for $26.79 cash
Each share Common $0.0001 par exchanged for 15.244 cash

SIZEMORE ENVIRONMENTAL GROUP INC (DE)
Merged into EnClean, Inc. 6/28/91
Each share Common $0.001 par exchanged for (0.0361) share Common 1¢ par
(See EnClean, Inc.)

SIZER STEEL CORP. (NY)
Charter revoked for failure to file reports and pay fees 12/16/29

SIZMEK INC (DE)
Acquired by Solomon Holding, LLC 09/27/2016
Each share Common $0.001 par exchanged for $3.90 cash

SIZZLER INTL INC (DE)
Name changed to Worldwide Restaurant Concepts Inc. 9/4/2001
(See Worldwide Restaurant Concepts Inc.)

SIZZLER RESTAURANTS INTL INC (DE)
Reincorporated 8/26/85
Common no par split (2) for (1) by issuance of (1) additional share 7/1/83
Common no par split (3) for (2) by issuance of (0.5) additional share 7/12/85
State of incorporation changed from (CA) to (DE) 8/26/85
Common no par changed to 1¢ par in August 1986
Common 1¢ par split (3) for (2) by issuance of (0.5) additional share 9/16/86
Merged into Collins Foods, Inc. 4/25/91
Each share Common 1¢ par exchanged for (1.25) shares Common 1¢ par
Collins Foods, Inc. name changed to Sizzler International, Inc. 5/6/91 which name changed to Worldwide Restaurant Concepts, Inc. 9/4/2001
(See Worldwide Restaurant Concepts Inc.)

SJ ELECTRONICS INC (NV)
SEC revoked common stock registration 10/14/2011

SJ RES LTD (BC)
Name changed to Ark La Tex Industries Ltd. 07/11/1984
Ark La Tex Industries Ltd. recapitalized as Landstar Properties Inc. 06/17/1992

SJG CAP TR (DE)
Issue Information - 1,400,000 shares 8.35% PFD SECS offered at $25 per share on 04/29/1997
8.35% Preferred Securities called for redemption at $25 on 11/5/2003

SJI GROUP INC (DE)
Name changed to iCOMMERCE Group, Inc. 06/10/1999
(See iCOMMERCE Group, Inc.)

SJNB FINL CORP (CA)
Stock Dividend - 10% 04/23/1990
Merged into Greater Bay Bancorp 10/23/2001
Each share Common no par exchanged for (1.82) shares Common no par
Greater Bay Bancorp merged into Wells Fargo & Co. (New) 10/01/2007

SJOSTROM AUTOMATIONS INC (FL)
Merged into First Research Corp. 09/09/1968
Each share Class A Common 10¢ par exchanged for (4) shares Common 10¢ par
(See First Research Corp.)

SJS BANCORP INC (DE)
Merged into Shoreline Financial Inc. 6/13/97
Each share Common 1¢ par exchanged for $27 cash

SJTC LIQUIDATING CO., INC. (VT)
Liquidation completed
Each share Common $1 par exchanged for initial distribution of $20.72 cash 10/02/1975
Each share Class B Common $1 par exchanged for initial distribution of $20.72 cash 10/02/1975
Each share Common $1 par received second and final distribution of $1.14 cash 07/02/1976
Each share Class B Common $1 par received second and final distribution of $1.14 cash 07/02/1976

SJW CORP (CA)
Common $6.25 par changed to $3.125 par and (1) additional share issued 07/24/1985
4.625% Preferred Ser. G $25 par called for redemption 06/01/1990
4.75% Preferred Ser. A $25 par called for redemption 06/01/1990
4.75% Conv. Preferred Ser. B $25 par called for redemption 06/01/1990
4.7% Conv. Preferred Ser. C $25 par called for redemption 06/01/1990
4.7% Preferred Ser. D $25 par called for redemption 06/01/1990
5.5% Preferred Ser. E $25 par called for redemption 06/01/1990
Common $3.125 par changed to $1.042 par and (2) additional shares issued payable 03/01/2004 to holders of record 02/10/2004
Common $1.042 par changed to $0.521 par and (1) additional share issued payable 03/16/2006 to holders of record 03/02/2006
Ex date - 03/17/2006
Reincorporated under the laws of Delaware as SJW Group and Common $0.521 par changed to $0.001 par 11/16/2016

SK CORP (KOREA)
GDR agreement terminated 06/21/2007
Each 144 GDR for Non-Vtg. Ordinary exchanged for $30.87853 cash
Each 144A GDR for Ordinary exchanged for $64.582116 cash

SK RLTY VENTURES INC (NV)
Charter revoked for failure to file reports and pay fees 12/31/2009

SK TECHNOLOGIES CORP (DE)
Each share Common $0.0001 par exchanged for (0.1) share old Common $0.001 par 12/18/1989
Each share old Common $0.001 par exchanged for (0.1) share new Common $0.001 par 06/01/1993
Each share new Common $0.001 par exchanged again for (0.01) share new Common $0.001 par 05/12/2004
Name changed to Cirilium Holdings, Inc. (DE) 07/19/2004
Cirilium Holdings, Inc. (DE) reorganized in Florida 01/09/2007 which name changed to Cambridge Park Limited, Inc. 02/22/2007 which recapitalized as Family Entertainment Corp. 11/30/2007 which recapitalized as Airborne Security & Protective Services, Inc. (Ctfs. dated prior to 09/30/2009) 09/16/2008 which name changed to Harbor Brewing Co., Inc. 09/30/2009 which name changed to CTGX Mining, Inc. 02/28/2013

SKAGGS COS INC (DE)
Common $1 par split (3) for (2) by issuance of (0.5) additional share 2/27/76
Under plan of merger name changed to American Stores Co. (New) 7/26/79
American Stores Co. (New) merged into Albertson's, Inc. 6/23/99 which merged into Supervalu Inc. 6/2/2006

SKAGGS DRUG CTRS INC (DE)
5% Conv. Preferred $20 par called for redemption 6/7/68
Common $1 par and Class B Common $1 par split (3) for (2) by issuance of (0.5) additional share respectively 7/1/68

SKAGGS (continued)
Stock Dividend - Common and Class B Common - 10% 6/15/70
Under plan of merger name changed to Skaggs Companies, Inc. and Class B Common $1 par reclassified as Common $1 par 12/31/70
Skaggs Companies, Inc. name changed to American Stores Co. (New) 7/26/79 which merged into Albertson's, Inc. 6/23/99 which merged into Supervalu Inc. 6/2/2006

SKAGGS PAY LESS DRUG STORES (CA)
Common $1 par split (5) for (4) by issuance of (0.25) additional share 4/17/67
Common $1 par changed to no par and (1) additional share issued 3/1/68
Name changed to Pay Less Drug Stores 5/12/71
(See Pay Less Drug Stores)

SKAHA INC (UT)
Reincorporated under the laws of Delaware as Haben Industries, Inc. 06/16/1988
Haben Industries, Inc. recapitalized as Embrace Systems Corp. 04/29/1992
(See Embrace Systems Corp.)

SKAIST MINES LTD (BC)
Capital Stock 50¢ par changed to no par 02/10/1975
Recapitalized as Intercoast Resources Corp. 06/15/1977
Each share Capital Stock no par exchanged for (1/3) share Class A Stock no par
(See Intercoast Resources Corp.)

SKALBANIA ENTERPRISES LTD (BC)
Name changed to Selco International Properties Inc. 03/03/1988
(See Selco International Properties Inc.)

SKAMPER CORP (IN)
Common no par split (3) for (2) by issuance of (0.5) additional share 7/30/71
Merged into AMF Inc. 4/14/72
Each share Common no par exchanged for (0.75) share Common $1.75 par
(See AMF Inc.)

SKANA CAP CORP (BC)
Reincorporated under the laws of Alberta as MENA Hydrocarbons Inc. 06/22/2011

SKANDINAVISKA ENSKILDA BANKEN (SWEDEN)
ADR agreement terminated 04/20/2009
No ADR's remain outstanding (Additional Information in Active)

SKANEATELES BANCORP INC (DE)
Common no par split (3) for (2) by issuance of (0.5) additional share payable 11/28/1997 to holders of record 11/12/1997
Merged into BSB Bancorp, Inc. 07/01/1999
Each share Common 1¢ par exchanged for (0.97) share Common 1¢ par
BSB Bancorp, Inc. merged into Partners Trust Financial Group, Inc. (DE) 07/14/2004 which merged into M&T Bank Corp. 11/30/2007

SKANEATELES SVGS BK (SKANEATELES, NY)
Reorganized under the laws of Delaware as Center Banks Inc. and Common $1 par changed to 1¢ par 04/17/1990
Center Banks Inc. name changed to Skaneateles Bancorp, Inc. 04/16/1997 which merged into BSB Bancorp, Inc. 07/01/1999 which merged into Partners Trust Financial Group, Inc. (DE) 07/14/2004 which merged into M&T Bank Corp. 11/30/2007

SKAT RES LTD (BC)
Merged into Stand-Skat Resources Ltd. 10/16/1978
Each share Capital Stock no par exchanged for (0.64689) share Capital Stock no par
Stand-Skat Resources Ltd. merged into Ramrod Energy Corp. 03/01/1983 which recapitalized as Consolidated Ramrod Gold Corp. 08/27/1986 which name changed to Quest International Resources Corp. 04/09/1996 which recapitalized as Standard Mining Corp. 06/16/1999 which merged into Doublestar Resources Ltd. (YT) 11/01/2001 which reincorporated in British Columbia 10/10/2002 which merged into Selkirk Metals Corp. 07/23/2007
(See Selkirk Metals Corp.)

SKB BANKA D D (SLOVAKIA)
GDR agreement terminated 09/20/2001
Each 144A GDR for Ordinary exchanged for $10.1577 cash
Each Reg. S GDR for Ordinary exchanged for $10.1577 cash

SKEENA RES LTD (BC)
Merged into Golden Nevada Resources Inc. 08/19/1987
Each share Common no par exchanged for (1) share Common no par
Golden Nevada Resources Inc. recapitalized as Goldnev Resources Inc. 06/19/1989

SKEENA SILVER MINES LTD. (BC)
Recapitalized as Consolidated Skeena Mines Ltd. 7/9/65
Each share Capital Stock no par exchanged for (0.2) share Common no par
Consolidated Skeena Mines Ltd. merged into International Mariner Resources Inc. 2/9/71
(See International Mariner Resources Ltd.)

SKELLY OIL CO (DE)
Common $25 par changed to $15 par 00/00/1936
Common $15 par changed to $25 par 00/00/1950
Common $25 par changed to $10 par and (1.5) additional shares issued 11/18/1966
Stock Dividends - 10% 09/24/1948; 10% 03/10/1949; 10% 08/24/1949; 100% 05/18/1950; 10% 03/05/1952; 100% 09/04/1953
Merged into Getty Oil Co. 01/31/1977
Each share Common $10 par exchanged for (0.5875) share Common $4 par
(See Getty Oil Co.)

SKELLY RES LTD (BC)
Name changed to Bel Pac Industries Ltd. 8/31/87
(See Bel Pac Industries Ltd.)

SKG INTERACTIVE INC (CANADA)
Cease trade order effective 04/18/2002
Stockholders' equity unlikely

SKI FREE MARINE INC (AB)
Struck off register and declared dissolved for failure to file reports 09/01/1992

SKI PARK CITY WEST INC (UT)
Charter suspended for failure to pay taxes 09/30/1975

SKIATRON CORP.
Name changed to Skiatron Electronics & Television Corp. in 1950
(See Skiatron Electronics & Television Corp.)

SKIATRON ELECTRS & TELEVISION CORP (NY)
Dissolved by proclamation 3/24/93

SKIBO FINL CORP (USA)
Merged into Northwest Bancorp, Inc. (USA) 4/30/2004
Each share Common 10¢ par exchanged for $17 cash

SKIBSAKSJESELSKAPET STORLI (NORWAY)
Name changed to Odfjell ASA 1/22/98

SKIDAGATE EXPL LTD (BC)
Name changed to Granada Exploration Corp. 6/26/81
(See Granada Exploration Corp.)

SKIL CORP (DE)
Common $2 par split (3) for (1) by issuance of (2) additional shares 6/25/62
Stock Dividend - 25% 12/20/59
Merged into Emerson Electric Co. 3/23/79
Each share Common $2 par exchanged for (0.895) share Common $1 par

SKILES OIL CORP (DE)
6% Conv. Preferred $10 par called for redemption 02/16/1962
Name changed to Davis (Alva C.) Petroleum, Inc. 06/26/1968
(See Davis (Alva C.) Petroleum, Inc.)

SKILL RES LTD (AB)
Recapitalized as Unicorp Resources Ltd. 6/27/84
Each (0.25) share Class B Preferred $5 par exchanged for (0.5) share Conv. Class A no par and (0.5) share Class B no par
Each share Common no par exchanged for (0.5) share Conv. Class A no par and (0.5) share Class B no par
Unicorp Resources Ltd. merged into Asamera Inc. 5/1/86 which was acquired by Gulf Canada Resources Ltd. 8/4/88
(See Gulf Canada Resources Ltd.)

SKILLED HEALTHCARE GROUP INC (DE)
Name changed to Genesis Healthcare, Inc. 02/03/2015

SKILLSOFT CORP (DE)
Issue Information - 3,100,000 shares COM offered at $14 per share on 01/31/2000
Merged into SmartForce PLC 09/09/2002
Each share Common $0.001 par exchanged for (2.3674) Sponsored ADR's for Ordinary
SmartForce PLC name changed to SkillSoft PLC 11/19/2002
(See SkillSoft PLC)

SKILLSOFT PLC (IRELAND)
Acquired by SSI Investments III Ltd. 05/26/2010
Each Sponsored ADR for Ordinary EUR 0.11 par exchanged for $11.20 cash
Each Sponsored 144A ADR for Ordinary EUR 0.11 par exchanged for $11.20 cash

SKILSAW, INC. (DE)
Stock Dividends - 200% 12/12/47; 20% 12/14/50
Name changed to Skil Corp. in 1952
Skil Corp. merged into Emerson Electric Co. 3/23/79

SKIN CTL SYS INC (DE)
Charter cancelled and declared inoperative and void for non-payment of taxes 3/1/91

SKIN TIGHT INC (FL)
Name changed to Callmate Telecom International, Inc. 12/21/1998
Callmate Telecom International, Inc. name changed to BankEngine Technologies, Inc. (FL) 03/21/2001 which reincorporated in Delaware 05/23/2002 which recapitalized as Syscan Imaging, Inc. 04/02/2004 which name changed to Sysview Technology, Inc. 06/27/2006 which name changed to Document Capture Technologies, Inc. 01/08/2008
(See Document Capture Technologies, Inc.)

SKINNER CHUCK CO. (CT)
Stock Dividends - 100% 4/11/51; 100% 6/1/58
Name changed to Skinner Precision Industries, Inc. 10/20/60
Skinner Precision Industries, Inc. merged into Honeywell Inc. 2/13/79 which merged into Honeywell International Inc. 12/1/99

SKINNER CO.
Acquired by Nebraska-Iowa Packing Co. in 1938 which completed liquidation in 1958

SKINNER MACARONI CO (NE)
Each share 8% Preferred $100 par exchanged for (2) shares 5% Preferred $100 par 11/16/1961
Merged into Hershey Foods Corp. 01/03/1979
Each share 5% Preferred $100 par exchanged for $105 cash

SKINNER PACKING CO.
Acquired by Nebraska-Iowa Packing Co. in 1927 liquidation of which was completed in 1958

SKINNER PRECISION INDS INC (CT)
Each (5) shares old Common $20 par exchanged for (4) shares new Common $20 par plus $58 cash 7/22/63
Stock Dividend - 100% 4/18/66
Merged into Honeywell Inc. 2/13/79
Each share Common $20 par exchanged for (2.6163) shares Common $1.50 par
Honeywell Inc. merged into Honeywell International Inc. 12/1/99

SKINNY NUTRITIONAL CORP (NV)
Assets sold for the benefit of creditors 08/20/2014
No stockholders' equity

SKINNY TECHNOLOGIES INC (BC)
Recapitalized as Pediment Exploration Ltd. 09/22/2004
Each (15) shares Common no par exchanged for (1) share Common no par
Pediment Exploration Ltd. name changed to Pediment Gold Corp. 02/26/2009 which merged into Argonaut Gold Inc. 02/01/2011

SKINS INC (NV)
Chapter 7 bankruptcy proceedings terminated 08/19/2013
No stockholders' equity

SKINTEK LABS INC (DE)
Each share old Common $0.001 par exchanged for (0.002) share new Common $0.001 par 04/18/2002
Name changed to Hunno Technologies Inc. 09/18/2002
Hunno Technologies Inc. name changed to Abazias, Inc. 10/08/2003 which was acquired by OmniReliant Holdings, Inc. 08/27/2009

SKINZWRAPS INC (DE)
Common $0.001 par split (3) for (1) by issuance of (2) additional shares payable 05/21/2007 to holders of record 05/17/2007 Ex date - 05/22/2007
Recapitalized as Evolution Technology Resources, Inc. 04/24/2014
Each share Common $0.001 par exchanged for (0.00016666) share Common $0.001 par

SKIPPERS INC (WA)
Common 10¢ par split (3) for (2) by

issuance of (0.5) additional share 5/5/83
Merged into National Pizza Co. 1/12/90
Each share Common 10¢ par exchanged for $11.50 cash

SKLAR COMMUNICATIONS SVCS INC (NY)
Name changed to American Multimedia, Inc. 05/11/1970
(See American Multimedia, Inc.)

SKLAR CORP. (PA)
Each (50,000) shares old Common 10¢ par exchanged for (1) share new Common 10¢ par 1/30/2001
Note: In effect holders received $0.46 cash per share and public interest was eliminated

SKLAR MFG LTD (ON)
Merged into PCL Industries Ltd. 10/01/1982
Each share Common no par exchanged for (1) share Class A Preference Ser. 2 no par, (1.25) shares Common no par and $1.70 cash
(See PCL Industries Ltd.)

SKLAR'S INC. (MN)
Foreclosed and out of business in March, 1978
No stockholders' equity

SKN RES LTD (BC)
Name changed to Silvercorp Metals Inc. 05/02/2005

SKOGAN FOODS INC (NV)
Name changed to Sino Express Travel, Ltd. 11/01/2005
(See Sino Express Travel, Ltd.)

SKOKIE FED SVGS & LN ASSN ILL (USA)
Placed in receivership 02/06/1990
No stockholders' equity

SKOOBINS RES INC (AB)
Reincorporated under the laws of Ontario as Medipattern Corp. 05/06/2005
(See Medipattern Corp.)

SKOOKUM MNG LTD (AB)
Issue Information - 2,000,000 shares COM offered at $0.15 per share on 09/30/1997
Merged into Matrix Petroleum Inc. 07/15/2003
Each share Common no par exchanged for (0.180574) share Common no par
Matrix Petroleum Inc. acquired by Berens Energy Ltd. 12/12/2003
(See Berens Energy Ltd.)

SKOOKUM URANIUM INC. (WA)
Involuntarily dissolved by law for non-payment of corporate fees 7/1/64

SKOPE ENERGY INC (AB)
Reorganized under Companies Creditors Arrangement Act 02/19/2013
No stockholders' equity

SKOR FOOD GROUP INC (ON)
Each share old Common no par exchanged for (1) share new Common no par to reflect a (1) for (100) reverse split followed by a (100) for (1) forward split 03/05/2010
Note: Holders of (99) or fewer pre-split shares received $0.36 cash per share
Acquired by Colabor Group Inc. 06/23/2011
Each share new Common no par exchanged for $1.33 cash

SKOURAS BROTHERS ENTERPRISES, INC.
Bankrupt in 1936

SKRCO INC (FL)
Name changed to Diversity Group International, Inc. 06/18/2007
Diversity Group International, Inc. recapitalized as Automotive Resource Network Holdings, Inc. 01/06/2012

SKREEM COM CORP (NV)
Name changed to Waterford Sterling Corp. 12/12/2000
Waterford Sterling Corp. recapitalized as Eternal Technologies Group, Inc. 12/13/2002
(See Eternal Technologies Group, Inc.)

SKREEM ENTMT CORP (DE)
Each share Common $0.001 par received distribution of (1) share Skreem Entertainment Corp. (NV) Common $0.001 par payable 02/02/2007 to holders of record 01/29/2007
Name changed to SKRM Interactive, Inc. 02/05/2007
SKRM Interactive, Inc. name changed to Sector 10, Inc. 04/14/2008

SKREEM ENTMT CORP (NV)
Recapitalized as Diversified Global Holdings, Inc. (NV) 09/24/2008
Each share Common $0.001 par exchanged for (0.1) share Common $0.001 par
Diversified Global Holdings, Inc. (NV) reincorporated in Delaware as Winwheel Bullion Inc. 11/25/2008 which name changed to Verdant Automotive Corp. 06/09/2011 which name changed to VRDT Corp. 02/09/2012
(See VRDT Corp.)

SKRM INTERACTIVE INC (DE)
Name changed to Sector 10, Inc. 04/14/2008

SKTF ENTERPRISES INC (FL)
Name changed to Speedemissions Inc. 8/27/2003

SKUKUM GOLD INC (BC)
Struck off register and declared dissolved for failure to file returns 4/29/94

SKUKUM VENTURES INC (BC)
Name changed to Skukum Gold Inc. 3/30/88
(See Skukum Gold Inc.)

SKULLCANDY INC (DE)
Acquired by MRSK Hold Co. 10/03/2016
Each share Common $0.0001 par exchanged for $6.35 cash

SKUNK WK TECHNOLOGIES INC (NV)
Name changed to Genoray Advanced Technologies Ltd. 02/29/2004
Genoray Advanced Technologies Ltd. recapitalized as Fennel Resources, Inc. 11/07/2005 which recapitalized as 3P Networks, Inc. 09/20/2006 which recapitalized as Kender Energy Inc. 10/07/2008 which recapitalized as Bettwork Industries Inc. 07/02/2014

SKY CITY ENTMT GROUP LTD OLD (NEW ZEALAND)
Each Unsponsored ADR for Ordinary exchanged for (1) SKYCITY Entertainment Group Ltd. (New) Sponsored ADR for Ordinary 09/04/2015

SKY CITY STORES INC (KY)
Merged into Interco Inc. (Old) 2/1/77
Each share Common $1 par exchanged for (0.3115) share Common no par
(See Interco Inc. (Old))

SKY DEUTSCHLAND AG (GERMANY)
ADR agreement terminated 10/22/2015
Each ADR for Ordinary issued by Bank of New York exchanged for $7.384258 cash
Note: Citibank issued ADR's received $7.401118 cash
Deutsche Bank issued ADR's received $7.411879 cash

SKY DIGITAL STORES CORP (NV)
Recapitalized as Qualis Innovations, Inc. 02/14/2018
Each share Common $0.001 par exchanged for (0.001) share Common $0.001 par

SKY FGHT INC (FL)
Name changed to Caldera Corp. 09/09/1994
Caldera Corp. name changed to Level Jump Financial Group, Inc. 12/28/1999
(See Level Jump Financial Group, Inc.)

SKY FINL GROUP INC (OH)
Stock Dividends - 10% payable 12/10/1998 to holders of record 11/30/1998; 10% payable 11/01/1999 to holders of record 10/15/1999; 10% payable 11/10/2000 to holders of record 10/30/2000 Ex date - 10/26/2000
Merged into Huntington Bancshares Inc. 07/02/2007
Each share Common no par exchanged for (1.098) shares Common no par and $3.023 cash

SKY GAMES INTL LTD (BERMUDA)
Name changed to Interactive Entertainment Ltd. 05/13/1997
Interactive Entertainment Ltd. name changed to Creator Capital Ltd. 10/16/2000

SKY HARVEST WINDPOWER CORP (NV)
Name changed to Sky Harvest Energy Corp. 08/13/2013

SKY-HY, INC. (ME)
Charter suspended for failure to file annual reports 10/4/78

SKY-MOBI LTD (CAYMAN ISLANDS)
Acquired by Amber Shining Investment Ltd. 11/16/2016
Each Sponsored ADS for Ordinary exchanged for $2.15 cash

SKY NETWORK TELEVISION LTD (NEW ZEALAND)
ADR agreement terminated 06/28/2005
Each Sponsored ADR for Ordinary exchanged for $49.50378 cash

SKY PWR SOLUTIONS CORP (NV)
Recapitalized as Clean Enviro Tech Corp. 01/18/2013
Each share Common $0.001 par exchanged for (0.02) share Common $0.001 par
Clean Enviro Tech Corp. recapitalized as Cyber Apps World Inc. 04/30/2015

SKY RIDGE RES LTD (BC)
Each share old Common no par exchanged for (0.33333333) share new Common no par 11/14/2011
Each share new Common no par exchanged again for (0.33333333) share new Common no par 02/03/2014
Recapitalized as Japan Gold Corp. 09/19/2016
Each share new Common no par exchanged for (0.5) share Common no par

SKY SCIENTIFIC INC (CA)
Each share old Common no par exchanged for (0.1) share new Common no par 04/24/1995
Charter suspended for failure to file reports and pay fees 10/15/1997

SKY SPECIALTIES CORP.
Acquired by Mueller Brass Co. in 1933
Details not available

SKYBERRY CAP CORP (AB)
Reorganized under the laws of British Columbia as Lipari Energy, Inc. 03/14/2011
Each share Common no par exchanged for (0.03448276) share Common no par
(See Lipari Energy, Inc.)

SKYBOX INTL INC (DE)
Merged into Marvel Entertainment Group, Inc. 5/1/95
Each share Common $1 par exchanged for $16 cash

SKYBRIDGE DEV CORP (ON)
Reincorporated 10/28/2008
Place of incorporation changed from (BC) to (ON) 10/28/2008
Merged into Mega Silver Inc. (BC) 05/27/2009
Each share Common no par exchanged for (0.4) share Common no par
Mega Silver Inc. (BC) reincorporated in Ontario as Mega Precious Metals Inc. 09/14/2009 which merged into Yamana Gold Inc. 06/24/2015

SKYBRIDGE INTL INC (BC)
Name changed to International Potential Explorations Inc. 04/30/1987
International Potential Explorations Inc. name changed to Banyan Industries International Inc. 04/12/1991 which name changed to Incentive Design Group Ltd. 11/19/1991 which recapitalized as Envoy Communications Group Inc. 01/22/1996 which name changed to Envoy Capital Group Inc. 04/05/2007 which merged into Merus Labs International Inc. (New) 12/22/2011
(See Merus Labs International Inc. (New))

SKYBRIDGE WIRELESS INC (NV)
Each share old Common $0.001 par exchanged for (10) shares new Common $0.001 par 9/25/2003
Recapitalized as SkyBridge Technology Group, Inc. 3/21/2006
Each share new Common $0.001 par exchanged for (0.005) share Common $0.001 par

SKYCREEK MINERALS INC (BC)
Recapitalized as Spectra Group of Great Restaurants Inc. 12/16/1993
Each share Common no par exchanged for (0.01) share Common no par
Spectra Group of Great Restaurants Inc. merged into Madison Pacific Properties Inc. 06/28/2007

SKYDOOR MEDIA & ENTMT INC (DE)
Name changed to Ice Holdings, Inc. (DE) 10/09/1996
Ice Holdings, Inc. (DE) reorganized in Nevada as Gaia Resources, Inc. 10/20/2006 which recapitalized as Ram Gold & Exploration, Inc. 02/08/2008 which name changed to DPollution International Inc. 08/31/2010 which recapitalized as Ecrid, Inc. 10/16/2017

SKYE INTL INC (NV)
Each share old Common $0.001 par exchanged for (0.25) share new Common $0.001 par 05/21/2008
Filed a petition under Chapter 7 Federal Bankruptcy Code 04/28/2011
Stockholders' equity unlikely

SKYE PHARMATECH INC (ON)
Name changed to SYN-X Pharma Inc. 4/4/2000
SYN-X Pharma Inc. was acquired by Nanogen, Inc. 4/21/2004

SKYE RES INC (BC)
Acquired by HudBay Minerals Inc. 08/26/2008
Each share Common no par exchanged for (0.61) share Common no par and $0.001 cash

SKYE RES LTD (CANADA)
Merged into Campbell Resources Inc. (Old) 01/25/1982
Each share Capital Stock no par exchanged for (1.125) shares Common $1 par
Campbell Resources Inc. (Old) merged into Campbell Resources Inc. (New) 06/08/1983
(See Campbell Resources Inc. (New))

SKYEPHARMA PLC (ENGLAND & WALES)
Each old Sponsored ADR for Ordinary exchanged for (0.1) new Sponsored ADR for Ordinary 10/02/2008
Basis changed from (1:10) to (1:1) 10/02/2008
ADR agreement terminated 06/27/2016
Each new Sponsored ADR for Ordinary exchanged for $6.243414 cash

SKYFLYER INC (NV)
Name changed to Blackstone Lake Minerals Inc. 01/23/2008
Blackstone Lake Minerals Inc. name changed to Caleco Pharma Corp. 08/31/2009
(See Caleco Pharma Corp.)

SKYFRAMES COMMUNICATIONS INC (PA)
Name changed to Princeton Holdings, Inc. 06/13/2007
Princeton Holdings, Inc. name changed to Axiom Management, Inc. 07/24/2007
(See Axiom Management, Inc.)

SKYFRAMES INC (UT)
Each share Common 10¢ par exchanged for (0.01) share Common $0.001 par 03/31/2006
SEC revoked common stock registration 10/24/2008

SKYGAME INC (ON)
Reincorporated 04/20/1994
Place of incorporation changed from (Canada) to (ON) 04/20/1994
Recapitalized as Alpha Group Industries Inc. 05/16/1997
Each share Common no par exchanged for (0.25) share Common no par

SKYGIVERS INC (NV)
SEC revoked common stock registration 05/18/2006

SKYGOLD RES LTD (BC)
Name changed to Canadian Water Corp. 01/13/1992
Canadian Water Corp. recapitalized as Aumine Resources Ltd. 11/07/1996 which name changed to PetroReal Oil Corp. 08/06/1998 which recapitalized as International PetroReal Oil Corp. (BC) 09/13/2002 which reorganized in Alberta 06/28/2007 which name changed to PetroReal Energy Inc. 09/15/2008

SKYGOLD VENTURES LTD (BC)
Reincorporated 08/13/2004
Issue Information - 2,000,000 shares COM offered at $0.10 per share on 02/11/1997
State of incorporation changed from (AB) to (BC) 08/13/2004
Name changed to Spanish Mountain Gold Ltd. 01/14/2010

SKYHARBOUR DEVS LTD (BC)
Name changed to Skyharbour Resources Ltd. 10/25/2002

SKYHAWK RES INC (BC)
Struck off register and declared dissolved for failure to file returns 12/3/93

SKYHIGH RES LTD (BC)
Common no par split (4) for (1) by issuance of (3) additional shares 07/17/1986
Name changed to MIU Industries Ltd. 08/17/1989

MIU Industries Ltd. recapitalized as Secured Communication Canada 95 Inc. 05/01/1995
(See Secured Communication Canada 95 Inc.)

SKYJACK INC (ON)
Acquired by Linamar Corp. 10/1/2002
Each share Common no par exchanged for $2.13 cash

SKYLAND LIFE INSURANCE CO. (NC)
Stock Dividends - 100% 4/15/57; 25% 4/10/59
Merged into Guaranty Savings Life Insurance Co. in 1960
(See Guaranty Savings Life Insurance Co.)

SKYLANDS CMNTY BK (HACKETTSTOWN, NJ)
Stock Dividends - 5% payable 2/25/98 to holders of record 2/4/98; 5% payable 4/16/99 holders of record 3/31/99
Under plan of reorganization name changed to Skylands Financial Corp. 9/17/99
Skylands Financial Corp. merged into Fulton Financial Corp. 8/1/2000

SKYLANDS FINL CORP (NJ)
Merged into Fulton Financial Corp. 8/1/2000
Each share Common $2.50 par exchanged for (0.819) share Common $2.50 par

SKYLANDS PK MGMT INC (NJ)
Common no par split (3) for (1) by issuance of (2) additional shares 01/24/1994
Each share old Common no par exchanged for (0.1) share new Common no par 11/07/1996
Name changed to Millennium Sports Management, Inc. 09/18/1997
(See Millennium Sports Management, Inc.)

SKYLARK RES LTD (BC)
Recapitalized as GMD Resource Corp. 07/27/1992
Each share Common no par exchanged for (0.142857) share Common no par
GMD Resource Corp. recapitalized as Chatworth Resources Inc. 10/14/2004 which merged into ComWest Enterprise Corp. 12/12/2005 which name changed to Unisync Corp. 08/01/2014

SKYLINE CHILI INC (OH)
Merged into Skyline Acquisition Corp. 4/28/98
Each share Common no par exchanged for $6.75 cash

SKYLINE CORP. (DE)
Merged into Pryor Manufacturing Co. 09/30/1954
Details not available

SKYLINE CORP (IN)
Common 25¢ par changed to $0.08333333 par and (2) additional shares issued 09/12/1968
Common $0.08333333 par changed to $0.0277 par and (2) additional shares issued 10/08/1969
Name changed to Skyline Champion Corp. 06/04/2018

SKYLINE ENTMT INC (NV)
Name changed to Quotemedia.com, Inc. 08/19/1999
Quotemedia.com, Inc. name changed to QuoteMedia, Inc. 03/11/2003

SKYLINE EXPLS LTD (BC)
Name changed to Skyline Gold Corp. 03/06/1989
Skyline Gold Corp. reorganized as Skycreek Minerals Inc. 07/14/1993 which recapitalized as Spectra Group of Great Restaurants Inc. 12/16/1993 which merged into

Madison Pacific Properties Inc. 06/28/2007

SKYLINE GOLD CORP (BC)
Recapitalized as SnipGold Corp. 05/24/2012
Each share Common no par exchanged for (0.1) share Common no par
SnipGold Corp. merged into Seabridge Gold Inc. 06/21/2016

SKYLINE GOLD CORP (BC)
Reorganized as Skycreek Minerals Inc. 07/14/1993
Each share Common no par exchanged for (1) share Common no par
Note: Holders also received (1) share International Skyline Gold Corp. Common no par for each share surrendered
Skycreek Minerals Inc. recapitalized as Spectra Group of Great Restaurants Inc. 12/16/1993 which merged into Madison Pacific Properties Inc. 06/28/2007

SKYLINE HOMES, INC. (IN)
Class A Common $1 par and Class B Common $1 par changed to 50¢ par respectively and (1) additional share issued 09/10/1962
Class A Common 50¢ par and Class B Common 50¢ par reclassified as Common 50¢ par 03/12/1964
Common 50¢ par changed to 25¢ par and (1) additional share issued 09/24/1964
Name changed to Skyline Corp. 08/22/1966
Skyline Corp. name changed to Skyline Champion Corp. 06/04/2018

SKYLINE HOTELS LTD (ON)
Common no par split (2) for (1) by issuance of (1) additional share 10/5/72
Merged into York-Hannover Ltd. 5/16/80
Each share Common no par exchanged for $5.50 cash

SKYLINE MED INC (DE)
Reincorporated 12/18/2013
State of incorporation changed from (MN) to (DE) 12/18/2013
Each share old Common 1¢ par exchanged for (0.01333333) share new Common no par 10/28/2014
Each share new Common 1¢ par exchanged again for (0.04) share new Common 1¢ par 10/28/2016
Name changed to Precision Therapeutics Inc. 02/02/2018

SKYLINE NAT RES LTD (AB)
Recapitalized as Stellarton Energy Corp. 09/06/1996
Each (12.4) shares Common no par exchanged for (1) share Class A Common no par
(See Stellarton Energy Corp.)

SKYLINE OIL CO (NV)
Merged into Texas Eastern Corp. 4/29/77
Each share Capital Stock $1 par exchanged for (0.3817244) share Common $3.50 par
Texas Eastern Corp. merged into Panhandle Eastern Corp. 6/28/89 which name changed to Panenergy Corp. 4/26/96 which merged into Duke Energy Corp. (NC) 6/18/97 which merged into Duke Energy Corp. (DE) 4/3/2006

SKYLINE OILS LTD.
Merged into Consolidated Mic Mac Oils Ltd. 00/00/1953
Each share Common exchanged for (0.1666666) share new Common no par
Consolidated Mic Mac Oils Ltd. merged into Mic Mac Oils (1963) Ltd. 02/17/1964
(See Mic Mac Oils (1963) Ltd.)

SKYLINE URANIUM & MINERALS CORP. LTD. (ON)
Charter cancelled in November, 1961

SKYLINK AMER INC (TX)
Reincorporated 09/28/1989
State of incorporation changed from (AL) to (TX) 09/28/1989
Name changed to Crown Casino Corp. 11/09/1993
Crown Casino Corp. name changed to Crown Group, Inc. 10/02/1997 which name changed to America's Car-Mart, Inc. 03/28/2002

SKYLINK COMMUNICATIONS CORP (OR)
Involuntarily dissolved for failure to file reports and pay fees 05/18/2001

SKYLINK COMMUNICATIONS INC (AB)
Struck off register for failure to file annual returns 09/01/1996

SKYLINK TELECOMMUNICATIONS CORP (NV)
Reorganized under the laws of Oregon as Skylink Communications Corp. 6/15/98
Each share Common 1¢ par exchanged for (1) share Common 1¢ par
(See Skylink Communications Corp.)

SKYLON ALL ASSET TR (ON)
Trust terminated 12/31/2014
Each Unit received $18.5927 cash

SKYLON CAP YIELD TR (ON)
Merged into High Yield & Mortgage Plus Trust 05/01/2007
Each Unit Ser. 2007 no par received (0.699308) Unit no par and $7.146 cash
(See High Yield & Mortgage Plus Trust)

SKYLON GLOBAL CAP YIELD TR (ON)
Trust terminated 08/03/2012
Each Series 2012 Unit received $25.0492 cash

SKYLON GLOBAL CAP YIELD TR II (ON)
Trust terminated 08/03/2012
Each Series 2012 Unit received $20.3555 cash

SKYLON INTL ADVANTAGE YIELD TR (ON)
Trust terminated 12/31/2013
Each Ser. A Unit received $23.5746 cash
Each Ser. B Unit received USD $9.8165 cash

SKYLYNX COMMUNICATIONS INC (CO)
Reincorporated under the laws of Delaware as Inforum Communications, Inc. 04/19/2000
(See Inforum Communications, Inc.)

SKYLYNX COMMUNICATIONS INC (DE)
Recapitalized as PawsPlus, Inc. 01/29/2009
Each (15) shares Common $0.0001 par exchanged for (1) share Common $0.0001 par
(See PawsPlus, Inc.)

SKYMALL INC (NV)
Merged into Gemstar-TV Guide International, Inc. 07/18/2001
Each share Common $0.001 par exchanged for (0.03759) share Common 1¢ par and $1.50 cash
Gemstar-TV Guide International, Inc. merged into Macrovision Solutions Corp. 05/05/2008 which name changed to Rovi Corp. 07/16/2009 which name changed to TiVo Corp. 09/08/2016

SKYMARK AIRLS INC (CA)
Completely liquidated 11/14/69
Each share Common $1 par exchanged for first and final

SKYMARK HLDGS INC (DE)
distribution of (0.25) share Golden West Airlines, Inc. Common $1 par Golden West Airlines, Inc. name changed to Old GWAL, Inc. 6/12/77
(See Old GWAL, Inc.)

SKYMARK HLDGS INC (DE)
Chapter 11 bankruptcy proceedings converted to Chapter 7 on 05/17/2010
No stockholders' equity

SKYMORE RES INC (AB)
Reorganized under the laws of Ontario as Seven Clans Resources Ltd. 11/20/2001
Each share Common no par exchanged for (0.33333333) share Common no par
Seven Clans Resources Ltd. recapitalized as Mexgold Resources Inc. 09/15/2003 which was acquired by Gammon Lake Resources Inc. 08/08/2006 which name changed to Gammon Gold Inc. (QC) 06/19/2007 which reincorporated in Ontario as AuRico Gold Inc. 06/14/2011 which merged into Alamos Gold Inc. (New) 07/06/2015

SKYNET HLDGS INC (DE)
Chapter 11 bankruptcy proceedings terminated 08/20/2003
Stockholders' equity unlikely

SKYNET TELEMATICS INC (NV)
Recapitalized as Brisam Corp. 08/10/2007
Each share Common $0.001 par exchanged for (0.01) share Common $0.001 par
Note: No holder will receive fewer than (10) post-split shares

SKYPEOPLE FRUIT JUICE INC (FL)
Each share old Common $0.001 par exchanged for (0.66666666) share new Common $0.001 par 10/29/2009
Each share new Common $0.001 par exchanged again for (0.125) share new Common $0.001 par 03/16/2016
Name changed to Future FinTech Group Inc. 06/12/2017

SKYPOSTAL NETWORKS INC (NV)
Name changed to SkyShop Logistics, Inc. 08/16/2010

SKYROCKET EXPL & RES INC (BC)
Reorganized under the laws of Nevada as Titans Titanium Corp. 6/30/2000
Each share Common no par exchanged for (1) share Common and (1) Common Stock Purchase Warrant expiring 1/31/2005
Note: Failure to surrender certificates prior to 5/16/2000 may result in holders retaining an interest in (BC) company which will be dissolved

SKYSAT COMMUNICATIONS NETWORK CORP (DE)
Charter cancelled and declared inoperative and void for non-payment of taxes 03/01/2006

SKYTALK COMMUNICATIONS INC (NV)
Name changed to SMO Multimedia Corp. 02/15/2002
SMO Multimedia Corp. name changed to Strategic Management & Opportunity Corp. (Old) 09/02/2004 which reorganized as Strategic Management & Opportunity Corp. (New) 09/25/2018

SKYTEL COMMUNICATIONS INC (DE)
Merged into MCI Worldcom, Inc. 10/1/99
Each share $2.25 Conv. Exchangeable Preferred 1¢ par exchanged for (1) share $2.25 Conv. Exchangeable Preferred 1¢ par
Each share Common 1¢ par exchanged for (0.2566) share Common 1¢ par
MCI Worldcom, Inc. name changed to WorldCom Inc. (New) 5/1/2000
(See WorldCom Inc. (New))

SKYTERRA COMMUNICATIONS INC (DE)
Each share Common 1¢ par received distribution of (0.5) share Hughes Communications, Inc. Common $0.001 par payable 02/21/2006 to holders of record 02/13/2006
Ex date - 02/13/2006
Merged into Sol Private Corp. 03/29/2010
Each share Common 1¢ par exchanged for $5 cash

SKYTEX INTL INC (NV)
Name changed to Majestic Companies, Ltd. 12/11/1998
(See Majestic Companies, Ltd.)

SKYTRADER CORP (UT)
Chapter 11 bankruptcy proceedings converted to Chapter 7 on 8/23/89
Stockholders' equity unlikely

SKYWAY COMMUNICATIONS HLDG CORP (FL)
Plan of reorganization under Chapter 11 Federal Bankruptcy Code effective 06/04/2007
No stockholders' equity

SKYWAY DRIVE-IN THEATRES, LTD. (ON)
Completely liquidated 10/16/63
Each share Capital Stock no par exchanged for first and final distribution of $2.50 cash

SKYWAY ENGINEERING CO., INC. (IN)
Name changed to United Technical Industries Corp. 11/18/1966
(See United Technical Industries Corp.)

SKYWAY RES LTD (BC)
Recapitalized as Burrard Ventures Inc. 7/24/89
Each share Common no par exchanged for (0.5) share Common no par
(See Burrard Ventures Inc.)

SKYWELL CORP (DE)
Charter cancelled and declared inoperative and void for non-payment of taxes 3/1/90

SKYWEST ENERGY CORP (AB)
Recapitalized as Marquee Energy Ltd. (Old) 12/09/2011
Each share Common no par exchanged for (0.125) share Common no par
Marquee Energy Ltd. (Old) merged into Marquee Energy Ltd. (New) 12/08/2016

SKYWEST RES CORP (AB)
Merged into Summit Resources Ltd. 6/30/87
Each (1.75) shares Common no par exchanged for (1) share Common no par
(See Summit Resources Ltd.)

SKYWORLD RES & DEV LTD (BC)
Recapitalized as Whitewater Resources Ltd. 03/20/1990
Each share Common no par exchanged for (0.3030303) share Common no par

SL GREEN RLTY CORP (MD)
Each Preferred Income Equity Share exchanged for (1.0215) shares Common 1¢ par 10/1/2003
7.875% Preferred Ser. D 1¢ par called for redemption at $25 plus $0.4922 accrued dividends on 07/13/2012
7.625% Preferred Ser. C 1¢ par called for redemption at $25 plus $0.0349479 accrued dividends on 06/21/2013
(Additional Information in Active)

SL INDS INC (DE)
Reincorporated 06/20/2013
Common 20¢ par split (4) for (3) by issuance of (0.33333333) additional share 02/05/1986
Preferred Stock Purchase Rights declared for Common stockholders of record 12/13/1987 were redeemed at $0.00792 per right 11/29/1994 for holders of record 11/14/1994
State of incorporation changed from (NJ) to (DE) 06/20/2013
Acquired by Handy & Harman Ltd. 06/01/2016
Each share Common 20¢ par exchanged for $40 cash

SL SPLIT CORP (ON)
Issue Information - 1,055,000 PFD SHS offered at $25.78 per share on 10/31/2007
Issue Information - 2,110,000 CAP SHS offered at $15.26 per share on 10/31/2007
Class A Preferred Shares called for redemption at $25.78 on 01/31/2013
Class A Capital Shares called for redemption at $1.55 on 01/31/2013

SLABSDIRECT COM INC (DE)
Name changed to CTT International Distributors Inc. 1/5/2005
CTT International Distributors Inc. name changed to SK3 Group, Inc. 5/23/2007

SLADE ENERGY INC (AB)
Name changed to Westpoint Energy Inc. 4/10/2000
(See Westpoint Energy Inc.)

SLADEN MALARCTIC MINES LTD. (ON)
Completely liquidated 00/00/1952
Each (100) shares Common received (50) Barnat Mines Ltd. 5% Debentures, (50) shares Capital Stock $1 par and (10) shares Sladen (Quebec) Ltd. Common
(See each company's listing)

SLADEN-MALARTIC MINES LTD.
Reorganized as Sladen (Quebec) Ltd. and each (100) shares Capital Stock $1 par exchanged for (10) shares new Capital Stock $1 par and $50 of Debenture Notes of Barnat Mines Ltd. in 1952
Sladen (Quebec) Ltd. charter cancelled 11/2/74

SLADEN QUE LTD. (QC)
Charter cancelled for failure to file reports and pay fees 11/02/1974

SLADES FERRY BANCORP (MA)
Stock Dividends - 5% payable 02/11/1998 to holders of record 01/30/1998; 5% payable 02/09/2000 to holders of record 01/21/2000
Merged into Independent Bank Corp. 03/01/2008
Each share Common 1¢ par exchanged for (0.818) share Common 1¢ par

SLANT FIN CORP (NY)
Shares reacquired 07/14/1993
Each share Common $0.025 par exchanged for $52 cash

SLAP INC (NV)
Common $0.001 par split (9) for (1) by issuance of (8) additional shares payable 11/09/2009 to holders of record 11/02/2009 Ex date - 11/10/2009
Name changed to Estate Coffee Holdings Corp. 02/09/2010
Estate Coffee Holdings Corp. name changed to Fresh Traffic Group Inc. 11/04/2010 which recapitalized as Synergetics, Inc. 08/31/2012

SLATE CREEK MINING CO. (WA)
Name changed to Western Gold Mining Inc. 04/18/1952
Western Gold Mining Inc. recapitalized as Lundell Technologies, Inc. 07/26/1996 which name changed to Worldtek Corp. 12/17/2003
(See Worldtek Corp.)

SLATECO INTL GROUP INC (NV)
Each share old Common 1¢ par exchanged for (0.0005) share new Common 1¢ par 05/19/2003
Reincorporated under the laws of Wyoming as Terrablock Development, Inc. 02/21/2006
Terrablock Development, Inc. name changed to Linked Media Group, Inc. 12/30/2008
(See Linked Media Group, Inc.)

SLATER-CARTER-STEVENS CO.
Merged into Stevens (J.P.) & Co., Inc. in 1946
Each share Preferred exchanged for (6.18132) shares Capital Stock $15 par
Each share Common exchanged for (0.63555) share Capital Stock $15 par
(See Stevens (J.P.) & Co., Inc.)

SLATER (N.) CO., LTD. (CANADA)
Each share Common $20 par exchanged for (3) shares Common no par in 1954
Acquired by Slater Steel Industries Ltd. 3/3/61
Each share Common no par exchanged for (2) shares Common no par and $12.50 cash
Preferred $50 par called for redemption 3/19/63
Slater Steel Industries Ltd. name changed to Slater Steel Corp. 7/27/84 which name changed to Slater Industries Inc. 10/2/86 which name changed to Slater Steel Inc. 6/25/96
(See Slater Steel Inc.)

SLATER DEV CORP (NY)
Name changed 1/20/88
Class A Common 20¢ par reclassified as Common 20¢ par 4/4/72
Name changed from Slater Electric Inc. to Slater Development Corp. 1/20/88
Completely liquidated 10/16/2006
Each share Common 20¢ par exchanged for first and final distribution of $3.70107 cash

SLATER INDS INC (ON)
Each share Class A no par exchanged for (1.1) shares Common no par 3/10/95
Each share Non-Vtg. Class B no par exchanged for (1) share Common no par 3/10/95
Name changed to Slater Steel, Inc. 6/25/96
(See Slater Steel Inc.)

SLATER INDUSTRIES LTD. (ON)
Merged into Slater Steel Industries Ltd. 2/22/62
Each share 6-1/2% Preferred Ser. A $20 par exchanged for (1) share 6-1/4% Preferred Ser. A $20 par
Each share Common no par exchanged for (2) shares Common no par
Slater Steel Industries Ltd. name changed to Slater Steel Corp. 7/27/84 which name changed to Slater Industries Inc. 10/2/86 which name changed to Slater Steel Inc. 6/25/96
(See Slater Steel Inc.)

SLATER MNG CORP (BC)
Recapitalized as Libero Mining Corp. 02/05/2016
Each share Common no par exchanged for (0.5) share Common no par
Libero Mining Corp. name changed to Libero Copper Corp. 11/01/2017

SLATER STEEL INDUSTRIES LTD. (ON)
6-1/4% Preferred Ser. A $20 par called for redemption 2/1/65
Common no par split (2) for (1) by issuance of (1) additional share 2/8/65
Common no par reclassified as Class A no par 1/27/84
Each share Class A no par received distribution of (1) share Class B no par 2/1/84
Name changed to Slater Steel Corp. 7/27/84
Slater Steel Corp. name changed to Slater Industries Inc. 10/2/86 which name changed to Slater Steel Inc. 6/25/96
(See Slater Steel Inc.)

SLATER STL CORP (ON)
Name changed to Slater Industries Inc. and each share 5-1/2% Class A Preference $1.10 Ser. $20 par, 5-1/2% Class B Preference $1.10 2nd Ser. $20 par and 6% Preference $1.20 Ser. $20 par reclassified as (1) share 7% Preference 1st Ser. $20 par, 7% Preference 2nd Ser. $20 par and 7-1/2% Preference 1st Ser. $20 par respectively 10/02/1986
Note: Class A no par and Class B no par not affected except for the change of name
Slater Industries Inc. name changed to Slater Steel Inc. 06/25/1996
(See Slater Steel Inc.)

SLATER STL INC (ON)
7% Preferred 1st Ser. $20 par called for redemption 12/31/96
7% Preferred 2nd Ser. $20 par called for redemption 12/31/96
7.5% Preferred $20 par called for redemption 12/31/96
Placed in receivership 8/30/2004
No stockholders' equity

SLATER WALKER AMER LTD (DE)
Name changed to Cornwall Equities, Ltd. 10/17/1974
(See Cornwall Equities, Ltd.)

SLATER WALKER CDA LTD (CANADA)
Common no par split (3) for (1) by issuance of (2) additional shares 8/9/71
Under plan of merger each share Common no par received (1) additional share Common no par 7/14/72
Name changed to Talcorp Associates Ltd. 3/10/76
Talcorp Associates Ltd. name changed to Talcorp Ltd. 9/14/82 which reorganized as Consolidated Talcorp Ltd. 8/7/86 which name changed to Sound Insight Enterprises Ltd. 12/7/90 which merged into CamVec Corp. 9/11/92 which name changed to AMJ Campbell Inc. 8/14/2001
(See AMJ Campbell Inc.)

SLATER WALKER SECS LTD (ENGLAND)
Ordinary 5s par changed to 25p par per currency change 02/15/1971
Stock Dividend - 33-1/3% 06/25/1972
Reported out of business 00/00/1974
Details not available

SLATTERY GROUP INC (NJ)
Each share Common $10 par exchanged for (0.01) share Common $1,000 par 6/15/90
Acquired by SGI Acquisition Corp. 1/31/95
Each share Common $1,000 par exchanged for $4,674 cash

SLAUGHTER BROS INC (TX)
Merged into STK Enterprises, Inc. 06/07/1984
Each share Common 10¢ par exchanged for $10.50 cash

SLAVE POINT CONS MINES LTD (BC)
Name changed to Amparo Development Corp. 1/24/77
(See Amparo Development Corp.)

SLAVE POINT MINES LTD. (BC)
Recapitalized as Slave Point Consolidated Mines Ltd. 03/07/1972
Each share Capital Stock $1 par exchanged for (0.1) share Capital Stock no par
Slave Point Consolidated Mines name changed to Amparo Development Corp. 01/24/1977
(See Amparo Development Corp.)

SLAVIA CORP (NV)
Name changed to Mobetize Corp. 08/14/2013

SLAVNEFT-MEGIONNEFTEGAZ OPEN JT STK CO (RUSSIA)
Sponsored GDR's for Reg. S Preferred split (15) for (1) by issuance of (14) additional GDR's payable 09/30/2002 to holders of record 09/27/2002 Ex date - 09/25/2002
Sponsored GDR's for Reg. S Ordinary split (15) for (1) by issuance of (14) additional GDR's payable 09/30/2002 to holders of record 09/27/2002 Ex date - 09/25/2002
Basis changed from (1:30) to (1:2) 09/30/2002
GDR agreement terminated 04/19/2018
No GDR's remain outstanding

SLC, INC. (UT)
Liquidation completed
Each share Capital Stock $1 par received initial distribution of $2 cash 08/30/1967
Each share Capital Stock $1 par received second distribution of $1.20 cash 11/30/1967
Each share Capital Stock $1 par received third distribution of $0.65 cash 03/01/1968
Each share Capital Stock $1 par exchanged for fourth and final distribution of $0.1055 cash 02/17/1972

SLC CAP INC (CANADA)
Name changed to Conporec Inc. 06/23/2005
(See Conporec Inc.)

SLEAHCIM CORP. (NY)
Completely liquidated for cash in 1954

SLED DOGS CO (CO)
Plan of reorganization under Chapter 11 Federal Bankruptcy Code effective 09/10/1998
Each share old Common 1¢ par exchanged for (0.01851851) share new Common 1¢ par
Reincorporated under the laws of Nevada as Xdogs.com, Inc. 05/10/1999
Xdogs.com, Inc. recapitalized as Xdogs Inc. 08/22/2000 which name changed to Avalon Oil & Gas, Inc. 07/22/2005 which name changed to Groove Botanicals, Inc. 05/14/2018

SLEEMAN BREWERIES LTD (BC)
Acquired by Sapporo Breweries Ltd. 10/18/2006
Each share Common no par exchanged for $17.50 cash

SLEEP CTRY CDA INCOME FD (ON)
Acquired by 7019416 Canada Inc. 09/24/2008
Each Trust Unit no par received $22 cash

SLEEP HEALERS HLDGS INC (NV)
Name changed to Sleep Holdings, Inc. 10/09/2006
Sleep Holdings, Inc. name changed to ALL-Q-TELL Corp. 11/03/2010
(See ALL-Q-TELL Corp.)

SLEEP HLDGS INC (NV)
Name changed to ALL-Q-TELL Corp. 11/03/2010
(See ALL-Q-TELL Corp.)

SLEEPING GOLD LTD (BC)
Recapitalized as Achieva Development Corp. 09/14/1992
Each (3.5) shares Common no par exchanged for (1) share Common no par
Achieva Development Corp. recapitalized as Angus Ventures Corp. 07/09/2008 which name changed to Encanto Potash Corp. 07/15/2009

SLEEPING WITH THE ENEMY INC (CO)
Name changed to Healthy Coffee International, Inc. 12/13/2007

SLEEPSOURCE INTL LTD (NV)
Charter permanently revoked 1/1/2005

SLEMON YELLOWKNIFE MINES LTD. (ON)
Merged into Pardee Amalgamated Mines Ltd. in December 1954
Each share Capital Stock $1 par exchanged for (0.05) share Common $1 par
Pardee Amalgamated Mines Ltd. liquidated for Rio Algom Mines Ltd. 11/9/61 which name changed to Rio Algom Ltd. 4/30/75
(See Rio Algom Ltd.)

SLENT COMPUTER CORP (TX)
Charter cancelled for failure to maintain a resident agent 03/18/1971

SLH CALIF MUNS FD INC (MD)
Name changed to Shearson Lehman Brothers California Municipals Fund Inc. 8/10/90
Shearson Lehman Brothers California Municipals Fund Inc. name changed to Smith Barney Shearson California Municipals Fund Inc. 8/2/93 which name changed to Smith Barney California Municipals Fund 10/14/94

SLH CORP (KS)
Common $1 par split (3) for (1) by issuance of (2) additional shares payable 07/21/1997 to holders of record 07/14/1997
Common $1 par split (2) for (1) by issuance of (1) additional share payable 02/09/1998 to holders of record 02/02/1998
Name changed to Syntroleum Corp. (KS) 08/07/1998
Syntroleum Corp. (KS) reincorporated in Delaware 06/00/1999
(See Syntroleum Corp.)

SLH GLOBAL OPPORTUNITIES FD (MA)
Name changed to Shearson Lehman Brothers Global Opportunities Fund 08/10/1990
(See Shearson Lehman Brothers Global Opportunities Fund)

SLH HIGH YIELD FD INC (MD)
Voluntarily dissolved 02/01/1994
Details not available

SLH MANAGED MUNS FD INC (MD)
Name changed to Shearson Lehman Brothers Managed Municipals Fund Inc. 8/10/90
Shearson Lehman Brothers Managed Municipals Fund Inc. name changed to Smith Barney Shearson Managed Municipals Fund Inc. 8/2/93 which name changed to Smith Barney Managed Municipals Fund Inc. 10/14/94

SLH MICH MUNS FD (MA)
Trust terminated 03/30/1994
Details not available

SLH OHIO MUNS FUND (MA)
Trust terminated 03/30/1994
Details not available

SLH TELECOMMUNICATIONS TR (MA)
Name changed to Shearson Lehman Brothers Telecommunications Trust 03/06/1991
(See Shearson Lehman Brothers Telecommunications Trust)

SLI INC (OK)
Plan of reorganization under Chapter 11 Federal Bankruptcy Code effective 6/30/2003
No stockholders' equity

SLICK AIRWAYS, INC. (DE)
Capital Stock $10 par changed to no par 11/10/54
Capital Stock no par changed to $5 par 11/2/56
Capital Stock $5 par changed to no par 5/24/60
Name changed to Slick Corp. 5/1/62
Slick Corp. merged into United States Filter Corp. 8/3/72
(See United States Filter Corp.)

SLICK CORP (DE)
Merged into United States Filter Corp. 08/03/1972
Each share $1.75 Conv. Preferred Ser. A no par exchanged for (2.3) shares Common no par
Each share Common no par exchanged for (1) share Common no par
(See United States Filter Corp.)

SLICK ROCK URANIUM DEVELOPMENT CORP. (UT)
Name changed to International Technical Development Corp. 2/26/69
International Technical Development Corp. dissolved 11/9/74

SLIPPERY ROCK FINL CORP (PA)
Common $1 par changed to 25¢ par and (3) additional shares issued payable 06/28/1996 to holders of record 06/03/1996
Common 25¢ par split (2) for (1) by issuance of (1) additional share payable 12/30/1998 to holders of record 12/04/1998 Ex date - 12/31/1998
Stock Dividend - 10% payable 12/28/1995 to holders of record 11/15/1995 Ex date - 11/13/1995
Merged into F.N.B. Corp. (FL) 10/08/2004
Each share Common 25¢ par exchanged for either (1.3395) shares Common 1¢ par and $0.075 cash or $28 cash
Note: Option to receive stock and cash expired 09/23/2004

SLM CORP (DE)
Each share Mandatory Conv. Preferred Ser. C 20¢ par exchanged for (50.8906) shares Common 20¢ par 12/15/2010
6.97% Preferred Ser. A 20¢ par called for redemption at $50 plus $0.038722 accrued dividends on 05/05/2017
(Additional Information in Active)

SLM HLDGS INC (DE)
SEC revoked common stock registration 10/09/2013

SLM HLDG CORP (DE)
Common 20¢ par split (7) for (2) by issuance of (2.5) additional shares payable 01/02/1998 to holders of record 12/12/1997 Ex date - 01/05/1998
Name changed to USA Educational Inc. 07/31/2000
USA Educational Inc. name changed to SLM Corp. 05/17/2002

SLM INTL INC (DE)
Old Common 1¢ par split (3) for (2) by issuance of (0.5) additional share 12/03/1993
Plan of reorganization under Chapter

11 Federal Bankruptcy Code effective 04/11/1997
Each (67) shares old Common 1¢ par exchanged for (1) Common Stock Purchase Warrant expiring 04/02/2002
Name changed to Hockey Co. 02/03/2000
(See Hockey Co.)

SLM SOFTWARE INC (ON)
Reorganized as Slmsoft.Com Inc. 7/23/99
Each share Common no par exchanged for (0.5) share Limited Voting Stock no par and (0.5) share Variable Multiple Voting no par
Slmsoft.Com Inc. name changed to SLMsoft Inc. 6/14/2002

SLMSOFT INC (ON)
Name changed 6/14/2002
Name changed from SLMsoft.Com Inc. to SLMsoft Inc. 6/14/2002
Placed in receivership 10/31/2003
Stockholders' equity unlikely

SLN VENTURES CORP (BC)
Recapitalized as Pan Ocean Explorations Inc. 04/01/1997
Each share Common no par exchanged for (1/6) share Common no par
(See Pan Ocean Explorations Inc.)

SLOAN ELECTRONICS INC (DE)
Name changed to Salient Cybertech Inc. 06/03/1999
Salient Cybertech Inc. name changed to BrandAid Marketing Corp. 12/24/2001
(See BrandAid Marketing Corp.)

SLOAN TECHNOLOGY CORP (CA)
Common 10¢ par split (2) for (1) by issuance of (1) additional share 02/24/1986
Merged into Veeco Instruments, Inc. 06/25/1986
Each share Common 10¢ par exchanged for (0.395) share Common $1 par
(See Veeco Instruments, Inc.)

SLOANE (W & J) CORP. (DE)
See - W & J Sloane Corp.

SLOANE MINING CO. LTD. (ON)
Merged into Gerrard Realty Inc. 1/28/76
Each (17) shares Common no par exchanged for (1) share Common no par

SLOANE PETROLEUMS INC (BC)
Merged into Gentry Resources Ltd. 03/01/2001
Each share Common no par exchanged for (0.1) share Common no par and $0.72 cash
Gentry Resources Ltd. merged into Crew Energy Inc. 08/22/2008

SLOANS SUPERMARKETS INC (NY)
Stock Dividend - 10% 1/20/95
Name changed to Gristede's Sloan's, Inc. 10/30/97
Gristede's Sloan's, Inc. name changed to Gristede's Foods, Inc. 10/21/99
(See Gristede's Foods, Inc.)

SLOCAN DEV LTD (BC)
Recapitalized as International Slocan Development Ltd. 10/07/1992
Each share Common no par exchanged for (1/3) share Common no par
International Slocan Development Ltd. recapitalized as Slocan Holdings Ltd. 08/15/1995 which recapitalized as Galaxy Energy Corp. 10/26/1999 which recapitalized as Galaxy Sports Inc. 08/10/2001
(See Galaxy Sports Inc.)

SLOCAN FOREST PRODS LTD (BC)
Common no par split (2) for (1) by issuance of (1) additional share 5/11/90
Common no par split (2) for (1) by issuance of (1) additional share 5/24/94
Acquired by Canfor Corp. (Old) 4/1/2004
Each share Common no par exchanged for (1.3147) shares Common no par
(See Canfor Corp. (Old))

SLOCAN HLDGS LTD (BC)
Recapitalized as Galaxy Energy Corp. 10/26/1999
Each share Common no par exchanged for (0.5) share Common no par
Galaxy Energy Corp. recapitalized as Galaxy Sports Inc. 08/10/2001
(See Galaxy Sports Inc.)

SLOCAN IDAHO MINES CORP.
Bankrupt in 1941

SLOCAN KING MINES LTD.
Acquired by Silversmith Mines Ltd. on a (1) for (4) basis in 1937
(See Silversmith Mines Ltd.)

SLOCAN LODE MINES LTD. (BC)
Struck off register and declared dissolved for failure to file reports and pay fees 9/19/68

SLOCAN OTTAWA MINES LTD. (BC)
Name changed to Slocan Development Corp. Ltd. 04/19/1972
Each share Common no par exchanged for (1) share Common no par
Slocan Development Corp. Ltd. recapitalized as International Slocan Development Ltd. 10/07/1992 which recapitalized as Slocan Holdings Ltd. 08/15/1995 which recapitalized as Galaxy Energy Corp. 10/26/1999 which recapitalized as Galaxy Sports Inc. 08/10/2001
(See Galaxy Sports Inc.)

SLOCAN SOVEREIGN (1897) MINING CO. LTD.
Dissolved in 1948

SLOCAN UNITED MINES LTD. (BC)
Name changed to Ottawa Uranium Mines Ltd. 00/00/1955
Ottawa Uranium Mines Ltd. name changed to Ottawa Silver Mines Ltd. 05/00/1961 which recapitalized as Slocan Ottawa Mines Ltd. 05/06/1965 which name changed to Slocan Development Corp. Ltd. 04/19/1972 which recapitalized as International Slocan Development Ltd. 10/07/1992 which recapitalized as Slocan Holdings Ltd. 08/15/1995 which recapitalized as Galaxy Energy Corp. 10/26/1999 which recapitalized as Galaxy Sports Inc. 08/10/2001
(See Galaxy Sports Inc.)

SLOCAN VAN ROI MINES LTD. (BC)
Recapitalized as Kopan Developments Ltd. 5/19/60
Each share Capital Stock no par exchanged for (0.25) share Capital Stock no par
Kopan Developments Ltd. recapitalized as Jordesco Resources Ltd. 8/14/72
(See Jordesco Resources Ltd.)

SLOPE ENERGY INC (UT)
Recapitalized as Comnet, Inc. 3/21/85
Each share Common $0.01 par exchanged for (0.25) share Common $0.001 par
(See Comnet, Inc.)

SLOPE TRACTOR, INC. (KS)
Filed a petition under Section 4 Federal Bankruptcy Act 1/18/79
Details not available

SLOPESTYLE CORP (TX)
Reincorporated under the laws of Nevada as Remediation Services, Inc. 01/30/2008
Remediation Services, Inc. name changed to LianDi Clean Technology Inc. 04/21/2010

SLOSS-SHEFFIELD STEEL & IRON CO. (NJ)
Merged into United States Pipe & Foundry Co. on a share for share basis in 1952
United States Pipe & Foundry Co. merged into Walter (Jim) Corp. 8/30/69
(See Walter (Jim) Corp.)

SLOUD INC (NV)
Name changed to Leone Asset Management, Inc. 11/21/2013

SLOVAKIAN GRAM MINERALS CORP (CANADA)
Name changed to Gram Minerals Corp. 10/16/2000
(See Gram Minerals Corp.)

SLOVAKOFARMA A S (SLOVAKIA)
GDR agreement terminated 03/16/2004
Each 144A GDR for Ordinary exchanged for $3.0357 cash
Each Reg. S GDR for Ordinary exchanged $3.0357 cash

SLOVNAFT A.S. (SLOVAKIA)
GDR agreement terminated 08/17/2004
No GDR's remain outstanding

SLP ASSOCIATES, INC. (NC)
Liquidation completed
Each share Common no par exchanged for initial distribution of (0.328502) share American Home Products Corp.
Common $1 par and a receipt for future distributions 10/17/1967
Each receipt exchanged for second and final distribution of (0.01759) share American Home Products Corp. Common $1 par 12/15/1970
American Home Products Corp. name changed to Wyeth 03/11/2002 which was acquired by Pfizer Inc. 10/15/2009

SLS ASSOC INC (NY)
Reorganized under the laws of Delaware as Service Corp. of America 08/14/1972
Each share Common 1¢ par exchanged for (0.294118) share Common 1¢ par
(See Service Corp. of America)

SLS INDS INC (NV)
SEC revoked common stock registration 08/15/2011

SLS INTL INC (DE)
Chapter 11 bankruptcy proceedings converted to Chapter 7 on 12/11/2009
No stockholders' equity

SLUMACH LOST CREEK MINE, LTD. (BC)
Struck off register and declared dissolved for failure to file returns 2/9/56

SLUMBER LODGE DEV LTD (BC)
Name changed to Western Dominion Investment Ltd. 7/17/91
(See Western Dominion Investment Ltd.)

SLUMBER MAGIC ADJUSTABLE BED LTD (BC)
Name changed to Victory Ventures Inc. 5/7/96
Victory Ventures Inc. name changed to Global Investment.com Financial Inc. 7/28/99 which name changed to Global Investment Financial Group Inc. 4/4/2001 which recapitalized as Global Financial Group Inc. 3/4/2002 which name changed to egX Group Inc. 4/17/2007

SLUMBERLAND INC (MN)
Completely liquidated 06/01/1978
Each share Common 5¢ par exchanged for first and final distribution of $2.50 cash

SLW ENTERPRISES INC (WA)
Common $0.0001 par split (6.17) for (1) by issuance of (5.17) additional shares payable 03/06/2002 to holders of record 03/04/2002
Ex date - 03/07/2002
Name changed to HiEnergy Technologies, Inc. (WA) 04/30/2002
HiEnergy Technologies, Inc. (WA) reincorporated in Delaware 10/16/2002
(See HiEnergy Technologies, Inc.)

SLY INDUSTRIES, INC. (DE)
Charter revoked for non-payment of taxes 4/1/63

SLYCE INC (AB)
Recapitalized as Pounce Technologies Inc. 01/30/2017
Each share Common no par exchanged for (0.05) share Common no par

SM PRIME HLDGS INC (PHILIPPINES)
Stock Dividends - 25.2106% payable 08/20/2007 to holders of record 06/28/2007; 25% payable 06/25/2012 to holders of record 05/29/2012
GDR agreement terminated 08/30/2018
Each Reg. S GDR for Common exchanged for (50) shares Common
Each 144A GDR for Common exchanged for (50) shares Common

SM&A (DE)
Reincorporated 11/30/2006
State of incorporation changed from (CA) to (DE) and Common no par changed to $0.0001 par 11/30/2006
Acquired by Project Victor Holdings, Inc. 12/29/2008
Each share Common no par exchanged for $6.25 cash

SM&A CORP (CA)
Name changed to Emergent Information Technologies Inc. 05/04/2000
Emergent Information Technologies Inc. name changed to SM&A (CA) 01/29/2002 which reincorporated in Delaware 11/30/2006
(See SM&A (DE))

SM&R BALANCED FD INC (MD)
Merged into California Investment Trust 07/09/2010
Each share Class A 1¢ par automatically became (0.95149202) share Equity Income Fund Class A no par
Each share Class B 1¢ par automatically became (0.96851497) share Equity Income Fund Class B no par
Merged into California Investment Trust II 07/09/2010
Each share Class T 1¢ par automatically became (0.99640968) share Equity Income Fund Direct Class
(See California Investment Trust II)

SM&R CAP FDS INC (MD)
Name changed to SM&R Investments, Inc. 01/01/1999

SM&R EQUITY INCOME FD INC (MD)
Merged into California Investment Trust 07/09/2010
Each share Class A 1¢ par automatically became (1.01972168) shares Equity Income Fund Class A no par
Each share Class B 1¢ par automatically became (0.98578453) share Equity Income Fund Class B no par
Merged into California Investment Trust II 07/09/2010
Each share Class T 1¢ par automatically became (1.07234109)

shares Equity Income Fund Direct Class
(See California Investment Trust II)

SM&R GROWTH FD INC (MD)
Merged into California Investment Trust 07/09/2010
Each share Class A 1¢ par automatically became (0.22361164) share Equity Income Fund Class A no par
Each share Class B 1¢ par automatically became (0.21840724) share Equity Income Fund Class B no par
Merged into California Investment Trust II 07/09/2010
Each share Class T 1¢ par automatically became (0.22899341) share Equity Income Fund Direct Class
(See California Investment Trust II)

SM&R INVTS INC (MD)
Completely liquidated 02/26/2014
Each share SM&R Primary Fund Class A 1¢ par received net asset value
Each share SM&R Tax Free Fund Class A 1¢ par received net asset value
Each share SM&R Tax Free Fund Class B 1¢ par received net asset value
Each share SM&R Tax Free Fund Class T 1¢ par received net asset value
(Additional Information in Active)

SMACK SPORTSWEAR (NV)
Each share old Common $0.001 par exchanged for (0.33333333) share new Common $0.001 par 04/14/2015
Name changed to Almost Never Films Inc. 03/02/2016

SMALL BUSINESS DEV CORP (UT)
Name changed to American Professional Sports Products Inc. 11/22/1974
American Professional Sports Products Inc. reorganized as Dyna Graphics International, Inc. 03/27/1975
(See Dyna Graphics International, Inc.)

SMALL BUSINESS INVT CO NEW YORK INC (NY)
Name changed to Columbia Ventures, Inc. 6/27/73

SMALL CAP PREM & DIVID INCOME FD INC (MD)
Issue Information - 17,000,000 shares COM offered at $20 per share on 07/26/2005
Completely liquidated 05/24/2010
Each share Common $0.001 par exchanged for first and final distribution of $10.379375 cash

SMALL CAP STRATEGIES INC (NV)
Each share old Common $0.001 par exchanged for (0.05) share new Common $0.001 par 12/21/2006
Each share new Common $0.001 par exchanged again for (0.05) share new Common $0.001 par 06/04/2007
Recapitalized as Bay Street Capital, Inc. 08/31/2010
Each share new Common $0.001 par exchanged for (0.02) share Common $0.001 par
Bay Street Capital, Inc. name changed to Los Angeles Syndicate of Technology, Inc. 10/14/2010 which name changed to Invent Ventures, Inc. 09/19/2012

SMALL (P. A. & S.) CO. (PA)
Common $10 par changed to $5 par 3/6/69
Merged into Flickinger (S.M.) Co., Inc. 3/15/76
Each share Common $5 par exchanged for (1) share Conv. Preferred no par
(See Flickinger (S.M.) Co., Inc.)

SMALL FRY SNACK FOODS LTD (ON)
Name changed to Humpty Dumpty Snack Foods Inc. 10/23/2000
(See Humpty Dumpty Snack Foods Inc.)

SMALL TOWN RADIO INC (NV)
Recapitalized as Tombstone Western Resources, Inc. 5/12/2006
Each share Common no par exchanged for (0.01) share Common no par
Tombstone Western Resources, Inc. name changed to Dutch Gold Resources, Inc. 12/12/2006

SMALL TUBE PRODS INC (CT)
5% Preferred $20 par called for redemption 04/01/1969
Completely liquidated 11/14/1969
Each share Class A Common no par or Class B Common no par exchanged for first and final distribution of (1.892243) shares National Distillers & Chemical Corp. Common $2.50 par
National Distillers & Chemical Corp. name changed to Quantum Chemical Corp. 01/04/1988 which merged into Hanson PLC (Old) 10/01/1993 which reorganized as Hanson PLC (New) 10/15/2003
(See Hanson PLC (New))

SMALLCAP FD INC (MD)
Name changed to Investors First Fund, Inc. 10/16/2003
Investors First Fund, Inc. merged into Cornerstone Strategic Value Fund, Inc. 6/28/2004

SMALLS OILFIELD SVCS CORP (DE)
Name changed to Superior Energy Services, Inc. 12/20/1995

SMALLWOOD STONE CO.
Reorganized in 1942
New company subsequently dissolved
No stockholders' equity

SMALLWORLDWIDE PLC (ENGLAND & WALES)
Merged into General Electric Co. 12/27/2000
Each Sponsored ADR for Ordinary exchanged for $20 cash

SMART & FINAL INC (DE)
Common 1¢ par split (3) for (2) by issuance of (0.5) additional share 02/05/1993
Merged into Apollo Management, L.P. 05/31/2007
Each share Common 1¢ par exchanged for $22 cash

SMART & FINAL IRIS CORP (CA)
Acquired by Casino USA Inc. 01/25/1985
Each share 5% Part. Class A $1 par exchanged for $123.50 cash
Each share 5% Non-Cum. Part. Class B $1 par exchanged for $123.50 cash

SMART API VENTURE CAP CORP (CANADA)
Name changed to Vigil Locating Systems Corp. 02/03/2003
(See Vigil Locating Systems Corp.)

SMART BALANCE INC (DE)
Name changed to Boulder Brands, Inc. 01/02/2013
(See Boulder Brands, Inc.)

SMART CHOICE AUTOMOTIVE GROUP INC (FL)
Each share old Common 1¢ par exchanged for (0.5) share new Common 1¢ par 08/24/1998
Each share new Common 1¢ par exchanged for (0.05) share new Common 1¢ par 07/26/2000
SEC revoked common stock registration 02/20/2007

SMART COMM INTL LTD (NV)
SEC revoked common stock registration 03/21/2014

SMART ENERGY SOLUTIONS INC (NV)
Each share old Common no par exchanged for (0.00066666) share new Common no par 01/20/2015
New Common no par changed to $0.0001 par 12/23/2013
Name changed to CannaPowder, Inc. 07/11/2018

SMART FIT FNDTNS INC (FL)
Reincorporated 05/10/1982
State of incorporation changed from (NY) to (FL) 05/10/1982
Name changed to Cyberfast Systems Inc. 10/27/1998
Cyberfast Systems Inc. recapitalized as GulfStream Industries, Inc. 04/05/2005 which recapitalized as Single Source Investment Group, Inc. 01/03/2006
(See Single Source Investment Group, Inc.)

SMART GAMES INTERACTIVE, INC. (DE)
Name changed to Yifan Communications, Inc. 07/28/2000
(See Yifan Communications, Inc.)

SMART HLDGS INC (NV)
Old Common $0.0001 par split (16) for (1) by issuance of (15) additional shares payable 05/06/2010 to holders of record 04/29/2010
Ex date - 05/07/2010
Each share old Common $0.0001 par exchanged for (0.01111111) share new Common $0.0001 par 10/15/2012
Recapitalized as SStartrade Tech, Inc. 11/28/2017
Each share new Common $0.0001 par exchanged for (0.1) share Common $0.0001 par

SMART HOME CONCEPTS INC (NV)
Name changed to AfO International, Inc. 06/03/2005
AfO International, Inc. name changed to Human Unitec International, Inc. 12/15/2008

SMART KIDS GROUP INC (FL)
Each share old Common $0.0001 par exchanged for (0.01) share new Common $0.0001 par 12/12/2011
Name changed to WMX Group Holdings, Inc. 07/26/2012
WMX Group Holdings, Inc. name changed to Oxford City Football Club, Inc. 08/05/2013
(See Oxford City Football Club, Inc.)

SMART KIDS INC (NV)
Each share old Common $0.003 par exchanged for (0.002) share new Common $0.003 par 4/15/2002
Name changed to Beneficial Holdings, Inc. and (2) additional shares issued 10/9/2003

SMART MODULAR TECHNOLOGIES INC (CA)
Common no par split (2) for (1) by issuance of (1) additional share payable 12/17/1997 to holders of record 12/03/1997
Merged into Solectron Corp. 12/01/1999
Each share Common no par exchanged for (0.51) share Common $0.001 par
Solectron Corp. merged into Flextronics International Ltd. 10/01/2007 which name changed to Flex Ltd. 09/28/2016

SMART MODULAR TECHNOLOGIES WWH INC (CAYMAN ISLANDS)
Issue Information - 18,181,818 ORD shs. offered at $9 per share on 02/02/2006
Acquired by Saleen Holdings, Inc. 08/26/2011
Each share Ordinary $0.00016667 par exchanged for $9.25 cash

SMART MOVE INC (DE)
Assets forclosed upon 05/06/2009
Stockholders' equity unlikely

SMART ONLINE INC (DE)
Name changed to MobileSmith, Inc. 09/25/2013

SMART REAL ESTATE INVT TR (AB)
Name changed to SmartCentres Real Estate Investment Trust 10/24/2017

SMART SERVER INC (NV)
Name changed to RumbleON, Inc. and Common $0.001 par reclassified as Class B Common $0.001 par 02/21/2017

SMART TECHNOLOGIES HLDG CORP (FL)
Name changed to EM Quantum Technologies Inc. 07/07/2016

SMART TECHNOLOGIES INC (AB)
Class A Subordinate no par reclassified as old Common no par 09/15/2014
Each share old Common no par exchanged for (0.1) share new Common no par 05/12/2016
Acquired by Hon Hai Precision Industry Co., Ltd. 09/19/2016
Each share new Common no par exchanged for USD$4.50 cash
Note: Unexchanged certificates will be cancelled and become without value 09/17/2021

SMART TEK SOLUTIONS INC (NV)
Each share old Common $0.001 par exchanged for (0.004) share new Common $0.001 par 03/31/2009
Name changed to Trucept, Inc. 01/03/2013

SMART TRUCK SYS INC (NV)
Recapitalized as Speechphone, Inc. 05/20/2008
Each share Common $0.001 par exchanged for (0.004) share Common $0.001 par
Speechphone, Inc. name changed to Hallmark Venture Group, Inc. 08/12/2008

SMARTALK TELESERVICES INC (CA)
Issue Information - 4,200,000 shares COM offered at $14.50 per share on 10/23/1996
Plan of reorganization under Chapter 11 Federal Bankruptcy proceedings effective 06/30/2001
Stockholders' equity unlikely

SMARTCARD INTL INC (NY)
Name changed to IX Systems, Inc. 10/01/1991
IX Systems, Inc. recapitalized as Guwo Holdings, Inc. 02/02/2007 which name changed to QED Connect, Inc. 07/23/2007

SMARTCARDESOLUTIONS COM LTD (ON)
Ceased operations 06/30/2001
Stockholders' equity unlikely

SMARTDATA CORP NEW (NV)
Each share old Common $0.001 par exchanged for (0.02564102) share new Common $0.001 par 02/26/2013
Note: Holders of between (100) to (3,900) shares received (100) shares
Holders of (99) or fewer shares were not affected
Name changed to Stratean, Inc. 12/01/2014
Stratean, Inc. name changed to Cleanspark, Inc. 11/14/2016

SMARTDATA CORP OLD (NV)
Each share old Common $0.001 par exchanged for (0.1) share new Common $0.001 par 01/25/2000

SMARTDATA CORP (Cont.)
Name changed to Ride Motors Inc. 12/18/2002
Ride Motors Inc. name changed to Smartdata Corp. (New) 06/15/2012 which name changed to Stratean, Inc. 12/01/2014 which name changed to Cleanspark, Inc. 11/14/2016

SMARTDATA INC (CA)
Name changed to Coastal Technologies Inc. 10/10/2005
Coastal Technologies Inc. recapitalized as Cyclone Power Technologies, Inc. 07/02/2007

SMARTDISK CORP (DE)
Name changed to SMDK Corp. 08/09/2007
(See SMDK Corp.)

SMARTEC HLDGS INC (NV)
Each share old Common $0.001 par exchanged for (20) shares new Common $0.001 par 11/26/2007
Name changed to MabCure Inc. 01/22/2008

SMARTEK INC (ID)
Each share old Common $0.001 par exchanged for (0.05) share new Common $0.001 par 03/05/1997
New Common $0.001 par split (2) for (1) by issuance of (1) additional share payable 04/24/1998 to holders of record 04/17/1998
Administratively dissolved 02/17/2000

SMARTEL COMMUNICATIONS CORP (ON)
Name changed to Intasys Corp. 07/29/1996
Intasys Corp. name changed to Mamma.com Inc. 01/12/2004 which name changed to Copernic Inc. 06/21/2007 which merged into Comamtech Inc. (ON) 11/04/2010 which reincorporated in Delaware as DecisionPoint Systems, Inc. (New) 06/22/2011

SMARTERKIDS COM INC (DE)
Issue Information - 4,500,000 shares COM offered at $14 per share on 11/23/1999
Merged into LearningStar Corp. 4/30/2001
Each share Common 1¢ par exchanged for (0.125) share Common 1¢ par.
LearningStar Corp. name changed to Excelligence Learning Corp. 5/3/2002
(See Excelligence Learning Corp.)

SMARTFLEX SYS INC (DE)
Merged into Saturn Electronics & Engineering, Inc. 08/26/1999
Each share Common $0.0025 par exchanged $10.50 cash

SMARTFORCE PLC (IRELAND)
Name changed to SkillSoft PLC 11/19/2002
(See SkillSoft PLC)

SMARTGATE INC (NV)
Name changed to Invisa, Inc. 02/25/2002
Invisa, Inc. name changed to Uniroyal Global Engineered Products, Inc. 07/16/2012

SMARTIRE SYS INC (BC)
Reincorporated 02/06/2003
Reincorporated 12/20/2006
Place of incorporation changed from (BC) to (YT) 02/06/2003
Place of incorporation changed back from (YT) to (BC) 12/20/2006
Name changed to TTC Technology Corp. 04/14/2010
(See TTC Technology Corp.)

SMARTLOGIK GROUP PLC (UNITED KINGDOM)
Each old Sponsored ADR for Ordinary exchanged for (0.1) new Sponsored ADR for Ordinary 08/17/2001
ADR basis changed from (1:4) to (1:40) 08/17/2001
ADR agreement terminated 12/29/2003
No ADR holders' equity

SMARTOR PRODS INC (AB)
Delisted from Canadian Venture Stock Exchange 03/19/2002

SMARTPAY EXPRESS INC (NV)
Each share old Common $0.001 par exchanged for (0.02) share new Common $0.001 par 11/21/2008
Name changed to Blue Water Ventures International, Inc. 07/03/2012

SMARTPROS LTD (DE)
Merged into DF Institute, LLC 12/23/2015
Each share Common $0.0001 par exchanged for $3.57 cash

SMARTS OIL & GAS INC (NV)
Name changed to Dynamic Natural Resources, Inc. 08/27/2007
Dynamic Natural Resources, Inc. name changed to Universal Tracking Solutions, Inc. 10/31/2008

SMARTSALES INC (ON)
Notice of termination given to all staff and trustee in bankruptcy appointed 11/12/2002
Stockholders' equity unlikely

SMARTSERV ONLINE INC (DE)
Each share old Common 1¢ par exchanged for (0.16666666) share new Common 1¢ par 10/26/1998
Each share new Common 1¢ par exchanged again for (0.16666666) share new Common 1¢ par 11/25/2003
Name changed to Uphonia, Inc. 01/25/2006
(See Uphonia, Inc.)

SMARTSOURCES COM INC (CO)
Reincorporated under the laws of Washington as Infertek, Inc. and Common 1¢ par changed to no par 06/15/2001
Infertek, Inc. name changed to Metarunner, Inc. 06/15/2004
(See Metarunner, Inc.)

SMARTSTOP SELF STORAGE INC (MD)
Acquired by Extra Space Storage Inc. 10/01/2015
Each share Common $0.001 par exchanged for $13.75 cash

SMARTVIDEO TECHNOLOGIES INC (DE)
Name changed to uVuMobile, Inc. 06/04/2007
(See uVuMobile, Inc.)

SMASH MINERALS CORP (BC)
Merged into Prosperity Goldfields Corp. (BC) 04/24/2012
Each share Common no par exchanged for (0.625) share Common no par
Prosperity Goldfields Corp. (BC) recapitalized as Northern Empire Resources Corp. 12/12/2014 which merged into Coeur Mining, Inc. 10/01/2018

SMC COMPUTER SVCS INC (TX)
Name changed to Britco, Inc. 12/21/1971
(See Britco, Inc.)

SMC CORP (OR)
Merged into Monaco Coach Corp. 08/06/2001
Each share Common no par exchanged for $3.70 cash

SMC INDS INC (TX)
Common 50¢ par split (3) for (2) by issuance of (0.5) additional share 03/08/1972
Stock Dividend - 50% 11/02/1971
Merged into Dimark, Inc. 08/08/1978

Each share Common 50¢ par exchanged for $5.75 cash

SMC INVT CORP (DE)
Recapitalized as Source Capital, Inc. 10/16/1972
Each share Common $1 par exchanged for (0.2) share $2.40 Preferred $3 par and (0.4) share Common $1 par

SMC RECORDINGS INC (NV)
Stock Dividend - 10% payable 01/31/2011 to holders of record 01/07/2011 Ex date - 02/22/2011
Recapitalized as SMC Entertainment, Inc. 05/06/2011
Each share Common $0.001 par exchanged for (0.02) share Common $0.001 par

SMD INDS INC (MA)
Common $1 par changed to 50¢ par and (1) additional share issued 9/20/68
Common 50¢ par split (3) for (2) by issuance of (0.5) additional share 1/31/83
Merged into American Greetings Corp. 12/31/86
Each share Common 50¢ par exchanged for $8.50 cash

SMDK CORP. (DE)
Certificate of dissolution filed 10/28/2014
No stockholders' equity

SMED INTL INC (AB)
Merged into Haworth, Inc. 03/14/2000
Each share Common no par exchanged for $24 cash

SMED MFG INC (AB)
Merged into SMED International Inc. 7/1/96
Each share Common no par exchanged for (1) share Common no par
(See SMED International Inc.)

SMEDVIG A S (NORWAY)
Sponsored ADR's for A Shares NOK 1.50 par split (2) for (1) by issuance of (1) additional ADR payable 10/24/2000 to holders of record 10/17/2000 Ex date - 10/25/2000
Sponsored ADR's for B Shares NOK 1.50 par split (2) for (1) by issuance of (1) additional ADR payable 10/24/2000 to holders of record 10/17/2000 Ex date - 10/25/2000
Sponsored ADR for A Shares NOK 1.50 par changed to NOK 10 par 05/18/2002
Sponsored ADR for B Shares NOK 1.50 par changed to NOK 10 par 05/18/2002
Acquired by Seadrill Ltd. 06/15/2006
Each Sponsored ADR for A Shares NOK 10 par exchanged for $32.5026 cash
Each Sponsored ADR for B Shares NOK 10 par exchanged for $26.15087 cash

SMELTERS CORP. OF CANADA LTD. (ON)
Charter cancelled for failure to file reports and pay taxes in 1949

SMELTERS DEVELOPMENT CORP. (DE)
Dissolved and each share Common $1 par exchanged for (1) share of Patino Enterprises of Canada Ltd. Capital Stock $5 par 8/18/54
Patino Enterprises of Canada Ltd. merged into Patino of Canada Ltd. 10/6/55 which merged into Patino Corp. Ltd. 6/11/52 which merged into Patino Mining Corp. 11/26/62 which reorganized as Patino N.V. 12/20/71
(See Patino N.V.)

SMETHPORT RAILROAD
Dissolved in 1932

SMF ENERGY CORP (DE)
Each share old Common 1¢ par exchanged for (0.22222222) share new Common 1¢ par 10/01/2009
Plan of reorganization under Chapter 11 Federal Bankruptcy proceedings effective 12/28/2012
No stockholders' equity

SMG CAP CORP (SK)
Merged into CAPA Software Publishing Corp. 07/12/1990
Each share Common no par exchanged for (0.6) share Class A Common no par
(See CAPA Software Publishing Corp.)

SMG INDIUM RES LTD (DE)
Units separated 05/31/2013
Name changed to SMG Industries Inc. 04/03/2018

SMI FINL GROUP INC (NV)
Name changed to AmeraMex International Inc. 5/30/2001

SMI INTL INC (TX)
Name changed to SMI/USA, Inc. 10/01/1990
(See SMI/USA, Inc.)

SMI LIQUIDATING CORP. (NY)
Completely liquidated 5/22/86
Each share Common 50¢ par received first and final distribution of $1.60 cash

SMI OIL & GAS INC (CANADA)
Merged into Canadian Leader Energy Inc. 11/2/95
Each share Class A Common no par exchanged for (0.454) share Common no par
Canadian Leader Energy Inc. merged into Centurion Energy International Inc. 5/20/97
(See Centurion Energy International Inc.)

SMI PRODS INC (DE)
Reincorporated 02/09/2007
Place of incorporation changed from (NV) to (DE) 02/09/2007
Each share Common $0.001 par exchanged for (0.1) share Common $0.001 par
Name changed to Nile Therapeutics, Inc. 10/11/2007
Nile Therapeutics, Inc. recapitalized as Capricor Therapeutics, Inc. 11/21/2013

SMI USA INC (TX)
Merged into SMI TEM Corp. 10/6/92
Each share Common 50¢ par exchanged for $0.50 cash

SMILEN FOOD STORES, INC. (NY)
Merged into Big Apple Supermarkets, Inc. 2/26/65
Each share Common $1 par exchanged for (0.28) share Common 10¢ par
Big Apple Supermarkets, Inc. merged into Foodarama Supermarkets, Inc. 5/15/70
(See Foodarama Supermarkets, Inc.)

SMILES INC (DE)
Filed petition under Chapter 7 Federal Bankruptcy Code 1/9/86
Stockholders' equity unlikely

SMITH, INC. (MN)
Each share Common $25 par exchanged for (5) shares Common $5 par in 1949
Reorganized 6/10/66
Preferred and Common deemed worthless

SMITH (ELWIN G.) & CO., INC. (PA)
Merged into Cyclops Corp. 1/13/72
Each share Common $5 par exchanged for (1) share $1.15 Conv. Preferred Ser. B $1 par
(See Cyclops Corp.)

SMITH (L.C.) & CORONA TYPEWRITERS, INC. (NY)
Each share 7% Preferred $100 par exchanged for (1-4/11) shares $6 Preferred no par in 1935
Name changed to Smith-Corona, Inc. in 1953
Smith-Corona, Inc. name changed to Smith- Corona Marchant, Inc. 6/30/58 which merged into SCM Corp. 11/30/62
(See SCM Corp.)

SMITH & DAVIS MANUFACTURING CO. (MO)
Acquired by AFSCO Corp. 06/00/1971
Details not available

SMITH & DOVE MANUFACTURING CO.
Acquired by Ludlow Manufacturing Associates in 1928
Details not available

SMITH (ALEXANDER) & SONS CARPET CO. (NY)
Name changed to Smith (Alexander), Inc. 5/1/51
Smith (Alexander), Inc. name changed to Mohasco Industries, Inc. 12/31/55 which name changed to Mohasco Corp. 5/3/74
(See Mohasco Corp.)

SMITH & WESSON, INC. (MA)
Each share Capital Stock $100 par exchanged for (20) shares Capital Stock $5 par 00/00/1944
Bangor Punta Alegre Sugar Corp. acquired 100% through purchase offer as of 10/01/1967
Public interest eliminated

SMITH & WESSON HLDG CORP (NV)
Name changed to American Outdoor Brands Corp. 01/03/2017

SMITH & WOLLENSKY RESTAURANT GROUP INC (DE)
Issue Information - 5,295,972 shares COM offered at $8.50 per share on 05/22/2001
Merged into Project Grill, LLC 08/28/2007
Each share Common 1¢ par exchanged for $11 cash

SMITH A O CORP (DE)
Reincorporated 10/10/1986
Common no par changed to $10 par 00/00/1936
Common $10 par split (2) for (1) by issuance of (1) additional share 09/20/1957
Common $10 par changed to $5 par 04/09/1970
Common $5 par split (2) for (1) by issuance of (1) additional share 05/15/1972
Common $5 par reclassified as Class A Common $5 par 09/20/1983
Each share Class A Common $5 par received distribution of (0.5) share Class B $1 par 09/30/1983
Stock Dividend - 100% 04/12/1948
State of incorporation changed from (NY) to (DE) 10/10/1986
$2.125 Conv. Exchangeable Preferred $1 par called for redemption 04/23/1992
(Additional Information in Active)

SMITH AGRICULTURAL CHEMICAL CO. (OH)
Each share Common $100 par exchanged for (10) shares old Common no par 00/00/1929
Each share old Common no par exchanged for (3) shares new Common no par 01/31/1955
Merged into Smith-Douglass Co., Inc. 09/01/1959
Each share 6% Preferred $100 par exchanged for (1.2) shares 5% Preferred $100 par
Each share new Common no par exchanged for (0.1) share 5% 2nd Preferred Ser. A $100 par

Smith-Douglass Co., Inc. acquired by Borden Co. 12/30/1964 which name changed to Borden, Inc. 04/17/1968 which merged into RJR Nabisco Holdings Corp. 03/14/1995 which name changed to Nabisco Group Holdings Corp. 06/15/1999
(See Nabisco Group Holdings Corp.)

SMITH ALSOP PAINT & VARNISH CO (IN)
Each share Common no par exchanged for (1) share Capital Stock $20 par 00/00/1953
Stock Dividend - 50% 03/12/1956
Acquired by Bruder (M.A.) & Sons, Inc. 00/00/1969
Details not available

SMITH BARNEY APPRECIATION FD INC (MD)
Name changed 10/14/1994
Name changed from Smith Barney Shearson Appreciation Fund Inc. to Smith Barney Appreciation Fund Inc. 10/14/1994
Name changed to Legg Mason Partners Appreciation Fund, Inc. 05/01/2006
(See Legg Mason Partners Appreciation Fund, Inc.)

SMITH BARNEY CALIF MUNS FD (MD)
Name changed from Smith Barney Shearson California Municipals Fund Inc. to Smith Barney California Municipals Fund Inc. 10/14/1994
Name changed to Legg Mason Partners California Municipals Fund, Inc. 04/07/2006 Legg Mason Partners California Municipals Fund, Inc. name changed to Legg Mason Partners Income Trust 04/16/2007

SMITH BARNEY HIGH INCOME OPPORTUNITY FD INC (MD)
Name changed to High Income Opportunity Fund Inc. 12/20/94
High Income Opportunity Fund Inc. name changed to Western Asset High Income Opportunity Fund Inc. 10/9/2006

SMITH BARNEY INTER MUN FD INC (MD)
Name changed to Intermediate Muni Fund, Inc. 12/28/2000
Intermediate Muni Fund, Inc. name changed to Western Asset Intermediate Muni Fund, Inc. 10/09/2006

SMITH BARNEY MUN FD INC (MD)
Merged into Intermediate Muni Fund, Inc. 12/28/2000
Each share Common $0.001 par exchanged for (1.45437) shares Common $0.001 par
Intermediate Muni Fund, Inc. name changed to Western Asset Intermediate Muni Fund, Inc. 10/09/2006

SMITH BARNEY TELECOMMUNICATIONS INCOME FD (MA)
Completely liquidated 3/12/2004
Each Share of Bene. Int. received net asset value

SMITH BERGER MFG CORP (WA)
Merged into American Hoist & Derrick Co. 7/27/78
Each share Common $1 par exchanged for (0.342856) share Common $1 par
An additional and final distribution of (0.085715) share Common $1 was made 9/12/79
American Hoist & Derrick Co. name changed to Amdura Corp. 2/13/89
(See Amdura Corp.)

SMITH BROTHERS REFINERY CO., INC.
Acquired by Warren Petroleum Corp. 00/00/1946
Details not available

SMITH CANNERY MACHINES CO. (WA)
Name changed to Smith-Berger Manufacturing Corp. in November 1962
Smith-Berger Manufacturing Corp. merged into American Hoist & Derrick Co. 7/27/78 which name changed to Amdura Corp. 2/13/89
(See Amdura Corp.)

SMITH CHARLES E RESIDENTIAL RLTY INC (MD)
Issue Information - 7,848,000 shares COM offered at $24 per share on 06/23/1994
Merged into Archstone-Smith Trust 10/31/2001
Each share Conv. Preferred Ser. A exchanged for (1) share Conv. Preferred Ser. H 1¢ par
Each share Conv. Preferred Ser. E exchanged for (1) share Conv. Preferred Ser. J 1¢ par
Each share Conv. Preferred Ser. F exchanged for (1) share Conv. Preferred Ser. K 1¢ par
Each share Conv. Preferred Ser. G exchanged for (1) share Preferred Ser. L 1¢ par
Each share Common 1¢ par exchanged for (1.975) Common Units 1¢ par
(See Archstone-Smith Trust)

SMITH COBALT MINES LTD. (ON)
Charter cancelled for failure to pay taxes and file returns 3/16/76

SMITH (J. HUNGERFORD) CO. (NY)
Each share Common no par exchanged for (5) shares Common $5 par 00/00/1946
Merged into United Fruit Co. 04/20/1966
Each share Common $5 par exchanged for (1) share $2 Conv. Preferred Ser. A no par
United Fruit Co. merged into United Brands Co. 06/30/1970 which name changed to Chiquita Brands International, Inc. 03/20/1990
(See Chiquita Brands International, Inc.)

SMITH (T.L.) CO. (WI)
Each share Common no par exchanged for (6) shares Common $1 par in 1942
Merged into Smith-Essick, Inc. 5/2/66
Each share Common $1 par exchanged for (2) shares Common $2 par
Smith-Essick, Inc. name changed to Essick Investment Co. 5/1/67
(See Essick Investment Co.)

SMITH (WERNER G.) CO.
Acquired by Archer-Daniels-Midland Co. in 1929

SMITH (F.H.) CO. (DE)
Proclaimed inoperative and void for non-payment of taxes 4/1/32

SMITH (S. MORGAN) CO., INC. (PA)
Acquired by Allis-Chalmers Manufacturing Co. 01/28/1959
Each share Capital Stock $10 par exchanged for (1.1) shares Common $10 par
Allis-Chalmers Manufacturing Co. name changed to Allis-Chalmers Corp. 05/28/1971 which name changed to Allis-Chalmers Energy, Inc. 01/01/2005
(See Allis-Chalmers Energy, Inc.)

SMITH-CORONA, INC. (NY)
Common no par changed to $10 par in 1954
Common $10 par changed to $5 par and (1) additional share issued 10/18/57
Under plan of merged name changed to Smith-Corona Marchant, Inc. 6/30/58
Smith-Corona Marchant, Inc. name changed to SCM Corp. 11/30/62

(See SCM Corp.)

SMITH CORONA CORP (DE)
Reorganized under Chapter 11 Federal Bankruptcy Code 02/28/1997
Each share old Common 1¢ par exchanged for (0.05) Common Stock Purchase Warrant expiring 09/28/1999
Plan of reorganization under Chapter 11 Federal Bankruptcy proceedings effective 03/30/2001
No new Common stockholders' equity

SMITH-CORONA MARCHANT, INC. (NY)
Name changed to SCM Corp. 11/30/62
(See SCM Corp.)

SMITH DIETERICH CORP (NY)
Charter cancelled and proclaimed dissolved for failure to pay taxes 12/16/1974

SMITH-DOUGLASS CO., INC. (VA)
Acquired by Borden Co. 12/30/1964
Each share Common $5 par exchanged for (0.9) share Capital Stock $7.50 par
5% Preferred $100 par called for redemption 01/29/1965
5% Conv. 2nd Preferred Ser. B $100 par called for redemption 01/29/1965
Borden Co. name changed to Borden, Inc. 04/17/1968 which merged into RJR Nabisco Holdings Corp. 03/14/1995 which name changed to Nabisco Group Holdings Corp. 06/15/1999
(See Nabisco Group Holdings Corp.)

SMITH ENGINEERING WORKS (WI)
Each share Capital Stock $100 par exchanged for (10) shares Capital Stock $10 par in 1946
Merged into Barber-Greene Co. (Ill.) 5/31/60
Each share Capital Stock $10 par exchanged for (6) shares Common $5 par
Barber-Greene Co. (Ill.) reincorporated under the laws of Delaware 1/2/69 which merged into Astec Industries, Inc. 12/29/86

SMITH ESSICK INC. (CA)
Name changed to Essick Investment Co. 5/1/67
(See Essick Investment Co.)

SMITH-FAUS DRUG CO. (UT)
Acquired by Brunswig Drug Co. in 1952
Each share Common $100 par exchanged for (12.8723) shares Common no par
Brunswig Drug Co. merged into Bergen Brunswig Corp. 3/26/69 which merged into AmeriSourceBergen Corp. 8/29/2001

SMITH (B.) FLOORING, INC. (UT)
Recapitalized as Ophir International, Inc. 11/2/84
Each share Common $0.001 par exchanged for (8) shares Common $0.001 par

SMITH (EDSON B.) FUND (MA)
Liquidation completed 09/17/1963
Total distribution per Certificate of Beneficial Interest $1 par was (1) share Foursquare Fund, Inc. Common $1 par and $0.0367 cash
Foursquare Fund, Inc. merged into Eaton Vance Investors Fund, Inc. 09/12/1983 which name changed to Eaton Vance Investors Trust 09/29/1993
(See Eaton Vance Investors Trust)

SMITH-GARDNER & ASSOCS INC (FL)
Issue Information - 4,410,000 shares COM offered at $12 per share on 01/29/1999

Name changed to Ecometry Corp.
12/4/2000

SMITH HAYES TR INC (MN)
Convertible Preferred Portfolio $0.001 par liquidated 2/21/89
Covered Option Writing Portfolio $0.001 par liquidated 6/30/90
Defensive Growth Portfolio $0.001 par liquidated 6/30/90
Opportunity Portfolio name changed to Value Portfolio 6/30/90
Value Portfolio $0.001 par liquidated 3/30/92
(Additional Information in Active)

SMITH HOWARD LTD (AUSTRALIA)
Each Unsponsored ADR for Ordinary AUD $1 par exchanged for (1) Sponsored ADR for Ordinary AUD $1 par 04/21/1997
Stock Dividend - 10% 09/03/1987
ADR agreement terminated 12/12/2001
Each Sponsored ADR for Ordinary AUD $1 par exchanged for $15.2339 cash

SMITH (ALEXANDER), INC. (NY)
Common $20 par changed to $5 par 5/21/54
Under plan of merger name changed to Mohasco Industries, Inc. 12/31/55
Mohasco Industries, Inc. name changed to Mohasco Corp. 5/3/74
(See Mohasco Corp.)

SMITH INDS INTL INC (CA)
Capital Stock no par split (3) for (2) by issuance of (0.5) additional share 06/24/1966
Capital Stock no par split (2) for (1) by issuance of (1) additional share 12/15/1967
Capital Stock no par reclassified as Common no par 04/12/1968
Name changed to Smith International, Inc. (CA) 05/13/1969
Smith International, Inc. (CA) reincorporated in Delaware 05/19/1983
(See Smith International, Inc.)

SMITH INTL INC (DE)
Reincorporated 05/19/1993
Common no par split (2) for (1) by issuance of (1) additional share 06/01/1973
Common no par split (2) for (1) by issuance of (1) additional share 05/27/1980
State of incorporation changed from (CA) to (DE) and Common no par changed to $1 par 05/19/1983
Plan of reorganization under Chapter 11 Federal Bankruptcy proceedings confirmed 11/12/1987
Each (4.7194) shares Common $1 par received distribution of (1) Common Stock Purchase Warrant Class B expiring 02/28/1995
8.75% Conv. Preferred $1 par called for redemption 06/21/1993
Common $1 par split (2) for (1) by issuance of (1) additional share payable 07/08/2002 to holders of record 06/20/2002 Ex date - 07/09/2002
Common $1 par split (2) for (1) by issuance of (1) additional share payable 08/24/2005 to holders of record 08/05/2005 Ex date - 08/25/2005
Merged into Schlumberger Ltd. 08/27/2010
Each share Common $1 par exchanged for (0.6966) share Common 1¢ par

SMITH INVT CO (NV)
Reincorporated 10/01/1997
Each share Capital Stock $10 par exchanged for (5) shares Capital Stock $2 par 08/31/1959
Each share Capital Stock $2 par exchanged for (185) shares Capital Stock 10¢ par 06/10/1970

State of incorporation changed from (DE) to (NV) 10/01/1997
Capital Stock 10¢ par split (2) for (1) by issuance of (1) additional share payable 06/01/1998 to holders of record 05/15/1998
Each share new Common 10¢ par received distribution of (1) share Smith Investment Co. LLC Membership Unit payable 01/19/2009 to holders of record 12/22/2008
Merged into Smith (A.O.) Corp. 04/22/2009
Each share Common 10¢ par exchanged for (2.396) shares Restricted Class A Common $5 par and (0.306) Common $1 par
Note: Each share Common 10¢ par received an additional (0.157) share Common $1 par from escrow 11/29/2011

SMITH J C MARKETING CORP (BC)
Name changed to Devin Energy Corp. 10/19/98

SMITH KLINE & FRENCH LABS (PA)
Each share Common no par exchanged for (20) shares Common no par 00/00/1947
Each share Common no par exchanged for (2) shares Common $1 par 00/00/1950
Common $1 par changed to 33-1/3¢ par and (2) additional shares issued 00/00/1954
Common 33-1/3¢ par changed to no par and (2) additional shares issued 05/29/1959
Common no par changed to $1 par 04/24/1973
Name changed to SmithKline Corp. 07/01/1973
SmithKline Corp. name changed to SmithKline Beckman Corp. 03/04/1982 which merged into SmithKline Beecham PLC 07/26/1989 which merged into GlaxoSmithKline PLC 12/27/2000

SMITH LABS INC (IL)
Merged into Columbia Hospital Corp. (NV) 5/17/90
Each share Common no par exchanged for (1) share Common 1¢ par
Columbia Hospital Corp. (NV) reincorporated in Delaware as Columbia Healthcare Corp. 9/1/93 which merged into Columbia/HCA Healthcare Corp. 2/10/94 which name changed to HCA - The Healthcare Co. 5/25/2000 which name changed to HCA Inc. (Ctfs. dated after 6/29/2001) 6/29/2001
(See HCA Inc. (Ctfs. dated after 6/29/2001))

SMITH (H.D.) MANUFACTURING CORP.
In receivership in 1950

SMITH MILLER & PATCH INC (NJ)
Merged into Cooper Laboratories, Inc. 03/16/1972
Each share Capital Stock 10¢ par exchanged for (1) share Common 10¢ par
(See Cooper Laboratories, Inc.)

SMITH NEWS PLC (UNITED KINGDOM)
Name changed to Connect Group PLC 04/22/2014

SMITH (E.L.) OIL CO., INC.
Merged into Lion Oil Refining Co. on a (0.1) for (1) basis in 1938
Lion Oil Refining Co. name changed to Lion Oil Co. in 1945 which merged into Monsanto Chemical Co. 9/30/55 which name changed to Monsanto Co. 4/1/64 which name changed to Pharmacia Corp. 3/31/2000 which merged into Pfizer Inc. 4/16/2003

SMITH (H.C.) OIL TOOL CO. (CA)
Name changed to Smith Tool Co. 09/01/1959
Smith Tool Co. name changed to Smith Industries International, Inc. 11/17/1960 which name changed to Smith International, Inc. (CA) 05/13/1969 which reincorporated in Delaware 05/19/1983
(See Smith International, Inc.)

SMITH (FRANK) PAPER CO.
Merged into Sorg Paper Co. in 1930
Details not available

SMITH (FLETCHER) STUDIOS, INC. (NY)
See - Fletcher Smith Studios Inc.

SMITH TECHNOLOGY CORP (DE)
Name changed 09/23/1996
Name changed from Smith Environmental Technologies Corp. to Smith Technology Corp. 09/23/1996
Chapter 11 bankruptcy proceedings terminated 05/21/2003
Stockholders' equity unlikely

SMITH TOOL CO. (CA)
Name changed to Smith Industries International, Inc. 11/17/1960
Smith Industries International, Inc. name changed to Smith International, Inc. (CA) 05/13/1969 which reincorporated in Delaware 05/19/1983
(See Smith International, Inc.)

SMITH-WARING CORP. (DE)
Charter cancelled and declared inoperative and void for non-payment of taxes 3/22/22

SMITH YOUNG TOWER CORP.
Name changed to San Antonio Transit Co. in 1942
San Antonio Transit Co. name changed to San Antonio Corp. 10/1/59
(See San Antonio Corp.)

SMITHFIELD CDA LTD (ON)
Exchangeable Shares no par split (2) for (1) by issuance of (1) additional share payable 09/14/2001 to holders of record 09/06/2001
Each Exchangeable Share no par exchanged for (1) share Smithfield Foods, Inc. Common 50¢ par and $3.25 cash 03/31/2014
(See Smithfield Foods, Inc.)

SMITHFIELD COS INC (VA)
Common no par split (2) for (1) by issuance of (1) additional share payable 1/30/98 to holders of record 1/5/98
Merged into Smithfield Foods, Inc. 7/31/2001
Each share Common no par exchanged for $8.50 cash

SMITHFIELD FOODS INC (VA)
Reincorporated 06/10/1971
Reincorporated 09/02/1997
State of incorporation changed from (FL) to (DE) 06/10/1971
6.75% Conv. Preferred $1 par called for redemption 11/23/1971
Common $1 par split (2) for (1) by issuance of (1) additional share 10/03/1986
Common $1 par changed to 50¢ par and (1) additional share issued 09/20/1988
Common 50¢ par split (2) for (1) by issuance of (1) additional share 05/31/1991
State of incorporation changed from (DE) to (VA) 09/02/1997
Common 50¢ par split (2) for (1) by issuance of (1) additional share payable 06/26/1997 to holders of record 09/12/1997
Common 50¢ par split (2) for (1) by issuance of (1) additional share payable 09/14/2001 to holders of record 09/06/2001 Ex date - 09/17/2001

Acquired by Shuanghui International Holdings Ltd. 09/26/2013
Each share Common 50¢ par exchanged for $34 cash

SMITHKLINE BEECHAM CORP
Name changed 03/04/1982
Common $1 par changed to 50¢ par and (1) additional share issued 05/31/1977
Common 50¢ par changed to 25¢ par and (1) additional share issued 05/31/1979
Name changed from SmithKline Corp. to SmithKline Beckman Corp. 03/04/1982
Common 25¢ par split (2) for (1) by issuance of (1) additional share 06/12/1987
Merged into SmithKline Beecham PLC 07/26/1989
Each share Common 25¢ par exchanged for (1) Equity Unit
Note: In addition each share Common 25¢ par received distribution of (0.5) share Allergan, Inc. Common 1¢ par, (0.18326) share Beckman Instruments, Inc. Common 10¢ par and $5.50 cash 07/31/1989
SmithKline Beecham PLC merged into GlaxoSmithKline PLC 12/27/2000
144A Flexible Auction Rate Preferred Ser. K called for redemption at $500,000 on 02/26/2001
Money Market Preferred Ser. J called for redemption at $500,000 on 03/01/2001
144A Flexible Auction Rate Preferred Ser. L called for redemption at $500,000 on 03/05/2001
144A Flexible Auction Rate Preferred Ser. M called for redemption at $500,000 on 03/08/2001
Money Market Preferred Ser. A called for redemption at $500,000 on 03/12/2001
Money Market Preferred Ser. B called for redemption at $500,000 on 03/12/2001
Money Market Preferred Ser. C called for redemption at $500,000 on 03/15/2001
Money Market Preferred Ser. D called for redemption at $500,000 on 03/19/2001

SMITHKLINE BEECHAM HLDGS CORP (DE)
Flexible Auction Rate Preferred Ser. A-1 called for redemption at $100,000 on 7/15/99
Flexible Auction Rate Preferred Ser. A-2 called for redemption at $100,000 on 7/15/99
Money Market Preferred Ser. E called for redemption at $100,000 on 3/8/2004
Money Market Preferred Ser. F called for redemption at $100,000 on 3/8/2004
Money Market Preferred Ser. G called for redemption at $100,000 on 3/12/2004
Flexible Auction Rate Preferred Ser. B-1 called for redemption at $100,000 on 3/17/2004
Money Market Preferred Ser. H called for redemption at $100,000 on 3/19/2004
Flexible Auction Rate Preferred Ser. B-2 called for redemption at $100,000 on 3/24/2004
Money Market Preferred Ser. I called for redemption at $100,000 on 3/26/2004
Flexible Auction Rate Preferred Ser. C-1 called for redemption at $100,000 on 3/22/2004
Flexible Auction Rate Preferred Ser. C-2 called for redemption at $100,000 on 3/29/2004
Flexible Auction Rate Preferred Ser. B-3 called for redemption at $100,000 on 3/31/2004

FINANCIAL INFORMATION, INC. SMI-SMU

Flexible Auction Rate Preferred Ser. C-3 called for redemption at $100,000 on 4/5/2004

SMITHKLINE BEECHAM P L C (ENGLAND)
ADR's for Equity Units split (2) for (1) by issuance of (1) additional ADR 07/24/1992
Sponsored ADR's for A Ordinary 25p par split (2) for (1) by issuance of (1) additional ADR 07/24/1992
Each ADR for Equity Units exchanged for (1) ADR for A Ordinary and $1.1255 cash 04/15/1996
Sponsored ADR's for A Ordinary 25p par split (2) for (1) by issuance of (1) additional ADR payable 08/28/1997 to holders of record 08/25/1997 Ex date - 08/29/1997
Stock Dividend - 1.85% payable 04/14/1996 to holders of record 04/12/1996
Merged into GlaxoSmithKline PLC 12/27/2000
Each Sponsored ADR for A Ordinary 25p par exchanged for (1.138) Sponsored ADR's for Ordinary

SMITHS FOOD & DRUG CTRS INC (DE)
Merged into Meyer (Fred), Inc. (New) 9/9/97
Each share Preferred Ser. 1 1¢ par exchanged for $0.33333333 cash
Each share Class A Common 1¢ par exchanged for (1.05) shares Common 1¢ par
Each share Class B Common 1¢ par exchanged for (1.05) shares Common 1¢ par

SMITHS TRANSFER CORP (VA)
Name changed 04/21/1969
Name changed from Smith's Transfer Corp. of Staunton to Smith's Transfer Corp. 04/21/1969
Stock Dividends - 50% 11/27/1970; 75% 01/14/1972
Merged into ARA Services, Inc. 01/28/1980
Each share Common $2.50 par exchanged for (0.9) share Common 50¢ par
(See ARA Services, Inc.)

SMITHTOWN BANCORP INC (NY)
Common $5 par changed to $2.50 par and (1) additional share issued payable 05/06/1998 to holders of record 04/22/1998
Common $2.50 par changed to $1.25 par and (1) additional share issued payable 05/04/2001 to holders of record 04/20/2001 Ex date - 05/07/2001
Common $1.25 par split (2) for (1) by issuance of (1) additional share payable 04/17/2003 to holders of record 04/04/2003 Ex date - 04/21/2003
Common $1.25 changed to 1¢ par and (1) additional share issued payable 05/07/2004 to holders of record 04/23/2004 Ex date - 05/10/2004
Common 1¢ par split (3) for (2) by issuance of (0.5) additional share payable 05/05/2006 to holders of record 04/21/2006 Ex date - 05/08/2006
Stock Dividend - 10% payable 04/02/2007 to holders of record 03/16/2007 Ex date - 03/14/2007
Merged into People's United Financial, Inc. 11/30/2010
Each share Common 1¢ par exchanged for (0.1596) share Common 1¢ par and $1.79 cash

SMITHVILLE LIQUIDATING CORP. (NJ)
Completely liquidated 12/19/74
Each share Common 10¢ par exchanged for first and final distribution of $7 cash

SMITHWAY MTR XPRESS CORP (NV)
Merged into Western Express, Inc. 10/29/2007
Each share Class A Common 1¢ par exchanged for $10.63 cash

SMITTEN PRESS LOC LORE & LEGENDS INC (NV)
Reincorporated 07/13/2007
Place of incorporation changed from (ON) to (NV) and Common no par changed to $0.001 par 07/13/2007
Recapitalized as Datamill Media Corp. 08/23/2010
Each share Common $0.001 par exchanged for (0.01) share Common $0.001 par
Datamill Media Corp. name changed to AvWorks Aviation Corp. (NV) 11/30/2011 which reincorporated in Florida as Vapor Group, Inc. 04/29/2014

SMJ INVTS INC (FL)
Name changed to Monarch Holdings, Inc. 12/19/2005
Monarch Holdings, Inc. recapitalized as ProConcept Marketing Group, Inc. 12/24/2007
(See ProConcept Marketing Group, Inc.)

SMK SPEEDY INTL INC (ON)
Plan of arrangement effective 1/7/2004
Each share Common no par exchanged for $1.73 principal amount of Sr. Secured Subordinated Notes due 2009, $0.65 principal amount of US$ T-Notes due 7/2/2010 and $3.53 cash

SMLX TECHNOLOGIES INC (CO)
Filed a general assignment for the benefit of creditors under Chapter 727 of the Florida Statutes 12/31/2002
No stockholders' equity

SMM ENTERPRISES LTD (BC)
Name changed to Acuvision Systems Inc. 02/20/1987
Acuvision Systems Inc. recapitalized as International Acuvision Systems Inc. (BC) 08/27/1991 which reincorporated in Delaware 09/15/1993 which recapitalized as AcuBid.Com, Inc. 03/18/1999 which name changed to Asia Web Holdings, Inc. 06/01/2000 which name changed to Case Financial, Inc. 05/22/2002
(See Case Financial, Inc.)

SMO MULTIMEDIA CORP (NV)
Name changed to Strategic Management & Opportunity Corp. (Old) 09/02/2004
Strategic Management & Opportunity Corp. (Old) reorganized as Strategic Management & Opportunity Corp. (New) 09/25/2018

SMOKE CRAFT INC (OR)
Merged into International Multifoods Corp. 09/03/1976
Each share Capital Stock no par exchanged for (1.090778) share Common $1 par
Note: Above ratio includes a (2) for (1) split paid to holders of International Multifoods Corp. 09/03/1976
International Multifoods Corp. merged into Smucker (J.M.) Co. 06/18/2004

SMOKE WATCHERS INTL INC (NY)
Charter cancelled and proclaimed dissolved for failure to pay taxes and file reports 12/15/1972

SMOKERS LOZENGE INC (NV)
Name changed to Cybermesh International Corp. 04/03/2008

SMOKEY RES LTD (AB)
Name changed to General Leisure Corp. and Common no par reclassified as Class A Common no par 04/06/1989
General Leisure Corp. name changed to Westgroup Corporations Inc. 05/13/1991 which recapitalized as Beaumont Select Corps., Inc. 02/28/1995
(See Beaumont Select Corporations Inc.)

SMOKIN CONCEPTS DEV CORP (CO)
Name changed to Bourbon Brothers Holding Corp. 01/29/2014
Bourbon Brothers Holding Corp. name changed to Southern Concepts Restaurant Group, Inc. 03/13/2015

SMOKY HILL SVCS INC (NV)
Name changed to LearnCom, Inc. and (124) additional shares issued 05/10/2000
(See LearnCom, Inc.)

SMOOFI INC (NV)
Common $0.001 par split (3) for (1) by issuance of (2) additional shares payable 05/07/2015 to holders of record 04/25/2015 Ex date - 05/08/2015
Name changed to NuLife Sciences Inc. 12/08/2016

SMRT CORP LTD (SINGAPORE)
ADR agreement terminated 11/14/2016
Each ADR for Common exchanged for $11.986965 cash

SMS GROUP INC (FL)
Name changed to Natural Resources Recovery Inc. 11/8/90
Natural Resources Recovery Inc. name changed to Rare Earth Metals, Inc. (FL) 3/13/92 which reorganized in Delaware as Americare Health Group Inc. 3/3/93 which name changed to Zagreus Inc. 3/26/99

SMSA BALLINGER ACQUISITION CORP (NV)
Name changed to Blackboxstocks Inc. 03/09/2016

SMSA EL PASO I ACQUISITION CORP (NV)
Name changed to Latin America Ventures, Inc. 01/26/2009
Latin America Ventures, Inc. name changed to Chile Mining Technologies Inc. 07/23/2010

SMSA EL PASO II ACQUISITION CORP (NV)
Name changed to Resource Holdings, Inc. 06/30/2010

SMSA GAINESVILLE ACQUISITION CORP (NV)
Common $0.001 par split (13.3935) for (1) by issuance of (12.3935) additional shares payable 07/07/2014 to holders of record 06/23/2014 Ex date - 07/08/2014
Name changed to Titanium Healthcare, Inc. 10/09/2014

SMSA KATY ACQUISITION CORP (NV)
Name changed to L2 Medical Development Co. 07/03/2012
L2 Medical Development Co. name changed to Enerpulse Technologies, Inc. 10/04/2013

SMSA KERRVILLE ACQUISITION CORP (NV)
Name changed to Guwenhua International Co. 03/11/2013
Guwenhua International Co. name changed to Tyin Group Holdings Ltd. 01/29/2014

SMSA PALESTINE ACQUISITION CORP (NV)
Reorganized as Asia Green Agriculture Corp. 01/25/2011
Each share Common $0.001 par exchanged for (2.5) shares Common $0.001 par
(See Asia Green Agriculture Corp.)

SMSACTIVE TECHNOLOGIES CORP (NV)
Recapitalized as Exchange Mobile Telecommunications Corp. 11/17/2006
Each share Common $0.001 par exchanged for (0.01) share Common $0.001 par
Exchange Mobile Telecommunications Corp. recapitalized as Anything Technologies Media, Inc. 09/20/2010

SMSMOBILITY INC (NV)
Each share old Common $0.001 par exchanged for (0.002) share new Common $0.001 par 02/17/2005
Name changed to Star Petroleum Corp. 07/25/2005
Star Petroleum Corp. recapitalized as Exact Energy Resources, Inc. 12/11/2007
(See Exact Energy Resources, Inc.)

SMT HEALTH SVCS INC (DE)
Merged into Three Rivers Acquisition Corp. 9/29/97
Each share Common 1¢ par exchanged for $11.75 cash

SMT S A (POLAND)
Name changed to iAlbatros Group S.A. 08/18/2016

SMTC MFG CORP CDA (ON)
Issue Information - 4,375,000 EXCHANGEABLE SHARES offered at $16 per share on 07/20/2000
Each Exchangeable Share no par exchanged for (1) share SMTC Corp. Common 1¢ par 05/25/2012

SMTEK INTL INC (DE)
Each share old Common 1¢ par exchanged for (0.05) share new Common 1¢ par 05/25/1999
Merged into CTS Corp. 02/01/2005
Each share new Common 1¢ par exchanged for (0.2913) share Common 1¢ par and $10.725 cash

SMTP INC (DE)
Each share old Common $0.001 par exchanged for (0.2) share new Common $0.001 par 12/27/2013
Name changed to SharpSpring, Inc. 12/01/2015

SMUGGLER DIVIDE MINING CO.
Name changed to Smuggler Mining Co., Ltd. in 1930
Smuggler Mining Co., Ltd. name changed to American Environmental Sciences Ltd. 3/16/70
(See American Environmental Sciences, Inc.)

SMUGGLER MNG LTD (NV)
Name changed to American Environmental Sciences, Inc. 3/16/70
(See American Environmental Sciences, Inc.)

SMUGGLER UNION MINING CO.
Dissolved in 1930

SMUGGLERS ATTIC INC (DE)
Adjudicated bankrupt 04/02/1975
Stockholders' equity unlikely

SMURFIT-STONE CONTAINER CORP NEW (DE)
Merged into Rock-Tenn Co. 05/27/2011
Each share Common $0.001 par exchanged for (0.30605) share Class A Common 1¢ par and $17.50 cash
Rock-Tenn Co. merged into WestRock Co. 07/01/2015

SMURFIT-STONE CONTAINER CORP OLD (DE)
Reorganized under Chapter 11 Federal Bankruptcy proceedings as Smurfit-Stone Container Corp. (New) 06/30/2010
Each share 7% Conv. Exchangeable Preferred Ser. A 1¢ par received (0.472284) share Common $0.001 par

SMV-SNO — **FINANCIAL INFORMATION, INC.**

Each share Common 1¢ par received (0.008442) share Common $0.001 par
Note: Certificates were not required to be surrendered and are without value
Smurfit-Stone Container Corp. (New) merged into Rock-Tenn Co. 05/27/2011 which merged into WestRock Co. 07/01/2015

SMV MINERALS INC (CA)
Merged into Guadalupe Minerals Inc. 10/15/1990
Each share Common $1 par exchanged for $3 cash

SMX CORP (FL)
Each share old Common $0.0001 par exchanged for (0.1) share new Common $0.0001 par 12/12/2000
Administratively dissolved 10/01/2004

SMYTH MFG CO (CT)
Each share Common $100 par exchanged for (4) shares Common $25 par 00/00/1928
Each share Common $25 par exchanged for (5) shares Common $5 par 00/00/1957
Stock Dividend - 200% 03/15/1963
Name changed to S Corp. 08/18/1972
(See S Corp.)

SN STRATEGIES CORP (NV)
Common $0.001 par split (1.316984) for (1) by issuance of (0.316984) additional shares payable 07/09/2009 to holders of record 07/08/2009 Ex date - 07/10/2009
Name changed to China SHESAYS Medical Cosmetology Inc. 07/06/2010

SN UTD ENTERPRISES INC (DE)
Name changed to Itzyourmall, Inc. 06/08/2006

SNA RES LTD (BC)
Recapitalized as Enterprise Development Corp. 10/29/79
Each share Common no par exchanged for (0.2) share Common no par
Enterprise Development Corp. recapitalized as Magenta Development Corp. 3/28/84
(See Magenta Development Corp.)

SNACK FACTORY, INC. (UT)
Name changed to Maid-Rite Industries Inc. 3/28/85
Maid-Rite Industries Inc. name changed to Delta Rental Systems Inc. 12/15/87
(See Delta Rental Systems Inc.)

SNACKHEALTHY INC (NV)
Name changed to Amaize Beverage Corp. 08/19/2015
Amaize Beverage Corp. name changed to Curative Biosciences, Inc. 03/14/2018

SNACKIE JACKS LTD (ON)
Reorganized under the laws of Nevada as Rocky Mountain Brands Inc. 12/23/2004
Each share Common no par exchanged for (0.125) share Common no par
Rocky Mountain Brands Inc. name changed to The Estate Vault, Inc. 01/24/2008
(See The Estate Vault, Inc.)

SNAK-N-POP VENDING INC (FL)
Name changed to Eurasia Gold Fields, Inc. 03/02/1998
(See Eurasia Gold Fields, Inc.)

SNAKE EYES GOLF CLUBS INC (DE)
SEC revoked common stock registration 08/15/2011

SNAM RETE GAS SPA (ITALY)
Name changed to Snam S.p.A. 01/03/2012

SNAP INTERACTIVE INC (DE)
Old Common $0.001 par split (3) for (1) by issuance of (2) additional shares payable 01/22/2010 to holders of record 01/14/2010 Ex date - 01/25/2010
Each share old Common $0.001 par exchanged for (0.02857142) share new Common $0.001 par 01/06/2017
Name changed to PeerStream, Inc. 03/12/2018

SNAP N SOLD CORP (FL)
Name changed to Hot Web, Inc. 09/25/2006
Hot Web, Inc. name changed to Gold Coast Mining Corp. 07/02/2009 which name changed to Green Leaf Innovations, Inc. 03/10/2015

SNAP ON TOOLS CORP (DE)
Common $1 par split (2) for (1) by issuance of (1) additional share 05/31/1957
Common $1 par split (2) for (1) by issuance of (1) additional share 05/14/1969
Common $1 par split (3) for (1) by issuance of (2) additional shares 06/30/1972
Common $1 par split (2) for (1) by issuance of (1) additional share 05/11/1979
Common $1 par split (2) for (1) by issuance of (1) additional share 07/25/1986
Stock Dividends - 100% 06/29/1946; 100% 03/11/1963
Name changed to Snap-on Inc. 04/22/1994

SNAP ONLINE MARKETING INC (NV)
Name changed to LifeLogger Technologies Corp. 01/27/2014

SNAPER PATENT TECHNOLOGIES INC (BC)
Recapitalized as Emerging Growth Technologies Inc. 05/19/1992
Each share Common no par exchanged for (0.2) share Common no par
Emerging Growth Technologies Inc. name changed to Mandorin Goldfields, Inc. (BC) 04/23/1996 which reincorporated in Yukon 06/11/1999 which name changed to Sphere Resources Inc. 11/27/2007

SNAPPLE BEVERAGE CORP (DE)
Common 1¢ par split (2) for (1) by issuance of (1) additional share 6/11/93
Common 1¢ par split (2) for (1) by issuance of (1) additional share 9/24/93
Merged into Quaker Oats Co. 12/6/94
Each share Common 1¢ par exchanged for $14 cash

SNAP2 CORP (NV)
Each share old Common $0.001 par exchanged for (0.1) share new Common $0.001 par 09/10/2003
Recapitalized as Vertigo Theme Parks, Inc. 02/16/2007
Each share Common $0.001 par exchanged for (0.02) share Common $0.001 par
(See Vertigo Theme Parks, Inc.)

SNB BANCSHARES INC (GA)
Common $1 par split (5) for (4) by issuance of (0.25) additional share payable 09/25/1997 to holders of record 09/25/1997
Name changed to Security Bank Corp. 06/03/2003
(See Security Bank Corp.)

SNB BANCSHARES INC (TX)
Issue Information - 4,727,273 shares COM offered at $10.50 per share on 08/17/2004
Merged into Prosperity Bancshares, Inc. 4/1/2006
Each share Common 1¢ par exchanged for (0.3577) share Common $1 par and $7.50 cash

SNB BK & TR (BATTLE CREEK, MI)
Merged into Detroitbank Corp. 9/1/81
Each share Common $10 par exchanged for $35 principal amount of 10% Unsecured Conv. Subordinated Debentures due 1993/2000 plus $5.54 cash

SNB CAP CORP (BC)
Name changed to Protox Therapeutics Inc. 07/14/2004
Protox Therapeutics Inc. name changed to Sophiris Bio Inc. 04/05/2012

SNB CORP (OH)
Merged into Park National Corp. 4/30/2000
Each share Common no par exchanged for (5.367537) shares Common no par

SNC EQUITY INC (AB)
Name changed to RenoWorks Software Inc. 9/19/2002

SNC-LAVALIN GROUP INC (CANADA)
Name changed 5/12/93
Name changed from SNC Group Inc. to SNC-Lavalin Group Inc. 5/12/93
Class A Subordinate no par split (3) for (1) by issuance of (2) additional shares payable 6/3/96 to holders of record 5/30/96 Ex date - 5/28/96
Class A Subordinate no par reclassified as Common no par 5/6/97
(Additional Information in Active)

SND ENERGY LTD (CANADA)
Recapitalized as Boyuan Construction Group, Inc. 02/24/2009
Each share Common no par exchanged for (0.00079489) share Common no par

SNEED OIL CO. (NV)
Liquidated 5/8/64

SNELLING & SNELLING INC (PA)
Common 5¢ par reclassified as Class B Common 5¢ par 00/00/1990
99% acquired at $20.84 cash per share through purchase offer that expired 07/29/1996
Public interest eliminated

SNELLING TRAVEL INC (NV)
Reorganized 07/29/2002
Reorganized from under the laws of (CO) to (NV) 07/29/2002
Each share Common $0.001 par exchanged for (0.01) share Common $0.001 par
Name changed to Global Vision Holdings Inc. 08/30/2002
Global Vision Holdings Inc. recapitalized as Asiana Corp. 01/24/2008

SNH CAP TR I (DE)
10.25% Trust Preferred Securities called for redemption at $25 on 6/15/2006

SNIA SPA (ITALY)
Name changed 04/20/1999
Stock Dividend - 20% 11/02/1962
Name changed from Snia Viscosa (Societa Nazionale Industria Applicazioni Viscosa) to Snia S.p.A. 04/20/1999
ADR agreement terminated 10/16/2000
Each ADR for Ordinary 1200 Lire par exchanged for $0.897 cash

SNIDER PACKING CORP.
Acquired by General Foods Corp. on a (0.8) for (1) basis 7/7/43
(See General Foods Corp.)

SNIF SEC INC (BC)
Merged into Acme Protective Systems Ltd. 5/12/2014
Each share Common no par exchanged for $0.09 cash

SNIFFEX INC (NV)
Name changed to Homeland Safety International, Inc. 10/2/2006

SNIPER ENTERPRISES INC (BC)
Name changed to TransAmerican Energy Inc. 08/16/2005
TransAmerican Energy Inc. recapitalized as American Biofuels Inc. 09/12/2018

SNIPGOLD CORP (BC)
Merged into Seabridge Gold Inc. 06/21/2016
Each share Common no par exchanged for (0.01587301) share Common no par
Note: Unexchanged certificates will be cancelled and become without value 06/21/2022

SNL ENTERPRISES LTD (BC)
Name changed to Logan Copper Inc. 02/19/2010

SNL FINL CORP (UT)
Common $1 par reclassified as either (1) share Class A Common $1 par or (5) shares Class C Common 20¢ par 04/00/1986
Each share Class A Common $1 par exchanged for (0.5) share Class A Common $2 par 07/23/1987
Each share Class C Common 20¢ par exchanged for (0.5) share Class C Common 40¢ par 07/23/1987
Name changed to Security National Financial Corp. 12/27/1990

SNOBRO ENTERPRISES INC (BC)
Name changed to SIQ Mountain Industries Inc. 10/05/2017

SNOCONE SYS INC (NV)
Each share old Common $0.001 par exchanged for (0.2) share new Common $0.001 par 03/14/2005
Name changed to Who's Your Daddy, Inc. 04/21/2010
Who's Your Daddy, Inc. name changed to FITT Highway Products, Inc. 07/19/2010 which name changed to Global Future City Holding Inc. 10/29/2014

SNOOSE ENERGY & DEVELOPMENT INC. (ID)
Name changed to Terra International Inc. in 1983
Terra International name changed to Sans Prix Cosmetics, Inc. 11/1/87 which name changed to International Jet Engine Supply, Inc. 9/25/91

SNOOSE MINING CO. (ID)
Each share Common 25¢ par exchanged for (0.25) share Common $1 par 7/22/64
Name changed to Snoose Energy & Development Inc. in 1981
Snoose Energy & Development Inc. name changed to Terra International Inc. in 1983 which name changed to Sans Prix Cosmetics, Inc. 11/1/87 which name changed to International Jet Engine Supply, Inc. 9/25/91

SNOOZEBOX HLDGS PLC (UNITED KINGDOM)
ADR agreement terminated 09/24/2018
ADR holders' equity unlikely

SNOW & SAIL SPORTS INC (DE)
Common $0.001 par split (28.5) for (1) by issuance of (27.5) additional shares payable 09/06/2006 to holders of record 08/28/2006 Ex date - 09/07/2006
Name changed to Andover Medical, Inc. 09/15/2006
Andover Medical, Inc. recapitalized as Hot Mama's Foods, Inc. 08/06/2013

SNOW EAGLE RES LTD (BC)
Recapitalized as FluroTech Ltd. 06/12/2018
Each share Common no par

exchanged for (0.22222222) share Common no par

SNOW LAKE GOLD MINES LTD. (ON)
Name changed to Snow Lake Mines Ltd. in 1956 which was recapitalized as Phoenix Canada Oil Co. Ltd. 3/8/60

SNOW LAKE MINES LTD. (ON)
Recapitalized as Phoenix Canada Oil Co. Ltd. on a (1) for (15) basis 3/8/60

SNOW MOUNTAIN WATER & POWER CO.
Acquired by Pacific Gas & Electric Co. in 1929
Details not available

SNOW SPORTS PUBLICATIONS, INC. (MN)
Attorney reported company out of business 00/00/1979
Details not available

SNOW SUMMIT SKI CORP (CA)
Acquired by Mammoth Resorts LLC 02/27/2015
Each share Common no par exchanged for $592.70161427 cash

SNOWBALL COM INC (DE)
Recapitalized 09/24/2001
Issue Information - 6,250,000 shares COM offered at $11 per share on 03/20/2000
Each share old Common $0.001 par exchanged for (0.33333333) share new Common $0.001 par 03/06/2001
Recapitalized from Snowball, Inc. to Snowball.com, Inc. 09/24/2001
Each share new Common $0.001 par exchanged for (0.16666666) share Common $0.001 par 09/24/2001
Name changed to IGN Entertainment, Inc. 05/10/2002
(See IGN Entertainment, Inc.)

SNOWBIRD INVTS LTD (AB)
Struck off register for failure to file annual returns 10/01/1995

SNOWBIRD VACATIONS INTERNATIONAL INC (ON)
Reincorporated 11/12/1997
Place of incorporation changed from (BC) to (ONT) 11/12/1997
Name changed to inTRAVELnet.Com Inc. 03/22/1999
inTRAVELnet.Com Inc. recapitalized as Forum National Investments Ltd. 07/05/2002

SNOWCAP WATERS LTD (BC)
Recapitalized as Seacrest Development Corp. 4/30/98
Each share Common no par exchanged for (0.1) share Common no par
Seacrest Development Corp. recapitalized as Norzan Enterprises Ltd. 3/18/2004

SNOWDEN YELLOWKNIFE MINES, LTD. (ON)
Dissolved 3/30/59

SNOWDON MINING & EXPLORATIONS LTD. (QC)
Dissolved for failure to file reports and pay fees 8/29/92

SNOWDON RES CORP (NV)
SEC revoked common stock registration 02/22/2013

SNOWDRIFT BASE METAL MINES LTD. (ON)
Merged into Indian Mountain Metal Mines Ltd. 06/24/1971
Each share Capital Stock $1 par exchanged for (0.117647) share Capital Stock $1 par
Indian Mountain Metal Mines Ltd. merged into Initiative Explorations Inc. 02/13/1980 which merged into Canhorn Chemical Corp. 04/26/1995 which merged into Nayarit Gold Inc. 05/02/2005 which merged into Capital Gold Corp. 08/02/2010 which merged into Gammon Gold Inc. (QC) 04/08/2011 which reincorporated in Ontario as AuRico Gold Inc. 06/14/2011 which merged into Alamos Gold Inc. (New) 07/06/2015

SNOWFIELD RES LTD (BC)
Recapitalized as Snowfield Development Corp. 4/28/2000
Each share Common no par exchanged for (0.25) share Common no par

SNOWRUNNER INC (CO)
Name changed to Sled Dogs Co. (CO) 11/29/1994
Sled Dogs Co. (CO) reincorporated in Nevada as Xdogs.com, Inc. 05/10/1999 which recapitalized as Xdogs Inc. 08/22/2000 which name changed to Avalon Oil & Gas, Inc. 07/22/2005 which name changed to Groove Botanicals, Inc. 05/14/2018

SNOWSHOE GOLD MINES LTD. (QC)
Completely liquidated 08/12/1963
Each share Capital Stock $1 par exchanged for (0.25) share Western Quebec Mines Co. Ltd. Capital Stock $1 par
Western Quebec Mines Co. Ltd. name changed to Western Quebec Mines Inc. 06/00/1986 which merged into Wesdome Gold Mines Ltd. 07/18/2007

SNOWSTORM HYDRAULIC CO. (CO)
Charter revoked for failure to pay taxes 09/03/1913

SNOWY PEAK FINL INC (CO)
Name changed to Consolidated Builders Supply Corp. 5/7/98
Consolidated Builders Supply Corp. recapitalized as Global Business Information Directory, Inc. 3/24/99 which recapitalized as Jimmy Vu's Take Out, Inc. 3/4/2005
(See Jimmy Vu's Take Out, Inc.)

SNP HEALTH SPLIT CORP (ON)
Issue Information - 6,600,000 CAP SHS offered at $11.15 per share and 3,300,000 PFD offered at $25 per share on 01/28/2002
Preferred Shares no par called for redemption at $25 on 02/11/2009
Capital Shares no par called for redemption at $2.6507 on 02/11/2009

SNP SPLIT CORP (ON)
Preferred called for redemption at USD$25 on 06/02/2006
Class B Preferred Ser. 1 called for redemption at USD$10.25 on 06/03/2011
Capital Shares no par called for redemption at USD$3.9418 on 06/03/2011

SNRG CORP (NV)
SEC revoked common stock registration 06/21/2012

SNS PRECIOUS METALS INC (BC)
Recapitalized as Gold Finder Explorations Ltd. 10/08/2010
Each share Common no par exchanged for (0.1) share Common no par
Gold Finder Explorations Ltd. recapitalized as Venzee Technologies Inc. 01/05/2018

SNS SILVER CORP (BC)
Name changed to SNS Precious Metals Inc. 05/17/2010
SNS Precious Metals Inc. recapitalized as Gold Finder Explorations Ltd. 10/08/2010 which recapitalized as Venzee Technologies Inc. 01/05/2018

SNT CLEANING INC (NV)
Common $0.001 par split (6) for (1) by issuance of (5) additional shares payable 05/19/2009 to holders of record 05/15/2009 Ex date - 05/20/2009
Name changed to Orofino Gold Corp. 12/23/2009
Orofino Gold Corp. name changed to Bakken Energy Corp. 09/03/2014

SNT LTD (ON)
Completely liquidated 02/08/1996
Each Capital Share no par exchanged for first and final distribution of $19.1775 cash
Each Equity Dividend Share no par exchanged for first and final distribution of $12.6067 cash

SNTL CORP (DE)
Under plan of reorganization each share Common no par automatically became (1) SNTL Litigation Trust Trust Unit no par 7/18/2002

SNYDER CHEMICAL CORP. (NY)
Name changed to Synco Resins, Inc. 1/1/56
(See Synco Resins, Inc.)

SNYDER COMMUNICATIONS INC (DE)
Each share Common $0.001 par received distribution of (1/3) share Ventiv Health, Inc. Common $0.001 par payable 09/27/1999 to holders of record 09/20/1999 Ex date - 09/28/1999
Common $0.001 par reclassified as SNC Common $0.001 par 10/28/1999
Each share SNC Common $0.001 par received distribution of (0.25) share Circle.Com Common $0.001 par 10/28/1999
Merged into Havas Advertising S.A. 09/26/2000
Each share SNC Common $0.001 par exchanged for (1.371) Sponsored ADR's for Ordinary
Merged into Havas Advertising S.A. 06/27/2001
Each share Circle Com Common $0.001 par exchanged for (0.0937) Sponsored ADR for Ordinary
Havas Advertising S.A. name changed to Havas S.A. 05/24/2002
(See Havas S.A.)

SNYDER CORP (MI)
Stock Dividends - 10% 10/13/1967; 10% 10/18/1968; 10% 10/24/1969; 20% 10/17/1975; 20% 10/15/1976; 20% 10/14/1977; 20% 10/12/1979; 20% 10/17/1980
Merged into Giddings & Lewis, Inc. (Old) 03/02/1981
Each share Common $1 par exchanged for (0.478054) share Common $2 par
(See Giddings & Lewis, Inc. (Old))

SNYDER CNTY TR CO (SELINSGROVE, PA)
Common $10 par changed to $5 par and (1) additional share issued 06/28/1976
Stock Dividend - 100% 06/30/1976
Reorganized as Sun Bancorp, Inc. (PA) and Common $5 par changed to $2.50 par 11/26/1982
Sun Bancorp, Inc. (PA) merged into Omega Financial Corp. 10/01/2004 which merged into F.N.B. Corp. 04/01/2008

SNYDER OIL CORP (DE)
$4 Conv. Exchangeable Preferred 1¢ par called for redemption 1/3/95
$6 Depositary Conv. Preferred called for redemption at $25.90 on 12/1/97
Merged into Santa Fe Snyder Corp. 5/5/99
Each share Common 1¢ par exchanged for (2.05) shares Common 1¢ par
Santa Fe Snyder Corp. merged into Devon Energy Corp. (New) 8/29/2000

SNYDER OIL PARTNERS (DE)
Reincorporated 7/10/86
State of incorporation changed from (TX) to (DE) 7/10/86
Reorganized as Snyder Oil Corp. 3/23/90
Each Preference A Unit exchanged for (1.35) shares Common 1¢ par
Note: Holdings of (74) or fewer Preference A Units exchanged for $13.18 cash per Unit
Each Unit of Ltd. Partnership exchanged for (0.5) share Common 1¢ par
Note: Holdings of (199) or fewer Units exchanged for $4.88 cash per Unit
Snyder Oil Corp. merged into Santa Fe Snyder Corp. 5/5/99 which merged into Devon Energy Corp. (New) 8/29/2000

SNYDER STRYPES TR (DE)
Each share Structured Yield Product exchanged for (1.4426488) Havas Advertising S.A. Sponsored ADR for Ordinary, (0.2630651) share Snyder Communications Inc. Circle.Com Common $0.001 par and $0.4175 cash 10/18/2000
(See each company's listing)

SNYDER TOOL & ENGINEERING CO. (MI)
Each share Common no par exchanged for (2) shares Common $10 par 00/00/1935
Each share Common $10 par exchanged for (5) shares Common $1 par 00/00/1940
Stock Dividends - 20% 11/30/1950; 10% 06/29/1951; 10% 12/17/1951
Name changed to Snyder Corp. 11/19/1958
(See Snyder Corp.)

SNYDERS-LANCE INC (NC)
Acquired by Campbell Soup Co. 03/26/2018
Each share Common $0.83333333 par exchanged for $50 cash

SO ACT NETWORK INC (DE)
Name changed to Max Sound Corp. 03/15/2011

SOAPSTONE NETWORKS INC (DE)
Liquidation completed
Each share Common $0.0001 par received initial distribution of $0.76 cash payable 04/07/2010 to holders of record 07/31/2009
Each share Common $0.0001 par received second and final distribution of $0.00925 cash payable 12/21/2012 to holders of record 07/31/2009
Note: Certificates were not required to be surrendered and are without value

SOBEYS INC (NS)
Name changed 06/01/1999
Name changed from Sobeys Canada Inc. to Sobeys Inc. 06/01/1999
Merged into Empire Co., Ltd. 06/15/2007
Each share Common no par exchanged for $58 cash

SOBEYS STORES LTD (NS)
Class A Common no par split (2) for (1) by issuance of (1) additional share 10/13/66
Class B Common no par split (2) for (1) by issuance of (1) additional share 10/13/66
Class A Common no par split (3) for (1) by issuance of (2) additional shares 2/25/81
Class B Common no par split (3) for (1) by issuance of (2) additional shares 2/25/81
9% Conv. Preference 1981 Ser. $20 par for redemption 6/1/85
Class A Common no par split (3) for (1) by issuance of (2) additional shares 11/6/85
Class B Common no par split (3) for

(1) by issuance of (2) additional shares 11/6/85
Merged into Empire Co. Ltd. 5/15/87
Each share Class A Common no par exchanged for (1.6) shares Non-Vtg. Class A no par
Each share Class B Common no par exchanged for (1.6) shares Non-Vtg. Class A no par
(Additional Information in Active)

SOBIESKI BANCORP INC (DE)
Liquidation completed
Each share Common 1¢ par received initial distribution of $5.75 cash payable 09/30/2005 to holders of record 09/19/2005 Ex date - 10/03/2005
Each share Common 1¢ par received second distribution of $2.25 cash payable 10/02/2006 to holders of record 09/22/2006 Ex date - 10/03/2006
Each share Common 1¢ par received third distribution of $1 cash payable 03/30/2009 to holders of record 03/19/2009 Ex date - 03/31/2009
Each share Common 1¢ par received fourth distribution of $1 cash payable 12/22/2011 to holders of record 12/12/2011 Ex date - 12/23/2011
Each share Common 1¢ par received fifth and final distribution of $0.455 cash payable 07/24/2012 to holders of record 07/21/2012
Note: Certificates were not required to be surrendered and are without value

SOBIGA MINES LTD (QC)
Cease trade order effective in December 1980
Stockholders' equity unlikely

SOBIKS INTL FRANCHISING INC (FL)
Name changed to Quality Restaurant Ventures, Inc. and (24) additional shares issued 01/12/2004
Quality Restaurant Ventures, Inc. name changed to Airborne Security & Protective Services, Inc. (Ctfs. dated after 05/25/2010) 05/25/2010

SOBIKS SUBS (NV)
Each share old Common $0.001 par exchanged for (1/3) share new Common $0.001 par 12/5/95
Name changed to Interfoods of America Inc. 9/11/96
(See Interfoods of America Inc.)

SOCAL CAP CORP (BC)
Name changed to Empyrean Diagnostics Ltd. (BC) 08/05/1993
Empyrean Diagnostics Ltd. (BC) reincorporated in Wyoming 12/31/1996 which name changed to Empyrean Bioscience, Inc. (WY) 02/08/1999 which reincorporated in Delaware 03/21/2001
(See Empyrean Bioscience, Inc. (DE))

SOCAL-EQUITIES HOLDING CO. (UT)
Recapitalized as Micro-Thermology Corp. 09/26/1983
Each share Common $0.001 par exchanged for (0.2) share Common $0.005 par
Micro-Thermology Corp. name changed to Designers International Corp. 01/12/1985
(See Designers International Corp.)

SOCAL OIL & REFINING CO. (CA)
Each share Capital Stock $1 par exchanged for (18.2) shares Capital Stock 50¢ par 7/6/60
In process of liquidation
Each share Capital Stock 50¢ par exchanged for initial distribution of $0.50 cash 11/9/64
Each share Capital Stock 50¢ par received second distribution of $0.25 cash 4/26/65

Name changed to S.O.R. Liquidating Co. 5/5/65
(See S.O.R. Liquidating Co.)

SOCAL RES INC (NV)
Recapitalized as Art Guard Inc. 6/7/90
Each share Common $0.001 par exchanged for (0.02) share Common $0.001 par
Art Guard Inc. reorganized in Delaware as Computer Integration Corp. 4/27/94
(See Computer Integration Corp.)

SOCHINSKAYA TPS OJSC (RUSSIA)
Name changed to Inter RAO UES 10/06/2008
Inter RAO UES name changed to Inter RAO UES PJSC 09/29/2015

SOCHRYS COM INC (NV)
Name changed to Validian Corp. 2/6/2003

SOCIALWISE INC (CO)
Name changed to BillMyParents, Inc. 06/13/2011
BillMyParents, Inc. name changed to SpendSmart Payments Co. (CO) 02/28/2013 which reincorporated in Delaware as SpendSmart Networks, Inc. 06/20/2014

SOCIEDAD EMPRESA DE ESTONA DE ARACA
Acquired by Patino Mines & Enterprises Consolidated (Inc.) in 1932
Details not available

SOCIEDAD QUIMICA Y MINERA DE CHILE S A (CHILE)
ADR agreement terminated 06/05/2008
Each Sponsored ADR for Ser. A exchanged for $262.266372 cash

SOCIETA EDISON (ITALY)
Merged into Montecatini Edison S.p.A. 7/7/66
Each ADR for Capital Stock 2000 Lire par exchanged for (2) ADR's for Capital Stock 1000 Lire par
Montecatini Edison S.P.A. recapitalized as Montedison S.p.A. 6/19/87
(See Montedison S.p.A.)

SOCIETA FINANZIARI SIDERURGICA (ITALY)
Liquidated 00/00/1988
Details not available

SOCIETA GENERALE IMMOBILIARE DI LAVORI (ITALY)
Depositary agreement terminated 03/00/1973
Each CDR for Bearer 250 Lire par exchanged for (10) shares Italian Bearer 250 Lire par

SOCIETA INIZIATIVE AUTOSTRADALI E SERVIZI S P A (ITALY)
ADR agreement terminated 12/26/2017
No ADR's remain outstanding

SOCIETE ANONYME DES AUTOMOBILES PEUGEOT (FRANCE)
Each ADR for Bearer 62.50 Frcs. par exchanged for (2) ADR's for Bearer 31.25 Frcs. par 08/05/1963
ADR's for Bearer 31.25 Frcs. par changed to 35 Frcs. par 06/30/1964
Name changed to Peugeot S.A. 11/08/1966
Peugeot S.A. name changed to Peugeot-Citroen S.A. 09/30/1976
(See Peugeot-Citroen S.A.)

SOCIETE ANONYME FRANCAISE FERODO (FRANCE)
Name changed to Valeo 02/09/1990

SOCIETE D EXPL MINIERE MAZARIN INC (QC)
Name changed to Mazarin Mining Corp. Inc. 11/4/93

Mazarin Mining Corp. Inc. name changed to Mazarin Inc. 9/26/2000

SOCIETE DES AUTOMOBILES SIMCA (FRANCE)
ADR agreement terminated 01/17/1968
Each ADR for Capital Stock 100 Frcs. par exchanged for (1) share Capital Stock 100 Frcs. par
Note: Unexchanged ADR's were sold and the proceeds, if any, held for claim after 01/16/1969

SOCIETE EN COMMANDITE VENOIR I (QC)
Recapitalized as Coveinor Mines Inc. 03/03/1995
Each share Common no par exchanged for (0.25) share Common no par
(See Coveinor Mines Inc.)

SOCIETE EUROPEENE DE COMMUNICATION S A (LUXEMBOURG)
Merged into Netcom AB 11/6/2000
Each Sponsored ADR for Class A exchanged for (0.08695652) Sponsored ADR for Class A
Each Sponsored ADR for Class B exchanged for (0.08695652) Sponsored ADR for Class A
Netcom AB name changed to Tele2 AB 2/20/2001
(See Tele2 AB)

SOCIETE INDUSTRIELLE DE MECANIQUE CARROSSERIE AUTOMOBILE (FRANCE)
Name changed to Simca, S.A. 03/24/1959
(See Simca, S.A.)

SOCIETE MINIERE LOUVEM INC (QC)
Merged into Richmont Mines Inc. 06/30/2010
Each share Common no par exchanged for (0.18518519) share Common no par
Richmont Mines Inc. merged into Alamos Gold Inc. (New) 11/24/2017

SOCIETE NATIONALE DES PETROLES D'AQUITAINE (FRANCE)
Name changed to Societe Nationale Elf Aquitaine 07/09/1976
Societe Nationale Elf Aquitaine name changed to ELF Aquitaine 02/22/1994

SOCIETE NATIONALE ELF AQUITAINE (FRANCE)
Each Unsponsored ADR for Bearer 50 Frcs. par exchanged for (0.5) Sponsored ADR for Bearer 50 Frcs. par 06/27/1988
Sponsored ADR's for Bearer 50 Frcs. par split (2) for (1) by issuance of (1) additional ADR 12/14/1990
Stock Dividend - 20% 03/30/1979
Name changed to ELF Aquitaine 02/22/1994
ELF Aquitaine acquired by Total Fina Elf S.A. 9/18/2000 which name changed back to Total S.A. 05/07/2003

SOCIETY BRAND CLOTHES, INC. (IL)
Name changed to Industrial Development Corp. 00/00/1954
(See Industrial Development Corp.)

SOCIETY CORP (OH)
Voting Trust Agreement terminated 9/16/68
Each VTC for Common $1 par exchanged for (1) share Common $1 par
Common $1 par split (2) for (1) by issuance of (1) additional share 7/15/70
$4 Conv. Preferred Ser. A $100 par called for redemption 5/15/78
$4 Conv. Preferred Ser. B $100 par called for redemption 5/15/78

$4.50 Conv. Preferred Ser. C $100 par called for redemption 5/15/78
Common $1 par split (2) for (1) by issuance of (1) additional share 2/24/87
Common $1 par split (2) for (1) by issuance of (1) additional share 3/22/93
Stock Dividend - 100% 9/15/78
Under plan of merger name changed to KeyCorp (New) 3/1/94

SOCIETY FDS (MA)
Earnings Momentum Equity Fund no par merged into Growth Stock Fund 03/30/1994
Details not available
Reincorporated under the laws of Delaware as Victory Portfolios and Growth Stock Fund no par, Ohio Tax Free Bond Fund no par, Special Growth Stock Fund no par, Tax Exempt Fund no par, U.S. Government Income Fund no par, and Value Stock Fund no par reclassified as Growth Fund $0.001 par, Ohio Municipal Bond Fund $0.001 par, Special Growth Fund $0.001 par, Tax Free Money Market Fund $0.001 par, Government Mortgage Fund $0.001 par and Value Fund $0.001 par respectively 09/01/1994
Note: Balanced Fund no par, Diversified Stock Fund no par, Intermediate Income Fund no par, International Growth Fund no par, Investment Quality Bond Fund no par, Limited Term Income Fund no par, Ohio Regional Stock Fund no par, Prime Obligations Fund no par, Special Value Fund no par, Stock Index Fund no par, and U.S. Government Obligations Fund no par all changed to $0.001 par 09/01/1994

SOCIETY FOR SVGS (HARTFORD, CT)
Common $1 par split (2) for (1) by issuance of (1) additional share 03/03/1986
Stock Dividend - 10% 12/19/1986
Reorganized under the laws of Delaware as Society for Savings Bancorp, Inc. 06/01/1987
Each share Common $1 par exchanged for (1) share Common $1 par
Society for Savings Bancorp, Inc. merged into Bank of Boston Corp. 07/09/1993 which name changed to BankBoston Corp. 04/25/1997 which merged into Fleet Boston Corp. 10/01/1999 which name changed to FleetBoston Financial Corp. 04/18/2000 which merged into Bank of America Corp. 04/01/2004

SOCIETY FOR SVGS BANCORP INC (DE)
Merged into Bank of Boston Corp. 07/09/1993
Each share Common $1 par exchanged for (0.8) share Common $2.25 par
Bank of Boston Corp. name changed to BankBoston Corp. 04/25/1997 which merged into Fleet Boston Corp. 10/01/1999 which name changed to FleetBoston Financial Corp. 04/18/2000 which merged into Bank of America Corp. 04/01/2004

SOCKET COMMUNICATIONS INC (DE)
Issue Information - 500,000 UNITS consisting of (2) shares COM and (1) WT offered at $12 per Unit on 06/06/1995
Name changed to Socket Mobile, Inc. 05/01/2008

SOCKEYE SEAFOOD GROUP INC (NV)
Name changed to Stargold Mines, Inc. 11/24/2006

FINANCIAL INFORMATION, INC.   SOC-SOF

(See Stargold Mines, Inc.)

SOCONY MOBIL OIL CO (NY)
Stock Dividend - 25% 6/18/56
Name changed to Mobil Oil Corp. 5/18/66
Mobil Oil Corp. reorganized as Mobil Corp. 6/21/76 which merged into Exxon Mobil Corp. 11/30/99

SOCONY-VACUUM CORP.
Name changed to Socony-Vacuum Oil Co., Inc. and Capital Stock $25 par changed to $15 par in 1934
Socony-Vacuum Oil Co., Inc. name changed to Socony Mobil Oil Co., Inc. 4/29/55 which name changed to Mobil Oil Corp. 5/18/66 which reorganized as Mobil Corp. 6/21/76 which merged into Exxon Mobil Corp. 11/30/99

SOCONY VACUUM OIL INC (NY)
Name changed to Socony Mobil Oil Co., Inc. 4/29/55
Socony Mobil Oil Co., Inc. name changed to Mobil Oil Corp. 5/18/66 which reorganized as Mobil Corp. 6/21/76 which merged into Exxon Mobil Corp. 11/30/99

SOCRATES TECHNOLOGIES CORP (DE)
SEC revoked common stock registration 11/16/2005
Stockholders' equity unlikely

SODAK GAMING INC (SD)
Common no par split (2) for (1) by issuance of (1) additional share payable 09/27/1996 to holders of record 09/13/1996
Merged into International Game Technology 09/01/1999
Each share Common $0.001 par exchanged for $10 cash

SODAK URANIUM & MINING CO., INC. (DE)
Charter forfeited 7/1/61

SODARCAN INC (CANADA)
Acquired by Aon Reed Stenhouse Acquisition Corp. 07/03/1997
Each share Common no par exchanged for $3.85 cash

SODEN (G.A.) & CO.
Bankrupt in 1934

SODEXHO ALLIANCE S A (FRANCE)
Name changed to Sodexo 02/13/2008

SODEXHO MARRIOTT SVCS INC (DE)
Merged into Sodexho Alliance, S.A. 06/20/2001
Each share Common $1 par exchanged for $32 cash

SODISCO-HOWDEN GROUP INC (QC)
Each share $0.65 Conv. 1st Preferred Ser. 2 no par exchanged for (71.79) shares Common no par 5/13/99
Each share old Common no par exchanged for (0.05) share new Common no par 5/19/2000
Acquired by CanWel Building Materials Ltd. 2/22/2005
Each share new Common no par exchanged for $3.25 cash

SODISCO INC (QC)
Acquired by Unigesco Inc. 6/25/89
Each share Common no par exchanged for $10.75 cash

SOEFL INC (NV)
Name changed to Surepure, Inc. 09/14/2011

SOFAMOR/DANEK GROUP INC (IN)
Merged into Medtronic, Inc. (MN) 01/27/1999
Each share Common no par exchanged for (1.65159) shares Common 10¢ par
Medtronic, Inc. (MN) reincorporated in Ireland as Medtronic PLC 01/27/2015

SOFICAP ACQUISITIONS INC (AB)
Issue Information - 2,000,000 shares COM offered at $0.15 per share on 11/15/2001
Delisted from NEX 10/03/2006

SOFT LANDING LABS LTD (IL)
Each share old Common $0.000001 par exchanged for (0.000002) share new Common $0.000001 par 02/02/2016
Note: In effect holders received $0.30 cash per share and public interest was eliminated

SOFT-LITE BAY STATE OPTICAL CO., INC. (ME)
Liquidation completed 3/22/57
Details not available

SOFTBANK (POLAND)
Sponsored Reg. S GDR's for Ordinary split (2) for (1) by issuance of (1) additional GDR payable 07/07/2000 to holders of record 07/05/2000 Ex date - 07/06/2000
Name changed to Asseco Poland S.A. 02/07/2007

SOFTBANK CORP (JAPAN)
ADR's for Common split (20) for (1) by issuance of (19) additional ADR's payable 02/14/2011 to holders of record 02/11/2011 Ex date - 02/15/2011
Basis changed from (1:10) to (1:0.5) 02/15/2011
Name changed to SoftBank Group Corp. 07/06/2015

SOFTBRANDS INC (DE)
Merged into Steel Holdings, Inc. 08/13/2009
Each share Common 1¢ par exchanged for $0.92 cash
Note: An additional distribution of $0.00736146 cash per share was made from escrow 12/31/2012

SOFTCAN DISTRG LTD (BC)
Name changed to Sona Systems (Canada) Ltd. 3/3/86
Sona Systems (Canada) Ltd. recapitalized as Startec Marketing Corp. 5/13/88 which recapitalized as Vitality Products Inc. 2/9/93

SOFTCARE EC INC (BC)
Name changed 10/05/2001
Name changed from Softcare EC.com, Inc. to Softcare EC Inc. 10/05/2001
Recapitalized as Open EC Technologies, Inc. 06/23/2003
Each share Common no par exchanged for (0.1) share Common no par
(See Open EC Technologies, Inc.)

SOFTCHOICE CORP NEW (CANADA)
Acquired by Goliath Acquisition Inc. 06/20/2013
Each share Common no par exchanged for $20 cash

SOFTCHOICE CORP OLD (CANADA)
Merged into Softchoice Corp. (New) 05/15/2002
Each share Common no par exchanged for (0.421) share Common no par
(See Softchoice Corp. (New))

SOFTCOP CORP (ON)
Delisted from Canadian Dealer Network 5/31/96

SOFTDESK INC (DE)
Merged into Autodesk Inc. 3/31/97
Each share Common 1¢ par exchanged for (0.477327) share Common no par

SOFTEN TECHNOLOGY CORP (NY)
Dissolved by proclamation 12/24/91

SOFTFUND CAP PARTNERS INC (BC)
Recapitalized as Sand River Resources Ltd. 06/30/1994
Each share Common no par exchanged for (0.25) share Common no par
Sand River Resources Ltd. recapitalized as Rio Fortuna Exploration Corp. 11/30/1999 which recapitalized as Fortune River Resource Corp. 12/21/2005 which merged into Bravada Gold Corp. (New) 01/07/2011

SOFTGUARD SYS INC (NV)
Each share Common $0.001 par exchanged for (0.1) share Common 1¢ par 02/08/1988
Charter revoked for failure to file reports and pay fees 05/01/1993

SOFTIMAGE INC (QC)
Acquired by Microsoft Corp. 6/27/94
Each share Common no par exchanged for either (0.458) share Softimage Inc. Non-Vtg. Exchangeable Share or (0.458) share Microsoft Corp. Common $0.001 par

SOFTKEY INTL INC (DE)
Name changed to Learning Co. Inc. 10/24/1996
Learning Co. Inc. merged into Mattel, Inc. 05/13/1999

SOFTKEY SOFTWARE PRODS INC NEW (ON)
Merged into Mattel, Inc. 01/07/2003
Each Non-Vtg. Exchangeable Share no par exchanged for (1.2) shares Common $1 par

SOFTKEY SOFTWARE PRODS INC OLD (ON)
Merged into SoftKey International Inc. 02/04/1994
Each share Common no par and Non-Vtg. Exchangeable Share no par exchanged for either (0.36) share SoftKey International Inc. Common 1¢ par or (0.36) share SoftKey Software Products Inc. (New) Non-Vtg. Exchangeable Share no par
Note: Each SoftKey Software Products Inc. (New) Non-Vtg. Exchangeable Share is exchangeable share-for-share with SoftKey International Inc. Common
SoftKey International Inc. name changed to Learning Co. Inc. 10/24/1996 which merged into Mattel, Inc. 05/13/1999

SOFTLEAD INC (NV)
Recapitalized as Sysorex Global Holdings Corp. 06/03/2011
Each share Common $0.001 par exchanged for (0.05) share Common $0.001 par
Sysorex Global Holdings Corp. name changed to Sysorex Global 01/04/2016 which recapitalized as Inpixon 03/01/2017

SOFTLINK INC (NV)
Name changed to Inchorus.com 03/24/2000
Inchorus.com recapitalized as Lifestyle Enhancement Systems Inc. 09/12/2002 which name changed to Australian Agricultural & Property Development Inc. 12/08/2003 which name changed to WorldSource, Inc. 06/21/2005
(See WorldSource, Inc.)

SOFTLOCK COM INC (DE)
Chapter 11 bankruptcy proceedings converted to Chapter 7 on 12/17/2002
Stockholders' equity unlikely

SOFTNET INDS INC (DE)
Name changed to I Crystal, Inc. 07/29/1999
I Crystal, Inc. name changed to ICrystal, Inc. 06/15/2000 which name changed to ALL Fuels & Energy Co. 05/07/2007 which recapitalized as All Energy Corp. 01/17/2012

SOFTNET SYS INC (DE)
Reincorporated 04/13/1999
State of incorporation changed from (NY) to (DE) 04/13/1999
Name changed to American Independence Corp. 11/14/2002
(See American Independence Corp.)

SOFTNET TECHNOLOGY CORP (NV)
Each share old Common $0.001 par exchanged for (0.1) share new Common $0.001 par 04/18/2008
Note: Holders of (9) or fewer pre-split shares will receive $0.10 cash per share upon written request
Charter revoked for failure to file reports and pay taxes 02/28/2010

SOFTPOINT INC (NV)
Each share old Common 1¢ par exchanged for (0.1) share new Common 1¢ par 11/8/91
Recapitalized as Acquest Corp. 11/4/96
Each share new Common 1¢ par exchanged for (0.1) share Common 1¢ par

SOFTQUAD INTL INC (NB)
Reincorporated 08/31/1994
Reincorporated 09/18/1998
Place of incorporation changed from (BC) to (ON) 08/31/1994
Each share old Common no par exchanged for (0.4) share new Common no par 01/25/1996
Place of incorporation changed from (ON) to (NB) 09/18/1998
Name changed to NewKidco International Inc. 01/28/1999
(See NewKidco International Inc.)

SOFTQUAD SOFTWARE LTD (DE)
Merged into Corel Corp. 3/15/2002
Each share Common $0.001 par exchanged for (0.519) share Common no par
(See Corel Corp.)

SOFTROCK PETE LTD (AB)
Name changed to Softrock Minerals Ltd. 8/27/97

SOFTSEL COMPUTER PRODS INC (DE)
Name changed to Merisel, Inc. 08/28/1990
(See Merisel, Inc.)

SOFTSTONE INC (DE)
Recapitalized as TS Electronics, Inc. 08/15/2003
Each (21.8045) shares Common $0.001 par exchanged for (1) share Common $0.001 par
TS Electronics, Inc. name changed to China Pharma Holdings, Inc. (DE) 05/04/2006 which reincorporated in Nevada 12/27/2012

SOFTWALL EQUIP CORP (UT)
Each share old Common $0.001 par exchanged for (0.01) share new Common $0.001 par 07/12/2002
Note: Holders of (101) to (10,000) shares will receive (100) shares only
Holders of (100) shares or fewer were not affected by the reverse split
Name changed to Inncardio, Inc. 02/28/2005
Inncardio, Inc. name changed to Long-e International, Inc. 01/11/2007
(See Long-e International, Inc.)

SOFTWARE AG INTERNATIONAL, INC. (DE)
Name changed to Software AG Systems Group Inc. 12/22/81
Software AG Systems Group Inc. name changed to Software AG Systems Inc. (Old) 10/26/83
(See Software AG Systems Inc. (Old))

SOFTWARE AG SYS INC NEW (DE)
Issue Information - 7,700,000 shares COM offered at $10 per share on 11/18/1997
Name changed to Saga Systems, Inc. 5/24/99
(See Saga Systems, Inc.)

SOF-SOL

SOFTWARE AG SYS INC OLD (DE)
Merged into Jupiter Acquisition Corp. in 1988
Each share Common 1¢ par exchanged for $11.50 cash

SOFTWARE AG SYSTEMS GROUP INC. (DE)
Name changed to Software AG Systems Inc. (Old) 10/26/83
(See Software AG Systems Inc. (Old))

SOFTWARE APPLICATIONS CORP (NY)
Name changed to Kairos Corp. 06/24/1971
(See Kairos Corp.)

SOFTWARE ARTISTRY INC (IN)
Merged into International Business Machines Corp. 1/27/98
Each share Common no par exchanged for $24.50 cash

SOFTWARE COM INC (DE)
Merged into Phone.com, Inc. 11/17/2000
Each share Common $0.001 par exchanged for (1.6105) shares Common $0.001 par
Phone.com, Inc. name changed to Openwave Systems Inc. 11/20/2000 which name changed to Unwired Planet, Inc. 05/09/2012 which name changed to Great Elm Capital Group, Inc. 06/17/2016

SOFTWARE CONNECTION INC (NV)
Name changed to Swissoil Corp. 06/07/1984
(See Swissoil Corp.)

SOFTWARE CTL SYS INTL INC (AB)
Delisted from Canadian Venture Exchange 05/31/2001

SOFTWARE DELIVERY SYS CORP (FL)
Name changed to Boyle International Inc. 6/20/97

SOFTWARE DEVELOPERS INC (DE)
Name changed to Netegrity Inc. 07/08/1996
(See Netegrity Inc.)

SOFTWARE DISTR NETWORK INC (CO)
Plan of reorganization under Chapter 11 Federal Bankruptcy proceedings confirmed 02/24/1986
Stockholders' equity unlikely

SOFTWARE ETC STORES INC (DE)
Merged into NeoStar Retail Group, Inc. 12/19/94
Each share Common 1¢ par exchanged for (1) share Common 1¢ par
(See NeoStar Retail Group, Inc.)

SOFTWARE GAMING CORP (ON)
Recapitalized as Xperia Corp. 11/09/2001
Each share Common no par exchanged for (0.16666666) share Common no par
Xperia Corp. recapitalized as Xgen Ventures Inc. 11/26/2004
(See Xgen Ventures Inc.)

SOFTWARE HOLDRS TR (DE)
Trust terminated
Each Depositary Receipt received first and final distribution of $53.091175 cash payable 01/08/2013 to holders of record 12/24/2012

SOFTWARE NET CORP (DE)
Issue Information - 5,000,000 shares COM offered at $9 per share on 06/17/1998
Name changed to Beyond.com Corp. 12/21/98
(See Beyond.com Corp.)

SOFTWARE OF EXCELLENCE INTL INC (FL)
Name changed to Systems of Excellence Inc. 2/9/96
(See Systems of Excellence Inc.)

SOFTWARE PROFESSIONALS INC (CA)
Issue Information - 1,000,000 shares COM offered at $5.50 per share on 04/20/1994
Name changed to Enlighten Software Solutions, Inc. (CA) 05/21/1996
Enlighten Software Solutions, Inc. (CA) reorganized in Delaware as Diversified Opportunities, Inc. 02/12/2008 which name changed to Sugarmade, Inc. 07/15/2011

SOFTWARE PUBG CORP (CA)
Common no par split (3) for (2) by issuance of (0.5) additional share 11/20/1989
Merged into Allegro New Media, Inc. 12/27/1996
Each share Common no par exchanged for (0.26805) share Common $0.001 par
Allegro New Media, Inc. name changed to Software Publishing Corporation Holdings, Inc. 06/16/1997 which name changed to Vizacom Inc. 07/15/1999
(See Vizacom Inc.)

SOFTWARE PUBG CORP HLDGS INC (DE)
Each share old Common $0.001 par exchanged for (1/3) share new Common $0.001 par 05/27/1998
Name changed to Vizacom Inc. 07/15/1999
(See Vizacom Inc.)

SOFTWARE SEC SYS INC (UT)
Each share old Common $0.0005 par exchanged for (0.02) share new Common $0.0005 par 04/20/1992
Charter expired 02/13/2002

SOFTWARE SVCS AMER INC (MA)
Stock Dividend - 25% 2/28/85
Involuntarily dissolved 8/31/98

SOFTWARE SPECTRUM INC (TX)
Merged into Level 3 Communications, Inc. 06/18/2002
Each share Common 1¢ par exchanged for $37 cash

SOFTWARE SYS INC (DE)
Charter forfeited for failure to maintain a resident agent 12/30/1973

SOFTWARE TECHNOLOGIES CORP (CA)
Issue Information - 4,000,000 shares OC-COM offered at $12 per share on 04/27/2000
Name changed to SeeBeyond Technology Corp. (CA) 11/1/2000
SeeBeyond Technology Corp. (CA) reincorporated in Delaware 7/9/2001
(See Sun Microsystems, Inc.)

SOFTWARE TOOLWORKS INC (DE)
Each (150) shares Common $0.001 par exchanged for (1) share Common 1¢ par 9/12/88
Common 1¢ par split (2) for (1) by issuance of (1) additional share 4/4/90
Merged into Pearson Inc. 5/2/94
Each share Common 1¢ par exchanged for $14.75 cash

SOFTWARE 2000 INC (MA)
Name changed to Infinium Software, Inc. 2/17/97
(See Infinium Software, Inc.)

SOFTWORKS INC (DE)
Merged into EMC Corp. 01/27/2000
Each share Common $0.001 par exchanged for $10 cash

SOGELEC AMER (ID)
Name changed to Allmine Inc. 12/00/1994
Allmine Inc. recapitalized as Ad Art Electronic Sign Corp. 10/22/1996
(See Ad Art Electronic Sign Corp.)

SOGEMINES LTD (CANADA)
Each share 6% Preferred $10 par exchanged for (1) share Common no par 09/09/1965
Each share Ordinary $1 par exchanged for (0.1) share Common no par 09/09/1965
Name changed to Genstar Ltd. 02/25/1969
Genstar Ltd. name changed to Genstar Corp. 06/15/1981
(See Genstar Corp.)

SOGEN FDS INC (MD)
Overseas Fund $0.001 par reclassified as Overseas Fund Class A $0.001 par 04/24/1998
Name changed to First Eagle SoGen Funds, Inc. 01/07/2000
First Eagle SoGen Funds, Inc. name changed to First Eagle Funds, Inc. (MD) 12/30/2002 which reincorporated in Delaware as First Eagle Funds 11/04/2004

SOGEN INTL FD INC (DE)
Reincorporated 07/17/1985
State of incorporation changed from (DE) to (MD) and Common $1 par changed to $0.001 par 07/17/1985
Under plan of reorganization each share Common $0.001 par automatically became (1) share SoGen Funds, Inc. International Fund Class A $0.001 par 07/31/1998
SoGen Funds, Inc. name changed to First Eagle SoGen Funds, Inc. 01/07/2000
(See First Eagle SoGen Funds, Inc.)

SOGENA INC (QC)
Each share Common $5 par exchanged for (5) shares Common $1 par 7/19/72
Company wound up in 1987
Details not available

SOGEPET LTD (ON)
Reincorporated under the laws of Alberta as High Bullen Resources Ltd. 01/20/1995
High Bullen Resources Ltd. merged into Highridge Exploration Ltd. 07/31/1996 which merged into Talisman Energy Inc. 08/05/1999
(See Talisman Energy Inc.)

SOGEVEX INC (QC)
Merged into Les Tourbieres Premier Ltee/ Premier Peat Moss Ltd. 05/27/1989
Details not available

SOGO CAP INC (AB)
Struck off the register for failure to file annual returns 08/01/1999

SOHIO EXPL CORP (BC)
Recapitalized as Sensat Technologies Ltd. 04/17/1986
Each (3.5) shares Common no par exchanged for (1) share Common no par
(See Sensat Technologies Ltd.)

SOHN BREWING CO.
Bankrupt in 1935

SOHO RES CORP (BC)
Recapitalized as Telson Resources Inc. 01/17/2013
Each share Common no par exchanged for (0.125) share Common no par
Telson Resources Inc. name changed to Telson Mining Corp. 02/21/2018

SOHR GAS & OIL, INC. (UT)
Name changed to Hi-tec Mineral Recovery, Inc. 8/25/86
(See Hi-tec Mineral Recovery, Inc.)

SOHU COM INC (DE)
Completely liquidated 06/01/2018
Each share Common $0.001 par received first and final distribution of (1) Sohu.com Ltd. Sponsored ADR for Ordinary

SOIL BUILDERS INTERNATIONAL CORP. (DE)
Name changed to Aluminum & Chemical Corp. 11/7/56
(See Aluminum & Chemical Corp.)

SOIL SOLIDIFIERS, INC. (MN)
Adjudicated bankrupt 10/10/68
No stockholders' equity

SOILIFE HUMUS CO. (DE)
Charter cancelled and declared inoperative and void for non-payment of taxes 10/1/36

SOJITZ CORP (JAPAN)
ADR agreement terminated 03/23/2010
No ADR's remain outstanding

SOJOURN VENTURES INC (BC)
Recapitalized as Sojourn Explorations Inc. 08/24/2017
Each share Common no par exchanged for (0.33333333) share Common no par

SOK PPTYS LTD (CANADA)
Name changed to Impact Telemedia International Ltd. 08/03/1990
Impact Telemedia International Ltd. name changed to UC'NWIN Systems Ltd. (Canada) 07/17/1992 which reincorporated in Delaware as UC'NWIN Systems Corp. 12/11/1995 which recapitalized as Winner's Edge.com, Inc. 10/29/1999 which name changed to Sealant Solutions Inc. 08/06/2001 which name changed to PowerChannel, Inc. 07/28/2003 which recapitalized as Qualibou Energy Inc. 02/05/2008

SOKO FITNESS & SPA GROUP INC (DE)
Acquired by Queen Beauty & Wellness Group Ltd. 07/27/2011
Each share Common $0.001 par exchanged for $4.50 cash

SOL MELIA S A (SPAIN)
144A Sponsored ADR's for Ordinary split (3) for (1) by issuance of (2) additional ADR's payable 08/11/1999 to holders of record 08/06/1999
Reg. S Sponsored ADR's for Ordinary split (3) for (1) by issuance of (2) additional ADR's payable 08/11/1999 to holders of record 08/06/1999
Name changed to Melia Hotels International S.A. 03/07/2014
(See Melia Hotels International S.A.)

SOL PETROLEO S A (ARGENTINA)
Stock Dividends - 156.6213% payable 01/17/1998 to holders of record 01/16/1998; 4.96% payable 10/20/2011 to holders of record 07/15/2011; 4.9639% payable 02/11/2015 to holders of record 02/06/2015 Ex date - 02/04/2015; 8.9868% payable 02/20/2015 to holders of record 02/17/2015 Ex date - 02/12/2015
Name changed to Carboclor, S.A. 06/19/2015
(See Carboclor, S.A.)

SOL-VENTURES INC (UT)
Name changed to Sara Care, Inc. 01/25/1988
(See Sara Care, Inc.)

SOLA BASIC INDS INC (WI)
Common $1 par split (3) for (2) by issuance of (0.5) additional share 10/30/1967
Common $1 par split (3) for (2) by issuance of (0.5) additional share 11/12/1976
Merged into General Signal Corp. 09/30/1977
Each share Common $1 par exchanged for (0.7) share Common $1 par
Each share 4.5% Preferred Ser. A $25 par exchanged for $20.10 principal amount of 8.85% 10-Year Promissory Notes or $20.10 cash 00/00/1979
General Signal Corp. merged into SPX Corp. 10/06/1998

SOLA INTL INC (DE)
Merged into Sun Acquisition, Inc. 3/22/2005

FINANCIAL INFORMATION, INC.

Each share Common 1¢ par exchanged for $28 cash

SOLA RESOURCE CORP (AB)
Reincorporated 07/28/2004
Place of incorporation changed from (BC) to (AB) 07/28/2004
Recapitalized as Cancana Resources Corp. (AB) 01/24/2011
Each share Common no par exchanged for (0.1) share Common no par
Cancana Resources Corp. (AB) reincorporated in British Columbia 08/12/2015 which reorganized as Meridian Mining S.E 11/28/2016

SOLACE RES CORP (BC)
Name changed to First Graphite Corp. 03/27/2012
First Graphite Corp. recapitalized as Desert Star Resources Ltd. (Old) 01/21/2013 which merged into Desert Star Resources Ltd. (New) 04/15/2015 which name changed to Kutcho Copper Corp. 12/21/2017

SOLAIA VENTURES INC (BC)
Recapitalized as Trivello Ventures Inc. 01/22/2003
Each share Common no par exchanged for (0.08333333) share Common no par
Trivello Ventures Inc. name changed to Trivello Energy Corp. 05/04/2006 which name changed to Equitas Resources Corp. 10/19/2010 which name changed to Altamira Gold Corp. 04/18/2017

SOLANA PETE CORP (AB)
Recapitalized as Q-Gold Resources Ltd. (AB) 06/02/2005
Each share Common no par exchanged for (1/9) share Common no par
Q-Gold Resources Ltd. (AB) reincorporated in British Columbia 12/30/2011

SOLANA RES LTD (AB)
Merged into Gran Tierra Energy Inc. (NV) 11/17/2008
Each share Common no par exchanged for (0.9527918) share Common $0.001 par
Gran Tierra Energy Inc. (NV) reincorporated in Delaware 10/31/2016

SOLANBRIDGE GROUP INC (NV)
Reincorporated under the laws of Maryland and Common $0.001 par changed to $0.00001 par 10/16/2013

SOLANEX MGMT INC (NV)
Name changed to Solanbridge Group, Inc. (NV) 04/11/2011
Solanbridge Group, Inc. (NV) reincorporated in Maryland 10/16/2013

SOLAR ACQUISITION CORP (FL)
SEC revoked common stock registration 12/24/2015

SOLAR AGE MFG CORP (DE)
Reincorporated under the laws of Nevada as Solar Age Industries, Inc. 08/20/1984
Solar Age Industries, Inc. name changed to Solar Group, Inc. 07/17/1998 which name changed to Forex365, Inc. 08/28/2008 which name changed to Fuer International Inc. 08/30/2010
(See Fuer International Inc.)

SOLAR AIRCRAFT CO. (CA)
Stock Dividend - 10% 4/15/54
Completely liquidated 8/26/63
Each share Common $1 par exchanged for first and final distribution of $14.169 cash

SOLAR AMER CORP (WY)
Name changed to Horizon Energy Corp. 06/19/2013

Horizon Energy Corp. recapitalized as Technovative Group, Inc. 03/02/2015

SOLAR CORP.
Merged into Gamble-Skogmo, Inc. on a (34) for (1) basis in 1946
Gamble-Skogmo, Inc. merged into Wickes Companies, Inc. 1/26/85 which name changed to Collins & Aikman Group Inc. 7/17/92
(See Collins & Aikman Group Inc.)

SOLAR CTL CORP (CO)
Merged into United Solar Associates, Inc. 3/13/81
Each share Common 1¢ par exchanged for (0.2) share Common 10¢ par
(See United Solar Associates, Inc.)

SOLAR DESIGN SYS INC (UT)
Name changed to Biopetrol, Inc. (UT) 06/15/1981
Biopetrol, Inc. (UT) reincorporated in Nevada as Kensington International, Inc. 04/17/1996
(See Kensington International, Inc.)

SOLAR DYNAMICS INC (UT)
Name changed to Goldynamics 03/27/1978
Goldynamics name changed to Nugget Gold Mines, Inc. 10/25/1979
(See Nugget Gold Mines, Inc.)

SOLAR ELEC ENGR INC (CA)
Each share old Common no par exchanged for (0.04) share new Common no par 12/6/82
Name changed to U.S. Electricar, Inc. 1/12/94
U.S. Electricar, Inc. recapitalized as Enova Systems Inc. 11/17/99

SOLAR ENERGY LTD (DE)
Each share old Common $0.0001 par exchanged for (0.1) share new Common $0.0001 par 07/20/2001
SEC revoked common stock registration 06/12/2013

SOLAR ENERGY RESH CORP (CO)
Each share old Common no par exchanged for (0.02) share new Common no par 12/10/1993
Reorganized under the laws of California as Telegen Corp. 10/28/1996
Each share new Common no par exchanged for (0.13793103) share Common no par
Telegen Corp. name changed to Vu1 Corp. 06/05/2008

SOLAR ENERGY SOURCES INC (DE)
Name changed to SES Solar, Inc. 8/21/2006

SOLAR ENERGY SYS INC (NJ)
Charter revoked for failure to file reports and pay fees 08/05/1995

SOLAR ENERTECH CORP (NV)
Reincorporated under the laws of Delaware 08/13/2008

SOLAR ENGR GROUP (NJ)
Recapitalized as Solar Financial Services Inc. 03/14/1990
Each share Common no par exchanged for (0.05) share Common no par

SOLAR FARM INDS INC (CO)
Merged into Evolution Technologies, Inc. 04/20/1981
Each (2.7525456) shares Common 1¢ par exchanged for (1) share Common 1¢ par
(See Evolution Technologies, Inc.)

SOLAR GROUP INC (NV)
Name changed 07/17/1998
Each share old Common 1¢ par exchanged for (0.18181818) share new Common 1¢ par 07/09/1998
Name changed from Solar Age Industries, Inc. to Solar Group, Inc. 07/17/1998
Name changed to Forex365, Inc. 08/28/2008

Forex365, Inc. name changed to Fuer International Inc. 08/30/2010
(See Fuer International Inc.)

SOLAR INDS INC (CO)
Merged into United Solar Associates, Inc. 3/13/81
Each share Common $0.001 par exchanged for (0.2) share Common 10¢ par
(See United Solar Associates, Inc.)

SOLAR INDS INC (FL)
Name changed to Pan American Gold, Inc. 4/10/87
(See Pan American Gold, Inc.)

SOLAR MANUFACTURING CORP. (NY)
Completely liquidated in 1950
No stockholders' equity

SOLAR-MATES INC (NY)
Name changed to Serengeti Eyewear Inc. 2/13/97

SOLAR METRICS INC (CO)
Charter dissolved for failure to file annual reports 1/1/88

SOLAR MICRO INC (DE)
Recapitalized as Cambridge Equities Ltd. 08/16/1984
Each share Common $0.001 par exchanged for (0.2) share Common $0.005 par
(See Cambridge Equities Ltd.)

SOLAR NIGHT INDS INC (NV)
Old Common $0.00001 par split (2) for (1) by issuance of (1) additional share payable 05/08/2006 to holders of record 05/08/2006 Ex date - 05/09/2006
Each share old Common $0.00001 par exchanged for (0.004) share new Common $0.00001 par 02/11/2013
Name changed to Premium Beverage Group, Inc. 10/23/2013

SOLAR PHYSICS CORP (UT)
Name changed to LeJay Corp. 08/28/1980
LeJay Corp. name changed to Drumm Corp. 09/24/1983 which name changed to Horti-Tech Inc. 01/07/1986
(See Horti-Tech Inc.)

SOLAR PWR INC (CA)
Merged into SPI Energy Co., Ltd. 01/04/2016
Each share Common $0.0001 par exchanged for (0.1) Sponsored ADR for Ordinary
Note: Shares acquired after 11/05/2015 received (1) share Ordinary USD$0.000001 par
(See SPI Energy Co., Ltd.)

SOLAR REFINING CO.
Acquired by Standard Oil Co. (Ohio) in 1931
(See Standard Oil Co. (Ohio))

SOLAR SATELLITE COMMUNICATION INC (CO)
Each share old Common $0.001 par exchanged for (0.1) share new Common $0.001 par 01/16/1989
Each share new Common $0.001 par exchanged again for (0.14285714) share new Common $0.001 par 08/30/2001
Merged into Solar Satellite Communication Inc. (DE) 10/22/2007
Details not available

SOLAR SHELTER INC (DE)
Name changed 03/20/1980
Name and state of incorporation changed from Solar Shelter Engineering Co., Inc. (PA) to Solar Shelter, Inc. (DE) 03/20/1980
Charter cancelled and declared inoperative and void for non-payment of taxes 03/01/1987

SOLAR SILVER MINES INC (WA)
Company believed out of business 00/00/1987
Details not available

SOLAR SPECTRUM INC (UT)
Name changed to Parmax, Inc. 07/15/1986
Parmax, Inc. recapitalized as Nise Inc. 09/14/1993
(See Nise Inc.)

SOLAR SYS BY SUN DANCE INC (DE)
Name changed to Eurocapital Corp. 3/25/87
Eurocapital Corp. recapitalized as Alternative Distributors Corp. 12/26/91
(See Alternative Distributors Corp.)

SOLAR SYSTEMS, INC. (DE)
Charter revoked for non-payment of taxes 4/1/64

SOLAR TECHNOLOGY CORP (CO)
Charter suspended for failure to file annual reports 09/30/1985

SOLARA EXPL LTD (AB)
Each Class B Share no par exchanged for (10) Class A Shares no par 12/31/2010
Placed in receivership and all officers and directors resigned 12/19/2012
Stockholders' equity unlikely

SOLARBROOK WTR & PWR CORP (NC)
Each share old Common 1¢ par exchanged for (0.00002) share new Common 1¢ par 11/21/2008
New Common 1¢ par split (7) for (1) by issuance of (6) additional shares payable 06/16/2009 to holders of record 06/08/2009 Ex date - 06/17/2009
Administratively dissolved 04/04/2012

SOLARCELL CORP (CO)
Each share old Common no par exchanged for (0.1) share new Common no par 1/16/89
Recapitalized as 4Front Software International Inc. 1/4/93
Each share new Common no par exchanged for (0.0075187) share Common no par
4Front Software International Inc. name changed to 4Front Technologies Inc. 12/11/97
(See 4Front Technologies Inc.)

SOLARCITY CORP (DE)
Merged into Tesla Motors, Inc. 11/21/2016
Each share Common $0.0001 par exchanged for (0.11) share Common $0.001 par
Tesla Motors, Inc. name changed to Tesla, Inc. 02/02/2017

SOLARFLEX CORP (DE)
Common $0.0001 par split (10) for (1) by issuance of (9) additional shares payable 12/02/2013 to holders of record 11/26/2013 Ex date - 12/03/2013
Recapitalized as KinerjaPay Corp. 03/10/2016
Each share Common $0.0001 par exchanged for (0.03333333) share Common

SOLARFUN PWR HLDGS CO LTD (CAYMAN ISLANDS)
Name changed to Hanwha SolarOne Co., Ltd. 02/15/2011
Hanwha SolarOne Co., Ltd. name changed to Hanwha Q CELLS Co., Ltd. 02/09/2015

SOLARGEN ENERGY INC (NV)
Name changed to Nevo Energy, Inc. 05/12/2011

SOLARGY SYS INC (NV)
SEC revoked common stock registration 06/29/2011

SOL-SOL

SOLARON CORP (CO)
Under plan of reorganization name changed to First Exploration Co. and each share Common 1¢ par received (0.5) Common Stock Purchase Warrant Ser. A expiring 02/22/1991 and (0.5) Common Stock Purchase Warrant Ser. B expiring 02/22/1992 on 02/22/1990
(See First Exploration Co.)

SOLARTE HOTEL CORP (BRITISH VIRGIN ISLANDS)
Reincorporated under the laws of Wyoming as Windaus Global Energy, Inc. 02/22/2013
Windaus Global Energy, Inc. name changed to WindStream Technologies, Inc. 03/27/2014

SOLAR3D INC (DE)
Each share old Common $0.001 par exchanged for (0.03846153) share new Common $0.001 par 02/25/2015
Name changed to Sunworks, Inc. 03/01/2016

SOLARWINDS INC (DE)
Acquired by SolarWinds Holdings, Inc. 02/05/2016
Each share Common $0.001 par exchanged for $60.10 cash

SOLARWORLD AG (GERMANY)
Each old ADR for Common exchanged for (0.01333333) new ADR for Common 02/10/2014
Basis changed from (1:0.5) to (1:0.25) 02/10/2014
ADR agreement terminated 10/15/2018
Each new ADR for Common exchanged for (0.25) share Common
Note: Company is insolvent. Depositary will attempt to sell unexchanged ADR's after 04/15/2019.

SOLAZYME INC (DE)
Name changed to TerraVia Holdings, Inc. 05/11/2016
(See TerraVia Holdings, Inc.)

SOLBEC PHARMACEUTICALS LTD (AUSTRALIA)
Name changed to Freedom Eye Ltd. 01/09/2009
(See Freedom Eye Ltd.)

SOLDI VENTURES INC (BC)
Recapitalized as Vega Mining Inc. 12/16/2013
Each share Common no par exchanged for (0.1) share Common no par

SOLEBURY NATL BK (NEW HOPE, PA)
Common $5 par changed to $2.50 par and (1) additional share issued 09/20/1978
Stock Dividends - 10% 04/10/1973; 25% 06/02/1975
Merged into Continental Bank (Norristown, PA) 09/29/1980
Each share Common $2.50 par exchanged for (1.05) shares Capital Stock $5 par
Continental Bank (Norristown, PA) reorganized as Continental Bancorp, Inc. 05/01/1982 which merged into Midlantic Corp. 01/30/1987 which merged into PNC Bank Corp. 12/31/1995 which name changed to PNC Financial Services Group, Inc. 03/15/2000

SOLECTRIC CORP (CO)
Merged into Alpha Solarco Inc. 8/28/92
Each share Common no par exchanged for (1) share Common no par
Alpha Solarco Inc. recapitalized as Fiber Application Systems Technology Ltd. 3/17/2003

SOLECTRON CORP (DE)
Reincorporated 02/25/1997
Common no par split (2) for (1) by issuance of (1) additional share 04/20/1992
Common no par split (2) for (1) by issuance of (1) additional share 11/17/1993
State of incorporation changed from (CA) to (DE) and Common no par changed to $0.001 par 02/25/1997
Common $0.001 par split (2) for (1) by issuance of (1) additional share payable 08/04/1997 to holders of record 07/21/1997 Ex date - 08/05/1997
Common $0.001 par split (2) for (1) by issuance of (1) additional share payable 02/24/1999 to holders of record 02/10/1999 Ex date - 02/25/1999
Common $0.001 par split (2) for (1) by issuance of (1) additional share payable 03/08/2000 to holders of record 02/23/2000 Ex date - 03/09/2000
Each Adjustable Rate Equity Security Unit received (2.5484) shares Common $0.001 par 11/15/2004
Merged into Flextronics International Ltd. 10/01/2007
Each share Common $0.001 par exchanged for either (0.305877) share Ordinary S$0.01 par and $0.441126 cash or $3.89 cash
Note: Option to receive stock expired 09/27/2007
Flextronics International Ltd. name changed to Flex Ltd. 09/28/2016

SOLECTRON GLOBAL SVCS CDA INC (CANADA)
Merged into Flextronics International Ltd. 10/01/2007
Each Exchangeable Share exchanged for either (0.305877) share Ordinary S$0.01 par and $0.441126 cash or $3.89 cash
Note: Option to receive stock expired 09/27/2007
Flextronics International Ltd. name changed to Flex Ltd. 09/28/2016

SOLEGEAR BIOPLASTIC TECHNOLOGIES INC (AB)
Name changed to good natured Products Inc. 10/31/2017

SOLEIL CAP CORP (BC)
Recapitalized as Goldplay Exploration Ltd. 03/06/2018
Each share Common no par exchanged for (0.5) share Common no par

SOLEIL CAP L P (DE)
Name changed to VPR Brands, L.P. 09/21/2015

SOLEIL FILM INC (CA)
Reorganized 07/13/2004
Reorganized from Soleil Film & Television, Inc. to Soleil Film, Inc. 07/13/2004
Each (30) shares Common $0.001 par exchanged for (1) share Common $0.001 par
Name changed to Imperia Entertainment, Inc. (CA) 08/04/2005
Imperia Entertainment, Inc. (CA) reincorporated in Nevada 08/28/2006 which recapitalized as Viratech Corp. 10/11/2011

SOLENERGY CORP (CO)
Recapitalized as Carnegie International Corp. 5/3/96
Each share Common no par exchanged for (0.1) share Common no par
(See Carnegie International Corp.)

SOLERA HLDGS INC (DE)
Acquired by Summertime Acquisition Corp. 03/03/2016
Each share Common 1¢ par exchanged for $55.85 cash

SOLEX CAP INC (ON)
Name changed to Farini Group Inc. 9/13/96
Farini Group Inc. recapitalized as Farini Companies Inc. 9/8/97

SOLEX RES CORP (CANADA)
Recapitalized as Southern Andes Energy Inc. 05/17/2010
Each share Common no par exchanged for (0.33333333) share Common no par
Southern Andes Energy Inc. merged into Macusani Yellowcake Inc. 04/13/2012 which recapitalized as Plateau Uranium Inc. 05/01/2015 which changed to Plateau Energy Metals Inc. 03/16/2018

SOLEXA INC (DE)
Merged into Illumina, Inc. 1/26/2007
Each share Common 1¢ par exchanged for (0.344) share Common 1¢ par

SOLID CTLS INC (MN)
Common 10¢ par changed to 5¢ par and (1) additional share issued 07/31/1979
Common 5¢ par split (2) for (1) by issuance of (1) additional share 01/31/1985
Common 5¢ par changed to $0.001 par 10/31/2016
Recapitalized as Korver Corp. 06/15/2018
Each share Common $0.001 par exchanged for (0.01) share Common $0.001 par

SOLID GOLD CAP CORP (BC)
Merged into Consolidated Ruskin Developments Ltd. (New) 03/31/1992
Each (1.2) shares Common no par exchanged for (1) share Common no par
Consolidated Ruskin Developments Ltd. (New) name changed to Leisureways Marketing Ltd. (BC) 11/23/1992 which reincorporated in Yukon 11/10/1997 which name changed to LML Payment Systems Inc. (YT) 07/15/1998 which reincorporated in British Columbia 09/07/2012

SOLID PHOTOGRAPHY INC (DE)
Name changed to Robotic Vision Systems, Inc. 07/31/1981
(See Robotic Vision Systems, Inc.)

SOLID RES LTD (AB)
Name changed to Iberian Minerals Ltd. 06/13/2014
Iberian Minerals Ltd. name changed to Mineworx Technologies Ltd. 06/06/2017

SOLID ST GEOPHYSICAL INC (AB)
Class A Common no par reclassified as Common no par 4/6/94
Acquired by SSGI Acquisition 12/19/97
Each share Common no par exchanged for $3.50 cash

SOLID ST TECHNOLOGY INC (MA)
Involuntarily dissolved 8/31/98

SOLID STATE SCIENTIFIC DEVICES CORP. (DE)
Name changed to Solid State Scientific Inc. 12/1/71
(See Solid State Scientific Inc.)

SOLID ST SCIENTIFIC INC (DE)
Each share Common 10¢ par exchanged for (0.25) share Common 40¢ par 6/1/72
Acquired by Penn Central Corp. 5/14/84
Each share Common 40¢ par exchanged for $8.82 cash

SOLIDAY'S HOLIDAYS INTERNATIONAL LTD. (IA)
Charter cancelled for failure to maintain a registered agent 4/28/76

SOLIDOR RES INC (BC)
Recapitalized as Sheffield Resources Inc. (BC) 03/12/1997
Each share Common no par exchanged for (0.2) share Common no par
Sheffield Resources Inc. (BC) reincorporated in Nova Scotia as Globalstore.com, Inc. 04/27/1999 which name changed to GSO Solutions, Inc. 03/24/2000
(See GSO Solutions, Inc.)

SOLIDYNE INC (NY)
Common 10¢ par split (5) for (4) by issuance of (0.25) additional share 10/20/72
Stock Dividend - 25% 1/22/72
Merged into Til Acquisition Corp. 6/3/83
Each share Common 10¢ par exchanged for $4.75 cash

SOLIGEN TECHNOLOGIES INC (WY)
Reincorporated 04/13/1993
Place of incorporation changed from (BC) to (WY) 04/13/1993
Administratively dissolved 05/31/2006

SOLIMAR ENERGY LTD (AUSTRALIA)
Each share old Ordinary exchanged for (0.04) share new Ordinary 12/19/2013
Ceased operations 01/12/2015
Assets held by trustee for the benefit of creditors

SOLIS TEK INC (NV)
Common $0.001 par split (6) for (1) by issuance of (5) additional shares payable 09/02/2015 to holders of record 09/02/2015
Name changed to Generation Alpha, Inc. 09/27/2018

SOLITAIRE MINERALS CORP (BC)
Each share old Common no par exchanged for (0.2) share new Common no par 03/10/2009
Recapitalized as Pistol Bay Mining Inc. 11/06/2012
Each share new Common no par exchanged for (0.05) share Common no par

SOLITARIO EXPL & RTY CORP (CO)
Name changed to Solitario Zinc Corp. 07/18/2017

SOLITARIO RES CORP (CO)
Name changed to Solitario Exploration & Royalty Corp. 06/17/2008
Solitario Exploration & Royalty Corp. name changed to Solitario Zinc Corp. 07/18/2017

SOLITE PRODS CORP (NY)
Merged into Continental Strategics Corp. 01/02/1969
Each share Common 1¢ par exchanged for (0.0715) share Common 14¢ par
Continental Strategics Corp. merged into Chadbourn Inc. 04/27/1970 which reorganized as Stanwood Corp. 06/12/1975 which was acquired by Delta Woodside Industries, Inc. (DE) 09/07/1988 which merged into Delta Woodside Industries, Inc. (SC) 11/15/1989
(See Delta Woodside Industries, Inc. (SC))

SOLITEC INC (CA)
Each share old Common no par exchanged for (0.05) share new Common no par 3/2/92
Reorganized under the laws of Nevada as Turn Technology, Inc. 2/14/94
Each share new Common no par exchanged for (0.1) share Common no par
(See Turn Technology Inc.)

SOLITRON DEVICES, INC. (NY)
Common 5¢ par split (2) for (1) by

issuance of (1) additional share 4/7/66
Common 5¢ par changed to $1 par 6/14/66
Common $1 par split (5) for (1) by issuance of (4) additional shares 4/19/68
Reincorporated under the laws of Delaware 8/20/87

SOLLBERGER ENGINEERING CO., INC.
Name changed to Smith Steel Casting Co. in 1952

SOLO INTL RES LTD (BC)
Recapitalized as Regent Ventures Ltd. 02/01/1991
Each share Common no par exchanged for (0.5) share Common no par

SOLO PETES LTD (AB)
Recapitalized as ETC Transaction Corp. (ALTA) 3/12/96
Each share Class A Common no par exchanged for (0.2) share Common no par
ETC Transaction Corp. (ALTA) reincorporated in Delaware as Electronic Transmission Corp. 2/11/97

SOLO RES & ENERGY INC (ON)
Merged into Flying Cross Resources Ltd. 12/04/1985
Each share Common no par exchanged for (0.166666) share Common no par
Flying Cross Resources Ltd. merged into International Larder Minerals Inc. 05/01/1986 which merged into Explorers Alliance Corp. 10/13/2000
(See Explorers Alliance Corp.)

SOLO SERVE CORP (DE)
Each share old Common 1¢ par exchanged for (0.5) share new Common 1¢ par 7/18/95
Assets sold for the benefit of creditors 4/26/99
No stockholders' equity

SOLOMINO GOLD MINES LTD. (ON)
Charter revoked for failure to file reports and pay fees 9/8/66

SOLOMON DEV LTD (BC)
Recapitalized 07/26/1971
Recapitalized from Solomon Mines Ltd. to Solomon Development Ltd. 07/26/1971
Each share Capital Stock 50¢ par exchanged for (1) share Capital Stock no par
Struck off register and declared dissolved for failure to file returns 06/27/1977

SOLOMON GOLD CORP (AB)
Merged into Solomon Resources Ltd. 08/01/1989
Each share Common no par exchanged for (0.66666666) share Common no par
Solomon Resources Ltd. recapitalized as Damara Gold Corp. 10/01/2014

SOLOMON INC (AR)
Charter revoked for failure to file reports and pay fees in 1986

SOLOMON-PAGE GROUP LTD (DE)
Merged into TSPGL Merger Corp. 10/30/2000
Each share Common $0.001 par exchanged for $5.25 cash

SOLOMON RES LTD (BC)
Each share old Common no par exchanged for (0.1) share new Common no par 06/29/2009
Recapitalized as Damara Gold Corp. 10/01/2014
Each share Common no par exchanged for (0.1) share Common no par

SOLOMON SAM INC (DE)
Common 10¢ par split (3) for (2) by issuance of (0.5) additional share 6/15/78
Acquired by Service Merchandise Co., Inc. 8/10/82
Each share Common 10¢ par exchanged for (0.4) share Common $1 par
(See Service Merchandise Co., Inc.)

SOLOMON SOFTWARE INC (OH)
Merged into Great Plains Software, Inc. 6/9/2000
Each share Class A Common exchanged for (0.6544) share Common 1¢ par and $3.77 cash
Note: Additional shares were placed in an escrow account for possible future distribution
Great Plains Software, Inc. merged into Microsoft Corp. 4/5/2001

SOLOMON TECHNOLOGIES INC (DE)
Recapitalized as Technipower Systems, Inc. 09/29/2009
Each share Common $0.001 par exchanged for (0.01) share Common $0.001 par
(See Technipower Systems, Inc.)

SOLOMON TRADING LTD (CO)
Recapitalized as Voyageur First Inc. 11/17/1994
Each share Common no par exchanged for (0.05555555) share Common no par
Voyageur First Inc. name changed to North American Resorts Inc. 03/30/1995 which name changed to Immulabs Corp. 09/15/2000 which name changed to Xerion EcoSolutions Group, Inc. (CO) 04/07/2003 which reorganized in Nevada as SINO-American Development Corp. 06/19/2006 which recapitalized as Harvest Bio-Organic International Co., Ltd. 12/07/2010
(See Harvest Bio-Organic International Co., Ltd.)

SOLOMONS PILLARS MINES LTD (ON)
Charter cancelled for failure to pay taxes and file returns 03/16/1976

SOLON AUTOMATED SVCS INC (DE)
Common 10¢ par split (2) for (1) by issuance of (1) additional share 4/28/72
Common 10¢ par split (7) for (4) by issuance of (0.75) additional share 12/21/72
Common 10¢ par split (4) for (3) by issuance of (1/3) additional share 5/23/83
Merged into ARA Services, Inc. 8/26/83
Each share Common 10¢ par exchanged for $25.25 cash

SOLON INDUSTRIES, INC. (OH)
Stock Dividend - 10% 12/31/61
Completely liquidated 11/21/67
Each share Common no par exchanged for first and final distribution of (0.231481) share Whittaker Corp. (Calif.) $1.25 Conv. Preferred Ser. A no par
(See Whittaker Corp. (Calif.))

SOLOPOINT INC (CA)
Name changed 10/26/1999
Each share old Common no par exchanged for (0.25) share new Common no par 07/07/1998
Name changed from SoloPoint, Inc. to SoloPoint.com, Inc. 10/26/1999
Reincorporated under the laws of Delaware as Borneo Energy USA, Inc. and Common no par changed to $0.001 par 12/28/2010
Borneo Energy USA, Inc. name changed to AAP, Inc. 09/28/2011

SOLPOWER CORP (NV)
Each share old Common $0.001 par exchanged for (0.1) share new Common $0.001 par 01/14/2008
Name changed to Bitcoin Collect, Inc. 06/10/2014
Bitcoin Collect, Inc. name changed to Good Vibrations Shoes Inc. 09/09/2014

SOLSTICE NAT RESOURCE CORP (AB)
Name changed to Cayo Resources Inc. 04/02/1996
Cayo Resources Inc. merged into Pure Gold Minerals Inc. 11/20/1997 which recapitalized as Pure Diamonds Exploration Inc. 12/05/2006 which recapitalized as Burnstone Ventures Inc. 08/14/2009

SOLSTICE RESORTS INC (MN)
SEC revoked common stock registration 06/14/2011

SOLTA MED INC (DE)
Acquired by Valeant Pharmaceuticals International, Inc. 01/23/2014
Each share Common $0.001 par exchanged for $2.92 cash

SOLTORO LTD (CANADA)
Merged into Agnico Eagle Mines Ltd. 06/10/2015
Each share Common no par exchanged for (0.00793) share Common no par, (1) share Palamina Corp. Common no par and $0.01 cash
Note: Unexchanged certificates will be cancelled and become without value 06/10/2021

SOLTRAX INC (NM)
Charter voluntarily suspended 03/12/1997
Details not available

SOLUCORP INDS LTD (BC)
Reincorporated under the laws of Yukon 04/04/1997

SOLUMINAIRE SYS CORP. (BC)
Struck off register and declared dissolved for failure to file returns 05/11/1990

SOLUTEC CORP (FL)
Became defunct 00/00/1971
Stockholders' equity unlikely

SOLUTIA INC (DE)
Plan of reorganization under Chapter 11 Federal Bankruptcy Code effective 02/28/2008
Each share old Common 1¢ par received (0.005766) share new Common 1¢ par and (0.042909) Common Stock Purchase Warrant expiring 12/31/2013
Note: No stock distribution made to holders of (174) or fewer shares
No warrant distribution made to holders of (24) or fewer shares
Certificates were not required to be surrendered and are without value
Merged into Eastman Chemical Co. 07/02/2012
Each share new Common 1¢ par exchanged for (0.12) share Common 1¢ par and $22 cash

SOLUTION TECHNOLOGY INTL INC (DE)
Recapitalized as Reinsurance Technologies Ltd. 06/01/2009
Each share Common 1¢ par exchanged for (0.0025) share Common 1¢ par
(See Reinsurance Technologies Ltd.)

SOLUTIONINC TECHNOLOGIES LTD (BC)
Reincorporated under the laws of Nova Scotia 02/24/2004

SOLUTIONNET INTERNATIONAL INC (MN)
SEC revoked common stock registration 08/23/2010
Stockholders' equity unlikely

SOLUTIONS SOFTWARE 2001 INC (DE)
Recapitalized 04/20/2001
Recapitalized from Solutions Software Inc. to Solutions Software 2001 Inc. 04/20/2001
Each share Common $0.001 par exchanged for (0.2) share Common $0.001 par
Recapitalized as EMC Development Corp. 01/14/2003
Each share Common $0.001 par exchanged for (0.02) share Common $0.001 par
EMC Development Corp. recapitalized as EM International Enterprises Corp. 01/24/2008
(See EM International Enterprises Corp.)

SOLUTIONS TECHNOLOGY INC (NV)
Merged into International Mercantile Corp. 1/12/2002
Each share Common $0.001 par exchanged for (1) share new Common 1¢ par

SOLUTIONS4CO2 INC (ON)
Name changed to BlueOcean NutraSciences Inc. 06/05/2014
BlueOcean NutraSciences Inc. name changed to CO2 Gro Inc. 04/12/2018

SOLV-EX CORP NEW (NM)
SEC revoked common stock registration 11/16/2007
Stockholders' equity unlikely

SOLV EX CORP OLD (NM)
Plan of reorganization under Chapter 11 Federal Bankruptcy Code effective 08/31/1998
Each share Common 1¢ par exchanged for (1) share Solv-Ex Corp. (New) Common 1¢ par and (1/3) Common Stock Purchase Warrant expiring 08/31/2002
Note: Unexchanged certificates were cancelled and became without value 12/01/1998
(See Solv-Ex Corp. (New))

SOLVAY S A (BELGIUM)
ADR agreement terminated 08/23/2010
Each Sponsored ADR for Ordinary exchanged for $111.428513 cash
(Additional Information in Active)

SOLVAY-SODI AD (BULGARIA)
GDR agreement terminated 06/21/2018
Each Reg. S GDR for Ordinary exchanged for (1) share Ordinary
Note: Unexchanged GDR's will be sold and the proceeds, if any, held for claim after 12/21/2018

SOLVENTOL CHEM PRODS INC (MI)
Stock Dividends - 10% 11/30/1961; 10% 11/23/1962; 10% 12/02/1963; 10% 09/30/1965
Name changed to S.C. Products, Inc. 05/07/1974
(See S.C. Products, Inc.)

SOLVIS GROUP INC (NV)
SEC revoked common stock registration 07/08/2008

SOLVISTA GOLD CORP (ON)
Name changed to Rockcliff Copper Corp. 10/21/2015
Rockcliff Copper Corp. name changed to Rockcliff Metals Corp. 11/02/2017

SOM RES INC (NV)
Name changed to Century Petroleum Corp. and (6) additional shares issued 08/09/2006

SOMA DUVERNY GOLD MINES LTD. (QC)
Recapitalized as Dolsan Mines Ltd. 10/08/1957
Each share Common $1 par exchanged for (0.25) share Common $1 par
Dolsan Mines Ltd. recapitalized as

Consolidated Dolsan Mines Ltd.
03/04/1968
(See Consolidated Dolsan Mines Ltd.)

SOMANETICS CORP (MI)
Conv. Preferred 1¢ par called for redemption 02/28/1996
Each share old Common 1¢ par exchanged for (0.1) share new Common 1¢ par 04/11/1997
Merged into Covidien PLC 07/27/2010
Each share new Common 1¢ par exchanged for $25 cash

SOMAR LIQUIDATING CORP. (MD)
Dissolved 4/4/62

SOMATIX THERAPY CORP (DE)
Merged into Cell Genesys, Inc. 05/30/1997
Each share Preferred Ser. A-1 1¢ par exchanged for (2.4062) shares Common $0.001 par
Each share Preferred Ser. A-2 1¢ par exchanged for (2.4062) shares Common $0.001 par
Each share Common 1¢ par exchanged for (0.385) share Common $0.001 par
Cell Genesys, Inc. merged into BioSante Pharmaceuticals, Inc. 10/14/2009 which recapitalized as ANI Pharmaceuticals, Inc. 07/18/2013

SOMATOGEN INC (DE)
Merged into Baxter International Inc. 5/4/98
Each share Common $0.001 par exchanged for (0.16849) share Common 1¢ par and (1) Contingent Payment Right

SOMATRONICS INC (NY)
Dissolved by proclamation 3/27/79

SOMAXON PHARMACEUTICALS INC (DE)
Issue Information - 5,000,000 shares COM offered at $11 per share on 12/14/2005
Each share old Common $0.0001 par exchanged for (0.125) share new Common $0.0001 par 10/12/2012
Merged into Pernix Therapeutics Holdings, Inc. 03/06/2013
Each share new Common $0.0001 par exchanged for (0.47773006) share Common 1¢ par

SOMBRIO CAP CORP (NV)
Common $0.001 par split (8) for (1) by issuance of (7) additional shares payable 05/05/2011 to holders of record 05/02/2011 Ex date - 05/06/2011
Name changed to Hotcloud Mobile, Inc. 05/16/2011
(See Hotcloud Mobile, Inc.)

SOMEBOX INC (DE)
Name changed to Boxwoods, Inc. 10/20/2006
Boxwoods, Inc. name changed to Duke Mining Co., Inc. 07/13/2009 which reorganized as KaChing KaChing, Inc. 06/07/2010 which name changed to KS International Holdings Corp. 12/02/2013

SOMEDIA NETWORKS INC (CANADA)
Name changed to VidWRX Inc. 09/09/2015

SOMERA COMMUNICATIONS INC (DE)
Issue Information - 8,500,000 shares COM offered at $12 per share on 11/12/1999
Each share old Common $0.001 par exchanged for (0.1) share new Common $0.001 par 4/12/2006
Merged into Telmar Network Technology 9/1/2006
Each share new Common $0.001 par exchanged for $4.60 cash

SOMERSET BANCORP INC (NJ)
Capital Stock $5 par changed to $2.50 par and (1) additional share issued 8/14/85
Acquired by Summit Bancorporation 12/15/88
Each share Capital Stock $2.50 par exchanged for (2.21375) shares Common no par
Summit Bancorporation merged into Summit Bancorp 3/1/96 which merged into FleetBoston Financial Corp. 3/1/2001 which merged into Bank of America Corp. 4/1/2004

SOMERSET BANKSHARES INC (MA)
Under plan of reorganization each share Common $1 par automatically became (1) share Somerset Savings Bank (New) (Somerville, MA) Common $1 par 9/28/92
Somerset Savings Bank (New) (Sommerville, MA) merged into UST Corp. 7/15/98
(See UST Corp.)

SOMERSET CAP CORP (DE)
Charter cancelled and declared inoperative and void for non-payment of taxes 3/1/74

SOMERSET GROUP INC (IN)
Common no par split (5) for (4) by issuance of (0.25) additional share 04/01/1987
Common no par split (5) for (4) by issuance of (0.25) additional share payable 03/11/1996 to holders of record 02/29/1996
Common no par split (5) for (4) by issuance of (0.25) additional share payable 03/14/1997 to holders of record 02/26/1997
Merged into First Indiana Corp. 09/29/2000
Each share Common no par exchanged for either (1.21) shares Common 1¢ par or $24.70 cash
Note: Option to receive stock expired 09/14/2000
(See First Indiana Corp.)

SOMERSET HILLS & CNTY NATL BK (BASKING RIDGE, NJ)
Merged into First National State Bancorporation 04/19/1973
Each share Common $5 par exchanged for (0.875) share Common $6.25 par
First National State Bancorporation name changed to First Fidelity Bancorporation (Old) 05/01/1985 which merged into First Fidelity Bancorporation (New) 02/29/1988 which merged into First Union Corp. 01/01/1996 which name changed to Wachovia Corp. (Ctfs. dated 09/01/2001) 09/01/2001 which merged into Wells Fargo & Co. (New) 12/31/2008

SOMERSET HILLS BANCORP (NJ)
Stock Dividends - 5% payable 05/15/2002 to holders of record 04/30/2002 Ex date - 05/03/2002; 5% payable 06/30/2003 to holders of record 06/02/2003 Ex date - 05/29/2003; 5% payable 06/02/2004 to holders of record 05/17/2004; 5% payable 06/30/2005 to holders of record 05/17/2005 Ex date - 05/13/2005; 5% payable 05/31/2006 to holders of record 05/15/2006 Ex date - 05/11/2006; 5% payable 05/31/2007 to holders of record 05/15/2007 Ex date - 05/11/2007; 5% payable 05/30/2008 to holders of record 05/16/2008 Ex date - 05/14/2008; 5% payable 05/28/2010 to holders of record 05/17/2010 Ex date - 05/13/2010
Merged into Lakeland Bancorp, Inc. 05/31/2013
Each share Common no par exchanged for (1.1962) shares Common no par

SOMERSET HILLS NATIONAL BANK (BASKING RIDGE, NJ)
Capital Stock $25 changed to $7.50 par and (3) additional shares issued 02/07/1967
Merged into Somerset Hills & County National Bank (Basking Ridge, NJ) 01/13/1969
Each share Capital Stock $7.50 par exchanged for (2) shares Common $5 par
Somerset Hills & County National Bank (Basking Ridge, NJ) merged into First National State Bancorporation 04/19/1973 which name changed to First Fidelity Bancorporation (Old) 05/01/1985 which merged into First Fidelity Bancorporation (New) 02/29/1988 which merged into First Union Corp. 01/01/1996 which name changed to Wachovia Corp. (Ctfs. dated after 09/01/2001) 09/01/2001 which merged into Wells Fargo & Co. (New) 12/31/2008

SOMERSET HILLS NATL BK (BERNARDSVILLE, NJ)
Legal domicile changed to Somerset Hills National Bank (Basking Ridge, NJ) 00/00/1963
Somerset Hills National Bank (Basking Ridge, NJ) merged into Somerset Hills & County National Bank (Basking Ridge, NJ) 01/13/1969 which merged into First National State Bancorporation 04/19/1973 which name changed to First Fidelity Bancorporation (Old) 05/01/1985 which merged into First Fidelity Bancorporation (New) 02/29/1988 which merged into First Union Corp. 01/16/1996 which name changed to Wachovia Corp. (Ctfs. dated after 09/01/2001) 09/01/2001 which merged into Wells Fargo & Co. (New) 12/31/2008

SOMERSET INTL GROUP INC (DE)
SEC revoked common stock registration 10/03/2011

SOMERSET LIMITED, INC. (MN)
Merged into Landvest Development Corp. 9/20/72
Each share Common 10¢ par exchanged for (0.5) share Common 5¢ par
(See Landvest Development Corp.)

SOMERSET PRESS, INC. (NJ)
Company advised privately held 00/00/1976
Details not available

SOMERSET SVGS BK (SOMERVILLE, MA)
Reorganized as Somerset Bankshares Inc. 10/3/88
Each share Common $1 par exchanged for (1) share Common $1 par
Somerset Bankshares Inc. reorganized as Somerset Savings Bank (New) (Somerville, MA) 9/28/92 merged into UST Corp. 7/15/98
(See UST Corp.)

SOMERSET SVGS BK NEW (SOMERVILLE, MA)
Each share old Common $1 par exchanged for (0.4) share new Common $1 par 7/12/93
Merged into UST Corp. 7/15/98
Each share new Common $1 par exchanged for (0.19) share Common $0.625 par

SOMERSET TEL CO (ME)
5% Preferred $5 par called for redemption at $5 on 6/25/97
Public interest eliminated

SOMERSET TR CO (SOMERSET, PA)
Under plan of reorganization each share Common $10 par automatically became (4) shares Somerset Trust Holding Co. Common no par 08/31/2000

SOMERSET TR CO (SOMERVILLE, NJ)
Capital Stock $25 par changed to $5 par and (4) additional shares issued 12/18/70
Stock Dividends - 25% 1/31/62; 20% 1/31/63
Reorganized as Somerset Bancorp Inc. 10/1/84
Each share Capital Stock $5 par exchanged for (1) share Capital Stock $5 par
Somerset Bancorp Inc. acquired by Summit Bancorporation 12/15/88 which merged into Summit Bancorp 3/1/96 which merged into FleetBoston Financial Corp. 3/1/2001 which merged into Bank of America Corp. 4/1/2004

SOMERSET UNION & MIDDLESEX LIGHTING CO.
Merged into Public Service Electric & Gas Co. in 1937
(See Public Service Electric & Gas Co.)

SOMERSET VY BK (SOMERVILLE, NJ)
Merged into SVB Financial Services, Inc. 8/30/96
Each share Common $4.17 par exchanged for (1.2) shares Common no par
SVB Financial Services, Inc. merged into Fulton Financial Corp. 7/1/2005

SOMERVILLE BELKIN INDS LTD (CANADA)
$2.80 Preferred $50 par called for redemption 8/4/87
Public interest eliminated

SOMERVILLE CAP INC (AB)
Reincorporated under the laws of Canada as Book4Golf.com Corp. 10/14/1999
Book4Golf.com Corp. (Canada) reorganized in Alberta as B-for-G Capital Inc. 10/26/2004 which recapitalized as Parkbridge Lifestyle Communities Inc. 12/23/2004
(See Parkbridge Lifestyle Communities Inc.)

SOMERVILLE INDUSTRIES LTD. (CANADA)
Name changed to Somerville Belkin Industries Ltd./Les Industries Somerville Belkin Ltee. 11/2/77
(See Somerville Belkin Industries Ltd./Les Industries Somerville Belkin Ltee.)

SOMERVILLE LTD. (CANADA)
Name changed to Somerville Industries Ltd. 5/16/61
Somerville Industries Ltd. name changed to Somerville Belkin Industries Ltd./Les Industries Somerville Belkin Ltee. 11/2/77
(See Somerville Belkin Industries Ltd./Les Industries Somerville Belkin Ltee.)

SOMERVILLE NATIONAL BANK (SOMERVILLE, MA)
Merged into County Bank N.A. (Cambridge, MA) 02/24/1967
Each share Capital Stock $10 par exchanged for (2) shares Common $10 par
County Bank N.A. (Cambridge, MA) name changed to Shawmut County Bank, N.A. (Cambridge, MA) 04/01/1975
(See Shawmut County Bank, N.A. (Cambridge, MA)

SOMERVILLE TRUST CO. (SOMERVILLE, NJ)
Each share Capital Stock $100 par exchanged for (4) shares Capital Stock $25 par 1/15/60
Stock Dividends - 25% 2/2/53; 20% 11/15/54; 16-2/3% 12/14/55

Name changed to Somerset Trust Co. (Somerville, NJ) 4/18/60
Somerset Trust Co. (Somerville, NJ) reorganized as Somerset Bancorp Inc. 10/1/84 which was acquired by Summit Bancorporation 12/15/88 which merged into Summit Bancorp 3/1/96 which merged into FleetBoston Financial Corp. 3/1/2001 which merged into Bank of America Corp. 4/1/2004

SOMNUS MED TECHNOLOGIES INC (DE)
Merged into Gyrus Group PLC 06/20/2001
Each share Common $0.001 par exchanged for $3.11 cash

SOMO INC (NV)
Name changed to Enterprise Energy, Inc. 05/02/2016

SONA DEV CORP (TX)
Name changed to Sibling Entertainment Group Holdings, Inc. 06/15/2007
Sibling Entertainment Group Holdings, Inc. recapitalized as Sibling Group Holdings, Inc. 08/21/2012

SONA MOBILE HLDGS CORP (DE)
Chapter 7 bankruptcy proceedings terminated 09/09/2016
Stockholders' equity unlikely

SONA RES CORP (BC)
Merged into Skeena Resources Ltd. 09/16/2016
Each share Common no par exchanged for (0.5111) share Common no par
Note: Unexchanged certificates will be cancelled and become without value 09/16/2022

SONA RES INC (NV)
Common $0.001 par split (40) for (1) by issuance of (39) additional shares payable 06/30/2010 to holders of record 06/30/2010
Ex date - 07/01/2010
Name changed to Marine Drive Mobile Corp. 06/30/2011
Marine Drive Mobile Corp. name changed to Gamzio Mobile, Inc. 11/15/2013

SONA SYS CDA LTD (BC)
Recapitalized as Startec Marketing Corp. 5/13/88
Each share Common no par exchanged for (0.25) share Common no par
Startec Marketing Corp. recapitalized as Vitality Products Inc. 2/9/93

SONAE INDUSTRIA SGPS S A (PORTUGAL)
ADR agreement terminated 08/09/2017
No ADR's remain outstanding

SONARTEC NORTH AMER INC (ON)
Name changed to Sonatel Telecommunications Corp. 12/24/1987
Sonatel Telecommunications Corp. name changed to Cycomm International Inc. (ON) 02/26/1992 which reincorporated in Wyoming 11/03/1995
(See Cycomm International Inc.)

SONAT INC (DE)
Common $1 par split (2) for (1) by issuance of (1) additional share 09/14/1993
Merged into El Paso Energy Corp. 10/25/1999
Each share Common $1 par exchanged for (1) share Common $3 par
El Paso Energy Corp. name changed to El Paso Corp. 02/05/2001 which merged into Kinder Morgan, Inc. (New) 05/25/2012

SONAT OFFSHORE DRILLING INC (DE)
Name changed to Transocean Offshore Inc. (DE) 09/04/1996
Transocean Offshore Inc. (DE) reincorporated in the Cayman Islands 05/14/1999 which name changed to Transocean Sedco Forex Inc. 12/31/1999 which name changed to Transocean Inc. (Old) 05/09/2002 which merged into Transocean Inc. (New) (Cayman Islands) 11/27/2007 which reorganized in Switzerland as Transocean Ltd. 12/18/2008

SONATEL TELECOMMUNICATIONS CORP (ON)
Name changed to Cycomm International Inc. (ON) 02/26/1992
Cycomm International Inc. (ON) reincorporated in Wyoming 11/03/1995
(See Cycomm International Inc.)

SONATRON TUBE CO.
Merged into National Union Radio Corp. in 1929
National Union Radio Corp. name changed to National Union Electric Corp. in 1954
(See National Union Electric Corp.)

SONDE RES CORP (AB)
Each share old Common no par exchanged for (0.9) share new Common no par and (0.34) share Marquee Energy Ltd. Common no par 01/03/2014
Filed a petition under Bankruptcy & Insolvency Act 02/02/2015
Stockholders' equity unlikely

SONDERLING BROADCASTING CORP (DE)
Reincorporated 5/29/69
State of incorporation changed from (IL) to (DE) and Capital Stock no par changed to 10¢ par 5/29/69
Capital Stock 10¢ par split (3) for (2) by issuance of (0.5) additional share 1/14/77
Merged into Viacom International, Inc. 3/25/80
Each share Capital Stock 10¢ par exchanged for (1) share $2.10 Conv. Preferred no par plus $4.50 cash or $28 cash
Note: Option to receive cash is applicable to not more than 49% and not less than 40% of the outstanding shares and such option expired 4/9/80
(See Viacom International, Inc.)

S1 CORP (DE)
Acquired by ACI Worldwide, Inc. 02/13/2012
Each share Common 1¢ par exchanged for (0.1064) share Common $0.005 par and $6.62 cash

SONERA CORP (FINLAND)
ADR agreement terminated 12/31/1999
Each 144A Sponsored ADR for Ordinary exchanged for (1) share 144A Ordinary
Note: Unexchanged ADR's will be sold and the proceeds, if any, distributed after 06/30/2000
Acquired by TeliaSonera AB 12/09/2002
Each Sponsored ADR for Ordinary exchanged for $6.0386204 cash

SONESTA INTL HOTELS CORP (NY)
5% Preferred $25 par conversion privilege expired 04/01/1961
Under plan of partial liquidation each share Common $1 par changed to 80¢ par and stamped to indicate distribution of $1.66 cash 12/03/1973
Stamped Common 80¢ par split (3) for (1) by issuance of (2) additional shares 07/06/1981
Each share Stamped Common 80¢ par exchanged for (0.75) share Class A Common 80¢ par 10/04/1983
Class A Common 80¢ par split (2) for (1) by issuance of (1) additional share 07/07/1986
Class A Common 80¢ par split (2) for (1) by issuance of (1) additional share payable 07/30/1999 to holders of record 07/16/1999
5% Preferred $25 par called for redemption at $27.50 on 08/15/2001
Acquired by Sonesta Acquisition Corp. 01/31/2012
Each share Class A Common 80¢ par exchanged for $31 cash

SONESTA RES LTD (BC)
Recapitalized as SNA Resources Ltd. 9/13/76
Each share Capital Stock no par exchanged for (0.2) share Common Stock no par
SNA Resources Ltd. recapitalized as Enterprise Development Corp. 10/29/79 which recapitalized as Magenta Development Corp. 3/28/84
(See Magenta Development Corp.)

SONEX INC (PA)
Common 25¢ par split (3) for (2) by issuance of (0.5) additional share 05/06/1969
Reorganized as Marketline Systems, Inc. 03/10/1978
Each share Common 25¢ par exchanged for (0.1) share Common 25¢ par

SONEX RESH INC (MD)
Common 1¢ par split (2) for (1) by issuance of (1) additional share 04/28/1986
SEC revoked common stock registration 07/13/2007
Stockholders' equity unlikely

SONG CORP (ON)
Filed an assignment under Bankruptcy and Insolvency Act 5/4/2007
No stockholders' equity

SONG NETWORKS HLDG AKTIEBOLAG (SWEDEN)
ADR agreement terminated 12/17/2002
Each Sponsored ADR for Ordinary exchanged for (0.01) Ordinary Share
Note: Unexchanged ADR's will be sold and proceeds held for claim after 6/17/2003

SONGBIRD DEV INC (NV)
Name changed to Knowledge Machine International, Inc. 11/10/2014
Knowledge Machine International, Inc. recapitalized as Dthera Sciences 11/02/2016

SONGZAI INTL HLDG GROUP INC (NV)
Each share old Common $0.001 par exchanged for (0.1) share new Common $0.001 par 01/10/2008
Name changed to U.S. China Mining Group, Inc. 07/27/2010

SONIC DRYING SYSTEMS LTD. (BC)
Dissolved 7/27/82
Details not available

SONIC ELEC ENERGY CORP (CO)
Common no par split (3) for (1) by issuance of (2) additional shares 4/27/88
Proclaimed dissolved for failure to pay taxes and file reports 1/1/92

SONIC ENVIRONMENTAL SOLUTIONS INC (BC)
Name changed to Sonic Technology Solutions Inc. 06/27/2007
Sonic Technology Solutions Inc. name changed to Sonoro Energy Ltd. (BC) 07/07/2010 which reincorporated in Alberta 08/07/2013

SONIC ENVIRONMENTAL SYS INC (DE)
Name changed 03/10/1971
Name changed 08/09/1989
Name changed from Sonic Development Corp. of America to Sonic Development Corp. 03/10/1971
Name changed from Sonic Development Corp. to Sonic Environmental Systems, Inc. 08/09/1989
Common 10¢ par split (2) for (1) by issuance of (1) additional share 05/27/1994
Reorganized under Chapter 11 Federal Bankruptcy Code as Turbosonic Technologies Inc. 08/26/1997
Each share Common 10¢ par exchanged for (0.1328) share Common 10¢ par
(See Turbosonic Technologies Inc.)

SONIC INDS INC (OK)
Merged into New Sonic, Inc. 04/24/1986
Each share Capital Stock $1 par exchanged for $4.75 cash

SONIC INNOVATIONS INC (DE)
Name changed to Otix Global, Inc. 06/15/2009
(See Otix Global, Inc.)

SONIC JET PERFORMANCE INC (CO)
Common no par split (2) for (1) by issuance of (1) additional share payable 03/26/1999 to holders of record 03/12/1999
Name changed to Force Protection, Inc. (CO) 09/30/2003
Force Protection, Inc. (CO) reorganized in Nevada 02/04/2005
(See Force Protection, Inc.)

SONIC MEDIA CORP (NV)
Name changed to Larrea BioSciences Corp. 6/1/2004

SONIC PETROLEUM, INC. (UT)
Name changed to Mason Oil Co., Inc. 06/08/1981
Mason Oil Co., Inc. name changed to Brandmakers Inc. 11/16/1999

SONIC RAY RES LTD (BC)
Recapitalized as Stryker Resources Ltd. 09/25/1979
Each share Common no par exchanged for (0.25) share Common no par
Stryker Resources Ltd. recapitalized as Stryker Ventures Corp. 08/25/1997
(See Stryker Ventures Corp.)

SONIC RESEARCH CORP. (MA)
Declared dissolved by Court decree for failure to pay taxes and file reports 10/14/64

SONIC SOLUTIONS (CA)
Merged into Rovi Corp. 02/17/2011
Each share Common no par exchanged for (0.112) share Common $0.001 par and $7.70 cash
Rovi Corp. name changed to TiVo Corp. 09/08/2016

SONIC SYS CORP (DE)
Name changed to Unity Wireless Corp. 07/20/2000
(See Unity Wireless Corp.)

SONIC SYS INC (NY)
Charter cancelled and proclaimed dissolved for failure to pay taxes and file reports 12/16/1968

SONIC TAPE PUB LTD CO (UNITED KINGDOM)
Each ADR for Ordinary 25p par exchanged for (0.1) ADR for Ordinary 2.50p par 07/15/1988
Name changed to Systems Connections Group PLC 07/18/1989
(See Systems Connections Group PLC)

SONIC TECHNOLOGY SOLUTIONS INC (BC)
Name changed to Sonoro Energy Ltd. (BC) 07/07/2010
Sonoro Energy Ltd. (BC) reincorporated in Alberta 08/07/2013

SONICBLUE INC (DE)
Plan of Liquidation under Chapter 11 Federal Bankruptcy proceedings effective 12/04/2008
No stockholders' equity

SONICPORT INC (NV)
Reincorporated 02/00/2000
Name changed 02/07/2001
State of incorporation changed from (CO) to (NV)02/00/2000
Name changed from SonicPort.com, Inc. to SonicPort, Inc. 02/07/2001
Name changed to US Dataworks, Inc. 03/27/2002
(See US Dataworks, Inc.)

SONICS INTL INC (TX)
Name changed to Ozite Corp. (TX) 5/7/81
Ozite Corp. (TX) reincorporated in Delaware 8/28/90
Ozite Corp. (DE) merged into Pure Tech International, Inc. (New) 7/31/95 which name changed to Puretec Corp. 5/7/96
(See Puretec Corp.)

SONICWALL INC (CA)
Common no par split (2) for (1) by issuance of (1) additional share payable 09/15/2000 to holders of record 08/25/2000 Ex date - 09/18/2000
Acquired by PSM Holdings 2, Inc. 07/23/2010
Each share Common no par exchanged for $11.50 cash

SONIKA INC (NV)
Name changed to Cavio International Inc. 3/4/2002
Cavio International Inc. name changed to Allied Energy Inc. 9/18/2003 which name changed to FloodSmart, Inc. 9/29/2005 which name changed to Axis Energy Corp. 8/1/2006

SONO RES INC (NV)
Name changed to Alaska Gold Corp. 06/27/2012
(See Alaska Gold Corp.)

SONOCHEM INC (DE)
Recapitalized as Digital Dictation, Inc. 10/10/1995
Each share Common 1¢ par exchanged for (0.1) share Common 1¢ par
Digital Dictation, Inc. merged into MedQuist Inc. 07/31/1998 which merged into MedQuist Holdings Inc. 10/18/2011 which name changed to MModal Inc. 01/25/2012
(See MModal Inc.)

SONOCO PRODS CO (SC)
$2.25 Conv. Preferred Ser. A no par called for redemption at $51.575 plus $0.363 accrued dividend on 9/28/97
(Additional Information in Active)

SONOMA COLLEGE INC (CA)
SEC revoked common stock registration 05/23/2011

SONOMA COUNTY SAVINGS & LOAN ASSOCIATION (CA)
Merged into Great American Federal Savings & Loan Association 6/30/82
Each share Guarantee Stock $10 par exchanged for $28.16 cash

SONOMA INTL INC (NV)
Recapitalized as Sonoma Mines, Inc. 11/13/1968
Each share Capital Stock 10¢ par exchanged for (0.25) share Capital Stock 40¢ par
Sonoma Mines, Inc. name changed to Sonoma International (Old) 06/23/1971 which recapitalized as Sonoma International (New) 12/27/1996
(See Sonoma International (New))

SONOMA INTL NEW (NV)
SEC revoked common stock registration 10/03/2011

SONOMA INTL OLD (NV)
Recapitalized as Sonoma International (New) 12/27/1996
Each share Common 40¢ par exchanged for (0.005) share Common $0.001 par
(See Sonoma International (New))

SONOMA MINES INC (NV)
Name changed to Sonoma International (Old) 06/23/1971
Sonoma International (Old) recapitalized as Sonoma International (New) 12/27/1996
(See Sonoma International (New))

SONOMA QUICKSILVER MINES, INC. (NV)
Name changed to Sonoma International, Inc. 9/20/62
Sonoma International, Inc. recapitalized as Sonoma Mines, Inc. 11/13/68 which name changed to Sonoma International (Old) 6/23/71 which recapitalized as Sonoma International (New) 12/27/96

SONOMA RESOURCE CORP (BC)
Reincorporated under the laws of Wyoming as Biometric Security Corp. 10/09/1998
Biometric Security Corp. recapitalized as Safeguard Biometric Corp. (WY) 12/29/1999 which reincorporated in British Columbia 11/30/2001 which name changed to Devon Ventures Corp. 02/11/2002 which name changed to Pender Financial Group Corp. 06/23/2004
(See Pender Financial Group Corp.)

SONOMA RES INC (BC)
Name changed to Element Lifestyle Retirement Inc. 12/04/2015

SONOMA VY BK (SONOMA, CA)
Common no par split (2) for (1) by issuance of (1) additional share payable 4/30/98 to holders of record 4/10/98
Stock Dividends - 10% payable 6/28/96 to holders of record 6/14/96; 5% payable 8/31/99 to holders of record 8/16/99, 5% payable 9/25/2000 to holders of record 9/8/2000 Ex date - 9/6/2000
Under plan of reorganization each share Common no par automatically became (1) share Sonoma Valley Bancorp Common nopar 10/31/2000

SONOMA VINEYARDS (CA)
Merged into Field Acquisition Corp. 01/23/1985
Each share Common 25¢ par exchanged for $2 cash

SONOMAWEST HLDGS INC (DE)
Reincorporated 11/15/2004
State of incorporation changed from (CA) to (DE) and Common no par changed to $0.0001 par 11/15/2004
Each share Common $0.0001 par received distribution of (0.679) share MetroPCS Communications, Inc. Common $0.0001 par payable 01/09/2008 to holders of record 12/24/2007 Ex date - 01/11/2008
Each share Common $0.0001 par received distribution of (0.12071) share MetroPCS Communications, Inc. Common $0.0001 par payable 08/18/2008 to holders of record 07/28/2008 Ex date - 08/19/2008
Acquired by Stapleton Acquisition Co. 06/24/2011
Each share Common $0.0001 par exchanged for $10.05 cash
06/23/1971 which recapitalized as Sonoma International (New) 12/27/1996
(See Sonoma International (New))

SONOMAX HEARING HEALTHCARE INC (CANADA)
Merged into Sonomax Technologies Inc. 03/02/2010
Each share Common no par exchanged for (1) share Common no par
(See Sonomax Technologies Inc.)

SONOMAX TECHNOLOGIES INC (CANADA)
Assets surrendered to creditors 12/03/2014
No stockholders' equity

SONOMED INC (QC)
Plan of arrangement effective 06/29/2007
Each share Common no par exchanged for (1) share SND Energy Ltd. Common no par and $0.102595 cash
Each share Common no par received an additional distribution of approximately $0.003 cash 11/00/2007
SND Energy Ltd. recapitalized as Boyuan Construction Group, Inc. 02/24/2009

SONOR RES CORP (CANADA)
Name changed 04/17/1986
Name changed from Sonor Petroleum Corp. to Sonor Resources Corp. and Common no par reclassified as Class B Subordinate no par 04/17/1986
Name changed to Home Capital Group Inc. (Canada) 01/21/1987
Home Capital Group Inc. (Canada) reincorporated in Ontario 07/18/1988

SONORA DIAMOND CORP (ON)
Reincorporated 05/28/1989
Name changed 06/03/1997
Place of incorporation changed from (BC) to (ON) 05/28/1989
Name changed from Sonora Gold Corp. to Sonora Diamond Corp. 06/03/1997
Reincorporated under the laws of Bermuda as Sonora Diamond Corp. Ltd. 01/25/1999
(See Sonora Diamond Corp. Ltd.)

SONORA DIAMOND CORP LTD (BERMUDA)
Cease trade order effective 06/29/2001
Stockholders' equity unlikely

SONORA ELECTROMATICS, INC. (NJ)
Adjudicated bankrupt 10/21/64
No stockholders' equity

SONORA GOLD CORP (BC)
Recapitalized as MetalQuest Minerals Inc. 10/17/2007
Each share Common no par exchanged for (0.33333333) share Common no par
MetalQuest Minerals Inc. recapitalized as Canada Gold Corp. 09/01/2009 which name changed to STEM 7 Capital Inc. 07/12/2013 which name changed to South Star Mining Corp. 12/22/2017

SONORA PHONOGRAPH CO., INC.
Bankrupt in 1929

SONORA PRODUCTS CORP. OF AMERICA
Adjudicated bankrupt in 1929
No stockholders' equity

SONORAN ENERGY INC (WA)
Each share Common no par received distribution of (0.08) share Common no par and (0.08) Common Stock Purchase Warrant expiring 07/25/2005 payable 08/22/2003 to holders of record 07/25/2003 Ex date - 07/23/2003
Chapter 11 bankruptcy proceedings dismissed 12/31/2009
No stockholders' equity

SONORAN GROUP INC (UT)
Recapitalized as Zorro International Inc. 04/29/1994
Each share Common $0.001 par exchanged for (0.03333333) share Common $0.001 par
Zorro International Inc. recapitalized as Health & Wealth Inc. 07/12/1994 which recapitalized as Twenty First Century Health Inc. 05/23/1995 which name changed to Bio-Tech Industries Inc. 05/21/1997
(See Bio-Tech Industries Inc.)

SONORO ENERGY LTD (BC)
Each share old Common no par exchanged for (0.1) share new Common no par 12/09/2013
Reincorporated under the laws of Alberta 08/07/2013

SONOSITE INC (WA)
Name changed 11/24/1998
Name changed from SonoSight, Inc. to SonoSite, Inc. 11/24/1998
Acquired by FUJIFILM Holdings Corp. 03/29/2012
Each share Common 1¢ par exchanged for $54 cash

SONOTONE CORP. (NY)
Merged into Clevite Corp. 10/27/67
Each share Common $1 par exchanged for $10.50 cash

SONS OF GWALIA LTD (WESTERN AUSTRALIA)
Name changed 07/22/1992
Name changed from Sons of Gwalia N.L. to Sons of Gwalia Ltd. 07/22/1992
Stock Dividends - 100% 12/28/1994; 100% 12/28/1994
Company placed into voluntary administration under a Deed of Company Arrangement Act 08/29/2004
ADR's holders' equity unlikely

SONTAG CHAIN STORES CO. LTD.
Liquidated in 1947

SONTECH INC (NV)
Name changed to Wellness America Online, Inc. 11/06/2000
Wellness America Online, Inc. name changed to General Ventures, Inc. 04/15/2005
(See General Ventures, Inc.)

SONTERRA RES INC (DE)
Name changed to Velocity Energy Inc. 04/14/2009

SONTRA MED CORP (MN)
Each share old Common 1¢ par exchanged for (0.1) share new Common 1¢ par 08/10/2006
Name changed to Echo Therapeutics, Inc. (MN) 10/08/2007
Echo Therapeutics, Inc. (MN) reincorporated in Delaware 06/09/2008

SONTRIX INC (CO)
In process of liquidation
Each share Common 4¢ par exchanged for initial distribution of $1.40 cash 12/19/75
Note: Holders could advise agent to retain certificates or to return Stamped certificates
Each share Common 4¢ par received second distribution of $0.85 cash 6/30/76
Each share Common 4¢ par received third distribution of $0.21 cash 11/14/77
Details on subsequent distibutions, if any, are not available

SONUS COMMUNICATION HLDGS INC (DE)
Plan of reorganization under Chapter 11 Federal Bankruptcy Code effective 01/31/2003
No stockholders' equity

SONUS CORP (AB)
Liquidation completed

Each share Common no par received first and final liquidation of $1 cash payable 10/28/2002 to holders of record 10/24/2002
Note: Certificates were not required to be surrendered and are valueless

SONUS NETWORKS INC NEW (DE)
Name changed to Ribbon Communications Inc. 11/29/2017

SONUS NETWORKS INC OLD (DE)
Old Common $0.001 par split (3) for (1) by issuance of (2) additional shares payable 10/06/2000 to holders of record 09/29/2000 Ex date - 10/10/2000
Each share old Common $0.001 par exchanged for (0.2) share new Common $0.001 par 01/30/2015
Under plan of merger each share new Common $0.001 par automatically became (1) share Sonus Networks, Inc. (New) Common $0.0001 par 10/27/2017
Sonus Networks, Inc. (New) name changed to Ribbon Communications Inc. 11/29/2017

SONUS PHARMACEUTICALS INC (DE)
Recapitalized as OncoGenex Pharmaceuticals, Inc. 08/21/2008
Each share Common $0.001 exchanged for (0.05555555) share Common $0.001 par
OncoGenex Pharmaceuticals, Inc. recapitalized as Achieve Life Sciences, Inc. 08/03/2017

SONUS VENTURE CAP CORP (QC)
Issue Information - 2,966,666 shares COM offered at $0.15 per share on 04/26/2002
Reorganized under the laws of Ontario as ACE/Security Laminates Corp. 05/25/2004
Each share Common no par exchanged for (0.4) share Common no par
(See ACE/Security Laminates Corp.)

SOO LINE CORP (MN)
Merged into Soo Line Acquisition Corp. 04/09/1990
Each share Common $3-1/3 par exchanged for $21.50 cash

SOO LINE RR CO (MN)
Common no par split (2) for (1) by issuance of (1) additional share 5/26/72
Common no par changed to $3-1/3 par and (2) additional shares issued 2/14/79
Under plan of reorganization each share Common $3-1/3 par automatically became (1) share Soo Line Corp. Common $1 par 12/31/84
(See Soo Line Corp.)

SOO-TOMIC URANIUM MINES, LTD. (ON)
Charter cancelled for failure to file returns and pay taxes 9/21/59

SOOCANA EXPLS LTD (ON)
Merged into Plata-Peru Resources Inc. 8/8/97
Each share Common no par exchanged for (0.5) share Common no par
(See Plata-Peru Resources Inc.)

SOONER DEFENSE FLA INC (FL)
Chapter 11 bankruptcy proceedings converted to Chapter 7 on 12/16/88
Stockholders' equity unlikely

SOONER ENERGY CORP (BC)
Reincorporated under the laws of Oklahoma as Tatonka Energy, Inc. and Common no par changed to $0.001 par 10/07/1994
Takonka Energy, Inc. recapitalized as Phymed, Inc. 03/12/1999
(See Phymed, Inc.)

SOONER FED SVGS & LN ASSN TULSA OKLA (USA)
Placed in conservatorship 11/16/1989
No stockholders' equity

SOONER HLDGS INC (OK)
Recapitalized as FlyingEagle PU Technical Corp. 01/30/2012
Each share Common $0.001 par exchanged for (0.05467261) share Common $0.001 par

SOONER LIFE INS CO (OK)
Stock Dividends - 25% 04/17/1972; 25% 04/19/1974; 20% 04/11/1975; 20% 04/26/1976; 50% 04/01/1977; 20% 03/22/1978
Merged into USLIFE Corp. 07/02/1979
Each share Common $1 par exchanged for (0.25) share $3.33 Preferred Ser. C $1 par
USLIFE Corp. merged into American General Corp. 06/17/1997 which merged into American International Group, Inc. 08/29/2001

SOONER ST FARMS INC (OK)
Charter cancelled for failure to pay taxes 2/23/90

SOONER STATE OIL CO., INC. (DE)
Name changed to Todd Group, Inc. and Common 10¢ par changed to 1¢ par 11/20/70
Todd Group, Inc. name changed to Charmec Group, Inc. 3/12/80 which reorganized as Charme Properties Inc. 6/1/83
(See Charme Properties Inc.)

SOOOO GOOD INTL LTD (NV)
Common $0.001 par split (2) for (1) by issuance of (1) additional share payable 07/18/2005 to holders of record 07/15/2005 Ex date - 07/19/2005
Charter revoked for failure to file reports and pay taxes 07/31/2009

SOPAC CELLULAR SOLUTIONS INC (NV)
Name changed to iTalk Inc. 12/21/2012

SOPHA MILLER GOLD MINES LTD. (ON)
Charter revoked for failure to file reports and pay fees 4/22/65

SOPHEON PLC (UNITED KINGDOM)
ADR agreement terminated 01/26/2015
No ADR's remain outstanding

SOPHIA CAP CORP (BC)
Reorganized as Folkstone Capital Corp. 09/10/2013
Each share Common no par exchanged for (1.09) share Common no par

SOPRO FOODS INC (NY)
Name changed 01/09/1984
Name changed from Sopro Products, Inc. to Sopro Foods, Inc. 01/09/1984
Filed a petition under Chapter 7 Federal Bankruptcy Code 01/20/1988
No stockholders' equity

SORA CAP CORP (BC)
Name changed to ProSmart Enterprises Inc. 07/12/2017

SORANZO INTL SPIRITS INC (BC)
Recapitalized as FirstLine Ventures Ltd. 11/21/1997
Each share Common no par exchanged for (0.2) share Common no par
FirstLine Ventures Ltd. recapitalized as Aeon Ventures Ltd. 11/18/1999 which recapitalized as Statesman Resources Ltd. 06/28/2004

SORBENT TECHNOLOGIES CORP (OH)
Stock Dividend - 5% payable 11/26/2002 to holders of record 10/26/2002 Ex date - 12/18/2002
Merged into Albemarle Corp. 08/04/2008
Each share Common no par exchanged for $6.4326 cash

SOREL ELEVATORS LTD.-LES ELEVATEURS DE SOREL LTEE. (CANADA)
Acquired by Intercolonial Trading Corp., Ltd. 06/15/1982
Each share Preferred $100 par exchanged for $197.08 cash
Each share Common no par exchanged for $135 cash

SORELL INC (NV)
Name changed to Emporia, Inc. 02/27/2008

SORENSEN INDUSTRIES CORP. (CO)
Merged into Amglobal Corp. 3/17/89
Each share Common $0.0001 par exchanged for (0.1) share Common $0.001 par
Amglobal Corp. charter cancelled 3/1/90

SORG INC (NY)
Filed a petition under Chapter 11 Federal Bankruptcy Code 8/8/89
Stockholders' equity unlikely

SORG (PAUL A.) PAPER CO.
Name changed to Sorg Paper Co. in 1930

SORG PAPER CO (OH)
Common $100 par changed to no par 00/00/1931
Each share Preferred Ser. A $100 par exchanged for (1.2) shares 5.5% Preferred $100 par, (0.5) share Common $10 par and $2.50 cash 00/00/1947
Each share Preferred Ser. B $100 par exchanged for (1.125) shares 5.5% Preferred $100 par, (0.5) share Common $10 par and $2.50 cash 00/00/1947
Each share Common no par exchanged for (10) shares Common $10 par 00/00/1947
Each share Common $10 par exchanged for (2) shares Common $5 par 03/25/1971
Stock Dividend - 10% 12/28/1979
Acquired by Mosinee Paper Corp. 08/22/1983
Each share Common $5 par exchanged for $25 cash

SORG PRTG INC (NY)
Stock Dividend - 100% 08/02/1971
Name changed to Sorg Inc. 09/24/1986
(See Sorg Inc.)

SORICON CORP (DE)
Acquired by International Verifact Inc. 12/30/94
Each share Common 1¢ par exchanged for (0.5) share new Common no par and (0.375) Common Stock Purchase Warrant expiring 12/30/97
International Verifact Inc. merged into IVI Checkmate Corp. 6/25/98
(See IVI Checkmate Corp.)

SOROBAN ENGINEERING, INC. (FL)
Each share Class A Common $1.25 par exchanged for (3) shares Class A Common $1 par 9/28/59
Each share Class B Common $1.25 par exchanged for (3) shares Class B Common $1 par 9/28/59
Completely liquidated 5/29/68
Each share Class A Common $1 par exchanged for first and final distribution (0.25) share Mohawk Data Sciences Corp. Common 10¢ par
Mohawk Data Sciences Corp. name changed to Qantel Corp. 9/17/87
(See Qantel Corp.)

SOROCABANA RAILWAY CO.
Liquidated in 1949

SORORITY INDS (NV)
Charter revoked for failure to file reports and pay fees 02/01/1983

SORREL RES LTD (AB)
Struck off register for failure to file annual returns 03/01/1994

SORRENTO NETWORKS CORP (DE)
Reincorporated 06/04/2003
Each share old Common 30¢ par exchanged for (0.05) share new Common 30¢ par 10/28/2002
State of incorporation changed from (NJ) to (DE) 06/04/2003
Merged into Zhone Technologies, Inc. 07/01/2004
Each share new Common 30¢ par exchanged for (0.9) share Common $0.001 par
Zhone Technologies, Inc. name changed to DASAN Zhone Solutions, Inc. 09/12/2016

SOS CONS INC (NV)
Common $1 par split (2) for (1) by issuance of (1) additional share 3/16/73
Name changed to Core Industries Inc. 1/10/78
(See Core Industries Inc.)

SOS INTL INC (NV)
Recapitalized as DuraSwitch Industries Inc. 01/12/1998
Each share Common $0.001 par exchanged for (0.05) share Common $0.001 par
DuraSwitch Industries Inc. name changed to InPlay Technologies, Inc. 06/15/2005
(See InPlay Technologies, Inc.)

SOS STAFFING SVCS INC (UT)
Secondary Offering - 4,000,000 shares COM offered at $16.75 per share on 10/15/1997
Each share Common 1¢ par exchanged for (0.2) share Common $0.002 par 8/28/2003
Merged into Hire Calling Holding Co. 11/4/2003
Each share Common $0.002 par exchanged for $1.3789 cash

SOSS MFG CO (NV)
Reincorporated 3/1/65
Each share Common $10 par exchanged for (10) shares Common $1 par in 1936
Stock Dividends - 20% 12/16/49; 100% 12/11/64
State of incorporation changed from (ME) to (NV) 3/1/65
Common $1 par split (4) for (3) by issuance of (1/3) additional share 10/29/68
Stock Dividends - 20% 12/16/49; 100% 12/11/64; 10% 3/21/67; 33-1/3% 9/19/67; 10% 3/19/68
Name changed to SOS Consolidated Inc. 1/27/69
SOS Consolidated Inc. name changed to Core Industries Inc. 1/10/78
(See Core Industries Inc.)

SOSSIN SYS INC (FL)
Each (50,000) shares Common 10¢ par exchanged for (1) share Common $5,000 par 05/07/1979
Note: In effect holders received $0.20 cash per share and public interest eliminated

SOTECH CORP (FL)
Name changed to VNI Communications, Inc. 03/22/1990
(See VNI Communications, Inc.)

SOTECH INC (NV)
Name changed to Qnective, Inc. 03/08/2007
(See Qnective, Inc.)

SOTHABYS INVT CORP (UT)
Involuntarily dissolved 08/01/1988

SOT-SOU   **FINANCIAL INFORMATION, INC.**

SOTHEBY PARKE BERNET GROUP PLC (ENGLAND)
Acquired by Taubman U.K. Investments, Inc. 04/21/1984
Each ADR for Ordinary 5p par exchanged for $9.95 cash

SOTHEBYS HLDGS INC (MI)
Class A Limited Voting Common 10¢ par split (2) for (1) by issuance of (1) additional share 7/17/89
Class B Common 10¢ par split (2) for (1) by issuance of (1) additional share 7/17/89
Reincorporated under the laws of Delaware as Sotheby's, Class A Limited Voting 10¢ par and Class B Common 10¢ par reclassified as Common 1¢ par 6/30/2006

SOTON HLDGS GROUP INC (NV)
Name changed to Rio Bravo Oil, Inc. 01/26/2012

SOUFUN HLDGS LTD (CAYMAN ISLANDS)
ADR's for Class A Ordinary split (4) for (1) by issuance of (3) additional ADR's payable 02/17/2011 to holders of record 02/10/2011 Ex date - 02/18/2011
Basis changed from (1:4) to (1:1) 02/18/2011
ADR's for Class A Ordinary split (5) for (1) by issuance of (4) additional ADR's payable 04/04/2014 to holders of record 03/28/2014 Ex date - 04/07/2014
Basis changed from (1:1) to (0.2) 04/07/2014
Name changed to Fang Holdings Ltd. 09/23/2016

SOUHEGAN NATL BK (MILFORD, NH)
Common $20 par changed to $10 par 12/31/1978
Common $10 par changed to $5 par 02/07/1984
Stock Dividends - 100% 02/06/1979; 10% 04/15/1984
Acquired by Amoskeag Bank Shares, Inc. 11/30/1985
Each share Common $5 par exchanged for $76.45 cash

SOULFOOD CONCEPTS INC (DE)
SEC revoked common stock registration 11/22/2004

SOUND & VISUAL ED INC (UT)
Name changed to Tanner Petroleum, Inc. 05/28/1974
Tanner Petroleum, Inc. recapitalized as Solar Design Systems, Inc. 10/13/1978 which name changed to Biopetrol, Inc. (UT) 06/15/1981 which reincorporated in Nevada as Kensington International, Inc. 04/17/1996
(See Kensington International, Inc.)

SOUND ADVICE INC (FL)
Merged into Tweeter Home Entertainment Group, Inc. 08/01/2001
Each share Common 1¢ par exchanged for (1) share Common 1¢ par
(See Tweeter Home Entertainment Group, Inc.)

SOUND BKG CO (MOREHEAD CITY, NC)
Reclassification effective 10/26/2005
Each share Common $5 par held by holders of (249) shares or fewer exchanged for (1) share Ser. A Preferred $5 par
Each share Ser. A Preferred $5 par exchanged for (1) share Common $5 par 11/03/2014
Stock Dividends - in Preferred to holders of Preferred 20% payable 08/30/2007 to holders of record 08/15/2007 Ex date - 08/27/2007; 10% payable 03/14/2014 to holders of record 02/14/2014 Ex date - 02/12/2014; in Common to holders of Common 20% payable 08/30/2007 to holders of record 08/15/2007 Ex date - 08/27/2007; 10% payable 03/14/2014 to holders of record 02/14/2014 Ex date - 02/12/2014
Merged into West Town Bancorp, Inc. 09/05/2017
Each share Common $5 par exchanged for $12.75 cash

SOUND CAP INC (ON)
Merged into Luminart Inc. 04/30/1994
Each share Common no par exchanged for (0.1) share Common no par
(See Luminart Inc.)

SOUND CITY ENTMT GROUP INC (CO)
Company became private 06/28/2006
Details not available

SOUND COMMUNICATION CORP (AB)
Struck off register and delcared dissolved for failure to file returns 12/01/1993

SOUND DESIGNS INC (NV)
Each share old Common $0.001 par exchanged for (13) shares new Common $0.001 par 01/24/2000
Name changed to Plus Solutions, Inc. 06/06/2000
(See Plus Solutions, Inc.)

SOUND ENERGY TR (AB)
Merged into Advantage Energy Income Fund 09/06/2007
Each Trust Unit exchanged for (0.3) Trust Unit no par
Advantage Energy Income Fund reorganized as Advantage Oil & Gas Ltd. 07/09/2009

SOUND FED BANCORP (DE)
Reorganized as Sound Federal Bancorp, Inc. 01/06/2003
Each share Common 1¢ par exchanged for (2.7667) shares Common 1¢ par
(See Sound Federal Bancorp, Inc.)

SOUND FED BANCORP INC (DE)
Merged into Hudson City Bancorp, Inc. 07/14/2006
Each share Common 1¢ par exchanged for $20.75 cash

SOUND FINL INC (USA)
Reorganized under the laws of Maryland as Sound Financial Bancorp, Inc. 08/22/2012
Each share Common 1¢ par exchanged for (0.87423) share Common 1¢ par

SOUND IDEAS INC (BC)
Name changed to SID Energy Inc. 07/03/1990
(See SID Energy Inc.)

SOUND INDS INC (UT)
Reorganized under the laws of Delaware as Scottsdale Technologies, Inc. 3/31/97
Each share new Common $0.001 par exchanged for (1) share Common $0.001 par
(See Scottsdale Technologies, Inc.)

SOUND INDS LTD (UT)
Recapitalized as Sound Industries, Inc. (UT) 1/10/97
Each share Common $0.001 par exchanged for (0.01) share Common $0.001 par
Sound Industries, Inc. (UT) reorganized in Delaware as Scottsdale Technologies, Inc. 3/31/97
(See Scottsdale Technologies, Inc.)

SOUND INSIGHT ENTERPRISES LTD (CANADA)
Merged into CamVec Corp. 9/11/92
Each share Common no par exchanged for (0.093) share Common no par
CamVec Corp. name changed to AMJ Campbell Inc. 8/14/2001
(See AMJ Campbell Inc.)

SOUND MONEY INVS INC (NV)
Charter revoked for failure to file reports and pay fees 6/1/2002

SOUND OF MUSIC INC (MN)
Name changed to Best Buy Co., Inc. 2/18/83

SOUND ONE CORP (NY)
Common 1¢ par split (2) for (1) by issuance of (1) additional share 12/31/82
Merged into Todd-AO Corp. 6/22/99
Each share Common 1¢ par exchanged for $11.50 cash

SOUND REVOLUTION INC (DE)
Each (42) shares old Common $0.0001 par exchanged for (1) share new Common $0.0001 par 06/26/2008
Name changed to On4 Communications, Inc. 08/20/2009

SOUND SOURCE INTERACTIVE INC (DE)
Each (5.976) shares Common $0.001 par exchanged for (1) share Common $0.001 par 10/25/95
Name changed to TDK Mediactive Inc. 12/1/2000
(See TDK Mediactive Inc.)

SOUND TECHNOLOGY INC (UT)
Reorganized under the laws of Delaware as S D I Holding Co. 3/28/88
Each share Common $0.001 par exchanged for (0.1) share Common $0.001 par

SOUND WHSE INC (DE)
Acquired by Shamrock Holdings Inc. 5/4/89
Each share Common 1¢ par exchanged for $25.65 cash

SOUND WORLDWIDE HLDGS INC (DE)
Name changed to Chatter Box Call Center Ltd. 04/14/2011
(See Chatter Box Call Center Ltd.)

SOUNDBITE COMMUNICATIONS INC (DE)
Issue Information - 5,202,022 shares COM offered at $8 per share on 11/01/2007
Acquired by Genesys Telecommunications Laboratories, Inc. 07/03/2013
Each share Common $0.001 par exchanged for $5 cash

SOUNDCACHE COM INC (AB)
Name changed to Genoray Advanced Technologies Ltd. 05/09/2002
(See Genoray Advanced Technologies Ltd.)

SOUNDESIGN CORP (DE)
Common $1 par split (3) for (2) by issuance of (0.5) additional share 9/21/72
Common $1 par split (3) for (2) by issuance of (0.5) additional share 11/1/76
Merged into SDN Corp. 1/26/82
Each share Common $1 par exchanged for $17 cash

SOUNDS 24-7 INC (NV)
Each share old Common $0.001 par exchanged for (0.0002) share new Common $0.001 par 11/26/2004
Recapitalized as Allied Energy Corp. 1/26/2006
Each share new Common $0.001 par exchanged for (1/6) share Common $0.001 par

SOUNDSCRIBER CORP (CT)
Common no par changed to $4 par 00/00/1954
Common $4 par changed to no par 08/26/1965
5% Conv. Preferred $10 par called for redemption 12/20/1971
Name changed to Dual-Lite, Inc. 12/04/1975
(See Dual-Lite, Inc.)

SOUNDVEST EQUITY FD (ON)
Trust terminated 06/14/2018
Each Trust Unit received $4.5612 cash

SOUNDVIEW PULP CO.
Merged into Scott Paper Co. in 1951
Each share Common $5 par exchanged for (1.25) shares Common no par
Scott Paper Co. merged into Kimberly- Clark Corp. 12/12/95

SOUNDVIEW TECHNOLOGY GROUP INC (DE)
Each share old Common 1¢ par exchanged for (0.2) share new Common 1¢ par 06/30/2003
Merged into Schwab (Charles) Corp. 01/16/2004
Each share new Common 1¢ par exchanged for $15.50 cash

SOUNDWORKS ENTMT INC (DE)
Recapitalized as Data Evolution Holdings, Inc. 4/12/2004
Each share Common $0.001 par exchanged for (0.1) share Common $0.001 par

SOUNDWORKS INTL INC (NV)
Old Common $0.001 par split (5) for (1) by issuance of (4) additional shares payable 02/15/1999 to holders of record 02/11/1999
Each share old Common $0.001 par exchanged for (0.2) share new Common $0.001 par 08/15/2002
Each share new Common $0.001 par exchanged for (0.5) share Common 1¢ par 01/16/2004
Name changed to Global Triad, Inc. 01/16/2004
Global Triad, Inc. recapitalized as Miracle Applications Corp. 12/03/2007 which name changed to Outfront Companies 01/26/2011
(See Outfront Companies)

SOUNDYNAMICS SYS LTD (DE)
Name changed to Electronic Specialty Products, Inc. 07/15/1983
Electronic Specialty Products, Inc. (DE) 08/29/1991 which name changed to Sport of Kings, Inc. (DE) 08/29/1991 which reorganized in Nevada as Triad North America, Inc. 04/27/2006 which name changed to Kingslake Energy, Inc. 06/07/2006
(See Kingslake Energy, Inc.)

SOUP NUTSY CORP (NY)
Each share old Common $0.0001 par exchanged for (5) shares new Common $0.0001 par 05/21/1998
Name changed to Swindbourne (Leonard) Second Acquisition Corp. 11/16/1998
Swindbourne (Leonard) Second Acquisition Corp. recapitalized as Montt International Corp. 06/01/1999
(See Montt International Corp.)

SOURCE CAP & INVT CORP (AB)
Name changed to Berwick Retirement Communities Ltd. 4/8/98
(See Berwick Retirement Communities Ltd.)

SOURCE CAP CORP (AB)
Recapitalized as Source Capital & Investment Corp. 10/15/92
Each share Common no par exchanged for (0.1) share Common no par
Source Capital & Investment Corp. name changed to Berwick Retirement Communities Ltd. 4/16/98
(See Berwick Retirement Communities Ltd.)

SOURCE CAP CORP (WA)
Each share Class B Common no par

exchanged for (0.33333333) share Class A Common no par 05/27/1994
Each share Class A Common no par exchanged for (0.2) share Common no par 06/03/1996
Merged into Sterling Financial Corp. 09/28/2001
Each share Common no par exchanged for (0.475) share Common $1 par
Sterling Financial Corp. merged into Umpqua Holdings Corp. 04/18/2014

SOURCE CAP INC (DE)
$2.40 Preferred $3 par called for redemption at $27.50 on 06/29/2012
(Additional Information in Active)

SOURCE CO (MO)
Name changed to Source Information Management Co. 07/07/1997
Source Information Management Co. name changed to Source Interlink Companies, Inc. (MO) 08/02/2002 which reincorporated in Delaware 02/28/2005
(See Source Interlink Companies, Inc.)

SOURCE DATA AUTOMATION INC (DE)
Charter cancelled and declared inoperative and void for non-payment of taxes 1/30/73

SOURCE DIRECT HLDGS INC (NV)
Each share old Common $0.001 par exchanged for (0.04) share new Common $0.001 par 12/04/2006
Charter permanently revoked 07/30/2010

SOURCE ENERGY CORP (UT)
Each share old Common $0.00025 par exchanged for (0.025) share new Common $0.00025 par 04/10/2000
Name changed to Innuity, Inc. (UT) 12/20/2005
Innuity, Inc. (UT) reincorporated in Washington 11/21/2008
(See Innuity, Inc.)

SOURCE ETF TR (DE)
Trust terminated 04/17/2015
Each share EURO STOXX 50 ETF received $48.00987363 cash

SOURCE EXPL CORP (ON)
Reincorporated 01/17/2011
Place of incorporation changed from (AB) to (ON) 01/17/2011
Each share old Common no par exchanged for (0.1) share new Common no par 09/09/2016
Name changed to Mexican Gold Corp. 04/26/2017

SOURCE FINL INC (DE)
Name changed to Alltemp, Inc. 04/27/2017

SOURCE GOLD CORP (NV)
Common $0.001 par split (4) for (1) by issuance of (3) additional shares payable 10/14/2009 to holders of record 10/14/2009
Common $0.001 par changed to $0.00001 par 03/24/2014
Each share old Common $0.00001 par exchanged for (0.0005) share new Common $0.00001 par 10/15/2015
Recapitalized as Golden Matrix Group, Inc. 04/07/2016
Each share new Common $0.00001 par exchanged for (0.00066666) share Common $0.00001 par

SOURCE INTERLINK COS INC (DE)
Name changed 08/02/2002
Reincorporated 02/28/2005
Each (1.21) shares old Common 1¢ par exchanged for (1) share new Common 1¢ par 10/07/1997
Name changed from Source Information Management Co. to Source Interlink Companies, Inc. 08/02/2002
State of incorporation changed from (MO) to (DE) 02/28/2005
Plan of reorganization under Chapter 11 Federal Bankruptcy Code effective 06/19/2009
No stockholders' equity

SOURCE INVT INC (UT)
Each share old Common $0.005 par exchanged for (0.1) share new Common $0.005 par 08/08/1978
Involuntarily dissolved for failure to pay taxes 09/12/1991

SOURCE LIFE SCIENCES INC (CANADA)
Delisted from Toronto Venture Stock Exchange 01/13/2009

SOURCE MEDIA INC (DE)
Each share old Common $0.001 par exchanged for (0.5) share new Common $0.001 par 10/10/95
Assets sold by foreclosure 3/14/2002
Stockholders' equity unlikely

SOURCE ONE INC (NV)
SEC revoked common stock registration 10/23/2008

SOURCE ONE MTG SVCS CORP (DE)
9.375% Quarterly Income Capital Securities Preferred called for redemption at $25 on 6/2/99
8.42% Preferred Ser. A 1¢ par called for redemption at $25 on 6/3/99

SOURCE PERRIER S A (FRANCE)
Stock Dividends - 25% 06/23/1972; 25% 07/29/1974; 33.33333333% 08/30/1980
Acquired by Demilac 08/28/1992
Each ADR for Bearer exchanged for $68.09 cash

SOURCE PETE INC (NV)
Chapter 7 bankruptcy proceedings terminated 09/11/2007
No stockholders' equity

SOURCE RES LTD (YT)
Reincorporated 09/08/1993
Place of incorporation changed from (BC) to (Yukon) 09/08/1993
Recapitalized as Namibian Minerals Corp. 10/12/1993
Each share Common no par exchanged for (0.666) share Common no par
(See Namibian Minerals Corp.)

SOURCE SCIENTIFIC INC (CA)
Acquired by Boston Biomedica, Inc. 07/02/1997
Each share Common no par exchanged for approximately $0.05 cash

SOURCE SVCS CORP (DE)
Common 2¢ par split (3) for (2) by issuance of (0.5) additional share payable 11/15/97 to holders of record 11/3/97
Merged into Romac International, Inc. 4/20/98
Each share Common 2¢ par exchanged for (1.1351) shares Common 1¢ par
Romac International, Inc. name changed to kforce.com, Inc. 5/16/2000 which name changed to Kforce Inc. 6/20/2001

SOURCE VENTURE CAP INC (NV)
Each share Common $0.001 par exchanged for (0.002) share old Common 50¢ par 03/04/1992
Each share old Common 50¢ par exchanged for (0.04) share new Common 50¢ par 03/20/2007
Name changed to ConnectAJet.com, Inc. 07/18/2007
(See ConnectAJet.com, Inc.)

SOURCECORP INC (DE)
Merged into Apollo Management, L.P. 7/12/2006
Each share Common 1¢ par exchanged for $25 cash

SOURCEFIRE INC (DE)
Issue Information - 5,770,000 shares COM offered at $15 per share on 03/08/2007
Acquired by Cisco Systems, Inc. 10/07/2013
Each share Common $0.001 par exchanged for $76 cash

SOURCEFORGE INC (DE)
Name changed to Geeknet, Inc. 11/04/2009
(See Geeknet, Inc.)

SOURCESMITH INDS INC (BC)
Cease trade order effective 03/24/2006
Stockholders' equity unlikely

SOURIS VALLEY OIL CO. LTD. (MB)
Acquired by Landa Oil Co. (Old) 03/24/1959
Each share Common no par exchanged for (0.04) share Common 10¢ par
Landa Oil Co. (Old) name changed to Landa Industries, Inc. 04/07/1967 which recapitalized as Surveyor Companies, Inc. 11/12/1971 which name changed to Forum Companies, Inc. 09/23/1974
(See Forum Companies, Inc.)

SOUSA (JOHN PHILIP) ENTERPRISES, LTD. (NY)
Charter cancelled and proclaimed dissolved for failure to pay taxes 9/2/77

SOUTH AFRICAN BREWERIES LTD (SOUTH AFRICA)
Each Unsponsored ADR for Ordinary Rand-20 par exchanged for (1) Sponsored ADR for Ordinary Rand-20 par 11/7/94
Each Sponsored Reg. S ADR for Ordinary Rand-20 par exchanged for (1) Sponsored ADR for Ordinary Rand-20 par 11/19/96
Reorganized in England & Wales as South African Breweries PLC 3/8/99
Each Sponsored ADR for Ordinary Rand-20 par exchanged for approximately (2) Sponsored ADR's for Ordinary
South African Breweries PLC name changed to SABMiller PLC 7/9/2002

SOUTH AFRICAN BREWERIES PLC (ENGLAND & WALES)
Name changed to SABMiller PLC 07/09/2002
(See SABMiller PLC)

SOUTH AFRICAN LD & EXPL LTD (SOUTH AFRICA)
Name changed to Sallies Ltd. 11/15/1999
(See Sallies Ltd.)

SOUTH ALA BANCORPORATION INC NEW (AL)
Common 1¢ par split (3) for (2) by issuance of (0.5) additional share payable 07/01/1998 to holders of record 06/15/1998
Name changed to BancTrust Financial Group, Inc. 05/15/2002
BancTrust Financial Group, Inc. merged into Trustmark Corp. 02/15/2013

SOUTH AMERICAN AIR LINE, INC.
Liquidated in 1931

SOUTH AMERN GOLD & COPPER LTD (CANADA)
Reincorporated 05/03/2007
Place of incorporation changed from (Bermuda) to (Canada) 05/03/2007
Recapitalized as Cerro Grande Mining Corp. 04/14/2011
Each share Common no par exchanged for (0.1) share Common no par

SOUTH AMERICAN GOLD & PLATINUM CO. (DE)
Common $5 par changed to $1 par in 1933
Merged into International Mining Corp. 10/7/63
Each share Common $1 par exchanged for (1) share Common $1.66-2/3 par
(See International Mining Corp.)

SOUTH AMERICAN GOLD AREAS LTD. (ENGLAND)
Dissolved 02/08/1957
Details not available

SOUTH AMERN GOLDFIELDS INC (CANADA)
Merged into Golden Star Resources Ltd. (Canada) 05/20/1992
Each share Common no par exchanged for (0.1538461) share Common no par

SOUTH AMERICAN MINING LTD. (ON)
Merged into Able Land & Minerals Ltd. on a (0.8) for (1) basis 9/16/59
Able Land & Minerals Ltd. acquired by Canaveral International Corp. 5/1/63 which recapitalized as Madison Group Associates Inc. 2/2/93
(See Madison Group Associates Inc.)

SOUTH AMERN PPTYS INC (NV)
Name changed to USA Restaurant Funding Inc. 11/17/2014
USA Restaurant Funding Inc. name changed to Chron Organization, Inc. 03/24/2016 which name changed to Zenergy Brands, Inc. 12/01/2017

SOUTH AMERN SILVER CORP (BC)
Reincorporated 12/24/2013
Place of incorporation changed from (Canada) to (BC) 12/24/2013
Each share Common no par exchanged for (1) share Common no par and (1) Non-Vtg. Class B Share no par
Name changed to TriMetals Mining Inc. 03/19/2014

SOUTH AMERICAN UTILITIES CORP.
Property sold at foreclosure 00/00/1941
No stockholders' equity

SOUTH ATLANTIC CO. (DE)
Each share old Common $1 par exchanged for (0.2) share new Common $1 par 10/25/1965
Charter cancelled and declared inoperative and void for non-payment of taxes 04/15/1976

SOUTH ATLANTIC FINL CORP (FL)
Merged into Stamford Capital Group, Inc. 11/04/1987
Each share Common 1¢ par exchanged for (1) share Common $1 par
Stamford Capital Group, Inc. name changed to Independence Holding Co. (New) 09/10/1990

SOUTH ATLANTIC GAS CO. (GA)
Reorganized as Savannah Gas Co. 10/01/1964
Each share Common $5 par exchanged for (2) shares Common $2.50 par
Savannah Gas Co. merged into Atlanta Gas Light Co. 01/31/1966 which reorganized as AGL Resources Inc. 03/06/1996
(See AGL Resources Inc.)

SOUTH ATLANTIC LIFE INSURANCE CO. (FL)
Merged into Kennesaw Life & Accident Insurance Co. 09/28/1966
Each share Common $1 par exchanged for (0.740741) share Common $1 par
Kennesaw Life & Accident Insurance Co. merged into Lykes-Youngstown Financial Corp. 11/14/1969 which name changed to LifeSurance Corp. 05/10/1971 which merged into Regan Holding Corp. 10/31/1991
(See Regan Holding Corp.)

SOUTH ATLANTIC RES LTD (CANADA)
Name changed 7/30/96
Name changed from South Atlantic Diamonds Corp. to South Atlantic Resources Ltd. 7/30/96
Recapitalized as South Atlantic Ventures Ltd. 4/2/2002
Each share Common no par exchanged for (1/6) share Common no par
South Atlantic Ventures Ltd. name changed to Lundin Mining Corp. 8/12/2004

SOUTH ATLANTIC TR (MA)
Reorganized under the laws of Florida as South Atlantic Financial Corp. 08/01/1979
Each Share of Bene. Int. no par exchanged for (1) share Common 1¢ par
South Atlantic Financial Corp. merged into Stamford Capital Group, Inc. 11/04/1987 which name changed to Independence Holding Co. (New) 09/10/1990

SOUTH ATLANTIC VENTURES LTD (BC)
Name changed to Southern Copper Corp. 6/15/93
(See Southern Copper Corp.)

SOUTH ATLANTIC VENTURES LTD (CANADA)
Name changed to Lundin Mining Corp. 8/12/2004
Each share Common no par exchanged for (1) share Common no par

SOUTH BACHELOR MINING CO., LTD. (QC)
Charter annulled for failure to file annual reports 10/28/78

SOUTH BAY BK (TORRANCE, CA)
Merged into National Mercantile Bancorp 12/14/2001
Each share Common exchanged for $10.52 cash

SOUTH BAY CORP. LIQUIDATING TRUST (NY)
In process of liquidation
Each share Stamped Capital Stock $10 par exchanged for fourth distribution of $1 cash 8/13/82
Details on subsequent distributions, if any, are not available
(See South Bay Corp. for previous distributions)

SOUTH BAY CORP (NY)
In process of liquidation
Each share Capital Stock $10 par stamped to indicate initial distribution of (0.6626) share Elgin National Industries, Inc. Common $1 par; (0.9115) share Giant Portland Cement Co. Common $1 par and $5.19 cash 6/30/75
(See each company's listing)
Each share Capital Stock $10 par stamped to indicate second distribution of $1.55 cash 12/15/76
Each share Capital Stock $10 par stamped to indicate third distribution of $1 cash 1/5/78
Assets transferred to South Bay Corp. Liquidating Trust 3/31/79
(See South Bay Corp. Liquidating Trust)

SOUTH BAY HLDGS INC (CA)
Under plan of merger each share Common no par exchanged for $2.20 cash 6/28/96
Note: Each share Common no par received an additional final distribution of $0.29 cash per share 5/21/99

SOUTH BAY INDUSTRIES, INC. (DE)
Out of business 8/3/63
No stockholders' equity

SOUTH BAY SVGS & LN ASSN (CA)
Placed in receivership 00/00/1986

No stockholders' equity

SOUTH BEND LATHE WORKS (IN)
Stock Dividends - 50% 7/25/45; 66-2/3% 9/16/46
Acquired by American Steel Foundries on a (0.5) for (1) basis 6/12/59
American Steel Foundries name changed to Amsted Industries Inc. (N.J.) 1/25/62 which was reincorporated under the laws of Delaware 1/31/68
(See Amsted Industries Inc. (Del.))

SOUTH BEND PALACE THEATRE, INC. (IN)
Liquidation completed 10/16/61

SOUTH BOSTON SVGS BK (BOSTON, MA)
Common $1 par split (3) for (2) by issuance of (0.5) additional share 2/28/85
Under plan of reorganization each share Common $1 par automatically became (1) share Boston Bancorp Common $1 par 3/1/85
Boston Bancorp merged into Bank of Boston Corp. 6/28/96 which name changed to BankBoston Corp. 4/25/97 which merged into Fleet Boston Corp. 10/1/99 which name changed to FleetBoston Financial Corp. 4/18/2000 which merged into Bank of America Corp. 4/1/2004

SOUTH BOULDER MINES LTD (AUSTRALIA)
Each Sponsored ADR for Ordinary received distribution of $0.057126 cash payable 09/02/2014 to holders of record 08/25/2014 Ex date - 08/21/2014
Name changed to Danakali Ltd. 06/15/2015

SOUTH BRAZEAU PETES LTD (AB)
Under plan of merger each share Capital Stock no par exchanged for $0.268 cash 07/29/1977

SOUTH BRH VY BANCORP INC (WV)
Name changed to Summit Financial Group, Inc. 12/30/1999

SOUTH CAROLINA COMMUNITY BANCSHARES INC (DE)
Merged into Union Financial Bancshares Inc. 11/12/1999
Each share Common 1¢ par exchanged for (0.98) share Common 1¢ par and $6.54 cash
(See Union Financial Bancshares Inc.)

SOUTH CAROLINA CONTINENTAL TELEPHONE CO. (DE)
5-1/2% Preferred $25 par called for redemption 9/12/57
Public interest eliminated

SOUTH CAROLINA ELEC & GAS CO (SC)
Common $7.50 par changed to $4.50 par 00/00/1948
5-1/2% Conv. Preferred $50 par called for redemption 05/10/1950
Common $4.50 par split (2) for (1) by issuance of (1) additional share 07/01/1965
6-7/8% Preferred $100 par called for redemption 01/31/1979
Under plan of reorganization each share Common $4.50 par automatically became (1) share SCANA Corp. (Old) Common no par 12/31/1984
10-3/4% Preferred $100 par called for redemption 07/01/1986
11.08% Preferred $100 par called for redemption 07/01/1986
13.88% Preferred $100 par called for redemption 07/01/1987
7.70% Preferred $100 par called for redemption at $101 plus $1.176 accrued dividend on 11/26/1997
8.12% Preferred $100 par called for redemption at $102.03 plus $1.241 accrued dividend on 11/26/1997
8.40% Preferred $100 par called for redemption at $101 plus $1.283 accrued dividend on 11/26/1997
8.72% Preferred $50 par called for redemption at $51 plus $0.68222 accrued dividend on 11/26/1997
9.40% Preferred $50 par called for redemption at $51.175 plus $0.718 accrued dividend on 11/26/1997
SCANA Corp. (Old) merged into SCANA Corp. (New) 02/10/2000
4.50% Preferred $50 par called for redemption at $51 on 12/30/2009
4.60% Preferred Ser. A $50 par called for redemption at $51 on 12/30/2009
4.60% Preferred Ser. B $50 par called for redemption at $50.50 on 12/30/2009
5% Preferred $50 par called for redemption at $52.50 on 12/30/2009
5.125% Preferred $50 par called for redemption at $51 on 12/30/2009
6.52% Preferred $50 par called for redemption at $100 on 12/30/2009

SOUTH CAROLINA FED CORP (USA)
Stock Dividends - 10% 01/20/1989; 10% 09/18/1991
Merged into First Union Corp. 01/15/1993
Each share Common $1 par exchanged for (0.745) share Common $3.33-1/3 par
Note: Each share Common $1 par received an additional distribution of (0.015) share Common $3.33-1/3 par 12/31/1993
First Union Corp. name changed to Wachovia Corp. (Ctfs. dated after 09/01/2001) 09/01/2001 which merged into Wells Fargo & Co. (New) 12/31/2008

SOUTH CAROLINA INS CO (SC)
Common $8 par changed to $10 par in 1942
Common $10 par changed to $5 par 3/31/67
Common $5 par changed to $1.60 par and (1) additional share issued 4/1/70
Common $1.60 par changed to $1 par and (1) additional share issued 2/1/72
Stock Dividends - 11-1/9% 12/28/66; 10% 2/26/71; 25% 4/1/75
Under plan of reorganization each share Common $1 par automatically became (1) share Seibels Bruce Group, Inc. Common $1 par 10/31/78

SOUTH CAROLINA NATL BK (CHARLESTON, SC)
Each share Common $100 par exchanged for (10) shares Common $10 par 00/00/1941
Common $10 par changed to $5 par and (1) additional share issued 02/20/1959
Stock Dividends - 20% 05/21/1940; 33-1/3% 03/11/1946; 25% 09/16/1949; 12-1/2% 11/01/1955; 10% 01/26/1962; 10% 03/10/1967; 10% 08/05/1969; 20% 02/15/1971
Reorganized as South Carolina National Corp. 07/01/1972
Each share Common $5 par exchanged for (2) shares Common $5 par
South Carolina National Corp. merged into Wachovia Corp. (New) (Ctfs. dated between 05/20/1991 and 09/01/2001) 12/06/1991 which merged into Wachovia Corp. (Ctfs. dated after 09/01/2001) 09/01/2001 which merged into Wells Fargo & Co. (New) 12/31/2008

SOUTH CAROLINA NATL CORP (SC)
Common $5 par split (2) for (1) by issuance of (1) additional share 01/02/1985
Common $5 par split (2) for (1) by issuance of (1) additional share 10/01/1986
Stock Dividends - 10% 01/02/1979; 10% 01/02/1980
Merged into Wachovia Corp. (New) (Ctfs. dated between 05/20/1991 and 09/01/2001) 12/06/1991
Each share Common $5 par exchanged for (0.675) share Common $5 par
Wachovia Corp. (New) (Ctfs. dated between 05/20/1991 and 09/01/2001) merged into Wachovia Corp. (Ctfs. dated after 09/01/2001) 09/01/2001 which merged into Wells Fargo & Co. (New) 12/31/2008

SOUTH CAROLINA WATER & UTILITY CO. (SC)
Proclaimed dissolved for failure to maintain a registered agent 1/8/81

SOUTH CENT BANCSHARES INC (KY)
Acquired by First Southern Bancorp, Inc. 2/20/2003
Each share Common exchanged for $423.35 cash

SOUTH CENT INDS INC (FL)
Proclaimed dissolved for failure to file reports and pay fees 07/11/1972

SOUTH CENTREMAQUE GOLD MINES LTD.
Acquired by Centremaque Gold Mines 00/00/1950
Each share Capital Stock $1 par exchanged for (0.25) share Capital Stock $1 par
Centremaque Gold Mines Ltd. recapitalized as Norsyncomaque Mining Ltd. 08/07/1956 which recapitalized as Silvermaque Mining Ltd. 07/04/1961 which recapitalized as Geomaque Explorations Ltd./Explorations Geomaque Ltee. 09/19/1986 which merged into Defiance Mining Corp. 06/25/2003 which merged into Rio Narcea Gold Mines, Ltd. 09/03/2004
(See Rio Narcea Gold Mines, Ltd.)

SOUTH CHICAGO SVGS BK (CHICAGO, IL)
Capital Stock $100 par changed to $62.50 par in 1940
Reorganized under the laws of Delaware as Advance Bancorp, Inc. 3/12/87
Each share Capital Stock $62.50 par exchanged for (10) shares Common 1¢ par
Advance Bancorp, Inc. merged into Charter One Financial, Inc. 6/6/2003
(See Charter One Financial, Inc.)

SOUTH CHINA INDS INC (CANADA)
Name changed to TriNorth Capital Inc. 06/30/1999
TriNorth Capital Inc. recapitalized as Difference Capital Funding Inc. 06/01/2012 which recapitalized as Difference Capital Financial Inc. 06/17/2013

SOUTH CHINA MORNING POST HLDGS LTD (BERMUDA)
Name changed to SCMP Group Ltd. 12/05/2001
SCMP Group Ltd. name changed to Armada Holdings Ltd. 07/06/2016 which name changed to Great Wall Pan Asia Holdings Ltd. 01/20/2017
(See Great Wall Pan Asia Holdings Ltd.)

SOUTH COAST BK (COSTA MESA, CA)
Declared insolvent and bank closed by California Superintendent of Banking 4/12/85
Stockholders' equity unlikely

SOUTH COAST CO.
Reorganized as South Coast Corp. in 1935
Details not available

SOUTH COAST CORP (DE)
Each share old Common $1 par exchanged for (2) shares new Common $1 par in 1937
Stock Dividend - 50% 1/31/62
Completely liquidated 6/24/68
Each share new Common $1 par exchanged for first and final distribution of (0.6) share Walter (Jim) Corp. Common 16-2/3¢ par
(See Walter (Jim) Corp.)

SOUTH COAST LIFE INSURANCE CO. (TX)
Capital Stock no par changed to $1 par 3/10/64
Acquired by USLIFE Holding Corp. 7/25/67
Each share Capital Stock $1 par exchanged for (0.2) share Capital Stock $2 par
USLIFE Holding Corp. name changed to USLIFE Corp. 5/22/70 which merged into American General Corp. 6/17/97 which merged into American International Group, Inc. 8/29/2001

SOUTH COAST NATL BK (COSTA MESA, CA)
Name changed to South Coast Bank (Costa Mesa, CA) 8/1/79
(See South Coast Bank (Costa Mesa, CA))

SOUTH COLO NATL BK (DENVER, CO)
Merged into Colorado National Bankshares, Inc. 09/27/1982
Each share Common $5 par exchanged for (2.4) shares Common no par
Colorado National Bankshares, Inc. merged into First Bank System, Inc. 05/28/1993 which name changed to U.S. Bancorp 08/01/1997

SOUTH COMSTOCK CORP. (NV)
Name changed to Comstock Industries, Inc. (NV) 08/18/1983
Comstock Industries, Inc. (NV) reincorporated in Florida 07/21/2000
(See Comstock Industries, Inc.)

SOUTH CNTY BK N A (RANCHO SANTA MARGARITA, CA)
Under plan of reorganization each share Common $5 par automatically became (1) share CalWest Bancorp Common $5 par 07/31/2003

SOUTH CROFTY HLDGS LTD (BC)
Name changed to North Pacific GeoPower Corp. 12/05/2001
North Pacific GeoPower Corp. recapitalized as Western GeoPower Corp. 10/09/2003 which merged into Ram Power, Corp. 10/20/2009 which recapitalized as Polaris Infrastructure Inc. 05/19/2015

SOUTH DAKOTA CORP (SD)
Reincorporated under the laws of Delaware as Western Empire Financial Inc. 08/27/1971
(See Western Empire Financial Inc.)

SOUTH DAKOTA DEVELOPMENT & REFINING CO. (SD)
Charter expired by time limitations 2/16/70

SOUTH DOME LAKE MINES, LTD.
Dissolved in 1951
Each share Capital Stock $1 par received (0.538) share of Midcamp Mines Ltd. Capital Stock $1 par and $0.012 in cash
Midcamp Mines Ltd. completed liquidation 5/5/59

SOUTH EAST NATL BK (CHICAGO, IL)
Each share Common $100 par exchanged for (4) shares Common $25 par in 1947
Common $25 par changed to $10 par 1/12/62
Stock Dividends - 100% 7/1/47; 25% 2/1/54; 40% 1/25/61; 14-2/7% 1/12/62
Merged into Chicago Bank of Commerce (Chicago, IL) 1/3/72
Each share Common $10 par exchanged for (2) shares Common Capital Stock $10 par
Chicago Bank of Commerce (Chicago, IL) name changed to Associated Bank Chicago (Chicago, IL) 10/17/88
(See Associated Bank Chicago (Chicago, IL))

SOUTH END BK & TR CO (HARTFORD, CT)
Stock Dividend - 10% 01/15/1969
Name changed to Guaranty Bank & Trust Co. (Hartford, CT) 06/05/1972
Guaranty Bank & Trust Co. (Hartford, CT) acquired by Connecticut BancFederation, Inc. 12/28/1973
(See Connecticut BancFederation, Inc.)

SOUTH END PETROLEUMS LTD. (CANADA)
Deemed not to be subsisting company for failure to file returns 2/5/55

SOUTH END VENTURES INC (NV)
Name changed to Shore Group, Inc. (NV) 02/09/1993
Shore Group, Inc. (NV) reincorporated in Delaware 01/18/1994
(See Shore Group, Inc.)

SOUTH FINL GROUP INC (SC)
Each share Mandatory Conv. Preferred Ser. 2008D-V no par exchanged for (153.84541985) shares Common $1 par 05/17/2010
Each share Mandatory Conv. Preferred Ser. 2008D-NV no par exchanged for (153.84591893) shares Common $1 par 05/17/2010
Merged into Toronto-Dominion Bank (Toronto, ON) 09/30/2010
Each share Common $1 par exchanged for (0.004) share Common no par

SOUTH FLA BK HLDG CORP (FL)
Merged into Fifth Third Bancorp 6/11/99
Each share Common 1¢ par exchanged for (0.348) share Common no par

SOUTH FLA BKG CORP (FL)
Merged into Colonial BancGroup, Inc. 02/12/1998
Each share Common $1 par exchanged for (1.5746) shares Common $2.50 par
(See Colonial BancGroup, Inc.)

SOUTH FLA FINL CORP (FL)
Merged into SouthTrust Corp. 10/29/90
Each share Class A Common 10¢ par exchanged for $24.50 cash

SOUTH FORK MINING & LEASING CO. (ID)
Liquidation completed 12/1/60

SOUTH FORK OIL & GAS CO (NV)
Recapitalized as Tejas Oil & Gas Co. 5/28/85
Each share Common $0.001 par exchanged for (0.25) share Common $0.001 par
Tejas Oil & Gas Co. charter revoked 4/1/89

SOUTH GEORGIA NATURAL GAS CO. (GA)
Common $1 par split (5) for (4) by issuance of (0.25) additional share 06/15/1966
Common $1 par split (6) for (5) by issuance of (0.2) additional share 06/15/1967
Acquired by Southern Natural Gas Co. 07/18/1969
Each share Common $1 par exchanged for (1) share Conv. Preference Ser. 1 $1 par
Southern Natural Gas Co. reorganized as Southern Natural Resources, Inc. 05/25/1973
(See Southern Natural Resources, Inc.)

SOUTH GIROUX MINES LTD. (ON)
Recapitalized as Professor Silver Mines Ltd. on a (1/3) for (1) basis 2/23/60
Professor Silver Mines Ltd. merged into Consolidated Professor Mines Ltd. 3/9/64
(See Consolidated Professor Mines Ltd.)

SOUTH HILLS BANK (CHARLESTON, WV)
Merged into Wesbanco, Inc. 4/20/87
Each share Common Capital $5 par exchanged for (1.2) shares Common $4.1666 par

SOUTH HILLSBOROUGH CMNTY BK (APOLLO BEACH, FL)
Merged into Provident Bancorp Inc. 2/11/97
Each share Common $2 par exchanged for (0.4345) share Common no par

SOUTH JERSEY FINL CORP INC (DE)
Merged into Richmond County Financial Corp. 7/31/2000
Each share Common no par exchanged for $20 cash

SOUTH JERSEY GAS, ELECTRIC & TRACTION CO.
Merged into Public Service Electric & Gas Co. and stock exchanged for a like amount of First and Refunding Mortgage Bonds in 1938

SOUTH JERSEY GAS CO (NJ)
Common $5 par changed to $2.50 par and (1) additional share issued 05/26/1959
Stock Dividend - 10% 05/19/1958
Reorganized as South Jersey Industries, Inc. 04/20/1970
Each share Common $2.50 par exchanged for (1) share Common $2.50 par

SOUTH JERSEY NATL BK (CAMDEN, NJ)
Reorganized as Heritage Bancorporation 11/01/1971
Each share Common $5.625 par exchanged for (1) share Common no par
(See Heritage Bancorporation)

SOUTH JERSEY TITLE & FINANCE CO. (NJ)
Name changed to South Jersey Title Insurance Co. 00/00/1946
South Jersey Title Insurance Co. acquired by Commonwealth Land Title Insurance Co. 12/31/1964 which was acquired by Provident National Corp. 10/31/1969 which merged into PNC Financial Corp. 01/19/1983 which name changed to PNC Bank Corp. 02/08/1993 which name changed to PNC Financial Services Group, Inc. 03/15/2000

SOUTH JERSEY TITLE INSURANCE CO. (NJ)
Acquired by Commonwealth Land Title Insurance Co. 12/31/1964
Each share Capital Stock $20 par exchanged for (1.2) shares Common $1.66-2/3 par
Commonwealth Land Title Insurance Co. acquired by Provident National Corp. 10/31/1969 which merged into PNC Financial Corp. 01/19/1983 which name changed to PNC Bank Corp. 02/08/1993 which name changed to PNC Financial Services Group, Inc. 03/15/2000

SOUTH KEORA MINES LTD. (ON)
Charter cancelled for failure to file reports and pay fees in 1965

SOUTH LAKE MINING CO.
Dissolved in 1935

SOUTH MALARTIC GOLD MINES LTD. (QC)
Bankrupt in 1946

SOUTH MCKENZIE ISLAND MINES LTD. (ON)
Charter cancelled and declared dissolved 8/9/72
No stockholders' equity

SOUTH-MONT CORP (CO)
Recapitalized as Black Cat Entertainment Corp. 06/15/1990
Each share Common no par exchanged for (0.005) share Common no par
Black Cat Entertainment Corp. name changed to Mobile Airwaves Corp. 08/15/2005 which recapitalized as American Community Development, Inc. 11/04/2009 which recapitalized as UMF Group Inc. 02/23/2017

SOUTH OKLAHOMA TOWN CO. (OK)
Voluntarily dissolved 6/5/81
Details not available

SOUTH PAC GOLD CORP (BC)
Name changed to Western Carlyle Concepts Inc. 2/9/89
(See Western Carlyle Concepts Inc.)

SOUTH PAC MINERALS CORP (BC)
Recapitalized as Tribune Resources Corp. 07/28/2006
Each share Common no par exchanged for (0.125) share Common no par
Tribune Resources Corp. name changed to Tribune Uranium Corp. 06/13/2007 which name changed to Tribune Minerals Corp. 07/18/2008 which name changed to Stratton Resources Inc. 09/14/2011 which name changed to Torq Resources Inc. 03/15/2017

SOUTH PAC RES CORP (CANADA)
Name changed 10/24/1994
Name changed from South Pacific Resources Inc. to South Pacific Resources Corp. 10/24/1994
Each share old Common no par exchanged for (1/3) share new Common no par 02/22/1995
Recapitalized as Lexacal Investment Corp. 07/24/1998
Each share new Common no par exchanged for (0.25) share Common no par
Lexacal Investment Corp. name changed to New West Energy Services Inc. 10/26/2007

SOUTH PARK NATL BK (HOUSTON, TX)
Common $20 par changed to $10 par and (1) additional share issued plus a 10% stock dividend paid 03/15/1968
Stock Dividend - 15% 03/18/1970
Name changed to Gulf Freeway National Bank (Houston, TX) 09/12/1973
Gulf Freeway National Bank (Houston, TX) acquired by Southwest Bancshares, Inc. 03/29/1979 which merged into MCorp. 10/11/1984
(See MCorp)

SOUTH PARKWAY BUILDING CORP. (IL)
Completely liquidated 11/2/61
Each share Common no par exchanged for first and final distribution of $97 cash

SOUTH PENN COLLIERIES CO.
Reorganized as Penn Anthracite Collieries Co. in 1931
Details not available

SOUTH PENN OIL CO. (PA)
Each share Capital Stock $100 par exchanged for (4) shares Common $25 par in 1926
Each share Common $25 par exchanged for (2) shares Common $12.50 par in 1946
Under plan of merger name changed to Pennzoil Co. (PA) (New) and Common $12.50 par changed to $5 par 7/3/63
Pennzoil Co. (PA) (New) merged into Pennzoil United, Inc. 4/1/68 which name changed to Pennzoil Co. (DE) 6/1/72 which name changed to PennzEnergy Co. 12/30/98

SOUTH PENN TEL CO (PA)
6% 1st Preferred $100 par called for redemption 10/01/1967
6% Preferred Ser. A $100 par called for redemption 11/20/1967
Merged into Mid-Continent Telephone Corp. 12/07/1967
Each share Common $100 par exchanged for (43) shares Common no par
Note: Certificates surrendered between 12/07/1969 and 12/07/1971 received cash
Unexchanged certificates were cancelled and became without value 12/07/1971
Mid-Continent Telephone Corp. name changed to Alltel Corp. (OH) 10/25/1983 which reincorporated in Delaware 05/15/1990
(See Alltel Corp.)

SOUTH PITTSBURGH WTR CO (PA)
Name changed to Western Pennsylvania Water Co. 06/02/1972
Western Pennsylvania Water Co. name changed to Pennsylvania-American Water Co. 02/01/1989
(See Pennsylvania-American Water Co.)

SOUTH POINTE ENTERPRISES INC (FL)
Name changed to Metro Global Media, Inc. (FL) 2/21/96
Metro Global Media, Inc. (FL) reincorporated in Delaware 11/8/96

SOUTH PORTO RICO SUGAR CO. (NJ)
Each share Common $100 par exchanged for (4) shares Common no par 00/00/1927
Each share 8% Preferred $100 par exchanged for (4) shares 8% Preferred $25 par 00/00/1947
Common no par changed to $5 par 12/01/1955
Stock Dividends - 25% 01/01/1955; 10% 09/30/1957
Name changed to South Puerto Rico Sugar Co. 04/01/1959
(See South Puerto Rico Sugar Co.)

SOUTH PUERTO RICO SUGAR CO. (NJ)
Stock Dividend - 10% 08/15/1963
Merged into Gulf & Western Industries, Inc. (DE) 07/12/1967
Each share 8% Preferred $25 par exchanged for $50 principal amount of 6% Non-Conv. Subord. Debentures due 07/01/1987
Each share Common $5 par exchanged for $38 principal amount of 5-1/4% Conv. Subord. Debentures due 07/01/1987

SOUTH SANGAMON BANC SHARES, INC. (IL)
Merged into Illini Community Bancorp, Inc. 09/14/1984
Each share Common $1 par exchanged for (0.1435) share Common $10 par
Illini Community Bancorp, Inc. name changed to Illini Corp. 04/21/1994
(See Illini Corp.)

SOUTH SEA ENERGY CORP (NV)
Name changed to Ameriwest Energy Corp. 09/11/2007
(See Ameriwest Energy Corp.)

SOUTH SEAS MNG LTD (ON)
Charter cancelled and declared dissolved for failure to file returns and pay fees 03/16/1976

SOUTH SEMINOLE BK (FERN PARK, FL)
Name changed to Combank/Casselberry (Fern Park, FL) 02/27/1973
(See Combank/Casselberry (Fern Park, FL))

SOUTH SHORE BANK (CHICAGO, IL)
Merged into ShoreBank (Detroit, MI) 01/31/2001
Details not available

SOUTH SHORE NATL BK (CHICAGO, IL)
Each share Capital Stock $100 par changed for $10 par and (9) additional shares issued 05/02/1961
Stock Dividends - 150% 11/26/1954; 33.03333333% 09/28/1958; 50% 09/21/1961; 33.03333333% 12/14/1965
Name changed to South Shore Bank (Chicago, IL) 12/19/1978

SOUTH SHORE NATL BK (QUINCY, MA)
Capital Stock $100 par changed to $25 par and (3) additional shares issued 12/11/1958
Capital Stock $25 par changed to $6.25 par and (3) additional shares issued 03/08/1966
Stock Dividend - 25% 05/15/1958
Merged into Shorebank, Inc. 11/13/1968
Each share Capital Stock $6.25 par exchanged for (1) share Common $6.25 par
Shorebank, Inc. name changed to Multibank Financial Corp. 11/21/1972 which was acquired by Bank of Boston Corp. 07/13/1993 which name changed to BankBoston Corp. 04/25/1997 which merged into Fleet Boston Corp. 10/01/1999 which name changed to FleetBoston Financial Corp. 04/18/2000 which merged into Bank of America Corp. 04/01/2004

SOUTH SHORE OIL & DEV CO (DE)
Completely liquidated 10/1/68
Each share Capital Stock 10¢ par exchanged for first and final distribution of (0.6) share Walter (Jim) Corp. Common 16-23¢ par
(See Walter (Jim) Corp.)

SOUTH SHORE PUBG INC (MA)
Stock Dividend - 33.03333333% 08/18/1972
Each share Common 10¢ par exchanged for (0.00006711) share Common $1,490 par 10/06/1978
Note: In effect holders received $5.10 cash per share and public interest eliminated

SOUTH SHORE RES INC (NV)
Old Common $0.001 par split (4) for (1) by issuance of (3) additional shares payable 04/30/2007 to holders of record 04/27/2007
Ex date - 05/01/2007
Each share old Common $0.001 par exchanged for (0.01) share new Common $0.001 par 06/20/2011
Name changed to E-Buy Home Inc. 02/06/2013

SOUTH SIDE BK & TR CO (SCRANTON, PA)
Capital Stock $25 par changed to $10 par and (1.5) additional shares issued plus a 100% stock dividend paid 01/05/1970
Name changed to Penn Security Bank & Trust Co. (Scranton, PA) 03/01/1971
Penn Security Bank & Trust Co. (Scranton, PA) recapitalized as Penseco Financial Services Corp. 12/31/1997 which merged into Peoples Financial Services Corp. 12/02/2013

SOUTH SIDE NATL BK (ST LOUIS, MO)
Capital Stock $20 par changed to $10 par and (1) additional share issued 2/10/65
Stock Dividend - 100% 2/20/68
Reorganized as Southside Bancshares Corp. 1/3/83
Each share Capital Stock $10 par exchanged for (1) share Common $10 par
Southside Bancshares Corp. merged into Allegiant Bancorp, Inc. 9/28/2001 which merged into National City Corp. 4/9/2004

SOUTH SOUND NATIONAL BANK (LACEY, WA)
Merged into Rainier Bancorporation 6/1/86
Each share Common $1.25 par exchanged for (0.746) share Common $2.50 par
Rainier Bancorporation acquired by Security Pacific Corp. 8/31/87 which merged into BankAmerica Corp. (Old) 4/22/92 which merged into BankAmerica Corp. (New) 9/30/98 which name changed to Bank of America Corp. 4/28/99

SOUTH STATE URANIUM MINES LTD. (ON)
Charter revoked for failure to file reports and pay fees 11/30/64

SOUTH STS OIL & GAS CO (TX)
Merged into American Exploration Co. 11/15/1983
Each share Common $1 par exchanged for (1.2) shares Common 5¢ par
American Exploration Co. merged into Louis Dreyfus Natural Gas Corp. 10/14/1997 which merged into Dominion Resources, Inc. (New) 11/01/2001 which name changed to Dominion Energy, Inc. 05/11/2017

SOUTH STD MNG CO (UT)
Merged into Chief Consolidated Mining Co. 07/01/1996
Each share Common 10¢ par exchanged for (0.3) share Common 50¢ par
(See Chief Consolidated Mining Co.)

SOUTH STR FINL CORP (NC)
Recapitalized 03/22/2007
Each share Common no par held by holders of (749) or fewer shares exchanged for (1) share Ser. A Preferred no par
Merged into BNC Bancorp 04/01/2014
Each share Ser. A Preferred no par exchanged for $8.85 cash
Each share Common no par exchanged for $8.85 cash

SOUTH STREET TRUST
Liquidation completed in 1948

SOUTH TERMINAL TRUST (MA)
Merged into Sears (David) Real Estate Trust on a share for share basis 3/31/61
Sears (David) Real Estate Trust acquired by Real Estate Trust of America 12/30/66
(See Real Estate Trust of America)

SOUTH TEX BANCSHARES INC (TX)
Merged into Prosperity Acquisition Corp. 10/1/99
Each share Common exchanged for $93.40 cash

SOUTH TEX DEV CO (DE)
Each share Class B Common $20 par exchanged for (10) shares Common $2 par 01/16/1962
Each share Class A Common $20 par exchanged for (0.5) share Common $2 par and $40 cash 02/01/1962
Merged into Sabine Royalty Corp. 08/31/1972
Each share Common $2 par exchanged for (1) share Common no par
Each Certificate of Bene. Int. no par exchanged for $1 cash
Sabine Royalty Corp. reincorporated in Louisiana as Sabine Corp. 01/03/1977
(See Sabine Corp.)

SOUTH TEX DRILLING & EXPL INC (TX)
Name changed 06/30/1981
Name changed from South Texas Drilling Co. to South Texas Drilling & Exploration, Inc. 06/30/1981
Name changed to Pioneer Drilling Co. 08/17/2001
Pioneer Drilling Co. name changed to Pioneer Energy Services Corp. 07/30/2012

SOUTH TEX OIL CO (NV)
Chapter 7 bankruptcy proceedings terminated 11/18/2016
Stockholders' equity unlikely

SOUTH TEXAS COTTON OIL CO.
Acquired by Wesson Oil & Snowdrift Co., Inc. in 1932
Details not available

SOUTH TEXAS DEVELOPMENT CO. (NY)
Each share Common $100 par exchanged for (3) shares Class A Common $20 par and (2) shares Class B Common $20 par in 1952
Merged into South Texas Development Co. (Del.) share for share 8/1/60
South Texas Development Co. (Del.) merged into Sabine Royalty Corp. 8/31/72 which was reincorporated in Louisiana as Sabine Corp. 1/3/77
(See Sabine Corp.)

SOUTH TEXAS GAS CO.
Dissolved in 1932

SOUTH TEXAS OIL & GAS CO. (DE)
Adjudicated bankrupt 11/15/58

SOUTH UMPQUA BK (ROSEBURG, OR)
Name changed 4/29/98
Each share Common $2.50 par exchanged for (3) shares Common 83-1/3¢ par 1/1/79
Name changed from South Umpqua State Bank (Roseburg, OR) to South Umpqua Bank (Roseburg, OR) 4/29/98
Under plan of reorganization each share Common 83-1/3¢ par automatically became (1) share Umpqua Holdings Corp. Common 83-1/3¢ par 3/12/99

SOUTH UMPQUA STATE BANK (CANYONVILLE, OR)
Each share Common $100 par exchanged for (10) shares Common $10 par 01/01/1969
Each share Common $10 par exchanged for (4) shares Common $2.50 par 01/01/1973
Location changed to Roseburg, OR 00/00/1973

SOUTH UNUK GOLD CORP (BC)
Recapitalized as Unuk Gold Corp. 7/26/94
Each share Common no par exchanged for (0.25) share Common no par
Unuk Gold Corp. name changed to Auterra Ventures Inc. 10/1/98 which name changed Global Hunter Corp. 2/24/2005

SOUTH VY BANCORPORATION (CA)
Stock Dividend - 10% payable 02/23/1996 to holders of record 02/16/1996

Merged into Pacific Capital Bancorp (Old) 11/20/1996
Each share Common no par exchanged for (0.92) share Common no par
Pacific Capital Bancorp (Old) merged into Pacific Capital Bancorp (New) (CA) 12/30/1998 which reorganized in Delaware 12/29/2010
(See Pacific Capital Bancorp (New))

SOUTH VERMILLION GOLD MINES, LTD. (ON)
Charter cancelled for failure to file reports and pay taxes in 1956

SOUTH WALES ELECTRICITY PLC (UNITED KINGDOM)
ADR agreement terminated 5/3/96
Each Final Installment Sponsored ADR for Ordinary 50p par exchanged for $125.60 cash

SOUTH WEST BOX CO. (DE)
Name changed to Hoerner Boxes of Sand Springs, Inc. 4/1/54
Hoerner Boxes of Sand Springs, Inc. merged into Hoerner Boxes, Inc. 11/1/54 which merged into Hoerner Waldorf Corp. 5/17/66 which merged into Champion International Corp. 2/24/77 which merged into International Paper Co. 6/20/2000

SOUTH WEST GOLD CORP (BC)
Name changed to Helix Biotech Corp. 09/28/1987
Helix Biotech Corp. recapitalized as International Helix Biotechnologies Inc. 10/22/1993 which merged into Helix BioPharma Corp. 08/15/1995

SOUTH WEST PENNSYLVANIA PIPE LINES (PA)
Capital Stock $100 par changed to $50 par in 1928
Capital Stock $50 par changed to $10 par in 1939
Liquidation completed 11/22/54

SOUTH WEST PPTY TR INC (MD)
Merged into United Dominion Realty Trust, Inc. (VA) 12/31/1996
Each share Common 1¢ par exchanged for (1.0833) shares Common $1 par
United Dominion Realty Trust, Inc. (VA) reincorporated in Maryland 06/11/2003 which name changed to UDR, Inc. 03/14/2007

SOUTH WEST WATER CO.
Merged into Uniontown Water Co. in 1938 which is all owned by Pennsylvania State Water Corp. a subsidiary of American Water Works Co., Inc.

SOUTH WESTN ELECTRICITY PLC (UNITED KINGDOM)
ADR agreement terminated 9/18/95
Each Final Installment Sponsored ADR for Ordinary 50p par exchanged for approximately $137.90 cash

SOUTH WINDSOR BK & TR CO (SOUTH WINDSOR, CT)
Common $5 par changed to $1.666 par by issuance of (2) additional shares 2/15/73
Merged into Bank of New England Corp. 12/21/87
Each (3.2) shares Common $1.666 par exchanged for (1) shares Common $5 par
(See Bank of New England Corp.)

SOUTHAM CO. LTD. (CANADA)
Common no par split (4) for (1) by issuance of (3) additional shares 6/3/60
Name changed to Southam Press Ltd. 4/30/64
Southam Press Ltd. name changed to Southam Inc. 12/21/78
(See Southam Inc.)

SOUTHAM INC (CANADA)
Name changed 12/21/78
Common no par split (4) for (1) by issuance of (3) additional shares 1/17/72
Common no par reclassified as Conv. Class A Common no par 2/15/74
Name changed from Southam Press Ltd. to Southam Inc. and Class A Common no par and Conv. Class B Common no par reclassified as Common no par 12/21/78
Common no par split (4) for (1) by issuance of (3) additional shares 8/21/85
Acquired by Hollinger Canadian Publishing Holdings Inc. 1/22/99
Each share Common no par exchanged for $25.25 cash

SOUTHAMPTON LMBR CORP (NY)
Voluntarily dissolved 6/27/97
Details not available

SOUTHAMPTON VENTURES INC (ON)
Recapitalized as Quetzal Energy Ltd. 04/21/2009
Each share Common no par exchanged for (0.5) share Common no par
Quetzal Energy Ltd. recapitalized as Santa Maria Petroleum Inc. (ON) 06/11/2012 which reorganized in British Columbia as Kalytera Therapeutics, Inc. 01/11/2017

SOUTHBANC SHS INC (DE)
Merged into National Commerce Financial Corp. 11/19/2001
Each share Common 1¢ par exchanged for (1.1142) shares Common $2 par
National Commerce Financial Corp. merged into SunTrust Banks, Inc. 10/1/2004

SOUTHBAR MINES LTD. (ON)
Charter cancelled for failure to file reports and pay taxes 12/1/60

SOUTHBORROUGH VENTURES INC (NV)
Common $0.001 par split (4) for (1) by issuance of (3) additional shares payable 01/27/2003 to holders of record 01/22/2003 Ex date - 01/28/2003
Name changed to AmeriChip International, Inc. 12/09/2003
(See AmeriChip International, Inc.)

SOUTHBRIDGE PLASTIC PRODUCTS INC. (NY)
Acquired by Grace (W.R.) & Co. (CT) 07/14/1965
Each share Class A $1 par exchanged for (0.2545) share Common $1 par
Grace (W.R.) & Co. (CT) reincorporated in New York 05/19/1988
(See Grace (W.R.) & Co.)

SOUTHBRIDGE RES CORP (BC)
Name changed to Vodis Pharmaceuticals Inc. 07/29/2014

SOUTHBROOK INTL TELEVISION PLC (ENGLAND)
ADR agreement terminated 00/00/1987
No ADR's remain outstanding

SOUTHCAM PETROLEUM CORP. (DE)
Charter cancelled and declared inoperative and void for non-payment of taxes 4/1/66

SOUTHCAN MNG LTD (BC)
Recapitalized as Capella Resources Ltd. 8/18/81
Each share Common no par exchanged for (0.25) share Common no par
(See Capella Resources Ltd.)

SOUTHCOAST CMNTY BK (MT PLEASANT, SC)
Stock Dividend - 10% payable 03/26/1999 to holders of record 03/11/1999
Under plan of reorganization each share Common $5 par automatically became (1) share Southcoast Financial Corp. Common no par 04/29/1999
Southcoast Financial Corp. merged into BNC Bancorp 06/17/2016 which merged into Pinnacle Financial Partners, Inc. 06/16/2017

SOUTHCOAST FINL CORP (SC)
Stock Dividends - 10% payable 04/16/2001 to holders of record 03/15/2001; 10% payable 05/13/2002 to holders of record 04/22/2002; 10% payable 05/30/2003 to holders of record 05/09/2003 Ex date - 05/07/2003; 5% payable 08/15/2003 to holders of record 07/21/2003 Ex date - 07/17/2003; 10% payable 05/28/2004 to holders of record 05/07/2004 Ex date - 05/05/2004; 10% payable 06/24/2005 to holders of record 05/27/2005 Ex date - 05/25/2005; 10% payable 05/26/2006 to holders of record 05/05/2006 Ex date - 05/03/2006; 10% payable 06/22/2007 to holders of record 06/01/2007 Ex date - 05/30/2007; 10% payable 06/29/2011 to holders of record 06/15/2011 Ex date - 06/13/2011; 15% payable 01/17/2013 to holders of record 12/31/2012 Ex date - 12/27/2012; 15% payable 06/21/2013 to holders of record 05/31/2013 Ex date - 05/29/2013
Merged into BNC Bancorp 06/17/2016
Each share Common no par exchanged for (0.6068) share Common $0.001 par
BNC Bancorp merged into Pinnacle Financial Partners, Inc. 06/16/2017

SOUTHCORP LTD (AUSTRALIA)
Name changed 01/15/1998
Name changed from Southcorp Holdings Ltd. to Southcorp Ltd. 01/15/1998
Merged into Foster's Group Ltd. 08/08/2005
Each Sponsored ADR for Ordinary exchanged for $16.01445 cash

SOUTHDOWN INC (LA)
$1.80 Conv. Preferred $10 par called for redemption 10/23/78
$3.75 Conv. Exchangeable Preferred Ser. B no par called for redemption 11/21/96
Each share $2.875 Conv. Preferred Ser. D 5¢ par exchanged for (1.511) shares Common $1.25 par 9/2/97
Merged into Cemex, S.A. de C.V. 11/16/2000
Each share Common $1.25 par exchanged for $73 cash
(See Southdown Sugars, Inc.)

SOUTHDOWN SUGARS, INC. (LA)
Common $5 par changed to $2.50 par 9/21/56
Stock Dividends - 25% 6/14/54; 10% 4/29/55; 10% 4/15/57; 10% 4/13/59
Name changed to Southdown, Inc. 5/12/59
(See Southdown, Inc.)

SOUTHEAST ACQUISITIONS LTD PARTNERSHIP (DE)
Completely liquidated 03/15/2004
Each Unit of Ltd. Partnership Int. III received first and final distribution of $238 cash
Completely liquidated 12/01/2006
Each Unit of Ltd. Partnership Int. II received first and final distribution of $740 cash

SOUTHEAST BANCORPORATION INC (FL)
Name changed to Southeast Banking Corp. 04/22/1971
(See Southeast Banking Corp.)

SOUTHEAST BANK (TAMPA, FL)
Through voluntary exchange offer 98% held by Southeast Bancorporation, Inc. as of 9/16/77
Public interest eliminated

SOUTHEAST BANK OF GALT OCEAN MILE (FORT LAUDERDALE, FL)
100% acquired by Southeast Banking Corp. through exchange offer as of 07/13/1973
Public interest eliminated

SOUTHEAST BKG CORP (FL)
Common $5 par split (2) for (1) by issuance of (1) additional share 05/15/1972
Limited Div. Conv. Preferred Ser. A no par called for redemption 06/29/1979
Common $5 par split (3) for (2) by issuance of (0.5) additional share 02/06/1987
$4.06 Conv. Preferred no par called for redemption 03/02/1987
10% Conv. Preferred Ser. C $1 par called for redemption 07/31/1989
Stock Dividend - 10% 05/03/1971
Chapter 7 bankruptcy proceedings terminated 08/04/2017
No stockholders equity

SOUTHEAST COMM HLDG CO (GA)
Name changed to ebank.com, Inc. 04/20/1999
ebank.com, Inc. name changed to ebank Financial Services, Inc. 01/01/2003
(See ebank Financial Services, Inc.)

SOUTHEAST EQUITY MGMT INC (DE)
Name changed to Nationwide Power Corp. 9/7/82
Nationwide Power Corp. merged into Brooks Satellite Inc. 5/29/86
(See Brooks Satellite Inc.)

SOUTHEAST EXPL CORP (UT)
Proclaimed dissolved for failure to pay taxes 09/30/1982

SOUTHEAST FIRST BANK (JACKSONVILLE, FL)
Through voluntary exchange offer 98.5% held by Southeast Bancorporation, Inc. as of 3/18/71
Public interest eliminated

SOUTHEAST FIRST BANK OF LARGO (LARGO, FL)
99% held by Southeast Banking Corp. through exchange offer which expired 07/31/1974
Public interest eliminated

SOUTHEAST FIRST NATIONAL BANK (MIAMI SPRINGS, FL)
97.9% held by Southeast Banking Corp. as of 12/31/1967
Public interest eliminated

SOUTHEAST MISSOURI LEAD CO.
Dissolved in 1938

SOUTHEAST NATL BANCSHARES PA INC (PA)
Stock Dividend - 10% 03/17/1982
Merged into Fidelcor, Inc. 06/30/1983
Each share Common $1 par exchanged for (1.86) shares $3.25 Conv. Preferred Ser. A $1 par
Fidelcor, Inc. merged into First Fidelity Bancorporation (New) 02/29/1988
(See First Fidelity Bancorporation (New))

SOUTHEAST NATIONAL BANK (DUNEDIN, FL)
96.8% held by Southeast Banking Corp. as of 04/27/1972
Public interest eliminated

SOU-SOU

SOUTHEAST NATL BK (HAMMOND, LA)
Merged into Hancock Holding Co. 01/15/1997
Each share Common no par exchanged for (0.267) share Common $3.33 par and $8.0522 cash
Hancock Holding Co. name changed to Hancock Whitney Corp. 05/25/2018

SOUTHEAST NATIONAL BANK OF NAPLES (NAPLES, FL)
Over 99% acquired by Southeast Banking Corp. through exchange offer as of 01/17/1974
Public interest eliminated

SOUTHEAST NATL BK PA (CHESTER, PA)
Common $3.33333333 par changed to $6 par 03/01/1971
Stock Dividend - 10% 04/21/1981
Under plan of reorganization each share Common $6 par automatically became (1) share Southeast National Bancshares of Pennsylvania Common $1 par 01/04/1982
Southeast National Bancshares of Pennsylvania merged into Fidelcor, Inc. 06/30/1983 which merged into First Fidelity Bancorporation (New) 02/29/1988
(See First Fidelity Bancorporation (New))

SOUTHEAST RLTY CORP (FL)
Name changed to Crocker Realty Trust, Inc. 06/30/1995
(See Crocker Realty Trust, Inc.)

SOUTHEAST TIRE RECYCLING INC (FL)
Name changed to Clearworks Technologies, Inc. 05/14/1998
Clearworks Technologies, Inc. name changed to Clearworks.Net Inc. 04/29/1999 which merged into Eagle Wireless International, Inc. 02/05/2001 which name changed to Eagle Broadband, Inc. 03/04/2002
(See Eagle Broadband, Inc.)

SOUTHEAST TITLE & INSURANCE CO. (FL)
Common $7.50 par changed to $2.50 par 05/01/1961
Each share Common $2.50 par exchanged for (1) share Common $4 par 06/16/1969
Merged into Associated Industries Insurance Company, Inc. 06/10/1996
Details not available

SOUTHEASTERN AGRIC INDS INC (NY)
Charter cancelled and proclaimed dissolved for failure to pay taxes 06/27/1979

SOUTHEASTERN AIRWAYS, INC. (FL)
Proclaimed dissolved and charter cancelled for non-payment of taxes 5/1/62

SOUTHEASTERN BANCORP INC (TN)
Each share old Common exchanged for (0.2) share new Common 4/26/2000

SOUTHEASTERN BK FINL CORP (GA)
Stock Dividend - 10% payable 06/02/2008 to holders of record 05/22/2008 Ex date - 05/20/2008
Merged into South State Corp. 01/03/2017
Each share Common $3 par exchanged for (0.7307) share Common $2.50 par

SOUTHEASTERN CAP CORP (GA)
Reincorporated 07/31/1976
State of incorporation changed from (TN) to (GA) 07/31/1976

Each share old Common $1 par exchanged for (0.0004) share new Common $1 par 11/01/1996
Note: In effect holders received $19.94 cash per share and public interest was eliminated
Note: Unexchanged certificates were cancelled and became without value 11/01/2001
$1.40 Preferred Ser. A called for redemption at $14 on 10/15/1997
Public interest eliminated

SOUTHEASTERN COAL CO.
In process of liquidation in 1942

SOUTHEASTERN CORP.
Dissolved in 1947

SOUTHEASTERN CTL SYS INC (DE)
Charter forfeited for failure to maintain a registered agent 11/04/1990

SOUTHEASTERN DRILLING INC (TX)
Common $1 par split (2) for (1) by issuance of (1) additional share 6/28/67
Name changed to Sedco, Inc. 12/30/68
Sedco, Inc. merged into Schlumberger Ltd. 12/24/84

SOUTHEASTERN FACTORS CORP. (NC)
Merged into American Discount Co. on a (0.125) for (1) basis 10/2/61
American Discount Co. merged into American Credit Corp. 12/31/64 which merged into Wachovia Corp. (Old) 7/1/70
Wachovia Corp. (Old) merged into First Wachovia Corp. 12/5/85 which name changed to Wachovia Corp. (New) 5/20/91 which merged into Wachovia Corp. (Ctfs. dated after 9/1/2001) 9/1/2001

SOUTHEASTERN FIDELITY FIRE INSURANCE CO. (GA)
Name changed to Southeastern Fidelity Insurance Co. 2/1/67

SOUTHEASTERN FUND (SC)
Each share Common $2.50 par exchanged for (3) shares Common $1 par 00/00/1952
Acquired by American Investors Corp. (TN) 09/15/1958
Each share Common $1 par exchanged for (1.1) shares Common $1 par
American Investors Corp. (TN) reincorporated in Delaware as AIC Corp. 12/31/1964 which name changed to Crutcher Resources Corp. 12/31/1968
(See Crutcher Resources Corp.)

SOUTHEASTERN GAS & WATER CO.
Name changed to Southeastern Corp. in 1944 which dissolved in 1947

SOUTHEASTERN GEN CORP (FL)
Charter cancelled and proclaimed dissolved for non-payment of taxes 06/10/1968

SOUTHEASTERN GREYHOUND LINES
Acquired by Greyhound Corp. (DE) in 1951
Each share Common $5 par exchanged for (1.3) shares Common $3 par
Greyhound Corp. (DE) reincorporated in (AZ) 3/3/78 which name changed to Greyhound Dial Corp. 5/8/90 which name changed to Dial Corp. (AZ) 5/14/91 which reincorporated in (DE) 3/18/92 which name changed to Viad Corp. 8/15/96

SOUTHEASTERN ICE UTILITIES CORP.
Acquired by Atlantic Ice & Coal Co. in 1931
Details not available

SOUTHEASTERN IND BANCORP (IN)
Merged into First Financial Bancorp 6/1/97

Each share Common no par exchanged for $261.3153 cash

SOUTHEASTERN INDIANA CORP.
Liquidated in 1942

SOUTHEASTERN INNS CORP (TN)
Charter revoked for non-payment of taxes 10/22/1976

SOUTHEASTERN INVESTMENT TRUST, INC.
Liquidated in 1950
No Common stockholders' equity

SOUTHEASTERN LIFE INSURANCE CO. (SC)
Under plan of merger name changed to Liberty Life Insurance Co. (S.C.) 1/1/42

SOUTHEASTERN MICH GAS CO (MI)
Stock Dividends - 50% 10/15/1957; 25% 10/15/1958; 20% 12/15/1970; 25% 03/22/1979
Under plan of reorganization each share Common $10 par automatically became (1) share Southeastern Michigan Gas Enterprises, Inc. Common $10 par 11/01/1977
Southeastern Michigan Gas Enterprises, Inc. name changed to Semco Energy Inc. 04/24/1997
(See Semco Energy Inc.)
Name changed to SEMCO Energy Gas Co. 04/30/1997

SOUTHEASTERN MICH GAS ENTERPRISES INC (MI)
Common $10 par split (0.55) for (1) to reflect a (3) for (2) split and the payment of a 5% stock dividend 05/15/1986
Common $10 par split (4) for (3) by issuance of (1/3) additional share 01/15/1989
Stock Dividends - 10% 05/15/1978; 10% 05/15/1979; 10% 02/15/1980; 10% 05/15/1981; 5% payable 05/15/1996 to holders of record 05/05/1996
Name changed to Semco Energy Inc. 04/24/1997
(See Semco Energy Inc.)

SOUTHEASTERN MICH HLDG CO (DE)
Stock Dividend - 100% 10/02/1972
Name changed to Security Bancorp, Inc. (DE) 01/16/1973
Security Bancorp, Inc. (DE) reincorporated in Michigan 01/31/1983 which merged into First of America Bank Corp. 05/01/1992 which merged into National City Corp. 03/31/1998 which was acquired by PNC Financial Services Group, Inc. 12/31/2008

SOUTHEASTERN MODULAR INDS INC (DE)
Name changed to Pneucyclic Sciences, Inc. 1/28/74
(See Pneucyclic Sciences, Inc.)

SOUTHEASTERN MTG INVS TR (MA)
Name changed to Universal Investors Trust 05/23/1969
Universal Investors Trust name changed to Universal Housing & Development Co. 03/17/1971
(See Universal Housing & Development Co.)

SOUTHEASTERN NEWSPAPERS CORP (GA)
6% Preferred $10 par called for redemption 6/30/66
6-1/2% Conv. Preference $7 par called for redemption 6/30/66
Class A Common 50¢ par called for redemption 5/3/71
Public interest eliminated

SOUTHEASTERN POWER & LIGHT CO.
Acquired by Commonwealth & Southern Corp. in 1930 which was dissolved 10/1/49

(See Commonwealth & Southern Corp.)

SOUTHEASTERN PROPANE GAS CO (FL)
Name changed to Public Gas Co. 08/21/1981
(See Public Gas Co.)

SOUTHEASTERN PUB SVC CO (DE)
Common 10¢ par changed to $1 par 02/01/1962
Common $1 par split (4) for (3) by issuance of (1/3) additional share 07/02/1979
Merged into Triarc Companies, Inc. (OH) 04/14/1994
Each share Common $1 par exchanged for (0.8) share Class A Common 10¢ par
Triarc Companies, Inc. (OH) reincorporated in Delaware 06/30/1994 which name changed to Wendy's/Arby's Group, Inc. 09/29/2008 which name changed to Wendy's Co. 07/11/2011

SOUTHEASTERN SVGS BK INC CHARLOTTE (NC)
Name changed 7/13/88
Name changed from Southeastern Savings & Loan Co. to Southeastern Savings Bank, Inc. 7/13/88
Stock Dividends - 10% 12/2/85; 10% 3/3/87
Taken over by the RTC 11/18/90
Stockholders' equity unlikely

SOUTHEASTERN SECURITY INSURANCE CO. (TN)
Merged into Lincoln American Life Insurance Co. 8/1/63
Each share Common $1 par exchanged for (1) share Common Capital Stock $1 par
Lincoln American Life Insurance Co. reorganized as Lincoln American Corp. (TN) 4/1/69 which merged into Lincoln American Corp. (NY) 5/1/72 which merged into American General Corp. 9/1/80 which merged into American International Group, Inc. 8/29/2001

SOUTHEASTERN STATE BANK (TULSA, OK)
Name changed to Bank of Tulsa (Tulsa, OK) 3/10/77
Bank of Tulsa (Tulsa, OK) reorganized as Tulbancorp, Inc. 12/29/78
(See Tulbancorp, Inc.)

SOUTHEASTERN SURETY CO. (FL)
Common $15 par changed to $10 par 00/00/1956
Common $10 par changed to $7.50 par 00/00/1958
Name changed to Southeast Title & Insurance Co. 03/31/1959
(See Southeast Title & Insurance Co.)

SOUTHEASTERN SURGICAL SUPPLY CO (DE)
Name changed to American Home Patient Centers Inc. 03/15/1983
American Home Patient Centers Inc. name changed to Wessex Corp. 05/27/1986 which name changed to Diversicare Corp. of America 05/01/1989
(See Diversicare Corp. of America)

SOUTHEASTERN TEL CO (FL)
Common no par changed to $10 par in 1949
5.6% Preferred $25 par called for redemption 3/22/65
Common $10 par split (3) for (2) by issuance of (0.5) additional share 5/24/67
Merged into Central Telephone Co. (New) 12/1/71
Each share $6 Div. Ser. Preferred no par exchanged for (1) share $6 Preferred Ser. 2 no par
Each share Common $10 par

exchanged for (0.91) share Conv. Jr. Preferred no par
(See Central Telephone Co. (New))

SOUTHEASTERN THRIFT & BK FD INC (MD)
Name changed 10/28/1991
Name changed from Southeastern Savings Institutions Fund, Inc. to Southeastern Thrift & Bank Fund, Inc. 10/28/1991
Common $0.001 par split (2) for (1) by issuance of (1) additional share 11/30/1995
Name changed to Hancock (John) Financial Trends Fund, Inc. 03/26/2001
Hancock (John) Financial Trends Fund, Inc. name changed to Financial Trends Fund, Inc. 11/20/2007 which name changed to Diamond Hill Financial Trends Fund, Inc. 01/15/2008
(See Diamond Hill Financial Trends Fund, Inc.)

SOUTHERN ACCEP CORP (GA)
Recapitalized as Efficiency Lodge, Inc. 12/31/96
Each share Common 10¢ par exchanged for (0.01) share Common 10¢ par

SOUTHERN ACID & SULPHUR CO., INC.
Acquired by Mathieson Chemical Corp. on a (5.5) for (8) basis in 1949
Mathieson Chemical Corp. merged into Olin Mathieson Chemical Corp. in 1954 which name changed to Olin Corp. 9/1/69

SOUTHERN ADVANCE BAG & PAPER CO. INC. (ME)
Common no par changed to $1 par 00/00/1945
Stock Dividends - 100% 10/00/1946; 100% 12/00/1948
Acquired by Gair (Robert) Co., Inc. 05/02/1955
Each share Common $1 par exchanged for (0.23) share $4.50 Preferred $100 par and (0.666666) share Common $1 par
(See Gair (Robert) Co., Inc.)

SOUTHERN AFRICA FD INC (MD)
Completely liquidated 11/23/2004
Each share Common 1¢ par exchanged for first and final distribution of $22.86481 cash

SOUTHERN AFRICA MINERALS CORP (CANADA)
Name changed to Tango Mineral Resources Inc. 7/2/2002
Tango Mineral Resources Inc. recapitalized as RNC Gold Inc. 12/4/2003 which merged into Yamana Gold Inc. 2/28/2006

SOUTHERN AIR TRANSPORT, INC.
Liquidated in 1931

SOUTHERN AIRLS INC (FL)
Proclaimed dissolved for failure to file reports and pay fees 11/1/85

SOUTHERN AMERN FIRE INS CO (FL)
Stock Dividends - 10% 12/30/1963; 90% 12/31/1964
Proclaimed dissolved for failure to file reports and pay fees 12/11/1976

SOUTHERN ANDES ENERGY INC (CANADA)
Each share Common no par received distribution of (0.449) share Caracara Silver Inc. Common no par payable 04/12/2012 to holders of record 04/10/2012 Ex date - 04/05/2012
Merged into Macusani Yellowcake Inc. 04/13/2012
Each share Common no par exchanged for (0.8) share Common no par
Macusani Yellowcake Inc. recapitalized as Plateau Uranium Inc. 05/01/2015 which changed to Plateau Energy Metals Inc. 03/16/2018

SOUTHERN ARIZ BANCORP INC (AZ)
Merged into Zions Bancorporation 06/01/1996
Each share Common no par exchanged for (0.287347) share Common no par
Zions Bancorporation merged into Zions Bancorporation, N.A. (Salt Lake City, UT) 10/01/2018

SOUTHERN ARIZ BK & TR CO (TUCSON, AZ)
Capital Stock $100 par changed to $10 par and (9) additional shares issued 4/24/56
Capital Stock $10 par changed to $12 par 6/7/71
Merged into First National Bank of Arizona (Phoenix, AZ) 5/14/75
Each share Capital Stock $12 par exchanged for (0.85) share Capital Stock $10 par
First National Bank of Arizona (Phoenix, AZ) merged into Western Bancorporation 7/1/80 which name changed to First Interstate Bancorp 6/1/81 which merged into Wells Fargo & Co. (Old) 4/1/96 which merged into Wells Fargo & Co. (New) 11/2/98

SOUTHERN ARIZ MNG & SMLT CORP (CANADA)
Recapitalized as Unirom Technologies Inc. 03/12/1997
Each share Common no par exchanged for (0.02083333) share Common no par
(See Unirom Technologies Inc.)

SOUTHERN ATLANTIC CORP (FL)
Proclaimed dissolved for failure to file reports and pay fees 11/01/1985

SOUTHERN AWYS INC (DE)
Each share Common $1 par exchanged for (0.33333333) share Common $3 par 00/00/1949
Common $3 par changed to $2 par and (0.5) additional share issued 06/10/1966
$0.36 Conv. Preferred Ser. B $1 par reclassified as Common $2 par 12/31/1974
$0.36 Conv. Preferred Ser. A $1 par called for redemption 10/20/1978
Stock Dividend - 10% 10/31/1963
Merged into Republic Airlines, Inc. 07/01/1979
Each share Common $2 par exchanged for (2.1) shares Common 20¢ par
(See Republic Airlines, Inc.)

SOUTHERN BAKERIES CO (DE)
Each share Common no par exchanged for (2) shares Common $7 par 7/1/59
Under plan of reorganization each share Preferred no par and Common $7 par automatically became (1) share Southern Daisy Industries, Inc. (GA) Ser. A Preferred no par or Common $1 par respectively 3/7/72
(See Southern Daisy Industries, Inc.)

SOUTHERN BAKING CO.
Succeeded by Columbia Baking Co. 00/00/1928
Details not available

SOUTHERN BANCORPORATION (DE)
Name changed to Southern Bancorporation of Alabama 04/21/1975
Southern Bancorporation of Alabama name changed to SouthTrust Corp. 09/18/1981 which merged into Wachovia Corp. (Ctfs. dated after 09/01/2001) 11/01/2004 which merged into Wells Fargo & Co. (New) 12/31/2008

SOUTHERN BANCORPORATION ALA (DE)
Common $5 par changed to $2.50 par and (1) additional share issued 05/06/1977
Name changed to SouthTrust Corp. 09/18/1981
SouthTrust Corp. merged into Wachovia Corp. (Ctfs. dated after 09/01/2001) 11/01/2004 which merged into Wells Fargo & Co. (New) 12/31/2008

SOUTHERN BANCORPORATION INC (SC)
Stock Dividends - 20% 01/25/1980; 10% 10/31/1985
Acquired by First Union Corp. 04/01/1986
Each share $6.28 Conv. Preferred $10 par exchanged for $327.36 cash
Each share Common $2.50 par exchanged for $30 cash

SOUTHERN BANCSHARES LTD (IL)
Merged into Old National Bancorp 1/29/99
Each share Common $2 par exchanged for (2.8875) shares Common no par

SOUTHERN BK & TR CO (GREENVILLE, SC)
Common $10 par changed to $5 par and (1) additional share issued 12/31/1970
Reorganized as Southern Bancorporation, Inc. 10/31/1973
Each share Common $5 par exchanged for (2) shares Common $2.50 par
(See Southern Bancorporation, Inc.)

SOUTHERN BK & TR CO (RICHMOND, VA)
Capital Stock $15 par changed to $10 par and (1) additional share issued plus a 33-1/3% stock dividend paid 01/31/1964
Stock Dividends - 20% 02/14/1949; 25% 07/20/1950; 100% 04/15/1952; 100% 02/03/1958; 25% 12/30/1969
Reorganized as Southern Bankshares, Inc. 05/01/1970
Each share Capital Stock $10 par exchanged for (1) share Common $10 par
Southern Bankshares, Inc. merged into Jefferson Bankshares, Inc. 12/31/1979 which merged into Wachovia Corp. (New) (Ctfs. dated between 05/20/1991 and 09/01/2001) 10/31/1997 which merged into Wachovia Corp. (Ctfs. dated after 09/01/2001) 09/01/2001 which merged into Wells Fargo & Co. (New) 12/31/2008

SOUTHERN BANK (WEST PALM BEACH, FL)
96.6% held by Barnett Banks of Florida, Inc. through exchange offer which expired 11/15/1973
Public interest eliminated

SOUTHERN BK GROUP INC (GA)
Merged into SouthTrust Corp. 06/30/1995
Each share Common $1 par exchanged for (0.5275665) share Common $2.50 par
SouthTrust Corp. merged into Wachovia Corp. (Ctfs. dated after 09/01/2001) 11/01/2004 which merged into Wells Fargo & Co. (New) 12/31/2008

SOUTHERN BK NORFOLK (NORFOLK, VA)
Through exchange offer First Virginia Corp. acquired all but (268) shares of Capital Stock $10 par as of 01/09/1963
Public interest eliminated

SOUTHERN BANKERS INVT CO (TX)
Each share Common $1 par exchanged for (2) shares Common no par 8/17/70
Charter forfeited for failure to pay taxes 2/26/73

SOUTHERN BANKERS SECURITIES CORP.
Assets sold to Carriers & General Corp. in 1936
Details not available

SOUTHERN BANKSHARES INC (VA)
Stock Dividend - 25% 06/29/1973
Merged into Jefferson Bankshares, Inc. 12/31/1979
Each share $3.50 Conv. Preferred $10 par exchanged for (2.7969) shares Common $2.50 par
Each share Common $10 par exchanged for (1.79) shares Common $2.50 par
Jefferson Bankshares, Inc. merged into Wachovia Corp. (New) (Ctfs. dated between 05/20/1991 and 09/01/2001) 10/31/1997 which merged into Wachovia Corp. (Ctfs. dated after 09/01/2001) 09/01/2001 which merged into Wells Fargo & Co. (New) 12/31/2008

SOUTHERN BANKSHARES INC (WV)
Stock Dividend - 200% 10/20/86
Acquired by Key Centurion Bancshares, Inc. 5/1/91
Each share Common $2.50 par exchanged for $60.06 cash

SOUTHERN BAR MINERALS CORP (ON)
Name changed to Texas Gulf Petroleum Corp. (ON) 01/26/1996
Texas Gulf Petroleum Corp. (ON) reincorporated in British Columbia 06/11/1996 which recapitalized as Portrush Petroleum Corp. 03/15/2000 which recapitalized as Westbridge Energy Corp. 12/11/2009

SOUTHERN BELLA INC (DE)
Common $0.000001 par split (80) for (1) by issuance of (79) additional shares payable 08/30/2011 to holders of record 08/29/2011
Ex date - 08/31/2011
Name changed to Great American Energy, Inc. 09/09/2011
Great American Energy, Inc. recapitalized as Sovereign Lithium, Inc. 07/12/2013

SOUTHERN BELLE ELECTRICAL INDS INC (FL)
Charter cancelled and proclaimed dissolved for non-payment of taxes 05/23/1973

SOUTHERN BERKSHIRE POWER & ELECTRIC CO. (MA)
Merged into New England Electric System on a (3.4) for (1) basis 6/30/59
(See New England Electric System)

SOUTHERN BIOTECH INC (FL)
Chapter 11 bankruptcy proceedings converted to Chapter 7 on 12/19/86
Stockholders' equity unlikely

SOUTHERN BISCUIT CO., INC.
Acquired by Weston (George) Ltd. in 1944

SOUTHERN BLEACHERY, INC.
Acquired by Southern Bleachery & Print Works, Inc. 00/00/1931
Details not available

SOUTHERN BLEACHERY & PRINT WORKS, INC. (DE)
Stock Dividend - 400% 2/48
Merged into Burlington Industries, Inc. on a (1) for (2.25) basis 1/2/65
(See Burlington Industries, Inc.)

SOUTHERN BOND & SHARE CORP.
Merged into Pacific Southern Investors, Inc. 00/00/1932
Details not available

SOUTHERN BREWERIES, INC.
Dissolved in 1946

SOUTHERN BUSINESS & INDL DEV CORP (MS)
Charter suspended for failure to file reports and pay taxes 06/02/1976

SOUTHERN CALIFORNIA AVIATION CORP. (DE)
Dissolved 00/00/1935
Details not available

SOUTHERN CALIF BEVERAGE CORP (FL)
Name changed to Tropical Beverage, Inc. 09/12/2003
Tropical Beverage, Inc. recapitalized as ViviCells International, Inc. 05/09/2008

SOUTHERN CALIFORNIA DUROX, INC. (CA)
Charter suspended for failure to file reports and pay fees 12/01/1982

SOUTHERN CALIF EDISON CO (CA)
Name changed 00/00/1947
5% Original Preferred $100 par and Common $100 par changed to $25 par and (3) additional shares issued respectively 04/01/1926
Name changed from Southern California Edison Co. to Southern California Edison Co., Ltd. 00/00/1930 and back to Southern California Edison Co. 00/00/1947
6% Ser. B $25 par called for redemption 06/23/1947
5.5% Ser. C $25 par called for redemption 06/23/1947
4.88% Preferred $25 par called for redemption 12/20/1961
5% Original Preferred $25 par and Common $25 par changed to $8.33333333 par and (2) additional shares issued respectively 01/19/1962
4.48% Conv. Preference $25 par called for redemption 07/31/1963
4.56% Conv. Preference $25 par called for redemption 07/31/1963
Common $8.33333333 par changed to $4.16666666 par and (1) additional share issued 08/10/1984
12% Preferred $100 par called for redemption 02/28/1986
8.85% Preferred $25 par called for redemption 03/04/1986
9.2% Preferred $25 par called for redemption 03/04/1986
7.375% Preference $25 par called for redemption 02/29/1988
5.2% Conv. Preference $25 par called for redemption 05/31/1988
Under plan of reorganization each share 5% Original Preferred $8.33333333 par exchanged for (2.1) shares SCEcorp Common $4.16666666 par 07/01/1988
Under plan of reorganization each share Common $4.16666666 par automatically became (1) share SCEcorp Common $4.16666666 par 07/01/1988
8.7% Preferred $100 par called for redemption 02/26/1992
8.96% Preferred $100 par called for redemption 02/26/1992
8.54% Preferred $100 par called for redemption 08/12/1992
8.7% Preferred Ser. A $100 par called for redemption 08/12/1992
7.325% Preferred $100 par called for redemption 04/30/1993
7.8% Preferred $100 par called for redemption 04/30/1993
7.58% Preferred $100 par called for redemption 06/30/1995
7.36% Preferred $25 par called for redemption at $25 plus $0.46 accrued dividends on 04/30/1997
5.8% Preferred $25 par called for redemption at $25.25 plus $0.1208 accrued dividends on 06/30/1998
6.45% Preferred $100 par called for redemption at $100 on 06/30/2002
7.23% Preferred $100 par called for redemption at $100 on 04/30/2005
6.05% Preferred $100 par called for redemption at $100 on 05/20/2005
6% Preference Ser. C no par called for redemption at $100 on 02/28/2013
6.125% Preference Ser. B no par called for redemption at $100 on 02/28/2013
Adjustable Rate Preference Ser. A no par called for redemption at $100 plus $0.567334 accrued dividends on 09/16/2015
6.5% Preference Ser. B no par called for redemption at $100 plus $0.541667 accrued dividends on 03/31/2016
(Additional Information in Active)

SOUTHERN CALIF 1ST NATL CORP (CA)
Stock Dividend - 10% 02/15/1970
Completely liquidated 10/06/1975
Each share Common $5 par exchanged for first and final distribution of $18.50 cash

SOUTHERN CALIF 1ST NATL BK (SAN DIEGO, CA)
Reorganized as Southern California First National Corp. 02/28/1969
Each share Common $5 par exchanged for (2) shares Common $5 par
(See Southern California First National Corp.)

SOUTHERN CALIF GAS CO (CA)
$10 Preferred no par called for redemption 04/30/1990
Flexible Auction Preferred Ser. A no par called for redemption 03/28/1996
Flexible Auction Preferred Ser. C no par called for redemption 04/18/1996
7.75% Preferred $25 par called for redemption at $25 on 02/02/1998
(Additional Information in Active)

SOUTHERN CALIFORNIA GAS CORP.
Dissolved in 1935

SOUTHERN CALIFORNIA IRON & STEEL CO.
Acquired by Bethlehem Steel Corp. (NJ) in 1929
(See Bethlehem Steel Corp. (NJ))

SOUTHERN CALIFORNIA LAND DEVELOPMENT CORP. (UT)
Charter revoked for failure to file reports and pay fees 3/31/67

SOUTHERN CALIF MINORITY CAP CORP (CA)
Voluntarily dissolved 02/05/1979
Details not available

SOUTHERN CALIF MTG & LN CORP (CA)
Name changed to Western Pacific Financial Corp. 07/02/1973
(See Western Pacific Financial Corp.)

SOUTHERN CALIF PETE CORP (CA)
Each share Class A $10 par exchanged for (3) shares Common no par or (1) share 6% Preferred $10 par 00/00/1949
Each share Class B $10 par exchanged for (2) shares Common no par 00/00/1949
Common no par changed to $2 par 00/00/1950
6% Conv. Preferred $25 par called for redemption 07/29/1964
Name changed to Scope Industries 11/30/1964

SOUTHERN CALIF PLASTIC CO (CA)
Common $1 par changed to no par 10/09/1968
Name changed to Maxad, Inc. 12/26/1968
Maxad, Inc. name changed to Morehouse Industries, Inc. 01/25/1974 which recapitalized as Summa Industries 12/22/1993
(See Summa Industries)

SOUTHERN CALIF WTR CO (CA)
Each share Common $100 par exchanged for (4) shares Common $25 par 00/00/1938
Each share Common $25 par exchanged for (5) shares Common $5 par 00/00/1950
5.44% Preferred $25 par called for redemption 12/15/1961
Common $5 par split (3) for (2) by issuance of (0.5) additional share 03/28/1962
Common $5 par changed to $2.50 par and (1) additional share issued 10/05/1993
Under plan of reorganization each share 4% Preferred $25 par, 4-1/4% Preferred $25 par and Common $2.50 par automatically became (1) share American States Water Co. 4% Preferred $25 par, 4.25% Preferred $25 par and Common no par respectively 06/30/1998

SOUTHERN CAN CO.
Acquired by Continental Can Co., Inc. 00/00/1928
Details not available

SOUTHERN CDA PWR LTD (CANADA)
Each share old Common no par exchanged for (4) shares new Common no par 00/00/1928
Acquired by Quebec Hydro-Electric Commission 11/05/1963
Each share 6% Part. Preferred $100 par exchanged for $100 principal amount of 6% 10 year Debentures and $15 cash
Each share new Common no par exchanged for $56.75 cash 06/12/1967

SOUTHERN CAP TR I (DE)
8.25% Capital Securities called for redemption at $10 on 4/29/2005

SOUTHERN CARGO INC (FL)
Name changed to Accufacts Pre-Employment Screening Inc. 10/15/98
(See Accufacts Pre-Employment Screening Inc.)

SOUTHERN CHEMICAL COTTON CO., INC. (TN)
Stock Dividend - 200% 11/1/48
Liquidation completed
Each share Common no par exchanged for initial distribution of $9 cash 4/19/65
Each share Common no par received second distribution of $2 cash 8/16/65
Each share Common no par received third distribution of $2 cash 1/10/66
Each share Common no par received fourth and final distribution of $1.4556 cash 2/1/66

SOUTHERN CITIES POWER CO.
Acquired by Tennessee Electric Power Co. in 1929 which was dissolved in 1939

SOUTHERN CITIES SUPPLY CO.
Bankrupt in 1930

SOUTHERN CITIES UTILITIES CO.
Assets sold to Central Public Service Corp. in 1930 which reorganized under the laws of Delaware as Central Public Utility Corp. (Old) in 1935 which reorganized in 1952
(See listing for Central Public Utility Corp. (Old) company)

SOUTHERN CO CAP TR IV (DE)
7.125% Guaranteed Trust Preferred Securities called for redemption at $25 on 6/30/2003

SOUTHERN COAL & IRON CORP. (VA)
Charter revoked and annulled for failure to file reports and pay fees 5/31/26

SOUTHERN COLORADO POWER CO. (CO)
Each share 7% Preferred $100 par exchanged for (0.1) shares Common no par 00/00/1945
Each share Class A Common $25 par exchanged for (0.2) share Common no par 00/00/1945
Common no par changed to $7.50 par 00/00/1952
Merged into Western Power & Gas Co. on a share for share basis 05/01/1961
Western Power & Gas Co. name changed to Western Power & Gas Co., Inc. 07/01/1965 which name changed to Central Telephone & Utilities Corp. 06/05/1968 which name changed to Centel Corp. 04/30/1982 which was acquired by Sprint Corp. (KS) 03/09/1993 which name changed to Sprint Nextel Corp. 08/12/2005 which merged into Sprint Corp. (DE) 07/10/2013

SOUTHERN CMNTY BANCSHARES INC (GA)
Common no par split (4) for (3) by issuance of (0.33333333) additional share payable 11/21/2003 to holders of record 10/21/2003 Ex date - 11/24/2003
Common no par split (4) for (3) by issuance of (0.33333333) additional share payable 09/15/2004 to holders of record 09/01/2004 Ex date - 09/16/2004
Filed a petition under Chapter 7 Federal Bankruptcy Code 09/01/2009
No stockholders' equity

SOUTHERN CMNTY BK & TR (WINSTON-SALEM, NC)
Common $5 par split (5) for (4) by issuance of (0.25) additional share payable 12/29/1997 to holders of record 12/24/1997
Common $5 par split (2) for (1) by issuance of (1) additional share payable 06/01/1999 to holders of record 05/03/1999
Stock Dividends - 10% payable 11/18/1998 to holders of record 10/30/1998; 10% payable 10/18/2000 to holders of record 10/06/2000; 5% payable 10/15/2001 to holders of record 10/01/2001 Ex date - 09/28/2001
Under plan of reorganization each share Common $5 par automatically became (1) share Southern Community Financial Corp. Common no par 10/01/2001
(See Southern Community Financial Corp.)

SOUTHERN CMNTY CAP TR I (DE)
7.25% Conv. Guaranteed Trust Preferred Securities called for redemption at $10 on 03/12/2004

SOUTHERN CMNTY CAP TR II (DE)
7.95% Trust Preferred Securities called for redemption at $10 on 03/18/2013

SOUTHERN CMNTY FINL CORP (NC)
Stock Dividend - 5% payable 10/15/2002 to holders of record 10/01/2002 Ex date - 09/27/2002
Merged into Capital Bank Financial Corp. 10/02/2012
Each share Common no par exchanged for $3.11 cash and (1) Contingent Value Right

SOUTHERN CMNTY FINL CORP (VA)
Name changed to Village Bank & Trust Financial Corp. 5/18/2005

SOUTHERN CO CAP TR III (DE)
7.75% Quarterly Income Preferred Securities called for redemption at $25 on 8/23/2003

SOUTHERN CO CAP TR V (DE)
6.875% Quarterly Income Preferred Securities called for redemption at $25 on 12/23/2003

SOUTHERN CO CAP TR VI (DE)
7.125% Guaranteed Trust Preferred Securities called for redemption at $25 on 07/31/2007

SOUTHERN CONN BANCORP INC (CT)
Stock Dividend - 5% payable 05/09/2005 to holders of record 04/26/2005
Acquired by Liberty Bank (Middletown, CT) 06/21/2013
Each share Common 1¢ par exchanged for $3.76 cash

SOUTHERN CONN GAS CO (CT)
Common $20 par changed to $13-1/3 par and (0.5) additional share issued 06/19/1974
Under plan of reorganization each share Common $13-1/3 par automatically became (1) share Connecticut Energy Corp. Common $13-1/3 par 05/01/1979
11% Preferred $100 par called for redemption 10/01/1986
4.75% Preferred $100 par called for redemption 12/00/1993
Connecticut Energy Corp. merged into Energy East Corp. 02/08/2000
(See Energy East Corp.)

SOUTHERN CONNECTICUT & LONG ISLAND TELEVISION CO. INC. (CT)
Dissolved 10/31/56

SOUTHERN CONSTRUCTION & MORTGAGE CO., INC. (FL)
Charter cancelled and company declared dissolved for non-payment of taxes 4/24/59

SOUTHERN CONTAINER CORP (NY)
Merged out of existence 05/14/1991
Details not available

SOUTHERN COPPER CORP (BC)
Under plan of reorganization each share Common no par exchanged for (1.666) shares Santa Catalina Mining Corp. and (2.5) shares South Atlantic Diamonds Corp. Common no par 11/1/94
Santa Catalina Mining Corp. recapitalized as Valkyries Petroleum Corp. 4/25/2002
(See each company's listing)

SOUTHERN COSMETICS INC (NV)
Name changed to Revenge Designs, Inc. 12/18/2007
Revenge Designs, Inc. name changed to Cartel Blue, Inc. 09/18/2015

SOUTHERN CR ACCEP INC (FL)
Adjudicated bankrupt 03/09/1967
No stockholders' equity

SOUTHERN CRESCENT FINL CORP (GA)
Merged into Eagle Bancshares Inc. 3/26/97
Each share Common $1 par exchanged for (1.162) shares Common $1 par
(See Eagle Bancshares Inc.)

SOUTHERN CROSS GOLD INC (BC)
Struck off register and declared dissolved for failure to file returns 12/9/94

SOUTHERN CROSS INDS INC (GA)
Proclaimed dissolved for failure to file annual reports 5/13/88

SOUTHERN CROSS RES INC (CANADA)
Reincorporated 03/17/2005
Place of incorporation changed from (ON) to (Canada) 03/17/2005
Recapitalized as sxr Uranium One Inc. 12/19/2005
Each share Common no par exchanged for (0.2) share Common no par
sxr Uranium One Inc. name changed to Uranium One Inc. 06/18/2007
(See Uranium One Inc.)

SOUTHERN CROSS VENTURES INC (UT)
Reorganized under the laws of Nevada as Centra Corp. 01/20/1989
Each share Common 1¢ par exchanged for (0.25) share Common $0.001 par
Centra Corp. recapitalized as Greenway Environmental Systems, Inc. 05/10/1991 which merged into Travel Dynamics, Inc. 01/13/1999 which name changed to TRU Dynamics International, Inc. 02/14/2001
(See TRU Dynamics International, Inc.)

SOUTHERN DAIRIES, INC. (DE)
Merged into National Dairy Products Corp. 6/12/57
Each share Class A no par exchanged for (2.1) shares Common $5 par
Each share Class B no par exchanged for (1.1) shares Common $5 par
National Dairy Products Corp. name changed to Kraftco Corp. 4/18/69 which name changed to Kraft, Inc. (Old) 10/27/26 which reorganized as Dart & Kraft, Inc. 9/25/80 which name changed to Kraft, Inc. (New) 11/21/86
(See Kraft, Inc. (New))

SOUTHERN DAISY INDS INC (GA)
Administratively dissolved 5/13/88

SOUTHERN DEV INC NEW (NV)
Name changed to EssxSport Corp. 09/10/1998
EssxSport Corp. name changed to Giant Jr. Investments, Corp. 05/28/2004 which name changed to Financial Media Group, Inc. 09/14/2005 which name changed to Clicker Inc. 07/08/2009
(See Clicker Inc.)

SOUTHERN DEVELOPMENT INC OLD (NV)
Name changed to Integrated Communications Access Network Inc. 12/23/1994
Integrated Communications Access Network Inc. name changed to Southern Development Inc. (New) 03/05/1996 which name changed to EssxSport Corp. 09/10/1998 which name changed to Giant Jr. Investments, Corp. 05/28/2004 which name changed to Financial Media Group, Inc. 09/14/2005 which name changed to Clicker Inc. 07/08/2009
(See Clicker Inc.)

SOUTHERN DISC CO (GA)
Merged into Industrial National Corp. 02/27/1973
Each share Common $1 par exchanged for $23.4066 cash

SOUTHERN DIVERSIFIED INDS INC (FL)
Merged into P.H.C., Inc. 4/22/85
Each share Common 10¢ par exchanged for (2) shares Common 10¢ par
(See P.H.C., Inc.)

SOUTHERN EAGLE ENTERPRISES INC (ON)
Merged into Equican Ventures Corp. 12/4/87
Each (38) shares Class A no par exchanged for (23) shares Class A no par
Each (38) shares Common no par exchanged for (23) shares Common no par
Equican Ventures Corp. recapitalized as Equican Capital Corp. 1/27/88 which name changed to Genterra Capital Corp. (Old) 8/23/95 which merged into Genterra Capital Corp. (New) 2/28/97 which recapitalized as Genterra Capital, Inc. 6/30/98 which name changed to Genterra Investment Corp. 4/30/99 which merged into Genterra Inc. 12/31/2003

SOUTHERN EAGLE PETE CORP (ON)
Conv. Preferred Ser. Y no par called for redemption 5/11/87
Merged into Southern Eagle Enterprises Inc. 10/1/87
Each share Non-Vtg. Class A no par exchanged for (1) share Non-Vtg. Class A no par
Each share Common no par exchanged for (1) share Common no par
Southern Eagle Enterprises Inc. merged into Equican Ventures Corp. 12/4/87 which recapitalized as Equican Captial Corp. 1/27/88 which name changed to Genterra Capital Corp. (Old) 8/23/95 which merged into Genterra Capital Corp. (New) 2/28/97 which recapitalized as Genterra Capital, 6/30/98 which name changed to Genterra Investment Corp. 4/30/99 which merged into Genterra Inc. 12/31/2003

SOUTHERN EAGLE PETE INC (ON)
Merged into Southern Eagle Petroleum Corp. 4/23/86
Each share Common no par exchanged for (0.94) share Conv. Preference Ser. Y no par, (0.47) share Non-Vtg. Class A no par and (0.47) share Common no par
Southern Eagle Petroleum Corp. merged into Southern Eagle Enterprises Inc. 10/1/87 which merged into Equican Ventures Corp. 12/4/87 which recapitalized as Equican Capital Corp. 1/27/88 which name changed to Genterra Capital Corp. (Old) 8/23/95 which merged into Genterra Capital Corp. (New) 2/28/97 which recapitalized as Genterra Capital, Inc. 6/30/98 which name changed to Genterra Investment Corp. 4/30/99 which merged into Genterra Inc. 12/31/2003

SOUTHERN EDUCATORS CORP. (LA)
Voluntarily dissolved 12/31/79
Details not available

SOUTHERN EDUCATORS LIFE INS CO (GA)
Stock Dividend - 15% 6/8/84
Each share Common 50¢ par exchanged for (0.001) share Common $600 par 9/27/93
Note: In effect holders received $8.10 cash per share and public interest was eliminated

SOUTHERN ELEC PLC (UNITED KINGDOM)
Stock Dividend - 400% 03/25/1994
Merged into Scottish & Southern Energy PLC 12/14/1998
Each Sponsored ADR for Ordinary 50p par exchanged for (1) Sponsored ADR for Ordinary
Scottish & Southern Energy PLC name changed to SSE PLC 10/11/2011

SOUTHERN ELECTRICAL CORP. (TN)
Each share Common no par exchanged for (7) shares Common $3 par in 1950
Merged into Olin Mathieson Chemical Corp. on a (0.635) for (1) basis 5/6/57
Olin Mathieson Chemical Corp. name changed to Olin Corp. 9/1/69

SOUTHERN ELECTRS CORP (DE)
Common 1¢ par split (3) for (2) by issuance of (0.5) additional share 02/20/1992
Common 1¢ par split (3) for (2) by issuance of (0.5) additional share 02/01/1993
Name changed to SED International Holdings, Inc. (DE) 11/12/1997
SED International Holdings, Inc. (DE) reincorporated in Georgia 11/10/1998

SOUTHERN ENERGY CO INC (NV)
Reincorporated 12/13/2007
State of incorporation changed from (CA) to (NV) 12/13/2007
SEC revoked common stock registration 10/14/2009
Stockholders' equity unlikely

SOUTHERN ENERGY HOMES INC (DE)
Common $0.0001 par split (5) for (4) by issuance of (0.25) additional share 08/21/1995
Common $0.0001 par split (3) for (2) by issuance of (0.5) additional share payable 07/03/1996 to holders of record 06/19/1996
Merged into Berkshire Hathaway Inc. 10/20/2006
Each share Common $0.0001 par exchanged for $8.50 cash

SOUTHERN ENERGY INC (DE)
Name changed to Mirant Corp. (Old) 01/22/2001
Mirant Corp. (Old) reorganized as Mirant Corp. (New) 01/03/2006 which merged into GenOn Energy, Inc. 12/03/2010 which merged into NRG Energy, Inc. 12/14/2012

SOUTHERN EQUITABLE LIFE INSURANCE CO. (AR)
Common 5¢ par changed to 10¢ par 12/00/1960
Each share Common 10¢ par exchanged for (0.33333333) share Class A Common 10¢ par and (0.66666666) share Class B Common 10¢ par 10/25/1961
Merged into United Founders Life Insurance Co. 12/01/1966
Each share Class A Common 10¢ par or Class B Common 10¢ par exchanged for (1) share Common 10¢ par
(See United Founders Life Insurance Co.)

SOUTHERN EXPL & DEV CORP (QC)
Recapitalized as Calvin Exploration & Development Corp. 01/01/1973
Each share Capital Stock $1 par exchanged for (1) share Capital Stock no par
(See Calvin Exploration & Development Corp.)

SOUTHERN EXTRUSIONS INC (AR)
Completely liquidated 12/21/1971
Each share Common $1 par exchanged for first and final distribution of (0.38943) share Howmet Corp. Common $1 par
(See Howmet Corp.)

SOUTHERN FILM EXTRUDERS INC (NC)
Common $2.50 par changed to $2 par 02/28/1975
Common $2 par changed to no par 09/23/1983
Stock Dividends - 25% 04/15/1975; 25% 04/07/1977
Merged into a private company 03/27/1986
Each share Common no par exchanged for $3.25 cash

SOUTHERN FINANCE CO., INC. (NC)
Assets sold under execution of judgement 2/7/62
No Preferred or Common Stockholders' equity

SOUTHERN FINL BANCORP INC (VA)
Stock Dividends - 10% payable 08/30/1996 to holders of record

08/16/1996; 10% payable 12/28/2001 to holders of record 12/14/2001; 15% payable 02/20/2003 to holders of record 02/05/2003 Ex date - 02/03/2003; 10% payable 10/31/2003 to holders of record 10/15/2003 Ex date - 10/10/2003
Merged into Provident Bankshares Corp. 04/30/2004
Each share Common 1¢ par exchanged for (1.0875) shares Common $1 par and $11.125 cash
Provident Bankshares Corp. acquired by M&T Bank Corp. 05/26/2009

SOUTHERN FINL CAP TR I (DE)
$0.55 Capital Securities called for redemption at $5 plus $0.4125 accrued dividends on 7/15/2005

SOUTHERN FINL FED SVGS BK (WARRENTON, VA)
Common $8 par split (4) for (3) by issuance of (1/3) additional share 02/15/1995
Stock Dividend - 10% 08/30/1995
Under plan of merger each share Common $8 par automatically became (1) share Southern Financial Bancorp, Inc. Common 1¢ par 12/01/1995
Southern Financial Bancorp, Inc. merged into Provident Bankshares Corp. 04/30/2004 which was acquired by M&T Bank Corp. 05/26/2009

SOUTHERN FIRE & CASUALTY CO. (TN)
Common no par changed to $2 par in 1953
Name changed to Southern Title Insurance Co. 3/31/65
Southern Title Insurance Co. name changed to Fidelity National Title Insurance Co. of Tennessee 4/28/89
(See Fidelity National Title Insurance Co. of Tennessee)

SOUTHERN FIRE INSURANCE CO. (NC)
Each share Capital Stock $25 par exchanged for (1.19) shares Capital Stock $10 par 00/00/1933
Stock Dividends - 100% 03/15/1946; 50% 06/28/1951; 33-1/3% 12/05/1956
Merged into United States Fire Insurance Co. 12/31/1956
Each share Capital Stock $10 par exchanged for (1) share Capital Stock $20 par
(See United States Fire Insurance Co.)

SOUTHERN FIRE INSURANCE CO. OF NEW YORK
Name changed to Gibraltar Fire & Marine Insurance Co. in 1937
Gilbraltar Fire & Marine Insurance Co. merged into Home Insurance Co. in 1948
(See Home Insurance Co.)

SOUTHERN "500" INDUSTRIES, INC. (SC)
Merged into Dealers Discount Corp. 5/31/67
Each share Common $1 par exchanged for (0.1) share Common $5 par and 50¢ principal amount of 6-1/2% Debentures due 6/1/72
Dealers Discount Corp. name changed to Develco, Inc. 8/1/68 which name changed to Southern "500" Truck Stops, Inc. 10/31/74
(See Southern "500" Truck Stops, Inc.)

SOUTHERN "500" TRUCK STOPS, INC. (SC)
Involuntarily dissolved 12/28/1977

SOUTHERN FRANKLIN PROCESS CO. (DE)
7% Preferred $100 par called for redemption 12/31/56
Completely liquidated 12/31/56
Each share Common no par exchanged for (0.7) share Franklin Process Co. Common no par
(See Franklin Process Co.)

SOUTHERN FRONTIER FIN CO (DE)
Name changed to Telerent Leasing Corp. 1/1/69
(See Telerent Leasing Corp.)

SOUTHERN FRONTIER RES INC (ON)
Merged into Planetsafe Enviro Corp. 04/18/1995
Each share Common no par exchanged for (1.5) shares Common no par and (1) share Inland National Capital Ltd. Common no par
(See each company's listing)

SOUTHERN GAS & WATER CO. (WV)
Common no par changed to $1 par 06/14/1961
$4.50 Preferred no par called for redemption 04/29/1965
$5 Preferred no par called for redemption 04/29/1965
Name changed to West Virginia Water Co. 05/19/1965
West Virginia Water Co. name changed to West Virginia-American Water Co. 01/01/1987
(See West Virginia-American Water Co.)

SOUTHERN GAS CO.
Acquired by United Gas Corp. in 1930
(See United Gas Corp.)

SOUTHERN GAS UTILITIES, INC.
Acquired by United Gas Corp. in 1930
(See United Gas Corp.)

SOUTHERN GENERAL CORP. (SC)
Involuntarily dissolved for failure to pay taxes 04/20/1983

SOUTHERN GENERAL INSURANCE CO. (GA)
Name changed to First General Insurance Co. 10/4/72

SOUTHERN GOLD RES LTD (BC)
100% reacquired by the company through purchase offer as of 06/00/1991
Public interest eliminated

SOUTHERN GOLDFIELDS LTD (AUSTRALIA)
Recapitalized as Australian Gold Fields NL 04/18/1997
Each Sponsored ADR for Ordinary exchanged for (0.05) Sponsored ADR for Ordinary
(See Australian Gold Fields NL)

SOUTHERN GOLDS, LTD. (ON)
Charter cancelled for failure to file reports and pay taxes 3/13/57

SOUTHERN GOURMET PRODS INC (FL)
Each share Common $0.001 par exchanged for (0.001) share Common 10¢ par 05/19/1993
Administratively dissolved 08/26/1994

SOUTHERN GROCERY STORES, INC.
Merged into Colonial Stores, Inc. on a (2) for (1) basis 12/19/40
(See Colonial Stores, Inc.)

SOUTHERN GROUP INTL INC (FL)
Name changed to National Coal Corp. 08/04/2003
(See National Coal Corp.)

SOUTHERN GROWTH INDUSTRIES, INC. (SC)
Placed in receivership in April 1964
Assets sold for benefit of creditors
No stockholders' equity

SOUTHERN GULF UTILITIES, INC. (FL)
Name changed to Ecological Science Corp. 06/19/1968
Ecological Science Corp. name changed to Amicor Inc. 05/20/1974 which recapitalized as Keystone Camera Products Corp. 06/20/1984
(See Keystone Camera Products Corp.)

SOUTHERN HERITAGE BANCSHARES INC (TN)
Merged into First Citizens Bancshares, Inc. 10/01/2014
Each share Common $1 par exchanged for (0.2876) share Common no par and $12.25 cash

SOUTHERN HERITAGE INSURANCE CO. (GA)
Acquired by GEICO Corp. in 1991
Details not available

SOUTHERN HOLDING & SECURITIES CORP.
Liquidation completed in 1943

SOUTHERN HOME MED EQUIP INC (NV)
Each share old Common $0.001 par exchanged for (0.001) share new Common $0.001 par 06/27/2008
Name changed to Southern Home Medical, Inc. 07/27/2012

SOUTHERN HOME SVGS BK (PENSACOLA, FL)
Stock Dividend - 20% 01/20/1986
Merged into Great Western Financial Corp. 08/28/1987
Each share Common $1 par exchanged for (1.14) shares Common $1 par
Great Western Financial Corp. merged into Washington Mutual Inc. 07/01/1997
(See Washington Mutual, Inc.)

SOUTHERN HOSPITALITY CORP (TN)
Under plan of reorganization each share Common 8-1/3¢ par exchanged for subscription right to purchase (1) share Common no par until 05/22/1989
Note: Unexchanged certificates were cancelled and became without value 05/23/1989
Each share old Common no par exchanged for (0.0005) share new Common no par 04/21/1992
Note: In effect holders received $0.87 cash per share and public interest was eliminated

SOUTHERN HOSPITALITY DEV CORP (CO)
Name changed to Smokin Concepts Development Corp. 05/09/2013
Smokin Concepts Development Corp. name changed to Bourbon Brothers Holding Corp. 01/29/2014 which name changed to Southern Concepts Restaurant Group, Inc. 03/13/2015

SOUTHERN ICE & UTILITIES CO.
Name changed to Southern Ice Co., Inc. (Texas) in 1935 which was liquidated in 1950

SOUTHERN ICE CO., INC. (TX)
Liquidated in 1950

SOUTHERN ICE CO (DE)
Each share 7% Preferred Ser. A $100 par exchanged for (1) share $7 Preferred no par and (1) share Common $1 par 00/00/1934
Common no par changed to $1 par 00/00/1934
Name changed to Southern-Piedmont Ice Co. 04/10/1979

SOUTHERN ILL NATL BK (EAST ST LOUIS, IL)
Capital Stock $100 par changed to $25 par and (3) additional shares issued plus a 100% stock dividend paid 01/22/1959
Name and location changed to Firstar Bank N.A. (Fairview Heights, IL) 03/03/1975
Firstar Bank, N.A. (Fairview Heights, IL) name changed to Southern Illinois Bank (Fairview Heights, IL) 05/12/1978
(See Southern Illinois Bank (Fairview Heights, IL))

SOUTHERN ILLINOIS NATIONAL BANK (FAIRVIEW HEIGHTS, IL)
Name changed to Southern Illinois Bank (Fairview Heights, IL) 5/12/78
Southern Illinois Bank (Fairview Heights, IL) acquired by Firstar Bank, N.A. (Chicago, IL) 6/29/83

SOUTHERN IND GAS & ELEC CO (IN)
Common no par split (2) for (1) by issuance of (1) additional share 03/26/1964
Common no par split (2) for (1) by issuance of (1) additional share 03/11/1977
Common no par split (3) for (2) by issuance of (0.5) additional share 03/15/1985
Common no par split (4) for (3) by issuance of (0.33333333) additional share 03/11/1988
Common no par split (4) for (3) by issuance of (0.33333333) additional share 04/16/1992
8.75% Preferred $100 par called for redemption 12/09/1992
Under plan of reorganization each share Common no par automatically became (1) share SIGCORP, Inc. Common no par 01/01/1996
SIGCORP, Inc. merged into Vectren Corp. 03/31/2000
4.8% Preferred $100 par called for redemption at $110 plus $1.35 accrued dividends on 10/16/2001
4.75% Preferred $100 par called for redemption at $101 plus $0.97 accrued dividends on 10/16/2001
6.5% Preferred called for redemption at $104.23 plus $0.73 accrued dividends on 10/16/2001

SOUTHERN INDIANA TELEPHONE & TELEGRAPH CO.
Acquired by Indiana Telephone Corp. in 1935
No stockholders' equity

SOUTHERN INDIANA TELEPHONE CO., INC. (IN)
5% Preferred Ser. A $100 par called for redemption 01/02/1964
Acquired by United Utilities, Inc. 03/01/1965
Each share 5-1/2% 1st Preferred Ser. A $20 par exchanged for (0.9) share Common $2.50 par
United Utilities, Inc. name changed to United Telecommunications, Inc. 06/02/1972 which name changed to Sprint Corp. (KS) 02/26/1992 which name changed to Sprint Nextel Corp. 08/12/2005 which merged into Sprint Corp. (DE) 07/10/2013

SOUTHERN INDL BK (JACKSONVILLE, FL)
Name changed to Beneficial Savings Bank of Jacksonville (Jacksonville, FL) 04/26/1982
(See Beneficial Savings Bank of Jacksonville (Jacksonville, FL))

SOUTHERN INDUSTRIAL SAVINGS BANK (MIAMI, FL)
Name changed to Bank of Miami (Miami, FL) 9/5/67
Bank of Miami (Miami, FL) merged into Southeast Banking Corp. 4/15/87

SOUTHERN INDS CORP (AL)
Each share Common $100 par exchanged for (20) shares Common no par 12/7/55
Common no par split (4) for (1) by issuance of (3) additional shares 4/15/58
Common no par split (5) for (4) by issuance of (0.25) additional share 12/31/63
Common no par changed to 10¢ par

and (1) additional share issued 7/11/78
Merged into Dravo Corp. 6/1/79
Each share Common 10¢ par exchanged for (0.6552) share Common $1 par
(See Dravo Corp.)

SOUTHERN INDUSTRIES FUND, INC. (GA)
Stock Dividend - 100% 4/25/56
Name changed to Fund of America, Inc. (GA) 9/20/60 which reincorporated in New York 10/21/63 which name changed to American Capital Growth & Income Fund, Inc. (NY) 7/23/90 which reincorporated in Maryland 7/6/93 which reincorporated in Delaware as Van Kampen American Capital Growth & Income Fund 7/31/95 which name changed to Van Kampen Growth & Income Fund 7/14/98

SOUTHERN INK & LACQUER CO., INC. (GA)
Completely liquidated 08/31/1967
Each share Capital Stock no par exchanged for first and final distribution of (1-13/15) shares Martin Marietta Corp. (Old) Common $1 par
Martin Marietta Corp. (Old) merged into Martin Marietta Corp. (New) 04/02/1993 which merged into Lockheed Martin Corp. 03/15/1995

SOUTHERN INVS SVC INC (DE)
Plan of reorganization under Chapter 11 Federal Bankruptcy Code effective 11/1/2005
No stockholders' equity

SOUTHERN INVTS INC (OK)
Recapitalized as Global Warming Solutions, Inc. 07/06/2007
Each share Common $0.001 par exchanged for (0.1) share Common $0.001 par

SOUTHERN JERSEY BANCORP (NJ)
Stock Dividend - 3% payable 01/01/1999 to holders of record 12/21/1998
Merged into Hudson United Bancorp 12/01/1999
Each share Common $5 par exchanged for (1.2978) shares Common no par
Hudson United Bancorp merged into TD Banknorth Inc. 01/31/2006
(See TD Banknorth Inc.)

SOUTHERN KANSAS GAS CO.
Acquired by Oklahoma Natural Gas Corp. (Md.) in 1928 which was reorganized as Oklahoma Natural Gas Co. (Del.) 12/1/33 which name changed to Oneok Inc. 12/10/80

SOUTHERN LD & EXPL INC (NV)
Name changed to Investment & Consulting International, Inc. (Old) 06/22/1991
Investment & Consulting International, Inc. (Old) name changed to Currentsea 07/02/1991 which name changed to Investment & Consulting International, Inc. (New) 06/02/1993 which recapitalized as KleenAir Systems, Inc. 04/11/1995 which recapitalized as Migami, Inc. 03/02/2006

SOUTHERN LEGACY MINERALS INC (BC)
Reorganized under the laws of Alberta as Regulus Resources Inc. (New) 10/03/2014
Each share Common no par exchanged for (0.1883) share Common no par
Note: Unexchanged certificates will be cancelled and become without value 10/03/2020

SOUTHERN LIBERTY INVESTMENT CORP. (TX)
Charter forfeited for failure to pay taxes 2/15/65

SOUTHERN LIFE & HEALTH INSURANCE CO. (AL)
Merged into Standard Security Holding Corp. 4/2/81
Each share Common $1 par exchanged for $42 cash

SOUTHERN LIFE INSURANCE CO. OF GEORGIA (GA)
Stock Dividends - 100% 04/01/1957; 20% 09/15/1959
Merged into Piedmont Southern Life Insurance Co. 07/11/1960
Each share Common exchanged for (1) share Common
Piedmont Southern Life Insurance Co. acquired by Piedmont Management Co. Inc. 07/11/1968 which merged into Chartwell RE Corp. 12/13/1995 which merged into Trenwick Group Inc. 10/27/1999 which merged into Trenwick Group Ltd. 09/27/2000
(See Trenwick Group Ltd.)

SOUTHERN LIFE INVT CORP (TX)
Merged into Mischer Corp. (TX) 10/31/69
Each share Common no par exchanged for (1) share Common no par
Mischer Corp. (TX) reincorporated in Delaware 8/31/72 which name changed to Southern Investors Service Co., Inc. 5/21/93
(See Southern Investors Service Co., Inc.)

SOUTHERN LITHIUM CORP (BC)
Each share old Common no par exchanged for (0.1) share new Common no par 12/13/2017
Name changed to Le Mare Gold Corp. 02/02/2018

SOUTHERN LTS RES LTD (BC)
Recapitalized as Balsam Resources Inc. 03/27/1987
Each share Common no par exchanged for (1/3) share Common no par
Balsam Resources Inc. recapitalized as Consolidated Balsam Resources Inc. 01/18/1990 which recapitalized as Bluebird Explorations Ltd. 10/01/1991 which recapitalized as Spire Ventures Ltd. 10/24/1995 which recapitalized as Consolidated Spire Ventures Ltd. 01/04/2001 which recapitalized as Berkwood Resources Ltd. 12/01/2010

SOUTHERN MANUFACTURING CO.
Properties sold in 1933

SOUTHERN MARYLAND AGRICULTURAL ASSOCIATION OF PRINCE GEORGE'S COUNTY, MARYLAND (MD)
Capital Stock 50¢ par changed to 5¢ par 12/9/58
Name changed to Somar Liquidating Corp. 2/7/62
(See Somar Liquidating Corp.)

SOUTHERN MATERIALS CO., INC. (VA)
Common $2 par split (3) for (2) by issuance of (0.5) additional share 6/14/62
Acquired by Lone Star Cement Corp. (ME) on a (0.6) for (1) basis 8/15/62
Lone Star Cement Corp. (ME) reincorporated under the laws of Delaware 5/29/69 which name changed to Lone Star Industries, Inc. 5/20/71
(See Lone Star Industries, Inc.)

SOUTHERN MD AGRIC ASSN PRINCE GEORGES CNTY MD INC (MD)
Name changed to Gibraltar Pari-Mutuel, Inc. 6/25/73
(See Gibraltar Pari-Mutuel, Inc.)

SOUTHERN MD BK & TR CO (HILLCREST HEIGHTS, MD)
Name changed to Bank of Maryland (Hillcrest Heights, MD) in June 1974
(See Bank of Maryland (Hillcrest Heights, MD))

SOUTHERN MED & PHARMACEUTICAL CORP (FL)
Name changed to Southern Biotech, Inc. 10/23/1981
(See Southern Biotech, Inc.)

SOUTHERN MEMORIAL LIFE INSURANCE CO. (AL)
Merged into Vulcan Life & Accident Insurance Co. 5/22/62
Each share Capital Stock $1 par exchanged for (0.0625) share Capital Stock $2.50 par
Vulcan Life & Accident Insurance Co. name changed to Vulcan Life Insurance Co. 4/21/71
(See Vulcan Life Insurance Co.)

SOUTHERN METALS CORP (YT)
Name changed to EPICentrix Technologies, Inc. 11/22/2000
EPICentrix Technologies, Inc. name changed to Ventura Gold Corp. (YT) 07/05/2004 which reincorporated in British Columbia 10/07/2004 which merged into International Minerals Corp. 01/20/2010
(See International Minerals Corp.)

SOUTHERN MINERAL CORP (MS)
Reorganized from under the laws of (MS) to (NV) 6/10/82
Each share Class A 5¢ par exchanged for (5) shares Common 1¢ par Old Common 1¢ par split (4) for (3) by issuance of (1/3) additional share 1/4/85
Each share old Common 1¢ par exchanged for (0.2) share new Common 1¢ par 8/1/2000
Merged into PetroCorp Inc. 6/7/2001
Each share new Common 1¢ par exchanged for $4.71 cash

SOUTHERN MO BANCORP INC (DE)
Reincorporated under the laws of Missouri 4/1/99

SOUTHERN MO BANCSHARES INC (MO)
Merged into Southern Missouri Bancorp, Inc. 02/23/2018
Each share Common $1 par exchanged for (9.2498) shares Common 1¢ par and $98.05 cash

SOUTHERN MONTANA OIL CO. (MT)
Charter expired by time limitation 10/30/36

SOUTHERN MORTGAGE INVESTMENT CO., INC. (SC)
Out of business and dissolved 6/10/76

SOUTHERN NAT GAS CO (DE)
Each share Class A no par exchanged for (1) share Common $7.50 par 00/00/1939
Each share Class B no par exchanged for (0.5) share Common $7.50 par 00/00/1939
Common $7.50 par changed to $3.75 par and (1) additional share issued 05/21/1965
Stock Dividend - 100% 11/07/1952
Under plan of reorganization each share Conv. Preference Ser. 1 $1 par, Conv. Preference Ser. 2 $1 par and Common $3.75 par automatically became (1) share Southern Natural Resources, Inc. Conv. Preference Ser. 1 $1 par, Conv. Preference Ser. 2 $1 par and Common $3.75 par respectively 05/25/1973
Southern Natural Resources, Inc. name changed to Sonat Inc. 01/01/1982 which merged into El Paso Energy Corp. 10/25/1999 which name changed to El Paso Corp. 02/05/2001 which merged into Kinder Morgan, Inc. (New) 05/25/2012

SOUTHERN NAT RES INC (DE)
Common $3.75 par split (2) for (1) by issuance of (1) additional share 09/14/1977
Conv. Preference Ser. 1 $1 par called for redemption 07/14/1980
Conv. Preference Ser. 2 $1 par called for redemption 07/14/1980
Common $3.75 par split (2) for (1) by issuance of (1) additional share 09/14/1981
Common $3.75 par changed to $1 par 11/06/1981
Name changed to Sonat Inc. 01/01/1982
Sonat Inc. merged into El Paso Energy Corp. 10/25/1999 which name changed to El Paso Corp. 02/05/2001 which merged into Kinder Morgan, Inc. (New) 05/25/2012

SOUTHERN NATL BK (HOUSTON, TX)
Stock Dividend - 10% 02/05/1966
Reorganized as Southern National Corp. (TX) 03/31/1969
Each share Common Capital Stock $10 par exchanged for (2.5) shares Common $4 par
Southern National Corp. (TX) merged into Texas American Bancshares Inc. 05/01/1974
(See Texas American Bancshares Inc.)

SOUTHERN NATL BK N C (LUMBERTON, NC)
Reorganized as Southern National Corp. (NC) 11/12/1968
Each share Common $5 par exchanged for (1) share Common $5 par
Southern National Corp. name changed to BB&T Corp. 05/19/1997

SOUTHERN NATIONAL BANK OF SOUTH CAROLINA (GREENVILLE, SC)
Acquired by Branch Banking & Trust Co. of South Carolina (Greenville, SC) 05/27/1995
Details not available

SOUTHERN NATIONAL CORP.
Dissolved in 1936

SOUTHERN NATL CORP (NC)
Common $5 par split (5) for (4) by issuance of (0.25) additional share 2/28/73
Common $5 par split (2) for (1) by issuance of (1) additional share 4/26/85
Common $5 par split (3) for (2) by issuance of (0.5) additional share 6/22/87
Common $5 par split (3) for (2) by issuance of (0.5) additional share 6/30/89
6.75% Depositary Preferred Ser. A called for redemption 3/29/96
6.75% Conv. Preferred Ser. A $5 par called for redemption 3/29/96
Name changed to BB&T Corp. 5/19/97

SOUTHERN NATL CORP (TX)
Merged into Texas American Bancshares Inc. 05/01/1974
Each share Common $4 par exchanged for (1) share Common $5 par
(See Texas American Bancshares Inc.)

SOUTHERN NATURAL GAS CORP.
Reorganized as Southern Natural Gas Co. in 1936
(See Southern Natural Gas Co.)

SOUTHERN NEV PWR CO (NV)
Common $5 par changed to $1 par 6/25/56
Stock Dividend - 50% 1/18/61

Name changed to Nevada Power Co. 6/1/61

SOUTHERN NEVADA TELEPHONE CO. (NV)
Merged into Central Telephone Co. (Old) 09/21/1961
5.44% Preferred $25 par and 5.48% Preferred $25 par exchanged respectively on a share for share basis
Each share Common $8 par exchanged for (1.6) share Common $10 par
Central Telephone Co. (Old) merged into Central Telephone Co. (New) 12/01/1971
(See Central Telephone Co. (New))

SOUTHERN NEW ENGLAND ICE CO.
Reorganized as Southern New England Ice Co., Inc. in 1936
Details not available

SOUTHERN NEW ENGLAND TEL CO (CT)
Each share Common $100 par exchanged for (4) shares Common $25 par in 1949
Common $25 par changed to $12.50 par and (1) additional share issued 10/15/83
Under plan of reorganization each share Common $12.50 par automatically became (1) share Southern New England Telecommunications Corp. Common $1 par 7/1/86
$3.82 Preferred Ser. A $50 par called for redemption 9/12/86
$4.625 Preferred Ser. B $50 par called for redemption 9/12/86
Southern New Enlgand Telecommunications Corp. merged into SBC Communications Inc. 10/26/98 which name changed to AT&T Inc. 11/18/2005

SOUTHERN NEW ENGLAND TELECOMMUNICATIONS CORP (CT)
Common $1 par split (2) for (1) by issuance of (1) additional share 1/12/90
Merged into SBC Communications, Inc. 10/26/98
Each share Common $1 par exchanged for (1.7568) shares Common $1 par
SBC Communications, Inc. name changed to AT&T Inc. 11/18/2005

SOUTHERN NEW JERSEY TITLE & MORTGAGE GUARANTY CO.
Liquidated in 1935
Details not available

SOUTHERN NEW YORK INVESTMENT CORP.
Dissolved and final liquidating payment made in 1940
Details not available

SOUTHERN NITES PETE CORP (BC)
Name changed to Oracle Energy Corp. 7/11/2000

SOUTHERN NITROGEN INC (DE)
Merged into Kaiser Aluminum & Chemical Corp. 11/3/66
Each share Common 10¢ par exchanged for (0.074) share 4-3/4% Conv. Preference 1966 Ser. $100 par and (0.4) share Common 33-1/3¢ par
(See Kaiser Aluminum & Chemical Corp.)

SOUTHERN OHIO BK (CINCINNATI, OH)
Capital Stock $20 par changed to $10 par and (1) additional share issued plus a 10% stock dividend paid effected by a (2.2) for (1) exchange 03/01/1963
100% held by Western & Southern Life Insurance Co. prior to 06/04/1973
Public interest eliminated

SOUTHERN OHIO CMNTY BANCORPORATION (OH)
Merged into United Bancorp, Inc. 7/7/98
Each share Common $5 par exchanged for (11) shares Common $10 par

SOUTHERN OHIO ELECTRIC CO.
Merged into Columbus & Southern Ohio Electric Co. in 1937
(See Columbus & Southern Ohio Electric Co.)

SOUTHERN OIL & TRANSPORT CO.
Dissolved in 1927

SOUTHERN OIL CORP. (DE)
No longer in existence having become inoperative and void for non-payment of taxes 4/1/54

SOUTHERN OIL CORP. (MT)
Suspended for failure to file returns and pay taxes 5/4/59

SOUTHERN ORAL LABORATORIES, INC. (FL)
Charter cancelled and proclaimed dissolved for non-payment of taxes 6/28/71

SOUTHERN OXYGEN CO., INC. (VA)
Reorganized under the laws of Delaware as Southern Oxygen Co. and each share Common $25 par exchanged for (2) shares Common $12.50 par 10/1/51
Southern Oxygen Co. merged into Air Products & Chemicals, Inc. 7/13/61

SOUTHERN OXYGEN CO. (DE)
Common $12.50 par changed to $6.25 par and (1) additional share issued 1/10/58
Merged into Air Products & Chemicals, Inc. on a (1/3) for (1) basis 7/13/61

SOUTHERN PA BK (YORK, PA)
Name changed 07/15/1974
Common $10 par changed to $5 par and (1) additional share issued plus a 50% stock dividend paid 10/01/1971
Stock Dividend - 10% 03/12/1974
Name changed from Southern Pennsylvania National Bank (York, PA) to Southern Pennsylvania Bank 07/15/1974
Common $5 par changed to $2.50 par 03/25/1980
Merged into Dauphin Deposit Corp. 10/01/1982
Each share Common $2.50 par exchanged for (0.64) share Common $10 par
Dauphin Deposit Corp. merged into Allied Irish Banks, PLC 07/08/1997
(See Allied Irish Banks, PLC)

SOUTHERN PAC DEV CORP (BC)
Recapitalized as Southern Pacific Resource Corp. (BC) 03/03/2006
Each share Common no par exchanged for (1/3) share Common no par
Southern Pacific Resource Corp. (BC) reincorporated in Alberta 11/17/2006

SOUTHERN PAC FDG CORP (CA)
Common no par split (3) for (2) by issuance of (0.5) additional share payable 01/23/1997 to holders of record 01/09/1997 Ex date - 01/24/1997
Plan of reorganization under Chapter 11 Federal Bankruptcy Code effective 07/30/1999
No stockholders' equity

SOUTHERN PAC PETE LTD (BC)
Recapitalized as Sonic-Ray Resources Ltd. 05/01/1972
Each share Common $1 par exchanged for (0.1) share Common no par
Sonic-Ray Resources Ltd. recapitalized as Stryker Resources Ltd. 09/25/1979 which recapitalized as Stryker Ventures Corp. 08/25/1997
(See Stryker Ventures Corp.)

SOUTHERN PAC PETE N L (AUSTRALIA)
Each old ADR for Ordinary exchanged for (5) new ADR's for Ordinary 03/12/1980
Each new ADR for Ordinary exchanged for (0.05) old Sponsored ADR for Ordinary 03/01/2002
Each old Sponsored ADR for Ordinary exchanged for (0.04) new Sponsored ADR for Ordinary 08/06/2008
Stock Dividend - 900% 10/31/1980
Name changed to Laguna Resources NL 02/12/2010
(See Laguna Resources NL)

SOUTHERN PAC RAIL CORP (DE)
Merged into Union Pacific Corp. 9/11/96
Each share Common $0.001 par exchanged for $25 cash

SOUTHERN PAC RESOURCE CORP (BC)
Reincorporated under the laws of Alberta 11/17/2006

SOUTHERN PACIFIC CO (DE)
Reincorporated 00/00/1947
Common $100 par changed to no par 00/00/1940
State of incorporation changed from (KY) to (DE) 00/00/1947
Common no par split (2) for (1) by issuance of (1) additional share 08/27/1952
Common no par split (3) for (1) by issuance of (2) additional shares 11/12/1959
Common no par split (2) for (1) by issuance of (1) additional share 06/30/1983
Merged into Santa Fe Southern Pacific Corp. 12/23/1983
Each share Common no par exchanged for (1.543) shares Common $1 par
Santa Fe Southern Pacific Corp. name changed to Santa Fe Pacific Corp. 04/25/1989 which merged into Burlington Northern Santa Fe Corp. 09/22/1995
(See Burlington Northern Santa Fe Corp.)

SOUTHERN PACIFIC GOLDEN GATE CO.
Out of business 00/00/1943
Details not available

SOUTHERN PACIFIC GOLDEN GATE FERRIES, INC.
Bankrupt in 1940

SOUTHERN PACKING CORP.
Dissolved in 1933

SOUTHERN PERU COPPER CORP (DE)
Name changed to Southern Copper Corp. 9/20/2005

SOUTHERN PETRO CORP (BC)
Recapitalized as Can Am Industries Corp. 08/11/1987
Each share Capital Stock no par exchanged for (1) share Capital Stock no par
CanAm Industries Corp. recapitalized as Save-On Automotive Industries Corp. 04/05/1990 which name changed to MIS Multimedia Interactive Services Inc. (BC) 09/08/1993 which reincorporated in Delaware as MIS International, Inc. 07/01/1997 which name changed to Cosmoz.Com, Inc. 12/07/1998 which name changed to Cosmoz Infrastructure Solutions, Inc. 04/16/2001 which recapitalized as FinancialContent, Inc. 11/13/2001
(See FinancialContent, Inc.)

SOUTHERN PETROLEUM & REFINING CORP. (DE)
Charter cancelled and declared inoperative and void for non-payment of taxes 3/17/26

SOUTHERN PHOSPHATE CORP. (DE)
Name changed to Carey, Baxter & Kennedy, Inc. in 1947
Carey, Baxter & Kennedy, Inc. name changed to CBK Industries, Inc. 4/17/64 which name changed to CBK Agronomics, Inc. 4/24/69 which name changed to General Energy Corp. (Del.) 10/10/72 which merged into Kirby Exploration Co. 7/15/83 which reorganized as Kirby Exploration Co. Inc. 8/1/84 which name changed to Kirby Corp. 5/1/90

SOUTHERN PINE CHEMICAL CO.
Dissolved in 1938

SOUTHERN PIPE LINE CO. (PA)
Capital Stock $50 par changed to $10 par in 1928
Each share Capital Stock $10 par exchanged for (1) share Capital Stock $1 par and $5 cash 7/11/47
Merged into Ashland Oil & Refining Co. 12/31/66
Each share Capital Stock $1 par exchanged for $6.25 cash

SOUTHERN PLASTICS ENGR CORP (NC)
Each share Common $1 par exchanged for (0.002) share Common $500 par 09/22/1980
Merged into Electro-Shield Corp. 09/22/1982
Each share Common $500 par exchanged for $175 cash

SOUTHERN PLATINUM CORP (ON)
Merged into Lonmin PLC 7/28/2005
Each share Common no par exchanged for $2.66 cash

SOUTHERN POWER CO.
Merged into Duke Power Co. in 1928
(See Duke Power Co.)

SOUTHERN PRECISION INDS INC (AR)
Acquired by Transogram Co., Inc. 04/16/1970
Each share Common $1 par exchanged for (0.522957) share Common $1 par

SOUTHERN PRODS INC (NV)
Common $0.001 par split (4) for (1) by issuance of (3) additional shares payable 09/14/2011 to holders of record 09/14/2011 Ex date - 09/15/2011
Common $0.001 par split (5) for (1) by issuance of (4) additional shares payable 12/31/2012 to holders of record 12/28/2012 Ex date - 01/02/2013
Name changed to Co-Signer, Inc. 08/13/2013
Co-Signer, Inc. name changed to Cross Click Media Inc. 07/14/2014

SOUTHERN PRODUCTION CO., INC. (DE)
Stock Dividend - 10% 7/25/52
Liquidation completed 8/9/57

SOUTHERN PROPERTIES, INC. (TX)
Dissolved 10/29/57

SOUTHERN RADIO CORP. (NC)
6% Preferred $50 par called for redemption in June 1963
Voluntarily dissolved 11/1/95
Details not available

SOUTHERN RLTY & UTILS CORP (DE)
Merged into Sorel Realty Corp. 06/27/1975
Each share Common $1 par exchanged for $5.20 cash

SOUTHERN REEF VENTURES INC (ON)
Cease trade order effective 05/26/2003

SOUTHERN REPUBLIC LIFE INSURANCE CO. (TX)
Merged into Southwest American Life Insurance Co. 02/21/1958
Each share Common exchanged for (12.73846) share Common
Southwest American Life Insurance Co. merged into Union Bankers Insurance Co. 02/14/1961
(See Union Bankers Insurance Co.)

SOUTHERN RES LTD (AUSTRALIA)
ADR agreement terminated 04/22/2009
No ADR holders' equity

SOUTHERN RESV INC (NJ)
Name changed 9/30/83
Each share old Common 1¢ par exchanged for (1/3) share new Common 1¢ par 7/16/83
Name changed from Southern Reserve Oil Corp. to Southern Reserve, Inc. 9/30/83
Charter declared void for non-payment of taxes 7/30/93

SOUTHERN RETAIL MKTG CORP (DE)
Charter cancelled and declared inoperative and void for non-payment of taxes 3/1/89

SOUTHERN RIO RES LTD (BC)
Recapitalized as Silver Quest Resources Ltd. 12/15/2005
Each share Common no par exchanged for (0.2) share Common no par
(See Silver Quest Resources Ltd.)

SOUTHERN RY CO (VA)
Each share Common $100 par exchanged for (1) share Common no par 00/00/1938
Each share Preferred $100 par exchanged for (2) shares Preferred $50 par 06/11/1953
Common no par split (2) for (1) by issuance of (1) additional share 06/25/1953
Each share 5% Preferred $50 par exchanged for (2.5) shares 5% Preferred $20 par 05/28/1956
Common no par split (5) for (2) by issuance of (1.5) additional shares 06/11/1956
5% Preferred $20 par changed to $10 par and (1) additional share issued 07/07/1972
Common no par split (2) for (1) by issuance of (1) additional share 07/07/1972
Each share 5% Preferred $10 par exchanged for (0.2) share $2.60 Preferred Ser. A no par 02/01/1979
$3 3-Yr. Conv. Preference Ser. A no par reclassified as $3 Conv. Preference Ser. A no par
$3 Conv. Preference Ser. A no par called for redemption 10/31/1979
Merged into Norfolk Southern Corp. 06/01/1982
Each share Common no par exchanged for (1.9) shares Common $1 par

SOUTHERN SAUCE CO INC (FL)
Each share old Common $0.001 par exchanged for (0.5) share new Common $0.001 par 04/15/2008
Name changed to Shengkai Innovations, Inc. 10/23/2008

SOUTHERN SCOTTISH INNS INC (LA)
Stock Dividend - 10% 11/01/1979
SEC revoked common stock registration 07/23/2013

SOUTHERN SEC BK CORP (DE)
Class A Common 1¢ par reclassified as Common 1¢ par 11/12/2001
Non-Vtg. Class B 1¢ par reclassified as Common 1¢ par 11/12/2001
Name changed to PanAmerican Bancorp (New) 07/30/2002
PanAmerican Bancorp (New) name changed to Sun American Bancorp 01/23/2006
(See Sun American Bancorp)

SOUTHERN SEC LIFE INS CO (FL)
Stock Dividends - 20% 9/28/89; 5% payable 5/1/2002 to holders of record 4/1/2002 Ex date - 3/27/2002; 5% payable 4/10/2003 to holders of record 4/5/2003 Ex date - 4/2/2003
Merged into SSLIC Holding Co. 2/28/2005
Each share Class A Common $1 par exchanged for $3.84 cash

SOUTHERN SECS CORP (IN)
Administratively dissolved 01/31/1994

SOUTHERN SIERRAS POWER CO.
Merged into Nevada-California Electric Corp. in 1937
(See Nevada California Electric Corp.)

SOUTHERN SOFTWARE GROUP INC (DE)
Name changed to SecureD Services, Inc. 07/30/2003
(See SecureD Services, Inc.)

SOUTHERN SPRING BED CO. (GA)
Name changed to Southern Cross Industries, Inc. 3/15/66
(See Southern Cross Industries, Inc.)

SOUTHERN STAR ENERGY INC (NV)
Common $0.001 par split (7.5) for (1) by issuance of (6.5) additional shares payable 11/13/2006 to holders of record 11/13/2006
Common $0.001 par split (3) for (2) by issuance of (0.5) additional share payable 04/04/2007 to holders of record 04/04/2007
SEC revoked common stock registration 06/11/2014

SOUTHERN STAR RES-LTD (BC)
Name changed to Cheers International Telemarketing Ltd. 10/06/1988
Cheers International Telemarketing Ltd. recapitalized as American Highland Mining Corp. 01/04/1990 which name changed to Cryocon Containers Inc. 02/26/1992 which recapitalized as Cryocon-Pacific Containers Inc. 06/17/1993 which recapitalized as Alda Industries Corp. 05/06/1996 which recapitalized as Crux Industries Inc. 07/14/1999 which name changed to Mont Blanc Resources Inc. 11/18/2005 which name changed to Sonora Gold & Silver Corp. 07/17/2008

SOUTHERN STAR RES INC (ON)
Merged into Gold Eagle Mines Ltd. 12/27/2006
Each share Common no par exchanged for (1) share Common no par
Note: Unexchanged certificates were cancelled and became without value 12/27/2008
Gold Eagle Mines Ltd. acquired by Goldcorp Inc. 09/25/2008

SOUTHERN STARR BROADCASTING GROUP INC (DE)
Stock Dividend - 10% 04/25/1994
Merged into Multi-Market Radio Inc. 03/27/1995
Each share Common 10¢ par exchanged for $13.61 cash

SOUTHERN STATES INVESTMENT CO. (SC)
Completely liquidated 7/15/65
Each share Common $1 par received (0.055555) share Farmers National Life Insurance Co. (Fla.) Common $1 par
Certificates were not required to be surrendered and are now valueless

SOUTHERN STATES IRON ROOFING CO. (GA)
Name changed to Reynolds Aluminum Supply Co. 11/01/1957
Reynolds Aluminum Supply Co. liquidated for Reynolds Metals Co. 10/04/1964 which merged into Alcoa Inc. 05/03/2000 which name changed to Arconic Inc. (PA) 11/01/2016 which reincorporated in Delaware 12/31/2017

SOUTHERN STATES LIFE INSURANCE CO. (TX)
Common no par changed to $1 par 10/14/1958
Common $1 par changed to no par 04/25/1962
Stock Dividends - 50% 05/01/1954; 10% 04/25/1962
Merged into Alabama National Life Insurance Co. 06/15/1966
Each share Preferred $100 par exchanged for (1) share Preferred $100 par
Each share Common no par exchanged for (4) shares Common 25¢ par
(See Alabama National Life Insurance Co.)

SOUTHERN STATES OIL CO. (MS)
Liquidation completed 5/4/64

SOUTHERN STATES OIL CORP. (DE)
Charter cancelled and declared inoperative and void for non-payment of taxes 4/1/33

SOUTHERN STATES TRANSPORTATION CO.
Dissolved in 1936

SOUTHERN STORES CORP.
Reorganized as Southern Food Stores, Inc. in 1933 which name was changed to Margaret Ann Super Markets, Inc. in 1942

SOUTHERN STS LENDERS INC (GA)
Under plan of reorganization each share Common $0.001 par automatically became (1) share HOM Corp. Common no par 7/5/2000
HOM Corp. name changed to R Wireless Inc. 1/22/2003 which name changed to TX Holdings, Inc. 9/19/2005

SOUTHERN STS PETE CORP (NV)
Recapitalized as Southern States Corp. 02/01/1983
Each share Common 10¢ par exchanged for (0.2) share Common 10¢ par

SOUTHERN STS PWR INC (DE)
Each share old Common $0.001 par exchanged for (0.06666666) share new Common $0.001 par 03/18/2004
Name changed to Interfoundry, Inc. 10/17/2005

SOUTHERN SUGAR CO.
Reorganized as United States Sugar Corp. in 1931
(See United States Sugar Corp.)

SOUTHERN SUN MINERALS INC (BC)
Name changed to Nevada Energy Metals Inc. 02/02/2016

SOUTHERN SURETY CO. (IA)
Succeeded by Southern Surety Co. of New York in 1928 which was taken over by New York State Superintendent of Insurance for liquidation in 1932

SOUTHERN SURETY CO. OF NEW YORK
Taken over by New York State Superintendent of Insurance for liquidation in 1932
Details not available

SOUTHERN SYND INC (GA)
Under plan of merger each share Common $1 par exchanged for (2) shares Common 50¢ par and $1 in cash 3/23/61
Under plan of liquidation assets transferred to Southern Syndicate, Inc. Liquidating Trust 7/2/74
Each share Common 50¢ par received initial distribution of $0.71 cash 12/20/74
Each share Common 50¢ par received second distribution of $0.35 cash 1/31/76
Each share Common 50¢ par received third distribution of $0.12 cash 6/20/77
Each share Common 50¢ par received fourth distribution of $0.30 cash 2/17/78
Each share Common 50¢ par received fifth distribution of $0.37 cash 12/12/78
Each share Common 50¢ par received sixth distribution of $0.38 cash 6/8/79
Each share Common 50¢ par received seventh distribution of $0.03 cash 2/28/80
Details on subsequent distributions, if any, are not available

SOUTHERN TELECOMMUNICATIONS CO J S C (RUSSIA)
Stock Dividend - 9% payable 01/29/2002 to holders of record 01/18/2002 Ex date - 01/16/2002
Merged into Rostelecom OJSC 04/13/2011
Each Sponsored ADR for Ordinary RUB 35,970 par exchanged for $13.995733 cash

SOUTHERN TITLE INS CO (TN)
$1.50 Conv. Preferred $25 par called for redemption 6/13/83
Conv. 2nd Preferred $1 par called for redemption 6/13/83
Name changed to Fidelity National Title Insurance Co. of Tennessee 4/28/89
(See Fidelity National Title Insurance Co. of Tennessee)

SOUTHERN TOY & HOBBY, INC. (GA)
Adjudicated bankrupt 4/11/63
No stockholders' equity

SOUTHERN TRANSPORTATION CO. (DE)
Dissolved in 1948

SOUTHERN TRANSPORTATION CO. (NJ)
Reorganized as Southern Transportation Co. (Del.) in 1936 which was dissolved in 1948

SOUTHERN UN CO NEW (DE)
10% Preferred Ser. A no par called for redemption 06/15/1993
Common $1 par split (3) for (2) by issuance of (0.5) additional share 03/09/1994
Common $1 par split (4) for (3) by issuance of (1/3) additional share payable 03/11/1996 to holders of record 02/23/1996 Ex date - 03/12/1996
Common $1 par split (3) for (2) by issuance of (0.5) additional share payable 07/13/1998 to holders of record 06/30/1998 Ex date - 07/14/1998
Each 5.75% Corporate Unit received (2.9652) shares Common $1 par 08/16/2006
Each 5% Corporate Unit received (1.846) shares Common $1 par 02/19/2008
7.55% Depositary Preferred Ser. A no par called for redemption at $25 on 07/30/2010
Stock Dividends - 5% payable 12/10/1996 to holders of record

11/22/1996; 5% payable 12/10/1997 to holders of record 11/21/1997; 5% payable 12/09/1998 to holders of record 11/23/1998; 5% payable 08/06/1999 to holders of record 07/23/1999; 5% payable 06/30/2000 to holders of record 06/19/2000; 5% payable 08/30/2001 to holders of record 08/16/2001; 5% payable 07/14/2002 to holders of record 07/1/2002; 5% payable 07/31/2003 to holders of record 07/17/2003 Ex date - 07/15/2003; 5% payable 08/31/2004 to holders of record 08/20/2004; 5% payable 09/01/2005 to holders of record 08/22/2005 Ex date - 09/01/2005
Merged into Energy Transfer Equity, L.P. 03/26/2012
Each share Common $1 par exchanged for (1) Common Unit
Energy Transfer Equity, L.P. name changed to Energy Transfer L.P. 10/19/2018

SOUTHERN UN CO OLD (DE)
Conv. Jr. Preferred $7.50 par called for redemption 11/30/76
Common $1 par split (5) for (4) by issuance of (0.25) additional share 1/23/78
Common $1 par split (3) for (2) by issuance of (0.5) additional share 12/15/80
4-3/4% Preferred $100 par called for redemption 9/15/82
5% Preferred $100 par called for redemption 9/15/82
5.35% Preferred $100 par called for redemption 5/1/87
12-1/4% Preferred $1 par called for redemption 5/29/87
$2.56 Preferred no par called for redemption 6/1/87
4-1/4% Preferred $100 par called for redemption 6/1/87
4-1/2% Preferred $100 par called for redemption 6/1/87
4.55% Preferred $100 par called for redemption 6/1/87
5.05% Preferred $100 par called for redemption 6/1/87
Merged into Metro Mobile CTS, Inc. 2/7/90
Each share old 10% Preferred no par exchanged for $108 cash
Each share old Common $1 par exchanged for $13.80 cash

SOUTHERN UN OILS LTD (ON)
Charter cancelled for failure to pay taxes and file returns 04/00/1975

SOUTHERN UN PRODTN CO (DE)
Stock Dividend - 50% 05/01/1974
Name changed to Supron Energy Corp. 04/18/1977
(See Supron Energy Corp.)

SOUTHERN UN RES INC (BC)
Recapitalized as Skeena Resources Ltd. 09/14/1984
Each share Common no par exchanged for (0.33333333) share Common no par
Skeena Resources Ltd. merged into Golden Nevada Resources Inc. 08/19/1987 which recapitalized as Goldnev Resources Inc. 06/19/1989

SOUTHERN UN FING I (DE)
9.48% Trust Originated Preferred Securities called for redemption at $25 on 10/31/2003

SOUTHERN UNION GAS CO. NEW (DE)
$1 Preference Common $1 par called for redemption 9/24/56
4.64% Conv. 2nd Preferred $25 par called for redemption 3/20/62
Common $1 par split (5) for (4) by issuance of (0.25) additional share 7/13/62
6-1/4% Preferred $100 par called for redemption 12/16/63
Common $1 par split (5) for (4) by issuance of (0.25) additional share 1/15/65
Name changed to Southern Union Co. (Old) 5/7/76
(See Southern Union Co. (Old))

SOUTHERN UNION GAS CO. OLD (DE)
Reorganized as Southern Union Gas Co. (DE) (New) 11/24/42
7% and Class A 8% Preference $25 par received a like amount of 6% 25-year Debentures and cash for accrued dividends
Each share Common no par exchanged for (1) share Common $1 par
Southern Union Gas Co. (DE) (New) name changed to Southern Union Co. (Old) 5/7/76
(See Southern Union Co. (Old))

SOUTHERN UNION LIFE INSURANCE CO. (TX)
Merged into Kennesaw Life & Accident Insurance Co. 09/28/1966
Each share Common no par exchanged for (0.065147) share Common $1 par
Kennesaw Life & Accident Insurance Co. merged into Lykes-Youngstown Financial Corp. 11/14/1969 which name changed to LifeSurance Corp. 05/10/1971 which merged into Regan Holding Corp. 10/31/1991
(See Regan Holding Corp.)

SOUTHERN UNITED, INC. (AL)
Merged into Southern United Life Insurance Co. on a (0.6) for (1) basis 12/16/1964
(See Southern United Life Insurance Co.)

SOUTHERN UNITED GAS CO.
Name changed to Arkansas-Oklahoma Gas Co. 00/00/1944
(See Arkansas-Oklahoma Gas Co.)

SOUTHERN UNITED ICE CO. (NJ)
Merged into Atlantic Co. on a (0.666666) for (1) basis in 1954
Atlantic Co. merged into JacksonAtlantic, Inc. 11/15/68 which name changed to Munford, Inc. 5/11/71
(See Munford, Inc.)

SOUTHERN UTD LIFE INS CO (AL)
Common 20¢ par changed to $1 par 10/03/1972
Stock Dividend - 10% 05/26/1972
Dissolved 08/21/1998
Details not available

SOUTHERN UTAH POWER CO. (UT)
Common no par changed to $10 par 04/00/1954
Merged into California-Pacific Utilities Co. 06/19/1958
Each share Common $10 par exchanged for (2/3) share Common $10 par
California-Pacific Utilities Co. name changed to CP National Corp. 05/08/1978 which was acquired by Alltel Corp. (OH) 12/30/1988 which reincorporated in Delaware 05/15/1990
(See Alltel Corp.)

SOUTHERN WEAVING CO (SC)
Each share Common $100 par exchanged for (10) shares Common no par in 1930
Common no par split (5) for (1) by issuance of (4) additional shares 5/26/58
Stock Dividend - 25% 2/24/67
Acquired by Woven Electronics Corp. 8/27/82
Each share Common no par exchanged for $55 cash

SOUTHERN WEBBING MLS INC (NC)
In process of liquidation
Each share Common $10 par received initial distribution of $1.25 cash payable 12/08/2004 to holders of record 12/01/2004 Ex date - 01/07/2005
Each share Common $10 par received second distribution of $0.55 cash payable 12/22/2005 to holders of record 12/15/2005 Ex date - 01/10/2006
Each share Common $10 par received third distribution of $0.55 cash payable 12/22/2006 to holders of record 12/19/2006 Ex date - 12/27/2006
Each share Common $10 par received fourth and final distribution of $1.12 cash payable 10/28/2011 to holders of record 10/28/2011
Note: Certificates were not required to be surrendered and are without value

SOUTHERN WHOLESALERS, INC. (DE)
No longer in existence having become inoperative and void for non-payment of taxes 4/1/64

SOUTHERN WISCONSIN ELECTRIC CO.
Acquired by Wisconsin Power & Light Co. in 1929
Details not available

SOUTHERNERA DIAMONDS INC (CANADA)
Acquired by Mwana Africa PLC 12/21/2007
Each share Common no par exchanged for (0.43859649) share Ordinary 10p par

SOUTHERNERA RES LTD (CANADA)
Reincorporated 06/06/2002
Place of incorporation changed from (ONT) to (Canada) 06/06/2002
Name changed to SouthernEra Diamonds Inc. 08/30/2004
SouthernEra Diamonds Inc. acquired by Mwana Africa PLC 12/21/2007

SOUTHERNNET INC (DE)
Reincorporated 11/17/1988
State of incorporation changed from (SC) to (DE) 11/17/1988
Merged into Telecom USA, Inc. 12/14/1988
Each share Common 1¢ par exchanged for (1) share Common 1¢ par
(See Telecom USA, Inc.)

SOUTHERTON CORP (DE)
Charter cancelled and declared inoperative and void for non-payment of taxes 3/1/81

SOUTHESK ENERGY LTD (AB)
Ser. A Preferred no par called for redemption at $7.50 on plus $0.1125 accrued dividends on 6/30/2004
Merged into 1120754 Alberta Corp. 12/1/2004
Each share Common no par exchanged for $2.50 cash

SOUTHFORK ENERGY CORP (CANADA)
Recapitalized as United Southfork Energy Inc. 4/21/82
Each share Common no par exchanged for (1/3) share Common no par
(See United Southfork Energy Inc.)

SOUTHGATE BANK (PRAIRIE VILLAGE, KS)
Name changed 01/24/1984
Stock Dividend - 12.5% 00/00/1977
Name changed from Southgate Bank & Trust Co. (Prairie Village, KS) to Southgate Bank (Prairie Village, KS) 01/24/1984
Acquired by Bank IV Kansas, N.A. (Wichita, KS) 02/13/1993
Details not available

SOUTHGATE RES LTD (BC)
Name changed to Consolidated CBA Corp. Ltd. 08/30/1985
(See Consolidated CBA Corp. Ltd.)

SOUTHGATE STATE BANK & TRUST CO. (PRAIRIE VILLAGE, KS)
Stock Dividends - 19.0476% 00/00/1969; 20% 00/00/1971; 38.4% 00/00/1975
Name changed to Southgate Bank & Trust Co. (Prairie Village, KS) 01/13/1976
Southgate Bank & Trust Co. (Prairie Village, KS) name changed to Southgate Bank (Prairie Village, KS) 01/24/1984
(See Southgate Bank (Prairie Village, KS))

SOUTHGATE STATE BANK (PRAIRIE VILLAGE, KS)
Stock Dividend - 100% 03/01/1967
Name changed to Southgate State Bank & Trust Co. (Prairie Village, KS) 07/01/1967
Southgate State Bank & Trust Co. (Prairie Village, KS) name changed to Southgate Bank & Trust Co. (Prairie Village, KS) 01/13/1976 which name changed to Southgate Bank (Prairie Village, KS) 01/24/1984
(See Southgate Bank (Prairie Village, KS))

SOUTHGOBI ENERGY RES LTD (BC)
Name changed to SouthGobi Resources Ltd. 05/17/2010

SOUTHHAMPTON ENTERPRISES CORP (BC)
Recapitalized as Antigua Enterprises Inc. (BC) 06/13/1997
Each share Common no par exchanged for (0.2) share Common no par
Antigua Enterprises Inc. (BC) reincorporated in Yukon 07/17/1998
(See Antigua Enterprises Inc.)

SOUTHHOLD SUMMER THEATRE, INC. (NY)
Charter cancelled and proclaimed dissolved for failure to pay taxes and file returns 12/15/72

SOUTHINGTON BK & TR CO (SOUTHINGTON, CT)
Common $12.50 par changed to $6.25 par and (1) additional share issued 04/30/1979
Merged into CBT Corp. 02/01/1982
Each share Common $6.25 par exchanged for (2.5738) shares Common $10 par
CBT Corp. merged into Bank of New England Corp. 06/14/1985
(See Bank of New England Corp.)

SOUTHINGTON HARDWARE CO.
Name changed to Southington Hardware Manufacturing Co. in 1940
Southington Hardware Manufacturing Co. merged into Pittsburgh Screw & Bolt Corp. 8/31/57 which name changed to Screw & Bolt Corp. of America 4/16/59 which name changed to Ampco-Pittsburgh Corp. 12/31/70

SOUTHINGTON HARDWARE MANUFACTURING CO. (CT)
Capital Stock $25 par changed to $5 par and (4) additional shares issued in 1955
Merged into Pittsburgh Screw & Bolt Corp. 8/31/57
Each share Capital Stock $25 par exchanged for (1.45) shares Capital Stock $1 par
Pittsburgh Screw & Bolt Corp. name changed to Screw & Bolt Corp. of America 4/16/59 which name changed to Ampco- Pittsburgh Corp. 12/31/70

SOUTHINGTON SVGS BK (SOUTHINGTON, CT)
Common $1 par split (3) for (2) by issuance of (0.5) additional share 12/30/86

Common $1 par split (6) for (5) by issuance of (0.2) additional share 6/1/93
Under plan of reorganization each share Common $1 par automatically became (1) share Bancorp Connecticut, Inc. (DE)
Common $1 par 11/17/94
(See Bancorp Connecticut, Inc. (DE))

SOUTHLAND APARTMENTS
Liquidated in 1947

SOUTHLAND BANCORPORATION (DE)
Name changed to Colonial BancGroup, Inc. 12/31/1981
(See Colonial BancGroup, Inc.)

SOUTHLAND BK CORP (GA)
Acquired by First Liberty Financial Corp. 6/19/98
Each share Common no par exchanged for (5.265) shares Common $1 par
First Liberty Financial Corp. merged into BB&T Corp. 11/19/99

SOUTHLAND BUSINESS BK (IRWINDALE, CA)
Merged into Vineyard National Bancorp 07/03/2003
Each share Common no par exchanged for (0.31505) share Common no par
(See Vineyard National Bancorp)

SOUTHLAND CAP INVS INC (FL)
Class A Common 10¢ par reclassified as Common 5¢ par 2/28/82
Recapitalized as Laurentian Capital Corp. (FL) 5/17/84
Each share Common 5¢ par exchanged for (0.25) share Common 5¢ par
Laurentian Capital Corp. (FL) reincorporated in Delaware 7/24/87
(See Laurentian Capital Corp.)

SOUTHLAND CORP. (DE)
Name changed 00/00/1946
Name changed from Southland Ice Co. to Southland Corp. 00/001946
Stock Dividend - 50% 11/15/1947
Merged into Southland Corp. of Texas 12/27/1960
Details not available

SOUTHLAND CORP (TX)
Name changed 00/00/1963
Name changed from Southland Corp. of Texas to Southland Corp. 00/00/1963
Common 1¢ par split (3) for (2) by issuance of (0.5) additional share 06/01/1971
Common 1¢ par split (3) for (2) by issuance of (0.5) additional share 01/28/1983
Stock Dividends - 320% 12/10/1963; 50% 02/20/1968
Merged into JT Acquisition Corp. 12/15/1987
Each share $4 Conv. Exchangeable Preferred Ser. A no par exchanged for $90.27 cash
Each share Common 1¢ par exchanged for (0.6672) share Southland Corp. 15% Exchangeable Preferred no par and $61.32 cash
Each share 15% Exchangeable Preferred no par exchanged for (1) share Common $0.0001 par and (0.073) Common Stock Purchase Warrant expiring 02/26/1996 on 03/05/1991
Name changed to 7-Eleven Inc. 04/28/1999
(See 7-Eleven Inc.)

SOUTHLAND ENERGY CORP (OK)
Reincorporated 06/25/1980
Each share old Common no par exchanged for (0.2) share new Common no par 05/31/1978
State of incorporation changed from (WA) to (OK) and new Common no par changed to Common $0.0002 par 06/25/1980

Common $0.0002 par split (2) for (1) by issuance of (1) additional share 01/07/1983
Plan of reorganization under Chapter 11 Federal Bankruptcy Code confirmed 04/25/1988
No stockholders' equity

SOUTHLAND EQUITY CORP (FL)
Common $1 par changed to 33-1/3¢ par and (2) additional shares issued 6/26/72
Common 33-1/3¢ par changed to 16-2/3¢ par and (1) additional share issued 6/15/73
Stock Dividend - 33-1/3% 12/22/72
Merged into Southland Capital Investors, Inc. 2/28/82
Each share Class A Common 16-2/3¢ par exchanged for (0.55) share Common 5¢ par
Southland Capital Investors, Inc. recapitalized as Laurentian Capital Corp. (FL) 5/17/84 which reincorporated in Delaware 7/24/87
(See Laurentian Capital Corp.)

SOUTHLAND FINL CORP (DE)
Common $1 par split (2) for (1) by issuance of (1) additional share 12/12/1973
8-1/2% Preferred Ser. A no par called for redemption 00/00/1984
Stock Dividend - 50% 02/22/1980
Completely liquidated 06/30/1989
Each share Common $1 par exchanged for first and final distribution of $2 cash

SOUTHLAND FINL INC (NV)
Each share old Common 1¢ par exchanged for (0.0016666) share new Common 1¢ par 01/31/1998
Name changed to StarBridge Global Inc. 11/20/2000
StarBridge Global Inc. recapitalized as China Mulans Nano Technology Corp., Ltd. 01/29/2007

SOUTHLAND GREYHOUND LINES, INC.
Dissolution approved in 1934

SOUTHLAND INVT CORP (GA)
Completely liquidated 06/25/1978
Each share Common $1 par exchanged for first and final distribution of $1.03 cash

SOUTHLAND LIFE INS CO (TX)
Capital Stock $10 par changed to no par 00/00/1938
Capital Stock no par changed to $5 par 03/02/1956
Capital Stock $5 par changed to $3 par and (2/3) additional share issued plus a 25% stock dividend paid 04/16/1962
Stock Dividends - 100% 03/11/1947; 100% 03/09/1948; 50% 03/15/1956; 33-1/3% 04/27/1959; 25% 04/16/1964; 60% 04/19/1966; 25% 04/14/1970
Merged into Southland Financial Corp. 12/31/1971
Each share Capital Stock $3 par exchanged for (2) shares Common $1 par
(See Southland Financial Corp.)

SOUTHLAND NATL INS CORP (AL)
Each share Common $1 par exchanged for (0.25) share Common $4 par 8/15/92
Merged into Collateral Investment Corp. 12/5/96
Each share Common $4 par exchanged for $38 cash

SOUTHLAND PAPER MLS INC (TX)
Common no par split (25) for (1) by issuance of (24) additional shares 10/29/71
Merged into St. Regis Paper Co. 12/1/77
Each share Common no par exchanged for (1.1) shares Common $5 par
St. Regis Paper Co. name changed to

St. Regis Corp. 4/28/83 which merged into Champion International Corp. 11/20/84 which merged into International Paper Co. 6/20/2000

SOUTHLAND RTY CO (DE)
Common no par changed to $5 par 00/00/1932
Common $5 par changed to $2 par and (2) additional shares issued 06/14/1967
Common $2 par changed to $1 par and (1) additional share issued 11/30/1973
Common $1 par changed to 50¢ par and (1) additional share issued 11/26/1976
Common 50¢ par changed to 25¢ par and (1) additional share issued 06/15/1979
Common 25¢ par changed to $0.125 par and (1) additional share issued 06/20/1980
Each share Common $0.125 par received distribution of (1) San Juan Basin Royalty Trust Unit of Bene. Int. payable 11/18/1980 to holders of record 11/03/1980 Ex date - 11/19/1980
Merged into Burlington Northern Inc. 12/13/1985
Each share Common $0.125 par exchanged for $17 cash

SOUTHLANDS MNG CORP (BC)
Recapitalized as Euro-Pacific Resource Group Inc. 05/27/1991
Each share Common no par exchanged for (0.2) share Common no par
Euro-Pacific Resource Group Inc. recapitalized as Holt International Investments Ltd. 05/21/1996 which name changed to Argent Resources Ltd. 11/04/1998 which recapitalized as Argent Mining Corp. 04/07/2006 which recapitalized as Avion Resources Corp. 06/21/2007 which name changed to Avion Gold Corp. (BC) 06/05/2009 which reincorporated in Ontario 06/14/2011 which merged into Endeavour Mining Corp. 10/18/2012

SOUTHLIFE HLDG CO (TN)
Merged into Capital Holding Corp. 09/08/1989
Each share 12.50% Class A Preferred $10 par exchanged for $11 cash
Each share Common 5¢ par exchanged for (0.2108) share Common $1 par and $2.10 cash

SOUTHMARK CORP (GA)
Conv. Preferred Ser. A $2 par called for redemption 09/30/1983
Increasing Rate Preferred Ser. F $2 par called for redemption 12/01/1986
Each share 7% Conv. Preferred Ser. G $2 par exchanged for (0.76) share 9-1/4% Conv. Preferred Ser. H $2 par 11/30/1987
Reorganized under Chapter 11 Federal Bankruptcy Code 08/10/1990
Each share Adjustable Rate Preferred Ser. D $2 par exchanged for (0.2775) share new Common $1 par
Each share 9-1/4% Conv. Preferred Ser. H $2 par exchanged for (0.1369) share new Common $1 par
Each share old Common $1 par exchanged for (0.03) share new Common $1 par
Stock Dividends - 10% 10/29/1982; 10% 09/15/1983; 10% 09/16/1985; 15% 05/07/1986
(Additional Information in Active)

SOUTHMARK EQUITY PARTNES LTD L P (CA)
Name changed to McNeil Real Estate Fund 4/13/92
(See McNeil Real Estate Fund)

SOUTHMARK INCOME INVS LTD L P (CA)
Name changed to McNeil Real Estate Fund XX, L.P. 4/13/92
(See McNeil Real Estate Fund XX, L.P.)

SOUTHMARK PETE LTD (ON)
Charter cancelled and declared dissolved for failure to file returns and pay fees 03/16/1976

SOUTHMARK PPTYS (MD)
Reorganized under the laws of Georgia as Southmark Corp. and Conv. Preferred Ser. A Shares of Bene. Int. $5 par, Common Shares of Bene. Int. $1 par reclassified as Conv. Preferred Ser. A $2 par or Common $1 par respectively 05/01/1982
(See Southmark Corp.)

SOUTHMARK PRIME PLUS L P (DE)
Name changed to McNeil Real Estate Fund XXVII L.P. 4/13/92
(See McNeil Real Estate Fund XXVII L.P.)

SOUTHMAYD CORP (NY)
Reincorporated under the laws of Delaware as Medical Fiduciaries Inc. 12/27/72
Medical Fiduciaries, Inc. name changed to Global Health Services, Inc. 9/20/76 which name changed to American West Financial, Inc. 5/28/86
(See American West Financial, Inc.)

SOUTHMOOR BANK & TRUST CO. (CHICAGO, IL)
Name changed to Guaranty Bank & Trust Co. (Chicago, IL) 03/00/1960
(See Guaranty Bank & Trust Co. (Chicago, IL))

SOUTHMOOR HOTEL CO.
Liquidated in 1947

SOUTHMOST SVGS & LN ASSN (TX)
Taken over by the RTC in October 1990
Stockholders' equity unlikely

SOUTHMOUNT INVESTMENT CO. LTD.
Liquidation completed in 1950

SOUTHOLD SVGS BK (SOUTHOLD, NY)
Merged into North Fork Bancorporation, Inc. 8/1/88
Each share Common $1 par exchanged for (0.75) share Common $2.50 par and $10 cash
North Fork Bancorporation, Inc. merged into Capital One Financial Corp. 12/1/2006

SOUTHPOINT RES LTD (AB)
Name changed to E4 Energy Inc. 08/23/2005
E4 Energy Inc. merged into Twin Butte Energy Ltd. 02/08/2008

SOUTHPORT CAP CORP (BC)
Recapitalized as VP Group Media Ltd. (BC) 04/04/2002
Each share Common no par exchanged for (0.5) share Common no par
VP Group Media Ltd. (BC) reincorporated in Ontario 01/06/2005 which recapitalized as DVD Investments Ltd. 02/03/2006 which name changed to Mooncor Oil & Gas Corp. 10/22/2007 which recapitalized as Sensor Technologies Inc. 10/24/2018

SOUTHPORT COML CORP (NY)
Charter cancelled and declared dissolved for failure to pay taxes 03/23/1999

SOUTHPORT RES INC (BC)
Recapitalized as Olds Industries Inc. 06/03/1992
Each share Common no par

SOU-SOU

SOUTHSHORE CMNTY BK (APOLLO BEACH, FL)
Bank failed 07/22/2011
No stockholders' equity

SOUTHSHORE CORP (CO)
Name changed to IRV Inc. 04/18/2000
IRV Inc. name changed to Scarab Systems, Inc. 03/24/2003 which name changed to Torrent Energy Corp. 07/30/2004 which recapitalized as 1pm Industries, Inc. 04/06/2015

SOUTHSIDE ATLANTIC BK (JACKSONVILLE, FL)
Name changed to Atlantic Bank of South Jacksonville (Jacksonville, FL) 07/24/1974
(See Atlantic Bank of South Jacksonville (Jacksonville, FL))

SOUTHSIDE BANCSHARES CORP (MO)
Common $10 par split (10) for (1) by issuance of (9) additional shares payable 2/15/96 to holders of record 1/31/96
Common $10 par split (3) for (1) by issuance of (2) additional shares payable 11/15/98 to holders of record 11/2/98
Merged into Allegiant Bancorp, Inc. 9/28/2001
Each share Common $10 par exchanged for either (0.54789823) share Common 1¢ par and $6.30 cash or $14 cash
Note: Option to receive stock and cash expired 10/29/2001
Allegiant Bancorp, Inc. merged into National City Corp. 4/9/2004

SOUTHSIDE BK (TAPPAHANNOCK, VA)
Merged into Eastern Virginia Bankshares, Inc. 12/29/97
Each share Common $10 par exchanged for (2.5984) shares Common $2 par 12/29/1997
Eastern Virginia Bankshares, Inc. merged into Southern National Bancorp of Virginia, Inc. 06/23/2017

SOUTHSIDE CAP TR I (DE)
8.5% Guaranteed Trust Preferred Securities called for redemption at $10 on 10/6/2003

SOUTHSIDE CAP TR II (DE)
8.75% Conv. Trust Preferred Securities called for redemption at $11.50 on 12/31/2003

SOUTHSIDE FINL GROUP INC (GA)
Merged into Newman Holdings Inc. 8/22/96
Each share Common $10 par exchanged for $41 cash

SOUTHSIDE STATE BANK (TYLER, TX)
Under plan of reorganization each share Common $5 par automatically became (1) share SoBank, Inc. Common $5 par 11/17/82

SOUTHSTAR PRODTNS INC (FL)
Each share old Common no par exchanged for (0.01) share new Common no par 05/31/1995
Name changed to Medical Technology & Innovations, Inc. (FL) 09/12/1995
Medical Technology & Innovations, Inc. (FL) reincorporated in Delaware as itLinkz Group, Inc. 04/05/2007 which recapitalized as China YCT International Group, Inc. 11/26/2007 which name changed to Spring Pharmaceutical Group, Inc. 08/31/2018

SOUTHTECH CAP CORP (AB)
Recapitalized as Vogogo Inc. 09/15/2014

Each share Common no par exchanged for (0.2) share Common no par

SOUTHTRUST CORP (DE)
Common $2.50 par split (3) for (2) by issuance of (0.5) additional share 10/31/1983
Common $2.50 par split (5) for (3) by issuance of (2/3) additional share 06/21/1985
Common $2.50 par split (3) for (2) by issuance of (0.5) additional share 01/24/1992
Common $2.50 par split (3) for (2) by issuance of (0.5) additional share 05/19/1993
Common $2.50 par split (3) for (2) by issuance of (0.5) additional share payable 02/26/1998 to holders of record 02/13/1998
Common $2.50 par split (2) for (1) by issuance of (1) additional share payable 05/11/2001 to holders of record 04/30/2001 Ex date - 05/14/2001
Merged into Wachovia Corp. (Ctfs. dated after 09/01/2001) 11/01/2004
Each share Common $2.50 par exchanged for (0.89) share Common $3.33-1/3 par
Wachovia Corp. (Ctfs. dated after 09/01/2001) merged into Wells Fargo & Co. (New) 12/31/2008

SOUTHVAAL HLDGS LTD (SOUTH AFRICA)
Merged into Anglogold Ltd. 6/29/98
Each ADR for Foreign Rand-50 par exchanged for (2) Sponsored ADR's for Ordinary Rand-50 par
AngloGold Ltd. name changed to AngloGold Ashanti Ltd. 4/26/2004

SOUTHVIEW RES INC (AB)
Recapitalized 05/05/1998
Recapitalized from Southview Capital Corp. to Southview Resources Inc. 05/05/1998
Each share Common no par exchanged for (0.33333333) share Common no par
Recapitalized as Elgin Resources Inc. (AB) 11/28/2000
Each share Common no par exchanged for (0.33333333) share Common no par
Elgin Resources Inc. (AB) reincorporated in British Columbia 01/24/2005 which merged into Eastern Platinum Ltd. 04/26/2005

SOUTHVUE MINES LTD. (ON)
Charter cancelled 11/27/68
No stockholders' equity

SOUTHWALL TECHNOLOGIES INC (DE)
Each share old Common $0.001 par exchanged for (0.2) share new Common $0.001 par 03/17/2011
Acquired by Solutia Inc. 11/28/2011
Each share new Common $0.001 par exchanged for $13.60 cash

SOUTHWARD ENERGY LTD (AB)
Acquired by Matco Investments Ltd. 04/30/2003
Each share Common no par exchanged for $4.77 cash

SOUTHWARD RES LTD (AB)
Recapitalized as Southward Energy Ltd. 4/23/87
Each share Common no par exchanged for (1/3) share Common no par
(See Southward Energy Ltd.)

SOUTHWARD VENTURES DEPOSITARY TR (FL)
In process of liquidation
Each share Common 1¢ par exchanged for initial distribution of (1) old Unit of Bene. Int. no par 05/13/1982
Each old Unit of Bene. Int. no par received initial distribution of $2.70 cash 10/15/1984

Each (110) old Units of Bene. Int. exchanged for (1) new Unit of Bene. Int. 11/17/1997
Note: Holders of (109) or fewer pre-split Units received $1 cash per Unit
Details on subsequent distributions, if any are not available

SOUTHWARD VENTURES INC (FL)
Assets transferred to Southward Ventures Depositary Trust 5/13/82
(See Southward Ventures Depositary Trust)

SOUTHWAY UTILITY CORP. (IN)
Common $200 par changed to $20 par 11/14/60
Reorganized 2/6/70
No stockholders' equity

SOUTHWEST AIRMOTIVE CO (TX)
Common $1 par changed to 66-2/3¢ par and (0.5) additional share issued 10/21/68
Merged into Cooper Airmotive, Inc. 9/28/73
Each share Common 66-2/3¢ par exchanged for $11.50 cash

SOUTHWEST AIRWAYS CO. (AZ)
Stock Dividend - 2500% 7/15/48
Name changed to Pacific Air Lines, Inc. (AZ) 1/30/58
Pacific Air Lines, Inc. (AZ) in Delaware 7/14/66 which name changed to Air West, Inc. 4/17/68 which name changed to AW Liquidating Co. 4/1/70
(See AW Liquidating Co.)

SOUTHWEST AMALGAMATED PROPERTIES & SECURITIES, INC. (TX)
Charter forfeited for failure to pay taxes 5/8/72

SOUTHWEST AMERICAN HOUSES, INC. (TX)
Liquidation completed
Each share Common 10¢ par received initial distribution of $0.30 cash 9/29/77
Each share Common 10¢ par received second distribution of $0.10 cash 2/16/79
Each share Common 10¢ par exchanged for third and final distribution of $0.13 cash 7/7/82

SOUTHWEST AMERICAN LIFE INSURANCE CO. (TX)
Under plan of merger each share Common no par exchanged for (0.04) share Common $1 par 2/21/58
Merged into Union Bankers Insurance Co. on a (1) for (2.25) basis 2/14/61
(See Union Bankers Insurance Co.)

SOUTHWEST BANCORP (CA)
$2.50 Conv. Preferred no par called for redemption 4/24/89
Acquired by Security Pacific Corp. 10/19/89
Each share Common no par exchanged for (0.15948963) share Common $10 par
Security Pacific Corp. merged into BankAmerica Corp. (Old) 4/22/92 which merged into BankAmerica Corp. (New) 9/30/98 which name changed to Bank of America Corp. 4/28/99

SOUTHWEST BANCORP INC (OK)
Preferred Ser. A $1 par called for redemption at $25 on 09/01/1998
Common $1 par split (3) for (2) by issuance of (0.5) additional share payable 08/29/2001 to holders of record 08/15/2001 Ex date - 08/30/2001
Common $1 par split (2) for (1) by issuance of (1) additional share payable 08/29/2003 to holders of record 08/15/2003 Ex date - 09/02/2003

Merged into Simmons First National Corp. 10/19/2017
Each share Common $1 par exchanged for (0.3903) share Class A Common 1¢ par and $5.11 cash

SOUTHWEST BANCORPORATION TEX INC (TX)
Common $1 par split (2) for (1) by issuance of (1) additional share payable 05/29/1998 to holders of record 05/15/1998
Common $1 par split (2) for (1) by issuance of (1) additional share payable 07/15/2004 to holders of record 07/01/2004
Name changed to Amegy Bancorporation, Inc. 05/05/2005
Amegy Bancorporation, Inc. merged into Zions Bancorporation 12/03/2005 which merged into Zions Bancorporation, N.A (Salt Lake City, UT) 10/01/2018

SOUTHWEST BANCSHARES INC (DE)
Ctfs. dated prior to 10/11/84
Common $10 par changed to $5 par and (1) additional share issued 10/18/72
Common $5 par split (3) for (2) by issuance of (0.5) additional share 8/21/81
$4.75 Conv. Preferred Ser. A $1 par called for redemption 10/9/84
Merged into MCorp 10/11/84
Each share Common $5 par exchanged for (1.05) shares Common $5 par
(See MCorp)

SOUTHWEST BANCSHARES INC (DE)
Ctfs. dated after 2/11/92
Common 1¢ par split (3) for (2) by issuance of (0.5) additional share payable 11/13/96 to holders of record 10/22/96
Merged into Alliance Bancorp 6/30/98
Each share Common 1¢ par exchanged for (1.1981) shares Common 1¢ par
Alliance Bancorp merged into Charter One Financial, Inc. 7/2/2001
(See Charter One Financial, Inc.)

SOUTHWEST BK (FT WORTH, TX)
Reorganized as SWB Bancshares, Inc. 01/05/1998
Each share Common $1 par held by Texas residents exchanged for (6) shares 7% Preferred $1 par and (1) share Common $1 par
Each share Common $1 par held by non-Texas residents exchanged for $14.25 cash
(See SWB Bancshares, Inc.)

SOUTHWEST BK (ST LOUIS, MO)
Common $10 par changed to $5 par and (1) additional share issued 3/14/73
Common $5 par changed to $2.50 par and (1) additional share issued 4/18/77
Acquired by Mississippi Valley Investment Co. 10/12/84
Each share Common $2.50 par exchanged for $11 cash

SOUTHWEST BK (VISTA CA)
Common $3 par changed to $1.50 par and (1) additional share issued 6/1/76
Stock Dividends - 10% 7/15/76; 10% 12/11/78
Under plan of reorganization each share $2.50 Conv. Preferred no par and Common $1.50 par automatically became (1) share Southwest Bancorp $2.50 Conv. Preferred no par and Common no par respectively 10/31/81
Southwest Bancorp acquired by Security Pacific Corp. 10/19/89 which merged into BankAmerica Corp. (Old) 4/22/92 which merged

into BankAmerica Corp. (New) 9/30/98 which name changed to Bank of America Corp. 4/28/99

SOUTHWEST BK TEX NATL ASSN (HOUSTON, TX)
Under plan of reorganization each share Common $5 par automatically became (1) share Southwest Bancorporation, Inc. Common $1 par 7/1/96

SOUTHWEST BKS INC (FL)
Merged into F.N.B. Corp. 1/21/97
Each share Common no par exchanged for (0.819) share Common $2 par

SOUTHWEST BORDER CORP (UT)
Reorganized under the laws of Nevada as EFO, Inc. 04/30/1993
Each share Common 2¢ par exchanged for (0.2) share Common 2¢ par
EFO, Inc. name changed to Think.com, Inc. 03/03/1999 which name changed to Go Think.com, Inc. 06/14/1999 which recapitalized as Knowledge Transfer Systems Inc. 04/24/2001 which name changed to Global General Technologies, Inc. 07/08/2005 which recapitalized as Turbine Aviation, Inc. 12/19/2014

SOUTHWEST CAFES INC (TX)
Name changed to El Chico Restaurants, Inc. 10/12/92
(See El Chico Restaurants, Inc.)

SOUTHWEST CAP CORP (CO)
Name changed to Design Institute America, Inc. 4/4/88
(See Design Institute America, Inc.)

SOUTHWEST CAP CORP (NM)
Each share old Common $1 par exchanged for (0.6349) share new Common $1 par 3/15/2002
Name changed to Scanner Technologies Corp. 7/31/2002

SOUTHWEST CAP TR II (DE)
10.50% Trust Preferred Securities called for redemption at $25 on 09/15/2013

SOUTHWEST CMNTY BANCORP (CA)
Common no par split (2) for (1) by issuance of (1) additional share payable 05/28/2003 to holders of record 05/14/2003 Ex date - 05/29/2003
Common no par split (3) for (2) by issuance of (0.5) additional share payable 06/04/2004 to holders of record 05/20/2004
Stock Dividend - 5% payable 05/18/2005 to holders of record 04/25/2005 Ex date - 04/21/2005
Merged into Placer Sierra Bancshares 06/12/2006
Each share Common no par exchanged for (1.58) shares Common no par
Placer Sierra Bancshares merged into Wells Fargo & Co. (New) 06/04/2007

SOUTHWEST CMNTY BK (ENCINITAS, CA)
Common no par split (3) for (2) by issuance of (0.5) additional share payable 12/03/1999 to holders of record 11/19/1999
Common no par split (5) for (4) by issuance of (0.25) additional share payable 03/15/2002 to holders of record 02/28/2002 Ex date - 03/18/2002
Under plan of reorganization each share Common no par automatically became (1) share Southwest Community Bancorp Common no par 04/01/2003
Southwest Community Bancorp merged into Placer Sierra Bancshares 06/12/2006 which merged into Wells Fargo & Co. (New) 06/04/2007

SOUTHWEST CONSOLIDATED CORP.
Liquidation completed in 1946
Details not available

SOUTHWEST CONSOLIDATED GAS UTILITIES CORP.
Name changed to Southwest Consolidated Corp. in 1939
(See Southwest Consolidated Corp.)

SOUTHWEST DAIRY PRODUCTS CO.
Merged into Foremost Dairies, Inc. (DE) 00/00/1946
Details not available

SOUTHWEST EQUITIES INC (DE)
Name changed to NSC Service Group Inc. 4/12/89
NSC Service Group Inc. name changed to Fibercorp International, Inc. 2/1/91
(See Fibercorp International, Inc.)

SOUTHWEST FACTORIES INC (OK)
7% Conv. Preferred $10 par called for redemption 8/31/64
Merged into Hinderliter Industries, Inc. 10/12/82
Each share Common 40¢ par exchanged for (1) share 1982 Preferred 1¢ par and (0.5) Common Stock Purchase Warrant expiring 10/11/87
(See Hinderliter Industries, Inc.)

SOUTHWEST FACTORING CORP. (AR)
Liquidation completed
Each share Common 10¢ par exchanged for initial distribution of $0.30 cash 7/20/66
Each share Common 10¢ par received second distribution of $0.10 cash 12/20/67
Each share Common 10¢ par received third and final distribution of $0.5611 cash 7/29/70

SOUTHWEST FGHT LINES INC (MO)
Reorganized as Scotch-Deluxe Industries, Inc. 4/6/70
Each share Class A Common 25¢ par exchanged for (1) share Common no par and $8.50 cash
(See Scotch-Deluxe Industries, Inc.)

SOUTHWEST FINL CORP (IL)
Merged into Suburban Bank & Trust Co. (Elmhurst, IL) 10/17/97
Each share Common $2.50 par exchanged for $49.50 cash

SOUTHWEST FLA BKS INC (FL)
$2.1875 Conv. Preferred $1 par called for redemption 12/31/82
Merged into Landmark Banking Corp. of Florida 5/31/84
Each share Common $1 par exchanged for (1.55) shares Common $1 par
Landmark Banking Corp. of Florida merged into Citizens & Southern Georgia Corp. 8/30/85 which name changed to Citizens & Southern Corp. 5/20/86 which merged into C&S/Sovran Corp. 9/1/90 which merged into NationsBank Corp. 12/31/91 which reincorporated in Delaware as BankAmerica Corp. (Old) 9/25/98 which merged into BankAmerica Corp. (New) 9/30/98 which name changed to Bank of America Corp. 4/28/99

SOUTHWEST FLA ENTERPRISES INC (FL)
Shares reacquired 12/23/2013
Each share 6% Preferred $10 par exchanged for $10 cash
Each share Common 10¢ par exchanged for $70 cash

SOUTHWEST FOREST INDS INC (NV)
$1.32 Conv. Preferred $1 par called for redemption 06/15/1978
$1.04 Conv. Preferred $1 par called for redemption 10/12/1978
$1.24 Conv. Preferred $1 par called for redemption 10/12/1978
$1.50 Conv. Preferred $1 par called for redemption 06/18/1979
$1.20 Conv. Preferred Ser. A $1 par called for redemption 10/01/1979
Merged into Stone Container Corp. 04/16/1987
Each share Common $1 par exchanged for $32.25 cash

SOUTHWEST GAS CAP I (DE)
9.125% Trust Originated Preferred Securities called for redemption at $25 on 9/24/2003

SOUTHWEST GAS CO.
Reorganized as Southwest Gas Co. of Oklahoma in 1935
Details not available

SOUTHWEST GAS CO. OF OKLAHOMA
Merged into Southwest Natural Gas Co. in 1937
Each share 7% Preferred exchanged for $50 in Debentures and (0.5) share $6 Preferred
Each share Common exchanged for (10) shares new Common
Southwest Natural Gas Co. merged into Arkansas Louisiana Gas Co. 10/2/61 which name changed to Arkla, Inc. 11/23/81 which name changed to NorAm Energy Corp. 5/11/94 which merged into Houston Industries Inc. 8/6/97 which name changed to Reliant Energy Inc. 2/8/99 which reorganized as CenterPoint Energy, Inc. 8/31/2002

SOUTHWEST GAS CORP (CA)
Capital Stock $1 par reclassified as Common $1 par 11/30/1955
$1.50 Preferred $25 par called for redemption 12/31/1963
Common $1 par split (2) for (1) by issuance of (1) additional share 06/10/1964
$1.20 Conv. Prior Preferred $9 par called for redemption 09/30/1964
$1 Conv. Preferred $5 par called for redemption 04/09/1979
$2.30 Preference $20 par called for redemption 12/22/1986
Preferred Stock Purchase Rights declared for Common stockholders of record 04/15/1996 were redeemed at $0.01 per right 03/03/2003 to holders of record 02/18/2003
Name changed to Southwest Gas Holdings, Inc. 01/03/2017

SOUTHWEST GAS PRODUCING INC (LA)
Liquidation completed
Each share Common $1 par exchanged for initial distribution of $0.40 cash 7/2/73
Each share Common $1 par received second distribution of $9.80 cash 8/10/73
Each share Common $1 par received third distribution of $0.50 cash 12/31/73
Each share Common $1 par received fourth and final distribution of $0.57 cash 1/28/76

SOUTHWEST GAS UTILITIES CORP. (DE)
Reorganized as Southwest Consolidated Gas Utilities Corp. in 1934
Details not available

SOUTHWEST GAS UTILITIES CORP. OF OKLAHOMA
Merged into Southwest Natural Gas Co. in 1937
Each share $6 Preferred exchanged for $50 in Debentures and (0.5) share $6 Preferred
Each share Common exchanged for (74) shares new Common
Southwest Natural Gas Co. merged into Arkansas Louisiana Gas Co. 10/2/61 which name changed to Arkla, Inc. 11/23/81 which name changed to NorAm Energy Corp. 5/11/94 which merged into Houston Industries Inc. 8/6/97 which name changed to Reliant Energy Inc. 2/8/99 which reorganized as CenterPoint Energy, Inc. 8/31/2002

SOUTHWEST GREASE & OIL INC (KS)
Each share Common $7.50 par exchanged for (4) shares Common no par 02/15/1969
Recapitalized as Southwest Petro-Chem, Inc. 05/06/1970
Each share Common no par exchanged for (1) share Common no par
(See Southwest Petro-Chem, Inc.)

SOUTHWEST HOLDINGS CO. (DE)
Class A Preferred $1 par called for redemption in 1970
Public interest was eliminated

SOUTHWEST ICE & DAIRY PRODUCTS CO. (DE)
Merged into Central Dairy Products Co. 8/31/55
Each share Common no par exchanged for (5) shares Common $1 par 8/31/55

SOUTHWEST INDTY & LIFE INS CO (TX)
Each share Common no par exchanged for (0.25) share Common $2 par 5/15/61
Reorganized under the laws of Nevada as Silco, Inc. 8/1/68
Each share Common $2 par or VTC for Common $2 par exchanged for (1) share Common $1 par
(See Silco, Inc.)

SOUTHWEST INDL PRODS INC (MN)
Recapitalized as Aubryn International, Inc. 08/17/1998
Each share Common no par exchanged for (1/6) share Common no par
Aubryn International, Inc. recapitalized as Pacific Sunset Investments, Inc. 01/21/2004 which name changed to Gen-ID Lab Services, Inc. 10/10/2005 which recapitalized as Adventura Corp. 11/01/2009

SOUTHWEST LD CORP (TX)
Stock Dividend - 100% 8/6/71
Charter forfeited for failure to pay taxes 3/10/75

SOUTHWEST LEASE & ROYALTY CO. (TX)
Charter forfeited for failure to pay taxes 7/10/68

SOUTHWEST LEASING CORP (CA)
Stock Dividends - 50% 1/9/73; 10% 10/22/76; 10% 10/21/77; 10% 10/20/78
Merged into SW Leasing of California 2/14/91
Each share Common 10¢ par exchanged for $8 cash

SOUTHWEST LUMBER MILLS, INC. (NV)
Common $20 par changed to $10 par in 1936 and to $1 par in 1947
Name changed to Southwest Forest Industries, Inc. 12/11/59
(See Southwest Forest Industries Inc.)

SOUTHWEST MANUFACTURING CO. (AR)
Liquidation completed 11/15/57
Details not available

SOUTHWEST MFG CORP (MN)
Name changed to Data Acquisition Technologies, Inc. 09/29/1998
Data Acquisition Technologies, Inc.

SOU-SOU

name changed to Autoco.com, Inc. 05/18/1999

SOUTHWEST MFG INC (NM)
Name changed to Aztech International Ltd. 8/20/73
(See Aztech International Ltd.)

SOUTHWEST MTG & RLTY INVS (TX)
In process of liquidation
Each share of Bene. Int. $1 par exchanged for initial distribution of $8.25 cash 12/8/82
Assets transferred to Southwest Mortgage & Realty Investors Shareholders' Liquidating Trust 12/22/82
(See Southwest Mortgage & Realty Investors Shareholders' Liquidating Trust)

SOUTHWEST MORTGAGE & REALTY INVESTORS SHAREHOLDERS' LIQUIDATING TRUST (CA)
In process of liquidation
Each Non-Transferable Share of Bene. Int. received iniital distribution of $4.75 cash 6/17/83
Each Non-Transferable Share of Bene. Int. received second distribution of $1 cash 7/29/84
Details on subsequent distributions, if any, are not available
(See Southwest Mortgage & Realty Investors for previous distribution)

SOUTHWEST NATL BK (EL PASO, TX)
Stock Dividend - 20% 2/10/60
100% owned by First City Bancorporation of Texas, Inc. (TX) as of 8/31/72
(See First City Bancorporation of Texas, Inc. (TX))

SOUTHWEST NATL BK PA (GREENSBURG, PA)
Stock Dividends - 25% 5/20/77; 10% 9/25/81
Under plan of reorganization each share Common $10 par automatically became (1) share Southwest National Corp. (PA) Common $10 par 11/6/81
Southwest National Corp. merged into First Commonwealth Financial Corp. 12/31/98

SOUTHWEST NATL CORP (PA)
Common $10 par changed to $2.50 par and (3) additional shares issued 06/02/1986
Stock Dividends - 20% 08/23/1985; 20% 06/03/1994
Merged into First Commonwealth Financial Corp. 12/31/1998
Each share Common $2.50 par exchanged for (2.9) shares Common $1 par

SOUTHWEST NATURAL GAS CO. (DE)
Stock Dividend - 50% 7/1/50
Merged into Arkansas Louisiana Gas Co. on a (0.2) for (1) basis 10/2/61
Arkansas Louisiana Gas Co. name changed to Arkla, Inc. 11/23/81 which name changed to NorAm Energy Corp. 5/11/94 which merged into Houston Industries Inc. 8/6/97 which name changed to Reliant Energy Inc. 2/8/99 which reorganized as CenterPoint Energy, Inc. 8/31/2002

SOUTHWEST OIL CO. (WY)
Charter revoked for failure to file reports and pay fees 7/19/27

SOUTHWEST OIL CORP. (DE)
Name changed to Melo-Sonics Corp. 05/08/1961
(See Melo-Sonics Corp.)

SOUTHWEST OVERTHRUST OIL & GAS INC (NV)
Name changed to SW Capital Corp. 6/30/86
(See SW Capital Corp.)

SOUTHWEST PENNSYLVANIA GAS CORP. (PA)
Reorganized in 1953
No stockholders' equity

SOUTHWEST PETRO CHEM INC (KS)
Merged into Witco Chemical Corp. 08/31/1978
Each share Common no par exchanged for $12.50 cash

SOUTHWEST PETROLEUM CO. LTD. (CANADA)
Merged into Commonwealth Petroleum Services Ltd. 07/21/1967
Each share Capital Stock no par exchanged for (1) share Common no par
Commonwealth Petroleum Services Ltd. acquired by Westburne International Industries Ltd. (AB) 09/30/1969 which reincorporated in Canada 10/18/1977
(See Westburne International Industries Ltd. (Canada))

SOUTHWEST POWER CO.
Dissolved in 1928
Details not available

SOUTHWEST PUBLIC SERVICE CO.
Reorganized as Central Diary Products Co. 12/1/36
No stockholders' equity

SOUTHWEST RLTY & DEV INC NEW (DE)
Name changed 6/24/77
Under plan of merger name changed from Southwest Realty & Development Co., Inc. (Old) to Southwest Realty & Development Co., Inc. (New) and each (500) old Common 20¢ par exchanged for (1) share new Common 20¢ par 6/24/77
Completely liquidated
Each share Common 20¢ par exchanged for first and final distribution of (1) Southwest Stockholders' Liquidating Trust Share of Bene. Int. $100 par 6/5/78

SOUTHWEST RLTY LTD (TX)
Reorganized under the laws of Maryland as Southwestern Property Trust Inc. 10/01/1992
Each 12% Conv. Preferred Depositary Receipt exchanged for $21 cash
Each Common Depositary Receipt exchanged for (0.2) share Common 1¢ par
Southwestern Property Trust Inc. name changed to South West Property Trust, Inc. 06/01/1994 which merged into United Dominion Realty Trust, Inc. (VA) 12/31/1996 which reincorporated in Maryland 06/11/2003 which name changed to UDR, Inc. 03/14/2007

SOUTHWEST RESERVE LIFE INSURANCE CO. (TX)
Merged into National Empire Life Insurance Co. on a (2.625) for (1) basis 8/1/63
National Empire Life Insurance Co. merged into Empire Life Insurance Co. of America (AL) 6/30/66
(See Empire Life Insurance Co. of America (AL))

SOUTHWEST RES INC (DE)
Reorganized under the laws of Nevada as Puration, Inc. 02/29/2012
Each share Common $0.001 par exchanged for (0.00029069) share Common $0.001 par

SOUTHWEST RES INC (NM)
Merged into Cobb Resources Corp. 09/02/1983
Each (12.8) shares Common $0.001 par exchanged for (1) share Common 1¢ par
Cobb Resources Corp. name changed to Family Room Entertainment Corp. 04/26/2000

SOUTHWEST RTY CORP (DE)
Name changed to Classicvision Entertainment Inc. 6/17/96
Classicvision Entertainment Inc. recapitalized as Allixion International Corp. 7/20/2005

SOUTHWEST SVGS & LN ASSN (CA)
Placed in conservatorship 04/27/1989
No stockholders' equity

SOUTHWEST SCOTTISH INNS INC (AR)
Merged into Mid-Continent, Inc. 01/24/1975
Each share Common $1 par exchanged for (0.625) share Common 4¢ par
Mid-Continent, Inc. name changed to Mid Continent Systems, Inc. 09/24/1976
(See Mid Continent Systems, Inc.)

SOUTHWEST SECS GROUP INC (DE)
Common 10¢ par split (3) for (2) by issuance of (0.5) additional share 07/01/1993
Stock Dividends - 10% payable 10/01/1997 to holders of record 09/15/1997; 5% payable 08/03/1998 to holders of record 07/15/1998; 10% payable 08/02/1999 to holders of record 07/15/1999; 10% payable 08/01/2000 to holders of record 07/14/2000; 10% payable 08/01/2001 to holders of record 7/13/2001 Ex date - 07/11/2001
Name changed to SWS Group, Inc. 11/07/2001
SWS Group, Inc. merged into Hilltop Holdings Inc. 01/01/2015

SOUTHWEST SERVICE CO. (DE)
Merged into Southwest Ice & Dairy Products Co. in 1955
Details not available

SOUTHWEST SILVER MINES (NV)
Under plan of merger each share Capital Stock 15¢ par automatically became (1) share General Oil & Mining Corp. Capital Stock no par 4/28/71
General Oil & Mining Corp. merged into Control Metals Corp. 7/20/71
(See Control Metals Corp.)

SOUTHWEST TECHNOLOGIES INC (BC)
Cease trade order effective 12/04/1989
Stockholders' equity unlikely

SOUTHWEST TEXAS NATIONAL BANK (SAN ANTONIO, TX)
Merged into Republic of Texas Corp. 2/1/80
Each share Common Capital Stock $10 par exchanged for $34.50 cash

SOUTHWEST TEXAS OIL & GAS CO. (TX)
Charter forfeited for failure to pay taxes 3/21/66

SOUTHWEST TITLE & TRUST CO., INC. (OK)
Common $10 par changed to $50 par 03/17/1981
Merged into First American Title & Trust Co. 04/17/2007
Details not available

SOUTHWEST UNION SECURITIES CORP. (CA)
Charter forfeited for failure to file reports and pay fees 00/00/1929

SOUTHWEST UTILITY DAIRY PRODUCTS CO.
Reorganized as Central Diary Products Co. 12/1/36
No stockholders' equity

SOUTHWEST UTILITY ICE CO.
Name changed to Southwest Utility Dairy Products Co. in 1931
(See Southwest Utility Dairy Products Co.)

SOUTHWEST VIRGINIA INVESTMENT CORP. (VA)
Merged into Estate Life Insurance Co. of America 12/31/65
Each share Common $1 par exchanged for (1) share Common 25¢ par
Estate Life Insurance Co. of America merged into Founders Financial Corp. (FL) 6/30/81 which merged into Laurentian Capital Corp. (FL) 12/1/86 which reincorporated in Delaware 7/24/87
(See Laurentian Capital Corp.)

SOUTHWEST WHEEL & MANUFACTURING CO. (TX)
Merged into National City Lines, Inc. 03/28/1969
Each share Common $1 par exchanged (0.4083167) share Common 50¢ par
(See National City LInes, Inc.)

SOUTHWEST WTR CO (DE)
Reincorporated 06/30/1988
Common $50 par changed to $10 par and (4) additional shares issued 10/00/1960
Common $10 par changed to $1 par 09/30/1975
Common $1 par split (2) for (1) by issuance of (1) additional share 04/30/1984
Common $1 par split (2) for (1) by issuance of (1) additional share 07/31/1986
$4 Preferred Ser. C $50 par called for redemption 00/00/1987
Stock Dividends - 10% 00/00/1983; 25% 07/20/1985
State of incorporation changed from (CA) to (DE) and Common $1 par changed to 1¢ par 06/30/1988
Common 1¢ par split (5) for (4) by issuance of (0.25) additional share payable 10/20/1998 to holders of record 10/01/1998
Common 1¢ par split (3) for (2) by issuance of (0.5) additional share payable 10/20/1999 to holders of record 10/01/1999
Common 1¢ par split (5) for (4) by issuance of (0.25) additional share payable 01/19/2001 to holders of record 01/01/2001 Ex date - 01/22/2001
Common 1¢ par split (4) for (3) by issuance of (1/3) additional share payable 01/20/2004 to holders of record 01/01/2004 Ex date - 01/21/2004
Stock Dividends - 5% payable 01/20/1996 to holders of record 01/02/1996; 20% payable 01/20/1997 to holders of record 01/02/1997; 5% payable 01/20/1998 to holders of record 01/02/1998; 5% payable 10/22/2001 to holders of record 10/01/2001 Ex date - 09/27/2001; 5% payable 01/20/2003 to holders of record 01/01/2003; 5% payable 01/21/2005 to holders of record 01/03/2005 Ex date - 12/30/2004; 5% payable 01/20/2006 to holders of record 01/02/2006 Ex date - 12/28/2005
Merged into SW Merger Acquisition Corp. 09/13/2010
Each share Common 1¢ par exchanged for $11 cash
$2.625 Preferred Ser. A 1¢ par called for redemption at $52 plus $1.34 accrued dividends on 10/03/2010
Public interest eliminated

SOUTHWESTERN ASSOCIATED TELEPHONE CO. (DE)
Name changed to General Telephone Co. of the Southwest in 1952
General Telephone Co. of the Southwest name changed to GTE Southwest Inc. 1/1/88

SOUTHWESTERN BANK (TUCSON, AZ)
Closed by Superintendent of Banks and receiver appointed 9/25/81
No stockholders' equity

SOUTHWESTERN BELL CORP (DE)
Common $1 par split (3) for (1) by issuance of (2) additional shares 5/22/87
Common $1 par split (2) for (1) by issuance of (1) additional share 5/25/93
Name changed to SBC Communications, Inc. 4/28/95
SBC Communications, Inc. name changed to AT&T Inc. 11/18/2005

SOUTHWESTERN CAPITAL CORP. (CA)
Name changed to Intermark Investing, Inc. 9/19/68
Intermark Investing, Inc. name changed to Intermark, Inc. (CA) 10/4/71 which reincorporated in Delaware 9/13/83 which reorganized as Triton Group Ltd. (New) 6/25/93 which name changed to Alarmguard Holdings, Inc. 4/16/97
(See Alarmguard Holdings, Inc.)

SOUTHWESTERN DEVELOPMENT CO. (CO)
Completely liquidated in 1954
Each share Common $5 par exchanged for (2) shares Pioneer Natural Gas Co. Common $7.50 par
Pioneer Natural Gas Co. name changed to Pioneer Corp. (Tex.) 4/18/75 which liquidated for Mesa Limited Partnership 6/30/86

SOUTHWESTERN DEVELOPMENT CO. (ME)
Charter revoked for failure to file reports and pay fees in 1913

SOUTHWESTERN DRUG CORP (TX)
Common no par changed to $1 par 7/29/58
Common $1 par split (3) for (1) by issuance of (2) additional shares 7/28/59
5% 1st Preferred no par called for redemption 1/15/65
Stock Dividends - 10% 7/15/57; 10% 8/15/69; 50% 6/28/76
Acquired by Gulf United Corp. 9/24/79
Each share Common $1 par exchanged for (1) share Common $1 par
(See Gulf United Corp.)

SOUTHWESTERN ELEC PWR CO (DE)
9.72% Preferred $100 par called for redemption 10/31/1985
8.84% Preferred $100 par called for redemption 04/01/1987
8.16% Preferred $100 par called for redemption 05/01/1987
9.60% Preferred $100 par called for redemption 11/01/1988
6.95% Preferred $100 par called for redemption at $102.34 on 04/01/1998
4.28% Preferred $100 par called for redemption at $103.904 on 12/01/2011
4.65% Preferred $100 par called for redemption at $102.75 on 12/01/2011
5% Preferred $100 par called for redemption at $109 on 12/01/2011

SOUTHWESTERN ELEC SVC CO (TX)
Stock Dividend - 100% 11/07/1958
4.40% Preferred $100 par called for redemption 02/26/1993
4-3/4% Preferred $100 par called for redemption 02/26/1993
5.95% Preferred $100 par called for redemption 02/26/1993
Merged into Texas Utilities Co. 07/01/1993
Each share Common $1 par exchanged for (2.2) share Common no par
Texas Utilities Co. reorganized as Texas Utilities Co. (Holding Co.) 08/05/1997 which name changed to TXU Corp. 05/16/2000
(See TXU Corp.)

SOUTHWESTERN ENERGY CO (DE)
Reincorporated 06/30/2006
Common $2.50 par split (2) for (1) by issuance of (1) additional share 08/05/1981
Common $2.50 par changed to 10¢ par 06/09/1993
Common 10¢ par split (3) for (1) by issuance of (2) additional shares 08/05/1993
Common 10¢ par split (2) for (1) by issuance of (1) additional share payable 06/03/2005 to holders of record 05/20/2005 Ex date - 06/06/2005
Common 10¢ par split (2) for (1) by issuance of (1) additional share payable 11/17/2005 to holders of record 11/03/2005 Ex date - 11/18/2005
State of incorporation changed from (AR) to (DE) and Common 10¢ par changed to 1¢ par 06/30/2006
Each share 6.25% Depositary Mandatory Conv. Preferred Ser. B received distribution of (0.05924) share Common 1¢ par payable 10/17/2016 to holders of record 10/01/2016 Ex date - 09/28/2016
Each share 6.25% Depositary Mandatory Conv. Preferred Ser. B automatically became (2.17391) shares Common 1¢ par 01/12/2018
(Additional Information in Active)

SOUTHWESTERN ENGINEERING CO. (CA)
Name changed to Sweco, Inc. 1/2/68
Sweco, Inc. merged into Emerson Electric Co. 3/23/79

SOUTHWESTERN ENGINEERING CORP.
Dissolved in 1934

SOUTHWESTERN ENVIRONMENTAL CORP (CO)
Each share old Common 1¢ par exchanged for (0.66666666) share new Common 1¢ par 08/13/1998
Name changed CITA Biomedical, Inc. (CO) 11/30/1998
CITA Biomedical, Inc. (CO) reincorporated in Delaware 05/29/2002 which recapitalized as Xino Corp. 01/07/2005 which reorganized as AsherXino Corp. 08/19/2009
(See AsherXino Corp.)

SOUTHWESTERN FINANCIAL CORP. (DE)
Acquired by Hathaway Instruments, Inc. (Del.) on a (0.2) for (1) basis 3/10/60
Hathaway Instruments, Inc. (Del.) merged into Lionel Corp. 11/3/61

SOUTHWESTERN FINL CORP (ID)
Name changed to Univest Technologies, Inc. 10/11/1985
Univest Technologies, Inc. name changed to Outpatient Treatment Centers, Inc. 12/22/1986
(See Outpatient Treatment Centers, Inc.)

SOUTHWESTERN GAS & ELEC CO (DE)
Name changed to Southwestern Electric Power Co. 10/01/1958
(See Southwestern Electric Power Co.)

SOUTHWESTERN GOLD CORP (BC)
Name changed to Southwestern Resources Corp. 06/05/2001
(See Southwestern Resources Corp.)

SOUTHWESTERN GROUP FINL INC (DE)
Merged into Kaneb Services, Inc. 02/28/1979
Each share Common $1 par exchanged for (0.95) share Common no par
Kaneb Services, Inc. name changed to Xanser Corp. 08/07/2001 which name changed to Furmanite Corp. 05/17/2007 which merged into Team, Inc. 02/29/2016

SOUTHWESTERN GROUP INC (OK)
Stock Dividend - 20% 02/27/1970
Charter suspended for failure to pay taxes 02/10/1986

SOUTHWESTERN GROUP INVS INC (DE)
Name changed to Southwestern Group Financial Inc. 09/19/1975
Southwestern Group Financial Inc. merged into Kaneb Services, Inc. 02/28/1979 which name changed to Xanser Corp. 08/07/2001 which name changed to Furmanite Corp. 05/17/2007 which merged into Team, Inc. 02/29/2016

SOUTHWESTERN INDUSTRIAL IRON & CHEMICAL CO., INC. (AZ)
Charter revoked for failure to file reports and pay fees 4/4/60

SOUTHWESTERN INSURANCE CO. (OK)
Stock Dividends - 20% 03/01/1966; 10% 03/01/1967
Completely liquidated 11/17/1967
Each share Common $1 par exchanged for first and final distribution of (1) share Southwestern Group, Inc. Capital Stock $1 par
(See Southwestern Group, Inc.)

SOUTHWESTERN INVT CO (TX)
Each share Common no par exchanged for (2) shares Common $5 par 00/00/1953
Each share Common $5 par exchanged for (2) shares Common $2.50 par 11/08/1955
$1 Preferred Ser. A no par called for redemption 08/00/1962
$1 Preferred Ser. B $20 par called for 09/01/1962
6% Preferred $20 par called for redemption 08/00/1965
5-1/4% Preferred $20 par reclassified as 5-1/4% Class A, S.F. Preferred Ser. II $20 par, 5-1/2% Preferred 1964 Ser. A $20 par reclassified as 5-1/2% Class A, S.F. Preferred Ser. III $20 par and 5-3/4% Preferred $20 par reclassified as 5-3/4% Class A, S.F. Preferred Ser. IV $20 par 08/25/1965
5.25% Class A Preferred Ser. 1 $20 par called for redemption 07/23/1973
5.25% Class A Preferred Ser. 2 $20 par called for redemption 07/23/1973
5.5% Class A Preferred Ser. 3 $20 par called for redemption 07/23/1973
5.75% Class A Preferred Ser. 4 $20 par called for redemption 07/23/1973
6% Class A Preferred Ser. 4 $20 par called for redemption 07/23/1973
Acquired by Beatrice Foods Co. 07/24/1973
Each share Common $2.50 par exchanged for (1.6) shares Common no par
Beatrice Foods Co. name changed to Beatrice Companies, Inc. 06/05/1984
(See Beatrice Companies, Inc.)

SOUTHWESTERN INVS GROWTH FD (DE)
Merged into Plitrend Fund, Inc. 07/23/1982
Each share Common $1 par exchanged for (0.7527915537) share Common 1¢ par
Plitrend Fund, Inc. name changed to U.S. Trend Fund, Inc. (PA) 02/00/1986 which reincorporated in Maryland as Capstone U.S. Trend Fund, Inc. 05/11/1992 which name changed to Capstone Growth Fund, Inc. 08/26/1994 which name changed to Capstone Series Fund, Inc. 01/22/2002

SOUTHWESTERN INVS INC (DE)
Common $1 par changed to 50¢ par and (1) additional share issued 08/15/1961
Name changed to Investors Income Fund, Inc. 06/04/1986
Investors Income Fund, Inc. name changed to Capstone Government Income Trust, Inc. (DE) 01/08/1991 which reincorporated in Maryland as Capstone Fixed Income Series Inc. 05/11/1992
(See Capstone Fixed Income Series Inc.)

SOUTHWESTERN LIFE CORP (DE)
Stock Dividend - 50% 2/11/77
Completely liquidated 5/1/80
Each share Common $2.50 par exchanged for first and final distribution of (0.2) share Tenneco Inc. $11 Preference no par and (0.75) share Common $5 par
Tenneco Inc. merged into El Paso Natural Gas Co. 12/12/96 which reorganized as El Paso Energy Corp. 8/1/98 which name changed to El Paso Corp. 2/5/2001

SOUTHWESTERN LIFE CORP NEW (DE)
Name changed to I.C.H. Corp. (New) 10/10/95
(See I.C.H. Corp. (New))

SOUTHWESTERN LIFE HLDGS INC (DE)
Merged into Swiss Re Life & Health America Holding Co. 6/21/2001
Each share Common 1¢ par exchanged for $18.50 cash

SOUTHWESTERN LIFE INS CO (TX)
Each share Capital Stock $100 par exchanged for (10) shares Capital Stock $10 par 00/00/1930
Capital Stock $10 par changed to $5 par and (1) additional share issued plus a 33.33333333% stock dividend paid 12/15/1959
Capital Stock $5 par changed to $2.50 par and (1) additional share issued plus a 36.36% stock dividend paid 04/13/1965
Stock Dividends - 25% 12/20/1950; 50% 03/23/1956; 10% 04/09/1962; 33.33333333% 11/01/1968; 30% 05/05/1972
Under plan of reorganization each share Capital Stock $2.50 par automatically became (1) share Southwestern Life Corp. Common $2.50 par 12/28/1972
Southwestern Life Corp. liquidated for Tenneco Inc. 05/01/1980 which merged into El Paso Natural Gas Co. 12/12/1996 which reorganized as El Paso Energy Corp. 08/01/1998 which name changed to El Paso Corp. 02/05/2001

SOUTHWESTERN LIGHT & POWER CO.
Dissolved in 1944

SOUTHWESTERN MIAMI DEVELOPMENT CO.
Acquired by Inspiration Consolidated Copper Co. in 1929
(See Inspiration Consolidated Copper Co.)

SOUTHWESTERN MINES CORP. (AZ)
Charter revoked for failure to file annual reports 12/8/27

SOU-SOV

SOUTHWESTERN OIL PRODUCERS, INC. (NV)
Charter revoked for failure to file reports and pay fees 3/4/63

SOUTHWESTERN OKLAHOMA OIL CO. (DE)
Charter cancelled and declared inoperative and void for non-payment of taxes 4/15/70

SOUTHWESTERN PPTY TR INC (MD)
Name changed to South West Property Trust, Inc. 06/01/1994
South West Property Trust, Inc. merged into United Dominion Realty Trust, Inc. (VA) 12/31/1996 which reincorporated in Maryland 06/11/2003 which name changed to UDR, Inc. 03/14/2007

SOUTHWESTERN PUB SVC CO (NM)
12.50% Preferred $100 par called for redemption in 1986
9.68% Preferred $100 par called for redemption 12/28/92
$3.70 Preferred Ser. A $100 par called for redemption 12/27/95
3.90% Preferred $100 par called for redemption 12/27/95
4.15% Preferred $100 par called for redemption 12/27/95
4.25% Preferred $100 par called for redemption 12/27/95
4.36% Preferred $25 par called for redemption 12/27/95
4.40% Preferred $25 par called for redemption 12/27/95
4.40% Preferred $100 par called for redemption 12/27/95
4.60% Preferred $100 par called for redemption 12/27/95
4.75% Preferred $100 par called for redemption 12/27/95
5% Preferred $25 par called for redemption 12/27/95
5 5/8% Preferred $100 par called for redemption 12/27/95
6.50% Preferred $100 par called for redemption 12/27/95
8% Preferred $100 par called for redemption 12/27/95
8.88% Preferred $25 par called for redemption 12/27/95
$3.70 Preferred $100 par called for redemption 12/27/95
Merged into New Century Energies, Inc. 8/1/97
Each share Common $1 par exchanged for (0.95) share Common $1 par
New Century Energies, Inc. merged into Xcel Energy Inc. 8/18/2000

SOUTHWESTERN PUBLIC SVC CAP I (DE)
Issue Information - 4,000,000 PFD SECS SER A 7.85% shares offered at $25 per share on 10/16/1996
7.85% Preferred Securities Ser. A called for redemption at $25 plus $0.239861 accrued dividend on 10/15/2003

SOUTHWESTERN RESEARCH & DEVELOPMENT CO. (AZ)
Name changed to Southwestern Research & General Investment Co. (AZ) 10/27/1961
Southwestern Research & General Investment Co. (AZ) reincorporated in Delaware as Southwestern Research Corp. 11/26/1969 which name changed to Toltec Real Estate Corp. 11/15/1980
(See Toltec Real Estate Corp.)

SOUTHWESTERN RESH & GEN INVT CO (AZ)
Reincorporated under the laws of Delaware as Southwestern Research Corp. 11/26/1969
Southwestern Research Corp. name changed to Toltec Real Estate Corp. 11/15/1980
(See Toltec Real Estate Corp.)

SOUTHWESTERN RESH CORP (DE)
Common $5 par split (5) for (4) by issuance of (0.25) additional share 12/05/1969
Name changed to Toltec Real Estate Corp. 11/15/1980
(See Toltec Real Estate Corp.)

SOUTHWESTERN RES CORP (BC)
Common no par split (2) for (1) by issuance of (1) additional share payable 06/21/2004 to holders of record 06/17/2004
Acquired by Hochschild Mining PLC 05/26/2009
Each share Common no par exchanged for $0.50 cash

SOUTHWESTERN SVGS ASSN (TX)
99.8519% acquired by Southwestern Group Investors, Inc. through exchange offer which expired 07/31/1971
Public interest eliminated

SOUTHWESTERN SEWER CO. (TX)
Liquidated in 1956

SOUTHWESTERN STS GAS CO (NM)
Each share Common no par exchanged for (0.1) share Class A Common no par 7/12/68
Name changed to Midwest Energy Corp. 7/20/73
Midwest Energy Corp. reorganized as Swab- Fox Companies 9/23/83 which name changed to Tribune/Swab Fox Companies, Inc. 10/1/84 which recapitalized as T/SF Communications Corp. 5/24/95

SOUTHWESTERN STATES GAS CORP. (DE)
Merged into Tesoro Petroleum Corp. (DE) 12/20/1965
Each share Common 6¢ par exchanged for (0.007692) share Common $1 par
Tesoro Petroleum Corp. (DE) merged into Tesoro Petroleum Corp. (CA) 02/01/1968 which reincorporated back in Delaware 03/03/1969 which name changed to Tesoro Corp. 11/08/2004 which name changed to Andeavor 08/01/2017 which merged into Marathon Petroleum Corp. 10/01/2018

SOUTHWESTERN STATES TELEPHONE CO. (DE)
Reorganized 06/10/1937
Each share Preferred $100 par exchanged for (0.5) share Common $1 par
No old Common stockholders' equity
Common $1 par split (2) for (1) by issuance of (1) additional share 06/24/1963
Merged into General Telephone & Electronics Corp. share for share 06/30/1964
$1.44 Conv. Preferred $25 par called for redemption 06/29/1964
1960 Ser. Preferred called for redemption 07/22/1964
$1.18 Preferred $25 par called for redemption 07/22/1964
$1.20 Preferred $25 par called for redemption 07/22/1964
$1.25 Preferred $25 par called for redemption 07/22/1964
$1.28 Preferred $25 par called for redemption 07/22/1964
$1.32 Preferred $25 par called for redemption 07/22/1964
General Telephone & Electronics Corp. name changed to GTE Corp. 07/01/1982 which merged into Verizon Communications Inc. 06/30/2000

SOUTHWESTERN TELECOM INC. (NV)
Merged into J-E Too, Inc. 1/24/92
Each share Common $0.001 par exchanged for $0.02 cash

SOUTHWESTERN UTILITIES CORP.
Merged into Union Gas Corp. in 1926
Union Gas Corp. property was acquired by Union Gas System, Inc. in 1933
(See Union Gas System, Inc.)

SOUTHWESTERN WTR EXPL CO (CO)
Reincorporated under the laws of Nevada as Fuquan Financial Co. 04/23/2018

SOUTHWIND RES EXPLS LTD (ON)
Delisted from Alberta Stock Exchange 10/11/1989

SOUTHWOOD EXPLORATION CO., INC. (DE)
Merged into Petro-Lewis Corp. in September 1969
Each share Common $1 par exchanged for (0.091) share 44¢ Conv. Preferred Ser. A no par
(See Petro-Lewis Corp.)

SOUVALL-PAGE & CO INC (UT)
Each share old Class A Common no par exchanged for (0.001) share new Class A no par in September 1998
Note: No holder received fewer than (100) shares
New Class A Common no par reclassified as old Common no par and (3) additional shares issued 6/5/2006
Old Common no par split (11) for (1) by issuance of (10) additional shares payable 10/10/2006 to holders of record 10/10/2006
Name changed to American Basketball Association, Inc. 1/4/2007

SOVEREIGN AMERN ARTS CORP (NY)
Each share old Common 10¢ par exchanged for (0.2) share new Common 10¢ par 10/26/1976
Completely liquidated 03/05/1999
Details not available

SOVEREIGN BANCORP INC (VA)
Reincorporated 01/30/2009
Common $1 par split (5) for (4) by issuance of (0.25) additional share 12/20/1989
Common $1 par split (5) for (4) by issuance of (0.25) additional share 05/15/1991
Common $1 par changed to no par 06/30/1991
Common no par split (5) for (4) by issuance of (0.25) additional share 07/15/1991
Common no par split (5) for (4) by issuance of (0.25) additional share 10/04/1991
Common no par split (6) for (5) by issuance of (0.2) additional share 11/16/1992
Common no par split (6) for (5) by issuance of (0.2) additional share 05/17/1993
Common no par split (6) for (5) by issuance of (0.2) additional share 11/17/1993
Common no par split (6) for (5) by issuance of (0.2) additional share payable 03/14/1997 to holders of record 03/03/1997
Common no par split (6) for (5) by issuance of (0.2) additional share payable 04/15/1998 to holders of record 03/31/1998
6.25% Conv. Preferred Ser. B no par called for redemption at $52.188 plus $0.78125 accrued dividends on 05/15/1998
Stock Dividends - 20% 02/15/1991; 10% 03/02/1992; 10% 05/15/1992; 10% 08/14/1992; 10% 05/16/1994; 5% payable 02/15/1996 to holders of record 02/01/1996; 5% payable 07/06/2006 to holders of record 06/15/2006 Ex date - 06/13/2006
State of incorporation changed from (PA) to (VA) 01/30/2009
Merged into Banco Santander, S.A. 01/30/2009
Each share Common no par exchanged for (0.3206) ADR for Ordinary Euro 50 par
Name changed to Santander Holdings USA, Inc. 02/24/2010
(See Santander Holdings USA, Inc.)

SOVEREIGN CAP TR II (DE)
7.5% Capital Preferred Securities called for redemption at $32.79 on 08/25/2003

SOVEREIGN CAP TR III (DE)
8.75% Capital Preferred Securities called for redemption at $25 on 01/30/2007

SOVEREIGN CAP TR IV
Contingent Conv. Trust Preferred Income Equity Securities called for redemption at $50 plus $1.604375 accrued dividends on 02/28/2014

SOVEREIGN CAP TR V (DE)
7.75% Capital Securities called for redemption at $25 on 06/13/2011

SOVEREIGN CHEM & PETE PRODS INC (DE)
Charter cancelled and declared inoperative and void for non-payment of taxes 6/24/91

SOVEREIGN CHIEF VENTURES LTD (BC)
Name changed to Saxon Oil Co. Ltd. 04/21/2006
(See Saxon Oil Co. Ltd.)

SOVEREIGN CORP (DE)
Stock Dividends - 25% 12/21/1970; 25% 12/29/1971; 25% 12/20/1972; 25% 12/27/1973; 20% 12/31/1980; 25% 12/31/1981
Merged into Chubb Corp. 03/31/1987
Each share Common $1 par exchanged for (0.1365) share Common $1 par
Chubb Corp. merged into Chubb Ltd. 01/15/2016

SOVEREIGN ENTERPRISES INC (NY)
Reincorporated under the laws of Delaware as Varlen Corp. and Common 1¢ par changed to 10¢ par 01/30/1970
(See Varlen Corp.)

SOVEREIGN HOTEL CO.
Merged into Rockefeller Park Hotel Corp. and each share Capital Stock no par exchanged for (1) share new Preferred $55 par in 1951
Rockefeller Park Hotel Corp. charter cancelled 4/1/58

SOVEREIGN INDS INC (CO)
Assets ordered liquidated by Court appointed receiver 03/09/1982
No stockholders' equity

SOVEREIGN INVT CORP (TX)
Completely liquidated 3/30/70
Each share Common $1 par received first and final distribution of (0.370787) share Coaches of America, Inc. Common no par
Note: Certificates were not required to be surrendered and are now valueless

SOVEREIGN INVS INC (MD)
Reincorporated 05/01/1990
Each share Common 10¢ par exchanged for (0.1) share Common $1 par 00/00/1940
Common $1 par changed to 50¢ par and (1) additional share issued 04/29/1987
State of incorporation changed from (DE) to (MD) and Common 50¢ par changed to 1¢ par 05/01/1990
Trust terminated 03/19/1997
Details not available

SOVEREIGN LIFE ASSURANCE CO. OF CANADA (CANADA)
Through purchase offer of CAD $450 cash

100% was acquired by Industrial Acceptance Corp. Ltd. as of 12/31/1962
Public interest eliminated

SOVEREIGN LIFE INS CO CALIF (CA)
Each share Capital Stock $375 par exchanged for (20) shares Capital Stock $18.75 par 03/30/1964
Each share Capital Stock $18.75 par exchanged for (4) shares Capital Stock $4.75 par 03/14/1966
Merged into Sovereign Corp. 03/15/1970
Each share Capital Stock $4.75 par exchanged for (5) shares Common $1 par
Sovereign Corp. merged into Chubb Corp. 03/31/1987 which merged into Chubb Ltd. 01/15/2016

SOVEREIGN METALS CORP (BC)
Recapitalized as Barytex Resources Corp. 04/29/1986
Each share Capital Stock no par exchanged for (0.33333333) share Capital Stock no par
Barytex Resources Corp. recapitalized as International Barytex Resources Ltd. 07/06/1993 which merged into Kobex Minerals Inc. 09/30/2009 which name changed to Kobex Capital Corp. 08/29/2014 which name changed to Itasca Capital Ltd. 06/23/2016

SOVEREIGN RESOURCES, INC. (CO)
Each share Common 1¢ par exchanged for (0.05) share Common 4¢ par 09/11/1958
Name changed to Sovereign Industries, Inc. 08/02/1967
(See Sovereign Industries, Inc.)

SOVEREIGN THOROUGHBREDS INC (NY)
Name changed to Equine Corp. 06/25/1985
Equine Corp. name changed to Lexington Group, Inc. 04/24/1986 which name changed to Harris & Harris Group, Inc. 08/15/1988 which name changed to 180 Degree Capital Corp. 03/27/2017

SOVEREIGN URANIUM GAS & OIL CO. (CO)
Name changed to Sovereign Resources, Inc. 11/20/1956
Sovereign Resources, Inc. name changed to Sovereign Industries, Inc. 08/02/1967
(See Sovereign Industries, Inc.)

SOVEREIGN WEALTH CORP (DE)
Name changed to Lenco Mobile Inc. 02/25/2009
(See Lenco Mobile Inc.)

SOVEREIGN-WESTERN CORP. (NV)
Merged into Westgate-California Corp. 2/26/62
5% Preferred $70 par exchanged share for share
Each share Common $1 par exchanged for (1) share Class A Common $5 par
(See Westgate-California Corp.)

SOVRAN FINL CORP (VA)
Common $5 par split (3) for (2) by issuance of (0.5) additional share 08/23/1985
$2.37 Conv. Preferred Ser. A $25 par called for redemption 11/20/1989
Merged into C&S/Sovran Corp. 09/01/1990
Each share Common $5 par exchanged for (1.23) shares Common $1 par
C&S/Sovran Corp. merged into NationsBank Corp. (NC) 12/31/1991 which reincorporated in Delaware as BankAmerica Corp. (Old) 09/25/1998 which merged into BankAmerica Corp. (New) 09/30/1998 which name changed to Bank of America Corp. 04/28/1999

SOVRAN GROUP LTD (NV)
Name changed to Hystar Aerospace Corp. 11/5/2000
Hystar Aerospace Corp. name changed to Angus Energy Corp. 6/19/2003

SOVRAN SELF STORAGE INC (MD)
9.85% Preferred Ser. B 1¢ par called for redemption at $25 plus $0.2052 accrued dividends on 08/01/2004
Name changed to Life Storage, Inc. 08/15/2016

SOY ENVIRONMENTAL PRODS INC (DE)
Each share old Common $0.001 par exchanged for (0.04) share new Common $0.001 par 2/27/2007
Name changed to MetaPower International, Inc. 6/6/2007

SOYA CORP. OF AMERICA (MD)
Charter annulled for failure to pay taxes and file reports 10/27/55

SOYERS CAP LTD (ON)
Name changed to BlueRush Media Group Corp. 12/21/2007
BlueRush Media Group Corp. name changed to BlueRush Inc. 04/30/2018

SOYODO GROUP HLDGS INC (DE)
Reorganized under the laws of Nevada as Omphalos, Corp. 04/30/2008
Each share Common $0.0001 par exchanged for (1/3) share Common $0.0001 par

SP ACQUISITION HLDGS INC (DE)
Issue Information - 40,000,000 UNITS consisting of (1) share COM and (1) WT offered at $10 per Unit on 10/10/2007
Completely liquidated 10/15/2009
Each Unit exchanged for initial distribution of $9.84503002 cash
Each share Common $0.001 par exchanged for initial distribution of $9.84503002 cash
Each Unit received second and final distribution of $0.03785177 cash payable 06/07/2013 to holders of record 10/14/2009
Each share Common $0.001 par received second and final distribution of $0.03785177 cash payable 06/07/2013 to holders of record 10/14/2009

SP BANCORP INC (MD)
Acquired by Green Bancorp, Inc. 10/17/2014
Each share Common 1¢ par exchanged for $29.5536 cash

SP HLDG CORP (DE)
Each share old Common $0.001 par exchanged for (0.00333333) share new Common $0.001 par 11/21/2005
Name changed to Organic To Go Food Corp. 05/21/2007
(See Organic To Go Food Corp.)

SP VENTURES INC (DE)
Name changed to McKesson Corp. (New) 12/1/94
McKesson Corp. (New) name changed to McKesson HBOC Inc. 1/12/99 which name changed to McKesson Corp. 7/30/2001

SPA FAUCET INC (UT)
Each share old Common $0.001 par exchanged for (3) shares new Common $0.001 par 10/21/1996
SEC revoked common stock registration 08/22/2007

SPA INTL INC (NV)
Each share old Common $0.001 par exchanged for (0.5) share new Common $0.001 par 08/11/1995
Charter permanently revoked 01/31/2001

SPA-KING MOUNT CLEMENS WATER PRODUCTS CORP. (DE)
Charter revoked for non-payment of taxes 4/1/59

SPA LADY CORP (DE)
Charter cancelled and declared inoperative and void for non-payment of taxes 6/27/89

SPA MINES LTD (BC)
Recapitalized as Copperust Mines Ltd. 09/24/1973
Each share Capital Stock no par exchanged for (1/3) share Common no par
Copperust Mines Ltd. name changed to Ark Energy Ltd. 10/20/1978 which recapitalized as Arcanna Industries Corp. 06/27/1990 which merged into Mercana Industries Ltd. (BC) 12/17/1993 which reincorporated in Ontario 06/28/1995
(See Mercana Industries Ltd.)

SPACARB, INC. (DE)
Liquidated in 1954

SPACE & LEISURE TIME LTD (DE)
Stock Dividend - 10% 08/01/1975
Merged into Hadato Properties Inc. 07/14/1980
Each share Common 1¢ par exchanged for $5 cash

SPACE AGE MATERIALS CORP. (NY)
Completely liquidated 4/6/66
Each share Common 10¢ par exchanged for first and final distribution of (0.053965) share Pfizer (Chas.) & Co., Inc. (Del.) Common 33-1/3¢ par
Pfizer (Chas.) & Co., Inc. (Del.) name changed to Pfizer Inc. 4/27/70

SPACE AGE TECHNOLOGY INC (UT)
Common 1¢ par changed to $0.002 par and and (2) additional shares issued 02/02/1987
Name changed to East Coast Water Refining Co., Inc. 02/12/1987

SPACE CITY U.S.A., INC. (AL)
Adjudicated bankrupt 9/20/67

SPACE COMPONENTS INC (DC)
Capital Stock 10¢ par changed to 5¢ par and (0.5) additional shares issued 03/13/1970
Charter revoked for failure to file reports and pay fees 09/13/1971

SPACE CORP (TX)
Stock Dividend - 10% 06/16/1972
Merged into Interstate Corp. 06/20/1973
Each share Common $1 par exchanged for $7 cash

SPACE CRAFT INC (DE)
Stock Dividend - 50% 07/01/1969
Name changed to SCI Systems, Inc. 01/01/1970
SCI Systems, Inc. merged into Sanmina Corp. 12/06/2001 which name changed to Sanmina-SCI Corp. 12/10/2001 which name changed back to Sanmina Corp. 11/15/2012

SPACE DATA INDS INC (CO)
Recapitalized as Golden Spike Petroleum Inc. 02/10/1981
Each share Common 1¢ par exchanged for (0.33333333) share Common 3¢ par
(See Golden Spike Petroleum Inc.)

SPACE FINANCIAL CORP. (AZ)
Under plan of merger name changed to Western Energy Corp. 6/21/67
Western Energy Corp. recapitalized as United Western Energy Corp. 11/29/78
(See United Western Energy Corp.)

SPACE LAUNCHES FING INC (NV)
Common $0.0001 par split (4) for (1) by issuance of (3) additional shares payable 02/19/2002 to holders of record 02/11/2002 Ex date - 02/20/2002
Reorganized under the laws of Wyoming as Crown Marketing 12/02/2010
Each share Common $0.0001 par exchanged for (0.001) share Common no par
Crown Marketing name changed to America Great Health 06/29/2017

SPACE METALS, INC. (DE)
Charter cancelled and declared inoperative and void for non-payment of taxes 04/15/1972

SPACE MICROWAVE LABS INC (CA)
Charter suspended for failure to file reports and pay fees 09/01/1988

SPACE ORDNANCE SYS INC (CA)
Name changed to TransTechnology Corp. (CA) 01/23/1974
TransTechnology Corp. (CA) reincorporated in Delaware 07/18/1986 which name changed to Breeze-Eastern Corp. 10/12/2006
(See Breeze-Eastern Corp.) 08/03/1966)

SPACE-PAK INTERNATIONAL LTD. (ON)
Plan for reorganization not approved and deemed a bankrupt company by Court 12/7/70

SPACE PLASTICS INC (AZ)
Proclaimed dissolved 12/15/81

SPACE PRODUCTS, INC. (NH)
Adjudicated bankrupt 10/25/63
No stockholders' equity

SPACE RESH & DEV CORP (OR)
Name changed to P & G Manufacturing Co. 02/28/1966
P & G Manufacturing Co. name changed to Oswego Liquidating Corp. 03/08/1971
(See Oswego Liquidating Corp.)

SPACE RESH CTR INC (AZ)
Charter revoked for failure to file reports or pay fees 12/26/1972

SPACE STRUCTURES, INC. (MN)
Merged into Resco, Inc. 1/1/62
Each share Capital Stock $1 par exchanged for (0.555555) share Common 10¢ par
Resco, Inc. merged into Interplastic Corp. 5/1/62
(See Interplastic Corp.)

SPACE SYS INTL CORP
Acquired by Stratcomm Media Ltd. (BC) 12/10/2001
Each share Common exchanged for (0.5181) share Common no par Stratcomm Media Ltd. (BC) reincorporated in Yukon 11/12/97
(See Stratcomm Media Ltd.)

SPACE SYS LAB INC (FL)
Name changed to MTX International Inc. 3/9/94
MTX International Inc. name changed to AmeriNet Financial Systems, Inc. 10/31/95

SPACE TECHNOLOGY & RESH CORP (CO)
Charter suspended for failure to file annual reports 10/20/1964

SPACE TECHNOLOGY LABORATORIES, INC. (DE)
Merged into Thompson Ramo Wooldridge Inc. 9/29/63

SPACE-TONE ELECTRONICS CORP. (MD)
Bankrupt 6/25/63; stock worthless

SPACE WIF CORP (DE)
Recapitalized as Gateways To Space Inc. 5/1/92
Each share Common $0.001 par exchanged for (0.02) share Common $0.001 par
Gateways To Space Inc. recapitalized as eMax Corp. 2/18/2000 which

recapitalized as eMax Holdings Corp. 5/27/2004

SPACEDEV INC (DE)
Reincorporated 08/20/2007
State of incorporation changed from (CO) to (DE) 08/20/2007
Acquired by Sierra Nevada Corp. 12/16/2008
Each share Common $0.0001 par exchanged for $0.72658 cash

SPACEHAB INC (WA)
Each share Conv. Preferred Ser. C no par exchanged for (146.1) shares new Common no par 11/29/2007
Each share old Common no par exchanged for (0.1) share new Common no par 11/29/2007
Name changed to Astrotech Corp. (WA) 02/17/2009
Astrotech Corp. (WA) reincorporated in Delaware 12/22/2017

SPACELABS INC (CA)
Merged into Squibb Corp. 04/29/1980
Each share Capital Stock $1 par exchanged for (1.56) shares Common $1 par
Squibb Corp. merged into Bristol-Myers Squibb Co. 10/04/1989

SPACELABS MED INC (DE)
Merged into Instrumentarium Corp. 7/3/2002
Each share Common 1¢ par exchanged for $14.25 cash

SPACELINK LTD (CO)
Name changed back to Jones Spacelink, Ltd. 11/26/1985
(See Jones Spacelink, Ltd.)

SPACEMASTER RES LTD (CANADA)
Recapitalized 11/04/1977
Recapitalized from Spacemaster Minerals Ltd. to Spacemaster Resources Ltd. 11/04/1977
Each share Capital Stock no par exchanged for (0.1) share Common no par
Name changed to Exmoor Oil & Gas Corp. 09/26/1988
Exmoor Oil & Gas Corp. recapitalized as Koala Kreme Inc. 02/16/1990 which recapitalized as Sur American Gold Corp. (Canada) 06/15/1995 which reincorporated in British Columbia as Cadan Resources Corp. 08/28/2007 which name changed to Rizal Resources Corp. 10/07/2016

SPACEONICS, INC. (IL)
Merged into Portable Electric Tools, Inc. 01/31/1964
Each share Common no par exchanged for (0.2) share Common $1 par
Portable Electric Tools, Inc. merged into Murphy (G.W.) Industries, Inc. 10/17/1967 which name changed to Reed Tool Co. 09/15/1972 which merged into Baker Oil Tools, Inc. 11/26/1975 which name changed to Baker International Corp. (CA) 01/28/1976 which reincorporated in Delaware 01/27/1983 which merged into Baker Hughes Inc. 04/03/1987 which merged into Baker Hughes, a GE company 07/05/2017

SPACEPATH INC (NV)
Recapitalized as KTL Bamboo International Corp. 03/26/2015
Each share Common $0.001 par exchanged for (0.5) share Common $0.001 par
KTL Bamboo International Corp. name changed to Miramar Labs, Inc. 06/16/2016
(See Miramar Labs, Inc.)

SPACEPLEX AMUSEMENT CTRS INTL LTD (NV)
Each share old Common $0.001 par exchanged for (1/30) share new Common $0.001 par 02/28/1995
Each share new Common $0.001 par exchanged again for (1/30) share new Common $0.001 par 01/02/1996
Recapitalized as Air Energy Inc. 05/24/1996
Each share new Common $0.001 par exchanged for (0.4) share Common $0.001 par
Air Energy Inc. name changed to Powerhouse International Corp. 12/24/1997 which name changed to iLive, Inc. 10/21/1999
(See iLive, Inc.)

SPACERAYS INC (NY)
Adjudicated bankrupt 02/25/1975
Stockholders' equity unlikely

SPACESONICS INC (CA)
Charter suspended for failure to file reports and pay fees 06/09/1972

SPACETEC IMC CORP (MA)
Recapitalized as Labtec Inc. 2/19/99
Each share Common 1¢ par exchanged for (1/3) share Common 1¢ par
Labtec Inc. merged into Logitech International S.A. 3/23/2001

SPACIAL CORP (DE)
Name changed to Alliance Environmental Technologies, Inc. 10/31/2001
(See Alliance Environmental Technologies, Inc.)

SPACO, INC. (AL)
Merged into AC Equipment Co., Inc. 09/29/1989
Details not available

SPADA GOLD LTD (BC)
Name changed to Awale Resources Ltd. 01/03/2018

SPAGHETTI JOES, INC. (UT)
Recapitalized as Delta Petroleum Corp. 2/28/79
Each share Common 1¢ par exchanged for (10) shares Common 1¢ par
Delta Petroleum Corp. reincorporated in Delaware as Delta Petroleum & Energy Corp. 9/24/80 which name changed to PNX Industries, Inc. 12/15/86
(See PNX Industries, Inc.)

SPAGHETTI WHSE INC (TX)
Common 1¢ par split (3) for (2) by issuance of (0.5) additional share 6/27/91
Merged into Consolidated Restaurants Companies 1/22/99
Each share Common 1¢ par exchanged for $8 cash

SPAIN FD INC (MD)
Name changed to Ibero-America Fund, Inc. 01/25/2010
(See Ibero-America Fund, Inc.)

SPALDING (A.G.) & BROTHERS (NJ)
Recapitalized under the laws of Delaware as Spalding (A.G.) & Bros., Inc. in 1939
Each share 7% 1st Preferred $100 par exchanged for (1) share new 1st Preferred no par and $1.92 in cash
Each share 8% 2nd Preferred $100 par exchanged for (12) shares new Common $1 par
Each share Common no par exchanged for (1) share new Common $1 par
Spaulding (A.G.) & Bros., Inc. merged into Questor Corp. 4/21/69
(See Questor Corp.)

SPALDING A G & BROS INC (DE)
1st Preferred no par changed to Preferred $50 par in 1945
Merged into Questor Corp. 4/21/69
Each share Common $1 par exchanged for (1) share $2 Conv. Prior Preferred Ser. A no par
(See Questor Corp.)

SPAN AIR INC (NY)
Charter cancelled and proclaimed dissolved for failure to pay taxes 06/24/1981

SPAN AMERICA BOAT CO., INC. (DE)
Charter revoked for non-payment of taxes 4/1/64

SPAN AMER MED SYS INC (SC)
Common no par split (2) for (1) by issuance of (1) additional share 02/20/1986
Acquired by Savaria Corp. 06/16/2017
Each share Common no par exchanged for $29 cash

SPAN CORP. (DE)
Merged into Two Pesos Inc. 2/5/87
Each share Common 1¢ par exchanged for (0.1) share Common 1¢ par
Two Pesos Inc. assets transferred to TPI Dissolution Corp. 6/30/93
(See TPI Dissolution Corp.)

SPAN MINERALS OF CANADA LTD. (CANADA)
Deemed defunct 01/00/1957
Stockholders' equity unlikely

SPANDEX CORP. (DE)
Acquired by Fibre Research & Development Corp. for cash 11/21/63

SPANEX CAP INC (ON)
Recapitalized as SAMSys Technologies, Inc. (ONT) 04/24/1997
Each share Common no par exchanged for (1/3) share Common no par
SAMSys Technologies, Inc. (ONT) reincorporated in Canada 03/27/2002
(See SAMSys Technologies, Inc.)

SPANG, CHALFANT & CO., INC.
Merged into National Supply Co. (PA) in 1937
Each share Preferred exchanged for (1) share Prior Preferred
Each share Common exchanged for (1.5) shares new Common
National Supply Co. (PA) merged into Armco Steel Corp. 4/30/58 which name changed to Armco Inc. 7/1/78 which merged into AK Steel Holding Corp. 9/30/99

SPANG INDS INC (PA)
Merged into Spang & Co. 01/31/1983
Each share Common $1 par exchanged for $20 cash

SPANG STORES INC (PA)
Acquired by Adams Drug Co., Inc. 11/20/1979
Details not available

SPANISH ADVERTISING & MKTG SVC (NY)
Dissolved by proclamation 3/15/85

SPANISH AMERICAN MINES LTD. (ON)
Merged into Northspan Uranium Mines Ltd. 7/5/56
Each share Capital Stock $1 par exchanged for (0.5) share Capital Stock $1 par
Northspan Uranium Mines Ltd. merged into Rio Algom Mines Ltd. 6/30/60 which name changed to Rio Algom Ltd. 4/30/75
(See Rio Algom Ltd.)

SPANISH LANGUAGE TELEVISION ARIZ INC (AZ)
Adjudicated bankrupt 06/03/1970
Stockholders' equity unlikely

SPANISH RIVER PULP & PAPER MILLS LTD.
Acquired by Abitibi Power & Paper Co. Ltd. in 1928
(See Abitibi Power & Paper Co. Ltd.)

SPANISH TRAIL (UT)
Name changed to Unified Telecommunications Corp. 08/24/1984
(See Unified Telecommunications Corp.)

SPANISH TRAIL URANIUM CO. (UT)
Merged into Twentieth Century Fuels, Inc. on a (1) for (5) basis 6/15/56
Twentieth Century Fuels, Inc. recapitalized as Twentieth Century Engineering Corp. 8/30/63 which merged into Radiant Industries, Inc. 12/29/69 which name changed to Caltem Liquidating, Inc. 6/30/80
(See Caltem Liquidating, Inc.)

SPANLINK COMMUNICATIONS INC (MN)
Issue Information - 1,900,000 shares COM offered at $4 per share 04/29/1996
Merged into Spanlink Acquisition Corp. 4/13/2000
Each share Common no par exchanged for $10.50 cash

SPANSION INC (DE)
Plan of reorganization under Chapter 11 Federal Bankruptcy proceedings effective 05/10/2010
No old Class A Common stockholders' equity
Merged into Cypress Semiconductor Corp. 03/12/2015
Each share new Class A Common $0.001 par exchanged for (2.457) shares Common 1¢ par

SPANTEL COMMUNICATIONS INC (FL)
Recapitalized as Systems America, Inc. 05/27/2010
Each share Common $0.001 par exchanged for (0.002) share Common $0.001 par
(See Systems America, Inc.)

SPANTEL CORP (DE)
Charter cancelled and declared inoperative and void for non-payment of taxes 03/01/1994

SPANTEL CORP (NE)
Reorganized under the laws of Delaware 07/30/1985
Each share Common $0.001 par exchanged for (1/3) share Common 1¢ par
(See SpanTel Corp. (DE))

SPAR AEROSPACE LTD (CANADA)
Name changed 09/06/1978
Name changed from Spar Aerospace Products to Spar Aerospace Ltd. 09/06/1978
$1.08 Conv. Preferred Ser. A no par called for redemption 07/02/1982
Jr. Preferred Initial Ser. no par called for redemption 09/07/1979
Jr. Preferred Second Ser. no par called for redemption 04/18/1983
Old Common no par reclassified as Subordinate Shares no par 05/31/1983
Subordinate Shares no par split (2) for (1) by issuance of (1) additional share 06/08/1983
Subordinate Shares no par reclassified as new Common no par 05/26/1993
Stock Dividend - In Jr. Pfd. Initial Ser. to Common holders 200% 06/14/1979
Merged into L-3 Communications Holdings, Inc. 01/23/2002
Each share new Common no par exchanged for $15.50 cash

SPAR-MICA CORP. LTD. (QC)
Declared bankrupt 00/00/1960
No stockholders' equity

SPARA ACQUISITION ONE CORP (CANADA)
Completely liquidated
Each share Common no par received first and final distribution of (0.5297) share Digital Shelf Space Corp. Common no par and (0.5297) Common Stock Purchase Warrant expiring 07/03/2016 payable

07/09/2013 to holders of record 06/25/2013

SPARCAP ONE LTD (ON)
Completely liquidated
Each share Common no par received first and final distribution of $0.0492 cash payable 02/28/2014 to holders of record 02/21/2014

SPARCRAFT, INC. (MI)
Voluntarily dissolved 2/20/75
Details not available

SPARE BACKUP INC (DE)
SEC revoked common stock registration 01/13/2017

SPARGOS MNG N L (AUSTRALIA)
Name changed 05/26/1988
Each Unsponsored ADR for Ordinary AUD$0.25 par exchanged for (1) Sponsored ADR for Ordinary AUD$0.25 par 04/22/1988
Stock Dividend - 10% 07/10/1987
Name changed from Spargos Exploration N.L. to Spargos Mining N.L. 05/26/1988
Acquired by Beach Petroleum N.L. 05/22/1994
Each Sponsored ADR for Ordinary AUD$0.25 par exchanged for $0.065 cash

SPARK NETWORKS INC (DE)
Merged into Spark Networks S.E. 11/03/2017
Each share Common $0.001 par exchanged for (0.1) Sponsored ADR for Ordinary

SPARK NETWORKS PLC (ENGLAND & WALES)
Reorganized under the laws of Delaware as Spark Networks, Inc. 07/09/2007
Each Reg. S Sponsored GDR for Ordinary exchanged for (1) share Common $0.001 par
Each Sponsored ADR for Ordinary exchanged for (1) share Common $0.001 par
Spark Networks, Inc. merged into Spark Networks S.E. 11/03/2017

SPARK STOVES CO. (NV)
In process of liquidation 7/1/55

SPARKING EVENTS INC (NV)
Common $0.001 par split (3) for (1) by issuance of (2) additional shares payable 06/15/2009 to holders of record 06/15/2009
Name changed to Xodtec Group USA, Inc. 07/20/2009
Xodtec Group USA, Inc. name changed to Xodtec LED, Inc. 04/16/2010 which name changed to Cala Energy Corp. 10/21/2013 which name changed to Lingerie Fighting Championships, Inc. 04/29/2015

SPARKLETTS ARTESIAN WATER CO.
Acquired by Sparkletts Bottled Water Corp. in 1928 which was dissolved in 1934

SPARKLETTS BOTTLED WATER CORP.
Dissolved in 1934

SPARKLETTS DRINKING WATER CORP. (CA)
Acquired by Foremost Dairies, Inc. on a (3-3/8) for (1) basis 4/9/64

SPARKLING WTR AUSTRIA INC (DE)
Recapitalized as Dairy Whey Foods Corp. 7/27/83
Each share Common 1¢ par exchanged for (0.5) share Common 1¢ par
Dairy Whey Foods Corp. name changed to Novar International Corp. 6/8/84
(See Novar International Corp.)

SPARKMAN ENERGY CORP (NV)
Name changed to Eskey Inc. 07/29/1985
Eskey Inc. merged into Yankee Companies, Inc. 01/02/1985 which reorganized as National Environmental Group Inc. 10/11/1989 which reorganized as Key Energy Group, Inc. 12/04/1992 which name changed to Key Energy Services Inc. (MD) 12/09/1998
(See Key Energy Services Inc. (MD))

SPARKMAN PRODUCING CO (TX)
Name changed to Arch Petroleum Inc. (TX) 06/06/1985
Arch Petroleum Inc. (TX) merged into USENCO Inc. 06/01/1988 which name changed to Arch Petroleum Inc. (NV) 06/01/1988 which reincorporated in Delaware 12/31/1991 which merged into Pogo Producing Co. 08/14/1998 which merged into Plains Exploration & Production Co. 11/06/2007 which merged into Freeport-McMoRan Copper & Gold Inc. 05/31/2013 which name changed to Freeport-McMoRan Inc. 07/14/2014

SPARKS (A.J.) & CO. (MI)
Became private 06/05/1991
Details not available

SPARKS INDS INC (DE)
Each share old Capital Stock $0.0004 par exchanged for (0.33333333) share new Capital Stock $0.0004 par 08/00/1979
Each share new Capital Stock $0.0004 par exchanged again for (0.1) share new Capital Stock $0.0004 par 01/00/1983
Name changed to J.E.I. Airlines, Inc. 10/17/1984
(See J.E.I. Airlines, Inc.)

SPARKS ST BK (SPARKS, MD)
Merged into Mercantile Bankshares Corp. 11/1/1995
Each share Common $10 par exchanged for (2.33333333) shares Common $2 par
Mercantile Bankshares Corp. merged into PNC Financial Services Group, Inc. 03/02/2007

SPARKS-WITHINGTON CO. (OH)
Common no par changed to $2.50 par 8/18/55
Name changed to Sparton Corp. 10/31/56

SPARKYS VIRGIN ISLANDS INC (VIRGIN ISLANDS)
Completely liquidated 12/29/1972
Each share Common 5¢ par exchanged for first and final distribution of (0.473489) share Host International, Inc. Common $2.50 par
(See Host International, Inc.)

SPARLING CAP CORP (AB)
Name changed to Red-Tail Infotech Inc. 09/29/2000
Red-Tail Infotech Inc. name changed to Life Sciences Institute Inc. 03/27/2003 which recapitalized as Quattro Exploration & Production Ltd. 11/23/2011

SPARLING GEORGE LTD (BC)
Placed in receivership 11/30/1976
No stockholders' equity

SPARMAC PETROLEUMS LTD. (AB)
Merged into Tidal Petroleum Corp. Ltd. 07/14/1958
Each share Capital Stock exchanged for (0.25) share Capital Stock 10¢ par
(See Tidal Petroleum Corp. Ltd.)

SPARROW RES LTD (BC)
Struck off register and declared dissolved for failure to file returns 10/26/84

SPARROW VENTURES CORP (BC)
Recapitalized as Westcot Ventures Corp. 09/14/2017
Each share Common no par exchanged for (0.1) share Common no par

SPARROWTECH MULTIMEDIA INC (ON)
Reorganized under the laws of Wyoming as RV Wireless Inc. 09/01/2004
Each share Common no par exchanged for (0.1) share Common no par
RV Wireless Inc. recapitalized as Mobicom Communications Inc. 05/24/2006 which reorganized as Resource Group International, Inc. 11/08/2007

SPARROWTECH RESOURCES INC (NV)
Name changed 03/28/2007
Name changed from Sparrowtech Multimedia Corp. to Sparrowtech Resources, Inc. 03/28/2007
Merged into Converge Global, Inc. (Old) 10/26/2009
Each share Common $0.001 par exchanged for (0.03333333) share Common $0.001 par
Converge Global, Inc. (Old) recapitalized as Converge Global, Inc. (New) 09/03/2010 which name changed to Marijuana Co. of America, Inc. 12/01/2015

SPARTA FOODS INC (MN)
Each share old Common 1¢ par exchanged for (1/3) share new Common 1¢ par 11/18/93
Merged into Cenex Harvest States Cooperatives 6/1/2000
Each share new Common 1¢ par exchanged for $1.41 cash

SPARTA FOUNDRY CO.
Merged into Muskegon Piston Ring Co. on a share for share basis in 1936
Muskegon Piston Ring Co. name changed to AP Parts Corp. 4/1/66 which merged into Dunhill International, Inc. 10/31/67 which name changed to Questor Corp. 12/1/68
(See Questor Corp.)

SPARTA PHARMACEUTICALS INC (DE)
Each share old Common $0.001 par exchanged for (0.2) share new Common $0.001 par 05/13/1998
Merged into SuperGen Inc. 08/12/1999
Each share Common $0.001 par exchanged for (0.02518) share Common $0.001 par and (0.01296) Common Stock Purchase Warrant expiring 08/12/2001
SuperGen Inc. name changed to Astex Pharmaceuticals, Inc. 09/12/2011
(See Astex Pharmaceuticals, Inc.)

SPARTA ST BK (SPARTA, MI)
Reorganized as 1st Community Bancorp, Inc. 4/7/87
Each share Common $10 par exchanged for (1) share Common $10 par
1st Community Bancorp, Inc. name changed to ChoiceOne Financial Services Inc. 5/30/97

SPARTA SURGICAL CORP (DE)
Each share old Common $0.002 par exchanged for (0.125) share new Common $0.002 par 02/04/1994
Each share new Common $0.002 par exchanged again for (1/6) share new Common $0.002 par 03/28/1997
Chapter 11 bankruptcy proceedings dismissed 02/07/2011
No stockholders' equity

SPARTA VENTURES CORP (FL)
Name changed to Thermal Ablation Technologies Corp. 10/23/1998
Thermal Ablation Technologies Corp. name changed to Poker.com Inc. 08/09/1999 which name changed to LegalPlay Entertainment Inc. 09/15/2003 which recapitalized as Synthenol Inc. (FL) 12/18/2006 which reincorporated in Nevada as SinoCubate, Inc. 11/25/2008 which name changed to Viking Investments Group, Inc. 07/16/2012 which name changed to Viking Energy Group, Inc. 05/08/2017

SPARTA WTR CORP (AB)
Recapitalized as Base of the Bridge Technology Ltd. 08/04/2006
Each share Common no par exchanged for (0.25) share Common no par
(See Base of the Bridge Technology Ltd.)

SPARTACUS CAP INC (BC)
Name changed to Rare Element Resources Ltd. 7/17/2003

SPARTAN AIR POLLUTION CONTROL, LTD. (NY)
Charter cancelled and proclaimed dissolved for failure to file reports and pay taxes 12/15/1973

SPARTAN AIR SVCS LTD (CANADA)
Name changed to Spartan Capital Corp. Ltd. 05/28/1973
Spartan Capital Corp. name changed to Akers Medical Technology Ltd. 07/09/1986 which recapitalized as Digital Fusion Multimedia Corp. 10/26/1994
(See Digital Fusion Multimedia Corp.)

SPARTAN AIRCRAFT CO. (DE)
Name changed to Minnehoma Financial Co. 5/31/68
Minnehoma Financial Co. merged into New Minnehoma Co. 8/1/72

SPARTAN BANKCORP, INC. (MI)
Merged into Banc One Corp. (DE) 1/2/87
Each share Common $10 par exchanged for (2.4121) shares Common no par
Banc One Corp. (DE) reincorporated in Ohio 5/1/89 which merged into Bank One Corp. 10/2/98 merged into J.P. Morgan Chase & Co. 12/31/2000 which name changed to JPMorgan Chase & Co. 7/20/2004

SPARTAN BUSINESS SVCS CORP (NV)
Name changed to Gunpowder Gold Corp. 11/19/2010

SPARTAN CAP LTD (CANADA)
Name changed to Akers Medical Technology Ltd. 07/09/1986
Akers Medical Technology Ltd. recapitalized as Digital Fusion Multimedia Corp. 10/26/1994
(See Digital Fusion Multimedia Corp.)

SPARTAN ENERGY CORP (AB)
Each share old Common no par exchanged for (0.33333333) share new Common no par 06/23/2017
Merged into Vermilion Energy Inc. 05/31/2018
Each share new Common no par exchanged for (0.1476) share Common no par
Note: Unexchanged certificates will be cancelled and become without value 05/31/2021

SPARTAN EXPL LTD (AB)
Merged into Spartan Oil Corp. 06/03/2011
Each share Common no par exchanged for (1) share Common no par, (0.1667) Common Stock Purchase Warrant expiring 07/01/2011 and $4 cash
Note: Unexchanged certificates were

cancelled and became without value 06/03/2014
Spartan Oil Corp. merged into Bonterra Energy Corp. (New) 01/29/2013

SPARTAN EXPLS LTD (BC)
Recapitalized as Nuspar Resources Ltd. 10/7/74
Each share Common 50¢ par exchanged for (0.2) share Common no par
(See Nuspar Resources Ltd.)

SPARTAN FDG CO (ID)
Each share old Common $0.001 par exchanged for (1/6) share new Common $0.001 par 07/01/1991
Name changed to Venture Tech, Inc. (ID) 06/01/1995
Venture Tech, Inc. (ID) reincorporated in Nevada as VentureQuest Group, Inc. 05/10/2001 which name changed to Northwater Resources, Inc. 02/15/2006 which name changed to Dex-Ray Resources, Inc. 03/27/2008
(See Dex-Ray Resources, Inc.)

SPARTAN FOOD SYS INC (SC)
Common 10¢ par split (5) for (4) by issuance of (0.25) additional share 6/24/77
Common 10¢ par split (5) for (4) by issuance of (0.25) additional share 10/2/78
Stock Dividend - 100% 2/29/72
Merged into Trans World Corp. (DE) 7/10/79
Each share Common 10¢ par exchanged for $28 cash

SPARTAN MFG CORP (DE)
Name changed to Spartech Corp. 05/16/1983
Spartech Corp. merged into PolyOne Corp. 03/13/2013

SPARTAN OIL CORP (AB)
Merged into Bonterra Energy Corp. (New) 01/29/2013
Each share Common no par exchanged for (0.1169) share Common no par
Note: Unexchanged certificates were cancelled and became without value 01/29/2016

SPARTAN PPTYS INC (GA)
Out of business 12/31/1977
No stockholders' equity

SPARTAN REFINING CO.
Succeeded by Atlas Pipe Line Corp. in 1941
(See Atlas Pipe Line Corp.)

SPARTAN STORES INC (MI)
Name changed to SpartanNash Co. 05/29/2014

SPARTAN URANIUM CORP. (UT)
Name changed to Process Energy Inc. and Common 1¢ par changed to $0.001 par 6/1/82
Process Energy Inc. name changed to Auta-Tronics International, Inc. 6/1/84

SPARTANBURG BK & TR CO (SPARTANBURG, SC)
Common $10 par changed to $5 par and (1) additional share issued plus a 10% stock dividend paid 4/1/71
Common $5 par changed to $2.50 par and (1) additional share issued in August 1973
Stock Dividends - 10% 4/1/68; 10% 4/1/69; 10% 4/1/70; 10% 4/1/72; 10% 3/28/73; 10% 2/26/74; 20% 9/4/80
Merged into Bankers Trust of South Carolina (Columbia, SC) 5/1/81
Each share Common $2.50 par exchanged for (0.6436) share Common $10 par
Bankers Trust of South Carolina (Columbia, SC) acquired by NCNB Corp. 1/2/86 which name changed to NationsBank Corp. 12/31/91

which reincorporated in Delaware as BankAmerica Corp. (Old) 9/25/98 which merged into BankAmerica Corp. (New) 9/30/98 which name changed to Bank of America Corp. 4/28/99

SPARTANS INDUSTRIES, INC. (DE)
Common $1 par split (2) for (1) by issuance of (1) additional share 06/03/1966
Stock Dividend - 50% 05/16/1960
Merged into Spartans Industries, Inc. (NY) 09/25/1966
Each share Common $1 par exchanged for (1) share Class A $1 par
Spartans Industries, Inc. (NY) merged into Arlen Realty & Development Corp. 02/26/1971 which name changed to Arlen Corp. 10/16/1985
(See Arlen Corp.)

SPARTANS INDS INC (NY)
Merged into Arlen Realty & Development Corp. 02/26/1971
Each share 4% Conv. Preferred $10 par exchanged for (1) share 4% Conv. Preferred $10 par
Each share Class A $1 par exchanged for (1) share Common
Each share Common $1 par exchanged for (1) share Common
Arlen Realty & Development Corp. name changed to Arlen Corp. 10/16/1985
(See Arlen Corp.)

SPARTECH CORP (DE)
Each share Common 50¢ par automatically became (0.2) share Common 75¢ par 04/08/1987
Merged into PolyOne Corp. 03/13/2013
Each share Common 75¢ par exchanged for (0.3167) share Common 1¢ par and $2.67 cash

SPARTEK INC (DE)
Conv. Preferred Ser. A no par called for redemption 08/15/1977
Stock Dividend - 10% 07/15/1977
Name changed to SPR Fund, Inc. and Common $5 par changed to 1¢ par 03/30/1979
SPR Fund, Inc. liquidated for Fidelity Municipal Bond Fund 11/09/1984

SPARTEX OIL & GAS LTD (ON)
Merged into Newore Developments Ltd. 03/19/1973
Each share Capital Stock $1 par exchanged for (0.28571428) shares Capital Stock
(See Newore Developments Ltd.)

SPARTON ASBESTOS MINES LTD. (ON)
Name changed to Sparton Mining & Development Ltd. in February 1974
Sparton Mining & Development Ltd. merged into Sparton Resources Inc. 12/30/82

SPARTON CORP (OH)
6% Preferred $100 par called for redemption 6/15/70
(Additional Information in Active)

SPARTON MINING & DEVELOPMEMT LTD. (ON)
Merged into Sparton Resources Inc. 12/30/82
Each share Capital Stock $1 par exchanged for (1) share Common no par

SPARX ENERGY CORP (BC)
Name changed to Provenance Gold Corp. 01/16/2017

SPATIAL TECHNOLOGY INC (DE)
Issue Information - 3,000,000 shares COM offered at $5 per share on 10/17/1996
Name changed to PlanetCAD Inc. 11/10/2000
PlanetCAD Inc. name changed to Avatech Solutions, Inc. 11/19/2002

which name changed to Rand Worldwide, Inc. 12/30/2010

SPATIALIGHT INC (NY)
Each share old Common 1¢ par exchanged for (0.02) share new Common 1¢ par 08/24/2007
Filed a petition under Chapter 7 Federal Bankruptcy Code 02/21/2008
No stockholders' equity

SPATIALIZER AUDIO LABS INC (DE)
Reincorporated 07/27/1994
Place of incorporation changed from (YT) to (DE) and Common no par changed to 1¢ par 07/27/1994
Each share old Common 1¢ par exchanged for (0.1) share new Common 1¢ par 12/17/2008
Recapitalized as AMERI Holdings, Inc. 05/26/2015
Each share new Common 1¢ par exchanged for (0.05678591) share Common 1¢ par

SPAWNING GROUND INC (NV)
Name changed to CandleWealth International, Inc. 12/21/2004
CandleWealth International, Inc. recapitalized as Promethean Corp. 06/18/2007

SPC INTL INVTS LTD (ON)
Merged into Eighty-Eight Corp. 8/31/90
Each share Common no par exchanged for $22 cash

SPDR INDEX SHS FDS (MA)
Trust terminated 03/31/2015
Each share S&P Small Cap Emerging Asia Pacific ETF received $40.236409 cash
Trust terminated 08/31/2016
Each share MSCI Beyond BRIC ETF received $53.181495 cash
Each share MSI EM 50 ETF received $44.18222 cash
Each share Russell/Nomura PRIME Japan ETF received $47.244311 cash
Each share Russell/Nomura Small Cap Japan ETF received $56.828096 cash
Each share S&P BRIC 40 ETF received $20.990868 cash
Each share S&P International Mid Cap ETF received $30.550502 cash
Trust terminated 11/21/2016
Each share MSCI International Real Estate Currency Hedged ETF received $34.85718 cash
Each share MSCI Mexico StrategicFactors ETF received $19.504463 cash
Each share MSCI South Korea StrategicFactors ETF received $24.941118 cash
Each share MSCI Taiwan StrategicFactors ETF received $54.144386 cash
(Additional Information in Active)

SPDR SER TR (MA)
Lehman California Municipal Bond ETF reclassified as Barclays Capital California Municipal Bond ETF 01/06/2009
Lehman New York Municipal Bond ETF reclassified as Barclays Capital New York Municipal Bond ETF 01/06/2009
S&P VRDO Municipal BOND ETF reclassified as Nuveen S&P VRDO Municipal Bond ETF 04/01/2010
KBW Mortgage Finance ETF reclassified as S&P Mortgage Finance ETF 10/24/2011
Nuveen Barclays Capital Build American Bond ETF reclassified as Nuveen Barclays Build American Bond ETF 10/31/2012
Nuveen Barclays Capital California Municipal Bond ETF reclassified as Nuveen Barclays California Municipal Bond ETF 10/31/2012
Nuveen Barclays Capital New York

Municipal Bond ETF reclassified as Nuveen Barclays New York Municipal Bond ETF 10/31/2012
Trust terminated 03/31/2015
Each Nuveen S&P VRDO Municipal Bond ETF received $29.958572 cash
Each S&P Mortgage Finance ETF received $58.564773 cash
Trust terminated 08/31/2016
Each BofA Merrill Lynch Emerging Markets Corporate Bond ETF received $29.663739 cash
Each Barclays International High Yield Bond ETF received $23.690673 cash
Each Nuveen Barclays Build America Bond ETF received $67.097342 cash
Each Nuveen Barclays California Municipal Bond ETF received $25.271343 cash
Each Nuveen Barclays New York Municipal Bond ETF received $24.569846 cash
(Additional Information in Active)

SPEAKOPHONE INC. (DE)
No longer in existence having become inoperative and void for non-payment of taxes 4/1/32

SPEAR, INC. (MA)
Completely liquidated 8/30/68
Each share Common 10¢ par exchanged for first and final distribution of (0.2) share Becton, Dickinson & Co. Common $1 par

SPEAR & CO. (NJ)
Each share 7% 1st Preferred $100 par exchanged for (1.25) shares $5.50 Preferred no par and $5 in cash in 1936
Each share 2nd Preferred $100 par exchanged for (1.25) shares $5.50 2nd Preferred no par in 1936
Each share Common no par exchanged for (1) share Common $1 par in 1936
$5.50 2nd Preferred no par changed to $5 2nd Preferred no par in 1951
Common $1 par changed to 10¢ par 7/17/58
Name changed to Acme-Hamilton Manufacturing Corp. 1/19/60
(See Acme-Hamilton Manufacturing Corp.)

SPEAR & JACKSON INC (NV)
Merged into United Pacific Industries Ltd. 10/18/2007
Each share Common $0.001 par exchanged for $1.96 cash

SPEAR FINL SVCS INC (CA)
Name changed to JMC Group Inc. 06/21/1993
JMC Group Inc. name changed to Fechtor, Detwiler, Mitchell & Co. Inc. 08/30/1999 which recapitalized as Detwiler, Mitchell & Co. 03/27/2001 which name changed to Detwiler Fenton Group, Inc. 10/20/2008

SPEAR HEAD INDS INC (TX)
Stock Dividend - 100% 12/06/1971
Adjudicated bankrupt 03/19/1973
Stockholders' equity unlikely

SPEARHEAD ENERGY INC (CO)
Merged into Universal Fuels Co. 04/23/1982
Each share Common no par exchanged for (1) share Common 1¢ par
Universal Fuels Co. recapitalized as Remington-Hall Capital Corp. 02/06/1998 which name changed to Ault Glazer & Co., Inc. 03/12/2008 which name changed to Tytan Holdings Inc. 10/02/2009

SPEARHEAD EXPLORATIONS LTD. (ON)
Charter revoked for failure to file reports and pay fees 4/1/65

SPEARHEAD INDS INC (MN)
Common 5¢ par split (2) for (1) by issuance of (1) additional share 11/06/1987
Stock Dividend - 10% 11/01/1985
Acquired by Paper Magic Group 12/30/1991
Each share Common 5¢ par exchanged for $2.72 cash

SPEARHEAD LTD INC (FL)
Recapitalized as Heritage Action Corp. 01/08/2016
Each share Common $0.001 par exchanged for (0.002) share Common $0.001 par
Heritage Action Corp. name changed to Heritage Printing Technology Corp. 06/28/2016 which recapitalized as Comerton Corp. 11/07/2017

SPEARHEAD RES INC (AB)
Merged into Arctos Petroleum Corp. 10/04/2004
Each share Common no par exchanged for (1) share Common no par
Arctos Petroleum Corp. recapitalized as Stetson Oil & Gas Ltd. (AB) 11/12/2007 which reincorporated in Ontario 08/21/2014 which name changed to Magnolia Colombia Ltd. 06/14/2017

SPECIAL DEVICES INC (DE)
Merged into SDI Acquisition 12/15/98
Each share Common 1¢ par exchanged for $34 cash

SPECIAL DIVERSIFIED OPPORTUNITES INC (DE)
Recapitalized as Standard Diversified Opportunities Inc. 06/02/2017
Each share Common 1¢ par exchanged for (0.04) share Class A Common 1¢ par Standard Diversified Opportunities Inc. name changed to Standard Diversified Inc. 04/25/2018

SPECIAL INVESTMENTS & SECURITIES, INC. (DE)
Liquidation completed
Each share Common 10¢ par exchanged for initial distribution consisting of (0.3902) share California Packing Corp. Capital Stock $2.50 par; (0.0328) share Canada Dry Corp. Common $1.66-2/3 par (0.0261) share McCall Corp. Common no par; (0.0224) share Pennsalt Chemicals Corp. $2.50 Conv. Preference $1 par; (0.0159) share Wheeling Steel Corp. Common $10 par and $8.60 cash 12/28/66
Each share Common 10¢ par received second and final distribution of $0.61 cash 3/31/67
(See each company's listing)

SPECIAL METALS, INC. (DE)
Merged into Allegheny Ludlum Steel Corp. 1/4/65
Each (4.35) shares Common $2 par exchanged for (1) share Common $1 par
Allegheny Ludlum Steel Corp. name changed to Allegheny Ludlum Industries, Inc. 4/24/70 which name changed to Allegheny International Inc. 4/29/81
(See Allegheny International Inc.)

SPECIAL METALS CORP (DE)
Issue Information - 3,850,000 shares COM offered at $16.50 per share on 02/26/1997
Plan of reorganization under Chapter 11 Federal Bankruptcy Code effective 11/26/2003
No stockholders' equity

SPECIAL OPPORTUNITIES FD INC (MD)
3% Conv. Preferred Ser. A $0.001 par conversion privilege expired 02/28/2014
3% Preferred Ser. A $0.001 par called for redemption at $50 on 03/03/2014
(Additional Information in Active)

SPECIAL PORTFOLIOS INC (MN)
Cash Portfolio 1¢ par completely liquidated 03/01/1996
Details not available
Merged into Fortis Growth Fund, Inc. 03/01/1996
Each share Stock Portfolio 1¢ par exchanged for Class Z 1¢ par on a net asset basis
(See Fortis Growth Fund, Inc.)

SPECIAL RES INC (BC)
Name changed to Trigon Technologies Inc. 2/23/84
(See Trigon Technologies Inc.)

SPECIAL STUDIES INC (NY)
Name changed to Spectex Industries Inc. 07/07/1972
(See Spectex Industries Inc.)

SPECIAL TRANSN SVCS INC (MN)
Name changed to Kaiser Corp. 02/01/1972
Kaiser Corp. name changed to Pilot Industries Corp. 07/12/1977

SPECIAL VALUE EXPANSION FD LLC (DE)
144A Money Market Preferred Ser. A called for redemption at $50,000 on 12/14/2010
144A Money Market Preferred Ser. B called for redemption at $50,000 on 12/14/2010

SPECIAL WASTE MGMT INC (BC)
Struck off register and declared dissolved for failure to file returns 7/10/92

SPECIALISTICS INC (DE)
Each share old Common $0.00001 par exchanged for (0.14285714) share new Common $0.00001 par 06/27/1996
Name changed to Eastern Group International Co. Ltd. 07/26/1996
Eastern Group International Co. Ltd. name changed to Telespace Ltd. 01/07/1997 which name changed to Qinnet.com, Inc. 01/10/2000 which name changed to Q-Net Technologies, Inc. 08/13/2001
(See Q-Net Technologies, Inc.)

SPECIALIZED BUSINESS SVCS INC (NY)
Name changed to SBS Industries, Inc. 05/03/1971
(See SBS Industries, Inc.)

SPECIALIZED DATA SVCS CORP (NY)
Name changed to Programmed Tax South Inc. 04/27/1970
Programmed Tax South Inc. merged into Programmed Proprietary Systems, Inc. 07/16/1971 which name changed to Programmed Tax Systems, Inc. 01/28/1975 which merged into Automatic Data Processing, Inc. 01/22/1980

SPECIALIZED EDUCATIONAL TRANSN CORP (DE)
Name changed to Service Group, Inc. 06/09/1969
Service Group, Inc. name changed to American Protection Industries Inc. 11/01/1971
(See American Protection Industries Inc.)

SPECIALIZED HEALTH PRODS INTL INC (DE)
Merged into Bard (C.R.), Inc. 06/09/2008
Each share Common 2¢ par exchanged for $1 cash

SPECIALIZED HOME MED SVCS INC (NV)
Name changed to IGSM Group, Inc. 11/23/2007
IGSM Group, Inc. recapitalized as Continental Rail Corp. 08/09/2013 which recapitalized as MediXall Group, Inc. 11/22/2016

SPECIALIZED LEASING INC (NV)
Each share old Common $0.001 par exchanged for (0.1) share new Common $0.001 par 01/28/2003
Name changed to Sassoon Group, Inc. 09/19/2003
Sassoon Group, Inc. name changed to BIB Holdings, Ltd. 12/15/2003 which name changed to Incode Technologies Corp. (NV) 02/07/2005 which reincorporated in Delaware as Inseq Corp. 07/13/2005 which name changed to GS Energy Corp. 07/19/2006 which recapitalized as EcoSystem Corp. 02/12/2008 which recapitalized as Adarna Energy Corp. 07/07/2011
(See Adarna Energy Corp.)

SPECIALIZED MED SVCS INC (FL)
Name changed to SMS Group Inc. 12/18/89
SMS Group Inc. name changed to Natural Resources Recovery Inc. 11/8/90 which name changed to Rare Earth Metals, Inc. (FL) 3/13/92 which reorganized in Delaware as Americare Health Group Inc. 3/3/93 which name changed to Zagreus Inc. 3/26/99

SPECIALIZED SVCS INC (DE)
Merged into Home Acquisition Co. 03/15/1985
Each share Common $1 par exchanged for $10.50 cash

SPECIALIZED SVCS INC (MI)
Each share old Common $0.0001 par exchanged for (0.1) share new Common $0.0001 par 11/13/2007
Each share new Common $0.0001 par exchanged again for (0.02) share new Common $0.0001 par 01/09/2009
Name changed to Exergetic Energy, Inc. 01/12/2011

SPECIALIZED SYS INC (CA)
Name changed to Kentana Development, Inc. 02/23/1990
Kentana Development, Inc. reorganized as Silicon Disk Corp. 03/01/1992 which recapitalized as Canadian Piper Air Corp. 06/23/1992

SPECIALIZER INC (NV)
Name changed to Anpulo Food Development, Inc. 02/28/2013

SPECIALTY CARE NETWORK INC (DE)
Issue Information - 3,198,062 shares COM offered at $8 per share on 02/06/1997
Name changed to Healthgrades.com, Inc. 01/05/2000
Healthgrades.com, Inc. name changed to Health Grades Inc. 11/21/2000
(See Health Grades Inc.)

SPECIALTY CATALOG CORP (DE)
Merged into Specialty Acquisition Corp. 11/14/2001
Each share Common 1¢ par exchanged for $3.75 cash

SPECIALTY CHEM RES INC (DE)
Each (14) shares old Common 10¢ par exchanged for (1) share new Common 10¢ par 02/26/1992
Company terminated registration of common stock and is no longer public as of 10/17/2005

SPECIALTY COMPOSITES CORP (DE)
Acquired by Cabot Corp. 03/22/1989
Each share Common 1¢ par exchanged for $3.50 cash

SPECIALTY CONTRACTORS INC (NV)
Name changed to CIAO Group, Inc. 06/06/2014

SPECIALTY CONVERTERS, INC. (DE)
8% Conv. Preferred $5 par called for redemption 3/25/65
Name changed to Specialty Composites, Inc. 5/16/73
(See Specialty Composites Corp.)

SPECIALTY ELECTRONICS DEVELOPMENT CORP. (NY)
Each share Common 4¢ par exchanged for (0.5) share Common 8¢ par 11/25/66
Name changed to Spedcor Electronics, Inc. 11/21/67
Spedcor Electronics, Inc. merged into Entron, Inc. 12/31/69
(See Entron, Inc.)

SPECIALTY EQUIP COS INC (DE)
Merged into SPE Acquisition, Inc. 9/14/88
Each share old Common 1¢ par exchanged for $33 cash
Merged into United Technologies Corp. 11/20/2000
Each share new Common 1¢ par exchanged for $30.50 cash

SPECIALTY EQUITIES CORP (NV)
Charter revoked for failure to file reports and pay fees 01/07/1974

SPECIALTY LABORATORIES INC (CA)
Issue Information - 5,000,000 shares COM offered at $16 per share on 12/07/2000
Merged into AmeriPath Inc. 1/31/2006
Each share Common no par exchanged for $13.25 cash

SPECIALTY MED PRODS INC (BC)
Recapitalized as Fedora Industries Inc. 10/20/1997
Each share Common no par exchanged for (0.2) share Common no par
Fedora Industries Inc. name changed to Airbomb.com Marketing Ltd. (BC) 02/21/2000 which reincorporated in Delaware as airbomb.com, Inc. 05/09/2000 which name changed to RT Petroleum Inc. 05/18/2005
(See RT Petroleum Inc.)

SPECIALTY PAPERBOARD INC (DE)
Name changed to Fibermark, Inc. 4/1/97
(See Fibermark, Inc.)

SPECIALTY PAPERS CO. (OH)
Acquired by James River Corp. of Virginia 12/15/86
Each share Common no par exchanged for (2) shares Common 10¢ par

SPECIALTY PRODS & INSULATION CO (PA)
Acquired by Superior Plus Corp. 09/28/2009
Details not available

SPECIALTY RESTAURANTS CORP (CA)
Company went private in 1981
Stock is repurchased at a price equal to 75% of book value
Contact: Lynn Kellum, 8191 E Kaiser Blvd, Anaheim, CA 92808 (714) 279-6100

SPECIALTY RETAIL CONCEPTS INC (BC)
Recapitalized as Altoro Gold Corp. 01/09/1997
Each share Common no par exchanged for (0.2) share Common no par
Altoro Gold Corp. merged into Solitario Resources Corp. 10/18/2000 which name changed to Solitario Exploration & Royalty Corp. 06/17/2008 which name changed to Solitario Zinc Corp. 07/18/2017

SPECIALTY RETAIL CONCEPTS INC (NC)
Stock Dividend - 10% 10/27/1986

Filed for Chapter 11 bankruptcy
proceedings 04/11/1988
Details not available

SPECIALTY RETAIL GROUP INC (FL)
Recapitalized as TBM Holdings, Inc.
06/15/1999
Each (412.92) shares Common
$0.001 par exchanged for (1) share
Common $0.001 par
(See TBM Holdings, Inc.)

SPECIALTY RETAIL SVCS INC (DE)
Each share old Common 1¢ par
exchanged for (0.1) share new
Common 1¢ par 12/30/1997
Name changed to Global A, Inc.
08/11/1998
(See Global A, Inc.)

SPECIALTY RETAIL VENTURES INC (DE)
Charter cancelled and declared
inoperative and void for
non-payment of taxes 3/1/93

SPECIALTY STORES CO., INC. (NY)
Name changed to Diversified
Specialty Stores Corp. 5/27/58
Diversified Specialty Stores Corp.
name changed to Diversified Stores
Corp. 1/9/59 which merged into City
Stores Co. 1/30/60 which name
changed to CSS Industries, Inc.
9/24/85

SPECIALTY TELECONSTRUCTORS INC (NV)
Reincorporated under the laws of
Delaware as Omniamerica Inc.
09/15/1998
Omniamerica Inc. merged into
American Tower Corp. (Old)
02/25/1999 which reorganized as
American Tower Corp. (New)
01/03/2012

SPECIALTY UNDERWRITERS ALLIANCE INC (DE)
Merged into Tower Group, Inc.
11/13/2009
Each share Common 1¢ par
exchanged for (0.28) share Common
1¢ par
Tower Group, Inc. merged into Tower
Group International, Ltd. 03/14/2013
(See Tower Group International, Ltd.)

SPECIALTY WOODS INC (AB)
Recapitalized as Sheffield Resources
Ltd. (AB) 01/12/2005
Each share Common no par
exchanged for (0.5) share Common
no par
Sheffield Resources Ltd. (AB)
reincorporated in British Columbia
04/06/2006 which was acquired by
Nevoro Inc. 07/29/2008 which was
acquired by Starfield Resources Inc.
10/08/2009

SPECOPS LABS INC (CANADA)
Recapitalized as Link Linux Inc.
3/10/2006
Each (15) shares Common no par
exchanged for (1) share Common
no par

SPECS MUSIC INC (FL)
Common 1¢ par split (5) for (4) by
issuance of (0.25) additional share
12/22/86
Common 1¢ par split (3) for (2) by
issuance of (0.5) additional share
10/2/87
Common 1¢ par split (4) for (3) by
issuance of (1/3) additional share
8/21/89
Merged into Camelot Music 7/29/98
Each share Common 1¢ par
exchanged for $3.30 cash

SPECTAIR INDS INC (BC)
Recapitalized as International
Spectair Resources Inc. 12/1/89
Each share Common no par
exchanged for (1/3) share Common
no par
International Spectair Resources Inc.
name changed to Camden Oil Corp.

11/5/91 which name changed to
Maxwell Resources Inc. 12/2/92
which name changed to Maxwell
Energy Corp. (BC) 5/12/93 which
reincorporated in Alberta 9/12/96
which recapitalized as Maxwell Oil &
Gas Ltd. 11/18/96
(See Maxwell Oil & Gas Ltd.)

SPECTEX INDS INC (NY)
Merged out of existence 06/24/1997
Details not available

SPECTOR FREIGHT SYSTEM, INC. (MO)
99.95% held by Spector Industries,
Inc. as of 8/3/73
Merged into Telecom Corp. 12/31/80
Each share Class A Common $1 par
exchanged for (1) share Common
$1 par
Telecom Corp. name changed to TCC
Industries, Inc. 6/1/94
(See TCC Industries, Inc.)

SPECTOR INDS INC (DE)
Merged into Telecom Corp. 12/31/80
Each share Common $1 par
exchanged for (1) share Common
$1 par
Telecom Corp. name changed to TCC
Industries, Inc. 6/1/94
(See TCC Industries, Inc.)

SPECTOR (EDWARD) PRODUCTIONS, INC. (NY)
Voluntarily dissolved in April 1972
Former transfer agent opined in
December 1972 that there was no
stockholders' equity

SPECTRA CORP (IL)
Merged into Spectra McIntosh Corp.
06/30/1969
Each share Preferred Ser. A $3 par
exchanged for (1) share Preferred
Ser. A $3 par
Each share Common $1 par
exchanged for (1) share Common
$1 par
Spectra McIntosh Corp. name
changed to McIntosh Corp.
09/27/1973 which merged into
Norris Industries, Inc. 06/30/1977
(See Norris Industries, Inc.)

SPECTRA ENERGY CDA EXCHANGECO INC (CANADA)
Each Spectra Energy Exchangeable
Share no par exchanged for (1)
share Spectra Energy Corp.
Common $0.001 par 03/17/2010
Each Duke Energy Exchangeable
Share no par exchanged for (1)
share Duke Energy Corp. Common
$0.001 par 03/17/2010
(See each company's listing)

SPECTRA ENERGY CORP (DE)
Merged into Enbridge Inc. 02/27/2017
Each share Common $0.001 par
exchanged for (0.984) share
Common no par

SPECTRA ENERGY INCOME FD (AB)
Acquired by Spectra Energy Corp.
05/06/2008
Each Trust Unit exchanged for $11.25
cash

SPECTRA GROUP GREAT RESTAURANTS INC (BC)
Common no par reclassified as Class
A Common no par 06/19/2002
Merged into Madison Pacific
Properties Inc. 06/28/2007
Each share Non-Vtg. Common no par
exchanged for (1) share Class B
Common no par
Each share Class A Common no par
exchanged for (1) share Class B
Common no par

SPECTRA INDUSTRIES, INC. (IL)
Name changed to Spectra Corp.
9/25/68
Spectra Corp. merged into Spectra
McIntosh Corp. 6/30/69 which name
changed to McIntosh Corp. 9/27/73

which merged into Norris Industries,
Inc. 6/30/77
(See Norris Industries, Inc.)

SPECTRA McINTOSH CORP (DE)
Conv. Preferred Ser. A $3 par called
for redemption 2/15/72
Name changed to McIntosh Corp.
9/27/73
McIntosh Corp. merged into Norris
Industries, Inc. 6/30/77
(See Norris Industries, Inc.)

SPECTRA MED INC (NM)
Charter revoked for failure to file
reports and pay fees 7/2/2002

SPECTRA PHARMACEUTICAL SVCS INC (MD)
Plan of reorganization under Chapter
11 Federal Bankruptcy proceedings
confirmed 08/21/1991
No stockholders' equity

SPECTRA-PHYSICS, INC. (CA)
Capital Stock 33-1/3¢ par changed to
20¢ par and (1) additional share
issued 3/21/73
Reincorporated under the laws of
Delaware as Spectra-Physics
(Delaware) Inc. 1/28/87
Spectra-Physics (Delaware) Inc.
name changed to Spectra-Physics,
Inc. (DE) 3/10/87
(See Spectra-Physics, Inc. (DE))

SPECTRA PHYSICS INC (DE)
Ctfs. dtd. prior to 8/5/87
Merged into Ciba-Geigy Corp. 8/5/87
Each share Capital Stock 20¢ par
exchanged for $36.50 cash

SPECTRA-PHYSICS INC (DE)
Name changed 6/18/2001
Name changed from Spectra-Physics
Lasers, Inc. to Spectra-Physics, Inc.
6/18/2001
Merged into Thermo Electron Corp.
2/26/2002
Each share Common no par
exchanged for $17.50 cash

SPECTRA-PHYSICS (DELAWARE) INC. (DE)
Name changed to Spectra-Physics,
Inc. (DE) 3/10/87
(See Spectra-Physics, Inc. (DE))

SPECTRA PREM INDS INC (CANADA)
Merged into 6551399 Canada Inc.
1/18/2007
Each share Subordinate no par
exchanged for $2.85 cash

SPECTRA SPORTS, INC. (CA)
Merged into Checchi & Co.
01/29/1971
Each share Capital Stock $1 par
exchanged for (0.08) share Common
$1.60 par
(See Checchi & Co.)

SPECTRA VENTURES LTD (BC)
Recapitalized as Consolidated
Spectra Ventures Ltd. 1/12/94
Each share Common no par
exchanged for (1/3) share Common
no par
Consolidated Spectra Ventures Ltd.
name changed to Tiger International
Resources Inc. 12/27/96

SPECTRADYNE INC (TX)
Common no par split (3) for (2) by
issuance of (0.5) additional share
11/17/80
Common no par split (3) for (2) by
issuance of (0.5) additional share
7/10/81
Common no par split (3) for (2) by
issuance of (0.5) additional share
2/3/84
Common no par split (3) for (2) by
issuance of (0.5) additional share
6/13/86
Acquired by SPI Holding, Inc. 10/8/87
Each share Common no par
exchanged for (0.28) share 16%
Preferred 1¢ par and $39 cash

Note: Option to receive (1) Common
Stock Purchase Warrant in lieu of
$1.50 cash expired 11/12/87
SPI Holding, Inc. name changed to
Spectravision Inc. 5/25/94 which
reorganized as On Command Corp.
10/8/96 which merged into Liberty
Media Corp. (New) 12/8/2003 which
reorganized as Liberty Media Corp.
(Incorporated 2/28/2006) 5/10/2006

SPECTRAFAX CORP (FL)
Reincorporated under the laws of
Delaware as Serefex Corp.
04/02/2002

SPECTRAL CAP CORP (AB)
Name changed to Mount Real
Financial Corp. 05/04/1994
Mount Real Financial Corp. name
changed to Mount Real Corp. (AB)
08/25/1995 which reincorporated in
Canada 07/10/1998
(See Mount Real Corp.)

SPECTRAL DIAGNOSTICS INC (ON)
Name changed to Spectral Medical
Inc. 12/31/2014

SPECTRAL DYNAMICS CORP (CA)
Name changed 8/11/77
Common no par split (2) for (1) by
issuance of (1) additional share
3/30/72
Common no par split (3) for (2) by
issuance of (0.5) additional share
10/22/73
Name changed from Spectral
Dynamics Corp. of San Diego to
Spectral Dynamics Corp. 8/11/77
Merged into Scientific-Atlanta, Inc.
1/31/78
Each share Common no par
exchanged for (0.65) share Common
50¢ par
(See Scientific-Atlanta, Inc.)

SPECTRALINK CORP (DE)
Merged into Polycom, Inc. 03/26/2007
Each share Common 1¢ par
exchanged for $11.75 cash

SPECTRAMED INC (DE)
Merged into BOC Acquisition Corp.
09/06/1988
Each share Common 1¢ par
exchanged for $12 cash

SPECTRAMETRICS INC (MA)
Merged into Beckman Instruments,
Inc. 05/28/1980
Each share Common 33-1/3¢ par
exchanged for (0.17235) share
Common $1 par
Beckman Instruments, Inc. merged
into SmithKline Beckman Corp.
03/04/1982 which merged into
SmithKline Beecham PLC
07/26/1989 which merged into
GlaxoSmithKline PLC 12/27/2000

SPECTRAN CORP (DE)
Merged into Lucent Technologies Inc.
2/1/2000
Each share Common 1¢ par
exchanged for $9 cash

SPECTRAN INC (CA)
Adjudicated bankrupt 6/14/72

SPECTRANETICS CORP (DE)
Acquired by Koninklijke Philips N.V.
08/09/2017
Each share Common $0.001 par
exchanged for $38.50 cash

SPECTRASCAN INC (CO)
Name changed to International
Horizons, Inc. 11/29/95
(See International Horizons, Inc.)

SPECTRASEARCH INC (NY)
Recapitalized as Arcus Inc.
09/29/1989
Each share Common $0.001 par
exchanged for (0.25) share Common
1¢ par
(See Arcus Inc.)

SPECTRASITE HLDGS INC (DE)
Plan of reorganization under Chapter

SPECTRASITE INC (DE)
11 Federal Bankruptcy Code effective 2/10/2003
Each share Common $0.001 par exchanged for (0.00752294) SpectraSite, Inc. Common Stock Purchase Warrant expiring 02/10/2010

SPECTRASITE INC (DE)
Common 1¢ par split (2) for (1) by issuance of (1) additional share payable 08/21/2003 to holders of record 08/14/2003 Ex date - 08/22/2003
Merged into American Tower Corp. (Old) 08/08/2005
Each share Common 1¢ par exchanged for (3.575) shares Class A Common 1¢ par
American Tower Corp. (Old) reorganized as American Tower Corp. (New) 01/03/2012

SPECTRASOURCE CORP (NV)
Recapitalized as China Yibai United Guarantee International Holding, Inc. 06/17/2009
Each (15) shares Common $0.001 par exchanged for (1) share Common $0.001 par

SPECTRATEK INC (UT)
Each share Common $0.001 par exchanged for (0.005) share new Common $0.001 par 12/15/1993
Reincorporated under the laws of Delaware as Teltran International Group Ltd. 10/06/1997
Teltran International Group Ltd. recapitalized as CelebDirect, Inc. 09/10/2007 which name changed to Muscle Flex, Inc. 10/01/2008 which name changed to Bravada International, Ltd. 07/19/2010

SPECTRAVIDEO INC (DE)
Charter cancelled and declared inoperative and void for non-payment of taxes 6/17/93

SPECTRAVISION INC (DE)
Plan of reorganization under Chapter 11 Federal Bankruptcy Code effective 10/08/1996
Each share Class B Common $0.001 par exchanged for an undetermined amount of On Command Corp. Common 1¢ par and Common Stock Purchase Warrants
On Command Corp. merged into Liberty Media Corp. (New) 12/08/2003 which reorganized as Liberty Media Corp. (Incorporated 02/28/2006) 05/10/2006 which name changed to Liberty Interactive Corp. 09/26/2011 which name changed to Qurate Retail, Inc. 04/10/2018

SPECTRE GAMING INC (MN)
SEC revoked common stock registration 03/21/2017

SPECTRE INDS INC (NV)
Each share old Common $0.001 par exchanged for (0.06666666) share new Common $0.001 par 06/08/2004
Name changed to Sensor System Solutions, Inc. 12/08/2004
Sensor System Solutions, Inc. recapitalized as Victor Mining Industry Group Inc. 04/15/2014

SPECTRE MTR CARS INC (NV)
Recapitalized as Spectre Industries, Inc. 11/06/1997
Each share Common $0.001 par exchanged (0.2) share Common $0.001 par
Spectre Industries, Inc. name changed to Sensor System Solutions, Inc. 12/08/2004 which recapitalized as Victor Mining Industry Group Inc. 04/15/2014

SPECTRIAN CORP (DE)
Reincorporated 10/03/1997
Issue Information - 2,425,000 shares COM offered at $12.50 per share on 08/03/1994
State of incorporation changed from (CA) to (DE) 10/03/1997
Merged into REMEC, Inc. 12/20/2002
Each share Common $0.001 par exchanged for (1) share Common 1¢ par
(See REMEC, Inc.)

SPECTRO INDS INC (DE)
Common $1 par split (2) for (1) by issuance of (1) additional share 01/24/1983
Common $1 par split (2) for (1) by issuance of (1) additional share 02/26/1985
Merged into McKesson Corp. (MD) 06/04/1985
Each share Common $1 par exchanged for $20 cash

SPECTROAIR EXPLS LTD (BC)
Recapitalized as Channel Gold Resources Corp. 10/06/1975
Each share Common no par exchanged for (0.2) share Common no par
Channel Gold Resources Corp. recapitalized as St. Elias Exploration Corp. 04/17/1979 which name changed to Bigstone Minerals Ltd. 01/19/1984 which recapitalized as Adamas Resources Corp. 08/30/1993 which recapitalized as Britannica Resources Corp. 08/27/2002 which name changed to Trinity Valley Energy Corp. 10/08/2013 which recapitalized as Smooth Rock Ventures Corp. 11/15/2017

SPECTRON, INC. (FL)
Proclaimed dissolved for non-payment of taxes 6/30/66

SPECTRONICS INC (TX)
Merged into Honeywell Inc. 8/25/78
Each share Common 15¢ par exchanged for (0.41587) share Common $1.50 par
Honeywell Inc. merged into Honeywell International Inc. 12/1/99

SPECTRUM ACQUISITION HLDGS INC (NV)
Each share old Common $0.001 par exchanged for (0.05) share new Common $0.001 par 03/17/2008
Each share new Common $0.001 par exchanged again for (0.0001) share new Common $0.001 par 10/05/2011
Stock Dividend - 20% payable 01/31/2012 to holders of record 01/16/2012 Ex date - 01/11/2012
Recapitalized as Nouveau Holdings, Ltd. 04/30/2013
Each share new Common $0.001 par exchanged for (0.00125) share Common $0.001 par

SPECTRUM BRANDS CORP (FL)
Common $0.001 par split (6) for (1) by issuance of (5) additional shares payable 11/05/2001 to holders of record 10/30/2001 Ex date - 11/06/2001
Administratively dissolved 10/04/2002

SPECTRUM BRANDS HLDGS INC OLD (DE)
Merged into Spectrum Brands Holdings, Inc. (New) 07/16/2018
Each share Common 1¢ par exchanged for (1) share Common 1¢ par

SPECTRUM BRANDS INC (WI & DE)
Plan of reorganization under Chapter 11 Federal Bankruptcy proceedings effective 08/28/2009
No stockholders' equity
Note: Spectrum Brands, Inc. (DE) issued to Noteholders through Chapter 11 reorganization 08/28/2009
Merged into Spectrum Brands Holdings, Inc. (Old) 06/16/2010
Each share Common 1¢ par exchanged for (1) share Common 1¢ par
Spectrum Brands Holdings, Inc. (Old) merged into Spectrum Brands Holdings, Inc. (New) 07/16/2018

SPECTRUM CAP TR I (DE)
Name changed to GWB Capital Trust I 5/29/2003
(See GWB Capital Trust I)

SPECTRUM CAP TR II (DE)
Name changed to GWB Capital Trust II 5/29/2003
(See GWB Capital Trust II)

SPECTRUM CELLULAR CORP (DE)
Under plan of reorganization each share Common $0.001 par automatically became (1) share Spectrum Information Technologies, Inc. Common $0.001 par 9/22/89
Spectrum Information Technologies, Inc. name changed to SITI-Sites.com, Inc. 3/10/2000

SPECTRUM COMMUNICATIONS CORP (CO)
Administratively dissolved 1/1/90

SPECTRUM CTL INC (PA)
Common no par split (2) for (1) by issuance of (1) additional share 11/03/1978
Common no par split (2) for (1) by issuance of (1) additional share 03/07/1980
Common no par split (2) for (1) by issuance of (1) additional share 12/17/1980
Acquired by API Technologies Corp. 06/02/2011
Each share Common no par exchanged for $20 cash

SPECTRUM DATATECH INC (CO)
Each share old Common $0.0001 par exchanged for (1/7) share new Common $0.0001 par 06/29/1990
Name changed to Spindle Oil & Gas, Inc. 06/07/1991
(See Spindle Oil & Gas, Inc.)

SPECTRUM DIGITAL CORP (DE)
Class A Common $0.001 par reclassified as Common $0.001 par 09/30/1985
Merged into Micom Systems, Inc. 12/08/1987
Each share 8% Conv. Exchangeable Preference $1 par exchanged for $8.33 cash
Each share Common $0.001 par exchanged for (0.0769) share Common no par
Note: An additional and final undetermined distribution was paid 05/13/1988

SPECTRUM ENTERPRISES INC (DE)
Recapitalized as Money Radio Inc. 03/19/1990
Each share Common $0.0001 par exchanged for (0.1) share Common $0.0001 par
(See Money Radio Inc.)

SPECTRUM EQUITIES INC (DE)
Recapitalized as Imtek Office Solutions Inc. 04/22/1997
Each share Common $0.001 par exchanged for (0.0025) share Common $0.001 par
(See Imtek Office Solutions Inc.)

SPECTRUM FINL CORP (DE)
Common $20 par changed to $5 par and (3) additional shares issued 5/12/87
Merged into Key Centurion Bancshares, Inc. 1/31/91
Each share Common $5 par exchanged for (3) shares Common $3 par
Key Centurion Bancshares, Inc. merged into Banc One Corp. 5/3/93 which merged into Bank One Corp. 10/2/98 which merged into J.P. Morgan Chase & Co. 12/31/2000 which name changed to JPMorgan Chase & Co. 7/20/2004

SPECTRUM GAMES CORP (BC)
Name changed to Playdium Entertainment Corp. 02/26/2001
(See Playdium Entertainment Corp.)

SPECTRUM GLOBAL SOLUTIONS INC (BC)
Reincorporated under the laws of Nevada 02/05/2018

SPECTRUM GOLD CORP (CANADA)
Recapitalized as Scarlett Minerals Inc. 12/30/91
Each share Class A Common no par exchanged for (0.5) share Class A Common no par
Scarlett Minerals Inc. name changed to SMI Oil & Gas, Inc. 9/20/94 which merged into Canadian Leader Energy Inc. 11/2/95 which merged into Centurion Energy International Inc. 5/20/97
(See Centurion Energy International Inc.)

SPECTRUM GROUP INC (FL)
Common 1¢ par split (3) for (2) by issuance of (0.5) additional share 12/2/85
Acquired by Chesebrough-Pond's, Inc. 12/4/86
Each share Common 1¢ par exchanged for $13.1069 cash

SPECTRUM HOLOBYTE INC (MD)
Name changed to MicroProse, Inc. (New) 9/22/97
(See MicroProse, Inc. (New))

SPECTRUM INDL RES LTD (BC)
Recapitalized as International Data Service Corp. 11/26/1987
Each share Capital Stock no par exchanged for (0.33333333) share Common no par
(See International Data Service Corp.)

SPECTRUM INFORMATION TECHNOLOGIES INC (DE)
Plan of reorganization under Chapter 11 Federal Bankruptcy Code effective 03/31/1997
Each share old Common $0.001 par exchanged for (0.01333333) share new Common $0.001 par
Name changed to SITI-Sites.com, Inc. 03/10/2000

SPECTRUM LABS INC (CA)
Each share old Common no par exchanged for (1/3) share new Common no par 02/27/1992
Reorganized under the laws of Delaware 09/30/1998
Each share new Common no par exchanged for (0.1) share Common 1¢ par
(See Spectrum Laboratories, Inc. (DE))

SPECTRUM LABS INC (DE)
Each share old Common 1¢ par exchanged for (0.00004) share new Common 1¢ par 11/28/2005
Note: In effect holders received $2.56 cash per share and public interest was eliminated

SPECTRUM LTD (NJ)
Common 5¢ par changed to 1-2/3¢ par and (2) additional shares issued 11/29/1968
Charter voided for non-payment of taxes 01/08/1970

SPECTRUM MGMT UNDERWRITERS GROUP (NV)
Recapitalized as Academy Insurance & Financial Services Inc. 6/27/95
Each share Common $0.001 par exchanged for (0.05) share Common $0.001 par
Academy Insurance & Financial Services Inc. name changed to Guardian Insurance & Financial Services Inc. 1/2/96 which name

SPECTRUM MICROWAVE CORP (DE)
changed to Genesis Insurance & Financial Services, Inc. 6/7/96
(See Genesis Insurance & Financial Services, Inc.)

SPECTRUM MICROWAVE CORP (DE)
Name changed to Spectrum Digital Corp. 02/14/1985
Spectrum Digital Corp. merged into Micom Systems, Inc. 12/08/1987
(See Micom Systems, Inc.)

SPECTRUM OIL CORP (DE)
Each share old Common $0.001 par exchanged for (0.1) share new Common $0.001 par 7/12/96
Each share new Common $0.001 par exchanged again for (0.01) share new Common $0.001 par 9/5/2001
Charter cancelled and declared inoperative and void for non-payment of taxes 3/1/2003

SPECTRUM ORGANIC PRODS INC (CA)
Merged into Hain Celestial Group, Inc. 12/19/2005
Each share Common no par exchanged for (0.01792929) share Common 1¢ par and $0.3485 cash

SPECTRUM PHARMACEUTICAL CORP (FL)
Recapitalized as WorldWideWeb Institute.com, Inc. 07/01/1999
Each share Common $0.001 par exchanged for (0.1) share Common $0.001 par

SPECTRUM RES CORP (DE)
Name changed to Transmarine Resources, Inc. 06/03/1970
Each share Capital Stock 1¢ par exchanged for (1) share Capital Stock 1¢ par
(See Transmarine Resources, Inc.)

SPECTRUM RES INC (CO)
Each share old Common $0.0001 par exchanged for (0.04) share new Common $0.0001 par 07/14/1989
Name changed to Spectrum Datatech, Inc. 07/24/1989
Spectrum Datatech, Inc. name changed to Spindle Oil & Gas, Inc. 06/07/1991
(See Spindle Oil & Gas, Inc.)

SPECTRUM RES INC (DE)
Reincorporated 4/18/89
State of incorporation changed from (UT) to (DE) 4/18/89
Charter cancelled and declared inoperative and void for non-payment of taxes 3/1/90

SPECTRUM RESOURCES LTD. (BC)
Recapitalized as Spectrum Industrial Resources Ltd. 1/9/70
Each share Capital Stock no par exchanged for (0.5) share Capital Stock no par
Spectrum Industrial Resources Ltd. recapitalized as International Data Service Corp. 11/26/87

SPECTRUM SCIENCES & SOFTWARE HLDGS CORP (DE)
Name changed to Horne International, Inc. 09/12/2006
(See Horne International, Inc.)

SPECTRUM SIGNAL PROCESSING INC (BC)
Merged into Vecima Networks Inc. 5/2/2007
Each share Common no par exchanged for (0.04) share Common no par and $0.4915 cash

SPECTRUM 2000 INC (CO)
Administratively dissolved 02/01/2001

SPECTRUM VENTURES INC (NV)
Recapitalized as Cobra Technologies Inc. 2/18/99
Each (24) shares Common $0.001 par exchanged for (1) share Common $0.001 par
Cobra Technologies Inc. name changed to Celexx Corp. 10/19/99

SPECTRUM VENTURES LTD (CO)
Reorganized under the laws of Nevada as Nxtech Wireless & Cable Systems, Inc. 03/06/2002
Each share Common no par exchanged for (0.16666666) share Common no par
Nxtech Wireless & Cable Systems, Inc. recapitalized as Chimera Technology Corp. 09/26/2002 which recapitalized as Oriens Travel & Hotel Management Corp. 08/21/2007 which recapitalized as Pure Hospitality Solutions, Inc. 11/12/2014

SPECTRUMEDICAL INC (UT)
Merged out of existence 6/18/84
Details not available

SPECTRUMEDIX CORP (DE)
Company terminated common stock registration and is no longer public as of 07/13/2001

SPECTRUMGOLD INC (BC)
Acquired by NovaGold Resources Inc. (NS) 07/15/2004
Each share Common no par exchanged for (0.74074074) share new Common no par
NovaGold Resources Inc. (NS) reincorporated in British Columbia 06/12/2013

SPECTRX INC (DE)
Issue Information - 2,201,699 shares COM offered at $7 per share on 07/01/1997
Name changed to Guided Therapeutics, Inc. 05/07/2008

SPECULATORS FD LTD (AB)
Name changed to Newmark Resources Ltd. 1/18/74
Newmark Resources Ltd. recapitalized as Trinity Resources Ltd. 5/10/77 which merged into Enscor Inc. 7/18/91 which name changed to Rose Corp. 6/1/98
(See Rose Corp.)

SPEDCOR ELECTRS INC (NY)
Merged into Entron, Inc. 12/31/1969
Each share Common 8¢ par exchanged for (1) share Common 30¢ par
(See Entron, Inc.)

SPEECH PHONE INC (NV)
Name changed to Hallmark Venture Group, Inc. 08/12/2008

SPEECHLINK COMMUNICATIONS CORP (DE)
Recapitalized as Eros Enterprises, Inc. 12/15/2005
Each share Common 1¢ par exchanged for (0.001) share Common $0.001 par
Eros Enterprises, Inc. name changed to IQ Webquest, Inc. 03/03/2006

SPEECHSWITCH INC (NJ)
Name changed to Kenergy Scientific, Inc. 02/25/2011

SPEECHWORKS INTL INC (DE)
Issue Information - 4,750,000 shares COM offered at $20 per share on 07/31/2000
Merged into ScanSoft, Inc. 8/12/2003
Each share Common $0.001 par exchanged for (0.86) share Common $0.001 par
ScanSoft, Inc. name changed to Nuance Communications, Inc. (New) 11/21/2005

SPEED BUILDING, INC. (KY)
Liquidated in 1957

SPEED COMM INC (MN)
Each share old Common no par exchanged for (0.0625) share new Common no par 04/18/2016
Note: Holders of (15) or fewer pre-split shares received $0.01 cash per share
Assets foreclosed upon 06/08/2016
No stockholders' equity

SPEED EQUIP WORLDS AMER INC (TX)
Adjudicated bankrupt 02/24/1975
Stockholders' equity unlikely

SPEED O LAQ CHEMS CORP (MN)
Liquidation completed
Each share Common 60¢ par received initial distribution of $0.90 cash 05/29/1974
Each share Common 60¢ par received second distribution of $0.60 cash 01/31/1975
Each share Common 60¢ par received third distribution of $0.30 cash 04/29/1975
Each share Common 60¢ par exchanged for fourth and final distribution of $0.0375799 cash 10/13/1978

SPEED O PRINT BUSINESS MACH CORP (DE)
Reincorporated 05/10/1985
State of incorporation changed from (IL) to (DE) 05/10/1985
Name changed to SBM Industries, Inc. 08/26/1992
SBM Industries, Inc. name changed to Star Struck, Ltd. 05/03/1999
(See Star Struck, Ltd.)

SPEED QUEEN CORP. (DE)
Acquired by McGraw Electric Co. 09/30/1956
Preferred $25 par received $25.50 cash
Each share Common $1 par exchanged for (0.44247787) share Common $1 par
McGraw Electric Co. name changed to McGraw-Edison Co. 01/02/1957
(See McGraw-Edison Co.)

SPEED WAY FOOD STORES INC (NY)
Charter cancelled and proclaimed dissolved for failure to pay taxes 06/26/1996

SPEED WRAP INC. (CO)
Charter revoked for failure to file reports and pay fees 9/8/54

SPEEDATA INC (NY)
Charter cancelled and proclaimed dissolved for failure to pay taxes and file reports 12/15/1975

SPEEDCOM WIRELESS CORP (DE)
Name changed to SP Holding Corp. 07/05/2005
SP Holding Corp. name changed to Organic To Go Food Corp. 05/21/2007
(See Organic To Go Food Corp.)

SPEEDCOM WIRELESS INTL CORP (DE)
Merged into SPEEDCOM Wireless Corp. 09/27/2000
Each share Common $0.001 par exchanged for (1.146) shares Common $0.001 par
SPEEDCOM Wireless Corp. name changed to SP Holding Corp. 07/05/2005 which name changed to Organic To Go Food Corp. 05/21/2007
(See Organic To Go Food Corp.)

SPEEDEE MART, INC. (CA)
Liquidation completed
Each share Common no par exchanged for initial distribution of $10.25 cash 9/17/64
Each share Common no par received second and final distribution of $1.4049 cash 10/12/65

SPEEDFAM INTL INC (IL)
Issue Information - 2,850,000 shares COM offered at $11 per share on 10/09/1995
Under plan of merger name changed to SPEEDFAM-IPEC, Inc. 04/06/1999
SPEEDFAM-IPEC, Inc. merged into Novellus Systems, Inc. 12/06/2002 which merged into Lam Research Corp. 06/04/2012

SPEEDFAM-IPEC INC (IL)
Merged into Novellus Systems, Inc. 12/06/2002
Each share Common 1¢ par exchanged for (0.1818) share Common no par
Novellus Systems, Inc. merged into Lam Research Corp. 06/04/2012

SPEEDHAUL HLDGS INC (NJ)
Each share old Common $0.0001 par exchanged for (0.33333333) share new Common $0.0001 par 01/23/2007
Reincorporated under the laws of Florida as Gold Horse International, Inc. 11/23/2007
(See Gold Horse International, Inc.)

SPEEDRING CORP. (DE)
Name changed to Schiller Corp. 11/7/68
Schiller Corp. name changed to Schiller Industries, Inc. 12/23/69
(See Schiller Industries, Inc.)

SPEEDRY CHEMICAL PRODUCTS INC. (NY)
Name changed to Magic Marker Corp. (NY) and Class A Common 50¢ par reclassified as Common 50¢ par 05/23/1966
Magic Marker Corp. (NY) reincorporated in Delaware 09/00/1975
(See Magic Marker Corp. (DE))

SPEEDSPORT BRANDING INC (NV)
Name changed to CannLabs, Inc. 06/12/2014

SPEEDUS COM (DE)
Name changed to Speedus Corp. 06/06/2002

SPEEDWARE CORP (CANADA)
Merged into Activant Solutions Inc. 4/5/2005
Each share Common no par exchanged for $3.91 cash

SPEEDY MUFFLER KING INC (ON)
Name changed to SMK Speedy International, Inc. 7/20/98
(See SMK Speedy International, Inc.)

SPEER CARBON CO. (NY)
Recapitalized 7/31/59
Common $2.50 par changed to $1.25 par and (1) additional share issued
Acquired by Air Reduction Co., Inc. 8/31/61
7% Preferred $100 par received $101.75 cash; Common exchanged on a (1) for (2.25) basis

SPEER CARBON CO. (PA)
Reincorporated under laws of New York under plan of merger in 1952
Each share 7% Preferred $100 par exchanged for (1) share new 7% Preferred $100 par
Each share Common no par exchanged for (1) share Common $2.50 par
Speer Carbon Co. (N.Y.) was acquired by Air Reduction Co., Inc. 8/31/61

SPEER DARROW MGMT INC (ON)
Name changed to Rex Diamond Mining Corp. (ON) 09/14/1995
Rex Diamond Mining Corp. (ON) reincorporated in Yukon 07/13/2000 which reorganized in Ontario as Rex Opportunity Corp. 11/09/2011

SPEIDEL NEWSPAPERS INC (DE)
Merged into Gannett Co., Inc. (Old) 05/11/1977
Each share Common $1 par exchanged for (0.8) share Common $1 par
Gannett Co., Inc. (Old) name changed to TEGNA Inc. 06/26/2015

SPEIZMAN INDS INC (DE)
Reincorporated 03/29/1974
State of incorporation changed from (NC) to (DE) and Common no par changed to 10¢ par 03/29/1974
Plan of reorganization under Chapter 11 Federal Bankruptcy Code effective 02/08/2005
No stockholders' equity

SPELLING AARON PRODTNS INC (CA)
Reorganized under the laws of Delaware as Spelling Entertainment, Inc. and Class A Common no par changed to 1¢ par 03/01/1989
Spelling Entertainment, Inc. merged into Charter Co. 07/30/1992 which name changed to Spelling Entertainment Group Inc. (FL) 10/14/1992 which reincorporated in Delaware 05/30/1995
(See Spelling Entertainment Group Inc.)

SPELLING ENTMT GROUP INC (DE)
Reincorporated 05/30/1995
State of incorporation changed from (FL) to (DE) 05/30/1995
Merged into Viacom Inc. (Old) 06/23/1999
Each share Common 10¢ par exchanged for $9.75 cash

SPELLING ENTMT INC (DE)
Merged into Charter Co. 07/30/1992
Each share Class A Common 1¢ par exchanged for (1) share Common 10¢ par
Charter Co. name changed to Spelling Entertainment Group Inc. (FL) 10/14/1992 which reincorporated in Delaware 05/30/1995
(See Spelling Entertainment Group Inc.)

SPELLMAN ENGR INC (FL)
Plan of Arrangement under Chapter XI bankruptcy proceedings confirmed 07/08/1966
No stockholders' equity

SPELNA CAP CORP (CANADA)
Name changed to NX Phase Capital Inc. 11/28/2007

SPENCAR EXPLS LTD (BC)
Name changed to American Fibre Corp. 04/17/1986
American Fibre Corp. merged into Heritage American Resource Corp. 07/25/1994 which recapitalized as Heritage Explorations Ltd. 09/17/2001 which merged into St Andrew Goldfields Ltd. 08/22/2005 which merged into Kirkland Lake Gold Inc. 01/29/2016 which merged into Kirkland Lake Gold Ltd. 12/06/2016

SPENCE & GREEN CHEM CO (TX)
Charter forfeited for failure to pay taxes 12/2/85

SPENCER CHAIN STORES, INC.
Name changed to Spencer Shoe Corp. in 1937
Spencer Shoe Corp. name changed to Spencer Companies, Inc. 9/22/70 which was acquired by Baker (J.), Inc. 4/15/89

SPENCER CHEMICAL CO. (MO)
4.20% Preferred $100 par called for redemption 1/23/54
Each share Common $2 par exchanged for (1.25) shares Common $6 par in 1949
Common $6 par split (2) for (1) by issuance of (1) additional share 7/1/60
Completely liquidated 5/4/64
Each share Common $6 par exchanged for first and final distribution of $41 cash

SPENCER COS INC (MA)
2% Conv. Participating Preferred $100 par called for redemption 11/11/70
Acquired by Baker (J), Inc. 4/15/89
Each share Common $1 par exchanged for (0.04) share Common 50¢ par
Baker (J) Inc. name changed to Casual Male Corp. 2/26/2001
(See Casual Male Corp.)

SPENCER FOODS INC (DE)
Each share Common $1 par exchanged for (1/43,000) share Common $43,000 par 01/27/1979
Note: In effect holders received $12 cash per share and public interest eliminated

SPENCER GIFTS, INC. (NJ)
Common 25¢ par split (5) for (3) by issuance of (2/3) additional share 3/25/65
Common 25¢ par split (5) for (4) by issuance of (0.25) additional share 4/29/66
Stock Dividend - 10% 2/28/64
Merged into MCA Inc. 4/30/68
Each share Common 25¢ par exchanged for (1/3) share Common no par
(See MCA Inc.)

SPENCER GREAN FUND, INC. (NY)
Name changed to Heritage Fund, Inc. 08/15/1956
Heritage Fund, Inc. name changed to American Heritage Fund, Inc. 08/30/1976
(See American Heritage Fund, Inc.)

SPENCER KELLOGG & SONS, INC. (NY)
See - Kellogg (Spencer) & Sons, Inc.

SPENCER KENNEDY LABS INC (MA)
Completely liquidated 11/21/79
Each share Common $1 par exchanged for first and final distribution of (0.03362) share Computer Devices, Inc. (MA) Common 1¢ par
Computer Devices, Inc. reorganized in Maryland 6/30/86
(See Computer Devices, Inc. (MD))

SPENCER LABORATORIES, INC. (NJ)
Merged into Unimed, Inc. 9/6/62
Each share Class A and/or B Common exchanged for (44) shares Common $1 par
Unimed, Inc. name changed to Unimed Pharmaceuticals Inc. 5/2/94
(See Unimed Pharmaceuticals Inc.)

SPENCER MILLS, INC.
Reorganized as Spindale Mills, Inc. in 1939

SPENCER PACKING CO (IA)
Reincorporated under the laws of Delaware as Spencer Foods, Inc. 03/01/1970
(See Spencer Foods, Inc.)

SPENCER SHOE CORP (MA)
Common no par changed to $1 par in 1952
Common $1 par split (5) for (4) by issuance of (0.25) additional share 9/29/61
Common $1 par split (2) for (1) by issuance of (1) additional share 4/17/69
Name changed to Spencer Companies, Inc. 9/22/70
Spencer Companies, Inc. acquired by Baker (J.), Inc. 4/15/89 which name changed to Casual Male Corp. 2/26/2001
(See Casual Male Corp.)

SPENCER TELEFILM, INC. (TX)
Dissolved 12/21/61
No stockholders' equity

SPENCER TURBINE CO (CT)
Merged into Matrix Capital 05/02/2007
Each share Common no par exchanged for $21.863114 cash
Each share Common no par received an initial additional distribution of $1.9745 cash from escrow 12/01/2008
Each share Common no par received a second additional distribution of $0.08906073 cash from escrow 02/11/2009
Each share Common no par received a third additional distribution of $0.30169994 cash from escrow 03/13/2009
Each share Common no par received a fourth additional distribution of $0.0017783 cash from escrow 05/26/2010
Each share Common no par received a fifth additional distribution of $1.4033149 cash from escrow 06/07/2012
Each share Common no par received a sixth additional distribution of $0.129176 cash from escrow 08/07/2013

SPENCER URANIUM CORP. (UT)
Charter suspended for non-payment of taxes 9/30/60

SPENCERS RESTAURANTS INC (DE)
Recapitalized as WSR Energy Resources Inc. 07/02/2001
Each share Common $0.001 par exchanged for (0.01) share Common $0.001 par
WSR Energy Resources Inc. recapitalized as Biomass Resources Corp. 02/17/2006 which recapitalized as Eagle Resource Holdings, Inc. 05/31/2007

SPENDSMART PMTS CO (CO)
Each share old Common $0.001 par exchanged for (0.06666666) share new Common $0.001 par 04/25/2013
Reincorporated under the laws of Delaware as SpendSmart Networks, Inc. 06/20/2014

SPENDTHRIFT FARM INC (KY)
Administratively dissolved 11/1/91

SPERRY & HUTCHINSON CO (NJ)
$3 Conv. Preference no par called for redemption 06/15/1981
Merged into Baldwin-United Corp. 10/28/1981
Each share Common $1 par exchanged for $36 cash

SPERRY CORP. OLD (DE)
Common $1 par split (2) for (1) by issuance of (1) additional share 00/00/1954
Merged into Sperry Rand Corp. 06/30/1955
Each share Common $1 par exchanged for (3.25) shares Common 50¢ par
Sperry Rand Corp. name changed to Sperry Corp. (New) 08/01/1979 which merged into Burroughs Corp. (DE) 09/16/1986 which name changed to Unisys Corp. 11/13/1986

SPERRY CORP NEW (DE)
Merged into Burroughs Corp. (DE) 09/16/1986
Each share Common 50¢ par exchanged for (0.918) share Conv. Preferred Ser. A $1 par and $30.60 cash
Burroughs Corp. (DE) name changed to Unisys Corp. 11/13/1986

SPERRY FLOUR CO.
Acquired by General Mills, Inc. in 1929
Details not available

SPERRY RAND CORP. (DE)
$4.50 Preferred $25 par called for redemption 07/01/1968
Name changed to Sperry Corp. (New) 08/01/1979
Sperry Corp. (New) merged into Burroughs Corp. (DE) 09/16/1986 which name changed to Unisys Corp. 11/13/1986

SPERTI DRUG CORP (DE)
Under plan of merger each share Common 10¢ par automatically became (1) share Sperti Drug Products, Inc. Common 10¢ par 8/31/70
(See Sperti Drug Products, Inc.)

SPERTI DRUG PRODS INC (OH)
Common no par split (2) for (1) by issuance of (1) additional share 2/27/86
Charter forfeited for failure to maintain a registered agent 6/17/91

SPERTI FOODS, INC.
Name changed to Sperti Products, Inc. in 1950
(See Sperti Products, Inc.)

SPERTI PRODS INC (OH)
Common $1 par changed to 50¢ par and (1) additional share issued 6/7/61
5% Conv. Preferred $10 par called for redemption 3/1/63
Merged into Sperti Drug Products, Inc. 8/31/70
Each share Common 50¢ par exchanged for (1) share Common no par
(See Sperti Drug Products, Inc.)

SPERZEL NV INC (NV)
Reorganized as Asia Media Communications Ltd. 02/17/1994
Each share Common 1¢ par exchanged for (0.1) share Common 1¢ par
Asia Media Communications Ltd. name changed to MyWeb Inc.com 04/28/1999
(See MyWeb Inc.com)

SPESCOM SOFTWARE INC (CA)
Name changed to Enterprise Informatics, Inc. 5/16/2007

SPEX GROUP INC (DE)
Merged into a private company 7/1/88
Each share Common 1¢ par exchanged for $0.236 cash

SPEX INDS INC (NJ)
Common 10¢ par split (5) for (4) by issuance of (0.25) additional share 3/23/81
Stock Dividend - 100% 4/23/69
Merged into Spex Group, Inc. 2/27/84
Each share Common 10¢ par exchanged for (4.75) shares Common 1¢ par
(See Spex Group, Inc.)

SPEYSIDE VENTURES INC (BC)
Name changed to Trandirect.com Technologies Inc. 7/19/99
Trandirect.com Technologies Inc. recapitalized as Consolidated Trandirect.com Technologies Inc. 8/14/2000 which name changed to International Samuel Exploration Corp. 6/20/2001

SPG PPTYS INC (MD)
Under plan of merger each share 8.75% Preferred Ser. B $0.0001 par and 7.89% Step Up Preferred Ser. C $0.0001 par automatically became (1) share Simon Property Group, Inc. 8.75% Preferred Ser. F or 7.89% Step Up Preferred Ser. G respectively
Each share Common exchanged for $26.28 cash 7/1/2001

SPHERE DEV LTD (BC)
Struck off register and declared dissolved for failure to file returns 01/17/1977

SPHERE DRAKE HLDGS LTD (BERMUDA)
Merged into Fairfax Financial Holdings Ltd. 12/03/1997
Each share Common 1¢ par

SPHERE FTSE ASIA SUSTAINABLE YIELD INDEX ETF (ON)
Under plan of merger each Hedged Common Unit automatically became (1.015327) Sphere FTSE Canada Sustainable Yield Index ETF Unhedged Common Units 01/11/2018

SPHERE FTSE US SUSTAINABLE YIELD INDEX ETF (ON)
Under plan of merger each Hedged Common Unit automatically became (0.925575) Sphere FTSE Canada Sustainable Yield Index ETF Unhedged Common Unit 01/11/2018

SPHERE OF LANGUAGE (NV)
Reorganized as Clean Power Technologies, Inc. 06/16/2006
Each share Common $0.001 par exchanged for (4) shares Common $0.001 par

SPHERE 3D CORP OLD (ON)
Under plan of reorganization each share Common no par automatically became (1) share Sphere 3D Corp. (New) Common no par 03/24/2015

SPHERION CORP (DE)
Name changed to SFN Group, Inc. 03/01/2010
(See SFN Group, Inc.)

SPHINX INTL INC (FL)
Liquidation completed
Each share Common 1¢ par received initial distribution of $0.65 cash payable 5/18/2001 to holders of record 5/10/2001
Each share Common 1¢ par received second distribution of $1 cash payable 5/9/2002 to holders of record 5/2/2002 Ex date - 5/10/2002
Each share Common 1¢ par received third distribution of $0.50 cash payable 11/12/2002 to holders of record 11/1/2002 Ex date - 11/18/2002
Each share Common 1¢ par exchanged for fourth and final distribution of $0.5268 cash 8/8/2003

SPHINX NAT RES INC (DE)
Reincorporated 05/04/1990
Name changed 06/28/1991
Each share Common no par exchanged for (0.1) share Common $0.001 par 12/26/1989
Place of incorporation changed from (BC) to (DE) 05/04/1990
Common $0.001 par split (5) for (1) by issuance of (4) additional shares 01/22/1991
Name changed from Sphinx Mining Inc. to Sphinx Natural Resources, Inc. 06/28/1991
Each share new Common $0.001 par exchanged for (0.1) share Common no par 05/24/1993
Stock Dividend - 20% payable 08/09/1991 to holders of record 07/10/1991
Name changed to Malvy Technology, Inc. 06/16/1993
Malvy Technology, Inc. name changed to Metal Recovery Technologies Inc. 06/30/1995
(See Metal Recovery Technologies Inc.)

SPHINX PHARMACEUTICALS CORP (DE)
Merged into Lilly (Eli) & Co. 09/09/1994
Each share Common 1¢ par exchanged for $6 cash

SPI ACQUISITION CORP. (MA)
Involuntarily dissolved 1/4/91
Details not available

SPI ENERGY CO LTD (CAYMAN ISLANDS)
ADS agreement terminated 09/18/2017
Each Sponsored ADS for Ordinary exchanged for (10) shares Ordinary $0.000001 par

SPI HLDG INC (DE)
Reorganized under Chapter 11 Federal Bankruptcy Code 11/23/1992
Each share 16% Preferred 1¢ par exchanged for (0.30785) share Class B Common $0.001 par and (0.38717) Contingent Value Right which expired 11/23/1995
Name changed to Spectravision Inc. 05/25/1994
Spectravision Inc. reorganized as On Command Corp. 10/08/1996 which merged into Liberty Media Corp. (New) 12/08/2003 which reorganized as Liberty Media Corp. (Incorporated 02/28/2006) 05/10/2006 which name changed to Liberty Interactive Corp. 09/26/2011 which name changed to Qurate Retail, Inc. 04/10/2018

SPI PHARMACEUTICALS INC (DE)
Common 1¢ par split (2) for (1) by issuance of (1) additional share 04/22/1985
Common 1¢ par split (6) for (5) by issuance of (0.2) additional share 08/14/1989
Stock Dividends - 10% 04/11/1991; 15% 08/05/1991
Merged into ICN Pharmaceuticals, Inc. (New) 11/10/1994
Each share Common 1¢ par exchanged for (1) share Common 1¢ par
ICN Pharmaceuticals, Inc. (New) name changed to Valeant Pharmaceuticals International 11/12/2003 which merged into Valeant Pharmaceuticals International, Inc. (Canada) 09/28/2010 which reincorporated in British Columbia 08/09/2013

SPI SAFETY PACKAGING INTL LTD (BC)
Struck from the register and dissolved 06/21/1991

SPI-SUSPENSION & PTS INDS LTD (ISRAEL)
Each share Ordinary IS 0.25 par exchanged for (0.2) share Ordinary IS 1.25 par 01/13/1997
Ordinary IS 1.25 par changed to ILS 0.25 par 02/01/2000
Name changed to Crow Technologies 1977 Ltd. 08/31/2000

SPI WORLDWIDE INC (DE)
Name changed to Talent Alliance, Inc. 06/30/2008
Talent Alliance, Inc. name changed to Hire International, Inc. 09/24/2010 which recapitalized as TruLan Resources Inc. 11/20/2012 which recapitalized as Trinity Resources Inc. 09/18/2015

SPIC & SPAN INC (WI)
Each share Common $1 par exchanged for (0.004) share Common $1 par 05/04/1974
Note: In effect holders received $4 cash per share and public interest was eliminated

SPICE DEPOT INC (NV)
Each share old Common $0.001 par exchanged for (0.25) share new Common $0.001 par 05/29/2007
Charter revoked for failure to file reports and pay taxes 02/28/2011

SPICE ENTMT INC (DE)
Merged into Playboy Enterprises Inc. 03/15/1999
Each share Common 1¢ par exchanged for (0.1133) share Class B Common 1¢ par, (0.125) share Directrix, Inc. Common 1¢ par and $3.60 cash
(See each company's listing)

SPICER MANUFACTURING CORP.
Reorganized as Dana Corp. 00/00/1946
Each share Common no par exchanged for (3) shares Common $1 par
(See Dana Corp.)

SPICOLOGY INC (CA)
Each share old Common $0.001 par exchanged for (2) shares new Common $0.001 par 11/13/2001
Name changed to Leftbid Corp. 11/28/2001

SPICY GOURMET MFG INC (DE)
Name changed to BullsNBears.com, Inc. 11/16/2012
BullsNBears.com, Inc. name changed to Michael James Enterprises, Inc. 12/11/2015

SPICY PICKLE FRANCHISING INC (CO)
Name changed to Capital Franchising, Inc. (CO) 10/08/2013
Capital Franchising, Inc. (CO) reorganized in Delaware as Jubilee4 Gold, Inc. 05/27/2014 which recapitalized as Helix TCS, Inc. 11/03/2015

SPIDER RES INC (CANADA)
Merged into Cliffs Natural Resources Inc. 10/06/2010
Each share Common no par exchanged for $0.19 cash

SPIDER URANIUM MINING CO., INC. (ID)
Recapitalized as Standard Systems International, Inc. 12/8/69
Each share Capital Stock 10¢ par exchanged for (0.2) share Capital Stock 50¢ par
Standard Systems International, Inc. charter forfeited 11/30/73

SPIDERBOY INTL INC (MN)
Reorganized under the laws of Delaware as Charys Holding Co., Inc. 07/20/2004
Each share Common no par exchanged for (0.1) share Common $0.001 par
(See Charys Holding Co., Inc.)

SPIEGEL, INC. (DE)
Ctfs. dated prior to 11/1/65
Each share Common no par exchanged for (5) shares Common $2 par in 1937
Common $2 par changed to no par and (0.5) additional share issued 10/7/59
Stock Dividend - 10% 1/2/59
Acquired by Beneficial Finance Co. 11/1/65
Each share $4.50 Preferred no par exchanged for (1) share 4-1/2% Preferred $100 par or $102.50 in cash plus accrued dividends to 11/1/65 option to receive
4-1/2% Preferred expires after 11/22/65
Each share Common no par exchanged for (1/3) share Common $1 par and (0.25) share $4.30 Conv. Preferred no par
Beneficial Finance Co. name changed to Beneficial Corp. (New) 5/1/70 which merged into Household International, Inc. 6/30/98 which merged into HSBC Holdings PLC 3/28/2003

SPIEGEL, MAY, STERN CO., INC.
Name changed to Spiegel, Inc. in 1937
Spiegel, Inc. was acquired by Beneficial Finance Co. 11/1/65 which name changed to Beneficial Corp. (New) 5/1/70

SPIEGEL INC (DE)
Ctfs. dated after 10/14/87
Non-Vtg. Class A Common $1 par split (2) for (1) by issuance of (1) additional share 11/2/93
Plan of reorganization under Chapter 11 Federal Bankruptcy Code effective 6/21/2005
No stockholders' equity

SPIEGL FARMS INC (DE)
Recapitalized as Spiegl Foods, Inc. 1/2/66
Each share Common no par exchanged for (0.25) share Common $1 par
(See Spiegl Foods, Inc.)

SPIEGL FOODS INC (DE)
Common $1 par changed to 50¢ par and (1) additional share issued 04/06/1971
Common 50¢ par changed to 33-1/3¢ par and (0.5) additional share issued 12/15/1972
100% acquired by Balfour, Guthrie & Co. through purchase offer which expired 06/24/1974
Public interest eliminated

SPIEKER PPTYS INC (MD)
Merged into Equity Office Properties Trust 7/2/2001
Each share 9.45% Preferred Ser. B $0.001 par exchanged for (1) share Preferred Ser. D 1¢ par
Each share 7.875% Preferred Ser. C $0.001 par exchanged for (1) share Preferred Ser. E 1¢ par
Each share 8% Preferred Ser. E $0.001 par exchanged for (1) share Preferred Ser. F 1¢ par
Each share Common $0.0001 par exchanged for (1.49586) shares Common 1¢ par and $13.50 cash
(See Equity Office Properties Trust)

SPIGADORO INC (DE)
Charter cancelled and declared inoperative and void for non-payment of taxes 03/01/2004

SPIKE-REDWATER OIL CO., LTD. (ON)
Charter reported cancelled in 1959

SPILLANE-FELLOWS PRODUCTIONS, INC. (TN)
Charter revoked for non-payment of taxes 1/30/75

SPINA INC (DE)
Name changed to Piccard Medical Corp. 08/31/1999
(See Piccard Medical Corp.)

SPINA PORCUPINE MINES, LTD. (ON)
Name changed to Coloma Resources Ltd. 7/7/82
(See Coloma Resources Ltd.)

SPINDALE MLS INC (DE)
Stock Dividend - Payable to holders of Common in shares of Common - 10% 6/15/67; Payable to holders of Common and Class B Common in shares of Class B Common - 15% 10/1/68; 100% 2/20/74
Liquidation completed
Each share Common $10 par received initial distribution of $8.64 cash 2/27/98
Each share Common $10 par received second and final distribution of $1.95 cash in 1999
Note: It is unknown if holders were required to surrender certificates to receive payment

SPINDLE OIL & GAS INC (CO)
Administratively dissolved 11/01/1998

SPINDLE TOP ENERGY & RES INC (ON)
Merged into Flying Cross Resources Ltd. 12/04/1985
Each share Common no par exchanged for (1/3) share Common no par

Flying Cross Resources Ltd. merged into International Larder Minerals Inc. 05/01/1986 which merged into Explorers Alliance Corp. 10/13/2000
(See Explorers Alliance Corp.)

SPINDLETOP OIL & GAS CO (UT)
Merged into Spindletop Oil & Gas Co. (TX) 7/13/90
Each share Common 1¢ par exchanged for (1) share Common $0.001 par

SPINE PAIN MGMT INC (DE)
Name changed to Spine Injury Solutions, Inc. 10/08/2015

SPINE-TECH INC (MN)
Issue Information - 3,500,000 shares COM offered at $9 per share on 06/22/1995
Merged into Sulzer Medica Ltd. 1/30/98
Each share Common 1¢ par exchanged for $52 cash

SPINET GOLD MINES LTD. (ON)
Charter cancelled for non-compliance with corporation laws 4/29/63
Capital Stock worthless

SPINET MINING CO. LTD.
Succeeded by Spinet Gold Mines Ltd. in 1946
(See Spinet Gold Mines Ltd.)

SPINK ARMS BUILDING CO.
Reorganized as Spink Arms Hotel Corp. in 1943
Each share Preferred exchanged for (1) share Common or $2.87 in cash
Spink Arms Hotel Corp. charter revoked 6/30/78

SPINK ARMS HOTEL CORP. (IN)
Charter revoked for failure to file annual reports 6/30/78

SPINNAKER DEV CORP (ON)
Delisted from Toronto Stock Exchange 9/2/94

SPINNAKER EXPL CO (DE)
Issue Information - 8,000,000 shares COM offered at $14.50 per share on 09/28/1999
Merged into Norsk Hydro A.S.A. 12/13/2005
Each share Common 1¢ par exchanged for $65.50 cash

SPINNAKER INDS INC (DE)
Common no par split (3) for (2) by issuance (0.5) additional share 12/30/94
Common no par split (3) for (2) by issuance (0.5) additional share 12/29/95
Common no par reclassified as Class A Common no par 8/1/96
Plan of reorganization under Chapter 11 Federal Bankruptcy Code effective 6/6/2003
No stockholders' equity

SPINNAKER RECREATIONAL DEV CORP (CANADA)
Name changed to Health Development Services Inc. (Canada) 12/5/86
Health Development Services Inc. (Canada) reincorporated in Ontario as Spinnaker Development Corp. 10/30/90
(See Spinnaker Development Corp.)

SPINNAKER SOFTWARE CORP (MN)
Merged into SoftKey International Inc. 02/04/1994
Each share Common 1¢ par exchanged for (0.1624) share Common 1¢ par
SoftKey International Inc. name changed to Learning Co. Inc. 10/24/1996 which merged into Mattel, Inc. 05/13/1999

SPINNER CORP (UT)
Each share old Common $0.001 par exchanged for (0.025) share new Common $0.001 par 05/01/1986

Name changed to American Confectionery Corp. 03/15/1990
(See American Confectionery Corp.)

SPINRITE INCOME FD (ON)
Trust Units no par called for redemption at $2.25 on 11/21/2007

SPINROCKET COM INC (DE)
Name changed to Connectivcorp 09/11/2000
Connectivcorp name changed to Majesco Holdings Inc. 04/14/2004 which name changed to Majesco Entertainment Co. 04/11/2005 which name changed to PolarityTE, Inc. 01/11/2017

SPINTEK GAMING TECHNOLOGIES INC (NV)
Reincorporated 08/24/1998
State of incorporation changed from (CA) to (NV) 08/24/1998
Assets sold for the benefit of creditors 03/28/2001
Stockholders' equity unlikely

SPIRAL ENERGY TECH INC (NV)
Recapitalized as Exactus, Inc. 03/22/2016
Each share Common $0.0001 par exchanged for (0.03380102) share Common $0.0001 par

SPIRAL ENGR CORP (BC)
Name changed to Spiral Optics Inc. 1/17/89
(See Spiral Optics Inc.)

SPIRAL METAL INC (DE)
Reincorporated 05/30/1975
State of incorporation changed from (NJ) to (DE) and Common 10¢ par changed to 1¢ par 05/30/1975
Stock Dividends - 100% 06/05/1968; 50% 03/20/1969
Under plan of merger each share Common 1¢ par exchanged for $0.0152 cash 07/05/1985

SPIRAL OPTICS INC. (BC)
Struck off register and declared dissolved for failure to file returns 7/24/92

SPIRATONE INTERNATIONAL, INC. (DE)
Charter cancelled and declared inoperative and void for non-payment of taxes 3/1/90

SPIRE ENERGY LTD (AB)
Acquired by Quintana Minerals Resources Corp. 6/6/2002
Each share Common no par exchanged for $2.41 cash

SPIRE INC (MD)
Each Corporate Unit automatically became (0.8712) share Common $1 par 04/03/2017
(Additional Information in Active)

SPIRE INTL INC (UT)
Name changed to Sento Technical Innovations Corp. 09/10/1996
Sento Technical Innovations Corp. name changed to Sento Corp. 08/11/1998
(See Sento Corp.)

SPIRE VENTURES LTD (BC)
Recapitalized as Consolidated Spire Ventures Ltd. 01/04/2001
Each share Common no par exchanged for (0.5) share Common no par
Consolidated Spire Ventures Ltd. recapitalized as Berkwood Resources Ltd. 12/01/2010

SPIRELLA INTERNATIONAL INC.
Dissolved in 1957

SPIRENT PLC (UNITED KINGDOM)
Each share old Sponsored ADR for Ordinary exchanged for (0.5) new Sponsored ADR for Ordinary 07/10/2001
Basis changed from (1:2) to (1:4) 07/10/2001
Name changed to Spirent Communications PLC 05/08/2006

SPIRIT CAP CORP (AB)
Reorganized as Spirit Corp. 8/30/91
Each share 1st Preferred Ser. 1 $10 par automatically became (1) share 1st Preferred Ser. 1 $10 par
Each share Common no par exchanged for (0.0625) share Common no par
Each share Class A no par automatically became (1) share Class A no par
Each share Class B no par automatically became (1) share Class B no par
Each share Class C $10 par automatically became (1) share Class C $10 par
Each share Class D $10 par automatically became (1) share Class D $10 par
Each share Class E $10 par automatically became (1) share Class E $10 par
Each share Class F $10 par automatically became (1) share Class F $10 par
Spirit Corp. merged into Best Pacific Resources Ltd. 4/22/97
(See Best Pacific Resources Ltd.)

SPIRIT CORP (AB)
Merged into Best Pacific Resources Ltd. 4/22/97
Each share Common no par exchanged for (0.15384615) share Common no par and (0.7692307) Common Stock Purchase Warrant expiring 6/30/98
(See Best Pacific Resources Ltd.)

SPIRIT ENERGY CORP. LTD. (AB)
Name changed to Spirit Capital Corp. 1/29/87
Spirit Capital Corp. reorganized as Spirit Corp. 8/30/91 which merged into Best Pacific Resources Ltd. 4/22/97

SPIRIT ENERGY CORP (BC)
Name changed to Canadian Spirit Resources Inc. (BC) 06/23/2004
Canadian Spirit Resources Inc. (BC) reincorporated in Alberta 05/25/2012

SPIRIT EXPLS LTD (BC)
Recapitalized as Cannon Resources Ltd. 07/03/1975
Each share Capital Stock 50¢ par exchanged for (0.25) share Capital Stock no par
Cannon Resources Ltd. recapitalized as Samson Gold Corp. 12/13/1983 which name changed to Kinghorn Energy Corp. 09/20/1989 which recapitalized as Kinghorn Petroleum Corp. 04/30/1991 which recapitalized as Triple 8 Energy Corp. (BC) 11/17/1992 which reincorporated in Alberta 02/24/1994 which name changed to Oilexco Inc. 03/01/1994 which recapitalized as ScotOil Petroleum Ltd. (AB) 06/09/2011 which reincorporated in British Columbia as 0915988 B.C. Ltd. 07/27/2011
(See 0915988 B.C. Ltd.)

SPIRIT FIN CORP (MD)
Issue Information - 26,086,957 shares COM offered at $11 per share on 12/15/2004
Merged into Macquarie Bank Ltd. 08/01/2007
Each share Common 1¢ par exchanged for $14.50 cash

SPIRIT INTL INC (NV)
Name changed to Jiucaitong Group Ltd. 12/07/2017

SPIRIT LAKE EXPLS LTD (ON)
Name changed to VenCan Gold Corp. 02/21/1994
VenCan Gold Corp. name changed to Red Pine Exploration Inc. 03/02/2009

SPIRIT LAKE MINES LTD (ON)
Recapitalized as Spirit Lake Explorations Ltd. 03/08/1976
Each share Capital Stock $1 par exchanged for (0.2) share Capital Stock no par
Spirit Lake Explorations Ltd. name changed to VenCan Gold Corp. 02/21/1994 which name changed to Red Pine Exploration Inc. 03/02/2009

SPIRIT PETE CORP (BC)
Recapitalized as Dryden Resource Corp. 12/16/1987
Each share Common no par exchanged for (0.33333333) share Common no par
Dryden Resource Corp. merged into Leicester Diamond Mines Ltd. 06/01/1993 which recapitalized as Target Exploration & Mining Corp. 04/30/2004 which merged into Crosshair Exploration & Mining Corp. 03/31/2009 which name changed to Crosshair Energy Corp. 11/02/2011 which recapitalized as Jet Metal Corp. (BC) 09/23/2013 which reorganized in Canada as Canada Jetlines Ltd. 03/07/2017

SPIRIT RLTY CAP INC OLD (MD)
Issue Information - 29,000,000 shares COM offered at $15 per share on 09/19/2012
Merged into Spirit Realty Capital, Inc. (New) 07/17/2013
Each share Common 1¢ par exchanged for (1.9048) shares Common 1¢ par

SPIRIT RES LTD (BC)
Reincorporated under the laws of Delaware as Hygeia Holdings Ltd. 03/03/1993
Hygeia Holdings Ltd. name changed to Novopharm Biotech Inc. (DE) 07/28/1995 which merged into Novopharm Biotech Inc. (BC) 08/25/1997 which name changed to Viventia Biotech Inc. 09/11/2000
(See Viventia Biotech Inc.)

SPIROS DEV CORP II INC (DE)
Issue Information - 5,500,000 UNITS consisting of (1) share Callable COM of Spiros Development Corp. II, Inc. and (1) WT to purchase (0.25) share of Dura Pharmaceuticals, Inc. COM offered at $16 per Unit on 12/16/1997
Units separated 12/31/1999
Merged into Dura Pharmaceuticals, Inc. 08/31/2000
Each share Common $0.001 par exchanged for (1) Common Stock Purchase Warrant expiring 09/01/2005 and $13.25 cash

SPITFIRE ENERGY LTD (AB)
Issue Information - 1,000,000 shares COM offered at $0.20 per share on 12/14/2001
Name changed to Whitecap Resources Inc. 07/12/2010

SPLASH TECHNOLOGY HLDGS INC (DE)
Merged into Electronics for Imaging, Inc. 10/23/2000
Each share Common $0.001 par exchanged $10 cash

SPLENTEX INC (DE)
Merged into Splendor Form International, Inc. 04/07/1981
Each share Common $1 par exchanged for $8 cash

SPLINEX TECHNOLOGY INC (DE)
Name changed to TOT Energy, Inc. 06/02/2008
TOT Energy, Inc. name changed to Net Element, Inc. (Old) 11/26/2010 which merged into Net Element International, Inc. 10/03/2012 which name changed to Net Element, Inc. (New) 12/09/2013

SPLINTERNET HLDGS INC (DE)
Name changed to Defenect Group, Inc. 04/05/2010

SPLIT REIT OPPORTUNITY TR (ON)
Merged into Criterion REIT Income Fund 01/04/2012
Each Preferred Security received $10.14375 cash
Each Capital Unit received (1.52) Class A Units

SPLIT ROCK LODGE INC (PA)
Name changed to Big Boulder Corp. 09/16/1975
Big Boulder Corp. merged into Blue Ridge Real Estate Co. 11/01/2013

SPLIT ROCK MINES LTD. (ON)
Charter revoked for failure to file reports and pay fees 4/22/65

SPLIT YIELD CORP (ON)
Class I Preferred no par called for redemption at $18.6989 on 02/01/2012
Class II Preferred no par called for redemption 02/01/2012
No payment will be made
Capital Shares no par called for redemption 02/01/2012
No payment will be made

SPLITDORF-BETHLEHEM ELECTRICAL CO.
Merged into Splitdorf Electrical Co. in 1931 which dissolved in 1932

SPLITDORF ELECTRICAL CO.
Dissolved in 1932

SPLITROCK SVCS INC (DE)
Merged into McLeodUSA Inc. 04/03/2000
Each share Common $0.001 par exchanged for (0.5347) share Common $0.001 par
(See McLeodUSA Inc.)

SPM GROUP INC (CO)
Each share old Common no par exchanged for (0.0002) share new Common no par 06/28/2000
Name changed to Zamage Digital Imaging Inc. (CO) 11/20/2001
Zamage Digital Imaging Inc. (CO) reorganized in Nevada as Provectus Pharmaceuticals, Inc. 04/11/2002 which reincorporated in Delaware as Provectus Biopharmaceuticals, Inc. 01/23/2014

SPO MED INC (DE)
Recapitalized as SPO Global Inc. 10/07/2013
Each share Common 1¢ par exchanged for (0.05) share Common 1¢ par

SPOKANE ENTERPRISES, INC. (WA)
Liquidation effected by transfer of liabilities to Spokane Pres-To-Log, Inc. 4/13/62
No stockholders' equity

SPOKANE-IDAHO COPPER CO.
Succeeded by Columbia Mines Corp. 00/00/1935
Details not available

SPOKANE INTERNATIONAL RAILWAY CO. (WA)
Reorganized as Spokane International Railroad Co. in 1941.
No stockholders' equity

SPOKANE MINING SYNDICATE, INC. (WA)
Automatically dissolved and declared non-existent by State of Washington for non-payment of license fees 7/1/63

SPOKANE NATURAL GAS CO. (WA)
Merged into Washington Water Power Co. on a (0.2174) for (1) basis 6/2/58
Washington Water Power Co. name changed to Avista Corp. 12/2/98

SPOKANE PORTLAND CEMENT CO. (WA)
Reorganized in 1937
Each share 7% Preferred $100 par exchanged for (2) shares Common $25 par
Each share Common $100 par received $1.50 in cash
Recapitalized in 1949
Each share Common $25 par exchanged for (4) shares Common $2 par
Dissolution approved 1/6/56

SPOKANE RES LTD (BC)
Recapitalized as SKN Resources Ltd. 7/26/2001
Each share Common no par exchanged for (0.1) share Common no par
SKN Resources Ltd. name changed to Silvercorp Metals Inc. 5/2/2005

SPOKANE SILVER & LEAD CO.
Insolvent in 1938

SPOKANE WAREHOUSE & STORAGE CO. (WA)
Charter revoked for failure to file reports and pay fees 7/1/65

SPONDA PLC (FINLAND)
ADR agreement terminated 08/06/2018
No ADR's remain outstanding

SPONGETECH DELIVERY SYS INC (DE)
Chapter 7 bankruptcy proceedings terminated 08/28/2014
No stockholders' equity

SPOOFEM COM INC (OK)
Name changed to Spoofem.com USA, Inc. 04/06/2010
Spoofem.com USA, Inc. recapitalized as Hi-Tech Crime Solutions, Corp. 10/07/2011 which name changed to Montague International Holding Ltd. 07/20/2012

SPOOFEM USA (OK)
Recapitalized as Hi-Tech Crime Solutions, Corp. 10/07/2011
Each share Common $0.001 par exchanged for (0.002) share Common $0.001 par

SPOONER GOLD MINES LTD.
Aquired by Norex Mines Ltd. on a (1) for (4) basis in 1939
Norex Mines Ltd. charter revoked 9/24/56

SPOONER MINES & OILS LTD (CANADA)
Common no par changed to 30¢ par 07/18/1956
Common 30¢ par changed to no par 03/02/1959
Recapitalized as Canadian Spooner Resources Inc. 01/09/1986
Each share Common no par exchanged for (0.33333333) share Common no par

SPOONER OILS LTD. (CANADA)
Name changed to Spooner Mines & Oils Ltd. in 1956
Spooner Mines & Oils Ltd. recapitalized as Canadian Spooner Resources Inc. 1/9/86

SPOOZ INC (NV)
Charter permanently revoked 06/01/2010

SPORRAN MINES LTD (ON)
Charter cancelled for failure to file reports and pay fees 03/16/1976

SPORT ACTIVE TELEVISION NETWORK INC (AB)
Recapitalized 03/11/1997
Recapitalized from Sports Active Inc. to Sport Active Television Network Inc. 03/11/1997
Each share Common no par exchanged for (0.25) share Common no par

Delisted from Alberta Stock Exchange 04/23/1999

SPORT CHALET INC (DE)
Each share Common 1¢ par exchanged for (0.25) share Class B Common 1¢ par 09/21/2005
Each share Class B Common 1¢ par received distribution of (7) shares Class A Common 1¢ par payable 09/29/2005 to holders of record 09/22/2005
Acquired by Vestis Retail Group, LLC 08/19/2014
Each share Class A Common 1¢ par exchanged for $1.20 cash
Each share Class B Common 1¢ par exchanged for $1.20 cash

SPORT CTRS INC NEW ENG (MA)
Voluntarily dissolved 04/27/1982
Details not available

SPORT-HALEY INC (CO)
Reincorporated under the laws of Delaware as Sport-Haley Holdings, Inc. 11/10/2011

SPORT OF KINGS INC (DE)
Reorganized under the laws of Nevada as Triad North America, Inc. 04/27/2006
Each share Common 1¢ par exchanged for (0.001) share Common $0.001 par
Triad North America, Inc. name changed to Kingslake Energy, Inc. 06/07/2006
(See Kingslake Energy, Inc.)

SPORT SHACKS INC (MN)
Name changed to Regent Enterprises, Inc. 9/2/87
(See Regent Enterprises, Inc.)

SPORT SPECIFIC INTL INC (AB)
Delisted from Alberta Stock Exchange 6/11/97

SPORT SUPPLY GROUP INC NEW (DE)
Merged into Sage Parent Co., Inc. 08/05/2010
Each share Common 1¢ par exchanged for $13.55 cash

SPORT SUPPLY GROUP INC OLD (DE)
Common 1¢ par split (5) for (4) by issuance of (0.25) additional share 03/10/1994
Merged into Collegiate Pacific Inc. 11/13/2006
Each share Common 1¢ par exchanged for $8.80 cash

SPORT TECH ENTERPRISES INC (DE)
Name changed to Online Internet Network, Inc. 06/19/2012

SPORT-TRONIX USA INC (DE)
Each share old Common $0.0001 par exchanged for (0.01) share new Common $0.0001 par 12/8/97
Name changed to Creative Gourmet Inc. 4/7/98

SPORTAN UTD INDS INC (TX)
Each share Common $0.001 par exchanged for (0.02) share Common 5¢ par 04/14/2004
Name changed to PharmaFrontiers Corp. 07/20/2004
PharmaFrontiers Corp. recapitalized as Opexa Therapeutics, Inc. 06/19/2006 which recapitalized as Acer Therapeutics Inc. (TX) 09/21/2017 which reincorporated in Delaware 05/15/2018

SPORTCO (UT)
Name changed to Pan American Investments, Inc. 12/24/79
Pan American Investments, Inc. name changed to Oxtec Medical Industries, Inc. 11/18/83 which recapitalized as Federal Medical Industries, Inc. 5/12/86
(See Federal Medical Industries, Inc.)

SPORTECH PLC (SCOTLAND)
ADR agreement terminated 1/12/2004
Each ADR for Ordinary 5p par exchanged for $0.1633 cash

SPORTECULAR INC (NY)
Each share old Common $0.0005 par exchanged for (0.1) share new Common $0.0005 par 11/21/85
Dissolved by proclamation 3/25/92

SPORTEK INTL INC (NV)
Charter revoked for failure to file reports and pay taxes 10/13/86

SPORTING GOODS, INC.
Liquidated in 1948

SPORTING LIFE INC (DE)
Charter cancelled and declared inoperative and void for non-payment of taxes 3/1/94

SPORTING MAGIC INC (DE)
Each share old Common $0.001 par exchanged for (0.8333333) share new Common $0.001 par 06/28/2001
Note: No holder of (101) shares or more will receive fewer than (100) post-split shares
Holders of (100) shares or fewer were not affected by the reverse split
New Common $0.001 par split (2) for (1) by issuance of (1) additional share payable 12/27/2001 to holders of record 12/21/2001 Ex date - 12/28/2001
Name changed to Next, Inc. 12/27/2002
(See Next, Inc.)

SPORTMART INC (DE)
Secondary Offering - 2,500,000 shares CL A offered at $14 per share on 10/19/1994
Each share old Common 1¢ par exchanged for (0.5) share new Common 1¢ par and (0.5) share Class A Common 1¢ par 9/27/94
Merged into Gart Sports Co. 1/9/98
Each share Class A Common 1¢ par exchanged for (0.165014) share Common 1¢ par 1/9/98
Each share new Common 1¢ par exchanged for (0.165014) share Common 1¢ par
Gart Sports Co. name changed to Sports Authority, Inc. (New) 8/4/2003
(See Sports Authority, Inc. (New))

SPORTO CORP (MA)
Merged out of existence 9/12/89
Details not available

SPORTS & REC INC (DE)
Common 1¢ par split (3) for (2) by issuance of (0.5) additional share 9/23/94
Reincorporated under the laws of Florida as JumboSports Inc. 2/19/97
(See JumboSports Inc.)

SPORTS ALUMNI INC (NV)
Recapitalized as CoMedia Corp. 05/17/2007
Each share Common $0.001 par exchanged for (0.00231379) share Common $0.001 par
(See CoMedia Corp.)

SPORTS ARENAS (DELAWARE) INC. (DE)
Name changed to Sports Arenas, Inc. 10/19/60

SPORTS ARENAS INC (DE)
Name changed 10/19/1960
Name changed from Sports Arenas (Delaware) Inc. to Sports Arenas, Inc. 10/19/1960
SEC revoked common stock registration 07/13/2007
Stockholders' equity unlikely

SPORTS ASSOC INC (CT)
Completely liquidated 06/20/1980
Each share Class B Common no par received first and final distribution of $0.5250 cash

FINANCIAL INFORMATION, INC.

SPORTS ASYLUM INC (NV)
Name changed to Cell MedX Corp. 10/09/2014

SPORTS AUTH INC NEW (DE)
Merged into Green Equity Investors IV, LP 05/03/2006
Each share Common 1¢ par exchanged for $37.25 cash

SPORTS AUTH INC OLD (DE)
Common 1¢ par split (3) for (2) by issuance of (0.5) additional share payable 07/16/1996 to holders of record 07/01/1996 Ex date - 07/17/1996
Merged into Sports Authority, Inc. (New) 08/04/2003
Each share Common 1¢ par exchanged for (0.37) share Common 1¢ par
(See Sports Authority, Inc. (New))

SPORTS CLUB INC (DE)
Acquired by Five Star Club Services, Inc. 03/11/2014
Each share Common 1¢ par exchanged for $1.61 cash

SPORTS CONCEPTS INC (NV)
Charter revoked for failure to file reports and pay fees 06/30/2009

SPORTS ENTMT ENTERPRISES INC (CO)
Each share old Common no par received distribution of (0.27658) share All-American SportPark, Inc. Common $0.001 par payable 05/08/2002 to holders of record 05/03/2002 Ex date - 05/01/2002
Each share old Common no par exchanged for (0.5) share new Common no par 07/15/2002
Reincorporated under the laws of Delaware as CKX, Inc. and Common no par changed to 1¢ par 03/25/2005
(See CKX, Inc.)

SPORTS/ENTMT GROUP INC (DE)
Merged into SEG Merger Corp. 2/29/96
Each share Common 1¢ par exchanged for $0.001 cash

SPORTS FILMS & TALENTS INC (MN)
Liquidation completed
Each share Common 5¢ par exchanged for $1 cash 01/10/1980
Each share Common 5¢ par received second and final distribution of $0.14957 cash 12/10/1981

SPORTS GAMING INC (FL)
Name changed to CyberGames, Inc. 04/29/1998
CyberGames, Inc. recapitalized as River Creek Holdings, Inc. 07/23/2004 which name changed to EQ Labs, Inc. 02/05/2009

SPORTS GROUP INTL INC (FL)
Name changed to Kahala Corp. (FL) 01/22/2001
Kahala Corp. (FL) reincorporated in Delaware 12/31/2012
(See Kahala Corp.)

SPORTS-GUARD INC (DE)
Recapitalized as Colmena Corp. 11/10/1997
Each share Common 1¢ par exchanged for (0.1) share Common 1¢ par
Colmena Corp. recapitalized as NetWorth Technologies, Inc. 12/16/2004 which recapitalized as Solution Technology International, Inc. 08/22/2006 which recapitalized as Reinsurance Technologies Ltd. 06/01/2009
(See Reinsurance Technologies Ltd.)

SPORTS HEROES INC (DE)
Filed a petition under Chapter 7 Federal Bankruptcy Code 10/28/96
Stockholder's equity unlikely

SPORTS INFORMATION & PUBG CORP (CO)
Name changed to In Vivo Medical Diagnostics, Inc. 9/27/2004
In Vivo Medical Diagnostics, Inc. name changed to In Veritas Medical Diagnostics, Inc. 4/8/2005

SPORTS INFORMATION DATA BASE INC (DE)
Charter cancelled and declared inoperative and void for non-payment of taxes 6/23/86

SPORTS INTL INC (OH)
Name changed to Startec Inc. 11/19/92

SPORTS INTL LTD (DE)
Name changed to Interactive Gaming & Communications Corp. (Old) 2/26/96
Interactive Gaming & Communications Corp. (Old) name changed to GlobSpan Technology Partners, Inc. 2/2/2000 which name changed to GlobeSpan Technology Partners, Inc. 2/10/2000 which name changed to Interactive Gaming & Communications Corp. (New) 9/27/2000 which recapitalized as Great American Financial Corp. 4/1/2003

SPORTS LD CORP (DE)
Name changed to Hawaii Land Corp. 03/08/1974
(See Hawaii Land Corp.)

SPORTS MGMT & REC INC (NV)
Common $0.001 par split (10) for (1) by issuance of (9) additional shares payable 8/6/2004 to holders of record 8/6/2004 Ex date - 8/11/2004
Name changed to Lauraan Corp. 8/11/2004
Lauraan Corp. recapitalized as Special Projects Group, Ltd. 2/17/2006

SPORTS MEDIA INC (DE)
Charter cancelled and declared inoperative and void for non-payment of taxes 3/1/97

SPORTS MKTG INC (MN)
Proclaimed dissolved for failure to file annual reports 12/31/93

SPORTS PPTYS ACQUISITION CORP (DE)
Liquidation completed
Each Unit exchanged for initial distribution of $9.91021907 cash 01/27/2010
Each share Common $0.001 par exchanged for initial distribution of $9.91021907 cash 01/27/2010
Each Unit received second distribution of $0.06958523 cash payable 04/20/2010 to holders of record 01/27/2010
Each share Common $0.001 par received second distribution of $0.06958523 cash payable 04/20/2010 to holders of record 01/27/2010
Each Unit received third and final distribution of $0.0557672 cash payable 02/23/2011 to holders of record 01/27/2010
Each share Common $0.001 par received third and final distribution of $0.0557672 cash payable 02/23/2011 to holders of record 01/27/2010

SPORTS RESORTS INTL INC (MI)
Common 10¢ par split (2) for (1) by issuance of (1) additional share payable 9/6/2001 to holders of record 8/9/2001 Ex date - 9/7/2001
Under plan of merger each share Common 10¢ par exchanged for $1 cash 3/30/2006

SPORTS RESTAURANTS INC (DE)
Charter cancelled and declared inoperative and void for non-payment of taxes 03/01/2000

SPORTS RESTAURANTS INC (NV)
Charter revoked for failure to file reports and pay fees 04/01/1990

SPORTS SCIENCES INC (OH)
Reincorporated under the laws of Delaware as Smart Games Interactive, Inc. and Common no par changed to $0.0002 par 10/11/1996
Smart Games Interactive, Inc. name changed to Yifan Communications, Inc. 07/28/2000
(See Yifan Communications, Inc.)

SPORTS SOURCE INC (DE)
Common $0.001 par split (2) for (1) by issuance of (1) additional share payable 3/6/2006 to holders of record 3/3/2006 Ex date - 3/7/2006
Name changed to New Oriental Energy & Chemical Corp. 11/22/2006

SPORTS-STUFF COM INC (NV)
Name changed to Mobilized Entertainment, Inc. 03/03/2008

SPORTS SUPPLEMENT GROUP INC (NV)
Name changed to CarSmartt, Inc. 02/14/2018

SPORTS SYS INC (DE)
Name changed to Ora Industries, Inc. 04/06/1973
Ora Industries, Inc. name changed to Hospitality Health Care, Inc. 09/28/1977
(See Hospitality Health Care, Inc.)

SPORTS-TECH INC (NV)
Recapitalized as All-Comm Media Corp. 08/23/1995
Each share Common 1¢ par exchanged for (0.25) share Common 1¢ par
All-Comm Media Corp. name changed to Marketing Services Group, Inc. 07/01/1997 which name changed to MKTG Services, Inc. 03/26/2002 which name changed to Media Services Group, Inc. 12/26/2003 which name changed to MSGI Security Solutions, Inc. 02/09/2005
(See MSGI Security Solutions, Inc.)

SPORTS TECH INTL INC (DE)
Merged into Bristol Holdings Inc. 3/31/92
Each share Common 1¢ par exchanged for (1.2) shares Common 1¢ par
Bristol Holdings Inc. name changed to Sports-Tech, Inc. 4/20/92 which recapitalized as All-Comm Media Corp. 8/23/95 which name changed to Marketing Services Group, Inc. 7/1/97 which name changed to MKTG Services, Inc. 3/26/2002 which name changed to Media Services Group, Inc. 12/26/2003 which name changed to MSGI Security Solutions, Inc. 2/9/2005

SPORTS TIME INC (NV)
Each share Common $0.001 par exchanged for (1/6) share Common $0.005 par 11/09/1993
Each share old Common $0.005 par exchanged for (0.25) share new Common $0.005 par 05/06/1996
Name changed to Group Seven Communications Inc. 02/27/1997
Group Seven Communications Inc. recapitalized as Zcom Networks, Inc. 03/12/2007 which recapitalized as Global Gateway Media & Communications, Inc. 12/02/2009

SPORTS UNDERWRITERS INC (TX)
Charter forfeited for failure to pay taxes 03/10/1975

SPORTS WHEELS INC (NV)
Common 2¢ par split (10) for (1) by issuance of (9) additional shares payable 04/17/2003 to holders of record 04/09/2003 Ex date - 04/21/2003
Common 2¢ par split (10) for (1) by issuance of (9) additional shares payable 11/05/2003 to holders of record 10/20/2003 Ex date - 11/06/2003
Recapitalized as Automotive Specialty Concepts, Inc. 02/01/2005
Each share Common 2¢ par exchanged for (0.01) share Common 2¢ par
Automotive Specialty Concepts, Inc. name changed to Drake Gold Resources, Inc. 02/13/2006 which name changed to Universal Apparel & Textile Co. 04/27/2015

SPORTSCENE RESTAURANTS INC (CANADA)
8% Non-Vtg. Preferred called for redemption at $2.25 on 05/01/2003
Class A Common no par split (3) for (2) by issuance of (0.5) additional share 01/29/2004
Name changed to Sportscene Group Inc. 01/23/2006

SPORTSCLICK INC (AB)
Assets sold for the benefit of creditors 08/05/2010
Stockholders' equity unlikely

SPORTSCOACH CORP (CA)
Name changed to Transtec Corp. 07/03/1978
Transtec Corp. name changed to Automoco Corp. 06/14/1979
(See Automoco Corp.)

SPORTSEND INC (NV)
SEC revoked common stock registration 11/24/2010

SPORTSLAND SALES INC (NV)
Recapitalized as Medtex Corp. 11/13/94
Each share Common $0.001 par exchanged for (1/30) share Common $0.001 par
Medtex Corp. recapitalized as Opal Technologies Inc. 7/7/97

SPORTSLINE COM INC (DE)
Name changed 11/19/99
Issue Information - 3,500,000 shares COM offered at $8 per share on 11/13/1997
Name changed from Sportsline USA, Inc. to Sportsline.com Inc. 11/19/99
Merged into Viacom Inc. (Old) 12/10/2004
Each share Common 1¢ par exchanged for $1.75 cash

SPORTSMAN CAMPING CTRS AMER INC (UT)
Name changed to Sportco 12/2/76
Sportco name changed to Pan American Investments, Inc. 12/24/79 which name changed to Oxtec Medical Industries, Inc. 11/18/83 which recapitalized as Federal Medical Industries, Inc. 5/12/86
(See Federal Medical Industries, Inc.)

SPORTSMANS GUIDE INC (MN)
Each share old Common 1¢ par exchanged for (0.1) share new Common 1¢ par 3/5/97
New Common 1¢ par split (3) for (2) by issuance of (0.5) additional share payable 4/15/2005 to holders of record 3/25/2005 Ex date - 4/18/2005
Merged into Redcats USA, Inc. 8/31/2006
Each share new Common 1¢ par exchanged for $31 cash

SPORTSMANS RESORTS INTL INC (NV)
Name changed to Business Resources Inc. 06/04/1986
(See Business Resources Inc.)

SPORTSMANS WHSL CO (NV)
Each share old Common $0.0001 par exchanged for (1.6) shares new Common $0.0001 par 02/12/2001
Name changed to Cetalon Corp. 03/13/2001

(See Cetalon Corp.)

SPORTSMATE INTL INC (AB)
Delisted from Alberta Stock Exchange 06/15/1998

SPORTSNUTS INC (DE)
Name changed 10/06/2003
Each share Common $0.0001 par exchanged for (0.05) share Common $0.002 par 06/26/2000
Name changed from Sportsnuts.com International, Inc. to SportsNuts, Inc. 10/06/2003
Each share Common $0.002 par received distribution of (0.00449155) share Synerteck Inc. Common $0.001 par payable 11/24/2004 to holders of record 11/15/2004
Each share Common $0.002 par received distribution of (0.00412133) share Secure Netwerks, Inc. Common $0.001 par payable 03/08/2007 to holders of record 03/01/2007 Ex date - 02/27/2007
Recapitalized as FuelStream, Inc. 05/13/2010
Each share Common $0.002 par exchanged for (0.01) share Common $0.002 par

SPORTSOTRON INC (NY)
Merged into Sportsotron Sales, Inc. 11/10/1978
Each share Common 1¢ par exchanged for $3.50 cash

SPORTSPARK OF AMERICA, INC. (DE)
Recapitalized as Argos Energy Texas, Inc. 7/16/90
Each share Common $0.0001 par exchanged for (0.04) share Common $0.0025 par which changed its name to First American Energy, Inc. 8/21/90
(See First American Energy, Inc.)

SPORTSPLEX INC (NV)
Charter revoked for failure to file reports and pay fees 08/01/2005

SPORTSPRIZE ENTMT INC (NV)
Filed a petition under Chapter 7 Federal Bankruptcy Code 12/01/2000
No stockholders' equity

SPORTSPUBLICATION NET INC (CO)
Reincorporated 08/02/2004
Name and state of incorporation changed from sport-publication.net Inc. (CO) to Sportspublication.Net Inc. (NV) 08/02/2004
Common $0.001 par split (65) for (1) by issuance of (64) additional shares payable 09/27/2004 to holders of record 09/17/2004 Ex date - 09/24/2004
Name changed to Bio-Safe Natural Technologies, Inc. 09/29/2004
Bio-Safe Natural Technologies, Inc. name changed to Equal Trading Inc. 12/08/2004

SPORTSSTAR MARKETING INC (CO)
Name changed to College Bound Student Alliance, Inc. (CO) 08/03/1999
College Bound Student Alliance, Inc. (CO) reincorporated in Nevada 08/28/2000 which name changed to College Partnership, Inc. (NV) 06/03/2003 which reincorporated in Delaware as College Partnership Merger Co. 12/19/2007 which name changed to NPI08, Inc. 02/07/2008 which name changed to BlackStar Energy Group, Inc. 02/09/2010 which name changed to BlackStar Enterprise Group, Inc. 09/30/2016

SPORTSTOWN INC (DE)
Plan of liquidation approved 11/30/95
No stockholders' equity

SPORTSWAYS, INC. (CA)
Each share old Common no par exchanged for (0.5) share new Common no par 3/6/62
Name changed to Wershow (Milton J.) Enterprises 1/27/69
Wershow (Milton J.) Enterprises name changed to Jilco Industries, Inc. 7/26/72

SPORTSWORLD COMMUNICATIONS CORP. (DE)
Name changed to World Industries, Inc. (DE) 9/12/74
World Industries, Inc. (DE) recapitalized as World Corp. 3/31/76
(See World Corp.)

SPORTSWORLD 2000 INC (FL)
Administratively dissolved for failure to file annual reports 8/26/94

SPOT MOBILE INTL LTD (DE)
Each share old Common $0.001 par exchanged for (0.03333333) share new Common $0.001 par 10/29/2010
SEC revoked common stock registration 02/21/2017

SPOTLESS INC (VA)
Charter terminated 05/31/2007

SPOTTS FLORAFAX CORP (DE)
Name changed to Florafax International, Inc. 8/29/74
Florafax International, Inc. name changed to Gerald Stevens Inc. 4/30/99
(See Gerald Stevens Inc.)

SPOTTS INTL INC (MN)
Reincorporated under the laws of Delaware as Spotts Florafax Corp. and Common 20¢ par changed to 10¢ par 12/15/70
Spotts Florafax Corp. name changed to Florafax International, Inc. 8/29/74 which name changed to Gerald Stevens Inc. 4/30/99
(See Gerald Stevens Inc.)

SPR FD INC (DE)
Completely liquidated 11/09/1984
Each share Common 1¢ par exchanged for first and final distribution of (2.518) Fidelity Municipal Bond Fund Shares of Bene. Int. 1¢ par

SPR INC (DE)
Issue Information - 2,600,000 shares COM offered at $16 per share on 10/01/1997
Common 1¢ par split (3) for (2) by issuance of (0.5) additional share payable 8/28/98 to holders of record 8/14/98
Merged into Leapnet, Inc. 5/1/2000
Each share Common 1¢ par exchanged for (1.085) shares Common 1¢ par
(See Leapnet, Inc.)

SPRAGUE ELEC CO (MA)
Common $2.50 par changed to $1.25 par and (1) additional share issued 05/01/1967
Stock Dividends - 50% 12/15/1952; 50% 12/20/1954
Merged into GK Technologies, Inc. 05/26/1979
Each share Common $1.25 par exchanged for $27.50 cash

SPRAGUE ENGINEERING CORP. (CA)
Merged into Teledyne, Inc. 10/31/1963
Each (3.53) shares Common $1 par exchanged for (1) share $1 Conv. Preferred Ser. A $1 par
(See Teledyne, Inc.)

SPRAGUE-SELLS CORP.
Acquired by Bean (John) Manufacturing Co. 00/00/1928
Details not available

SPRAGUE TECHNOLOGIES INC (DE)
Name changed to STI Group, Inc. 05/29/1992
STI Group, Inc. merged into American Annuity Group, Inc. 01/07/1993 which name changed to Great American Financial Resources, Inc. 06/13/2000
(See Great American Financial Resources, Inc.)

SPRAGUE WARNER-KENNY CORP. (MD)
Name changed to Consolidated Grocers Corp. 05/29/1945
Consolidated Grocers Corp. name changed to Consolidated Foods Corp. 02/24/1954 which name changed to Sara Lee Corp. 04/02/1985 which recapitalized as Hillshire Brands Co. 06/29/2012
(See Hillshire Brands Co.)

SPRAY-AIR INTL INC (AB)
Name changed to Epicore Networks Inc. 12/23/1991
Epicore Networks Inc. recapitalized as Epicore BioNetworks Inc. 08/28/2000

SPRAY BILT INC (FL)
Name changed to Enviromatics, Inc. (FL) and Class A Common 10¢ par reclassified as Common 10¢ par 11/05/1969
Enviromatics, Inc. (FL) merged into Enviromatics, Inc. (DE) 12/21/1970 which name changed to Familian Corp. 04/14/1971
(See Familian Corp.)

SPRAY PAINTING CO. (FL)
Name changed to Kanco Tech Inc. 5/2/69
Kanco Tech Inc. name changed to Hotsy Corp. 2/27/76
(See Hotsy Corp.)

SPRAY RESORTS CORP (AB)
Recapitalized as Petrolian Resources Corp. 11/5/90
Each share Common no par exchanged for (0.25) share Common no par
Petrolian Resources Corp. merged into Startech Energy Ltd. 8/19/91

SPRAY TECH, INC. (UT)
Name changed to U.S. Ener-Mark Corp. 06/27/1978
(See U.S. Ener-Mark Corp.)

SPRAYFOIL INDL CORP (MN)
Statutorily dissolved 10/05/1991

SPREADTRUM COMMUNICATIONS INC (CAYMAN ISLANDS)
Issue Information - 8,992,700 ADR's offered at $14 per ADR on 06/26/2007
Acquired by Tsinghua Unigroup Ltd. 12/23/2013
Each Sponsored ADR for Ordinary exchanged for $31 cash

SPRECKELS INDS INC (DE)
Plan of reorganization under Chapter 11 Federal Bankruptcy Code effective 9/2/93
Shares of old Class A Common 1¢ par were cancelled and replaced by a like number of new Class A Common 1¢ par
Merged into Columbus McKinnon Corp. 5/29/96
Each share new Class A Common 1¢ par exchanged for $24 cash

SPRECKELS SUGAR CORP.
Property and assets sold at public auction in 1934

SPRING & MERCER CAP CORP (BC)
Name changed to Genview Capital Corp. 07/08/2010
Genview Capital Corp. recapitalized as Hempco Food & Fiber Inc. 04/20/2016

SPRING APARTMENT HOTEL CO. (WA)
Name changed to Emel Motor Hotel, Inc. 6/1/59
Emel Motor Hotel, Inc. completely liquidated for cash 9/10/69

SPRING BRANCH BK (HOUSTON, TX)
Common $5 par changed to $2 par and (0.5) additional share issued 03/01/1974
Stock Dividends - 20% 03/14/1975; 20% 03/23/1978; 50% 03/12/1979; 10% 03/10/1980
Merged into Republic of Texas Corp. 05/01/1981
Each share Common $2 par exchanged for (0.92) share Common $5 par
Republic of Texas Corp. name changed to RepublicBank Corp. 06/30/1982 which merged into First RepublicBank Corp. 06/06/1987
(See First RepublicBank Corp.)

SPRING BROOK WATER SUPPLY CO.
Acquired by Scranton-Spring Brook Water Service Co. 00/00/1928
Details not available

SPRING COULEE OIL CORP. LTD. (AB)
Recapitalized as New Spring Coulee Oil & Minerals Ltd. on a (1) for (4) basis in 1954
New Spring Coulee Oil & Minerals Ltd. recapitalized as Native Minerals Ltd. 11/3/60
(See Native Minerals Ltd.)

SPRING CREEK ACQUISITION CORP (CAYMAN ISLANDS)
Name changed to AutoChina International Ltd. 06/16/2009
AutoChina International Ltd. name changed to Fincera Inc. 08/05/2015 which name changed back to AutoChina International Ltd. 09/02/2015 which name changed back to Fincera Inc. 08/31/2017

SPRING CREEK CAP CORP (NV)
Common $0.001 par split (3) for (1) by issuance of (2) additional shares payable 01/23/2009 to holders of record 01/15/2009 Ex date - 01/26/2009
Name changed to Spring Creek Healthcare Systems, Inc. 09/30/2010
(See Spring Creek Healthcare Systems, Inc.)

SPRING CREEK HEALTHCARE SYS INC (NV)
SEC revoked common stock registration 10/09/2013

SPRING KIST CORP. (UT)
Charter revoked for failure to file reports and pay fees 10/14/63

SPRING STR CAP CO (CA)
Each share Common $100 par exchanged for (100) shares Common $1 par 06/22/1961
Completely liquidated 02/14/1972
Each share Common $1 par exchanged for first and final distribution of $6.58 cash

SPRING VALLEY CO. LTD. (CA)
Liquidation completed in 1952

SPRING VY FOODS INC (DE)
Merged into Heublein, Inc. 09/30/1972
Each share Common $1 par exchanged for (0.147634) share Common no par
Heublein, Inc. merged into Reynolds (R.J.) Industries, Inc. 10/13/1982 which name changed to RJR Nabisco, Inc. 04/25/1986 which merged into RJR Holdings Group, Inc. 04/28/1989
(See RJR Holdings Group, Inc.)

SPRING VALLEY WATER CO.
Name changed to Spring Valley Co., Ltd. in 1930 which was liquidated in 1952

SPRINGBANK RES INC (NV)
Name changed to Location Based Technologies, Inc. 10/23/2007

SPRINGBANK VENTURES INC (BC)
Name changed to Ondine Biopharma Corp. 04/02/2004
Ondine Biopharma Corp. recapitalized as Ondine Biomedical Inc. 10/14/2010
(See Ondine Biomedical Inc.)

SPRINGBAY OIL CO INC (NY)
Name changed to Monolith Athletic Club, Inc. 7/7/2005

SPRINGBOARD RES LTD (BC)
Recapitalized as Summex Mines Ltd. (BC) 08/17/1993
Each share Common no par exchanged for (0.25) share Common no par
Summex Mines Ltd. (BC) reincorporated in Yukon 10/15/1997
(See Summex Mines Ltd.)

SPRINGBOARD SOFTWARE INC (MN)
Name changed to Spinnaker Software Corp. 07/20/1989
Spinnaker Software Corp. merged into SoftKey International Inc. 02/04/1994 which name changed to Learning Co. Inc. 10/24/1996 which merged into Mattel, Inc. 05/13/1999

SPRINGER CORP (NM)
Acquired by Springer Investors, Inc. 08/31/1973
Each share Common $2 par exchanged for $4.75 cash

SPRINGER RES LTD (BC)
Recapitalized as Bristol Explorations Ltd. 05/14/1992
Each share Common no par exchanged for (0.2) share Common no par
Bristol Explorations Ltd. recapitalized as Afrasia Mineral Fields Inc. 07/17/1996 which recapitalized as Westbay Ventures Inc. 01/24/2017 which name changed to Cryptanite Blockchain Technologies Corp. 03/12/2018

SPRINGER STURGEON GOLD MINES LTD.
Name changed to Barymin Co. Ltd. 00/00/1949
(See Barymin Co. Ltd.)

SPRINGFIELD & XENIA RAILWAY
Out of business 00/00/1928
Details not available

SPRINGFIELD ASSOCIATES
Liquidated in 1944

SPRINGFIELD ATLANTIC BK (JACKSONVILLE, FL)
99.75% acquired by Atlantic Bancorporation through exchange offer which expired 10/22/1973
Public interest eliminated

SPRINGFIELD BREWERIES CO.
Liquidated in 1945

SPRINGFIELD CAP CORP (CO)
Reorganized as Bio-Dental Technologies Corp. 09/26/1990
Each share Common $0.001 par exchanged for (4) shares Common 1¢ par
Bio-Dental Technologies Corp. merged into Zila, Inc. 01/08/1997
(See Zila, Inc.)

SPRINGFIELD CITY WATER CO. (ME)
Liquidation completed 12/12/58

SPRINGFIELD CO INC (DE)
SEC revoked common stock registration 01/12/2011

SPRINGFIELD FIRE & MARINE INSURANCE CO. (MA)
Capital Stock $100 par changed to $25 par 00/00/1927
Each share Capital Stock $25 par exchanged for (2.5) shares Capital Stock $10 par 00/00/1947
Capital Stock $10 par reclassified as Common $10 par and distribution of (0.1) share $6.50 Preferred $10 par and (3/7ths) share Common $10 par paid 06/16/1958
Common $10 par changed to $2 par 07/01/1958
Name changed to Springfield Insurance Co. 12/31/1960
Springfield Insurance Co. merged into Monarch Life Insurance Co. 05/28/1965
(See Monarch Life Insurance Co.)

SPRINGFIELD GAS & ELECRIC CO.
Liquidated in 1945

SPRINGFIELD GAS LT CO (MA)
Each share Capital Stock $25 par exchanged for (2.5) shares Capital Stock $10 par 5/15/61
Capital Stock $10 par reclassified as Common $10 par 7/1/64
Name changed to Bay State Gas Co. (Old) 11/14/73
Bay State Gas Co. (Old) merged into Bay State Gas Co. (New) 11/19/74 which merged into Nipsco Industries, Inc. 2/12/99 which name changed to NiSource Inc. (IN) 4/14/99 which reincorporated in Delaware 11/1/2000

SPRINGFIELD GREENE INDUSTRIES, INC. (OH)
Name changed to Mid-Continent Manufacturing Co. (OH) 08/18/1964
Mid-Continent Manufacturing Co. (OH) reincorporated in Delaware as Mid-Con Inc. 10/31/1968 which merged into A-T-O Inc. 10/29/1969 which name changed to Figgie International Inc. (OH) 06/01/1981 which reorganized in Delaware as Figgie International Holdings Inc. 07/18/1983 which name changed to Figgie International Inc. 12/31/1986 which name changed to Scott Technologies, Inc. 05/20/1998 which merged into Tyco International Ltd. (Bermuda) 05/03/2001 which reincorporated in Switzerland 03/17/2009 which merged into Johnson Controls International PLC 09/06/2016

SPRINGFIELD ICE CO.
Reorganized as Springfield Ice & Fuel Co. in 1937

SPRINGFIELD INSTN FOR SVGS BK (SPRINGFIELD, MA)
Under plan of reorganization each share Common $1 par automatically became (1) share SIS Bancorp, Inc. Common 1¢ par 6/21/96
(See SIS Bancorp, Inc.)

SPRINGFIELD INSURANCE CO. (MA)
Merged into Monarch Life Insurance Co. 5/28/65
Each share Common $2 par exchanged for (1) share Capital Stock $2 par
(See Monarch Life Insurance Co.)

SPRINGFIELD INVT CORP (UT)
Name changed to Sun Bay Group, Inc. 12/06/1989

SPRINGFIELD MANUFACTURING CORP.
Liquidated in 1936

SPRINGFIELD MARINE BK (SPRINGFIELD, IL)
Each share Capital Stock $100 par exchanged for (4) shares Capital Stock $25 par 2/16/53
Capital Stock $25 par changed to $12.50 par and (1) additional share issued 1/21/77
Stock Dividends - 100% 2/14/56; 100% 1/15/68; 100% 2/1/75
Merged into Marine Bancorp, Inc. 10/3/80
Each share Capital Stock $12.50 par exchanged for (1) share Common $12.50 par
Marine Bancorp, Inc. name changed to Marine Corp. 7/1/84 which merged into Banc One Corp. 1/1/92 which merged into Bank One Corp. 10/2/98 which merged into J.P. Morgan Chase & Co. 12/31/2000 which name changed to JPMorgan Chase & Co. 7/20/2004

SPRINGFIELD RAILWAY & LIGHT CO.
Reorganized as Springfield Gas & Electric Co. 00/00/1927
Details not available

SPRINGFIELD RAILWAY COMPANIES
Merged into New York, New Haven & Hartford Railroad Co. under plan of reorganization on basis of (1) share Common no par for each $100 allowed claims 5/26/48
New York, New Haven & Hartford Railroad Co. declared insolvent 12/24/68

SPRINGFIELD RES LTD (BC)
Struck off register and declared dissolved for failure to file returns 4/22/94

SPRINGFIELD SAFE DEPOSIT & TRUST CO. (SPRINGFIELD, MA)
Each share Capital Stock $100 par exchanged for (4) shares Capital Stock $25 par 01/29/1930
Capital Stock $25 par changed to $10 par and (1.5) additional shares issued plus a 20% stock dividend paid 01/26/1960
Stock Dividends - 100% 01/20/1927; 25% 06/20/1961
Under plan of merger name changed to Safe Deposit Bank & Trust Co. (Springfield, MA) 03/05/1962
Safe Deposit Bank & Trust Co. (Springfield, MA) name changed to First Bank & Trust Co. of Hampden County (Springfield, MA) 05/06/1968 which name changed to Shawmut First Bank & Trust Co. (Springfield, MA) 04/01/1975

SPRINGFIELD TELEVISION BROADCASTING CORP (MA)
Name changed to Springfield Television Corp. 3/17/78

SPRINGHURST COPPER MINES LTD. (ON)
Charter revoked for failure to file reports and pay fees 8/19/65

SPRINGLAKE RES LTD (CANADA)
Recapitalized as Savoy Minerals Ltd. 12/08/1988
Each share Common no par exchanged for (0.08) share Common no par
(See Savoy Minerals Ltd.)

SPRINGLEAF HLDGS INC (DE)
Name changed to OneMain Holdings, Inc. 11/27/2015

SPRINGMAN PAPER PRODUCTS CO.
Acquired by Detroit Gasket & Manufacturing Co. in 1928
Details not available

SPRINGPOINT RES LTD (AB)
Recapitalized as Canadian Platinum Refineries Inc. 06/24/1986
Each share Common no par exchanged for (0.1) share Common no par
(See Canadian Platinum Refineries Inc.)

SPRINGPOLE MINES LTD. (ON)
Merged into Milestone Exploration Ltd. 07/23/1968
Each share Common $1 par exchanged for (0.131491) share Capital Stock no par
Milestone Exploration Ltd. merged into Jubilee Gold Inc. 01/01/2010 which merged into Jubilee Gold Exploration Inc. 01/25/2013

SPRINGROCK CAP INC (ON)
Recapitalized as ThermoCeramix Corp. 04/07/2014
Each share Common no par exchanged for (0.4) share Common no par

SPRINGS INDS INC (SC)
Name changed 4/20/82
Name changed from Springs Mills, Inc. to Springs Industries, Inc. 4/20/82
Common 50¢ par changed to 25¢ par and (1) additional share issued 5/15/87
Common 25¢ par reclassified as Class A Common 25¢ par 6/28/88
Merged into Heartland Industries Partners LP 9/5/2001
Each share Class A Common 25¢ par exchanged for $46 cash
Each share Class B Common 25¢ par exchanged for $46 cash

SPRINGSYDE RES LTD (AB)
Merged into Courage Energy Inc. 9/1/95
Each share Common no par exchanged for (1) share Common no par
(See Courage Energy Inc.)

SPRINGTON CAP CORP (DE)
Recapitalized as Naturade, Inc. 05/01/1989
Each share Common $0.001 par exchanged for (0.05) share Common $0.001 par

SPRINGWOOD RES INC (NV)
Each share old Common $0.001 par exchanged for (0.001) share new Common $0.001 par 5/19/99
Name changed to Innovative Coatings Corp. 10/22/99
Innovative Coatings Corp. name changed to Capital Fund Investment Inc. 12/29/2000
(See Capital Fund Investment Inc.)

SPRINT NEXTEL CORP (KS)
Name changed 08/12/2005
Each share Common no par received distribution of (0.33333333) share 360 Communications Co. Common 1¢ par payable 03/07/1996 to holders of record 02/27/1996 Ex date - 03/08/1996
Common $2.50 par reclassified as FON Common Ser. 1 $2 par 11/23/1998
Each share FON Common Ser. 1 $2 par received distribution of (0.5) share PCS Common Ser. 1 $1 par payable 11/24/1998 to holders of record 11/23/1998 Ex date - 11/24/1998
FON Common Ser. 1 $2 par split (2) for (1) by issuance of (1) additional share payable 06/04/1999 to holders of record 05/13/1999 Ex date - 06/07/1999
PCS Common Ser. 1 $1 par split (2) for (1) by issuance of (1) additional share payable 02/04/2000 to holders of record 01/14/2000 Ex date - 02/07/2000
$1.50 Conv. Preferred Ser. 1 no par called for redemption at $42.50 on 05/25/2000
$1.25 to $1.50 Conv. Preferred Ser. 2 no par called for redemption at $50 on 05/25/2000
Each share PCS Common Ser. 1 $1 par exchanged for (0.5) share FON Common Ser. 1 $2 par 04/23/2004
Each Equity Unit $2 par received (0.5102) share FON Common Ser. 1 $2 par 08/17/2004
Under plan of merger name changed from Sprint Corp. to Sprint Nextel Corp. 08/12/2005
Each share Common Ser. 1 $2 par received distribution of (0.05) share

Embarq Corp. Common 1¢ par payable 05/17/2006 to holders of record 05/08/2006 Ex date - 05/18/2006
Merged into Sprint Corp. (DE) 07/10/2013
Each share Common no par exchanged for (0.26174405) share Common 1¢ par and $5.647658 cash

SPRINT RES LTD (ON)
Name changed to Meacon Bay Resources Inc. 3/9/87
Meacon Bay Resources Inc. recapitalized as Advantex Marketing International Inc. 9/16/91

SPRIZA MEDIA INC (BC)
Each share old Common no par exchanged for (0.2) share new Common no par 02/22/2017
Name changed to Fanlogic Interactive Inc. 03/29/2017

SPROATT SILVER MINES LTD (ON)
Reorganized under the laws of British Columbia as Hecate Gold Corp. 07/06/1977
Each share Capital Stock no par exchanged for (0.2) share Capital Stock no par
Hecate Gold Corp. merged into Host Ventures Ltd. 06/29/1982 which recapitalized as Hot Resources Ltd. 04/30/1984 which name changed to Inter-Globe Resources Ltd. 04/16/1985
(See Inter-Globe Resources Ltd.)

SPROTT ENERGY OPPORTUNITIES TR (ON)
Name changed to Ninepoint Energy Opportunities Trust 03/29/2018

SPROTT MOLYBDENUM PARTN CORP (ON)
Each share Common no par received distribution of $1.76 cash payable 07/10/2009 to holders of record 07/10/2009
Name changed to Cadomin Capital Corp. 07/10/2009
(See Cadomin Capital Corp.)

SPROTT PWR CORP (CANADA)
Name changed to Renewable Energy Developers Inc. 07/02/2013
Renewable Energy Developers Inc. merged into Capstone Infrastructure Corp. 10/07/2013
(See Capstone Infrastructure Corp.)

SPROTT RESOURCE CORP (CANADA)
Merged into Sprott Resource Holdings Inc. 02/13/2017
Each share Common no par exchanged for (3) shares Common no par
Note: Unexchanged certificates will be cancelled and become without value 02/13/2023

SPROTT RESOURCE LENDING CORP (CANADA)
Merged into Sprott Inc. 07/24/2013
Each share Common no par exchanged for (0.5) share Common no par and $0.15 cash

SPROTT STRATEGIC FIXED INCOME FD (ON)
Trust terminated 09/30/2015
Each Trust Unit received $5.84144947 cash

SPROUL HOMES CORP. (NV)
Name changed to National Environment Corp. 07/15/1968
(See National Environment Corp.)

SPROUSE REALTY CORP. (OR)
Called for redemption 2/1/77
Public interest eliminated

SPROUSE REITZ STORES INC (OR)
Reorganized 03/14/1986
Reorganized from Sprouse-Reitz Co., Inc. to Sprouse-Reitz Stores, Inc. 03/14/1986

Each share Common $100 par exchanged for (10) shares Common $10 par
Each share Non-Vtg. Common $100 par exchanged for (10) shares Non-Vtg. Common $10 par
Liquidation completed
Each share Common $10 par received initial distribution of $2.0572 cash 09/30/1994
Each share Non-Vtg. Common $10 par received initial distribution of $2.0572 cash 09/30/1994
Each share Common $10 par received second distribution of $0.41842 cash 01/31/1995
Each share Non-Vtg. Common $10 par received second distribution of $0.41842 cash 01/31/1995
Each share Common $10 par received third distribution of $0.1264 cash 03/00/1997
Each share Non-Vtg. Common $10 par received third distribution of $0.1264 cash 03/00/1997
Each share Common $10 par received fourth and final distribution of $0.542 cash 12/19/1997
Each share Non-Vtg. Common $10 par received fourth and final distribution of $0.542 cash 12/19/1997
Note: Certificates were not required to be surrendered and are without value

SPROUT DEV INC (AB)
Name changed to VioSolar Inc. 07/10/2007

SPRUCE FALLS ACQUISITION CORP (ON)
Merged into Tembec Inc. (QC) 05/20/1997
Each share Class 2 Restricted Voting Special Share exchanged for (1) share Class A Common no par
Each share Class 3 Restricted Voting Special Share exchanged for (1) share Class A Common no par
Tembec Inc. (QC) reorganized in Canada 02/29/2008 which merged into Rayonier Advanced Materials Inc. 11/21/2017

SPRUCE STR MED BLDG INC (PA)
Liquidation completed
Each share Capital Stock no par received initial distribution of $50 cash 11/01/1967
Each share Capital Stock no par exchanged for second and final distribution of $31.535 cash 03/18/1968

SPRYLOGICS INTL CORP (CANADA)
Each share old Common no par exchanged for (0.1) share new Common no par 09/06/2013
Name changed to Breaking Data Corp. 09/14/2015

SPS INDS LTD (AB)
Recapitalized as Landover Energy Inc. 6/23/99
Each share Common no par exchanged for (0.25) share Common no par
(See Landover Energy Inc.)

SPS TECHNOLOGIES INC (PA)
Common $1 par split (2) for (1) by issuance of (1) additional share payable 08/29/1997 to holders of record 08/20/1997 Ex date - 09/02/1997
Stock Dividend - 10% 10/06/1980
Merged into Precision Castparts Corp. 12/09/2003
Each share Common $1 par exchanged for (0.354558) share Common $1 par and $31.789 cash
(See Precision Castparts Corp.)

SPS TRANSACTION SVCS INC (DE)
Common 1¢ par split (2) for (1) by issuance of (1) additional share 11/16/94

Merged into Novus Credit Services Inc. 10/16/98
Each share Common 1¢ par exchanged for $32.02 cash

SPSS INC (DE)
Merged into International Business Machines Corp. 10/02/2009
Each share Common 1¢ par exchanged for $50 cash

SPT SULPHUR POLYMER TECHNOLOGIES INC (BC)
Name changed to LeenLife Pharma International Inc. 12/03/2015
LeenLife Pharma International Inc. name changed to LeanLife Health Inc. 01/15/2018

SPUD OIL & GAS CO. OF CANADA LTD. (CANADA)
Name changed to Span Minerals of Canada Ltd. 00/00/1953
(See Span Minerals of Canada Ltd.)

SPUD VALLEY GOLD MINES LTD. (BC)
Name changed to Valley Explorations Ltd. 7/4/57 which was dissolved 7/13/61

SPUR DISTRIBUTING CO., INC. (DE)
Liquidation completed 7/17/59

SPUR OIL CO. (DE)
Merged into Murphy Corp. (La.) on a (0.7) for (1) basis 12/29/60 which was reincorporated in Delaware 1/1/64

SPUR PETES LTD (AB)
Struck off register for failure to file annual returns 12/15/1975

SPUR RANCH INC (FL)
Name changed to Rounder, Inc. 01/24/2012
Rounder, Inc. name changed to Fortitude Group, Inc. 01/08/2013

SPUR VENTURES INC (BC)
Name changed to Atlantic Gold Corp. 08/20/2014

SPURLOCK INDS INC (VA)
Merged into Borden Chemical, Inc. 5/12/99
Each share Common $0.001 par exchanged for $3.40 cash

SPUTNIK INC (NV)
Name changed to Sputnik Enterprises, Inc. 05/16/2008

SPVC CAP CORP (SK)
Voluntarily dissolved 09/02/2010
Details not available

SPW CORP (TX)
Plan of reorganization under Chapter 11 Federal Bankruptcy proceedings confirmed 12/29/1987
No stockholders' equity

SPY DEPOT INTL INC (DE)
Name changed to Fortune Graphite Inc. (DE) 01/07/2003
Fortune Graphite Inc. (DE) reorganized in British Columbia 05/01/2010

SPY HILL ROYALTIES LTD.
Merged into Amalgamated Oils Ltd. in 1941 liquidation of which was completed 10/15/58

SPYGLASS INC (DE)
Issue Information - 2,000,000 shares COM offered at $17 per share on 06/26/1995
Common 1¢ par split (2) for (1) by issuance of (1) additional share 12/20/1995
Merged into OpenTV Corp. 07/25/2000
Each share Common 1¢ par exchanged for (0.7236) share Class A Ordinary no par
(See OpenTV Corp.)

SPYN CORP (NV)
Company's sole asset filed an assignment in bankruptcy 03/26/2003

Stockholders' equity unlikely

SQA INC (DE)
Merged into Rational Software Corp. 2/26/97
Each share Common 1¢ par exchanged for (0.86) share Common 1¢ par
(See Rational Software Corp.)

SQD CO. (DE)
Liquidation completed
Each share Common 10¢ par exchanged for initial distribution of (1) share Kar Nut Products Co. Common $2 par and $5.65 cash 12/23/77
(See Kar Nut Products Co.)
Each share Common 10¢ par received second distribution of (1) Share of Bene. Int. and $0.33 cash 9/21/78
Each Share of Bene. Int. received third distribution of $0.19 cash 6/11/80
Each Share of Bene. Int. received fourth distribution of $1.25 cash 9/19/80
Each Share of Bene. Int. exchanged for fifth and final distribution of $0.211 cash 2/18/83

SQL FINANCIALS INTL INC (DE)
Name changed to Clarus Corp. 09/01/1998
Clarus Corp. name changed to Black Diamond, Inc. 01/20/2011 which name changed back to Clarus Corp. 08/14/2017

SQRIBE TECHNOLOGIES CORP (DE)
Merged into Brio Technology, Inc. 08/03/1999
Each share Conv. Preferred Ser. B exchanged for (0.77659397) share Common $0.001 par
Each share Common exchanged for (0.87) share Common $0.001 par
Brio Technology, Inc. name changed to Brio Software, Inc. 09/07/2001 which merged into Hyperion Solutions Corp. 10/16/2003
(See Hyperion Solutions Corp.)

SQUARE D CO (DE)
Reincorporated 06/16/1989
Class B Common no par changed to Common $1 par 00/00/1937
Each share Common $1 par exchanged for (3) shares Common $5 par 00/00/1946
Common $5 par split (3) for (1) by issuance of (2) additional shares 10/05/1956
Common $5 par split (5) for (4) by issuance of (0.25) additional share 12/30/1961
Common $5 par changed to $1.66-2/3 par and (2) additional shares issued 05/20/1966
State of incorporation changed from (MI) to (DE) 06/16/1989
Common Stock Purchase Rights declared for Common stockholders of record 09/15/1988 were redeemed at $0.01 per right 06/03/1991 for holders of record 05/28/1991
Merged into SQD Acquisition Co. 08/22/1991
Each share Common $1.66-2/3 par exchanged for $88 cash

SQUARE H INDS INC (TX)
Recapitalized as Oakmont Corp. 03/10/1971
Each share Common 25¢ par exchanged for (0.2) share Common no par
Oakmont Corp. name changed to Oakmont Marine Corp. 09/12/1975 which name changed to Lorain Telecom Corp. (TX) 11/07/1983 which reorganized in Delaware 04/10/1985
(See Lorain Telecom Corp.)

SQUARE INDS INC (NY)
Stock Dividends - 10% 6/30/83; 10% 8/31/84
Merged into Central Parking Corp. 1/20/97
Each share Common 1¢ par exchanged for $28.50 cash
Each share Common 1¢ par received an additional distribution of $0.51 cash 2/24/97
Each share Common 1¢ par received a second additional distribution of $2.00883 cash 4/7/97
Each share Common 1¢ par received a third and final additional distribution of $0.210885 cash 5/9/97

SQUARE-KNOT INC (MN)
Recapitalized as RLD Enterprises, Inc. 10/31/97
Each (14.4) shares Common no par exchanged for (1) share Common no par
RLD Enterprises, Inc. name changed to Go-Rachels.com Corp. 1/27/99 which name changed to Rachel's Gourmet Snacks Inc. 9/17/2001
(See Rachel's Gourmet Snacks Inc.)

SQUARE 1 FINL INC (DE)
Merged into PacWest Bancorp 10/06/2015
Each share Class A Common 1¢ par exchanged for (0.5997) share Common 1¢ par

SQUARE ROOT INDUSTRIES, INC. (DE)
Became inoperative and void for non-payment of taxes 04/01/1957

SQUARE SHOOTER INC (NV)
Recapitalized as VisiTrade, Inc. 12/07/2006
Each share Common $0.001 par exchanged for (0.2) share Common $0.001 par
VisiTrade, Inc. recapitalized as BlackBox SemiConductor, Inc. 01/19/2011 which name changed to Vision Dynamics Corp. 01/16/2013 which recapitalized as Secured Technology Innovations Corp. 02/14/2014

SQUARE SHOOTER INTL LTD (DE)
Company terminated common stock registration and is no longer public as of 04/10/2001

SQUAREMOON INC (NV)
Each share old Common $0.001 par exchanged for (0.05) share new Common $0.001 par 11/07/2001
Name changed to KidSational Inc. 12/17/2002
KidSational Inc. name changed to Stratton Holdings Inc. 02/09/2009 which name recapitalized as Profitable Developments, Inc. 12/24/2012

SQUIBB (E.R.) & SONS (NY)
Acquired by Mathieson Chemical Corp. 00/00/1952
Each share $4 Preferred no par exchanged for $100 principal amount of Ser. A Debentures
Each share Common 5¢ par exchanged for (0.6) share Common $5 par
Mathieson Chemical Corp. merged into Olin Mathieson Chemical Corp. 00/00/1954 which name changed to Olin Corp. 09/01/1969

SQUIBB BEECH NUT INC (DE)
Under plan of merger name changed to Squibb Corp. 04/30/1971
Squibb Corp. merged into Bristol-Myers Squibb Co. 10/04/1989

SQUIBB CORP (DE)
$2 Conv. Preferred $1 par called for redemption 08/02/1971
Common $1 par split (2) for (1) by issuance of (1) additional share 06/20/1974
Common $1 par changed to 10¢ par and (1) additional share issued 06/29/1987
Merged into Bristol-Myers Squibb Co. 10/04/1989
Each share Common 10¢ par exchanged for (2.4) shares Common 10¢ par

SQUIBB-PATTISON BREWERIES, INC.
Properties sold in 1936

SQUIRE (JOHN P.) & CO.
Liquidated in 1936

SQUIRE FOR MEN INC (CA)
Name changed to Consolidated Hair Products, Inc. 6/6/66
(See Consolidated Hair Products, Inc.)

SQUIRT DETROIT BOTTLING CO (DE)
Name changed to SQD Co. 11/22/1977
(See SQD Co.)

SRA INTL INC (DE)
Issue Information - 5,000,000 shares CL A offered at $18 per share on 05/23/2002
Class A Common $0.004 par split (2) for (1) by issuance of (1) additional share payable 05/27/2005 to holders of record 05/13/2005 Ex date - 05/31/2005
Acquired by Sterling Parent Inc. 07/20/2011
Each share Class A Common $0.004 par exchanged for $31.25 cash

SREI INFRASTRUCTURE FIN LTD (INDIA)
144A GDR's for Equity split (9) for (5) by issuance of (0.8) additional GDR payable 03/21/2011 to holders of record 02/11/2011
Reg. S GDR's for Equity split (9) for (5) by issuance of (0.8) additional GDR payable 03/21/2011 to holders of record 02/11/2011
GDR agreement terminated 05/16/2016
Each 144A GDR for Equity Shares exchanged for (4) Equity Shares
Each Reg. S GDR's for Equity Shares exchanged for (4) Equity Shares

SRF FUND, INC. (MD)
Name changed to SteinRoe Special Fund, Inc. 9/17/79
SteinRoe Special Fund, Inc. merged into SteinRoe Equity Trust 12/31/87 which name changed to SteinRoe Investment Trust 6/30/89

SRI / SURGICAL EXPRESS INC (FL)
Acquired by Synergy Health US Holdings Ltd. 07/16/2012
Each share Common $0.001 par exchanged for $3.70 cash

SRI CORP (NJ)
Common $4 par changed to $2 par and (1) additional share issued 12/15/1979
Common $2 par split (3) for (2) by issuance of (0.5) additional share 04/01/1981
Common $2 par split (2) for (1) by issuance of (1) additional share 09/01/1983
Name changed to Selective Insurance Group, Inc. 05/02/1986

SRI TRANG AGRO-IND PUB CO LTD (THAILAND)
ADR agreement terminated 05/21/2018
No ADR's remain outstanding

SRKP 6 INC (DE)
Name changed to Vicor Technologies, Inc. 03/31/2007

SRM NETWORKS INC (DE)
Reincorporated 08/21/2002
Common $0.001 par split (11) for (1) by issuance of (10) additional shares payable 02/15/2002 to holders of record 02/14/2002
Ex date - 02/19/2002
State of incorporation changed from (NV) to (DE) 08/21/2002
Name changed to Hy-Tech Technology Group Inc. 02/03/2003
Hy-Tech Technology Group Inc. name changed to Innova Holdings, Inc. 07/29/2004 which recapitalized as Innova Robotics & Automation, Inc. 11/20/2006 which name changed to CoroWare, Inc. 05/12/2008

SRO ENTMT INTL INC (BC)
Recapitalized as PacRim Entertainment Group Inc. 1/30/90
Each share Common no par exchanged for (0.4) share Common no par
PacRim Entertainment Group Inc. name changed to Evergreen International Technology Inc. 1/9/91 which name changed to Jot-It! Software Corp. 2/1/97 which name changed to Sideware Systems Inc. (BC) 2/18/98 which reincorporated in Yukon 1/2/2002 which reincorporated in Delaware as Knowledgemax, Inc. 5/21/2002
(See Knowledgemax, Inc.)

SRR MERCANTILE INC (BC)
Delisted from Toronto Venture Stock Exchange 7/4/2002

SRS CAP CORP (AB)
Name changed to Postec Systems Inc. 8/20/96

SRS LABS INC (DE)
Merged into DTS, Inc. 07/20/2012
Each share Common $0.001 par exchanged for (0.31127) share Common $0.0001 par
(See DTS, Inc.)

SRS TECHNICAL INC (NV)
Name changed to Composite Design, Inc. 5/14/87
Composite Design, Inc. recapitalized as Centraxx Inc. 5/18/99

SRSI CAP GROUP INC (DE)
Name changed to Sector Associates, Ltd. 01/17/1989
Sector Associates, Ltd. recapitalized as Viragen (Europe) Ltd. 04/24/1996 which name changed to Viragen International, Inc. 03/27/2002
(See Viragen International, Inc.)

SRX POST HLDGS INC (CANADA)
Plan of Arrangement under Companies' Creditors Arrangement Act effective 11/12/2008
No stockholders' equity

SS&C TECHNOLOGIES INC (DE)
Common 1¢ par split (3) for (2) by issuance of (0.5) additional share payable 3/5/2004 to holders of record 2/20/2004 Ex date - 3/8/2004
Merged into Carlyle Group 11/23/2005
Each share Common 1¢ par exchanged for $37.25 cash

SSA GLOBAL TECHNOLOGIES INC (DE)
Merged into Magellan Holdings, Inc. 07/28/2006
Each share Common 1¢ par exchanged for $19.50 cash

SSBCITI FDS INC (NY)
Completely liquidated 09/27/2002
Each Humane Equity Fund received first and final distribution of $5.50 cash

SSBH CAP I (DE)
7.20% Trust Preferred Securities called for redemption at $25 on 3/3/2003

SSC CORP (UT)
Name changed to Texas Bio Scan, Inc. 2/21/84

SSE TELECOM INC (DE)
Chapter 11 Federal Bankruptcy proceedings converted to Chapter 7 on 11/02/2001
Stockholders' equity unlikely

SSF INC (CO)
Reorganized under the laws of Pennsylvania as Micro Diagnostics Corp. 07/31/1989
Each share Common no par exchanged for (0.01) share Common no par

SSGA ACTIVE TR (MA)
Name changed 12/05/2014
Name changed from SSgA Active ETF Trust to SSgA Active Trust 12/05/2014
Trust terminated 08/31/2016
Each share SPDR SSgA Risk Aware ETF received $40.704544 cash
(Additional Information in Active)

SSGA DOW JONES CDA TITANS 40 INDEX PARTN FD (ON)
Name changed 3/28/2002
Name changed from SSgA Dow Jones Canada 40 Index Participation Fund to SSgA Dow Jones Canada Titans 40 Index Participation Fund 3/28/2002
Completely liquidated
Each Unit no par received first and final distribution of $37 cash payable 11/1/2002 to holders of record 11/1/2002
Note: Certificates were not required to be surrendered and are now valueless

SSI CAP CORP (NY)
Reorganized under the laws of Colorado as Oralabs Holding Corp. 08/26/1997
Each share Common 1¢ par exchanged for (0.5) share Common 1¢ par
Oralabs Holding Corp. name changed to China Precision Steel, Inc. (CO) 12/28/2006 which reincorporated in Delaware 11/16/2007

SSI COMPUTER CORP (DE)
Under plan of merger name changed to Itel Corp. (Old) 6/17/69
Itel Corp. (Old) reorgananized as Itel Corp. (New) 9/19/83 which name changed to Anixter International Inc. 9/1/95

SSI INTL LTD (NV)
SEC revoked common stock registration 04/05/2016

SSI LTD (INDIA)
Name changed to PVP Ventures Ltd. 07/09/2008

SSI SURGICAL SVCS INC (NY)
Merged into Teleflex Inc. 5/17/2007
Each share Common 1¢ par exchanged for $1 par

SSL FINANCIAL CORP. (GA)
Name changed to Sentry Bancshares Corp. 6/29/87

SSL INTL PLC (UNITED KINGDOM)
ADR agreement terminated
No ADR's remain outstanding

SSMC INC N V (NETHERLANDS ANTILLES)
Name changed 3/29/91
Under plan of merger each share Common $1 par exchanged for (1) share 15% Preferred Ser. B no par 4/6/90
Name changed from SSMC Inc. (DE) to SSMC Inc. N.V. (Netherlands Antilles) 3/29/91
15% Preferred Ser. B no par called for redemption 8/9/91
Public interest eliminated

SSP INDS (CA)
Capital Stock $1 par reclassified as Common $1 par 11/00/1968
Stock Dividends - 20% 07/15/1968; 10% 06/05/1972; 20% 02/23/1973; 25% 05/31/1974; 10% 03/25/1980

Merged into TransTechnology Corp. (CA) 11/17/1983
Each share Common $1 par exchanged for $6.70 cash

SSP OFFSHORE INC (AB)
In process of liquidation
Each share Common no par received initial distribution of USD$0.175 cash payable 09/30/2014 to holders of record 09/25/2014 Ex date - 10/01/2014
Note: Details on additional distributions, if any, are not available

SSP SOLUTIONS INC (DE)
Merged into Saflink Corp. 08/09/2004
Each share Common 1¢ par exchanged for (0.6) share new Common 1¢ par
Saflink Corp. recapitalized as IdentiPHI, Inc. 02/19/2008
(See IdentiPHI, Inc.)

SSQ ACQUISITIONS INC (ON)
Reorganized under the laws of Canada as Craig Wireless Systems Ltd. 09/01/2007
Each share Common no par exchanged for (1/6) share Subordinate no par

SSTL INC (NV)
Name changed to Zenovia Digital Exchange Corp. 06/05/2015

ST ASSEMBLY TEST SVCS LTD (SINGAPORE)
Issue Information - 153,000,000 ADR'S offered at $21 per ADR on 01/28/2000
Under plan of merger name changed to STATS ChipPAC Ltd. 08/05/2004
(See STATS ChipPAC Ltd.)

ST LIQUIDATING CO. (MN)
Liquidation completed
Each share Common $1 par exchanged for initial distribution of $3.40 cash 3/7/79
Each share Common $1 par received second distribution of $0.40 cash 10/2/79
Each share Common $1 par received third and final distribution of $0.1457 cash 9/2/81

ST LIQUIDATING CORP. (IN)
Liquidation completed
Each share Capital Stock $1 par received initial distribution of (0.25) share Associated Brewing Co. old Common $1 par and $16 cash 7/20/64
Each share Capital Stock $1 par received second distribution of $2 cash 1/13/65
Each share Capital Stock $1 par received third distribution of $1.85 cash 6/25/65
Each share Capital Stock $1 par received fourth and final distribution of $0.155 cash 5/5/69

ST ONLINE CORP (NV)
Name changed to Park Place Energy Corp. (NV) 07/09/2007
Park Place Energy Corp. (NV) reincorporated in Delaware as Park Place Energy Inc. 12/22/2015

ST SYS CORP (BC)
Recapitalized as Sky Ridge Resources Ltd. 12/24/2007
Each share Common no par exchanged for (0.14285714) share Common no par
Sky Ridge Resources Ltd. recapitalized as Japan Gold Corp. 09/19/2016

ST SYS INC (DE)
Charter cancelled and declared inoperative and void for non-payment of taxes 3/1/91

STA-BRITE FLUORESCENT MANUFACTURING CO. (FL)
Name changed to Ultra-Jet Industries, Inc. 03/19/1968

(See Ultra-Jet Industries, Inc.)

STA KLEEN BAKERY INC (VA)
Class A Common $1 par reclassified as Common $1 par 00/00/1947
Completely liquidated 06/01/1977
Each share Common $1 par exchanged for first and final distribution of $4.24 cash

STA RITE INDS INC (WI)
Common $2 par split (3) for (2) by issuance of (0.5) additional share 05/12/1969
Common $2 par split (4) for (3) by issuance of (1/3) additional share 10/13/1978
Stock Dividend - 10% 07/15/1976
Merged into Wicor, Inc. 08/31/1982
Each share Common $2 par exchanged for (0.9) share Common $1 par
5% Conv. Preferred Ser. A $25 par called for redemption 11/04/1982
5% Conv. Preferred Ser. D $25 par called for redemption 11/04/1982
Public interest eliminated
(See Wicor Inc.)

STA-RITE PRODUCTS, INC. (WI)
Stock Dividend - 100% 10/15/64
Merged into Sta-Rite Industries, Inc. 5/31/66
Each share 5% Preferred $10 par exchanged for (0.4) share 5% Conv. Preferred Ser. $25 par
Common $2 par exchanged share for share Sta-Rite Industries, Inc. merged into Wicor, Inc. 8/31/82
(See Wicor, Inc.)

STA-TITE CONDUIT CORP. (NY)
Name changed to Cadillac Conduit Corp. 08/30/1961
Cadillac Conduit Corp. name changed to Cadillac Cable Corp. 11/27/1968 which merged into Ag-Met, Inc. 08/29/1974 which name changed to Refinemet International Co. 09/18/1980
(See Refinemet International Co.)

STA-TITE CORP (MN)
Common 10¢ par split (5) for (1) by issuance of (4) additional shares 12/31/93
Name changed to STI, Inc. 4/27/95
(See STI, Inc.)

STAAR SURGICAL CO (CA)
Common no par split (2) for (1) by issuance of (1) additional share 7/2/84
Common no par split (2) for (1) by issuance of (1) additional share 11/8/84
Reincorporated under the laws of Delaware in April 1986

STABELL RES INC (CANADA)
Reincorporated 7/17/87
Place of incorporation changed from (BC) to (Canada) 7/17/87
Dissolved 6/23/97
Details not available

STABILITY LIFE INSURANCE CO.-LA STABILITE CIE D'ASSURANCE-VIE (QC)
Capital Stock $100 par changed to $5 par and (19) additional shares issued 10/20/65
Completely liquidated 2/2/70
Each share Capital Stock $5 par exchanged for first and final distribution $6.95 cash

STAC SOFTWARE INC (CA)
Name changed 10/24/95
Name changed 12/17/98
Name changed from Stac Electronics to Stac Inc. 10/24/95
Each share Common no par received distribution of (3.9156) shares Hi/fn Inc. Common no par payable 12/16/98 to holders of record 12/1/98
Name changed from Stac Inc. to Stac Software Inc. 12/17/98

Each share old Common no par exchanged for (0.25) share new Common no par 5/7/99
Name changed to Previo, Inc. 4/25/2000
(See Previo, Inc.)

STACCATO GOLD RES LTD (BC)
Acquired by Timberline Resources Corp. 06/02/2010
Each share Common no par exchanged for (0.14285714) share Common $0.001 par and USD$0.0001 cash
Note: Unexchanged certificates were cancelled and became without value 06/02/2016

STACCATOS INC (AB)
Name changed to Gravity West Mining Corp. 04/14/2005
Gravity West Mining Corp. recapitalized as Rock Tech Resources Inc. (AB) 03/09/2009 which reincorporated in British Columbia as Rock Tech Lithium Inc. 05/12/2010

STACEYS BUFFET INC (FL)
Each share old Common 1¢ par exchanged for (0.2) share new Common 1¢ par 07/17/1996
Chapter 7 bankruptcy proceedings terminated 10/31/2001
Stockholders' equity unlikely

STACIA VENTURES INC (CANADA)
Reincorporated 03/25/1993
Place of incorporation changed from (BC) to (Canada) 03/25/1993
Name changed to Environmental Applied Research Technology House Earth (Canada) Corp. 12/12/1995
Environmental Applied Research Technology House Earth (Canada) Corp. recapitalized as TORR Canada Inc. 11/08/2005 which name changed to ProSep Inc. 05/23/2008

STACK-IT STORAGE INC (NV)
Name changed to Manufactured Housing Properties Inc. 12/08/2017

STACKPAL INTL INC (ON)
Name changed to Innomat Solutions Corp. 10/09/1997
Innomat Solutions Corp. recapitalized as Carber Capital Corp. 11/26/1999 which recapitalized as Ba Ba Capital Inc. 08/17/2010 which recapitalized as Imex Systems Inc. 05/13/2016

STACKPOLE LTD (ON)
Acquired by Tomkins PLC 6/25/2003
Each share Common no par exchanged for $33.25 cash

STACKPOOL ENTERPRISES LTD (QC)
Name changed to Geneva Capital Ventures Inc.-Entreprises de Placements Geneve Inc. 4/25/73
(See Geneva Capital Ventures Inc.-Entreprises de Placements Geneve Inc.)

STACKPOOL MINING & HOLDING CORP. LTD. (ON)
Completely liquidated 7/30/71
Each share Common $1 par exchanged for first and final distribution of (1) share Stackpool Enterprises Ltd. Common no par
Stackpool Enterprises Ltd. name changed to Geneva Capital Ventures Inc.- Entreprises de Placements Geneve Inc. 4/25/73
(See Geneva Capital Ventures Inc.-Entreprises de Placements Geneve Inc.)

STACKPOOL MINING CO. LTD. (ON)
Recapitalized as Stackpool Mining & Holding Corp. Ltd. 09/19/1962
Each share Common $1 par exchanged for (0.05) share Common $1 par
Stackpool Mining & Holding Corp. Ltd. liquidated for Stackpool Enterprises

Ltd. 07/30/1971 which name changed to Geneva Capital Ventures Inc.-Entreprises de Placements Geneve Inc. 04/25/1973
(See Geneva Capital Ventures Inc.-Entreprises de Placements Geneve Inc.)

STACKPOOL RES LTD (BC)
Recapitalized as Britt Resources Ltd. 03/16/1990
Each share Common no par exchanged for (0.33333333) share Common no par
Britt Resources Ltd. recapitalized as La Cieba Minerals Corp. (BC) 07/15/1992 which reincorporated in Canada as Lowell Petroleum Inc. 09/26/1995 which recapitalized as Hedong Energy, Inc. 08/17/1998 which recapitalized as Benchmark Energy Corp. 02/09/2004 which name changed to Bolivar Energy Corp. (Canada) 10/29/2010 which reorganized in Alberta as Anatolia Energy Corp. 12/13/2011 which merged into Cub Energy Inc. 07/01/2013

STACO INC (DE)
Reincorporated 11/15/1973
State of incorporation changed from (MN) to (DE) 11/15/1973
Merged into Components Corp. of America 08/02/1979
Each share Common 50¢ par exchanged for $2.55 cash

STACY INDS INC (DE)
Charter forfeited for failure to maintain a registered agent 02/25/1991

STADACONA MINES 1944 LTD (CANADA)
Declared dissolved for failure to file reports or pay fees 09/19/1970

STADACONA ROUYN MINES LTD.
Recapitalized as Stadacona Mines (1944) Ltd. share for share 00/00/1944
(See Stadacona Mines (1944) Ltd.)

STADE EXPL INC (AB)
Name changed to Tessex Energy Inc. 7/14/97
Tessex Energy Inc. merged into Encounter Energy Inc. 6/10/98 which merged into Impact Energy Inc. (Canada) 10/21/2002 which merged into Thunder Energy Inc. 4/30/2004
(See Thunder Energy Inc.)

STADIUM PRODTNS INC (NY)
Charter cancelled and proclaimed dissolved for failure to pay taxes 12/15/1975

STADIUM RLTY TR (MA)
Completely liquidated 01/20/1982
Each Share of Bene. Int. no par exchanged for first and final distribution of $12.06 cash

STADLER FERTILIZER CO. (OH)
Liquidation completed
Each share Common no par exchanged for initial distribution of $60 cash 6/19/70
Each share Common no par received second distribution of $10 cash 7/24/70
Each share Common no par received third and final distribution of $15 cash 5/1/73

STADLER PRODUCTS CO.
Name changed to Stadler Fertilizer Co. in 1948
Stadler Fertilizer Co. completely liquidated 5/1/73

STAFF, BUSINESS & DATA AIDS, INC. (NY)
Stock Dividend - 10% 9/28/64
Name changed to Staff Builders Inc. (NY) 6/15/67
Staff Builders Inc. (NY) merged into Tender Loving Care Health Care

Services, Inc. (Old) 5/14/87 which name changed to Staff Builders, Inc. (New) (DE) 12/1/87 which name changed to ATC Healthcare, Inc. 8/2/2001

STAFF BLDRS INC (DE)
Each share Common 1¢ par exchanged for (1) share Class A Common 1¢ par 01/03/1996
Each share Class A Common 1¢ par received distribution of (0.5) share Tender Loving Care Health Services, Inc. (New) Common 1¢ par payable 10/21/1999 to holders of record 10/12/1999
Name changed to ATC Healthcare, Inc. 08/02/2001
(See ATC Healthcare, Inc.)

STAFF BLDRS INC (NY)
Capital Stock 10¢ par split (2) for (1) by issuance of (1) additional share 12/08/1969
Capital Stock 10¢ par split (5) for (4) by issuance of (0.25) additional share 09/06/1978
Capital Stock 10¢ par split (4) for (3) by issuance of (0.33333333) additional share 06/04/1979
Capital Stock 10¢ par split (3) for (2) by issuance of (0.5) additional share 04/03/1980
Stock Dividends - 25% 02/21/1968; 33.333333% 11/08/1968; 50% 04/07/1969
Merged into Tender Loving Care Health Care Services, Inc. (Old) 05/14/1987
Each share Capital Stock 10¢ par exchanged for (1.6) shares Common 1¢ par
Tender Loving Care Health Care Services, Inc. (Old) name changed to Staff Builders, Inc. (DE) 12/01/1987 which name changed to ATC Healthcare, Inc. 08/02/2001

STAFF LEASING INC (FL)
Secondary Offering - 3,100,000 shares COM offered at $29 per share on 04/23/1998
Name changed to Gevity HR, Inc. 06/03/2002
(See Gevity HR, Inc.)

STAFFING RES INC (DE)
Name changed to Career Blazers Inc. 04/01/1998
Career Blazers Inc. name changed to Immedient Corp. 12/21/1999
(See Immedient Corp.)

STAFFING 360 SOLUTIONS INC (NV)
Each share old Common $0.00001 par exchanged for (0.1) share new Common $0.00001 par 09/17/2015
Reincorporated under the laws of Delaware 06/20/2017

STAFFMARK INC (DE)
Name changed to Edgewater Technology, Inc. 6/29/2000

STAFFORD CO.
Liquidated in 1935

STAFFORD ENERGY INC (NV)
Recapitalized as Nucon-RF, Inc. 05/23/2006
Each (275) shares Common $0.001 par exchanged for (1) share Common $0.001 par
Nucon-RF, Inc. name changed to NNRF, Inc. 09/10/2007

STAFFORD FOODS LTD (ON)
Acquired by Canbra Foods Ltd. in July 1978
Each share Common no par exchanged for $4.25 cash

STAFFORD INDS LTD (BC)
Recapitalized as New Stafford Industries Ltd. 07/21/1997
Each share Common no par exchanged for (0.25) share Common no par
New Stafford Industries Ltd. name changed to Grandcru Resources

Corp. 07/10/2003 which merged into Bell Copper Corp. (Old) 05/12/2008 which reorganized as Bell Copper Corp. (New) 07/23/2013

STAFFORD LOWDON INC (DE)
Merged into American Standard Inc. 09/13/1979
Each share Common $1 par exchanged for $26.75 cash

STAFFORD VENTURES INC (NV)
Name changed to Stafford Energy Inc. 08/01/2002
Stafford Energy Inc. recapitalized as Nucon-RF, Inc. 05/23/2006 which name changed to NNRF, Inc. 09/10/2007

STAG HLDGS LTD (BC)
Name changed 11/30/90
Name changed from Stag Explorations Ltd. to Stag Holdings Ltd. 11/30/90
Name changed to Unidex Communications Corp. (BC) 2/8/93
Unidex Communications Corp. (BC) reincorporated in Wyoming 4/13/95 which recapitalized as United Digital Network, Inc. 7/9/96 which merged into Star Telecommunications, Inc. 3/24/99
(See Star Telecommunications, Inc.)

STAG INDL INC (MD)
9% Preferred Ser. A 1¢ par called for redemption at $25 plus $0.19375 accrued dividends on 11/02/2016
6.625% Preferred Ser. B 1¢ par called for redemption at $25 on 07/11/2018
(Additional Information in Active)

STAGE CAP INC (BC)
Name changed to Trueclaim Exploration Inc. 02/23/2009

STAGE DELICATESSEN & RESTAURANT INC (NY)
Name changed to Stage Industries, Inc. 01/12/1970
(See Stage Industries, Inc.)

STAGE INDS INC (NY)
Each share Common 10¢ par exchanged for (0.1) share Common $1 par 05/26/1972
Merged into RAJ Restaurant Corp. 07/28/1977
Each share Common $1 par exchanged for $3 cash

STAGE STORES INC (DE)
Plan of reorganization under Chapter 11 Federal Bankruptcy Code confirmed 08/08/2001
No stockholders' equity

STAGE II APPAREL CORP (NY)
Name changed to JKC Group Inc. 04/18/2002
JKC Group Inc. name changed to Magic Lantern Group, Inc. 11/08/2002
(See Magic Lantern Group, Inc.)

STAGGS BILT HOMES INC (AZ)
Recapitalized 10/20/1971
Recapitalized from Staggs Enterprises, Inc. to Staggs-Bilt Homes, Inc. 10/20/1971
Each share Common no par exchanged for (0.1) share Common no par
Name changed to SBH, Inc. 01/30/1973
(See SBH, Inc.)

STAGING CONNECTIONS GROUP LTD (AUSTRALIA)
ADR agreement terminated 04/11/2014
No ADR's remain outstanding

STAHL METAL PRODUCTS, INC. (OH)
Acquired by Scott & Fetzer Co. 4/28/67
Each share Common $1 par exchanged for (1.3) shares Common no par
(See Scott & Fetzer Co.)

STAHL-MEYER, INC. (NY)
Adjudicated bankrupt 11/15/62
No stockholders' equity

STAHL (H.A.) PROPERTIES CO.
Properties acquired by bondholders committee in 1931

STAHLWERKE PEINE SALZGITTER A G (GERMANY)
ADR agreement terminated 00/00/1989
No ADR's remain outstanding

STAINLESS STEEL PRODUCTS INC. (CA)
Stock Dividend - 50% 03/17/1964
Name changed to SSP Industries 04/10/1968
(See SSP Industries)

STAIRS EXPL & MNG LTD (ON)
Charter cancelled for failure to pay taxes and file returns 03/25/1980

STAKE TECHNOLOGY LTD (CANADA)
Name changed to SunOpta Inc. 10/31/2003

STAKED PLAINS TRUST LTD. (MA)
Liquidation completed 12/12/55

STAKHANOV FERROALLOY PLT JSC (UKRAINE)
Each GDR agreement terminated 05/20/2016
Each Reg. S Sponsored GDR for Ordinary exchanged for (100) shares Ordinary
Note: Unexchanged GDR's will be sold and the proceeds, if any, held for claim after 05/25/2017

STAKOOL INC (NV)
Common $0.001 par changed to $0.00001 par 07/23/2012
Each share old Common $0.00001 par exchanged for (0.01) share new Common $0.00001 par 09/20/2013
Name changed to Fresh Promise Foods, Inc. 11/12/2013

STAKTEK HLDGS INC (DE)
Name changed to Entorian Technologies Inc. 02/27/2008
(See Entorian Technologies Inc.)

STALEY A E MFG CO (DE)
Each share Common $100 par exchanged for (10) shares Common $10 par in 1937
Common $10 par changed to no par and (1) additional share issued 6/11/75
Common no par split (2) for (1) by issuance of (1) additional share 3/22/76
Common no par split (3) for (2) by issuance of (0.5) additional share 12/22/80
Stock Dividends - 100% 7/1/46; 100% 6/6/51
Under plan of reorganization each share $3.75 Preference no par and Common no par automatically became (1) share Staley Continental, Inc. $3.75 Preference 1¢ par and Common 1¢ par respectively 2/12/85
(See Staley Continental, Inc.)

STALEY CONTL INC (DE)
$3.75 Preference 1¢ par called for redemption 7/1/88
Merged into RP Acquisition Corp. 6/6/88
Each share Common 1¢ par exchanged for $36.50 cash

STALL LAKE MINES LTD (MB)
Shares reacquired 7/23/2002
Each share Common no par exchanged for $1.868 cash

STALLION GROUP (NV)
Each share old Common $0.001 par exchanged for (3) shares new Common $0.001 par 10/02/2006
New Common $0.001 par split (2) for (1) by issuance of (1) additional

share payable 04/17/2007 to holders of record 04/17/2007 Ex date - 04/18/2007
Completely liquidated 12/31/2010
Each share new Common $0.001 par exchanged for first and final distribution of CAD $0.00013626 cash

STALLION RES LTD (BC)
Struck off register and declared dissolved for failure to file returns 7/16/93

STALLONE (JACQUELINE), INC. (NV)
Name changed back to Twentieth Century International, Inc. 09/27/1985
(See Twentieth Century International, Inc.)

STALLONE ENTMT INC (UT)
Name changed 5/31/91
Name changed from Stallone/McComb Inc. to Stallone Entertainment, Inc. 5/31/91
Name changed to American Steinwinter, Inc. 10/2/92
American Steinwinter, Inc. name changed to Lo Boy Inc. 7/1/94
(See Lo Boy Inc.)

STAMBAUGH ESTATES, INC. (OH)
Liquidation completed
Each share Common par exchanged for initial distribution of $70 cash 12/6/67
Each share Common no par received second distribution of $5 cash 5/13/68
Each share Common no par received third and final distribution of $2.49212 cash 12/13/68

STAMBAUGH THOMPSON CO (OH)
Name changed to EFT & Co. Inc. 6/18/97

STAMFORD & WESTERN GAS CO.
Dissolved in 1935

STAMFORD BANCORP INC (ON)
Recapitalized as Stamford International Inc. 04/15/1996
Each share Common no par exchanged for (0.16666666) share Common no par
(See Stamford International Inc.)

STAMFORD BK CORP (NY)
Stock Dividend - 5% payable 03/15/1996 to holders of record 02/01/1996
Acquired by Delaware Bancshares, Inc. 11/09/2007
Each share Common $5 par exchanged for $50.50 cash

STAMFORD CAP GROUP INC (DE)
Name changed to Independence Holding Co. (New) 09/10/1990

STAMFORD CHEMICAL INDUSTRIES, INC. (DE)
Completely liquidated 10/4/65
Each share Common 25¢ par exchanged for first and final distribution of $4.36 cash

STAMFORD FID BK & TR CO (STAMFORD, CT)
Each share Capital Stock $50 par exchanged for (5) shares Capital Stock $10 par 6/9/59
Recapitalized as Fidelity Trust Co. (Stamford, CT) 10/1/69
Each share Capital Stock $10 par exchanged for (2.5) shares Capital Stock $5 par to effect a (2) for (1) split and 25% stock dividend
Fidelity Trust Co. (Stamford, CT) acquired by Shawmut Corp. 11/24/86 which merged into Shawmut National Corp. 2/29/88 which merged into Fleet Financial Group, Inc. (New) 11/30/95 which name changed to Fleet Boston Corp. 10/1/99 which name changed to FleetBoston Financial Corp.

4/18/2000 which merged into Bank of America Corp. 4/1/2004

STAMFORD GAS & ELECTRIC CO.
Merged into Connecticut Power Co. 00/00/1936
Details not available

STAMFORD INDL GROUP INC (DE)
Each share old Common $0.0001 par exchanged for (0.2) share new Common $0.0001 par 03/13/2009
Chapter 7 bankruptcy proceedings terminated 07/28/2014
No stockholders' equity

STAMFORD INTL INC (ON)
Delisted from Canadian Dealers Network 10/13/2000

STAMFORD LD CORP LTD (SINGAPORE)
ADR agreement terminated 04/14/2016
No ADR's remain outstanding

STAMFORD WTR CO (CT)
Each share Capital Stock $100 par exchanged for (5) shares Capital Stock $20 par 00/00/1937
Capital Stock $20 par changed to $10 par and (1) additional share issued 02/15/1979
Stock Dividend - 100% 04/01/1983
Merged into Hydraulic Co. 03/15/1984
Each share Capital Stock $10 par exchanged for $19.50 cash

STAMPEDE ENTMT INC (NV)
Name changed to Global Affiliate Network, Inc. 10/31/2005
(See Global Affiliate Network, Inc.)

STAMPEDE INTL RES INC (BC)
Merged into International H.R.S. Industries Inc. 05/15/1984
Each share Class A Common no par exchanged for (0.66666666) share Common no par
International H.R.S. Industries Inc. name changed to Glenex Industries Inc. 05/25/1987 which merged into Quest Investment Corp. 07/04/2002 which merged into Quest Capital Corp. (BC) 06/30/2003 which reincorporated in Canada 05/27/2008 which name changed to Sprott Resource Lending Corp. 09/10/2010 which merged into Sprott Inc. 07/24/2013

STAMPEDE INTL RES LTD (BC)
Merged into Stampede International Resources Inc. 05/31/1982
Each share Capital Stock no par exchanged for (1) share Class A Common no par
Stampede International Resources Inc. merged into International H.R.S. Industries Inc. 05/15/1984 which name changed to Glenex Industries Inc. 05/25/1987 which merged into Quest Investment Corp. 07/04/2002 which merged into Quest Capital Corp. (BC) 06/30/2003 which reincorporated in Canada 05/27/2008 which name changed to Sprott Resource Lending Corp. 09/10/2010 which merged into Sprott Inc. 07/24/2013

STAMPEDE OILS INC (AB)
Assets sold for the benefit of creditors 12/19/2006
No stockholders' equity

STAMPEDE OILS LTD (AB)
Merged into United Bata Resources Ltd. 03/24/1969
Each share Common 50¢ par exchanged for (2) shares Common 50¢ par
(See United Bata Resources Ltd.)

STAMPEDER EXPL LTD (AB)
Acquired by Gulf Canada Resources Ltd. 09/10/1997
Each share Common no par exchanged for (0.69124) share Common no par
(See Gulf Canada Resources Ltd.)

STAN LEE MEDIA INC (CO)
Stock Dividend - 10% payable 02/13/2001 to holders of record 11/13/2000
Each share old Common $0.001 par exchanged for (0.01) share new Common $0.001 par 01/12/2007
Note: Company has advised it is considered private and will only provide information directly to shareholders

STAN WEST MNG CORP (DE)
Name changed to FIAC, Inc. 05/28/1992
(See FIAC, Inc.)

STANADYNE INC (DE)
Common $10 par changed to $5 par and (1) additional share issued 08/21/1972
Common $5 par changed to $2.50 par and (1) additional share issued 09/07/1984
Common $2.50 par split (3) for (2) by issuance of (0.5) additional share 11/19/1987
Merged into FLSI Acquisition Corp. 03/11/1988
Each share Common $2.50 par exchanged for $55 cash

STANBURY-PIOCHE SILVER MINING CO. (UT)
Merged into Black Hawk Resources Co. 8/17/69
Each share Common 50¢ par exchanged for (2.5) shares Common no par
Black Hawk Resources Co. name changed to Trionics, Inc. 7/2/90

STANCAN URANIUM CORP. (DE)
Recapitalized as Stanward Corp. 8/30/60
Each share Common 1¢ par exchanged for (0.2) share Common 5¢ par
Stanward Corp. acquired by Stanrock Uranium Mines Ltd. 6/7/67 which merged into Denison Mines Ltd. 2/12/73 which recapitalized as Denison Energy Inc. (ONT) 5/30/2002 which reorganized in Alberta 3/8/2004 which name changed to Calfrac Well Services Ltd. 3/29/2004

STANCIL HOFFMAN CORP (CA)
Merged into Stancil Corp. 04/01/1981
Each share Capital Stock no par exchanged for $1.81 cash

STANCOR LTD. (ON)
Reorganized as Sklar Manufacturing Ltd. 07/31/1968
Each share 6% Conv. 1st Preference 1966 Ser. $10 par exchanged for (4) shares Common no par
Each share Common no par exchanged for (0.4) share Common no par plus (0.6) share Common Stock Purchase Warrant expiring 07/02/1978
Sklar Manufacturing Ltd. merged into PCL Industries Ltd. 10/01/1982
(See PCL Industries Ltd.)

STANCORP FINL GROUP INC (OR)
Common no par split (2) for (1) by issuance of (1) additional share payable 12/09/2005 to holders of record 11/25/2005 Ex date - 12/12/2005
Acquired by Meiji Yasuda Life Insurance Co. 03/07/2016
Each share Common no par exchanged for $115 cash

STAND N SNACK AMER INC (FL)
Name changed to Servamerica, Inc. 12/31/69
(See Servamerica, Inc.)

STAND PETROLEUM LTD. (BC)
Merged into Stand-Skat Resources Ltd. 10/16/1978
Each share Capital Stock no par exchanged for (0.09154) share Capital Stock no par
Stand-Skat Resources Ltd. merged into Ramrod Energy Corp. 03/01/1983 which recapitalized as Consolidated Ramrod Gold Corp. 08/27/1986 which name changed to Quest International Resources Corp. 04/09/1996 which recapitalized as Standard Mining Corp. 06/16/1999 which merged into Doublestar Resources Ltd. (YT) 11/01/2001 which reincorporated in British Columbia 10/10/2002 which merged into Selkirk Metals Corp. 07/23/2007
(See Selkirk Metals Corp.)

STAND SKAT RES LTD (BC)
Merged into Ramrod Energy Corp. 03/01/1983
Each share Capital Stock no par exchanged for (1/3) share Common no par
Ramrod Energy Corp. recapitalized as Consolidated Ramrod Gold Corp. 08/27/1986 which name changed to Quest International Resources Corp. 04/09/1996 which recapitalized as Standard Mining Corp. 06/16/1999 which merged into Doublestar Resources Ltd. (YT) 11/01/2001 which reincorporated in British Columbia 10/10/2002 which merged into Selkirk Metals Corp. 07/23/2007
(See Selkirk Metals Corp.)

STANDARD & POOR'S CORP. (NY)
Merged into McGraw-Hill, Inc. 02/15/1966
Each share Common $1 par exchanged for (1) share $1.20 Conv. Preference $10 par
(See McGraw-Hill, Inc.)

STANDARD & POORS INTERCAPITAL DYNAMICS FD INC (DE)
Acquired by Tudor Hedge Fund 09/30/1975
Each share Capital Stock 10¢ par exchanged for (0.49146) share Common $1 par
Tudor Hedge Fund name changed to Tudor Fund 06/18/1980 which name changed to WPG Tudor Fund 12/29/1989
(See WPG Tudor Fund)

STANDARD & POORS INTERCAPITAL INCOME SECS INC (MD)
Name changed to Intercapital Income Securities, Inc. 09/01/1977
Intercapital Income Securities, Inc. name changed to Morgan Stanley Dean Witter 12/21/1998 which name changed to Morgan Stanley Trusts 12/20/2001
(See Morgan Stanley Trusts)

STANDARD & SHELL HOMES CORP. (FL)
Name changed to Standard Investment Corp. of Florida 08/09/1963
Standard Investment Corp. of Florida recapitalized as Industrial-America Corp. 02/26/1965
(See Industrial-America Corp.)

STANDARD ACCIDENT INSURANCE CO. (MI)
Common $50 par changed to $20 par in 1932 and to $10 par in 1933
Merged into Reliance Insurance Co. on a (2) for (1) basis 12/31/63
(See Reliance Insurance Co.)

STANDARD AIRCRAFT EQUIP INC (NY)
Stock Dividend - 10% 09/29/1966
Merged into Stanair Equipment, Inc. 08/11/1975
Each share Common 50¢ par exchanged for $3.38 cash

STANDARD AIRCRAFT PRODUCTS, INC.
Name changed to Standard-Thomson Corp. in 1946
(See Standard-Thomson Corp.)

STANDARD AIRWAYS, INC. (MD)
Declared insolvent by court 5/10/70
Stock declared worthless

STANDARD ALL AMERICA TRUST SHARES
Trust terminated in 1933

STANDARD ALLIANCE INDS INC (DE)
5.25% Conv. Preferred Ser. A $100 par changed to no par 06/02/1971
5.25% Conv. Preferred Ser. A no par called for redemption 08/26/1981
Merged into Walco National Corp. 12/09/1981
Each share Common $1 par exchanged for $40 cash

STANDARD AMER FINL CORP (DE)
Merged into Sundstrand Corp. (DE) 8/5/77
Each share Common $1 par exchanged for (0.457) share Common $1 par
Sundstrand Corp. (DE) merged into United Technologies Corp. 6/10/99

STANDARD AMER LIFE INS CO (IL)
Reorganized under the laws of Delaware as Standard of America Financial Corp. 1/8/69
Each share Common $1 par exchanged for (1) share Common $1 par
Standard of America Financial Corp. merged into Sundstrand Corp. (DE) 8/5/77 which merged into United Technologies Corp. 6/10/99

STANDARD AMERICAN TRUST SHARES
Trust terminated in 1940

STANDARD ANNUITY & LIFE INS CO (IL)
Over 99% acquired by Columbia National Corp. through exchange offer which expired 06/27/1968
Public interest eliminated

STANDARD AUTOMOTIVE CORP (DE)
Issue Information - 1,000,000 shares SR PFD CONV 8.50% offered at $12 per share on 01/22/1998
Issue Information - 1,300,000 shares COM offered at $10 per share on 01/22/1998
Chapter 11 bankruptcy proceedings dismissed 05/13/2004
No stockholders' equity

STANDARD BANCSHARES INC (IL)
Stock Dividend - 5% payable 01/26/2001 to holders of record 01/09/2001 Ex date - 02/05/2001
Merged into First Midwest Bancorp, Inc. 12/06/2016
Each share Common $10 par exchanged for (0.435) share Common 1¢ par

STANDARD BK & TR CO (CHICAGO, IL)
Stock Dividend - 162.58% 04/30/1970
Name changed to Heritage/Standard Bank & Trust Co. (Chicago, IL) 11/01/1974
Heritage/Standard Bank & Trust Co. (Chicago, IL) reorganized as Standard Bancshares, Inc. 11/14/1984 which merged into First Midwest Bancorp, Inc. 12/06/2016

STANDARD BK & TR CO (DUNN, NC)
Merged into Triangle Bancorp Inc. 3/31/95
Each share Common $5 par exchanged for (2) shares Common no par 3/31/95
Triangle Bancorp Inc. merged into Centura Banks, Inc. 2/18/2000

FINANCIAL INFORMATION, INC. STA-STA

which merged into Royal Bank of Canada (Montreal, QC) 6/5/2001

STANDARD BERYLLIUM CORP (NY)
Charter cancelled and proclaimed dissolved for failure to pay taxes 12/20/1977

STANDARD BRANDS AMER INC (DE)
Name changed to Lionshare Group, Inc. 05/07/1998
(See Lionshare Group, Inc.)

STANDARD BRANDS INC (DE)
Each share old Common no par exchanged for (0.25) share new Common no par 09/10/1943
New Common no par split (2) for (1) by issuance of (1) additional share 11/04/1959
New Common no par split (2) for (1) by issuance of (1) additional share 05/31/1966
New Common no par split (2) for (1) by issuance of (1) additional share 02/07/1972
New Common no par split (2) for (1) by issuance of (1) additional share 10/10/1975
Merged into Nabisco Brands, Inc. 07/06/1981
Each share $3.50 Preferred no par exchanged for (1) share $3.50 Preferred $1 par
Each share Common no par exchanged for (1) share Common $2 par
(See Nabisco Brands, Inc.)

STANDARD BRANDS PAINT CO (DE)
Reincorporated 6/12/87
Common $1 par split (2) for (1) by issuance of (1) additional share 05/05/1964
Common $1 par split (2) for (1) by issuance of (1) additional share 02/05/1969
Common $1 par split (2) for (1) by issuance of (1) additional share 02/07/1972
Common $1 par split (2) for (1) by issuance of (1) additional share 04/29/1983
State of incorporation changed from (MD) to (DE) and Common $1 par changed to 1¢ par 06/12/1987
Each share old Common no par exchanged for (0.1) share new Common 1¢ par 05/16/1995
Plan of Liquidation under Chapter 11 Federal Bankruptcy Code effective 11/01/1997
Stockholders' equity unlikely

STANDARD BRASS & MFG CO (TX)
100% acquired by Unimet Corp. as of 03/15/1973
Public interest eliminated

STANDARD BRED PACERS & TROTTERS INC (NY)
Dissolved by proclamation 5/17/90

STANDARD BREWING CO. OF SCRANTON (PA)
Common no par changed to $2.78 par 00/00/1941
Common $2.78 par changed to $1 par 00/00/1952
Name changed to Standard Industries, Inc. (PA) 00/00/1954
Standard Industries, Inc. (PA) name changed to Crane Carrier Industries, Inc. (PA) 10/31/1957 which reincorporated in Delaware 10/23/1959 which name changed to CCI Corp. 10/14/1963 which name changed to CCI Marquardt Corp. 06/12/1968 which name changed to CCI Corp. 09/26/1969
(See CCI Corp.)

STANDARD BROADCASTING LTD (CANADA)
Common no par split (5) for (1) by issuance of (4) additional shares 7/10/68
Merged into Slaight Broadcasting Inc. 1/14/86

Each share Common no par exchanged for $22 cash

STANDARD BUSINESS INDUSTRIES, LTD. (MO)
Charter revoked for failure to file reports and pay fees 1/1/64

STANDARD CABLE CORP.
Out of business 00/00/1953
Details not available

STANDARD CAP & SEAL CORP.
Name changed to Standard Packaging Corp. in 1952

STANDARD CAP CORP (DE)
Name changed to VolitionRX Ltd. 10/11/2011

STANDARD CHEMICAL CO., LTD. (CANADA)
Acquired by Dominion Tar & Chemical Co. Ltd. 00/00/1951
Each share Common no par exchanged for (0.4) share new Common no par and $0.584 cash
Dominion Tar & Chemical Co. Ltd. name changed to Domtar Ltd. 07/01/1965 which name changed to Domtar Ltd.-Domtar Ltee. 01/13/1972 which name changed to Domtar Inc. 02/23/1978 which reorganized as Domtar Corp. (DE) 03/07/2007

STANDARD CLAY PRODUCTS, LTD. (CANADA)
Acquired by Feralco Industries Ltd. in 1957
Details not available

STANDARD COAL CO.
Sold at auction in 1939
No stockholders' equity

STANDARD COATED PRODUCTS CORP.
Merged into Interchemical Corp. in 1944
Each (10) shares Preferred exchanged for (1) share 6% Preferred and (1) share new Common
Each (35) shares old Common exchanged for (1) share new Common
Interchemical Corp. name changed to Inmont Corp. 4/15/69 which merged into Carrier Corp. 12/27/77 which was acquired by United Technologies Corp. 7/6/79

STANDARD COIL PRODUCTS CO. (IL)
Name changed to Standard Kollsman Industries Inc. 06/16/1960
Standard Kollsman Inustries Inc. merged into Sun Chemical Corp. 12/29/1972 which name changed to Sequa Corp. 05/08/1987
(See Sequa Corp.)

STANDARD COLLATERAL TRUSTEED COMMON STOCK SHARES
Trust terminated in 1934

STANDARD COMM INC (DE)
Recapitalized as China Jianye Fuel, Inc. 01/18/2008
Each share Common $0.001 par exchanged for (0.15384615) share Common $0.001 par
(See China Jianye Fuel, Inc.)

STANDARD COML CORP (NC)
Reincorporated 03/11/1983
Name changed 08/25/1987
Each share Preferred $100 par exchanged for (20) shares Common $1 par 00/00/1935
Each share Common no par exchanged for (1) share Common $1 par 00/00/1935
Common $1 par changed to 20¢ par and (4) additional shares issued 12/30/1977
Common 20¢ par split (5) for (3) by issuance of (0.66666666) additional share 11/01/1982

State of incorporation changed from (DE) to (NC) 03/11/1983
Common 20¢ par split (3) for (2) by issuance of (0.5) additional share 02/10/1986
Name changed from Standard Commercial Tobacco Co. to Standard Commericial Corp. 08/25/1987
Common 20¢ par split (3) for (2) by issuance of (0.5) additional share 10/01/1988
Stock Dividends - 1% payable 03/15/1996 to holders of record 03/01/1996; 1% payable 06/17/1996 to holders of record 05/31/1996; 1% payable 09/16/1996 to holders of record 08/30/1996; 1% payable 12/16/1996 to holders of record 11/29/1996; 1% payable 03/17/1997 to holders of record 02/28/1997; 1% payable 06/16/1997 to holders of record 05/30/1997
Merged into Alliance One International, Inc. 05/13/2005
Each share Common 20¢ par exchanged for (3) shares Common no par
Alliance One International, Inc. name changed to Pyxus International, Inc. 09/12/2018

STANDARD COMPUTER & PICTURES CORP (DE)
Charter cancelled and declared inoperative and void for non-payment of taxes 4/15/72

STANDARD COMPUTER CORP (CA)
Each share old Common no par exchanged for (0.13333333) share new Common no par 05/19/1975
Name changed to SCC Liquidating Corp. 11/05/1976
SCC Liquidating Corp. liquidated for United Telecommunications, Inc. 05/15/1981 which name changed to Sprint Corp. (KS) 02/26/1992 which name changed to Sprint Nextel Corp. 08/12/2005 which merged into Sprint Corp. (DE) 07/10/2013

STANDARD COMPUTERS INC (PA)
Merged into Computer Leasing Co. (DE) 10/31/68
Each share Common $1 par exchanged for (1.9) shares Common no par
Computer Leasing Co. (DE) merged into University Computing Co. (TX) 12/17/69 which reincorporated under the laws of Delaware 6/30/72 which name changed to Wyly Corp. 5/25/73 which name changed to Uccel Corp. 5/22/84 which merged into Computer Associates International, Inc. 8/19/87 which name changed to CA, Inc. 2/1/2006

STANDARD CONTAINER CO (GA)
Stock Dividends - 10% 12/22/1975; 10% 01/14/1977; 10% 01/12/1978; 10% 01/11/1979
Merged into Brockway Glass Co., Inc. 08/31/1979
Each share Common $1 par exchanged for $13.70 cash

STANDARD CONTAINER TRANS CORP (DE)
Adjudicated bankrupt 02/10/1975
Stockholders' equity unlikely

STANDARD CONVEYOR CO (MN)
Each share Common $10 par exchanged for (0.0001) share Common $100 par 4/28/81
Note: In effect holders received $0.10 cash per share and public interest was eliminated

STANDARD COOSA THATCHER CO (TN)
Each share Common $25 par exchanged for (4) shares Common $10 par 00/00/1950
Under plan of acquisition each share

Common $10 par exchanged for $53 cash 07/30/1982

STANDARD CORPORATIONS, INC. (NJ)
Charter declared void for non-payment of taxes 1/23/39

STANDARD COUPLER CO.
Dissolution approved in 1938

STANDARD CREAMERIES, INC.
Acquired by Borden Co. 00/00/1929
Details not available

STANDARD DIVERSIFIED OPPORTUNITIES INC (DE)
Each share Class A Common 1¢ par received distribution of (1) share Class B Common 1¢ par payable 06/02/2017 to holders of record 06/02/2017
Name changed to Standard Diversified Inc. 04/25/2018

STANDARD DREDGING CO.
Merged into Standard Dredging Corp. 00/00/1937
Each share Preferred no par exchanged for (1) share $1.60 Preferred $20 par and $15 in Liquidating Notes of Dredging Realization Corp.
Each share Common no par exchanged for (1) share Common $1 par
(See Standard Dredging Corp.)

STANDARD DREDGING CORP (NJ)
Charter declared void for non-payment of taxes 01/14/1982

STANDARD DRILLING CO. (DE)
Recapitalized as Standard Systems & Technology, Inc. 09/09/1983
Each (17.25) shares Common $0.0001 par exchanged for (1) share Common $0.0001 par
(See Standard Systems & Technology, Inc.)

STANDARD DRILLING INC (NV)
Recapitalized as EFactor Group Corp. 11/04/2013
Each share Common $0.001 par exchanged for (0.025) share Common $0.001 par

STANDARD ELEC INC (TX)
Common $25 par changed to $12.50 par and (1) additional share issued 06/01/1962
Name changed to Standard Industries, Inc. (TX) 01/05/1978

STANDARD ELECTRICAL PRODUCTS CO. (OH)
Stock Dividend - 10% 6/10/57
Acquired by General Electronic Control, Inc. 7/27/62
Each share Common 25¢ par exchanged for (1) share Class A Common 10¢ par
General Electronic Control, Inc. recapitalized as Staco, Inc. (Minn.) 9/10/65 which reincorporated in Delaware 11/15/73
(See Staco, Inc. (Del.))

STANDARD ELECTRONICS CORP. (MN)
Merged into California Data Systems Corp. 5/1/69
Each share Common 25¢ par exchanged for (0.1) share Common 10¢ par
California Data Systems Corp. name changed to Interscan, Inc. 6/16/71 which assets were sold in March 1972

STANDARD ELECTRONICS RESEARCH CORP. (DE)
Charter revoked for non-payment of taxes 04/01/1964

STANDARD EQUITIES CORP. (DE)
Name changed to Sheraton Corp. in 1943
Sheraton Corp. name changed to United States Realty-Sheraton Corp.

5/17/46 which name changed to Sheraton Corp. of America 8/19/46 which was acquired by International Telephone & Telegraph Corp. (DE) 2/29/68 which name changed to ITT Corp. 12/31/83 which reorganized in Indiana as ITT Industries, Inc. 12/19/95 which name changed to ITT Corp. 7/1/2006

STANDARD ETAC CORP (CANADA)
Merged into Etac Sales Ltd. 07/04/1988
Each share Common no par exchanged for (0.3606) share Common no par

STANDARD FABRICS INC (MN)
Stock Dividend - 50% 08/21/1970
Common 10¢ par changed to 5¢ par 04/04/1973
Recapitalized as Minnetonka Mills, Inc. 04/01/1976
Each share Common 5¢ par exchanged for (0.1) share Common 50¢ par
(See Minnetonka Mills, Inc.)

STANDARD FACTOR & FIN CO (GA)
Proclaimed dissolved for failure to file annual reports 05/01/1981

STANDARD FACTORS CORP. (NY)
Name changed to Standard Financial Corp. 6/7/57
Standard Financial Corp. name changed to SFC Financial Corp. 12/31/62 which name changed back to Standard Financial Corp. 4/22/64
(See Standard Financial Corp.)

STANDARD FDG CORP (NY)
Merged into Atlantic Premium 6/17/99
Each share Common $0.001 par exchanged for $3.50 cash

STANDARD FED BANCORPORATION INC (MI)
Merged into ABN AMRO North America Inc. 5/1/97
Each share Common $1 par exchanged for $59 cash

STANDARD FED BK (TROY, MI)
Under plan of reorganization each share Common $1 par automatically became (1) share Standard Federal Bancorporation, Inc. Common $1 par 4/25/95
(See Standard Federal Bancorporation, Inc.)

STANDARD FEDERAL FIRE INSURANCE CO.
Liquidated in 1930

STANDARD FINL CORP (MD)
Under plan of merger name changed to Standard AVB Financial Corp. 04/10/2017

STANDARD FINL CORP (NY)
Voting Trust Agreement terminated 07/00/1955
Each VTC for Common $1 par exchanged for (1) share Common $1 par
$0.75 Preferred called for redemption 08/30/1961
Name changed to SFC Financial Corp. 12/31/1962 which name changed back to Standard Financial Corp. 04/22/1964
$3 Conv. Preferred no par called for redemption 05/28/1965
$5.80 Preferred Ser. A-2 no par called for redemption 05/28/1965
$5.80 Preferred Ser. A-3 no par called for redemption 05/28/1965
Each share Common $1 par exchanged for (0.001) share Common $1000 par 12/17/1979
Note: In effect holders received $10 cash per share and public interest was eliminated

STANDARD FINL INC (DE)
Merged into TCF Financial Corp. 09/04/1997
Each share Common no par exchanged for either (0.49359) share Common 1¢ par or $25.81 cash
Note: Option to receive stock expired 09/29/1997

STANDARD FIRE INSURANCE CO. OF NEW JERSEY (NJ)
Capital Stock $12.50 par changed to $17.50 par 9/12/57
Stock Dividend - 66-2/3% 11/5/51
Merged into Reliance Insurance Co. on a (2.2) for (1) basis 6/30/62
(See Reliance Insurance Co.)

STANDARD FORGINGS CORP. (DE)
Each share Class A no par exchanged for (4) shares Common no par in 1935
Common no par changed to $1 par in 1945
Stock Dividend - 10% 5/29/52
Under plan of merger name changed to Standard Alliance Industries, Inc. 5/16/66
(See Standard Alliance Industries, Inc.)

STANDARD FRUIT & STEAMSHIP CO. (DE)
$3 Participating Preference no par called for redemption 02/23/1968
Merged into Castle & Cooke, Inc. (Old) 12/23/1968
Each share Common $2.50 par exchanged for (3) shares Common $10 par
Castle & Cooke, Inc. (Old) name changed to Dole Food Co., Inc. (HI) 07/30/1991 which reincorporated in Delaware 07/01/2001
(See Dole Food Co., Inc. (Old) (DE))

STANDARD FRUIT & STEAMSHIP CORP. (DE)
Recapitalized 00/00/1933
Each share old $7 Preferred no par exchanged for (1) share $3 Part. Preference no par and (0.5) share Common $10 par
Each share Non-Assenting $7 Preferred no par exchanged for (1) share new $7 Preferred no par
Each share Common no par exchanged for (0.1) share Common $10 par
Recapitalized as Standard Fruit & Steamship Co. 03/30/1955
Each share Common $10 par exchanged for (4) shares Common $2.50 par
Each share $3 Part. Preference no par exchanged for (1) share $3 Part. Preference no par
Standard Fruit & Steamship Co. merged into Castle & Cooke, Inc. (Old) 12/23/1968 which name changed to Dole Food Co., Inc. (HI) 07/30/1991 which reincorporated in Delaware 07/01/2001
(See Dole Food Co., Inc. (Old) (DE))

STANDARD FUEL LTD (CANADA)
Completely liquidated 00/00/1974
Each share 4.50% Preferred $50 par received first and final distribution of $53 cash
Each share Common no par received first and final distribution of $48.50 cash

STANDARD GAS & ELEC CO (DE)
Recapitalized in 1928 $7 Prior Preference $100 par changed to no par
Each share 8% Preferred $50 par exchanged for (1) share $4 Preferred no par
Liquidation completed
Each share $7 Prior Preference no par exchanged for first and final distribution of (4.7) shares Wisconsin Public Service Corp. Common $10 par, (2.9) shares Oklahoma Gas & Electric Co. Common $10 par and (2.1) shares Duquesne Light Co. Common $10 par 12/1/52
Each share $6 Prior Preference no par exchanged for first and final distribution of (4.4) shares Wisconsin Public Service Corp. Common $10 par, (2.6) shares Oklahoma Electric Co. Common $10 par and (1.8) shares Duquesne Light Co. Common $10 par 12/1/52
Final date to exchange stock was 12/1/57, after which date unexchanged $6 & $7 Preference ctfs. became worthless
Each share $4 Preferred no par exchanged for first and final distribution (4) shares Duquesne Light Co. Common $10 par 4/27/53
Final date to exchange stock was 4/27/58, after which date unexchanged $4 Preferred ctfs. became worthless
Each share Common no par received initial distribution of (0.25) share Duquesne Light Co. Common $10 par 9/3/53
Common no par changed to $1 par 2/16/55
Common $1 par changed to 10¢ par 4/26/57
Each share Common 10¢ par received second distribution of (0.08) share Duquesne Light Co. Common $5 par, (0.01) share Duquesne Light Co. Preferred $50 par, (0.03) share Wisconsin Public Service Corp. Common $10 par and $1.30 cash 7/28/61
Each share Common 10¢ par exchanged for third distribution of $1.20 cash 3/10/69
Final date to exchange stock was 6/30/70 after which date unexchanged Common ctfs. became worthless

STANDARD GAS CO. OF AMERICA
Property sold in 1934

STANDARD GAS LIGHT CO. OF NEW YORK
Merged into Consolidated Edison Co. of New York, Inc. 00/00/1936
Details not available

STANDARD GILSONITE CO. (UT)
Acquired by Mesa Petroleum Co. 9/10/65
Each share Common 10¢ par exchanged for (0.01929004) share Capital Stock $1 par
(See Mesa Petroleum Corp.)

STANDARD GOLD HOLDINGS INC (NV)
Name changed 03/06/2013
Name and place of incorporation changed from Standard Gold, Inc. (CO) to Standard Gold Holdings, Inc. (NV) 03/06/2013
Name changed to Standard Metals Processing, Inc. 12/06/2013

STANDARD GOLD MINES LTD (BC)
Merged into HLX Resources Ltd. 09/01/1989
Each share Common no par exchanged for (0.2735) share Common no par
HLX Resources Ltd. recapitalized as Emperor Gold Corp. 03/30/1992 which name changed to Emgold Mining Corp. 08/01/1997

STANDARD GOLD MINES LTD (QC)
Recapitalized as S.G.M. Corp.-Corporation S.G.M. 12/17/1976
Each share Capital Stock $1 par exchanged for (0.2) share Capital Stock no par
(See S.G.M. Corp.-Corporation S.G.M.)

STANDARD GRAPHITE CORP (BC)
Name changed to Choom Holdings Inc. 11/22/2017

STANDARD GYPSUM CO. OF CALIFORNIA (DE)
Liquidation completed in 1953

STANDARD GYPSUM CORP (TX)
Each share old Common 1¢ par exchanged for (0.1) share new Common 1¢ par 05/16/1988
Acquired by Caraustar Industries, Inc. 00/00/1996
Details not available

STANDARD HAVENS INC (MO)
Common 5¢ par reclassified as Class A Common 5¢ par 05/10/1983
Class A Common 5¢ par split (2) for (1) by issuance of (1) additional share 06/06/1983
Stock Dividend - 100% 02/22/1982
Merged into Raytheon Co. 06/07/1989
Each share Class A Common 5¢ par exchanged for $3.58 cash

STANDARD HLDGS GROUP LTD (DE)
Company notified SEC no longer operating or now private 04/11/2016

STANDARD INDUSTRIALS, INC.
Liquidated in 1936

STANDARD INDUSTRIES, INC. (PA)
Common $1 par changed to 50¢ par 04/11/1955
Name changed to Crane Carrier Industries, Inc. (PA) 10/31/1957
Crane Carrier Industries, Inc. (PA) reincorporated under the laws of Delaware 10/23/1959 which name changed to CCI Corp. 10/14/1963 which name changed to CCI Marquardt Corp. 06/12/1968 which name changed to CCI Corp. 09/26/1969
(See CCI Corp.)

STANDARD INDS LTD (ON)
Common no par reclassified as Class A Conv. Common no par 07/07/1975
Class A Conv. Common no par split (2) for (1) by issuance of (1) additional share 09/21/1979
Class B Conv. Common no par split (2) for (1) by issuance of (1) additional share 09/21/1979
Preference $10 par called for redemption 11/25/1983
Under plan of merger each share Class A Conv. Common no par and Class B Conv. Common no par automatically became (1) share Canada Cement Lafarge Ltd. - Ciments Canada Lafarge Ltee. Exchangeable Preference no par respectively 12/30/1983
Note: An additional (0.45) share was distributed 01/01/1984
Canada Cement Lafarge Ltd. - Ciments Canada Lafarge Ltee. name changed to Lafarge Canada Inc. 01/12/1988
(See Lafarge Canada Inc.)

STANDARD INSTALLMENT FIN CO (OK)
Adjudicated bankrupt 04/12/1965
No stockholders' equity

STANDARD INSTRUMENT CORP. (NY)
Each share Common 20¢ par exchanged for (1) share Class A 20¢ par 09/23/1960
Name changed to H-T Products Corp. 07/12/1967
(See H-T Products Corp.)

STANDARD INTL CORP (OH)
Common no par split (5) for (4) by issuance of (0.25) additional share 12/02/1968
Name changed to Standex International Corp. (OH) 07/24/1973
Standex International Corp. (OH) reincorporated in Delaware 06/30/1975

STANDARD INTERNATIONAL SECURITIES CORP.
Acquired by Atlantic & Pacific International Corp. in 1929
Details not available

STANDARD INVESTING CORP. (MD)
Merged into Standard Equities Corp. in May 1941
Each share Preferred exchanged for (2) shares Common $1 par
Each share Common exchanged for (0.014) share Common $1 par
Standard Equities Corp. name changed to Sheraton Corp. in 1943 which name changed to United States Realty-Sheraton Corp. 5/17/46 which name changed to Sheraton Corp. of America 8/19/46 which was acquired by International Telephone & Telegraph Corp. (DE) 2/29/68 which name changed to ITT Corp. 12/31/83 which reorganized in Indiana as ITT Industries, Inc. 12/19/95 which name changed to ITT Corp. 7/1/2006

STANDARD INVESTMENT CO., INC. (MD)
Liquidated in 1954

STANDARD INVESTMENT CORP. OF FLORIDA (FL)
Recapitalized as Industrial-America Corp. 02/26/1965
Each share Common 25¢ par exchanged for (0.2) share Common $1.25 par
(See Industrial-America Corp.)

STANDARD KNITTING MLS INC (TN)
Acquired by Chadbourn Inc. 04/22/1970
Each share 7% Preferred $100 par exchanged for (11) shares 46-2/3¢ Conv. Jr. Preferred Ser. A $10 par
Each share Common $8-1/3 par exchanged for (1.5) shares 46-2/3¢ Conv. Jr. Preferred Ser. A $10 par
Chadbourn Inc. reorganized as Stanwood Corp. 06/12/1975 which was acquired by Delta Woodside Industries, Inc. (DE) 09/07/1988 which merged into Delta Woodside Industries, Inc. (SC) 11/15/1989
(See Delta Woodside Industries, Inc. (SC))

STANDARD KOLLSMAN INDS INC (IL)
Merged into Sun Chemical Corp. 12/29/1972
Each share Capital Stock $1 par exchanged for (0.222222) share Common $1 par
Sun Chemical Corp. name changed to Sequa Corp. 05/08/1987
(See Sequa Corp.)

STANDARD LABORATORIES, INC. (IL)
Charter dissolved 1/27/27

STANDARD LIFE & ACC INS CO (OK)
Reorganized as Standard Life Corp. 01/02/1973
Each share Common $1 par exchanged for (1) share Common 10¢ par
Standard Life Corp. reorganized as National Guaranty Insurance Co. 04/06/1981
(See National Guaranty Insurance Co.)

STANDARD LIFE CORP (OK)
Under plan of reorganization each share Common 10¢ par automatically became (1) share National Guaranty Insurance Co. Common Capital Stock 25¢ par 04/06/1981
(See National Guaranty Insurance Co.)

STANDARD LIFE INSURANCE CO. OF THE SOUTH (MS)
Name changed to Standard Life Insurance Co. 3/16/66
(See Standard Life Insurance Co.)

STANDARD LIFE INS CO (MS)
Stock Dividends - 100% 04/02/1966; 20% 02/26/1977
Merged into New Standard Life Insurance Co. 11/14/1986
Each share Common $10 par exchanged for $547.97 cash

STANDARD LIFE INS CO IND (IN)
Class A $5 par and Class B $5 par reclassified as Common $5 par 02/02/1962
Common $5 par changed to $1 par and (4) additional shares issued 12/28/1964
Common $1 par changed to $1.50 par 06/23/1972
Stock Dividends - 10% 03/16/1962; 10% 05/01/1964; 10% 04/22/1966; 10% 04/14/1972; 10% 11/04/1977
Merged into INA Standard, Inc. 09/22/1980
Each share Common $1.50 par exchanged for $28 cash

STANDARD LIFE PLC (UNITED KINGDOM)
Each old ADR for Ordinary exchanged for (0.81818181) new ADR for Ordinary 03/16/2015
Name changed to Standard Life Aberdeen PLC 08/28/2017

STANDARD LOGIC INC (CA)
Common 10¢ par changed to 5¢ par and (1) additional share issued 11/19/1973
Common 5¢ par changed to 2-1/2¢ par and (1) additional share issued 10/20/1978
Name changed to Appoint Technologies, Inc. 04/12/1993
(See Appoint Technologies, Inc.)

STANDARD MAGNESIUM & CHEMICAL CO. (DE)
Liquidation completed
Each share Common 10¢ par exchanged for initial distribution of (0.14) share Kaiser Aluminum & Chemical Corp. Common $0.33333333 par 03/16/1964
Each share Common 10¢ par received second distribution of (0.007736) share Kaiser Aluminum & Chemical Corp.
Common $0.33333333 par and $0.01 cash 06/02/1967
Each share Common 10¢ par received a special third and final distribution of $0.085699 cash 12/16/1969
(See Kaiser Aluminum & Chemical Corp.)

STANDARD MAGNESIUM CORP. (NY)
Recapitalized under the laws of Delaware as Standard Magnesium & Chemical Co. 5/31/63
Each share Common 10¢ par exchanged for (0.2) share Common 10¢ par
Standard Magnesium & Chemical Co. completed liquidation 12/16/69

STANDARD MGMT CORP (IN)
Stock Dividend - 5% payable 06/21/1996 to holders of record 05/17/1996
Conv. Class S Preferred no par called for redemption at $10 plus $1.6274 accrued dividends on 08/01/1997
SEC revoked common stock registration 10/07/2013

STANDARD MANUFACTURING CORP. (IL)
Completely liquidated 10/25/65
Each share Class A Common 10¢ par exchanged for first and final distribution of $0.755 cash

STANDARD METALS CO. (NV)
Charter revoked for failure to file reports and pay fees 2/28/24

STANDARD METALS CORP (DE)
Each share Common 1¢ par exchanged for (1/3) share Common 3¢ par 07/26/1961
Stock Dividends - 10% 05/07/1975; 10% 11/27/1980
Name changed to American Holdings, Inc. 11/22/2005
(See American Holdings, Inc.)

STANDARD MICROSYSTEMS CORP (DE)
Common 10¢ par split (3) for (2) by issuance of (0.5) additional share 07/29/1983
Acquired by Microchip Technology Inc. 08/03/2012
Each share Common 10¢ par exchanged for $37 cash

STANDARD MILLING CO.
Acquired by Gold Dust Corp. 00/00/1929
Details not available

STANDARD MILLING CO. NEW (IL)
Reincorporated under the laws of Delaware 5/31/55
Each share Common $1 par exchanged for (2) shares Class A Common $1 par and (1) share Class B Common $1 par
Standard Milling Co. (DE) name changed to Uhlmann Co. 1/10/83
(See Uhlmann Co.)

STANDARD MNG CORP (BC)
Merged into Doublestar Resources Ltd. (YT) 11/01/2001
Each share Common no par exchanged for (0.2) share Common no par
Doublestar Resources Ltd. (YT) reincorporated in British Columbia 10/10/2002 which merged into Selkirk Metals Corp. 07/23/2007
(See Selkirk Metals Corp.)

STANDARD MNG INC (AB)
Merged into Quest International Resources Corp. 04/03/1999
Each share Common no par exchanged for (1) share Common no par
Quest International Resources Corp. recapitalized as Standard Mining Corp. 06/16/1999 which merged into Doublestar Resources Ltd. (YT) 11/01/2001 which reincorporated in British Columbia 10/10/2002 which merged into Selkirk Metals Corp. 07/23/2007
(See Selkirk Metals Corp.)

STANDARD MLG CO (DE)
Name changed to Uhlmann Co. 01/10/1983
(See Uhlmann Co.)

STANDARD MODERN TECHNOLOGIES CORP (ON)
Placed in receivership 10/00/1987
No stockholders' equity

STANDARD MOTELS INC (CA)
Class A Common $1 par reclassified as Class B Common $1 par 00/00/1956
Adjudicated bankrupt 02/15/1972
Stockholders' equity unlikely

STANDARD MOTOR CONSTRUCTION CO. (NJ)
Charter revoked for failure to file reports and pay fees 12/30/32

STANDARD NATIONAL CORP.
Liquidation completed in 1947

STANDARD OF THE SOUTHWEST LIFE INSURANCE CO. (NM)
Merged into American Home Security Life Insurance Co. 6/18/65
Each share Capital Stock $1 par exchanged for (1.5) shares Class A Common 20¢ par
American Home Security Life Insurance Co. merged into S.N.L. Financial Corp. 4/16/82 which name changed to Security National Financial Corp. 12/27/90

STANDARD OIL & EXPL DEL INC (DE)
Each share old Common $0.001 par exchanged for (0.25) share new Common $0.001 par 8/14/89
Plan of reorganization under Chapter 11 Federal Bankruptcy Code effective 4/22/93
Each share new Common $0.001 par exchanged for (1) American Resources of Delaware, Inc. Common Stock Purchase Warrant expiring 4/24/95

STANDARD OIL CO. (KY)
Each share Common $25 par exchanged for (2.5) shares Common $10 par in 1928
Merged into Standard Oil Co. of California 9/29/61
Each share Common $10 par exchanged for (1) share $3.30 Preferred no par
(See Standard Oil Co. of California)

STANDARD OIL CO. (NE)
Acquired by Standard Oil Co. (Indiana) for $17.50 per share in cash in 1939

STANDARD OIL CO. OF NEW YORK
Merged into Socony-Vacuum Corp. share for share in 1931
Socony-Vacuum Corp. name changed to Socony-Vacuum Oil Co., Inc. in 1934 which name changed to Socony Mobil Oil Co., Inc. 4/29/55 which name changed to Mobil Oil Corp. 5/18/66 which reorganized as Mobil Corp. 6/21/76 which merged into Exxon Mobil Corp. 11/30/99

STANDARD OIL CO (IN)
Capital Stock $25 par changed to $12.50 par and (1) additional share issued 10/16/1964
Capital Stock $12.50 par split (2) for (1) by issuance of (1) additional share 12/16/1974
Capital Stock $12.50 par reclassified as Common no par 04/23/1980
Common no par split (2) for (1) by issuance of (1) additional share 05/27/1980
Stock Dividend - 100% 12/01/1954
Name changed to Amoco Corp. 04/23/1985
Amoco Corp. merged into BP Amoco p.l.c. 12/31/1998 which name changed to BP PLC 05/01/2001

STANDARD OIL CO (NJ)
Each share Capital Stock $25 par exchanged for (2) shares Capital Stock $15 par 00/00/1951
Capital Stock $15 par changed to $7 par and (2) additional shares issued 03/16/1956
Name changed to Exxon Corp. 11/01/1972
Exxon Corp. name changed to Exxon Mobil Corp. 11/30/1999

STANDARD OIL CO (OH)
Each share Common $100 par exchanged for (4) shares Common $25 par 00/00/1927
Each share Common $25 par exchanged for (2.5) shares Common $10 par 00/00/1945
4-1/4% Conv. Preferred $100 par called for redemption 09/04/1945
5% Preferred $100 par called for redemption 09/04/1945
Common $10 par changed to $5 par and (1) additional share issued 07/31/1964
Common $5 par changed to no par and (1) additional share issued 12/17/1973
Common no par split (2) for (1) by issuance of (1) additional share 06/30/1978
4% Conv. Preferred Ser. B $100 par called for redemption 07/16/1979
Common no par split (2) for (1) by

issuance of (1) additional share 06/20/1980
3-3/4% Preferred Ser. A $100 par called for redemption 06/28/1987
Stock Dividends - 20% 06/25/1956; 10% 06/24/1963; 10% 12/26/1967
Merged into BP America Inc. 06/29/1987
Each share Common no par exchanged for (0.2) ADR Purchase Warrant expiring 01/31/1993 of British Petroleum Co. p.l.c. and $71.50 cash

STANDARD OIL CO CALIF (DE)
Capital Stock no par split (2) for (1) by issuance of (1) additional share 3/14/51
Capital Stock no par changed to $6.25 par and (1) additional share issued 6/18/56
Capital Stock $6.25 par reclassified as Common $6.25 par 9/12/61
$3.30 Conv. Preferred no par called for redemption 10/1/66
Common $6.25 par changed to $3.125 par and (1) additional share issued 12/10/73
Common $3.125 par changed to $3 par and (1) additional share issued 3/10/81
Name changed to Chevron Corp. 7/1/84
Chevron Corp. name changed to ChevronTexaco Corp. 10/9/2001 which name changed back to Chevron Corp. 5/9/2005

STANDARD OIL CO USA INC (FL)
Name changed to Gold Mining USA Inc. 05/24/2012
Gold Mining USA Inc. name changed to Vita Mobile Systems, Inc. 01/31/2018

STANDARD OIL INVESTMENT SHARES
Dissolved in 1932

STANDARD OIL TRUST SHARES
Series A and B Trusts terminated and liquidated 00/00/1936
Details not available

STANDARD PAC CORP NEW (DE)
Common 1¢ par split (2) for (1) by issuance of (1) additional share payable 08/29/2005 to holders of record 08/08/2005 Ex date - 08/30/2005
Merged into CalAtlantic Group, Inc. 10/01/2015
Each share Common 1¢ par exchanged for (0.2) share Common 1¢ par
CalAtlantic Group, Inc. merged into Lennar Corp. 02/12/2018

STANDARD PAC CORP OLD (DE)
Reincorporated 08/31/1981
Common 25¢ par split (3) for (2) by issuance of (0.5) additional share 12/15/1977
Stock Dividend - 10% 12/15/1978
State of incorporation changed from (CA) to (DE) 08/31/1981
Common 25¢ par split (3) for (2) by issuance of (0.5) additional share 03/04/1985
Common 25¢ par split (3) for (2) by issuance of (0.5) additional share 03/11/1986
Assets transferred to Standard Pacific, L.P. 12/30/1986
Each share Common 25¢ par exchanged for (1) Depository Receipt
Standard Pacific, L.P. reorganized as Standard Pacific Corp. (New) 12/31/1991 which merged into CalAtlantic Group, Inc. 10/01/2015 which merged into Lennar Corp. 02/12/2018

STANDARD PAC FINL CORP (NV)
Recapitalized as Standard General Group 09/11/1990
Each share Common $0.001 par exchanged for (0.16666666) share Common $0.001 par

STANDARD PAC L P (DE)
Depositary Receipts split (2) for (1) by issuance of (1) additional Receipt 05/06/1987
Under plan of reorganization each Depositary Receipt automatically became (1) share Standard Pacific Corp. (New) Common 1¢ par 12/31/1991
Standard Pacific Corp. (New) merged into CalAtlantic Group, Inc. 10/01/2015 which merged into Lennar Corp. 02/12/2018

STANDARD PACKAGING CORP (VA)
Common $1 par split (3) for (1) by issuance of (2) additional shares 12/27/1955
Under plan of merger each share Preference $10 par exchanged for (1) share $1.60 Conv. Preferred $20 par 09/15/1958
Each share $1.20 Conv. Preferred $20 par or 6% Conv. Preferred $20 par exchanged for $24 principal amount of 5.25% 25-Year Conv. Subord. Debentures due 1990 or 6% Non-Conv. Subord. Debentures due 1990 on 04/30/1965
Note: Option to receive 5.25% Conv. Subord. Debentures expired 05/25/1965
Merged into Saxon Industries, Inc. (NY) 10/22/1970
Each share $1.60 Conv. Preferred $20 par exchanged for (1.761) shares Common 25¢ par
Each share Common $1 par exchanged for (0.5) share Common 25¢ par
Saxon Industries, Inc. (NY) reincorporated in Delaware 10/03/1975 which reorganized as Paper Corp. of America 04/01/1985
(See Paper Corp. of America)

STANDARD PAPER CO.
Acquired by Sutherland Paper Co. 00/00/1928
Details not available

STANDARD PAPER MFG CO (VA)
Each share 7.5% Preferred $100 par exchanged for (2) shares 6% Conv. Preferred $50 par and (1.2) shares Common $50 par 00/00/1941
Each share Common $100 par and Class B Common $100 par exchanged for (1) share Common $50 par 00/00/1941
6% Conv. Preferred $50 par called for redemption 01/02/1964
Common $50 par changed to $10 par and (4) additional shares issued 12/10/1964
Charter cancelled and proclaimed dissolved for failure to file reports 06/01/1978

STANDARD PARTS CO. (OH)
Incorporated 11/2/16
Charter cancelled for non-payment of taxes 2/14/25

STANDARD PATENTS & DEVICES INC (NY)
Merged into Intercontinental Industries Corp. 06/26/1972
Each share Common 1¢ par exchanged for (1) share Common 1¢ par
(See Intercontinental Industries Corp.)

STANDARD PAV & MATLS LTD (ON)
Each share 7% Preferred $100 par exchanged for (4) shares Preferred no par and (2) shares Common no par 00/00/1939
Common no par split (3) for (1) by issuance of (2) additional shares 08/11/1959
Common no par split (3) for (1) by issuance of (2) additional shares 12/07/1972
Name changed to Standard Industries Ltd. 01/01/1974
Standard Industries Ltd. merged into Canada Cement Lafarge Ltd. - Ciments Canada Lafarge Ltee. 12/30/1983 which name changed to Lafarge Canada Inc. 01/12/1988
(See Lafarge Canada Inc.)

STANDARD PAVING, LTD.
Merged into Standard Paving & Materials Ltd. 00/00/1929
Details not available

STANDARD PETROLEUM CORP. (DE)
Name changed to Guardian Oil Co., Inc. 00/00/1954
Guardian Oil Co., Inc. merged into Consolidated Rimrock Oil Corp. 10/01/1956 which merged into Consolidated Oil & Gas, Inc. (CO) 04/30/1958 which was acquired by Hugoton Energy Corp. 09/07/1995 which merged into Chesapeake Energy Corp. 03/10/1998

STANDARD PKG CORP (DE)
Issue Information - 4,500,000 shares COM offered at $11.50 per share on 05/27/2004
Common $0.001 par split (2) for (1) by issuance of (1) additional share payable 01/17/2008 to holders of record 01/08/2008 Ex date - 01/18/2008
Name changed to SP Plus Corp. 12/02/2013

STANDARD PLATE GLASS CO.
Liquidated in 1933

STANDARD PLYWOOD CORP (CA)
Charter suspended for failure to file reports and pay fees 11/03/1980

STANDARD POWER & LIGHT CORP. (DE)
Common no par changed to $1 par in 1936
Recapitalized as Standard Shares, Inc. 3/27/56
Each share Class B Common no par or Common $1 par exchanged for (1) share Common $1 par
Standard Shares, Inc. name changed to Pittway Corp. (DE) 12/28/89
(See Pittway Corp. (DE))

STANDARD PRESSED STL CO (PA)
Common $10 par changed to $1 par 06/11/1956
Common $1 par split (2) for (1) by issuance of (1) additional share 03/14/1968
Stock Dividend - 250% 12/28/1956
Name changed to SPS Technologies, Inc. 04/25/1978
SPS Technologies, Inc. merged into Precision Castparts Corp. 12/09/2003
(See Precision Castparts Corp.)

STANDARD PRODS CO (OH)
Common $1 par split (2) for (1) by issuance of (1) additional share 10/10/55
Common $1 par split (3) for (2) by issuance of (0.5) additional share 12/28/71
Common $1 par split (3) for (2) by issuance of (0.5) additional share 7/20/73
Common $1 par split (3) for (2) by issuance of (0.5) additional share 2/25/83
Common $1 par split (3) for (1) by issuance of (2) additional shares 8/25/83
Common $1 par split (3) for (2) by issuance of (0.5) additional share 4/25/86
Common $1 par split (5) for (4) by issuance of (0.25) additional share 9/18/87
Common $1 par split (5) for (4) by issuance of (0.25) additional share 6/3/93
Merged into Cooper Tire & Rubber Co. 10/27/99
Each share Common $1 par exchanged for $36.50 cash

STANDARD PRUDENTIAL CORP. OLD (NY)
Class B 4¢ par called for redemption 06/30/1965
Merged into Standard Prudential United Corp. 08/18/1966
Each share Class A $1.20 par exchanged for (0.7) share Common $1 par
Each share Class C 10¢ par exchanged for (0.7) share Conv. Preference 10¢ par
Standard Prudential United Corp. name changed to Standard Prudential Corp. (New) 10/22/1968 which name changed to Sterling Bancorp (NY) 10/24/1978 which merged into Sterling Bancorp (DE) 11/01/2013

STANDARD PRUDENTIAL CORP NEW (NY)
10¢ Conv. Preferred no par called for redemption 11/30/1979
Name changed to Sterling Bancorp (NY) 10/24/1978
Sterling Bancorp (NY) merged into Sterling Bancorp (DE) 11/01/2013

STANDARD PRUDENTIAL UNITED CORP. (OLD) (NY)
Name changed to Standard Prudential Corp. (New) 10/22/1968
Standard Prudential Corp. (New) name changed to Sterling Bancorp (NY) 10/24/1978 which merged into Sterling Bancorp (DE) 11/01/2013

STANDARD RADIO LTD. (CANADA)
Common no par split (5) for (1) by issuance of (4) additional shares 7/19/62
Name changed to Standard Broadcasting Corp. Ltd. 7/5/68
(See Standard Broadcasting Corp. Ltd.)

STANDARD RAILWAY EQUIPMENT MANUFACTURING CO. (DE)
Name changed to Stanray Corp. 05/02/1960
Stanray Corp. merged into IC Industries, Inc. 04/26/1977
(See IC Industries, Inc.)

STANDARD REALTY CO. OF BALTIMORE (MD)
Charter forfeited for failure to file annual reports 10/14/82

STANDARD RLTY INVS CORP (DE)
Became defunct 06/30/1974
Attorney opined no stockholders' equity

STANDARD RECTIFIER CORP. (NV)
Name changed to Newbar Televonics, Inc. 5/27/68
Newbar Televonics, Inc. recapitalized as Emerson Films, Inc. 11/6/70
(See Emerson Films, Inc.)

STANDARD REGISTER CO (OH)
Common $1 par changed to 50¢ par and (1) additional share issued 05/11/1962
Common 50¢ par changed to no par and (2) additional shares issued 06/03/1983
Common no par split (2) for (1) by issuance of (1) additional share 06/04/1985
Common no par changed to $1 par and (1) additional share issued 06/05/1987
Each share old Class A $1 par exchanged for (0.2) new Class A $1 par 05/10/2013
Each share old Common $1 par exchanged for (0.2) share new Common $1 par 05/10/2013
Plan of reorganization under Chapter 11 Federal Bankruptcy proceedings effective 12/18/2015

No stockholders' equity

STANDARD RES CORP (DE)
Reincorporated 11/28/69
State of incorporation changed from (NY) to (DE) 11/28/69
Name changed to Microsemiconductor Corp. 3/22/72
Microsemiconductor Corp. name changed to Microsemi Corp. 2/10/83

STANDARD RES INC (NV)
Name changed to Veta Grande Companies, Inc. (Old) and Common $1 par changed to 1¢ par 06/17/1980
Veta Grande Companies, Inc. (Old) recapitalized as Veta Grande Companies, Inc. (New) 07/28/1986 which name changed to Forum Re Group Inc. 07/29/1988 which name changed to THE Group, Inc. 02/05/1990
(See THE Group, Inc.)

STANDARD SANITARY MANUFACTURING CO. (NJ)
Merged into American Radiator & Standard Sanitary Corp. 3/26/29
(See American Radiator & Standard Sanitary Corp.)

STANDARD SAVINGS INVESTMENT CO. (CO)
Declared defunct and inoperative for failure to file reports and pay taxes 10/15/74

STANDARD SAVINGS LIFE INSURANCE CO. (CO)
Name changed to Standard Savings Investment Co. 7/7/66
Standard Savings Investment Co. declared defunct 10/15/74

STANDARD SCREW CO (DE)
Reincorporated 5/29/69
Each share Common $100 par exchanged for (5) shares Common $20 par in 1937
Each share 6% Class A Preferred $100 par exchanged for (3) shares Common $20 par in 1951
Common $20 par split (3) for (1) by issuance of (2) additional shares 3/10/60
Common $20 par changed to $10 par and (2) additional shares issued 7/31/67
State of incorporation changed from (NJ) to (DE) 5/29/69
Name changed to Stanadyne, Inc. 4/1/70
(See Stanadyne, Inc.)

STANDARD SEC HLDG CORP (DE)
Name changed to Geneve Capital Group, Inc. 06/25/1981
Geneve Capital Group, Inc. liquidated for Stamford Capital Group, Inc. 08/05/1988 which name changed to Independence Holding Co. (New) 09/01/1990

STANDARD SEC LIFE INS CO N Y (NY)
Class A $2 par and Common $2 par changed to $1 par 06/19/1964
Class A $1 par and Common $1 par changed to $1.10 par 05/06/1970
Merged into Standard Security Holding Corp. 03/15/1979
Each share Class A $1.10 par exchanged for $13.75 cash
Each share Common $1.10 par exchanged for $13.75 cash

STANDARD SHS INC (DE)
Stock Dividend - 100% 12/28/64
Each share Common $1 par received distribution of (1.63) shares Pittway Corp. Class A $1 par and $7.11 cash 11/9/89
Under plan of merger name changed to Pittway Corp. (DE) 12/28/89
(See Pittway Corp. (DE))

STANDARD SIGN & SIGNAL CO. (TX)
Reorganized as A.R.C. Industries, Inc. 3/12/69

Each share Common 10¢ par exchanged for (0.2) share Common 50¢ par
A.R.C. Industries, Inc. name changed to Appalachian Resources, Inc. 9/8/71

STANDARD SILICA CORP. (DE)
Assets sold and in process of liquidation in 1955

STANDARD SILICA CORP. (IL)
Each share Common $10 par exchanged for (3) shares Common $1 par in 1937
Reincorporated under laws of Delaware in 1953 which company was in process of liquidation in 1955

STANDARD SILVER CORP (NV)
Each share old Common 1¢ par exchanged for (0.5) share new Common 1¢ par 04/17/2007
Name changed to Texas Rare Earth Resources Corp. (NV) 09/29/2010
Texas Rare Earth Resources Corp. (NV) reincorporated in Delaware 08/24/2012 which name changed to Texas Mineral Resources Corp. 03/21/2016

STANDARD SILVER-LEAD MINING CO. (WA)
Placed in receivership in 1960
Liquidation of assets insufficient to pay creditors in full
No stockholders' equity

STANDARD SLAG CO (OH)
6% 1st Preferred $50 par called for redemption 12/22/89
6% 2nd Preferred $50 par called for redemption 12/22/89

STANDARD STATE BANK (CHICAGO, IL)
Name changed to Standard Bank & Trust Co. (Chicago, IL) 06/01/1962
Standard Bank & Trust Co. (Chicago, IL) name changed to Heritage/Standard Bank & Trust Co. (Chicago, IL) 11/01/1974 which reorganized as Standard Bancshares, Inc. 11/14/1984 which merged into First Midwest Bancorp, Inc. 12/06/2016

STANDARD STEEL CONSTRUCTION CO., LTD.
Acquired by United Steel Corp. Ltd. on a share for share basis in 1941
United Steel Corp. Ltd. recapitalized as James United Steel Ltd. 6/28/65 which name changed to James United Industries, Ltd. 9/25/69
(See James United Industries, Ltd.)

STANDARD STEEL SPRING CO. (PA)
Each share Common $100 par exchanged for (10) shares Common no par in 1929
Common no par changed to $5 par in 1937
Each share Common $5 par exchanged for (5) shares Common $1 par in 1943
Stock Dividend - 10% 12/10/50
Merged into Rockwell Spring & Axle Co.
(See Rockwell Spring & Axle Co.)

STANDARD STOKER CO., INC.
Name changed to Read Standard Corp. in 1951
Read Standard Corp. merged into Capitol Products Corp. 11/3/56
(See Capitol Products Corp.)

STANDARD STRUCTURAL STL LTD (QC)
Common no par split (2) for (1) by issuance of (1) additional share 10/13/1965
100% acquired by International Utilities Corp. through purchase offer which expired 02/12/1971
Public interest eliminated

STANDARD SULPHUR CO. (DE)
Recapitalized as Inter World TV

Films, Inc. on a (0.2) for (1) basis 9/5/58
(See Inter World TV Films, Inc.)

STANDARD SYS & TECHNOLOGY INC (DE)
Charter cancelled and declared inoperative and void for non-payment of taxes 06/27/1989

STANDARD SYS INTL INC (ID)
Charter forfeited for failure to file reports and pay fees 11/30/1973

STANDARD TANK CAR CO.
Assets sold in 1929
No stockholders' equity

STANDARD TELEPHONE CO.
Reorganized as Investors Telephone Co. in 1936
No stockholders' equity

STANDARD TELEVISION & ELECTRIC CORP.
Dissolution approved in 1934

STANDARD TEXTILE PRODUCTS CO.
Reorganized as Standard Coated Products Corp. 00/00/1937
Each share $7 Preferred Ser. A exchanged for (0.5) share Common
Each share $5 Preferred Ser. B exchanged for (0.2) share Common
Each share Common exchanged for (0.02) share new Common
Standard Coated Products Corp. merged into Interchemical Corp. 00/00/1944 which name changed to Inmont Corp. 04/15/1969 which merged into Carrier Corp. 12/27/1977 which was acquired by United Technologies Corp. 07/06/1979

STANDARD THOMSON CORP (DE)
Each share Common 2¢ par exchanged for (1/3) share Common $1 par 00/00/1947
5-1/2% Preferred $12.50 par called for redemption 04/01/1975
Stock Dividend - 25% 12/31/1972
Merged into Allegheny Ludlum Industries, Inc. 02/28/1975
Each share Common $1 par exchanged $18 cash

STANDARD TIE & TIMBER WESTERN, LTD. (AB)
Name changed to Penny Spruce Mills Ltd. in 1952, which liquidated in July, 1961

STANDARD-TOCH CHEMICALS, INC. (NY)
Common no par changed to $1 par and (1) additional share issued 3/12/56
Merged into Standard Toch Industries, Inc. 7/1/60
Each share Common 1¢ par exchanged for (10) shares Class A Common 1¢ par
(See Standard Toch Industries, Inc.)

STANDARD TOCH INDUSTRIES, INC. (PA)
Merged into Kenrich Petrochemicals, Inc. 03/16/1962
Each share Class A Common 1¢ par exchanged for (0.15) share Class A Common 20¢ par, (0.08) Class A Common Stock Purchase Warrant and (0.1) share Panel-Lift Door Corp. Class A Common 1¢ par
(See each company's listing)

STANDARD TOLLING CORP (BC)
Each share old Common no par exchanged for (0.33333333) share new Common no par 11/25/2014
Voluntarily dissolved 04/24/2017
No stockholders' equity

STANDARD TOOL CO.
In process of liquidation in 1949

STANDARD TRUST BANK (CLEVELAND, OH)
Dissolved 12/21/31

No stockholders' equity

STANDARD TR CO (TORONTO, ON)
Over 95% acquired by Standard Trustco Ltd. through exchange offer as of 11/24/1980
Public interest eliminated

STANDARD TRUSTCO LTD (ON)
Common no par split (3) for (1) by issuance of (2) additional shares 5/25/82
14-1/4% 1st Preferred Ser. B $20 par called for redemption 7/1/87
Common no par split (2) for (1) by issuance of (1) additional share 8/21/87
Company placed in bankruptcy 4/17/91
Common no par delisted from Toronto Stock Exchange 6/17/92
Stockholders' equity unlikely

STANDARD TUBE CO. (MI)
Merged into Michigan Seamless Tube Co. (DE) 07/01/1968
Each share Class B Common $1 par exchanged for (0.5) share Common $5 par
Michigan Seamless Tube Co. (DE) name changed to Quanex Corp. 02/24/1977
(See Quanex Corp.)

STANDARD TUNGSTEN CORP (DE)
Charter cancelled and declared inoperative and void for non-payment of taxes 4/15/73

STANDARD UNDERGROUND CABLE CO.
Merged into General Cable Corp. 00/00/1927
Details not available

STANDARD URANIUM CORP. (DE)
Name changed to Standard Metals Corp. 05/19/1960
Standard Metals Corp. name changed to American Holdings, Inc. 11/22/2005
(See American Holdings, Inc.)

STANDARD URANIUM INC (BC)
Merged into Energy Metals Corp. 03/13/2006
Each share Common no par exchanged for (0.64) share Common no par
Energy Metals Corp. merged into Uranium One Inc. 08/10/2007
(See Uranium One Inc.)

STANDARD UTILITIES, INC.
Name changed to Standard Investment Co., Inc. in 1948 which was liquidated in 1954

STANDARD VARNISH WORKS (NY)
Name changed to Standard-Toch Chemicals, Inc. in 1951
Standard-Toch Chemicals, Inc. merged into Standard Toch Industries, Inc. 7/1/60
(See Standard Toch Industries, Inc.)

STANDARD WALL PAPER CO. (DE)
Acquired by United Wall Paper Factories Inc. 00/00/1927
Details not available

STANDARD WHOLESALE PHOSPHATE & ACID WORKS, INC.
Merged into Mathieson Chemical Corp. on a (3) for (2) basis in 1949
Mathieson Chemical Corp. merged into Olin Mathieson Chemical Corp. in 1954 which name changed to Olin Corp. 9/1/69

STANDART BROTHERS HARDWARE CORP.
Property sold and certificate holders received $9.70 per unit in 1944

STANDBY RESV FD INC (MD)
Name changed to Cowen Standby Reserve Fund, Inc. 07/02/1992
Cowen Standby Reserve Fund, Inc. name changed to Cowen (SG)

Standby Reserve Fund, Inc. 07/01/1998
(See Cowen (SG) Standby Reserve Fund, Inc.)

STANDBY TAX EXEMPT RESV FD INC (MD)
Name changed to Cowen Standby Tax-Exempt Reserve Fund, Inc. 12/15/1992
Cowen Standby Tax-Exempt Reserve Fund, Inc. name changed to Cowen (SG) Standby Tax-Exempt Reserve Fund, Inc. 07/01/1998
(See Cowen (SG) Standby Tax-Exempt Reserve Fund, Inc.)

STANDEX INTL CORP (OH)
Reincorporated under the laws of Delaware 06/30/1975

STANDISH CARE CO (DE)
Recapitalized as CareMatrix Corp. 10/14/1996
Each share Common 1¢ par exchanged for (0.2) share Common 5¢ par
Preferred not affected except for change of name
(See CareMatrix Corp.)

STANDISH CUTLERY CORP. (NJ)
Charter revoked for failure to file reports and pay fees 1/22/25

STANDUN INC (CA)
Common no par changed to $1 par 5/6/69
Common $1 par split (5) for (4) by issuance of (0.25) additional share 4/9/71
Common $1 par split (4) for (3) by issuance of (1/3) additional share 2/9/73
Common $1 par split (5) for (4) by issuance of (0.25) additional share 8/15/83
Stock Dividend - 25% 3/10/72
Acquired by a group of investors 11/1/85
Each share Common $1 par exchanged for $7.75 cash

STANFIELD ARBITRAGE CDO LTD (CAYMAN ISLANDS)
144A 3c7 Preferred called for redemption at $1,000 on 07/16/2007

STANFIELD EDL ALTERNATIVES INC (FL)
Each share old Common no par exchanged for (0.0125) share new Common no par 02/23/2001
Each share new Common no par exchanged again for (0.01) share new Common no par 09/02/2003
Name changed to North American Liability Group, Inc. 10/07/2003
North American Liability Group, Inc. name changed to NorMexSteel, Inc. 04/13/2005 which recapitalized as BioChem Solutions Inc. 07/07/2006 which name changed to Balmoral FX Systems Inc. 07/29/2010 which recapitalized as Amalgamated Gold & Silver, Inc. 08/01/2012 which recapitalized as Rainforest Resources Inc. 03/15/2016

STANFORD BANCORPORATION (DE)
Name changed 05/19/1970
Name and state of incorporation changed from Stanford Bancorporation (CA) to Stanford Bancorporation, Inc. (DE) 05/19/1970
Merged into Unionamerica, Inc. (CA) 03/29/1971
Each share Common $12 par exchanged for (1.7) shares Common no par
(See Unionamerica, Inc. (CA))

STANFORD BK (PALO ALTO, CA)
100% acquired by Stanford Bancorporation, Inc. through exchange offer which expired 09/06/1969
Public interest eliminated

STANFORD CAP CORP (DE)
Recapitalized as Skreem Entertainment Corp. (DE) 03/16/2004
Each share Common $0.001 par exchanged for (0.2) share Common $0.001 par
Skreem Entertainment Corp. (DE) name changed to SKRM Interactive, Inc. 02/05/2007 which name changed to Sector 10, Inc. 04/14/2008

STANFORD ENERGY CORP (BC)
Recapitalized as Stanford Oil & Gas Ltd. 07/10/1998
Each share Common no par exchanged for (0.5) share Common no par
Stanford Oil & Gas Ltd. merged into Hilton Petroleum Ltd. (BC) 03/31/1999 which reincorporated in Yukon 04/01/1999 which name changed to Hilton Resources Ltd. (YT) 03/02/2004 which reincorporated in British Columbia 11/23/2004 which recapitalized as Rochester Resources Ltd. 08/26/2005

STANFORD MGMT LTD (DE)
Common $0.001 par split (20) for (1) by issuance of (19) additional shares payable 01/18/2008 to holders of record 01/18/2008 Ex date - 01/18/2008
Name changed to Allezoe Medical Holdings Inc. (DE) 02/17/2011
Allezoe Medical Holdings Inc. (DE) reorganized in Florida as Novation Holdings, Inc. 11/07/2012

STANFORD MICRODEVICES INC (DE)
Name changed to Sirenza Microdevices, Inc. 10/04/2001
Sirenza Microdevices, Inc. merged into RF Micro Devices, Inc. 11/13/2007 which merged into Qorvo, Inc. 01/02/2015

STANFORD MINES LTD. (ON)
Capital Stock no par reclassified as Conv. Class A Common no par 12/16/76
Name changed to Stanford Resources Ltd. and Conv. Class A Common no par reclassified as Common no par 9/23/80
Stanford Resources Ltd. recapitalized as Consolidated Stanford Corp. 8/4/89

STANFORD OIL & GAS LTD (BC)
Merged into Hilton Petroleum Ltd. (BC) 03/31/1999
Each share Common no par exchanged for (0.5263157) share Common no par
Hilton Petroleum Ltd. (BC) reincorporated in Yukon 04/01/1999 which name changed to Hilton Resources Ltd. (YT) 03/02/2004 which reincorporated in British Columbia 11/23/2004 which recapitalized as Rochester Resources Ltd. 08/26/2005

STANFORD RES LTD (ON)
Recapitalized as Consolidated Stanford Corp. 8/4/89
Each share Common no par exchanged for (0.1) share Common no par
(See Consolidated Stanford Corp.)

STANFORD TELECOMMUNICATIONS INC (CA)
Common no par split (5) for (4) by issuance of (0.25) additional share 6/16/86
Common no par split (2) for (1) by issuance of (1) additional share payable 2/28/97 to holders of record 2/10/97
Merged into Newbridge Networks Corp. 12/15/99

Each share Common no par exchanged for $34.22 cash

STANFORD'S LTD.
Bankrupt in 1931

STANG HYDRONICS INC (DE)
Stock Dividend - 20% 09/18/1974
Merged into Stang Dewatering Inc. 03/26/1986
Details not available

STANGE CO (DE)
Reincorporated 08/19/1968
State of incorporation changed from (IL) to (DE) 08/19/1968
Common $1 par split (3) for (1) by issuance of (2) additional shares 08/29/1968
Common $1 par split (2) for (1) by issuance of (1) additional share 05/30/1975
Merged into McCormick & Co., Inc. 02/24/1981
Each share Common $1 par exchanged for (0.65) share Non-Vtg. Common no par

STANGE (WM. J.) CO. (IL)
Stock Dividend - 100% 6/28/63
Name changed to Stange Co. (Ill.) 6/26/64
Stange Co. (Ill.) reincorporated under the laws of Delaware 8/19/68 which merged into McCormick & Co., Inc. 2/24/81

STANHILL CONSOLIDATED LTD. (AUSTRALIA)
Name changed 07/07/1959
Name changed from Stanhill Holdings Ltd. to Stanhill Consolidated Ltd. 07/07/1959
Wound up 05/04/1965
Stockholders' equity unlikely

STANHOME INC (MA)
Non-Vtg. Common $1 par changed to 50¢ par and (1) additional share issued 11/01/1984
Common $1 par changed to 50¢ par and (1) additional share issued 11/01/1984
Each share Non-Vtg. Common 50¢ par exchanged for (2) shares Common 25¢ par 09/05/1986
Each share Vtg. Common 50¢ par exchanged for (2) shares Common 25¢ par 09/05/1986
Common 25¢ par changed to $0.125 par and (1) additional share issued 06/01/1988
Name changed to Enesco Group, Inc. (MA) 04/30/1998
Enesco Group, Inc. (MA) reincorporated in Illinois 07/31/2003
(See Enesco Group, Inc.)

STANLEIGH URANIUM MINING CORP. LTD. (ON)
Merged into Preston Mines Ltd. 8/31/60
Each share Capital Stock $1 par exchanged for (1) share 4% Preference 50¢ par
(See Preston Mines Ltd.)

STANLEY AVIATION CO. (CO)
Name changed to Sacol, Inc. 9/8/58
(See Sacol, Inc.)

STANLEY AVIATION CORP (NY)
Stock Dividends - 50% 03/15/1968; 10% 06/22/1979
Acquired by Flight Refuelling (Holdings) Ltd. 06/29/1981
Each share Common 10¢ par exchanged for $24 cash

STANLEY BLACK & DECKER INC (CT)
Each Corporate Unit automatically became (1) share 4.75% Conv. Perpetual Preferred Ser. B no par 11/17/2015
4.75% Conv. Perpetual Preferred Ser. B no par called for redemption at $100 plus $0.49 accrued dividends on 12/24/2015
(Additional Information in Active)

STANLEY FURNITURE CO (VA)
Common $5 par split (3) for (2) by issuance of (0.5) additional share 01/05/1967
Acquired by Mead Corp. 09/30/1969
Each share Common $5 par exchanged for (2.125) shares Common no par
Mead Corp. merged into MeadWestvaco Corp. 01/29/2002 which merged into WestRock Co. 07/01/2015

STANLEY FURNITURE INC (DE)
Each share old Common 2¢ par exchanged for (0.5) share new Common 2¢ par 07/01/1993
New Common 2¢ par split (2) for (1) by issuance of (1) additional share payable 05/15/1998 to holders of record 05/01/1998
New Common 2¢ par split (2) for (1) by issuance of (1) additional share payable 06/06/2005 to holders of record 05/13/2005 Ex date - 06/07/2005
Name changed to HG Holdings, Inc. 03/20/2018

STANLEY HOME PRODS INC (MA)
Each share Common $5 par exchanged for (1) share Common $1 par and (4) shares Non-Voting Common $1 par 00/00/1948
Common $1 par and Non-Voting Common $1 par changed to $15 par 00/00/1949
Each share Common $15 par or Non-Voting Common $15 par exchanged for (3) shares Common $5 par or Non-Voting Common $5 par respectively 00/00/1951
Common $5 par and Non-Voting Common $5 par changed to $2.50 par respectively and (1) additional share issued 05/27/1966
Common $2.50 par and Non-Voting Common $2.50 par changed to $1.25 par respectively and (1) additional share issued 05/27/1968
Common $1.25 par and Non-Voting Common $1.25 par changed to $1 par respectively and (0.25) additional share issued 05/28/1971
Name changed to Stanhome Inc. 07/01/1982
Stanhome Inc. name changed to Enesco Group, Inc. (MA) 04/30/1998 which reincorporated in Illinois 07/31/2003
(See Enesco Group, Inc.)

STANLEY INC (DE)
Issue Information - 6,300,000 shares COM offered at $13 per share on 10/17/2006
Merged into CGI Group Inc. 08/17/2010
Each share Common 1¢ par exchanged for $37.50 cash

STANLEY INDUSTRIES CORP. (NY)
Name changed to Amcare Centers Inc. and Common 10¢ par reclassified as Class A Common 10¢ par 12/05/1967
(See Amcare Centers Inc.)

STANLEY INTERIORS CORP (DE)
Under plan of merger each share Common 1¢ par exchanged for (1) share 10% Preferred 1¢ par and $9 cash 01/17/1989
Merged into Stanley Furniture Co. Inc. 11/09/1992
Each share 10% Preferred 1¢ par exchanged for (0.05759814) share Common 2¢ par
Stanley Furniture Co. Inc. name changed to HG Holdings, Inc. 03/20/2018

STANLEY JOHN MINES INC (WA)
Name changed to Consolidated Nuclear Inc. 1/19/78
Consolidated Nuclear, Inc. merged into FP Investments, Inc. 1/20/83

which name changed to FP Industries, Inc. 7/29/85
(See FP Industries, Inc.)

STANLEY MARK STRAND, INC.
Acquired by Warner Brothers Pictures, Inc. 00/00/1929
Details not available

STANLEY RESOURCE MANAGEMENT GROUP LTD. (BC)
Name changed to Stanley Resources Ltd. 07/04/1980
Stanley Resources Ltd. name changed to Equi Ventures Inc. 09/22/1986
(See Equi Ventures Inc.)

STANLEY RES LTD (BC)
Name changed to Equi Ventures Inc. 09/22/1986
(See Equi Ventures Inc.)

STANLEY TECHNOLOGY GROUP INC (CANADA)
Name changed to Stantec Inc. 11/3/98

STANLEY WARNER CORP. (DE)
See - Warner (Stanley) Corp.

STANLEY WELL SVC INC (TX)
Merged into Alliance Well Service, Inc. 09/28/1984
Each share Common 1¢ par exchanged for (0.0941) share Common 1¢ par
Alliance Well Service, Inc. recapitalized as Alliance Northwest Industries, Inc. 07/30/1993
(See Alliance Northwest Industries, Inc.)

STANLEY WKS (CT)
Common $25 par changed to $10 par and (1.5) additional shares issued 12/18/1959
Common $10 par changed to $5 par and (1) additional share issued 06/24/1971
Common $5 par split (3) for (2) by issuance of (0.5) additional share 10/02/1978
Common $5 par changed to $2.50 par and (1) additional share issued 05/20/1980
Common $2.50 par split (3) for (2) by issuance of (0.5) additional share 09/27/1986
Common $2.50 par split (2) for (1) by issuance of (1) additional share payable 06/03/1996 to holders of record 05/13/1996 Ex date - 06/04/1996
Stock Dividends - 16-2/3% 05/01/1947; 33-1/3% 05/01/1950; 33-1/3% 02/02/1956
Under plan of merger name changed to Stanley Black & Decker, Inc. 03/12/2010
Each Equity Unit automatically became (16.19) shares Stanley Black & Decker, Inc. Common $2.50 par and $30 cash 05/17/2010
Each Treasury Unit automatically became (16.19) shares Stanley Black & Decker, Inc. Common $2.50 par and $30 cash 05/17/2010

STANLIFT CORP (MA)
Common 50¢ par split (5) for (4) by issuance of (0.25) additional share 12/9/68
Completely liquidated 11/27/70
Each share Common 50¢ par exchanged for first and final distribution of (0.85) share Varlen Corp. Common 10¢ par
(See Varlen Corp.)

STANLINE INC (CA)
Acquired by Bunzl PLC 04/29/1988
Each share Common 1¢ par exchanged for $13.50 cash

STANLY CAP CORP (NC)
Name changed to Uwharrie Capital Corp. 04/22/1997

STANMAR RES LTD (BC)
Merged into Tandem Resources Ltd. (New) 11/15/1985
Each share Common no par exchanged for (0.25) share Common no par
Tandem Resources Ltd. (New) (BC) reincorporated in Ontario 01/03/1997 which recapitalized as OPEL International Inc. (ON) 09/26/2006 which reincorporated in New Brunswick 01/30/2007 which reincorporated in Ontario as OPEL Solar International Inc. 12/01/2010 which name changed to OPEL Technologies Inc. 08/29/2011 which name changed to POET Technologies Inc. 07/25/2013

STANNDCO DEVELOPERS INC (NY)
Trustee discharged and bankruptcy proceedings closed 06/10/1991
No stockholders' equity

STANNEX MINERALS LTD (BC)
Recapitalized as Ryker Resources Ltd. 05/00/1973
Each share Common 50¢ par exchanged for (0.33333333) share Common 50¢ par
(See Ryker Resources Ltd.)

STANRAY CORP (DE)
Merged into IC Industries, Inc. 04/26/1977
Each share Common $1 par exchanged for (0.48) share $3.50 Conv. 2nd Preferred Ser. 1 no par or $20 cash
Note: Option to receive cash expired 05/17/1977
(See IC Industries, Inc.)

STANROCK URANIUM MINES LTD (ON)
Acquired by Denison Mines Ltd. 2/12/73
Each share Common $1 par exchanged for (0.014285) share Capital Stock $1 par
Denison Mines Ltd. recapitalized as Denison Energy Inc. (ONT) 5/30/2002 which reorganized in Alberta 3/8/2004 which name changed to Calfrac Well Services Ltd. 3/29/2004

STANSBURY HLDGS CORP (UT)
Name changed 03/22/1990
Each share Common 1¢ par exchanged for (0.04) share Common 25¢ par 04/27/1985
Name changed from Stansbury Mining Corp. to Stansbury Holdings Corp. 03/22/1990
SEC revoked common stock registration 08/05/2003

STANSTEAD CAP INC (CANADA)
Name changed to Blue Tree Wireless Data Inc. 09/19/2004
(See Blue Tree Wireless Data Inc.)

STANT CORP (DE)
Merged into Tomkins PLC 05/08/1997
Each share Common 1¢ par exchanged for $21.50 cash

STANTEX CORP. (PA)
Charter revoked for failure to file reports and pay fees 8/2/66

STANTON INDUSTRIES, INC. (NY)
Name changed to International Monetary Funding Corp. 06/28/1982
International Monetary Funding Corp. recapitalized as Hawaiian Sugar Technologies, Inc. 01/20/1983 which recapitalized as Entertainment Inns of America, Inc. 10/21/1983 which name changed to Tiger Marketing, Inc. 11/08/1984 which recapitalized as U.S. Health Services, Inc. 04/08/1986 which name changed to Diamond Trade Center, Inc. 10/30/1990
(See Diamond Trade Center, Inc.)

STANTON LEAD MINES LTD. (ON)
Charter cancelled for failure to file reports and pay taxes May 1957

STANWARD CORP. (DE)
Each share Common 5¢ par exchanged for (0.1) share Common 50¢ par 4/26/66
Completely liquidated 6/7/67
Each share Common 50¢ par exchanged for first and final distribution of (5) shares Stanrock Uranium Mines Ltd. Common $1 par
Stanrock Uranium Mines Ltd. acquired by Denison Mines Ltd. 2/12/73 which recapitalized as Denison Energy Inc. (ONT) 5/30/2002 which reorganized in Alberta 3/8/2004 which name changed to Calfrac Well Services Ltd. 3/29/2004

STANWELL OIL & GAS LTD. (ON)
Recapitalized as Cordwell International Developments Ltd. 12/16/66
Each share Capital Stock $1 par exchanged for (0.2) share Capital Stock no par
Cordwell International Developments Ltd. charter cancelled 11/28/73

STANWICK CORP (DE)
Liquidation completed
Each share Common 10¢ par received initial distribution of $1 cash 10/24/1986
Each share Common 10¢ par received second distribution of $1 cash 02/20/1987
Each share Common 10¢ par received third distribution of $0.50 cash 10/01/1988
Each share Common 10¢ par exchanged for fourth and final distribution of $2.07 cash 10/05/1990

STANWOOD CORP (NC)
Acquired by Delta Woodside Industries, Inc. (DE) 09/07/1988
For holdings of (26) shares or more each share Common $1 par exchanged for (0.6473) share Common 1¢ par and $0.66 cash
For holdings of (25) shares of fewer each share Common $1 par exchanged for $11.9625 cash
Note: Option for holders of (25) or fewer shares to elect to receive stock and cash expired 11/06/1988
Delta Woodside Industries, Inc. (DE) merged into Delta Woodside Industries, Inc. (SC) 11/15/1989
(See Delta Woodside Industries, Inc. (SC))

STANWOOD OIL CORP (PA)
Each share Common $1 par exchanged for (5) shares Common 20¢ par 00/00/1945
Common 20¢ par changed to 5¢ par 00/00/1951
Common 5¢ par changed to 2-1/2¢ par 00/00/1954
Common 2-1/2¢ par changed to 1-1/4¢ par 00/00/1955
Each share old Common 1-1/4¢ par exchanged for (0.16666666) share new Common 1-1/4¢ par 08/01/1975
Name changed to Penn Star Oil Corp., Inc. 11/13/1980

STANWOOD RUBBER CO. (DE)
Charter cancelled for non-payment of taxes in 1923

STAODYN INC (CO)
Name changed 9/11/90
Name changed from Staodynamics, Inc. to Staodyn Inc. 9/11/90
Merged into Rehabilicare Inc. 3/17/98
Each share Common 1¢ par exchanged for (0.829) share Common 10¢ par
Rehabilicare Inc. name changed to Compex Technologies, Inc.

12/16/2002 which merged into Encore Medical Corp. 2/24/2006
(See Encore Medical Corp.)

STAPLE MINES & MINERALS LTD. (ON)
Charter cancelled for failure to file reports and pay taxes in 1955

STAPLE MNG LTD (ON)
Merged into Gerrard Realty Inc. 01/28/1976
Each share Capital Stock no par exchanged for (0.1282051) share Common no par

STAPLES INC (DE)
COM ($0.0006) 855030 10 2
Common $0.0006 par split (3) for (2) by issuance of (0.5) additional share 07/10/1991
Common $0.0006 par split (3) for (2) by issuance of (0.5) additional share 12/13/1993
Common $0.0006 par split (3) for (2) by issuance of (0.5) additional share 10/28/1994
Common $0.0006 par split (3) for (2) by issuance of (0.5) additional share 07/24/1995
Common $0.0006 par split (3) for (2) by issuance of (0.5) additional share payable 03/25/1996 to holders of record 03/15/1996
Common $0.0006 par split (3) for (2) by issuance of (0.5) additional share payable 01/30/1998 to holders of record 01/20/1998
Common $0.0006 par split (3) for (2) by issuance of (0.5) additional share payable 01/28/1999 to holders of record 01/18/1999
Common $0.0006 par split (3) for (2) by issuance of (0.5) additional share payable 04/15/2005 to holders of record 03/29/2005 Ex date - 04/18/2005
Acquired by Arch Parent Inc. 09/12/2017
Each share Common $0.0006 par exchanged for $10.25 cash

STAPLING MACHS CO (DE)
Common no par split (8) for (1) by issuance of (7) additional shares 4/1/66
Name changed to Rockaway Corp. 5/4/71
(See Rockaway Corp.)

STAR ALLY INC (NV)
Name changed to DKG Capital Inc. 03/24/2017

STAR AMUSEMENT CO (NV)
Name changed to Comet Enterprises Inc. 8/29/86
Comet Enterprises Inc. name changed to Comet Entertainment, Inc. 5/8/89 which recapitalized as Texoil Inc. (New) 3/16/93
(See Texoil Inc. (New))

STAR BANC CORP (DE)
Common $5 par split (3) for (1) by issuance of (2) additional shares payable 01/15/1997 to holders of record 12/31/1996 Ex date - 01/16/1997
Merged into Firstar Corp. (New) 11/20/1998
Each share Common $5 par exchanged for (1) share Common 1¢ par
Firstar Corp. (New) merged into U.S. Bancorp (DE) 02/27/2001

STAR BRITE CORP (FL)
Name changed to Ocean Bio-Chem, Inc. 10/12/1984

STAR CAP CORP (PA)
Acquired by Abacus Fund, Inc. 12/09/1969
Each share Common $1 par exchanged for (0.285714) share Common 33-1/3¢ par
Abacus Fund, Inc. merged into Paine, Webber, Jackson & Curtis Inc.

04/03/1972 which reorganized as Paine Webber Inc. 02/01/1974 which name changed to Paine Webber Group Inc. 05/21/1984 which merged into UBS AG 11/03/2000
(See UBS AG)

STAR CASINOS INTL INC (CO)
Chapter 11 Federal Bankruptcy proceedings converted to Chapter 7 on 3/18/97
Stockholders' equity unlikely

STAR CENTY PANDAHO CORP (NV)
Recapitalized as International Leaders Capital Corp. 10/04/2017
Each share Common $0.001 par exchanged for (0.02) share Common $0.001 par

STAR CHOICE COMMUNICATIONS INC (CANADA)
Merged into Canadian Satellite Communications Inc. 08/31/1999
For Canadian Residents: Each share Common no par exchanged for (4.8) shares Common no par
For Non-Canadian Residents: Each share Common no par exchanged for C$15.65 cash
Canadian Satellite Communications Inc. acquired by Shaw Communications Inc. 04/02/2001

STAR CITY HLDGS LTD (AUSTRALIA)
ADR agreement terminated 01/17/2000
Each Sponsored ADR for Ordinary exchanged for $10.06949517 cash

STAR CLASSICS INC (NY)
Name changed to Starmark Inc. (NY) 12/11/1991
Starmark Inc. (NY) reorganized in Delaware as Babystar Inc. 03/23/1993 which name changed to Datatrend Services Inc. 11/27/1995
(See Datatrend Services Inc.)

STAR COMPUTING LTD (NV)
Each share old Common $0.001 par exchanged for (4) shares new Common $0.001 par 03/09/2004
Name changed to VitroTech Corp. 04/01/2004
(See VitroTech Corp.)

STAR DANCE RES LTD (BC)
Recapitalized as Dancing Star Resources Ltd. 01/13/1999
Each (8.5) shares Common no par exchanged for (1) share Common no par
Dancing Star Resources Ltd. recapitalized as Alcor Resources Ltd. 07/09/2003 which name changed to Balto Resources Ltd. 06/16/2008

STAR DATA SYS INC (ON)
Each share old Common no par exchanged for (0.1) share new Common no par 5/27/93
Acquired by CGI Group Inc. 1/31/2001
Each share Common no par exchanged for (0.737) share Class A Subordinate no par

STAR DOLPHIN INC (NV)
Charter revoked for failure to file reports and pay fees 12/31/1997

STAR E MEDIA CORP (NV)
Recapitalized as Demobag Brands, Inc. 01/19/2007
Each share Common $0.001 par exchanged for (0.00266666) share Common $0.001 par
Demobag Brands, Inc. recapitalized as China Gold Resource, Inc. 08/16/2007 which name changed to WiseMobi, Inc. 05/13/2008 which recapitalized as New Infinity Holdings, Ltd. 02/23/2015

STAR ENERGY CORP (NV)
Each share old Common $0.001 par exchanged for (5) shares new Common $0.001 par 12/30/2005
SEC revoked common stock registration 06/06/2013

STAR ENTMT GROUP INC (UT)
Charter expired by time limitation 07/11/2001

STAR GLO INDS INC (UT)
Under Court Order holders of Common 10¢ par (Green or Yellow certificates) were required to surrender their certificates for Common 10¢ par (Red or Blue certificates) on a share for share basis by 12/31/1974
Note: Unexchanged certificates were cancelled and became without value
Completely liquidated 07/01/1986
Each share Common 10¢ par exchanged for first and final distribution of $5.65 cash

STAR GROUP NEWSPAPER NETWORKS INC (ON)
Name changed to TKN Interactive Marketing Systems, Inc. 04/07/1998
TKN Interactive Marketing Systems, Inc. name changed to eStation.com Inc. 04/22/1999 which name changed to eStation Network Services Inc. 10/30/2001
(See eStation Network Services Inc.)

STAR HEDGE MANAGERS CORP (ON)
Fund terminated 04/24/2015
Each Class A Share received $5.5833 cash

STAR HEDGE MANAGERS CORP II (ON)
Combined Units separated 05/06/2011 Fund terminated 04/24/2015
Each Class A Share received $4.6468 cash

STAR INDS INC (NY)
Acquired by Newstar Industries, Inc. 12/21/1971
Each share Class A $1 par exchanged for $155.20 cash

STAR LAKE GOLD MINES LTD (MB)
Recapitalized as Winnipeg Gold Ltd. 01/31/1974
Each share Capital Stock no par exchanged for (0.5) share Capital Stock no par
(See Winnipeg Gold Ltd.)

STAR LAND & EXPLORATION LTD. (AB)
Name changed to Victoria Land & Minerals Ltd. 11/29/1961
Victoria Land & Minerals Ltd. acquired by Plains Petroleums Ltd. 07/22/1966
(See Plains Petroleums Ltd.)

STAR MARITIME ACQUISITION CORP (DE)
Issue Information - 18,867,000 UNITS consisting of (1) share COM and (1) WT offered at $10 per Unit on 12/15/2005
Merged into Star Bulk Carriers Corp. 12/05/2007
Each share Common $0.0001 par exchanged for (1) share Common 1¢ par

STAR MARKET CO. (MA)
Merged into Jewel Tea Co., Inc. 1/31/64
Each share Common $1 par exchanged for (0.4) share Common $1 par
Jewel Tea Co., Inc. name changed to Jewel Companies, Inc. 6/15/66 which merged into American Stores Co. (New) 11/16/84 which merged into Albertson's, Inc. 6/23/99 which merged into Supervalu Inc. 6/2/2006

STAR MED CORP (UT)
Each share old Common $0.001 par exchanged for (0.002) share new Common $0.001 par 3/21/97
Name changed to Netmaster Group, Inc. 8/1/97
Netmaster Group, Inc. name changed to Zulu Tek, Inc. 1/15/98

STAR METRO CORP (NV)
Name changed to BioPack Environmental Solutions Inc. 02/27/2007
BioPack Environmental Solutions Inc. recapitalized as Tristar Wellness Solutions Inc. 01/18/2013

STAR MINERALS GROUP LTD (BC)
Each share old Common no par exchanged for (0.33333333) share new Common no par 12/27/2013
Name changed to Navis Resources Corp. 04/11/2016

STAR MNG INC (NY)
Name changed to Tech-Star International Inc. 3/29/84
(See Tech-Star International Inc.)

STAR MULTI CARE SVCS INC (NY)
Old Common $0.001 par split (3) for (2) by issuance of (0.5) additional share 05/12/1994
Each share old Common $0.001 par exchanged for (0.33333333) share new Common $0.001 par 12/13/1999
Each share new Common $0.001 par exchanged again for (0.33333333) share new Common $0.001 par 01/25/2001
Stock Dividends - 6% payable 01/12/1996 to holders of record 12/22/1995; 5% payable 11/04/1996 to holders of record 10/11/1996
Each (55,000) shares new Common $0.001 par exchanged again for (1) share new Common $0.001 par 05/28/2004
Note: In effect holders received $0.126 cash per share and public interest was eliminated

STAR OF HOPE MINING CO. (CO)
Charter revoked for failure to file reports and pay fees 09/16/1913

STAR OF MINETA LTD (BC)
Recapitalized as International Star Resources Ltd. 08/24/1995
Each share Common no par exchanged for (0.5) share Common no par
(See International Star Resources Ltd.)

STAR ONE RES INC (BC)
Name changed to Hyder Gold Inc. 06/26/1989
Hyder Gold Inc. recapitalized as Gleichen Resources Ltd. (BC) 08/03/2006 which reincorporated in Ontario as Torex Gold Resources Inc. 05/04/2010

STAR PAGING INTL HLDGS LTD (BERMUDA)
Name changed to Star Telecom International Holding Ltd. 03/28/1996
Star Telecom International Holding Ltd. name changed to China Online (Bermuda) Ltd. 08/02/1999 which name changed to COL Capital Ltd. 07/09/2004 which name changed to China Medical & HealthCare Group Ltd. 03/11/2016
(See China Medical & HealthCare Group Ltd.)

STAR PETE CORP (NV)
Recapitalized as Exact Energy Resources, Inc. 12/11/2007
Each share Common $0.001 par exchanged for (0.00666666) share Common $0.001 par
(See Exact Energy Resources, Inc.)

STAR PETROLEUM CO. (TX)
Charter forfeited for failure to pay taxes 5/19/50

STAR PETROLEUM CO. OF CALIFORNIA LTD.
Name changed to Calstar Petroleum Co. in 1941
(See Calstar Petroleum Co.)

STAR PHOENIX AIRCRAFT CORP (NV)
Name changed to Judgement Recovery Network, Inc. 4/12/96

STAR PORTFOLIO CORP (ON)
Combined Units separated 11/16/2010
Under plan of reorganization each Star Yield Managers Class Trust Unit automatically became (1) Star Yield Managers Trust, Unit 01/20/2016
(See Star Yield Managers Trust)

STAR RES CORP (BC)
Each share old Common no par exchanged for (0.14285714) share new Common no par 11/27/2001
Name changed to Jaguar Resources Corp. 09/18/2003
Jaguar Resources Corp. name changed to Brazauro Resources Corp. 09/08/2004
(See Brazauro Resources Corp.)

STAR RES INC (DE)
Each (82.85) shares old Common 1¢ par exchanged for (1) share new Common 1¢ par 10/25/96
Name changed to Logiphone Group Inc. 10/25/96
(See Logiphone Group Inc.)

STAR RUBBER CO.
Liquidated in 1929

STAR SVGS & LN ASSN (PA)
Merged into Citizens Financial Services, Inc. 11/16/1990
Each share Common $1 par exchanged for (1.25) shares Common $1 par

STAR SCIENTIFIC INC (DE)
Common 1¢ par changed to $0.0001 par 09/21/2001
Name changed to Rock Creek Pharmaceuticals, Inc. 06/04/2014

STAR SVCS GROUP INC (FL)
Merged into Allied Waste North America, Inc. 7/2/2001
Each share Common 1¢ par exchanged for $2.70 cash
Note: An initial additional distribution of $0.21 cash per share was made 2/1/2002
A second additional distribution of $0.067941 cash was made 4/28/2005

STAR STATES CORP (DE)
Name changed to WSFS Financial Corp. 06/01/1993

STAR STRUCK LTD (DE)
Company terminated common stock registration and is no longer public as of 03/07/2003

STAR SUPER MARKETS, INC. (FL)
Class A Common $2 par changed to $1.67 par and Class B Common 50¢ par changed to 38¢ par 12/29/59
Name changed to United Star Companies, Inc. 1/15/62 which was adjudicated bankrupt 9/5/63

STAR SUPERMARKETS INC (NY)
Each share Class A $10 par exchanged for (315) shares Common $1 par 07/06/1965
Each share Class B $10 par exchanged for (197) shares Common $1 par 07/06/1965
Stock Dividends - 10% 01/13/1975; 10% 01/12/1976; 25% 07/23/1979
Name changed to Martek Investors, Inc. 12/07/1982
Martek Investors, Inc. name changed to Rochester Fund Municipals, Inc. 03/31/1986

STAR TANK & BOAT CO. (IN)
Name changed to Starcraft Corp. 1/1/66
Starcraft Corp. merged into Bangor Punta Corp. 9/30/68
(See Bangor Punta Corp.)

STAR TECHNOLOGIES INC (DE)
SEC revoked common stock registration 11/10/2005
Stockholders' equity unlikely

STAR TELECOM INTL HLDG LTD (BERMUDA)
Sponsored ADR's for Ordinary split (2) for (1) by issuance of (1) additional ADR payable 03/31/1998 to holders of record 02/20/1998
Name changed to China Online (Bermuda) Ltd. 08/02/1999
China Online (Bermuda) Ltd. name changed to COL Capital Ltd. 07/09/2004 which name changed to China Medical & HealthCare Group Ltd. 03/11/2016
(See China Medical & HealthCare Group Ltd.)

STAR TELECOMMUNICATIONS INC (DE)
Issue Information - 4,000,000 shares COM offered at $9 per share on 06/12/1997
Secondary Offering - 6,000,000 shares COM offered at $27 per share on 04/29/1998
Plan of reorganization under Chapter 11 Federal Bankruptcy Code effective 08/13/2002
No stockholders' equity

STAR URANIUM CORP (BC)
Name changed to Star Minerals Group Ltd. 10/11/2013
Star Minerals Group Ltd. name changed to Navis Resources Corp. 04/11/2016

STAR URANIUM LTD. (AB)
Recapitalized as Star Land & Exploration Ltd. in November, 1959
Each share Capital Stock no par exchanged for (0.5) share Capital Stock $1 par
Star Land & Exploration Ltd. name changed to Victoria Land & Minerals Ltd. 11/29/61 which was acquired by Plains Petroleums Ltd. 7/22/66
(See Plains Petroleums Ltd.)

STAR VALLEY RES CORP (BC)
Name changed to Western Pinnacle Mining Ltd. (BC) 11/26/1996
Western Pinnacle Mining Ltd. (BC) reincorporated in Yukon 05/15/1997 which recapitalized as WPN Resources Ltd. 01/08/2002 which name changed to Grove Energy Ltd. (YT) 06/01/2004 which reincorporated in British Columbia 06/02/2005 which was acquired by Stratic Energy Corp. 04/24/2007
(See Stratic Energy Corp.)

STAR VENTURES INC (CO)
Name changed to Tele-Matic Industries, Inc. 8/1/90
Tele-Matic Industries, Inc. recapitalized as Tele-Matic Corp. 3/25/92 which name changed to T-NETIX, Inc. (CO) 10/23/95 which reincorporated in Delaware 9/7/2001
(See T-NETIX, Inc.)

STAR WORLD PRODTNS INC (DE)
Charter cancelled and declared inoperative and void for non-payment of taxes 03/01/1988

STAR YIELD MANAGERS TR (ON)
Trust terminated 09/22/2017
Each Unit received $11.4206 cash

STARBASE-1 COFFEE LTD (NV)
Recapitalized as Nu Star Holdings, Inc. 4/23/2004
Each share Common $0.001 par exchanged for (0.1) share Common $0.001 par

STARBASE CORP (DE)
Each share old Common 1¢ par exchanged for (1/3) share new Common 1¢ par 3/20/95
Each share new Common 1¢ par exchanged again for (0.1) share new Common 1¢ par 7/31/2002
Merged into Borland Software Corp. 1/8/2003
Each share new Common 1¢ par exchanged for $2.75 cash

STARBEC INC (AB)
Acquired by a private company 10/18/96
Each share Common no par exchanged for $0.10 cash

STARBERRYS CORP (NV)
Name changed to Visualant Inc. 08/18/2004
Visualant Inc. name changed to Know Labs, Inc. 05/25/2018

STARBIRD MINES LTD. (MB)
Charter forfeited for failure to file annual reports 12/19/62

STARBIRD MINES LTD (BC)
Name changed to Camrelco Resources Group Ltd. 4/21/76
Camrelco Resources Group Ltd. recapitalized as Canadian Beaver Resources Ltd. 1/6/82
(See Canadian Beaver Resources Ltd.)

STARBOW HLDGS LTD (BERMUDA)
Name changed to Town Health Medical Technology Holdings Co. Ltd. 09/13/2006
Town Health Medical Technology Holdings Co. Ltd. name changed to Hong Kong Health Check & Laboratory Holdings Co. Ltd. 07/20/2007 which name changed to China Gogreen Assets Investment Ltd. 09/02/2011
(See China Gogreen Assets Investment Ltd.)

STARBRIDGE GLOBAL INC (NV)
Recapitalized as China Mulans Nano Technology Corp., Ltd. 1/29/2007
Each (30) shares Common $0.001 par exchanged for (1) share Common $0.001 par

STARBRIDGE VENTURE CAP INC (AB)
Merged into Intermap Technologies Ltd. 3/13/97
Each share Common no par exchanged for (1) share Class A Common no par
Intermap Technologies Ltd. recapitalized as Intermap Technologies Corp. 5/25/99

STARBRIGHT VENTURE CAP INC (ON)
Merged into Grasslands Entertainment Inc. (AB) 07/11/2001
Each share Common no par exchanged for (1) share Common no par
Grasslands Entertainment Inc. (AB) reorganized in Ontario as Lakeside Minerals Inc. 01/04/2012 which name changed to Lineage Grow Co. Ltd. 07/25/2017

STARBURST ENERGY CORP (BC)
Recapitalized as National Scientific Products Corp. 09/09/1987
Each share Common no par exchanged for (0.25) share Common no par
(See National Scientific Products Corp.)

STARBURST INC (UT)
Name changed to Solar Spectrum, Inc. 06/09/1978
Solar Spectrum, Inc. name changed to Parmax, Inc. 07/15/1986 which name recapitalized as Nise Inc. 09/14/1993
(See Nise Inc.)

STARCAST CORP (AB)
Recapitalized as Sat-Tel Corp. 05/06/1999
Each (1.75) shares Common no par exchanged for (1) share Common no par
Sat-Tel Corp. merged into IROC Systems Corp. (Canada) 02/28/2003 which name changed to IROC Energy Services Corp. 05/22/2007 which merged into Western Energy Services Corp. 04/22/2013

STARCH INRA HOOPER INC (NY)
Name changed 02/27/1974
Name changed from Starch (Daniel) & Staff, Inc. to Starch/Inra/Hooper, Inc. 02/27/1974
Each share Common 10¢ par exchanged for (0.01) share Common $2 par 06/07/1985
Name changed to Roper Starch Worldwide, Inc. 03/11/1993
(See Roper Starch Worldwide, Inc.)

STARCHILD CORP (UT)
Each share old Class A Common 1¢ par exchanged for (0.25) share new Class A Common 1¢ par 8/26/91
Reorganized under the laws of Texas as Ferex Corp. 7/29/94
Each share new Class A Common 1¢ par exchanged for (0.75) share Class A Common 1¢ par
(See Ferex Corp.)

STARCOM INC (CO)
Chapter 11 Federal Bankruptcy Code converted to Chapter 7 on 7/10/87
Stockholders' equity unlikely

STARCOM WIRELESS NETWORKS INC (DE)
Name changed to SkyLynx Communications, Inc. 09/29/2003
SkyLynx Communications, Inc. recapitalized as PawsPlus, Inc. 01/29/2009
(See PawsPlus, Inc.)

STARCORE INTL VENTURES LTD (BC)
Name changed to Starcore International Mines Ltd. 02/01/2008

STARCORE RES LTD (BC)
Recapitalized as Starcore International Ventures Ltd. 02/02/2004
Each share Common no par exchanged for (0.1) share Common no par
Starcore International Ventures Ltd. name changed to Starcore International Mines Ltd. 02/01/2008

STARCORP INC (DE)
Recapitalized as Fidelity First Financial Corp. 2/3/97
Each share Common $0.0015 par exchanged for (1/3) share Common $0.0015 par

STARCOURT GOLD MINES LTD. (ON)
Charter revoked for failure to file reports and pay fees 8/24/64

STARCRAFT AUTOMOTIVE CORP (IN)
Name changed to Starcraft Corp. (Ctfs. dated after 3/16/95) 3/16/95
Starcraft Corp. (Ctfs. dated after 3/16/95) merged into Quantum Fuel Systems Technology Worldwide, Inc. 3/4/2005

STARCRAFT CORP (IN)
Ctfs. dated prior to 9/30/68
Merged into Bangor Punta Corp. 9/30/68
Each share Common $1 par exchanged for (2/3) share Common $1 par
(See Bangor Punta Corp.)

STARCRAFT CORP (IN)
Ctfs. dated after 3/16/95
Stock Dividends - 5% payable 3/7/2003 to holders of record 2/21/2003 Ex date - 2/19/2003; 5% payable 3/19/2004 to holders of record 2/20/2004 Ex date - 2/18/2004
Merged into Quantum Fuel Systems Technology Worldwide, Inc. 3/4/2005
Each share Common no par exchanged for (2.341) shares Common $0.001 par

STARDRILL-KEYSTONE CO. (PA)
Recapitalized 12/15/1955
Each share 6% Preferred $10 par exchanged for (1) share 60¢ Preferred $10 par and (1) share 45¢ Prior Preferred $7.20 par or (1) share 60¢ Preferred $10 par and (2) shares new Common $1 par
Each share old Common $1 par exchanged for (1) share new Common $1 par or (1/3) share 60¢ Preferred $10 par
60¢ Preferred $10 par called for redemption 08/19/1959
45¢ Prior Preferred $7.20 par called for redemption 08/19/1959
Completely liquidated 09/15/1959
Each share new Common $1 par exchanged for first and final distribution of $8.76 cash

STARDRIVE SOLUTIONS INC (WA)
Charter cancelled and proclaimed dissolved for failure to pay fees 11/19/2001

STARDUST, INC. (NV)
Voluntarily dissolved 5/18/65
Details not available

STARDUST INC (NY)
Under plan of merger name changed to Sanmark-Stardust Inc. and Common $1 par changed to 1¢ par 03/12/1981
Sanmark-Stardust Inc. name changed to Movie Star, Inc. 01/04/1993 which recapitalized as Frederick's of Hollywood Group Inc. 01/29/2008
(See Frederick's of Hollywood Group Inc.)

STARDUST INC PRODTN-RECORDING-PROMOTION (UT)
Recapitalized as Hartcourt Investments USA Inc. 11/21/94
Each share Common $0.001 par exchanged for (0.1) share Common $0.001 par
Hartcourt Investments USA Inc. recapitalized as Hartcourt Companies, Inc. 10/6/95

STARDUST VENTURES INC (BC)
Delisted from Vancouver Stock Exchange 10/31/1994

STARENT NETWORKS CORP (DE)
Issue Information - 10,534,841 shares COM offered at $12 per share on 06/05/2007
Merged into Cisco Systems, Inc. 12/18/2009
Each share Common $0.001 par exchanged for $35 cash

STARFEST INC (CA)
Name changed to Concierge Technologies, Inc. (CA) 4/2/2002
Concierge Technologies, Inc. (CA) reincorporated in Nevada 10/5/2006

STARFIELD COMMUNICATIONS GROUP INC (AB)
Name changed to Starfield Resources Inc. 12/18/97

STARFIRE BOAT CORP. (OK)
Adjudicated bankrupt 10/18/1963
No stockholders' equity

STARFIRE INDS LTD (BC)
Name changed 6/1/85
Name changed from Starfire Resources Ltd. to Starfire Industries Ltd. 6/1/85
Capital Stock no par split (5) for (4) by issuance of (0.25) additional share 1/5/87

STA-STA

Delisted from Vancouver Stock
Exchange 10/9/87

STARFIRE TECHNOLOGIES INTL INC (BC)
Delisted from Toronto Venture Stock
Exchange 04/30/2003

STARFLICK COM (NV)
Old Common $0.00001 par split (30)
for (1) by issuance of (29) additional
shares payable 06/26/2014 to
holders of record 06/26/2014
Name changed to Lotus
Bio-Technology Development Corp.
04/07/2016

STARGAZER RES LTD (AB)
Recapitalized as Stockmen Energy
Ltd. 12/31/1984
Each share Common no par
exchanged for (0.2) share Common
no par
Stockmen Energy Ltd. recapitalized
as Stockmen Oil & Gas Ltd.
04/14/1987 which merged into Prime
Petroleum Corp. 05/01/1989 which
merged into Senex Petroleum Corp.
12/31/1989 which merged into
Devran Petroleum Ltd. 03/01/1993
which name changed to Reserve
Royalty Corp. 11/16/1995 which
merged into PrimeWest Energy
Trust 07/27/2000
(See PrimeWest Energy Trust)

STARGOLD MINES INC (NV)
Common $0.001 par split (40) for (1)
by issuance of (39) additional
shares payable 11/24/2006 to
holders of record 11/24/2006
SEC revoked common stock
registration 12/01/2011

STARI LTD (UT)
Involuntarily dissolved 5/1/98

STARICH INC (UT)
Each share old Common $0.001 par
exchanged for (0.05) share new
Common $0.001 par 02/08/1994
Voluntarily dissolved 10/02/1996
Details not available

STARINVEST GROUP INC (NV)
Each share Common $0.001 par
received distribution of (0.5) share
GoIP Global, Inc. Common $0.001
par payable 08/31/2005 to holders
of record 06/30/2005
Each share Common $0.001 par
received distribution of (0.0333)
share Rep Retail E-Promotion Inc.
Common payable 03/10/2006 to
holders of record 02/15/2006
Note: Holders of (29) shares or fewer
received $5 cash per share
Charter cancelled 10/01/2012

STARK BEN INC (DE)
Name changed to China Greenstar
Corp. 01/22/2015

STARK ELECTRIC RAILROAD CO.
Sold at auction 00/00/1939
Details not available

STARK MILLS
Merged into New England Southern
Corp. 00/00/1928
Details not available

STARK-TUSCARAWAS CO.
Dissolved 00/00/1928
Details not available

STARK WETZEL FOODS INC (IN)
Name changed 05/11/1972
Name changed from Stark Wetzel &
Co., Inc. to Stark-Wetzel Foods Inc.
05/11/1972
Name changed to SW, Inc.
11/06/1974
(See SW, Inc.)

STARKIVES INC (NY)
Charter cancelled and proclaimed
dissolved for failure to pay taxes
3/25/92

STARLETTA MINES LTD (BC)
Name changed to Golden Star Mines
Ltd. 03/24/1977
Golden Star Mines Ltd. name
changed to Golden State Resources
Ltd. 04/21/1981 which recapitalized
as Golden Maritime Resources Ltd.
05/12/1997
(See Golden Maritime Resources Ltd.)

STARLIGHT ACQUISITIONS INC (CO)
Each share Common no par
exchanged for (0.005) share
Common 2¢ par 08/01/1995
Reincorporated under the laws of
Delaware as Toucan Gold Corp. and
Common 2¢ par changed to 1¢ par
07/29/1996
Toucan Gold Corp. name changed to
Authoriszor, Inc. 08/26/1999 which
recapitalized as GreenGro
Technologies, Inc. 02/10/2010

STARLIGHT ENERGY CORP (BC)
Recapitalized as Hansa International
Resources Ltd. 07/23/1990
Each share Common no par
exchanged for (0.28571428) share
Common no par
(See Hansa International Resources Ltd.)

STARLIGHT INTL HLDGS LTD (BERMUDA)
Sponsored ADR's for Ordinary split
(3) for (2) by issuance of (0.5)
additional ADR payable 10/14/1997
to holders of record 09/11/1997
ADR agreement terminated
04/13/2015
No ADR's remain outstanding

STARLIGHT MINES LTD. (ON)
Charter cancelled for failure to file
reports and pay fees 11/12/69

STARLIGHT RES INC (NV)
Name changed to Essential
Technologies, Inc. 12/01/1989
Essential Technologies, Inc. name
changed to Forbidden City Holdings,
Inc. 02/03/1995 which name
changed to Life Industries Inc.
05/26/1995 which recapitalized as
Quill Industries Inc. 09/19/1997
which recapitalized as Ostrich
Products of America, Inc.
06/01/2005 which name changed to
PayPro, Inc. 07/11/2005 which name
changed to Panamersa Corp.
02/16/2007 which recapitalized as
Eagle Worldwide Inc. 01/12/2012

STARLIGHT U S MULTI-FAMILY CORE FD (ON)
Merged into Starlight U.S.
Multi-Family (No. 5) Core Fund
10/18/2016
Each Class A Unit exchanged for
(2.4187) Class A Ltd. Partnership
Units
Each Class U Unit exchanged for
(1.8324) Class U Ltd. Partnership
Units
Each Class C Unit exchanged for
(2.5515) Class C Ltd. Partnership
Units
Each Class F Unit exchanged for
(2.4941) Class F Ltd. Partnership
Units
Each Class I Unit exchanged for
(2.4175) Class D Ltd. Partnership
Units
Note: Unexchanged certificates will
be cancelled and become without
value 10/18/2022

STARLIGHT U S MULTI-FAMILY NO 2 CORE FD (ON)
Merged into Starlight U.S.
Multi-Family (No. 5) Core Fund
10/18/2016
Each Class A Unit exchanged for
(2.4615) Class A Ltd. Partnership
Units
Each Class U Unit exchanged for
(1.9081) Class U Ltd. Partnership
Units
Each Class C Unit exchanged for
(2.6191) Class C Ltd. Partnership
Units
Each Class D Unit exchanged for
(2.4697) Class D Ltd. Partnership
Units
Each Class F Unit exchanged for
(2.5558) Class F Ltd. Partnership
Units
Note: Unexchanged certificates will
be cancelled and become without
value 10/18/2022

STARLIGHT U S MULTIFAMILY NO 3 CORE FD (ON)
Merged into Starlight U.S.
Multi-Family (No. 5) Core Fund
10/18/2016
Each Class A Unit exchanged for
(1.7804) Class A Ltd. Partnership
Units
Each Class U Unit exchanged for
(1.4074) Class U Ltd. Partnership
Units
Each Class C Unit exchanged for
(1.901) Class C Ltd. Partnership
Units
Each Class D Unit exchanged for
(1.7924) Class D Ltd. Partnership
Units
Each Class F Unit exchanged for
(1.8545) Class F Ltd. Partnership
Units
Note: Unexchanged certificates will
be cancelled and become without
value 10/18/2022

STARLIGHT U S MULTI-FAMILY NO 4 CORE FD (ON)
Merged into Starlight U.S.
Multi-Family (No. 5) Core Fund
10/18/2016
Each Class A Unit exchanged for
(1.3532) Class A Ltd. Partnership
Units
Each Class U Unit exchanged for
(1.2801) Class U Ltd. Partnership
Units
Each Class C Unit exchanged for
(1.4404) Class C Ltd. Partnership
Units
Each Class D Unit exchanged for
(1.3591) Class D Ltd. Partnership
Units
Each Class E Unit exchanged for
(1.2873) Class E Ltd. Partnership
Units
Each Class F Unit exchanged for
(1.3788) Class F Ltd. Partnership
Units
Each Class H Unit exchanged for
(1.3334) Class H Ltd. Partnership
Units
Note: Unexchanged certificates will
be cancelled and become without
value 10/18/2022

STARLIMS TECHNOLOGIES LTD (ISRAEL)
Issue Information - 2,100,000 ORD
shs. offered at $13.50 per share on
05/23/2007
Acquired by Abbot Laboratories
03/22/2010
Each share Ordinary NIS 1 par
exchanged for $14 cash

STARLINE, INC. (IL)
Acquired by Chromalloy American
Corp. (DE) 02/19/1969
Each share Capital Stock no par
exchanged for (0.2903927) share $5
Conv. Preferred $1 par and
(1.207115) shares Common $1 par
Chromalloy American Corp. (DE)
merged into Sun Chemical Corp.
12/23/1986 which name changed to
Sequa Corp. 05/08/1987
(See Sequa Corp.)

STARLING CORP. (CA)
Charter suspended for failure to file
reports and pay taxes 03/01/1965

STARLINK CAP CORP (AB)
Name changed 12/08/2000
Name changed from Starlink
Communications Corp. to Starlink
Capital Corp. 12/08/2000
Recapitalized as Nevis Energy
Services Ltd. 10/05/2001
Each share Class A Common no par
exchanged for (0.1) share Class A
Common no par
Nevis Energy Services Ltd. was
acquired by Phoenix Technlogy
Services Inc. 11/01/2002 which
recapitalized as Phoenix Technology
Income Fund 07/01/2004 which
reorganized as PHX Energy
Services Corp. 01/06/2011

STARLITE GOLD MINES LTD. (BC)
Name changed to Camela Mines &
Oils Ltd. 8/21/69
Camela Mines & Oils Ltd. declared
dissolved in 1976

STARLITE PETROLEUMS LTD. (BC)
Name changed to Starlite Gold Mines
Ltd. 9/16/65
Starlite Gold Mines Ltd. name
changed to Camela Mines & Oils
Ltd. 8/21/69
(See Camela Mines & Oils Ltd.)

STARLOG FRANCHISE CORP (NJ)
Recapitalized as Retail Entertainment
Group, Inc. 07/09/1998
Each share Common $0.0001 par
exchanged for (0.1) share Common
1¢ par
(See Retail Entertainment Group, Inc.)

STARMARK INC (NY)
Reorganized under the laws of
Delaware as Babystar Inc.
03/23/1993
Each share Common 1¢ par
exchanged for (0.19) share new
Common 1¢ par
Babystar Inc. name changed to
Datatrend Services Inc. 11/27/1995
(See Datatrend Services Inc.)

STARMARK INDS INC (UT)
Reorganized under the laws of
Delaware as Starmark Energy
Systems, Inc. 7/8/85
Each share Common 1¢ par
exchanged for (0.04) share Common
10¢ par

STARMARK RES LTD (BC)
Recapitalized as Transglobe
Resources Ltd. 03/26/1987
Each share Common no par
exchanged for (1/3) share Common
no par
Transglobe Resources Ltd. name
changed to Transglobe Real Estate
Corp. 06/19/1990 which name
changed to Ultra Petroleum Corp.
(BC) 10/21/1993 which
reincorporated in Yukon 03/01/2000

STARMASTER TROPHIES, INC. (OR)
Liquidated in March 1971
No stockholders' equity

STARMAX TECHNOLOGIES INC (ON)
Each old share Common no par
exchanged for (10) shares new
Common no par 12/16/2002
Name changed to MedCap Corp.
(ON) 11/24/2004
MedCap Corp. (ON) reorganized in
Nevada as Fortune Market Media,
Inc. 11/13/2007
(See Fortune Market Media, Inc.)

STARMED GROUP INC (NV)
Each share old Common 1¢ par
exchanged for (0.025) share new
Common 1¢ par 08/13/2007
Name changed to Westmoore
Holdings, Inc. 01/28/2008
Westmoore Holdings, Inc. name
changed to Rockwall Holdings, Inc.
04/22/2010
(See Rockwall Holdings, Inc.)

STARMEDIA NETWORK INC (DE)
Issue Information - 7,000,000 shares COM offered at $15 per share on 05/25/1999
Recapitalized as CycleLogic, Inc. 4/3/2003
Each share Common $0.001 par exchanged for (0.001) share Common $0.001 par
(See CycleLogic, Inc.)

STARMET CORP (MA)
Petition filed under Chapter 11 Federal Bankruptcy Code dismissed 12/20/2002
No stockholders' equity

STARMIN MNG INC (ON)
Recapitalized as First Dynasty Mines Ltd. 08/16/1994
Each share Common no par exchanged for (1/3) share Common no par
First Dynasty Mines Ltd. name changed to Sterlite Gold Ltd. 05/21/2002
(See Sterlite Gold Ltd.)

STARNET COMMUNICATIONS INTL INC (DE)
Reincorporated under the laws of England & Wales as World Gaming PLC and Common $0.001 par changed to Sponsored ADR for Ordinary 05/29/2001
(See World Gaming PLC)

STARNET FINL INC (DE)
Each share old Common 1¢ par exchanged for (0.01) share new Common 1¢ par 3/17/2006
Name changed to Mobile Ready Entertainment Corp. 5/9/2006

STARNET INTL CORP (FL)
Recapitalized as Prime Time Group, Inc. 07/22/2004
Each share Common $0.0001 par exchanged for (0.02) share Common $0.0001 par
Prime Time Group, Inc. recapitalized as Hunt Gold Corp. 11/30/2007
(See Hunt Gold Corp.)

STARNET UNIVERSE INTERNET INC (CA)
Merged into Staruni Corp. 12/30/1996
Each share Common no par exchanged for (0.5) share Common 25¢ par
Staruni Corp. recapitalized as Elephant Talk Communications, Inc. (CA) 01/22/2002 which reincorporated in Delaware 09/26/2011 which name changed to Pareteum Corp. 11/03/2016

STARONT TECHNOLOGIES INC (ON)
Delisted from NEX 08/01/2008

STARPOINT ENERGY LTD (AB)
Under plan of merger each share Common no par exchanged for (0.11111111) share Mission Oil & Gas Inc. Common no par and (0.25) StarPoint Energy Ltd. Trust Unit no par 01/07/2005
Note: Canadian residents option to receive Exchangeable Shares in lieu of Trust Units expired 01/03/2005
Each Exchangeable Share no par exchanged for (1) 1198330 Alberta Ltd. Special Share 01/05/2006

STARPOINT ENERGY TR (AB)
Acquired by Canetic Resources Trust 01/05/2006
Each Trust Unit exchanged for (1) Trust Unit no par, (0.1) share TriStar Oil & Gas Ltd. Common no par and (0.021) Common Stock Purchase Warrant expiring 02/06/2006
(See each company's listing)

STARPOINT GOLDFIELDS INC (BC)
Name changed 05/27/1996
Name changed from Starpoint Systems Inc. to Starpoint Goldfields Inc. 05/27/1996

Delisted from Toronto Venture Stock Exchange 03/13/2002

STARPOINTE SVGS BK (FRANKLIN, NJ)
Location changed 07/01/1988
Stock Dividends - 10% 05/29/1987; 10% 05/27/1988
Location changed from (Plainfield, NJ) to (Franklin, NJ) 07/01/1988
Acquired by Dime Savings Bank of New York, FSB (New York, NY) 12/01/1989
Each share Common $2 par exchanged for $21 cash

STARR BROADCASTING GROUP INC (DE)
Reincorporated 03/31/1970
State of incorporation changed from (NE) to (DE) 03/31/1970
Non-Voting Conv. Preferred Ser. M $20 par called for redemption 11/06/1978
Non-Voting Preferred Ser. P $20 par called for redemption 11/06/1978
Acquired by Shamrock Broadcasting Inc. 07/18/1979
Each share Common $1 par exchanged for $15.25 cash

STARRATT NICKEL MINES LTD (ON)
Recapitalized as Starratt Resources Ltd. 10/31/1994
Each share Common $1 par exchanged for (0.2) share Common no par
(See Starratt Resources Ltd.)

STARRATT OLSEN GOLD MINES LTD. (ON)
Name changed to Starratt Nickel Mines Ltd. 00/00/1957
Starratt Nickel Mines Ltd. recapitalized as Starratt Resources Ltd. 10/31/1994
(See Starratt Resources Ltd.)

STARRATT RES LTD (ON)
Delisted from Canadian Dealer Network 10/13/2000

STARRETT BROS & EKEN INC (NY)
Voting Trust Agreement terminated 2/28/63
Each VTC for Common $7.50 par exchanged for (1) share Common $7.50 par
Common $7.50 par changed to $3.75 par and (1) additional share issued 6/7/63
Common $3.75 par split (2) for (1) by issuance of (1) additional share 6/28/66
Common $3.75 par changed to $1 par and (1.2) additional shares issued 6/28/68
Stock Dividends - 10% 7/19/66; 10% 6/25/69
Name changed to Starrett Housing Corp. 5/26/71
Starrett Housing Corp. name changed to Starrett Corp. 6/23/95
(See Starrett Corp.)

STARRETT CORP. (DE)
Recapitalized in 1933
6% Preferred $50 par changed to $10 par
Preferred $10 par changed to $2 par
Common no par changed to $1 par
Reorganized in 1936
Each share Preferred $10 par exchanged for (1) share Common $1 par
Each share Preferred $2 par exchanged for (0.2) share Common $1 par
Each share Common $1 par exchanged for (0.1) share new Common $1 par
Recapitalized 4/30/57
Common $1 par changed to 10¢ par
Recapitalized as Parvin-Dohrmann Co. 6/3/63
Each share Preferred 50¢ par exchanged for (0.2) share Preferred $2.50 par

Each share Common 10¢ par exchanged for (0.2) share Common 50¢ par
Parvin/Dohrmann Co. name changed to Recrion Corp. 12/14/70 which merged into Argent Corp. 8/31/74

STARRETT CORP (NY)
Name changed 6/23/95
Common $1 par split (3) for (2) by issuance of (0.5) additional share 4/20/72
Common $1 par split (3) for (2) by issuance of (0.5) additional share 6/15/78
Name changed from Starrett Housing Corp. to Starrett Corp. 6/23/95
Merged into Startt Acquisition, Inc. 12/30/97
Each share Common $1 par exchanged for $12.25 cash

STARREX MNG LTD (CANADA)
Name changed to Starrex International Ltd. 05/01/2014

STARS GROUP INC (ON)
Each share Conv. Class A Preferred no par automatically became approximately (52.7085) shares Common no par 07/18/2018
(Additional Information in Active)

STARS INCOME FD (ON)
Merged into MINT Income Fund 09/25/2009
Each Trust Unit no par exchanged for (1.34864982) Trust Units no par

STARS TO GO INC (CA)
SEC revoked common stock registration 10/01/2012

STARSHIP CRUISE LINE INC (DE)
Company terminated registration of common stock and is no longer public as of 12/14/2000

STARSIGHT TELECAST INC (CA)
Merged into Gemstar International Group Ltd. (British Virgin Islands) 05/08/1997
Each share Common no par exchanged for (0.6062) share Ordinary £1 par
Gemstar International Group Ltd. (British Virgin Islands) reincorporated in Delaware 02/09/2000 which name changed to Gemstar-TV Guide International, Inc. 07/12/2000 which merged into Macrovision Solutions Corp. 05/05/2008 which name changed to Rovi Corp. 07/16/2009 which name changed to TiVo Corp. 09/08/2016

STARSTREAM COMMUNICATIONS GROUP INC (DE)
Name changed to Catalyst Energy Services Inc. 8/16/94
(See Catalyst Energy Services Inc.)

START CALL COM INC (FL)
Common $0.000666 par split (11) for (1) by issuance of (10) additional shares payable 02/08/2002 to holders of record 02/04/2002 Ex date - 02/11/2002
Each share old Common $0.000666 par exchanged for (0.04) share new Common $0.000666 par 12/16/2002
Name changed to Visator, Inc. 01/01/2003
Visator, Inc. name changed to GoldSpring, Inc. (FL) 03/18/2003 which reincorporated in Nevada 11/12/2008 which name changed to Comstock Mining Inc. 07/21/2010

STARTALE GROUP INC (NV)
Common $0.001 par split (3) for (1) by issuance of (2) additional shares payable 06/24/2008 to holders of record 05/22/2008 Ex date - 06/25/2008
Name changed to Alco Energy Corp. 06/25/2008
Alco Energy Corp. name changed to A & J Venture Capital Group, Inc.

08/21/2009 which recapitalized as ReliaBrand Inc. 02/24/2011

STARTEC GLOBAL COMMUNICATIONS CORP (DE)
Reincorporated 03/26/1999
Place of incorporation changed from (MD) to (DE) 03/26/1999
Plan of reorganization under Chapter 11 Federal Bankruptcy Code effective 05/17/2004
No stockholders' equity

STARTEC MARKETING CORP (BC)
Recapitalized as Vitality Products Inc. 2/9/93
Each share Common no par exchanged for (0.2) share Common no par

STARTECH ENERGY INC (AB)
Merged into Impact Energy Inc. Canada 1/31/2001
Each share Common no par held by Canadian Residents exchanged for (1) share Common no par and (0.96) ARC Energy Trust Unit no par
Each share Common no par held by Non-Canadian residents exchanged for (1) share Common no par and (0.96) ARC Resources Ltd. Exchangeable Share
(See each company's listing)

STARTECH ENERGY INC (SK)
Merged into Startech Energy Inc. 7/6/94
Each (8.58) shares Common no par exchanged for (1) share Common no par
Startech Energy Inc. merged into Impact Energy Inc. Canada 1/31/2001 which merged into Thunder Energy Inc. 4/30/2004
(See Thunder Energy Inc.)

STARTECH ENVIRONMENTAL CORP (CO)
Stock Dividend - 5% payable 11/29/1996 to holders of record 11/11/1996
SEC revoked common stock registration 10/09/2013

STARTECK INDS LTD (BC)
Recapitalized as International StarTeck Industries Ltd. 09/24/1999
Each share Common no par exchanged for (0.25) share Common no par
(See International StarTeck Industries Ltd.)

STARTEK COM INC (FL)
Name changed to Bentley Communications Corp. 11/29/1999
Bentley Communications Corp. name changed to Bentley Commerce Corp. 01/12/2004
(See Bentley Commerce Corp.)

STARTEL CORP (CA)
Stock Dividend - 20% 12/11/1986
Merged into Converse Technology, Inc. 08/10/1992
Each share Common no par exchanged for (0.5778) share Common 1¢ par
Converse Technology, Inc. merged into Verint Systems Inc. 02/05/2013

STARTER CORP (DE)
Plan of reorganization under Chapter 11 Federal Bankruptcy Code effective 5/16/2000
No stockholders' equity

STARTIGAN CORP (CANADA)
Reincorporated under the laws of Yukon as Ecuadorian Minerals Corp. 02/14/1994
Ecuadorian Minerals Corp. name changed to International Minerals Corp. 01/24/2002
(See International Minerals Corp.)

STARTRONIX INTL INC (DE)
Each share old Common $0.001 par exchanged for (0.05) share new Common $0.001 par 05/21/1999

Charter cancelled and declared inoperative and void for non-payment of taxes 03/01/2002

STARUNI CORP (CA)
Recapitalized as Elephant Talk Communications, Inc. (CA) 01/22/2002
Each share Common no par exchanged for (0.1) share Common no par
Elephant Talk Communications, Inc. (CA) reincorporated in Delaware 09/26/2011 which name changed to Pareteum Corp. 11/03/2016

STARVIDEO PRODTNS INC (CO)
Name changed to Pantheon Industries, Inc. 08/01/1987
(See Pantheon Industries, Inc.)

STARVOX COMMUNICATIONS INC (DE)
Filed a petition under Chapter 7 Federal Bankruptcy Code 03/26/2008
No stockholders' equity

STARWAVE CORP (WA)
Merged into Infoseek Corp. 11/18/98
Each share Common no par exchanged for (0.26) share Common no par

STARWOOD FINL INC (MD)
Stock Dividend - 0.01905% payable 11/18/1999 to holders of record 11/03/1999
Name changed to iStar Financial Inc. 05/01/2000
iStar Financial Inc. name changed to iStar Inc. 08/19/2015

STARWOOD FINL TR (CA)
Merged into Starwood Financial Trust (MD) 06/18/1998
Each Class A Share of Bene Int. $1 par exchanged for (0.16666666) Class A Share of Bene. Int. $1 par
Starwood Financial Trust (MD) name changed to Starwood Financial Inc. 11/04/1999 which name changed to iStar Financial Inc. 05/01/2000 which name changed to iStar Inc. 08/19/2015

STARWOOD FINL TR (MD)
Under plan of merger name changed to Starwood Financial Inc. 11/04/1999
Starwood Financial Inc. name changed to iStar Financial Inc. 05/01/2000 which name changed to iStar Inc. 08/19/2015

STARWOOD HOTELS & RESORTS (MD)
Name changed 01/02/1998
Name changed 02/24/1998
Each old Combined Certificate exchanged for (0.16666666) new Combined Certificate 06/19/1995
New Combined Certificates split (3) for (2) by issuance of (0.5) additional Certificate payable 01/27/1997 to holders of record 12/30/1996 Ex date - 01/28/1997
Under plan of merger name changed from Starwood Lodging Trust to Starwood Hotels & Resorts Trust 01/02/1998
Name changed from Starwood Hotels & Resorts Trust to Starwood Hotels & Resorts 02/24/1998
Reorganized as Starwood Hotels & Resorts Worldwide, Inc. 01/06/1999
Each Combined Certificate exchanged for (1) Combined Certificate
Starwood Hotels & Resorts Worldwide, Inc. merged into Marriott International, Inc. (New) 09/23/2016

STARWOOD HOTELS & RESORTS WORLDWIDE INC (MD)
Paired certificates separated 4/10/2006
Each Starwood Hotels & Resorts Class B Share of Bene. Int. 1¢ par exchanged for (0.6122) share Host Marriott Corp. Common $1 par and $0.503 cash
Note: Holders retained Common Stock portion of paired certificate
Each share Common 1¢ par received distribution of (0.4309) share Interval Leisure Group, Inc. Common 1¢ par payable 04/30/2016 to holders of record 03/28/2016 Ex date - 05/13/2016
Merged into Marriott International, Inc. (New) 09/23/2016
Each share Common 1¢ par exchanged for (0.8) share Class A Common $1 par and $21 cash

STARWOOD INDS INC (ON)
Ceased operations 09/30/2008
Details not available

STARWOOD VENTURES INC (CO)
Name changed to Cine-Source, Inc. (CO) 05/17/1989
Cine-Source, Inc. (CO) reorganized in Nevada as First Quantum Ventures, Inc. 05/21/2004 which name changed to DiMi Telematics International, Inc. 03/16/2012 which name changed to Bespoke Extracts, Inc. 03/10/2017

STARWOOD WAYPOINT HOMES (MD)
Merged into Invitation Homes Inc. 11/16/2017
Each Common Share of Bene. Int. 1¢ par exchanged for (1.614) shares Common 1¢ par

STARWOOD WAYPOINT RESIDENTIAL TR (MD)
Name changed to Colony Starwood Homes 01/06/2016
Colony Starwood Homes name changed to Starwood Waypoint Homes 07/31/2017 which merged into Invitation Homes Inc. 11/16/2017

STARX RESOURCE CORP (BC)
Reincorporated under the laws of Yukon as Gabriel Resources Ltd. 04/16/1997

STARZ (DE)
Liberty Capital Common Ser. A 1¢ par reclassified as Common Ser. A 1¢ par 06/10/2013 Liberty Capital Common Ser. B 1¢ par reclassified as Common Ser. B 1¢ par 06/10/2013
Merged into Lions Gate Entertainment Corp. 12/08/2016
Each share Common Ser. A 1¢ par exchanged for (0.6784) Non-Vtg. Class B Share no par and $18 cash
Each share Common Ser. B 1¢ par exchanged for (0.6321) Class A Share no par, (0.6321) Non-Vtg. Class B Share no par and $7.26 cash

STASSAL INDS INC (NY)
Dissolved by proclamation 9/30/81

STASSI INTERAXX INC (DE)
Plan of reorganization under Chapter 11 Federal Bankruptcy Code effective 10/30/2007
Each share Conv. Preferred Ser. A received distribution of (1/6) share Aviation Holdings Group, Inc. Common, (1/6) share Geo Finance Corp. Common, (1/6) share Harbrew Imports, Ltd. Common, (1/6) share Southern Cross Resource Group, Inc. Common, (1/6) share Transferorbit Corp. Common, and (1/6) share Voicenetworkx, Inc. Common
Note: Unexchanged certificates were cancelled and became without value 02/09/2017

STAT HEALTHCARE INC (DE)
Merged into Stat Healthcare Inc. (New) 6/24/96
Each share Common 1¢ par exchanged for (1) share Common 1¢ par
Stat Healthcare Inc. (New) merged into American Medical Response, Inc. 12/10/96
(See American Medical Response, Inc.)

STAT HEALTHCARE INC NEW (DE)
Merged into American Medical Response, Inc. 12/10/96
Each share Common 1¢ par exchanged for (0.25) share Common 1¢ par
(See American Medical Response, Inc.)

STAT-TECH INTL CORP (CO)
Each share Common $0.0001 par exchanged for (0.025) share Common 1¢ par 11/19/1991
Plan of reorganization under Chapter 11 Federal Bankruptcy proceedings confirmed 03/16/1993
Stockholders' equity unlikely

STATE AUTOMOTIVE CORP (PA)
Name changed 5/3/74
Name changed from State Automotive Distributors, Inc. to State Automotive Corp. 5/3/74
Name changed to State Products Corp. 4/23/76
(See State Products Corp.)

STATE BANCORP INC (NY)
Common $5 par split (2) for (1) by issuance of (1) additional share 07/03/1989
Common $5 par split (6) for (5) by issuance of (0.2) additional share payable 07/03/1997 to holders of record 06/13/1997
Common $5 par split (6) for (5) by issuance of (0.2) additional share payable 07/08/2005 to holders of record 06/17/2005 Ex date - 07/11/2005
Common $5 par changed to 1¢ par 04/28/2009
Stock Dividends - 10% 07/10/1987; 10% 07/08/1988; 10% 07/02/1990; 10% 07/12/1991; 10% 07/10/1992; 10% 07/30/1993 10% 07/05/1994; 10% 07/05/1995; 8% payable 07/05/1996 to holders of record 06/14/1996; 5% payable 07/03/1998 to holders of record 06/12/1998; 6% payable 07/02/1999 to holders of record 06/11/1999; 8% payable 07/06/2000 to holders of record 06/09/2000; 5% payable 07/06/2001 to holders of record 06/08/2001 Ex date - 06/06/2001; 5% payable 07/12/2002 to holders of record 06/14/2002; 5% payable 07/11/2003 to holders of record 06/13/2003 Ex date - 06/11/2003; 5% payable 07/09/2004 to holders of record 06/11/2004
Merged into Valley National Bancorp 01/01/2012
Each share Common 1¢ par exchanged for (1) share Common no par

STATE BANCSHARES INC (PA)
Name changed to JeffBanks, Inc. 05/22/1995
JeffBanks, Inc. merged into Hudson United Bancorp 11/30/1999 which merged into TD Banknorth Inc. 01/31/2006
(See TD Banknorth Inc.)

STATE BANK & TRUST CO. (EVANSTON, IL)
Common $60 par changed to $50 par and (0.5) additional share issued plus a 25-875/3993% stock dividend paid 01/15/1960
Common $50 par changed to $25 par and (1) additional share issued 01/20/1964
Stock Dividends - 20% 11/18/1954; 10% 01/18/1957; 10% 01/17/1958; 10% 01/16/1959; 10% 01/13/1961; 10% 01/12/1962; 10% 01/14/1963; 87.8% 01/20/1967
Name changed to State National Bank (Evanston, IL) 02/18/1967
State National Bank (Evanston, IL) reorganized as State National Corp. (DE) 02/01/1973
(See State National Corp. (DE))

STATE BK & TR CO (DEFIANCE, OH)
Reorganized as Rurban Financial Corp. 01/01/1984
Each share Common $10 par exchanged for (1) share Common no par
Rurban Financial Corp. name changed to SB Financial Group, Inc. 04/25/2013

STATE BK & TR CO (GREENWOOD, SC)
Stock Dividends - 10% 8/15/66; 10% 8/1/67
Name changed to Bankers Trust of South Carolina (Columbia, SC) 9/5/69
Bankers Trust of South Carolina (Columbia, SC) merged into Bankers Trust of South Carolina, N.A. (Columbia, SC) 10/15/73 which name changed back to Bankers Trust of South Carolina (Columbia, SC) 12/10/74
Bankers Trust of South Carolina (Columbia, SC) acquired by NCNB Corp. 1/2/86 which name changed to NationsBank Corp. 12/31/91 which reincorporated in Delaware as BankAmerica Corp. (Old) 9/25/98 which merged into BankAmerica Corp. (New) 9/30/98 which name changed to Bank of America Corp. 4/28/99

STATE BK & TR CO (PETOSKEY, MI)
Capital Stock $20 par changed to $10 par to effect a (2) for (1) split and a 25% stock dividend by issuance of (1.5) additional shares 2/28/77
Merged into Old Kent Financial Corp. 1/2/80
Each share Capital Stock $10 par exchanged for $118 principal amount of 9-1/4% Installment Notes due 1/15/81

STATE BK & TR CO (WELLSTON, MO)
Capital Stock $25 par changed to $10 par and (1.5) additional shares issued 11/01/1960
Capital Stock $10 par changed to $5 par and (1) additional share issued 02/14/1964
Stock Dividends - 33-1/3% 02/03/1948; 50% 11/30/1951; 33-1/3% 12/21/1953; 10% 02/07/1956; 12-1/2% 02/14/1957; 10% 02/23/1960; 10% 02/14/1967; 40% 06/03/1968
Name changed to First State Bank & Trust Co. (Wellston, MO) 04/14/1971
First State Bank & Trust Co. (Wellston, MO) name changed to Landmark Central Bank & Trust Co. (Wellston, MO) 11/01/1976
(See Landmark Central Bank & Trust Co. (Wellston, MO))

STATE BK & TR CO LAKE CNTY (MENTOR, OH)
Merged into BancOhio National Bank (Columbus, OH) 09/01/1981
Each share Capital Stock $10 par exchanged for $41 cash

STATE BK (ALLEGHENIES, VA)
Merged into F & M National Corp. 1/3/2000
Each share Common exchanged for (0.646) share Common $2 par
F & M National Corp. merged into BB&T Corp. 8/9/2001

STATE BK (FAYETTEVILLE, NC)
Merged into First Citizens Bancshares, Inc. 3/2/95

Each share Common $2.50 par exchanged for $5 cash

STATE BK (JACKSONVILLE, FL)
Stock Dividend - 10% 01/21/1967
Name changed to Flagship Bank of Jacksonville (Jacksonville, FL) 04/03/1978
(See Flagship Bank of Jacksonville (Jacksonville, FL))

STATE BK (SOUTH ORANGE, NJ)
Merged into United National Bancorp 9/30/98
Each share Common $5 par exchanged for (1.245) shares Common $2.50 par
(See United National Bancorp)

STATE BK ALBANY (ALBANY, NY)
Each share Capital Stock $100 par exchanged for (10) shares Capital Stock $10 par in 1946
Capital Stock $10 par changed to $5 par and (1) additional share issued 12/1/67
Stock Dividend - 50% 3/1/49
Reorganized as United Bank Corp. of New York 12/31/71
Each share Capital Stock $5 par exchanged for (1.5) shares Common $5 par
United Bank Corp. of New York name changed to Norstar Bancorp Inc. 1/4/82 which merged into Fleet/Norstar Financial Group, Inc. 1/1/88 which name changed to Fleet Financial Group, Inc. (New) 4/15/92 which name changed to Fleet Boston Financial Corp. 10/1/99 which name changed to FleetBoston Financial Corp. 4/18/2000 which merged into Bank of America Corp. 4/1/2004

STATE BK CHITTENANGO (CHITTENANGO, NY)
Reorganized as SBC Financial Corp. 6/17/85
Each share Common $15 par exchanged for (3) shares Common $15 par
(See SBC Finanical Corp.)

STATE BK COLOMA (COLOMA, MI)
Merged into Shoreline Financial Corp. 7/30/98
Each share Common no par exchanged for (80.77) shares Common $1 par
Shoreline Financial Corp. merged into Chemical Financial Corp. 1/9/2001

STATE BK EAST FT WORTH (FORT WORTH, TX)
Name changed to Fort Worth Bank & Trust (Fort Worth, TX) 12/30/1975
Fort Worth Bank & Trust (Fort Worth, TX) name changed to MBank Fort Worth East (Fort Worth, TX) 10/15/1984
(See MBank Fort Worth East (Fort Worth, TX))

STATE BK EASTN PA (KINGSTON, PA)
Merged into First Valley Corp. 5/1/72
Each share Common $10 par exchanged for (1.8) shares Common $1 par
First Valley Corp. acquired by United Jersey Banks 1/29/88 which name changed to UJB Financial Corp. 6/30/89 which name changed to Summit Bancorp 3/1/96 which merged into FleetBoston Financial Corp. 3/1/2001 which merged into Bank of America Corp. 4/1/2004

STATE BK LONG ISLAND (NEW HYDE PARK, NY)
Common $10 par changed to $5 par and (1) additional shares issued 06/15/1972
Stock Dividends - 10% 06/15/1973; 10% 06/13/1974; 10% 07/15/1975; 10% 07/20/1976; 10% 6/15/1977; 10% 09/28/1978; 10% 07/20/1979; 10% 07/18/1980; 10% 07/17/1981; 10% 07/16/1982; 10% 06/30/1983;
10% 06/29/1984; 10% 07/19/1985; 20% 07/31/1986
Under plan of reorganization each share Common $5 par automatically became (1) share State Bancorp, Inc. Common $5 par 06/24/1986
State Bancorp, Inc. merged into Valley National Bancorp 01/01/2012

STATE BK MAYVILLE (MAYVILLE, WI)
Acquired by Marshall & Ilsley Bank Stock Corp. 09/01/1971
Each share Common $20 par exchanged for (3.5) shares Common $2.50 par
Marshall & Ilsley Bank Stock Corp. name changed to Marshall & Ilsley Corp. (Old) 12/30/1971
(See Marshall & Ilsley Corp. (Old))

STATE BK N J (FORT LEE, NJ)
Liquidation completed
Each share Capital Stock $5 par exchanged for initial distribution of $6.50 cash 08/26/1980
Each share Capital Stock $5 par received second and final distribution of $0.23 cash 05/03/1984

STATE BANK OF FRASER (FRASER, MI)
Capital Stock $100 par split (4) for (3) by issuance of (1/3) additional share 5/1/68
Merged into Commerce Bancorp, Inc. (Mich.) 4/1/83
Each share Capital Stock $100 par exchanged for $1,050 cash

STATE BANK OF LONG BEACH (LONG BEACH, NY)
Merged into Commercial Bank of North America (New York, NY) 03/30/1962
Each share Capital Stock $10 par exchanged for (0.8) share Capital Stock $5 par
Commerical Bank of North America (New York, NY) name changed to Bank of North America (New York, NY) (New) 03/15/1965
(See Bank of North America (New York, NY) (New))

STATE BANK OF MANVILLE (MANVILLE, NJ)
Merged into Somerset Trust Co. (Somerville, NJ) 6/1/77
Each share Common $10 par exchanged for (0.25) share Capital Stock $5 par
Somerset Trust Co. (Somerset, NJ) reorganized as Somerset Bancorp Inc. 10/1/84 which was acquired by Summit Bancorporation 12/15/89 which merged into Summit Bancorp 3/1/96 which merged into FleetBoston Financial Corp. 3/1/2001 which merged into Bank of America Corp. 4/1/2004

STATE BANK OF RALEIGH (RALEIGH, NC)
Merged into United Carolina Bancshares Corp. 9/1/84
Each share Common $6 par exchanged for (1.9195) shares Common $4 par
United Carolina Bancshares Corp. merged into BB&T Corp. 7/1/97

STATE BANK OF RARITAN VALLEY (RARITAN, NJ)
Acquired by Heritage Bank North (Jamesburg, N.J.) 8/31/81
Each share Common $12.50 par exchanged for $23.50 cash

STATE BANK OF SUFFOLK (BAY SHORE, NY)
Merged into Franklin National Bank of Long Island (Mineola, NY) 10/25/1974
Each share Capital Stock $4 par exchanged for (0.918) share Common $5 par
Franklin National Bank of Long Island (Mineola, NY) name changed to Franklin National Bank (Mineola, NY) 10/16/1962 which reorganized as Franklin New York Corp. 09/22/1969
(See Franklin New York Corp.)

STATE BK OF WESTCHESTER (WHITE PLAINS, NY)
Name changed to Reliance Bank (White Plains, NY) 03/30/1993
(See Reliance Bank (White Plains, NY))

STATE BK REMINGTON INC (REMINGTON, VA)
Merged into James River Bankshares, Inc. 8/16/99
Each share Common $10 par exchanged for (2.9) shares Common $5 par
James River Bankshares, Inc. merged into First Virginia Banks, Inc. 7/2/2001 which merged into BB&T Corp. 7/1/2003

STATE BK SOMERSET CNTY (RARITAN, NJ)
Name changed to State Bank of Raritan Valley (Raritan, NJ) 08/05/1970
(See State Bank of Raritan Valley (Raritan, NJ))

STATE BD & MTG CO (MN)
Common 31-1/4¢ par changed to 15-5/8¢ par and (1) additional share issued 03/15/1973
Name changed to SBM Co. 04/03/1992
(See SBM Co.)

STATE BD CASH MGMT FD INC (MD)
Charter forfeited 10/06/1998

STATE BD COM STK FD INC (MD)
Charter forfeited 10/06/1998

STATE BD DIVERSIFIED FD INC (MD)
Charter forfeited 10/06/1998

STATE BD PROGRESS FD INC (MD)
Voluntarily dissolved 07/19/1994
Details not available

STATE BD TAX-FREE INCOME FD INC (MD)
Charter forfeited 10/06/1998

STATE CAP LIFE INS CO (NC)
Common $5 par changed to $2.50 par and (1) additional share issued 03/30/1964
Stock Dividend - 25% 04/11/1969
Merged into Durham Life Insurance Co. 01/01/1970
Each share Common $2.50 par exchanged for (2/3) share Capital Stock $5 par
Durham Life Insurance Co. reorganized as Durham Corp. 12/31/1979 which merged into Capital Holding Corp. 11/14/1991 which name changed to Providian Corp. 05/12/1994 which merged into Aegon N.V. 06/10/1997

STATE CEDAR CORP.
Property sold and distribution of $79.20 per share made in 1943

STATE CENT SVGS BK (KEOKUK, IA)
Common $20 par split (2) for (1) by issuance of (1) additional share payable 10/3/97 to holders of record 6/16/97
Acquired by Logan Investment Corp. in March 2006
Details not available

STATE EXPL CO (CA)
Name changed to Statex Petroleum, Inc. 11/01/1976
(See Statex Petroleum, Inc.)

STATE FARM BALANCE FD INC (MD)
Merged into State Farm Associates' Funds Trust 04/01/2001
Details not available

STATE FARM GROWTH FD INC (MD)
Merged into State Farm Associates' Funds Trust 04/01/2001
Details not available

STATE FARM INCOME FD INC (MD)
Name changed to State Farm Balanced Fund, Inc. 03/18/1976
(See State Farm Balanced Fund, Inc.)

STATE FARM INTERIM FD INC (MD)
Merged into State Farm Associates' Funds Trust 04/01/2001
Details not available

STATE FARM MUN BD FD INC (MD)
Merged into State Farm Associates' Funds Trust 04/01/2001
Details not available

STATE FINL SVCS CORP (WI)
Class A Common 10¢ par split (6) for (5) by issuance of (0.2) additional share 4/9/93
Class A Common 10¢ par split (6) for (5) by issuance of (0.2) additional share payable 2/28/98 to holders of record 2/14/98
Stock Dividend - 20% payable 2/29/96 to holders of record 2/14/96
Merged into Associated Banc-Corp 10/3/2005
Each share Class A Common 10¢ par exchanged for (1.2) shares Common 1¢ par

STATE FIRE & CAS CO (FL)
Under plan of merger each share Class A Common $1 par or Class B Common $1 par exchanged for (0.12) share Common $5 par 12/31/1965
Common $5 par changed to $2 par 12/31/1967
Stock Dividends - Paid on Class A & B Common in Class A Common: 20% 06/29/1956; 11-1/9% 06/14/1957; 40% 05/20/1965
Declared insolvent 06/13/1969
No stockholders' equity

STATE 1ST NATL BK (TEXARKANA, AR)
Stock Dividend - 33-1/3% 3/1/74
Under plan of reorganization each share Capital Stock $10 par automatically became (1) share State First Financial Corp. Capital Stock $10 par 3/31/87

STATE FRANKLIN BANCSHARES INC (TN)
Each share old Common $1 par exchanged for (1) share new Common $1 par to reflect a (1) for (3,001) reverse split followed by a (3,001) for (1) forward split 09/28/2005
Note: Holders of (3,000) or fewer pre-split shares received $25.25 cash per share
Merged into Jefferson Bancshares, Inc. 10/31/2008
Each share Common $1 par exchanged for either (1.1287) shares Common 1¢ par, (0.8977) share Common 1¢ par and $2.05 cash or $10 cash
Note: Option to receive stock and cash expired 12/01/2008
Non-residents of Tennessee will receive cash
Jefferson Bancshares, Inc. merged into HomeTrust Bancshares, Inc. 05/31/2014

STATE FRANKLIN SVGS BK (JOHNSON CITY, TN)
Under plan of reorganization each share Common $1 par automatically became (1) share State of Franklin Bancshares, Inc. Common $1 par 05/15/1998
Franklin Bancshares, Inc. merged into Jefferson Bancshares, Inc. 10/31/2008 which merged into HomeTrust Bancshares, Inc. 05/31/2014

STATE GTY AUXILIARY CORP (CA)
Completely liquidated 05/12/1976
Each share Capital Stock $1 par exchanged for first and final distribution of (1) share Allied Properties Common no par
Allied Properties assets transferred to Allied Properties Liquidating Trust 03/31/1977
(See Allied Properties Liquidating Trust)

STATE GUARANTY CORP. (DE)
Preferred and Common no par exchanged (7) for (1) in 1929
Merged into Allied Properties 9/12/62
Each share Preferred no par exchanged for (1) share 4-1/2% Conv. Preferred $50 par and (1) share of Common no par
Each share Common no par exchanged on a share for share basis
Allied Properties assets transferred to Allied Properties Liquidating Trust 3/31/77
(See Allied Properties Liquidating Trust)

STATE INDS (CA)
Each share Common $1 par exchanged for (0.1) share Common no par 6/1/65
Common no par split (3) for (2) by issuance of (0.5) additional share 1/20/70
Name changed to State Recreation, Inc. 1/14/76
State Recreation, Inc. name changed to State Products Inc. 5/26/92

STATE INVESTORS, INC. (AL)
Merged into Teleprompter Corp. 10/23/70
Each share Common $1 par exchanged for (1) Ctf. of Right or $2 cash

STATE INVS BANCORP INC (LA)
Acquired by First NBC Bank Holding Co. 11/30/2015
Each share Common 1¢ par exchanged for $21.51 cash

STATE LIFE & HEALTH INS INC (NC)
Preferred $1 par called for redemption 08/01/1972
Merged into National Savings Corp. 01/01/1973
Each share Common $1 par exchanged for (1.5) shares Common $1 par
(See National Savings Corp.)

STATE LIFE INS CO COLO (CO)
Common $1 par changed to 35¢ par 11/3/61
Voting Trust Agreement terminated 4/17/62
Each VTC for Common 35¢ par exchanged for (1) share Common 35¢ par Common 35¢ par changed to 40¢ par 6/11/68
Common 40¢ par changed to 50¢ par 5/15/70
Acquired by Bankers Life & Casualty Co. 10/1/79
Each share Common 50¢ par exchanged for $3.84 cash

STATE LIFE OF ILLINOIS (IL)
Common 17-1/2¢ par changed to 27-1/2¢ par 08/17/1962
Completely liquidated 08/31/1967
Each share Common 27-1/2¢ par exchanged for first and final distribution of (0.166666) share Franklin Life Insurance Co. Capital Stock $2 par
Franklin Life Insurance Co. name changed to FDS Holding Co. 12/30/1978 which merged into American Brands, Inc. (NJ) 02/14/1979 which reincorporated in Delaware 01/01/1986 which name changed to Fortune Brands, Inc. 05/30/1997 which name changed to Beam Inc. 10/04/2011

STATE LN & FIN CORP (DE)
Recapitalized in 1951
Each share Class A Common no par exchanged for (2) shares Class A Common $1 par
Each share Class B Common no par exchanged for (2) shares Class B Common $1 par
Class A Common $1 par and Class B Common $1 par split (2) for (1) respectively by issuance of (1) additional share 10/1/54
Name changed to American Finance System Inc. 5/1/68
American Finance System Inc. merged into Security Pacific Corp. 12/15/78 which merged into BankAmerica Corp. (Old) 4/22/92 which merged into BankAmerica Corp. (New) 9/30/98 which name changed to Bank of America Corp. 4/28/99

STATE MUT INVS INC (DE)
Reincorporated 01/31/1980
State of incorporation changed from (MA) to (DE) and Shares of Bene. Int. no par reclassified as Common 10¢ par 01/31/1980
Name changed to First City Properties Inc. 06/25/1981
First City Properties Inc. name changed to First City Industries Inc. (Old) 05/31/1985
(See First City Industries Inc. (Old))

STATE MUT SECS TR (MA)
Name changed 7/1/86
Name changed from State Mutual Securities, Inc. to State Mutual Securities Trust and Common $1 par reclassified as Shares of Bene. Int. $1 par 7/1/86
Name changed to Allmerica Securities Trust 6/1/94
(See Allmerica Securities Trust)

STATE NATIONAL BANCORP, INC. (KY)
Merged into Trans Financial Bancorp, Inc. 04/01/1994
Each share Common no par exchanged for (5.3) shares Common no par
Trans Financial Bancorp, Inc. name changed to Trans Financial, Inc. 04/24/1995 which merged into Star Banc Corp. 08/21/1998 which merged into Firstar Corp. (New) 11/20/1998 which merged into U.S. Bancorp (DE) 02/27/2001

STATE NATL BANCORP INC (DE)
Merged into CBT Corp. 12/29/1982
Each share Common $1 par exchanged for $43 cash

STATE NATL BANCSHARES (DE)
Name changed to PanNational Group Inc. 07/27/1972
PanNational Group Inc. merged into Mercantile Texas Corp. 04/08/1982 which name changed to MCorp 10/11/1984
(See MCorp)

STATE NATL BANCSHARES INC (TX)
Issue Information - 1,907,692 shares COM offered at $26 per share on 09/29/2005
Merged into Banco Bilbao Vizcaya Argentaria, S.A. 1/3/2007
Each share Common $1 par exchanged for $38.50 cash

STATE NATIONAL BANK (DECATUR, AL)
Stock Dividends - 33-1/3% 12/30/44; 75% 6/21/46; 30.9% 12/28/48; 25% 12/27/50; 10% 6/5/58; 10% 2/6/61; 10% 2/6/63
Name changed to State National Bank of Alabama (Decatur, Ala.) 2/1/64
State National Bank of Alabama (Decatur, Ala.) name changed to Central Bank of Alabama, N.A. (Decatur, Ala.) 6/4/73

(See Central Bank of Alabama, N.A. (Decatur, Ala.))

STATE NATL BK (DENISON, TX)
Merged into First International Bancshares, Inc. 11/15/1973
Each share Capital Stock $25 par exchanged for (3.37) shares Common $5 par
First International Bancshares, Inc. name changed to InterFirst Corp. 12/31/1981 which merged into First RepublicBank Corp. 06/06/1987
(See First RepublicBank Corp.)

STATE NATL BK (EL PASO, TX)
Capital Stock $100 par changed to $20 par and (4) additional shares issued plus a 100% stock dividend paid 05/23/1967
Stock Dividends - 100% 12/31/1945; 100% 11/01/1948; 25% 12/19/1950; 100% 03/01/1955; 25% 04/01/1971
Reorganized as State National Bancshares, Inc. 04/03/1972
Each share Capital Stock $20 par exchanged for (2) shares Common $10 par
State National Bancshares, Inc. name changed to PanNational Group Inc. 07/27/1972 which merged into Mercantile Texas Corp. 04/08/1982 which name changed to MCorp 10/11/1984
(See MCorp)

STATE NATL BK (EVANSTON, IL)
Common $25 par changed to $12.50 par and (1) additional share issued 02/15/1968
Stock Dividends - 20% 02/03/1969; 10% 02/06/1970; 10% 02/09/1972
Under plan of reorganization each share Common $12.50 par automatically became (1) share State National Corp. (DE) Common $12.50 par 02/01/1973
(See State National Corp. (DE))

STATE NATL BK (MAYSVILLE, KY)
Common $25 par changed to $5 par and (4) additional shares issued 12/04/1982
Reorganized as State National Bancorp, Inc. (KY) 12/04/1982
Each share Common $5 par exchanged for (1) share Common no par and $28 principal amount of Variable Rate Debentures due 12/27/2007
State National Bancorp, Inc. (KY) merged into Trans Financial Bancorp, Inc. 04/01/1994 which name changed to Trans Financial, Inc. 04/24/1995 which merged into Star Banc Corp. 08/21/1998 which merged into Firstar Corp. (New) 11/20/1998 which merged into U.S. Bancorp (DE) 02/27/2001

STATE NATIONAL BANK (TEXARKANA, AR)
Each share Capital Stock $100 par exchanged for (10) shares Capital Stock $10 par and 100% stock dividend paid 00/00/1954
Stock Dividend - 50% 01/16/1961
Name changed to State First National Bank (Texarkana, AK) 02/15/1966
State First National Bank (Texarkana, AR) reorganized as State First Financial Corp. 03/31/1987

STATE NATL BK ALA (DECATUR, AL)
Stock Dividends - 10% 02/28/1966; 16-2/3% 03/29/1968
Name changed to Central Bank of Alabama, N.A. (Decatur, AL) 06/04/1973
(See Central Bank of Alabama, N.A. (Decatur, AL))

STATE NATL BK CONN (BRIDGEPORT, CT)
Stock Dividend - 150% 03/29/1974
100% acquired by State National Bancorp Inc. 00/00/1979
Public interest eliminated

STATE NATL BK MD (BETHESDA, MD)
Name changed 02/16/1971
Name changed from State National Bank (Bethesda, MD) to State National Bank of Maryland (Bethesda, MD) 02/16/1971
Common $15 par changed to $2.50 par and (5) additional shares issued 03/15/1972
Location changed to State National Bank of Maryland (Rockville, MD) 03/06/1973
State National Bank of Maryland (Rockville, MD) acquired by Dominion Bankshares Corp. 05/03/1986 which merged into First Union Corp. 03/01/1993 which name changed to Wachovia Corp. (Ctfs. dated after 09/01/2001) 09/01/2001 which merged into Wells Fargo & Co. (New) 12/31/2008

STATE NATL BK MD (ROCKVILLE, MD)
Acquired by Dominion Bankshares Corp. 05/03/1986
Each share Common $2.50 par exchanged for (0.8283) share Common $5 par
Dominion Bankshares Corp. merged into First Union Corp. 03/01/1993 which name changed to Wachovia Corp. (Ctfs. dated after 09/01/2001) 09/01/2001 which merged into Wells Fargo & Co. (New) 12/31/2008

STATE NATIONAL CORP. (LA)
Merged into Louisiana Bancshares, Inc. 4/16/85
Each share Common $10 par exchanged for (8.12757) shares Common no par
Louisiana Bancshares, Inc. name changed to Premier Bancorp, Inc. 4/15/87 which merged into Banc One Corp. 1/2/96 which merged into Bank One Corp. 10/2/98 which merged into J.P. Morgan Chase & Co. 12/31/2000 which name changed to JPMorgan Chase & Co. 7/20/2004

STATE NATL CORP (DE)
Common $12.50 par split (3) for (2) by issuance of (0.5) additional share 05/22/1978
Common $12.50 par changed to no par and (1) additional share issued 05/04/1984
Common no par received distribution of (1.5) additional shares to reflect a (2) for (1) split and the payment of a 25% stock dividend 05/15/1986
Stock Dividends - 10% 01/10/1974; 50% 10/15/1975; 20% 04/25/1980
Merged into NBD Bancorp, Inc. 12/17/1987
Each share Common no par exchanged for $25 cash

STATE NATL COS INC (DE)
Acquired by Markel Corp. 11/17/2017
Each share Common $0.001 par exchanged for $21 cash

STATE NATIONAL SECURITIES CO. (MO)
Dissolved in 1953

STATE O MAINE INC (DE)
Common 10¢ par split (5) for (4) by issuance of (0.25) additional share 8/6/87
Common 10¢ par split (6) for (5) by issuance of (0.2) additional share 2/23/89
Common 10¢ par split (5) for (4) by issuance of (0.25) additional share 12/14/89
Common 10¢ par split (3) for (2) by issuance of (0.5) additional share 3/16/92
Stock Dividends - 100% 7/15/76; 20% 1/9/87
Name changed to Nautica Enterprises, Inc. 7/14/93

(See Nautica Enterprises, Inc.)

STATE OF THE ART INC (CA)
Merged into Sage Group PLC 3/30/98
Each share Common no par exchanged for $22 cash

STATE-PLANTERS BANK & TRUST CO. (RICHMOND, VA)
Stock Dividends - 20% 10/1/45; 33-1/3% 10/15/47; 25% 8/2/54
Name changed to State-Planters Bank of Commerce & Trusts (Richmond, Va.) and Capital Stock $12.50 par changed to $20 par 1/1/56
State-Planters Bank of Commerce & Trusts (Richmond, Va.) name changed to United Virginia Bank/State Planters (Richmond, Va.) 2/15/69 which name changed to United Virginia Bank (Richmond, Va.) 12/15/71
(See United Virginia Bank (Richmond, Va.))

STATE PLANTERS BK COMM & TRS (RICHMOND, VA)
Each share Capital Stock $20 par exchanged for (0.8772) shares Capital Stock $50 par 01/15/1968
Name changed to United Virginia Bank/ State Planters (Richmond, VA) 02/15/1969
United Virginia Bank/State Planters (Richmond, VA) name changed to United Virginia Bank (Richmond, VA) 12/15/1971
(See United Virginia Bank (Richmond, VA))

STATE POLICEMAN ANNUAL MAGAZINE INC (UT)
Name changed to National Health & Safety Corp. 02/02/1993
National Health & Safety Corp. recapitalized as ADS Media Group, Inc. 02/06/2003
(See ADS Media Group, Inc.)

STATE PRODS CORP (PA)
Each share Common 5¢ par exchanged for (1/6500) share Common $325 par 5/29/84
In effect holders received $4 cash per share and public interest was eliminated

STATE REAL ESTATE INVESTMENT TRUST (SC)
Liquidation completed
Each Share of Beneficial Interest no par exchanged for $0.730736 in 1983
Note: Certificates were not required to be surrendered and are now valueless

STATE REC INC (CA)
Name changed to State Products Inc. 5/26/92

STATE SVGS & LN ASSN (CA)
Guarantee Stock 50¢ par changed to 40¢ par and (0.25) additional share issued 06/11/1973
Guarantee Stock 40¢ par changed to 50¢ par 12/03/1981
Name changed to American Savings & Loan Association 08/05/1983
(See American Savings & Loan Association)

STATE SVGS BANCORP INC (MI)
Merged into Chemical Financial Corp. 5/1/96
Each share Common $20 par exchanged for (5) shares Common $10 par

STATE SAVINGS BANK (COUNCIL BLUFFS, IA)
Name changed to State Bank & Trust (Council Bluffs, IA) 8/8/67

STATE SVGS BK (OWOSSO, MI)
Stock Dividend - 10% 02/28/1975
Name changed to Key State Bank (Owosso, MI) 10/01/1977
Key State Bank (Owosso, MI)

acquired by Chemical Financial Corp. 10/21/1993

STATE SEC LIFE INS CO (IN)
Administratively dissolved 3/4/92

STATE STR BK & TR CO (BOSTON, MA)
Under plan of merger each share Capital Stock $20 par exchanged for (2) shares Capital Stock $10 par 4/17/61
Reorganized as State Street Boston Financial Corp. 6/15/70
Each share Capital Stock $10 par exchanged for (1) share Common $10 par
State Street Boston Financial Corp. name changed to State Street Boston Corp. 5/3/77 which name changed to State Street Corp. 4/16/97

STATE STR BOSTON CORP (MA)
Common $10 par split (2) for (1) by issuance of (1) additional share 5/19/82
Common $10 par changed to $1 par and (1) additional share issued 5/18/83
Common $1 par split (2) for (1) by issuance of (1) additional share 8/15/85
Common $1 par split (2) for (1) by issuance of (1) additional share 8/5/86
Common $1 par split (2) for (1) by issuance of (1) additional share 5/13/92
Name changed to State Street Corp. 4/16/97

STATE STR CORP (MA)
Each 6.75% SPACES received (5.0505) shares Common $1 par 11/15/2005
(Additional Information in Active)

STATE STR GROWTH FD INC (MA)
Voluntarily dissolved 09/07/1990
Details not available

STATE STR INVT TR (MA)
Name changed 05/01/1989
Common no par changed to $10 par and (1) additional share issued 10/15/1955
Common $10 par changed to $2.50 par 03/06/1973
Stock Dividend - 100% 04/15/1944
Name changed from State Street Investment Corp. to State Street Investment Trust and Common $2.50 par reclassified as Shares of Bene. Int. $0.001 par 05/01/1989
Shares of Bene. Int. $0.001 par split (5) for (1) by issuance of (4) additional shares 05/04/1990
Shares of Bene. Int. $0.001 par split (2) for (1) by issuance of (1) additional share 11/06/1992
Name changed to State Street Master Investment Trust 12/14/1989
State Street Master Investment Trust name changed to State Street Research Master Investment Trust 05/25/1995
(See State Street Research Master Investment Trust)

STATE STR LIFE INS CO (MA)
Acquired by New Jersey Life Insurance Co. 12/31/70
Each share Common no par exchanged for (0.363636) share New Jersey Life Co. Common 1¢ par
New Jersey Life Insurance Co. acquired by New Jersey Life Co. 8/1/73
(See New Jersey Life Co.)

STATE STR RESH EQUITY TR (MA)
Merged into BlackRock Funds 01/28/2005
Details not available

STATE STR RESH FINL TR (MA)
Merged into BlackRock Funds 01/28/2005
Details not available

STATE STR RESH INCOME TR (MA)
Merged into BlackRock Funds 01/28/2005
Details not available

STATE STR RESH MONEY MKT TR (MA)
Merged into BlackRock Funds 01/28/2005
Details not available

STATE STR RESH TAX-EXEMPT TR (MA)
Merged into Strong Income Funds 03/07/2003
Details not available

STATE STREET ASSOCIATES (MA)
Merged into Bradley Real Estate Trust (MA) on a (1.1979) for (1) basis 2/3/61
Bradley Real Estate Trust (MA) reorganized in Maryland as Bradley Real Estate, Inc. 10/17/94

STATE STREET BOSTON FINANCIAL CORP. (MA)
Name changed to State Street Boston Corp. 5/3/77

STATE STREET EXCHANGE (MA)
Name changed to 53 State Street Corp. in 1954 53 State Street Corp. completed liquidation 10/31/68

STATE STREET MASTER INVESTMENT TRUST (MA)
Name changed to State Street Research Master Investment Trust 05/25/1995
(See State Street Research Master Investment Trust)

STATE STREET RESEARCH MASTER INVESTMENT TRUST (MA)
Merged into BlackRock Funds 01/28/2005
Details not available

STATE STREET THEATRE CO. (IL)
Involuntarily dissolved 7/2/35

STATE STREET TRUST CO. (BOSTON, MA)
Each share Capital Stock $100 par exchanged for (5) shares Capital Stock $20 par in 1945
Stock Dividend - 37-1/2% 2/18/55
Under plan of merger name changed to Second Bank-State Street Trust Co. (Boston, MA) 2/21/55
Second Bank-State Street Trust Co. (Boston, MA) name changed to State Street Bank & Trust Co. (Boston, MA) 4/15/60 which reorganized as State Street Boston Financial Corp. 6/15/70 which name changed to State Street Boston Corp. 5/3/77 which name changed to State Street Corp. 4/16/97

STATE TELEPHONE CO. OF TEXAS
Name changed to Southwestern Associated Telephone Co. in 1931
Southwestern Associated Telephone Co. name changed to General Telephone Co. of the Southwest in 1952 which name changed to GTE Southwest Inc. 1/1/88

STATE THEATRE CO. (MA)
Dissolved 1/3/39

STATE WHOLESALE CO. (OH)
Charter cancelled for failure to pay taxes 2/15/22

STATECOURT ENTERPRISES, INC. (DE)
Merged into Romax Realty Corp. and each share Common 25¢ par received $9.50 in cash 1/23/61

STATEFED FINL CORP (IA)
Common 1¢ par split (2) for (1) by issuance of (1) additional share

payable 11/14/97 to holders of record 10/31/97
Merged into Liberty Banshares, Inc. 3/11/2004
Each share Common 1¢ par exchanged for $13.47 cash

STATEN IS BANCORP INC (DE)
Issue Information - 38,333,333 shares COM offered at $10 per share on 09/12/1997
Common 1¢ par split (2) for (1) by issuance of (1) additional share payable 11/19/2001 to holders of record 11/5/2001 Ex date - 11/20/2001
Merged into Independence Community Bank Corp. 4/13/2004
Each share Common 1¢ par exchanged for (0.605863) share Common 1¢ par
(See Independence Community Bank Corp.)

STATEN ISLAND NATIONAL BANK & TRUST CO. (PORT RICHMOND, NY)
Merged into Chase Manhattan Bank (New York, NY) 7/22/57
Each share Common $50 par exchanged for (6) shares Capital Stock $12.50 par
Chase Manhattan Bank (New York, NY) name changed to Chase Manhattan Bank (N.A.), (New York, NY) 9/23/65 which reorganized as Chase Manhattan Corp. (Old) 6/4/69 which merged into Chase Manhattan Corp. (New) 3/31/96 which name changed to J.P. Morgan Chase & Co. 12/31/2000 which name changed to JPMorgan Chase & Co. 7/20/2004

STATER BROS. MARKETS (CA)
Merged into Petrolane Gas Service, Inc. 7/1/68
Each share Common no par exchanged for (0.484) share $1.375 Conv. Preferred Ser. A $1 par and (0.33) share Common $1 par
Petrolane Gas Service, Inc. name changed to Petrolane, Inc. 2/7/69
(See Petrolane, Inc.)

STATER BROS INC (DE)
Merged into Craig Corp. 12/21/87
Each share Common 1¢ par exchanged for $25.50 cash

STATES EXPL LTD (CANADA)
Reincorporated 10/27/1982
Place of incorporation changed from (BC) to (Canada) 10/27/1982
Dissolved 05/06/2004
Details not available

STATES GEN LIFE INS CO (TX)
Stock Dividends - 33-1/3% 05/28/1965; 20% 05/25/1966; 25% 05/19/1967
Merged into Rosewood Life Insurance Co. 01/31/1980
Each share Capital Stock $1 par exchanged for $15.25 cash

STATES OIL CORP.
Liquidated in 1949

STATESIDE OIL CORP (BC)
Recapitalized 3/10/94
Recapitalized from States Energy Corp to Stateside Oil Corp. 3/10/94
Each share Common no par exchanged for (0.5) share Common no par
Merged into 528140 B.C. Ltd. 2/26/97
Each share Common no par exchanged for $1.45 cash

STATESMAN GROUP INC (DE)
Non-Cum. Conv. Preference $1 par called for redemption 5/10/76
Stock Dividends - 10% 6/28/79; 10% 6/27/80; 10% 6/29/81; 10% 6/29/82; 10% 6/29/83; 10% 7/9/84; 10% 6/28/85; 10% 6/27/86; 10% 6/26/87; 10% 6/24/88; 10% 12/19/89; 10% 2/14/94

Merged into Conseco Capital
Partners II, L.P. 9/29/94
Each share Common $1 par
exchanged for $15.25 cash plus a
non-transferable contingent payment
right to receive additional cash
based upon outcome of litigation

STATESMAN INS CO (IN)
Common $5 par changed to $6.50 par
11/20/1973
Each share Common $6.50 par
exchanged for (0.002) share
Common $3,250 par 07/01/1987
Stock Dividends - 27% 12/18/1980;
20% 04/04/1984 Administratively
dissolved 02/22/2008

STATESMAN LIFE INS CO (IA)
Merged into American Liberty Life
Insurance Co. 12/31/1982
Each share Common $1 par
exchanged for $5.71 cash

STATESWEST AIRLS INC (DE)
Each (6) shares old Common 5¢ par
exchanged for (1) share new
Common 5¢ par 6/15/90
Chapter 11 bankruptcy proceedings
dismissed 9/27/94
No stockholders' equity

STATEWIDE BANCORP (NJ)
$2.20 Conv. Preferred Ser. A no par
called for redemption 7/15/86
Common $5 par changed to $2.50 par
and (1) additional share issued
7/28/86
Filed petition under Chapter 11
Federal Bankruptcy Code 5/22/91
Stockholders' equity unlikely

STATEWIDE CORP (NV)
Plan of reorganization effective
09/15/1997
Each (4-2/3) shares Common no par
exchanged for (1) share Dalab
Holdings, Inc. Common no par and
(1) share Restove Industries Inc.
Common no par
(See each company's listing)

STATEWIDE FINL CORP (NJ)
Merged into Independence
Community Bank Corp. 1/7/2000
Each share Common no par
exchanged for either (2.07) shares
Common 1¢ par, $25.14 cash, or a
combination thereof

STATEWIDE SECURITY CORP. (DE)
Charter cancelled and declared
inoperative and void for
non-payment of taxes 5/1/35

STATEX PETE INC (CA)
Common $1 par changed to 50¢ par
and (1) additional share issued
10/15/1980
Merged into PS Group, Inc.
12/31/1986
Each share $2.55 Conv. Preferred
Ser. A $20 par exchanged for $18.50
cash
Each share Common 50¢ par
exchanged for $9 cash

STATHAM INSTRS INC (CA)
Stock Dividends - 50% 10/14/66; 40%
2/27/70
Merged into Gould Inc. 7/2/74
Each share Common $1 par
exchanged for (1) share $1.35 Conv.
Preferred $1 par
(See Gould Inc.)

STATIA TERMINALS GROUP N V (NETHERLANDS ANTILLES)
Issue Information - 7,600,000 shares
CL A COM offered at $20 per share
on 04/23/1999
Completely liquidated
Each share Class A Common 1¢ par
received first and final distribution of
$18.4998 cash payable 02/28/2002
to holders of record 02/28/2002
Note: Certificates were not required to
be surrendered and are without
value

STATION CASINOS INC (NV)
$3.50 Conv. Preferred 1¢ par called
for redemption at $100 on
06/14/1999
Common 1¢ par split (3) for (2) by
issuance of (0.5) additional share
payable 07/17/2000 to holders of
record 06/30/2000 Ex date -
07/18/2000
Merged into Fertitta Colony Partners
LLC 11/07/2007
Each share Common 1¢ par
exchanged for $90 cash

STATION ONE WEST INC (UT)
Reincorporated under the laws of
Delaware as Continental Heritage
Corp. 02/22/1974
Continental Heritage Corp. name
changed to Visionquest Worldwide
Holdings Corp. 08/12/1999
(See Visionquest Worldwide Holdings Corp.)

STATIONDIGITAL CORP (DE)
Common $0.001 par split (17.6471)
for (1) by issuance of (16.6471)
additional shares payable
08/22/2014 to holders of record
08/21/2014 Ex date - 08/25/2014
SEC revoked common stock
registration 10/06/2017

STATIONS HLDG INC
Plan of reorganization under Chapter
11 Federal Bankruptcy Code
effective 10/25/2002
Each share Exchangeable Preferred
exchanged for initial distribution of
$855.9186353 cash 10/28/2002
Each share Exchangeable Preferred
received second and final
distribution of $21.9135393 cash
payable 3/3/2003 to holders of
record 10/25/2002 Ex date -
3/11/2003

STATISTICAL ECONOMIC PLANNING INC (NY)
Charter cancelled and proclaimed
dissolved for failure to pay taxes
9/30/81

STATISTICS MGMT DATA PROCESSING INC (NY)
Merged into Itel Corp. (Old) 6/17/69
Each share Common 10¢ par
exchanged for (1.5) shares Common
$1 par
Itel Corp. (Old) reorganized as Itel
Corp. (New) 9/19/83 which name
changed to Anixter International Inc.
9/1/95

STATLER HOTELS DELAWARE CORP. (DE)
Common $1 par changed to 10¢ par
02/17/1958
Merged into Hilton Hotels Corp. on a
(0.2) for (1) basis 07/23/1962
(See Hilton Hotels Corp.)

STATMASTER CORP (NY)
Adjudicated bankrupt 05/12/1967
No stockholders' equity

STATOIL ASA (NORWAY)
Name changed 10/01/2007
Name changed 11/02/2009
Name changed from Statoil A.S.A. to
StatoilHydro A.S.A. 10/01/2007
StatoilHydro A.S.A. name changed
back to Statoil A.S.A. 11/02/2009
Name changed to Equinor A.S.A.
05/16/2018

STATOR CORP.
Dissolved in 1950

STATOR REFRIGERATION, INC.
Acquired by Stator Corp. in 1937
which was dissolved in 1950

STATORDYNE CORP (DE)
Filed a petition under Chapter 11
Federal Bankruptcy Code
08/00/1995
Stockholders' equity unlikely

STATS CHIPPAC LTD (SINGAPORE)
ADR agreement terminated
04/30/2008
Each 144A Sponsored ADR for
Ordinary exchanged for $7.191519
cash

STATTON FURNITURE MFG CO (MD)
Completely liquidated 06/30/2009
Each share Preferred $100 par
exchanged for first and final
distribution of $214.36 cash

STATUS GAME CORP (DE)
Stock Dividend - 10% 12/10/1986
Charter forfeited for failure to maintain
a registered agent 11/00/1998

STATUS MARKETING CORP (NY)
Dissolved by proclamation 3/25/92

STATUS WINES TUSCANY INC (NV)
Recapitalized as Mariner's Choice
International Inc. (NV) 06/04/2007
Each share Common $0.001 par
exchanged for (0.002) share
Common $0.001 par
Note: No holders will receive fewer
than (500) post-split shares
Mariner's Choice International Inc.
(NV) reorganized in Wyoming
09/02/2014 which name changed to
Han Tang Technology, Inc.
09/28/2015

STAUFFER CHEM CO (DE)
Common $10 par changed to $5 par
and (1) additional share issued
05/08/1959
$1.80 Conv. Preference Ser. A no par
called for redemption 12/26/1975
Common $5 par changed to $2.50 par
and (1) additional share issued
05/27/1976
3.5% Preferred $100 par called for
redemption 10/18/1976
Common $2.50 par changed to $1.25
par and (1) additional share issued
05/25/1979
Merged into Chesebrough-Pond's,
Inc. 03/28/1985
Each share Common $1.25 par
exchanged for $28 cash

STAUFFER COMMUNICATIONS INC (DE)
Merged into Morris Communications
Corp. 6/14/95
Each share Common $1 par
exchanged for $283.43 cash

STAUFFER PUBLICATIONS, INC. (DE)
Preferred $50 par called for
redemption 4/16/73
Name changed to Stauffer
Communications, Inc. 6/1/77

STAV ELECTRICAL SYSTEMS (1994) LTD (ISRAEL)
Issue Information - 800,000 ORD
shares offered at $6 per share on
11/25/1998
Name changed to Marnetics
Broadband Technologies Ltd.
01/01/2001
(See Marnetics Broadband Technologies Ltd.)

STAVELY APARTMENTS LTD. (ON)
Recapitalized as Stavely Realties Ltd.
and each share Common no par
exchanged for (13) shares 5%
Preferred $1 par and (1) share new
Common no par in 1952
(See Stavely Realties Ltd.)

STAVELY REALTIES LTD. (ON)
5% Preferred $1 par called for
redemption 2/28/73
Liquidation completed
Each share Common no par received
initial distribution of $50 cash
1/11/82
Each share Common no par
exchanged for second and final
distribution of $18.20 cash 4/11/83

STAVID ENGINEERING, INC. (NJ)
6% Preferred $100 par called for
redemption 09/21/1959
Acquired by Lockheed Aircraft Corp.
(CA) 10/02/1959
Each share Common no par
exchanged for (2.5) shares Capital
Stock $1 par
Lockheed Aircraft Corp. (CA) name
changed to Lockheed Corp. (CA)
09/30/1997 which reincorporated in
Delaware 06/30/1986 which merged
into Lockheed Martin Corp.
03/15/1995

STAYTON OIL CO.
Liquidation completed in 1949

STB SYS INC (TX)
Issue Information - 2,000,000 shares
COM offered at $12 per share on
02/14/1997
Common 1¢ par split (3) for (2) by
issuance of (0.5) additional share
payable 7/17/97 to holders of record
6/23/97
Common 1¢ par split (3) for (2) by
issuance of (0.5) additional share
payable 2/20/98 to holders of record
2/11/98
Merged into 3dfx Interactive, Inc.
5/13/99
Each share Common 1¢ par
exchanged for (0.65) share Common
no par
(See 3dfx Interactive, Inc.)

STC PLC (ENGLAND)
Acquired by Northern Telecom
Ltd.-Northern Telecom Ltee.
00/00/1991
Details not available

STEADFAST HLDGS GROUP INC (NV)
Each share old Common $0.001 par
exchanged for (0.00025) share new
Common $0.001 par 09/26/2008
Recapitalized as Scorpex, Inc.
05/20/2011
Each share new Common $0.001 par
exchanged for (0.001) share
Common $0.001 par

STEADFAST VENTURES INC (BC)
Delisted from Canadian Dealer
Network 05/31/2000

STEADMAN AMERN IND FD (DC)
Stock Distributions - 100% 11/8/67;
100% 9/11/70
Name changed to Ameritor Industry
Fund 9/23/98
(See Ameritor Industry Fund)

STEADMAN ASSD FD (DC)
Reincorporated 12/27/1974
Place of incorporation changed from
(MO) to (DC) 12/27/1974
Name changed Ameritor Security
Trust 09/23/1998
(See Ameritor Security Trust)

STEADMAN FIDUCIARY INVT FD INC (DE)
Stock Dividend - 100% 11/8/67
Merged into Steadman Investment
Fund, Inc. (New) 1/25/73
Each share Common $1 par
exchanged for (4) shares Common
25¢ par
Steadman Investment Fund, Inc.
(New) changed to Ameritor
Investment Fund 9/23/98

STEADMAN INDS LTD (ON)
Name changed to Interpool
International Ltd. 06/08/1971
Interpool International Ltd. liquidated
for Interpool Ltd. 12/08/1971
(See Interpool Ltd.)

STEADMAN INVT FD NEW (DC)
Name changed 11/02/1967
Name changed from Steadman
Fiduciary Investment Fund, Inc. to
Steadman Investment Fund, Inc.
(Old) 11/02/1967
Steadman Fiduciary Investment Fund,
Inc. (Old) merged into Steadman

Investment Fund, Inc. (New) 01/25/1973
Name changed to Ameritor Investment Fund 09/23/1998
(See Ameritor Investment Fund)

STEADMAN OCEANOGRAPHIC TECHNOLOGY & GROWTH FD (DC)
Completely liquidated 6/9/98
Each Share of Bene. Int. $1 par exchanged for first and final distribution of $0.47 cash

STEADMAN SCIENCE & GROWTH FD INC (DE)
Acquired by Steadman American Industry Fund, Inc. 9/14/70
Each share Capital Stock 33-1/3¢ par received (0.87461) share Common $1 par
Note: Shares were automatically credited to holders' account evidencing ownership
Certificates were not surrendered and are now without value
Steadman American Industry Fund, Inc. name changed to Ameritor Industry Fund 9/23/98
(See Ameritor Industry Fund)

STEADMAN'S SHARES IN AMERICAN INDUSTRY, INC. (DE)
Name changed to Steadman American Industry Fund, Inc. 10/19/67
Steadman American Industry Fund, Inc. name changed to Ameritor Industry Fund 9/23/98
(See Ameritor Industry Fund)

STEADYMED LTD (ISRAEL)
Merged into United Therapeutics Corp. 08/30/2018
Each share Ordinary ILS 0.01 par exchanged for (1) Contingent Value Right and $4.46 cash

STEAK & ALE RESTAURANTS AMER INC (DE)
Common 5¢ par split (2) for (1) by issuance of (1) additional share 05/02/1972
Merged into Pillsbury Co. 05/28/1976
Each share Common 5¢ par exchanged for (0.6) share Common no par
(See Pillsbury Co.)

STEAK & BREW INC (DE)
Name changed to Beefsteak Charlie's, Inc. 4/1/76
Beefsteak Charlie's, Inc. name changed to Lifestyle Restaurants, Inc. 4/29/85 which merged into Bombay Palace Restaurants, Inc. 9/14/87
(See Bombay Palace Restaurants, Inc.)

STEAK N SHAKE, INC. NEW (DE)
Common 50¢ par split (2) for (1) by issuance of (1) additional share 03/30/1972
Common 50¢ par changed to no par and (1) additional share issued 04/01/1977
Reincorporated under the laws of Indiana 04/01/1977
Steak n Shake, Inc. (IN) reorganized as Consolidated Products, Inc. 05/15/1984 which name changed to Steak n Shake Co. 02/12/2001 which name changed to Biglari Holdings Inc. 04/08/2010

STEAK N SHAKE, INC. OLD (DE)
Reorganized 00/00/1951
Each share Common 50¢ par exchanged for (1) share Steak n Shake of Illinois, Inc. Common 50¢ par and (1) share Steak n Shake of Missouri, Inc. Common 50¢ par
(See each company's listing)

STEAK N SHAKE CO (IN)
Each share old Common no par exchanged for (0.05) share new Common no par 12/21/2009

Name changed to Biglari Holdings Inc. 04/08/2010

STEAK N SHAKE INC (IN)
Under plan of reorganization each share Common no par automatically became (1) share Consolidated Products, Inc. Common no par 05/15/1984
Consolidated Products, Inc. name changed to Steak n Shake Co. 02/12/2001 which name changed to Biglari Holdings Inc. 04/08/2010

STEAK N SHAKE OF ILLINOIS, INC. (DE)
Merged into Steak n Shake, Inc. (DE) (New) 00/00/1954
Each share Common 50¢ par exchanged for (1) share Common 50¢ par
Steak n Shake, Inc. (DE) (New) reincorporated in Indiana 04/01/1977 which reorganized as Consolidated Products, Inc. 05/15/1984 which name changed to Steak n Shake Co. 02/12/2001 which name changed to Biglari Holdings Inc. 04/08/2010

STEAK N SHAKE OF MISSOURI, INC. (DE)
Merged into Steak n Shake, Inc. (DE) (New) 00/00/1954
Each share Common 50¢ par exchanged for (1.25) shares Common 50¢ par
Steak n Shake, Inc. (DE) (New) reincorporated in Indiana 04/01/1977 which reorganized as Consolidated Products, Inc. 05/15/1984 which name changed to Steak n Shake Co. 02/12/2001 which name changed to Biglari Holdings Inc. 04/08/2010

STEAKHOUSE PARTNERS INC (DE)
Plan of reorganization under Chapter 11 Bankruptcy Code effective 12/31/2003
No old Common stockholders' equity
Chapter 7 bankruptcy proceedings terminated 07/14/2016
New Common stockholders' equity unlikely

STEALTH ENERGY INC (BC)
Recapitalized as Blackstream Energy Corp. 05/04/2012
Each share Common no par exchanged for (0.1) share Common no par
Blackstream Energy Corp. name changed to SunOil Ltd. 10/11/2013

STEALTH INDS INC (NV)
Reincorporated 11/22/2000
Each share old Common $0.001 par exchanged for (0.01) share new Common $0.001 par 10/28/2000
State of incorporation changed from (MN) to (NV) 11/22/2000
Recapitalized as Precious Metals Exchange Corp. 01/23/2009
Each share new Common $0.001 par exchanged for (0.1) share Common $0.001 par
Precious Metals Exchange Corp. name changed to Legends Food Corp. 07/19/2011 which name changed to Republic of Texas Brands, Inc. 11/07/2011 which name changed to Totally Hemp Crazy Inc. 08/05/2014 which name changed to Rocky Mountain High Brands Inc. 10/16/2015

STEALTH MEDIALABS INC (NV)
Each (300) shares old Common $0.001 par exchanged for (1) share new Common $0.001 par 10/27/2009
Reincorporated under the laws of Oklahoma as Crosswind Renewable Energy Corp. 09/24/2010

STEALTH MINERALS LTD (AB)
Reincorporated under the laws of British Columbia 02/25/2005

STEALTH MNG CORP (AB)
Issue Information - 3,500,000 shares COM offered at $0.25 per share on 03/27/1997
Recapitalized as Stealth Minerals Ltd. (AB) 06/01/2001
Each share Common no par exchanged for (2/3) share Common no par
Stealth Minerals Ltd. (AB) reincorporated in British Columbia 02/25/2005

STEALTH RES INC (NV)
Reorganized as US Tungsten Corp. 08/09/2012
Each share Common $0.001 par exchanged for (30) shares Common $0.001 par
US Tungsten Corp. recapitalized as Aziel Corp. 01/23/2018

STEALTH VENTURES INC (BC)
Name changed to Annova International Holdings Corp. 05/12/1994
Annova International Holdings Corp. recapitalized as Annova Business Group Inc. 04/27/1995 which recapitalized as Capital Alliance Group Inc. 11/27/1998 which name changed to CIBT Education Group Inc. 11/14/2007

STEALTH VENTURES LTD (BC)
Reorganized under the laws of Alberta as Stealth Ventures Inc. 08/23/2012
Each share Common no par exchanged for (0.06666666) share Common no par

STEAM CLEANING USA INC (DE)
Recapitalized as Humana Trans Services Holding Corp. 08/11/2003
Each share Common $0.0001 par exchanged for (0.125) share Common $0.0001 par
Humana Trans Services Holding Corp. name changed to Accountabilities, Inc. 12/06/2005 which name changed to Corporate Resource Services, Inc. 04/21/2010

STEAM ENGINE SYS CORP (MA)
Common $1 par split (3) for (1) by issuance of (2) additional shares 04/01/1970
Common $1 par changed to 10¢ par and (1) additional share issued 05/05/1972
Name changed to Scientific Energy Systems Corp. 01/01/1973
Scientific Energy Systems Corp. name changed to PMC/Beta Corp. 06/01/1979
(See PMC/Beta Corp.)

STEAM MOTORS CO. (MA)
Proclaimed dissolved for failure to file reports and pay taxes 3/31/24

STEAMPUNK WIZARDS INC (NV)
Name changed to Tianci International Inc. 01/31/2017

STEARMAN AIRCRAFT CO.
Merged into United Aircraft & Transport Corp. in 1929
Details not available

STEARNS (FREDERICK) & CO.
Acquired by Sterling Drug Inc. on a (1) for (2) basis in 1944
(See Sterling Drug Inc.)

STEARNS & FOSTER CO. (OH)
Merged into Ohio Mattress Co. (Ohio) 12/22/83
Each share Common no par exchanged for (1.5) shares Common $1 par
Ohio Mattress Co. (Ohio) reorganized in Delaware 7/11/84
(See Ohio Mattress Co. (Del.))

STEARNS & LEHMAN INC (OH)
Merged into Kerry Holding Co. 3/6/2002

Each share Common $0.001172 par exchanged for $7.7177 cash

STEARNS (F.B.) CO.
Dissolved in 1929

STEARNS MFG CO (MN)
Merged into SMCA, Inc. 06/06/1985
Each share Common 1¢ par exchanged for $8 cash

STEARNS MFG INC (MI)
Stock Dividend - 25% 02/15/1945
Merged into Conergics Corp. 12/30/1977
Each share Common $1 par exchanged for $1 cash

STEBAR NATL CORP (DE)
Each share Common 1¢ par exchanged for (0.05) share Common 20¢ par 02/05/1974
Reincorporated under the laws of Oklahoma as Tetra International Corp. 03/07/1983
(See Tetra International Corp.)

STEC INC (CA)
Acquired by Western Digital Corp. 09/13/2013
Each share Common $0.001 par exchanged for $6.85 cash

STECHER TRAUNG SCHMIDT CORP (NY)
Name changed 2/4/66
Each share Common no par exchanged for (4) shares Common $10 par in 1937
7-1/2% Preferred $100 par changed to 5% Preferred $100 par in 1939
Stock Dividend - 50% 1/24/61
Name changed from Stecher-Traung Lithograph Corp. to Stecher-Traung-Schmidt Corp. 2/24/66
Common $10 par changed to $5 par and (1) additional share issued 1/16/67
5% Preferred $100 par called for redemption 6/30/83
Common $5 par changed to 50¢ par 7/1/83
Merged into IP-STS Acquisition Corp.
Each share Common 50¢ par exchanged for $16.50 cash

STECK-VAUGHN PUBG CORP (DE)
Merged into Harcourt General, Inc. 1/30/98
Each share Common 1¢ par exchanged for $14.75 cash

STEDMAN BROTHERS, LTD. (ON)
Common no par exchanged (4) for (1) in 1946
Common no par split (3) for (1) by issuance of (2) additional shares 10/24/61
Acquired by Gamble-Skogmo, Inc. by purchase offer in 1964
Each share Common no par exchanged for $20 cash

STEDMAN PRODUCTS CO.
Name changed to Stedman Rubber Flooring Co. in 1930
Stedman Rubber Flooring Co. acquired by Armstrong Cork Co. in 1936
(See Armstrong Cork Co.)

STEDMAN RUBBER FLOORING CO.
Acquired by Armstrong Cork Co. 00/00/1936
Details not available

STEED VENTURES CORP (BC)
Delisted from Vancouver Stock Exchange 07/07/1989

STEEGO CORP (DE)
Acquired by Industrial Equity (Pacific) Ltd. 12/20/1991
Each share Common 10¢ par exchanged for $2.625 cash

STEEL & TUBE HLDGS LTD (NEW ZEALAND)
ADR agreement terminated 03/13/2018
No ADR's remain outstanding

STEEL & TUBES, INC.
Acquired by Republic Iron & Steel Co. 00/00/1928
Details not available

STEEL CITY NATL BK (CHICAGO, IL)
Name and location changed to U.S. Bank (Lansing, IL) 8/22/94

STEEL CITY PRODS INC (DE)
Each share old Common 1¢ par exchanged for (0.00000333) share new Common 1¢ par 03/31/2004
Note: In effect holders received $0.0168 cash per share and public interest was eliminated

STEEL CO CDA LTD (CANADA)
Each share Preference $100 par exchanged for (4) shares 7% Preference $25 par 00/00/1928
Each share Ordinary $100 par exchanged for (4) shares old Ordinary no par 00/00/1928
Each share 7% Preference $25 par exchanged for (5) shares 7% Preference $5 par 00/00/1950
Each share old Ordinary no par exchanged for (5) shares new Ordinary no par 00/00/1950
Recapitalized 07/15/1953
Each share 7% Preference $5 par exchanged for (1.066666) shares Common no par
Each share new Ordinary no par exchanged for (1) share Common no par
Common no par split (4) for (1) by issuance of (3) additional shares 05/15/1962
Common no par reclassified as Conv. Class A Common no par 05/21/1974
Name changed to Stelco Inc. 07/09/1980
(See Stelco Inc.)

STEEL CO WALES LTD (ENGLAND)
Nationalized by the United Kingdom 08/08/1967
Each ADR for Ordinary £1 par exchanged for £1-5s-4.0336d principal amount of 6-1/2% Treasury Stock due 01/28/1971

STEEL CREST HOMES INC (PA)
Each share Common no par exchanged for (0.05) share Common 1¢ par 11/17/1969
Stock Dividend - 10% 11/01/1962
Reincorporated under the laws of Delaware as Residex Corp. 07/03/1970
(See Residex Corp.)

STEEL EXCEL INC (DE)
Old Common $0.001 par split (50) for (1) by issuance of (49) additional shares payable 10/05/2011 to holders of record 10/05/2011
Each share old Common $0.001 par exchanged for (1) share new Common $0.001 par to reflect a (1) for (500) reverse split followed by a (500) for (1) forward split 06/19/2014
Note: Holders of (499) or fewer pre-split shares received $33.90 cash per share
Merged into Steel Partners Holdings L.P. 02/15/2017
Each share new Common $0.001 par exchanged for (0.712) 6% Preferred Unit Ser. A no par

STEEL HEDDLE MFG CO (PA)
Common $100 par changed to no par 00/00/1935
Each share Common no par exchanged for (4) shares Common $1 par 00/00/1948
Acquired by SHMC Acquisition Corp. 12/06/1988
Each share Common $1 par exchanged for $111.3689 cash

STEEL IMPT & FORGE CO (OH)
Common $1 par split (3) for (1) by issuance of (2) additional shares 07/17/1957
Common $1 par split (2) for (1) by issuance of (1) additional share 10/25/1967
Name changed to SIFCO Industries, Inc. 02/01/1969

STEEL MATERIALS CORP.
In process of liquidation in 1948

STEEL MELTING CORP. (IA)
Liquidation completed
Each share Common $1 par exchanged for initial distribution of $10 cash 2/18/75
Each share Common $1 par received second distribution of $1 cash 11/6/75
Each share Common $1 par received third and final distribution of $0.3732971 cash 8/12/76

STEEL PARTNERS LTD (DE)
Each share old Common $0.0001 par exchanged for (0.2) share new Common $0.0001 par 02/26/2004
Each share new Common $0.0001 par exchanged for (0.02) share Common $0.001 par 01/24/2005
Note: In effect holders received $1,000 cash per share and public interest was eliminated

STEEL PARTS CORP. (IN)
Capital Stock $5 par changed to no par and (0.5) additional share issued 4/2/62
Completely liquidated for cash 11/30/64

STEEL PLT EQUIP CORP (PA)
Under plan of merger each share Common no par exchanged for $8.25 cash 11/12/2003

STEEL PRODUCTS ENGINEERING CO. (OH)
Acquired by Kelsey-Hayes Wheel Co. 10/31/55
Each share Common $1 par exchanged for (0.67308) share Common $1 par
Kelsey-Hayes Wheel Co. name changed to Kelsey-Hayes Co. 12/20/56 which merged into Fruehauf Corp. (MI) 10/31/73 which merged into Fruehauf Corp. (DE) 12/23/86 which name changed to K-H Corp. 8/4/89 which merged into Varity Corp. (Canada) 12/1/89 which reorganized in Delaware 8/1/91 which merged into LucasVarity PLC 9/6/96
(See LucasVarity PLC)

STEEL REALTY DEVELOPMENT CORP. (DE)
No longer in existence having become inoperative and void for non-payment of taxes 3/18/25

STEEL TECHNOLOGIES INC (KY)
Common no par split (3) for (2) by issuance of (0.5) additional share 1/9/87
Common no par split (3) for (2) by issuance of (0.5) additional share 3/11/88
Common no par split (3) for (2) by issuance of (0.5) additional share 6/4/93
Merged into Mitsui & Co. Ltd. 6/1/2007
Each share Common no par exchanged for $30 cash

STEEL VAULT CORP (DE)
Merged into PositiveID Corp. 11/10/2009
Each share Common 1¢ par exchanged for (0.5) share Common 1¢ par

STEEL WEST VA INC (DE)
Merged into Roanoke Electric Steel Corp. 12/17/98
Each share Common 1¢ par exchanged for $10.75 cash

STEEL'S DEPARTMENT STORES, INC. (MA)
Proclaimed dissolved for failure to file reports and pay taxes 3/31/26

STEELCLOUD INC (VA)
Name changed 08/14/2001
Name changed from SteelCloud Co. to SteelCloud Inc. 08/14/2001
Assets transferred to creditor and company dissolved 07/16/2014
No stockholders' equity

STEELE RECORDING CORP (NV)
Common $0.001 par split (10) for (1) by issuance of (9) additional shares payable 07/08/2010 to holders of record 07/01/2010 Ex date - 07/09/2010
Name changed to Steele Resources Corp. (NV) 09/01/2010
Steele Resources Corp. (NV) reorganized in Oklahoma as Steele Oceanic Corp. 03/17/2017

STEELE RES CORP (NV)
Each share old Common $0.001 par exchanged for (0.33333333) share new Common $0.001 par 05/02/2011
Reorganized under the laws of Oklahoma as Steele Oceanic Corp. 03/17/2017
Each share new Common $0.001 par exchanged for (0.00025) share Common $0.0001 par

STEELHAWK ENERGY INC (BC)
Name changed 09/01/1990
Name changed from Steelhawk Resources Ltd. to Steelhawk Energy Inc. 09/01/1990
Name changed to Nucell Energy Canada Inc. 11/27/1990
(See Nucell Energy Canada Inc.)

STEELMAN GAS LTD. (SK)
Acquired by Provo Gas Products Ltd. in May 1965
Each share Common $1 par exchanged for (1) share Capital Stock no par
Provo Gas Producers Ltd. acquired by Dome Petroleum Ltd. 6/28/67
(See Dome Petroleum Ltd.)

STEELMET INC (PA)
Stock Dividends - 100% 01/30/1970; 10% 01/29/1976; 10% 01/25/1980; 10% 01/30/1981
Plan of reorganization under Chapter 11 on the Federal Bankruptcy Code confirmed 04/04/1985
Each share Common 50¢ par exchanged for $0.05 cash

STEELOY MINING CORP. LTD. (ON)
Recapitalized as Texore Mines Ltd. on a (0.25) for (1) basis 8/14/64

STEELS CONSOLIDATED, INC.
Business discontinued 00/00/1930
Details not available

STEELTON BANCORP INC (PA)
Stock Dividends - 5% payable 1/15/2001 to holders of record 12/31/2000; 5% payable 12/15/2001 to holders of record 12/1/2001 Ex date - 11/28/2001
Merged into Sun Bancorp, Inc. 4/23/2003
Each share Common 10¢ par exchanged for $22.04 cash

STEELY GROUP INC (AB)
Ceased operations 6/15/2001
No stockholders' equity

STEEP ROCK IRON MINES LTD. (ON)
Common no par changed to $1 par in 1943
Each share 5% Preference Ser. B $100 par exchanged for (33-1/3) shares Common $1 par 4/1/55
Name changed to Steep Rock Resources, Inc. 6/30/83
(See Steep Rock Resources, Inc.)

STEEP ROCK RES INC (ON)
Acquired by MAS Minerals Corp. 09/06/1988
Each share Common $1 par exchanged for $2.55 cash

STEEPLEJACK INDL GROUP INC (AB)
Merged into Brock Holdings III, Inc. 09/26/2007
Each share Common no par exchanged for $11.50 cash

STEERING CTL SYS INC (UT)
Name changed to Indwest, Inc. in 1995
Indwest, Inc. name changed to Medi-Hut Co., Inc. (UT) 1/28/98 which reincorporated in Delaware 2/27/98 which reincorporated in Nevada 10/31/2001 which name changed to Scivanta Medical Corp. 1/4/2007

STEETLEY INDS LTD (ON)
Each share old Common no par exchanged for (5) shares new Common no par 6/7/71
Merged into Steetley of Canada (Holdings) Ltd. 12/31/78
Each share new Common no par exchanged for (1) share Class A Preference $19 par or (1) share Class B Preference 1¢ par
Note: Preference shares were subsequently redeemed for $19 cash

STEETLEY OF CANADA LTD. (CANADA)
100% acquired by Steetley Co. Ltd. in 1956
Public interest eliminated

STEFAN RES INC (BC)
Recapitalized as Tugold Resources Inc. 02/14/1985
Each share Common no par exchanged for (0.33333333) share Ser. A Common no par
Tugold Resources Inc. recapitalized as Gold Power Resources Corp. 12/28/1988 which recapitalized as Triple Force Industries Inc. 12/06/1991 which recapitalized as Petrock Ventures Inc. 01/08/1997 which recapitalized as Croydon Mercantile Corp. 02/31/2002 which name changed to World Mahjong Ltd. 12/01/2015

STEIGER TRACTOR INC (MN)
Merged into Tenneco Inc. 11/10/86
Each share Common $1 par exchanged for $3.50 cash

STEIN (A.) & CO. (IL)
Stock Dividend - 100% 4/29/46
Merged into Apparel Industries, Inc. and each share Common no par exchanged for $34.375 of 5-1/2% Debentures 11/18/60

STEIN BLOCH CO.
Merged into Fashion Park Associates, Inc. in 1929 whose assets were sold at bankruptcy sale in 1933

STEIN COSMETICS CO., INC.
Bankrupt in 1935

STEIN HALL & CO INC (NY)
Common $1 par changed to 66-2/3¢ par and (0.5) additional share issued 05/17/1963
Merged into Celanese Corp. 04/13/1971
Each share Common 66-2/3¢ par exchanged for (0.25) share Common no par
(See Celanese Corp.)

STEIN INDS INC (WI)
Stock Dividend - 100% 4/27/79
Merged into Stein Holdings Inc. 7/23/99
Each share Common 10¢ par exchanged for $16.15 cash

STEIN ROE & FARNHAM BALANCED FD INC (MD)
Capital Stock $1 par split (2) for (1) by issuance of (1) additional share 3/11/66
Name changed to SteinRoe Total Return Fund, Inc. 12/15/83
SteinRoe Total Return Fund, Inc. merged into SteinRoe Equity Trust 12/31/87 which name changed to SteinRoe Investment Trust 6/30/89

STEIN ROE & FARNHAM CAP OPPORTUNITIES FD INC (MD)
Capital Stock 34¢ par changed to $1 par and (0.5) additional share issued 3/31/70
Under plan of merger each share Capital Stock $1 par automatically became (1) SteinRoe Equity Trust Capital Opportunities Fund Share of Bene. Int. $1 par 12/31/87
SteinRoe Equity Trust name changed to SteinRoe Investment Trust 6/30/89

STEIN ROE & FARNHAM FUND, INC. (MD)
Capital Stock $25 par changed to $1 par and (2) additional shares issued in 1952
Name changed to Stein Roe & Farnham Balanced Fund, Inc. 2/18/59
Stein Roe & Farnham Balanced Fund, Inc. name changed to SteinRoe Total Return Fund, Inc. 12/15/83 which merged into SteinRoe Equity Trust 12/31/87 which name changed to SteinRoe Investment Trust 6/30/89

STEIN ROE & FARNHAM INTL FD INC (MD)
Name changed to Stein Roe & Farnham Capital Opportunities Fund, Inc. 3/24/69
Stein Roe & Farnham Capital Opportunities Fund, Inc. merged into SteinRoe Equity Trust 12/31/87 which name changed to SteinRoe Investment Trust 6/30/89

STEIN ROE & FARNHAM STK FD INC (MD)
Capital Stock $1 par split (3) for (1) by issuance of (2) additional shares 3/11/66
Under plan of merger each share Common $1 par automatically became (1) SteinRoe Equity Trust Stock Fund Share of Bene. Int. $1 par 12/31/87
SteinRoe Equity Trust name changed to SteinRoe Investment Trust 6/30/89

STEINBERG DRUG STORES, INC.
Acquired by Crown Drug Stores, Inc. 00/00/1930
Details not available

STEINBERG INC (QC)
Class A no par split (2) for (1) by issuance of (1) additional share 7/10/85
Common no par split (2) for (1) by issuance of (1) additional share 7/10/85
U.S. $2.875 Retractable 2nd Preference Ser. B no par called for redemption 12/31/87
$2.72 Conv. 3rd Preferred Ser. I no par called for redemption 5/24/88
Acquired by Corporation d'Acquisition Socanav-Caisse Inc. 10/11/89
Each share Class A no par exchanged for $51 cash
Variable Rate 2nd Preference Ser. 2 no par called for redemption 11/21/90
5-1/4% Preferred Ser. A $100 par called for redemption 11/30/90
$1.95 2nd Preferred Ser. 1 $25 par called for redemption 11/30/90
$2.9375 Retractable 2nd Preference Ser. A no par called for redemption 11/30/90
Public interest eliminated

STEINBERGS LTD (QC)
Class A $1 par changed to no par and (1) additional share issued 02/01/1966
Name changed to Steinberg Inc. 09/15/1978
(See Steinberg Inc.)

STEINBRECHER CORP (DE)
Acquired by Tellabs, Inc. 04/17/1996
Each share Common 1¢ par exchanged for $4.46 cash

STEINER LEISURE LTD (BAHAMAS)
Common 1¢ par split (3) for (2) by issuance of (0.5) additional share payable 10/24/1997 to holders of record 10/13/1997
Common 1¢ par split (3) for (2) by issuance of (0.5) additional share payable 04/28/1998 to holders of record 04/14/1998
Acquired by Nemo Parent, Inc. 12/09/2015
Each share Common 1¢ par exchanged for $65 cash

STEINER OPTICS INTL INC (DE)
Each share old Common $0.00001 par exchanged for (0.001) share new Common $0.00001 par 06/30/2000
Note: In effect holders received $10 cash per share and public interest was eliminated

STEINHOFF INTL HLDGS LTD (SOUTH AFRICA)
ADR agreement terminated 02/26/2016
Each ADR for Ordinary issued by Bank of New York exchanged for $26.035479 cash
Note: Additional exchange rates vary upon issuing depositary

STEINMETZ ELECTRIC MOTOR CAR CORP.
Out of business in 1927

STEINROE BD FD INC (MD)
Name changed to SteinRoe Managed Bonds, Inc. 12/31/85
Steinroe Managed Bonds, Inc. merged into Steinroe Income Trust 12/31/87

STEINROE CASH RESVS INC (MD)
Under plan of merger each share Common 10¢ par automatically became (1) SteinRoe Income Trust Cash Reserves Share of Bene. Int. 10¢ par 12/31/87

STEINROE DISCOVERY FD INC (MD)
Under plan of merger each share Common 1¢ par automatically became (1) SteinRoe Equity Trust Discovery Fund Share of Bene. Int. 1¢ par 12/31/87
SteinRoe Equity Trust name changed to SteinRoe Investment Trust 6/30/89

STEINROE EQUITY PORTFOLIO (MA)
Under plan of merger each Prime Equities Share of Bene. Int. no par automatically became (1) SteinRoe Equity Trust Prime Equities Share of Bene. Int. no par 12/31/87
SteinRoe Equity Trust name changed to SteinRoe Investment Trust 6/30/89

STEINROE GOVT RESVS INC (MD)
Under plan of merger each share Common 1¢ par automatically became (1) SteinRoe Income Trust Government Reserves Share of Bene. Int. 1¢ par 12/31/87

STEINROE GOVTS PLUS (MA)
Under plan of merger each Share of Bene. Int. no par automatically became (1) SteinRoe Income Trust Government Income Fund no par 12/31/87

STEINROE HIGH-YIELD BONDS (MA)
Under plan of merger each share of Bene. Int. no par automatically became (1) SteinRoe Income Trust High-Yield Bonds Share of Bene. Int. no par 12/31/87
SteinRoe Income Trust High-Yield Bonds reclassified as SteinRoe Income Trust Income Fund Shares 11/1/89

STEINROE HIGH YIELD MUNS INC (MD)
Under plan of merger each share Common 1¢ par automatically became (1) SteinRoe Tax-Exempt Income Trust High-Yield Municipals Share of Bene. Int. 1¢ par 12/31/87
SteinRoe Tax-Exempt Income Trust name changed to SteinRoe Municipal Trust 8/1/91

STEINROE INCOME TR (MA)
High-Yield Bonds Shares of Bene. Int. no par reclassified as Income Fund Shares of Bene. Int. no par 11/1/89
Governments Plus Shares of Bene. Int. no par reclassified as Government Income Fund Shares of Bene. Int. no par 4/2/90
Managed Bonds Shares of Bene. Int. $1 par reclassified as Intermediate Bond Fund Shares of Bene. Int. $1 par 4/2/90
(Additional Information in Active)

STEINROE INTER MUNS INC (MD)
Under plan of merger each share Common 1¢ par automatically became (1) SteinRoe Tax-Exempt Income Trust Intermediate Municipals Share of Bene. Int. 1¢ par 12/31/87
SteinRoe Tax-Exempt Income Trust name changed to SteinRoe Municipal Trust 8/1/91

STEINROE INVT TR (MA)
Name changed 6/30/89
Each (2.596) Discovery Fund Shares of Bene. Int. $1 par exchanged for (1) Capital Opportunities Fund Share of Bene. Int. $1 par 6/30/89
Each (1.726) Universe Fund Shares of Bene. Int. $1 par exchanged for (1) Capital Opportunities Fund Share of Bene. Int. $1 par 6/30/89
Name changed from Steinroe Equity Trust to Steinroe Investment Trust 6/30/89
Growth & Income Fund reorganized as Prime Equities Fund 6/29/90
Each (1.066) Shares of Bene. Int $1 par exchanged for (1) share of Bene. Int. $1 par
(Additional Information in Active)

STEINROE MANAGED BDS INC (MD)
Under plan of merger each share Capital Stock $1 par automatically became (1) SteinRoe Income Trust Managed Bonds Share of Bene. Int. $1 par 12/31/87

STEINROE MANAGED MUNS INC (MD)
Under plan of merger each share Common $1 par automatically became (1) SteinRoe Tax-Exempt Income Trust Managed Municipals Share of Bene. Int. $1 par 12/31/87
SteinRoe Tax-Exempt Income Trust name changed to SteinRoe Municipal Trust 8/1/91

STEINROE RADIO CO. (DE)
Charter cancelled and declared inoperative and void for non-payment of taxes 4/1/34

STEINROE SPL FD INC (MD)
Common $1 par changed to 10¢ par 9/17/79
Under plan of merger each share Common 10¢ par automatically became (1) SteinRoe Equity Trust Special Fund Share of Bene. Int. 10¢ par 12/31/87
SteinRoe Equity Trust name changed to SteinRoe Investment Trust 6/30/89

STEINROE TAX EXEMPT BD FD INC (MD)
Name changed to SteinRoe Managed Municipals, Inc. 7/31/86
SteinRoe Managed Municipals, Inc. merged into SteinRoe Tax-Exempt Income Trust 12/31/87 which name changed to SteinRoe Municipal Trust 8/1/91

STEINROE TAX EXEMPT INCOME TR (MA)
Name changed to SteinRoe Municipal Trust 8/1/91

STEINROE TAX EXEMPT MONEY FD INC (MD)
Under plan of merger each share Common 1¢ par automatically became (1) SteinRoe Tax-Exempt Income Trust Tax-Exempt Money Fund Share of Bene. Int. 1¢ par 12/31/87
SteinRoe Tax-Exempt Income Trust name changed to SteinRoe Municipal Trust 8/1/91

STEINROE TOTAL RETURN FD INC (MD)
Under plan of merger each share Common $1 par automatically became (1) SteinRoe Equity Trust Total Return Fund Share of Bene. Int. $1 par 12/31/87
SteinRoe Equity Trust name changed to SteinRoe Investment Trust 6/30/89

STEINROE UNIVERSE FD INC (MD)
Capital Stock $1 par split (4) for (1) by issuance of (3) additional shares 6/17/83
Under plan of merger each Capital Stock $1 par automatically became (1) Steinroe Investment Trust Capital Opportunities Share of Bene. Int. $1 par 12/31/87

STEINS HLDGS INC (NV)
Name changed to Crown Partners Inc. 01/22/2002
Crown Partners Inc. recapitalized as TaxMasters, Inc. 08/12/2009
(See TaxMasters, Inc.)

STEINTRON INTL ELECTRS LTD (BC)
Acquired by Omnitron Investments Ltd. 10/03/1979
Each share Common no par exchanged for $8 cash

STEINWAY & SONS (NY)
Common $100 par changed to no par in 1941
Acquired by Columbia Broadcasting System, Inc. 4/27/72
Each share Common no par exchanged for (7.1159) shares Common $2.50 par
Columbia Broadcasting System, Inc. name changed to CBS Inc. 4/18/74
(See CBS Inc.)

STEINWAY MUSICAL INSTRS INC (DE)
Acquired by Pianissimo Holdings Corp. 09/19/2013
Each share Ordinary Common $0.001 par exchanged for $40 cash

STEKOLL PETROLEUM CORP. (DE)
Name changed to Sunac Petroleum Corp. 06/11/1962
(See Sunac Petroleum Corp.)

STELBER CYCLE CORP (NY)
Name changed to Stelber Industries, Inc. 9/27/68
Stelber Industries, Inc. adjudicated bankrupt 6/24/77

STELBER INDS INC (NY)
Stock Dividend - 100% 04/10/1969
Adjudicated bankrupt 06/24/1977

STELCANUS IRON ORE LTD.
Name changed to Femco Mines Ltd. 00/00/1950
(See Femco Mines Ltd.)

STELCO INC (CANADA)
$3.625 Preferred Ser. E no par called for redemption 08/01/1988
$2.50 Preferred Ser. D no par called for redemption 11/01/1988
Total holdings of $1.94 Conv. Preferred Ser. C $25 par exchanged for (i) $1.94 Redeemable Preferred Ser. C $25 par and (ii) $1.94 Non-Redeemable Preferred Ser. C $25 par at a rate determined by lot 03/09/1998
$1.94 Preferred Ser. B $25 par called for redemption 05/01/1998
$1.94 Preferred Ser. C $25 par called for redemption 05/01/1998
$1.94 Non-Redeemable Preferred Ser. C $25 par called for redemption 11/01/1999
Plan of Arrangement under Companies' Creditors Arrangement Act effective 03/31/2006
No stockholders' equity
Acquired by U.S. Steel Corp. 10/31/2007
Each share Common no par exchanged for $38.50 cash

STELLA BELLA CORP U S A (NV)
Each share old Common 1¢ par exchanged for (0.005) share new Common 1¢ par 04/16/1997
Name changed to International Brands Inc. 10/10/1997
(See International Brands Inc.)

STELLA BLU INC (NV)
Reorganized as Xalles Holdings Inc. 08/24/2015
Each share Common $0.0001 par exchanged for (3) shares Common $0.0001 par

STELLAKO MNG LTD (BC)
Recapitalized as Arizako Mines Ltd. 07/02/1976
Each share Capital Stock no par exchanged for (0.2) share Common no par
Arizako Mines Ltd. merged into Goldrich Resources Inc. 10/22/1984
(See Goldrich Resources Inc.)

STELLAR BUSINESS BK (COVINA, CA)
Merged into AltaPacific Bancorp 02/17/2012
Each share Common no par exchanged for (0.8443) share Common no par

STELLAR COMMUNICATIONS INC (NV)
Name changed to Medical Home Supplies Inc. 12/29/1989
Medical Home Supplies, Inc. name changed to ADS Systems, Inc. 05/10/2004 which recapitalized as Remington Ventures, Inc. 11/18/2004
(See Remington Ventures, Inc.)

STELLAR INDS INC (DE)
Reincorporated 01/06/1970
State of incorporation changed from (CO) to (DE) and Common no par changed to 10¢ par 01/06/1970
Common 10¢ par changed to 1¢ par 10/26/1977
Completely liquidated 06/30/1980
Each share Common 1¢ par received first and final distribution of $0.0189 cash
Note: Certificates were not required to be surrendered are without value

STELLAR INTL INC (ON)
Name changed to Stellar Pharmaceuticals Inc. 01/01/2005
Stellar Pharmaceuticals Inc. name changed to Tribute Pharmaceuticals Canada Inc. 01/02/2013 which merged into Aralez Pharmaceuticals Inc. 02/09/2016

STELLAR METALS INC (BC)
Name changed 09/23/1996
Name changed from Stellar Gold Corp. to Stellar Metals Inc. 09/23/1996
Recapitalized as Geostar Metals Inc. 10/07/1999
Each share Common no par exchanged for (1/9) share Common no par
Geostar Metals Inc. name changed to Skana Capital Corp. (BC) 11/27/2006 which reincorporated in Alberta as MENA Hydrocarbons Inc. 06/22/2011

STELLAR PAC VENTURES INC (CANADA)
Reincorporated 04/24/2006
Place of incorporation changed from (BC) to (Canada) 04/24/2006
Each share old Common no par received distribution of (0.04) share Stelmine Canada Ltd. Common no par payable 02/04/2008 to holders of record 01/30/2008 Ex date - 01/28/2008
Each share old Common no par exchanged for (0.4) share new Common no par 10/20/2009
Each share new Common no par received distribution of (0.1268) share TomaGold Corp. Common no par payable 05/04/2012 to holders of record 04/30/2012 Ex date - 04/26/2012
Recapitalized as Stellar AfricaGold Inc. 04/01/2013
Each share new Common no par exchanged for (0.1) share Common no par

STELLAR PHARMACEUTICALS INC (ON)
Name changed to Tribute Pharmaceuticals Canada Inc. 01/02/2013
Tribute Pharmaceuticals Canada Inc. merged into Aralez Pharmaceuticals Inc. 02/09/2016

STELLAR RESOURCE CORP (BC)
Recapitalized as Maesa Petroleum Inc. 12/15/89
Each share Common no par exchanged for (0.125) share Common no par
Maesa Petroleum Inc. name changed to Maesa Gaming Management Inc. (BC) 5/4/94 which reincorporated in Delaware 7/30/96 which recapitalized as Mako Capital Inc. 7/15/98 which name changed to O Media, Inc. 4/7/99 which name changed to Original Media, Inc. 1/4/2000 which recapitalized as OMDA Oil & Gas Inc. 6/7/2002

STELLAR TECHNOLOGIES INC (CO)
Reincorporated under the laws of Delaware as GeM Solutions, Inc. 10/24/2006
(See GeM Solutions, Inc.)

STELLARONE CORP (VA)
Merged into Union First Market Bankshares Corp. 01/02/2014
Each share Common $1 par exchanged for (0.9739) share Common $1.33 par
Union First Market Bankshares Corp. name changed to Union Bankshares Corp. 04/28/2014

STELLARTON ENERGY CORP (AB)
Acquired by Tom Brown Resources Ltd. 1/15/2001
Each share Class A Common no par exchanged for $5 cash

STELLENT INC (MN)
Merged into Oracle Corp. 12/14/2006
Each share Common 1¢ par exchanged for $13.50 cash

STELLEX INDS INC (NY)
Dissolved by proclamation 12/29/82

STELMA INC (DE)
Stock Dividend - 100% 11/18/1960
Merged into Data Products Corp. 05/08/1969
Each share Common 10¢ par exchanged for (2.25) shares Common 10¢ par
Data Products Corp. name changed to Dataproducts Corp. 08/23/1974
(See Dataproducts Corp.)

STELMAR SHIPPING LTD (LIBERIA)
Merged into Overseas Shipholding Group, Inc. 01/20/2005
Each share Common 2¢ par exchanged for $48 cash

STELWAY FOOD SVCS INC (BC)
Struck off register and declared dissolved for failure to file returns 7/9/93

STEM CELL ASSURN INC (NV)
Name changed to BioRestorative Therapies, Inc. (NV) 09/16/2011
BioRestorative Therapies, Inc. (NV) reincorporated in Delaware 01/01/2015

STEM CELL INNOVATIONS INC (DE)
SEC revoked common stock registration 01/26/2012

STEM CELL THERAPEUTICS CORP (ON)
Reincorporated 11/07/2013
Each share old Common no par exchanged for (0.1) share new Common no par 02/06/2013
Place of incorporation changed from (AB) to (ON) 11/07/2013
Name changed to Trillium Therapeutics Inc. 06/06/2014

STEM CELL THERAPY INTL INC (NV)
Name changed 10/18/2005
Name changed from Stem Cell International, Inc. to Stem Cell Therapy International, Inc. 10/18/2005
Name changed to AmStem Corp. 02/23/2010
(See AmStem Corp.)

STEM CELL VENTURES INC (NV)
Recapitalized as Pipejoin Technologies, Inc. 09/11/2007
Each (60) shares Common $0.001 par exchanged for (1) share Common $0.001 par

STEM DEV CORP (DE)
Charter cancelled and declared inoperative and void for non-payment of taxes 3/1/77

STEM INDS INC (DE)
Charter cancelled and declared inoperative and void for non-payment of taxes 3/1/88

STEM 7 CAP INC (BC)
Each share old Common no par exchanged for (0.1) share new Common no par 01/12/2015
Name changed to South Star Mining Corp. 12/22/2017

STEMCELL GLOBAL RESH INC (NV)
Charter permanently revoked 01/31/2005

STEMCELLS INC (DE)
Each share old Common 1¢ par exchanged for (0.1) share new Common 1¢ par 07/06/2011
Each share new Common 1¢ par exchanged again for (0.08333333) share new Common 1¢ par 05/09/2016
Recapitalized as Microbot Medical, Inc. 11/29/2016
Each share new Common 1¢ par exchanged for (0.11111111) share Common 1¢ par

STEMEN LABORATORIES, INC. (OK)
Merged into IHC Inc. 8/26/68
Each share Common 10¢ par exchanged for (0.112) share Common $1 par and $0.07 cash
IHC Inc. name changed to Portage Industries Corp. 7/23/73 which name changed to Sweitzer Holdings, Inc. 3/18/76
(See Sweitzer Holdings, Inc.)

STENDIG INDS INC (DE)
Name changed to Cantel Industries, Inc. 4/17/89
Cantel Industries, Inc. name changed to Cantel Medical Corp. 4/7/2000

STEP OUT INC (NV)
Name changed to IDS Solar Technologies, Inc. 10/12/2012
IDS Solar Technologies, Inc. name changed to IDS Industries, Inc. 06/10/2013 which name changed to Aja Cannafacturing, Inc. 08/11/2014

STEP SAVER DATA SYS INC (PA)
Chapter 11 bankruptcy proceedings converted to Liquidating Chapter 11 on 02/27/1990
Stockholders equity unlikely

STEP 2 SOFTWARE CORP (BC)
Recapitalized as Emergo Software Corp. 11/01/1999
Each share Common no par exchanged for (0.2) share Common no par
Emergo Software Corp. name changed to eTVtech.com Communications Inc. 03/21/2000 which name changed to eTV Technology Inc. 05/02/2001 which recapitalized as Ocean Park Ventures Corp. 04/02/2009 which recapitalized as Dunnedin Ventures Inc. 08/06/2013

STEPAN CO (DE)
Reincorporated 03/31/1959
Name changed 01/01/1984
State of incorporation changed from (IL) to (DE) 03/31/1959
Common $1 par split (2) for (1) by issuance of (1) additional share 09/29/1972
Common $1 par split (2) for (1) by issuance of (1) additional share 12/31/1981
Name changed from Stepan Chemical Co. to Stepan Co. 01/01/1984
5.50% Conv. Preferred no par split (8) for (1) by issuance of (7) additional shares 05/10/1993
5.50% Conv. Preferred no par called for redemption at $25 plus $0.267361 accrued dividends on 08/09/2013

STEPAN FERMENTATION CHEMICALS, INC. (DE)
5-1/2% Conv. Preferred $33.33 par called for redemption 11/25/66
Public interest eliminated

STEPHEN F. WHITMAN & SON, INC.
See - Whitman (Stephen F.) & Son, Inc.

STEPHEN REALTY INVESTMENT CO. (CO)
Completely liquidated 5/23/66
Each share of Bene. Int. $1 par exchanged for first and final distribution of $5.51 cash

STEPHENS WIN COMPANIES INC (MN)
Name changed 10/9/80
Name changed from Stephens (Win) Leasing Co. to Stephens (Win) Companies, Inc. 10/9/80
Each share Common $1 par exchanged for initial distribution of $4 cash 1/20/83
Each share Common $1 par received second distribution of $1 cash 4/12/83
Each share Common $1 par received third distribution of $0.50 cash 6/30/86
Each share Common $1 par received

fourth and final distribution of $0.15 cash 3/10/88

STEPHENS JOHN & CO INC (MN)
Name changed to Chi-Chi's, Inc. and Common 2¢ par changed to 1¢ par 10/08/1979
(See Chi-Chi's, Inc.)

STEPHENSON COUNTY ABSTRACT CO. (IL)
Merged into Wilkinson (H.B.) Title Co. of Stephenson County 05/31/2005
Details not available

STEPHENSON FIN INC (SC)
Recapitalized 00/00/1952
Each share 6-1/2% Preferred $25 par exchanged for $25 principal amount of Debentures
Each share Common $10 par exchanged for (4) shares Common $2.50 par
Common $2.50 par changed to $2 par and (0.25) additional share issued 01/15/1964
5.50% Preferred $25 par called for redemption 03/01/1970
6% Preferred $25 par called for redemption 03/01/1970
Completely liquidated 03/01/1970
Each share Common $2 par exchanged for first and final distribution of $45 cash

STEPHENSON NATL BANCORP INC (WI)
Under plan of merger each share Common $1 par received $112 cash 12/22/2006

STEPHENSON NATL BK & TR (MARINETTE, WI)
Stock Dividend - 50% 05/15/1980
Under plan of reorganization each share Capital Stock $5 par automatically became (1) share Stephenson National Bancorp, Inc. Common $1 par 08/15/1984
(See Stephenson National Bancorp, Inc.)

STEPHENSON NATIONAL BANK (MARINETTE, WI)
Stock Dividend - 50% 01/30/1976
Name changed to Stephenson National Bank & Trust (Marinette, WI) 01/27/1978
Stephenson National Bank & Trust (Marinette, WI) reorganized as Stephenson National Bancorp, Inc. 08/15/1984
(See Stephenson National Bancorp, Inc.)

STEPHENSONS RENT SVCS INCOME FD (ON)
Acquired by Edgestone Capital Equity Fund III (Canada), LP 07/19/2007
Each Trust Unit Class A no par received $6.875 cash
Each Trust Unit Class B no par received $6.875 cash

STEPPE GOLD RES LTD (YUKON)
Name changed 6/7/96
Reincorporated 8/12/96
Name changed from Steppe Gold International Inc. to Steppe Gold Resources Ltd. 6/7/96
Place of incorporation changed from (Canada) to (Yukon) 8/12/96
Assets foreclosed upon 5/20/99
No stockholders' equity

STEPSTONE ENTERPRISES LTD NEW (BC)
Name changed to ACT360 Solutions Ltd. 09/03/2004
ACT360 Solutions Ltd. recapitalized as Kona Bay Technologies Inc. 06/03/2016

STEPSTONE ENTERPRISES LTD OLD (BC)
Under plan of merger name changed to Stepstone Enterprises Ltd. (New) 06/30/2003
Stepstone Enterprises Ltd. (New) name changed to ACT360 Solutions Ltd. 09/03/2004 which recapitalized as Kona Bay Technologies Inc. 06/03/2016

STERCHI BROS STORES INC (DE)
Each share Preferred $100 par exchanged for (1) share 6% 1st Preferred $50 par, (1) share 5% 2nd Preferred $20 par and (4) shares Common no par in 1936
Common no par changed to $1 par in 1941
5% 2nd Preferred $20 par called for redemption 1/15/46
6% 1st Preferred $50 par called for redemption 1/15/46
Common $1 par split (2) for (1) by issuance of (1) additional share 1/6/69
Stock Dividends - 100% 8/23/46; 10% 9/14/73
Merged into Heilig-Meyers Co. 2/13/86
Each share Common $1 par exchanged for $33 cash

STEREO VLG INC (GA)
Common 1¢ par split (3) for (2) by issuance of (0.5) additional share 5/30/85
Plan of reorganization under Chapter 11 confirmed 3/24/88
No stockholders' equity

STEREOSCAPE COM INC (NV)
Each share old Common $0.001 par exchanged for (0.06666666) share new Common $0.001 par 10/15/2002
Name changed to Marx Toys & Entertainment Corp. 03/21/2003
Marx Toys & Entertainment Corp. recapitalized as Toyshare, Inc. 07/03/2007 which name changed to Capital Financial Global, Inc. 05/27/2011

STERI-CORP. OF AMERICA (FL)
Charter revoked for failure to file reports and pay fees 6/30/67

STERICYCLE INC (DE)
Each share 5.25% Depositary Preferred Ser. A automatically became (0.73394) share Common 1¢ par 09/14/2018
(Additional Information in Active)

STERIGENICS INTL INC (DE)
Issue Information - 2,000,000 shares COM offered at $12 per share on 08/13/1997
Merged into Ion Beam Applications S.A. 7/20/99
Each share Common $0.001 par exchanged for $27 cash

STERILE CONCEPTS HLDGS INC (VA)
Issue Information - 5,437,000 shares COM offered at $17 per share on 09/27/1994
Merged into Maxxim Medical, Inc. 9/18/96
Each share Common no par exchanged for $20 cash

STERILE RECOVERIES INC (FL)
Name changed to SRI/Surgical Express, Inc. 01/16/2001
(See SRI/Surgical Express, Inc.)

STERILON CORP. (NY)
Acquired by Gillette Co. on a (2/3) for (1) basis 9/28/62
Gillette Co. merged into Procter & Gamble 10/1/2005

STERILSEAT CORP. OF AMERICA (DE)
Common 10¢ par changed to 15¢ par in 1948
Recapitalized in 1951
Each share Preferred no par exchanged for (7) shares new Common no par
Each share Common 15¢ par exchanged for (0.01) share new Common no par
No longer in existence having become inoperative and void for non-payment of taxes 4/1/53

STERION INC (MN)
Name changed to STEN Corp. 1/31/2005

STERIS CORP (OH)
Common no par split (2) for (1) by issuance of (1) additional share 08/24/1995
Common no par split (2) for (1) by issuance of (1) additional share payable 08/24/1998 to holders of record 08/10/1998
Merged into STERIS PLC 11/03/2015
Each share Common no par exchanged for for (1) share Ordinary £0.10 par

STERISYSTEMS LTD (CANADA)
Common no par split (3) for (1) by issuance of (2) additional shares 12/7/72
Merged into Sterivest Holdings, Inc. 12/25/81
Each share Common no par exchanged for $5.25 cash

STERITEK INC (NJ)
Merged into Steritel Acquisition 5/14/99
Each share Common no par exchanged for $1.39 cash

STERIVET LABS LTD (ON)
Common no par split (3) for (1) by issuance of (2) additional shares 05/28/1987
Reorganized as Hyal Pharmaceutical Corp. (ON) 05/09/1990
Each share Common no par exchanged for (1) share Common no par
Hyal Pharmaceutical Corp. (ON) reorganized in Yukon as Cade Struktur Corp. 07/27/2001 which was acquired by KHD Humboldt Wedag International Ltd. 10/23/2006 which reorganized as Terra Nova Royalty Corp. 03/30/2010 which name changed to MFC Industrial Ltd. 09/30/2011 which name changed to MFC Bancorp Ltd. (BC) 02/16/2016
(See MFC Bancorp Ltd. (BC))

STERLING, INC. (NY)
Stock Dividend - 10% 12/30/52
Name changed to Weiman Co., Inc. (N.Y.) 4/25/57
Weiman Co., Inc. (N.Y.) reincorporated in Delaware 4/30/69
(See Weiman Co., Inc. (Del.))

STERLING & WELCH CO.
Acquired by Allied Stores Corp. and each share held was exchanged for (13) shares new 4% Preferred $100 par in 1949
(See Allied Stores Corp.)

STERLING ALUMINUM PRODUCTS, INC. (MO)
Each share Capital Stock no par exchanged for (100) shares Capital Stock $1 par 00/00/1936
Capital Stock $1 par changed to $5 par 00/00/1950
Stock Dividends - 50% 12/30/1948; 25% 01/16/1956
Merged into Federal-Mogul Corp. (MI) on a (1) for (2.25) basis 04/30/1965
(See Federal-Mogul Corp. (MI))

STERLING BANCORP (NY)
Preferred Stock Purchase Rights declared for Common stockholders of record 03/03/1989 were redeemed at $0.01 per right 06/30/1998 for holders of record 06/15/1998
Conv. Preferred Ser. B $5 par called for redemption at $28 plus $0.05 accrued dividends on 06/29/2001
Common $1 par split (5) for (4) by issuance of (0.25) additional share payable 09/10/2003 to holders of record 09/01/2003 Ex date - 09/11/2003
Common $1 par split (6) for (5) by issuance of (0.2) additional share payable 12/08/2004 to holders of record 11/29/2004 Ex date - 12/09/2004
Stock Dividends - 5% payable 12/14/1999 to holders of record 12/14/1999; 10% payable 12/11/2000 to holders of record 12/01/2000; 10% payable 12/10/2001 to holders of record 11/30/2001; 20% payable 12/09/2002 to holders of record 12/02/2002; 5% payable 12/12/2005 to holders of record 11/30/2005 Ex date - 11/28/2005
Merged into Sterling Bancorp (DE) 11/01/2013
Each share Common $1 par exchanged for (1.2625) shares Common 1¢ par

STERLING BANCORP TR I (DE)
8.375% Trust Preferred Securities called for redemption at $10 plus $0.14 accrued dividends on 06/01/2014

STERLING BANCORPORATION (CA)
Stock Dividends - 10% 7/10/87; 10% 8/9/88
Name changed to Sterling West Bancorp 5/27/92
Sterling West Bancorp merged into Pacific Bank, N.A. (San Francisco, CA) 7/3/98

STERLING BANCSHARES CAP TR I (DE)
9.50% Trust Preferred Securities called for redemption at $25 on 11/01/2002

STERLING BANCSHARES CAP TR II (DE)
9.2% Trust Preferred Securities called for redemption at $25 on 05/08/2006

STERLING BANCSHARES CAP TR III (DE)
8.30% Trust Preferred Securities called for redemption at $25 on 10/27/2011

STERLING BANCSHARES CORP (DE)
Merged into Fleet Financial Group, Inc. (New) 8/15/94
Each share Common 10¢ par exchanged for (1.096) shares Common $1 par
Fleet Financial Group, Inc. (New) name changed to Fleet Boston Corp. 10/1/99 which name changed to FleetBoston Financial Corp. 4/18/2000 which merged into Bank of America Corp. 4/1/2004

STERLING BANCSHARES INC (TX)
Common $1 par split (3) for (2) by issuance of (0.5) additional share 02/10/1995
Common $1 par split (3) for (2) by issuance of (0.5) additional share payable 02/14/1996 to holders of record 02/02/1996
Common $1 par split (3) for (2) by issuance of (0.5) additional share payable 02/24/1997 to holders of record 02/10/1997
Common $1 par split (3) for (2) by issuance of (0.5) additional share payable 02/20/1998 to holders of record 02/06/1998
Common $1 par split (3) for (2) by issuance of (0.5) additional share payable 09/18/2001 to holders of record 09/04/2001 Ex date - 09/19/2001
Common $1 par split (3) for (2) by issuance of (0.5) additional share payable 12/15/2006 to holders of record 12/01/2006 Ex date - 12/18/2006
Merged into Comerica, Inc. 07/28/2011

Each share Common $1 par exchanged for (0.2365) share Common $5 par

STERLING BK (MOUNT LAUREL, NJ)
Stock Dividends - 5% payable 08/31/1998 to holders of record 07/31/1998; 5% payable 07/31/1999 to holders of record 06/30/1999; 5% payable 09/30/2000 to holders of record 07/31/2000; 5% payable 08/22/2001 to holders of record 06/30/2001 Ex date - 08/16/2001; 5% payable 07/31/2002 to holders of record 06/30/2002 Ex date - 07/29/2002; 5% payable 07/31/2004 to holders of record 06/30/2004; 5% payable 08/12/2005 to holders of record 07/29/2005 Ex date - 07/27/2005; 5% payable 09/08/2006 to holders of record 08/25/2006 Ex date - 08/23/2006
Under plan of reorganization each share Common $10 par automatically became (1) share Sterling Banks, Inc. Common $2 par 03/19/2007
(See Sterling Banks, Inc.)

STERLING BANK (LOS ANGELES, CA)
Under plan of reorganization each share Common no par automatically became (1) share Sterling Bancorporation Common no par 12/16/82
Sterling Bancorporation name changed to Sterling West Bancorp 5/27/92 which merged into Pacific Bank, N.A. (San Francisco, CA) 7/3/98

STERLING BKS INC (NJ)
Stock Dividend - 5% payable 09/07/2007 to holders of record 08/24/2007 Ex date - 08/22/2007
Acquired by Roma Financial Corp. 07/16/2010
Each share Common $2 par exchanged for $2.52 cash

STERLING BERYLLIUM & OIL CO. (UT)
Merged into Elgin Gas & Oil Co. on a (4.5) for (1) basis 06/12/1959
(See Elgin Gas & Oil Co.)

STERLING BIOTECH LTD (INDIA)
Sponsored Reg. S GDR's for Ordinary split (2) for (1) by issuance of (1) additional GDR payable 03/30/2005 to holders of record 03/25/2005
GDR agreement terminated 03/06/2017
Each Sponsored Reg. S GDR's for Ordinary exchanged for (6) shares Ordinary

STERLING BREWERS, INC. (IN)
Name changed to ST Liquidating Corp. 6/30/64
(See ST Liquidating Corp.)

STERLING CABLE FD INC (CO)
Charter forfeited for failure to maintain a registered agent 11/26/1991

STERLING CAP CORP (NY)
Merged into Gabelli Equity Trust, Inc. 9/12/2005
Each share Common $1 par exchanged for (0.7914) share Common $0.001 par

STERLING CAP GROUP INC (DE)
Reorganized as Xi Tec, Inc. 05/12/1989
Each share Common $0.0001 par exchanged for (0.1) share Common $0.001 par
(See Xi Tec, Inc.)

STERLING CAP INVT GROUP INC (NV)
Recapitalized as Crystal Properties Holdings Inc. 09/17/2018
Each share Class A Common no par exchanged for (0.001) share Class A Common no par

(See Crystal Properties Holdings Inc.)

STERLING CAP TR I (DE)
9.50% Capital Securities called for redemption at $25 on 5/16/2003

STERLING CENTRECORP INC (ON)
Acquired by SCI Acquisition Inc. 06/15/2007
Each share Common no par exchanged for $1.26 cash

STERLING CHEMICALS INC NEW (DE)
Acquired by Eastman Chemical Co. 08/09/2011
Each share Common 1¢ par exchanged for $2.50 cash

STERLING CHEMS HLDGS INC (DE)
Plan of reorganization under Chapter 11 Federal Bankruptcy Code effective 12/6/2002
No stockholders' equity

STERLING CHEMS INC OLD (DE)
Merged into STX Acquisition Corp. 8/21/96
Each share Common 1¢ par exchanged for $12 cash

STERLING COAL CO. LTD.
Name changed to Conger Lehigh Fuels Ltd. 00/00/1950
Each share Common $100 par exchanged for (1) share Capital Stock no par
(See Conger Lehigh Fuels Ltd.)

STERLING COMM INC (DE)
Merged into SBC Communications, Inc. 3/24/2000
Each share Common 1¢ par exchanged for $44.25 cash

STERLING COMMUNICATIONS INC (NY)
Completely liquidated 09/07/1973
Each share Common 10¢ par exchanged for first and final distribution of $2.625 cash

STERLING COMPUTER SYS INC (NV)
Each share old Common 50¢ par exchanged for (0.33333333) share new Common 50¢ par 10/06/1972
Completely liquidated 11/01/1984
Each share new Common 50¢ par exchanged for first and final distribution of $3.52 cash

STERLING CONTL CORP (UT)
Proclaimed dissolved for failure to pay taxes 3/1/93

STERLING DISCOUNT CORP. (GA)
Completely liquidated for cash 7/21/64

STERLING DRUG INC (DE)
Each share Capital Stock $10 par exchanged for (2) shares Common $5 par 00/00/1945
Common $5 par split (2) for (1) by issuance of (1) additional share 01/04/1957
Common $5 par changed to $2.50 par and (2) additional shares issued 07/01/1963
Common $2.50 par split (3) for (2) by issuance of (0.5) additional share 12/02/1968
$1.50 Conv. Preferred $2.50 par called for redemption 02/24/1972
Common $2.50 par split (3) for (2) by issuance of (0.5) additional share 06/09/1972
Merged into Eastman Kodak Corp. 02/29/1988
Each share Common $2.50 par exchanged for $89.50 cash

STERLING ELECTRIC MOTORS, INC. (CA)
Name changed to 5401 Telegraph Road Co. 7/8/60
5401 Telegraph Road Co. liquidation for cash was completed 1/23/61

STERLING ELECTRONICS, INC. (TX)
Common 50¢ par split (3) for (2) by issuance of (0.5) additional share 8/18/67
Stock Dividend - 20% 2/4/63
Reincorporated under the laws of Nevada as Sterling Electronics Corp. 10/18/67
(See Sterling Electronics Corp.)

STERLING ELECTRS CORP (NV)
75¢ Conv. Preferred Ser. A $2.50 par called for redemption 10/00/1968
20¢ Conv. Preferred Ser. B $2.50 par called for redemption 12/06/1968
Common 50¢ par split (3) for (2) by issuance of (0.5) additional share 01/09/1969
Stock Dividend - 5% payable 12/30/1996 to holders of record 12/09/1996
Merged into Marshall Industries 01/16/1998
Each share Common 50¢ par exchanged for $21 cash

STERLING ENERGY CORP (BC)
Recapitalized as International Sterling Holdings Inc. 10/21/85
Each share Common no par exchanged for (0.2) share Common no par
(See International Sterling Holdings Inc.)

STERLING ENGINE CO. (NY)
Each share $0.55 Preferred $8 par received a Stock Dividend of (1) share Common 10¢ par in 1951
Each share Common $1 par exchanged for (1) share Common 10¢ par in 1951
Recapitalized in 1953
Each (2) shares 5% Prior Preferred $10 par exchanged for (1) share new 5% Preferred $10 par and (3.5) shares Common 10¢ par in 1953
Each share $0.55 Preferred $8 par exchanged for (2.25) shares Common 10¢ par in 1953
Name changed to Sterling Precision Instrument Corp. in 1955
Sterling Precision Instrument Corp. merged into Sterling Precision Corp. 1/3/56 which name changed to Steego Corp. 8/23/79
(See Steego Corp.)

STERLING ENTERPRISES INC (CO)
Recapitalized as Humanus Corp. 10/31/91
Each share Common $0.0001 par exchanged for (0.1) share Common $0.0001 par

STERLING EQUITY HLDGS INC (NV)
SEC revoked common stock registration 11/24/2010

STERLING EXPL INC (NV)
Name changed to Winchester International Resorts Inc. 09/14/2009

STERLING EXTRUDER CORP (NJ)
Stock Dividend - 25% 10/20/1967
Merged into Baker Perkins PLC 05/07/1986
Each share Common 10¢ par exchanged for $23.50 cash

STERLING FIN CORP CALIF (CA)
Charter cancelled for failure to file reports and pay taxes 7/1/96

STERLING FINANCIAL CORP. (IL)
Involuntarily dissolved for failure to pay taxes and file reports 12/01/1997

STERLING FINL CORP (PA)
Common $5 par split (3) for (2) by issuance of (0.5) additional share 11/30/1992
Common $5 par split (5) for (4) by issuance of (0.25) additional share payable 11/15/1999 to holders of record 11/01/1999
Common $5 par split (5) for (4) by issuance of (0.25) additional share payable 06/03/2002 to holders of record 05/15/2002
Common $5 par split (5) for (4) by issuance of (0.25) additional share payable 02/20/2004 to holders of record 02/06/2004 Ex date - 02/23/2004
Common $5 par split (5) for (4) by issuance of (0.25) additional share payable 06/01/2005 to holders of record 05/13/2005 Ex date - 06/02/2005
Stock Dividends - 100% 09/01/1994; 5% payable 07/22/1996 to holders of record 07/10/1996; 5% payable 06/01/1998 to holders of record 05/19/1998; 10% payable 11/27/2000 to holders of record 11/06/2000 Ex date - 11/02/2000
Merged into PNC Financial Services Group, Inc. 04/04/2008
Each share Common $5 par exchanged for $18.05 cash

STERLING FINL CORP (WA)
$1.8125 Conv. Preferred Ser. A $1 par called for redemption at $26.07 on 09/05/1997
Common $1 par split (3) for (2) by issuance of (0.5) additional share payable 08/31/2005 to holders of record 08/17/2005 Ex date - 09/01/2005
Common $1 par changed to no par 08/26/2010
Stock Dividends - 10% 08/31/1993; 10% 08/31/1994; 10% 08/31/1995; 10% payable 11/27/2000 to holders of record 11/06/2000; 10% payable 11/30/2001 to holders of record 11/08/2001 Ex date - 11/06/2001; 10% payable 05/31/2002 to holders of record 05/03/2002 Ex date - 05/01/2002; 10% payable 05/30/2003 to holders of record 05/05/2003 Ex date - 05/01/2003; 10% payable 05/28/2004 to holders of record 05/10/2004
Each share old Common no par exchanged for (0.01515151) share new Common no par 11/19/2010
Merged into Umpqua Holdings Corp. 04/18/2014
Each share new Common no par exchanged for (1.671) shares Common no par and $2.18 cash

STERLING FINL CORP CDA (ON)
Name changed to Sterling Centrecorp Inc. 06/08/2001
(See Sterling Centrecorp Inc.)

STERLING-FORBES CAPITAL CORP. (CO)
Involuntarily dissolved for failure to file reports and pay taxes 1/1/90

STERLING GEN INC (DE)
Name changed to Carnaby Shops of Florida, Inc. 10/26/1976
(See Carnaby Shops of Florida, Inc.)

STERLING GOLD CORP (NV)
Name changed to iDcentrix, Inc. 03/13/2008
iDcentrix, Inc. name changed to North China Horticulture, Inc. 09/01/2010
(See North China Horticulture, Inc.)

STERLING HEALTHCARE GROUP INC (FL)
Merged into FPA Medical Management Inc. 10/31/96
Each share Common $0.0001 par exchanged for (0.951) shares Common no par
(See FPA Medical Management Inc.)

STERLING HSE CORP (KS)
Acquired by Alternative Living Services, Inc. 10/23/97
Each share Common no par exchanged for (1.1) shares Common 1¢ par
Alternative Living Services, Inc. name changed to Alterra Healthcare Corp. 5/19/99
(See Alterra Healthcare Corp.)

STERLING INC (OH)
Merged into Ratners Group PLC 08/21/1987
Each share Common no par exchanged for $41 cash

STERLING INVESTMENT FUND, INC. (NC)
Merged into Nation-Wide Securities Co. Inc. 11/1/68
Each share Common $1 par exchanged for (1.213) shares Capital Stock $1 par
Nation-Wide Securities Co. Inc. name changed to Bullock Balanced Shares, Inc. 1/14/85 which name changed to Alliance Balanced Shares, Inc. 3/13/87 which name changed to AllianceBernstein Balanced Shares, Inc. 3/31/2003

STERLING INVT INC (UT)
Recapitalized as Sterling Medical Devices, Inc. 02/07/1983
Each share Common $0.001 par exchanged for (0.25) share Common $0.001 par
Sterling Medical Devices, Inc. recapitalized as Sterling Medical Systems, Inc. 12/07/1987

STERLING INVTS LTD (CO)
Each (420) shares old Common no par exchanged for (1) share new Common no par 4/1/92
Reincorporated under the laws of Oklahoma as Molly Murphy's, Inc. 10/12/92
Molly Murphy's, Inc. name changed to Sterling Diversified Holdings, Inc. 1/26/94

STERLING LEAF INCOME TR (AB)
Delisted from Toronto Venture Stock Exchange 06/23/2006

STERLING MEDIA CAP GROUP INC (PA)
Each share old Class A Common no par exchanged for (0.0328409) share new Class A Common no par 11/03/2000
Reincorporated under the laws of Nevada as Sterling Capital Investment Group, Inc. 01/18/2001
Sterling Capital Investment Group, Inc. recapitalized as Crystal Properties Holdings Inc. 09/17/2008
(See Crystal Properties Holdings Inc.)

STERLING MEDICAL DEVICES, INC. (UT)
Recapitalized as Sterling Medical Systems, Inc. 12/7/87
Each share Common $0.001 par exchanged for (0.1) share Common $0.001 par

STERLING MNG CO (ID)
Capital Stock 10¢ par changed to 5¢ par and (1) additional share issued 01/24/1969
Under Chapter 11 plan of reorganization each share Common 5¢ par received $0.06 cash payable 08/00/2012 to holders of record 07/22/2011

STERLING MOTOR TRUCK CO.
Assets sold to Sterling Motor Truck Co., Inc. in 1933
Details not available

STERLING MOTOR TRUCK CO., INC.
Acquired by White Motor Co. in 1951
Each share Common $1 par exchanged for (0.25) share Common $1 par
White Motor Co. name changed to White Motor Corp. 4/26/65 which reorganized as Northeast Ohio Axle, Inc. 11/15/83 which name changed to NEOAX, Inc. (OH) 5/13/86 which reincorporated in Delaware 5/21/87 which name changed to EnviroSource, Inc. 11/14/89 which recapitalized as Envirosource, Inc. 6/22/98
(See Envirosource, Inc.)

STERLING MOVIES U.S.A., INC. (NY)
Name changed to Sterling Communications Inc. 12/12/67
Sterling Communications Inc. completely liquidated 9/7/73

STERLING NATL BK & TR CO (NEW YORK, NY)
Capital Stock $25 par changed to $15 par and (0.666) additional share issued plus a 200% stock dividend paid 11/21/1956
Capital Stock $15 par changed to $30 par 09/00/1970
99.9% acquired by Standard Financial Corp. 00/00/1980
Public interest eliminated

STERLING NATL BK DAVIE (FORT LAUDERDALE, FL)
Over 95.9% acquired by American Bancshares, Inc. as of 12/23/1977
Public interest eliminated

STERLING OIL & DEVELOPMENT CO.
Liquidated in 1941

STERLING OIL & GAS CO. (TX)
Name changed to Tennessee Production Co. (TX) in 1951
Tennessee Production Co. (TX) acquired by Tennessee Production Co. (DE) in 1952 which merged into Tennessee Gas Transmission Co. in 1954 which name changed to Tenneco Inc. 4/11/66 which merged into El Paso Natural Gas Co. 12/12/96 which reorganized as El Paso Energy Corp. 8/1/98 which name changed to El Paso Corp. 2/5/2001

STERLING OIL & GAS CO (NV)
Recapitalized as Landstar Development Group, Inc. 04/21/2014
Each share Common $0.00001 par exchanged for (0.03333333) share Common $0.00001 par
Landstar Development Group, Inc. recapitalized as Solar Integrated Roofing Corp. 11/12/2015

STERLING OIL & REFINING CORP.
Name changed to Sterling Oil & Gas Co. in 1950
Sterling Oil & Gas Co. name changed to Tennessee Production Co. (TX) in 1951 which was acquired by Tennessee Production Co. (DE) in 1952 which merged into Tennessee Gas Transmission Co. in 1954 which name changed to Tenneco Inc. 4/11/66 which merged into El Paso Natural Gas Co. 12/12/96 which reorganized as El Paso Energy Corp. 8/1/98 which name changed to El Paso Corp. 2/5/2001

STERLING OIL CO. (AZ)
Company officers arrested for fraud in 1910
No stockholders' equity

STERLING OIL OKLA INC (DE)
Charter cancelled and declared void for failure to pay franchise taxes 3/1/2004

STERLING OPTL CORP (NY)
Plan of reorganization under Chapter 11 Federal Bankruptcy Code effective 01/12/1995
No stockholders' equity

STERLING PAC RES INC (BC)
Recapitalized as Tres-Or Resources Ltd. 1/11/99
Each share Common no par exchanged for (0.2) share Common no par

STERLING-PACIFIC OIL CO. LTD.
Liquidated in 1934

STERLING PARTNERS INC (DE)
Each share old Common $0.001 par exchanged for (0.25) share new Common $0.001 par 01/14/1999

Name changed to GourmetMarket.com Inc. 01/22/1999
GourmetMarket.com Inc. recapitalized as TargitInteractive Inc. 08/09/2001 which recapitalized as NetSpace International Holdings, Inc. 06/11/2007 which recapitalized as Alternative Fuels Americas, Inc. 10/13/2010 which name changed to Kaya Holdings, Inc. 04/07/2015

STERLING PETROLEUM CO., INC.
Merged into Midland Oil Corp. on a (1) for (400) basis in 1946
Midland Oil Corp. charter cancelled 3/1/76

STERLING PIPE & SUPPLY CO (OK)
Merged into Foster (L.B.) Co. 06/29/1985
Each share Common 1¢ par exchanged for $0.50 cash

STERLING PRECISION CORP (DE)
5% Conv. Preferred Ser. A $10 par called for redemption 02/15/1968
5% Conv. Preferred Ser. B $10 par called for redemption 02/15/1968
5% Conv. Preferred Ser. C $10 par called for redemption 02/15/1968
Name changed to Steego Corp. 08/23/1979
(See Steego Corp.)

STERLING PRECISION INSTRUMENT CORP. (NY)
Merged into Sterling Precision Corp. share for share 1/3/56
Sterling Precision Corp. name changed to Steego Corp. 8/23/79
(See Steego Corp.)

STERLING PRODUCTS, INC.
Name changed to Sterling Drug Inc. 00/00/1942
(See Sterling Drug Inc.)

STERLING RES CORP (UT)
Reorganized under the laws of Delaware as Saratoga Resources Inc. 1/21/94
Each share Common 25¢ par exchanged for (1/30) share Common 25¢ par
Saratoga Resources Inc. recapitalized as OptiCare Health Systems, Inc. 8/10/99 which merged into Refac Optical Group 3/6/2006
(See Refac Optical Group)

STERLING RES LTD (AB)
Each share old Common no par exchanged for (0.01) share new Common no par 07/07/2016
Name changed to PetroTal Corp. 06/06/2018

STERLING SALT CO.
Acquired by International Salt Co. in 1929
Details not available

STERLING SVGS & LN ASSN (CA)
Name changed to USLIFE Savings & Loan Association 03/01/1971
(See USLIFE Savings & Loan Association)

STERLING SVGS ASSN SPOKANE (WA)
Each share $2.50 Conv. Preferred Ser. B $1 par exchanged for (2.2) shares Common $10 par 11/30/1991
Stock Dividend - 10% 12/01/1988
Name changed to Sterling Financial Corp. 11/01/1992
Sterling Financial Corp. merged into Umpqua Holdings Corp. 04/18/2014

STERLING SEAL CO (PA)
Stock Dividends - 25% 5/3/68; 10% 2/17/69; 10% 9/5/69
Acquired by VCA Corp. 11/1/71
Each share Common $1 par exchanged for (0.64) share Common 25¢ par
VCA Corp. merged into Ethyl Corp. 10/30/74 which reorganized as NewMarket Corp. 6/18/2004

STERLING SECURITIES CORP.
Merged into Atlas Corp. 10/31/1936
Each share $3 1st Preferred exchanged for (1) share 6% Preferred $50 par
Each share $1.20 Preference exchanged for (0.15) share 6% Preferred $50 par and (0.4) share Common $5 par
Each share Class A Common exchanged for (0.23) share Common $5 par
Each share Class B Common exchanged for (0.05) share Common $5 par
(See Atlas Corp.)

STERLING SHOES INCOME FD (BC)
Under plan of reorganization each Unit no par automatically became (1) share Sterling Shoes Inc. (Canada) Common no par 07/08/2010

STERLING SILVER MINES LTD. (BC)
Acquired by Gem Explorations Ltd. 11/00/1964
Each share Capital Stock 50¢ par exchanged for (0.6666666) share Capital Stock 50¢ par
Gem Explorations Ltd. recapitalized as Consolidated Gem Explorations Ltd. 01/08/1968 which recapitalized as Brendon Resources Ltd. 02/13/1973 which recapitalized as Brendex Resources Ltd. 09/10/1976
(See Brendex Resources Ltd.)

STERLING SOFTWARE INC (DE)
$7.20 Exchangeable Preferred 10¢ par called for redemption 12/04/1991
Each share Common 10¢ par received distribution of (1.5926) shares Sterling Commerce, Inc. Common 1¢ par payable 10/07/1996 to holders of record 09/30/1996 Ex date - 10/08/1996
Common 10¢ par split (2) for (1) by issuance of (1) additional share payable 04/03/1998 to holders of record 03/20/1998 Ex date - 04/06/1998
Merged into Computer Associates International, Inc. 04/07/2000
Each share Common 10¢ par exchanged for (0.5634) share Common 10¢ par
Computer Associates International, Inc. name changed to CA, Inc. 02/01/2006

STERLING STORES AMER INC (RI)
Each share Common 30¢ par exchanged for (0.1) share Common $3 par 08/15/1963
Reorganized under the laws of Delaware as Sterling General, Inc. 03/07/1969
Each share Common $3 par exchanged for (1) share Common 5¢ par
Sterling General, Inc. name changed to Carnaby Shops of Florida, Inc. 10/26/1976
(See Carnaby Shops of Florida, Inc.)

STERLING STORES INC (AR)
Merged into Duckwall-Alco Stores Inc. 05/27/1983
Each share Preferred no par exchanged for (1.457) shares Common $2.50 par or $25.50 cash
Each share Common $1 par exchanged for (0.3057) share Common $2.50 par
(See Duckwall-Alco Stores Inc.)

STERLING SUGARS INC (LA)
Reincorporated 02/08/2000
State of incorporation changed from (DE) to (LA) 02/08/2000
Each (2,000) shares old Common $1 par exchanged for (1) share new Common $1 par 07/01/2005
Each share new Common $1 par

exchanged again for (1) share new Common $1 par 08/20/2010
Note: In effect holders received $19,300 cash per share and public interest was eliminated

STERLING TELECASTING CO. (SC)
Dissolved in 1954

STERLING TELEVISION CO., INC. (NY)
Merged into Walter Reade/Sterling, Inc. 7/1/63
Each share Class A 25¢ par or Class B 25¢ par exchanged for (1) share Common 25¢ par
Walter Reade/Sterling, Inc. name changed to Reade (Walter) Organization, Inc. 9/8/66
(See Reade (Walter) Organization, Inc.)

STERLING TR CORP (TORONTO, ON)
Name changed 08/03/1977
Each share Capital Stock $100 par exchanged for (5) shares Capital Stock $20 par 00/00/1951
Each share Capital Stock $20 par exchanged for (2) shares Capital Stock $10 par 11/14/1961
Each share Capital Stock $10 par exchanged for (5) shares Capital Stock $2 par 04/28/1966
Name changed from Sterling Trusts Corp. to Sterling Trust Corp. 08/03/1977
Name changed to General Trust Corp. of Canada (Toronto, ON) 06/13/1988
(See General Trust Corp. of Canada (Toronto, ON))

STERLING URANIUM CORP. (UT)
Capital Stock 25¢ par changed to 1¢ par 12/7/57
Recapitalized as Sterling Beryllium & Oil Co. 2/4/58
Each share Capital Stock 1¢ par exchanged for (0.05) share Capital Stock 20¢ par
Sterling Beryllium & Oil Co. merged into Elgin Gas & Oil Co. 6/12/59
(See Elgin Gas & Oil Co.)

STERLING VARNISH CO (PA)
Completely liquidated 01/18/1969
Each share Common $100 par exchanged for first and final distribution of (150) shares Reichhold Chemicals, Inc. Common $1 par
(See Reichhold Chemicals, Inc.)

STERLING VENTURE CORP (CO)
Name changed to Fun Rentals USA, Inc. 09/13/1988

STERLING VISION INC (NY)
Name changed to Emerging Vision, Inc. 04/17/2000
(See Emerging Vision, Inc.)

STERLING WEST BANCORP (CA)
Merged into Pacific Bank, N.A. (San Francisco, CA) 7/3/98
Each share Common no par exchanged for $7.11 cash

STERLING WORLDWIDE CORP (NV)
Each share old Common 10¢ par exchanged for (0.25) share new Common 10¢ par 04/24/1997
Each share new Common 10¢ par exchanged for (0.005) share Common no par 07/25/1997
Each share Common no par exchanged for (0.005) share Common $0.001 par 07/25/1998
Name changed to Sun Quest Holdings Inc. 12/23/1999
Sun Quest Holdings Inc. name changed to Sunrise Consulting Group, Inc. 12/04/2007

STERLINGMARC MNG LTD (BC)
Recapitalized as West Oak Resource Corp. 06/23/1999
Each share Common no par exchanged for (1/6) share Common no par
West Oak Resource Corp. name changed to Telesis North Communications Inc. 03/06/2001
(See Telesis North Communications Inc.)

STERLINGSOUTH BK & TR CO (GREENSBORO, NC)
Merged into BNC Bancorp 07/20/2006
Each share Common no par exchanged for (1.21056) shares Common no par
BNC Bancorp merged into Pinnacle Financial Partners, Inc. 06/16/2017

STERLITE GOLD LTD (ON)
Acquired by GeoProMining Ltd. 10/18/2007
Each share Common no par exchanged for $0.3845 cash

STERLITE INDS INDIA LTD (INDIA)
144A GDR's for Equity Shares split (2) for (1) by issuance of (1) additional GDR payable 03/08/2004 to holders of record 02/06/2004
Ex date - 02/04/2004
GDR agreement terminated 09/24/2007
Each 144A GDR for Equity Shares exchanged for (1) Equity Share
Note: Unexchanged GDR's were sold and the proceeds distributed on a pro-rata basis
ADR basis changed from (1:1) to (1:4) 06/28/2010
Merged into Sesa Goa Ltd. 09/09/2013
Each ADR for Equity Share exchanged for (0.6) ADR for Equity Share
Sesa Goa Ltd. name changed to Sesa Sterlite Ltd. 09/25/2013 which name changed to Vedanta Ltd. 05/05/2015

STERN & STERN TEXTILES INC (NY)
4-1/2% Preferred $50 par called for redemption 03/14/1950
Name changed to Sterns Holdings Inc. 11/03/1977
(See Sterns Holdings Inc.)

STERN BROTHERS (NY)
Common no par changed to $1 par in 1934
Merged into Allied Stores Corp. through the payment of $24 cash for each share Common and/or VTC for Common $1 par 7/23/59

STERN HASKELL INC (NY)
Charter cancelled and proclaimed dissolved for failure to pay taxes 09/29/1983

STERN METALS CORP (NY)
Common $1 par split (2) for (1) by issuance of (1) additional share 3/20/70
Name changed to Sterndent Corp. 6/22/72
(See Sterndent Corp.)

STERNCO INDS INC (NJ)
Class A 10¢ par split (5) for (4) by issuance of (0.25) additional share 10/10/1965
Class A 10¢ par changed to 5¢ par and (1) additional share issued 05/07/1968
Class A 5¢ par changed to 2-1/2¢ par and (1) additional share issued 05/12/1969
Class A 2-1/2¢ par changed to 1-2/3¢ par and (0.5) additional share issued 05/21/1970
Merged into Hartz Mountain Corp. 05/31/1973
Each share Class A 1-2/3¢ par exchanged for (1.25) shares Common 1¢ par
(See Hartz Mountain Corp.)

STERNDENT CORP (NY)
Acquired by Cooper Laboratories, Inc. 12/18/1981

Each share Common $1 par exchanged for $25 principal amount of 12% Conv. Subordinated Debentures due 01/01/2007 or $22.50 cash
Note: Option to receive Debentures expired 03/05/1982

STERNE STACKHOUSE INC (AB)
Name changed 11/27/96
Name changed from Sterne Software Inc. to Sterne Stackhouse Inc. 11/27/96
Name changed to Labrador Technologies Inc. 6/17/2004

STERNER LIGHTING, INC. (MN)
Name changed to Sterner Lighting Systems Inc. 4/22/74
(See Sterner Lighting Systems Inc.)

STERNER LTG SYS INC (MN)
Common 10¢ par split (5) for (4) by issuance of (0.25) additional share 4/18/83
Stock Dividend - 25% 12/3/82
Merged into Churchill Companies 8/4/89
Each share Common 10¢ par exchanged for $17 cash

STERNS HLDGS INC (NY)
Under plan of merger each share Common $1 par exchanged for $23.10 cash 07/22/1983

STEROIDOGENESIS INHIBITORS INTL INC (NV)
Name changed to Samaritan Pharmaceuticals, Inc. 4/25/2001

STET HELLAS TELECOMMUNICATIONS S A (GREECE)
Name changed to TIM Hellas Telecommunications S.A. 11/4/2004
(See TIM Hellas Telecommunications S.A.)

STET SOCIETA FINANZIARIA TELEFONICA S P A (ITALY)
ADR's for Ordinary split (3) for (2) by issuance of (0.5) additional ADR 08/17/1990
Each Unsponsored ADR for Ordinary exchanged for (1) Sponsored ADR for Ordinary 02/27/1995
Name changed to Telecom Italia S.p.A. (Old) 07/18/1997
Telecom Italia S.p.A. (Old) merged into Telecom Italia S.p.A. (New) 08/04/2003

STETSON JOHN B CO (DE)
Reincorporated 04/30/1966
State of incorporation changed from (PA) to (DE) 04/30/1966
Common no par changed to $1 par 11/26/1971
Merged into JBS Acquisition Corp. 12/19/1988
Each share $2 Preferred $25 par exchanged for $33 cash
Each share $2.80 Preferred Ser. A $1 par exchanged for $44.50 cash
Each share Common $1 par exchanged for $29.50 cash

STETSON OIL & GAS LTD (ON)
Reincorporated 08/21/2014
Each share old Common no par received distribution of (1) share Preference Ser. 1 no par payable 11/17/2008 to holders of record 11/10/2008
Each share old Common no par exchanged for (0.09090909) share new Common no par 02/27/2012
Preference Ser. 1 no par called for redemption at $0.0001 on 01/20/2014
Place of incorporation changed from (AB) to (ON) 08/21/2014
Name changed to Magnolia Colombia Ltd. 06/14/2017

STETSON OIL EXCHANGE INC (UT)
Recapitalized as Telecom Wireless Corp. (UT) 04/23/1998
Each share Common $0.006 par exchanged for (0.02) share Common $0.006 par
Telecom Wireless Corp. (UT) reincorporated in Delaware as TCOM Ventures Corp. 06/15/2000
(See TCOM Ventures Corp.)

STEUBEN TR CO (HORNELL, NY)
Under plan of reorganization each share Common $50 par automatically became (1) share Steuben Trust Corp. Common $1 par 02/05/1990

STEUBENVILLE, EAST LIVERPOOL & BEAVER VALLEY TRACTION CO.
Dissolved in 1939

STEUBENVILLE HOTEL CORP (OH)
Charter cancelled for failure to pay taxes 05/30/1975

STEVCOKNIT INC (DE)
Common $1 par changed to 10¢ par 06/26/1975
Merged into Stevens (J.P.) & Co., Inc. 02/01/1983
Each share Common 10¢ par exchanged for (0.1145) share Capital Stock $7.50 par
(See Stevens (J.P.) & Co., Inc.)

STEVEN MYERS & ASSOC INC (CA)
Issue Information - 3,150,000 shares COM offered at $12 per share on 01/28/1998
Name changed to SM&A Corp. 08/18/1998
SM&A Corp. name changed to Emergent Information Technologies Inc. 05/04/2000 which name changed to SM&A (CA) 01/29/2002 which reincorporated in Delaware 11/30/2006
(See SM&A (DE))

STEVENS, (M.T.) & SONS CO.
Merged into Stevens (J.P.) & Co., Inc. in 1946
Each share Common $100 par exchanged for (23.9829) shares new Capital Stock $15 par
(See Stevens (J.P.) & Co., Inc.)

STEVENS & THOMPSON PAPER CO (NY)
Each share Common $10 par exchanged for (0.5) share Common $10 par 00/00/1939
Merged into Dixico, Inc. 04/05/1976
Each share Common $10 par exchanged for (1.645) shares Common $1 par
(See Dixico, Inc.)

STEVENS ANN INC (NY)
Merged into ASI Apparel, Inc. 05/29/1980
Each share Common 1¢ par exchanged for $3.14 cash

STEVENS DURYEA, INC. (DE)
Charter cancelled and declared inoperative and void for non-payment of taxes 3/19/24

STEVENS ELECTROTECH INC (CA)
Name changed to Lightwave Cablevision Systems, Inc. 11/27/1990
(See Lightwave Cablevision Systems, Inc.)

STEVENS GREASE & OIL CO. (OH)
Charter revoked for failure to file reports and pay fees 11/15/59

STEVENS HOTEL CORP.
Liquidated 1945

STEVENS INTERNATIONAL INC (DE)
Name changed 05/18/1995
Each share Common 10¢ par exchanged for (0.5) share Common Ser. A 10¢ par and (0.5) share Conv. Common Ser. B 10¢ par 08/24/1988
Common Ser. A 10¢ par split (3) for (2) by issuance of (0.5) additional share 07/28/1989
Conv. Common Ser. B 10¢ par split

(3) for (2) by issuance of (0.5) additional share 07/28/1989
Name changed from Stevens Graphics Corp. to Stevens International, Inc. 05/18/1995
Chapter 11 bankruptcy proceedings converted to Chapter 7 on 03/06/2003
No stockholders' equity

STEVENS J P & CO INC (DE)
Common $15 par changed to $7.50 par and (1) additional share issued 06/26/1974
Stock Dividends - 10% 11/14/1962; 10% 11/18/1964; 10% 02/15/1979; 10% 02/15/1980
Merged into Magnolia Partners, L.P. 06/30/1988
Each share Common $7.50 par exchanged for $68.50 cash

STEVENS LINEN WORKS
Liquidated in 1940

STEVENS MARKETS, INC. (FL)
Name changed to S.L.S., Inc. 5/3/64 which completed liquidation 4/28/65
(See listing for S.L.S., Inc.)

STEVENS RES INC (NV)
Name changed to Nova Lifestyle, Inc. 06/27/2011

STEVENSON ENGINEERING CORP.
Name changed to Sealol Corp. in 1943
Sealol Corp. name changed to Sealol, Inc. in 1960 which merged into EG&G, Inc. 10/15/68 which name changed to PerkinElmer, Inc. 10/25/99

STEVENSON HOTEL
Property sold and holders received $1.27 per Unit in 1940

STEVES FAMOUS HOT DOGS INC (NV)
Dissolved 08/01/1994
Details not available

STEVES HOMEMADE ICE CREAM INC (NJ)
Name changed to Integrated Brands Inc. 08/08/1995
Integrated Brands Inc. merged into Yogen Fruz World-Wide Inc. 03/18/1998 which name changed to CoolBrands International Inc. (NS) 10/06/2000 which reincorporated in Canada 03/27/2006 which reorganized in Delaware as Swisher Hygiene Inc. 11/04/2010

STEVIA AGRITECH CORP (NV)
Common $0.001 par split (15) for (1) by issuance of (14) additional shares payable 05/07/2012 to holders of record 05/07/2012
Name changed to Rightscorp, Inc. 07/17/2013

STEVIA FIRST CORP (NV)
Common $0.001 par split (7) for (1) by issuance of (6) additional shares payable 10/12/2011 to holders of record 10/12/2011
Recapitalized as Vitality Biopharma, Inc. 07/20/2016
Each share Common $0.001 par exchanged for (0.1) share Common $0.001 par

STEVIA INC (IL)
Involuntarily dissolved for failure to pay taxes and file reports 4/1/2000

STEVRON INDS INC (DE)
Reincorporated 5/20/85
State of incorporation changed from (CT) to (DE) 5/20/85
Merged into Renew Entertainment Corp. 9/6/85
Details not available

STEWART & STEVENSON SVCS INC (TX)
Common no par split (3) for (2) by issuance of (0.5) additional share 07/15/1988

Common no par split (2) for (1) by issuance of (1) additional share 07/14/1989
Common no par split (2) for (1) by issuance of (1) additional share 05/13/1992
Stock Dividend - 50% 01/08/1982
Merged into Armor Holdings, Inc. 05/25/2006
Each share Common no par exchanged for $36.50 cash

STEWART APARTMENTS
Trust terminated in 1950
Details not available

STEWART CONCRETE & MATERIAL CO. (MO)
Out of business 01/01/1969
Details not available

STEWART CREEK MINING CO. LTD.
Dissolved in 1948

STEWART ENTERPRISES INC (LA)
Class A Common no par split (3) for (2) by issuance of (0.5) additional share 12/01/1993
Class A Common no par split (3) for (2) by issuance of (0.5) additional share payable 06/21/1996 to holders of record 05/28/1996
Class A Common no par split (2) for (1) by issuance of (1) additional share payable 04/24/1998 to holders of record 04/10/1998
Acquired by Service Corporation International 12/23/2013
Each share Class A Common no par exchanged for $13.25 cash

STEWART FOODS INC (VA)
Charter terminated 01/02/1999

STEWART FORM INC. (CA)
Name changed to Stewart Products Corp. 05/13/1966
(See Stewart Products Corp.)

STEWART INTL PRODTNS INC (NY)
Charter cancelled and proclaimed dissolved for failure to pay taxes 06/24/1981

STEWART IRON WORKS CO., INC. (KY)
7% Preferred $25 par called for redemption 04/01/1961
(Additional Information in Active)

STEWART LAKE RES INC (ON)
Name changed 06/27/1986
Recapitalized 09/16/1986
Name changed from Stewart Lake Iron Mines of Ontario Ltd. to Stewart Lake Mines Inc.-Mines de Lac Stewart Inc. 06/27/1986
Recapitalized from Stewart Lake Mines Inc.-Mines de Lac Stewart Inc. to Stewart Lake Resources Inc.-Ressources de Lac Stewart Inc. 09/16/1986
Each share Capital Stock $1 par exchanged for (1/3) share Common no par
Delisted from Canadian Dealer Network 01/03/1995

STEWART MORGAN CORP (CA)
Merged into Axion System Science, Inc. 01/26/1989
Each share Common 1¢ par exchanged for (2) shares Common 1¢ par
Axion System Science, Inc. recapitalized as Wordcraft Systems, Inc. (CA) 06/15/1994 which reorganized in Delaware as Wake Up Now, Inc. 12/01/2010

STEWART OIL & GAS CO. (DE)
Name changed to National Diversified Industries, Inc. 07/25/1963
(See National Diversified Industries, Inc.)

STEWART PRODUCTS CORP. (CA)
Charter suspended for failure to pay taxes 02/02/1970

STEWART SANDWICHES INC (VA)
Common $1 par split (3) for (2) by issuance of (0.5) additional share 01/03/1972
Common $1 par split (3) for (2) by issuance of (0.5) additional share 01/12/1973
Stock Dividends - 10% 02/27/1974; 10% 01/16/1975
Name changed to Stewart Foods Inc. 12/05/1991
(See Stewart Foods Inc.)

STEWART TITLE & TR PHOENIX INC (DE)
Each share old Common $100 par exchanged for (0.002) share new Common $100 par 04/13/1999
Note: In effect holders received $4 cash per share and public interest was eliminated

STEWART TITLE GTY CO (TX)
Each share 8% Preferred $100 par exchanged for (10) shares 6% Conv. Preferred $10 par and (10) shares new Common $1 par 04/26/1964
Each share old Common exchanged for (10) shares new Common $1 par or Class B
Common $1 par at holders' option which expired 05/28/64 after which exchangeable for Class B Common $1 par on 04/26/1964
100% reacquired as of 01/01/1973
Public interest eliminated

STEWART URANIUM DRILLING CO., INC. (DE)
Merged into Shawano Development Corp. 06/01/1955
Each share Common 1¢ par exchanged for (0.6) share Common 25¢ par
(See Shawano Development Corp.)

STEWART W P & CO LTD (DE)
Reincorporated 06/18/2010
Place of Incorporation changed from (Bermuda) to (DE) 06/18/2010
Merged into AllianceBernstein L.P. 12/12/2013
Each share Common 1¢ par exchanged for (1) Contingent Value Right and $12 cash

STEWART WARNER CORP (VA)
Capital Stock $10 par changed to $5 par 00/00/1934
Capital Stock $5 par changed to $2.50 par and (1) additional share issued 01/12/1960
Capital Stock $2.50 par reclassified as Common $2.50 par 05/08/1968
Common $2.50 par split (5) for (4) by issuance of (0.25) additional share 06/07/1979
Common $2.50 par split (5) for (4) by issuance of (0.25) additional share 12/07/1981
Merged into BTR plc 12/17/1987
Each share Common $2.50 par exchanged for $33 cash

STEWART-WARNER SPEEDOMETER CORP.
Name changed to Stewart-Warner Corp. 00/00/1929
(See Stewart-Warner Corp.)

STEWARTS & LLOYDS LTD (ENGLAND)
Stock Dividend - 50% 02/25/1964
Nationalized by the United Kingdom 08/08/1967
Each ADR for Ordinary £1 par exchanged for £1-11s-8.102d principal amount of 6-1/2% Treasury Stock due 01/28/1971

S3 INC (DE)
Common $0.0001 par split (2) for (1) by issuance of (1) additional share 12/17/1993
Common $0.0001 par split (2) for (1) by issuance of (1) additional share 09/29/1995

Name changed to SONICblue Inc. 11/15/2000
(See SONICblue Inc.)

S3 INVT CO INC (CA)
Name changed from S31 Holdings Inc. to S3 Investment Co., Inc. 10/21/2004
Each (150) shares old Common $0.001 par exchanged for (1) share new Common $0.001 par 02/12/2007
Name changed to Redwood Group International 05/09/2011

STI GROUP INC (DE)
Merged into American Annuity Group, Inc. 01/07/1993
Each share Common $1 par exchanged for (1) share Common $1 par
American Annuity Group, Inc. name changed to Great American Financial Resources, Inc. 06/13/2000
(See Great American Financial Resources, Inc.)

STI HLDGS INC (NV)
Name changed to Grand Perfecta, Inc. 04/22/2013

STI INC (MN)
Proclaimed dissolved for failure to file annual reports and pay fees 03/24/2003

STICKELBER & SONS INC (MO)
Merged into Marion Corp. 02/01/1965
Each share Common exchanged for (1) share Common no par
(See Marion Corp.)

STICKY WEB INC (FL)
Name changed to Perfect Web Technologies, Inc. 12/22/2006
Perfect Web Technologies, Inc. name changed to Ovation Music & Studios, Inc. 02/03/2015 which recapitalized as TLD3 Entertainment Group, Inc. 01/19/2017

STIFEL (J.L.) & SONS, INC. (WV)
Stock Dividend - 166.66666666% 08/28/1957
Merged into Indian Head Mills, Inc. (MA) 09/13/1957
Each share Common $5 par exchanged for (0.25) share $1.50 Preferred $20 par
(See Indian Head Mills, Inc. (MA))

STIFEL FINL CAP TR I (DE)
9% Trust Preferred Securities called for redemption at $25 on 07/13/2007

STIG CORP., INC. (FL)
Proclaimed dissolved for failure to file reports and pay fees 06/28/1971

STIKINE EXPLORATIONS LTD. (BC)
Struck off register and proclaimed dissolved for failure to file returns 09/23/1974

STIKINE GOLD CORP (BC)
Name changed to Stikine Energy Corp. 08/03/2010

STIKINE IRON MINES LTD (BC)
Recapitalized as Petrogold Resources Corp. 02/18/1975
Each share Common 50¢ par exchanged for (0.1) share Common no par
Petrogold Resources Corp. name changed to Petrogold Financial Corp. 02/14/1986 which name changed to Columbia Leisure Corp. 10/11/1988
(See Columbia Leisure Corp.)

STIKINE RES LTD (BC)
Acquired by Prime Resources Group Inc. 12/14/1993
Each share Common no par exchanged for (7.35) shares Common no par
Prime Resources Group Inc. merged into HomeStake Mining Co.

12/03/1998 which merged into Barrick Gold Corp. 12/14/2001

STIKINE RIVER MINES LTD (BC)
Name changed to Canadian Hidrogas Resources Ltd. 02/28/1969
(See Canadian Hidrogas Resources Ltd.)

STIKINE SILVER LTD (BC)
Recapitalized as Consolidated Stikine Silver Ltd. 01/08/1985
Each share Common 50¢ par exchanged for (0.33333333) share Common no par
Consolidated Stikine Silver Ltd. name changed to Stikine Resources Ltd. 09/20/1989 which was acquired by Prime Resources Group Inc. 12/14/1993 which merged into HomeStake Mining Co. 12/03/1998 which merged into Barrick Gold Corp. 12/14/2001

STILFONTEIN GOLD MNG LTD (SOUTH AFRICA)
ADR agreement terminated 02/16/2010
No ADR holders' equity

STILL MAN MFG CORP (NY)
Merged into Teledyne, Inc. 03/04/1968
Each share Class A 75¢ par exchanged for $12.50 cash

STILLWATER MINING CO. LTD.
Dissolved 00/00/1938
Details not available

STILLWATER MNG CO (DE)
Common 1¢ par split (3) for (2) by issuance of (0.5) additional share payable 12/31/1998 to holders of record 12/21/1998 Ex date - 01/04/1999
Acquired by Sibanye Gold Ltd. 05/04/2017
Each share Common 1¢ par exchanged for $18 cash

STILWELL FINL INC (DE)
Name changed to Janus Capital Group Inc. 01/01/2003
Janus Capital Group Inc. merged into Janus Henderson Group PLC 05/30/2017

STIMSONITE CORP (DE)
Merged into Avery Dennison Corp. 07/13/1999
Each share Common 1¢ par exchanged for $14.75 cash

STIMUTECH INC (DE)
Name changed to Valiant International Inc. 05/29/1992
Valiant International Inc. name changed to Techno Dynamics Inc. 11/22/1993
(See Techno Dynamics Inc.)

STINA RES LTD (BC)
Name changed to CellCube Energy Storage

STINGRAY COPPER INC (CANADA)
Merged into Mercator Minerals Ltd. 12/21/2009
Each share Common no par exchanged for (0.25) share Common no par

STINGRAY RES INC (CANADA)
Name changed to Stingray Copper Inc. 07/18/2007
Stingray Copper Inc. merged into Mercator Minerals Ltd. 12/21/2009

STINSON & FARR THOROUGHBRED MGMT CO (UT)
Involuntarily dissolved 05/01/1990

STINSON AIRCRAFT CORP.
Dissolved 00/00/1938
Details not available

STIRLING COOKE BROWN HOLDINGS LTD (BERMUDA)
Name changed to AlphaStar Insurance Group Ltd. 09/10/2002
(See AlphaStar Insurance Group Ltd.)

STIRLING EXPL LTD (BC)
Name changed to Luiri Gold Ltd. (BC) 06/26/2006
Luiri Gold Ltd. (BC) reincorporated in Bermuda 09/13/2012

STIRLING HOMEX CORP (DE)
Adjudicated insolvent 06/13/1977
No stockholders' equity

STIROL (UKRAINE)
Sponsored ADR's for Common split (5) for (1) by issuance of (4) additional ADR's payable 11/02/2005 to holders of record 11/01/2005
Basis changed from (1:5) to (1:1) 11/02/2005
ADR agreement terminated 07/03/2014
Each Sponsored ADR for Common exchanged for (1) share Common
Note: Unexchanged ADR's will be sold and the proceeds, if any, held for claim after 07/03/2015

STIRRUP CREEK GOLD LTD (BC)
Recapitalized as Adanac Gold Corp. 07/28/2003
Each share Common no par exchanged for (0.2) share Common no par
Adanac Gold Corp. name changed to Adanac Moly Corp. 11/04/2004 which name changed to Adanac Molybdenum Corp. 11/06/2006
(See Adanac Molybdenum Corp.)

STIRUS RESH & DEV INC (FL)
Recapitalized as Mecaserto, Inc. 11/19/1998
Each share Common $0.0001 par exchanged for (0.05) share Common $0.0001 par
Mecaserto, Inc. recapitalized as National Business Holdings, Inc. 05/25/2004 which name changed to Union Dental Holdings, Inc. 01/21/2005

STIX, BAER & FULLER CO. (MO)
Common no par changed to $10 par 00/00/1935
Each share Common $10 par exchanged for (2) shares Common $5 par 00/00/1946
Acquired by Associated Dry Goods Corp. 03/04/1963
Each share 7% Preferred $25 par exchanged for $27.50 cash
Each share Common $5 par exchanged for (0.875) share Common 50¢ par

STM CORP (NV)
Reorganized as Kramer & Lee International 09/07/1988
Each share Common $0.001 par exchanged for (10) shares Common $0.001 par
Kramer & Lee International name changed to Water U.S.A., Inc. 07/31/1992
(See Water U.S.A., Inc.)

STM WIRELESS INC (DE)
Plan of reorganization under Chapter 11 Federal Bankruptcy Code effective 09/23/2005
No stockholders' equity

STN INC (AB)
Placed in receivership and assets sold for the benefit of creditors 00/00/1995
No stockholders' equity

STN SHOP TELEVISION NETWORK LTD (BC)
Reincorporated under the laws of Delaware as Shop Television Network Inc. 12/21/1987
(See Shop Television Network Inc.)

STO-MED INC (NV)
Name changed to Advanced Technologies Inc. (NV) 08/23/1997
(See Advanced Technologies Inc. (UT))

STOCHASTIC MODELS INC (DE)
Chapter 11 bankruptcy proceedings converted to a Liquidating Chapter 11 on 01/05/1989
No stockholders' equity

STOCK & BD FD INC (MD)
Each share Class C Common no par exchanged for (1) share Class A Common no par 08/31/1994
Name changed to Federated Stock & Bond Fund, Inc. (New) (MD) 03/31/1996
Federated Stock & Bond Fund, Inc. (New) (MD) reincorporated in Massachusetts as Federated Stock & Bond Fund 09/05/2008

STOCK ACCUMULATION FD INC (IA)
Merged into Princor Capital Accumulation Fund, Inc. 05/01/1990
Each share Common $0.001 par exchanged for (0.87) share Common 1¢ par
Princor Capital Accumulation Fund, Inc. name changed to Principal Capital Value Fund, Inc. 01/01/1998
(See Principal Capital Value Fund, Inc.)

STOCK AVERAGE FD INC (MD)
Completely liquidated 00/00/1979
Details not available

STOCK BLDG SUPPLY HLDGS INC (DE)
Name changed to BMC Stock Holdings, Inc. 12/02/2015

STOCK FD AMER INC (DE)
Merged into Investment Co. of America, Inc. 06/25/1976
Each share Capital Stock $1 par exchanged for (0.550704) share Common $1 par

STOCK MKT SOLUTIONS INC (NV)
Each share old Common $0.001 par exchanged for (0.1) share new Common $0.001 par 04/10/2006
Name changed to YTXP Corp. 04/21/2006
YTXP Corp. name changed to TXP Corp. 07/10/2006
(See TXP Corp.)

STOCK-TRAK GROUP INC (NV)
Name changed from Media Survivors, Inc. 09/02/2009

STOCK WATCH MAN INC (NV)
Name changed to Nuclear Solutions, Inc. and Common $0.001 par changed to $0.0001 par 09/21/2001
Nuclear Solutions, Inc. name changed to U.S. Fuel Corp. 10/07/2011
(See U.S. Fuel Corp.)

STOCK YARDS NATIONAL BANK OF SOUTH ST. PAUL (SOUTH ST. PAUL, MN)
Stock Dividends - 20% 01/19/1956; 20% 01/16/1962
Name changed to Northwestern National Bank of South St. Paul (South St. Paul, MN) 04/10/1968
(See Northwestern National Bank of South St. Paul (South St. Paul, MN))

STOCK YDS BK & TR CO (LOUISVILLE, KY)
Name changed 07/20/1972
Name changed from Stock Yards Bank to Stock Yards Bank & Trust Co. (Louisville, KY) 07/20/1972
Stock Dividends - 100% 06/30/1983; 100% 05/01/1985
Reorganized as S.Y. Bancorp, Inc. 10/04/1988
Each share Common $10 par exchanged for (3) shares Common no par
S.Y. Bancorp, Inc. name changed to Stock Yards Bancorp, Inc. 04/25/2014

STOCKBERGER MACHINERY, INC. (IN)
Class A no par and Class B no par reclassified as Common no par 00/00/1960
Assets sold at auction 00/00/1984
No stockholders' equity

STOCKBRIDGE CAP LTD (DE)
Name changed to Export Tyre Holding Co. (Old) 05/22/1989
Export Tyre Holding Co. (Old) merged into Export Tyre Holding Co. (New) 01/31/1995
(See Export Tyre Holding Co. (New))

STOCKDALE SAVINGS & LOAN ASSOCIATION (CA)
Under plan of reorganization each share Guarantee Stock $8 par automatically became (1) share Bank of Stockdale, F.S.B. (Glendale, CA) Guarantee Stock $4 par 06/30/1991
Bank of Stockdale, F.S.B. (Bakersfield, CA) merged into VIB Corp. 01/28/1999
(See VIB Corp.)

STOCKER & YALE INC OLD (MA)
Common no par changed to $1 par 02/18/1962
Common $1 par split (2) for (1) by issuance of (1) additional share 02/20/1981
Common $1 par split (3) for (2) by issuance of (0.5) additional share 09/16/1983
Stock Dividends - 33.33333333% 05/23/1980; in Conv. Class A Common to holders of Common 100% 08/08/1986
Acquired by S&Y Acquisition Corp. 06/14/1989
Each share Common $1 par exchanged for $12 cash
Each share Conv. Class A Common $1 par exchanged for $12 cash

STOCKERYALE INC (MA)
Name changed 07/03/2000
Each share old Common no par exchanged for (0.2) share new Common no par 12/28/1995
Name changed from Stocker & Yale, Inc. (New) to StockerYale, Inc. 07/03/2000
Common no par split (2) for (1) by issuance of (1) additional share payable 07/31/2000 to holders of record 07/17/2000
Name changed to ProPhotonix Ltd. 07/23/2010

STOCKGROUP INFORMATION SYS, INC. (CO)
Name changed 09/20/2001
Name changed from Stockgroup.com Holdings, Inc. to Stockgroup Information Systems, Inc. 09/20/2001
Name changed to Stockhouse, Inc. 07/21/2008
Stockhouse, Inc. name changed to Invictus Financial Inc. 04/01/2010

STOCKGUARD CORP (ON)
Charter cancelled 01/22/2007

STOCKHOLDER SYS INC (GA)
Acquired by NYNEX Corp. 09/19/1990
Each share Class A Common 5¢ par exchanged for (0.2174) share Common $1 par
NYNEX Corp. merged into Bell Atlantic Corp. 08/14/1997

STOCKHOUSE INC (CO)
Name changed to Invictus Financial Inc. 04/01/2010

STOCKMAN LIFE INSURANCE CO. (SD)
Name changed to Stockman National Life Insurance Co. 03/31/1964
Stockman National Life Insurance Co. merged into World Service Life Insurance Co. (TX) 12/31/1970 which merged into World Service Life Insurance Co. (CO) 07/31/1978

which merged into Western Preferred Corp. 02/21/1979
(See Western Preferred Corp.)

STOCKMAN NATIONAL LIFE INSURANCE CO. (SD)
Merged into World Service Life Insurance Co. (TX) 12/31/1970
Each share Common 50¢ exchanged for either (0.25) share Common $1 par or $2.26 cash
Note: Option to receive stock expired 04/15/1971
World Service Life Insurance Co. (TX) merged into World Service Life Insurance Co. (CO) 07/31/1978 which merged into Western Preferred Corp. 02/21/1979
(See Western Preferred Corp.)

STOCKMANS BK COMM (ELK GROVE, CA)
Common no par split (4) for (3) by issuance of (0.33333333) additional share payable 10/21/1996 to holders of record 10/01/1996
Acquired by SFG Merger Co. 05/14/1999
Each share Common no par exchanged for $16.55 cash

STOCKMANS LIFE INS CO AMER (OR)
Merged into First Pacific Corp. 05/31/1968
Each share Common $1 par exchanged for (1) share Common $1 par
First Pacific Corp. liquidated for American Guaranty Financial Corp. 06/03/1971 which name changed to Encore Group Inc. 07/18/1990
(See Encore Group Inc.)

STOCKMEN ENERGY LTD (AB)
Recapitalized as Stockmen Oil & Gas Ltd. 04/14/1987
Each share Common no par exchanged for (0.1) share Common no par
Stockmen Oil & Gas Ltd. merged into Prime Petroleum Corp. 05/01/1989 which merged into Senex Petroleum Corp. 12/31/1989 which merged into Devran Petroleum Ltd. 03/01/1993 which name changed to Reserve Royalty Corp. 11/16/1995 which merged into PrimeWest Energy Trust 07/27/2000
(See PrimeWest Energy Trust)

STOCKMEN MINERALS LTD (AB)
Name changed to Indigo Gold Mines Inc. 08/18/1988
Indigo Gold Mines Inc. recapitalized as New Indigo Resources Inc. 10/05/1992 which merged into Tahera Corp. 03/01/1999 which name changed to Tahera Diamond Corp. 06/23/2004
(See Tahera Diamond Corp.)

STOCKMEN OIL & GAS LTD (AB)
Merged into Prime Petroleum Corp. 05/01/1989
Each share Common no par exchanged for (0.5) share Common no par
Prime Petroleum Corp. merged into Senex Petroleum Corp. 12/31/1989 which merged into Devran Petroleum Ltd. 03/01/1993 which name changed to Reserve Royalty Corp. 11/16/1995 which merged into PrimeWest Energy Trust 07/27/2000
(See PrimeWest Energy Trust)

STOCKMEN RES CORP (BC)
Recapitalized as Panhandle Resources Corp. 10/16/1992
Each share Common no par exchanged for (0.2) share Common no par
Panhandle Resources Corp. name changed to Abacan Resource Corp. (Old) 01/27/1993 which merged into Abacan Resource Corp. (New) 02/10/1995
(See Abacan Resource Corp. (New))

STOCKMENS BANCORP (AZ)
Merged into Zions Bancorporation 01/17/2007
Each share Common no par exchanged for (7.3831) shares Common no par
Zions Bancorporation merged into Zions Bancorporation, N.A (Salt Lake City, UT) 10/01/2018

STOCKMENS CAP TR (DE)
9% Trust Preferred Securities called for redemption at $100 on 02/23/2007

STOCKPORT EXPL INC (CANADA)
Name changed to Sona Nanotech Inc. 10/04/2018

STOCKS & STOCKS LTD (SOUTH AFRICA)
ADR agreement terminated 10/19/2004
No ADR holders' equity

STOCKSCAPE COM TECHNOLOGIES INC (BC)
Merged into Quest Investment Corp. 07/04/2002
Each share Common no par exchanged for (0.24162176) share Common no par
Quest Investment Corp. merged into Quest Capital Corp. (BC) 06/30/2003 which reincorporated in Canada 05/27/2008 which name changed to Sprott Resource Lending Corp. 09/10/2010 which merged into Sprott Inc. 07/24/2013

STOCKTON, WHATLEY, DAVIN & CO. (FL)
Stock Dividends - 10% 07/15/1955; 10% 07/31/1956
Acquired by General American Oil Co. of Texas 05/19/1964
Each share Common $4 par exchanged for (0.37840928) share Common $5 par
(See General American Oil Co. of Texas)

STOCKTON FIRE BRICK CO.
Acquired by Gladding, McBean & Co. 00/00/1943
Details not available

STOCKTON SVGS & LN ASSN (CA)
Capital Stock $1 par changed to $0.33333333 par and (2) additional shares issued 05/15/1985
Capital Stock $0.33333333 par changed to no par and (1) additional share issued 06/16/1986
Under plan of reorganization each share Capital Stock no par automatically became (1) share Common 1¢ par California Financial Holding Co. (DE) 06/01/1988
California Financial Holding Co. merged into Temple-Inland Inc. 06/27/1997
(See Temple-Inland Inc.)

STOCKTON WHITE & CO (NC)
Common $1 par split (4) for (3) by issuance of (0.33333333) additional share 02/26/1975
Merged into WhiteStock Corp. 12/31/1982
Each share Common $1 par exchanged for (1) share Common $1 par
WhiteStock Corp. liquidated for First Citizens Corp. (NC) 01/03/1985 which reorganized in Delaware as First Citizens BancShares, Inc. 10/20/1986

STOCKUP COM INC (NV)
Common no par split (2) for (1) by issuance of (1) additional share payable 09/20/1999 to holders of record 09/14/1999
Reorganized as Preference Technologies Inc. 02/23/2000
Each share Common no par exchanged for (2) shares Common no par
(See Preference Technologies Inc.)

STOCKWALK GROUP INC (MN)
Name changed 01/01/2001
Name changed from Stockwalk.com Group, Inc. to Stockwalk Group, Inc. 01/01/2001
Plan of reorganization under Chapter 11 Federal Bankruptcy Code effective 05/31/2002
Each share Common no par exchanged for $0.005 cash
Note: Unexchanged certificates were cancelled and became without value 05/21/2007

STOCO INC (UT)
Name changed to RSM Industries 10/16/1985

STOICO RESTAURANT GROUP INC (DE)
Charter cancelled and declared inoperative and void for non-payment of taxes 01/09/2002

STOKELY BROTHERS & CO., INC.
Name changed to Stokely-Van Camp, Inc. 00/00/1944
Stokely-Van Camp, Inc. merged into Quaker Oats Co. 10/31/1983
(See Stokely-Van Camp, Inc.)

STOKELY FOODS, INC.
Merged into Stokely-Van Camp, Inc. 05/29/1952
Each share $1.50 Preferred $1 par exchanged for (1.5) shares 5% Prior Preference $20 par
Each share Common 50¢ par exchanged for (2) shares Common $1 par
(See Stokely-Van Camp, Inc.)

STOKELY USA INC (WI)
Merged into Chiquita Brands International Inc. 01/16/1998
Each share Common 5¢ par exchanged for (0.066537) share Common 33¢ par
(See Chiquita Brands International, Inc.)

STOKELY VAN CAMP INC (IN)
Stock Dividends - 10% 09/20/1945; 10% 10/20/1947; 10% 10/01/1955; 10% 10/01/1956; 10% 10/02/1961
Merged into Quaker Oats Co. 10/31/1983
Each share Common $1 par exchanged for $77 cash
5% Prior Preference called for redemption at $21 plus $0.269 accrued dividends on 12/21/2001
5% Conv. 2nd Preferred $20 par called for redemption at $21 on 12/21/2001
Public interest eliminated

STOLLWERCK CHOCOLATE CO.
Liquidated 00/00/1929
Details not available

STOLT NIELSEN S A (LUXEMBOURG)
Each share Common no par received distribution of (0.5) Sponsored ADR for Class B payable 12/29/1995 to holders of record 12/26/1995
ADR agreement terminated 05/24/2007
Each Sponsored ADR for Class B exchanged for $27.92893 cash
ADR agreement terminated 02/09/2011
Each ADR for Common exchanged for $22.71414 cash

STOLT OFFSHORE S A (LUXEMBOURG)
Name changed 05/11/2000
Each share Common $2 par received distribution of (0.5) Sponsored ADR for Class A payable 06/25/1998 to holders of record 06/22/1998
Sponsored ADR's for Class A reclassified as Sponsored ADR's for Common 03/07/2001
Name changed from Stolt Comex Seaway S.A. to Stolt Offshore S.A. 05/11/2000
Name changed to Acergy S.A. 04/10/2006
Acergy S.A. name changed to Subsea 7 S.A. 01/10/2011

STOLT TANKERS & TERMS HLDGS SA (LUXEMBOURG)
Name changed to Stolt-Nielsen S.A. 06/16/1993
(See Stolt-Nielsen S.A.)

STOMPY BOT CORP (BC)
Name changed to Blocplay Entertainment Inc. 02/02/2018

STONADA MINES LTD.
Merged into Argyll Gold Mines Ltd. 00/00/1946
Each share Common exchanged for (5) shares Common
(See Argyll Gold Mines Ltd.)

STONE & THOMAS CO (WV)
Merged into Elder Beerman Acquisition Corp. 07/27/1998
Each Unit of Ltd. Partnership exchanged for $568.39 cash
Note: Details on subsequent distributions from escrow account are not available

STONE & WEBSTER INC (DE)
Capital Stock no par changed to $1 par 05/19/1958
Capital Stock $1 par split (2) for (1) by issuance of (1) additional share 01/12/1968
Capital Stock $1 par reclassified as Common $1 par 05/16/1969
Common $1 par split (2) for (1) by issuance of (1) additional share 02/27/1981
Common $1 par split (2) for (1) by issuance of (1) additional share 07/28/1989
Plan of reorganization under Chapter 11 Federal Bankruptcy Code effective 01/27/2004
Each share Common $1 par exchanged for $0.62 cash
Note: Unexchanged certificates were cancelled and became without value 01/27/2006

STONE AGRIBUSINESS FD (ON)
Trust terminated 12/16/2015
Each Trust Unit received $7.95 cash

STONE ARCADE ACQUISITION CORP (DE)
Name changed to KapStone Paper & Packaging Corp. 03/01/2007

STONE CABIN MINING CO. (NV)
Charter revoked for failure to file reports and pay fees 03/04/1929

STONE CONS CORP (CANADA)
$21.50 Class A Preferred Ser. 1 no par called for redemption 08/29/1996
Merged into Abitibi-Consolidated Inc. 05/30/1997
Each share Common no par exchanged for (1.0062) shares Common no par
Abitibi-Consolidated Inc. merged into AbitibiBowater Inc. 10/29/2007
(See AbitibiBowater Inc.)

STONE CONTAINER CORP (DE)
Reincorporated 05/20/1987
Common $1 par split (2) for (1) by issuance of (1) additional share 06/12/1962
Common $1 par split (2) for (1) by issuance of (1) additional share 04/30/1968
Common $1 par split (3) for (2) by issuance of (0.5) additional share 06/04/1976
Common $1 par split (3) for (2) by issuance of (0.5) additional share 03/13/1981
Common $1 par split (5) for (4) by issuance of (0.25) additional share 03/12/1982

STO-STO FINANCIAL INFORMATION, INC.

Common $1 par changed to no par 05/11/1982
$3.50 Conv. Exchangeable Preferred Ser. C no par called for redemption 04/27/1987
State of incorporation changed from (IL) to (DE) and Common no par changed to 1¢ par 05/20/1987
Common no par split (2) for (1) by issuance of (1) additional share 06/12/1987
Common no par split (3) for (2) by issuance of (0.5) additional share 03/11/1988
Merged into Smurfit-Stone Container Corp. (Old) 11/18/1998
Each share Common 1¢ par exchanged for (0.99) share Common 1¢ par
Merged into Smurfit-Stone Container Corp. (Old) 11/15/2000
Each share $1.75 Exchangeable Conv. Preferred Ser. E 1¢ par exchanged for (1) share 7% Exchangeable Conv. Preferred Ser. A 1¢ par
Smurfit-Stone Container Corp. (Old) reorganized as Smurfit-Stone Container Corp. (New) 06/30/2010 which merged into Rock-Tenn Co. 05/27/2011 which merged into WestRock Co. 07/01/2015

STONE E B FIN INC (NC)
98.8% acquired by Security Finance Corp. of Spartanburg through purchase offer which expired 10/13/1975
Public interest eliminated

STONE ENERGY CORP (DE)
Each share old Common 1¢ par exchanged for (0.1) share new Common 1¢ par 06/13/2016
Each share new Common 1¢ par exchanged again for (0.176263) share new Common 1¢ par and (0.622009) Common Stock Purchase Warrant expiring 02/28/2021 on 03/01/2017
Name changed to Talos Energy Inc. 05/10/2018

STONE FIELD MGMT CO (WY)
Name changed to American Radio Empire, Inc. 02/08/2006
(See American Radio Empire, Inc.)

STONE GRILL INTL INC (NV)
Name changed to Definition Ltd. 01/13/1995
Definition Ltd. name changed to Epersonnelmanagement.com 05/01/2000 which name changed to Monogram Pictures, Inc. 10/03/2000 which name changed to Vitallabs, Inc. 05/20/2002 which name changed to America Asia Corp. (NV) 10/19/2004 which reincorporated in Washington as America Asia Energy Corp. 11/08/2005 which name changed to Renegade Energy Corp. 09/14/2006 which recapitalized as Carson Development Corp. 10/20/2008
(See Carson Development Corp.)

STONE HARBOR INVESTMENTS INC (NV)
Name changed to LTS Nutraceuticals, Inc. 05/13/2011

STONE INTERNATIONAL, INC. (NV)
Recapitalized as Armas International Manufacturing Co., Inc. 05/01/1990
Each share Common $0.005 par exchanged for (0.05) share Common $0.005 par
Armas International Manufacturing Co., Inc. recapitalized as Inter-Link Communications Group, Inc. 10/23/1998 which name changed to EnterTech Media Group, Inc. 04/22/1999
(See EnterTech Media Group, Inc.)

STONE MARK CAP LTD (YT)
Reincorporated 06/21/1993
Place of incorporation changed from (Canada) to (YT) 06/21/1993
Delisted from Vancouver Stock Exchange 03/04/1994

STONE MED SUPPLY CORP (NY)
Merged into Micro Bio Medics, Inc. 01/22/1996
Each share Common 1¢ par exchanged for (0.0818) share Common 1¢ par
Micro Bio Medics, Inc. merged into Schein (Henry), Inc. 08/01/1997

STONE MOUNTAIN SCENIC RR INC (GA)
Capital Stock $1 par changed to 50¢ par and (1) additional share issued 02/15/1966
Liquidation completed
Each share Capital Stock 50¢ par received initial distribution of $1.60 cash 07/16/1981
Each share Capital Stock 50¢ par received second and final distribution of $0.1743 cash 09/10/1985
Note: Certificates were not required to be surrendered and are without value

STONE MTN HLDGS INC (BC)
Delisted from NEX 06/08/2010

STONE MTN INDS INC (CO)
Recapitalized as Indemnity Holdings, Inc. 06/30/1992
Each share Common $0.0001 par exchanged for (0.00666666) share Common $0.015 par
Indemnity Holdings, Inc. name changed to Star Casinos International, Inc. 03/01/1994
(See Star Casinos International, Inc.)

STONE MTN RES INC (DE)
Name changed to Kandi Technologies, Corp. 08/27/2007
Kandi Technologies, Corp. name changed to Kandi Technologies Group, Inc. 12/31/2012

STONE PRINTING & MANUFACTURING CO. (VA)
100% acquired by Hickory Printing Group, Inc. 00/00/1977
Public interest eliminated

STONE RIDGE EXPL CORP (BC)
Recapitalized as Sproutly Canada Inc. 07/09/2018
Each share Common no par exchanged for (0.5) share Common no par

STONE STR BANCORP INC (NC)
Merged into CCB Financial Corp. 10/02/1999
Each share Common no par exchanged for (0.48) share Common $5 par
CCB Financial Corp. merged into National Commerce Bancorporation 07/05/2000 which name changed to National Commerce Financial Corp. 04/25/2001 which merged into SunTrust Banks, Inc. 10/01/2004

STONE TAN CHINA ACQUISITION CORP (DE)
Completely liquidated 10/16/2009
Each Unit exchanged for first and final distribution of $7.98311799 cash
Each share Common $0.0001 par exchanged for first and final distribution of $7.98311799 cash

STONE TOTAL RETURN UNIT TR (ON)
Trust terminated 06/12/2009
Each Trust Unit received first and final distribution of $2.28 cash 06/12/2009

STONECHURCH INC (NV)
Each share old Common $0.001 par exchanged for (5) shares new Common $0.001 par 11/14/2005
Name changed to Gulf United Energy, Inc. 03/02/2006

STONECLIFFE CAP INC (AB)
Name changed to Ruby Red Resources Inc. 12/27/2006
Ruby Red Resources Inc. recapitalized as SG Spirit Gold Inc. (AB) 10/20/2010 which reincorporated in British Columbia 12/20/2011 which name changed to DOJA Cannabis Co. Ltd. 08/09/2017 which name changed to Hiku Brands Co. Ltd. 01/31/2018 which merged into Canopy Growth Corp. 09/06/2018

STONECUTTER MLS CORP (NC)
Name changed 00/00/1943
Name changed from Stonecutter Mills Co. to Stonecutter Mills Corp. 00/00/1943
Class A $5 par and Class B $5 par changed to $10 par 00/00/1948
Stock Dividend - (1) share Class B for each (4) shares Class A and/or Class B 03/30/1950
Out of business 06/02/1999
Details not available

STONEFIRE ENERGY CORP (AB)
Acquired by Angle Energy Inc. 01/18/2010
Each share Class A Common no par exchanged for $2 cash
Each share Class B Common no par exchanged for $10 cash

STONEGA COKE & COAL CO. (DE)
Common $100 par changed to $60 par 00/00/1940
Common $60 par changed to $15 par and (3) additional shares issued 06/04/1957
Stock Dividend - 11.11111111% 12/21/1948
Merged into Westmoreland Coal Co. (DE) 04/30/1964
Each share Common $15 par exchanged for (1.5) shares Common $10 par

STONEGATE AGRICOM LTD (ON)
Merged into Itafos 07/21/2017
Each share Common no par exchanged for (0.008) share Ordinary CAD $0.001 par
Note: Unexchanged certificates will be cancelled and become without value 07/21/2023

STONEGATE BK (POMPANO BEACH, FL) Location changed 02/13/2014
Location changed from Ft. Lauderdale, FL to Pompano Beach, FL 02/13/2014
Merged into Home BancShares, Inc. 09/26/2017
Each share Common $5 par exchanged for (2.0145) shares Common 1¢ par and $3.27 cash

STONEGATE DISTILLERY, INC. (IL)
Completely liquidated 04/30/1966
Details not available

STONEGATE MTG CORP (OH)
Acquired by Home Point Financial Corp. 06/01/2017
Each share Common 1¢ par exchanged for $8 cash

STONEHAM DRILLING TR (AB)
Merged into Western Energy Services Corp. 06/15/2011
Each Trust Unit Class A no par exchanged for (61.538) shares Common no par
Note: Unexchanged certificates were cancelled and became without value 06/15/2017

STONEHAVEN EXPL LTD (AB)
Name changed to Front Range Resources Ltd. 08/11/2016
Front Range Resources Ltd. recapitalized as Arrow Exploration Corp. 10/05/2018

STONEHAVEN RLTY TR (MD)
Name changed to Paragon Real Estate Equity & Investment Trust 07/01/2003
Paragon Real Estate Equity & Investment Trust name changed to Pillarstone Capital REIT 06/20/2016

STONELEIGH PARTNERS ACQUISITION CORP (DE)
Completely liquidated 09/08/2009
Each Unit exchanged for first and final distribution of $8.04 cash
Each share Common $0.0001 par exchanged for first and final distribution of $8.04 cash

STONEPOINT ENERGY INC (AB)
Acquired by Endurance Energy Ltd. 09/04/2015
Each share Common no par exchanged for $0.078125 cash
Note: Unexchanged certificates were cancelled and became without value 09/04/2018

STONEPOINT GROUP LTD (AB)
Reorganized under the laws of British Columbia as StonePoint Global Brands Inc. 06/30/2005
Each share Common no par exchanged for (0.1) share Common no par

STONERIDGE RES INC (DE)
Recapitalized as Acceptance Insurance Companies Inc. 12/22/1992
Each share Common 10¢ par exchanged for (0.25) share Common 40¢ par
(See Acceptance Insurance Companies Inc.)

STONES STORES, INC. (NV)
Recapitalized as Stone International, Inc. 05/01/1987
Each share Common $0.001 par exchanged for (0.2) share Common $0.005 par
Stone International, Inc. recapitalized as Armas International Manufacturing Co., Inc. 05/01/1990 which recapitalized as Inter-Link Communications Group, Inc. 10/23/1998 which name changed to EnterTech Media Group, Inc. 04/22/1999
(See EnterTech Media Group, Inc.)

STONESHIELD CAP CORP (BC)
Recapitalized as Wolfeye Resource Corp. 04/17/2013
Each share Common no par exchanged for (0.33333333) share Common no par
Wolfeye Resource Corp. name changed to Lexagene Holdings Inc. 10/19/2016

STONEWALL JACKSON LIFE INS CO (WV)
Common $1 par changed to 25¢ par 09/27/1965
Completely liquidated 09/24/1969
Each share Common 25¢ par exchanged for first and final distribution of (0.102367) share United Founders Life Insurance Co. Common $1 par
(See United Founders Life Insurance Co.)

STONEWALL RES INC (BC)
Name changed to Terra Health Corp. 04/23/1992
Terra Health Corp. recapitalized as T.H.C. Medical Inc. 12/09/1993
(See T.H.C. Medical Inc.)

STONEY CREEK MINES LTD (BC)
Recapitalized as Cyn-Tech Ventures Ltd. 07/02/1992
Each share Common no par exchanged for (0.33333333) share Common no par
Cyn-Tech Ventures Ltd. recapitalized

as Consolidated Cyn-Tech Ventures Ltd. 06/29/1995 which name changed to Trans-Orient Petroleum Ltd. (BC) 06/27/1996 which reincorporated in Yukon 09/26/1997 which reincorporated back in British Columbia 01/16/2006 which merged into TAG Oil Ltd. 12/16/2009

STONINGTON CAP CORP (CANADA)
Dividend Shares no par called for redemption at $0.40 plus $0.006055 accrued dividends on 12/31/2004
Merged into Pyxis Capital Inc. 02/27/2006
Each Multiple Share no par exchanged for (1) share Common no par
Each Subordinate Share no par exchanged for (1) Non-Vtg. Share no par
(See Pyxis Capital Inc.)

STONY CREEK RAILROAD CO.
Merged into Reading Co. 12/31/1945
Each share Common exchanged for (0.04) share Common $50 par
Reading Co. merged into Reading Entertainment Inc. (DE) 10/15/1996 which reincorporated in Nevada 12/29/1999 which merged into Reading International, Inc. 12/31/2001

STONY HILL CORP (NV)
Name changed to Applied Biosciences Corp. 03/29/2018

STONY ISLAND CORP. (IL)
Completely liquidated 01/13/1948
Each Participating Certificate no par exchanged for first and final distribution of $35 cash

STONY PASS MINING CO. (CO)
Charter dissolved for failure to pay taxes and file annual reports 01/01/1919

STONY POINT REC CORP (NY)
Chapter 11 Federal Bankruptcy proceedings converted to Chapter 7 on 01/07/1988
Stockholders' equity unlikely

STOP & SHOP, INC. (MA)
Common $1 par split (3) for (1) by issuance of (2) additional shares 05/21/1956
Stock Dividends - 10% 11/20/1950; 10% 02/15/1952; 10% 02/16/1953; 25% 11/16/1959; 25% 11/01/1960
Name changed to Stop & Shop Companies, Inc. 05/26/1970
(See Stop & Shop Companies, Inc.)

STOP & SHOP COS INC (MA)
Common $1 par split (5) for (4) by issuance of (0.25) additional share 04/01/1976
Common $1 par split (5) for (4) by issuance of (0.25) additional share 10/29/1982
Common $1 par split (2) for (1) by issuance of (1) additional share 06/30/1983
Common $1 par split (2) for (1) by issuance of (1) additional share 07/01/1987
Merged into SSC Acquisition Corp. 06/22/1988
Each share Common $1 par exchanged for $44 cash

STOP & SHOP COS INC NEW (DE)
Merged into Koninklijke Ahold N.V. 07/24/1996
Each share Common 1¢ par exchanged for $33.50 cash

STOP & SHOP LTD.
Liquidation completed 00/00/1950
Details not available

STOP CONVENIENCE FOOD STORES INC (NJ)
Name changed to Hubbard's Cupboard Inc. 05/16/1977
(See Hubbard's Cupboard Inc.)

STOP N GO FOODS INC (OH)
Merged into Sun Co., Inc. 09/10/1976
Each share Common no par exchanged for (0.274) share Common $1 par
Sun Co., Inc. name changed to Sunoco, Inc. 11/06/1998 which merged into Energy Transfer Partners, L.P. (Old) 10/05/2012 which merged into Energy Transfer Partners, L.P. (New) 02/01/2017 which merged into Energy Transfer L.P. 10/19/2018

STOP-N-SOCK LTD (NV)
Name changed to CostplusFive.Com Inc. 03/01/1999
CostplusFive.Com Inc. name changed to Computerxpress.com Inc. 03/24/2000 which name changed to Aurora Precious Metals Inc. 02/12/2003 which name changed to V-Net Beverage, Inc. 09/03/2003 which name changed to RushNet, Inc. 07/08/2005
(See RushNet, Inc.)

STOPWATCH INC (DE)
Name changed to Tirex America, Inc. 03/10/1993
Tirex America, Inc. name changed to Tirex Corp. 07/11/1997

STOR FURNISHINGS INTL INC (DE)
Merged into IKEA US West, Inc. 02/14/1992
Each share Common 1¢ par exchanged for $3.10 cash

STORAGE ACCESS TECHNOLOGIES INC (YT)
Recapitalized as BluePoint Data Storage, Inc. 01/31/2003
Each share Common no par exchanged for (0.16666666) share Common no par
BluePoint Data Storage, Inc. name changed to BluePoint Data, Inc. 07/27/2009
(See BluePoint Data, Inc.)

STORAGE ALLIANCE INC (NV)
Recapitalized as ReBuilder Medical, Inc. 11/27/2006
Each share Common $0.0001 par exchanged for (0.01) share Common $0.0001 par
ReBuilder Medical, Inc. name changed to Pizza International, Inc. 12/14/2006 which name changed to Look Entertainment, Inc. 05/23/2007 which recapitalized as VTEC, Inc. 07/05/2007 which name changed to United Consortium, Ltd. (Old) 03/10/2008 which reorganized as United Consortium, Ltd. (New) 05/05/2010

STORAGE COMPUTER CORP (DE)
Charter cancelled and declared inoperative and void for non-payment of taxes 03/01/2006

STORAGE DIMENSIONS INC (DE)
Name changed to Artecon, Inc. 04/01/1998
Artecon, Inc. merged into Dot Hill Systems Corp. (NY) 08/02/1999 which reincorporated in Delaware 09/19/2001

STORAGE ENGINE INC (NJ)
Plan of reorganization under Chapter 11 Federal Bankruptcy Code effective 07/10/2004
No stockholders' equity

STORAGE EQUITIES INC (CA)
Name changed to Public Storage, Inc. (CA) 11/16/1995
Public Storage, Inc. (CA) reincorporated in Maryland as Public Storage 06/04/2007

STORAGE INNOVATION TECHNOLOGIES INC (NV)
Reorganized under the laws of Florida as Connectyx Technologies Holdings Group, Inc. 10/29/2007
Each share Common $0.001 par exchanged for (0.001) share Common $0.001 par

STORAGE ONE INC (ON)
Name changed to EcomPark Inc. 05/19/1999
EcomPark Inc name changed to NAME Inc. 09/27/2000 which merged into itemus inc. 06/08/2001
(See itemus inc.)

STORAGE PPTYS INC (CA)
Merged into Public Storage, Inc. (CA) 06/27/1996
Each share Common 5¢ par exchanged for (0.344) share Common 5¢ par and $0.18 cash
Public Storage, Inc. (CA) reincorporated in Maryland as Public Storage 06/04/2007

STORAGE SUITES AMER INC (DE)
Each share Class A Common 50¢ par received distribution of (0.01) share Medical Career Colleges Common payable 05/30/2003 to holders of record 05/22/2003 Ex date - 06/02/2003
Recapitalized as Bio-Matrix Scientific Group, Inc. 12/20/2004
Each share Class A Common 50¢ par exchanged for (0.1) share Class A Common 50¢ par
Bio-Matrix Scientific Group, Inc. name changed to BMXP Holdings, Inc. 08/28/2006 which recapitalized as Freedom Environmental Services, Inc. 06/11/2008

STORAGE SYS INC (CO)
Name changed to Fisher Television Corp. 03/05/1999
Fisher Television Corp. recapitalized as MBC Food Corp. 04/15/2002 which recapitalized as Concorde America, Inc. 06/30/2004

STORAGE TECHNOLOGY CORP (DE)
Common 10¢ par split (2) for (1) by issuance of (1) additional share 06/14/1978
Common 10¢ par split (2) for (1) by issuance of (1) additional share 05/29/1979
Common 10¢ par changed to 1¢ par 07/28/1987
Each share Common 1¢ par exchanged for (0.1) share Common 10¢ par 05/22/1989
Each share $3.50 Conv. Exchangeable Preferred 1¢ par exchanged for (2.128) shares Common 1¢ par 12/15/1995
Note: Certificates surrendered after 12/15/1995 will receive $50 principal amount of 7% Convertible Subordinated Debenture due 03/15/2008
Common 10¢ par split (2) for (1) by issuance of (1) additional share payable 06/26/1998 to holders of record 06/05/1998 Ex date - 06/29/1998
Merged into Sun Microsystems, Inc. 08/31/2005
Each share Common 10¢ par exchanged for $37 cash

STORAGE TR RLTY (MD)
Merged into Public Storage, Inc. (CA) 03/12/1999
Each Share of Bene. Int. 1¢ par exchanged for (0.86) share Common 10¢ par
Public Storage, Inc. (CA) reincorporated in Maryland as Public Storage 06/04/2007

STORAGE USA INC (TN)
Merged into Security Capital Group Inc. 04/26/2002
Each share Common 1¢ par exchanged for $42.70 cash

STORAGEFLOW SYS CORP (AB)
Reincorporated 06/19/2002
Place of incorporation changed from (BC) to (AB) 06/19/2002

Recapitalized as Northern Pine Ventures Inc. (AB) 11/21/2003
Each share Common no par exchanged for (0.2) share Common no par
Northern Pine Ventures Inc. (AB) reincorporated in British Columbia as Landmark Minerals Inc. 07/18/2005 which merged into Ucore Uranium Inc. 08/17/2007 which name changed to Ucore Rare Metals Inc. 06/29/2010

STORAGENETWORKS INC (DE)
In process of liquidation
Each share Common 1¢ par received initial distribution of $1.6529 cash payable 11/03/2003 to holders of record 10/28/2003 Ex date - 11/04/2003
Note: Amount or number of additional distribution(s), if any, are not available

STORER COMMUNICATIONS INC (OH)
Name changed 01/01/1983
Common $1 par split (2) for (1) by issuance of (1) additional share 02/25/1955
7% Conv. Preferred $100 par called for redemption 07/01/1955
Common $1 par split (2) for (1) by issuance of (1) additional share 12/28/1965
Common $1 par split (5) for (4) by issuance of (0.25) additional share 10/29/1976
Common $1 par split (2) for (1) by issuance of (1) additional share 11/19/1979
Name changed from Storer Broadcasting Co. to Storer Communications, Inc. 01/01/1983
Merged into SCI Holdings, Inc. 12/05/1985
Each share Common $1 par exchanged for (1) Common Stock Purchase Warrant expiring 12/05/1995 and $91 cash

STORESCOPE TV INC (DE)
Proclaimed inoperative and void for non-payment of taxes 04/15/1970

STORIMIN EXPL LTD (CANADA)
Each share Common no par reclassified as (1) share Common no par and (1) share Class B no par 09/26/1995
Plan of arrangement effective 09/28/1995
Each share Class B no par exchanged for (0.5) share Moss Lake Gold Mines Ltd. Common no par
(See Moss Lake Gold Mines Ltd.)
Recapitalized as Storimin Resources Ltd. (Canada) 03/31/1997
Each share Common no par exchanged for (0.33333333) share Common no par
Storimin Resources Ltd. (Canada) reincorporated in Ontario 10/30/1998 which recapitalized as Digital Rooster.com Inc. 01/19/2000 which recapitalized as Digital Rooster.com Ltd. 12/02/2002 which name changed to Phinder Technologies Inc. (ON) 02/07/2005 which reincorporated in Florida 01/19/2007 which name changed to Zupintra Corp., Inc. 06/21/2007
(See Zupintra Corp., Inc.)

STORIMIN RES LTD (ON)
Recapitalized as Digital Rooster.com Inc. 01/19/2000
Each share Common no par exchanged for (0.08333333) share Common no par
Digital Rooster.com Inc. recapitalized as Digital Rooster.com Ltd. 12/02/2002 which name changed to Phinder Technologies Inc. (ON) 02/07/2005 which reincorporated in Florida 01/19/2007 which name

changed to Zupintra Corp., Inc. 06/21/2007
(See Zupintra Corp., Inc.)

STORKLINE CORP. (IL)
Common $10 par changed to $5 par and (1) additional share issued 12/07/1960
Common $5 par split (5) for (1) by issuance of (4) additional shares 11/26/1963
Name changed to MPI Industries, Inc. (IL) 03/31/1964
MPI Industries, Inc. (IL) reincorporated in Delaware 04/05/1968 which merged into DeSoto, Inc. 11/03/1969 which merged into Keystone Consolidated Industries, Inc. 09/27/1996
(See Keystone Consolidated Industries, Inc.)

STORKLINE FURNITURE CORP. (IL)
Each share 8% Preference $25 par exchanged for (2) shares Common $10 par and $2 cash 00/00/1936
Each share Common no par exchanged for (0.5) share Common $10 par 00/00/1936
Name changed to Storkline Corp. 11/30/1960
Storkline Corp. name changed to MPI Industries, Inc. (IL) 03/31/1964 which reincorporated in Delaware 04/05/1968 which merged into DeSoto, Inc. 11/03/1969 which merged into Keystone Consolidated Industries, Inc. 09/27/1996
(See Keystone Consolidated Industries, Inc.)

STORM CLOUD DEV CORP (BC)
Struck off register and declared dissolved for failure to file returns 06/10/1983

STORM DRILLING & MARINE INC (DE)
Merged into Odeco Drilling Inc. 05/30/1975
Each share Common $4 par exchanged for $29 cash

STORM ENERGY INC (AB)
Each share old Common no par exchanged for (0.2) share new Common no par 03/23/1999
Plan of arrangement effective 08/23/2002
Each share new Common no par exchanged for (1) Focus Energy Trust, Trust Unit no par and (1) share Storm Energy Ltd. Common no par
Note: Canadian residents had the option to receive (1) FET Resources Ltd. Exchangeable share in lieu of Focus Energy Trust, Trust Unit
(See each company's listing)

STORM ENERGY LTD (AB)
Plan of arrangement effective 6/25/2004
Each share Common no par exchanged for (0.05905) Harvest Energy Trust Trust Unit no par, (0.053) share Rock Energy Inc. Common no par, (1) share Storm Explorations Inc. Common no par, (1) Warrant Note with a principal amount of $0.02 and $3.2779 cash
(See each company's listing)

STORM EXPL INC (CANADA)
Merged into ARC Energy Trust 08/17/2010
Each share Common no par exchanged for (0.57) Trust Unit, (0.33333333) share Storm Resources Ltd. Common no par and (0.13332) Storm Resources Ltd. Common Stock Purchase Warrant expiring 09/08/2010 and $1 cash
(See each company's listing)

STORM HIGH PERFORMANCE SOUND CORP (FL)
Reincorporated under the laws of Nevada as Magellan Filmed Entertainment, Inc. 09/26/2000
Magellan Filmed Entertainment, Inc. recapitalized as Magellan Industries, Inc. 09/21/2004
(See Magellan Industries, Inc.)

STORM KING MINES INC (CO)
Name changed to New Castle Energy Corp. 08/16/1985
(See New Castle Energy Corp.)

STORM VENTURES INTL INC (AB)
Under plan of merger name changed to Chinook Energy Inc. (Old) 07/05/2010
(See Chinook Energy Inc. (Old))

STORMEDIA INC (DE)
Class A Common $0.013 par split (3) for (2) by issuance of (0.5) additional share payable 05/28/1996 to holders of record 05/13/1996
Plan of reorganization under Chapter 11 Federal Bankruptcy proceedings effective 03/00/2000
No stockholders' equity

STORMFELTZ-LOVELEY CO. FORECLOSURE TRUST
Liquidation completed 00/00/1947
Details not available

STORMIN RES INC (BC)
Name changed to Biocoll Medical Corp. 12/22/1992
Biocoll Medical Corp. merged into GenSci Regeneration Sciences Inc. 08/12/1997
(See GenSci Regeneration Sciences Inc.)

STORMKING AIRCRAFT CORP., INC. (NV)
Charter revoked for failure to file reports and pay fees 03/05/1934

STORMONT GOLD MINES LTD. (ON)
Charter cancelled 10/21/1957

STORNAWAY CAP DEV CORP (BC)
Name changed 01/07/1988
Name changed from Stornaway Resources Corp. to Stornaway Capital Development Corp. 01/07/1988
Delisted from Vancouver Stock Exchange 05/02/1991

STORNOWAY DIAMOND CORP (BC)
Each share old Common no par exchanged for (0.25) share new Common no par 02/22/2011
Reincorporated under the laws of Canada 10/28/2011

STORNOWAY VENTURES LTD (BC)
Merged into Stornoway Diamond Corp. (BC) 07/10/2003
Each share Common no par exchanged for (0.8734) share Common no par
Stornoway Diamond Corp. (BC) reincorporated in Canada 10/28/2011

STORY CHEM CORP (GA)
Merged into Swanton Corp. 01/31/1983
Each share Common no par exchanged for (0.01538461) share Common 10¢ par
(See Swanton Corp.)

STORYBOOK VLG INC (NY)
Dissolved by proclamation 06/27/1979

STOTLER GROUP INC (IL)
Filed a petition under Chapter 7 Federal Bankruptcy Code 08/24/1990
Stockholders' equity unlikely

STOUFFER CORP (OH)
Each share old Class B no par exchanged for (5) shares new Class B no par 00/00/1940
New Class B no par reclassified as Common $5 par 00/00/1946
Each share Common $5 par exchanged for (2) shares Common $2.50 par 00/00/1949
Common $2.50 par changed to $1.25 par and (1) additional share issued 04/01/1957
Name changed to Stouffer Foods Corp. 10/13/1961
Stouffer Foods Corp. merged into Litton Industries, Inc. 10/04/1967
(See Litton Industries, Inc.)

STOUFFER FOODS CORP. (OH)
Common $1.25 par changed to no par 10/11/1962
Common no par split (2) for (1) by issuance of (1) additional share 08/31/1965
Merged into Litton Industries, Inc. 10/04/1967
Each share Common no par exchanged for (0.312) share Common $1 par
(See Litton Industries, Inc.)

STOUT-D. & C. AIRLINES, INC.
Assets purchased by North American Aviation Corp. and company liquidated 00/00/1930
Details not available

STOUT OIL CO. (CO)
Declared defunct and inoperative for failure to pay taxes and file reports 03/23/1957

STOVALL TWENTY FIRST CONSISTENT RETURN TR (MA)
Merged into Eaton Vance Total Return Trust 02/24/1989
Details not available

STOVE CREEK DOME OIL & REFINING CO. (UT)
Merged into Big Piney Oil & Uranium Co. on a share for share basis 07/01/1955
Big Piney Oil & Uranium Co. name changed to Big Piney Oil & Gas Co. 03/29/1957 which merged into National Energy Group, Inc. 06/11/1991
(See National Energy Group, Inc.)

STOVEL-ADVOCATE PRESS LTD. (CANADA)
Acquired by Lawson & Jones Ltd. 00/00/1960
Each share Common exchanged for $1.75 cash

STOVEL PRESS, LTD. (CANADA)
Merged into Stovel-Advocate Press Ltd. 00/00/1952
Each share Common exchanged for (1) share Common
(See Stovel-Advocate Press Ltd.)

STOVER GOLD MINES LTD. (ON)
Charter cancelled and declared dissolved for failure to file returns and pay fees 11/22/1972

STOW RES LTD (BC)
Merged into Leicester Diamond Mines Ltd. 06/01/1993
Each share Common no par exchanged for (1) share Common no par
Leicester Diamond Mines Ltd. recapitalized as Target Exploration & Mining Corp. 04/30/2004 which merged into Crosshair Exploration & Mining Corp. 03/31/2009 which name changed to Crosshair Energy Corp. 11/02/2011 which recapitalized as Jet Metal Corp. (BC) 09/23/2013 which reorganized in Canada as Canada Jetlines Ltd. 03/07/2017

STOWE-FULLER REFRACTORIES CO.
Dissolved 00/00/1952
Details not available

STOWE R L MLS INC (NC)
Acquired 03/25/1998
Each share Common $10 par exchanged for $45 cash

STOWE SPINNING CO (NC)
Merged into Stowe (R.L.) Mills, Inc. 09/28/1985
Each share Capital Stock $100 par exchanged for (20) shares Common $10 par
(See Stowe (R.L.) Mills, Inc.)

STOWE-WOODWARD, INC. (MA)
Name changed to S W Industries, Inc. 03/23/1965
(See S W Industries, Inc.)

STOX COM INC (CANADA)
Dissolved for non-compliance 07/06/2005
Stockholders' equity unlikely

STOX INFOLINK SYS INC (CANADA)
Name changed to stox.com Inc. 02/24/1999
(See Stox.Com Inc.)

STP CORP (DE)
Merged into Esmark, Inc. (Inc. 03/14/1969) 05/11/1978
Each share Common $1 par exchanged for $22.50 cash

STRACHAN INC (NV)
Reorganized as Lighttouch Vein & Laser, Inc. 11/15/1999
Each share Common $0.001 par exchanged for (1.6304347) shares Common $0.001 par
LightTouch Vein & Laser, Inc. name changed to Grow Solutions Holdings, Inc. 07/09/2015

STRACHAN RES LTD (BC)
Name changed to Lotus Ventures Inc. 12/08/2014

STRADER CONSTR INC (DE)
Charter cancelled and declared inoperative and void for non-payment of taxes 04/15/1973

STRAIGHT PATH COMMUNICATIONS INC (DE)
Merged into Verizon Communications Inc. 02/28/2018
Each share Class B Common 1¢ par exchanged for (3.7969) shares Common 10¢ par

STRAINWISE INC (UT)
Reincorporated under the laws of Colorado as STWC Holdings, Inc. and Common no par changed to $0.00001 par 11/14/2016

STRAIT GOLD CORP (ON)
Name changed to Strait Minerals Inc. 08/01/2012
Strait Minerals Inc. recapitalized as Montan Mining Corp. 03/09/2015

STRAIT MINERALS INC (ON)
Recapitalized as Montan Mining Corp. 03/09/2015
Each share Common no par exchanged for (0.1) share Common no par

STRAITS ASIA RES LTD (SINGAPORE)
Name changed to Sakari Resources Ltd. 08/25/2011
(See Sakari Resources Ltd.)

STRAITS OIL & GAS LTD (AUSTRALIA)
Each share old Ordinary A AUD $0.20 par exchanged for (0.4) share new Ordinary A AUD $0.20 par 10/08/1991
Name changed to Pyrenees Gold Corp. 10/02/1994
(See Pyrenees Gold Corp.)

STRAITS TOWING LTD (BC)
Merged into Rivtow Straits Ltd. 11/16/1970
Each share Class A no par exchanged for (3) shares Common $1 par
Each share Class B no par exchanged for (5.08336) shares Common $1 par
(See Rivtow Straits Ltd.)

STRALEM FD (DE)
Name changed 04/30/1999
Name changed from Stralem Fund, Inc. to Stralem Fund 04/30/1999

Common $1 par reclassified as Balanced Fund $1 par 03/26/2003
Balanced Fund $1 par completely liquidated 03/15/2007
Details not available
(Additional Information in Active)

STRALEM TECHNOLOGY FUND, INC. (DE)
Name changed to Stralem Fund, Inc. 03/28/1974
Stralem Fund, Inc. name changed to Stralem Fund 04/30/1999
(See Stralem Fund)

STRAND OIL & GAS LTD (AB)
Recapitalized as Bowtex Energy (Canada) Corp. 01/23/1987
Each share Common no par exchanged for (0.2) share Common no par
Bowtex Energy (Canada) Corp. name changed to Luscar Oil & Gas Ltd. 10/21/1993 which merged into Encal Energy Ltd. 07/13/1994 which merged into Calpine Canada Holdings Ltd. 04/19/2001 which was exchanged for Calpine Corp. 05/27/2002
(See Calpine Corp.)

STRAND RES INC (BC)
Reorganized as under the laws of Canada as Tri-Star Gold Corp. 10/24/1996
Each share Common no par exchanged for (1) share Common no par
(See Tri-Star Gold Corp.)

STRANDTEK INTL INC (DE)
Charter cancelled and declared inoperative and void for non-payment of taxes 03/01/2004

STRANNAR MINES LTD. (ON)
Dissolved 11/01/1965
Details not available

STRAT PETE LTD (NV)
Each share old Common no par exchanged for (0.07692307) share new Common no par 12/10/2004
Charter revoked for failure to file reports and pay fees 09/30/2008

STRATA CAP CORP (DE)
Each (15) shares Common $0.001 par exchanged for (1) share old Common $0.000001 par 05/28/2010
Note: No holder will receive fewer than (100) post-split shares
Each share old Common $0.000001 par exchanged for (0.001) share new Common $0.000001 par 07/09/2010
Note: No holder will receive fewer than (100) post-split shares
Name changed to Metrospaces, Inc. 02/13/2013

STRATA COAL CO (NV)
Name changed to Delmar Management Inc. 11/26/2002
Delmar Management Inc. name changed to 2energia Inc. 01/31/2003 which name changed to Coastal Holdings, Inc. 07/02/2003 which name changed to Canadian Blue Gold, Inc. 10/18/2007 which recapitalized as Boreal Water Collection, Inc. 03/19/2008
(See Boreal Water Collection, Inc.)

STRATA CORP (DE)
Name changed to B.T. Energy Corp. 09/07/1989
(See B.T. Energy Corp.)

STRATA CORP (OH)
Class A Common no par split (5) for (4) by issuance of (0.25) additional share 10/15/1982
Reorganized under the laws of Delaware 08/02/1983
Each share Class A Common no par exchanged for (1) share Class A Common no par
Strata Corp. (DE) name changed to B.T. Energy Corp. 09/07/1989
(See B.T. Energy Corp.)

STRATA ENERGY CORP (BC)
Name changed to U.S. Platinum Inc. 07/20/1987
U.S. Platinum Inc. name changed to Universal Energy Corp. 01/10/2006 which name changed to Supreme Resources Ltd. 02/09/2007 which name changed to Supreme Pharmaceuticals Inc. (BC) 03/14/2014 which reincorporated in Canada 12/21/2015 which name changed to Supreme Cannabis Co. Inc. 12/29/2017

STRATA MINERALS INC (CANADA)
Reincorporated 03/27/2017
Each share old Common no par exchanged for (0.1) share new Common no par 01/13/2014
Place of incorporation changed from Canada to Ontario 03/27/2017
Each share new Common no par exchanged for (0.1) share Common no par
Name changed to Revival Gold Inc. 07/10/2017

STRATA SEARCH INC (DE)
Charter forfeited for failure to maintain a registered agent 02/25/1991

STRATA-X LTD (AB)
Reincorporated under the laws of British Columbia as Strata-X Energy Ltd. 10/12/2012

STRATABASE (NV)
Name changed 03/30/2001
Name changed from Stratabase.Com to Stratabase 03/30/2001
Reincorporated under the laws of Canada as Stratabase Inc. and Common $0.001 par changed to no par 08/17/2004
Stratabase Inc. name changed to Strata Oil & Gas Inc. 07/15/2005

STRATABASE INC (CANADA)
Name changed to Strata Oil & Gas Inc. 07/15/2005

STRATABID COM INC (DE)
Name changed to Bodisen Biotech, Inc. 03/01/2004
(See Bodisen Biotech, Inc.)

STRATACOM INC (DE)
Common 1¢ par split (2) for (1) by issuance of (1) additional share 12/15/1994
Common 1¢ par split (2) for (1) by issuance of (1) additional share payable 02/15/1996 to holders of record 02/01/1996
Merged into Cisco Systems, Inc. 07/09/1996
Each share Common 1¢ par exchanged for (1) share Common no par

STRATACOM TECHNOLOGY INC (BC)
Name changed to Strategic Oil & Gas Ltd. (BC) 03/31/2005
Strategic Oil & Gas Ltd. (BC) reincorporated in Alberta 09/09/2010

STRATAGENE CORP (DE)
Merged into Agilent Technologies, Inc. 06/07/2007
Each share Common $0.0001 par exchanged for $10.94 cash

STRATAGOLD CORP (BC)
Acquired by Victoria Gold Corp. 06/08/2009
Each share Common no par exchanged for (0.1249) share Common no par

STRATAMERICA CORP (UT)
Name changed to Dreams, Inc. 04/09/1996
(See Dreams, Inc.)

STRATAPROP INVTS LTD (AB)
Recapitalized as Allied Equities Ltd. 10/28/1991
Each share Class A Common no par exchanged for (0.33333333) share Class A Common no par
(See Allied Equities Ltd.)

STRATAS LTD (ON)
Charter cancelled for failure to file reports and pay taxes 12/31/1990

STRATASYS INC (DE)
Common 1¢ par split (3) for (2) by issuance of (0.5) additional share payable 12/19/2003 to holders of record 11/20/2003 Ex date - 12/22/2003
Common 1¢ par split (2) for (1) by issuance of (1) additional share payable 08/29/2007 to holders of record 08/15/2007 Ex date - 08/30/2007
Merged into Stratasys Ltd. 12/03/2012
Each share Common 1¢ par exchanged for (1) share Ordinary ILS 0.01 par

STRATCOMM MEDIA LTD (YT)
Reincorporated 11/12/1997
Place of incorporation changed from (BC) to (YT) 11/12/1997
Common no par split (10) for (1) by issuance of (9) additional shares payable 02/08/2002 to holders of record 01/25/2002
Delisted from Canadian Venture Stock Exchange 02/08/2002

STRATEAN INC (NV)
Common $0.001 par split (3) for (1) by issuance of (2) additional shares payable 05/13/2015 to holders of record 05/13/2015
Name changed to Cleanspark, Inc. 11/14/2016

STRATEGABIZ INC (DE)
Name changed to CryptoSign, Inc. 07/06/2015
CryptoSign, Inc. name changed to NABUfit Global, Inc. 12/10/2015 which name changed to NewBridge Global Ventures, Inc. 12/12/2017

STRATEGIA CORP (KY)
Under plan of partial liquidation each share Common no par received initial distribution of $1.95 cash 10/27/2000
Each share Common no par received second distribution of $0.115 cash payable 12/01/2000 to holders of record 11/30/2000
Each share Common no par received third distribution of $0.11 cash payable 12/06/2000 to holders of record 12/01/2000
Reorganized under the laws of Nevada as Catthai Corp. 08/20/2008
Each share Common no par exchanged for (0.01) share Common $0.001 par
(See Catthai Corp.)

STRATEGIC ABSTRACT & TITLE CORP (DE)
Recapitalized as SA Holdings, Inc. 02/18/1992
Each share Common $0.0001 par exchanged for (0.1) share Common $0.0001 par
SA Holdings, Inc. name changed to SA Telecommunications, Inc. 08/03/1995
(See SA Telecommunications, Inc.)

STRATEGIC ACQUISITIONS INC (CO)
Name changed to National Securities Holding Corp. 11/30/1989
National Securities Holding Corp. recapitalized as New Frontier Media Inc. 09/15/1995
(See New Frontier Media Inc.)

STRATEGIC ALLIANCE GROUP INC (FL)
Each share old Common 10¢ par exchanged for (0.004) share new Common 10¢ par 11/04/2003
Name changed to CruiseCam International, Inc. 07/30/2004
Each share new Common 10¢ par exchanged for (1) share Common 10¢ par

STRATEGIC AMERN OIL CORP (NV)
Recapitalized as Duma Energy Corp. 04/04/2012
Each share Common $0.001 par exchanged for (0.04) share Common $0.001 par
Duma Energy Corp. name changed to Hydrocarb Energy Corp. 02/18/2014

STRATEGIC AUTOMATED SYS INC (UT)
Name changed to Strategic Medical Research Corp. (UT) 10/25/1971
Strategic Medical Research Corp. (UT) merged into Strategic Medical Research Corp. (DE) 08/04/1972 which name changed to Greenwich Pharmaceuticals Inc. 03/20/1979 which name changed to Boston Life Sciences, Inc. 06/15/1995 which name changed to Alseres Pharmaceuticals, Inc. 06/11/2007

STRATEGIC AUTOMATED SYS INTL INC (DE)
Reincorporated 03/07/1972
State of incorporation changed from (UT) to (DE) 03/07/1972
Name changed to Superblock Industries Inc. 06/30/1978
Superblock Industries Inc. recapitalized as Trilogy Gaming Corp. 01/31/1996 which name changed to TELnet go 2000, Inc. 01/01/2000
(See TELnet go 2000, Inc.)

STRATEGIC CAP BANCORP INC (IL)
Company's sole asset placed in receivership 05/22/2009
Stockholders' equity unlikely

STRATEGIC CAP GAINS INC (TX)
Name changed to Strategic Gold/Minerals Fund, Inc. 07/28/1988
(See Strategic Gold/Minerals Fund, Inc.)

STRATEGIC CAP RES INC (FL)
Reincorporated 8/14/2003
Each share old Common $0.001 par exchanged for (0.005) share new Common $0.001 par 6/17/2002
State of incorporation changed from (DE) to (FL) 8/14/2003
Merged into Mergerco, Inc. 2/4/2004
Each share new Common $0.001 par exchanged for $25 cash

STRATEGIC COMMUNICATIONS LTD (BC)
Recapitalized as Stratcomm Media Ltd. (BC) 07/05/1991
Each share Common no par exchanged for (0.2) share Common no par
Stratcomm Media Ltd. (BC) reincorporated in Yukon 11/12/1997
(See Stratcomm Media Ltd.)

STRATEGIC DATA CTRS INC (NY)
Merged into Strategic Industries, Inc. (New) 10/09/1969
Each share Common 1¢ par exchanged for (1) share Common 1¢ par
(See Strategic Industries, Inc. (New))

STRATEGIC DATA LTD (AB)
Recapitalized 01/17/1997
Recapitalized from Strategic Data Inc. to Strategic Data Ltd. 01/17/1997
Each share Common no par exchanged for (0.25) share Common no par
Name changed to Securex Ltd. 06/18/2001
(See Securex Ltd.)

STRATEGIC DATA TRANS INC (NY)
Merged into Strategic Industries, Inc. (New) 10/09/1969
Each share Common 1¢ par exchanged for (0.285714) share Common 1¢ par
(See Strategic Industries, Inc. (New))

STRATEGIC DENTAL MGMT CORP (CO)
Reorganized under the laws of Delaware as Drywave Technologies, Inc. 07/16/2013
Each share Common $0.001 par exchanged for (22.75) shares Common $0.001 par
Drywave Technologies, Inc. recapitalized as Bionik Laboratories Corp. 02/13/2015

STRATEGIC DIAGNOSTICS INC NEW (DE)
Name changed to Special Diversified Opportunities Inc. 09/19/2013
Special Diversified Opportunities Inc. recapitalized as Standard Diversified Opportunities Inc. 06/02/2017 which name changed to Standard Diversified Inc. 04/25/2018

STRATEGIC DIAGNOSTICS INC OLD (DE)
Merged into EnSys Environmental Products Inc. 12/30/1996
Each share Conv. Preferred Ser. A 1¢ par exchanged for (0.7392048) share Conv. Preferred Ser. A 1¢ par
Each share Common 1¢ par exchanged for (0.7392048) share Common 1¢ par
EnSys Environmental Products Inc. name changed to Strategic Diagnostics Inc. (New) 01/02/1997 which name changed to Special Diversified Opportunities Inc. 09/19/2013 which recapitalized as Standard Diversified Opportunities Inc. 06/02/2017 which name changed to Standard Diversified Inc. 04/25/2018

STRATEGIC DISTR INC (DE)
Each share old Common 10¢ par exchanged for (0.1) share new Common 10¢ par 05/17/2001
Merged into Project Eagle Holding Corp. 03/29/2007
Each share new Common 1¢ par exchanged for $10 cash

STRATEGIC ENERGY FD (ON)
Each Trust Unit received distribution of (1) SEF Private Issuers Trust Unit payable 02/24/2009 to holders of record 02/04/2009
Under plan of reorganization each Trust Unit automatically became (1) Sentry Select Energy Income Fund Ser. A Unit 02/24/2009

STRATEGIC EQUITIES INC (NY)
Recapitalized as Southeastern Agricultural Industries, Inc. 08/01/1975
Each share Common 1¢ par exchanged for (0.33333333) share Common 1¢ par
(See Southeastern Agricultural Industries, Inc.)

STRATEGIC EXPL INC (CANADA)
Dissolved for non-compliance 07/23/2009

STRATEGIC FACS INC (NY)
Merged into Strategic Industries, Inc. (New) 10/09/1969
Each share Common 1¢ par exchanged for (0.33333333) share Common 1¢ par
(See Strategic Industries, Inc. (New))

STRATEGIC GAMING INVTS INC (DE)
Each share Common $0.001 par received distribution of (2) shares Strategic Gaming Investments, Inc. (NV) Restricted Common payable 09/10/2008 to holders of record 09/03/2008
Recapitalized as Amerigo Energy, Inc. 09/11/2008
Each share Common $0.001 par exchanged for (0.05) share Common $0.001 par
Amerigo Energy, Inc. name changed to Quest Solution, Inc. 06/10/2014

STRATEGIC GLOBAL INCOME FD INC (MD)
Completely liquidated
Each share Common $0.001 par received first and final distribution of $9.0767 cash payable 05/25/2016 to holders of record 05/18/2016

STRATEGIC GOLD/MINERALS FUND, INC. (TX)
Voluntarily dissolved 01/12/1993
Details not available

STRATEGIC GROWTH VENTURES INC (NV)
Recapitalized as Beere Financial Group, Inc. 05/31/2006
Each share Common $0.001 par exchanged for (0.2) share Common $0.001 par
Beere Financial Group, Inc. recapitalized as Steadfast Holdings Group, Inc. 10/01/2007 which recapitalized as Scorpex, Inc. 05/20/2011

STRATEGIC HOTELS & RESORTS INC (MD)
Name changed 03/15/2006
Name changed from Strategic Hotel Capital, Inc. to Strategic Hotels & Resorts, Inc. 03/15/2006
8.5% Preferred Ser. A 1¢ par called for redemption at $25 plus $0.548959 accrued dividends on 04/03/2014
8.25% Preferred Ser. C 1¢ par called for redemption at $25 plus $0.01719 accrued dividends on 07/03/2014
8.25% Preferred Ser. B 1¢ par called for redemption at $25 plus $0.028646 accrued dividends on 01/05/2015
Acquired by BRE Diamond Hotel Holdings LLC 12/11/2015
Each share Common 1¢ par exchanged for $14.25 cash

STRATEGIC INCOME ALLOCATION FD (ON)
Trust terminated 03/24/2017
Each Trust Unit received $7.32779 cash

STRATEGIC INDUSTRIES INC. (DE)
Reincorporated 01/22/1990
State of incorporation changed from (WY) to (DE) 01/22/1990 Company bankrupt 03/01/1991
Details not available

STRATEGIC INDS INC NEW (NY)
Merged 10/09/1969
Merged from Strategic Industries, Inc. (Old) into Strategic Industries, Inc. (New) 10/09/1969
Each share Common 1¢ par exchanged for (1) share Common 1¢ par
Assignment for benefit of creditors instituted 07/13/1971
Attorney opined that there will be no stockholders' equity

STRATEGIC INFORMATION INC (DE)
Name changed to Strategic Distribution, Inc. and Conv. Class A Common 10¢ par,
Class B Common 10¢ par reclassified as Common 10¢ par 11/09/1990
(See Strategic Distribution, Inc.)

STRATEGIC LD MGMT INC (FL)
Recapitalized as China Now, Inc. 07/13/2006
Each share Common $0.001 par exchanged for (0.002) share Common $0.001 par
(See China Now, Inc.)

STRATEGIC MGMT & OPPORTUNITY CORP OLD (NV)
Stock Dividend - 3% payable 02/22/2011 to holders of record 01/19/2011
Reorganized as Strategic Management & Opportunity Corp. (New) 09/25/2018
Each share Common $0.001 par exchanged for (0.0002) share Common $0.001 par

STRATEGIC MGMT INC (UT)
Name changed to Solar-Physics Corp. 12/16/1975
Solar-Physics Corp. name changed to LeJay Corp. 08/28/1980 which name changed to Drumm Corp. 09/24/1983 which name changed to Horti-Tech Inc. 01/07/1986
(See Horti-Tech Inc.)

STRATEGIC MATLS CORP (NY)
Adjudicated bankrupt 05/09/1969
Trustee's opinion: Common Stock has no value

STRATEGIC MED RESH CORP (DE)
Name changed to Greenwich Pharmaceuticals Inc. 03/20/1979
Greenwich Pharmaceuticals Inc. name changed to Boston Life Sciences, Inc. 06/15/1995 which name changed to Alseres Pharmaceuticals, Inc. 06/11/2007

STRATEGIC MED RESH CORP (UT)
Merged into Strategic Medical Research Corp. (DE) 08/04/1972
Each share Common $1 par exchanged for (3) shares Common 10¢ par
Strategic Medical Research Corp. (DE) name changed to Greenwich Pharmaceuticals Inc. 03/20/1979 which name changed to Boston Life Sciences, Inc. 06/15/1995 which name changed to Alseres Pharmaceuticals, Inc. 06/11/2007

STRATEGIC MERCHANT BANCORP INC (BC)
Name changed to Strategic Nevada Resources Corp. 08/03/2006
Strategic Nevada Resources Corp. name changed to SNS Silver Corp. 02/26/2007 which name changed to SNS Precious Metals Inc. 05/17/2010 which recapitalized as Gold Finder Explorations Ltd. 10/08/2010 which recapitalized as Venzee Technologies Inc. 01/05/2018

STRATEGIC METALS CORP (BC)
Merged into Consolidated Strategic Metals Inc. 03/29/1982
Each share Common no par exchanged for (0.75) share Common no par
Consolidated Strategic Metals Inc. name changed to New Strategic Metals Inc. 05/25/1983 which name changed to P.S.M. Technologies Inc. 12/29/1986
(See P.S.M. Technologies Inc.)

STRATEGIC METALS LTD OLD (BC)
Each share old Common no par received distribution of (0.25) share Zinccorp Resources Inc. Common no par and (0.25) Common Stock Purchase Warrant expiring 10/02/2009 payable 07/10/2008 to holders of record 07/09/2008
Each share old Common no par received distribution of (0.33333333) share Silver Range Resources Ltd. Common no par and (0.16666667) Common Stock Purchase Warrant expiring 02/10/2013 payable 08/10/2011 to holders of record 07/27/2011
Old Common no par reclassified as new Common no par 08/10/2011
Plan of arrangement effective 06/15/2017
Each share new Common no par automatically became (1) share Strategic Metals Ltd. (New) Common no par and received distribution of (0.22222222) share Trifecta Gold Ltd. Common no par

STRATEGIC METALS RESH INC (UT)
Capital Stock 1¢ par changed to 10¢ par 12/26/1959
Merged into Worldcom, Inc. 02/17/1972
Each share Capital Stock 10¢ par exchanged for (0.062165) share Common 10¢ par
Worldcom, Inc. name changed to Charter West Corp. 06/28/1982 which name changed to Sellinger Pharmaceuticals Inc. 06/22/1983 which name changed to Promedica Inc. 06/28/1988 which name changed to Zhou Lin International Inc. 11/28/1994 which name changed to Renu-U-International Inc. 12/24/1996 which name changed to Colormax Technologies, Inc. 09/07/1999
(See Colormax Technologies, Inc.)

STRATEGIC MINERALS PLC (UNITED KINGDOM)
ADR agreement terminated 10/09/2018
Each Sponsored ADR for Ordinary exchanged for (100) shares Ordinary
Note: Unexchanged ADR's will be sold and the proceeds, if any, held for claim after 04/09/2019

STRATEGIC MTG INVTS INC (MD)
Merged into Capstead Mortgage Corp. 11/06/1989
Each share Common 1¢ par exchanged for (1) share $1.60 Non-Vtg. Preferred Ser. A 1¢ par and $0.18 cash

STRATEGIC NEV RES CORP (BC)
Name changed to SNS Silver Corp. 02/26/2007
SNS Silver Corp. name changed to SNS Precious Metals Inc. 05/17/2010 which recapitalized as Gold Finder Explorations Ltd. 10/08/2010 which recapitalized as Venzee Technologies Inc. 01/05/2018

STRATEGIC OIL & GAS LTD (BC)
Reincorporated under the laws of Alberta 09/09/2010

STRATEGIC OILS (UT)
Charter suspended for failure to pay taxes 09/15/1972

STRATEGIC PARTNERS EQUITY FD INC (MD)
Name changed to Jennison Blend Fund, Inc. 03/23/2005

STRATEGIC PLANNING ASSOC INC (DE)
Class B Common 10¢ par split (4) for (3) by issuance of (1/3) additional share 08/10/1988
Acquired by Marsh & McLennan Companies, Inc. 02/14/1990
Each share Class B Common 10¢ par exchanged for (0.1785) share Common $1 par

STRATEGIC RARE EARTH METALS INC (NV)
Each share old Common $0.001 par exchanged for (0.1) share new Common $0.001 par 04/30/2013
Stock Dividend - 4% payable 02/21/2011 to holders of record 01/17/2011
Name changed to Affinity Beverage Group, Inc. 04/13/2016

STRATEGIC RECOVERY CORP (UT)
Name changed to Lance Systems, Inc. 02/26/1987
Lance Systems, Inc. name changed to Conspiracy Entertainment Holdings, Inc. 08/01/2003
(See Conspiracy Entertainment Holdings, Inc.)

STRATEGIC RESOURCE ACQUISITION CORP (ON)
Issue Information - 12,371,300 shares COM offered at $4.85 per share on 05/11/2007
Each (12) shares old Common no par

exchanged for (1) share new
Common no par 05/28/2010
Name changed to Portex Minerals
Inc. 04/21/2011

STRATEGIC RES INC (ON)
Each share old Common no par
exchanged for (0.06666666) share
new Common no par 01/16/2015
Reincorporated under the laws of
British Columbia 06/07/2016

STRATEGIC RES LTD (NV)
Charter revoked for failure to file
reports and pay fees 03/31/2010

STRATEGIC SILVER FD INC (TX)
Reincorporated under the laws of
Maryland as Lexington Strategic
Silver Fund, Inc. 06/08/1992
Lexington Strategic Silver Fund, Inc.
name changed to Lexington Silver
Fund Inc. 05/10/1999 which name
changed to Pilgrim Silver Fund, Inc.
08/07/2000 which merged into
Pilgrim Gold Fund, Inc. 02/20/2001
which name changed to Pilgrim
Precious Metals Fund, Inc.
03/01/2001 which name changed to
ING Precious Metals Fund, Inc.
03/01/2002
(See ING Precious Metals Fund, Inc.)

STRATEGIC SOLUTIONS GROUP INC (DE)
Recapitalized as Southern Software
Group, Inc. 03/13/2003
Each (35) shares Common $0.0001
par exchanged for (1) share
Common $0.0001 par
Southern Software Group, Inc. name
changed to SecureD Services, Inc.
07/30/2003
(See SecureD Services, Inc.)

STRATEGIC SYS INC (NY)
Assignment for benefit of creditors
only instituted 08/13/1971
No stockholders' equity

STRATEGIC TECHNOLGIES INC (BC)
Name changed to Wireless2
Technologies, Inc. 10/24/2006
Wireless2 Technologies, Inc. name
changed to Nanotech Security Corp.
04/15/2010

STRATEGIC TECHNOLOGY DEV INC (DE)
Name changed to
Telecommunications Designs, Inc.
02/01/1987
(See Telecommunications Designs, Inc.)

STRATEGIC TREAS POSITIONS INC (TX)
Voluntarily dissolved 02/12/1993
Details not available

STRATEGIC VALUE AMERICAN EQUITY FUND LTD. (CANADA)
Name changed to StrategicNova U.S.
Large Cap Growth Fund Ltd.
09/26/2000
(See StrategicNova U.S. Large Cap Growth Fund Ltd.)

STRATEGIC VALUE CANADIAN EQUITY FUND LTD. (CANADA)
Name changed to StrategicNova
Canadian Large Cap Value Fund
Ltd. 09/26/2000
(See StrategicNova Canadian Large Cap Value Fund Ltd.)

STRATEGIC VALUE COMMONWEALTH FUND LTD. (CANADA)
Name changed to StrategicNova
Commonwealth Fund Ltd.
09/26/2000
(See StrategicNova Commonwealth Fund Ltd.)

STRATEGIC VALUE CORP (ON)
Merged into Nova Bancorp Group
(Canada) Ltd. 06/08/2000
Each share Common no par
exchanged for $3 cash

STRATEGIC VALUE DIVIDEND FUND LTD. (CANADA)
Name changed to StrategicNova
Canadian Dividend Fund Ltd.
09/26/2000
(See StrategicNova Canadian Dividend Fund Ltd.)

STRATEGIC VALUE INTERNATIONAL FUND LTD. (CANADA)
Name changed to StrategicNova
World Large Cap Fund Ltd.
09/26/2000
(See StrategicNova World Large Cap Fund Ltd.)

STRATEGIC VENTURES INC (FL)
Name changed to Internet Venture
Group Inc. (FL) 10/19/1999
Internet Venture Group Inc. (FL)
reincorporated in Delaware as IVG
Corp. 02/28/2001 which
recapitalized as Group Management
Corp. (DE) 12/17/2001 which
reincorporated in Georgia as Silver
Screen Studios, Inc. 09/05/2003
which name changed to Global 1
Investment Holdings Corp.
11/13/2006
(See Global 1 Investment Holdings Corp.)

STRATEGIC VISTA INTL INC (ON)
Name changed to Lorex Technology
Inc. 03/20/2006
(See Lorex Technology Inc.)

STRATEGICNOVA CANADIAN BOND FUND (ON)
Merged into Dynamic Canadian Bond
Fund 03/01/2004
Details not available

STRATEGICNOVA CANADIAN DIVIDEND FUND LTD. (CANADA)
Merged into Dynamic Canadian
Dividend Fund Ltd. 08/26/2003
Details not available

STRATEGICNOVA CANADIAN LARGE CAP VALUE FUND LTD. (CANADA)
Merged into Dynamic Focus &
Canadian Fund 10/02/2003
Details not available

STRATEGICNOVA COMMONWEALTH FUND LTD. (CANADA)
Merged into Commonwealth World
Balanced Fund Ltd. 08/26/2003
Details not available

STRATEGICNOVA INCOME FUND (ON)
Name changed to StrategicNova
Canadian Bond Fund 12/00/2001
(See StrategicNova Canadian Bond Fund)

STRATEGICNOVA U.S. LARGE CAP GROWTH FUND LTD. (CANADA)
Merged into Dynamic Power
American Growth Fund Ltd.
08/26/2003
Details not available

STRATEGICNOVA WORLD LARGE CAP FUND LTD. (CANADA)
Completely liquidated 09/19/2005
Details not available

STRATEGIKA INC (DE)
Name changed to Tiens Biotech
Group (USA), Inc. 02/17/2004
(See Tiens Biotech Group (USA), Inc.)

STRATEGINET INC (DE)
Common $0.001 par split (5) for (2)
by issuance of (1.5) additional
shares payable 06/20/2000 to
holders of record 05/31/2000
Each share old Common $0.001 par
exchanged for (0.1) share new
Common $0.001 par 11/15/2001
Recapitalized as Cemtrex Inc.
12/28/2014
Each share Common $0.001 par
exchanged for (0.5) share Common
$0.001 par

STRATEGY SHS (DE)
Trust terminated 05/30/2018
Each share Active Alts Contrarian
ETF received $25.65 cash
(Additional Information in Active)

STRATEGY X INC (NV)
Each share old Common $0.001 par
exchanged for (0.008) share new
Common $0.001 par 05/30/2006
Recapitalized as Alliance
Transcription Services, Inc.
08/14/2007
Each share new Common $0.001 par
exchanged for (0.00028392) share
Common $0.001 par
(See Alliance Transcription Services, Inc.)

STRATERA INC (NV)
Recapitalized as Gulf West
Investment Properties, Inc.
12/16/2009
Each share Common $0.001 par
exchanged for (0.01) share Common
$0.001 par

STRATESEC INC (DE)
Chapter 11 bankruptcy proceedings
terminated 08/11/2009
Stockholders' equity unlikely

STRATEVEST FDS (DE)
Name changed to Banknorth Funds
11/01/2001
(See Banknorth Funds)

STRATEX NETWORKS INC (DE)
Merged into Harris Stratex Networks,
Inc. 01/26/2007
Each share Common 1¢ par
exchanged for (0.25) share Class A
Common 1¢ par
Harris Stratex Networks, Inc. name
changed to Aviat Networks, Inc.
01/27/2010

STRATFORD ACQUISITION CORP (MN)
Reincorporated under the laws of
New York as Novex Systems
International, Inc. 04/29/1999
Novex Systems International, Inc.
recapitalized as American Home
Food Products Inc. 06/08/2005
which name changed to Artisanal
Brands, Inc. 11/04/2010

STRATFORD AMERN CORP (AZ)
Each share old Common 1¢ par
exchanged for (0.06666666) share
new Common 1¢ par 07/20/1998
Merged into Stratford Holdings
Investment, LLC 05/30/2006
Each share Common 1¢ par
exchanged for $0.90 cash

STRATFORD CORP. (NY)
Name changed to Universal Cigar
Corp. and Common $1 par changed
to 10¢ par 03/07/1964
(See Universal Cigar Corp.)

STRATFORD ENTERPRISES CO (OK)
Name changed to American Gilsonite
Co. 08/00/1991
(See American Gilsonite Co.)

STRATFORD FINL GROUP LTD (DE)
Each share old Common $0.001 par
exchanged for (0.01) share new
Common $0.001 par 10/31/1990
Name changed to SFG Corp.
01/19/1993
SFG Corp. name changed to SFG
Financial Corp. 08/04/2000
(See SFG Financial Corp.)

STRATFORD INC (MN)
Adjudicated bankrupt 04/15/1971
Stockholders' equity unlikely

STRATFORD INDS INC (FL)
Acquired by Equipment Co. of
America 09/01/1972
Each share Common 10¢ par
exchanged for $0.75 cash

STRATFORD OF TEXAS, INC. LIQUIDATING TRUST (DE)
Liquidation completed

Each share Common 10¢ par
exchanged for initial distribution of
$0.09 cash 03/06/1979
Each share Common 10¢ par
received second distribution of $0.50
cash 07/31/1982
Each share Common 10¢ par
received third and final distribution
of $0.13 cash 10/29/1985

STRATFORD PEN CORP. (NY)
Name changed to Stratford Corp. and
Common $1 par changed to 10¢ par
04/24/1956
Stratford Corp. name changed to
Universal Cigar Corp. 03/07/1964
(See Universal Cigar Corp.)

STRATFORD SOFTWARE CORP (BC)
Merged into Bow-Flex, Inc.
01/26/1993
Each share Common no par
exchanged for (0.28571428) share
Common no par
Bow-Flex, Inc. name changed to
Direct Focus, Inc. 06/17/1998 which
name changed to Nautilus Group,
Inc. 05/21/2002 which name
changed to Nautilus, Inc. 03/14/2005

STRATFORD TEX INC (DE)
Reincorporated 05/24/1973
State of incorporation changed from
(TX) to (DE) 05/24/1973
Assets transferred to Stratford of
Texas, Inc. Liquidating Trust
06/05/1978
(See Stratford of Texas, Inc. Liquidating Trust)

STRATFORD VENTURES LTD (BC)
Name changed to MRC Metall
Resources Corp. (BC) 08/29/1997
MRC Metall Resources Corp. (BC)
reincorporated in Canada as Mount
Dakota Energy Corp. 08/24/1998
which reincorporated in British
Columbia 08/07/2015

STRATHCLAIR VENTURES LTD (BC)
Name changed to SilverCrest Mines
Inc. 05/28/2003
SilverCrest Mines Inc. merged into
First Majestic Silver Corp.
10/07/2015

STRATHCONA BREWING INVTS INC (AB)
Struck off register and declared
dissolved for failure to file returns
08/01/1994

STRATHCONA RES INDS LTD (AB)
Recapitalized as Clarepine Industries
Inc. 05/24/1988
Each share Common no par
exchanged for (0.1) share Common
no par
(See Clarepine Industries Inc.)

STRATHEARN HOUSE GROUP LTD (ON)
Delisted from Toronto Stock
Exchange 03/05/1993

STRATHFIELD OIL & GAS LTD (AB)
Class A Common no par reclassified
as Common no par 09/17/1984
Merged into Inverness Petroleum Ltd.
12/31/1991
Each share 7% Conv. 1st Preferred
Ser. C no par exchanged for (1)
share 7% Conv. Class A Preferred
Ser. 3 no par
Each share Common no par
exchanged for (0.925) share
Common no par
Inverness Petroleum Ltd. merged into
Rigel Energy Corp. 01/10/1996
which merged into Talisman Energy
Inc. 10/05/1999
(See Talisman Energy Inc.)

STRATHMORE GOLD MINES LTD.
Name changed to Strathmore Mines
Ltd. 00/00/1947
(See Strathmore Mines Ltd.)

STRATHMORE INDS INC (NY)
Merged into Transworld Investment Corp. 01/08/1971
Each share Common 1¢ par exchanged for (0.33333333) share Common 1¢ par
(See Transworld Investment Corp.)

STRATHMORE MINERALS CORP (BC)
Each share Common no par received distribution of (0.33333333) share Fission Energy Corp. Common no par payable 07/20/2007 to holders of record 07/13/2007 Ex date - 07/11/2007
Merged into Energy Fuels Inc. 08/30/2013
Each share Common no par exchanged for (1.47) shares Common no par

STRATHMORE MINES LTD. (ON)
Charter cancelled and company declared dissolved for default in filing returns 09/28/1964

STRATHMORE RES LTD (BC)
Recapitalized as Strathmore Minerals Corp. 09/18/2000
Each share Common no par exchanged for (0.2) share Common no par
Strathmore Minerals Corp. merged into Energy Fuels Inc. 08/30/2013

STRATIC ENERGY CORP (YT)
Merged into EnQuest PLC 11/05/2010
Each share Common no par exchanged for (0.089626) share Ordinary
Note: Unexchanged certificates were cancelled and became without value 11/05/2015

STRATIVATION INC (DE)
Each share old Common $0.001 par exchanged for (0.02) share new Common $0.001 par 01/10/2007
Name changed to CNS Response, Inc. 03/09/2007
CNS Response, Inc. name changed to MYnd Analytics, Inc. 01/12/2016

STRATMIN INC (CANADA)
Each share old Class A Common no par exchanged for (0.33333333) share new Class A Common no par 07/27/1994
Name changed to Strategic Exploration (Strex) Inc. 04/26/1996
(See Strategic Exploration (Strex) Inc.)

STRATO INDUSTRIES INC. (FL)
Charter revoked for failure to file reports and pay fees 06/07/1966

STRATO-MISSILES, INC. (DE)
Name changed to American Checkmaster System, Inc. 10/31/1966
(See American Checkmaster System, Inc.)

STRATOFLEX INC (TX)
Merged into Parker-Hannifin Corp. 06/17/1988
Each share Common $2.50 par exchanged for $61.04 cash
Each share Class B Common $2.50 par exchanged for $61.04 cash

STRATOS BIOTECHNOLOGIES INC (BC)
Merged into SNB Capital Corp. 05/20/2003
Each share Common no par exchanged for (0.33333333) share Common no par
SNB Capital Corp. name changed to Protox Therapeutics Inc. 07/14/2004 which name changed to Sophiris Bio Inc. 04/05/2012

STRATOS GLOBAL CORP (NL)
Merged into Communications Investment Partners Ltd. 12/11/2007
Each share Common no par exchanged for $7 cash

STRATOS INTL INC (DE)
Name changed 11/06/2003
Each share old Common 1¢ par exchanged for (0.1) share new Common 1¢ par 10/21/2002
Name changed from Stratos Lightwave, Inc. to Stratos International, Inc. 11/06/2003
Merged into Emerson Electric Co. 07/12/2007
Each share Common 1¢ par exchanged for $8 cash

STRATOSPHERE COMMUNICATIONS CORP (DE)
Recapitalized as Multicast Interactive Corp. 11/27/2000
Each share Common $0.001 par exchanged for (0.05) share Common $0.001 par
Multicast Interactive Corp. recapitalized as MPD Development Corp. 03/15/2010 which recapitalized as Astor Explorations Corp. 05/19/2010

STRATOSPHERE CORP (DE)
Plan of reorganization under Chapter 11 Federal Bankruptcy Code effective 10/14/98
No old Common stockholders' equity
Merged into Strat Merger Corp. 12/19/2002
Each share new Common 1¢ par exchanged for $45.32 cash

STRATTON & TERSTEGGE INC (KY)
Stock Dividends - 25% 09/05/1946; 100% 03/01/1948
Name changed to S&T Industries, Inc. 03/05/1975
(See S&T Industries, Inc.)

STRATTON CAP CORP (ON)
Recapitalized as Millennial Esports Corp. 10/27/2016
Each share Common no par exchanged for (0.25) share Common no par

STRATTON CORP (VT)
Each share old Capital Stock $1 par exchanged for (0.000004) share new Capital Stock $1 par 05/11/1983
Note: In effect holders received $7.50 cash per share and public interest was eliminated

STRATTON ENGINE CO. (MA)
Out of business in 1909
Charter subsequently dissolved in 1910

STRATTON FUND, INC. (MD)
Acquired by Empire Fund, Inc. 08/03/1964
Each share Common exchanged for (0.6786819) share Capital Stock $1 par
Empire Fund, Inc. merged into American Leaders Fund, Inc. 04/09/1979 which name changed to Federated American Leaders Fund Inc. 03/31/1996 which reorganized as Federated Equity Funds 09/18/2009

STRATTON GROUP LTD (NY)
Adjudicated bankrupt 05/13/1976
Stockholders' equity unlikely

STRATTON GROWTH FD INC (MD)
Reincorporated 06/21/1985
Common 10¢ par split (2) for (1) by issuance of (1) additional share 04/21/1983
Stock Dividend - 100% 03/30/1976
State of incorporation changed from (DE) to (MD) 06/21/1985
Name changed to Stratton Multi-Cap Fund, Inc. 05/01/2006

STRATTON HLDGS INC (NV)
Recapitalized as Profitable Developments, Inc. 12/24/2012
Each share Common $0.001 par exchanged for (0.00083333) share Common $0.001 par

STRATTON MONTHLY DIVID REIT SHS INC (MD)
Name changed 12/09/1997
Name changed from Stratton Monthly Dividend Shares, Inc. to Stratton Monthly Dividend REIT Shares, Inc. 12/09/1997
Name changed to Stratton Real Estate Fund, Inc. 09/30/2009

STRATTON RES INC (BC)
Common no par split (2) for (1) by issuance of (1) additional share payable 09/21/2011 to holders of record 09/13/2011
Name changed to Torq Resources Inc. 03/15/2017

STRATUM HLDGS INC (NV)
Each share Common $0.001 par exchanged for (0.1) share Common 1¢ par 12/17/2009
Name changed to Caprock Oil, Inc. 03/25/2014
Caprock Oil, Inc. recapitalized as Stack-It Storage, Inc. 07/23/2015 which name changed to Manufactured Housing Properties Inc. 12/08/2017

STRATUM RES LTD (AB)
Struck from register and dissolved 07/01/1993

STRATUS COMPUTER INC (MA)
Merged into Ascend Communications Inc. 10/19/1998
Each share Common 1¢ par exchanged for (0.75) share Common $0.001 par
Ascend Communications, Inc. merged into Lucent Technologies Inc. 06/24/1999 which merged into Alcatel-Lucent S.A. 11/30/2006
(See Alcatel-Lucent S.A.)

STRATUS ENTMT INC (NV)
Common $0.001 par split (5) for (1) by issuance of (4) additional shares payable 07/30/2007 to holders of record 07/25/2007 Ex date - 07/31/2007
Name changed to Latin Television, Inc. (New) 09/10/2007
Latin Television, Inc. (New) recapitalized as Pure Play Music, Ltd. 07/10/2008
(See Pure Play Music, Ltd.)

STRATUS MEDIA GROUP INC (NV)
Recapitalized as RestorGenex Corp. (NV) 03/10/2014
Each share Common $0.001 par exchanged for (0.01) share Common $0.001 par
RestorGenex Corp. (NV) reincorporated in Delaware 06/18/2015 which name changed to Diffusion Pharmaceuticals Inc. 01/25/2016

STRATUS SVCS GROUP INC (DE)
Each share Common 1¢ par exchanged for (0.25) share Common 4¢ par 07/14/2004
SEC revoked common stock registration 12/22/2011

STRAUS (NATHAN)-DUPARQUET, INC. (NY)
Each share Common no par exchanged for (2) shares Common $3 par 00/00/1951
Merged into Standard Factors Corp. 06/30/1955
Each share Common $3 par exchanged for for (2) shares Common $1 par
Standard Factors Corp. name changed to Standard Financial Corp. 06/07/1957 which name changed to SFC Financial Corp. 12/31/1962 which name changed back to Standard Financial Corp. 04/22/1964
(See Standard Financial Corp.)

STRAUS (S.W.) & CO., INC.
Liquidated 00/00/1938
No stockholders' equity

STRAUS DUPARQUET INC (NY)
Name changed to Guardian Development Corp. 01/25/1971
(See Guardian Development Corp.)

STRAUS (S.W.) INVESTING CO.
Liquidated 00/00/1938
No stockholders' equity

STRAUSS (ROBERT S.) & CO.
Bankrupt 00/00/1930
No stockholders' equity

STRAUSS STORES CORP (NY)
Each share Common 10¢ par exchanged for (0.5) share Common 20¢ par 06/15/1971
Common 20¢ par changed to $0.001 par 04/03/1979
Each share Common $0.001 par exchanged for (0.01) share Common 10¢ par 01/25/1982
Merged into Strauss Merchandising Corp. 08/31/1982
Each share Common 10¢ par exchanged for $95 cash

STRAWBERRY VY ESTATES OF THE OZARKS (UT)
Name changed to Continental Industries, Inc. 02/02/1982

STRAWBRIDGE & CLOTHIER (PA)
Each share Common no par exchanged for (3) shares Common $5 par 00/00/1946
5% Preferred $100 par called for redemption 01/30/1946
6% Prior Preference Ser. A $100 par called for redemption 03/01/1947
5% Preferred $100 par called for redemption 04/01/1995
Common $5 par changed to $1 par and (1) additional share issued 05/14/1984
Common $1 par split (3) for (2) by issuance of (0.5) additional share 05/16/1985
Common $1 par reclassified as Common Ser. A $1 par 07/23/1986
In process of liquidation
Each share Common Ser. A $1 par exchanged for initial distribution of (0.2) share May Department Stores Co. Common 50¢ par payable 07/18/1997 to holders of record 07/15/1997
Each share Common Ser. B $1 par exchanged for initial distribution of (0.2) share May Department Stores Co. Common 50¢ par payable 07/18/1997 to holders of record 07/15/1997
Each share Common Ser. A $1 par received second distribution of $0.054 cash payable 09/15/1997 to holders of record 07/15/1997
Each share Common Ser. B $1 par received second distribution of $0.054 cash payable 09/15/1997 to holders of record 07/15/1997
Note: Details on subsequent distributions, if any, are not available

STRAY HORSE RES INC (BC)
Name changed to Oriole Communications Inc. 07/28/1987
Oriole Communications Inc. recapitalized as Consolidated Oriole Communications Inc. 09/10/1993 which name changed to Oriole Systems Inc. 03/26/1996
(See Oriole Systems Inc.)

STRAYER ED INC (MD)
Common 1¢ par split (3) for (2) by issuance of (0.5) additional share payable 11/18/1997 to holders of record 11/04/1997
Under plan of merger name changed to Strategic Education, Inc. 08/01/2018

STRAZA INDUSTRIES (CA)
Completely liquidated 04/03/1968
Each share Capital Stock $1 par exchanged for first and final distribution of (0.193) share

AMETEK, Inc. (Old) Capital Stock no par
AMETEK, Inc. (Old) merged into Culligan Water Technologies, Inc. 07/31/1997 which merged into United States Filter Corp. (New) 06/15/1998
(See United States Filter Corp. (New))

STREAM COMMUNICATIONS NETWORK & MEDIA INC (BC)
SEC revoked common stock registration 07/13/2012

STREAM COMMUNICATIONS NETWORK INC (BC)
Name changed to Stream Communications Network & Media Inc. 08/17/2004
(See Stream Communications Network & Media Inc.)

STREAM EXCHANGE TRADED TR (DE)
Trust terminated 10/24/2013
Each S&P Dynamic Roll Global Commodities Fund Common Unit of Bene. Int. received $26.28 cash

STREAM FLOW MEDIA INC (CO)
Name changed to Blue Water Bar & Grill, Inc. 10/16/2015
Blue Water Bar & Grill, Inc. name changed to Tiger Reef, Inc. 02/01/2017

STREAM GLOBAL SVCS INC (DE)
Acquired by SGS Holdings L.L.C. 04/27/2012
Each share Common $0.001 par exchanged for $3.25 cash

STREAM OIL & GAS LTD (BC)
Merged into TransAtlantic Petroleum Ltd. 11/20/2014
Each share Common no par exchanged for (0.04812) share new Common USD $0.10 par
Note: Holders may receive an additional contingent distribution

STREAM TRACK INC (WY)
Recapitalized as Total Sports Media, Inc. 12/06/2016
Each share Common $0.001 par exchanged for (0.00125) share Common $0.001 par

STREAM VENTURES INC (ON)
Recapitalized as Beleave Inc. 12/31/2015
Each share Common no par exchanged for (0.1) share Common no par

STREAMEDIA COMMUNICATIONS INC (DE)
Recapitalized as XXIS Corp. (DE) 10/26/2001
Each share Common $0.001 par exchanged (0.00333333) share Common $0.001 par
XXIS Corp. (DE) reincorporated in Florida 12/03/2007 which name changed to 141 Capital Inc. 01/21/2009

STREAMLINE COM INC (DE)
Company ceased operations 11/22/2000
Stockholders' equity unlikely

STREAMLINE WEB BROADCASTING INC (BC)
Recapitalized as Kavalmedia Services Ltd. 05/17/2005
Each share Common no par exchanged for (0.33333333) share Common no par
Kavalmedia Services Ltd. name changed to EmerGeo Solutions Worldwide Inc. 08/05/2008
(See EmerGeo Solutions Worldwide Inc.)

STREAMLOGIC CORP (DE)
Plan of reorganization under Chapter 11 Federal Bankruptcy Code effective 03/31/1998
No stockholders' equity

STREAMSCAPE MINERALS INC (NV)
Recapitalized as VeruTEK Technologies, Inc. (NV) 05/03/2007
Each (4.462) shares Common $0.001 par exchanged for (1) share Common $0.001 par
VeruTEK Technologies, Inc. (NV) reincorporated in Delaware 05/26/2009

STREAMSCAPE NETWORKS INC (DE)
Reported insolvent 00/00/2001
Stockholders' equity unlikely

STREAMSIDE RES INC (ON)
Recapitalized as Ring Sights Worldwide Inc. 10/14/1987
Each share Common no par exchanged for (0.2) share Common no par
(See Ring Sights Worldwide Inc.)

STREET RES INC (ON)
Name changed to EXMIN Resources Inc. 07/19/2005
EXMIN Resources Inc. merged into Dia Bras Exploration Inc. 10/01/2009 which name changed to Sierra Metals Inc. 12/07/2012

STREETLIGHT INTELLIGENCE INC (AB)
Assets sold for the benefit of creditors 11/18/2011
No stockholders' equity

STREETTRACKS GOLD TR (NY)
Name changed to SPDR Gold Trust 05/21/2008

STREETTRACKS SER TR (MA)
Completely liquidated
Each SPDR O-Strip Exchange Traded Fund received first and final distribution of $52.042885 cash payable 09/25/2006 to holders of record 09/20/2006
Dow Jones U.S. Large Cap Value Index Fund 1¢ par split (2) for (1) by issuance of (1) additional share payable 09/21/2005 to holders of record 09/19/2005 Ex date - 09/22/2005
Dow Jones U.S. Small Cap Value Index Fund 1¢ par split (3) for (1) by issuance of (2) additional shares payable 09/21/2005 to holders of record 09/19/2005 Ex date - 09/22/2005
Wilshire Reit Index Fund 1¢ par split (3) for (1) by issuance of (2) additional shares payable 09/21/2005 to holders of record 09/19/2005 Ex date - 09/22/2005
Dow Jones U.S. Large Cap Value Index Fund 1¢ par reclassified as streetTracks DJ Wilshire Large Cap Value ETF 1¢ par 11/01/2005
Dow Jones U.S. Small Cap Value Index Fund 1¢ par reclassified as streetTracks DJ Wilshire Small Cap Value ETF 1¢ par 11/01/2005
Wilshire Reit Index Fund 1¢ par reclassified as streetTracks DJ Wilshire REIT ETF 1¢ par 11/01/2005
Name changed to SPDR Series Trust 08/01/2007

STREETWEAR CORP (ON)
Name changed to BitRush Corp. 09/10/2015

STREICHER MOBILE FUELING INC (FL)
Reincoporated under the laws of Delaware as SMF Energy Corp. 02/14/2007
(See SMF Energy Corp.)

STRESSGEN BIOTECHNOLOGIES CORP (BC)
Name changed to Nventa Biopharmaceuticals Corp. 06/07/2006
Nventa Biopharmaceuticals Corp. acquired by Akela Pharma Inc. 05/21/2009
(See Akela Pharma Inc.)

STRESSGEN BIOTECHNOLOGIES CORP (YT)
Plan of arrangement effective 03/28/2006
Each share Class A Common no par exchanged for (1) share GVIC Publications Ltd. Class B Common no par, (0.05263157) share Non-Vtg. Class C Common no par, and (0.10526315) share Stressgen Biotechnologies Corp. (BC) Common no par
(See each company's listing)

STREVELL-PATERSON FINANCE CORP. (UT)
Stock Dividend - 20% 04/25/1959
Completely liquidated 07/00/1969
Each share Common 50¢ par exchanged for first and final distribution of $0.50 cash
American Finance System Inc. acquired 99% prior to the liquidation and will purchase the remaining minority shares at $0.73 per share, however, the offer may be discontinued at anytime

STRIA CAP INC (CANADA)
Name changed to Stria Lithium Inc. 05/09/2014

STRICK, INC. (DE)
Name changed to Distribution International Corp. 05/09/1975
(See Distibution International Corp)

STRIDE RITE CORP (MA)
Each share Conv. Preferred Ser. A $1 par exchanged for (4.5) shares Common $1 par 03/15/1972
Each share Conv. Preferred Ser. B $1 par exchanged for (4.5) shares Common $1 par 03/15/1972
Each share Conv. Preferred Ser. C $1 par exchanged for (4.5) shares Common $1 par 03/15/1972
Common $1 par split (2) for (1) by issuance of (1) additional share 04/28/1972
Common $1 par split (2) for (1) by issuance of (1) additional share 02/18/1983
Common $1 par split (2) for (1) by issuance of (1) additional share 12/30/1987
Common $1 par split (2) for (1) by issuance of (1) additional share 07/18/1989
Common $1 par split (2) for (1) by issuance of (1) additional share 12/18/1991
Merged into Collective Brands, Inc. 08/17/2007
Each share Common $1 par exchanged for $20.50 cash

STRIKE AXE INC (DE)
SEC revoked common stock registration 04/05/2016

STRIKE CAP CORP (AB)
Name changed to Strike Petroleum Ltd. 11/17/2004
Strike Petroleum Ltd. merged into FairWest Energy Corp. 05/30/2007
(See FairWest Energy Corp.)

STRIKE DIAMOND CORP (BC)
Recapitalized as Sunvest Minerals Corp. 03/15/2016
Each share Common no par exchanged for (0.1) share Common no par

STRIKE ENERGY INC (CANADA)
Merged into Tarragon Oil & Gas Ltd. 05/01/1996
Each share Common no par exchanged for (0.02717391) share new Common no par
Tarragon Oil & Gas Ltd. merged into Marathon Oil Canada Ltd. 09/11/1998
(See Marathon Oil Canada Ltd.)

STRIKE GRAPHITE CORP (BC)
Each share old Common no par exchanged for (0.1) share new Common no par 07/22/2013
Name changed to Strike Diamond Corp. 11/24/2014
Strike Diamond Corp. recapitalized as Sunvest Minerals Corp. 03/15/2016

STRIKE PETROLEUM LTD (AB)
Merged into FairWest Energy Corp. 05/30/2007
Each share Common no par exchanged for (0.55617352) share Common no par
(See FairWest Energy Corp.)

STRIKE RES LTD (BC)
Name changed to Cleanfield Alternative Energy Inc. 09/20/2006
(See Cleanfield Alternative Energy Inc.)

STRIKEFORCE TECHNOLOGIES INC (NJ)
Each share old Common $0.0001 par exchanged for (0.1) share new Common $0.0001 par 11/03/2008
Reincorporated under the laws of Wyoming 11/15/2010

STRIKEPOINT GOLD INC (AB)
Reincorporated under the laws of British Columbia 08/12/2015

STRIKER CAP CORP (CO)
Reincorporated under the laws of Nevada as Petro Plus USA Inc. 07/21/2006
Petro Plus USA Inc. name changed to Petroleum Consolidators of America, Inc. (NV) 09/08/2006 which reincorporated in Delaware as CTX Virtual Technologies, Inc. 04/19/2010

STRIKER ENERGY CORP (NV)
Old Common $0.0001 par split (2) for (1) by issuance of (1) additional share payable 09/15/2008 to holders of record 09/15/2008
Name changed to PediatRx Inc. 12/28/2010
PediatRx Inc. name changed to Quint Media Inc. 08/07/2013 which recapitalized as OncBioMune Pharmaceuticals, Inc. 08/28/2015

STRIKER EXPL CORP (AB)
Merged into Gear Energy Ltd. 07/29/2016
Each share Common no par exchanged for (2.325) shares Common no par
Note: Unexchanged certificates will be cancelled and become without value 07/26/2019

STRIKER INDS INC (DE)
Reincorporated 07/02/1985
Recapitalized 09/27/1993
State of incorporation changed from (CO) to (DE) 07/02/1985
Each share Common 1¢ par exchanged for (0.02) share Common 50¢ par 11/01/1985
Recapitalized from Striker Petroleum Corp. to Striker Industries Inc. 09/27/1993
Each share new Common 50¢ par exchanged for (0.05) share Common 1¢ par
Common 1¢ par changed to 20¢ par 09/30/1993
Each share Common 20¢ par exchanged for (0.4) share Common 50¢ par 06/26/1997
Charter cancelled and declared inoperative and void for non-payment of taxes 03/01/2000

STRIKER OIL & GAS INC (NV)
Charter permanently revoked 05/31/2010

STRIKER RES N L (AUSTRALIA)
Name changed to North Australian Diamonds Ltd. 09/22/2005
North Australian Diamonds Ltd. name changed to Merlin Diamonds Ltd. 02/06/2013

STRIKEZONE MINERALS CDA LTD (BC)
Recapitalized as Gold World Resources Inc. (BC) 01/31/2006
Each (5.5) shares Common no par exchanged for (1) share Common no par
Gold World Resources Inc. (BC) reincorporated in Ontario 04/18/2007

STRINGS LTD (DE)
Charter cancelled and declared void for non-payment of taxes 03/01/1993

STRINTZIS LINES SHIPPING S A (GREECE)
Name changed to Blue Star Maritime S.A. 07/21/2004
(See Blue Star Maritime S.A.)

STROBER ORGANIZATION INC (DE)
Acquired by Hamilton Acquisition LLC 03/26/1997
Each share Common 1¢ par exchanged for $6 cash

STROBRIDGE LITHOGRAPHING CO. (OH)
Name changed to Merten Co. 10/31/1960
(See Merten Co.)

STROEHMAN BROS CO (PA)
Merged into Weston (George) Ltd. 01/03/1980
Each share Common $12.50 par exchanged for $38 cash

STROLEE OF CALIFORNIA, INC. (CA)
Merged into U.S. Industries, Inc. 06/28/1968
Each share Common no par exchanged for (0.1517) share Special Conv. Preference Ser. A $2.50 par
(See U.S. Industries, Inc.)

STROMBERG CARBURETOR CO. OF AMERICA
Acquired by Bendix Aviation Corp. 00/00/1929
Details not available

STROMBERG-CARLSON CO. (NY)
Common no par changed to $10 par 00/00/1946
Stock Dividends - 10% 01/03/1949; 10% 02/01/1951
Merged into General Dynamics Corp. 06/30/1955
Each share Common $10 par exchanged for (1) share Common $1 par

STROMBERG-CARLSON TELEPHONE MANUFACTURING CO.
Name changed to Stromberg-Carlson Co. 00/00/1943
Stromberg-Carlson Co. merged into General Dynamics Corp. 06/30/1955

STRONG, CARLISLE & HAMMOND CO. (IL)
Name changed to CRF Corp. 04/02/1956
(See CRF Corp.)

STRONG, COBB & CO., INC. (DE)
Each share old Common $1 par exchanged for (38) shares new Common $1 par 04/03/1951
Merged into Strong Cobb Arner Inc. 06/08/1959
Each share Preferred $100 par exchanged for (4) shares Preferred $25 par
Each share Common $1 par exchanged for (1) share Common $1 par
(See Strong Cobb Arner Inc.)

STRONG ADVANTAGE FD INC (WI)
Common $0.0001 par reclassified as Ultra Short-Term Income Fund Investors Series $0.0001 par 02/25/2002
Merged into Wells Fargo Funds Trust 04/11/2005
Details not available

STRONG BALANCED FD INC (WI)
Name changed 06/06/2000
Name changed from Strong Asset Allocation Fund Inc. to Strong Balanced Fund, Inc. 06/06/2000
Merged into Wells Fargo Funds Trust 04/11/2005
Details not available

STRONG BALANCED STK FD INC (WI)
Name changed 03/12/2001
Name changed from Strong Schafer Funds, Inc. to Strong Balanced Stock Fund, Inc. 03/12/2001
Merged into Strong Balanced Fund, Inc. 03/28/2003
Details not available

STRONG COBB ARNER INC. (NY)
5% Preferred $25 par called for redemption 07/15/1964
Completely liquidated 07/14/1965
Each share Common $1 par exchanged for $3 principal amount of Foremost Dairies, Inc. 5.5% Conv. Capital Subord. Debentures due 09/01/1980 and $4.80564 cash

STRONG CORPORATE BOND FD INC (WI)
Common $0.001 par reclassified as Investor Class 08/31/1999
Merged into Wells Fargo Funds Trust 04/11/2005
Details not available

STRONG DISCOVERY FD INC (WI)
Merged into Wells Fargo Funds Trust 04/11/2005
Details not available

STRONG (NICHOLAS) FUND, INC. (MD)
See - Nicholas Strong Fund Inc

STRONG GOVT SECS FD INC (WI)
Common $0.001 par reclassified as Investor Class $0.001 par 08/31/1999
Merged into Wells Fargo Funds Trust 04/11/2005
Details not available

STRONG INCOME FD INC (WI)
Name changed to Strong Corporate Bond Fund Inc. 05/01/1995
(See Strong Corporate Bond Fund Inc.)

STRONG INVT FD INC (WI)
Name changed to Strong Asset Allocation Fund Inc. 12/30/1994
Strong Asset Allocation Fund Inc. name changed to Strong Balanced Fund, Inc. 06/06/2000
(See Strong Balanced Fund, Inc.)

STRONG LARGE CAP GROWTH FD INC (WI)
Merged into Wells Fargo Funds Trust 04/11/2005
Details not available

STRONG MONEY MKT FD INC (WI)
Merged into Wells Fargo Funds Trust 04/11/2005
Details not available

STRONG MULTI CAP VALUE FD INC (MD)
Name changed 05/15/2001
Name changed from Strong Schafer Value Fund to Strong Multi Capital Value Fund Inc. 05/15/2001
Reorganized as Strong Equity Funds II, Inc. 06/01/2001
Details not available

STRONG MUN BD FD INC (WI)
Advisor Class completely liquidated 10/18/2001
Details not available
Institutional Class completely liquidated 10/18/2001
Details not available
Merged into Wells Fargo Funds Trust 04/11/2005
Details not available

STRONG MUN FDS INC (WI)
Name changed 01/05/1989
Name changed 10/27/1995
Name changed from Strong Tax-Free Money Market Fund, Inc. to Strong Municipal Money Market Fund, Inc. 01/05/1989
Name changed from Strong Municipal Money Market Fund, Inc. to Strong Municipal Funds, Inc. and Common $0.0001 par reclassified as Money Market Investor Series 10/27/1995
Merged into Wells Fargo Funds Trust 04/11/2005
Details not available

STRONG OPPORTUNITY FD INC (WI)
Merged into Wells Fargo Funds Trust 04/11/2005
Details not available

STRONG SHORT TERM BD FD INC (WI)
Merged into Wells Fargo Funds Trust 04/11/2005
Details not available

STRONG TAX FREE INCOME FD INC (WI)
Name changed to Strong Municipal Bond Fund, Inc. and Common $0.001 par reclassified as Investor Class 12/28/1988
(See Strong Municipal Bond Fund, Inc.)

STRONG TECHNICAL INC (DE)
Recapitalized as Zhongpin Inc. 02/17/2006
Each (35.349) shares Common $0.001 par exchanged for (1) share Common $0.001 par

STRONG TOTAL RETURN FD INC (WI)
Name changed to Strong Large Cap Growth Fund, Inc. and Common 1¢ par reclassified as Investor Class 1¢ par 04/26/2006
(See Strong Large Cap Growth Fund, Inc.)

STRONG WEAR HOSIERY INC (PA)
Adjudicated bankrupt 07/24/1974
Stockholders' equity unlikely

STRONGBOW RESOURCE CORP (BC)
Merged into Consolidated Ramrod Gold Corp. 12/14/1989
Each share Common no par exchanged for (0.20546537) share Common no par
Consolidated Ramrod Gold Corp. recapitalized as Quest International Resources Corp. 04/09/1996 which recapitalized as Standard Mining Corp. 06/16/1999 which merged into Doublestar Resources Ltd. (YT) 11/01/2001 which reincorporated in British Columbia 10/10/2002 which merged into Selkirk Metals Corp. 07/23/2007
(See Selkirk Metals Corp.)

STRONGBOW RES INC (BC)
Reorganized under the laws of Canada as Strongbow Exploration Inc. 05/03/2004
Each share Common no par exchanged for (0.5) share Common no par
Notes: Holders entitled to (99) shares or fewer received $1.06 cash per share
No distributions under $10 will be made

STRONGBOW RES INC (NV)
Each share old Common $0.001 par exchanged for (0.25) share new Common $0.001 par 03/17/2014
Name changed to Fortem Resources Inc. 03/30/2017

STRONGCO INC (ON)
Reorganized as Strongco Income Fund 05/06/2005
Each share Common no par exchanged for (1) Unit no par
Strongco Income Fund reorganized as Strongco Corp. 07/02/2010

STRONGCO INCOME FD (ON)
Under plan of reorganization each Unit no par automatically became (1) share Strongco Corp. Common no par 07/02/2010

STRONGHOLD INDS INC (CO)
Recapitalized as Image Worldwide, Inc. 11/30/2007
Each share Common $0.001 par exchanged for (0.1) share Common $0.001 par
Image Worldwide, Inc. recapitalized as STL Marketing Group, Inc. 09/03/2009

STRONGHOLD METALS INC (BC)
Recapitalized as Eagle Mountain Gold Corp. 07/26/2012
Each share Common no par exchanged for (0.2) share Common no par
Eagle Mountain Gold Corp. merged into Goldsource Mines Inc. 03/05/2014

STRONGHOLD TECHNOLOGIES INC (NV)
Name changed to DealerAdvance, Inc. 10/13/2006
(See DealerAdvance, Inc.)

STRONGSVILLE SVGS BK (STRONGSVILLE, OH)
Common $100 par split (2) for (1) by issuance of (1) additional share 02/22/1994
Under plan of reorganization each share Common $100 par automatically became (1) share Emerald Financial Corp. Common no par 03/06/1997
Emerald Financial Corp. merged into Fifth Third Bancorp 08/06/1999

STROOCK (S.) & CO., INC. (NY)
Capital Stock no par exchanged (3) for (1) 00/00/1944
Name changed to Ramco Enterprises, Inc. 12/30/1960
Ramco Enterprises, Inc. liquidated for Stetson (John B.) Co. 12/15/1971
(See Stetson (John B.) Co.)

STROTHER DRUG CO (VA)
Stock Dividend - 10% 09/15/1976
Merged into Alco Standard Corp. 12/31/1981
Each share Common $2 par exchanged for $16 cash

STROUDS INC (DE)
Plan of reorganization under Chapter 11 Federal Bankruptcy Code effective 03/20/2002
No stockholders' equity

STROUSS-HIRSCHBERG CO.
Merged into May Department Stores Co. on a (0.8) for (1) basis in 1948
May Department Stores Co. merged into Federated Department Stores, Inc. 8/30/2005 which name changed to Macy's, Inc. 6/1/2007

STROUT PLASTICS INC (MN)
Merged into S S S & P, Inc. 09/27/1979
Each share Common 10¢ par exchanged for $7 cash

STRUCTOFAB INC (GA)
Recapitalized as Tessa Complete Health Care Inc. 02/12/1998
Each share Common 2¢ par exchanged for (0.04) share Common 2¢ par
(See Tessa Complete Health Care Inc.)

FINANCIAL INFORMATION, INC. STR-STU

STRUCTURAL CONCRETE SYSTEMS, INC. (OH)
Charter cancelled for failure to pay taxes 04/15/1977

STRUCTURAL CONCRETE UNIT CORP. (DE)
Charter cancelled and declared inoperative and void for non-payment of taxes 04/01/1934

STRUCTURAL DYNAMICS RESH CORP (OH)
Class A Common no par split (4) for (1) by issuance of (3) additional shares 09/10/1987
Class A Common no par split (2) for (1) by issuance of (1) additional share 05/11/1990
Class A Common no par split (2) for (1) by issuance of (1) additional share 08/09/1991
Merged into Electronic Data Systems Corp. (DE) 08/31/2001
Each share Common no par exchanged for $25 cash

STRUCTURAL ENHANCEMENT TECHNOLOGIES CORP (DE)
Recapitalized as Eco-Petroleum Solutions, Inc. 02/07/2013
Each share Common $0.0001 par exchanged for (0.002) share Common $0.0001 par
Eco-Petroleum Solutions, Inc. name changed to Enzolytics Inc. 03/22/2018

STRUCTURAL FIBERS INC (OH)
Common $10 par changed to no par 10/10/1960
Common no par split (3) for (2) by issuance of (0.5) additional share 01/03/1972
Name changed to ESSEF Industries, Inc. 01/04/1982
ESSEF Industries, Inc. name changed to ESSEF Corp. 02/05/1985
(See ESSEF Corp.)

STRUCTURAL FOAM PRODS INC (DE)
Charter cancelled and declared inoperative and void for non-payment of taxes 03/01/1976

STRUCTURAL INSTRUMENTATION INC (DE)
Name changed to SI Technologies Inc. 02/12/1996
(See SI Technologies Inc.)

STRUCTURAL PLASTICS CORP (MN)
Statutorily dissolved 10/04/1991

STRUCTURED BIOLOGICALS INC (ON)
Recapitalized as Ben-Abraham Technologies Inc. 12/06/1996
Each share Common no par exchanged for (0.28571428) share Common no par
Ben-Abraham Technologies Inc. name changed to BioSante Pharmaceuticals, Inc. (WY) 12/17/1999 which reincorporated in Delaware 06/26/2001 which recapitalized as ANI Pharmaceuticals, Inc. 07/18/2013

STRUTHERS CAP CORP (NY)
Name changed to Vega Capital Corp. 05/08/1978
(See Vega Capital Corp.)

STRUTHERS FURNACE CO.
Reorganized as Struthers Iron & Steel Co. 00/00/1927
Details not available

STRUTHERS INC (NV)
Each share old Common $0.001 par exchanged for (0.001) share new Common $0.001 par 08/16/1998
New Common $0.001 par split (10) for (1) by issuance of (9) additional shares payable 09/30/1998 to holders of record 09/01/1998
Each (1,500) shares new Common $0.001 par exchanged again for (1) share new Common $0.001 par 01/12/2004
Name changed to Global Marine Ltd. 08/02/2004
(See Global Marine Ltd.)

STRUTHERS INDS INC (DE)
Each share Common 10¢ par exchanged for (0.425) share Common 1¢ par 01/21/1997
Plan of reorganization under Chapter 11 Federal Bankruptcy Code effective 11/30/2007
No stockholders' equity

STRUTHERS INTL RESH CORP (DE)
Each share Common $0.001 par received distribution of (0.1) share Struthers Inc. Common $0.001 par payable 12/29/1998 to holders of record 09/01/1998
Charter cancelled and declared inoperative and void for non-payment of taxes 03/01/1999

STRUTHERS IRON & STEEL CO.
Liquidated 00/00/1950
Details not available

STRUTHERS OIL & GAS CORP (DE)
Common 10¢ par split (3) for (1) by issuance of (2) additional shares 02/05/1980
Name changed to Struthers Industries, Inc. 11/28/1991
(See Struthers Industries, Inc.)

STRUTHERS SCIENTIFIC & INTL CORP (DE)
Stock Dividend - in Class A to holders of Class A 10% 01/31/1964
Charter cancelled and declared inoperative and void for non-payment of taxes 03/01/1995

STRUTHERS THERMO FLOOD CORP (DE)
Name changed to Struthers Oil & Gas Corp. 08/31/1977
Struthers Oil & Gas Corp. name changed to Struthers Industries, Inc. 11/28/1991
(See Struthers Industries, Inc.)

STRUTHERS-WELLS CO.
Acquired by Struthers-Wells Titusville Corp. 00/00/1928
Details not available

STRUTHERS WELLS CORP (MD)
Each share Common no par exchanged for (2) shares Common $2.50 par 00/00/1949
Common $2.50 par changed to $1 par and (2) additional shares issued 11/02/1961
Common $1 par split (3) for (2) by issuance of (0.5) additional share 11/30/1965
Adjudicated bankrupt 02/00/1994
Stockholders' equity unlikely

STRUTHERS-WELLS TITUSVILLE CORP.
Name changed to Struthers Wells Corp. 00/00/1942
(See Struthers Wells Corp.)

STRUTWEAR, INC. (MN)
Common $5 par changed to $1 par 05/15/1958
Merged into Kayser-Roth Corp. 05/26/1960
Each share 5% Preferred $100 par exchanged for (3) shares Common $5 par
Each share Common $1 par exchanged for (0.01851851) share Common $5 par
(See Kayser-Roth Corp.)

STRUTWEAR KNITTING CO.
Reorganized as Strutwear, Inc. 00/00/1944
Details not available

STRYKER VENTURES CORP (BC)
Recapitalized 08/25/1997
Recapitalized from Stryker Resources Ltd. to Stryker Ventures Corp. 08/25/1997
Each share Common no par exchanged for (0.1) share Common no par
Cease trade order effective 07/10/2002

STS PWR PEDAL CORP (BC)
Recapitalized as Mark-Can Investment Corp. 01/31/2001
Each share Common no par exchanged for (0.14285714) share Common no par
Mark-Can Investment Corp. recapitalized as Yale Resources Ltd. 09/30/2003 which recapitalized as Alta Vista Ventures Ltd. 05/29/2013 which name changed to Global UAV Technologies Ltd. 05/17/2017

STSC INC (DE)
Merged into Continental Telecom Inc. 09/02/1982
Each share Common 10¢ par exchanged for $11 cash

STT ENVIRO CORP (CANADA)
Acquired by Carmeuse Lime (Canada) Ltd. 07/04/2017
Each share Common no par exchanged for $0.315 cash

STUART CO. (CA)
Stock Dividends - 10% 12/15/1956; 100% 01/10/1957
Merged into Atlas Chemical Industries, 05/31/1961
Each share Common exchanged for (1.5) shares Common $1 par
(See Atlas Chemical Industries, Inc.)

STUART D A LTD (ON)
Name changed 10/20/1986
Each share Preference no par exchanged for (2) shares new Common no par 00/00/1953
Each share old Common no par exchanged for (1.5) shares new Common no par 00/00/1953
New Common no par split (4) for (1) by issuance of (3) additional shares 11/09/1967
Name changed from Stuart (D.A.) Oil Co. Ltd. to Stuart (D.A.) Ltd. 10/20/1986
Common no par split (3) for (1) by issuance of (2) additional shares 06/13/1988
Acquired by Werhahn International Inc. 01/31/1995
Each share Common no par exchanged for $8.50 cash

STUART ENERGY SYS CORP (CANADA)
Merged into Hydrogenics Corp. (Old) 01/21/2005
Each share Common no par exchanged for (0.74) share Common no par
Hydrogenics Corp. (Old) reorganized as Hydrogenics Corp. (New) 10/27/2009

STUART ENTMT INC (DE)
Plan of reorganization under Chapter 11 Federal Bankruptcy Code effective 02/08/2000
Each share Common 1¢ par will receive $0.0216 cash

STUART HALL INC (MO)
Common $1 par changed to $0.66666666 par and (0.5) additional share issued 07/15/1976
Common $0.66666666 par changed to $0.33333333 par and (1) additional share issued 10/22/1980
Common $0.33333333 par changed to 25¢ par and (0.33333333) additional share issued 12/18/1989
Stock Dividend - 10% 08/15/1986
Acquired by Newell Co. 07/08/1992
Each share Common 25¢ par exchanged for (0.3986) share Common $1 par
Newell Co. name changed to Newell Rubbermaid Inc. 03/24/1999

STUART HOUSE INTL LTD (CANADA)
6% Preferred Ser. A $8 par conversion privilege expired 05/01/1974
6% Preferred Ser. A $8 par called for redemption 08/01/1978
Merged into Vanctor Investments Ltd. 01/01/1985
Each share Common no par exchanged for $5 cash

STUART-JAMES VENTURE PARTNERS I, L.P. (DE)
Name changed to Westwood Technology Ventures L.P. 02/28/1991

STUART LYLE INC (DE)
Acquired by Carol Communication Corp. 01/09/1989
Each share Common 10¢ par exchanged for $13.50 cash

STUART McGUIRE INC (VA)
Common 5¢ par split (2) for (1) by issuance of (1) additional share 08/30/1983
Merged into Home Shopping Network Realty, Inc. 10/27/1986
Each share Common 5¢ par exchanged for $5 cash

STUART NATIONAL BANK (STUART, FL)
Merged into Florida National Banks of Florida, Inc. 08/01/1980
Each share Common $5 par exchanged for $95 cash

STUARTS DEPT STORES INC (DE)
Common 1¢ par split (3) for (2) by issuance of (0.5) additional share 08/30/1985
Chapter 11 bankruptcy proceedings converted to Chapter 7 on 02/14/1996
No stockholders' equity

STUBNITZ GREENE CORP. (MI)
Stock Dividend - 10% 02/28/1957
Merged into Hoover Ball & Bearing Co. (MI) 08/31/1964
Each share Common $1 par exchanged for (0.455) share Common $2.50 par
Hoover Ball & Bearing Co. (MI) reincorporated in Delaware 12/31/1968 which reincorporated back in Michigan 08/01/1976 which name changed to Hoover Universal Inc. 01/17/1978 which merged into Johnson Controls, Inc. 05/12/1985 which merged into Johnson Controls International PLC 09/06/2016

STUBNITZ GREENE SPRING CORP. (MI)
Name changed to Stubnitz Greene Corp. 06/23/1955
Stubnitz Greene Corp. merged into Hoover Ball & Bearing Co. (MI) 08/31/1964 which reincorporated in Delaware 12/31/1968 which reincorporated back in Michigan 08/01/1976 which name changed to Hoover Universal Inc. 01/17/1978 which merged into Johnson Controls, Inc. 05/12/1985 which merged into Johnson Controls International PLC 09/06/2016

STUDEBAKER CORP. (DE)
Merged into Studebaker-Packard Corp. 00/00/1954
Each share Common $1 par exchanged for (1.5) shares Common $10 par
Studebaker-Packard Corp. name changed to Studebaker Corp. (MI) 06/29/1962 which merged into Studebaker-Worthington, Inc. 11/27/1967
(See Studebaker-Worthington, Inc.)

STUDEBAKER CORP. (MI)
Each share Common $1 par exchanged for (0.2) share Common $5 par 05/24/1965

STU-STY

Merged into Studebaker-Worthington, Inc. 11/27/1967
Each share 5% Conv. Preferred $100 par exchanged for (14) shares $1.40 Conv. Preferred Ser. A no par
Each share $2.50 2nd Preferred Ser. A $10 par exchanged for (0.5) share $5 Conv. Preferred Ser. B no par
Each share Common $5 par exchanged for (1) share Common $1 par
(See Studebaker-Worthington, Inc.)

STUDEBAKER CORP. (NJ)
Reorganized as Studebaker Corp. (DE) 00/00/1935
No stockholders' equity

STUDEBAKER MAIL ORDER CO.
Liquidation completed 00/00/1934
Details not available

STUDEBAKER-PACKARD CORP. (MI)
Common 10 par changed to $1 par 11/02/1956
Name changed to Studebaker Corp. (MI) 06/29/1962
Studebaker Corp. (MI) merged into Studebaker-Worthington, Inc. 11/27/1967
(See Studebaker-Worthington, Inc.)

STUDEBAKER WORTHINGTON INC (DE)
Common $1 par split (3) for (2) by issuance of (0.5) additional share 09/03/1976
$1.40 Conv. Preferred Ser. A no par called for redemption 03/30/1978
$5 Conv. Preferred Ser. B no par called for redemption 03/30/1978
Common $1 par split (2) for (1) by issuance of (1) additional share 12/19/1978
Acquired by McGraw-Edison Co. 10/24/1979
Each share Common $1 par exchanged for $51.50 cash

STUDEBAKERS RESOURCE DEV LTD (BC)
Delisted from Vancouver Stock Exchange 02/21/1989

STUDENT ADVANTAGE INC (DE)
Each share old Common 1¢ par exchanged for (0.1) share new Common 1¢ par 06/28/2002
Each share new Common 1¢ par exchanged again for (0.1) share new Common 1¢ par 06/30/2003
Merged into Athena Ventures Parent, Inc. 03/16/2004
Each share new Common 1¢ par exchanged for $1.05 cash

STUDENT AIDE CTRS AMER INC (NJ)
Name changed to TCA International, Inc. 02/25/1988

STUDENT LOAN CORP (DE)
Acquired by Discover Financial Services 12/31/2010
Each share Common 1¢ par exchanged for $30 cash
Note: Each share Common 1¢ par received an initial additional distribution of $2.50 cash 12/23/2011

STUDENT LN MARKETING ASSN (USA)
Each share Common $100 par exchanged for (6) shares Common $16.67 par 03/31/1981
Each share Common $16.67 par exchanged for (35) shares Common 50¢ par 09/29/1983
Common 50¢ par split (5) for (2) by issuance of (1.5) additional shares 06/30/1989
Non-Vtg. Common 50¢ par split (5) for (2) by issuance of (1.5) additional shares 06/30/1989
Each share Common 50¢ par exchanged for (1) share Unrestricted Common 50¢ par 07/23/1992
Each share Non-Vtg. Common 50¢ par exchanged for (1) share Unrestricted Common 50¢ par 07/23/1992
Under plan of reorganization each share Common 50¢ par automatically became (1) share SLM Holding Corp. (DE) Common 20¢ par 08/08/1997
SLM Holding Corp. (DE) name changed to USA Educational Inc. 07/31/2000
Adjustable Rate Preferred Ser. A $50 par called for redemption at $50 on 12/10/2001
USA Educational Inc. name changed to SLM Corp. 05/17/2002

STUDENT TRANSN AMER LTD (ON)
Name changed to Student Transportation Inc. 11/19/2009

STUDENT TRANSN INC (ON)
Income Participating Securities separated 12/21/2009
Acquired by Spinner Can AcquireCo Inc. 04/27/2018
Each share Common no par exchanged for USD$7.50 cash
Note: Unexchanged certificates will be cancelled and become without value 04/27/2024

STUDIO APT INC (NY)
Each share Common $1 par exchanged for (0.1) share Common $10 par 04/30/1965
Completely liquidated 09/30/1972
Each share Common $10 par exchanged for first and final distribution of $492 cash

STUDIO BROMONT INC (FL)
Name changed to United American Corp. 03/01/2004

STUDIO CITY HLDG CORP (NY)
SEC revoked Preferred and Common stock registration 09/09/2005

STUDIO EIGHT LTG INC (NY)
Adjudicated bankrupt 01/23/1978
Stockholders' equity unlikely

STUDIO ONE MEDIA INC (DE)
Name changed to AfterMaster, Inc. 10/14/2015

STUDIO PLUS HOTELS INC (VA)
Common 1¢ par split (3) for (2) by issuance of (0.5) additional share payable 07/09/1996 to holders of record 06/20/1996
Merged into Extended Stay America, Inc. 04/11/1997
Each share Common 1¢ par exchanged for (1.2272) shares Common 1¢ par
(See Extended Stay America, Inc.)

STUDIO RE LTD
144A Preference called for redemption at $1.01 on 01/07/2004

STUDIO II PRODUCTIONS INC (FL)
Recapitalized as Studio II Brands, Inc. 09/01/2009
Each share Common $0.001 par exchanged for (0.5) share Common $0.001 par

STUFF YER FACE INC (NJ)
Recapitalized as Tubby's, Inc. 04/02/1990
Each share Common $0.00001 par exchanged for (0.33333333) share Common $0.001 par
(See Tubby's Inc.)

STUPIDPC INC (GA)
Name changed to Webcatalyst, Inc. 10/20/2000
(See Webcatalyst, Inc.)

STURDIVANT LIFE INS CO (NC)
Common $10 par and Non-Vtg. Common $10 par reclassified as Common $2 par 05/01/1966
Common $2 par split (5) for (1) by issuance of (4) additional shares 05/13/1966
Common $2 par changed to no par 12/15/1978
Acquired by Heritage Life Insurance Co. 07/06/1989
Each share Common no par exchanged for $12.07129 cash

STURDY MINES LTD (ON)
Capital Stock $1 par changed to no par 04/01/1971
Charter cancelled for failure to pay taxes and file returns 03/14/1978

STURGEON BASIN MINES LTD. (ON)
Charter cancelled for failure to file reports and pay taxes in 1970

STURGEON KING MINING CORP. LTD. (ON)
Merged into Bayfor Corp. Inc. 05/00/1972
Each share Capital Stock no par exchanged for (0.181818) share Capital Stock no par
(See Bayfor Corp. Inc.)

STURGEON PETES LTD (AB)
Struck off register for failure to file annual returns 04/01/1982

STURGEON RIVER GOLD MINES LTD. (ON)
Name changed to Sturgeon River Mines Ltd. 10/18/1955
Sturgeon River Mines Ltd. recapitalized as Quebec Sturgeon River Mines Ltd. 06/04/1964 which merged into QSR Ltd. 09/07/1993 which name changed to Coniagas Resources Ltd. 06/25/1999 which name changed to Lithium One Inc. 07/23/2009
(See Lithium One Inc.)

STURGEON RIVER MINES LTD. (ON)
Recapitalized as Quebec Sturgeon River Mines Ltd. on a (0.25) for (1) basis 06/04/1964
Quebec Sturgeon River Mines Ltd. merged into QSR Ltd. 09/07/1993 which name changed to Coniagas Resources Ltd. 06/25/1999 which name changed to Lithium One Inc. 07/23/2009
(See Lithium One Inc.)

STURGEX MINES LTD (ON)
Merged into Royex Sturgex Mining Ltd. 07/31/1974
Each share Common no par exchanged for (0.5882352) share Common no par
Royex Sturgex Mining Ltd. name changed to Royex Gold Mining Corp. 06/08/1984 which merged into Corona Corp. 07/01/1988 which recapitalized as International Corona Corp. 06/11/1991
(See International Corona Corp.)

STURGIS BK & TRUST CO (STURGIS, MI)
Name changed 07/28/1998
Common $1 par split (2) for (1) by issuance of (1) additional share payable 06/15/1998 to holders of record 05/15/1998
Name changed from Sturgis Federal Savings Bank (Sturgis, MI) to Sturgis Bank & Trust Co. (Sturgis, MI) 07/28/1998
Under plan of reorganization each share Common $1 par automatically became (1) share Sturgis Bancorp, Inc. Common $1 par 01/01/2002

STURTEVANT (B.F.) CO. (MA)
Acquired by Westinghouse Electric Corp. 09/00/1945
Details not available

STUTZ MOTOR CAR CO. OF AMERICA (DE)
Adjudicated bankrupt 03/00/1938
No stockholders' equity

STUYVESANT BUFFALO, INC.
Out of business 00/00/1938
Details not available

STUYVESANT INS CO (NY)
Each share Capital Stock $100 par exchanged for (4) shares Capital Stock $25 par 00/00/1929
Capital Stock $25 par changed to $10 par 00/00/1932
Capital Stock $10 par changed to $5 par 00/00/1935
Capital Stock $5 par changed to $3 par 03/18/1964
Stock Dividend - 60.1% 12/15/1956
Over 99% held by GAC Corp. (DE) and balance held by directors as of 01/01/1974
Public interest eliminated

STUYVESANT LIFE INS CO (PA)
Over 99% held by GAC Corp. (DE) and balance held by directors as of 01/01/1974
Public interest eliminated

STV, INC. (PA)
Name changed to STV Engineers, Inc. 02/05/1979
STV Engineers, Inc. name changed to STV Group, Inc. 06/25/1991

STV GRP INC (PA)
Name changed 06/25/1991
Common $1 par split (2) for (1) by issuance of (1) additional share 08/15/1983
Name changed from STV Engineers, Inc. to STV Group, Inc. 06/25/1991
Common $1 par split (2) for (1) by issuance of (1) additional share payable 04/01/1998 to holders of record 03/31/1998
Company went private 08/30/2001
Each share Common $1 par exchanged for $11.25 cash

S2 GOLF INC (NJ)
Each share old Common 1¢ par exchanged for (0.25) share new Common 1¢ par 06/28/1991
Name changed to Women's Golf Unlimited, Inc. 06/19/2001
(See Women's Golf Unilimited, Inc.)

S2C GLOBAL SYS INC (NV)
Recapitalized as VIPR Corp. 08/06/2014
Each share Common $0.001 par exchanged for (0.00333333) share Common $0.001 par

STX EUROPE ASA (NORWAY)
ADR agreement terminated 03/19/2014
No ADR's remain outstanding

STYLE CENTER BUILDING CORP. (IL)
Liquidated 00/00/1946
No stockholders' equity

STYLE-RITE HOMES CORP. (OH)
Charter revoked for failure to file reports and pay fees 06/25/1959

STYLECLICK COM INC (CA)
Merged into Styleclick, Inc. 07/27/2000
Each share Common no par exchanged for (1) share Common 1¢ par
(See Styleclick, Inc.)

STYLECLICK INC (DE)
Company terminated registration of common stock and is no longer public as of 03/21/2003

STYLES ON VIDEO INC (DE)
Common $0.001 par split (3) for (2) by issuance of (0.5) additional share 10/14/1993
Each share old Common $0.001 par exchanged for (0.1) share new Common $0.001 par 06/13/1997
Charter forfeited for failure to maintain a registered agent 11/20/1998

STYLESITE MARKETING INC (DE)
Chapter 11 bankruptcy proceedings dismissed 06/11/2002
No stockholders' equity

STYLEX HOMES INC (NY)
Each share old Common 10¢ par exchanged for (0.1) share new Common 10¢ par 10/30/1992
Recapitalized as Cytation.Com Inc. (NY) 02/12/1999
Each share new Common 10¢ par exchanged for (0.5) share Common 10¢ par
Cytation.Com Inc. (NY) reincorporated in Delaware as Collegelink, Inc. 11/16/1999 which name changed to Cytation Corp. 06/21/2001

STYLING TECHNOLOGY CORP (DE)
Plan of reorganization under Chapter 11 Federal Bankruptcy Code effective 09/13/2002
No stockholders' equity

STYLON CORP (DE)
Reincorporated 04/29/1960
State of incorporation changed from (MA) to (DE) 04/29/1960
Each share Common $1 par exchanged for (0.25) share Common $4 par 10/31/1962
Name changed to DCA Development Corp. 05/25/1970
(See DCA Development Corp.)

STYLUS ENERGY INC (AB)
Acquired by Compton Petroleum Corp. 08/15/2007
Each share Common no par exchanged for $2.70 cash

STYNRO DEV LTD (BC)
Name changed to Syn-Trac Industries Ltd. 10/22/1976
Syn-Trac Industries Ltd. name changed to Austra Resources Corp. 08/07/1984 which name changed to Austar Resources Inc. 11/01/1990 which recapitalized as Austpro Energy Corp. 01/31/1996

SU MARK BOATS (DE)
Reincorporated 11/08/1991
State of incorporation changed from (MA) to (DE) 11/08/1991
Charter cancelled and declared inoperative and void for non-payment of taxes 03/01/1996

SUARRO COMMUNICATIONS INC (NV)
Name changed to E-Net Corp. 02/12/1999
E-Net Corp. name changed to E-Net Financial Corp. 05/12/1999 which name changed to e-Net.com Corp. 01/18/2000 which name changed to e-Net.Financial.Com Corp. 02/02/2000 which name changed to Anza Capital, Inc. 01/01/2002 which recapitalized as Renhuang Pharmaceutical, Inc. 08/11/2006 which name changed to China Botanic Pharmaceutical Inc. 11/22/2010

SUAVE SHOE CORP (FL)
Common 1¢ par split (3) for (2) by issuance of (0.5) additional share 01/10/1972
Stock Dividend - 10% 04/15/1981
Name changed to French Fragrances Inc. 12/01/1995
French Fragrances Inc. name changed to Elizabeth Arden, Inc. 01/25/2001
(See Elizabeth Arden, Inc.)

SUB CAP INC (CANADA)
Each share old Common no par exchanged for (0.1) share new Common no par 11/25/2009
Name changed to Inca One Metals Corp. 05/11/2011
Inca One Metals Corp. name changed to Inca One Resources Inc. 10/26/2011 which name changed to Inca One Gold Corp. 09/17/2014

SUB NIGEL LTD (SOUTH AFRICA)
Name changed to Gold Fields Property Co. Ltd. 01/28/1972
Gold Fields Property Co. Ltd. name changed to Mawenzi Resources Ltd. 06/08/1998 which name changed to Zarara Energy Ltd. 10/27/2000
(See Zarara Energy Ltd.)

SUB ZERO FREEZER CO., INC. (WI)
Called for redemption 06/15/1976
Public interest eliminated

SUBARU AMER INC (NJ)
Reincorporated 03/21/1977
State of incorporation changed from (PA) to (NJ) 03/21/1977
Common 1¢ par split (8) for (1) by issuance of (7) additional shares 05/01/1986
Merged into Fuji Heavy Industries Ltd. 08/31/1990
Each share Common 1¢ par exchanged for $9 cash

SUBDIVISION DEVELOPMENT CORP. (GA)
Completely liquidated 12/27/1974
Each share Common 25¢ par or Class A Common 25¢ par received first and final distribution of $3 cash

SUBEO LTD (ON)
Charter cancelled for failure to pay taxes and file returns 03/00/1976

SUBEX AZURE LTD (INDIA)
Name changed to Subex Ltd. 11/30/2007

SUBEX SYS LTD (INDIA)
Name changed to Subex Azure Ltd. 08/21/2006
Subex Azure Ltd. name changed to Subex Ltd. 11/30/2007

SUBJEX CORP (MN)
SEC revoked common stock registration 10/10/2014

SUBLINGUAL PRODS INTL INC (NV)
Name changed to Pharmaceutical Labs, Inc. (NV) 03/27/1992
Pharmaceutical Labs, Inc. (NV) reorganized in Delaware as Annapolis Capital Holdings Inc. 07/14/2006 which name changed to Podium Venture Group, Inc. 08/30/2006 which name changed to Capital Oil & Gas, Inc. 08/07/2008 which recapitalized as Southcorp Capital, Inc. 01/28/2009

SUBLOO INTL RESOURCE CORP (CANADA)
Reincorporated 08/18/1994
Place of incorporation changed from (BC) to (Canada) 08/18/1994
Name changed to Goldminco Mining Corp. 10/07/1996
Goldminco Mining Corp. recapitalized as Goldminco Consolidated Mining Corp. 12/22/1997 which recapitalized as Goldminco Corp. 04/06/2000
(See Goldminco Corp.)

SUBMARINE BOAT CORP.
Liquidated 00/00/1935
No stockholders' equity

SUBMARINE OIL & GAS LTD. (ON)
Acquired by Camerina Petroleum Corp. 12/08/1960
Each share Capital Stock no par exchanged for (0.4) share Capital Stock no par
(See Camerina Petroleum Corp.)

SUBMARINE SIGNAL CO.
Merged into Raytheon Manufacturing Co. on a (5.5) for (1) basis in 1946 which name was changed to Raytheon Co. 5/4/59

SUBMARINO S A (BRAZIL)
Merged into Americanas.com 06/05/2007
Each 144A Sponsored GDR for Common exchanged for $69.34755 cash
Each Reg. S Sponsored GDR for Common exchanged for $69.34755 cash

SUBMICRON SYS CORP (DE)
Liquidating plan of reorganization under Chapter 11 Federal Bankruptcy Code effective 05/16/2000
No stockholders' equity

SUBPRIME ADVANTAGE INC (NV)
Reorganized as Citadel Exploration, Inc. 03/18/2011
Each share Common $0.001 par exchanged for (12) shares Common $0.001 par

SUBSCRIPTION TELEVISION INC (DE)
Common $1 par changed to 1¢ par 06/30/1967
Each share Common 1¢ par exchanged for (0.1) share Common 10¢ par 12/31/1970
Name changed to Burnley Corp. 10/23/1978
(See Burnley Corp.)

SUBSTANCE ABUSE TECHNOLOGIES INC (DE)
Plan of reorganization under Chapter 11 Federal Bankruptcy Code effective 05/26/1998
No stockholders' equity

SUBSURFACE RESV CORP (TX)
Vountarily dissolved 03/30/2000
Details not available

SUBURBAN AIRLS INC (DE)
Acquired by US Airways Group, Inc. 04/30/1986
Each share Common $1 par exchanged for $46.60 cash

SUBURBAN BANCORP, INC. (DE)
Merged into Bank of Montreal (Montreal, QC) 09/30/1994
Each share Class A Common $1 par exchanged for (3.9352) shares Common no par

SUBURBAN BANCORP (MD)
Name changed 12/31/1981
Common $5 par split (3) for (2) by issuance of (0.5) additional share 06/07/1974
Name changed from Suburban Bancorporation to Suburban Bancorp 12/31/1981
Merged into Sovran Financial Corp. 03/31/1986
Each share Common $5 par exchanged for (2.926) shares Common $5 par
Sovran Financial Corp. merged into C&S/Sovran Corp. 09/01/1990 which merged into NationsBank Corp. 12/31/1991 which reincorporated in Delaware as BankAmerica Corp. (Old) 09/25/1998 which merged into BankAmerica Corp. (New) 09/30/1998 which name changed to Bank of America Corp. 04/28/1999

SUBURBAN BANCORPORATION INC (DE)
Merged into Fifth Third Bancorp 07/25/1997
Each share Common 1¢ par exchanged for (0.36536) share Common no par

SUBURBAN BANCSHARES INC (DE)
Merged into Columbia Bancorp 03/08/2000
Each share Common 1¢ par exchanged for (0.2338) share Common 1¢ par
Columbia Bancorp merged into Fulton Financial Corp. 02/01/2006

SUBURBAN BK (NORRISTOWN, PA)
Merged into American Bank & Trust Co. of Pennsylvania (Reading, PA) 12/31/1980
Each share Capital Stock $10 par exchanged for (1.65) shares Capital Stock $5 par
American Bank & Trust Co. of Pennsylvania (Reading, PA) reorganized as American Bancorp, Inc. 09/02/1981 which merged into Meridian Bancorp, Inc. 06/30/1983 which merged into CoreStates Financial Corp 04/09/1996 which merged into First Union Corp. 04/28/1998 which name changed to Wachovia Corp. (Ctfs. dated after 09/01/2001) 09/01/2001 which merged into Wells Fargo & Co. (New) 12/31/2008

SUBURBAN BANKSHARES INC (FL)
Merged into 1st United Bancorp 06/03/1994
Each share Class A Common 10¢ par exchanged for (0.44) share Common no par
1st United Bancorp merged into Wachovia Corp. (New) (Ctfs. dated between 05/20/1991 and 09/01/2001) 11/11/1997 which merged into Wachovia Corp. (Ctfs. dated after 09/01/2001) 09/01/2001 which merged into Wells Fargo & Co. (New) 12/31/2008

SUBURBAN BROADCASTING CORP (NY)
Acquired by Wometco Enterprises, Inc. 01/06/1981
Details not available

SUBURBAN CASUALTY INSURANCE CO.
Dissolved 00/00/1930
Details not available

SUBURBAN CMNTY BK (CHALFONT, PA)
Merged into Univest Corp. of Pennsylvania 10/03/2003
Each share Common $5 par exchanged for $20 cash

SUBURBAN COS (CA)
Merged into Williams Brothers Co. 01/08/1971
Each share Common $1 par exchanged for $11 principal amount of 10-Year Ser. A Debentures due 01/01/1981 and (0.6) Ser. A Warrant which expired 01/01/1976

SUBURBAN DIRECTORY PUBLISHERS, INC. (PA)
Name changed to Suburban Publishers, Inc. 05/10/1966
Suburban Publishers, Inc. name changed to Jewelcor, Inc. 04/13/1970
(See Jewelcor, Inc.)

SUBURBAN ELECTRIC CO. (MA)
Acquired by New England Electric System 06/30/1959
Each share Common $25 par exchanged for (5.5) shares Common $1 par
(See New England Electric System)

SUBURBAN ELECTRIC DEVELOPMENT CO.
Acquired by Electric Products Corp. 00/00/1930
Details not available

SUBURBAN ELECTRIC SECURITIES CO. (MA)
Merged into Middlesex & Boston Street Railway Co. 12/00/1954
Each share Common no par exchanged for (2) shares Capital Stock $10 par
(See Middlesex & Boston Street Railway Co.)

SUBURBAN FED SVGS BK (COLLINGDALE, PA)
Merged into Main Line Federal Savings Bank (Villanova, PA) 12/29/1995
Each share Common $1 par exchanged for $10.25 cash

SUBURBAN GAS & ELECTRIC CO. (MA)
Under plan of merger each share Common $25 par exchanged for (0.5) share Common $25 par of Mystic Valley Gas Co. and (0.5)

SUB-SUD

share Common $25 par of Suburban Electric Co. 00/00/1953
(See each company's listing)

SUBURBAN GAS (CA)
Common $1 par split (2) for (1) by issuance of (1) additional share 03/02/1960
Common $1 par split (2) for (1) by issuance of (1) additional share 03/24/1961
5.5% Preferred $25 par called for redemption 10/31/1961
Name changed to Suburban Companies 09/05/1969
(See Suburban Companies)

SUBURBAN GAS SERVICE, INC. (CA)
Common $1 par split (3) for (2) by issuance of (0.5) additional share 02/24/1958
Name changed to Suburban Gas 12/16/1960
Suburban Gas name changed to Suburban Companies 09/05/1969
(See Suburban Companies)

SUBURBAN LIFE INSURANCE CO. (MD)
Merged into Chesapeake Life Insurance Co. 09/11/1964
Each share Common $1 par exchanged for (0.18181818) share Class A $1 par and (0.18181818) share Class B $1 par
Chesapeake Life Insurance Co. (MD) recapitalized under the laws of Oklahoma 09/27/1993
(See Chesapeake Life Insurance Co.)

SUBURBAN LODGES AMER INC (GA)
Merged into Intown Holding Co., L.L.C. 05/02/2002
Each share Common 1¢ par exchanged for $8.25 cash
Note: Each share Common 1¢ par received an initial additional distribution of $0.25 cash 06/02/2003
Each share Common 1¢ par received a second distribution of $0.43 cash 06/01/2004
Each share Common 1¢ par received a third and final distribution of approximately $0.048 cash 01/03/2005

SUBURBAN NATL BK VA (MCLEAN, VA)
Merged into First & Merchants Corp. 08/01/1970
Each share Capital Stock $10 par exchanged for (1.38) shares Common 10¢ par
First & Merchants Corp. merged into Sovran Financial Corp. 12/31/1983 which merged into C&S/Sovran Corp. 09/01/1990 which merged into NationsBank Corp. 12/31/1991 which reincorporated in Delaware as BankAmerica Corp. (Old) 09/25/1998 which merged into BankAmerica Corp. (New) 09/30/1998 which name changed to Bank of America Corp. 04/28/1999

SUBURBAN NATL CORP (MA)
Acquired by Lexington Savings Bank (Lexington, MA) 12/23/1993
Each share Common $100 par exchanged for $184.06 cash

SUBURBAN OSTOMY SUPPLY INC (MA)
Merged into Invacare Corp. 01/28/1998
Each share Common no par exchanged for $11.75 cash

SUBURBAN PROPANE GAS CORP (NJ)
5% Preferred $50 par called for redemption 00/00/1951
5.2% Preferred 1951 Ser. $50 par called for redemption 04/19/1963
5.2% Preferred 1952 Ser. $50 par called for redemption 04/19/1963
Common $1 par split (3) for (2) by issuance of (0.5) additional share 03/22/1971
Common $1 par split (3) for (2) by issuance of (0.5) additional share 05/22/1972
Stock Dividend - 10% 03/29/1982
Merged into National Distillers & Chemical Corp. 02/17/1983
Each share Common $1 par exchanged for $51 cash

SUBURBAN PUBLISHERS INC (PA)
Stock Dividends - 50% 01/24/1969; 100% 12/31/1969
Name changed to Jewelcor, Inc. 04/13/1970
(See Jewelcor, Inc.)

SUBURBAN RAPID TRANSIT STREET RAILWAY CO.
Merged into Pittsburgh Railway Co. 09/30/1950
Details not available

SUBURBAN TR CO (HYATTSVILLE, MD)
Stock Dividends - 10% 07/15/1954; 100% 01/19/1962; 10% 04/11/1969; 25% 04/16/1971
Reorganized as Suburban Bancorporation 07/01/1972
Each share Capital Stock $10 par exchanged for (2) shares Common $5 par
Suburban Bancorporation name changed to Suburban Bancorp 12/31/1981 which merged into Sovran Financial Corp. 03/31/1986 which merged into C&S/Sovran Corp. 09/01/1990 which merged into NationsBank Corp. (NC) 12/31/1991 which reincorporated in Delaware as BankAmerica Corp. (Old) 09/25/1998 which merged into BankAmerica Corp. (New) 09/30/1998 which name changed to Bank of America Corp. 04/28/1999

SUBURBAN TR CO (WESTFIELD, NJ)
Common $25 par changed to $5 par and (4) additional shares issued 03/29/1968
Stock Dividends - 10% 09/20/1962; 100% 11/12/1963; 10% 10/26/1964; 10% 09/09/1966
Merged into Fidelity Union Bancorporation 12/22/1972
Each share Common $5 par exchanged for $43 cash

SUBURBAN WTR SVC INC (CT)
Under plan of merger name changed to Connecticut Water Service, Inc. 04/10/1975

SUBURBAN WTR SYS (CA)
Each share Common $1 par exchanged for (3) shares Common $5 par 05/22/1973
Merged into SouthWest Water Co. (CA) 09/30/1975
Each share $2.62 Preferred Ser. A $50 par exchanged for $35 principal amount of 9.5% Conv. Debentures due 08/15/1995
Each share $1.50 Preferred Ser. B $50 par exchanged for $21 principal amount of 9.5% Conv. Debentures due 08/15/1995
Each share Common $5 par exchanged for (0.8) share Common $1 par and $1.50 cash
SouthWest Water Co. (CA) reincorporated in Delaware 06/30/1988
(See SouthWest Water Co.)

SUBURBFED FINL CORP (DE)
Common 1¢ par split (3) for (2) by issuance of (0.5) additional share 11/03/1995
Merged into CFS Bancorp Inc. (DE) 07/24/1998
Each share Common 1¢ par exchanged for (3.6) shares Common 1¢ par
CFS Bancorp Inc. (DE) reincorporated in Indiana 06/30/2005 which merged into First Merchants Corp. 11/12/2013

SUCAMPO PHARMACEUTICALS INC (DE)
Acquired by Mallinckrodt PLC 02/13/2018
Each share Class A Common 1¢ par exchanged for $18 cash

SUCCESS BANCSHARES INC (DE)
Merged into BankFinancial Corp. 11/16/2001
Each share Common $0.001 par exchanged for $19 cash

SUCCESS CAP TR I (DE)
8.95% Trust Preferred Securities called for redemption at $10 on 12/15/2003

SUCCESS DEV GROUP INC (NV)
SEC revoked common stock registration 01/18/2008
Stockholders' equity unlikely

SUCCESS DEV INTL INC (FL)
Name changed to International Media Holdings, Inc. 04/01/1999
(See International Media Holdings, Inc.)

SUCCESS EXPL & RES INC (NV)
Name changed to FileWarden.com 03/11/2014

SUCCESS FINL SVCS GROUP INC (NV)
Old Common $0.002 par split (6) for (1) by issuance of (5) additional shares payable 08/09/2002 to holders of record 08/02/2002
Ex date - 08/12/2002
Each share old Common $0.002 par exchanged for (0.01) new share Common $0.002 par 02/10/2003
Name changed to Consolidated American Industries Corp. 03/01/2005

SUCCESS MOTIVATION INST INC (TX)
Common 50¢ par split (2) for (1) by issuance of (1) additional share 12/15/1969
Name changed to SMI International, Inc. 03/29/1979
SMI International, Inc. name changed to SMI/USA, Inc. 10/01/1990
(See SMI/USA, Inc.)

SUCCESSFACTORS INC (DE)
Acquired by SAP AG 02/22/2012
Each share Common $0.001 par exchanged for $40 cash

SUCCESSORIES INC (MN)
Merged into S.I. Acquisition LLC 06/19/2003
Each share Common 1¢ par exchanged for $0.30 cash

SUCRE AGRIC CORP (NV)
Recapitalized as Bluefire Ethanol Fuels, Inc. 06/22/2006
Each share Common $0.001 par exchanged for (1/3) share Common $0.001 par
Bluefire Ethanol Fuels, Inc. name changed to BlueFire Renewables, Inc. 10/25/2010

SUCREST CORP (NY)
Common Stock $1 par reclassified as Common Shares $1 par 08/23/1965
Common Shares $1 par split (3) for (2) by issuance of (0.5) additional share 09/10/1965
Common Shares $1 par split (2) for (1) by issuance of (1) additional share 08/15/1974
Name changed to Ingredient Technology Corp. (NY) 12/15/1977
Ingredient Technology Corp. (NY) reincorporated in Delaware 06/30/1978

(See Ingredient Technology Corp. (DE))

SUDAMET VENTURES INC (CANADA)
Recapitalized as Avigo Resources Corp. 05/05/2005
Each share Common no par exchanged for (0.5) share Common no par
Avigo Resources Corp. name changed to Carbon Friendly Solutions Inc. 08/08/2008 which changed name to MicroCoal Technologies Inc. 07/22/2013 which reorganized as Targeted Microwave Solutions Inc. 05/22/2015

SUDAMTEX DE VENEZUELA C A S A C A (VENEZUELA)
Each old Sponsored ADR for Ordinary VEB 20 par exchanged for (0.25) new Sponsored ADR for Ordinary VEB 20 par 08/25/1997
Stock Dividends - 10% 12/16/1994; 5% payable 03/11/1996 to holders of record 03/07/1996; 12% payable 01/07/1998 to holders of record 12/24/1997; 1% payable 12/17/1998 to to holders of record 11/27/1998
ADR agreement terminated 04/25/2007
No ADR holders' equity

SUDBAY BERYLLIUM MINES LTD. (ON)
Charter revoked for failure to file reports and pay fees 08/19/1965

SUDBAY EXPLORATION & MINING LTD. (ON)
Name changed to Sudbay Beryllium Mines Ltd. 04/04/1960
(See Sudbay Beryllium Mines Ltd.)

SUDBURY BASIN MINES LTD.
Acquired by Ventures, Ltd. 00/00/1943
Each share Capital Stock exchanged for (0.33333333) share Ventures Ltd. Capital Stock no par and (1) share Ontario Pyrites Co. Capital Stock no par
(See each company's listing)

SUDBURY CAP CORP (ON)
Recapitalized as NiCo Mining Ltd. 03/18/2008
Each share Common no par exchanged for (0.1) share Common no par
NiCo Mining Ltd. name changed to Red Crescent Resources Ltd. 11/11/2010

SUDBURY CONTACT MINES LTD (ON)
Capital Stock $1 par changed to no par 06/09/1971
Name changed to Contact Diamond Corp. 09/30/2004
Contact Diamond Corp. acquired by Stornoway Diamond Corp. (BC) 01/17/2007 which reincorporated in Canada 10/28/2011

SUDBURY INC (DE)
Reorganized 05/27/1987
Under plan of reorganization each share Sudbury Holdings, Inc. Common 1¢ par automatically became (1) share Sudbury, Inc. Common 1¢ par 05/27/1987
Reorganized under Chapter 11 Federal Bankruptcy Code 08/31/1992
For each (46.9) shares old Common 1¢ par holders received (1) share new Common 1¢ par; for each (44.56) shares old Common 1¢ par (1) Participating Certificate Ser. A; for each (42.33) shares old Common 1¢ par (1) Participating Certificate Ser. B and for each (19.05) shares old Common 1¢ par (1) Participating Certificate Ser. C
Merged into Intermet Corp. 01/02/1997

Each share new Common 1¢ par exchanged for $12.50 cash

SUDBURY MIDZONE MINES LTD. (ON)
Merged into Midrim Mining Co. Ltd. 04/18/1955
Each share Capital Stock $1 par exchanged for (0.5) share Capital Stock $1 par
Midrim Mining Co. Ltd. merged into Plasma Environmental Technologies, Inc. 05/31/1996 which recapitalized as Blue Vista Technologies Inc. 08/17/2007 which recapitalized as Arbitrage Exploration Inc. 01/16/2015 which name changed to Argo Gold Inc. 09/22/2016

SUDBURY NORTHRIM EXPLORATION CO. LTD. (ON)
Merged into Midrim Mining Co. Ltd. 04/18/1955
Each share Capital Stock $1 par exchanged for (0.33333333) share Capital Stock $1 par
Midrim Mining Co. Ltd. merged into Plasma Environmental Technologies, Inc. 05/31/1996 which recapitalized as Blue Vista Technologies Inc. 08/17/2007 which recapitalized as Arbitrage Exploration Inc. 01/16/2015 which name changed to Argo Gold Inc. 09/22/2016

SUDBURY OFFSETS LTD. (CANADA)
Recapitalized as Nickel Offsets Ltd. 00/00/1938
Each share Common no par exchanged for (0.2) share Common no par
Nickel Offsets Ltd. merged into Canhorn Mining Corp. 01/09/1986 which merged into Canhorn Chemical Corp. 04/26/1995 which merged into Nayarit Gold Inc. 05/02/2005 which merged into Capital Gold Corp. 08/02/2010 which merged into Gammon Gold Inc. (QC) 04/08/2011 which reincorporated in Ontario as AuRico Gold Inc. 06/14/2011 which merged into Alamos Gold Inc. (New) 07/06/2015

SUDONTA GOLD MINES, LTD. (ON)
Charter surrendered for failure to file reports and pay taxes 00/00/1958

SUDORE GOLD MINES LTD. (ON)
Charter revoked for failure to file reports and pay fees 11/10/1966 00/00/1946)

SUE ANN INC (TX)
Stock Dividends - 50% 02/14/1975; 50% 06/16/1975; 50% 08/26/1976
Name changed to CS Group, Inc. 08/06/1980
CS Group, Inc. recapitalized as DeCorp Inc. 10/29/1987
(See DeCorp Inc.)

SUE WONG INTL INC (AZ)
Reorganized under the laws of Colorado as Amalgamated Explorations, Inc. 08/03/1995
Each share Common $0.0015 par exchanged for (0.1) share Common $0.0001 par
(See Amalgamated Explorations, Inc.)

SUEZ (FRANCE)
Merged into GDF Suez S.A. 07/22/2008
Each Sponsored ADR for Ordinary exchanged for (0.9545) Sponsored ADR for Ordinary and $6.3588174 cash
GDF Suez S.A. name changed to Engie 07/31/2015

SUEZ ENVIRONNEMENT CO S A (FRANCE)
Name changed to SUEZ 05/27/2016

SUEZ PETE CORP (BC)
Name changed to Overseas Platinum Corp. 04/29/1987
Overseas Platinum Corp.

recapitalized as Broadlands Resources Ltd. (Old) 05/28/1991 which merged into International Broadlands Resources Ltd. 04/06/1995 which recapitalized as Broadlands Resources Ltd. (New) 03/15/1999 which recapitalized as Pinnacle Mines Ltd. (Ctfs. dated after 07/16/2003) 07/16/2003 which name changed to Jayden Resources Inc. (BC) 06/29/2010 which reincorporated in Cayman Islands 10/03/2012

SUFFER (NV)
Recapitalized as Ophir Resources Co. 01/23/2013
Each share Common $0.001 par exchanged for (0.001) share Common $0.001 par
(See Ophir Resources Co.)

SUFFIELD FINL CORP (DE)
Name changed to First Coastal Corp. 05/15/1992
(See First Coastal Corp.)

SUFFIELD SVGS BK (SUFFIELD, CT)
Common $1 par split (2) for (1) by issuance of (1) additional share payable 12/20/1985
Under plan of reorganization each share Common $1 par automatically became (1) share Suffield Financial Corp. Common $1 par 01/30/1987
Suffield Financial Corp. name changed to First Coastal Corp. 05/15/1992
(See First Coastal Corp.)

SUFFOLK BANCORP (NY)
Common $5 par split (5) for (1) by issuance of (4) additional shares 07/31/1986
Common $5 par split (2) for (1) by issuance of (1) additional share 05/22/1987
Common $5 par changed to $2.50 par and (1) additional share issued payable 05/15/1997 to holders of record 05/01/1997
Common $2.50 par split (2) for (1) by issuance of (1) additional share payable 01/02/2002 to holders of record 12/14/2001 Ex date - 01/03/2002
Merged into People's United Financial, Inc. 04/01/2017
Each share Common $2.50 par exchanged for (2.225) shares Common 1¢ par

SUFFOLK CNTY NATL BK (RIVERHEAD, NY)
Common $10 par changed to $5 par and (1) additional share issued 05/07/1969
Stock Dividend - 100% 04/20/1972
Reorganized as Suffolk Bancorp 01/02/1985
Each share Common $5 par exchanged for (1) share Common $5 par
Suffolk Bancorp merged into People's United Financial, Inc. 04/01/2017

SUFFOLK FIRST BK (SUFFOLK, VA)
Stock Dividend - 10% payable 01/31/2007 to holders of record 01/03/2007 Ex date - 12/29/2006
Under plan of reorganization each share Common $3.20 par automatically became (1) share First Bankshares, Inc. Common $3.20 par 08/15/2008
First Bankshares, Inc. merged into Xenith Bankshares, Inc. (Old) 12/22/2009 which merged into Xenith Bankshares, Inc. (New) 08/01/2016 which merged into Union Bankshares Corp. 01/01/2018

SUFFOLK REAL ESTATE TRUST
Liquidated 00/00/1949
Details not available

SUFFOLK RES LTD (BC)
Delisted from Alberta Stock Exchange 10/12/1989

SUFFOLK TITLE & GUARANTEE CO.
Name changed to Greater New York Suffolk Title & Guarantee Co. 00/00/1930
(See Greater New York Suffolk Title & Guarantee Co.)

SUGAR CREEK FINL CORP (USA)
Reorganized under the laws of Maryland 04/09/2014
Each share Common 1¢ par exchanged for (1.0453) shares Common 1¢ par

SUGAR CREEK OIL & GAS INC (AB)
Merged into Petrostar Petroleums Inc. (New) 06/11/1992
Each share Common no par exchanged for (0.2105263) share Common no par
Petrostar Petroleums Inc. (New) merged into Crestar Energy Inc. 06/07/1996 which was acquired by Gulf Canada Resources Ltd. 11/13/2000
(See Gulf Canada Resources Ltd.)

SUGAR ESTATE OF THE ORIENTE, INC.
Reorganized as West Indies Sugar Corp. 00/00/1931
Details not available

SUGAR FINANCE CORP. (DE)
Charter cancelled and declared inoperative and void for non-payment of taxes 03/21/1923

SUGAR PINE LUMBER CO.
Bankrupt 00/00/1933
No stockholders' equity

SUGARBUSH VALLEY CORP. (VT)
100% acquired by Solon Automated Services, Inc. as of 04/14/1978
Public interest eliminated

SUGARDALE FOODS INC (OH)
Name changed to Morgan's Restaurants, Inc. 03/04/1976
Morgan's Restaurants, Inc. name changed to Mortronics Inc. 06/30/1982 which name changed to Morgan's Foods, Inc. 09/19/1986
(See Morgan's Foods, Inc.)

SUGARLOAF MTN CORP (ME)
Common $10 par changed to $1 par and (9) additional shares issued 10/25/1982
Reorganized under Chapter 11 Federal Bankruptcy Code 04/03/1987
Each share Common $1 par exchanged for (1) share Class B Common $1 par and $1 in Shareholder Credits or $5 in Shareholder Credits
Note: Option to receive Class B Common shares expired 05/22/1987 (Additional Information in Active)

SUGEN INC (DE)
Merged into Pharmacia & Upjohn Inc. 08/31/1999
Each share Common 1¢ par exchanged for (0.6091) share Common 1¢ par
Pharmacia & Upjohn Inc. merged into Pharmacia Corp. 03/31/2000 which merged into Pfizer Inc. 04/16/2003

SUISSE INTL ENTMT CORP (UT)
Involuntarily dissolved 01/01/1988

SUISUN VALLEY BANK (FAIRFIELD, CA)
Merged into Napa Valley Bancorp 04/17/1989
Each share Common $10 par exchanged for (1.133) shares Common no par
Napa Valley Bancorp acquired by Westamerica Bancorporation 04/15/1993

SUITE101 COM INC (DE)
Name changed to GeoGlobal Resources Inc. 02/02/2004

SUITOMAT CORP (DE)
Assets assigned for the benefit of creditors 10/16/1973
No stockholders' equity

SUIZA FOODS CORP (DE)
Under plan of merger name changed to Dean Foods Co. (New) 12/21/2001

SUJA MINERALS CORP (NV)
Name changed to GEI Global Energy Corp. 09/17/2013

SUJANA UNVL INDS LTD (INDIA)
ADR agreement terminated 03/26/2015
No GDR's remain outstanding

SUKARI VENTURES CORP (BC)
Name changed to Gravis Energy Corp. 03/31/2010
Gravis Energy Corp. recapitalized as Biocure Technology Inc 11/29/2017

SUKHA BALKA JSC (UKRAINE)
GDR agreement terminated 08/24/2017
Each Reg. S Sponsored GDR for Ordinary exchanged for (25) shares Ordinary
Note: Unexchanged GDR's will be sold and the proceeds, if any, held for claim after 08/27/2018

SUKUMA EXPLS LTD (BC)
Recapitalized as S.M.A. Resources Ltd. 08/29/1991
Each share Common no par exchanged for (1/3) share Common no par
S.M.A. Resources Ltd. name changed to Biomin Therapeutic Corp. 02/15/1994 which name changed to Pharmex Industries Inc. 11/06/1996 which name changed to PanGeo Pharma Inc. (BC) 08/21/2000 which reincorporated in Canada 09/21/2000 which recapitalized as Silvio Ventures Inc. 01/09/2006 which name changed to Regency Gold Corp. 07/17/2008

SULCUS HOSPITALITY TECHNOLOGIES CORP (PA)
Name changed 08/27/1997
Conv. Preferred no par called for redemption 12/30/1992
Name changed from Sulcus Computer Corp. to Sulcus Hospitality Technologies Corp. 08/27/1997
Merged into Eltrax Systems, Inc. 03/25/1999
Each share Common no par exchanged for (0.55) share Common 1¢ par
Eltrax Systems, Inc. name changed to Verso Technologies, Inc. 10/02/2000
(See Verso Technologies, Inc.)

SULLAIR CORP (IN)
Common no par split (3) for (2) by issuance of (0.5) additional share 05/25/1973
Common no par split (2) for (1) by issuance of (1) additional share 05/06/1981
Stock Dividends - 100% 09/22/1978; 10% 03/15/1980
Acquired by Sundstrand Corp. 11/13/1984
Each share Common no par exchanged for $8.50 cash

SULLICO MINES LTD (QC)
Merged into Sullivan Mining Group Ltd. 09/02/1969
Each share Capital Stock $1 par exchanged for (1) share Capital Stock no par
Sullivan Mining Group Ltd. merged into Sullivan Mines Inc.-Mines Sullivan Inc. 07/01/1983
(See Sullivan Mines Inc.-Mines Sullivan Inc.)

SULLICO RES LTD (ON)
Name changed to Sullivan Resources Ltd. 06/23/1982

SULLIDEN GOLD CORP LTD (QC)
Plan of arangement effective 08/08/2014
Each share Common no par exchanged for (0.525) share Rio Alto Mining Ltd. Common no par and (0.1) share Sulliden Mining Capital Inc. Common no par
(See each company's listing)
Note: Unexchanged certificates will be cancelled and become without value 08/08/2020

SULLIVAN/BOURLAMAQUE GOLD MINES LTD. (QC)
Charter cancelled and declared dissolved for failure to file reports and pay fees 08/18/1973

SULLIVAN BROADCAST HLDGS INC (TN)
Merged into Sinclair Broadcast Group, Inc. 07/01/1998
Each share Common no par exchanged for $33.24 cash

SULLIVAN COMPUTER CORP (DE)
Name changed to CHoPP Computer Corp. 11/19/1986
CHoPP Computer Corp. name changed to ANTs software.com 02/18/1999 which name changed to ANTs software, inc. 04/05/2001
(See ANTs software inc.)

SULLIVAN CONS MINES LTD (QC)
Name changed to Sullivan Mines Ltd. and Common $1 par changed to no par 11/28/1968
Sullivan Mines Ltd. merged into Sullivan Mining Group Ltd. 09/02/1969 which merged into Sullivan Mines Inc.-Mines Sullivan Inc. 07/01/1983
(See Sullivan Mines Inc.-Mines Sullivan Inc.)

SULLIVAN CNTY HARNESS RACING ASSN INC (NY)
Each share Class B Stock $1 par exchanged for $2.25 cash 04/04/1985
Each share Class C Stock 60¢ par exchanged for $2.25 cash 04/04/1984
Merged into Berenson Pari-Mutual of New York, Inc. 06/24/1985
Each share Class A Stock $1 par exchanged for $3.50 cash

SULLIVAN CNTY NATL BK (LIBERTY, NY)
Acquired by United Bank Corp. of New York 06/01/1981
Each share Common $5 par exchanged for $8 principal amount 10% Non-Assignable Debentures due 1981-1986 and $27 cash

SULLIVAN DENTAL PRODS INC (DE)
Common 1¢ par split (3) for (2) by issuance of (0.5) additional share 05/17/1991
Common 1¢ par split (3) for (2) by issuance of (0.5) additional share 01/29/1992
Merged into Schein (Henry), Inc. 11/12/1997
Each share Common 1¢ par exchanged for (0.735) share Common 1¢ par

SULLIVAN GOLD MINES LTD.
Acquired by Sullivan Consolidated Mines Ltd. 00/00/1934
Each share Common exchanged for (0.87) share Common $1 par
Sullivan Consolidated Mines Ltd. name changed to Sullivan Mines Ltd. 11/22/1968 which merged into Sullivan Mining Group Ltd. 09/02/1969 which merged into Sullivan Mines Inc.-Mines Sullivan Inc. 07/01/1983
(See Sullivan Mines Inc.-Mines Sullivan Inc.)

SULLIVAN MACHINERY CO.
Merged into Joy Manufacturing Co. 00/00/1946
Each share Common no par exchanged for (1.25) shares Common $1 par
Joy Manufacturing Co. merged into Joy Technologies Inc. 06/24/1987
(See Joy Technologies Inc.)

SULLIVAN MINES INC (QC)
Acquired by Cambior Inc. 10/15/1987
Each share Common no par exchanged for $7.50 cash

SULLIVAN MINES LTD (QC)
Merged into Sullivan Mining Group Ltd. 09/02/1969
Each share Common no par exchanged for (1) share Capital Stock no par
Sullivan Mining Group Ltd. merged into Sullivan Mines Inc.-Mines Sullivan Inc. 07/01/1983
(See Sullivan Mines Inc.-Mines Sullivan Inc.)

SULLIVAN MNG GROUP LTD (QC)
Capital Stock no par reclassified as Conv. Class A Capital Stock no par 10/30/1974
Conv. Class A Capital Stock no par and Conv. Class B Capital Stock no par reclassified as Common no par 02/05/1980
Merged into Sullivan Mines Inc.-Mines Sullivan Inc. 07/01/1983
Each share Common no par exchanged for (1) share Common no par
(See Sullivan Mines Inc.-Mines Sullivan Inc.)

SULLIVAN PACKING CO.
Acquired by Hygrade Food Products Corp. 00/00/1931
Details not available

SULLIVAN POCAHONTAS COAL CO.
Merged into Comago Smokeless Fuel Co. 00/00/1927
Details not available

SULPETRO LTD (AB)
7% 1st Preferred Ser. A $20 par called for redemption 09/21/1981
Class A Common no par reclassified as Common no par 11/22/1984
Class B Common no par reclassified as Common no par 11/22/1984
Placed in receivership 06/17/1987
No stockholders' equity

SULPHCO INC (NV)
Filed a petition under Chapter 7 Federal Bankruptcy Code 09/16/2011
Stockholders' equity unlikely

SULPHUR CONVERTING CORP. (QC)
Company ceased reporting 00/00/1955

SULPHUR-DAVIS OIL CO. (OK)
Charter revoked for failure to file reports and pay fees 06/10/1919

SULPHUR EXPL CO (DE)
Charter cancelled and declared inoperative and void for non-payment of taxes 03/01/1979

SULPHUR PROCESSING CORP (DE)
Charter cancelled and declared inoperative and void for non-payment of taxes 04/15/1972

SULPHUR SPRINGS LN & BLDG ASSN (TX)
Under plan of reorganization each share Common 1¢ par automatically became (1) share L & B Financial, Inc. Common 1¢ par 11/13/1995
L & B Financial, Inc. merged into Jefferson Savings Bancorp, Inc. 02/28/1997 which merged into Union Planters Corp. 02/12/2001 which merged into Regions Financial Corp. (New) 07/01/2004

SULPHURETS GOLD CORP (BC)
Acquired by Placer Dome Inc. 12/14/1989
Each share Common no par exchanged for $0.95 cash

SULRAY, INC. (NY)
Name changed to Holmes (Thomas) Corp. (NY) 06/22/1964
Holmes (Thomas) Corp. (NY) reincorporated in Delaware 06/16/1969 which merged into Rite Aid Corp. 03/15/1973

SULTAN CORP LTD (AUSTRALIA)
Name changed to Balamara Resources, Ltd. 02/07/2012

SULTAN GOLD MINING CO. INC. (ID)
Charter forfeited for failure to file annual reports 11/30/1938

SULTAN MINERALS INC (BC)
Recapitalized as Apex Resources Inc. 07/18/2016
Each share Common no par exchanged for (0.1) share Common no par

SULTANA OIL & GAS CO. (OK)
Charter cancelled for failure to pay taxes 08/08/1921

SULZER MEDICA (SWITZERLAND)
Name changed to Centerpulse Ltd. 06/01/2002
Centerpulse Ltd. merged into Zimmer Holdings, Inc. 10/02/2003 which name changed to Zimmer Biomet Holdings, Inc. 06/29/2015

SULZINC MINES LTD. (ON)
Charter cancelled for failure to file reports and pay taxes 00/00/1959

SUM INVESTMENT CORP. (UT)
Name changed to Astron Innovations, Inc. 12/31/1976
Astron Innovations, Inc. name changed to Astron Energy Co., Inc. 03/13/1977

SUMAC VENTURES INC (BC)
Struck off register and declared dissolved for failure to file returns 04/16/1993

SUMACH RES INC (ON)
Company dissolved 08/28/1989
Details not available

SUMBURGH DEVS LTD (CANADA)
Recapitalized as Access Banking Network Inc. 09/24/1984
Each share Common no par exchanged for (0.5) share Common no par
Access Banking Network Inc. recapitalized as Access ATM Network Inc. 05/24/1985 which merged into Ancom ATM International Inc. 01/18/1988
(See Ancom ATM International Inc.)

SUMEX CORP (UT)
Each share old Common $0.001 par exchanged for (0.05) share new Common $0.001 par 05/20/1993
Recapitalized as Ezix.Com, Inc. 03/18/1999
Each share new Common $0.001 par exchanged for (0.025) share Common $0.001 par
Ezix.Com, Inc. name changed to E-Center.com Inc. 07/19/1999 which name changed to Merlin Software Technologies Holdings Inc. 11/30/1999 which name changed to Optika Investment Co. Inc. (NV) 01/25/2000 which reincorporated in Delaware as USA Broadband, Inc. 07/10/2001

SUMITOMO BK CALIF (SAN FRANCISCO, CA)
8.125% Depositary Preferred Ser. A called for redemption at $25 on 04/30/1998
Common $20 par changed to $10 par and (1) additional share issued 12/28/1970
Common $10 par changed to $5 par and (1) additional share issued 01/18/1973
Merged into Zions Bancorporation 10/01/1998
Each share Common $5 par exchanged for $38.25 cash

SUMITOMO BK LTD (JAPAN)
Stock Dividend - 10% 07/18/1989
Name changed to Sumitomo Mitsui Banking Corp. 04/16/2001
Sumitomo Mitsui Banking Corp. merged into Sumitomo Mitsui Financial Group, Inc. 01/15/2003

SUMITOMO METAL INDS LTD (JAPAN)
Each Unsponsored ADR for Common exchanged for (2) Sponsored ADR's for Common 07/13/1993
Merged into Nippon Steel & Sumitomo Metal Corp. 10/01/2012
Each Sponsored ADR for Common exchanged for (0.735) Sponsored ADR for Common

SUMITOMO MITSUI BKG CORP (JAPAN)
Basis changed from (1:10) to (1:1) 04/18/2001
Merged into Sumitomo Mitsui Financial Group, Inc. 01/15/2003
Each ADR for Common exchanged for (1) ADR for Common
Note: Unexchanged ADR's will be sold and the proceeds, if any held for claim after 08/17/2003

SUMITOMO TR & BKG LTD (JAPAN)
Merged into Sumitomo Mitsui Trust Holdings Inc. 04/01/2011
Each Sponsored ADR for Common exchanged for (1.49) Sponsored ADR's for Common

SUMMA FOUR INC (DE)
Merged into Cisco Systems, Inc. 11/4/98
Each share Common 1¢ par exchanged for (0.268491) share Common no par

SUMMA INDS (CA)
Merged into Habasit Holding AG 10/16/2006
Each share Common no par exchanged for $15 cash

SUMMA MED CORP (NM)
Each share old Common 1¢ par exchanged for (0.25) share new Common 1¢ par 05/25/1982
Chapter 7 bankruptcy proceedings terminated 04/08/1994
Stockholders' equity unlikely

SUMMA METALS CORP (CO)
Name changed to Casmyn Corp. (CO) 10/26/1994
Casmyn Corp. (CO) reorganized in Nevada as Aries Ventures Inc. 04/11/2000 which reincorporated in Delaware as Cardium Therapeutics, Inc. 01/23/2006 which name changed to Taxus Cardium Pharmaceuticals Group, Inc. 10/07/2014

SUMMA PPTYS CORP (NV)
Reincorporated under the laws of Delaware as Nevatech Industries Inc. 12/14/1989
Each share Common $0.001 par exchanged for (0.25) share Common $0.001 par

SUMMA RX LABS INC (DE)
Each share old Common 1¢ par exchanged for (0.1) share new Common 1¢ par 07/07/1993
Company terminated registration of common stock and is no longer public as of 03/03/2003
Details not available

SUMMA TECHNOLOGIES INC (CA)
Charter suspended for failure to file reports and pay fees 3/3/86

SUMMA VEST INC (UT)
Each (350) shares old Common $0.001 par exchanged for (1) share new Common $0.001 par 11/05/1996
Name changed to Applied Voice Recognition Inc. (UT) 01/13/1997
Applied Voice Recognition Inc. (UT) reincorporated in Delaware 02/03/1998 which name changed to E-Docs.MD, Inc. 02/23/1999
(See E-Docs.MD, Inc.)

SUMMAGRAPHICS CORP (DE)
Name changed to Calcomp Technology Inc. 7/24/96
(See Calcomp Technology Inc.)

SUMMARY CORP (NV)
Name changed to Luma Net Corp. 9/13/96
Luma Net Corp. recapitalized as Riviera International Casinos Inc. 8/22/97 which name changed to International Casino Cruises Inc. 11/21/97 which name changed to Mountain Energy Inc. 5/26/98
(See Mountain Energy Inc.)

SUMMCORP (IN)
Common no par split (3) for (2) by issuance of (0.5) additional share 11/26/85
Common no par split (2) for (1) by issuance of (1) additional share 6/10/86
$2.88 Conv. Preferred $10 par called for redemption 9/30/87
Stock Dividend - 20% 1/30/85
Merged into NBD Bancorp, Inc. 7/1/92
Each share Common no par exchanged for (1.35) shares Common $1 par
NBD Bancorp, Inc. name changed to First Chicago NBD Corp. 12/1/95 which merged into Bank One Corp. 10/2/98 which merged into J.P. Morgan Chase & Co. 12/31/2000 which name changed to JPMorgan Chase & Co. 7/20/2004

SUMMEDIA COM INC (CO)
SEC revoked common stock registration 09/11/2008

SUMMER & CO (DE)
Merged into SC Acquisition Corp. 5/20/97
Each share Class A Common no par exchanged for $6.65 cash

SUMMER STREET TRUST (MA)
Liquidation completed 4/27/60
Details not available

SUMMERS (JOHN) & SONS LTD. (ENGLAND)
Nationalized by the United Kingdom 08/08/1967
Each ADR for Ordinary £1 par exchanged for £1-11s-0.1029d principal amount of 6-1/2% Treasury Stock due 01/28/1971

SUMMERS ELEC CO (NV)
Common $1 par and Class A Common $1 par split (3) for (2) by issuance of (0.5) additional share respectively 11/22/1968
Each share Class A Common $1 par exchanged for (1) share Common $1 par 02/02/1970
Merged into Thomas Tilling Ltd. 04/25/1979
Each share Common $1 par exchanged for $30 cash

SUMMERS GYROSCOPE CO. (CA)
Capital Stock $1 par changed to 10¢ par 7/28/58
Name changed to Guidance Technology, Inc. 5/16/61
Guidance Technology, Inc. merged into Rospatch Corp. (DE) 11/5/82 which reincorporated in Michigan 6/3/85 which name changed to Ameriwood Industries International Corp. 12/13/91

(See Ameriwood Industries International Corp.)

SUMMERS INDS INC (DE)
Charter cancelled and declared inoperative and void for non-payment of taxes 3/1/76

SUMMERTON BUILDING
Property sold and distribution of $64.05 per share made in 1943

SUMMERWOOD INDS INC (AB)
Name changed to Recycled Solutions for Industry Inc. 09/17/1998
Recycled Solutions for Industry Inc. name changed to Resin Systems Inc. 05/05/2000 which name changed to RS Technologies Inc. 06/23/2010
(See RS Technologies Inc.)

SUMMEX MINES LTD (YUKON)
Reincorporated 10/15/1997
Place of incorporation changed from (BC) to (Yukon) 10/15/1997
Delisted from Vancouver Stock Exchange 03/17/1998

SUMMIT & ELIZABETH TR CO (SUMMIT, NJ)
Stock Dividends - 100% 10/9/67; 10% 10/17/73
Under plan of reorganization each share Capital Stock $8 par automatically became (1) share Summit Bancorporation 1/15/74
Summit Bancorporation merged into Summit Bancorp 3/1/96 which merged into FleetBoston Financial Corp. 3/1/2001 which merged into Bank of America Corp. 4/1/2004

SUMMIT AMER TELEVISION INC (TN)
Merged into Scripps (E.W.) Co. 04/14/2004
Each share Ser. A Preferred $10 par exchanged for $10 cash
Each share Common $0.0025 par exchanged for $4.05 cash

SUMMIT AUTONOMOUS INC (MA)
Name changed 5/19/2000
Common 1¢ par split (3) for (2) by issuance of (0.5) additional share 12/1/95
Each share Common 1¢ par received distribution of (0.2857) share LCA-Vision Inc. new Common $0.0001 par payable 12/29/97 to holders of record 12/18/97
Name changed from Summit Technology, Inc. to Summit Autonomous, Inc. 5/19/2000
Merged into Alcon Holdings Inc. 8/31/2000
Each share Common 1¢ par exchanged for $19 cash

SUMMIT BANCORP (IN)
Under plan of merger each share Common $10 par automatically became (1) share SummCorp Common $10 par 4/24/84
SummCorp merged into NBD Bancorp, Inc. 7/1/92 which name changed to First Chicago NBD Corp. 12/1/95 which merged into Bank One Corp. 10/2/98 which merged into J.P. Morgan Chase & Co. 12/31/2000 which name changed to JPMorgan Chase & Co. 7/20/2004

SUMMIT BANCORP (NJ)
Adjustable Rate Preferred Ser. B no par called for redemption 12/15/1996
Adjustable Rate Preferred Ser. C no par called for redemption 12/15/1996
Common $1.20 par changed to 80¢ par and (0.5) additional share issued payable 09/24/1997 to holders of record 09/03/1997 Ex date - 09/25/1997
Merged into FleetBoston Financial Corp. 03/01/2001
Each share Common 80¢ par exchanged for (1.02) shares Common 1¢ par
FleetBoston Financial Corp. merged into Bank of America Corp. 04/01/2004

SUMMIT BANCORP (OH)
Merged into FirstFederal Financial Services Corp. 07/08/1997
Each share Common no par exchanged for (2.3375) shares Common $1 par
FirstFederal Financial Services Corp. name changed to Signal Corp. 06/16/1998 which merged into FirstMerit Corp. 02/12/1999 which merged into Huntington Bancshares Inc. 08/16/2016

SUMMIT BANCORP INC (WA)
Merged into Washington Mutual Savings Bank (Seattle, WA) 11/15/1994
Each share Common $8 par exchanged for (0.646) share Common $1 par
Washington Mutual Savings Bank (Seattle, WA) reorganized as Washington Mutual Inc. 11/29/1994
(See Washington Mutual, Inc.)

SUMMIT BANCORPORATION (NJ)
Common no par split (3) for (2) by issuance of (0.5) additional share 9/15/78
Common no par split (3) for (2) by issuance of (0.5) additional share 4/21/83
Common no par split (3) for (2) by issuance of (0.5) additional share 12/31/84
Common no par split (3) for (2) by issuance of (0.5) additional share 12/31/85
$2.20 Conv. Preferred Ser. A no par called for redemption 7/15/86
Merged into Summit Bancorp 3/1/96
Each share Adjustable Rate Preferred Ser. B no par exchanged for (1) share Adjustable Rate Preferred Ser. B no par
Each share Common no par exchanged for (0.9) share Common $1.20 par
Summit Bancorp merged into FleetBoston Financial Corp. 3/1/2001 which merged into Bank of America Corp. 4/1/2004

SUMMIT BANCSHARES INC (TX)
Common $1.25 par split (2) for (1) by issuance of (1) additional share payable 12/9/97 to holders of record 11/19/97
Common $1.25 par split (2) for (1) by issuance of (1) additional share payable 12/31/2004 to holders of record 12/20/2004 Ex date - 1/3/2005
Merged into Cullen/Frost Bankers, Inc. 12/8/2006
Each share Common $1.25 par exchanged for $27.64 cash

SUMMIT BK CORP (GA)
Common 1¢ par split (2) for (1) by issuance of (1) additional share payable 11/18/2002 to holders of record 11/13/2002 Ex date - 11/19/2002
Stock Dividends - 20% payable 02/16/2001 to holders of record 02/15/2001 Ex date - 02/13/2001; 50% payable 02/17/2004 to holders of record of 02/09/2004 Ex date - 02/18/2004
Merged into UCBH Holdings, Inc. 12/29/2006
Each share Common 1¢ par exchanged for $24.50 cash

SUMMIT BANKING CORP. (FL)
Stock Dividend - 10% 6/1/79
Acquired by Gulfstream Banks, Inc. 9/30/81
Each share Common 30¢ par exchanged for $4.55 cash

SUMMIT BANKSHARES INC (VA)
Merged into One Valley Bancorp, Inc. 8/7/98
Each share Common $1 par exchanged for (1.36) shares Common $10 par
One Valley Bancorp, Inc. merged into BB&T Corp. 7/6/2000

SUMMIT BROKERAGE SVCS INC (FL)
Name changed to Summit Financial Services Group, Inc. 03/02/2004
Summit Financial Services Group, Inc. merged into RCS Capital Corp. 06/11/2014
(See RCS Capital Corp.)

SUMMIT BROOKLYN CORP (NY)
Merged into Daylin-Summit, Inc. 9/7/72
Details not available

SUMMIT CAP FD INC (DE)
Acquired by Selected Special Shares, Inc. 09/19/1974
Each share Common $1 par exchanged for (0.2917) share Common 25¢ par
Selected Special Shares, Inc. name changed to Selected International Fund, Inc. 05/01/2011

SUMMIT CARE CORP (CA)
Merged into Fountain View, Inc. 4/16/98
Each share Common no par exchanged for $21 cash

SUMMIT COACHES INC (UT)
Each share old Common $0.0001 par exchanged for (0.01) share new Common $0.0001 par 01/31/2005
Name changed to Madison Bay Holdings, Inc. 07/11/2005
Madison Bay Holdings, Inc. recapitalized as Middle East Oil Corp. 01/08/2010
(See Middle East Oil Corp.)

SUMMIT CORP.
Merged into Connecticut Investment Management Corp. 00/00/1931
Details not available

SUMMIT DENTAL CLINICS INC (DE)
Recapitalized as AyreTrade, Inc. 08/14/2012
Each share Common $0.0001 par exchanged for (0.004) share Common $0.0001 par
AyreTrade, Inc. name changed to Rocky Mountain Ayre, Inc. 02/05/2015

SUMMIT DESIGN INC (DE)
Name changed to Innoveda Inc. 03/23/2000
(See Innoveda Inc.)

SUMMIT DIVERSIFIED LTD (ON)
Merged into Sumtra Diversified Inc. 08/30/1978
Each share Capital Stock no par exchanged for (2/3) shares Capital Stock no par

SUMMIT ENERGY INC (NV)
Each share Common 10¢ par exchanged for (0.2) share Common 50¢ par 10/11/1976
Stock Dividend - 50% 02/28/1980
Name changed to Caspen Oil, Inc. 09/13/1988
(See Caspen Oil, Inc.)

SUMMIT ENTMT GROUP CORP INC (NV)
Name changed to Extreme Innovations, Inc. 09/30/2005
Extreme Innovations, Inc. recapitalized as Silverhawk Entertainment Group, Inc. 07/27/2006 which name changed to Acme Sports & Entertainment, Inc. 06/27/2007 which recapitalized as Casa Havana, Inc. 06/17/2008 which name changed to Design Marketing Concepts, Inc. 12/09/2009

(See Design Marketing Concepts, Inc.)

SUMMIT EXPLORATIONS & HOLDINGS LTD. (ON)
Name changed to Summit Diversified Ltd. 03/03/1972
Summit Diversified Ltd. merged into Sumtra Diversified Inc. 08/30/1978

SUMMIT FAMILY RESTAURANTS INC (DE)
Merged into CKE Restaurants, Inc. 07/15/1996
Each share Common 10¢ par exchanged for (0.1043) share Common 1¢ par and $2.63 cash
(See CKE Restaurants, Inc.)

SUMMIT FINL CORP (SC)
Common $1 par split (2) for (1) by issuance of (1) additional share payable 08/24/1998 to holders of record 08/10/1998
Stock Dividends - 5% payable 02/05/1996 to holders of record 01/22/1996; 5% payable 02/03/1997 to holders of record 01/20/1997; 5% payable 12/30/1997 to holders of record 12/15/1997; 5% payable 12/28/1998 to holders of record 12/14/1998; 5% payable 11/29/1999 to holders of record 11/15/1999; 5% payable 11/20/2000 to holders of record 11/06/2000 Ex date - 11/02/2000; 5% payable 11/09/2001 to holders of record 10/29/2001 Ex date - 10/25/2001; 5% payable 12/05/2002 to holders of record 11/22/2002 Ex date - 11/20/2002; 5% payable 12/05/2003 to holders of record 11/21/2003 Ex date - 11/19/2003
Merged into First Citizens Bancorporation, Inc. 07/01/2005
Each share Common $1 par exchanged for $22 cash

SUMMIT FINL GROUP INC (WV)
Each share 8% Non-Cum Preferred Ser. 2009 $1 par exchanged for (181.8182) shares Common $2.50 par 03/12/2015
Each share 8% Non-Cum Preferred Ser. 2011 $1 par exchanged for (125) shares Common $2.50 par
(Additional Information in Active)

SUMMIT FINL SVCS GROUP INC (FL)
Merged into RCS Capital Corp. 06/11/2014
Each share Common $0.0001 par exchanged for (0.01137) share Common $0.001 par and $1.35 cash
Note: Each share Common $0.0001 par received $0.060896 cash from escrow 07/20/2015
(See RCS Capital Corp.)

SUMMIT FINISHING CO., INC. (CT)
Merged into Beryllium Corp. 07/15/1966
Each share Common no par exchanged for (2.1176) shares Common 50¢ par
Beryllium Corp. merged into Kawecki Berylco Industries, Inc. 10/15/1968
(See Kawecki Berylco Industries, Inc.)

SUMMIT GLOBAL LOGISTICS INC (DE)
Chapter 11 bankruptcy proceedings converted to Chapter 7 on 11/12/2008
No stockholders' equity

SUMMIT GOLD MINES INC (BC)
Recapitalized as Paragon Entertainment Corp. 06/23/1993
Each share Common no par exchanged for (0.2) share Common no par
(See Paragon Entertainment Corp.)

SUMMIT GROUP INC (DE)
Merged into Ciber, Inc. 05/05/1998
Details not available

SUMMIT HEALTH LTD (CA)
Merged into OrNda HealthCorp. 04/19/1994
Each share Common no par exchanged for (0.2157) share Common 1¢ par and $5.50 cash

SUMMIT HILL TR CO (SUMMIT HILL, PA)
Acquired by Harleysville National Corp. 06/01/1992
Each share Capital Stock $25 par exchanged for (31) shares Common $1 par
Harleysville National Corp. merged into First Niagara Financial Group, Inc. (New) 04/09/2010 which merged into KeyCorp (New) 08/01/2016

SUMMIT HLDG CORP (WV)
Common $2.50 par changed to $1.25 par and (1) additional share issued 06/26/1986
Common 1.25 par changed to $0.625 par and (1) additional share issued 12/24/1987
Merged into United Bankshares, Inc. 10/21/1992
Each share Common $0.625 par exchanged for (0.8) share Common $2.50 par and $8.60 cash
Note: An additional payment of $0.281437 cash was made 11/08/1993

SUMMIT HLDG SOUTHEAST INC (FL)
4% Preferred Ser. A $10 par called for redemption at $10 on 09/28/1998
Merged into Liberty Mutual Group 09/30/1998
Each share Common 1¢ par exchanged for $33 cash

SUMMIT HOTEL PPTYS INC (MD)
9.25% Preferred Ser. A 1¢ par called for redemption at $25 plus $0.37257 accrued dividends on 10/28/2016
7.875% Preferred Ser. B 1¢ par called for redemption at $25 plus $0.05469 accrued dividends on 12/11/2017
7.125% Preferred Ser. C 1¢ par called for redemption at $25 plus $0.09401 accrued dividends on 03/20/2018
(Additional Information in Active)

SUMMIT LIFE CORP (OK)
Each share old Common 1¢ par exchanged for (0.01) share new Common 1¢ par 01/30/2004
Note: In effect holders received $0.50 cash per share and public interest was eliminated

SUMMIT MED SYS INC (MN)
Name changed to Celeris Corp. 11/18/1998
(See Celeris Corp.)

SUMMIT MINING CORP. (PA)
Name changed to Summit Industries Inc. 08/01/1960
Summit Industries Inc. name changed to Pennsylvania Mineral & Mining Co. 03/03/1973

SUMMIT MTG INVS (MA)
Liquidation completed
Each Share of Bene. Int. no par exchanged for initial distribution of $5 cash 11/15/1985
Each Share of Bene. Int. no par received second and final distribution of $0.48 cash 10/08/1986

SUMMIT NATL BK (TORRINGTON, CT)
Declared insolvent 04/03/1992
No stockholders' equity

SUMMIT NATL CONSLDTN GROUP INC (DE)
Name changed to Superwipes, Inc. 10/12/2004
(See Superwipes, Inc.)

SUMMIT NATL HLDG CO (OH)
Common $1 par changed to 50¢ par and (1) additional share issued 03/03/1966
Merged into Cargill, Inc. 12/31/1974
Each share Common 50¢ par exchanged for $4.50 cash

SUMMIT OILFIELD CORP (NV)
Under plan of reorganization each share old Common 1¢ par exchanged for (0.07417) share new Common 1¢ par, (0.07417) Class A Common Stock Purchase Warrant expiring 12/22/1992 and (0.07417) Class B Common Stock Purchase Warrant expiring 12/22/1996 on 03/12/1990
Recapitalized as Grasso Corp. 12/21/1990
Each share new Common 1¢ par exchanged for (0.1) share Common 1¢ par
Grasso Corp. merged into Offshore Logistics, Inc. 09/16/1994 which name changed to Bristow Group, Inc. 02/01/2006

SUMMIT ORGANIZATION INC (NY)
Under plan of merger each share Common 10¢ par exchanged for $1.63 cash 08/15/1979

SUMMIT PASS RES CORP (BC)
Merged into Oklahoma Crude Ltd. 07/12/1982
Each share Common no par exchanged for (0.33333333) share Common no par
Oklahoma Crude Ltd. recapitalized as International Telesis Industries Corp. 03/04/1986 which name changed to Madonna Educational Group of Canada Ltd. 02/06/1989
(See Madonna Educational Group of Canada Ltd.)

SUMMIT PETE CORP (CO)
Each share old Common 1¢ par exchanged for (0.05) share Common 1¢ par 02/21/1995
Merged into MRI Acquisition Corp. 12/20/1996
Each share Common 1¢ par exchanged for $0.70 cash

SUMMIT PPTYS (OH)
Merged into IRT Property Co. 06/20/1979
Each Share of Bene. Int. exchanged for (0.48243) share Common $1 par
Note: Contingency trust fund terminated and additional shares distributed 11/07/1979
IRT Property Co. merged into Equity One, Inc. 02/13/2003 which merged into Regency Centers Corp. 03/01/2017

SUMMIT PPTYS INC (MD)
Merged into Camden Property Trust 02/28/2005
Each share Common 1¢ par exchanged for $31.20 cash

SUMMIT PPTY GROUP INC (NV)
Name changed to Corbel Holdings Inc. 04/30/2001
Corbel Holdings Inc. name changed to BioTech Medics, Inc. 11/30/2004

SUMMIT REAL ESTATE INVT TR (ON)
Trust terminated 01/25/2007
Each Trust Unit received $30 cash

SUMMIT RES LTD (AB)
Common no par split (2) for (1) by issuance of (1) additional share 09/21/1987
Common no par split (2) for (1) by issuance of (1) additional share 08/18/1993
Acquired by Paramount Resources Ltd. 08/02/2002
Each share Common no par exchanged for $7.40 cash

SUMMIT SVGS BK (BELLEVUE, WA)
Name changed 11/27/1990
Common $8 par split (2) for (1) by issuance of (1) additional share 02/21/1986
Stock Dividend - 10% 09/05/1984
Name changed from Summit Savings Association to Summit Savings Bank (Bellevue, WA) 11/27/1990
Under plan of reorganization each share Common $8 par automatically became (1) share Summit Bancorp Inc. Common $8 par 05/26/1992
Summit Bancorp Inc. merged into Washington Mutual Savings Bank (Seattle, WA) 11/15/1994 which reorganized as Washington Mutual Inc. 11/29/1994
(See Washington Mutual, Inc.)

SUMMIT SVGS FSB (ROHNERT PARK, CA)
Acquired by a private investor 07/31/1998
Each share Common $4 par exchanged for $10.4363 cash

SUMMIT SEMICONDUCTOR INC (DE)
Name changed to Summit Wireless Technologies, Inc. 09/21/2018

SUMMIT SILVER INC (ID)
Each share old Common 10¢ par exchanged for (0.16666666) share new Common 10¢ par 07/01/1998
Recapitalized as Elite Logistics Inc. 11/05/1999
Each share new Common 10¢ par exchanged for (0.16666666) share Common 10¢ par
(See Elite Logistics Inc.)

SUMMIT SYS INC (NV)
Charter revoked for failure to file reports and pay taxes 06/01/1998

SUMMIT TAX EXEMPT BD FD L P (DE)
Each Unit of Ltd. Partnership automatically became (0.9560) share Charter Municipal Mortgage Acceptance Co. Common Share of Bene. Int. no par 10/01/1997
Charter Municipal Mortgage Acceptance Co. name changed to CharterMac 11/17/2003 which name changed to Centerline Holding Co. 04/02/2007
(See Centerline Holding Co.)

SUMMIT TAX EXEMPT L P (DE)
Each Beneficial Unit Certificate II automatically became (1.0811) share Charter Municipal Mortgage Acceptance Co. Common Share of Bene. Int. no par 10/01/1997
Each Beneficial Unit Certificate III automatically became (0.9170) share Charter Municipal Mortgage Acceptance Co. Common Share of Bene. Int. no par 10/01/1997
Charter Municipal Mortgage Acceptance Co. name changed to CharterMac 11/17/2003 which name changed to Centerline Holding Co. 04/02/2007
(See Centerline Holding Co.)

SUMMIT TRUST CO. (SUMMIT, NJ)
Capital Stock $20 par changed to $8 par and (1.5) additional shares issued 06/08/1964
Stock Dividends - 20% 12/04/1953; 11.11111111% 11/16/1960
Merged into Summit & Elizabeth Trust Co. (Summit, NJ) 12/31/1964
Each share Capital Stock $8 par exchanged for (1) share Capital Stock $8 par
Summit & Elizabeth Trust Co. (Summit, NJ) reorganized as Summit Bancorporation 01/15/1974 which merged into Summit Bancorp 03/01/1996 which merged into FleetBoston Financial Corp. 03/01/2001 which merged into Bank of America Corp. 04/01/2004

SUMMIT URANIUM MINES, INC. (NV)
Charter revoked for failure to file reports and pay fees 03/04/1957

SUMMIT VENTURES INC (BC)
Name changed to Sumac Ventures Inc. 09/09/1986
(See Sumac Ventures Inc.)

SUMMIT WATER CO.
Merged into Williamsport Water Co. 00/00/1941
Details not available

SUMMIT WORLD VENTURES INC (DE)
Name changed to iNetEvents Inc. 06/30/2000
iNetEvents Inc. recapitalized as International Card Establishment, Inc. 10/29/2003

SUMMO MINERALS CORP (BC)
Reorganized under the laws of Canada as Constellation Copper Corp. 07/19/2002
Each share Common no par exchanged for (0.1) share Common no par
(See Constellation Copper Corp.)

SUMMUS CAP CORP (AB)
Recapitalized as Mongolia Growth Group Ltd. 02/04/2011
Each share Common no par exchanged for (0.5) share Common no par

SUMMUS INC (DE)
Reorganized 03/16/2005
Reorganized from under the laws of (FL) to (DE) 03/16/2005
Each share Common $0.001 par exchanged for (0.1) share Common $0.001 par
Name changed to Oasys Mobile, Inc. 02/06/2006
(See Oasys Mobile, Inc.)

SUMMUS WKS INC (DE)
Recapitalized as XTend Medical Corp. 09/26/2007
Each (8,334) shares Common $0.000001 par exchanged for (1) share Common $0.000001 par
XTend Medical Corp. name changed to MultiCorp International Inc. 08/28/2012

SUMOTEXT INC (NV)
Common $0.0001 par split (11) for (1) by issuance of (10) additional shares payable 09/27/2010 to holders of record 09/27/2010
Name changed to Sebring Software, Inc. 12/01/2010
(See Sebring Software, Inc.)

SUMTOTAL SYS INC (DE)
Merged into Amber Holding Inc. 07/21/2009
Each share Common $0.001 par exchanged for $4.85 cash

SUMY NVO FRUNZE PJSC (UKRAINE)
GDR agreement terminated 04/21/2017
No GDR's remain outstanding

SUN & SURF INC (NY)
Common $0.001 par split (10) for (1) by issuance of (9) additional shares payable 09/02/2003 to holders of record 08/29/2003 Ex date - 09/03/2003
Each share Common $0.001 par received distribution of (0.1) share Surf Franchise, Inc. Common payable 12/11/2003 to holders of record 09/08/2003 Ex date - 09/04/2003
Reincorporated under the laws of Delaware as IJJ Corp. 02/26/2004

SUN-AIRE LABORATORIES INC. (FL)
Voluntarily dissolved 05/24/1963
Details not available

SUN AIRL CORP (MO)
Adjudicated bankrupt 10/29/1969
No stockholders' equity

SUN AMERN BANCORP (DE)
Each share Common 1¢ par exchanged for (0.4) share Common $0.025 par 05/23/2007
SEC revoked common stock registration 10/07/2014

SUN BANCORP INC (NJ)
Common $1 par split (3) for (2) by issuance of (0.5) additional share payable 09/25/1997 to holders of record 09/11/1997
Common $1 par split (3) for (2) by issuance of (0.5) additional share payable 03/18/1998 to holders of record 03/04/1998
Each share Common $1 par exchanged for (0.2) share Common $5 par 08/11/2014
Stock Dividends - 5% payable 10/30/1996 to holders of record 10/15/1996; 5% payable 06/25/1997 to holders of record 06/02/1997; 5% payable 05/26/1998 to holders of record 05/05/1998; 5% payable 06/21/1999 to holders of record 06/07/1999; 5% payable 06/21/2000 to holders of record 06/07/2000; 5% payable 06/13/2001 to holders of record 05/31/2001 Ex date - 05/29/2001; 5% payable 05/23/2002 to holders of record 05/09/2002 Ex date - 05/07/2002; 5% payable 04/21/2003 to holders of record 04/07/2003 Ex date - 04/03/2003; 5% payable 04/20/2004 to holders of record 04/06/2004 Ex date - 04/02/2004; 5% payable 04/20/2005 to holders of record 04/06/2005 Ex date - 04/04/2005; 5% payable 05/18/2006 to holders of record 05/08/2006 Ex date - 05/04/2006; 5% payable 05/24/2007 to holders of record 05/14/2007 Ex date - 05/10/2007; 5% payable 05/23/2008 to holders of record 05/13/2008 Ex date - 05/09/2008; 5% payable 05/14/2009 to holders of record 04/30/2009 Ex date - 04/28/2009
Merged into OceanFirst Financial Corp. 01/31/2018
Each share Common $5 par exchanged for (0.9289) share Common 1¢ par

SUN BANCORP INC (PA)
Common $2.50 par split (2) for (1) by issuance of (1) additional share 12/11/1992
Common $2.50 par split (3) for (2) by issuance of (0.5) additional share 12/16/1994
Common $2.50 par split (3) for (2) by issuance of (0.5) additional share payable 12/12/1997 to holders of record 11/28/1997
Common $2.50 par split (3) for (2) by issuance of (0.5) additional share payable 03/18/1998 to holders of record 03/04/1998
Stock Dividends - 10% 12/10/1993; 10% 12/15/1995; 5% payable 06/06/1997 to holders of record 05/23/1997; 5% payable 06/05/1998 to holders of record 05/22/1998; 5% payable 06/11/1999 to holders of record 05/28/1999
Merged into Omega Financial Corp. 10/01/2004
Each share Common $2.50 par exchanged for (0.664) share Common $5 par
Omega Financial Corp. merged into F.N.B. Corp. 04/01/2008

SUN BANCSHARES INC (SC)
Merged into SCBT Financial Corp. 11/18/2005
Each share Common no par exchanged for (0.464516) share Common $2.50 par and $3.60 cash
SCBT Financial Corp. name changed to First Financial Holdings, Inc. 07/30/2013 which name changed to South State Corp. 06/30/2014

SUN BANK (JACKSONVILLE, FL)
Name changed to Sun Bank/North Florida, N.A. (Jacksonville, FL) 01/01/1984
(See Sun Bank/North Florida, N.A. (Jacksonville, FL))

SUN BANK/MIAMI, N.A. (MIAMI, FL)
Name changed to SunTrust Bank, Miami, N.A. (Miami, FL) 10/06/1995
(See SunTrust Bank, Miami, N.A. (Miami, FL))

SUN BANK/NORTH FLORIDA, N.A. (JACKSONVILLE, FL)
Acquired by SunTrust Banks, Inc. 01/01/2000
Details not available

SUN BANK OF COCOA, N.A. (COCOA, FL)
Acquired by Sun First National Bank of Brevard County (Melbourne, FL) 06/01/1979
Details not available

SUN BANK OF TAMPA BAY (TAMPA, FL)
Acquired by SunTrust Banks, Inc. 01/01/2000
Details not available

SUN BANK/TALLAHASSEE, N.A. (TALLAHASSEE, FL)
Merged into SunTrust Bank, Tallahassee, N.A. (Tallahassee, FL) 07/00/1985
Each share Common exchanged for (1.1) shares Common
(See SunTrust Bank, Tallahassee, N.A. (Tallahassee, FL))

SUN BKS INC (FL)
Merged into SunTrust Banks, Inc. 07/01/1985
Each share Common $2.50 par exchanged for (1.1) shares Common $1 par

SUN BANKS OF FLORIDA, INC. (FL)
$4.375 Conv. Preferred no par called for redemption 12/10/1982
Name changed to Sun Banks, Inc. 05/02/1983
Sun Banks, Inc. merged into SunTrust Banks, Inc. 07/01/1985

SUN BEAR MINES LTD (ON)
Charter cancelled for failure to pay taxes and file returns 03/16/1976

SUN BELT PETE INC (TX)
Charter forfeited for failure to pay taxes 06/17/1991

SUN BIOPHARMA INC (UT)
Reincorporated under the laws of Delaware 05/25/2016

SUN BREWING LTD (CHANNEL ISLANDS)
Name changed to SUN Interbrew Ltd. (Channel Islands) 05/03/1999
Sun Interbrew Ltd. (Channel Islands) reincorporated in Cyprus as SUN Interbrew PLC 01/20/2011

SUN CAL ENERGY INC (NV)
SEC revoked common stock registration 12/22/2011

SUN CAP TR (DE)
9.85% Preferred Sercurities called for redemption at $25 on 04/01/2002

SUN CAP TR II (DE)
8.875% Preferred Securities called for redemption at $10 on 12/31/2003

SUN CHEM CORP (DE)
$4.50 Preferred Ser. A no par called for redemption 03/31/1970
Common $1 par split (3) for (2) by issuance of (0.5) additional share 03/01/1977
Common $1 par split (4) for (3) by issuance of (0.33333333) additional share 11/07/1979
Common $1 par split (3) for (2) by issuance of (0.5) additional share 03/31/1981
Each share Common $1 par exchanged for (0.5) share Class A Common no par and (0.5) share Conv. Class B Common no par 12/19/1986
Name changed to Sequa Corp. 05/08/1987
(See Sequa Corp.)

SUN CITY DAIRY PRODS INC (DE)
Name changed to Sun City Industries, Inc. 05/20/1969
Sun City Industries, Inc. name changed to Worldwide Biotech & Pharmaceutical Co. 01/12/2005
(See Worldwide Biotech & Pharmaceutical Co.)

SUN CITY INDS INC (DE)
Old Common 10¢ par split (3) for (2) by issuance of (0.5) additional share 07/15/1983
Old Common 10¢ par split (3) for (2) by issuance of (0.5) additional share 04/15/1987
Old Common 10¢ par split (3) for (2) by issuance of (0.5) additional share 07/26/1991
Each share old Common 10¢ par exchanged for (0.01) share new Common 10¢ par 08/20/2003
Stock Dividend - 100% 06/16/1969
Name changed to Worldwide Biotech & Pharmaceutical Co. 01/12/2005
(See Worldwide Biotech & Pharmaceutical Co.)

SUN CITY VENTURES INC (AB)
Recapitalized as Conor Pacific Environmental Technologies Inc. 05/04/1995
Each share Common no par exchanged for (0.1) share Common no par
Conor Pacific Environmental Technologies Inc. name changed to Conor Pacific Group Inc. 12/20/2001 which name changed to Precision Assessment Technology Corp. 08/20/2003
(See Precision Assessment Technology Corp.)

SUN CMNTYS INC (MD)
7.125% Preferred Ser. A 1¢ par called for redemption at $25 plus $0.14349 accrued dividends on 11/14/2017
(Additional Information in Active)

SUN COAST DEVELOPMENT CO. (DE)
No longer in existence having become inoperative and void for non-payment of taxes 04/01/1967

SUN COAST INDS INC (DE)
Name changed 03/04/1994
Each share old Common 1¢ par exchanged for (0.2) share new Common 1¢ par 01/02/1992
Name changed from Sun Coast Plastics, Inc. to Sun Coast Industries, Inc. 03/04/1994
Merged into Saffron Acquisition Corp. 03/04/1998
Each share Common 1¢ par exchanged for $10.75 cash

SUN CMNTY BANCORP LTD (AZ)
Merged into Capitol Bancorp Ltd. 03/31/2002
Each share Common no par exchanged for (0.734) share Common no par
(See Capitol Bancorp Ltd.)

SUN CORP (OH)
In process of liquidation
Each share Common no par or VTC's for Common no par exchanged for initial distribution of (0.24976) share Talley Industries, Inc. Common $1 par 08/11/1969
Note: Amount or number of subsequent distributions, if any, are unavailable
(See Talley Industries, Inc.)

SUN CTRY BK (APPLE VALLEY, CA)
Merged into America Bancshares Inc. 08/21/2003

Each share Common no par exchanged for $12.50 cash

SUN CUT FLORAL NETWORK INC (NV)
Recapitalized as Avis Financial Corp. 12/09/2005
Each share Common $0.001 par exchanged for (0.05) share Common $0.001 par
Note: Holders of between (20) and (399) shares will receive (20) shares Holders of (19) or fewer shares were not affected by the reverse split

SUN DEV CO (MN)
Out of business 06/01/1972
No stockholders' equity

SUN DEVIL GOLD CORP (BC)
Name changed to Cardero Resource Corp. 05/13/1999

SUN DISTRS L P (DE)
Name changed to SunSource L.P. 04/15/1996
(See SunSource L.P.)

SUN DRUG INC (PA)
Name changed to Spang Stores, Inc. 01/03/1968
(See Spang Stores, Inc.)

SUN ELEC CORP (DE)
Common $1 par split (2) for (1) by issuance of (1) additional share 05/13/1966
Common $1 par split (5) for (4) by issuance of (0.25) additional share 06/17/1968
6% Preferred $100 par called for redemption 12/09/1968
Common $1 par split (3) for (2) by issuance of (0.5) additional share 01/12/1976
Common $1 par split (3) for (2) by issuance of (0.5) additional share 06/15/1978
Stock Dividend - 25% 03/15/1973
Common Stock Purchase Rights declared for Common stockholders of record 06/23/1988 were redeemed at $0.01 per right 10/02/1992 for holders of record 09/25/1992
Merged into Snap-On Tools Corp. 10/02/1992
Each share Common $1 par exchanged for $11.25 cash

SUN ENERGY INC (DE)
Each share old Common 1¢ par exchanged for (0.1) share new Common 1¢ par 03/23/1989
Reorganized under the laws of Nevada as STO-MED Inc. 02/23/1996
Each share new Common 1¢ par exchanged for (0.2) share Common 1¢ par
STO-MED Inc. name changed to Advanced Technologies Inc. (NV) 08/23/1997
(See Advanced Technologies Inc. (NV))

SUN ENERGY PARTNERS L P (DE)
Merged into Kerr-McGee Corp. 06/30/1999
Each Depositary Unit exchanged for $4.52 cash
Each Depositary Unit received an additional final distribution of $1.28 cash 06/07/2000

SUN ENTERPRISES, INC. (MN)
Name changed to World Wide Petroleum Corp. and Common 25¢ par changed to 10¢ par 09/22/1966
World Wide Petroleum Corp. name changed to World Wide Industries, Inc. 10/08/1968
(See World Wide Petroleum Corp.)

SUN ENTMT HLDG CORP (BC)
Became private 12/04/2014
Each share Common no par received $0.10 cash
Note: Certificates were not required to be surrendered and are without value

SUN EQUITIES CORP (DE)
Merged into Ergon Corp. 08/22/1989
Each share Common 1¢ par exchanged for $2.60 cash

SUN EXPL & PRODTN CO (DE)
Name changed to Oryx Energy Co. 05/03/1989
Oryx Energy Co. merged into Kerr-McGee Corp. 02/26/1999

SUN EXPRESS GROUP INC (FL)
Name changed to Sun Network Group, Inc. 10/01/2001
Sun Network Group, Inc. name changed to Aventura Holdings, Inc. 11/04/2005 which recapitalized as Zolon Corp. 03/15/2010 which name changed to Quadrant 4 Systems Corp. (FL) 05/31/2011 which reincorporated in Illinois 04/25/2013
(See Quadrant 4 Systems Corp.)

SUN FIN & LN CO (FL)
6% Preferred $10 par called for redemption 05/31/1969
Completely liquidated 05/31/1969
Each share Common $1 par exchanged for first and final distribution of (0.25) share Gulf Life Holding Co. Common $2.50 par
Gulf Life Holding Co. name changed to Gulf United Corp. 05/16/1977
(See Gulf United Corp.)

SUN FINANCE & LOAN CO. (OH)
Through exchange offer Sunamerica Corp. acquired 100% of Common $1 par as of 06/07/1969
6% Preferred $100 par called for redemption 12/31/1974
Public interest eliminated

SUN FING I
Plan of reorganization under Chapter 11 Federal Bankruptcy Code effective 02/28/2002
No stockholders' equity

SUN FIRST NATIONAL BANK (DUNEDIN, FL)
100% held by Sun Banks of Florida, Inc. as of 12/31/1991
Public interest eliminated

SUN FIRST NATIONAL BANK OF LAKE WALES (LAKE WALES, FL)
Acquired by Sun First National Bank of Polk County (Winter Haven, FL) 12/01/1979
Details not available

SUN FREE ENTERPRISES LTD (BC)
Cease trade order effective 07/10/1996
Stockholders' equity unlikely

SUN FRUIT LTD (NV)
Federal Equity Receivership imposed 03/03/1977
No stockholders' equity

SUN GLO PRODS CORP (FL)
Voluntarily dissolved 11/29/1982
Details not available

SUN GLOW INDUSTRIES, INC.
Liquidated 00/00/1947
Details not available

SUN GOD RES LTD (BC)
Name changed to Infotec Industries Inc. 04/14/1986
Infotec Industries Inc. recapitalized as Sellectek Industries Inc. 11/13/1986 which name changed to Global-Pacific Minerals Inc. (BC) 08/29/1989 which reorganized in Wyoming as UNIREX Technologies Inc. 04/23/2001 which recapitalized as UNIREX Corp. 07/19/2001
(See UNIREX Corp.)

SUN GOLD DEVS INTL CORP (BC)
Recapitalized as Gridiron Resources Ltd. 01/20/1994
Each share Common no par exchanged for (0.33333333) share Common no par
(See Gridiron Resources Ltd.)

SUN GOLD INDUSTRIES OF NEW YORK INC (NY)
Dissolved by proclamation 06/24/1981

SUN GRO HORTICULTURE INC (CANADA)
Acquired by 1582956 Alberta Ltd. 03/09/2011
Each share Common no par exchanged for $6.60 cash
Each share 144A Common no par exchanged for $6.60 cash

SUN GRO HORTICULTURE INCOME FD (BC)
Under plan of reorganization each Trust Unit no par automatically became (1) share Sun Gro Horticulture Inc. (Canada) Common no par 01/10/2011
(See Sun Gro Horticulture Inc.)

SUN HEALTHCARE GROUP INC NEW (DE)
Acquired by Genesis HealthCare LLC 12/04/2012
Each share Common 1¢ par exchanged for $8.50 cash

SUN HEALTHCARE GROUP INC OLD (DE)
Plan of reorganization under Chapter 11 Federal Bankruptcy Code effective 02/28/2002
No old Common stockholders' equity
Each share new Common 1¢ par received distribution of (0.33333333) share Sun Healthcare Group, Inc. (New) Common 1¢ par and $0.1335 cash payable 11/15/2010 to holders of record 11/05/2010
Under plan of reorganization each share new Common 1¢ par automatically became (0.33333333) share Sabra Health Care REIT, Inc. (MD) Common 1¢ par 11/15/2010

SUN HEET INC (CO)
Charter suspended for failure to file annual reports 06/28/1982

SUN HLDG CORP (NV)
Charter revoked for failure to file reports and pay fees 03/31/2000

SUN ICE LTD (AB)
Name changed to Sylre Ltd. 01/30/2004
Sylre Ltd. acquired by Northern Financial Corp. 01/17/2005 which recapitalized as Added Capital Inc. 07/23/2014

SUN INC (PA)
Common $1 par split (2) for (1) by issuance of (1) additional share 06/19/1980
$2.25 Conv. Preferred $1 par called for redemption 08/10/1988
Each share $1.80 Depositary Preference Ser. A exchanged for (0.949837) share Common $1 par and $0.03758 cash 05/28/1998
Name changed to Sunoco, Inc. 11/06/1998
Sunoco, Inc. merged into Energy Transfer Partners, L.P. (Old) 10/05/2012 which merged into Energy Transfer Partners, L.P. (New) 05/01/2017 which merged into Energy Transfer L.P. 10/19/2018

SUN INTERBREW LTD (CHANNEL ISLANDS)
Reincorporated under the laws of Cyprus as SUN Interbrew PLC 01/20/2011

SUN INTL HOTELS LTD (BAHAMAS)
Name changed to Kerzner International Ltd. 07/01/2002
(See Kerzner International Ltd.)

SUN INTL INC (UT)
Involuntarily dissolved 12/31/1986

SUN INTL LTD (SOUTH AFRICA)
ADR agreement terminated 03/19/2018
No ADR's remain outstanding

SUN INVESTING CO.
Dissolved 00/00/1936
Details not available

SUN INVESTMENT CO. (CA)
Dissolved 01/23/1974
Details not available

SUN-KRAFT, INC. (DE)
Bankrupt 00/00/1951
Stockholders' equity unlikely

SUN LIFE & PROVINCIAL HLDGS PLC (UNITED KINGDOM)
Acquired by AXA S.A. 07/26/2000
Each Sponsored ADR for Ordinary exchanged for 505p cash

SUN LIFE ASSURANCE CO OF CDA (CANADA)
6.5% Class E Ser. 1 Preferred called for redemption at $25 plus $0.40625 accrued dividends on 06/30/2005

SUN LIFE CAP TR (ON)
ExchangEable Capital Securities Ser. A called for redemption at $1,000 plus $34.325 accrued dividends on 01/03/2012

SUN LIFE FINL INC (CANADA)
Name changed from Sun Life Financial Services of Canada Inc. to Sun Life Financial Inc. 07/02/2003
Class A 5-Yr. Rate Reset Preferred Ser. 6 no par called for redemption at $25 on 06/30/2014
(Additional Information in Active)

SUN LIFE GROUP AMER INC (DE)
Name changed to Sunamerica Corp. 05/01/1989
Sunamerica Corp. merged into Sunamerica Inc. 08/13/1993

SUN LIFE INS CO AMER (MD)
Stock Dividends - 20% 04/26/1965; 10% 05/01/1968
Acquired by Kaufman & Broad, Inc. 11/19/1971
Each share Voting or Non-Vtg. Common $2.50 par exchanged for (0.2) share $1.50 Conv. Preferred Ser. A no par and (0.65) share Common $1 par
Kaufman & Broad, Inc. name changed to Broad, Inc. 03/08/1989 which name changed to SunAmerica Inc. 02/01/1993 which merged into American International Group, Inc. 01/01/1999

SUN LINE HELICOPTERS INC. (FL)
Charter cancelled and proclaimed dissolved for non-payment of taxes 05/13/1969

SUN-MARK INTL CORP (NV)
Charter revoked for failure to file reports and pay fees 05/01/1990

SUN MASTR CORP (KS)
Proclaimed dissolved for failure to file annual reports 02/15/1978

SUN MEDIA CORP (ON)
Merged into Quebecor Inc. 01/07/1999
Each share Common no par exchanged for $21 cash

SUN MICROSYSTEMS INC (DE)
Reincorporated 09/17/1986
State of incorporation changed from (CA) to (DE) 09/17/1986
Common $0.00067 par split (2) for (1) by issuance of (1) additional share 12/20/1988
Common $0.00067 par split (2) for (1) by issuance of (1) additional share 12/11/1995
Common $0.00067 par split (2) for (1) by issuance of (1) additional share payable 12/10/1996 to holders of record 11/18/1996
Common $0.00067 par split (2) for (1) by issuance of (1) additional share payable 04/08/1999 to holders of record 03/18/1999
Common $0.00067 par split (2) for (1)

by issuance of (1) additional share
payable 12/07/1999 to holders of
record 11/11/1999
Common $0.00067 par split (2) for (1)
by issuance of (1) additional share
payable 12/05/2000 to holders of
record 11/09/2000 Ex date -
12/06/2000
Each share Common $0.00067 par
exchanged for (0.25) share Common
$0.001 par 11/12/2007
Acquired by Oracle Corp. 01/26/2010
Each share Common $0.001 par
exchanged for $9.50 cash

SUN MORTGAGE CO.
Bankrupt 00/00/1939
Stockholders' equity unlikely

SUN MTR INTL INC (WY)
SEC revoked common stock
registration 12/22/2011

SUN MUSIC GROUP INC (DE)
Recapitalized as Banyan Healthcare
Services Inc. 12/21/1997
Each share Common $0.001 par
exchanged (0.33333333) share
Common $0.001 par
Banyan Healthcare Services Inc.
recapitalized as Netoy.com Corp.
03/15/1999 which name changed to
SafePay Solutions, Inc. 03/03/2006
which name changed to Emaji, Inc.
03/11/2008 which name changed to
Broadside Enterprises, Inc.
12/01/2016

SUN NETWORK GROUP INC (FL)
Name changed to Aventura Holdings,
Inc. 11/04/2005
Aventura Holdings, Inc. recapitalized
as Zolon Corp. 03/15/2010 which
name changed to Quadrant 4
Systems Corp. (FL) 05/31/2011
which reincorporated in Illinois
04/25/2013
(See Quadrant 4 Systems Corp.)

SUN NEW MEDIA INC (MN)
Reincorporated under the laws of
Delaware as NextMart, Inc.
05/08/2007

SUN OIL & GAS CORP (NV)
Each share old Common $0.001 par
exchanged for (0.2) share new
Common $0.001 par 09/19/2005
Recapitalized as China 3C Group
12/20/2005
Each share new Common $0.001 par
exchanged for (0.05) share Common
$0.001 par
China 3C Group recapitalized as
Yosen Group, Inc. 12/31/2012

SUN OIL CO. OF CALIFORNIA (CA)
Adjudicated bankrupt 06/22/1970
No stockholders' equity

SUN OIL CO (PA)
Reincorporated 09/30/1971
Common no par split (6) for (5) by
issuance of (0.2) additional share
05/16/1947
Common no par split (5) for (4) by
issuance of (0.25) additional share
12/30/1954
4.5% Preferred Ser. A $100 par called
for redemption 02/01/1956
Common no par split (7) for (3) by
issuance of (0.333) additional share
06/10/1966
Under plan of merger Common no par
changed to $1 par 10/25/1968
Stock Dividends - 10% 12/29/1941;
10% 12/15/1944; 10% 12/15/1945;
10% 01/30/1948; 10% 12/30/1948;
10% 12/15/1949; 10% 12/15/1950;
10% 12/15/1951; 10% 12/10/1974
State of incorporation changed from
(NJ) to (PA) 09/30/1971
Name changed to Sun Co., Inc.
04/27/1976
Sun Co., Inc. name changed to
Sunoco, Inc. 11/06/1998 which
merged into Energy Transfer
Partners, L.P. (Old) 10/05/2012
which merged into Energy Transfer
Partners, L.P. (New) 05/01/2017
which merged into Energy Transfer
L.P. 10/19/2018

SUN PEAKS ENERGY INC (NV)
Charter revoked for failure to file
reports and pay fees 03/31/2008

SUN PWR CORP (NV)
Recapitalized as Cardinal Minerals,
Inc. 01/16/2004
Each share Common no par
exchanged for (0.33333333) share
Common no par
Cardinal Minerals, Inc. recapitalized
as Universal Food & Beverage Co.
03/04/2005
(See Universal Food & Beverage Co.)

SUN PUBG LTD (BC)
Each share Common $10 par
exchanged for (5) shares Common
$2 par 10/03/1955
Each share Common $2 par
exchanged for (1) share Class A no
par and (1) share Class B no par
07/09/1956
Merged into F.P. Publications
(Western) Ltd. 07/27/1978
Each share Class A no par
exchanged for $69 cash
Each share Class B no par
exchanged for $69 cash

SUN QUEST HLDGS INC (NV)
Name changed to Sunrise Consulting
Group, Inc. 12/04/2007

SUN RAY DRUG CO. (PA)
Each share Common $1 par
exchanged for (4) shares Common
25¢ par 00/00/1947
Merged into Consolidated Sun Ray,
Inc. 02/02/1959
Each share Common 25¢ par
exchanged for (8) shares Common
$1 par
Consolidated Sun Ray, Inc.
recapitalized as Penrose Industries
Corp. 10/23/1964
(See Penrose Industries Corp.)

SUN RAYZ PRODS INC (FL)
Name changed to Trivos, Inc.
06/22/2006
(See Trivos, Inc.)

SUN RED CAP CORP (AB)
Merged into Compass Petroleum Ltd.
06/04/2010
Each share Common no par
exchanged for (0.025) share
Common no par
Note: Unexchanged certificates were
cancelled and became without value
06/04/2015
Compass Petroleum Ltd. merged into
Whitecap Resources Inc.
02/10/2012

SUN RIV GOLD CORP (BC)
Recapitalized as Yellow Point Mining
Corp. 03/11/1991
Each share Common no par
exchanged for (0.16666666) share
Common no par
Yellow Point Mining Corp.
recapitalized as Desert Sun Mining
Corp. (BC) 08/26/1994 which
reincorporated in Canada
03/20/2003 which was acquired by
Yamana Gold Inc. 04/05/2006

SUN RIV MNG INC (CO)
Recapitalized as XsunX, Inc.
10/07/2003
Each share Common 1¢ par
exchanged for (0.05) share Common
1¢ par

SUN RUBBER CO. (OH)
Name changed to Sun Corp.
01/17/1966
(See Sun Corp.)

SUN-RYPE PRODS LTD (BC)
Each share Class B Common no par
exchanged for (1) share Common
no par 07/11/2000

Acquired by Great Pacific Industries
Inc. 10/03/2013
Each share Common no par
exchanged for $7.50 cash

SUN SVGS & LN ASSN (CA)
Guarantee Stock $8 par changed to
$4 par and (1) additional share
issued 05/15/1983
Placed in receivership by FSLIC
07/18/1986
No stockholders' equity

SUN SCIENTIFIC GROUP INC (DE)
Charter cancelled and declared
inoperative and void for
non-payment of taxes 03/01/1989

SUN SOURCE INC (NV)
Reorganized as PayStar
Communications Corp. 11/16/1998
Each share Common $0.001 par
exchanged for (2) shares Common
$0.001 par
PayStar Communications Corp. name
changed to PayStar Corp.
10/04/2001
(See PayStar Corp.)

SUN-SPORT INDS INC (WA)
Charter cancelled and proclaimed
dissolved for failure to pay fees
10/19/1987

SUN SPORTSWEAR INC (WA)
Merged into Brazos Sportswear, Inc.
03/14/1997
For 50% of holdings:
Each share Common no par
exchanged for (0.2) share Common
$0.001 par and $2.20 cash for the
remaining 50%
Brazos Sportswear, Inc. recapitalized
as Marinas International Inc.
08/29/2005
(See Marinas International Inc.)

SUN ST CAP CORP (NV)
Merged into Zions Bancorporation
10/17/1997
Each share Common no par
exchanged for either (3.341) shares
Common no par, $131.23 cash or a
combination thereof
Note: Option to receive anything other
than cash expired 10/31/1997
(See Zions Bancorporation)

SUN ST SVGS & LN ASSN (AZ)
Guaranty Stock $5 par changed to $1
par and (9) additional shares issued
to effect a (5) for (1) split and 100%
stock dividend 12/30/1983
Guaranty Stock $1 par split (4) for (3)
by issuance of (0.33333333)
additional share 03/17/1986
Stock Dividend - 50% 12/28/1984
Placed in receivership 06/14/1989
No stockholders' equity

SUN TECH ENTERPRISES (NV)
Each share old Common $0.001 par
exchanged for (0.01) share new
Common $0.001 par 05/07/1996
Name changed to Medtrak
Electronics, Inc. 07/29/1996
(See Medtrak Electronics, Inc.)

**SUN TELEVISION & APPLIANCES
INC (DE)**
Common 1¢ par split (2) for (1) by
issuance of (1) additional share
07/22/1993
Plan of reorganization under Chapter
11 Federal Bankruptcy Code
effective 12/22/1999
No stockholders' equity

SUN TIDE CORP (UT)
Name changed to Maxa Corp.
04/13/1974
(See Maxa Corp.)

SUN-TIMES MEDIA GROUP INC (DE)
Plan of reorganization under Chapter
11 Federal Bankruptcy proceedings
effective 10/01/2011
No stockholders' equity

SUN TZU CORP (WA)
Charter expired 10/31/2009

SUN URANIUM CO. (UT)
Merged into Sun Uranium Mining Co.
12/15/1954
Each share Common 1¢ par
exchanged for (0.25) share Capital
Stock 50¢ par
Sun Uranium Mining Co. recapitalized
as Sun Tide Corp. 07/22/1955 which
recapitalized as Maxa Corp.
04/13/1974
(See Maxa Corp.)

SUN URANIUM MINING CO. (UT)
Name changed to Sun Tide Corp. and
Capital Stock 50¢ par changed to
10¢ par 07/22/1955
Sun Tide Corp. name changed to
Maxa Corp. 04/13/1974
(See Maxa Corp.)

SUN VACATION PPTYS CORP (NV)
SEC revoked common stock
registration 07/16/2008

SUN VY BANCORP (ID)
Company's sole asset placed in
receivership 04/24/2009
No stockholders' equity

SUN VY GOLD MINES LTD (BC)
Struck off register and declared
dissolved for failure to file returns
11/01/1991

**SUN VY ID & RED LAKE RES LTD
(BC)**
Name changed to Red Lake & Sun
Valley Resources Ltd. 09/04/1987
Red Lake & Sun Valley Resources
Ltd. recapitalized as International
R.S.V. Resource Corp. 12/27/1989
which recapitalized as Harambee
Mining Corp. 05/05/1997 which
recapitalized as Neuer Kapital Corp.
01/03/2002 which name changed to
Crescent Resources Corp.
08/03/2005 which recapitalized as
Coventry Resources Inc. 01/09/2013
(See Coventry Resources Inc.)

**SUN VY LEAD SILVER MINES INC
(ID)**
Name changed to Smartek, Inc.
02/12/1996
(See Smartek, Inc.)

SUN VALLEY MINING CORP. (DE)
Proclaimed inoperative and void for
non-payment of taxes 04/01/1958

SUN VALLEY RANCH INC. (ON)
Name changed to Tri-Lateral Free
Trade Inc. 03/25/1991
Tri-Lateral Free Trade Inc.
recapitalized as Tri-Lateral
Investments Corp. 06/19/1995 which
recapitalized as Tri-Lateral Venture
Corp. 11/11/1998 which name
changed to Pan American Gold
Corp. 05/06/2004 which
recapitalized as Newcastle
Resources Ltd. (ON) 11/28/2008
which reincorporated in British
Columbia as RepliCel Life Sciences
Inc. 07/01/2011

SUN-WEST MINERALS LTD. (BC)
Struck off register and declared
dissolved for failure to file returns
07/08/1974

SUN WORLD PARTNERS INC (NV)
Name changed to PreAxia Health
Care Payment Systems, Inc.
01/15/2009

SUNAC PETROLEUM CORP. (DE)
Acquired by Sunset International
Petroleum Corp. 09/01/1964
Each share Capital Stock $1 par
received $0.37 cash

SUNAIR SVCS CORP (FL)
Name changed 11/30/2005
Common 10¢ par split (4) for (3) by
issuance of (0.33333333) additional
share 06/09/1972
Common 10¢ par split (2) for (1) by
issuance of (1) additional share
06/17/1983

Stock Dividends - 10% 06/26/1978; 100% 01/02/1981
Name changed from Sunair Electronics, Inc. to Sunair Services Corp. 11/30/2005
Acquired by Massey Services, Inc. 12/16/2009
Each share Common 10¢ par exchanged for $2.75 cash

SUNALTA ENERGY INC (AB)
Merged into a private company 07/02/1996
Each share Common no par exchanged for $0.94 cash

SUNAMERICA CAP TR I (DE)
9.95% Trust Originated Preferred called for redemption at $25 on 06/16/1997

SUNAMERICA CAP TR II (DE)
8.35% Trust Originated Preferred Securities called for redemption at $25 plus $0.475486 accrued dividends on 03/23/2001

SUNAMERICA CAP TR III (DE)
8.30% Trust Originated Preferred Securities called for redemption at $25 on 12/20/2001

SUNAMERICA CORP (DE)
Merged into Chemical New York Corp. 06/30/1975
Each share Common $1 par exchanged for (0.84) share Common $12 par
Chemical New York Corp. name changed to Chemical Banking Corp. 04/29/1988 which name changed to Chase Manhattan Corp. (New) 03/31/1996 which name changed to J.P. Morgan Chase & Co. 12/31/2000 which name changed to JPMorgan Chase & Co. 07/20/2004

SUNAMERICA CORP NEW (DE)
Merged into Sunamerica Inc. 8/13/93
Each share Adjustable Rate Preferred Ser. A no par exchanged for (1) share Adjustable Rate Preferred Ser. C no par

SUNAMERICA FOCUSED ALPHA GROWTH FD INC (MD)
Under plan of reorganization each share Common $0.001 par automatically became (1) SunAmerica Specialty Series Focused Alpha Growth Fund Class A 01/23/2012

SUNAMERICA FOCUSED ALPHA LARGE-CAP FD INC (MD)
Under plan of reorganization each share Common $0.001 par automatically became (1) SunAmerica Specialty Series Focused Alpha Large-Cap Fund Class A 01/23/2012
No stockholders' equity

SUNAMERICA INC (MD)
Depositary Shares Ser. A called for redemption 8/16/94
Mandatory Conversion Premium Preferred Ser. A no par called for redemption 8/16/94
Issue Information - 4,000,000 PFD MAN CONV PREM DIVID SER E $3.10 offered at $62 per share on 10/26/95
Common $1 par split (3) for (2) by issuance of (0.5) additional share 11/10/95
$2.78 Depositary Preferred Ser. D no par called for redemption 1/2/96
$2.78 Mandatory Conversion Premium Preferred Ser. D no par called for redemption 1/2/96
Common $1 par split (2) for (1) by issuance of (1) additional share payable 8/30/96 to holders of record 8/21/96 Ex date - 9/3/96
Class B Common $1 par split (2) for (1) by issuance of (1) additional share payable 8/30/96 to holders of record 8/21/96
Adjustable Rate Preferred Ser. C

$100 par called for redemption 10/4/96
9.25% Preferred Ser. B $25 par called for redemption at $25 plus accrued dividend on 6/16/97
Common $1 par split (3) for (2) by issuance (0.5) additional share payable 8/29/97 to holders of record 8/20/97 Ex date - 9/2/97
Depositary Preferred Ser. E called for redemption at (2.812677255) shares Common $1 par plus $0.3875 accrued dividend on 10/30/98
$3.10 Mandatory Conv. Preferred Premium Dividend Ser. E called for redemption at (140.633862734) shares Common $1 par plus $19.375 accrued dividend on 10/30/98
8.50% Equity Redeemable Security Unit Preferred called for redemption at (0.87897647) share Common $1 par plus $0.036986301 accrued dividend and unpaid contract fees on 10/30/98
Each share Class B Common $1 par exchanged for (1) share Common $1 par 1/1/99
Merged into American International Group, Inc. 1/1/99
Each share Common $1 par exchanged for (0.855) share Common $2.50 par

SUNAMERICA INCOME PLUS FD INC (MD)
Merged into SunAmerica Fund Group 06/11/1992
Details not available

SUNASCO INC. (PA)
Name changed to Scientific Resources Corp. 10/11/68
(See Scientific Resources Corp.)

SUNATCO DEV CORP (BC)
Recapitalized as International Sunatco Industries Ltd. 01/14/1991
Each share Capital Stock no par exchanged for (1/3) share Common no par

SUNBASE ASIA INC (NV)
Name changed to Centire International, Inc. (NV) 06/08/2007
Centire International, Inc. (NV) reincorporated in Florida as Jericho Energy Co., Inc. 07/18/2008

SUNBEAM CORP NEW (DE)
Name changed 5/22/95
Name changed from Sunbeam-Oster Inc. to Sunbeam Corp. (New) 5/22/95
Plan of reorganization under Chapter 11 Federal Bankruptcy Code effective 12/18/2002
No stockholders' equity

SUNBEAM CORP OLD (DE)
Reincorporated 7/18/69
Common no par changed to $1 par and (0.5) additional share issued 8/15/55
Common $1 par split (5) for (4) by issuance of (0.25) additional share 4/25/62
Common $1 par split (5) for (4) by issuance of (0.25) additional share 4/29/64
Common $1 par split (4) for (3) by issuance of (1/3) additional share 4/30/65
Common $1 par changed to no par 6/7/65
Stock Dividends - 25% 4/11/49; 33-1/3% 4/15/50; 100% 4/7/52; 10% 1/31/54
State of incorporation changed from (IL) to (DE) 7/18/69
Common no par changed to $1 par and (0.5) additional share issued 8/12/69
Merged into Allegheny International Inc. 1/2/82
Each share Common $1 par

exchanged for (0.36) share $11.25 Conv. Preferred no par
(See Allegheny International Inc.)

SUNBEAM EXPLORATION CO. LTD. (ON)
Charter cancelled for failure to file reports and pay taxes in 1970

SUNBEAM KIRKLAND GOLD MINES LTD.
Bankrupt in 1941

SUNBEAM SOLAR INC. (UT)
Reincorporated under the laws of Nevada as GamePlan, Inc. 12/31/1991
Each share Common $0.001 par exchanged for (0.2) share Common $0.001 par 12/31/1991

SUNBELT AIRLS INC (NY)
Common 1¢ par split (10) for (1) by issuance of (9) additional shares 7/31/79
Recapitalized as Florida Publishers, Inc. 10/15/80
Each share Common 1¢ par exchanged for (0.1) share Common 1¢ par
(See Florida Publishers, Inc.)

SUNBELT BANK & TRUST CO. (TULSA, OK)
Name changed to Central Bank & Trust of Tulsa (Tulsa, OK) 11/19/1984
(See Central Bank & Trust of Tulsa (Tulsa, OK))

SUNBELT CAP CORP (CO)
Name changed to AFG, Inc. 11/19/1986

SUNBELT COS INC (DE)
Merged into Pelican Companies Inc. 12/22/95
Each share Common 1¢ par exchanged for $7.95 cash

SUNBELT DEV CORP (BC)
Name changed to Plaser Light Corp. 4/8/88
(See Plaser Light Corp.)

SUNBELT EXPL INC (NV)
Liquidating plan of reorganization under Chapter 11 Federal Bankruptcy Code effective 02/00/1989
No old Common stockholders' equity
Recapitalized as iExalt, Inc. 09/13/1999
Each share new Common $0.001 par exchanged for (0.1) share Common $0.001 par

SUNBELT INTL CORP (NV)
Each share old Common $0.001 par exchanged for (0.001) share new Common $0.001 par 08/29/2012
Recapitalized as Nevcor Business Solutions Inc. 02/06/2014
Each share new Common $0.001 par exchanged for (0.01) share Common $0.001 par
Nevcor Business Solutions Inc. name changed to CPSM, Inc. 07/15/2014 which name changed to Astro Aerospace Ltd. 04/24/2018

SUNBELT NATL BK (HOUSTON, TX)
Merged into Prime Bancshares, Inc. 5/22/98
Each share Common no par exchanged for (1.625) shares Common 25¢ par
Prime Bancshares, Inc. merged into Wells Fargo & Co. (New) 1/28/2000

SUNBELT NURSERY GROUP (DE)
Acquired by Pier 1 Imports, Inc. 11/21/90
Each share Common 1¢ par exchanged for $12 cash

SUNBELT NURSERY GROUP INC (DE)
Filed a petition under Chapter 11 Federal Bankruptcy Code 04/01/1998

Stockholders' equity unlikely

SUNBELT OIL & GAS INC (DE)
Name changed to Dallas Sunbelt Oil & Gas, Inc. 05/08/1981
(See Dallas Sunbelt Oil & Gas, Inc.)

SUNBELT PROFESSIONAL SVCS INC (CO)
Each share Common $0.0001 par exchanged for (0.025) share Common $0.004 par 12/29/89
Name changed to Magnum Resources International, Inc. 3/30/90

SUNBERTA RES INC (NV)
Old Common $0.001 par split (20) for (1) by issuance of (19) additional shares payable 01/14/2008 to holders of record 01/14/2008
Name changed to Grid Petroleum Corp. 12/16/2009
Grid Petroleum Corp. name changed to Simlatus Corp. 04/26/2016

SUNBIRD TECHNOLOGIES INC (UT)
Proclaimed dissolved for failure to pay taxes 1/1/96

SUNBLUSH TECHNOLOGIES CORP (BC)
Recapitalized as FreshXtend Technologies Corp. 12/31/2003
Each share Common no par exchanged for (0.2) share Common no par
(See FreshXtend Technologies Corp.)

SUNBURST, INC. (NV)
Charter revoked for failure to file reports and pay fees 03/03/1975

SUNBURST ACQUISITIONS I INC (CO)
Name changed to Invu, Inc. 03/05/1997
(See Invu, Inc.)

SUNBURST ACQUISITIONS II INC (TX)
Recapitalized as Vector Energy Corp. (TX) 06/23/1998
Each (3.33) shares Common no par exchanged for (1) share Common no par
Preferred affected only by name change
Vector Energy Corp. (TX) reorganized in Nevada as VTEX Energy, Inc. 11/15/2002
(See VTEX Energy, Inc.)

SUNBURST ACQUISITIONS III INC (NV)
Reincorporated 09/30/2008
Common no par split (16.16) for (1) by issuance of (15.16) additional shares payable 09/14/1999 to holders of record 09/13/1999
State of incorporation changed from Colorado to Nevada and Common no par changed to $0.0001 par 09/30/2008
Recapitalized as Percipio Biotherapeutics, Inc. 10/29/2008
Each share Common $0.0001 par exchanged for (0.01492537) share Common $0.0001 par
(See Percipio Biotherapeutics, Inc.)

SUNBURST ACQUISITIONS IV INC (CO)
Common no par split (20) for (1) by issuance of (19) additional shares payable 08/18/1999 to holders of record 08/16/1999
Recapitalized as Mexoro Minerals Ltd. (CO) 02/15/2006
Each share Common no par exchanged for (0.02) share Common no par
Mexoro Minerals Ltd. (CO) reincorporated in Delaware as Pan American Goldfields Ltd. 07/22/2010

SUNBURST ALLIANCE INC (NV)
Common $0.001 par split (5) for (1) by issuance of (4) additional shares

payable 02/18/2005 to holders of record 02/17/2005
Charter revoked for failure to file reports and pay fees 11/30/2008

SUNBURST EXPL LTD (ON)
Recapitalized as Sunburst Resources 1991 Inc. 11/14/1991
Each share Common no par exchanged for (0.1) share Common no par
Sunburst Resources 1991 Inc. name changed to Sunburst M.C. Ltd. 02/16/1994 which name changed to Channel I Canada Inc. 01/10/1997 which recapitalized as Zaurak Capital Corp. 12/01/1999
(See Zaurak Capital Corp.)

SUNBURST HOSPITALITY CORP (DE)
Merged into Nova Finance Co. LLC 01/05/2001
Each share Common 1¢ par exchanged for $7.375 cash

SUNBURST INDS INC (NV)
Charter revoked for failure to file reports and pay fees 03/06/1978

SUNBURST M C LTD (ON)
Name changed to Channel I Canada Inc. 01/10/1997
Channel I Canada Inc. recapitalized as Zaurak Capital Corp. 12/01/1999
(See Zaurak Capital Corp.)

SUNBURST MADISON OIL CORP (DE)
No longer in existence having become inoperative and void for non-payment of taxes 10/01/1963

SUNBURST NUCLEAR CORP (UT)
Name changed to Becos Industries, Inc. (UT) 08/25/1980
Becos Industries, Inc. (UT) reorganized in Nevada 10/31/1984 which name changed to Softpoint Inc. 09/01/1989 which recapitalized as Acquest Corp. 11/04/1996
(See Acquest Corp.)

SUNBURST OIL & GAS INC (AB)
Assets sold for the benefit of creditors 08/21/2001
No stockholders' equity

SUNBURST OIL & REFINING CO.
Property sold 00/00/1936
Details not available

SUNBURST OIL CO. LTD.
Acquired by Newalta Petroleums Ltd. on a (1) for (4) basis 00/00/1951
(See Newalta Petroleums Ltd.)

SUNBURST PETROLEUM CORP. (NV)
Name changed to Sunburst Industries, Inc. 03/06/1970
(See Sunburst Industries, Inc.)

SUNBURST RES 1991 INC (ON)
Name changed to Sunburst M.C. Ltd. 02/16/1994
Sunburst M.C. Ltd. name changed to Channel I Canada Inc. 01/10/1997 which recapitalized as Zaurak Capital Corp. 12/01/1999
(See Zaurak Capital Corp.)

SUNBURST URANIUM CORP. (NV)
Name changed to Sunburst, Inc. 00/00/1958
(See Sunburst, Inc.)

SUNBURY BRIDGE CO.
Acquired by Commonwealth of Pennsylvania 00/00/1949
Details not available

SUNBURY FOODS INC (PA)
Common $2.50 par changed to $1.25 par 08/13/1969
Name changed to Foodcraft, Inc. 05/03/1978
(See Foodcraft, Inc.)

SUNBURY MILK PRODUCTS CO. (PA)
Capital Stock $25 par reclassified as Common $25 par 03/27/1957
Each share Common $25 par exchanged for (5) shares Common $5 par 03/15/1960
Common $5 par changed to $2.50 par and (1) additional share issued 06/15/1964
Name changed to Sunbury Foods, Inc. 06/01/1964
Sunbury Foods, Inc. name changed to Foodcraft, Inc. 05/03/1978
(See Foodcraft, Inc.)

SUNCAST NETWORK INC (DE)
SEC revoked common stock registration 01/19/2012

SUNCL INC (DE)
Name changed to netValue Holdings, Inc. 11/24/1998
netValue Holdings, Inc. name changed to Stonepath Group, Inc. 09/25/2000

SUNCOAST BANCORP INC (FL)
Stock Dividend - 5% payable 09/30/2004 to holders of record 09/20/2004 Ex date - 09/16/2004
Merged into Cadence Financial Corp. 08/17/2006
Each share Common 1¢ par exchanged for (1.19) shares Common $1 par
(See Cadence Financial Corp.)

SUNCOAST NATURALS INC (DE)
Name changed to Intelligent Security Networks, Inc. 08/22/2005
Intelligent Security Networks, Inc. name changed to Gambino Apparel Group, Inc. 04/10/2006 which recapitalized as Patient Portal Technologies, Inc. 09/01/2006

SUNCOAST PETE CORP (BC)
Delisted from Vancouver Stock Exchange 11/03/1992

SUNCOAST SVGS & LN ASSN (FL)
Class A Common $3.55 par reclassified as Common $3.55 par 07/01/1988
Stock Dividend - 10% 02/21/1989
Merged into BankUnited Financial Corp. 11/15/1996
Each share 8% Conv. Preferred Ser. A $5 par exchanged for (1) share 8% Conv. Preferred 1¢ par
Each share Common $1.10 par exchanged for (1) share Class A Common 1¢ par
(See BankUnited Financial Corp.)

SUNCOM TELECOMMUNICATIONS INC (CANADA)
Name changed to VirtualSellers.com, Inc. 06/01/1999
VirtualSellers.com, Inc. name changed to Healthtrac, Inc. 03/25/2002
(See Healthtrac, Inc.)

SUNCOM WIRELESS HLDGS INC (DE)
Each share old Class A Common 1¢ par exchanged for (0.1) share new Class A Common 1¢ par 05/16/2007
Merged into T-Mobile USA, Inc. 02/22/2008
Each share Class A Common 1¢ par exchanged for $27 cash

SUNCOOK MILLS
In process of liquidation 00/00/1943
Details not available

SUNCOR ENERGY INC OLD (CANADA)
Name changed 04/18/1997
$1.92 Preferred Ser. A no par called for redemption 09/01/1992
Name changed from Suncor Inc. to Suncor Energy Inc. (Old) 04/18/1997
Common no par split (2) for (1) by issuance of (1) additional share payable 05/12/1997 to holders of record 05/08/1997 Ex date - 05/13/1997
Common no par split (2) for (1) by issuance of (1) additional share payable 05/15/2000 to holders of record 05/10/2000 Ex date - 05/16/2000
Common no par split (2) for (1) by issuance of (1) additional share payable 05/22/2002 to holders of record 05/15/2002 Ex date - 05/23/2002
9.05% Canadian Dollar Preferred Securities called for redemption at $25 on 03/15/2004
9.125% U.S. Dollar Preferred Securities called for redemption at $25 on 03/15/2004
Common no par split (2) for (1) by issuance of (1) additional share payable 05/27/2008 to holders of record 05/14/2008 Ex date - 05/27/2008
Merged into Suncor Energy Inc. (New) 08/01/2009
Each share Common no par exchanged for (1) share Common no par
Note: Unexchanged certificates were cancelled and became without value 08/01/2015

SUNCORP-METWAY LTD (AUSTRALIA)
Name changed to Suncorp Group Ltd. 02/03/2011

SUNCREST ENERGY INC (AB)
Recapitalized 07/06/1993
Recapitalized from Suncrest Capital Corp. to Suncrest Energy Inc. 07/06/1993
Each share Class A Common no par exchanged for (0.5) share Common no par
Recapitalized as Nextra Technologies Inc. 10/18/1994
Each share Common no par exchanged for (0.33333333) share Common no par
Nextra Technologies Inc. name changed to NUVO Network Management Inc. 06/27/1997
(See NUVO Network Management Inc.)

SUNCREST ENERGY INC (WY)
Each share old Common no par exchanged for (0.001) share new Common no par 07/19/2004
Each share new Common no par exchanged again for (0.01) share new Common no par 10/01/2004
Each share new Common no par exchanged for (10) shares new Common no par 10/06/2005
Name changed to Amerossi International Group, Inc. 01/30/2006
Amerossi International Group, Inc. recapitalized as Bio-Med Technologies, Inc. 11/19/2007
(See Bio-Med Technologies, Inc.)

SUNCREST GLOBAL ENERGY CORP (NV)
Each share old Common $0.001 par exchanged for (0.076923) share new Common $0.001 par 12/29/2006
Name changed to Beacon Enterprise Solutions Group, Inc. 02/15/2008
Beacon Enterprise Solutions Group, Inc. name changed to FTE Networks, Inc. 03/18/2014

SUNCROSS EXPL CORP (NV)
Each share old Common $0.001 par exchanged for (19) shares new Common $0.001 par 05/19/2008
Name changed to Team Nation Holdings Corp. 07/07/2008
Team Nation Holdings Corp. name changed to Top Shelf Brands Holdings Corp. 11/17/2014

SUNDANCE ENERGY CORP. (NV)
Charter revoked for failure to file reports and pay fees 12/18/1990

SUNDANCE ENERGY CORP (AB)
Each share old Common no par exchanged for (0.2) share new Common no par 09/30/2013
Name changed to Ceno Energy Ltd. 06/23/2014
Ceno Energy Ltd. name changed to Vital Energy Inc. 10/10/2014

SUNDANCE ENERGY RES LTD (CANADA)
Name changed to Sunmist Energy Resources Ltd. 03/25/1980
Sunmist Energy Resources Ltd. recapitalized as Sunmist Energy '84 Inc. 06/04/1984 which name changed to Sunmist Energy '86 Inc. 03/05/1987
(See Sunmist Energy '86 Inc.)

SUNDANCE GOLD LTD (BC)
Recapitalized as Argrel Resources Ltd. 11/06/1985
Each share Capital Stock no par exchanged for (0.2) share Common no par
(See Argrel Resources Ltd.)

SUNDANCE GOLD MNG & EXPL INC (DE)
Name changed to Sundance International, Inc. 05/02/1983
Sundance International, Inc. name changed to Burzynski Research Institute, Inc. 07/13/1984

SUNDANCE HOMES INC (IL)
Proclaimed dissolved for failure to pay taxes and file reports 08/01/2002

SUNDANCE INTL INC (DE)
Name changed to Burzynski Research Institute, Inc. 07/13/1984

SUNDANCE MNG CO (OR)
Name changed to Quantum Systems Industries, Inc. 12/20/1971
Quantum Systems Industries, Inc. name changed to Balboa Development Inc. 12/13/1985
(See Balboa Development Inc.)

SUNDANCE OIL CO (UT)
Common 10¢ par split (2) for (1) by issuance of (1) additional share 07/17/1978
Common 10¢ par split (2) for (1) by issuance of (1) additional share 09/22/1980
Acquired by Societe Quebecoise d'Initiatives Petrolieres 12/21/1984
Each share Common 10¢ par exchanged for $10 cash

SUNDANCE RES INC (AB)
Merged into True Energy Inc. 08/31/2000
Each share Common no par exchanged for (0.444) share Common no par
(See True Energy Inc.)

SUNDANCE RES LTD (BC)
Recapitalized as Mammoth Energy Inc. 08/23/1995
Each share Common no par exchanged for (0.1) share Common no par
Mammoth Energy Inc. recapitalized as Cierra Pacific Ventures Ltd. 02/25/1998 which recapitalized as Alange Energy Corp. 07/15/2009 which recapitalized as PetroMagdalena Energy Corp. 07/19/2011
(See PetroMagdalena Energy Corp.)

SUNDANCE ROYALTIES, LTD.
Merged into Amalgamated Oils, Ltd. 00/00/1941
Details not available

SUNDAY COMMUNICATIONS LTD (CAYMAN ISLANDS)
Each old Sponsored ADR for Ordinary

exchanged for (0.3) new Sponsored ADR for Ordinary 07/25/2002
Basis changed from (1:30) to (1:100) 07/25/2002
Acquired by PCCW Mobile 12/04/2006
Each new Sponsored ADR for Ordinary exchanged for $8.30728 cash

SUNDBY BATTERY & MANUFACTURING CO. (ND)
Charter revoked for failure to file reports and pay fees 10/30/1925

SUNDBY BATTERY CO. (WI)
Charter revoked for failure to file reports and pay fees 01/01/1926

SUNDERLAND CORP (DE)
Name changed to Vestin Group Inc. 07/03/2000
(See Vestin Group Inc.)

SUNDEW INTL INC (DE)
Name changed to Legend International Holdings, Inc. 04/16/2003
(See Legend International Holdings, Inc.)

SUNDOG TECHNOLOGIES INC (DE)
Each share old Common $0.001 par exchanged for (0.5) share new Common $0.001 par 12/15/2000
Name changed to Arkona Inc. 02/22/2001
(See Arkona Inc.)

SUNDOWN MINING CO. (UT)
Name changed to Sundown Petroleum Co. 01/03/1957
Sundown Petroleum Co. name changed to United Tele-Tronics, Inc. 07/12/1961 which name changed to United Resources Inc. (UT) 04/24/1967 which name changed to Pacific Air Transport Inc. 01/31/1968 which name changed to Pacific Air Transport International Inc. 09/28/1970 which recapitalized as Chase Hanover Corp. 09/17/1983
(See Chase Hanover Corp.)

SUNDOWN PETROLEUM CO. (UT)
Name changed to United Tele-Tronics, Inc. 07/12/1961
United Tele-Tronics, Inc. name changed to United Resources Inc. (UT) 04/24/1967 which name changed to Pacific Air Transport Inc. 01/31/1968 which name changed to Pacific Air Transport International Inc. 09/28/1970 which recapitalized as Chase Hanover Corp. 09/17/1983
(See Chase Hanover Corp.)

SUNDOWNER OFFSHORE SVCS INC (NV)
Merged into Nabors Industries, Inc. (DE) 10/27/1994
Each share Common 1¢ par exchanged for (2.8) shares Common 10¢ par
Nabors Industries, Inc. (DE) reincorporated in Bermuda as Nabors Industries Ltd. 06/24/2002

SUNDSTRAND CORP (DE)
Reincorporated 12/15/1966
State of incorporation changed from (IL) to (DE) 12/15/1966
Common $5 par changed to $1 par and (1) additional share issued 12/29/1966
Common $1 par split (2) for (1) by issuance of (1) additional share 11/15/1978
$3.50 Conv. Preferred no par called for redemption 02/09/1982
Common $1 par changed to 50¢ par and (1) additional share issued 06/20/1990
Common 50¢ par split (2) for (1) by issuance of (1) additional share payable 03/19/1996 to holders of record 03/05/1996
Merged into United Technologies Corp. 06/10/1999

Each share Common 50¢ par exchanged for (0.558) share Common $1 par and $35 cash

SUNDSTRAND MACHINE TOOL CO. (IL)
Common no par changed to $5 par 00/00/1937
Common $5 par split (2) for (1) by issuance of (1) additional share 12/20/1955
Stock Dividends - 50% 11/05/1941; 100% 06/25/1948
Name changed to Sundstrand Corp. (IL) 04/28/1959
Sundstrand Corp. (IL) reincorporated in Delaware 12/15/1956 which merged into United Technologies Corp. 06/10/1999

SUNEDISON INC (DE)
Plan of reorganization under Chapter 11 Federal Bankruptcy proceedings effective 12/29/2017
No stockholders' equity

SUNEDISON SEMICONDUCTOR LTD (SINGAPORE)
Acquired by GlobalWafers Co., Ltd. 12/02/2016
Each share Ordinary no par exchanged for $12 cash

SUNERGY CMNTYS INC (DE)
Recapitalized as River Oaks Industries, Inc. 06/30/1983
Each share Common $0.005 par exchanged for (0.5) share Common 1¢ par
(See River Oaks Industries, Inc.)

SUNEVA RES LTD (BC)
Recapitalized as International Suneva Resources Ltd. 01/20/1989
Each share Common no par exchanged for (0.28571428) share Common no par
International Suneva Resources Ltd. recapitalized as Nevsun Reources Ltd. 12/19/1991

SUNEXCO ENERGY CORP (BC)
Recapitalized as Selena Research Corp. 01/16/1986
Each share Common no par exchanged for (0.25) share Common no par
Selena Research Corp. recapitalized as SLN Ventures Corp. 03/01/1994 which recapitalized as Pan Ocean Explorations Inc. 04/01/1997
(See Pan Ocean Explorations Inc.)

SUNF INC (MN)
Liquidation completed
Each share Common 50¢ par received initial distribution of $4.25 cash 04/23/1990
Each share Common 50¢ par received second distribution of $0.75 cash 05/00/1991
Each share Common 50¢ par exchanged for third and final distribution of $0.1225 cash 11/25/1992

SUNFIRE ENERGY CORP (AB)
Merged into Tusk Energy Inc. 07/02/2003
Each share Class A Common no par exchanged for $3.41 cash

SUNFLOWER STATE OIL CO., INC. (DE)
Recapitalized as Petrosur Oil Corp. 11/01/1957
Each share Common 10¢ par exchanged for (0.1) share Common 10¢ par
Petrosur Oil Corp. merged into Techtro-Matic Corp. 08/24/1961
(See Techtro-Matic Corp.)

SUNFLOWER USA LTD (NV)
Recapitalized 03/01/1999
Recapitalized from Sunflower Ltd. to Sunflower (USA) Ltd. 03/01/1999
Each share Common no par exchanged for (0.33333333) share Common no par

SEC revoked common stock registration 09/22/2008

SUNGAME CORP (DE)
Each share old Common $0.001 par exchanged for (0.025) share new Common $0.001 par 01/10/2011
SEC revoked common stock registration 10/11/2017

SUNGARD DATA SYS INC (DE)
Common 1¢ par split (2) for (1) by issuance of (1) additional share 07/07/1995
Common 1¢ par split (2) for (1) by issuance of (1) additional share payable 09/22/1997 to holders of record 09/02/1997 Ex date - 09/23/1997
Common 1¢ par split (2) for (1) by issuance of (1) additional share payable 06/18/2001 to holders of record 05/25/2000 Ex date - 06/19/2001
Merged into Solar Capital Corp. 08/11/2005
Each share Common 1¢ par exchanged for $36 cash

SUNGATE RES LTD (CANADA)
Merged into Barrick Resources Corp. 10/14/1983
Each share Capital Stock no par exchanged for (0.1897397) share Conv. 1st Preferred Ser. A no par and (0.3890525) share Conv. Exchangeable 2nd Preferred Ser. A no par
Barrick Resources Corp. recapitalized as American Barrick Resources Corp. 12/06/1985 which name changed to Barrick Gold Corp. 01/18/1995

SUNGLASS HUT INTL INC (DE)
Common 1¢ par split (2) for (1) by issuance of (1) additional share 11/30/1994
Common 1¢ par split (2) for (1) by issuance of (1) additional share 10/16/1995
Merged into Luxottica Group S.p.A. 04/04/2001
Each share Common 1¢ par exchanged for $11.50 cash

SUNGLOBE FIBER SYS CORP (NV)
Charter permanently revoked 11/30/2007

SUNGOLD ENTMT CORP (BC)
Name changed 05/26/1997
Name changed 03/20/2000
Stock Dividend - 5% payable 09/08/2003 to holders of record 09/01/2003 Ex date - 10/06/2003
Name changed from Sungold Gaming Inc. to Sungold Gaming International Ltd. and (2) additional shares issued 05/26/1997
Name changed from Sungold Gaming International Ltd. to Sungold Entertainment Corp. 03/20/2000
Reincorporated under the laws of Canada as Sungold International Holdings Corp. 12/12/2003

SUNGOLD INC (UT)
Proclaimed dissolved for failure to pay taxes 05/01/1990

SUNGRO MINERALS INC (NV)
Each share old Common $0.001 par exchanged for (5) shares new Common $0.001 par 08/03/2009
Recapitalized as American Mineral Group, Inc. 04/24/2013
Each share new Common $0.001 par exchanged for (0.008) share Common $0.001 par
American Mineral Group, Inc. name changed to Telco Cuba Inc. 07/21/2015

SUNGROUP INC (TN)
Common $1 par split (2) for (1) by issuance of (1) additional share 03/29/1985
Voluntarily dissolved 12/30/1999

Details not available

SUNGWON PIPE CO LTD (KOREA)
Name changed to BnB Sungwon Co., Ltd. 05/11/2011

SUNGY MOBILE LTD (CAYMAN ISLANDS)
Acquired by Sunflower Parent Ltd. 11/18/2015
Each Sponsored ADR for Class A Ordinary exchanged for $4.85 cash

SUNHAWK COM CORP (WA)
Name changed to Stardrive Solutions Inc. 08/06/2001
(See Stardrive Solutions Inc.)

SUNLAND ENTMT INC (DE)
Reorganized 08/09/2002
Reorganized from California to under the laws of Delaware 08/09/2002
Each share Common no par exchanged for (0.1) share Common $0.001 par
Name changed to Trestle Holdings, Inc. 09/17/2003
Trestle Holdings, Inc. recapitalized as MogiZone Holding Corp. 08/31/2009 which name changed to Balincan USA, Inc. 09/30/2015

SUNLAND INDS INC (AZ)
Merged into Photocomm, Inc. (AZ) 09/26/1988
Each share Common 10¢ par exchanged for (0.25) share Common 10¢ par and (1) Common Stock Purchase Warrant expiring 09/26/1989
Photocomm, Inc. (AZ) reincorporated in Delaware as Golden Genesis Co. 06/25/1998
(See Golden Genesis Co.)

SUNLAND MEDIA GROUP (NV)
Name changed to Homestead Gold & Silver Ltd. 09/09/2011

SUNLIGHT COAL CO. (IN)
Completely liquidated 04/30/1947
Each share Preferred $25 par exchanged for first and final distribution of $27.50 cash

SUNLIGHT OILS, LTD.
Acquired by Mercury Oils, Ltd. 00/00/1929
Details not available

SUNLIGHT SYS LTD (NV)
Recapitalized as NanoPierce Technologies Inc. 02/27/1998
Each share Common $0.0001 par exchanged for (1/3) share Common $0.0001 par
NanoPierce Technologies Inc. recapitalized as VYTA Corp. (NV) 01/31/2006 which reincorporated in Delaware 08/20/2010 which recapitalized as Bio Lab Naturals, Inc. 11/05/2010

SUNLITE ENERGY CORP (NJ)
Recapitalized as Developers of Energy Systems Corp. 05/15/1987
Each share Common $0.0001 par exchanged for (0.25) share Common $0.002 par
(See Developers of Energy Systems Corp.)

SUNLITE INC (DE)
Charter cancelled and declared inoperative and void for non-payment of taxes 03/01/1995

SUNLITE OIL CO (DE)
Name changed 12/31/1982
Name changed from Sunlite Oil Co. of Delaware to Sunlite Oil Co. 12/31/1982
Merged into Anret, Inc. 09/21/1983
Each share Common $1 par exchanged for (1) share Common 20¢ par
Anret, Inc. name changed to Sunlite Inc. 12/13/1983
(See Sunlite Inc.)

SUN-SUN

SUNLITE OIL LTD (AB)
Merged into Sunlite Oil Co. of Delaware 07/08/1982
Each share Common no par exchanged for (1) share Common $1 par
Sunlite Oil Co. of Delaware name changed to Sunlite Oil Co. 12/13/1982 which merged into Anret, Inc. 09/21/1983 which name changed to Sunlite Inc. 12/13/1983
(See Sunlite Inc.)

SUNLITE TECHNOLOGIES CORP (DE)
Recapitalized as Discover Capital Holdings Corp. 09/24/2001
Each (150) shares Common $0.0001 par exchanged for (1) share Common $0.0001 par
Discover Capital Holdings Corp. name changed to FSBO Media Holdings, Inc. 11/04/2005 which recapitalized as Guard Dog, Inc. 10/28/2008

SUNLOCH MINES LTD (BC)
Over 84% owned by Cominco Ltd. as of 00/00/1982
Public interest eliminated

SUNLOGIC INC (NV)
Name changed to Dawson Science Corp. (NV) 03/17/1995
Dawson Science Corp. (NV) reorganized in Delaware as Integrated Transportation Network Group Inc. 06/30/1998
(See Integrated Transportation Network Group Inc.)

SUNMADE ELEC CORP (NY)
Name changed to Van Wyck International Corp. 08/25/1970
Van Wyck International Corp. name changed to Robeson Industries Corp. (NY) 07/26/1982 which reincorporated in Delaware 10/23/1984
(See Robeson Industries Corp.)

SUNMAKERS TRAVEL GROUP INC (BC)
Name changed to Setanta Ventures Inc. 01/24/1996
(See Setanta Ventures Inc.)

SUNMARK INDS I INC (DE)
Each share old Common $0.001 par exchanged for (0.01) share new Common $0.001 par 06/21/1996
Each share new Common $0.001 par exchanged again for (0.01) share new Common $0.001 par 02/16/1998
Name changed to Mark I Industries, Inc. 05/14/1998 which name changed to Foodvision.com Inc. 06/00/1999
(See Foodvision.com Inc.)

SUNMARK INTL INDS INC (DE)
Reorganized under the laws of Washington as Royal Sunmark Energy Corp. 08/22/2005
Each share Common $0.001 par exchanged for (0.05) share Common $0.001 par
Royal Sunmark Energy Corp. name changed to Detex Security Systems, Inc. 10/19/2005 which name changed to Detection Security Systems, Inc. 05/15/2006 which recapitalized as Nexis International Industries, Inc. 08/30/2007
(See Nexis International Industries, Inc.)

SUNMIST ENERGY 84 INC (CANADA)
Recapitalized 06/04/1984
Recapitalized from Sunmist Energy Resources Ltd. to Sunmist Energy '84 Inc. 06/04/1984
Each share Common no par exchanged for (0.33333333) share Common no par
Name changed to Sunmist Energy '86 Inc. 03/05/1987
(See Sunmist Energy '86 Inc.)

SUNMIST ENERGY 86 INC (CANADA)
Struck off register and declared dissolved for failure to file returns 08/01/1992

SUNNCOMM INC (NV)
Stock Dividend - 4% payable 06/15/2001 to holders of record 06/06/2001
Reorganized as SunnComm Technologies Inc. 11/21/2002
Each share Common $0.001 par exchanged for (1) share Common $0.001 par
SunnComm Technologies Inc. name changed to SunnComm International, Inc. 05/03/2004 which name changed to Amergence Group, Inc. 06/01/2007 which name changed to Altitude Organic Corp. 05/16/2011 which name changed to Tranzbyte Corp. 02/22/2012 which name changed to American Green, Inc. 07/01/2014

SUNNCOMM INTL INC (NV)
Each share Common $0.001 par received distribution of (0.056) share Quiet Tiger, Inc. Common $0.001 par payable 10/22/2004 to holders of record 09/30/2004 Ex date - 09/28/2004
Name changed to Amergence Group, Inc. 06/01/2007
Amergence Group, Inc. name changed to Altitude Organic Corp. 05/16/2011 which name changed to Tranzbyte Corp. 02/22/2012 which name changed to American Green, Inc. 07/01/2014

SUNNCOMM TECHNOLOGIES INC (DE)
Name changed to SunnComm International, Inc. 05/03/2004
SunnComm International, name changed to Amergence Group, Inc. 06/01/2007 which name changed to Altitude Organic Corp. 05/16/2011 which name changed to Tranzbyte Corp. 02/22/2012 which name changed to American Green, Inc. 07/01/2014

SUNNINGDALE INC (DE)
Name changed to AdAl Group, Inc. 11/05/2004
(See AdAl Group, Inc.)

SUNNINGDALE OILS LTD (AB)
Acquired by Kerr-McGee Corp. 12/09/1976
Each share Common no par exchanged for $17 cash

SUNNY HILL MINES INC (UT)
Name changed to Bagley Corp. 07/31/1981
(See Bagley Corp.)

SUNNY HILLS MUTUAL WATER CO.
Liquidated 00/00/1952
Details not available

SUNNY LD TOURS INC (NV)
Recapitalized as InterAllied Restaurant Group, Inc. 11/15/1993
Each share Common 1¢ par exchanged for (0.1) share Common 1¢ par
InterAllied Restaurant Group, Inc. name changed to InterAllied Group, Inc. (NV) 02/08/1999 which reincorporated in Delaware as Pilot Therapeutics Holdings, Inc. 12/06/2001
(See Pilot Therapeutics Holdings, Inc.)

SUNNY PEAK MINING CO. (ID)
Class A 20¢ par and Class B 20¢ par reclassified as Capital Stock 20¢ par 06/20/1969
Charter revoked for failure to file reports and pay fees 11/30/1971

SUNNY VALLEY OIL CO. (CO)
Charter revoked for failure to file reports and pay fees 10/19/1964

SUNNYDALE FARMS INC (NY)
Each share Common 50¢ par exchanged for (0.05) share Common $10 par 10/10/1975
Each share Common $10 par exchanged for (0.05) share Common $200 par 10/03/1979
Each share Common $200 par exchanged for (0.1) share Common $2,000 par 02/06/1980
Note: In effect holders received $800 cash per share and public interest was eliminated

SUNNYSIDE ACRES MOBILE ESTATES (NV)
Common $0.001 par split (9) for (1) by issuance of (8) additional shares payable 10/11/2007 to holders of record 10/10/2007 Ex date - 10/12/2007
Name changed to Sino-Bon Entertainment, Inc. 07/19/2010
(See Sino-Bon Entertainment, Inc.)

SUNNYSIDE DEV CORP (UT)
Merged into National Energy Corp. (NV) 02/09/1972
Each share Common $1 par exchanged for (3) shares Common $1 par
(See National Energy Corp. (NV))

SUNNYSIDE TEL CO (OR)
Acquired by Continental Telephone Corp. 10/15/1969
Each share Common $1 par exchanged for (0.307692) share Common $1 par
Continental Telephone Corp. name changed to Continental Telecom Inc. 05/06/1982 which name changed to Contel Corp. 05/01/1986 which merged into GTE Corp. 03/14/1991 which merged into Verizon Communications Inc. 06/30/2000

SUNOCO INC (PA)
Common $1 par split (2) for (1) by issuance of (1) additional share payable 08/01/2005 to holders of record 07/18/2005 Ex date - 08/02/2005
Each share Common $1 par received distribution of (0.53046456) share SunCoke Energy, Inc. Common 1¢ par payable 01/17/2012 to holders of record 01/05/2012 Ex date - 01/18/2012
Merged into Energy Transfer Partners, L.P. (Old) 10/05/2012
Each share Common $1 par exchanged for (0.5245) Common Unit and $25 cash
Energy Transfer Partners, L.P. (Old) merged into Energy Transfer Partners, L.P. (New) 05/01/2017 which merged into Energy Transfer L.P. 10/19/2018

SUNOCO LOGISTICS PARTNERS L P (DE)
Common Units split (3) for (1) by issuance of (2) additional Units payable 12/02/2011 to holders of record 11/18/2011 Ex date - 12/05/2011
Common Units split (2) for (1) by issuance of (1) additional Unit payable 06/12/2014 to holders of record 06/05/2014 Ex date - 06/13/2014
Under plan of merger name changed to Energy Transfer Partners, L.P. (New) 05/01/2017 Energy Transfer Partners, L.P. (New) merged into Energy Transfer L.P. 10/19/2018

SUNORCA DEV CORP (BC)
Name changed to Wildflower Marijuana Inc. 06/16/2014
Wildflower Marijuana Inc. name changed to Wildflower Brands Inc. 05/03/2018

SUNOVIA ENERGY TECHNOLOGIES INC (NV)
Name changed to Evolucia Inc. 08/16/2012
(See Evolucia Inc.)

SUNPEAKS VENTURES INC (NV)
Each share old Common $0.001 par exchanged for (45) shares new Common $0.001 par 12/07/2011
Name changed to Pharmagen, Inc. 01/15/2013

SUNPHARM CORP (DE)
Merged into GelTex Pharmaceuticals Inc. 11/17/1999
Each share Common $0.0001 par exchanged for (0.14525) share Common 1¢ par
(See GelTex Pharmaceuticals Inc.)

SUNPOINT SECS INC (TX)
Common no par split (2) for (1) by issuance of (1) additional share payable 10/02/1997 to holders of record 09/29/1997
Assets taken over by the Securities Investor Protection Corp. 11/19/1999
Stockholders' equity unlikely

SUNPORT MED CORP (WY)
Name changed 06/29/1992
Reincorporated 02/25/1998
Name changed from Sunport Metals Corp. to Sunport Medical Corp. 06/29/1992
Place of incorporation changed from (BC) to (WY) 02/25/1998
Reorganized under the laws of Nevada as Argent Capital Corp. 02/27/1998
Each share Common no par exchanged for (0.03333333) share Common $0.001 par
Argent Capital Corp. name changed to Sequoia Interests Corp. 12/08/2003 which name changed to Baby Bee Bright Corp. (New) 05/02/2006 which name changed to Fusion Pharm, Inc. 04/08/2011

SUNQUEST INFORMATION SYS INC (PA)
Merged into Misys PLC 08/01/2001
Each share Common no par exchanged for $24 cash

SUNRAY DX OIL CO (DE)
4.5% Preferred Ser. A $25 par called for redemption 06/08/1962
Merged into Sun Oil Co. (NJ) 10/25/1968
Each share Common $1 par exchanged for (1) share $2.25 Conv. Preferred no par to 03/20/1972 after which holders received $50.48 cash only
Sun Oil Co. (NJ) reincorporated in Pennsylvania 09/30/1971 which name changed to Sun Co., Inc. 04/27/1976
(See Sun Co., Inc.)

SUNRAY INDS INC (NY)
Charter cancelled and proclaimed dissolved for failure to pay taxes 06/24/1981

SUNRAY MID-CONTINENT OIL CO. (DE)
Name changed to Sunray DX Oil Co. 04/27/1962
5.5% Conv. 2nd Preferred $30 par called for redemption 05/08/1962
Sunray DX Oil Co. merged into Sun Oil Co. (NJ) 10/25/1968 which reincorporated in Pennsylvania 09/30/1971 which name changed to Sun Co., Inc. 04/27/1976
(See Sun Co., Inc.)

SUNRAY MINES LTD. (BC)
Liquidated 00/00/1979
Details not available

SUNRAY OIL CORP. (DE)
Common $5 par changed to $1 par 00/00/1934
Each share 6% Preferred $100 par

exchanged for (2) shares 5.5%
Preferred $50 par 00/00/1936
Each share 4.25% Preferred Ser. A
$100 par exchanged for (4) shares
4.25% Preferred Ser. A $25 par
00/00/1948
Under plan of merger name changed
to Sunray Mid-Continent Oil Co.
05/16/1955
Sunray Mid-Continent Oil Co. name
changed to Sunray DX Oil Co.
04/27/1962 which merged into Sun
Oil Co. (NJ) 10/25/1968 which
reincorporated in Pennsylvania
09/30/1971 which name changed to
Sun Co., Inc. 04/27/1976
(See Sun Co., Inc.)

SUNRAY RES INC (AB)
Acquired by Pipestone Petroleums
Inc. 01/31/1990
Each share Common no par
exchanged for (1) share Common
no par
Pipestone Petroleums Inc. merged
into Blue Range Resource Corp.
07/11/1995 which merged into Big
Bear Exploration Ltd. 02/12/1999
which merged into Avid Oil & Gas
Ltd. 02/02/2000
(See Avid Oil & Gas Ltd.)

SUNRESORTS LTD N V (NETHERLANDS ANTILLES)
Petition under Section 304 of the U.S.
Bankruptcy Code dismissed
09/13/2006
Stockholders' equity unlikely

SUNRIDGE ENERGY CORP (BC)
Recapitalized as Golden Coast
Energy Corp. 07/30/2013
Each share Common no par
exchanged for (0.25) share Common
no par
(See Golden Coast Energy Corp.)

SUNRIDGE GOLD CORP (BC)
Liquidation completed
Each share Common no par received
initial distribution of $0.36 cash
payable 05/26/2016 to holders of
record 05/18/2016
Each share Common no par received
second and final distribution of
$0.03 cash payable 12/08/2016 to
holders of record 12/05/2016
Ex date - 12/09/2016

SUNRIDGE INVTS CORP (BC)
Name changed to Sunridge Energy
Corp. 03/16/2011
Sunridge Energy Corp. recapitalized
as Golden Coast Energy Corp.
07/30/2013
(See Golden Coast Energy Corp.)

SUNRISE ASSISTED LIVING INC (DE)
Name changed to Sunrise Senior
Living, Inc. 05/30/2003
(See Sunrise Senior Living, Inc.)

SUNRISE BANCORP (CA)
Merged into First Banks America, Inc.
10/31/1996
Each share Common no par
exchanged for $4 cash

SUNRISE BANCORP INC (DE)
Certificates dated prior to 09/04/1992
Merged into PNC Financial Corp.
09/04/1992
Each share Common 10¢ par
exchanged for (0.557) share
Common $5 par
PNC Financial Corp. name changed
to PNC Bank Corp. 02/08/1993
which name changed to PNC
Financial Services Group, Inc.
03/15/2000

SUNRISE BANCORP INC (DE)
Certificates dated after 04/05/1993
Merged into Reliance Bancorp Inc.
01/11/1996
Each share Common 10¢ par
exchanged for $32 cash

SUNRISE CONSOLIDATED OIL CO. (CA)
Charter suspended for failure to file
reports and pay fees 02/28/1925

SUNRISE EDL SVCS INC (DE)
Each share 9% Preferred Ser. C 1¢
par received distribution of (0.23)
share Common 1¢ par payable
09/30/1997 to holders of record
09/01/1997
Merged into TesseracT Group, Inc.
01/21/1998
Each share 9% Preferred Ser. C
exchanged for (3.069) shares
Common 1¢ par
Each share Common 1¢ par
exchanged for (0.393) share
Common 1¢ par
(See TesseracT Group, Inc.)

SUNRISE ENERGY RESOURCES INC (DE)
Recapitalized as Green Technology
Solutions, Inc. (DE) 11/19/2010
Each share Common $0.001 par
exchanged for (0.005) share
Common $0.001 par
Green Technology Solutions, Inc.
(DE) reorganized in Nevada
09/02/2014

SUNRISE ENERGY SVCS INC (DE)
Under plan of reorganization each
share old Common $1 par
automatically became (0.1) share
new Common $1 par 09/17/1997
Name changed to Sunrise Energy
Resources, Inc. and Common $1
par changed to $0.001 par
10/01/2004
Sunrise Energy Resources, Inc.
recapitalized as Green Technology
Solutions, Inc. (DE) 11/19/2010
which reorganized in Nevada
09/02/2014

SUNRISE EXPRESS INC (NV)
Name changed to World Commerce
Online, Inc. (NV) 09/29/1998
World Commerce Online, Inc. (NV)
reincorporated in Delaware
10/15/1999
(See World Commerce Online, Inc.)

SUNRISE FED SVGS & LN ASSN NEWPORT KY (USA)
Under plan of reorganization each
share Common $1 par automatically
became (1) share Sunrise Bancorp,
Inc. Common 10¢ par 04/26/1989
Sunrise Bancorp, Inc. merged into
PNC Financial Corp. 09/04/1992
which name changed to PNC Bank
Corp. 02/08/1993 which name
changed to PNC Financial Services
Group, Inc. 03/15/2000

SUNRISE FUND INC. (NY)
Name changed to Trinity Place Fund,
Inc. 06/26/1968
(See Trinity Place Fund, Inc.)

SUNRISE GLOBAL INC (NV)
Name changed to Greenkraft, Inc.
12/27/2013

SUNRISE HLDGS LTD (NV)
Name changed to Event Cardio
Group Inc. 11/07/2014

SUNRISE INTL INC (AB)
Delisted from Toronto Venture Stock
Exchange 03/11/2008

SUNRISE INTL LEASING CORP (DE)
Name changed 02/13/1995
Reincorporated 10/17/1997
Name changed from Sunrise Leasing
Corp. to Sunrise Resources, Inc.
02/13/1995
Name changed from Sunrise
Resources, Inc. to Sunrise
International Leasing Corp. and
state of incorporation changed from
(MN) to (DE) 10/17/1997
Merged into King Management Corp.
06/28/2000
Each share Common 1¢ par
exchanged for $5.25 cash

SUNRISE INVT HLDG CDA CORP (AB)
Recapitalized as Amerpro Industries
Inc. (AB) 07/24/1995
Each share Class A no par
exchanged for (0.2) share Class A
Common no par
Amerpro Industries Inc. (AB)
reorganized in British Columbia as
Amerpro Resources Inc. 03/06/2009
which name changed to Electric
Metals Inc. 10/14/2009 which
merged into Moimstone Corp.
09/12/2013 which name changed to
Apivio Systems Inc. 05/23/2014
(See Apivio Systems Inc.)

SUNRISE MED INC (DE)
Common $1 par split (2) for (1) by
issuance of (1) additional share
09/09/1992
Merged into V.S.M. Acquisition Corp.
12/13/2000
Each share Common $1 par
exchanged for $10 cash

SUNRISE METALS CORP (BC)
Recapitalized as Pacific Sun
Resource Corp. 01/24/1990
Each share Common no par
exchanged for (0.25) share Common
no par
Pacific Sun Resource Corp. name
changed to Masterpiece Quality
Products, Inc. 08/16/1993 which
recapitalized as Aruma Ventures,
Inc. 03/21/1997 which recapitalized
as Dot.Com Technologies Inc.
09/07/1999 which recapitalized as
BCS Collaborative Solutions Inc.
07/12/2002 which recapitalized as
BCS Global Networks Inc.
09/02/2003
(See BCS Global Networks Inc.)

SUNRISE MINERALS INC (BC)
Recapitalized as Cronus Resources
Ltd. (BC) 03/10/2008
Each share Common no par
exchanged for (0.25) share Common
no par
Cronus Resources Ltd. (BC)
reincorporated in Ontario
06/25/2009 which merged into
Continental Gold Ltd. (New)
(Bermuda) 03/30/2010 which
reorganized in Ontario as
Continental Gold Inc. 06/12/2015

SUNRISE MNG CORP (NV)
Name changed to Sunrise Holdings
Ltd. 03/27/2008
Sunrise Holdings Ltd. name changed
to Event Cardio Group Inc.
11/07/2014

SUNRISE PETE RES INC (WA)
Each share old Common $0.001 par
exchanged for (2) shares new
Common $0.001 par 11/01/2006
SEC revoked common stock
registration 11/02/2006

SUNRISE PRESCHOOLS INC (DE)
Name changed to Sunrise
Educational Services, Inc.
01/31/1997
Sunrise Educational Services, Inc.
merged into TesseracT Group, Inc.
01/21/1998
(See TesseracT Group, Inc.)

SUNRISE PRODS CORP (CA)
Recapitalized as Gila Mines Corp.
07/12/1982
Each share Common no par
exchanged for (0.2) share Common
no par
(See Gila Mines Corp.)

SUNRISE REAL ESTATE DEV GROUP INC (TX)
Name changed to Sunrise Real
Estate Group, Inc. 05/23/2006

SUNRISE SVGS & LN ASSN FLA (FL)
Class A Common 1¢ par split (6) for
(5) by issuance of (0.2) additional
share 08/31/1981
Class B Common $3.75 par split (6)
for (5) by issuance of (0.2)
additional share 08/31/1981
Class A Common 1¢ par split (6) for
(5) by issuance of (0.2) additional
share 08/31/1982
Class B Common $3.75 par split (6)
for (5) by issuance of (0.2)
additional share 08/31/1982
Class A Common 1¢ par split (5) for
(4) by issuance of (0.25) additional
share 09/30/1983
Class B Common $3.75 par split (5)
for (4) by issuance of (0.2)
additional share 09/30/1983
Class A Common 1¢ par split (6) for
(5) by issuance of (0.2) additional
share 12/12/1984
Class B Common $3.75 par split (6)
for (5) by issuance of (0.2)
additional share 12/12/1984
Declared insolvent by the Federal
Home Loan Bank Board 07/18/1985
No stockholders' equity

SUNRISE SILVER MINES LTD. (BC)
Recapitalized as Sunrise Metals
Corp. 01/17/1977
Each share Common 50¢ par
exchanged for (0.25) share Common
no par
Sunrise Metals Corp. recapitalized as
Pacific Sun Resource Corp.
01/24/1990 which name changed to
Masterpiece Quality Products, Inc.
08/16/1993 which recapitalized as
Aruma Ventures, Inc. 03/21/1997
which recapitalized as Dot.Com
Technologies Inc. 09/07/1999 which
recapitalized as BCS Collaborative
Solutions Inc. 07/12/2002 which
recapitalized as BCS Global
Networks Inc. 09/02/2003
(See BCS Global Networks Inc.)

SUNRISE SOLAR CORP (NV)
SEC revoked common stock
registration 06/20/2013

SUNRISE SR LIVING REAL ESTATE INVT TR (ON)
Acquired by Ventas, Inc. 04/27/2007
Each Unit no par received $16.50
cash

SUNRISE TECHNOLOGIES INTL INC (DE)
Reincorporated 07/31/1993
Reincorporated from Sunrise
Technologies, Inc. (CA) to Sunrise
Technologies International Inc. (DE)
07/31/1993
Filed plan of liquidation under
Chapter 7 Federal Bankruptcy Code
09/23/2002
Stockholders' equity unlikely

SUNRISE TELECOM INC (DE)
Reincorporated 07/10/2000
State of incorporation changed from
(CA) to (DE) 07/10/2000
Name changed to SRTI BlockChain
Generation, Inc. 02/13/2018

SUNRISE TOURS INC (NV)
Name changed to Luboa Group, Inc.
02/12/2016

SUNRIVER CORP (DE)
Name changed to Boundless Corp.
05/27/1997
(See Boundless Corp.)

SUNS GROUP LTD (HONG KONG)
Each Sponsored ADR for Ordinary
exchanged for (0.001) Sponsored
ADR for Ordinary 02/16/2007
Name changed to Loudong General
Nice Resources (China) Holdings
Ltd. 07/15/2009
*(See Loudong General Nice
Resources (China) Holdings Ltd.)*

SUNSAV INC (MA)
Reincorporated under the laws of
Nevada as Highline Industries, Inc.
07/10/1986
(See Highline Industries, Inc.)

SUNSET BRANDS INC (NV)
Each share old Common $0.001 par exchanged for (0.5) share new Common $0.001 par 02/07/2005
Each share new Common $0.001 par exchanged for (0.002) share Common $0.0001 par 01/26/2012
Name changed to Sunset Capital Assets, Inc. 02/02/2015

SUNSET COLOR LABS INC (NY)
Proclaimed dissolved for failure to file reports and pay fees 12/15/1967

SUNSET COVE MNG INC (BC)
Each share old Common no par exchanged for (0.1) share new Common no par 09/02/2014
Each share new Common no par exchanged again for (0.1) share new Common no par 08/26/2016
Name changed to Manganese X Energy Corp. 12/02/2016

SUNSET DEV CO (NV)
Charter revoked for failure to file reports and pay fees 03/06/1972

SUNSET FINL RES INC (MD)
Name changed to Alesco Financial Inc. 10/09/2006
Alesco Financial Inc. recapitalized as Cohen & Co. Inc. (Old) 12/16/2009 which name changed to Institutional Financial Markets, Inc. 01/24/2011 which reorganized as Cohen & Co. Inc. (New) 09/05/2017

SUNSET HOUSE (CA)
Stock Dividend - 20% 09/15/1966
Acquired by Broadway-Hale Stores, Inc. (DE) 01/15/1969
Each share Common $1 par exchanged for (0.5) share $2 Conv. Preferred Ser. A $5 par
Broadway-Hale Stores, Inc. (DE) merged into Broadway-Hale Stores, Inc. (CA) 08/27/1970 which name changed to Carter Hawley Hale Stores Inc. (CA) 05/30/1974 which reincorporated in Delaware 07/26/1984 which name changed to Broadway Stores, Inc. 06/17/1994 which merged into Federated Department Stores, Inc. 10/11/1995 which name changed to Macy's, Inc. 06/01/2007

SUNSET HOUSE DISTRIBUTING CORP. (CA)
Name changed to Sunset House 06/09/1966
Sunset House acquired by Broadway-Hale Stores, Inc. (DE) 01/15/1969 which merged into Broadway-Hale Stores, Inc. (CA) 08/27/1970 which name changed to Carter Hawley Hale Stores Inc. (CA) 05/30/1974 which reincorporated in Delaware 07/26/1984 which name changed to Broadway Stores, Inc. 06/17/1994 which merged into Federated Department Stores, Inc. 10/11/1995 which name changed to Macy's, Inc. 06/01/2007

SUNSET INDS INC (CA)
Common no par split (3) for (2) by issuance of (0.5) additional share 09/30/1968
Common no par changed to $1 par 06/27/1969
Common $1 par split (3) for (2) by issuance of (0.5) additional share 05/22/1972
Merged into New Sunset Inc. 11/01/1982
Each share Common $1 par exchanged for $5 cash

SUNSET INTL PETE CORP (DE)
Merged into Sunasco Inc. 04/30/1966
Each share Common $1 par exchanged for (0.050984) share $1.65 Conv. Preferred 10¢ par and (0.260279) share Common 10¢ par
Sunasco Inc. name changed to Scientific Resources Corp. 10/11/1968

(See Scientific Resources Corp.)

SUNSET MINERALS, INC. (WA)
Incorporated 08/27/1943
Completely liquidated 07/10/1954
Each share Capital Stock 5¢ par received first and final distribution of (1) share Sunset Mines, Inc. Capital Stock 10¢ par
(See Sunset Mines, Inc.)

SUNSET MINES, INC. (ID)
Merged into Spokane National Mines, Inc. on a (0.2) for (1) basis 02/15/1964

SUNSET MINING CORP. LTD. (BC)
Struck off register and declared dissolved for failure to file returns 01/27/1975

SUNSET OIL CO. (CA)
Common no par changed to $1 par 00/00/1949
Merged into Sunset International Petroleum Corp. 09/01/1956
Each share Common exchanged for (3) shares Common $1 par
Sunset International Petroleum Corp. merged into Sunasco Inc. 04/30/1966 which name changed to Scientific Resources Corp. 10/11/1968
(See Scientific Resources Corp.)

SUNSET OILS LTD. (AB)
Capital Stock 25¢ par changed to $0.235 par by distribution of $0.015 per share 00/00/1947
Merged into Alberta Pacific Consolidated Oils Ltd. 05/31/1955
Each share Capital Stock $0.235 par exchanged for (1) share Capital Stock no par
Alberta Pacific Consolidated Oils Ltd. merged into Canadian Industrial Gas & Oil Ltd. 03/08/1965 which merged into Norcen Energy Resources Ltd. (AB) 10/28/1975 which reincorporated in Canada 04/15/1977
(See Norcen Energy Resources Ltd.)

SUNSET PACIFIC OIL CO. (DE)
Reorganized as Sunset Oil Co. 00/00/1930
Details not available

SUNSET SUITS HLDGS INC (NV)
Name changed to Honsen Energy & Resources International Ltd. 07/06/2016

SUNSET SYSTEM (TX)
Incorporated 10/15/1915
Charter forfeited for failure to pay taxes 03/07/1930

SUNSET SYSTEM (TX)
Incorporated 04/11/1939
Charter forfeited for failure to pay taxes 05/19/1950

SUNSET YELLOWKNIFE MINES LTD (ON)
Charter cancelled for failure to file reports and pay fees 01/28/1972

SUNSHINE BANCORP INC (MD)
Merged into CenterState Bank Corp. 01/01/2018
Each share Common 1¢ par exchanged for (0.89) share Common 1¢ par

SUNSHINE BISCUITS, INC. (NY)
Capital Stock $12.50 par changed to $6.25 par and (1) additional share issued 04/30/1963
Merged into American Tobacco Co. 05/31/1966
Each share Capital Stock $6.25 par exchanged for (1.4) shares Common $6.25 par
American Tobacco Co. name changed to American Brands, Inc. (NJ) 07/01/1969 which reincorporated in Delaware 01/01/1986 which name changed to Fortune Brands, Inc. 05/30/1997 which name changed to Beam Inc. 10/04/2011

(See Beam Inc.)

SUNSHINE CAP CORP (AB)
Recapitalized as Open Source Health Inc. 02/10/2014
Each share Common no par exchanged for (0.16666666) share Common no par
Open Source Health Inc. recapitalized as Weekend Unlimited Inc. 10/15/2018

SUNSHINE CAP INC (UT)
Reincorporated under the laws of Nevada and Common no par changed to 1¢ par 01/04/1989

SUNSHINE CAP I INC (FL)
Name changed to Rubber Technology International Inc. (FL) 02/28/1997
Rubber Technology International Inc. (FL) reincorporated in Nevada 05/31/2001
(See Rubber Technology International Inc.)

SUNSHINE COLUMBIA RES LTD (BC)
Recapitalized as K-2 Resources Inc. 02/23/1987
Each share Common no par exchanged for (0.5) share Common no par
K-2 Resources Inc. name changed to Jazz Resources Inc. 05/29/1996

SUNSHINE COMSTOCK MINES LTD. (BC)
Name changed to Sunshine Columbia Resources Ltd. 12/10/1974
Sunshine Columbia Resources Ltd. recapitalized as K-2 Resources Inc. 02/23/1987 which name changed to Jazz Resources Inc. 05/29/1996

SUNSHINE CONS INC (ID)
Merged into Sunshine Mining Co. 12/30/1981
Each share Common 25¢ par exchanged for (0.55) share Capital Stock 50¢ par
Sunshine Mining Co. name changed to Sunshine Mining & Refining Co. 06/20/1994
(See Sunshine Mining & Refining Co.)

SUNSHINE CORP (CO)
Common 10¢ par changed to 1¢ par 03/10/1970
Declared defunct and inoperative for failure to file reports and pay taxes 10/16/1971

SUNSHINE FIFTY INC (MI)
Each share old Common $1 par exchanged for (0.2) share new Common $1 par 08/11/1972
Stock Dividends - 10% 02/18/1983; 10% 02/17/1984; 20% 02/15/1985; 10% 02/14/1986
Each share new Common $1 par held by holders of (200) or fewer shares exchanged for $3.50 cash 06/30/1993
Public interest eliminated

SUNSHINE FINL INC (MD)
Acquired by The First Bancshares, Inc. 04/02/2018
Each share Common 1¢ par exchanged for $27 cash

SUNSHINE HEART INC (DE)
Each share old Common $0.0001 par exchanged for (0.03333333) share new Common $0.0001 par 01/13/2017
Name changed to CHF Solutions, Inc. 05/24/2017

SUNSHINE JR STORES INC (FL)
Stock Dividends - 15% 05/15/1974; 10% 03/31/1976; 25% 04/02/1980
Merged into E-Z Serve Corp. 07/21/1995
Each share Common 10¢ par exchanged for $12 cash

SUNSHINE LARDEAU MINES LTD. (BC)
Name changed to Sunshine Comstock Mines Ltd. 10/08/1965

Sunshine Comstock Mines Ltd. name changed to Sunshine Columbia Resources Ltd. 12/10/1974 which recapitalized as K-2 Resources Inc. 02/23/1987 which name changed to Jazz Resources Inc. 05/29/1996

SUNSHINE MNG & REFNG CO (DE)
Reincorporated 03/12/1980
Name changed 06/20/1994
Capital Stock 10¢ par split (5) for (4) by issuance of (0.25) additional share 12/28/1967
Capital Stock 10¢ par changed to 5¢ par and (1) additional share issued 08/09/1968
State of incorporation changed from (WA) to (DE) 03/12/1980
Common 5¢ par changed to 50¢ par and (1.5) additional shares issued 03/19/1980
Common 50¢ par changed to 1¢ par 00/00/1993
Name changed from Sunshine Mining Co. to Sunshine Mining & Refining Co. 06/20/1994
Each share $11.94 Preferred $1 par exchanged for approximately (6) shares old Common 1¢ par and (2) Common Stock Purchase Warrants expiring 05/22/2001 on 05/22/1996
Each share old Common 1¢ par exchanged for (0.125) share new Common 08/06/1999
Plan of reorganization under Chapter 11 Federal Bankruptcy proceedings effective 02/05/2001
Each share new Common 1¢ par received (0.352) share new Common 1¢ par payable 02/28/2001 to holders of record 02/23/2001
Ex date - 03/01/2001
Note: Holdings of (99) shares or fewer pre-reorganization shares were cancelled and are without value
SEC revoked common stock registration 07/16/2008

SUNSHINE OIL, INC. (WA)
Charter dissolved for non-payment of fees 07/01/1956

SUNSHINE OIL CO. (OK)
Charter forfeited for failure to file reports 00/00/1938

SUNSHINE OIL CO. (TX)
Charter expired by time limitations 12/27/1930

SUNSHINE PARK RACING ASSN INC (FL)
$4.80 Preferred 25¢ par called for redemption 03/15/1960
Each share Common 10¢ par exchanged for (2) shares Common 5¢ par 07/01/1955
Name changed to Florida Downs, Inc. 12/28/1965
(See Florida Downs, Inc.)

SUNSHINE PCS CORP (DE)
Under plan of partial liquidation each share Class A Common $0.0001 par received received distribution of $0.83 cash payable 03/19/2004 to holders of record 03/12/2004
Ex date - 03/22/2004
Each share old Class A Common $0.0001 par exchanged for (0.001) share new Class A Common $0.0001 par 01/27/2010
Note: Holders of (999) or fewer pre-split shares will receive $0.05 cash per share
Name changed to ICTC Group, Inc. 10/26/2011
(See ICTC Group, Inc.)

SUNSHINE PWR CORP (FL)
Common 1¢ par split (2) for (1) by issuance of (1) additional share 06/15/1983
Name changed to Mayfair Financial Corp. 12/19/1986
(See Mayfair Financial Corp.)

SUNSHINE RES INTL INC (FL)
Involuntarily dissolved for failure to maintain a registered agent 12/30/1988

SUNSHINE TRADING CORP (FL)
Name changed to Sunshine Power Corp. 12/06/1982
Sunshine Power Corp. name changed to Mayfair Financial Corp. 12/19/1986
(See Mayfair Financial Corp.)

SUNSHINE VENTURES INC (NV)
Name changed to Christine's Precious Petals Inc. 07/14/2003
Christine's Precious Petals Inc. name changed to Global Business Markets, Inc. 09/05/2003 which name changed to GREM USA 03/03/2005

SUNSI ENERGIES INC (NV)
Each share old Common $0.001 par exchanged for (0.5) share new Common $0.001 par 10/09/2012
Name changed to ForceField Energy Inc. 02/28/2013

SUNSOURCE CAP TR (DE)
Name changed to Hillman Group Capital Trust 03/19/2002

SUNSOURCE INC (DE)
Merged into Allied Capital Corp. (New) 09/26/2001
Each share Common 1¢ par exchanged for $10.375 cash

SUNSOURCE L P (DE)
Merged into SunSource Inc. 09/30/1997
Each Depositary Receipt Class A exchanged for (0.38) share SunSource Capital Trust, 11.6% Preferred Security and $1.30 cash
Each Depositary Receipt Class B exchanged for (0.25) share Common no par
(See each company's listing)

SUNSTAR FOODS INC (MN)
Name changed to SUNF, Inc. 12/19/1989
(See SUNF, Inc.)

SUNSTAR HEALTHCARE INC (DE)
Company's sole asset liquidated by Florida Department of Insurance 02/02/2000
Stockholders' equity unlikely

SUNSTAR RES LTD (AB)
Recapitalized as Stade Exploration Inc. 07/17/1991
Each share Class A no par exchanged for (0.25) share Class A no par
Stade Exploration Inc. name changed to Tessex Energy Inc. 07/14/1997 which merged into Encounter Energy Inc. 06/10/1998 which merged into Impact Energy Inc. (Canada) 10/21/2002 which merged into Thunder Energy Inc. 04/30/2004
(See Thunder Energy Inc.)

SUNSTATE INTL LTD (ON)
Recapitalized as Hyberlab Teknologies Corp. 11/12/1997
Each share Common no par exchanged for (0.1) share Common no par
(See Hyberlab Teknologies Corp.)

SUNSTATE RES LTD (BC)
Recapitalized as International Sunstate Ventures Ltd. 12/06/1999
Each share Common no par exchanged for (0.16666666) share Common no par
International Sunstate Ventures Ltd. recapitalized as Thelon Ventures Ltd. 05/23/2002 which recapitalized as Thelon Capital Ltd. 02/04/2010 which name changed to THC BioMed Intl Ltd. 04/29/2015 which name changed to Global Li-Ion Graphite Corp. 07/14/2017

SUNSTATES CORP (FL)
$3.75 Preferred $100 par changed to $25 par and (3) additional shares issued 08/01/1985
Each share $15 Preferred $100 par reclassified as (4) shares $3.75 Preferred $25 par 08/01/1985
Common 10¢ par split (2) for (1) by issuance of (1) additional share 02/05/1988
Merged into Acton Corp. 05/04/1988
Each share Preferred Class A Ser. I 10¢ par exchanged for (1) share Preferred Class E Ser. I 10¢ par
Each share Preferred Class A Ser. II 10¢ par exchanged for (1) share Preferred Class E Ser. II 10¢ par
Each share $3.75 Preferred $25 par exchanged for (1) share $3.75 Preferred $25 par
Each share Conv. Accumulating Class B 10¢ par exchanged for (1) share Conv. Accumulating Class B 10¢ par
Each share Common 10¢ par exchanged for (0.8125) share Common 33-1/3¢ par
Acton Corp. name changed to Sunstates Corp. (New) 01/03/1994
(See Sunstates Corp. (New))

SUNSTATES CORP NEW (DE)
Charter cancelled and declared inoperative and void for non-payment of taxes 03/01/2003

SUNSTATES CORP OLD (DE)
Merged into Sunstates Corp. (FL) 01/30/1985
Each share Common $1 par exchanged for (0.075) share $15 Preferred $100 par
Sunstates Corp. (FL) merged into Acton Corp. 05/04/1988 which name changed to Sunstates Corp. (New) 01/03/1994
(See Sunstates Corp. (New))

SUNSTONE HOTEL INVS INC NEW (MD)
8% Preferred Ser. A 1¢ par called for redemption at $25 plus $0.33 accrued dividends on 03/01/2013
8% Preferred Ser. D 1¢ par called for redemption at $25 plus $0.027778 accrued dividends on 04/06/2016
(Additional Information in Active)

SUNSTONE HOTEL INVS INC OLD (MD)
Merged into SHP Acquisition 11/22/1999
Each share Common 1¢ par exchanged for $10.3761 cash

SUNSTYLE CORP (FL)
Completely liquidated 03/28/2003
No stockholders' equity

SUNTAC MINERALS CORP (BC)
Merged into Canarc Resource Corp. 06/01/1993
Each share Common no par exchanged for (0.2857142) share Common no par

SUNTEC CAP INC (AB)
Name changed to Suntec Pure Water Technologies Inc. (AB) 07/26/2004
Suntec Pure Water Technologies Inc. (AB) reorganized in British Columbia as Mira Resources Corp. 04/10/2008 which recapitalized as Serrano Resources Ltd. 06/08/2015

SUNTEC PURE WTR TECHNOLOGIES INC (AB)
Reorganized under the laws of British Columbia as Mira Resources Corp. 04/10/2008
Each share Common no par exchanged for (0.35714285) share Common no par
Mira Resources Corp. recapitalized as Serrano Resources Ltd. 06/08/2015

SUNTEC SYS INC (MN)
Involuntarily dissolved 10/10/1991

SUNTEC VENTURES LTD NEW (BC)
Merged 01/30/1986
Suntec Ventures Ltd. (Old) merged into Suntec Ventures Ltd. (New) 01/30/1986
Each share Common no par exchanged for (1) share Common no par
Recapitalized as Consolidated Suntec Ventures Ltd. 05/19/1987
Each share Common no par exchanged for (0.25) share Common no par
Consolidated Suntec Ventures Ltd. name changed to Vortex Energy Systems Inc. 10/03/1990 which recapitalized as Autumn Industries Inc. 09/16/1994 which name changed to Altek Power Corp. 03/07/2001

SUNTECH PWR HLDGS CO LTD (CAYMAN ISLANDS)
ADR agreement terminated 09/14/2015
ADR holders' equity unlikely

SUNTERRA CORP (MD)
Plan of reorganization under Chapter 11 Federal Bankruptcy Code effective 07/29/2002
No old Common stockholders' equity
Merged into Diamond Resorts, LLC 04/27/2007
Each share new Common 1¢ par exchanged for $16 cash

SUNTIDE REFINING CO. (DE)
Merged into Sunray Mid-Continent Oil 10/30/1959
Each share Common 1¢ par exchanged for (0.33333333) share Common $1 par
Sunray Mid-Continent Oil Co. name changed to Sunray DX Oil Co. 04/27/1962 which merged into Sun Oil Co. (NJ) 10/25/1968 which reincorporated in Pennsylvania 09/30/1971 which name changed to Sun Co., Inc. 04/27/1976
(See Sun Co., Inc.)

SUNTREE INVTS INTL CORP (AB)
Struck off register and declared dissolved for failure to file annual returns 01/01/1996

SUNTRON CORP (DE)
Merged into Sunn Acquisition Corp. 12/12/2007
Each share Common 1¢ par exchanged for $1.15 cash

SUNTRUST BANK, MIAMI, N.A. (MIAMI, FL)
Acquired by SunTrust Banks, Inc. 01/01/2000
Details not available

SUNTRUST BANK, TALLAHASSEE, N.A. (TALLAHASSEE, FL)
Acquired by SunTrust Bank, Northwest Florida (Tallahassee, FL) 07/07/1999
Details not available

SUNTRUST BKS INC (GA)
5.875% Depositary Preferred Ser. E called for redemption at $25 on 03/15/2018
(Additional Information in Active)

SUNTRUST CAP IV (DE)
7.125% Trust Preferred Securities called for redemption at $25 on 11/13/2006

SUNTRUST CAP V (DE)
7.05% Trust Preferred Securities called for redemption at $25 on 12/08/2006

SUNTRUST CAP IX (DE)
7.875% Trust Preferred Securities called for redemption at $25 on 07/11/2012

SUNVENTURES RES INC (AB)
Name changed 12/02/1993
Name changed from Sunventures Corp. to Sunventures Resources Inc. 12/02/1993
Recapitalized as Commonwealth Energy Inc. 01/13/1995
Each share Common no par exchanged for (0.2) share Common no par
Commonwealth Energy Inc. name changed to Scimitar Hydrocarbons Corp. 02/08/1996 which was acquired by Rally Energy Corp. 07/10/2002
(See Rally Energy Corp.)

SUNVEST RESORTS INC (DE)
Reorganized under the laws of Florida 08/06/1996
Each share Common $0.0001 par exchanged for (0.005) share Common $0.0001 par
Sunvest Resorts, Inc. (FL) name changed to US Data Authority, Inc. 06/23/2000
(See US Data Authority, Inc.)

SUNVEST RESORTS INC (FL)
Each share old Common $0.0001 par exchanged for (0.27777777) share new Common $0.0001 par 04/28/2000
Name changed to US Data Authority, Inc. 06/23/2000
(See US Data Authority, Inc.)

SUNWALKER DEV INC (UT)
Reorganized under the laws of Nevada as iShopper.com, Inc. 10/12/1999
Each share Common $0.001 par exchanged for (0.001) share Common $0.001 par
iShopper.com, Inc. name changed to Ensurge, Inc. 10/16/2000

SUNWARD RES LTD (BC)
Merged into NovaCopper Inc. 06/24/2015
Each share Common no par exchanged for (0.3) share Common no par
Note: Unexchanged certificates will be cancelled and become without value 06/24/2021
NovaCopper Inc. name changed to Trilogy Metals Inc. 09/08/2016

SUNWARD TECHNOLOGIES INC (DE)
Each share Common 1¢ par exchanged for (0.2) share Common 5¢ par 01/10/1994
Merged into Read-Rite Corp. 08/22/1994
Each share Common 5¢ par exchanged for (1.077) shares Common $0.0001 par
(See Read-Rite Corp.)

SUNWAY GLOBAL INC (NV)
Each share old Common $0.0000001 par exchanged for (0.1) share new Common $0.0000001 par 12/30/2014
Each share new Common $0.0000001 par exchanged again for (0.000025) share new Common $0.0000001 par 03/02/2016
Note: In effect holders received $0.18 cash per share and public interest was eliminated

SUNWEST BK NEW (TUSTIN, CA)
Each share old Common no par exchanged for (0.03333333) share new Common no par 12/20/2004
Each share new Common no par exchanged again for (0.1) share new Common no par 01/10/2012
Acquired by Sunwest Bancorp, Inc. 01/06/2016
Each share new Common no par exchanged for $56,300 cash

SUNWEST BANK OLD (TUSTIN, CA)
Merged into Centennial Beneficial Corp. 06/18/1985
Each share Capital Stock $5 par exchanged for $50.75 cash

SUNWEST FINL SVCS INC (NM)
Common $5 par changed to no par 03/26/1986
Common no par split (2) for (1) by issuance of (1) additional share 08/20/1986
Merged into Boatmen's Bancshares, Inc. 10/01/1992
Each share Common no par exchanged for (0.7722) share Common $1 par
Boatmen's Bancshares, Inc. merged into NationsBank Corp. 01/07/1997 which reincorporated in Delaware as BankAmerica Corp. (Old) 09/25/1998 which merged into BankAmerica Corp. (New) 09/30/1998 which name changed to Bank of America Corp. 04/28/1999

SUNWEST INDS INC (UT)
Recapitalized as International Training & Educational Corp. 07/05/1994
Each share Common $0.001 par exchanged for (0.002) share Common $0.001 par
International Training & Educational Corp. name changed to Digimedia USA Inc. 02/12/1996 which name changed to Algorythm Technologies Corp. 07/24/1997 which name changed to Quikbiz Internet Group, Inc. 07/07/1998
(See Quikbiz Internet Group, Inc.)

SUNWIN INTL NEUTRACEUTICALS INC (NV)
Name changed to Sunwin Stevia International, Inc. 04/20/2012

SUNWOOD CORP (DE)
Charter cancelled and declared inoperative and void for non-payment of taxes 03/01/1990

SUNWORLD INTL AWYS INC (NV)
Filed petition under Chapter 11 Federal Bankruptcy Code 04/11/1988
No stockholders' equity

SUNX ENERGY INC (NV)
Recapitalized as Suntex Enterprises, Inc. 01/23/2017
Each share Common $0.001 par exchanged for (0.0001) share Common $0.00001 par

SUPARNA GOLD CORP (BC)
Name changed to Scientific Metals Corp. 05/09/2016
Scientific Metals Corp. name changed to US Cobalt Inc. 05/25/2017 which merged into First Cobalt Corp. (BC) 06/05/2018 which reincorporated in Canada 09/04/2018

SUPER BLUE DOMAIN TECHNOLOGIES INC (NV)
Name changed to Golden Energy Corp. 06/16/2009
Golden Energy Corp. name changed to Golden Grail Technology Corp. 12/31/2014

SUPER-COLD CORP. (CA)
Liquidation completed 05/20/1959
Details not available

SUPER-CORPORATIONS OF AMERICA TRUST SHARES
Series A (Maximum Return Series) trust terminated 00/00/1940 and liquidation completed 00/00/1943
Series B (Capital Accumulation Series) trust terminated 00/00/1940 and liquidation completed 00/00/1942
Series BB trust terminated 00/00/1938 and liquidation completed 00/00/1940
Series C (Maximum Return Series) trust terminated 00/00/1948 and liquidation completed 00/00/1949
Series D (Capital Accumulation Series) trust terminated 00/00/1948 and liquidation completed 00/00/1949

Series AA trust terminated 00/00/1949 and liquidation completed 00/00/1952
Details not available

SUPER DISTRIBUTING CORP. (NY)
Charter cancelled and proclaimed dissolved for failure to file reports and pay taxes 12/16/1929

SUPER DLR STORES INC (NC)
Stock Dividend - 33.33333333% 05/21/1979
99% acquired by Variety Wholesalers, Inc. through purchase offer which expired 06/18/1981
Public interest eliminated

SUPER DRUG MARKETS LTD. (SK)
Assets liquidated for benefit of creditors 09/17/1965
No stockholders' equity

SUPER DUPES INC (MN)
Reorganized under Chapter 11 bankruptcy proceedings 05/18/1982
No stockholders' equity

SUPER ELECTRIC PRODUCTS CORP. (NJ)
Each share Common $2 par exchanged for (2) shares Common $1 par 12/15/1949
Recapitalized as Union Spring & Manufacturing Co. and Common $1 par changed to 10¢ par 01/07/1952
Union Spring & Manufacturing Co. name changed to Union Corp. (NJ) 01/19/1966 which reincorporated in Delaware 07/24/1987
(See Union Corp. (DE))

SUPER ENERGY INVTS CORP (NV)
Recapitalized as USA Signal Technology, Inc. 04/17/2006
Each share Common $0.0004 par exchanged for (0.05) share Common $0.0004 par
USA Signal Technology, Inc. name changed to Icon Media Holdings, Inc. 06/10/2011

SUPER FOOD SVCS INC (DE)
Class B 1¢ par reclassified as Common 1¢ par 11/12/1958
$1.50 Preferred $1 par reclassified as Conv. Preferred no par 11/14/1961
Common 1¢ par changed to $1 par and (1) additional share issued 11/22/1961
Conv. Preferred no par called for redemption 01/15/1962
$1.20 Preferred $1 par reclassified as Preferred 1st Ser. no par 11/14/1962
Common $1 par split (3) for (2) by issuance of (0.5) additional share 06/27/1983
Common $1 par split (2) for (1) by issuance of (1) additional share 12/15/1985
Common $1 par split (3) for (2) by issuance of (0.5) additional share 12/13/1989
$1.20 Preferred 1st Ser. no par called for redemption 09/15/1992
Merged into Nash-Finch Corp. 11/22/1996
Each share Common $1 par exchanged for $15.50 cash

SUPER GROUP LTD (SOUTH AFRICA)
Each Unsponsored ADR for Ordinary exchanged for (1) Sponsored ADR for Ordinary 08/15/2011
Basis changed from (1:50) to (1:5) 06/02/2014
ADR agreement terminated 09/26/2016
Each Sponsored ADR for Ordinary exchanged for (5) shares Ordinary

SUPER JET INC (UT)
Name changed to Fullerton Zip Nut, Inc. (UT) 11/29/1982
Fullerton Zip Nut, Inc. (UT) reincorporated in Nevada as Fullerton Inc. 02/25/1985 which recapitalized as Pacific Power

Group, Inc. 10/24/1994 which name changed to LP Holdings, Inc. 12/20/2005 which name changed to Tanke, Inc. 10/17/2007

SUPER LT INC (DE)
Common $0.0001 par split (20.2931) for (1) by issuance of (19.2931) additional shares payable 08/17/2012 to holders of record 08/13/2012 Ex date - 08/20/2012
Name changed to Be Active Holdings, Inc. 01/07/2013

SUPER LUCK INC (DE)
Name changed to Beijing Century Health Medical, Inc. 05/04/2010

SUPER MAID CORP. (IL)
Name changed to Advance Aluminum Castings Corp. 00/00/1933
Advance Aluminum Castings Corp. name changed to Advance Ross Electronics Corp. 07/29/1959 which was acquired by Byllesby (H.M.) & Co. 05/16/1963 which name changed to Advance Ross Corp. (Old) 04/23/1964 which reorganized as Advance Ross Corp. (New) 06/17/1993 which merged into CUC International Inc. 01/10/1996 which name changed to Cendant Corp. 12/17/1997 which reorganized as Avis Budget Group, Inc. 09/01/2006

SUPER MARKET DEVELOPERS, INC. (MO)
Through voluntary purchase offer 100% acquired by Associated Wholesale Grocers, Inc. 00/00/1966
Public interest eliminated

SUPER MARKET DISTRIBUTING, INC. (MA)
Name changed to SMD Industries, Inc. 08/03/1967
(See SMD Industries, Inc.)

SUPER MKT VIDEO INC (NV)
Name changed to L.A. Entertainment, Inc. 11/01/1989
L.A. Entertainment, Inc. name changed to Gerant Industries, Inc. 12/28/1992 which reorganized as Xplorer, S.A. 12/16/1996 which name changed to Netholdings.com Inc. 12/08/1999 which name changed to Global Axcess Corp. 05/09/2001
(See Global Axcess Corp.)

SUPER MOLD CORP. OF CALIFORNIA (CA)
Common $10 par changed to $25 par and (3) additional shares issued 00/00/1952
Name changed to Super Mold Corp. 07/17/1968
Super Mold Corp. name changed to Intercole Automation, Inc. (CA) 09/22/1972 which name changed to Intercole Inc. 12/08/1980
(See Intercole Inc.)

SUPER MOLD CORP (CA)
Under plan of merger name changed to Intercole Automation, Inc. (CA) 09/22/1972
Intercole Automation, Inc. (CA) name changed to Intercole Inc. 12/08/1980
(See Intercole Inc.)

SUPER NATURE CORP (IL)
Name changed to L T C Pharmaceuticals Corp. 03/20/1970
(See L T C Pharmaceuticals Corp.)

SUPER NOVA MINERALS CORP (BC)
Each share Common no par received distribution of (1) share Ole Remediation Ltd. Common no par payable 10/22/2012 to holders of record 10/01/2012 Ex date - 09/26/2012
Name changed to Super Nova Petroleum Corp. 04/03/2014
Super Nova Petroleum Corp. name changed to Koios Beverage Corp. 05/01/2018

SUPER NOVA PETE CORP (BC)
Each share old Common no par exchanged for (0.1) share new Common no par 01/14/2016
Name changed to Koios Beverage Corp. 05/01/2018

SUPER PHONE INTL INC (DE)
Recapitalized as Mega Com Group, Inc. 01/16/1997
Each share Common $0.001 par exchanged for (0.1) share Common $0.001 par
Mega Com Group, Inc. name changed to X-Stream Network, Inc. 07/28/1998
(See X-Stream Network, Inc.)

SUPER RITE CORP (DE)
Name changed 06/21/1991
Name changed from Super Rite Food Holdings Corp. to Super Rite Corp. 06/21/1991
$1.50 Sr. Exchangeable Preferred 1¢ par called for redemption 06/15/1992
Merged into Richfood Holdings, Inc. 10/15/1995
Each share Common no par exchanged for (1.0205) shares Common no par
Richfood Holdings, Inc. merged into Supervalu Inc. 08/31/1999
(See Supervalu Inc.)

SUPER RITE FOODS INC (DE)
Acquired by Super Rite Foods Holdings Corp. 09/20/1989
Each share Common 5¢ par exchanged for (0.2) share $1.50 Sr. Exchangeable Preferred 1¢ par, (0.0468) Common Stock Purchase Warrant expiring 04/01/1996 and $25.25 cash
Super Rite Foods Holdings Corp. name changed to Super Rite Corp. 06/21/1991 which merged into Richfood Holdings, Inc. 10/15/1995 which merged into Supervalu Inc. 08/31/1999

SUPER SCOOP ICE CREAM CORP (BC)
Name changed to Trojan Energy Corp. 01/07/1983
Trojan Energy Corp. recapitalized as International Trojan Development Corp. 04/18/1985 which recapitalized as Trojan Ventures Inc. 06/20/1991 which reorganized in Cayman Islands as Alcanta International Education Ltd. 03/26/1999 which name changed to Access International Education Ltd. 01/17/2001

SUPER SVC DRUG INC (CO)
Charter suspended for failure to file corporate reports 12/06/1977

SUPER-SERVICE STATIONS LTD. (NS)
Called for redemption 12/29/1971
Public interest eliminated

SUPER SKY INTL INC (WI)
Common 10¢ par split (5) for (4) by issuance of (0.25) additional share 12/08/1986
Stock Dividend - 25% 06/16/1986
Acquired by Koru Holdings, Inc. 11/10/1987
Each share Common 10¢ par exchanged for $10 cash

SUPER SOL LTD (ISRAEL)
Common I£19.800 par changed to IS 2 par 06/29/1980
Stock Dividends - 1000% 09/29/1980; 50% 03/24/1981
ADR agreement terminated 12/24/2002
Each Sponsored ADR for Ordinary ILS 0.1 par exchanged for $13.16417 cash

SUPER STORES INC (DE)
Common no par changed to $1 par 10/12/1970

Each share Common $1 par exchanged for (0.33333333) share Common 1¢ par 01/01/1974
Charter cancelled and declared inoperative and void for non-payment of taxes 03/01/1987

SUPER-TEMP CORP. (CA)
Completely liquidated 06/23/1966
Each share Common no par exchanged for first and final distribution of $5 cash

SUPER TWINS RES LTD (BC)
Name changed to Whitegold Resource Corp. 02/13/1997
Whitegold Resource Corp. recapitalized as Whitegold Natural Resource Corp. 04/09/2001 which recapitalized as Spirit Energy Corp. 05/28/2002 which name changed to Canadian Spirit Resources Inc. (BC) 06/23/2004 which reincorporated in Alberta 05/25/2012

SUPER VALU STORES INC (DE)
5.4% Preferred 1954 Ser. $50 par called for redemption 07/01/1957
Common $5 par and VTC's for Common $5 par changed to $1.66666666 par and (2) additional shares issued respectively 08/28/1961
Voting Trust Agreement terminated 11/22/1963
Each VTC for Common $1.66666666 par exchanged for (1) share Common $1.66666666 par
Common $1.66666666 par split (3) for (2) by issuance of (0.5) additional share 12/28/1971
5% Preferred 1948 Ser. $50 par called for redemption 08/08/1972
2nd Conv. Preferred Ser. A no par called for redemption 08/08/1972
Common $1.66666666 par changed to $1 par and (1) additional share issued 08/05/1976
Common $1 par split (2) for (1) by issuance of (1) additional share 08/07/1978
Common $1 par split (2) for (1) by issuance of (1) additional share 08/07/1981
Common $1 par split (2) for (1) by issuance of (1) additional share 08/08/1985
Stock Dividend - Common & VTC's for Common - 100% 01/22/1959
Name changed to Supervalu Inc. 06/30/1992
(See Supervalu Inc.)

SUPER VISION INTL INC (DE)
Name changed to Nexxus Lighting, Inc. and Class A Common $0.001 par reclassified as Common $0.001 par 04/16/2007
Nexxus Lighting, Inc. name changed to Revolution Lighting Technologies, Inc. 11/15/2012

SUPERBLOCK INDS INC (DE)
Recapitalized as Trilogy Gaming Corp. 01/31/1996
Each share Common 1¢ par exchanged for (0.01) share Common $0.001 par
Trilogy Gaming Corp. name changed to TELnet go 2000, Inc. 01/01/2000
(See TELnet go 2000, Inc.)

SUPERBURN SYS LTD (BC)
Merged into Conpress Investments B.V. 02/28/1990
Each share Common no par exchanged for $0.70 cash

SUPERCART INTL INC (NV)
Each share old Common $0.001 par exchanged for (0.1) share new Common $0.001 par 03/17/1994
Charter revoked for failure to file reports and pay fees 04/01/2000

SUPERCLICK INC (WA)
Acquired by AT&T Inc. 01/18/2012
Each share Common $0.0006 par exchanged for $0.268 cash

SUPERCOM LTD (ISRAEL)
Recapitalized as Vuance Ltd. 05/14/2007
Each (5.88235) shares Ordinary ILS 0.001 par exchanged for (1) share Ordinary ILS 0.0588235 par
Vuance Ltd. name changed to SuperCom, Ltd. 03/15/2013

SUPERCOMPUTING SOLUTIONS INC (DE)
Charter cancelled and declared inoperative and void for non-payment of taxes 03/01/1994

SUPERCONDUCTIVE COMPONENTS INC (OH)
Each share old Common no par exchanged for (0.1) share new Common no par 05/15/1996
Name changed to SCI Engineered Materials, Inc. 08/08/2008

SUPERCRETE LTD (MB)
Each share Common 25¢ par exchanged for (0.33333333) share Common 75¢ par 10/27/1969
Merged into Supercrete Inc. 11/23/1978
Each share Common 75¢ par exchanged for $5.85 cash

SUPERCUTS INC (DE)
Common 1¢ par split (3) for (2) by issuance of (0.5) additional share 04/01/1992
Merged into Regis Corp. (New) 10/25/1996
Each share Common 1¢ par exchanged for (0.4) share Common 5¢ par

SUPERDIRECTORIES INC (WY)
Reincorporated 08/12/2010
State of incoporation changed from (DE) to (WY) and Common 1¢ par changed to $0.00000001 par 08/12/2010
Each share old Common $0.00000001 par exchanged for (0.001) share new Common $0.00000001 par 01/11/2011
Each share new Common $0.00000001 par exchanged again for (0.0004) share new Common $0.00000001 par 06/04/2012
SEC revoked common stock registration 12/07/2016

SUPERDRAULIC CORP. (MI)
Charter revoked for failure to file reports and pay fees 05/15/1955

SUPERFLY ADVERTISING INC (DE)
SEC revoked common stock registration 07/20/2010

SUPERGEN INC (DE)
Reincorporated 11/05/1997
State of incorporation changed from (CA) to (DE) 11/05/1997
Name changed to Astex Pharmaceuticals, Inc. 09/12/2011
(See Astex Pharmaceuticals, Inc.)

SUPERGROUP PLC (ENGLAND)
Name changed to Superdry PLC 01/19/2018

SUPERHEATER CO.
Merged into Combustion Engineering-Superheater, Inc. 12/31/1948
Each share Common exchanged for (1) share Capital Stock $1 par
Combustion Engineering-Superheater, Inc. name changed to Combustion Engineering, Inc. 04/15/1953
(See Combustion Engineering, Inc.)

SUPERIOR ACCEP LTD (ON)
Acquired by Great Universal Stores PLC 02/24/1987
Each share Class A no par exchanged for $14.513 cash
Each share Class B no par exchanged for $14.513 cash

SUPERIOR ACID & CHEMS LTD (ON)
Charter cancelled for failure to pay taxes and file returns 03/16/1976

SUPERIOR ACID & IRON LTD. (ON)
Recapitalized as Superior Acid & Chemicals Ltd. 11/24/1971
Each share Capital Stock no par exchanged for (0.25) share Capital Stock no par
(See Superior Acid & Chemicals Ltd.)

SUPERIOR BANCORP (DE)
Each share old Common $0.001 par exchanged for (0.25) share new Common $0.001 par 04/28/2008
Principal asset placed in receivership 04/15/2011
Stockholders' equity unlikely

SUPERIOR BENEFIT LIFE INS CO (NE)
Merged into Superior Equity Corp. 02/28/1972
Each share Common 50¢ par exchanged for (0.608) share Common no par
(See Superior Equity Corp.)

SUPERIOR CABLE CORP. (NC)
Stock Dividend - 10% 09/01/1965
Completely liquidated 04/03/1967
Each share Common $1 par exchanged for first and final distribution of (2.05) shares Continental Telephone Corp. Common $1 par
Continental Telephone Corp. name changed to Continental Telecom Inc. 05/06/1982 which name changed to Contel Corp. 05/01/1986 which merged into GTE Corp. 03/14/1991 which merged into Verizon Communications Inc. 06/30/2000

SUPERIOR CALIFORNIA FARM LANDS CO. (DE)
Dissolved 01/30/1946
No stockholders' equity

SUPERIOR CALIFORNIA OIL CO. (NV)
Charter revoked for failure to file reports and pay fees 01/05/1931

SUPERIOR CAP INC (QC)
Name changed to Emerging Africa Gold EAG Inc. 06/27/1996
Emerging Africa Gold EAG Inc. merged into Diagem International Resources Corp. (BC) 05/31/2002 which reincorporated in Canada as Diagem Inc. 11/18/2004
(See Diagem Inc.)

SUPERIOR CARE INC (DE)
Name changed to Lifetime Corp. 10/28/1986
Lifetime Corp. acquired by Olsten Corp. 07/30/1993 which merged into Adecco S.A. 03/15/2000 which name changed to Adecco Group AG 06/03/2016

SUPERIOR COACH CORP (OH)
Merged into Sheller-Globe Corp. 06/02/1969
Each share Common $1.25 par exchanged for (0.4) share $1.40 Conv. Preferred no par and (0.37) share Common no par
(See Sheller-Globe Corp.)

SUPERIOR COML CORP (DE)
Each share Class A Common 1¢ par exchanged for (0.5) share Class A Common 2¢ par 12/01/1962
Company believed out of business 00/00/1984
Details not available

SUPERIOR COMPUTER CORP (NJ)
Placed in receivership 11/15/1972
No stockholders' equity

SUPERIOR CONSULTANT HLDGS CORP (DE)
Merged into Affiliated Computer Services, Inc. 01/28/2005
Each share Common 1¢ par exchanged for $8.50 cash

SUPERIOR COPPER CORP (ON)
Merged into Nighthawk Gold Corp. 05/30/2016

Each share Common no par exchanged for (0.32493545) share Common no par
Note: Unexchanged certificates will be cancelled and become without value 05/30/2022

SUPERIOR DIAMONDS INC (BC)
Reincorporated 06/30/2004
Each share old Common no par exchanged for (0.5) share new Common no par 11/27/2003
Place of incorporation changed from (YT) to (BC) 06/30/2004
Name changed to Northern Superior Resources Inc. 04/15/2008

SUPERIOR ELEC CO (CT)
Common $1 par split (2) for (1) by issuance of (1) additional share 03/15/1974
Stock Dividends - 10% 12/15/1972; 10% 05/24/1985
Merged into Dana Corp. 06/19/1989
Each share Common $1 par exchanged for $16.50 cash

SUPERIOR ELECTRONICS CO. (MN)
Recapitalized as Whitlock Corp. 09/00/1970
Each share Class A Common 10¢ par exchanged for (0.5) share Common 10¢ par
(See Whitlock Corp.)

SUPERIOR ELECTRS INDS LTD (CANADA)
Placed into receivership 06/08/1979
No stockholders' equity

SUPERIOR ELEVATOR & FORWARDING CORP.
Dissolved 00/00/1939
Details not available

SUPERIOR ELEVATOR CORP.
Reorganized as Superior Elevator & Forwarding Corp. 00/00/1930
Details not available

SUPERIOR ENERGY CORP. (UT)
Name changed to Skytrader Corp. 09/19/1984
(See Skytrader Corp.)

SUPERIOR EQUITY CORP (DE)
Charter cancelled and declared inoperative and void for non-payment of taxes 03/01/1975

SUPERIOR ESSEX INC (DE)
Merged into LS Corp. 08/07/2008
Each share Common 1¢ par exchanged for $45 cash

SUPERIOR FIBER PRODUCTS, INC. (WI)
Acquired by Gold Bond Stamp 00/00/1974
Details not available

SUPERIOR FINL CORP (DE)
Merged into Arvest Bank Group, Inc. 08/28/2003
Each share Common 1¢ par exchanged for $23.75 cash

SUPERIOR FINL CORP (MI)
Acquired by an investor group 12/16/1985
Each share Common $10 par exchanged for $30 cash

SUPERIOR FINL HLDGS INC (QC)
Recapitalized as Superior Capital Inc. 12/23/1991
Each share Common $1 par exchanged for (0.33333333) Common no par
Superior Capital Inc. name changed to Emerging Africa Gold EAG Inc. 06/27/1996 which merged into Diagem International Resource Corp. (BC) 05/31/2002 which reincorporated in Canada as Diagem Inc. 11/18/2004
(See Diagem Inc.)

SUPERIOR FLASHER CORP (NY)
Name changed to Vestec Corp. 02/11/1983
(See Vestec Corp.)

SUPERIOR FOODS INC (TX)
Stock Dividends - 10% 07/29/1977; 10% 07/10/1981
Merged into Texas American Acquisition Corp. 11/21/1984
Each share Common $1 par exchanged for $4 principal amount of 11% Non-transferable Notes due 11/21/1988 and $1 cash

SUPERIOR FORWARDING CO., INC.
Reorganized as Superior Elevator & Forwarding Corp. 00/00/1930
Details not available

SUPERIOR GALLERIES INC (DE)
Merged into DGSE Companies, Inc. 05/31/2007
Each share Common $0.001 par exchanged for (0.2731) share Common 1¢ par
Note: Holders received an additional distribution of (0.038483) share Common 1¢ par per share from escrow 07/25/2008

SUPERIOR HEALTH SVCS INC (CO)
Name changed to Wyndon Corp. 02/10/1972
(See Wyndon Corp.)

SUPERIOR HLDG CORP (GA)
Common $1 par changed to 1¢ par 03/25/1985
Name changed to Superior TeleTec Inc. 08/21/1989
Superior TeleTec Inc. merged into Alpine Group, Inc. 11/10/1993
(See Alpine Group, Inc.)

SUPERIOR INDUSTRIES CORP. (NY)
Completely liquidated 09/29/1967
Each share Common 10¢ par exchanged for first and final distribution of (0.166666) share Diversified Products Corp. Common 50¢ par
Diversified Products Corp. merged into Liggett Group Inc. 02/17/1977
(See Liggett Group Inc.)

SUPERIOR INDS INTL INC (CA)
Reincorporated 07/01/1994
Common 50¢ par split (5) for (4) by issuance of (0.25) additional share 07/14/1978
Common 50¢ par split (5) for (4) by issuance of (0.25) additional share 07/12/1979
Common 50¢ par split (5) for (4) by issuance of (0.25) additional share 07/29/1985
Common 50¢ par split (5) for (4) by issuance of (0.25) additional share 07/21/1989
Common 50¢ par split (2) for (1) by issuance of (1) additional share 08/07/1992
Common 50¢ par split (3) for (2) by issuance of (0.5) additional share 07/20/1993
Stock Dividends - 10% 12/15/1975; 10% 12/15/1976; 10% 09/19/1977; 10% 07/01/1993; 10% 07/24/1986; 10% 06/24/1988; 10% 06/29/1990; 10% 08/09/1991
State of incorporation changed from (DE) to (CA) and Common 50¢ par changed to no par 07/01/1994
Reincorporated under the laws of Delaware and Common no par changed to 1¢ par 05/20/2015

SUPERIOR LOAN CORP. (MO)
Charter forfeited for failure to file reports 01/01/1976

SUPERIOR LUBE INC (NV)
Each (27) shares old Common $0.001 par exchanged for (1) share new Common $0.001 par 12/20/1996
Name changed to Telpac Industries, Inc. 08/06/1997

SUPERIOR MFG & INSTR CORP (NY)
Common 50¢ par split (5) for (4) by issuance of (0.25) additional share 05/20/1968
Stock Dividend - 20% 03/15/1967
Liquidation completed
Each share Common 50¢ par exchanged for initial distribution of $17.45 cash 09/21/1984
Assets transferred to SMI Liquidating Corp. 09/21/1984
(See SMI Liquidating Corp.)

SUPERIOR MARKETING RESH CORP (UT)
Common no par split (3) for (1) by issuance of (2) additional shares 05/01/1986
Proclaimed dissolved for failure to pay taxes 01/01/1995

SUPERIOR MED CONCEPTS INC (DE)
Charter cancelled and declared inoperative and void for non-payment of taxes 03/01/1996

SUPERIOR MINES CO. (DE)
No longer in existence having become inoperative and void for non-payment of taxes 04/01/1934

SUPERIOR MNG CORP (YT)
Recapitalized as Superior Mining International Corp. (Yukon) 05/10/2006
Each share Common no par exchanged for (0.2) share Common no par
Superior Mining International Corp. (Yukon) reincorporated in British Columbia 02/18/2008

SUPERIOR MNG INTL CORP (YT)
Reincorporated under the laws of British Columbia 02/18/2008

SUPERIOR MOTORS, INC. (NV)
Charter revoked for failure to file reports and pay fees 03/02/1931

SUPERIOR NATL BK & TR CO (HANCOCK, MI)
Reorganized as Keweenaw Financial Corp. 06/30/1990
Each share Common $12.50 par exchanged for (2) shares Common no par

SUPERIOR NATL CAP TR I (DE)
Note: Superior National Capital Trust I is registered as a Trust which exists for the sole purpose of issuing equity securities and investing the proceeds in an equivalent amount of 10.75% Sr. Sub. Notes due 12/01/2017
SNTL Corp., Guarantor of Trust, Chapter 11 bankruptcy proceedings effective 07/18/2002
Holders received an undetermined amount of SNTL Litigation Trust Units

SUPERIOR NATL INS GROUP INC (CA)
Each share old Common no par exchanged for (0.25) share new Common no par 05/25/1995
Reincorporated under the laws of Delaware 04/11/1997
Superior National Insurance Group, Inc. (DE) name changed to SNTL Corp. 04/18/2001 which reorganized as SNTL Litigation Trust 07/18/2002

SUPERIOR NATL INS GROUP INC (DE)
Name changed to SNTL Corp. 04/18/2001
SNTL Corp. reorganized as SNTL Litigation Trust 07/18/2002

SUPERIOR NETWORKS INC (NV)
Common $0.001 par split (3) for (1) by issuance of (2) additional shares payable 03/13/2002 to holders of record 03/11/2002 Ex date - 03/14/2002
Name changed to L.Air Holding Inc. 10/28/2002
L.Air Holding Inc. recapitalized as Hansheng Industrial Equipment Manufacturing (USA) Inc. 10/03/2006

SUPERIOR OFFSHORE INTL INC (DE)
Plan of liquidation under Chapter 11 Federal Bankruptcy Code effective 02/11/2009
No stockholders' equity

SUPERIOR OIL CO. (CA)
Under plan of consolidation each share Preferred $25 par exchanged for (1.48) shares Capital Stock $25 par 00/00/1937
Each share Common $25 par exchanged for (1) share Capital Stock $25 par
Under plan of merger state of incorporation changed to Nevada and Capital Stock $25 par became Common $25 par 04/24/1963
(See Superior Oil Co. (NV))

SUPERIOR OIL CO (NV)
Common $25 par changed to $2.50 par and (9) additional shares issued 06/15/1965
Common $2.50 par changed to 50¢ par and (4) additional shares issued 11/07/1979
Common 50¢ par changed to 10¢ par and (4) additional shares issued 07/10/1981
Stock Dividend - 90% 12/27/1983
Merged into Mobil Corp. 09/28/1984
Each share Common 10¢ par exchanged for $25 principal amount of 13.765% Debentures 2nd Ser. due 09/15/2004 and $20 cash

SUPERIOR OIL CORP.
Acquired by Sunray Oil Corp. 00/00/1943
Each share Common $1 par exchanged for (0.6) share Common $1 par
Sunray Oil Corp. name changed to Sunray Mid-Continent Oil Co. 05/16/1955 which name changed to Sunray DX Oil Co. 04/27/1962 which merged into Sun Oil Co. (NJ) 10/25/1968 which reincorporated in Pennsylvania 09/30/1971 which name changed to Sun Co., Inc. 04/27/1976
(See Sun Co., Inc.)

SUPERIOR OILS, LTD. (AB)
Name changed to Superior Oils of Canada Ltd. 05/00/1951
Superior Oils of Canada Ltd. recapitalized as New Superior Oils of Canada Ltd. 04/00/1952 which was acquired by Canadian Petrofina Ltd. 06/29/1960 which name changed to Petrofina Canada Ltd. 08/01/1968 which name changed to Petrofina Canada Inc. 09/26/1979 which name changed to Petro-Canada Enterprises Inc./Entreprises Petro-Canada Inc. 11/16/1981
(See Petro-Canada Enterprises Inc./Entreprises Petro-Canada Inc.)

SUPERIOR OILS OF CANADA LTD. (AB)
Recapitalized as New Superior Oils of Canada Ltd. 04/00/1952
Each share Capital Stock no par exchanged for (0.33333333) share Capital Stock $1 par
New Superior Oils of Canada Ltd. acquired by Canadian Petrofina Ltd. 06/29/1960 which name changed to Petrofina Canada Ltd. 08/01/1968 which name changed to Petrofina Canada Inc. 09/26/1979 which name changed to Petro-Canada Enterprises Inc./Entreprises Petro-Canada Inc. 11/16/1981
(See Petro-Canada Enterprises Inc./Entreprises Petro-Canada Inc.)

SUPERIOR PIPELINE CORP (BC)
Reincorporated under the laws of Yukon as Superior Mining Corp. 02/10/1998
Superior Mining Corp. recapitalized as Superior Mining International Corp. (Yukon) 05/10/2006 which reincorporated in British Columbia 02/18/2008

SUPERIOR PLUS INCOME FD (AB)
Name changed 02/26/2003
Name changed from Superior Propane Income Fund to Superior Plus Income Fund 02/26/2003
Plan of arrangement effective 12/31/2008
Each Trust Unit no par exchanged for (1) share Superior Plus Corp. Common no par

SUPERIOR PORTLAND CEMENT, INC. (WA)
Recapitalized 00/00/1945
Each share Class A Preferred no par exchanged for $50 principal amount of 5% Debentures and (0.5) share old Common no par plus all unpaid Class A Preferred dividends accrued through 06/30/1945
Each share Class B Common no par exchanged for (1) share old Common no par
Each share old Common no par exchanged for (2) shares new Common no par 00/00/1954
Merged into Lone Star Cement Corp. (ME) 04/01/1957
Each share new Common no par exchanged for (1.75) shares Common $4 par
Lone Star Cement Corp. (ME) reincorporated in Delaware 05/29/1969 which name changed to Lone Star Industries, Inc. 05/20/1971
(See Lone Star Industries, Inc.)

SUPERIOR SCREW & BOLT MANUFACTURING CO.
Acquired by Federal Screw Works 00/00/1929
Details not available

SUPERIOR SEPARATOR CO. (DE)
Under plan of merger name changed to Daffin Corp. 06/30/1960
Daffin Corp. name changed to Farmhand, Inc. 09/21/1966 which merged into Arizona-Colorado Land & Cattle Co. 06/09/1972 which name changed to AZL Resources, Inc. 05/17/1977
(See AZL Resources, Inc.)

SUPERIOR SVCS INC (WI)
Merged into Vivendi 11/10/1999
Each share Common 1¢ par exchanged for $27 cash

SUPERIOR SILVER MINES INC (ID)
Name changed 12/04/1964
Name changed from Superior Mines, Inc. to Superior Silver Mines, Inc. 12/04/1964
Reincorporated under the laws of Nevada as Clean Wind Energy Tower, Inc. 01/24/2011
Clean Wind Energy Tower, Inc. name changed to Solar Wind Energy Tower, Inc. 03/11/2013

SUPERIOR STEAMSHIP CO.
Dissolved 00/00/1936
Details not available

SUPERIOR STEEL CORP. (VA)
Each share Common $100 par exchanged for (2) shares Common $50 par 00/00/1946
Stock Dividend - 10% 10/13/1955
Merged into Copperweld Steel Co. 11/30/1957
Each share Common $50 par exchanged for (0.75) share Common $5 par
Copperweld Steel Co. name changed to Copperweld Corp. (PA) 04/27/1973 which reincorporated in Delaware 01/16/1987
(See Copperweld Corp. (DE))

SUP-SUP   **FINANCIAL INFORMATION, INC.**

SUPERIOR SUGAR REFINING CO. (MI)
Dissolved 12/14/1955
Details not available

SUPERIOR SUPPLEMENTS INC (DE)
Company terminated common stock registration and is no longer public as of 01/09/2001

SUPERIOR TELECOM INC (DE)
Common 1¢ par split (5) for (4) by issuance of (0.25) additional share payable 02/02/1998 to holders of record 01/23/1998 Ex date - 02/03/1998
Common 1¢ par split (5) for (4) by issuance of (0.25) additional share payable 02/03/1999 to holders of record 01/20/1999 Ex date - 02/04/1999
Stock Dividend - 3% payable 02/11/2000 to holders of record 02/03/2000
Plan of Reorganization under Chapter 11 Federal Bankruptcy Code effective 11/10/2003
No stockholders' equity

SUPERIOR TELETEC INC (GA)
Merged into Alpine Group, Inc. 11/10/1993
Each share Common 1¢ par exchanged for either (0.696) share Common 10¢ par or (0.461) share Common 10¢ par and $2.50 cash
Note: Option to receive stock and cash expired 01/10/1994
(See Alpine Group, Inc.)

SUPERIOR TOOL & DIE CO. (MI)
Merged into Bethlehem Corp. on a share for share basis 08/31/1962

SUPERIOR TR I (DE)
Plan of reorganization under Chapter 11 Federal Bankruptcy Code effective 11/10/2003
No stockholders' equity

SUPERIOR UNIFORM GROUP INC (FL)
Reincorporated 05/08/1998
Common $1 par split (3) for (2) by issuance of (0.5) additional share 02/05/1969
Common $1 par split (2) for (1) by issuance of (1) additional share 03/15/1982
Common $1 par split (4) for (1) by issuance of (3) additional shares 06/22/1992
Name and state of incorporation changed from Superior Surgical Mfg. Co., Inc. (NY) to Superior Uniform Group, Inc. (FL) and Common $1 par changed to $0.001 par 05/08/1998
Common $0.001 par split (2) for (1) by issuance of (1) additional share payable 02/04/2015 to holders of record 01/12/2015 Ex date - 02/05/2015
Name changed to Superior Group of Companies, Inc. 05/15/2018

SUPERIOR VENTURE CORP (NV)
Recapitalized as Ilustrato Pictures International Inc. 03/11/2013
Each share Common $0.001 par exchanged for (0.02) share Common $0.001 par

SUPERIOR WELL SVCS INC (DE)
Merged into Nabors Industries Ltd. 09/10/2010
Each share Common 1¢ par exchanged for $22.12 cash

SUPERIOR WINDOW CO (FL)
Each share 70¢ Conv. Preferred $8 par exchanged for (5) shares Class A Common 10¢ par 12/14/1966
Name changed to Suwinco, Inc. 06/17/1980
(See Suwinco, Inc.)

SUPERIOR WIRELESS COMMUNICATIONS INC (NV)
Recapitalized as JustWebit.Com, Inc. 08/16/1999
Each share Common no par exchanged for (0.05) share Common no par
JustWebit.Com, Inc. name changed to Synthetic Turf Corp. of America 11/12/2002 which recapitalized as City Capital Corp. 12/15/2004

SUPERIORCLEAN INC (NV)
Name changed to Megola, Inc. 10/01/2003

SUPERLATTICE PWR INC (NV)
Each share old Common $0.001 par exchanged for (3) shares new Common $0.001 par 10/19/2009
Recapitalized as Sky Power Solutions Corp. 04/25/2011
Each share new Common $0.001 par exchanged for (0.00333333) share Common $0.001 par
Sky Power Solutions Corp. recapitalized as Clean Enviro Tech Corp. 01/18/2013 which recapitalized as Cyber Apps World Inc. 04/30/2015

SUPERMAC TECHNOLOGY INC (DE)
Merged into Radius Inc. 08/31/1994
Each share Common $0.001 par exchanged for (0.738158) share new Common no par
Radius Inc. name changed to Digital Origin Inc. 03/01/1999 which merged into Media 100 Inc. 05/09/2000
(See Media 100 Inc.)

SUPERMAIL INTL INC (UT)
Each share old Common 1¢ par exchanged for (0.16666666) share new Common 1¢ par 12/15/1992
Name changed to First Automated, Inc. 10/27/2003
First Automated, Inc. recapitalized as PBHG, Inc. 07/19/2004
(See PBHG, Inc.)

SUPERMARKET INVT INC (MO)
98% acquired by Super Market Developers, Inc. through purchase offer which expired 02/16/1976
Public interest eliminated

SUPERMARKET SERVICES, INC. (DE)
Name changed to Ross Viking Merchandise Corp. 08/22/1990
(See Ross Viking Merchandise Corp.)

SUPERMARKETS GEN CORP (DE)
Common $1 par split (2) for (1) by issuance of (1) additional share 08/27/1971
$1.30 Conv. Preferred no par called for redemption 02/01/1980
Common $1 par split (2) for (1) by issuance of (1) additional share 08/22/1983
Common $1 par split (2) for (1) by issuance of (1) additional share 08/22/1986
Merged into Supermarkets General Holdings Corp. 10/05/1987
Each share Common $1 par exchanged for $52 principal amount of 13.125% Jr. Subord. Discount Debentures due 10/05/2003 and (0.709) share $3.52 Exchangeable Preferred no par
(See Supermarkets General Holdings Corp.)

SUPERMARKETS GEN HLDGS CORP (DE)
Plan of reorganization under Chapter 11 Federal Bankruptcy proceedings effective 09/19/2000
Each share $3.52 Exchangeable Preferred 1¢ par received pro rata distribution of $500,000 cash
Note: Certificates were not required to be surrendered and are without value

SUPERMARKETS OPERATING CO. (NJ)
Common 50¢ par split (2) for (1) by issuance of (1) additional share 06/30/1965
Merged into Supermarkets General Corp. 04/27/1966
Each share Common 50¢ par exchanged for (1) share Common $1 par
(See Supermarkets General Corp.)

SUPERMEDIA INC (DE)
Merged into Dex Media, Inc. (New) 04/30/2013
Each share Common 1¢ par exchanged for (0.4386) share Common $0.001 par
(See Dex Media, Inc. (New))

SUPERMERCADOS UNIMARC S A (CHILE)
ADR agreement terminated 09/24/2009
Each Sponsored ADR for Common exchanged for $0.636233 cash

SUPERNOVA CAP CORP (BC)
Merged into Panoro Minerals Ltd. 06/05/2003
Each share Common no par exchanged for (1) share Common no par

SUPERPACK LTD (ON)
Name changed to SPC International Investments Ltd. 7/17/89
(See SPC International Investments Ltd.)

SUPERPACK VENDING LTD. (ON)
Name changed to Superpack Corp. Ltd. 04/19/1963
Superpack Corp. Ltd. name changed to SPC International Investments Ltd. 07/17/1989
(See SPC International Investments Ltd.)

SUPERPRO VENDING GROUP INC (DE)
Name changed to AFA Music Group Ltd. (DE) 10/08/2007
AFA Music Group Ltd. (DE) reincorporated in Florida as AFA Music Group, Inc. 01/17/2008 which name changed to 3D Eye Solutions, Inc. 09/16/2008

SUPERSCOPE INC (CA)
Common $1 par split (3) for (2) by issuance of (0.5) additional share 04/05/1968
Name changed to Marantz Co., Inc. (CA) 06/22/1984
Marantz Co., Inc. (CA) reincorporated in Delaware 07/17/1986
(See Marantz Co., Inc. (DE))

SUPERSILK HOSIERY MILLS LTD.
Name changed to General Products Manufacturing Corp. Ltd. 00/00/1944
(See General Products Manufacturing Corp. Ltd.)

SUPERSTAR PETES LTD (ON)
Charter cancelled and declared dissolved for failure to file returns and pay fees 11/09/1976

SUPERSTITION CONSOLIDATED MINING CO. (AZ)
Charter expired by time limitation 01/07/1940

SUPERSTITION GOLD MINES LTD. (ON)
Charter cancelled 00/00/1953

SUPERTECH INDS INC (BC)
Name changed 07/24/1987
Name changed from Supertech Industries Ltd. to Supertech Industries Inc. 07/24/1987
Recapitalized as Encore Products Inc. 10/11/1989
Each share Common no par exchanged for (0.2) share Common no par
(See Encore Products Inc.)

SUPERTEL COMMUNICATIONS LTD (CO)
Name changed to Premier Platforms Holding Co., Inc. 09/24/2002
Premier Platforms Holding Co., Inc. name changed to Paolo Nevada Enterprises, Inc. (CO) 02/17/2005 which reorganized in Nevada as David Loren Corp. 11/13/2006 which recapitalized as Kibush Capital Corp. 08/23/2013

SUPERTEL HOSPITALITY INC (DE)
Merged into Humphrey Hospitality Trust, Inc. 10/26/1999
Each share Common 1¢ par exchanged for (1.3) shares Common 1¢ par
Humphrey Hospitality Trust, Inc. name changed to Supertel Hospitality, Inc. (VA) 05/27/2005 which reincorporated in Maryland 11/20/2014 which name changed to Condor Hospitality Trust, Inc. 07/21/2015

SUPERTEL HOSPITALITY INC (MD)
Name changed to Condor Hospitality Trust, Inc. 07/21/2015

SUPERTEL HOSPITALITY INC (VA)
Each share old Common 1¢ par exchanged for (0.125) share new Common 1¢ par 08/15/2013
Reincorporated under the laws of Maryland 11/20/2014
Supertel Hospitality, Inc. (MD) name changed to Condor Hospitality Trust, Inc. 07/21/2015

SUPERTEST PETE LTD (ON)
Ordinary and Common no par exchanged (5) for (1) 00/00/1951
Common no par exchanged (10) for (1) 03/01/1956
Merged into BP Canada Ltd. (Canada) 12/23/1971
Each share 5% Preference $100 par exchanged for (1) share 5% Preference $100 par
Each share Ordinary no par exchanged for (5) shares Common no par and (0.5) share Class A no par
Each share Common no par exchanged for $16.50 cash 01/25/1972
BP Canada Ltd. (Canada) reincorporated under the laws of Ontario 10/18/1972 which name changed to BP Canada Ltd.-BP Canada Ltee. 04/27/1973 which reincorporated in Canada as BP Canada Inc. 07/06/1979
(See BP Canada Inc.)

SUPERTEX INC (CA)
Acquired by Microchip Technology Inc. 04/01/2014
Each share Common $0.001 par exchanged for $33 cash

SUPERVALU INC (DE)
Common $1 par split (2) for (1) by issuance of (1) additional share payable 08/18/1998 to holders of record 07/20/1998 Ex date - 08/19/1998
Common $1 par changed to 1¢ par 07/17/2012
Each share old Common 1¢ par exchanged for (0.14285714) share new Common 1¢ par 08/02/2017
Acquired by United Natural Foods, Inc. 10/22/2018
Each share new Common 1¢ par exchanged for $32.50 cash

SUPERVISED EXECUTIVE FUND (1955) LTD. (CANADA)
Voluntarily dissolved 10/28/1965
Details not available

SUPERVISED INVS GROWTH FD INC (MD)
Name changed to Kemper Growth Fund, Inc. (MD) 02/17/1977
Kemper Growth Fund, Inc. (MD) reincorporated in Massachusetts as

Kemper Growth Fund 01/31/1986 which name changed to Scudder Growth Fund 06/25/2001 which name changed to Scudder Growth Trust 01/15/2003
(See Scudder Growth Trust)

SUPERVISED INVS INCOME FD INC (MD)
Name changed to Kemper Total Return Fund, Inc. (MD) 02/17/1977
Kemper Total Return Fund, Inc. (MD) reincorporated in Massachusetts as Kemper Total Return Fund 01/31/1986 which name changed to Scudder Total Return Fund 06/08/2001 which name changed to DWS Balanced Fund 02/06/2006

SUPERVISED INVS SVCS INC (DE)
Merged into Kemperco, Inc. 05/22/1970
Each share Common 1¢ par exchanged for (0.8) share Common $5 par and (0.2) Common Stock Purchase Warrant expiring 00/00/1975
Kemperco, Inc. name changed to Kemper Corp. (Old) 01/15/1974
(See Kemper Corp. (Old))

SUPERVISED INVS SUMMIT FD INC (MD)
Name changed to Kemper Summit Fund, Inc. (MD) 02/17/1977
Kemper Summit Fund, Inc. (MD) reincorporated in Massachusetts as Kemper Summit Fund 01/31/1986
(See Kemper Summit Fund)

SUPERVISED SHARES, INC. (DE)
Name changed to Massachusetts Investors Second Fund, Inc. 00/00/1940
Massachusetts Investors Second Fund, Inc. name changed to Massachusetts Investors Growth Stock Fund, Inc. (DE) 00/00/1952 which reincorporated in Massachusetts 02/27/1959

SUPERVISED SHS INC (IA)
Merged into Mutual of Omaha Income Fund, Inc. 12/28/1970
Each share Capital Stock 25¢ par exchanged for (0.14863) share Common 1¢ par
Mutual of Omaha Income Fund, Inc. name changed to Pioneer Income Fund, Inc. (NE) 12/01/1993 which reincorporated in Delaware as Pioneer Income Fund 06/30/1994 which name changed to Pioneer Balanced Fund 02/01/1997 which merged into Pioneer Series Trust IV 11/10/2006

SUPERVISION ENTMT INC (NV)
Name changed to BioNeutra International, Ltd. 11/04/2013

SUPERWIPES INC (DE)
SEC revoked common stock registration 05/25/2006

SUPERWIRE INC (NV)
Name changed 07/12/2002
Name changed from Superwire.Com, Inc. to Superwire, Inc. 07/12/2002
Each share old Common $0.001 par exchanged for (0.025) share new Common $0.001 par 04/02/2007
Recapitalized as Cannalink, Inc. 09/09/2014
Each share new Common $0.001 par exchanged for (0.02) share Common $0.00001 par

SUPPLY RES INC (NY)
Each share Common 10¢ par exchanged for (1/600) share Common $60 par 06/01/1979
Note: In effect holders received $5 cash per share and public interest eliminated

SUPPORTSAVE SOLUTIONS INC (NV)
Name changed to Golden Time Network Marketing Ltd. 01/03/2017

SUPPORTSOFT INC (DE)
Name changed 03/28/2002
Issue Information - 4,250,000 shares COM offered at $14 per share on 07/18/2000
Name changed from support.com, Inc. to SupportSoft, Inc. 03/28/2002
Name changed back to support.com, Inc. 06/22/2009

SUPPORTSPAN INC (NV)
Merged into Adex Media, Inc. 06/02/2008
Each share Common $0.0001 par exchanged for (19.362442) shares Common $0.0001 par
(See Adex Media, Inc.)

SUPRA COLOR INC (MN)
91% reacquired by the company as of 09/00/1979
Public interest eliminated

SUPRADUR COS INC (DE)
Name changed 07/18/1983
Common no par changed to 1¢ par 05/02/1973
Name changed from Supradur Manufacturing Corp. to Supradur Companies, Inc. 07/01/1983
Chapter 11 bankruptcy proceedings terminated 05/03/2004
Stockholders' equity unlikely

SUPREMA INTL INC (DE)
Each share Common $0.001 par exchanged for (0.05) share Common $0.002 par 07/16/1984
Charter cancelled and declared inoperative and void for non-payment of taxes 03/01/1986

SUPREMA SPECIALTIES INC (NY)
Chapter 11 bankruptcy proceedings converted to Chapter 7 on 03/20/2002
Stockholders' equity unlikely

SUPREME CORP (TX)
Merged into ESI Industries, Inc. (TX) 04/30/1987
Each share Common 1¢ par exchanged for (0.7) share Class A Common 10¢ par
ESI Industries, Inc. (TX) reincorporated in Delaware 09/18/1989 which name changed to Supreme Industries, Inc. 06/17/1993
(See Supreme Industries, Inc.)

SUPREME CORP BERHAD (SINGAPORE)
Name changed to Lion Land Berhad 11/01/1991
Lion Land Berhad name changed to Lion Industries Corp. Berhad 04/08/2003
(See Lion Industries Corp. Berhad)

SUPREME EQUIP & SYS CORP (NY)
Common $1 par changed to 66-2/3¢ par and (0.5) additional share issued 07/05/1972
SEC revoked common stock registration 10/21/2008

SUPREME GAS & OIL LTD (AB)
Struck off register for failure to file annual returns 11/15/1978

SUPREME HLDGS INC (NV)
Name changed 12/03/2002
Name changed from Supreme Hospitality to Supreme Holdings, Inc. 12/03/2002
Name changed to Systems Management Solutions, Inc. 08/20/2004
Systems Management Solutions, Inc. recapitalized as Sunrise Solar Corp. 07/25/2008
(See Sunrise Solar Corp.)

SUPREME INDS INC (DE)
Stock Dividends - 10% payable 12/22/1995 to holders of record 12/15/1995 Ex date - 12/13/1995; 5% payable 05/19/1997 to holders of record 05/12/1997; 5% payable 11/17/1997 to holders of record 11/10/1997 Ex date - 11/06/1997; 5% payable 06/01/1998 to holders of record 05/25/1998 Ex date - 05/20/1998; 5% payable 11/20/1998 to holders of record 11/13/1998; 5% payable 07/19/1999 to holders of record 07/12/1999 Ex date - 07/08/1999; 5% payable 12/06/1999 to holders of record 11/29/1999; 5% payable 05/22/2000 to holders of record 05/15/2000 Ex date - 05/11/2000; 10% payable 10/16/2003 to holders of record 10/06/2003 Ex date - 10/02/2003; 2% payable 08/29/2008 to holders of record 08/22/2008 Ex date - 08/20/2008; 6% payable 11/28/2008 to holders of record 11/21/2008 Ex date - 11/19/2008; 5% payable 06/03/2013 to holders of record 05/20/2013 Ex date - 05/16/2013
Acquired by Wabash National Corp. 09/27/2017
Each share Class A Common 10¢ par exchanged for $21 cash

SUPREME INTL CORP (FL)
Common 1¢ par split (3) for (2) by issuance of (0.5) additional share payable 08/15/1997 to holders of record 07/31/1997
Name changed to Perry Ellis International, Inc. 06/21/1999
(See Perry Ellis International, Inc.)

SUPREME LIBERTY LIFE INSURANCE CO. (IL)
Name changed to Supreme Life Insurance Co. of America 11/04/1960
(See Supreme Life Insurance Co. of America)

SUPREME LIFE INS CO AMER (IL)
Common $10 par changed to $5 par 06/29/1965
Common $5 par changed to $2.50 par 12/07/1965
Common $2.50 par changed to $3 par 06/14/1966
Common $3 par changed to $4 par 00/00/1972
Common $4 par changed to $1.50 par 04/18/1979
Common $1.50 par changed to $1.94 par 12/03/1979
Common $1.94 par changed to $1.43 par 09/15/1982
Common $1.43 par changed to $2 par 12/19/1984
Each share Common $1.40 par exchanged for (0.01) share Common $140 par 09/30/1992
Issued an order of liquidation 07/00/1995
No stockholders equity

SUPREME MINES LTD. (QC)
Charter cancelled 06/00/1973

SUPREME OIL & GAS CORP (CA)
Name changed to Pan American Energy Corp. (CA) and Common $2 par changed to 10¢ par 09/28/1990
Pan American Energy Corp. (CA) reorganized in Nevada as Pan American Industries, Inc. 10/11/1994 which name changed to Sunbase Asia Inc. 01/31/1995 which name changed to Centire International, Inc. (NV) 06/08/2007 which reincorporated in Florida as Jericho Energy Co., Inc. 07/18/2008

SUPREME OIL & GAS LTD (AB)
Recapitalized as Supreme Gas & Oil Ltd. 11/05/1968
Each share Capital Stock no par exchanged for (0.666666) share Capital Stock no par
(See Supreme Gas & Oil Ltd.)

SUPREME PHARMACEUTICALS INC (CANADA)
Reincorporated 12/21/2015
Each share old Common no par exchanged for (0.2) share new Common no par 07/29/2014
Place of incorporation changed from (BC) to (Canada) 12/21/2015
Name changed to Supreme Cannabis Co. Inc. 12/29/2017

SUPREME PPTY INC (IL)
Merged into Supreme Realty Investments, Inc. 09/09/2004
Each share Common $0.001 par exchanged for (1.3953) shares Common $0.001 par
Supreme Realty Investments, Inc. name changed to Home System Group 10/04/2006

SUPREME RLTY INVT INC (NV)
Each share old Common $0.001 par exchanged for (0.1) share new Common $0.001 par 07/05/2005
Each share new Common $0.001 par exchanged again for (0.1) share new Common $0.001 par 07/24/2006
Name changed to Home System Group 10/04/2006

SUPREME RES INC (BC)
Struck off register and declared dissolved for failure to file returns 10/28/1994

SUPREME RES LTD (BC)
Name changed to Supreme Pharmaceuticals Inc. (BC) 03/14/2014
Supreme Pharmaceuticals Inc. (BC) reincorporated in Canada 12/21/2015 which name changed to Supreme Cannabis Co. Inc. 12/29/2017

SUPREME SPECIALTIES, INC. (NY)
Name changed to Educational Applications, Inc. 08/06/1968
(See Educational Applications, Inc.)

SUPREME SUNRISE FOOD EXCHANGE INC. (NY)
Name changed to Sunrise Supermarkets Corp. 00/00/1953

SUPREMEX INCOME FD (QC)
Under plan of reorganization each Trust Unit no par automatically became (1) share Supremex Inc. (Canada) Common no par 01/04/2011

SUPREX ENERGY CORP (AB)
Delisted from Canadian Venture Stock Exchange 03/20/2002

SUPRON ENERGY CORP (DE)
Common $1 par split (3) for (2) by issuance of (0.5) additional share 08/01/1979
Common $1 par split (3) for (2) by issuance of (0.5) additional share 06/15/1980
Common $1 par split (2) for (1) by issuance of (1) additional share 06/15/1981
Stock Dividend - 100% 06/15/1977
Merged into Allied Corp. 04/23/1982
Each share Common $1 par exchanged for $35 cash

SUPRONICS CORP (NJ)
Adjudicated bankrupt 09/31/1977
Stockholders' equity unlikely

SUQUASH COLLIERIES LTD. (BC)
Dissolved 01/00/1961
No stockholders' equity

SUR AMERN GOLD CORP (CANADA)
Reincorporated under the laws of British Columbia as Cadan Resources Corp. 08/28/2007
Cadan Resources Corp. name changed to Rizal Resources Corp. 10/07/2016

SURAJ VENTURES INC (NV)
Name changed to Ironwood Gold Corp. 10/27/2009

SURAMERICANA DE INVERSIONES SA (COLOMBIA)
Name changed to Grupo de Inversiones S.A. 05/27/2009

SURAMINA RES INC (CANADA)
Merged into Canadian Gold Hunter Corp. 04/21/2009
Each share Common no par exchanged for (0.7541) share Common no par
Canadian Gold Hunter Corp. name changed to NGEx Resources Inc. 09/22/2009

SURE ENERGY INC (AB)
Merged into Tamarack Valley Energy Ltd. 10/15/2013
Each share Common no par exchanged for (0.105) share Common no par

SURE HAIR INC (CO)
Recapitalized as Palmer Medical Inc. 07/16/1997
Each share Common $0.001 par exchanged for (0.002) share Common $0.001 par
Palmer Medical Inc. recapitalized as Edatenow.Com, Inc. 02/03/1999
Edatenow.Com, Inc. name changed to Encounter.Com, Inc. 05/31/1999 which name changed to Encounter Technologies Inc. 02/18/2010

SURE INVT CO (UT)
Name changed to Globesat Holding Corp. 10/22/1987
(See Globesat Holding Corp.)

SURE SERVICE FILLING STATIONS, INC. (NJ)
Charter declared void for non-payment of taxes 00/00/1929

SURE SHOT INTL INC (FL)
Common no par split (3) for (2) by issuance of (0.5) additional share 02/01/1995
Chapter 11 bankruptcy proceedings terminated 05/04/1998
Stockholders' equity unlikely

SUREBEAM CORP (DE)
Filed a petition under Chapter 7 Federal Bankruptcy Code 01/19/2004
No stockholders' equity

SUREBET CASINOS INC (UT)
Charter expired 09/16/2002

SURECARE INC (DE)
SEC revoked common stock registration 10/17/2008

SUREFIRE COMM INC (CANADA)
Each share old Common no par exchanged for (0.1) share new Common no par 04/01/2003
Name changed to Terra Payments Inc. 09/25/2003
Terra Payments Inc. merged into Optimal Group Inc. 04/06/2004
(See Optimal Group Inc.)

SUREQUEST SYS INC (DE)
Reorganized 04/23/2003
Reorganized from Nevada to under the laws of Delaware 04/23/2003
Each share old Common $0.001 par for (0.025) share new Common $0.001 par
Acquired by MealSuite, Inc. 05/18/2018
Each share new Common $0.001 par exchanged for $0.0245 cash

SURETY BK (VALLEJO, CA)
Merged into First Banks America Inc. 12/01/1997
Each share Preferred Ser. A $1 par exchanged for either (2.2016) shares Common 15¢ par, $30.73 cash, or a combination thereof
Each share Common $1 par exchanged for either (2.5879) shares Common 15¢ par, $36.12 cash, or a combination thereof
Note: Option to receive stock only or stock and cash expired 12/18/1997

SURETY CAP CORP (DE)
Reincorporated 06/12/2014
Each share old Common 1¢ par exchanged for (0.1) share new Common 1¢ par 06/14/1993
Under Chapter 11 Federal Bankruptcy proceedings each share new Common 1¢ par received $0.0135 cash payable 01/15/2009 to holders of record 01/15/2009
State of incorporation changed from (DE) to (TX) 06/12/2014
Each share new Common 1¢ par exchanged again for (0.00000066) share new Common 1¢ par 07/22/2016
Note: In effect holders received $0.00010037 cash per share and public interest was eliminated
No payment of less than $5 will be made

SURETY FED SVGS & LN ASSN MORGANTON N C (USA)
Placed in receivership 07/09/1991
No stockholders' equity

SURETY FED SVGS BK (VALLEJO, CA)
Name changed to Surety Bank (Vallejo, CA) 11/01/1994
(See Surety Bank (Vallejo, CA))

SURETY FINL CORP (UT)
Merged into Witter (Dean) Organization Inc. 12/30/1976
Each share Common $1 par exchanged for (0.35) share Common $1 par
Witter (Dean) Organization Inc. name changed to Witter (Dean) Reynolds Organization Inc. 01/03/1978 which merged into Sears, Roebuck & Co. 12/31/1981 which merged into Sears Holdings Corp. 03/24/2005

SURETY GROUP, INC. (CO)
Declared defunct and inoperative for failure to file reports and pay taxes 10/16/1971

SURETY HLDGS CORP (FL)
Each share old Common $0.001 par exchanged for (0.1) share new Common $0.001 par 06/08/1999
Reincorporated under the laws of Delaware 06/09/1999

SURETY INVT CO (SC)
Acquired by Liberty Corp. (SC) 12/31/1968
Each share Common $10 par exchanged for (3.666666) shares Common $2 par
(See Liberty Corp. (SC))

SURETY LIFE INS CO (UT)
Common $10 par changed to $1 par and (9) additional shares issued 07/01/1961
Stock Dividends - 100% 06/01/1959; 50% 08/02/1960; 10% 06/15/1962
Acquired by Surety Financial Corp. 05/02/1972
Each share Common $1 par exchanged for (1) share Common $1 par
Surety Financial Corp. merged into Witter (Dean) Organization Inc. 12/30/1976 which name changed to Witter (Dean) Reynolds Organization Inc. 01/03/1978 which merged into Sears, Roebuck & Co. 12/31/1981 which merged into Sears Holdings Corp. 03/24/2005

SURETY NATL BK (ENCINO, CA)
Common $5 par and VTC's for Common $5 par changed to $4 par respectively and (0.25) additional share issued 02/15/1970
Merged into California Overseas Bank (Encino, CA) 11/08/1979
Each share Common $4 par and VTC's for Common $4 par exchanged for $6 cash

SURETY OIL CO. (NV)
Charter revoked for failure to file reports and pay fees 03/02/1964

SURETY OIL CO. LTD. (ON)
Name changed to Surety Oils & Minerals Ltd. 12/30/1954
Surety Oils & Minerals Ltd. name changed to Woodgreen Copper Mines Ltd. 11/30/1956 which recapitalized as Consolidated Woodgreen Mines Ltd. 02/00/1959 which recapitalized as Cumberland Mining Co. Ltd. 04/20/1964
(See Cumberland Mining Co. Ltd.)

SURETY OILS & MINERALS LTD. (ON)
Name changed to Woodgreen Copper Mines Ltd. 11/30/1956
Woodgreen Copper Mines Ltd. recapitalized as Consolidated Woodgreen Mines Ltd. 02/00/1959 which recapitalized as Cumberland Mining Co. Ltd. 04/20/1964
(See Cumberland Mining Co. Ltd.)

SURETY SAVINGS & LOAN ASSOCIATION (AZ)
Merged into Century Bank (Phoenix, AZ) 01/02/1981
Each share Guaranty Stock $1 par exchanged for (1) share Common $1 par
(See Century Bank (Phoenix, AZ))

SUREWEST COMMUNICATIONS (CA)
Merged into Consolidated Communications Holdings, Inc. 07/02/2012
Each share Common no par exchanged for (1.40565) shares Common no par

SUREWIN RES INC (BC)
Struck off register and declared dissolved for failure to file returns 10/30/1992

SURF A MOVIE SOLUTIONS INC (NV)
Each share Common $0.001 par exchanged for (50) shares Common $0.0001 par 09/27/2012
Name changed to Frac Water Systems, Inc. 09/12/2013
Frac Water Systems, Inc. name changed to Cannabis Therapy Corp. 03/24/2014 which name changed to Peak Pharmaceuticals, Inc. 02/05/2015

SURF APARTMENTS
Trust terminated 00/00/1950
Details not available

SURF FRANCHISE INC (NY)
Name changed to China Voice Holding Corp. (NY) 05/21/2004
China Voice Holding Corp. (NY) reincorporated in Nevada 07/22/2008
(See China Voice Holding Corp.)

SURF GROUP INC (NY)
Common $0.001 par split (18) for (1) by issuance of (17) additional shares payable 01/06/2003 to holders of record 12/30/2002
Ex date - 01/07/2003
Name changed to tds (Telemedicine) Inc. (NY) 02/13/2003 tds (Telemedicine) Inc. (NY) reincorporated in Delaware as GS EnviroServices Inc. 06/14/2007
(See GS EnviroServices, Inc.)

SURF INLET CONSOLIDATED GOLD MINES LTD. (BC)
Capital Stock no par changed to 50¢ par 00/00/1938
Name changed to Surf Inlet Consolidated Mines Ltd. 11/02/1954
Surf Inlet Consolidated Mines Ltd. recapitalized as Western Surf Inlet Mines Ltd. 06/15/1959 which was acquired by Matachewan Consolidated Mines, Ltd. 04/26/1966

SURF INLET CONSOLIDATED MINES LTD. (BC)
Recapitalized as Western Surf Inlet Mines Ltd. 04/03/1959
Each share Capital Stock 50¢ par exchanged for (0.25) share Class A Common 50¢ par
Western Surf Inlet Mines Ltd. acquired by Matachewan Consolidated Mines, Ltd. 04/26/1966

SURF INLET MINES LTD (BC)
Recapitalized as Princess Resources Ltd. 03/02/1993
Each share Common no par exchanged for (0.1) share Common no par
(See Princess Resources Ltd.)

SURF MINING CO. (WA)
Proclaimed dissolved for non-payment of fees 07/01/1923

SURF OILS LTD (AB)
Common no par split (3) for (2) by issuance of (0.5) additional share 06/25/1981
Recapitalized as Shannon Energy Ltd. 09/10/1985
Each share Common no par exchanged for (0.1) share Common no par
Shannon Energy Ltd. recapitalized as Shannon Environmental Ltd. 03/02/1993
(See Shannon Environmental Ltd.)

SURFACE TECH INC (NV)
Recapitalized as BrandQuest Development Group, Inc. 10/30/2006
Each share Common $0.001 par exchanged for (0.1) share Common $0.001 par
BrandQuest Development Group, Inc. name changed to Novus Acquisition & Development Corp. 07/27/2009

SURFCONTROL PLC (UNITED KINGDOM)
Acquired by Websense, Inc. 10/03/2007
Each Sponsored 144A ADR for Ordinary exchanged for $43.0357 cash
Each Sponsored Reg. S ADR for Ordinary exchanged for $43.0357 cash

SURFECT HLDGS INC (DE)
Filed a petition under Chapter 7 Federal Bankrutpcy Code 08/17/2009
Stockholders' equity unlikely

SURFER CORP (NV)
Merged into Edifice American Corp. 09/15/1988
Each share Common $0.001 par exchanged for (1) share Common $0.001 par
(See Edifice American Corp.)

SURFNET MEDIA GROUP INC (DE)
Name changed to Modavox, Inc. 09/15/2005
Modavox, Inc. name changed to Augme Technologies, Inc. 03/23/2010 which name changed to Hipcricket, Inc. 08/26/2013
(See Hipcricket, Inc.)

SURFORAMA COM INC (NV)
Name changed to eRXSYS Inc. 08/29/2003
eRXSYS Inc. name changed to Assured Pharmacy, Inc. 11/07/2005
(See Assured Pharmacy, Inc.)

SURG O FLEX AMER INC (DE)
Charter cancelled and declared inoperative and void for non-payment of taxes 03/01/1974

SURG II INC (MN)
Each share Common no par exchanged for (0.025) share Common 1¢ par 10/04/2002
Name changed to Chiral Quest Inc. 02/14/2003
Chiral Quest Inc. name changed to VioQuest Pharmaceuticals, Inc. (MN) 08/27/2004 which reincorporated in Delaware 10/06/2005

SURGE COMPONENTS INC NEW (NY)
Reincorporated under the laws of Nevada 08/31/2010

SURGE COMPONENTS INC OLD (NY)
Merged into Surge Components Inc. (New) 02/19/1996
Each share Common $0.001 par exchanged for (0.08333333) share Common $0.001 par
Surge Components Inc. (New) (NY) reincorporated in Nevada 08/31/2010

SURGE ENTERPRISES INC (NV)
Name changed to Southern Star Energy Inc. Inc. 11/13/2006
(See Southern Star Energy Inc.)

SURGE PETE INC (AB)
Merged into Innova Exploration Ltd. 04/16/2004
Each share Common no par exchanged for (1.9738) shares Common no par
(See Innova Exploration Ltd.)

SURGE RES INC (AB)
Name changed to Eaglewood Energy Inc. 11/05/2007
(See Eaglewood Energy Inc.)

SURGERY CTRS CORP (OK)
Name changed to Interwest Medical Corp. 04/04/1985
(See Interwest Medical Corp.)

SURGICAL APPLIANCE INDS INC (OH)
Common $100 par split (5) for (1) by issuance of (4) additional shares 02/25/1974
Each share Common $100 par exchanged for (0.00002) share Common no par 10/01/1984
Note: In effect holders received cash per share and public interest was eliminated

SURGICAL CARE AFFILIATES INC (DE)
Merged into UnitedHealth Group Inc. 03/27/2017
Each share Common 1¢ par exchanged for (0.269154) share Common 1¢ par and $11.40 cash

SURGICAL CARE AFFILIATES INC (TN)
Common 25¢ par split (5) for (4) by issuance of (0.25) additional share 09/09/1987
Common 25¢ par split (5) for (4) by issuance of (0.25) additional share 07/11/1988
Common 25¢ par split (3) for (2) by issuance of (0.5) additional share 06/19/1989
Common 25¢ par split (2) for (1) by issuance of (1) additional share 8/17/90
Common 25¢ par split (3) for (2) by issuance of (0.5) additional share 08/19/1991
Merged into HealthSouth Corp. 01/17/1996
Each share Common 25¢ par exchanged for (1.1726) shares Common 1¢ par
HealthSouth Corp. name changed to Encompass Health Corp. 01/02/2018

SURGICAL HEALTH CORP (DE)
Merged into HealthSouth Corp. 06/21/1995
Each share Common $0.0025 par exchanged for (0.2633) Common 1¢ par
HealthSouth Corp. name changed to Encompass Health Corp. 01/02/2018

SURGICAL LASER TECHNOLOGIES INC (DE)
Each share old Common 1¢ par exchanged for (0.2) share new Common 1¢ par 01/11/1999
Stock Dividend - 50% 12/28/1990
Merged into PhotoMedex, Inc. (DE) 12/30/2004
Each share new Common 1¢ par exchanged for (1.12) shares Common 1¢ par
PhotoMedex, Inc. (DE) reincorporated in Nevada 12/29/2010 which name changed to FC Global Realty Inc. 11/01/2017

SURGICAL PRODUCTS CORP. (UT)
Name changed to Jamaica Marble Inc. (UT) 10/19/1993
Jamaica Marble Inc. (UT) recapitalized as Jamaica Holding Co. Inc. (UT) 08/08/1994 which recapitalized as Klein Engineered Competition Components Inc. (UT) 05/21/1996 which reorganized in Delaware as Automotive Performance Group, Inc. 04/09/1998

SURGICAL SAFETY PRODS INC (NY)
Recapitalized as Power3 Medical Products, Inc. 09/24/2003
Each share Common $0.001 par exchanged for (0.02) share Common $0.001 par

SURGICAL TECHNOLOGIES INC (UT)
Reincorporated 01/24/1994
State of incorporation changed from (DE) to (UT) 01/24/1994
Merged into 4Health Inc. 07/16/1996
Each share Common 1¢ par exchanged for (0.5) share Common 1¢ par and (0.25) Common Stock Purchase Warrant expiring 01/16/1998
4Health Inc. name changed to Irwin Naturals/4Health, Inc. 07/01/1998 which name changed to Omni Nutraceuticals, Inc. 08/23/1999
(See Omni Nutraceuticals, Inc.)

SURGICARE CORP (TX)
Merged into Medical Care International, Inc. 03/07/1984
Each share Common 1¢ par exchanged for (0.818) share Common 1¢ par
Medical Care International, Inc. merged into Medical Care America, Inc. 09/09/1992 which merged into Columbia/HCA Healthcare Corp. 09/16/1994 which name changed to HCA - The Healthcare Co. 05/25/2000 which name changed to HCA Inc. (Ctfs. dated after 06/29/2001) 06/29/2001
(See HCA Inc. (Ctfs. dated after 06/29/2001))

SURGICARE INC (DE)
Reorganized as Orion HealthCorp, Inc. 12/15/2004
Each share Class A Common $0.005 par exchanged for (0.1) share Common $0.001 par

SURGICARE INC (MO)
Charter forfeited for failure to maintain a registered agent 09/17/1981

SURGICOT INC (CT)
Common $1 par changed to 1¢ par 11/06/1974
Merged into Squibb Corp. 06/22/1979
Each share Common $1 par exchanged for (0.502) share Common $1 par
Squibb Corp. merged into Bristol-Myers Squibb Co. 10/04/1989

SURGIDYNE INC (MN)
Name changed to Surg II, Inc. 01/23/2002
Surg II, Inc. name changed to Chirlal Quest Inc. 02/14/2003 which name changed to VioQuest Pharmaceuticals, Inc. (MN) 08/27/2004 which reincorporated in Delaware 10/06/2005

SURGILIGHT INC (FL)
Reincorporated 02/11/2002
Common $0.0001 par split (2) for (1) by issuance of (1) additional share payable 01/26/2000 to holders of record 01/25/2000
State of incorporation changed from (DE) to (FL) 02/11/2002
Chapter 7 bankruptcy proceedings terminated 06/14/2012
Stockholders' equity unlikely

SURGIMED INTL INC (UT)
Name changed to NLB Capital Corp. 06/00/1987
NLB Capital Corp. recapitalized as Integrated Masonry Systems International 11/01/1997
(See Integrated Masonry Systems International)

SURGIMETRICS USA INC (WY)
Each share old Common $0.001 par exchanged for (0.33333333) share new Common $0.001 par 10/28/1996
Administratively dissolved 06/28/1999

SURGITUBE PRODS CORP (NY)
Completely liquidated 09/25/1973
Each share Class A $1 par or Class B 10¢ par exchanged for $1.056 cash

SURGUTNEFTEGAZ JSC (RUSSIA)
Sponsored ADR's for Preferred split (10) for (1) by issuance of (9) additional ADR's payable 04/17/2008 to holders of record 04/15/2008 Ex date - 04/18/2008
Sponsored ADR's for Ordinary split (5) for (1) by issuance of (4) additional ADR's payable 04/17/2008 to holders of record 04/15/2008 Ex date - 04/18/2008
Basis changed from (1:100) to (1:10) 04/17/2008
Name changed to Surgutneftegas PJSC 07/23/2018

SURINAM RES LTD (BC)
Merged into Suntec Ventures Ltd. (New) 01/30/1986
Each share Common no par exchanged for (1) share Common no par
Suntec Ventures Ltd. (New) recapitalized as Consolidated Suntec Ventures Ltd. 05/19/1987 which name changed to Vortex Energy Systems Inc. 10/03/1990 which recapitalized as Autumn Industries Inc. 09/16/1994 which name changed to Altek Power Corp. 03/07/2001

SURLUGA GOLD MINES LTD (ON)
Capital Stock $1 par changed to no par 12/17/1963
Recapitalized as Pursides Gold Mines Ltd. 07/31/1973
Each share Capital Stock no par exchanged for (0.1) share Capital Stock no par
Pursides Gold Mines Ltd. recapitalized as Citadel Gold Mines Inc. 07/22/1980 which recapitalized as Anconia Resources Corp. 06/20/2011

SUROCO ENERGY INC (AB)
Merged into Petroamerica Oil Corp. 07/21/2014
Each share Common no par exchanged for (2.2161) shares Common no par
(See Petroamerica Oil Corp.)

SURPASS CHEMS LTD (ON)
Merged into Witco Chemical Corp. 08/31/1979
Each share Common no par exchanged for (0.4018) share Class B no par or (0.4018) share Common $5 par
Note: Option to receive Class B no par expired 10/09/1979
Witco Chemical Corp. name changed to Witco Corp. 10/01/1985 which merged into CK Witco Corp. 09/01/1999 which name changed to Crompton Corp. 04/27/2000 which name changed to Chemtura Corp. 07/01/2005
(See Chemtura Corp.)

SURPASS PETROCHEMICALS LTD. (ON)
Recapitalized as New Surpass Petrochemicals Ltd. 06/25/1958
Each share Common no par exchanged for (0.1) share Common no par
New Surpass Petrochemicals Ltd. name changed to Surpass Chemicals Ltd. 08/01/1968 which merged into Witco Chemical Corp. 08/31/1979 which name changed to Witco Corp. 10/01/1985 which merged into CK Witco Corp. 09/01/1999 which name changed to Crompton Corp. 04/27/2000 which name changed to Chemtura Corp. 07/01/2005
(See Chemtura Corp.)

SURPASS PETROLEUMS LTD. (ON)
Acquired by Surpass Petrochemicals Ltd. 02/15/1954
Each share Common no par exchanged for (1) share Common no par
Surpass Petrochemicals Ltd. recapitalized as New Surpass Petrochemicals Ltd. 06/25/1958 which name changed to Surpass Chemicals Ltd. 08/01/68 which merged into Witco Chemical Corp. 08/31/1979 which name changed to Witco Corp. 10/01/1985 which merged into CK Witco Corp. 09/01/1999 which name changed to Crompton Corp. 04/27/2000 which name changed to Chemtura Corp. 07/01/2005
(See Chemtura Corp.)

SURREY BK & TR (MT AIRY, NC)
Stock Dividends - 20% payable 02/26/1999 to holders of record 02/01/1999; 20% payable 03/15/2000 to holders of record 02/15/2000; 10% payable 01/31/2002 to holders of record 12/31/2001 Ex date - 12/27/2001
Under plan of reorganization each share Common no par automatically became (1) share Surrey Bancorp Common no par 05/01/2003

SURREY CAP CORP (ON)
Name changed to Subscribe Technologies Inc. 01/11/2017

SURREY INC (TX)
Reincorporated under the laws of Wyoming as Payless Communication Holdings, Inc. 04/15/2005
Payless Communication Holdings, Inc. recapitalized as Integrated Telecom, Inc. 11/10/2005 which name changed to Payless Telecom Solutions, Inc. 12/01/2005 which name changed to WOW Holdings, Inc. 04/14/2008
(See WOW Holdings, Inc.)

SURREY METRO SVGS CR UN (BC)
Non-Vtg. Shares 1¢ par split (2) for (1) by issuance of (1) additional share 05/02/1994
Merged into Coast Capital Savings Credit Union 06/27/2002
Each Non-Vtg. Share 1¢ par exchanged for $21 cash

SURREY OIL & GAS CORP. (DE)
Merged into Tex-Star Oil & Gas Corp. 06/15/1960
Each share Common $1 par exchanged for (0.2) share Common $1 par
Tex-Star Oil & Gas Corp. name changed to Texas Oil & Gas Corp. 12/21/1964 which merged into United States Steel Corp. (Old) 02/11/1986 which name changed to USX Corp. 07/08/1986 which reorganized as USA-Marathon

SUR-SUT

Group Inc. 05/06/1991 which name changed to Marathon Oil Corp. 12/31/2001

SURVEYOR COS INC (DE)
Name changed to Forum Companies, Inc. 09/23/1974
(See Forum Companies, Inc.)

SURVEYOR FD INC (DE)
Each share Common 10¢ par exchanged for (0.25) share Common 40¢ par 05/01/1972
Merged into Surveyor Fund, Inc. (MD) 09/10/1973
Each share Common 40¢ par exchanged for (2.34) shares Common $1 par
Surveyor Fund, Inc. (MD) name changed to Alliance Global Small Capital Fund, Inc. 09/17/1990 which name changed to AllianceBernstein Global Small Capital Fund, Inc. 03/31/2003
(See AllianceBernstein Global Small Capital Fund, Inc.)

SURVEYOR FD INC (MD)
Name changed to Alliance Global Small Capital Fund, Inc. and Common $1 par reclassified as Class A $1 par 09/17/1990
Alliance Global Small Capital Fund, Inc. name changed to AllianceBernstein Global Small Capital Fund, Inc. 03/31/2003
(See AllianceBernstein Global Small Capital Fund, Inc.)

SURVEYOR INDS INC (CA)
Charter cancelled for failure to file reports and pay taxes 01/02/1992

SURVIV-ALL, INC. (NY)
Charter cancelled and proclaimed dissolved for failure to pay taxes 12/15/1965

SURVIVAL TECHNOLOGY INC (DE)
Name changed to Meridian Medical Technologies, Inc. 11/21/1996
(See Meridian Medical Technologies, Inc.)

SURVIVORS BENEFIT INS CO (MO)
Common $1.25 par changed to $2.40 par 12/07/1979
Each (2,500) shares Common $2.40 par exchanged for (1) share Common $6,000 par 11/30/1980
Note: In effect holders received $6.61 cash per share and public interest was eliminated

SUSA CORP (CO)
Charter suspended for failure to file annual reports 08/01/1991

SUSAN THOMAS INC (NY)
Completely liquidated 09/23/1968
Each share Common $1 par exchanged for first and final distribution of (0.25) share Genesco Inc. $2.40 Preferred Ser. 2 no par and (0.3) share Common $1 par

SUSHEE INC (DE)
Name changed to VidShadow, Inc. 04/10/2008
VidShadow, Inc. recapitalized as OneScreen Inc. 03/06/2009

SUSIE GOLD MINES LTD (BC)
Name changed to Suzie Mining Explorations Ltd. 11/02/1988
(See Suzie Mining Explorations Ltd.)

SUSQUEHANNA BANCSHARES INC (PA)
Common $5 par changed to $2 par and (2) additional shares issued 07/18/1986
Common $2 par split (5) for (4) by issuance of (0.25) additional share 08/27/1993
$1.80 Conv. Preferred Ser. A no par called for redemption 02/07/1994
Common $2 par split (3) for (2) by issuance of (0.5) additional share payable 07/02/1997 to holders of record 06/10/1997
Common $2 par split (3) for (2) by issuance of (0.5) additional share payable 07/01/1998 to holders of record 06/15/1998
Merged into BB&T Corp. 08/01/2015
Each share Common $2 par exchanged for (0.253) share Common $5 par and $4.05 cash

SUSQUEHANNA CAP I (DE)
9.375% Capital Securities called for redemption at $25 on 09/18/2012

SUSQUEHANNA CORP (DE)
Capital Stock $1 par split (2) for (1) by issuance of (1) additional share 09/28/1959
Capital Stock $1 par reclassified as Common $1 par 04/21/1967
Each share Class A Conv. Preferred $5 par exchanged for (2.46) shares Common $1 par 09/16/1983
Stock Dividend - 100% 07/30/1956
Acquired by S.A. Financiere Eternit 02/18/1988
Each share Common $1 par exchanged for $5.85 cash

SUSQUEHANNA MILLS, INC. (NY)
Each share Common 50¢ par exchanged for (2) shares Common 25¢ par 00/00/1946
Merged into H & B American Machine Co., Inc. 03/31/1954
Each share Common 25¢ par exchanged for (1) share Common 10¢ par
H & B American Machine Co., Inc. name changed to H & B American Corp. 07/23/1959 which merged into Teleprompter Corp. 09/17/1970
(See Teleprompter Corp.)

SUSQUEHANNA SILK MILLS
Dissolved 00/00/1941
Details not available

SUSQUEHANNA VALLEY BK & TR CO (SUNBURY, PA)
Merged into Northern Central Bank & Trust Co. (Williamsport, PA) 05/06/1974
Each share Capital Stock $10 par exchanged for (0.55) share Common $10 par
Northern Central Bank & Trust Co. (Williamsport, PA) name changed to Northern Central Bank (Williamsport, PA) 07/01/1975 which merged into NCB Financial Corp. 07/29/1983 which merged into Keystone Financial, Inc. 12/31/1984 which merged into M&T Bank Corp. 10/06/2000

SUSSER HLDGS CORP (DE)
Merged into Energy Transfer Partners, L.P. (Old) 08/29/2014
Each share Common 1¢ par exchanged for (0.7253) Common Unit and $40.125 cash
Energy Transfer Partners, L.P. (Old) merged into Energy Transfer Partners, L.P. (New) 05/01/2017 which merged into Energy Transfer L.P. 10/19/2018

SUSSER PETE PARTNERS LP (DE)
Name changed to Sunoco L.P. 10/27/2014

SUSSEX & MERCHANTS NATL BK (NEWTON, NJ)
Common $25 par changed to $10 par and (1.5) additional shares issued plus a 33-1/3% stock dividend paid 04/01/1968
Stock Dividends - 50% 00/00/1947; 25% 00/00/1949
Reorganized as Midlantic Banks Inc. 06/12/1970
Each share Common $10 par exchanged for (1.25) shares Common $10 par
Midlantic Banks Inc. merged into Midlantic Corp. 01/30/1987 which merged into PNC Bank Corp. 12/31/1995 which name changed to PNC Financial Services Group, Inc. 03/15/2000

SUSSEX BANCORP (NJ)
Common no par split (2) for (1) by issuance of (1) additional share payable 08/03/1998 to holders of record 07/03/1998 Ex date - 08/04/1998
Stock Dividends - 5% payable 07/28/2000 to holders of record 07/05/2000 Ex date - 06/30/2000; 5% payable 11/24/2003 to holders of record 11/03/2003 Ex date - 10/30/2003; 5% payable 11/29/2005 to holders of record 11/03/2005 Ex date - 11/01/2005; 6.5% payable 11/12/2008 to holders of record 10/29/2008 Ex date - 10/27/2008
Name changed to SB One Bancorp 05/02/2018

SUSSEX CNTY ST BK (FRANKLIN, NJ)
Common $5 par changed to $2.50 par and (1) additional share issued 08/01/1991
Stock Dividend - 3% payable 05/01/1996 to holders of record 04/01/1996
Under plan of reorganization each share Common $2.50 par automatically became (1) share Sussex Bancorp Common no par 11/20/1996
Sussex Bancorp name changed to SB One Bancorp 05/02/2018

SUSSEX EXPLS LTD (ON)
Recapitalized as Print Three Express International Inc. 06/30/1993
Each share Common no par exchanged for (0.25) share Common no par
Print Three Express International Inc. recapitalized as Le Print Express International Inc. 12/15/1993
(See Le Print Express International Inc.)

SUSSEX FIRE INSURANCE CO. (NJ)
Acquired by Eagle Fire Insurance Co. 09/29/1939
Details not available

SUSSEX RAILROAD CO.
Merged into Delaware, Lackawanna & Western Railroad Co. 00/00/1946
Each share exchanged for $12 cash

SUSSEX TR CO (LAUREL, DE)
Common $10 par changed to $5 par and (1) additional share issued 01/02/1985
Stock Dividends - 100% 12/30/1977; 100% 12/31/1981
Merged into Wilmington Trust Corp. 01/29/1992
Each share Common $5 par exchanged for (0.8) share Common 1¢ par
Wilmington Trust Corp. merged into M&T Bank Corp. 05/16/2011

SUSSEX VENTURES LTD (CO)
Reincorporated under the laws of Nevada as AgriBioTech, Inc. 06/29/1994
(See AgriBioTech, Inc.)

SUSSMAN PROPERTIES LTD. (ON)
Name changed to Corporate Properties Ltd. 05/31/1971
Corporate Properties Ltd. name changed to Seamiles Ltd. 11/29/2006 which name changed to Intellectual Capital Group Ltd. 04/03/2012

SUSSMAN REALTY CORP. LTD. (ON)
Recapitalized as Sussman Properties Ltd. 09/30/1968
Each share Common no par exchanged for (0.25) share Common no par
Sussman Properties Ltd. name changed to Corporate Properties Ltd. 05/31/1971 which name changed to Seamiles Ltd. 11/29/2006 which name changed to Intellectual Capital Group Ltd. 04/03/2012

SUSTAINABLE DEV INTL INC (NV)
Name changed to Clean Energy Inc. 09/19/2002
(See Clean Energy Inc.)

SUSTAINABLE ENERGY DEV INC (DE)
Recapitalized as United States Oil & Gas Corp. 04/17/2008
Each (30) shares Common $0.0001 par exchanged for (1) share Common $0.0001 par

SUSTAINABLE ENERGY TECHNOLOGIES LTD (AB)
Each share old Common no par exchanged for (0.1) share new Common no par 12/27/2012
Name changed to Eguana Technologies Inc. 11/18/2013

SUSTAINABLE ENVIRONMENTAL TECHNOLOGIES CORP (CA)
Each share old Common $0.001 par exchanged for (0.06666666) share new Common $0.001 par 01/25/2012
Acquired by HJG Holdings, LLC 12/11/2013
Each share Common $0.001 par exchanged for $0.11 cash

SUSTAINABLE PETE GROUP INC (NV)
Name changed to Sustainable Projects Group Inc. 10/26/2017

SUSTAINABLE PWR CORP (NV)
SEC revoked common stock registration 05/22/2014

SUSTAINABLE PRODTN ENERGY TR (AB)
Merged into Energy Income Fund 10/04/2010
Each Trust Unit no par automatically became (1) Trust Unit no par

SUSTUT EXPL INC (DE)
Each share old Common $0.001 par exchanged for (0.99026242) share new Common $0.001 par 05/02/2008
New Common $0.001 par split (5) for (2) by issuance of (1.5) additional shares payable 03/12/2009 to holders of record 03/12/2009 Ex date - 03/13/2009
Name changed to Optex Systems Holdings, Inc. 05/01/2009

SUTCLIFFE CO. (KY)
Acquired by Davidson Supply Co. 12/31/1968
Details not available

SUTCLIFFE RES LTD (AB)
Name changed to Zoloto Resources Ltd. 07/05/2007

SUTHERLAND ASSET MGMT CORP (MD)
Name changed to Ready Capital Corp. 10/01/2018

SUTHERLAND PAPER CO. (MI)
Each share Common $10 par exchanged for (2) shares Common $5 par 06/08/1951
Merged into KVP Sutherland Paper Co. 01/04/1960
Each share Common $5 par exchanged for (1) share Common $5 par
KVP Sutherland Paper Co. merged into Brown Co. (DE) 05/12/1966
(See Brown Co. (DE))

SUTHERLAND PPTYS INC (TX)
Company became private 00/00/1985
Details not available

SUTHERLAND RES LTD (BC)
Recapitalized as Suntec Ventures Ltd. (Old) 09/05/1985
Each share Common no par exchanged for (0.25) share Common no par

Suntec Ventures Ltd. (Old) merged into Suntec Ventures Ltd. (New) 01/30/1986 which recapitalized as Consolidated Suntec Ventures Ltd. 05/19/1987 which name changed to Vortex Energy Systems Inc. 10/03/1990 which recapitalized as Autumn Industries Inc. 09/16/1994 which name changed to Altex Power Corp. 03/07/2001

SUTHERLAND URANIUM MINING CO. (CO)
Charter dissolved for failure to file annual reports 01/01/1982

SUTRO MTG INVT TR (CA)
Shares of Bene. Int. $1 par reclassified as Common $1 par 06/28/1977
Stock Dividend - 500% 03/31/1969
Acquired by PNB Mortgage & Realty Investors 11/01/1979
Each share Common $1 par exchanged for (1) Share of Bene. Int. $1 par
PNB Mortgage & Realty Investors name changed to Mortgage & Realty Trust 12/17/1984 which name changed to Value Property Trust 10/27/1995 which merged into Wellsford Real Properties, Inc. 02/23/1998 which name changed to Reis, Inc. 06/01/2007
(See Reis, Inc.)

SUTRON CORP (VA)
Acquired by Danaher Corp. 07/28/2015
Each share Common 1¢ par exchanged for $8.50 cash

SUTTER BASIN CO.
Acquired by Sutter Basin Corp. 00/00/1928
Details not available

SUTTER BASIN CORP (DE)
Voting Trust Agreement terminated 00/00/1958
Each VTC for Capital Stock no par exchanged for (1) share Capital Stock no par
72% held by Sutter Land Sales Co. as of 01/00/1983
Public interest eliminated

SUTTER BUTTE CANAL CO. (CA)
Dissolved 00/00/1957
Details not available

SUTTER BUTTES LAND CO. (CA)
Liquidation completed 11/06/1964
Details not available

SUTTER BUTTES SVGS & LN ASSN (CA)
Merged into TriCo Bancshares 10/16/1996
Each share Common $10 par exchanged for (0.16791325) shares Common $5 par

SUTTER HLDG INC (DE)
Each share old Common $0.0001 par exchanged for (0.05) share new Common $0.0001 par 06/13/2002
Name changed to CIC Holding Co., Inc. 12/06/2006
CIC Holding Co., Inc. recapitalized as Global Wear Ltd. 01/10/2008 which recapitalized as Sovereign Wealth Corp. 03/12/2008 which name changed to Lenco Mobile Inc. 02/25/2009
(See Lenco Mobile Inc.)

SUTTON CORP (DE)
Charter cancelled and declared inoperative and void for non-payment of taxes 03/01/1976

SUTTON (O.A.) CORP., INC. (KS)
Merged into Vornado, Inc. (KS) on a (0.02) for (1) basis 11/5/59
Vornado, Inc. (KS) reincorporated in Delaware 6/30/65 which reincorporated as Vornado Realty Trust (MD) 5/6/93

SUTTON ENGINEERING CO. (PA)
Merged into SMS Demag Inc. 07/06/1979
Details not available

SUTTON GROUP RLTY SVCS LTD (CANADA)
Reorganized 01/24/1992
Reorganized from Sutton Group Realty Services Ltd. to Sutton Group Financial Services Ltd. 01/24/1992
Each share old Common no par exchanged for (2) shares new Common no par
New Common no par split (2) for (1) by issuance of (1) additional share 10/08/1993
Merged into SGFS Acquisition Inc. 02/19/2004
Each share new Common no par exchanged for $0.15 cash

SUTTON-HORSLEY CO. LTD.
Liquidated 00/00/1944
Details not available

SUTTON INDUSTRIES, INC. (NY)
Reorganized under the laws of Delaware as ABG Industries, Inc. 09/16/1968
Each share Common 25¢ par exchanged for (1) share Common 1¢ par
(See ABG Industries, Inc.)

SUTTON LEASING CORP. (NY)
Name changed to Sutton Industries, Inc. (NY) 11/06/1961
Sutton Industries, Inc. (NY) reorganized in Delaware as ABG Industries, Inc. 09/16/1968
(See ABG Industries, Inc.)

SUTTON RES LTD (BC)
Each share old Common no par exchanged for (2) shares new Common no par 04/30/1997
Merged into Barrick Gold Corp. 06/07/1999
Each share new Common no par exchanged for (0.463) share Common no par

SUTTON TRADING SOLUTIONS INC (NV)
Recapitalized as Global Diversified Acquisition Corp. 04/24/2003
Each share Common $0.001 par exchanged for (0.0025) share Common $0.001 par
Global Diversified Acquisition Corp. name changed to Mailkey Corp. 04/13/2004 which name changed to IElement Corp. 08/25/2005
(See IElement Corp.)

SUVAL INDS INC (NY)
Completely liquidated 03/12/1969
Each share Common 50¢ par exchanged for first and final distribution of (0.412) share Whittaker Corp. (CA) Common $1 par
Whittaker Corp. (CA) reincorporated in Delaware 06/16/1986
(See Whittaker Corp. (DE))

SUWINCO, INC. (FL)
Assets sold for the benefit of stockholders and company voluntarily dissolved 12/14/1984
Details not available

SUZANO BAHIA SUL PAPEL E CELULOSE S A (BRAZIL)
Name changed to Suzano Papel e Celulose S.A. 08/04/2006

SUZANO PETROQUIMICA S A (BRAZIL)
Acquired by Dapean Participacoes S.A. 06/11/2008
Each Sponsored ADR for Preferred exchanged for $69.59119 cash

SUZIE MNG EXPLS LTD (BC)
Delisted from Vancouver Stock Exchange 11/02/1988

SUZY SHIER LTD (CANADA)
Name changed to La Senza Corp. 07/20/2001
(See La Senza Corp.)

SVB CAP I (DE)
8.25% Trust Preferred Securities called for redemption at $25 on 12/01/2003

SVB CAP II (DE)
7% Trust Preferred Securities called for redemption at $25 plus $0.320833 accrued dividends on 12/21/2017

SVB FINL SVCS INC (NJ)
Stock Dividends - 5% payable 11/19/1999 to holders of record 11/04/1999; 5% payable 11/21/2000 to holders of record 11/07/2000 Ex date - 11/03/2000; 5% payable 11/20/2001 to holders of record 11/06/2001 Ex date - 11/02/2001; 5% payable 11/29/2002 to holders of record 11/14/2002 Ex date - 11/12/2002; 5% payable 12/03/2003 to holders of record 11/17/2003 Ex date - 11/13/2003; 5% payable 12/01/2004 to holders of record 11/15/2004
Merged into Fulton Financial Corp. 07/01/2005
Each share Common no par exchanged for (1.1899) shares Common $2.50 par

SVEDALA INDUSTRI AB (SWEDEN)
Acquired by Metso Corp. 09/29/2001
Details not available

SVENSKA CELLULOSA AKTIEBOLAGET SCA (SWEDEN)
Each ADR for Non-Restricted B, Skr.25 par exchanged for (1.5) ADR's for Non-Restricted B, Skr.10 par 07/03/1989
ADR agreement terminated 06/30/1990
Details not available
(Additional Information in Active)

SVH LIQUIDATING CORP. (CA)
Liquidated 08/14/1964
Each share Common $1 par exchanged for (0.2) share Occidental Petroleum Corp. (CA) Capital Stock 20¢ par and $0.05 cash
Occidental Petroleum Corp. (CA) reincorporated in Delaware 05/21/1986

SVI MEDIA INC (NV)
Chapter 11 bankruptcy proceedings converted to Chapter 7 on 06/16/2008
No stockholders' equity

SVI SOLUTIONS INC (DE)
Reincorporated 03/26/2001
Reincorporated from SVI Holdings, Inc. (NV) to SVI Solutions Inc. (DE) 03/26/2001
Name changed to Island Pacific Inc. 07/11/2003
Island Pacific Inc. name changed to Retail Pro, Inc. 01/29/2008
(See Retail Pro, Inc.)

SVIT GOLD CORP (BC)
Name changed to Catalyst Copper Corp. 02/02/2010
Catalyst Copper Corp. merged into NewCastle Gold Ltd. 05/27/2016 which merged into Equinox Gold Corp. 12/22/2017

SVL HOLDINGS LTD. (ON)
Each share old Common no par exchanged for (0.0005) share new Common no par 02/14/2011
Note: In effect holders received $11 cash per share and public interest was eliminated

SVT CAP CORP (BC)
Name changed to Delta 9 Cannabis Inc. 11/06/2017

SVT INC (DE)
SEC revoked common stock registration 03/06/2007

SW CAP CORP (NV)
Completely liquidated 08/14/1989
Each share Common $0.001 par received first and final distribution of $0.00925 cash

SW CHINA IMPORTS INC (NV)
Name changed to Med-Cannabis Pharma, Inc. 07/01/2014
Med-Cannabis Pharma, Inc. name changed to Mansfield-Martin Exploration Mining, Inc. 03/14/2017

SW INC (IN)
Administratively dissolved 02/13/1991

SW VENTURES INC (NV)
Reorganized under the laws of Delaware as New Generation Plastic, Inc. 06/11/1899
Each share Common $0.001 par exchanged for (0.06666666) share Common $0.001 par
New Generation Plastic, Inc. name changed to New Generation Holdings, Inc. 08/08/2000
(See New Generation Holdings, Inc.)

SWAB FOX COS INC (NM)
Name changed to Tribune/Swab Fox Companies, Inc. 10/01/1984
(See Tribune/Swab Fox Companies, Inc.)

SWABETTES INC (NJ)
Acquired by Becton, Dickenson & Co. 07/14/1972
Each share Common 10¢ par exchanged for (0.031552) share Common $1 par

SWAIN (R.L.) TOBACCO CO., INC.
Declared bankrupt 00/00/1947
No stockholders' equity

SWALLOW MINING CORP. (NV)
Charter revoked 03/02/1964

SWAN APARTMENT BUILDING LIQUIDATION TRUST
Liquidated 00/00/1952
Details not available

SWAN FINCH OIL CORP (NY)
7% Preferred $25 par reclassified as 6% Preferred $25 par 00/00/1935
Common $25 par changed to $15 par 00/00/1935
Each share Common $15 par exchanged for (3) shares Common $5 par 09/15/1955
Liquidation completed
Each share 4% Conv. 2nd Preferred $10 par exchanged for first and final distribution of $14.18 cash 06/15/1968
Each share 6% Preferred $25 par exchanged for first and final distribution of $40.70 cash 06/15/1968
Each share Common $5 par exchanged for initial distribution of $0.25 cash 06/15/1968
Each share Common $5 par received second distribution of $0.20 cash 05/25/1970
Each share Common $5 par received third and final distribution of $0.20 cash 09/09/1974
Note: Unexchanged certificates were cancelled and became without value 11/01/1973

SWAN HILLS ENERGY LTD PARTNERSHIP (AB)
Each old Limited Partnership Unit no par exchanged for (0.000001) new Limited Partnership Unit no par 06/02/2010
Note: In effect holders received $1.80 cash per Unit and public interest was eliminated

SWAN RES LTD (AUSTRALIA)
Reorganized as Rhodes Mining N.L. 10/27/1993
Each Unsponsored ADR for Ordinary

exchanged for (1) Sponsored ADR for Ordinary

SWAN RUBBER CO. (OH)
Stock Dividend - 300% 07/25/1951
Assets acquired by Amerace Corp. 05/19/1961
Details not available

SWAN RYAN INTL LTD (ENGLAND)
Name changed to Ryan Hotels PLC 00/00/1980
Ryan Hotels PLC name changed to Gresham Hotel Group PLC 04/18/2001
(See Gresham Hotel Group PLC)

SWAN VY SNOWMOBILES INC (NV)
Recapitalized as Nettaxi, Inc. 09/30/1998
Each share Common $0.001 par exchanged for (0.660066) share Common $0.001 par
Nettaxi, Inc. name changed to Nettaxi.com 11/09/1999 which reorganized in Delaware as RAE Systems Inc. 04/09/2002
(See RAE Systems Inc.)

SWANEE PAPER CORP (DE)
Stock Dividend - 50% 08/06/1962
Merged into Potlatch Forests, Inc. (DE) 12/23/1968
Each share Common $1 par exchanged for (0.44) share Common $1 par
Potlatch Forests, Inc. (DE) name changed to Potlatch Corp. (Old) 04/27/1973 which reorganized as Potlatch Corp. (New) 02/03/2006 which name changed to PotlatchDeltic Corp. 02/23/2018

SWANK INC (DE)
Old Common $1 par split (2) for (1) by issuance of (1) additional share 07/15/1961
Old Common $1 par split (2) for (1) by issuance of (1) additional share 05/01/1965
Plan of recapitalization effective 02/29/1988
Each share Common $1 par exchanged for (1) share old Common 10¢ par and $17 cash
Each share old Common 10¢ par received additional distribution of $1.10 cash 07/19/1988
Each share old Common 10¢ par exchanged for (0.33333333) share new Common 10¢ par 08/04/2000
Acquired by Randa Accessories Leather Goods L.L.C. 05/18/2012
Each share new Common 10¢ par exchanged for $10 cash

SWANN CORP.
Acquired by Monsanto Chemical Co. 00/00/1935
Details not available
(See Monsanto Chemical Co.)

SWANNELL MINERALS CORP (BC)
Recapitalized as Globenet Resources Inc. 04/01/1997
Each share Common no par exchanged for (0.1) share Common no par
Globenet Resources Inc. name changed to Terra Nova Gold Corp. 01/28/2003 which name changed to Terra Nova Minerals Inc. (BC) 02/19/2008 which reincorporated in Canada 02/05/2009 which reincorporated in Alberta as Terra Nova Energy Ltd. 08/21/2012 which reincorporated in British Columbia 10/31/2016 which recapitalized as Claren Energy Ltd. 11/14/2016

SWANSEA CONS MNG CO (UT)
Merged into North Lily Mining Co. 12/01/1976
Each share Common 10¢ par exchanged for (0.047) share Capital Stock 10¢ par
(See North Lily Mining Co.)

SWANSON MINES LTD. (QC)
Assets acquired by Gibson Mines Ltd. 00/00/1958
Each share Common exchanged for (0.5) share Common
(See Gibson Mines Ltd.)

SWANTON (NORMAN F.) ASSOCIATES, INC. (DE)
Stock Dividend - 10% 09/16/1975
Name changed to Swanton Corp. 08/09/1976
(See Swanton Corp.)

SWANTON CORP (DE)
Common 10¢ par split (2) for (1) by issuance of (1) additional share 07/01/1983
Stock Dividends - 10% 11/16/1979; 10% 06/02/1980; 25% 07/01/1981
Charter cancelled and declared inoperative and void for non-payment of taxes 06/24/1992

SWAP-A-DEBT INC (DE)
Name changed to WikiLoan Inc. 06/26/2009
WikiLoan Inc. name changed to Wiki Group, Inc. 03/26/2012 which recapitalized as Source Financial, Inc. 03/21/2013 which name changed to Alltemp, Inc. 04/27/2017

SWARTWOUT CO. (OH)
Common no par changed to $1 par 03/25/1957
Name changed to DKS Co. which liquidated 11/30/1960

SWAV ENTERPRISES LTD (NV)
Name changed to GBS Enterprises Inc. 09/07/2010
GBS Enterprises Inc. recapitalized as Marizyme, Inc. 07/27/2018

SWAY RES INC (BC)
Name changed to Orion International Minerals Corp. 01/26/1996
Orion International Minerals Corp. recapitalized as Laurier Resources, Inc. 05/04/1998 which name changed to Zarcan International Resources Inc. 11/08/1999 which name changed to Bighorn Petroleum Ltd. 01/30/2006 which recapitalized as Sunset Pacific Petroleum Ltd. 05/07/2009

SWB BANCSHARES INC (TX)
Each share 7% Ser. A Preferred $1 par exchanged for $1 cash 12/02/2002
Each share Common $1 par held by holders of (1,499) shares or fewer exchanged for $25 cash 12/02/2002
Acquired by First Texas BHC, Inc. 07/17/2007
Each share Common $1 par exchanged for $60 cash

SWEANY GOLD CORP (UT)
Involuntarily dissolved 05/01/1990

SWEAT-COMINGS CO. (VT)
Capital Stock $100 par changed to $1 par 01/30/1963
Preferred $4 par called for redemption 05/15/1974

SWEATER BEE BY BANFF LTD (NY)
Stock Dividend - 50% 10/09/1972
Merged into RAB Knits, Ltd. 04/20/1977
Each share Common 1¢ par exchanged for $2.75 cash

SWECO INC (CA)
Each VTC for Common $4 par exchanged for (1) share Common $4 par 09/23/1973
Merged into Emerson Electric Co. 03/23/1979
Each share Common $4 par exchanged for (13.119465) shares Common $1 par

SWEDESBORO TR CO (SWEDESBORO, NJ)
Common $50 par changed to $10 par and (4) additional shares issued 01/29/1973
Merged into Guarantee Bank (Atlantic City, NJ) 07/28/1978
Each share Common $10 par exchanged for (1.35) shares Capital Stock $1 par
Guarantee Bank (Atlantic City, NJ) reorganized as Guarantee Bancorp Inc. 01/02/1981 which merged into First Jersey National Corp. 01/17/1984
(See First Jersey National Corp.)

SWEDISH AMERICAN FILM CORP. (DE)
No longer in existence having become inoperative and void for non-payment of taxes 03/21/1923

SWEDISH MATCH AB (SWEDEN)
ADR agreement terminated 10/18/2004
Each Sponsored ADR for Ordinary exchanged for $120.2442 cash (Additional Information in Active)

SWEDISH MTRS CORP PUB LTD (THAILAND)
ADR agreement terminated 12/17/2012
No ADR's remain outstanding

SWEDISHVEGAS INC (DE)
Company terminated common stock registration and is no longer public as of 04/03/2008

SWEDLOW AEROPLASTICS CORP.
Acquired by Shellmar Products Corp. 00/00/1945
Details not available

SWEDLOW INC (CA)
Common $1 par split (3) for (2) by issuance of (0.5) additional share 08/06/1973
Under plan of partial liquidation each share old Common $1 par exchanged for (0.5) share new Common $1 par and $8 cash 02/02/1976
New Common $1 par split (3) for (2) by issuance of (0.5) additional share 12/10/1981
Acquired by Pilkington Brothers PLC 12/18/1986
Each share new Common $1 par exchanged for $32.60 cash

SWEENEY (B.K.) CO. (CO)
Name changed to Sweeney (B.K.) Manufacturing Co. 03/04/1964
(See Sweeney (B.K.) Manufacturing Co.)

SWEENEY (B.K.) MANUFACTURING CO. (CO)
Reverted to private company 01/00/1966
Details not available

SWEEPRITE MFG INC (SK)
Ceased operations 08/30/2005
Stockholders' equity unlikely

SWEET CORP., MINING & MILLING (UT)
Name changed to Ronden Food Systems, Inc. and Capital Stock $1 par changed to no par 6/25/69
(See Ronden Food Systems, Inc.)

SWEET CREAMS UNLIMITED INC (DE)
Recapitalized as U.S. Asset Corp. 05/21/1991
Each share Common $0.0025 par exchanged for (0.1) share Common $0.001 par
U.S. Asset Corp. name changed to Securitek International Corp. 07/02/1996
(See Securitek International Corp.)

SWEET GRASS OILS LTD. (ON)
Capital Stock no par changed to 25¢ par 12/00/1952
Recapitalized as Great Sweet Grass Oils Ltd. 04/22/1954
Each share Capital Stock 25¢ par exchanged for (0.2) share Capital Stock $1 par
Great Sweet Grass Oils Ltd. recapitalized as Kardar Canadian Oils Ltd. 06/29/1962
(See Kardar Canadian Oils Ltd.)

SWEET (ALFRED J.) INC.
Dissolved in 1932

SWEET LITTLE DEAL INC (MN)
Recapitalized as Physicians Insurance Services, Ltd. (MN) 03/26/1992
Each share Common no par exchanged for (0.1) share Common no par
Physicians Insurance Services, Ltd. (MN) reincorporated in Nevada as PI Services, Inc. 01/12/2009 which recapitalized as China Lithium Technologies, Inc. 07/23/2010
(See China Lithium Technologies, Inc.)

SWEET N LEGAL USA INC (OK)
Name changed to SWLG Corp. 3/1/83
(See SWLG Corp.)

SWEET OIL REFINING CO.
Acquired by Osceola Refining Co., Inc. 00/00/1943
Details not available

SWEET SPOT GAMES INC (NV)
Reorganized as Greenfield Farms Food, Inc. 04/04/2011
Each share Common $0.001 par exchanged for (40) shares Common $0.001 par

SWEET STUFF INC (NV)
Name changed to U.S. Network Funding Inc. 04/21/1994
U.S. Network Funding Inc. name changed to Apple Ventures Inc. 03/23/1995 which recapitalized as Kelcord International Inc. 10/26/1997
(See Kelcord International Inc.)

SWEET SUCCESS ENTERPRISES INC (NV)
Charter revoked for failure to file reports and pay fees 10/01/2008

SWEET URANIUM CORP. MINING & MILLING (UT)
Name changed to Sweet Corp., Mining & Milling 3/21/56
Sweet Corp., Mining & Milling name changed to Ronden Food Systems, Inc. 6/25/69
(See Ronden Food Systems, Inc.)

SWEET VICTORY INC (NY)
Dissolved by proclamation 3/24/93

SWEETBRIER CORP (NV)
Name changed to Dippy Foods Inc. 9/29/98

SWEETS & EATS INC (FL)
Common $0.001 par split (4) for (1) by issuance of (3) additional shares payable 05/01/2000 to holders of record 04/19/2000
Name changed to Safe Transportation Systems, Inc. 01/23/2001
(See Safe Transportation Systems, Inc.)

SWEETS & TREATS INC (DE)
Common $0.00001 par split (16) for (1) by issuance of (15) additional shares payable 04/22/2016 to holders of record 04/14/2016
Ex date - 04/25/2016
Name changed to Atlas Technology International, Inc. 11/16/2016

SWEETS CO. OF AMERICA, INC. (VA)
Capital Stock $50 par changed to $12.50 par 00/00/1941
Each share Capital Stock $12.50 par exchanged for (3) shares Capital Stock $4.16-2/3 par 00/00/1946
Capital Stock $4.16-2/3 par changed to Common $1.38-8/9 par and (2) additional shares issued 02/14/1962
Common $1.38-8/9 par changed to

69-4/9¢ par and (1) additional share issued 05/19/1964
Name changed to Tootsie Roll Industries, Inc. 05/02/1966

SWEETSKINZ HLDGS INC (DE)
Plan of reorganization under Chapter 11 Federal Bankruptcy Code effective 06/05/2007
No stockholders' equity

SWEETWATER INC (DE)
Name changed to SWWT Inc. 02/06/1998
SWWT Inc. recapitalized as SVT Inc. 02/06/2002
(See SVT Inc.)

SWEETWATER PETE CORP (BC)
Merged into Consolidated Ascot Petroleum Corp. 02/08/1982
Each share Common no par exchanged for (0.65) share Common no par
Consolidated Ascot Petroleum Corp. name changed to Ascot Investment Corp. 03/03/1987 which recapitalized as Pacific Western Investments Inc. 08/03/1990 which merged into Revenue Properties Co. Ltd. 01/01/1992 which merged into Morguard Corp. 12/01/2008

SWEETWATER RES INC (NV)
Common $0.001 par split (25) for (1) by issuance of (24) additional shares payable 07/19/2010 to holders of record 06/30/2010
Ex date - 07/20/2010
Name changed to Centaurus Diamond Technologies, Inc. 07/09/2012

SWEETWATER WATER CORP.
Name changed to California Water & Telephone Co. in 1935
(See California Water & Telephone Co.)

SWEITZER HLDGS INC (OH)
Merged into Phillips Group, Inc. 01/24/1983
Each share Common 66-2/3¢ par exchanged for $0.35 cash

SWENKO RESH & DEV INC (MN)
Common 10¢ par changed to 1¢ par and (4) additional shares issued 10/27/71
Involuntarily dissolved 10/4/91

SWENSENS INC (DE)
Merged into Steve's Homemade Ice Cream, Inc. 08/23/1988
Each (6) shares Common 10¢ par exchanged for (2) shares Class A Common 1¢ par and (1) Class B Common Stock Purchase Warrant expiring 08/23/1993
Steve's Homemade Ice Cream, Inc. name changed to Integrated Brands Inc. 08/08/1995 which merged into Yogen Fruz World-Wide Inc. 03/18/1998 which name changed to CoolBrands International Inc. (NS) 10/06/2000 which reincorporated in Canada 03/27/2006 which reorganized in Delaware as Swisher Hygiene Inc. 11/04/2010

SWEPCO CAP I (DE)
7.875% Trust Preferred Securities Ser. A called for redemption at $25 plus $0.169531 accrued dividend on 10/31/2003

SWI STEELWORKS INC (BC)
Delisted from Toronto Venture Stock Exchange 06/06/2004

SWIFT & CO (DE)
Reincorporated 03/14/1969
Each share Capital Stock $100 par exchanged for (4) shares Capital Stock $25 par 00/00/1930
Capital Stock $25 par changed to $12.50 par and (1) additional share issued 06/05/1967
State of incorporation changed from (IL) to (DE) and Capital Stock $12.50 par reclassified as Common $1 par 03/14/1969
Reorganized as Esmark, Inc. (Inc. 03/14/1969) 04/30/1973
Each share 4-3/4% Conv. Preferred Ser. A Class 1 $100 par exchanged for (1) share 4-3/4% Conv. Preferred Ser. A Class 1 $100 par
Each share Common $1 par exchanged for (1) share Common $1 par
(See Esmark, Inc. (Inc. 03/14/1969))

SWIFT BUSINESS MACHINES CORP. (DE)
Capital Stock $1 par changed to 1¢ par in 1941
No longer in existence having become inoperative and void for non-payment of taxes 4/1/63

SWIFT COPPER MINES LTD. (ON)
Charter dissolved 8/19/65

SWIFT ENERGY CO (DE)
Name changed to SilverBow Resources, Inc. 05/05/2017

SWIFT ENERGY CO (TX)
Stock Dividends - 10% 09/29/1994; 10% payable 10/23/1997 to holders of record 10/13/1997
Under plan of reorganization each share Common 1¢ par automatically became (0.00892078) share Swift Energy Co. (DE) Common 1¢ par, (0.04778898) Common Stock Purchase Warrant expiring 04/22/2019 and (0.04778898) Common Stock Purchase Warrant expiring 04/22/2020
Note: Holders of (56) or fewer shares are not entitled to stock; holders of (10) or fewer shares are not entitled to Warrants
Swift Energy Co. (DE) name changed to SilverBow Resources, Inc. 05/05/2017

SWIFT HOMES, INC. (PA)
Name changed to Swift Industries, Inc. 07/21/1965
(See Swift Industries, Inc.)

SWIFT INDPT CORP (DE)
Acquired by a partnership 02/27/1986
Each share Common 10¢ par exchanged for (1) share Swift Independent Packing Co. Exchangeable Preferred Ser. A 1¢ par and $21 cash
Swift Independent Packing Co. name changed to SIPCO, Inc. 10/25/1988
(See SIPCO, Inc.)

SWIFT INDPT PACKING CO (DE)
Name changed to SIPCO, Inc. 10/25/1988
(See SIPCO, Inc.)

SWIFT INDS INC (PA)
Chapter 11 bankruptcy proceedings closed 12/12/1977
No stockholders' equity

SWIFT MINERALS LTD (BC)
Merged into Agritek Bio Ingredients Corp. 12/23/1992
Each share Common no par exchanged for (0.5) share Common no par
Agritek Bio Ingredients Corp. name changed to Innovium Capital Corp. 12/15/1999 which name changed to Innovium Media Properties Corp. 09/24/2007

SWIFT PWR CORP (BC)
Acquired by Fort Chicago Energy Partners L.P. 08/26/2010
Each share Common no par exchanged for $0.35 cash

SWIFT RES INC (BC)
Each share old Common no par exchanged for (0.1) share new Common no par 10/22/2013
Name changed to Guyana Goldstrike Inc. 03/21/2017

SWIFT START CORP (DE)
Name changed to BioHiTech Global, Inc. 09/16/2015

SWIFT TRANSN CO (DE)
Merged into Knight-Swift Transportation Holdings Inc. 09/11/2017
Each share Class A Common 1¢ par exchanged for (0.72) share Class A Common 1¢ par

SWIFT TRANSN INC (NV)
Reincorporated 07/13/1993
State of incorporation changed from (DE) to (NV) 07/13/1993
Common $0.001 par split (3) for (2) by issuance of (0.5) additional share 11/18/1993
Common $0.001 par split (2) for (1) by issuance of (1) additional share 11/18/1994
Common $0.001 par split (3) for (2) by issuance of (0.5) additional share payable 03/12/1998 to holders of record 03/02/1998
Common $0.001 par split (3) for (2) by issuance of (0.5) additional share payable 04/10/1999 to holders of record 03/31/1999
Merged into Saint Corp. 05/10/2007
Each share Common $0.001 par exchanged for $31.55 cash

SWIFTKNOWLEDGE INC (MN)
Assets sold for the benefit of creditors 12/29/2008
No stockholders' equity

SWIFTYNET COM INC (FL)
Name changed 10/22/1999
Name changed from Swifty Carwash & Quick-Lube, Inc. to Swiftynet.com, Inc. 10/22/1999
Name changed to Yseek, Inc. 02/01/2001
Yseek, Inc. name changed to Advanced 3-D Ultrasound Services, Inc. 05/12/2003 which name changed to World Energy Solutions, Inc. 11/18/2005 which name changed to EClips Energy Technologies, Inc. (FL) 03/26/2009 which reincorporated in Delaware as EClips Media Technologies, Inc. 05/13/2010 which name changed to Silver Horn Mining Ltd. (DE) 04/27/2011 which reorganized in Nevada as Great West Resources, Inc. 04/21/2014 which name changed to Orbital Tracking Corp. 02/20/2015

SWIM LAKE MINES LTD (BC)
Capital Stock 50¢ par changed to no par 09/11/1974
Recapitalized as Karma Ventures Inc. 10/30/1978
Each share Capital Stock no par exchanged for (0.2) share Common no par
Karma Ventures Inc. name changed to Donner Resources Ltd. 12/21/1982
(See Donner Resources Ltd.)

SWIMMING POOL DEVELOPMENT CO., INC. (DE)
Name changed to Diverco Inc. 10/25/1963
(See Diverco Inc.)

SWINDBOURNE LEONARD SECOND ACQUISITION CORP (NY)
Recapitalized as Montt International Corp. 06/01/1999
Each share Common $0.0001 par exchanged for (0.01) share Common $0.001 par
(See Montt International Corp.)

SWING BIKE INC (UT)
Reorganized as Horizon Energy Corp. 12/24/79
Each share Common $0.002 par exchanged for (3) shares Common 1¢ par
Horizon Energy Corp. name changed to New Horizon Education, Inc.
6/1/93 which name changed to American Hospital Resources, Inc. 6/26/2002 which name changed to HAPS USA, Inc. 5/12/2005 which name changed to PGMI, Inc. 3/16/2006

SWING-N-SLIDE CORP (DE)
Name changed to Playcore, Inc. 4/28/98
(See Playcore, Inc.)

SWINGERS INTL INC (DE)
Reincorporated 8/30/70
State of incorporation changed from (WY) to (DE) and each share Common $1 par exchanged for (0.2) share Common 1¢ par 8/30/70
Charter cancelled and declared inoperative and void for non-payment of taxes 3/1/76

SWINGING PIG PRODUCTIONS INC (FL)
Name changed to Heavy Earth Resources, Inc. 10/17/2011

SWINGLES FURNITURE RENT INC (DE)
Charter forfeited for failure to maintain a registered agent 01/02/2005

SWINGLINE INC (NY)
Class A $1 par reclassified as Common $1 par 12/04/1964
Common $1 par split (2) for (1) by issuance of (1) additional share 01/17/1966
Common $1 par split (2) for (1) by issuance of (1) additional share 01/24/1968
Merged into American Brands, Inc. 09/01/1970
Each share Common $1 par exchanged for $35 cash

SWIRE PPTYS LTD (HONG KONG)
Merged into Swire Pacific Ltd. 07/07/1984
Each ADR for Ordinary HKD $1 par exchanged for (0.13) ADR for A Ordinary HKD $0.60 par and $0.41 cash
(Additional Information in Active)

SWISHER INTL GROUP INC (DE)
Merged into Sigi Acquisition Corp. 06/14/1999
Each share Class A Common 1¢ par exchanged for $9.50 cash

SWISHER INTL INC (NV)
Each share old Common $0.001 par exchanged for (0.33333333) share new Common $0.001 par 01/28/1993
Merged into HB Fairview Holdings LLC 03/16/2006
Each share new Common $0.001 par exchanged for $7 cash

SWISS ARMY BRANDS INC (DE)
Merged into Victorinox AG 08/28/2002
Each share Common 10¢ par exchanged for $9 cash

SWISS BK CORP (SWITZERLAND)
Each Sponsored ADR for Bearer SWF 100 par exchanged for (2) new Sponsored ADR's for Bearer SWF 50 par 05/13/1996
ADR agreement terminated 00/00/1998
Details not available

SWISS CDN RES INC (AB)
Name changed to Western Star Energy Corp. 08/20/1992
Western Star Energy Corp. recapitalized as Western Star Exploration Ltd. 08/30/1994 which merged into EnerMark Income Fund 01/25/2000 which merged into Enerplus Resources Fund 06/22/2001 which reorganized as Enerplus Corp. 01/03/2011

SWISS CHALET INC (PR)
Reorganized under Chapter 11 Federal Bankruptcy Code 06/14/1985

SWI-SYD   FINANCIAL INFORMATION, INC.

Each share 70¢ 1st Preferred $9 par exchanged for (18) shares Common no par
Each share 6% Conv. Preferred $20 par exchanged for (40) shares Common no par
Merged into SCI Acquisition Inc. 08/02/2000
Each share Common no par exchanged for $15.946433 cash

SWISS MEDICA INC (DE)
SEC revoked common stock registration 12/22/2011

SWISS OIL CORP. (KY)
Merged into Ashland Oil & Refining Co. on a share for share basis 10/31/36
Ashland Oil & Refining Co. name changed to Ashland Oil, Inc. 2/2/70 which name changed to Ashland Inc. (Old) 1/27/95
(See Ashland Inc. (Old))

SWISS REINS CO (SWITZERLAND)
ADR agreement terminated 03/21/2011
Each Sponsored ADR for Ordinary exchanged for $60.320495 cash

SWISS TECHNIQUE INC (NV)
Name changed to NuTek, Inc. 03/03/1995
NuTek, Inc. name changed to Datascension, Inc. 01/26/2004
(See Datascension, Inc.)

SWISS WTR DECAFFEINATED COFFEE INCOME FD (BC)
Under plan of reorganization each Trust Unit no par automatically became (1) share Ten Peaks Coffee Co. Inc. (Canada) Common no par 01/04/2011
Ten Peaks Coffee Co. Inc. name changed to Swiss Water Decaffeinated Coffee Inc. 10/22/2018

SWISSOIL CORP (NV)
Charter revoked for failure to file reports and pay fees 02/01/1985

SWISSRAY INTL INC (DE)
Reincorporated 07/11/2002
Each share old Common no par exchanged for (0.1) share new Common no par 10/01/1998
State of incorporation changed from (NY) to (DE) 07/11/2002
Each share new Common 1¢ par exchanged for (0.00133333) share Common $0.0001 par 12/01/2003
Under plan of merger each share Common $0.0001 par exchanged for $0.01 cash 04/12/2006

SWISSTRONICS INC (TX)
Name changed to Rimco Financial Corp. 02/20/1985
Rimco Financial Corp. name changed to Rimco Capital Corp. 04/12/1986

SWITCH & DATA FACS CO INC (DE)
Issue Information - 11,666,667 shares COM offered at $17 per share on 02/07/2007
Merged into Equinix, Inc. 04/30/2010
Each share Common $0.0001 par exchanged for (0.11321688) share Common $0.001 par and $7.94189104 cash

SWITCHBOARD INC (DE)
Merged into InfoSpace, Inc. 06/03/2004
Each share Common 1¢ par exchanged for $7.75 cash

SWITCHCO INC (DE)
Completely liquidated 8/14/91
Each share Common 1¢ par exchanged for first and final distribution of $0.42 cash 8/14/91

SWITSON INDS LTD (ON)
Merged into Regina Products Canada Ltd. 06/30/1966
Each share Common no par received (1) share 5% Preference $3 par

Note: Certificates were not required to be surrendered and are without value
(See Regina Products Canada Ltd.)

SWK ACQUISITION CORP (DE)
Name changed to Aerometals, Inc. 09/09/1989
(See Aerometals, Inc.)

SWLG CORP (OK)
Charter cancelled for failure to pay taxes 2/10/86

SWOPE ENTERPRISES, INC. (UT)
Name changed to Commedia Pictures Productions, Inc. 6/6/83
Each share Common $0.001 par exchanged for (1) share Common $0.001 par
(See Commedia Pictures Productions, Inc.)

SWORDFISH FINL INC (MN)
Each share Common 16¢ par exchanged for (10) shares Common $0.0001 par 06/13/2011
Recapitalized as SoOum, Corp. 10/01/2015
Each share Common $0.0001 par exchanged for (0.001) share Common $0.0001 par

SWS GROUP INC (DE)
Each share Common 10¢ par received distribution of (0.25) share Westwood Holdings Group, Inc. Common 1¢ par payable 06/28/2002 to holders of record 06/17/2002 Ex date - 07/01/2002
Common 10¢ par split (3) for (2) by issuance of (0.5) additional share payable 01/02/2007 to holders of record 12/15/2006 Ex date - 01/03/2007
Merged into Hilltop Holdings Inc. 01/01/2015
Each share Common 10¢ par exchanged for (0.2496) share Common 1¢ par and $1.94 cash

SWUNG INC (NV)
Recapitalized as American Capital Holdings 11/15/2002
Each share Common $0.001 par exchanged for (0.01) share Common $0.001 par
American Capital Holdings name changed to Symphony Investments, Inc. 05/09/2003 which name changed to International Pharmacy Outlets Inc. 09/29/2003 which name changed to Bionic Products, Inc. 12/11/2006 which recapitalized as Texas Oil & Minerals Inc. 02/01/2012

SWVA BANCSHARES INC (VA)
Merged into FNB Corp. 05/01/2001
Each share Common 10¢ par exchanged for either (1.1952) shares Common $5 par, $20.25 cash, or a combination thereof
Note: Option to receive stock and cash or cash only expired 05/09/2001
FNB Corp. merged into StellarOne Corp. 02/28/2008 which merged into Union First Market Bankshares Corp. 01/02/2014 which name changed to Union Bankshares Corp. 04/28/2014

SWWT INC (DE)
Recapitalized as SVT Inc. 02/06/2002
Each share Common $0.001 par exchanged for (0.5) share Common $0.001 par
(See SVT Inc.)

SXC HEALTH SOLUTIONS CORP (YT)
Common no par split (2) for (1) by issuance of (1) additional share payable 09/17/2010 to holders of record 09/14/2010 Ex date - 09/10/2010
Name changed to Catamaran Corp. 07/11/2012

(See Catamaran Corp.)

SXR URANIUM ONE INC (CANADA)
Name changed to Uranium One Inc. 06/18/2007
(See Uranium One Inc.)

SXT RES LTD (BC)
Struck off register and declared dissolved for failure to file reports 10/23/1992

SYBASE INC (DE)
Common $0.001 par split (2) for (1) by issuance of (1) additional share 11/19/1993
Merged into SAP AG 07/29/2010
Each share Common $0.001 par exchanged for $65 cash

SYBRA INC (DE)
Acquired by Valhi, Inc. 05/14/1990
Each share Common 10¢ par exchanged for (1.6) shares Common 1¢ par

SYBRON CHEMS INC (DE)
Name changed 01/29/1993
Name changed from Sybron Chemical Industries Inc. to Sybron Chemicals Inc. 01/29/1993
Merged into Bayer AG 10/23/2000
Each share Common 1¢ par exchanged for $35 cash

SYBRON CORP (NY)
Merged into SC Acquisition Corp. 05/06/1986
Each share $2.40 Conv. Preferred $4 par exchanged for $42 cash
Each share Common $2.50 par exchanged for $26.25 cash

SYBRON DENTAL SPECIALTIES INC (DE)
Merged into Danaher Corp. 05/19/2006
Each share Common 1¢ par exchanged for $47 cash

SYBRON INTL CORP (WI)
Reincorporated 1/31/94
Name changed 1/31/94
Reincorporated from Sybron Corp. (DE) to Sybron International Corp. (WI) 1/31/94
Common 1¢ par split (2) for (1) by issuance of (1) additional share 12/15/95
Common 1¢ par split (2) for (1) by issuance of (1) additional share payable 2/20/98 to holders of record 2/12/98
Each share Common 1¢ par received distribution of (1/3) share Sybron Dental Specialties, Inc. Common 1¢ par payable 12/11/2000 to holders of record 11/30/2000 Ex date - 12/12/2000
Name changed to Apogent Technologies, Inc. 12/12/2000
Apogent Technologies, Inc. merged into Fisher Scientific International Inc. 8/2/2004 which merged into Thermo Fisher Scientific Inc. 11/9/2006

SYCAMORE DEV GROUP INC (NV)
Name changed to ReBuilder Medical Technologies, Inc. 03/20/2007
ReBuilder Medical Technologies, Inc. name changed to Lion Gold Brazil, Inc. 08/23/2012 which recapitalized as Cannabiz Mobile, Inc. 06/24/2014

SYCAMORE NETWORKS INC (DE)
Old Common $0.001 par split (3) for (1) by issuance of (2) additional shares payable 02/11/2000 to holders of record 02/04/2000
Each share old Common $0.001 par exchanged for (0.1) share new Common $0.001 par 12/22/2009
Liquidation completed
Each share new Common $0.001 par received initial distribution of $0.24 cash payable 07/29/2014 to holders of record 07/18/2014 Ex date - 07/30/2014
Each share new Common $0.001 par

received second distribution of $0.29 cash payable 04/29/2016 to holders of record 04/22/2016 Ex date - 05/02/2016
Each share new Common $0.001 par received third and final distribution of $0.2261 cash payable 11/21/2016 to holders of record 11/12/2016 Ex date - 11/22/2016
Note: Certificates were not required to be surrendered and are without value

SYCO COMICS & DISTR INC (DE)
Name changed to Syconet.Com Inc. (DE) 02/17/1999
Syconet.Com Inc. (DE) reincorporated in Nevada 10/04/2002 which name changed to Point Group Holdings Inc. 12/06/2002 which name changed to GameZnFlix, Inc. 02/05/2004 which name changed to TBC Global News Network, Inc. 07/30/2009 which name changed to InCapta, Inc. 11/10/2015

SYCO INC (DE)
Reincorporated under the laws of Colorado as Marine Exploration, Inc. 05/11/2007
Marine Exploration, Inc. recapitalized as In Ovations Holdings Inc. 10/15/2013

SYCON CORP (ON)
Delisted from Canadian Dealer Network 12/31/2003

SYCON ENERGY CORP. (ON)
Name changed to Sycon Corp. 11/00/1987
(See Sycon Corp.)

SYCONET COM INC (NV)
Reincorporated 10/04/2002
State of incorporation changed from (DE) to (NV) and Common $0.0001 par changed to $0.001 par 10/04/2002
Name changed to Point Group Holdings Inc. 12/06/2002
Point Group Holdings Inc. name changed to GameZnFlix, Inc. 02/05/2004 which name changed to TBC Global News Network, Inc. 07/30/2009 which name changed to InCapta, Inc. 11/10/2015

SYCOR INC (DE)
Merged into Northern Telecom Ltd.-Northern Telecom Ltee. 05/26/1978
Each share Common 50¢ par exchanged for (0.9072) share Common no par
Northern Telecom Ltd.-Northern Telecom Ltee. name changed to Nortel Networks Corp. (Old) 04/30/1999 which reorganized as Nortel Networks Corp. (New) 05/01/2000
(See Nortel Networks Corp. (New))

SYDENHAM CAP INC (AB)
Merged into Learning Library Inc. 07/05/2002
Each share Common no par exchanged for (1) share Common no par
Learning Library Inc. recapitalized as Street Resources Inc. 01/05/2005 which name changed to EXMIN Resources Inc. 07/19/2005 which merged into Dia Bras Exploration Inc. 10/01/2009 which name changed to Sierra Metals Inc. 12/07/2012

SYDNEY DEV CORP (BC)
Reorganized under the laws of Canada as SDC Sydney Development Corp. 09/18/1986
Each share 9% Conv. Preference no par exchanged for (1) share 9% Conv. Preference no par
Each share Common no par exchanged for (0.2) share Common no par

(See SDC Sydney Development Corp.)

SYDNEY OIL LTD (AUSTRALIA)
Acquired by Command Petroleum 09/23/1988
Each ADR for Ordinary AUD $0.25 par exchanged for $0.214 cash

SYDNEY RES CORP (BC)
Merged into West Timmins Gold Corp. 09/18/2006
Each share Common no par exchanged for (1) share Common no par
West Timmins Gold Corp. merged into Lake Shore Gold Corp. 11/05/2009 which merged into Tahoe Resources Inc. 04/07/2016

SYDNOR BARENT SCANNER CORP (NM)
Charter revoked for failure to file reports and pay fees 01/23/2001

SYER CORP. (DE)
Charter cancelled and declared inoperative and void for non-payment of taxes 04/01/1935

SYH CORP (ON)
Recapitalized as Consolidated SYH Corp. 08/20/1990
Each share Common no par exchanged for (0.1) share Common no par
(See Consolidated SYH Corp.)

SYKES DATATRONICS INC (NY)
Common 10¢ par split (3) for (1) by issuance of (2) additional shares 06/19/1981
Stock Dividends - 50% 03/10/1980; 100% 11/14/1980
Dissolved by proclamation 01/25/2012

SYLOGIST INC (AB)
Recapitalized as Sylogist Ltd. 12/04/2002
Each share Common no par exchanged for (0.14285714) share Common no par

SYLRE LTD (AB)
Acquired by Northern Financial Corp. 01/17/2005
Each share Common no par exchanged for (8.8) shares Common no par and $0.17 cash
Northern Financial Corp. recapitalized as Added Capital Inc. 07/23/2014

SYLVAN INC (NV)
Reincorporated 07/01/1994
Name and state of incorporation changed from Sylvan Foods Holdings Inc. (DE) to Sylvan Inc. (NV) 07/01/1994
Merged into Snyder Associated Companies, Inc. 06/10/2004
Each share Common $0.001 par exchanged for $12.25 cash

SYLVAN LAKE TELEPHONE CO., INC. (NY)
Merged into Rochester Telephone Corp. 02/28/1974
Each share 5% Preferred $100 par exchanged for $100 cash
Each share Common no par exchanged for (2.2348) shares 5% Conv. Preferred $100 par
Rochester Telephone Corp. name changed to Frontier Corp. 01/01/1995 which merged into Global Crossing Ltd. 09/28/1999
(See Global Crossing Ltd.)

SYLVAN LEARNING CORP (WA)
Common 1¢ par split (2) for (1) by issuance of (1) additional share 01/31/1986
Merged into Kinder-Care, Inc. 02/08/1988
Each share Common 1¢ par exchanged for (1) share Common 50¢ par
Kinder-Care, Inc. name changed to Enstar Group, Inc. (DE) 11/06/1989
(See Enstar Group, Inc. (DE))

SYLVAN LEARNING SYS INC (MD)
Common 1¢ par split (3) for (2) by issuance of (0.5) additional share payable 11/07/1996 to holders of record 10/07/1996
Common 1¢ par split (3) for (2) by issuance of (0.5) additional share payable 05/22/1998 to holders of record 04/01/1998 Ex date - 05/26/1998
Name changed to Laureate Education, Inc. 05/17/2004
(See Laureate Education, Inc.)

SYLVAN LIFE INSURANCE CO. (UT)
Common $10 par changed to $5 par and (1) additional share issued 07/31/1961
Each share Common $5 par exchanged for (2.5) shares Common $2 par 11/30/1963
Merged into Bonneville-Sylvan Life Insurance Co. 04/01/1965
Each share Common $2 par exchanged for (1) share Capital Stock $2 par
Bonneville-Sylvan Life Insurance Co. reorganized as Bonneville Financial Corp., Inc. 12/01/1972 which merged into Professional Investors Corp. 03/31/1975 which name changed to Professional Investors Insurance Group, Inc. 03/11/1985
(See Professional Investors Insurance Group, Inc.)

SYLVANIA BANCORP INC (OH)
Acquired by Toledo Trustcorp, Inc. 12/31/1985
Each share Common $6.25 par exchanged for $30 cash

SYLVANIA ELEC PRODS INC (MA)
Common no par changed to $7.50 par 00/00/1951
Stock Dividend - 10% 12/18/1953
Merged into General Telephone & Electronics Corp. 03/05/1959
Each share $4 Preferred no par exchanged for (2) shares 4.36% Preferred $50 par
Each share Common $7.50 par exchanged for (1) share Common $10 par
General Telephone & Electronics Corp. name changed to GTE Corp. 07/01/1982 which merged into Verizon Communications Inc. 06/30/2000

SYLVANIA HOTEL (PA)
Reorganized 00/00/1947
No stockholders' equity

SYLVANIA INDUSTRIAL CORP.
Acquired by American Viscose Corp. 00/00/1946
Each share Common exchanged for (0.75) share Common $14 par
American Viscose Corp. name changed to A.V.C. Corp. 08/06/1963 which merged into Raybestos-Manhattan, Inc. (CT) 04/30/1981 which name changed to Raymark Corp. 06/28/1982 which reorganized in Delaware as Raytech Corp. 10/15/1986
(See Raytech Corp.)

SYLVANIA INSURANCE CO. OF PHILADELPHIA
Merged into Globe Insurance Co. of America 00/00/1930
Details not available

SYLVANIA SVGS BK (SYLVANIA, OH)
Each share Capital Stock $25 par exchanged for (4) shares Capital Stock $6.25 par 04/16/1974
Stock Dividends - 100% 00/00/1948; 10% 10/03/1955; 10% 03/01/1960; 10% 00/00/1963
Reorganized as Sylvania BanCorp, Inc. 02/01/1985
Each share Capital Stock $6.25 par exchanged for (1) share Common $6.25 par
(See Sylvania BanCorp, Inc.)

SYLVANITE GOLD MINES, LTD. (ON)
Capital Stock $1 par changed to 35¢ par 07/12/1960
Liquidation completed 11/27/1963
Details not available

SYLVERITE MINES LTD. (BC)
Acquired by Slocan Base Metals Ltd. and liquidated 00/00/1950
Details not available

SYM TEK SYS INC (CA)
Common no par split (3) for (1) by issuance of (2) additional shares 03/10/1980
Common no par split (2) for (1) by issuance of (1) additional share 05/23/1983
Plan of reorganization under Chapter 11 Federal Bankruptcy Code confirmed 08/29/1995
Stockholders' equity unlikely

SYMAX LIFT HLDG CO LTD (BC)
Reincorporated 10/05/2010
Place of incorporation changed from (AB) to (BC) 10/05/2010
Acquired by 1060719 B.C. Ltd. 04/05/2016
Each share Common no par exchanged for $0.25 cash
Note: Unexchanged certificates will be cancelled and become without value 04/05/2019

SYMBIAT INC (DE)
Filed a petition under Chapter 7 Federal Bankruptcy Code 03/29/2004
Stockholders' equity unlikely

SYMBID CORP (NV)
Recapitalized as Sincerity Applied Materials Holdings Corp. 06/14/2017
Each share Common $0.001 par exchanged for (0.01666666) share Common $0.001 par

SYMBIO CAP CORP (BC)
Name changed to Blackeagle Development Corp. 08/07/2014
Blackeagle Development Corp. name changed to EVI Global Group Developments Corp. 07/13/2016

SYMBION HEALTH LTD (AUSTRALIA)
Acquired by Primary Health Care Ltd. 04/28/2008
Each ADR for Ordinary exchanged for $19.26648 cash

SYMBION INC (DE)
Merged into Crestview Partners, L.P. 08/23/2007
Each share Common 1¢ par exchanged for $22.35 cash

SYMBION INC (UT)
Liquidation completed
Each share Common 1¢ par received initial distribution of $0.10 cash 02/28/1992
Each share Common 1¢ par received second and final distribution of $0.05 cash 10/24/1994

SYMBOL TECHNOLOGIES INC (DE)
Reincorporated 11/20/1987
State of incorporation changed from (NY) to (DE) 11/20/1987
Common 1¢ par split (2) for (1) by issuance of (1) additional share 05/31/1988
Common 1¢ par split (3) for (2) by issuance of (0.5) additional share payable 04/01/1997 to holders of record 03/10/1997 Ex date - 04/02/1997
Common 1¢ par split (3) for (2) by issuance of (0.5) additional share payable 04/03/1998 to holders of record 03/17/1998 Ex date - 04/06/1998
Common 1¢ par split (3) for (2) by issuance of (0.5) additional share payable 06/14/1999 to holders of record 06/01/1999 Ex date - 06/15/1999
Common 1¢ par split (3) for (2) by issuance of (0.5) additional share payable 04/05/2000 to holders of record 03/13/2000
Common 1¢ par split (3) for (2) by issuance of (0.5) additional share payable 04/16/2001 to holders of record 03/26/2001 Ex date - 04/17/2001
Merged into Motorola, Inc. 01/09/2007
Each share Common 1¢ par exchanged for $15 cash

SYMBOLIC DISPLAYS INC (NV)
Reorganized 03/23/1979
Each share Common 10¢ par exchanged for (1/6) share Common 60¢ par 02/14/1977
Reorganized from (CA) to under the laws of Nevada 03/23/1979
Each share Common 60¢ par exchanged for (1) share Common 60¢ par
Name changed to SDI Investors, Inc. 05/23/1980
(See SDI Investors, Inc.)

SYMBOLICS INC (DE)
Each share Common 1¢ par exchanged for (0.1) share Common 10¢ par 12/03/1990
Chapter 11 bankruptcy proceedings dismissed 05/07/1996
No stockholders' equity

SYMBOLLON PHARMACEUTICALS INC (DE)
Name changed 06/26/2001
Name changed from Symbollon Corp. to Symbollon Pharmaceuticals, Inc. 06/26/2001
SEC revoked common stock registration 08/26/2014

SYMC RES LTD (BC)
Recapitalized as G4G Resources Ltd. 10/15/2007
Each share Common no par exchanged for (0.5) share Common no par
G4G Resources Ltd. recapitalized as G4G Capital Corp. (BC) 01/23/2015 which reincorporated in Ontario as White Gold Corp. 12/23/2016

SYMES RES LTD (BC)
Struck off register and declared dissolved for failure to file returns 10/02/1992

SYMETRA FINL CORP (DE)
Acquired by Sumitomo Life Insurance Company of Japan 02/01/2016
Each share Common 1¢ par exchanged for $32 cash

SYMETRICS ENGR CORP (FL)
Name changed 02/23/1968
Name changed from Symetrics Engineering Corp. of Florida to Symetrics Engineering Corp. 02/23/1968
Name changed to Symetrics Industries, Inc. 07/07/1970
(See Symetrics Industries, Inc.)

SYMETRICS INDS INC (FL)
Common 25¢ par split (3) for (2) by issuance of (0.5) additional share 05/15/1995
Stock Dividend - 10% 04/30/1986
Merged into Tel-Save Holdings, Inc. 02/03/1998
Each share Common 25¢ par exchanged for $15 cash

SYMETRIX INC (DE)
Charter cancelled and declared inoperative and void for non-payment of taxes 04/15/1972

SYMINGTON CO.
Reorganized as Symington-Gould Corp. 00/00/1936
Each share Class A exchanged for (1.5) shares Common $1 par
Each share Common exchanged for (0.2) share Common $1 par
Symington-Gould Corp. name changed to Symington Wayne Corp. 03/12/1958 which merged into

Dresser Industries, Inc. (New) 04/30/1968 which merged into Halliburton Co. 09/29/1998

SYMINGTON-GOULD CORP. (MD)
Under plan of merger name changed to Symington Wayne Corp. 03/12/1958
Symington Wayne Corp. merged into Dresser Industries, Inc. (New) 04/30/1968 which merged into Halliburton Co. 09/29/1998

SYMINGTON WAYNE CORP (MD)
Merged into Dresser Industries, Inc. (New) 04/30/1968
Each share Common $1 par exchanged for (1.1) shares $2 Conv. Preferred Ser. B no par
Dresser Industries, Inc. (New) merged into Halliburton Co. 09/29/1998

SYMIX SYS INC (OH)
Common no par split (2) for (1) by issuance of (1) additional share payable 09/27/1996 to holders of record 09/10/1996
Name changed to Frontstep Inc. 11/10/2000
Frontstep Inc. merged into MAPICS, Inc. 02/19/2003
(See MAPICS, Inc.)

SYMMAR INC (DE)
Common 10¢ par changed to 1¢ par 09/26/1973
Name changed to Aspir-Air Inc. 05/23/1990
(See Aspir-Air Inc.)

SYMMETRICOM INC (DE)
Reincorporated 01/07/2002
Common no par split (3) for (2) by issuance of (0.5) additional share payable 08/18/2000 to holders of record 08/07/2000
State of incorporation changed from (CA) to (DE) and Common no par changed to $0.0001 par 01/07/2002
Acquired by Microsemi Corp. 11/26/2013
Each share Common $0.0001 par exchanged for $7.18 cash

SYMMETRY HLDGS INC (DE)
Name changed to Novamerican Steel Inc. 12/07/2007
Novamerican Steel Inc. name changed to Barzel Industries Inc. 02/13/2009
(See Barzel Industries Inc.)

SYMMETRY MED INC (DE)
Merged into Symmetry Surgical Inc. 12/05/2014
Each share Common $0.0001 par exchanged for (0.25) share Common $0.0001 par and $7.50 cash
(See Symmetry Surgical Inc.)

SYMMETRY RES INC (AB)
Merged into Berkley Petroleum Corp. 01/31/2000
Each share Common no par exchanged for (0.081) share Common no par
(See Berkley Petroleum Corp.)

SYMMETRY SURGICAL INC (DE)
Acquired by Symmetry Surgical Holdings, Inc. 07/01/2016
Each share Common $0.0001 par exchanged for $13.10 cash

SYMONS BROS & CO (MI)
Charter declared inoperative and void for failure to file reports 05/15/1984

SYMONS INTL GROUP INC (IN)
SEC revoked common stock registration 07/20/2010

SYMPHONIX DEVICES INC (DE)
Plan of liquidation approved 06/19/2003
Distribution information was provided only to holders of record 07/02/2003

SYMPHONY CAP CORP (AB)
Recapitalized as Kensbrook Development Corp. 09/23/1991

Each share Common no par exchanged for (0.33333333) share Common no par
(See Kensbrook Development Corp.)

SYMPHONY HLDG CO (UT)
Reorganized under the laws of Nevada as Symphony Ventures Inc. 03/23/1994
Each share Common $0.001 par exchanged for (0.02) share Common $0.001 par
Symphony Ventures Inc. recapitalized as Micro-ASI International Inc. 09/06/1996 which name changed to McHenry Metals Golf Corp. 04/01/1997

SYMPHONY INVTS INC (NV)
Each share old Common $0.001 par exchanged for (0.0004) share new Common $0.001 par 09/03/2003
Name changed to International Pharmacy Outlets Inc. 09/29/2003
International Pharmacy Outlets Inc. name changed to Bionic Products, Inc. 12/11/2006 which recapitalized as Texas Oil & Minerals Inc. 02/01/2012

SYMPHONY TELECOM CORP. (DE)
SEC revoked common stock registration 09/18/2008

SYMPHONY TELECOM INTL INC (UT)
Common $0.001 par split (3) for (2) by issuance of (0.5) additional share payable 04/01/2001 to holders of record 03/30/2001 Ex date - 04/02/2001
Reincorporated under the laws of Delaware as Symphony Telecom Corp. 07/18/2001
(See Symphony Telecom Corp.)

SYMPHONY VENTURES INC (NV)
Recapitalized as Micro-ASI International Inc. 09/06/1996
Each share Common $0.001 par exchanged for (0.1) share Common $0.001 par
Micro-ASI International Inc. name changed to McHenry Metals Golf Corp. 04/01/1997

SYMPLEX COMMUNICATIONS CORP (DE)
Cease trade order effective 10/12/2001
Stockholders' equity unlikely

SYMPOSIUM CORP (DE)
Name changed 5/20/99
Each share old Common $0.001 par exchanged for (0.5) share new Common $0.001 par 11/13/1998
Name changed from Symposium Telecom Corp. to Symposium Corp. 05/20/1999
Name changed to Cross Media Marketing Corp. 12/29/2000
(See Cross Media Marketing Corp.)

SYMPOSIUM PRODUCTIONS CORP (FL)
Common $0.001 par split (12) for (1) by issuance of (11) additional shares payable 09/27/2006 to holders of record 09/27/2006
Name changed to Grid Cloud Solutions, Inc. 12/14/2010
Grid Cloud Solutions, Inc. recapitalized as Great Rock Development Corp. 02/29/2012 which recapitalized as Comepay, Inc. 03/01/2018

SYMS CORP (NJ)
Under plan of reorganization each share Common 5¢ par automatically became (1) share Trinity Place Holdings Inc. Common 1¢ par 09/14/2012

SYMYX TECHNOLOGIES INC (DE)
Merged into Accelrys, Inc. 07/01/2010
Each share Common $0.001 par exchanged for (0.7802) share Common $0.0001 par
(See Accelrys, Inc.)

SYN TRAC INDS LTD (BC)
Name changed to Austra Resources Corp. 08/07/1984
Austra Resources Corp. name changed to Austar Resources Inc. 11/01/1990 which recapitalized as Austpro Energy Corp. 01/31/1996

SYN TREK INC (NJ)
Charter declared void for non-payment of taxes 09/01/1988

SYNAGEVA BIOPHARMA CORP (DE)
Merged into Alexion Pharmaceuticals, Inc. 06/22/2015
Each share Common $0.001 par exchanged for (0.6581) share Common $0.0001 par and $115 cash

SYNAGRO TECHNOLOGIES INC (DE)
Reincorporated 05/28/1996
Each share old Common $0.002 par exchanged for (0.06666666) share new Common $0.002 par 07/13/1995
State of incorporation changed from (NV) to (DE) 05/28/1996
Merged into Synatech Holdings, Inc. 04/02/2007
Each share new Common $0.002 par exchanged for $5.76 cash

SYNALLOY CORP (SC)
Common $1 par split (5) for (4) by issuance of (0.25) additional share 03/29/1968
Common $1 par split (5) for (4) by issuance of (0.25) additional share 02/27/1981
Common $1 par split (5) for (4) by issuance of (0.25) additional share 03/12/1982
Common $1 par split (5) for (4) by issuance of (0.25) additional share 03/16/1984
Reincorporated under the laws of Delaware 06/03/1988

SYNAPTEC A KNOWLEDGE ENGR CORP (BC)
Delisted from Vancouver Stock Exchange 01/10/1990

SYNAPTIC PHARMACEUTICAL CORP (DE)
Merged into H. Lundbeck A/S 03/06/2003
Each share Common 1¢ par exchanged for $6.50 cash

SYNAPTIX SYS CORP (CO)
Name changed to Affiliated Resources Corp. 01/12/1999

SYNAPTX WORLDWIDE INC (UT)
Reincorporated under the laws of Delaware as Paladyne Corp. and Common $0.00004 par changed to $0.001 par 03/05/1999
Paladyne Corp. name changed to Market Central, Inc. 02/05/2003 which name changed to Scientigo, Inc. 02/17/2006 which recapitalized as Incumaker, Inc. 06/01/2011

SYNAVANT INC (DE)
Merged into Dendrite International, Inc. 06/17/2003
Each share Common 1¢ par exchanged for $3.22 cash

SYNBIOTICS CORP (CA)
Old Common no par split (2) for (1) by issuance of (1) additional share 02/20/1986
Each share old Common no par exchanged for (1) share new Common no par to reflect a (1) for (2,000) reverse split followed by a (2,000) for (1) forward split 11/03/2005
Note: Holders of (1,999) or fewer pre-split shares will receive $0.13 cash per share
Merged into Pfizer Inc. 12/30/2010
Each share new Common no par exchanged for $0.2867385 cash
Note: An additional distribution of $0.01885 cash per share was paid 01/17/2012 to holders of record 12/30/2010

SYNC RESH INC (DE)
Each share old Common $0.001 par exchanged for (0.2) share new Common $0.001 par 6/25/99
Name changed to Entrada Networks Inc. 8/31/2000

SYNC2 ENTERTAINMENT CORP (NV)
Recapitalized as iGen Networks Corp. 06/30/2009
Each share Common $0.001 par exchanged for (0.01) share Common $0.001 par

SYNCFEED INC (NV)
Name changed to Affinity Gold Corp. 02/13/2009

SYNCHRONEX CORP (DE)
Charter cancelled and declared inoperative and void for non-payment of taxes 03/01/1974

SYNCLINE, INC. (UT)
Recapitalized as Pipesaver Technologies, Inc. 02/03/1983
Each share Common $0.001 par exchanged for (1.5) shares Common $0.001 par

SYNCO DEV CORP (BC)
Delisted from Vancouver Stock Exchange 10/06/1989

SYNCO RESINS, INC. (NY)
Completely liquidated 12/21/1965
Each share Common $1 par exchanged for first and final distribution of $3.44 cash

SYNCOM CORP (DE)
Common 1¢ par split (4) for (1) by issuance of (3) additional shares 03/20/1984
Charter cancelled and declared inoperative and void for non-payment of taxes 03/01/1988

SYNCOM IMAGE DISPLAY SYS INC (CANADA)
Recapitalized as Syncom Imaging Systems Inc. 10/08/1998
Each share Common no par exchanged for (0.2) share Common no par
(See Syncom Imaging Systems Inc.)

SYNCOM IMAGING SYS INC (CANADA)
Assets sold for the benefit of creditors 06/00/2002
No stockholders' equity

SYNCOM INC. (NY)
Reincorporated 09/01/1972
State of incorporation changed from (TX) to (NY) and Common no par changed to 2¢ par 09/01/1972
Name changed to Disc-Tape Liquidating Corp. 07/27/1979
(See Disc-Tape Liquidating Corp.)

SYNCOR INTL CORP (CA)
Common 1¢ par split (3) for (2) by issuance of (0.5) additional share 04/30/1981
Merged into Nuclear Pharmacy Inc. (NM) 08/05/1985
Each share Common 1¢ par exchanged for (0.729) share Common 5¢ par
Nuclear Pharmacy Inc. (NM) reincorporated in Delaware 10/15/1985 which name changed to Syncor International Corp. 02/03/1986 which merged into Cardinal Health, Inc. 01/01/2003

SYNCOR INTL CORP NEW (DE)
Common 5¢ par split (2) for (1) by issuance of (1) additional share payable 08/09/2000 to holders of record 07/26/2000
Merged into Cardinal Health, Inc. 01/01/2003
Each share Common 5¢ par exchanged for (0.47) share Common no par

FINANCIAL INFORMATION, INC. SYN-SYN

SYNCRETE TECHNOLOGIES INC (AB)
Struck off register for failure to file annual returns 12/01/1994

SYNCRO GROWTH FD INC (WA)
Name changed to Safeco Growth Fund, Inc. (WA) 01/30/1974
Safeco Growth Fund, Inc. (WA) reincorporated in Delaware 09/30/1993
(See Safeco Growth Fund, Inc.)

SYNCRO INCOME FD INC (WA)
Name changed to Safeco Income Fund, Inc. (WA) 01/30/1974
Safeco Income Fund, Inc. (WA) reincorporated in Delaware 09/30/1993
(See Safeco Income Fund, Inc.)

SYNCRONYS ALTERNATIVE ENERGY INC (NV)
Charter revoked for failure to file reports and pay taxes 11/30/2009

SYNCRONYS INTL INC (NV)
Each share old Common $0.001 par exchanged for (0.03571428) share new Common $0.001 par 06/19/2008
Each share new Common $0.001 par received distribution of (1) share Lectric, Inc. Restricted Common payable 04/17/2013 to holders of record 03/29/2013
Name changed to Seeker Tec International, Inc. 04/24/2013

SYNCRONYS SOFTCORP (NV)
Name changed to Syncronys Alternative Energy, Inc. 07/27/2007
(See Syncronys Alternative Energy, Inc.)

SYNC2 NETWORKS CORP (NV)
Common $0.001 par split (17) for (1) by issuance of (16) additional shares payable 05/13/2009 to holders of record 04/23/2009
Ex date - 05/14/2009
Recapitalized as Trex Acquisition Corp. 03/20/2014
Each share Common $0.001 par exchanged for (0.001) share Common $0.001 par

SYNDEOS GROUP INC (FL)
Recapitalized as Air Media Now!, Inc. 04/10/2002
Each share Common $0.001 par exchanged for (0.2) share Common $0.001 par

SYNDICATE MINING & MILLING CO.
Liquidated 00/00/1928
Details not available

SYNDICATED FOOD SVC INTL INC (FL)
Plan of reorganization under Chapter 11 Federal Bankruptcy Code effective 07/21/2007
No stockholders' equity

SYNDICATION INC (DE)
Each share old Common $0.0001 par exchanged for (0.005) share new Common $0.0001 par 11/06/2008
Each share new Common $0.0001 par exchanged again for (0.005) share new Common $0.0001 par 02/28/2014
Each share new Common $0.0001 par exchanged again for (0.002) share new Common $0.0001 par 02/23/2015
Recapitalized as Day Tradexchange, Inc. 04/07/2017
Each share new Common $0.0001 par exchanged for (0.005) share Common $0.0001 par

SYNEAR FOOD HLDGS LTD (BERMUDA)
ADR agreement terminated 01/25/2016
No ADR's remain outstanding

SYNECO SYS INC (MN)
Merged into Syneco Acquisition Corp. 12/30/2009
Each share Common 1¢ par exchanged for $0.05 cash

SYNEGRATE CORP (FL)
Recapitalized as Papa Bello Enterprises, Inc. 06/24/2008
Each share Common no par exchanged for (0.00333333) share Common $0.0001 par
Papa Bello Enterprises, Inc. name changed to WO Group, Inc. 08/03/2017

SYNENCO ENERGY INC (AB)
Acquired by Total S.A. 08/11/2008
Each share Class A Common no par exchanged for $10.25 cash

SYNER DATA INC (MA)
Adjudicated bankrupt 12/05/1973
Stockholders' equity unlikely

SYNER-SEIS TECHNOLOGIES INC (AB)
Recapitalized as Intequest Corp. 06/25/2004
Each share Common no par exchanged for (0.125) share Common no par
(See Intequest Corp.)

SYNERCOM TECHNOLOGY INC (DE)
Name changed to Alpha Technologies Group, Inc. 04/19/1995
(See Alpha Technologies Group, Inc.)

SYNERCON CORP (TN)
Acquired by Corroon & Black Corp. 04/30/1976
Each share Common $1 par exchanged for (0.6412) share Common 50¢ par
Corroon & Black Corp. merged into Willis Corroon PLC 10/08/1990 which name changed to Willis Corroon Group PLC 01/22/1992
(See Willis Corroon Group PLC)

SYNERGEN INC (DE)
Common 1¢ par split (3) for (2) by issuance of (0.5) additional share 10/29/1991
Merged into Amgen Acquisition Subsidiary, Inc. 12/29/1994
Each share Common 1¢ par exchanged for $9.25 cash

SYNERGETIC SCIENCES INC (NM)
Filed for Chapter 7 Federal Bankruptcy Code 09/29/1980
Stockholders' equity unlikely

SYNERGETIC TECHNOLOGIES INC (NV)
Each share old Common $0.001 par exchanged for (0.1) share new Common $0.001 par 10/08/2004
Recapitalized as Praebius Communications, Inc. 12/11/2007
Each share Common $0.001 par exchanged for (0.005) share Common $0.001 par
Praebius Communications, Inc. recapitalized as Adaptive Ad Systems, Inc. 07/18/2014

SYNERGETICS CORP (MA)
Assets sold to Search Corp. 10/00/1970
Details not available

SYNERGETICS INTL INC (CO)
Reorganized under the laws of Nevada as Presidential Holdings, Inc. 04/20/2003
Each share Common 1¢ par exchanged for (0.02) share Common 1¢ par
Presidential Holdings, Inc. name changed to Kewl International, Inc. 11/14/2003 which recapitalized as Meg Athletic Corp. 11/15/2004 which recapitalized as Pure H2O Inc. 05/10/2006 which recapitalized as Newron Sport 10/03/2008

SYNERGETICS USA INC (DE)
Acquired by Valeant Pharmaceuticals International, Inc. 10/15/2015
Each share Common $0.001 par exchanged for $6.50 cash and (1) Contingent Value Right

SYNERGEX CORP (CA)
Acquired by Bergen Brunswig Corp. 01/03/1985
Each share Common no par exchanged for $18 cash

SYNERGIE HLDGS LTD INC (FL)
Name changed to Synergie Wellness Products, Inc. 03/15/2004

SYNERGISTIC CAP CORP (DE)
Recapitalized as Americanino Capital Corp. 01/26/1990
Each share Common $0.001 par exchanged for (0.025) share Common $0.001 par
(See Americanino Capital Corp.)

SYNERGISTIC COMMUNICATIONS GROUP INC (MO)
Common no par split (2) for (1) by issuance of (1) additional share 11/04/1974
Common no par split (3) for (2) by issuance of (0.5) additional share 04/15/1982
Common no par split (3) for (2) by issuance of (0.5) additional share 02/01/1985
Liquidation completed
Each share Common no par received initial distribution of $0.7112 cash 01/03/1989
Each share Common no par received second and final distribution of $0.062 cash 08/01/1990
Note: Certificates were not required to be surrendered and are without value

SYNERGISTIC HLDGS CORP (DE)
Name changed to Salex Holding Corp. 03/03/1998
(See Salex Holding Corp.)

SYNERGISTICS INC (MA)
Merged into Synergistics Acquisition Corp. 10/02/2002
Each share Common no par exchanged for $0.025 cash

SYNERGISTICS INDS LTD (ON)
Acquired by Geon Co. 11/17/1997
Each share Non-Vtg. Class A no par exchanged for $22 cash

SYNERGX SYS INC (DE)
Common $0.001 par split (2) for (1) by issuance of (1) additional share payable 07/25/2003 to holders of record 07/18/2003 Ex date - 07/28/2003
Merged into Firecom, Inc. 07/27/2010
Each share Common $0.001 par exchanged for $0.70 cash

SYNERGY ACQUISITION CORP (AB)
Each share old Common no par exchanged for (0.16666666) share new Common no par 05/13/2011
Reincorporated under the laws of Canada as Genius Properties Ltd. 02/13/2014
Genius Properties Ltd. name changed to Cerro de Pasco Resources Inc. 10/18/2018

SYNERGY BRANDS INC (DE)
Each share old Common $0.001 par exchanged for (0.2) share new Common $0.001 par 04/20/2001
Each share new Common $0.001 par exchanged again for (0.25) share new Common $0.001 par 02/20/2003
Filed a petition under Chapter 7 Federal Bankruptcy Code 01/28/2011
No stockholders' equity

SYNERGY FINL GROUP INC (NJ)
Merged into New York Community Bancorp, Inc. 10/01/2007

Each share Common 10¢ par exchanged for (0.8) share Common 1¢ par

SYNERGY FINL GROUP INC (USA)
Reorganized under the laws of New Jersey 01/20/2004
Each share Common 10¢ par exchanged for (3.7231) shares Common 10¢ par
Synergy Financial Group, Inc. (NJ) merged into New York Community Bancorp, Inc. 10/01/2007

SYNERGY INTL LTD (BC)
Struck off register and declared dissolved for failure to file returns 08/28/1987

SYNERGY MEDIA INC (NV)
Recapitalized as VIPR Industries, Inc. 02/06/2008
Each share Common $0.001 par exchanged for (0.00008) share Common $0.001 par

SYNERGY PHARMACEUTICALS INC (FL)
Each share Common $0.0001 par exchanged for (0.5) share new Common $0.0001 par 12/01/2011
Reincorporated under the laws of Delaware 02/16/2012

SYNERGY RENEWABLE RES INC (BC)
Recapitalized 01/09/1997
Recapitalized from Synergy Resource Technologies Inc. to Synergy Renewable Resources Inc. 01/09/1997
Each share Common no par exchanged for (0.2) share Common no par
SEC revoked common stock registration 07/20/2010

SYNERGY RES CORP (CO)
Name changed to SRC Energy Inc. 03/06/2017

SYNERGY RESOURCES LTD. (BC)
Name changed to Synergy International Ltd. 03/01/1976
(See Synergy International Ltd.)

SYNERGY SOFTWARE DEV INC (FL)
Name changed to Universal Media Holdings, Inc. 11/15/2004
Universal Media Holdings, Inc. name changed to Lyric Jeans, Inc. 03/08/2006

SYNERGY STRIPS CORP (NV)
Name changed to Synergy CHC Corp. 08/18/2015

SYNERGY TECHNOLOGIES CORP (CO)
Plan of reorganization under Chapter 11 Federal Bankruptcy Code effective 08/11/2003
Each share Common $0.002 par received (0.01) share Australian Oil & Gas Corp. (DE) Common $0.001 par payable 09/26/2003 to holders of record 08/11/2003
Note: Certificates were not required to be exchanged and are without value

SYNERON MED LTD (ISRAEL)
Acquired by a group of investors 07/17/2017
Each share Ordinary ILS 0.01 par exchanged for $11 cash

SYNERTECK INC (DE)
Name changed to IFSA Strongman, Inc. 12/28/2005
(See IFSA Strongman, Inc.)

SYNESI INC (DE)
Name changed to Carefree Group, Inc. 10/25/2007

SYNETIC INC (DE)
Common 1¢ par split (2) for (1) by issuance of (1) additional share 02/26/1993
Under plan of merger name changed to Medical Manager Corp. (New) 07/23/1999

Medical Manager Corp. (New) merged into WebMD Corp. 09/12/2000 which name changed to Emdeon Corp. 10/17/2005 which name changed to HLTH Corp. 05/21/2007 which merged into WebMD Health Corp. 10/23/2009
(See WebMD Health Corp.)

SYNETIX GROUP INC (NV)
Reincorporated 12/31/2008
Each share Common $0.001 par exchanged for (0.05) share Common 2¢ par 03/08/1984
State of incorporation changed from (UT) to (NV) and Common 2¢ par changed to $0.001 par 12/31/2008
Merged out of existence 11/20/2015
Details not available

SYNFUEL TECHNOLOGY INC (NV)
Each share old Common 10¢ par exchanged for (0.025) share new Common 10¢ par 08/27/1997
Recapitalized as Rigid Airship USA Inc. 11/10/1998
Each share Common 10¢ par exchanged for (0.33333333) share Common 10¢ par
(See Rigid Airship USA Inc.)

SYNGAS INTL CORP (NV)
Recapitalized as Energy Quest Inc. 05/31/2007
Each share Common $0.001 par exchanged for (0.05) share Common $0.001 par

SYNGENTA AG (SWITZERLAND)
ADR agreement terminated 01/16/2018
Each Sponsored ADR for Common exchanged for $92.95 cash

SYNGOLD EXPL INC (ON)
Each share old Common no par exchanged for (0.2) share new Common no par 06/01/1989
Merged into Thunderwood Resources Inc.- Les Ressources Thunderwood Inc. 06/01/1989
Each share new Common no par exchanged for (0.71428571) share Common no par
Each share Class A $1 par exchanged for (1) share Class B no par
Thunderwood Resources Inc.-Les Ressources Thunderwood Inc. merged into Thundermin Resources Inc. 11/01/1998 which merged into Rambler Metals & Mining PLC 01/12/2016

SYNIVERSE HLDGS INC (DE)
Acquired by Buccaneer Holdings, Inc. 01/13/2011
Each share Common $0.001 par exchanged for $31 cash

SYNODON INC (AB)
Placed in receivership 11/30/2016
Stockholders' equity unlikely

SYNOPTIC SYS CORP (DE)
Charter cancelled and declared inoperative and void for non-payment of taxes 04/15/1972

SYNOPTICS COMMUNICATIONS INC (CA)
Common no par split (2) for (1) by issuance of (1) additional share 07/20/1990
Common no par split (3) for (1) by issuance of (2) additional shares 06/11/1993
Merged into Bay Networks, Inc. 10/21/1994
Each share Common no par exchanged for (0.725) share Common 1¢ par
Bay Networks, Inc. merged into Northern Telecom Ltd.-Northern Telecom Ltee. 08/31/1998 which name changed to Nortel Networks Corp. (Old) 04/30/1999 which reorganized as Nortel Networks Corp. (New) 05/01/2000
(See Nortel Networks Corp. (New))

SYNOVA HEALTHCARE GROUP INC (NV)
Chapter 11 bankruptcy proceedings converted to Chapter 7 on 12/28/2007
No stockholders' equity

SYNOVIS LIFE TECHNOLOGIES INC (MN)
Acquired by Baxter International Inc. 02/15/2012
Each share Common 1¢ par exchanged for $28 cash

SYNOVUS FINL CORP (GA)
Fixed-to-Floating Rate Non-Cum Perpetual Preferred Ser. C no par called for redemption at $25 on 08/01/2018
(Additional Information in Active)

SYNPLICITY INC (CA)
Merged into Synopsys, Inc. 05/15/2008
Each share Common no par exchanged for $8 cash

SYNPRO ENVIRONMENTAL SVCS INC (DE)
Charter cancelled and declared inoperative and void for non-payment of taxes 03/01/1994

SYNQUEST INC (GA)
Each share old Common 1¢ par exchanged for (0.1) share new Common 1¢ par 07/30/2002
Name changed to Viewlocity Inc. 01/07/2003
(See Viewlocity, Inc.)

SYNREAL SVCS CORP (NV)
Name changed to Experiential Agency, Inc. and (12) additional shares issued 02/02/2004
Experiential Agency, Inc. recapitalized as XA, Inc. 12/09/2004
(See XA, Inc.)

SYNSORB BIOTECH INC (AB)
Each share old Common no par exchanged for (0.125) share new Common no par 05/08/2002
Each share new Common no par received distribution of (0.1008125) share Oncolytics Biotech Inc. Common no par payable 05/16/2002 to holders of record 05/08/2002
Name changed to Hawker Resources Inc. 04/13/2003
Hawker Resources Inc. name changed to Iteration Energy Ltd. 07/11/2005 which merged into Chinook Energy Inc. (Old) 07/05/2010
(See Chinook Energy Inc. (Old))

SYNTA PHARMACEUTICALS CORP (DE)
Recapitalized as Madrigal Pharmaceuticals, Inc. 07/25/2016
Each share Common $0.0001 par exchanged for (0.02857142) share Common $0.0001 par

SYNTAVCO, INC. (WA)
Reorganized as Jenex Gold Corp. 05/08/1974
Each share Common $0.001 par exchanged for (1) share Common $0.001 par
Jenex Gold Corp. recapitalized as Sun Tzu Corp. 01/15/2009
(See Sun Tzu Corp.)

SYNTAX-BRILLIAN CORP (DE)
Plan of reorganization under Chapter 11 Federal Bankruptcy Code effective 07/07/2009
No stockholders' equity

SYNTECH DIAMOND FILMS INC (ON)
Merged into Structured Biologicals Inc. 07/27/1993
Each share Common no par exchanged for (0.2) share Common no par
Structured Biologicals Inc. recapitalized as Ben-Abraham Technologies Inc. 12/06/1996 which name changed to BioSante Pharmaceuticals, Inc. (WY) 12/17/1999 which reincorporated in Delaware 06/26/2001 which recapitalized as ANI Pharmaceuticals, Inc. 07/18/2013

SYNTECH INTL INC (DE)
Reorganized under Chapter 11 Federal Bankruptcy Code 12/31/1991
Each share $2.75 Conv. Preferred $1 par exchanged for (5) shares new Common 10¢ par
Each (1.5) shares old Common 10¢ par exchanged for (1) share new Common 10¢ par
Recapitalized as IDS Worldwide Solutions, Inc. 06/21/2005
Each share new Common 10¢ par exchanged for (0.01) share Common 10¢ par
IDS Worldwide Solutions, Inc. name changed to IDS Worldwide, Inc. (DE) 10/19/2005 which reincorporated in Nevada as Avalon Technology Group, Inc. 06/16/2008

SYNTEGRA INVT CORP (BC)
Merged into VendTek Systems Inc. 04/26/2002
Each share Common no par exchanged for (0.23294819) share Common no par
(See VendTek Systems Inc.)

SYNTEL INC (MI)
Common no par split (3) for (2) by issuance of (0.5) additional share payable 04/22/1998 to holders of record 04/06/1998
Common no par split (2) for (1) by issuance of (1) additional share payable 11/03/2014 to holders of record 10/20/2014 Ex date - 11/04/2014
Acquired by Atos S.E. 10/09/2018
Each share Common no par exchanged for $41 cash

SYNTELLECT INC (DE)
Merged into Enghouse Systems Ltd. 12/17/2002
Each share Common 1¢ par exchanged for $0.72 cash

SYNTELLO INC (DE)
Each share old Common 1¢ par exchanged for (0.0005) share new Common 1¢ par 01/05/1996
Reorganized as Maxim Pharmaceuticals, Inc. 10/09/1996
Each share new Common 1¢ par exchanged for (66.6666) shares Common $0.001 par
Maxim Pharmaceuticals, Inc. merged into EpiCept Corp. 01/05/2006 which recapitalized as Immune Pharmaceuticals Inc. 08/21/2013

SYNTEX CORP (PANAMA)
Common $2 par changed to $1 par and (2) additional shares issued 11/22/1963
Common $1 par split (2) for (1) by issuance of (1) additional share 01/04/1966
Common $1 par split (2) for (1) by issuance of (1) additional share 01/03/1974
Class A Conv. Preferred no par called for redemption 01/14/1981
Common $1 par split (2) for (1) by issuance of (1) additional share 03/12/1982
Common $1 par split (2) for (1) by issuance of (1) additional share 12/13/1985
Common $1 par split (2) for (1) by issuance of (1) additional share 06/12/1987
Class C Preferred no par called for redemption 06/30/1987
Class B Conv. Preferred no par called for redemption 05/30/1989
Common $1 par split (2) for (1) by issuance of (1) additional share 04/18/1991
Merged into Roche Capital Corp. 10/28/1994
Each share Common $1 par exchanged for $24 cash

SYNTHATRON CORP (DE)
Charter cancelled and declared inoperative and void for non-payment of taxes 03/01/1988

SYNTHEMED CORP (DE)
Ceased operations 04/00/1982
No stockholders' equity

SYNTHEMED INC (DE)
Name changed to Pathfinder Cell Therapy, Inc. 09/16/2011

SYNTHENOL INC (FL)
Reincorporated under the laws of Nevada as SinoCubate, Inc. and Common 1¢ par changed to $0.001 par 11/25/2008
SinoCubate, Inc. name changed to Viking Investments Group, Inc. 07/16/2012 which name changed to Viking Energy Group, Inc. 05/08/2017

SYNTHES INC (DE)
Name changed 05/21/2004
Name changed from Synthes-Stratec Inc. to Synthes, Inc., 144A Common CHF 0.01 par changed to CHF 0.001 par and (9) additional shares issued 05/21/2004
Merged into Johnson & Johnson 06/14/2012
Each share 144A Common CHF 0.001 par exchanged for (1.717) shares Common $1 par and CHF 55.65 cash

SYNTHESIS ENERGY SYS INC (MS)
Reincorporated under the laws of Delaware and Common $0.001 par changed to 1¢ par 07/26/2005

SYNTHETECH INC (OR)
Reincorporated 06/20/1991
State of incorporation changed from (CO) to (OR) 06/20/1991
Acquired by Grace (W.R.) & Co. (New) 11/22/2010
Each share Common $0.001 par exchanged for $1.163286 cash

SYNTHETIC BLOOD & MED TECHNOLOGIES INC (DE)
Each share old Common $0.00001 par exchanged for (0.01) share new Common $0.00001 par 11/27/1989
Each share new Common $0.00001 par exchanged for (0.4) share Common $0.0001 par 01/22/1996
Name changed to RFI Recycled Fibre Industries Inc. 12/04/1996
RFI Recycled Fibre Industries Inc. name changed to Strandtek International, Inc. 10/28/1998
(See Strandtek International, Inc.)

SYNTHETIC BLOOD INTL INC (NJ)
Reincorporated under the laws of Delaware as Oxygen Biotherapeutics, Inc. and Common 1¢ par changed to $0.0001 par 07/01/2008
Oxygen Biotherapeutics, Inc. name changed to Tenax Therapeutics, Inc. 09/19/2014

SYNTHETIC FLOWERS AMER INC (FL)
Name changed to Pinecrest Investment Group Inc. 03/01/1999
Pinecrest Investment Group Inc. recapitalized as Acology Inc. 02/14/2014 which name changed to Medtainer, Inc. 10/05/2018

SYNTHETIC INDS INC (DE)
Merged into Investcorp S.A. 12/14/99
Each share Common $1 par exchanged for $33 cash

SYNTHETIC TURF CORP AMER (NV)
Recapitalized as City Capital Corp. 12/15/2004

Each share Common $0.001 par exchanged for (0.01) share Common $0.001 par

SYNTHONICS TECHNOLOGIES INC (UT)
Reincorporated under the laws of Delaware 12/23/99

SYNTHOS S A (POLAND)
ADR agreement terminated 02/01/2018
Each ADR for Ordinary issued by Bank of New York exchanged for $14.401126 cash

SYNTONIC TECHNOLOGY INC (PA)
Acquired by Control Data Corp. (DE) 08/10/1972
Each share Common 50¢ par exchanged for (0.222222) share Common $5 par
Control Data Corp. (DE) name changed to Ceridian Corp. (Old) 06/03/1992
(See Ceridian Corp. (Old))

SYNTREX INC (NJ)
Plan of reorganization under Chapter 11 Federal Bankruptcy proceedings effective 12/31/1992
No stockholders' equity

SYNTRO CORP (DE)
Merged into Mallinckrodt Group Inc. 11/06/1995
Each share Common 1¢ par exchanged for $3.55 cash

SYNTROLEUM CORP (DE)
Reincorporated 06/00/1999
State of incorporation changed from (KS) to (DE) 06/00/1999
Each share old Common 1¢ par exchanged for (0.1) share new Common 1¢ par 04/12/2013
Liquidation completed
Each share new Common 1¢ par received initial distribution of (0.2103) share Renewable Energy Group, Inc. Common $0.0001 par payable 07/30/2014 to holders of record 06/11/2014
Each share new Common 1¢ par received second distribution of (0.104) share Renewable Energy Group, Inc. Common $0.0001 par payable 10/03/2014 to holders of record 06/11/2014
Each share new Common 1¢ par received third distribution of $0.191157 cash payable 01/20/217 to holders of record 06/11/2014
Each share new Common 1¢ par received fourth and final distribution of (0.0161276) share Renewable Energy Group, Inc. Common $0.0001 par and $0.12039 cash payable 08/31/2017 to holders of record 06/11/2014

SYNTRON COMMUNICATIONS INC (DE)
Reincorporated 1/12/90
State of incorporation changed from (NV) to (DE) 1/12/90
Charter cancelled and declared inoperative and void for non-payment of taxes 3/1/92

SYNUTRA INTL INC (DE)
Acquired by Beams Power Investment Ltd. 05/16/2017
Each share Common $0.0001 par exchanged for $6.05 cash

SYNVION CORP (CO)
SEC enforcement proceedings concluded 12/8/99
No stockholders' equity

SYNVISTA THERAPEUTICS INC (DE)
Company terminated common stock registration and is no longer public as of 03/19/2009

SYNX PHARMA INC (ON)
Acquired by Nanogen, Inc. 04/21/2004
Each share Common no par exchanged for (0.123) share Common no par
(See Nanogen, Inc.)

SYPHER RES LTD (AB)
Name changed to Atlas Cloud Enterprises Inc. (AB) 07/25/2014
Atlas Cloud Enterprises Inc. (AB) reincorporated in British Columbia as Atlas Blockchain Group Inc. 07/27/2018

SYQUEST TECHNOLOGY INC (DE)
Assets sold for the benefit of creditors 04/22/1999
No stockholders' equity

SYRA-CORD TIRE & RUBBER CORP. (NY)
Charter cancelled and proclaimed dissolved for failure to file reports and pay taxes 12/15/32

SYRACUSE, BINGHAMTON & NEW YORK RAILROAD CO.
Merged into Delaware, Lackawanna & Western Railroad Co. through payment of $175 per share in 1946

SYRACUSE CAP CORP (BC)
Name changed to Natcore Technology Inc. 05/19/2009

SYRACUSE CHINA CORP (DE)
Merged into Canadian Pacific Investments Ltd.-Investissements Canadien Pacifique Ltee. 04/28/1978
Each share Common 5¢ par exchanged for $26.75 cash

SYRACUSE CHINA CORP (NY)
Name changed to Fayette-Court Corp. 11/23/1971
(See Fayette-Court Corp.)

SYRACUSE LIGHTING CO.
Merged into Niagara Hudson Public Service Corp. which name changed to Central New York Power Corp. 7/31/37
Each share 8% Preferred exchanged for (1.2) shares 5% Preferred $100 par
Each share 6-1/2% Preferred exchanged for (1.1) shares 5% Preferred $100 par
Each share 6% Preferred exchanged for (1.05) shares 5% Preferred $100 par
Central New York Power Corp. merged into Niagara Mohawk Power Corp. 1/5/50

SYRACUSE MORTGAGE CORP. (NY)
Liquidated 12/21/1959
Each share 7% Preferred $10 par exchanged for $5 cash
Common and Class A Common no par declared worthless

SYRACUSE NORTHERN ELECTRIC RAILWAY, INC.
Dissolved in 1938

SYRACUSE OILS LTD (AB)
Merged into Bow Valley Industries Ltd. 4/30/71
Each share Common no par exchanged for (0.2) share Common no par
Bow Valley Industries Ltd. name changed to Bow Valley Energy Inc. 6/7/93 which was acquired by Talisman Energy Inc. 8/11/94

SYRACUSE SUPPLY CO (NY)
Common $8 par changed to $4 par 12/15/65
Common $4 par split (3) for (2) by issuance of (0.5) additional share 3/11/85
Stock Dividends - 10% 12/1/74; 100% 12/11/79; 10% 6/8/87; 10% 6/6/88
Acquired by a management group 2/7/90
Each share Common $4 par exchanged for $16.25 cash

SYRACUSE TRAN CORP (NY)
Liquidation completed

Each share Common no par exchanged for initial distribution of (1) Non-Tranferable Ctf. of Bene. Int. 07/17/1972
Each Ctf. of Bene. Int. received initial distribution of $1.92 cash 06/29/1973
Each Ctf. of Bene. Int. received second distribution of $5.50 cash 06/28/1974
Each Ctf. of Bene. Int. received third distribution of $5.50 cash 06/30/1975
Each Ctf. of Bene. Int. received fourth distribution of $5.50 cash 06/30/1976
Each Ctf. of Bene. Int. received fifth distribution of $50 cash 01/31/1977
Each Ctf. of Bene. Int. received sixth distribution of $1 cash 06/29/1978
Each Ctf. of Bene. Int. received seventh and final distribution of $17.764 cash 12/07/1979

SYRACUSE WASHING MACHINE CORP.
Name changed to Easy Washing Machine Corp. 00/00/1932
Easy Washing Machine Corp. merged into Union Chemical & Materials Corp. 08/31/1955 which merged into Vulcan Materials Co. 12/31/1957

SYRATECH CORP (DE)
Merged into Syratech Corp. (New) 04/16/1997
Each share Common 1¢ par exchanged for $32 cash
Note: Holders had the right to retain 34.75% of total holdings in stock
Acquired by Lifetime Brands, Inc. 04/27/2006
Details not available

SYRINGA BANCORP (ID)
Common no par split (2) for (1) by issuance of (1) additional share payable 01/15/2007 to holders of record 01/02/2007 Ex date - 01/19/2007
Administratively dissolved 05/14/2014

SYRINGA BK (BOISE, ID)
Under plan of reorganization each share Common $5 par automatically became (1) share Syringa Bancorp Common no par 08/24/2005
(See Syringa Bancorp)

SYRUS CAP CORP (BC)
Recapitalized as New Syrus Capital Corp. 11/19/96
Each share Common no par exchanged for (0.5) share Common no par
New Syrus Capital Corp. name changed to Player Petroleum Corp. (BC) 2/25/97 which reincorporated in Alberta 4/29/98
(See Player Petroleum Corp.)

SYSCAN IMAGING INC (DE)
Name changed to Sysview Technology, Inc. 06/27/2006
Sysview Technology, Inc. name changed to Document Capture Technologies, Inc. 01/08/2008
(See Document Capture Technologies, Inc.)

SYSCAN INTL INC (CANADA)
Each share old Common no par exchanged for (0.025) share new Common no par 11/05/2008
Assets sold for the benefit of creditors 02/19/2009
Stockholders' equity unlikely

SYSCOMM INTL CORP (DE)
Issue Information - 1,250,000 shares COM offered at $5 per share on 06/17/1997
Name changed to InfoTech USA, Inc. 04/09/2003
InfoTech USA, Inc. name changed to IFTH Acquisition Corp. 12/04/2008 which name changed to Steel Vault Corp. 03/18/2009 which merged into PositiveID Corp. 11/10/2009

SYSCON CORP (DC)
Common 5¢ par split (3) for (2) by issuance of (0.5) additional share 11/30/1985
Merged into Harnischfeger Industries, Inc. 12/30/1986
Each share Common 5¢ par exchanged for $19.50 cash

SYSKA & HENNESSY INC (NY)
Acquired by a management group 00/00/2000
Details not available

SYSOREX GLOBAL (NV)
Name changed 01/04/2016
Each share old Common $0.001 par exchanged for (0.5) share new Common $0.001 par 04/09/2014
Name changed from Sysorex Global Holdings Corp. to Sysorex Global 01/04/2016
Recapitalized as Inpixon 03/01/2017
Each share new Common $0.001 par exchanged for (0.06666666) share Common $0.001 par

SYSPOWER MULTIMEDIA INDS INC (BRITISH VIRGIN ISLANDS)
Reincorporated 02/15/1995
Place of incorporation changed from (BC) to (British Virgin Islands) 02/15/1995
Delisted from Vancouver Stock Exchange 03/05/1996

SYSTECH RETAIL SYS CORP (ON)
Name changed 09/24/2002
Name and place of incorporation changed from Systech Retail Systems Inc. (BC) to Systech Retail Systems Corp. (ONT) 09/24/2002
Merged into Torex Retail PLC 11/02/2005
Each share Common no par exchanged for $0.0031947 cash

SYS (CA)
4% Conv. Preferred 50¢ par called for redemption 05/15/2002
Merged into Kratos Defense & Security Solutions, Inc. 06/30/2008
Each share Common no par exchanged for (1.2582) shares Common $0.001 par

SYS COMPUTER CORP (NY)
Placed in receivership 10/23/1975
No stockholders' equity

SYSTEM CTL CO (GA)
Involuntarily dissolved for failure to pay taxes 01/06/1990

SYSTEM CTRLS INC (NV)
Each share old Common 1¢ par exchanged for (0.01) share new Common 1¢ par 01/21/1993
Each share new Common 1¢ par received distribution of (1) share Quantum Communications Group, Inc. 04/15/1994
Charter revoked for failure to file reports and pay fees 05/31/2000

SYSTEM DEV CORP (DE)
Reincorporated 09/20/1974
State of incorporation changed from (CA) to (DE) 09/20/1974
Merged into Burroughs Corp. (MI) 01/05/1981
Each share Common $1 par exchanged for $69 cash

SYSTEM INDS INC (DE)
Reincorporated 00/00/1987
Common 1¢ par split (2) for (1) by issuance of (1) additional share 06/23/1981
State of incorporation changed from (CA) to (DE) 00/00/1987
Reorganized as Anchor Pacific Underwriters Inc. 01/03/1995
Each share Common 1¢ par exchanged for (0.0236244) share Common 2¢ par and (0.0236244) Common Stock Purchase Warrant expiring 01/06/1996
Anchor Pacific Underwriters Inc.

recapitalized as CGrowth Capital, Inc. 02/23/2010

SYSTEM INTEGRATORS INC (CA)
Acquired by a group of investors 02/06/1989
Each share Common no par exchanged for $10 cash

SYSTEM MEAT CO. (WY)
Assets liquidated for benefit of creditors 11/21/1966
No stockholders' equity

SYSTEM SOFTWARE ASSOC INC (DE)
Common $0.0033 par split (3) for (2) by issuance of (0.5) additional share 01/17/1989
Common $0.0033 par split (3) for (2) by issuance of (0.5) additional share 01/12/1990
Common $0.0033 par split (3) for (2) by issuance of (0.5) additional share 12/23/1991
Common $0.0033 par split (3) for (2) by issuance of (0.5) additional share 12/24/1992
Common $0.0033 par split (3) for (2) by issuance of (0.5) additional share payable 01/10/1996 to holders of record 12/28/1995
Each share old Common $0.0033 par exchanged for (0.25) share new Common $0.0033 par 09/02/1999
Assets sold for benefit of creditors 07/31/2000
No stockholders' equity

SYSTEMATIC BAKERIES INC (NY)
Name changed to S.Y.S. Industries, Inc. 01/30/1970
S.Y.S. Industries, Inc. name changed to Rhine Industries Inc. 02/11/1977
(See Rhine Industries Inc.)

SYSTEMATIC TAX INC (DE)
Under plan of reorganization each share Common 10¢ par automatically became (1) share Physiodata, Inc. Common 1¢ par 09/09/1975
Physiodata, Inc. recapitalized as Petro Nicholas, Inc. 06/30/1980 which name changed to Mariah Oil & Gas Corp. 01/01/1981
(See Mariah Oil & Gas Corp.)

SYSTEMATICS GEN CORP (DC)
Common $0.01333333 par split (7) for (4) by issuance of (0.75) additional share 11/04/1983
Merged into Atlantic Research Corp. (DE) 09/30/1985
Each share Common $0.01333333 par exchanged for (0.4) share Common 10¢ par
(See Atlantic Research Corp. (DE))

SYSTEMATICS INC (AR)
Common $0.025 par split (2) for (1) by issuance of (1) additional share 10/21/1983
Merged into Alltel Corp. 05/31/1990
Each share Common $0.025 par exchanged for (1.325) shares Common $1 par
(See Alltel Corp.)

SYSTEMATION INC (DE)
Charter cancelled and declared inoperative and void for non-payment of taxes 03/01/1989

SYSTEMED INC (DE)
Merged into Merck & Co., Inc. 07/19/1996
Each share Common 10¢ par exchanged for $3 cash
8% Conv. Preferred $1 par called for redemption 09/16/1996
Public interest eliminated

SYSTEMED INC (UT)
Reincorporated under the laws of Delaware as Knowledge Data Systems, Inc. 03/16/1987
(See Knowledge Data Systems, Inc.)

SYSTEMEDICS INC (NJ)
Merged into Equifax Inc. 05/24/1978
Each share Common 10¢ par exchanged for (0.1119) share Common $2.50 par

SYSTEMETRICS INC (DE)
Insolvent and ceased operations 07/01/1970
No stockholders' equity

SYSTEMEYES INTL INC (UT)
Involuntarily dissolved for failure to maintain a registered agent 02/28/1991

SYSTEMHOUSE LTD (CANADA)
Class A Common no par split (2) for (1) by issuance of (1) additional share 01/05/1981
Reorganized as SHL Systemhouse Inc. 01/31/1985
Each share Conv. 1st Preference Ser. I no par exchanged for (0.6) share Common no par
Each share Class A Common no par exchanged for (0.2) share Common no par
(See SHL Systemhouse Inc.)

SYSTEMIX INC (DE)
Acquired by Novartis AG 02/19/1997
Each share Common 1¢ par exchanged for $19.50 cash

SYSTEMONE TECHNOLOGIES INC (FL)
Plan of reorganization under Chapter 11 Federal Bankruptcy proceedings effective 11/25/2009
No stockholders' equity

SYSTEMS & COMPUTER TECHNOLOGY CORP (DE)
Common 1¢ par split (2) for (1) by issuance of (1) additional share payable 05/15/1998 to holders of record 05/01/1998
Merged into SunGard Data Systems Inc. 02/13/2004
Each share Common 1¢ par exchanged for $16.50 cash

SYSTEMS AIR LTD (ON)
Charter cancelled for failure to pay taxes and file returns 03/16/1976

SYSTEMS AMER INC (FL)
Common $0.001 par changed to $0.0001 par and (4) additional shares issued payable 08/20/2012 to holders of record 08/20/2012
Administratively dissolved 09/25/2015

SYSTEMS ASSOC INC (DE)
Merged into First Data Resources Inc. 12/31/1986
Each share Common 1¢ par exchanged for $13.25 cash

SYSTEMS ASSOC INC CALIF (CA)
Name changed to SYS 03/18/1985
SYS merged into Kratos Defense & Security Solutions, Inc. 06/30/2008

SYSTEMS ASSOCIATES, INC. (CA)
Name changed to Systems Associates, Inc. of California 11/28/1979
Systems Associates, Inc. of California name changed to SYS 03/18/1985 which merged into Kratos Defense & Security Solutions, Inc. 06/30/2008

SYSTEMS ASSURN CORP (DE)
Each share old Common 1¢ par exchanged for (1/70) share new Common 1¢ par 01/24/1997
Each share new Common 1¢ par exchanged again for (0.2) share new Common 1¢ par 12/19/1997
Name changed to Digital Commerce International, Inc. 06/11/1999
Digital Commerce International, Inc. name changed to NetCare Health Group, Inc. 04/05/2002
(See NetCare Health Group, Inc.)

SYSTEMS CAP CORP (DE)
Name changed to NRG Inc. 05/24/1973

(See NRG Inc.)

SYSTEMS CAPITAL, INC. (VA)
Automatically dissolved for failure to file reports 06/02/1969

SYSTEMS COMMUNICATIONS INC (FL)
Recapitalized as Hitsgalore.com, Inc. 03/19/1999
Each share Common $0.001 par exchanged for (0.14285714) share Common $0.001 par
Hitsgalore.com, Inc. name changed to Diamond Hitts Production, Inc. (FL) 05/01/2001 which reincorporated in Nevada 09/04/2001
(See Diamond Hitts Production, Inc.)

SYSTEMS CONNECTIONS GROUP PLC (UNITED KINGDOM)
ADR agreement terminated 05/25/1994
Details not available

SYSTEMS CORP (HI)
Involuntarily dissolved 11/16/1998

SYSTEMS CTR INC (DE)
Merged into Sterling Software, Inc. 07/01/1993
Each share Common 1¢ par exchanged for (0.5417) share Common 10¢ par and $0.01 cash
Sterling Software, Inc. merged into Computer Associates International, Inc. 04/07/2000 which name changed to CA, Inc. 02/01/2006

SYSTEMS DATA SVCS CORP (NY)
Involuntarily dissolved 09/28/1994

SYSTEMS DIMENSIONS LTD (CANADA)
Acquired by Coastal Enterprises Ltd. 04/04/1978
Each share Common no par exchanged for $4.60 cash

SYSTEMS DISPLAY INTL INC (OR)
Involuntarily dissolved for failure to file reports and pay fees 05/15/1990

SYSTEMS ENGR & MFG CORP (DE)
Common 20¢ par changed to 14¢ par and (0.5) additional share issued 05/01/1978
Common 14¢ par changed to 1¢ par and (0.5) additional share issued 06/16/1978
Common 1¢ par split (3) for (2) by issuance of (0.5) additional share 05/18/1981
Common 1¢ par split (5) for (3) by issuance of (2/3) additional share 03/12/1985
Merged into SEM Acquisition Corp. 01/20/1989
Each share Common 1¢ par exchanged for $6 cash

SYSTEMS ENGR LABS INC (FL)
Common $1 par split (2) for (1) by issuance of (1) additional share 03/29/1968
Merged into Gould Inc. 12/18/1980
Each share Common $1 par exchanged for (2) shares Common $4 par
(See Gould Inc.)

SYSTEMS EQUIP CORP (NY)
Merged into Firetector Inc. 08/23/1991
Each share Common 1¢ par exchanged for (0.25) share new Common $0.001 par
Firetector Inc. name changed to Synergx Systems Inc. 05/24/2002
(See Synergx Systems Inc.)

SYSTEMS EVOLUTION INC (ID)
Each share old Common no par exchanged for (0.03333333) share new Common no par 09/10/2007
Each share new Common no par exchanged again for (0.002) share Common $0.0001 par 03/03/2009
Name changed to Highline Technical Innovations, Inc. 04/19/2010
Highline Technical Innovations, Inc.

name changed to SPO Networks, Inc. 01/12/2017

SYSTEMS FOR ADVANCED INFORMATION INC (DE)
Merged into Gilman Services, Inc. 07/01/1975
Each share Common 1¢ par exchanged for (0.25) share Common 10¢ par
(See Gilman Services, Inc.)

SYSTEMS FOR HEALTH CARE INC (UT)
Chapter 11 bankruptcy proceedings converted to Chapter 7 on 11/30/1988
Stockholders' equity unlikely

SYSTEMS INC (FL)
Common $2 par changed to $1 par 06/26/1968
Completely liquidated 07/30/1971
No stockholders' equity

SYSTEMS LIAISON INC (DE)
Charter cancelled and declared inoperative and void for non-payment of taxes 04/15/1972

SYSTEMS MGMT SOLUTIONS INC (NV)
Each share old Common $0.0001 par exchanged for (0.4) share new Common $0.0001 par 04/05/2005
Recapitalized as Sunrise Solar Corp. 07/25/2008
Each share Common $0.0001 par exchanged for (0.2) share Common $0.0001 par
(See Sunrise Solar Corp.)

SYSTEMS OF EXCELLENCE INC (FL)
Administratively dissolved for failure to file annual reports 10/16/1998

SYSTEMS PLANNING CORP (CA)
Name changed to Greiner Engineering Inc. (CA) 05/11/1984
Greiner Engineering Inc. (CA) reincorporated in Nevada 12/18/1986 which merged into URS Corp. (DE) 03/29/1996 which merged into AECOM Technology Corp. 10/17/2014 which name changed to AECOM 01/06/2015

SYSTEMS WEST CONSULTANTS LTD (AB)
Recapitalized as Siocta Ventures Inc. 03/20/1991
Each share Common no par exchanged for (0.33333333) share Common no par
Siocta Ventures Inc. name changed to TradeRef Software Corp. (AB) 07/11/1994 which reincorporated in Anguilla 12/11/1996 which name changed to Hansa.net Global Commerce, Inc. 02/20/1997 which name changed to KMT-Hansa Corp. 09/27/2013

SYSTEMS WEST I INC (CO)
Name changed to Systems West Inc. 03/26/1990

SYSTEMS XCELLENCE INC (CANADA)
Each share old Common no par exchanged for (0.25) share new Common no par 06/09/2006
Reincorporated under the laws of Yukon as SXC Health Solutions Corp. 08/01/2007
SXC Health Solutions Corp. name changed to Catamaran Corp. 07/11/2012
(See Catamaran Corp.)

SYSTEMSOFT CORP (DE)
Common 1¢ par split (2) for (1) by issuance of (1) additional share payable 07/17/1996 to holders of record 07/03/1996
Plan of reorganization under Chapter 11 Federal Bankruptcy Code effective 03/01/2000
No stockholders' equity

SYSTEX CORP (TAIWAN)
Stock Dividends - approximately 28.55% payable 06/28/2001 to holders of record 04/24/2001; 20% payable 09/23/2002 to holders of record 07/18/2002 Ex date - 07/16/2002; 10% payable 08/21/2003 to holders of record 06/19/2003 Ex date - 06/19/2003; 5.13% payable 12/17/2004 to holders of record 10/14/2004
Merged into Sysware Corp. 01/02/2007
Each 144A Sponsored GDR for Common exchanged for $1.02271 cash
Each Reg. S Sponsored GDR for Common exchanged for $1.02271 cash

SYSTOMATION INC (NY)
Common $1 par changed to 20¢ par and (4) additional shares issued 05/06/1970
Filed a petition under Chapter XI bankruptcy proceedings 07/22/1976
No stockholders' equity

SYSTONETICS INC (CA)
Common 10¢ par changed to 5¢ par and (1) additional share issued 08/22/1983
Filed a petition under Chapter 7 Federal Bankruptcy Code 01/11/1991
No stockholders' equity

SYSTREX CORP (NY)
Dissolved by proclamation 03/25/1992

SYSTRON DONNER CORP (CA)
Capital Stock no par split (3) for (2) by issuance of (0.5) additional share 02/26/1968
Merged into Thorn Electrical Industries of London 09/12/1979
Each share Capital Stock no par exchanged for $15 cash

SYSVIEW TECHNOLOGY INC (DE)
Name changed to Document Capture Technologies, Inc. 01/08/2008
(See Document Capture Technologies, Inc.)

SYSWIN INC (CAYMAN ISLANDS)
Acquired by Brilliant Strategy Ltd. 04/08/2013
Each Sponsored ADR for Ordinary exchanged for $2 cash

SYTECH CORP (DE)
Name changed to 87 Acquisition Corp. (DE) 09/30/1987 87 Acquisition Corp. (DE) reincorporated in Louisiana 01/24/1994
(See 87 Acquisition Corp.)

SYTJES PANNEKOEKEN HUIS FAMILY RESTAURANTS INC (MN)
Chapter 11 bankruptcy proceedings converted to Chapter 7 on 10/21/1996
No stockholders' equity

SYTRON INC (PA)
Chapter 7 Federal Bankruptcy proceedings terminated 08/15/2006
Stockholders' equity unlikely

SZABO FOOD SVC INC (DE)
5% Preferred $10 par reclassified as Preferred Ser. A $1 par 03/14/1974
Name changed to Oakbrook Consolidated, Inc. 08/19/1975
(See Oakbrook Consolidated, Inc.)

SZEKELY (O.E.) CORP.
Succeeded by Szekely Aircraft & Engine Co. 00/00/1929
Details not available

SZEKELY AIRCRAFT & ENGINE CO.
Assets sold 00/00/1932
Details not available

SZEMCO, INC. (FL)
Adjudicated bankrupt 04/16/1965
No stockholders' equity

SZL SPORTSIGHT INC (BC)
Name changed to QuesTec Imaging, Inc. (BC) 04/29/1996
QuesTec Imaging, Inc. (BC) reincorporated in Wyoming 03/18/1998 which name changed to QuesTec.com, Inc. 01/18/2000 which name changed to QuesTec, Inc. 01/17/2001
(See QuesTec, Inc.)

SZM DISTRS INC (NV)
Common $0.001 par split (8.25) for (1) by issuance of (7.25) additional shares payable 07/19/2002 to holders of record 07/18/2002 Ex date - 07/22/2002
Common $0.001 par split (3) for (1) by issuance of (2) additional shares payable 02/18/2003 to holders of record 02/15/2003 Ex date - 02/19/2003
Reorganized under the laws of Delaware as TNX Television Holdings, Inc. 02/17/2004
Each share Common $0.001 par exchanged for (1) share Common $0.001 par
(See TNX Television Holdings, Inc.)

SZYDS VENTURES INC (AB)
Name changed to Commonwealth Energy Corp. 12/12/1997
Commonwealth Energy Corp. merged into Empire Energy Corp. (UT) 06/29/2001 which reorganized in Nevada as Empire Energy Corp. International 04/26/2004

T

T / F PURIFINER INC (DE)
Common $0.001 par split (5) for (2) by issuance of (1.5) additional share payable 01/14/1997 to holders of record 01/01/1997
Name changed to Puradyn Filter Technologies Inc. 02/03/1998

T / R SYS INC (GA)
Merged into Electronics For Imaging, Inc. 11/03/2003
Each share Common 1¢ par exchanged for $1.5748 cash

T. ROWE PRICE ASSOCIATES, INC. (MD)
See - Price T Rowe Assoc Inc

T & E INDS INC (NJ)
Merged into Vacutronics, Inc. 09/22/1981
Each share Common 10¢ par exchanged for $1.375 cash

T & E THEATRE COM INC (CANADA)
Recapitalized as Manele Bay Ventures Inc. 02/28/2002
Each share Common no par exchanged for (0.33333333) share Common no par
Manele Bay Ventures Inc. name changed to MBA Gold Corp. 07/15/2003 which name changed to MBA Resources Corp. 10/14/2005 which name changed to Thunderbird Energy Corp. 07/27/2006 which recapitalized as Gordon Creek Energy Inc. 10/24/2013

T & F MGMT ASSOC INC (DE)
Name changed to Swiss Sun International, Ltd. 03/21/1990

T & H RES LTD (ON)
Each share Common no par received distribution of (1) share Aurado Exploration Ltd. Common no par payable 11/17/1997 to holders of record 11/14/1997
Reorganized under the laws of Canada as LAB International Inc. 05/16/2002
Each share Common no par exchanged for (0.05) share Common no par
LAB International Inc. name changed to Akela Pharma Inc. 07/13/2007
(See Akela Pharma Inc.)

T & I COMPANIES, INC. (DE)
Charter cancelled and declared inoperative and void for non-payment of taxes 03/01/1974

T & N PLC (ENGLAND)
Merged into Federal-Mogul Corp. (MI) 03/06/1998
Each Sponsored ADR for Ordinary exchanged for approximately $16.88 cash

T & W FINL CORP (WA)
Plan of reorganization under Chapter 11 Federal Bankruptcy Code effective 02/17/2001
No stockholders' equity

T.A.G. INC. (OR)
Involuntarily dissolved for failure to file reports and pay fees 12/03/1993

T A MATLS INC (DE)
Name changed to Tekology Corp. 06/11/1971
(See Tekology Corp.)

T & G2 (NV)
Name changed to Softnet Technology Corp. 08/04/2004
Each share Common $0.001 par exchanged for (1) share Common $0.001 par

T B & T INC (DE)
Merged into Colonial BancGroup, Inc. 11/30/1998
Each share Common no par exchanged for (0.6406) share Common $2.50 par
(See Colonial BancGroup, Inc.)

T B MNG VENTURES INC (ON)
Recapitalized as Sphere 3D Corp. (Old) 12/28/2012
Each share Common no par exchanged for (0.25) share Common no par
Sphere 3D Corp. (Old) reorganized as Sphere 3D Corp. (New) 03/24/2015

T-BAMM (NV)
Name changed to China VTV Ltd. 06/29/2018

T BANCSHARES INC (TX)
Acquired by T Acquisition, Inc. 05/15/2017
Each share Common 1¢ par exchanged for $8.0275 cash

T-BAR INC (MD)
Common 25¢ par split (7) for (5) by issuance of (0.4) additional share 04/25/1980
Common 25¢ par split (3) for (2) by issuance of (0.5) additional share 06/04/1982
Stock Dividends - 25% 04/19/1976; 20% 04/21/1978; 25% 04/20/1979; 25% 06/26/1981
Merged into Data Switch Corp. 07/01/1987
Each share Common 25¢ par exchanged for $8.25 cash

T BAR M INC (TX)
Each share Common 1¢ par exchanged for (1/180,000) share Common $1,800 par 08/04/1986
Note: In effect holders received $1.03 cash per share and public interest was eliminated

T-BAY HLDGS INC (NV)
Each share old Common $0.001 par exchanged for (0.05) share new Common $0.001 par 01/18/2005
Note: No holder will receive fewer than (100) shares
Each share new Common $0.001 par exchanged again for (0.01) share new Common $0.001 par 03/06/2013
Recapitalized as TOCCA Life Holdings, Inc. 01/12/2015
Each share new Common $0.001 par exchanged for (0.002) share Common $0.001 par

T-BIRD PHARMA INC (BC)
Name changed to Emerald Health Therapeutics, Inc. 06/19/2015

T BOONE PICKENS ENERGY FD (ON)
Class A Combined Units separated 02/12/2010
Completely liquidated
Each Class A Unit received $7.66 cash payable 03/20/2013 to holders of record 03/15/2013
Each Class F Unit received $7.79 cash payable 03/20/2013 to holders of record 03/15/2013
Each Class U Unit received USD $8.04 cash payable 03/20/2013 to holders of record 03/15/2013

T-BOWL INTERNATIONAL, INC. (NJ)
Name changed to TX Industries, Inc. 04/26/1968
(See TX Industries, Inc.)

T.C.C., INC. (NY)
Ceased operations 00/00/1987
Details not available

T C C INC (MI)
Charter declared inoperative and void for failure to file reports 05/15/1998

T C EXPLS LTD (BC)
Recapitalized as Decca Resources Ltd. 10/20/1970
Each share Common no par exchanged for (0.2) share Common no par
Decca Resources Ltd. name changed to Sceptre Resources Ltd. (B.C.) 12/27/1977 which reincorporated in Canada 10/31/1979 which merged into Canadian Natural Resources Ltd. 08/15/1996

T C I TRAVEL CORP (CA)
Common no par split (2) for (1) by issuance of (1) additional share 11/27/1972
Name changed to First Travel Corp. 11/01/1974
(See First Travel Corp.)

T-CAP INC (AB)
Recapitalized as Eastern Stone Products Ltd. (AB) 06/16/1992
Each share Common no par exchanged for (0.33333333) share Common no par
Eastern Stone Products Ltd. (AB) reincorporated in Ontario 07/07/1995 which recapitalized as Greenshield Resources Inc. 08/18/1995 which was acquired by Greenshield Resources Ltd. 11/11/2002 which recapitalized as Greenshield Explorations Ltd. (ON) 06/13/2006 which reincorporated in British Columbia 10/19/2007

T CELL SCIENCES INC (DE)
Under plan of merger name changed to AVANT Immunotherapeutics, Inc. 08/21/1998
AVANT Immunotherapeutics, Inc. name changed to Celldex Therapeutics, Inc. 10/01/2008

T.E.C. INC. (PA)
Dissolved 00/00/1959
Details not available

T E N PRIVATE CABLE SYS INC (CANADA)
Recapitalized as Cinema Internet Networks Inc. (Canada) 07/27/1999
Each share Common no par exchanged for (0.2) share Common no par
Cinema Internet Networks Inc. (Canada) reincorporated in British Columbia as Quentin Ventures Ltd. 06/27/2014 which name changed to Identillect Technologies Corp. 05/25/2016

T EATON LTD (ON)
Plan of Arrangement effective 12/30/1999
Each share Common no par

automatically became (1) Participating Unit representing pro rata interest in a Sears Canada Inc. Variable Rate Promissory Note
Each Participating Unit received initial distribution of approximately $0.81866 cash payable 06/30/2006 to holders of record 06/28/2006

T F H PUBNS INC (NY)
Common 10¢ par split (3) for (2) by issuance of (0.5) additional share 09/15/1966
Stock Dividend - 50% 11/15/1963
Name changed to Miracle Pet Products, Inc. 01/08/1969
(See Miracle Pet Products, Inc.)

T.F.M. CORP.
Liquidation completed 00/00/1952
Details not available

T G BANCSHARES CO (MO)
Merged into County National Bancorporation 12/23/1981
Each share Common $5 par exchanged for (0.6227) share Common $5 par and $1.016 cash
County National Bancorporation name changed to County Tower Corp. 12/23/1981
(See County Tower Corp.)

T G S PPTYS LTD (AB)
Plan of arrangement effective 12/06/2002
Each share Common no par exchanged for (1) share TGS Properties Inc. Common no par and (0.0911) TGS North American Real Estate Investment Trust Trust Unit no par
(See TGS Properties Inc.)

T H C MED INC (BC)
Delisted from Vancouver Stock Exchange 10/19/2000

T H E FITNESS CTRS INC (DE)
Charter cancelled and declared inoperative and void for non-payment of taxes 03/01/1985

T HSE & CO LTD (DE)
Each share old Common $0.0001 par exchanged for (0.1) share new Common $0.0001 par 03/05/1999
Name changed to Team Labs Systems Group Inc. 08/28/2000
Team Labs Systems Group Inc. name changed to SciLabs Holdings, Inc. 07/17/2001
(See SciLabs Holdings, Inc.)

T I C INDS CORP. (DE)
Recapitalized 07/07/1972
Recapitalized from T.I.C. Mining Corp. to T.I.C. Industries, Inc. 07/07/1972
Each share Common 10¢ par exchanged for (0.2) share Common 50¢ par
Charter cancelled and declared inoperative and void for non-payment of taxes 03/01/2000

T I CORP CALIF (CA)
Name changed to Ticor 04/27/1977
(See Ticor)

T I ENERGY INC (KS)
Name changed to Cidco Group, Inc, 08/02/1983
(See Cidco Group, Inc.)

T.I.M.E. INC. (DE)
Name changed to T.I.M.E. Freight, Inc. 08/24/1960
T.I.M.E. Freight, Inc. merged into T.I.M.E.-DC, Inc. 01/17/1969
(See T.I.M.E.-DC, Inc.)

T I M E DC INC (DE)
Merged into Contran Corp. 06/21/1989
Each share 72¢ Conv. Preferred Ser A $10 par exchanged for $0.25 cash
Each share Common $2 par exchanged for $0.25 cash

T I M E FGHT INC (DE)
Common $2 par changed to $1 par and (1) additional share issued 06/30/1965
Merged into T.I.M.E.-DC, Inc. 01/17/1969
Each share Common $1 par exchanged for (0.75) share 72¢ Conv. Preferred Ser. A $10 par and (0.5) share Common $2 par
(See T.I.M.E.-DC, Inc.)

T I TRAVEL INTL INC (BC)
Each share Common no par received distribution of (0.04) share Class B Common no par 07/08/1988
Delisted from Vancouver Stock Exchange 03/02/1990

T J CINNAMONS INC (DE)
Name changed to Paramark Enterprises Inc. 09/09/1996
Paramark Enterprises Inc. name changed to Raptor Investments Inc. (DE) 11/01/2001 which reincorporated in Florida 12/04/2001 which name changed to Snap 'N' Sold Corp. 07/22/2005 which name changed to Hot Web, Inc. 09/25/2006 which name changed to Gold Coast Mining Corp. 07/02/2009 which name changed to Green Leaf Innovations, Inc. 03/10/2015

T.K. PRODUCTS, INC. (MN)
Completely liquidated 04/09/1984
Details not available

T.K.C.L., INC. (NY)
Recapitalized as Outdoor Sportsman's Travel, Ltd. 09/06/1977
Each share Common 10¢ par exchanged for (0.0833) share Common 10¢ par
Outdoor Sportsman's Travel, Ltd. name changed to Anglo American Properties, Inc. 03/31/1978
(See Anglo American Properties, Inc.)

T L COMMUNICATIONS INC (CA)
Charter cancelled for failure to file reports and pay taxes 09/04/1990

T M P INVTS LTD (ON)
Name changed to Grey Goose Corp. Ltd. (ON) 06/20/1972
Grey Goose Corp. Ltd. (ON) reincorporated in Canada 01/15/1980
(See Grey Goose Corp. Ltd. (Canada))

T.M.T. TRAILER FERRY, INC. (DE)
Each share Common 10¢ par exchanged for (0.2) share Common 10¢ par 03/31/1958
Reorganized under Chapter X bankruptcy proceedings 01/07/1975
Each share Common 10¢ par exchanged for $3 cash

T M T RES INC (BC)
Each share old Common no par exchanged for (0.28571428) share new Common no par 11/30/2011
New Common no par split (3) for (2) by issuance of (0.5) additional share payable 06/20/2014 to holders of record 06/10/2014 Ex date - 06/23/2014
Recapitalized as Ladera Ventures Corp. 08/28/2017
Each share new Common no par exchanged for (0.1) share Common no par
Ladera Ventures Corp. recapitalized as MedMen Enterprises Inc. 05/29/2018

T-MOBILE US INC (DE)
Each share 5.5% Mandatory Conv. Preferred Ser. A $0.00001 par automatically became (1.6119) shares Common $0.00001 par 12/15/2017
(Additional Information in Active)

T N B FINL CORP (MA)
Common $1 par split (3) for (2) by issuance of (0.5) additional share 06/16/1978
Merged into New England Merchants Co., Inc. 09/30/1981
Each share Common $1 par exchanged for (0.9) share Common $5 par
New England Merchants Co., Inc. name changed to Bank of New England Corp. 05/01/1982
(See Bank of New England Corp.)

T-NETIX INC (DE)
Reincorporated 09/07/2001
State of incorporation changed from (CO) to (DE) 09/07/2001
Merged into TZ Holdings, Inc. 03/04/2004
Each share Common 1¢ par exchanged for $4.60 cash

T O D TASTE ON DEMAND INC (NV)
Recapitalized as China Environmental Protection, Inc. 03/25/2010
Each share Common $0.001 par exchanged for (0.2164989) share Common $0.001 par

T O N M OIL & GAS EXPL CORP (NM)
Reorganized as Tellus Industries, Inc. (NM) 09/10/1985
Each share Common 1¢ par exchanged for (0.1) share Common 1¢ par and (0.02) Class A Common Stock Purchase Warrant expiring 09/30/1988
Tellus Industries, Inc. (NM) reincorporated in Nevada 08/14/1986
(See Tellus Industries, Inc.)

T O PLASTICS INC (MN)
Merged into Top Acquisitions, Inc. 06/12/1985
Each share Common 40¢ par exchanged for $9 cash

T P C CORP (DE)
Merged into Pacificorp Holdings, Inc. 04/15/1997
Each share Common 1¢ par exchanged for $13.41 cash

T P C HOME CARE SVCS INC (NY)
Merged into Star Multi Care Services, Inc. 09/09/1997
Each share Common 1¢ par exchanged for (0.1214102302) share Common $0.001 par and $0.299113511 cash
(See Star Multi Care Services, Inc.)

T R FINL CORP (DE)
Common 1¢ par split (2) for (1) by issuance of (1) additional share payable 05/14/1997 to holders of record 05/01/1997
Merged into Roslyn Bancorp, Inc. 02/17/1999
Each share Common 1¢ par exchanged for (2.05) shares Common 1¢ par
Roslyn Bancorp, Inc. merged into New York Community Bancorp, Inc. 11/03/2003

T R INDS INC (UT)
Merged into Tenakill Associates, Inc. 10/02/1975
Each share Common 1¢ par exchanged for (1) share Common 1¢ par
(See Tenakill Associates, Inc.)

TR 3 CHEM CORP (NV)
Recapitalized 03/25/1975
Recapitalized from TR-3 International, Inc. to TR-3 Chemical Corp. 03/25/1975
Each share Common 1¢ par exchanged for (0.1) share Common 10¢ par
Recapitalized as TR-3 Industries Inc. 09/30/1979
Each share Common 10¢ par exchanged for (0.25) share Common 40¢ par
TR-3 Industries Inc. name changed to Diversified American Industries Inc. 06/14/1990 which name changed to Thunderstone Group Inc. 11/13/1995 which name changed to Cronus Corp. 03/04/1996
(See Cronus Corp.)

T R V MINERALS CORP (BC)
Struck off register and declared dissolved for failure to file returns 10/30/1992

T RAY SCIENCE INC (BC)
Name changed to Verisante Technology, Inc. 01/18/2011

T.S.C. LIQUIDATING CORP. (PA)
Liquidation completed
Each share Common 1¢ par exchanged for initial distribution of $0.50 cash 03/06/1978
Each share Common 1¢ par received second and final distribution of $0.011463 cash 10/30/1978

T S FISHER INC (CO)
Name changed to Bio-Tech Systems International, Inc. 04/11/1989

T-S INVESTORS CORP.
Dissolved 00/00/1938
Details not available

T S TELECOM LTD (ON)
Reorganized under the laws of British Columbia as Quanta Resources Inc. 03/09/2009
Each share Common no par exchanged for (0.2) share Common no par

T T A RES CORP (BC)
Name changed to Minefund Development Corp. 08/26/1999

T T ACQUISITIONS INC (CO)
Name changed to Financial Resources Marketing Corp. 08/19/1989

T T C INDS INC (NY)
Dissolved by proclamation 12/16/1974

T-3 ENERGY SVCS INC (DE)
Merged into Robbins & Myers, Inc. 01/10/2011
Each share Common $0.001 par exchanged for (0.894) share Common no par and $7.95 cash
(See Robbins & Myers, Inc.)

T V DEV CORP (NY)
Completely liquidated 09/12/1969
Each share Common 5¢ par exchanged for first and final distribution of (1) share Acquisition Newsletter, Inc. Common 1¢ par
Acquisition Newsletter, Inc. merged into National Modular Housing Components Inc. 06/28/1971
(See National Modular Housing Components Inc.)

T.V.S. INDUSTRIES LTD. (BC)
Name changed to GBX Mines Ltd. 02/11/1974
GBX Mines Ltd. recapitalized as El Paso Energy Corp. 08/20/1979 which recapitalized as E.L.E. Energy Corp. 10/05/1984 which recapitalized as Maple Leaf Springs Water Corp. 11/12/1992 which recapitalized as International Maple Leaf Springs Ltd. 02/24/1998
(See International Maple Leaf Springs Ltd.)

T W A R INC (UT)
Recapitalized as Lentec Imaging Inc. (UT) 06/01/1995
Each share Common no par exchanged for (0.03769231) share Common no par
Lentec Imaging Inc. (UT) reorganized in Nevada as RTO Holdings, Inc. 06/21/2006 which name changed to Orion Ethanol, Inc. 11/07/2006

T W CHRISTIAN INC (MN)
SEC revoked common stock registration 05/18/2009

T&G APOTHECARY INC (NV)
Reorganized as Biologix Hair Inc. 12/13/2012

Each share Common $0.001 par exchanged for (7) shares Common $0.001 par

TAB PRODS CO (DE)
Reincorporated 11/26/1986
Each share 7% Conv. Preferred $10 par exchanged for (10) shares 7% Conv. Preferred $1 par 03/04/1968
Each share old Common no par exchanged for (10) shares new Common no par 03/04/1968
7% Conv. Preferred $1 par called for redemption 09/02/1968
New Common no par split (3) for (2) by issuance of (0.5) additional share 10/28/1977
New Common no par split (3) for (2) by issuance of (0.5) additional share 10/17/1980
New Common no par split (3) for (2) by issuance of (0.5) additional share 02/25/1983
New Common no par split (3) for (2) by issuance of (0.5) additional share 03/30/1984
New Common no par split (3) for (2) by issuance of (0.5) additional share 05/26/1986
State of incorporation changed from (CA) to (DE) 11/26/1986
Merged into HS Morgan Ltd. Partnership 10/23/2002
Each share Common no par exchanged for $5.85 cash

TAB VENTURES CORP (BC)
Name changed to Nu-Sky Exploration Inc. 06/26/1989
Nu-Sky Exploration Inc. recapitalized as Consolidated Nu-Sky Exploration Inc. (BC) 05/22/1991 which reorganized in Alberta as Nu-Sky Energy Inc. 03/01/1995
(See Nu-Sky Energy Inc.)

TABACALERAYSIDRON INC (NV)
Common $0.0001 par split (5.75) for (1) by issuance of (4.75) additional shares payable 07/09/2015 to holders of record 07/06/2015 Ex date - 07/10/2015
Name changed to Mount TAM Biotechnologies, Inc. 08/31/2015

TABACH INDUSTRIES, INC. (CA)
Name changed to Continental Consolidated Inc. 03/22/1967
(See Continental Consolidated Inc.)

TABATHA V INC NEW (CO)
Common $0.001 par split (4) for (1) by issuance of (3) additional shares payable 12/14/2006 to holders of record 12/14/2006 Ex date - 12/15/2006
SEC revoked common stock registration 02/10/2011

TABATHA V INC OLD (CO)
Recapitalized as Power-Save Energy Corp. 11/14/2005
Each share Common $0.001 par exchanged for (0.01) share Common $0.001 par
Power-Save Energy Corp. name changed to Tabatha V, Inc. (New) 01/06/2006
(See Tabatha V, Inc. (New))

TABBYS INTL INC (FL)
Name changed to Gulf Leasing Corp. 12/14/1971
(See Gulf Leasing Corp.)

TABCORP HLDGS LTD (AUSTRALIA)
ADR agreement terminated 04/30/2010
Each Sponsored 144A ADR for Ordinary exchanged for $82.61057 cash
Each Sponsored ADR for Ordinary exchanged for $82.61057 cash (Additional Information in Active)

TABER MILLS CORP.
Bankrupt 00/00/1940
No stockholders' equity

TABLE MESA OIL CO.
Merged into Holly Oil Co. 01/29/1954
Each share Capital Stock $1 par exchanged for (0.16666666) share Capital Stock $1 par
Holly Oil Co. name changed to Holly Resources Corp. 11/01/1968
(See Holly Resources Corp.)

TABLE ROCK LABS INC (SC)
Voluntarily dissolved 06/07/1974
Details not available

TABOR ENVIRONMENTAL SVCS INC (DE)
Each share Common $0.001 par exchanged for (0.16) share Common $0.00625 par 01/18/1988
Recapitalized as Wastec Inc. 10/14/1991
Each share Common $0.00625 par exchanged for (0.125) share Common $0.00625 par
Wastec Inc. name changed to Environmental Services Group Inc. 01/10/1994
(See Environmental Services Group Inc.)

TABOR LAKE GOLD MINES, LTD. (ON)
Charter cancelled and declared dissolved for failure to file returns and pay fees 11/09/1976

TABULATING & BUSINESS SERVICES, INC. (NY)
Name changed to TBS Computer Centers Corp. 07/01/1967
(See TBS Computer Centers Corp.)

TABULATING & DATA PROCESSING CORP (NY)
Merged into Datatab, Inc. 06/30/1969
Each share Common 10¢ par exchanged for (0.5) share Common $1 par
(See Datatab, Inc.)

TABULATING MACHINE CO.
Merged into International Business Machine Corp. 00/00/1933
Details not available

TABULATING STK FORMS INC (NY)
Charter cancelled and proclaimed dissolved for failure to pay taxes 03/31/1982

TAC ACQUISITION CORP (DE)
Units separated 02/14/2007
Liquidation completed
Each share Common $0.00001 par exchanged for initial distribution of $5.6941 cash 02/14/2007
Each share Common $0.00001 par received second and final distribution of $0.041786 cash payable 07/01/2008 to holders of record 02/14/2007 Ex date - 07/02/2008

TAC CAP CORP (BC)
Name changed to TAC Gold Corp. 12/21/2009

TAC INC (UT)
Each share old Common $0.001 par exchanged for (0.005) share new Common $0.001 par 04/16/1998
Recapitalized as Innovative Property Development Corp. 08/27/1998
Each share new Common $0.001 par exchanged for (0.005) share Common $0.001 par
Innovative Property Development Corp. name changed to ChinaMallUSA.com, Inc. 06/01/1999
(See ChinaMallUSA.com, Inc.)

TACA AIRWAYS, S.A.
Recapitalized as Taca Corp. 00/00/1951
Each share Capital Stock $1 par exchanged for (1) share Common 10¢ par
Taca Corp. was acquired by Taca International Airlines, S.A. 12/05/1960
(See Taca International Airlines, S.A.)

TACA CORP. (DE)
Acquired by Taca International Airlines, S.A. 12/05/1960
Each share Common 10¢ par exchanged for (1) share Capital Stock 25 Centavos par
(See Taca International Airlines, S.A.)

TACA INTL AIRLS S A (EL SALVADOR)
Each share Capital Stock 25 Centavos par exchanged for (0.00000769) share Capital Capital Stock 7,500 Colones par 01/00/1985
Note: Under Salvadorian law holders not entitled to receive (1) full share will be aggregated with like holders until the combined interest entitles them to a full share. Holders will then be considered as owning an undivided interest as tenants-in-common.
Public interest eliminated

TACHE LAKE MINES LTD (QC)
Recapitalized as Consolidated Tache Mines & Investments Ltd. 08/17/1972
Each share Capital Stock $1 par exchanged for (0.1) share Capital Stock no par
Consolidated Tache Mines & Investments Ltd. name changed to Tache Resources Inc. 09/13/1982 which recapitalized as United North American Resources, Inc. 02/15/1985 which reorganized in the United Kingdom as Alliance Resources PLC 02/11/1991 which merged into AROC Inc. 12/08/1999
(See AROC Inc.)

TACHE RES INC (QC)
Recapitalized as United North American Resources, Inc. (QC) 02/15/1985
Each share Capital Stock no par exchanged for (0.16666666) share Common no par
United North American Resources, Inc. (QC) reorganized in United Kingdom as Alliance Resources PLC 02/11/1991 which merged into AROC Inc. 12/08/1999
(See AROC Inc.)

TACHTRONIC INSTRS INC (MN)
Name changed to QMC Technologies Inc. 12/07/1987
(See QMC Technologies Inc.)

TACITUS VENTURES INC (DE)
Name changed to World Wide Stone Corp. (DE) 11/15/1989
World Wide Stone Corp. (DE) reincorporated in Nevada 11/30/1989

TACO BELL (CA)
Common 10¢ par split (2) for (1) by issuance of (1) additional share 03/05/1976
Merged into PepsiCo, Inc. (DE) 06/20/1978
Each share Common 10¢ par exchanged for (1.43) shares Capital Stock 5¢ par
PepsiCo, Inc. (DE) reincorporated in North Carolina 12/04/1986

TACO CABANA INC (DE)
Class A Common 1¢ par split (3) for (2) by issuance of (0.5) additional share 10/18/1993
Merged into Carrols Corp. 12/20/2000
Each share Class A Common 1¢ par exchanged for $9.04 cash

TACO CHARLEY INC (CA)
Acquired by PepsiCo, Inc. 02/04/1983
Each share Common no par exchanged for $1.80 cash

TACO CORP (SC)
Each share Common $1 par exchanged for (0.002) share Common no par 09/20/1974
Note: In effect holders received $15 cash per share and public interest was eliminated

TACO INC (NV)
Name changed to Communique Wireless Corp. 04/10/1997
Communique Wireless Corp. name changed to Communique Corp. 10/10/1997 which name changed to Formal Systems America Inc. 12/17/1998
(See Formal Systems America Inc.)

TACO KING INC (DE)
Assets sold for benefit of creditors 10/00/1971
No stockholders' equity

TACO SI INC (MN)
Involuntarily dissolved 10/04/1991

TACO TICO INC. (KS)
Merged into Foley Family Corp. 07/21/1975
Each share Common no par exchanged for $1.60 cash

TACO TOWNE INTL INC (MN)
Merged into Colonial Services Co. 09/00/1970
Each share Common 25¢ par received (0.33333333) share Common 1¢ par
Note: Certificates were not required to be surrendered and are without value
(See Colonial Services Co.)

TACO VILLA INC (DE)
Name changed to Del Taco Restaurants, Inc. 05/25/1989
(See Del Taco Restaurants, Inc.)

TACO VIVA INC (FL)
Common 1¢ par split (3) for (2) by issuance of (0.5) additional share 06/01/1983
Common 1¢ par split (3) for (2) by issuance of (0.5) additional share 03/29/1985
Name changed to QSR, Inc. 10/23/1989
QSR, Inc. merged into Miami Subs Corp. 10/01/1991 which merged into Nathan's Famous, Inc. 10/01/1999

TACOMA BOATBUILDING INC (WA)
Common $1 par split (3) for (2) by issuance of (0.5) additional share 12/06/1982
Reorganized under Chapter 11 Federal Bankruptcy Code 09/10/1987
Each share Common $1 par received (0.209899) share Common 1¢ par
Note: Common $1 par certificates were not required to be surrendered and are without value
Each share Common 1¢ par exchanged for (0.1) share Common 10¢ par 05/16/1990
Stock Dividend - 50% 07/07/1981
Filed a petition under Chapter 11 Federal Bankruptcy Code 02/24/1992
Stockholders' equity unlikely

TACOMA RAILWAY & POWER CO.
Name changed to Tacoma Transit Co. 00/00/1941
(See Tacoma Transit Co.)

TACOMA RES LTD (BC)
Struck off register and declared dissolved for failure to file returns 11/29/1985

TACOMA-SEATTLE CO-OPERATIVE RARE METALS CO. (WA)
Charter cancelled and proclaimed dissolved for failure to pay fees 07/01/1934

TACOMA TRANSIT CO. (NJ)
Each share Capital Stock no par exchanged for (10) shares Capital Stock $5 par 00/00/1946
Capital Stock $5 par changed to $4 par 00/00/1954
Capital Stock $4 par changed to $1 par 00/00/1955

Liquidation completed 06/15/1961
Details not available

TACONIC INVESTMENT CORP. (MA)
Liquidation completed
Each share Common $25 par exchanged for initial distribution of $62 cash 11/06/1972
Each share Common $25 par received second distribution of $3 cash 06/25/1974
Each share Common $25 par received third and final distribution of $1 cash 08/22/1977

TACONIC RACING & BREEDING ASSN INC (VT)
Completely liquidated 01/15/1973
Each share Capital Stock $1 par exchanged for $6 cash

TACONY-PALMYRA FERRY CO.
Liquidated in 1929

TACONY STEEL CO.
Property sold 00/00/1928
No stockholders' equity

TACTEX CTLS INC (AB)
Ceased operations 11/00/2008
Stockholders' equity unlikely

TACTICAL SOLUTION PARTNERS INC (DE)
Name changed to Brekford International Corp. 05/13/2008
Brekford International Corp. name changed to Brekford Corp. 07/21/2010 which name changed to Brekford Traffic Safety, Inc. 06/08/2017 which merged into Novume Solutions, Inc. 08/28/2017

TAD CAP CORP (BC)
Name changed to TAD Mineral Exploration Inc. 03/10/2010
TAD Mineral Exploration Inc. recapitalized as Everest Ventures Inc. 01/19/2016 which name changed to Halio Energy Inc. 06/28/2016

TAD MINERAL EXPL INC (BC)
Recapitalized as Everest Ventures Inc. 01/19/2016
Each share Common no par exchanged for (0.1) share Common no par
Everest Ventures Inc. name changed to Halio Energy Inc. 06/28/2016

TADDEO CONSTR & LEASING CORP (NY)
Merged into Sound One Corp. 09/29/1981
Each share Common 10¢ par exchanged for (1) share Common 1¢ par
(See Sound One Corp.)

TADEO HLDGS INC (DE)
Name changed to TekInsight.com Inc. 12/03/1999
TekInsight.com Inc. name changed to DynTek Inc. 12/31/2001

TADIRAN LTD (ISRAEL)
Acquired by Koor Industries Ltd. 12/18/1998
Each Sponsored ADR for Ordinary exchanged for $36.375 cash

TADS ENTERPRISES INC (DE)
Acquired by Tad's Interim Corp. 05/05/1988
Each share Common 20¢ par exchanged for $13.25 cash

TAEL CAP INC (AB)
Merged into Torch River Resources Ltd. 06/17/2004
Each share Common no par exchanged for (1) share Common no par
Torch River Resources Ltd. name changed to Saint Jean Carbon Inc. 11/04/2013

TAEWOONG CO LTD (KOREA)
GDR agreement terminated 07/02/2012
Each Sponsored 144A GDR for Common exchanged for (5) shares Common
Each Sponsored Reg. S GDR for Common exchanged for (5) shares Common

TAFFET ELECTRS INC (NY)
Adjudicated bankrupt 10/23/1970
Stockholders' equity unlikely

TAFT BROADCASTING CO (DE)
Common $1 par changed to 50¢ par and (1) additional share issued 08/03/1965
Common 50¢ par split (2) for (1) by issuance of (1) additional share 08/14/1978
Acquired by FMI Financial Corp. 10/06/1987
Each share Common 50¢ par exchanged for $157.10 cash

TAFT BUILDING CO. (CA)
Liquidation completed 00/00/1955
Details not available

TAFT ELECTROSYSTEMS INC (NJ)
Liquidated 12/23/1974
No stockholders' equity

TAFT NATL BK (TAFT, CA)
Merged into United Security Bancshares 04/23/2004
Each share Common $4 par exchanged for (0.90314316) share Common no par

TAG-ALDER MINES LTD. (ON)
Charter revoked for failure to file reports and pay fees 04/01/1965

TAG EVENTS CORP (NV)
Name changed to Deer Consumer Products, Inc. 09/29/2008

TAG GROUP INC (FL)
Proclaimed dissolved for failure to file reports and pay fees 09/14/2007

TAG HEUER INTL S A (SWITZERLAND)
ADR agreement terminated 05/17/2000
Each Sponsored ADR for Ordinary exchanged for $11.952 cash

TAG-IT PAC INC (DE)
Name changed to Talon International, Inc. 07/23/2007

TAG OIL LTD (YUKON)
Common no par split (3) for (2) by issuance of (0.5) additional share payable 05/03/2004 to holders of record 04/27/2004 Ex date - 05/04/2004
Reincorporated under the laws of British Columbia 10/12/2006

TAGALDER INC (ON)
Recapitalized as Tagalder (2000) Inc. 09/01/2000
Each share Common no par exchanged for (0.1) share Common no par

TAGAMI MINES LTD (QC)
Merged into CDA International Inc. 12/09/1999
Each share Common $1 par exchanged for (0.1) share Common no par
(See CDA International Inc.)

TAGGART BROTHERS CO., INC.
Acquired by Taggart Corp. 00/00/1928
Details not available

TAGGART CAP CORP (ON)
Reorganized as PRO Real Estate Investment Trust 03/13/2013
Each share Common no par exchanged for (0.1) Trust Unit
Note: Unexchanged certificates will be cancelled and become without value 03/13/2019

TAGGART CORP.
Merged into St. Regis Paper Co. 00/00/1949
Details not available

TAGISH LAKE GOLD CORP (BC)
Merged into New Pacific Metals Corp. 12/23/2010
Each share Common no par exchanged for $0.10 cash
Note: Unexchanged certificates were cancelled and became without value 12/23/2016

TAGO INC (CA)
Each share old Common no par exchanged for (0.1) share new Common $0.001 par 12/06/1989
Stock Dividend - 10% 08/03/1992
Merged into BioSource International, Inc. 05/19/1993
Each share Common $0.001 par exchanged for (1) share Common $0.001 par
(See BioSource International, Inc.)

TAGUS RES LTD (BC)
Common 50¢ par changed to no par 00/00/1983
Recapitalized as High Reserve Resources Ltd. 04/26/1984
Each share Common no par exchanged for (0.33333333) share Common no par
(See High Reserve Resources Ltd.)

TAHERA CORP (BC)
Name changed to Tahera Diamond Corp. 06/23/2004
(See Tahera Diamond Corp.)

TAHERA DIAMOND CORP (BC)
Each share old Common no par exchanged for (0.2) share new Common no par 05/18/2006
Assets sold for the benefit of creditors 07/27/2010
Stockholders' equity unlikely

TAHITI RESORT HOTELS INC (BC)
Cease trade order effective 03/14/1989
Details not available

TAHOE PAC CORP (NV)
Name changed to Ameri-First Financial Group, Inc. (NV) 01/06/2000
Ameri-First Financial Group, Inc. (NV) reincorporated in Delaware 03/22/2000 which reincorporated in Nevada as Eight Dragons Co. 12/07/2007 which name changed to Rokk3r Inc. 06/18/2018

TAHTSA MINES LTD (BC)
Name changed to Tatsa Resources Ltd. 02/11/1982
Tatsa Resources Ltd. name changed to Acorn Resources Ltd. 07/06/1983 which recapitalized as Consolidated Acorn Resources Ltd. 07/23/1990
(See Consolidated Acorn Resources Ltd.)

TAI CHEUNG HLDGS LTD (HONG KONG)
Stock Dividend - 10% 08/28/1994
ADR agreement terminated 08/07/2017
Each Sponsored ADR for Ordinary exchanged for $5.322391 cash

TAI ENERGY CORP (BC)
Acquired by Maxx Petroleum Ltd. 03/17/1995
Each share Common no par exchanged for (0.334) share Common no par and $0.18 cash
Maxx Petroleum Ltd. acquired by Provident Energy Trust 05/25/2001 which reorganized as Provident Energy Ltd. (New) 01/03/2011 which merged into Pembina Pipeline Corp. 04/02/2012

TAI ENERGY RES CORP (BC)
Merged into Tai Energy Corp. 06/30/1993
Each share Common no par exchanged for (0.489112) share Common no par
Tai Energy Corp. acquired by Maxx Petroleum Ltd. 03/17/1995 which was acquired by Provident Energy Trust 05/21/2001 which reorganized as Provident Energy Ltd. (New) 01/03/2011 which merged into Pembina Pipeline Corp. 04/02/2012

TAI FAN VENTURES INC (CANADA)
Name changed to La Ronge Resources Inc. 07/19/1988
La Ronge Resources Inc. name changed to IAE Hong Kong Equities Inc. 01/04/1991
(See IAE Hong Kong Equities Inc.)

TAIG VENTURES INC (UT)
Recapitalized as Viper Networks Inc. (UT) 01/11/2001
Each (12) shares Common $0.001 par exchanged for (1) share Common $0.001 par
Viper Networks, Inc. (UT) reincorporated in Nevada 05/18/2005

TAIGA FST PRODS LTD (BC)
Common no par split (2) for (1) by issuance of (1) additional share payable 08/06/2002 to holders of record 08/02/2002
Reorganized as Taiga Building Products Ltd. 09/01/2005
Each share Common no par exchanged for (4) Stapled Units

TAIGA MINES LTD (BC)
Struck off register and declared dissolved for failure to file returns 08/06/1974

TAILOR AQUAPONICS WORLD WIDE INC (NV)
Each share old Common $0.001 par exchanged for (1.01) shares new Common $0.001 par 12/21/2006
Note: No holder will receive fewer than (100) post-split shares
Each share new Common $0.001 par exchanged again for (0.1) share new Common $0.001 par 03/19/2007
Note: No holder will receive fewer than (100) post-split shares
Recapitalized as Diversified Acquisitions, Inc. 08/20/2007
Each (1,200) shares new Common $0.001 par exchanged for (1) share new Common $0.001 par
Note: No holder will receive fewer than (100) post-split shares
Diversified Acquisitions, Inc. recapitalized as Vitalcare Diabetes Treatment Centers, Inc. 03/24/2008 which recapitalized as China Advanced Technology 06/23/2010 which name changed to Goliath Film & Media Holdings 01/20/2012

TAILWIND FINL INC (DE)
Completely liquidated 04/20/2009
Each Unit exchanged for first and final distribution of $8.17733907 cash
Each share Common $0.001 par exchanged for first and final distribution of $8.17733907 cash

TAINA DEVS CORP (BC)
Name changed to Double Eagle Entertainment Corp. 01/06/1994
(See Double Eagle Entertainment Corp.)

TAINA GOLD INC (BC)
Name changed to Oxin Industries Ltd. 02/19/1986
(See Oxin Industries Ltd.)

TAIPAN CAP CORP (BC)
Name changed to Taipan Resources Inc. 11/03/2009
Taipan Resources Inc. name changed to Molori Energy Inc. 01/06/2017

TAIPAN RES INC (BC)
Each share old Common no par exchanged for (0.1) share new Common no par 09/15/2015
Name changed to Molori Energy Inc. 01/06/2017

TAISHO MARINE & FIRE INS LTD (JAPAN)
Name changed to Mitsui Marine & Fire Insurance Co., Ltd. 04/01/1991
Mitsui Marine & Fire Insurance Co., Ltd. name changed to Mitsui Sumitomo Insurance Co. 11/30/2001 which reorganized as Mitsui Sumitomo Insurance Group Holdings, Inc. 04/01/2008 which name changed to MS&AD Insurance Group Holdings, Inc. 04/01/2010

TAIT PAPER & COLOR INDUSTRIES, INC. (NY)
Name changed to Imperial Paper & Color Corp. 00/00/1929
(See Imperial Color Chemical & Paper Corp.)

TAIWAN EQUITY FD INC (MD)
Liquidation completed
Each share Common 1¢ par received initial distribution of $20.40 cash payable 05/11/2000 to holders of record 05/05/2000
Each share Common 1¢ par received second and final distribution of $0.37 cash 06/27/2000

TAIWAN GTR CHINA FD (MA)
Name changed to Shelton Greater China Fund 06/13/2011

TAJ MAHAL HLDG CORP (DE)
Merged into Trump Hotels & Casino Resorts, Inc. 04/17/1996
Each share Class A Common 1¢ par exchanged for approximately (1.04) shares Common 1¢ par
Trump Hotels & Casino Resorts, Inc. reorganized as Trump Entertainment Resorts, Inc. 05/20/2005
(See Trump Entertainment Resorts, Inc.)

TAJEE RES LTD (BC)
Struck off register and dissolved for failure to file returns 06/16/1995

TAJEN RES CORP (AB)
Name changed to Syncrete Technologies Inc. 08/24/1988
(See Syncrete Technologies Inc.)

TAJIRI VENTURES CORP (BC)
Name changed to Tajiri Resources Corp. 04/26/2011

TAKAMINE FERMENT CO. (WV)
Liquidation for cash completed 01/11/1965
Six cash distributions were paid to holders of record of various dates without presentation of certificates which are now of no value

TAKARA HLDGS INC (JAPAN)
ADR agreement terminated 03/13/2018
No ADR's remain outstanding

TAKARA RES INC (CANADA)
Each share old Common no par exchanged for (0.33333333) share new Common no par 04/23/2010
Each share new Common no par exchanged again for (0.1) share new Common no par 12/31/2013
Name changed to Castle Silver Resources Inc. 11/28/2016
Castle Silver Resources Inc. name changed to Canada Cobalt Works Inc. 02/23/2018

TAKATA CORP (JAPAN)
Notice of Acquisition of Issued Shares without Contribution published 06/20/2018
No ADR holders' equity

TAKE TO AUCTION COM INC (FL)
Name changed to Nimbus Group Inc. 09/14/2001
Nimbus Group Inc. name changed to Taylor Madison Corp. 04/01/2004 which recapitalized as Telzuit Medical Technologies, Inc. 08/19/2005
(See Telzuit Medical Technologies, Inc.)

TAKECARE INC (DE)
Merged into FHP International Corp. 06/17/1994
Each share Common 10¢ par exchanged for either (1.6) shares Conv. Preferred Ser. A $1 par and (0.4800) share Common 5¢ par or (1.096) shares Adjustable Rate Preferred Ser. B $1 par and $27.40 cash
Note: Option to receive Ser. B and cash expired 11/30/1993
FHP International Corp. merged into PacifiCare Health Systems, Inc. (New) 02/14/1997 which merged into UnitedHealth Group Inc. 12/20/2005

TAKEDOWN ENTMT INC (NV)
Common $0.001 par split (5) for (1) by issuance of (4) additional shares payable 06/30/2010 to holders of record 06/30/2010
Recapitalized as Green Hygienics Holdings Inc. 07/24/2012
Each share Common $0.001 par exchanged for (0.0005) share Common $0.001 par

TAKEFUJI CORP (JAPAN)
ADR agreement terminated 12/23/2014
No ADR holders' equity

TAKEOUTMUSIC COM HLDGS CORP (WA)
Each share old Common no par exchanged for (0.04) share new Common no par 02/09/2001
Company terminated common stock registration and is no longer public as of 03/28/2002

TAKEPOINT VENTURES LTD (BC)
Reorganized under the laws of Yukon as Consolidated Takepoint Ventures Ltd. 06/25/2002
Each share Common no par exchanged for (0.33333333) share Common no par
Consolidated Takepoint Ventures Ltd. name changed to Lake Shore Gold Corp. (YT) 12/18/2002 which reincorporated in British Columbia 06/30/2004 which reincorporated in Canada 07/18/2008 which merged into Tahoe Resources Inc. 04/07/2016

TAKLA GOLD MINES LTD (CANADA)
Recapitalized as Canard Resources Ltd. 01/24/1994
Each share Common no par exchanged for (0.125) share Common no par
(See Canard Resources Ltd.)

TAKLA SILVER MINES LTD (BC)
Struck off register and declared dissolved for failure to file returns 10/28/1974

TAKLA STAR RES LTD (AB)
Reincorporated under the laws of Canada as North Group Ltd. 08/30/2002
North Group Ltd. (Canada) reincorporated in British Columbia as North Group Finance Ltd. 12/22/2005 which recapitalized as Peekaboo Beans Inc. 09/29/2016

TAKO RES LTD (BC)
Recapitalized as Consolidated Tako Resources Ltd. 03/27/1998
Each share Common no par exchanged for (0.1428571) share Common no par
Consolidated Tako Resources Ltd. recapitalized as International Tako Industries Inc. (BC) 01/18/2000 which reincorporated in Alberta 11/26/2002 which name changed to Ironhorse Oil & Gas Inc. 05/14/2004 which recapitalized as Pond Technologies Holdings Inc. 02/06/2018

TAKU RIVER GOLD MINES LTD. (BC)
Merged into New Taku Mines Ltd. 04/22/1954
Each share Common no par exchanged for (0.25) share Common no par
New Taku Mines Ltd. name changed to Rembrandt Gold Mines Ltd. (ON) 10/17/1974 which reincorporated in Canada 08/04/1992 which reincorporated in Cayman Islands 05/16/1996
(See Rembrandt Gold Mines Ltd.)

TAKURA MINERALS INC (BC)
Recapitalized as Consolidated African Mining Corp. (BC) 08/28/1997
Each share Common no par exchanged for (0.5) share Common no par
Consolidated African Mining Corp. (BC) reincorporated in Yukon 12/08/1997 which recapitalized as Excam Developments Inc. 01/19/2000
(See Excam Developments Inc.)

TAL CAP INC (MN)
Common 50¢ par changed to 20¢ par 06/09/1970
Company believed out of business 00/00/1990
Details not available

TAL INTL GROUP INC (DE)
Merged into Triton International Ltd. 07/12/2016
Each share Common $0.001 par exchanged for (1) share Common 1¢ par

TAL WIRELESS NETWORKS INC (DE)
Charter forfeited for failure to maintain a registered agent 02/25/1998

TALARIAN CORP (DE)
Merged into TIBCO Software Inc. 04/23/2002
Each share Common $0.001 par exchanged for (0.21793) share Common $0.001 par and $2.65 cash
(See TIBCO Software Inc.)

TALBERT MED MGMT HLDGS CORP (DE)
Merged into MedPartners, Inc. (New) 09/23/1997
Each share Common no par exchanged for $63 cash

TALBORNE CAP CORP (CANADA)
Assets sold for the benefit of creditors 00/00/1994
No stockholders' equity

TALBOT BANCSHARES INC (MD)
Merged into Shore Bancshares, Inc. 12/01/2000
Each share Common 1¢ par exchanged for (2.85) shares Common 1¢ par

TALBOT BK (EASTON, MD)
Under plan of reorganization each share Common 1¢ par automatically became (2) shares Talbot Bancshares Inc. Common 1¢ par 05/01/1997
Talbot Bancshares Inc. merged into Shore Bancshares, Inc. 12/01/2000

TALBOTS INC (DE)
Common 1¢ par split (2) for (1) by issuance of (1) additional share payable 11/07/2000 to holders of record 10/25/2000 Ex date - 11/08/2000
Acquired by TLB Holdings L.L.C. 08/03/2012
Each share Common 1¢ par exchanged for $2.75 cash

TALBRYN FINL CORP (NY)
Name changed to Zuccarelli Holophonics Corp. 02/17/1988

TALCORP ASSOCIATES LTD. (CANADA)
Common no par reclassified as Conv. Class A Common no par 12/13/1976
Conv. Class A Common no par split (2) for (1) by issuance of (1) additional share 05/16/1980
Conv. Class B Common no par split (2) for (1) by issuance of (1) additional share 05/16/1980
Conv. Class C Common no par split (2) for (1) by issuance of (1) additional share 05/16/1980
Conv. Class A Common no par split (2) for (1) by issuance of (1) additional share 05/21/1981
Conv. Class B Common no par split (2) for (1) by issuance of (1) additional share 05/21/1981
Conv. Class C Common no par split (2) for (1) by issuance of (1) additional share 05/21/1981
Name changed to Talcorp Ltd. 09/14/1982
Talcorp Ltd. reorganized as Consolidated Talcorp Ltd. 08/07/1986 which name changed to Sound Insight Enterprises Ltd. 12/07/1990 which merged into CamVec Corp. 09/11/1992 which name changed to AMJ Campbell Inc. 08/14/2001
(See AMJ Campbell Inc.)

TALCORP LTD (CANADA)
Conv. Class A Common no par reclassified as Common no par 01/27/1983
Conv. Class B Common no par reclassified as Common no par 01/27/1983
Conv. Class C Common no par reclassified as Non-Vtg. Common no par 01/27/1983
Reorganized as Consolidated Talcorp Ltd. 08/07/1986
Each share $3 Conv. Preference no par exchanged for (0.4) share Common no par
Each share Common no par exchanged for (0.1) share Common no par
Each share Non-Vtg. Common no par exchanged for (0.1) share Common no par
Consolidated Talcorp Ltd. name changed to Sound Insight Enterprises Ltd. 12/07/1990 which merged into CamVec Corp. 09/01/1992 which name changed to AMJ Campbell Inc. 08/14/2001
(See AMJ Campbell Inc.)

TALCOTT JAMES INC (NY)
Each share Class A $50 par exchanged for (9.9989) shares Common $9 par 00/00/1936
Each share Class B $50 par exchanged for (5) shares Common $9 par 00/00/1936
Each share Common no par exchanged for (5) shares Common $9 par 00/00/1936
5.25% Preferred Ser. A $50 par reclassified as 5.75% Preferred Ser. I-A $50 par 00/00/1954
4.5% Preferred $50 par reclassified as 5% Preferred $50 par 00/00/1954
5% Preferred $50 par called for redemption 10/01/1959
Common $9 par changed to $4.50 par and and (1) additional share issued 04/25/1961
Reorganized 10/04/1968
Each share 4.5% Conv. Preferred Ser. I-F $50 par exchanged for (1) share Talcott National Corp. $2.25 Conv. Preferred Ser. A $1 par
Each share 5.5% Conv. Preferred Ser. I-G $50 par exchanged for (1) share Talcott National Corp. $2.75 Conv. Preferred Ser. B $1 par
Each share $5.50 Conv. Preferred Ser. I-I $50 par exchanged for (1) share Talcott National Corp. $5.50 Conv. Preferred Ser. C $1 par
Each share Common $4.50 par exchanged for (1) share Talcott National Corp. Common $1 par

TAL-TAL

(See Talcott National Corp.)
5.25% Conv. Preferred Ser. I-D $50 par called for redemption 09/01/1970
6.25% Preferred Ser. I-C $50 par called for redemption 02/00/1974
6.25% Preferred Ser. I-H $50 par called for redemption 02/00/1975
5.5% Preferred Ser. I-B $50 par called for redemption 04/01/1975
5.25% Preferred Ser. I-E $50 par called for redemption 04/30/1979
$8 Preferred Ser. I-J $50 par called for redemtpion 04/30/1979
$8 Preferred Ser. I-K $50 par called for redemption 04/30/1979
Stock Dividends - 10% 12/28/1950; 10% 12/31/1953; 10% 12/31/1956; 10% 12/31/1958
Name changed to Leucadia Inc. 05/27/1980
(See Leucadia Inc.)

TALCOTT NATL CORP (NY)
$2.75 Preferred Ser. B $1 par called for called for redemption 00/00/1979
$2.25 Preferred Ser. A $1 par called for redemption 00/00/1974
Name changed to Leucadia National Corp. 05/27/1980
Leucadia National Corp. name changed to Jefferies Financial Group Inc. 05/24/2018

TALECRIS BIOTHERAPEUTICS HLDGS CORP (DE)
Merged into Grifols, S.A. 06/02/2011
Each share Common 1¢ par exchanged for (1.297) Sponsored ADR's for Non-Vtg. Class B Ordinary and $19 cash

TALEMON INVTS LTD (BC)
Struck off register and declared dissolved for failure to file returns 03/11/1994

TALEN ENERGY CORP (DE)
Acquired by Riverstone Holdings LLC 12/06/2016
Each share Common $0.001 par exchanged for $14 cash

TALENT ALLIANCE INC (DE)
Name changed to Hire International, Inc. 09/24/2010
Hire International, Inc. recapitalized as TruLan Resources Inc. 11/20/2012 which recapitalized as Trinity Resources Inc. 09/18/2015

TALENT SILVER MINES LTD. (ON)
Charter cancelled and company declared dissolved for failure to file reports and pay fees 08/24/1964

TALEO CORP (DE)
Acquired by Oracle Corp. 04/09/2012
Each share Class A Common $0.00001 par exchanged for $46 cash

TALISMAN ENERGY INC (CANADA)
9% Preferred Securities called for redemption at $25 on 02/17/2004
Common no par split (3) for (1) by issuance of (2) additional shares payable 05/25/2004 to holders of record 05/19/2004 Ex date - 05/26/2004
8.9% Preferred Securities called for redemption at $25 plus $0.55625 accrued dividend on 06/15/2004
Common no par split (3) for (1) by issuance of (2) additional shares payable 05/30/2006 to holders of record 05/25/2006 Ex date - 05/31/2006
Acquired by Repsol S.A. 05/08/2015
Each share Rate Reset 1st Preferred Ser. 1 exchanged for $25 cash
Each share Common no par exchanged for USD$8 cash
Note: Unexchanged certificates were cancelled and became without value 05/08/2018

TALISMAN ENTERPRISES INC (ON)
Each share old Common no par exchanged for (0.04) share new Common no par 01/27/1999
Filed an assignment under the Bankruptcy and Insolvency Act 02/02/2001
Stockholders' equity unlikely

TALISMAN HLDGS INC (CO)
Each share old Common $0.0001 par exchanged for (0.0001) share new Common $0.0001 par 01/22/2013
Recapitalized as Fidelity Holding Corp. 08/20/2014
Each share new Common $0.0001 par exchanged for (0.0001) share Common $0.0001 par

TALISMAN MINING & LEASING CO. (WA)
Charter cancelled and proclaimed dissolved for non-payment of taxes 07/01/1960

TALISON LITHIUM EXCHANGECO LTD (BC)
Each Exchangeable Share automatically became (1) share Talison Lithium Ltd. Ordinary 05/31/2012
(See Talison Lithium Ltd.)

TALISON LITHIUM LTD (AUSTRALIA)
Acquired by Chengdu Tianqi Industry (Group) Co., Ltd. 03/12/2013
Each share Ordinary exchanged for CAD $7.50 cash

TALK AMER HLDGS INC (DE)
Each share old Common 1¢ par exchanged for (0.33333333) share new Common 1¢ par 10/16/2002
Acquired by Cavalier Telephone Corp. 12/15/2006
Each share new Common 1¢ par exchanged for $8.10 cash

TALK CITY INC (DE)
Name changed to LiveWorld, Inc. 05/08/2001

TALK COM INC (DE)
Name changed to Talk America Holdings Inc. 04/10/2001
(See Talk America Holdings Inc.)

TALK VISUAL CORP (NV)
Reincorporated 06/24/1999
State of incorporation changed from (DE) to (NV) 06/24/1999
Name changed to TVC Telecom, Inc. 09/19/2003

TALKEETNA GOLD EXPL LTD (NV)
Recapitalized as Founders Equity Corp. 01/08/1986
Each share Common $0.001 par exchanged for (0.1) share Common 10¢ par
(See Founders Equity Corp.)

TALKING RINGS ENTMT INC (DE)
Recapitalized as TRE Group Inc. 06/01/1994
Each share Common $0.00001 par exchanged for (0.001) share Common $0.00001 par
TRE Group Inc. name changed to Merchandise Entertainment Television Holdings, Inc. 08/04/1994 which recapitalized as World Sports Licensing Corp. 11/29/1999 which reorganized as Choice Sports Network, Inc. 03/14/2000 which name changed to Sports Entertainment & Learning Network Inc. 09/15/2000

TALKPOINT COMMUNICATIONS INC (DE)
Chapter 11 bankruptcy proceedings converted to Chapter 7 on 09/21/2005
Stockholders' equity unlikely

TALL FEATHERS FARMS, INC. (DE)
Charter cancelled and declared inoperative and void for non-payment of taxes 03/01/1992

TALL TREES LED CO (FL)
Recapitalized as Light Engine Design Corp. 12/21/2016
Each share Common $0.001 par exchanged for (0.16666666) share Common $0.001 par

TALLAGIUM CORP (AB)
Cease trade order effective 05/07/2008

TALLAHASSEE BK & TR CO (TALLAHASSEE, FL)
Common $100 par changed to $20 par and (4) additional shares issued plus a 25% stock dividend paid 01/10/1955
Stock Dividend - 200% 06/11/1966
98.6% held by Barnett Banks of Florida, Inc. as of 12/23/1970
Public interest eliminated

TALLEY INDS INC (DE)
Common $1 par split (2) for (1) by issuance of (1) additional share 09/30/1968
Common $1 par split (5) for (4) by issuance of (0.25) additional share 07/08/1987
Merged into Carpenter Technology Corp. 02/19/1998
Each share $1.10 Conv. Preferred Ser. A $1 par exchanged for $11.70 cash
Each share $1 Conv. Preferred Ser. B $1 par exchanged for $16 cash
Each share Common $1 par exchanged for $12 cash

TALLGRASS ENERGY CORP (AB)
Discharged from receivership 04/04/2014
Stockholders' equity unlikely

TALLGRASS ENERGY GP LP (DE)
Name changed to Tallgrass Energy, L.P. 07/02/2018

TALLGRASS ENERGY PARTNERS LP (DE)
Merged into Tallgrass Energy, L.P. 07/02/2018
Each Common Unit exchanged for (2) Class A Shares

TALLMAN INDS INC (DE)
Merged into Data-Design Laboratories (CA) 04/30/1980
Each share Common 10¢ par exchanged for (1) share Capital Stock $0.33333333 par
Data-Design Laboratories (CA) reincorporated in Delaware as Data-Design Laboratories, Inc. 12/01/1986 which name changed to DDL Electronics, Inc. 12/17/1993 which name changed to SMTEK International, Inc. 10/09/1998 which merged into CTS Corp. 02/01/2005

TALLOU GOLD CORP (BC)
Cease trade order effective 04/08/1991
Stockholders' equity unlikely

TALLTREE RES LTD (BC)
Name changed to Peer 1 Network Enterprises, Inc. 07/23/2002
(See Peer 1 Network Enterprises, Inc.)

TALLY CORP (WA)
Common $1 par changed for 50¢ and (1) additional share issued 04/30/1963
Common 50¢ par changed to $0.33333333 par and (0.5) additional share issued 05/05/1965
Common $0.33333333 par changed to $0.16666666 par and (1) additional share issued 04/20/1966
Merged into Mannesmann AG 10/31/1979
Each share Common $0.16666666 par exchanged for $14 cash

TALLY HO EXPL LTD (BC)
Struck off register and declared dissolved for failure to file returns 11/23/1990

TALLY-HO VENTURES INC (DE)
Each share old Common $0.001 par exchanged for (0.03333333) share new Common $0.001 par 05/09/2005
Name changed to Premier Wealth Management, Inc. 10/10/2007
(See Premier Wealth Management, Inc.)

TALLY REGISTER CORP. (WA)
Name changed to Tally Corp. 04/30/1963
(See Tally Corp.)

TALLY RES INC (BC)
Recapitalized as Sequoia Resources Ltd. 08/02/1984
Each share Capital Stock no par exchanged for (0.33333333) share Common no par
Sequoia Resources Ltd. name changed to American Technology & Information, Inc. 08/07/1985
(See American Technology & Information, Inc.)

TALMAN FIN CORP A (DE)
Market Auction Preferred no par called for redemption 12/23/1991
Public interest eliminated

TALMAN FIN CORP B (DE)
Market Auction Preferred no par called for redemption 11/18/1991
Public interest eliminated

TALMAN FIN CORP C (DE)
Market Auction Preferred no par called for redemption 12/02/1991
Public interest eliminated

TALMAN FIN CORP D (DE)
Stated Rate Auction Preferred no par called for redemption 05/28/1992
Public interest eliminated

TALMAN FIN CORP E (DE)
Market Auction Preferred no par called for redemption 12/09/1991
Public interest eliminated

TALMAN FIN CORP F (DE)
Market Auction Preferred no par called for redemption 12/30/1991
Public interest eliminated

TALMAN FIN CORP G (DE)
Fixed Dividend/Market Auction Preferred no par called for redemption 12/16/1991
Public interest eliminated

TALMAN FIN CORP H (DE)
Fixed Dividend/Market Auction Preferred no par called for redemption 11/25/1991
Public interest eliminated

TALMAN HOME FED SVGS & LN ASSN ILL (USA)
Acquired by LaSalle National Corp. 02/28/1992
Each share Common 1¢ par exchanged for $10 cash

TALMER BANCORP INC (MI)
Merged into Chemical Financial Corp. 08/31/2016
Each share Class A Common $1 par exchanged for (0.4725) share Common $1 par and $1.61 cash

TALMORA LONGLAC GOLD MINES LTD.
Assets acquired by Tombill Gold Mines Ltd. 00/00/1949
Details not available

TALMORA RES INC (AB)
Merged into Talmora Diamond Inc. 01/23/2007
Each share Common no par exchanged for (1) share Common no par

TALON, INC. (PA)
Each share old Common $5 par exchanged for (0.5) share Class A Common $5 par and (0.5) share Class B Common $5 par 00/00/1951
Each share Class A Common $5 par

or Class B Common $5 par exchanged for (1) share new Common $5 par 03/19/1963
New Common $5 par changed to $2.50 par and (1) additional share issued 07/10/1964
Common $2.50 par changed to $1.25 par and (1) additional share issued 04/11/1966
Completely liquidated 07/15/1968
Each share Common $1.25 par exchanged for first and final distribution of (1) share Textron Inc. (DE) $1.40 Conv. Preferred Ser. B no par

TALON INDS INC (UT)
Administratively dissolved 12/31/85

TALON INTL ENERGY LTD (YT)
Reorganized under the laws of Alberta as Canadian Energy Exploration Inc. 01/20/2010
Each share Common no par exchanged for (0.1) share new Common no par
Canadian Energy Exploration Inc. acquired by Standard Exploration Ltd. 10/22/2012

TALON PETROLEUMS LTD (AB)
Acquired by Ventus Energy Ltd. 09/21/1999
Each share Common no par exchanged for either (0.0857) share Common no par or $0.60 cash
Ventus Energy Ltd. name changed to Navigo Energy Inc. 05/24/2002
(See Navigo Energy Inc.)

TALON THERAPEUTICS INC (DE)
Acquired by Spectrum Pharmaceuticals, Inc. 07/17/2013
Each share Common $0.001 par exchanged for (1) Contingent Value Right and $0.05609 cash

TALOS INDS INC (BC)
Struck off register and declared dissolved for failure to file returns 4/16/92

TALUS VENTURES CORP (BC)
Name changed to SolutionInc Technologies Ltd. (BC) 6/26/2002
SolutionInc Technologies Ltd. (BC) reincorporated in Nova Scotia 2/24/2004

TALVEST FDS (PE)
Charter surrendered and dissolved 12/23/1996
Details not available

TALVEY METAL MINES LTD. (ON)
Charter cancelled and company declared dissolved for default in filing returns 11/30/64

TALWARE NETWORX INC (AB)
Each share old Common no par exchanged for (0.1) share new Common no par 10/17/2005
Cease trade order effective 09/19/2009

TALX CORP (MO)
Common 1¢ par split (3) for (2) by issuance of (0.5) additional share payable 01/19/2001 to holders of record 12/22/2000 Ex date - 01/22/2001
Common 1¢ par split (3) for (2) by issuance of (0.5) additional share payable 02/17/2005 to holders of record 01/20/2005 Ex date - 02/18/2005
Common 1¢ par split (3) for (2) by issuance of (0.5) additional share payable 01/17/2006 to holders of record 12/19/2005 Ex date - 01/18/2006
Stock Dividends - 10% payable 10/19/2000 to holders of record 09/21/2000; 10% payable 10/18/2001 to holders of record 09/20/2001
Merged into Equifax, Inc. 05/15/2007
Each share Common 1¢ par exchanged for (0.861) share Common $1.25 par

TAM HENDERSON INC (NV)
Name changed to Universal Travel Group 8/23/2006

TAM RESTAURANTS INC (DE)
SEC revoked common stock registration 02/06/2008
Note: Aerofoam Metals Inc. was dismissed from revocation proceedings and is not related to this company

TAM S A (BRAZIL)
Acquired by LAN Airlines S.A. 07/23/2012
Each Sponsored ADR for Preferred exchanged for $22.293908 cash
Each Sponsored ADR for Common exchanged for $22.293908 cash

TAMA PACKING CO. (IA)
Completely liquidated 12/15/68
Each share Common $1 par exchanged for first and final distribution of $0.51 cash

TAMALPAIS BANCORP (CA)
Company's principal asset placed in receivership 04/16/2010
Stockholders' equity unlikely

TAMALPAIS SAVINGS & LOAN ASSOCIATION (CA)
Completely liquidated 03/16/1970
Each share Guarantee Stock $1 par exchanged for first and final distribution (1.562549) shares Golden West Financial Corp. (CA) Common 50¢ par
Golden West Financial Corp. (CA) reincorporated in Delaware 10/31/1975 which merged into Wachovia Corp. (Ctfs. dated after 09/01/2001) 10/02/2006 which merged into Wells Fargo & Co. (New) 12/31/2008

TAMAN CORP (ON)
Placed in receivership 00/00/1989
No stockholders' equity

TAMAN RES LTD (ON)
Capital Stock $1 par reclassified as Common no par 07/29/1983
Recapitalized as Taman Corp. 12/23/1986
Each share Common no par exchanged for (0.2) share Common no par and (0.2) share Class A no par
(See Taman Corp.)

TAMAN URANIUM MINES LTD. (ON)
Name changed to Taman Resources Ltd. 7/10/70
Taman Resources Ltd. recapitalized as Taman Corp. 12/23/86
(See Taman Corp.)

TAMANDARE EXPLORATIONS INC (NV)
Name changed to Tonix Pharmaceuticals Holding Corp. 10/19/2011

TAMAR ELECTRS INDS INC (DE)
Merged into LTV Ling Altec, Inc. 04/20/1971
Each share Common 25¢ par exchanged for (2.3) shares Common 50¢ par
LTV Ling Altec, Inc. name changed to Altec Corp. 04/27/1972
(See Altec Corp.)

TAMARA MNG LTD (QC)
Charter annulled for failure to file annual reports 06/01/1974

TAMARA RES INC (BC)
Recapitalized as Matrix Energy Inc. 2/18/94
Each share Common no par exchanged for (0.4) share Common no par
Matrix Energy Inc. recapitalized as Promax Energy Inc. (BC) 2/3/99 which reincorporated in Alberta 6/8/2000
(See Promax Energy Inc.)

TAMARAC GAS & OIL CO., INC. (DE)
No longer in existence having become inoperative and void for non-payment of taxes 4/1/62

TAMARAC VENTURES LTD (NV)
Recapitalized as NeuroCorp, Ltd. 11/30/1994
Each share Common $0.001 par exchanged for (0.025) share Common $0.001 par
(See NeuroCorp, Ltd.)

TAMARACK & CUSTER CONSOLIDATED MINING CO.
Merged into Day Mines, Inc. 00/00/1947
Details not available

TAMARAK INC (NV)
SEC revoked common stock registration 03/31/2005

TAMARIND HLDG CORP (BC)
Name changed to Canarctic Ventures Ltd. 03/23/1983
Canarctic Ventures Ltd. recapitalized as Consolidated Canarctic Industries Ltd. 02/21/1985
(See Consolidated Canarctic Industries Ltd.)

TAMARIND INDS INC (UT)
Involuntarily dissolved 07/11/2001

TAMARON OIL & GAS INC NEW (CO)
Name changed to Pacific Development Corp. (CO) 08/10/1995
Pacific Development Corp. (CO) reincorporated in Delaware as Cheshire Distributors Inc. 03/24/2000 which recapitalized as LMIC, Inc. 07/21/2003 which name changed to Z Holdings Group, Inc. 10/15/2012 which name changed to Ariel Clean Energy, Inc. 08/20/2015

TAMARON OIL & GAS INC OLD (CO)
Each share Common $0.001 par exchanged (0.04) share Common $0.001 par 10/15/1985
Charter revoked for failure to file reports and pay fees 01/01/1990

TAMASEK CORP LTD (NV)
Recapitalized as Demert & Dougherty, Inc. 01/26/1998
Each share Common $0.002 par exchanged for (1/6) share Common $0.002 par
(See Demert & Dougherty, Inc.)

TAMAVACK RES INC (BC)
Merged into Eurus Resource Corp. 5/1/90
Each (7.5) shares Common no par exchanged for (1) share Common no par
Eurus Resource Corp. merged into Crystallex International Corp. (BC) 9/29/95 which reincorporated in Canada 1/23/98

TAMBANG BATUBARA BUKIT ASAM TBK (INDONESIA)
Basis changed from (1:5) to (1:25) 12/19/2017
Name changed to PT Bukit Asam (Persero) Tbk 12/27/2017

TAMBLYN G LTD (CANADA)
Common no par exchanged (4) for (1) 00/00/1936
Common no par exchanged (2) for (1) 07/15/1957
Acquired by Loblaw Companied Ltd. 08/11/1975
Each share Common no par exchanged for $20 cash
Name changed to Boots Drug Stores (Canada) Ltd. 12/11/1978
(See Boots Drug Stores (Canada) Ltd.)

TAMBORIL CIGAR CO (DE)
Reorganized as Axion Power International Inc. 6/7/2004
Each share Common $0.001 par exchanged for (0.0625) share Common $0.001 par to reflect a (1) for (1,600) reverse split followed by a (100) for (1) forward split
Note: No holder will receive fewer than (100) shares

TAMBORIL CIGAR CO (WA)
Reincorporated under the laws of Delaware 1/15/97
Tamboril Cigar Co. (DE) reorganized as Axion Power International, Inc. 6/7/2004

TAMBORINE HLDGS INC (MS)
Name changed to Synthesis Energy Systems, Inc. (MS) 5/20/2005
Synthesis Energy Systems, Inc. (MS) reincorporated in Delaware 7/26/2005

TAMBRANDS INC (DE)
Common 25¢ par split (2) for (1) by issuance of (1) additional share 12/23/86
Common 25¢ par split (2) for (1) by issuance of (1) additional share 12/15/90
Merged into Procter & Gamble Co. 7/21/97
Each share Common 25¢ par exchanged for $50 cash

TAMERLANE VENTURES INC (CANADA)
Reincorporated 07/26/2010
Place of incorporation changed from (BC) to (Canada) 07/26/2010
Assets sold for the benefit of creditors 12/16/2016
No stockholders' equity

TAMI INC (DE)
Merged into Athlone Industries, Inc. 12/20/1974
Each share Common 10¢ par exchanged for $2 cash
Each share Class B Common 10¢ par exchanged for $2 cash

TAMICON IRON MINES LTD. (ON)
Declared dissolved 10/22/62
No stockholders' equity

TAMIJA GOLD & DIAMOND EXPL INC (DE)
SEC revoked common stock registration 01/30/2013

TAMINCO CORP (DE)
Acquired by Eastman Chemical Co. 12/05/2014
Each share Common $0.001 par exchanged for $26 cash

TAMIR BIOTECHNOLOGY INC (DE)
SEC revoked common stock registration 06/20/2013

TAMPA BAY CORP (NV)
Recapitalized as Sun Holding Corp. 09/03/1997
Each (21) shares Common $0.001 par exchanged for (1) share Common $0.001 par
(See Sun Holding Corp.)

TAMPA ELEC CO (FL)
Each share Common $100 par exchanged for (5) shares Common no par 00/00/1926
Common no par changed to $7 par and (2) additional shares issued 00/00/1954
Common $7 par changed to no par and (1) additional share issued 12/11/1959
Common no par split (2) for (1) by issuance of (1) additional share 05/09/1963
5.1% Preferred Ser. C $100 par called for redemption 09/30/1964
Under plan of reorganization each share Common no par automatically became (1) share TECO Energy, Inc. Common $1 par 04/14/1981
9.75% Preferred Ser. G $100 par called for redemption 02/15/1990

TAM-TAN

FINANCIAL INFORMATION, INC.

7.44% Preferred Ser. F $100 par called for redemption 04/29/1996
8% Preferred Ser. E $100 par called for redemption 04/29/1996
4.16% Preferred Ser. B $100 par called for redemption at $102.875 on 07/16/1997
4.32% Preferred Ser. A $100 par called for redemption at $103.75 on 07/16/1997
(See TECO Energy, Inc.)

TAMPA MARINE CO. (FL)
Acquired by DeBardeleben Marine Corp. 04/25/1963
Each share Class A $1 par or Class B $1 par exchanged for (1) share Common 50¢ par
(See DeBardeleben Marine Corp.)

TAMPA UNION TERMINAL, INC.
Assets sold in reorganization 00/00/1941
No stockholders' equity

TAMPAX INC (DE)
Common $1 par changed to 25¢ par and (3) additional shares issued 05/26/1972
Stock Dividends - 200% 05/29/1952; 200% 05/28/1962
Name changed to Tambrands Inc. 04/24/1984
(See Tambrands Inc.)

TAMPAX SALES CORP. (CO)
Each share Common 50¢ par exchanged for (5) shares Common 10¢ par 00/00/1948
Acquired by Tampax, Inc. 01/15/1960
Each share Class A or Class B Common exchanged for (0.28571428) share Common $1 par Tampax, Inc. name changed to Tambrands Inc. 04/24/1984
(See Tambrands Inc.)

TAMPICO CAP CORP (BC)
Delisted from Vancouver Stock Exchange 03/06/1995

TAMPICO DEVS LTD (BC)
Recapitalized as Pico Resources Ltd. 12/20/1979
Each share Capital Stock 50¢ par exchanged for (0.25) share Common no par
Pico Resources Ltd. name changed to Tampico Capital Corp. 07/31/1992
(See Tampico Capital Corp.)

TAMPICO-TEXAS OIL CO. (AZ)
Charter revoked for failure to file reports or pay fees 10/29/1952

TAN RANGE EXPL CORP (AB)
Class A Common no par reclassified as Common no par 05/09/1996
Name changed to Tanzanian Royalty Exploration Corp. 03/08/2006

TANAGER RES LTD (ON)
Recapitalized as Consolidated Tanager Ltd. 01/27/1993
Each share Common no par exchanged for (0.2) share Common no par

TANAR GOLD MINES LTD. (BC)
Completely liquidated 2/17/66
Each share Capital Stock 50¢ par received first and final distribution of (0.8) share Calmac Mines Ltd. Common $1 par (of which (0.45) is escrowed share) and (0.605) share Peso Silver Mines Ltd. Capital Stock $1 par
Stock certificates were not surrendered and are now worthless

TANARIS PWR HLDGS INC (NV)
Recapitalized as Hammer Fiber Optics Holdings Corp. 05/03/2016
Each share Common $0.001 par exchanged for (0.001) share Common $0.001 par

TANAUR YELLOWKNIFE MINES LTD. (ON)
Charter revoked for failure to file reports and pay fees 09/09/1958

TANAWAH GOLD MINING CO. (NV)
Charter revoked for failure to file reports and pay fees 03/03/1924

TANBRIDGE CORP (CANADA)
Assets sold for the benefit of creditors 00/00/2004
No stockholders' equity

TANCOR INTL INC (NV)
Each share Common $0.025 par exchanged for (0.00001) share Common $2,500 par 08/19/1977
Note: In effect holders received $0.03 cash per share and public interest was eliminated

TANCORD INDS LTD (CANADA)
Each share old Common no par exchanged for (1) share 6% Non-Cum. Preferred $4 par and (1) share new Common no par 12/30/63
6% Non-Cum. Preferred $4 par called for redemption 12/21/73
New Common no par reclassified as 6% Class A Preferred $3.50 par and simultaneously called for redemption 03/22/1974
Public interest eliminated

TANDBERG ASA (NORWAY)
Acquired by Cisco Systems, Inc. 07/13/2010
Each ADR for Common exchanged for $26.104 cash

TANDEM COMPUTERS INC (DE)
Reincorporated 02/01/1980
State of incorporation changed from (CA) to (DE) 02/01/1980
Common 5¢ par changed to $0.025 par and (1) additional share issued 07/18/1980
Common $0.025 par split (3) for (1) by issuance of (2) additional shares 07/20/1981
Common $0.025 par split (2) for (1) by issuance of (1) additional share 06/12/1987
Merged into Compaq Computer Corp. 08/29/1997
Each share Common $0.025 par exchanged for (0.525) share Common 1¢ par
Compaq Computer Corp. merged into Hewlett-Packard Co. 05/03/2002 which name changed to HP Inc. 11/02/2015

TANDEM ENERGY HLDGS INC (NV)
Completely liquidated
Each share Common $0.001 par received first and final distribution of (0.5769) share Platinum Energy Resources, Inc. Common $0.0001 par payable 08/07/2008 to holders of record 06/24/2008 Ex date - 08/08/2008
Note: Certificates were not required to be surrendered and are without value

TANDEM MINES LTD. (ON)
Recapitalized as Halmon Mining & Processing Ltd. on a (1) for (5) basis 04/03/1958
(See Halmon Mining & Processing Ltd.)

TANDEM RES LTD NEW (ON)
Reincorporated 01/03/1997
Place of incorporation changed from (BC) to (ON) 01/03/1997
Recapitalized as OPEL International Inc. (ON) 09/26/2006
Each share Common no par exchanged for (0.05) share Common no par
OPEL International Inc. (ON) reincorporated in New Brunswick 1/30/2007 which reincorporated in Ontario as OPEL Solar International Inc. 12/01/2010 which name changed to OPEL Technologies Inc. 08/29/2011 which name changed to POET Technologies Inc. 07/25/2013

TANDEM RES LTD OLD (BC)
Merged into Tandem Resources Ltd. (New) (BC) 11/15/1985
Each share Common no par exchanged for (1) share Common no par
Tandem Resources Ltd. (New) (BC) reincorporated in Ontario 01/03/1997 which recapitalized as OPEL International Inc. (ON) 09/26/2006 which reincorporated in New Brunswick 01/30/2007 which reincorporated in Ontario as OPEL Solar International Inc. 12/01/2010 which name changed to OPEL Technologies Inc. 08/29/2011 which name changed to POET Technologies Inc. 07/25/2013

TANDON CORP (DE)
Reincorporated 07/1988
Common 1¢ par changed to no par and (1) additional share issued 04/12/1983
State of incorporation changed from (CA) to (DE) 07/00/1988
Stock Dividend - 100% 08/20/1982
Name changed to TSL Holdings Inc. 12/24/1992
(See TSL Holdings Inc.)

TANDY BRANDS INC (DE)
Common $1 par split (3) for (2) by issuance of (0.5) additional share 12/12/1980
Common $1 par split (3) for (2) by issuance of (0.5) additional share 10/01/1987
Stock Dividend - 100% 05/16/1977
Name changed to Bombay Co. Inc. 11/09/1990
(See Bombay Co. Inc.)

TANDY CORP (DE)
Reincorporated 02/27/1968
6% Preferred called for redemption 01/31/1961
State of incorporation changed from (NJ) to (DE) 02/27/1968
Common $1 par split (2) for (1) by issuance of (1) additional share 04/08/1969
Common $1 par split (2) for (1) by issuance of (1) additional share 07/28/1971
Common $1 par split (2) for (1) by issuance of (1) additional share 01/09/1976
Common $1 par split (2) for (1) by issuance of (1) additional share 06/30/1978
Common $1 par split (2) for (1) by issuance of (1) additional share 12/30/1980
Common $1 par split (2) for (1) by issuance of (1) additional share 05/29/1981
Each share Common $1 par received distribution of (0.1) share InterTAN, Inc. Common $1 par 01/16/1987
$2.14 Depositary Preferred called for redemption 03/10/1995
Common $1 par split (2) for (1) by issuance of (1) additional share payable 09/22/1997 to holders of record 08/29/1997 Ex date - 09/23/1997
Common $1 par split (2) for (1) by issuance of (1) additional share payable 06/21/1999 to holders of record 06/01/1999 Ex date - 06/22/1999
Name changed to RadioShack Corp. 05/18/2000
RadioShack Corp. name changed to RS Legacy Corp. 09/23/2015
(See RS Legacy Corp.)

TANDYCRAFTS INC (DE)
Common $1 par split (2) for (1) by issuance of (1) additional share 10/01/1992
Common $1 par split (2) for (1) by issuance of (1) additional share 02/25/1993
Plan of reorganization under Chapter 11 Federal Bankruptcy Code effective 06/03/2003
No stockholders' equity

TANG INDS INC (DE)
Company believed private 00/00/1977
Details not available

TANGANYIKA CONCESSIONS LTD (ENGLAND)
Stock Dividend - 100% 03/12/1958
Name changed to Tanks Consolidated Investments Ltd. 07/24/1978
(See Tanks Consolidated Investments Ltd.)

TANGANYIKA OIL LTD (CANADA)
Acquired by Sinopec International Petroleum Exploration & Production Corp. 12/23/2008
Each share Common no par exchanged for $31.50 cash

TANGARINE PMT SOLUTIONS CORP (CANADA)
Acquired by 4491157 Canada Inc. 03/24/2009
Each share Common no par exchanged for $0.22 cash

TANGELO GAMES CORP (BC)
Acquired by GoGel Holdiings Inc. 09/20/2018
Each share Common no par exchanged for $0.02565 cash
Note: Unexchanged certificates will be cancelled and become without value 09/20/2024

TANGENT OIL & GAS LTD (BC)
Name changed to Pacific Star Communications Corp. 05/06/1987

TANGENT SOLUTIONS INC (DE)
Each share old Common $0.001 par exchanged for (0.3) share new Common $0.001 par 02/11/2002
SEC revoked common stock registration 04/26/2010

TANGER FACTORY OUTLET CTRS INC (NC)
Issue Information - 3,000,000 DEPOSITARY SH REP 1/10 PFD SER A CONV $15.75 offered at $25 per share on 12/09/1993
$15.75 Depositary Preferred Ser. A 1¢ par called for redemption at $25 plus $2.46 accrued dividends on 06/20/2003
7.5% Class C Preferred 1¢ par called for redemption at $25 plus $0.198 accrued dividends on 12/09/2010
(Additional Information in Active)

TANGER INDS (CA)
Common $1 par split (3) for (1) by issuance of (2) additional shares 10/10/1968
Name changed to Verit Industries (CA) 04/02/1973
Verit Industries (CA) reincorporated in Delaware as Verit Industries, Inc. 01/02/1992
(See Verit Industries, Inc.)

TANGIBLE ASSET GALLERIES INC (NV)
Reorganized under the laws of Delaware as Superior Galleries, Inc. 06/30/2003
Each share Common $0.001 par exchanged for (0.05) share Common $0.001 par
(See Superior Galleries, Inc.)

TANGIBLE DATA INC (CO)
Name changed to TDI Holding Corp. 10/25/2002
TDI Holding Corp. recapitalized as Fashion House Holdings, Inc. 08/30/2005
(See Fashion House Holdings, Inc.)

TANGIERS PETE LTD (AUSTRALIA)
Name changed to 88 Energy Ltd. 04/17/2015

TANGLEWOOD CONS RES INC (ON)
Recapitalized as FCMI Financial Corp. 12/15/1986

FINANCIAL INFORMATION, INC. TAN-TAP

Each share Common no par exchanged for (0.08) share Common no par
(See FCMI Financial Corp.)

TANGLEWOOD PETROLEUM CORP. (ON)
Recapitalized as Tanglewood Consolidated Resources Inc. 11/09/1982
Each share Common no par exchanged for (0.5) share Common no par
Tanglewood Consolidated Resources Inc. recapitalized as FCMI Financial Corp. 12/15/1986
(See FCMI Financial Corp.)

TANGO ENERGY INC (AB)
Issue Information - 1,500,000 shares COM offered at $0.20 per share on 04/24/2002
Name changed to Tamarack Valley Energy Ltd. 06/25/2010

TANGO GOLD MINES INC (BC)
Name changed to Tango Mining Ltd. 11/24/2014

TANGO INC (FL)
Recapitalized as AutoBidXL Inc. 10/24/2005
Each share Common $0.001 par exchanged for (0.005) share Common $0.001 par
AutoBidXL Inc. name changed to Trophy Resources, Inc. 2/28/2006

TANGO MINERAL RES INC (CANADA)
Recapitalized as RNC Gold Inc. 12/04/2003
Each share Common no par exchanged for (0.04) share Common no par and (0.02) Common Stock Purchase Warrant expiring 12/05/2005
RNC Gold Inc. merged into Yamana Gold Inc. 02/28/2006

TANGOE INC (DE)
Acquired by Asentinel, LLC 06/16/2017
Each share Common $0.0001 par exchanged for $6.50 cash

TANGRAM ENTERPRISE SOLUTIONS INC (PA)
Acquired by Opsware Inc. 02/20/2004
Each share Common 1¢ par exchanged for (0.02288) share Common $0.001 par
(See Opsware Inc.)

TANISYS TECHNOLOGY INC (WY)
Each share old Common 1¢ par exchanged for (0.5) share new Common 1¢ par 0/25/2000
Acquired by ATESub, Inc. 09/24/2004
Each share new Common 1¢ par exchanged for $0.001 cash

TANKER OIL & GAS LTD (BC)
Recapitalized as Tyson Financial Corp. 05/23/1990
Each share Common no par exchanged for (0.33333333) share Common no par
Tyson Financial Corp. recapitalized as Midd Financial Corp. 06/01/1992
(See Midd Financial Corp.)

TANKLESS SYS WORLDWIDE INC (NV)
Name changed to Skye International, Inc. 11/11/2005
(See Skye International, Inc.)

TANKNOLOGY ENVIRONMENTAL INC (TX)
Name changed to TEI Inc. 08/06/1997
TEI Inc. merged into Pinnacle Global Group, Inc. 01/29/1999 which name changed to Sanders Morris Harris Group Inc. 05/23/2001 which name changed to Edelman Financial Group Inc. 05/27/2011
(See Edelman Financial Group Inc.)

TANKNOLOGY-NDE INTL INC (DE)
Voluntarily dissolved 04/00/2009

Details not available

TANKS CONS INVTS LTD (ENGLAND)
Acquired by Societe-Generale Holdings S.A. 03/22/1982
Each ADR for Ordinary exchanged for $7.81 cash

TANNER ARCTIC ENTERPRISES LTD (AB)
Recapitalized 06/23/1991
Recapitalized from Tanner Arctic Oil Ltd. to Tanner Arctic Enterprises Ltd. 06/23/1991
Each share Common no par exchanged for (0.1) share Common no par
Name changed to Kuma Resources Ltd. 08/01/1993
Kuma Resources Ltd. name changed to Algonquin Petroleum Corp. 03/18/1997 which recapitalized as Algonquin Oil & Gas Ltd. 04/10/2000 which recapitalized as PetroShale Inc. 03/19/2012

TANNER PETE INC (UT)
Recapitalized as Solar Design Systems, Inc. 10/13/1978
Each share Common 10¢ par exchanged for (0.1) share Common 1¢ par
Solar Design Systems, Inc. name changed to Biopetrol, Inc. (UT) 06/15/1981 which reincorporated in Nevada as Kensington International, Inc. 04/17/1996
(See Kensington International, Inc.)

TANNER PRUIT EXPL INC (CO)
Name changed to TPEX Exploration Inc. 12/02/1980
TPEX Exploration Inc. name changed to Kestrel Energy Inc. 03/14/1995
(See Kestrel Energy, Inc.)

TANNERS NATL BK (CATSKILL, NY)
Common $50 par changed to $10 par and (4) additional shares issued 02/17/1970
Merged into Bank of New York Co., Inc. 03/01/1972
Each share Common $10 par exchanged for (2.75) shares Common $7.50 par
Bank of New York Co., Inc. merged into Bank of New York Mellon Corp. 07/01/2007

TANNERS NATL BK (WOBURN, MA)
Completely liquidated 04/28/1983
Each share Capital Stock $50 par exchanged for first and final distribution of $45 cash

TANNERS PRODUCTS CO. (DE)
Name changed to American Hair & Felt Co. 00/00/1929
American Hair & Felt Co. name changed to Ozite Corp. 06/29/1962 which merged into Brunswick Corp. 08/16/1974

TANNERS RESTAURANT GROUP INC (TX)
Name changed to Corzon Inc. 09/18/2000
Corzon Inc. recapitalized as LecStar Corp. 03/29/2001
(See LecStar Corp.)

TANNETICS INC (PA)
Stock Dividends - 10% 11/02/1981; 10% 12/01/1982
Name changed to TNT Liquidating Co. 11/18/1983
(See TNT Liquidating Co.)

TANNING TECHNOLOGY CORP (DE)
Merged into Platinum Equity, LLC 06/12/2003
Each share Common 1¢ par exchanged for $1.15 cash

TANNISSE URANIUM MINING CO. OF NEVADA (NV)
Name changed to Palm Beach Partners Inc. 08/26/1992
Palm Beach Partners Inc. name changed to Datcha Holdings of America Inc. 03/01/1993
(See Datcha Holdings of America Inc.)

TANO CORP (LA)
Merged into Rexnord Inc. 07/05/1984
Each share Common 10¢ par exchanged for $4.50 cash

TANOS PETE CORP (BC)
Recapitalized as Cypango Ventures Ltd. 11/10/1992
Each share Common no par exchanged for (0.2) share Common no par
Cypango Ventures Ltd. recapitalized as Techsite Strategies Corp. 02/24/2000 which name changed to Sola Resource Corp. (BC) 07/17/2003 which reincorporated in Alberta 07/28/2004 which recapitalized as Cancana Resources Corp. (AB) 01/24/2011 which reincorporated in British Columbia 08/12/2015 which reorganized as Meridian Mining S.E 11/28/2016

TANOX INC (DE)
Merged into Genentech, Inc. 08/02/2007
Each share Common 1¢ par exchanged for $20 cash

TANQ CAP CORP (ON)
Recapitalized as True North Commercial Real Estate Investment Trust 12/14/2012
Each share Common no par exchanged for (0.125) Trust Unit

TANQUERAY EXPL LTD (AB)
Each share old Common no par exchanged for (0.33333333) share new Common no par 09/02/2016
Name changed to ImmunoPrecise Antibodies Ltd. 12/29/2016

TANQUERAY RES LTD (AB)
Recapitalized as Tanqueray Exploration Ltd. 09/13/2011
Each share Common no par exchanged for (0.1) share Common no par
Tanqueray Exploration Ltd. name changed to ImmunoPrecise Antibodies Ltd. 12/29/2016

TANSY RES INC (BC)
Reorganized as Cabot Resources Corp. 03/22/1990
Each share Common no par exchanged for (1) share Common no par
Cabot Resources Corp. merged into Emtech Technology Corp. 08/16/1993 which reorganized as Emtech Ltd. (Bermuda) 07/18/1994 which name changed to Ashurst Technology Ltd. 07/09/1996
(See Ashurst Technology Ltd.)

TANTALUM REFINING & MINING CORP. OF AMERICA LTD. (ON)
Assets acquired by Nationwide Minerals Ltd. 00/00/1952
Each share Common exchanged for (0.25) share Common
(See Nationwide Minerals Ltd.)

TANTALUS RES LTD (BC)
Recapitalized as Tapango Resources Ltd. 11/22/1996
Each share Common no par exchanged for (0.33333333) share Common no par
Tapango Resources Ltd. merged into CarbonOne Technologies Inc. 07/27/2015 which name changed to CarbonOne Technologies Inc. 10/12/2016 which recapitalized as Lincoln Ventures Inc. 07/16/2018

TANTATO RES LTD (BC)
Name changed to Interactive Communications Corp. 07/25/1989
Interactive Communications Corp. recapitalized as ICM Ventures Inc. 12/13/1993 which name changed to RMS Medical Systems Inc.

04/30/1996 which recapitalized as Pacific Genesis Technologies Inc. (BC) 12/21/1999 which reincorporated in Alberta as Ware Solutions Corp. 10/01/2001
(See Ware Solutions Corp.)

TANTIVY GROUP INC (NV)
Each share old Common $0.001 par exchanged for (0.2) share new Common $0.001 par 11/27/2002
Recapitalized as Oretech, Inc. 04/01/2003
Each share new Common $0.001 par exchanged for (0.1) share Common $0.001 par
(See Oretech, Inc.)

TANYA HAWAII CORP (HI)
Merged into Bristol-Myers Co. 02/28/1970
Each share Common $10 par exchanged for (0.310848) share Common $1 par
Note: Additional escrowed shares were distributed before 03/31/1975
Bristol-Myers Co. name changed to Bristol-Myers Squibb Co. 10/04/1989

TANZILLA EXPLS LTD (BC)
Name changed to Regis Development Corp. 07/24/1974
Regis Development Corp. recapitalized as Manus Industries Inc. 01/10/1992 which recapitalized as Consolidated Manus Industries Inc. 11/10/1992 which recapitalized as Westmount Resources Ltd. (New) 02/08/1996 which recapitalized as Mt. Tom Minerals Corp. 05/20/1998 which name changed to Global Net Entertainment Corp. 10/14/1999 which recapitalized as Guildhall Minerals Ltd. 02/21/2006 name changed to Edge Resources Inc. 07/28/2009
(See Edge Resources Inc.)

TAO PARTNERS INC (DE)
Name changed to Inetvisionz.Com Inc. 05/12/1999
(See Inetvisionz.Com Inc.)

TAOMEE HLDGS LTD (CAYMAN ISLANDS)
Acquired by Orient TM Parent Ltd. 06/21/2016
Each Sponsored ADR for Ordinary exchanged for $3.717 cash

TAOS CAP INC (CANADA)
Name changed to TransGaming Inc. 11/18/2005
TransGaming Inc. recapitalized as Findev Inc. 12/06/2016

TAP CAP CORP (ON)
Class A Subordinate no par reclassified as Class A no par 06/28/1990
Delisted from Toronto Stock Exchange 03/04/1994

TAPAJOS GOLD INC (BC)
Merged into Brasilca Mining Corp. 04/03/2000
Each share Common no par exchanged for (1) share Common no par
(See Brasilca Mining Corp.)

TAPANGO RES LTD (BC)
Old Common no par split (7) for (1) by issuance of (6) additional shares payable 01/22/2007 to holders of record 01/15/2007 Ex date - 01/11/2007
Each share old Common no par exchanged for (0.5) share new Common no par 11/21/2011
Each share new Common no par exchanged again for (0.1) share new Common no par 01/16/2015
Merged into CarbonOne Technologies Inc. 07/27/2015
Each share new Common no par exchanged for (1.071) shares Common no par
Note: Unexchanged certificates will

TAP-TAR — FINANCIAL INFORMATION, INC.

be cancelled and become without value 07/27/2022
CarbonOne Technologies Inc. name changed to TekModo Industries Inc. 10/12/2016 which recapitalized as Lincoln Ventures Ltd. 07/16/2018

TAPARKO CAP CORP (CANADA)
Name changed to Odyssey Energy Corp. 12/12/2000
(See Odyssey Energy Corp.)

TAPE-LICATOR, INC. (UT)
Recapitalized as American Aurum, Inc. 08/08/1981
Each share Common 1¢ par exchanged for (0.025) share Common 5¢ par

TAPE NETWORKS, INC. (CA)
Charter suspended for failure to file reports and pay taxes 06/01/1976

TAPE PRODUCTION CORP. (FL)
Dissolved 06/27/1960
Details not available

TAPECON INC (NY)
Merged into Davis-Hale Holdings 01/01/1993
For holdings of (101) shares or more each share Common 1¢ par exchanged for $6.60 principal amount of Tapecon Inc. Adjustable Rate Subordinated Debentures due 00/00/1996 and $4.40 cash
For holdings of (100) shares or fewer each share Common 1¢ par exchanged for $11 cash

TAPESTRY PHARMACEUTICALS INC (DE)
Each share old Common $0.0075 par exchanged for (0.1) share new Common $0.0075 par 02/03/2006
Plan of reorganization under Chapter 11 Federal Bankruptcy proceedings effective 03/13/2012
No stockholders' equity

TAPESTRY RESOURCE CORP (BC)
Common no par split (4) for (1) by issuance of (3) additional shares payable 06/15/2010 to holders of record 06/15/2010 Ex date - 06/11/2010
Name changed to Gran Colombia Gold Corp. 08/24/2010

TAPESTRY VENTURES LTD (BC)
Recapitalized as Tapestry Resource Corp. 12/23/2004
Each share Common no par exchanged for (0.25) share Common no par
Tapestry Resource Corp. name changed to Gran Colombia Gold Corp. 08/24/2010

TAPIMMUNE INC (NV)
Each share old Common $0.001 par exchanged for (0.1) share new Common $0.001 par 07/27/2009
Each share new Common $0.001 par exchanged again for (0.01) share new Common $0.001 par 02/25/2014
Each share new Common $0.001 par exchanged again for (0.08333333) share new Common $0.001 par 09/16/2016
Reincorporated under the laws of Delaware as Marker Therapeutics, Inc. 10/18/2018

TAPIN COPPER MINES LTD (BC)
Placed in bankruptcy 03/11/1977
No stockholders' equity

TAPIOCA CORP (NV)
Name changed to Sino Fortune Holding Corp. 04/19/2016
Sino Fortune Holding Corp. name changed to Hui Ying Financial Holdings Corp. 12/04/2017

TAPISTRON INTL INC (GA)
Chapter 11 bankruptcy proceedings terminated 01/04/2005
No stockholders' equity

TAPPAN CO (OH)
Common $5 par split (2) for (1) by issuance of (1) additional share 06/01/1959
Common $5 par changed to $2.50 par and (1) additional share issued 04/29/1969
Merged into N.U.E. Inc. 02/20/1981
Each share Common $2.50 par exchanged for $18 cash

TAPPAN GURNEY LTD (CANADA)
$1.60 Preferred $30 par called for redemption 02/15/1974
Acquired by Corpex (1977) Inc. 12/00/1968
Details not available

TAPPAN STOVE CO. (OH)
Each share Common no par exchanged for (15) shares Common $5 par 00/00/1937
Stock Dividend - 100% 05/28/1947
Name changed to Tappan Co. 11/25/1957
(See Tappan Co.)

TAPPAN ZEE FINL INC (DE)
Merged into U.S.B. Holding Co., Inc. 08/31/1998
Each share Common 1¢ par exchanged for (1.12) shares Common 1¢ par
U.S.B. Holding Co., Inc. merged into KeyCorp (New) 01/01/2008

TAPPAN ZEE NATL BK (NYACK, NY)
Stock Dividend - 25% 03/19/1969
Acquired by Chemical New York Corp. 02/01/1972
Each share Capital Stock $5 par exchanged for (0.5752) share Common $12 par
Chemical New York Corp. name changed to Chemical Banking Corp. 04/29/1988 which name changed to Chase Manhattan Corp. (New) 03/31/1996 which name changed to J.P. Morgan Chase & Co. 12/31/2000 which name changed to JPMorgan Chase & Co. 07/20/2004

TAPPIT RES LTD (CANADA)
Each share old Common no par exchanged for (0.5) share new Common no par 12/28/2000
Under plan of merger each share Common no par exchanged for (0.1) share Starpoint Energy Ltd. Common no par, (0.19) Crescent Point Energy Trust Trust Unit no par and $0.36 cash 09/10/2003
(See each company's listing)

TAR BABY MINING CO. (UT)
Each share Capital Stock 20¢ par exchanged for (0.2) share Capital Stock $1 par 04/28/1956
Name changed to Tar Baby Oil Co. 11/20/1957
Tar Baby Oil Co. name changed to Paramount Oil Co. 02/28/1959 which name changed to Paramount General Corp. 05/12/1965
(See Paramount General Corp.)

TAR BABY OIL CO. (UT)
Each share old Capital Stock $1 par exchanged for (0.15) share new Capital Stock $1 par 10/24/1958
Name changed to Paramount Oil Co. 02/28/1959
Paramount Oil Co. name changed to Paramount General Corp. 05/12/1965
(See Paramount General Corp.)

TAR POINT OIL CO. (QC)
Acquired by New Associated Developments Ltd. 04/17/1963
Each share Capital Stock $1 par exchanged for (0.02040816) share Capital Stock $1 par
New Associated Developments Ltd. recapitalized as Consolidated Developments Ltd. 05/10/1971
(See Consolidated Developments Ltd.)

TARA BANKSHARES CORP (GA)
Merged into First Citizens Corp. 04/10/1997
Each share Common $10 par exchanged for $15 cash

TARA EXPL & DEV LTD (ON)
Capital Stock $1 par changed to no par 07/21/1982
Acquired by Outokumpu Oy 05/02/1986
Each share Capital Stock no par exchanged for $19 cash

TARA GOLD RES CORP (NV)
Each share Common $0.001 par received distribution of (0.38843) share Firma Holdings Corp. Common $0.001 par payable 02/05/2015 to holders of record 01/28/2015
Charter revoked 10/31/2016

TARA MINERALS CORP (NV)
Name changed to Firma Holdings Corp. 06/23/2014

TARA PRODTNS CORP (DE)
Each share Common $0.0001 par exchanged for (0.01) share Common $0.01 par 01/09/1973
Charter cancelled and declared inoperative and void for non-payment of taxes 03/01/1977

TARANTELLA INC (CA)
Each share old Common no par exchanged exchanged for (0.2) share new Common no par 06/06/2003
Merged into Sun Microsystems, Inc. 07/13/2005
Each share new Common no par exchanged for $0.90 cash

TARBELL MINES LTD. (ON)
Charter revoked for failure to file reports and pay fees 12/10/1962

TARBUTT MINES LTD. (ON)
Charter revoked for failure to file reports and pay fees 03/03/1966

TARGA OIL & GAS INC (NV)
Merged into Chapman Energy, Inc. 08/11/1983
Each share Common 1¢ par exchanged for (0.14285714) share Common $0.001 par
Chapman Energy, Inc. name changed to Coda Energy, Inc. 10/10/1989
(See Coda Energy, Inc.)

TARGA RESOURCE CORP (AB)
Struck off register for failure to file annual returns 09/01/1993

TARGA RESOURCES (UT)
Name changed to Warren-Randall Corp. (UT) 11/25/1985
Warren-Randall Corp. (UT) reorganized in Nevada as Pacific Snax Corp. 06/23/1994
(See Pacific Snax Corp.)

TARGA RES PARTNERS LP (DE)
Merged into Targa Resources Corp. 02/17/2016
Each Common Unit exchanged for (0.62) share Common $0.001 par
(Additional Information in Active)

TARGACEPT INC (DE)
Each share Common $0.001 par received distribution of $1.08 principal amount of Conv. Notes due 02/19/2018 payable 08/19/2015 to holders of record 08/14/2015 Ex date - 08/20/2015
Merged into Catalyst Biosciences, Inc. 08/21/2015
Each share Common $0.001 par exchanged for (0.14285714) share Common $0.001 par

TARGANTA THERAPEUTICS CORP (DE)
Acquired by Medicines Co. 02/26/2009
Each share Common $0.0001 par exchanged for $2 cash

TARGAS RES INC (BC)
Struck off register and declared dissolved for failure to file returns 10/22/1993

TARGET CAP INC (NV)
Name changed to BioElectric, Inc. 02/01/1994
BioElectric, Inc. recapitalized as NexMed, Inc. 10/02/1995 which name changed to Apricus Biosciences, Inc. 09/14/2010

TARGET DEV GROUP INC (DE)
Reincorporated under the laws of Wyoming 04/13/2009

TARGET DEV GROUP INC (WY)
Name changed to Hannover House, Inc. 04/03/2012

TARGET ENERGY INC (AB)
Recapitalized as Olympia Financial Group Inc. 01/24/2002
Each share Common no par exchanged for (0.004) share Common no par

TARGET EXPL & MNG CORP (BC)
Merged into Crosshair Exploration & Mining Corp. 03/31/2009
Each share Common no par exchanged for (1.2) shares Common no par
Crosshair Exploration & Mining Corp. name changed to Crosshair Energy Corp. 11/02/2011 which recapitalized as Jet Metal Corp. (BC) 09/23/2013 which reorganized in Canada as Canada Jetlines Ltd. 03/07/2017

TARGET LOGISTICS INC (DE)
Merged into Mainfreight Ltd. 10/31/2007
Each share Common 1¢ par exchanged for $2.50 cash

TARGET MACHINES, INC. (KS)
Charter cancelled for failure to file annual reports 04/15/1977

TARGET MINES LTD (BC)
Struck off register and declared dissolved for failure to file returns 09/30/1974

TARGET OIL & GAS INC (CO)
Name changed to Egret Energy Corp. 12/31/1984
Egret Energy Corp. recapitalized as Territorial Resources Inc. 07/08/1988
(See Territorial Resources Inc.)

TARGET PETROLEUMS LTD. (ON)
Merged into Savanna Creek Gas & Oil Ltd. 04/24/1957
Each share Common $1 par exchanged for (0.16666666) share Common 50¢ par
Savanna Creek Gas & Oil Ltd. recapitalized as Savanna Resources Ltd. (ON) 09/19/1973 which reincorporated in Alberta 02/25/1980 which recapitalized as Hansa Corp. 02/12/2001 which name changed to Azteca Gold Corp. 12/28/2006

TARGET RES LTD (BC)
Name changed to Grand China Resources Ltd. 05/16/1986
Grand China Resources Ltd. recapitalized as New China Resources Ltd. 09/07/1989 which name changed to Sino Pac International Investments Inc. 02/06/1991 which recapitalized as Paron Resources Inc. 12/16/1996

TARGET TECHNOLOGIES INC (NY)
Name changed to C-Phone Corp. 08/22/1996
(See C-Phone Corp.)

TARGET THERAPEUTICS INC (DE)
Common $0.0025 par split (2) for (1) by issuance of (1) additional share 12/18/1995
Merged into Boston Scientific Corp. 04/08/1997
Each share Common $0.0025 par

exchanged for (1.07) shares Common $0.0025 par

TARGET VANGUARD CAP INC (CANADA)
Recapitalized as Coretek Vencap Inc. 02/22/1995
Each share Common no par exchanged for (0.5) share Common no par
Coretek Vencap Inc. recapitalized as Ungava Minerals Corp. 12/04/1996 which name changed to Nearctic Nickel Mines Inc. 09/07/2007

TARGET VENTURE CORP (CO)
Company became private 09/02/1992
Details not available

TARGETED GENETICS CORP (WA)
Each share old Common 1¢ par exchanged for (0.1) share new Common 1¢ par 05/11/2006
Name changed to AmpliPhi Biosciences Corp. 03/09/2011

TARGETS TR I (DE)
Targeted Growth Enhanced Terms Securities called for redemption at $50.375 on 08/15/2000

TARGETVIEWZ INC (FL)
Recapitalized as Greenway Energy 11/15/2007
Each share Common $0.0001 par exchanged for (0.005) share Common $0.0001 par
Greenway Energy name changed to Greenway Technology 09/19/2008

TARGITINTERACTIVE INC (DE)
Recapitalized as NetSpace International Holdings, Inc. 06/11/2007
Each share Common $0.001 par exchanged for (0.01) share Common $0.001 par
NetSpace International Holdings, Inc. recapitalized as Alternative Fuels Americas, Inc. 10/13/2010 which name changed to Kaya Holdings, Inc. 04/07/2015

TARI CO. (TX)
Charter forfeited for failure to pay taxes 02/18/1998

TARI GROUP INC (UT)
Name changed to Microshare Corp. 11/12/1986

TARI INC (NV)
Name changed to Sunridge International, Inc. 09/23/2009

TARIS INC (DE)
Name changed to Advanced Sensor Industries Inc. 03/00/1994
Advanced Sensor Industries, Inc. name changed to Fonix Corp. 05/13/1994
(See Fonix Corp.)

TARN PURE TECHNOLOGIES CORP (BC)
Struck from the register and declared dissolved for failure to file returns 07/21/1995

TARO INDS LTD (AB)
Each share old Common no par exchanged for (0.1) share new Common no par 07/04/1995
Merged into EVI, Inc. 01/15/1998
Each share new Common no par exchanged for (0.123) share Common no par
EVI, Inc. name changed to EVI Weatherford, Inc. 05/27/1998 which name changed to Weatherford International Inc. (New) (DE) 09/21/1998 which reincorporated in Bermuda as Weatherford International Ltd. 06/26/2002 which reincorporated in Switzerland 02/25/2009 which reincorporated in Ireland as Weatherford International PLC 06/18/2014

TARO VIT INDS LTD (ISRAEL)
Name changed to Taro Pharmaceutical Industries Ltd. 02/27/1994

TARONGA RESOURCES LTD. (BC)
Struck off register and declared dissolved for failure to file returns 02/25/1983

TARPON COAST BANCORP INC (FL)
Merged into First Busey Corp. 07/29/2005
Each share Common 1¢ par exchanged for approximately (0.71933) share Common $0.001 par and $12.80 cash

TARPON FINL CORP (FL)
Merged into Community National Bancorporation 02/28/2000
Each share Common exchanged for (1.6) shares Common no par
(See Community National Bancorporation)

TARPON INDS INC (MI)
Plan of reorganization under Chapter 11 Federal Bankruptcy Code effective 10/31/2008
No stockholders' equity

TARPON OIL CO (DE)
Charter cancelled and declared inoperative and void for non-payment of 04/15/1973

TARQUIN FINL CORP (DE)
Name changed to International Hardware, Inc. 06/05/1990
(See International Hardware, Inc.)

TARQUIN GROUP INC (ON)
Assets sold for the benefit of creditors 07/07/2008
Stockholders' equity unlikely

TARRAGON CORP. (NV)
Recapitalized as Sunray Minerals Inc. 12/23/1991
Each share Common $0.001 par exchanged for (0.01666666) share Common $0.001 par

TARRAGON CORP (NV)
Name changed 07/01/2004
Common 1¢ par split (3) for (2) by issuance of (0.5) additional share payable 02/14/2003 to holders of record 02/04/2003 Ex date - 02/18/2003
Common 1¢ par split (5) for (4) by issuance of (0.25) additional share payable 01/15/2004 to holders of record 01/01/2004 Ex date - 01/16/2004
Name changed from Tarragon Realty Investors Inc. to Tarragon Corp. 07/01/2004
Common 1¢ par split (3) for (2) by issuance of (0.5) additional share payable 02/10/2005 to holders of record 02/01/2005 Ex date - 02/11/2005
Stock Dividends - 10% payable 02/15/2001 to holders of record 02/01/2001 Ex date - 01/30/2001; 10% payable 04/26/2002 to holders of record 04/15/2002 Ex date - 04/11/2002
Plan of reorganization under Chapter 11 Federal Bankruptcy proceedings effective 07/06/2010
No stockholders' equity

TARRAGON OIL & GAS LTD (ON)
Each share old Common no par exchanged for (0.125) share new Common no par 07/05/1991
New Common no par split (2) for (1) by issuance of (1) additional share 06/09/1993
Merged into Marathon Oil Canada Ltd. 08/11/1998
Each share new Common no par exchanged for either (0.2814) share Common no par, $14.25 cash or a combination of stock and cash
Note: Option to receive stock or combination of stock and cash expired 08/10/1998
(See Marathon Oil Canada Ltd.)

TARRANT APPAREL GROUP (CA)
Common no par split (2) for (1) by issuance of (1) additional share payable 06/01/1998 to holders of record 05/08/1998
Acquired by Sunrise Acquisition Co., LLC 08/20/2009
Each share Common no par exchanged for $0.85 cash

TARRON INDS LTD (BC)
Name changed 06/29/1988
Name changed from Tarron Resources Ltd. to Tarron Industries Ltd. 06/29/1988
Name changed to Orko Gold Corp. 05/16/1997
Orko Gold Corp. name changed to Orko Silver Corp. 04/10/2006 which was acquired by Coeur d'Alene Mines Corp. (ID) 04/16/2013 which reincorporated in Delaware as Coeur Mining, Inc. 05/17/2013

TARSIS CAP CORP (BC)
Name changed to Tarsis Resources Ltd. 06/18/2009
Tarsis Resources Ltd. recapitalized as Alianza Minerals Ltd. 04/30/2015

TARSIS RES LTD (BC)
Reorganized as Alianza Minerals Ltd. 04/30/2015
Each share Common no par exchanged for (0.1) share Common no par

TARTAN ENERGY INC (AB)
Reincorporated 08/01/2001
Place of incorporation changed from (BC) to (AB) 08/01/2001
Merged into Nations Energy Co. Ltd. 02/02/2006
Each share Common no par exchanged for $0.63 cash

TARTAN LAKE GOLD MINES LTD. (ON)
Charter cancelled and declared dissolved for failure to file returns and pay fees 11/08/1977

TARTAN PETROLEUMS LTD. (AB)
Struck off register for failure to file returns 02/15/1962

TARTISAN RES CORP (ON)
Name changed to Tartisan Nickel Corp. 03/23/2018

TARXIEN CORP (ON)
Recapitalized 01/31/1989
Recapitalized from Tarxien International Inc. to Tarxien Corp. 01/31/1989
Each share old Common no par exchanged for (0.05) share new Common no par
Merged into Gecamex Acquisitions 12/09/1996
Each share new Common no par exchanged for $15.40 cash

TARZAN GOLD INC (ON)
Merged into Glen Auden Resources Ltd. 01/24/1990
Each share Common no par exchanged for (0.6) share Common no par
Glen Auden Resources Ltd. recapitalized as Maple Minerals Inc. 06/28/1996 which recapitalized as Maple Minerals Corp. 11/09/2001 which name changed to Mega Uranium Ltd. 10/19/2005

TASCO HLDGS INTL INC (DE)
Reorganized 8/29/2005
Reorganized from Tasco International, Inc. to Tasco Holdings International, Inc. 08/29/2005
Each share Common $0.0001 par exchanged for (10) shares Common $0.0001 par
Name changed to Bio-Matrix Scientific Group, Inc. (New) 09/05/2006

TASEKO MINES LTD (BC)
Name changed to Taseko Mines Ltd. (N.P.L.) 03/22/1990

TASER INTL INC (DE)
Common $0.00001 par split (3) for (1) by issuance of (2) additional shares payable 02/10/2004 to holders of record 01/26/2004 Ex date - 02/11/2004
Common $0.00001 par split (2) for (1) by issuance of (1) additional share payable 04/29/2004 to holders of record 04/15/2004 Ex date - 04/30/2004
Common $0.00001 par split (2) for (1) by issuance of (1) additional share payable 11/29/2004 to holders of record 11/15/2004
Name changed to Axon Enterprise, Inc. 04/06/2017

TASEX CAP LTD (BC)
Name changed to Flinders Resources Ltd. 02/27/2012
Flinders Resources Ltd. name changed to Leading Edge Materials Corp. 08/26/2016

TASH-ORN MINES LTD.
Sold to Tashota Goldfields Ltd. 00/00/1932
Details not available

TASHOTA GOLD MINES LTD.
Name changed to Kowkash Holdings Ltd. 00/00/1934
(See Kowkash Holdings Ltd.)

TASHOTA GOLDFIELDS LTD.
Bankrupt 00/00/1938
No stockholders' equity

TASHOTA NIPIGON MINES LTD (ON)
Merged into McAdam Resources Inc. 12/01/1988
Each share Capital Stock $1 par exchanged for (0.5) share Common no par
McAdam Resources Inc. recapitalized as Boulder Mining Corp. (ON) 05/09/1995 which reincorporated in British Columbia as Opal Energy Corp. 01/09/2007 which name changed to Versus Systems Inc. 07/13/2016

TASK MGMT INC (DE)
Name changed to Integra Distribution, Inc. 05/27/2004
Integra Distribution, Inc. recapitalized as Powerlock International Corp. 08/25/2005

TASKER PRODS CORP (DE)
Name changed 08/18/2006
Reincorporated 07/16/2007
Name changed from Tasker Capital Corp. to Tasker Products Corp. 08/18/2006
State of incorporation changed from (NV) to (DE) 07/16/2007
SEC revoked common stock registration 10/05/2011
Stockholders' equity unlikely

TASMAN METALS LTD (BC)
Merged into Leading Edge Materials Corp. 08/26/2016
Each share Common no par exchanged for (0.5) share Common no par
Note: Unexchanged certificates will be cancelled and become without value 08/26/2022

TASMAQUE GOLD MINES LTD. (ON)
Charter cancelled for failure to pay taxes and file returns 02/12/1970

TASSAWAY INC (DE)
Charter cancelled and declared inoperative and void for non-payment of taxes 03/01/1977

TASSETTE, INC. (DE)
Name changed to Tassaway, Inc. 08/10/1971
(See Tassaway, Inc.)

TASTE IT PRESENTS INC (NY)
Each share Common $0.0001 par exchanged for (0.0000125) share Common no par 09/04/1992
Note: In effect holders received $0.02 cash per share and public interest was eliminated

TASTEE FREEZ INDS INC (DE)
Name changed to TFI Companies, Inc. 12/04/1969
TFI Companies, Inc. name changed to Cardiff Equities Corp. 07/30/1982
(See Cardiff Equities Corp.)

TASTY BAKING CO (PA)
Class A Common 50¢ par reclassified as Common 50¢ par 12/20/1985
Class B Common 50¢ par reclassified as Common 50¢ par 12/20/1985
Common 50¢ par split (3) for (2) by issuance of (0.5) additional share 12/01/1986
Common 50¢ par split (3) for (2) by issuance of (0.5) additional share 12/01/1987
Common 50¢ par split (5) for (4) by issuance of (0.25) additional share payable 12/01/1997 to holders of record 11/07/1997
Acquired by Flowers Foods, Inc. 05/24/2011
Each share Common 50¢ par exchanged for $4 cash

TASTY FRIES INC (NV)
Each share old Common $0.001 par exchanged for (0.05) share new Common $0.001 par 12/23/1996
Voluntarily dissolved 10/11/2011
Details not available

TASTYEAST, INC. (DE)
Reorganized under the laws of New Jersey 00/00/1941
Company insolvent, no stockholders' equity

TASTYEAST, INC. (MA)
Acquired by Tastyeast, Inc. (DE) 00/00/1934
Details not available

TASU RES LTD (BC)
Name changed to Imtrex Industries & Recycling Inc. 10/15/1990
(See Imtrex Industries & Recycling Inc.)

TATA COMMUNICATIONS LTD (INDIA)
ADR agreement terminated 07/14/2013
Each Sponsored ADR for Equity Shares exchanged for $2.710779 cash

TATA ELEC COS (INDIA)
Name changed to Tata Power Co. Ltd. 02/09/2007

TATA ENGR & LOCOMOTIVE LTD (INDIA)
Stock Dividend - 60% payable 02/07/1996 to holders of record 10/31/1995
Each old GDR for Ordinary automatically became (1) new GDR for Ordinary 09/03/1997
Name changed to Tata Motors Ltd. 10/16/2003

TATA IRON & STEEL CO LTD (INDIA)
Name changed to Tata Steel Ltd. 09/01/2005

TATA TEA LTD (INDIA)
144A GDR's for Equity split (10) for (1) by issuance of (9) additional GDR's payable 07/13/2010 to holders of record 07/01/2010
Ex date - 07/14/2010
Reg. S GDR's for Equity split (10) for (1) by issuance of (9) additional GDR's payable 07/13/2010 to holders of record 07/01/2010
Ex date - 07/14/2010
Name changed to Tata Global Beverages Ltd. 07/22/2010

TATHACUS RES LTD (CANADA)
Name changed to Pan Terra Industries Inc. 04/20/2004
Pan Terra Industries Inc. name changed to Kombat Copper Inc. 04/30/2012 which name changed to Trigon Metals Inc. 12/28/2016

TATHAM OFFSHORE INC (DE)
Each share old Common 1¢ par exchanged for (0.1) share new Common 1¢ par 11/24/1997
Mandatory Redeemable Preferred called for redemption at $0.50 on 02/23/1998
Recapitalized as Patriot Energy Corp. 11/20/2006
Each share new Common 1¢ par exchanged for (0.001) share Common 1¢ par

TATLAR RES LTD (BC)
Recapitalized as Opact Resources Ltd. 07/22/1991
Each share Common no par exchanged for (0.25) share Common no par
Opact Resources Ltd. recapitalized as Blue Lightning Ventures Inc. 07/21/1999 which name changed to Universal Uranium Ltd. 05/03/2005 which name changed to Expedition Mining Inc. 07/07/2010 which name changed to Imagin Medical Inc. 02/24/2016

TATMAR VENTURES INC (BC)
Name changed to Highway 50 Gold Corp. 07/29/2011

TATONKA ENERGY INC (OK)
Recapitalized as Phymed, Inc. 03/12/1999
Each share Common $0.001 par exchanged for (0.1) share Common 1¢ par
(See Phymed, Inc.)

TATONKA OIL & GAS INC (CO)
SEC revoked common stock registration 07/19/2012

TATRASS INTL LTD (AB)
Merged into Vitreous Environmental Group Inc. 11/09/1992
Each share Common no par exchanged for (1) share Common no par
Vitreous Environmental Group Inc. recapitalized as Vitreous Capital Inc. 03/06/1998 which name changed to Vitreous Glass Inc. 02/15/2007

TATSA RES LTD (BC)
Name changed to Acorn Resources Ltd. 07/06/1983
Acorn Resources Ltd. recapitalized as Consolidated Acorn Resources Ltd. 07/23/1990
(See Consolidated Acorn Resources Ltd.)

TATUM INDUSTRIES, INC. (CO)
Recapitalized as Modern Technologies Mining Corp. 8/4/83
Each share Common no par exchanged for (8) shares Common no par

TATUM PETE CORP (CA)
Merged into Tatum Petroleum Corp. (DE) 6/30/86
Each share Common no par exchanged for (6) shares Common 1¢ par
(See Tatum Petroleum Corp. (DE))

TATUM PETE CORP (DE)
Liquidation completed
Each share Common 1¢ par received initial distribution of $0.70 cash payable 09/23/2005 to holders of record 09/01/2005
Each share Common 1¢ par received second and final distribution of $0.094 cash payable 07/24/2006 to holders of record 07/18/2006
Ex date - 09/21/2006

TAUBMAN CTRS INC (MI)
8.30% Preferred Ser. A 1¢ par called for redemption at $25 plus $0.270902 accrued dividends on 05/18/2006
7.625% Preferred Ser. H 1¢ par called for redemption at $25 plus $0.333594 accrued dividends on 09/04/2012
8% Preferred Ser. G 1¢ par called for redemption at $25 plus $0.35 accrued dividends on 09/04/2012
(Additional Information in Active)

TAUBMAN STORES CORP.
Bankrupt 00/00/1929
No stockholders' equity

TAUNTON GAS LIGHT CO.
Merged into Brockton Taunton Gas Co. 00/00/1952
Each share Capital Stock $50 par exchanged for (1.4) shares $3.80 Preferred $50 par
Brockton Taunton Gas Co. merged into Bay State Gas Co. (New) 11/19/1974
(See Bay State Gas Co. (New))

TAUNTON-NEW BEDFORD COPPER CO.
Acquired by Republic Brass Corp. 00/00/1928
Details not available

TAUNTON SVGS BK (TAUNTON, MA)
Acquired by New Bedford Institution for Savings (New Bedford, MA) 08/19/1988
Each share Common 10¢ par exchanged for $17 cash

TAUNTON TECHNOLOGIES INC (DE)
Name changed to VISX, Inc. (DE) 11/28/1990
VISX, Inc. (DE) merged into Advanced Medical Optics, Inc. 05/27/2005
(See Advanced Medical Optics, Inc.)

TAURCANIS MINES LTD. (ON)
Recapitalized as Tundra Gold Mines Ltd. (ON) 04/30/1963
Each share 6% Preference $35 par exchanged for (1) share 6% Conv. Preference $35 par
Each share Common $1 par exchanged for (0.25) share Common $1 par Tundra Gold Mines Ltd. (ON) reincorporated in British Columbia 02/05/1982
(See Tundra Gold Mines Ltd.)

TAURUS ENTMT COS (CO)
Name changed to Bluestar Health, Inc. 08/20/2004
(See Bluestar Health, Inc.)

TAURUS EXPL LTD (BC)
Name changed to Trans Asia Resources Inc. 11/28/1997
Trans Asia Resources Inc. name changed to Municipal Solutions Group, Inc. 01/14/2002 which reorganized as CloudBench Applications, Inc. 07/21/2008 which name changed to BasicGov Systems, Inc. 12/24/2009 which name changed to Pedro Resources Ltd. 09/30/2010

TAURUS FOOTWEAR INC (CANADA)
Dissolved for non-compliance 12/09/1999

TAURUS INDUSTRIES, INC. (NV)
Recapitalized as Pharmical, Inc. 01/05/1973
Each share Common 1¢ par exchanged for (3) shares Common 3¢ par
Pharmical, Inc. name changed to Bonneville Raceway Park, Inc. 06/06/1974 which merged into International Teledata II Corp. 03/01/1981 which name changed to International Teledata Corp. 06/12/1984
(See International Teldata Corp.)

TAURUS MINERALS INC (UT)
Completely liquidated 05/16/2012
Each share Common 1¢ par exchanged for first and final distribution of $0.0548 cash

TAURUS MUNICALIFORNIA HLDGS INC (MD)
Merged into MuniYield California Fund, Inc. 02/09/1998
Each share Adjustable Dividend Auction Market Preferred 10¢ par exchanged for (0.750863) share Common 10¢ par
Each share Common 10¢ par exchanged for (0.750863) share Common 10¢ par
MuniYield California Fund, Inc. name changed to BlackRock MuniYield California Fund, Inc. 10/02/2006

TAURUS MUNINEWYORK HLDGS INC (MD)
Merged into MuniYield New York Insured Fund II, Inc. 02/09/1998
Each share Auction Market Preferred Adjustable Divided 10¢ par exchanged for (0.7958) share Common 10¢ par
Each share Common 10¢ par exchanged for (0.7958) share Common 10¢ par
MuniYield New York Insured Fund II, Inc. reorganized as MuniYield New York Insured Fund, Inc. 03/06/2000 which name changed to BlackRock MuniYield New York Insured Fund, Inc. 10/02/2006 which name changed to BlackRock MuniYield New York Quality Fund, Inc. 11/09/2010

TAURUS OIL CORP. (CO)
Common no par split (10) for (1) by issuance of (9) additional shares 05/01/1980
Reorganized as Taurus Petroleum, Inc. 11/19/1984
Each share Common no par exchanged for (0.023337) share Common $0.001 par
Taurus Petroleum, Inc. recapitalized as Taurus Entertainment Companies, Inc. 11/24/1997 which name changed to Bluestar Health, Inc. 08/20/2004
(See Bluestar Health, Inc.)

TAURUS PETE INC (CO)
Recapitalized as Taurus Entertainment Companies, Inc. 11/24/1997
Each share Common $0.001 par exchanged for (0.00333333) share Common $0.001 par
Taurus Entertainment Companies, Inc. name changed to Bluestar Health, Inc. 08/20/2004
(See Bluestar Health, Inc.)

TAURUS RES LTD (BC)
Capital Stock no par split (2) for (1) by issuance of (1) additional share 03/16/1981
Capital Stock no par reclassified as Class A Common no par 10/28/1982
Recapitalized as International Taurus Resources Inc. 11/24/1988
Each share Class A Common no par exchanged for (0.1) share Class A Common no par
International Taurus Resources Inc. merged into American Bonanza Gold Corp. 03/31/2005 which merged into Kerr Mines Inc. 07/07/2014

TAUSSIG, DAY & CO., INC. (MO)
Completely liquidated 09/30/1969
Each share Capital Stock $1 par exchanged for first and final distribution of $1.594 cash

TAVA TECHNOLOGIES INC (CO)
Merged into Real Software N.V. 07/23/1999
Each share Common $0.0001 par exchanged for $8 cash

TAVART CO. (CA)
Name changed to Wread, Inc. 05/26/1965
(See Wread, Inc.)

TAWA PORCUPINE GOLD MINES LTD. (ON)
Charter cancelled for failure to file reports and pay taxes 00/00/1955

TAWSHO MNG INC (ON)
Merged into Genesis Metals Corp. 03/02/2016
Each share Common no par exchanged for (0.2297) share Common no par
Note: Unexchanged certificates will be cancelled and become without value 03/02/2022

TAX CONSULTANTS INC (CA)
Name changed to T C I, Enterprises 03/09/1973
T C I, Enterprises name changed to Frontier Adjusters, Inc. 03/02/1978 which merged into Frontier Financial Corp. 05/07/1984 which name changed to Frontier Adjusters of America, Inc. 10/17/1986
(See Frontier Adjuster of America, Inc.)

TAX CORP AMER (DC)
Completely liquidated 05/29/1970
Each share Common 1¢ par exchanged for first and final distribution of (1) share Automation Technology, Inc. Common 1¢ par
Automation Technology, Inc. name changed to Tax Corp. of America (MD) 03/11/1971
(See Tax Corp. of America (MD)

TAX CORP AMER (MD)
Ceased operations 07/09/1980
No stockholders' equity

TAX DEFD CAP CORP (MD)
Voluntarily dissolved 12/21/1982
Details not available

TAX EXEMPT CALIF MONEY MKT FD (MA)
Shares of Bene. Int. no par reclassified as Premier Shares no par 09/09/2008
Completely liquidated 04/08/2016
Each Institutional Share no par received $1 cash
Each Premier Share no par received $1 cash

TAX FREE MONEY FD INC (MD)
Reorganized as Smith Barney Tax Free Money Funds Inc. 10/14/1994
Details not available

TAX FREE MUN LEASE FD INC (MD)
Name changed to Limited Term Municipal Fund, Inc. 07/01/1985
(See Limited Term Municipal Fund, Inc.)

TAX-FREE PUERTO RICO TARGET MAT FD INC (PR)
Preferred Linked to S&P Index 2002 Ser. B called for redemption at $25 on 06/07/2008

TAX MAN INC (MA)
Class A Common $1 par changed to 50¢ par and (1) additional share issued 08/15/1969
8.5% Conv. Preferred Ser. A $95 par called for redemption 05/31/1978
8.5% Conv. Preferred Ser. B $95 par called for redemption 08/00/1981
Each share old Common 50¢ par exchanged for (0.0002) share new Common 50¢ par 10/31/1997
Note: In effect holders received $0.75 cash per share and public interest was eliminated

TAX MANAGED FD FOR UTIL SHS INC (MD)
Capital Stock 10¢ par split (6) for (5) by issuance of (0.2) additional share 11/29/1979
Capital Stock 10¢ par split (6) for (5) by issuance of (0.2) additional share 12/02/1980
Name changed to ABT Utility Income Fund 12/01/1984
(See ABT Utility Income Fund)

TAX OPTIMIZED RETURN ORIENTED SECS TR (ON)
Name changed to Aston Hill Capital Growth Fund 01/24/2011

TAX SECURITY CORP. (DE)
Charter cancelled and declared inoperative and void for non-payment of taxes 03/01/1974

TAX SPECIALIST INC (CO)
Each share Common 1¢ par exchanged for (0.1) share Common 10¢ par 12/06/1973
Declared defunct and inoperative for failure to pay taxes and file annual reports 01/31/1977

TAXMASTERS (NV)
Chapter 11 bankruptcy proceedings converted to Chapter 7 on 05/09/2012
Stockholders' equity unlikely

TAXTRONICS INC (NY)
Stock Dividend - 10% 07/15/1970
Name changed to Indiaports, Inc. 04/29/1977
(See Indiaports, Inc.)

TAXX CORP (DE)
Name changed to World Marketing & Travel, Inc. 07/06/1995
World Marketing & Travel, Inc. recapitalized as Savant Biotechnology Inc. 02/10/1997 which name changed to Children's Beverage Group, Inc. 05/13/1997
(See Children's Beverage Group, Inc.)

TAY RIV PETE LTD (BC)
Name changed to Butec International Chemical Corp. 11/27/1985
Butec International Chemical Corp. recapitalized as International Butec Industries Corp. 05/05/1988 which recapitalized as WebSmart.com Communications, Inc. 10/17/2000 which name changed to Gold Reach Resources Ltd. 10/13/2004 which name changed to Surge Copper Corp. 02/21/2018

TAY RIVER MINES LTD. (BC)
Name changed to Tay River Petroleum Ltd. and Common 50¢ par changed to no par 08/08/1980
Tay River Petroleum Ltd. name changed to Butec International Chemical Corp. 11/27/1985 which recapitalized as International Butec Industries Corp. 05/05/1988 which recapitalized as WebSmart.com Communications, Inc. 10/17/2000 which name changed to Gold Reach Resources Ltd. 10/13/2004 which name changed to Surge Copper Corp. 02/21/2018

TAYC CAP TR I (DE)
9.75% Trust Preferred Securities called for redemption at $25 plus $0.555209 accured dividends on 09/22/2014

TAYCO DEVS INC (NY)
Each share Common 50¢ par exchanged for (10) shares Common 5¢ par 09/15/1961
Stock Dividend - 10% 04/27/1973
Merged into Taylor Devices, Inc. 03/31/2008
Each share Common 5¢ par exchanged for (1) share Common 2-1/2¢ par

TAYGETUS IMPORTED FOODS, INC. (IL)
Proclaimed dissolved for failure to pay taxes and file reports 12/01/1983

TAYLOR, HARKINS & LEA, INC. (PA)
Liquidation completed

Each share Common 1¢ par received initial distribution of $0.157 cash 04/27/1965
Each share Common 1¢ par received second and final distribution of $0.072 cash 06/30/1966

TAYLOR, PEARSON & CARSON (CANADA), LTD. (CANADA)
Acquired by Prairie Pacific Distributors Ltd. 11/20/1959
Each share Common exchanged for $21 cash
5% Preference called for redemption 03/27/1961
Public interest eliminated

TAYLOR BISCUIT CO. (DE)
Acquired by Fairmont Foods Co. 11/20/1968
Each share Common $1 par exchanged for (0.166666) share Common 50¢ par
Fairmont Foods Co. merged into American Financial Corp. 07/24/1980
(See American Financial Corp.)

TAYLOR CAP GROUP INC (DE)
Perpetual Preferred Ser. A 1¢ par called for redemption at $25.10 on 07/16/2004
5% Perpetual Preferred Ser. B 1¢ par called for redemption at $1,000 on 12/23/2013
Merged into MB Financial, Inc. 08/18/2014
Each share 8% Perpetual Non-Cum Preferred Ser. A 1¢ par exchanged for (1) share Perpetual Non-Cum Preferred Ser. A 1¢ par
Each share Common 1¢ par exchanged for (0.64318) share Common 1¢ par and $4.08 cash

TAYLOR CHEMICAL FOAM INDUSTRIES LTD. (CANADA)
Proclaimed dissolved for failure to file reports 06/12/1968

TAYLOR (E.E.) CO.
Liquidated 00/00/1927
Details not available

TAYLOR CORP (DE)
Each share 4% Preferred $100 par acquired by Alco Standard Corp. for $70 cash 04/02/1968
Acquired by Alco Standard Corp. 10/16/1968
Each share Common $3 par exchanged for (0.5) share Common no par
Alco Standard Corp. name changed to IKON Office Solutions, Inc. 01/24/1997
(See IKON Office Solutions, Inc.)

TAYLOR (WILLIAM) CORP.
In process of liquidation 00/00/1942
Details not available

TAYLOR (E.E.) CORP. (MA)
Preferred $100 par and Prior Preference
$100 par called for redemption 05/09/1969
Public interest eliminated

TAYLOR CREEK MINING CO., LTD. (BC)
Name changed to Zenda Gold Mining (Canada) Ltd. 04/27/1950
Zenda Gold Mining (Canada) Ltd. name changed to Zenda Exploration Co., Ltd. 01/08/1953
(See Zenda Exploration Co., Ltd.)

TAYLOR ENGINES, INC. (NV)
Charter revoked for failure to file reports and pay fees 03/01/1965

TAYLOR EQUITIES INC (DE)
Recapitalized as Freight Connection, Inc. 01/07/1992
Each share old Common $0.001 par exchanged for (0.2) share new Common $0.001 par
(See Freight Connection, Inc.)

TAYLOR FARM OIL CO. (WV)
Dissolved 10/24/1911
Details not available

TAYLOR FIBRE CO. (DE)
Name changed to Taylor Corp. 09/01/1962
Taylor Corp. acquired by Alco Standard Corp. 10/16/1968 which name changed to IKON Office Solutions, Inc. 01/24/1997
(See IKON Office Solutions, Inc.)

TAYLOR FOOD CO. (DE)
Name changed to Taylor Biscuit Co. 00/00/1952
Taylor Biscuit Co. acquired by Fairmont Foods Co. 11/20/1968 which merged into American Financial Corp. 07/24/1980
(See American Financial Corp.)

TAYLOR GAS LIQUIDS FD (AB)
Reorganized under the laws of Ontario as Taylor NGL Limited Partnership 08/16/2000
Each Trust Unit no par exchanged for (1) Unit of Ltd. Partnership no par
Taylor NGL Limited Partnership acquired by AltaGas Income Trust 01/10/2008 which reorganized as AltaGas Ltd. 07/06/2010

TAYLOR GROUP INC (MO)
Merged into Seven-Up Co. 05/01/1980
Each share Common $1 par exchanged for $51 cash

TAYLOR INSTR COS (NY)
Each share Common $100 par exchanged for (5) shares Common $20 par 00/00/1945
Each share Common $20 par exchanged for (2) shares Common $10 par 08/30/1957
Common $10 par changed to $5 par and (1) additional share issued 08/31/1960
Common $5 par split (5) for (3) by issuance of (0.66666666) additional share 11/13/1964
Merged into Sybron Corp. 10/07/1968
Each share Common $5 par exchanged for (1) share $2.40 Conv. Preferred $4 par
(See Sybron Corp.)

TAYLOR INTL CORP (NV)
Reincorporated 05/27/1971
Capital Stock $10 par changed to $5 par and (1) additional share issued 12/23/1959
Each share Capital Stock $5 par exchanged for (0.1) share Capital Stock $1.50 par 06/22/1965
State of incorporation changed from (NY) to (NV) 05/27/1971
Merged into Mason Corp. 04/16/1984
Each share Capital Stock $1.50 par exchanged for $1.40 cash

TAYLOR INVESTMENT CO. (DE)
Voluntarily dissolved 12/21/1954
Details not available

TAYLOR JACK DEV CORP (DE)
Stock Dividend - 10% 08/15/1973
Name changed to Taylor Realty Enterprises, Inc. 06/28/1974
(See Taylor Realty Enterprises, Inc.)

TAYLOR LOGAN CO.
Dissolved in 1942

TAYLOR MACHINE WORKS, INC. (MS)
Name changed to Taylor Group, Inc. 12/28/1991

TAYLOR MADISON CORP (FL)
Recapitalized as Telzuit Medical Technologies, Inc. 08/19/2005
Each share Common $0.001 par exchanged for (0.03225806) share Common $0.001 par
(See Telzuit Medical Technologies, Inc.)

TAYLOR MILLING CORP.
Liquidation completed 00/00/1946

Details not available

TAYLOR (BRIDGE RIVER) MINES, LTD. (BC)
Name changed to Inter-Tech Development & Resources Ltd. 05/09/1969
Inter-Tech Development & Resources Ltd. name changed to Inter-Tech Resources Ltd. 06/24/1971
(See Inter-Tech Resources Ltd.)

TAYLOR NELSON SOFRES PLC (UNITED KINGDOM)
Name changed 06/16/1998
Name changed from Taylor Nelson AGB PLC to Taylor Nelson Sofres PLC 06/16/1998
Sponsored ADR's for Ordinary split (3.75) for (1) by issuance of (2.75) additional ADR's payable 01/03/2006 to holders of record 12/30/2005 Ex date - 01/04/2006
Basis changed from (1:15) to (1:4) 01/03/2006
Acquired by WPP PLC (Old) 12/12/2008
Each Sponsored ADR for Ordinary exchanged for $14.60477 cash

TAYLOR NGL LTD PARTNERSHIP (ON)
Acquired by AltaGas Income Trust 01/10/2008
Each Unit of Ltd. Partnership no par exchanged for (0.42) Trust Unit no par
AltaGas Income Trust reorganized as AltaGas Ltd. 07/06/2010

TAYLOR OIL & GAS CO. (DE)
Merged into Delhi-Taylor Oil Corp. 00/00/1955
Each share Common exchanged for (1.37) shares Common $1 par
(See Delhi-Taylor Oil Corp.)

TAYLOR PUBLISHING CO. (TX)
Each share Common $2 par exchanged for (2) shares Common $1 par 03/20/1961
Stock Dividend - 10% 11/24/1961
Merged into International Silver Co. (CT) 09/18/1967
Each share Common $1 par exchanged for (1) share Conv. 2nd Preferred Ser. A no par
International Silver Co. (CT) name changed to Insilco Corp. 04/10/1969
(See Insilco Corp.)

TAYLOR RAND INC (ON)
Recapitalized as Sheridan Reserve Inc. 06/25/1996
Each share Common no par exchanged for (0.1) share Common no par
Sheridan Reserve Inc. name changed to Nevadabobs.com, Inc. 08/04/2000 which name changed to Nevada Bob's International Inc. 08/27/2001 which name changed to Loncor Resources Inc. 12/02/2008

TAYLOR RLTY ENTERPRISES INC (DE)
Each share Common 1¢ par exchanged for (0.00025) share Common $250 par 06/30/1976
Note: In effect holders received $3.75 cash per share and public interest was eliminated

TAYLOR RENTAL CORP (MA)
Stock Dividend - 25% 05/28/1981
Merged into Stanley Works 06/03/1983
Each share Common $1 par exchanged for (0.465) share Common $2.50 par
Stanley Works name changed to Stanley Black & Decker, Inc. 03/12/2010

TAYLOR S COS INC (UT)
Chapter 11 bankruptcy proceedings converted to Chapter 7 on 12/6/88
Stockholders' equity unlikely

TAYLOR WHARTON IRON & STEEL CO. (NJ)
Recapitalized 00/00/1934
Each share Preferred $100 par exchanged for (3) shares Capital Stock no par
Each share Common no par exchanged for (1) share Capital Stock no par
Assets sold and name changed to Twisco Corp. 00/00/1953
(See Twisco Corp.)

TAYLOR WINDFALL GOLD MNG LTD (BC)
Merged into Taywin Resources Ltd. 11/15/1972
Each share Common $1 par exchanged for (0.1) share Common 70¢ par
Taywin Resources Ltd. recapitalized as Consolidated Taywin Resources Ltd. 08/26/1994 which name changed to Inspiration Mining Corp. (BC) 04/29/1996 which reincorporated in Ontario 08/18/2008

TAYLOR WINE INC (NY)
Common $2 par split (3) for (1) by issuance of (2) additional shares 08/19/1971
Merged into Coca-Cola Co. 01/21/1977
Each (3.75) shares Common $2 par exchanged for (1) share Common no par

TAYLOR-YOUNG AIRPLANE CO.
Name changed to Taylorcraft Aviation Corp. in 1939
(See Taylorcraft Aviation Corp.)

TAYLORCRAFT AVIATION CORP. (DE)
Bankrupt in 1947

TAYSAN GOLD MINING CORP. (PHILIPPINES)
Dissolved 05/31/1954
Details not available

TAYWIN RES LTD (BC)
Common 70¢ par changed to no par 11/05/1985
Recapitalized as Consolidated Taywin Resources Ltd. 08/26/1994
Each share Common no par exchanged for (0.2) share Common no par
Consolidated Taywin Resources Ltd. name changed to Inspiration Mining Corp. (BC) 04/29/1996 which reincorporated in Ontario 08/18/2008

TAZIN MINES LTD (CANADA)
Recapitalized as Zinat Mines Ltd. 8/14/70
Each share Capital Stock no par exchanged for (0.25) share Capital Stock no par
Zinat Mines Ltd. name changed to Newport Mining & Land Development Ltd. 1/15/73
(See Newport Mining & Land Development Ltd.)

TAZIN URANIUM MINES LTD. (BC)
Dissolved by default and stricken from register 8/30/62

TB ADVISORS INC (AB)
Issue Information - 2,000,000 shares COM offered at $0.10 per share on 09/12/1997
Reincorporated under the laws of Canada as Honeybee Technology Inc. 03/30/1999
(See Honeybee Technology Inc.)

TB HLDG CO (PA)
Liquidation completed
Each share Capital Stock $10 par exchanged for initial distribution of $32.72 cash 3/12/90
Each share Common $10 par received second and final distribution of $2.82 cash 4/27/94

TB WOODS CORP (DE)
Merged into Altra Holdings, Inc. 04/06/2007
Each share Common 1¢ par exchanged for $24.80 cash

TBA ENTMT CORP (DE)
Merged into TBA Holdings, LLC 6/29/2004
Each share Common no par exchanged for $0.681783 cash

TBC CORP NEW (DE)
Merged into Sumitomo Corp. 11/17/2005
Each share Common 10¢ par exchanged for $35 cash

TBC CORP OLD (DE)
Common 10¢ par split (3) for (2) by issuance of (0.5) additional share 2/26/87
Common 10¢ par split (3) for (2) by issuance of (0.5) additional share 9/8/87
Common 10¢ par split (3) for (2) by issuance of (0.5) additional share 10/27/89
Common 10¢ par split (3) for (2) by issuance of (0.5) additional share 11/15/91
Common 10¢ par split (3) for (2) by issuance of (0.5) additional share 12/11/92
Under plan of reorganization each share Common 10¢ par automatically became (1) share TBC Corp. (New) Common 10¢ par 11/19/2004
(See TBC Corp. (New))

TBC GLOBAL NEWS NETWORK INC (NV)
Each share old Common $0.001 par exchanged for (0.00033333) share new Common $0.001 par 04/27/2015
Name changed to InCapta, Inc. 11/10/2015

TBC INVTS INC (AB)
Issue Information - 1,200,000 shares COM offered at $0.25 per share on 11/12/1996
Name changed to Warwick Communications Inc. 11/11/97

TBM ENTERPRISES INC (WA)
Merged into Antioch Resources, Inc. 04/23/1984
Each share Common $0.001 par exchanged for (0.5) share Common 1¢ par and (0.5) share Class A Common 1¢ par
Antioch Resources, Inc. recapitalized as Antioch Resources Ltd. 03/01/1988 which merged into Consolidated Nevada Goldfields Corp. 06/25/1991 which recapitalized as Real Del Monte Mining Corp. 05/14/1998
(See Real Del Monte Mining Corp.)

TBM HLDGS INC (FL)
Proclaimed dissolved for failure to file reports and pay fees 10/01/2004

TBS COMPUTER CTRS CORP (NY)
Merged into NCSS Holding Co., Inc. 03/11/1974
Each share Common 10¢ par exchanged for $9 cash

TBS INTERNATIONAL LTD (BERMUDA)
Issue Information - 8,160,000 shares CL A COM offered at $10 per share on 07/05/2005
Reincorporated under the laws of Ireland as TBS International PLC and Class A Common 1¢ par reclassified as Class A Ordinary 1¢ par 01/07/2010
(See TBS International PLC)

TBS INTERNATIONAL PLC (IRELAND)
Plan of reorganization under Chapter 11 Federal Bankruptcy proceedings confirmed 03/29/2012

No stockholders' equity

TBS INVTS LTD (CO)
Name changed to Sprung & Wise Capital Group, Inc. 06/24/1987

TBX RES INC (TX)
Each share old Common 1¢ par received distribution of (0.2) share GULFTEX Drilling Inc. Common 1¢ par payable 09/15/2001 to holders of record 08/15/2001 Ex date - 08/13/2001
Each share old Common 1¢ par exchanged for (0.1) share new Common 1¢ par 09/29/2005
Name changed to Frontier Oilfield Services, Inc. 02/17/2012

TC PWR MGMT CORP (NV)
Common $0.001 par split (4) for (1) by issuance of (3) additional shares payable 11/16/2010 to holders of record 11/16/2010
Name changed to Axiom Gold & Silver Corp. 05/16/2011
Axiom Gold & Silver Corp. recapitalized as Axiom Oil & Gas Corp. 10/16/2013

TC X CALIBUR INC (NV)
Each share old Common $0.001 par exchanged for (0.05) share new Common $0.001 par 03/21/2001
Note: Holders of (100) or fewer pre-split shares received share for share Holders of between (101) and (2,000) shares received (100) shares only
Each share new Common $0.001 par exchanged again for (2.3943) shares new Common $0.001 par 12/31/2007
Each share new Common $0.001 par exchanged again for (0.25) share new Common $0.001 par 11/26/2010
Name changed to Medican Enterprises, Inc. 09/18/2013

TCA CABLE TV INC (TX)
Common 10¢ par split (5) for (4) by issuance of (0.25) additional share 4/24/86
Common 10¢ par split (2) for (1) by issuance of (1) additional share 7/11/89
Common 10¢ par split (2) for (1) by issuance of (1) additional share payable 8/5/98 to holders of record 7/15/98
Stock Dividend - 20% 1/17/83
Merged into Cox Communications, Inc. (DE) 8/12/99
Each share Common 10¢ par exchanged for (0.7418) share Class A Common $1 par and $31.25 cash
(See Cox Communications, Inc. (DE))

TCBY ENTERPRISES INC (DE)
Merged into Capricorn Investors III, L.P. 06/01/2000
Each share Common 10¢ par exchanged for $6 cash

TCC BEVERAGES LTD (CANADA)
Reincorporated 07/27/1987
Place of incorporation changed from (ONT) to (Canada) 07/27/1987
Name changed to Coca Cola Beverages Ltd. 08/20/1990
(See Coca Cola Beverages Ltd.)

TCC EQUIP INCOME FD (CA)
Completely liquidated 08/02/2005
Each Depositary Unit received first and final distribution of $0.21 cash
Note: Certificates were not required to be surrendered and are without value

TCC INC (TX)
Each share Common 10¢ par exchanged for (0.1) share Common $1 par 5/12/75
Common $1 par changed to 10¢ par 4/1/76
Name changed to Continuum Co., Inc. (TX) 12/7/79

Continuum Co., Inc. (TX) reincorporated in (DE) 8/20/87 which merged into Computer Sciences Corp. 8/1/96

TCC INDS INC (TX)
Company reported out of business 00/00/1999
No stockholders' equity

TCEH CORP (DE)
Name changed to Vistra Energy Corp. 11/07/2016

TCENET INC (AB)
Acquired by WNS Emergent Inc. 09/30/2003
Each share Common no par exchanged for (0.32669026) share Common no par
WNS Emergent Inc. name changed to CriticalControl Solutions Corp. 06/14/2004 which name changed to Critical Control Energy Services Corp. 07/03/2015

TCF CAP I (DE)
10.75% Capital Securities Ser. I called for redemption at $25 on 07/30/2012

TCF ENERGY INC (QC)
Merged into TriGas Exploration Inc. 07/01/1996
Each share Common no par exchanged for (1) share Common no par or $1 cash
(See TriGas Exploration Inc.)

TCF FINL CORP (DE)
Reorganized 11/27/1987
Reorganized from TCF Banking & Savings, F.A. (Minneapolis, MN) to TCF Financial Corp. (DE) 11/27/1987
Each share Common 1¢ par exchanged for (1) share Common 1¢ par
Preferred Ser. A 1¢ par called for redemption 07/03/1995
7.5% Depositary Preferred Ser. A called for redemption at $25.234375 on 10/16/2017
6.45% Non-Cum. Perpetual Preferred Ser. B 1¢ par called for redemption at $25 on 03/01/2018

TCG INTL INC (BC)
Each share Common no par exchanged for (0.5) share Class A Multiple Stock no par and (0.5) share Class B Subordinate no par 9/14/92
Plan of recapitalization effective 5/9/96
Each share Class A Multiple Stock no par exchanged for (1) share Preference no par which was subsequently redeemed for $3.48 cash
Each share Class B Subordinate no par exchanged for (1) share Preference no par which was subsequently redeemed for $3.48 cash

TCHAIKAZAN ENTERPRISES LTD (BC)
Struck off register and declared dissolved for failure to file returns 08/02/1991

TCI COMMUNICATIONS FING I (DE)
8.72% Trust Originated Preferred Securities called for redemption at $25 on 02/28/2002

TCI COMMUNICATIONS FINANCING II (DE)
10% Trust Originated Preferred Securities called for redemption at $25 on 02/28/2002

TCI COMMUNICATIONS FING IV (DE)
9.72% Trust Originated Preferred Securities called for redemption at $25 plus $0.006 accrued dividends on 04/01/2002

TCI COMMUNICATIONS INC (DE)
Merged into AT&T Corp. 3/9/99

Each share Exchangeable Preferred 1¢ par exchanged for (1.6437) shares Common $1 par
AT&T Corp. merged into AT&T Inc. 11/18/2005

TCI ENTERPRISES (CA)
Name changed to Frontier Adjusters, Inc. 03/02/1978
Frontier Adjusters, Inc. merged into Frontier Financial Corp. 05/07/1984 which name changed to Frontier Adjusters of America, Inc. 10/17/1986
(See Frontier Adjusters of America, Inc.)

TCI INTL INC (DE)
Stock Dividend - 10% 09/30/1988
Merged into General Signal Corp. 03/23/2001
Each share Common no par exchanged for $11.25 cash

TCI MUSIC INC (DE)
Conv. Preferred Ser. A 1¢ par called for redemption at $23.175 on 06/11/1999
Name changed to Liberty Digital Inc. 09/10/1999
Liberty Digital Inc. merged into Liberty Media Corp. (New) 03/14/2002 which reorganized as Liberty Media Corp. (Incorporated 02/28/2006) 05/10/2006 which name changed to Liberty Interactive Corp. 09/26/2011 which name changed to Qurate Retail, Inc. 04/10/2018

TCI PAC COMMUNICATIONS INC (DE)
Sr. Preferred Class A called for redemption at $102.50 on 04/26/2002

TCI SATELLITE ENTMT INC (DE)
Name changed to Liberty Satellite & Technology, Inc. 08/15/2000
Liberty Satellite & Technology, Inc. merged into Liberty Media Corp. (New) 11/12/2003 which reorganized as Liberty Media Corp. (Incorporated 02/28/2006) 05/10/2006 which name changed to Liberty Interactive Corp. 09/26/2011 which name changed to Qurate Retail, Inc. 04/10/2018

TCI SOLUTIONS INC (DE)
Merged into Retalix Ltd. 11/21/2005
Each share Preferred Ser. A $0.001 par exchanged for $0.8409 cash
Each share Preferred Ser. B $0.001 par exchanged for $0.7573 cash
Each share Common $0.001 par exchanged for $0.132 cash

TCN INC (NV)
Charter revoked for failure to file reports and pay fees 11/01/1988

TCO INDS INC (DE)
Merged into Holiday Inns of America, Inc. 02/27/1969
Each share $1 Conv. Preferred $20 par exchanged for (0.2) share Conv. Special Ser. A $1.125 par and (0.25) share Common $1.50 par
Each share Common $1 par exchanged for (0.5) share Conv. Special Ser. A $1.125 par and (0.59375) share Common $1.50 par
Holiday Inns of America, Inc. name changed to Holiday Inns, Inc. 05/22/1969 which reorganized in Delaware as Holiday Corp. 05/15/1985 which merged into Bass PLC 02/07/1990 which name changed to Six Continents PLC 07/31/2001
(See Six Continents PLC)

TCOM VENTURES CORP (DE)
Charter cancelled and declared inoperative and void for non-payment of taxes 03/01/2002

TCP CAP CORP (DE)
Name changed to BlackRock TCP Capital Corp. 08/14/2018

TCP INTERNATIONAL HOLDINGS LTD (SWITZERLAND)
Acquired by Quality Light Source GmbH 02/28/2018
Each share Common CHF 1 par exchanged for $1 cash

TCP RELIABLE INC (NJ)
Acquired by TCP Parent, Inc. 06/23/2014
Each share Common $0.001 par exchanged for $0.13 cash

TCPI INC (FL)
Recapitalized as Packaged Home Solutions Inc. 07/27/2006
Each share Common $0.001 par exchanged for (0.001) share Common $0.001 par
(See Packaged Home Solutions Inc.)

TCR ENVIRONMENTAL CORP (ON)
Delisted from Canadian Venture Stock Exchange 05/31/2001

TCR SVC INC (NY)
Each share old Common 1¢ par exchanged for (0.09090909) share new Common 1¢ par 11/06/1978
Merged into ITII Merger Corp. 06/30/1984
Each share new Common 1¢ par exchanged for $123.9946 cash
Note: Additional cash distribution from escrow account may have been made but details not available

TCS ENERGY SYS LTD (ON)
Name changed to Advanced Pultrusion Technologies Inc. 06/29/1993
(See Advanced Pultrusion Technologies Inc.)

TCS ENTERPRISES INC (CA)
Reorganized under the laws of Nevada as American Home Capital Corp. 11/25/1998
Each share Common no par exchanged for (0.1) share Common $0.001 par
(See American Home Capital Corp.)

TCSB BANCORP INC (MI)
Merged into Independent Bank Corp. 04/01/2018
Each share Common no par exchanged for (1.1166) shares new Common no par

TCSI CORP (NV)
Common $0.0067 par split (3) for (2) by issuance of (0.5) additional share payable 06/14/1996 to holders of record 05/28/1996
Merged into Rocket Software, Inc. 03/12/2003
Each share Common $0.0067 par exchanged for $0.52 cash

TCT FINL GROUP B INC (NV)
Name changed to Mirador Diversified Services Inc. 05/25/2000
(See Mirador Diversified Services Inc.)

TCT LOGISTICS INC (AB)
Placed in receivership 01/24/2002
Stockholders' equity unlikely

TCW CONV SECS FD INC (MD)
Name changed to TCW Strategic Income Fund, Inc. 12/27/2005

TCW/DW TERM TR 2002 (MA)
Trust terminated 12/23/2002
Each Share of Bene. Int. 1¢ par received first and final distribution of $10.68 cash

TCW/DW TERM TR 2003 (MA)
Liquidation completed
Each Share of Bene. Int. 1¢ par received initial distribution of $0.03 cash payable 05/23/2003 to holders of record 05/09/2003
Each Share of Bene. Int. 1¢ par received second distribution of $0.03 cash payable 06/20/2003 to holders of record 06/06/2003
Each Share of Bene. Int. 1¢ par received third distribution of $0.03 cash payable 08/22/2003 to holders of record 08/08/2003
Each Share of Bene. Int. 1¢ par received fourth distribution of $0.03 cash payable 09/19/2003 to holders of record 09/05/2003
Each Share of Bene. Int. 1¢ par received fifth distribution of $0.03 cash payable 10/17/2003 to holders of record 10/03/2003
Each Share of Bene. Int. 1¢ par exchanged for sixth and final distribution of $10 cash 12/15/2003

TCW/DW TERM TR 2000 (MA)
Each Share of Bene. Int. received distribution of $0.02 cash payable 11/17/2000 to holders of record 11/06/2000
Trust terminated 12/18/2000
Each Share of Bene. Int. 1¢ par exchanged for $10.102124 cash

TCW GEM V LTD
144A Class A Preference Shares called for redemption at $710.681304 on 03/13/2006

TD BANKNORTH INC (DE)
Merged into Toronto-Dominion Bank (Toronto, ON) 04/20/2007
Each share Common 1¢ par exchanged for $32.33 cash

TD CAP CORP (DE)
Name changed to USAsia International Publications, Inc. 12/28/1989
USAsia International Publications, Inc. name changed to NJS Acquisition Corp. 12/07/1995 which name changed to KIWI Holdings Inc. 11/21/1997 which name changed to Chariot International Holdings Inc. 04/30/1999
(See Chariot International Holdings Inc.)

TD RLTY INVTS (ON)
Name changed 11/19/1980
Name changed from TD Realty Investments to TD Realty Investments/Les Placements Immobiliers TD 11/19/1980
Acquired by Toronto-Dominion Bank (Toronto, ON) 09/21/1981
Each Trust Unit no par exchanged for $24 cash

TD SPLIT INC (ON)
Class A Preferred no par called for redemption at $14.70 plus $0.2205 accrued dividends on 11/15/2005
Under plan of merger each share Class A Capital Share no par exchanged for $41.2953 cash 11/15/2005
Class B Preferred no par called for redemption at $28.10 plus $0.298563 accrued dividends on 11/15/2010
Each Class B Capital Share no par received $45.2674 cash 11/15/2010
Class C Preferred no par called for redemption at $10 on 11/13/2015
Class C Capital Share no par called for redemption at $28.7964 on 11/13/2015

TD TSE 300 CAPPED INDEX FD (ON)
Name changed to TD S&P/TSX Capped Composite Index Fund 05/01/2002

TD TSE 300 INDEX FD (ON)
Name changed to TD S&P/TSX Composite Index Fund 05/01/2002

TD WATERHOUSE GROUP INC (DE)
Merged into Toronto-Dominion Bank (Toronto, ON) 11/27/2001
Each share Common 1¢ par exchanged for $9.50 cash

TDA INDS INC (NY)
Each share Common 10¢ par exchanged for (0.2) share Common 20¢ par 10/25/1974

Merged into TDA Acquisition Corp. 05/15/1989
Each share Common 20¢ par exchanged for $18 cash

TDC A/S (DENMARK)
ADR agreement terminated 09/26/2006
Each Sponsored ADR for Ordinary exchanged for $17.73233 cash

TDI HLDG CORP (CO)
Recapitalized as Fashion House Holdings, Inc. 08/30/2005
Each share Common no par exchanged for (0.04587155) share Common no par
Note: Holders of between (100) and (2,179) shares received (100) shares
Holders of (99) or fewer shares were not affected by the reverse split
(See Fashion House Holdings, Inc.)

TDI VENTURE EQUITIES LTD (ON)
Recapitalized as VTL Venture Equities Ltd. 05/00/1983
Each share Class A Preference no par exchanged for (2) shares Common no par
Each share Common no par exchanged for (2) shares Common no par
VTL Venture Equities Ltd. name changed to VTL Venture Corp. 07/07/1986 which name changed to Allcorp United Inc. 07/06/1994 which recapitalized as NTEX Inc. 11/07/1997
(See NTEX Inc.)

TDK ELECTRS LTD (JAPAN)
Each old ADR for Common exchanged for (5) new ADR's for Common 04/30/1981
Each new ADR for Common exchanged again for (1) new ADR for Common 04/01/1982
Name changed to TDK Corp. 03/01/1983

TDK MEDIACTIVE INC (DE)
Merged into Take-Two Interactive Software, Inc. 12/02/2003
Each share Common $0.001 par exchanged for $0.55 cash

TDS CAP I (DE)
8.5% Trust Originated Preferred Sercurities called for redemption at $25 on 09/02/2003

TDS CAP II (DE)
8.04% Guaranteed Trust Originated Preferred Securities called for redemption at $25 on 09/02/2003

TDS TELEMEDICINE INC (NY)
Each share old Common $0.001 par exchanged for (0.01) share new Common $0.001 par 10/05/2006
Reincorporated under the laws of Delaware as GS EnviroServices Inc. 06/14/2007
(See GS EnviroServices, Inc.)

TDT DEV INC (NV)
Name changed to Stronghold Technologies, Inc. 07/11/2002
Stronghold Technologies, Inc. name changed to DealerAdvance, Inc. 10/13/2006
(See DealerAdvance, Inc.)

TDX CORP (DE)
Company terminated common stock registration and is no longer public as of 04/29/1996

TDZ HLDGS INC (ON)
Contingent Value Rights called for redemption 08/09/2004
Completely liquidated
Each share Common no par received first and final distribution of $$0.097 cash payable 10/03/2013 to holders of record 08/27/2013

TEACHERS INS CO (CA)
Merged into INA Corp. 12/31/1976

Each share Capital Stock $1 par exchanged for $5 cash

TEACHERS NATL LIFE INS CO (KY)
Merged into Western Pioneer Life Insurance Co. 11/16/1972
Each share Common $1 par exchanged for (0.535617) share Common $1 par
Western Pioneer Life Insurance Co. merged into I.C.H. Corp. (Old) 04/18/1985 which name changed to Southwestern Life Corp. (New) 06/15/1994 which name changed to I.C.H. Corp. (New) 10/10/1995
(See I.C.H. Corp. (New))

TEACHERS PET INC (NV)
Each share old Common $0.001 par exchanged for (15) shares new Common $0.001 par 07/30/2010
Name changed to Giggles N' Hugs, Inc. 09/17/2010

TEACHERS PET PRODTNS INC (WA)
Name changed to Highland Resources, Inc. 06/20/1988
(See Highland Resources, Inc.)

TEACHING MACHINES, INC. (NM)
Adjudicated bankrupt 12/23/1965
No stockholders' equity

TEACHING NETWORK CORP (FL)
Reorganized as Phoenix BioPharm Inc. 10/03/2006
Each share Common $0.0001 par exchanged for (2) shares Common $0.0001 par

TEACHING TECHNOLOGY CORP (CA)
Name changed to Stewart Morgan Corp. and Common 10¢ par changed to 1¢ par 08/07/1980
Stewart Morgan Corp. merged into Axion System Science, Inc. 01/26/1989 which recapitalized as Wordcraft Systems, Inc. (CA) 06/15/1994 which reorganized in Delaware as Wake Up Now, Inc. 12/01/2010

TEACHING TIME INC (FL)
Name changed to Red Mountain Resources, Inc. (FL) 04/04/2011
Red Mountain Resources, Inc. (FL) reorganized in Texas 01/31/2014

TEAL EXPL & MNG INC (YT)
Acquired by African Rainbow Minerals Ltd. 03/25/2009
Each share Common no par exchanged for $3 cash

TEAL EXPLORATION LTD. (ON)
Charter revoked for failure to file reports and pay fees 12/27/1967

TEAL INDS LTD (BC)
Name changed 12/05/1986
Name changed from Teal Minerals Ltd. to Teal Industries Ltd. 12/05/1986
Petitioned into bankruptcy 03/00/1993
No stockholders' equity

TEAM AMER CORP (OH)
Name changed to Team Mucho, Inc. 01/02/2001
Team Mucho, Inc. name changed to Team America, Inc. 05/30/2002
(See Team America, Inc.)

TEAM AMER INC (OH)
Chapter 11 bankruptcy proceedings dismissed 11/07/2008
No stockholders' equity

TEAM COMMUNICATIONS GROUP INC (CA)
Filed a petition under Chapter 7 Federal Bankruptcy Code 04/16/2002
Stockholders' equity unlikely

TEAM ENERGY & MINERALS INC. (ON)
Delisted from Canadian Dealer Network 08/31/1992

TEAM FINL CAP TR I (DE)
9.5% Trust Preferred Securities called for redemption at $10 on 09/18/2006

TEAM FINL INC (KS)
Chapter 11 bankruptcy proceedings dismissed 03/27/2014
No stockholders' equity

TEAM HEALTH HOLDINGS INC (DE)
Acquired by Tennessee Parent, Inc. 02/06/2017
Each share Common 1¢ par exchanged for $43.50 cash

TEAM INC (TX)
Common 30¢ par split (2) for (1) by issuance of (1) additional share payable 08/29/2007 to holders of record 08/15/2007 Ex date - 08/30/2007
Reincorporated under the laws of Delaware 12/01/2011

TEAM LABS SYS GROUP INC (DE)
Each share old Common $0.0001 par exchanged for (0.02) share new Common $0.0001 par 10/10/2000
New Common $0.0001 par split (3) for (1) by issuance of (2) additional shares payable 03/15/2001 to holders of record 03/05/2001 Ex date - 03/16/2001
Name changed to SciLabs Holdings, Inc. 07/17/2001
(See SciLabs Holdings, Inc.)

TEAM MUCHO INC (OH)
Name changed to Team America, Inc. 05/30/2002
(See Team America, Inc.)

TEAM NATION HLDGS CORP (NV)
Name changed to Top Shelf Brands Holdings Corp. 11/17/2014

TEAM RENT GROUP INC (DE)
Name changed to Budget Group, Inc. 04/29/1997
(See Budget Group, Inc.)

TEAM RES CORP (BC)
Recapitalized as Consolidated Team Resources Corp. 03/07/1994
Each share Common no par exchanged for (0.33333333) share Common no par
Consolidated Team Resources Corp. name changed to QHR Technologies Inc. (BC) 06/27/2000 which reincorporated in Canada as QHR Corp. 07/08/2013
(See QHR Corp.)

TEAM SPORTS ENTMT INC (DE)
Name changed to Idea Sports Entertainment Group, Inc. 11/09/2004
Idea Sports Entertainment Group, Inc. recapitalized as HealthSport, Inc. 05/16/2006
(See HealthSport, Inc.)

TEAMASIA SEMICONDUCTOR INDIA LTD (INDIA)
GDR agreement terminated 01/23/2009
No GDR holders' equity

TEAMLINK COM INC (FL)
Reincorporated under the laws of Georgia as Teamlink, Inc. 08/25/2004
(See Teamlink, Inc.)

TEAMLINK INC (GA)
Proclaimed dissolved for failure to file annual reports 07/09/2005

TEAMSTAFF INC (NJ)
Each share old Common $0.001 par exchanged for (0.28571428) share new Common $0.001 par 06/02/2000
Each share new Common $0.001 par exchanged again for (0.25) share new Common $0.001 par 04/21/2008
Name changed to DLH Holdings Corp. 06/27/2012

TEAMUPSPORT INC (NV)
Name changed to KonaRed Corp. 09/09/2013

TEAMWAY INC (UT)
Name changed to Health & Fitness Retreats, Inc. 08/01/1984
Health & Fitness Retreats, Inc. name changed to Ormc Laboratories, Inc. 01/11/1985
(See Ormc Laboratories, Inc.)

TEARDROP GOLF CO (DE)
Recapitalized as Digital Info Security Co. 03/28/2007
Each share Common 1¢ par exchanged for (0.2) share Common $0.0001 par

TEAVANA HLDGS INC (DE)
Acquired by Starbucks Corp. 12/31/2012
Each share Common $0.00003 exchanged for $15.50 cash

TEC FACTORY INC (DE)
Name changed to HeartSTAT Technology, Inc. 02/26/2004
HeartSTAT Technology, Inc. name changed to Verdant Technology Corp. 03/01/2006
(See Verdant Technology Corp.)

TEC INC (MN)
Name changed to Jones Plumbing Systems, Inc. 04/28/1989
(See Jones Plumbing Systems, Inc.)

TEC TECHNOLOG ENTERPRISES CORP (BC)
Struck off register and declared dissolved for failure to file returns 03/26/1993

TEC TECHNOLOGY INC (NV)
Reincorporated 06/30/2012
State of incorporation changed from (DE) to (NV) 06/30/2012
Recapitalized as Telidyne Inc. 04/03/2018
Each share Common $0.001 par exchanged for (0.001) share Common $0.001 par

TEC TORCH INC (NJ)
Merged into Star-Glo Industries, Inc. 01/23/1981
Each share Common 10¢ par exchanged for (0.25) share new Common 10¢ par
(See Star-Glo Industries, Inc.)

TECCOR ELECTRS INC (TX)
Acquired by Ranco Inc. 09/28/1979
Each share Common 20¢ par exchanged for $12 cash

TECH ACHIEVERS GROWTH & INCOME ETF (ON)
Name changed to Harvest Tech Achievers Growth & Income ETF 06/19/2018

TECH ACHIEVERS GROWTH & INCOME FD (ON)
Under plan of reorganization each Unit automatically became (1) Tech Achievers Growth & Income ETF Class A Unit 06/22/2017
Tech Achievers Growth & Income ETF name changed to Harvest Tech Achievers Growth & Income ETF 06/19/2018

TECH AEROFOAM PRODS INC (FL)
Common 10¢ par changed to 1¢ par and (1) additional share issued 03/01/1968
Merged into Arlen Realty & Development Corp. 11/28/1972
Each share Common 1¢ par exchanged for (0.66666666) share Common $1 par
Arlen Realty & Development Corp. name changed to Arlen Corp. 10/16/1985
(See Arlen Corp.)

TECH AMERN RES CORP (FL)
In process of liquidation
Each share Common 1¢ par

exchanged for initial distribution of $0.28 cash 08/02/1985
Note: Details on additional distributions, if any, are not available

TECH ANTARES CORP. (DE)
Merged into Anagraphic Corp. 12/11/1962
Each share Common no par exchanged for (0.5) share Common 10¢ par
(See Anagraphic Corp.)

TECH ASSETS LTD (NV)
Charter permanently revoked 06/01/2003

TECH CREATIONS INC (DE)
Reorganized as iJoin Systems, Inc. 05/04/2001
Each share Common $0.001 par exchanged for (8) shares Common no par
(See iJoin Systems, Inc.)

TECH ELECTRO INDS INC (TX)
Each share Common $0.001 par exchanged for (0.16666666) share Common 1¢ par 12/04/1995
Each share Class A Preferred received distribution of (0.41) share Common 1¢ par payable 12/31/2000 to holders of of record 11/30/2000
Name changed to Zunicom, Inc. 10/17/2002

TECH FDRY VENTURES INC (NV)
Each share old Common $0.0001 par exchanged for (10) shares new Common $0.0001 par 04/28/2016
Name changed to Nevada Canyon Gold Corp. 07/28/2016

TECH GIANTS COVERED CALL ETF (ON)
Name changed to First Asset Tech Giants Covered Call ETF 06/06/2012

TECH-HLDGS INC (DE)
Recapitalized as Prostar Holdings Inc. 05/26/1994
Each share Common $0.001 par exchanged for (0.02985074) share Common $0.001 par
(See Prostar Holdings Inc.)

TECH LABS INC (DE)
Reincorporated 07/19/2007
Old Common 1¢ par split (3) for (1) by issuance of (2) additional shares 08/12/1968
Each share old Common 1¢ par exchanged for (0.03333333) share new Common 1¢ par par 12/13/2006
Stock Dividend - 10% 06/01/1968
State of incorporation changed from (NJ) to (DE) 07/09/2007
Recapitalized as Renewal Fuels, Inc. 08/01/2007
Each share new Common 1¢ par exchanged for (0.06666666) share Common 1¢ par

TECH LEADERS INCOME FD (ON)
Under plan of reorganization each Unit automatically became (1) Tech Leaders Income ETF Unit 04/03/2018

TECH LINE CORP (NJ)
Recapitalized as First World Corp. 03/02/1970
Each share Class A Common 5¢ par exchanged for (0.33333333) share Class A Common 15¢ par
(See First World Corp.)

TECH-NET COMMUNICATIONS INC (NV)
Name changed to Knightsbridge Fine Wines, Inc. 09/25/2003
Knightsbridge Fine Wines, Inc. name changed to 360 Global Wine Co. 02/15/2005
(See 360 Global Wine Co.)

TECH OHM ELECTRS INC (NY)
Name changed to International Citrus Corp. 12/05/1975
International Citrus Corp.

recapitalized as Princeton Commercial Holdings, Inc. 03/03/2004 which name changed to EuroWind Energy, Inc. 04/28/2004 which name changed to First Petroleum & Pipeline Inc. 03/31/2005 which recapitalized as Luke Entertainment, Inc. 11/15/2007 which name changed to Greene Concepts, Inc. 01/14/2011

TECH OPS INC (DE)
Common no par split (3) for (1) by issuance of (2) additional shares 12/16/1985
Under plan of reorganization and dissolution each share Common no par exchanged for first and final distribution of (1) share Tech/Ops Landauer, Inc. Common $1 par, (1) share Tech/Ops Sevcon, Inc. Common no par and $2.70 cash 02/01/1988
(See each company's listing)

TECH OPS LANDAUER INC (DE)
Common $1 par split (2) for (1) by issuance of (1) additional share 12/29/1988
Name changed to Landauer, Inc. 02/07/1991
(See Landauer, Inc.)

TECH OPS SEVCON INC (DE)
Common no par changed to 10¢ par 01/27/1993
Common 10¢ par split (2) for (1) by issuance of (1) additional share 08/28/1995
Name changed to Sevcon, Inc. 06/08/2011
(See Sevcon, Inc.)

TECH-PANEL CO., INC. (NC)
Name changed to Capri Industries, Inc. 04/05/1967
(See Capri Industries, Inc.)

TECH SERV INC (MD)
Common $0.16666666 par changed to 10¢ par and (0.66666666) additional share issued 01/13/1969
Common 10¢ par split (3) for (2) by issuance of (0.5) additional share 04/21/1986
Charter forfeited for failure to file annual reports 10/03/1994

TECH SOLUTIONS CAP CORP (BC)
Name changed to Upper Canyon Minerals Corp. 02/07/2008

TECH SQUARED INC (MN)
In process of liquidation
Each share Common no par exchanged for initial distribution of (0.17586) share Digital River Inc. Common 1¢ par 12/17/1999
Assets transferred to Tech Squared Liquidating Trust 12/17/1999
(See Tech Squared Liquidating Trust)

TECH SQUARED LIQUIDATING TRUST (MN)
Liquidation completed
Each Share of Bene. Int. no par received an undetermined amount of cash on a pro rata basis payable 12/00/2003 to holders of record 12/17/1999

TECH STAR INTL INC (NY)
Dissolved by proclamation 06/23/1993

TECH SYM CORP (NV)
Merged into Integrated Defense Technologies, Inc. 09/29/2000
Each share Common 10¢ par exchanged for $30 cash

TECH TEAM GLOBAL INC (DE)
Acquired by Stefanini International Holdings, Ltd. 01/05/2011
Each share Common 1¢ par exchanged for $8.35 cash

TECH TIME INC (FL)
Name changed to Uniquest, Inc. 03/28/1991
(See Uniquest, Inc.)

TECH TOWN HLDGS INC (NV)
Name changed to Hash Labs Inc. 03/06/2018

TECH TRAINER CORP (DE)
Common 10¢ par split (2) for (1) by issuance of (1) additional share 05/03/1971
Name changed to Southeastern Modular Industries, Inc. 09/23/1971
Southeastern Modular Industries, Inc. name changed to Pneucyclic Sciences, Inc. 01/28/1974
(See Pneucyclic Sciences, Inc.)

TECHALT INC (NV)
Each share old Common $0.001 par exchanged for (0.01) share new Common $0.001 par 10/02/2008
Each share new Common $0.001 par exchanged again for (0.0002) share new Common $0.001 par 05/04/2011
Name changed to All American Energy Holding, Inc. 10/23/2012
All American Energy Holding, Inc. recapitalized as All American Energy Corp. 11/14/2017 which name changed to Core Lithium Corp. 04/11/2018

TECHAMERICA GROUP INC (DE)
Acquired by Fermenta AB 11/09/1987
Each share Common 10¢ par exchanged for $4 cash

TECHBUILT HOMES, INC. (DE)
Name changed to Techbuilt, Inc. 09/24/1964
Techbuilt, Inc. acquired by Riegel Paper Corp. (DE) 04/15/1970
(See Riegel Paper Corp. (DE))

TECHBUILT INC (DE)
Completely liquidated 04/15/1970
Each share Common 10¢ par exchanged for first and final distribution of (0.21) share Riegel Paper Corp. (DE) Common $5 par
(See Riegel Paper Corp. (DE))

TECHBYTE INTL INC (CANADA)
Name changed 06/11/1990
Name changed from Techbyte Inc. to Techbyte International Inc. 06/11/1990
Declared bankrupt 08/30/1995
Details not available

TECHCO HLDGS INC (DE)
Adjudicated bankrupt 04/07/1976
Stockholders' equity unlikely

TECHCORP INDS INC (AB)
Name changed 06/22/1998
Name changed from Techcorp Rentals Inc. to Techcorp Industries Inc. 06/22/1998
Acquired by Alpine Oil Services Corp. 11/09/1999
Each share Common no par exchanged for (1/3) share Common no par
Alpine Oil Services Corp. merged into Weatherford Oil Services, Inc. 08/10/2000 which was exchanged for Weatherford International Inc. (New) (DE) 04/20/2001 which reincorporated in Bermuda 06/26/2002

TECHDYNE INC (FL)
Name changed to Simclar, Inc. 09/01/2003

TECHE HLDG CO (LA)
Merged into IBERIABANK Corp. 05/30/2014
Each share Common 1¢ par exchanged for (1.162) shares Common $1 par

TECHEDGE INC (DE)
Name changed to China Biopharma, Inc. 09/25/2006

TECHFORCE CORP (GA)
Merged into Equant Holdings U.S., Inc. 08/06/1999
Each share Common 1¢ par exchanged for $8.50 cash

TECHGROUP VENTURES INC (BC)
Name changed to eReservation Systems Corp. 11/17/2000
eReservation Systems Corp. name changed to Cobre Exploration Corp. 10/25/2007 which name changed to Calico Resources Corp. 01/28/2011 which merged into Paramount Gold Nevada Corp. 07/07/2016

TECHKNITS INC (NY)
Each share Common $0.001 par exchanged for (1/3) share Common $0.003 par 12/19/1990
Chapter 11 bankruptcy proceedings terminated 08/17/2000
Stockholders' equity unlikely

TECHMARINE INTL PLC (UNITED KINGDOM)
ADR agreement terminated 08/18/2003
Each Sponsored ADR for Ordinary exchanged for (10) shares Ordinary

TECHMATION CORP (NY)
Name changed to Instasan Pharmaceuticals, Inc. 10/27/1978
(See Instasan Pharmaceuticals, Inc.)

TECHMEDIA ADVERTISING INC (NV)
SEC revoked common stock registration 02/27/2013

TECHMIRE LTD (CANADA)
Acquired by EXCO Technologies Ltd. 01/15/2001
Each share Common no par exchanged for $3.85 cash

TECHNALYSIS CORP (MN)
Common 10¢ par split (3) for (2) by issuance of (0.5) additional share 05/10/1985
Stock Dividends - 30% 06/12/1981; 50% 03/11/1983; 50% 05/04/1989
Merged into Compuware Corp. 04/30/1996
Each share Common 10¢ par exchanged for $14 cash

TECHNAMATION HOLDINGS LTD. (ON)
Charter cancelled for failure to pay taxes and file returns 02/21/1973

TECHNAMATION INC (NY)
Adjudicated bankrupt 04/17/1972
Stockholders' equity unlikely

TECHNAPOWER INDS CORP (DE)
83.6% acquired by API Enterprises, Inc. as of 09/17/1990
Public interest eliminated

TECHNATURE INC (NV)
Name changed back to Richmond Services Inc. 01/25/2000
Richmond Services Inc. name changed to eKnowledge.com Inc. 04/28/2000 which name changed to eKnowledge Group Inc. 05/09/2000 which recapitalized as Amazon Oil & Energy Corp. 09/21/2006 which name changed to AEC Holdings, Corp. 02/20/2007
(See AEC Holdings, Corp.)

TECHNE CORP (MN)
Common 1¢ par split (2) for (1) by issuance of (1) additional share payable 11/17/1997 to holders of record 11/10/1997
Common 1¢ par split (2) for (1) by issuance of (1) additional share payable 12/01/2000 to holders of record 11/24/2000 Ex date - 12/04/2000
Name changed to Bio-Techne Corp. 11/04/2014

TECHNEDYNE INC (UT)
Proclaimed dissolved for failure to pay taxes 03/31/1986

TECHNEST HLDGS INC (NV)
Each (211.18) shares old Common $0.001 par exchanged for (1) share new Common $0.001 par 07/20/2005
Each share new Common $0.001 par

received distribution of (1) Contingent Value Right payable 02/02/2011 to holders of record 01/25/2011
Each Contingent Value Right received distribution of $0.103739 cash payable 05/08/2012 to holders of record 01/25/2011
Reincorporated under the laws of Delaware as AccelPath, Inc. 05/09/2012

TECHNI ELECTRS INC (NJ)
Common 10¢ par changed to 1¢ par 08/20/1963
Completely liquidated 02/23/1967
Each share Common 1¢ par exchanged for first and final distribution of $0.2241 cash

TECHNIBIOTICS INC (NY)
Charter cancelled and proclaimed dissolved for failure to pay taxes 03/25/1981

TECHNICAL ANIMATIONS, INC. (NY)
Class A Capital Stock 10¢ par and Class B Capital Stock 10¢ par changed to 5¢ par 12/00/1960
Name changed to Technamation, Inc. 12/02/1968
(See Technamation, Inc.)

TECHNICAL CHEMICALS & PRODS INC (FL)
Common $0.001 split (2) for (1) by issuance of (1) additional share 08/02/1995
Name changed to TCPI, Inc. 07/21/2000
TCPI, Inc. recapitalized as Packaged Home Solutions Inc. 07/27/2006
(See Packaged Home Solutions Inc.)

TECHNICAL COATINGS INC (DE)
Each share old Common $0.005 par exchanged for (0.2) share new Common $0.005 par 01/17/1992
Name changed to Surgicare, Inc. 07/07/1999
Surgicare, Inc. recapitalized as Orion HealthCorp, Inc. 12/15/2004

TECHNICAL COATINGS INC (UT)
Reincorporated under the laws of Delaware 01/20/1984
Technical Coatings, Inc. (DE) name changed to Surgicare, Inc. 07/07/1999 which reorganized as Orion HealthCorp Inc. 12/15/2004

TECHNICAL CRAFTS CORP. (CA)
Liquidation completed
Each share Capital Stock $1 par received initial distribution of $0.20 cash 07/17/1954
Eash share Capital Stock $1 par received second distribution of $0.13 cash 12/08/1954
Each share Capital Stock $1 par received third and final distribution of $0.1045 cash 12/10/1965

TECHNICAL EQUIP LEASING CORP (DE)
Merged into Libsub, Inc. 05/11/1984
Each share Common 5¢ par exchanged for $7 cash

TECHNICAL EQUITIES CORP (CA)
Capital Stock $1 par split (2) for (1) by issuance of (1) additional share 08/15/1984
Plan of reorganization under Chapter 11 Federal Bankruptcy proceedings confirmed 07/13/1987
No stockholders' equity

TECHNICAL FD INC (DE)
Name changed to Van Strum & Towne Stock Fund, Inc. 00/00/1953
Van Strum & Towne Stock Fund, Inc. acquired by Institutional Shares, Ltd. 11/07/1957 which name changed to Channing Shares, Inc. (DE) 04/01/1964 which reincorporated in Maryland 10/09/1973 which merged into American General Shares, Inc. 09/02/1975 which merged into American General Enterprise Fund,

Inc. 08/31/1979 which name changed to American Capital Enterprise Fund, Inc. (MD) 09/09/1983 which reincorporated in Delaware as Van Kampen American Capital Enterprise Fund 08/03/1995 which name changed to Van Kampen Enterprise Fund 08/31/1998

TECHNICAL INDS & ENERGY CORP (DE)
Name changed to Energy & Technology Corp. 09/09/2008

TECHNICAL INDS INC (CA)
Acquired by Thermal Systems, Inc. 11/28/1969
Each share Capital Stock 25¢ par exchanged for (0.36885) share Common 10¢ par
Thermal Systems, Inc. name changed to Axial Corp. 10/05/1970 which name changed to Axial Liquidating Corp. 05/31/1973 which liquidated for Sierracin Corp. (CA) 06/06/1973 which reincorporated in Delaware 05/31/1977
(See Sierracin Corp. (DE))

TECHNICAL INFORMATION CORP (NY)
Each share Common 10¢ par exchanged for (0.1) share Common $1 par 05/15/1966
Charter cancelled and proclaimed dissolved for failure to pay taxes 12/15/1975

TECHNICAL MAINTENANCE CORP (NV)
Name changed to TouchTunes Music Corp. (NV) 12/14/1998
TouchTunes Music Corp. (NV) reorganized in Delaware 11/09/2006 which name changed to Touchtunes Holdings Corp. 12/10/2007

TECHNICAL MANAGERS, INC.
Dissolved 00/00/1951
Details not available

TECHNICAL MATERIEL CORP (NY)
Common 50¢ par changed to 25¢ par and (1) additional share issued 05/04/1961
Each share Common 25¢ par exchanged for (2) shares Common $0.125 par 02/14/1962
Plan of reorganization under Chapter 11 Federal Bankruptcy Code effective 11/29/1995
No stockholders' equity

TECHNICAL MEASUREMENT CORP (DE)
Adjudicated bankrupt 01/22/1968
No stockholders' equity

TECHNICAL METALS INC (MA)
Out of business 00/00/1972
No stockholders' equity

TECHNICAL OLYMPIC USA INC (DE)
Common 1¢ par split (3) for (2) by issuance of (0.5) additional share payable 05/31/2004 to holders of record 05/14/2004 Ex date - 06/01/2004
Common 1¢ par split (5) for (4) by issuance of (0.25) additional share payable 03/31/2005 to holders of record 03/11/2005 Ex date - 04/01/2005
Name changed to TOUSA, Inc. 05/08/2007
(See TOUSA, Inc.)

TECHNICAL OPERATIONS INC (DE)
Common 10¢ par changed to no par and (1.5) additional shares issued 06/01/1959
Name changed to Tech/Ops, Inc. 01/22/1981
(See Tech/Ops, Inc.)

TECHNICAL PRODUCERS INC. (NV)
Charter revoked for failure to file reports and pay fees 03/02/1964

TECHNICAL PUBG CO (DE)
Stock Dividends - 10% 06/07/1976; 10% 06/13/1977
Merged into Dun & Bradstreet Companies, Inc. 01/19/1978
Each share Common 30¢ par exchanged for (1) share Common $1 par
Dun & Bradstreet Companies, Inc. name changed to Dun & Bradstreet Corp. 04/17/1979 which name changed to R.H. Donnelley Corp. 07/01/1998
(See R.H. Donnelley Corp.)

TECHNICAL RESEARCH CO. (WA)
Acquired by Guardsman Chemicals, Inc. 07/31/1980
Each share Common 10¢ par exchanged for $1.536 cash

TECHNICAL RES INC (NV)
Name changed to Earth Energy Inc. 07/01/1974
(See Earth Energy Inc.)

TECHNICAL SVCS GROUP INC (NY)
Company believed out of business 00/00/1988
Details not available

TECHNICAL SOLUTIONS LTD (NV)
Name changed to American Coal Corp. (Old) 01/26/1990
American Coal Corp. (Old) recapitalized as US Jet, Inc. 08/25/1998 which recapitalized as American Coal Corp. (New) 10/29/1999 which name changed to Kevcorp Services, Inc. 06/22/2004 which recapitalized as Center For Wound Healing, Inc. 02/15/2006
(See Center For Wound Healing, Inc.)

TECHNICAL TAPE INC (MI)
Stock Dividends - 15% 07/15/1977; 15% 07/14/1978; 15% 02/15/1979; 15% 06/15/1981
Acquired by Beiersdorf AG 09/26/1988
Each share Common $1 par exchanged for $16 cash

TECHNICAL VENTURES INC (NY)
Name changed to Amfil Technologies Inc. 05/28/2010

TECHNICAL VENTURES RX CORP (AB)
Merged into Hemostemix Inc. 11/10/2014
Each share Common no par exchanged for (0.2) share Common no par
Note: Unexchanged certificates will be cancelled and become without value 11/10/2020

TECHNICARE CORP (DE)
Common 50¢ par split (2) for (1) by issuance of (1) additional share 09/01/1977
Merged into Johnson & Johnson 02/21/1979
Each share Common 50¢ par exchanged for (0.175) share Common $2.50 par

TECHNICLONE CORP (DE)
Reincorporated 04/24/1997
Each share old Common no par exchanged for (0.01) share new Common no par 03/12/1987
State of incorporation and name changed from Techniclone International Corp. (CA) to Techniclone Corp. (DE) and Common no par changed to $0.001 par 04/24/1997
Name changed to Peregrine Pharmaceuticals, Inc. 11/07/2000
Peregrine Pharmaceuticals, Inc. name changed to Avid Bioservices, Inc. 01/08/2018

TECHNICOIL CORP (AB)
Merged into Essential Energy Services Ltd. 05/31/2011
Each share Common no par

exchanged for (0.7111) share Common no par and $0.80 cash
Note: Unexchanged certificates were cancelled and became without value 05/31/2017

TECHNICOLOR INC (DE)
Each share Capital Stock no par exchanged for (2) shares Capital Stock $1 par 00/00/1953
Capital Stock $1 par split (3) for (2) by issuance of (0.5) additional share 10/03/1980
Merged into MacAndrews & Forbes Group, Inc. 01/24/1983
Each share Capital Stock $1 par exchanged for $23 cash

TECHNICOM INTL INC (DE)
Common 1¢ par split (2) for (1) by issuance of (1) additional share 12/20/1982
Common 1¢ par split (2) for (1) by issuance of (1) additional share 03/21/1983
Stock Dividend - 50% 10/18/1982
Merged into TIE/Communications, Inc. 10/30/1984
Each share Common 1¢ par exchanged for (0.29) share Common 5¢ par
(See TIE/Communications, Inc.)

TECHNICON CORP (DE)
Merged into Revlon, Inc. 05/02/1980
Each share Common 5¢ par exchanged for $18 cash

TECHNICRAFT LABORATORIES INC. (CT)
Liquidation completed 08/14/1959
Details not available

TECHNIFOAM CORP. (DE)
Name changed to Master Industries, Inc. 08/31/1964
(See Master Industries, Inc.)

TECHNIGEN CORP (CANADA)
Name changed 06/09/1987
Name changed from Technigen Platinum Corp. to Technigen Corp. 06/09/1987
Each share old Class A Common no par exchanged for (0.2) share new Class A Common no par 07/09/1993
Reorganized under the laws of Nevada as Mammoth Energy Group, Inc. 07/19/2006
Each share new Class A Common no par exchanged for (0.01) share Common $0.0001 par
Mammoth Energy Group, Inc. (NV) reorganized in Wyoming 08/19/2013 which recapitalized as Strategic Asset Leasing Inc. 11/12/2014

TECHNILAB PHARMA INC (CANADA)
Acquired by Merckle GmbH 07/31/2000
Each share Common no par exchanged for $6.10 cash

TECHNIMAR INDS INC (DE)
Chapter 11 bankruptcy proceedings converted to Chapter 7 on 03/02/1999
No stockholders' equity

TECHNIMED CORP (DE)
Charter cancelled and declared inoperative and void for non-payment of taxes 01/06/1996

TECHNIP (FRANCE)
Name changed 10/11/2001
Under plan of merger name changed from Technip to Technip-Coflexip 10/11/2001
ADR agreement terminated 05/30/2003
Each ADR for Ordinary exchanged for $65.5284 cash
Name changed from Technip-Coflexip to Technip 07/14/2003
Basis changed from (1:0.25) to (1:1) 05/18/2005
Sponsored ADR's for Ordinary split (4) for (1) by issuance of (3) additional ADR's payable 03/21/2011

to holders of record 03/18/2011
Ex date - 03/22/2011
Basis changed from (1:1) to (1:0.25) 03/21/2011
Merged into TechnipFMC PLC 01/17/2017
Each Sponsored ADR for Ordinary exchanged for (0.5) share Ordinary $1 par

TECHNIPOWER SYS INC (DE)
SEC revoked common stock registration 07/08/2014

TECHNIPURE INC (AB)
Name changed to Terra Mannix Inc. 11/14/1997
(See Terra Mannix Inc.)

TECHNIQUE DENTAL LAB INC (NY)
Name changed to Metropolitan Health Care Co., Inc. 08/18/1970
(See Metropolitan Health Care Co., Inc.)

TECHNIQUEST INTL INC (DE)
Charter cancelled and declared inoperative and void for non-payment of taxes 03/01/1989

TECHNISCOPE DEV CORP (BC)
Delisted from Vancouver Stock Exchange 03/05/1993

TECHNISOURCE INC (FL)
Merged into IM Acquisition, Inc. 07/23/2002
Each share Common 1¢ par exchanged for $4 cash

TECHNITREND INC (NJ)
Charter declared void for non-payment of taxes 04/14/1975

TECHNITROL INC (PA)
Common 25¢ par changed to $0.125 par and (1) additional share issued 02/13/1967
Common $0.125 par split (2) for (1) by issuance of (1) additional share 01/24/1984
Common $0.125 par split (3) for (1) by issuance of (2) additional shares 09/18/1994
Common $0.125 par split (2) for (1) by issuance of (1) additional share payable 02/28/1997 to holders of record 02/07/1997 Ex date - 03/03/1997
Common $0.125 par split (2) for (1) by issuance of (1) additional share payable 11/27/2000 to holders of record 11/06/2000 Ex date - 11/28/2000
Name changed to Pulse Electronics Corp. 11/15/2010
(See Pulse Electronics Corp.)

TECHNIVEST FD (MD)
Reincorporated 04/01/1973
State of incorporation changed from (DE) to (MD) 04/01/1973
Acquired by Ivest Fund, Inc. (MD) 11/30/1973
Each share Common 10¢ par exchanged for (0.8489) share Common $1 par
Ivest Fund, Inc. (MD) name changed to Vanguard World Fund, Inc. (MA) 09/30/1985 which reorganized in Delaware as Vanguard World Fund 06/30/1998

TECHNO CORP (PA)
Each share Common 10¢ par exchanged for (0.00005) share Common $2,000 par 03/28/1977
Note: In effect holders received $1.25 cash per share and public interest was eliminated

TECHNO DYNAMICS INC (DE)
Charter cancelled and declared inoperative and void for non-payment of taxes 03/01/1996

TECHNO FD INC (OH)
Assets sold for benefit of creditors 12/00/1969
No stockholders' equity

TECHNO TRAINING INC (UT)
Reincorporated under the laws of Delaware as Tabor Environmental Services, Inc. 02/18/1987
Tabor Environmental Services, Inc. recapitalized as Wastec Inc. 10/14/1991 which name changed to Environmental Services Group Inc. 01/10/1994
(See Environmental Services Group Inc.)

TECHNO-VENDING CORP. (DE)
Insolvent 00/00/1963
No stockholders' equity

TECHNOCONCEPTS INC (CO)
Recapitalized as Alexandria Advantage Warranty Co. 01/16/2015
Each share Common $0.001 par exchanged for (0.00011764) share Common $0.001 par

TECHNODYNE INC (DE)
Common $1 par changed to 50¢ par and (1) additional share issued 12/29/1980
Common 50¢ par changed to 5¢ par 11/03/1988
Charter cancelled and declared inoperative and void for non-payment of taxes 03/01/1992

TECHNOGENETICS INC (DE)
Merged into Leeco Diagnostics, Inc. 05/10/1989
Each share Common 1¢ par exchanged for (0.5) share Common 1¢ par
Leeco Diagnostics, Inc. merged into Endogen, Inc. 03/19/1993
(See Endogen, Inc.)

TECHNOGRAPH INC (NC)
Administratively dissolved 03/07/1994

TECHNOGRAPH PRINTED ELECTRONICS, INC. (NC)
Name changed to Technograph Inc. 02/03/1965
(See Technograph Inc.)

TECHNOGRAPH PRINTED ELECTRONICS, INC. (NY)
Reincorporated under the laws of North Carolina and Common 40¢ par changed to 1¢ par 02/01/1958
Technograph Printed Electronics, Inc. (NC) name changed to Technograph Inc. 02/03/1965
(See Technograph Inc.)

TECHNOIR INC (NV)
Name changed to Global Satellite Network USA, Inc. 06/12/1997
(See Global Satellite Network USA, Inc.)

TECHNOL FUEL CONDITIONERS INC (CO)
Reorganized under the laws of Florida as Allied Energy Group, Inc. 08/18/2006
Each share Common $0.001 par exchanged for (0.1) share Common $0.001 par
Allied Energy Group, Inc. name changed to Allied Energy, Inc. 04/22/2010

TECHNOLOGIA SYS CORP (BC)
Common no par split (2) for (1) by issuance of (1) additional share 06/07/1990
Recapitalized as Master Player Home Entertainment Corp. 02/11/1994
Each share Common no par exchanged for (0.25) share Common no par
Master Player Home Entertainment Corp. recapitalized as International Player Enterprises Inc. 03/17/1997

TECHNOLOGICAL DEVICES INC (NY)
Merged into TDI Holding Corp. 09/01/1987
Each share Common 1¢ par exchanged for $7.50 cash

TECHNOLOGICAL INDS CORP (DE)
Reincorporated 05/27/1971
State of incorporation changed from (FL) to (DE) 05/27/1971
Name changed to T & I Companies, Inc. (DE) 06/16/1972
(See T & I Companies, Inc. (DE))

TECHNOLOGICAL PRODS INC (MD)
Declared bankruptcy and went out of business 06/29/1971
No stockholders' equity

TECHNOLOGIES SCAN CORP (NV)
Name changed to PetVivo Holdings, Inc. 04/29/2014

TECHNOLOGIES STERILIZATION OZONE TSO3 INC (QC)
Name changed to TSO3 Inc. 05/30/2002

TECHNOLOGY & RESOURCE CAP CORP (BC)
Name changed to P2P Health Systems Inc. 10/10/2003
P2P Health Systems Inc. recapitalized as Salares Lithium Inc. 11/26/2009 which merged into Talison Lithium Ltd. 09/22/2010
(See Talison Lithium Ltd.)

TECHNOLOGY ACQUISITION CORP (NV)
Each share old Common $0.001 par exchanged for (0.1) share new Common $0.001 par 10/28/2003
Name changed to Minrad International, Inc. (NV) 12/21/2004
Minrad International, Inc. (NV) reincorporated in Delaware 04/25/2005
(See Minrad International, Inc.)

TECHNOLOGY APPLICATIONS INTL CORP (FL)
Name changed to Rejuvel Bio-Sciences, Inc. 06/11/2015

TECHNOLOGY ASSETS INC (NV)
Each share old Common no par exchanged for (10) shares new Common no par 09/24/2004
Name changed to Sierra Explorations, Inc. 10/28/2008
(See Sierra Explorations, Inc.)

TECHNOLOGY ASSOC INC (MA)
Common 1¢ par changed to $0.001 par 12/23/1982
Proclaimed dissolved for failure to file reports and pay taxes 12/31/1990

TECHNOLOGY CONNECTIONS INC (NC)
Each share old Common $0.001 par exchanged for (0.05) share new Common $0.001 par 01/15/2004
Name changed to HouseRaising, Inc. 08/31/2004
(See HouseRaising, Inc.)

TECHNOLOGY CONSULTING PARTNERS INC (CO)
Name changed to TechnoConcepts, Inc. 04/16/2004
TechnoConcepts, Inc. recapitalized as Alexandria Advantage Warranty Co. 01/16/2015

TECHNOLOGY DEV CORP (TX)
Charter forfeited for failure to pay taxes 08/27/1996

TECHNOLOGY ENTERPRISES INC (NV)
Reorganized as Life Exchange, Inc. 01/20/2006
Each share Common $0.001 par exchanged for (10) shares Common $0.001 par

TECHNOLOGY EQUIP CORP (NY)
Recapitalized as Systems Equipment Corp. 10/10/1986
Each share Common 10¢ par exchanged for (3) shares Common 1¢ par
Systems Equipment Corp. merged into Firetector Inc. 08/23/1991 which

name changed to Synergx Systems Inc. 05/24/2002
(See Synergx Systems Inc.)

TECHNOLOGY EQUITY CORP (DE)
Name changed to Portuguese Realty Investment Corp. 04/21/1983
Portuguese Realty Investment Corp. name changed to Phorum Re Investment Corp. 05/22/1987
(See Phorum Re Investment Corp.)

TECHNOLOGY EXCHANGE INC (NY)
Name changed to Charlotte-Sheldon, Inc. 04/02/1982
Charlotte-Sheldon, Inc. name changed to Data Cablevision, Inc. 08/13/1982 which name changed to T.C.C., Inc. 07/22/1983
(See T.C.C., Inc.)

TECHNOLOGY EXPOSITIONS LTD (DE)
Recapitalized as World-Wide Patents, Ltd. 05/15/1978
Each share Common $0.001 par exchanged for (5) shares Common $0.001 par

TECHNOLOGY FD (MA)
Reincorporated 01/31/1986
State of incorporation changed from (DE) to (MA) 01/31/1986
Name changed to Kemper Technology Fund 02/01/1988
Kemper Technology Fund name changed to Scudder Technology Fund 06/25/2001 which name changed to DWS Technology Fund 02/06/2006

TECHNOLOGY FLAVORS & FRAGRANCES INC (DE)
Merged into FFG Industries, Inc. 06/27/2005
Each share Common 1¢ par exchanged for $1.55 cash

TECHNOLOGY FOR COMMUNICATIONS INTL INC (DE)
Name changed 03/27/1987
Name changed from Technology for Communications International (CA) to Technology for Communications International, Inc. (DE) and Common no par changed to 1¢ par 03/27/1987
Name changed to TCI International, Inc. 05/12/1988
(See TCI International, Inc.)

TECHNOLOGY FDG PARTNERS L P (CA & DE)
Trust terminated 12/29/1995
Units of Ltd. Partnership I details not available
Units of Ltd. Partnership II details not available
Units of Ltd. Partnership III assets transferred to Units of Ltd. Partnership III Liquidating Trust 07/07/2006
Trust terminated 11/30/2007
Units of Ltd. Partnership III Liquidating Trust details not available
Note: Units of Ltd. Partnership III formed under the laws of Delaware

TECHNOLOGY GROUP INC (CA)
Name changed to Union Reserves, Inc. 01/01/1983
(See Union Reserves, Inc.)

TECHNOLOGY GROWTH PARTNERS CORP (BC)
Name changed to VantagePoint Systems, Inc. 08/21/2001
(See VantagePoint Systems, Inc.)

TECHNOLOGY GUARDIAN INC (NV)
Name changed to eSAT, Inc. 02/04/1999
(See eSAT, Inc.)

TECHNOLOGY HORIZONS CORP (DE)
Name changed to CDKnet.com, Inc. 12/16/1998
CDKnet.com, Inc. name changed to

Arkados Group, Inc. 09/06/2006 which name changed to Solbright Group, Inc. 11/07/2017

TECHNOLOGY INC (OH)
Common no par split (3) for (2) by issuance of (0.5) additional share 08/30/1967
Common no par split (3) for (2) by issuance of (0.5) additional share 04/22/1969
Common no par split (2) for (1) by issuance of (1) additional share 01/18/1982
Common no par split (5) for (4) by issuance of (0.25) additional share 07/29/1982
Common no par split (2) for (1) by issuance of (1) additional share 07/27/1984
Common no par split (5) for (4) by issuance of (0.25) additional share 07/14/1986
Name changed to Krug International Corp. 07/22/1986
Krug International Corp. name changed to SunLink Health Systems, Inc. 08/20/2001

TECHNOLOGY INSTRUMENT CORP. (MA)
Merged into Bowmar Instrument Corp. on a (1) for (3.3) basis 10/02/1961
Bowmar Instrument Corp. merged into White Electronic Designs Corp. 10/23/1998
(See White Electronic Designs Corp.)

TECHNOLOGY INTEGRATION GROUP INC (DE)
Common $0.001 par split (9.5) for (1) by issuance of (8.5) additional shares payable 08/31/2006 to holders of record 08/21/2006 Ex date - 09/01/2006
Name changed to Odyne Corp. 10/19/2006
(See Odyne Corp.)

TECHNOLOGY INTL LTD (NM)
Each share old Common no par exchanged for (0.02) share new Common no par 11/01/1993
Charter revoked for failure to file reports and pay fees 12/27/1993

TECHNOLOGY INVT CAP CORP (MD)
Name changed to TICC Capital Corp. 12/03/2007
TICC Capital Corp. name changed to Oxford Square Capital Corp. 03/23/2018

TECHNOLOGY INVTS INC (UT)
Reorganized under the laws of Delaware as Medical Communications, Inc. 06/20/1989
Each share Common $0.001 par exchanged for (0.2) share Common 1¢ par
Medical Communications, Inc. recapitalized as 1-800-Consumer International Inc. 04/29/1997 which recapitalized as ISA Internationale Inc. 05/09/1998

TECHNOLOGY LEASING & CAP CORP (NY)
Dissolved by proclamation 12/24/1991

TECHNOLOGY LIBERATION CAP INC (UT)
Proclaimed dissolved for failure to pay taxes 08/01/1988

TECHNOLOGY LOGISTICS SYS INC (NV)
Recapitalized as Interactive Business Development, Inc. (New) 01/03/2006
Each share Common $0.001 par exchanged for (0.02) share Common $0.001 par
Interactive Business Development, Inc. (New) name changed to American Biodiesel Fuels Corp. 02/02/2007 which name changed to Planet Resource Recovery, Inc. 03/09/2007

TECHNOLOGY MGMT & MARKETING INC (CO)
Recapitalized as NetUSA, Inc. 02/17/1996
Each share Common $0.000011 par exchanged for (0.00125) share Common $0.000011 par

TECHNOLOGY MARKETING INC (CA)
Charter suspended for failure to file reports and pay fees 11/18/1996

TECHNOLOGY MODELING ASSOCS INC (CA)
Merged into Avant! Corp. 01/16/1998
Each share Common no par exchanged for (0.662045) share Common $0.0001 par
Avant! Corp. merged into Synopsys, Inc. 06/06/2002

TECHNOLOGY MONITORING SOLUTIONS INC (DE)
Completely liquidated
Each share Common $0.001 par received first and final distribution of $0.005323 cash payable 12/19/2014 to holders of record 12/12/2014 Ex date - 12/22/2014

TECHNOLOGY PUBG INC (NV)
Common $0.001 par split (8) for (1) by issuance of (7) additional shares payable 09/24/2009 to holders of record 09/24/2009
Name changed to Nexaira Wireless, Inc. 11/02/2009

TECHNOLOGY RESH CORP (FL)
Each share Common 17¢ par exchanged for (0.33333333) share Common 51¢ par 09/15/1995
Acquired by Coleman Cable, Inc. 05/16/2011
Each share Common 51¢ par exchanged for $7.20 cash

TECHNOLOGY RES INC (FL)
Common $0.001 par split (15) for (1) by issuance of (14) additional shares payable 09/07/2007 to holders of record 09/03/2007 Ex date - 09/10/2007
Name changed to Shaka Shoes, Inc. 07/23/2009
Shaka Shoes, Inc. name changed to Renuen Corp. 02/09/2012

TECHNOLOGY SELECTION INC (NV)
Name changed to TSET, Inc. 06/04/1999
TSET, Inc. name changed to Kronos Advanced Technologies Inc. 01/18/2002
(See Kronos Advanced Technologies Inc.)

TECHNOLOGY SVC GROUP INC (DE)
Merged into Elcotel Inc. 12/18/1997
Each share Common 1¢ par exchanged for (1.05) shares Common 1¢ par
(See Elcotel Inc.)

TECHNOLOGY SYS INC (MD)
Out of business 07/16/1971
No stockholders' equity

TECHNOLOGY SYS INTL INC (FL)
Name changed to ITS Networks, Inc. 01/29/2001
ITS Networks, Inc. name changed to Teleconnect, Inc. 02/28/2005

TECHNOLOGY TRANSFER INTL INC (CO)
Each share old Common $0.001 par exchanged for (0.25) share new Common $0.001 par 09/03/1987
Name changed to Transnational Technologies, Inc. 01/28/1993
(See Transnational Technologies, Inc.)

TECHNOLOGY TRANSFER LTD (DE)
Stock Dividend - 200% 05/05/1972
Charter cancelled and declared inoperative and void for non-payment of taxes 03/01/1977

TECHNOLOGY VISIONS GROUP INC (DE)
Recapitalized as Sutura, Inc. 08/22/2005
Each share Common $0.001 par exchanged for (0.08333333) share Common $0.001 par

TECHNOMIC INC (DE)
Reincorporated 06/09/1970
Name changed 06/26/1978
State of incorporation changed from (IL) to (DE) 06/09/1970
Name changed from Technomic Research Associates, Inc. to Technomic, Inc. 06/26/1978
Company advised private 12/00/1988
Details not available

TECHNOPRISES LTD (ISRAEL)
SEC revoked Ordinary stock registration 07/02/2010
No stockholders' equity

TECHNOR INTL INC (NV)
Name changed to CellPoint Inc. 10/04/1999
(See CellPoint Inc.)

TECHNOVISION SYS INC (BC)
Under plan of merger each share old Common no par exchanged for (1) share new Common no par 12/01/2002
Merged into Uniserve Communications Corp. 11/20/2003
Each share new Common no par exchanged for (1) share Common no par

TECHO CORP (CA)
Charter suspended for failure to file reports and pay fees 07/01/1981

TECHOLDMIN LTD (ON)
Merged into Enviro Waste Technologies Inc. 02/25/2000
Each share Common no par exchanged for (1) share Common no par
Enviro Waste Technologies Inc. merged into Compressario Corp. 03/07/2002
(See Compressario Corp.)

TECHRICH CORP (NM)
Charter revoked for failure to file reports and pay fees 04/25/1991

TECHS LOANSTAR INC (NV)
Common $0.001 par split (4) for (1) by issuance of (3) additional shares payable 04/29/2008 to holders of record 04/29/2008
Common $0.001 par split (3) for (1) by issuance of (2) additional shares payable 07/19/2010 to holders of record 07/16/2010 Ex date - 07/20/2010
Name changed to Quture International, Inc. 09/05/2012

TECHSCIENCE INDS INC (DE)
Each share old Common 1¢ par exchanged for (0.16666666) share new Common 1¢ par 03/26/1999
Name changed to PetPlanet.Com Inc. 05/26/1999
PetPlanet.Com Inc. name changed to eMemberDirect, Inc. 10/02/2000
(See eMemberDirect, Inc.)

TECHSECURE PARTNERS INC (NV)
Name changed to Poker TV Network Inc. 08/11/2005
Poker TV Network Inc. recapitalized as PC Universe, Inc. 07/05/2006
(See PC Universe, Inc.)

TECHSITE STRATEGIES CORP (BC)
Name changed to Sola Resource Corp. (BC) 07/17/2003
Solo Resource Corp. (BC) reincorporated in Alberta 07/28/2004 which recapitalized as Cancana Resources Corp. (AB) 01/24/2011 which reincorporated in British Columbia 08/12/2015 which reorganized as Meridian Mining S.E 11/28/2016

TECHSYS INC (NJ)
Each share old Common no par exchanged for (0.00001052) share new Common no par 01/07/2005
Note: In effect holders received $0.02 cash per share and public interest was eliminated

TECHTANA CAP LTD (BC)
Recapitalized as Forum Ventures Ltd. 12/21/1995
Each share Common no par exchanged for (0.14285714) share Common no par
Forum Ventures Ltd. recapitalized as Forum Development Corp. 10/15/2001 which name changed to Forum Uranium Corp. 06/27/2006 which name changed to Forum Energy Metals Corp. 02/28/2018

TECHTOWER GROUP INC (WY)
Charter revoked for failure to pay taxes 01/27/1988

TECHTRAN INDS INC (NY)
Merged into Photographic Sciences Corp. 11/10/1986
Each share Common 1¢ par exchanged for (0.5) share Common 1¢ par
Photographic Sciences Corp name changed to PSC Inc. 05/28/1992
(See PSC Inc.)

TECHTRO-MATIC CORP. (NY)
Under plan of merger each share Common $1 par exchanged for (1.25) shares Common 10¢ par 08/24/1961
Proclaimed dissolved for failure to file reports and pay taxes 12/15/1969

TECHTRON INC (DE)
Under plan of merger each share Common 1¢ par exchanged for $0.125 cash 10/15/1988

TECHVEN ASSN INC (MA)
Name changed to Computer Devices, Inc. (MA) 05/25/1979
Computer Devices, Inc. (MA) reorganized in Maryland 06/30/1986
(See Computer Devices, Inc. (MD))

TECHVEND INC (DE)
Recapitalized as Hemi Energy Group, Inc. 06/21/2005
Each share Common $0.001 par exchanged for (0.02631578) share Common $0.001 par

TECHWELL INC (DE)
Acquired by Intersil Corp. 04/27/2010
Each share Common $0.001 par exchanged for $18.50 cash

TECK COMINCO LTD (CANADA)
Name changed 11/21/1978
Name changed 09/12/2001
Capital Stock no par reclassified as Class A Common no par 05/29/1969
Name changed from Teck Corp. Ltd. to Teck Corp. 11/21/1978
Class B Common no par reclassified as Class B Subordinate no par 02/16/1983
7.25% Conv. Preferred Ser. F no par called for redemption 11/06/1987
Class A Common no par split (2) for (1) by issuance of (1) additional share 02/19/1988
Class B Subordinate no par split (2) for (1) by issuance of (1) additional share 02/19/1988
9.25% Preferred Ser. E no par called for redemption 12/17/1990
Name changed from Teck Corp. to Teck Cominco Ltd. 09/12/2001
Class A Common no par split (2) for (1) by issuance of (1) additional share payable 05/10/2007 to holders of record 05/07/2007 Ex date - 05/03/2007
Class B Subordinate no par split (2) for (1) by issuance of (1) additional share payable 05/10/2007 to holders of record 05/07/2007 Ex date - 05/11/2007

Stock Dividend - 100% 03/05/1980
Name changed to Teck Resources
Ltd. 04/27/2009

TECK-HUGHES GOLD MINES, LTD. (ON)
Merged into Teck Corp. Ltd. on a (0.4) for (1) basis 09/11/1963
Teck Corp. Ltd. name changed to Teck Corp. Ltd. 11/21/1978 which name changed to Teck Cominco Ltd. 09/12/2001 which name changed to Teck Resources Ltd. 04/27/2009

TECK WORLD INDS INC (AB)
Struck off register for failure to file annual returns 12/01/1997

TECKLA INC (DE)
Charter forfeited for failure to maintain a registered agent 02/05/1979

TECKMINE INDS INC (NV)
Name changed to Victory Electronic Cigarettes Corp. 07/15/2013
Victory Electronic Cigarettes Corp. name changed to Electronic Cigarettes International Group, Ltd. 07/11/2014

TECKTON INC (MA)
Involuntarily dissolved 12/31/1990

TECMA LABS INC (NJ)
Recapitalized as Lightpaths TP Technologies Inc. 04/21/1997
Each share Common no par exchanged for (0.1) share Common no par
Lightpaths TP Technologies Inc. name changed to mPhase Technologies Inc. 05/15/1997

TECMAR TECHNOLOGIES INTL INC (CANADA)
Each share Common no par received distribution of (1.1) shares Storage One Inc. Common no par payable 4/3/97 to holders of record 4/2/97 Ex date - 3/31/97
Name changed to Xencet Investments Inc. 3/31/98
Xencet Investments Inc. name changed to Games Trader Inc. 11/11/98 which name changed to GTR Group Inc. 6/29/99 which name changed to Mad Catz Interactive, Inc. 9/5/2001

TECNICA ED CORP (CA)
Charter suspended for failure to file reports and pay taxes 05/01/1974

TECNOL MED PRODS INC (DE)
Common $0.001 par split (3) for (2) by issuance of (0.5) additional share 02/24/1993
Merged into Kimberly-Clark Corp. 12/18/1997
Each share Common $0.001 par exchanged for (0.42) share Common $1.25 par

TECNOMATIX TECHNOLOGIES LTD (ISRAEL)
Acquired by UGS Corp. 04/01/2005
Each share Ordinary NIS 0.01 par exchanged for $17 cash

TECNOPETROL INC (YT)
Each share old Common no par exchanged for (0.16666666) share new Common no par 08/01/2002
Name changed to Bolivar Gold Corp. 01/24/2003
(See Bolivar Gold Corp.)

TECO CAP TR I (DE)
8.50% Trust Preferred Securities called for redemption at $25 on 12/20/2006

TECO ELEC & MACHY LTD (TAIWAN)
Stock Dividends - In 144A GDR's for Common payable to holders of 144A GDR's for Common 22.46% payable 08/31/1998 to holders of record 06/24/1998; 9.5498% payable 11/01/1999 to holders of record 07/26/1999; 13.5327% payable 09/09/2000 to holders of record 05/30/2000; 7.7846% payable 07/27/2001 to holders of record 06/25/2001 Ex date - 06/21/2001; in Reg. S GDR's for Common payable to holders of Reg. S GDR's for Common 7.7846% payable 07/27/2001 to holders of record 06/25/2001
GDR agreement terminated 10/20/2017
Each 144A GDR for Common exchanged for $9.114419 cash
Each Reg. S GDR for Common exchanged for $9.114419 cash

TECO ENERGY INC (FL)
Common $1 par split (2) for (1) by issuance of (1) additional share 08/15/1987
Common $1 par split (2) for (1) by issuance of (1) additional share 08/30/1993
Each Equity Security Unit received (0.9509) share Common $1 par 01/14/2005
Acquired by Emera Inc. 07/01/2016
Each share Common $1 par exchanged for $27.55 cash

TECO INC (IL)
Common $10 par changed to $1.25 par and (7) additional shares issued 09/21/1970
Reincorporated under the laws of Delaware as Pay Television Corp. and Common $1.25 par changed to no par 05/12/1972
(See Pay Television Corp.)

TECO MINES & OILS LTD. (ON)
Charter cancelled for failure to pay taxes and file returns 05/18/1976

TECOGEN INC (MA)
Name changed to Thermo Power Corp. 03/12/1993
(See Thermo Power Corp.)

TECON INC (UT)
Each share old Common $0.001 par exchanged for (0.25) share new Common $0.001 par 04/11/1989
Each share new Common $0.001 par exchanged again for (0.01935658) share new Common $0.001 par 11/20/1995
Name changed to Buyit.com Inc. 05/06/1999
Buyit.com Inc. name changed to Craftclick.com, Inc. (UT) 01/10/2000 which reorganized under the laws of Delaware 05/07/2000 which name changed to Mobilepro Corp. 06/19/2001

TECOR INC (DE)
Merged into Tracey-Locke Co., Inc. 01/31/1974
Each share Common 25¢ par exchanged for $0.25 cash

TECSCAN INTL INC (NV)
Name changed to Bio-Life Labs, Inc. 05/19/2004
(See Bio-Life Labs, Inc.)

TECSYN INTL INC (ON)
Non-Vtg. Stock no par split (2) for (1) by issuance of (1) additional share 12/31/1986
Each share Preference Ser. 1 Class C exchanged for (5) shares 6.5% Conv. 1st Preferred Ser. A $30 par 10/18/1991
Each share 6.5% Conv. 1st Preferred Ser. A $30 par exchanged for (6) shares 1st Preference $5 par 10/18/1991
Each share Non-Vtg. Stock no par exchanged for (1) share new Common no par 10/18/1991
1st Preference $5 par called for redemption 03/15/1994
Each share new Common no par exchanged for (0.33333333) share Common no par 02/03/1998
Merged into EXCO Technologies Ltd. 09/01/2000

Each share Common no par exchanged for $2.70 cash

TECTEL INC (CO)
Plan of reorganization under Chapter 11 Federal Bankruptcy proceedings confirmed 06/09/1988
No stockholders' equity for holders of old Common no par

TECTON CORP (CT)
Voluntarily dissolved 12/26/1973
Details not available

TECTON CORP (NV)
Each share old Common $0.0001 par exchanged for (0.025) share new Common $0.0001 par 06/06/2013
Name changed to Endurance Exploration Group, Inc. 02/03/2014

TECTONIC CAP CORP (BC)
Name changed to Tectonic Minerals Corp. 04/24/2009
Tectonic Minerals Corp. name changed to Comstock Metals Ltd. 10/14/2011

TECTONIC ENERGY CORP (DE)
Merged into ENERTEC Corp. 05/04/1984
Each share Common 1¢ par exchanged for (0.1) share Common 1¢ par
(See ENERTEC Corp.)

TECTONIC MINERALS CORP (BC)
Name changed to Comstock Metals Ltd. 10/14/2011

TECTONIC NETWORK INC (DE)
Plan of reorganization under Chapter 11 Federal Bankruptcy proceedings effective 07/17/2006
No stockholders' equity

TECTONICS, INC. (NY)
Incorporated 01/01/1966
Charter cancelled and proclaimed dissolved for failure to pay taxes 12/16/1974

TECTRA INDS INC (DE)
Charter cancelled and declared inoperative and void for non-payment of taxes 06/26/1985

TECTUM CORP. (OH)
Name changed to American Enterprises, Inc. 03/06/1963
(See American Enterprises, Inc.)

TECUMESEH RES LTD (BC)
Name changed to Thrust Resources Inc. 02/25/1985
Thrust Resources Inc. recapitalized as Balaclava Industries Ltd. 07/06/1993 which name changed to Balaclava Mines Inc. 11/08/1996 which recapitalized as Pillar Resources Inc. 06/07/2001 which name changed to PilaGold Inc. 10/21/2003 which merged into Radius Gold Inc. 07/02/2004

TECUMSEH DEVELOPMENTS LTD. (ON)
Acquired by Trans-Canada Explorations Ltd. 00/00/1955
Each share Capital Stock no par exchanged for (0.2) share Capital Stock $1 par
Trans-Canada Explorations Ltd. merged into Roman Corp. Ltd. 11/27/1964
(See Roman Corp. Ltd.)

TECUMSEH PETROLEUMS LTD. (AB)
Struck off register for failure to file annual returns 11/15/1967

TECUMSEH PRODS CO (MI)
Common $1 par split (3) for (1) by issuance of (2) additional shares 04/27/1973
Common $1 par reclassified as Class B Common $1 par 04/22/1992
Each share Class B Common $1 par received distribution of (1) share Non-Vtg. Class A Common $1 par 05/29/1992
Non-Vtg. Class A Common $1 par split (2) for (1) by issuance of (1) additional share 06/30/1993
Each share Class B Common $1 par received distribution of (1) share Non-Vtg. Class A Common $1 par 06/30/1993
Non-Vtg. Class A Common $1 par reclassified as Common no par 05/02/2014
Class B Common $1 par reclassified as Common no par 05/02/2014
Stock Dividends - 300% 04/11/1949; 100% 04/19/1957; 50% 04/22/1960
Acquired by MA Industrial JV LLC 09/21/2015
Each share Common no par exchanged for $5 cash

TEDA TRAVEL GROUP INC (DE)
Name changed to Network CN, Inc. 08/15/2006

TEDDY BEAR VY MINES LTD (ON)
Company wound up 05/25/2007
No stockholders' equity

TEDDY MINING & MILLING CO. LTD. (ID)
Charter forfeited for failure to file reports 11/30/1977

TEDDYS HOUSE SEAFOOD INC (NY)
Name changed to Foodways National, Inc. 06/29/1971
(See Foodways National, Inc.)

TEDESCO, INC. (MN)
Name changed to Norseman Broadcasting Corp. 12/08/1966
(See Norseman Broadcasting Corp.)

TEDOM CAP INC (DE)
Common $0.001 par split (3) for (1) by issuance of (2) additional shares payable 04/05/2010 to holders of record 03/26/2010 Ex date - 04/06/2010
Name changed to eLayaway, Inc. 05/24/2010

TEE COMM ELECTRS INC (CANADA)
Assets sold for benefit of creditors 04/00/1999
No stockholders' equity

TEE RIFIK CORP (NV)
Recapitalized as Shop TV Inc. 07/06/1998
Each share Common $0.001 par exchanged for (0.66666666) share Common $0.001 par
Shop TV Inc. recapitalized as Site2Shop.com, Inc. 02/23/1999 which name changed to Intermedia Marketing Solutions, Inc. 04/20/2001
(See Intermedia Marketing Solutions, Inc.)

TEECO PPTYS L P (DE)
Liquidation completed
Each Unit of Ltd. Partnership received initial distribution of $0.50 cash 01/24/1979
Each Unit of Ltd. Partnership received second distribution of $0.15 cash 04/24/1979
Each Unit of Ltd. Partnership received third distribution of $0.15 cash 10/24/1979
Each Unit of Ltd. Partnership received fourth distribution of $6.50 cash 12/27/1979
Each Unit of Ltd. Partnership received fifth distribution of $5 cash 01/07/1980
Each Unit of Ltd. Partnership received sixth distribution of $0.15 cash 04/24/1980
Each Unit of Ltd. Partnership received seventh distribution of $0.15 cash 07/24/1980
Each Unit of Ltd. Partnership received eighth distribution of $0.50 cash 10/27/1980
Each Unit of Ltd. Partnership received ninth distribution of $0.20 cash 01/26/1981
Each Unit of Ltd. Partnership received

tenth distribution of $1 cash 04/27/1981
Each Unit of Ltd. Partnership received eleventh distribution of $0.10 cash 07/27/1981
Each Unit of Ltd. Partnership received twelfth distribution of $0.10 cash 10/26/1981
Each Unit of Ltd. Partnership received thirteenth distribution of $0.10 cash 01/25/1982
Each Unit of Ltd. Partnership received fourteenth distribution of $0.10 cash 04/26/1982
Each Unit of Ltd. Partnership received fifteenth distribution of $0.10 cash 10/25/1982
Each Unit of Ltd. Partnership received sixteenth distribution of $0.10 cash 01/24/1983
Each Unit of Ltd. Partnership received seventeenth distribution of $0.10 cash 04/26/1983
Each Unit of Ltd. Partnership received eighteenth distribution of $0.10 cash 07/25/1983
Each Unit of Ltd. Partnership received nineteenth distribution of $0.10 cash 10/24/1983
Each Unit of Ltd. Partnership received twentieth distribution of $0.10 cash 01/23/1984
Each Unit of Ltd. Partnership received twenty-first distribution of $0.10 cash 04/23/1984
Each Unit of Ltd. Partnership received twenty-second distribution of $0.10 cash 06/30/1984
Each Unit of Ltd. Partnership received twenty-third distribution of $0.10 cash 10/22/1984
Each Unit of Ltd. Partnership received twenty-fourth distribution of $0.10 cash 01/22/1985
Each Unit of Ltd. Partnership received twenty-fifth distribution of $0.10 cash 04/22/1985
Twenty-sixth distribution of $0.10 cash 07/22/1985
Twenty-seventh distribution of $0.10 cash 10/21/1985
Twenty-eighth distribution of $0.10 cash 01/21/1986
Twenty-ninth distribution of $0.10 cash 04/21/1986
Thirtieth distribution of $0.10 cash 07/21/1986
Thirty-first distribution of $0.10 cash 10/20/1986
Thirty-second distribution of $0.10 cash 01/20/1987
Thirty-third distribution of $0.10 cash 04/20/1987
Thirty-fourth distribution of $0.10 cash 07/20/1987
Thirty-fifth distribution of $0.10 cash 10/19/1987
Thirty-sixth distribution of $0.10 cash 01/00/1988
Thirty-seventh distribution of $0.10 cash 04/00/1988
Thirty-eighth and final distribution of $0.10 cash 07/00/1988

TEEKAY PETROJARL ASA (NORWAY)
Acquired by TPO Investments 07/09/2008
Each Sponsored ADR for Ordinary exchanged for $9.355283 cash

TEEKAY SHIPPING CORP (MARSHALL ISLANDS)
Reincorporated 12/20/1999
Place of incorporation changed from (Liberia) to (Marshall Islands) 12/20/1999
Each 7.25% Premium Equity Participating Unit received (1.1364) Common Units 02/16/2006
Name changed to Teekay Corp. 05/30/2007

TEEN ED GROUP INC (DE)
Name changed to Vomart International Auto Parts, Inc. 06/27/2011

TEEN GLOW MAKEUP INC (NV)
Reorganized as American Power Corp. 06/18/2010
Each share Common $0.001 par exchanged for (340) shares Common $0.001 par
(See American Power Corp.)

TEESHIN RES LTD (ON)
Recapitalized as Habsburg Resources Inc. 05/08/1991
Each share Common no par exchanged for (0.125) share Common no par
Habsburg Resources Inc. name changed to Dome Mountain Resources Ltd. 09/14/1994 which recapitalized as DMR Resources Ltd. 11/06/1996
(See DMR Resources Ltd.)

TEGAL CORP (DE)
Each share old Common 1¢ par exchanged for (0.08333333) share new Common 1¢ par 07/25/2006
Each share new Common 1¢ par exchanged again for (0.2) share new Common 1¢ par 06/17/2011
Name changed to CollabRx, Inc. 09/27/2012
CollabRx, Inc. recapitalized as Rennova Health, Inc. 11/03/2015

TEGL SYS CORP (BC)
Struck off register and declared dissolved for failure to file returns 09/02/1994

TEGO SILVER COBALT MINES LTD. (ON)
Charter revoked for failure to file reports and pay fees 04/15/1965

TEGRA ENTERPRISES INC (BC)
Recapitalized as Pacific Video Canada Ltd. 08/21/1989
Each share Common no par exchanged for (0.2) share Common no par
Pacific Video Canada Ltd. reorganized as Command Post & Transfer Corp. (BC) 05/01/1999 which reincorporated in Ontario 06/24/1999
(See Command Post & Transfer Corp. (ONT))

TEHAMA BANCORP (CA)
Stock Dividend - 10% payable 05/15/2000 to holders of record 04/10/2000
Merged into Humboldt Bancorp 03/09/2001
Each share Common no par exchanged for (1.775) shares Common no par
Humboldt Bancorp merged into Umpqua Holdings Corp. 07/10/2004

TEHAMA BK (RED BLUFF, CA)
Name changed 02/18/1997
Common no par split (2) for (1) by issuance of (1) additional share 09/30/1994
Stock Dividend - 10% payable 05/01/1996 to holders of record 04/10/1996
Name changed from Tehama County Bank (Red Bluff, CA) to Tehama Bank (Red Bluff, CA) 02/18/1997
Under plan of reorganization each share Common no par automatically became (1) share Tehama Bancorp Common no par 07/01/1997
Tehama Bancorp merged into Humboldt Bancorp 03/09/2001 which merged into Umpqua Holdings Corp. 07/10/2004

TEI INC (TX)
Merged into Pinnacle Global Group, Inc. 01/29/1999
Each share Common 1¢ par exchanged for (0.25) share Common 1¢ par
Pinnacle Global Group, Inc. name changed to Sanders Morris Harris Group Inc. 05/23/2001 which name changed to Edelman Financial Group Inc. 05/27/2011
(See Edelman Financial Group Inc.)

TEIG ROSS INC (MN)
Statutorily dissolved 11/13/1991

TEIG ROSS KLENERT & CHICA INC (MN)
Name changed to Teig Ross, Inc. 08/31/1972
(See Teig Ross, Inc.)

TEIJIN SEIKI LTD (JAPAN)
Merged into Nabtesco Corp. 09/22/2003
Each ADR for Common exchanged for $4.4854 cash
Note: Due to ADR's being unsponsored exchange rate may vary among agents

TEJAS GAS CORP (DE)
Common 25¢ par split (3) for (2) by issuance of (0.5) additional share 03/30/1993
Common 25¢ par split (3) for (2) by issuance of (0.5) additional share payable 05/10/1996 to holders of record 04/26/1996 Ex date - 05/13/1996
Stock Dividend - 10% 08/24/1995
5.25% Depositary Preferred called for redemption at $51.575 plus $0.0656 accrued dividends on 11/10/1997
5.25% Preferred $1 par called for redemption at $257.875 plus $0.3281 accrued dividends on 11/10/1997
Merged into Shell Oil Co. 01/12/1998
Each share Common 25¢ par exchanged for $61.50 cash
9.96% Depositary Preferred called for redemption at $25 on 02/02/1998
Public interest eliminated

TEJAS GAS CORP (TX)
Stock Dividend - 25% 06/15/1977
Under plan of merger each share Common $0.33333333 par exchanged for $28 cash 11/16/1979

TEJAS INC (DE)
Name changed to Westech Capital Corp. 08/05/2010

TEJAS OIL & GAS CO (NV)
Charter revoked for failure to file reports and pay taxes 04/01/1989

TEJAS PWR CORP (DE)
Name changed to TPC Corp. 05/06/1996
(See TPC Corp.)

TEJON RANCH CO (CA)
Common $1 par split (10) for (1) by issuance of (9) additional shares payable 03/10/1986
Reincorporated under the laws of Delaware 06/10/1987
Stock Dividend - 900% 05/02/1951

TEK NET INTL CDA LTD (BC)
Delisted from Vancouver Stock Exchange 09/01/1988

TEK SYS INC (UT)
Charter expired 06/02/2005

TEKA-TECELAGEM KUEHNRICH S A (BRAZIL)
ADR agreement terminated 05/04/2014
Each Sponsored ADR for Preferred exchanged for (5,000) Preferred Shares
Each Sponsored ADR for Ordinary exchanged for (5,000) Ordinary Shares

TEKELEC (CA)
Common no par split (2) for (1) by issuance of (1) additional share 03/29/1995
Common no par split (2) for (1) by issuance of (1) additional share payable 08/22/1997 to holders of record 08/08/1997
Common no par split (2) for (1) by issuance of (1) additional share payable 07/06/1998 to holders of record 06/19/1998
Acquired by Siris Capital Group, L.L.C. 01/27/2012
Each share Common no par exchanged for $11 cash

TEKERRA GAS INC (AB)
Merged into Del Roca Energy Ltd. 10/31/1998
Each share Common no par exchanged for (0.6) share Common no par
Del Roca Energy Ltd. merged into Tusk Energy Inc. 02/01/2003
(See Tusk Energy Inc.)

TEKGRAF INC (GA)
Reincorporated 07/31/1998
State of incorporation changed from (DE) to (GA) 07/31/1998
Name changed to Centiv, Inc. (GA) 12/31/2001
Centiv, Inc. (GA) reincorporated in Delaware 06/12/2002 which reorganized in Nevada as CNTV Entertainment Group, Inc. 11/19/2004 which recapitalized as Degama Software Solutions, Inc. 05/29/2008

TEKINSIGHT COM INC (DE)
Name changed to DynTek Inc. 12/31/2001

TEKLOGIX INTL INC (ON)
Merged into Psion Canada Inc. 09/20/2000
Each share Common no par exchanged for (2.021) Exchangeable Shares no par
(See Psion Canada Inc.)

TEKMAR CORP (DE)
Charter cancelled and declared inoperative and void for non-payment of taxes 03/01/1977

TEKMIRA PHARMACEUTICALS CORP (BC)
Each share old Common no par exchanged for (0.2) share new Common no par 11/04/2010
Name changed to Arbutus Biopharma Corp. 08/03/2015

TEKMODO INDS INC (BC)
Each share old Common no par exchanged for (0.4) share new Common no par 06/30/2017
Each share new Common no par exchanged again for (0.25) share new Common no par 09/28/2017
Recapitalized as Lincoln Ventures Ltd. 07/16/2018
Each share new Common no par exchanged for (0.1) share Common no par

TEKNEKRON COMMUNICATIONS SYS INC (NV)
Name changed to TCSI Corp. 01/21/1995
(See TCSI Corp.)

TEKNIK DIGITAL ARTS INC (NV)
Name changed to Halitron, Inc. and Common $0.001 par changed to $0.0001 par 08/13/2014

TEKNION CORP (ON)
Merged into 2158436 Ontario Ltd. 02/27/2008
Each Subordinate Share no par exchanged for $3.15 cash

TEKNOL MNG LTD (BC)
Recapitalized as Marco Resources Ltd. 09/08/1975
Each share Common no par exchanged for (0.5) share Common no par
(See Marco Resources Ltd.)

TEKNOR INDL COMPUTERS INC (CANADA)
Name changed to Saco Smartvision Inc. 09/01/1999
(See Saco Smartvision Inc.)

TEKNOWLEDGE CORP NEW (DE)
Each share old Common 1¢ par exchanged for (0.2) share new Common 1¢ par 12/22/1998
Chapter 7 bankruptcy proceedings terminated 06/05/2013
No stockholders' equity

TEKNOWLEDGE INC (DE)
Stock Dividend - 27.5% 02/10/1989
Name changed to Cimflex Teknowledge Corp. 02/24/1989
Cimflex Teknowledge Corp. name changed to Teknowledge Corp. 06/30/1994
(See Teknowledge Corp.)

TEKOIL & GAS CORP (DE)
Each share old Common $0.000000001 par exchanged for (0.01) share new Common $0.000000001 par 10/13/2005
Plan of reorganization under Chapter 11 Federal Bankruptcy proceedings effective 03/31/2010
No stockholders' equity

TEKOIL CORP. (DE)
Merged into Consolidated Oil & Gas, Inc. (CO) 02/23/1962
Each share Common exchanged for (0.4) share Common 20¢ par
Consolidated Oil & Gas, Inc. (CO) was acquired by Hugoton Energy Corp. 09/07/1995 which merged into Chesapeake Energy Corp. 03/10/1998

TEKOLOGY CORP (DE)
Charter cancelled and declared inoperative and void for non-payment of taxes 03/01/1976

TEKTRONIX INC (OR)
Common no par split (2) for (1) by issuance of (1) additional share 05/09/1977
Common no par split (2) for (1) by issuance of (1) additional share 01/26/1987
Common no par split (3) for (2) by issuance of (0.5) additional share payable 10/31/1997 to holders of record 10/10/1997 Ex date - 11/03/1997
Common no par split (2) for (1) by issuance of (1) additional share payable 10/31/2000 to holders of record 10/10/2000 Ex date - 11/01/2000
Merged into Danaher Corp. 11/21/2007
Each share Common no par exchanged for $38 cash

TEKWERKS SOLUTIONS INC (BC)
Name changed to Hudson Resources Inc. 12/09/2002

TEL A SIGN INC (DE)
Reorganized 07/22/1968
Common 20¢ par changed to no par 07/20/1960
Reorganized from under the laws of (IL) to (DE) 07/22/1968
Each share Common no par exchanged for (0.33333333) share Common 10¢ par
Name changed to Randy Industries, Inc. 01/29/1969
(See Randy Industries, Inc.)

TEL AVIV RES LTD (BC)
Name changed to Moran Resources Corp. 11/30/1981
Moran Resources Corp. recapitalized as Stornaway Resources Corp. 03/25/1985 which name changed to Stornaway Capital Development Corp. 01/07/1988
(See Stornaway Capital Development Corp.)

TEL-COM WIRELESS CABLE TV CORP (FL)
Name changed to 5th Avenue Channel Corp. 03/25/1999
5th Avenue Channel Corp. recapitalized as Simulated Environment Concepts, Inc. 01/16/2008

TEL ELECTRS INC (UT)
Each share Common $0.005 par exchanged for (0.025) share Common 2¢ par 07/10/1990
Name changed to TELS Corp. 09/13/1994
TELS Corp. name changed to Hampton Consulting Corp. 10/01/2004
(See Hampton Consulting Corp.)

TEL GOLD MINES, LTD. (ON)
Charter cancelled for failure to file reports and pay taxes 00/00/1955

TEL MAN INC (SC)
Name changed to SouthernNet, Inc. (SC) 12/31/1986
SouthernNet, Inc. (SC) reincorporated in Delaware 11/17/1988 which merged into Telecom USA, Inc. 12/14/1988
(See Telecom USA, Inc.)

TEL NT LTD (AB)
Capital Shares no par called for redemption at $22.0113 on 07/31/1998
Equity Dividend Shares no par called for redemption at $13.4362 on 07/31/1998
Public interest eliminated

TEL O TRONIC INDS INC (DE)
Name changed to American Swiss International Corp. 06/20/1986
(See American Swiss International Corp.)

TEL-ONE INC (FL)
Name changed to Teleon Corp. 05/28/2002
Teleon Corp. name changed to Auto Centrix Inc. 06/21/2004 which recapitalized as Greenstone Holdings, Inc. 01/03/2006
(See Greenstone Holdings, Inc.)

TEL PAGE CORP (NY)
Reincorporated under the laws of Delaware as Mobile Communications Corp. of America 3/1/73
Mobile Communications Corp. of America acquired by BellSouth Corp. 4/4/89 which merged into AT&T Inc. 12/29/2006

TEL-SAVE COM INC (DE)
Name changed 11/16/1998
Common 1¢ par split (3) for (2) by issuance of (0.5) additional share payable 03/15/1996 to holders of record 02/29/1996
Common 1¢ par split (2) for (1) by issuance of (1) additional share payable 01/31/1997 to holders of record 01/17/1997
Name changed from Tel-Save Holdings, Inc. to Tel-Save.Com Inc. 11/16/1998
Name changed to Talk.Com Inc. 04/26/1999
Talk.Com Inc. name changed to Talk America Holdings Inc 04/10/2001
(See Talk America Holdings Inc.)

TEL-STAN COMMUNICATION INC (UT)
Proclaimed dissolved for failure to file reports 12/31/1986

TEL-VOICE COMMUNICATIONS INC (NV)
Recapitalized as Home Services International, Inc. 01/08/2003
Each (28.9) shares Common $0.001 par exchanged for (1) share Common $0.001 par
Home Services International, Inc. name changed to Internal Hydro International, Inc. (NV) 01/02/2004 which reincorporated in Florida 02/04/2004 which name changed to Renewable Energy Resources, Inc. 02/20/2007 which name changed to New Green Technologies, Inc. 07/03/2008 which recapitalized as Spur Ranch, Inc. 08/25/2010 which name changed to Rounder, Inc. 01/24/2012 which name changed to Fortitude Group, Inc. 01/08/2013

TELALERT INTL INC (NV)
Recapitalized as Fingerware Corp. 6/9/2005
Each share Common $0.001 par exchanged for (0.001) share Common $0.001 par
Fingerware Corp. name changed to Seamless Technology, Inc. 10/25/2005

TELANETIX INC (DE)
Each share old Common $0.0001 par exchanged for (0.01333333) share new Common $0.0001 par 06/01/2011
Acquired by Intermedia Holdings, Inc. 08/30/2013
Each share new Common $0.0001 par exchanged for $7.284 cash

TELATINOS INC (TX)
Each share old Common $0.0001 par exchanged for (30) shares new Common $0.0001 par 11/30/2004
Each share new Common $0.0001 par exchanged again for (5) shares new Common $0.0001 par 12/29/2004
Each share new Common $0.0001 par exchanged again for (1.2) shares new Common $0.0001 par 02/11/2005
Each share new Common $0.0001 par exchanged again for (33) shares new Common $0.0001 par 05/25/2005
Each share new Common $0.0001 par exchanged again for (0.00033613) share new Common $0.0001 par 08/26/2005
Name changed to Netco Investments, Inc. 11/04/2005
(See Netco Investments, Inc.)

TELAUTOGRAPH CORP (VA)
Common no par changed to $5 par 00/00/1933
Each share Common $5 par exchanged for (2) shares Common $1 par 05/04/1956
Merged into Arden-Mayfair, Inc. 12/31/1971
Each share Common $1 par exchanged for (0.7) share Common $1 par
Arden-Mayfair, Inc. reorganized as Arden Group, Inc. 12/19/1978
(See Arden Group, Inc.)

TELAVA NETWORKS INC (CA)
Name changed back to Transnational Financial Network, Inc. 03/00/2009
Note: Action taken due to rescinding of merger agreement, this company is private and no longer related to Transnational Financial Network, Inc.

TELAXIS COMMUNICATIONS CORP (MA)
Issue Information - 4,000,000 shares COM offered at $17 per share on 02/01/2000
Reorganized under the laws of Delaware as YDI Wireless, Inc. 07/09/2003
Each share Common 1¢ par exchanged for (0.25) share Common 1¢ par
Note: Holders of (99) or fewer shares received cash
YDI Wireless, Inc. name changed to Terabeam, Inc. 11/07/2005 which name changed to Proxim Wireless Corp. 09/10/2007

TELCO COMMUNICATIONS GROUP INC (VA)
Merged into Excel Communications, Inc. (VA) 10/14/97
Each share Common no par exchanged for (0.7595) share Common $0.001 par and $15 cash

TELCO COMMUNICATIONS INC (CO)
Chapter 11 bankruptcy proceedings converted to Chapter 7 on 05/10/1994
Stockholders' equity unlikely
Recapitalized as Smartsources.Com Inc. (CO) 11/09/1998
Each share new Common no par exchanged for (0.01333333) share Common no par
Smartsources.Com Inc. (CO) reincorporated in Washington as Infertek, Inc. 06/15/2001 which name changed to Metarunner, Inc. 06/15/2004
(See Metarunner, Inc.)

TELCO MARKETING SVCS INC (DE)
Name changed to Technical Equipment Leasing Corp. 12/28/1979
(See Technical Equipment Leasing Corp.)

TELCO PRODS CORP (NY)
Charter cancelled and proclaimed dissolved for failure to pay taxes 09/25/1991

TELCO RESH CORP (CANADA)
Merged into Peregrine Systems, Inc. 03/30/2000
Each share Common no par exchanged for (0.082511) share Common no par
(See Peregrine Systems, Inc.)

TELCO SPLIT CORP (ON)
Preferred no par called for redemption at $25.50 on 08/31/2001
Capital Shares no par called for redemption at $4.28 on 08/30/2002
Public interest eliminated

TELCO SYS INC (CA)
Merged into World Access Inc. 11/30/1998
Each share Common no par exchanged for (0.5862) share Common 1¢ par
(See World Access Inc.)

TELCO-TECHNOLOGY INC (DE)
Reincorporated 01/00/1998
Each share old Common $0.001 par exchanged for (0.001) share new Common $0.001 par 08/07/1995
State of incorporation changed from (NV) to (DE) 01/00/1998
Recapitalized as GreenWorks Corp. 12/29/2004
Each share Common $0.001 par exchanged for (0.02) share Common $0.001 par
GreenWorks Corp. name changed to GreenShift Corp. 05/17/2005 which recapitalized as Carbonics Capital Corp. 02/12/2008 which recapitalized as Westport Energy Holdings Inc. 12/03/2012

TELCOBLUE INC (WY)
Reincorporated 12/23/2004
Each share old Common $0.001 par exchanged for (0.05) share new Common $0.001 par 11/20/2003
State of incorporation changed from (DE) to (WY) 12/23/2004
Administratively dissolved 03/14/2009

TELCOM INC (DE)
Stock Dividend - 10% 10/16/1972
Merged into xonics, inc. (CA) 03/31/1975
Each share Common 10¢ par exchanged for (0.25) share Common 10¢ par xonics, inc. (CA) reincorporated in Delaware 03/24/1980
(See xonics, inc.)

TELCOM SEMICONDUCTOR INC (DE)
Issue Information - 3,600,000 shares COM offered at $8.50 per share on 07/27/1995

Merged into Microchip Technology Inc. 01/16/2001
Each share Common $0.001 par exchanged for (0.53) share Common $0.001 par

TELCOMAR COMMUNICATIONS INC (NY)
Name changed to Sentry Investigation Corp. 07/24/1975
Sentry Investigation Corp. name changed to Sentry Armored Courier Corp. 02/23/1978 which name changed to Grant Enterprise Ltd. 03/30/1987

TELCOPLUS ENTERPRISES INC (BC)
Name changed to Yamiri Gold & Energy Inc. 12/05/2005
Yamiri Gold & Energy Inc. name changed to Cannon Point Resources Ltd. 04/27/2010 which merged into Northern Dynasty Minerals Ltd. 10/29/2015

TELE ART INC (VIRGIN ISLANDS)
Each share old Common no par exchanged for (0.01) share new Common no par 03/31/1989
High Court of Justice of the British Virgin Islands granted order to wind up company 07/17/1998
Stockholders' equity unlikely
Note: Liquidation still proceeding as of 05/06/2008

TELE-BROADCASTERS INC (DE)
Voluntarily dissolved 08/15/1986
Details not available

TELE CAPITAL INC (CANADA)
Name changed to Pathonic Network Inc. 10/02/1986
(See Pathonic Network Inc.)

TELE CAPITAL LTD (CANADA)
Merged into La Verendrye Management Corp.-Corp. Gestion La Verendrye 06/11/1982
Each share Class A Common no par exchanged for $35 cash

TELE CELULAR SUL PARTICIPACOES S A (BRAZIL)
Under plan of merger name changed to TIM Participacoes S.A. 08/30/2004

TELE CENTRO OESTE CELULAR PARTICIPACOES S A (BRAZIL)
ADR basis changed from (1:3,000) to (1:1) 05/04/2005
Merged into Vivo Participacoes S.A. 03/31/2006
Each Sponsored ADR for Preferred exchanged for (3.083) Sponsored ADR's for Preferred
Vivo Participacoes S.A. merged into Telecomunicacoes de Sao Paulo S.A. - Telesp 06/07/2011 which name changed to Telefonica Brasil, S.A. 10/11/2011

TELE CENTRO SUL PARTICIPACOES S A (BRAZIL)
Name changed to Brasil Telecom Participacoes S.A. 07/05/2000
Brasil Telecom Participacoes S.A. merged into Brasil Telecom S.A. 11/16/2009 which name changed to Oi S.A. 02/28/2012

TELE COMMUNICATIONS INC NEW (DE)
Class A Common $1 par reclassified as TCI Group Ser. A Common $1 par 8/10/95
Class B Common $1 par reclassified as TCI Group Ser. B Common $1 par 8/10/95
Each share TCI Group Ser. A Common $1 par received distribution of (0.1) share TCI Satellite Entertainment Inc. Class A Common $8 par payable 12/4/96 to holders of record 11/12/96 Ex date - 12/5/96
Each share TCI Group Ser. B Common $1 par received distribution of (0.1) share TCI Satellite Entertainment Inc. Class B Common $8 par payable 12/4/96 to holders of record 11/12/96 Ex date - 12/5/96
Liberty Media Group Ser. A Common $1 par split (2) for (1) by issuance of (1) additional share payable 1/13/97 to holders of record 12/27/96
Each share Liberty Media Group Ser. B Common $1 par received distribution of (0.5) share Liberty Media Group Ser. A Common $1 par payable 1/13/97 to holders of record 12/27/96
Liberty Media Group Ser. A Common $1 par split (3) for (2) by issuance of (0.5) additional share payable 2/6/98 to holders of record 1/30/98
Liberty Media Group Ser. B Common $1 par split (3) for (2) by issuance of (0.5) additional share payable 2/6/98 to holders of record 1/30/98
Preferred Ser. D 1¢ par called for redemption at $304.0233 on 4/1/98
Stock Dividend - in Liberty Media Group Ser. A Common to holders of Liberty Media Group Ser. A Common 25% 8/10/95
Merged into AT&T Corp. 3/9/99
Each share Liberty Media Group Conv. Preferred Ser. H 1¢ par exchanged for (0.590625) share Liberty Media Group Class A Common $1 par
Each share TCI Group Conv. Preferred Ser. G 1¢ par exchanged for (0.923083) share Common $1 par
Each share Liberty Media Group Ser. A Common $1 par exchanged for (1) share Liberty Media Group Class A Common $1 par
Each share Liberty Media Group Ser. B Common $1 par exchanged for (1) share Liberty Media Group Class B Common $1 par
Each share TCI Group Ser. A Common $1 par exchanged for (0.7757) share Common $1 par
Each share TCI Group Ser. B Common $1 par exchanged for (0.8533) share Common $1 par
Each share TCI Ventures Group Ser. A Common $1 par exchanged for (0.52) share Liberty Media Group Class A Common $1 par
Each share TCI Ventures Group Ser. B Common $1 par exchanged for (0.52) share Liberty Media Group Class B Common $1 par
6% Exchangeable Class B Jr. Preferred 1¢ par called for redemption at $100 on 2/22/2000
AT&T Corp. merged into AT&T Inc. 11/18/2005

TELE COMMUNICATIONS INC OLD (DE)
Common $1 par reclassified as Class A Common $1 par and (1) share Class B Common $1 par issued 08/31/1979
Class A Common $1 par split (2) for (1) by issuance of (1) additional share 07/15/1983
Class B Common $1 par split (2) for (1) by issuance of (1) additional share 07/15/1983
Class B Common $1 par reclassified as Conv. Class B Common $1 par 05/20/1986
Class A Common $1 par split (2) for (1) by issuance of (1) additional share 07/11/1986
Conv. Class B Common $1 par split (2) for (1) by issuance of (1) additional share 07/11/1986
Class A Common $1 par split (3) for (2) by issuance of (0.5) additional share 07/31/1987
Conv. Class B Common $1 par split (3) for (2) by issuance of (0.5) additional share 07/31/1987
Class A Common $1 par split (2) for (1) by issuance of (1) additional share 09/29/1989
Conv. Class B Common $1 par split (2) for (1) by issuance of (1) additional share 09/29/1989
12.875% Compounding Preferred Ser. A $1 par called for redemption 02/01/1993
Stock Dividend - In Class A Common 100% 07/15/1980
Merged into Tele-Communications, Inc. (New) 08/05/1994
Each share Class A Common $1 par exchanged for (1) share Class A Common $1 par
Each share Conv. Class B Common $1 par exchanged for (1) share Conv. Class B Common $1 par
Tele-Communications, Inc. (New) merged into AT&T Corp. 03/09/1999 which merged into AT&T Inc. 11/18/2005

TELE-COMMUNICATIONS INTL INC (DE)
Merged into Tele-Communications, Inc. (New) 11/19/98
Each share Ser. A Common $1 par exchanged for (0.58) share Liberty Media Group Ser. A Common $1 par
Tele-Communications, Inc. (New) merged into AT&T Corp. 3/9/99 which merged into AT&T Inc. 11/18/2005

TELE DANMARK A/S (DENMARK)
Sponsored ADR's for Class split (2) for (1) by issuance of (1) additional ADR payable 06/07/1999 to holders of record 06/04/1999
Name changed to TDC A/S and Sponsored ADR's for Class B reclassified as Sponsored ADR's for Ordinary 06/27/2001
(See TDC A/S)

TELE DYNAMICS INC (NV)
Name changed to Classic Rarities Inc. 03/06/1987

TELE-FILM ELECTRONICS ENGINEERING CORP. (CO)
Merged into Risk (George) Industries, Inc. 09/01/1966
Each share Common 10¢ par exchanged for (1) share Common 10¢ par

TELE-LAWYER INC (NV)
Merged into Legal Access Technologies, Inc. 6/12/2001
Each share Common $0.001 par exchanged for (1) share Common $0.001 par

TELE-MATIC CORP (CO)
Recapitalized 3/25/92
Recapitalized from Tele-Matic Industries, Inc. to Tele-Matic Corp. 03/25/1992
Each share Common no par exchanged for (0.05) share Common 1¢ par
Name changed to T-NETIX, Inc. (CO) 10/23/1995
T-NETIX, Inc. (CO) reincorporated in Delaware 09/07/2001
(See T-NETIX, Inc.)

TELE METROPOLE INC (QC)
Name changed 07/05/1973
Each share Common $1 par exchanged for (1) share Class A Common 20¢ par and (4) shares Class B Common 20¢ par 04/07/1967
Name changed from Tele-Metropole Corp. to Tele-Metropole Inc. 07/05/1973
Class A Common 20¢ par and Class B 20¢ par changed to no par and (1) additional share issued respectively 08/29/1973
Class A Common no par split (2) for (1) by issuance of (1) additional share 10/15/1980
Class B no par split (2) for (1) by issuance of (1) additional share 10/15/80 10/15/1980
Name changed to TVA Group Inc. 02/17/1998

TELE NORDESTE CELULAR PARTICIPACOES S A (BRAZIL)
Merged into TIM Participacoes S.A. 8/30/2004
Each Sponsored ADR for Preferred no par exchanged for (1.8522) Sponsored ADR's for Preferred no par

TELE NORTE CELULAR PARTICIPACOES S A (BRAZIL)
ADR basis changed from (1:50,000) to (1:1) 08/17/2007
ADR agreement terminated 10/26/2008
Each Sponsored ADR for Preferred exchanged for $14.59482 cash

TELE NORTE LESTE PARTICIPACOES S A (BRAZIL)
ADR basis changed from (1:1,000) to (1:1) 08/30/2004
Each Sponsored ADR for Preferred received distribution of (1) Contax Participacoes S.A. Sponsored ADR for Preferred payable 09/06/2005 to holders of record 08/31/2005 Ex date - 08/30/2005
Merged into Oi S.A. 04/09/2012
Each Sponsored ADR for Preferred exchanged for (0.642) Sponsored ADR for Preferred and (0.1879) Sponsored ADR for Common

TELE-OPTICS INC (DE)
Common 1¢ par changed to Common $0.001 par 10/00/1999
Recapitalized as Velocity Asset Management, Inc. 04/12/2004
Each (13) shares Common $0.001 par exchanged for (1) share Common $0.001 par
Velocity Asset Management, Inc. recapitalized as Velocity Portfolio Group, Inc. 11/17/2008

TELE PAC INTL COMMUNICATIONS CORP (BC)
Name changed to Pacific AD-Link Corp. 12/17/1997
Pacific AD-Link Corp. name changed to Pacific E-Link Corp. 07/15/1999
(See Pacific E-Link Corp.)

TELE RADIO SYS LTD (CANADA)
Discharged from bankruptcy 06/00/1998
No stockholders' equity

TELE SUDESTE CELULAR PARTICIPACOES S A (BRAZIL)
ADR basis changed from (1:5,000) to (1:1) 05/04/2005
Merged into Vivo Participacoes S.A. 03/31/2006
Each Sponsored ADR for Preferred exchanged for (3.2879) Sponsored ADR's for Preferred
Vivo Participacoes S.A. merged into Telecomunicacoes de Sao Paulo S.A. - Telesp 06/07/2011 which name changed to Telefonica Brasil, S.A. 10/11/2011

TELE TALK INC (ON)
Recapitalized as Stackpal International, Inc. 09/12/1995
Each share Common no par exchanged for (0.06666666) share Common no par
Stackpal International, Inc. name changed to Innomat Solutions Corp. 10/09/1997 which recapitalized as Carber Capital Corp. 11/26/1999 which recapitalized as Ba Ba Capital Inc. 08/17/2010 which recapitalized as Imex Systems Inc. 05/13/2016

TELE-TAPE PRODUCTIONS, INC. (DE)
Reincorporated 12/31/1969
Common no par split (2) for (1) by issuance of (1) additional share 08/10/1968

FINANCIAL INFORMATION, INC.   TEL-TEL

State of incorporation changed from (IL) to (DE) 12/31/1969
Name changed to Tele-Tape Corp. 11/30/1970
Tele-Tape Corp. name changed to Teletape Corp. 03/01/1971 which name changed to Reeves Teletape Corp. 11/16/1976 which name changed to Reeves Communications Corp. 12/06/1979
(See Reeves Communications Corp.)

TELE-TONE RADIO TAPE CORP. (NY)
Bankruptcy proceedings instituted 00/00/1952
Stockholders' equity unlikely

TELE-TRIP POLICY CO., INC. (NY)
Name changed to Founders Corp. 8/1/55

TELE-TRONICS CO. (PA)
Reorganized as Winslow Tele-Tronics, Inc. 11/18/63
Each share Common 40¢ par exchanged for (0.2) share Common no par
Winslow Tele-Tronics, Inc. name changed to Winslow Technology, Inc. 5/20/70

TELE 2000 S A (PERU)
Name changed to Bellsouth Peru S.A. 06/19/2000
(See Bellsouth Peru S.A.)

TELE VIDEO COMMUNICATIONS INC (DE)
Name changed to Venture Music Group International, Ltd. 10/19/2001
Venture Music Group International, Ltd. name changed to Standard Holdings Group, Ltd. 2/2/2005

TELE-VIDEO CORP. (DE)
Charter revoked for non-payment of taxes 04/01/1960

TELEAUCTIONS AMER INC (FL)
Name changed to Puma Energy, Inc. (FL) 6/29/98
Puma Energy, Inc. (FL) reincorporated in Delaware as Blue Diamond Ventures, Inc. 10/26/2004

TELEBACKUP EXCHANGECO INC (AB)
Each Exchangeable Share no par exchanged for (5.0589) shares Symantec Corp. Common 1¢ par 03/02/2006

TELEBACKUP SYS INC (AB)
Merged into Telebackup Exchangeco Inc. 06/10/1999
Each share Common no par exchanged for (0.13233) Exchangeable Share no par Telebackup Exchangeco Inc. exchanged for Symantec Corp. 03/02/2006

TELEBANC CAP TR II (DE)
9% Guaranteed Beneficial Unsecured Securities Ser. A called for redemption at $25 on 07/08/2004

TELEBANC FINL CORP (DE)
Secondary Offering - 4,500,000 shares COM offered at $14.50 per share on 07/23/1998
Common 1¢ par split (2) for (1) by issuance of (1) additional share payable 6/8/99 to holders of record 5/28/99
Stock Dividend - 100% payable 6/22/98 to holders of record 5/27/98
Merged into E*Trade Group, Inc. 1/13/2000
Each share Common 1¢ par exchanged for (1.05) shares Common 1¢ par
E*Trade Group, Inc. name changed to E*Trade Financial Corp. 10/1/2003

TELEBEC LTD (QC)
Name changed to Bell Nordiq Group Inc. 04/10/2002
(See Bell Nordiq Group Inc.)

TELEBIT CORP (CA)
Merged into Cisco Systems, Inc. 10/24/1996
Each share Common no par exchanged for $13.35 cash

TELEBYTE INC (DE)
Reincorporated 00/00/1987
Reincorporated 06/28/1999
State of incorporation changed from (NY) to (NV) 00/00/1987
Reincorporated from Telebyte Technology Inc. (NV) to under the laws of Delaware as Telebyte, Inc. 06/28/1999
Merged into TBTIA, Inc. 09/01/2006
Each share Common 1¢ par exchanged for $1.02 cash

TELECAKE INTL INC (NM)
Name changed to First American Investors 1/20/78

TELECAKE INTL INC (UT)
Proclaimed dissolved for failure to pay taxes 02/28/1991

TELECALC INC (WA)
Filed a petition under Chapter 11 Federal Bankruptcy Code 12/22/1989
Stockholders' equity unlikely

TELECASH INDS INC (DE)
Chapter 11 bankruptcy proceedings converted to Chapter 7 on 04/14/1991
No stockholders' equity

TELECAST INC (MI)
Charter declared inoperative and void for failure to file reports 05/15/1992

TELECEL COMUNICACOES PESSOAIS SA (PORTUGAL)
Acquired by Vodafone Group Plc (New) 04/04/2003
Each 144A Sponsored ADR for Ordinary exchanged for approximately $7.90 cash
Each Reg. S Sponsored ADR for Ordinary exchanged for approximately $7.90 cash

TELECHECK INTL INC (DE)
Reincorporated 12/01/1970
Stock Dividend - 50% 03/12/1969
State of incorporation changed from (HI) to (DE) 12/01/1970
Adjudicated bankrupt 05/15/1974
Stockholders' equity unlikely

TELECHIPS CORP (NV)
Each share old Common 1¢ par exchanged for (0.06666666) share new Common 1¢ par 03/07/1997
Chapter 7 bankruptcy proceedings closed 07/28/2004
Stockholders' equity unlikely

TELECHROME MANUFACTURING CORP. (NY)
Name changed to L.I. Chromatel, Inc. 01/03/1962
(See L.I. Chromatel, Inc.)

TELECI INC (TX)
Reincorporated 11/30/1983
State of incorporation changed from (TN) to (TX) 11/30/1983
Charter forfeited for failure to pay taxes 02/15/1994

TELECITY GROUP PLC (UNITED KINGDOM)
Each Unsponsored ADR for Ordinary exchanged for (1) Sponsored ADR for Ordinary 07/30/2010
Merged into Equinix, Inc. 01/15/2016
Each Sponsored ADR for Ordinary exchanged for (0.0672) share new Common $0.001 par and $16.35976 cash

TELECO OILFIELD SVCS INC (DE)
Stock Dividend - 100% 04/15/1981
Merged into Sonat Inc. 02/24/1984
Each share Common $0.001 par exchanged for $17 cash

TELECOIN CORP. (DE)
No longer in existence having become inoperative and void for non-payment of taxes 04/01/1957

TELECOM ARGENTINA STET-FRANCE TELECOM S A (ARGENTINA)
Sponsored ADR's for Class B split (2) for (1) by issuance of (1) additional ADR payable 08/27/1997 to holders of record 08/21/1997 Ex date - 08/28/1997
Name changed to Telecom Argentina S.A. 04/20/2004

TELECOM COMMUNICATIONS INC (DE)
Reincorporated 02/28/2005
State of incorporation changed from (IN) to (DE) 02/28/2005
Name changed to MyStarU.com, Inc. 07/30/2007
MyStarU.com, Inc. recapitalized as Subaye, Inc. 10/26/2009

TELECOM CORP (TX)
Name changed to TCC Industries, Inc. 06/01/1994
(See TCC Industries, Inc.)

TELECOM CORP NEW ZEALAND LTD (NEW ZEALAND)
Sponsored ADR's for Ordinary split (2) for (1) by issuance of (1) additional ADR payable 04/08/1997 to holders of record 04/01/1997
ADR basis changed from (1:8) to (1:5) 09/24/2007
Stock Dividend - 42.22222% payable 09/24/2007 to holders of record 09/21/2007 Ex date - 09/25/2007
Name changed to Spark New Zealand Ltd. 08/08/2014

TELECOM EIREANN (IRELAND)
Name changed to Eircom PLC 09/06/1999
(See Eircom PLC)

TELECOM EQUIPMENT CORP. (NJ)
Common 1¢ par split (3) for (2) by issuance of (0.5) additional share 06/18/1982
Name changed to Telecom Plus International, Inc. 10/01/1982
Telecom Plus International, Inc. name changed to TPI Enterprises, Inc. 04/01/1987 which merged into Shoney's Inc. 09/09/1996
(See Shoney's Inc.)

TELECOM HOLDRS TR (DE)
Trust terminated
Each Depositary Receipt received first and final distribution of $31.773553 cash payable 01/08/2013 to holders of record 12/24/2012

TELECOM ITALIA SPA OLD (ITALY)
Each Sponsored ADR for Ordinary 1000 Lire par received distribution of (0.56) SEAT Pagine Gialle S.p.A. Ordinary share payable 11/20/2000 to holders of record 11/15/2000 Ex date - 11/13/2000
Each Sponsored ADR for Savings 1000 Lire par received distribution of (0.56) SEAT Pagine Gialle S.p.A Ordinary share payable 11/20/2000 to holders of record 11/15/2000 Ex date - 11/13/2000
Note: Option to receive Ordinary expired 11/20/2000 after which time holders received $1.3495 cash per share
Sponsored ADR's for Ordinary 1000 Lire par changed to Euro 0.55 par 05/03/2001
Sponsored ADR's for Savings 1000 Lire par changed to Euro 0.55 par 05/31/2001
Merged into Telecom Italia S.p.A. (New) 08/04/2003
Each Sponsored ADR for Ordinary Euro 0.55 par exchanged for (3.300871) Sponsored ADR's for Ordinary
Each Sponsored ADR for Savings Euro 0.55 par exchanged for (3.300871) Sponsored ADR's for Ordinary

TELECOM MIDWEST CORP. (MO)
Adjudicated bankrupt 05/15/1972
No stockholders' equity

TELECOM PLUS INTL INC (NJ)
Common 1¢ par split (2) for (1) by issuance of (1) additional share 07/29/1983
Name changed to TPI Enterprises, Inc. 04/01/1987
TPI Enterprises, Inc. merged into Shoney's Inc. 09/09/1996
(See Shoney's Inc.)

TELECOM TECHNOLOGIES INC (TN)
Name changed to Precise Positioning Products Inc. and (1) additional share issued 08/02/2002
Precise Positioning Products Inc. recapitalized as Free DA Connection Services, Inc. 02/14/2005 which recapitalized as Earthshine International Ltd. 09/11/2007

TELECOM USA INC (DE)
Preferred Stock Purchase Rights declared for Common stockholders of record 02/15/1990 were redeemed at $0.01 per right 08/15/1990 for holders of record 08/14/1990
Acquired by MCI Communications Corp. 08/14/1990
Each share Common 1¢ par exchanged for $42 cash

TELECOM WIRELESS CORP (UT)
Each share old Common $0.006 par exchanged for (0.2) share new Common $0.006 par 05/04/1999
Reincorporated under the laws of Delaware as TCOM Ventures Corp. 06/15/2000
(See TCOM Ventures Corp.)

TELECOMASIA CORP PUB LTD (THAILAND)
ADR agreement terminated 12/18/2003
Each 144A Sponsored GDR for Ordinary exchanged for $1.373873 cash

TELECOMM COM INC (DE)
Name changed to Lion Capital Holdings, Inc. 07/24/2003
Lion Capital Holdings, Inc. name changed to DeFi Global, Inc. 06/11/2010
(See DeFi Global, Inc.)

TELECOMM INDS INC (DE)
Chapter 11 bankruptcy proceedings terminated 03/13/2002
Stockholders' equity unlikely

TELECOMM SALES NETWORK INC (DE)
Name changed to Anpath Group, Inc. 03/06/2007
Anpath Group, Inc. name changed to Q2Power Technologies, Inc. 12/11/2015 which name changed to Q2Earth, Inc. 08/31/2017

TELECOMMERCE CORP (ON)
Recapitalized as E Ventures Inc. 02/25/1999
Each share Common no par exchanged for (0.1) share Common no par
(See E Ventures Inc.)

TELECOMMUNICATION DESIGNS INC (DE)
Charter cancelled and declared inoperative and void for non-payment of taxes 03/01/1989

TELECOMMUNICATION PRODS INC (CO)
Each share old Common no par exchanged for (0.05) share new Common no par 11/05/2001
Reincorporated under the laws of Delaware as B2Digital, Inc. and Common no par changed to $0.001 par 07/23/2004

TELECOMMUNICATION SYS INC (MD)
Acquired by Comtech Telecommunications Corp. 02/23/2016
Each share Class A Common 1¢ par exchanged for $5 cash

TELECOMMUNICATIONS INDS INC (NY)
Stock Dividend - 100% 03/08/1971
Reorganized under the laws of Delaware as TII Corp. 01/19/1976
Each share Common 1¢ par exchanged for (1) share Common 1¢ par
TII Corp. name changed to TII Industries, Inc. 01/27/1979 which name changed to Tii Network Technologies, Inc. 12/10/2001
(See Tii Network Technologies, Inc.)

TELECOMMUNICATIONS NETWORK INC (DE)
Common 1¢ par split (3) for (2) by issuance of (0.5) additional share 07/10/1986
Merged into Infopage, Inc. 03/28/1990
Each share Common 1¢ par exchanged for $7 cash

TELECOMMUNICATIONS SPECIALISTS INC (DE)
Charter cancelled and declared inoperative and void for non-payment of taxes 03/01/1990

TELECOMMUNICATIONS TECHNOLOGIES LTD (NV)
Recapitalized as PNG Ventures Inc. (Old) 03/04/1998
Each share Common $0.001 par exchanged for (0.025) share Common no par
PNG Ventures Inc. (Old) name changed to Paper Computer Corp. 05/01/2000 which recapitalized as PNG Ventures Inc. (New) 07/05/2001
(See PNG Ventures Inc. (New))

TELECOMPUTING CORP. (CA)
Stock Dividend - 200% 12/15/1952
Name changed to Whittaker Corp. (CA) 05/04/1964
Whittaker Corp. (CA) reincorporated in Delaware 06/16/1986
(See Whittaker Corp. (DE))

TELECOMUNICACOES BRASILEIRAS S A (BRAZIL)
Each Sponsored ADR for Ordinary no par received distribution of (0.2) Tele Centro Sul Participacoes S.A. Sponsored ADR for Preferred no par 11/00/1998
ADR agreement terminated 01/31/2000
Each Sponsored ADR for Ordinary no par exchanged for $0.0101 cash 05/31/2002
Each Sponsored ADR for Preferred received distribution of (0.3333334) Tele Centro Oeste Celular Participacoes S.A. Sponsored ADR for Preferred payable 12/12/2003 to holders of record 12/10/2003 Ex date - 12/15/2003
Each Sponsored ADR for Preferred received distribution of (1) Contax Participacoes S.A. Sponsored ADR for Preferred payable 09/06/2005 to holders of record 08/31/2005 Ex date - 08/30/2005
Each Sponsored ADR for Preferred received distribution of (1) Tele Norte Leste Participacoes S.A. Sponsored ADR for Preferred payable 07/10/2007 to holders of record 07/05/2007 Ex date - 07/11/2007
Each Sponsored ADR for Preferred received distribution of (0.02) Tele Norte Celular Participacoes S.A. Sponsored ADR for Preferred payable 07/30/2008 to holders record 07/28/2008 Ex date - 07/24/2008
Each Sponsored ADR for Preferred received distribution of (0.3032056) Brasil Telecom S.A. Sponsored ADR for Preferred and (0.1720066) Brasil Telecom S.A. Sponsored ADR for Common payable 11/23/2009 to holders of record 11/20/2009 Ex date - 11/24/2009
Each Sponsored ADR for Preferred received distribution of (0.155) Telecomunicacoes de Sao Paulo S.A. Sponsored ADR for Preferred payable 06/15/2011 to holders record 06/10/2011 Ex date - 06/08/2011
ADR agreement terminated 07/15/2011
Each Sponsored ADR for Preferred exchanged for approximately $4.10 cash

TELECOMUNICACOES BRASILEIRAS S A TELEBRAS BASKET (BRAZIL)
ADR agreement terminated 03/19/2001
Each Sponsored ADR for Units exchanged for $34.5378 cash

TELECOMUNICACOES DE SAO PAULO S A - TELESP (BRAZIL)
Each Sponsored ADR for Preferred received distribution of (0.02) Telefonica Data Brasil Holdings S.A. Sponsored ADR for Preferred payable 06/01/2001 to holders of record 05/31/2001 Ex date - 06/07/2001
ADR basis changed from (1:1,000) to (1:1) 06/30/2005
Name changed to Telefonica Brasil, S.A. 10/11/2011

TELECONCEPTS CORP (DE)
Common 10¢ par split (3) for (2) by issuance of (0.5) additional share 07/15/1978
Common 10¢ par split (2) for (1) by issuance of (1) additional share 02/14/1983
Stock Dividends - 25% 07/29/1981; 25% 07/29/1982
Name changed to Virology Testing Sciences, Inc. 10/07/1992
Virology Testing Sciences, Inc. name changed to Viral Testing Systems Corp. 12/31/1992
(See Viral Testing Systems Corp.)

TELECONFERENCING SYS INTL INC (CO)
Recapitalized as GS Telecom Ltd. 01/06/1998
Each share Common no par exchanged for (0.00666666) share Common no par
(See GS Telecom Ltd.)

TELECONNECT CO (IA)
Merged into Telecom USA, Inc. 12/14/1988
Each share Common 7¢ par exchanged for (1) share Common 1¢ par
(See Telecom USA, Inc.)

TELECOR INC. SHAREHOLDERS LIQUIDATING TRUST (DE)
Liquidation completed
Each Share of Bene. Int. 50¢ par received fourth distribution of $0.0275 cash 03/29/1982
Each Share of Bene. Int. 50¢ par received fifth distribution of $0.025 cash 09/27/1982
Each Share of Bene. Int. 50¢ par received sixth and final distribution of $0.169 cash 03/24/1983
Note: Certificates were not required to be surrendered and are without value
(See Telecor, Inc. for previous distributions)

TELECOR INC (DE)
Common 50¢ par split (3) for (2) by issuance of (0.5) additional share 04/28/1972
Common 50¢ par split (3) for (2) by issuance of (0.5) additional share 03/24/1977
Stock Dividend - 50% 02/02/1971
In process of liquidation
Each share Common 50¢ par received initial distribution of $5.60 cash 05/29/1979
Each share Common 50¢ par received second distribution of $1 cash 07/24/1979
Each share Common 50¢ par received third distribution of (1) share Common 50¢ par and $1.786985 principal amount of 10% Subordinated Debentures due 04/01/1994 of Electro Rent Corp. plus $1.21 cash 03/31/1980
Assets transferred to Telecor Inc. Shareholders Liquidating Trust and Common 50¢ par reclassified as Share of Bene. Int. 50¢ par 04/01/1980
(See Telecor Inc. Shareholders Liquidating Trust)

TELECORP INC (ON)
Each share old Common $0.0001 par exchanged for (0.00028571) share new Common $0.0001 par 09/16/2014
Each share new Common $0.0001 par exchanged again for (0.0002) share new Common $0.0001 par 10/14/2016
Reincorporated under the laws of Delaware as Exxe Group Inc. 04/18/2018

TELECORP PCS INC NEW (DE)
Merged into AT&T Wireless Services, Inc. 2/15/2002
Each share Class A Common 1¢ par exchanged for (0.9) share Common 1¢ par
Each share Class A Common 1¢ par received an initial escrow distribution of approximately $0.28 cash payable 12/9/2003 to holders of record 2/15/2002
Each share Class A Common 1¢ par received second distribution of $0.00198159 cash 10/20/2006
(See AT&T Wireless Services, Inc.)

TELECORP PCS INC OLD (DE)
Merged into TeleCorp PCS, Inc. (New) 11/13/2000
Each share Class A Common 1¢ par exchanged for (1) share Common 1¢ par
TeleCorp PCS, Inc. (New) merged into AT&T Wireless Services, Inc. 2/15/2002
(See AT&T Wireless Services, Inc.)

TELECRAFTER CORP (DE)
Name changed to Wegener Corp. 05/09/1989

TELECREDIT INC (DE)
Common 1¢ par split (3) for (2) by issuance of (0.5) additional share 03/12/1981
Common 1¢ par split (2) for (1) by issuance of (1) additional share 03/06/1987
Stock Dividend - 50% 01/27/1983
Merged into Equifax Inc. 12/28/1990
Each share Common 1¢ par exchanged for (2.8625) shares Common $2.50 par

TELECTRO INDUSTRIES CORP. (NY)
Name changed to Pilot Radio-Television Corp. 05/25/1967
Pilot Radio-Television Corp. name changed to Pilot Radio Corp. 11/01/1973
(See Pilot Radio Corp.)

TELECTRO MEK INC (DE)
Charter cancelled and declared inoperative and void for non-payment of taxes 4/15/71

TELEDATA COMMUNICATIONS LTD (ISRAEL)
Acquired by ADC Telecommunications, Inc. 11/05/1998
Each share Ordinary ILS 0.10 par exchanged for $15.75 cash

TELEDATA INC (NY)
Name changed to TDA Industries, Inc. 12/02/1970
(See TDA Industries, Inc.)

TELEDATA INFORMATICS LTD (INDIA)
GDR agreement terminated 11/12/2013
No GDR's remain outstanding

TELEDATA INTL INC (DE)
Each share old Common $0.001 par exchanged for (0.1) share new Common $0.001 par 09/01/1986
Reincorporated under the laws of Utah as US Fax, Inc. 06/15/1987

TELEDATA VENTURES CORP (BC)
Reincorporated under the laws of Yukon as CTF Technologies Inc. 04/06/1998
CTF Technologies Inc. (YT) reincorporated in British Columbia 08/11/2008
(See CTF Technologies Inc.)

TELEDIGITAL INC (DE)
Company terminated registration of common stock and is no longer public as of 09/09/2005

TELEDYNE CDA LTD (ON)
Merged into Teledyne Newco Inc. 11/19/1993
Each share Common no par exchanged for $18.875 cash

TELEDYNE INC (DE)
Capital Stock $1 par reclassified as Common $1 par 10/29/1963
$1 Conv. Preferred Ser. A $1 par called for redemption 04/06/1966
Common $1 par split (2) for (1) by issuance of (1) additional share 07/18/1967
Common $1 par split (2) for (1) by issuance of (1) additional share 03/24/1969
$3.50 Conv. Preferred $1 par called for redemption 07/30/1971
Conv. Preferred Ser. C $1 par called for redemption 01/23/1973
Conv. Preferred Ser. B $1 par called for redemption 11/23/1975
$6 Conv. Preferred $1 par called for redemption 04/26/1978
Common $1 par split (5) for (4) by issuance of (0.25) additional share 04/15/1980
Common $1 par split (3) for (2) by issuance of (0.5) additional share 03/25/1981
Common $1 par split (5) for (1) by issuance of (4) additional shares 03/01/1990
Each share Common $1 par received distribution of (0.01) share Ser. E Preferred $1 par payable 03/08/1996 to holders of record 02/20/1996
Preferred Ser. E $1 par called for redemption 08/14/1996
Stock Dividend - 10% 06/02/1978
Merged into Allegheny Teledyne Inc. 08/15/1996
Each share Common 10¢ par exchanged for (1.925) shares Common 10¢ par
Allegheny Teledyne Inc. name changed to Allegheny Technologies Inc. 11/29/1999

TELEFFICIENCY HLDG CORP (DE)
Recapitalized as Media City Corp. 02/06/2007
Each share Class A Common $0.0001 par exchanged for (0.04) share Class A Common $0.0001 par
Media City Corp. name changed to

Effective Control Transport, Inc. 12/04/2007

TELEFILE COMPUTER CORP (MA)
Proclaimed dissolved for failure to file reports and pay fees 10/19/83

TELEFLEX LTD. (CANADA)
Under plan of liquidation each share Common no par exchanged for (1) share Teleflex Inc. Common no par plus cash 12/20/61

TELEFONICA CZECH REP A S (CZECH REPUBLIC)
GDR agreement terminated 05/15/2015
Each Reg. S Sponsored GDR for Ordinary exchanged for $9.405156 cash
Each Reg. S Sponsored GDR for Ordinary received distribution of $7.063423 cash payable 06/26/2015 to holders of record 05/29/2015 Ex date - 06/29/2015

TELEFONICA DATA BRASIL HLDG SA (BRAZIL)
ADR agreement terminated 10/05/2006
Each Sponsored ADR for Preferred exchanged for (0.663227) Telecomunicacoes de Sao Paulo S.A. - Telesp Sponsored ADR for Preferred and $0.886215 cash
Note: Unexchanged ADR's were sold and holders received $17.62226 cash after 10/05/2007
Telecomunicacoes de Sao Paulo S.A. - Telesp name changed to Telefonica Brasil, S.A. 10/11/2011

TELEFONICA DE ARGENTINA S A (ARGENTINA)
Old Sponsored ADR's for Class B 1 Peso par split (2) for (1) by issuance of (1) additional ADR 02/27/1995
ADR agreement terminated 09/24/1998
Each 144A Sponsored ADR for Class B 1 Peso par exchanged for $40.8579236 cash
Each old Sponsored ADR for Class B 1 Peso par received (0.00303035) share Advance Telecomunicaciones S.A. Ordinary and (1.54105387) shares Telefonica Moviles Argentina S.A. payable 12/12/2001 to holders of record 12/11/2001
Note: Due to no ADR facility being established shares will be sold and proceeds distributed after 12/28/2001
Each old Sponsored ADR for Class B 1 Peso par exchanged for (0.8156) new Sponsored ADR for Class B 1 Peso par 12/12/2001
Acquired by Telefonica, S.A. 01/25/2010
Each new Sponsored ADR for Class B 1 Peso par exchanged for $10.4967591 cash

TELEFONICA DE ESPANA S A (SPAIN)
Name changed to Telefonica, S.A. 4/15/98

TELEFONICA DEL PERU S A (PERU)
Each Sponsored ADR S/100 par received distribution of (1.695457872) shares Telefonica Moviles Peru Holdings S.A.A. Class B payable and (0.121298619) share Telefonica Data Peru S.A.A. Class B payable 12/31/2001 to holders of record 6/15/2001 or $0.2791 cash
Note: Option to receive shares expired 6/25/2001
Each old Sponsored ADR S/100 par exchanged for (0.8183252) new Sponsored ADR S/100 6/19/2001
ADR agreement terminated 2/27/2004
Each Sponsored ADR for Class B S/100 par exchanged for $3.56282 cash

TELEFONICA MOVILES S A (SPAIN)
Issue Information - 300,000,000 SPONSORED ADR's offered at $9.3346 per ADR on 11/21/2000
Merged into Telefonica, S.A. 7/29/2006
Each Sponsored ADR for Ordinary exchanged for (0.26666666) Sponsored ADR for Ordinary P500 par

TELEFONICA O2 CZECH REP A S (CZECH REPUBLIC)
Name changed to Telefonica Czech Republic, A.S. 06/10/2011
(See Telefonica Czech Republic, A.S.)

TELEFONOS DE MEXICO S A B DE C V (MEXICO)
Name changed 12/05/2006
ADR's for Bearer Shares P100 par reclassified as ADR's for Nominative Shares P100 par 03/31/1980
ADR's for Nominative Shares P100 par split (2) for (1) by issuance of (1) additional ADR payable 02/04/2000 holders of record 01/31/2000
Sponsored ADR's for Ser. L no par split (2) for (1) by issuance of (1) additional ADR payable 02/04/2000 to holders of record 01/31/2000
Each ADR for Nominative Shares P100 par exchanged for (0.05) Sponsored ADR for Ser A P100 par 12/04/2000
Each Sponsored ADR for Ser. A no par received distribution of (1) America Movil Sponsored ADR for Ordinary L payable 02/07/2001 to holders of record 02/06/2001 Ex date - 02/08/2001
Each Sponsored ADR for Ordinary L no par received distribution of (1) America Movil Sponsored ADR for Ordinary L payable 02/07/2001 to holders of record 02/06/2001 Ex date - 02/08/2001
Sponsored ADR's for Ser. A no par split (2) for (1) by issuance of (1) additional ADR payable 05/27/2005 to holders of record 05/24/2005 Ex date - 05/31/2005
Sponsored ADR's for Ser. L no par split (2) for (1) by issuance of (1) additional ADR payable 05/27/2005 to holders of record 05/24/2005 Ex date - 05/31/2005
Stock Dividend - 20% 07/29/1977
Name changed from Telefonos de Mexico, S.A. de C.V. to Telefonos de Mexico, S.A.B. de C.V. 12/05/2006
Each Sponsored ADR for Ser. A no par received distribution of (1) Telmex Internacional, S.A.B. de C.V. Sponsored ADR for Ser. A no par payable 06/10/2008 to holders of record 06/09/2008 Ex date - 06/11/2008
Each Sponsored ADR for Ser. L no par received distribution of (1) Telmex Internacional, S.A.B. de C.V. Sponsored ADR for Ser. L no par payable 06/10/2008 to holders of record 06/09/2008 Ex date - 06/11/2008
ADR agreement terminated 01/30/2012
Each Sponsored ADR for Ser. A no par exchanged for $16.1076 cash
Each Sponsored ADR for Ser. L no par exchanged for $16.1076 cash

TELEGEN CORP (CA)
Each share old Common no par exchanged for (0.0625) share new Common no par 10/03/2000
Name changed to Vu1 Corp. 06/05/2008

TELEGENERAL CORP (DE)
Charter cancelled and declared inoperative and void for non-payment of taxes 03/01/1978

TELEGIFT INTERNATIONAL, INC. (UT)
Name changed to Turbotron Corp. 08/11/1972

TELEGLOBE INC (CANADA)
Conv. 2nd Preferred Ser. 81 no par called for redemption at $25 plus $0.00548 accrued dividends on 05/02/1997
Common no par split (2) for (1) by issuance of (1) additional share payable 06/16/1998 to holders of record 06/15/1998 Ex date - 06/17/1998
Acquired by BCE Inc. 11/01/2000
Each share Common no par exchanged for (0.907) share Common no par and $0.10 cash
5.4% Ser. Conv. 3rd Preferred called for redemption at $25 plus $0.2219 accrued dividends on 04/02/2001

TELEGLOBE INTL HLDGS LTD (BERMUDA)
Acquired by Videsh Sanchar Nigam Ltd. 02/13/2006
Each share Common U.S. $0.01 par exchanged for $4.50 cash

TELEGRAPH COMMUNICATIONS LTD (ISRAEL)
Name changed to Hilan Tech Ltd. 11/01/2000

TELEGRAPH GOLD CORP (UT)
Proclaimed dissolved for failure to pay taxes 01/01/1995

TELEGRAPH SVGS & LN ASSN (IL)
Closed by Federal Savings & Loan Insurance Corp. 05/23/1980
No stockholders' equity

TELEGROUP INC (IA)
Plan of reorganization under Chapter 11 Federal Bankruptcy Code effective 03/20/2000
No stockholders' equity

TELEGUARD SYS INTL INC (BC)
Struck from the register and dissolved 05/01/1992

TELEHEALTHCARE INC (WY)
Common $0.001 par split (3) for (1) by issuance of (2) additional shares payable 06/22/2016 to holders of record 05/07/2016 Ex date - 06/23/2016
Name changed to XSport Global, Inc. 06/05/2018

TELEHOP COMMUNICATIONS INC (ON)
Name changed to ADYA Inc. 02/10/2017

TELEHUBLINK CORP (DE)
SEC revoked common stock registration 10/15/2010
Stockholders' equity unlikely

TELEKOMUNIKACJA POLSKA S A (POLAND)
Name changed to Orange Polska S.A. 01/24/2014
(See Orange Polska S.A.)

TELELESTE CELULAR PARTICIPACOES S A (BRAZIL)
ADR basis changed from (1:50,000) to (1:1) 05/04/2005
Merged into Vivo Participacoes S.A. 03/31/2006
Each Sponsored ADR for Preferred exchanged for (3.8998) Sponsored ADR's for Preferred
Vivo Participacoes S.A. merged into Telecomunicacoes de Sao Paulo S.A. - Telesp 06/07/2011 which name changed to Telefonica Brasil, S.A. 10/11/2011

TELELINK COMMUNICATIONS CORP NEW (BC)
Reorganized under the laws of Canada as Ignition Point Technologies Corp. 04/20/2001
Each share Common no par exchanged for (1/3) share Common no par
Ignition Point Technologies Corp. recapitalized as Tilting Capital Corp. 08/24/2009

TELELINK COMMUNICATIONS CORP OLD (BC)
Merged into Telelink Communications Corp. (New) (BC) 08/01/1996
Each share Common no par exchanged for (1) share Common no par
Telelink Communications Corp. (New) (BC) reorganized in Canada as Ignition Point Technologies Corp. 04/20/2001 which recapitalized as Tilting Capital Corp. 08/24/2009

TELEMAC CELLULAR INTL INC (BC)
Name changed to Cancall Cellular Communications Inc. 12/06/1994
(See Cancall Cellular Communications Inc.)

TELEMAIS TELECOMMUNICATIONS INC (NV)
Each share old Common $0.001 par exchanged for (0.01) share new Common $0.001 par 05/17/2002
Each share new Common $0.001 par exchanged again for (0.05) share new Common $0.001 par 10/11/2002
Recapitalized as WebSky, Inc. 01/20/2004
Each share new Common $0.001 par exchanged for (0.1) share Common $0.001 par

TELEMALL COMMUNICATIONS INC (NV)
Recapitalized as Stein's Holdings, Inc. 04/22/1999
Each share Common $0.001 par exchanged for (0.005) share Common $0.001 par
Stein's Holdings, Inc. name changed to Crown Partners Inc. 01/22/2002 which recapitalized as TaxMasters, Inc. 08/12/2009
(See TaxMasters, Inc.)

TELEMATE NET SOFTWARE INC (GA)
Merged into Verso Technologies, Inc. 11/19/2001
Each share Common 1¢ par exchanged for (2.62) shares Common 1¢ par
(See Verso Technologies, Inc.)

TELEMATICS INTL INC (DE)
Merged into ECI Telecom Ltd. 12/22/1993
Each share Common 1¢ par exchanged for (0.66) share Ordinary NIS0.12 par
(See ECI Telecom Ltd.)

TELEMATION INC (NV)
Stock Dividend - 300% 10/24/1986
Name changed to TLM Corp. 06/30/1989
(See TLM Corp.)

TELEMAX GLOBAL COMMUNICATIONS INC (WA)
Each share old Common no par exchanged for (0.01) share new Common no par 11/16/2005
Name changed to ICBS, Ltd. 06/01/2006

TELEMED CORP (MD)
Common 5¢ par split (5) for (4) by issuance of (0.25) additional share 12/15/1976
Stock Dividends - 100% 12/30/1974; 20% 01/29/1976
Merged into Becton, Dickinson & Co. 02/22/1979
Each share Common 5¢ par exchanged for (0.229) share Common $1 par

TELEMEDIA INC (CANADA)
Acquired by Telemedia Acquisition 10/31/1997
Each share Class A Subordinate no par exchanged for $7.50 cash

TELEMEDIA INTL INC (CO)
Name changed to Precision Micro-Devices, Inc. 12/31/1986

TELEMEDICUS INC (TX)
Recapitalized as National Wind Solutions Inc. 10/01/2008
Each share Common $0.001 par exchanged for (0.05) share Common $0.001 par
National Wind Solutions Inc. recapitalized as National Clean Fuels Inc. 03/17/2010 which recapitalized as Quantum International Corp. 01/20/2012

TELEMET, INC. (NJ)
Charter cancelled and became void for non-payment of taxes 03/27/1972

TELEMETER MAGNETICS, INC. (NY)
Merged into Ampex Corp. 12/30/1960
Each share Common 10¢ par exchanged for (0.5) share Common $1 par
Ampex Corp. merged into Signal Companies, Inc. 01/15/1981 which merged into Allied-Signal Inc. 09/19/1985 which name changed to AlliedSignal Inc. 04/26/1993 which name changed to Honeywell International Inc. 12/01/1999

TELEMETRIX INC (DE)
Chapter 11 bankruptcy proceedings dismissed 03/11/2009
No stockholders' equity

TELEMETRY CTLS INC (FL)
Proclaimed dissolved for failure to file reports and pay fees 08/13/1993

TELEMIG CELULAR PARTICIPACOES S A (BRAZIL)
ADR basis changed from (1:20,000) to to (1:2) 08/14/2007
Merged into Vivo Participacoes S.A. 09/04/2009
Each Sponsored ADR for Preferred exchanged for (2.74) Sponsored ADR's for Preferred
Vivo Participacoes S.A. merged into Telecomunicacoes de Sao Paulo S.A. - Telesp 06/07/2011 which name changed to Telefonica Brasil, S.A. 10/11/2011

TELEMINE INC (NY)
Each share old Common 1¢ par exchanged for (0.05) share new Common 1¢ par 11/01/1994
Name changed to Comedco Inc. 04/03/1995
(See Comedco Inc.)

TELEMONDE INC (DE)
Reincorporated 11/09/1999
State of incorporation changed from (NV) to (DE) 11/09/1999
SEC revoked common stock registration 11/16/2005

TELEMUNDO GROUP INC NEW (DE)
Reorganized 12/30/1994
Telemundo Group, Inc. (Old) reorganized under Chapter 11 of the Federal Bankruptcy Code effective 12/30/1994
No stockholders' equity
Merged into Sony Pictures Entertainment, Inc. 08/12/1998
Each share Class A Common 1¢ par exchanged for $44.12537 cash
Each share Class B Common 1¢ par exchanged for $44.12537 cash

TELENET CORP (DE)
Merged into General Telephone & Electronics Corp. 06/13/1979
Each share Common $1 par exchanged for (0.7652) share Common $3.33333333 par
General Telephone & Electronics Corp. name changed to GTE Corp. 07/01/1982 which merged into Verizon Communications Inc. 06/30/2000

TELENETICS CORP (CA)
Each share old Common no par exchanged for (0.2) share new Common no par 01/08/1999

SEC revoked common stock registration 04/30/2010

TELEON CORP (FL)
Each share old Common $0.0001 par exchanged for (0.01) share new Common $0.0001 par 06/14/2004
Name changed to Auto Centrix Inc. 06/21/2004
Auto Centrix Inc. recapitalized as Greenstone Holdings, Inc. 01/03/2006
(See Greenstone Holdings, Inc.)

TELE1 EUROPE HLDG AB (SWEDEN)
Name changed to Song Networks Holding AB 06/21/2001
(See Song Networks Holding AB)

TELEPAD CORP (DE)
Plan of reorganization under Chapter 11 Federal Bankruptcy Code effective 11/08/1999
No stockholders' equity

TELEPANEL SYS INC (CANADA)
Recapitalized 07/12/1989
Recapitalized from Telepanel, Inc. to Telepanel Systems Inc. 07/12/1989
Each share Common no par exchanged for (0.02127659) share Common no par
Filed a proposal under the Bankruptcy and Insolvency Act 11/17/2005
No stockholders' equity

TELEPARTNER A/S (DENMARK)
Name changed to Euro909.com A/S 10/18/1999
Euro909.com A/S name changed to EuroTrust A/S 12/10/2001
(See EuroTrust A/S)

TELEPHONE & DATA SYS INC (DE)
Reincorporated 05/22/1998
Common $1 par split (3) for (2) by issuance of (0.5) additional share 03/17/1988
Common $1 par split (3) for (2) by issuance of (0.5) additional share 12/16/1988
State of incorporation changed from (IA) to (DE), Common $1 par and Ser. A Common $1 par changed to 1¢ par 05/22/1998
Preferred Ser. EE called for redemption 04/05/2017
Preferred Ser. OO called for redemption 04/05/2017
(Additional Information in Active)

TELEPHONE & ELECTRONICS CORP. (NJ)
Adjudicated bankrupt in August 1962
No stockholders' equity

TELEPHONE BOND & SHARE CO. (DE)
Each share 7% 1st Preferred $100 par exchanged for (5) shares 5% Preferred $20 par and (5) shares Common $1 par in 1953
Each share $4 Part. Preferred no par exchanged for (6) shares 5% Preferred $20 par in 1953
Each share Class A Common no par exchanged for (1) share 5% Preferred $20 par and (1) share Common $1 par in 1953
Name changed to Continental Telephone Co. (Old) 2/11/55
Continental Telephone Co. (Old) merged into General Telephone Corp. 8/8/56 which name changed to General Telephone & Electronics Corp. 3/5/59 which name changed to GTE Corp. 7/1/82 which merged into Verizon Communications Inc. 6/30/2000

TELEPHONE CO., INC. (UT)
Name changed to Beehive Telephone Co., Inc. 11/16/77

TELEPHONE EMPLOYEES INSURANCE CO. (MD)
Common $10 par changed to $2.50 par and (3) additional shares issued 4/16/62

Merged into Bankers & Telephone Employees Insurance Co. on a (0.5) for (1) basis 12/31/63
(See Bankers & Telephone Employees Insurance Co.)

TELEPHONE EMPLOYEES LIFE INSURANCE CO. (MD)
Under plan of merger, each share Capital Stock $10 par exchanged for (1) share Capital Stock $5 par 9/20/63
Name changed to First Federated Life Insurance Co. (New) 9/30/63
(See First Federated Life Insurance Co. (New))

TELEPHONE EXPRESS CORP (SD)
Charter cancelled for failure to file annual reports 7/1/92

TELEPHONE INVESTMENT CORP.
Liquidated 00/00/1937
Details not available

TELEPHONE SECURITIES, INC. (NJ)
Common $50 par changed to $1 par 00/00/1932
Dissolved 00/00/1944
Details not available

TELEPHONE SERVICE CO. OF OHIO (DE)
Class A Common $1 par and Class B Common $1 par split (8) for (1) respectively by issuance of (7) additional shares 07/15/1960
Class A Common $1 par and Class B Common $1 par split (2) for (1) respectively by issuance of (1) additional share 07/15/1964
$5 Preferred $5 par called for redemption 09/30/1965
Acquired by United Utilities, Inc. 01/25/1967
Each share Class A Common $1 par or Class B Common $1 par exchanged for (1.3) shares Common $2.50 par
United Utilities, Inc. name changed to United Telecommunications, Inc. 06/02/1972 which name changed to Sprint Corp. (KS) 02/26/1992 which name changed to Sprint Nextel Corp. 08/12/2005 which merged into Sprint Corp. (DE) 07/10/2013

TELEPHONE SPECIALISTS INC (MN)
Statutorily dissolved 12/30/94

TELEPHONE SUPPORT SYS INC (NY)
Proclaimed dissolved 12/29/99

TELEPHONE UTILS INC (WA)
Common $1 par split (5) for (4) by issuance of (0.25) additional share 3/10/66
Name changed to Pacific Telecom, Inc. 4/26/82
(See Pacific Telecom, Inc.)

TELEPHONE UTILS PA INC (PA)
5% Preferred Ser. A $50 par called for redemption 03/14/1979
Merged into Mid-Continent Telephone Corp. 07/12/1979
Each share Common 50¢ par exchanged for $35 cash
Each share Class A Common 50¢ par exchanged for (1) share $2.25 Conv. Preferred Ser. D no par
Mid-Continent Telephone Corp. name changed to Alltel Corp. (OH) 10/25/1983 which reincorporated in Delaware 05/15/1990
(See Alltel Corp.)

TELEPHONES, INC. (IA)
Merged into Continental Telephone Corp. 4/15/66
Each share Common $1 par exchanged for (1) share Common $1 par
Continental Telephone Corp. name changed to Continental Telecom Inc. 5/6/82 which name changed to Contel Corp. 5/1/86 which merged into GTE Corp. 3/14/91 which

merged into Verizon Communications Inc. 6/30/2000

TELEPHONY COMMUNICATIONS INTL INC (ON)
Delisted from Alberta Stock Exchange 05/22/1991

TELEPICTURES CORP (NY)
Common 1¢ par split (3) for (2) by issuance of (0.5) additional share 09/30/1985
Under plan of merger name changed to Lorimar-Telepictures Corp. 02/18/1986
Lorimar-Telepictures Corp. acquired by Warner Communications Inc. 01/11/1989 which merged into Time Warner Inc. (Old) 01/10/1990 which merged into AOL Time Warner Inc. 01/11/2001 which name changed to Time Warner Inc. (New) 10/16/2003 which merged into AT&T Inc. 06/15/2018

TELEPIZZA S A (SPAIN)
ADR agreement terminated 03/05/2007
Each Sponsored ADR for Ordinary exchanged for $4.21512 cash

TELEPLUS CONSUMER SVCS INC (NV)
Reincorporated 04/10/2003
State of incorporation changed from (CO) to (NV) 04/10/2003
Recapitalized as Scrip Advantage, Inc. 01/05/2005
Each share Common $0.001 par exchanged for (0.4) share Common $0.001 par
(See Scrip Advantage, Inc.)

TELEPLUS WORLD CORP (NV)
Name changed 10/30/2006
Name changed from Teleplus Enterprises, Inc. to Teleplus World, Corp. 10/30/2006
Chapter 11 bankruptcy proceedings dismissed 08/10/2009
No stockholders' equity

TELEPORT COMMUNICATIONS GROUP INC (DE)
Merged into AT&T Corp. 7/24/98
Each share Class A Common 1¢ par exchanged for (0.943) share Common $1 par
AT&T Corp. merged into AT&T Inc. 11/18/2005

TELEPOST COMMUNICATIONS INC (BC)
Delisted from Toronto Venture Stock Exchange 04/20/2004

TELEPRO INDS INC (NJ)
Each share Common 1¢ par exchanged for (0.125) share Common 8¢ par 11/01/1973
Name changed to Harvel Industries Corp. 05/30/1975
(See Harvel Industries Corp.)

TELEPROBE SYS INC (DE)
Under plan of reorganization name changed to Intercom Systems, Inc. and Common 1¢ par changed to $0.0005 par 10/31/1989
(See Intercom Systems, Inc.)

TELEPROMPTER CORP (NY)
Common $1 par split (5) for (2) by issuance of (1.5) additional shares 7/26/57
Common $1 par split (4) for (1) by issuance of (3) additional shares 3/24/72
Each Ctf. of Right (issued per merger of State Investors, Inc.) exchanged for (1/44) share Common $1 par or $2.272 cash 3/14/74
Merged into Westinghouse Electric Corp. 8/18/81
Each share Common $1 par exchanged for $38 cash

TELEQUEST INC (CA)
Charter cancelled for failure to file reports and pay taxes 3/2/92

TELEQUIPMENT INC (NV)
Name changed to Green Dolphin Systems Corp. 09/00/1999
Green Dolphin Systems Corp. name changed to Home/Office Express, Inc. 02/25/2000 which name changed to IAMG Holdings, Inc. 04/27/2000 which name changed to Curv Entertainment Group, Inc. 11/26/2007 which name changed to SuperBox, Inc. 09/01/2011

TELERAM COMMUNICATIONS CORP (NY)
Chapter 11 bankruptcy proceedings converted to Chapter 7 on 10/16/85
Stockholders' equity unlikely

TELERATE INC (DE)
Common 1¢ par split (2) for (1) by issuance of (1) additional share 10/13/87
Merged into Dow Jones & Co., Inc. 1/3/90
Each share Common 1¢ par exchanged for $21 cash

TELEREGISTER CORP (DE)
Name changed to Bunker-Ramo Corp. (Old) 7/9/64
Bunker-Ramo Corp. (Old) merged into Bunker Ramo Corp. (New) 6/3/68 which merged into Allied Corp. 7/31/81 which merged into Allied-Signal Inc. 9/19/85 which name changed to AlliedSignal Inc. 4/26/93 which name changed to Honeywell International Inc. 12/1/99

TELERENT LEASING CORP (DE)
Stock Dividends - 25% 3/19/76; 10% 3/14/80
Merged into Aviation Group, Inc. 1/19/84
Each share Common 50¢ par exchanged for $13.75 cash

TELERGY INC (UT)
Merged out of existence 1/8/98
Details not available

TELESCAN INC (DE)
Merged into INVESTools Inc. 12/06/2001
Each share Common $0.0001 par exchanged for (0.55531) share Common 1¢ par
INVESTools Inc. name changed to thinkorswim Group Inc. 06/06/2008 which merged into TD AMERITRADE Holding Corp. 06/11/2009

TELESCENE FILM GROUP INC (CANADA)
Filed a Notice of Intention to make a Proposal under the Bankruptcy and Insolvency Act 12/01/2000
Details not available

TELESCIENCES INC (DE)
Each share old Common 1¢ par exchanged for (0.25) share new Common 1¢ par 10/15/1999
Merged into EDB Business Partner ASA 12/09/1999
Each share new Common 1¢ par exchanged for $8.79 cash

TELESCIENCES INC (NJ)
Name changed to Marlton Technologies, Inc. (NJ) 1/18/88
Marlton Technologies, Inc. (NJ) reincorporated in Pennsylvania 11/20/2001
(See Marlton Technologies, Inc. (PA))

TELESCRIPT-CSP INC. (NY)
Name changed to Telescript Industries Corp. 4/26/84
(See Telescript Industries Corp.)

TELESCRIPT INDS CORP (NY)
Each share old Common 1¢ par exchanged for (0.1) share new Common 1¢ par 10/15/87
Charter cancelled and proclaimed dissolved for failure to pay taxes 3/24/93

TELESELL, LTD. (OK)
Charter suspended for failure to file reports and pay fees 2/28/75

TELESERVICES INTERNET GROUP INC (FL)
Name changed 07/12/1999
Name changed from Teleservices International Group, Inc. to Teleservices Internet Group, Inc. 07/12/1999
Each share old Common $0.0001 par exchanged for (0.1) share new Common $0.0001 par 06/23/2000
Recapitalized as Opus Magnum Ameris, Inc. 02/16/2012
Each share new Common $0.0001 par exchanged for (0.01) share Common $0.0001 par
(See Opus Magnum Ameris, Inc.)

TELESHARES INC (DE)
Charter cancelled and declared inoperative and void for non-payment of taxes 3/1/79

TELESIS COMPUTER NETWORKING INC (BC)
Recapitalized as NT Network Systems Inc. 8/9/93
Each share Common no par exchanged for (0.25) share Common no par
NT Network Systems Inc. recapitalized as Network Telemetrics Ltd. 1/12/96 which name changed to Belvedere Resources Ltd. 10/14/97

TELESIS INC (AB)
Recapitalized as P.C. Ventures Ltd. 02/23/1989
Each share Common no par exchanged for (0.1) share Common no par
(See P.C. Ventures Ltd.)

TELESIS INDL GROUP INC (AB)
Name changed to Merendon Canada Inc. 10/09/1998
Merendon Canada Inc. recapitalized as Richfield Explorations Inc. 03/08/2000
(See Richfield Explorations Inc.)

TELESIS NORTH COMMUNICATIONS INC (BC)
Delisted from Toronto Venture Stock Exchange 06/16/2004

TELESIS SYS CORP (DE)
Merged into Valid Logic Systems Inc. (DE) 05/11/1987
Each share Common 10¢ par exchanged for (0.925) share Common no par
Valid Logic Systems Inc. (DE) merged into Cadence Design Systems Inc. 12/31/1991

TELESIS TECHNOLOGY CORP (FL)
Reorganized under the laws of Nevada as Iteknik Holding Corp. 01/31/2007
Each share Common $0.001 par exchanged for (0.02) share Common $0.0001 par
Iteknik Holding Corp. (NV) reincorporated in Wyoming 11/30/2010

TELESOFT CORP (AZ)
Each (110,000) shares old Common no par exchanged for (1) share new Common no par 12/10/2003
Note: In effect holders received $1.82 cash per share and public interest was eliminated

TELESOURCE INTL INC (DE)
Name changed to Pernix Group, Inc. 11/18/2009

TELESP CELULAR PARTICIPACOES S A (BRAZIL)
ADR basis changed from (1:2,500) to (1:1) 05/04/2005
Name changed to Vivo Participacoes S.A. 03/31/2006
Vivo Participacoes S.A. merged into Telecomunicacoes de Sao Paulo S.A. - Telesp 06/07/2011 which name changed to Telefonica Brasil, S.A. 10/11/2011

TELESP PARTICIPACOES S A (BRAZIL)
Name changed to Telecomunicacoes de Sao Paulo S.A. - Telesp 01/10/2000
Telecomunicacoes de Sao Paulo S.A. - Telesp name changed to Telefonica Brasil, S.A. 10/11/2011

TELESPACE LTD (DE)
Each share old Common $0.00001 par exchanged for (0.125) share new Common $0.00001 par 08/03/1999
Name changed to Qinnet.com, Inc. 01/10/2000
Qinnet.com, Inc. name changed to Q-Net Technologies, Inc. 08/13/2001
(See Q-Net Technologies, Inc.)

TELESPECTRUM WORLDWIDE INC (DE)
Each share old Common 1¢ par exchanged for (0.001) share new Common 1¢ par 03/17/2003
Note: In effect holders received $10 cash per share and public interest was eliminated

TELESPHERE COMMUNICATIONS INC (DE)
Name changed 09/27/1989
Common 1¢ par split (3) for (2) by issuance of (0.5) additional share 09/17/1981
Common 1¢ par split (3) for (2) by issuance of (0.5) additional share 11/13/1981
Stock Dividend - 50% 01/10/1983
Name changed from Telesphere International, Inc. to Telesphere Communications, Inc. 09/27/1989
Plan of reorganization under Chapter 11 Federal Bankruptcy proceedings confirmed 05/17/1994
No stockholders' equity

TELESSO TECHNOLOGIES LTD (AUSTRALIA)
ADR agreement terminated 04/16/2018
No ADR holders' equity

TELESTA THERAPEUTICS INC (CANADA)
Merged into ProMetic Life Sciences Inc. 11/01/2016
Each share Common no par exchanged for (0.04698) share Common no par
Note: Unexchanged certificates will be cancelled and become without value 11/01/2022

TELESTONE TECHNOLOGIES CORP (DE)
SEC revoked common stock registration 12/21/2016

TELESTUDIOS, INC. (NY)
Merged into National Telefilm Associates, Inc. (NY) 07/20/1959
Each share Class A 10¢ par exchanged for (0.1944) share Common 10¢ par
National Telefilm Associates, Inc. (NY) reorganized in Delaware as Republic Pictures Corp. 12/28/1984
(See Republic Pictures Corp. (DE))

TELESYSTEM INTL WIRELESS INC (CANADA)
Each old Subordinate no par exchanged for (0.2) share new Subordinate no par 06/27/2001
New Subordinate no par reclassified as Common no par 05/17/2002
Each share old Common no par exchanged for (0.2) share new Common no par 06/30/2003
Liquidation completed
Each share new Common no par received initial distribution of $17.01 cash payable 09/27/2005 to holders of record 09/08/2005 Ex date - 09/06/2005
Each share new Common no par received second distribution of $1.79 cash payable 09/27/2005 to holders of record 09/21/2005 Ex date - 09/19/2005
Each share new Common no par received third and final distribution of $1.1614 cash payable 01/31/2006 to holders of record 12/14/2005 Ex date - 12/12/2005
Note: Certificates were not required to be surrendered and are without value

TELESYSTEM TELECOM LTD (QC)
1% Ranking Preferred 1st Ser. no par called for redemption at $25 on 10/05/1998
Public interest eliminated

TELETAPE CORP (DE)
Name changed 03/01/1971
Name changed from Tele-Tape Corp. to Teletape Corp. 03/01/1971
Name changed to Reeves Teletape Corp. 11/16/1976
Reeves Teletape Corp. name changed to Reeves Communications Corp. 12/06/1979
(See Reeves Communications Corp.)

TELETEC DEV INC (BC)
Name changed to Great Weighs! Industries Inc. 04/27/1987
(See Great Weighs! Industries Inc.)

TELETECH HLDGS INC (DE)
Name changed to TTEC Holdings, Inc. 01/10/2018

TELETEK INC (NV)
Reincorporated 04/09/1993
Each share Common 1¢ par exchanged for (0.1) share old Common $0.0001 par 05/27/1988
Each share old Common $0.0001 par exchanged for (0.03333333) share new Common $0.0001 par 07/20/1992
State of incorporation changed from (CO) to (NV) 04/09/1993
Each share new Common $0.0001 par exchanged again for (0.05) share new Common $0.0001 par 10/07/1993
Recapitalized as Trans Global Group, Inc. (NV) 10/15/2007
Each share Common $0.0001 par exchanged for (0.0025) share Common $0.0001 par
Trans Global Group, Inc. (NV) reincorporated in Florida 03/28/2014

TELETEK LTD (DE)
Name changed to Black Warrior Wireline Corp. 06/22/1989
Black Warrior Wireline Corp. name changed to Warrior Energy Services Corp. 02/08/2006 which merged into Superior Energy Services, Inc. 12/12/2006

TELETIMER INTL INC (DE)
Each share old Common $0.001 par exchanged for (0.1) share new Common $0.001 par 03/31/1989
Charter cancelled and declared inoperative and void for non-payment of taxes 03/01/2002

TELETOUCH COMMUNICATIONS INC (DE)
Each share old Common $0.001 par exchanged for (0.66666666) share new Common $0.001 par 06/25/1998
Filed a petition under Chapter 7 Federal Bankruptcy Code 10/03/2013
Stockholders' equity unlikely

TELETRAK ADVANCED TECHNOLOGY SYS INC (DE)
Recapitalized as Teletrak Environmental Systems Inc. 09/28/1998
Each share Common 1¢ par

TEL-TEL FINANCIAL INFORMATION, INC.

exchanged for (0.1) share Common $0.001 par and (0.5) Common Stock Purchase Warrant expiring 00/00/2001

TELETRANS INDS INC (DE)
Charter cancelled and declared inoperative and void for non-payment of taxes 03/01/1982

TELETRAY ELECTRONIC SYSTEMS, INC. (MD)
Stock Dividend - 33.33333333% 12/22/1960
Charter revoked for failure to file reports and pay fees 12/01/1964

TELETRONICS, INC. (WA)
Charter cancelled and declared dissolved for failure to pay fees 07/01/1973

TELETRONICS INC (DE)
Name changed to National Integrated Industries, Inc. 01/11/1974

TELETRONICS INDS INC (DE)
Charter cancelled and declared inoperative and void for non-payment of taxes 04/15/1972

TELETRONICS INTL INC (DE)
Stock Dividend - 10% 01/31/1977
Name changed to Video Corp. of America 12/20/1977
(See Video Corp. of America)

TELE2 AB (SWEDEN)
ADR agreement terminated 04/25/2005
Each Sponsored ADR for Class A share SEK5 par exchanged for $34.50176 cash
Each Sponsored ADR for Class B share SEK5 par exchanged for $34.79347 cash
(Additional Information in Active)

TELETYPE CORP. OF CHICAGO
Acquired by American Telephone & Telegraph Co. 00/00/1930
Details not available

TELEVIDEO INC (DE)
Each share old Common 1¢ par exchanged for (0.25) share new Common 1¢ par 04/22/1998
Plan of reorganization under Chapter 11 Federal Bankruptcy Code effective 07/28/2006
No stockholders' equity

TELEVISION & ELECTRIC CORP. OF AMERICA (DE)
No longer in existence having become inoperative and void for non-payment of taxes 04/01/1939

TELEVISION & RADAR CORP. (DE)
Name changed to Plastoid Corp. of America 09/09/1961
Plastoid Corp. of America name changed to Plastoid Cable Corp. of America 06/18/1964 which name changed to Cable Liquidation Corp. 02/10/1969 which liquidated for Babbitt (B.T.), Inc. 03/04/1969 which name changed to B.T.B. Corp. 12/05/1969 which name changed to International Banknote Co., Inc. 01/02/1973 which merged into United States Banknote Corp. (NY) 07/25/1990 which reincorporated in Delaware 09/21/1993 which name changed to to American Banknote Corp. 07/03/1995
(See American Banknote Corp.)

TELEVISION & RADIO BROADCASTING CORP (DE)
Merged into Patriot Broadcasting Corp. 02/24/1984
Each share Common 10¢ par exchanged for $1.23 cash

TELEVISION COMMUNICATIONS CORP (DE)
Merged into Kinney Services, Inc. 01/31/1972
Each share Capital Stock $1 par exchanged for (0.32) share Common $1 par
Kinney Services, Inc. name changed to Warner Communications Inc. 02/11/1972
(See Warner Communications Inc.)

TELEVISION CONCEPTS 3 INC (NV)
Each share old Common $0.001 par exchanged for (0.00005) share new Common $0.001 par 07/15/1996
Note: In effect holders received $0.01125 cash per share and public interest was eliminated

TELEVISION CORP AMER (CO)
Charter suspended for failure to file annual reports 09/30/1983

TELEVISION DIABLO, INC. (CA)
Name changed to Metropolitan Broadcasting Corp. of California 04/01/1960
Metropolitan Broadcasting Corp. of California name changed to KOVR Broadcasting Co. 09/09/1964
(See KOVR Broadcasting Co.)

TELEVISION-ELECTRONICS FD INC (DE)
Common $1 par split (2) for (1) by issuance of (1) additional share 01/30/1954
Common $1 par changed to 50¢ par and (1) additional share issued 02/29/1960
Name changed to Technology Fund, Inc. (DE) 01/19/1968
Technology Fund, Inc. (DE) reincorporated in Massachusetts 01/31/1986 which name changed to Kemper Technology Fund 02/01/1988 which name changed to Scudder Technology Fund 06/25/2001 which name changed to DWS Technology Fund 02/06/2006

TELEVISION EQUIPMENT CORP. (DE)
Each share Common 10¢ par exchanged for (2) shares Common 5¢ par 00/00/1950
No longer in existence having become inoperative and void for non-payment of taxes 04/01/1955

TELEVISION FUND, INC. (DE)
Name changed to Television-Electronics Fund, Inc. 00/00/1950
Television-Electronics Fund, Inc. name changed to Technology Fund, Inc. (DE) 01/19/1968 which reincorporated in Massachusetts 01/31/1986 which name changed to Kemper Technology Fund 02/01/1988 which name changed to Scudder Technology Fund 06/25/2001 which name changed to DWS Technology Fund 02/06/2006

TELEVISION INDUSTRIES, INC. (DE)
Name changed to Trans-Beacon Corp. 05/05/1966
(See Trans-Beacon Corp.)

TELEVISION LABORATORIES, LTD.
Name changed to Farnsworth Television, Inc. 00/00/1935
Farnsworth Television, Inc. reorganized as Farnsworth Television & Radio Corp. 00/00/1939 which name changed to F.A.R. Liquidating Corp. 00/00/1949
(See F.A.R. Liquidating Corp.)

TELEVISION MFRS AMER CO (DE)
Name changed to TMA Co. 01/26/1970
(See TMA Co.)

TELEVISION NETWORKING INC (NV)
Name changed to Global Teledata Corp. 10/29/1998
(See Global Teledata Corp.)

TELEVISION SHARES MANAGEMENT CORP. (DE)
Name changed to Supervised Investors Services, Inc. 06/03/1963
Supervised Investors Services, Inc. merged into Kemperco, Inc. 05/22/1970 which name changed to Kemper Corp. (Old) 01/15/1974
(See Kemper Corp. (Old))

TELEVISION TECHNOLOGY CORP (DE)
Each share Common 1¢ par exchanged for (0.25) share Common 4¢ par 09/25/1992
Name changed to Larcan-TTC Inc. 02/03/1994
(See Larcan-TTC Inc.)

TELEVISO CORP. (DE)
Acquired by Doughboy Industries, Inc. 09/18/1961
Each share Common exchanged for (0.478) share Common $1 par
Doughboy Industries, Inc. name changed to Domain Industries, Inc. 06/18/1970
(See Domain Industries, Inc.)

TELEVOLT CORP. (DE)
Charter cancelled and declared inoperative and void for non-payment of taxes 03/01/1974

TELEWEST COMMUNICATIONS NEW PLC (UNITED KINGDOM)
Name changed 10/02/1995
Name changed 05/16/1996
Name changed from Telewest Communications PLC (Old) to Telewest, PLC 10/02/1995
Name changed from Telewest, PLC to Telewest Communications PLC (New) 05/16/1996
Each old Sponsored ADR for Ordinary exchanged for (0.05) new Sponsored ADR for Ordinary 09/30/2002
Basis changed from (1:10) to (1:200) 09/30/2002
Under plan of reorganization each new Sponsored ADR for Ordinary automatically became (0.24863239) share Telewest Global Inc. (DE) Common 1¢ par 07/14/2004
Telewest Global Inc. merged into NTL Inc. (Ctfs. dated after 03/03/2006) 03/03/2006 which name changed to Virgin Media, Inc. 02/06/2007 which merged into Liberty Global PLC 06/10/2013

TELEWEST GLOBAL INC (DE)
Merged into NTL Inc. (Ctfs. dated after 03/03/2006) 03/03/2006
Each share Common 1¢ par exchanged for (0.2875) share Common 1¢ par and $16.25 cash
NTL Inc. (Ctfs. dated after 03/03/2006) name changed to Virgin Media, Inc. Inc. 02/06/2007 which merged into Liberty Global PLC 06/10/2013

TELEWORLD ENTERPRISES INC (NY)
Reorganized under the laws of Nevada as 1Twoe.Com, Inc. 08/05/1999
Each share Common $0.001 par exchanged for (0.25) share Common $0.001 par
1Twoe.Com, Inc. recapitalized as DMT Energy Inc. 06/23/2003
(See DMT Energy Inc.)

TELEWORLD INC (NY)
Merged into Union Corp. (NJ) 10/30/1972
Each share Common 2¢ par exchanged for (0.21) share Common 50¢ par
Union Corp. (NJ) reincorporated in Delaware 07/24/1987
(See Union Corp. (DE))

TELEX-CHILE S A (CHILE)
Each old Sponsored ADR for Ordinary exchanged for (0.1) new Sponsored ADR for Ordinary 08/29/2002
Name changed to Chilesat Corp. 02/14/2003
(See Chilesat Corp.)

TELEX CORP (DE)
Reincorporated 03/31/1963
Name and state of incorporation changed from Telex, Inc. (MN) to Telex Corp. (DE) 03/31/1963
Common $1 par split (5) for (1) by issuance of (4) additional shares 05/01/1970
Merged into Memorex Telex Corp. 06/29/1988
Each share Common $1 par exchanged for (10.33) shares Exchangeable Preferred Ser. A 1¢ par
Memorex Telex Corp. reorganized as Memorex Telex N.V. (Old) 02/18/1992
(See Memorex Telex N.V. (Old))

TELFAIR STOCKTON & CO., INC.
Each share Capital Stock $1 par exchanged for (2) shares Common $4 par 00/00/1946
Merged into Stockton, Whatley, Davin & Co. 00/00/1952
Each share Common $4 par exchanged for (1) share Common $4 par
Stockton, Whatley, Davin & Co. was acquired by General American Oil Co. of Texas 05/19/1964
(See General American Oil Co. of Texas)

TELFERSCOT RES INC (CANADA)
Recapitalized as Canntab Therapeutics Ltd. 04/20/2018
Each share Common no par exchanged for (0.005) share Common no par

TELFORD SVCS GROUP (AB)
Name changed 07/25/2001
Name changed from Telford Resources Ltd. to Telford Services Group Inc. 07/25/2001
Acquired by Aviation Acquisitions Inc. 08/11/2009
Each share Common no par exchanged for $0.10 cash

TELIA AB (SWEDEN)
Name changed to TeliaSonera AB 12/02/2002
(See TeliaSonera AB)

TELIASONERA AB (SWEDEN)
ADR agreement terminated 08/06/2004
Each Sponsored ADR for Ordinary exchanged for $29.46217 cash
Name changed to Telia Co. AB 04/28/2016

TELICONICS INC (DE)
Each share old Common $0.001 par exchanged for (0.1) share new Common $0.001 par 04/14/1993
Reported out of business 00/00/1994
Stockholders' equity unlikely

TELIDENT INC (MN)
Each share old Common 1¢ par exchanged for (0.5) share new Common 1¢ par 06/04/1996
Each share new Common 1¢ par exchanged for (0.25) share Common 8¢ par 01/13/1998
Each share Common 8¢ par received distribution of (0.13157894) share Teltronics Inc. new Common $0.001 par payable 06/02/2000 to holders of record 05/30/2000
Completely liquidated 09/28/2000
Each share Common 8¢ par exchanged for first and final distribution of $0.014 cash

TELIGENT INC (DE)
Incorporated 09/26/1997
Plan of reorganization under Chapter 11 Federal Bankruptcy proceedings effective 09/12/2002
No stockholders' equity

TELIK INC (DE)
Each share old Common 1¢ par exchanged for (0.03333333) share new Common 1¢ par 04/02/2012

Recapitalized as MabVax
Therapeutics Holdings, Inc.
09/10/2014
Each share new Common 1¢ par
exchanged for (0.125) share
Common 1¢ par

TELIOS PHARMACEUTICALS INC (CA)
Reorganized as Integra Lifesciences
Corp. 08/16/1995
Each share Conv. Preferred 1¢ par
exchanged for initial distribution of
(0.549133) share Common 1¢ par
Each share Common no par
exchanged for initial distribution of
(0.02) share Common 1¢ par
Each share Conv. Preferred 1¢ par
received second and final
distribution of (0.0085) share
Common 1¢ par 02/21/1996
Each share Common no par received
second and final distribution of
(0.0085) share Common 1¢ par
02/21/1996
Integra Lifesciences Corp. name
changed to Integra Lifesciences
Holdings Corp. 05/17/1999

TELKOM SA LTD (SOUTH AFRICA)
Each Sponsored ADR for Ordinary
received distribution of $24.777879
cash payable 06/29/2009 to holders
of record 06/18/2009 Ex date -
06/30/2009
Name changed to Telkom SA SOC
Ltd. 04/15/2013

TELKWA GOLD CORP (AB)
Reincorporated under the laws of
Ontario as Honey Badger
Exploration Inc. 06/23/2008

TELKWA MTN MINES LTD (BC)
Struck off register and declared
dissolved for failure to file returns
04/04/1977

TELL CITY NATL BANCORP (IN)
Name changed to National Bancorp
03/00/1988
National Bancorp merged into CNB
Bancshares Inc. 08/03/1998 which
merged into Fifth Third Bancorp
10/29/1999

TELLABS INC (DE)
Reincorporated 04/26/1992
Common no par split (2) for (1) by
issuance of (1) additional share
08/12/1983
State of incorporation changed from
(IL) to (DE) and Common no par
changed to to 1¢ par 04/26/1992
Common 1¢ par split (3) for (2) by
issuance of (0.5) additional share
11/19/1993
Common 1¢ par split (2) for (1) by
issuance of (1) additional share
05/20/1994
Common 1¢ par split (2) for (1) by
issuance of (1) additional share
05/19/1995
Common 1¢ par split (2) for (1) by
issuance of (1) additional share
payable 11/15/1996 to holders of
record 10/31/1996
Common 1¢ par split (2) for (1) by
issuance of (1) additional share
payable 05/17/1999 to holders of
record 05/03/1999
Acquired by Blackhawk Holding
Vehicle LLC 12/03/2013
Each share Common 1¢ par
exchanged for $2.45 cash

TELLCO INFORMATION SVCS INC (UT)
Proclaimed dissolved for failure to
pay taxes 12/31/1979

TELLERIAN CAP CORP (ON)
Name changed to Cogient Corp.
03/23/2001
(See Cogient Corp.)

TELLING-BELLE VERNON CO.
Acquired by National Dairy Products
Corp. 00/00/1928

Details not available

TELLIS GOLD MNG CO (CO)
Each share old Common $0.001 par
exchanged for (0.25) share new
Common $0.001 par 04/03/1987
Recapitalized as Bannockburn
Resources Inc. 03/21/2002
Each share Common $0.001 par
exchanged for (0.33333333) share
Common $0.001 par
Bannockburn Resources Inc. (CO)
reorganized in British Columbia as
Bannockburn Resources Ltd.
04/02/2004 which name changed to
Lucara Diamond Corp. 08/14/2007

TELLIUM INC (DE)
Recapitalized as Zhone Technologies,
Inc. 11/14/2003
Each share Common $0.001 par
exchanged for (0.25) share Common
$0.001 par
Zhone Technologies, Inc. name
changed to DASAN Zhone
Solutions, Inc. 09/12/2016

TELLURIAN INC (DE)
Incorporated 01/25/1996
Company terminated registration of
common stock and is no longer
public as of 11/16/1998

TELLURIDE BLACK BEAR MINES, INC.
Dissolved 00/00/1946
Details not available

TELLUS INDS INC (NV)
Reincorporated 08/14/1996
State of incorporation changed from
(NM) to (NV) 08/14/1986
Reorganized under Chapter 11
Federal Bankruptcy Code
01/18/1990
Each share old Common 1¢ par
exchanged for (0.04) share new
Common 1¢ par
Note: Unexchanged certificates were
cancelled and became without value
07/16/1997
SEC revoked common stock
registration 05/26/2010

TELLZA COMMUNICATIONS INC (ON)
Each share old Common no par
exchanged for (0.06666666) share
new Common no par 06/20/2016
Name changed to Tellza Inc.
12/13/2017

TELMED INC (DE)
Each share Common $0.001 par
exchanged for (1/7) share Common
$0.007 par 02/28/1997
Charter cancelled and declared
inoperative and void for
non-payment of taxes 03/01/1999

TELMEX INTERNACIONAL S A B DE C V (MEXICO)
ADR agreement terminated
09/10/2010
Each Sponsored ADR for Ser. A
exchanged for $18.617234 cash
Each Sponsored ADR for Ser. L
exchanged for $18.617234 cash

TELMONT CORP (MN)
Merged into Cosmetex Industries, Inc.
(DE) 12/30/1975
Each share Common $0.33333333
par exchanged for (0.8) share
Non-Vtg. Class A Conv. Preferred 1¢
par
(See Cosmetex Industries, Inc. (DE))

TELNETGO2000 INC (DE)
SEC revoked common stock
registration 05/26/2010

TELNET WORLD COMMUNICATIONS INC (UT)
Each (36) shares old Common $0.001
par exchanged for (1) share new
Common $0.001 par 05/28/1999
Each share new Common $0.001 par
exchanged again for (3.5) shares

new Common $0.001 par
11/29/2000
Reincorporated under the laws of
Nevada as Givemepower Corp.
07/05/2001

TELOCITY INC (DE)
Merged into Hughes Electronics Corp.
04/03/2001
Each share Common $0.001 par
exchanged for $2.15 cash

TELOR OPHTHALMIC PHARMACEUTICALS INC (DE)
Each share old Common $0.001 par
exchanged for (0.1) share new
Common $0.001 par 11/15/1995
Name changed to Occupational
Health & Rehabilitation, Inc.
06/06/1996
(See Occupational Health &
Rehabilitation, Inc.)

TELOS CORP (CA)
Acquired by Contel Corp. 02/21/1990
Each share Common 1¢ par
exchanged for $15.50 cash

TELPAC INTL INC (NV)
Reincorporated under the laws of
Utah as Intermarket Ventures Inc.
09/05/1997
(See Intermarket Ventures Inc.)

TELS CORP (UT)
Name changed to Hampton
Consulting Corp. 10/01/2004
Each share Common 2¢ par
exchanged for (1) share Common
2¢ par
(See Hampton Consulting Corp.)

TELSCAPE INTL INC NEW (TX)
Petition under Chapter 11 Federal
Bankruptcy Code dismissed
12/03/2004
No stockholders' equity

TELSCAPE INTL INC OLD (TX)
Under plan of merger each share
Common $0.001 par automatically
became (1) share Telscape
International Inc. (New) Common
$0.001 par 06/02/2000
(See Telscape International Inc.
(New))

TELSHARE INTL INC (DE)
Recapitalized as Sunvest Resorts,
Inc. (DE) 07/16/1996
Each share Common $0.0001 par
exchanged for (0.005) share
Common $0.0001 par
Sunvest Resorts, Inc. (DE)
reorganized in Florida 08/06/1996
which name changed to US Data
Authority, Inc. 06/23/2000
(See US Data Authority, Inc.)

TELSOFT MOBILE DATA INC (BC)
Merged into MDSI Mobile Data
Solutions Inc. 12/15/1995
Each share Preferred Ser. 3 no par
exchanged for (0.16703548) share
Common no par
Each share Common no par
exchanged for (0.1604235) share
Common no par
(See MDSI Mobile Data Solutions
Inc.)

TELSON RES INC (BC)
Each share old Common no par
exchanged for (0.5) share new
Common no par 10/20/2015
Name changed to Telson Mining
Corp. 02/21/2018

TELSTAR CORP (NV)
Charter revoked for failure to file
reports and pay fees 05/01/1990

TELSTAR INC (DE)
Adjudicated bankrupt 02/07/1972
Stockholders' equity unlikely

TELSTAR RESOURCE CORP (BC)
Recapitalized 11/18/82
Recapitalized from Telstar Petroleum
& Minerals Inc. to Telstar Resource
Corp. 11/18/1982

Each share Common no par
exchanged for (0.25) share Common
no par
Struck from register and declared
dissolved for failure to file returns
03/20/1992

TELSTAR RES LTD (AB)
Acquired by majority shareholders
04/11/2006
Each share Common no par
exchanged for $0.11 cash

TELTECH RESOURCE NETWORK CORP (MN)
Merged into Sopheon PLC
09/18/2000
Each share Common exchanged for
(0.24238) share Ordinary and
$1.05838 cash

TELTONE CORP (WA)
Each share old Common no par
exchanged for (0.00111111) share
new Common no par 01/03/2003
Note: Holders of (899) or fewer
pre-split shares received $0.24 cash
per share
New Common no par split (10) for (1)
by issuance of (9) additional shares
payable 06/30/2003 to holders of
record 06/13/2003 Ex date -
07/10/2003
In process of liquidation
Each share new Common no par
received initial distribution of $2
cash payable 09/25/2008 to holders
of record 09/25/2008
Note: Details on subsequent
distributions, if any, are not available

TELTRAN INTL GROUP LTD (DE)
Each share old Common $0.001 par
exchanged for (0.05) share new
Common $0.001 par 12/01/1997
Stock Dividends - 5% payable
07/01/1999 to holders of record
05/30/1999; 5% payable 10/15/1999
to holders of record 09/01/1999; 5%
payable 04/15/2000 to holders of
record 03/31/2000; 5% payable
10/15/2000 to holders of record
09/29/2000 Ex date - 09/27/2000
Recapitalized as CelebDirect, Inc.
09/10/2007
Each share new Common $0.001 par
exchanged for (0.02) share Common
$0.001 par
CelebDirect, Inc. name changed to
Muscle Flex, Inc. 10/01/2008 which
name changed to Bravada
International, Ltd. 07/19/2010

TELTREND INC (DE)
Merged into Westell Technologies,
Inc. 03/17/2000
Each share Common 1¢ par
exchanged for (3.3) shares Class A
Common 1¢ par

TELTRONICS INC (DE)
Each share old Common $0.001 par
exchanged for (0.04) share new
Common $0.001 par 06/20/1994
Plan of reorganization under Chapter
11 Federal Bankruptcy proceedings
effective 02/17/2012
No stockholders' equity

TELULAR CDA INC (ON)
Each share Common no par received
distribution of (1) Lava Systems Inc.
Common Stock Purchase Warrant
expiring 07/31/1997 payable
06/11/1997 to holders of record
06/09/1997
Name changed to GDI Global Data
Inc. 12/16/1998

TELULAR CORP (DE)
Each share old Common 1¢ par
exchanged exchanged for (0.25)
share new Common 1¢ par
01/27/1999
Acquired by ACP Tower Holdings,
LLC 06/24/2013
Each share new Common 1¢ par
exchanged for $12.61 cash

TEL-TEM FINANCIAL INFORMATION, INC.

TELUM INTL CORP (ON)
SEC revoked common stock registration 02/25/2008

TELUS COMMUNICATIONS BC INC (CANADA)
Name changed to Telus Communications Inc. 1/22/2001
(See Telus Communications Inc.)

TELUS COMMUNICATIONS INC (CANADA)
$1.21 Preferred called for redemption at $26 on 07/01/2004
$4.50 Preferred called for redemption at $104 on 07/01/2004
$5.75 Preferred called for redemption at $104 on 07/01/2004
$6 Preference Shares called for redemption 07/01/2004
$4.75 Preferred called for redemption at $105 on 07/15/2004
$4.75 Preferred 1956 Ser. called for redemption 07/15/2004
$5.15 Preferred Shares called for redemption 07/15/2004
$4.375 Preferred called for redemption at $104 on 08/01/2004
$6 Preferred called for redemption at $105 on 08/01/2004
Public interest eliminated

TELUS CORP (AB)
Merged into BCT.TELUS Communications Inc. 01/31/1999
Each share Common no par exchanged for (0.582975) share Common no par and (0.194325) Non-Vtg. Share no par
Note: Unexchanged certificates were cancelled and became without value 01/31/2005
BCT.Telus Communications Inc. name changed to Telus Corp. (Canada) 05/08/2000

TELVENT GIT S A (SPAIN)
Acquired by Schneider Electric S.A. 12/15/2011
Each share Ordinary EUR 3.00505 par exchanged for USD$33.54 cash

TELVUE CORP (DE)
Each share old Common 1¢ par exchanged for (0.005) share new Common 1¢ par 03/22/2012
Voluntarily dissolved 01/29/2018
Each share new Common 1¢ par received distribution of (1) TVC, LLC Class B Unit
Note: Unitholders are not expected to receive any distributions

TELXON CORP (DE)
Common 1¢ par split (3) for (2) by issuance of (0.5) additional share 06/21/1985
Common 1¢ par split (3) for (2) by issuance of (0.5) additional share 05/12/1986
Merged into Symbol Technologies, Inc. 12/01/2000
Each share Common 1¢ par exchanged for (0.5) share Common 1¢ par
(See Symbol Technologies, Inc.)

TELYNX INC (DE)
Each share old Class A Common 1¢ par exchanged for (0.5) share new Class A Common 1¢ par 06/04/2001
Each share new Class A Common 1¢ par exchanged again for (0.1) share new Class A Common 1¢ par 07/14/2004
SEC revoked common stock registration 02/07/2007

TELZUIT MED TECHNOLOGIES INC (FL)
Proclaimed dissolved for failure to file reports and pay fees 09/26/2008

TEMAGAMI MINING CO. LTD. (ON)
Name changed to Copperfields Mining Corp. Ltd. 11/10/1964
Copperfields Mining Corp. Ltd. name changed to Copperfields Mining Corp. (ON) 04/04/1974 which reincorporated in Canada 08/31/1983 which merged into Teck Corp. 09/02/1983 which name changed to Teck Cominco Ltd. 09/12/2001 which name changed to Teck Resources Ltd. 04/27/2009

TEMAGAMI OIL & GAS LTD (BC)
Common no par split (3) for (1) by issuance of (2) additional shares 12/29/1980
Common no par called for redemption at $0.041 on 01/07/2000

TEMANDA MINES LTD. (ON)
Merged into Can-Con Enterprises & Explorations Ltd. 11/30/1970
Each share Capital Stock $1 par exchanged for (0.03333333) share Capital Stock no par
Can-Con Enterprises & Explorations Ltd. name changed to Aubet Resources Inc. 09/08/1981 which recapitalized as Aubet Explorations Ltd. 09/30/1998 which name changed to Visa Gold Explorations Inc. 08/25/1999
(See Visa Gold Explorations Inc.)

TEMBA RES LTD (AB)
Merged into Westlinks Resources Ltd. 06/30/1998
Each share Common no par exchanged for (0.2) share Common no par
Westlinks Resources Ltd. name changed to Enterra Energy Corp. 12/18/2001 which recapitalized as Enterra Energy Trust 11/25/2003 which reorganized as Equal Energy Ltd. 06/03/2010
(See Equal Energy Ltd.)

TEMBEC INC (CANADA)
Merged into Rayonier Advanced Materials Inc. 11/21/2017
Each share Common no par exchanged for (0.16839419) share Common 1¢ par and $1.60337355 caah
Note: Unexchanged certificates will be cancelled and become without value 11/21/2023

TEMBEC INC (QC)
Class A Common no par reclassified as Common no par 02/24/2000
Contingent Value Rights expired without value 03/31/2000
Reorganized under the laws of Canada 02/29/2008
Each share Common no par exchanged for (0.0584) share Common no par and (0.129778) Common Stock Purchase Warrant expiring 02/29/2012
Tembec Inc. (Canada) merged into Rayonier Advanced Materials Inc. 11/21/2017

TEMBLOR OIL CO. OF MASSACHUSSETTS
Dissolved 00/00/1943
Details not available

TEMCO AIRCRAFT CORP. (DE)
Stock Dividend - 50% 12/21/1953
Merged into Ling-Temco Electronics, Inc. 07/19/1960
Each share Common $1 par exchanged for (0.12) share 4.5% Preferred Ser. A $30 par and (0.48) share Common 50¢ par
Ling-Temco Electronics, Inc. name changed to Ling-Temco-Vought, Inc. 08/16/1961 which name changed to LTV Corp. (Old) 05/05/1972 which reorganized as LTV Corp. (New) 06/28/1993
(See LTV Corp. (New))

TEMCO HOME HEALTH CARE PRODS INC (NJ)
Common 1¢ par split (3) for (2) by issuance of (0.5) additional share 12/09/1985
Reincorporated under the laws of Delaware as Temco National Corp. 03/02/1989
Temco National Corp. name changed to Wendt-Bristol Health Services Corp. 10/26/1992
(See Wendt-Bristol Health Services Corp.)

TEMCO NATL CORP (DE)
Stock Dividend - 10% 11/29/1990
Name changed to Wendt-Bristol Health Services Corp. 10/26/1992
(See Wendt-Bristol Health Services Corp.)

TEMCO SVC INDS INC (DE)
Acquired by Atalian Global Services Inc. 01/08/2016
Each share Common $1 par exchanged for $59.572882 cash

TEMECULA VY BANCORP INC (CA)
Reincorporated 12/18/2003
State of incorporation changed from (DE) to (CA) and Common $0.001 par changed to no par 12/18/2003
Common no par split (2) for (1) by issuance of (1) additional share payable 12/23/2003 to holders of record 12/18/2003 Ex date - 12/24/2003
Chapter 7 bankruptcy proceedings terminated 07/13/2016
Stockholders' equity unlikely

TEMECULA VY BK N A (TEMECULA, CA)
Common $1.25 par split (2) for (1) by issuance of (1) additional share payable 05/01/1999 to holders of record 04/28/1999
Under plan of reorganization each share Common $1.25 par automatically became (1) share Temecula Valley Bancorp Inc. (DE) Common $0.001 par 06/01/2002
Temecula Valley Bancorp Inc. (DE) reincorporated in California 12/23/2003
(See Temecula Valley Bancorp Inc. (CA))

TEMENOS GROUP AG (SWITZERLAND)
Each Unsponsored ADR for Ordinary exchanged for (1) Sponsored ADR for Ordinary 04/08/2013
Name changed to Temenos AG 05/24/2018

TEMEX RES CORP (ON)
Merged into Lake Shore Gold Corp. 09/21/2015
Each share Common no par exchanged for (0.105) share Common no par
Note: Unexchanged certificates will be cancelled and become without value 09/21/2021
Lake Shore Gold Corp. which merged into Tahoe Resources Inc. 04/07/2016

TEMISCA RES INC (CANADA)
Recapitalized as Tom Exploration Inc. 05/17/1996
Each share Common no par exchanged for (0.1) share Common no par
Tom Exploration Inc. name changed to Excel Gold Mining Inc. 04/22/2008

TEMISKAMING MINING CO. LTD.
Liquidated 00/00/1951
Details not available

TEMORIS RES INC (CANADA)
Name changed to Glen Eagle Resources Inc. 09/10/2008

TEMP STIK CORP (CA)
Company reported out of business 12/29/1995
Details not available

TEMPCO BUSINESS SVCS INC (MI)
Charter declared inoperative and void for failure to file reports 07/15/1979

TEMPCO INC (NV)
Name changed to Esio Water & Beverage Development Corp. 01/18/2013
Esio Water & Beverage Development Corp. name changed to UPD Holding Corp. 03/01/2017

TEMPERATURE ENGR CORP (NJ)
Name changed to Opt-Sciences Corp. 12/31/1968

TEMPEST ENERGY CORP (AB)
Each share Class B Common no par exchanged for (1.7941) shares Class A Common no par 11/22/2005
Plan of arrangement effective 11/30/2005
Each share Class A Common no par exchanged for (0.4255) Daylight Energy Trust, Trust Unit no par, (0.1344) share Open Range Energy Corp. (Old) Common no par and (0.02688) Common Stock Purchase Warrant expiring 12/30/2005
(See each company's listing)

TEMPEST TECHNOLOGIES INC (MD)
In process of liquidation
Each share Common 1¢ par received initial distribution of $0.60 cash 03/06/1991
Each share Common 1¢ par received second distribution of $0.26 cash 01/24/1992
Note: Details on subsequent distribution(s), if any, are not available

TEMPEST TRADING TECHNOLOGIES INC (CA)
Reorganized under the laws of Nevada as Humble Energy, Inc. 02/25/2009
Each (150) shares Common no par exchanged for (1) share Common $0.001 par

TEMPLAR ENERGY LTD (AB)
Delisted from Alberta Stock Exchange 07/24/1998

TEMPLAR MNG CORP (BC)
Struck off register and declared dissolved for failure to file returns 10/19/1990

TEMPLAR MOTOR CAR CO. (OH)
Charter cancelled for failure to pay taxes 2/15/26

TEMPLAR MOTORS CORP. (DE)
Dissolved 06/17/1921
Details not available

TEMPLAR RES CORP (BC)
Recapitalized as Moneta Resources Inc. 06/07/2007
Each share Common no par exchanged for (0.5) share Common no par
Moneta Resources Inc. name changed to Border Petroleum Inc. (BC) 08/08/2008 which reorganized in Alberta as Border Petroleum Corp. 09/14/2010 which recapitalized as Border Petroleum Ltd. 03/24/2014

TEMPLATE SOFTWARE INC (VA)
Merged into Level 8 Systems, Inc. 12/27/1999
Each share Common 1¢ par exchanged for (0.2838) share Common 1¢ par and $4 cash
Level 8 Systems, Inc. recapitalized as Cicero, Inc. 01/16/2007

TEMPLE ANTHRACITE COAL CO.
Reorganized as East Temple Corp. 00/00/1936
Stockholders received nothing but rights

TEMPLE COAL CO. (PA)
Liquidation completed 06/19/1956
Each share Preferred no par received (1) share Common $1 par of Azalea Homes, Inc. and $3 cash
Common $1 par had no equity
(See Azalea Homes, Inc.)

TEMPLE CORP.
Bankrupt 00/00/1930
Stockholders' equity unlikely

TEMPLE EXPLS INC (ON)
Recapitalized as Burgess Point Resources Inc. 07/10/1987
Each share Common no par exchanged for (0.2) share Common no par
Burgess Point Resources Inc. recapitalized as Metallica Resources Inc. 01/14/1994 which merged into New Gold Inc. 06/30/2008

TEMPLE GOLD MINES, LTD. (ON)
Charter cancelled and company declared dissolved for failure to file reports and pay fees 08/24/1964

TEMPLE INDS INC (TX)
Each share Common $10 par exchanged for (3) shares Common $3.33333333 par 06/27/1968
Each share Common $3.33333333 par exchanged for (2) shares Common $0.16666666 par 04/02/1969
Merged into Time Inc. (NY) 08/17/1973
Each share Common $0.16666666 par exchanged for (0.5) share Common $1 par
Time Inc. (NY) reincorporated in Delaware 12/07/1983 which name changed to Time Warner Inc. (Old) 07/25/1989 which merged into AOL Time Warner Inc. 01/11/2001 which name changed to Time Warner Inc. (New) 10/16/2003

TEMPLE-INLAND INC (DE)
Common $1 par split (5) for (4) by issuance of (0.25) additional share 03/31/1987
Common $1 par split (2) for (1) by issuance of (1) additional share 03/15/1990
Common $1 par split (2) for (1) by issuance of (1) additional share payable 04/01/2005 to holders of record 03/01/2005 Ex date - 04/04/2005
Each share Common $1 par received distribution of (0.33333333) share Forestar Real Estate Group Inc. Common $1 par payable 12/28/2007 to holders of record 12/14/2007 Ex date - 12/31/2007
Each share Common $1 par received distribution of (0.33333333) share Guaranty Financial Group Inc. Common $1 par payable 12/28/2007 to holders of record 12/14/2007 Ex date - 12/31/2007
Acquired by International Paper Co. 02/13/2012
Each share Common $1 par exchanged for $32 cash

TEMPLE MOUNTAIN URANIUM CO. (UT)
Name changed to Temple Mountain Industries, Inc. 01/15/1972
Each share Common $0.025 par exchanged for (1) share Common $0.025 par

TEMPLE NATL BK (TEMPLE, TX)
Merged into First International Bancshares, Inc. 09/21/1973
Each share Capital Stock $100 par exchanged for (47) shares Common $5 par
First International Bancshares, Inc. name changed to Interfirst Corp. 12/31/1981 which merged into First RepublicBank Corp. 06/06/1987
(See First RepublicBank Corp.)

TEMPLE OIL CO. (UT)
Liquidation completed
Each share Common 5¢ par received initial distribution of $3.50 cash 12/16/1968
Each share Common 5¢ par received second and final distribution of $3.89 cash 03/24/1969

TEMPLE REAL ESTATE INVT TR (MB)
Under plan of reorganization each Trust Unit automatically became (1) share Temple Hotels Inc. (Canada) Common no par 12/31/2012

TEMPLE SUMMIT FINL PROJS INC (NV)
Reincorporated 08/15/1994
State of incorporation changed from (TX) to (NV) 08/15/1994
Each share old Common $0.0001 par exchanged for (0.005) share new Common $0.0001 par 07/25/2000
Name changed to Wintech Digital Systems Technology Corp. 09/11/2000

TEMPLETON, DAMROTH CORP. (NY)
Recapitalized 05/25/1960
Each share Common 10¢ par exchanged for (1) share Class A Common 10¢ par and (0.1) share Class B Common 10¢ par
Name changed to Lexington Research & Management Corp. 12/28/1964
(See Lexington Research & Management Corp.)

TEMPLETON & LIDDELL FUND, INC. (NJ)
Common $1 par split (3) for (1) by issuance of (2) additional shares 05/05/1955
Common $1 par split (5) for (1) by issuance of (4) additional shares 01/30/1959
Name changed to Securities Fund, Inc. (NJ) 02/11/1959
Securities Fund, Inc. (NJ) reincorporated in Pennsylvania 03/01/1967 which name changed to Hedberg & Gordon Fund, Inc. 02/25/1969 which name changed to Plitrend Fund, Inc. 02/20/1974 which name changed to U.S. Trend Fund, Inc. (PA) 02/00/1986 which reincorporated in Maryland as Capstone U.S. Trend Fund, Inc. 05/11/1992 which name changed to Capstone Growth Fund, Inc. 08/26/1994 which name changed to Capstone Series Fund, Inc. 01/22/2002

TEMPLETON CHINA WORLD FD INC (MD)
Reincorporated under the laws of Delaware as Templeton China World Fund and Common 1¢ par reclassified as Advisor Class 08/08/2003

TEMPLETON DEVELOPING MKTS TR (MA)
Common 1¢ par reclassified as Class I 1¢ par 05/01/1995
Class I 1¢ par reclassified as Class A 1¢ par 01/01/1995
Class II 1¢ par reclassified as Class C 1¢ par 01/01/1995
Reincorporated under the laws of Delaware 09/27/2002

TEMPLETON EMERGING MKTS APPRECIATION FD (ON)
Merged into Templeton Management Ltd. 9/21/2001
Each Unit no par exchanged for (1.87879931) Emerging Markets Fund Deferred Load Units no par

TEMPLETON EMERGING MKTS APPRECIATION FUND INC (MD)
Merged into Templeton Developing Markets Trust (MA) 9/26/2002
Each share Common 1¢ par exchanged for (1.1) Advisor Class Shares of Bene. Int.
Templeton Developing Markets Trust (MA) reincorporated in Delaware 9/27/2002

TEMPLETON EMERGING MKTS FD INC (MD)
Reincorporated under the laws of Delaware as Templeton Emerging Markets Fund and Common 1¢ par reclassified as Shares of Bene. Int. no par 11/01/2002

TEMPLETON EMERGING MKTS INCOME FD INC (MD)
Reincorporated under the laws of Delaware as Templeton Emerging Markets Income Fund 6/1/2004

TEMPLETON ENERGY INC (DE)
Name changed to TGX Corp. 06/02/1987
(See TGX Corp.)

TEMPLETON GALBRAITH & HANSBERGER LTD. (CAYMAN ISLANDS)
Acquired by Franklin Resources, Inc. 10/30/1992
Details not available

TEMPLETON GLOBAL FDS INC (MD)
Name changed to Templeton Smaller Companies Growth Fund, Inc. 01/01/1991
Templeton Smaller Companies Growth Fund, Inc. name changed to Templeton Global Smaller Companies Fund, Inc. (MD) 05/14/1996 which reincorporated in Delaware as Templeton Global Smaller Companies Fund 06/01/2004

TEMPLETON GLOBAL GOVTS INCOME TR (MA)
Merged into Templeton Global Income Fund, Inc. (MD) 8/30/2002
Each Share of Bene. Int. 1¢ par exchanged for (0.92244897) share Common 1¢ par
Templeton Global Income Fund, Inc. (MD) reincorporated in Delaware as Templeton Global Income Fund 6/1/2004

TEMPLETON GLOBAL INCOME FD INC (MD)
Reincorporated under the laws of Delaware as Templeton Global Income Fund 6/1/2004

TEMPLETON GLOBAL OPPORTUNITIES TR (MA)
Reincorporated 10/10/2006
Shares of Bene. Int. 1¢ par reclassified as Shares of Bene. Int. Class A 1¢ par 05/01/1995
State of organization changed from (MA) to (DE) and Class A Shares of Bene. Int. 1¢ par changed to no par 10/10/2006
Under plan of reorganization each Class A, C or Advisor Class Share of Bene. Int. no par automatically became (0.71014776), (0.70870342) or (0.70684482) Templeton Growth Fund, Inc. Class A, Class C1 or Advisor Class Share of Bene. Int. 1¢ par respectively 08/24/2018

TEMPLETON GLOBAL REAL ESTATE FD (MA)
Name changed 05/15/1996
Name changed from Templeton Real Estate Securities Fund to Templeton Global Real Estate Fund 05/15/1996
Merged into Franklin Real Estate Securities Trust 09/23/1999
Details not available

TEMPLETON GLOBAL SMALLER COS FD INC (MD)
Name changed 05/14/1996
Common 20¢ par reclassified as Class I 20¢ par 05/01/1995
Name changed from Templeton Smaller Companies Growth Fund, Inc. to Templeton Global Smaller Companies Fund, Inc. 05/14/1996
Class I 20¢ par reclassified as Class A 20¢ par 01/01/1999
Class II 20¢ par reclassified as Class C 20¢ par 01/01/1999
Reincorporated under the laws of Delaware as Templeton Global Smaller Companies Fund and Class A 20¢ par and Class C 20¢ par changed to no par 06/01/2004

TEMPLETON GROWTH FD LTD (CANADA)
Name changed to Axe-Templeton Growth Fund of Canada Ltd. 9/10/57
Axe-Templeton Growth Fund of Canada Ltd. name was changed back to Templeton Growth Fund of Canada Ltd. 7/3/63 which name changed to Templeton Growth Fund, Ltd. 7/2/64

TEMPLETON INCOME TR (MA)
Income Fund Class I 1¢ par reclassified as Global Bond Fund Class I 1¢ par 05/15/1996
Money Fund 1¢ par acquired by Franklin Money Fund on a net asset basis 12/31/1996
Global Bond Fund Class I 1¢ par reclassified as Global Bond Fund Class A 1¢ par 01/01/1999
Reincorporated under the laws of Delaware and 1¢ par changed to no par 08/01/2007

TEMPLETON NATL BK (TEMPLETON, CA)
Merged into Bank of Santa Maria (Santa Maria, CA) 03/10/1995
Each share Common $5 par exchanged for (1.2439) shares Common no par
Bank of Santa Maria (Santa Maria, CA) reorganized as BSM Bancorp 03/11/1997 which merged into Mid-State Bancshares 07/10/1998
(See Mid-State Bancshares)

TEMPLETON RUSSIA & EAST EUROPEAN FD INC (MD)
Name changed 07/31/2002
Name changed from Templeton Russia Fund, Inc. to Templeton Russia & East European Fund, Inc. 07/31/2002
Completely liquidated
Each share Common 1¢ par received first and final distribution of $10.1286 cash payable 12/18/2015 to holders of record 11/20/2015

TEMPLETON VALUE FD INC (MD)
Merged into Templeton Smaller Companies Growth Fund, Inc. 11/19/1993
Details not available

TEMPLETON VIETNAM & SOUTHEAST ASIA FD (MD)
Name changed 4/24/98
Name changed from Templeton Vietnam Opportunities Fund Inc. to Templeton Vietnam & Southeast Asia Fund, Inc. 4/24/98
Merged into Templeton Developing Markets Trust (MA) 9/26/2002
Each share Common no par exchanged for (0.921) Advisor Class Share of Bene. Int.
Templeton Developing Markets Trust (MA) reincorporated in Delaware 9/27/2002

TEMPLOR GOLD MINES LTD.
Succeeded by Templor Mines Ltd. 00/00/1945
Each share Capital Stock $1 par exchanged for (1) share Capital Stock $1 par
(See Templor Mines Ltd.)

TEMPLOR MINES LTD. (ON)
Dissolved by default 11/05/1962
No stockholders' equity

TEMPO DEVICES INC. (DE)
Name changed to Tempo Instruments & Controls Corp. 05/15/1973
(See Tempo Instruments & Controls Corp.)

TEMPO ENTERPRISES INC (OK)
Merged into Tele-Communications, Inc. (Old) 12/20/1988
Each share Common 1¢ par exchanged for (0.381) share Class A Common $1 par

Tele-Communications, Inc. (Old)
merged into Tele-Communications, Inc. (New) 08/05/1994 which merged into AT&T Corp. 03/09/1999 which merged into AT&T Inc. 11/18/2005

TEMPO INSTRS & CTLS CORP (DE)
Merged into Bowthorpe International Inc. 05/09/1983
Each share Common 1¢ par exchanged for $25.816 cash
Note: $3.184 cash per share was placed in escrow pending possible future distribution. Company refused to provide additional information.

TEMPO INSTRUMENT INC. (NY)
Merged into Allen Electric & Equipment Corp. (MI) 07/13/1967
Each share Common 5¢ par exchanged for (0.071287) share Common $1 par
Allen Electric & Equipment Co. (MI) reincorporated in Delaware 05/01/1969 which name changed to Allen Group Inc. 05/05/1972 which name changed to Allen Telecom Inc. 02/28/1997 which merged into Andrew Corp. 07/15/2003 which merged into CommScope, Inc. 12/27/2007
(See CommScope, Inc.)

TEMPO PARTICIPACOES S A (BRAZIL)
GDR agreement terminated 11/27/2015
Each 144A GDR for Common exchanged for (3) shares Common
Each Reg. S GDR for Common exchanged for (3) shares Common

TEMPO RES LTD (BC)
Name changed to Hystar Aerospace Corp. 09/26/1989
(See Hystar Aerospace Corp.)

TEMPORARY FINL SVCS INC (WA)
Each share Common $0.001 received distribution of (1) share Genesis Financial Inc. Common $0.001 payable 11/28/2003 to holders of record 11/20/2003
Common $0.001 par split (5) for (1) by issuance of (4) additional shares payable 08/19/2005 to holders of record 08/09/2005 Ex date - 08/22/2005
Name changed to Command Center, Inc. 01/09/2006

TEMPORARY INVT FD INC (MD)
Common $1 par changed to $0.001 par and (999) additional shares issued 06/01/1975
Common $0.001 par reclassified as Class A Common $0.001 par 04/12/1979
Note: Class A Common $0.001 par reclassified as TempFund Class B 04/12/1979
Under plan of reorganization each TempFund Class B share automatically became Provident Institutional Funds TempFund shares on a net asset basis 02/10/1999
Under plan of reorganization each TempCash Class C share automatically became Provident Institutional Funds TempCash Dollar shares on a net asset basis 02/10/1999
Provident Institutional Funds name changed to BlackRock Provident Institutional Funds 01/29/2001 which name changed to BlackRock Liquidity Funds 11/19/2003

TEMPORARY TIME CAP CORP (CO)
Each share old Common $0.001 par exchanged for (1/6) share new Common $0.001 par 04/02/1993
Name changed to Hybred International, Inc. 04/29/2008
Hybred International, Inc.

recapitalized as All Grade Mining, Inc. 11/23/2011

TEMPUR-PEDIC INTL INC (DE)
Name changed to Tempur Sealy International, Inc. 06/26/2013

TEMPUS CORP (CANADA)
Reincorporated 03/14/2003
Place of incorporation changed from (MB) to (Canada) 03/14/2003
Name changed to Acadian Gold Corp. 03/20/2003
Acadian Gold Corp. name changed to Acadian Mining Corp. 06/28/2007
(See Acadian Mining Corp.)

TEMTEX INDS INC (DE)
Each share Common 10¢ par exchanged for (0.5) share Common 20¢ par 12/23/1972
Common 20¢ par split (3) for (2) by issuance of (0.5) additional share 06/06/1983
Common 20¢ par split (3) for (2) by issuance of (0.5) additional share 03/20/1984
Stock Dividend - 10% 06/15/1978
Recapitalized as Wanderport Corp. 03/13/2007
Each share Common 20¢ par exchanged for (0.04) share Common $0.001 par

TEN & 10 INC (NV)
Recapitalized as Globalite Group, Inc. 05/14/2007
Each share Common $0.001 par exchanged for (0.0025) share Common $0.001 par
Globalite Group, Inc. recapitalized as Language 2 Language Universal Holdings, Inc. 11/04/2008

TEN DA BRAND FROZEN FOODS INC (NJ)
Liquidation completed
Each share Common 10¢ par exchanged for initial distribution of $0.75 cash 12/23/1977
Each share Common 10¢ par received second and final distribution of $0.86 cash 07/10/1978

10 EAST 40TH ST. BUILDING, INC. (NY)
Class A 10¢ par changed to Common 10¢ par 00/00/1950
Liquidation completed 02/21/1956
Details not available

1088 PARK AVENUE CORP. (NY)
Completely liquidated 00/00/1953
No stockholders' equity

TEN FORTY TAX INC (NY)
Name changed to Rusco Development Corp. (NY) 01/05/1971
Rusco Development Corp. (NY) reincorporated in Delaware as Atlantic Medical Corp. 01/20/1972 which recapitalized as I-Rock Industries, Inc. 04/05/1999 which name changed to IR Operating Corp. 04/26/1999 which name changed to Digi Link Technologies, Inc. 02/12/2001
(See Digi Link Technologies, Inc.)

10 GROUP PLC (UNITED KINGDOM)
ADR agreement terminated 06/13/2005
No ADR's remain outstanding

TEN KEYS, INC. (RI)
Name changed to First Mutual Fund of Rhode Island, Inc. 09/13/1965
First Mutual Fund of Rhode Island, Inc. name changed to First Mutual Fund, Inc. 11/14/1972 which name changed to First Mutual Funds 07/03/1992
(See First Mutual Funds)

TEN MILE MINING CO. (AZ)
Charter expired by time limitation 10/10/1931

10 MINUTE PIT STOP USA INC (NV)
Recapitalized as Pit Stop Auto Centers, Inc. 05/18/1990
Each share Common 5¢ par exchanged for (0.02) share Common 5¢ par
Pit Stop Auto Centers, Inc. recapitalized as Resources of the Pacific Corp. 08/04/1995 which name changed to Semper Resources Corp. (NV) 06/21/1996 which reincorporated in Oklahoma 00/00/2005 which name changed to Cyberfund, Inc. (OK) 09/01/2006 which reincorporated in Delaware as ROK Entertainment Group Inc. 12/31/2007
(See ROK Entertainment Group Inc.)

TEN PEAKS COFFEE CO (CANADA)
Name changed to Swiss Water Decaffeinated Coffee Inc. 10/22/2018

1061 ROSEMONT AVENUE BUILDING CORP.
Reorganized as Coronado Apartment Hotel Corp. in 1952
Each share Common no par exchanged for (1) share Preferred $80 par
Coronado Apartment Hotel Corp. dissolved 2/13/59

TEN STIX INC (NV)
Reincorporated 08/05/2004
State of incorporation changed from (CO) to (NV) 08/05/2004
Name changed to Motorsports Emporium, Inc. 12/07/2004
Motorsports Emporium, Inc. name changed to International Building Technologies Group, Inc. 08/16/2007
(See International Building Technologies Group, Inc.)

1010 FIFTH AVENUE, INC.
Dissolved in 1948

TEN-TEX INC (MN)
Statutorily dissolved 10/01/1991

TEN YEAR NOTEHOLDERS CORP.
Dissolved in 1945

TENACITY RES CORP (BC)
Delisted from Toronto Venture Stock Exchange 06/05/2002

TENAJON RES CORP (BC)
Name changed 09/15/1988
Name changed from Tenajon Silver Corp. to Tenajon Resources Corp. 09/15/1988
Plan of Arrangement effective 10/17/2014
Each share Common no par held by holders of (500) or more shares exchanged for (1) share Class A no par and (0.21276595) share Pinnacle Mines Ltd. Common no par
Each share Common no par held by holders of (499) or fewer shares exchanged for either (1) share Class A no par and (0.21276595) share Pinnacle Mines Ltd. Common no par or $0.23 cash per Tenajon share and $0.20 cash per Pinnacle share
Note: Option to receive cash expired 11/17/2014
Note: Unexchanged certificates of fewer than (499) shares were cancelled and became without value 11/17/2014
Merged into Creston Moly Corp. 08/26/2009
Each share Common no par exchanged for (0.84) share Common no par
Creston Moly Corp. merged into Mercator Minerals Ltd. 06/21/2011

TENAKILL ASSOC INC (DE)
Charter cancelled and declared inoperative and void for non-payment of taxes 03/01/1983

TENAX, INC. (NY)
Adjudicated bankrupt 7/30/63
No stockholders' equity

TENBY DEVS LTD (BC)
Name changed to Porcher Island Gold Corp. 10/18/1996
Porcher Island Gold Corp. recapitalized as Tetra Metals Ltd. 01/08/1999 which recapitalized as Palladon Ventures Ltd. 11/02/2000

TENCOR INSTRS (CA)
Common no par split (2) for (1) by issuance of (1) additional share 6/21/95
Merged into KLA-Tencor Corp. 4/30/97
Each share Common no par exchanged for (1) share Common $0.001 par

TENDER LOVING CARE HEALTH CARE SVCS INC OLD (DE)
Name changed to Staff Builders, Inc. 12/01/1987
Staff Builders, Inc. name changed to ATC Healthcare, Inc. 08/02/2001
(See ATC Healthcare, Inc.)

TENDER LOVING CARE HEALTH SVCS INC NEW (DE)
Merged into Med Diversified, Inc. 02/13/2002
Each share Common 1¢ par exchanged for $1 cash

TENDER SENDER INC (OR)
Involuntarily dissolved for failure to file reports and pay fees 5/31/91

TENDERCARE INTL INC (CO)
Merged into Hain Celestial Group, Inc. 12/10/2007
Each share Common 1¢ par exchanged for $0.4449 cash

TENDERFOOR GOLD MINING & MILLING CO. (SD)
Charter expired by time limitation 1/8/22

TENDERFOOT INTL INC (IL)
Reorganized under Chapter 11 Bankruptcy Act as Wimpy's USA, Inc. 1/29/82
Each share Common no par exchanged for (0.5) share Common no par
Note: For holdings sold pursuant to the May 3, 1978 prospectus each (3) shares Common no par exchanged for (2) shares Common no par
(See Wimpy's USA, Inc.)

TENENDO MINING CORP. LTD. (ON)
Charter cancelled for failure to file reports and pay taxes 1/20/58

TENERA INC (DE)
Company terminated common stock registration and is no longer public as of 01/13/2004

TENERA L P (DE)
Recapitalized as TENERA, Inc. 06/30/1995
Each Depositary Unit exchanged for (1) share Common $0.001 par
(See TENERA, Inc.)

TENERE GROUP INC (MO)
Merged into TGI Acquisition 3/17/99
Each share Common 1¢ par exchanged for $9.4416 cash

TENERGY LTD (AB)
Acquired by Quintana Canada Corp. 3/29/2006
Each share Common no par exchanged for $6.30 cash

TENET HEALTHCARE CORP (NV)
Each share 7% Mandatory Conv. Preferred 15¢ par exchanged for (170.9402) shares Common 5¢ par 10/02/2012
(Additional Information in Active)

TENET INFORMATION SVCS INC (UT)
Each share old Common $0.001 par exchanged for (0.05) share new Common $0.001 par 1/23/2004

Name changed to LGA Holdings, Inc. 11/7/2005

TENFOLD CORP (DE)
Acquired by Versata Enterprises, Inc. 05/30/2008
Each share Class A Conv. Preferred $0.001 par exchanged for $0.5418793 cash
Each share Common $0.001 par exchanged for $0.0400092 cash

TENGA LABS INC (AB)
Recapitalized as TLT Resources Ltd. 08/06/1998
Each share Common no par exchanged for (0.1) share Common no par
TLT Resources Ltd. recapitalized as Buffalo Diamonds Ltd. 12/01/1998 which recapitalized as Buffalo Gold Ltd. 02/17/2003
(See Buffalo Gold Ltd.)

TENGASCO INC (TN)
Each share old Common $0.001 par exchanged for (1) share new Common $0.001 par 08/11/1998
Stock Dividend - 5% payable 10/01/2001 to holders of record 09/04/2001 Ex date - 08/30/2001
Reincorporated under the laws of Delaware 06/28/2011

TENGTU INTL CORP (DE)
SEC revoked common stock registration 04/15/2010

TENGUY WORLD INTL INC (CO)
Recapitalized as CMK Gaming International, Inc. 10/23/2013
Each share Common $0.0001 par exchanged for (0.00057045) share Common $0.0001 par

TENISON DRILLING CO., INC. (MT)
Became inoperative in 1958
Common Stock valueless

TENKE MNG CORP (CANADA)
Each share old Common no par exchanged for (0.2) share new Common no par new Common no par 06/22/1999
Merged into Lundin Mining Corp. 07/03/2007
Each share new Common no par exchanged for (1.73) shares Common no par, (1) share Suramina Resources Inc. Common no par and $0.001 cash
(See each company's listing)

TENKOM GROUP INC (NV)
Recapitalized as VMT Scientific, Inc 8/15/2005
Each (75) share Common $0.001 par exchanged for (1) share Common $0.001 par

TENN ARK FURNITURE WORLD CORP (DE)
Name changed to Donald Corp. 05/18/1973
(See Donald Corp.)

TENN-FLAKE CORP. (TN)
Assets sold for benefit of creditors 9/17/76
No stockholders' equity

TENNA CORP (OH)
Common no par split (2) for (1) by issuance of (1) additional share 10/28/68
Common no par split (2) for (1) by issuance of (1) additional share 8/11/69
Filed for Chapter 7 bankruptcy proceedings 9/25/80
No stockholders' equity

TENNALTA PETE CORP (NV)
Recapitalized as GRIT International Groups Inc. 07/10/2007
Each share Common $0.001 par exchanged for (0.001) share Common $0.001 par
GRIT International Groups Inc. recapitalized as GRIT International Inc. 12/23/2008

TENNECO AUTOMOTIVE INC (DE)
Name changed to Tenneco Inc. 10/20/2005

TENNECO CORP (DE)
$1.60 2nd Preferred no par called for redemption 11/1/79
Public interest eliminated

TENNECO INC (DE)
4.72% Conv. 2nd Preferred $100 par reclassified as 4.72% 2nd Preferred $100 par 04/01/1969
4.1% Preferred $100 par called for redemption 04/01/1976
4.25% Preferred $100 par called for redemption 04/01/1976
4.65% Preferred $100 par called for redemption 04/01/1976
5.36% Conv. 2nd Preferred $100 par called for redemption 11/01/1979
$5.50 Conv. Preference $100 par called for redemption 11/01/1979
4.6% Preferred $100 par called for redemption 04/01/1980
4.64% Preferred $100 par called for redemption 04/01/1981
5.1% Preferred $100 par called for redemption 10/01/1981
5.25% Preferred $100 par called for redemption 10/01/1982
5.12% Preferred $100 par called for redemption 04/01/1984
$11 Preference no par called for redemption 04/08/1987
4.5% 2nd Preferred $100 par called for redemption 11/19/1987
4.72% 2nd Preferred $100 par called for redemption 11/19/1987
4.92% 2nd Preferred $100 par called for redemption 11/19/1987
5% 2nd Preferred $100 par called for redemption 11/19/1987
5.04% Preferred $100 par called for redemption 11/19/1987
5.08% Preferred $100 par called for redemption 11/19/1987
5.14% Preferred $100 par called for redemption 11/19/1987
5.24% Preferred $100 par called for redemption 11/19/1987
7.25% Preferred $100 par called for redemption 11/19/1987
7.94% Preferred $100 par called for redemption 11/19/1987
8.52% Preferred $100 par called for redemption 11/19/1987
4.9% Preferred $100 par called for redemption 10/16/1989
Variable Rate Preferred no par called for redemption 06/28/1993
Each share $2.80 Depositary Preferred Ser. A exchanged for (0.970488) share Common $5 par 12/16/1994
8.25% Jr. Preferred Ser. A name changed to El Paso Tennessee Pipeline Co. 12/11/1996
(See El Paso Tennessee Pipeline Co.)
Each share Common $5 par received distribution of (0.2) share Newport News Shipbuilding Inc. Common 1¢ par and (1) share Tenneco Inc. (New) Common 1¢ par payable 12/12/1996 to holders of record 12/11/1996
Merged into El Paso Natural Gas Co. 12/12/1996
Each share $4.50 Preferred no par exchanged for (2.365) shares new Common $3 par
Each share $7.40 Preference no par exchanged for (2.365) shares new Common $3 par
Each share Common $5 par exchanged for (0.093) share Common $3 par
El Paso Natural Gas Co. reorganized as El Paso Energy Corp. 08/01/1998 which name changed to El Paso Corp. 02/05/2001 which merged into Kinder Morgan, Inc. (New) 05/25/2012

TENNECO INC NEW (DE)
Each share Common 1¢ par received distribution of (1) share of Tenneco Automotive Inc. Common 1¢ par payable 11/4/99 to holders of record 10/29/99
Recapitalized as Tenneco Automotive Inc. 11/5/99
Each share Common 1¢ par exchanged for (0.2) share Common 1¢ par
Tenneco Automotive Inc. name changed to Tenneco Inc. 10/20/2005

TENNECO MFG CO (DE)
Merged into Tenneco Chemicals, Inc. 12/31/67
Each share Common $5 par exchanged for $36 cash

TENNECO OFFSHORE INC (DE)
Liquidation completed
Each share Common $1 par exchanged for initial distribution of (1) TEL Offshore Trust Unit of Bene. Int. 01/14/1983
Each share Common $1 par received second distribution of $1.10 cash 03/15/1983
Each share Common $1 par received third and final distribution of $0.10181 cash 09/15/1983

TENNECO PACKAGING INC (DE)
Name changed to Pactiv Corp. 11/05/1999
(See Pactiv Corp.)

TENNESSEE ALA & GA RY CO (DE)
Capital Stock $5 par and VTC's for Capital Stock $5 par changed to $2.50 par and (1) additional share or VTC respectively issued 05/27/1964
Each VTC for Capital Stock $2.50 par stamped to indicate extension of Voting Trust Agreement to 10/31/1977
100% acquired by Southern Railway Co. through voluntary exchange offer which expired 01/01/1971
Public interest eliminated

TENNESSEE AMERN WTR CO (TN)
5% Preferred $100 par called for redemption at $105 plus $0.486111 accrued dividends on 07/06/2012
Public interest eliminated

TENNESSEE BANCORP INC (TN)
Merged into Union Planters Corp. 05/01/1994
Each share Common $1 par exchanged for $23.65 cash

TENNESSEE BANK & TRUST CO. (HOUSTON, TX)
Merged into Houston National Bank (Houston, TX) 10/16/1964
Each share Capital Stock $5 par exchanged for (1) share Common $5 par
Houston National Bank (Houston, TX) reorganized as Houston National Co. 03/27/1969 which merged into Republic of Texas Corp. 04/23/1975 which name changed to RepublicBank Corp. 06/30/1982 which merged into First RepublicBank Corp. 06/06/1987
(See First RepublicBank Corp.)

TENNESSEE COMM BANCORP INC (TN)
SEC revoked common stock registration 05/16/2014

TENNESSEE COPPER & CHEMICAL CORP. (NY)
Name changed to Tennessee Corp. 00/00/1930
(See Tennessee Corp.)

TENNESSEE CORP. (NY)
Common no par changed to $5 par 00/00/1933
Common $5 par changed to $2.50 par and (1) additional share issued 00/00/1954
Common $2.50 par changed to $1.25 par and (1) additional share issued 10/07/1959
Acquired by Cities Service Co. 06/14/1963
Each share Common $1.25 par exchanged for (0.9) share $2.25 Conv. Preference no par
(See Cities Service Co.)

TENNESSEE EASTERN ELECTRIC CO.
Reorganized as East Tennessee Light & Power Co. 07/15/1940
Each share 6% Preferred exchanged for (1.335) shares new Preferred
Each share $7 Preferred exchanged for (1.39083333) shares new Preferred
(See East Tennessee Light & Power Co.)

TENNESSEE ELECTRIC POWER CO.
Dissolved 00/00/1939
Details not available

TENNESSEE FORGING STL CORP (VA)
Preferred $100 par changed to $10 par and (9) additional shares issued 11/13/1969
Common $1 par split (2) for (1) by issuance of (1) additional share 09/03/1974
Charter cancelled and proclaimed dissolved for failure to file reports 09/01/1986

TENNESSEE GAS & TRANSMISSION CO. (TN)
Reincorporated under the laws of Delaware as Tennessee Gas Transmission Co. 07/18/1947
Tennessee Gas Transmission Co. name changed to Tenneco Inc. 04/11/1966 which merged into El Paso Natural Gas Co. 12/12/1996 which reorganized as El Paso Energy Corp. 08/01/1998 which name changed to El Paso Corp. 02/05/2001

TENNESSEE GAS TRANSMISSION CO (DE)
5.85% Preferred called for redemption 07/15/1955
5.16% 2nd Preferred called for redemption 03/06/1959
5% 2nd Preferred called for redemption 06/01/1959
Stock Dividends - 33.33333333% 11/12/1948; 25% 11/10/1949; 25% 12/15/1950; 20% 07/18/1952; 33.33333333% 11/18/1955; 20% 03/05/1958; 50% 06/16/1960
Name changed to Tenneco Inc. 04/11/1966
Tenneco Inc. merged into El Paso Natural Gas Co. 12/12/1996 which reorganized as El Paso Energy Corp. 08/01/1998 which name changed to El Paso Corp. 02/05/2001

TENNESSEE INVESTORS, INC. (TN)
Recapitalized as Southeastern Capital Corp. (TN) 06/07/1961
Each share Common exchanged for (0.9) share Common $1 par
Southeastern Capital Corp. (TN) reincorporated in Georgia 07/31/1976
(See Southeastern Capital Corp. (GA))

TENNESSEE LIFE & SERVICE INSURANCE CO. (TN)
Each share Common $5 par exchanged for (5) shares Common $1 par 05/28/1956
Merged into Allied Security Insurance Co. 07/15/1958
Each share Common $1 par exchanged for (0.25) share Common $1 par
Allied Security Insurance Co. merged into United Family Life Insurance Co. 12/03/1963 which reorganized as Interfinancial Inc. 07/01/1969

TENNESSEE LIFE INSURANCE CO. (TX)
Merged into Philadelphia Life Insurance Co. 8/24/67
Each share Capital Stock $1 par exchanged for (0.81818) share Capital Stock $1 par
Philadelphia Life Insurance Co. merged into Tenneco Inc. 3/1/78 which merged into El Paso Natural Gas Co. 12/12/96 which reorganized as El Paso Energy Corp. 8/1/98 which name changed to El Paso Corp. 2/5/2001

TENNESSEE NAT GAS LINES INC (TN)
Common $1 par split (6) for (5) by issuance of (0.2) additional share 06/02/1967
Stock Dividends - 25% 06/19/1958; 10% 01/10/1966; 10% 05/22/1970
Under plan of reorganization each share Common $1 par automatically became (1) share Tennessee Natural Resources, Inc. Common $1 par 09/30/1983
(See Tennessee Natural Resources, Inc.)

TENNESSEE NAT RES INC (TN)
Merged into Piedmont Natural Gas Co., Inc. 03/15/1985
Each share Common $1 par exchanged for $16.50 cash

TENNESSEE NATIONAL LIFE INSURANCE CO. (TN)
Merged into Tidelands Capital Corp. 12/31/1968
Each share Common $1 par exchanged for (4) shares Common no par
Tidelands Capital Corp. merged into Western Preferred Corp. 03/06/1981
(See Western Preferred Corp.)

TENNESSEE ODIN INSURANCE CO.
Name changed to Southern Fire & Casualty Co. 00/00/1949
Southern Fire & Casualty Co. name changed to Southern Title Insurance Co. 03/31/1965 which name changed to Fidelity National Title Insurance Co. of Tennessee 04/28/1989
(See Fidelity National Title Insurance Co. of Tennessee)

TENNESSEE PRODS & CHEM CORP (TN)
Liquidation completed
Each share Common $5 par stamped to indicate initial distribution of $8.60 cash 12/06/1967
Each share Stamped Common $5 par stamped to indicate second distribution of $4 cash 05/08/1968
Each share Stamped Common $5 par stamped to indicate third distribution of $1.20 cash 10/02/1968
Each share Stamped Common $5 par stamped to indicate fourth distribution of $6 cash 12/02/1969
Each share Stamped Common $5 par exchanged for fifth and final distribution of $5.44 cash 09/30/1970

TENNESSEE PRODUCTION CO. (DE)
Reorganized 00/00/1952
Reorganized from Texas to under the laws of Delaware 00/00/1952
Each share Common no par exchanged for (5) shares Common $5 par
Merged into Tennessee Gas Transmission Co. 00/00/1954
Each share Common $5 par exchanged for (0.6) Common $5 par
Tennessee Gas Transmission Co. name changed to Tenneco Inc. 04/11/1966 which merged into El Paso Natural Gas Co. 12/12/1996 which reorganized as El Paso Energy Corp. 08/01/1998 which name changed to El Paso Corp. 02/05/2001

TENNESSEE PRODUCTS CORP. (TN)
Name changed to Tennessee Products & Chemical Corp. 05/28/1947
(See Tennessee Products & Chemical Corp.)

TENNESSEE PUBLIC SERVICE CO.
Dissolved 00/00/1939
Details not available

TENNESSEE-SCHUYLKILL CORP. (DE)
Charter cancelled and declared inoperative and void for non-payment of taxes 04/01/1955

TENNESSEE STOVE WORKS (TN)
Name changed to Modern Maid, Inc. 09/01/1965
(See Modern Maid, Inc.)

TENNESSEE VA ENERGY CORP (TN & VA)
Acquired by United Cities Gas Co. 12/04/1986
Each share Common $1 par exchanged for (0.586) share Common $3.33333333 par
United Cities Gas Co. merged into Atmos Energy Corp. 07/31/1997

TENNESSEE VALLEY BANCORP INC (TN)
Common $10 par split (5) for (4) by issuance of (0.25) additional share 01/02/1973
Common $10 par changed to $6.66666666 par and (0.5) additional share issued 02/26/1973
Name changed to Commerce Union Corp. 04/20/1982
Commerce Union Corp. merged into Sovran Financial Corp. 11/01/1987 which merged into C&S/Sovran Corp. 09/01/1990 which merged into NationsBank Corp. 12/31/1991 which reincorporated in Delaware as BankAmerica Corp. (Old) 09/25/1998 which merged into BankAmerica Corp. (New) 09/30/1998 which name changed to Bank of America Corp. 04/28/1999

TENNESSEE VALLEY BANK (KNOXVILLE, TN)
Merged into Valley Fidelity Bank & Trust Co. (Knoxville, TN) 05/01/1964
Each share Capital Stock $10 par exchanged for (1) share Common $16 par
(See Valley Fidelity Bank & Trust Co. (Knoxville, TN))

TENNESSEE VALLEY LIFE INSURANCE CO. (TN)
Merged into National American Life Insurance Co. 12/31/1963
Each share Common exchanged for (0.77) share Common 50¢ par
(See National American Life Insurance Co.)

TENNESSEE WATER CO.
Acquired by Tennessee Electric Power Co. 00/00/1929
Details not available

TENNEY CORP. (DE)
Name changed to Omega Equities Corp. 04/24/1967
Omega Equities Corp. recapitalized as Ben Wa International Inc. 06/29/1981 which name changed to CEC Properties, Inc. 03/01/1996
(See CEC Properties, Inc.)

TENNEY ENGR INC (NJ)
Common 10¢ par split (5) for (4) by issuance of (0.25) additional share 06/15/1979
Common 10¢ par split (5) for (4) by issuance of (0.25) additional share 06/13/1980
Common 10¢ par split (4) for (3) by issuance of (1/3) additional share 06/19/1981
Common 10¢ par split (4) for (3) by issuance of (1/3) additional share 06/21/1982
Common 10¢ par split (5) for (4) by issuance of (0.25) additional share 06/20/1983
Common 10¢ par split (5) for (4) by issuance of (0.25) additional share 06/22/1984
Common 10¢ par reclassified as Class B Common 10¢ par 05/27/1997
Each share Class B Common 10¢ par received distribution of (1) share of Class A Common 10¢ par payable 05/27/1997 to holders of record 04/10/1997
Stock Dividend - 10% 06/16/1978
Petition under Chapter 11 Federal Bankruptcy Code converted to Chapter 7 on 05/31/2000
No stockholders' equity

TENNIS LADY INC (DE)
Common 1¢ par split (5) for (4) by issuance of (0.25) additional share 05/15/1984
Charter forfeited 02/25/1991

TENNIS UNLIMITED INC (NY)
Name changed to Sinnet Industries, Inc. and Common 10¢ par changed to 1¢ par 01/5/1973
Sinnet Industries, Inc. name changed to Alpha Petroleum Exploration Corp. 12/01/1980
(See Alpha Petroleum Exploration Corp.)

TENNYSON HLDGS LTD (AUSTRALIA)
Name changed to Tennyson Networks Ltd. 00/00/2000
(See Tennyson Networks Ltd.)

TENNYSON NETWORKS LTD (AUSTRALIA)
ADR agreement terminated 06/23/2004
Details not available

TENO-BOSTON GOLD MINES LTD. (ON)
Charter cancelled for failure to file reports and pay taxes 00/00/1955

TENON LTD (NEW ZEALAND)
ADR agreement terminated 09/30/2004
Each Sponsored ADR for Forest Division exchanged for $15.3456 cash
Each Sponsored ADR for Ser. A Forest Division Shares exchanged for $15.3456 cash

TENORE RESOURCE CORP (BC)
Name changed 12/18/1986
Name changed from Tenore Oil & Gas Ltd. to Tenore Resource Corp. 12/18/1986
Merged into Golden Nevada Resources Inc. 08/19/1987
Each share Common no par exchanged for (1) share Common no par
Golden Nevada Resources Inc. recapitalized as Goldnev Resources Inc. 06/19/1989

TENQUILLE RES LTD (BC)
Struck off register and declared dissolved for failure to file returns 07/03/1992

TENSAS DELTA LD CO (MI)
Reincorporated 07/27/1978
State of incorporation changed from (MI) to (LA) 07/27/1978
Merged into Tensas Delta Exploration Co., L.L.C. 04/09/2002
Details not available

TENSAS INC (DE)
Common $0.001 par changed to 1¢ par and (2) additional shares issued payable 02/22/2011 to holders of record 02/15/2011 Ex date - 02/23/2011
Name changed to PGI Energy, Inc. 02/28/2011

TENSLEEP COM INC (CO)
Name changed 04/27/1999
Name changed 11/10/1999
Name changed 09/08/2000
Name changed from Tensleep Design Inc. to Tensleep Technologies, Inc. (Old) 04/27/1999
Name changed from Tensleep Technologies, Inc. (Old) to Tensleep.com, Inc. 11/10/1999
Name changed from Tensleep.com, Inc. (Old) to Tensleep Corp. 09/08/2000
Stock Dividend -.10% payable 06/15/2000 to holders of record 03/31/2000
Each share Common 1¢ par received distribution of (0.1) share Tensleep Technologies, Inc. (New) Common $0.001 par payable 08/15/2002 to holders of record 07/19/2002 Ex date - 07/17/2002
Name changed to Epic Corp. 10/05/2007

TENSLEEP TECHNOLOGIES INC NEW (CO)
Name changed to Yeahronimo Media Ventures, Inc. 03/17/2005
Yeahronimo Media Ventures, Inc. name changed to Commodore International Corp. 10/10/2005

TENSOR CORP (NY)
Name changed to Magicsilk, Inc. 05/09/1986
Magicsilk, Inc. name changed to Vader Group Inc. 04/13/1988 which name changed to SoftNet Systems, Inc. (NY) 06/29/1993 which reincorporated in Delaware 04/13/1999 which name changed to American Independence Corp. 11/14/2002
(See American Independence Corp.)

TENSOR ELECTRIC DEVELOPMENT CO., INC. (NY)
Name changed to Tensor Corp. 01/17/1964
Tensor Corp. name changed to Magicsilk, Inc. 05/09/1986 which name changed to Vader Group Inc. 04/13/1988 which name changed to SoftNet Systems, Inc. (NY) 06/29/1993 which reincorporated in Delaware 04/13/1999 which name changed to American Independence Corp. 11/14/2002
(See American Independence Corp.)

TENTH PWR TECHNOLOGIES CORP (ON)
Each share old Common no par exchanged for (0.2) share new Common no par 08/18/2009
Acquired by 2372052 Ontario Ltd. 05/16/2013
Each share new Common no par exchanged for $0.01 cash

TENTHGATE INTL INC (DE)
Recapitalized as TGI Solar Power Group, Inc. 07/25/2008
Each share Common 2¢ par exchanged for (0.01) share Common $0.001 par

TEO LT AB (LITHUANIA)
GDR agreement terminated 07/01/2010
Each 144A GDR for Ordinary exchanged for $7.44562 cash
Each Reg. S GDR for Ordinary exchanged for $7.44562 cash

TEP FD INC (DE)
Merged into TEP Acquisition, Inc. 11/28/2006
Each share Common 10¢ par exchanged for $18.089 cash

TEPPCO PARTNERS L P (DE)
Units of Ltd. Partnership Int. no par split (2) for (1) by issuance of (1) additional Unit payable 08/21/1998

to holders of record 08/10/1998
Ex date - 08/24/1998
Merged into Enterprise Products Partners L.P. 10/26/2009
Each Unit of Ltd. Partnership Int. no par exchanged for (1.24) Common Units no par

TEQUILA MINERALS CORP (BC)
Name changed to Santa Fe Metals Corp. 03/06/2008

TEQUILABERRYS INC (MN)
Statutorily dissolved 12/30/1994

TER THERMAL RETRIEVAL SYS LTD (AB)
Delisted from Toronto Venture Stock Exchange 10/07/2004

TERA COMPUTER CO (WA)
Name changed to Cray Inc. 04/04/2000

TERA CORP (CA)
Completely liquidated 12/03/1986
Each share Common no par exchanged for first and final distribution of (1) TENERA, L.P. Depositary Receipt, (1) Tera Liquidating Trust Unit of Bene. Int. $0.80 cash
(See each company's listing)

TERA LIQUIDATING TRUST (CA)
In process of liquidation
Details not available

TERA WEST VENTURES INC (NV)
Name changed to American Diversified Group Inc. (NV) 03/15/1995
American Diversified Group Inc. (NV) reincorporated in Delaware as GlobeTel Communications Corp. 07/24/2002 which name changed to Sanswire Corp. 09/24/2008 which name changed to World Surveillance Group Inc. 04/27/2011

TERABEAM INC (DE)
Name changed to Proxim Wireless Corp. 09/10/2007

TERABIT ACCESS TECHNOLOGY INTL LTD (HONG KONG)
Name changed to Ruili Holdings Ltd. 01/06/2005
Ruili Holdings Ltd. name changed to See Corp. Ltd. 11/07/2005
(See See Corp. Ltd.)

TERACOM INC (DE)
Recapitalized as Dix Hills Equities Group, Inc. 01/27/1988
Each share Common $0.001 par exchanged for (0.1) share Common $0.001 par
Dix Hills Equities Group, Inc. name changed to Millennium Quest Inc. 03/22/2002 which recapitalized as American Lorain Corp. (DE) 07/25/2007 which reincorporated in Nevada 11/09/2009 which recapitalized as Planet Green Holdings Corp. 10/01/2018

TERADATA CORP (DE)
Merged into American Telephone & Telegraph Co. 02/28/1992
Each share Common 1¢ par exchanged for (0.802) share Common $1 par
American Telephone & Telegraph Co. name changed to AT&T Corp. 04/20/1994 which merged into AT&T Inc. 11/18/2005

TERAFORCE TECHNOLOGY CORP (DE)
Plan of reorganization under Chapter 11 Federal Bankruptcy Code effective 04/18/2004
No stockholders' equity

TERAFOX CORP (NV)
Name changed to Star Wealth Group Inc. 12/28/2017

TERAGLOBAL COMMUNICATIONS CORP (DE)
Reincorporated 08/26/1999
State of incorporation changed from (WY) to (DE) 08/26/1999
Each share old Common no par exchanged for (0.04) share new Common no par 03/18/2002
Each share new Common no par exchanged again for (0.001) share new Common no par 11/06/2002
Note: In effect holders received $290 cash per share and public interest was eliminated

TERAK CORP (DE)
Merged into Sanders Associates, Inc. (DE) 07/30/1985
Each share Common 1¢ par exchanged for $0.54689 cash

TERANET IA INC (BC)
Name changed to Triant Technologies Inc. 05/06/1996
Triant Technologies Inc. recapitalized as Triant Holdings, Inc. 12/12/2005
(See Triant Holdings, Inc.)

TERANET INCOME FD (ON)
Acquired by Borealis Acquisition Corp. 11/14/2008
Each Trust Unit no par received $10.25 cash

TERASEN INC (BC)
Common no par split (2) for (1) by issuance of (1) additional share payable 06/14/2004 to holders of record 06/07/2004
Acquired by Kinder Morgan, Inc. (KS) 11/30/2005
Each share Common no par exchanged for (0.1635) share Common $5 par and $18.20 cash
(See Kinder Morgan, Inc. (KS))

TERATO RES LTD (AB)
Struck off register for failure to file annual returns 07/01/1989

TERAYON COMMUNICATION SYS INC (DE)
Common $0.001 par split (2) for (1) by issuance of (1) additional share payable 05/05/2000 to holders of record 04/25/2000
Merged into Motorola, Inc. 07/20/2007
Each share Common $0.001 par exchanged for $1.80 cash

TERCICA INC (DE)
Merged into Ipsen S.A. 10/16/2008
Each share Common $0.001 par exchanged for $9 cash

TERENCENET INC (NV)
Name changed to Atlantic Synergy, Inc. 10/01/2003
Atlantic Synergy, Inc. name changed to Acies Corp. 11/16/2004
(See Acies Corp.)

TEREX CORP (NV)
Common Capital Stock no par changed to $1 par 07/10/1969
Company reported out of business 09/22/1989
Stockholders' equity unlikely

TEREX RES INC (AB)
Recapitalized as United Terrex Corp. 04/18/1994
Each share Common no par exchanged for (0.25) share Common no par
United Terrex Corp. name changed to Siberian Pacific Resources Inc. 12/21/1994
(See Siberian Pacific Resources Inc.)

TEREX RES INC (ON)
Name changed to Trelawney Resources Inc. 11/07/2006
Trelawney Resources Inc. recapitalized as Trelawney Mining & Exploration Inc. 04/17/2009
(See Trelawney Mining & Exploration Inc.)

TERITON RES LTD (BC)
Recapitalized as Mashiach Capital Inc. 02/11/1992
Each share Common no par exchanged for (0.25) share Common no par
Mashiach Capital Inc. recapitalized as Animatronix Entertainment Corp. 03/26/1993 which name changed to Creative Entertainment Technologies Inc. 07/13/1995
(See Creative Entertainment Technologies Inc.)

TERLINGUA MERCURY CORP. (TX)
Out of business 00/00/1959
No stockholders' equity

TERMEX RES INC (BC)
Name changed to TME Resources Inc. 02/04/1987
TME Resources Inc. recapitalized as International TME Resources Inc. 07/19/1994 which merged into Chelsea Oil & Gas Ltd. 10/07/2013

TERMIFLEX CORP (MA)
Merged into WPI Group, Inc. 05/04/1994
Each share Common 10¢ par exchanged for (1.2) shares Common 1¢ par
WPI Group, Inc. name changed to Nexiq Technologies Inc. 11/13/2000
(See Nexiq Technologies Inc.)

TERMINAL APPLICATIONS GROUP INC (NY)
Proclaimed dissolved 06/23/1999

TERMINAL DATA CORP (DE)
Reincorporated 09/02/1987
State of incorporation changed from (CA) to (DE) 09/02/1987
Stock Dividends - 10% 02/15/1978; 10% 01/08/1979; 10% 12/07/1979; 10% 02/20/1981; 50% 11/23/1981; 25% 01/06/1983; 25% 01/11/1984; 10% 02/08/1985
Acquired by Bantec, Inc. 02/28/1994
Each share Common $1 par exchanged for $3.375 cash

TERMINAL EQUIP CORP (DE)
Name changed to Tycom Corp. 05/01/1973
(See Tycom Corp.)

TERMINAL HUDSON CORP (NY)
Reincorporated under the laws of Nevada as Titmus Optical Corp. 07/10/1972
Titmus Optical Corp. name changed to King Optical Corp. 05/17/1974
(See King Optical Corp.)

TERMINAL-HUDSON ELECTRONICS, INC. (NY)
Name changed to Terminal-Hudson Corp. (NY) 05/05/1971
Terminal-Hudson Corp. (NY) reincorporated Nevada as Titmus Optical Corp. 07/10/1972 which name changed to King Optical Corp. 05/17/1974
(See King Optical Corp.)

TERMINAL PROMOTIONS INC (CA)
Charter cancelled for failure to file reports and pay taxes 07/01/1988

TERMINAL PROPERTIES, INC.
Merged into Goldblatt Bros., Inc. 00/00/1952
Each share Common no par exchanged for (4) shares Common $8 par or $100 cash
Note: Option to receive stock expired (60) days after the effective date

TERMINAL REFRIGERATING & WAREHOUSING CORP. (DE)
Each share Capital Stock $50 par exchanged for (0.004) share Capital Stock no par 10/23/1980
Note: In effect holders received $446.21 cash per share and public interest was eliminated

TERMINAL TOWER CO. (OH)
Each share old Capital Stock $1 par exchanged (0.1) share new Capital Stock $1 par 00/00/1948
Liquidated 02/20/1956
Details not available

TERMINAL TRANSPORT CO., INC. (IN)
Name changed to JK Corp. 03/25/1966
(See JK Corp.)

TERMINAL WAREHOUSE CO. (NY)
Dissolved 00/00/1947
Details not available

TERMINALS & TRANSPORTATION CORP.
Acquired by Merchants Refrigerating Co. 00/00/1945
Details not available

TERMINALS & TRANSPORTATION CORP. OF AMERICA
Reorganized as Terminals & Transportation Corp. 00/00/1935
Details not available

TERMINALS CORP.
Dissolved 00/00/1949
Details not available

TERMO LTD. (CANADA)
Charter surrendered and company dissolved 03/20/1972
No stockholders' equity

TERRA BLOCK INTL INC (NV)
Name changed to EarthBlock Technologies, Inc. 04/01/2005

TERRA CHEMS INC (DE)
Merged into Hudson Bay Mining & Smelting Co., Ltd. 06/16/1981
Each share Common $1 par exchanged for $21 cash

TERRA CORP (NM)
Acquired by Trimble Navigation Ltd. (CA) 07/02/1996
Each share Common 50¢ par exchanged for (0.08) share Common no par
Trimble Navigation Ltd. (CA) reincorporated in Delaware as Trimble Inc. 10/03/2016

TERRA COTTA PRODUCTS CORP.
Reorganized as Eastern Terra Cotta Co. 00/00/1931
Details not available

TERRA FIRMA RES INC (BC)
Recapitalized as Apple Capital Inc. 11/25/2014
Each share Common no par exchanged for (0.1) share Common no par
Apple Capital Inc. name changed to YDreams Global Interactive Technologies Inc. 07/22/2016

TERRA HEALTH CORP (BC)
Recapitalized as T.H.C. Medical Inc. 12/09/1993
Each share Common no par exchanged for (0.33333333) share Common no par
(See T.H.C. Medical Inc.)

TERRA INDS INC (MD)
Each share Ser. B Preferred exchanged for (12.3762) shares Common no par 07/25/2005
Each share 4.25% Conv. Perpetual Preferred Ser. A exchanged for (120.4819) shares Common no par 03/15/2010
Merged into CF Industries Holdings, Inc. 04/15/2010
Each share Common no par exchanged for (0.0953) share Common 1¢ par and $37.15 cash

TERRA INTERNATIONAL INC. (ID)
Name changed to Sans Prix Cosmetics, Inc. 11/01/1987
Sans Prix Cosmetics, Inc. name changed to International Jet Engine Supply Inc. 09/25/1991

TERRA INTL PHARMACEUTICALS INC (FL)
Recapitalized as Americabilia.Com Inc. (FL) 09/15/1999
Each share Common $0.001 par exchanged for (0.01213592) share Common $0.001 par
Americabilia.Com Inc. (FL) reincorporated in Nevada as Crystalix Group International Inc. 12/06/2002 which recapitalized as Seaena, Inc. 03/31/2006
(See Seaena, Inc.)

TERRA INVENTIONS CORP (NV)
SEC revoked common stock registration 08/08/2016

TERRA LINDA CORP (DE)
Charter cancelled and declared inoperative and void for non-payment of taxes 06/27/1989

TERRA MANNIX INC (AB)
Delisted from Canadian Venture Exchange 05/31/2000

TERRA MEDIA LTD (DE)
Reorganized as Terra Energy Resources, Ltd. 08/29/2008
Each share Common $0.001 par exchanged for (71) shares Common $0.001 par

TERRA MINES LTD (BC)
Name changed 08/20/1982
Stock Dividends - 10% 01/30/1978; 10% 02/25/1980; 10% 01/16/1981
Name from Terra Mining & Exploration Ltd. to Terra Mines Ltd. 08/20/1982
Company went bankrupt 02/03/1994
No stockholders' equity

TERRA NETWORKS S A (SPAIN)
Merged into Telefonica, S.A. 7/18/2005
Each Sponsored ADR for Ordinary exchanged for (0.07407407) Sponsored ADR for Ordinary

TERRA NITROGEN CO L P (DE)
Senior Preference Units called for redemption at $22.105 on 05/27/1997
Acquired by CF Industries Holdings, Inc. 04/02/2018
Each Common Unit exchanged for $84.033 cash

TERRA NOSTRA RES CORP (NV)
Plan of reorganization under Chapter 11 Federal Bankruptcy proceedings effective 07/01/2009
No stockholders' equity

TERRA NOSTRA TECHNOLOGY LTD (NV)
Name changed 04/02/2003
Name changed from Terra Nostra Resources Ltd. to Terra Nostra Technology Ltd. 04/02/2003
Recapitalized as Terra Nostra Resources Corp. 01/20/2005
Each share Common $0.001 par exchanged for (0.1) share Common $0.001 par
(See Terra Nostra Resources Corp.)

TERRA NOVA (BERMUDA) HLDGS LTD (BERMUDA)
Merged into Markel Corp. 03/24/2000
Each share Ordinary $1 par exchanged for (0.07027) share Common no par, (0.07027) Contingent Value Right and $13 cash

TERRA NOVA ACQUISITION CORP (DE)
Name changed to ClearPoint Business Resources, Inc. 02/12/2007

TERRA NOVA ENERGY INC (BC)
Recapitalized as Sato Stevia International Inc. 12/08/1987
Each share Common no par exchanged for (0.33333333) share Common no par
(See Sato Stevia International Inc.)

TERRA NOVA ENERGY LTD (BC)
Reincorporated 10/31/2016
Place of incorporation changed from (AB) to (BC) 10/31/2016
Recapitalized as Claren Energy Corp. 11/14/2016
Each share Common no par exchanged for (0.25) share Common no par

TERRA NOVA FINL GROUP INC (IL)
Reincorporated 06/20/2008
Each share old Common 1¢ par exchanged for (0.1) share new Common 1¢ par 08/01/2007
State of incorporation changed from (TX) to (IL) 06/20/2008
Name changed to TNFG Corp. 10/25/2010
(See TNFG Corp.)

TERRA NOVA GOLD CORP (BC)
Name changed to Terra Nova Minerals Inc. (BC) 02/19/2008
Terra Nova Minerals Inc. (BC) reincorporated in Canada 02/05/2009 which reincorporated in Alberta as Terra Nova Energy Ltd. 08/21/2012 which reincorporated in British Columbia 10/31/2016 which recapitalized as Claren Energy Corp. 11/14/2016

TERRA NOVA MINERALS INC (CANADA)
Reincorporated 02/05/2009
Place of incorporation changed from (BC) to (Canada) 02/05/2009
Each share old Common no par exchanged for (0.07407407) share new Common no par 12/30/2010
Reincorporated under the laws of Alberta as Terra Nova Energy Ltd. 08/21/2012
Terra Nova Energy Ltd. (AB) reincorporated in British Columbia 10/31/2016 which recapitalized as Claren Energy Corp. 11/14/2016

TERRA NOVA RTY CORP (BC)
Each share Common no par received distribution of (0.25) share KHD Humboldt Wedag International A.G. Ordinary payable 07/01/2010 to holders of record 07/01/2010 Ex date - 06/29/2010
Each share Common no par received distribution of (0.25) share KHD Humboldt Wedag International A.G. Ordinary payable 09/23/2010 to holders of record 09/23/2010 Ex date - 09/21/2010
Name changed to MFC Industrial Ltd. 09/30/2011
MFC Industrial Ltd. name changed to MFC Bancorp Ltd. (BC) 02/16/2016
(See MFC Bancorp Ltd. (BC))

TERRA PMTS INC (CANADA)
Merged into Optimal Group Inc. 04/06/2004
Each share Common no par exchanged for (0.4532) share Class A Common no par
(See Optimal Group Inc.)

TERRA RES INC (DE)
Merged into CRA, Inc. 11/01/1976
Each share Common $1 par exchanged for $31 cash

TERRA RICHE MINES LTD (ON)
Charter cancelled and declared dissolved for failure to file returns and pay fees 04/16/1976

TERRA SANTA AGRO S A (BRAZIL)
ADR agreement terminated 01/02/2018
Each 144A Sponsored ADR for Ordinary exchanged for $2.555313 cash
Each Reg. S Sponsored ADR for Ordinary exchanged for $2.555313 cash

TERRA TURNAROUND SPECIALISTS INC (FL)
Proclaimed dissolved for failure to file reports and pay fees 10/13/1989

TERRA VENTURES INC (BC)
Each share Common no par received distribution of (0.5) share Terrex Energy Inc. Common no par payable 06/11/2010 to holders of record 06/11/2010 Ex date - 06/09/2010
Merged into Hathor Exploration Ltd. 08/05/2011
Each share Common no par exchanged for (0.2) share Common no par
Note: Unexchanged certificates were cancelled and became without value 08/05/2017
(See Hathor Exploration Ltd.)

TERRA VISTA INC (UT)
Proclaimed dissolved for failure to file annual reports 07/01/1993

TERRABLOCK DEV INC (WY)
Each share old Common 1¢ par exchanged for (0.02) share new Common 1¢ par 05/12/2006
Name changed to Linked Media Group, Inc. 12/30/2008
(See Linked Media Group, Inc.)

TERRACAMP DEVS LTD (BC)
Struck off register and declared dissolved for failure to file returns 07/10/1992

TERRACE BK FLA (TAMPA, FL)
Reorganized as Pilot Bancshares Inc. 10/01/1995
Each share Common 10¢ par exchanged for (2) shares Common 10¢ par

TERRACE BAY INDS LTD (BC)
Name changed 04/14/1989
Name changed from Terrace Bay Resources Ltd. to Terrace Bay Industries Ltd. 04/14/1989
Name changed to PlanVest Capital Corp. 01/11/1991
PlanVest Capital Corp. name changed to C.M. Oliver Inc. 04/10/1997 which recapitalized as Datawest Solutions Inc. 02/22/2000
(See Datawest Solutions Inc.)

TERRACE FOOD GROUP INC (DE)
Each share old Common $0.001 par exchanged for (0.1) share new Common $0.001 par 3/18/99
Under plan of merger each share new Common $0.001 par exchanged for approximately $0.09 cash 12/23/2005

TERRACE HLDGS INC (DE)
Name changed to Terrace Food Group, Inc. 1/13/98
(See Terrace Food Group, Inc.)

TERRACE RES INC NEW (BC)
Name changed to Terrace Energy Corp. 06/24/2011

TERRACE RES INC OLD (BC)
Recapitalized as Terrace Resources Inc. (New) 06/01/2009
Each share Common no par exchanged for (0.58613898) share Common no par
Terrace Resources Inc. (New) name changed to Terrace Energy Corp. 06/24/2011

TERRACO GOLD CORP (AB)
Name changed 05/12/2003
Name changed from Terraco Energy Corp. to Terraco Gold Corp. 05/12/2003
Reincorporated under the laws of British Columbia 06/08/2011

TERRACOM INC (CO)
Each share old Common no par exchanged for (0.01) share new Common no par 02/14/2001
Recapitalized as EurAsiaCom, Inc. 12/14/2001
Each share new Common no par exchanged for (0.0005) share Common no par
EurAsiaCom, Inc. recapitalized as Supertel Communications, Ltd. 06/24/2002 which name changed to Premier Platforms Holding Co., Inc. 09/24/2002 which name changed to Paolo Nevada Enterprises, Inc. (CO) 02/17/2005 which reincorporated in Nevada as David Loren Corp. 11/13/2006 which recapitalized as Kibush Capital Corp. 08/23/2013

TERRACOM INC (DE)
Charter cancelled and declared inoperative and void for non-payment of taxes 03/01/1994

TERRACOPIA INC (UT)
Charter expired 01/16/2008

TERRADYNE ENERGY CORP (AB)
Assets sold for the benefit of creditors in 2003
No stockholders' equity

TERRAFORM GLOBAL INC (DE)
Acquired by Brookfield Asset Management Inc. 12/28/2017
Each share Class A Common 1¢ par exchanged for $5.10 cash

TERRAGOLD EXPLS INC (BC)
Reorganized 6/15/98
Reorganized from Terragold Resources Inc. (NFLD) to Terragold Exploration Inc. (BC) 6/15/95
Each share Common no par exchanged for (1) share Common no par
Name changed to Terramin Resources Ltd. (BC) 1/9/98
Terramin Resources Ltd. (BC) reorganized in Canada as Terramin Mining Inc. 8/12/99
(See Terramin Mining Inc.)

TERRALENE FUELS CORP (DE)
Recapitalized as Golden Star Enterprises Ltd. 07/16/2013
Each share Common $0.0001 par exchanged for (0.025) share Common $0.0001 par

TERRAMAR CORP (TX)
Common no par changed to 10¢ par 01/19/1982
Acquired by Boundary Oil Co. 07/09/1986
Details not available

TERRAMAR RES CORP (BC)
Struck off register and declared dissolved for failure to file returns 09/23/1994

TERRAMIN MNG INC (CANADA)
Dissolved for non-compliance 02/09/2006

TERRAMIN RES LTD (BC)
Reorganized under the laws of Canada as Terramin Mining Inc. 8/12/99
Each share Common no par exchanged for (0.25) share Common no par
(See Terramin Mining Inc.)

TERRANE METALS CORP (BC)
Merged into Thompson Creek Metals Co., Inc. 10/20/2010
Each share Common no par exchanged for (0.052) share Common no par and $0.90 cash
Note: Unexchanged certificates were cancelled and became without value 10/20/2016

TERRANO CORP (NE)
Name changed to Dynamic Healthcare Technologies, Inc. (NE) 6/13/95
Dynamic Healthcare Technologies, Inc. (NE) reincorporated in Florida 7/1/96 which merged into Cerner Corp. 12/17/2001

TERRANOVA INC (AB)
Name changed to Kevin Sports Toys International Inc. 6/19/90

Kevin Sports Toys International Inc. recapitalized as Gobi Oil & Gas Ltd. 12/31/93 which merged into Dominion Explorers Inc. (New) 12/31/94 which merged into Neutrino Resources Inc. 2/28/97
(See Neutrino Resources Inc.)

TERRAPET ENERGY CORP (DE)
Charter cancelled and declared inoperative and void for non-payment of taxes 03/01/1993

TERRAPIN ENTERPRISES INC (NV)
Name changed to Black Sea Oil, Inc. (New) 12/19/2006
Black Sea Oil, Inc. (New) recapitalized as Clearview Acquisitions, Inc. 11/14/2008 which name changed to Helix Wind, Corp. 04/24/2009

TERRAPIN 3 ACQUISITION CORP (DE)
Merged into Yatra Online, Inc. 12/19/2016
Each Unit exchanged for (1) share Ordinary $0.0001 par and (1) Class A Common Stock Purchase Warrant expiring 12/16/2021
Each share Class A Common $0.0001 par exchanged for (1) share Ordinary $0.0001 par

TERRAQUEST ENERGY CORP (AB)
Recapitalized as Masters Energy Inc. 03/02/2004
Each (12) shares Common no par exchanged for (1) share Common no par
Masters Energy Inc. merged into Zargon Energy Trust 04/29/2009 which reorganized as Zargon Oil & Gas Ltd. (New) 01/07/2011

TERRASOL HLDGS LTD (NV)
Name changed to Alternative Energy Development Corp. 06/11/2009

TERRASTAR DEV CORP (BC)
Struck off register and declared dissolved for failure to file returns 8/23/96

TERRASTAR RES CORP (BC)
Name changed to Pine Point Mines Inc. 03/07/2002
Pine Point Mines Inc. name changed to Mineworks Resources Corp. 01/23/2004 which name changed to Tower Energy Ltd. 07/25/2005 which recapitalized as Tower Resources Ltd. 09/20/2011

TERRATECH RES INC (ON)
Delisted from Toronto Stock Exchange 07/09/1992

TERRAVEST CAP INC (AB)
Name changed to TerraVest Industries Inc. (New) 02/28/2018

TERRAVEST INCOME FD (AB)
Plan of arrangement effective 11/05/2012
Each Trust Unit exchanged for (1) share TerraVest Capital Inc. Common no par
TerraVest Capital Inc. name changed to TerraVest Industries Inc. (New) 02/28/2018

TERRAVEST INDS INC OLD (AB)
Subordinated Exchangeable Shares Ser. 2 no par reclassified as Exchangeable Shares no par 07/09/2006
Exchangeable Shares no par called for redemption at approximately $8.7942605 on 08/31/2008

TERRAVIA HLDGS INC (DE)
Plan of reorganization under Chapter 11 Federal Bankruptcy proceedings effective 01/26/2018
No stockholders' equity

TERRAWEST INDS INC (BC)
Delisted from Canadian Venture Exchange 05/31/2000

TERRE AUX BOUEFS LD CO (DE)
Capital Stock $5 par changed to $1 par and (4) additional shares issued 08/11/1978
Company advised only (2) holders as of 00/00/1980
Public interest eliminated

TERRE HAUTE ELECTRIC CO., INC.
Merged into Public Service Co. of Indiana, Inc. 09/06/1941
Each share Preferred exchanged for (1) share 5% Preferred $100 par, (0.2) share Common no par and $0.08 cash
(See Public Service Co. of Indiana, Inc.)

TERRE HAUTE FIRST CORP (IN)
Name changed to First Financial Corp. 03/19/1985

TERRE HAUTE 1ST NATL BK (TERRE HAUTE, IN)
Stock Dividends - 33-1/3% 7/25/46; 200% 3/15/73
Under plan of reorganization each share Common $20 par automatically became (1) share Terre Haute First Corp. Common no par 5/2/83
Terre Haute First Corp. name changed to First Financial Corp. (IN) 3/19/85

TERRE HAUTE MALLEABLE & MFG CORP (IN)
Capital Stock no par changed to $5 par 00/00/1937
Stock Dividends - 20% 01/29/1951; 10% 01/28/1952; 10% 01/28/1953
Acquired by United Industrial Syndicate, Inc. 00/00/1969
Details not available

TERRE HAUTE TRACTION & LIGHT CO.
Name changed to Terre Haute Electric Co., Inc. 00/00/1931
Terre Haute Electric Co., Inc. merged into Public Service Co. of Indiana, Inc. 09/06/1941
(See Public Service Co. of Indiana, Inc.)

TERREBONE CORP (LA)
Stock Dividend - 20% 12/17/80
Merged into Louisiana Bancshares, Inc. 1/17/86
Each share Capital Stock $5 par exchanged for (3.02164) shares Common no par
Louisiana Bancshares, Inc. name changed to Premier Bancorp, Inc. 4/15/87 which merged into Banc One Corp. 1/2/96 which merged into Bank One Corp. 10/2/98 which merged into J.P. Morgan Chase & Co. 12/31/2000 which name changed to JPMorgan Chase & Co. 7/20/2004

TERREBONNE MINES, LTD. (ON)
Charter cancelled for failure to file reports and pay taxes 00/00/1952

TERREMARK WORLDWIDE INC (DE)
Each share old Common $0.001 par exchanged for (0.1) share new Common $0.001 par 05/10/2005
Acquired by Verizon Communications Inc. 04/11/2011
Each share new Common $0.001 par exchanged for $19 cash

TERRENEX ACQUISITION CORP (AB)
Plan of Arrangement effective 11/27/2007
Each share Class B Preferred no par exchanged for (1) share Terrenex Ltd. Class B Preferred no par
Each share Common no par exchanged for (1) share Common no par
Note: Unexchanged certificates were cancelled and became without value 11/27/2013

Terrenex Ltd. acquired by Questerre Energy Corp. 04/29/2008

TERRENEX LTD (AB)
Acquired by Questerre Energy Corp. 04/29/2008
Each share Class B Preferred no par exchanged for (4.7) shares Common no par
Each share Common no par exchanged for (4.7) shares Common no par

TERRENEX VENTURES INC (AB)
Merged into Terrenex Acquisition Corp. 08/22/1995
Each share Common no par exchanged for (1) share Common no par
Terrenex Acquisition Corp. reorganized as Terrenex Ltd. 11/27/2007 which was acquired by Questerre Energy Corp. 04/29/2008

TERRENO RLTY CORP (MD)
7.75% Preferred Ser. A 1¢ par called for redemption at $25 plus $0.096875 accrued dividends on 07/19/2017
(Additional Information in Active)

TERRESTAR CORP (DE)
Each share 144A Conv. Preferred Ser. B 1¢ par received distribution of (3.331) shares Common 1¢ par payable 10/15/2007 to holders of record 10/05/2007 Ex date - 10/11/2007
Each share 144A Conv. Preferred Ser. B 1¢ par received distribution of (5.962) shares Common 1¢ par payable 04/15/2008 to holders of record 04/04/2008 Ex date - 04/07/2008
Each share 144A Conv. Preferred Ser. B 1¢ par received distribution of (50.314) shares Common 1¢ par payable 04/15/2009 to holders of record 04/03/2009 Ex date - 04/01/2009
Plan of reorganization under Chapter 11 Federal Bankruptcy proceedings effective 03/07/2013
No Common stockholders' equity

TERREX ENERGY INC (AB)
Acquired by Anterra Energy Inc. 03/14/2013
Each share Common no par exchanged for (0.307) share Class A Common no par

TERREX MNG LTD (ON)
Charter cancelled and declared dissolved for failure to file returns and pay fees 03/16/1976

TERREX RES N L (AUSTRALIA)
ADR agreement terminated 01/24/2000
Each ADR for Ordinary exchanged for $0.036 cash

TERRITORIAL GENERATION CO NO 9 (RUSSIA)
GDR agreement terminated 11/01/2013
Each Sponsored 144A GDR for Ordinary exchanged for $1.54826 cash
Each Sponsored Reg. S GDR for Ordinary exchanged for $1.54826 cash

TERRITORIAL GOLD PLACERS LTD. (BC)
Dissolved 09/21/1984

TERRITORIAL PETE VENTURES LTD (BC)
Recapitalized as First Medical Management Ltd. 10/16/1987
Each share Common no par exchanged for (0.33333333) share Common no par
(See First Medical Management Ltd.)

TERRITORIAL RES INC (CO)
Each share old Common no par exchanged for (0.33333333) share new Common no par 05/12/1997
Each share new Common no par exchanged again for (0.0000277) share new Common no par 05/28/1998
Note: In effect holders received $1.40 cash per share and public interest was eliminated

TERRITORIAL URANIUM MINES LTD (ON)
Acquired by New Territorial Uranium Mines Ltd. 12/10/1968
Each share Capital Stock $1 par exchanged for (1) share Capital Stock no par
New Territorial Uranium Mines Ltd. name changed to Mid-West Energy Inc. 08/02/1977 which recapitalized as Millrock Development Corp. 11/19/1984 which recapitalized as Delta Gold Mining Corp. 09/05/1991 which merged into Chase Resource Corp. (New) 05/30/1997
(See Chase Resource Corp. (New))

TERRITORY MINING CO. LTD. (QC)
Merged into St. Fabien Copper Mines Ltd. 07/27/1967
Each share Capital Stock $1 par exchanged for (1) share Common $1 par
St. Fabien Copper Mines Ltd. name changed to St. Fabien Explorations Inc. 02/11/1981 which recapitalized as Fabien Explorations Inc. 07/18/1983
(See Fabien Explorations Inc.)

TERRITORY MNG LTD (BC)
Struck off register and declared dissolved for failure to file returns 01/17/1977

TERRY CORP CONN (CT)
Merged into Ingersoll-Rand Co. (NJ) 10/16/1974
Each share Common $5 par exchanged for (0.37) share Common $2 par
Ingersoll-Rand Co. (NJ) reorganized in Bermuda as Ingersoll-Rand Co. Ltd. 12/31/2001 which reincorporated in Ireland as Ingersoll-Rand PLC 07/01/2009

TERRY HOME DESIGNS INC (NV)
Each share Common $0.001 par exchanged for (0.5) share Common $0.002 par 10/29/1990
Name changed to RS Imaging, Inc. 11/09/1992
RS Imaging, Inc. name changed to Commonwealth Associates Inc. 08/25/1993 which name changed to KCD Holdings Inc. 10/25/1994 which name changed to Sequester Holdings Inc. 04/01/1997 which recapitalized as China Biolife Enterprises Inc. 06/19/2006 which recapitalized as Asia Pacific Energy Inc. 12/07/2007

TERRY INDS INC (DE)
Charter cancelled and declared inoperative and void for non-payment of taxes 04/15/1968

TERRY SHOPS, INC. (NJ)
Adjudicated bankrupt 07/16/1963
No stockholders' equity

TERRY STEAM TURBINE CO (CT)
Each share Common $100 par exchanged for (12.5) shares Common no par and (0.75) share Preferred $100 par 00/00/1930
Common no par changed to $5 par and (4) additional shares issued 11/13/1958
Preferred called for redemption 06/15/1961
Common $5 par split (3) for (1) by issuance of (2) additional shares 04/15/1971
Name changed to Terry Corp. of Connecticut 08/03/1971
Terry Corp. of Connecticut merged

TER-TET

into Ingersoll-Rand Co. (NJ) 10/16/1974 which reorganized in Bermuda as Ingersoll-Rand Co. Ltd. 12/31/2001 which reincorporated in Ireland as Ingersoll-Rand PLC 07/01/2009

TERRYDALE RLTY TR (MO)
In process of liquidation
Each Share of Bene. Int. $1 par received initial distribution of $24 cash 02/23/1981
Each Share of Bene. Int. $1 par received second distribution of $9.50 cash 01/12/1982
Assets transferred to Terrydale Liquidating Trust 02/02/1982
Each Share of Bene. Int. $1 par received third and final distribution of $0.35 cash 02/04/1982

TERRYPHONE CORP. (PA)
Acquired by International Telephone & Telegraph Corp. (MD) 09/30/1964
Each share Common exchanged for (0.087) share Capital Stock no par
International Telephone & Telegraph Corp. (MD) reincorporated in Delaware 01/31/1968 which name changed to ITT Corp. 12/31/1983 which reorganized in Indiana as ITT Industries, Inc. 12/19/1995 which name changed to ITT 07/01/2006

TERRYVILLE TR CO (TERRYVILLE, CT)
Capital Stock $100 par changed to $10 par and (9) additional shares issued plus a 20% stock dividend paid 09/27/1965
Reorganized as Connecticut BancFederation, Inc. 12/28/1973
Each share Capital Stock $10 par exchanged for (4.5593) shares Common $10 par
(See Connecticut BancFederation, Inc.)

TERTIARY MINES LTD (AB)
Acquired by Song Corp. 11/23/1999
Each share Common no par exchanged for (0.36363636) share Common no par
(See Song Corp.)

TERTM TECHNOLOGY CORP (MN)
Name changed 00/00/1990
Name changed from TERTM, Inc. to TERTM Technology Corp. 00/00/1990
Reorganized as DynEco Corp. 01/10/1994
Each share Common 1¢ par exchanged for (0.1) share Common 1¢ par and (1) Unit consisting of (1) Common Stock Purchase Warrant, Class A expiring 06/15/1994, (1) Common Stock Purchase Warrant, Class B expiring 09/15/1994 and (1) Common Stock Purchase Warrant, Class C expiring 12/13/1994
DynEco Corp. recapitalized as Dynamic Leisure Corp. 03/06/2006
(See Dynamic Leisure Corp.)

TESCO AMERN INC (UT)
Each share Common $0.001 par exchanged for (0.02) share Common 5¢ par 08/20/1982
Merged into a private corporation 05/07/1990
Each share Common 5¢ par exchanged for $0.08 cash

TESCO CORP (AB)
Merged into Nabors Industries Ltd. 12/15/2017
Each share Common no par exchanged for (0.68) share Common $0.001 par

TESCO STORES HLDGS LTD (UNITED KINGDOM)
Stock Dividends - 20% 10/18/1962; 50% 08/06/1963; 33.33333333% 08/09/1965; 100% 02/16/1968; 12.5% 02/22/1972; 12.5% 08/17/1973
Name changed to Tesco PLC 07/29/1983

TESCORP INC (DE)
10% Conv. Preferred $1 par called for redemption at $5 on 02/09/1998
Merged into Supercanal Holding S.A. 03/13/1998
Each share 8% Conv. Preferred $1 par exchanged for $144 cash
Each share Common $1 par exchanged for $4.50 cash

TESDATA SYS CORP (DE)
Merged into Infinet Inc. 09/15/1987
Each share Common 1¢ par exchanged for $0.15 cash

TESLA EXPLS LTD (BC)
Dissolved 08/29/2005

TESLA MAGNETIC HOLDINGS INC. (IN)
Administratively dissolved 08/26/1999

TESLA MTRS INC (DE)
Name changed to Tesla, Inc. 02/02/2017

TESLA VISION CORP (NV)
SEC revoked common stock registration 09/11/2009
Stockholders' equity unlikely

TESLIN RIV RES CORP (BC)
Each share old Common no par exchanged for (0.2) share new Common no par 11/22/2012
Each share new Common no par exchanged again for (0.25) share new Common no par 09/09/2014
Recapitalized as Siyata Mobile Inc. 07/29/2015
Each share new Common no par exchanged for (0.45454545) share Common no par

TESMA INTL INC (ON)
Merged into Magna International Inc. 02/06/2005
Each share Class A Subordinate no par exchanged for (0.44) share Class A Subordinate no par

TESMARK INC (NV)
Name changed to 5 G Wireless Communications, Inc. 02/05/2001
5 G Wireless Communications, Inc. name changed to Clean Energy & Power, Inc. 06/26/2009
(See Clean Energy & Power, Inc.)

TESORO CORP (DE)
Reorganized 02/01/1968
Reincorporated 03/03/1969
Name changed 11/08/2004
Reorganized from Delaware to under the laws of California 02/01/1968
Each share Common $1 par exchanged for (2.7) shares Common $0.33333333 par
State of incorporation changed from (CA) back to (DE) 03/03/1969
Common $0.33333333 par changed to $0.16666666 par and (1) additional share issued 03/11/1974
Each share $2.16 Conv. Preferred no par exchanged for (4.9) shares Common $0.16666666 par 02/09/1994
Note: An additional (0.1) share Common $0.16666666 par was issued for each share Preferred held to pay certain legal fees and expenses
Each Premium Income Equity Security exchanged for (1) share Common $0.16666666 par 07/01/2001
Name changed from Tesorp Petroleum Corp. to Tesoro Corp. 11/08/2004
Common $0.16666666 par split (2) for (1) by issuance of (1) additional share payable 05/29/2007 to holders of record 05/14/2007 Ex date - 05/30/2007
Name changed to Andeavor 08/01/2017

Andeavor merged into Marathon Petroleum Corp. 10/01/2018

TESORO DISTRS INC (OK)
Name changed to Tesoro Enterprises, Inc. 03/11/2010

TESORO ENERGY CORP (AB)
Recapitalized as Peregrine Energy Ltd. 07/23/2004
Each share Common no par exchanged for (0.05) share Common no par
Peregrine Energy Ltd. merged into Mahalo Energy Ltd. 06/05/2006
(See Mahalo Energy Ltd.)

TESORO LOGISTICS LP (DE)
Name changed to Andeavor Logistics L.P. 08/01/2017

TESS, INC. (UT)
Name changed to Ashford Financial Group, Inc. 12/00/1986

TESSA COMPLETE HEALTH CARE INC (GA)
Each share old Common 2¢ par exchanged for (0.005) share new Common 2¢ par 12/12/2001
Each share new Common 2¢ par exchanged again for (0.03333333) share new Common 2¢ par 06/03/2002
SEC revoked common stock registration 01/25/2007

TESSA VENTURES LTD (BC)
Recapitalized as International Tessa Capital Corp. 02/23/1993
Each share Common no par exchanged for (0.5) share Common no par
International Tessa Capital Corp. name changed to Apex Resorts Corp. 10/05/1993 which recapitalized as A.M.R. Corporate Group Ltd. 11/12/1996 which recapitalized as Consolidated A.M.R. Corporate Ltd. 12/03/1998 which recapitalized as Consolidated A.M.R. Development Corp. 10/17/2000 which recapitalized as West Hawk Development Corp. 01/09/2002

TESSENDERLO CHEMIE NV (BELGIUM)
ADR agreement terminated 10/12/2004
Each Sponsored ADR for Ordinary exchanged for (0.2) share Ordinary

TESSERA HLDG CORP (DE)
Name changed to Xperi Corp. 02/23/2017

TESSERA TECHNOLOGIES INC (DE)
Name changed to Tessera Holding Corp. 12/01/2016
Tessera Holding Corp. name changed to Xperi Corp. 02/23/2017

TESSERACT GROUP INC (MN)
Plan of reorganization under Chapter 11 Federal Bankruptcy Code effective 12/03/2002
No stockholders' equity

TESSEX ENERGY INC (AB)
Merged into Encounter Energy Inc. 06/10/1998
Each share Class A Common no par exchanged for (0.33333333) share Common no par
Encounter Energy Inc. merged into Impact Energy Inc. (Canada) 10/21/2002 which merged into Thunder Energy Inc. 04/30/2004
(See Thunder Energy Inc.)

TEST CORP (FL)
Charter cancelled and proclaimed dissolved for non-payment of taxes 07/02/1973

TEST EQUIPMENT CORP. (TX)
Merged into Westec Corp. 05/13/1968
Details not available

TESTAMATIC CORP (NY)
Dissolved by proclamation 03/24/1993

TETHYS ENERGY INC (AB)
Merged into Unocal Corp. 07/18/2001
Each share Common no par exchanged for $4.25 cash

TETHYS PETE LTD (GUERNSEY)
Reincorporated under the laws of Cayman Islands 07/28/2008

TETON ENERGY CORP (DE)
Plan of reorganization under Chapter 11 Federal Bankruptcy proceedings effective 01/22/2010
No stockholders' equity

TETON INDS INC (BC)
Recapitalized as Grand Teton Industries Inc. 03/20/1986
Each share Common no par exchanged for (0.5) share Common no par
(See Grand Teton Industries Inc.)

TETON INVTS INC (CO)
Declared defunct and inoperative for failure to pay taxes and file annual reports 04/03/1995

TETON PETE CO (DE)
Each share old Common $0.001 par exchanged for (0.08333333) share new Common $0.001 par 04/28/2003
Name changed to Teton Energy Corp. 07/01/2005
(See Teton Energy Corp.)

TETONKA DRILLING INC (AB)
Merged into Bonus Resource Services Corp. 11/02/2000
Each share Common no par exchanged for (1.507) shares Common no par
Bonus Resource Services Corp. recapitalized as Enserco Energy Service Co. Inc. 05/15/2001
(See Enserco Energy Service Co. Inc.)

TETRA INTL CORP (OK)
Charter suspended for failure to pay taxes 02/19/1985

TETRA METALS LTD (BC)
Recapitalized as Palladon Ventures Ltd. 11/02/2000
Each share Common no par exchanged for (0.25) share Common no par

TETRA SYS INC (DE)
Charter cancelled and declared inoperative and void for non-payment of taxes 06/25/1987

TETRA TECH INC (CA)
Common 50¢ par split (3) for (2) by issuance of (0.5) additional share 11/10/1981
Merged into Honeywell Inc. 04/28/1982
Each share Common 50¢ par exchanged for (0.28037) share Common $1.50 par
Honeywell Inc. merged into Honeywell International Inc. 12/01/1999

TETRA URANIUM MINES LTD. (ON)
Merged into Continental Consolidated Mines & Oils Co. Ltd. 10/04/1957
Each share Common no par exchanged for (0.1) share Common no par
(See Continental Consolidated Mines & Oils Co. Ltd.)

TETRAFLUOR, INC. (CA)
Merged into Amerco, Inc. 02/28/1963
Each share Common no par exchanged for (0.2) share Common $1 par
Amerco, Inc. merged into Royal Industries, Inc. (DE) 06/02/1969
(See Royal Industries, Inc. (DE))

TETRAGENEX PHARMACEUTICALS INC (DE)
SEC revoked common stock registration 01/16/2014

TETRARCH INC (NV)
Charter revoked for failure to file reports and pay fees 10/01/2000

TETRATEL INC (AB)
Reincorporated 08/15/2000
Place of incorporation changed from (ON) to (AB) 08/15/2000
Cease trade order effective 01/22/2002

TETRIDYN SOLUTIONS INC (NV)
Each share old Common $0.001 par exchanged for (0.004) share new Common $0.001 par 03/28/2017
Name changed to Ocean Thermal Technology Corp. 05/25/2017

TEUCRIUM COMMODITY TR (DE)
Trust terminated 12/23/2014
Each Natural Gas Fund Common Share of Bene. Int. received $10.74064 cash
Each WTI Crude Oil Fund Common Share of Bene. Int. received $26.77999 cash
(Additional Information in Active)

TEUTONIA AVENUE STATE BANK (MILWAUKEE, WI)
Name changed to Teutonia Bank (Milwaukee, WI) 03/00/1950
Teutonia Bank (Milwaukee, WI) name changed to Milwaukee Western Bank (Milwaukee, WI) 10/01/1957
(See Milwaukee Western Bank (Milwaukee, WI))

TEUTONIA BANK (MILWAUKEE, WI)
Name changed to Milwaukee Western Bank (Milwaukee, WI) 10/01/1957
(See Milwaukee Western Bank (Milwaukee, WI))

TEVANA TRADERS CORP (ON)
Delisted from Vancouver Stock Exchange 03/03/1997

TEVERE INC (FL)
Each share Common $0.00001 par exchanged for (0.01) share new Common $0.00001 par 02/25/1985
Proclaimed dissolved for failure to file reports and pay fees 08/25/1995

TEX-AG CO. (TX)
Merged into Tanger Industries 06/30/1971
Each share Common $1 par exchanged for (1.25723) shares Common $1 par
Tanger Industries name changed to Verit Industries (CA) 04/02/1973 which reincorporated in Delaware as Verit Industries, Inc. 01/02/1992
(See Verit Industries, Inc.)

TEX-CAN MINES LTD. (BC)
Merged into Bright Star Trio Mining Ltd. 08/06/1971
Each share Common no par exchanged for (1) share Common no par
Bright Star Trio Mining Ltd. merged into Salem Mines Ltd. 06/15/1972 which name changed to Salem Resources Ltd. 11/19/1973
(See Salem Resources Ltd.)

TEX GOLD RES LTD (BC)
Name changed to Genesys Pharma Inc. 11/13/1992
Genesys Pharma Inc. merged into Novopharm Biotech Inc. (New) 08/25/1997 which name changed to Viventia Biotech Inc. 09/11/2000
(See Viventia Biotech Inc.)

TEX-LA-HOMA OIL CORP. (DE)
Charter cancelled for non-payment of taxes 01/23/1924

TEX N PETROLEUM CORP. (DE)
Dissolved 03/24/1967
No stockholders' equity

TEX-O-KAN FLOUR MILLS CO.
Name changed to Burrus Mills Inc. 00/00/1951
(See Burrus Mills, Inc.)

TEX SOL EXPLS LTD (ON)
Capital Stock $1 par changed to no par 03/31/1971
Merged into Dominion Explorers Inc. (Old) 07/19/1985
Each share Capital Stock no par exchanged for (0.4) share Subordinate no par
Dominion Explorers Inc. (Old) merged into Dominion Explorers Inc. (New) 12/31/1994 which merged into Neutrino Resources Inc. 02/28/1997
(See Neutrino Resources Inc.)

TEX-STAR OIL & GAS CORP. (DE)
Common $1 par changed to 50¢ par and (1) additional share issued 01/09/1962
Name changed to Texas Oil & Gas Corp. 12/21/1964
Texas Oil & Gas Corp. merged into United States Steel Corp. (Old) 02/11/1986 which name changed to USX Corp. 07/08/1986 which reorganized as USX-Marathon Group Inc. 05/06/1991 which name changed to Marathon Oil Corp. 12/31/2001

TEX-TUBE, INC. (TX)
Completely liquidated 05/21/1964
Each share Common $1 par exchanged for first and final distribution of (0.4) share Detroit Steel Corp. Common $1 par
6% Conv. Preferred $10 par called for redemption 05/25/1964
Detroit Steel Corp. name changed to Cliffs-St. Clair Corp. 11/16/1970 which liquidated for Cleveland-Cliffs Iron Co. 03/15/1972 which reorganized as Cleveland-Cliffs Inc. (Old) 07/01/1985 which name changed to Cliffs Natural Resources Inc. 10/15/2008 which name changed to Cleveland-Cliffs Inc. (New) 08/25/2017

TEX U S OIL & GAS INC (ON)
Recapitalized as Orex Resources Ltd. 12/29/1986
Each share Common no par exchanged for (0.2) share Common no par
Orex Resources Ltd. name changed to Carlin Gold Co. Inc. 07/20/1988 which recapitalized as Altair International Gold Inc. 03/08/1994 which name changed to Altair International Inc. (ON) 11/06/1996 which reincorporated in Canada 07/02/2002 which name changed to Altair Nanotechnologies Inc. 07/17/2002

TEXACAL RES LTD (BC)
Recapitalized as Rainier Energy Resources Inc. 06/19/1974
Each share Capital Stock no par exchanged for (0.2) share Capital Stock no par
(See Rainier Energy Resources Inc.)

TEXACAN ENERGY LTD (BC)
Struck off register and declared dissolved for failure to file returns 11/19/1988

TEXACO CDA INC (CANADA)
Common no par split (4) for (1) by issuance of (3) additional shares 08/25/1980
6% 1st Preferred Ser. A $100 par called for redemption 11/15/1983
Merged into Imperial Oil Ltd.-Compagnie Petroliere Imperial Ltee. 04/19/1989
Each share Common no par exchanged for $34.36 cash

TEXACO CDA LTD (CANADA)
Name changed 07/14/1975
Common no par split (3) for (1) by issuance of (2) additional shares 02/02/1967
Name changed from Texaco Canada Ltd. to Texaco Canada Ltd.-Texaco Canada Ltee. 07/14/1975

4% Preferred $100 par reclassified as 6% 1st Preferred Ser. A $100 par 06/01/1978
Name changed to Texaco Canada Inc. 07/25/1978
Texaco Canada Inc. merged into Imperial Oil Ltd.-Compagnie Petroliere Imperial Ltee. 04/19/1989

TEXACO CDA PETE INC (CANADA)
Merged into Texaco Acquisition 06/12/1995
Each share Common no par exchanged for $1.48 cash

TEXACO CAPITAL LLC (TURKS & CAICOS ISLANDS)
6.875% Guaranteed Monthly Income Preferred Ser. A called for redemption at $25 on 11/30/2001
Adjustable Rate Monthly Income Preferred Ser. B called for redemption at $25 on 11/30/2001
Deferred Preferred Ser. C called for redemption at $25 plus $22.28 accrued dividends on 02/28/2005

TEXACO INC (DE)
Capital Stock $25 par changed to $12.50 par and (1) additional share issued 08/10/1961
Capital Stock $12.50 par changed to $6.25 par and (1) additional share issued 08/08/1969
Capital Stock $6.25 par reclassified as Common $6.25 par 04/22/1980
Variable Rate Preferred Ser. C $50 par called for redemption 09/30/1994
Common $6.25 par changed to $3.125 par and (1) additional share issued payable 09/29/1997 to holders of record 09/11/1997
Ex date - 09/30/1997
Merged into ChevronTexaco Corp. 10/09/2001
Each share Common $3.125 par exchanged for (0.77) share Common 75¢ par
ChevronTexaco Corp. name changed to Chevron Corp. 05/09/2005

TEXACO INC BOOK ENTRY BANK (NY)
Market Auction Preferred Ser. G-1 called for redemption at $250,000 on 06/21/2001

TEXACO INC BOOK ENTRY BANK (NY)
Market Auction Preferred Ser. H-1 called for redemption at $250,000 on 06/21/2001

TEXACO INC BOOK ENTRY BANK (NY)
Market Auction Preferred Ser. J-1 called for redemption at $250,000 on 06/21/2001

TEXACO INC BOOK ENTRY BANK (NY)
Market Auction Preferred Ser. I-1 called for redemption at $250,000 on 06/21/2001

TEXADA CAP CORP (BC)
Name changed to Petro Vista Energy Corp. 04/11/2008

TEXADA RES LTD (AB)
Name changed to Ramarro Resources Inc. 11/11/1987
(See Ramarro Resources Inc.)

TEXADA SOFTWARE INC (ON)
Reorganized 11/05/2008
Reorganized under the laws of Ontario 11/05/2008
Each share Common no par exchanged for (0.1) share Common no par
Recapitalized as Noble Iron Inc. 07/23/2012
Each share Common no par exchanged for (0.2) share Common no par

TEXADA VENTURES INC (NV)
Old Common $0.001 par split (5) for

(1) by issuance of (4) additional shares payable 11/20/2006 to holders of record 11/20/2006
Each share new Common $0.001 par exchanged for (0.4) share new Common $0.001 par 03/30/2009
Name changed to Black Sea Metals, Inc. 11/07/2011

TEXAL DEVS LTD (BC)
Name changed 05/16/1974
Name changed from Texal Development Ltd. to Texal Developments Ltd. and Capital Stock 50¢ par changed to no par 05/16/1974
Recapitalized as T X Resources Ltd. 05/21/1976
Each share Capital Stock no par exchanged for (0.5) share Common no par
(See T X Resources Ltd.)

TEXALTA PETE LTD (AB)
Merged into PetroFrontier Corp. 06/03/2011
Each share Class A Common no par exchanged for (0.45) share Common no par
Note: Unexchanged certificates were cancelled and became without value 06/03/2015

TEXAM OIL & GAS CO. (DE)
Merged into Texas National Petroleum Co. 09/01/1955
Each share Common exchanged for (1) share Common $1 par
(See Texas National Petroleum Co.)

TEXAM OIL CORP. (NV)
Each share old Common $1 par exchanged for (0.1) share new Common $1 par 03/29/1963
Name changed to Energy Resources Corp. 10/23/1967
Energy Resources Corp. merged into ENERTEC Corp. 05/04/1984
(See ENERTEC Corp.)

TEXANA CAPITAL CORP. (TX)
Charter forfeited for failure to pay taxes 01/09/1989

TEXARKANA FIRST FINL CORP (TX)
Acquired by First United Bancshares, Inc. 10/31/2000
Each share Common 1¢ par exchanged for $23.35208 cash

TEXARKANA NATL BANCSHARES INC (TX)
Merged into Hibernia Corp. 12/31/1996
Each share Common $10 par exchanged for (8.2) shares Class A Common no par
Hibernia Corp. merged into Capital One Financial Corp. 11/16/2005

TEXARKANA NATIONAL BANK (TEXARKANA, TX)
Each share Capital Stock $100 par exchanged for (15) shares Capital Stock $10 par to effect a (10) for (1) split and a 50% stock dividend 01/21/1958
Stock Dividends - 33.33333333% 01/27/1960; 10% 02/17/1971
Merged into Texarkana National Bancshares, Inc. 11/26/1975
Each share Capital Stock $10 par exchanged for (1.333333) shares Capital Stock $10 par
Texarkana National Bancshares, Inc. merged into Hibernia Corp. 12/31/1996 which merged into Capital One Financial Corp. 11/16/2005

TEXAS & PAC RY CO (USA)
Merged into Missouri Pacific Railroad Co. 10/15/1976
Each share Common $100 par exchanged for (9.5) shares Common no par
Missouri Pacific Railroad Co. merged into Missouri Pacific Corp.

11/01/1978 which merged into Union Pacific Corp. 12/22/1982

TEXAS ADAMS OIL CO., INC. (DE)
Declared bankrupt 00/00/1957
No stockholders' equity

TEXAS AIR CORP (DE)
$2.25 Conv. Preferred 10¢ par called for redemption 08/12/1985
15% Preferred 10¢ par called for redemption 01/30/1987
Name changed to Continental Airlines Holdings, Inc. 06/11/1990
(See Continental Airlines Holdings, Inc.)

TEXAS AMERN BANCSHARES INC (TX)
Stock Dividends - 10% 08/29/1980; 25% 08/31/1981
Plan of liquidation under Chapter 11 Federal Bankruptcy proceedings confirmed 06/07/1990
No stockholders' equity

TEXAS AMERN ENERGY CORP (DE)
$2.575 Conv. Exchangeable Preferred no par called for redemption 05/01/1988
Name changed to Kent Financial Services, Inc. (DE) 07/27/1990
Kent Financial Services, Inc. (DE) reincorporated in Nevada 12/15/2006
(See Kent Financial Services, Inc.)

TEXAS AMERN GROUP INC (TX)
Each (60) shares old Common 10¢ par exchanged for (1) share new Common 10¢ par 12/13/1995
Name changed to New Texas American Group Inc. 05/16/2008
New Texas American Group Inc. recapitalized as Zana Acquisition Co. 06/26/2008

TEXAS AMERN OIL CORP (DE)
Under plan of reorganization each share Common 10¢ par automatically became (1) share Texas American Energy Corp. Common 10¢ par 06/13/1980
Texas American Energy Corp. name changed to Kent Financial Services, Inc. (DE) 07/27/1990 which reincorporated in Nevada 12/15/2006
(See Kent Financial Services, Inc.)

TEXAS AMERN RES INC (TX)
Each share Common no par exchanged for (10) shares Common 1¢ par 02/13/1981
Each share old Common 1¢ par exchanged for (0.5) share new Common 1¢ par 07/01/1983
Name changed to Tari Co. 12/20/1994
(See Tari Co.)

TEXAS AMERN SULPHUR CO (TX)
Name changed to Texas American Group Inc. 11/02/1988
Texas American Group Inc. name changed to New Texas American Group Inc. 05/16/2008 which recapitalized as Zana Acquisition Co. 06/26/2008

TEXAS ANADARKO OIL CORP. (DE)
Charter revoked for non-payment of taxes 10/01/1958

TEXAS-ARKANSAS FUND
Liquidated 00/00/1949
Details not available

TEXAS BANCSHARES INC (TX)
Merged into Wells Fargo & Co. 12/16/1999
Each share Common no par exchanged for (0.8366826) share Common $1-2/3 par

TEXAS BK & TR CO (DALLAS, TX)
Each share Capital Stock $20 par exchanged for (2) shares Capital Stock $10 par 07/12/1956
Stock Dividend - 10% 07/23/1956
Merged into First City Bancorporation of Texas, Inc. (TX) 01/01/1974

Each share Capital Stock $10 par exchanged for (1.125) shares Common $6.50 par
(See First City Bancorporation of Texas, Inc. (TX))

TEXAS BK (SAN ANTONIO, TX)
Reorganized as Texas Bancorp Shares, Inc. 07/15/1988
Details not available

TEXAS BIOTECHNOLOGY CORP (DE)
Name changed to Encysive Pharmaceuticals Inc. 05/16/2003
(See Encysive Pharmaceuticals Inc.)

TEXAS BUTADIENE & CHEMICAL CORP. (DE)
Liquidation completed
Each share Common $1 par stamped to indicate initial distribution of $10 cash 08/03/1962
Each share Stamped Common $1 par received second and final distribution of $3.80 cash 07/16/1963
Note: Certificates were not required to be surrendered and are without value

TEXAS CALGARY CO. (DE)
Capital Stock $1 par changed to 25¢ par 01/25/1956
Acquired by Texstar Corp. 10/02/1959
Each share Capital Stock 25¢ par exchanged for (0.125) share Common 10¢ par
(See Texstar Corp.)

TEXAS CAP CORP (TX)
Name changed to Telecom Corp. 10/19/1968
Telecom Corp. name changed to TCC Industries, Inc. 06/01/1994
(See TCC Industries, Inc.)

TEXAS CITY CHEMICALS, INC. (TX)
Assets sold for benefit of creditors 05/10/1957
No stockholders' equity

TEXAS CITY NATL BK (TEXAS CITY, TX)
Merged into Merchants Bank Inc. 01/08/1996
Each share Common $5 par exchanged for $42.50 cash

TEXAS CLAY INDS INC (TX)
Merged into Temtex Industries, Inc. 08/06/1971
Each share Common no par exchanged for (1) share Common 10¢ par
Temtex Industries, Inc. recapitalized as Wanderport Corp. 03/13/2007

TEXAS CO. (OLD)
Succeeded by Texas Corp. 00/00/1927
Details not available

TEXAS CO. NEW (DE)
Capital Stock $25 par split (2) for (1) by issuance of (1) additional share 06/11/1951
Capital Stock $25 par split (2) for (1) by issuance of (1) additional share 06/09/1956
Name changed to Texaco Inc. 05/01/1959
Texaco Inc. merged into ChevronTexaco Corp. 10/09/2001 which name changed to Chevron Corp. 05/09/2005

TEXAS COMM BANCSHARES INC (DE)
Common $10 par changed to $4 par and (1.5) additional share issued 12/04/1972
$2.20 Conv. Special Preferred Ser. A $10 par called for redemption 12/01/1978
Common $4 par split (2) for (1) by issuance of (1) additional share 12/31/1980
$1.80 Conv. Preferred $10 par called for redemption 02/25/1986

Acquired by Chemical New York Corp. 05/01/1987
Each share Common $4 par exchanged for (1) share Adjustable Rate Preferred Ser. C no par, (0.09) share Common $12 par, (1) share Conv. Class B Common no par and $7 cash
Note: Holders also received (1) share National Loan Bank (Houston, TX) Common 1¢ par upon exchange
Chemical New York Corp. name changed to Chemical Banking Corp. 04/29/1988 which name changed to Chase Manhattan Corp. (New) 03/31/1996 which name changed to J.P. Morgan Chase & Co. 12/31/2000 which name changed to JPMorgan Chase & Co. 07/20/2004

TEXAS COMM BK (HOUSTON, TX)
Stock Dividend - 10.34% 02/26/1971
Under plan of reorganization each share Common $10 par automatically became (1) share Texas Commerce Bancshares, Inc. Common $10 par 07/07/1971
Texas Commerce Bancshares, Inc. acquired by Chemical New York Corp. 05/01/1987 which name changed to Chemical Banking Corp. 04/29/1988 which name changed to Chase Manhattan Corp. (New) 03/31/1996 which name changed to J.P. Morgan Chase & Co. 12/31/2000 which name changed to JPMorgan Chase & Co. 07/20/2004

TEXAS COML RES INC (TX)
Reincorporated under the laws of Delaware as Petrosearch Corp. 08/28/2003
Petrosearch Corp. (DE) reorganized in Nevada as Petrosearch Energy Corp. 12/31/2004 which merged into Double Eagle Petroleum Co. 08/06/2009

TEXAS COMWLTH RES CORP (BC)
Recapitalized as Black Jade Resources Ltd. 08/28/1984
Each share Common no par exchanged for (0.33333333) share Common no par
Black Jade Resources Ltd. name changed to International Magnetics Corp. 00/00/1985 which name changed to United Southern Minerals Corp. 11/01/1988
(See United Southern Minerals Corp.)

TEXAS CONSOLIDATED OILS (TX)
Assets sold to satisfy First Mortgage Noteholders 11/01/1960
No stockholders' equity

TEXAS CONSUMER FIN CORP (TX)
Each share Common 50¢ par exchanged for (0.0001) share Common $5000 par 12/07/1972
Note: In effect holders received $1.41 cash per share and public interest was eliminated

TEXAS CONSUMERS WATER CO.
Dissolved 00/00/1937
Details not available

TEXAS CONTINENTAL LIFE INSURANCE CO. (TX)
Merged into National Western Life Insurance Co. (CO) 12/31/1964
Each share Common no par exchanged for (0.0713623) share Common 10¢ par
National Western Life Insurance Co. (CO) reincorporated in Delaware as National Western Life Group, Inc. 10/02/2015

TEXAS CORP. (DE)
Name changed to Texas Co. (New) 00/00/1941
Texas Co. (New) name changed to Texaco Inc. 05/01/1959 which merged into ChevronTexaco Corp. 10/09/2001 which name changed to Chevron Corp. 05/09/2005

TEXAS CREEK MINES LTD. (BC)
Recapitalized as Tex-Can Mines Ltd. 03/22/1971
Each share Common no par exchanged for (0.33333333) share Common no par
Tex-Can Mines Ltd. merged into Bright Star Trio Mining Ltd. 08/06/1971 which merged into Salem Mines Ltd. 06/15/1972 which name changed to Salem Resources Ltd. 11/05/1979
(See Salem Resources Ltd.)

TEXAS CRUDE OIL CO. (TX)
Company went into bankruptcy and assets sold 00/00/1920
No stockholders' equity

TEXAS DIVERSIFIED DISTRS INC (DE)
Name changed to Black Dragon Resources, Inc. 03/10/2004
Black Dragon Resources, Inc. recapitalized as Black Dragon Resource Companies, Inc. 01/05/2005

TEXAS DOME RESOURCE CORP (BC)
Name changed to Microkey Communications Systems Inc. 06/06/1994
(See Microkey Communications Systems Inc.)

TEXAS E-SOLUTIONS INC (NV)
Name changed to Wireless Synergies Inc. 08/27/2001
Wireless Synergies Inc. name changed to 2KSounds Corp. 05/21/2002
(See 2KSounds Corp.)

TEXAS EAGLE OIL AND REFINING CO. (DE)
Charter cancelled for non-payment of taxes 01/01/1926

TEXAS EAGLE OIL CO (OK)
Merged into Dallas Oil & Minerals, Inc. 07/01/1984
Each share Common $0.002 par exchanged for (0.09905045) share Common 2¢ par
Dallas Oil & Minerals, Inc. merged into Lomak Petroleum, Inc. 12/19/1990 which name changed to Range Resources Corp. 08/25/1998

TEXAS EASTERN PRODUCTION CORP. (DE)
Merged into Texas Eastern Transmission Corp. 11/30/1955
Each share Common exchanged for (0.38461538) share Common $7 par
(See Texas Eastern Transmission Corp.)

TEXAS EASTN CORP (DE)
Common $3.50 par split (2) for (1) by issuance of (1) additional share 05/31/1984
Merged into Panhandle Eastern Corp. 06/28/1989
Each share Common $3.50 par exchanged for (2.304) shares Common $1 par
Panhandle Eastern Corp. name changed to Panenergy Corp. 04/26/1996 which merged into Duke Energy Corp. (NC) 06/18/1997 which merged into Duke Energy Corp. (DE) 04/03/2006

TEXAS EASTN TRANSMISSION CORP (DE)
Common $7 par changed to $3.50 par (1) additional share issued 06/01/1961
$5.50 1st Preferred $100 par called for redemption 09/01/1963
5.85% 1st Preferred $100 par called for redemption 01/17/1964
5.80% Preferred $100 par called for redemption 07/30/1964
4.50% Preferred $100 par called for redemption 06/05/1975

4.75% Preferred $100 par called for redemption 06/05/1975
5.35% Subord. Preferred $100 par called for redemption 06/05/1975
5.75% Subord. Preferred $100 par called for redemption 06/05/1975
5.125% Subord. Preferred $100 par called for redemption 06/05/1975
Under plan of merger each share Common $3.50 par automatically became (1) share Texas Eastern Corp. Common $3.50 par 08/31/1976
(See Texas Eastern Corp.)
6.70% Preferred $100 par called for redemption 05/31/1983
14% Preferred $1 par called for redemption 02/07/1985
14.85% Preferred $1 par called for redemption 02/07/1985
$2.40 Preferred $1 par called for redemption 02/11/1985
$2.875 Preferred $1 par called for redemption 02/11/1985
5% Preferred $100 par called for redemption 05/31/1985
Adjustable Rate Preferred Ser. A $1 par called for redemption 03/23/1988
5.52% Preferred $100 par called for redemption 05/31/1989
5.60% Preferred $100 par called for redemption 05/31/1989
5% 2nd Preferred 1964 Ser. $100 par called for redemption 10/01/1993

TEXAS ELEC SVC CO (TX)
Under plan of merger each share $4 Preferred no par, $4.56 Preferred no par, $4.64 Preferred no par, $5.08 Preferred no par, $7.44 Preferred no par, $8.32 Preferred no par, $8.44 Preferred no par, $8.92 Preferred no par, $9.36 Preferred no par, $10.08 Preferred no par and $10.12 Preferred no par automatically became (1) share Texas Utilities Electric Co. $4 Preferred no par, $4.56 Preferred no par, $4.64 Preferred no par, $5.08 Preferred no par, $7.44 Preferred no par, $8.32 Preferred no par, $8.44 Preferred no par, $8.92 Preferred no par, $9.36 Preferred no par, $10.08 Preferred no par and $10.12 Preferred no par respectively 01/01/1984
Texas Utilities Electric Co. name changed to TXU Electric Co. 06/14/1999 which name changed to TXU US Holdings Co. 01/01/2002
(See TXU US Holdings Co.)

TEXAS ELECTRIC RAILWAY CO. (TX)
Liquidation completed 09/30/1955
Details not available

TEXAS ENERGIES INC (TX)
Merged into Sunshine Mining Co. 01/17/1985
Each share Common 10¢ par exchanged for (0.4227) share Capital Stock 50¢ par
Sunshine Mining Co. name changed to Sunshine Mining & Refining Co. 06/20/1994
(See Sunshine Mining & Refining Co.)

TEXAS ENERGY & MFG CO (DE)
Name changed to Southern Retail Marketing Corp. 05/23/1986
(See Southern Retail Marketing Corp.)

TEXAS ENGINEERING & MANUFACTURING CO., INC.
Name changed to Temco Aircraft Corp. and a stock dividend of 20% distributed 00/00/1952
Temco Aircraft Corp. merged into Ling-Temco Electronics, Inc. 07/19/1960 which name was changed to Ling-Temco-Vought, Inc. 08/16/1961 which name changed to LTV Corp. (Old) 05/05/1972 which reorganized as LTV Corp. (New) 06/28/1993
(See LTV Corp. (New))

TEXAS EQUIP CORP (NV)
Each share old Common $0.001 par exchanged for (0.14285714) share new Common $0.001 par 09/08/1999
Charter revoked 09/01/2004

TEXAS EQUITIES (AZ)
Name changed to Continental Diversified Industries 04/06/1973
(See Continental Diversified Industries)

TEXAS FD INC (DE)
Stock Dividend - 200% 03/31/1952
Name changed to Commerce Fund, Inc. (DE) 12/05/1968
Commerce Fund, Inc. (DE) reincorporated in Texas 03/30/1973 which name changed to Commerce Income Shares Inc. 10/14/1977 which reorganized in Massachusetts as Commerce Income Shares 08/26/1985

TEXAS FED FINL CORP (DE)
Stock Dividend - 20% 12/20/1983
Merged into Trinity Banc Savings Association 12/31/1984
Each share Common 1¢ par exchanged for $44 cash

TEXAS FED SVGS & LN ASSN DALLAS (USA)
Reorganized as Texas Federal Financial Corp. 09/08/1983
Each share Common 1¢ par exchanged for (1) share Common 1¢ par
(See Texas Federal Financial Corp.)

TEXAS FIRST MTG REIT (TX)
Name changed 07/06/1971
Name changed from Texas First Mortgage Investors to Texas First Mortgage Real Estate Investment Trust 07/06/1971
Name changed to Parkway Co. (TX) 09/26/1979
Parkway Co. (TX) reincorporated in Maryland as Parkway Properties, Inc. 08/02/1996 which merged into Cousins Properties Inc. 10/06/2016

TEXAS GAS & OIL INC (BC)
Name changed to Legend Power Systems Inc. 07/03/2008

TEXAS GAS CORP. (DE)
Name changed to Texas Gas Resources Corp. 05/12/1983
Texas Gas Resources Corp. merged into CSX Corp. 09/30/1983

TEXAS GAS DISTRIBUTING CO.
Dissolved 00/00/1941
Details not available

TEXAS GAS PRODUCING CO. (TX)
Acquired by Landa Oil Co. (Old) 10/15/1965
Each share Common 25¢ par exchanged for (0.666666) share Common 10¢ par and $2 principal amount of 5% Conv. Debentures due 10/01/1980
Landa Oil Co. (Old) name changed to Landa Industries, Inc. 04/07/1967 which recapitalized as Surveyor Companies, Inc. 11/12/1971 which name changed to Forum Companies, Inc. 09/23/1974
(See Forum Companies, Inc.)

TEXAS GAS RES CORP (DE)
Merged into CSX Corp. 09/30/1983
Each share Common $5 par exchanged for (0.684) share Common $1 par

TEXAS GAS TRANSMISSION CORP (DE)
Common no par changed to $5 par 00/00/1948
5.25% 2nd Preferred $100 par called for redemption 10/01/1975
Common $5 par split (3) for (2) by issuance of (0.5) additional share 06/22/1966

5.4% Preferred $100 par called for redemption 10/01/1975
Common $5 par split (2) for (1) by issuance of (1) additional share 09/15/1979
$1.50 Conv. Preference $5 par called for redemption 10/30/1979
Under plan of reorganization each share Common $5 par automatically became (1) share Texas Gas Corp. Common $5 par 01/01/1983
(See Texas Gas Corp.)
4.96% Preferred $100 par called for redemption 08/01/1983
9.375% Preferred $100 par called for redemption 01/30/1987
8.25% Preferred $100 par called for redemption 04/01/1989
Public interest eliminated

TEXAS GAS UTILITIES CO. (DE)
Reorganized as Texas Gas Utilities Corp. 01/03/1956
Each share Common $1 par exchanged for (0.75) share Common $2 par
Texas Gas Utilities Corp. merged into Associated Oil & Gas Co. 12/21/1962 which name changed to AO Industries, Inc. 05/05/1969 which name changed to Aegis Corp. 06/01/1974
(See Aegis Corp.)

TEXAS GAS UTILITIES CORP. (TX)
Merged into Associated Oil & Gas Co. 12/21/1962
Each share Common $2 par exchanged for (1.18919) shares Common 1¢ par
Associated Oil & Gas Co. name changed to AO Industries, Inc. 05/05/1969 which name changed to Aegis Corp. 06/01/1974
(See Aegis Corp.)

TEXAS GENCO HLDGS INC (TX)
Acquired by GC Power Acquisition LLC 12/14/2004
Each share Common $0.001 par exchanged for $47 cash

TEXAS GENERAL GROUP, INC. (TX)
Name changed to Texas General Resources, Inc. 03/23/1981
(See Texas General Resources, Inc.)

TEXAS GENL RES INC (TX)
Plan of reorganization under Chapter 11 Federal Bankruptcy proceedings confirmed 01/24/1989
No stockholders' equity

TEXAS GLASS FIBER CORP. (TX)
Declared bankrupt 04/05/1960
No stockholders' equity

TEXAS GULF BANCSHARES INC (TX)
Merged into Texas Regional Bancshares, Inc. 01/02/2004
Each share Common $10 par exchanged for $83.20 cash

TEXAS GULF INC (TX)
Name changed to Texasgulf Inc. 04/27/1973
(See Texasgulf Inc.)

TEXAS GULF INDS INC (TX)
Charter forfeited for failure to pay taxes 02/14/1995

TEXAS GULF PETE CORP (BC)
Reincorporated 06/11/1996
Place of incorporation changed from (ON) to (BC) 06/11/1996
Recapitalized as Portrush Petroleum Corp. 03/15/2000
Each share Common no par exchanged for (0.2) share Common no par
Portrush Petroleum Corp. recapitalized as Westbridge Energy Corp. 12/11/2009

TEXAS GULF PRODUCING CO. (DE)
Common no par changed to $1 par 00/00/1945

Common $1 par changed to $10 par 00/00/1949
Common $10 par changed to $3.33333333 par and (2) additional shares issued 04/29/1955
Stock Dividend - 10% 12/16/1953
Liquidation completed
Each share Common $3.33333333 par received initial distribution of $1 cash 06/08/1964
Each share Common $3.33333333 par stamped to indicate second distribution of $59 cash 12/10/1964
Each share Stamped Common $3.33333333 par exchanged for third distribution of $3.75 cash 04/22/1965
Each share Stamped Common $3.33333333 par received fourth distribution of $0.25 cash 01/11/1967
Each share Stamped Common $3.33333333 par received fifth and final distribution of $0.7053951 cash 11/14/1969

TEXAS GULF SULPHUR CO (TX)
Each share Capital Stock $10 par exchanged for (4) shares Capital Stock no par in 1926
Capital Stock no par split (3) for (1) by issuance of (2) additional shares in 1955
Capital Stock no par split (3) for (1) by issuance of (2) additional shares 6/3/68
Name changed to Texas Gulf, Inc. and Capital Stock no par reclassified as Common no par 4/28/72
Texas Gulf, Inc. name changed to Texasgulf Inc. 4/27/73
(See Texasgulf Inc.)

TEXAS HANOVER OIL CO. (TX)
Charter forfeited for failure to pay taxes 6/28/68

TEXAS HERITAGE SVGS ASSN/BANC (TX)
Merged into Jefferson Savings Bancorp, Inc. 12/31/96
Each share Common $2.50 par exchanged for (0.3976) share Common 1¢ par
Jefferson Savings Bancorp, Inc. merged Union Planters Corp. 2/12/2001 which merged into Regions Financial Corp. (New) 7/1/2004

TEXAS HILL CTRY BARBECUE INC (NV)
Name changed to South American Properties, Inc. 04/10/2013
South American Properties, Inc. name changed to USA Restaurant Funding Inc. 11/17/2014 which name changed to Chron Organization, Inc. 03/24/2016 which name changed to Zenergy Brands, Inc. 12/01/2017

TEXAS HITECH INC (DE)
Each share Common $0.001 par exchanged for (0.1) share Common 1¢ par 8/26/86
Recapitalized as THT Lloyd's Inc. 10/25/86
Each share Common 1¢ par exchanged for (0.1) share Common 1¢ par
THT Lloyd's Inc. name changed to THT Inc. 5/4/88
(See THT Inc.)

TEXAS HOMER OIL CO. (AZ)
Charter revoked for failure to file reports and pay fees 6/28/27

TEXAS HYDRO ELECTRIC CORP. (TX)
Common no par changed to $1 par 3/3/55
Liquidation completed 3/11/64

TEXAS-ILLINOIS NATURAL GAS PIPELINE CO. (TX)
Acquired by Peoples Gas Light & Coke Co. on a (0.5) for (1) basis 11/30/59

TEX-TEX   **FINANCIAL INFORMATION, INC.**

Peoples Gas Light & Coke Co. acquired by Peoples Gas Co. 9/26/68 which name changed to Peoples Energy Corp. 2/1/80 which merged into Integrys Energy Group, Inc. 2/21/2007

TEXAS INDS INC (DE)
Common $1 par split (2) for (1) by issuance of (1) additional share 02/10/1953
Common $1 par split (2) for (1) by issuance of (1) additional share 11/30/1978
5% Preferred no par called for redemption at $105 on 03/29/1996
Common $1 par split (2) for (1) by issuance of (1) additional share payable 02/28/1997 to holders of record 02/03/1997 Ex date - 03/03/1997
Each share Common $1 par received distribution of (1) share Chaparral Steel Co. Common 1¢ par payable 07/29/2005 to holders of record 07/20/2005 Ex date - 08/01/2005
Stock Dividend - 100% 05/25/1955
Merged into Martin Marietta Materials, Inc. 07/01/2014
Each share Common $1 par exchanged for (0.7) share Common 1¢ par

TEXAS INSTRS INC (DE)
4.48% Preferred Ser. A $25 par called for redemption 08/01/1957
4% Preferred 1959 Ser. $25 par called for redemption 11/25/1963
Conv. Money Market Preferred Ser. C-3 called for redemption 04/09/1991
Depositary Preferred Ser. A $25 par called for redemption 09/27/1993
Conv. Preferred Ser. A $25 par called for redemption 09/27/1993
(Additional Information in Active)

TEXAS INTL AIRLS INC (DE)
Common $2 par changed to 1¢ par 04/26/1972
Under plan of reorganization each share Common 1¢ par automatically became (1) share Texas Air Corp. Common 1¢ par 06/11/1980
Texas Air Corp. name changed to Continental Airlines Holdings, Inc. 06/11/1990
(See Continental Airlines Holdings, Inc.)

TEXAS INTL CO (DE)
Common 10¢ par split (2) for (1) by issuance of (1) additional share 02/20/1981
Reorganized under Chapter 11 Federal Bankruptcy Code as Phoenix Resource Companies, Inc. 04/09/1990
Each share Common 10¢ par exchanged for (0.125) Common Stock Purchase Warrant Ser. A expiring 04/09/1991
Phoenix Resource Companies, Inc. merged into Apache Corp. 05/20/1996

TEXAS INTERNATIONAL PETROLEUM CORP. (DE)
Name changed to Texas International Co. 01/03/1972
Texas International Co. reorganized as Phoenix Resource Companies, Inc. 04/09/1990 which merged into Apache Corp. 05/20/1996

TEXAS INTL SPEEDWAY INC (TX)
Adjudicated bankrupt 09/00/1971
Stockholders' equity unlikely

TEXAS INTERNATIONAL SULPHUR CO. (DE)
No longer in existence having become inoperative and void for non-payment of taxes 4/1/64

TEXAS LAND & MORTGAGE CO. LTD.
In process of liquidation in 1945

TEXAS LAND SYNDICATE NO. 1
Liquidated in 1940

TEXAS LAND SYNDICATE NO. 3
Liquidation completed in 1942

TEXAS LIFE INS CO (TX)
Stock Dividend - 50% 06/10/1983
Acquired by Metropolitan Life Insurance Co. 07/31/1988
Each share Capital Stock $2 par exchanged for $18.71 principal amount of MetLife Texas Holdings, Inc. 9.41% Contingent Payment Notes due 12/31/1997 and $69 cash

TEXAS-LOUISIANA POWER CO.
Reorganized as Community Public Service Co. in 1935
No stockholders' equity

TEXAS MERIDIAN RES CORP (TX)
Name changed to Meridian Resource Corp. 06/19/1997
(See Meridian Resource Corp.)

TEXAS MERIDIAN RES LTD (TX)
Merged into Texas Meridian Resources Corp. 12/18/1990
Each Unit of Ltd. Partnership Int. exchanged for (0.2) share Common 1¢ par
Texas Meridian Resources Corp. name changed to Meridian Resources Corp. 06/19/1997
(See Meridian Resource Corp.)

TEXAS METALS INC (TX)
Merged into Pearsall Corp. 06/23/1971
Each share Common 20¢ par exchanged for (1) share Common 20¢ par
Pearsall Corp. recapitalized as Pearsall Chemical Corp. 04/25/1973
(See Pearsall Chemical Corp.)

TEXAS MICRO INC (DE)
Merged into RadiSys Corp. 8/13/99
Each share Common 40¢ par exchanged for (0.20146) share Common no par

TEXAS MONEY FUND, INC. (TX)
Ceased operations 04/29/1983
Details not available

TEXAS NATIONAL BANK (DALLAS, TX)
Merged into First Security National Corp. 01/18/1974
Each share Common Capital Stock $5 par exchanged for (1.8) shares Common $2.50 par
First Security National Corp. merged into First City Bancorporation of Texas, Inc. (TX) 12/03/1979
(See First City Bancorporation of Texas, Inc. (TX))

TEXAS NATIONAL BANK (HOUSTON, TX)
Capital Stock $20 par changed to $10 par and (1) additional share issued 02/09/1960
Stock Dividend - 16.66666666% 02/01/1957
Merged into Texas National Bank of Commerce (Houston, TX) 01/17/1964
Each share Capital Stock $10 par exchanged for (1) share Capital Stock $10 par
Texas National Bank of Commerce (Houston, TX) name changed to Texas Commerce Bank N.A. (Houston, TX) 01/20/1970 which reorganized as Texas Commerce Bancshares, Inc. 07/07/1971 which was acquired by Chemical New York Corp. 05/01/1987 which name changed to Chemical Banking Corp. 04/29/1988 which name changed to Chase Manhattan Corp. (New) 03/31/1996 which name changed to J.P. Morgan Chase & Co. 12/31/2000 which name changed to JPMorgan Chase & Co. 07/20/2004

TEXAS NATL BK COMM (HOUSTON, TX)
Name changed to Texas Commerce Bank N.A. (Houston, TX) 01/20/1970
Texas Commerce Bank N.A. (Houston, TX) reorganized as Texas Commerce Bancshares, Inc. 07/07/1971 which was acquired by Chemical New York Corp. 05/01/1987 which name changed to Chemical Banking Corp. 04/29/1988 which name changed to Chase Manhattan Corp. (New) 03/31/1996 which name changed to J.P. Morgan Chase & Co. 12/31/2000 which name changed to JPMorgan Chase & Co. 07/20/2004

TEXAS NATIONAL OIL CO. (TX)
Charter revoked for failure to file reports and pay fees 9/30/53

TEXAS NATIONAL PETROLEUM CO. (DE)
Liquidation completed
Each share Common $1 par stamped to indicate initial distribution of $3.50 cash 12/14/1962
Each share Stamped Common $1 par exchanged for second distribution of $3.90 cash 02/04/1963
Each share Stamped Common $1 par received third distribution of $0.15 cash 04/24/1963
Each share Stamped Common $1 par received fourth and final distribution of $0.00375 cash 03/21/1972

TEXAS NATURAL GASOLINE CORP. (DE)
Common $1 par split (2) for (1) by issuance of (1) additional share 1/30/58
Merged into Union Texas Natural Gas Corp. 3/3/60
Each share Common $1 par exchanged for (0.75) share Class A $1 par and (0.375) share Class B $1 par
Union Texas Natural Gas Corp. merged into Allied Chemical Corp. 2/20/62 which name changed to Allied Corp. 4/27/81 which merged into Allied-Signal Inc. 9/19/85 which name changed to AlliedSignal Inc. 4/26/93 which name changed to Honeywell International Inc. 12/1/99

TEXAS NEVADA OIL & GAS CO. (TX)
Merged into Houston American Energy Corp. 01/18/2002
Each share Common no par exchanged for (1) share Common $0.001 par

TEXAS NEW MEX PWR CO (TX)
Reorganized as TNP Enterprises, Inc. 10/3/84
Each share Common $10 par exchanged for (2) shares Common no par
4.65% Preferred Ser. B $100 par called for redemption at $100 on 9/15/2000
(See TNP Enterprises, Inc.)

TEXAS NORTHERN OIL CORP. (DE)
Merged into Gulf Coast Leaseholds, Inc. 05/24/1954
Each share Common 10¢ par exchanged for (0.36363636) share Capital Stock
Gulf Coast Leaseholds, Inc. name changed to Coronet Petroleum Corp. 09/04/1964 which liquidated for Texstar Corp. 04/15/1965
(See Texstar Corp.)

TEXAS NORTHN MINERAL LTD (BC)
Name changed 11/18/87
Name changed from Texas Northern Oil & Gas Inc. to Texas Northern Minerals Ltd. 11/18/87
Recapitalized as Consolidated Texas Northern Minerals Ltd. 3/23/92
Each share Common no par exchanged for (0.2) share Common no par

Consolidated Texas Northern Minerals recapitalized as Rio Verde Industries Inc. 6/28/2000

TEXAS-OHIO GAS CO. (DE)
Name changed to Colonial Natural Gas Corp. in 1955 which completed liquidation 10/12/64

TEXAS OIL & GAS CORP (DE)
Common 50¢ par split (2) for (1) by issuance of (1) additional share 02/14/1969
Common 50¢ par split (2) for (1) by issuance of (1) additional share 03/01/1971
Common 50¢ par split (2) for (1) by issuance of (1) additional share 06/30/1972
Common 50¢ par split (2) for (1) by issuance of (1) additional share 01/14/1980
Common 50¢ par split (2) for (1) by issuance of (1) additional share 01/14/1981
Common 50¢ par split (2) for (1) by issuance of (1) additional share 01/12/1984
Stock Dividends - 10% 05/16/1975; 10% 01/16/1979; 10% 10/31/1980; 10% 07/15/1983
Merged into United States Steel Corp. (Old) 02/11/1986
Each share Common 50¢ par exchanged for (0.6333) share Common $1 par
United States Steel Corp. (Old) name changed to USX Corp. 07/08/1986 which reorganized as USX-Marathon Group Inc. 05/06/1991 which name changed to Marathon Oil Corp. 12/31/2001

TEXAS OIL PRODUCING & REFINING CO. (TX)
Charter revoked for failure to file reports and pay fees 05/19/1950

TEXAS PACIFIC COAL & OIL CO. (TX)
Capital Stock $10 par split (2) for (1) by issuance of (1) additional share 10/21/1955
Stock Dividend - 100% 09/03/1948
Liquidation completed
Each share Capital Stock $10 par stamped to indicate initial distribution of $68 cash 11/12/1963
Each share Stamped Capital Stock $10 par exchanged for second distribution of $0.53 cash 08/31/1964
Each share Stamped Capital Stock $10 par received third and final distribution of $0.44 cash 10/01/1964

TEXAS PETE CO (TX)
Charter forfeited for failure to pay taxes 01/09/1989

TEXAS PETE CORP (BC)
Recapitalized as North American Equity Corp. 03/07/1989
Each share Common no par exchanged for (0.33333333) share Common no par
(See North American Equity Corp.)

TEXAS PETE CORP (CO)
Name changed to E.T. Network, Inc. 11/18/1993
E.T. Network, Inc. recapitalized as E.T. Capital Inc. 02/08/1995 which recapitalized as eCom.com, Inc. (CO) 10/15/1999 which reincorporated in Nevada 06/10/2000 which recapitalized as E.T. Corp. 04/12/2002 which recapitalized as ParaFin Corp. 10/15/2004

TEXAS PETROCHEMICALS INC (DE)
Name changed to TPC Group Inc. 03/25/2010
(See TPC Group Inc.)

TEXAS PHARMACAL CO. (TX)
Stock Dividend - 100% 04/01/1964

Acquired by Warner-Lambert Pharmaceutical Co. 04/11/1966
Each share Common $5 par exchanged for (1.2) shares Common $1 par
Warner-Lambert Pharmaceutical Co. name changed to Warner-Lambert Co. 11/13/1970 which merged into Pfizer Co. 06/19/2000

TEXAS PWR & LT CO (TX)
Under plan of merger each share $4 Preferred no par, $4.44 Preferred no par, $4.56 Preferred no par, $4.76 Preferred no par, $4.84 Preferred no par, $7.24 Preferred no par, $7.80 Preferred no par, $8.16 Preferred no par, $8.20 Preferred no par, $8.68 Preferred no par, $8.84 Preferred no par, $9.32 Preferred no par and $10.92 Preferred no par automatically became (1) share Texas Utilities Electric Co. $4 Preferred no par, $4.44 Preferred no par, $4.56 Preferred no par, $4.76 Preferred no par, $4.84 Preferred no par, $7.24 Preferred no par, $7.80 Preferred no par, $8.16 Preferred no par, $8.20 Preferred no par, $8.68 Preferred no par, $8.84 Preferred no par, $9.32 Preferred no par and $10.92 Preferred no par respectively 01/01/1984
Texas Utilities Electric Co. name changed to TXU Electric Co. 06/14/1999 which name changed to TXU US Holdings Co. 01/01/2002
(See TXU US Holdings Co.)

TEXAS POWER CORP. (TX)
Each share Common no par exchanged for (8) shares Common $1 par 03/03/1955
Liquidation completed 03/11/1964
Details not available

TEXAS PUBLIC SERVICE CO.
Merged into Southern Union Gas Co. (DE) (New) 07/21/1949
Each share Common exchanged for $12 principal amount of 3.25% 15-year Debentures and (1) share $1 Preference Common $1 par
(See Southern Union Gas Co. (DE) (New))

TEXAS RARE EARTH RES CORP (DE)
Reincorporated 08/24/2012
State of incorporation changed from (NV) to (DE) 08/24/2012
Name changed to Texas Mineral Resources Corp. 03/21/2016

TEXAS REGL BANCSHARES INC (TX)
Class A $1 par split (3) for (2) by issuance of (0.5) additional share payable 08/21/1997 to holders of record 07/31/1997
Class A Common $1 par split (3) for (2) by issuance of (0.5) additional share payable 06/28/2002 to holders of record 06/21/2002 Ex date - 07/01/2002
Class A Common $1 par split (3) for (2) by issuance of (0.5) additional share payable 08/30/2004 to holders of record 08/23/2004
Stock Dividends - 10% payable 01/12/2001 to holders of record 01/02/2001; 10% payable 04/15/2003 to holders of record 04/01/2003 Ex date - 03/28/2003
Merged into Banco Bilbao Vizcaya Argentaria, S.A. 11/10/2006
Each share Class A Common $1 par exchanged for $38.90 cash

TEXAS RESEARCH & ELECTRONIC CORP. (MN)
Class A Common 10¢ par reclassified as Common 10¢ par 08/25/1961
Name changed to United States Brass Corp. 05/15/1963
United States Brass Corp. liquidated for Hydrometals, Inc. 12/07/1967
(See Hydrometals, Inc.)

TEXAS RESV LIFE INS CO (TX)
Each share Capital Stock no par exchanged for (0.2) share Common $1 par 00/00/1962
Merged into Great Southwest Life Insurance Co. 12/31/1964
Each share Preferred exchanged for (22) shares Common no par
Each share Common $1 par exchanged for (3) shares Common no par
(See Great Southwest Life Insurance Co.)

TEXAS SCIENTIFIC INDUSTRIES, INC. (DE)
Name changed to Bridgestone Capital Corp. 01/06/1988
Bridgestone Capital Corp. name changed to Imagetrust Inc. 10/13/1992
(See Imagetrust Inc.)

TEXAS SCIENTIFIC INDS INC (UT)
Merged into Emory Capital Corp. 08/14/1989
Each share Common exchanged for (0.05) share Common 1¢ par
Emory Capital Corp. name changed to Sargent, Inc. (Old) 11/29/1990 which reorganized as Sargent, Inc. (New) 07/25/1994 which name changed to National Quality Care Inc. 05/28/1996

TEXAS SEC BANCSHARES INC (TX)
Name changed to Central Bancorporation, Inc. 04/05/1995
Central Bancorporation, Inc. merged into Norwest Corp. 01/28/1997 which name changed to Wells Fargo & Co. (New) 11/02/1998

TEXAS SEVENS RES INC (BC)
Recapitalized as Canadian Eagle Explorations Ltd. 07/14/1989
Each share Common no par exchanged for (0.2) share Common no par
Canadian Eagle Explorations Ltd. recapitalized as Eaglecrest Explorations Ltd. 02/01/1993 which name changed to Colombia Crest Gold Corp. 02/14/2011

TEXAS SIDEWINDER OIL CORP (BC)
Name changed to Archon Minerals Ltd. 05/29/1995

TEXAS SOUTHEASTERN GAS CO. (DE)
Liquidation completed 07/29/1960
Details not available

TEXAS SOUTHERN OIL & GAS CO. (DE)
No longer in existence having become inoperative and void for non-payment of taxes 04/01/1960

TEXAS ST BK (AUSTIN, TX)
Common $10 par split (2) for (1) by issuance of (1) additional share 03/15/1972
Acquired by Republic of Texas Corp. 01/03/1979
Each share Common $10 par exchanged for $30 cash

TEXAS ST BK (SAN ANGELO, TX)
Under plan of reorganization each share Common no par automatically became (1) share Texas Bancorp, Inc. Common no par 01/02/1997

TEXAS ST BK (SAN ANTONIO, TX)
Name changed to Texas Bank (San Antonio, TX) 02/16/1978
(See Texas Bank (San Antonio, TX))

TEXAS ST NETWORK INC (TX)
Name changed to TSN Liquidating, Inc. 02/29/1972
(See TSN Liquidating, Inc.)

TEXAS ST VIDEO CO (TX)
Reincorporated under the laws of Delaware as TSV Corp. 02/27/1986
(See TSV Corp.)

TEXAS STANDARD OIL CO. (TX)
Charter forfeited for failure to pay taxes 05/19/1950

TEXAS STAR RES CORP (BC)
Name changed to Star Resources Corp. 10/30/1996
Star Resources Corp. name changed to Jaguar Resources Corp. 09/18/2003 which name changed to Brazauro Resources Corp. 09/08/2004
(See Brazauro Resources Corp.)

TEXAS STATE PETROLEUM, INC. (DE)
Merged into Appell Petroleum Corp. 09/17/1957
Each share Common 10¢ par exchanged for (0.066666) share Common $1 par
(See Appell Petroleum Corp.)

TEXAS SUGAR REFINING CO.
Acquired by Texas Sugar Refining Corp. 00/00/1929
Details not available

TEXAS SUGAR REFINING CORP.
Assets sold 00/00/1942
Details not available

TEXAS SWEET CRUDE OIL CORP (DE)
SEC revoked common stock registration 02/19/2014

TEXAS T MINERALS INC (BC)
Acquired by Grandcru Resources Corp. 05/23/2006
Each share Common no par exchanged for (1) share Common no par
Grandcru Resources Corp. merged into Bell Copper Corp. (Old) 05/12/2008 which reorganized as Bell Copper Corp. (New) 07/23/2013

TEXAS T RES INC (AB)
Reincorporated 08/23/2001
Place of incorporation changed from (BC) to (AB) 08/23/2001
Recapitalized as Texas T Minerals Inc. 02/19/2004
Each share Common no par exchanged for (0.1) share Common no par
Texas T Minerals Inc. Inc. acquired by Grandcru Resources Corp. 05/23/2006 which merged into Bell Copper Corp. (Old) 05/12/2008 which reorganized as Bell Copper Corp. (New) 07/23/2013

TEXAS TENN INDS INC (TX)
Name changed to Igloo Corp. and Class A Common 20¢ par reclassified as Common 20¢ par 08/25/1971
Igloo Corp. merged into Coca-Cola Bottling Co. of New York, Inc. 12/21/1972
(See Coca-Cola Bottling Co. of New York, Inc.)

TEXAS TEXTILE MILLS (TX)
Each share old Common no par exchanged for (10) shares new Common no par 00/00/1947
Name changed to Miller (G.E.) & Co. 00/00/1955
(See Miller (G.E.) & Co.)

TEXAS TORTILLA BAKERY INC (DE)
Each share Common $0.0001 par exchanged for (0.04) share Common $0.0025 par 11/24/1989
Charter cancelled and declared inoperative and void for non-payment of taxes 06/24/1991

TEXAS TOY CO. (DE)
No longer in existence having become inoperative and void for non-payment of taxes 04/01/1960

TEXAS UNION OIL CORP. (DE)
Charter revoked for non-payment of taxes 10/01/1959

TEXAS UTD BANCORP INC (TX)
Stock Dividend - 15% 09/30/1981
Merged into Allied Bancshares, Inc. (TX) 06/01/1984
Each share Common $1 par exchanged for (1.373875) shares Common $1 par
Allied Bancshares, Inc. (TX) reincorporated in Delaware 04/22/1987 which merged into First Interstate Bancorp 01/29/1988 which merged into Wells Fargo & Co. (Old) 04/01/1996 which merged into Wells Fargo & Co. (New) 11/02/1998

TEXAS UTD BANCSHARES INC (TX)
Common $1 par split (3) for (2) by issuance of (0.5) additional share payable 10/15/2003 to holders of record 10/1/2003 Ex date - 10/16/2003
Merged into Prosperity Bancshares, Inc. 2/1/2007
Each share Common $1 par exchanged for (1) share Common $1 par

TEXAS UNITED OIL & REFINING CO. (DE)
No longer in existence having become inoperative and void for non-payment of taxes 03/18/1925

TEXAS URANIUM CORP (UT)
Proclaimed dissolved for failure to pay taxes 11/09/1974

TEXAS UTILS CO (HOLDING CO) (TX)
Reorganized 08/05/1997
Common no par split (2) for (1) by issuance of (1) additional share 10/28/1955
Common no par split (2) for (1) by issuance of (1) additional share 06/05/1962
Common no par split (2) for (1) by issuance of (1) additional share 06/06/1972
Reorganized from Texas Utilities Co. to Texas Utilities Co. (Holding Co.) 08/05/1997
Name changed to TXU Corp. 05/16/2000
(See TXU Corp.)

TEXAS UTILS ELEC CO (TX)
$10.12 Preferred no par called for redemption 04/21/1993
$10.92 Preferred no par called for redemption 04/30/1993
$11.32 Preferred no par called for redemption 05/03/1993
Flexible Adjustable Rate Preferred Ser. A no par called for redemption 06/30/1993
Flexible Adjustable Rate Preferred Ser. B no par called for redemption 06/30/1993
$9.32 Preferred no par called for redemption 08/05/1993
$9.36 Preferred no par called for redemption 08/05/1993
$10 Preferred no par called for redemption 08/05/1993
$10.08 Preferred no par called for redemption 08/05/1993
$9.48 Preferred no par called for redemption 09/23/1993
$7.44 Preferred no par called for redemption 07/01/1994
$7.48 Preferred no par called for redemption 07/01/1994
$7.80 Preferred no par called for redemption 07/01/1994
$10.375 Preferred no par called for redemption 04/01/1995
Adjustable Rate Preferred Ser. B no par called for redemption at $100 on 04/21/1997
$6.84 Preferred no par called for redemption 05/01/1997
$7.20 Preferred no par called for redemption 05/01/1997
$7.24 Preferred no par called for redemption 05/01/1997
Adjustable Rate Preferred Ser. A no

par called for redemption at $100 on 07/10/1997
$8.20 Depositary Preferred called for redemption at $25 on 01/01/1998
Name changed to TXU Electric Co. 06/14/1999
TXU Electric Co. name changed to TXU US Holdings Co. 1/1/2002
(See TXU US Holdings Co.)

TEXAS VANGUARD OIL CO (TX)
Each share old Common 5¢ par exchanged for (0.25) share new Common 5¢ par 02/16/1990
Acquired by Texas Vanguard Restructuring Co. 10/17/2014
Each share new Common 5¢ par exchanged for $13.11 cash

TEXAS WESTERN OIL CO., INC. (DE)
No longer in existence having become inoperative and void for non-payment of taxes 04/01/1959

TEXAS WESTN INC (UT)
Proclaimed dissolved for failure to pay taxes 10/10/1978

TEXAS WINERY PRODS INC (TX)
Charter forfeited for failure to pay taxes 02/02/1993

TEXAS WYO DRILLING INC (DE)
Each share old Common $0.001 par exchanged for (2) shares new Common $0.001 par 01/23/2012
Each share new Common $0.001 par exchanged again for (0.00666666) share new Common $0.001 par 02/25/2016
Recapitalized as Drone USA, Inc. 05/19/2016
Each share new Common $0.001 par exchanged for (0.08333333) share Common $0.001 par

TEXASGULF INC (TX)
Common no par split (2) for (1) by issuance of (1) additional share 06/01/1981
$3 Conv. Preferred Ser. A $1 par called for redemption 09/18/1981
Merged into Societe Nationale Elf Aquitaine 09/25/1981
Each share Common no par exchanged for $56 cash

TEXAUST INC (TX)
Each share Common $0.0001 par exchanged for (0.1) share Common 1¢ par 08/01/1985
Charter forfeited for failure to pay taxes 11/18/1991

TEXAVADA OIL CO. (NV)
Charter revoked for failure to file reports and pay fees 03/03/1924

TEXBEAU INDS INC (AB)
Name changed to SGI Super Grass Inc. 12/21/1987
SGI Super Grass Inc. name changed to Canadian-Star Industries Inc. 05/24/1989
(See Canadian-Star Industries Inc.)

TEXCALOKAN OIL & GAS CO., INC. (ME)
Charter suspended for non-payment of taxes 00/00/1922

TEXCAN ENERGY & RES INC (ON)
Name changed to Geovex Petroleum Corp. 10/29/1981
Geovex Petroleum Corp. merged into Flying Cross Resources Ltd. 12/04/1985 which merged into International Larder Minera Inc. 05/01/1986 which merged into Explorers Alliance Corp. 10/13/2000
(See Explorers Alliance Corp.)

TEXCAN TECHNOLOGY CORP (BC)
Recapitalized as International Texcan Technology Corp. 01/29/1987
Each share Common no par exchanged for (0.33333333) share Common no par
(See International Texcan Technology Corp.)

TEXCEL INTL INC (DE)
Each share old Common 1¢ par exchanged for (0.4) share new Common 1¢ par 02/28/1989
Charter cancelled and declared inoperative and void for non-payment of taxes 03/01/1991

TEXCOM INC (TX)
Reincorporated under the laws of Nevada 01/03/2012

TEXCRETE STRUCTURAL PRODUCTS CO. (DE)
Assets acquired by Texas Industries, Inc. 02/06/1958
Each share Common 10¢ par exchanged for (0.33333333) share Common $1 par
Texas Industries, Inc. merged into Martin Marietta Materials, Inc. 07/01/2014

TEXDAHL CORP (TX)
Charter forfeited for failure to pay taxes 03/15/1976

TEXEN OIL & GAS INC (NV)
Common $0.00001 par split (5) for (2) by issuance of (1.5) additional shares payable 05/22/2002 to holders of record 05/21/2002
Ex date - 05/23/2002
Name changed to SNRG Corp. 08/02/2005
(See SNRG Corp.)

TEXFI INDS INC (DE)
Stock Dividend - 50% 02/12/1971
Common $1 par split (4) for (3) by issuance of (0.33333333) additional share 07/23/1987
$1.10 Preferred 1987 Ser. $1 par called for redemption 10/08/1993
Adjustable Rate Preferred 1988B Ser. $1 par called for redemption 10/08/1993
Chapter 11 bankruptcy petition dismissed 03/29/2007
No stockholders' equity

TEXIZE CHEMICALS, INC. (DE)
Reincorporated 01/27/1960
Common $1 par split (4) for (1) by issuance of (3) additional shares 01/19/1959
Class B Common $1 par split (4) for (1) by issuance of (3) additional shares 01/19/1959
State of incorporation changed from (SC) to (DE) and Class B Common $1 par reclassified as Common $1 par 01/27/1960
Stock Dividend - 100% 02/01/1960
Merged into Norwich Pharmacal Co. 12/06/1967
Each share Common $1 par exchanged for (0.66) share Common $0.3125 par
Norwich Pharmacal Co. merged into Morton-Norwich Products, Inc. (NY) 04/25/1969 which reincorporated in Delaware 11/28/1969 which merged into Morton Thiokol, Inc. 09/24/1982 which reorganized as Thiokol Corp. (DE) (New) 07/01/1989 which name changed to Cordant Technologies Inc. 05/07/1998
(See Cordant Technologies Inc.)

TEXLA OIL CORP.
Merged into Salt Dome Oil Corp. 00/00/1936
Details not available

TEXMASS PETROLEUM CO. (TX)
Name changed to Texas Consolidated Oils 05/00/1950
(See Texas Consolidated Oils)

TEXMEX CORP. (TX)
Charter forfeited for failure to pay taxes 05/21/1964

TEXMONT MINES LTD (ON)
Capital Stock $1 par changed to no par 11/19/1971
Recapitalized as New Texmont Explorations Ltd. (ON) 03/20/1979
Each share Capital Stock no par exchanged for (0.25) share Capital Stock no par
New Textmont Explorations Ltd. (ON) reincorporated in Canada 03/19/1982
(See New Texmont Explorations Ltd.)

TEXO OIL CORP (OK)
Acquired by Discovery Oil, Ltd. 12/18/1981
Each share Common 1¢ par exchanged for (0.8) share Common 1¢ par
(See Discovery Oil, Ltd.)

TEXOIL INC NEW (NV)
Each share old Common 1¢ par exchanged for (0.5) share new Common 1¢ par 11/22/1993
Each share new Common 1¢ par exchanged again for (0.16666666) share new Common 1¢ par 06/25/1999
Merged into Ocean Energy Inc. (New) 03/22/2001
Each share new Common 1¢ par exchanged for $8.25 cash

TEXOIL INC OLD (NV)
Recapitalized as Unicorp, Inc. (Old) 10/10/1988
Each shares Common $0.002 par exchanged for (0.02857142) share Common 1¢ par
Unicorp, Inc. (Old) name changed to Unicorp, Inc. (New) 03/03/2000 which recapitalized as Striker Oil & Gas, Inc. 04/24/2008
(See Striker Oil & Gas, Inc.)

TEXOLINA OIL CO. (DE)
Merged into Tekoil Corp. 11/04/1957
Each share Common exchanged for (0.2) share Common
Tekoil Corp. merged into Consolidated Oil & Gas, Inc. 02/23/1962 which was acquired by Hugoton Energy Corp. 09/07/1995 which merged into Chesapeake Energy Corp. 03/10/1998

TEXON ENERGY CORP (TX)
SEC revoked common stock registration 10/13/2010
Stockholders' equity unlikely

TEXON OIL & LAND CO.
Merged into Continental Oil Co. (DE) 00/00/1948
Each share Capital Stock $2 par exchanged for (0.27) share Capital Stock $5 par
Continental Oil Co. (DE) name changed to Conoco Inc. 07/02/1979 which was acquired by Du Pont (E.I.) De Nemours & Co. 09/30/1981

TEXOR, INC. (DE)
Name changed to Texor/Cab Industries, Inc. 11/08/1978
(See Texor/Cab Industries, Inc.)

TEXOR CAB INDS INC (DE)
Charter cancelled and declared inoperative and void for non-payment of taxes 03/01/1980

TEXORO RES LTD (BC)
Recapitalized as International Texoro Resources Ltd. 12/08/1989
Each share Common no par exchanged for (0.2) share Common no par
International Texoro Resources Ltd. recapitalized as Great Western Gold Corp. 07/24/1991 which name changed to Great Western Minerals Group Ltd. (BC) 08/14/2002 which reincorporated in Canada 12/12/2007
(See Great Western Minerals Group Ltd.)

TEXOTA OIL CO. (DE)
Each share Common 1¢ par exchanged for (0.2) share Common 5¢ par 04/10/1962
Name changed to North America Resources Corp. 12/15/1968

TEXPACK LTD. (ON)
Acquired by American Hospital Supply Corp. 10/10/1967
Each share Common no par exchanged for $12.35 cash

TEXPEZ OIL & GAS CORP (BC)
Name changed to CCW Systems Ltd. 12/09/1986
(See CCW Systems Ltd.)

TEXSCAN CORP (DE)
Reincorporated 05/03/1985
Capital Stock no par split (7) for (5) by issuance of (0.4) additional share 11/04/1968
Capital Stock no par split (6) for (5) by issuance of (0.2) additional share 09/11/1980
Capital Stock no par split (2) for (1) by issuance of (1) additional share 05/11/1981
Capital Stock no par split (5) for (4) by issuance of (0.25) additional share 06/14/1982
State of incorporation changed from (IN) to (DE) 05/03/1985
Plan of reorganization under Chapter 11 Federal Bankruptcy proceeding confirmed 11/24/1987
No Capital stockholders' equity
Old Common 1¢ par issued to Debentureholders only
Each share old Common 1¢ par exchanged for (0.2) share new Common 1¢ par 10/29/1990
Stock Dividend - 10% 01/21/1980
Reorganized under the laws of Nevada as TSX Corp. 04/28/1993
Each share new Common 1¢ par exchanged for (1) share Common 1¢ par and (1) Common Stock Purchase Warrant expiring 04/28/2003
TSX Corp. merged into ANTEC Corp. 02/07/1997 which name changed to Arris Group, Inc. (Old) 08/03/2001 which reorganized as ARRIS Group, Inc. (New) 04/16/2013 which merged into ARRIS International PLC 01/05/2016

TEXSCAN ELECTR MFG CO (IN)
Adjudicated bankrupt 09/17/1969
No stockholders' equity

TEXSCAN LTD (IN)
Merged into Texscan Corp. (IN) 01/26/1973
Each share Common no par exchanged for (0.066666) share Capital Stock no par
Texscan Corp. (IN) reincorporated in Delaware 05/03/1985 which reorganized as TSX Corp. (NV) 04/28/1993 which merged into ANTEC Corp. 02/07/1997 which name changed to Arris Group, Inc. (Old) 08/03/2001 which reorganized as ARRIS Group, Inc. (New) 04/16/2013 which merged into ARRIS International PLC 01/05/2016

TEXSTAR CORP (DE)
Each share Common 10¢ par exchanged for (0.1) share Common $1 par 03/18/1964
Merged into Hillman Co. 01/16/1978
Each share 6% Conv. Preferred $10 par exchanged for $10.13 cash
Each share 6% Preferred $5 par exchanged for $5.06 cash
Each share Common $1 par exchanged for $9 cash

TEXSTYRENE CORP (DE)
Name changed to Aris Corp. 10/28/1988
Aris Corp. name changed to Lamonts Corp. 04/12/1991 which name changed to Lamonts Apparel, Inc. 11/02/1992
(See Lamonts Apparel, Inc.)

TEXSUN CORP (TX)
Acquired by Royal Crown Cola Co. 11/24/1970
Each share Class C Capital Stock no

par exchanged for (5) shares Common $1 par
Royal Crown Cola Co. name changed to Royal Crown Companies, Inc. 03/07/1978
(See Royal Crown Companies, Inc.)

TEXT 2 WIN INTL (NV)
Each (1.5) shares old Common $0.001 par exchanged (1) share new Common $0.001 par 02/07/2005
Name changed to Entertainment Factory, Inc. (NV) 09/20/2005
Entertainment Factory, Inc. (NV) reorganized in Delaware as Tri-Hub International, Ltd. 07/16/2008

TEXTAINER EQUIP INCOME FD L P (CA)
Completely liquidated 08/02/2005
Each Unit of Ltd. Partnership II received first and final distribution of $0.19 cash
Each Unit of Ltd. Partnership III received first and final distribution of $0.20 cash
Each Unit of Ltd. Partnership IV received first and final distribution of $0.25 cash
Each Unit of Ltd. Partnership V received first and final distribution of $0.39 cash
Each Unit of Ltd. Partnership VI received first and final distribution of $0.47 cash
Note: Certificates were not required to be surrendered and are without value

TEXTECHNOLOGIES INC (DE)
Name changed to We-R-You Corp. 04/25/2008

TEXTILE CRAFTS BUILDING, INC. (NY)
Liquidation completed 00/00/1954
Details not available

TEXTILE DISTRS INC (MO)
Class A Common 10¢ par split (3) for (2) by issuance of (0.5) additional share 05/15/1969
Reincorporated under the laws of Delaware as Apparel Retailers, Inc. and Class A Common 10¢ par reclassified as Common 10¢ par 06/16/1969
(See Apparel Retailers, Inc.)

TEXTILE FINISHING MACHINERY CO.
Name changed to T.F.M. Corp. 00/00/1952
(See T.F.M. Corp.)

TEXTILE PROPERTIES, INC.
Reorganized as Textile Realty Corp. 00/00/1944
No stockholders' equity

TEXTILE REALTY CORP. (NY)
Acquired by Manhattan Properties, Inc. 10/11/1963
Details not available

TEXTILE SECURITIES CO.
Liquidated 00/00/1928
Details not available

TEXTILEATHER CORP. (DE)
Each share Common no par exchanged for (5) shares Common $1 par 00/00/1948
Merged into General Tire & Rubber Co. 04/30/1954
Each share Common $1 par exchanged for (0.10638297) share 5.5% Preference $100 par
(See General Tire & Rubber Co.)

TEXTILES DIONNE INC (QC)
Merged into Dominion Textile Inc. 05/07/1990
Each share Common no par exchanged for either (0.3125) share Common no par or $4.75 cash
(See Dominion Textile Inc.)

TEXTILES INC (NC)
Each share Class B Preferred $50 par exchanged for (3) shares 4% Preferred $25 par 00/00/1941
Each share Common $10 par exchanged for (1) share Common $1 par 00/00/1941
Common $1 par split (2) for (1) by issuance of (1) additional share 02/26/1966
Common $1 par split (5) for (4) by issuance of (0.25) additional share 03/10/1972
Name changed to Ti-Caro Inc. 09/30/1978
(See Ti-Caro Inc.)

TEXTILFOAM, INC. (DE)
Adjudicated bankrupt 03/15/1963
No stockholders' equity

TEXTONE INC (DE)
Merged into Nortek, Inc. (RI) 07/09/1985
Each share Common 20¢ par exchanged for (1.09) shares Common $1 par
Nortek, Inc. (RI) reincorporated in Delaware 04/23/1987 which reorganized as Nortek Holdings, Inc. 11/20/2002
(See Nortek Holdings, Inc.)

TEXTRABET INC (NV)
Recapitalized as First Platinum Card Corp. 09/26/2006
Each share Common no par exchanged for (0.0005) share Common no par
First Platinum Card Corp. recapitalized as First Platinum Retail Innovations, Inc. 02/16/2007
(See First Platinum Retail Innovations, Inc.)

TEXTRON, INC. (NH)
Liquidated 00/00/1953
Details not available

TEXTRON CAP I (DE)
7.92% Trust Preferred Securities called for redemption at $25 on 07/17/2003

TEXTRON ELECTRONICS, INC. (DE)
Merged into Textron Industries, Inc. 01/01/1968
Each share Common 50¢ par exchanged for $8 cash

TEXTRON INC (DE)
Name changed 02/24/1955
Name changed 05/15/1956
Reincorporated 01/02/1968
Each share Common $1 par exchanged for (2) shares Common 50¢ par 09/10/1945
$2.50 Prior Preferred called for redemption 02/01/1946
Each share 5% Preferred $25 par exchanged for (1) share $1.25 Preferred no par 07/23/1947
Under plan of merger name changed from Textron, Inc. to Textron American, Inc. 02/24/1955
Name changed from Textron American, Inc. to Textron, Inc. 05/15/1956
4% Preferred Ser. A $100 par called for redemption 06/12/1959
4% Preferred Ser. B $100 par called for redemption 06/12/1959
Common 50¢ par changed to 25¢ par and (1) additional share issued 12/31/1965
Common 25¢ par split (2) for (1) by issuance of (1) additional share 09/01/1967
State of incorporation changed from (RI) to (DE) 01/02/1968
$1.40 Conv. Preferred Ser. B no par called for redemption at $45 plus $0.05 accrued dividends on 01/13/2010
$2.08 Conv. Preferred no par called for redemption at $50 plus $0.07 accrued dividends on 01/13/2010
(Additional Information in Active)

TEXTURA CORP (DE)
Acquired by Oracle Corp. 06/10/2016

Each share Common $0.001 par exchanged for $26 cash

TEXTURED FIBRES INC (DE)
Name changed to Texfi Industries, Inc. 07/01/1969
(See Texfi Industries, Inc.)

TEXTURED PRODS INC (DE)
Name changed to Pyro Technology Corp. 10/12/1983
(See Pyro Technology Corp.)

TEXXON INC (OK)
Reorganized under the laws of Nevada as Continan Communications, Inc. 12/01/2006
Each share Common $0.001 par exchanged for (0.05) share Common $0.001 par
Continan Communications, Inc. recapitalized as XXX Acquisition Corp. 06/09/2009 which name changed to NightCulture, Inc. 09/20/2011
(See NightCulture, Inc.)

TF FINL CORP (PA)
Reincorporated 04/29/2011
Stock Dividend - 5% payable 02/28/2011 to holders of record 02/15/2011 Ex date - 02/11/2011
State of incorporation changed from (DE) to (PA) 04/29/2011
Merged into National Penn Bancshares, Inc. 10/24/2014
Each share Common 10¢ par exchanged for (4.22) shares Common np par
National Penn Bancshares, Inc. merged into BB&T Corp. 04/01/2016

TFB BANCORP INC (AZ)
Common $5 par split (3) for (1) by issuance of (2) additional shares payable 04/21/2015 to holders of record 04/21/2015
Merged into Glacier Bancorp, Inc. 05/01/2017
Each share Common $5 par exchanged for (0.59809) share Common 1¢ par and $7.36152 cash

TFC ENTERPRISES INC (DE)
Merged into Consumer Portfolio Services, Inc. 05/20/2003
Each share Common 1¢ par exchanged for $1.87 cash

TFC HLDG CO (DE)
Each share old Common $0.005 par exchanged for (0.2) share new Common $0.005 par 08/16/2006
Acquired by RBB Bancorp 02/19/2016
Each share new Common $0.005 par exchanged for $15.6272 cash

TFC INTL INC (DE)
Charter forfeited for failure to maintain a registered agent 09/21/1993

TFC TELESERVICES CORP (GA)
Name changed to Central Corp. 03/31/1987
Central Corp. reorganized as Resurgens Communications Group, Inc. 05/16/1989 which name changed to LDDS Communications, Inc. 09/15/1993 which name changed to WorldCom, Inc. 05/26/1995 which name changed to MCI WorldCom, Inc. 09/14/1998 which name changed to WorldCom Inc. (New) 05/01/2000
(See WorldCom Inc. (New))

TFH INTL INC (CANADA)
Name changed to Highbourne Capital Corp. 08/17/1995
Highbourne Capital Corp. recapitalized as A & E Capital Funding Corp. 08/12/1996 which recapitalized as E & E Capital Funding Inc. 10/18/2005 which merged into GC-Global Capital Corp. 01/09/2006 which name changed to Fountain Asset Corp. 09/02/2015

TFI COS INC (DE)
Name changed to Cardiff Equities Corp. 07/30/1982
(See Cardiff Equities Corp.)

T5 CORP (CO)
Voluntarily dissolved 02/28/2016
Details not available

TFS (SWITZERLAND)
ADR agreement terminated 07/27/2004
Each Sponsored ADR for Ordinary exchanged for (0.2) share Ordinary
Note: Unexchanged ADR's will be sold and proceeds held for claim after 07/27/2005

TFS CORP LTD (AUSTRALIA)
ADR agreement terminated 06/19/2017
No ADR's remain outstanding

TG WORLD ENERGY CORP (AB)
Merged into TVI Pacific Inc. 03/10/2011
Each share Common no par exchanged for (0.458) share Common no par
Note: Unexchanged certificates were cancelled and became without value 03/10/2014

TGC INC (NJ)
Recapitalized as Equion Corp. 01/31/1985
Each share Common $1 par exchanged for (0.01) share Common 1¢ par
(See Equion Corp.)

TGC INDS INC (TX)
Each share Common 10¢ par exchanged for (0.33333333) share Common 30¢ par 11/09/1998
Common 30¢ par changed to 1¢ par 06/12/2003
8% Conv. Exchangeable Preferred Ser. C $1 par called for redemption at $7 plus $0.20 accrued dividends on 06/30/2005
Stock Dividends - 5% payable 04/25/2006 to holders of record 04/11/2006 Ex date - 04/07/2006; 5% payable 04/27/2007 to holders of record 04/13/2007 Ex date - 04/11/2007; 5% payable 04/28/2008 to holders of record 04/14/2008 Ex date - 04/10/2008; 5% payable 05/12/2009 to holders of record 04/28/2009 Ex date - 04/24/2009; 5% payable 05/14/2010 to holders of record 04/30/2010 Ex date - 04/28/2010; 5% payable 05/14/2012 to holders of record 04/30/2012 Ex date - 04/26/2012; 5% payable 05/14/2013 to holders of record 04/30/2013 Ex date - 04/26/2013
Reorganized as Dawson Geophysical Co. (New) 02/12/2015
Each share Common 1¢ par exchanged for (0.33333333) share Common 1¢ par

TGFIN HLDGS INC (DE)
Recapitalized as Redify Group, Inc. 02/28/2014
Each share Common 1¢ par exchanged for (0.1) share Common 1¢ par
Preferred not affected except for change of name

TGI FRIDAYS INC (NY)
Merged into Carlson Hospitality Group, Inc. 02/20/1990
Each share Common 1¢ par exchanged for $14.875 cash

TGK 10 JSC (RUSSIA)
Name changed to Fortum Open Joint Stock Co. 07/14/2009
(See Fortum Open Joint Stock Co.)

TGS NORTH AMERN REAL ESTATE INVT TR (AB)
Acquired by Red Mile Acquisitions, Inc. 06/21/2006
Each Trust Unit no par exchanged for $9.15 cash

TGS PPTYS INC (AB)
Acquired by Airstate Ltd. 04/09/2003
Each share Common no par
exchanged for $1.20 cash

TGV SOFTWARE INC (DE)
Merged into Cisco Systems, Inc.
03/29/1996
Each share Common $0.001 par
exchanged for (0.4) share Common
no par

TGW CORP (QC)
Reincorporated under the laws of
Canada as GlobeStar Mining Corp.
12/18/2002
(See GlobeStar Mining Corp.)

TGX CORP (DE)
Plan of reorganization under Chapter
11 Federal Bankruptcy Code
effective 06/12/1997
Each share Sr. Preferred Ser. A 1¢
par exchanged for (0.5) share
Sheridan Energy Inc. Common 1¢
par
No Common stockholders' equity
(See Sheridan Energy Inc.)

TGX FIN CORP (DE)
Short Term Auction Rate Preferred
Ser. C no par called for redemption
03/20/1990
Short Term Auction Rate Preferred
Ser. D no par called for redemption
03/27/1990
Public interest eliminated

THACKERAY CORP (DE)
$4.15 Preferred 10¢ par called for
redemption 07/11/1986
Liquidation completed
Each share Common 10¢ par
received initial distribution of $0.80
cash payable 01/12/2005 to holders
of record 01/11/2005 Ex date -
01/13/2005
Each share Common 10¢ par
received second and final
distribution of $0.42 cash payable
06/17/2005 to holders of record
01/11/2005

THADDEUS GOLD MINES, LTD. (ON)
Charter cancelled for failure to file
reports and pay taxes 00/00/1955

THAI FD INC (MD)
Completely liquidated
Each share Common 1¢ par received
first and final distribution of $11.307
cash payable 01/26/2018 to holders
of record 01/19/2018

THAI ONE ON INC (NV)
Reorganized as Index Oil & Gas, Inc.
12/16/2005
Each share Common $0.001 par
exchanged for (11) shares Common
$0.001 par
(See Index Oil & Gas, Inc.)

THAI PLASTIC & CHEMICALS PUB CO LTD (THAILAND)
ADR agreement terminated
02/13/2017
No ADR's remain outstanding

THAI TAP WTR SUPPLY (THAILAND)
Name changed to TTW Public
Company Ltd. 04/07/2014

THAI TEL & TELECOMMUNICATION PUB CO LTD (THAILAND)
Stock Dividend - 40.995% payable
07/12/1996 to holders of record
05/14/1996
Name changed to TT&T Public Co.
Ltd. 04/19/2002
(See TT&T Public Co. Ltd.)

THAI UN FROZEN PRODS PUB CO LTD (THAILAND)
Name changed to Thai Union Group
Public Co. Ltd. 10/13/2015

THAICOM PUB CO LTD (THAILAND)
ADR agreement terminated
05/21/2018
Each Sponsored ADR for Common
exchanged for (4) shares Common
Note: Unexchanged ADR's will be
sold and the proceeds, if any, held
for claim after 05/24/2019

THAILASKA EXPLS LTD (BC)
Name changed to James Industries
Inc. 09/27/1976
James Industries Inc. recapitalized as
International James Industries Inc.
04/28/1987 which name changed to
CDIS Software Inc. 07/08/1988
which recapitalized as International
CDIS Software Inc. 03/06/1989
which name changed to A.T.H. Fund
Inc. 07/24/1990
(See A.T.H. Fund Inc.)

THALES (FRANCE)
ADR agreement terminated
11/24/2017
Each ADR for Ordinary exchanged for
$128.311225 cash
(Additional Information in Active)

THALHEIM EXPOSITION MGMT CORP (DE)
Common 10¢ par changed to 8¢ par
and (0.25) additional share issued
11/02/1970
Common 8¢ par changed to $0.064
par and (0.25) additional share
issued 11/12/1971
Common $0.064 par changed to
$0.04267 par and (0.5) additional
share issued 10/31/1972
Merged into Jay & Beth Enterprises,
Inc. 06/22/1979
Each share Common $0.04267 par
exchanged for $4.50 cash

THALHIMER BROS INC (VA)
Each share Common $10 par
exchanged for (2) shares Common
$5 par 00/00/1952
Common $5 par changed to $2.50 par
and (1) additional share issued
01/15/1969
Common $2.50 par changed to
$1.66666666 par and (0.5)
additional share issued 04/29/1977
3.65% Preferred $100 par called for
redemption 07/31/1978
Stock Dividends - 10% 01/29/1965;
10% 01/28/1966; 10% 04/30/1974;
10% 04/30/1975; 10% 01/30/1976;
10% 01/27/1978
Merged into Carter Hawley Hale
Stores Inc. (CA) 08/14/1978
Each share Common $1.66666666
par exchanged for (0.975) share
Common $5 par
Carter Hawley Hale Stores Inc. (CA)
reincorporated in Delaware
07/26/1984 which name changed to
Broadway Stores, Inc. 06/17/1994
which merged into Federated
Department Stores, Inc. 10/11/1995
which name changed to Macy's, Inc.
06/01/2007

THALIA INC (CO)
Name changed to Video Superstores
of America, Inc. 10/19/1987
(See Video Superstores of America, Inc.)

THALLION PHARMACEUTICALS INC NEW (CANADA)
Merged into BELLUS Health Inc.
08/15/2013
Each share Common no par
exchanged for (1) Contingent Value
Right and $0.1889 cash
Note: Unexchanged certificates will
be cancelled and become without
value 08/15/2019

THALLION PHARMACEUTICALS INC OLD (CANADA)
Each share Common no par
exchanged for (1) share Thallion
Pharmaceuticals Inc. (New)
Common no par 07/27/2009
(See Thallion Pharmaceuticals Inc. (New))

THANDS RES CORP (WV)
Proclaimed dissolved for
non-payment of taxes 12/16/1987

THANE INTL INC (DE)
Merged into Direct Marketing
Holdings, Inc. 02/12/2004
Each share Common no par
exchanged for $0.35 cash

THAON COMMUNICATIONS INC (NV)
Common $0.001 par split (2) for (1)
by issuance of (1) additional share
payable 11/27/2000 to holders of
record 11/20/2000
Each share old Common $0.001 par
exchanged for (0.02) share new
Common $0.001 par 01/10/2003
Recapitalized as PracticeXpert, Inc.
07/21/2003
Each share new Common $0.001 par
exchanged for (0.05) share Common
$0.001 par 07/21/2003
(See PracticeXpert, Inc.)

THARPE & BROOKS, INC. (GA)
Acquired by First National Holding
Corp. (GA) 04/30/1970
Details not available

THATCHER GLASS MANUFACTURING CO., INC. (NY)
$2.40 Preference no par called for
redemption 08/15/1958
Common $5 par changed to $2.50 par
and (1) additional share issued
01/08/1965
Merged into Rexall Drug & Chemical
Co. 06/30/1966
Each share Common $2.50 par
exchanged for (1) share $2 Conv.
Preferred Ser. A $5 par
Rexall Drug & Chemical Co. name
changed to Dart Industries, Inc.
04/22/1969 which reorganized as
Dart & Kraft, Inc. 09/25/1980 which
name changed to Kraft, Inc. (New)
11/21/1986
(See Kraft, Inc. (New))

THATCHER MANUFACTURING CO. (NY)
Recapitalized as Thatcher Glass
Manufacturing Co., Inc. 00/00/1946
Each share Common no par
exchanged for (2) shares Common
$5 par
Thatcher Glass Manufacturing Co.,
Inc. merged into Rexall Drug &
Chemical Co. 06/30/1966 which
name changed to Dart Industries,
Inc. 04/22/1969 which reorganized
as Dart & Kraft, Inc. 09/25/1980
which name changed to Kraft, Inc.
(New) 11/21/1986
(See Kraft, Inc. (New))

THATCHER SECURITIES CORP.
Liquidated 00/00/1931
Details not available

THATLOOK COM INC (NV)
Filed plan of liquidation under
Chapter 7 Federal Bankruptcy Code
10/29/2003
No stockholders' equity

THAXTON GROUP INC (SC)
Plan of reorganization under Chapter
11 Federal Bankruptcy Code
effective 04/16/2007
No stockholders' equity

THAYER-FOSS CO.
Dissolved 00/00/1935
Details not available

THAYER TELKEE CORP.
Dissolved 00/00/1950
Details not available

THAYER-WEST POINT HOTEL CO.
Liquidated 00/00/1948
Details not available

THAYER WEST POINT HOTEL CORP.
Succeeded by Thayer-West Point
Hotel Co. with no stockholders'
equity 00/00/1929

THAYERS, LTD. (ON)
Merged into Reliance Petroleum Ltd.
00/00/1949
Each share Preferred no par
exchanged for (1) share Preferred
$50 par and $16.875 cash
Each share Common no par
exchanged for (0.33333333) share
Class A no par
(See Reliance Petroleum Ltd.)

THC BIOMED INTL LTD (BC)
Name changed to Global Li-Ion
Graphite Corp. 07/14/2017

THC COMMUNICATIONS INC (DE)
SEC revoked common stock
registration 10/15/2010

THC HOMECARE INC (UT)
Each share old Common $0.001 par
exchanged for (0.125) share new
Common $0.001 par 12/24/1996
Involuntarily dissolved 09/01/1998

THC THERAPEUTICS INC (NV)
Name changed to Millennium
BlockChain, Inc. 02/07/2018

THCG INC (DE)
Reincorporated 05/16/2000
State of incorporation changed from
(UT) to (DE) 05/16/2000
Name changed to THCG Liquidating
Trust and Common 1¢ par
reclassified as Non-transferable
Units of Bene. Int. 07/16/2001
(See THCG Liquidating Trust)

THCG LIQUIDATING TR (DE)
Liquidation completed
Each Non-transferable Unit of Bene.
Int. received first and final
distribution of $0.09659168 cash
payable 04/12/2007 to holders of
record 03/21/2007 Ex date -
04/25/2007
Note: Certificates were not required to
be surrendered and are without
value

THE EMPLOYER INC (NV)
Recapitalized as Vana Blue, Inc.
02/21/2008
Each share Common $0.001 par
exchanged for (0.05) share Common
$0.001 par
Vana Blue, Inc. name changed to
Osyka Corp. 05/19/2010

THE ESTATE VAULT INC (NV)
SEC revoked common stock
registration 05/09/2013

THE 1411 HLDG CO (DE)
Charter cancelled and declared
inoperative and void for
non-payment of taxes 03/01/1987

THE GROUP INC (NV)
Dissolved 02/10/2004
Details not available

THE LEAGUE PUBLISHING INC (NV)
Name changed to Good Life China
Corp. 04/08/2008

THEAMERICANWEST COM INC (NV)
Each share old Common $0.001 par
exchanged for (6) shares new
Common $0.001 par 2/12/2003
Name changed to WordLogic Corp.
04/10/2003

THEATER NEAR YOU CORP (NV)
Name changed to Siberian Industries
Ltd. 04/14/2000
Siberian Industries Ltd. name
changed to Midastrade.com, Inc.
08/23/2000
(See Midastrade.com Inc.)

THEATER XTREME ENTMT GROUP INC (FL)
Filed a petition under Chapter 7
Federal Bankruptcy Code
12/15/2008
No stockholders' equity

THEATRE CORP. OF AMERICA (NY)
Charter cancelled and proclaimed
dissolved for failure to file reports
and pay taxes 12/15/1964

THEATRE OF MICHIGAN CO. (MI)
Charter voided for failure to file
reports and pay fees 05/15/1965

THEATRE PROPERTIES (HAMILTON) LTD. (ON)
Acquired by General Theatres Investment Co. Ltd. through purchase offer which expired 11/00/1953
Public interest eliminated

THEATRE 200, INC. (NY)
Name changed to Spector (Edward) Productions, Inc. 11/07/1958
(See Spector (Edward) Productions, Inc.)

THEATRES LAURENTIDE, INC. (QC)
Recapitalized as Theatres Independants Inc. 10/01/1965
Each share Preference $25 par exchanged for (1) share Preference $25 par
Each share Common no par exchanged for (5) shares Common $1 par

THEATRICAL SUBSIDIARIES, INC. (NY)
Merged into Golden West Markets, Inc. 05/28/1959
Each share Common 10¢ par exchanged for (0.1) share Capital Stock $1 par
(See Golden West Markets, Inc.)

THECOMICSTORE COM INC (NV)
Reorganized as CMI Holdings Group Inc. 03/01/2001
Each share Common $0.001 par exchanged for (50) shares Common $0.001 par
CMI Holdings Group Inc. recapitalized as RFMR Acquisition Corp. 04/02/2004 which name changed to Great Northern Oilsands, Inc. (NV) 11/14/2006 which reorganized in Florida as New Asia Gold Corp. 06/05/2008 which recapitalized as New World Gold Corp. 05/08/2009

THEHEALTHCHANNEL COM INC (DE)
Each share old Common $0.001 par exchanged for (2) shares new Common $0.001 par 08/06/1999
Each share new Common $0.001 par exchanged again for (0.33333333) share new Common $0.001 par 11/17/2000
SEC revoked common stock registration 12/09/2005

THEIL INC (NY)
Liquidated and assets sold for benefit of creditors only 00/00/1972
No stockholders' equity

THEIL PUBLICATIONS, INC. (NY)
Name changed to Theil, Inc. 07/01/1965
(See Theil, Inc.)

THEINTERNETCORP.NET, INC. (NV)
Name changed to Bear Aerospace, Inc. 05/22/2001
(See Bear Aerospace, Inc.)

THELON CAP LTD (BC)
Each share old Common no par exchanged for (0.16666666) share new Common no par 12/23/2014
Name changed to THC BioMed Intl Ltd. 04/29/2015
THC BioMed Intl Ltd. name changed to Global Li-Ion Graphite Corp. 07/14/2017

THELON VENTURES LTD (BC)
Recapitalized as Thelon Capital Ltd. 02/04/2010
Each share Common no par exchanged for (0.1) share Common no par
Thelon Capital Ltd. name changed to THC BioMed Intl Ltd. 04/29/2015 which name changed to Global Li-Ion Graphite Corp. 07/14/2017

THEME FACTORY INC (NV)
Each share old Common $0.001 par exchanged for (0.4) share new Common $0.001 par 04/19/1991
Each share new Common $0.001 par exchanged again for (0.01) share new Common $0.001 par 10/12/1999
New Common $0.001 par split (4) for (1) by issuance of (3) additional shares payable 03/22/2001 to holders of record 03/12/2001 Ex date - 03/23/2001
Name changed to Geyser Group, Ltd. 03/12/2001
Geyser Group, Ltd. recapitalized as XStream Beverage Group Ltd. 10/16/2001 which name changed to XStream Beverage Network, Inc. 10/06/2004 which name changed to Hull Energy, Inc. 05/12/2008 which name changed to Gemini Group Global Corp. 11/04/2013

THEME HOSIERY CO., INC. (IN)
In process of liquidation 00/00/1959
Details not available

THEME RESTAURANTS INC (ON)
Charter cancelled for failure to file reports and pay taxes 12/10/1990

THEMESCAPES INC (DE)
Name changed to Cyclone Holdings, Inc. 05/17/2006
Cyclone Holdings, Inc. recapitalized as digitiliti, Inc. 03/07/2007

THENETDIGEST COM INC (DE)
Each share old Class A Common $0.001 par exchanged for (0.05263157) share new Class A Common $0.001 par 06/07/2002
SEC revoked common stock registration 09/09/2009

THEODORE GAMES INC (NV)
Reincorporated under the laws of Texas as Interamericas Communications Corp. 10/07/1994
Interamericas Communications Corp. name changed to Firstcom Corp. 10/22/1998 which merged into AT&T Latin America Corp. 08/29/2000
(See AT&T Latin America Corp.)

THEODORE GARY & CO. (MO)
See - Gary (Theodore) & Co.

THEOLIA SA (FRANCE)
Name changed to Futuren S.A. 11/18/2015

THEORETICS INC (DE)
Name changed to Safetek International Inc. 01/04/1989

THERABIOGEN INC (NV)
SEC revoked common stock registration 04/21/2016

THERADYNE CORP (MN)
Each share Common 50¢ par exchanged for (0.005) share old Common $100 par 07/01/1983
Each share old Common $100 par exchanged for (0.02) share new Common $100 par 06/18/1986
Public interest eliminated

THERAGENICS CORP (DE)
Common 1¢ par split (2) for (1) by issuance of (1) additional share payable 04/15/1998 to holders of record 03/31/1998
Acquired by Juniper Investment Co., LLC 10/29/2013
Each share Common 1¢ par exchanged for $2.20 cash

THERAMED CAP CORP (BC)
Name changed to Vigil Health Solutions Inc. 04/11/2003

THERAPEUTIC ANTIBODIES INC (DE)
Merged into Protherics PLC 09/15/1999
Each share Common $0.001 par exchanged for (1.163) shares Ordinary 2p par

THERAPEUTIC DISCOVERY CORP (DE)
Acquired by Alza Corp. 09/29/1997
Each share Class A Common 1¢ par exchanged for $12.3011 cash

THERAPEUTIC MEDCO, INC. (OR)
Involuntarily dissolved 04/02/1987

THERAPEUTIC TECHNOLOGIES INC (FL)
Proclaimed dissolved 12/21/1982

THERAPY LASERS INC (NV)
Each share old Common $0.001 par exchanged for (0.1) share new Common $0.001 par 04/25/2000
Name changed to SpectraSource Corp. 08/17/2000
SpectraSource Corp. recapitalized as China Yibai United Guarantee International Holding, Inc. 06/17/2009

THERASENSE INC (DE)
Merged into Abbott Laboratories 04/06/2004
Each share Common $0.001 par exchanged for $27 cash

THERATECH INC (DE)
Common 1¢ par split (3) for (2) by issuance of (0.5) additional share payable 06/28/1996 to holders of record 06/14/1996
Merged into Watson Pharmaceuticals Inc. 01/15/1999
Each share Common 1¢ par exchanged for (0.2663) share Common $0.0033 par
Watson Pharmaceuticals Inc. name changed Actavis, Inc. (NV) 01/24/2013 which reorganized in Ireland as Actavis PLC 10/01/2013

THERATECH INC (NV)
Charter revoked for failure to file reports and pay fees 11/01/1990

THERATRON CORP. (MN)
Assets sold on foreclosure of chattel mortgages and liens 09/18/1963
No stockholders' equity

THERATX INC (DE)
Merged into Vencor Inc. (Old) 03/21/1997
Each share Common $0.001 par exchanged for $17.10 cash

THERAVANCE INC (DE)
Each share Common 1¢ par received distribution of (0.28571428) share Theravance Biopharma, Inc. Ordinary $0.00001 par payable 06/02/2014 to holders of record 05/15/2014 Ex date - 06/03/2014
Name changed to Innoviva, Inc. 01/11/2016

THERM AIR MFG INC (NY)
Merged into Radon Manufacturing Co., Inc. 05/10/1983
Each share Common 10¢ par exchanged for $0.25 cash

THERM-O-DISC, INC. (OH)
Common $1 par split (3) for (2) by issuance of (0.5) additional share 02/09/1962
Completely liquidated 02/26/1968
Each share Common $1 par exchanged for first and final distribution of (0.76) share Emerson Electric Co. Common $1 par

THERMA FREEZE INC (DE)
Name changed to Enviro-Energy Corp. 07/03/2001
(See Enviro-Energy Corp.)

THERMA-WAVE INC (DE)
Acquired by KLA-Tencor Corp. 05/25/2007
Each share Class B Preferred 1¢ par exchanged for $1,064.516129 cash
Each share Common 1¢ par exchanged for $1.65 cash

THERMACELL TECHNOLOGIES INC (FL)
Each share old Common $0.0001 par exchanged for (0.25) share new Common $0.0001 par 04/14/2000
Plan of reorganization under Chapter 11 Federal Bankruptcy Code effective 08/30/2002
Each share new Common $0.0001 par exchanged again for (0.0787) share new Common $0.0001 par
Name changed to Absolute Waste Services, Inc. 07/31/2003
Absolute Waste Services, Inc. recapitalized as Absolute Potential, Inc. 11/03/2006

THERMACOR TECHNOLOGY INC (NV)
Each share old Common $0.001 par exchanged for (0.001) share new Common $0.001 par 12/11/1992
Recapitalized as Applied Technology Inc. 05/06/1994
Each share new Common $0.001 par exchanged for (0.02) share Common $0.001 par
Applied Technology Inc. recapitalized as Golden Panther Resources Ltd. 03/22/1997 which name changed to Panther Resources Ltd. 03/13/1998 which recapitalized as PhantomFilm.Com 06/15/1999 which recapitalized as Komodo, Inc. 10/08/2001
(See Komodo, Inc.)

THERMACTOR CO. (DE)
No longer in existence having become inoperative and void for non-payment of taxes 04/01/1967

THERMADYNE HLDGS CORP NEW (DE)
Merged 05/22/1998
Thermadyne Holdings Corp. (Old) merged into Thermadyne Holdings Corp. (New) 05/22/1998
Each share Common 1¢ par exchanged for either (1) share old Common 1¢ par or $34.50 cash
Note: Option to retain stock expired 05/20/1998
Plan of reorganization under Chapter 11 Federal Bankruptcy Code effective 05/23/2003
No old Common stockholders' equity
Acquired by Thermadyne Technologies Holdings, Inc. 12/03/2010
Each share new Common 1¢ par exchanged for $15 cash

THERMADYNE INDS INC (DE)
Plan of reorganization under Chapter 11 Federal Bankruptcy proceedings confirmed 01/19/1994
Each share Increasing Dividend Sr. Exchangeable Preferred no par exchanged for (0.08) share Thermadyne Holdings Corp. (Old) Common 1¢ par
Thermadyne Holdings Corp. (Old) merged into Thermadyne Holdings Corp. (New) 05/22/1998
(See Thermadyne Holdings Corp. (New))

THERMAGE INC (DE)
Name changed to Solta Medical, Inc. 01/12/2009
(See Solta Medical, Inc.)

THERMAL & ELECTRONICS INDUSTRIES, INC. (NJ)
Name changed to T & E Industries, Inc. 06/28/1966
(See Vacutronics, Inc.)

THERMAL ABLATION TECHNOLOGIES CORP (FL)
Name changed to Poker.com Inc. 08/09/1999
Poker.com Inc. name changed to LegalPlay Entertainment Inc. 09/15/2003 which recapitalized as Synthenol Inc. (FL) 12/18/2006 which reincorporated in Nevada as SinoCubate, Inc. 11/25/2008 which name changed to Viking Investments Group, Inc. 07/16/2012 which name changed to Viking Energy Group, Inc. 05/08/2017

THERMAL AIRE AMER INC (DE)
Reorganized as Ceco Systems, Inc. 12/04/1972
Each share Common 10¢ par exchanged for (0.5) share Common 20¢ par
(See Ceco Systems, Inc.)

THERMAL CTL TECHNOLOGIES CORP (AB)
Delisted from Canadian Venture Exchange 05/31/2000

THERMAL ENERGY STORAGE INC (CO)
SEC revoked common stock registration 12/30/2011

THERMAL EXPL CO (CA)
Merged into Western Copper Holdings Ltd. 10/07/1996
Each share Common 1¢ par exchanged for (0.2) share Western Copper Holdings Ltd. Common no par and (0.2) share Pacific Cascade Resources Corp. Common no par
(See each company's listing)

THERMAL INDS INC (PA)
Common 5¢ par changed to 1¢ par and (1) additional share issued 02/20/1984
Stock Dividends - 100% 07/26/1981; 100% 05/01/1986
Merged into H.I.G. Investment Group, L.P. 05/30/1997
Each share Common 1¢ par exchanged for $15 cash

THERMAL MATERIALS, INC. (DE)
Charter cancelled and declared inoperative and void for non-payment of taxes 04/15/1968

THERMAL PWR CO (CA)
Common $1 par changed to no par and (0.5) additional share issued 06/04/1969
Common no par split (2) for (1) by issuance of (1) additional share 05/30/1973
Merged into Natomas Co. 02/27/1979
Each share Common no par exchanged for $34.35 cash

THERMAL PROFILES INC (NY)
Common $0.015 par changed to 1¢ par 11/22/1983
Charter cancelled and proclaimed dissolved for failure to pay taxes 09/29/1993

THERMAL RESEARCH & ENGINEERING CORP. (DE)
Completely liquidated 12/08/1967
Each share Capital Stock $1 par exchanged for first and final distribution of (0.33333333) share Cosmodyne Corp. Common no par
Cosmodyne Corp. reorganized as Cordon International Corp. 07/30/1971
(See Cordon International Corp.)

THERMAL SYS INC (WA)
Charter cancelled and proclaimed dissolved for failure to pay fees 03/23/1998

THERMAL SYSTEMS, INC. (CA)
Name changed to Axial Corp. 10/05/1970
Axial Corp. name changed to Axial Liquidating Corp. 05/31/1973 which liquidated for Sierracin Corp. (CA) 06/06/1973 which reincorporated in Delaware 05/31/1977
(See Sierracin Corp. (DE))

THERMAL TENNIS INC (NV)
Name changed to CannaSys, Inc. 12/01/2014

THERMALATOR FINL CORP (NY)
Charter cancelled and proclaimed dissolved for failure to pay taxes 09/29/1993

THERMALECTRIC, INC. (NY)
Charter cancelled and proclaimed dissolved for failure to file reports and pay taxes 12/15/1972

THERMALENE PRODS INC (DE)
Charter cancelled and declared inoperative and void for non-payment of taxes 03/01/1991

THERMALTEC INTL CORP (DE)
Name changed to TTI Holdings of America Corp. 05/17/2001
TTI Holdings of America Corp. recapitalized as Steam Cleaning USA, Inc. 09/03/2002 which recapitalized as Humana Trans Services Holding Corp. 08/11/2003 which name changed to Accountabilities, Inc. 12/06/2005 which name changed to Corporate Resource Services, Inc. 04/21/2010

THERMASCAN INC (DE)
Acquired by Virology Testing Sciences, Inc. 12/30/1992
Each share Common $0.003 par exchanged for (0.15) share Common 10¢ par and (0.075) share Lone Star Casino Corp. Common 10¢ par
(See each company's listing)

THERMATEST LABORATORIES, INC. (CA)
Dissolved 02/28/1966
No stockholders' equity

THERMATOMIC CARBON CO. (DE)
Merged into Commercial Solvents Corp. 04/30/1957
Each share Common no par exchanged for (0.055555) share Common $1 par
(See Commercial Solvents Corp.)

THERMATOOL CORP (MA)
Under plan of merger each share Common 1¢ par exchanged for $0.33 cash 01/14/2005

THERMATRIX INC (DE)
Plan of reorganization under Chapter 11 Federal Bankruptcy Code effective 02/26/2001
No stockholders' equity

THERMATROL NEW YORK INC (DE)
Recapitalized as General Business Data Centers, Inc. 10/10/1973
Each share Common 10¢ par exchanged for (0.4) share Common 1¢ par
(See General Business Data Centers, Inc.)

THERMATRON CORP. LTD. (ON)
Name changed to Mytolon Chemical Inc. 09/15/1971
Each share Common no par exchanged for (1) share Common no par
Mytolon Chemical Inc. merged into Elkins Productions of Canada Ltd. 00/00/1972 which merged into Life Investors International Ltd. 06/00/1973 which merged into Life Investors International Ltd. 07/14/1973
(See Life Investors International Ltd.)

THERMATRON INC (DE)
Common 1¢ par split (10) for (1) by issuance of (9) additional shares 11/30/1979
Charter cancelled and declared inoperative and void for non-payment of taxes 03/01/1988

THERMAX INTL CORP (AB)
Delisted from Toronto Venture Stock Exchange 06/20/2003

THERMEDICS DETECTION INC (MA)
Merged into Thermedics Inc. 04/12/2000
Each share Common 10¢ par exchanged for $8 cash

THERMEDICS INC (MA)
Common 10¢ par split (4) for (3) by issuance of (0.33333333) additional share 09/16/1985
Common 10¢ par split (3) for (2) by issuance of (0.5) additional share 10/31/1986
Common 10¢ par split (3) for (2) by issuance of (0.5) additional share 11/01/1993
Stock Dividend - 25% 01/15/1985
Merged into Thermo Electron Corp. 06/30/2000
Each share Common 10¢ par exchanged for (0.45) share Common $1 par
Thermo Electron Corp. name changed to Thermo Fisher Scientific, Inc. 11/09/2006

THERMEX INC (DE)
Charter cancelled and declared inoperative and void for non-payment of taxes 03/01/1980

THERMICEDGE CORP (AB)
Common no par split (10) for (1) by issuance of (9) additional shares payable 03/12/1998 to holders of record 12/31/1997
Reincorporated under the laws of Ontario as Fuel Cell Technologies Corp. 05/19/2000
(See Fuel Cell Technologies Corp.)

THERMO ANALYTICAL INC. (MA)
Name changed to Thermo Environmental Corp. 10/05/1987
Thermo Environmental Corp. merged into Thermo Instrument Systems Inc. 01/17/1990 which merged into Thermo Electron Corp. 06/30/2000 which name changed to Thermo Fisher Scientific, Inc. 11/09/2006

THERMO BIOANALYSIS CORP (DE)
Merged into Thermo Instrument Systems Inc. 04/14/2000
Each share Common 1¢ par exchanged for $28 cash

THERMO BIOMEDICAL INC (DE)
Name changed to Viasys Healthcare Inc. 04/05/2001
(See Viasys Healthcare Inc.)

THERMO CARDIOSYSTEMS INC (MA)
Common 10¢ par split (3) for (2) by issuance of (0.5) additional share 01/15/1990
Common 10¢ par split (5) for (4) by issuance of (0.25) additional share 05/07/1990
Under plan of recapitalization each share Common 10¢ par exchanged for (1) share Non-Redeemable Common 10¢ par and (1) Redemption Right expiring 12/31/1993 on 05/23/1990
Non-Redeemable Common 10¢ par split (2) for (1) by issuance of (1) additional share 11/01/1993
Non-Redeemable Common 10¢ par split (3) for (2) by issuance of (0.5) additional share payable 05/15/1996 to holders of record 05/01/1996 Ex date - 05/16/1996
Merged into Thoratec Corp. 02/14/2001
Each share Non-Redeemable Common 10¢ par exchanged for (0.835) share Common 10¢ par
(See Thoratec Corp.)

THERMO ECOTEK CORP (DE)
Common 10¢ par split (3) for (2) by issuance of (0.5) additional share payable 10/16/1996 to holders of record 10/02/1996 Ex date - 10/17/1996
Merged into Thermo Electron Corp. 08/10/2000
Each share Common 10¢ par exchanged for (0.431) share Common $1 par
Thermo Electron Corp. name changed to Thermo Fisher Scientific, Inc. 11/09/2006

THERMO ELECTRON CORP (DE)
Common $1 par split (3) for (2) by issuance of (0.5) additional share 01/03/1984
Common $1 par split (3) for (2) by issuance of (0.5) additional share 09/16/1985
Common $1 par split (3) for (2) by issuance of (0.5) additional share 10/31/1986
Common $1 par split (3) for (2) by issuance of (0.5) additional share 10/28/1993
Common $1 par split (3) for (2) by issuance of (0.5) additional share 05/24/1995
Preferred Stock Purchase Rights redeemed at $0.009 per right 02/12/1996 for holders of record 01/29/1996
Common $1 par split (3) for (2) by issuance of (0.5) additional share payable 06/05/1996 to holders of record 05/22/1996 Ex date - 06/06/1996
Each share Common $1 par received distribution of (0.0612) share Kadant Inc. Common 1¢ par payable 08/08/2001 to holders of record 07/30/2001 Ex date - 08/09/2001
Each share Common $1 par received distribution of (0.1461) share Viasys Healthcare Inc. Common 1¢ par payable 11/15/2001 to holders of record 11/07/2001 Ex date - 11/16/2001
Stock Dividends - 100% 12/17/1973; 50% 08/01/1979
Under plan of merger name changed to Thermo Fisher Scientific Inc. 11/09/2006

THERMO ELECTRON ENGINEERING CORP. (DE)
Name changed to Thermo Electron Corp. 08/28/1967
Thermo Electron Corp. name changed to Thermo Fisher Scientific, Inc. 11/09/2006

THERMO ELECTRON TECHNOLOGIES CORP (DE)
Name changed to ThermoTrex Corp. 06/10/1992
ThermoTrex Corp. merged into Thermo Electron Corp. 08/15/2000 which name changed to Thermo Fisher Scientific, Inc. 11/09/2006

THERMO ENVIRONMENTAL CORP (MA)
Stock Dividend - 50% 09/07/1988
Merged into Thermo Instrument Systems Inc. 01/17/1990
Each share Common 10¢ par exchanged for (0.5) share Common 10¢ par
Thermo Instrument Systems Inc. merged into Thermo Electron Corp. 06/30/2000 which name changed to Thermo Fisher Scientific, Inc. 11/09/2006

THERMO FIBERGEN INC (DE)
Merged into Kadant Inc. 12/27/2001
Each share Common 1¢ par exchanged for $12.75 cash

THERMO FIBERTEK INC (DE)
Common 1¢ par split (3) for (2) by issuance of (0.5) additional share 09/15/1995
Common 1¢ par split (3) for (2) by issuance of (0.5) additional share payable 06/26/1996 to holders of record 06/12/1996 Ex date - 06/27/1996
Recapitalized as Kadant Inc. 07/12/2001
Each share Common 1¢ par exchanged for (0.2) share Common 1¢ par

THERMO FLEX CORP. (CA)
Charter suspended for non-payment of taxes 10/01/1962

THERMO INSTR SYS INC (DE)
Common 10¢ par split (3) for (2) by issuance of (0.5) additional share 01/29/1988
Common 10¢ par split (3) for (2) by

issuance of (0.5) additional share 07/22/1993
Common 10¢ par split (3) for (2) by issuance of (0.5) additional share 04/14/1995
Common 10¢ par split (5) for (4) by issuance of (0.25) additional share 12/29/1995
Common 10¢ par split (5) for (4) by issuance of (0.25) additional share payable 10/31/1997 to holders of record 10/20/1997 Ex date - 11/03/1997
Merged into Thermo Electron Corp. 06/30/2000
Each share Common 10¢ par exchanged for (0.85) share Common $1 par
Thermo Electron Corp. name changed to Thermo Fisher Scientific, Inc. 11/09/2006

THERMO KINETIC CORP (AZ)
Capital Stock $1 par changed to no par 10/19/1970
Reorganized under Chapter X bankruptcy proceedings 11/12/1980
Each share Capital Stock no par exchanged for $0.3832 cash

THERMO KING CORP. (MN)
Acquired by Westinghouse Electric Corp. 08/12/1961
Each share Capital Stock $1 par exchanged for (0.77777777) share Common $6.25 par
Westinghouse Electric Corp. name changed to CBS Corp. 12/01/1997 which merged into Viacom Inc. (Old) 05/04/2000
(See Viacom Inc. (Old))

THERMO-KING RAILWAY CORP. (MN)
Completely liquidated 06/09/1965
Each share Common $1 par exchanged for first and final distribution of $1.2213 cash

THERMO MAGNETICS INC (MA)
Name changed to Thermatool Corp. 05/17/1974
(See Thermatool Corp.)

THERMO MGMT ASSOC INC (NJ)
Charter declared void for non-payment of taxes 09/01/1988

THERMO-MIZER ENVIRONMENTAL CORP (DE)
Recapitalized as Laminaire Corp. 06/29/1998
Each share Common $0.001 par exchanged for (0.25) share Common $0.001 par
Laminaire Corp. recapitalized as Agent 155 Media Group, Inc. 11/19/2004 which recapitalized as Cavico Corp. 05/12/2006
(See Cavico Corp.)

THERMO NATL INDS INC (NJ)
Majority shares acquired through purchase offer which expired 04/15/1991
Public interest eliminated

THERMO OPPORTUNITY FD INC (MD)
Completely liquidated 07/24/2000
Each share Common $0.001 par exchanged for first and final distribution of $13.39 cash

THERMO OPTEK CORP (DE)
Merged into Thermo Electron Corp. 05/12/2000
Each share Common 1¢ par exchanged for $15 cash

THERMO PWR CORP (MA)
Merged into Thermo Electron Corp. 10/28/1999
Each share Common 10¢ par exchanged for $12 cash

THERMO PROCESS SYS INC (DE)
Common 10¢ par split (6) for (5) by issuance of (0.2) additional share 07/20/1988
Common 10¢ par split (3) for (2) by issuance of (0.5) additional share 09/28/1989
Stock Dividend - 20% 03/16/1989
Name changed to Thermo Terratech Inc. 12/18/1995
Thermo Terratech Inc. merged into Thermo Electron Corp. 09/25/2000 which name changed to Thermo Fisher Scientific, Inc. 11/09/2006

THERMO REMEDIATION INC (CA)
Common 1¢ par split (3) for (2) by issuance of (0.5) additional share 03/31/1995
Name changed to ThermoRetec Corp. 09/15/1998
(See ThermoRetec Corp.)

THERMO SENTRON INC (DE)
Merged into Thermedics Inc. 04/04/2000
Each share Common 1¢ par exchanged for $15.50 cash

THERMO SYS INC (MN)
Common 10¢ par split (1.333) for (1) by issuance of (0.333) additional share 04/14/1976
Name changed to TSI Inc. 06/30/1977
(See TSI Inc.)

THERMO TECH INTL INC (BC)
Recapitalized as Consolidated Thermo Tech International Inc. 09/08/1989
Each share Common no par exchanged for (0.2) share Common no par
Consolidated Thermo Tech International Inc. recapitalized as Thermo Tech Technologies Inc. (BC) 06/09/1992 which reincorporated in Yukon 04/11/2000

THERMO TECH TECHNOLOGIES INC (YT)
Reincorporated 12/02/1997
Reincorporated 07/25/2000
Place of incorporation changed from (BC) to (Canada) 12/02/1997
Place of incorporation changed from (Canada) to (YT) 07/25/2000
Struck off register 05/20/2005

THERMO TERRATECH INC (DE)
Merged into Thermo Electron Corp. 09/25/2000
Each share Common 10¢ par exchanged for (0.3945) share Common $1 par
Thermo Electron Corp. name changed to Thermo Fisher Scientific, Inc. 11/09/2006

THERMO VISION CORP (DE)
Merged into Thermo Instrument Systems Inc. 01/07/2000
Each share Common 1¢ par exchanged for $7 cash

THERMO VOLTEK CORP (DE)
Common 5¢ par split (3) for (2) by issuance of (0.5) additional share 11/01/1993
Common 5¢ par split (3) for (2) by issuance of (0.5) additional share payable 08/23/1996 to holders of record 08/09/1996
Merged into TV Acquisition Corp. 03/25/1999
Each share Common 5¢ par exchanged for $7 cash

THERMOBIOS PHARMACEUTICALS INC (NY)
Name changed to Interconnect Resources Corp. 10/03/1972

THERMODYNAMICS, INC. (CO)
Adjudicated bankrupt and assets sold to satisfy creditors 09/12/1963
No stockholders' equity

THERMODYNE INTL LTD (DE)
Each share Common 10¢ par exchanged for (0.1) share Common $1 par 06/15/1979
Merged into Thermodyne Newco, Inc. 07/17/1981
Each share Common $1 par exchanged for $22.50 cash

THERMODYNETICS INC (DE)
Each share old Common 1¢ par exchanged for (0.2) share new Common 1¢ par 04/18/2005
Reincorporated under the laws of Nevada 12/11/2008

THERMOELASTIC TECHNOLOGIES INC (CO)
Each share old Common $0.0001 par exchanged for (0.002) share new Common $0.0001 par 01/29/2003
Name changed to Wannigan Capital Corp. 06/30/2003
(See Wannigan Capital Corp.)

THERMOENERGY CORP (AR)
Common Ser. A $0.001 par reclassified as Common $0.001 par 06/27/2000
Common Ser. B $0.001 par reclassified as Common $0.001 par 06/27/2000
Stock Dividend - 10% payable 06/21/2002 to holders of record 06/10/2002 Ex date - 06/06/2002
Reincorporated under the laws of Delaware 06/25/2007

THERMOGAS CO. (IA)
Common $2 par changed to $1 par and (1) additional share issued 07/24/1962
Merged into Mid-America Pipeline Co. 03/01/1966
Each share Common $1 par exchanged for (0.5) share $1.12 Conv. Preferred Ser. A no par
Mid-America Pipeline Co. name changed to Mapco Inc. 05/14/1968
(See Mapco Inc.)

THERMOGENESIS CORP (DE)
Each share old Common $0.001 par exchanged for (0.5) share new Common $0.001 par 06/14/1996
Each share new Common $0.001 par exchanged again for (0.25) share new Common $0.001 par 08/27/2010
Name changed to Cesca Therapeutics Inc. 02/20/2014

THERMOID CO. (DE)
Common no par changed to $1 par 00/00/1933
Each share 7% Preferred $100 par exchanged for (1.33333333) shares $3 Preferred $10 par 00/00/1936
$3 Preferred $10 par changed to $2.50 Preferred $50 par 00/00/1945
Merged into Porter (H.K.) Co., Inc. (DE) 12/11/1958
Each share Common $1 par exchanged for (0.16666666) share 5.5% Preference $100 par
(See Porter (H.K.) Co., Inc.)

THERMOLASE CORP (CA)
Common 1¢ par split (2) for (1) by issuance of (1) additional share 06/06/1995
Merged into Thermo Electron Corp. 08/15/2000
Each share Common 1¢ par exchanged for (0.132) share Common $1 par
Thermo Electron Corp. name changed to Thermo Fisher Scientific, Inc. 11/09/2006

THERMOMETER CORP. OF AMERICA (OH)
Name changed to Springfield Greene Industries, Inc. 09/25/1959
Springfield Greene Industries, Inc. name changed to Mid-Continent Manufacturing Co. (OH) 08/18/1964 which reincorporated in Delaware as Mid-Con Inc. 10/31/1968 which merged into A-T-O Inc. 10/29/1969 which name changed to Figgie International Inc. (OH) 06/01/1981 which reorganized in Delaware as Figgie International Holdings Inc. 07/18/1983 which name changed to Figgie International Inc. 12/31/1986 which name changed to Scott Technologies, Inc. 05/20/1998 which merged into Tyco International Ltd. (Bermuda) 05/03/2001 which reincorporated in Switzerland 03/17/2009 which merged into Johnson Controls International PLC 09/06/2016

THERMOPLASTICS CORP. (NC)
Completely liquidated 05/15/1968
Each share Capital Stock $1 par exchanged for first and final distribution of (0.051472) share Whittaker Corp. (CA) Common $1 par
Whittaker Corp. (CA) reincorporated in Delaware 06/16/1986
(See Whittaker Corp. (DE))

THERMOQUEST CORP (DE)
Merged into Thermo Electron Corp. 05/12/2000
Each share Common 1¢ par exchanged for $17 cash

THERMORETEC CORP (CA)
Merged into Thermo Electron Corp. 06/06/2000
Each share Common 1¢ par exchanged for $7 cash

THERMOSPECTRA CORP (DE)
Merged into TS Acquisition Corp. 12/09/1999
Each share Common 1¢ par exchanged for $16 cash

THERMOTECH INDS INC (MN)
Acquired by International Telephone & Telegraph Corp. 09/11/1970
Each share Common 35¢ par exchanged for (0.1535) share Common $1 par
International Telephone & Telegraph Corp. name changed to ITT Corp. 12/31/1983 which reorganized in Indiana as ITT Industries, Inc. 12/19/1995 which name changed to ITT Corp. 07/01/2006 which name changed to ITT Inc. 05/17/2016

THERMOTEK INTL INC (DE)
Name changed to Eagle Worldwide Marketing, Inc. (DE) 02/25/2003
Eagle Worldwide Marketing, Inc. (DE) reincorporated in Washington 04/27/2005 which recapitalized as IPhone2, Inc. 07/18/2005
(See IPhone2, Inc.)

THERMOTREX CORP (DE)
Common 1¢ par split (3) for (2) by issuance of (0.5) additional share 10/20/1993
Merged into Thermo Electron Corp. 08/15/2000
Each share Common 1¢ par exchanged for (0.5503) share Common $1 par
Thermo Electron Corp. name changed to Thermo Fisher Scientific, Inc. 11/09/2006

THERMOTRONICS CORP., INC. (FL)
Charter revoked for failure to file reports and pay fees 08/28/1964

THERMOVIEW INDS INC (DE)
Reincorporated 05/22/1998
State of incorporation changed from (NV) to (DE) 05/22/1998
Each share old Common $0.001 par exchanged for (0.33333333) share new Common $0.001 par 10/06/1999
Chapter 11 bankruptcy proceedings converted to Chapter 7 on 10/03/2006
Stockholders' equity unlikely

THERMOVOLT LTD. (ON)
Name changed to National Controls (Canada) Ltd. 12/28/1962
(See National Controls (Canada) Ltd.)

THERON HLDGS LTD (SOUTH AFRICA)
ADR agreement terminated 00/00/1985
Details not available

THESEUS CAP INC (QC)
Name changed to GDG Environment Group Ltd. 08/01/2008
(See GDG Environment Group Ltd.)

THESPORTSCOLLECTION COM INC (CO)
Reorganized under the laws of Nevada as Braz Diamond Mining, Inc. 09/24/2004
Each share Common no par exchanged for (65) shares Common $0.001 par
(See Braz Diamond Mining, Inc.)

THESTREET COM INC (DE)
Name changed to TheStreet, Inc. 05/31/2011

THETFORD CORP (DE)
Merged into Dyson-Moran Corp. 12/15/1988
Each share Common 25¢ par exchanged for $33 cash

THEW SHOVEL CO. (OH)
Each share Common no par exchanged for (2) shares Common $5 par 00/00/1937
Stock Dividend - 200% 05/08/1948
Merged into Koehring Co. 02/07/1964
Each share Common $5 par exchanged for (1.33333333) shares Common $2 par
(See Koehring Co.)

THIEM CORP (WI)
Merged into Koppers Co., Inc. 05/21/1976
Each share Common $1 par exchanged for (0.35) share Common $2.50 par
(See Koppers Co., Inc.)

THILMANY PULP & PAPER CO (WI)
Merged into Hammermill Paper Co. 04/01/1969
Each share Common $10 par exchanged for (1) share Common $1.25 par
(See Hammermill Paper Co.)

THIN EXPRESS INC (NV)
Recapitalized as CyberKey Corp. 02/18/2003
Each share Common $0.002 par exchanged for (0.001) share Common $0.002 par
CyberKey Corp. name changed to CyberKey Solutions, Inc. 04/24/2006
(See CyberKey Solutions, Inc.)

THIN FILM BATTERY INC (CO)
Name changed to Global Acquisition, Inc. 04/17/2001
Global Acquisition, Inc. name changed to Oak Ridge Micro-Energy, Inc. 02/21/2002 which name changed to Oak Ridge Energy Technologies, Inc. 08/28/2013 which name changed to Oakridge Global Energy Solutions, Inc. 11/07/2014

THINK AGAIN INC (DE)
Name changed to Caribbean Developments, Inc. 11/12/2004
Caribbean Developments, Inc. recapitalized as VShield Software Corp. 01/30/2007

THINK COM INC (NV)
Name changed to Go Think.com, Inc. 06/14/1999
Go Think.com, Inc. recapitalized as Knowledge Transfer Systems Inc. 04/24/2001 which name changed to Global General Technologies, Inc. 07/08/2005 which recapitalized as Turbine Aviation, Inc. 12/19/2014

THINK NEW IDEAS INC (DE)
Merged into AnswerThink Consulting Group, Inc. 11/05/1999
Each share Common $0.0001 par exchanged for (0.7) share Common $0.001 par
AnswerThing Consulting Group, Inc. name changed to Answerthink, Inc. 06/20/2000 which name changed to Hackett Group, Inc. 01/01/2008

THINK PARTNERSHIP INC (NV)
Name changed to Kowabunga! Inc. 10/01/2008
Kowabunga! Inc. name changed to Inuvo, Inc. 07/30/2009

THINKA WEIGHT-LOSS CORP (NV)
Name changed to TransWorld Benefits International, Inc. (NV) 10/28/2003
TransWorld Benefits International, Inc. (NV) reincorporated in California 01/15/2008
(See TransWorld Benefits International, Inc.)

THINKENGINE NETWORKS INC (DE)
Filed a petition under Chapter 7 Federal Bankruptcy Code 01/14/2009
Stockholders' equity unlikely

THINKING TOOLS INC (DE)
Recapitalized as GVI Security Solutions, Inc. 04/14/2004
Each (65) shares Common $0.001 par exchanged for (1) share Common $0.001 par
(See GVI Security Solutions, Inc.)

THINKORSWIM GROUP INC (DE)
Merged into TD AMERITRADE Holding Corp. 06/11/2009
Each share Common 1¢ par exchanged for (0.398) share Common 1¢ par and $3.34 cash

THINKPATH INC (ON)
Name changed 06/06/2001
Name changed from Thinkpath.com Inc. to Thinkpath Inc. 06/06/2001
Each share old Common no par exchanged for (0.0002) share new Common no par 06/30/2005
Plan of reorganization under Chapter 11 Federal Bankruptcy proceedings effective 12/25/2008
No stockholders' equity

THIOKOL CORP (VA)
Name changed 00/00/1953
Name changed 11/20/1973
Each share Capital Stock no par exchanged for (3) shares Capital Stock $1 par 00/00/1943
Name changed from Thiokol Corp. (Old) (DE) to Thiokol Chemical Corp. (DE) 00/00/1953
Capital Stock $1 par split (2) for (1) by issuance of (1) additional share 01/22/1958
Voting Trust terminated and each VTC exchanged for Capital Stock $1 par share for share 10/31/1958
Capital Stock $1 par split (3) for (1) by issuance of (2) additional shares 04/30/1959
Capital Stock $1 par reclassified as Common $1 par 04/25/1967
Name and state of incorporation changed from Thiokol Chemical Corp. (DE) to Thiokol Corp. (VA) 11/20/1973
Common $1 par split (2) for (1) by issuance of (1) additional share 08/01/1980
Merged into Morton Thiokol, Inc. 09/24/1982
Each share Common $1 par exchanged for (1.3507) shares Common $1 par
Morton Thiokol, Inc. reorganized as Thiokol Corp. (DE) (New) 07/01/1989 which name changed to Cordant Technologies Inc. 05/07/1998
(See Cordant Techologies Inc.)

THIOKOL CORP NEW (DE)
Common $1 par split (2) for (1) by issuance of (1) additional share payable 03/13/1998 to holders of record 02/27/1998
Name changed to Cordant Technologies Inc. 05/07/1998
(See Cordant Technologies Inc.)

THIOS RES INC (BC)
Recapitalized as Ellios Resources Ltd. 09/17/1993
Each share Common no par exchanged for (0.1) share Common no par
Ellios Resources Ltd. name changed to Fjordland Minerals Ltd. 10/08/1996 which recapitalized as Fjordland Exploration Inc. 05/03/2002

THIRD & BRADY STREETS LIQUIDATION TRUST
In process of liquidation 00/00/1948
Details not available

THIRD AVE FD INC (MD)
Reincorporated under the laws of Delaware as Third Avenue Trust and Common $0.001 par reclassified as Value Trust $0.001 par 03/31/1997

THIRD AVENUE RAILWAY CO.
Merged into Third Avenue Transit Corp. 00/00/1942
Each share Common exchanged for (1) share Common
(See Third Avenue Transit Corp.)

THIRD AVENUE TRANSIT CORP. (NY)
Reorganized 04/10/1957
No stockholders' equity

THIRD CDN GEN INVT TR LTD (CANADA)
Common $5 par changed to no par 00/00/1933
$2.50 Preferred $50 par called for redemption 04/15/1994
Common no par split (6) for (1) by issuance of (5) additional shares 05/19/1994
Acquired by Third Canadian Holdings #1 Ltd. 10/05/2011
Each share Common no par exchanged for $41.07 cash
Note: Unexchanged certificates were cancelled and became without value 10/05/2017

THIRD CENTY VENTURE CORP (IN)
Charter revoked for failure to file annual reports 07/31/1987

THIRD DIMENSION INDS LTD (ON)
Name changed to TDI Venture Equities Ltd. 08/22/1979
TDI Venture Equities Ltd. recapitalized as VTL Venture Equities Ltd. 05/00/1983 which name changed to VTL Venture Corp. 07/07/1986 which name changed to Allcorp United Inc. 07/06/1994 which recapitalized as NTEX Inc. 11/07/1997
(See NTEX Inc.)

THIRD DIVERSIFIED STANDARD SECURITIES LTD.
Merged into Consolidated Diversified Standard Securities Ltd. 00/00/1932
Details not available

THIRD EMPIRE FD INC (MD)
Merged into Fifth Empire Fund, Inc. 05/15/1974
Each share Capital Stock $1 par exchanged for (0.6350) share Capital Stock $1 par
Fifth Empire Fund, Inc. merged into Fourth Empire Fund, Inc. 11/27/1974 which merged into American Leaders Fund, Inc. 04/09/1979 which name changed to Federated American Leaders Fund, Inc. 03/31/1996

THIRD FINL CORP (OH)
Merged into Security Banc Corp. 10/21/1996
Each share Common no par exchanged for $33.41 cash

THIRD INVESTMENT COUNSEL CORP.
Name changed to Scudder, Stevens & Clark Common Stock Fund, Inc. and (1) additional share issued 00/00/1950
Scudder, Stevens & Clark Common Stock Fund, Inc. name changed to Scudder Common Stock Fund, Inc. 03/07/1979 which name changed to Scudder Growth & Income Fund 12/31/1984
(See Scudder Growth & Income Fund)

THIRD MILLENNIUM INDS INC (NV)
Recapitalized as Millennium Energy Corp. 03/11/2014
Each share Common $0.001 par exchanged for (0.002) share Common $0.001 par

THIRD MILLENNIUM SOFTWARE CORP (NV)
Recapitalized as BidHit.com, Inc. 05/17/1999
Each share Common $0.001 par exchanged for (1/6) share Common $0.001 par
BidHit.com, Inc. name changed to U.S. National Commercial Partners Inc. 09/11/2001 which recapitalized as Data-Fit, Inc. 09/10/2003 which recapitalized as Real Security Co., Inc. 12/12/2005
(See Real Security Co., Inc.)

THIRD MILLENNIUM TELECOMMUNICATIONS INC (FL)
Reincorporated under the laws of Delaware as TMTM Merger Co. 09/04/2009
TMTM Merger Co. recapitalized as Green Processing Technologies, Inc. 06/16/2010 which recapitalized as Umbra Applied Technologies Group, Inc. 01/13/2014

THIRD NATIONAL BANK & TRUST CO. (SPRINGFIELD, MA)
Each share Capital Stock $100 par exchanged for (10) shares Capital Stock $10 par 00/00/1941
Stock Dividend - 25% 11/08/1957
Name changed to Third National Bank of Hampden County (Springfield, MA) 11/17/1961
Third National Bank of Hampden County (Springfield, MA) reorganized as T.N.B. Financial Corp. 10/17/1972 which merged into New England Merchants Co., Inc. 09/30/1981 which name changed to Bank of New England Corp. 05/01/1982
(See Bank of New England Corp.)

THIRD NATL BK & TR CO (CAMDEN, NJ)
Under plan of reorganization each share Capital Stock $6.25 par exchanged for (0.69) share United Jersey Banks Common $5 par 10/01/1970
United Jersey Banks name changed to UJB Financial Corp. 06/30/1989 which name changed to Summit Bancorp 03/01/1996 which merged into FleetBoston Financial Corp. 03/01/2001 which merged into Bank of America Corp. 04/01/2004

THIRD NATL BK & TR CO (DAYTON, OH)
Each share Common $25 par exchanged for (2) shares Common $12.50 par and a 33.33333333% stock dividend paid 07/17/1945
Common $12.50 par changed to $6.25 par and (1) additional share issued 06/28/1963
Stock Dividends - 20% 11/16/1941; 25% 01/15/1951; 10% 01/30/1952; 10% 01/18/1954; 13.6363% 01/18/1956; 20% 02/11/1959; 10% 01/24/1961; 19.203% 06/29/1964

THIRD NATL BK & TR CO (SCRANTON, PA)

Reorganized as Interstate Financial Corp. (OH) 01/06/1982
Each share Common $6.25 par exchanged for (1.25) shares Common $5 par
(See Interstate Financial Corp.)

THIRD NATL BK & TR CO (SCRANTON, PA)

Common $100 par changed to $25 par and (3) additional shares issued 12/30/1930
Common $25 par changed to $10 par and (1.5) additional shares issued 03/13/1968
Stock Dividends - 50% 01/28/1963; 10% 02/16/1970; 100% 03/30/1973; 10% 12/31/1985
Merged into Independence Bancorp, Inc. (PA) 03/19/1987
Each share Common $10 par exchanged for (4.06) shares Common $2.50 par
Independence Bancorp, Inc. (PA) merged into CoreStates Financial Corp 06/27/1994 which merged into First Union Corp. 04/28/1998 which name changed to Wachovia Corp. (Ctfs. dated after 09/01/2001) 09/01/2001 which merged into Wells Fargo & Co. (New) 12/31/2008

THIRD NATIONAL BANK (NASHVILLE, TN)

Certificates dated prior to 12/31/1968
Each share Capital Stock $100 par exchanged for (12) shares Capital Stock $10 par to effect a (10) for (1) split and a 20% stock dividend 07/02/1962
Stock Dividends - 100% 01/13/1950; 20% 09/02/1952; 16.6666666% 10/07/1955; 25% 06/04/1959; 48.4781% 03/01/1967
Merged into NLT Corp. (DE) 12/31/1968
Each share Capital Stock $10 par exchanged for (2.1) shares Common $5 par
NLT Corp. (DE) reincorporated in Tennessee 01/01/1981 which merged into American General Corp. 11/04/1982

THIRD NATL BK HAMPDEN CNTY (SPRINGFIELD, MA)

Stock Dividends - 121.238938% 05/01/1963; 10% 02/14/1969
Under plan of reorganization each share Common $10 par automatically became (1) share T.N.B. Financial Corp. Common $1 par 10/17/1972
T.N.B. Financial Corp. merged into New England Merchants Co., Inc. 09/30/1981 which name changed to Bank of New England Corp. 05/01/1982
(See Bank of New England Corp.)

THIRD NATL BK NEW (NASHVILLE, TN)

Certificates dated after 05/28/1970
Stock Dividend - 100% 03/01/1971
Under plan of reorganization each share Capital Stock $10 par automatically became (1) share Third National Corp. Common $10 par 01/01/1972
Third National Corp. merged into SunTrust Banks, Inc. 12/29/1986

THIRD NATL CORP (TN)

Common $10 par changed to $7.50 par and (0.5) additional share issued 05/10/1984
Common $7.50 par changed to $3.75 par and (1) additional share issued 09/12/1985
Stock Dividends - 20% 02/20/1981; 20% 02/24/1982
Merged into SunTrust Banks, Inc. 12/29/1986
Each share Common $3.75 par exchanged for (1.67) shares Common $1 par

THIRD NATIONAL INVESTORS CORP.

Merged into National Investors Corp. (MD) 00/00/1937
Each share Common exchanged for (4.49) shares new Capital Stock $1 par
National Investors Corp. (MD) name changed to Seligman Growth Fund, Inc. 05/01/1982

THIRD ORDER NANOTECHNOLOGIES INC (NV)

Name changed to Lightwave Logic, Inc. 03/10/2008

THIRD UNITED CITIES REALTY CORP. (NY)

Liquidation completed 07/03/1956
Details not available

THIRD WAVE COMMERCE CORP (AB)

Merged into International Hospitality Inc. 07/07/1993
Each share Common no par exchanged for (0.2) share Common no par
International Hospitality Inc. (Old) reorganized as International Hospitality Inc. (New) 12/05/1996
(See International Hospitality Inc. (New))

THIRD WAVE TECHNOLOGIES INC (DE)

Merged into Hologic, Inc. 07/24/2008
Each share Common $0.001 par exchanged for $11.25 cash

THIRDCOAST LTD (ON)

Acquired by Parrish & Heimbecker, Ltd. 09/04/2012
Each share Common no par exchanged for $155 cash

13 COINS RESTAURANTS LTD (BC)

Name changed to M.C. Beverages, Ltd. 12/18/1987
(See M.C. Beverages, Ltd.)

1347 CAP CORP (DE)

Units separated 08/03/2016
Note: Rights portion received (0.1) share Common
Name changed to Limbach Holdings, Inc. 08/03/2016

THIRTEEN MILE GOLD LTD (AB)

Recapitalized 05/28/1990
Recapitalized from Thirteen Mile Resources Ltd. to Thirteen Mile Gold Ltd. 05/28/1990
Each share Common no par exchanged for (0.2) share Common no par
Name changed to Bow River Exploration Ltd. 04/18/1995
(See Bow River Exploration Ltd.)

1325 UN CORP (NY)

Adjudicated bankrupt 08/07/1970
Stockholders' equity unlikely

13TH & 15TH STREETS PASSENGER RAILWAY CO.

Acquired by Philadelphia Transportation Co. 00/00/1940
Each share Common exchanged for $86.45 principal amount of 3%-6% Consolidated Mortage Bonds and (0.7235) share $1 Part. Preferred $20 par
(See Philadelphia Transportation Co.)

THIRTY FEDERAL STREET CORP.

Liquidated 00/00/1954
Details not available

3500 LAKE SHORE DRIVE BLDG. CORP.

Liquidated 00/00/1950
Details not available

THIRTY-FIVE SPLIT CORP (ON)

Preferred Shares no par called for redemption at $25 on 03/31/2008
Capital Shares no par called for redemption at $58.9432 on 03/31/2008
Public interest eliminated

34 EAST 51ST STREET, INC.

Dissolved 00/00/1947
Details not available

3400 SHERIDAN CORP. (IL)

Liquidation approved 12/03/1956
Details not available

3434 BROADWAY CORP. (IL)

Liquidation completed 05/20/1956
Details not available

THIRTY FOURTH STREET CROSSTOWN RAILWAY

Sold to New York Railways Corp. 00/00/1934
Details not available

31E CELLULAR CORP (NV)

Recapitalized as Capital Acquisitions Holdings Ltd. 12/05/2005
Each share Common $0.0001 par exchanged for (0.01) share Common $0.0001 par
Capital Acquisitions Holdings Ltd. name changed to Sun Peaks Energy, Inc. 02/13/2007
(See Sun Peaks Energy, Inc.)

37POINT9 (NV)

Recapitalized as Global Medical Products Holdings, Inc. 11/25/2002
Each share Common $0.001 par exchanged for (0.02) share Common $0.001 par
(See Global Medical Products Holdings, Inc.)

3206 AINSLIE STREET BUILDING CORP. (IL)

Completely liquidated
Each share Common $10 par exchanged for first and final distribution of $3.230247 cash 06/00/1973

THIS CANT BE YOGURT INC (DE)

Common 10¢ par split (3) for (2) by issuance of (0.5) additional share 10/25/1984
Common 10¢ par split (3) for (2) by issuance of (0.5) additional share 02/22/1985
Common 10¢ par split (3) for (2) by issuance of (0.5) additional share 05/24/1985
Name changed to TCBY Enterprises, Inc. 07/30/1985
(See TCBY Enterprises, Inc.)

THISTLE GROUP HLDGS CO (PA)

Merged into Citizens Bank of Pennsylvania (Philadelphia, PA) 01/05/2004
Each share Common 1¢ par exchanged for $26 cash

THISTLE MNG INC (YT)

Each share old Common no par exchanged for (0.005) share new Common no par 07/08/2005
Ceased operations 06/26/2009
No stockholders' equity

THISTLETOWN CAP INC (ON)

Reincorporated under the laws of Alberta as Kelso Energy Inc. 07/14/2003
Kelso Energy Inc. recapitalized as COSTA Energy Inc. 04/28/2006 which recapitalized as Artek Exploration Ltd. 01/20/2010 which merged into Kelt Exploration Ltd. 04/21/2015

THITEC RECOVERY SYS LTD (BC)

Struck off register and dissolved for failure to file returns 12/30/1994

THIZ TECHNOLOGY GROUP LTD (HONG KONG)

ADR agreement terminated 04/27/2015
No ADR's remain outstanding

THOMAS & BETTS CORP (TN)

Name changed 04/25/1968
Reincorporated 05/03/1996
$5 Preferred $100 par called for redemption 03/31/1964
Common $1 par changed to 50¢ par and (1) additional share issued 01/10/1966
Stock Dividends - 10% 09/30/1964; 10% 03/31/1965
Name changed from Thomas & Betts Co. to Thomas & Betts Corp. 04/25/1968
Common 50¢ par split (2) for (1) by issuance of (1) additional share 10/08/1973
Common 50¢ par split (2) for (1) by issuance of (1) additional share 07/06/1984
Common 50¢ par split (2) for (1) by issuance of (1) additional share payable 04/09/1996 to holders of record 03/08/1996 Ex date - 04/10/1996
State of incorporation changed from (NJ) to (TN) and Common 50¢ par changed to no par 05/03/1996
Common no par changed to 10¢ par 05/06/1998
Acquired by ABB Ltd. 05/16/2012
Each share Common 10¢ par exchanged for $72 cash

THOMAS & SKINNER, INC. (IN)

Name changed to Tesla Magnetic Holdings Inc. 01/02/1979
(See Tesla Magentic Holdings Inc.)

THOMAS ALLEC CORP. (NV)

Bankrupt 00/00/1953
No stockholders' equity

THOMAS (I.P.) & SON CO. (NJ)

Each share Common $100 par exchanged for (2) shares Common no par 00/00/1947
Merged into Pennsylvania Salt Manufacturing Co. 03/31/1955
Each share Preferred $100 par exchanged for $100 market value of Common $10 par
Each share Common no par exchanged for (1.135) shares Common $10 par
Pennsylvania Salt Manufacturing Co. name changed to Pennsalt Chemicals Corp. 04/24/1957 which merged into Pennwalt Corp. 03/31/1969
(See Pennwalt Corp.)

THOMAS CO., INC. (MI)

Capital Stock $1 par reclassified as Common no par 6/30/70
Name changed to Epic Manufacturing Corp. 2/1/71
Epic Manufacturing Corp. adjudicated bankrupt 12/7/71

THOMAS CO. (MI)

Name changed to Thomas Co., Inc. 09/25/1968
Thomas Co., Inc. name changed to Epic Manufacturing Corp. 02/01/1971
(See Epic Manufacturing Corp.)

THOMAS EDISON INNS INC (MI)

Name changed to Meritage Hospitality Group Inc. 05/21/1996

THOMAS (RICHARD) ENTERPRISES, INC.

Succeeded by Thomascolor, Inc. 00/00/1947
Details not available

THOMAS EQUIP INC (DE)

Name changed to Osiris Corp. 01/29/2008

THOMAS FURNACE CO.

Liquidated 00/00/1927
Details not available

THOMAS GROUP INC (DE)

Each share old Common 1¢ par exchanged for (0.2) share new Common 1¢ par 08/16/2010 Chapter 7 Bankruptcy proceedings terminated 07/13/2017
No stockholders' equity

THOMAS HOLMES CORP (DE)
Reincorporated 06/16/1969
State of incorporation changed from (NY) to (DE) 06/16/1969
Merged into Rite Aid Corp. 03/15/1973
Each share Common 10¢ par exchanged for $4.75 cash
Note: An additional initial distribution of $0.269113 cash per share was paid from escrow 04/01/1974

THOMAS (SUSAN) INC. (NY)
See - Susan Thomas Inc.

THOMAS INDS INC (DE)
5% Preferred Ser. B $10 par called for redemption 12/00/1973
$5 Preferred Ser. A $100 par called for redemption 09/15/1965
Each share Class B Common $10 par exchanged for (10) shares Common $1 par 02/29/1960
Class A Common $1 par reclassified as Common $1 par 04/20/1960
Common $1 par split (4) for (3) by issuance of (0.3333333) additional share 04/01/1967
Common $1 par split (2) for (1) by issuance of (1) additional share 07/01/1969
Common $1 par split (3) for (2) by issuance of (0.5) additional share payable 12/01/1997 to holders of record 11/14/1997 Ex date - 12/02/1997
Stock Dividends - 25% 07/01/1964; 25% 01/01/1966; 10% 01/01/1978; 10% 01/01/1979; 10% 01/01/1980; 10% 01/01/1981; 10% 01/01/1982; 10% 01/01/1984; 10% 01/01/1985; 10% 01/01/1987
Merged into Gardner Denver, Inc. 07/01/2005
Each share Common $1 par exchanged for $40 cash

THOMAS INTL CORP (DE)
Acquired by Whirlpool Corp. (DE) 11/28/1979
Each share Common 5¢ par exchanged for $2 cash
Note: An additional distribution yet to be determined will be made pending settlement of stockholder litigation

THOMAS NATIONWIDE TRANS LTD (AUSTRALIA)
Stock Dividends - (Canadian Registry) 10% 01/31/1974; 10% 12/16/1974; 10% 12/07/1979; 10% 04/16/1982
Name changed to TNT Ltd. 12/16/1985
(See TNT Ltd.)

THOMAS PPTYS GROUP, INC. (DE)
Merged into Parkway Properties, Inc. 12/19/2013
Each share Common 1¢ par exchanged for (0.3822) share Common $0.001 par
Parkway Properties, Inc. merged into Cousins Properties Inc. 10/06/2016

THOMAS STEEL CO. (DE)
Acquired by Pittsburgh Steel Co. 00/00/1951
Each share Common $1 par exchanged for (0.33333333) share 5.5% Prior Preferred $100 par and (0.33333333) share Common no par
Pittsburgh Steel Co. merged into Wheeling-Pittsburgh Steel Corp. 12/05/1968 which reorganized as Wheeling-Pittsburgh Corp. 01/03/1991 which reorganized as WHX Corp. 07/26/1994
(See WHX Corp.)

THOMAS-TODD PRODUCTIONS, INC. (NY)
Recapitalized as Cinerama Productions Corp. (NY) 00/00/1953
Each share Common 5¢ par exchanged for (2) shares Common 1¢ par
Cinerama Productions Corp. (NY) reincorporated in Delaware as Amedco, Inc. 09/30/1960 which recapitalized as Gulf States Industries, Inc. 05/15/1962
(See Gulf States Industries, Inc.)

THOMAS WEISEL PARTNERS GROUP INC (DE)
Merged into Stifel Financial Corp. 07/01/2010
Each share Common 1¢ par exchanged for (0.1364) share Common 15¢ par

THOMASCOLOR, INC.
Bankrupt 00/00/1950
Stockholders' equity unlikely

THOMASSON (L.), INC. (DE)
Class A Common no par and Class B Common no par reclassified as Common no par 00/00/1960
Merged into Krylon, Inc. 08/03/1961
Each share Common no par exchanged for (8) shares Common no par
Krylon, Inc. acquired by Borden Co. 01/18/1966 which name changed to Borden, Inc. 04/17/1968 which merged into RJR Nabisco Holdings Corp. 03/14/1995 which name changed to Nabisco Group Holdings Corp. 06/15/1999
(See Nabisco Group Holdings Corp.)

THOMASTON COTTON MLS INC (GA)
Stock Dividends - 100% 03/21/1951; 10% 10/24/1977
Name changed to Thomaston Mills, Inc. 10/05/1978
(See Thomaston Mills, Inc.)

THOMASTON FED SVGS BK (THOMASTON, GA)
Common $1 par split (3) for (2) by issuance of (0.5) additional share payable 03/15/1998 to holders of record 03/01/1998
Merged into Flag Financial Corp. 08/27/1999
Each share Common $1 par exchanged for (1.7275) shares Common $1 par
(See Flag Financial Corp.)

THOMASTON MLS INC (GA)
Common $10 par reclassified as Class B Common $1 par 06/02/1988
Each share Class B Common $1 par received distribution of (3) shares Class A Common $1 par 06/15/1988
Class A Common $1 par split (2) for (1) by issuance of (1) additional share 05/15/1992
Class B Common $1 par split (2) for (1) by issuance of (1) additional share 05/15/1992
Assets sold for the benefit of creditors 12/18/2001
No stockholders' equity

THOMASVILLE FURNITURE INDUSTRIES, INC. (NC)
Common $5 par changed to $2.50 par and (1) additional share issued 05/25/1964
Acquired by Armstrong Cork Co. 11/01/1968
Each share Common $2.50 par exchanged for (0.7) share Common $1 par
Armstrong Cork Co. name changed to Armstrong World Industries, Inc. (Old) 05/15/1980 which reorganized as Armstrong Holdings, Inc. 05/01/2000
(See Armstrong Holdings, Inc.)

THOMPSON & SUTHERLAND LTD. (NS)
Formal assignment in bankruptcy filed 02/10/1984
No stockholders' equity

THOMPSON AUTOMATIC ARMS CORP.
Merged into Auto-Ordnance Corp. 00/00/1941
Each share Capital Stock $1 par exchanged for (4) shares Common $1 par
Auto-Ordnance Corp. name changed to Maguire Industries, Inc. 00/00/1944 which name changed to Components Corp. of America 04/03/1961
(See Components Corp. of America)

THOMPSON BOUSQUET GOLD MINES LTD (QC)
Name changed to Les Mines d'Or Thompson- Bousquet Ltee. 04/30/1980
Les Mines d'Or Thompson-Bousquet Ltee. merged into Long Lac Minerals Ltd. 11/02/1981 which merged into Lac Minerals Ltd. (Old) 12/31/1982 which merged into LAC Minerals Ltd. (New) 07/29/1985 which was acquired by American Barrick Resources Corp. 10/17/1994 which name changed to Barrick Gold Corp. 01/18/1995

THOMPSON CADILLAC MINING CORP.
Bankrupt 00/00/1939
Details not available

THOMPSON CREEK METALS CO INC (BC)
Reincorporated 07/29/2008
Place of incorporation changed from (ON) to (BC) 07/29/2008
Each Tangible Equity Unit automatically became (5.3879) shares Common no par 05/15/2015
Merged into Centerra Gold Inc. 10/21/2016
Each share Common no par exchanged for (0.0988) share Common no par
Note: Unexchanged certificates will be cancelled and become without value 10/21/2022

THOMPSON DESIGNS INC (NV)
Name changed to BioPharmX Corp. (NV) 03/03/2014
BioPharmX Corp. (NV) reincorporated in Delaware 05/16/2014

THOMPSON DIVERSACORP LTD (ON)
Acquired by Trinity Managed Investments Ltd. 07/07/1976
Each share Common no par exchanged for $7 cash

THOMPSON (H.I.) FIBER GLASS CO. (CA)
Capital Stock $1 par changed to no par and (1) additional share issued 10/23/1959
Capital Stock no par reclassified as Common no par 02/27/1963
Stock Dividends - 50% 02/15/1957; 50% 10/15/1958; 25% 10/21/1960
Name changed to Hitco 02/19/1965
Hitco merged into Armco Steel Corp. 12/31/1969 which name changed to Armco Inc. 07/01/1978 which merged into AK Steel Holding Corp. 09/30/1999

THOMPSON INDS INC (MA)
Common $1 par split (6) for (1) by issuance of (5) additional shares 03/15/1957
Merged into International Telephone & Telegraph Corp. (DE) 06/03/1969
Each share Common $1 par exchanged for $28.25 cash

THOMPSON INTL CORP (UT)
Name changed to Inland Western Corp. 10/24/1974
(See Inland Western Corp.)

THOMPSON J WALTER CO (DE)
Under plan of reorganization each share Common 10¢ par automatically became (1.5) shares JWT Group, Inc. Common 10¢ par 06/04/1980
(See JWT Group, Inc.)

THOMPSON JOHN R CO (DE)
Reincorporated 06/30/1970
Capital Stock $25 par changed to $15 par 00/00/1947
Capital Stock $15 par changed to $7.50 par and (1) additional share issued 09/23/1959
Capital Stock $7.50 par changed to $3.75 par and (1) additional share issued 05/16/1969
State of incorporation changed from (WV) to (DE) 06/30/1970
Completely liquidated 04/06/1972
Each share Capital Stock $3.75 par exchanged for (0.25) share Green Giant Co. (MN) $1.76 Conv. Preference Ser. D $1 par
Green Giant Co. (MN) reincorporated in Delaware 11/01/1973 which was acquired by 03/09/1979
(See Pillsbury Co.)

THOMPSON LUNDMARK GOLD MINES LTD (CANADA)
Merged into Consolidated Thompson-Lundmark Gold Mines Ltd. 01/16/1986
Each (2.03043) shares Capital Stock no par exchanged for (1) share Common no par
Consolidated Thompson-Lundmark Gold Mines Ltd. name changed to Consolidated Thompson Iron Mines Ltd. 08/24/2006
(See Consolidated Thompson Iron Mines Ltd.)

THOMPSON MED INC (NY)
Common 10¢ par split (5) for (4) by issuance of (0.25) additional share 12/31/1982
Common 10¢ par split (2) for (1) by issuance of (1) additional share 08/01/1983
Acquired by a management group 11/09/1988
Each share Common 10¢ par exchanged for $22.50 cash

THOMPSON PAPER BOX LTD (ON)
3% 2nd Preference $1 par called for redemption 05/01/1968
Name changed to Thompson Diversacorp Ltd. 07/11/1975
(See Thompson Diversacorp Ltd.)

THOMPSON PBE INC (DE)
Merged into FinishMaster, Inc. 11/21/1997
Each share Common $0.001 par exchanged for $8 cash

THOMPSON PRODS INC (OH)
Each share Common $100 par exchanged for (8) shares Class A no par and (2) shares Class B no par 00/00/1927
Each share Class A or B no par exchanged for (1) share Common no par 00/00/1930
Each share Common no par exchanged for (1.2) shares Common $5 par 00/00/1950
Common $5 par split (2) for (1) by issuance of (1) additional share 00/00/1954
Stock Dividends - 100% 11/17/1950; 10% 09/15/1953
Name changed to Thompson Ramo Wooldridge, Inc. 10/31/1958
Thompson Ramo Wooldridge, Inc. name changed to TRW Inc. 04/30/1965 which merged into Northrop Grumman Corp. 12/11/2002

THOMPSON RAMO WOOLDRIDGE INC (OH)
Common $5 par changed to $2.50 par and (1) additional share issued 01/08/1965
Stock Dividend - 10% 01/31/1963
Name changed to TRW Inc. 04/30/1965
TRW Inc. merged into Northrop Grumman Corp. 12/11/2002

THOMPSON-STARRETT CO.
Reorganized as Thompson-Starrett Co., Inc. 00/00/1928
Details not available

THOMPSON STARRETT INC (DE)
Recapitalized 00/00/1954
Each share $3.50 Preference no par exchanged for (7) shares Common 10¢ par
Each share Common no par exchanged for (0.2) share Common 10¢ par
70¢ Conv. Preferred $10 par called for redemption 01/11/1966
Name changed to TST Industries, Inc. 05/01/1968
TST Industries, Inc. merged into Elgin National Industries, Inc. 02/28/1969
(See Elgin National Industries, Inc.)

THOMPSON'S MALTED MILK CO.
Acquired by Borden Co. 00/00/1928
Details not available

THOMPSON'S SPA, INC. (MA)
Name changed to Thompson Industries, Inc. 00/00/1949
(See Thompson Industries, Inc.)

THOMSON ADVISORY GROUP L P (DE)
Stock Dividend - 106% 10/09/1994
Merged into PIMCO Advisors L.P. 11/15/1994
Each Unit of Ltd. Partnership exchanged for (1) Class A Unit of Ltd. Partnership
PIMCO Advisors L.P. exchanged for Oppenheimer Capital L.P. 12/31/1997 which name changed to PIMCO Advisors Holdings L.P. 01/01/1998
(See PIMCO Advisors Holdings L.P.)

THOMSON BRANDT (FRANCE)
Nationalized 00/00/1982
Details not available

THOMSON CORP (ON)
$1.84375 Preference Ser. IV no par called for redemption 06/21/1993
$1.85 Preference Ser. I no par called for redemption 10/18/1993
$1.825 Retractable Preference Ser. III no par called for redemption 12/31/1993
Floating Rate Preference Ser. V called for redemption at $25.50 on 04/14/2003
Name changed to Thomson Reuters Corp. 04/17/2008

THOMSON CSF (FRANCE)
Each old ADR for Ordinary exchanged for (1) new ADR for Ordinary 03/16/1988
Name changed to Thales S.A. 12/06/2000
(See Thales S.A.)

THOMSON DRILLING LTD (ON)
Name changed to Thomson Industries Ltd. 07/01/1973
(See Thomson Industries Ltd.)

THOMSON ELECTRIC WELDER CO. (MA)
Name changed to Pleasant Street Co., Inc. 07/17/1959
(See Pleasant Street Co., Inc.)

THOMSON ELECTRIC WELDING CO. (MA)
Merged into Thomson Electric Welder Co. 06/29/1946
Each share Capital Stock $20 par exchanged for (0.1806391) share Common $5 par
Thomson Electric Welder Co. name changed to Pleasant Street Co., Inc. 07/17/1959
(See Pleasant Street Co., Inc.)

THOMSON-GIBB ELECTRIC WELDING CO.
Merged into Thomson Electric Welder Co. 06/29/1946
Each share Capital Stock $20 par exchanged for (1) share Capital Stock $20 par
Thomson Electric Welder Co. name changed to Pleasant Street Co., Inc. 07/17/1959
(See Pleasant Street Co., Inc.)

THOMSON GOLD LTD (BC)
Struck off register and declared dissolved for failure to file returns 10/09/1992

THOMSON INDS LTD (ON)
Capital Stock no par split (2) for (1) by issuance of (1) additional share 02/17/1978
Merged into ATCO Industries Ltd. 03/03/1978
Each share Capital Stock no par exchanged for USD$20 cash

THOMSON MCKINNON ASSET MGMT LP (DE)
Name changed to Thomson Advisory Group L.P. 09/11/1990
Thomson Advisory Group L.P. merged into PIMCO Advisors L.P. 11/15/1994 which was exchanged for Oppenheimer Capital, L.P. 12/31/1997 which name changed to PIMCO Advisors Holdings L.P. 01/01/1998
(See PIMCO Advisors Holdings L.P.)

THOMSON NEWSPAPERS LTD (ON)
Common no par split (3) for (1) by issuance of (2) additional shares 12/11/1968
Common no par split (3) for (1) by issuance of (2) additional shares 10/23/1972
Common no par reclassified as Conv. Class A no par 06/04/1974
Conv. Class A no par split (3) for (1) by issuance of (2) additional shares 05/31/1985
Conv. Class B no par split (3) for (1) by issuance of (2) additional shares 05/31/1985
6-3/4% Preference Ser. A $50 par called for redemption 02/28/1989
Merged into Thomson Corp. 06/05/1989
Each share Conv. Class A no par exchanged for (1.67) shares Common no par
Each share Conv. Class B no par exchanged for (1.67) shares Common no par
Thomson Corp. name changed to Thomson Reuters Corp. 04/17/2008

THOMSON REUTERS PLC (ENGLAND & WALES)
Each Sponsored ADR for Ordinary exchanged for (6) shares Thomson Reuters Corp. Common no par 09/10/2009

THOMSON S A (FRANCE)
Name changed 10/16/2002
Sponsored ADR's for Ordinary split (2) for (1) by issuance of (1) additional ADR payable 06/22/2000 to holders of record 06/15/2000
Ex date - 06/23/2000
Name changed from Thomson Multimedia to Thomson S.A. 10/16/2002
Name changed to Technicolor S.A. 02/03/2010

THOR CORP. (IL)
Common $5 par changed to $20 par 00/00/1951
Stock Dividends - 10% 01/10/1948; 10% 07/05/1956
Name changed to Allied Paper Corp. 10/05/1956
(See Allied Paper Corp.)

THOR CORP (DE)
Name changed to Thor Energy Resources, Inc. 07/31/1981
(See Thor Energy Resources Inc.)

THOR ENERGY CORP (OK)
Reincorporated 12/28/1981
State of incorporation changed from (NY) to (OK) 12/28/1981
Merged into Burton-Hawks, Inc. 06/27/1983
Each share Common 1¢ par exchanged for (8.67) shares Common 1¢ par
Burton-Hawks, Inc. reincorporated in Delaware as Hawks Industries, Inc. 12/29/1998 which reorganized in Wyoming 02/02/1998 which reincorporated in Nevada 02/18/2000 which name changed to Emex Corp. 02/20/2001
(See Emex Corp.)

THOR ENERGY RES INC (DE)
Preferred Ser. A $1 par called for redemption 08/31/1981
Plan of reorganization under Chapter 11 Federal Bankruptcy proceedings effective 09/20/1995
Preferred Ser. B $1 par was cancelled and deemed worthless
Each share Common $1 par exchanged for $0.175 cash

THOR EXPLS LTD OLD (BC)
Merged into Thor Explorations Ltd. (New) 09/01/2009
Each share Common no par exchanged for (0.5) share Common no par

THOR GOLD CORP (AB)
Name changed to Solomon Gold Corp. 04/11/1989
Solomon Gold Corp. merged into Solomon Resources Inc. 08/01/1989 which recapitalized as Damara Gold Corp. 10/01/2014

THOR MGMT GROUP INC (CO)
Name changed to AXYN Corp. 06/26/1998
AXYN Corp. name changed to Chef Selections, Inc. 04/27/2004 which recapitalized as Talisman Holdings, Inc. 04/14/2010 which recapitalized as Fidelity Holding Corp. 08/20/2014

THOR PWR TOOL CO (DE)
Voting Trust Agreement terminated 05/16/1960
Each VTC for Capital Stock no par exchanged for (1) share Capital Stock no par
Merged into S-W Power Tool Co. 04/02/1973
Each share Capital Stock no par exchanged for $5 cash

THOR URANIUM MINES LTD. (ON)
Merged into Consolidated Thor Mines Ltd. 09/30/1955
Each share Common $1 par exchanged for (1) share Capital Stock $1 par
Thor Mines Ltd. name changed to Nealon Mines Ltd. 01/18/1957
(See Nealon Mines Ltd.)

THOR VENTURES CORP (FL)
Recapitalized as Jure Holdings, Inc. 12/09/2002
Each share Common 1¢ par exchanged for (0.1) share Common 1¢ par
Jure Holdings, Inc. name changed to OpenLimit, Inc. 11/14/2003 which recapitalized as SunVesta, Inc. 08/27/2007

THORATEC CORP (CA)
Name changed 02/14/2001
Each share old Common no par exchanged for (0.33333333) share new Common no par 06/03/1996
Under plan of merger name changed from Thoratec Laboratories Corp. to Thoratec Corp. 02/14/2001
Acquired by St. Jude Medical, Inc. 10/08/2015
Each share new Common no par exchanged for $63.50 cash

THORCO GOLD FINDERS INC. (ON)
Name changed to Thorco Resources Inc. 06/29/1987
Thorco Resources Inc. merged into Caledonia Mining Corp. (BC) 02/04/1992 which reincorporated in Canada 03/29/1995 which reincorporated in Jersey as Caledonia Mining Corp. PLC 03/24/2016

THORCO RES INC (ON)
Merged into Caledonia Mining Corp. (BC) 02/04/1992
Each share Common no par exchanged for (0.19426) share Common no par
Caledonia Mining Corp. (BC) reincorporated in Canada 03/29/1995 which reincorporated in Jersey as Caledonia Mining Corp. PLC 03/24/2016

THORIUM ENERGY INC (NV)
Name changed to Monolith Ventures, Inc. 04/28/2008
Monolith Ventures, Inc. name changed to Zero Gravity Solutions, Inc. 03/13/2013

THORIUM EXPLORATION & GOLD LTD. (ON)
Charter cancelled for failure to file reports and pay taxes 00/00/1952

THORIUM PWR LTD (NV)
Recapitalized as Lightbridge Corp. 09/29/2009
Each (30) shares Common $0.001 par exchanged for (1) share Common $0.001 par

THORMOOR COPPER MINES LTD.
Bankrupt 00/00/1928
No stockholders' equity

THORN APPLE VY INC (DE)
Common 10¢ par split (3) for (2) by issuance of (0.5) additional share 06/14/1991
Common 10¢ par split (3) for (2) by issuance of (0.5) additional share 12/23/1992
Chapter 11 bankruptcy proceedings converted to Chapter 7 on 07/31/2001
No stockholders' equity

THORN EMI P L C (ENGLAND)
Each Unsponsored ADR for Ordinary exchanged for (1) Sponsored ADR for Ordinary 03/04/1991
Name changed to EMI Group PLC 08/19/1996
(See EMI Group PLC)

THORN HILL GOLD MINES LTD. (ON)
Merged into Landmark Mines Ltd. 05/00/1956
Each share Common exchanged for (0.1) share Common
(See Landmark Mines Ltd.)

THORN PLC (UNITED KINGDOM)
Each Sponsored ADR for Ordinary exchanged for (0.8571) Sponsored ADR for Class B 07/18/1997
Acquired by Future Rentals PLC 11/06/1998
Each Sponsored ADR for Class B exchanged for $16.947 cash

THORNAPPLE CAP INC (CAYMAN ISLANDS)
Recapitalized as Agility Health, Inc. 10/11/2013
Each share Common CAD $0.001 par exchanged for (0.5) share Common CAD $0.001 par

THORNBURG MTG INC (MD)
Name changed 04/27/2000
Name changed from Thornburg Mortgage Asset Corp. to Thornburg Mortgage, Inc. 04/27/2000
Each share 9.68% Conv. Preferred Ser. A 1¢ par exchanged for (1) share Common 1¢ par 08/18/2003
Each share old Common 1¢ par

THO-THR   FINANCIAL INFORMATION, INC.

exchanged for (0.1) share new
Common 1¢ par 09/29/2008
Name changed to TMST, Inc.
08/07/2009
(See TMST, Inc.)

THORNBURY CAP CORP (ON)
Recapitalized as International
Uranium Corp. 05/16/1997
Each share Common no par
exchanged for (0.2) share Common
no par
International Uranium Corp. name
changed to Denison Mines Corp.
12/06/2006

THORNCLIFFE MINES LTD. (ON)
Charter revoked for failure to file
reports and pay fees 01/26/1967

THORNCLIFFE PARK LTD. (ON)
Name changed to Canadianwide
Properties Ltd. 01/01/1962
(See Canadianwide Properties Ltd.)

THORNCREST EXPLS LTD (ON)
Common $1 par changed to no par
12/28/1972
Name changed to New Concept
Technologies International Inc. (ON)
03/10/1994
New Concept Technologies
International Inc. (ON)
reincorporated in Bermuda as New
Concept Technologies International
Ltd. 12/15/1994 which name
changed to NTI Resources Ltd.
(Bermuda) 08/16/1996 which
reincorporated in Alberta 05/28/1997
(See NTI Resources Ltd.)

THORNCREST OIL & GAS CO. LTD. (ON)
Name changed to Thorncrest
Explorations Ltd. 06/08/1954
Thorncrest Explorations Ltd. name
changed to New Concept
Technologies International Inc.
(ONT) 03/10/1994 which
reincorporated in Bermuda as New
Concept Technologies International
Ltd. 12/15/1994 which name
changed to NTI Resources Ltd.
(Bermuda) 08/16/1996 which
reincorporated in Alberta 05/28/1997
(See NTI Resources Ltd.)

THORNCREST OILS & GAS LTD. (ON)
Name changed to Thorncrest
Explorations Ltd. 00/00/1954
Thorncrest Explorations Ltd. name
changed to New Concept
Technologies International Inc. (ON)
03/10/1994 which reincorporated in
Bermuda as New Concept
Technologies International Ltd.
12/15/1994 which name changed to
NTI Resources Ltd. (Bermuda)
08/16/1996 which reincorporated in
Alberta 05/28/1997
(See NTI Resources Ltd.)

THORNECLIFF VENTURES LTD (CANADA)
Reincorporated under the laws of
Yukon as eMobile Data Corp.
03/22/2001
(See eMobile Data Corp.)

THORNLOE PORCUPINE GOLD MINES, LTD. (ON)
Charter cancelled for failure to file
reports and pay taxes 05/13/1957

THORNYCROFT APARTMENTS, INC. (NY)
Liquidation completed 07/02/1954
Details not available

THOROFARE CORP (DE)
Name changed 05/21/1982
Common 25¢ par split (3) for (1) by
issuance of (1) additional share
05/17/1955
Common 25¢ par changed to $5 par
04/12/1972
Common $5 par changed to $1 par
01/15/1980
Stock Dividend - 10% 01/02/1952

Name changed from Thorofare
Markets, Inc. to Thorofare Corp.
05/21/1982
Name changed to Casablanca
Industries Inc. 01/31/1983
(See Casablanca Industries Inc.)

THOROUGHBRED BREEDERS INC (FL)
Proclaimed dissolved for failure to file
reports and pay fees 10/13/89

THOROUGHBRED CAP INC (ON)
Name changed to Sunora Foods Inc.
12/17/2013

THOROUGHBRED ENTERPRISES, INC. (FL)
Name changed to International
Beauty Corp. 03/12/1964
International Beauty Corp. name
changed to Cement International
Corp. 03/15/1966 which name
changed to Comp-Tronics, Inc.
09/09/1969 which name changed to
Silvatex, Inc. 01/07/1980 which
name changed to Grandma's Inc.
07/30/1982
(See Grandma's Inc.)

THOROUGHBRED HORSE CO (DE)
Name changed to Alco International
Group Group, Inc. 01/14/1986
(See Alco International Group, Inc.)

THOROUGHBRED INTS INC (NV)
Each share old Common $0.001 par
exchanged for (0.1) share new
Common $0.001 par 01/09/2004
Name changed to Phoenix Interests,
Inc. 05/27/2004
Phoenix Interests, Inc. name changed
to NuMobile, Inc. 07/15/2009 which
recapitalized as Priority Aviation,
Inc. 01/06/2014

THOROUGHBRED INVTS INC (FL)
Name changed to Jameson
Investments Inc. 01/27/1988
Jameson Investments Inc. name
changed to Meadowlands
Investments Inc. 03/03/1988
(See Meadowlands Investments Inc.)

THOROUGHBREDS U S A INC (NY)
Name changed to New Sky
Communications, Inc. 09/15/1986
New Sky Communications, Inc. name
changed to Document Security
Systems, Inc. 02/03/2003

THORP FIN CORP (WI)
Each share Common $5 par
exchanged for (5) shares Common
$1 par 05/29/1959
Acquired by International Telephone &
Telegraph Corp. (DE) 01/03/1969
Each share 5% 1st Preferred Ser. A
$100 par exchanged for (1) share $6
Preferred Ser. M no par
Each share $1.56 Conv. Preference
$1 par exchanged for (0.435) share
$4 Conv. Preferred Ser. K no par
Each share Common $1 par
exchanged for (0.2) share $4 Conv.
Preferred Ser. K no par
International Telephone & Telegraph
Corp. (DE) name changed to ITT
Corp. 12/31/1983 which reorganized
in Indiana as ITT Industries, Inc.
12/19/1995 which name changed to
ITT Corp. 07/01/2006

THORPE BAY EXPLORATIONS LTD. (ON)
Merged into Tri-Bridge Consolidated
Gold Mines Ltd. 10/13/1973
Each share Capital Stock no par
exchanged for (0.1) share Common
no par
Tri-Bridge Consolidated Gold Mines
Ltd. merged into Lobo Gold &
Resources Inc. 07/06/1983 which
recapitalized as Lobo Capital Inc.
06/11/1992 which name changed to
Q & A Communications Inc.
03/01/1993 which recapitalized as Q
& A Capital Inc. 11/05/1997 which

recapitalized as Leader Capital
Corp. 08/17/1998
(See Leader Capital Corp.)

THORREZ & MAES MANUFACTURING CO.
Dissolved 00/00/1949
Details not available

THORSDEN GROUP LTD (DE)
Name changed to Sundog
Technologies Inc. 07/14/1999
Sundog Technologies Inc. name
changed to Arkona Inc. 02/22/2001
(See Arkona Inc.)

THORTEC INTL INC (DE)
Under plan of reorganization name
changed back to URS Corp. (DE)
02/21/1990
Each share Common 25¢ par
exchanged for (0.1) share Common
1¢ par

THO2 & RARE METALS EXPL INC (ID)
Name changed to Golf-Technology
Holding, Inc. (ID) 01/13/1995
Golf-Technology Holding, Inc. (ID)
reincorporated in Delaware as
Snake Eyes Golf Clubs, Inc.
12/18/1997
(See Snake Eyes Golf Clubs, Inc.)

THOUGHTSHARE COMMUNICATIONS INC (AB)
Recapitalized as Qumana Software
Inc. 12/06/2004
Each share Common no par
exchanged for (0.05) share Common
no par

THOUSAND TRAILS INC (DE)
Merged into KTTI Holding Co., Inc.
7/22/2003
Each share Common no par
exchanged for $14.50 cash

THOUSAND TRAILS INC (WA)
Common no par split (3) for (2) by
issuance of (0.5) additional share
02/21/1983
Common no par split (3) for (2) by
issuance of (0.5) additional share
06/08/1984
Stock Dividend - 10% 06/30/1980
Merged into U.S. Trails 03/29/1994
Each share Common no par
exchanged for $1.55 cash

THQ INC (DE)
Name changed 12/31/1997
Each share old Common $0.0001 par
exchanged for (0.06666666) share
new Common $0.0001 par
02/15/1995
Name and place of incorporation
changed from T.HQ, Inc. (NY) to
THQ Inc. (DE) and Common
$0.0001 par changed to 1¢ par
12/31/1997
Old Common 1¢ par split (3) for (2)
by issuance of (0.5) additional share
payable 08/24/1998 to holders of
record 08/20/1998
Old Common 1¢ par split (3) for (2)
by issuance of (0.5) additional share
payable 12/01/1999 to holders of
record 11/15/1999
Old Common 1¢ par split (3) for (2)
by by issuance of (0.5) additional
share payable 04/09/2002 to holders
of record 03/26/2002 Ex date -
04/10/2002
Old Common 1¢ par split (3) for (2)
by issuance of (0.5) additional share
payable 09/01/2005 to holders of
record 08/19/2005 Ex date -
09/02/2005
Each share old Common 1¢ par
exchanged for (0.1) share new
Common 1¢ par 07/09/2012
Plan of reorganization under Chapter
11 Federal Bankruptcy proceedings
effective 08/02/2013
Shareholder interest was placed in a
Stock Trust for possible future
distribution

THREE BROTHERS MINING EXPLORATION LTD. (ON)
Merged into Consolidated Professor
Mines Ltd. 03/09/1964
Each share Common no par
exchanged for (0.2) share Common
no par
(See Consolidated Professor Mines
Ltd.)

THREE CNTY RECYCLING & COMPOSTING INC (ON)
Name changed to TCR Environmental
Corp. 12/05/1997
(See TCR Environmental Corp.)

THREE D DEPTS INC (DE)
Common 25¢ par split (3) for (2) by
issuance (0.5) additional share
08/31/1983
Common 25¢ par reclassified as
Conv. Class B Common 25¢ par
12/13/1983
Each share Conv. Class B Common
25¢ par received distribution of (1)
share Class A Common 25¢ par
12/22/1983
Stock Dividends - 20% 05/09/1977;
10% 11/19/1979
Chapter 11 bankruptcy proceedings
terminated 08/22/2000
Stockholders' equity unlikely

3-D GEOPHYSICAL INC (DE)
Merged into Western Atlas Inc.
04/30/1998
Each share Common 1¢ par
exchanged for $9.65 cash

3D IMAGE TECHNOLOGY INC (DE)
Company ceased operations due to
financial difficulties 3/31/99

3-D SYS INC (BC)
Reincorporated under the laws of
Delaware as 3D Systems Corp. and
Common no par changed to $0.001
par 08/12/1993

THREE DIMENSIONAL CIRCUITS INC (DE)
Bankruptcy proceedings under
Chapter 11 dismissed 03/26/1984
No stockholders' equity

3 DIMENSIONAL PHARMACEUTICALS INC (DE)
Merged into Johnson & Johnson
3/31/2003
Each share Common $0.001 par
exchanged for $5.74 cash

3 E INTL CORP (DE)
Recapitalized as Mobilestream, Inc.
8/15/2005
Each share Common 1¢ par
exchanged for (0.001) share
Common 1¢ par
Mobilestream, Inc. name changed to
Mobilestream Oil, Inc. 3/31/2006

318 ADAMS BUILDING, INC.
Liquidated in 1947

THREE-FIVE SYS INC (DE)
Common 1¢ par split (2) for (1) by
issuance of (1) additional share
05/04/1994
Common 1¢ par split (4) for (3) by
issuance of (1/3) additional share
payable 12/17/1999 to holders of
record 12/03/1999 Ex date -
12/20/1999
Common 1¢ par split (3) for (2) by
issuance of (0.5) additional share
payable 05/12/2000 to holders of
record 05/01/2000 Ex date -
05/15/2000
Each share Common 1¢ par received
distribution of (0.25) share Brillian
Corp. Common $0.001 par payable
09/15/2003 to holders of record
09/04/2003 Ex date - 09/16/2003
Under plan of reorganization each
share Common 1¢ par received first
and final distribution of $0.111 cash
payable 02/24/2010 to holders of
record 01/29/2010 Ex date -
02/12/2010
Note: Holders of (90) or fewer shares

COPYRIGHTED MATERIAL   2596   NO UNAUTHORIZED REPRODUCTION

will not qualify for a distribution; their shares will be allocated to qualified holders
Certificates were not required to be surrendered and are without value

THREE HUNDRED ADAMS BLDG INC (IL)
Completely liquidated 12/30/1969
Each share Common no par exchanged for first and final distribution of $85 cash

360 COMMUNICATIONS CO (DE)
Merged into Alltel Corp. 07/01/1998
Each share Common 1¢ par exchanged for (0.74) share Common $1 par
(See Alltel Corp.)

300 SUNRISE, INC. (NY)
Completely liquidated 5/11/66
Each share Common $5 par exchanged for first and final distribution of (0.021646) share Spencer Shoe Corp. Conv. Part. Preferred $100 par
Spencer Shoe Corp. name changed to Spencer Companies, Inc. 9/22/70 which was acquired by Baker (J.), Inc. 4/15/89

300 WEST 97TH STREET CORP.
Property sold in 1945
No stockholders' equity

3 I CO INFORMATION INTERSCIENCE INC (PA)
Class A Common 10¢ par split (3) for (1) by issuance of (2) additional shares 1/31/69
Merged into Insyte Corp. 9/4/73
Each share Class A Common 10¢ par exchanged for (0.2) share Common 1¢ par
Insyte Corp. name changed to Insyte Energy Corp. 1/28/83 which merged into Shannon Group Inc. (TX) 7/27/84

THREE L ENTERPRISES INC (DE)
Name changed to Intelicom International Corp. 09/10/1996
Intelicom International Corp. name changed to IntraTel Group, Ltd. 04/01/1997
(See IntraTel Group, Ltd.)

THREE M'S WEST (UT)
Name changed to Modern Mining & Milling Co., Inc. 2/28/73
Modern Mining & Milling Co., Inc. recapitalized as Copper Mountain Energy, Inc. 12/1/78
(See Copper Mountain Energy, Inc.)

THREE POINTS, INC. (MN)
Each share Common 5¢ par exchanged for (0.25) share Common 20¢ par 2/27/78
Merged into C K Subsidiary, Inc. 12/27/79
Each share Common 20¢ par exchanged for $0.50 cash

THREE RIVERS BK & TR CO (JEFFERSON BOROUGH, PA)
Merged into USBANCORP, Inc. 06/30/1984
Each share Common $20 par exchanged for (1.5) shares Common $2.50 par and $270 cash
USBANCORP, Inc. name changed to AmeriServ Financial, Inc. 05/07/2001

THREE RIVS BANCORP INC (PA)
Merged into Sky Financial Group, Inc. 10/01/2002
Each share Common 1¢ par exchanged for (0.296) share Common no par and $11.5101 cash
Sky Financial Group, Inc. merged into Huntington Bancshares Inc. 07/02/2007

THREE RIVS FINL CORP (MI)
Stock Dividend - 10% payable 12/11/1998 to holders of record 11/11/1998

Merged into Peoples Bancorp 02/29/2000
Each share Common 1¢ par exchanged for (1.08) shares Common $1 par
Peoples Bancorp merged into Horizon Bancorp 07/01/2015

THREE ROSES INC (DE)
Name changed to Transcolor Corp. 01/25/1990
(See Transcolor Corp.)

3 SHINE TECHNOLOGIES INC (NV)
Name changed to Rorine International Holding Corp. 10/07/2015

360 CAP FINL SVCS GRP INC (BC)
Name changed to 360 Blockchain Inc. 10/10/2017

360 GLOBAL WINE CO (NV)
Each (150) shares old Common $0.001 par exchanged for (1) share new Common $0.001 par 03/01/2006
Note: No holder will receive fewer than (100) shares
Plan of reorganization under Chapter 11 Federal Bankruptcy proceedings effective 06/18/2010
Holders of (9,300) shares or more will receive pro-rata distribution of new Common
Holders of (9,299) shares or fewer will not receive a distribution

THREE SIXTY INC (DE)
Name changed to IAHL Corp. 11/30/2007

360 INTERCHANGE INC (NV)
Name changed to ecoSolutions Intl 04/14/2008 ecoSolutions Intl name changed to Hedgebrook 12/10/2012

360 VOX CORP (ON)
Merged into Dundee Corp. 07/03/2014
Each share Class A Common no par exchanged for (0.01221) share Class A Subordinate no par
Note: Unexchanged certificates will be cancelled and become without value 07/03/2020

THREE-STATES NATURAL GAS CO. (DE)
Merged into Delhi-Taylor Oil Corp. on (1) for (4.75) basis 5/31/61
(See Delhi-Taylor Oil Corp.)

THREE STATES URANIUM CORP. (DE)
Merged into Consolidated Uranium Mines, Inc. 11/09/1954
Each share Common exchanged for (0.2) share Common $0.075 par
(See Consolidated Uranium Mines, Inc.)

310 FIFTH AVENUE CORP.
Merged into International Business Machines Corp. 00/00/1933
Details not available

310 HLDGS INC (NV)
Name changed to JBI, Inc. 10/19/2009
JBI, Inc. name changed to Plastic2Oil, Inc. 08/06/2014

312-FUTURES INC (IL)
Name changed to Jack Carl/312 Futures, Inc. (IL) 08/29/1986
Jack Carl/312 Futures, Inc. (IL) reincorporated in Delaware 05/03/1994 which name changed to IFX Corp. 06/02/1997
(See IFX Corp.)

324, INC. (MN)
Liquidation completed
Each share Common 10¢ par exchanged for initial distribution of $3.21 cash 04/30/1981
Each share Common 10¢ par received second distribution of $1.16 cash 01/05/1982
Each share Common 10¢ par

received third and final distribution of $0.068 cash 01/03/1983

322 EIGHTH AVENUE CORP.
Reorganized 00/00/1947
No stockholders' equity

THREE YEAR NOTEHOLDERS CORP.
Dissolved 00/00/1945
Details not available

3C GEN CORP (NY)
Common 1¢ par split (2) for (1) by issuance of (1) additional share 01/04/1993
Merged into Monroe Acquisition Corp. 08/21/2003
Each share Common 1¢ par exchanged for $6.35 cash

3CI COMPLETE COMPLIANCE CORP (DE)
Merged into Stericycle, Inc. 04/26/2006
Each share Common 1¢ par exchanged for $0.60 cash

3CI INC (DE)
Stock Dividend - 33-1/3% 02/16/1987
Recapitalized as Cordero Industries Inc. 06/01/1990
Each share Common 1¢ par exchanged for (0.1) share Common 1¢ par
(See Cordero Industries Inc.)

3COM CORP (DE)
Reincorporated 06/11/1997
Common no par split (2) for (1) by issuance of (1) additional share 08/31/1994
Common no par split (2) for (1) by issuance of (1) additional share 08/25/1995
State of incorporation changed from (CA) to (DE) and Common no par changed to 1¢ par 06/11/1997
Each share Common 1¢ par received distribution of (1.484) shares Palm, Inc. (Old) Common 1¢ par payable 07/27/2000 to holders of record 07/11/2000
Acquired by Hewlett-Packard Co. 04/12/2010
Each share Common 1¢ par exchanged for $7.90 cash

3D VISIT INC (CANADA)
Recapitalized as Focus Metals Inc. 12/09/2008
Each share Common no par exchanged for (0.25) share Common no par
Focus Metals Inc. name changed to Focus Graphite Inc. 05/25/2012

3DFX INTERACTIVE INC (CA)
Chapter 11 bankruptcy proceedings converted to Chapter 7 on 05/19/2015
Stockholders' equity unlikely

3DICON CORP (OK)
Each share old Common $0.0002 par exchanged for (0.02857142) share new Common $0.0002 par 04/27/2012
Recapitalized as Coretec Group Inc. 06/29/2017
Each share new Common $0.0002 par exchanged for (0.00333333) share Common $0.0002 par

3DM WORLDWIDE PLC (ENGLAND)
Name changed to Environmental Recycling Technologies PLC 10/16/2007
(See Environmental Recycling Technologies PLC)

3DO CO (DE)
Each share old Common 1¢ par exchanged for (0.125) share new Common 1¢ par 08/22/2002
Chapter 11 bankruptcy proceedings converted to Chapter 7 on 11/07/2003
No stockholders' equity

3DX TECHNOLOGIES INC (DE)
Merged into Esenjay Exploration, Inc. 09/24/1999
Each share Common 1¢ par exchanged for (0.30769237) share Common 1¢ par
(See Esenjay Exploration, Inc.)

3EEE INC (DE)
Recapitalized as Digital Utilities Ventures Inc. 05/12/2009
Each share Common $0.001 par exchanged for (0.2) share Common $0.001 par

3H BLDG CORP (DE)
Reincorporated 11/12/1970
State of incorporation changed from (IL) to (DE) and Common no par changed to $1 par 11/12/1970
Merged into U.S. Home Corp. 10/03/1972
Each share Common $1 par exchanged for (0.51467) share Common 10¢ par
U.S. Home Corp. (Old) reorganized as U.S. Home Corp. (New) 06/21/1993 which merged into Lennar Corp. 05/02/2000

THREEMAN MINING CO. (NY)
Charter cancelled and proclaimed dissolved for failure to file reports and pay fees 12/15/1973

3MV ENERGY CORP (CANADA)
Lender realized on Security 01/21/2016
No stockholders' equity

3NET MEDIA CORP (AB)
Recapitalized as Everton Resources Inc. (AB) 11/04/2002
Each share Common no par exchanged for (0.25) share Common no par
Everton Resources Inc. (AB) reincorporated in Canada 04/16/2004

3NET SYS INC (DE)
Recapitalized as Alternative Technology Resources, Inc. 11/29/1996
Each share Common 1¢ par exchanged for (0.1) share Common 1¢ par
Alternative Technology Resources, Inc. name changed to National Healthcare Exchange Services, Inc. 02/09/2004
(See National Healthcare Exchange Services, Inc.)

3P INTL ENERGY CORP (ON)
Name changed to Cub Energy Inc. (ON) 01/30/2012
Cub Energy Inc. (ON) reincorporated in Canada 02/28/2012

3P NETWORKS INC (NV)
Recapitalized as Kender Energy Inc. 10/07/2008
Each share Common $0.001 par exchanged for (0.005) share Common $0.001 par
Kender Energy Inc. recapitalized as Bettwork Industries Inc. 07/02/2014

3PAR INC (DE)
Acquired by Hewlett-Packard Co. 09/27/2010
Each share Common $0.001 par exchanged for $33 cash

3SBIO INC (CAYMAN ISLANDS)
Acquired by Decade Sunshine Ltd. 05/30/2013
Each Sponsored ADR for Ordinary exchanged for $16.70 cash

3 SI HLDGS INC (WY)
Reorganized under the laws of Florida as Bulova Technologies Group, Inc. 02/25/2009
Each share Common 1¢ par exchanged for (0.06666666) share Common $0.001 par

360NETWORKS CORP (BC)
Majority of shares acquired through

purchase offer which expired 03/22/2005
Public interest eliminated

360NETWORKS INC (NS)
Plan of reorganization under Chapter 11 Federal Bankruptcy Code effective 11/12/2002
No stockholders' equity

3TEC ENERGY CORP (DE)
Each share old Common 2¢ par exchanged for (0.33333333) share new Common 2¢ par 01/18/2000
Conv. Preferred Ser. C 2¢ par called for redemption at $5 plus $0.25 accrued dividends on 09/30/2000
Merged into Plains Exploration & Production Co. 06/04/2003
Each share new Common 2¢ par exchanged old (0.85) share Common 1¢ par and $8.50 cash
Plains Exploration & Production Co. merged into Freeport-McMoRan Copper & Gold Inc. 05/31/2013 which name changed to Freeport-McMoRan Inc. 07/14/2014

333 BLDG CORP (DE)
Acquired by 333 Holdings Co. 11/30/2012
Each share Common $1 par exchanged for $0.22 cash

3TL TECHNOLOGIES CORP (BC)
Each share old Common no par exchanged for (0.1) share new Common no par 05/23/2017
Name changed to Datable Technologies Corp. 05/18/2018

THRESHOLD PHARMACEUTICALS INC (DE)
Each share old Common $0.001 par exchanged for (0.16666666) share new Common $0.001 par 08/20/2008
Recapitalized as Molecular Templates, Inc. 08/02/2017
Each share new Common $0.001 par exchanged for (0.09090909) share Common $0.001 par

THRESHOLD TECHNOLOGY INC (DE)
Charter cancelled and declared inoperative and void for non-payment of taxes 03/01/1986

THRIFT COURTS OF AMERICA, INC. (DE)
Adjudicated bankrupt 02/12/1965
No stockholders' equity

THRIFT DRUG CO PA (PA)
Common $1 par split (4) for (3) by issuance of (0.33333333) additional share 12/09/1966
Common $1 par split (4) for (3) by issuance of (0.33333333) additional share 12/18/1967
Stock Dividends - 33.33333333% 12/19/1964; 50% 12/03/1965
Acquired by Penney (J.C.) Co., Inc. 03/12/1969
Each share Common $1 par exchanged for (1.35) shares Common 50¢ par

THRIFT INC (ND)
Name changed to Valdak Corp. 09/06/1967

THRIFT INTERSTATE CORP. (PA)
Name changed to Signal Finance Corp. 01/11/1967
Signal Finance Corp. name changed to Signet Corp. 01/09/1969 which merged into Philadelphia National Corp. 06/29/1973 which merged into CoreStates Financial Corp 05/02/1983 which merged into First Union Corp. 04/28/1998 which name changed to Wachovia Corp. (Ctfs. dated after 09/01/2001) 09/01/2001 which merged into Wells Fargo & Co. (New) 12/31/2008

THRIFT INVESTMENT CORP. (PA)
Recapitalized 00/00/1947

Each share 6% Preferred $10 par exchanged for (2.165) shares new Class A Common no par
Each share old Class A Common no par exchanged for (1) share new Class A Common no par
Each share old Common no par exchanged for (0.172) share new Class B Common no par
New Class A Common no par and new Class B Common no par changed to $1 par 00/00/1952
$0.60 Preferred 1952 Ser. no par called for redemption 12/31/1955
$0.60 Preferred 1953 Ser. no par called for redemption 12/31/1956
Recapitalized 05/20/1967
Each share Class A Common $1 par exchanged for (1) share Common $1 par
Each share Class B Common $1 par exchanged for (8) shares Common $1 par
Under plan of merger name changed to Thrift Interstate Corp. 04/15/1965
Thrift Interstate Corp. name changed to Signal Finance Corp. 01/11/1967 which name changed to Signet Corp. 01/09/1969 which merged into Philadelphia National Corp. 06/29/1973 which merged into CoreStates Financial Corp 05/02/1983 which merged into First Union Corp. 04/28/1998 which name changed to Wachovia Corp. (Ctfs. dated after 09/01/2001) 09/01/2001 which merged into Wells Fargo & Co. (New) 12/31/2008

THRIFT MGMT INC (FL)
Name changed to TMI Holdings, Inc. 08/27/2001
TMI Holdings, Inc. name changed to Total Identity Corp. 09/12/2003 which recapitalized as 247MGI, Inc. 12/21/2006 which name changed to Baron Capital Enterprise, Inc. 12/16/2011

THRIFTIMART INC (CA)
Name changed to Smart & Final Iris Corp. 07/20/1984
(See Smart & Final Iris Corp.)

THRIFTWAY FOODS INC. (PA)
Merged into Fleming Co., Inc. 08/26/1965
Each share Common $2 par exchanged for (0.86) share Common $2.50 par
Fleming Co., Inc. name changed to Fleming Companies, Inc. (KS) 04/28/1972 which reincorporated in Oklahoma 04/29/1981
(See Fleming Companies, Inc. (OK))

THRIFTWAY LEASING CO (NJ)
Common 50¢ par changed to $0.16666666 par and (2) additional shares issued 05/26/1972
Merged into Interway Corp. 07/01/1979
Each share Common $0.16666666 par exchanged for $7.875 cash

THRIFTY CORP (CA)
Common no par split (2) for (1) by issuance of (1) additional share 06/10/1983
Acquired by Pacific Lighting Corp. 08/05/1986
Each share Common no par exchanged for (0.802) share Common no par
Pacific Lighting Corp. name changed to Pacific Enterprises 02/16/1988
(See Pacific Enterprises)

THRIFTY DRUG STORES CO., INC. (CA)
Each share Preferred $25 par exchanged for (0.3) share 4.50% Ser. A Preferred $100 par 00/00/1945
Common no par changed to $1 par 00/00/1945
Each share Common $1 par

exchanged for (2) shares Common 50¢ par 00/00/1947
Common 50¢ par changed to no par and (1) additional share issued 02/16/1959
4.50% Preferred Ser. A $100 par called for redemption 06/30/1965
4.50% Preferred Ser. B $100 par called for redemption 06/30/1965
Common no par split (2) for (1) by issuance of (1) additional share 03/31/1972
Stock Dividends - 50% 12/15/1955; 100% 06/30/1965
Name changed to Thrifty Corp. 02/05/1977
Thrifty Corp. acquired by Pacific Lighting Corp. 08/05/1986 which name changed to Pacific Enterprises 02/16/1988
(See Pacific Enterprises)

THRIFTY PAYLESS HLDGS INC (DE)
Each share Class C Common 1¢ par exchanged for (20) shares Class B Common 1¢ par 04/22/1996
Merged into Rite Aid Corp. 12/12/1996
Each share Class A Common 1¢ par exchanged for (0.65) share Common $1 par
Each share Class B Common 1¢ par exchanged for (0.65) share Common $1 par

THRIFTY PRTG INC (NV)
Each share old Common $0.001 par exchanged for (6) shares new Common $0.001 par 6/12/2006
Name changed to Anavex Life Sciences Corp. 1/25/2007

THRIFTY RENT-A-CAR SYS INC (OK)
Common 5¢ par split (3) for (2) by issuance of (0.5) additional share 09/30/1988
Merged into Chrysler Corp. 06/23/1989
Each share Common 5¢ par exchanged for $27.75 cash

THRIFTY TEL INC (DE)
Chapter 11 bankruptcy proceedings converted to Chapter 7 on 3/8/95
Stockholders' equity unlikely

THRILLTIME ENTMT INTL INC (BC)
Name changed to Advanced Proteome Therapeutics Corp. 10/25/2006

THRIVE DEV INC (NV)
Name changed to Green Parts International, Inc. 5/25/2005

THRUSH INDS INC (BC)
Name changed to Miranda Diamond Corp. 3/15/2002

THRUST CAP CORP (AB)
Merged into Zaio Corp. 02/23/2004
Each share Common no par exchanged for (1) share Common no par
Zaio Corp. name changed to Clarocity Corp. 10/17/2016

THRUST ENERGY CORP (NV)
Each share old Common $0.0001 par exchanged for (0.05) share new Common $0.0001 par 09/30/2010
Name changed to American Mining Corp. 05/05/2011
American Mining Corp. name changed to Cannabics Pharmaceuticals Inc. 06/20/2014

THRUST RES INC (BC)
Recapitalized as Balaclava Industries Ltd. 7/6/93
Each share Common no par exchanged for (0.2173913) share Common no par
Balaclava Industries Ltd. name changed to Balaclava Mines Inc. 11/8/96 which recapitalized as Pillar Resources Inc. 6/7/2001 which name changed to PilaGold Inc. 10/21/2003 which merged into Radius Gold Inc. 7/2/2004

THRUST VENTURES INC (UT)
Name changed to Bio-Thrust Inc. (UT) 03/27/1987
Bio-Thrust Inc. (UT) reorganized in Nevada as Easy Golf Corp. 04/22/2005 which name changed to China Bio-Immunity Corp. 02/25/2008

THRUSTMASTER INC (OR)
Stock Dividend - 3% payable 02/28/1997 to holders of record 02/14/1997
Name changed to CenterSpan Communications Corp. (OR) 10/29/1999
CenterSpan Communications Corp. (OR) reorganized in Nevada as Suvanza 03/19/2010

THT INC (DE)
Name changed 5/4/88
Name changed from THT Lloyd's Inc. to THT Inc. 5/4/88
Each share old Common 1¢ par exchanged for (0.2) share new Common 1¢ par 9/1/92
Merged into PH II Acquisition Sub Inc. 3/4/99
Each share new Common 1¢ par exchanged for $3.75 cash

THUMPER RES CORP (BC)
Recapitalized as Arequipa Resources Ltd. 9/8/93
Each share Common no par exchanged for (1/3) share Common no par
(See Arequipa Resources Ltd.)

THUNANDER CORP (DE)
Common 1¢ par split (5) for (4) by issuance of (0.25) additional share 05/15/1987
Stock Dividend - 25% 07/08/1983
Merged into Shelter Components Corp. 02/05/1988
Each share Common 1¢ par exchanged for (1) share Common 1¢ par
(See Shelter Components Corp.)

THUNDELARRA EXPL LTD (WESTERN AUSTRALIA)
Reincorporated 01/23/2001
Reincorporated 09/08/2003
Place of incorporation changed from (BC) to (YT) 01/23/2001
Place of incorporation changed from (YT) to (Western Australia) 09/08/2003
Name changed to Thundelarra Ltd. 03/21/2013

THUNDER BAY AMETHYST MINING CO. LTD. (ON)
Wound up 00/00/1981
Details not available

THUNDER BAY CAP CORP (AB)
Struck off register for failure to file annual returns 04/01/1996

THUNDER BAY GOLD MINES LTD. (ON)
Name changed to Gold Island Porcupine Mines Ltd. 00/00/1943
Gold Island Porcupine Mines Ltd. name changed to Milmar-Island Mines Ltd. 01/09/1959 which name changed to Milmar-Island Metals & Holdings Ltd. 12/22/1970
(See Milmar-Island Metals & Holdings Ltd.)

THUNDER BAY NICKEL MINING CORP. LTD. (ON)
Merged into Great Lakes Nickel Ltd. 08/29/1969
Each share Common $1 par exchanged for (0.5) share Common $1 par
(See Great Lakes Nickel Ltd.)

THUNDER CREEK MINES LTD (BC)
Name changed to Excalibur Development Ltd. (BC) 07/19/1979
Excalibur Development Ltd. (BC) reincorporated in Canada as Excalibur Energy Corp. 02/23/1981

(See Excalibur Energy Corp.)

THUNDER ENERGY INC (AB)
Plan of arrangement effective 07/12/2005
Each share Common no par exchanged for (0.5) Thunder Energy Trust, Trust Unit no par, (0.33333333) share Alberta Clipper Energy Inc. Common no par and (0.33333333) share Ember Resources Inc. Common no par
(See each company's listing)

THUNDER ENERGY TR (AB)
Acquired by Aston Hill Financial Inc. 06/26/2007
Each Trust Unit no par received $4 cash

THUNDER ENGINES CORP (BC)
Recapitalized as Golden Thunder Resources Ltd. 05/02/1996
Each share Common no par exchanged for (0.2) share Common no par
Golden Thunder Resources Ltd. recapitalized as Consolidated Golden Thunder Resources Ltd. 12/04/2000 which name changed to GHG Resources Ltd. 05/10/2004 which name changed to Los Andes Copper Ltd. 03/29/2007

THUNDER EXPLS LTD (BC)
Name changed to Cam-Net Communications Network Inc. 04/22/1985
Cam-Net Communications Network Inc. name changed to Suncom Telecommunications Inc. 08/01/1997 which name changed to VirtualSellers.com, Inc. 06/01/1999 which name changed to Healthtrac, Inc. 03/25/2002
(See Healthtrac, Inc.)

THUNDER GROUP INC (DE)
Charter cancelled and declared inoperative and void for non-payment of taxes 03/01/1994

THUNDER MTN GOLD INC (ID)
Reincorporated under the laws of Nevada and Common 5¢ par changed to $0.001 par 02/19/2008

THUNDER OIL & GAS INC (DE)
Recapitalized as Command Entertainment Inc. 12/14/1995
Each share Common $0.00001 par exchanged for (0.1) share Common $0.00001 par
Command Entertainment Inc. recapitalized as International Industries Inc. 01/21/1998 which name changed to International Internet Inc. 02/25/1999 which name changed to Evolve One, Inc. 11/30/2000 which name changed to China Direct, Inc. (DE) 09/19/2006 which reincorporated in Florida 06/21/2007 which name changed to China Direct Industries, Inc. 05/29/2009 which name changed to CD International Enterprises, Inc. 02/29/2012

THUNDER SWORD RES INC (BC)
Recapitalized as Rainmaker Mining Corp. 11/23/2009
Each share Common no par exchanged for (0.1) share Common no par
Rainmaker Mining Corp. name changed to Rainmaker Resources Ltd. (BC) 05/08/2014 which reorganized in Ontario as Indiva Ltd. 12/19/2017

THUNDER VY MINES LTD (BC)
Struck off register and declared dissolved for failure to file returns 01/09/1978

THUNDER VY RES LTD (ON)
Merged into Castlestar Capital Developments Corp. 03/30/1990
Each share Common no par exchanged for (1.1) shares Common no par
Castlestar Capital Developments Corp. recapitalized as Southern Frontier Resources Inc. 11/11/1993
(See Southern Frontier Resources Inc.)

THUNDERBALL ENTMT INC (NV)
Name changed to Ready Credit Corp. 08/26/2005

THUNDERBIRD BANK (GLENDALE, AZ)
Location changed to Phoenix, AZ 09/00/1972
Thunderbird Bank (Phoenix, AZ) reorganized as Thunderbird Capital Corp. 06/30/1984 which merged into Marshall & Ilsley Corp. (Old) 10/01/1986
(See Marshall & Ilsley Corp. (Old))

THUNDERBIRD BK GLENDALE ARIZ (PHOENIX, AZ)
Under plan of reorganization each share Common $10 par automatically became (1) share Thunderbird Capital Corp. Common $10 par 06/30/1984
Thunderbird Capital Corp. merged into Marshall & Ilsley Corp. (Old) 10/01/1986
(See Marshall & Ilsley Corp. (Old))

THUNDERBIRD CAPITAL CORP. (AZ)
Merged into Marshall & Ilsley Corp. (Old) 10/01/1986
Each share Common $10 par exchanged for (18.41) shares Common $1 par
(See Marshall & Ilsley Corp. (Old))

THUNDERBIRD DEVELOPMENT, INC. (CO)
Charter revoked for failure to file reports and pay fees 10/17/1963

THUNDERBIRD ENERGY CORP (CANADA)
Recapitalized as Gordon Creek Energy Inc. 10/24/2013
Each share Common no par exchanged for (0.06666666) share Common no par

THUNDERBIRD EXPLORATIONS INC. (ON)
Name changed to Thunderbolt Gas & Oil Explorations Ltd. 11/25/1977
Thunderbolt Gas & Oil Explorations Ltd. merged into Parapet Petroleum Inc. 12/29/1982 which merged into D'Eldona Resources Ltd. 10/15/1984 which recapitalized as Western D'Eldona Resources Ltd. 06/01/1988
(See Western D'Eldona Resources Ltd.)

THUNDERBIRD HOMES INC (SC)
Charter revoked for failure to maintain a registered agent 02/28/1990

THUNDERBIRD LEASING CORP. (AZ)
Incorporated 04/07/1959
Charter revoked for failure to pay fees 11/03/1965

THUNDERBIRD PARK DEVELOPMENT CO. (CO)
Involuntarily dissolved 01/01/1980

THUNDERBIRD PROJS LTD (BC)
Recapitalized as Consolidated Thunderbird Projects Ltd. 12/17/1998
Each share Common no par exchanged for (0.2) share Common no par
Consolidated Thunderbird Projects Ltd. name changed to Jenosys Enterprises, Inc. 08/16/1999 which recapitalized as Fintry Enterprises Inc. 12/10/2004 which recapitalized as Mesa Uranium Corp. 12/23/2005 which name changed to Mesa Exploration Corp. 03/30/2011

THUNDERBIRD RESORTS INC (YT)
Reorganized under the laws of British Virgin Islands 11/20/2007
Each share Common no par exchanged for (0.33333333) share Common no par

THUNDERBOLT GAS & OIL EXPLS INC (ON)
Merged into Parapet Petroleum Inc. 12/29/1982
Each share Common no par exchanged for (1) share Common no par
Parapet Petroleum Inc. merged into D'Eldona Resources Ltd. 10/15/1984 which recapitalized as Western D'Eldona Resources Ltd. 06/01/1988
(See Western D'Eldona Resources Ltd.)

THUNDERBOLT OIL CORP. (DE)
No longer in existence having become inoperative and void for non-payment of taxes 10/01/1965

THUNDERBOLT RES LTD (BC)
Name changed to Warwick Petroleum Ltd. 03/18/1982
Warwick Petroleum Ltd. merged into Europa Petroleum Ltd. 02/22/1983 which merged into Orbit Oil & Gas Ltd. 11/08/1984
(See Orbit Oil & Gas Ltd.)

THUNDERBOLT URANIUM CORP. (UT)
Merged into Resource Ventures Corp. 12/01/1958
Each share Capital Stock 1¢ par exchanged for (0.013333) share Common 25¢ par
Resource Ventures Corp. merged into Petroleum Resources Corp. 06/30/1965 which name changed to PRC Corp. 11/09/1970 which name changed to Corterra Corp. 11/28/1972 which assets were transferred to CorTerra Corp. Liquidating Corp. 10/08/1980
(See CorTerra Corp. Liquidating Corp.)

THUNDERHEAD GOLD MINES LTD (ON)
Name changed to Caratel Ltd. 03/31/1990
Caratel Ltd. recapitalized as Juritel Systems, Inc. 08/24/1992 which name changed to Huntington Rhodes, Inc. 09/23/1993
(See Huntington Rhodes Inc.)

THUNDERMIN RES INC (ON)
Merged into Rambler Metals & Mining PLC 01/12/2016
Each share Common no par exchanged for (0.06126051) share Ordinary 1p par

THUNDERSPIKE RES LTD (AB)
Struck off register for failure to file annual returns 01/01/1997

THUNDERSTONE GROUP INC (NV)
Name changed to Cronus Corp. 03/04/1996
(See Cronus Corp.)

THUNDERWOOD EXPLS LTD (BC)
Recapitalized as International Thunderwood Explorations Ltd. (BC) 07/14/1983
Each share Capital Stock no par exchanged for (0.2) share Common no par
International Thunderwood Explorations Ltd. (BC) reincorporated in Canada 04/27/1987 which reorganized in Ontario as Thunderwood Resources Inc.-Les Ressources Thunderwood Inc. 06/01/1989 which merged into Thundermin Resources Inc. 11/01/1998 which merged into Rambler Metals & Mining PLC 01/12/2016

THUNDERWOOD RES INC (ON)
Class B no par called for redemption 08/31/1989
Merged into Thundermin Resources Inc. 11/01/1998
Each share Common no par exchanged for (0.16666666) share Common no par and (0.16666666) Common Stock Purchase Warrant expiring 06/30/2000
Thundermin Resources Inc. merged into Rambler Metals & Mining PLC 01/12/2016

THURBER EARTHEN PRODUCTS CO.
Liquidated 00/00/1939
Details not available

THURBOIS MINES LTD. (ON)
Recapitalized as New Thurbois Mines Ltd. on a (0.25) for (1) basis 00/00/1948
New Thurbois Mines Ltd. name changed to Canadian Thorium Corp. Ltd. 10/10/1956 which recapitalized as Quebec Mattagami Minerals Ltd. 10/11/1961 which name changed to Q.M.G. Holdings Inc. 10/03/1977
(See Q.M.G. Holdings Inc.)

THURLOW GOLD MINES LTD. (BC)
Dissolved 00/00/1948
Details not available

THUROW ELECTRONICS, INC. (FL)
Each share Class A Common $2.50 par exchanged for (1) share Common $2.50 par 01/15/1966
Completely liquidated 11/01/1967
Each share Common $2.50 par exchanged for first and final distribution of $4.60 cash

THURSBY (REED A.) & CO. (FL)
Charter cancelled and proclaimed dissolved for non-payment of taxes 06/28/1965

THURSTON CHEMICAL CO. (MO)
Acquired by Grace (W.R.) & Co. (CT) 00/00/1953
Each share Common $5 par exchanged for (0.45) share Common no par
Grace (W.R.) & Co. (CT) reincorporated in New York 05/19/1988
(See Grace (W.R.) & Co.)

THURSTON FINANCIAL CORP. (DE)
Name changed to Professional Investors Corp. 03/05/1973
Professional Investors Corp. name changed to Professional Investors Insurance Group, Inc. 03/11/1985
(See Professional Investors Insurance Group, Inc.)

THURSTON INC (FL)
Liquidation completed
Each share Common 10¢ par exchanged for initial distribution of $21.68 cash 04/06/1979
Each share Common 10¢ par received second and final distribution of $0.25 cash 12/17/1979

THURSTON NATIONAL INSURANCE CO. (OK)
Reorganized as Thurston Financial Corp. 12/31/1972
Each share Common $1 par exchanged for (1) share Common 10¢ par
Thurston Financial Corp. name changed to Professional Investors Corp. 03/05/1973 which name changed to Professional Investors Insurance Group, Inc. 03/11/1985
(See Professional Investors Insurance Group, Inc.)

THURSTON NATL LIFE INS CO (OK)
Merged into Thurston Financial Corp. 12/31/1972
Each share Common $1 par exchanged for (2.5) shares Common 10¢ par
Thurston Financial Corp. name changed to Professional Investors Corp. 03/05/1973 which name changed to Professional Investors Insurance Group, Inc. 03/11/1985

THYER MANUFACTURING CORP. (OH)
(See Professional Investors Insurance Group, Inc.)

THYER MANUFACTURING CORP. (OH)
Charter revoked for failure to file reports and pay fees 08/16/1963

THYSSEN A G (GERMANY)
Each old ADR for Ordinary exchanged for (5) new ADR's for Ordinary 04/20/1987
Merged into Thyssen Krupp AG 03/25/1999
Each new ADR for Ordinary exchanged for $38.362 cash

THYSSEN MNG EXPL INC (BC)
Name changed to Trilogy Metals Inc. (BC) 12/08/2000
Trilogy Metals Inc. (BC) reincorporated in Canada as NWest Energy Inc. 03/07/2008 which recapitalized as NWest Energy Corp. 11/04/2010 which name changed to Ceylon Graphite Corp. 01/03/2017

THYSSENKRUPP BUDD CDA INC (ON)
Acquired by Thyssenkrupp Budd Co. 04/28/2005
Each share Common no par exchanged for $9 cash

TI CARO INC (NC)
Recapitalized
Common $1 par split (2) for (1) by issuance of (1) additional share 03/31/1981
Common $1 par split (3) for (2) by issuance of (0.5) additional share 07/01/1983
Acquired by a group of investors 05/06/1984
Each share Common $1 par exchanged for $23.12 cash
4% Preferred $25 par called for redemption 06/04/1984
Public interest eliminated

TI GROUP PLC (ENGLAND)
Each ADR for Ordinary exchanged for (2) ADR's for Ordinary 05/26/1987
Each Unsponsored ADR for Ordinary exchanged for (1) Sponsored ADR for Ordinary 07/12/1990
Merged into Smiths Group PLC 12/04/2000
Each Sponsored ADR for Ordinary exchanged for (0.92) share Ordinary

TI-MAIL INC (NV)
Reincorporated 12/10/1998
State of incorporation changed from (OR) to (NV) 12/10/1998
Recapitalized as Desert Winds Entertainment Corp. 02/02/1999
Each share Common $0.001 par exchanged for (0.02) share Common $0.001 par
Desert Winds Entertainment Corp. name changed to SunnComm, Inc. 07/06/2000 which reorganized as SunnComm Technologies Inc. 11/21/2002 which name changed to SunnComm International, Inc. 05/03/2004 which name changed to Amergence Group, Inc. 06/01/2007 which name changed to Altitude Organic Corp. 05/16/2011 which name changed to Tranzbyte Corp. 02/22/2012 which name changed to American Green, Inc. 07/01/2014

TIA MARIA INC (CA)
Name changed to North Point Pier Inc. 08/08/1977
North Point Pier Inc. name changed to Pier 39, Inc. 03/15/1979
(See Pier 39, Inc.)

TIANHE UN HLDGS LTD (NV)
Recapitalized as National Art Exchange, Inc. 08/24/2017
Each share Common $0.001 par exchanged for (0.01) share Common $0.001 par

TIANJIN CAP ENVIRONMENTAL PROTN GROUP CO LTD (CHINA)
Name changed 11/25/2008
Name changed from Tianjin Capital Environmental Protection Co., Ltd. to Tianjin Capital Environmental Protection Group Co., Ltd. 11/25/2008
ADR agreement terminated 01/25/2018
Each Sponsored ADR for H Shares exchanged for (20) H Shares
Note: Unexchanged ADR's will be sold and the proceeds, if any, held for claim after 01/28/2019

TIANLI AGRITECH INC (BRITISH VIRGIN ISLANDS)
Name changed to Aoxin Tianli Group, Inc. 07/29/2014
Aoxin Tianli Group, Inc. name changed to Renmin Tianli Group, Inc. 11/13/2017

TIANRONG BLDG MATL HLDGS LTD (UT)
Charter expired 01/05/2007

TIANXIN MNG USA INC (NV)
Charter cancelled 01/31/2011

TIARA CORP. (ID)
Charter forfeited for failure to file reports 12/01/1980

TIARA ENTERPRISES LTD (BC)
Recapitalized 02/28/1986
Recapitalized from Tiara Resources Ltd. to Tiara Enterprises Ltd. 02/28/1986
Each share old Common no par exchanged for (2) shares new Common no par
Struck off register and declared dissolved for failure to file returns 07/07/1989

TIARA MINES LTD. (ON)
Recapitalized as Tormont Mines Ltd. 08/04/1961
Each share Common exchanged for (3.5) shares Common
(See Tormont Mines Ltd.)

TIARCO CORP (NJ)
Name changed to Inter-Ocean Holdings, Inc. 00/00/1983
(See Inter-Ocean Holdings, Inc.)

TIB BK (KEY LARGO, FL)
Common $2.50 par split (2) for (1) by issuance of (1) additional share payable 05/14/1996 to holders of record 05/02/1996
Under plan of reorganization each share Common $2.50 par automatically became (1) share TIB Financial Corp. Common 10¢ par 08/31/1996
TIB Financial Corp. merged into Capital Bank Financial Corp. 09/21/2012 which merged into First Horizon National Corp. 11/30/2017

TIB EXPLS LTD (ON)
Charter cancelled for failure to pay taxes and file returns 05/00/1974

TIB FINL CORP (FL)
Old Common 10¢ par split (2) for (1) by issuance of (1) additional share payable 10/23/2006 to holders of record 10/09/2006 Ex date - 10/24/2006
Each share old Common 10¢ par exchanged for (0.01) share new Common 10¢ par 12/16/2010
Stock Dividends - 1% payable 07/17/2008 to holders of record 07/07/2008 Ex date - 07/02/2008; 1% payable 10/10/2008 to holders of record 09/30/2008 Ex date - 09/26/2008; 1% payable 01/10/2009 to holders of record 12/31/2008 Ex date - 12/29/2008; 1% payable 04/10/2009 to holders of record 03/31/2009 Ex date - 03/27/2009; 1% payable 07/10/2009 to holders of record 06/30/2009 Ex date - 06/26/2009; 1% payable 10/10/2009 to holders of record 09/30/2009 Ex date - 09/28/2009
Merged into Capital Bank Financial Corp. 09/21/2012
Each share new Common 10¢ par exchanged for (0.7205) share Class A Common 1¢ par
Capital Bank Financial Corp. merged into First Horizon National Corp. 11/30/2017

TIBBERON, INC. (UT)
Name changed to Krutex Energy Corp. in 11/00/1984
Krutex Energy Corp. merged into Foreland Corp. 06/28/1991
(See Foreland Corp.)

TIBCO SOFTWARE INC (DE)
Common $0.001 par split (3) for (2) by issuance of (0.5) additional share payable 02/18/2000 to holders of record 02/07/2000
Acquired by Balboa Intermediate Holdings, LLC 12/05/2014
Each share Common $0.001 par exchanged for $24 cash

TIBER ENERGY CORP (BC)
Acquired by LASMO Holdings Inc. 04/17/1989
Each share Common no par exchanged for $5.25 cash

TIBER RES LTD (AB)
Merged into Tiber Energy Corp. 02/19/1982
Each share Common no par exchanged for (0.33333333) share Common no par and (0.11111111) Common Stock Purchase Warrant expiring 02/29/1984
(See Tiber Energy Corp.)

TIBERON MINERALS LTD (CANADA)
Reincorporated 06/03/2002
Place of incorporation changed from (AB) to (Canada) 06/03/2002
Acquired by Dragon Capital Management Ltd. 04/03/2007
Each share Common no par exchanged for $3.65 cash

TIBERON RES LTD (NV)
Name changed to ePromo.com 08/22/2000
ePromo.com recapitalized as Asia Pacific Entertainment, Inc. 05/23/2007 which name changed to Access Beverage Inc. 01/06/2009 which name changed to Unity Auto Parts Inc. 09/22/2009 which name changed to Unity Management Group, Inc. 01/08/2010 which name changed to Petrotech Oil & Gas, Inc. 03/26/2013

TIBLEMACO GOLD MINES, LTD. (ON)
Charter cancelled for failure to file reports and pay taxes 03/11/1957

TIBLEMONT GOLDFIELDS LTD. (ON)
Name changed to Tib Exploration Ltd. 07/19/1956
(See Tib Exploration Ltd.)

TIBLEMONT IS MNG CO LTD (CANADA)
Declared dissolved for failure to file reports or pay fees 10/19/1999

TIBURON PETE CORP (BC)
Name changed to Bristol Trading Co. Ltd. 05/12/1987

TIBURON VINTNERS INC (CA)
Name changed to Sonoma Vineyards 12/28/1973
(See Sonoma Vineyards)

TIC INTL CORP (DE)
Each share Common 25¢ par exchanged for (0.0166666) share Common $25.25 par 03/12/1991
Each share Common $25.25 par exchanged for (0.01666666) share Common $25.25 par 12/18/1995
Note: In effect holders received $550 cash per share and public interest was eliminated

TICC CAP CORP (MD)
Name changed to Oxford Square Capital Corp. 03/23/2018

TICE TECHNOLOGY INC (DE)
Name changed to Atmospheric Glow Technologies, Inc. 03/12/2004
(See Atmospheric Glow Technologies, Inc.)

TICINO RES CORP (BC)
Recapitalized as Neuro Discovery Inc. (BC) 12/31/2001
Each share Common no par exchanged for (0.5) share Common no par
Neuro Discovery Inc. (BC) reincorporated in Canada 06/28/2002 which name changed to Allon Therapeutics Inc. 09/29/2004
(See Allon Therapeutics Inc.)

TICKER TAPE RES LTD (BC)
Recapitalized as International Ticker Tape Resources Ltd. 12/13/1991
Each share Common no par exchanged for (0.27027027) share Common no par
International Ticker Tape Resources Ltd. name changed to Econogreen Environmental Systems Ltd. 09/03/1993 which name changed to Voisey Bay Resources Inc. 06/28/1995 which merged into Twin Gold Corp. 04/04/1997 which name changed to Twin Mining Corp. 03/15/2000 which recapitalized as Atlanta Gold Inc. 03/28/2007

TICKET TO SEE INC (NV)
Name changed to Cell Source, Inc. 06/27/2014

TICKETCART INC (NV)
Recapitalized as Innovative Beverage Group Holdings, Inc. (NV) 08/29/2007
Each share Common $0.001 par exchanged for (0.01) share Common $0.001 par
Innovative Beverage Group Holdings, Inc. (NV) reorganized in Delaware as Quantum Computing Inc. 07/03/2018

TICKETMASTER ENTMT INC (DE)
Name changed 01/31/2001
Name changed 10/29/2008
Issue Information - 7,000,000 shares CL B offered at $14 per share on 12/02/1998
Name changed from Tickemaster Online-Citysearch, Inc. to Ticketmaster (Ctfs. dated prior to 01/31/2001) 01/31/2001
Merged into USA Interactive 01/17/2003
Each share Class B 1¢ par exchanged for (0.935) share Common 1¢ par
USA Interactive name changed to InterActiveCorp 06/23/2003 which name changed to IAC/InterActiveCorp 07/14/2004
TICKETMASTER (Ctfs. dated after 08/20/2008)
Name changed from Ticketmaster (Ctfs. dated after 08/20/2008) to Ticketmaster Entertainment, Inc. 10/29/2008
Merged into Live Nation Entertainment, Inc. 01/27/2010
Each share Common 1¢ par exchanged for (1.4743728) shares Common 1¢ par

TICKETMASTER GROUP INC (IL)
Merged into USA Networks, Inc. 06/24/1998
Each share Common no par exchanged for (1.126) shares Common 1¢ par
USA Networks, Inc. name changed to USA Interactive 05/09/2002 which name changed to InterActiveCorp 06/23/2003 which name changed to IAC/InterActiveCorp 07/14/2004

TICKETS COM INC (DE)
Each share old Common $0.000225 par exchanged for (0.125) share new Common $0.000225 par 07/23/2001
Merged into MLB Advanced Media, L.P. 03/21/2005
Each share new Common $0.000225 exchanged for $1.10 cash

TICKLE ME INC (NY)
Dissolved by proclamation 09/25/2002

TICOR (CA)
Merged into Southern Pacific Co. 07/27/1979
Each share Common $1 par exchanged for $22 principal amount of 10.35% Debentures due 07/01/1994 and $18 cash

TIDAL MARINE INTL CORP (DE)
Ceased operations late 00/00/1972
A major shareholder advised stock is valueless

TIDAL OSAGE OIL CORP.
Acquired by Darby Petroleum Corp. 00/00/1929
Details not available

TIDAL PETROLEUM CORP. LTD. (AB)
Capital Stock $1 par changed to 10¢ par 07/14/1958
Acquired by Delhi-Taylor Oil Corp. 12/10/1962
Details not available

TIDAL RES INC (AB)
Acquired by Chauvco Resources Ltd. 1/8/97
Each share Common no par exchanged for $2.05 cash

TIDALWAVE HLDGS INC (FL)
Each share old Common $0.001 par exchanged for (0.00066666) share new Common $0.001 par 02/20/2008
Note: No holder of between (30,000) and (749,999) pre-split shares will receive fewer than (500) shares
Each share new Common $0.001 par received distribution of (10) shares Restricted Preferred Ser. 2 payable 02/28/2008 to holders of record 02/21/2008
SEC revoked Preferred and Common stock registration 01/29/2009

TIDBIT ALLEY INC (NJ)
Chapter 11 Bankruptcy proceedings converted to Chapter 7 on 11/24/1987
Stockholders' equity unlikely

TIDE LAKE LITHIUM MINES LTD. (ON)
Charter revoked for failure to file reports and pay fees 09/28/1964

TIDE WATER ASSOCIATED OIL CO. (DE)
Common no par changed to $10 par 00/00/1937
Stock Dividend - 100% 06/03/1952
Name changed to Tidewater Oil Co. 05/04/1956
Tidewater Oil Co. merged into Getty Oil Co. 09/30/1967
(See Getty Oil Co.)

TIDE WATER OIL CO. (DE)
Merged into Tide Water Associated Oil Co. 00/00/1937
Each share Capital Stock exchanged for (3) shares Common $10 par
Tide Water Associated Oil Co. name changed to Tidewater Oil Co. 05/04/1956 which merged into Getty Oil Co. 09/30/1967
(See Getty Oil Co.)

TIDE WATER OIL CO. (NJ)
Dissolved and assets acquired by Tide Water Oil Co. (DE) 00/00/1936
Details not available

TIDE WATER POWER CO.
Merged into Carolina Power & Light Co. 00/00/1952

Each share $1.35 Preferred $25 par exchanged for (0.25) share $5 Preferred no par
Each share Common no par exchanged for (0.275) share new Common no par
Carolina Power & Light Co. reorganized as CP&L Energy, Inc. 06/19/2000 which name changed to Progress Energy, Inc. 12/11/2000 which merged into Duke Energy Corp. 07/02/2012

TIDE WEST OIL INC (DE)
Reincorporated 11/20/1992
Each share old Common no par exchanged for (1/93.3125) share new Common no par 02/28/1986
State of incorporation changed from (CO) to (DE) 11/20/1992
Each share new Common no par exchanged for (0.1) share Common 1¢ par 01/28/1993
Merged into HS Resources Inc. 06/17/1996
Each share Common 1¢ par exchanged for (0.6295) share Common $0.001 par and $8.704 cash
HS Resources Inc. merged into Kerr-McGee Corp. 08/01/2001
(See Kerr-McGee Corp.)

TIDEL TECHNOLOGIES INC (DE)
Name changed to Secure Alliance Holdings Corp. 06/19/2007
Secure Alliance Holdings Corp. recapitalized as aVinci Media Corp. 06/09/2008
(See aVinci Media Corp.)

TIDELANDS BANCSHARES INC (SC)
Acquired by United Community Banks, Inc. 07/01/2016
Each share Common 1¢ par exchanged for $0.52 cash

TIDELANDS CAP CORP (LA)
Merged into Western Preferred Corp. 03/06/1981
Each share Common no par exchanged for (0.34602076) share Common 20¢ par
(See Western Preferred Corp.)

TIDELANDS COPPER MINES LTD. (ON)
Charter revoked for failure to file reports and pay fees 09/28/1964

TIDELANDS OIL CORP. (DE)
Merged into Commonwealth Oil Co. 12/31/1957
Each share Common 50¢ par exchanged for for (0.11111111) share Common 1¢ par
Commonwealth Oil Co. merged into Jupiter Corp. 03/01/1962 which merged into Jupiter Industries, Inc. 11/12/1971
(See Jupiter Industries, Inc.)

TIDEMARK BANCORP INC (VA)
Acquired by Crestar Financial Corp. 03/24/1995
Each share Common $1 par exchanged for (0.131) share Common $5 par
Crestar Financial Corp. merged into SunTrust Banks, Inc. 12/31/1998

TIDEWATER INC OLD (DE)
Common 50¢ par split (3) for (2) by issuance of (0.5) additional share 10/28/1980
Common 50¢ par changed to 10¢ par 12/12/1991
Reorganized as Tidewater Inc. (New) 07/31/2017
Each share Common 10¢ par exchanged for (0.03183263) share Common $0.001 par, (0.0516) Common Stock Purchase Warrant, Ser. A expiring 07/31/2023 and (0.0558) Common Stock Purchase Warrant, Ser. B expiring 07/31/2023

TIDEWATER MARINE SVC INC (DE)
Conv. Preferred Ser. A no par called for redemption 10/03/1967
$1.50 Conv. Preferred Ser. A no par called for redemption 02/11/1969
Common $1 par changed to 50¢ par and (1) additional share issued 09/20/1976
Stock Dividends - 100% 12/15/1964; 25% 01/20/1966; 50% 11/29/1968
Name changed to Tidewater Inc. (Old) 08/12/1977
Tidewater Inc. (Old) reorganized as Tidewater Inc. (New) 07/31/2017

TIDEWATER NATURAL GAS CO. (NC)
Name changed 07/14/1958
Name changed from Tidewater Gas Co. to Tidewater Natural Gas Co. 07/14/1958
Merged into North Carolina Natural Gas Corp. 12/11/1964
Each share 6% Preferred $20 par exchanged for (3) shares Common $2.50 par
Each share Common $1 par exchanged for (0.6) share Common $2.50 par
North Carolina Natural Gas Corp. merged into Carolina Power & Light Co. 07/15/1999 which reorganized as CP&L Energy, Inc. 06/19/2000 which name changed to Progress Energy, Inc. 12/11/2000 which merged into Duke Energy Corp. 07/02/2012

TIDEWATER OIL CO (DE)
Merged into Getty Oil Co. 09/30/1967
Each share $1.20 Preferred $25 par exchanged for (1) share $1.20 Preferred $25 par
Each share Common $10 par exchanged for (1.186) shares Common $4 par
Note: Exchange for stock made through 09/30/1971 after which holders received cash only
(See Getty Oil Co.)

TIDEWATER RES INC (NV)
Reorganized as Precision Petroleum Corp. 01/08/2009
Each share Common $0.001 par exchanged for (12) shares Common $0.001 par

TIDEWATER TEL CO (VA)
5% Conv. Preferred Class A $20 par called for redemption 03/10/1966
Common $20 par changed to $10 par and (1) additional share issued 04/22/1966
Merged into Continental Telephone Corp. 08/01/1972
Each share Common $10 par exchanged for (1.98) shares Common $1 par
Continental Telephone Corp. name changed to Continental Telecom Inc. 05/06/1982 which name changed to Contel Corp. 05/01/1986 which merged into GTE Corp. 03/14/1991 which merged into Verizon Communications Inc. 06/30/2000

TIDWELL INDS INC (DE)
Reincorporated 08/15/1979
State of incorporation changed from (AL) to (DE) 08/15/1979
Common 10¢ par split (3) for (2) by issuance of (0.5) additional share 10/19/1981
Stock Dividends - 10% 07/31/1980; 10% 07/30/1981
Chapter 11 bankruptcy proceedings converted to Chapter 7 on 10/16/1989
No stockholders' equity

TIE COMMUNICATIONS INC (DE)
Common 5¢ par split (3) for (2) by issuance of (0.5) additional share 06/16/1980
Common 5¢ par split (3) for (2) by issuance of (0.5) additional share 11/10/1980
Common 5¢ par split (3) for (2) by issuance of (0.5) additional share 07/24/1981
Common 5¢ par split (2) for (1) by issuance of (1) additional share 07/18/1983
Reorganized under Chapter 11 Federal Bankruptcy proceedings 07/02/1991
Each share Common 5¢ par exchanged for (0.0285714) share Common 10¢ par
Merged into Tie Communications Corp. 12/13/1995
Each share Common 10¢ par exchanged for $8.60 cash

TIE TELECOMMUNICATIONS CDA LTD (CANADA)
Under plan of reorganization each share Common no par exchanged for $1.375 cash 06/14/1994

TIEMPO EQUITIES INC (MN)
Merged into Atrix International, Inc. 10/17/1990
Each share Common 1¢ par exchanged for (0.5) share Common 1¢ par
(See Atrix International, Inc.)

TIENS BIOTECH GROUP USA INC (DE)
Acquired by TIENS (USA) Investment Holdings Group Overseas Ltd. 08/11/2011
Each share Common $0.001 par exchanged for $1.72 cash

TIER ENVIRONMENTAL SVCS INC (DE)
Name changed to Gulfstar Industries, Inc. 01/04/1996
Gulfstar Industries, Inc. recapitalized as Media Vision Productions, Inc. 01/05/1999 which name changed to eCONTENT, Inc. 10/01/1999 which name changed to Earthworks Entertainment, Inc. 01/15/2004

TIER ONE ENERGY CORP (AB)
Acquired by Northrock Resources Ltd. 12/15/1999
Each share Class A Common no par exchanged for $4.50 cash
Each share Class B Common no par exchanged for $10 cash

TIER ONE PPTYS INC
144A Step Down Preferred called for redemption at $927.82 on 03/30/1999

TIER TECHNOLOGIES INC (DE)
Reincorporated 07/15/2005
State of incorporation changed from (CA) to (DE) and Class B Common no par reclassified as Common 1¢ par 07/15/2005
Name changed to Official Payments Holdings, Inc. 01/04/2012
(See Official Payments Holdings, Inc.)

TIERCO (MA)
Reorganized under the laws of Delaware as Tierco Group, Inc. and Shares of Bene. Int. $1 par reclassified as Common $1 par 06/04/1981
Tierco Group, Inc. name changed to Premier Parks Inc. 10/13/1994 which name changed to Six Flags, Inc. 06/30/2000
(See Six Flags, Inc.)

TIERCO GROUP INC (DE)
Name changed to Premier Parks Inc. 10/13/1994
Premier Parks Inc. name changed to Six Flags, Inc. 06/30/2000
(See Six Flags, Inc.)

TIERNEY MINING CO.
Acquired by Portsmouth Steel Corp. 00/00/1948
Details not available

TIERONE CORP (WI)
Chapter 7 bankruptcy proceedings terminated 02/19/2016
No stockholders' equity

TIERRA ENERGY CORP (UT)
Name changed to Tradestar Corp. (UT) 08/19/1985
Tradestar Corp. (UT) reorganized in Nevada as Tradestar Resources Corp. 06/29/2006
(See Tradestar Resources Corp.)

TIERRA ENVIRONMENTAL CORP (CO)
Name changed to Hallmark Properties Inc. 10/16/1998
Hallmark Properties Inc. name changed to Norton Motorcycles, Inc. 04/23/1999
(See Norton Motorcycles, Inc.)

TIERRA GRANDE RES INC (NV)
Name changed to VNUE, Inc. 07/20/2015

TIETOENATOR OYJ (FINLAND)
Name changed to Tieto OYJ 06/03/2009

TIEX INC (AB)
Recapitalized as Bullion Gold Resources Corp. (AB) 10/29/2012
Each share Common no par exchanged for (0.33333333) share Common no par
Bullion Gold Resources Corp. (AB) reincorporated in British Columbia 02/01/2016

TIFFANY & CO (NY)
Each share old Capital Stock no par exchanged for (16) shares new Capital Stock no par 00/00/1949
New Capital Stock no par split (4) for (1) by issuance of (3) additional shares 01/11/1962
New Capital Stock no par split (2) for (1) by issuance of (1) additional share 01/29/1964
New Capital Stock no par reclassified as Common $1 par 04/19/1965
Common $1 par split (3) for (2) by issuance of (0.5) additional share 07/06/1967
Common $1 par split (4) for (3) by issuance of (0.33333333) additional share 07/11/1968
Common $1 par split (5) for (4) by issuance of (0.25) additional share 01/05/1970
Merged into Avon Products, Inc. 04/25/1979
Each share Common $1 par exchanged for (0.845) share Capital Stock 50¢ par

TIFFANY ENTERPRISES, INC. (UT)
Merged into Western Corn Dog Factories 07/22/1977
Each share Common 1¢ par exchanged for (0.16666666) share Common 1¢ par
Western Corn Dog Factories merged into Resources West, Inc. 07/27/1981 which recapitalized as Magma Resources 01/27/1989 which name changed to Cellular Telecommunications & Technologies Inc. 07/15/1993 which recapitalized as China Biomedical Group Inc. 04/03/1995 which name changed to Internet Holdings Ltd. 06/30/1996 which name changed to HTTP Technology, Inc. (UT) 11/28/2000 which reincorporated in Delaware 12/19/2000 which name changed to Medicsight, Inc. 10/28/2002 which name changed to MGT Capital Investments, Inc. 01/24/2007

TIFFANY INDS INC (MO)
Common 10¢ par called for redemption 12/00/1986
Public interest eliminated

TIFFANY RES CORP (AB)
Reincorporated 05/19/1984
Place of incorporation changed from (AB) to (ON) 05/19/1984
Name changed to First Tiffany Resource Corp. 06/28/1984
(See First Tiffany Resource Corp.)

TIFFANY RES INC (BC)
Name changed 04/21/1983
Name changed from Tiffany Oil & Gas Corp. to Tiffany Resources Inc. 04/21/1983
Delisted from Vancouver Stock Exchange 05/02/1991

TIFFANY TILE CORP. (FL)
Adjudicated bankrupt 08/22/1967
No stockholders' equity

TIFFIN ART METAL CO. (OH)
Acquired by Springfield Greene Industries, Inc. 00/00/1961
Details not available

TIG HLDGS INC (DE)
Merged into Fairfax Financial Holdings Ltd. 04/13/1999
Each share Class A Common 1¢ par exchanged for $16.50 cash
Each share Common 1¢ par exchanged for $16.50 cash
$7.75 144A Preferred $100 par called for redemption at $100 on 05/15/2000
Public interest eliminated

TIGENIX (BELGIUM)
ADS agreement terminated 08/08/2018
Each Sponsored ADS for Ordinary exchanged for $41.570832 cash

TIGER CAP CORP (CO)
Name changed to Polydyne Industries Inc. 04/19/1989
Polydyne Industries Inc. name changed to Visicom International, Inc. 07/09/2008

TIGER-CAT ENERGY LTD (AB)
Merged into RMS Systems Inc. 09/29/2008
Each share Common no par exchanged for (0.33557046) share Common no par
RMS Systems Inc. merged into PHX Energy Services Corp. 12/02/2013

TIGER COAL & GAS INC (DE)
Name changed to Halal Financial Services, Inc. 06/00/2005

TIGER DIRECT INC (DE)
Merged into Global DirectMail Corp. 11/30/1995
Each share Common $0.001 par exchanged for (0.0095238) share Common 1¢ par
Global DirectMail Corp. name changed to Systemax Inc. 05/19/1999

TIGER ETHANOL INTL INC (NV)
Name changed to Tiger Renewable Energy Ltd. 02/29/2008
Tiger Renewable Energy Ltd. recapitalized as Cono Italiano, Inc. 08/10/2009

TIGER INTL INC (DE)
Each Depositary Conv. Preferred exchanged for (1) share Common $1 par 05/21/1985
Merged into Federal Express Corp. 02/15/1989
Each share Common $1 par exchanged for $20.875 cash

TIGER JIUJIANG MNG INC (WY)
Reorganized as VinCompass Corp. 12/15/2015
Each share Common $0.001 par exchanged for (5) shares Common $0.001 par

TIGER MARKETING INC (NY)
Recapitalized as U.S. Health Services, Inc. 04/08/1986
Each share Common 1¢ par exchanged for (0.25) share Common 1¢ par
U.S. Health Services, Inc. name changed to Diamond Trade Center, Inc. 10/30/1990
(See Diamond Trade Center, Inc.)

TIGER MEDIA INC (CAYMAN ISLANDS)
Reorganized under the laws of Delaware 03/20/2015
Each share Ordinary USD$0.0001 par exchanged for (0.2) share Common $0.0005 par
Tiger Media, Inc. (DE) name changed to IDI, Inc. 05/04/2015 which name changed to Cogint, Inc. 09/26/2016 which name changed to Fluent, Inc. 04/16/2018

TIGER MEDIA INC (DE)
Name changed to IDI, Inc. 05/04/2015
IDI, Inc. name changed to Cogint, Inc. 09/26/2016 which name changed to Fluent, Inc. 04/16/2018

TIGER OATS LTD (SOUTH AFRICA)
Name changed to Tiger Brands Ltd. 02/28/2000

TIGER OIL CORP (BC)
Merged into Palliser International Energy Inc. 06/01/1982
Each share Common no par exchanged for (0.45454545) share Common no par
Palliser International Energy Inc. recapitalized as Elan Industries Inc. 12/19/1986 which recapitalized as Trylox Environmental Corp. (BC) 08/17/1990 which reincorporated in Wyoming 09/14/1990
(See Trylox Environmental Corp. (WY))

TIGER OIL INTL INC (DE)
Common 10¢ par split (4) for (1) by issuance of (3) additional shares 11/21/1969
Merged into Cleveland-Cliffs Iron Co. 01/05/1979
Each share Common 10¢ par exchanged for $12.53 cash

TIGER PAC MNG CORP (BC)
Reincorporated 07/29/2004
Place of incorporation changed from (AB) to (BC) 07/29/2004
Recapitalized as Chantrell Ventures Corp. 08/31/2010
Each share Common no par exchanged for (0.4) share Common no par

TIGER PETE INC (QC)
Merged into Pan Orient Energy Corp. 12/08/2005
Each share Common no par exchanged for (0.23529411) share Common no par

TIGER RENEWABLE ENERGY LTD (NV)
Recapitalized as Cono Italiano, Inc. 08/10/2009
Each (60) shares Common $0.001 par exchanged for (1) share Common $0.001 par

TIGER RES INC (QC)
Delisted from Montreal Stock Exchange 09/26/1990

TIGER RIVER MINES, LTD. (CANADA)
Charter surrendered 00/00/1951

TIGER TEAM TECHNOLOGIES INC (NV)
Name changed to Physicians Healthcare Management Group, Inc. 07/12/2006

TIGER X MED INC (DE)
Name changed to BioCardia, Inc. 10/26/2016

TIGERA GROUP INC (DE)
Recapitalized as Connectivity Technologies Inc. 12/16/1996
Each share Common 1¢ par exchanged for (0.25) share Common 1¢ par
(See Connectivity Technologies Inc.)

TIGERLOGIC CORP (DE)
Liquidation completed
Each share Common 10¢ par received initial distribution of $0.09 cash payable 11/09/2016 to holders of record 10/31/2016 Ex date - 11/10/2016
Each share Common 10¢ par received second and final distribution of $0.0349 cash payable 07/26/2017 to holders of record 07/20/2017 Ex date - 07/27/2017

TIGERSHARK ENTERPRISES INC (NV)
Name changed to Great White Marine & Recreation, Inc. 05/14/1998
(See Great White Marine & Recreation, Inc.)

TIGERTEL COMMUNICATIONS INC (CANADA)
Acquired by 7212747 Canada Inc. 10/22/2009
Each share Common no par exchanged for $0.25 cash

TIGERTEL INC (CANADA)
Merged into AT&T Canada Corp. 01/06/2000
Each share Common no par exchanged for $9.25 cash 07/14/1999

TIGERTEL TELECOMMUNICATIONS CORP (BC)
Reincorporated under the laws of Canada as TigerTel Communications Inc. 05/01/2002
(See TigerTel Communications Inc.)

TIGNANELLO VENTURES CORP (BC)
Name changed to Bushman Resources Inc. 01/10/1997
(See Bushman Resources Inc.)

TIGRAY RES INC (CANADA)
Merged into East Africa Metals Inc. 05/07/2014
Each share Common no par exchanged as (0.55) share Common no par and (0.4) Common Stock Purchase Warrant expiring 05/06/2017
Note: Unexchanged certificates will be cancelled and become without value 05/07/2020

TIGRIS MINERALS CORP (BC)
Recapitalized as Vantex Oil, Gas & Minerals Ltd. (BC) 01/09/1996
Each share Common no par exchanged for (0.2) share Common no par
Vantex Oil, Gas & Minerals Ltd. (BC) reincorporated in Canada 06/19/1998 which name changed to Vantex Resources Ltd. 05/20/2004

TIGRIS URANIUM CORP (BC)
Recapitalized as Wolfpack Gold Corp. 05/21/2013
Each share Common no par exchanged for (0.33333333) share Common no par
Wolfpack Gold Corp. reorganized as enCore Energy Corp. 08/20/2014

TIGRSOFT INC (AB)
Recapitalized as Matrikon Inc. 04/17/2001
Each share Common no par exchanged for (0.2) share Common no par
(See Matrikon Inc.)

TII COMPUTER SYS INC (DE)
Name changed to Teleprobe Systems, Inc. 12/09/1985
Teleprobe Systems, Inc. reorganized as Intercom Systems, Inc. 10/31/1989
(See Intercom Systems, Inc.)

FINANCIAL INFORMATION, INC.

TII CORP (DE)
Name changed to TII Industries, Inc. 01/27/1979
TII Industries, Inc. name changed to Tii Network Technologies, Inc. 12/10/2001
(See Tii Network Technologies, Inc.)

TII NETWORK TECHNOLOGIES INC (DE)
Name changed 12/10/2001
Common 1¢ par split (2) for (1) by issuance of (1) additional share 07/15/1981
Each share old Common 1¢ par exchanged for (0.4) share new Common 1¢ par 04/26/1994
Stock Dividend - 10% 07/15/1983
Name changed from TII Industries, Inc. to Tii Network Technologies, Inc. 12/10/2001
Acquired by Kelta, Inc. 07/31/2012
Each share Common 1¢ par exchanged for $2.15 cash

TIKA CORP (NV)
Name changed to Paypad, Inc. 03/27/2006
Paypad, Inc. name changed to 3Pea International, Inc. 10/27/2006

TIKA RES LTD (BC)
Recapitalized as International Tika Resources Ltd. 08/29/1974
Each share Common no par exchanged for (0.5) share Common no par
(See International Tika Resources Ltd.)

TIKAL RES CORP (BC)
Acquired by BelAir Energy Corp. 12/14/2001
Each share Common no par exchanged for (0.4) share Common no par
BelAir Energy Corp. merged into Purcell Energy Ltd. (New) 09/04/2003
(See Purcell Energy Ltd. (New))

TIKAL RES INC (BC)
Merged into Tikal Resources Corp. 05/31/1999
Each share Common no par exchanged for (0.277777) share Common no par
Tikal Resources Corp. was acquired by BelAir Energy Corp. 12/14/2001 which merged into Purcell Energy Ltd. (New) 09/04/2003
(See Purcell Energy Ltd. (New))

TIKI DEV LTD (BC)
Name changed to Beermaster Distributors Ltd. 08/13/1973
Each share Capital Stock no par exchanged for (1) share Capital Stock no par
Beermaster Distributors Ltd. recapitalized as Sunatco Development Corp. 06/06/1977 which recapitalized as International Sunatco Industries Ltd. 01/14/1991

TILAR INDS INC (DE)
Charter cancelled and declared inoperative and void for non-payment of taxes 03/01/1976

TILCO INC (DE)
Reorganized in bankruptcy 01/30/1975
No stockholders' equity

TILDEN ASSOCS INC (DE)
Each share Common $0.0001 par exchanged for (0.2) share Common $0.0005 par 12/17/1997
Recapitalized as Carrier Alliance Holdings, Inc. 05/03/2012
Each share Common $0.0005 par exchanged for (0.1) share Common $0.0005 par

TILECAST CORP (PA)
Adjudicated bankrupt 06/14/1973
Stockholders' equity unlikely

TILINE INC (OR)
Name changed to Tiline Liquidating Co. 08/25/1970
(See Tiline Liquidating Co.)

TILINE LIQUIDATING CO. (OR)
Liquidation completed
Each share Common no par exchanged for initial distribution of (0.058479) share Whitaker Corp. Common $1 par 12/01/1970
Note: Details on subsequent distributions, if any, are not available

TILLER RES LTD (BC)
Each share old Common no par exchanged for (0.1) share new Common no par 12/11/2013
Each share new Common no par exchanged again for (0.1) share new Common no par 01/12/2017
Name changed to Blockchain Foundry Inc. 05/14/2018

TILLICIUM INDS LTD (BC)
Name changed 04/11/1987
Name changed from Tillicum Gold Mines Ltd. to Tillicum Industries Ltd. 04/11/1987
Struck off register and declared dissolved for failure to file returns 05/04/1994

TILLMAN INTL INC (UT)
Each share old Common $0.001 par exchanged for (0.01) share new Common $0.001 par 01/29/2004
Name changed to Quest Minerals & Mining Corp. 04/13/2004
Quest Minerals & Mining Corp. recapitalized as Kentucky Energy, Inc. 06/17/2010
(See Kentucky Energy, Inc.)

TILLMAN SURVEY INC (RI)
Liquidation completed
Each share Common 1¢ par received initial distribution of $0.30 cash 06/29/1987
Each share Common 1¢ par received second distribution of $0.20 cash 09/10/1987
Each share Common 1¢ par exchanged for third and final distribution of $0.065 cash 06/15/1990
Note: Unclaimed funds were escheated 09/01/1990

TILMORE CORP (DE)
Charter cancelled and declared inoperative and void for non-payment of taxes 04/15/1968

TILO ROOFING CO., INC. (DE)
Common no par changed to $1 par 00/00/1933
Common $1 par exchanged (4) for (1) 00/00/1936
$1.40 Preferred $25 par changed to $20 par 00/00/1939
Merged into Reynolds Metals Co. 08/01/1981
Each share Common exchanged for (0.1739) share 4.5% 2nd Preferred $100 par
(See Reynolds Metals Co.)

TIM HELLAS TELECOMMUNICATIONS S A (GREECE)
Merged into Troy GAC Telecommunications S.A. 11/03/2005
Each Sponsored ADR for Ordinary exchanged for $19.20614 cash

TIM HORTONS INC (CANADA)
Reincorporated 09/28/2009
Place of incorporation changed from (DE) to (Canada) and Common $0.001 par changed to no par 09/28/2009
Merged into Restaurant Brands International Inc. 12/15/2014
Each share Common no par exchanged for (0.8025) share Common no par and $65.50 cash

TIMAGAMI GOLD MINES LTD. (ON)
Charter cancelled for failure to file reports and pay taxes 00/00/1952

TIMBER LODGE STEAKHOUSE INC (MN)
Merged into Santa Barbara Restaurant Group, Inc. 09/01/1998
Each share Common $1 par exchanged for (0.9543) share Common 10¢ par
Santa Barbara Restaurant Group, Inc. merged into CKE Restaurants, Inc. 03/01/2002
(See CKE Restaurants, Inc.)

TIMBER REALIZATION CO. LIQUIDATING TRUST (MS)
Assets transferred from Timber Realization Co. to Timber Realization Co. Liquidating Trust 08/03/1987
Liquidation completed
Holdings of (300) or fewer Depositary Receipts received first and final distribution of $0.25 cash per Receipt 09/00/1987
Note: Details on subsequent distributions, if any, are not available

TIMBER RES INTL INC (DE)
Each share old Common $0.001 par exchanged for (0.03333333) share new Common $0.001 par 09/29/1999
New Common $0.001 par split (2) for (1) by issuance of (1) additional share payable 03/15/2000 to holders of record 03/10/2000
Each share new Common $0.001 par exchanged again for (0.01) share new Common $0.001 par 06/17/2002
Each share new Common $0.001 par exchanged again for (0.004) share new Common $0.001 par 10/15/2002
Each share new Common $0.001 par exchanged again for (0.01) share new Common $0.001 par 12/12/2002
Reincorporated under the laws of Wyoming as Amelot Holdings, Inc. and new Common $0.001 par changed to $0.0001 par 01/20/2005
Amelot Holdings, Inc. recapitalized as HLK Biotech Holding Group, Inc. 02/23/2018

TIMBERCRAFT INC (NY)
Adjudicated bankrupt 12/11/1975
Stockholders' equity unlikely

TIMBERCREEK GLOBAL REAL ESTATE FD (ON)
Under plan of merger each Class A and Class B Unit automatically became approximately (1.32) or (1.44) Timbercreek Global Real Estate Income Fund Ser. A or Ser. F Unit respectively 01/23/2018

TIMBERCREEK MTG INVT CORP (ON)
Class A no par reclassified as Common no par 11/29/2013
Each share Class B no par reclassified as (1.0638) shares Common no par 11/29/2013
Merged into Timbercreek Financial Corp. 07/05/2016
Each share Common no par exchanged for (1) share Common no par

TIMBERCREEK SR MTG INVT CORP (CANADA)
Class A reclassified as Common 11/29/2013
Merged into Timbercreek Financial Corp. 07/05/2016
Each share Common exchanged for (1.035) share Commonn no par

TIMBERJACK CORP (DE)
Merged into Rauma Acquisition Corp. 06/07/1989

Each share Common 1¢ par exchanged for $25 cash

TIMBERJACK SPORTING SUPPLIES INC (NV)
Recapitalized as China Wood, Inc. 11/16/2010
Each share Common $0.001 par exchanged for (0.00184973) share Common $0.001 par

TIMBERLAKE ENERGY SOLUTIONS INC (NV)
Charter revoked for failure to file reports and pay fees 05/31/2012

TIMBERLAND CO (DE)
Class A Common 1¢ par split (2) for (1) by issuance of (1) additional share payable 09/15/1999 to holders of record 08/31/1999 Ex date - 09/16/1999
Class A Common 1¢ par split (2) for (1) by issuance of (1) additional share payable 07/17/2000 to holders of record 06/30/2000 Ex date - 07/18/2000
Class A Common 1¢ par split (2) for (1) by issuance of (1) additional share payable 05/02/2005 to holders of record 04/14/2005 Ex date - 05/03/2005
Acquired by V.F. Corp. 09/13/2011
Each share Class A Common 1¢ par exchanged for $43 cash

TIMBERLAND INDS INC (WA)
Stock Dividends - 20% 06/20/1979; 20% 09/20/1984; 20% 09/09/1985
Merged into Weyerhaeuser Co. 11/19/1987
Each share Common 16¢ par exchanged for $9.20 cash

TIMBERLINE BANCSHARES INC (CA)
Merged into PremierWest Bancorp 04/16/2001
Each share Common no par exchanged for either (2.8257) shares Common no par, (1.69542) shares Common no par and $5.40 cash, or $13.50 cash
Note: Option to receive stock and cash or cash only expired 04/20/2001
Holders of (100) shares or fewer received cash
(See PremierWest Bancorp)

TIMBERLINE MINERALS INC (NV)
Reincorporated 04/21/1988
State of incorporation changed from (WY) to Nevada and Common 10¢ par changed to 1¢ par 04/21/1988
Charter revoked for failure to file reports and pay fees 03/15/1994

TIMBERLINE RES CORP (ID)
Reincorporated under the laws of Delaware 08/28/2008

TIMBERLINE SOFTWARE CORP (OR)
Name changed 04/21/1986
Name changed from Timberline Systems, Inc. to Timberline Software Corp. 04/21/1986
Common no par split (3) for (2) by issuance of (0.5) additional share 05/19/1995
Common no par split (3) for (2) by issuance of (0.5) additional share payable 05/17/1996 to holders of record 05/03/1996
Common no par split (5) for (4) by issuance of (0.25) additional share payable 11/21/1997 to holders of record 10/31/1997
Common no par split (4) for (3) by issuance of (0.33333333) additional share payable 11/20/1998 to holders of record 10/30/1998
Common no par split (4) for (3) by issuance of (0.33333333) additional share payable 11/19/1999 to holders of record 10/29/1999
Merged into Sage Group PLC 09/22/2003

Each share Common no par exchanged for $8.25 cash

TIMBERS CORP (DE)
Name changed to Ore-Best, Inc. 05/04/1987
(See Ore-Best, Inc.)

TIMBERWEST FST CORP (CANADA)
Reincorporated 06/14/2011
Old Stapled Units reclassified as new Stapled Units 05/11/2009
Each new Stapled Unit received distribution of (0.009852) new Stapled Unit payable 10/15/2010 to holders of record 10/15/2010
Ex date - 10/13/2010
Each new Stapled Unit received distribution of (0.008658) new Stapled Unit payable 01/17/2011 to holders of record 01/17/2011
Ex date - 01/13/2011
Each new Stapled Unit received distribution of (0.051572) new Stapled Unit payable 04/15/2011 to holders of record 04/15/2011
Place of incorporation changed from (BC) to (Canada) 06/14/2011
Acquired by British Columbia Investment Management Corp. 06/29/2011
Each new Stapled Unit exchanged for $6.16 cash
Note: Unexchanged certificates were cancelled and became without value 06/29/2017

TIMBERWEST FST LTD (BC)
Merged into TAL Acquisition Ltd. 06/23/1997
Each share Common no par exchanged for $22 cash

TIMBERWEST TIMBER TR (BC)
Each Installment Receipt plus final payment of $6 cash received (1) Trust Unit 11/12/1998
Plan of reorganization effective 10/09/1998
Holders had the option to exchange each Trust Unit for (1) TimberWest Forest Corp. Stapled Unit or retain their interests
(See TimberWest Forest Corp.)
Trust Units called for redemption 07/14/1999

TIMBUKTU GOLD CORP (AB)
Name changed to Marchmont Gold Corp. 06/11/1997
Marchmont Gold Corp. recapitalized as Adulis Minerals Corp. 05/18/2000 which recapitalized as Adulis Resources Inc. 05/01/2001 which name changed to Solana Resources Ltd. 10/18/2005 which merged into Gran Tierra Energy Inc. (NV) 11/17/2008 which reincorporated in Delaware 10/31/2016

TIMCO AVIATION SVCS INC (DE)
Each share old Common $0.001 par exchanged for (0.025) share new Common $0.001 par 11/23/2005
Merged into LJH, Ltd. 12/20/2006
Each share new Common $0.001 par exchanged for $4 cash

TIMCO ENTERPRISES, INC. (NV)
Recapitalized as Monarch Enterprises, Inc. (NV) 05/10/1966
Each share Capital Stock 2¢ par exchanged for (0.1) share Capital Stock 20¢ par
Monarch Enterprises, Inc. (NV) reincorporated in Delaware 11/05/1970 which merged into Uniflight, Inc. 06/02/1971
(See Uniflight, Inc.)

TIMCO INC. (NV)
Name changed to Timco Uranium, Inc. 08/04/1954
Timco Uranium, Inc. recapitalized as Timco Enterprises, Inc. 09/22/1961 which recapitalized as Monarch Enterprises Inc. (NV) 05/10/1966 which reincorporated in Delaware 11/05/1970 which merged into Uniflight, Inc. 06/02/1971
(See Uniflight, Inc.)

TIMCO URANIUM, INC. (NV)
Recapitalized as Timco Enterprises, Inc. 09/22/1961
Each share Capital Stock 1¢ par exchanged for (0.5) share Common 2¢ par
Timco Enterprises, Inc. recapitalized as Monarch Enterprises, Inc. (NV) 05/10/1966 which reincorporated in Delaware 11/05/1970 which merged into Uniflight, Inc. 06/02/1971
(See Uniflight, Inc.)

TIME AIR CORP (AB)
Merged into PWA Corp. 01/01/1991
Each share Common no par exchanged for (1.5191) shares Common no par
PWA Corp. recapitalized as Canadian Airlines Corp. 05/11/1995
(See Canadian Airlines Corp.)

TIME AIRLS INC (MI)
Completely liquidated 02/10/1972
Each share Common $1 par exchanged for first and final distribution of (0.1) share Caberfae, Inc. 7% Non-Cum. Conv. Preferred $10 par
(See Caberfae, Inc.)

TIME AMER INC (NV)
Name changed to NETtime Solutions, Inc. 05/11/2007
NETtime Solutions, Inc. name changed to Tempco, Inc. 10/14/2008 which name changed to Esio Water & Beverage Development Corp. 01/18/2013 which name changed to UPD Holding Corp. 03/01/2017

TIME ASSOCIATES INC (NV)
Each share old Common $0.001 par exchanged for (0.01428571) share new Common $0.001 par 08/19/2010
Name changed to Healthient, Inc. 12/14/2010
Healthient, Inc. recapitalized as SnackHealthy, Inc. 10/28/2013 which name changed to Amaize Beverage Corp. 08/19/2015 which name changed to Curative Biosciences, Inc. 03/14/2018

TIME BROKERS INC (NY)
Name changed to Computer Merchants Inc. 04/29/1976
(See Computer Merchants Inc.)

TIME ENERGY SYS INC (TX)
Common 1¢ par split (3) for (2) by issuance of (0.5) additional share 06/29/1984
Name changed to ACR Group, Inc. 02/22/1993
(See ACR Group, Inc.)

TIME FIN CORP (MA)
Common no par reclassified as Class B Common $5 par 08/18/1954
50¢ Preferred $5 par called for redemption 06/02/1959
Merged into Signet Corp. 05/12/1969
Each share Class A Common $5 par exchanged for (1) share 34¢ Conv. Preferred 1969 Ser. no par
Each share Class B Common $5 par exchanged for (0.75) share Common $1 par
Signet Corp. merged into Philadelphia National Corp. 06/29/1973 which merged into CoreStates Financial Corp 05/02/1983 which merged into First Union Corp. 04/28/1998 which name changed to Wachovia Corp. (Ctfs. dated after 09/01/2001) 09/01/2001 which merged into Wells Fargo & Co. (New) 12/31/2008

TIME FIN INC (MD)
Liquidation completed
Each share Preferred $100 par exchanged for first and final distribution of $100 cash 09/14/1970
Each share Class A Common $1 par or Class B Common $1 par exchanged for initial distribution of $9 cash 09/14/1970
Each share Class A Common $1 par or Class B Common $1 par received second distribution of $0.50 cash 07/01/1971
Each share Class A Common $1 par or Class B Common $1 par received third and final distribution of $0.8253473 cash 12/17/1974

TIME FINANCE CO. (KY)
Common $1 par changed to $5 par 00/00/1948
Common $5 par changed to $10 par 06/22/1956
Each share Common $10 par exchanged for (4) shares Common $2.50 par 10/02/1959
Stock Dividends - 50% 08/01/1957; 25% 01/15/1959
Acquired by C.I.T. Financial Corp. 05/31/1963
Each share Common $2.50 par exchanged for (0.3394) share Common no par
C.I.T. Financial Corp. merged into RCA Corp. 01/31/1980
(See RCA Corp.)

TIME FINL SVCS INC (NV)
Recapitalized as Interruption Television, Inc. 07/20/2000
Each share Common $0.001 par exchanged for (0.33333333) share Common $0.001 par
Interruption Television, Inc. name changed to Bongiovi Entertainment, Inc. 09/17/2002 which name changed to NewGen Technologies, Inc. 08/11/2005
(See NewGen Technologies, Inc.)

TIME HLDGS INC (NV)
$6.50 Conv. Preferred called for redemption 06/30/1972
Stock Dividends - 30% 03/31/1970; 10% 11/26/1973
Merged into N.V. Amev 01/09/1978
Each share Common $2 par exchanged for $35.25 cash

TIME HLDG INC (CA)
Recapitalized as Time-Lenders, Inc. 03/31/1975
Each share Class A Common $1 par exchanged for (0.01) share Class A Common $100 par
(See Time Lenders, Inc.)

TIME INC (DE)
Acquired by Meredith Corp. 01/31/2018
Each share Common 1¢ par exchanged for $18.50 cash

TIME INC (DE)
Reincorporated 12/07/1983
Each share old Common no par exchanged for (0.1) share Preferred no par and (1) share new Common no par 00/00/1933
Each share new Common no par exchanged for (4) shares Common $1 par 00/00/1941
Common $1 par split (3) for (1) by issuance of (2) additional shares 04/22/1964
Common $1 par split (2) for (1) by issuance of (1) additional share 10/01/1976
$1.575 Conv. Preferred Ser. A $1 par reclassified as $1.575 Conv. Preferred Ser. B $1 par 04/19/1979
Common $1 par split (2) for (1) by issuance of (1) additional share 10/01/1981
$4.50 Conv. Preferred Ser. C called for redemption 11/26/1982
State of incorporation changed from (NY) to (DE) 12/07/1983
$1.575 Conv. Preferred Ser. B $1 par called for redemption 07/01/1985
Stock Dividend - 100% 04/22/1949
Name changed to Time Warner Inc. (Old) 07/25/1989

Time Warner Inc. (Old) merged into AOL Time Warner Inc. 01/11/2001 which name changed to Time Warner Inc. (New) 10/16/2003

TIME INDS INC (DE)
Merged into Jefferson Smurfit Group Ltd. 02/15/1977
Each share Common 50¢ par exchanged for $8 cash

TIME INSURANCE CO. (CA)
Name changed to Time Fire & Casualty Co. 03/28/1962

TIME INS CO (WI)
Class A Common $2 par reclassified as Common $2 par 04/28/1969
Stock Dividends - Class A Common & Common - 10% 05/17/1967; 25% 04/19/1968; 20% 04/09/1969
Acquired by Time Holdings, Inc. 03/29/1971
Each share Common $2 par exchanged for (1) share Common $2 par
(See Time Holdings, Inc.)

TIME-LENDERS, INC. (CA)
Placed in receivership 03/03/1977
Details not available

TIME LENDING CALIF INC (NV)
Common $0.001 par split (4) for (1) by issuance of (3) additional shares payable 05/24/2005 to holders of record 05/20/2005 Ex date - 05/25/2005
Name changed to Time Associates, Inc. 06/08/2009
Time Associates, Inc. name changed to Healthient, Inc. 12/14/2010 which recapitalized as SnackHealthy, Inc. 10/28/2013 which name changed to Amaize Beverage Corp. 08/19/2015 which name changed to Curative Biosciences, Inc. 03/14/2018

TIME MGMT CORP (MN)
Merged into TMC Enterprises, Inc. 11/05/1992
Each share Common no par exchanged for $0.03 cash

TIME MGMT SOFTWARE INC (WA)
Each share Common 1¢ par exchanged for (0.2) share Common 5¢ par 02/22/1985
Reincorporated under the laws of Oklahoma as TMS, Inc. 06/01/1990
(See TMS, Inc.)

TIME-O-STAT CONTROLS CO.
Acquired by Minneapolis-Honeywell Regulator Co. 00/00/1931
Details not available

TIME OFF INC (NY)
Dissolved 02/22/2012
Details not available

TIME RES CORP (BC)
Reorganized under the laws of Alberta as J.C. International Petroleum Ltd. 11/30/1985
Each share Common no par exchanged for (1) share Class A no par
(See J.C. International Petroleum Ltd.)

TIME SAVER MKTS INC (CA)
Recapitalized as Alpine International Corp. (CA) 10/29/1973
Each share Common $1 par exchanged for (0.1) share Common 5¢ par
Alpine International Corp. (CA) reorganized in Delaware 09/28/1994 which recapitalized as Heng Fai China Industries, Inc. 11/10/1994 which name changed to Powersoft Technologies Inc. (DE) 04/03/1998 which reorganized in Colorado as Asia Supernet Corp. 12/22/1999

TIME SVGS & LN ASSN (CA)
Liquidation completed
Each share Guarantee Stock $10 par received initial distribution of $35 cash 03/12/1971

Each share Guarantee Stock $10 par exchanged for second and final distribution of $1.50 cash 08/16/1971

TIME SH CORP (MD)
Acquired by Houghton Mifflin Co. 07/29/1976
Each share Common no par exchanged for $1.40 cash

TIME SH PERIPHERALS CORP (CT)
Charter forfeited 05/30/1980

TIME SHARING RES INC (DE)
Common 1¢ par split (4) for (3) by issuance of (0.33333333) additional share 01/16/1981
Name changed to TSR, Inc. 02/27/1984

TIME SHARING TERMS INC (DE)
Name changed to TST Communications, Inc. 07/14/1971
(See TST Communications, Inc.)

TIME SVG HLDG INC (CA)
Name changed to Time Holding Co., Inc. 05/03/1971
Time Holding Co., Inc. recapitalized as Time-Lenders, Inc. 03/31/1975
(See Time-Lenders, Inc.)

TIME TABLE & FOLDER DISTRS INC (NY)
Voluntarily dissolved 03/18/1983
Details not available

TIME-TEL INTL CORP (CO)
Proclaimed dissolved for failure to file annual reports 01/01/1994

TIME WARNER CABLE INC (DE)
Each share Class A Common 1¢ par exchanged for (0.33333333) share Common 1¢ par 03/12/2009
Merged into Charter Communications, Inc. (New) 05/18/2016
Each share Common 1¢ par exchanged for (0.48908178) share Class A Common $0.001 par and $100 cash

TIME WARNER CAP I (DE)
8.875% Trust Preferred Securities called for redemption at $25 on 02/13/2001

TIME WARNER INC NEW (DE)
Each share old Common 1¢ par received distribution of (0.08367) share Time Warner Cable Inc. Common 1¢ par payable 03/27/2009 to holders of record 03/12/2009
Each share old Common 1¢ par exchanged for (0.33333333) share new Common 1¢ par 03/30/2009
Each share new Common 1¢ par received distribution of (0.09090909) share AOL Inc. Common 1¢ par payable 12/09/2009 to holders of record 11/27/2009 Ex date - 12/10/2009
Each share new Common 1¢ par received distribution of (0.125) share Time Inc. Common 1¢ par payable 06/06/2014 to holders of record 05/23/2014 Ex date - 06/09/2014
Merged into AT&T Inc. 06/15/2018
Each share new Common 1¢ par exchanged for (1.437) shares Common $1 par and $53.75 cash

TIME WARNER INC OLD (DE)
8.75% Conv. Exchangeable Depository Preferred Ser. C reclassified as 8.75% Conv. Exchangeable Preferred Ser. C $1 par 05/10/1990
11% Conv. Exchangeable Depositary Preferred Ser. D reclassified as 11% Conv. Exchangeable Preferred Ser. D $1 par 05/10/1990
Preferred Stock Purchase Rights declared for Common stockholders of record 04/29/1986 were redeemed at $0.05 per right 12/13/1991 for holders of record 12/06/1991
Common $1 par split (4) for (1) by issuance of (3) additional shares 09/10/1992
11% Conv. Exchangeable Preferred Ser. D $1 par called for redemption 02/12/1993
Each share 8.75% Conv. Exchangeable Preferred Ser. C $1 par exchanged for $50 principal amount of 8.75% Conv. Subordinated Debentures due 01/10/2005 on 04/01/1993
Common $1 par changed to 1¢ par 10/10/1996
Each share 10.25% Exchangeable Preferred Ser. M $1 par received distribution of (0.025625) additional share payable 09/30/1997 to holders of record 09/10/1997
Each share 10.25% Exchangeable Preferred Ser. M $1 par received distribution of (0.025625) additional share payable 12/30/1997 to holders of record 12/10/1997
Common 1¢ par split (2) for (1) by issuance of (1) additional share payable 12/15/1998 to holders of record 12/01/1998 Ex date - 12/16/1998
10.25% Exchangeable Preferred Ser. M $1 par called for redemption at $110,000 on 12/30/1998
Merged into AOL Time Warner Inc. 01/11/2001
Each share 11% Conv. Exchangeable Preferred Ser. D exchanged for (1) share 11% Conv. Exchangeable Preferred Ser. D
Each share Conv. Preferred Ser. E exchanged for (1) share Conv. Preferred Ser. E
Each share Conv. Preferred Ser. F exchanged for (1) share Conv. Preferred
Ser. F Each share Conv. Preferred Ser. J exchanged for (1) share Conv. Preferred
Ser. J Each share Ser. LMCN-V Common exchanged for (1.5) shares Ser. LMCN-V Common
Each share Common 1¢ par exchanged for (1.5) shares Common 1¢ par
AOL Time Warner Inc. name changed to Time Warner Inc. (New) 10/16/2003 which merged into AT&T Inc. 06/15/2018

TIME WARNER TELECOM INC (DE)
Name changed to tw telecom inc. 07/01/2008
tw telecom inc. merged into Level 3 Communications, Inc. 10/31/2014 which merged into CenturyLink, Inc. 11/01/2017

TIME WEALTH CORP (UT)
Proclaimed dissolved for failure to pay taxes 12/31/1975

TIMEBEAT COM ENTERPRISES INC (NV)
Reincorporated 10/16/2001
Place of incorporation changed from (YT) to (NV) 10/16/2001
Name changed to New Morning Corp. 09/30/2004
New Morning Corp. name changed to Window Rock Capital Holdings, Inc. 10/28/2005
(See Window Rock Capital Holdings, Inc.)

TIMED INVT FD LTD (CANADA)
Name changed to Industrial Dividend Fund Ltd. 12/19/1975

TIMELINE INC (WA)
Liquidation completed
Each share Common 1¢ par received initial distribution of $0.45 cash payable 06/25/2008 to holders of record 06/18/2008 Ex date - 06/26/2008
Each share Common 1¢ par received second and final distribution of $0.25 cash and pro rata interest in TMLN Royalty LLC payable 12/10/2008 to holders of record 12/01/2008 Ex date - 12/11/2008

TIMELY CLOTHES INC (NY)
Merged into Alligator Co., Inc. 06/10/1968
Each share Common $10 par exchanged for $20 cash

TIMEONE INC (NV)
Name changed to SunGlobe Fiber Systems Corp. 07/07/2000
(See SunGlobe Fiber Systems Corp.)

TIMEPLAN FINANCE CORP. (TN)
Acquired by Universal Finance Corp. (TX) 06/23/1960
Each share Common 10¢ par exchanged for (1) share Common 15¢ par
(See Universal Finance Corp. (TX))

TIMEPLEX INC (DE)
Common 1¢ par split (3) for (2) by issuance of (0.5) additional share 12/29/1980
Common 1¢ par split (5) for (4) by issuance of (0.25) additional share 12/23/1983
Stock Dividends - 20% 09/08/1980; 25% 12/15/1982
Acquired by Unisys Corp. 01/22/1988
Each share Common 1¢ par exchanged for (1) share Common $5 par

TIMER EXPLORATIONS INC (BC)
Name changed to Potash North Resource Corp. 05/30/2008
Potash North Resource Corp. merged into Potash One Inc. 04/17/2009
(See Potash One Inc.)

TIMES FIBER COMMUNICATIONS INC (DE)
Merged into LPL Investment Group 12/31/1985
Each share Common $1 par exchanged for $15.25 cash

TIMES MIRROR CO (DE)
Reincorporated 02/28/1986
Each share Capital Stock $1,000 par exchanged for (100) shares Capital Stock $10 par 04/26/1956
Capital Stock $10 par changed to no par and (2) additional shares issued 04/30/1960
Capital Stock no par reclassified as Common no par 05/04/1960
Common no par split (2) for (1) by issuance of (1) additional share 12/02/1966
Common no par split (2) for (1) by issuance of (1) additional share 11/28/1972
Conv. Preferred Ser. A no par called for redemption 10/13/1977
Common no par split (2) for (1) by issuance of (1) additional share 01/31/1984
State of incorporation changed from (CA) to (DE) 02/28/1986
Merged into Times Mirror Co. (New) 02/01/1995
Each share Ser. A Common $1 par exchanged for (1) share Ser. A Common $1 par and (0.615289) share Cox Communications, Inc. Class A Common $1 par
Each share Ser. C Common $1 par exchanged for (1) share Ser. C Common $1 par and (0.615289) share Cox Communications, Inc. Class A Common $1 par
Times Mirror Co. (New) merged into Tribune Co. 06/12/2000
(See Tribune Co.)

TIMES MIRROR CO NEW (DE)
Each share Preferred Ser. B $1 par exchanged for (0.57083) share Common Ser. A $1 par 04/02/1997
Merged into Tribune Co. 06/12/2000
Each 4.25% Premium Equity Participating Security automatically became (1) 4.25% Premium Equity Participating Security
Each share Common Ser. A $1 par exchanged for (2.5) shares Common 1¢ par
Each share Common Ser. C $1 par exchanged for (2.5) shares Common 1¢ par
(See Tribune Co.)

TIMES SQUARE ENERGY RES LTD (BC)
Recapitalized as New Hombre Resources Ltd. 01/27/1987
Each share Common no par exchanged for (0.5) share Common no par
New Hombre Resources Ltd. recapitalized as X.T.C. Resources Ltd. 03/20/1989
(See X.T.C. Resources Ltd.)

TIMES THREE WIRELESS INC (AB)
Ceased operations 02/21/2014

TIMESAVERS INC (MN)
Stock Dividend - 10% 07/15/1970
Merged into IMM Holding Co. 06/24/1974
Each share Common 50¢ par exchanged for $10 cash

TIMESHARE HLDGS INC (NV)
Name changed to TransGlobal Assets, Inc. 03/15/2011

TIMET CAP TR I (DE)
6.625% Conv. Preferred Securities called for redemption at $50.3313 plus $0.2116 accrued dividends on 03/03/2006

TIMEX CORP (DE)
Reincorporated 01/01/1970
State of incorporation changed from (CT) to (DE) 01/01/1970
Merged into TCN Corp. 03/15/1982
Each share Common no par exchanged for $65 cash

TIMIOS NATL CORP (DE)
Acquired by Timios Holdings Corp. 11/19/2015
Each share Common $0.001 par exchanged for $1.60 cash

TIMKEN-DETROIT AXLE CO. (OH)
Each share Common $10 par exchanged for (2) shares Common $5 par 00/00/1946
Merged into Rockwell Spring & Axle Co. 09/30/1953
Each share Common $5 par exchanged for (1) share Common $5 par
Rockwell Spring & Axle Co. name changed to Rockwell-Standard Corp. (PA) 04/21/1958 which reincorporated in Delaware 07/31/1964 which merged into North American Rockwell Corp. 09/22/1967 which merged into Rockwell International Corp. (Old) 02/16/1973 which merged into Boeing Co. 12/06/1996

TIMKEN ROLLER BEARING CO (OH)
Common no par split (2) for (1) by issuance of (1) additional share 06/04/1957
Common no par split (2) for (1) by issuance of (1) additional share 05/12/1965
Name changed to Timken Co. 05/01/1970

TIMM AIRCRAFT CORP. (CA)
Merged into International Glass Corp. 07/01/1957
Each share Capital Stock $1 par exchanged for (0.375) share Common $1 par
International Glass Corp. name changed to Monogram Precison Industries, Inc. 11/01/1957 which name changed to Monogram Industries, Inc. (CA) 12/03/1962 which reincorporated in Delaware 11/28/1969 which merged into Nortek, Inc. (RI) 08/26/1983 which reincorporated in Delaware

04/23/1987 which reorganized as Nortek Holdings, Inc. 11/20/2002
(See Nortek Holdings, Inc.)

TIMMAX RESOURCE CORP (BC)
Recapitalized as Metalline Resource Corp. 06/08/1994
Each share Common no par exchanged for (0.33333333) share Common no par
Metalline Resource Corp. name changed to Direct Choice T.V. Inc. (BC) 03/14/1995 which reincorporated in Canada as Star Choice Communications Inc. 12/11/1996 which merged into Canadian Satellite Communications 08/31/1999 which was acquired by Shaw Communications Inc. 04/02/2001

TIMMINS GOLD CORP (BC)
Recapitalized as Alio Gold Inc. 05/16/2017
Each share Common no par exchanged for (0.1) share Common no par

TIMMINS NICKEL INC (ON)
Delisted from Toronto Stock Exchange 02/11/1994

TIMPETE MNG CORP (BC)
Name changed to Entree Resources Inc. 02/05/2001
Entree Resources Inc. recapitalized as Entree Gold Inc. (BC) 10/10/2002 which reincorporated in Yukon 01/22/2003 which reincorporated back in British Columbia 05/27/2005 which reorganized as Entree Resources Ltd. 05/12/2017

TIMPTE INDS INC (DE)
Name changed 10/21/1970
Name changed from Timpte, Inc. to Timpte Industries, Inc. 10/21/1970
Each share Common 40¢ par exchanged for (0.5) share Common 80¢ par 05/03/1971
Merged into LGBW & B, Inc. 08/18/1977
Each share Common 80¢ par exchanged for $12 cash

TIMROD MNG LTD (QC)
Merged into Brominco Inc. 06/01/1976
Each share Common $1 par exchanged for (0.166667) share Capital Stock no par and $0.10 cash
Borminco Inc. merged into Aur Resources Inc. 05/16/1985 which was acquired by Teck Cominco Ltd. 08/30/2007

TIMVEST GROWTH FD INC (PE)
Name changed to Talvest Funds and Common no par reclassified as Growth Fund 03/23/1988
(See Talvest Funds)

TINDERBLOCK INC (UT)
Proclaimed dissolved for failure to maintain a registered agent 09/04/1990

TINEX DEVELOPMENT & EXPLORATION LTD. (ON)
Merged into Can-Con Enterprises & Explorations Ltd. 11/30/1970
Each share Capital Stock $1 par exchanged for (0.333333) share Capital Stock no par
Can-Con Enterprises & Explorations Ltd. name changed to Aubet Resources Inc. 09/08/1981 which recapitalized as Aubet Explorations Ltd. 09/30/1998 which name changed to Visa Gold Explorations Inc. 08/25/1999
(See Visa Gold Explorations Inc.)

TING PERIPHERALS INC (NV)
Recapitalized as Nimble Technologies International, Inc. 11/17/1992
Each share Common $0.001 par exchanged for (0.5) share Common $0.001 par
Nimble Technologies International,
Inc. recapitalized as CoreCare Systems Inc. (NV) 01/01/1995 which reincorporated in Delaware 01/27/1997
(See CoreCare Systems Inc.)

TINGLEFOOT MNG INC (UT)
Recapitalized as Mexico Investment Corp. 12/20/1995
Each share Common $0.001 par exchanged for (0.025) share Common $0.001 par
Mexico Investment Corp. name changed to Baja Pacific International, Inc. 02/26/1996 which name changed to Taig Ventures, Inc. 10/07/1998 which recapitalized as Viper Networks, Inc. (UT) 01/11/2001 which reincorporated in Nevada 05/18/2005

TINHORN RES LTD (AB)
Acquired by Redwood Energy Ltd. 03/18/2002
Each share Common no par exchanged for (0.9) share Common no par
(See Redwood Energy Ltd.)

TINKER NATL BK (EAST SETAUKET, NY)
Common $100 par changed to $25 par and (3) additional shares issued plus a 25% stock dividend paid 08/24/1956
Common $25 par changed to $10 par and (1.5) additional shares issued plus a 25% stock dividend paid 06/24/1960
Common $10 par changed to $5 par and (1) additional share issued 01/28/1964
Stock Dividends - 50% 11/04/1954; 16.66666666% 02/18/1957; 16.66666666% 07/09/1958; 12.5% 02/19/1959; 20% 01/22/1962; 20% 01/18/1963; 20% 02/04/1964; 20% 02/23/1965; 20% 02/28/1966; 20% 02/27/1967
Acquired by Marine Midland Tinker National Bank (East Setauket, NY) 05/16/1969
Details not available

TINNERMAN PRODS INC (OH)
Common $2 par changed to $1 par and (1) additional share issued 12/15/1965
Merged into Eaton Yale & Towne Inc. 01/31/1969
Each share Common $1 par exchanged for (1) share $2.30 Conv. Preferred Ser. A no par
Eaton Yale & Towne Inc. name changed to Eaton Corp. 04/21/1971

TINSLEY LABS INC (CA)
Common $0.16666666 par changed to no par 10/29/1968
Common no par split (3) for (2) by issuance of (0.5) additional share 05/31/1990
Common no par split (2) for (1) by issuance of (1) additional share payable 08/30/1996 to holders of record 08/15/1996
Merged into Silicon Valley Group Inc. 11/26/1997
Each share Common no par exchanged for (0.6594) share Common 1¢ par
Silicon Valley Group Inc. merged into ASM Lithography Holding N.V. 05/22/2001 which name changed to ASML Holding N.V. 06/00/2001

TINTA HILL MINES LTD (BC)
Name changed to Anchor Petroleum Corp. 04/30/1980
Anchor Petroleum Corp. recapitalized as Largo Resources Ltd. 05/30/1983

TINTAIR INC (DE)
Charter cancelled and declared inoperative and void for non-payment of taxes 04/15/1971

TINTIC CENT MNG CO (UT)
Merged into North Lily Mining Co. 12/01/1976
Each share Common 5¢ par exchanged for (0.0783) share Capital Stock 10¢ par
(See North Lily Mining Co.)

TINTIC CO.
Property sold 00/00/1936
No stockholders' equity

TINTIC COALITION MINES CORP (UT)
Recapitalized as Bio-Quant Inc. 09/15/2000
Each share Common no par exchanged for (0.25) share Common no par
(See Bio-Quant Inc.)

TINTIC DAVIS MINING CO. (UT)
Proclaimed dissolved for failure to pay taxes 11/09/1974

TINTIC DRAIN TUNNEL CO. (UT)
Merged into North Lily Mining Co. 12/01/1976
Each share Common 5¢ par exchanged for (0.0925) share Capital Stock 10¢ par
(See North Lily Mining Co.)

TINTIC ENTERPRISES INC (UT)
Name changed to Proteus Group, Inc. 02/24/1981
(See Proteus Group, Inc.)

TINTIC GOLD MNG CO (UT)
Common 10¢ par changed to $0.001 par 06/21/2001
Each share old Common $0.001 par exchanged for (0.1) share new Common $0.001 par 01/27/2003
Name changed to Kiwa Bio-Tech Products Group Corp. and (3) addiitonal shares issued 03/30/2004

TINTIC HUMBOLT MINING CO. (UT)
Recapitalized as Tintic Enterprises, Inc. 06/21/1973
Each share Capital Stock 10¢ par exchanged for (0.5) share Capital Stock 5¢ par
Tintic Enterprises, Inc. name changed to Proteus Group, Inc. 01/24/1981
(See Proteus Group, Inc.)

TINTIC LEAD CO (UT)
Under plan of merger Common $1 par changed to no par 12/22/1964
Name changed to Tintic Minerals Resources, Inc. 06/27/1969
Tintic Minerals Resources, Inc. merged into Horn Silver Mines, Inc. 07/20/1983
(See Horn Silver Mines, Inc.)

TINTIC MINERAL RES INC (UT)
Merged into Horn Silver Mines, Inc. 07/20/1983
Each share Common no par exchanged for (5) shares Common no par
(See Horn Silver Mines, Inc.)

TINTIC MTN MNG CORP (UT)
Proclaimed dissolved for failure to file annual reports 11/01/1991

TINTIC PRECIOUS METALS INC (UT)
Recapitalized as Tintic Coalition Mines Corp. 11/17/1995
Each share Common no par exchanged for (0.01) share Common no par
Tintic Coalition Mines Corp. recapitalized as Bio-Quant Inc. 09/15/2000
(See Bio-Quant Inc.)

TINTIC STD MNG CO (UT)
Merged into American Metal Climax, Inc. Inc. 06/27/1973
Each share Common $1 par exchanged for (0.110004) share Conv. Preferred Ser. A $1 par
American Metal Climax, Inc. name changed to Amax Inc. 07/01/1974 which merged into Cyprus Amax Minerals Co. 11/15/1993 which
merged into Phelps Dodge Corp. 12/02/1999 which merged into Freeport-McMoRan Copper & Gold Inc. 03/19/2007 which name changed to Freeport-McMoRan Inc. 07/14/2014

TINTINA RES INC (BC)
Name changed to Sandfire Resources America Inc. 02/02/2018

TINTINA SILVER MINES LTD. (CANADA)
Name changed to Tintina Mines Ltd. 07/09/1980

TINTINAGOLD RES INC (BC)
Each share Common no par received distribution of (1) share AsiaBaseMetals Inc. Common no par payable 10/08/2009 to holders of record 10/08/2009
Name changed to Tintina Resources Inc. 05/26/2011
Tintina Resources Inc. name changed to Sandfire Resources America Inc. 02/02/2018

TINTO GOLD CORP (BC)
Name changed to Ortho-Tronics Medical Technologies Ltd. 11/04/1988
Ortho-Tronics Medical Technologies Ltd. name changed to PlenTech Electronics Inc. 09/01/1993 which recapitalized as Consolidated Plentech Electronics Inc. 09/21/1998
(See Consolidated Plentech Electronics Inc.)

TINTON FALLS ST BK (TINTON FALLS, NJ)
Under plan of reorganization each share Common $5 par automatically became (1) share Community First Banking Co. Common $5 par 04/10/1996
Community First Banking Co. merged into Commerce Bancorp, Inc. 01/15/1999 which merged into Toronto-Dominion Bank (Toronto, ON) 03/31/2008

TINTORETTO INC (DE)
Charter cancelled and declared inoperative and void for non-payment of taxes 03/01/1993

TINYMASSIVE TECHNOLOGIES INC (BC)
Name changed to Pure Living Media Inc. 02/28/2011
Pure Living Media Inc. name changed to Scavo Resource Corp. 08/23/2012 which name changed to Brabeia Inc. 08/28/2015 which name changed to Seahawk Ventures Inc. 03/01/2016

TIO NETWORKS CORP (BC)
Acquired by PayPal Holdings, Inc. 07/18/2017
Each share Common no par exchanged for $3.35 cash
Note: Unexchanged certificates will be cancelled and become without value 07/18/2023

TIOGA COUNTY BELL TELEPHONE CO. (PA)
Merged into Commonwealth Telephone Co. (PA) 11/00/1953
Details not available

TIOGA LMBR CO (WV)
Merged into Pardee Resources Group, Inc. 09/06/2001
Details not available

TIOGA LUMBER CO. (NJ)
Charter cancelled and declared void for non-payment of taxes 02/28/1912

TIOGA PETROLEUM CORP.
Merged into Beaver Lodge Oil Corp. 00/00/1953
Each share Capital Stock exchanged for (0.25) share Common $1 par
Beaver Lodge Oil Corp. merged into Stekoll Petroleum Corp. 05/15/1959

FINANCIAL INFORMATION, INC. TIO-TIT

which name changed to Sunac
Petroleum Corp. 06/11/1962
(See Sunac Petroleum Corp.)

**TIOGA TECHNOLOGIES LTD
(ISRAEL)**
Name changed to Tikcro Technologies
Ltd. 09/02/2003

TIOMIN RES INC (CANADA)
Recapitalized as Vaaldiam Mining Inc.
03/26/2010
Each share Common no par
exchanged for (0.1) share Common
no par
(See Vaaldiam Mining Inc.)

TIONESTA PIPELINES INC. (DE)
Name changed to Greater Continental
Corp. 05/02/1968
(See Greater Continental Corp.)

TIP TOP PRODUCTS CO. (NE)
Class A Common $2 par changed to
$1 par and (1) additional share
issued 11/01/1960
Stock Dividend - Class A & B
Common - 200% 05/15/1962
Acquired by Rayette, Inc. 05/18/1964
Each share Class A or B Common $1
par exchanged for (0.22222222)
share Common 40¢ par
Rayette, Inc. name changed to
Rayette- Faberge, Inc. 06/15/65
which name changed to Faberge,
Inc. 06/30/1969
(See Faberge, Inc.)

TIP TOP TAILORS, INC.
Dissolved 00/00/1940
Details not available

TIP TOP TAILORS LTD. (CANADA)
Name changed to Dylex Diversified
(1967) Ltd. 08/01/1967
Dylex Diversified (1967) Ltd. name
changed to Dylex Diversified Ltd.
05/06/1969 which name changed to
Dylex Ltd. 08/01/1972
(See Dylex Ltd.)

TIP TOP URANIUM & OIL, INC. (CO)
Merged into Vista Petroleum Corp.
05/01/1960
Each share Common 1¢ par
exchanged for (0.0025) share
Common 25¢ par
(See Vista Petroleum Corp.)

TIPAZ INC (AR)
Reorganized 12/05/2003
Each share old Common no par
exchanged for (0.05) share new
Common no par 08/04/1999
Reorganized from under the laws of
(AZ) to (AR) 12/05/2003
Each share new Common no par
exchanged for (0.1) share Common
1¢ par
Note: Holders of between (999) and
(100) shares will receive (100)
shares only
Holders of (99) or fewer pre-split
shares not affected by split
Name changed to Valence Corp.
05/12/2004
(See Valence Corp.)

TIPHOOK PLC (UNITED KINGDOM)
Name changed to Central Transport
Rental Group PLC 12/15/1994
*(See Central Transport Rental Group
PLC)*

TIPPERARY CORP (TX)
Class A 50¢ par reclassified as
Common 50¢ par 01/24/1982
Common 50¢ par changed to 10¢ par
02/25/1986
Common 10¢ par changed to $0.001
par 02/24/1987
Each share Common $0.001 par
exchanged for (0.05) share Common
2¢ par 01/24/1990
Acquired by Santos International
Holdings Property Ltd. 10/28/2005
Each share Common 2¢ par
exchanged for $7.43 cash

**TIPPERARY LAND & EXPL CORP
(TX)**
Name changed 07/23/1969
Name changed from Tipperary Land
Corp. to Tipperary Land &
Exploration Corp. 07/23/1969
Name changed to Tipperary Corp.
03/07/1973
(See Tipperary Corp.)

**TIPPINGPOINT TECHNOLOGIES INC
(DE)**
Merged into 3Com Corp. 01/31/2005
Each share Common 1¢ par
exchanged for $47 cash

TIPTON CTRS INC (MO)
Merged into Dixons Group PLC
08/13/1987
Each share Common 10¢ par
exchanged for $9.50 cash

TIPTON INDUSTRIES, INC. (WA)
Charter cancelled and proclaimed
dissolved for failure to pay fees
07/01/1978

TIPTON INDS INC (CO)
Merged into FiberChem, Inc. (DE)
12/28/1988
Each share Common $0.0001 par
exchanged for (1) share Common
$0.0001 par
FiberChem, Inc. name changed to
DecisionLink, Inc. 12/05/2000
(See DecisionLink, Inc.)

TIPTREE FINL INC (MD)
Name changed to Tiptree Inc.
01/09/2017

TIR SYS LTD (BC)
Acquired by Koninklijke Philips
Electronics N.V. 06/08/2007
Each share Common no par
exchanged for $1.60 cash

TIRE TECH INTL INC (UT)
Name changed to Pinnacle
International Corp. 03/12/1986
(See Pinnacle International Corp.)

TIRELESS STEPS INC (NV)
Name changed to Meta Gold Inc.
07/18/2013
Meta Gold Inc. recapitalized as
Silverton Energy, Inc. 01/26/2015

TIRES INC (NV)
Name changed to Big O Tires, Inc.
12/26/1986
(See Big O Tires, Inc.)

TIREX AMER INC (DE)
Name changed to Tirex Corp.
07/11/1997

TIREX RES LTD (BC)
Recapitalized as European Electric
Metals Inc. 01/25/2018
Each share Common no par
exchanged for (0.1) share Common
no par

TIRON INC (DE)
Recapitalized as Access Healthnet,
Inc. 01/06/1989
Each share Common $0.001 par
exchanged for (0.25) share Common
$0.001 par
(See Access Healthnet, Inc.)

TIS MTG INVT CO (MD)
SEC revoked common stock
registration 04/26/2010

TISHMAN RLTY & CONSTR INC (NY)
Common no par changed to $1 par
00/00/1943
Common no par split (2) for (1) by
issuance of (1) additional share plus
a 10% stock dividend paid
01/05/1956
Common $1 par split (2) for (1) by
issuance of (1) additional share
07/15/1957
5% Preferred $20 par called for
redemption 12/22/1959
Common $1 par split (3) for (1) by
issuance of (2) additional shares
02/14/1969
Liquidation completed

Each share Common $1 par received
initial distribution of $11 cash
12/16/1977
Each share Common $1 par received
second distribution of $1 cash
04/26/1978
Each share Common $1 par received
third distribution of $1 cash
07/12/1978
Each share Common $1 par received
fourth distribution of $0.75 cash
09/27/1978
Each share Common $1 par
exchanged for fifth and final
distribution of (1) Teeco Properties
L.P. Unit of Ltd. Partnership
09/29/1978
Note: Under plan of liquidation assets
transferred to Teeco Properties L.P.
and name changed to Tishman
Liquidating Corp. 09/29/1978
(See Teeco Properties L.P.)

TISSERA INC (WA)
SEC revoked common stock
registration 03/21/2014

**TISZAI CHEMICAL GROUP PLC
(HUNGARY)**
Name changed 07/18/2006
Name changed from Tiszai Vegyi
Kombinat RT to Tiszai Chemical
Group PLC 07/18/2006
GDR agreement terminated
04/10/2015
Each 144A GDR for Ordinary
exchanged for $17.763358 cash
Each Reg. S GDR for Ordinary
exchanged for $17.763358 cash

TITAN COMPUTER SVCS INC (NY)
Name changed to Altitude
International, Inc. 08/07/2018

TITAN CONS INC (NV)
Name changed to Titan Oil & Gas,
Inc. (Ctfs. dated prior to 12/04/2008)
02/21/2005
Titan Oil & Gas, Inc. (Ctfs. dated prior
to 12/04/2008) name changed to
Green Star Energies, Inc.
12/04/2008 which recapitalized as
Rock Ridge Resources, Inc.
12/08/2011

TITAN CORP (DE)
$1 Conv. Preferred $1 par called for
redemption at $20 plus $0.03
accrued dividends on 03/15/2004
Each share Common 1¢ par received
distribution of (0.6986) share
SureBeam Corp. Common $0.001
par payable 08/05/2002 to holders
of record 07/26/2002 Ex date -
08/06/2002
Merged into L-3 Communications
Holdings Inc. 07/29/2005
Each share Common $0.001 par
exchanged for $23.10 cash

TITAN DEV CORP (DE)
Class A Common 10¢ par reclassified
as Common 10¢ par 09/24/1965
Recapitalized as Taylor (Jack)
Development Corp. 07/09/1971
Each share Common 10¢ par
exchanged for (0.125) share
Common 1¢ par
Taylor (Jack) Development Corp.
name changed to Taylor Realty
Enterprises, Inc. 06/28/1974
(See Taylor Realty Enterprises, Inc.)

TITAN DIGITAL CORP (AB)
Delisted from NEX 08/01/2008

**TITAN DIVERSIFIED VENTURES LTD
(AB)**
Recapitalized 07/12/1993
Recapitalized from Titan Diversified
Holdings Ltd. to Titan Diversified
Ventures Ltd. 07/12/1993
Each share Common no par
exchanged for (1/6) share Common
no par
Name changed to Trident Systems
Inc. 09/24/1993
Trident Systems Inc. recapitalized as
Loon Energy Inc. 12/01/1997

(See Loon Energy Inc.)

TITAN EMPIRE INC (ON)
Recapitalized as AWG
American-WestJava Gold Corp.
(ON) 11/02/1994
Each share Class A Subordinate no
par exchanged for (1) share
Common no par
Each share Class B Multiple no par
exchanged for (1) share Common
no par
AWG American-Westjava Gold Corp.
(ON) reincorporated in British
Columbia 01/04/1995 which
reorganized in Ontario as AWG
American-WestJava Gold Inc.
11/13/1995 which recapitalized as
Kalimantan Gold Corp. (ON)
05/03/1996 which reincorporated in
Bermuda as Kalimantan Gold Corp.
Ltd. 12/19/1997 which name
changed to Asiamet Resources Ltd.
07/27/2015
(See Asiamet Resources Ltd.)

**TITAN EMPLOYMENT SVCS LTD
(ON)**
Merged into Essex Oil Ltd.
11/14/2008
Each share Common no par
exchanged for (0.25) share Common
no par

TITAN ENERGY CORP (CO)
Reincorporated under the laws of
Nevada as Power Exploration, Inc.
07/01/1998
Power Exploration, Inc. name
changed to Matrix Energy Services
Corp. 05/25/2002 which name
changed to Shi Corp. 04/09/2009

TITAN ENERGY CORP (DE)
Charter cancelled and declared
inoperative and void for
non-payment of taxes 03/01/1985

TITAN ENERGY LTD (AUSTRALIA)
Name changed to TTE Petroleum Ltd.
09/25/2015
(See TTE Petroleum Ltd.)

**TITAN ENERGY WORLDWIDE INC
(NV)**
Each share old Common $0.0001 par
exchanged for (0.06666666) share
new Common $0.0001 par
08/10/2007
Acquired by Pioneer Power Solutions,
Inc. 12/31/2014
Each share new Common $0.0001
par exchanged for $0.0007 cash

TITAN EXPL INC (DE)
Merged into Pure Resources Inc.
05/25/2000
Each share Common 1¢ par
exchanged for (0.4302314) share
Common 1¢ par
Pure Resources Inc. merged into
Unocal Corp. 10/30/2002 which
merged into Chevron Corp.
08/10/2005

TITAN EXPL LTD (AB)
Each share Class B Common no par
exchanged for (3.861) shares Class
A Common no par 12/25/2007
Acquired by Penn West Energy Trust
01/11/2008
Each share Class A Common no par
exchanged for (0.1917) Trust Unit
Penn West Energy Trust reorganized
as Penn West Petroleum Ltd. (New)
01/03/2011 which name changed to
Obsidian Energy Ltd. 06/29/2017

TITAN GEN HLDGS INC (UT)
Reincorporated under the laws of
Delaware as Titan Global Holdings,
Inc. 11/14/2005

TITAN GLOBAL ENTMT INC (CO)
Old Common $0.001 par split (2) for
(1) by issuance of (1) additional
share payable 04/10/2006 to holders
of record 04/10/2006 Ex date -
04/11/2006
Each share old Common $0.001 par

exchanged for (0.00166666) share new Common $0.001 par 11/07/2007
Recapitalized as Sunset Island Group, Inc. 05/30/2008
Each share Common $0.001 par exchanged for (0.001) share Common $0.001 par

TITAN GOLDWORX RES INC (BC)
Name changed to Amana Copper Ltd. 09/10/2013
Amana Copper Ltd. name changed to International Wastewater Systems Inc. 10/28/2015 which recapitalized as Sharc International Systems Inc. 09/11/2017

TITAN GROUP INC (DE)
Each share old Common 1¢ par exchanged for (0.1) share new Common $1 par 07/31/1979
Name changed to Hanover Companies Inc. and new Common $1 par changed to Common 1¢ par 04/29/1985
(See Hanover Companies Inc.)

TITAN HLDGS INC (TX)
Stock Dividends - 5% payable 05/23/1996 to holders of record 05/13/1996; 5% payable 05/22/1997 to holders of record 05/12/1997
Merged into USF&G Corp. 12/22/1997
Each share Common 1¢ par exchanged for either (0.4951) share Common $2.50 par and $10.94 cash, (0.9902) share Common $2.50 par, or $21.88 cash
Note: Option to receive stock or cash only expired 02/11/1998

TITAN HLDG GROUP INC (FL)
Name changed to Powder River Coal Corp. 11/25/2011

TITAN INDUSTRIES, INC. (DE)
Name changed to Titan Group, Inc. 05/23/1967
Titan Group, Inc. name changed to Hanover Companies Inc. 04/29/1985
(See Hanover Companies Inc.)

TITAN INTL INC (CT)
Reorganized under the laws of Utah as Enrol Corp. 07/18/1997
Each share Common $1 par exchanged for (7) shares Common $1 par
Enrol Corp. name changed to E-Power International Inc. 01/22/2001 which recapitalized as Integrated Services Group Inc. 01/29/2003
(See Integrated Services Group Inc.)

TITAN INTL INC (IL)
Common no par split (5) for (4) by issuance of (0.25) additional share payable 08/15/2008 to holders of record 07/31/2008 Ex date - 08/18/2008
Reincorporated under the laws of Delaware and Common no par changed to $0.00001 par 06/26/2015

TITAN IRON MINES LTD. (ON)
Charter cancelled for failure to pay taxes and file returns 03/14/1978

TITAN IRON ORE CORP (NV)
Common $0.001 par split (37) for (1) by issuance of (36) additional shares payable 06/17/2011 to holders of record 06/17/2011
Recapitalized as iHookup Social, Inc. 04/29/2014
Each share Common $0.0001 par exchanged for (0.05) share Common $0.0001 par
iHookup Social, Inc. name changed to Friendable, Inc. 10/27/2015

TITAN LOGIX CORP (BC)
Name changed 06/01/2002
Name changed from Titan Pacific Resources Corp. to Titan Logix Corp. 06/01/2002

Reincorporated under the laws of Alberta 03/27/2013

TITAN METAL MANUFACTURING CO. (PA)
Merged into Cerro De Pasco Corp. 7/1/59
Each share Common $1 par exchanged for (0.78) share Common $5 par
Cerro De Pasco Corp. name changed to Cerro Corp. 1/1/61 which merged into Cerro-Marmon Corp. 2/24/76

TITAN MOTORCYCLE CO AMER INC (NV)
Each share old Common $0.001 par exchanged for (2) shares new Common $0.001 par 03/11/1997
Recapitalized as Feris International Inc. 08/03/2005
Each share new Common $0.001 par exchanged for (0.0025) share Common $0.001 par
Feris International Inc. name changed to Stratus Media Group, Inc. 07/10/2008 which recapitalized as RestorGenex Corp. (NV) 03/10/2014 which reincorporated in Delaware 06/18/2015 which name changed to Diffusion Pharmaceuticals Inc. 01/25/2016

TITAN OIL & GAS INC (NV)
Ctfs. dated prior to 12/04/2008
Name changed to Green Star Energies, Inc. 12/04/2008
Green Star Energies, Inc. recapitalized as Rock Ridge Resources, Inc. 12/08/2011

TITAN PETE LTD (AB)
Common $1 par changed to no par 11/13/1964
Struck off register for failure to file annual returns 05/14/1977

TITAN POLARIS MINES LTD (BC)
Recapitalized as Saxton Industries Ltd. 7/28/75
Each share Capital Stock no par exchanged for (0.25) share Capital Stock no par
Saxton Industries Ltd. name changed to Delbancor Industries Inc. 10/6/87
(See Delbancor Industries Inc.)

TITAN RES INC (NV)
Recapitalized as Palm Works Inc. 09/28/1999
Each share Common 2¢ par exchanged for (0.01) share Common 2¢ par
Palm Works Inc. name changed to Zydant Corp. 10/17/2000
(See Zydant Corp.)

TITAN RES LTD (BC)
Recapitalized as Golden Titan Resources Ltd. 09/08/1987
Each share Common no par exchanged for (0.5) share Common no par
Golden Titan Resources Ltd. merged into Titan Pacific Resources Ltd. 12/28/1989 which name changed to Titan Logix Corp. (BC) 06/01/2002 which reincorporated in Alberta 03/27/2013

TITAN TRADING ANALYTICS INC (BC)
Reincorporated 04/26/2005
Place of incorporation changed from (BC) to (AB) 04/26/2005
Ceased operations 08/22/2013
Stockholders' equity unlikely

TITAN URANIUM CORP (NM)
Name changed to Titan Technologies, Inc. 10/2/86

TITAN URANIUM INC (CANADA)
Name changed 06/27/2005
Reincorporated 02/19/2009
Name changed from Titan Uranium Exploration Inc. to Titan Uranium Inc. 06/27/2005
Place of incorporation changed from (BC) to (Canada) 02/19/2009

Merged into Energy Fuels Inc. 02/24/2012
Each share Common no par exchanged for (0.68) share Common no par
Note: Unexchanged certificates were cancelled and became without value 02/24/2015

TITAN WELLS INC (UT)
Each share Capital Stock 1¢ par exchanged for (0.1) share Capital Stock 10¢ par 08/27/1976
Capital Stock 10¢ par changed to 1¢ par 06/23/1982
Each share old Capital Stock 1¢ par exchanged for (0.0002) share new Capital Stock 1¢ par 12/10/1984
Proclaimed dissolved for failure to pay taxes 04/01/1994

TITAN WHEEL INTL INC (IL)
Common no par split (3) for (2) by issuance of (0.5) additional share 03/15/1995
Common no par split (3) for (2) by issuance of (0.5) additional share 08/31/1995
Name changed to Titan International, Inc. (IL) 05/22/1997
Titan International, Inc. (IL) reincorporated in Delaware 06/26/2015

TITANIC CAP CORP (FL)
Name changed to Admiral Transportation Group, Inc. 9/30/88
(See Admiral Transportation Group, Inc.)

TITANIC MINE HOLDINGS LTD. (CANADA)
Each share Capital Stock no par exchanged for (0.125) share New Royran Copper Mines Ltd. Capital Stock $1 par and (0.5) share Swanson Mines Ltd. Capital Stock $1 par 00/00/1956
(See each company's listing)

TITANIUM ASSET MANAGEMENT CORP (DE)
Acquired by TAMCO Holdings, LLC 10/22/2013
Each share Common $0.0001 par exchanged for $1.08 cash

TITANIUM CBO I LTD (CAYMAN ISLANDS)
144A Preference Shares called for redemption 4/25/2006

TITANIUM CORP INC (ON)
Reincorporated under the laws of Canada 03/19/2009

TITANIUM DEVELOPMENT CORP. (QC)
Adjudicated bankrupt 6/1/66
No stockholders' equity

TITANIUM FABRICATORS, INC. (CA)
Charter revoked for failure to file reports and pay fees 6/1/61

TITANIUM INTELLIGENCE INC (NV)
Each share old Common $0.001 par exchanged for (8) shares new Common $0.001 par 01/06/2004
Name changed to Liberty Star Gold Corp. 02/06/2004
Liberty Star Gold Corp. reorganized as Liberty Star Uranium & Metals Corp. 04/13/2007

TITANIUM METALLURGICAL INC (CA)
Adjudicated bankrupt 02/19/1974
Stockholders' equity unlikely

TITANIUM METALS CORP (DE)
6.75% Conv. Preferred Ser. A 1¢ par called for redemption at $50 on 06/28/2011
Each share old Common 1¢ par exchanged for (0.1) share new Common 1¢ par 02/14/2003
New Common 1¢ par split (5) for (1) by issuance of (4) additional shares payable 08/26/2004 to holders of

record 08/19/2004 Ex date - 08/27/2004
New Common 1¢ par split (2) for (1) by issuance of (1) additional share payable 09/06/2005 to holders of record 08/25/2005 Ex date - 09/07/2005
New Common 1¢ par split (2) for (1) by issuance of (1) additional share payable 02/16/2006 to holders of record 02/06/2006 Ex date - 02/17/2006
New Common 1¢ par split (2) for (1) by issuance of (1) additional share payable 05/15/2006 to holders of record 05/05/2006 Ex date - 05/16/2006
Acquired by Precision Castparts Corp. 01/07/2013
Each share Common 1¢ par exchanged for $16.50 cash

TITANIUM ORES CORP. (MD)
Charter revoked for failure to file reports and pay fees 11/27/63

TITANIUM ZIRCONIUM CO., INC. (NJ)
Name changed to Tizon Chemical Corp. 9/1/63
(See Tizon Chemical Corp.)

TITEFLEX, INC. (MA)
Recapitalized under plan of merger and each share Common $1 par exchanged for (2.5) shares new Common $1 par in 1951
Merged into Atlas Corp. on a (1.2) for (1) basis 8/17/62
(See Atlas Corp.)

TITLE & MORTGAGE GUARANTEE CO. OF BUFFALO
Liquidation ordered by Court in 1935

TITLE & TR CO FLA (FL)
Each share Capital Stock $100 par exchanged for (10) shares Capital Stock $10 par 07/26/1954
Each share Capital Stock $10 par exchanged for (2) shares Capital Stock $5 par 01/11/1961
Stock Dividends - 50% 01/12/1949; 33-1/3% 07/00/1954; 10% 01/16/1957; 10% 01/00/1958; 10% 01/14/1959; 10% 01/13/1960
100% acquired by GAC Corp. through voluntary exchange offer which expired 11/30/1973
Public interest eliminated

TITLE CONSULTING SVCS INC (DE)
Reincorporated under the laws of Nevada as Andiamo Corp. 07/05/2011
Andiamo Corp. (NV) reincorporated in Wyoming 10/12/2015

TITLE GTEE CO R I (RI)
Acquired by Commonwealth Land Title Insurance Co. 03/30/1970
Details not available

TITLE GUARANTEE & TRUST CO. (NY)
Capital Stock $12 par changed to $6 par 00/00/1944
Each (2) shares Capital Stock $6 par exchanged for (1) share Capital Stock $8 par 00/00/1952
Stock Dividend - 10% 02/26/1954
Name changed to Title Guarantee Co. 04/08/1959
(See Title Guarantee Co.)

TITLE GUARANTEE CO. (NY)
Stock Dividend - 50% 03/30/1962
Merged into Pioneer National Title Insurance Co. 06/30/1969
Details not available

TITLE GUARANTY & SURETY CO.
Liquidation completed in 1951

TITLE INSURANCE & TRUST CO. (CA)
Each share Capital Stock $100 par exchanged for (4) shares Capital Stock $25 par 01/00/1930
Each share Capital Stock $25 par

exchanged for (5) shares Capital Stock $5 par 01/18/1946
Each share Capital Stock $5 par exchanged for (2) shares Capital Stock $2.50 par 02/15/1956
Capital Stock $2.50 par reclassified as Common $2.50 par 01/14/1959
Common $2.50 par changed to $5 par 09/30/1959
7% Preferred $25 par called for redemption 12/30/1961
Common $5 par changed to $12.50 par 04/28/1967
Common $12.50 par changed to $1 par 04/11/1968
Common $1 par split (5) for (4) by issuance of (0.25) additional share 06/20/1968
Stock Dividends - 15% 06/10/1959; 10% 09/11/1961
Name changed to TI Corp. (of California) 06/28/1968
TI Corp. (of California) name changed to Ticor 04/27/1977
(See Ticor)

TITLE INS CO (ID)
Merged into Computing & Software, Inc. 02/10/1970
Each share Common $5 par exchanged for (0.7154) share Common no par
Computing & Software, Inc. name changed to Cordura Corp. (CA) 03/02/1973 which reincorporated in Delaware 06/27/1975
(See Cordura Corp. (DE))

TITLE INS CO MINN (MN)
Each share Capital Stock $100 par exchanged for (4) shares Capital Stock $25 par 01/13/1954
Each share Capital Stock $25 par exchanged for (5) shares Capital Stock $5 par 12/02/1963
Capital Stock $5 par changed to $2.50 par and (1) additional share issued 05/23/1969
Capital Stock $2.50 par changed to $1.25 par and (1) additional share issued 05/24/1972
Reorganized as Minnesota Title Financial Corp. 12/31/1973
Each share Capital Stock $1.25 par exchanged for (1) share Common $1.25 par
Minnesota Title Financial Corp. merged into Old Republic International Corp. 08/09/1978

TITLE STARTS ONLINE INC (NV)
Common $0.001 par split (14) for (1) by issuance of (13) additional shares payable 05/20/2010 to holders of record 05/17/2010
Ex date - 05/21/2010
Name changed to AMP Holding Inc. 05/26/2010
AMP Holding Inc. name changed to Workhorse Group Inc. 04/16/2015

TITLE TECHNOLOGIES INC (BC)
Recapitalized as Maxy Oil & Gas Inc. 10/26/1998
Each share Common no par exchanged for (0.2) share Common no par
Maxy Oil & Gas Inc. recapitalized as Maxy Gold Corp. 11/10/2003 which merged into Lara Exploration Ltd. 12/21/2009

TITLE WAVE STORES INC (MN)
Merged into Hollywood Entertainment Corp. 03/31/1995
Each share Common 1¢ par exchanged for $2 cash

TITLEIST PETES LTD (BC)
Recapitalized as Comp-Data International Inc. 09/10/1986
Each share Common no par exchanged for (0.2) share Common no par
Comp-Data International Inc. name changed to Armenian Express Canada Inc. 11/26/1987 which recapitalized as Armenex Resources Canada Inc. 07/04/1990 which recapitalized as Ecuadorean Copperfields. 08/31/1994 which recapitalized as Bronx Minerals Inc. 06/24/1996 which name changed to Las Vegas From Home.Com Entertainment Inc. 09/07/1999 which name changed to Jackpot Digital Inc. 06/18/2015

TITMUS OPTICAL CORP (NV)
Name changed to King Optical Corp. 05/17/1974
(See King Optical Corp.)

TITRODE CORP (DE)
Charter cancelled and declared inoperative and void for non-payment of taxes 03/01/1995

TITUS CAP CORP (BC)
Name changed to Titus Energy Corp. 07/08/2013
(See Titus Energy Corp.)

TITUS ENERGY CORP (BC)
Completely liquidated
Each share Common no par received first and final distribution of (0.25) share Term Oil Inc. Class A Common no par payable 08/30/2017 to holders of record 08/29/2017

TITUS FOODS INC (UT)
Charter expired 10/01/1998

TITUS INVESTMENT CORP. (UT)
Recapitalized as Titus Foods Inc. 05/16/1983
Each share Common $0.001 par exchanged for (0.01) share Common $0.001 par
(See Titus Foods Inc.)

TITUSVILLE IRON WORKS CO.
Acquired by Struthers-Wells Titusville Corp. 00/00/1928
Details not available

TITUSVILLE TRUST CO. (TITUSVILLE, PA)
Each share Capital Stock $100 par exchanged for (10) shares Capital Stock $10 par 00/00/1954
Stock Dividend - 100% 02/04/1963
Under plan of merger name changed to Pennsylvania Bank & Trust Co. (Titusville, PA) 05/03/1963
Pennsylvania Bank & Trust Co. (Titusville, PA) reorganized as Pennbancorp 12/31/1980 which merged into Integra Financial Corp. 01/26/1989 which merged into National City Corp. 05/03/1996 which was acquired by PNC Financial Services Group, Inc. 12/31/2008

TIVERTON PETES LTD (AB)
Class A Common no par split (2) for (1) by issuance of (1) additional share 01/21/1985
Merged into Arsenal Energy Inc. (New) 03/13/2006
Each share Class A Common no par exchanged for (0.23) share Common no par
Arsenal Energy Inc. (New) merged into Prairie Provident Resources Inc. 09/16/2016

TIVO INC (DE)
Merged into TiVo Corp. 09/08/2016
Each share Common $0.001 par exchanged for (0.3853) share Common $0.001 par and $2.75 cash

TIVOLI BREWING CO. (MI)
Name changed to Altes Brewing Co. 12/09/1948
Altes Brewing Co. name changed to National Brewing Co. of Michigan 01/28/1955 which merged into National Brewing Co. (MD) 05/01/1967 which name changed to O-W Fund, Inc. 10/31/1975 which merged into New York Venture Fund, Inc. 12/14/1988 which name changed to Davis New York Venture Fund, Inc. 10/01/1995

TIVOLI INDS INC (DE)
Reincorporated 03/29/1999
State of incorporation changed from (CA) to (DE) 03/29/1999
Each share old Common $0.001 par exchanged for (0.33333333) share new Common $0.001 par
Merged into Targetti Sankey SpA 11/30/1999
Each share new Common $0.001 par exchanged for $4.50 cash

TIVOLI SYS INC (TX)
Merged into International Business Machines Corp. 03/04/1996
Each share Common 1¢ par exchanged for $47.50 cash

TIW INDS LTD (CANADA)
Merged 12/31/1977
Merged from TIW Industries Ltd. into TIW Industries Ltd.-Les Industries TIW Ltee. 12/31/1977
Each share Common no par exchanged for (4) shares Common no par
Assets liquidated for benefit of creditors 06/04/1985
No stockholders' equity

TIWENZ GROUP (NV)
Name changed back to Silk Road Entertainment Inc. (Old) 02/01/2001
Silk Road Entertainment Inc. (Old) reorganized as Silk Road Entertainment Inc. (New) 09/05/2006

TIXFI INC (NV)
Name changed to IDdriven, Inc. 02/08/2016

TIZON CHEM CORP (NJ)
Stock Dividend - 25% 08/15/1968
Merged into Tandex Holding Co. 09/08/1977
Each share Capital Stock $1 par exchanged for $0.50 cash

TJ INTL INC (DE)
Common $1 par split (2) for (1) by issuance of (1) additional share 10/01/1993
Merged into Weyerhaeuser Co. 01/21/2000
Each share Common $1 par exchanged for $42 cash

TJ S HAMBURGERS INC (UT)
Proclaimed dissolved for failure to pay taxes 02/28/1991

TJ SYS CORP (DE)
Each share old Common 1¢ par exchanged for (0.125) share new Common 1¢ par 02/24/1994
Name changed to Leasing Edge Corp. 07/01/1995
Leasing Edge Corp. name changed to LEC Technologies, Inc. 03/20/1997 which name changed to Golf Entertainment, Inc. (DE) 02/18/1999 which reincorporated in Nevada as Contemporary Solutions, Inc. 05/02/2005
(See Contemporary Solutions, Inc.)

TJB ENTERPRISES INC (CA)
Name changed to Gallery Rodeo International, Inc. 09/00/1991
Gallery Rodeo International, Inc. name changed to Sierra-Rockies Corp. (CA) 11/15/1996 which reorganized in Nevada as Alpha Nutraceuticals Inc. 01/29/2004 which recapitalized as Alpha Nutra, Inc. 02/08/2005 which name changed to China Broadband, Inc. 05/16/2007 which name changed to YOU On Demand Holdings, Inc. 04/05/2011 which name changed to Wecast Network, Inc. 11/14/2016 which name changed to Seven Stars Cloud Group, Inc. 07/17/2017

TJS WOOD FLOORING INC (DE)
Name changed to China Advanced Construction Materials Group, Inc. (DE) 05/19/2008
China Advanced Construction Materials Group, Inc. (DE) reorganized in Nevada 08/02/2013

TJX COS INC (DE)
Certificates dated prior to 06/13/1989
Merged into Zayre Corp. 06/13/1989
Each share Common 1¢ par exchanged for (1.45) shares Common $1 par
Zayre Corp. name changed to TJX Companies, Inc. 06/20/1989

TJX COS INC NEW (DE)
Certificates dated after 06/20/1989
Preferred Stock Purchase Rights declared for Common stockholders were redeemed at $0.01 per right 03/07/1994 for holders of 02/17/1994
$3.125 Conv. Preferred Ser. C called for redemption 09/12/1996
Each share Conv. Preferred Ser. E exchanged for (21.592444) shares Common $1 par 11/17/1998
(Additional Information in Active)

TK STAR DESIGN INC (NV)
Name changed to China Global Media, Inc. 12/13/2011
(See China Global Media, Inc.)

TKE ENERGY TR (AB)
Recapitalized as True Energy Trust 11/07/2005
Each Trust Unit no par exchanged for (0.5) Trust Unit no par
True Energy Trust reorganized as Bellatrix Exploration Ltd. 11/02/2009

TKN INTERACTIVE MARKETING SYS INC (ON)
Name changed to eStation.com Inc. 04/21/1999
eStation.com Inc. name changed to eStation Network Services Inc. 10/30/2001
(See eStation Network Services Inc.)

TKO RES INC (BC)
Name changed to Canadian Imperial Venture Corp. 06/02/1999

TKS REAL ESTATE PUB CO LTD (UKRAINE)
GDR agreement terminated 06/13/2016
Each Sponsored GDR for Common exchanged for $0.20 cash

TL ADMIN CORP (DE)
Plan of reorganization under Chapter 11 Federal Bankruptcy proceedings effective 08/15/2005
No stockholders' equity

TL ENTERPRISES INC (CA)
Merged into Aquora Acquisition, Inc. 11/09/1984
Each share Common 10¢ par exchanged for $8.16 cash

TL INDS INC (DE)
Recapitalized as OT Computer Training Corp. 07/22/1998
Each share Common $0.001 par exchanged for (0.08333333) share Common $0.001 par
OT Computer Training Corp. recapitalized as COA Development Corp. 07/28/2000 which recapitalized as International Child Care Corp. 12/17/2001 which recapitalized as World Wide Child Care Corp. 05/21/2007

TLA, INC. (NY)
Dissolved by proclamation 06/27/2001

TLB INC (OH)
Name changed to Solomon Software, Inc. 00/00/1997
Solomon Software, Inc. merged into Great Plains Software, Inc. 06/09/2000 which merged into Microsoft Corp. 04/05/2001

TLC BEATRICE INTL HLDGS INC (DE)
In process of liquidation
Each share Common 1¢ par received initial distribution of $0.60 cash

payable 04/02/2003 to holders of record 03/19/2003 Ex date - 04/10/2003
Each share Common 1¢ par received second distribution of $0.48 cash payable 04/30/2003 to holders of record 04/21/2003 Ex date - 05/02/2003
Note: Number and amount of subsequent distribution(s), if any, are not available

TLC LASER EYE CTRS INC (ON)
Reincorporated under the laws of New Brunswick as TLC Vision Corp. 05/16/2002
(See TLC Vision Corp.)

TLC TEMP & STAFFING SVCS INC (NV)
Name changed to McBride Temporary Staffing Services 11/16/1998
(See McBride Temporary Staffing Services)

TLC THE LASER CTR INC (ON)
Name changed to TLC Laser Eye Centers Inc. (ON) 11/11/1999
TLC Laser Eye Centers Inc. (ON) reincorporated in New Brunswick as TLC Vision Corp. 05/16/2002
(See TLC Vision Corp.)

TLC VENTURES CORP (BC)
Name changed to Calibre Mining Corp. 06/18/2007

TLC VISION CORP (NB)
Plan of reorganization under Chapter 11 Federal Bankrtuptcy proceedings effective 05/20/2010
No stockholders' equity

TLII LIQUIDATING CORP (DE)
Completely liquidated 03/04/1998
Each share Common 1¢ par exchanged for first and final distribution of $10.17 cash

TLM CORP (NV)
Each share old Common $1 par exchanged for (0.01) share new Common $1 par 02/28/1997
Note: In effect holders received $1.31 cash per share and public interest was eliminated

TLNB FINL CORP (NY)
Merged into Community Bank System, Inc. 06/01/2007
Each share Common 40¢ par exchanged for $34.75 cash

TLO CAP CORP (BC)
Completely liquidated
Each share Common no par received first and final distribution of approximately (0.351) Eagle Graphite Inc. Unit consisting of (1) share Common no par and (0.5) Common Stock Purchase Warrant expiring 03/12/2020 payable 03/18/2015 to holders of record 03/09/2015

TLS CO (IA)
Merged into Norand Corp. 12/26/1985
Each share Common no par exchanged for $5 cash

TLT RES LTD (AB)
Recapitalized as Buffalo Diamonds Ltd. 12/01/1998
Each share Common no par exchanged for (0.1) share Common no par
Buffalo Diamonds Ltd. recapitalized as Buffalo Gold Ltd. 02/17/2003
(See Buffalo Gold Ltd.)

TM BIOSCIENCE CORP (ON)
Each share old Common no par exchanged for (0.2) share new Common no par 06/24/2004
Merged into Luminex Corp. 03/01/2007
Each share new Common no par exchanged for (0.06) share Common no par

TM CAP CORP (AB)
Name changed to TravellersMall.com Ltd. (AB) 10/23/2000
TravellersMall.com Ltd. (AB) reorganized in Canada as Oromonte Resources Inc. 03/29/2005 which recapitalized as Georox Resources Inc. 08/26/2008 which name changed to Prospera Energy Inc. 07/19/2018

TM CENTY INC (DE)
Name changed 10/01/1990
Name changed from TM Communications, Inc. to TM Century, Inc. 10/01/1990
Each share old Common 1¢ par exchanged for (0.125) share new Common 1¢ par 03/30/1992
Merged into Jones Media Group, Ltd. 09/29/2006
Each share new Common 1¢ par exchanged for $4.45 cash
Note: An additional distribution of $0.45987 cash was made from escrow 04/21/2010

TM ENTMT & MEDIA INC (DE)
Name changed to China MediaExpress Holdings, Inc. 10/16/2009
(See China MediaExpress Holdings, Inc.)

TM INDS INC (DE)
Adjudicated bankrupt 04/09/1973

TM MEDIA GROUP INC (NV)
SEC revoked common stock registration 07/14/2009

TM TECHNOLOGIES CORP (ON)
Name changed to TM Bioscience Corp. 07/29/1997
TM Bioscience Corp. merged into Luminex Corp. 03/01/2007

TMA CO (DE)
Adjudicated bankrupt 07/28/1972
Stockholders' equity unlikely

TMAN GLOBAL COM INC (FL)
Reorganized under the laws of Nevada as Franchise Holdings International, Inc. 05/08/2003
Each share Common $0.0001 par exchanged for (0.01) share Common $0.0001 par

TMB BANKSHARES INC (FL)
Merged into First Bankers Corp. of Florida 05/16/1986
Each share Common $1 par exchanged for $25.42 cash
Note: An additional $0.15 cash per share was distributed upon exchange of certificates

TMBR DRILLING INC (TX)
Name changed to TMBR/Sharp Drilling, Inc. 08/18/1986
TMBR/Sharp Drilling, Inc. merged into Patterson-UTI Energy, Inc. 02/12/2004

TMBR/SHARP DRILLING INC (TX)
Merged into Patterson-UTI Energy, Inc. 02/12/2004
Each share Common 10¢ par exchanged for (0.312166) share Common 10¢ par and $9.09 cash

TMC AGROWORLD CORP (DE)
Name changed to Dominican Cigar Corp. 08/22/1997
Dominican Cigar Corp. name changed to DCGR International Holdings, Inc. 06/01/1998 which recapitalized as American Way Home Based Business Systems, Inc. 04/12/2004 which name changed to American Way Business Development Corp. (DE) 09/30/2004 which reincorporated in Florida as Harvard Learning Centers, Inc. 10/30/2006 which name changed to Americas Learning Centers, Inc. 09/25/2007 which recapitalized as Hackett's Stores, Inc. 01/26/2009 which recapitalized as WiseBuys,

Inc. 06/17/2010 which name changed to Empire Pizza Holdings, Inc. 04/20/2011 which recapitalized as Vestiage, Inc. 03/22/2013

TMC INDS LTD (MA)
Reincorporated under the laws of Delaware as Middleby Corp. 05/15/1985

TMC MTG INVS (MA)
Under plan of reorganization each Share of Bene. Int. $1 par automatically became (1) share TMC Industries, Ltd. Common 1¢ par 02/27/1978
TMC Industries, Ltd. reincorporated in Delaware as Middleby Corp. 05/15/1985

TMC UTD INDS INC (FL)
Administratively dissolved for failure to file annual report 08/26/1994

TMD MGMT INC (NY)
Merged into Rondu Holdings Ltd. 08/01/1980
Each share Common 10¢ par exchanged for $0.10 cash

TME RES INC (BC)
Recapitalized as International TME Resources Inc. 07/19/1994
Each share Common no par exchanged for (0.33333333) share Common no par
International TME Resources Inc. merged into Chelsea Oil & Gas Ltd. 10/07/2013

TMEX USA INC (NV)
Recapitalized as Solargen Energy, Inc. 02/24/2009
Each share Common $0.001 par exchanged for (0.00049975) share Common $0.0001 par
Solargen Energy, Inc. name changed to Nevo Energy, Inc. 05/12/2011

TMI ALZHEIMERS CTRS INC (DE)
Recapitalized as New Generation Technology Holding, Inc. 11/26/2008
Each share Common $0.001 par exchanged for (0.1) share Common $0.001 par

TMI GROWTH PROPERTIES - '87, A CALIFORNIA LIMITED PARTNERSHIP (CA)
Charter suspended for failure to file reports and pay fees 06/17/1997

TMI HLDGS INC (FL)
Each share old Common 1¢ par exchanged for (0.1) share new Common 1¢ par 01/27/2003
Name changed to Total Identity Corp. 09/12/2003
Total Identity Corp. recapitalized as 247MGI, Inc. 12/21/2006 which name changed to Baron Capital Enterprise, Inc. 12/16/2011

TMI INC (MN)
Recapitalized as International Building Concepts Ltd. 01/24/1996
Each share Common 1¢ par exchanged for (0.25) share Common 1¢ par
(See International Building Concepts Ltd.)

TMI TECHNICAL MGMT INC (DE)
Charter forfeited for failure to maintain a resident agent 07/02/1984

TMK OAO (RUSSIA)
Name changed to PAO TMK 09/10/2015

TMK UNITED INC (DE)
Name changed to United Investors Management Co. 04/19/1988
(See United Investors Management Co.)

TML FOODS INC (SK)
Reorganized under the laws of British Columbia as TML Ventures Inc. 09/12/2001
Each share Common no par exchanged for (0.05) share Common no par
TML Ventures Inc. recapitalized as Range Metals Inc. 07/08/2005 which name changed to Range Energy Resources Inc. (Old) 01/13/2010 which name changed to Hawkstone Energy Corp. 09/01/2011 which name changed to Range Energy Resources Inc. (New) 11/17/2011

TML VENTURES INC (BC)
Each share Common no par received distribution of (2) shares Desert Gold Ventures Inc. Common no par payable 06/07/2004 to holders of record 06/03/2004
Recapitalized as Range Metals Inc. 07/08/2005
Each share Common no par exchanged for (0.1) share Common no par
Range Metals Inc. name changed to Range Energy Resources Inc. (Old) 01/13/2010 which name changed to Hawkstone Energy Corp. 09/01/2011 which name changed to Range Energy Resources Inc. (New) 11/17/2011

TMM INC OLD (NV)
Under plan of reorganization each share Common $0.001 par automatically became (1) share TMM Inc. (New) Common $0.001 par 01/27/1995

TMN CAP CORP (AB)
Recapitalized as Mayfair Media Corp. 09/06/1995
Each share Common no par exchanged for (0.5) share Common no par
Mayfair Media Corp. name changed to MF Media Corp. 12/15/1998
(See MF Media Corp.)

TMOC RES LTD (AUSTRALIA)
ADR agreement terminated 04/20/1989
No ADR's remain outstanding

TMP WORLDWIDE INC (DE)
Common $0.001 par split (2) for (1) by issuance of (1) additional share payable 02/29/2000 to holders of record 02/16/2000
Each share Common $0.001 par received distribution of (0.075) share Hudson Highland Group, Inc. Common $0.001 par payable 03/31/2003 to holders of record 03/14/2003 Ex date - 04/01/2003
Name changed to Monster Worldwide, Inc. 05/01/2003
(See Monster Worldwide, Inc.)

TMS INC (OK)
Completely liquidated 08/15/2005
Each share Common 5¢ par exchanged for first and final distribution of approximately $0.145 cash per share

TMS INTL CORP (DE)
Acquired by Crystal Acquisition Co., Inc. 10/16/2013
Each share Class A $0.001 par exchanged for $17.50 cash

TMSF HLDGS INC (DE)
Merged into TMSF Merger Corp. 11/19/2007
Each share Common $0.0001 par exchanged for $0.45 cash

TMSR HLDG CO LTD (DE)
Common $0.0001 par split (2) for (1) by issuance of (1) additional share payable 06/20/2018 to holders of record 06/14/2018 Ex date - 06/21/2018
Reincorporated under the laws of Nevada 06/21/2018

TMST INC (MD)
SEC revoked registration 05/01/2012

TMTM MERGER CO (DE)
Recapitalized as Green Processing Technologies, Inc. 06/16/2010
Each share Common $0.001 par exchanged (0.02) share Common $0.001 par
Green Processing Technologies, Inc. recapitalized as Umbra Applied Technologies Group, Inc. 01/13/2014

TMX GROUP INC (ON)
Merged into TMX Group Ltd. 09/14/2012
Each share Common no par exchanged for (1) share Common no par

TMX LTD (BERMUDA)
(Issued only as part of a unit consisting of (1) share TMX Ltd. Capital Stock BMD $0.12 par, (1) share International Time Corp. Common $0.001 par and (1) share Timex Corp. Common no par)
Merged into TCN Corp. 03/15/1982
Each share Capital Stock BMD $0.12 par exchanged for $65 cash

TN BANCSHARES, INC. (TX)
Declared insolvent and taken over by the FDIC 06/07/1990
Stockholders' equity unlikely

TN ENERGY SVCS ACQUISITION (DE)
Name changed to Zydeco Energy Inc. 12/21/1995
Zydeco Energy Inc. name changed to DTVN Holdings Inc. 12/26/2000
(See DTVN Holdings Inc.)

TNBANK (OAK RIDGE, TN)
Reorganized as Tennessee Valley Financial Holdings, Inc. 05/09/2002
Each share Common $1 par exchanged for (1) share Common $1 par

TNC MEDIA INC (DE)
Reincorporated 05/27/1994
State of incorporation changed from (NJ) to (DE) 05/27/1994
Name changed to Gothic Energy Corp. (DE) 04/18/1995
Gothic Energy Corp. (DE) reincorporated in Oklahoma 10/11/1996 which name changed to Chesapeake Energy Corp. 01/16/2001

TNE CASH MGMT TR (MA)
Name changed back to New England Cash Management Trust 04/11/1994
New England Cash Management Trust name changed to Nvest Cash Management Trust 02/01/2000 which name changed to CDC Nvest Cash Management Trust 05/01/2001 which name changed to Ixis Advisor Cash Management Trust 04/05/2005 which name changed to Natixis Cash Management Trust 06/20/2007

TNE FDS TR (MA)
Name changed back to New England Funds Trust II and Adjustable Rate U.S. Government Fund Class C, Limited Term U.S. Government Fund Class C, and Growth Opportunities Fund Class C reclassified as Adjustable Rate U.S. Government Fund Class Y, Limited Term U.S. Government Fund Class Y, and Growth Opportunities Fund Class Y respectively 04/18/1994
New England Funds Trust II name changed to Nvest Funds Trust II 02/01/2000 which name changed to CDC Nvest Funds Trust II 05/01/2001
(See CDC Nvest Funds Trust II)

TNE TAX EXEMPT MONEY MKT TR (MA)
Name changed to New England Tax Exempt Money Market Trust (New) 04/18/1994
New England Tax Exempt Money Market Trust (New) name changed to Nvest Tax Exempt Money Market Trust 02/01/2000 which name changed to CDC Nvest Tax Exempt Money Market Trust 05/01/2001
(See CDC Nvest Tax Exempt Money Market Trust)

TNFG CORP (IL)
Liquidation completed
Each share Common 1¢ par received initial distribution of $0.72 cash payable 11/18/2010 to holders of record 11/10/2010 Ex date - 11/19/2010
Each share Common 1¢ par received second distribution of $0.28 cash payable 03/22/2011 to holders of record 03/14/2011
Each share Common 1¢ par exchanged for third and final distribution of $0.103 cash 08/19/2011

TNI BIOTECH INC (FL)
Each share old Common $0.0001 par exchanged for (1) share new Common $0.0001 par 06/10/2013
Name changed to Immune Therapeutics, Inc. 12/11/2014

TNK RES INC (ON)
Recapitalized as Opus Minerals Inc. 05/18/1999
Each share Common no par exchanged for (0.1) share Common no par
Opus Minerals Inc. name changed to Investorlinks.com, Inc. 07/28/2000 which recapitalized as API Electronics Group Inc. (ON) 09/10/2001 which reorganized in Delaware as API Electronics Group Corp. 09/15/2004 which merged into API Nanotronics Corp. 11/07/2006 which name changed to API Technologies Corp. 10/27/2009
(See API Technologies Corp.)

TNP ENTERPRISES INC (TX)
Merged into SW Acquisition, L.P. 4/7/2000
Each share Common no par exchanged for $44 cash
Stock Dividends - 7.25% payable 10/1/2001 to holders of record 9/15/2001; 7.25% payable 4/1/2002 to holders of record 3/15/2002; 14.5% payable 4/1/2004 to holders of record 3/15/2004 Ex date - 3/30/2004; 7.25% payable 10/1/2004 to holders of record 9/15/2004 Ex date - 9/13/2004; 7.25% payable 4/1/2005 to holders of record 3/15/2005 Ex date - 3/11/2005
14.5% Ser. C Preferred 144A called for redemption at $1,100 plus $38.26 accrued dividends on 7/6/2005
14.5% Ser. D Preferred called for redemption at $1,100 plus $38.26 accrued dividends on 7/6/2005
Public interest eliminated

TNPC INC (DE)
Issue Information - 24,000,000 shares COM offered at $21 per share on 10/04/2000
Name changed to NewPower Holdings, Inc. 1/19/2001
(See NewPower Holdings, Inc.)

TNR GOLD CORP OLD (BC)
Reorganized as TNR Gold Corp. (New) 05/17/2011
Each share Common no par exchanged for (1) share Common no par
Note: Unexchanged certificates were cancelled and became without value 05/17/2017

TNR RES LTD (BC)
Recapitalized as TNR Gold Corp. (Old) 06/25/2003
Each share Common no par exchanged for (0.25) share Common no par
TNR Gold Corp. (Old) reorganized as TNR Gold Corp. (New) 05/17/2011

TNS INC (DE)
Issue Information - 4,420,000 shares COM offered at $18 per share on 03/16/2004
Acquired by Siris Capital Group, LLC 02/15/2013
Each share Common $0.001 par exchanged for $21 cash

TNT DESIGNS INC (DE)
Reincorporated under the laws of Nevada as Trim Holding Group 12/22/2009
Trim Holding Group name changed to HPIL Holding 06/11/2012

TNT EXPRESS N V (NETHERLANDS)
Each Sponsored ADR for Ordinary received distribution of $0.021452 cash payable 05/19/2014 to holders of record 04/15/2014 Ex date - 04/11/2014
Stock Dividends - 0.621118% payable 08/30/2011 to holders of record 08/11/2011 Ex date - 08/09/2011; 0.04494% payable 05/14/2012 to holders of record 04/12/2012 Ex date - 04/10/2012; 0.5291% payable 05/14/2013 to holders of record 04/11/2013 Ex date - 04/09/2013; 0.342465% payable 08/08/2013 to holders of record 08/06/2013; 0.90909% payable 09/02/2014 to holders of record 08/07/2014 Ex date - 08/05/2014
ADR agreement terminated 07/07/2016
Each Sponsored ADR for Ordinary exchanged for $8.916 cash

TNT FINL LTD (ON)
Capital Shares no par called for redemption 08/10/1995
Equity Dividend Shares no par called for redemption 08/10/1995

TNT FREIGHTWAYS CORP (DE)
Common 1¢ par split (3) for (2) by issuance of (0.5) additional share 9/22/93
Name changed to USFreightways Corp. 5/6/96
USFreightways Corp. name changed to USF Corp. 5/2/2003 which merged into Yellow Roadway Corp. 5/24/2005 which name changed to YRC Worldwide Inc. 1/4/2006

TNT LIQUIDATING CO. (PA)
Completely liquidated 11/25/83
Each share $5 Conv. Preferred $100 par exchanged for first and final distribution of cash
Each share Common $1 par exchanged for first and final distribution of $14 cash

TNT LTD (AUSTRALIA)
Each Unsponsored ADR for Ordinary exchanged for (1) Sponsored ADR for Ordinary 04/22/1991
Stock Dividends - 20% 07/17/1987; 20% 12/14/1988
Acquired by Koninklijke PTT Nederland NV 12/31/1996
Each Sponsored ADR for Ordinary exchanged for $9.5683 cash

TNT N V (NETHERLANDS)
Each Sponsored ADR for Ordinary received distribution of (0.01538462) ADR payable 05/06/2010 to holders of record 04/09/2010 Ex date - 04/07/2010
Each Sponsored ADR for Ordinary received distribution of (0.01388888) ADR payable 08/27/2010 to holders of record 08/09/2010 Ex date - 08/05/2010
Each Sponsored ADR for Ordinary received distribution of (0.01612903) ADR payable 03/18/2011 to holders of record 02/28/2011 Ex date - 02/24/2011
Stock Dividend - 2.5% payable 04/28/2009 to holders of record 04/13/2009 Ex date - 04/08/2009
Each Sponsored ADR for Ordinary received distribution of (1) TNT Express N.V. Sponsored ADR for Ordinary payable 05/31/2011 to holders of record 05/26/2011 Ex date - 06/01/2011
Name changed to PostNL N.V. 05/31/2011
(See PostNL N.V.)

TNT POST GROEP N V (NETHERLANDS)
Name changed to TPG N.V. 08/06/2001
TPG N.V. name changed to TNT N.V. 06/06/2005 which name changed to PostNL N.V. 05/31/2011
(See PostNL N.V.)

TNT-TELESET (RUSSIA)
GDR agreement terminated 12/31/2008
No GDR's remain outstanding

TNW INDS INC (DE)
Name changed to Gremor Motor Inns, Inc. 03/05/1974
(See Gremor Motor Inns, Inc.)

TNX TELEVISION HLDGS INC (DE)
Ceased operations 09/30/2005
Stockholders' equity unlikely

TO FITNESS INC (FL)
Common 1¢ par split (3) for (2) by issuance of (0.5) additional share 3/7/86
Proclaimed dissolved for failure to file reports and pay fees 10/11/91

TOA HBR WKS LTD (JAPAN)
ADR agreement terminated 02/21/2012
No ADR's remain outstanding

TOASTMASTER INC (MO)
Reincorporated 6/23/94
State of incorporation changed from (DE) to (MO) 6/23/94
Merged into Salton/Maxim Housewares, Inc. 1/7/99
Each share Common 10¢ par exchanged for $7 cash

TOBA INDS LTD (BC)
Name changed 10/15/1996
Name changed from Toba Gold Resources Ltd. to Toba Industries Ltd. 10/15/1996
Name changed to Beijing Marvel Cleansing Supplies Co., Ltd. 11/10/2008
Beijing Marvel Cleansing Supplies Co., Ltd. name changed to Brand Marvel Worldwide Consumer Products Corp. 02/11/2009

TOBA NICKEL & COPPER MINES LTD.
Merged into Transnorthern Nickel & Copper Mines Ltd. 00/00/1951
Each share Capital Stock $1 par exchanged for (0.4) share Capital Stock $1 par
(See Transnorthern Nickel & Copper Mines Ltd.)

TOBACCO & ALLIED STOCKS, INC. (DE)
Each share Common no par exchanged for (4) shares Common $5 par in 1953
Liquidation completed in 1955

TOBACCO ONE INC (DC)
SEC revoked common stock registration 09/18/2009
Stockholders' equity unlikely

TOBACCO PRODUCTS CORP. (VA)
Reorganized as Tobacco Products Corp. of New Jersey and Tobacco Products Corp. of Delaware in 1932, the latter company being liquidated in 1944

TOBACCO PRODUCTS CORP. OF DELAWARE
Liquidation completed in 1944

TOBACCO PRODUCTS EXPORT CORP. (OLD) (NY)
Each share Capital Stock no par exchanged for (0.1224) share Common of Morris (Philip) & Co. Ltd., Inc., 45¢ in cash and (0.1) share Tobacco Products Export Corp. (N.Y.) (New) Capital Stock no par 11/29/46
(See each company's listing)

TOBACCO PRODUCTS EXPORT CORP. NEW (NY)
Liquidation for cash completed 1/6/61
Details not available

TOBACCO SECS TR LTD (ENGLAND)
Each ADR for Ordinary Reg. £1 par exchanged for (4) ADR's for Ordinary Reg. 5s par 01/29/1962
Deferred Reg. 5s par and Ordinary Reg. 5s par changed to 25p par per currency change 02/15/1971
Merged into B.A.T Industries PLC 08/06/1976
Each share Deferred Reg. 25p par exchanged for (4) shares Ordinary Reg. 25p par
Each share Ordinary Reg. 25p par exchanged for (1) share Ordinary Reg. 25p par
Each ADR for Deferred Reg. 25p par exchanged for (4) ADR's for Ordinary Reg. 25p par
Each ADR for Ordinary Reg. 25p par exchanged for (1) ADR for Ordinary Reg. 25p par
(See B.A.T. Industries PLC)

TOBE MINES LTD (AB)
Name changed to Stratum Resources Ltd. 7/13/84
(See Stratum Resources Ltd.)

TOBEX RES LTD (BC)
Name changed to Langtec Capital Corp. 05/21/1992
Langtec Capital Corp. name changed to VisionQuest Enterprise Group Inc. 08/25/1997 which name changed to VisionQuest Energy Group Inc. 11/03/2006

TOBIAS KOTZIN CO (CA)
Stock Dividend - 25% 12/22/78
Merged into Dylex Ltd. 5/13/80
Each share Common 50¢ par exchanged for $6.50 cash

TOBICO CONS GOLD MINES LTD (ON)
Charter cancelled for failure to pay taxes and file returns 12/19/1979

TOBICO GOLD MINES LTD.
Recapitalized as Tobico Consolidated Gold Mines Ltd. 00/00/1949
Each share Capital Stock $1 par exchanged for (0.5) share Capital Stock $1 par
(See Tobico Consolidated Gold Mines Ltd.)

TOBIN CRAFT, INC. (DE)
Name changed to Dyna Ray Corp. and Class A 10¢ par and Class B 10¢ par reclassified as Common 1¢ par 06/19/1967
Dyna Ray Corp. name changed to Trans Delta Corp. 08/07/1972
(See Trans Delta Corp.)

TOBIN PACKING INC (DE)
7% Preferred $100 par called for redemption 9/30/54
Each share Common no par exchanged for (5) shares Common $3 par in 1947
Stock Dividend - (0.1) share 40¢ par Preferred for each share Common 2/11/80
Chapter 11 bankruptcy proceedings converted to Chapter 7 on 10/29/84
Stockholders' equity unlikely

TOBIRA THERAPEUTICS INC (DE)
Acquired by Allergan PLC 11/01/2016
Each share Common $0.001 par exchanged for (1) Non-transferrable Contingent Value Right and $28.35 cash

TOBURN-ALBERTA LTD (CANADA)
Dissolved 07/12/2004
Details not available

TOBURN GOLD MINES LTD. (ON)
Liquidation completed
Each share Capital Stock $1 par received initial distribution of $0.35 cash 8/1/53
Each share Capital Stock $1 par received second and final distribution of $0.0992 cash 6/15/54
Note: Certificates were not required to be surrendered and are without value

TOBY CREEK RES LTD (BC)
Recapitalized as Banff Resources Ltd. (BC) 10/29/93
Each share Common no par exchanged for (1/3) share Common no par
Banff Resources Ltd. (BC) reincorporated in Yukon 3/6/96
(See Banff Resources Ltd.)

TOBY VENTURES INC (BC)
Name changed to Storm Cat Energy Corp. 1/30/2004

TOCOM INC (TX)
Common 10¢ par split (3) for (2) by issuance of (0.5) additional share 11/30/1978
Common 10¢ par split (2) for (1) by issuance of (1) additional share 04/02/1980
Common 10¢ par split (5) for (4) by issuance of (0.25) additional share 06/15/1981
Merged into General Instrument Corp. (Incorporated 06/12/1967) 06/05/1984
Each share Common 10¢ par exchanged for (0.117647) share Common $1 par
(See General Instrument Corp. (Incorporated 06/12/1967))

TOCOR II INC (BRITISH VIRGIN ISLANDS)
Note: Units consist of (1) share Callable Common, (1) Callable Warrant, and (1) Ser. T Warrant to purchase Centocor, Inc. Common
Acquired by Centocor, Inc. 2/2/94
Each Unit exchanged for (3.2) shares Common 1¢ par
Centocor, Inc. merged into Johnson & Johnson 10/7/99

TOCOR INC (DE)
Merged into Centocor, Inc. 7/2/91
Each share Callable Common $1 par exchanged for (0.71562) share Common 1¢ par
Centocor, Inc. merged into Johnson & Johnson 10/7/99

TOCQUEVILLE TR (MA)
Under plan of reorganization each share Genesis Fund 1¢ par automatically became shares of Tocqueville Fund Class A 1¢ par on a net asset basis 10/31/2006
(Additional Information in Active)

TODAY COM INC (NV)
Each share old Common $0.001 par exchanged for (0.005) share new Common $0.001 par 05/14/2007
Recapitalized as Online Sales Strategies, Inc. 09/27/2007
Each share new Common $0.001 par exchanged for (0.5) share Common $0.001 par

TODAY HOME ENTMT INC (DE)
Charter cancelled and declared inoperative and void for non-payment of taxes 3/1/90

TODAYS BANCORP INC (DE)
Merged into Mercantile Bancorporation, Inc. 11/07/1996
Each share Common $5 par exchanged for (0.435) share Common $5 par and $11.44 cash
Mercantile Bancorporation, Inc. merged into Firstar Corp. (New) 09/20/1999 which merged into U.S. Bancorp (DE) 02/27/2001

TODAYS MAN INC (PA)
Each share old Common no par exchanged for (1) share new Common no par and (0.5) Common Stock Purchase Warrant expiring 12/31/1999 on 01/02/1998
Plan of reorganization under Chapter 11 Federal Bankruptcy Code effective 06/05/2004
No stockholders' equity

TODCO (DE)
Class A Common 1¢ par reclassified as Common 1¢ par 07/12/2006
Merged into Hercules Offshore Inc. 07/11/2007
Each share Common 1¢ par exchanged for (0.8535) share Common 1¢ par and $20.1601 cash
(See Hercules Offshore Inc.)

TODD AO CORP (DE)
Common 25¢ par reclassified as Conv. Class A 25¢ par 07/17/1987
Conv. Class A 25¢ par split (2) for (1) by issuance of (1) additional share 02/28/1992
Conv. Class A 25¢ par changed to 1¢ par 07/09/1996
Conv. Class B 25¢ par changed to 1¢ par 07/09/1996
Stock Dividend - Conv. Class A 10% 09/29/1995
Merged into Liberty Livewire Corp. 06/09/2000
Each share Conv. Class A Common 1¢ par exchanged for (0.4) share Class A Common 1¢ par and (0.5) share AT&T Corp. Liberty Media Group Class A Common $1 par
Each share Conv. Class B Common 1¢ par exchanged for (0.4) share Class A Common 1¢ par and (0.5) share AT&T Corp. Liberty Media Group Class A Common $1 par
(See each company's listing)

TODD CO., INC. (NY)
Acquired by Burroughs Corp. (Mich.) 6/11/55
Each share Class A and/or B Common $5 par exchanged for (1-1/3) shares Common $5 par
Burroughs Corp. (Mich.) reincorporated in Delaware 5/30/84 which name changed to Unisys Corp. 11/13/86

TODD COMMUNICATIONS INC (MN)
Merged into TCZ Inc. 02/28/1985
Each share Common 5¢ par exchanged for $2.25 cash

TODD GROUP INC (DE)
Name changed to Charmec Group, Inc. 3/12/80
Charmec Group, Inc. reorganized as Charme Properties Inc. 6/1/83
(See Charme Properties Inc.)

TODD INDS INC (FL)
Proclaimed dissolved for failure to file reports and pay fees 09/03/1976

TODD-JOHNSON DRY DOCKS, INC. (DE)
Merged into Todd Shipyards Corp. (NY) 00/00/1954
Each (3) shares Class A or B Common $1 par exchanged for (1) share Common $20 par
Todd Shipyards Corp. (NY) reorganized in Delaware 12/14/1990
(See Todd Shipyards Corp.)

TODD SHIPYARDS CORP (DE)
Reorganized 12/14/1990
Each share Common no par exchanged for (2) shares Common $20 par 00/00/1948
Common $20 par split (3) for (1) by issuance of (2) additional shares 06/25/1958
Common $20 par changed to $10 par and (1) additional share issued 07/15/1968
Common $10 par changed to $1 par 07/29/1977
Common $1 par split (2) for (1) by issuance of (1) additional share 01/05/1981
Reorganized from (NY) to under the laws of Delaware 12/14/1990
Each share $3.08 Conv. Exchangeable Preferred Ser. A $1 par exchanged for (6.75) shares Common 1¢ par
Common $1 par changed to 1¢ par 12/14/1990
Acquired by Vigor Industrial L.L.C. 02/15/2011
Each share Common 1¢ par exchanged for $22.27 cash

TODDY CORP.
Merged into Grocery Store Products, Inc. 00/00/1929
Details not available

TODEX CORP (NV)
Name changed to Global Smart Capital Corp. 02/03/2017

TODHUNTER INTL INC NEW (DE)
Name changed to Cruzan International, Inc. 5/2/2005
(See Cruzan International, Inc.)

TODHUNTER INTL INC OLD (DE)
Merged into TH Merger Co. 8/7/75
Each share Common $1 par exchanged for $3.50 principal amount of Todhunter International, Inc. 8% Subord. Debentures due 1985

TODWIND DEV CORP (BC)
Company placed in receivership 00/00/1984
Stockholders' equity unlikely

TOEN GROUP INC (NV)
Reorganized 06/17/1994
Reorganized from (CO) to under the laws of Nevada 06/17/1994
Each share Common no par exchanged for (0.001) share Common no par
Name changed to Virtual Enterprises, Inc. 10/08/1996
Virtual Enterprises, Inc. name changed to NetCommerce Inc. 09/08/1999
(See NetCommerce Inc.)

TOFF URANIUM MINES LTD. (ON)
Charter revoked for failure to file reports and pay fees 9/16/65

TOFINO GOLD MINING CO. LTD. (BC)
In liquidation in 1955

TOFINO MINES LTD (BC)
Each share Class B Common 50¢ par exchanged for (1) share Common 50¢ par 5/24/60
Name changed to Banqwest Resources Ltd. 5/10/78
Banqwest Resources Ltd. recapitalized as Universal Pre-Vent Inc. 11/4/86
(See Universal Pre-Vent Inc.)

TO4C CORP (UT)
Reorganized under the laws of Nevada as Aplox Corp. 4/27/2001
Each share Common $0.001 par exchanged for (0.1) share Common no par
Aplox Corp. name changed to Mirador Inc. 7/25/2001 which recapitalized as VWAY International 7/5/2004 which name to WorldWide Cannery & Distribution, Inc. 2/8/2006 which name changed to Global Diamond Exchange Inc. 9/22/2006

TOFRUZEN INC (CO)
Deliquent for failure to file a Periodic

TOFU TIME INC (DE)
Reincorporated 12/4/84
Common 1¢ par split (2) for (1) by issuance of (1) additional share 6/20/84
State of incorporation changed from (NY) to (DE) 12/4/84
Common 1¢ par split (3) for (2) by issuance of (0.5) additional share 7/9/85
Name changed to Tofutti Brands Inc. 3/13/86

TOGS FOR TYKES INC (NV)
Name changed to Biogentech Corp. 06/19/2003
Biogentech Corp. name changed to Cobalis Corp. 07/08/2004
(See Cobalis Corp.)

TOKAI BK LTD (JAPAN)
ADR agreement terminated 6/25/2001
Each ADR for Ordinary 50 yen par exchanged for approximately $66.702 cash
Note: Due to ADR's being unsponsored exchange rate may vary dependent upon depositary agent

TOKAI PHARMACEUTICALS INC (DE)
Recapitalized as Novus Therapeutics, Inc. 05/11/2017
Each share Common $0.001 par exchanged for (0.11111111) share Common $0.001 par

TOKAR LTD (QC)
Recapitalized as Canadian Tokar Ltd.-Tokar du Canada Ltee. 8/20/74
Each share Capital Stock no par exchanged for (0.5) share Capital Stock no par
Canadian Tokar Ltd.-Tokar du Canada Ltee. name changed to Interpublishing (Canada) Ltd.-Interpublication (Canada) Ltee. 4/21/76 which merged into Pagurian Corp. Ltd. 11/14/79 which name changed to Edper Group Ltd. 5/10/95

TOKENHOUSE YD HLDGS INC (AB)
Merged into Newgate Resources Ltd. 7/22/92
Each share Common no par exchanged for (1.2820512) shares Common no par
Newgate Resources Ltd. recapitalized as Para-Tech Energy Corp. 12/16/96

TOKHEIM CORP (IN)
Common no par changed to $5 par 5/2/56
Common $5 par split (2) for (1) by issuance of (1) additional share 4/30/68
Common $5 par split (2) for (1) by issuance of (1) additional share 5/1/72
Common $5 par changed to $1 par 4/4/73
Common $1 par split (2) for (1) by issuance of (1) additional share 11/30/78
Common $1 par split (3) for (2) by issuance of (0.5) additional share 2/27/81
Common $1 par changed to no par 5/1/81
Old Common no par split (3) for (2) by issuance of (0.5) additional share 3/15/85
Plan of reorganization under Chapter 11 Federal Bankruptcy Code effective 10/20/2000
Each share old Common no par exchanged for (1) Common Stock Purchase Warrant Ser. C expiring 10/20/2006
Note: Unexchanged certificates were cancelled and became without value 10/20/2001
Plan of reorganization under Chapter 11 Federal Bankruptcy Code effective 8/6/2003
No stockholders' equity

TOKHEIM OIL TANK & PUMP CO. (IN)
Each share Common $100 par exchanged for (40) shares Common $5 par in 1937
Each share Common $5 par exchanged for (1.5) shares Common no par in 1942
Name changed to Tokheim Corp. in 1953
(See Tokheim Corp.)

TOKIO MARINE & FIRE INS LTD (TOKIO KAIJO KASAI HOKEN KABUSHIKI KAISHA) (JAPAN)
Each old Common 50 Yen par exchanged for (10) new ADR's for Common 50 Yen par 01/02/1987
Stock Dividend - 10% 11/30/1976
Reorganized as Millea Holdings Inc. 04/02/2002
Each new ADR for Common 50 Yen par exchanged for (1) ADR for Common
Millea Holdings Inc. name changed to Tokio Marine Holdings, Inc. 07/01/2008

TOKLAN OIL CORP. (DE)
Assets acquired by Kirby Petroleum Co. (NV) on a (0.84) for (1) basis 1/22/58
Kirby Petroleum Co. name changed to Kirby Industries, Inc. 11/13/67

TOKLAN OIL CORP (OK)
Each share Capital Stock $0.001 par exchanged for (2) shares Capital Stock $0.0005 par 04/30/1982
Each share Capital Stock $0.0005 par exchanged for (0.05) share Capital Stock 1¢ par 01/29/1987
Merged into Cobb Oil & Gas Co. 03/31/1990
Each share Capital Stock 1¢ par exchanged for $0.3859 cash

TOKLAN ROYALTY CORP. (DE)
Recapitalized in 1946
Each share Class A Common no par exchanged for (1) share Common 70¢ par
Each share Class B Common no par exchanged for (20) shares Common 70¢ par
Name changed to Toklan Oil Corp. in 1955
Toklan Oil Corp. assets acquired by Kirby Petroleum Co. (NV) 1/22/58 which name changed to Kirby Industries, Inc. 11/13/67

TOKOS MED CORP (DE)
Merged into Matria Healthcare, Inc. 03/08/1996
Each share Common $0.001 par exchanged for (1) share Common 1¢ par
Matria Healthcare, Inc. merged into Inverness Medical Innovations, Inc. 05/09/2008 which name changed to Alere Inc. 07/14/2010
(See Alere Inc.)

TOKYO DOME CORP (JAPAN)
Stock Dividend - 10% 10/02/1991
ADR agreement terminated 12/12/2012
Each ADR for Common exchanged for (10) shares Common

TOKYO ELEC PWR CO INC (JAPAN)
Name changed to Tokyo Electric Power Co. Holdings, Inc. 04/01/2016

TOKYO RAIDERS (NV)
Name changed to Club USPN, Inc. 05/04/1990
Club USPN, Inc. name changed to XL Corp. 03/11/1994 which recapitalized as Commercial Labor Management, Inc. 03/20/1995 which name changed to Zeros & Ones, Inc. 07/01/1999 which name changed to Voyant International Corp. 04/30/2007
(See Voyant International Corp.)

TOKYO STAR BK LTD (JAPAN)
Acquired by Japan Blue Sky Capital Partners LP 07/31/2008
Each ADR for Ordinary exchanged for $9.03485 cash

TOKYO TRADING LTD (BC)
Delisted from Vancouver Stock Exchange 03/03/1997

TOKYU LD CORP (JAPAN)
ADR agreement terminated 10/31/2013
Each ADR for Common exchanged for approximately $104.126796 cash

TOLCHIN INSTRS INC (NY)
Stock Dividend - 100% 03/31/1971
Name changed to Buffet Crampon International, Inc. 12/22/1980
(See Buffet Crampon International, Inc.)

TOLEDO, BOWLING GREEN & SOUTHERN TRACTION CO.
Property sold and railway abandoned in 1930

TOLEDO EDISON CO (OH)
Each share Common $100 par exchanged for (10) shares Common no par in 1931
Each share Common no par exchanged for (2) shares Common $5 par in 1947
5% Preferred $100 par called for redemption 7/25/47
6% Preferred $100 par called for redemption 7/25/47
7% Preferred $100 par called for redemption 7/25/47
Merged into Centerior Energy Corp. 4/29/86
Each share Common $5 par exchanged for (1) share Common no par
$4.28 Preferred $25 par called for redemption 6/1/87
14.80% Preferred $100 par called for redemption 10/26/87
$3.72 Preferred $25 par called for redemption 11/6/87
$3.75 Preferred $25 par called for redemption 11/6/87
12.65% Preferred $100 par called for redemption 11/6/87
13-1/4% Preferred $100 par called for redemption 11/6/87
$3.47 Preferred $25 par called for redemption 4/16/88
11% Preferred $100 par called for redemption 4/3/92
$2.81 Preferred $25 par called for redemption 9/1/95
Centerior Energy Corp. merged into FirstEnergy Corp. 11/8/97
7.76% Preferred $100 par called for redemption at $102.437 plus $1.2933 accrued dividends on 2/1/2002
7.80% Preferred $100 par called for redemption at $101.65 plus $1.30 accrued dividends on 2/1/2002
8.32% Preferred $100 par called for redemption at $102.46 plus $1.3867 accrued dividends on 2/1/2002
8.84% Preferred $25 par called for redemption at $25.25 plus $0.3683 accrued dividends on 2/1/2002
10% Preferred $100 par called for redemption at $101 plus $1.6667 accrued dividends on 2/1/2002
Adjustable Rate Ser. A Preferred $25 par called for redemption at $25 plus $0.145833 accrued dividends on 7/1/2005
Adjustable Rate Ser. B Preferred $25 par called for redemption at $25 plus $0.243056 accrued dividends on 1/20/2006
$2.365 Preferred $25 par called for redemption at $27.75 plus $0.098542 accrued dividends on 12/15/2006
1947 4-1/4% Preferred $100 par called for redemption at $104.625 on 12/15/2006
1955 4.25% Preferred $100 par called for redemption at $102 on 12/15/2006
4.56% Preferred $100 par called for redemption at $101 on 12/15/2006
Public interest eliminated

TOLEDO FURNACE CO.
Merged into Interlake Iron Corp. 00/00/1929
Details not available

TOLEDO LIGHT & POWER CO.
Dissolved in 1941

TOLEDO MACHINE & TOOL CO.
Dissolved in 1939

TOLEDO MANAGEMENT CO. (OH)
Liquidation completed
Each share Common $5 par exchanged for first and final distribution of (0.2378686964) share Peter Hand Brewery Co. Common $1 par and (1) Toledo Management Co. Ctf. of Bene. Int. no par 05/27/1966
Peter Hand Brewery Co. name changed to Meister Brau, Inc. 06/01/1967
Each Ctf. of Bene. Int. no par exchanged for first and final distribution of (0.02) share Meister Brau, Inc. Common $1 par 11/28/1969
(See Meister Brau, Inc.)

TOLEDO MEDICAL CORP. (NV)
Recapitalized as Almaz Space Corp. 01/31/1991
Each share Common $0.001 par exchanged for (0.05) share Common $0.001 par
Almaz Space Corp. name changed to Ready When You Are Funwear, Inc. 04/14/1992 which recapitalized as Rhombic Corp. 02/17/1995 which recapitalized as Silverado Financial Inc. 04/29/2003 which name changed to MediaTechnics Corp. 05/23/2008

TOLEDO MNG CO (UT)
Each share Common 10¢ par exchanged for (0.2) share Common 50¢ par 05/28/1971
Name changed to Toledo Technology, Inc. 03/26/1984
Toledo Technology, Inc. recapitalized as HIPP International Inc. 08/31/1994 which name changed to Assembly & Manufacturing Systems Corp. 04/12/1995 which recapitalized as American Ship Inc. 09/05/1997 which name changed to Petshealth, Inc. 05/20/1998
(See Petshealth, Inc.)

TOLEDO NATL INS CO (OH)
Merged into Credit Life Insurance Co. 11/20/1974
Each share Class A $4 par exchanged for $0.46 cash
Each share Class B 50¢ par exchanged for $0.46 cash

TOLEDO SCALE CO. (NJ)
Merged into Toledo Scale Corp. on a (6) for (1) basis 11/19/57
Toledo Scale Corp. merged into Reliance Electric & Engineering Co. 12/29/67 which reincorporated in Delaware as Reliance Electric Co. 2/28/69
(See Reliance Electric Co.)

TOLEDO SCALE CORP. (OH)
Stock Dividend - 10% 5/31/67
Merged into Reliance Electric & Engineering Co. 12/29/67
Each share Common $1 par exchanged for (1) share $1.60 Conv. Preferred Ser. B no par
Reliance Electric & Engineering Co. reincorporated in Delaware as Reliance Electric Co. 2/28/69

TOL-TOM

(See Reliance Electric Co.)

TOLEDO SCALE MANUFACTURING CO.
Name changed to Toledo Scale Co. in 1940
Toledo Scale Co. merged into Toledo Scale Corp. 11/19/57 which merged into Reliance Electric & Engineering Co. 12/29/67 which reincorporated in Delaware as Reliance Electric Co. 2/28/69
(See Reliance Electric Co.)

TOLEDO SHIPBUILDING CO., INC.
Liquidation completed in 1948

TOLEDO SUGAR CO.
Dissolution approved in 1941

TOLEDO TECHNOLOGY INC (UT)
Recapitalized as HIPP International Inc. 08/31/1994
Each share Common 50¢ par exchanged for (0.02) share Common 50¢ par
HIPP International Inc. name changed to Assembly & Manufacturing Systems Corp. 04/12/1995 which recapitalized as American Ship Inc. 09/05/1997 which name changed to Petshealth, Inc. 05/20/1998
(See Petshealth, Inc.)

TOLEDO TRACTION LIGHT & POWER CO.
Name changed to Toledo Light & Power Co. in 1930 which was dissolved in 1941

TOLEDO TRAVELERS LIFE INSURANCE CO.
Acquired by Ohio National Life Insurance Co. 00/00/1930
Details not available

TOLEDO TR CO (TOLEDO, OH)
Common $50 par changed to $20 par and (1.5) additional shares issued 01/15/1962
Stock Dividends - 20% 11/20/1952; 12-1/2% 11/19/1954; 11-1/9% 05/22/1956; 10% 11/08/1957; 11-1/9% 11/16/1960; 10% 11/16/1964; 10% 12/06/1967
99.8% acquired by Trustcorp Bank, Ohio, N.A. through exchange offer which expired 07/02/1979
Public interest eliminated

TOLEDO TRUSTCORP INC (DE)
Common $20 par split (4) for (3) by issuance of (1/3) additional share 5/2/83
Common $20 par split (4) for (3) by issuance of (1/3) additional share 12/17/85
Stock Dividend - 20% 8/1/79
Name changed to Trustcorp, Inc. 4/10/86
Trustcorp, Inc. acquired by Society Corp. 1/5/90 which merged into KeyCorp (New) 3/1/94

TOLGECO GROUPE INC (CANADA)
Acquired by Placements Mecyva Inc./Mecyva Holdings Inc. 6/3/2002
Each share Common no par exchanged for $2.40 cash

TOLIN MANUFACTURING CORP. (FL)
Merged into Odell, Inc. 06/27/1967
Each share Common 10¢ par exchanged for (0.75) share Common 25¢ par
Odell, Inc. merged into Papercraft Corp. 03/26/1971
(See Papercraft Corp.)

TOLL HLDGS LTD (AUSTRALIA)
ADR agreement terminated 06/19/2015
Each ADR for Ordinary exchanged for $13.748655 cash

TOLLAND BK (TOLLAND, CT)
Name changed 09/04/1987
Name changed from Tolland Bank, F.S.B. (Tolland, CT) to Tolland Bank (Tolland, CT) 09/04/1987
Common $1 par split (4) for (3) by issuance of (0.33333333) additional share payable 07/17/1997 to holders of record 07/03/1997 Ex date - 07/18/1997
Under plan of reorganization each share Common $1 par automatically became (1) share Alliance Bancorp of New England, Inc. Common 1¢ par 10/03/1997
Alliance Bancorp of New England, Inc. merged into NewAlliance Bancshares, Inc. 04/02/2004 which merged into First Niagara Financial Group, Inc. (New) 04/15/2011 which merged into KeyCorp (New) 08/01/2016

TOLLEY INTL CORP (DE)
Reincorporated 3/31/76
State of incorporation changed from (NJ) to (DE) 3/31/76
Name changed to TIC International Corp. 11/6/81
(See TIC International Corp.)

TOLLGRADE COMMUNICATIONS INC (PA)
Common 20¢ par split (2) for (1) by issuance of (1) additional share payable 03/20/2000 to holders of record 02/28/2000
Acquired by Talon Holdings, Inc. 05/10/2011
Each share Common 20¢ par exchanged for $10.10 cash

TOLLTRECK SYS LTD (AUSTRALIA)
Name changed to Vanguard Petroleum Ltd. 10/18/1993
(See Vanguard Petroleum Ltd.)

TOLLYCRAFT CORP (WA)
Common $100 par changed to $5 par and (20) additional shares issued 9/23/59
Common $5 par split (3) for (1) by issuance of (2) additional shares 1/20/87
Stock Dividends - 20% 10/1/73; 20% 10/1/74
Merged into Olympic Equities, Inc. 7/10/87
Each share Common $5 par exchanged for $9 cash

TOLLYCRAFT YACHT CORP (NV)
Reorganized 12/29/96
State of incorporation changed from (MN) to (NV) 12/29/96
Each share old Common no par exchanged for (0.4) share new Common $0.001 par
Name changed to Childguard Corp. 3/27/2002
Childguard Corp. name changed to EWAN 1 Inc. 4/17/2002 which name changed to Advanced Technelix, Inc. 9/26/2006 which name changed to AccessKey IP, Inc. 3/26/2007

TOLMEX S A DE C V (MEXICO)
ADR agreement terminated 3/29/99
Each Sponsored ADR for Ordinary P1000 par exchanged for $35.49439 cash

TOLTEC AGRI NOMICS INC (AZ)
Charter revoked for failure to file reports and pay fees 5/10/77

TOLTEC CORP (DE)
Charter cancelled and declared inoperative and void for non-payment of taxes 3/1/74

TOLTEC MINES LTD (AB)
Struck off register for failure to file returns 08/00/1974

TOLTEC OIL & GAS INC (TX)
Reorganized under the laws of Nevada as Targa Oil & Gas, Inc. 11/24/82
Each share Common no par exchanged for (1) share Common 1¢ par
Targa Oil & Gas Inc. merged into Chapman Energy, Inc. 8/11/83 which name changed to Coda Energy, Inc. 10/10/89
(See Coda Energy, Inc.)

TOLTEC REAL ESTATE CORP (DE)
Plan of reorganization under Chapter 11 Federal Bankruptcy Code effective 02/28/1999
Each share Common $5 par exchanged for (1) Arizona Valley Inc. 5-yr. Common Stock Purchase Warrant
Note: Failure to exchange certificates prior to 09/27/1999 may result in loss of shareholder rights

TOLTEC RES LTD (BC)
Recapitalized as Canso Explorations Ltd. 11/13/1992
Each share Common no par exchanged for (0.2) share Common no par
Canso Explorations Ltd. name changed to Geonova Explorations Inc. 03/25/1994
Geonova Explorations Inc. merged into Campbell Resources Inc. (New) 06/30/2001
(See Campbell Resources Inc. (New))

TOLUCO INC (NV)
Reorganized 04/19/1976
Reorganized from (CA) to under the laws of (NV) 04/19/1976
Each share Common 10¢ par exchanged for (2) shares Common 5¢ par
Name changed to National Resources Group, Inc. 05/27/1980
(See National Resources Group, Inc.)

TOLUMA MNG & DEV LTD (BC)
Struck off register and declared dissolved for failure to file returns 01/21/1983

TOM BELL RTY CO (WY)
Common $1 par changed to no par 01/01/1969
Name changed to Bell Western Corp. 06/02/1969
Bell Western Corp. merged into Vanderbilt Energy Corp. 10/25/1978
(See Vanderbilt Energy Corp.)

TOM BROWN DRILLING INC (NV)
Name changed to Brown (Tom), Inc. and Common $1 par changed to 10¢ par 9/2/71
(See Brown (Tom), Inc.)

TOM EXPL INC (CANADA)
Name changed to Excel Gold Mining Inc. 04/22/2008

TOM HILL GOLF CO. (OR)
See - Hill (Tom) Golf Co.

TOM HUSTON PEANUT CO. (GA)
See - Huston (Tom) Peanut Co.

TOM JOHNSON-NIPIGON MINES LTD.
See - Johnson (Tom)-Nipigon Mines Ltd.

TOM KAT, INC. (KS)
Name changed to Kathol Petroleum, Inc. 4/17/67
(See Kathol Petroleum, Inc.)

TOM ONLINE INC (CAYMAN ISLANDS)
Issue Information - 11,250,000 ADR'S offered at $15.552 per ADR on 03/05/2004
Merged into TOM Group Ltd. 08/31/2007
Each Sponsored ADR for Ordinary HK$0.01 par exchanged for $15.607952 cash

TOM REED GOLD MINES CO. (AZ)
Acquired by Sawyer Petroleum Co. 11/30/1955
Details not available

TOMADELLI ELECTRONIC CORP. (DE)
Charter cancelled and declared inoperative and void for non-payment of taxes 4/1/33

TOMAHAWK CORP (AB)
Delisted from Canadian Dealer Network 5/31/2001

TOMAHAWK INDS INC (NV)
Each share old Common $0.001 par exchanged for (0.1) share new Common $0.001 par 9/26/2001
Name changed to Sparta Commercial Services, Inc. 8/25/2004

TOMAHAWK IRON MINES LTD.
Acquired by Mag-Iron Mining & Milling, Ltd. and each (20) shares exchanged for (1) new share in 1949
(See Mag-Iron Mining & Milling, Ltd.)

TOMAHAWK KRAFT PAPER CO.
Acquired by National Container Corp. (DE) 00/00/1947
Details not available

TOMAHAWK OIL & MINERALS, INC. (NV)
Name changed to Tomahawk Industries, Inc. 11/8/83
Tomahawk Industries, Inc. name changed to Sparta Commercial Services, Inc. 8/25/2004

TOMAHAWK RES LTD (BC)
Name changed to Sartis Medical Systems Canada Inc. 08/23/1993
Sartis Medical Systems Canada Inc. recapitalized as United Sartis Enterprises Inc. 12/05/1995 which name changed to Wellco Energy Services Inc. (BC) 02/11/1999 which reorganized in Alberta as Wellco Energy Services Trust 08/06/2002 which merged into Peak Energy Services Trust 03/12/2008 which reorganized as Peak Energy Services Ltd. (New) 01/06/2011
(See Peak Energy Services Ltd. (New))

TOMANET CORP (TX)
Name changed to Tomanet Mobile Parks, Inc. 1/22/72
Tomanet Mobile Parks, Inc. name changed to Tomanet Mobile Services, Inc. 11/28/72 which name changed back to Tomanet Corp. 11/4/74
In process of liquidation
Each share Common $1 par received initial distribution of (0.5) share Mid-West Steel Fabricating Corp. Common $1 par 3/31/77
Each share Common $1 par received second distribution of $0.50 cash 1/20/78
Each share Common $1 par received third distribution of $0.25 cash 1/18/79
Each share Common $1 par received fourth distribution of $0.25 cash 1/14/80
Each share Common $1 par received fifth distribution of $0.20 cash 12/10/80
Each share Common $1 par received sixth distribution of $0.10 cash 4/2/82
Each share Common $1 par received seventh distribution of $0.10 cash 10/22/82
Details on subsequent distributions, if any, are not available

TOMANET FINL CORP (TX)
Common $5 par changed to $1 par and (4) additional shares issued 05/27/1982
Name changed to Texana Capital Corp. 08/02/1984
(See Texana Capital Corp.)

TOMANET INC (AB)
Merged into Maxim Atlantic Corp. 8/19/2003
Each share Non-Vtg. Class A no par exchanged for (0.13018999) share Common no par
Each share Common no par exchanged for (0.13018999) share Common no par

TOMANET MOBILE PARKS, INC. (TX)
Name changed to Tomanet Mobile Services, Inc. 11/28/1972
Tomanet Mobile Services, Inc. name changed back to Tomanet Corp. 11/04/1974
(See Tomanet Corp.)

TOMANET MOBILE SERVICES, INC. (TX)
Name changed back to Tomanet Corp. 11/04/1974
(See Tomanet Corp.)

TOMAR TECHNOLOGY CORP (NY)
Dissolved by proclamation 06/24/1998

TOMATHEWS CORP (UT)
Recapitalized as USA Promotions, Inc. 05/27/1987
Each share Common $0.001 par exchanged for (0.1) share Common $0.001 par
USA Promotions, Inc. name changed to Prime Resources, Inc. 06/01/1990 which name changed to IPCOR, Ltd. 09/11/1990 which name changed to Luxury Seaside Resorts, Inc. (UT) 12/20/1991 which reincorporated in Nevada as RE/COMM Corp. 03/22/1992 which name changed to Metro Wireless Interactive Corp. 12/27/1993 which name changed to Red Rock International Corp. (NV) 04/01/1996 which reorganized in Kentucky as Page International Inc. 11/05/1977 which reincorporated in Nevada 12/31/1997 which name changed to China TianRen Organic Food, Inc. 06/14/2007

TOMBAC EXPLORATION LTD. (BC)
Merged into Magnum Consolidated Mining Co. Ltd. on a (2/7) for (1) basis 01/00/1962
Magnum Consolidated Mining Co. Ltd. liquidated for Brameda Resources Ltd. 03/11/1970 which merged into Teck Corp. 02/08/1979 which name changed to Teck Cominco Ltd. 09/12/2001 which name changed to Teck Resources Ltd. 04/27/2009

TOMBILL GOLD MINES LTD. (ON)
Name changed to Tombill Mines Ltd. 05/07/1959
(See Tombill Mines Ltd.)

TOMBILL MINES LTD (ON)
Each share Capital Stock no par exchanged for (0.25) share Conv. Class A Capital Stock no par and (0.75) shares Class B Capital Stock no par 8/20/81
Merged into Hornekids 1/15/98
Each share Conv. Class A Common no par exchanged for $7.69 cash
Each share Class B Common no par exchanged for $7.69 cash

TOMBIT RESOURCES LTD. (ON)
Name changed to Cliff Creek Resources Ltd. 04/26/1984
Cliff Creek Resources Ltd. name changed to Cliff Resources Corp. 00/00/1986 which name changed to Mineral Resources Corp. 09/13/1995 which name changed to Minroc Mines Inc. 06/10/1998 which name changed to Cassiar Mines & Metals, Inc. 06/10/1999 which name changed to Cassiar Magnesium Inc. 04/25/2000 which name changed to Cassiar Resources Inc. 07/25/2001 which name changed to Troutline Investments Inc. (ONT) 06/30/2003 which reorganized in Alberta as Innova Exploration Ltd. 04/16/2004
(See Innova Exploration Ltd.)

TOMBSTONE EXPLS LTD (AB)
Recapitalized as Mena Resources Inc. 4/17/2002
Each share Common no par exchanged for (0.1) share Common no par
Mena Resources Inc. merged into Rusoro Mining Ltd. 3/5/2007

TOMBSTONE MINERAL RESVS INC (AZ)
Recapitalized as Alanco Ltd. 9/17/80
Each share Capital Stock no par exchanged for (1/3) share Common no par
Alanco Ltd. recapitalized as Alanco Resources Corp. 7/3/90 which recapitalized as Alanco Environmental Resources Corp. 7/9/92 which name changed to Alanco Technologies, Inc. 11/12/99

TOMBSTONE TECHNOLOGIES INC (CO)
Name changed 08/08/2008
Name changed from Tombstone Cards, Inc. to Tombstone Technologies, Inc. 08/08/2008
Name changed to Hunt Global Resources, Inc. 02/03/2011
(See Hunt Global Resources, Inc.)

TOMBSTONE WESTN RES INC (NV)
Name changed to Dutch Gold Resources, Inc. 12/12/2006

TOMCAR MINES LTD. (ON)
Charter cancelled and company declared dissolved by default 2/12/62

TOMCOR ENTERPRISES (NV)
Name changed to Foxwedge, Inc. 08/15/1989

TOMICHI CREEK OUTFITTERS (NV)
Name changed to Healthcare Integrated Technologies Inc. 06/22/2018

TOMISKA COPPER MINES LTD. (QC)
Out of business in 1957
No stockholders' equity

TOMKINS PLC (UNITED KINGDOM)
Name changed 02/09/1988
Name changed from Tomkins (F.H.) PLC to Tomkins PLC 02/09/1988
Sponsored ADR's for Ordinary 5p par split (2) for (1) by issuance of (1) additional ADR 09/01/1992
Acquired by Pinafore Acquisitions Ltd. 09/24/2010
Each Sponsored ADR for Ordinary 5p par exchanged for $20.529002 cash

TOMLINSON OIL INC (KS)
Plan of reorganization effective 09/30/1985
Each (105.23814) shares Common no par exchanged for (1) share Common 1¢ par
Note: Unexchanged certificates were cancelled and became without value 09/20/1986
Each share Common 1¢ par exchanged for (0.005) share Common $2 par 03/20/1987
Stock Dividends - 10% 09/21/1979; 50% 09/30/1980
Merged into Tomlinson Acquisition Corp. 02/15/1988
Each share Common $2 par exchanged for $223 cash

TOMMY HILFIGER CORP (BRITISH VIRGIN ISLANDS)
Ordinary Stock 1¢ par split (2) for (1) by issuance of (1) additional share 01/17/1995
Ordinary Stock 1¢ par split (2) for (1) by issuance of (1) additional share payable 07/09/1999 to holders of record 06/18/1999 Ex date - 07/12/1999
Merged into Apax Partners Worldwide LLC 05/10/2006
Each share Common 1¢ par exchanged for $16.80 cash

TOMOKA BANCORP INC (FL)
Merged into Colonial BancGroup, Inc. 01/30/1997
Each share Common $5 par exchanged for (0.8062) share Common $2.50 par
(See Colonial BancGroup, Inc.)

TOMORROW INTL HLDGS LTD (BERMUDA)
ADR agreement terminated 05/11/2015
No ADR's remain outstanding

TOMORROWS MORNING INC (CA)
Reincorporated under the laws of Delaware as EKO International Corp. 04/08/2008

TOMOTHERAPY INC (WI)
Issue Information - 11,743,420 shares COM offered at $19 per share on 05/08/2007
Merged into Accuray Inc. 06/13/2011
Each share Common 1¢ par exchanged for (0.1648) share Common $0.001 par and $3.15 cash

TOMPKINS CNTY TR CO (ITHACA, NY)
Each share Capital Stock $25 par exchanged for (2.5) shares Capital Stock $10 par plus a 20% stock dividend paid 01/29/1948
Capital Stock $10 par changed to $5 par and (1) additional share issued 05/01/1985
Capital Stock $5 par changed to $2.50 par and (1) additional share issued 10/01/1986
Capital Stock $2.50 par changed to $1.66-2/3 par and (0.5) additional share issued 06/01/1989
Stock Dividends - 28.205% 01/21/1953; 25% 02/01/1962; 20% 02/17/1964; 20% 12/20/1967; 25% 04/15/1974; 11.111% 01/14/1977; 11.111% 06/01/1984; 10% 07/31/1987; 10% 12/01/1993; 10% 12/15/1995
Under plan of reorganization each share Common $1.66-2/3 par automatically became (1) share Tompkins County Trustco, Inc. 01/01/1996
Tompkins County Trustco, Inc. name changed to Tompkins Trustco, Inc. 05/10/1999 which name changed to Tompkins Financial Corp. 06/04/2007

TOMPKINS TRUSTCO INC (NY)
Name changed 05/10/1999
Common 10¢ par split (3) for (2) by issuance of (0.5) additional share payable 03/15/1998 to holders of record 03/01/1998 Ex date - 03/16/1998
Name changed from Tompkins Country Trustco Inc. to Tompkins Trustco Inc. 05/10/1999
Stock Dividends - 10% payable 08/15/2003 to holders of record 08/05/2003 Ex date - 08/01/2003; 10% payable 02/15/2005 to holders of record 02/04/2005, 10% payable 05/15/2006 to holders of record 05/03/2006 Ex date - 05/01/2006
Name changed to Tompkins Financial Corp. 06/04/2007

TOMPSON VY MNG & EXPL LTD (UT)
Involuntarily dissolved 05/01/1990

TOMRA SYS A / S (NORWAY)
Each old Sponsored ADR for Ordinary exchanged for (1) new Sponsored ADR for for Ordinary 5/23/94
Name changed to Tomra Systems A/S/A 12/10/99

TOMSUN FOODS INTL INC (DE)
Each share Common 10¢ par exchanged for (0.25) share Common 2¢ par 2/8/89
Charter cancelled and declared inoperative and void for non-payment of taxes 3/1/94

TONAWANDA SH CORP (NY)
Preferred no par called for redemption at $5.50 on 11/16/2012
(Additional Information in Active)

TONBRIDGE PWR INC (ON)
Each share old Common no par exchanged for (0.1) share new Common no par 11/06/2009
Acquired by Enbridge Inc. 10/13/2011
Each share new Common no par exchanged for $0.54 cash
Note: Unexchanged certificates were cancelled and became without value 10/13/2017

TONE-CRAFT PAINTS LTD. (ON)
Name changed to Tonecraft Ltd. 07/05/1971
Tonecraft Ltd. name changed to Color Your World Inc. 01/02/1980
(See Color Your World Inc.)

TONE IN TWENTY (NV)
Each share old Common $0.001 par exchanged for (0.16666666) share new Common $0.001 par 09/01/2009
Name changed to MusclePharm Corp. 03/25/2010

TONE PRODS INC (AR)
Each share old Common 10¢ par received distribution of (1) share Fun City Popcorn Inc. Common 1¢ par payable 10/25/2001 to holders of record 08/31/2001
Each share old Common 10¢ par exchanged for (0.01) share new Common 10¢ par 04/30/2002
Charter revoked for failure to pay taxes 12/31/2004

TONE RES LTD (YT)
Acquired by US Gold Canadian Acquisition Corp. 06/28/2007
Each share Common no par exchanged for (0.26) Exchangeable Share no par
US Gold Canadian Acquisition Corp. exchanged for McEwen Mining Inc. 05/29/2012

TONECRAFT LTD (ON)
Each share old Common no par exchanged for (3) shares new Common no par 09/27/1972
Name changed to Color Your World Inc. 01/02/1980
(See Color Your World Inc.)

TONECRAFT RLTY INC (ON)
Acquired by D.R. Strongman & Son Ltd. 04/30/1986
Each share Common no par exchanged for $8 cash

TONENGENERAL SEKIYU KABUSHIKI KAISHA (JAPAN)
ADR agreement terminated 04/24/2017
No ADR's remain outstanding

TONER SYS INTL INC (NV)
Reincorporated 02/09/1998
State of incorporation changed from (UT) to (NV) 02/09/1988
Reorganized as Trident Systems International, Inc. 01/25/2001
Each share Common $0.001 par exchanged for (0.25) share Common $0.001 par
Trident Systems International, Inc. name changed to AAMPRO Group, Inc. 01/07/2003
(See AAMPRO Group, Inc.)

TONGA CAP CORP (CO)
Each share Common $0.0001 par exchanged for (0.01) share Common 1¢ par 06/30/1992
Name changed to Momentum Biofuels, Inc. 11/01/2007

TONGJITANG CHINESE MEDICINES CO (CAYMAN ISLANDS)
Acquired by Hanmax Investment Ltd. 04/15/2011
Each Sponsored ADR for Ordinary exchanged for $4.50 cash

TONKA CORP (MN)
Common 66-2/3¢ par split (2) for (1) by issuance of (1) additional share 10/16/1967
Common 66-2/3¢ par split (2) for (1)

by issuance of (1) additional share 03/26/1985
Common 66-2/3¢ par split (2) for (1) by issuance of (1) additional share 07/12/1985
Common 66-2/3¢ par split (3) for (2) by issuance of (0.5) additional share 04/07/1986
Acquired by HIAC III Corp. 08/01/1991
Each share Common 66-2/3¢ par exchanged for $5 cash

TONKA TOYS, INC. (MN)
Common $1 par changed to 66-2/3¢ par and (0.5) additional share issued 10/02/1963
Name changed to Tonka Corp. 09/20/1965
(See Tonka Corp.)

TONKO DEV CORP (AB)
Each share old Common no par exchanged for (0.2) share new Common no par 07/13/2000
Acquired by Pyxis Real Estate Equities Inc. 03/15/2002
Each share new Common no par exchanged for $4.10 cash

TONOPAH BELMONT DEVELOPMENT CO.
Dissolved 00/00/1942
Details not available

TONOPAH EXTENSION MINING CO.
Property sold 00/00/1929
Details not available

TONOPAH GYPSY QUEEN MINING CO. (NV)
Common $1 par changed to 20¢ par 04/14/1956
Name changed to Twentieth Century Fuels, Inc. 06/15/1956
Twentieth Century Fuels, Inc. recapitalized as Twentieth Century Engineering Corp. 08/30/1963 which merged into Radiant Industries, Inc. 12/29/1969 which name changed to Caltem Liquidating, Inc. 06/30/1980
(See Caltem Liquidating, Inc.)

TONOPAH MINING CO. OF NEVADA (DE)
Liquidation completed
Each share Capital Stock $1 par exchanged for initial distribution of $5.52 cash 07/02/1964
Each share Capital Stock $1 par received second and final distribution of $0.1947 cash 10/15/1986

TONOPAH NORTH STAR TUNNEL & DEVELOPMENT CO. (NV)
Name changed to North Star Oil Co. 09/26/1956
North Star Oil Co. merged into North Star Oil Corp. 05/12/1961 which was acquired by Texam Oil Corp. 04/22/1964 which name changed to Energy Resources Corp. 10/23/1967 which merged into ENERTEC Corp. 05/04/1984
(See ENERTEC Corp.)

TONOPAH RES INC (BC)
Recapitalized as GoldZone Exploration Inc. 11/06/1996
Each share Common no par exchanged for (0.2) share Common no par
GoldZone Exploration Inc. recapitalized as Energulf Resources Inc. (BC) 08/13/2001 which reincorporated in Yukon 06/27/2003 which reincorporated in British Columbia 10/05/2004

TONS OF TOYS INC (DE)
Each share old Common 1¢ par exchanged for (0.02857142) share new Common 1¢ par 08/10/1990
Charter cancelled and declared inoperative and void for non-payment of taxes 03/01/1993

TONTINE MNG LTD (ON)
Merged into Coldstream Mines Ltd. 01/13/1972
Each share Capital Stock no par exchanged for (0.33333333) share Capital Stock no par
(See Coldstream Mines Ltd.)

TOO GOURMET INC (NV)
Common $0.001 par split (2) for (1) by issuance of (1) additional share payable 08/16/2002 to holders of record 08/15/2002 Ex date - 08/19/2002
Name changed to Global Life Sciences, Inc. 11/18/2003
Global Life Sciences, Inc. name changed to Nortia Capital Partners, Inc. 11/05/2004

TOO INC (DE)
Name changed to Tween Brands, Inc. 06/21/2006
Tween Brands, Inc. merged into Dress Barn, Inc. (CT) 11/25/2009 which reincorporated in Delaware as Ascena Retail Group, Inc. 01/03/2011

TOODOGGONE GOLD INC (BC)
Recapitalized as Tapajos Gold Inc. 06/06/1995
Each share Common no par exchanged for (0.25) share Common no par
Tapajos Gold Inc. merged into Brasilca Mining Corp. 04/03/2000
(See Brasilca Mining Corp.)

TOOKE BROS LTD (CANADA)
Recapitalized 00/00/1943
Each share 7% Preference $100 par exchanged for (2.8) shares Common no par
Each share Common no par exchanged for (0.2) share Common no par
Recapitalized 00/00/1954
Each share Common no par exchanged for (1) share Preferred $6 par, (1) share Common no par and $5 principal amount of 5% Debentures
Placed in bankruptcy 08/27/1973
No stockholders' equity

TOOL RESH & ENGR CORP (DE)
Common $1 par split (3) for (1) by issuance of (2) additional shares 02/26/1969
Name changed to TRE Corp. 12/14/1973
(See TRE Corp.)

TOOL SALES CO (MI)
Adjudicated bankrupt 11/18/1970
Stockholders' equity unlikely

TOOL STL GEAR & PINION CO (OH)
Common $5 par split (20) for (1) by issuance of (19) additional shares 01/01/1967
Name changed to XTEK, Inc. 12/06/1976
(See XTEK, Inc.)

TOOLEX INTL N V (NETHERLANDS)
Name changed 04/15/1998
Name changed from Toolex Alpha N.V. to Toolex International N.V. 04/15/1998
Declared bankruptcy 09/28/2001
No stockholders' equity

TOOTIE PIE CO INC (NV)
Plan of reorganization under Chapter 11 Federal Bankruptcy proceedings effective 08/22/2014
Each share old Common $0.001 par exchanged for (0.03440741) share new Common $0.001 par
Note: Company is now private

TOOTLE-ENRIGHT NATIONAL BANK (ST. JOSEPH, MO)
Merged into American National Bank (St. Joseph, MO) 12/06/1963
Each share Capital Stock $100 par exchanged for (1.2) shares Capital Stock $10 par

American National Bank (St. Joseph, MO) reorganized as Ameribanc, Inc. 03/10/1971
(See Ameribanc, Inc.)

TOOTSEE LAKE MINING CO. LTD. (ON)
Charter cancelled and company declared dissolved for default in filing returns 01/13/1971

TOP AIR MFG INC (IA)
Ceased operations and subsequently filed Notice of Termination of Registration 01/16/2001
No stockholders' equity

TOP BRASS ENTERPRISES INC (DE)
Ceased operations 04/20/1988
No stockholders' equity

TOP ENVIRONMENTAL CAP VENTURE INC (CANADA)
Name changed to Loubac Top Environmental Inc. (Canada) 06/11/2001
Loubac Top Environmental Inc. (Canada) reincorporated in British Columbia as Novus Gold Corp. 03/20/2009 which merged into PanTerra Gold Ltd. 04/19/2012

TOP FLIGHT GAMEBIRDS INC (DE)
Name changed to Global Pharm Holdings Group, Inc. 09/21/2010

TOP FLIGHT SOFTWARE INC (NV)
Name changed to Dendo Global Corp. 11/02/1998
Dendo Global Corp. name changed to TechAlt, Inc. 10/15/2004 which name changed to All American Energy Holding, Inc. 10/23/2012 which recapitalized as All American Energy Corp. 11/14/2017 which name changed to Core Lithium Corp. 04/11/2018

TOP GEAR INC (DE)
Common $0.0001 par split (17) for (1) by issuance of (16) additional shares payable 02/07/2012 to holders of record 01/03/2012 Ex date - 02/08/2012
Name changed to Luxeyard, Inc. 02/13/2012

TOP GROUP HLDGS INC (DE)
Common 1¢ par changed to $0.0001 par 01/21/2005
Name changed to Soyodo Group Holdings, Inc. (DE) 09/22/2005
Soyodo Group Holdings, Inc. (DE) reorganized in Nevada as Omphalos, Corp. 04/30/2008

TOP GUN CAP CORP (AB)
Recapitalized as Western Warrior Resources Inc. 07/04/2002
Each share Common no par exchanged for (0.4) share Common no par
Western Warrior Resources Inc. recapitalized as Whetstone Minerals Inc. (AB) 10/29/2008 which reincorporated in Channel Islands as Whetstone Minerals Ltd. 11/20/2009

TOP GUN EXPLS INC (BC)
Recapitalized as Consolidated Top Gun Explorations Inc. 04/13/1992
Each share Common no par exchanged for (0.456621) share Common no par
Consolidated Top Gun Explorations Inc. name changed to Sterling Pacific Resources Inc. 09/13/1993 which recapitalized as Tres-Or Resources Ltd. 01/11/1999

TOP-O'-THE-WORLD FARMS, INC. (CO)
Name changed to Upper Valley Farm & Land Co. 03/08/1963
(See Upper Valley Farm & Land Co.)

TOP SOURCE TECHNOLOGIES INC (DE)
Name changed 01/12/1990
Name changed 03/17/1994
Name changed from Top Sound

International Inc. to Top Source, Inc. 01/12/1990
Name changed from Top Source, Inc. to Top Source Technologies, Inc. 03/17/1994
Name changed to Global Technovations, Inc. 12/15/1999
(See Global Technovations, Inc.)

TOP TANKERS INC (MARSHALL ISLANDS)
Name changed to Top Ships Inc. 01/03/2008

TOP TO BOTTOM PRESSURE WASHING INC (FL)
Name changed to IBEX Advanced Mortgage Technology, Inc. 06/26/2014

TOP 20 DIVID TR (ON)
Trust terminated 05/31/2017
Each Trust Unit received $8.7232 cash

TOP 20 EUROPE DIVID TR (ON)
Trust terminated 01/31/2018
Each Unit received $8.835746 cash

TOPAZ ELECTRONICS (CA)
Name changed to Topaz, Inc. 8/1/79
(See Topaz, Inc.)

TOPAZ EXPL LTD (BC)
Common no par split (2) for (1) by issuance of (1) additional share 01/24/1986
Recapitalized as Consolidated Topaz Exploration Ltd. 08/01/1989
Each share Common no par exchanged for (0.33333333) share Common no par
Consolidated Topaz Exploration Ltd. recapitalized as Topaz Resources International Inc. 08/06/1991 which recapitalized as Pacific Topaz Resources Ltd. 07/21/1997 which recapitalized as Western Atlas Resources Inc. 06/20/2018

TOPAZ GROUP INC (NV)
Each share old Common $0.001 par exchanged for (0.33333333) share new Common $0.001 par 03/15/1999
Each share new Common $0.001 par exchanged again for (0.2) share new Common $0.001 par 11/22/2000
SEC revoked common stock registration 06/11/2009

TOPAZ INC (CA)
Common no par split (3) for (2) by issuance of (0.5) additional share 9/6/80
Common no par split (5) for (4) by issuance of (0.25) additional share 9/27/82
Stock Dividend - 10% 2/29/80
Merged into Square D Co. 2/14/83
Each share Common no par exchanged for $14.40 cash

TOPAZ RES INTL INC (BC)
Recapitalized as Pacific Topaz Resources Ltd. 07/21/1997
Each share Common no par exchanged for (0.5) share Common no par Pacific Topaz Resources Ltd. recapitalized as Western Atlas Resources Inc. 06/20/2018

TOPCALL INTL AG (AUSTRIA)
Sponsored ADR's for Ordinary AS100 par split (7) for (1) by issuance of (6) additional ADR's payable 02/04/1999 to holders of record 02/03/1999
Acquired by DICOM Group plc 11/00/2004
Each Sponsored ADR for Ordinary exchanged for approximately $0.508 cash
Note: Currency changed to Euro 01/01/1999

TOPCLICK INTL INC (DE)
Recapitalized as Datalogic International Inc. 7/30/2001
Each share Common no par

exchanged for (0.25) share Common no par

TOPJOBS NET PLC (ENGLAND & WALES)
Acquired by Scout24 AG 04/10/2001
Each Sponsored ADR for Ordinary 0.02p par exchanged for $1.50 cash

TOPKAPI RES LTD (BC)
Recapitalized as Owen Ventures Ltd. 08/13/1986
Each share Common no par exchanged for (0.4) share Common no par
(See Owen Ventures Ltd.)

TOPLEY CRISS MINES LTD (BC)
Struck off register and declared dissolved for failure to file returns 06/13/1977

TOPOX INC (DE)
Name changed to Supra Medical Corp. 10/26/92

TOPP INDUSTRIES, INC. (CA)
Reincorporated under the laws of Delaware as Topp Industries Corp. 10/07/1959
Topp Industries Corp. merged into United Industries Corp. (DE) 12/31/1959
(See United Industries Corp.)

TOPP INDUSTRIES CORP. (DE)
Merged into United Industrial Corp. (DE) share for share 12/31/1959
(See United Industrial Corp.)

TOPPER CORP (DE)
Adjudicated bankrupt 05/07/1973
Stockholders' equity unlikely

TOPPER GOLD CORP (BC)
Recapitalized as Consolidated Topper Gold Corp. 04/13/2000
Each share Common no par exchanged for (0.1) share Common no par
Consolidated Topper Gold Corp. name changed to Topper Resources Inc. (BC) 02/06/2002 which reincorporated in Alberta 05/03/2006 which name changed to Century Energy Ltd. (AB) 05/19/2006 which reincorporated in British Columbia 10/20/2016

TOPPER RES INC (AB)
Reincorporated 05/03/2006
Place of incorporation changed from (BC) to (AB) 05/03/2006
Name changed to Century Energy Ltd. (AB) 05/19/2006
Century Energy Ltd. (AB) reincorporated in British Columbia 10/20/2016

TOPPERS BRICK OVEN PIZZA INC (DE)
Name changed to Famous Food Group, Inc. 04/16/2003
Famous Food Group, Inc. recapitalized as Kootenai Corp. 07/05/2006 which reorganized as BizAuctions, Inc. 08/17/2006 which name changed to CannaGrow Holdings, Inc. 11/05/2014

TOPPS & TROWSERS (CA)
Common 10¢ par split (2) for (1) by issuance of (1) additional share 5/5/72
Stock Dividends - 50% 8/1/75; 50% 3/25/77
Name changed to Inmar Corp. 6/8/84
Inmar Corp. name changed to ACA Joe 7/16/85 which name changed to ACA Joe, Inc. 11/26/86
(See ACA Joe, Inc.)

TOPPS CHEWING GUM INC (NY)
Common 10¢ par split (2) for (1) by issuance of (1) additional share 4/29/83
Merged into Forstmann Little & Co. 2/22/84
Each share Common 10¢ par exchanged for $26.25 cash

TOPPS INC (DE)
Common 1¢ par split (3) for (2) by issuance of (0.5) additional share 03/31/1989
Common 1¢ par split (3) for (2) by issuance of (0.5) additional share 11/15/1989
Common 1¢ par split (3) for (2) by issuance of (0.5) additional share 08/01/1990
Merged into Tornante-MDP Joe Holding LLC 10/12/2007
Each share Common 1¢ par exchanged for $9.75 cash

TOPRO INC (CO)
Name changed to Tava Technologies, Inc. 1/30/98
(See Tava Technologies, Inc.)

TOPS APPLIANCE CITY INC (NJ)
Chapter 11 bankruptcy proceedings converted to Chapter 7 on 4/17/2000
No stockholders' equity

TOPS MKTS INC (DE)
Merged into RFS Buffalo Holding Corp. 09/17/1987
Each share Common 1¢ par exchanged for $33.50 cash

TOPSAIL ST BK (HAMPSTEAD, NC)
Merged into Anchor Financial Corp. 12/31/1993
Each share Common $3.50 par exchanged for (0.482) share Common $6 par
Anchor Financial Corp. merged into South Financial Group, Inc. 06/07/2000 which merged into Toronto-Dominion Bank (Toronto, ON) 09/30/2010

TOPSYS INTL INC (DE)
Stock Dividends - 10% 1/14/63; 10% 1/16/64; 50% 10/18/67; 100% 11/29/68
Name changed to TFC International, Inc. 1/26/88
(See TFC International, Inc.)

TOR AMERICAN OIL LTD. (QC)
Acquired by Tri-Tor Oils Ltd. 00/00/1953
Each share Capital Stock $1 par exchanged for (0.25) free and (1) escrowed share new Common $1 par
Tri-Tor Oils Ltd. merged into Bonnyville Oil & Refining Corp. 05/05/1955 which recapitalized as Consolidated Bonnyville Ltd. 03/02/1963 which was acquired by Cold Lake Pipe Line Co. Ltd. 02/26/1964 which recapitalized as Worldwide Energy Co. Ltd. (AB) 07/01/1967 which reincorporated in Delaware as Weco Development Corp. 07/17/1972 which name changed to Worldwide Energy Corp. 06/14/1977 which merged into Triton Energy Corp. (TX) 11/18/1986 which reincorporated in Delaware 05/12/1995 which merged into Triton Energy Ltd. 03/25/1996
(See Triton Energy Ltd.)

TOR CAL RES LTD (AB)
Name changed to Lidco Industries Inc. 2/23/88
(See Lidco Industries Inc.)

TOR EDUCATION INC (DE)
Completely liquidated 03/29/1967
Each share Capital Stock 10¢ par exchanged for first and final distribution of (0.151964) share Famous Artists Schools, Inc. Common 2¢ par
Famous Artists Schools, Inc. name changed to FAS International, Inc. 05/13/1969 which name changed to Bowline Corp. 04/20/1978
(See Bowline Corp.)

TOR INTL INC (CO)
Declared defunct and inoperative for failure to file reports and pay taxes 10/19/74

TORA TECHNOLOGIES INC (NV)
Common $0.001 par split (7.5) for (1) by issuance of (6.5) additional shares payable 02/16/2006 to holders of record 02/14/2006
Ex date - 02/17/2006
Name changed to Makeup.com, Ltd. 11/22/2006
Makeup.com, Ltd. name changed to LC Luxuries Ltd. 04/01/2010 which name changed to General Cannabis, Inc. 11/19/2010 which name changed to SearchCore, Inc. 01/06/2012 which name changed to Wisdom Homes of America, Inc. 03/05/2015

TORBAY HLDGS INC (DE)
Name changed to ICC Worldwide, Inc. 01/04/2008
(See ICC Worldwide, Inc.)

TORBRIT SILVER MINES LTD (BC)
Acquired by New York Oils Ltd. (B.C.) 8/31/70
Each share Capital Stock $1 par exchanged for (0.75) share Capital Stock no par
New York Oils Ltd. (BC) reincorporated in Alberta 7/19/82 which was acquired by Sceptre Resources Ltd. 3/14/89 which merged into Canadian Natural Resources Ltd. 8/15/96

TORBROOK IRON ORE MINES LTD. (NS)
Completely liquidated 12/30/63
Each share Capital Stock 10¢ par exchanged for first and final distribution $0.0015423 cash

TORC FINL CORP (AB)
Name changed to Vanguard Aviation Corp. 04/15/1999
(See Vanguard Aviation Corp.)

TORCAN EXPLS LTD (QC)
Charter cancelled 08/17/1985

TORCH ENERGY RTY TR (DE)
Liquidation completed 12/24/2014
No Unitholders' equity

TORCH EXECUTIVE SVCS LTD (NV)
Name changed to Harbin Electric, Inc. 01/24/2005
(See Harbin Electric, Inc.)

TORCH OFFSHORE INC (DE)
Issue Information - 5,000,000 shares COM offered at $16 per share on 06/06/2001
Plan of reorganization under Chapter 11 Federal Bankruptcy Code effective 7/14/2006
No stockholders' equity

TORCH RIV RES LTD (AB)
Each share old Common no par exchanged for (0.5) share new Common no par 11/28/2011
Name changed to Saint Jean Carbon Inc. 11/04/2013

TORCH RUBR INC (NY)
Adjudicated bankrupt 11/08/1973
Stockholders' equity unlikely

TORCHMAIL COMMUNICATIONS INC (DE)
Each share old Common $0.001 par exchanged for (5) shares new Common $0.001 par 03/18/2002
Name changed to Ohana Enterprises, Inc. 12/11/2002
Ohana Enterprises, Inc. recapitalized as Vinoble, Inc. 11/19/2004 which name changed to Matrixx Resource Holdings, Inc. 07/14/2006
(See Matrixx Resource Holdings, Inc.)

TORCHMARK CAP LLC (AL)
Guaranteed Monthly Income Preferred Securities Ser. A called for redemption at $25 plus $0.19125 accrued dividend on 11/30/2001

TORCHMARK CAP TR I (DE)
7.75% Guaranteed Trust Preferred Securities called for redemption at $25 plus $0.0054 accrued dividends on 11/02/2006

TORCHMARK CAP TR II (DE)
7.75% Guaranteed Trust Preferred Securities called for redemption at $25 plus $0.0054 accrued dividends on 11/02/2006

TORCHMARK CAP TR III (DE)
7.100% Trust Preferred Securities called for redemption at $25 plus $0.261319 accrued dividends on 10/24/2012

TORCHMARK CORP (DE)
Adjustable Rate Preferred Ser. A $1 par called for redemption 3/31/94
(Additional Information in Active)

TOREADOR RES CORP (DE)
Common Stock Purchase Rights declared for Common stockholders of record 04/13/1995 were redeemed at $0.01 per right 06/15/2000 for holders of record 06/05/2000
Merged into ZaZa Energy Corp. 02/22/2012
Each share Common 15-5/8¢ exchanged for (1) share Common 1¢ par

TOREADOR RTY CORP (DE)
Common 62-1/2¢ par changed to 15-5/8¢ par and (3) additional shares issued 04/06/1981
Name changed to Toreador Resources Corp. 06/05/2000
Toreador Resources Corp. merged into ZaZa Energy Corp. 02/22/2012

TORENE GOLD EXPL LTD (ON)
Name changed to AquaGold Resources Inc. (ONT) 04/05/1988
AquaGold Resources Inc. (ONT) reincorporated in Canada 01/19/1989 which name changed to Atlantic Industrial Minerals Inc. 11/19/1992

TOREX MINERALS LTD (BC)
Recapitalized as Corniche Resources Ltd. 1/27/87
Each share Common no par exchanged for (0.25) share Common no par
Corniche Resources Ltd. recapitalized as International Avalon Aircraft Inc. 4/18/88
(See International Avalon Aircraft Inc.)

TOREX RES INC (CANADA)
Merged into Summit Resources Ltd. 9/5/2000
Each share Common no par exchanged for $1.25 cash

TORGINOL INDS INC (NV)
Charter revoked for failure to file reports and pay fees 03/01/1981

TORHSEN ENERGY CORP (BC)
Name changed to Niagara Capital Corp. 2/23/87
(See Niagara Capital Corp.)

TORIC MINES CO. LTD.
Liquidation completed in 1949

TORIK CORP (NV)
Name changed to SmartGate, Inc. 10/15/1999
SmartGate, Inc. name changed to Invisa, Inc. 02/25/2002 which name changed to Uniroyal Global Engineered Products, Inc. 07/16/2015

TORIN CORP (CT)
Stock Dividend - 10% 4/28/1970
Merged into Clevepak Corp. 07/17/1982
Each share Common no par exchanged for $25 cash

TORINO OIL & GAS LTD (AB)
Placed in receivership 10/00/2002
Stockholders' equity unlikely

TORINO VENTURES INC (BC)
Each share old Common no par

TOR-TOR   FINANCIAL INFORMATION, INC.

exchanged for (0.2) share new Common no par 09/01/2015
Name changed to Torino Power Solutions Inc. 11/12/2015

TORK INC (DE)
Name changed 07/17/1975
Name changed from Tork Time Controls, Inc. to Tork Inc. 07/17/1975
Acquired by NSi Industries LLC 09/15/2006
Each share Common 1¢ par exchanged for $31.1021 cash consisting of $27.7562 merger consideration and $3.3459 initial distribution from escrow
Note: Each share Common 1¢ par received second distribution of $4.386256 cash from escrow 05/25/2007
Each share Common 1¢ par received third and final distribution of $3.0472294 cash from escrow 12/06/2007

TORM A S (DENMARK)
Each old Sponsored ADR for Common exchanged for (0.1) new Sponsored ADR for Common 11/27/2012
ADR basis changed from (1:1) to (1:10) 11/27/2012
ADR agreement terminated 07/19/2013
Each new Sponsored ADR for Common exchanged for $3.2458 cash

TORMEX MNG DEVELOPERS LTD (ON)
Merged into Lacana Mining Corp. 09/29/1975
Each share Capital Stock no par exchanged for (0.5) share Common no par
Lacana Mining Corp. merged into Corona Corp. 07/01/1988 which recapitalized as International Corona Corp. 06/11/1991 which merged into Homestake Mining Co. 08/17/1992
(See Homestake Mining Co.)

TORMONT MINES LTD (ON)
Charter cancelled 03/14/1978

TORNADO GOLD INTL CORP (NV)
Common $0.001 par split (6.82) for (1) by issuance of (5.82) additional shares payable 08/31/2004 to holders of record 08/30/2004
Ex date - 09/01/2004
State of incorporation changed from (NV) to (DE) 02/28/2007
SEC revoked common stock registration 02/24/2012

TORNADO RES LTD (BC)
Completely liquidated 08/03/2001
Each share Common no par received first and final distribution of $0.0725 cash

TORNADO TECHNOLOGIES INC (AB)
Merged into Empire Industries Ltd. (Old) 12/03/2007
Each share Common no par exchanged for (2.09) shares Common no par
Empire Industries Ltd. (Old) reorganized as Empire Industries Ltd. (New) 06/30/2016

TORNIER N V (NETHERLANDS)
Name changed to Wright Medical Group N.V. 10/02/2015

TORO CO (MN)
Common $1 par split (2) for (1) by issuance of (1) additional share 12/11/1978
Reincorporated under the laws of Delaware 12/15/1983

TORO ENERGY INC (AB)
Recapitalized as Sentra Resources Corp. 9/18/2003
Each share Common no par

exchanged for (0.25) share Class A Common no par
Sentra Resources Corp. acquired by Blue Mountain Energy Ltd. 9/30/2004
(See Blue Mountain Energy Ltd.)

TORO ENTERPRISES, INC. (OH)
Name changed to Torent Enterprises Inc. 8/31/81

TORO MANUFACTURING CORP. (MN)
Common $1 par split (2) for (1) by issuance of (1) additional share 8/17/55
Common $1 par split (2) for (1) by issuance of (1) additional share 6/9/67
Stock Dividends - 100% 3/19/65; 100% 7/20/71
Name changed to Toro Co. (MN) 10/29/71
Toro Co. (MN) reincorporated in Delaware 12/15/83

TORO MANUFACTURING CORP. OF MINNESOTA (DE)
Reincorporated under the laws of Minnesota 00/00/1936
Toro Manufacturing Corp. of Minnesota (MN) name changed to Toro Manufacturing Corp. 07/28/1955 which name changed to Toro Co. (MN) 10/29/1971 which reincorporated in Delaware 12/15/1983

TORO MANUFACTURING CORP. OF MINNESOTA (MN)
Common no par changed to $1 par 00/00/1946
Name changed to Toro Manufacturing Corp. 07/28/1955
Toro Manufacturing Corp. name changed to Toro Co. (MN) 10/29/1971 which reincorporated in Delaware 12/15/1983

TORO OIL & GAS LTD (AB)
Each share old Common no par exchanged for (0.04) share new Common no par 12/15/2014
Acquired by Steelhead Petroleum Ltd. 02/02/2017
Each share new Common no par exchanged for $0.37 cash
Note: Unexchanged certificates will be cancelled and become without value 02/02/2022

TORO RES CORP (BC)
Recapitalized as Big Wind Capital Inc. 06/17/2015
Each share Common no par exchanged for (0.2) share Common no par
Big Wind Capital Inc. name changed to Hilltop Cybersecurity Inc. 02/26/2018

TORO RES LTD (BC)
Name changed to British Medical Services Ltd. 05/02/1988
British Medical Services Ltd. recapitalized as BMD Enterprises Ltd. 10/05/1990
(See BMD Enterprises Ltd.)

TORO VENTURES INC (NV)
Recapitalized as Baying Ecological Holding Group Inc. 02/07/2014
Each share Common $0.001 par exchanged for (0.01) share Common $0.001 par

TORODE RLTY LTD (AB)
Name changed to CMQ Resources Inc. 01/29/2004
(See CMQ Resources Inc.)

TOROMONT INDUSTRIAL HOLDINGS LTD. (CANADA)
Name changed to Toromont Industries Ltd. 05/21/1974

TORONADO DEV CORP (BC)
Recapitalized as Cyclone Developments Ltd. 04/26/1977
Each share Capital Stock no par

exchanged for (0.25) share Capital Stock no par
Cyclone Developments Ltd. merged into Acheron Resources Ltd. 10/01/1982 which recapitalized as Abaddon Resources Inc. 09/12/1994 which recapitalized as Consolidated Abaddon Resources Inc. 01/31/2001 which name changed to Aben Resources Ltd. 01/13/2011

TORONADO MINES LTD (QC)
Charter annulled for failure to file annual reports 11/07/1981

TORONTO & LONDON INVT LTD (CANADA)
Acquired by Slater, Walker of Canada Ltd. 10/6/75
Details not available

TORONTO BREWING & MALTING CO., LTD.
Name changed to Canada Bud Breweries Ltd. 00/00/1928
Canada Bud Breweries merged into Canadian Breweries Ltd. 00/00/1943 which name changed to Carling O'Keefe Ltd. 11/09/1997
(See Carling O'Keefe Ltd.)

TORONTO BRICK CO. LTD. (ON)
Recapitalized in 1952
Each share Preference $100 par and all accrued dividends exchanged for (20) shares 1st Preference $10 par, (7) shares 2nd Preference $1 par, (6) shares Common no par and $1.50 in cash
Each share Common $100 par exchanged for (7) shares 2nd Preference $1 par and (20) shares Common no par
Recapitalized 6/13/55
Common no par exchanged (3) for (1)
Name changed to United Ceramics Ltd. 6/30/65

TORONTO CARPET MANUFACTURING CO. LTD. (ON)
Each share 8% Preferred $100 par exchanged for (1) share 6% Preferred $100 par in 1937
Each share Common $100 par exchanged for (1) share new Common $100 par in 1937
Name changed to Barrymore Carpet, Inc. 9/1/76

TORONTO DOMINION BK (TORONTO, ON)
Class A 1st Preferred Ser. C $25 par called for redemption 06/01/1986
$2.375 Class A 1st Preferred $25 par called for redemption 03/02/1988
$1.835 Class A 1st Preferred $25 par called for redemption 03/02/1992
Adjustable Rate 1st Preferred Class A Ser. F no par called for redemption 10/31/1994
Adjustable Rate 1st Preferred Class A Ser. E $25 par called for redemption 10/12/1995
Variable Rate 1st Preferred Class A Ser. D $25 par called for redemption 10/31/1995
Class A 1st Preferred Ser. K called for redemption at $25 on 02/03/2003
Class A 1st Preferred Ser. L called for redemption at $25 on 02/03/2003
Adjustable Dividend 1st Preferred Class A Ser. G called for redemption at $25 plus $0.003699 accrued dividend on 05/01/2003
Class A 1st Preferred Ser. H no par called for redemption at $25 plus $0.014589 accrued dividend on 05/03/2004
1st Preferred Class A Ser. J no par called for redemption at $25.80 plus $0.31875 accrued dividends on 10/31/2005
4.6% Class A 1st Preferred Ser. N no par called for redemption at $25 plus $0.2875 accrued dividends on 10/31/2011
4.7% Class A 1st Preferred Ser. M no

par called for redemption at $25 plus $0.29375 accrued dividends on 10/31/2011
Non-Cum. 5-Year Rate Reset Class A Preferred Ser. AA no par called for redemption at $25 on 01/31/2014
Non-Cum. 5-Year Rate Reset Class A Preferred Ser. AC no par called for redemption at $25 on 01/31/2014
Non-Cum. 5-Year Rate Reset Class A Preferred Ser. AE no par called for redemption at $25 on 04/30/2014
Non-Cum. 5-Year Rate Reset Class A Preferred Ser. AG no par called for redemption at $25 on 04/30/2014
Non-Cum. 5-Year Rate Reset Class A Preferred Ser. AI no par called for redemption at $25 on 07/31/2014
Non-Cum. 5-Year Rate Reset Class A Preferred Ser. AK no par called for redemption at $25 on 07/31/2014
Class A 1st Preferred Ser. O no par called for redemption at $25 on 10/31/2014
Non-Cum. Class A 1st Preferred Ser. P no par called for redemption at $25.50 plus $0.107877 accrued dividends on 03/02/2015
Non-Cum. Class A 1st Preferred Ser. Q no par called for redemption at $25.50 plus $0.115068 accrued dividends on 03/02/2015
Non-Cum. Class A 1st Preferred Ser. R no par called for redemption at $25 plus $0.003836 accrued dividends on 05/01/2015
Non-Cum. Class A 1st Preferred Ser. S no par called for redemption at $25 on 07/31/2018
Non-Cum. Class A 1st Preferred Ser. T no par called for redemption at $25 on 07/31/2018
(Additional Information in Active)

TORONTO ELEVATORS, LTD. (ON)
Common no par exchanged (4) for (1) in 1947
Common no par split (3) for (1) by issuance of (2) additional shares 6/19/59
Merged into Maple Leaf Mills Ltd. share for share 3/31/61
(See Maple Leaf Mills Ltd.)

TORONTO HARKER MINES LTD. (ON)
Charter cancelled in April 1958

TORONTO IRON WKS LTD (ON)
Each share Class A no par or old Common no par exchanged for (2) shares new Common no par 07/05/1966
Name changed to Toronto Iron Works Holdings Ltd. 05/15/1973
Toronto Iron Works Holdings Ltd. name changed to TIW Industries Ltd. 11/01/1976 which merged into TIW Industries Ltd.-Les Industries TIW Ltee. 12/31/1977
(See TIW Industries Ltd.-Les Industries TIW Ltee.)

TORONTO IRON WORKS HOLDINGS LTD. (ON)
Name changed to TIW Industries Ltd. 11/01/1976
TIW Industries Ltd. merged into TIW Industries Ltd.-Les Industries TIW Ltee. 12/31/1977
(See TIW Industries Ltd.-Les Industries TIW Ltee.)

TORONTO KIRKLAND MINES LTD.
Name changed to Toronto Harker Mines Ltd. in 1928
Toronto Harker Mines Ltd. charter cancelled in April 1928

TORONTO MAPLE LEAF HOCKEY CLUB LTD.
Acquired by Maple Leaf Gardens Ltd. 00/00/1931
Details not available

TORONTO MORTGAGE CO. (ON)
Assets acquired by Canada

Permanent Mortgage Corp. and completely liquidated 6/22/60
(See Canada Trustco Mortgage Co.)

TORONTO POWER CO. LTD.
Acquired by Hydro-Electric Power System of Ontario 00/00/1929
Details not available

TORONTO STAR LTD (ON)
6% 1st Part. Preference $50 par called for redemption 12/31/1966
6% 1st Conv. Preference $50 par called for redemption 12/31/1966
Common no par, Class B no par, Class C no par and Class D no par split (3) for (1) by issuance of (2) additional shares respectively 03/12/1973
Common no par reclassified as Conv. Class E no par 01/17/1974
Name changed to Torstar Corp. 01/24/1977

TORONTO SUN PUBG CORP (ON)
Common no par split (3) for (1) by issuance of (2) additional shares 05/29/1981
Common no par split (2) for (1) by issuance of (1) additional share 06/11/1987
Name changed to Sun Media Corp. 10/04/1996
(See Sun Media Corp.)

TORPEDO SPORTS USA INC (NV)
Name changed to Interactive Games, Inc. 03/09/2005
Interactive Games, Inc. name changed to China Nuvo Solar Energy, Inc. 08/13/2007 which name changed to SurgLine International, Inc. 01/27/2012

TORQ MEDIA CORP (BC)
Recapitalized as Quizam Media Corp. 05/18/2005
Each share Common no par exchanged for (0.25) share Common no par

TORQUAY OIL CORP (AB)
Acquired by CanEra Energy Corp. 12/21/2012
Each share Class A no par exchanged for $0.16 cash
Each share Class B no par exchanged for $1.60 cash
Note: Unexchanged certificates were cancelled and became without value 12/20/2017

TORQUE CTLS CORP (NY)
Completely liquidated 03/18/1969
Each share Common 1¢ par exchanged for first and final distribution of (1) share Triangle Corp. Common no par
Triangle Corp. name changed to Audits & Surveys Worldwide Inc. 03/28/1995
(See Audits & Surveys Worldwide Inc.)

TORQUE ENERGY INC (BC)
Merged into Dundee Energy Ltd. 08/03/2011
Each share Common no par exchanged for $0.50 cash
Note: Unexchanged certificates were cancelled and became without value 08/03/2017

TORQUE ENGR CORP (DE)
SEC revoked common stock registration 09/29/2009

TORQUE INDS INC (AB)
Name changed to BCB Holdings Inc. (AB) 03/31/1994
BCB Holdings Inc. (AB) reincorporated in Ontario 10/01/1996 which recapitalized as BCB Voice Systems Inc. 08/17/1998 which name changed to VoiceIQ Inc. (ON) 10/04/2000 which reorganized in Alberta as Yoho Resources Inc. (Old) 12/23/2004 which reorganized as Yoho Resources Inc. (New) 03/21/2014

(See Yoho Resources Inc. (New))

TORR CDA INC (CANADA)
Name changed to ProSep Inc. 05/23/2008

TORR LABS INC (CA)
Merged into Scanray Corp. 06/01/1984
Each share Common 4¢ par exchanged for $3 cash

TORRENCE EQUITY FD INC (DE)
Recapitalized as Standard & Poor's/Intercapital Dynamics Fund, Inc. 03/30/1972
Each share Capital Stock $1 par exchanged for (10) shares Capital Stock 10¢ par
Standard & Poor's/Intercapital Dynamics Fund, Inc. acquired by Tudor Hedge Fund 09/30/1975 which name changed to Tudor Fund 06/18/1980 which name changed to WPG Tudor Fund 12/29/1989
(See WPG Tudor Fund)

TORRENT CAP CORP (AB)
Delisted from Alberta Stock Exchange 09/23/1999

TORRENT ENERGY CORP (CO)
Recapitalized as 1pm Industries, Inc. 04/06/2015
Each share Common $0.0001 par exchanged for (0.001) share Common $0.0001 par

TORRENT RES LTD (BC)
Merged into Galveston Resources Ltd. 07/29/1986
Each share Common no par exchanged for (0.57142857) share Common no par
Galveston Resources Ltd. merged into Corona Corp. 07/01/1988 which recapitalized as International Corona Corp. 06/11/1991
(See International Corona Corp.)

TORRENTIAL ENERGY LTD (AB)
Recapitalized as Base Oil & Gas Ltd. 10/08/2009
Each share Common no par exchanged for (0.33333333) share Common no par
Base Oil & Gas Ltd. name changed to Marquee Petroleum Ltd. 09/20/2011 which merged into SkyWest Energy Corp. 12/09/2011 which recapitalized as Marquee Energy Ltd. (Old) 12/09/2011 which merged into Marquee Energy Ltd. (New) 12/08/2016

TORREON HLDGS INC (UT)
Recapitalized as Natvan Inc. 05/22/2001
Each share Common $0.001 par exchanged for (0.1) share Common $0.001 par
Natvan Inc. name changed to Prime Multimedia, Inc. 07/02/2003 which recapitalized as Eagle Rock Enterprises Inc. 07/01/2008 which name changed to Worldwide Food Services, Inc. 08/19/2009 which name changed to Global Holdings, Inc. 10/29/2013 which name changed to Element Global, Inc. 08/06/2015

TORREY PINES BANK (SOLANO BEACH, CA)
Under plan of reorganization each share Common $9 par automatically became (1) share Torrey Pines Group Common no par 01/01/1984
Torrey Pines Group acquired by Wells Fargo & Co. (Old) 04/01/1990 which merged into Wells Fargo & Co. (New) 11/02/1998

TORREY PINES GROUP (CA)
Acquired by Wells Fargo & Co. (Old) 04/01/1990
Each share Common no par exchanged for (0.44) share Common $5 par

Wells Fargo & Co. (Old) merged into Wells Fargo & Co. (New) 11/02/1998

TORREY PINES NEV INC (NV)
Merged into Netbet, Inc. 01/14/1998
Each share Common $0.001 par exchanged for (0.0666666) share Common $0.001 par
Netbet, Inc. name changed to Telemais Telecommunications, Inc. 05/17/2002 which recapitalized as WebSky, Inc. 01/20/2004

TORREY PINES PRODUCTIONS INC (NV)
Name changed to Mirage Computers Inc. 04/15/1999
Mirage Computers Inc. name changed to Mega Micro Technologies Group 04/14/2000
(See Mega Micro Technologies Group)

TORREYPINES THERAPEUTICS INC (DE)
Recapitalized as Raptor Pharmaceutical Corp. 09/29/2009
Each share Common $0.001 par exchanged for (0.05882353) share Common $0.001 par
(See Raptor Pharmaceutical Corp.)

TORREZ RES LTD (BC)
Name changed to WFI Industries Ltd. (BC) 05/11/1990
WFI Industries Ltd. (BC) reincorporated in Ontario 08/28/1997 which reincorporated in Canada 09/13/2004 which name changed to WaterFurnace Renewable Energy, Inc. 06/16/2008
(See WaterFurnace Renewable Energy, Inc.)

TORRIDON PLC (UNITED KINGDOM)
Placed in liquidation 07/30/2001
GDR holders' equity unlikely

TORRINGTON CO (ME)
Each share Capital Stock $25 par exchanged for (2) shares Capital Stock $12.50 par which was then changed to no par 00/00/1928
Common no par changed to $2.50 par and (1) additional share issued 10/13/1965
Merged into Ingersoll-Rand Co. (NJ) 01/02/1969
Each share Common $2.50 par exchanged for (1) share $2.35 Conv. Preference no par and (0.4) share Common $2 par
Ingersoll-Rand Co. (NJ) reorganized in Bermuda as Ingersoll-Rand Co. Ltd. 12/31/2001 which reincorporated in Ireland as Ingersoll-Rand PLC 07/01/2009

TORRINGTON ELECTRIC LIGHT CO.
Merged into Connecticut Power Co. 00/00/1947
Each share Common exchanged for $50 principal amount of bonds and (1.1) shares Common $25 par
Connecticut Power Co. merged into Hartford Electric Light Co. 01/01/1958
(See Hartford Electric Light Co.)

TORRINGTON MFG CO (CT)
Each share Common $25 par exchanged for (4) shares Common $6.25 par 00/00/1947
Common $6.25 par changed to no par and (1) additional share issued 03/29/1963
Common no par split (2) for (1) by issuance of (1) additional share 03/01/1965
Stock Dividends - 10% 03/27/1964; 10% 03/29/1966; 10% 03/26/1968; 10% 02/25/1969
Name changed to Torin Corp. 04/22/1979
(See Torin Corp.)

TORRINGTON RES LTD (AB)
Acquired by Magin Energy Inc. (New) 07/18/1998

Each share Common no par exchanged for (0.444) share Common no par and (0.5) Common Stock Purchase Warrant expiring 09/01/2000
Magin Energy Inc. (New) acquired by NCE Petrofund 07/03/2001 which name changed to Petrofund Energy Trust 11/01/2003 which merged into Penn West Energy Trust 07/04/2006 which reorganized as Penn West Petroleum Ltd. (New) 01/03/2011 which name changed to Obsidian Energy Ltd. 06/29/2017

TORSTAR CORP (ON)
$2.68 1st Preference 1981 Ser. $25 par called for redemption 07/02/1986
$1.70 Conv. 1st Preference 3rd Ser. $25 par called for redemption 04/05/1988
(Additional Information in Active)

TORTOISE CAP RES CORP (MD)
Issue Information - 5,740,000 shares COM offered at $15 per share on 02/01/2007
Name changed to CorEnergy Infrastructure Trust, Inc. 12/03/2012

TORTOISE ENERGY CAP CORP (MD)
Money Market Preferred Ser. II $0.001 par called for redemption at $25,000 plus $6 accrued dividends on 12/17/2009
Money Market Preferred Ser. I $0.001 par called for redemption at $25,000 plus $9.16 accrued dividends on 12/29/2009
Mandatory Redeemable Preferred Ser. 2016 $0.001 par called for redemption at $10.10 plus $0.06689 accrued dividends on 03/14/2011
5% Mandatory Redeemable Preferred Ser. B $0.001 par called for redemption at $10.10 plus $0.063890 accrued dividends on 05/17/2012
Merged into Tortoise Energy Infrastructure Corp. 06/23/2014
Each share 3.95% Mandatory Reedemable Preferred Ser. C $0.001 par exchanged for (1) share 3.95% Mandatory Reedemable Preferred Ser. C $0.001 par
Each share Common $0.001 par exchanged for (0.749479) share Common $0.001 par

TORTOISE ENERGY INFRASTRUCTURE CORP (MD)
Money Market Preferred Ser. IV $0.001 par called for redemption at $25,000 on 07/23/2008
Money Market Preferred Ser. III $0.001 par called for redemption at $25,000 on 07/24/2008
Money Market Preferred Ser. I $0.001 par called for redemption at $25,000 on 12/21/2009
Money Market Preferred Ser. II $0.001 par called for redemption at $25,000 on 12/21/2009
Mandatory Redeemable Preferred $0.001 par called for redemption at $10 plus $0.062501 accrued dividends on 01/07/2013
3.95% Mandatory Redeemable Preferred $0.001 par called for redemption at $10 plus $0.007681 accrued dividends on 01/08/2016
4.375% Mandatory Redeemable Preferred Ser. B $0.001 par called for redemption at $10 plus $0.015799 accrued dividends on 03/14/2016
(Additional Information in Active)

TORTOISE NORTH AMERN ENERGY CORP (MD)
Money Market Preferred Ser. I $0.001 par called for redemption at $25,000 on 12/26/2008
Merged into Tortoise Energy Infrastructure Corp. 06/23/2014
Each share Common $0.001 par

exchanged for (0.653958) share Common $0.001 par

TORTUGA MEXICAN IMPORTS INC (NV)
Common $0.001 par split (9) for (1) by issuance of (8) additional shares payable 04/05/2007 to holders of record 03/21/2007 Ex date - 04/09/2007
Name changed to Jetblack Corp. 04/05/2010

TORVEC INC (NY)
Name changed to CurAegis Technologies, Inc. 06/27/2016

TORWEST RES 1962 LTD (BC)
Recapitalized 01/10/1962
Recapitalized from Torwest Resources Ltd. to Torwest Resources (1962) Ltd. 01/10/1962
Each share Capital Stock 50¢ par exchanged for (0.2) share Capital Stock no par
Merged into Highmont Mining Corp. 07/04/1977
Each share Capital Stock no par exchanged for (0.125) share Common no par
Highmont Mining Corp. merged into Teck Corp. 09/28/1979 which name changed to Teck Cominco Ltd. 09/12/2001 which name changed to Teck Resources Ltd. 04/27/2009

TOSCA MNG CORP (BC)
Each share old Common no par exchanged for (0.25) share new Common no par 06/03/2013
Recapitalized as Tosca Resources Corp. 10/09/2014
Each share Common no par exchanged for (0.25) share Common no par
Tosca Resources Corp. name changed to Hatch Interactive Technologies Corp. 09/08/2015 which name changed to Fandom Sports Media Corp. 08/03/2016

TOSCA RES CORP (BC)
Name changed to Hatch Interactive Technologies Corp. 09/08/2015
Hatch Interactive Technologies Corp. name changed to Fandom Sports Media Corp. 08/03/2016

TOSCANA RES LTD (BC)
Recapitalized as TNR Resources Ltd. 04/15/1998
Each share Common no par exchanged for (0.2) share Common no par
TNR Resources Ltd. recapitalized as TNR Gold Corp. (Old) 06/25/2003 which reorganized as TNR Gold Corp. (New) 05/17/2011

TOSCANY IMPORTS LTD (NY)
Name changed to S.H.S. Funds, Inc. 04/05/1978
(See S.H.S. Funds, Inc.)

TOSCO, INC. (OK)
Charter cancelled for failure to pay taxes 05/01/1968

TOSCO CORP (NV)
$2.375 Conv. Preferred Ser. E $1 par called for redemption 09/10/1990
$4.375 Conv. Preferred Ser. F $1 par called for redemption 09/26/1994
Each share Common 15¢ par exchanged for (0.2) share Common 75¢ par 07/31/1989
Common 75¢ par split (3) for (1) by issuance of (2) additional shares payable 02/25/1997 to holders of record 02/13/1997 Ex date - 02/26/1997
Merged into Phillips Petroleum Co. 09/14/2001
Each share new Common 75¢ par exchanged for (0.8) share Common $1.25 par
Phillips Petroleum Co. name changed to ConocoPhillips 08/30/2002

TOSTEL CORP (CO)
Merged into Polus, Inc. 06/22/1998
Each share Common $0.025 par exchanged for (3) shares Common no par
(See Polus, Inc.)

TOT ENERGY INC (DE)
Name changed to Net Element, Inc. (Old) 11/26/2010
Net Element, Inc. (Old) merged into Net Element International, Inc. 10/03/2012 which name changed to Net Element, Inc. (New) 12/09/2013

TOTAL AMERN HLDG INC
Flex Money Market Preferred Ser. A called for redemption at $100,000 on 11/23/2004
Flex Money Market Preferred Ser. B called for redemption at $100,000 on 11/30/2004
Flex Money Market Preferred Ser. C called for redemption at $100,000 on 12/14/2004

TOTAL ASSETS PROTN INC (TX)
Charter forfeited for failure to pay taxes 2/2/93

TOTAL ASSETS PROTN LTD (AUSTRALIA)
ADR agreement terminated 04/02/1993
No stockholders' equity

TOTAL CDA OIL & GAS LTD (CANADA)
Name changed to Rigel Energy Corp. 06/09/1993
Rigel Energy Corp. merged into Talisman Energy Inc. 10/05/1999
(See Talisman Energy Inc.)

TOTAL COMMUNICATIONS NETWORK INC (UT)
Recapitalized as Enercell Corp. 10/20/1988
Each share Common $0.001 par exchanged for (3) shares Common $0.001 par
(See Enercell Corp.)

TOTAL CONTAINMENT INC (PA)
Reincorporated 05/15/1997
Issue Information - 1,644,000 shares COM offered at $9.50 per share on 02/25/1994
State of incorporation changed from (DE) to (PA) 05/15/1997
Company terminated registration of common stock and is no longer public as of 07/05/2001
Details not available

TOTAL CTL PRODS INC (IL)
Issue Information - 2,000,000 shares COM offered at $8 per share on 03/11/1997
Merged into General Electric Co. 2/16/99
Each share Common no par exchanged for $11 cash

TOTAL ED CORP (DE)
Charter cancelled and declared inoperative and void for non-payment of taxes 4/15/72

TOTAL ENERGOLD CORP (CANADA)
Acquired by Total Resources (Canada) Ltd. 03/16/1992
Each share Common no par exchanged for $1.55 cash

TOTAL ENERGY CAP INC
Money Market Preferred Ser. A called for redemption at $1,000,000 on 4/22/2005
Money Market Preferred Ser. B called for redemption at $1,000,000 on 4/29/2005
Money Market Preferred Ser. C called for redemption at $1,000,000 on 5/13/2005

TOTAL ENERGY LEASING CORP (DE)
Merged into Steinberg Subsidiary Corp. 03/27/1980

Each share Common $1 par exchanged for $0.50 cash

TOTAL ENERGY RES FIN INC
Auction Preferred Stock Ser. A called for redemption at $500,000 on 12/28/2004
Auction Preferred Stock Ser. B called for redemption at $500,000 on 2/22/2005

TOTAL ENERGY SVCS LTD (AB)
Merged into Total Energy Services Trust 04/28/2005
Each share Common no par exchanged for (1) Trust Unit no par
Total Energy Services Trust reorganized Total Energy Services Inc. 05/20/2009

TOTAL ENERGY SVCS TR (AB)
Plan of arrangement effective 05/20/2009
Each Trust Unit no par exchanged for (1) share Total Energy Services Inc. Common no par

TOTAL ENTMT RESTAURANT CORP (DE)
Issue Information - 2,100,000 shares COM offered at $9 per share on 07/17/1997
Name changed to Fox & Hound Restaurant Group 5/23/2005
(See Fox & Hound Restaurant Group)

TOTAL ERICKSON RES LTD (CANADA)
Merged into TOTAL Energold Corp. 09/19/1988
Each share Common no par exchanged for (0.357) share Common no par
Each share Legended Common no par exchanged for (0.357) share Common no par
(See TOTAL Energold Corp.)

TOTAL FINA ELF S A (FRANCE)
Name changed 06/14/1999
Name changed 03/22/2000
Name changed from Total S.A. to Total Fina S.A. 06/14/1999
Name changed from Total Fina S.A. to TotalFinaElf S.A. 03/22/2000
Name changed back to Total S.A. 05/07/2003

TOTAL FIRST AID INC (FL)
Name changed to Spearhead Ltd., Inc. and Common 1¢ par changed to $0.001 par 06/29/2004
Spearhead Ltd., Inc. recapitalized as Heritage Action Corp. 01/08/2016 which name changed to Heritage Printing Technology Corp. 06/28/2016 which recapitalized as Comerton Corp. 11/07/2017

TOTAL GLOBAL VENTURES INC (YT)
Recapitalized as JNB Developments Co. Ltd. 10/03/2001
Each share Common no par exchanged for (0.1) share Common no par
JNB Developments Co. Ltd. name changed to Cooper Minerals Inc. (YT) 07/14/2004 which reincorporated in British Columbia as United Coal Holdings Ltd. 05/28/2012

TOTAL HEALTH SYS INC (NY)
Common 1¢ par split (3) for (2) by issuance of (0.5) additional share 7/21/87
Acquired by Equicor Equitable HCA Corp. 2/20/90
Each share Common 1¢ par exchanged for $2.90 cash

TOTAL IDENTITY CORP (FL)
Recapitalized as 247MGI, Inc. 12/21/2006
Each share Common 1¢ par exchanged for (0.01) share Common 1¢ par 247MGI, Inc. name changed to Baron Capital Enterprise, Inc. 12/16/2011

TOTAL IMAGE CAP CORP (AB)
Delisted from Toronto Stock Venture Exchange 10/1/2002

TOTAL INVT CO (UT)
Recapitalized as Applied Industries, Inc. (UT) 04/29/1985
Each share Common no par exchanged for (0.1) share Common no par
Applied Industries, Inc. (UT) recapitalized as Asbestec Industries, Inc. (UT) 01/13/1986 which reorganized in Delaware as PDG Environmental, Inc. 12/17/1990

TOTAL LIFESTYLE CORP (DE)
Each share old Common $0.001 par exchanged for (0.1) share new Common $0.001 par 10/28/1997
Each share new Common $0.001 par exchanged again for (0.01) share new Common $0.001 par 04/28/1998
Name changed to Advanced Technologies Group Inc. 06/08/1998
Advanced Technologies Group Inc. name changed to Cra-Z Products, Inc. 09/11/1998 which recapitalized as Advanced Products Group, Inc. 05/15/1999 which name changed to Cloudtech Sensors, Inc. 06/25/2007

TOTAL LOGISTICS INC (WI)
Merged into Supervalu Inc. 02/07/2005
Each share Common $1 par exchanged for $28.50 cash

TOTAL LUXURY GROUP INC (IN)
Name changed 06/08/2004
Each share old Common $0.001 par exchanged for (0.01) share new Common $0.001 par 01/21/2003
Name changed from Total Entertainment Inc. to Total Luxury Group, Inc. (IN) 06/08/2004
Reincorporated under the laws of Nevada as Total Apparel Group, Inc. 08/27/2008

TOTAL MED ELECTIVE CARE CLINICS INC (NV)
Charter permanently revoked 12/31/2001

TOTAL NUTRACEUTICAL SOLUTIONS (NV)
Recapitalized as Entia Biosciences Inc. 02/15/2012
Each share Common $0.001 par exchanged for (0.1) share Common $0.001 par

TOTAL PETE NORTH AMER LTD (CANADA)
70¢ Non-Cum. Conv. Preferred Ser. A $20 par called for redemption 10/23/78
Common $1 par changed to no par 12/5/79
$2.88 Conv. Preferred no par called for redemption 12/30/93
Merged into Ultramar Diamond Shamrock Corp. 9/25/97
Each share Common no par exchanged for (0.322) share Common no par
Ultramar Diamond Shamrock Corp. merged into Valero Energy Corp. (New) 12/31/2001

TOTAL PHARMACEUTICAL CARE INC (CA)
Merged into Abbey Healthcare Group, Inc. 11/10/1993
Each share Common no par exchanged for (0.1706) share Common $0.001 par and $19 cash
Abbey Healthcare Group, Inc. merged into Apria Healthcare Group Inc. 06/28/1995
(See Apria Healthcare Group Inc.)

TOTAL PRODUCE PLC (IRELAND)
ADR agreement terminated 12/26/2017
No ADR's remain outstanding

TOTAL RENAL CARE HLDGS INC (DE)
Common $0.001 par split (5) for (3) by issuance of (0.66666666) additional share payable 10/20/1997 to holders of record 10/07/1997
Ex date - 10/21/1997
Name changed to DaVita, Inc. 10/09/2000
DaVita Inc. name changed to DaVita HealthCare Partners Inc. 11/02/2012 which name changed back to DaVita Inc. 09/01/2016

TOTAL RENAL CARE INC (DE)
Recapitalized as Total Renal Care Holdings Inc. 12/21/1995
Each share Non-Vtg. Class B $0.001 par exchanged for (0.66666666) share Common $0.001 par
Total Renal Care Holdings, Inc. name changed to DaVita, Inc. 10/09/2000 which name changed to DaVita HealthCare Partners Inc. 11/02/2012 which name changed back to DaVita Inc. 09/01/2016

TOTAL RESH CORP (DE)
Merged into Harris Interactive Inc. 11/01/2001
Each share Common $0.001 par exchanged for (1.2222) shares Common $0.001 par
(See Harris Interactive Inc.)

TOTAL RES INC (NY)
Merged into Northville Industries Corp. 01/28/1977
Each share Common 10¢ par exchanged for $4 cash

TOTAL SUPPLY SYS INC (FL)
Each share Common 10¢ par exchanged for (0.000025) share Common $4,000 par 07/01/1986
Note: In effect holders received $0.17 cash per share and public interest was eliminated

TOTAL-TEL USA COMMUNICATIONS INC (NJ)
Common 5¢ par split (2) for (1) by issuance of (1) additional share payable 07/01/1996 to holders of record 06/15/1996
Common 5¢ par split (2) for (1) by issuance of (1) additional share payable 07/15/1998 to holders of record 06/30/1998
Name changed to Covista Communications, Inc. 10/16/2000

TOTAL TELEVISION CABLE COMMUNICATIONS CORP (NV)
Charter revoked for failure to file reports and pay fees 8/1/81

TOTAL TRANSN COORDINATORS INC (NY)
Dissolved by proclamation 3/24/93

TOTAL WORLD TELECOMMUNICATIONS INC (DE)
Name changed to Whitehall Enterprises Inc. 02/10/1999
(See Whitehall Enterprises Inc.)

TOTALAXCESS COM INC (DE)
Each share old Common 1¢ par exchanged for (0.06666666) share new Common 1¢ par 02/11/2000
Chapter 7 bankruptcy proceedings terminated 05/05/2005
No stockholders' equity

TOTALLY HEMP CRAZY INC (NV)
Name changed to Rocky Mountain High Brands Inc. 10/16/2015

TOTALLY HIP INC (BC)
Recapitalized as Totally Hip Technologies Inc. 12/23/2003
Each share Common no par exchanged for (0.25) share Common no par

TOTALLY HIP SOFTWARE INC (BC)
Reincorporated 03/18/1999
Place of incorporation changed from (AB) to (BC) 03/18/1999
Recapitalized as Totally Hip Inc. 06/05/2002
Each share Common no par exchanged for (0.1) share Common no par
Totally Hip Inc. recapitalized as Totally Hip Technologies Inc. 12/23/2003

TOTALMED ASSOC INC (DE)
Charter cancelled and declared inoperative and void for non-payment of taxes 6/26/85

TOTALMED INC (DE)
Name changed to eNotes Systems, Inc. 06/15/2006
eNotes Systems, Inc. name changed to Veridigm, Inc. 12/07/2006 which recapitalized as Mobile Media Unlimited Holdings Inc. 02/02/2009 which recapitalized as EnableTS, Inc. 04/18/2011

TOTE-A-POKE FRIED CHICKEN, INC. (IN)
Bankruptcy proceedings closed 02/08/1979
No stockholders' equity

TOTEM INDS LTD (BC)
Recapitalized as Totem Capital Corp. 07/08/1988
Each share Common no par exchanged for (0.4) share Common no par
Totem Capital Corp. name changed to Totem Sciences Inc. 12/18/1989 which name changed to Totem Sciences Inc. 04/13/1994 which name changed to Totem Mining Corp. 03/03/1997 which recapitalized as Comcorp Ventures Inc. 07/06/2001 which name changed to Wildcat Silver Corp. 05/17/2006 which name changed to AZ Mining Inc. 06/05/2015 which name changed to Arizona Mining Inc. 10/28/2015
(See Arizona Mining Inc.)

TOTEM MINERALS INC (BC)
Name changed to Abzu Gold Ltd. 12/21/2010

TOTEM MNG CORP (BC)
Name changed 12/28/1989
Name changed 04/13/1994
Name changed 03/03/1997
Name changed from Totem Capital Corp. to Totem Health Sciences Inc. 12/18/1989
Name changed from Totem Health Sciences Inc. to Totem Sciences Inc. 04/13/1994
Name changed from Totem Sciences Inc. to Totem Mining Corp. 03/03/1997
Recapitalized as Comcorp Ventures Inc. 07/06/2001
Each share Common no par exchanged for (0.05917159) share Common no par
Comcorp Ventures Inc. name changed to Wildcat Silver Corp. 05/17/2006 which name changed to AZ Mining Inc. 06/05/2015 which name changed to Arizona Mining Inc. 10/28/2015
(See Arizona Mining Inc.)

TOTEM RES LTD (BC)
Name changed to Paragon Resources Ltd. 06/09/1978
Paragon Resources Ltd. recapitalized as SAMEX Mining Corp. 09/11/1995
(See SAMEX Mining Corp.)

TOTH ALUM CORP (LA)
SEC revoked common stock registration 06/11/2009

TOUCAN GOLD CORP (DE)
Name changed to Authoriszor, Inc. 08/26/1999
Authoriszor, Inc. recapitalized as GreenGro Technologies, Inc. 02/10/2010

TOUCH AMER HLDGS INC (DE)
Plan of reorganization under Chapter 11 Federal Bankruptcy Code effective 10/19/2004
Each share $6.875 Preferred 1¢ par received approximately $30.65 cash payable 03/25/2009 to holders of record 02/23/2009
Common holders may receive an undetermined amount of cash

TOUCH DIALOGUES INC (CO)
Recapitalized as InfoAmerica, Inc. 08/30/1989
Each share Common $0.0001 par exchanged for (0.004) share Common $0.025 par
Infoamerica, Inc. name changed to Las Americas Broadband Inc. 02/16/2001
(See Las Americas Broadband Inc.)

TOUCH INDS INC (GA)
Each share Common $0.0002 par exchanged for (0.5) share Common no par 08/28/1989
Plan of reorganization under Chapter 11 Federal Bankruptcy Code effective 07/01/2002
No stockholders' equity

TOUCH-IT INC (NV)
Each share old Common no par exchanged for (1/6) share new Common no par 01/04/1999
Name changed to Global Cyber Sports.Com Inc. 03/19/1999
Global Cyber Sports.Com Inc. recapitalized as International Group Holdings Inc. 04/04/2003 which was acquired by Energy Producers, Inc. 01/30/2004 which name changed to EGPI Firecreek, Inc. 01/30/2004

TOUCH TONE AMER INC (CA)
SEC revoked common stock registration 07/21/2009

TOUCHDOWN RES INC (BC)
Each share old Common no par exchanged for (0.1) share new Common no par 01/08/2013
Recapitalized as Letho Resources Corp. 03/03/2014
Each share new Common no par exchanged for (0.14285714) share Common no par

TOUCHFON INTL INC (CO)
Each share old Common $0.0001 par exchanged for (0.1) share new Common $0.0001 par 08/09/1989
Each share new Common $0.0001 par exchanged for (0.1) share Common $0.001 par 01/29/1990
Plan of reorganization under Chapter 11 Federal Bankruptcy proceedings confirmed 11/09/1993
No stockholders' equity

TOUCHIT TECHNOLOGIES INC (NV)
Recapitalized as Bitcoin Shop Inc. 02/05/2014
Each share Common $0.001 par exchanged for (0.00333333) share Common $0.001 par
Bitcoin Shop Inc. name changed to BTCS Inc. 08/03/2015

TOUCHPOINT METRICS INC (CA)
Name changed to McorpCX, Inc. 09/09/2015

TOUCHSTONE APPLIED SCIENCE ASSOC INC (DE)
Old Common $0.0001 par split (3) for (1) by issuance of (2) additional shares 10/12/1993
Each share old Common $0.0001 par exchanged for (0.25) share new Common $0.0001 par 03/04/1999
Name changed to Questar Assessment, Inc. 03/22/2007

TOUCHSTONE EXPLORATION INC (BC)
Merged into Touchstone Exploration Inc. (AB) 05/20/2014
Each share Common no par exchanged for (0.2355) share Common no par
Note: Unexchanged certificates were cancelled and became without value 05/20/2017

TOUCHSTONE GOLD LTD (ON)
Voluntarily dissolved 07/22/2016
Each share Common no par received first and final distribution of (1) share Intelicrypt Tactical Solutions Ltd. Ordinary £0.00001 par

TOUCHSTONE INVT TR (MA)
Bond Fund Class B no par reclassified as Core Bond Fund Class B no par 05/31/2003
Bond Fund Class C no par reclassified as Core Bond Fund Class C no par 05/31/2003
Intermediate Term Government Income Fund Class A no par reclassified as Intermediate Term U.S. Government Bond Fund Class A no par 05/31/2003
Intermediate Term Government Income Fund Class B no par reclassified as Intermediate Term U.S. Government Bond Fund Class B no par 05/31/2003
Intermediate Term Government Income Fund Class C no par reclassified as Intermediate Term U.S. Government Bond Fund Class C no par 05/31/2003
Short Term Government Income Fund no par reclassified as U.S. Government Money Market Fund no par 05/31/2003
Core Bond Fund Class B no par reclassified as Class A no par 05/24/2004
Completely liquidated 05/24/2004
Each share Intermediate Term U.S. Government Bond Fund Class A no par received shares of Core Bond Fund Class A no par on a net asset basis
Each share Intermediate Term U.S. Government Bond Fund Class B no par received shares of Core Bond Fund Class A no par on a net asset basis
Each share Intermediate Term U.S. Government Bond Fund Class C no par received shares of Core Bond Fund Class C no par on a net asset basis
Completely liquidated 10/31/2008
Each share U.S. Government Money Market Fund no par received net asset basis
(Additional Information in Active)

TOUCHSTONE MNG LTD (NV)
Common $0.0001 par split (2.782) for (1) by issuance of (1.782) additional shares payable 11/29/2010 to holders of record 11/29/2010
Ex date - 11/30/2010
Name changed to 22nd Century Group, Inc. 12/03/2010

TOUCHSTONE PETE INC (AB)
Name changed to Case Resources Inc. 05/17/2001
Case Resources Inc. merged into Fairborne Energy Ltd. (Old) 07/29/2004
(See Fairborne Energy Ltd. (Old))

TOUCHSTONE RES LTD (BC)
Each share old Common no par exchanged for (0.5) share new Common no par 04/04/2002
Recapitalized as Touchstone Exploration Inc. (BC) 07/06/2010
Each share new Common no par exchanged for (0.1) share Common no par
Touchstone Exploration Inc. (BC) merged into Touchstone Exploration Inc. (AB) 05/20/2014

TOUCHSTONE RES USA INC (DE)
Name changed to Cygnus Oil & Gas Corp. 06/09/2006

TOUCHSTONE SOFTWARE CORP (DE)
Reincorporated 01/17/1997
Each share old Common $0.001 par exchanged for (0.00666666) share new Common $0.001 par 05/01/1990
State of incorporation changed from (CA) to (DE) 01/17/1997
Merged into Phoenix Technologies Ltd. 07/01/2008
Each share Common $0.001 par exchanged for $1.48 cash

TOUCHTUNES MUSIC CORP (DE)
Name changed to Touchtunes Holdings Corp. 12/10/2007

TOUCHTUNES MUSIC CORP (NV)
Each share old Class A Common $0.001 par exchanged for (0.0005) share new Class A Common $0.001 par 01/24/2006
Note: Holders of (1,999) or fewer pre-split shares received $0.50 cash per share
Reorganized under the laws of Delaware 11/09/2006
Each share new Class A Common $0.001 par exchanged for (2,000) shares Common $0.001 par
Touchtunes Music Corp. (DE) name changed to Touchtunes Holdings Corp. 12/10/2007

TOUGH OAKES BURNSIDE GOLD MINES LTD.
Succeeded by Toburn Gold Mines Ltd. 00/00/1930
Details not available

TOUPS TECHNOLOGY LICENSING INC (FL)
Name changed to EarthFirst Technologies, Inc. 05/15/2000
(See EarthFirst Technologies, Inc.)

TOUR CFG INC (DE)
Each share Common 1¢ par received distribution of (7.8) shares Century Technologies Inc. (ON) Common no par payable 10/22/1997 to holders of record 07/01/1997
SEC revoked common stock registration 07/21/2009

TOUR DESIGN INTL INC (WY)
Name changed to Carolina Co. At Pinehurst Inc. 10/31/2001
(See Carolina Co. At Pinehurst Inc.)

TOURIST ENTERPRISES, INC. (UT)
Name changed to Turk Corp. and Common $1 par changed to no par 04/05/1978
(See Turk Corp.)

TOURNIGAN ENERGY LTD (BC)
Name changed 12/30/2002
Reincorporated 03/27/2008
Name changed 05/06/2008
Name and place of incorporation changed from Tournigan Ventures Corp. (BC) to Tournigan Gold Corp. (YT) 12/30/2002
Place of incorporation changed from (YT) to (BC) 03/27/2008
Name changed from Tournigan Gold Corp. to Tournigan Energy Ltd. 05/06/2008
Recapitalized as European Uranium Resources Ltd. 03/01/2012
Each share Common no par exchanged for (0.2) share Common no par
European Uranium Resources Ltd. recapitalized as Azarga Metals Corp. 05/31/2016

TOURNIGAN MNG EXPLS LTD (BC)
Recapitalized as International Tournigan Corp. 04/22/1992
Each share Capital Stock no par exchanged for (0.2) share Common no par
International Tournigan Corp. recapitalized as Tournigan Ventures Corp. (BC) 03/26/2001 which reincorporated in Yukon as Tournigan Gold Corp. 12/30/2002 which reincorporated back under the laws of British Columbia 03/27/2008 which name changed to Tournigan Energy Ltd. 05/06/2008 which recapitalized as European Uranium Resources Ltd. 03/01/2012 which recapitalized as Azarga Metals Corp. 05/31/2016

TOUSA INC (DE)
Plan of reorganization under Chapter 11 Federal Bankruptcy proceedings effective 08/21/2013
No stockholders' equity

TOV VENTURES LTD (NV)
Each share Common $0.001 par exchanged for (0.1) share Common 1¢ par 05/16/1986
Name changed to Fountain Powerboat Industries, Inc. 08/21/1986
(See Fountain Powerboat Industries, Inc.)

TOVA VENTURES II INC (ON)
Recapitalized as Enthusiast Gaming Holdings Inc. 10/04/2018
Each share Common no par exchanged for (0.23809523) share Common no par

TOVA VENTURES INC (BC)
Recapitalized as Auryx Gold Corp. 07/09/2010
Each share Common no par exchanged for (0.2) share Common no par
Auryx Gold Corp. merged into B2Gold Corp. 12/21/2011

TOVARICH LARDER GOLD MINES, LTD. (ON)
Charter surrendered 00/00/1953

TOVE GOLD MINES LTD. (ON)
Charter revoked for failure to file returns and pay fees 11/27/1961

TOWAGMAC EXPL LTD (QC)
Recapitalized as Tokar Ltd. 12/29/1969
Each share Capital Stock $1 par exchanged for (0.1) share Capital Stock no par
Tokar Ltd. recapitalized as Canadian Tokar Ltd. - Tokar du Canada Ltee. 08/20/1974 which name changed to Interpublishing (Canada) Ltd. - Interpublication (Canada) Ltee. 04/21/1976 which merged into Pagurian Corp. Ltd. 01/14/1979 which name changed to Edper Group Ltd. (Old) 05/10/1995 which name changed to EdperBrascan Corp. 08/01/1997 which name changed to Brascan Corp. 04/28/2000 which name changed to Brookfield Asset Management, Inc. 11/10/2005

TOWER ACCEPTANCE CORP. (DE)
Stock Dividend - 10% 3/20/60
Name changed to Tower Universal Corp. and Class A Common $1 par reclassified as Common $1 par 2/28/62
Tower Universal Corp. name changed to Tower Credit Corp. 7/9/64
(See Tower Credit Corp.)

TOWER AIR INC (DE)
Chapter 11 bankruptcy proceedings converted to Chapter 7 on 12/20/2000
Stockholders' equity unlikely

TOWER ANTENNAS INC (OH)
Merged into Citizens Financial Corp. (OH) 02/04/1969
Each $2 Conv. Preferred $1 par exchanged for (1) share $2 Conv. Preferred no par
Each share Common no par exchanged for (1.35) shares Common no par

TOWER AUTOMOTIVE CAP TR (DE)
Plan of reorganization under Chapter 11 Federal Bankruptcy Code effective 07/31/2007
No stockholders' equity

TOWER AUTOMOTIVE INC (DE)
Common 1¢ par split (2) for (1) by issuance of (1) additional share payable 07/15/1998 to holders of record 06/30/1998 Ex date - 07/16/1998
Plan of reorganization under Chapter 11 Federal Bankruptcy Code effective 07/31/2007
No stockholders' equity

TOWER BANCORP INC (PA)
Common $2.50 par split (2) for (1) by issuance of (1) additional share payable 05/15/1996 to holders of record 04/15/1996
Common $2.50 par changed to no par 04/01/1998
Stock Dividend - 10% 07/31/1995
Merged into Susquehanna Bancshares, Inc. 02/17/2012
Each share Common no par exchanged for $28 cash

TOWER BANK, N.A. (HIALEAH GARDENS, FL)
Assets liquidated by FDIC 11/01/1988
No stockholders' equity

TOWER BUILDING CORP. (IL)
Liquidation completed 6/7/60

TOWER CAP FD INC (DE)
Merged into Burnham Fund 10/29/1973
Each share Common $1 par exchanged for (0.55587) share Common $1 par
Burnham Fund merged into Drexel Burnham Fund 06/16/1975

TOWER COMMUNICATIONS CO. (IA)
Name changed to Tower Industries, Inc. 7/14/64 which completed liquidation 4/14/67
(See Tower Industries, Inc. (Old))

TOWER CORP (NV)
Reorganized under the laws of Virginia as Advanced Medical Sciences Inc. 03/01/1994
Each share Common $0.005 par exchanged for (0.04) share Common $0.005 par
Advanced Medical Sciences Inc. reorganized in Nevada as America's Shopping Mall, Inc. 07/14/1999 which name changed to Eagle Ventures International, Inc. 11/26/2007
(See Eagle Ventures International, Inc.)

TOWER CR CORP (DE)
Each share old Common $1 par exchanged for (0.25) share new Common $1 par 1/15/71
Charter cancelled and declared inoperative and void for non-payment of taxes 3/1/83

TOWER ENERGY LTD (BC)
Recapitalized as Tower Resources Ltd. 09/20/2011
Each share Common no par exchanged for (0.25) share Common no par

TOWER ENTERPRISES, INC. (UT)
Each share Capital Stock 5¢ par exchanged for (0.1) share Capital Stock 2nd Ser. 50¢ par 06/21/1968
Each share Capital Stock 2nd Ser. 50¢ par exchanged for (1) share Capital Stock 3rd Ser. 1¢ par 03/16/1971
Merged into Excalibur Industries 05/25/1971
Each share Capital Stock 3rd Ser. 1¢ par exchanged for (1) share Common 1¢ par

TOWER FD INC (DE)
Name changed to Tower Capital Fund, Inc. 10/29/1970
Tower Capital Fund, Inc. merged into Burnham Fund 10/29/1973 which merged into Drexel Burnham Fund 06/16/1975

TOWER FINL CORP (IN)
Merged into Old National Bancorp 04/25/2014
Each share Common no par exchanged for (1.2) shares Common no par and $6.75 cash

TOWER GARAGE, INC.
Liquidated in 1947

TOWER GROUP INC (DE)
Merged into Tower Group International, Ltd. 03/14/2013
Each share Common 1¢ par exchanged for (1.133) shares Common 1¢ par
(See Tower Group International, Ltd.)

TOWER GROUP INTL LTD (BERMUDA)
Acquired by ACP Re, Ltd. 09/15/2014
Each share Common 1¢ par exchanged for $2.50 cash

TOWER GROVE BK & TR CO (ST LOUIS, MO)
Capital Stock $20 par changed to $10 par and (1) additional share issued 01/22/1963
Stock Dividends - 100% 02/15/1955; 50% 01/28/1959
99.9% held by County Tower Corp. as of 00/00/1980
Public interest eliminated

TOWER HILL MINES LTD (BC)
Recapitalized as International Tower Hill Mines Ltd. (Old) 03/15/1991
Each share Common no par exchanged for (0.2) share Common no par
(See International Tower Hill Mines Ltd. (Old))

TOWER INDUSTRIES, INC. (OLD) (IA)
Ctfs. dated prior to 8/28/64
Liquidation completed
Each share Common no par stamped to indicate initial distribution of $2 cash 8/28/64
Each share Stamped Common no par received second distribution of $0.27 cash 2/28/66
Each share Stamped Common no par received third distribution of $0.09 cash 3/21/67
Each share Stamped Common no par exchanged for fourth and final distribution of (1) share Tower Industries, Inc. (New) Common no par 4/14/67
(See Tower Industries, Inc. (New))

TOWER INDS INC NEW (IA)
Ctfs. dated after 4/13/67
Each share old Common no par exchanged for (0.4) share new Common no par 6/11/69
Reacquired 8/31/87
Each share new Common no par exchanged for $5.50 cash

TOWER INSURANCE CO., INC. (WI)
100% acquired by Fiduciaries, Inc. 00/00/1975
Public interest eliminated

TOWER LINDEN BUILDING CORP.
Liquidated in 1941

TOWER MINES LTD. (BC)
Name changed to Tower Resources Ltd. 8/3/70
Tower Resources Ltd. recapitalized as Consolidated Tower Resources Ltd. 1/18/72
(See Consolidated Tower Resources Ltd.)

TOWER NATL BK (LIMA, OH)
Stock Dividends - 25% 05/22/1968; 20% 05/31/1972; 100% 06/01/1979
Merged into Banc One Corp. (DE) 04/02/1983
Each share Common Capital Stock $10 par exchanged for (1.185) shares Common no par

Banc One Corp. (DE) reincorporated in Ohio 05/01/1989 which merged into Bank One Corp. 10/02/1998 which merged into J.P. Morgan Chase & Co. 12/31/2000 which name changed to JPMorgan Chase & Co. 07/20/2004

TOWER NATIONAL LIFE INVESTMENT CO. (MO)
Completely liquidated 4/4/66
Each share Common $1 par exchanged for first and final distribution of (0.5) share Frontier-Tower Life Insurance Co. Common $1 par
Frontier-Tower Life Insurance Co. recapitalized as Frontier Insurance Co. 11/30/73 which recapitalized as Washington Security Life Insurance Co. 7/9/97

TOWER PETROLEUM, INC. (UT)
Name changed to Dura-Print Technologies 08/23/1983
(See Dura-Print Technologies)

TOWER PETROLEUMS LTD.
Acquired by Banff Oil Ltd. in 1952
Each share Capital Stock $1 par exchanged for (0.2) share Common 50¢ par
Banff Oil Ltd. completely liquidated for Aquitaine Co. of Canada Ltd.-Societe Aquitaine du Canada Ltee. 2/26/71
(See Aquitaine Co. of Canada Ltd.-Societe Aquitaine du Canada Ltee.)

TOWER PPTYS CO OLD (MO)
Merged into Commerce Bancshares, Inc. 01/29/1990
Each share Common $1 par exchanged for (7.88) shares Common $5 par

TOWER PRODS INC (IL)
Acquired by American Hospital Supply Corp. 11/24/1980
Each share Common $1 par exchanged for (0.3886) share Common no par
American Hospital Supply Corp. merged into Baxter Travenol Laboratories, Inc. 11/25/1985 which name changed to Baxter International Inc. 05/18/1988

TOWER RLTY TR INC (MD)
Issue Information - 12,015,000 shares COM offered at $26 per share on 10/09/1997
Merged into Reckson Associates Realty Corp. 5/24/99
Each share Common 1¢ par exchanged for (0.8364) share Class B Common 1¢ par
Reckson Associates Realty Corp. merged into SL Green Realty Corp. 1/25/2007

TOWER RES LTD (BC)
Recapitalized as Consolidated Tower Resources Ltd. 1/18/72
Each share Common no par exchanged for (0.2) share Common no par
(See Consolidated Tower Resources Ltd.)

TOWER TECH HLDGS INC (NV)
Name changed to Broadwind Energy, Inc. (NV) 03/04/2008
Broadwind Energy, Inc. (NV) reincorporated in Delaware 06/20/2008

TOWER TECH INC (OK)
Plan of reorganization under Chapter 11 Federal Bankruptcy proceedings effective 02/01/2002
Each share old Common $0.001 par exchanged for (0.02826) Common Stock Purchase Warrant expiring 1/31/2007
Company terminated common stock registration and is no longer public as of 07/13/2004

TOWER UNIVERSAL CORP. (DE)
Name changed to Tower Credit Corp. 7/9/64
(See Tower Credit Corp.)

TOWER'S MARTS, INC. (NY)
Merged into Towers Marts International, Inc. 09/29/1961
Each share Class A Stock 10¢ par exchanged for (1.25) share Capital Stock $1 par
(See Towers Marts International, Inc.)

TOWERMARC (MA)
Acquired by Freehold Investments Ltd. 10/31/84
Each Share of Bene. Int. $1 par exchanged for $10.65 cash

TOWERS FINL CORP (NJ)
Chapter 11 bankruptcy proceedings filed 3/26/93 and subseqently converted to Chapter 7
No stockholders' equity

TOWERS HOTEL CORP. (NY)
Liquidation completed 8/29/56

TOWERS MARTS & PPTYS LTD (ON)
Name changed to Towmart Holdings Ltd. 1/20/69
Towmart Holdings Ltd. recapitalized as T.M.P. Investments Ltd. 3/27/72 which name changed to Grey Goose Corp. Ltd. (ONT) 6/20/72 which reincorporated in Canada 1/15/80
(See Grey Goose Corp. Ltd. (Canada))

TOWERS MARTS INTERNATIONAL, INC. (DE)
Bankrupt 4/23/63
No stockholders' equity

TOWERS WATSON & CO (DE)
Merged into Willis Towers Watson PLC 01/05/2016
Each share Class A Common 1¢ par exchanged for (1) share Ordinary $0.000304635 par

TOWLE MFG CO (MA)
Common no par split (3) for (1) by issuance of (2) additional shares 6/30/48
Common no par split (2) for (1) by issuance of (1) additional share 4/15/64
Common no par split (2) for (1) by issuance of (1) additional share 4/14/67
Common no par split (2) for (1) by issuance of (1) additional share 8/5/68
Preferred Ser. A $1 par and Common no par split (2) for (1) by issuance of (1) additional share respectively 1/25/80
Completely liquidated in 1991
Each share Preferred Ser. A $1 par received first and final distribution of $0.05 cash
Each share Common no par received first and final distribution of $0.05 cash
Note: Certificates were not required to be surrendered and are now valueless

TOWMART HLDGS LTD (ON)
Recapitalized as T.M.P. Investments Ltd. 3/27/72
Each share Capital Stock no par exchanged for (0.1) share Capital Stock no par
T.M.P. Investments Ltd. name changed to Grey Goose Corp. Ltd. (ONT) 6/20/72 which reincorporated in Canada 1/15/80
(See Grey Goose Corp. Ltd. (Canada))

TOWMOTOR CORP. (OH)
Common $1 par split (2) for (1) by issuance of (1) additional share 11/1/55
Stock Dividends - 50% 4/25/62; 50% 10/1/64
Acquired by Caterpillar Tractor Co. (CA) 11/9/65
Each share Common $1 par exchanged for (1) share Common no par
Caterpillar Tractor Co. (CA) reorganized in Delaware as Caterpillar Inc. 5/22/86

TOWN & CAMPUS INC (NJ)
Charter revoked for failure to file annual reports 12/16/98

TOWN & CNTRY BK & TR CO (LUMBERTON, NC)
Merged into Wachovia Corp. (Old) 03/31/1977
Each share Capital Stock $5 par exchanged for (0.77) share Common $5 par
Wachovia Corp. (Old) merged into First Wachovia Corp. 12/05/1985 which name changed to Wachovia Corp. (New) (Ctfs. dated between 05/20/1991 and 09/01/2001) 05/20/1991 which merged into Wachovia Corp. (Ctfs. dated after 09/01/2001) 09/01/2001 which merged into Wells Fargo & Co. (New) 12/31/2008

TOWN & COUNTRY BANK & TRUST CO. (RESTON, VA)
Name changed to Enterprise Bank Corp. (Reston, Va.) 2/1/83
Enterprise Bank Corp. (Reston, Va.) merged into Washington Bancorporation 12/31/86

TOWN & COUNTRY BANK (SEAL BEACH, CA)
100% acquired by Farmers & Merchants Bank (Long Beach, CA) through purchase offer as of 10/15/1985
Public interest eliminated

TOWN & COUNTRY BANK (SPRINGFIELD, IL)
Under plan of reorganization each share Common $5 par automatically became (1) share Town & Country Bancorp Common $5 par in January 1985
Town & Country Bancorp name changed to Town & Country Financial Corp. 2/8/2005

TOWN & COUNTRY FOOD STORES, INC. (TX)
Merged into National Convenience Stores Inc. 1/1/68
Each share Common 50¢ par exchanged for (0.2) share $1.20 Preferred no par
(See National Convenience Stores Inc. (Tex.))

TOWN & CTRY BANCORP (IL)
Common $5 par split (2) for (1) by issuance of (1) additional share payable 2/28/2000 to holders of record 1/27/2000
Common $5 par split (3) for (2) by issuance of (0.5) additional share payable 9/30/2004 to holders of record 9/2/2004 Ex date - 10/1/2004
Stock Dividends - 10% payable 1/31/98 to holders of record 12/31/97; 10% payable 3/25/2002 to holders of record 1/23/2002 Ex date - 1/31/2002; 5% payable 3/31/2003 to holders of record 3/2/2003 Ex date - 2/26/2003
Name changed to Town & Country Financial Corp. 2/8/2005

TOWN & CTRY CORP (MA)
Plan of reorganization under Chapter 11 Federal Bankruptcy Code effective in June 1998
No stockholders' equity

TOWN & CTRY FOOD INC (IN)
Dissolved 03/28/1969
No stockholders' equity

TOWN & CTRY JEWELRY MFG CORP (MA)
Common 1¢ par reclassified as Class A Common 1¢ par 8/26/86
Each share Class A Common 1¢ par received distribution of (1) share Conv. Class B Common 1¢ par 6/1/87
Name changed to Town & Country Corp. 8/1/88
(See Town & Country Corp.)

TOWN & CTRY MOBILE HOMES INC (TX)
Common $1 par changed to 80¢ par and (0.25) additional share issued 2/27/67
Common 80¢ par split (2) for (1) by issuance of (1) additional share 3/14/69
Name changed to Brigadier Industries Corp. (TX) 4/5/82
Brigadier Industries Corp. (TX) merged into U.S. Home Corp. (Old) 1/7/83 which reorganized as U.S. Home Corp. (New) 6/21/93 which merged into Lennar Corp. 5/2/2000

TOWN & CTRY NURSING CTRS INC (NJ)
Name changed to Townco Medical Enterprises, Inc. 09/29/1972
(See Townco Medical Enterprises, Inc.)

TOWN & CTRY REPRODUCTIONS INC (NY)
Adjudicated bankrupt 10/10/1972
Stockholders' equity unlikely

TOWN & CTRY SECS CORP (IN)
Name changed to Kingsford Industries, Inc. 10/14/1970
(See Kingsford Industries, Inc.)

TOWN & CTRY TR (MD)
Merged into Magazine Acquisition GP LLC 3/31/2006
Each Share of Bene. Int. 1¢ par exchanged for $40.20 cash

TOWN BK (WESTFIELD, NJ)
Merged into Community Partners Bancorp 04/03/2006
Each share Common $5 par exchanged for (1.25) shares Common no par
Community Partners Bancorp name changed to Two River Bancorp 06/28/2013

TOWN CENTRE, LTD. (IA)
Completely liquidated in October, 1980
Each share Capital Stock $1 par exchanged for first and final distribution of $1 cash

TOWN CTR BANCORP (OR)
Common $5 par split (2) for (1) by issuance of (1) additional share payable 09/15/2006 to holders of record 09/01/2006 Ex date - 09/18/2006
Stock Dividends - 10% payable 02/18/2003 to holders of record 01/31/2003 Ex date - 01/29/2003; 10% payable 02/18/2004 to holders of record 01/30/2004 Ex date - 01/29/2004; 10% payable 04/15/2006 to holders of record 03/31/2006 Ex date - 03/29/2006
Merged into Columbia Banking System, Inc. 07/23/2007
Each share Common $5 par exchanged for (0.3391) share Common no par and $9.382 cash

TOWN CTR BK (PORTLAND, OR)
Stock Dividend - 10% payable 02/15/2002 to holders of record 02/01/2002 Ex date - 01/31/2002
Under plan of reorganization each share Common $5 par automatically became (1) share Town Center Bancorp Common $5 par 04/16/2002
Town Center Bancorp merged into Columbia Banking System, Inc. 07/23/2007

TOWN ENTERPRISES INC (DE)
Each share Class A Common 50¢ par exchanged for (0.2) share Class A Common $2.50 par 02/26/1968

TOW-TPI — FINANCIAL INFORMATION, INC.

Each share Class B Common 50¢ par exchanged for (0.2) share Class B Common $2.50 par 02/26/1968
Merged into Leucadia National Corp. 01/04/1984
Each share Preferred 10¢ par exchanged for $115 cash
Each share Class A Common $2.50 par exchanged for $0.15 cash
Each share Class B Common $2.50 par exchanged for $0.15 cash

TOWN HEALTH MED TECHNOLOGY HLDGS CO LTD (BERMUDA)
Name changed to Hong Kong Health Check & Laboratory Holdings Co. Ltd. 07/20/2007
Hong Kong Health Check & Laboratory Holdings Co. Ltd. name changed to China Gogreen Assets Investment Ltd. 09/02/2011
(See China Gogreen Assets Investment Ltd.)

TOWN PHOTOLAB, INC. (NY)
Acquired by Technicolor, Inc. on a (1) for (4.6) basis 12/11/63
(See Technicolor, Inc.)

TOWNCO MED ENTERPRISES INC (NJ)
Merged into Stanford Court Inc. 01/28/1982
Each share Common 1¢ par exchanged for $5.65 cash

TOWNE BANCORP INC (AZ)
Principal asset placed in receivership 05/07/2010
No stockholders' equity

TOWNE BANCORP INC (WA)
Reorganized 01/02/1997
Under plan of reorganization each share Towne Bank (Woodinville, WA) Common $10 par automatically became (1) share Towne Bancorp, Inc. Common $10 par 01/02/1997
Merged into First Savings Bank of Washington Bancorp, Inc. (DE) 04/01/1998
Each share Common $10 par exchanged for either (3.355) shares Common 1¢ par and $11.78 cash or $91.62 cash
Note: Option to receive stock and cash expired 03/17/1998
First Savings Bank of Washington Bancorp, Inc. (DE) reincorporated in Washington as First Washington Bancorp, Inc. 07/24/1998 which name changed to Banner Corp. 10/30/2000

TOWNE FINL CORP (OH)
Merged into Oak Hill Financial, Inc. 10/01/1999
Each share Common exchanged for (4.125) shares Common no par
Oak Hill Financial, Inc. merged into WesBanco, Inc. 11/30/2007

TOWNE LIMOUSINE SVC INC (NY)
Charter cancelled and proclaimed dissolved for failure to pay taxes 12/23/1992

TOWNE MANUFACTURING CO., INC. (VA)
Voluntarily dissolved 1/28/78
Details not available

TOWNE MINES CORP (DE)
$1.75 Prior Preferred $5 par called for redemption 01/01/1969
Liquidation completed
Each share Common 20¢ par received initial distribution of $14 cash 08/15/1975
Each share Common 20¢ par received second distribution of $6.50 cash 02/26/1976
Each share Common 20¢ par received third and final distribution of $6 cash 03/24/1977
Note: Certificates were not required to be surrendered and are without value

TOWNE-PAULSEN INC (CA)
Charter cancelled for failure to file reports and pay taxes 5/16/89
No stockholders' equity

TOWNE SECURITIES CORP. (DE)
Preferred $100 par changed to no par in 1944
Recapitalized in 1952
Preferred no par changed to $5 par
Common no par changed to 20¢ par
Name changed to Towne Mines Corp. in 1953
(See Towne Mines Corp.)

TOWNE SVCS INC (GA)
Issue Information - 4,000,000 shares CDT-COM offered at $8 per share on 07/30/1998
Each share old Common no par exchanged for (0.2) share new Common no par 12/21/2000
Merged into Private Business, Inc. 08/09/2001
Each share new Common no par exchanged for (0.9087) share new Common no par
Private Business, Inc. name changed to Goldleaf Financial Solutions, Inc. 05/05/2006
(See Goldleaf Financial Solutions, Inc.)

TOWNEBANK (PORTSMOUTH, VA)
Each share 8% Non-Cum. Conv. Preference Ser. A $5 par exchanged for (5.55) shares Common $1.667 par 09/01/2013
(Additional Information in Active)

TOWNER PETE CO (DE)
Common no par split (3) for (2) by issuance of (0.5) additional share 12/21/1979
Common no par split (4) for (3) by issuance of (1/3) additional share 09/02/1980
Common no par changed to $1 par and (0.5) additional share issued 08/27/1981
Plan of reorganization under Chapter 11 Federal Bankruptcy proceedings confirmed 11/25/1985
No stockholders' equity

TOWNPAGES NET COM PLC (UNITED KINGDOM)
Name changed to TPN Holdings PLC 03/02/2001
(See TPN Holdings PLC)

TOWNSEND (W.W.) & CO.
Bankrupt in 1930

TOWNSEND CO. (PA)
Acquired by Textron, Inc. (RI) (New) 03/01/1959
Details not available

TOWNSEND CORP. OF AMERICA (DE)
Under plan of merger name changed to Chatham Corp. 12/31/64

TOWNSEND GROWTH FUND, INC. (MD)
Liquidation completed
Each share Capital Stock 1¢ par exchanged for initial distribution of $5.25 cash 01/11/1965
Each share Capital Stock 1¢ par received second and final distribution of $1.01724 cash 12/01/1966

TOWNSEND INVESTMENT CO. (DE)
Name changed to Townsend Corp. of America 4/29/59 which name was changed to Chatham Corp. 12/31/64

TOWNSEND MANAGEMENT CO. (NJ)
Merged into Chatham Corp. on a (5.32) for (1) basis 12/31/64

TOWNSEND U.S. & INTERNATIONAL GROWTH FUND, INC. (MD)
Name changed to Townsend Growth Fund, Inc. 10/03/1960
(See Townsend Growth Fund, Inc.)

TOXIC CTL TECHNOLOGIES INC (DE)
Involuntary petition under Chapter 7 bankruptcy proceedings filed 12/27/86
No stockholders' equity

TOXIC DISP CORP (WY)
Recapitalized as Global Disposal Corp. 03/29/1996
Each share Common no par exchanged for (0.05) share Common no par
(See Global Disposal Corp.)

TOXIC WASTE CONTAINMENT INC (DE)
Charter cancelled and declared inoperative and void for non-payment of taxes 3/1/90

TOXICOM TECHNOLOGIES INC (MD)
Each share Common $0.001 par exchanged for (0.1) share Common 1¢ par 05/06/1985
Name changed to F&E Resource System Technology, Inc. 01/01/1990
F&E Resource System Technology, Inc. name changed to Wastemasters Inc. (MD) 06/05/1996 which reincorporated in Delaware as Environmental Energy Services Inc. 06/29/2001
(See Environmental Energy Services Inc.)

TOY BIZ INC (DE)
Merged into Marvel Enterprises Inc. 10/01/1998
Each share Class A Common 1¢ par exchanged for (1) share Common 1¢ par
Marvel Enterprises Inc. name changed to Marvel Entertainment, Inc. 09/16/2005 which merged into Disney (Walt) Co. 12/31/2009

TOY KING, INC. (FL)
Name changed to National Ventures, Inc. 11/1/68
National Ventures, Inc. name changed to Auto-Mission, Inc. 9/11/69
(See Auto-Mission, Inc.)

TOY POP CORP.
Bankrupt in 1950

TOYMAX INTL INC (DE)
Issue Information - 2,700,000 shares COM offered at $8.50 per share on 10/20/1997
Merged into JAKKS Pacific, Inc. 10/25/2002
Each share Common 1¢ par exchanged for (0.1258) share Common $0.001 par and $3 cash

TOYOTA MTR LTD (JAPAN)
Each old ADR for Common exchanged for (5) new ADR's for Common 03/15/1982
Stock Dividends - 10% 10/21/1977; 10% 03/11/1982
Name changed to Toyota Motor Corp. 07/01/1982

TOYS R US INC (DE)
Common 10¢ par split (3) for (2) by issuance of (0.5) additional share 07/28/1980
Common 10¢ par split (3) for (2) by issuance of (0.5) additional share 07/21/1981
Common 10¢ par split (3) for (2) by issuance of (0.5) additional share 07/22/1982
Common 10¢ par split (3) for (2) by issuance of (0.5) additional share 07/26/1983
Common 10¢ par split (3) for (2) by issuance of (0.5) additional share 01/08/1985
Common 10¢ par split (3) for (2) by issuance of (0.5) additional share 06/27/1986
Common 10¢ par split (3) for (2) by issuance of (0.5) additional share 05/26/1989
Common 10¢ par split (3) for (2) by issuance of (0.5) additional share 06/29/1990
Merged into Global Toys Acquisition, LLC 07/21/2005
Each share Common 10¢ par exchanged for $26.75 cash
Each Equity Security Unit Normal received $62.06535 cash 08/16/2005
Each Equity Security Unit Stripped received $62.06535 cash 08/16/2005

TOYSHARE INC (NV)
Name changed to Capital Financial Global, Inc. 05/27/2011

TOYZAP COM INC (TX)
Common $0.001 par split (2) for (1) by issuance of (1) additional share payable 06/01/2010 to holders of record 05/31/2010 Ex date - 06/02/2010
Name changed to Calpian Inc. 09/09/2010
Calpian Inc. name changed to MoneyOnMobile, Inc. 10/26/2016

TP RES LTD (BC)
Name changed to Crew Natural Resources Ltd. 09/28/1988
Crew Natural Resources Ltd. recapitalized as South Crofty Holdings Ltd. 10/05/1994 which name changed to North Pacific GeoPower Corp. 12/05/2001 which recapitalized as Western GeoPower Corp. 10/09/2003 which merged into Ram Power, Corp. 10/20/2009 which recapitalized as Polaris Infrastructure Inc. 05/19/2015

TPA AMER INC (DE)
Reincorporated 8/24/87
State of incorporation changed from (FL) to (DE) 8/24/87
Charter cancelled and declared inoperative and void for non-payment of taxes 3/1/93

TPB & T LTD (ON)
Dissolved 09/03/1994
Details not available

TPC GROUP INC (DE)
Acquired by Sawgrass Holdings Inc. 12/21/2012
Each share Common 1¢ par exchanged for $45 cash

TPEX EXPL INC (CO)
Each share old Common no par exchanged for (0.02) share new Common no par 6/10/92
Name changed to Kestrel Energy, Inc. 3/14/95
(See Kestrel Energy, Inc.)

TPG N V (NETHERLANDS)
Name changed to TNT N.V. 06/06/2005
TNT N.V. name changed to PostNL N.V. 05/31/2011
(See PostNL N.V.)

TPG PACE ENERGY HLDGS CORP (DE)
Units separated 08/01/2018
Name changed to Magnolia Oil & Gas Corp. 08/01/2018

TPI DISSOLUTION CORP. (TX)
In process of liquidation
Each share Common 1¢ par received initial distribution of (0.1) share Taco Cabana, Inc. Class A Common 1¢ par 8/5/93
Note: Details on subsequent distribution(s), if any, are not available

TPI ENTERPRISES INC (NJ)
Merged into Shoney's Inc. 9/9/96
Each share Common 1¢ par exchanged for (0.3283462) share Common $1 par
(See Shoney's Inc.)

TPI TRIUNFO PARTICIPACOES E INVESTIMENTOS S A (BRAZIL)
ADR agreement terminated 08/29/2016
Each ADR for Common exchanged for $1.037396 cash

TPN HLDGS PLC (UNITED KINGDOM)
ADR agreement terminated 11/10/2015
No ADR holders' equity

TRA VEL INC (DE)
Charter cancelled and declared inoperative and void for non-payment of taxes 3/1/77

TRABELLA URANIUM MINES, INC. (CO)
Name changed to Lamartine Mines, Inc. 1/8/63
Lamartine Mines, Inc. charter revoked 10/15/64

TRAC FINL GROUP INC (DE)
Name changed to FINI Group, Inc. 07/28/2006
FINI Group, Inc. name changed to Avalon Capital Holdings Corp 08/24/2007
(See Avalon Capital Holdings Corp.)

TRAC INDS INC (ON)
Name changed 6/11/87
Reincorporated 6/30/88
Name changed from Trac Resources Inc. to Trac Industries Inc. 6/11/87
Place of incorporation changed from (BC) to (ONT) 6/30/88
Recapitalized as Medical Resorts International Inc. 1/13/97
Each (12) shares Common no par exchanged for (1) share Common no par
Medical Resorts International Inc. recapitalized as Medical Services International Inc. 2/20/2001

TRACAN OIL & GAS LTD (BC)
Struck off register and declared dissolved for failure to file returns 8/22/94

TRACE PRODS (CA)
Merged into Circle Triangle Corp. 11/19/1990
Each share Common no par exchanged for $2 cash

TRACEABILITY SOLUTIONS INC (AB)
Delisted from Toronto Venture Stock Exchange 06/05/2002

TRACER PETE CORP (BC)
Issue Information - 1,600,000 Units consisting of (5) shares COM and (5) WTS offered at $5.625 per Unit on 09/20/1994
Each share old Common no par exchanged for (0.1) share new Common no par 5/27/98
Name changed to Forum Energy Corp. 7/21/2003
Forum Energy Corp. name changed to FEC Resources Inc. 6/9/2005

TRACER RES CORP (BC)
Struck off register and declared dissolved for failure to file returns 04/15/1988

TRACERLAB, INC. (MA)
Each share Common no par exchanged for (3) shares Common $1 par in 1949
Merged into Laboratory for Electronics, Inc. 10/30/61
Each (4.5) shares Common $1 par exchanged for (1) share Common $1 par
Laboratory for Electronics, Inc. name changed to LFE Corp. 11/3/69
(See LFE Corp.)

TRACK GROUP INC (UT)
Reincorporated under the laws of Delaware 08/05/2016

TRACK N TRAIL INC (DE)
Issue Information - 2,727,272 shares COM offered at $10.50 per share on 10/10/1997
Plan of reorganization under Chapter 11 Federal Bankruptcy Code effective 7/1/2002
No stockholders' equity

TRACKBETS INTL INC (NV)
SEC revoked common stock registration 10/23/2008

TRACKER EXPLS LTD (BC)
Recapitalized as Jentech Ventures Corp. 10/02/1987
Each share Common no par exchanged for (2) shares Common no par
Jentech Ventures Corp. recapitalized as Impact Travel Technology Inc. 04/26/1993 which recapitalized as MCF Enterprises, Inc. 03/12/1999 which name changed to Online Consortium Corp. 02/09/2001 which name changed to Equicap Financial Corp. 07/10/2003 which name changed to Zecotek Medical Systems, Inc. 02/10/2005 which name changed to Zecotek Photonics Inc. 11/26/2007

TRACKING CORP (NV)
Recapitalized as H-D International Holdings Group 01/05/2018
Each share Common $0.001 par exchanged for (0.001) share Common $0.001 par
Note: No holder will receive fewer than (100) shares

TRACKPOWER INC (WY)
Reorganized under the laws of Nevada as Gate to Wire Solutions, Inc. 09/26/2008
Each share Common $0.0001 par exchanged for (0.01) share Common $0.001 par
(See Gate to Wire Solutions, Inc.)

TRACKS INTL INC (CO)
Recapitalized as Nemdaco Inc. 12/22/1989
Each share Common $0.0001 par exchanged for (0.01) share Common $0.0001 par
(See Nemdaco, Inc.)

TRACKSOFT SYS INC (WY)
Name changed to Premier Brands, Inc. 06/08/2012
(See Premier Brands, Inc.)

TRACO CORP (NV)
Name changed to Energy International, Inc. 3/1/74
(See Energy International, Inc.)

TRACON INTL INC (NV)
Each share old Common exchanged for (5) shares new Common 01/13/1984
Charter revoked for failure to file reports and pay fees 09/01/1985

TRACOR COMPUTING CORP (TX)
Name changed to TCC, Inc. 5/15/72
TCC, Inc. name changed to Continuum Co., Inc. (TX) 12/7/79 which reincorporated in (DE) 8/20/87 which merged into Computer Sciences Corp. 8/1/96

TRACOR INC NEW (DE)
Merged into General Electric Co. P.L.C. 06/23/1998
Each share new Common 1¢ par exchanged for $40 cash

TRACOR INC OLD (DE)
Reincorporated 6/20/73
Common 50¢ par changed to 33-1/3¢ par and (0.5) additional share issued 5/24/67
State of incorporation changed from (TX) to (DE) 6/20/73
Common 33-1/3¢ par split (5) for (4) by issuance of (0.25) additional share 3/9/79
Common 33-1/3¢ par split (5) for (4) by issuance of (0.25) additional share 5/30/80
Common 33-1/3¢ par split (3) for (2) by issuance of (0.5) additional share 6/10/81
Common 33-1/3¢ par split (5) for (4) by issuance of (0.25) additional share 6/4/82
Common 33-1/3¢ par split (5) for (4) by issuance of (0.25) additional share 6/3/83
75¢ Conv. Preferred $1 par called for redemption 8/31/84
75¢ Conv. Preferred Ser. A $1 par called for redemption 8/31/84
Common 33-1/3¢ par split (5) for (4) by issuance of (0.25) additional share 5/31/85
Merged into Westmark Systems, Inc. 12/18/87
Each share Common 33-1/3¢ par exchanged for $32 cash

TRACTEBEL ENERGIA S A (BRAZIL)
Basis changed from (1:5,000) to (1:5) 05/23/2005
Each Sponsored ADR for Class B Preferred exchanged for (1) Sponsored ADR for Common 08/12/2005
Sponsored ADR's for Common split (5) for (1) by issuance of (4) additional ADR's payable 10/08/2008 to holders of record 10/07/2008 Ex date - 10/09/2008
Basis changed from (1:5) to (1:1) 10/08/2008
Name changed to Engie Brasil Energia S.A. 10/05/2016

TRACTOR SUPPLY CO. (IL)
Class A $1 par split (3) for (2) by issuance of (0.5) additional share 06/16/1961
Merged into TSC Industries, Inc. 02/19/1968
Each share Class A $1 par exchanged for (1) share Common $1 par
TSC Industries, Inc. acquired by National Industries, Inc. (KY) 12/06/1969 which merged into Fuqua Industries, Inc. 01/03/1978 which name changed to Actava Group Inc. 07/21/1993 which name changed to Metromedia International Group, Inc. 11/00/1995
(See Metromedia International Group, Inc.)

TRACY & AVERY, INC. (OH)
Preferred $25 par called for redemption 11/14/1980
Merged into Seaway Food Town, Inc. 12/15/1980
Each share Common $10 par exchanged for $30 cash
Note: An additional initial distribution of $6.10 cash was paid 12/15/1982
A second and final distribution of $0.42 cash was paid 09/06/1984

TRACY DRILLING CORP (CA)
Merged into Tracy Acquisition Corp. 6/24/85
Each share Capital Stock $1 par exchanged for $15 cash

TRACY FED BK FSB (TRACY, CA)
Merged into Tracy Bancshares, Inc. 5/9/97
Each share Common no par exchanged for $2.40 cash

TRACY SAVINGS & LOAN ASSOCIATION (CA)
Name changed to Tracy Federal Bank (Tracy, CA) in November, 1989
(See Tracy Federal Bank (Tracy, CA))

TRAD CABINET CORP. (DE)
Name changed to Robotape Corp. 6/17/58
Robotape Corp. name changed to Horne (Lena) Beauty Products, Inc. 2/24/60
(See Horne (Lena) Beauty Products, Inc.)

TRAD ELECTRONICS CORP. (DE)
Adjudicated bankrupt 9/21/60
No stockholders' equity

TRAD TELEVISION CORP. (DE)
Name changed to Trad Electronics Corp. 5/16/55
Trad Electronics Corp. was adjudicated bankrupt 9/21/60

TRADAMAX GROUP (NV)
Recapitalized 01/16/2001
Recapitalized from Tradamax (Asia) Group to Tradamax Group 01/16/2001
Each share Common $0.001 par exchanged for (0.25) share Common $0.001 par
SEC revoked common stock registration 07/26/2002

TRADE BK & TR CO (NEW YORK, NY)
Stock Dividends - 10% 3/1/54; 10% 2/17/59; 10% 4/22/69
Merged into National Bank of North America (West Hempstead, NY) 7/6/70
Each share Capital Stock $10 par exchanged for (0.4) share C.I.T. Financial Corp. $5.50 Conv. Preferred 1970 Ser. no par
(See C.I.T. Financial Corp.)

TRADE INDS INC (NV)
Recapitalized as Traco Corp. 03/21/1972
Each share Common no par exchanged for (0.2) share Common 5¢ par
Traco Corp. name changed to Energy International, Inc. 03/01/1974
(See Energy International, Inc.)

TRADE LINK WHSLRS INC (NV)
Name changed to China Modern Agricultural Information Inc. 04/11/2011

TRADE PUBLICATIONS, INC.
Bankrupt in 1930

TRADE STR RESIDENTIAL INC (MD)
Each share old Common 1¢ par exchanged for (0.00666666) share new Common 1¢ par 01/25/2013
Stock Dividend - 41.6667% payable 07/16/2012 to holders of record 05/17/2012
Merged into Independence Realty Trust, Inc. 09/17/2015
Each share new Common 1¢ par exchanged for (0.4108) share Common 1¢ par and $3.80 cash

TRADE THE PLANET CORP (MT)
Reincorporated under the laws of Nevada as Human Science Systems Inc. 04/04/2005
Human Science Systems Inc. recapitalized as Nutralogix Laboratories, Inc. 11/14/2005 which recapitalized as Matrix Denture Systems International, Inc. 10/09/2007

TRADE WINDS CO. (GA)
Stock Dividend - 10% 11/1/60
Merged into Grace (W.R.) & Co. (Conn.) 8/12/77
Each share Common $1 par exchanged for $7.97 cash

TRADE WINDS RES LTD (BC)
Recapitalized as Trade Winds Ventures Inc. 07/05/2002
Each share Common no par exchanged for (0.1) share Common no par
Trade Winds Ventures Inc. acquired by Detour Gold Corp. 12/01/2011

TRADE WINDS VENTURES INC (BC)
Acquired by Detour Gold Corp. 12/01/2011
Each share Common no par exchanged for (0.0142) share Common no par and $0.0001 cash
Note: Unexchanged certificates were

cancelled and became without value 12/01/2017

TRADEHOLD LTD (SOUTH AFRICA)
ADR agreement terminated 05/12/2014
No ADR's remain outstanding

TRADELINK INTL INC (FL)
Each share old Common $0.001 par exchanged for (0.2) share new Common $0.001 par 10/09/1996
Name changed to Bridgeport Communications, Inc. (FL) 09/03/1997
Bridgeport Communications, Inc. (FL) reincorporated in Delaware as WealthHound.com, Inc. 07/23/1999 which recapitalized as Eurosport Active World Corp. 04/07/2008

TRADEON INC (NV)
Name changed to China Green Energy Industries, Inc. 11/26/2010
China Green Energy Industries, Inc. recapitalized as Reelcause, Inc. 12/24/2014

TRADEPUBZ COM INC (NV)
Name changed to American Mobile Dental Corp. 9/1/2004

TRADEQUEST INTL INC (NV)
Reorganized 10/11/2005
Reorganized from (MS) to under the laws of Nevada 10/11/2005
Each (65) shares Common no par exchanged for (1) share Common $0.0001 par
SEC revoked common stock registration 10/14/2011

TRADER CLASSIFIED MEDIA N V (NETHERLANDS)
Issue Information - 13,000,000 shares CL A COM offered at $28.56 per share on 03/30/2000
Name changed from Trader.com N.V. to Trader Classified Media N.V. 09/12/2002
Liquidation completed
Each Class A New York Registry Share received initial distribution of $0.0443 cash payable 09/08/2008 to holders of record 08/27/2008
Ex date - 08/25/2008
Each Class A New York Registry Share received second and final distribution of approximately $0.02118 cash payable 12/26/2008 to holders of record 12/11/2008

TRADER RESOURCE CORP (BC)
Name changed to Mountain Minerals Co. Ltd. 1/1/95
Mountain Minerals Co. Ltd. merged into Highwood Resources Ltd. 8/12/96

TRADER SECRETS COM (NV)
Name changed to Voip Technology Inc. 3/13/2000
Voip Technology Inc. recapitalized as Oxford Ventures Inc. 1/30/2002 which recapitalized as Uluru Inc. 4/5/2006

TRADERADIUS ONLINE INC (BC)
Recapitalized as Jalna Resources Ltd. (New) 04/10/2003
Each share Common no par exchanged for (0.1) share Common no par
Jalna Resources Ltd. (New) reorganized as Jalna Minerals Ltd. 06/01/2006 which recapitalized as Papuan Precious Metals Corp. 10/01/2010 which name changed to Ironside Resources Inc. 04/21/2015

TRADERALERT COM INC (NV)
Name changed to Equityalert.Com, Inc. 6/2/99
Equityalert.Com, Inc. recapitalized as InnoTech Corp. 7/31/2001

TRADEREF SOFTWARE CORP (ANGUILLA)
Reincorporated 12/11/1996
Place of incorporation changed from (AB) to (Anguilla) 12/11/1996
Name changed to Hansa.net Global Commerce, Inc. 02/20/1997
Hansa.net Global Commerce, Inc. name changed to KMT-Hansa Corp. 09/27/2013

TRADERS FIN LTD (CANADA)
Class A Common no par and Class B Common no par exchanged (3) for (1) 00/00/1948
Class A Common no par and Class B Common no par exchanged (2) for (1) 00/00/1953
Class A Common no par and Class B Common no par split (3) for (1) respectively by issuance of (2) additional shares 05/25/1962
Name changed to Traders Group Ltd. 07/04/1966
(See Traders Group Ltd.)

TRADERS GROUP LTD (CANADA)
Acquired by Central Capital Corp. 10/23/1987
Each share Class A Common no par exchanged for (4.75) shares Class A Subordinate no par and $5 cash
4.50% Preferred $100 par called for redemption 01/31/1995
5% Preferred $40 par called for redemption 01/31/1995
5% Preferred Ser. A $30 par called for redemption 01/31/1995
7.50% Preferred $50 par called for redemption 01/31/1995
$2.16 Preferred Ser. B $30 par called for redemption 01/31/1995
10.25% Preferred $10 par called for redemption 01/31/1995
Central Capital Corp. recapitalized as YMG Capital Management Inc. 02/20/1998
(See YMG Capital Management Inc.)

TRADERS HOMEPLAN LTD. (CANADA)
Through purchase offer 99.9% acquired by Traders Group Ltd. as of 03/00/1974
Public interest eliminated

TRADERS INTL FRANCHISE SYS CORP (BC)
Recapitalized as NewQuest Ventures Corp. 05/22/1998
Each share Common no par exchanged for (0.33333333) share Common no par
NewQuest Ventures Corp. recapitalized as Aster Ventures Corp. 05/26/1999 which recapitalized as Knight Petroleum Corp. 03/22/2001 which name changed to Knight Resources Ltd. 03/07/2003 which recapitalized as Knight Metals Ltd. 05/25/2011 which name changed to Africa Hydrocarbons Inc. (BC) 02/02/2012 which reincorporated in Alberta 04/25/2013 which name changed to Blockchaink2 Corp. 05/30/2018

TRADERS NATL BK (KANSAS CITY, MO)
Capital Stock $62.50 par changed to $25 par and (1.5) additional shares issued plus a 16-2/3% stock dividend paid 02/25/1952
Capital Stock $25 par changed to $10 par and (1.5) additional shares issued 02/16/1968
Stock Dividends - 37% 00/00/1945; 12-1/2% 02/15/1956; 20% 02/16/1959
Acquired by General Bancshares Corp. 05/02/1975
Each share Capital Stock $10 par exchanged for $65 cash

TRADESMENS BK & TR CO (VINELAND, NJ)
Merged into Bank of New Jersey (Camden, NJ) 05/18/1970
Each share Common $10 par exchanged for (3.2) shares Common $5 par
Bank of New Jersey (Camden, NJ) reorganized as Bancshares of New Jersey 12/30/1972 which name changed to Northern National Corp. 05/28/1981 which merged into Horizon Bancorp 10/01/1983
(See Horizon Bancorp)

TRADESMENS NATL BK (NEW HAVEN, CT)
Each share Common $100 par exchanged for (5) shares Common $20 par 1/24/50
Each share Common $20 par exchanged for (2.2) shares Common $10 par 6/26/61
Stock Dividends - 10% 1/13/53; 14-2/7% 5/23/57; 12-1/2% 12/1/58; 11-1/9% 2/15/60; 11-1/9% 12/10/64; 12-1/2% 12/28/66; 11-1/9% 6/27/68
Merged into Connecticut Bank & Trust Co. (Hartford, CT) 12/29/69
Each share Common $10 par exchanged for (1) share Capital Stock $10 par
Connecticut Bank & Trust Co. (Hartford, CT) reorganized as CBT Corp. 2/27/70 which merged into Bank of New England Corp. 6/14/85
(See Bank of New England Corp.)

TRADESTAR CORP (UT)
Each share Common 1¢ par exchanged for (0.06666666) share Common $0.001 par 06/15/1998
Reorganized under the laws of Nevada as Tradestar Resources Corp. 06/29/2006
Each share Common $0.001 par exchanged for (0.05) share Common $0.001 par
(See Tradestar Resources Corp.)

TRADESTAR RES CORP (NV)
Charter revoked for failure to file reports and pay fees 06/28/2013

TRADESTAR SVCS INC (NV)
Name changed to Stratum Holdings, Inc. 03/06/2007
Stratum Holdings, Inc. name changed to Caprock Oil, Inc. 03/25/2014 which recapitalized as Stack-It Storage, Inc. 07/23/2015 which name changed to Manufactured Housing Properties Inc. 12/08/2017

TRADESTATION GROUP INC (FL)
Acquired by Monex Group, Inc. 06/10/2011
Each share Common 1¢ par exchanged for $9.75 cash

TRADESTREAM GLOBAL CORP (DE)
Recapitalized as Empire Global Corp. 09/30/2005
Each share Common $0.0001 par exchanged for (0.1) share Common $0.0001 par
Empire Global Corp. name changed to Newgioco Group, Inc. 02/16/2017

TRADEWINDS EXPLORATION, INC. (DE)
Recapitalized as Walter Amusements, Inc. on a (0.1) for (1) basis 5/19/64
Walter Amusements, Inc. name changed to Energy Systems United Corp. 11/6/80
(See Energy Systems United Corp.)

TRADEX GLOBAL FINL SVCS INC (DE)
SEC revoked preferred and common stock registration 01/14/2009
Stockholders' equity unlikely

TRADEZAP DIRECT INC (NV)
Name changed to World Bingo League Co., Inc. 01/19/2005
World Bingo League Co., Inc. name changed to World Entertainment Corp. 07/14/2005 which name changed to World Mobile Network Corp. 03/16/2006 which recapitalized as Guyana Gold Corp. 02/07/2008

TRADING HSE TSUM JT STK CO (RUSSIA)
Acquired by European Capital Investment Fund Inc. 12/26/2013
Each Sponsored ADR for Ordinary exchanged for $13.280783 cash

TRADING SOLUTIONS COM INC (NV)
Each (17) shares old Common 1¢ par exchanged for (1) share new Common 1¢ par 3/12/2004
Name changed to Chembio Diagnostics, Inc. 5/17/2004

TRADITION BK (HOUSTON, TX)
Merged into Tradition Bancshares Inc. 10/1/2003
Each share Common exchanged for $45.50 cash

TRADITIONAL INDS INC (CA)
Each share Common 20¢ par exchanged for (1/3) share Common 1¢ par 04/03/1986
Common 1¢ par split (4) for (3) by issuance of (1/3) additional share 06/29/1988
Filed a petition under Chapter 11 Federal Bankruptcy Code 03/28/1991
Stockholders' equity unlikely

TRADUS PLC (UNITED KINGDOM)
Acquired by Naspers Ltd. 03/07/2008
Each Sponsored ADR for Ordinary exchanged for $8,898.9512 cash

TRADUX CORP (DE)
Charter cancelled and declared inoperative and void for non-payment of taxes 03/01/1992

TRAFALGAR ENERGY LTD (AB)
Merged into Midway Energy Ltd. 07/31/2009
Each share Common no par exchanged for (1) share Common no par and (1/3) Common Stock Purchase Warrant expiring 08/31/2009
Midway Energy Ltd. merged into Whitecap Resources Inc. 04/26/2012

TRAFALGAR HOUSE PLC (UNITED KINGDOM)
Merged into Kvaerner AS 07/16/1996
Each Sponsored ADR for Ordinary 20p par exchanged for $3.8775 cash

TRAFALGAR HSG LTD (HONG KONG)
Under plan of recapitalization each ADR for Ordinary exchanged for $0.05 cash 03/06/1989

TRAFALGAR INC (UT)
Reincorporated under the laws of Nevada as Atlantic Funding Ltd. 11/13/1989

TRAFALGAR INDS INC (DE)
Merged into Triangle Industries, Inc. (Old) 05/16/1984
Each share Common 10¢ par exchanged for (0.020756) share $16.50 Preferred $1 par
Note: Holders of record 04/12/1984 also received (1) share Avery, Inc. Common 1¢ par
(See Triangle Industries, Inc. (Old))

TRAFALGAR LONG LAC GOLD MINES LTD. (ON)
Name changed to Trafalgar Mines & Oil Ltd. in 1942
(See Trafalgar Mines & Oil Ltd.)

TRAFALGAR MINES & OIL LTD. (ON)
Charter cancelled 3/19/69

TRAFALGAR RES INC (BC)
Recapitalized as WCN Investment Corp. 05/27/1987
Each share Common no par

exchanged for (3) shares Common no par
(See WCN Investment Corp.)

TRAFALGAR VENTURES INC (NV)
Reorganized under the laws of Delaware as Cyberkinetics Neurotechnology Systems, Inc. 10/07/2004
Each share Common $0.001 par exchanged for (0.4729729) share Common $0.001 par
(See Cyberkinetics Neurotechnology Systems, Inc.)

TRAFFIC & SAFETY CONTROL SYSTEMS, INC. (WA)
Name changed to Floscan Instrument Co., Inc. 7/19/72

TRAFFIC COM INC (DE)
Issue Information - 6,550,000 shares COM offered at $12 per share on 01/25/2006
Merged into NAVTEQ Corp. 03/06/2007
Each share Common 1¢ par exchanged for either (0.235) share Common $0.001 par or (0.098) share Common $0.001 par and $4.65 cash
Note: Option to receive stock and cash expired 03/27/2007
(See NAVTEQ Corp.)

TRAFFIC CONTROLS INC. (CA)
Charter revoked for failure to file reports and pay fees 1/3/67

TRAFFIC ENGINE HLDGS INC (FL)
Name changed to Syndeos Group Inc. 1/15/2002
Syndeos Group Inc. recapitalized as Air Media Now!, Inc. 4/10/2002

TRAFFIC SAFETY SYS INC (VA)
Merged into Virginia Tractor Co., Inc. 08/18/1980
Each share Common 10¢ par exchanged for $1 cash

TRAFFIC TECHNOLOGY INC (AZ)
Reorganized under the laws of Nevada as CalbaTech, Inc. 04/08/2003
Each share Common 1¢ par exchanged for (0.07142857) share Common $0.001 par
CalbaTech, Inc. recapitalized as LifeStem International, Inc. 05/02/2008 which recapitalized as International Aerospace Enterprises, Inc. 04/30/2009
(See International Aerospace Enterprises, Inc.)

TRAFFIX INC (DE)
Merged into New Motion, Inc. 02/04/2008
Each share Common $0.001 par exchanged for (0.676) share Common 1¢ par
New Motion, Inc. name changed to Atrinsic, Inc. 06/26/2009 which recapitalized as Protagenic Therapeutics, Inc. 07/27/2016

TRAFINA ENERGY LTD (AB)
Discharged from receivership 01/11/2017
No stockholders' equity

TRAGOES INC (ON)
Name changed to Rightsmarket.com Inc. 07/30/1999
(See Rightsmarket.com Inc.)

TRAI THIEN USA INC (NV)
Old Common $0.001 par split (7) for (1) by issuance of (6) additional shares payable 08/24/2010 to holders of record 08/24/2010
Each share old Common $0.001 par exchanged for (0.005) share new Common $0.001 par 02/06/2012
Name changed to Onassis Mining Group, Inc. 06/08/2015

TRAID CORP (CA)
Stock Dividend - 50% 04/15/1958

Merged into Acapulco y Los Arcos Restaurantes 01/28/1977
Each share Common $1 par exchanged for (1) share Common 10¢ par
Acapulco Los Arcos Restaurantes name changed to Acapulco Restaurants 03/26/1984 which merged into Restaurant Associates Industries, Inc. 02/04/1986
(See Restaurant Associates Industries, Inc.)

TRAIL AIRE INC (CA)
Adjudicated bankrupt 11/19/1963
Stockholders' equity unlikely

TRAIL MINES, INC. (CO)
Merged into Diversified Medical Investments Corp. 4/17/70
Each share Common 1¢ par exchanged for (0.02) share Common 1¢ par
(See Diversified Medical Investments Corp.)

TRAIL NATL BK (SARASOTA, FL)
Name changed to Popular Bank of Sarasota, N.A. (Sarasota, FL) 12/01/1975
Popular Bank of Sarasota, N.A., (Sarasota, FL) name changed to First Independent Bank, N.A. (Sarasota, FL) 10/13/1977
(See First Independent Bank, N.A. (Sarasota, FL))

TRAIL ONE INC (NV)
Recapitalized as Citius Pharmaceuticals, Inc. 09/12/2014
Each share Common $0.001 par exchanged for (0.625) share Common $0.001 par

TRAIL RUN MINES, INC. (CO)
Charter revoked for failure to file reports and pay fees 10/14/65

TRAILBLAZER OIL & GAS INC (UT)
Involuntarily dissolved 04/30/1987

TRAILCO CORP. (DE)
Liquidation completed 7/18/60

TRAILER BRDG INC (DE)
Plan of reorganization under Chapter 11 Federal Bankruptcy proceedings effective 04/02/2012
Each share Common 1¢ par exchanged for $0.15 cash
Note: Option for holders of (2,500) or more shares to elect to receive a pro rata share of new Common expired 04/16/2012

TRAILER CO. OF AMERICA
Reorganized as Trailmobile Co. 00/00/1944
Each share Common no par exchanged for (2) shares Common $5 par
Trailmobile Co. name changed to Wealden Co. 07/02/1951
(See Wealden Co.)

TRAILER HOST OF AMERICA, INC. (OR)
Involuntarily dissolved for failure to file reports 10/18/72

TRAILER LIFE PUBG INC (CA)
Name changed to TL Enterprises, Inc. 10/15/80
(See TL Enterprises, Inc.)

TRAILERANCHO CORP. LIQUIDATING TRUST (CA)
See - Trailerancho Corp.

TRAILERANCHO CORP (CA)
Common $1 par changed to 50¢ par 12/08/1971
Liquidation completed
Each share Common 50¢ par stamped to indicate initial distribution of $4.50 cash 09/15/1978
Each share Stamped Common 50¢ par received second distribution of $1.75 cash 01/08/1979
Each share Stamped Common 50¢

par exchanged for third distribution of $2.50 cash 01/26/1981
Each share Stamped Common 50¢ par received fourth distribution of $0.50 cash 05/08/1981
Each share Stamped Common 50¢ par received fifth and final distribution of $0.17 cash 10/08/1981

TRAILEROYAL PARK (CA)
Name changed to Electro-Care, Inc. 02/01/1968
Electro-Care, Inc. merged into Electro-Care Industries, Inc. 06/30/1969 which name changed to ECI Industries 12/16/1971
(See ECI Industries)

TRAILEUROP INC (DE)
Stock Dividend - 100% 10/14/65
Charter cancelled and declared inoperative and void for non-payment of taxes 3/1/90

TRAILMOBILE CDA LTD (ON)
Acquired by 1314385 Ontario Ltd. 05/13/2002
Each share Common no par exchanged for $0.10 cash

TRAILMOBILE CO.
Name changed to Wealden Co. 07/02/1951
(See Wealden Co.)

TRAIN TRAVEL HLDGS INC (NV)
Name changed to Turnkey Capital, Inc. 02/04/2016

TRAINING WITH PROS INC (NY)
Common 1¢ par split (3) for (1) by issuance of (2) additional shares 6/27/69
Name changed to Sensory Systems, Inc. 4/14/71
(See Sensory Systems, Inc.)

TRAK AUTO CORP (DE)
Merged into Halart 5/28/99
Each share Common 1¢ par exchanged for $9 cash

TRAK ELECTRONICS CO., INC. (CT)
Name changed to Wiltek, Inc. 03/17/1967
Wiltek, Inc. name changed to E-Sync Networks Inc. 07/28/1999
(See E-Sync Networks Inc.)

TRAKIT CORP (DE)
Charter cancelled and declared inoperative and void for non-payment of taxes 3/1/94

TRALEA GOLD MINES, LTD. (ON)
Charter surrendered 04/00/1959

TRAMFORD INTL LTD (BRITISH VIRGIN ISLANDS)
Name changed to China Technology Development Group Corp. 01/09/2006
China Technology Development Group Corp. recapitalized as Renewable Energy Trade Board Corp. (British Virgin Islands) 10/25/2012 which reincorporated in Cayman Islands as New Energy Exchange Ltd. 08/12/2015

TRAMMEL CROW REALTY TRUST (TX)
Completely liquidated 06/30/1966
Details not available

TRAMMELL CROW CO (DE)
Merged into CB Richard Ellis Group, Inc. 12/20/2006
Each share Common 1¢ par exchanged for $49.51 cash

TRAMMELL CROW REAL ESTATE INVS (TX)
Name changed to American Industrial Properties REIT 9/13/93
(See American Industrial Properties REIT)

TRAN-AIRE SYSTEMS, INC. (DE)
Each share Common 1¢ par exchanged for (0.2) share Common 5¢ par 1/30/70

Name changed to United Southwest Industries, Inc. 12/3/73
(See United Southwest Industries, Inc.)

TRAN ST FINL INC (UT)
Charter revoked for failure to pay taxes 09/15/1970

TRANCE GLOBAL ENTMT GROUP CORP (NV)
Name changed to Neuromama, Ltd. 05/22/2013

TRANCO RESEARCH CORP. (DE)
Charter cancelled and declared inoperative and void for non-payment of taxes 3/1/89

TRANCOR COMMUNICATIONS INC (NV)
Charter revoked for failure to file reports and pay fees 5/1/93

TRANCOR INDUSTRIES, INC. (NV)
Name changed to Trancor Communications Inc. 11/30/86
(See Trancor Communications Inc.)

TRANDIRECT COM TECHNOLOGIES INC (BC)
Recapitalized as Consolidated Trandirect.com Technologies Inc. 8/14/2000
Each share Common no par exchanged for (0.25) share Common no par
Consolidated Trandirect.com name changed to International Samuel Exploration Corp. 6/20/2001

TRANE CO (WI)
Each share Common $5 par exchanged for (2.5) shares Common $2 par in 1937
Common $2 par split (3) for (2) by issuance of (0.5) additional share 11/1/56
Common $2 par split (5) for (4) by issuance of (0.25) additional share 1/9/61
Common $2 par split (2) for (1) by issuance of (1) additional share 10/30/64
Common $2 par split (2) for (1) by issuance of (1) additional share 2/1/79
Stock Dividends - 100% 12/20/51; 100% 12/15/54
Merged into American Standard Inc. 2/24/84
Each share Common $2 par exchanged for (1.45) shares Common $1 par
(See American Standard Inc.)

TRANE INC (DE)
Merged into Ingersoll-Rand Co. Ltd. (Bermuda) 06/05/2008
Each share Common 1¢ par exchanged for (0.23) share Class A Common $1 par and $36.50 cash
Ingersoll-Rand Co. Ltd. (Bermuda) reincorporated in Ireland as Ingersoll-Rand PLC 07/01/2009

TRANQUILAIRE MENTAL HEALTH SVCS INC (TN)
Name changed to Tranquilaire Properties, Inc. 09/08/1975
(See Tranquilaire Properties, Inc.)

TRANQUILAIRE PROPERTIES, INC. (TN)
Charter revoked for non-payment of taxes 12/7/76

TRANS AIR FGHT SYS INC (NY)
Stock Dividends - 10% 01/07/1970; 10% 01/04/1973
Liquidation completed
Each share Common 10¢ par exchanged for initial distribution of (0.26041) share Air Express International Corp. Common 1¢ par and $1 cash 09/15/1980
Each share Common 10¢ par received second distribution of $2 cash 07/31/1981
Each share Common 10¢ par

received third and final distribution of $0.68 cash 02/18/1985

TRANS AIR SYS INC (NY)
Stock Dividend - 10% 01/06/1969
Name changed to Trans-Air Freight System Inc. 06/15/1969
(See Trans-Air Freight System Inc.)

TRANS AIRE ELECTRS INC (NY)
Each share Common 10¢ par exchanged for (0.1) share Class A Common no par 10/01/1973
Reorganized as Trinitech Systems, Inc. 06/24/1991
Each share Class A Common no par exchanged for (3) shares Class A Common $0.001 par
Trinitech Systems, Inc. name changed to NYFIX, Inc. (NY) 10/25/1999 which reincorporated in Delaware 12/16/2003
(See NYFIX, Inc. (DE))

TRANS ALASKA TEL CO (AK)
Completely liquidated 12/31/66
Each share Common $3 par exchanged for (1/9) share Continental Telephone Corp. Common $1 par
Continental Telephone Corp. name changed to Continental Telecom Inc. 5/6/82 which name changed to Contel Co. 5/1/86 which merged into GTE Corp. 3/14/91 which merged into Verizon Communications Inc. 6/30/2000

TRANS AM CAP CORP (DE)
Name changed to Pacific Animated Imaging Corp. 02/11/1991
Pacific Animated Imaging Corp. name changed to Strategic Solutions Group Inc. 05/23/1997 which recapitalized as Southern Software Group, Inc. 03/13/2003 which name changed to SecureD Services, Inc. 07/30/2003
(See SecureD Services, Inc.)

TRANS AMERICA CAPITAL CORP. (MO)
Liquidation completed
Each share Capital Stock $1 par received initial distribution of $0.53 cash 6/5/64
Each share Capital Stock $1 par received second distribution of $0.28 cash 1/4/65
Each share Capital Stock $1 par received third and final distribution of $0.045 cash 7/30/65
Certificates were not retired and are now without value

TRANS AMER INDS LTD (BC)
Merged into Primary Corp. 08/05/2008
Each share Common no par exchanged for (0.5) share Common no par
Primary Corp. name changed to Marret Resource Corp. 07/06/2012

TRANS-AMERICA PETROLEUMS LTD. (QC)
Charter annulled for failure to file annual reports 9/2/78

TRANS AMERN FDG CORP (DE)
Name changed to Hooker American Inc. 3/4/69
Hooker American Inc. name changed to Curtis-Hooker Corp. 9/23/70 which name changed back to Hooker American, Inc. 5/5/75
(See Hooker American, Inc.)

TRANS-AMERICAN MINERALS CORP. (CO)
Declared defunct and inoperative for failure to pay franchise taxes 10/26/60

TRANS-AMERICAN MINING CORP., LTD. (ON)
Charter cancelled for failure to file returns and pay fees 10/11/77

TRANS-AMERICAN PETROLEUM CORP. (DE)
No longer in existence having become inoperative and void for non-payment of taxes 4/1/59

TRANS-AMERICAN SECURITIES, INC. (GA)
Name changed to Interstate Credit Corp. (GA) 12/15/1965
(See Interstate Credit Corp. (GA))

TRANS ASIA RES INC (BC)
Name changed to Municipal Solutions Group, Inc. 01/14/2002
Municipal Solutions Group, Inc. reorganized as CloudBench Applications, Inc. 07/21/2008 which name changed to BasicGov Systems, Inc. 12/24/2009 which name changed to Pedro Resources Ltd. 09/30/2010

TRANS ASIAN RES LTD (BC)
Recapitalized as Pacific Falkon Resources Inc. 9/22/94
Each share Common no par exchanged for (1/3) share Common no par
Pacific Falkon Resources Inc. recapitalized as Pacific Consolidated Resources Corp. 6/29/98

TRANS ATLANTIC GAMES INC (NJ)
Charter declared void for non-payment of taxes 6/26/90

TRANS ATLANTIC RESOURCE CORP (NV)
Each share Capital Stock 1¢ par exchanged for (0.005) share Capital Stock $2 par 9/4/86
Charter revoked for failure to file reports and pay fees 3/1/89

TRANS ATLANTIC RES INC (BC)
Recapitalized as Trans Atlantic Enterprises Inc. 7/12/91
Each share Common no par exchanged for (0.25) share Common no par

TRANS-ATLANTIC VIDEO INC (NJ)
Name changed to Diamond Entertainment Corp. 07/15/1991
Diamond Entertainment Corp. name changed to Rx for Africa, Inc. 10/29/2007

TRANS ATLAS CORP (WA)
Common $1 par changed to 30¢ par and (2) additional shares issued 06/14/1973
Charter cancelled and proclaimed dissolved for failure to file reports 07/01/1977

TRANS BEACON CORP (DE)
Adjudicated bankrupt 03/22/1971
Stockholders' equity unlikely

TRANS BORDER ENERGY CORP (BC)
Recapitalized as Brownstone Investment Inc. 10/01/1992
Each share Common no par exchanged for (0.5) share Common no par
Brownstone Investment Inc. name changed to Brownstone Resources Inc. 01/20/1997 which name changed to Brownstone Ventures Inc. 12/23/2003 which name changed to Brownstone Energy Inc. (BC) 01/18/2011 which reincorporated in Canada 12/01/2011 which recapitalized as ThreeD Capital Inc. 06/23/2016

TRANS CDA CORP FD (QC)
Each share Common $10 par exchanged for (10) shares Common $1 par 12/29/1961
Each share Common $1 par exchanged for (1) share Power Corp. of Canada, Ltd. 5% Conv. 2nd Preferred Ser. A $12 par 09/19/1968
5% Preferred $20 par called for redemption 07/01/1976
6% Preferred $20 par called for redemption 07/01/1976
Public interest eliminated
(See Power Corp. of Canada, Ltd.)

TRANS-CANADA EXPLORATIONS LTD. (ON)
Merged into Roman Corp. Ltd. 11/27/64
Each share Capital Stock $1 par exchanged for (0.5) share Capital Stock no par
(See Roman Corp. Ltd.)

TRANS CDA FREEZERS LTD (CANADA)
Acquired by Warnock Hersey International Ltd. 10/30/1969
Each share Capital Stock no par exchanged for (1/3) share Common no par
Warnock Hersey International Ltd. name changed to TIW Industries Ltd.- Les Industries TIW Ltee. 12/31/1977
(See TIW Industries Ltd.- Les Industries TIW Ltee.)

TRANS CDA GLASS LTD (BC)
Common no par split (5) for (1) by issuance of (4) additional shares 6/12/86
Common no par split (3) for (1) by issuance of (2) additional shares 5/23/89
Name changed to TCG International Inc. 2/26/90
(See TCG International Inc.)

TRANS-CANADA MINES, LTD. (ON)
Dissolved 5/1/58

TRANS CDA MTG CORP WESTN LTD (AB)
Acquired by Melton Real Estate Ltd. 11/29/1968
Each share Capital Stock no par exchanged for (2) shares Common no par
Melton Real Estate Ltd. name changed to Melcor Developments Ltd. 06/11/1976

TRANS-CANADA OILS LTD. (BC)
Name changed to Trans-Canada Resources Ltd. (B.C.) 1/6/69
Trans-Canada Resources Ltd. (B.C.) reincorporated in Alberta 10/8/82 which merged into Trans-Canada Resources Ltd. (Alta.) (New) 11/1/82 which recapitalized as Consolidated Trans-Canada Resources Ltd. 9/22/88 which merged into Ranchmen's Resources Ltd. 9/30/89

TRANS-CANADA PETROLEUMS LTD. (QC)
Merged into Trans-Canada Explorations Ltd. on a (1) for (3) basis 10/13/55
Trans-Canada Explorations Ltd. merged into Roman Corp. Ltd. 11/27/64
(See Roman Corp. Ltd.)

TRANS CDA PIPE LINES LTD (CANADA)
Name changed to TransCanada PipeLines Ltd. and $2.75 Conv. Preferred Ser. A $50 par reclassified as $2.75 Conv. 1st Preferred Ser. A $50 par and $2.80 Preferred $50 par reclassified as $2.80 1st Preferred $50 par 04/19/1972
(See TransCanada PipeLines Ltd.)

TRANS-CANADA RESOURCES LTD. (BC)
Reincorporated under the laws of Alberta 10/08/1982
Trans-Canada Resources Ltd. (AB) (Old) merged into Trans-Canada Resources Ltd. (New) 11/01/1982 which recapitalized as Consolidated Trans-Canada Resources Ltd. 09/22/1988 which merged into Ranchmen's Resources Ltd. 09/30/1989 which merged into Crestar Energy Inc. 10/11/1995 which was acquired by Gulf Canada Resources Ltd. 11/13/2000
(See Gulf Canada Resources Ltd.)

TRANS CARIBBEAN AIR CARGO LINES, INC. (DE)
Name changed to Trans Caribbean Airways, Inc. 03/31/1952
Trans Caribbean Airways, Inc. name changed to Transportation Corp. of America 07/31/1959 which name changed back to Trans Caribbean Airways, Inc. 07/01/1964 which merged into American Airlines, Inc. 03/08/1971 which reorganized as AMR Corp. 10/01/1982 which reorganized as American Airlines Group Inc. 12/09/2013

TRANS CARIBBEAN AWYS INC (DE)
Class A Common 10¢ par split (5) for (4) by issuance of (0.25) additional share 01/15/1957
Class A Common 10¢ par split (5) for (4) by issuance of (0.25) additional share 01/26/1959
Name changed to Transportation Corp. of America 07/31/1959 which name changed back to Trans Caribbean Airways, Inc. Inc. 07/01/1964
Merged into American Airlines, Inc. 03/08/1971
Each share Class A Common 10¢ par exchanged for (0.146) share Common $1 par and a Depositary Receipt (representing fractional interest in escrowed shares)
American Airlines, Inc. reorganized as AMR Corp. 10/01/1982 which reorganized as American Airlines Group Inc. 12/09/2013

TRANS CARIBBEAN RESORTS INC (DE)
Name changed to Cornwall International Industries Inc. 10/16/1972
(See Cornwall International Industries Inc.)

TRANS-CDA RES LTD NEW (AB)
Name changed 11/1/82
Under plan of merger name changed from Trans-Canada Resources Ltd. (Old) to Trans-Canada Resources Ltd. (New) and each share $1.80 Conv. 1st Preferred Ser. A no par exchanged for (1) share $1.80 Conv. 1st Preferred Ser. A no par and each share Common no par exchanged for (1) share Class A Common no par 11/1/82
Each share $1.80 Conv. 1st Preferred Ser. A no par exchanged for (8) shares Class A Common no par 9/16/87
Recapitalized as Consolidated Trans-Canada Resources Ltd. 9/22/88
Each share Class A Common no par exchanged for (0.1) share Class A Common no par
Consolidated Trans-Canada Resources Ltd. merged into Ranchmen's Resources Ltd. 9/30/89 which merged into Crestar Energy Inc. 10/11/95 which was acquired by Gulf Canada Resources Ltd. 11/13/2000
(See Gulf Canada Resources Ltd.)

TRANS-CDA WORLD SEC CORP (CANADA)
Name changed to Garda World Security Corp. 08/21/2000
(See Garda World Security Corp.)

TRANS CENT AIRLS INC (CO)
Charter suspended for failure to file reports 12/06/1977

TRANS CENTRAL INDUSTRIES, INC. (DE)
Name changed to Vista Industries Corp. 8/5/63
Vista Industries Corp. charter cancelled 3/1/85

TRANS CENTRAL PETROLEUM CORP. (DE)
Name changed to Trans Central Industries, Inc. 6/1/60
Trans Central Industries, Inc. name changed to Vista Industries Corp. 8/5/63
(See Vista Industries Corp.)

TRANS-CHES MINES LTD. (ON)
Name changed to La Ronge Uranium Mines Ltd. 00/00/1949
(See La Ronge Uranium Mines Ltd.)

TRANS COAST INVT CO (CA)
Common $1 par changed to $5 par 02/29/1960
Common $5 par changed to $1 par 03/17/1961
Merged into California Financial Corp. 04/30/1973
Each share Common $1 par exchanged for (1) share Capital Stock $1 par
(See California Financial Corp.)

TRANS COASTAL RES CORP (BC)
Name changed 03/09/1998
Name changed from Trans Coastal Industries Inc. to Trans Coastal Resources Corp. 03/09/1998
Recapitalized as Transco Resources Corp. (BC) 01/11/2000
Each share Common no par exchanged for (0.25) share Common no par
Transco Resources Corp. (BC) reincorporated in Alberta 07/21/2006 which name changed to Bridge Resources Corp. 09/14/2006 which recapitalized as Idaho Natural Resources Corp. 04/24/2012
(See Idaho Natural Resources Corp.)

TRANS COLUMBIA EXPLS LTD (BC)
Recapitalized as Consolidated Trans Columbia Industries Ltd. 05/25/1973
Each share Common no par exchanged for (0.5) share Common no par
(See Consolidated Trans Columbia Industries Ltd.)

TRANS CONTL ENTMT GROUP INC (NV)
SEC revoked common stock registration 07/07/2006

TRANS CONTINENTAL INDUSTRIES, INC. (MI)
Each share Common $1 par exchanged for (0.25) share Common no par 10/12/1959
Name changed to Republic-Transcon Industries, Inc. 01/22/1960
Republic-Transcon Industries, Inc. acquired by Briggs Manufacturing Co. 10/19/1965 which name changed to Panacon Corp. 04/09/1970
(See Panacon Corp.)

TRANS CONTL INDS INC (NV)
Adjudicated bankrupt 07/27/1973
No stockholders' equity

TRANS CONTINENTAL INVESTMENT CO. (NV)
Merged into Bonneville Capital Corp. share for share 3/30/64
(See Bonneville Capital Corp.)

TRANS CONTL LEASING CORP (CA)
Merged into Worldwide Computer Services Inc. 12/28/1971
Each share Common no par exchanged for (1) share Common 1¢ par
Worldwide Computer Services Inc. name changed to Worldwide Commerce Inc. 02/24/1972
(See Worldwide Commerce Inc.)

TRANS CONTINENTAL LIFE INSURANCE CO. (IL)
Each share Common 25¢ par exchanged for (0.25) share Common $1 par 10/20/1964
Merged into Executive National Life Insurance Co. (IL) 03/31/1967
Each share Common $1 par exchanged for (0.6342937) share Common $1 par
Executive National Life Insurance Co. (IL) merged into Commonwealth Industries Corp. (IL) 08/10/1986 which reincorporated in Delaware 04/20/1981
(See Commonwealth Industries Corp.)

TRANS-CONTINENTAL TELEPHONE & ELECTRONICS, INC. (TX)
Merged into Continental Telephone Corp. 4/1/68
Each share Common $2 par exchanged for (1) share Common $1 par
Continental Telephone Corp. name changed to Continental Telecom Inc. 5/6/82 which name changed to Contel Corp. 5/1/86 which merged into GTE Corp. 3/14/91 which merged into Verizon Communications Inc. 6/30/2000

TRANS DELTA CORP (DE)
Merged into Petro-Lewis Corp. 09/24/1980
Each share Common 1¢ par exchanged for $21.43 cash

TRANS DOMINION ENERGY CORP (BC)
Recapitalized as Madison Oil Co. Inc. (BC) 05/25/2000
Each share Common no par exchanged for (0.02) share Common no par
Madison Oil Co. Inc. (BC) reincorporated in Delaware 07/12/2000 which merged into Torreador Resources Corp. 12/31/2001 which merged into ZaZa Energy Corp. 02/22/2012

TRANS DOMINION MINING & OILS CORP. (QC)
Acquired by International Mining & Development Corp. 07/01/1955
Each share Capital Stock $1 par exchanged for (0.2) share Common 1¢ par
(See International Mining & Development Corp.)

TRANS EAST AIR INC (NY)
Adjudicated bankrupt 06/15/1976
Stockholders' equity unlikely

TRANS EAST AIRLS INC (NY)
Name changed to Trans-East Air Inc. 08/26/1969
(See Trans-East Air Inc.)

TRANS EASTERN OIL & GAS LTD. (ON)
Merged into Erieshore Industries Inc. 05/10/1971
Each share Common $1 par exchanged for (0.222222) share Common no par
Erieshore Industries Inc. merged into Portfield Industries Inc. 10/22/1980 which recapitalized as Canmine Resources Corp. 05/01/1991
(See Canmine Resources Corp.)

TRANS EMPIRE OILS LTD. (CANADA)
Capital Stock no par changed to $1.25 par in 1954
Name changed to West Canadian Oil & Gas Ltd. 3/10/58
West Canadian Oil & Gas Ltd. merged into Canadian Delhi Oil Ltd. 1/1/62 which recapitalized as CanDel Oil Ltd. 1/10/72
(See CanDel Oil Ltd.)

TRANS ENERGY INC (NV)
Each share old Common $0.001 par exchanged for (0.25) share new Common $0.001 par 06/05/1998
Each share new Common $0.001 par exchanged again for (0.00666666) share new Common $0.001 par 01/28/2005
Acquired by EQT Corp. 12/05/2016
Each share new Common $0.001 par exchanged for $3.58 cash

TRANS-ERA OILS LTD. (ON)
Recapitalized as Rocky Petroleums Ltd. 11/15/1956
Each share Common no par exchanged for (0.166666) share Common 50¢ par
(See Rocky Petroleums Ltd.)

TRANS FINL BANCORP INC (KY)
Common $10 par changed to no par and (2) additional shares issued 09/24/1985
Common no par split (4) for (3) by issuance of (1/3) additional share 12/16/1991
Common no par split (4) for (3) by issuance of (1/3) additional share 02/01/1993
Stock Dividend - 50% 02/13/1989
Name changed to Trans Financial, Inc. 04/24/1995
Trans Financial, Inc. merged into Star Banc Corp. 08/21/1998 which merged into Firstar Corp. (New) 11/20/1998 which merged into U.S. Bancorp (DE) 02/27/2001

TRANS FINL INC (KY)
Merged into Star Banc Corp. 08/21/1998
Each share Common no par exchanged for (0.9003) share Common $5 par
Star Banc Corp. merged into Firstar Corp. (New) 11/20/1998 which merged into U.S. Bancorp (DE) 02/27/2001

TRANS FLA BANCSHARES INC (FL)
Completely liquidated 10/11/1982
Each share Capital Stock 1¢ par exchanged for first and final distribution of $2.15 cash

TRANS GLOBAL AIRLS INC (NJ)
Charter void by proclamation 6/26/90

TRANS GLOBAL GROUP INC (NV)
Reincorporated under the laws of Florida 03/28/2014

TRANS-GLOBAL HLDGS INC (NV)
Each share old Common $0.005 par exchanged for (0.1) share new Common $0.005 par 3/6/2006
Name changed to Clear Cut Film Technology Studios, Inc. 4/17/2006
Clear Cut Film Technology Studios, Inc. recapitalized as Trans-Global Capital Management, Inc. 2/13/2007

TRANS-GLOBAL INTERACTIVE LTD (AUSTRALIA)
Name changed 06/30/1999
Each Unsponsored ADR for Ordinary AUD $0.25 par exchanged for (0.05) old Sponsored ADR for Ordinary AUD $0.25 par 12/13/1993
Each old Sponsored ADR for Ordinary AUD $0.25 par exchanged for (0.2) new Sponsored ADR for Ordinary AUD $0.25 par 10/16/1995
Each new Sponsored ADR for Ordinary AUD $0.25 par exchanged again for (0.25) new Sponsored ADR for Ordinary AUD $0.25 par 06/15/1999
Name changed from Trans-Global Resources N.L. to Trans-Global Interactive Ltd. 06/30/1999
Each new Sponsored ADR for Ordinary AUD $0.25 par exchanged for (0.1) new Sponsored ADR 2002 for Ordinary AUD $0.25 par 06/17/2002
ADR agreement terminated 03/31/2003
Each new Sponsored ADR 2002 for Ordinary AUD $0.25 par exchanged for $10.8016 cash

TRANS GLOBAL LOGISTICS INC (MD)
Charter forfeited for failure to file annual reports 10/03/2008

TRANS GLOBAL SVCS INC (DE)
Each share old Common 1¢ par exchanged for (0.16666666) share new Common 1¢ par 06/19/1997
SEC revoked common stock registration 10/24/2008

TRANS GRAPHICS INC (DE)
Merged into Trans Graphics Acquisition Corp. 01/06/1986
Each share Common 1¢ par exchanged for $2 cash

TRANS GULF CORP (TX)
Charter forfeited for failure to pay taxes 04/09/1971

TRANS-GULF DEVELOPMENT CORP. (TX)
Old Common 25¢ par changed to 10¢ par 6/1/60
Each share Common 10¢ par exchanged for (0.1) share new Common 25¢ par 12/7/62
Name changed to Trans-Gulf Corp. and new Common 25¢ par changed to no par 12/1/67

TRANS-GULF OFFSHORE DRILLING, INC. (TX)
Name changed to Trans-Gulf Development Corp. 6/6/60
Trans-Gulf Development Corp. name changed to Trans-Gulf Corp. 12/1/67

TRANS HEX GROUP LTD (SOUTH AFRICA)
ADR agreement terminated 11/30/2017
Each Sponsored ADR for Common exchanged for (1) share Common
Note: Unexchanged ADR's will be sold and the proceeds, if any, held for claim after 12/03/2018

TRANS HEX INTL LTD (ON)
Reincorporated under the laws of Yukon as Tsodilo Resources Ltd. 6/14/2002

TRANS-INDIA ACQUISITION CORP (DE)
Completely liquidated 03/17/2009
Each Unit exchanged for first and final distribution of $7.9765704 cash
Each share Common $0.0001 par exchanged for first and final distribution of $7.9765704 cash

TRANS INDS INC (DE)
Common 10¢ par split (5) for (4) by issuance of (0.25) additional share 01/20/1986
Common 10¢ par split (3) for (2) by issuance of (0.5) additional share 07/07/1987
Stock Dividends - (1) for (7.792) 04/08/1972; 10% 01/10/1984; 10% 01/15/1985
Chapter 11 bankruptcy proceedings converted to Chapter 7 on 10/17/2006
No stockholders' equity

TRANS INTERNATIONAL AIRLINES CORP. (NV)
Common no par split (2) for (1) by issuance of (1) additional share 02/04/1966
Common no par split (2) for (1) by issuance of (1) additional share 09/22/1967
Stock Dividend - 50% 05/24/1966
Acquired by Transamerica Corp. 03/08/1968
Each share Common no par exchanged for (0.5) share Common $2 par
Transamerica Corp. merged into Aegon N.V. 07/21/1999

TRANS INTERNATIONAL CORP. (MO)
Name changed to Action Industries Inc. 06/29/1973
(See Action Industries Inc.)

TRANS INTL GOLD CORP (BC)
Recapitalized as Keaton Resources Ltd. 10/16/1991
Each share Common no par

exchanged for (0.5) share Common no par
Keaton Resources Ltd. name changed to GFM Resources Ltd. (BC) 11/07/1997 which reincorporated in Yukon 07/25/2000

TRANS LA GAS INC (LA)
Common no par split (3) for (2) by issuance of (0.5) additional share 11/30/83
Common no par split (4) for (3) by issuance of (1/3) additional share 5/22/85
Merged into Energas Co. 4/30/86
Each share Common no par exchanged for $21 cash

TRANS LEASING INTL INC (DE)
Name changed to TLII Liquidating Corp. 12/13/97
(See TLII Liquidating Corp.)

TRANS-LEDUC OILS LTD. (ON)
Charter cancelled and company declared dissolved for default in filing returns 09/28/1964

TRANS-LUX DAYLIGHT PICTURE SCREEN CORP.
Name changed to Trans-Lux-Corp. in 1937

TRANS MAX TECHNOLOGIES INC (NV)
Old Common $0.001 par split (6) for (1) by issuance of (5) additional shares payable 03/11/2004 to holders of record 03/02/2004 Ex date - 03/12/2004
Each share old Common $0.001 par exchanged for (0.005) share new Common $0.001 par 08/09/2004
Each share new Common $0.001 par exchanged again for (0.02) share new Common $0.001 par 04/22/2008
Name changed to Recovery Enterprises, Inc. 09/30/2008
Recovery Enterprises, Inc. name changed to KMT Global Holdings Inc. 05/03/2011 which recapitalized as StarPower ON Systems, Inc. 03/23/2017

TRANS-MICHIGAN AIRLINES, INC. (MI)
Charter declared inoperative and void for failure to file reports 5/15/74

TRANS-MOUNTAIN URANIUM CO., INC. (CO)
Declared defunct and inoperative for failure to pay Colorado taxes 10/14/63

TRANS MTN PIPE LINE LTD (CANADA)
Name changed 08/02/1972
Capital Stock no par split (5) for (1) by issuance of (4) additional shares 09/29/1958
Name changed from Trans Mountain Oil Pipe Line Co. to Trans Mountain Pipe Line Co. Ltd. 08/02/1972
Capital Stock no par reclassified as Conv. Class A Capital Stock no par 06/07/1976
Conv. Class A Capital Stock no par reclassified as Capital Stock no par 09/11/1979
Conv. Class B Capital Stock no par reclassified as Capital Stock no par 09/11/1979
Acquired by BC Gas Inc. (New) 11/14/1994
Each share Common no par exchanged for $24.50 cash

TRANS NATAL COAL CORP (SOUTH AFRICA)
ADR agreement terminated 00/00/1994
Details not available

TRANS NATION INC (ON)
9% Conv. Preference $10 par called for redemption 07/12/1976
Common no par 100% reacquired at $4 per share 00/00/1979

TRANS-NATION LAND CORP. (TORONTO) LTD. (ON)
Name changed to Trans-Nation Inc. 10/18/1974
(See Trans-Nation Inc.)

TRANS NATION MINERALS LTD. (NB)
Charter forfeited for failure to file annual returns 12/7/66

TRANS-NATION MOTELS, INC. (IN)
Charter revoked for failure to file annual reports 6/30/78

TRANS NATL COMMUNICATIONS INC (NY)
Charter cancelled and proclaimed dissolved for failure to pay taxes and file reports 12/20/1977

TRANS NATL CORP (FL)
Proclaimed dissolved for failure to file reports and pay fees 7/2/73

TRANS NATL LEASING INC (TX)
Merged into Associate Commercial Corp. 12/23/92
Each share Common 40¢ par exchanged for $4.25 cash

TRANS NATL MARKETING INDS INC (NY)
Adjudicated bankrupt 01/16/1976
Details not available

TRANS-NATIONAL MINERALS, INC. DELAWARE
No longer in existence having become inoperative and void for non-payment of taxes 4/1/58

TRANS NATL MINERALS INC (BC)
Name changed to IEMR Resources Inc. 09/10/2010

TRANS NEW ZEALAND OIL CO (NV)
Name changed to AMG Oil Ltd. (NV) 07/27/1998
AMG Oil Ltd. (NV) reincorporated in Canada 12/04/2008 which name changed to Adira Energy Ltd. 01/21/2010 which name changed to Empower Clinics Inc. 04/30/2018

TRANS-ORE MINES LTD. (BC)
Company dissolved and struck off register for failure to file reports 9/19/69

TRANS ORIENT PETE LTD (BC)
Reincorporated 09/26/1997
Reincorporated 01/16/2006
Old Common no par split (2) for (1) by issuance of (1) additional share payable 05/04/1998 to holders of record 05/04/1998
Each share old Common no par exchanged for (0.08333333) share new Common no par 03/01/2001
Each share new Common no par exchanged again for (0.33333333) share new Common no par 04/04/2002
Place of incorporation changed from (BC) to (YT) 09/26/1997 which changed back to (BC) 01/16/2006
Common no par split (7) for (1) by issuance of (6) additional shares payable 03/29/2006 to holders of record 03/20/2006 Ex date - 03/30/2006
Merged into TAG Oil Ltd. 12/16/2009
Each share Common no par exchanged for (0.35714285) share Common no par
Note: Unexchanged certificates were cancelled and became without value 12/16/2015

TRANS PAC BANCORP (CA)
Merged into TRP Acquisition Corp. 3/14/97
Each share Common no par exchanged for $8.19 cash
Note: An additional distribution of $0.42 cash per share was made 4/30/99

TRANS PAC DEVS LTD (DE)
Charter cancelled and declared inoperative and void for non-payment of taxes 04/15/1972

TRANS PAC FINL CORP (WA)
Merged into First Farwest Corp. 11/30/1976
Each share Common no par exchanged for $8.93 cash

TRANS PAC GROUP INC (UT)
Each share old Common $0.001 par exchanged for (0.4) share new Common $0.001 par 11/22/1996
Reincorporated under the laws of Nevada as Beverage Store, Inc. 02/05/1997
Beverage Store, Inc. recapitalized as Fortune Oil & Gas Inc. (NV) 04/17/1998 which reorganized in Wyoming as Manzo Pharmaceuticals, Inc. 09/17/2014

TRANS-PACIFIC AEROSPACE CO INC (NV)
Reincorporated under the laws of Wyoming 01/27/2017

TRANS-PACIFIC AIRLINES, LTD. (HI)
Name changed to Aloha Airlines, Inc. 11/18/58
Aloha Airlines, Inc. reorganized as Aloha, Inc. 3/30/84
(See Aloha, Inc.)

TRANS-PACIFIC INSURANCE CO. (AZ)
Adjudicated bankrupt in December 1962
No stockholders' equity

TRANS-PACIFIC LEASING, INC. (WA)
Name changed to Trans Pacific Financial Corp. 12/12/72
(See Trans Pacific Financial Corp.)

TRANS-PACIFIC RESEARCH & CAPITAL, INC. (WA)
Liquidation completed
Each share Common no par received initial distribution of $11 cash 10/22/86
Each share Common no par exchanged for second distribution of $1 cash 12/29/86
Each share Common no par received third and final distribution of $0.90 cash 6/30/87

TRANS PLAINS INSURANCE CO. (TX)
Charter cancelled 6/4/71
No stockholders' equity

TRANS PRAIRIE PIPELINES LTD (MB)
Common no par split (5) for (1) by issuance of (4) additional shares 5/26/62
6% Conv. Preferred Ser. A $50 par called for redemption 10/30/64
Name changed to Norcen Pipelines Ltd. 4/14/77
(See Norcen Pipelines Ltd.)

TRANS RAMPART INDS LTD (BC)
Name changed to Rampart Mercantile Inc. (BC) 05/28/1993
Rampart Mercantile Inc. (BC) reincorporated in Ontario 11/24/1999 which name changed to Aurquest Resources Inc. 04/14/2011 which name changed to Xanthic Biopharma Inc. 04/19/2018

TRANS-SCIENCE CORP (CA)
Reincorporated under the laws of Delaware as China Shuangji Cement, Ltd. and Common no par changed to $0.0001 par 11/09/2007
(See China Shuangji Cement, Ltd.)

TRANS SVCS CORP (UT)
Each share Common 1¢ par exchanged for (0.1) share Common 10¢ par 06/15/1972
Proclaimed dissolved for failure to pay taxes 03/31/1985

TRANS SONICS INC (MA)
Acquired by Foxboro Co. 12/20/1974
Each share Common $1 par exchanged for (0.25) share Common $1 par
(See Foxboro Co.)

TRANS-SOUTHERN CORP. (AL)
Merged into American Pyramid Companies Inc. in 1968
Each share Class A Common 30¢ par exchanged for (1.35) shares Common no par
American Pyramid Companies Inc. merged into American Consolidated Corp. 2/28/77 which merged into I.C.H. Corp. 4/18/85 which name changed to Southwestern Life Corp. (New) 6/15/94 which name changed to I.C.H. Corp. (New) 10/10/95
(See I.C.H. Corp. (New))

TRANS SOUTHN HLDG CORP (NY)
Charter cancelled and proclaimed dissolved for failure to file reports and pay taxes 12/15/1973

TRANS-STATE INVESTMENT CORP. (IL)
Merged into Investors Security Corp. (Ill.) 5/31/65
Each share Class A no par exchanged for (2.41608) shares Class A 25¢ par
Each share Class B no par exchanged for (2.11978) shares Class A 25¢ par
(See Investors Security Corp.)

TRANS-TEXAS AIRWAYS, INC. (TX)
Reincorporated under the laws of Delaware as Texas International Airlines, Inc. 10/01/1968
Texas International Airlines, Inc. reorganized as Texas Air Corp. 06/11/1980 which name changed to Continental Airlines Holdings, Inc. 06/11/1990
(See Continental Airlines Holdings, Inc.)

TRANS TEXAS BANCORPORATION (TX)
Common $10 par changed to $5 par and (1) additional share issued 1/1/77
Name changed to El Paso National Corp. 4/30/80
(See El Paso National Corp.)

TRANS UN CORP (DE)
Merged into Marmon Group, Inc. 02/10/1981
Each share Common $1 par exchanged for $55 cash

TRANS-UNION OIL & MINING CO. (UT)
Each share Capital Stock 5¢ par exchanged for (0.1) share Capital Stock 50¢ par 09/29/1959
Name changed to Water Wonderland Corp. 12/15/1960
Water Wonderland Corp. name changed to Progressive National Industries, Inc. 08/17/1972
(See Progressive National Industries, Inc.)

TRANS-UNITED INDUSTRIES, INC. (PA)
Reorganized 12/31/1965
No stockholders' equity

TRANS VALLEY GAS & OIL CORP. LTD. (ON)
Charter revoked for failure to file reports and pay fees 01/26/1967

TRANS-VIDEO PRODUCTIONS LTD. (ON)
Reorganized as Williams (Roger) Music Corp. Ltd. 08/30/1971
Each share 7% Preference $1 par exchanged for (0.05) share Common no par
Each share Common no par exchanged for (0.02) share Common no par
Williams (Roger) Music Corp. Ltd. name changed to RWMC Productions Ltd. 08/08/1974 which name changed to International

Phoenix Capital Corp. 01/18/1977 which name changed to Fairway Automotive Industries Ltd. 09/25/1986 which recapitalized as Fairway Industries Ltd. 02/26/1988 which recapitalized as Pharmaglobe Inc. (ON) 03/14/1994 which reincorporated in Delaware 03/01/2001 which name changed to Pharmaglobe America Group, Inc. 05/12/2004

TRANS WEST INC (DE)
Recapitalized as D-Vine Ltd. 02/20/1996
Each share Common 1¢ par exchanged for (0.00666666) share Common 1¢ par
D-Vine Ltd. name changed to Monsterdaata.Com Inc. 03/29/1999 which name changed to Monsterdaata Inc. 12/07/2000 which recapitalized as Enviro Global Corp. 08/08/2007

TRANS-WESTERN URANIUM CORP. (UT)
Recapitalized as Flying Diamond Land & Mineral Corp. 01/07/1969
Each share Common 2¢ par exchanged for (0.02) share Common $1 par
Flying Diamond Land & Mineral Corp. name changed to Flying Diamond Corp. 10/26/1971 which merged into Flying Diamond Oil Corp. 12/04/1974
(See Flying Diamond Oil Corp.)

TRANS WESTN EXPL INC (TX)
Old Common no par split (3) for (2) by issuance of (0.5) additional share 10/24/1980
Reorganized under Chapter 11 Federal Bankruptcy Code 08/19/1986
Each share old Common no par exchanged for (0.5) share new Common no par
Note: Unexchanged certificates were cancelled and became without value 11/18/1986
Recapitalized as United Trans-Western, Inc. (TX) 04/15/1987
Each share new Common no par exchanged for (1/3) share Ser. A Common no par
United Trans-Western, Inc. (TX) reincorporated in Delaware 07/26/1989
(See United Trans-Western, Inc.)

TRANS WESTN OIL & GAS CORP (DE)
Recapitalized as Transco Industries, Inc. 08/25/1969
Each share Common 25¢ par exchanged for (0.25) share Common 5¢ par

TRANS WORLD AIRLS INC (DE)
Ctfs. dated prior to 01/01/1979
Stock Dividend - 10% 01/15/1963
Under plan of reorganization name changed to Trans World Corp. (DE) 01/01/1979
Common $5 par, $2 Conv. Preferred no par and $1.90 Preferred Ser. B no par exchanged for Common $5 par, $2 Conv. Preferred no par and $1.90 Preferred Ser. B respectively
Trans World Corp. (DE) name changed to Transworld Corp. (DE) 04/25/1984
Assets were transferred to Transworld Corp. Liquidating Trust 12/31/1986
(See Transworld Corp. Liquidating Trust)
Ctfs. dated after 11/30/1982
$2.25 Conv. Preferred $0.001 par called for redemption 11/27/1985
Recapitalized 09/03/1988
Each share $6 Exchangeable Preferred $0.001 par exchanged for $50 principal amount of 12% Jr. Subordinated Debentures due 09/30/2008
Note: Unexchanged certificates were cancelled and deemed worthless by plan of reorganization under Chapter 11 Federal Bankruptcy proceedings confirmed 11/03/1993
Merged into TWA Acquisitions, Inc. 10/24/1988
Each share $2.25 Preferred $0.001 par exchanged for $0.25 cash
Each share Common 1¢ par exchanged for $20 cash and $30 principal amount of Trans World Airlines, Inc. 12% Jr. Subordinated Debentures due 09/30/2008
Note: Unexchanged certificates were cancelled and deemed worthless by plan of reorganization under Chapter 11 Federal Bankruptcy proceedings confirmed 11/03/1993
Plan of reorganization under Chapter 11 Federal Bankruptcy proceedings confirmed 11/03/1993
No stockholders' equity for holders of $0.05 Preference 50¢ par
Each share old Common 1¢ par exchanged for (0.0213) share new Common 1¢ par, (0.0426) Common Stock Purchase Warrant expiring 08/23/2002 and (0.0107) Equity Right 08/23/1995
Plan of reorganization under Chapter 11 Federal Bankruptcy proceedings confirmed 08/04/1995
Each share Preferred 1¢ par exchanged for (0.1024) share new Common 1¢ par, (0.1180) Common Stock Purchase Warrant expiring 08/23/2002, and (0.0512) Equity Right
Each Voting Trust Certificate exchanged for (0.0213) share new Common 1¢ par and (0.0246) Common Stock Purchase Warrants expiring 08/23/2002
12% Preferred 1¢ par called for redemption 04/26/1996
Plan of reorganization under Chapter 11 Federal Bankruptcy proceedings effective 06/25/2002
No stockholders' equity

TRANS WORLD ASSURN CO (CA)
Reorganized under the laws of Delaware as TWA Corp. and Common $1.06 par changed to $6 par 00/00/1983

TRANS WORLD ATTRACTIONS CORP (NY)
Name changed to Jenner Industries, Inc. 07/09/1979
(See Jenner Industries, Inc.)

TRANS WORLD BK (SHERMAN OAKS, CA)
Each share Capital Stock $3.50 par exchanged for (1.85153) shares Capital Stock $2 par 08/18/1972
Stock Dividends - 10% 12/05/1979; 10% 12/05/1980; 10% 12/04/1981
Under plan of reorganization each share Capital Stock $2 par automatically became (1) share Transworld Bancorp Common no par 10/01/1982
(See Transworld Bancorp)

TRANS WORLD CORP. (CO)
Recapitalized as International Recreation & Sports, Inc. 11/08/1968
Each share Common 10¢ par exchanged for (0.01) share Common $0.0001 par
(See International Recreation & Sports, Inc.)

TRANS WORLD CORP (DE)
Name changed to Transworld Corp. (DE) 04/25/1984
Transworld Corp. (DE) assets transferred to Transworld Corp. Liquidating Trust 12/31/1986
(See Transworld Corp. Liquidating Trust)

TRANS WORLD CORP (NV)
Each share old Common $0.001 par exchanged for (0.01) share new Common $0.001 par 04/05/2004
Acquired by FEC Overseas Investment (UK) Ltd. 04/30/2018
Each share new Common $0.001 par exchanged for $4.1886 cash

TRANS-WORLD ENTERPRISES INC (DE)
Each share old Common $0.001 par exchanged for (0.33333333) share new Common $0.001 par 03/01/1988
Name changed to RES-Q International, Inc. 08/23/1989
(See RES-Q International, Inc.)

TRANS WORLD FINL CO (DE)
Merged into Golden West Financial Corp. (DE) 10/31/1975
Each share Common $1 par exchanged for (0.9) share Conv. Preferred Ser. A no par
(See Golden West Financial Corp. (DE))

TRANS WORLD GAMING CORP (NV)
Name changed to Trans World Corp. 08/31/2000
(See Trans World Corp.)

TRANS WORLD LIFE INS CO (CA)
Name changed to Trans World Assurance Co. and Common $1 par changed to $1.06 par 03/30/1971
Trans World Assurance Co. reorganized in Delaware as TWA Corp. 00/00/1983

TRANS WORLD LIFE INS CO N Y (NY)
Common $2.50 par changed to $1.25 par 08/10/1966
Common $1.25 par changed to $1 par 12/15/1967
Each share Common $1 par exchanged for (0.25) share Common $2 par 05/17/1973
Acquired by American National Insurance Co. 05/02/1975
Each share Common $2 par exchanged for $10.50 cash

TRANS WORLD MEDIA (UT)
Proclaimed dissolved for failure to pay taxes 09/30/1978

TRANS WORLD MUSIC CORP (NY)
Common 1¢ par split (3) for (2) by issuance of (0.5) additional share 07/17/1987
Name changed to Trans World Entertainment Corp. 09/22/1994

TRANS WORLD TRADE INC (UT)
Merged into Transmerg Inc. 02/11/1988
Details not available

TRANS-WORLD URANIUM CORP. (UT)
Merged into Sterling Uranium Corp. share for share 03/01/1955
Sterling Uranium Corp. recapitalized as Sterling Beryllium & Oil Co. 02/04/1958 which merged into Elgin Gas & Oil Co. 06/12/1959
(See Elgin Gas & Oil Co.)

TRANS ZAMBEZI INDS LTD (BRITISH VIRGIN ISLANDS)
Name changed to TZI Ltd. 01/23/2002

TRANSAC ENTERPRISE CORP (BC)
Name changed to Evergreen Gaming Corp. 11/01/2006

TRANSACHROME CORP. (NY)
Charter cancelled and proclaimed dissolved for non-payment of taxes 12/15/1970

TRANSACT INTL INC (CT)
SEC revoked common stock registration 09/17/2009

TRANSACTION, INC. (MO)
Charter forfeited for failure to pay taxes 01/01/1975

TRANSACTION NETWORK SVCS INC (DE)
Common 1¢ par split (3) for (2) by issuance of (0.5) additional share payable 05/10/1996 to holders of record 04/30/1996
Merged into PSINet Inc. 11/22/1999
Each share Common 1¢ par exchanged for either (0.56226) share Common 1¢ par and $19.6983 cash or $45 cash
Note: Non-electors received (0.28113) share Common 1¢ par and $32.35 cash
(See PSINet Inc.)

TRANSACTION SYS ARCHITECTS INC (DE)
Class A Common $0.005 par split (2) for (1) by issuance of (1) additional share payable 07/01/1996 to holders of record 06/17/1996
Class A Common $0.005 par reclassified as Common $0.005 par 03/09/2005
Name changed to ACI Worldwide, Inc. 07/25/2007

TRANSAIR LTD (CANADA)
5% Preference no par called for redemption 03/11/1963
Class A $10 par reclassified as 70¢ Preference $10 par 11/29/1963
Class B no par reclassified as Common no par 11/29/1963
70¢ Preference $10 par called for redemption 09/21/1979
Under plan of arrangement each share Common no par exchanged for $3.02 cash 11/28/1979

TRANSAIRCO INC (DE)
Charter cancelled and declared inoperative and void for non-payment of taxes 03/01/1978

TRANSAKT CORP (AB)
Recapitalized as TransAKT Ltd. (AB) 08/04/2006
Each share Common no par exchanged for (0.5) share Common no par
TransAKT Ltd. (AB) reincorporated in Nevada 12/15/2010

TRANSAKT LTD (AB)
Reincorporated under the laws of Nevada and Common no par changed to $0.001 par 12/15/2010

TRANSALTA CORP (CANADA)
7.5% Canadian Originated Preferred Securities no par called for redemption at $25 plus $0.2363 accrued dividends on 02/15/2005
8.15% CDN$ Preferred Securities no par called for redemption at $25 plus $0.25678 accrued dividends on 02/15/2005
7.75% Preferred Securities no par called for redemption at $25 plus $0.01062 accrued dividends on 01/02/2007
(Additional Information in Active)

TRANSALTA PWR L P (ON)
Each Installment Receipt plus final payment of $4 cash received (1) Unit of Ltd. Partnership Int. prior to 04/01/1999
Merged into Cheung Kong Infrastructure Holdings Ltd. 12/06/2007
Each Unit of Ltd. Partnership Int. exchanged for $8.38 cash

TRANSALTA RES CORP (CANADA)
1st Preferred Ser. C no par called for redemption 1/1/89
1st Preferred Ser. B no par called for redemption 2/1/89
Public interest eliminated

TRANSALTA UTILS CORP (CANADA)
$2.36 1st Ser. 2nd Preferred no par called for redemption 01/06/1986
8-3/4% 10th Ser. 1st Preferred no par called for redemption 01/06/1986

TRA-TRA FINANCIAL INFORMATION, INC.

9-3/4% 9th Ser. 1st Preferred no par called for redemption 01/06/1986
9.80% 8th Ser. 1st Preferred no par called for redemption 01/06/1986
10% 7th Ser. 1st Preferred no par called for redemption 01/06/1986
12% 16th Ser. 1st Preferred no par called for redemption 09/30/1986
14.25% 17th Ser. 1st Preferred no par called for redemption 06/30/1987
$1.40 2nd Preferred no par called for redemption 10/01/1987
12-1/2% 1st Preferred no par called for redemption 10/01/1988
9% 1st Preferred no par called for redemption 07/01/1993
Conv. Class A Common no par reclassified as Common no par and (1) additional share issued 02/08/1988
Conv. Class B Common no par reclassified as Common no par and (1) additional share issued 02/08/1988
Under plan of reorganization each share new Common no par automatically became (1) share TransAlta Corp. Common no par 12/31/1992
8.40% 1st Preferred no par called for redemption at $25 on 03/27/2000
4% 1st Preferred no par called for redemption at $103 plus $0.778 accrued dividends on 09/10/2001
4.50% 1st Preferred no par called for redemption at $103 plus $0.875 accrued dividends on 09/10/2001
5% 1st Preferred no par called for redemption at $100 plus $0.972 accrued dividends on 09/10/2001
5.40% 1st Conv. Preferred no par called for redemption at $100 plus $1.05 accrued dividends on 09/10/2001
7% 1st Preferred no par called for redemption at $102 plus $1.361 accrued dividends on 09/10/2001
7.08% 1st Preferred no par called for redemption at $25 plus $0.344 accrued dividends on 09/10/2001
7.10% 1st Preferred no par called for redemption at $25 plus $0.345 accrued dividends on 09/10/2001
7.20% 1st Preferred no par called for redemption at $25 plus $0.35 accrued dividends on 09/10/2001
7.30% 1st Preferred no par called for redemption at $100 plus $1.419 accrued dividends on 09/10/2001
7.44% 1st Preferred 1977 Ser. no par called for redemption at $100 plus $1.447 accured dividends on 09/10/2001
7.44% 1st Preferred 1979 Ser. no par called for redemption at $100 plus $1.447 accured dividends on 09/10/2001
7.50% 1st Preferred no par called for redemption at $102 plus $1.458 accrued dividends on 09/10/2001
7.70% 1st Preferred no par called for redemption at $100 plus $1.497 accrued dividends on 09/10/2001

TRANSAMERICA BUSINESS CORP. (FL)
Filed for Chapter 11 bankruptcy proceedings 07/05/1985
No stockholders' equity

TRANSAMERICA CAP APPRECIATION FD (TX)
Name changed 04/19/1991
Name changed from Transamerica Technology Fund to Transamerica Capital Appreciation Fund 04/19/1991
Merged into Hancock (John) Capital Growth Fund 12/22/1994
Each share Class A $1 par exchanged for (1) share Class A $1 par
Each share Class B $1 par exchanged for (1) share Class B $1 par

(See Hancock (John) Capital Growth Fund)

TRANSAMERICA CAP FD (DE)
Name changed to FPA Capital Fund, Inc. 07/10/1984

TRANSAMERICA CAPITAL CORP. (GA)
Thru exchange offer 100% of Common $1 par was acquired by American Plan Corp. by 9/8/69

TRANSAMERICA CORP (DE)
Capital Stock $25 par changed to no par 00/00/1931
Each share Capital Stock no par exchanged for (0.5) share Capital Stock $2 par 00/00/1937
Capital Stock $2 par reclassified as Common $2 par 06/21/1961
Common $2 par split (5) for (4) by issuance of (0.25) additional share 04/03/1964
Common $2 par changed to $1 par and (1) additional share issued 02/28/1969
4.5% Conv. Preferred $100 par called for redemption 12/19/1979
$4.80 Conv. Preferred $100 par called for redemption 12/19/1979
Dutch Auction Rate Preferred Ser. B-1 $100 par called for redemption 01/08/1997
Dutch Auction Rate Preferred Ser. C-1 $100 par called for redemption 01/22/1997
Dutch Auction Rate Preferred Ser. A-1 $100 par called for redemption 02/12/1997
8.5% Preferred Ser. D $100 par called for redemption 02/15/1997
8.5% Depositary Preferred Ser. D called for redemption 02/15/1997
Common $1 par split (2) for (1) by issuance of (1) additional share payable 01/15/1999 to holders of record 12/31/1998 Ex date - 01/19/1999
Merged into Aegon N.V. 07/21/1999
Each share Common $1 par exchanged for (0.71813) share Ordinary Stock 2.50 Gldrs. par and $23.40 cash

TRANSAMERICA ENTERPRISES, INC. (UT)
Involuntarily dissolved 11/09/1974

TRANSAMERICA ENTERPRISES INC (TX)
Reincorporated under the laws of Delaware as Sea Venture Cruises, Inc. and Common $0.001 par changed to $0.0001 par 02/10/1989
Sea Venture Cruises, Inc. recapitalized as Internet Stock Exchange Corp. 04/14/1998 which name changed to Internet Stock Market Resources, Inc. 09/01/1998 which name changed to VentureNet, Inc. 06/26/2000 which name changed to VentureNet Capital Group, Inc. (DE) 11/06/2001 which reincorporated in Nevada 03/14/2003

TRANSAMERICA ENTMT CORP (DE)
Charter cancelled and declared inoperative and void for non-payment of taxes 3/1/88

TRANSAMERICA FINL CORP (DE)
Acquired by Transamerica Corp. 08/03/1961
Each share Common $10 par exchanged for (0.58) share 4.5% Conv. Preferred $100 par
(See Transamerica Corp.)

TRANSAMERICA INCOME SHS INC (DE)
Reincorporated 08/03/1979
State of incorporation changed from (DE) to (MD) 08/03/1979
Under plan of reorganization each share Common $1 par automatically became (2.3973619) Transamerica Funds Flexible Income Class I Shares no par 12/04/2015

TRANSAMERICA INVESTORS FUND, INC. (DE)
Name changed to Transamerica New Income, Inc. 3/12/82
Transamerica New Income, Inc. name changed to FPA New Income, Inc. 7/10/84

TRANSAMERICA NEW INCOME INC (DE)
Name changed to FPA New Income, Inc. 7/10/84

TRANSAMERICA RLTY INVS (CA)
Merged into Transamerica Corp. 09/30/1986
Each Share of Bene. Int. $1 par exchanged for (0.4143) share Common $1 par
Transamerica Corp. merged into Aegon N.V. 07/21/1999

TRANSAMERICA SHOE MACHINERY CORP (DE)
Merged into Katy Industries, Inc. 02/25/1971
Each share Common 75¢ par exchanged for (0.1828) share $1.46 Class B Conv. Preferred no par

TRANSAMERICA SPL SER INC (MD)
Voluntarily dissolved 03/19/1997
Details not available

TRANSAMERICA TAX FREE BD FD (MA)
Reorganized as Hancock (John) Tax Free Bond Fund 12/22/1994
Details not available

TRANSAMERICAN ENERGY CORP (DE)
12% Preferred Ser. A no par called for redemption at $100 on 6/17/97
Public interest eliminated

TRANSAMERICAN ENERGY INC (BC)
Each share old Common no par exchanged for (0.1) share new Common no par 02/17/2009
Recapitalized as American Biofuels Inc. 09/12/2018
Each share new Common no par exchanged for (0.1) share Common no par

TRANSAMERICAN HLDGS INC (NV)
Name changed to American Holding Investments, Inc. 10/14/2004
(See American Holding Investments, Inc.)

TRANSAMERICAN INSTR CORP (DE)
Charter cancelled and declared inoperative and void for non-payment of taxes 3/1/79

TRANSAMERICAN OIL & GAS INC (CO)
Name changed to Hanover Guaranty Inc. 06/10/1987
(See Hanover Guaranty Inc.)

TRANSAMERICAN PETE CORP (CO)
Recapitalized as Pre-Cell Solutions, Inc. 12/01/1998
Each share Common 1¢ par exchanged for (1/7) share Common 1¢ par
(See Pre-Cell Solutions, Inc.)

TRANSAMERICAN VENTURE CORP (FL)
Name changed to Higby's (J.), Inc. 12/01/1986
Higby's (J.), Inc. acquired by American Confectionery Corp. 03/09/1990
(See American Confectionery Corp.)

TRANSAMERICAN WASTE INDS INC (DE)
Merged into USA Waste Services, Inc. 5/6/98
Each share Common $0.001 par exchanged for (0.45232) share Common $0.001 par
USA Waste Services, Inc. merged into Waste Management, Inc. 7/16/98

TRANSARCTIC PETE CORP (ON)
Name changed to ivyNET Corp. 03/26/1999
ivyNET Corp. recapitalized as Saratoga Capital Corp. 08/25/2000
(See Saratoga Capital Corp.)

TRANSATLANTIC FD INC (MD)
Shares $1 par reclassified as Capital $1 par 00/00/1985
Reincorporated under the laws of Massachusetts as Kleinwort Benson Investment Strategies and Capital $1 par reclassified as International Equity Fund $1 par 01/12/1987
(See Kleinwort Benson Investment Strategies)

TRANSATLANTIC FUND LTD. (CANADA)
Merged into Transatlantic Fund Inc. (MD) 10/30/1963
Each Share $100 par exchanged for (50) Shares $1 par
Transatlantic Fund Inc. (MD) reincorporated in Massachusetts as Kleinwort Benson Investment Strategies 01/12/1987
(See Kleinwort Benson Investment Strategies)

TRANSATLANTIC HLDGS INC (DE)
Common $1 par split (3) for (2) by issuance of (0.5) additional share payable 07/18/1997 to holders of record 06/27/1997 Ex date - 07/21/1997
Common $1 par split (3) for (2) by issuance of (0.5) additional share payable 07/20/2001 to holders of record 06/29/2001 Ex date - 07/23/2001
Common $1 par split (5) for (4) by issuance of (0.25) additional share payable 07/16/2004 to holders of record 06/25/2004 Ex date - 07/19/2004
Merged into Alleghany Corp. 03/06/2012
Each share Common $1 par exchanged for $61.14 cash

TRANSATLANTIC PETE CORP (AB)
Each share old Common no par exchanged for (0.2) share new Common no par 01/21/2004
Reincorporated under the laws of Bermuda as TransAtlantic Petroleum Ltd. and Common no par changed to USD$0.01 par 10/01/2009

TRANSATOR EXPLORATIONS LTD. (ON)
Charter cancelled for failure to file reports and pay taxes in 1969

TRANSAURUM MINES LTD. (ON)
Merged into Garrison Creek Consolidated Mines Ltd. on a (1) for (15) basis 12/09/1954
Garrison Creek Consolidated Mines Ltd. merged into QSR Ltd. 09/07/1993 which name changed to Coniagas Resources Ltd. 06/25/1999 which name changed to Lithium One Inc. 07/23/2009
(See Lithium One Inc.)

TRANSAX INTL LTD (CO)
Recapitalized as Big Tree Group, Inc. 12/11/2012
Each (700) shares Common $0.00001 par exchanged for (1) share Common $0.00001 par

TRANSAXIS INC (DE)
SEC revoked common stock registration 07/07/2009

TRANSBANC DEPOSITORY RCPT & FDG CO (DE)
Charter cancelled and declared inoperative and void for non-payment of taxes 04/15/1973

TRANSBEC MINING CO., LTD. (ON)
Dissolved in 1958

TRANSBORDER CAP INC (AB)
Name changed to Eagle Rock
Exploration Ltd. 02/14/2006
Eagle Rock Exploration Ltd.
recapitalized as Wild Stream
Exploration Inc. 11/16/2009
(See Wild Stream Exploration Inc.)

TRANSBOTICS CORP (DE)
Company terminated common stock
registration and is no longer public
as of 08/19/2008

TRANSCANADA CAP (DE)
8.75% Trust Originated Preferred
Securities called for redemption at
$25 plus $0.0122 accrued dividend
on 7/3/2003

TRANSCANADA PIPELINES LTD (CANADA)
Common $1 par changed to
$0.33333333 par and (2) additional
shares issued 06/24/1974
$2.75 1st Preferred Ser. A $50 par
called for redemption 05/30/1978
$2.65 Conv. 2nd Preferred Ser. A $50
par called for redemption
05/31/1982
Common $0.33333333 par changed
to no par 11/20/1983
Common no par split (2) for (1) by
issuance of (1) additional share
02/22/1984
$4.50 1st Preferred Ser. B $50 par
called for redemption 03/22/1985
Retractable 1st Preferred Ser. D no
par called for redemption 11/01/1985
1st Preferred Ser. F no par called for
redemption 05/01/1987
$5.16 1st Preferred Ser. E no par
called for redemption 11/01/1989
$3.80 Retractable 1st Preferred Ser. J
no par called for redemption
10/01/1992
$3.90 Retractable 1st Preferred Ser. I
no par called for redemption
05/01/1993
$4.35 Retractable 1st Preferred Ser.
H no par called for redemption
05/01/1993
Each share 2nd Preferred Ser. B no
par exchanged for (1) share
Common no par 08/01/1995
$2.80 1st Preferred Ser. P no par
called for redemption on 06/01/1999
$3.95 1st Preferred Ser. O $50 par
called for redemption at $52 on
06/01/1999
$3.275 1st Preferred Ser. Q no par
called for redemption 12/15/1999
$2.80 1st Preferred no par called for
redemption at $50.50 on 01/12/2000
100% of 5.15% 1st Preferred Ser. S
no par acquired at $50 per share
through purchase offer which
expired 11/22/2000
Canadian Originated Preferred
Securities called for redemption at
$25 plus $0.2125 accrued dividends
on 11/07/2001
Under plan of reorganization each
share Common no par automatically
became (1) share TransCanada
Corp. Common no par 05/15/2003
8.25% Preferred Securities no par
called for redemption at $25 on
07/05/2007
5.60% 1st Preferred Ser. U no par
called for redemption at $50 plus
$0.5907 accrued dividends on
10/15/2013
5.60% 1st Preferred Ser. Y no par
called for redemption at $50 plus
$0.2455 accrued dividends on
03/05/2014

TRANSCANADA PWR L P (ON)
Name changed to EPCOR Power L.P.
09/06/2005
EPCOR Power L.P. name changed to
Capital Power Income L.P.
11/09/2009 which merged into
Atlantic Power Corp. 11/09/2011

TRANSCAPITAL FINL CORP (DE)
Taken over by the RTC 7/10/92

Stockholders' equity unlikely

TRANSCEIVER CORP AMER (DE)
Company became private 03/14/1983
Details not available

TRANSCEND CAP CORP (AB)
Name changed to Road New Media
Corp. 05/24/2002
Road New Media Corp. recapitalized
as Arian Resources Corp.
12/19/2012 which recapitalized as
Perisson Petroleum Corp.
12/19/2012

TRANSCEND SVCS INC (DE)
Each share Common 1¢ par
exchanged for (0.2) share Common
5¢ par 01/14/2000
Acquired by Nuance
Communications, Inc. (New)
04/26/2012
Each share Common 5¢ par
exchanged for $29.50 cash

TRANSCEND THERAPEUTICS INC (DE)
Issue Information - 1,800,000 shares
COM offered at $10 per share on
07/02/1997
Merged into KeraVision, Inc.
05/28/1999
Each share Common 1¢ par
exchanged for (0.16486) share
Common 1¢ par
(See KeraVision, Inc.)

TRANSCENDENT CORP (NV)
Each share old Common $0.0001 par
exchanged for (0.02) share new
Common $0.0001 par 11/14/1997
Recapitalized as Space Launches
Financing Inc. (NV) 11/18/1997
Each share new Common $0.0001
par exchanged for (0.25) share
Common $0.0001 par
Space Launches Financing, Inc. (NV)
reorganized in Wyoming as Crown
Marketing 12/02/2010 which name
changed to America Great Health
06/29/2017

TRANSCEPT PHARMACEUTICALS INC (DE)
Recapitalized as Paratek
Pharmaceuticals, Inc. 10/31/2014
Each share Common $0.001 par
exchanged for (0.08333333) share
Common $0.001 par

TRANSCISCO INDS INC (DE)
Reorganized under Chapter 11
Federal Bankruptcy Code as
Transcisco Industries, Inc. (New)
11/3/93
Each share Class A Common 1¢ par
exchanged for (1) share Common
1¢ par
Each share Class B Common 1¢ par
exchanged for (1) share Common
1¢ par
Transcisco Industries, Inc. (New)
merged into Trinity Industries, Inc.
9/3/96

TRANSCISCO INDS INC NEW (DE)
Merged into Trinity Industries, Inc.
9/3/96
Each share Common 1¢ par
exchanged for (0.1884) share
Common $1 par

TRANSCO COMPANIES, INC. (DE)
Name changed to Transco Energy
Co. 5/12/82
Transco Energy Co. merged into
Williams Companies Inc. 5/1/95

TRANSCO ENERGY CO (DE)
$3.875 Conv. Preferred no par called
for redemption 04/10/1987
Common Stock Purchase Rights
redeemed at $0.05 per right
02/08/1995 for holders of record
01/17/1995
$4.75 Conv. Preferred no par called
for redemption 03/20/1995
Merged into Williams Companies, Inc.
05/01/1995
Each share Common 50¢ par

exchanged for (0.625) share
Common $1 par

TRANSCO EXPL PARTNERS LTD (TX)
Liquidation completed
Each Depositary Unit received initial
distribution of $9.50 cash
09/18/1989
Each Depositary Unit received
second distribution of $0.35 cash
12/29/1989
Each Depositary Unit received third
and final distribution of $1.06 cash
09/30/1992

TRANSCO RESH CORP (DE)
Each share old Common 1¢ par
exchanged for (0.04) share new
Common 1¢ par 04/18/1996
Name changed to Geotele.Com Inc.
06/04/1999
Geotele.Com Inc. recapitalized as
Anthem Investment Corp.
10/18/2002 which recapitalized as
Wysak Petroleum Inc. 04/24/2003
which name changed to Wild Brush
Energy Inc. 04/11/2006

TRANSCO RES CORP (AB)
Reincorporated 07/21/2006
Place of incorporation changed from
(BC) to (AB) 07/21/2006
Name changed to Bridge Resources
Corp. 09/14/2006
Bridge Resources Corp. recapitalized
as Idaho Natural Resources Corp.
04/24/2012
(See Idaho Natural Resources Corp.)

TRANSCO STORAGE & TRANSPORTATION SERVICES LTD. (CANADA)
Reverted to a private company
00/00/1979
Details not available

TRANSCOASTAL INDS CORP (NJ)
Charter declared void for
non-payment of taxes 4/12/73

TRANSCOASTAL MARINE SVCS INC (DE)
Plan of liquidation under Chapter 7
Federal Bankruptcy Code filed
06/20/2000
No stockholders' equity

TRANSCOLOR CORP (DE)
Each (30) shares old Common
$0.0001 par exchanged for (1) share
new Common $0.0001 par
04/24/1991
Charter cancelled and declared
inoperative and void for
non-payment of taxes 03/01/1998

TRANSCOLT RES CORP (BC)
Merged into New Frontier Petroleum
Corp. 1/18/82
Each share Capital Stock no par
exchanged for (0.83) share Common
no par
New Frontier Petroleum Corp.
recapitalized as PetroMac Energy
Inc. 8/30/85
(See PetroMac Energy Inc.)

TRANSCOM INTL LTD (AUSTRALIA)
Each (100) Sponsored ADR's for
Ordinary A$0.20 par exchanged for
(83.3333) Sponsored ADR's for
Ordinary A$0.30 par 05/29/1998
Name changed to New Tel Ltd.
06/14/1999
(See New Tel Ltd.)

TRANSCOM WORLDWIDE S A (LUXEMBOURG)
ADR agreement terminated
12/19/2014
Each Sponsored ADR for Class A
exchanged for $0.696745 cash
Each Sponsored ADR for Class B
exchanged for $0.764252 cash

TRANSCOMMUNICATIONS CORP (DE)
Charter cancelled and declared
inoperative and void for
non-payment of taxes 4/15/72

TRANSCOMMUNITY FINL CORP (VA)
Name changed 05/25/2004
Name changed from TransCommunity
Bancshares Inc. to TransCommunity
Financial Corp. 05/25/2004
Each share Common 1¢ par
exchanged for (1) share Common
1¢ par
Merged into Community Bankers
Acquisition Corp. 05/31/2008
Each share Common 1¢ par
exchanged for (1.42) shares
Common 1¢ par
Community Bankers Acquisition Corp.
name changed to Community
Bankers Trust Corp. (DE)
06/02/2008 which reincorporated in
Virginia 04/30/2014

TRANSCON BLDRS INC (OH)
Merged into TCB Acquisition Inc.
4/8/86
Each share Common no par
exchanged for $9.50 cash

TRANSCON INC (CA)
Name changed to US 1 Industries,
Inc. (CA) 09/21/1994
US 1 Industries, Inc. (CA)
reincorporated in Indiana
02/00/1995
(See US 1 Industries, Inc. (IN))

TRANSCON LINES (CA)
Each share Common $10 par
exchanged for (2) shares Common
$5 par 00/00/1952
Each share Common $5 par
exchanged for (2) shares Common
$2.50 par 10/24/1957
Each share Common $2.50 par
exchanged for (2) shares Common
$1.25 par 05/22/1962
Common $1.25 par changed to
62-1/2¢ par and (1) additional share
issued 08/27/1965
Common 62-1/2¢ par changed to
31-1/4¢ par and (1) additional share
issued 08/01/1969
Under plan of reorganization each
share Common 31-1/4¢ par
automatically became (1) share
Transcon Inc. Common no par
05/01/1981
Transcon Inc. name changed to US 1
Industries, Inc. (CA) 09/21/1994
which reincorporated in Indiana
02/00/1995
(See US 1 Industries, Inc. (IN))

TRANSCONTINENT TELEVISION CORP. (NY)
Liquidation completed
Each share Class B Common $2.50
par stamped to indicate initial
distribution of $20 cash and
reduction of par value to $1 par
4/14/64
Each share Stamped Class B
Common $1 par received second
distribution of (1) share Northeastern
Pennsylvania Broadcasting, Inc.
Class B Common no par and
(0.015523) share VTC for Class A
Common no par 4/27/64
Each share Stamped Class B
Common $1 par stamped to indicate
third distribution of $1 cash and
reduction of par value to 10¢ par
2/18/65
Each share Stamped Class B
Common 10¢ par stamped to
indicate fourth distribution of $0.41
cash 6/26/67
Each share Stamped Class B
Common 10¢ par exchanged for fifth
and final distribution of $0.28 cash
8/29/69
*(See listing for Northeastern
Pennsylvania Broadcasting, Inc.)*

TRANSCONTINENTAL & WESTERN AIR, INC.
Name changed to Trans World Airlines, Inc. in 1950
Trans World Airlines, Inc. name changed to Trans World Corp. (Del.) 1/1/79 which name changed to Transworld Corp. (Del.) 4/25/84 which assets were transferred to Transworld Corp. Liquidating Trust 12/31/86
(See Transworld Corp. Liquidating Trust)

TRANSCONTINENTAL AIR TRANSPORT, INC. (DE)
Liquidation completed in 1946

TRANSCONTINENTAL BUS SYSTEM, INC. (DE)
Name changed to TCO Industries, Inc. 4/29/68
TCO Industries, Inc. merged into Holiday Inns of America, Inc. 2/27/69 which name changed to Holiday Inns, Inc. 5/22/69 which reorganized in Delaware as Holiday Corp. 5/15/85 which merged into Bass PLC 2/7/90 which name changed to Six Continents PLC 7/31/2001

TRANSCONTINENTAL ENERGY CORP (DE)
Reorganized under Chapter 11 Federal Bankruptcy Code as Regency Affiliates Inc. 12/31/87
Each share Common 10¢ par exchanged for (0.25) share Common 40¢ par

TRANSCONTINENTAL ENERGY CORP (NV)
Adjudicated bankrupt 10/05/1978
Stockholders' equity unlikely

TRANSCONTINENTAL GAS PIPE LINE CORP (DE)
Common 50¢ par split (2) for (1) by issuance of (1) additional share 2/1/56
$5.70 Preferred no par called for redemption 6/29/64
$5.96 Preferred no par called for redemption 6/29/64
$2.55 Preferred no par called for redemption 5/26/65
Common 50¢ par split (6) for (5) by issuance of (0.2) additional share 4/1/68
Stock Dividends - 10% 12/30/57; 20% 1/5/60; 20% 3/1/63; 20% 3/1/65
Under plan of reorganization each share Common 50¢ par automatically became (1) share Transco Companies, Inc. Common 50¢ par 9/11/73
(See Transco Companies, Inc. in Obsolete)
$4.90 Preferred no par called for redemption 5/1/85
$10.32 Preferred no par called for redemption 1/9/87
$13.62 Preferred no par called for redemption 8/2/88
$14.62 Preferred no par called for redemption 8/2/88
$5.60 Preferred no par called for redemption 8/1/89
$2.50 Preferred no par called for redemption 9/14/90
$5.26 Preferred no par called for redemption 5/1/92
$8.64 Preferred no par called for redemption 5/1/92
$5 Preferred no par called for redemption 5/2/94
$4.80 Preferred no par called for redemption 3/23/95
$6.65 Preferred no par called for redemption 3/23/95
$8.75 Preferred no par called for redemption 3/23/95
Public interest eliminated

TRANSCONTINENTAL HLDGS LTD (AUSTRALIA)
Struck off register 10/03/1990

TRANSCONTINENTAL INC (CANADA)
5-Yr. Rate Reset First Preferred Ser. D no par called for redemption at $25 on 10/15/2014
(Additional Information in Active)

TRANSCONTINENTAL INDS INC (DE)
Charter cancelled and declared inoperative and void for non-payment of taxes 4/15/73

TRANSCONTINENTAL INVESTING CORP (DE)
Class A Common $1 par reclassified as Common $1 par 10/29/1964
6-1/2% Preferred $25 par reclassified as Conv. Preference $28 par 07/01/1968
Merged into Omega-Alpha, Inc. 03/07/1972
Each share Conv. Preference $28 par exchanged for (6.76) shares Common $1 par
Each share Common $1 par exchanged for (1.45) shares Common $1 par
(See Omega-Alpha, Inc.)

TRANSCONTINENTAL MTR INNS INC (IN)
Merged into United Inns, Inc. 12/1/72
Each share Common $1 par exchanged for (0.307692) share Common Capital Stock $1 par
(See United Inns, Inc.)

TRANSCONTINENTAL OIL CO.
Acquired by Ohio Oil Co. 00/00/1930
Details not available

TRANSCONTINENTAL OIL CORP (DE)
Reorganized 05/05/1980
Each share Common 25¢ par exchanged for (0.25) share Common no par 10/22/1968
Common no par changed to 10¢ par 05/29/1969
$4 Ser. A Conv. Preferred called for redemption 10/31/1974
Under plan of reorganization each share Transcontinental Oil Corp. (Old) Common 10¢ par automatically became (1) share Transcontinental Oil Corp. (New) Common 10¢ par 05/05/1980
16% Preferred 10¢ par called for redemption 04/01/1981
Transcontinental Oil Corp. (New) name changed to Transcontinental Energy Corp. 05/15/1981 which reorganized as Regency Affiliates, Inc. 12/31/1987

TRANSCONTINENTAL PETROLEUM CORP.
Out of business in 1940

TRANSCONTINENTAL PWR CO (NV)
Merged into Transcontinental Energy Corp. 01/22/1973
Each share Common $1 par exchanged for (0.5) share Common 50¢ par
(See Transcontinental Energy Corp.)

TRANSCONTINENTAL RLTY INVS (DE)
Name changed 08/17/1990
Name changed from Transcontinental Realty Investors (CA) to Transcontinental Realty Investors, Inc. (DE) 08/17/1990
Each Share of Bene. Int. no par exchanged for (0.25) share Common 1¢ par
Reincorporated under the laws of Nevada 03/24/1992

TRANSCONTINENTAL RES LTD (ON)
Merged into Tatramar Holdings Ltd. 10/19/90
Each share Capital Stock no par exchanged for $1.80 cash

TRANSCONTINENTAL STORAGE & DISTRIBUTING CO. LTD. (CANADA)
Name changed to Transco Storage & Transportation Services Ltd. 6/25/59

TRANSCONTINENTAL VIDEO LTD (NM)
Charter revoked for failure to file reports and pay fees 07/25/1994

TRANSCONTINENTAL WASTE INDS INC (NV)
Name changed to Para Mas Internet Inc. 08/27/1999
(See Para Mas Internet Inc.)

TRANSCOR WASTE SVCS INC (FL)
Merged into Kimmins Corp. (New) 05/04/2007
Each share Common $0.001 par exchanged for $8.51 cash

TRANSCRYPT INTL INC (DE)
Issue Information - 2,900,000 shares COM offered at $8 per share on 01/22/1997
Secondary Offering - 4,500,000 shares COM offered at $21 per share on 10/15/1997
Name changed to EFJ, Inc. 06/13/2002
EFJ, Inc. name changed to EF Johnson Technologies, Inc. 05/28/2008
(See EF Johnson Technologies, Inc.)

TRANSCU GROUP LTD (SINGAPORE)
Name changed to OLS Enterprise Ltd. 07/28/2014
(See OLS Enterprise Ltd.)

TRANSDATA CORP (DE)
Each share Common 10¢ par exchanged for (0.25) share Common 1¢ par 10/11/73
Charter cancelled and declared inoperative and void for non-payment of taxes 3/1/83

TRANSDEL PHARMACEUTICALS INC (DE)
Recapitalized as Imprimis Pharmaceuticals, Inc. 02/24/2012
Each share Common $0.001 par exchanged for (0.125) share Common $0.001 par

TRANSDUCER CORP. OF AMERICA (NV)
Completely liquidated in 1989
Each share Capital Stock 1¢ par exchanged for first and final distribution of approximately $0.05 cash

TRANSDUCER SYS INC (PA)
Reincorporated 5/30/73
State of incorporation changed from (OH) to (PA) 5/30/73
Common no par split (5) for (4) by issuance of (0.25) additional share 12/15/80
Stock Dividend - 10% 10/15/84
Name changed to Xensor Corp. 1/1/95

TRANSDYNE CORP (NY)
Charter cancelled and proclaimed dissolved for failure to pay taxes 12/15/1975

TRANSEASTERN PWR TR (ON)
Name changed to Blockchain Power Trust 01/04/2018

TRANSFER SVCS INC (DE)
Charter cancelled and declared inoperative and void for non-payment of taxes 6/29/78

TRANSFER TECHNOLOGY INTL CORP (DE)
Each share old Common $0.001 par exchanged for (0.00333333) share new Common $0.001 par 02/28/2012
Name changed to Enviro-Serv, Inc. 04/23/2013

TRANSFIELD PETROLEUMS LTD. (AB)
Struck off register for failure to file annual returns 7/15/64

TRANSFINANCIAL HLDGS INC (DE)
Liquidation completed
Each share Common 1¢ par received initial distribution of $2.70 cash payable 6/28/2002 to holders of record 4/29/2002
Each share Common 1¢ par received second and final distribution of $0.1074 cash payable 4/28/2005 to holders of record 4/29/2002
Ex date - 4/29/2005
Each share Common 1¢ par received a litigation payment of $0.366317 cash payable 12/13/2005 to holders of record 4/29/2002
Note: Certificates were not required to be surrendered and are without value

TRANSFLORIDA BK (COOPER CITY, FL)
Merged into Union Planters Corp. 8/31/98
Each share Common no par exchanged for (0.8489) share Common $5 par
Union Planters Corp. merged into Regions Financial Corp. (New) 7/1/2004

TRANSFORCE INC (CANADA)
Name changed to TFI International Inc. 12/30/2016

TRANSFORCE INC (QC)
Reorganized as TransForce Income Fund (QC) 09/30/2002
Each share Common no par exchanged for (1) Trust Unit no par
TransForce Income Fund (QC) reorganized in Canada as TransForce Inc. 05/20/2008 which name changed to TFI International Inc. 12/30/2016

TRANSFORCE INCOME FD (QC)
Reorganized under the laws of Canada as TransForce Inc. and Trust Units reclassified as Common no par 05/20/2008
TransForce Inc. name changed to TFI International Inc. 12/30/2016

TRANSFORM LOGIC CORP (UT)
Each share old Common $0.0005 par exchanged for (1/6) share new Common $0.0005 par 06/15/1988
SEC revoked common stock registration 03/01/2012

TRANSFORM PACK INTERNATIONAL INC (MN)
Reorganized under the laws of Nevada as Quantum Group, Inc. (Ctfs. dtd. after 02/06/2004) 02/06/2004
Each share Common $0.004 par exchanged for (0.1) share Common $0.001 par
(See Quantum Group, Inc. (Ctfs. dtd. after 02/06/2004))

TRANSFORMA ACQUISITION GROUP INC (DE)
Issue Information - 12,500,000 UNITS consisting of (1) share COM and (1) WT offered at $8 per Unit on 12/20/2006
Liquidation completed
Each Unit exchanged for initial distribution of $8.13558484 cash 01/02/2009
Each share Common $0.0001 par exchanged for initial distribution of $8.13558484 cash 01/02/2009
Each Unit received second and final distribution of $0.0566114 cash payable 05/14/2009 to holders of record 12/29/2008
Each share Common $0.0001 par received second and final distribution of $0.0566114 cash payable 05/14/2009 to holders of record 12/29/2008

TRANSFORMATION PROCESSING INC (NV)
Each share old Common $0.001 par exchanged for (0.4) share new Common $0.001 par 10/15/1999
Name changed to eAutoclaims.com, Inc. 06/05/2000
eAutoclaims.com, Inc. name changed to eAutoclaims, Inc. 07/29/2004
(See eAutoclaims, Inc.)

TRANSFORMATIVE VENTURES LTD (BC)
Merged into Aztech Innovations Inc. 04/16/2010
Each share Common no par exchanged for (2/3) share Common no par

TRANSFORMER CORP.
Bankrupt in 1934

TRANSGAMING INC (CANADA)
Recapitalized as Findev Inc. 12/06/2016
Each share Common no par exchanged for (0.02857142) share Common no par

TRANSGENE S A (FRANCE)
ADR agreement terminated 11/14/2005
Each Sponsored ADR for Ordinary FF15 par exchanged for (0.33333333) share Ordinary
Note: Unexchanged ADR's will be sold and proceeds, if any, held for claim after 02/10/2006

TRANSGENIC SCIENCES INC (DE)
Name changed to TSI Corp. 11/05/1990
TSI Corp. acquired by Genzyme Transgenics Corp. 09/30/1994 which name changed to GTC Biotherapeutics, Inc. 06/03/2002
(See GTC Biotherapeutics, Inc.)

TRANSGENOMIC INC (DE)
Each share old Common 1¢ par exchanged for (0.08333333) share new Common 1¢ par 01/28/2014
Each share new Common 1¢ par exchanged again for (0.03333333) share new Common 1¢ par 06/13/2017
Name changed to Precipio, Inc. 06/30/2017

TRANSGLOBAL BUSINESS NEWS NETWORK INC (CANADA)
Recapitalized as Megasol Corp. 04/05/1993
Each share Common no par exchanged for (0.2) share Common no par
Megasol Corp. recapitalized as Clonus Corp. 09/17/1996 which name changed to San-Mar Environmental Corp. 09/22/1997 which recapitalized as Pure Zinc Technologies, Inc. 08/21/1998 which name changed to Charityville.com International Inc. 08/27/1999 which name changed to eNblast productions inc. 06/14/2000
(See eNblast productions inc.)

TRANSGLOBAL FINL SVCS LTD (ON)
Liquidation completed
Each share Capital Stock no par exchanged for initial distribution of $0.85 cash 9/24/85
Note: Details on subsequent distributions, if any, are not available

TRANSGLOBAL MNG CORP (NV)
Recapitalized as Ring Energy, Inc. 06/02/2008
Each (18) shares Common $0.001 par exchanged for (1) share Common $0.001 par

TRANSGLOBAL OIL CORP (DE)
Reincorporated under the laws of New Mexico 06/25/2007
(See Transglobal Oil Corp. (NM))

TRANSGLOBAL OIL CORP (NM)
Charter cancelled 03/15/2010

TRANSGLOBE APT REAL ESTATE INVT TR (ON)
Acquired by Starlight Investments Ltd. 06/29/2012
Each Unit received $14.25 cash

TRANSGLOBE ENERGY CORP (BC)
Reincorporated under the laws of Alberta 05/09/2004

TRANSGLOBE INTERNET & TELECOM CO LTD (BC)
Delisted from NEX 05/14/2015

TRANSGLOBE REAL ESTATE CORP. (BC)
Name changed to Ultra Petroleum Corp. (BC) 10/21/1993
Ultra Petroleum Corp. (BC) reincorporated in Yukon 03/01/2000

TRANSGLOBE RES LTD (BC)
Name changed to Transglobe Real Estate Corp. 06/19/1990
Transglobe Real Estate Corp. name changed to Ultra Petroleum Corp. (BC) 10/21/1993 which reincorporated in Yukon 03/01/2000

TRANSGOLD EXPLS & INVTS INC (ON)
Recapitalized 08/02/1991
Recapitalized from Transgold Resources Inc. to Transgold Explorations & Investments Inc. 08/02/1991
Each share old Common no par exchanged for (0.25) share new Common no par
Recapitalized as Temex Resources Corp. 04/07/2000
Each share new Common no par exchanged for (0.33333333) share Common no par
Temex Resources Corp. merged into Lake Shore Gold Corp. 09/21/2015 which merged into Tahoe Resources Inc. 04/07/2018

TRANSGULF CORP. (DE)
No longer in existence having become inoperative and void for non-payment of taxes 4/1/55

TRANSHORWOOD MINES LTD. (ON)
Name changed to Damascus Mines Ltd. in 1950
Damascus Mines Ltd. surrendered its charter in August 1959

TRANSIDYNE GEN CORP (DE)
Acquired by Customedix Corp. 08/25/1988
Each share Common 10¢ par exchanged for (1) share Common 1¢ par
(See Customedix Corp.)

TRANSIERRA EXPL CORP (CA)
Name changed to Belcor Inc. 07/01/1985
Belcor Inc. name changed to Silver Assets Inc. 08/19/1998
(See Silver Assets Inc.)

TRANSIERRA GOLD MINING CO. (CA)
Name changed to Transierra Exploration Corp. 00/00/1953
Transierra Exploration Corp. name changed to Belcor Inc. 07/01/1985 which name changed to Silver Assets Inc. 08/19/1998
(See Silver Assets Inc.)

TRANSIS-TRONICS, INC. (CA)
Recapitalized as Varadyne Industries, Inc. 3/19/68
Each share Common 25¢ par exchanged for (0.31) share Common 25¢ par
(See Varadyne Industries, Inc.)

TRANSISTOR APPLICATIONS, INC. (MA)
Name changed to New England Transformer Co., Inc. 06/30/1967
(See New England Transformer Co., Inc.)

TRANSISTOR ELECTRS CORP (MN)
Stock Dividend - 100% 1/9/69
Name changed to TEC, Inc. (MN) 8/29/69
TEC, Inc. (MN) name changed to Jones Plumbing Systems, Inc. 4/28/89
(See Jones Plumbing Systems, Inc.)

TRANSISTOR SPECIALTIES, INC. (NY)
Name changed to Darcy Industries, Inc. 3/15/67
Darcy Industries, Inc. declared insolvent 7/9/69

TRANSIT FINL HLDGS INC (CANADA)
Name changed to TFH International Inc. 06/21/1993
TFH International Inc. name changed to Highbourne Capital Corp. 08/17/1995 which recapitalized as A & E Capital Funding Corp. 08/12/1996 which recapitalized as E & E Capital Funding Inc. 10/18/2005 which merged into GC-Global Capital Corp. 01/09/2006 which name changed to Fountain Asset Corp. 09/02/2015

TRANSIT-FREEZE CORP. (NJ)
Charter declared void for non-payment of taxes 1/25/66

TRANSIT GROUP INC (FL)
Plan of reorganization under Chapter 11 Federal Bankruptcy Code effective 12/10/2002
No stockholders' equity

TRANSIT INVESTMENT CORP.
Liquidated in 1948

TRANSIT MGMT HLDG CORP (CO)
Name changed to China Green Lighting Ltd. 07/08/2011
(See China Green Lighting Ltd.)

TRANSITION ANALYSIS COMPONENT TECHNOLOGY INC (CA)
Merged into Aspect Development, Inc. 05/19/2000
Each share Common 1¢ par exchanged for (0.6647302) share Common 1¢ par
Aspect Development, Inc. merged into i2 Technologies, Inc. 06/12/2000 which merged into JDA Software Group, Inc. 01/28/2010
(See JDA Software Group, Inc.)

TRANSITION METALS & CHEMICALS, INC. (DE)
No longer in existence having become inoperative and void for non-payment of taxes 4/1/65

TRANSITION METALS INC (OR)
Recapitalized as Business Assets Management, Inc. 05/18/1989
Each share Common $0.001 par exchanged for (0.1) share Common $0.001 par
(See Business Assets Management, Inc.)

TRANSITION METALS CORP OLD (ON)
Reorganized as Transition Metals Corp. (New) 08/19/2013
Each share Common no par exchanged for (0.5) share Common no par

TRANSITION SYS INC (DE)
Name changed to Belair Financial Corp. 9/22/70
(See Belair Financial Corp.)

TRANSITION SYS INC (MA)
Merged into Eclipsys Corp. 12/31/1998
Each share Common 1¢ par exchanged for (0.525) share Common 1¢ par
Eclipsys Corp. merged into Allscripts Healthcare Solutions, Inc. 08/24/2010

TRANSITION THERAPEUTICS INC (ON)
Each share old Common no par exchanged for (0.11111111) share new Common no par 07/09/2007
Merged into OPKO Health, Inc. 08/31/2016
Each share new Common no par exchanged for (0.1657484) share Common 1¢ par
Note: Unexchanged certificates will be cancelled and become without value 08/30/2019

TRANSITIONAL HOSPS CORP (NV)
Merged into Vencor Inc. (Old) 08/26/1997
Each share Common $1 par exchanged for $16 cash

TRANSITRON ELECTR CORP (DE)
Completely liquidated 01/31/1987
No stockholders' equity

TRANSITUBES ELECTRONICS, INC. (FL)
Adjudicated bankrupt 4/4/67
No stockholders' equity

TRANSJERSEY BANCORP (NJ)
Stock Dividend - 10% 04/15/1975
Assets taken over by Commissioner of Banking of the State of New Jersey 01/10/1976
No stockholders' equity

TRANSKARYOTIC THERAPIES INC (DE)
Merged into Shire Pharmaceuticals Group PLC 07/28/2005
Each share Common 1¢ par exchanged for $37 cash

TRANSLAND INVTS INC (DE)
Charter cancelled and declared inoperative and void for non-payment of taxes 4/15/73

TRANSLAND URANIUM MINES LTD. (ON)
Charter cancelled for failure to file reports and pay taxes November 1961

TRANSLATION GROUP INC (NV)
Name changed to Omega Brands Inc. 06/10/2014

TRANSLATION GROUP LTD (DE)
Ceased operations 6/29/2004
Stockholders' equity unlikely

TRANSMAGNETICS INC (NY)
Liquidation completed
Each share Common 5¢ par exchanged for initial distribution of $1 cash 6/1/95
Each share Common 5¢ par received second distribution of $0.70 cash 3/5/96
Each share Common 5¢ par received third and final distribution of $0.22 cash 3/5/97

TRANSMARINE RES INC (DE)
Charter cancelled and declared inoperative and void for non-payment of taxes 04/15/1972

TRANSMARK USA INC (KY)
Administratively dissolved 11/3/97

TRANSMATION INC (OH)
Common no par changed to $1 par 8/21/69
Common $1 par changed to 50¢ par 9/7/76
Common 50¢ par split (2) for (1) by issuance of (1) additional share 8/2/82
Common 50¢ par split (2) for (1) by issuance of (1) additional share payable 7/22/97 to holders of record 7/1/97
Stock Dividend - 100% 8/3/81
Name changed to Transcat, Inc. 10/1/2002

TRANSMED EXPRESS INC (NY)
Name changed to American
Veterinary Products, Inc. 01/22/1990
American Veterinary Products, Inc.
name changed to GEN/Rx, Inc.
03/10/1993
(See GEN/Rx, Inc.)

TRANSMEDIA ASIA PAC INC (DE)
SEC revoked common stock
registration 10/13/2005
Stockholders' equity unlikely

TRANSMEDIA COMMUNICATIONS INC
Merged into Cisco Systems, Inc.
9/20/99
Each share Common exchanged for
(0.33581659) share Common no par

TRANSMEDIA EUROPE INC (DE)
SEC revoked common stock
registration 06/19/2009
Stockholders' equity unlikely

TRANSMEDIA INTL CORP (DE)
Charter cancelled and declared
inoperative and void for
non-payment of taxes 04/15/1971

TRANSMEDIA NETWORK INC (DE)
Reincorporated 07/20/1987
State of incorporation changed from
(CO) to (DE) 07/20/1987
Each share Common $0.001 par
exchanged for (0.0005) share
Common 2¢ par 10/05/1988
Note: Holders of (1,999) or fewer
pre-split shares received
$0.0854166 cash per share
Common 2¢ par split (100) for (1) by
issuance of (99) additional shares
10/05/1988
Stock Dividends - 50% 04/17/1992;
50% 10/21/1993; 50% 04/22/1994
Name changed to iDine Rewards
Network Inc. 02/01/2002
iDine Rewards Network Inc. name
changed to Rewards Network Inc.
12/09/2003
(See Rewards Network Inc.)

TRANSMEDICA ENTERPRISES INC (BC)
Common no par split (3) for (1) by
issuance of (2) additional shares
01/22/1986
Delisted from Vancouver Stock
Exchange 10/06/1989

TRANSMERIDIAN EXPL INC (DE)
Issue Information - 8,809,500 shares
COM offered at $2 per share on
11/07/2001
Plan of reorganization under Chapter
11 Federal Bankruptcy proceedings
confirmed 08/19/2009
No stockholders' equity

TRANSMETA CORP (DE)
Issue Information - 13,000,000 shares
COM offered at $21 per share on
11/06/2000
Each share old Common $0.00001
par exchanged for (0.05) share new
Common $0.00001 par 08/17/2007
Acquired by Novafora, Inc.
01/28/2009
Each share Common $0.00001 par
exchanged for $19.01 cash

TRANSMONTAIGNE INC (DE)
Name changed 08/26/1998
Name changed from Transmontaigne
Oil Co. to Transmontaigne Inc.
08/26/1998
Merged into Morgan Stanley Capital
Group Inc. 09/01/2006
Each share Conv. Ser. B Preferred
exchanged for $11.35 cash
Each share Common 1¢ par
exchanged for $11.35 cash

TRANSMOUNTAIN PRODUCTION CO. (DE)
Voluntarily dissolved 9/30/77
No stockholders' equity

TRANSNATION DEV CORP (DE)
Completely liquidated 03/11/1971

Each share Common $1 par
exchanged for first and final
distribution of (2.75) shares Madison
Square Garden Corp. (MI) Common
$1 par
(See Madison Square Garden Corp. (MI))

TRANSNATION RLTY CORP (DE)
Merged into Bowling Corp. of America
12/22/1969
Each share Common 10¢ par
exchanged for (1) share Common
40¢ par
Bowling Corp. of America name
changed to Charan Industries, Inc.
12/24/1969
(See Charan Industries, Inc.)

TRANSNATIONAL AUTOMOTIVE GROUP INC (NV)
Each share old Common $0.001 par
exchanged for (0.00333333) share
new Common $0.001 par
01/13/2012
Name changed to Transnational
Group, Inc. 07/24/2014

TRANSNATIONAL FINL NETWORK INC (CA)
Name changed 05/14/1999
Name changed from Transnational
Financial Corp. to Transnational
Financial Network, Inc. 05/14/1999
Name changed to Telava Networks,
Inc. 12/11/2007 which name
changed back to Transnational
Financial Network, Inc. 03/00/2009
Reorganized under the laws of
Oklahoma as Somerset Transition
Corp. 08/09/2013
Each share Common no par
exchanged for (0.00133333) share
Common $0.001 par

TRANSNATIONAL INDS INC (DE)
Each share old Common 1¢ par
exchanged for (0.05) share Common
20¢ par 08/15/1995
Completely liquidated 03/20/2007
Each share Common 20¢ par
received first and final distribution of
(1.0385) shares Evans & Sutherland
Computer Corp. Common 20¢ par
Note: Certificates were not required to
be surrendered and are without
value

TRANSNATIONAL RE CORP (DE)
Merged into PXRE Corp. (CT)
12/11/1996
Each share Class A Common 1¢ par
exchanged for (1.0575) shares
Common 1¢ par
PXRE Corp. (CT) reorganized in
Bermuda as PXRE Group Ltd.
10/05/1999 which merged into Argo
Group International Holdings, Ltd.
08/07/2007

TRANSNATIONAL TECHNOLOGIES, INC. (CO)
Proclaimed dissolved for failure to file
reports and pay fees 11/1/2002

TRANSNATIONAL VENTURES LTD. (LIBERIA)
(In combination with Dresser
Industries, Inc. (DE) Common 50¢
par)
Dissolved 05/10/1965
Each share of combined stock
exchanged for (1) share Dresser
Industries Inc. (DE) (Plain) (New)
Common 50¢ par

TRANSNORTHERN NICKEL & COPPER MINES LTD. (ON)
Charter cancelled 3/11/70
No stockholders' equity

TRANSOCEAN AIR LINES (CA)
Capital Stock no par split (10) for (1)
by issuance of (9) additional shares
in 1953
Name changed to Transocean Corp.
of California and Capital Stock no
par changed to Common $1 par
6/1/56

(See Transocean Corp. of California)

TRANSOCEAN CORP CALIF (CA)
Adjudicated bankrupt 4/16/64

TRANSOCEAN INC NEW (CAYMAN ISLANDS)
Reorganized under the laws of
Switzerland as Transocean Ltd.
12/18/2008
Each share Ordinary 1¢ par
exchanged for (1) Registered Share
CHF 15 par

TRANSOCEAN INC OLD (CAYMAN ISLANDS)
Name changed 05/09/2002
Name changed from Transocean
Sedco Forex Inc. to Transocean Inc.
(Old) 05/09/2002
Merged into Transocean Inc. (New)
(Cayman Islands) 11/27/2007
Each share Ordinary 1¢ par
exchanged for (0.6996) share
Ordinary 1¢ par and $33.03 cash
Transocean Inc. (New) (Cayman
Islands) reorganized in Switzerland
as Transocean Ltd. 12/18/2008

TRANSOCEAN OFFSHORE INC (CAYMAN ISLANDS)
Reincorporated 05/14/1999
Common 1¢ par split (2) for (1) by
issuance of (1) additional share
payable 09/19/1997 to holders of
record 09/05/1997 Ex date -
09/22/1997
Place of incorporation changed from
(DE) to (Cayman Islands)
05/14/1999
Name changed to Transocean Sedco
Forex Inc. 12/31/1999
Transocean Sedco Forex Inc. name
changed to Transocean Inc. (Old)
05/09/2002 which merged into
Transocean Inc. (New) (Cayman
Islands) 11/27/2007 which
reorganized in Switzerland as
Transocean Ltd. 12/18/2008

TRANSOCEAN OIL INC (DE)
Merged into Esmark, Inc. (Inc.
03/14/1969) 12/03/1979
Each share Common $1 par
exchanged for (0.88049) share
Common $1 par
(See Esmark, Inc. (Inc. 03/14/1969))

TRANSOCEAN PARTNERS LLC (MARSHALL ISLANDS)
Merged into Transocean Ltd.
12/09/2016
Each Common Unit exchanged for
(1.2) Registered Shares CHF 0.10
par

TRANSOFT TECHNOLOGIES INC (DE)
Name changed to Quri Resources
Inc. 02/05/2009

TRANSOHIO FINL CORP (DE)
Name changed to Transcapital
Financial Corp. 04/29/1986
(See Transcapital Financial Corp.)

TRANSOL CAP INC
Auction Market Preferred Stock called
for redemption at $1,000,000 on
6/30/98

TRANS1 INC (DE)
Name changed to Baxano Surgical,
Inc. 06/03/2013
(See Baxano Surgical, Inc.)

TRANSONIC, INC. (CA)
Merged into Jamieson Industries, Inc.
on a (0.593) for (1) basis 3/21/62
Jamieson Industries, Inc. liquidated
for Genisco Technology Corp.
(Calif.) 3/5/65 which reincorporated
in Delaware 4/9/84

TRANSPAC CONSTRUCTION CO., INC. (CA)
Name changed to Transpac
Industries, Inc. 5/28/76
(See Transpac Industries, Inc.)

TRANSPAC INDS (CA)
Liquidation completed
Each share Common 10¢ par
exchanged for initial distribution of
approximately $0.23 cash
06/05/1985
Each share Common 10¢ par
received second and final
distribution of $0.09 cash
08/15/1986

TRANSPACIFIC ASBESTOS, INC. (AB)
Name changed to Transpacific
Resources Inc. 09/06/1984
(See Transpacific Resources Inc.)

TRANSPACIFIC LIFE INSURANCE CO. (OR)
Merged into American Guaranty Life
Insurance Co. (OR) 10/04/1967
Each share Common 30¢ par
exchanged for (1/6) share Common
$1 par
American Guaranty Life Insurance
Co. (OR) reorganized as American
Guaranty Corp. (OR) 07/01/1969
which name changed to American
Guaranty Financial Corp.
12/04/1970 which name changed to
Encore Group Inc. 07/18/1990
(See Encore Group Inc.)

TRANSPACIFIC MINERALS INC (AB)
Issue Information - 1,500,000 shares
COM offered at $0.20 per share on
04/23/1997
Name changed to YFMC Healthcare
Inc. 06/26/1998
YFMC Healthcare Inc. acquired by
Med-Emerg International Inc.
12/22/1999 which was acquired by
AIM Health Group Inc. 01/30/2009
(See AIM Health Group Inc.)

TRANSPACIFIC RES INC (AB)
Delisted from Toronto Venture Stock
Exchange 06/20/2003

TRANSPIRATOR TECHNOLOGIES INC (DE)
Reorganized as CyGene
Laboratories, Inc. 10/01/2003
Each share Common 1¢ par
exchanged for (1.58) shares
Common 1¢ par
(See CyGene Laboratories, Inc.)

TRANSPORT CORP OF AMER INC (MN)
Merged into Patriot Holding Corp.
2/28/2006
Each share Common 1¢ par
exchanged for $10 cash

TRANSPORT DATA COMMUNICATIONS INC (DE)
Adjudicated bankrupt 09/18/1975
No stockholders' equity

TRANSPORT DEV GROUP LTD (ENGLAND)
ADR agreement terminated
12/24/1998
Each ADR for Ordinary 25p par
exchanged for $5.79 cash

TRANSPORT HLDGS INC (DE)
Merged into Conseco, Inc. 12/23/96
Each share Class A Common 1¢ par
exchanged for (1.4) shares Common
no par
(See Conseco, Inc.)

TRANSPORT INDEMNITY CO. (CA)
Acquired by Transport Underwriters
Association 00/00/1956
Details not available

TRANSPORT INDUSTRIES INC. (PA)
Out of business in 1966

TRANSPORT LIFE INS CO (TX)
Common $1 par split (2) for (1) by
issuance of (1) additional share
08/10/1981
Merged into American Can Co.
09/01/1982
Each share Common $1 par
exchanged for $26.50 cash

TRANSPORT MANAGEMENT CO. (TX)
Common $10 par changed to $1 par and (9) additional shares issued 5/18/65
Merged into Great American Insurance Co. 8/27/79
Each share Common $1 par exchanged for $25 cash

TRANSPORT MTR EXPRESS INC (IN)
Class B Common $1 par reclassified as Common $1 par 06/30/1968
Completely liquidated 06/19/1969
Each share Common $1 par exchanged for first and final distribution of (1/3) share Essex International, Inc. $2.84 Conv. Preferred Ser. A $1 par
Essex International, Inc. merged into United Aircraft Corp. 02/05/1974 which name changed to United Technologies Corp. 04/30/1975

TRANSPORT POOL CORP (DE)
Merged into Gelco-Feld Corp. 06/02/1975
Each share Common 10¢ par exchanged for $5 principal amount of 9-1/2% Subord. Debentures Ser. A or Ser. B due 08/15/1978 and $5 cash
Note: Non-electors received Ser. B Debentures

TRANSPORT UNDERWRITERS ASSOCIATION (CA)
Voluntarily dissolved 09/29/2000
Details not available

TRANSPORTACION MARITIMA MEXICANA S A DE C V (MEXICO)
Merged into Grupo TMM, S.A. de C.V. 12/26/2001
Each Sponsored ADR for Ordinary no par exchanged for (1) Sponsored ADR for Ordinary Ser. A no par
Each Sponsored ADR for L Shares exchanged for (1) Sponsored ADR for Ser. L Shares no par
Grupo TMM, S.A. de C.V. name changed to Grupo TMM, S.A. 10/15/2002 which name changed to Grupo TMM, S.A.B. 06/19/2007

TRANSPORTATION BLDG. CORP. OF CHICAGO (IL)
Liquidation completed 12/20/54

TRANSPORTATION BUILDING CO. (CA)
Liquidation completed 5/16/55

TRANSPORTATION CAP CORP (NY)
Merged into TCC Holding Corp. 8/30/94
Each share Common 50¢ par exchanged for $4.50 cash

TRANSPORTATION COMPONENTS INC (DE)
Plan of reorganization under Chapter 11 Federal Bankruptcy Code effective 06/11/2002
No stockholders' equity

TRANSPORTATION CONSULTANTS INTL (CA)
Name changed to TCI Travel Corp. 11/13/1972
TCI Travel Corp. name changed to First Travel Corp. 11/01/1974
(See First Travel Corp.)

TRANSPORTATION CORP. OF AMERICA (DE)
Class A Common 10¢ par split (6) for (5) by issuance of (0.2) additional share 1/26/60
Name changed back to Trans Caribbean Airways, Inc. 7/1/64
Trans Caribbean Airways, Inc. merged into American Airlines, Inc. 3/8/71 which reorganized as AMR Corp. 10/1/82

TRANSPORTATION CTLS & REDUCTIONS INC (NV)
Name changed to Canada Crown Investments Corp. 05/10/1990
Canada Crown Investments Corp. name changed to Global Aener/Cology Corp. 06/16/1996
(See Global Aener/Cology Corp.)

TRANSPORTATION DEVELOPMENT CORP. (DE)
No longer in existence having become inoperative and void for non-payment of taxes 4/1/57

TRANSPORTATION EQUIPMENT DEVELOPMENT CORP. (DE)
Charter cancelled and declared inoperative and void for non-payment of taxes 4/1/63

TRANSPORTATION EQUITIES INC (NV)
Charter revoked for failure to file reports and pay fees 02/25/1999

TRANSPORTATION HOLDING CO.
Liquidated in 1945

TRANSPORTATION INSURANCE CO. (NY)
Merged into North River Insurance Co. 00/00/1931
Details not available

TRANSPORTATION LOGISTICS INTL INC (CO)
Name changed to Global Concepts, Ltd. 11/08/2004
(See Global Concepts, Ltd.)

TRANSPORTATION RE-INSURANCE CO. OF NEW YORK
Merged into Transportation Insurance Co. 00/00/1929
Details not available

TRANSPORTATION SAFETY LTS INC (NV)
Name changed to ASGA Inc. 09/27/2001
ASGA Inc. name changed to ElectraCapital Inc. 09/02/2003
(See ElectraCapital Inc.)

TRANSPORTATION SAFETY SYS INC (UT)
Ceased operations and became insolvent 12/31/1977
Stockholders' equity unlikely

TRANSPORTATION SAFETY TECHNOLOGY INC (NV)
Recapitalized as Inca Designs, Inc. 03/26/2010
Each share Common $0.001 par exchanged for (0.1) share Common $0.0001 par

TRANSPORTATION TECHNOLOGIES INDS INC (DE)
Merged into Transportation Acquisition 1 Corp. 03/14/2000
Each share Common 1¢ par exchanged for $21.50 cash

TRANSPRO INC (DE)
Name changed to Proliance International, Inc. 07/22/2005
(See Proliance International, Inc.)

TRANSTAR HLDGS INC (NV)
Name changed 04/19/2001
Name changed from Transtar Communications Inc. to Transtar Holdings Inc. 04/19/2001
Recapitalized as MegaMania Interactive Inc. 12/19/2002
Each share Common 1¢ par exchanged for (0.01) share Common 1¢ par
MegaMania Interactive Inc. recapitalized as Latin Television, Inc. (Old) 02/09/2006 which name changed to The League Publishing Inc. 09/07/2007 which name changed to Good Life China Corp. 04/08/2008

TRANSTATES PETROLEUM INC. (NY)
Each share old Common 1¢ par exchanged for (0.1) share Common 10¢ par 04/04/1957
Each share 6% Conv. Preferred Ser. A $5 par exchanged for (5) shares new Common 1¢ par 02/14/1966
Each share Common 10¢ par exchanged for (1) share new Common 1¢ par 02/14/1966
Charter cancelled and proclaimed dissolved for failure to pay taxes and file reports 12/15/1971

TRANSTEC CORP (CA)
Name changed to Automoco Corp. 06/14/1979
(See Automoco Corp.)

TRANSTECH INDS INC (BC)
Recapitalized as International Transtech Inc. 09/23/1999
Each share Common no par exchanged for (0.2) share Common no par
International Transtech Inc. recapitalized as North American Vanadium Inc. 09/02/2005 which name changed to Veraz Petroleum Ltd. (BC) 06/26/2007 which reincorporated in Alberta 01/24/2008 which name changed to AlkaLi3 Resources Inc. 08/16/2016

TRANSTECH INDUSTRIES LTD. (BC)
Name changed to Canadian Transtech Industries Ltd. 08/18/1988
(See Canadian Transtech Industries Ltd.)

TRANSTECH SVCS PARTNERS INC (DE)
Completely liquidated 07/10/2009
Each Unit exchanged for first and final distribution of $7.87942028 cash
Each share Common $0.0001 par exchanged for first and final distribution of $7.87942028 cash

TRANSTECHNOLOGY CORP (DE)
Reincorporated 07/18/1986
State of incorporation changed from (CA) to (DE) 07/18/1986
Name changed to Breeze-Eastern Corp. 10/12/2006
(See Breeze-Eastern Corp.)

TRANSTECTOR SYS INC (DE)
Reincorporated 05/21/1987
State of incorporation changed from (CA) to (DE) and Common no par changed to 1¢ par 05/21/1987
Merged into Smiths Industries 11/30/1998
Each share Common 1¢ par exchanged for $8.7060134 cash

TRANSTEL COMMUNICATIONS CORP (BC)
Recapitalized as Consolidated T.C. Resources Ltd. 07/23/1990
Each share Common no par exchanged for (0.33333333) share Common no par
Consolidated T.C. Resources Ltd. name changed to Cyclone Capital Corp. 05/20/1992 which recapitalized as Nikos Explorations Ltd. 06/04/1996 which name changed to Labrador Gold Corp. 12/19/2017

TRANSTERRA MINES, LTD. (ON)
Charter cancelled 03/04/1957

TRANSTERRE EXPLS LTD (QC)
Name changed to Bayard Resources Ltd. 08/01/1973
(See Bayard Resources Ltd.)

TRANSTEXAS GAS CORP (DE)
Plan of reorganization under Chapter 11 Federal Bankruptcy Code effective 3/17/2000
Each share old Common 1¢ par will receive (0.00483118) share new Class A Common 1¢ and (0.0101617) Warrant expiring 6/30/2002
Note: Certificates were not required to be surrendered and are without value
Class B 1¢ par converted into Class A 1¢ par 5/29/2002
Each share old 10% Sr. Preferred exchanged for (0.5) share new 10% Sr. Preferred Ser. A and approximately (0.1798) share Class A Common 1¢ par 9/15/2002
Each share Jr. Preferred exchanged for approximately (0.1227) share Class A Common 1¢ par 9/15/2002
Stock Dividends - in Sr. Preferred to holders of Sr. Preferred 5% payable 12/1/2000 to holders of record 12/1/2000 Ex date - 11/29/2000; 5% payable 9/15/2001 to holders of record 9/1/2001 Ex date - 8/29/2001; 5% payable 3/15/2001 to holders of record 3/1/2001 Ex date - 2/27/2001; 5% payable 6/15/2001 to holders of record 6/1/2001 Ex date - 5/30/2001; 5% payable 3/15/2002 to holders of record 3/1/2002 Ex date - 3/5/2002; 5% payable 6/15/2002 to holders of record 6/1/2002 Ex date - 5/29/2002; in Jr. Preferred to holders of Jr. Preferred 2.5% payable 9/15/2000 to holders of record 9/1/2000; 2.5% payable 12/15/2000 to holders of record 12/1/2000 Ex date - 11/29/2000; 2.5% payable 12/15/2000 to holders of record 12/1/2000 Ex date - 11/29/2000; 2.5% payable 3/15/2001 to holders of record 3/1/2001 Ex date - 2/27/2001; 2.5% payable 6/15/2001 to holders of record 6/1/2001 Ex date - 5/30/2001; 5% payable 9/15/2001 to holders of record 9/1/2001 Ex date - 8/29/2001; 2.5% payable 12/15/2001 to holders of record 12/11/2001 Ex date - 11/28/2001; 2.5% payable 3/15/2002 to holders of record 3/1/2002 Ex date - 3/5/2002; 2.5% payable 6/15/2002 to holders of record 6/1/2002 Ex date - 5/29/2002; In Sr. Preferred to holders of Sr. Preferred 5% payable 9/15/2002 to holders of record 9/1/2002 Ex date - 8/28/2002; In Jr. Preferred to holders of Jr. Preferred 2.5% payable 9/15/2002 to holders of record 9/1/2002 Ex date - 8/28/2002
Plan of reorganization under Chapter 11 Federal Bankruptcy Code effective 8/28/2003
No stockholders' equity

TRANSTIDE INDS LTD (MB)
Delisted from Winnipeg Stock Exchange 02/21/1993

TRANSTRAK INC (NY)
Charter cancelled and declared inoperative and void for non-payment of taxes 03/24/1993

TRANSUE & WILLIAMS STEEL FORGING CORP. (DE)
Capital Stock no par split (2) for (1) by issuance of (1) additional share 12/29/1961
Stock Dividends - 10% 06/12/1952; 10% 12/10/1952
Merged into Standard Alliance Industries, Inc. 05/16/1966
Each share Capital Stock no par exchanged for (0.125) share 5.25% Conv. Preferred Ser. A $100 par and (0.625) share Common $1 par
(See Standard Alliance Industries, Inc.)

TRANSUN INTL AWYS INC (DE)
Name changed to Goldonline International Inc. 06/21/1999
Goldonline International Inc. name changed to SGD Holdings, Ltd. 02/05/2001

TRANSVAAL CONS LD & EXPL LTD (SOUTH AFRICA)
Name changed to Rand Mines Ltd. 11/14/1985
(See Rand Mines Ltd.)

TRANSVAAL EXPLORATIONS, LTD. (ON)
Charter cancelled for default in filing reports 04/24/1968

TRANSVAC INC (NY)
Name changed 08/23/1971
Name changed from Transvac Electronics, Inc. to Transvac, Inc. 08/23/1971
Charter cancelled and proclaimed dissolved for failure to pay taxes 12/20/1977

TRANSVAL ELECTRONICS CORP. (CA)
Charter revoked for failure to file reports and pay fees 07/01/1963

TRANSVISION, INC. (NY)
Each share old Common $1 par exchanged for (0.05) share new Common $1 par 09/12/1956
Name changed to Champion Pneumatic Machinery Co., Inc. 05/16/1960
(See Champion Pneumatic Machinery Co., Inc.)

TRANSVISION ELECTRONICS, INC. (NY)
Merged into Precision Apparatus, Inc. 03/12/1963
Each share Common $1 par exchanged for (1) share Common $1 par
Precision Apparatus, Inc. merged into Atlantic Services, Inc. 06/30/1966
(See Atlantic Services, Inc.)

TRANSVISION-TELEVISION (CANADA) LTD. (ON)
Recapitalized as Arcan Corp. Ltd. 00/00/1953
Each share Common no par exchanged for (0.05) share Common no par
(See Arcan Corp. Ltd.)

TRANSWAY INTL CORP (DE)
Merged into International Controls Corp. 12/27/1985
Each share Capital Stock no par exchanged for $48.33 principal amount of 14.50% Subord. Debentures due 01/01/2006 and $24 cash

TRANSWEST ENERGY INC (AB)
Merged into Jordan Petroleum Ltd. 02/28/1997
Each share Common no par exchanged for (0.14375) share Common no par
(See Jordan Petroleum Ltd.)
9.25% Conv. Preferred Ser. A no par called for redemption 04/07/1997
Public interest eliminated

TRANSWESTERN BOWLING CORP. (CA)
Charter revoked for failure to file reports and pay fees 01/02/1968

TRANSWESTERN LIFE INSURANCE CO. (NV)
Each share Capital Stock $10 par exchanged for (10) shares Capital Stock $1 par 12/29/1961
Merged into Transwestern Life Insurance Co. (MT) 01/11/1963
Each share Capital Stock $1 par exchanged for (3) shares Common 40¢ par
Transwestern Life Insurance Co. (MT) merged into Life of Montana Insurance Co. 04/15/1976 which name changed to American Plan Life Insurance Co. 12/01/1983
(See American Plan Life Insurance Co.)

TRANSWESTERN LIFE INS CO (MT)
Merged into Life of Montana Insurance Co. 04/15/1976
Each share Common 40¢ par exchanged for (0.15873015) share Common $1 par
Life of Montana Insurance Co. name changed to American Plan Life Insurance Co. 12/01/1983
(See American Plan Life Insurance Co.)

TRANSWESTERN OIL CO.
Merged into Sunray Oil Corp. 00/00/1946
Each share Capital Stock exchanged for (0.7) share 4.25% Preferred $100 par
(See Sunray Oil Corp.)

TRANSWESTERN PIPELINE CO (DE)
Merged into Texas Eastern Corp. 06/30/1983
Each share Common $1 par exchanged for (0.65) share Common $3.50 par
5.50% Preferred $100 par called for redemption 09/16/1985
Texas Eastern Corp. merged into Panhandle Eastern Corp. 06/28/1989 which name changed to Panenergy Corp. 04/26/1996 which merged into Duke Energy Corp. (NC) 06/18/1997 which merged into Duke Energy Corp. (DE) 04/03/2006

TRANSWESTERN ROYALTY CO.
Liquidated 00/00/1949
Details not available

TRANSWORLD BANCORP (CA)
Common no par split (2) for (1) by issuance (1) additional share 03/07/1995
Common no par split (5) for (4) by issuance (0.25) additional share payable 03/15/1996 to holders of record 02/23/1996
Stock Dividends - 10% 12/03/1982; 10% 01/06/1984
Merged into Glendale Federal Bank (Glendale, CA) 05/16/1997
Each share Common no par exchanged for $18.25 cash

TRANSWORLD BENEFITS INTL INC (CA)
Reincorporated 01/15/2008
State of incorporation changed from (NV) to (CA) 01/15/2008
SEC revoked common stock registration 02/20/2014

TRANSWORLD BUSINESS RESEARCH & DEVELOPMENT CORP. (IL)
Name changed to Transworld Corp. 6/6/67
(See Transworld Corp.)

TRANSWORLD CORP (DE)
$2.66 Conv. Preferred Ser. C no par called for redemption 12/03/1984
$1.90 Preferred Ser. B no par called for redemption 12/23/1985
Common $5 par split (3) for (2) by issuance of (0.5) additional share 05/30/1986
Under plan of liquidation each share $2 Conv. Preferred Ser. A no par exchanged for $50 cash 12/31/1986
Assets transferred to Transworld Corp. Liquidating Trust and Common $5 par reclassified as Units of Bene. Int. $5 par 12/31/1986
Completely liquidated 04/08/1987
Each Unit of Bene. Int. $5 par exchanged for first and final distribution of (0.051675) share UAL, Inc. Common $5 par and $17.29 cash
UAL, Inc. name changed to Allegis Corp. 04/30/1987 which name changed to UAL Corp. 05/27/1988
(See UAL Corp.)

TRANSWORLD CORP (IL)
Merged into Avenue Financial Corp. 8/31/84
Each share Class A 50¢ par exchanged for $2.38 cash

TRANSWORLD ENERGY CORP (NV)
Charter revoked for failure to file reports and pay fees 5/1/93

TRANSWORLD EQUIPMENT CORP. (NY)
Charter revoked for failure to file reports and pay fees 12/15/65

TRANSWORLD HEALTHCARE INC (NY)
Name changed 05/07/1997
Name changed from Transworld Home Healthcare, Inc. to Transworld Healthcare, Inc. 05/07/1997
Name changed to Allied Healthcare International Inc. 06/10/2002
(See Allied Healthcare International Inc.)

TRANSWORLD INVT CORP (DE)
100% acquired through purchase offer which expired 05/31/1979
Public interest eliminated

TRANSWORLD NETWORK CORP (NV)
Placed in receivership 10/18/1988
No stockholders' equity

TRANSWORLD OIL & GAS LTD (DE)
Each share Common 1¢ par received distribution of (0.1) share International Energy, Ltd. Common no par payable 05/01/2006 to holders of record 04/24/2006
Ex date - 04/20/2006
Recapitalized as Caribbean Exploration Ventures Inc. 01/16/2007
Each share Common 1¢ par exchanged for (0.001) share Common $0.001 par
Caribbean Exploration Ventures Inc. name changed to Siguiri Basin Mining, Inc. (DE) 03/28/2007 which reorganized in Nevada as Anything Brands Online Inc. 01/17/2008 which name changed to MyFreightWorld Technologies, Inc. 05/13/2010

TRANSWORLD SVCS INC (CA)
Merged into Raycomm Transworld Industries, Inc. 06/04/1986
Each share Common 10¢ par exchanged for (1.85) shares Common 1¢ par
(See Raycomm Transworld Industries, Inc.)

TRANSWORLD TEMPS INC (DE)
Out of business 3/1/93
No stockholders' equity

TRANSWORLD TRADING CORP (AB)
Recapitalized as Cylinder Enterprises Ltd. 07/30/1999
Each share Common no par exchanged for (1/3) share Common no par
Cylinder Enterprises Ltd. name changed to Mondev Senior Living Inc. 02/16/2000
(See Mondev Senior Living Inc.)

TRANSWORLD VENTURES CORP (DE)
Name changed to College Bound, Inc. 12/29/88
(See College Bound, Inc.)

TRANSYSTEM SVCS INC (NV)
Charter revoked for failure to file reports and pay fees 10/01/1990

TRANTER INC (MI)
Name changed 01/28/1974
Common $1 par split (3) for (1) by issuance of (2) additional shares 11/16/1984
Stock Dividends - 10% 11/30/1953; 20% 01/17/1966
Name changed from Tranter Manufacturing, Inc. to Tranter, Inc. 01/28/1974
Merged into Dover Corp. 01/05/1978
Each share Common $1 par exchanged for $38 cash

TRANZ RAIL HLDGS LTD (NEW ZEALAND)
ADR agreement terminated 8/2/2002
Each Sponsored ADR for Ordinary no par exchanged for $1.6707 cash

TRANZBYTE CORP (NV)
Name changed to American Green, Inc. 07/01/2014

TRANZCOM CHINA SEC NETWORKS INC (BC)
Name changed 06/25/2004
Name changed from Tranzcom Security Networks Inc. to Tranzcom China Security Networks Inc. 06/25/2004
Recapitalized as Pacific Link Mining Corp. 09/12/2007
Each share Common no par exchanged for (0.33333333) share Common no par

TRANZEO WIRELESS TECHNOLOGIES INC (CANADA)
Merged into Charlotte Resources Ltd. 07/04/2014
Each share Common no par exchanged for (0.13333333) share Common no par
Note: Unexchanged certificates will be cancelled and become without value 07/04/2020

TRANZONIC COS (OH)
Old Common no par split (2) for (1) by issuance of (1) additional share 10/16/87
Each share old Common no par received distribution of (0.5) share Class B Common no par 10/6/88
Old Common no par reclassified as Class A Common no par 6/18/92
Class B Common no par reclassified as Class A Common no par 8/7/96
Class A Common no par reclassified as new Common no par 8/7/96
Merged into Linsalata Capital Partners Fund II, L.P. 2/5/98
Each share Common no par exchanged for $29 cash

TRANZYME INC (DE)
Recapitalized as Ocera Therapeutics, Inc. 07/16/2013
Each share Common $0.00001 par exchanged for (0.08333333) share Common $0.00001 par
(See Ocera Therapeutics, Inc.)

TRAPPER RES LTD (AB)
Struck off register 03/01/1992

TRASCO WIND FORCE TECHNOLOGIES INC (BC)
Struck off register and declared dissolved for failure to file returns 08/25/1995

TRASK (SPENCER) FUND, INC.
Acquired by State Street Investment Corp. on a (1) for (2.876) basis 00/00/1944
State Street Investment Corp. name changed to State Street Investment Trust 05/01/1989 which name changed to State Street Master Investment Trust 12/14/1989 which name changed to State Street Research Master Investment Trust 05/25/1995
(See State Street Research Master Investment Trust)

TRASK CORP (BERMUDA)
Name changed to Med Net International Ltd. 1/8/96
(See Med Net International Ltd.)

TRATEC INC (CA)
Common 25¢ par split (3) for (2) by issuance of (0.5) additional share 11/22/76
Common 25¢ par split (3) for (2) by issuance of (0.5) additional share 6/29/77
Common 25¢ par split (3) for (2) by issuance of (0.5) additional share 7/21/78
Liquidation completed
Each share Common 25¢ par exchanged for initial distribution of $10.04 cash 6/7/79

Each share Common 25¢ par
received second distribution of $0.42
cash 3/20/81
Each share Common 25¢ par
received third and final distribution
of $0.0384 cash 7/17/81

TRATTNER ASSOCIATES, INC. (CA)
Acquired by Zale Corp. in May 1971
Each share Common $1 par
exchanged for (0.117845) share
Common $1 par
(See Zale Corp.)

TRAUNG LABEL & LITHOGRAPH CO.
Merged into Stecher-Traung
Lithograph Corp. 00/00/1932
Details not available

TRAV-LER INDUSTRIES, INC. (IL)
Liquidation completed
Each share Common $1 par
exchanged for initial distribution of
$5 cash 2/25/65
Each share Common $1 par received
second distribution of $0.85 cash
8/5/65
Each share Common $1 par received
third distribution of $0.20 cash
12/30/66
Each share Common $1 par received
fourth and final distribution of $0.22
cash 11/7/68

TRAV-LER RADIO CORP. (IL)
Name changed to Trav-Ler Industries,
Inc. 8/15/62
Trav-Ler Industries, Inc. completed
liquidation 11/7/68

TRAVEL AID & SAFETY ASSN INC (MO)
Charter forfeited for failure to pay
franchise tax 08/10/1987

TRAVEL AIR CO.
Name changed to Curtiss-Wright
Airplane Co. in 1930
(See Curtiss-Wright Airplane Co.)

TRAVEL CORRESPONDENTS AMER INC (NV)
Each share old Common $0.001 par
exchanged for (0.001) share new
Common $0.001 par 8/18/97
Name changed to Romanex Gas
Corp. 10/23/98
(See Romanex Gas Corp.)

TRAVEL DYNAMICS INC (NV)
Name changed to TRU Dynamics
International, Inc. 02/14/2001
(See TRU Dynamics International, Inc.)

TRAVEL EQUIP CORP (IN)
Reorganized under Chapter 11
Federal Bankruptcy Act 01/13/1981
No stockholders' equity

TRAVEL HUNT HLDGS INC (DE)
Reorganized 10/11/2007
Common $0.001 par split (7) for (1)
by issuance of (6) additional shares
payable 09/19/2005 to holders of
record 09/17/2005 Ex date -
09/20/2005
Reorganized from (FL) to under the
laws of Delaware 10/11/2007
Each share Common $0.001 par
exchanged for (0.1) share Common
$0.001 par
Name changed to China New Energy
Group Co. 05/28/2008

TRAVEL MGMT CORP (DE)
Charter cancelled and declared
inoperative and void for
non-payment of taxes 03/01/1974

TRAVEL MASTERS (NV)
Name changed to Progress Watch
Corp. 05/21/1999
Progress Watch Corp. name changed
to Mobile Broadcasting Holding, Inc.
11/26/2014 which name changed to
Medically Minded, Inc. 03/02/2016
which name changed to Sixty Six
Oilfield Services, Inc. 05/08/2017

TRAVEL PLAZA DEVS INC (AB)
Cease trade order in effect
04/28/2000

TRAVEL PORTS AMER INC (NY)
Stock Dividends - 6% payable 4/28/97
to holders of record 4/17/97; 8%
payable 4/23/98 to holders of record
4/10/98
Merged into TravelCenters of America
6/1/99
Each share Common 1¢ par
exchanged for $4.30 cash

TRAVEL SVCS INTL INC (DE)
Merged into Airtours plc 5/2/2000
Each share Common 1¢ par
exchanged for $26 cash

TRAVEL VENTURES INC (AB)
Name changed to TVI Copper Inc.
12/02/1992
TVI Copper Inc. name changed to TVI
Pacific Inc. 07/11/1994

TRAVELBYUS COM LTD (ON)
Each share Common no par
exchanged for (1) Exchangeable
share 1/25/2001
Note: Exchangeable into (1) share
Travelbyus, Inc. Common 1¢ par
(See Travelbyus, Inc.)

TRAVELBYUS INC (TX)
Charter forfeited for failure to pay
taxes 03/22/2002

TRAVELER SHOE CO.
Name changed to Traveler Shoe
Stores Corp. 00/00/1929
(See Traveler Shoe Stores Corp.)

TRAVELER SHOE STORES CORP.
Acquired by Melville Shoe Corp.
00/00/1930
Details not available

TRAVELERS/AETNA PPTY CAS CORP (CT)
Name changed to Travelers Property
Casualty Corp. 3/7/97
(See Travelers Property Casualty Corp.)

TRAVELERS CAP I (DE)
Name changed to Citigroup Capital I
10/08/1998
(See Citigroup Capital I)

TRAVELERS CAP IV (DE)
Name changed to Citigroup Capital IV
10/08/1998
(See Citigroup Capital IV)

TRAVELERS CORP (CT)
$2 Conv. Preferred no par called for
redemption 03/10/1982
Each share $4.16 Conv.
Exchangeable Preferred Ser. A no
par exchanged for $50 principal
amount of 8.32% Conv.
Subordinated Debentures due
03/10/2015 on 06/10/1988
Common $2.50 par changed to $1.25
par and (1) additional share issued
06/07/1982
Preference Stock Purchase Rights
declared for Common stockholders
of record 07/31/1986 were
redeemed at $0.05 per right
01/07/1994 for holders of record
12/30/1993
Merged into Travelers Inc. 12/31/1993
Each share 9.25% Depositary Share
Ser. B no par exchanged for (1)
9.25% Depositary Share Ser. D $1
par
Each share 9.25% Preference Ser. B
no par exchanged for (1) share
9.25% Preferred Ser. D $1 par
Each share Common $1.25 par
exchanged for (0.80423) share
Common 1¢ par
Travelers Inc. name changed to
Travelers Group Inc. 04/16/1995
which name changed to Citigroup
Inc. 10/08/1998

TRAVELERS CORPORATE LN FD INC (MD)
Name changed to Citigroup

Investments Corporate Loan Fund
Inc. 09/16/2002
Citigroup Investments Corporate Loan
Fund Inc. name changed to LMP
Corporate Loan Fund Inc.
10/09/2006 which name changed to
Western Asset Corporate Loan Fund
Inc. 04/04/2016

TRAVELERS EXPRESS CO., INC. (MN)
Acquired by Greyhound Corp. (DE)
7/1/65
Each share Common $1 par or Class
A Common $1 par exchanged (0.2)
share 3% 2nd Conv. Preference
$100 par
Greyhound Corp. (DE) reincorporated
in (AZ) 3/3/78 which name changed
to Greyhound Dial Corp. 5/8/90
which name changed to Dial Corp.
(AZ) 5/14/91 which reincorporated in
(DE) 3/18/92 which name changed
to Viad Corp. 8/15/96

TRAVELERS GROUP INC (DE)
Name changed 04/26/1995
Name changed from Travelers Inc. to
Travelers Group Inc. 04/26/1995
5.50% Conv. Preferred Ser. B $1 par
called for redemption 07/30/1996
Common 1¢ par split (3) for (2) by
issuance of (0.5) additional share
payable 05/24/1996 to holders of
record 05/06/1996 Ex date -
05/28/1996
Common 1¢ par split (4) for (3) by
issuance of (1/3) additional share
payable 11/22/1996 to holders of
record 11/04/1996 Ex date -
11/25/1996
9.25% Depositary Preferred Ser. D $1
par called for redemption at $25 on
07/01/1997
9.25% Preferred Ser. D $1 par called
for redemption at $50 on 07/01/1997
8.125% Depositary Preferred Ser. A
$1 par called for redemption at $25
on 07/28/1997
Common 1¢ par split (3) for (2) by
issuance of (0.5) additional share
payable 11/19/1997 to holders of
record 11/03/1997 Ex date -
11/20/1997
Under plan of merger name changed
to Citigroup Inc. 10/08/1998

TRAVELERS INFOCENTER INC (AL)
Reorganized under the laws of
Delaware as Green Dolphin
Systems Corp. 02/29/2000
Each share Common no par
exchanged for (0.1) share Common
no par
Green Dolphin Systems Corp. name
changed to Gold Coast Mining Corp.
(DE) 01/24/2007 which
reincorporated in Wyoming as
Strategic Mining Corp. 12/22/2009

TRAVELERS INSURANCE CO. (CT)
Common $100 par changed to $5 par
and (19) additional shares issued
plus a 25% stock dividend paid
8/15/55
Common $5 par changed to $2.50 par
and (1) additional share issued plus
a 100% stock dividend paid 4/1/64
Stock Dividend - 100% 12/15/49
Reorganized as Travelers Corp.
12/28/65
Each share Common $2.50 par
exchanged for (1) share Common
$2.50 par
Travelers Corp. merged into Travelers
Inc. 12/31/93 which name changed
to Travelers Group Inc. 4/16/95
which name changed to Citigroup
Inc. 10/8/98

TRAVELERS OIL & URANIUM CO., INC. (NV)
Charter cancelled for failure to file
reports and pay fees 3/4/68

TRAVELERS P&C CAP I (DE)
8.08% Trust Preferred Securities

called for redemption at $25 on
4/9/2003

TRAVELERS P&C CAP II (DE)
8% Trust Preferred Securities called
for redemption at $25 on 4/9/2003

TRAVELERS PPTY CAS CORP NEW (CT)
Issue Information - 210,000,000
shares CL A offered at $18.50 on
03/21/2002
Merged into St. Paul Travelers
Companies, Inc. 4/1/2004
Each share Class A Common 1¢ par
exchanged for (0.4334) share
Common 1¢ par
Each share Class B Common 1¢ par
exchanged for (0.4334) share
Common 1¢ par
St. Paul Travelers Companies, Inc.
name changed to Travelers
Companies, Inc. 2/27/2007

TRAVELERS PPTY CAS CORP OLD (CT)
Merged into Citigroup Inc. 4/20/2000
Each share Common 1¢ par
exchanged for $41.95 cash

TRAVELERS REAL ESTATE INVT TR (MA)
Acquired by Keystone Trats
Acquisition Corp. 05/19/1989
Each Share of Bene. Int. no par
exchanged for $8.50 cash

TRAVELERS RLTY INCOME INVS (MA)
Acquired by Keystone TRII
Acquisition Corp. 05/19/1989
Each Share of Bene. Int. no par
exchanged for $11.40 cash

TRAVELLERS OIL & DEVELOPMENT CO. (NV)
Charter revoked for failure to file
reports and pay fees 3/3/24

TRAVELLERSMALL COM LTD (AB)
Reorganized under the laws of
Canada as Oromonte Resources
Inc. 03/29/2005
Each share Common no par
exchanged for (0.1) share Common
no par
Oromonte Resources Inc.
recapitalized as Georox Resources
Inc. 08/26/2008 which name
changed to Prospera Energy Inc.
07/19/2018

TRAVELMAX INTL INC (DE)
Charter cancelled and declared
inoperative and void for
non-payment of taxes 3/1/90

TRAVELMAX INTL INC (UT)
Reincorporated under the laws of
Delaware as Network Holdings
International Inc. 1/26/98

TRAVELNET INTL CORP (DE)
Recapitalized as United Ventures
Group, Inc. 10/01/1998
Each share Common $0.001 par
exchanged for (0.05) share Common
$0.001 par
United Ventures Group, Inc. name
changed to American Jewelry Corp.
(DE) 10/13/2000 which
reincorporated in Nevada
01/31/2002 which name changed to
MSM Jewelry Corp. 06/24/2002
which name changed to GEMZ
Corp. 10/27/2003

TRAVELNOW COM INC (DE)
Reincorporated 10/19/2000
State of incorporation changed from
(FL) to (DE) 10/19/2000
Merged into Hotel Reservations
Network, Inc. 2/16/2001
Each share Common no par
exchanged for $4.16 cash

TRAVELOCITY COM INC (DE)
Merged into Sabre Holdings Corp.
4/11/2002
Each share Common $0.001 par
exchanged for $28 cash

TRA-TRE

TRAVELODGE CORP (CA)
Common 25¢ par changed to no par and (0.25) additional share issued 09/15/1961
Name changed to Travelodge International, Inc. 11/21/1969
(See Travelodge International, Inc.)

TRAVELODGE INTL INC (CA)
Merged into TrustHouse Forte PLC 02/12/1986
Each share Common no par exchanged for $44 cash

TRAVELPORT SYS INC (NV)
Each share old Common $0.001 par exchanged for (0.1) share new Common $0.001 par 6/25/2001
Name changed to American Petro-Hunter Inc. 9/7/2001

TRAVELSAFE INC (NV)
Name changed to Clone Algo Technologies Inc. and Common $0.00001 par changed to $0.001 par 10/16/2014

TRAVELSCAPE COM INC (DE)
Merged into Expedia, Inc. 3/17/2000
Each share Common exchanged for $5.122 cash

TRAVELSHORTS COM INC (WA)
Name changed to Sharps Elimination Technologies, Inc. 12/23/2002
Sharps Elimination Technologies, Inc. name changed to Quantum MRI, Inc. 09/13/2005

TRAVELSTAR INC (CA)
SEC revoked common stock registration 08/07/2014

TRAVELWAYS LTD (ON)
100% acquired by Laidlaw Transportation Ltd. as of 01/00/1980
Public interest eliminated

TRAVELZOO INC (DE)
Each share old Common 1¢ par exchanged for (1) share new Common 1¢ par to reflect a (1) for (25) reverse split followed by a (25) for for (1) forward split 11/07/2013
Note: Holders of (24) or fewer pre-split shares will receive $21 cash per share
Name changed to Travelzoo 05/12/2017

TRAVERSE CITY ST BK (TRAVERSE CITY, MI)
Capital Stock $100 par changed to $10 par and (9) additional shares issued plus a 100% stock dividend paid 02/17/1966
Reorganized as Pacesetter Financial Corp. (DE) 01/02/1973
Each share Capital Stock $10 par exchanged for (2.046) shares Common $10 par
Pacesetter Financial Corp. (DE) reincorporated in Michigan 03/10/1980
(See Pacesetter Financial Corp. (MI))

TRAVERSE LONGLAC MINES LTD. (ON)
Acquired by Consolidated Beta Gamma Mines Ltd. on a (1) for (2) basis in 1956
Consolidated Beta Gamma Mines Ltd. recapitalized as Beta Gamma Exploration & Development Ltd. 1/20/69 which was acquired by General Petroleums Drilling Ltd. 11/3/69

TRAVIS BOATS & MTRS INC (TX)
Merged into TMRC, L.L.P. 3/10/2005
Each share Common 1¢ par exchanged for $0.40 cash

TRAVIS INDS INC (CO)
Name changed 4/1/89
Name changed from Travis Investments, Inc. to Travis Industries, Inc. 4/1/89
Each share old Common $0.0001 par exchanged for (0.2) share new Common $0.0001 par 1/4/96

Name changed to Arete Corp. (CO) 10/1/98

TRAVLANG INC (DE)
Charter cancelled and declared inoperative and void for non-payment of taxes 03/01/2003

TRAVOO INC (FL)
Recapitalized as Yingtui Holdings Ltd. 04/05/2013
Each share Common $0.001 par exchanged for (0.05) share Common $0.001 par

TRAWLER PETE EXPLS LTD (BC)
Name changed to Fibrequest International Ltd. 12/06/1985
Fibrequest International Ltd. name changed to E.C.M. Paytel Ltd. 07/04/1988 which recapitalized as Consolidated Paytel Ltd. 02/22/1990 which recapitalized as Paytel Industries Ltd. 06/01/1994 which name changed to Rodera Diamond Corp. 04/19/1996 which merged into Pacific Rodera Ventures Inc. 03/01/1999 which name changed to Pacific Rodera Energy Inc. (BC) 06/22/2004 which reincorporated in Alberta 06/14/2006 which name changed to PRD Energy Inc. 08/12/2010

TRAX PETES LTD (BC)
Merged into Pacalta Resources Ltd. 2/9/96
Each share Common no par exchanged for $0.71 cash

TRAXION ENERGY INC (AB)
Name changed to Anglo Canadian Oil Corp. 04/23/2010
Anglo Canadian Oil Corp. merged into Tallgrass Energy Corp. 12/31/2012
(See Tallgrass Energy Corp.)

TRAXXEC INC (NV)
Name changed to Stem Cell Assurance, Inc. 08/14/2009
Stem Cell Assurance, Inc. name changed to BioRestorative Therapies, Inc. (NV) 09/16/2011 which reincorporated in Delaware 01/01/2015

TRAYLOR ENGINEERING & MANUFACTURING CO. (PA)
Each share 8% Preferred $100 par exchanged for (1.25) shares 5% Preferred $100 par and $13 in cash in 1937
Acquired by General American Transportation Corp. on a (1.2973) for (1) basis 4/15/59
General American Transportation Corp. name changed to GATX Corp. 6/27/75

TRAYMORE LTD.
Reorganized in 1935
No stockholders' equity

TRC COS INC (DE)
Common 10¢ par split (2) for (1) by issuance of (1) additional share 08/13/1985
Common 10¢ par split (3) for (2) by issuance of (0.5) additional share 03/07/1986
Common 10¢ par split (3) for (2) by issuance of (0.5) additional share 08/21/1999
Common 10¢ par split (3) for (2) by issuance of (0.5) additional share payable 03/05/2002 to holders of record 02/19/2002 Ex date - 03/06/2002
Stock Dividends - 10% 10/20/1978; 10% 10/19/1979
Acquired by Bolt Infrastructure Parent, Inc. 06/21/2017
Each share Common 10¢ par exchanged for $17.55 cash

TRE CORP (DE)
Common $1 par split (3) for (2) by issuance of (0.5) additional share 07/31/1979
Each share Common $1 par received

distribution of (1) Contingent Subordinated Obligation 11/14/1986
Merged into Aluminum Co. of America 01/30/1987
Each Contingent Subordinated Obligation exchanged for $1 cash
Each share Common $1 par exchanged for $46.38 cash

TRE GROUP INC (DE)
Name changed to Merchandise Entertainment Television Holdings, Inc. 08/04/1994
Merchandise Entertainment Television Holdings, Inc. recapitalized as World Sports Licensing Corp. 11/29/1999 which reorganized as Choice Sports Network, Inc. 03/14/2000 which name changed to Sports Entertainment & Learning Network Inc. 09/15/2000

TREADCO INC (DE)
Merged into Arkansas Best Corp. 06/10/1999
Each share Common 1¢ par exchanged for $9 cash

TREADWAY COS INC (NJ)
Merged into Fair Lanes, Inc. 08/31/1981
Each share Common $1 par exchanged for $12.50 cash

TREADWAY INNS INTERNATIONAL, INC. (DE)
Dissolved 10/14/1965
Details not available

TREADWELL CORP (NY)
Each share Common $10 par exchanged for $120 principal amount of 6% 7-Year Subord. Notes and $50 cash 02/21/1969

TREADWELL ENGINEERING CO. (PA)
Each share Common $100 par exchanged for (12) shares Common $10 par 02/28/1963
Merged into Treadwell Corp. 04/03/1963
Each share Common $10 par exchanged for (1) share Common $10 par
Treadwell Corp. reacquired all Common shares 02/21/1969
Public interest eliminated

TREADWELL YUKON CO., LTD.
Reorganized as Treadwell Yukon Corp., 02/07/1938
Each share Capital Stock exchanged for (0.1147052) share Capital Stock
(See Treadwell Yukon Corp., Ltd.)

TREADWELL YUKON CORP., LTD.
Liquidation approved 05/05/1942
Each share Capital Stock received (0.5) share Keno Hill Mining Co. Ltd. Capital Stock no par 10/01/1946
Cash liquidation completed 04/30/1947
Keno Hill Mining Co. Ltd. recapitalized as United Keno Hill Mines Ltd. 00/00/1948
(See United Keno Hill Mines Ltd.)

TREASURE, INC. (DE)
Name changed to Mature Concepts, Inc. 08/29/1986
(See Mature Concepts, Inc.)

TREASURE & EXHIBITS INTL INC (FL)
Name changed to Affinity International Marketing, Inc. 03/28/2001
Affinity International Marketing, Inc. name changed to Global Security & Intelligence Group Inc. 01/03/2003
(See Global Security & Intelligence Group Inc.)

TREASURE CACHE INC (NY)
Each share old Common $0.0001 par exchanged for (0.08333333) share new Common $0.0001 par 11/02/1999
Name changed to Wamex Holdings, Inc. 11/02/1999

(See Wamex Holdings, Inc.)

TREASURE COAST FED SVGS BK (PALM CITY, FL)
Merged into Harbor Federal Savings Bank (Fort Pierce, FL) 05/31/1996
Each share Common $8 par exchanged for $18.18 cash

TREASURE EXPLORATIONS INC (NV)
Name changed to Verify Smart Corp. 03/24/2009

TREASURE IS RES CORP (BC)
Struck off register and declared dissolved for failure to file returns 08/06/1993

TREASURE ISLE INC (FL)
Merged into TI Acquisition Co. 11/11/1988
Each share Common $1 par exchanged for $14.25 cash
Each share Class B Common $1 par exchanged for $14.25 cash

TREASURE MOUNTAIN GOLD MINING CO. (DE)
Charter became inoperative and void for non-payment of taxes 04/15/1972

TREASURE MTN HLDGS INC (NV)
Name changed 02/11/1997
Reincorporated 04/01/1997
Name changed from Treasure Mountain Mining Co. to Treasure Mountain Holdings, Inc. and Class A Common 10¢ par reclassified as Common $0.001 par 02/11/1997
State of incorporation changed from (UT) to (NV) 04/01/1997
Each share old Common $0.001 par exchanged for (0.01) share new Common $0.001 par 10/28/1997
Note: No holder will receive fewer than (50) shares
New Common $0.001 par split (2) for (1) by issuance of (1) additional share 10/30/2000
Recapitalized as Vyteris Holdings (Nevada), Inc. 05/03/2005
Each share new Common $0.001 par exchanged for (0.1) share Common $0.001 par
Vyteris Holdings (Nevada), Inc. name changed to Vyteris, Inc. 07/02/2007
(See Vyteris, Inc.)

TREASURE RES INC (NV)
Merged into a private company 07/29/1988
Details not available

TREASURE ROUYN MINES LTD. (ON)
Name changed to Centrefield Petroleums Ltd. 00/00/1951
Centrefield Petroleums Ltd. acquired by Ellesmere Oil & Development Ltd. 00/00/1952 which merged into New Concord Development Corp. Ltd. 00/00/1952
(See New Concord Development Corp. Ltd.)

TREASURE ST BK (MISSOULA, MT)
Merged into Glacier Bancorp, Inc. 08/31/2016
Each share Common 1¢ par exchanged for (0.1969) share Common 1¢ par and $1.957 cash

TREASURE ST INDS INC (MT)
Name changed to TSI, Inc. 04/18/2000
(See TSI, Inc.)

TREASURE STATE LIFE INSURANCE CO. (MT)
Merged into Southern Equitable Life Insurance Co. 06/03/1963
Each share Capital Stock 50¢ par exchanged for (0.5) share Class A Common 10¢ par and (1.25) shares Class B 10¢ par
Southern Equitable Life Insurance Co. merged into United Founders Life Insurance Co. 12/01/1966

(See United Founders Life Insurance Co.)

TREASURE URANIUM & RESOURCES, INC. (NV)
Name changed to Treasure Resources, Inc. 07/08/1960
(See Treasure Resources, Inc.)

TREASURE VY EXPLS LTD (ON)
Reincorporated 10/31/1984
Province of incorporation changed from (BC) to (ON) 10/31/1984
Name changed to TVX Mining Corp. 06/12/1986
TVX Mining Corp. recapitalized as Consolidated TVX Mining Corp. (ON) 12/01/1986 which reincorporated in Canada as TVX Gold Inc. 01/07/1991 which merged into Kinross Gold Corp. 01/31/2003

TREASURY FIRST INC (MD)
Charter forfeited 10/04/1996

TREASURY INTL INC (DE)
Each share old Common $0.0001 par exchanged for (0.01) share new Common 03/02/2001
SEC revoked common stock registration 06/19/2009

TREASURY VAULT URANIUM CORP. (CO)
Name changed to Sunshine Corp. 05/20/1969
(See Sunshine Corp.)

TREAT SYS INC (BC)
Name changed to Mega Silver Inc. (BC) 12/18/2007
Mega Silver Inc. (BC) reincorporated in Ontario as Mega Precious Metals Inc. 09/14/2009 which merged into Yamana Gold Inc. 06/24/2015

TREATS ENTERPRISES INC (DE)
Recapitalized as Jutland Enterprises, Inc. (New) 11/23/1992
Each share Common $0.001 par exchanged for (0.01) share Common $0.001 par
(See Jutland Enterprises, Inc. (New))

TREATS INC (CANADA)
Acquired by Triadon Capital Corp. 08/24/1990
Each share Common no par exchanged for $2 cash

TREATS INTL ENTERPRISES INC (DE)
Each share old Common $0.001 par exchanged for (0.33333333) share new Common $0.001 par 06/21/1993
Each share new Common $0.001 par exchanged again for (0.33333333) share new Common $0.001 par 07/10/2000
Merged into 1551053 Ontario Inc. 12/31/2002
Each share Common $0.001 par exchanged for $0.01 cash

TREATY RES LTD (AB)
Acquired by ALBA Petroleum Corp. 05/29/1990
Each share Common no par exchanged for (0.412678) share Class A Common no par
ALBA Petroleum Corp. merged into Alberta Oil & Gas Ltd. 12/31/1990 which recapitalized as Alberta Oil & Gas Petroleum Corp. 11/19/1997 which recapitalized as Edge Energy Inc. 04/14/1998 which merged into Ventus Energy Ltd. 08/11/2000 which name changed to Navigo Energy Inc. 05/24/2002
(See Navigo Energy Inc.)

TREBIT CORP. (MI)
Liquidation completed 12/08/1961
Details not available

TREBOR MINES, LTD. (ON)
Recapitalized as Ajax Minerals Ltd. 04/21/1961
Each share Capital Stock $1 par exchanged for (0.25) share Capital Stock $1 par
(See Ajax Minerals Ltd.)

TRECO INC (FL)
Name changed 05/03/1979
Reincorporated 06/25/1980
Name changed from Treco (FL) to Treco, Inc. (DE) 05/03/1979
State of incorporation changed from (DE) to (FL) 06/25/1980
Merged into Sunstates Corp. (FL) 01/30/1985
Each share Conv. Preferred Class A Ser. I 10¢ par and Preferred Class A Ser. II 10¢ par automatically became (1) share Conv. Preferred Class A Ser. I 10¢ par and Preferred Class A Ser. II 10¢ par
Each Share of Bene. Int. no par exchanged for (0.03) share $15 Preferred $100 par
Sunstates Corp. (FL) merged into Acton Corp. 05/04/1988 which name changed to Sunstates Corp. (New) 01/03/1994
(See Sunstates Corp. (New))

TRECO INC (QC)
Through purchase offer 100% acquired by Canam Manac Ltd. as of 09/26/1980
Public interest eliminated

TREDEGAR CO. (VA)
Merged into Albemarle Paper Manufacturing Co. 02/25/1957
Each share Common $100 par exchanged for (2) shares 6% Preferred B $100 par and (10.1) shares Class B Common $5 par
Albemarle Paper Manufacturing Co. name changed to Ethyl Corp. 11/30/1962 which reorganized as NewMarket Corp. 06/18/2004

TREDEGAR INDS INC (VA)
Common no par split (3) for (2) by issuance of (0.5) additional share payable 12/08/1995 to holders of record 01/01/1996
Common no par split (3) for (1) by issuance of (2) additional shares payable 07/01/1998 to holders of record 06/15/1998 Ex date - 06/15/1998
Name changed to Tredegar Corp. 05/20/1999

TREE COM INC (DE)
Name changed to LendingTree, Inc. 01/08/2015

TREE HOLDINGS 4, INC. (DE)
Voluntarily dissolved 12/31/1993
Details not available

TREE IS WIRE INCOME FD (BC)
Reorganized under the laws of Canada as Tree Island Steel Ltd. 10/03/2012
Each Trust Unit exchanged for (1) share Common no par
Note: Unexchanged certificates were cancelled and became without value 10/03/2018

TREE ISLAND INDS LTD (BC)
Name changed 10/08/1987
Name changed from Tree Island Steel Co. Ltd. to Tree Island Industries Ltd. 10/08/1987
Acquired by TX Acquisition, Inc. 04/21/1989
Each share Common no par exchanged for $14.92 cash

TREE PRESERVATION CO INC (DE)
Name changed to Tree Holdings 4, Inc. 11/16/1993
(See Tree Holdings 4, Inc.)

TREE TECHNOLOGY INTL INC (DE)
Charter cancelled and declared inoperative and void for non-payment of taxes 03/01/1994

TREE TOP INDS INC (NV)
Each share old Common $0.001 par exchanged for (0.01) share new Common $0.001 par 12/28/2012
Name changed to Global Tech Industries Group, Inc. 07/07/2016

TREEGENIC GOLD CORP (CANADA)
Name changed to Earth Alive Clean Technologies Inc. 04/17/2014

TREESDALE LABORATORIES, INC. (PA)
Name changed 07/22/1960
Common $3 par changed to 50¢ par 00/00/1953
Name changed from Treesdale Laboratories Textile Processing Co. to Treesdale Laboratories, Inc. 07/22/1960
Merged into American Gypsum Co. (NM) 10/09/1964
Each share 6% Preferred $3 par exchanged for (1) share 6% Preferred $3 par
Each share Common 50¢ par exchanged for (1) share Common $1 par
American Gypsum Co. (NM) was acquired by Susquehanna Corp. 12/13/1965
(See Susquehanna Corp.)

TREESOURCE INDS INC (OR)
Plan of reorganization under Chapter 11 Federal Bankruptcy Code effective 1/31/2002
No stockholders' equity

TREESWEET PRODUCTS CO. (CA)
Each share Common no par exchanged for (4) shares Common $1 par in 1937
Stock Dividend - 10% 2/26/54
Completely liquidated 2/28/66
Each share Common $1 par exchanged for first and final distribution of $18.07 cash

TREEV INC (DE)
Each share old Common $0.001 par exchanged for (0.25) share new Common $0.001 par 12/10/1998
Each share Conv. Preferred Ser. A $0.0001 par received distribution of (0.068993) share new Common $0.001 par payable 12/13/1999 to holders of record 10/26/1999
Each share Conv. Preferred Ser. A $0.0001 par received distribution of (0.034532) share new Common $0.001 par payable 06/26/2000 to holders of record 05/12/2000
Each share Conv. Preferred Ser. A $0.0001 par received distribution of (0.056471) share new Common $0.001 par payable 01/02/2001 to holders of record 11/14/2000 Ex date - 12/20/2000
Stock Dividend - in Preferred to holders of Preferred 6.8993% payable 10/21/1999 to holders of record 08/04/1999
Merged into CE Computer Equipment AG 01/22/2001
Each share Conv. Preferred Ser. A $0.001 par exchanged for (0.6391) Sponsored ADR for Ordinary
Each share new Common $0.001 par exchanged for (0.2626) Sponsored ADR for Ordinary
CE Computer Equipment AG name changed to Ceyoniq AG 03/02/2001
(See Ceyoniq AG)

TREGA BIOSCIENCES INC (DE)
Merged into LION Bioscience A.G. 3/14/2001
Each share Common $0.001 par exchanged for (0.01943271) Sponsored ADR for Ordinary
(See LION Bioscience A.G.)

TREGO ENERGY INC (AB)
Merged into Calibre Energy Inc. 3/24/98
Each share Common no par exchanged for (0.2) share Common no par and $1.20 cash
(See Calibre Energy Inc.)

TREGO INTL INC (AB)
Issue Information - 1,500,000 shares COM offered at $0.20 per share on 02/12/1997
Merged into TG World Energy Corp. 07/10/2001
Each share Common no par exchanged for (0.34268) share Common no par
TG World Energy Corp. merged into TVI Pacific Inc. 03/10/2011

TREK ENERGY INC (AB)
Delisted from Alberta Stock Exchange 10/13/1992

TREK MNG INC (BC)
Under plan of merger name changed to Equinox Gold Corp. 12/22/2017

TREK RES INC (UT)
Reincorporated under the laws of Delaware and Common $0.001 par changed to 1¢ par 2/7/2001

TREKLOGIC TECHNOLOGIES INC (ON)
Name changed to Brainhunter Inc. 06/22/2004
(See Brainhunter Inc.)

TRELAWNEY MNG & EXPL INC (ON)
Acquired by IAMGOLD Corp. 06/21/2012
Each share Common no par exchanged for $3.30 cash
Note: Unexchanged certificates were cancelled and became without value 06/21/2018

TRELAWNEY RES INC (ON)
Recapitalized as Trelawney Mining & Exploration Inc. 04/17/2009
Each share Common no par exchanged for (0.2) share Common no par
(See Trelawney Mining & Exploration Inc.)

TRELLIS TECHNOLOGY CORP (BC)
Delisted from Canadian Venture Stock Exchange 2/12/96
Stockholders' equity unlikely

TREMAR MINERALS LTD. (BC)
Recapitalized as Gary Mines Ltd. 1/22/71
Each share Capital Stock 50¢ par exchanged for (0.5) share Capital Stock $1 par
Gary Mines Ltd. struck off register 10/2/78

TREMCO INC (OH)
Common $1 par split (3) for (2) by issuance of (0.5) additional share 4/2/79
Merged into Goodrich (B.F.) Co. 1/11/80
Each share Common $1 par exchanged for $40 cash

TREMCO MANUFACTURING CO. (OH)
Each share Class B Common $1 par exchanged for (1) share Common $1 par 3/1/69
Common $1 par split (2) for (1) by issuance of (1) additional share 2/27/73
Name changed to Tremco Inc. 4/17/74
(See Tremco Inc.)

TREMINCO RES LTD (BC)
Name changed to Elkhorn Gold Mining Corp. 02/24/1999
Elkhorn Gold Mining Corp. recapitalized as Tulloch Resources Ltd. 03/09/2012 which recapitalized as Tidal Royalty Corp. 07/18/2017

TREMISIS ENERGY ACQUISITION CORP (DE)
Merged into RAM Energy Resources, Inc. 05/08/2006
Each share Common $0.0001 par exchanged for (1) share Common $0.0001 par
RAM Energy Resources, Inc.

recapitalized as Halcon Resources Corp. 02/10/2012

TREMISIS ENERGY ACQUISITION CORP II (DE)
Completely liquidated 12/07/2009
Each Unit exchanged for first and final distribution of $7.95337115 cash
Each share Common $0.0001 par exchanged for first and final distribution of $7.95337115 cash

TREMONT & SUFFOLK MILLS
Liquidation completed in 1930

TREMONT ADVISERS INC (DE)
Class A Common 1¢ par split (5) for (4) by issuance of (0.25) additional share payable 8/16/99 to holders of record 7/30/99
Class B Common 1¢ par split (5) for (4) by issuance of (0.25) additional share payable 8/16/99 to holders of record 7/30/99
Class A Common 1¢ par split (5) for (4) by issuance of (0.25) additional share payable 8/8/2000 to holders of record 7/31/2000
Class B Common 1¢ par split (5) for (4) by issuance of (0.25) additional share payable 8/8/2000 to holders of record 7/31/2000
Merged into Oppenheimer Acquisition Corp. 10/1/2001
Each share Class A Common 1¢ par exchanged for $19 cash
Each share Class B Common 1¢ par exchanged for $19 cash

TREMONT BUILDING TRUST (MA)
Merged into Boston Real Estate Trust share for share 1/31/55
Boston Real Estate Trust merged into Real Estate Investment Trust of America 6/1/56
(See Real Estate Investment Trust of America)

TREMONT CORP (DE)
Incorporated 5/23/55
Adjudicated bankrupt 11/15/66
Stockholders' equity unlikely

TREMONT CORP (DE)
Incorporated 1/3/86
Each share Common 10¢ par exchanged for (0.1) share Common $1 par 5/14/91
Merged into Valhi, Inc. 2/7/2003
Each share Common $1 par exchanged for (3.4) shares Common 1¢ par

TREMONT FAIR INC (NV)
Name changed to Vican Resources, Inc. 06/10/2011

TREMONT MOTEL CORP. (DE)
Stock Dividends - 10% 9/5/56; 10% 12/31/58
Name changed to Tremont Corp. 7/24/62
(See Tremont Corp.)

TREMOR ENTMT INC (NV)
Name changed to Durham Marketing Corp. 08/25/2003
(See Durham Marketing Corp.)

TREMOR VIDEO INC (DE)
Name changed to Telaria, Inc. 09/26/2017

TREN EXPL INC (WY)
Reincorporated 07/31/1998
Place of incorporation changed from (Canada) to (WY) 07/31/1998
Name changed to A Little Reminder (ALR) Inc. 08/03/1998
(See A Little Reminder (ALR) Inc.)

TREND CAP CORP (AB)
Name changed to Strategic Data Inc. 05/05/1995
Strategic Data Inc. recapitalized as Strategic Data Ltd. 01/17/1997 which name changed to Securex Ltd. 06/18/2001
(See Securex Ltd.)

TREND EXPLORATION & DEVELOPMENT LTD. (ON)
Charter cancelled for failure to file reports and pay taxes in 1970

TREND FD INC (MD)
Name changed to Twenty Five Fund, Inc. 04/17/1970
(See Twenty Five Fund, Inc.)

TREND INDS INC (GA)
Acquired by U.S. Plywood-Champion Papers Inc. 12/18/69
Each share Common no par exchanged for (0.9) share Common 50¢ par
U.S. Plywood-Champion Papers Inc. name changed to Champion International Corp. 5/12/72 which merged into International Paper Co. 6/20/2000

TREND LABS INC (DE)
Charter forfeited for failure to maintain a registered agent 02/25/1998

TREND-LINES INC (MA)
Class A Common 1¢ par split (3) for (2) by issuance of (0.5) additional share 09/01/1995
Plan of reorganization under Chapter 11 Federal Bankruptcy Code effective 10/29/2001
No stockholders' equity

TREND MNG CO (MT)
Reincorporated under the laws of Delaware 3/28/2001

TREND PETROLEUMS LTD. (ON)
Recapitalized as Wayne Petroleums Ltd. 10/2/56
Each share Capital Stock no par exchanged for (0.2) share Capital Stock no par
Wayne Petroleums Ltd. name changed to Anglo United Development Corp. Ltd. 3/19/62
(See Anglo United Development Corp. Ltd.)

TREND SET INDS INTL INC (BC)
Name changed to E.P.A. Enterprises Inc. 09/16/1993
E.P.A. Enterprises Inc. merged into Ecology Pure Air International Inc. 07/24/1996
(See Ecology Pure Air International Inc.)

TREND TECHNOLOGY CORP (NV)
Common $0.0001 par split (2) for (1) by issuance of (1) additional share payable 09/26/2007 to holders of record 09/25/2007 Ex date - 09/27/2007
Name changed to Americas Energy Co.-AECo 11/16/2009
(See Americas Energy Co.-AECo)

TREND VENTURES INC (CO)
Proclaimed dissolved for failure to file reports and pay fees 1/1/92

TREND VISION TECHNOLOGIES INC (BC)
Delisted from Vancouver Stock Exchange 03/07/1995

TRENDSETTER INDS INC (NV)
Charter revoked 09/30/2011

TRENDWEST RESORTS INC (OR)
Issue Information - 2,875,000 shares COM offered at $18 per share on 08/14/1997
Common no par split (3) for (2) by issuance of (0.5) additional share payable 3/28/2001 to holders of record 3/15/2001 Ex date - 3/30/2001
Common no par split (3) for (2) by issuance of (0.5) additional share payable 12/14/2001 to holders of record 11/29/2001 Ex date - 12/17/2001
Merged into Cedant Corp. 6/3/2002
Each share Common no par exchanged for (1.3074) shares CD stock 1¢ par

TRENHOLM INVT CORP (SC)
Liquidation completed
Each share Common $1 par exchanged for initial distribution of $1 cash 04/27/1978
Each share Common $1 par received second distribution of $0.25 cash 06/26/1979
Each share Common $1 par received third and final distribution of $0.73 cash 06/05/1981

TRENT PROCESS CORP. (DE)
Charter cancelled and declared inoperative and void for non-payment of taxes in 1933

TRENT-SEVERN WATERSHED LTD (AB)
Name changed to Fall River Resources Ltd. (AB) 11/14/2002
Fall River Resources Ltd. (AB) reincorporated in British Columbia 12/23/2004 which name changed to Earth Heat Resources Ltd. 07/29/2010 which name changed to Rampart Energy Ltd. 05/22/2013

TRENTON BK & TR CO (TRENTON, MI)
Acquired by Security Bancorp, Inc. (MI) 12/26/86
Each share Common $10 par exchanged for $68 cash

TRENTON BANKING CO. (TRENTON, NJ)
Each share Capital Stock $50 par exchanged for (2) shares Capital Stock $25 par 07/07/1952
Capital Stock $25 par changed to $12.50 par 06/01/1956
Merged into First Trenton National Bank (Trenton, NJ) 08/29/1958
Each share Capital Stock $12.50 par exchanged for (1) share Common $10 par
First Trenton National Bank (Trenton, NJ) name changed to New Jersey National Bank (Trenton, NJ) 05/11/1970 which reorganized as NJN Bancorporation 07/01/1971 which name changed to New Jersey National Corp. 03/21/1972 which was acquired by CoreStates Financial Corp 10/30/1986 which merged into First Union Corp. 04/28/1998 which name changed to Wachovia Corp. (Ctfs. dated after 09/01/2001) 09/01/2001 which merged into Wells Fargo & Co. (New) 12/31/2008

TRENTON CHEMICAL CO. (MI)
Acquired by Kish Industries, Inc. 12/7/56
Each share 5-1/2% Preference Common $1 par exchanged for 50¢ principal amount of 5% Debentures
Each share 6% Class B Preference Common $2 par exchanged for $1 principal amount of 5% Debentures
Each share Common $1 par exchanged for (0.1) share Common $1 par
(See Kish Industries, Inc.)

TRENTON CITIZENS SYSTEM CO. (NJ)
Name changed to Trenton Finance Co. in 1953 which name was changed to Citizens Finance Co. 1/21/54

TRENTON ENERGY INC (AB)
Acquired by 906727 Alberta Inc. 04/10/2001
Each share Common no par exchanged for $0.40 cash

TRENTON FINANCE CO. (NJ)
Name changed to Citizens Finance Co. 1/21/54

TRENTON FOODS, INC. (MO)
Merged into Carnation Co. 9/1/66
Each share Common 50¢ par exchanged for (0.2) share Common $2.75 par

(See Carnation Co.)

TRENTON GAS & OIL LTD (ON)
Charter cancelled and declared dissolved for failure to file returns and pay fees 5/9/77

TRENTON INDS INC (ON)
Deemed bankrupt 12/01/1995
No stockholders' equity

TRENTON MINES LTD. (SK)
Name changed to Trenton Petroleum & Mineral Corp. Ltd. 00/00/1959
Trenton Petroleum & Mineral Corp. Ltd. acquired by Paramount Petroleum & Mineral Corp. Ltd. 10/16/1959 which was acquired by Bison Petroleum & Minerals Ltd. 09/15/1960 which recapitalized as United Bison Resources Ltd. 12/22/1987 which merged into Nalcap Holdings Inc. 04/25/1991 which recapitalized as Arbatax International Inc. (Canada) 03/28/1996 which reincorporated in Yukon 08/06/1996 which name changed to MFC Bancorp Ltd. (YT) 03/03/1997 which reincorporated in British Columbia 11/03/2004 which name changed to KHD Humboldt Wedag International Ltd. 11/01/2005 which reorganized as Terra Nova Royalty Corp. 03/30/2010 which name changed to MFC Industrial Ltd. 09/30/2011 which name changed to MFC Bancorp Ltd. (BC) 02/16/2016
(See MFC Bancorp Ltd. (BC))

TRENTON MORTGAGE SERVICE CO.
Liquidation completed in 1949

TRENTON PETROLEUM & MINERAL CORP. LTD. (SK)
Acquired by Paramount Petroleum & Mineral Corp. Ltd. 10/16/1959
Each share Common no par exchanged for (4) shares Capital Stock $1 par
Paramount Petroleum & Mineral Corp. Ltd. acquired by Bison Petroleum & Minerals Ltd. 09/15/1960 which recapitalized as United Bison Resources Ltd. 12/22/1987 which merged into Nalcap Holdings Inc. 04/25/1991 which recapitalized as Arbatax International Inc. (Canada) 03/28/1996 which reincorporated in Yukon 08/06/1996 which name changed to MFC Bancorp Ltd. (YT) 03/03/1997 which reincorporated in British Columbia 11/03/2004 which name changed to KHD Humboldt Wedag International Ltd. 11/01/2005 which reorganized as Terra Nova Royalty Corp. 03/30/2010 which name changed to MFC Industrial Ltd. 09/30/2011 which name changed to MFC Bancorp Ltd. (BC) 02/16/2016
(See MFC Bancorp Ltd. (BC))

TRENTON SVGS BK FSB (TRENTON, NJ)
Under plan of reorganization each share Common 10¢ par automatically became (1) share Peoples Bancorp Inc. (NJ) Common 10¢ par 06/23/1997
Peoples Bancorp Inc. (NJ) reorganized as Peoples Bancorp Inc. (DE) 04/08/1998 which merged into Sovereign Bancorp, Inc. 07/01/1999 which merged into Banco Santander, S.A. 01/30/2009

TRENTON ST BK (TRENTON, MI)
Common $100 par changed to $20 par and (4) additional shares issued 1/13/48
Common $20 par changed to $10 par and (1) additional share issued 6/15/71
Name changed to Trenton Bank & Trust Co. (Trenton, MI) 4/17/80

(See Trenton Bank & Trust Co. (Trenton, MI))

TRENTON TR CO (TRENTON, NJ)
Class B Preferred $20 par changed to $56 par and (1) additional share issued 07/07/1958
Class A Preferred called for redemption 07/21/1958
Common $10 par changed to $5 par and (1) additional share issued 07/07/1958
Stock Dividends - 100% 11/01/1968; 50% 01/02/1970
Acquired by National State Bank (Elizabeth, NJ) 02/28/1972
Each share Class B Preferred $56 par exchanged for $56 cash
Each share Common $5 par exchanged for $60 cash

TRENTON VALLEY DISTILLERS CORP.
Name changed to Trenton Chemical Corp. in 1947
(See Trenton Chemical Co.)

TRENWICK GROUP INC (DE)
Common 10¢ par split (3) for (2) by issuance of (0.5) additional share payable 4/15/97 to holders of record 3/18/97
Merged into Trenwick Group Ltd. 9/27/2000
Each share Common 10¢ par exchanged for (1) share Common
(See Trenwick Group Ltd.)

TRENWICK GROUP LTD (BERMUDA)
Plan of reorganization under Chapter 11 Federal Bankruptcy Code effective 08/15/2005
No stockholders' equity

TREO INC (DE)
Merged into Bio-Manufacturing, Inc. 03/16/1990
Each share Common 1¢ par exchanged for (0.5) share Common 1¢ par
Bio-Manufacturing, Inc. merged into BioPlasty Inc. 05/29/1992
(See BioPlasty Inc.)

TRES ESTRELLAS ENTERPRISES INC (NV)
Name changed to IN Media Corp. 04/21/2010

TRESCO INC (PA)
Reincorporated under the laws of Delaware as Tresco Scientific Devices Corp. 03/05/1969
Tresco Scientific Devices Corp. name changed to Solid State Scientific Devices Corp. 12/02/1969 which name changed to Solid State Scientific Inc. 12/01/1971
(See Solid State Scientific Inc.)

TRESCO SCIENTIFIC DEVICES CORP (DE)
Name changed to Solid State Scientific Devices Corp. 12/02/1969
Solid State Scientific Devices Corp. name changed to Solid State Scientific Inc. 12/01/1971
(See Solid State Scientific Inc.)

TRESCOM INTL INC (FL)
Merged into Primus Telecommunications Group Inc. 06/09/1998
Each share Common $0.0419 par exchanged for (0.6147) Common 1¢ par
(See Primus Telecommunications Group Inc.)

TRESDOR LARDER MINES LTD (ON)
Charter cancelled and declared dissolved for failure to file returns and pay fees 05/18/1976

TRESORO MNG CORP (NV)
SEC revoked common stock registration 02/16/2016

TRESTLE HLDGS INC (DE)
Recapitalized as MoqiZone Holding Corp. 08/31/2009
Each share Common $0.001 par exchanged for (0.00392927) share Common $0.001 par
MoqiZone Holding Corp. name changed to Balincan USA, Inc. 09/30/2015

TREV CORP. (AB)
Name changed to Orogrande Resources Inc. 11/8/94
Orogrande Resources Inc. recapitalized as Volcanic Metals Exploration Inc. (ALTA) 7/9/2001 which reincorporated in Ontario 5/17/2005 which name changed to Energy Fuels Inc. 6/27/2006

TREVALI RES CORP (BC)
Under plan of merger name changed to Trevali Mining Corp. 04/07/2011

TREVCO OIL & GAS LTD (AB)
Name changed to Trev Corp. 9/18/90
Trev Corp. name changed to Orogrande Resources Inc. 11/8/94 which recapitalized as Volcanic Metals Exploration Inc. (ALTA) 7/9/2001 which reincorporated in Ontario 5/17/2005 which name changed to Energy Fuels Inc. 6/27/2006

TREVENEX RES INC (NV)
Name changed to Global MobileTech, Inc. 06/01/2010

TREVISTA ESTATES LTD. (CANADA)
Dissolved 00/00/1980
Details not available

TREVLAC RES INC (BC)
Recapitalized as Berkley Resources Inc. (Old) 07/30/1976
Each share Capital Stock no par exchanged for (0.2) share Capital Stock no par
Berkley Resources Inc. (Old) merged into Berkley Resources Inc. (New) 08/18/1986 which recapitalized as Berkley Renewables Inc. 04/16/2012

TREX MED CORP (DE)
Merged into Thermo Electron Corp. 11/29/2000
Each share Common 1¢ par exchanged for $2.15 cash

TREXAR CORP (DE)
Majority acquired by TR Acquisition Corp. as of 06/03/1983
Public interest eliminated

TREY RES INC (DE)
Recapitalized as SilverSun Technologies, Inc. 07/11/2011
Each share Class A Common $0.00001 par exchanged for (0.00055218) share Class A Common $0.00001 par

TREZAC CORP (TX)
Name changed to Trezac International Corp. 02/26/2003
Trezac International Corp. recapitalized as Millagro International Corp. 01/20/2004 which name changed to Telatinos Inc. 11/08/2004 which name changed to Netco Investments, Inc. 11/04/2005
(See Netco Investments, Inc.)

TREZAC INTL CORP (TX)
Each share old Common $0.001 par exchanged for (1.2) shares new Common $0.001 par 02/21/2003
Recapitalized as Millagro International Corp. 01/20/2004
Each share new Common $0.001 par exchanged for (0.001) share Common $0.001 par
Millagro International Corp. name changed to Telatinos Inc. 11/08/2004 which name changed to Netco Investments, Inc. 11/04/2005
(See Netco Investments, Inc.)

TRG INC. (NY)
Acquired by Control Data Corp. (MN) on a (1.9125) for (1) basis 12/09/1964
Control Data Corp. (MN) merged into Control Data Corp. (DE) 08/17/1968 which name changed to Ceridian Corp. (Old) 06/03/1992
(See Ceridian Corp. (Old))

TRI AID SCIENCES INC (NY)
Charter cancelled and proclaimed dissolved for failure to pay taxes 03/31/1982

TRI-ALPHA INVTS LTD (BC)
Name changed to Tri-Gold Resources Corp. 12/20/2004
Tri-Gold Resources Corp. recapitalized as Quadro Resources Ltd. 05/04/2009

TRI AMERN CORP (OH)
Common no par split (3) for (1) by issuance of (2) additional shares 9/30/77
Acquired by Scottish & York Holdings Ltd. 7/14/81
Each share Common no par exchanged for $11.50 cash

TRI ARC ENERGY LTD (AUSTRALIA)
Name changed to Triarc Corp. Ltd. 09/03/1987
Triarc Corp. Ltd. name changed to Central Bore NL 12/20/1994 which name changed to Central Exchange Ltd. 12/21/1999 which name changed to Orion Equities Ltd. 12/13/2005

TRI BASIN RES LTD (BC)
Name changed to Trian Equities Ltd. 12/21/1987
(See Trian Equities Ltd.)

TRI BRIDGE CONS GOLD MINES LTD (ON)
Merged into Lobo Gold & Resources Inc. 07/06/1983
Each share Common no par exchanged for (0.1) share Common no par
Lobo Gold & Resources Inc. recapitalized as Lobo Capital Inc. 06/11/1992 which name changed to Q & A Communications Inc. 03/01/1993 which recapitalized as Q & A Capital Inc. 11/05/1997 which recapitalized as Leader Capital Corp. 08/17/1998
(See Leader Capital Corp.)

TRI-BRIDGE MINES LTD. (ON)
Merged into Tri-Bridge Consolidated Gold Mines Ltd. 10/13/1973
Each share Capital Stock no par exchanged for (0.1) share Common no par
Tri-Bridge Consolidated Gold Mines Ltd. merged into Lobo Gold & Resources Inc. 07/06/1983 which recapitalized as Lobo Capital Inc. 06/11/1992 which name changed to Q & A Communications Inc. 03/01/1993 which recapitalized as Q & A Capital Inc. 11/05/1997 which recapitalized as Leader Capital Corp. 08/17/1998
(See Leader Capital Corp.)

TRI CAP CORP (NV)
Name changed to Advanced Appearance of America, Inc. 04/12/1988
Advanced Appearance of America, Inc. recapitalized as ATR Industries Inc. 01/06/1998 which name changed to Beautymerchant.com Inc. 09/17/1999 which name changed to National Beauty Corp. 03/30/2001 which recapitalized as Hairmax International, Inc. 08/01/2003 which name changed to China Digital Media Corp. 03/31/2005
(See China Digital Media Corp.)

TRI CHEM INC (DE)
Common 25¢ par changed to 20¢ par and (0.25) additional share issued 01/17/1969
Common 20¢ par split (3) for (2) by issuance of (0.5) additional share 02/18/1973
Common 20¢ par split (2) for (1) by issuance of (1) additional share 01/16/1976
Name changed to OCM Liquidating Corp. 05/31/1985
OCM Liquidating Corp. assets transferred to OCM Liquidating Trust 02/19/1986
(See OCM Liquidating Trust)

TRI-CITY BANCORP, INC. (TN)
Merged into First Virginia Banks, Inc. 05/28/1987
Each share Common $10 par exchanged for (3.75) shares Common $1 par
First Virginia Banks, Inc. merged into BB&T Corp. 07/01/2003

TRI-CITY BANK & TRUST CO. (BLOUNTVILLE, TN)
Under plan of reorganization each share Common $10 par automatically became (1) share Tri-City Bancorp, Inc. Common $10 par 05/11/1983
Tri-City Bancorp, Inc. merged into First Virginia Banks, Inc. 05/28/1987 which merged into BB&T Corp. 07/01/2003

TRI CITY BK (WARREN, MI)
Declared insolvent 09/27/1974
No stockholders' equity

TRI CITY NATIONAL BANK (OAK CREEK, WI)
Reorganized as Tri City Bankshares Corp. 01/29/1980
Each share Capital Stock $10 par exchanged for (1) share Common $1 par

TRI CITY RAILWAY & LIGHT CO.
Dissolved 00/00/1930
Details not available

TRI CITY RECORDING CO. (MI)
Out of business 05/00/1972
No stockholders' equity

TRI COAST FINL CORP (ON)
Common no par split (3) for (1) by issuance of (2) additional shares 09/27/1985
Recapitalized as Gold Medal Group Inc. 08/19/1987
Each share Common no par exchanged for (0.4) share Common no par
(See Gold Medal Group Inc.)

TRI COAST RES CORP (ON)
Reorganized as Tri-Coast Financial Corp. 12/07/1984
Each share Common no par exchanged for (2.5) shares Common no par
Tri-Coast Financial Corp. recapitalized as Gold Medal Group Inc. 08/19/1987
(See Gold Medal Group Inc.)

TRI COMMUNICATION SOLUTIONS INC (DE)
Ceased operations 11/22/2002
Stockholders' equity unlikely

TRI COMP SENSORS INC (CA)
Charter suspended for failure to file reports and pay fees 05/01/1989

TRI-CONTINENTAL ALLIED CO., INC.
Merged into Tri-Continental Corp. 00/00/1929
Details not available

TRI-CONTL CORP (MD)
$2.70 Preferred $50 par called for redemption 04/30/1963
(Additional Information in Active)

TRI-COR MINING CO. LTD. (ON)
Charter cancelled for failure to file reports and pay taxes 00/00/1968

TRI COUNTIES BANK (CHICO, CA)
Under plan of reorganization each share Common $5 par automatically

became (1) share TriCo Bancshares Common no par 09/07/1982

TRI-CNTY BANCORP INC (WY)
Common 10¢ par split (2) for (1) by issuance of (1) additional share payable 12/08/1997 to holders of record 11/18/1997
Merged into Platte Valley Financial Service Companies, Inc. 03/30/2001
Each share Common 10¢ par exchanged for $12.60 cash

TRI COUNTY BANKING CO. (OR)
Acquired by Citizens Bank (Corvallis, OR) 10/02/1993
Details not available

TRI-COUNTY CMNTY BK (LEHIGH ACRES, FL)
Merged into Florida Community Bank (Immokalee, FL) 07/26/1996
Each share Common $1 par exchanged for (0.6875) share Common $10 par
Florida Community Bank (Immokalee, FL) reorganized as Florida Community Banks, Inc. 04/16/2002
(See Florida Community Banks, Inc.)

TRI-CNTY FINL CORP (MD)
Common 1¢ par split (3) for (2) by issuance of (0.5) additional share payable 12/01/2004 to holders of record 11/05/2004
Common 1¢ par split (3) for (2) by issuance of (0.5) additional share payable 12/29/2005 to holders of record 12/12/2005 Ex date - 12/30/2005
Common 1¢ par split (3) for (2) by issuance of (0.5) additional share payable 11/27/2006 to holders of record 11/06/2006 Ex date - 11/28/2006
Name changed to Community Financial Corp. 10/18/2013

TRI CNTY NATL BK (MIDDLEBURG, PA)
Stock Dividends - 100% 08/03/1970; 100% 06/30/1971
Merged into NCB Financial Corp. 04/18/1984
Each share Capital Stock $10 par exchanged for (0.2125) share Common $5 par
NCB Financial Corp. merged into Keystone Financial, Inc. 12/31/1984 which merged into M&T Bank Corp. 10/06/2000

TRI CNTY SVGS & LN ASSN CAMDEN (NJ)
Each share Common $1 par exchanged for (4) shares Common $0.025 par 01/17/1983
Each share Common $0.025 par exchanged for (0.5) share Common 5¢ par 05/20/1983
Placed in receivership 11/13/1987
No stockholders' equity

TRI D AUTOMOTIVE LTD (ON)
Charter cancelled for failure to pay taxes and file returns 00/00/1989

TRI-DELTA CORP. (NY)
Completely liquidated 12/02/1988
Each share Common 1¢ par received first and final distribution of $0.41 cash
Note: Certificates were not required to be surrendered and are without value

TRI-EX MINES LTD. (ON)
Merged into Trimar Holdings & Explorations Ltd. 06/22/1967
Each share Capital Stock $1 par exchanged for (0.25) share Capital Stock no par
(See Trimar Holdings & Explorations Ltd.)

TRI-EX OIL & GAS LTD (AB)
Merged into Real Resources Inc. 01/09/1998
Each share Common no par exchanged for $0.87 cash

TRI FINANCIAL CORP. (CA)
Name changed to Crateo, Inc. 08/15/1967
(See Crateo, Inc.)

TRI FINANCIAL CORP. (NV)
Name changed to Santa Fe Financial Corp. 09/17/1970

TRI GOLD INDS INC (BC)
Name changed to Trimin Resources Inc. 03/06/1989
Trimin Resources Inc. name changed to Trimin Enterprises Inc. (BC) 11/01/1991 which reorganized as Trimin Enterprises Inc. (Canada) 07/27/1998
(See Trimin Enterprises Inc.)

TRI-GOLD RES CORP (BC)
Recapitalized as Quadro Resources Ltd. 05/04/2009
Each share Common no par exchanged for (0.14285714) share Common no par

TRI-ISTHMUS GROUP INC (DE)
Name changed to First Physicians Capital Group, Inc. 01/08/2010

TRI KAL INTERNATIONAL LTD. (ISLE OF MAN)
Dissolved 04/12/1995
Details not available

TRI-LATERAL VENTURE CORP (ON)
Name changed 06/19/1995
Recapitalized 11/11/1998
Name changed from Tri-Lateral Free Trade Inc. to Tri-Lateral Investments Corp. 06/19/1995
Recapitalized from Tri-Lateral Investments Corp. to Tri-Lateral Venture Corp. 11/11/1998
Each share Common no par exchanged for (0.1) share Common no par
Name changed to Pan American Gold Corp. and (6) additional shares issued 05/06/2004
Pan American Gold Corp. recapitalized as Newcastle Resources Ltd. (ON) 11/28/2008 which reincorporated in British Columbia as RepliCel Life Sciences Inc. 07/01/2011

TRI LINE EXPWYS LTD (AB)
Each share Common no par exchanged for (0.000001) share Common no par 08/10/1989
Note: In effect holders received $5.50 cash per share and public interest was eliminated

TRI LINK RES LTD (AB)
Acquired by Seneca Recources Corp. 06/16/2000
Each share Common no par exchanged for $7.05 cash

TRI LITE CORP (WA)
Charter cancelled and proclaimed dissolved for failure to pay fees 10/22/1990

TRI-LITE INC (PA)
Plan of reorganization under Chapter 11 Federal Bankruptcy proceedings confirmed 03/11/1997
Stockholders' equity unlikely

TRI-MARK MFG INC (CA)
Common $0.001 par changed to $0.0001 par and (7.34415909) additional shares issued payable 11/05/2010 to holders of record 10/28/2010 Ex date - 11/08/2010
Reincorporated under the laws of Delaware as FTOH Corp. 11/11/2010
FTOH Corp. name changed to 5to1 Holding Corp. 12/16/2010
(See 5To1 Holding Corp.)

TRI-METAL WORKS, INC. (NJ)
Common 25¢ par changed to $0.0625 par and (3) additional shares issued 08/01/1960
Adjudicated bankrupt 06/22/1965
No stockholders' equity

TRI-NATIONAL TRADING CORP.
Liquidated 00/00/1950
Details not available

TRI-NATL DEV CORP (WY)
Reincorporated 02/25/1997
Place of incorporation changed from (BC) to (WY) 02/25/1997
Each share Common no par received distribution of (0.04761904) share MRI Medical Diagnostics Inc. new Common no par payable 02/16/1998 to holders of record 01/27/1998
Filed a petition under Chapter 11 Federal Bankruptcy Code 08/23/2001
Stockholders' equity unlikely

TRI-NEM INC (DE)
Recapitalized as Innovus Corp. 09/07/1994
Each share Common $0.001 par exchanged for (0.1) share Common $0.001 par
Innovus Corp. name changed to Esynch Corp. 11/09/1998 which recapitalized as Mergence Corp. 02/13/2004

TRI-NITE MINING CO. (WA)
Name changed to American Trading & Exchange Corp. 05/22/1984
(See American Trading & Exchange Corp.)

TRI ORIGIN MINERALS LTD (AUSTRALIA)
Name changed to TriAusMin Ltd. 08/06/2010
TriAusMin Ltd. merged into Heron Resources Ltd. 08/19/2014
(See Heron Resources Ltd.)

TRI PAC RES LTD (BC)
Name changed to International Membership Marketing Inc. 05/01/1989
International Membership Marketing Inc. recapitalized as Internova Resources Ltd. 07/30/1991 which recapitalized as Parisco Foods Ltd. 01/22/1996
(See Parisco Foods Ltd.)

TRI POINT INDS INC (NY)
Merged into Farbwerke Hoechst AG 04/01/1971
Each share Common 10¢ par exchanged for $0.50 cash

TRI-POINT PLASTICS, INC. (NY)
Name changed to Tri-Point Industries, Inc. 2/24/61
(See Tri-Point Industries, Inc.)

TRI POINTE HOMES INC (DE)
Name changed to TRI Pointe Group, Inc. 07/08/2015

TRI-POWER MINERALS CORP. (BC)
Name changed to Tri-Power Petroleum Corp. (BC) 11/20/78
Tri-Power Petroleum Corp. (BC) reincorporated in Alberta 4/28/83 which recapitalized as Trical Resources Inc. 2/14/89 which recapitalized as Voyager Energy Inc. 2/19/90 which merged into Poco Petroleums Ltd. 6/1/91 which merged into Burlington Resources Inc. 11/18/99 which merged into ConocoPhillips 3/31/2006

TRI PWR PETE CORP (AB)
Reincorporated 04/20/1983
Common 50¢ par changed to no par 10/12/1979
Place of incorporation changed from (BC) to (AB) 04/20/1983
Recapitalized as Trical Resources Inc. 02/14/1989
Each share Common no par exchanged for (0.1) share Common no par
Trical Resources Inc. recapitalized as Voyager Energy Inc. 02/19/1990 which merged into Poco Petroleums Ltd. 06/01/1991 which merged into Burlington Resources Inc.

11/18/1999 which merged into ConocoPhillips 03/31/2006

TRI-PT MED CORP (DE)
Name changed to Closure Medical Corp. 01/13/1997
(See Closure Medical Corp.)

TRI-R SYS CORP (CO)
Company filed for Bankruptcy 4/3/91
Stockholders' equity unlikely

TRI-S SEC CORP (GA)
Company terminated common stock registration and is no longer public as of 09/08/2009

TRI SOUTH INVTS INC (GA)
Merged into Avalon Corp. 4/15/85
Each share Common 10¢ par exchanged for (1.18) shares Common $1 par
(See Avalon Corp.)

TRI-SOUTH MORTGAGE INVESTORS (MA)
Reorganized under the laws of Georgia as Tri-South Investments Inc. and Shares of Bene. Int. no par changed to Common 10¢ par 7/1/80
Tri-South Investments Inc. merged into Avalon Corp. 4/15/85
(See Avalon Corp.)

TRI ST BK & TR (MONTPELIER, ID)
Merged into Zions Bancorporation 07/11/1997
Each share Common no par exchanged for (9.6092) shares Common no par
Zions Bancorporation merged into Zions Bancorporation, N.A. (Salt Lake City, UT) 10/01/2018

TRI ST DISPLAYS INC (MN)
Name changed to Dynamic Merchandising, Inc. 01/01/1972
(See Dynamic Merchandising, Inc.)

TRI ST EXPL INC (UT)
Name changed to Cyntrox Corp. 12/01/1975
(See Cyntrox Corp.)

TRI ST FINL BANCORP INC (OH)
Merged into Mid Am, Inc. 03/04/1988
Each share Common no par exchanged for (2.237) shares Common no par
Mid Am, Inc. merged into Sky Financial Group, Inc. 10/02/1998 which merged into Huntington Bancshares Inc. 07/02/2007

TRI ST INC (UT)
Reorganized under the laws of Delaware as Energy Co. of North America 09/01/1978
Each share Common 10¢ par exchanged for (1) share Common 10¢ par
(See Energy Co. of North America)

TRI ST MTR TRAN CO DEL (DE)
Acquired by TRISM, Inc. 1/25/90
Each share Common 66-2/3¢ par exchanged for total value of $21.56 payable in 14.875% Notes due 12/15/96 (25%) and cash (75%)

TRI ST PETES INC (NV)
Recapitalized as Combined Companies, Inc. 2/12/80
Each share Common $1 par exchanged for (0.2) share Common 1¢ par
Combined Companies, Inc. name changed to Unisat Inc. 5/29/98 which name changed to Blagman Media International Inc. 5/6/99 which recapitalized as Innovation Holdings, Inc. 3/5/2003 which name changed to Marketing Concepts International 10/20/2006

TRI ST RES LTD (BC)
Cease trade order effective 01/11/1991
Stockholders' equity unlikely

TRI STAR GOLD CORP (CANADA)
Dissolved 06/17/2005

Details not available

TRI-STAR HLDGS INC (NV)
Recapitalized as Macada Holding, Inc. (NV) 08/20/2009
Each share Common $0.001 par exchanged for (0.002) share Common $0.0001 par
Macada Holding, Inc. (NV) reincorporated in Wyoming 02/22/2011 which recapitalized as KMA Holding, Inc. 03/17/2011
(See KMA Holding, Inc.)

TRI-STAR INTL LTD (NV)
Each share old Common $0.001 par exchanged for (0.025) share new Common $0.001 par 1/20/98
Each share new Common $0.001 par exchanged for (0.025) share old Common 1¢ par 3/10/98
Each share old Common 1¢ par exchanged for (0.004) share new Common 1¢ par 4/5/99
Name changed to Internationalstores.com Inc. 10/22/99

TRI STAR PICTURES INC (DE)
Name changed to Columbia Pictures Entertainment, Inc. 12/17/1987
(See Columbia Pictures Entertainment, Inc.)

TRI STAR RES LTD (BC)
Merged into United Tri-Star Resources Ltd. (BC) 12/31/1986
Each share Common no par exchanged for (0.2) share Common no par
United Tri-Star Resources Ltd. (BC) reincorporated in Canada 10/27/1994 which merged into UTS Energy Corp. 06/30/1998 which merged into SilverBirch Energy Corp. 10/01/2010 which merged into SilverWillow Energy Corp. 04/04/2012
(See SilverWillow Energy Corp.)

TRI ST EXPL & DEV CO (UT)
Name changed to Tri-State Exploration Inc. 06/05/1969
Tri-State Exploration Inc. name changed to Cyntrox Corp. 12/01/1975
(See Cyntrox Corp.)

TRI-ST 1ST BANC INC (OH)
Name changed 04/17/2002
Old Common no par split (5) for (4) by issuance of (0.25) additional share payable 08/25/1999 to holders of record 08/04/1999
Stock Dividend - 10% payable 01/11/2002 to holders of record 12/20/2001 Ex date - 12/18/2001
Name changed from Tri-State 1st Bank Inc. to Tri-State 1st Banc, Inc. 04/17/2002
Old Common no par split (5) for (4) by issuance of (0.25) additional share payable 01/24/2003 to holders of record 01/08/2003 Ex date - 01/27/2003
Each share old Common no par exchanged for (1) share new Common no par 04/30/2008
Note: Holders of (99) or fewer pre-split shares received $17 cash per share
Holders of between (100) and (499) shares received either (1) share Ser. A Preferred no par, $17 cash per share or a combination thereof. Option to receive stock or stock and cash expired 03/14/2008.
New Common no par split (5) for (4) by issuance of (0.25) additional share payable 01/14/2011 to holders of record 12/21/2010 Ex date - 01/18/2011
Merged into Farmers National Banc Corp. 10/01/2015
Each share Ser. A Preferred no par exchanged for $13.60 cash
Each share new Common no par exchanged for (1.747) shares Common no par

TRI ST MTR TRAN CO (DE)
Common $1 par changed to 66-2/3¢ par and (0.5) additional share issued 08/07/1968
Common 66-2/3¢ par split (3) for (2) by issuance of (0.5) additional share 03/15/1978
Stock Dividend - 10% 10/21/1966
Under plan of reorganization each share Common 66-2/3¢ par automatically became (1) share Tri-State Motor Transit Co. of Delaware Common 66-2/3¢ par 07/02/1984
(See Tri-State Motor Transit Co. of Delaware)

TRI-STATE OIL & GAS CORP.
Name changed to Tri-State Gas & Electric Corp. in 1931
(See Tri-State Gas & Electric Corp.)

TRI-STATE OIL & REFINING CO.
Merged into Crusader Corp. 00/00/1952
Each share Common 5¢ par exchanged for (0.8) share Capital Stock 5¢ par
Crusader Corp. merged into Crusader Oil & Uranium Co. 04/20/1955 which merged into Crusader Oil & Gas Co. 02/06/1959 which merged into Gold Empire Mining Co. 06/15/1968
(See Gold Empire Mining Co.)

TRI-STATE OIL CO. (TX)
Charter cancelled for non-payment of franchise taxes 5/19/50

TRI-STATE OIL CO. (WY)
Charter cancelled for non-payment of franchise taxes 7/19/27

TRI-STATE PETROLEUM & MINERALS, INC. (CO)
Recapitalized under the laws of Nevada as Tri-State Petroleum, Inc. 7/26/62
Tri-State Petroleum, Inc. recapitalized as Combined Companies, Inc. 2/12/80 which name changed to Unisat Inc. 5/29/98 which name changed to Blagman Media International Inc. 5/6/99 which recapitalized as Innovation Holdings, Inc. 3/5/2003 which name changed to Marketing Concepts International 10/20/2006

TRI-STATE ROYALTY CORP.
Acquired by Consolidated American Royalty Co. in 1931 which was dissolved in 1949

TRI-STATE URANIUM CO. (UT)
Recapitalized as Tri-State Exploration & Development Co. 08/26/1957
Each share Common 3¢ par exchanged for (0.2) share Common 3¢ par
Tri-State Exploration & Development Co. name changed to Tri-State Exploration Inc. 06/05/1969 which name changed to Cyntrox Corp. 12/01/1975
(See Cyntrox Corp.)

TRI TEC PLASTICS CORP (NY)
Merged into Secom General Corp. 12/17/1991
Each share Common 1¢ par exchanged for (0.0796) share Common 10¢ par
(See Secom General Corp.)

TRI TEX INC (FL)
Each (2.5033) shares old Common 1¢ par exchanged for (1) share new Common 1¢ par 5/26/89
Each (7) shares new Common 1¢ par exchanged for (1) share Common $0.001 par 4/12/91
Name changed to Enviromint International Inc. 6/30/92
(See Enviromint International Inc.)

TRI-TOR OILS LTD. (ON)
Merged into Bonnyville Oil & Refining Corp. 05/05/1955
Each share Common $1 par exchanged for (0.33333333) share Common $1 par
Bonnyville Oil & Refining Corp. recapitalized as Consolidated Bonnyville Ltd. 03/02/1963 which was acquired by Lake Pipe Line Co. Ltd. 02/26/1964 which recapitalized as Worldwide Energy Co. Ltd. (AB) 0/01/1967 which reincorporated in in Delaware as Weco Development Corp. 07/17/1972 which name changed to Worldwide Energy Corp. 06/14/1977 which merged into Triton Energy Corp. (TX) 11/18/1986 which reincorporated in Delaware 05/12/1995 which merged into Triton Energy Ltd. 03/25/1996
(See Triton Energy Ltd.)

TRI-UNITED PLASTICS CORP.
Property sold in 1948
No stockholders' equity

TRI-UTILITIES CORP.
Assets sold 00/00/1932
Details not available

TRI-VALLEY BK (SAN RAMON, CA)
Merged into Heritage Commerce Corp. 04/06/2018
Each share Common no par exchanged for (0.0489) share Common no par

TRI VY CORP (DE)
Common 1¢ par changed to $0.001 par 03/22/1997
Chapter 11 bankruptcy proceedings converted to Chapter 7 on 03/25/2013
Stockholders' equity unlikely

TRI-VISION INTL LTD (ON)
Merged into Wi-LAN Inc. (AB) 06/29/2007
Each share Common no par exchanged for (0.292) share Common no par
Note: Unexchanged certificates were cancelled and became without value 06/29/2009
Wi-LAN Inc. (AB) reincorporated in Canada 08/02/2007 which name changed to Quarterhill Inc. 06/05/2017

TRI-VY OIL & GAS CORP (DE)
Name changed to Tri-Valley Corp. 12/08/1986
(See Tri-Valley Corp.)

TRI WALL CONTAINERS INC (NY)
Merged into Indian Head Inc. 05/10/1974
Each share Common $1 par exchanged for $19 cash

TRI WAY LEISURE INDS INC (NJ)
Charter revoked for failure to file reports and pay fees 04/06/1995

TRI-WAY MEDIA & COMMUNICATIONS INC (FL)
Name changed 4/4/89
Name changed from Tri-Way Industries, Inc. to Tri-Way Media & Communications Inc. 4/4/89
Each share Common $0.0001 par exchanged for (0.1) share Common $0.001 par 4/30/89
Name changed to Rothchild Co., Inc. (FL) 11/27/89
Rothchild Co., Inc. (FL) reincorporated in Delaware 4/8/96 which name changed to Fremont Gold Corp. 7/30/96 which recapitalized as JSDC Inc. 1/28/2002 which recapitalized as Housing Solutions Hawaii Inc. 11/25/2002 which name changed to Home Solutions Health, Inc. 5/14/2004

TRI WEST PETROLEUMS LTD. (CANADA)
Acquired by Peak Oils Ltd. on a (7.871) for (1) basis 00/00/1952
Peak Oils Ltd. recapitalized as Consolidated Peak Oils Ltd. 00/00/1953 which was acquired by Western Allenbee Oil & Gas Co. Ltd. 06/20/1960 which name changed to Convoy Capital Corp. 04/28/1989 which recapitalized as Hariston Corp. 09/25/1992 which recapitalized as Midland Holland Inc. (Canada) 02/10/1999 which reincorporated in Yukon 03/11/1999 which name changed to Mercury Partners & Co. Inc. 02/22/2000 which name changed to Black Mountain Capital Corp. 05/02/2005 which recapitalized as Grand Peak Capital Corp. (YT) 11/20/2007 which reincorporated in British Columbia 04/27/2010

TRI WEST RES LTD (BC)
Recapitalized as Tri-Pacific Resources Ltd. 5/17/85
Each share Common no par exchanged for (0.2) share Common no par
Tri-Pacific Resources Ltd. name changed to International Membership Marketing Inc. 5/1/89 which recapitalized as Internova Resources Ltd. 7/30/91 which recapitalized as Parisco Foods Ltd. 1/22/96
(See Parisco Foods Ltd.)

TRI-WHITE CORP (CANADA)
Each share old Common no par exchanged for (0.5) share new Common no par 08/14/2003
Name changed to ClubLink Enterprises Ltd. 07/27/2009
ClubLink Enterprises Ltd. name changed to TWC Enterprises Ltd. 06/25/2014

TRI-X INTL LTD (BERMUDA)
Delisted from Canadian Dealer Network 05/31/2001

TRIACTOR RES CORP (BC)
Delisted from Vancouver Stock Exchange 03/01/1989

TRIAD AMERN CAP CORP (CA)
Merged into Triad Subsidiary Corp. 07/15/1976
Each share Common $1 par exchanged for $1.15 cash

TRIAD BK (GREENSBORO, NC)
Common $5 par changed to $2.50 par and (1) additional share issued in October 1984
Stock Dividend - 10% 3/24/87
Merged into United Carolina Bancshares Corp. 3/29/96
Each share Common $2.50 par exchanged for (0.854166) share Common $4 par
United Carolina Bancshares Corp. merged into BB&T Corp. 7/1/97

TRIAD COMPRESSOR INC (NV)
Name changed to Triad Innovations, Inc. 9/10/99

TRIAD DEV CORP (CO)
Name changed to Zootech 2000, Inc. (CO) 05/04/1999
Zootech 2000, Inc. (CO) reorganized in Wyoming as Premium Petroleum Corp. 02/24/2005 which recapitalized as Premium Energy Corp. 02/12/2013

TRIAD ENERGY CORP (DE)
Name changed to Global Gold Corp. 11/13/95

TRIAD HOSPS INC (DE)
Merged into Community Health Systems, Inc. 07/25/2007
Each share Common 1¢ par exchanged for $54 cash

TRIAD INDS INC (NV)
Each share old Common $0.001 par exchanged for (0.05) share new Common $0.001 par 3/3/2003
Name changed to Direct Equity International, Inc. 5/12/2006

TRIAD LEASES, LTD.
Merged into Triad Oil Co. Ltd. 10/17/51
Each share Capital Stock no par exchanged for (6.25) shares Capital Stock no par
Triad Oil Co. Ltd. name changed to BP Oil & Gas Ltd. 7/2/70 which merged into BP Canada Ltd. (Ont.) 10/18/72 which name changed to BP Canada Ltd.-BP Canada Ltee. 4/27/73 which reincorporated in Canada as BP Canada Inc. 7/6/79
(See BP Canada Inc.)

TRIAD LIFE INSURANCE CORP. (NC)
Acquired by Associated Madison Companies, Inc. 1/12/82
Each share Common Capital Stock $3 par exchanged for $40 cash

TRIAD MINERALS INC (NV)
Charter revoked for failure to file reports and pay fees 09/01/1988

TRIAD NORTH AMER INC (NV)
Name changed to Kingslake Energy, Inc. 06/07/2006
(See Kingslake Energy, Inc.)

TRIAD OIL LTD (AB)
Name changed to BP Oil & Gas Ltd. 07/02/1970
BP Oil & Gas Ltd. merged into BP Canada Ltd. (ON) 10/18/1972 which name changed to BP Canada Ltd.-BP Canada Ltee. 04/27/1973 which reincorporated in Canada as BP Canada Inc. 07/06/1979
(See BP Canada Inc.)

TRIAD PK LLC (DE)
Acquired by TKG Acquisition Corp. 5/29/98
Each Membership Interest exchanged for $1.90 cash

TRIAD SYS CORP (DE)
Reincorporated 3/9/87
State of incorporation changed from (CA) to (DE) 3/9/87
Under plan of recapitalization each share Common no par exchanged for (1) share Common $0.001 par and $15 cash 8/9/89
Each share Common $0.001 par received distribution of (1) Triad Park LLC Membership Interest payable 8/21/97 to holders of record 2/26/97
Merged into Cooperative Computing Inc. 2/27/97
Each share Common $0.001 par exchanged for $9.25 cash

TRIAD TECHNOLOGIES LTD (YUKON)
Reincorporated 5/20/94
Place of incorporation changed from (BC) to (Yukon) 5/20/94
Recapitalized as MPAC Industries Corp. (Yukon) 12/16/99
Each share Common no par exchanged for (0.1) share Common no par
MPAC Industries Corp. (Yukon) reincorporated in British Columbia 7/28/2006

TRIAD WARRANTY INC (NV)
Name changed to GTM Holdings, Inc. 05/30/2000
GTM Holdings, Inc. name changed to Asia Premium Television Group, Inc. 09/27/2002 which recapitalized as China Grand Resorts, Inc. 11/17/2009

TRIAM AUTOMOTIVE INC (ON)
Merged into Magma International Inc. 5/28/98
Each share Common no par exchanged for (0.0943) share Class A Common no par and $1.50 cash

TRIAM LTD (NV)
Name changed to WHY USA Financial Group, Inc. 12/16/1999
(See WHY USA Financial Group, Inc.)

TRIAN ACQUISITION I CORP (DE)
Issue Information - 80,000,000 UNITS consisting of (1) share COM and (1) WT offered at $10 per Unit on 01/23/2008
Completely liquidated 01/22/2010
Each Unit exchanged for first and final distribution of $9.876481 cash
Each share Common $0.0001 par exchanged for first and final distribution of $9.876481 cash

TRIAN EQUITIES LTD (BC)
Merged into AMT Investments Ltd. 1/29/2003
Each share Common no par exchanged for $4.20 cash

TRIAN HLDGS INC (DE)
$16.50 Preferred $1 par called for redemption 09/30/1989

TRIANGLE BANCORP INC (NC)
Common no par split (3) for (2) by issuance of (0.5) additional share payable 6/30/98 to holders of record 6/15/98 Ex date - 7/1/98
Merged into Centura Banks, Inc. 2/18/2000
Each share Common no par exchanged for (0.45) share Common no par
Centura Banks, Inc. merged into Royal Bank of Canada (Montreal, QC) 6/5/2001

TRIANGLE BK & TR CO (RALEIGH, NC)
Under plan of reorganization each share Common $5 par automatically became (1) share Triangle Bancorp, Inc. Common $4 par 11/26/91
Triangle Bancorp Inc. merged into Centura Banks, Inc. 2/18/2000 which merged into Royal Bank of Canada (Montreal, QC) 6/5/2001

TRIANGLE BRICK CO (NC)
Merged into Roeben-Klinkerwerke 02/06/1979
Each share Common $1 par exchanged for $14.25 cash

TRIANGLE BROADCASTING INC (NV)
Each share old Common $0.001 par exchanged for (0.2) share new Common $0.001 par 07/30/1998
Recapitalized as Coffaro Family Products, Inc. 01/31/2002
Each (60) shares new Common $0.001 par exchanged for (1) share Common $0.001 par
Coffaro Family Products, Inc. name changed to E-monee.com, Inc. 07/25/2006
(See E-monee.com, Inc.)

TRIANGLE BUSINESS MACHINES, INC. (CA)
Name changed to American Systems, Inc. 3/1/67
(See American Systems, Inc.)

TRIANGLE CAP CORP (MD)
Name changed to Barings BDC, Inc. 08/03/2018

TRIANGLE CAP ENERGY CORP (ON)
Recapitalized as Black Mountain Minerals Inc. 05/07/1997
Each share Common no par exchanged for (0.25) share Common no par
Black Mountain Minerals Inc. recapitalized as Augustine Ventures Inc. 11/30/2006 which merged into Red Pine Exploration Inc. 02/06/2017

TRIANGLE CASTINGS INC (NV)
Name changed to Prospect Global Resources Inc. 03/09/2011

TRIANGLE CONDUIT & CABLE CO. INC. (DE)
Name changed to Triangle Industries, Inc. (Old) 5/31/68
(See Triangle Industries, Inc. (Old))

TRIANGLE CORP. (NY)
Merged into Triangle-Pacific Forest Products Corp. 9/30/65
Each share Class A $1 par exchanged for (2) shares Common 50¢ par
Triangle-Pacific Forest Products Corp. name changed to Triangle Pacific Corp. 6/15/73
(See Triangle Pacific Corp.)

TRIANGLE CORP (DE)
Each share Common no par exchanged for (0.2) share Common 50¢ par 5/6/70
Common 50¢ par split (11) for (10) by issuance of (0.1) additional share 12/31/82
Common 50¢ par split (3) for (2) by issuance of (0.5) additional share 12/31/86
Stock Dividends - 10% 12/31/83; 10% 12/31/84; 10% 12/31/85; 10% 12/31/87; 10% 12/30/88
Name changed to Audits & Surveys Worldwide Inc. 3/28/95
(See Audits & Surveys Worldwide Inc.)

TRIANGLE EXPLS LTD (ON)
Recapitalized as Laser Expressions Inc. 03/17/1988
Each share Common no par exchanged for (0.1) share Common no par
Laser Expressions Inc. recapitalized as Speer Darrow Management Inc. 11/25/1992 which name changed to Rex Diamond Mining Corp. (ON) 09/14/1995 which reincorporated in Yukon 07/13/2000 which reorganized in Ontario as Rex Opportunity Corp. 11/09/2011

TRIANGLE GROUP INC (FL)
Each share Common $0.00001 par exchanged for (0.1) share Common $0.0001 par 08/14/1989
Each share Common $0.0001 par exchanged for (0.14285714) share Common $0.0007 par 10/06/1989
Recapitalized as Triangle Imaging Group, Inc. (FL) 04/13/1995
Each share Common $0.0007 par exchanged for (0.1) Common $0.0007 par
Triangle Imaging Group, Inc. (FL) reincorporated in Delaware as Electronic Business Services, Inc. 10/08/1999 which name changed to Tangent Solutions, Inc. 09/07/2001
(See Tangent Solutions, Inc.)

TRIANGLE HOME PRODS INC (DE)
Reincorporated 08/15/1987
Common no par changed to 45¢ par 09/12/1973
State of incorporation changed from (IL) to (DE) 08/15/1987
Common 45¢ par changed to 10¢ par 04/23/1993
Majority of shares acquired by purchase offer which expired 06/25/1998
Public interest eliminated

TRIANGLE IMAGING GROUP INC (FL)
Reincorporated under the laws of Delaware as Electronic Business Services, Inc. 10/08/1999
Electronic Business Services, Inc. name changed to Tangent Solutions, Inc. 09/07/2001
(See Tangent Solutions, Inc.)

TRIANGLE INC (CO)
Recapitalized as Pethealth Systems Inc. 02/19/1997
Each share Common no par exchanged for (0.005) share Common no par
Pethealth Systems Inc. name changed to Incubate This!, Inc. (CO) 03/01/2000 which reincorporated in Delaware 01/16/2001 which name changed to OrganiTECH USA Inc. 03/20/2001
(See OrganiTECH USA Inc.)

TRIANGLE INCOME FD INC (MD)
Name changed to Shearson High Yield Fund Inc. 11/18/1981
Shearson High Yield Fund Inc. name changed to SLH High Yield Fund Inc. 12/15/1988
(See SLH High Yield Fund Inc.)

TRIANGLE INDS INC NEW (DE)
15.75% Conv. Jr. Preferred $1 par called for redemption 1/12/89
Merged into Pechiney Corp. 1/13/89
Each share $2 Conv. Sr. Preferred $1 par exchanged for $101.92 cash
Each share Class A Common $1 par exchanged for $56 cash

TRIANGLE INDS INC OLD (DE)
Common no par split (2) for (1) by issuance of (1) additional share 08/05/1985
Common no par changed to $1 par 11/27/1985
$2.22 Conv. Preferred $1 par called for redemption 10/09/1986
Acquired by Triangle Industries, Inc. (New) 07/07/1988
Each share Adjustable Rate Part. Preferred $1 par exchanged for (1) share 15.75% Conv. Jr. Preferred $1 par and $25 cash
Each share Common $1 par exchanged for (1) share 15.75% Conv. Jr. Preferred $1 par and $25 cash
Each share $16.50 Preferred $1 par automatically became (1) share Trian Holdings Inc. $16.50 Preferred $1 par
(See each company's listing)

TRIANGLE INSTR INC (NY)
Dissolved by proclamation 12/16/1974

TRIANGLE J OIL CO. (CO)
Company dissolved 00/00/1988
Details not available

TRIANGLE LUMBER CORP. (NY)
Name changed to Triangle Corp. 06/05/1961
Triangle Corp. merged into Triangle-Pacific Forest Products Corp. 09/30/1965 which name changed to Triangle Pacific Corp. 06/15/1973
(See Triangle Pacific Corp.)

TRIANGLE MICROWAVE INC (NJ)
Common no par split (2) for (1) by issuance of (1) additional share 06/13/1983
Merged into KDI Corp. 08/21/1987
Each share Common no par exchanged for (1) Contingent Payment Obligation Unit and $6.50 cash
(See KDI Corp.)

TRIANGLE MINES INC. (UT)
Charter revoked for failure to file reports and pay fees 03/29/1957

TRIANGLE MOBILE HOME PRODS INC (IL)
Name changed to Triangle Home Products, Inc. (IL) 09/23/1971
Triangle Home Products, Inc. (IL) reincorporated in Delaware 08/15/1987
(See Triangle Home Products, Inc.)

TRIANGLE MULTI-MEDIA LTD INC (WA)
Recapitalized as Cinemax Pictures & Production Company International, Inc. 10/05/2007
Each share Common 1¢ par exchanged for (0.00002) share Common $0.001 par
Note: Holders of between (100) and

(4,999,999) shares received (100) shares
Holders of (99) shares or fewer were not affected by the reverse split
Cinemax Pictures & Production Company International, Inc. name changed to Circa Pictures & Production Company International, Inc. 04/03/2008

TRIANGLE MULTI-SERVICES CORP (ON)
Name changed to RXT 110 Inc. 04/28/2011
RXT 110 Inc. name changed to BIOSENTA Inc. 06/06/2012

TRIANGLE PAC CORP (DE)
Merged into Armstrong World Industries, Inc. (Old) 07/24/1998
Each share Common $1 par exchanged for $55.50 cash

TRIANGLE PAC CORP (NY)
Common 50¢ par split (2) for (1) by issuance of (1) additional share 06/30/1978
Merged into Beta Partners 05/16/1986
Each share Common 50¢ par exchanged for $53.50 cash

TRIANGLE-PACIFIC FOREST PRODUCTS CORP. (NY)
Name changed to Triangle Pacific Corp. 06/15/1973
(See Triangle Pacific Corp.)

TRIANGLE PETE CORP (NV)
Each share old Common $0.00001 par exchanged for (0.1) share new Common $0.00001 par 11/05/2010
Reincorporated under the laws of Delaware 12/03/2012

TRIANGLE PHARMACEUTICALS INC (DE)
Merged into Gilead Sciences, Inc. 01/23/2003
Each share Common $0.001 par exchanged for $6 cash

TRIANGLE RES INC (BC)
Recapitalized as Mortcorp Enterprises Inc. 10/19/1990
Each share Common no par exchanged for (1/3) share Common no par
Mortcorp Enterprises Inc. recapitalized as Licefa International Inc. 10/03/1994 which recapitalized as Continuum Arts Inc. 12/24/1996 which recapitalized as Continuum Resources Ltd. 05/13/1999 which was acquired by Fortuna Silver Mines Inc. 03/06/2009

TRIANGULUM CORP (AB)
Assets sold for the benefit of creditors 00/00/2004
No stockholders' equity

TRIANT HLDGS INC (BC)
Liquidation completed
Each share Common no par received first and final distribution of $0.20 cash payable 04/29/2009 to holders of record 04/17/2009
Note: Certificates were not required to be surrendered and are without value

TRIANT TECHNOLOGIES INC (BC)
Recapitalized as Triant Holdings, Inc. 12/12/2005
Each share Common no par exchanged for (0.1) share Common no par
(See Triant Holdings, Inc.)

TRIARC CORP LTD (AUSTRALIA)
Name changed to Central Bore NL 12/20/1994
Central Bore NL name changed to Central Exchange Ltd. 12/21/1999 which name changed to Orion Equities Ltd. 12/13/2005

TRIARC COS INC (DE)
Reincorporated 06/30/1994
State of incorporation changed from (OH) to (DE) 06/30/1994
Each share Class A Common 10¢ par received distribution of (2) shares Class B Ser 1 Common 10¢ par payable 09/04/2003 to holders of record 08/21/2003 Ex date - 09/05/2003
Under plan of merger name changed to Wendy's/Arby's Group, Inc. and Class B Common Ser. 1 10¢ par reclassified as Class A Common 10¢ par 09/29/2008
Wendy's/Arby's Group, Inc. name changed to Wendy's Co. 07/11/2011

TRIARX GOLD CORP (ON)
Delisted from Toronto Venture Stock Exchange 11/14/2002

TRIATHLON BROADCASTING CO (DE)
Merged into Capstar Radio Broadcasting Partners, Inc. 05/01/1999
Each share Conv. Mandatory Preferred 1¢ par exchanged for $108.30 cash
Each Conv. Mandatory Depositary Preferred par exchanged for $10.83 cash
Each share Class C Common 1¢ par exchanged for $13 cash
Each share Class A Common 1¢ par exchanged for $31 cash

TRIAUSMIN LTD (AUSTRALIA)
Merged into Heron Resources Ltd. 08/19/2014
Each share Ordinary exchanged for (0.42918454) share Ordinary
(See Heron Resources Ltd.)

TRIAX CARTS TR (ON)
Name changed to First Asset PowerGen Trust I 11/03/2006
First Asset PowerGen Trust I name changed to FA Power Fund 03/14/2007 which merged into First Asset PowerGen Fund 06/18/2008 which merged into Sprott Power Corp. 02/03/2011 which name changed to Renewable Energy Developers Inc. 07/02/2013 which merged into Capstone Infrastructure Corp. 10/07/2013

TRIAX CARTS III TR (ON)
Name changed to First Asset PowerGen Trust III 11/03/2006
First Asset PowerGen Trust III name changed to First Asset PowerGen Fund 03/14/2007 which merged into Sprott Power Corp. 02/03/2011 which name changed to Renewable Energy Developers Inc. 07/02/2013 which merged into Capstone Infrastructure Corp. 10/07/2013

TRIAX CARTS TECHNOLOGY TR (ON)
Name changed to First Asset Diversified Convertible Debenture Fund and Capital Repayment Target Securities reclassified as Units 02/22/2007

TRIAX DIVERSIFIED HIGH-YIELD TR (ON)
Each Installment Receipt plus final payment of $7 cash received (1) Trust Unit prior to 02/18/1998
Trust terminated 01/03/2017
Each Trust Unit received $7.8162 cash

TRIAX RESOURCE LTD PARTNERSHIP II (ON)
Name changed to First Asset Energy & Resource Income & Growth Fund 08/03/2006
First Asset Energy & Resource Income & Growth Fund merged into First Asset Energy & Resource Fund 10/04/2007

(See First Asset Energy & Resource Fund)

TRIAX RESOURCE LTD PARTNERSHIP (ON)
Name changed to First Asset Energy & Resource Fund 08/03/2006
(See First Asset Energy & Resource Fund)

TRIBAG MNG LTD (ON)
Recapitalized as Great Northern Financial Corp. 08/01/1975
Each share Capital Stock $1 par exchanged for (0.2) share Common no par
Great Northern Financial Corp. reorganized as Embassy Resources Ltd. 08/12/1983 which merged into Unicorp Canada Corp. 03/02/1984 which recapitalized as Unicorp Energy Corp. 06/25/1991 which name changed to Unicorp Inc. 05/28/1999 which name changed to Wilmington Capital Management Inc. 03/08/2002

TRIBAND ENTERPRISE CORP (AB)
Recapitalized as Wealth Minerals Ltd. 01/15/2004
Each share Common no par exchanged for (0.25) share Common no par

TRIBAND RES CORP (AB)
Name changed 02/14/1997
Name changed from Triband Capital Corp. to Triband Resource Corp. 02/14/1997
Recapitalized as Triband Enterprise Corp. 08/22/2001
Each share Common no par exchanged for (0.2) share Common no par
Triband Enterprise Corp. recapitalized as Wealth Minerals Ltd. 01/15/2004

TRIBEWORKS INC (DE)
Each share old Common $0.001 par exchanged for (0.25) share new Common $0.001 par 06/04/2004
Each share new Common $0.001 par exchanged again for (1/3) share new Common $0.001 par 09/07/2005
Name changed to Atlas Technology Group, Inc. 08/16/2007

TRIBORO COMMUNICATIONS INC (NY)
Merged into TBCM Communications, Inc. 03/19/1987
Each share Common 1¢ par exchanged for $4 cash

TRIBORO TELEPHONE PLANNING & INTERCONNECT, INC. (NY)
Name changed to Triboro Communications Inc. 12/20/1983
(See Triboro Communications Inc.)

TRIBRIDGE ENTERPRISES CORP (BC)
Each share old Common no par exchanged for (0.06666666) share new Common no par 05/29/1998
Recapitalized as Vision Gate Ventures Ltd. 03/16/1999
Each share new Common no par exchanged for (0.5) share Common no par
Vision Gate Ventures Ltd. name changed to Northern Lion Gold Corp. 07/10/2003

TRIBUNE CO NEW (DE)
4.25% Premium Equity Participating Securities called for redemption 03/15/2001
Common no par split (2) for (1) by issuance of (1) additional share 05/15/1987
Common no par split (2) for (1) by issuance of (1) additional share payable 01/15/1997 to holders of record 12/27/1996 Ex date - 01/16/1997
Common no par split (2) for (1) by issuance of (1) additional share payable 09/09/1999 to holders of record 08/19/1999 Ex date - 09/10/1999
Common no par changed to 1¢ par 06/12/2000
Merged into Sam Investment Trust 12/20/2007
Each share Common 1¢ par exchanged for $34 cash
Name changed to Tribune Media Co. 07/21/2014

TRIBUNE MINERALS CORP (BC)
Each share old Common no par exchanged for (0.05) share new Common no par 07/17/2009
Name changed to Stratton Resources Inc. 09/14/2011
Stratton Resources Inc. name changed to Torq Resources Inc. 03/15/2017

TRIBUNE OIL CORP (DE)
Merged into Sabine Corp. 02/10/1984
Each share Capital Stock 50¢ par exchanged for $20.02 cash

TRIBUNE PUBG CO OLD (DE)
Name changed to tronc, Inc. 06/20/2016
tronc, Inc. name changed to Tribune Publishing Co. (New) 10/10/2018

TRIBUNE RES CORP (BC)
Common no par split (2) for (1) by issuance of (1) additional share payable 03/30/2007 to holders of record 03/30/2007 Ex date - 03/28/2007
Name changed to Tribune Uranium Corp. 06/13/2007
Tribune Uranium Corp. name changed to Tribune Minerals Corp. 07/18/2008 which name changed to Stratton Resources Inc. 09/14/2011 which name changed to Torq Resources Inc. 03/15/2017

TRIBUNE SWAB FOX COS INC (NM)
Recapitalized as T/SF Communications Corp. 05/24/1995
Each share Common 10¢ par exchanged for (0.1255) share Common 10¢ par

TRIBUNE URANIUM CORP (BC)
Name changed to Tribune Minerals Corp. 07/18/2008
Tribune Minerals Corp. name changed to Stratton Resources Inc. 09/14/2011 which name changed to Torq Resources Inc. 03/15/2017

TRIBUTE MINERALS INC (ON)
Recapitalized as AurCrest Gold Inc. 12/03/2010
Each share Common no par exchanged for (0.2) share Common no par

TRIBUTE PHARMACEUTICALS CDA INC (ON)
Merged into Aralez Pharmaceuticals Inc. 02/09/2016
Each share Common no par exchanged for (0.1455) share Common no par
Note: Unexchanged certificates will be cancelled and become without value 02/09/2022

TRICAL RES INC (AB)
Recapitalized as Voyager Energy Inc. 02/19/1990
Each share Common no par exchanged for (0.25) share Common no par
Voyager Energy Inc. merged into Poco Petroleums Ltd. 06/01/1991 which merged into Burlington Resources Inc. 11/18/1999 which merged into ConocoPhillips 03/31/2006

TRICAN OILWELL SVC LTD (AB)
Name changed to Trican Well Service Ltd. 06/11/1997

TRICAN PETRO-CHEMICAL CORP. (QC)
Merged into Bonnyville Oil & Refining Corp. 05/05/1955
Each share Capital Stock $1 par exchanged for (0.33333333) share Common $1 par
Bonnyville Oil & Refining Corp. recapitalized as Consolidated Bonnyville Ltd. 03/02/1963 which was acquired by Cold Lake Pipe Line Co. Ltd. 02/26/1964 which recapitalized as Worldwide Energy Co. Ltd. (AB) 07/01/1967 which reincorporated in Delaware as Weco Development Corp. 07/17/1972 which name changed to Worldwide Energy Corp. 06/14/1977 which merged into Triton Energy Corp. (TX) 11/18/1986 which reincorporated in Delaware 05/12/1995 which merged into Triton Energy Ltd. 03/25/1996
(See Triton Energy Ltd.)

TRICARE INC (DE)
Common 1¢ par split (3) for (2) by issuance of (0.5) additional share 11/12/1991
Name changed to Transcend Services, Inc. 06/01/1995
(See Transcend Services, Inc.)

TRICELL INC (NV)
SEC revoked common stock registration 07/12/2012

TRICENTROL CANADA LTD. (AB)
Reincorporated under the laws of Ontario 11/28/1972
Tricentrol Canada Ltd. (ON) (Old) merged into Tricentrol Canada Ltd. (ON) (New) 12/28/1972
(See Tricentrol Canada Ltd. (ON) (New))

TRICENTROL CDA LTD NEW (ON)
Name changed 12/28/72
Under plan of merger name changed from Tricentrol Canada Ltd. (Old) to Tricentrol Canada Ltd. (New) and each share Common $2 par automatically became (1) share 6% Preference $15 par 12/28/72
6% Preference $15 par called for redemption 3/15/73
Public interest eliminated

TRICO INDS INC (CA)
Common 50¢ par split (2) for (1) by issuance of (1) additional share 03/27/1981
Acquired by PACCAR Inc 03/31/1987
Each share Common 50¢ par exchanged for $8 cash

TRICO MARINE SVCS INC (DE)
Old Common 1¢ par split (2) for (1) by issuance of (1) additional share payable 06/09/1997 to holders of record 05/23/1997
Plan of reorganization under Chapter 11 Federal Bankruptcy Code effective 03/15/2005
Each share old Common 1¢ par will receive (0.01351351) Common Stock Purchase Warrant Ser. A expiring 03/15/2010 and (0.01351351) Common Stock Purchase Warrant Ser. B expiring 03/15/2008
Note: Certificates were not required to be surrendered and are without value
Holders of (73) or fewer shares will not receive any distribution
Plan of reorganization under Chapter 11 Federal Bankruptcy proceedings effective 08/11/2011
No stockholders' equity

TRICO OIL & GAS CO. (CA)
Capital Stock $3 par changed to $2 par in 1937
Capital Stock $2 par changed to 50¢ par and (3) additional shares issued 11/3/59
Name changed to Trico Industries, Inc. 6/21/72
(See Trico Industries, Inc.)

TRICO PRODS CORP (NY)
Common no par split (4) for (1) by issuance of (3) additional shares 7/22/66
Merged into Stant Corp. 12/12/94
Each share Common no par exchanged for $85 cash

TRICO SECURITIES CORP. (DE)
Voluntarily dissolved 10/13/78
Details not available

TRICOM EQUITIES INC (AB)
Recapitalized as TCEnet Inc. 01/27/2000
Each share Common no par exchanged for (0.25) share Common no par
TCEnet Inc. acquired by WNS Emergent Inc. 09/30/2003 which name changed to CriticalControl Solutions Corp. 06/14/2004 which name changed to Critical Control Energy Services Corp. 07/03/2015

TRICOM INDIA LTD (INDIA)
Old Sponsored Reg. S GDR's for Equity Shares split (2) for (1) by issuance of (1) additional GDR payable 11/20/2006 to holders of record 10/26/2006
Old Sponsored Reg. S GDR's for Equity Shares split (5) for (2) by issuance of (1.5) additional GDR's issued payable 07/25/2008 to holders of record 07/24/2008
Basis changed from (1:1) to (1:2) 07/25/2008
Each old Sponsored Reg. S GDR for Equity Shares exchanged for (0.1) new Sponsored Reg. S GDR for Equity Shares 06/12/2014
GDR basis changed from (1:2) to (1:20) 06/12/2014
GDR agreement terminated 06/16/2015
Each new Sponsored Reg. S GDR for Equity Shares exchanged for (20) Equity Shares
Note: Unexchanged GDR's will be sold and the proceeds, if any, held for claim after 06/19/2015

TRICOM SA (DOMINICAN REPUBLIC)
ADR agreement terminated 03/28/2007
No ADRholders' equity

TRICOM TECHNOLOGY GROUP INC (NV)
Each share Common $0.001 par exchanged for (0.02) share old Common $0.0001 par 10/30/1998
Each share old Common $0.001 par exchanged for (0.002) share new Common $0.001 par 02/10/2000
Name changed to Omninet Media.com Inc. 02/18/2000
Omninet Media.com Inc. name changed to Omninet Media Corp. 06/01/2001 which name changed to Aquagold International, Inc. 03/28/2008

TRICON, INC. (DE)
Reincorporated 06/24/1970
State of incorporation changed from (CT) to (DE) and Common $1 par changed to 1¢ par 06/24/1970
Merged into Quality Care Nursing Centers, Inc. 11/30/1970
Each share Common 1¢ par exchanged for (1) share Common 1¢ par
Quality Care Nursing Centers, Inc. name changed to Quality Care Services, Inc. 04/01/1971 which name changed to Northwestern Service Corp. 01/24/1973
(See Northwestern Service Corp.)

TRICON GLOBAL RESTAURANTS INC (NC)
Name changed to Yum! Brands, Inc. 5/16/2002

TRICONEX CORP (CA)
Merged into TRX Corp. 11/18/94
Each share Common no par exchanged for $17.75 cash

TRICOR RES LTD (BC)
Delisted from Vancouver Stock Exchange 04/07/1986

TRICORD HURRICANE HLDGS INC (NV)
Name changed to Aria International Holdings, Inc. 03/09/2009
(See Aria International Holdings, Inc.)

TRICORD SYS INC (DE)
Plan of reorganization under Chapter 11 Federal Bankruptcy Code effective 06/05/2003
No stockholders' equity

TRIDAIR INDS (CA)
Merged into Rexnord Inc. 03/31/1976
Each share Common $1 par exchanged for (0.26) share Common $10 par
Each share Common $1 par received additional and final distribution of $0.23 cash 04/14/1978
Stock Dividend - 100% 06/12/1967
(See Rexnord Inc.)

TRIDEA INDS (CA)
Name changed to Relmar Industries 10/29/1969
Relmar Industries name changed to Technology Group, Inc. 03/20/1981 which name changed to Union Reserves, Inc. 01/01/1983
(See Union Reserves, Inc.)

TRIDEL ENTERPRISES INC (ON)
Merged into TDZ Holdings Inc. 04/28/1999
Each share Common no par exchanged for (1) share Common no par and (1) Contingent Right
Note: Unexchanged certificates were cancelled and became without value 04/28/2009
(See TDZ Holdings Inc.)

TRIDEN TELECOM INC (NV)
Each share old Common $0.001 par exchanged for (0.005) share new Common $0.001 par 10/04/2007
Name changed to Permanent Technologies, Inc. 12/10/2007

TRIDENT ENTERPRISES INC (CO)
Recapitalized as Corporate Vision Inc. (CO) 05/25/1995
Each (33) shares Common $0.001 par exchanged for (1) share Common 1¢ par
Corporate Vision Inc. (CO) reorganized in Oklahoma as Wastech, Inc. 03/18/2004
(See Wastech, Inc.)

TRIDENT ENVIRONMENTAL SYS INC (FL)
Recapitalized as Phoenix International Industries Inc. 09/18/1996
Each (15) shares Common $0.001 par exchanged for (1) share Common $0.001 par
Phoenix International Industries Inc. name changed to Epicus Communications Group, Inc. 05/07/2003
(See Epicus Communications Group, Inc.)

TRIDENT FINL SVC CORP (DE)
Name changed to Cosmos Futura, Inc. 04/12/1974
(See Cosmos Futura, Inc.)

TRIDENT GOLD CORP (ON)
Reorganized under the laws of British Columbia as Sebastiani Ventures Corp. 04/25/2017
Each share Common no par exchanged for (0.21052631) share Common no par

TRIDENT INTL INC (DE)
Merged into Illinois Tool Works Inc. 2/17/99
Each share Common 1¢ par exchanged for $16.50 cash

TRIDENT MEDIA GROUP INC (NV)
Each share old Common $0.001 par exchanged for (4) shares new Common $0.001 par 05/30/2000
Company terminated common stock registration and is no longer public as of 04/01/2002

TRIDENT NGL HLDG INC (DE)
Merged into NGC Corp. 03/15/1995
Each share Common 1¢ par exchanged for $11.75 cash
Note: Approximately 13% of outstanding shares were exchanged for NGC Corp. Common shares
NGC Corp. name changed to Dynegy Inc. (CO) 07/06/1998 which merged into Dynegy Inc. (IL) 02/01/2000 which merged into Dynegy Inc. (DE) (Old) 04/02/2007 which reorganized as Dynegy Inc. (DE) (New) 10/01/2012 which merged into Vistra Energy Corp. 04/09/2018

TRIDENT PERFORMANCE CORP (ON)
Completely liquidated 09/02/2016
Each Class A Share received first and final distribution of $9.6541 cash
Each Class F Share received first and final distribution of $10.2248 cash

TRIDENT PERFORMANCE CORP II (ON)
Completely liquidated 09/02/2016
Each Class A Share received first and final distribution of $7.5441 cash

TRIDENT PORCUPINE GOLD MINES LTD. (ON)
Charter cancelled in February, 1962
Stock worthless

TRIDENT RESOURCES CORP. (UT)
Charter suspended for failure to pay taxes 09/28/1973

TRIDENT RES INC (BC)
Recapitalized as Universal Trident Industries Ltd. 09/30/1996
Each share Common $1 par exchanged for (0.25) share Common no par
Universal Trident Industries Ltd. recapitalized as Poseidon Minerals Ltd. (BC) 08/29/1994 which reorganized in Canada as Stingray Resources Inc. 07/22/2003 which name changed to Stingray Copper Inc. 07/18/2007 which merged into Mercator Minerals Ltd. 12/21/2009

TRIDENT ROWAN GROUP INC (MD)
Name changed to Comtech Group Inc. 08/02/2004
Comtech Group Inc. name changed to Cogo Group, Inc. (MD) 05/13/2008 which reincorporated in Cayman Islands 08/03/2011 which name changed to Viewtran Group, Inc. 11/26/2013

TRIDENT SYS INC (AB)
Recapitalized as Loon Energy Inc. 12/01/1997
Each share Common no par exchanged for (0.25) share Common no par
(See Loon Energy Inc.)

TRIDENT SYS INTL INC (NV)
Each share old Common $0.001 par exchanged for (0.025) share new Common $0.001 par 10/16/2002
Name changed to AAMPRO Group, Inc. 01/07/2003
(See AAMPRO Group, Inc.)

TRIDEX CORP (CT)
Each share Common no par received distribution of (1.005) shares TransAct International Inc. Common

no par payable 03/31/1997 to
holders of record 03/14/1997
Under plan of reorganization each
share Common no par automatically
became (0.1) share Progressive
Software Holding Inc. (DE) Ser. A
Common no par 08/06/2002
(See Progressive Software Holding Inc.)

TRIDON ENTERPRISES INC (CO)
Recapitalized 04/19/1996
Recapitalized from Tridon Corp. to
Tridon Enterprises Inc. 04/19/1996
Each share Common $0.0001 par
exchanged for (0.1) share Common
$0.0001 par
Name changed to Alpha Spacecom,
Inc. (CO) 08/01/2002
Alpha Spacecom, Inc. (CO)
reorganized in Nevada 06/30/2005
which name changed to Beicang
Iron & Steel, Inc. 10/31/2006
(See Beicang Iron & Steel, Inc.)

TRIDON OIL & GAS LTD (BC)
Name changed to Energas Resources
Inc. (BC) 07/20/1992
Energas Resources Inc. (BC)
reincorporated in Delaware
08/20/2001 which recapitalized as
Enerlabs Inc. 01/25/2012 which
name changed to Energy &
Environmental Services, Inc.
12/30/2016

TRIDONT HEALTH CARE INC (ON)
Name changed to Phoenix Health
Group Inc. 02/14/1997
(See Phoenix Health Group Inc.)

TRIEX INTL CORP (DE)
Charter cancelled and declared
inoperative and void for
non-payment of taxes 04/15/1973

TRIEX MINERALS CORP (BC)
Merged into Canterra Minerals Corp.
12/11/2009
Each share Common no par
exchanged for (0.85) share Common
no par
Note: Unexchanged certificates were
cancelled and became without value
12/11/2015

TRIEX RES LTD (BC)
Ctfs. dtd. prior to 04/06/1988
Recapitalized as First Chartered
Development Corp. 04/06/1988
Each share Common no par
exchanged for (0.5) share Common
no par
First Chartered Development Corp.
recapitalized as APAC
Telecommunications Corp.
03/24/1995
(See APAC Telecommunications Corp.)

TRIEX RES LTD CDA (BC)
Ctfs. dtd. after 06/20/1994
Recapitalized as Triex Minerals Corp.
07/16/2002
Each share Common no par
exchanged for (1/3) share Common
no par
Triex Minerals Corp. merged into
Canterra Minerals Corp. 12/11/2009

TRIFIELD PETROLEUMS LTD. (ON)
Charter cancelled in January 1960

TRIFLEX FD INC (MD)
Name changed to SM&R Balanced
Fund, Inc. 01/01/1999
(See SM&R Balanced Fund, Inc.)

TRIFORM EXPLORATIONS (B.C.) LTD. (BC)
Recapitalized as Triform Mining Ltd.
10/24/1964
Each share Common no par
exchanged for (0.2) share Common
no par
Triform Mining Ltd. name changed to
Lucky Strike Mines Ltd. 10/04/1968
which name changed to Lucky Strike
Resources Ltd. 06/21/1980 which
recapitalized as Rojo Resources Ltd.
02/18/2015

TRIFORM EXPLORATIONS LTD. (ON)
Reincorporated under the laws of
British Columbia as Triform
Explorations (B.C.) Ltd. 00/00/1962
Triform Explorations (B.C.) Ltd.
recapitalized as Triform Mining Ltd.
10/24/1964 which name changed to
Lucky Strike Mines Ltd. 10/04/1968
which name changed to Lucky Strike
Resources Ltd. 06/21/1980 which
recapitalized as Rojo Resources Ltd.
02/18/2015

TRIFORM MINING LTD. (BC)
Name changed to Lucky Strike Mines
Ltd. 10/04/1968
Lucky Strike Mines Ltd. name
changed to Lucky Strike Resources
Ltd. 06/21/1980 which recapitalized
as Rojo Resources Ltd. 02/18/2015

TRIGAME ENTERPRISES INC (NJ)
Charter declared void for
non-payment of taxes 6/26/90

TRIGAS EXPL INC (AB)
Merged into Calpine Corp. 11/16/2000
Each share Common no par
exchanged for $3.20 cash

TRIGAS EXPL LTD (AB)
Merged into Pinnacle Resources Ltd.
(New) 11/22/1989
Each share Common no par
exchanged for (0.52631578) share
Common no par
Pinnacle Resources Ltd. (New)
merged into Renaissance Energy
Ltd. 07/16/1998 which merged into
Husky Energy Inc. 08/25/2000

TRIGATE ASSOC INC (NV)
Recapitalized as ATM Holdings Inc.
06/03/1996
Each share Common $0.001 par
exchanged for (0.08571918) share
Common $0.001 par
(See ATM Holdings Inc.)

TRIGEN ENERGY CORP (DE)
Acquired by T Acquisition Corp.
4/5/2000
Each share Common 1¢ par
exchanged for $23.50 cash

TRIGEN RES INC (BC)
Recapitalized as BlissCo Cannabis
Corp. 03/02/2018
Each share Common no par
exchanged for (0.44444444) share
Common no par

TRIGGER BLOCK INC (NV)
Recapitalized as Energy Systems
Solutions, Inc. 5/12/98
Each share Common $0.001 par
exchanged for (0.1) share Common
$0.001 par

TRIGOLD RES INC (BC)
Name changed to Crystal Exploration
Inc. 10/15/2015
Crystal Exploration Inc. recapitalized
as Benchmark Metals Inc.
05/29/2018

TRIGON EXPL CDA LTD (CANADA)
Name changed to Trigon Uranium
Corp. 12/13/2006
Trigon Uranium Corp. name changed
to IC Potash Corp. 12/17/2009
which name changed to Belgravia
Capital International Inc. 11/23/2017

TRIGON HEALTHCARE INC (VA)
Issue Information - 15,500,000 shares
COM offered at $13 per share on
01/30/1997
Merged into Anthem, Inc. 7/31/2002
Each share Common 1¢ par
exchanged for (1.062) shares
Common 1¢ par and $30 cash
Anthem, Inc. name changed to
WellPoint, Inc. 12/1/2004

TRIGON TECHNOLOGIES INC (BC)
Struck off register and declared
dissolved for failure to file returns
10/6/89

TRIGON URANIUM CORP (CANADA)
Each share old Common no par
exchanged for (0.25) share new
Common no par 11/12/2009
Name changed to IC Potash Corp.
12/17/2009
IC Potash Corp. name changed to
Belgravia Capital International Inc.
11/23/2017

TRIHOPE MINING & EXPLORATION LTD. (CANADA)
Name changed to Trihope Resources
Ltd. 1/2/68
(See Trihope Resources Ltd.)

TRIHOPE RES LTD (CANADA)
Dissolved 8/10/84
Details not available

TRIJET MNG CORP (BC)
Recapitalized as Umbral Energy
Corp. 03/08/2013
Each share Common no par
exchanged for (0.5) share Common
no par
Umbral Energy Corp. name changed
to Heritage Cannabis Holdings Corp.
01/10/2018

TRIKON TECHNOLOGIES INC (DE)
Reincorporated 05/17/2002
Each share Ser. I Preferred
automatically became (0.001) share
old Common no par 07/28/1998
Each share old Common no par
exchanged for (0.1) share new
Common no par 12/17/1999
Ser. H Preferred no par called for
redemption at $10 on 06/29/2001
State of incorporation changed from
(CA) to (DE) 05/17/2002
Stock Dividends - in Preferred to
holders of Preferred 4.0625%
payable 10/15/1999 to holders of
record 10/01/1999; 4.5625%
payable 04/16/2001 to holders of
record 04/02/2001
Merged into Aviza Technology, Inc.
12/01/2005
Each share new Common no par
exchanged for (0.29) share Common
$0.0001 par
(See Aviza Technology, Inc.)

TRIL-MEDIANET COM INC (DE)
Name changed to TEC Factory, Inc.
11/28/2000
TEC Factory, Inc. name changed to
HeartSTAT Technology, Inc.
02/26/2004 which name changed to
Verdant Technology Corp.
03/01/2006
(See Verdant Technology Corp.)

TRILAND INC (TX)
Proclaimed dissolved 10/1/90

TRILLIANT INC (NV)
Name changed to USA Uranium
Corp. 05/17/2007
(See USA Uranium Corp.)

TRILLING MED TECHNOLOGIES INC (NY)
Name changed to Water-Jel
Technologies Inc. (NY) 05/15/1991
Water-Jel Technologies Inc. (NY)
reincorporated in Delaware as
Xceed, Inc. 02/24/1998 which name
changed to Worldwide Xceed Group,
Inc. 11/29/2000
(See Worldwide Xceed Group, Inc.)

TRILLING RESOURCES, LTD. (NY)
Name changed to Trilling Medical
Technologies, Inc. 09/11/1987
Trilling Medical Technologies, Inc.
name changed to Water-Jel
Technologies Inc. (NY) 05/15/1991
which reincorporated in Delaware as
Xceed, Inc. 02/24/1998 which name
changed to Worldwide Xceed Group,
Inc. 11/29/2000
(See Worldwide Xceed Group, Inc.)

TRILLION CAP INC (CO)
Name changed to Signal-Hill Corp.
12/17/1987

TRILLION RES LTD (AB)
Recapitalized as Consolidated Trillion
Resources Ltd. 01/15/1999
Each share Common no par
exchanged for (1/6) share Common
no par
Consolidated Trillion Resources Ltd.
merged into Viceroy Exploration Ltd.
12/04/2003 which was acquired by
Yamana Gold Inc. 10/31/2006

TRILLIUM NORTH MINERALS LTD (BC)
Recapitalized as White Metal
Resources Corp. 06/04/2014
Each share Common no par
exchanged for (0.1) share Common
no par

TRILLIUM TEL SYS INC (CANADA)
Special Shares no par reclassified as
Common no par 12/31/85
Merged into Mitel Corp. 9/22/88
Each share Common no par
exchanged for $3 cash

TRILOCH RES INC (AB)
Issue Information - 9,179 UNITS
consisting of (600) CL A SHS and
(88) CL B SHS offered at $1,000 per
Unit
Acquired by Enerplus Resources
Fund 07/01/2005
Each share Class A no par
exchanged for (0.07151) Trust Unit
Ser. G and (0.1) share NuLoch
Resources Inc. Class A Common no
par
Each share Class B no par
exchanged for (0.23923) Trust Unit
Ser. G
Note: Holders received $0.35 cash
per share payable 07/20/2005 to
holders of record 07/10/2005
(See each company's listing)

TRILOG ASSOC INC (PA)
Common 1¢ par split (10) for (1) by
issuance of (9) additional shares
10/20/75
Merged into Comshare, Inc. 3/16/77
Each share Common 1¢ par
exchanged for (0.135108) share
Common $1 par
Note: An additional and final
distribution in stock and cash was
made in 1979
(See Comshare, Inc.)

TRILOGY ENERGY CORP (AB)
Merged into Paramount Resources
Ltd. 09/15/2017
Each share Common no par
exchanged for (0.26666666) share
Common no par
Note: Unexchanged certificates will
be cancelled and become without
value 09/15/2021

TRILOGY ENERGY TR (AB)
Reorganized as Trilogy Energy Corp.
02/10/2010
Each Trust Unit no par exchanged for
(1) share Common no par
Note: Unexchanged certificates were
cancelled and became without value
02/10/2015
Trilogy Energy Corp. merged into
Paramount Resources Ltd.
09/15/2017

TRILOGY ENTMT CORP (BC)
Recapitalized as Consolidated Trilogy
Ventures Ltd. 09/29/1993
Each share Common no par
exchanged for (0.2) share Common
no par
Consolidated Trilogy Ventures Ltd.
name changed to Thyssen Mining
Exploration Inc. 12/22/1998 which
name changed to Trilogy Metals Inc.
(BC) 12/08/2000 which
reincorporated in Canada as NWest
Energy Inc. 03/07/2008 which
recapitalized as NWest Energy

Corp. 11/04/2010 which name changed to Ceylon Graphite Corp. 01/03/2017

TRILOGY GAMING CORP (DE)
Name changed to TELnet go 2000, Inc. 01/01/2000
(See TELnet go 2000, Inc.)

TRILOGY LTD (BERMUDA)
Name changed to ELXSI Ltd. (Bermuda) 01/14/1987
ELXSI Ltd. (Bermuda) reincorporated in Delaware as ELXSI Corp. 08/13/1987

TRILOGY METALS INC (BC)
Incorporated 04/03/1986
Each share old Common no par exchanged for (0.2) share new Common no par 09/22/2006
Reincorporated under the laws of Canada as NWest Energy Inc. 03/07/2008
NWest Energy Inc. recapitalized as NWest Energy Corp. 11/04/2010 which name changed to Ceylon Graphite Corp. 01/03/2017

TRILOGY RES CORP (CANADA)
Each share old Common no par exchanged for (0.2) share new Common no par 6/26/91
Merged into Mannville Oil & Gas Ltd. 10/8/93
Each share new Common no par exchanged for (0.6) share Common no par
Mannville Oil & Gas Ltd. merged into Gulf Canada Resources Ltd. 8/14/95

TRILON FINL CORP (CANADA)
Class A no par split (3) for (2) by issuance of (0.5) additional share 5/15/87
Stock Dividend - 50% 7/2/85
Name changed to Brascan Financial Corp. 5/31/2002

TRILOS CORP (PA)
Name changed to Lifetime Products, Inc. 12/17/1990

TRILUCENT TECHNOLOGIES CORP (NV)
Each share old Common $0.001 par exchanged for (0.01) share new Common $0.001 par 12/14/2001
Recapitalized as Anza Innovations Inc. 12/03/2002
Each share new Common $0.001 par exchanged for (0.25) share Common $0.001 par
Note: No holder of (100) shares or more will receive fewer than (100) post-split shares
Holders of (99) shares or fewer will be rounded up to (100) post-split shares
Anza Innovations Inc. name changed to Goafeng Gold Corp. 02/17/2004 which recapitalized as Yosen Group, Inc. 12/31/2012

TRIM-A-LAWN CORP (NV)
Reincorporated 02/20/2004
Each share old Common no par exchanged for (0.33333333) share new Common no par 02/01/1996
State of incorporation changed from (TX) to (NV) 02/20/2004
Recapitalized as Litfiber, Inc. 02/26/2004
Each share new Common no par exchanged for (0.0005) share Common no par
Litfiber, Inc. recapitalized as Grifco International, Inc. 11/19/2004
(See Grifco International, Inc.)

TRIM HOLDING GROUP (NV)
Name changed to HPIL Holding 06/11/2012

TRIM IMAGE INC (NV)
Recapitalized as Karrington Holding Corp. 02/24/2005
Each share Common $0.001 par exchanged for (0.00017364) share Common $0.001 par

Karrington Holding Corp. name changed to World Wide Energy Corp. 03/23/2006 which recapitalized as Czech Republic Resource Corp. 10/30/2007 which name changed to Global Senior Enterprises Inc. 04/26/2013 which recapitalized as World Financial Holding Group 05/01/2018

TRIMAC CORP. (AB)
Name changed 02/01/1997
Common no par reclassified as Conv. Class A Common no par 07/19/1976
Conv. Class A Common no par and Conv. Class B Common no par reclassified as Common no par 01/31/1980
Common no par split (3) for (1) by issuance of (2) additional shares 02/15/1980
Common no par split (3) for (1) by issuance of (2) additional shares 05/22/1981
9.12% 1st Preferred Ser. A $25 par called for redemption on 09/30/1993
Name changed from Trimac Ltd. to Trimac Corp. 02/01/1997
Each share Common no par received distribution of (1) share Kenting Energy Services Inc. Common no par payable 02/11/1997 to holders of record 02/06/1997
Acquired by Trimac Holdings Ltd. 11/27/2000
Each share Common no par exchanged for $9.50 cash

TRIMAC INCOME FD (AB)
Under plan of reorganization each Trust Unit automatically became (1) share Trimac Transportation Ltd. Class A Common no par 01/07/2011
(See Trimac Transportation Ltd.)

TRIMAC PORCUPINE GOLD MINES LTD. (ON)
Charter cancelled for failure to file reports and pay taxes 00/00/1954

TRIMAC TRANSN LTD (AB)
Acquired by Trimac Holdings Ltd. 07/06/2016
Each share Class A Common no par exchanged for $6.25 cash

TRIMAINE HLDGS INC (WA)
Liquidation completed
Each share Common 1¢ par received initial distribution of (0.11598795) share MFC Bancorp Ltd. Common no par payable 4/27/2005 to holders of record 12/29/2004 Ex date - 12/30/2004
Each share Common 1¢ par received second and final distribution of (0.12288809) share Blue Earth Refineries Inc. Ordinary no par payable 5/5/2005 to holders of record 12/29/2004 Ex date - 12/30/2004
Note: Certificates were not required to be surrendered and are without value
(See each company's listing)

TRIMAR HLDGS & EXPLS LTD (ON)
Charter cancelled for failure to pay taxes and file returns 02/20/1980

TRIMARK ENERGY LTD (YT)
Name changed to Halo Resources Ltd. (YT) 02/23/2004
Halo Resources Ltd. (YT) reincorporated in British Columbia 11/16/2004 which merged into Sendero Mining Corp. 07/09/2013

TRIMARK FINL CORP (ON)
Common no par split (2) for (1) by issuance of (1) additional share 07/13/1995
Common no par split (2) for (1) by issuance of (1) additional share payable 07/09/1998 to holders of record 07/08/1998
Merged into AMVESCAP PLC 08/01/2000
Each share Common no par exchanged for approximately (1.05082) AMVESCAP Inc. Non-Vtg. Exchangeable Share and $1.57406 cash
AMVESCAP Inc. name changed to INVESCO Inc. (NS) 05/29/2007
(See INVESCO Inc.)

TRIMARK HLDGS INC (DE)
Merged into Lions Gate Entertainment Corp. 10/13/2000
Each share Common $0.001 par exchanged for (2.018) shares new Common no par and $4.50 cash

TRIMARK OIL & GAS LTD (YT)
Recapitalized as Trimark Energy Ltd. 03/21/2002
Each share Common no par exchanged for (0.14285714) share Common no par
Trimark Energy Ltd. name changed to Halo Resources Ltd. (YT) 02/23/2004 which reincorporated in British Columbia 11/16/2004 which merged into Sendero Mining Corp. 07/09/2013

TRIMARK RES LTD (YT)
Recapitalized as International Trimark Resources Ltd. 12/16/1996
Each share Common no par exchanged for (0.33333333) share Common no par
International Trimark Resources Ltd. recapitalized as Trimark Oil & Gas Ltd. 06/17/1997 which recapitalized as Trimark Energy Ltd. 03/21/2002 which name changed to Halo Resources Ltd. (YT) 02/23/2004 which reincorporated in British Columbia 11/16/2004 which merged into Sendero Mining Corp. 07/09/2013

TRIMAS CORP (DE)
Old Common 1¢ par split (2) for (1) by issuance of (1) additional share 02/28/1990
Old Common 1¢ par split (2) for (1) by issuance of (1) additional share 07/06/1993
Merged into Mascotech, Inc. 01/22/1998
Each share old Common 1¢ par exchanged for $34.50 cash
(Additional Information in Active)

TRIMATRIX, INC. (NY)
Charter cancelled and proclaimed dissolved for failure to pay taxes 12/15/1972

TRIMAX CONSULTING INC (NV)
Name changed to Xinda International Corp. 06/12/2017

TRIMBLE NAV LTD (CA)
Common no par split (3) for (2) by issuance of (0.5) additional share payable 03/04/2004 to holders of record 02/17/2004 Ex date - 03/05/2004
Common no par split (2) for (1) by issuance of (1) additional share payable 02/22/2007 to holders of record 02/08/2007 Ex date - 02/23/2007
Common no par split (2) for (1) by issuance of (1) additional share payable 03/20/2013 to holders of record 03/06/2013 Ex date - 03/21/2013
Reincorporated under the laws of Delaware as Trimble Inc. and Common no par changed to $0.001 par 10/03/2016

TRIMBLE RES CORP (CANADA)
Acquired by MFC Bancorp Ltd. 07/03/2002
Each share Common no par exchanged for $0.22 cash

TRIMBLE RES LTD (AB)
Merged into Grad & Walker Energy Corp. 09/30/1995
Each share Common no par exchanged for (0.02857142) Common no par
(See Grad & Walker Energy Corp.)

TRIMEDIA ENTMT GROUP INC (DE)
SEC revoked common stock registration 05/05/2014

TRIMEL CORP (ON)
Merged into Biovail Corp. International (New) 03/29/1994
Each share Common no par exchanged for (1) share Common no par
Biovail Corp. International (New) name changed to Biovail Corp. 02/18/2000 which merged into Valeant Pharmaceuticals International, Inc. (Canada) 09/28/2010 which reincorporated in British Columbia 08/09/2013 which name changed to Bausch Health Companies Inc. 07/16/2018

TRIMEL PHARMACEUTICALS CORP (ON)
Stock Dividend - 0.00818% payable 07/11/2011 to holders of record 07/11/2011
Name changed to Acerus Pharmaceuticals Corp. 09/11/2015

TRIMERIS INC (DE)
Recapitalized as Synageva BioPharma Corp. 11/03/2011
Each share Common $0.001 par exchanged for (0.2) share Common $0.001 par
Synageva BioPharma Corp. merged into Alexion Pharmaceuticals, Inc. 06/22/2015

TRIMFAST GROUP INC (NV)
Each share old Common $0.001 par exchanged for (0.1) share new Common $0.001 par 12/20/1998
Each share new Common $0.001 par exchanged again for (0.005) share new Common $0.001 par 10/21/2002
Each share new Common $0.001 par exchanged again for (0.11111111) share new Common $0.001 par 09/20/2004
Recapitalized as eDollars Inc. 11/21/2006
Each share new Common $0.001 par exchanged for (0.03333333) share new Common $0.001 par
eDollars Inc. recapitalized as Forex Inc. 06/18/2007 which name changed to Petrolgulf Inc. 03/26/2008 which name changed to Novagant Corp. 01/02/2014

TRIMIL CORP. (NC)
Liquidation completed 05/02/1960
Details not available

TRIMIN CAP CORP (CANADA)
Acquired by 6654134 Canada Inc. 01/01/2007
Each share Common no par exchanged for $3.25 cash

TRIMIN ENTERPRISES INC (CANADA)
Name changed 11/01/1991
Reorganized 07/27/1998
Name changed from Trimin Resources Inc. to Trimin Enterprises Inc. 11/01/1991
Reorganized from (BC) to under the laws of Canada 07/27/1998
Each share Common no par exchanged for (1) share Class A Common no par, (1) share Exchangeable Preferred no par and (1) share Trimin Capital Corp. Common no par
(See Trimin Capital Corp.)
Note: Each share Exchangeable Preferred no par was exchanged for either (0.2) share Class A Common no par or $0.25 cash
Note: Option to receive stock expired 08/14/198
Acquired by Carlyle Group 03/28/2000

Each share Class A Common no par exchanged for $7.35 cash

TRIMOCO PLC (ENGLAND)
Acquired by Hartwell PLC 09/10/1992
Each share Ordinary 10p par exchanged for 20p cash

TRIMOX ENERGY INC (AB)
Merged into Canext Energy Ltd. (New) 06/22/2007
Each share Class A no par exchanged for (1.0825) share Common no par
Each share Class B no par exchanged for (10.8247) shares Common no par
Canext Energy Ltd. (New) merged into TriOil Resources Ltd. 04/21/2010
(See TriOil Resources Ltd.)

TRIMTABS ETF TR (DE)
Trust terminated 11/03/2016
Each share Intl Free-Cash-Flow ETF no par received $21.68152 cash
(Additional Information in Active)

TRINA SOLAR LTD (CAYMAN ISLANDS)
Sponsored ADR's for Ordinary split (2) for (1) by issuance of (1) additional ADR payable 01/19/2010 to holders of record 01/15/2010
Ex date - 01/20/2010
Basis changed from (1:100) to (1:50) on 01/19/2010
Acquired by Fortune Solar Holdings Ltd. 03/13/2017
Each Sponsored ADR for Ordinary exchanged for $11.55 cash

TRINCANA RES LTD (BC)
Name changed to Bevo Agro Inc. 07/11/2000

TRINCOMALI LTD (DE)
Name changed to Global Explorations, Inc. 10/22/1999
Global Explorations, Inc. recapitalized as Malers, Inc. 05/17/2005 which name changed to Dot VN, Inc. 08/07/2006

TRINET CORP RLTY TR INC (MD)
Merged into Starwood Financial Inc. 11/04/1999
Each share 8% Preferred Ser. C 1¢ par exchanged for (1) share 8% Preferred Ser. D 1¢ par
Each share 9.2% Preferred Ser. B 1¢ par exchanged for (1) share 9.2% Preferred Ser. C 1¢ par
Each share 9.375% Preferred Ser. A 1¢ par exchanged for (1) share 9.375% Preferred Ser. B 1¢ par
Each share Common 1¢ par exchanged for (1.15) shares Common 1¢ par
Starwood Financial Inc. merged into iStar Financial Inc. 05/01/2000 which name changed to iStar Inc. 08/19/2015

TRINEXUS HLDGS LTD (ON)
Delisted from Toronto Venture Stock Exchange 06/05/2002

TRINIDAD CORP (CO)
Each (300) shares old Common 1¢ par exchanged for (1) share new Common 1¢ par 03/17/1995
Reorganized under the laws of Texas as Alpha Generation, Inc. 12/31/2001
Each share new Common 1¢ par exchanged for (1/3) share Common no par
Alpha Generation, Inc. name changed to Ouranos Resources Inc. 01/07/2005
(See Ouranos Resources Inc.)

TRINIDAD DRILLING LTD (AB)
Reincorporated 06/29/1999
Place of incorporation changed from (SK) to (AB) 06/29/1999
Recapitalized as Trinidad Energy Services Income Trust 09/17/2002
Each share Common no par exchanged for (1) Trust Unit no par
Trinidad Energy Services Income Trust reorganized back as Trinidad Drilling Ltd. 03/10/2008
(Additional Information in Active)

TRINIDAD ELECTRIC CO. LTD.
Acquired by City of Port of Spain, Trinidad 00/00/1936
Details not available

TRINIDAD ENERGY SVCS INCOME TR (AB)
Reorganized as Trinidad Drilling Ltd. 03/10/2008
Each Trust Unit no par exchanged for (1) share Common no par

TRINIDAD MINES, GAS & OIL LTD.
Bankrupt 00/00/1937
Stockholders' equity unlikely

TRINIDAD PETE DEV LTD (ENGLAND)
Ordinary Reg. 5s par and ADR's for Ordinary Reg. 5s par changed to £1 par respectively 06/28/1962
Liquidation completed
Each share Ordinary Reg. £1 par stamped to indicate initial distribution of 17s 6d cash 07/01/1969
Each ADR for Ordinary Reg. £1 par stamped to indicate initial distribution of $2.05 cash 07/01/1969
Each share Ordinary Reg. £1 par stamped to indicate second distribution of 5s 9d cash 10/06/1970
Each ADR for Ordinary Reg. £1 par stamped to indicate second distribution of $0.63 cash 10/08/1970
Each ADR for Ordinary Reg. £1 par exchanged for third and final distribution of $0.16 cash 03/16/1990

TRINITECH SYS INC (NY)
Name changed to NYFIX, Inc. (NY) 10/25/1999
NYFIX, Inc. (NY) reincorporated in Delaware 12/16/2003
(See NYFIX, Inc. (DE))

TRINITY ACQUISITION CORP (NY)
Ctfs. dated prior to 7/16/90
Reincorporated under the laws of Delaware as Sportspark of America, Inc. 7/16/90
Sportspark of America, Inc. recapitalized as Argos Energy Texas, Inc. 7/16/90 which changed its name to First American Energy, Inc. 8/21/90
(See First American Energy, Inc.)

TRINITY ACQUISITION CORP (NY)
Certificates dated after 09/07/1990
Name changed to T.HQ, Inc. (NY) 08/01/1991
T.HQ, Inc. (NY) reincorporated in Delaware as THQ Inc. 12/31/1997
(See THQ Inc.)

TRINITY AMERS INC (DE)
Merged into Brazil Fast Food Corp. 03/15/1996
Each share Common $0.0001 par exchanged (1) share Common $0.0001 par
(See Brazil Fast Food Corp.)

TRINITY ASSETS TR (MA)
Trust terminated 11/04/1993
Details not available

TRINITY CAP ENTERPRISES CORP (DE)
Name changed to SubMicron Systems Corp. 09/01/1993
(See SubMicron Systems Corp.)

TRINITY CAP OPPORTUNITY CORP (DE)
Name changed to Alliance Entertainment Corp. 11/30/93
(See Alliance Entertainment Corp.)

TRINITY CHIBOUGAMAU MINES LTD (QC)
Name changed to Trinity Mines Inc. 3/26/82
Trinity Mines Inc. recapitalized as Harlake Capital Group, Inc. 1/12/90 which name changed to Madison Grant Resources Inc. (QUE) 10/11/90 which reorganized under the laws of Canada as Banro International Capital Inc. 3/2/95 which name changed to Banro Resources Corp. (Canada) 5/6/96 which reincorporated in Ontario 10/24/96 which recapitalized as Banro Corp. (ONT) 1/22/2001 which reincorporated in Canada 4/2/2004

TRINITY COS INC (UT)
Reincorporated 05/07/2002
State of incorporation changed from (OK) to (UT) 05/07/2002
Common $0.001 par changed to no par 10/01/2002
Name changed to Trinity Learning Corp. 03/31/2003
Trinity Learning Corp. name changed to TWL Corp. (UT) 10/13/2006 which reorganized in Nevada 12/12/2007
(See TWL Corp.)

TRINITY CTL LTD (BC)
Name changed to Sunridge Gold Corp. 5/23/2002

TRINITY ENERGY RES INC (NV)
Under Chapter 11 plan of reorganization each share Common $0.001 par received approximately $0.0028 cash payable 06/10/2009 to holders of record 01/31/2003
Note: Certificates were not required to be surrendered and are without value

TRINITY EQUIP CORP (NJ)
Assets transferred to Pall Corp. 05/01/1961
Each share Common $1 par exchanged for (0.16666666) share Class A $1 par
(See Pall Corp.)

TRINITY FDG CO LLC
Money Market Preferred Ser. A called for redemption at $100,000 on 6/8/2004
Money Market Preferred Ser. B called for redemption at $100,000 on 6/8/2004

TRINITY GAS CORP. (NV)
Ctfs. dated prior to 7/8/93
Name changed to Petro-Sers Corp. 7/8/93
Petro-Sers Corp. name changed to Mid-Atlantic Home Health Network Inc. 12/9/94

TRINITY GAS CORP (NV)
Ctfs. dtd. after 07/09/1993
Plan of reorganization under Chapter 11 Federal Bankruptcy proceedings confirmed 10/27/1998
Each share old Common $0.001 par exchanged for either (1) share new Common $0.001 par and (1) Common Stock Purchase Right expiring 12/27/1999 or a pro rata share of any funds recovered from Civil Action No. 4-97CV-1018 filed in the U.S. District Court in the Northern District of Texas, Fort Worth Division
Note: Option to participate in Civil Action expired 06/01/1999
Note: Unexchanged certificates were cancelled and became without value 11/10/2000
Name changed to Trinity Energy Resources, Inc. 03/17/1999
(See Trinity Energy Resources, Inc.)

TRINITY INDUSTRIES, INC. (TX)
Common $1 par split (2) for (1) by issuance of (1) additional share 10/31/79
Common $1 par split (2) for (1) by issuance of (1) additional share 10/30/80
Stock Dividends - 60% 7/15/71; 100% 4/30/76
Reincorporated under the laws of Delaware 3/31/87

TRINITY INTL HLDGS PLC (UNITED KINGDOM)
Name changed to Trinity Public Ltd., Co. 05/05/1998
Trinity Public Ltd., Co, name changed to Trinity Mirror PLC 09/07/1999 which name changed to Reach PLC 05/23/2018

TRINITY LEARNING CORP (UT)
Each share old Common no par exchanged for (1) share new Common no par to reflect a (1) for (250) reverse split followed by a (250) for (1) forward split 06/16/2003
Name changed to TWL Corp. (UT) 10/13/2006
TWL Corp. (UT) reorganized in Nevada 12/12/2007
(See TWL Corp.)

TRINITY LIQUID ASSETS TR (MA)
Name changed to Trinity Assets Trust 11/16/1990
(See Trinity Assets Trust)

TRINITY LTD (HONG KONG)
ADR agreement terminated 01/24/2018
No ADR's remain outstanding

TRINITY MINES INC (QC)
Recapitalized as Harlake Capital Group, Inc. 1/12/90
Each share Capital Stock $1 par exchanged for (0.05) share Common $1 par
Harlake Capital Group, Inc. name changed to Madison Grant Resources Inc. (QUE) 10/11/90 which reorganized in Canada as Banro International Capital Inc. 3/2/95 which name changed to Banro Resources Corp. (Canada) 5/6/96 which reincorporated in Ontario 10/24/96 which recapitalized as Banro Corp. (ONT) 1/22/2001 which reincorporated in Canada 4/2/2004

TRINITY MIRROR PLC (UNITED KINGDOM)
Name changed to Reach PLC 05/23/2018

TRINITY OIL & GAS INC (CO)
Recapitalized as Questa Oil & Gas Co. 3/31/86
Each (125) shares Common $0.001 par exchanged for (1) share Common $0.001 par
Questa Oil & Gas Co. merged into Unit Corp. 3/21/2000

TRINITY OIL CORP (TX)
Merged into Amarco Resources Corp. (CO) 07/16/1979
Each share Common 1¢ par exchanged for (7) shares Common 1¢ par
Amarco Resources Corp. (CO) reorganized in Delaware 05/20/1980 which name changed to Bestway Rental, Inc. 03/28/1988 which reorganized as Bestway Inc. 06/07/1995
(See Bestway Inc.)

TRINITY PARTNERS ACQUISITION CO INC (DE)
Merged into FreeSeas Inc. 12/15/2005
Each share Class A Common $0.0001 par exchanged for (1) share Common $0.001 par
Each share Class B Common $0.0001 par exchanged for (1) share Common $0.001 par

TRINITY PETROLEUM CO.
Dissolved in 1951

TRINITY PLACE FUND, INC. (NY)
Charter cancelled and proclaimed dissolved for failure to pay taxes 6/27/79

TRINITY PLUMAS CAP CORP (BC)
Name changed to TrueStar Petroleum Corp. 5/16/2005

TRINITY PORTLAND CEMENT CO.
Merged into General Portland Cement Co. on a (29.3171) for (1) basis in 1947
General Portland Cement Co. name changed to General Portland Inc. 5/31/72
(See General Portland Inc.)

TRINITY PUB LTD CO (UNITED KINGDOM)
Name changed to Trinity Mirror PLC 09/07/1999
Trinity Mirror PLC name changed to Reach PLC 05/23/2018

TRINITY RESOURCES INC. (UT)
Name changed to Em Net Inc. 11/22/1987
Em Net Inc. recapitalized as American Ostrich Corp. (UT) 10/04/1995 which reincorporated in Delaware as CallNOW.com, Inc. 04/06/1999
(See CallNOW.com, Inc.)

TRINITY RES LTD (AB)
Merged into Enscor Inc. 7/18/91
Each share Capital Stock no par exchanged for (0.266) share Common no par
Enscor Inc. name changed to Rose Corp. 6/1/98
(See Rose Corp.)

TRINITY SIX INC (DE)
Name changed to USCI Inc. 05/15/1995
(See USCI Inc.)

TRINITY STL INC (TX)
Name changed to Trinity Industries, Inc. (Tex.) 6/15/66
Trinity Industries, Inc. (Tex.) reincorporated in Delaware 3/31/87

TRINITY TOWNE INVTS INC (CO)
Name changed to Dental Health of America, Inc. 6/24/89
Dental Health of America, Inc. (CO) reorganized in Delaware 9/18/89
(See Dental Health of America, Inc.)

TRINITY TRADE CORP (TX)
Charter forfeited for failure to pay taxes 2/21/83

TRINITY UNVL INS CO (TX)
Each share Capital Stock $100 par exchanged for (10) shares Capital Stock $10 par 00/00/1933
Capital Stock $10 par changed to $5 par and (1) additional share issued 03/10/1958
Stock Dividends - 25% 02/23/1953; 20% 02/25/1954; 33-1/3% 02/25/1955; 25% 02/24/1956; 10% 02/09/1962
100% acquired by Teledyne, Inc. through exchange offer which expired 07/11/1969
Public interest eliminated

TRINITY VY ENERGY CORP (BC)
Recapitalized as Smooth Rock Ventures Corp. 11/15/2017
Each share Common no par exchanged for (0.25) share Common no par

TRINITY VENTURES LTD (BC)
Acquired by Banks Ventures Ltd. 09/30/2002
Each share Common no par exchanged for (0.5) share Common no par
Banks Ventures Ltd. name changed to Banks Energy Inc. 07/26/2004 which merged into Arapahoe Energy Corp. (New) 10/20/2005 which name changed to Canadian Phoenix Resources Corp. 01/07/2008 which recapitalized as Knol Resources Corp. 03/11/2013

TRINITYCARE SR LIVING INC (NV)
Name changed to SeaBridge Freight Corp. 10/06/2010
SeaBridge Freight Corp. name changed to University General Health System, Inc. 03/29/2011
(See University General Health System, Inc.)

TRINITY3 CORP (DE)
SEC revoked common stock registration 12/30/2011

TRINON INC (NV)
Each share new Common $0.001 par exchanged for (0.25) share new Common $0.001 par 05/04/1998
Each share new Common $0.001 par exchanged again for (0.1) share new Common $0.001 par 06/01/1998
Name changed to Lexico Resources International Corp. 10/21/1998
(See Lexico Resources International Corp.)

TRINORTH CAP INC (CANADA)
Each share Common no par received distribution of (1) share Centiva Capital Inc. Common no par payable 10/22/2007 to holders of record 10/15/2007 Ex date - 10/11/2007
Recapitalized as Difference Capital Funding Inc. 06/01/2012
Each share Common no par exchanged for (0.1) share Common no par
Difference Capital Funding Inc. recapitalized as Difference Capital Financial Inc. 06/17/2013

TRINOVA CORP (OH)
Common $5 par split (3) for (2) by issuance of (0.5) additional share 12/1/86
$4.75 Conv. Preferred Ser. A no par called for redemption 3/2/87
Common $5 par split (2) for (1) by issuance of (1) additional share 9/15/87
Name changed to Aeroquip-Vickers, Inc. 4/17/97
(See Aeroquip-Vickers, Inc.)

TRINOVA RES EXPLS LTD (ON)
Name changed 09/05/1978
Name changed from Trinova Cobalt Silver Mines Ltd. to Trinova Resource Explorations Ltd. 09/05/1978
Merged into Flying Cross Resources Ltd. 12/04/1985
Each share Capital Stock no par exchanged for (0.2) share Common no par
Flying Cross Resources Ltd. merged into International Larder Minerals Inc. 05/01/1986 which merged into Explorers Alliance Corp. 10/13/2000
(See Explorers Alliance Corp.)

TRINSIC INC (DE)
Each share old Common 1¢ par exchanged for (0.1) share new Common 1¢ par 09/23/2005
Chapter 11 bankruptcy proceedings converted to Chapter 7 on 04/24/2007
Stockholders' equity unlikely

TRINTECH GROUP PLC (IRELAND)
Old Sponsored ADR's for Ordinary $0.0027 par split (2) for (1) by issuance of (1) additional ADR payable 03/22/2000 to holders of record 03/20/2000
Each old Sponsored ADR for Ordinary $0.0027 par exchanged for (0.25) new Sponsored ADR for Ordinary $0.0027 par 05/24/2002
ADR basis changed from (1:0.5) to (1:2) 05/24/2002
Acquired by Cerasus II Ltd. 12/31/2010
Each new Sponsored ADR for Ordinary $0.0027 par exchanged for $6.55 cash

TRINWALL BD FD INC (MD)
Merged into Putnam Income Fund Inc. 02/08/1980
Each share Common $1 par exchanged for (1.274216) shares Common $1 par
Putnam Income Fund Inc. name changed to Putnam Income Fund (New) 11/08/1982

TRINZIC CORP (DE)
Merged into PLATINUM Technology, Inc. 08/25/1995
Each share Common 1¢ par exchanged for (0.33333333) share Common $0.001 par
PLATINUM Technology, Inc. name changed to Platinum Technology International Inc. 01/04/1999 which merged into Computer Associates International, Inc. 06/29/1999 which name changed to CA, Inc. 02/01/2006

TRIO ARCHEAN DEV INC (BC)
Recapitalized as International Movie Group Inc. (BC) 07/10/1987
Each share Class B Special no par exchanged for (1) share Common no par
International Movie Group Inc. (BC) reincorporated in Canada 12/31/1990 which reincorporated in Delaware 05/16/1991 which merged into Lions Gate Entertainment Corp. 06/30/1998

TRIO INDS GROUP INC (FL)
Proclaimed dissolved for failure to file reports and pay fees 09/14/2007

TRIO INDS INC (CO)
Completely liquidated 02/16/1982
Each share Common $0.0025 par exchanged for first and final distribution of (0.2) share Pease (Willard) Oil & Gas Co. Common 50¢ par
Pease (Willard) Oil & Gas Co. recapitalized as Pease Oil & Gas Co. 07/05/1994 which name changed to Republic Resources, Inc. 07/12/2001
(See Republic Resources, Inc.)

TRIO KENWOOD CORP (JAPAN)
ADR agreement terminated 09/07/1982
Each ADR for Common JPY 50 par exchanged for (10) shares Common JPY 50 par

TRIO LABS INC (NY)
Dissolved by proclamation 1/14/82

TRIO MERGER CORP (DE)
Issue Information - 6,000,000 UNITS consisting of (1) share COM and (1) WT offered at $10 per Unit on 06/21/2011
Units separated 03/26/2012
Name changed to SAExploration Holdings, Inc. 06/25/2013

TRIO MINING EXPLORATION LTD. (ON)
Charter cancelled for failure to pay taxes and file returns in 1973

TRIO RES LTD (BC)
Acquired by Trio-Archean Developments Inc. 10/00/1980
Each share Common no par exchanged for (0.75) share Class B Special no par
Trio-Archean Developments Inc. recapitalized as International Movie Group Inc. (BC) 07/10/1987 which reincorporated in Canada 12/31/1990 which reincorporated in Delaware 05/16/1991 which merged into Lions Gate Entertainment Corp. 06/30/1998

TRIO TECH INC (DE)
Name changed to La Mar Technology, Inc. 05/11/1971
(See La Mar Technology, Inc.)

TRIO URANIUM MINES LTD. (ON)
Name changed to Trio Mining Exploration Ltd. 11/28/56
Trio Mining Exploration Ltd. charter cancelled in 1973

TRIOIL LTD NEW (AB)
Merged into Yangarra Resources Ltd. 11/9/2005
Each share Common no par exchanged for (1) share Common no par

TRIOIL LTD OLD (AB)
Reorganized as TriOil Ltd. (New) 8/13/2004
Each share Common no par exchanged for (1/3) share Common no par
TriOil Ltd. (New) merged into Yangarra Resources Ltd. 11/9/2005

TRIOIL RES LTD (AB)
Acquired by ORLEN Upstream sp. z o.o. 11/15/2013
Each share Class A Common no par exchanged for $2.85 cash
Note: Unexchanged certificates will be cancelled and become without value 11/14/2018

TRION CO.
Merged into Riegel Textile Corp. on a (2) for (1) basis in 1946

TRION INC (PA)
Common $2 par changed to 50¢ par in 1951
Common 50¢ par split (5) for (4) by issuance of (0.25) additional share 9/30/77
Common 50¢ par split (5) for (4) by issuance of (0.25) additional share 9/29/78
Common 50¢ par split (2) for (1) by issuance of (1) additional share 6/22/81
Common 50¢ par split (2) for (1) by issuance of (1) additional share 6/18/82
Common 50¢ par split (3) for (2) by issuance of (0.5) additional share 6/17/83
5% Preferred $5 par called for redemption 2/2/87
Common 50¢ par split (5) for (4) by issuance of (0.25) additional share 5/29/87
Common 50¢ par split (3) for (2) by issuance of (0.5) additional share 6/1/89
Stock Dividends - 100% 8/1/68; 10% 11/1/76
Merged into TI Acquisition Corp. 11/12/99
Each share Common 50¢ par exchanged for $5.50 cash

TRION TECHNOLOGY AG (GERMANY)
ADR agreement terminated 00/00/2002
Details not available

TRIONICS ENGR CORP (MD)
Adjudicated bankrupt 12/26/1974
Stockholders' equity unlikely

TRIONICS INDS LTD (BC)
Recapitalized 07/17/1994
Recapitalized from Trionics Technology Ltd. to Trionics Industries Ltd. 08/17/1994
Each share Common no par exchanged for (0.5) share Common no par
Name changed to Comptec Industries Ltd. 09/23/1996
Comptec Industries Ltd. recapitalized as Integrated Communications Industries Inc. 05/09/2000
(See Integrated Communications Industries Inc.)

TRIOPTIMUM CAP CORP (BC)
Name changed to Contec Innovations Inc. 7/29/2002

FINANCIAL INFORMATION, INC.   TRI-TRI

TRIOX LTD (HONG KONG)
Recapitalized as eQube Gaming Ltd. 11/04/2014
Each share Ordinary exchanged for (0.33333333) share Ordinary

TRIP TECH INC (TX)
Common $0.001 par split (1.48097397) for (1) by issuance of (0.48097397) additional share payable 06/13/2008 to holders of record 06/12/2008 Ex date - 06/16/2008
Common $0.001 par split (2) for (1) by issuance of (1) additional share payable 08/08/2008 to holders of record 08/08/2008 Ex date - 08/11/2008
Name changed to Winland Online Shipping Holdings Corp. 10/17/2008
Winland Online Shipping Holdings Corp. name changed to Winland Ocean Shipping Corp. 03/22/2011

TRIPAC ENGINEERING CORP. (MD)
Charter revoked for failure to file reports and pay fees 11/27/63

TRIPATH IMAGING INC (DE)
Merged into Becton, Dickinson & Co. 12/20/2006
Each share Common 1¢ par exchanged for $9.25 cash

TRIPATH TECHNOLOGY INC (DE)
Issue Information - 5,000,000 shares COM offered at $10 per share on 07/31/2000
Plan of reorganization under Chapter 11 Federal Bankruptcy Code effective 04/22/2008
No stockholders' equity

TRIPLE A & GOVT SER-1995 (MD)
Completely liquidated 6/29/95
Each share Common $0.001 par exchanged for first and final distribution of $10 cash

TRIPLE A & GOVT SER-1997 (MD)
Each share old Common $0.001 par exchanged for (0.9824) share new Common $0.001 par 12/26/95
Each share new Common $0.001 par exchanged again for (0.99104172) share new Common $0.001 par 12/27/96
Completely liquidated 6/29/97
Each share new Common $0.001 par exchanged for first and final distribution of $10 cash

TRIPLE A MED INC (NV)
Reorganized under the laws of Cayman Islands as Phoenix Medical Software, Inc. 01/28/2011
Each share Common $0.001 par exchanged for (2/3) share Common $0.001 par

TRIPLE BAY INDS INC (FL)
Name changed to Syzygy Entertainment, Ltd. 2/9/2007

TRIPLE CHECK INC (CA)
Stock Dividends - 10% 10/17/75; 10% 10/15/46; 12-1/2% 10/17/77; 10% 10/16/78; 10% 10/15/79; 10% 6/15/81
In process of liquidation
Each share Common $1 par received initial distribution of $0.25 cash 7/23/84
Each share Common $1 par received second distribution of $0.80 cash 6/10/85
Each share Common $1 par received third distribution of $1 cash 6/11/86
Each share Common $1 par received fourth distribution of $0.85 cash 7/13/87
Each share Common $1 par received fifth distribution of $0.05 cash 10/2/89
Note: Details on subsequent distribution(s), if any, are not available

TRIPLE CHIP SYS INC (DE)
Reincorporated under the laws of Tennessee as Miller Petroleum Inc. 01/13/1997
Miller Petroleum Inc. name changed to Miller Energy Resources, Inc. 04/12/2011
(See Miller Energy Resources, Inc.)

TRIPLE CROWN ELECTRS INC (ON)
Merged into CableServ Inc. 8/30/2000
Each share Common no par exchanged for (0.029598) share Common no par
(See CableServ Inc.)

TRIPLE CROWN MEDIA INC (DE)
Plan of reorganization under Chapter 11 Federal Bankruptcy proceedings effective 12/08/2009
No stockholders' equity

TRIPLE CROWN PETE LTD (AB)
Name changed to First Mountain Exploration Ltd. 12/22/2011
First Mountain Exploration Ltd. recapitalized as First Mountain Exploration Inc. 09/02/2014 which recapitalized as Point Loma Resources Ltd. 07/05/2016

TRIPLE CROWN RES INC (AB)
Recapitalized as Rangeland Resources Ltd. 10/5/89
Each share Common no par exchanged for (0.2) share Common no par
(See Rangeland Resources Ltd.)

TRIPLE CROWN RES LTD (BC)
Merged into Aurex Resources Inc. 7/11/85
Each share Common no par exchanged for (0.2) share Common no par
Aurex Resources Inc. merged into Galveston Resources Ltd. 7/29/86 which merged into Corona Corp. 7/1/88 which recapitalized as International Corona Corp. 6/11/91
(See International Corona Corp.)

TRIPLE D CT INC (WY)
Name changed to Video Stream International Inc. 12/19/97
Video Stream International Inc. name changed to TeraGlobal Communications Corp. (WY) 9/29/98 which reincorporated in Delaware 8/26/99
(See TeraGlobal Communications Corp. (DE))

TRIPLE DRAGON RESOURCES INC (BRITISH VIRGIN ISLANDS)
Name changed to Pasinex Resources Ltd. 03/30/2012

TRIPLE 8 ENERGY CORP (AB)
Reincorporated 02/24/1994
Place of incorporation changed from (BC) to (AB) 02/24/1994
Name changed to Oilexco Inc. 03/01/1994
Oilexco Inc. recapitalized as ScotOil Petroleum Ltd. (BC) 06/09/2011 which reincorporated in British Columbia as 0915988 B.C. Ltd. 07/27/2011
(See 0915988 B.C. Ltd.)

TRIPLE 8 ENERGY LTD (AB)
Common no par split (3) for (1) by issuance of (2) additional shares payable 02/25/2010 to holders of record 02/23/2010
Recapitalized as Hyperion Exploration Corp. 11/24/2010
Each share Common no par exchanged for (0.05) share Common no par
(See Hyperion Exploration Corp.)

TRIPLE 8 VENTURES LTD (AB)
Recapitalized as Triple 8 Energy Ltd. 10/30/2010
Each share Common no par exchanged for (0.125) share Common no par
Triple 8 Energy Ltd. recapitalized as Hyperion Exploration Corp. 11/24/2010
(See Hyperion Exploration Corp.)

TRIPLE FORCE INDS INC (BC)
Recapitalized as Petrock Ventures Inc. 01/08/1997
Each share Common no par exchanged for (0.25) share Common no par
Petrock Ventures Inc. recapitalized as Croydon Mercantile Corp. 12/31/2002 which name changed to World Mahjong Ltd. 12/01/2015

TRIPLE G SYS GROUP INC (ON)
Each share old Common no par exchanged for (0.2) share new Common no par 06/13/2001
Acquired by GE Canada Enterprises Co. 08/22/2003
Each share new Common no par exchanged for $3.30 cash

TRIPLE LAKE PORCUPINE GOLD MINES LTD. (ON)
Merged into Trimac Porcupine Gold Mines Ltd. 00/00/1945
Each share Capital Stock exchanged for (0.2) share Capital Stock
(See Trimac Porcupine Gold Mines Ltd.)

TRIPLE M MNG CORP (BC)
Name changed to S.E. Storage Express (International) Ltd. 06/30/1988
(See S.E. Storage Express (International) Ltd.)

TRIPLE O OIL CO. (OK)
Charter cancelled for failure to pay taxes 11/25/1925

TRIPLE O SEVEN CORP (UT)
Reincorporated under the laws of Nevada as Supervision Entertainment Inc. 04/01/2003
Supervision Entertainment Inc. name changed to BioNeutra International, Ltd. 11/04/2013

TRIPLE RIDGE MINES LTD. (ON)
Charter cancelled for failure to file reports and pay taxes 00/00/1959

TRIPLE S PLASTICS INC (MI)
Merged into Eimo Oyj 08/15/2001
Each share Common no par exchanged for (0.45) Sponsored ADR for Ser. A
Eimo Oyj recapitalized as Eimo Corp. 09/11/2002
(See Eimo Corp.)

TRIPLE STAR RESOURCE CORP (BC)
Recapitalized as Northern Plains Oil Corp. (BC) 08/06/1991
Each share Common no par exchanged for (0.33333333) share Common no par
Northern Plains Oil Corp. (BC) reorganized in Alberta as Gopher Oil & Gas Ltd. 01/22/1997 which recapitalized as Ventus Energy Ltd. 12/31/1998 which name changed to Navigo Energy Inc. 05/24/2002
(See Navigo Energy Inc.)

TRIPLE THREAT ENTERPRISES INC (NJ)
Name changed to Gaming Devices Funding Inc. 09/04/1992
Gaming Devices Funding Inc. name changed to Capital Gaming International Inc. 03/19/1993
(See Capital Gaming International Inc.)

TRIPLECROWN ACQUISITION CORP (DE)
Name changed to Cullen Agricultural Holding Corp. 10/22/2009
Cullen Agricultural Holding Corp. merged into Long Island Iced Tea Corp. 06/01/2015 which name changed to Long Blockchain Corp. 01/05/2018

TRIPLEPLAY SPORTS GROUP INC (ON)
Recapitalized as Bonanza Blue Corp. 08/16/2000
Each share Common no par exchanged for (0.1) share Common no par
Bonanza Blue Corp. recapitalized as CannaRoyalty Corp. 12/08/2016

TRIPLEX CORP. OF AMERICA (WA)
Acquired by Gera Corp. 00/00/1957
Each share Common $1 par exchanged for $3 principal amount of 6% Debentures Series A and $2.50 cash

TRIPOD INTL INC (NV)
Reorganized as Midex Gold Corp. (NV) 04/27/2009
Each share Common $0.001 par exchanged for (5) shares Common $0.001 par
Midex Gold Corp. (NV) reincorporated in Wyoming 09/15/2010 which name changed to Promithian Global Ventures, Inc. 05/14/2013

TRIPOINT MINES LTD. (ON)
Charter cancelled for failure to file reports and pay taxes 00/00/1969

TRIPOLI INC (PA)
Adjudicated bankrupt 1/26/73
No stockholders' equity

TRIPOS INC (UT)
Assets transferred 11/08/2007
Common 1¢ par split (2) for (1) by issuance of (1) additional share payable 02/02/2001 to holders of record 01/12/2001 Ex date - 02/05/2001
Liquidation completed
Each share Common 1¢ par exchanged for initial distribution of $0.47 cash 11/08/2007
Assets transferred from Tripos, Inc. to Tripos, Inc. Liquidating Trust 11/08/2007
Each Trust Beneficiary received second distribution of $0.15 cash payable 05/23/2008 to holders of record 11/08/2007
Each Trust Beneficiary received third and final distribution of $0.24894223 cash payable 07/16/2010 to holders of record 11/08/2007

TRIPPENSEE MFG. & SALES CORP. (DE)
Dissolved 10/23/1937
Details not available

TRIQUANTA INVTS LTD (AB)
Dissolved 01/05/2000
Details not available

TRIQUEST ENERGY CORP (AB)
Each share old Common no par exchanged for (0.25) share new Common no par 11/14/2002
Merged into Bonavista Energy Trust 01/29/2004
Each share new Common no par exchanged for $3.10 cash

TRIQUINT SEMICONDUCTOR INC (DE)
Reincorporated 02/12/1997
State of incorporation changed from (CA) to (DE) and Common no par changed to $0.001 par 02/12/1997
Common $0.001 par split (3) for (2) by issuance of (0.5) additional share payable 07/08/1999 to holders of record 06/22/1999
Common $0.001 par split (2) for (1) by issuance of (1) additional share payable 02/22/2000 to holders of record 02/01/2000
Common $0.001 par split (2) for (1) by issuance of (1) additional share payable 07/11/2000 to holders of record 06/19/2000
Merged into Qorvo, Inc. 01/02/2015
Each share Common $0.001 par exchanged for (0.4187) share Common $0.0001 par

TRI-TRI

TRIRAK INDS CORP (SK)
Cease trade order effective 03/25/1992

TRISM INC (DE)
Each share old Common 1¢ par exchanged for (0.01753728) share new Common 1¢ par 02/15/2000
Plan of reorganization under Chapter 11 Federal Bankruptcy Code effective 09/15/2003
No stockholders' equity

TRIST HLDGS INC (DE)
Name changed to AtheroNova, Inc. 05/25/2010

TRISTAR AEROSPACE CO (DE)
Merged into Honeywell International Inc. 12/10/1999
Each share Common 1¢ par exchanged for $9.50 cash

TRISTAR CORP (NY)
Plan of reorganization under Chapter 11 Federal Bankruptcy proceedings confirmed 11/05/2002
No stockholders' equity

TRISTAR OIL & GAS LTD NEW (AB)
Merged into PetroBakken Energy Ltd. (Old) 10/05/2009
Each share Common no par exchanged for (0.3617) share Class A Common no par and $4.7503 cash
PetroBakken Energy Ltd. (Old) reorganized as PetroBakken Energy Ltd. (New) 01/07/2013 which name changed to Lightstream Resources Ltd. 05/28/2013

TRISTAR OIL & GAS LTD OLD (AB)
Merged into TriStar Oil & Gas Ltd. (New) 08/16/2007
Each share Common no par exchanged for (0.4762) share Common no par
Note: Holders of (209) shares or fewer will receive approximately $3.59 cash per share
TriStar Oil & Gas Ltd. (New) merged into PetroBakken Energy Ltd. (Old) 10/05/2009 which reorganized as PetroBakken Energy Ltd. (New) 01/07/2013 which name changed to Lightstream Resources Ltd. 05/28/2013

TRISTATE BANCORP (OH)
Common $1 par split (2) for (1) by issuance of (1) additional share 03/15/1993
Merged into Fifth Third Bancorp 12/22/1993
Each share Common $1 par exchanged for (0.392) share Common no par

TRISTONE CMNTY BK (WINSTON-SALEM, NC)
Acquired by First Community Bancshares, Inc. (NV) 07/31/2009
Each share Common exchanged for (0.5262) share Common $1 par
First Community Bancshares, Inc. (NV) reincorporated in Virginia 10/09/2018

TRITEAL CORP (DE)
Plan of Reorganization under Chapter 11 Federal Bankruptcy Code effective 12/22/1999
Holders of record 10/15/2003 who exchanged their certificates prior to 12/15/2003 received $0.489406 cash per share
Note: Unexchanged certificates were cancelled and are without value

TRITECH INVTS INC (AB)
Name changed to InfoInterActive Inc. 01/31/1996
(See InfoInterActive Inc.)

TRITECH PRECISION INC (ON)
Acquired by Carlyle Group 03/28/2000
Each share Common no par exchanged for $33 cash

TRITEL INC (DE)
Merged into TeleCorp PCS, Inc. (New) 11/13/2000
Each share Class A Common 1¢ par exchanged for (0.76) share Class A Common 1¢ par
Each share Class B Common 1¢ par exchanged for (0.76) share Class A Common 1¢ par
TeleCorp PCS, Inc. (New) merged into AT&T Wireless Services, Inc. 02/15/2002
(See AT&T Wireless Services, Inc.)

TRITEX CORP (DE)
Acquired by Harbour Group 04/20/2007
Each share Preferred exchanged for $1.84619188 cash
Each share Class A exchanged for $10.448376 cash
Note: Each share Class A received an initial additional distribution of approximately $1.682 cash from escrow payable 02/25/2009 to holders of record 04/20/2007
Each share Class A received a second and final distribution of $1.1866512 cash from escrow payable 04/29/2013 to holders of record 04/20/2007

TRITEX PETE CORP (ON)
Recapitalized as Peregrine Instruments & Monitoring Inc. 02/05/1988
Each share Common no par exchanged for (0.125) share Common no par
Peregrine Instruments & Monitoring Inc. name changed to Justice Electronic Monitoring Systems Inc. 04/05/1990 which recapitalized as Jemtec Inc. 04/28/1994

TRITON ACQUISITION CORP. (NV)
Name changed 12/28/1998
Name changed from Triton Asset Management, Inc. to Bio-Chem Technology, Inc. 05/07/1991 which name changed back to Triton Asset Management, Inc. (FL) 09/24/1997
Triton Asset Management, Inc. (FL) reincorporated in Nevada as Triton Acquisition Corp. 12/28/1998
Name changed to Light Management Group, Inc. 05/20/1999

TRITON CANADA RES LTD (AB)
$1.20 Conv. Preferred Ser. B no par called for redemption 10/31/1993
10% Senior Preferred Ser. 1 no par called for redemption 10/31/1993
Name changed to Transwest Energy Inc. 11/16/1993
Transwest Energy Inc. merged into Jordan Petroleum Ltd. 02/28/1997
(See Jordan Petroleum Ltd.)

TRITON CAP CORP (AB)
Name changed to March Resources Corp. 09/30/2004
Each share Common no par exchanged for (1) share Common no par
March Resources Corp. recapitalized as Ranger Energy Ltd. (AB) 08/21/2009 which recapitalized in Ontario as North Sea Energy Inc. 10/21/2011

TRITON CORP (OK)
Out of business 00/00/1974
No stockholders' equity

TRITON DISTR SYS INC (CO)
Each share Common no par exchanged for (0.00666666) share old Common $0.001 par 09/16/2009
Each share old Common $0.001 par exchanged for (0.00990099) share new Common $0.001 par 06/24/2010
Each share new Common $0.001 par exchanged again for (0.01) share new Common $0.001 par 11/18/2010
Name changed to Green Cures & Botanical Distribution Inc. 05/27/2014

TRITON ENERGY CORP (AB)
Recapitalized as Waldron Energy Corp. 06/14/2010
Each share Common no par exchanged for (0.1) share Common no par

TRITON ENERGY CORP (DE)
Reincorporated 05/12/1995
Conv. Exchangeable Depositary Preferred no par called for redemption 11/25/1985
$2 Conv. Exchangeable Preferred no par called for redemption 08/22/1991
State of incorporation changed from (TX) to (DE) 05/12/1995
Preferred Stock Purchase Rights declared for Common stockholders of record 06/26/1990 were redeemed at $0.01 per right 06/16/1995 for holders of record 06/02/1995
Merged into Triton Energy Ltd. 03/25/1996
Each share 5% Conv. Preferred no par exchanged for (1) share 5% Conv. Preference 1¢ par
Each share Common $1 par exchanged for (1) share Ordinary 1¢ par
(See Triton Energy Ltd.)

TRITON ENERGY LTD (CAYMAN ISLANDS)
5% Conv. Preference 1¢ par called for redemption at $34.41 plus $0.15 accrued dividends on 10/31/2000
Acquired by Amerada Hess Corp. 08/20/2001
Each share Ordinary 1¢ par exchanged for $45 cash
8% Conv. Preferred called for redemption at $70 on 12/03/2001

TRITON EXPLS LTD (ON)
Charter cancelled for failure to pay taxes and file returns 02/06/1979

TRITON GROUP LTD (DE)
Name changed 01/30/1981
Name changed from Triton Group (MA) to Triton Group Ltd. (DE) 01/30/1981
Common $1 par changed to 10¢ par 12/19/1983
Each share Common 10¢ par exchanged for (0.1) share Common $1 par 10/15/1987
$1.20 Conv. Preferred Ser. C $1 par called for redemption 04/22/1988
Conv. Preferred Ser. A $1 par called for redemption 05/31/1989
Merged into Intermark, Inc. 08/30/1990
Each share Common $1 par exchanged for (1.4) shares Common $1 par
Intermark, Inc. reorganized as Triton Group Ltd. (New) 06/25/1993 which name changed to Alarmguard Holdings, Inc. 04/16/1997
(See Alarmguard Holding, Inc.)

TRITON GROUP LTD NEW (DE)
Stock Purchase Rights redeemed at $0.001 per right 00/00/1995
Recapitalized as Alarmguard Holdings, Inc. 04/16/1997
Each share Common $0.0001 par exchanged for (0.1) share Common $0.0001 par
(See Alarmguard Holding, Inc.)

TRITON INDS INC (QC)
Delisted from Montreal Stock Exchange 12/31/1993

TRITON INSURANCE CO. (OK)
Reorganized as Triton Corp. 03/01/1968
Each share Class A Common $1 par exchanged for (1) share Capital Stock $1 par
(See Triton Corp.)

TRITON MINES & METALS CORP. LTD. (ON)
Merged into Continental Consolidated Mines & Oils Co. Ltd. on a (0.2) for (1) basis 10/4/57
(See Continental Consolidated Mines & Oils Co. Ltd.)

TRITON MNG CORP (ON)
Merged into Black Hawk Mining Inc.-Compagnie Miniere Black Hawk Inc. 05/31/1998
Each share Common no par exchanged for (1) share Common no par
Black Hawk Mining Inc.-Compagnie Miniere Black Hawk Inc. merged into Glencairn Gold Corp. 10/20/2003 which recapitalized as Central Sun Mining Inc. 12/05/2007 which was acquired by B2Gold Corp. 03/31/2009

TRITON NETWORK SYS INC (DE)
Issue Information - 5,500,000 shares COM offered at $15 per share on 07/12/2000
Liquidation completed
Each share Common $0.001 par received initial distribution of $0.77 cash payable 03/09/2004 to holders of record 01/31/2002 Ex date - 03/10/2004
Each share Common $0.001 par received second and final distribution of $0.0272 cash payable 04/06/2012 to holders of record 03/30/2012
Note: Certificates were not required to be surrendered and are without value

TRITON OIL & GAS CORP (TX)
$1.96 Conv. Preferred no par called for redemption 7/25/80
Name changed to Triton Energy Corp. 12/1/81
Triton Energy Corp. (TX) reincorporated in Delaware 5/12/95

TRITON PCS HLDGS INC (DE)
Issue Information - 10,000,000 shares CL A offered at $18 per share on 10/27/1999
Name changed to SunCom Wireless Holdings, Inc. 05/04/2005
(See SunCom Wireless Holdings, Inc.)

TRITON RES INC (BC)
Struck off register and declared dissolved for failure to file returns 09/20/1985

TRITON RES INC (NV)
Common $0.001 par split (13) for (1) by issuance of (12) additional shares payable 09/30/2005 to holders of record 09/30/2005
Name changed to Skyflyer, Inc. 10/17/2006
Skyflyer, Inc. name changed to Blackstone Lake Minerals Inc. 01/23/2008 which name changed to Caleco Pharma Corp. 08/31/2009
(See Caleco Pharma Corp.)

TRITON TECHNOLOGIES INC (NV)
Each share old Common $0.00001 par exchanged for (0.005) share new Common $0.00001 par 12/23/2005
Reincorporated under the laws of Nevada as Solar Night Industries, Inc. 03/10/2006
Solar Night Industries, Inc. name changed to Premium Beverage Group, Inc. 10/23/2013

TRITON URANIUM MINES LTD. (ON)
Name changed to Triton Mines & Metals Corp. Ltd. 12/22/55
Triton Mines & Metals Corp. Ltd. merged into Continental Consolidated Mines & Oils Co. Ltd. 10/4/57
(See Consolidated Consolidated Mines & Oils Co. Ltd.)

TRIUMPH ACQUISITION CORP INC (CANADA)
Name changed to Chemaphor Inc. 08/04/2005
Chemaphor Inc. name changed to Avivagen Inc. 05/30/2012

TRIUMPH AMERN INC (DE)
Completely liquidated 06/20/1975
Each share Common $1 par exchanged for $2 cash

TRIUMPH APPAREL CORP (DE)
Controlling interest taken over by KSL Ventures, L.L.C. 04/29/2009
Details not available

TRIUMPH ASSOC LTD (NV)
Charter revoked 8/1/98

TRIUMPH CAP INC (FL)
Each share old Common $0.0001 par exchanged for (0.125) share new Common $0.0001 par 01/14/1988
Name changed to IRT Industries Inc. 12/06/1993
IRT Industries Inc. name changed to Xpedian, Inc. 01/26/2000 which name changed to Gala Hospitality Corp. 11/06/2001 which name changed to Gala Holding Corp. 09/04/2002 which recapitalized as Global TransNet Corp. 10/14/2003 which recapitalized as Legacy Brands Holding, Inc. (FL) 11/19/2009 which reincorporated in British Virgin Islands as Revelation MIS, Inc. 10/22/2010 which reincorporated in Florida as Jolen, Inc. 04/08/2015 which name changed to WOWI, Inc. 06/23/2016

TRIUMPH CORP (UT)
Merged into Monada Petroleum Corp. 3/24/69
Each share Common 10¢ par exchanged for (1) share Common 1¢ par

TRIUMPH DISHWASHERS, LTD. (ON)
Charter cancelled for failure to file reports and pay taxes 12/10/62

TRIUMPH ENERGY CORP (AB)
Each share Class A Common no par exchanged for (0.1) share Common no par 6/30/95
Acquired by Baytex Energy Ltd. 5/30/2001
Each share new Common no par exchanged for either (0.1267) share Common no par and $2.649597 cash or (0.3475) share Common no par
Note: Option to receive stock only expired 6/21/2001
(See Baytex Energy Ltd.)

TRIUMPH GOLD CORP (BC)
Reincorporated 08/26/2004
Place of incorporation changed from (YT) to (BC) 08/26/2004
Recapitalized as Kenai Resources Ltd. 05/01/2007
Each share Common no par exchanged for (0.16666666) Common no par
Kenai Resources Ltd. merged into Serabi Gold PLC 07/22/2013

TRIUMPH GROUP INC (CO)
Name changed to Novatek International, Inc. 12/28/90
Novatek International, Inc. name changed to Medical Diagnostic Products, Inc. 9/10/96
(See Medical Diagnostic Products, Inc.)

TRIUMPH INC (DE)
Charter cancelled and declared inoperative and void for non-payment of taxes 3/1/89

TRIUMPH INDS INC (TX)
Stock Dividend - 10% 01/20/1967
Adjudicated bankrupt 06/23/1978
Stockholders' equity unlikely

TRIUMPH INTL FOODS INC (NV)
Recapitalized as USLAB.Com, Inc. 05/03/1999
Each share Common $0.001 par exchanged for (0.005) share Common $0.001 par
USLAB.Com, Inc. name changed to Fly Networks Inc. 09/15/2000 which name changed to InterCommerceCorp 12/15/2003 which recapitalized as CipherPass Corp. 06/06/2005 which recapitalized as Javalon Technology Group, Inc. (NV) 09/06/2007 which reincorporated in British Virgin Islands as WorldVest Equity, Inc. 11/13/2008

TRIUMPH MGMT GROUP INC (NY)
Each share old Common $0.001 par exchanged for (1/7) share new Common $0.001 par 4/21/99
Administratively dissolved 6/27/2001

TRIUMPH OIL CORP. LTD. (ON)
Merged into Rio-Prado Consolidated Oils Ltd. in 1953
Each share Capital Stock $1 par exchanged for (0.45) share new Capital Stock $1 par
Rio-Prado Consolidated Oils Ltd. merged into Rio Palmer Oils Ltd. 7/25/55 which merged into Devon-Palmer Oils Ltd. 11/6/56 which merged into Triad Oil Manitoba Ltd. for cash 3/8/67

TRIUMPH PET INDS INC (NY)
Merged into TPI Merger Corp. 01/12/1981
Each share Common 10¢ par exchanged for $2.55 cash

TRIUMPH PETES LTD (BC)
Recapitalized as Arrowfield Resources Ltd. 08/04/1988
Each share Common no par exchanged for (0.25) share Common no par
Arrowfield Resources Ltd. recapitalized as ITL Capital Corp. 04/27/1992 which recapitalized as MPH Ventures Corp. 12/19/2005 which name changed to Cuba Ventures Corp. 03/21/2016 which name changed to CUV Ventures Corp. 03/01/2018

TRIUMPH RES LTD (BC)
Recapitalized as Jericho Resources Ltd. 10/02/1992
Each share Common no par exchanged for (0.25) share Common no par
Jericho Resources Ltd. name changed to Regia Resources Ltd. (BC) 04/18/1995 which reincorporated in Canada 07/07/1995
(See Regia Resources Ltd.)

TRIUMPH STORECRAFTERS CORP. (TX)
Stock Dividend - 20% 1/20/66
Name changed to Triumph Industries Inc. 2/8/66
Triumph Industries Inc. adjudicated bankrupt 6/23/78

TRIUMPH VENTURES II CORP (ON)
Completely liquidated
Each share Common no par received first and final distribution of $0.01165085 cash payable 08/28/2015 to holders of record 08/18/2015

TRIUMPH VENTURES III CORP (ON)
Recapitalized as Altitude Resources Inc. 02/15/2013
Each share Common no par exchanged for (0.5) share Common no par

TRIUMPH VENTURES CORP (ON)
Recapitalized as Highvista Gold Inc. 10/17/2011
Each share Common no par exchanged for (0.5) share Common no par

TRIUNE RES LTD (BC)
Delisted from Vancouver Stock Exchange 09/19/1995

TRIUS INVTS INC OLD (AB)
Name changed to eCycling Technologies Inc. 10/18/2006
eCycling Technologies Inc. name changed to Trius Investments Inc. (New) 10//18/2007

TRIUS THERAPEUTICS INC (DE)
Acquired by Cubist Pharmaceuticals, Inc. 09/11/2013
Each share Common $0.0001 par exchanged for (1) Non-Transferable Contingent Value Right and $13.50 cash

TRIVALENCE MNG CORP (BC)
Name changed to Azure Resources Corp. 03/26/2008
Azure Resources Corp. recapitalized as Panorama Petroleum Inc. 06/13/2014 which recapitalized as Stamper Oil & Gas Corp. 04/06/2017

TRIVANTAGE GROUP INC (NV)
Recapitalized as Proteo Inc. 1/28/2002
Each (150) shares Common $0.001 par exchanged for (1) share Common $0.001 par

TRIVASCULAR TECHNOLOGIES INC (DE)
Merged into Endologix, Inc. 02/03/2016
Each share Common 1¢ par exchanged for (0.6312) share Common $0.001 par and $0.34 cash

TRIVELLO ENERGY CORP (BC)
Each share old Common no par exchanged for (0.16666666) share new Common no par 12/22/2008
Name changed to Equitas Resources Corp. 10/19/2010
Equitas Resources Corp. name changed to Altamira Gold Corp. 04/18/2017

TRIVELLO VENTURES INC (BC)
Name changed to Trivello Energy Corp. 05/04/2006
Trivello Energy Corp. name changed to Equitas Resources Corp. 10/19/2010 which name changed to Altamira Gold Corp. 04/18/2017

TRIVEST EQUITIES LTD (NV)
Name changed to MCN Multicast Networks, Inc. 2/11/2005
MCN Multicast Networks, Inc. name changed to Downtown America Funding Corp. 9/8/2005 which name changed to Savior Energy Corp. 12/22/2006

TRIVOS INC (FL)
Each (97.98928) shares old Common $0.0001 par exchanged for (1) new Common $0.0001 par 06/30/2006
Proclaimed dissolved for failure to file reports and pay fees 09/26/2008

TRIWOOD CAP CORP (AB)
Name changed to Algae Biosciences Corp. 05/05/2011

TRIZAK CORP (GA)
SEC revoked common stock registration 09/17/2009

TRIZEC CDA INC (CANADA)
Merged into Brookfield Properties Corp. 10/05/2006
Each share Subordinate no par exchanged for $30.9809 cash

TRIZEC DEVELOPMENT LTD. (BC)
Name changed to Wavecom Development Ltd. 08/31/1971
Wavecom Development Ltd. recapitalized as Neptune Resources Corp. 06/21/1979 which merged into ABM Gold Corp. 12/05/1989 which reorganized as NorthWest Gold Corp. 06/01/1990 which merged into Northgate Exploration Ltd. (ON) 06/08/1993 which reincorporated in British Columbia 07/01/2001 which name changed to Northgate Minerals Corp. 05/20/2004 which merged into AuRico Gold Inc. 10/26/2011

TRIZEC HAHN CORP (ON)
Acquired by Trizec Canada Inc. 05/08/2002
Each share Subordinate no par exchanged for (0.89731519) Subordinate no par
(See Trizec Canada Inc.)

TRIZEC LTD (CANADA)
Name changed 04/01/1977
Common $1 par changed to no par 06/07/1968
Each share old Common no par exchanged for (0.1) share new Common no par 12/08/1971
Name changed from Trizec Corp. Ltd. to Trizec Corp. Ltd./La Corporation Trizec Ltee. 04/01/1977
Common no par split (2) for (1) by issuance of (1) additional share 05/05/1981
Common no par reclassified as Conv. Class B no par 01/24/1984
Each share Conv. Class B no par received distribution of (0.1) share Sr. Preferred Class B Ser. 3 no par and (1) share Class A no par 01/30/1984
Each share Sr. Preferred Class B Ser. 5 no par reclassified as (1) share Sr. Preferred Class B Ser. 4 no par 04/02/1986
Class A no par split (3) for (2) by issuance of (0.5) additional share 07/31/1986
Conv. Class B no par split (3) for (2) by issuance of (0.5) additional share 07/31/1986
Stock Dividend - 50% 07/31/1989
Recapitalized as Trizec Ltd. (New) 07/25/1994
Each share Sr. Adjustable Rate Preferred Class A Ser. 1 no par exchanged for (0.03783) share Common no par and (0.0794) Common Stock Purchase Warrant, Class A expiring 07/25/1999
Each share Sr. Adjustable Rate Preferred Class A Ser. 2 no par exchanged for (0.03783) share Common no par and (0.0794) Common Stock Purchase Warrant, Class A expiring 07/25/1999
Each share Sr. Adjustable Rate Preferred Class B Ser. 1 no par exchanged for (0.03783) share Common no par and (0.0794) Common Stock Purchase Warrant, Class A expiring 07/25/1999
Each share Sr. Adjustable Rate Preferred Class B Ser. 2 no par exchanged for (0.03783) share Common no par and (0.0794) Common Stock Purchase Warrant, Class A expiring 07/25/1999
Each share Variable Rate Sr. Preferred Class B Ser. 3 no par exchanged for (0.03783) share Common no par and (0.0794) Common Stock Purchase Warrant, Class A expiring 07/25/1999
Each share Variable Rate Sr. Preferred Class B. Ser. 4 no par exchanged for (0.03783) share Common no par and (0.0794) Common Stock Purchase Warrant, Class A expiring 07/25/1999
Each share Sr. Adjustable Rate Preferred Class B Ser. 5 no par exchanged for (0.03783) share Common no par and (0.0794) Common Stock Purchase Warrant, Class A expiring 07/25/1999
Each share Sr. Adjustable Rate Preferred Class B Ser. 6 no par

exchanged for (0.03783) share Common no par and (0.0794) Common Stock Purchase Warrant, Class A expiring 07/25/1999
Each share Class A Subordinate Ordinary no par exchanged for (0.030368) Common Stock Purchase Warrant expiring 07/25/1999 and (0.010902) Right to purchase Common
Each share Class A no par exchanged for (0.030368) Common Stock Purchase Warrant, Class A expiring 07/25/1999 and (0.010902) Right to purchase Common
Each share Class B no par exchanged for (0.030368) Common Stock Purchase Warrant, Class A expiring 07/25/1999 and (0.010902) Right to purchase Common
Trizec Ltd. (New) merged into Trizec Hahn Corp. 11/01/1996 which was acquired by Trizec Canada Inc. 05/08/2002
(See Trizec Canada Inc.)

TRIZEC LTD NEW (CANADA)
Merged into Trizec Hahn Corp. 11/1/96
Each share Common no par exchanged for (0.58) share Subordinate no par
Trizec Hahn Corp. was acquired by Trizec Canada Inc. 5/8/2002
(See Trizec Canada Inc.)

TRIZEC PPTYS INC (DE)
Merged into Grace Holdings LLC 10/5/2006
Each share Common 1¢ par exchanged for $29.0209 cash

TRIZETTO GROUP INC (DE)
Acquired by TZ Holdings, L.P. 08/04/2008
Each share Common $0.001 par exchanged for $22 cash

TRL RLTY INC (AB)
Name changed to Torode Realty Ltd. 01/22/1998
Torode Realty Ltd. name changed to CMQ Resources Inc. 01/29/2004
(See CMQ Resources Inc.)

TRM CORP (OR)
Name changed 09/11/1998
Name changed from TRM Copy Centers Corp. to TRM Corp. 09/11/1998
Reincorporated under the laws of Delaware as Access to Money, Inc. and Common no par changed to $0.001 par 06/25/2009
(See Access To Money, Inc.)

TRO LEARNING INC (DE)
Name changed to Plato Learning, Inc. 04/25/2000
(See Plato Learning, Inc.)

TROILUS EXPLORATIONS LTD. (QC)
Acquired by Muscocho Explorations Ltd. 04/29/1977
Each share Common $1 par exchanged for (0.1) share Capital Stock $1 par
Muscocho Explorations Ltd. merged into Golden Goose Resources Inc. 09/30/1996 which merged into Kodiak Exploration Ltd. 12/16/2010 which name changed to Prodigy Gold Inc. 01/04/2011

TROILUS MINES LTD (QC)
Name changed to Troilus Explorations Ltd. 07/06/1976
Troilus Explorations Ltd. acquired by Muscocho Explorations Ltd. 04/29/1977 which merged into Golden Goose Resources Inc. 09/30/1996 which merged into Kodiak Exploration Ltd. 12/16/2010 which name changed to Prodigy Gold Inc. 01/04/2011 which merged into Argonaut Gold Inc. 12/11/2012

TROJAN CONS MINES LTD (BC)
Recapitalized as B.X. Development Ltd. 11/01/1972
Each share Common $1 par exchanged for (0.2) share Common no par
B.X. Development Ltd. merged into Brent Petroleum Industries Ltd. 10/07/1981 which recapitalized as B.P.I. Resources Ltd. 05/20/1983 which name changed to Brent Resources Group Ltd. 03/22/1985

TROJAN ENERGY CORP (BC)
Recapitalized as International Trojan Development Corp. 4/18/85
Each share Capital Stock no par exchanged for (0.2) share Common no par
International Trojan Development Corp. recapitalized as Trojan Ventures Inc. 6/20/91 which reorganized in Cayman Islands as Alcanta International Education Ltd. 3/26/99 which name changed to Access International Education Ltd. 1/17/2001

TROJAN ENERGY CORP (NV)
Common 10¢ par changed to 1¢ par 11/10/1981
Name changed to Petro-Med, Inc. 09/10/1984
(See Petro-Med, Inc.)

TROJAN EXPLORATION LTD. (BC)
Merged into Trojan Consolidated Mines Ltd. 12/9/56
Each share Capital Stock 50¢ par exchanged for (2/3) share Common $1 par
Trojan Consolidated Mines Ltd. recapitalized as B.X. Development Ltd. 11/1/72 which merged into Brent Petroleum Industries Ltd. 10/7/81 which recapitalized as B.P.I. Resources Ltd. 5/20/83 which name changed to Brent Resources Group Ltd. 3/22/85

TROJAN INDS INC (DE)
Name changed to Leisure Trends, Inc. 05/04/1970
(See Leisure Trends, Inc.)

TROJAN OIL & GAS CO. (DE)
Liquidation completed 12/21/63

TROJAN TECHNOLOGIES INC (ON)
Merged into Danaher Corp. 11/10/2004
Each share Common no par exchanged for $10.65 cash

TROJAN VENTURES INC (BC)
Reorganized under the laws of Cayman Islands as Alcanta International Education Ltd. 3/26/99
Each share Common no par exchanged for (0.2) share Common no par
Alcanta International Education Ltd. name changed to Access International Education Ltd. 1/17/2001

TROLLEY CHEF INC (DE)
Recapitalized as Harbour Companies, Inc. 7/9/88
Each share Common 1¢ par exchanged for (3) shares Common $0.001 par
Harbour Companies, Inc. name changed to Castle Court Development Corp. 12/12/96

TROLLEY ENTERPRISES, INC. (UT)
Merged into Western Corn Dog Factories 7/22/77
Each share Common 1¢ par exchanged for (3.5) shares Common 1¢ par
Western Corn Dog Factories merged into Resources West, Inc. 7/27/81 which recapitalized as Magma Resources 12/27/89 which name changed to Cellular Telecommunications & Technologies Inc. 7/15/93 which recapitalized as China Biomedical Group Inc. 4/3/95 which name changed to Internet Holdings Ltd. 6/30/96 which name changed to HTTP Technology, Inc. (UT) 11/28/2000 which reincorporated in Delaware 12/19/2000 which name changed to Medicsight, Inc. 10/28/2002 which name changed to MGT Capital Investments, Inc. 1/24/2007

TROLLS SEAFOOD LTD (DE)
Name changed to Valdor Ltd. 05/00/1998
Valdor Ltd. name changed to Pear Technologies, Inc. 06/12/1998 which recapitalized as Sanswire Technologies Inc. 05/20/2002 which name changed to Wireless Holdings Group, Inc. 03/30/2005 which recapitalized as Vega Promotional Systems, Inc. (DE) 12/26/2006 which reorganized in Wyoming as Vega Biofuels, Inc. 07/29/2010

TRONC INC (DE)
Name changed to Tribune Publishing Co. (New) 10/10/2018

TRONCHEMICS RESH INC (MN)
Statutorily dissolved 09/25/1991

TRONIC PRODS INC (DE)
Each share Common 5¢ par exchanged for (0.5) share Common 1¢ par 11/20/1974
Name changed to Catania Bros. Foods, Inc. 12/28/1982
Catania Bros. Foods, Inc. name changed to Joedot Holdings, Inc. 12/10/1993
(See Joedot Holdings, Inc.)

TRONOMATIC CORP (NY)
Proclaimed dissolved for failure to file reports and pay fees 12/15/1970

TRONOX INC (DE)
Plan of reorganization under Chapter 11 Federal Bankruptcy proceedings effective 02/14/2011
Each share Class A Common 1¢ par automatically became (0.013148) Common Stock Purchase Warrant Ser. A expiring 01/25/2018 and (0.016245) Common Stock Purchase Warrant Ser. B expiring 01/25/2018
Each share Class B Common 1¢ par automatically became (0.013148) Common Stock Purchase Warrant Ser. A expiring 01/25/2018 and (0.016245) Common Stock Purchase Warrant Ser. B expiring 01/25/2018
Note: Certificates were not required to be surrendered and are without value
Merged into Tronox Ltd. 06/15/2012
Each share Common 1¢ par exchanged for (1) share Class A Ordinary and $12.50 cash

TROON ENTMT INC (UT)
Recapitalized 06/09/1986
Recapitalized from Troon Technology, Inc. to Troon Entertainment Corp. 06/09/1986
Each share Common $0.001 par exchanged for (0.25) share Common $0.001 par
Involuntarily dissolved 05/01/1988

TROON VENTURES LTD (BC)
Reorganized under the laws of Ontario as Grenville Strategic Royalty Corp. 02/21/2014
Each share Common no par exchanged for (0.6896) share Common no par and (0.3448) Common Stock Purchase Warrant expiring 02/19/2016
Note: Holders of (99) or fewer shares received $0.31 cash per share
Grenville Strategic Royalty Corp. merged into LOGiQ Asset Management Inc. (AB) 06/07/2018 which reorganized in British Columbia as Flow Capital Corp. 06/11/2018

TROOPER TECHNOLOGIES INC (BC)
Name changed 01/27/1995
Name changed from Trooper Explorations Ltd. to Trooper Technologies Inc. 01/27/1995
Name changed to Stream Communications Network, Inc. 10/19/2001
Stream Communications Network, Inc. name changed to Stream Communications Network & Media Inc. 08/17/2004
(See Stream Communications Network & Media Inc.)

TROPHY CAP INC (CANADA)
Recapitalized as LMS Medical Systems Inc. 04/01/2004
Each share Common no par exchanged for (0.05) share Common no par
LMS Medical Systems Inc. name changed to Maclos Capital Inc. 08/20/2012

TROPHY ENTERPRISES INC (NY)
Dissolved by proclamation 12/20/1977

TROPHY RES LTD (AB)
Name changed to Williston Wildcatters Oil Corp. 11/23/1993
(See Williston Wildcatters Oil Corp.)

TROPIC AIR CARGO INC (DE)
Recapitalized 10/06/1997
Recapitalized from Tropic Communications, Inc. to Tropic Air Cargo Inc. 10/06/1997
Each share Common 15¢ par exchanged for (0.16666666) share Common 90¢ par
SEC revoked common stock registration 09/17/2009

TROPIC ICE INC (PA)
Company liquidated 00/00/2002
Details not available

TROPIC INDS INC (UT)
Each share Common Capital 2¢ par exchanged for (0.1) share Common Capital Stock 20¢ par 03/04/1980
Each share Common Capital Stock 20¢ par exchanged for (0.2) share Common Capital Stock $1 par 09/11/1981
Recapitalized as United Datacopy, Inc. 02/19/1987
Each share Common Capital Stock $1 par exchanged for (0.2) share Common Capital Stock $1 par
United Datacopy, Inc. recapitalized as Pen International Inc. 03/21/1994 which recapitalized as Telnet World Communications, Inc. (UT) 03/02/1998 which reincorporated in Nevada as Givemepower Corp. 07/05/2001

TROPIC TRADING LTD (AB)
Struck off register and declared dissolved for failure to file returns 06/01/1997

TROPICAL BEVERAGE INC (FL)
Recapitalized as ViviCells International, Inc. 05/09/2008
Each (140) shares Common $0.001 par exchanged for (1) share Common $0.001 par

TROPICAL DEV INTL INC (UT)
Recapitalized as Impulse Energy Systems, Inc. 04/02/1990
Each share Common 1¢ par exchanged for (0.1) share Common 1¢ par
(See Impulse Energy Systems, Inc.)

TROPICAL GAS INC (PANAMA)
$5.24 Preferred $100 par called for redemption 05/01/1961
6% Conv. Preferred $100 par called for redemption 04/16/1962
Common 1¢ par changed to $1 par 04/25/1963

Common $1 par reclassified as Class A $1 par 01/05/1970
Merged into United States Freight Co. 01/14/1970
Each share Class A $1 par exchanged for (0.89) share Capital Stock no par
$6.25 Preferred $100 par called for redemption 02/11/1970
United States Freight Co. name changed to Transway International Corp. 06/03/174
(See Transway International Corp.)

TROPICAL LEISURE RESORTS INC (NV)
Recapitalized as eWorldMedia Holdings, Inc. 10/22/2002
Each share Common $0.001 par exchanged for (0.02) share Common $0.001 par
eWorldMedia Holdings, Inc. name changed to Liberty Diversified Holdings, Inc. 01/09/2006 which name changed to Nutripure Beverages, Inc. 01/17/2008

TROPICAL SPORTSWEAR INTL CORP (FL)
Plan of reorganation under Chapter 11 Federal Bankruptcy Code effective 07/18/2005
No stockholders' equity

TROPICAL SUBMARINE SAFARIS LTD (BC)
Recapitalized as International Submarine Safaris (Canada) Ltd. 08/02/1989
Each share Common no par exchanged for (0.2) share Common no par
(See International Submarine Safaris (Canada) Ltd.)

TROPICANA DEV CORP (BC)
Recapitalized as Santa Barbara Ventures Ltd. 09/08/1992
Each share Common no par exchanged for (0.125) share Common no par
Santa Barbara Ventures Ltd. name changed to Voodoo Ventures Ltd. 06/10/1994 which recapitalized as Pacific Royal Ventures Ltd. 03/01/1996 which merged into Pacific Rodera Ventures Inc. 03/01/1999 which name changed to Pacific Rodera Energy Inc. (BC) 06/22/2004 which reincorporated in Alberta 06/14/2006 which name changed to PRD Energy Inc. 08/12/2010

TROPICANA ENTMT INC (DE)
Acquired by Eldorado Resorts, Inc. 10/01/2018
Each share Common 1¢ par exchanged for $75.14 cash

TROPICANA POOLS INC (FL)
Merged into Goldfield Corp. (DE) 10/14/1975
Each share Common 1¢ par exchanged for $2.31 cash

TROPICANA PRODS INC (FL)
Common $1 par split (2) for (1) by issuance of (1) additional share 01/29/1971
Common $1 par split (2) for (1) by issuance of (1) additional share 03/31/1972
Merged into Beatrice Foods Co. 08/07/1978
Each share Common $1 par exchanged for (1) share $3.38 Conv. Preference Ser. A no par
Beatrice Foods Co. name changed to Beatrice Companies, Inc. 06/05/1984
(See Beatrice Companies, Inc.)

TROPICANA RES LTD (BC)
Name changed to Tropicana Development Corp. 10/19/1987
Tropicana Development Corp. recapitalized as Santa Barbara Ventures Ltd. 09/08/1992 which name changed to Voodoo Ventures Ltd. 06/10/1994 which recapitalized as Pacific Royal Ventures Ltd. 03/01/1996 which merged into Pacific Rodera Ventures Inc. 03/01/1999 which name changed to Pacific Rodera Energy Inc. (BC) 06/22/2004 which reincorporated in Alberta 06/14/2006 which name changed to PRD Energy Inc. 08/12/2010

TROPIKA INTL LTD (ON)
Each share old Common no par exchanged for (0.1) share new Common no par 05/07/1997
Delisted from Toronto Venture Stock Exchange 06/20/2003

TROPIX TOGS INC (FL)
Stock Dividend - 10% 03/25/1974
Merged into Nexus Industries, Inc. 03/04/1975
Each share Common 10¢ par exchanged for (0.25) Common Stock Purchase Warrant expiring 03/01/1980, $4 principal amount of 10% Subord. Sinking Fund Debentures due 03/01/1985 and $2.20 cash

TROPOL INC (DE)
Recapitalized as 21st Century Films, Corp. 03/15/1989
Each share Common $0.0001 par exchanged for (0.1) share Common 1¢ par
(See 21st Century Films, Corp.)

TROTT ELECTRS INC (NY)
Acquired by E.I.L. Newcorp 1987, Inc. 06/12/1987
Each share Common 5¢ par exchanged for $1.20 cash

TROUDOR RES INC (BC)
Recapitalized as Remington Creek Resources Inc. 03/14/1989
Each share Common no par exchanged for (1/3) share Common no par
Remington Creek Resources Inc. recapitalized as Grayd Resource Corp. 02/26/1996 which was acquired by Agnico-Eagle Mines Ltd. 01/24/2012 which name changed to Agnico Eagle Mines Ltd. 04/30/2013

TROUND INTL INC (DE)
Charter cancelled and declared inoperative and void for non-payment of taxes 05/30/1996

TROUP PORCUPINE MINES LTD. (ON)
Charter cancelled for failure to file reports and pay taxes 05/00/1958

TROUT LAKE MINES LTD. (AB)
Charter cancelled and declared dissolved by default 11/15/1958
No stockholders' equity

TROUT MNG CO (DE)
Charter cancelled and declared inoperative and void for non-payment of taxes 03/01/1994

TROUTLINE INVTS INC (ON)
Reorganized under the laws of Alberta as Innova Exploration Ltd. 04/16/2004
Each share Common no par exchanged for (0.11333371) share Common no par
(See Innova Exploration Ltd.)

TROVE INVT CORP (BC)
Name changed 02/11/1991
Name changed from Trove Resource Ltd. to Trove Investment Corp. 02/11/1991
Name changed to Net Nanny Software International Inc. (BC) 01/29/1997
Net Nanny Software International Inc. (BC) reincorporated in Yukon 11/15/2000
(See Net Nanny Software International Inc.)

TROVER SOLUTIONS INC (DE)
Acquired by Tailwind Capital Partners LLC 07/15/2004
Each share Common $0.001 par exchanged for $7 cash

TROY & BENNINGTON RAILROAD CO.
Acquired by Boston & Maine Railroad (ME, NH, MA, NY) 00/00/1946
Details not available

TROY BK & TR CO (TROY, AL)
Recapitalized as Henderson Bancshares, Inc. 10/01/1996
Each share Common $1 par exchanged for (2) shares Common $1 par

TROY CORP., INC. (UT)
Charter suspended for failure to pay taxes 04/30/1986

TROY COTTON & WOOLEN MANUFACTURING CO.
Liquidated 00/00/1929
Details not available

TROY ENERGY CORP (BC)
Reincorporated under the laws of Alberta 02/24/2011

TROY EXPL INC (UT)
Recapitalized as Troy Corp., Inc. 01/28/1985
Each share Common $0.005 par exchanged for (0.02) share Common no par
(See Troy Corp., Inc.)

TROY FINL CORP (DE)
Stock Dividend - 5% payable 03/29/2002 to holders of record 03/15/2002 Ex date - 03/13/2002
Merged into First Niagara Financial Group, Inc. (New) 01/16/2004
Each share Common $0.0001 par exchanged for (2.34323) shares Common 1¢ par
First Niagara Financial Group, Inc. (New) merged into KeyCorp (New) 08/01/2016

TROY GAS CO.
Merged into New York Power & Light Corp. 00/00/1927
Details not available

TROY GOLD INDS LTD (AB)
Reincorporated 09/06/1978
Place of incorporation changed from (Canada) to (AB) 09/06/1978
Struck off register for failure to file annual returns 06/01/1981

TROY GROUP INC (DE)
Each share old Common 1¢ par exchanged for (0.00001) share new Common 1¢ par 07/02/2009
Note: In effect holders received $2.26 cash per share and public interest was eliminated
An additional distribution of $0.2964 cash per share was made 08/01/2011

TROY HILL BANCORP INC (PA)
Merged into PennFirst Bancorp, Inc. 04/03/1997
Each share Common 1¢ par exchanged for (1.52) shares Common 1¢ par or (0.608) shares Common 1¢ par and $8.46 cash
Note: Option to receive stock and cash expired 05/06/1997
PennFirst Bancorp, Inc. name changed to ESB Financial Corp. 05/01/1998 which merged into WesBanco, Inc. 02/10/2015

TROY LAUNDRY MACHINERY CO., INC.
Merged into American Machine & Metals, Inc. 00/00/1934
Details not available

TROY LAUNDRY MACHINERY CO. LTD.
Succeeded by Troy Laundry Machinery Co., Inc. 00/00/1927
Details not available

TROY MINERALS & TECHNOLOGY CORP (BC)
Struck off register and declared dissolved for failure to file returns 09/18/1992

TROY RESOURCES LTD (AUSTRALIA)
Name changed 01/17/2012
Name changed from Troy Resources NL to Troy Resources Ltd. 01/17/2012
Shares transferred to Australian share register 05/15/2015

TROY SILVER MINES LTD (BC)
Struck off register and declared dissolved for failure to file returns 06/27/1977

TROYDEN CORP (NV)
Common $0.001 par split (31) for (1) by issuance of (30) additional shares payable 06/27/2000 to holders of record 06/26/2000
Name changed to Communicate.com Inc. 08/23/2000
Communicate.com Inc. name changed to Live Current Media Inc. 08/04/2008

TROYMIN RES LTD (AB)
Merged into Santoy Resources Ltd. (AB) (New) 04/24/2003
Each share Common no par exchanged for (0.6060606) share Common no par
Santoy Resources Ltd. (AB) (New) reorganized in British Columbia as Virginia Energy Resources Ltd. (Old) 07/24/2009 which reorganized as Anthem Resources Inc. 09/28/2012 which merged into Boss Power Corp. 07/23/2015 which name changed to Eros Resources Corp. 07/29/2015

TROYSCO MINES LTD (QC)
Voluntarily dissolved 02/15/1971
Details not available

TRP ENERGY SENSORS INC (NY)
Proclaimed dissolved 12/24/1991

TRP NT CORP (ON)
Preferred no par called for redemption at $16 on 08/18/2003
Capital Shares no par called for redemption at $8.76 on 08/18/2003

TRSG CORP (DE)
Recapitalized as Worldwide Holdings Corp. 05/21/2003
Each share Common $0.001 par exchanged for (0.00004) share Common $0.001 par

TR3 TR (ON)
Trust terminated 12/02/2004
Each Unit received $10 cash

TRU DYNAMICS INTL INC (NV)
Charter revoked for failure to file reports and pay fees 01/31/2006

TRU INC (UT)
Dissolved 09/00/1986
Each share Common 1¢ par received first and final distribution of $0.04 cash
Note: Certificates were not required to be surrendered and are without value

TRU-LINE DESIGN & ENGINEERING CO. (MN)
Adjudicated bankrupt 05/00/1963
No stockholders' equity

TRU WALL GROUP LTD (ON)
Name changed 05/11/1976
Name changed from Tru-Wall Concrete Forming Ltd. to Tru-Wall Group Ltd. 05/11/1976
Delisted from Toronto Stock Exchange 09/19/1997

TRUAX RES CORP (AB)
Common no par reclassified as Class A Common no par 10/09/1992
Merged into Elk Point Resources Inc. 06/06/1997

Each share Class A Common no par exchanged for (0.314) share new Class A Common no par
Elk Point Resources Inc. merged into Acclaim Energy Trust 01/28/2003
(See Acclaim Energy Trust)

TRUAX-TRAER COAL CO. (DE)
Common no par changed to $5 par 00/00/1948
Common $5 par changed to $1 par and stock dividend of (1) share $2.80 Conv. Preferred Ser. A $50 par for each (8.33333333) shares of Common paid 00/00/1951
Stock Dividend - 100% 11/21/1947
$2.80 Preferred Ser. A $50 par called for redemption 01/12/1960
Merged into Consolidation Coal Co. 04/30/1962
Each share Common $1 par exchanged for (1) share Common $1 par
(See Consolidation Coal Co.)

TRUAX-TRAER LIGNITE COAL CO.
Acquired by Truax-Traer Coal Co. 00/00/1936
Details not available

TRUAX VENTURES CORP (BC)
Recapitalized as Aries Resource Corp. 09/02/2004
Each share Common no par exchanged for (0.25) share Common no par
Aries Resource Corp. recapitalized as Alderon Resource Corp. 09/24/2008 which name changed to Alderon Iron Ore Corp. 10/05/2011

TRUBION PHARMACEUTICALS INC (DE)
Merged into Emergent BioSolutions Inc. 10/28/2010
Each share Common $0.001 par exchanged for (0.1641) share Common $0.001 par, (1) Contingent Value Right and $1.365 cash

TRUCK COMPONENTS INC (DE)
Merged into Johnstown America Industries Inc. 08/23/1995
Each share Common 1¢ par exchanged for $16 cash

TRUCK O MATIC INC (DE)
Filed for Chapter X bankruptcy proceedings 08/23/1974
No stockholders' equity

TRUCK OWNERS & OPERATORS NATIONAL ASSOCIATION, INC. (PA)
Name changed to Toona, Inc. and Common 1¢ par reclassified as Class A Common no par 05/21/1969

TRUCK UNDERWRITERS ASSN (CA)
Common $1 par split (5) for (4) by issuance of (0.25) additional share 06/11/1965
Stock Dividends - 100% 04/10/1956; 66.66666666% 06/10/1958
Merged into Farmers Group, Inc. 12/31/1970
Each share Common $1 par exchanged for (0.5) share $3 Conv. Preferred $1 par
(See Farmers Group, Inc.)

TRUCO INC (NV)
Recapitalized as Web Tech Inc. 04/04/1996
Each share Common $0.001 par exchanged for (0.16666666) share Common $0.001 par
Web Tech Inc. name changed to Cynergy Inc. 04/16/1997 which recapitalized as Mercantile Factoring Credit Online Corp. 09/29/1999 which name changed to Incitations Inc. 10/03/2000 which recapitalized as Osprey Gold Corp. 05/16/2003 which recapitalized as Gilla Inc. 03/30/2007

TRUDEV MINING & EXPLORATION LTD. (ON)
Charter revoked for failure to file reports and pay fees 05/13/1965

TRUDY CORP (WY)
Reincorporated 12/21/2010
State of incorporation changed from (DE) to (WY) 12/21/2010
Each share old Common $0.0001 par exchanged for (0.00006666) share new Common $0.0001 par 11/10/2011
SEC revoked common stock registration 05/28/2014

TRUE COLORS INTL (NV)
Name changed to AgTech Global International, Inc. 10/18/2017

TRUE ENERGY INC (AB)
Plan of arrangement effective 11/07/2005
Each share Common no par exchanged for (0.25) True Energy Trust, Trust Unit no par, (0.1) share Vero Energy Inc. Common no par and (1) Common Stock Purchase Warrant expiring 12/02/2005
(See each company's listing)

TRUE ENERGY TR (AB)
Reorganized as Bellatrix Exploration Ltd. 11/02/2009
Each Trust Unit no par exchanged for (1) share Common no par
Note: Unexchanged certificates were cancelled and became without value 11/02/2015

TRUE EXPL CORP (BC)
Name changed to Compusoft Canada Inc. 11/11/1998
Compusoft Canada Inc. name changed to TraceAbility Solutions Inc. 02/28/2001
(See TraceAbility Solutions Inc.)

TRUE GOLD MNG INC (BC)
Merged into Endeavour Mining Corp. 04/27/2016
Each share Common no par exchanged for (0.044) share Ordinary USD$0.01 par
Note: Unexchanged certificates will be cancelled and become without value 04/27/2022

TRUE HEALTH INC (UT)
Each share old Common 1¢ par exchanged for (0.1) share new Common 1¢ par 10/29/2001
Each share new Common 1¢ par exchanged for (0.01538461) share Common $0.001 par 03/03/2003
Each share new Common $0.001 par exchanged for (0.01666666) share Common 1¢ par 04/19/2004
Reorganized under the laws of Nevada as MediQuip Holdings, Inc. 05/01/2006
Each share Common 1¢ par exchanged for (1) share Common $0.001 par
MediQuip Holdings, Inc. name changed to Deep Down, Inc. 12/18/2006

TRUE NORTH APT REAL ESTATE INVT TR (ON)
Merged into Northview Apartment Real Estate Investment Trust 11/05/2015
Each Unit exchanged for (0.3908) Trust Unit
Note: Unexchanged certificates will be cancelled and become without value 11/05/2021

TRUE NORTH COMMUNICATIONS INC (DE)
Common 33-1/3 par split (2) for (1) by issuance of (1) additional share 2/17/95
Merged into Interpublic Group of Companies, Inc. 6/22/2001
Each share Common 33-1/3¢ par exchanged for (1.14) shares Common 10¢ par

TRUE NORTH CORP (AB)
Name changed to Empirical Inc. 11/30/2007
(See Empirical Inc.)

TRUE NORTH FILM & VIDEO PRODTNS INC (BC)
Struck off register and declared dissolved for failure to file returns 11/15/1996

TRUE NORTH WTR CORP (CANADA)
Reincorporated 12/12/2003
Place of incorporation changed from (AB) to (Canada) 12/12/2003
Name changed to Watertowne International Inc. 03/19/2004
Watertowne International Inc. recapitalized as Sightus Inc. 03/15/2006
(See Sightus Inc.)

TRUE RELIGION APPAREL INC (DE)
Reincorporated 08/19/2005
State of incorporation changed from (NV) to (DE) 08/19/2005
Acquired by TRLG Holdings, LLC 07/30/2013
Each share Common $0.00001 par exchanged for $32 cash

TRUE TASTE CORP. (TX)
Name changed to Magic Valley Frozen Foods, Inc. and Common $1 par changed to no par 02/15/1966
Magic Valley Frozen Foods, Inc. merged into Vahlsing, Inc. 10/31/1967
(See Vahlsing, Inc.)

TRUE TEMPER CORP. (OH)
Common no par changed to $20 par 00/00/1954
Common $20 par changed to $10 par and (1) additional share issued 08/20/1957
4.5% Preference $100 par called for redemption 07/15/1963
Common $10 par changed to $4 par and (1.5) additional shares issued 08/16/1965
Merged into Allegheny Ludlum Steel Corp. 07/31/1967
Each share Common $4 par exchanged for (0.5) share $3 Conv. Preferred $1 par
Allegheny Ludlum Steel Corp. name changed to Allegheny Ludlum Industries, Inc. 04/24/1970 which name changed to Allegheny International Inc. 04/29/1981
(See Allegheny International Inc.)

TRUE 2 BEAUTY INC (NV)
Each share old Common $0.001 par exchanged for (0.01) share new Common $0.001 par 01/13/2012
Name changed to LegacyXChange, Inc. 07/30/2015

TRUECONTEXT MOBILE SOLUTIONS CORP (ON)
Name changed to ProntoForms Corp. 06/19/2013

TRUECROSSING FDS (DE)
Name changed to NBP Truecrossing Funds 12/27/2000
(See NBP Truecrossing Funds)

TRUESDALE COAL CORP (DE)
Charter forfeited for failure to maintain a resident agent 08/01/1975

TRUESPORT ALLIANCES & ENTMT LTD (NV)
Recapitalized as ePunk, Inc. 07/05/2011
Each share Common $0.0001 par exchanged for (0.01) share Common $0.0001 par

TRUETIME INC (DE)
Merged into Symmetricon, Inc. 10/04/2002
Each share Common $0.001 par exchanged for (0.43697) share Common $0.0001 par and $0.84 cash
(See Symmetricom, Inc.)

TRUEVISION INC (CA)
Merged into Pinnacle Systems, Inc. 3/12/99
Each share Common no par exchanged for (0.0313) share Common no par
Pinnacle Systems, Inc. merged into Avid Technology, Inc. 8/9/2005

TRUEWEST CORP (NV)
Name changed to JD International Ltd. 12/05/2013

TRULAN RES INC (DE)
Recapitalized as Trinity Resources Inc. 09/18/2015
Each share Common $0.001 par exchanged for (0.00333333) share Common $0.001 par

TRULI MEDIA GROUP INC (OK)
Common $0.0001 par split (6) for (5) by issuance of (0.2) additional share payable 03/13/2013 to holders of record 02/25/2013 Ex date - 03/05/2013
Reorganized under the laws of Delaware 03/17/2015
Each share Common $0.0001 par exchanged for (0.02) share Common $0.0001 par

TRULIA INC (DE)
Merged into Zillow Group, Inc. 02/18/2015
Each share Common $0.00001 par exchanged for (0.444) share Class A Common $0.0001 par

TRUMARK RESOURCE CORP (BC)
Recapitalized as Tessa Ventures Ltd. 08/27/1991
Each share Common no par exchanged for (0.25) share Common no par
Tessa Ventures Ltd. recapitalized as International Tessa Capital Corp. 02/23/1993 which name changed to Apex Resorts Corp. 10/05/1993 which recapitalized as A.M.R. Corporate Group Ltd. 11/12/1996 which recapitalized as Consolidated A.M.R. Corporate Ltd. 12/03/1998 which recapitalized as Consolidated A.M.R. Development Corp. 10/17/2000 which recapitalized as West Hawk Development Corp. 01/09/2002

TRUMBULL FINL CORP (OH)
Merged into Second Bancorp Inc. 11/19/1998
Each share Common no par exchanged for (3.78) shares Common no par
Second Bancorp Inc. merged into Sky Financial Group, Inc. 07/02/2004 which merged into Huntington Bancshares Inc. 07/02/2007

TRUMBULL SVGS & LN CO (OH)
Under plan of reorganization each share Common no par automatically became (1) share Trumbull Financial Corp. Common no par 07/17/1997
Trumbull Financial Corp. merged into Second Bancorp Inc. 11/19/1998 which merged into Sky Financial Group, Inc. 07/02/2004 which merged into Huntington Bancshares Inc. 07/02/2007

TRUMBULL STEEL CO.
Merged into Republic Iron & Steel Co. 00/00/1928
Details not available

TRUMP ENTMT RESORTS INC (DE)
Plan of reorganization under Chapter 11 Federal Bankruptcy proceedings effective 07/16/2010
No stockholders' equity

TRUMP HOTELS & CASINO RESORTS INC (DE)
Issue Information - 10,000,000 shares COM offered at $14 per share on 06/07/1995
Reorganized as Trump Entertainment Resorts, Inc. 05/20/2005

FINANCIAL INFORMATION, INC.   TRU-TRU

Each share Common $0.001 par exchanged for first and final distribution of (0.001) share Common $0.001 par, (0.1106736) Class A Common Stock Purchase Warrant expiring 05/06/2006 and $0.88 cash
(See Trump Entertainment Resorts, Inc.)

TRUMP OIL CORP (NV)
Recapitalized as 20 / 20 Web Design Inc. 04/20/1999
Each share Common $0.001 par exchanged for (0.1) share Common $0.001 par
20 / 20 Web Design Inc. name changed to Bentleytel.com Inc. 04/16/2001 which name changed back to 20 / 20 Web Design Inc. 07/12/2001 which recapitalized as 20/20 Networks Inc. 02/14/2003 which name changed to Micro Bio-Medical Waste Systems, Inc. 01/02/2004 which name changed to Crown Equity Holdings Inc. 10/05/2006

TRUMP RESV MINERALS LTD (ON)
Recapitalized as TR Minerals Ltd. 1/7/93
Each share Common no par exchanged for (0.25) share Common no par
TR Minerals Ltd. recapitalized as Pangea Goldfields Inc. 1/11/94
(See Pangea Goldfields, Inc.)

TRUMPETER MINES LTD (BC)
Name changed to Loredi Resources Ltd. and Common $1 par changed to no par 09/28/1977
Loredi Resources Ltd. recapitalized as Marlin Developments Ltd. 01/15/1987 which name changed to Matrix Petroleum Inc. 12/13/2001 which was acquired by Berens Energy Ltd. 12/12/2003
(See Berens Energy Ltd.)

TRUMPETER YUKON GOLD INC (AB)
Merged into Tagish Lake Gold Corp. 12/01/2000
Each share Class A Subordinate no par exchanged for (0.1353) share Common no par
(See Tagish Lake Gold Corp.)

TRUNITY HLDGS INC (DE)
Recapitalized as True Nature Holding, Inc. 01/20/2016
Each share Common $0.0001 par exchanged for (0.00990099) share Common $0.0001 par

TRUNKBOW INTL HLDGS LTD (NV)
Acquired by Trunkbow Merger Group Ltd. 04/14/2014
Each share Common $0.001 par exchanged for $1.46 cash

TRUNKLINE GAS CO (DE)
5% Preferred Ser. A $100 par called for redemption 4/1/63
$5.60 Preferred Ser. B $100 par called for redemption 9/15/65
4.75% Preferred $100 par called for redemption 4/15/93
$5.15 Preferred Ser. C $100 par called for redemption 4/15/93
9.12% Preferred $100 par called for redemption 4/15/93

TRUNZ INC (NY)
Name changed 00/00/1941
Name changed from Trunz Pork Stores, Inc. to Trunz, Inc. 00/00/1941
Completely liquidated 03/31/1969
Each share Capital Stock no par exchanged for first and final distribution of (2.017) shares Horn & Hardart Co. (NY) Common no par
Horn & Hardart Co. (NY) reincorporated in Nevada 10/24/1980 which reincorporated in Delaware as Hanover Direct, Inc. 09/07/1993
(See Hanover Direct, Inc.)

TRUS JOIST CORP (DE)
Reincorporated 5/26/87
Common $1 par split (2) for (1) by issuance of (1) additional share 6/17/87
Stock Dividend - 100% 11/3/78
State of incorporation changed from (NV) to (DE) 5/26/87
Name changed to TJ International, Inc. 9/15/88
(See TJ International, Inc.)

TRUSCO SHARES, INC.
Dissolved in 1944

TRUSCON LABORATORIES, INC.
Acquired by Devoe & Raynolds Co., Inc. in 1945
Devoe & Raynolds Co., Inc. name changed to Revday Industries, Inc. 8/28/64 which completely liquidated 7/15/68

TRUSCON STEEL CO. (MI)
Dissolved 10/31/52

TRUSCON STEEL CO. OF CANADA LTD. (ON)
Acquired by Dominion Steel & Coal Corp., Ltd. in April 1958
Dominion Steel & Coal Corp., Ltd. acquired for cash by Sidbec 8/22/69

TR 3 INDS INC (NV)
Name changed to Diversified American Industries Inc. 06/14/1990
Diversified American Industries Inc. name changed to Thunderstone Group Inc. 11/13/1995 which name changed to Cronus Corp. 03/04/1996
(See Cronus Corp.)

TRUST AMER SVC CORP (FL)
Common 1¢ par split (3) for (2) by issuance of (0.5) additional share 9/25/87
Merged into Financial Resources Group Inc. 6/30/97
Each share Common 1¢ par exchanged for $1 cash

TRUST BK (MONTEREY PARK, CA)
Name changed 06/00/1999
Name changed from Trust Savings Bank F.S.B. (Monterey Park, CA) to Trust Bank (Monterey Park, CA) 06/00/1999
Acquired by East West Bancorp, Inc. 08/06/2004
Details not available

TRUST CTFS 2001-3 BEAR STEARNS DEPOSITOR (DE)
7.125% Trust Certificates Class A-1 called for redemption at $25 on 02/15/2007

TRUST CTFS 2001-4 BEAR STEARNS DEPOSITOR (DE)
7% Trust Certificates Class A-1 called for redemption at $25 on 02/15/2007

TRUST CO. OF GEORGIA (ATLANTA, GA)
Each share Capital Stock $100 par exchanged for (10) shares Capital Stock $10 par 8/23/58
Capital Stock $10 par changed to $5 par and (1) additional share issued 10/18/68
Stock Dividends - 100% 2/18/53; 22.2% 2/1/61; 100% 3/26/64; 100% 5/30/73
Under plan of merger each share Capital Stock $5 par automatically became (1) share Trust Co. of Georgia Common $5 par 11/12/74
Trust Co. of Georgia merged into SunTrust Banks, Inc. 7/1/85

TRUST CO. OF LARCHMONT (LARCHMONT, NY)
Merged into Bank of Westchester (Yonkers, NY) 12/20/1941
Each share Common $10 par exchanged for (1.428571) shares Common $10 par
Bank of Westchester (Yonkers, NY) merged into County Trust Co. (White Plains, NY) 07/30/1947 which merged into Bank of New York Co., Inc. 05/29/1969 which merged into Bank of New York Mellon Corp. 07/01/2007

TRUST CO. OF MORRIS COUNTY (MORRISTOWN, NJ)
Capital Stock $20 par changed to $10 par and (1) additional share issued plus a 10% stock dividend paid 10/16/64
Name changed to Trust Co. National Bank (Morristown, N.J.) 1/27/67
Trust Co. National Bank (Morristown, N.J.) merged into American National Bank & Trust (Montclair, N.J.) 7/10/70 which reorganized as Princeton American Bancorp. 1/1/72 which name changed to Horizon Bancorp 12/31/73
(See Horizon Bancorp)

TRUST CO AUSTRALIA LTD (AUSTRALIA)
ADR agreement terminated 09/11/2006
Details not available

TRUST CO GA (ATLANTA, GA)
Common $5 par split (3) for (2) by issuance of (0.5) additional share 1/30/84
Stock Dividends - 100% 1/12/81; 50% 1/14/83
Merged into SunTrust Banks, Inc. 7/1/85
Each share Common $5 par exchanged for (1) share Common $1 par

TRUST CO GA BK SAVANNAH N A (SAVANNAH, GA)
Stock Dividend - 50% 3/18/77
Merged into Trust Co. of Georgia 8/17/78
Each share Capital Stock $10 par exchanged for (1.1926) shares Common $5 par
Trust Co. of Georgia merged into SunTrust Banks, Inc. 7/1/85

TRUST CO N J NEW (JERSEY CITY, NJ)
Merged into North Fork Bancorporation, Inc. 05/17/2004
Each share Common $2 par exchanged for (1) share Common $0.001 par
North Fork Bancorporation, Inc. merged into Capital One Financial Corp. 12/01/2006

TRUST CO N J OLD (JERSEY CITY, NJ)
Each share Common $100 par exchanged for (4) shares Common $25 par 12/19/27
Common $25 par changed to $12.50 par 6/7/34
Common $12.50 par changed to $5 par 12/30/35
Common $5 par changed to $2.50 par 4/22/39
Common $2.50 par changed to $7.25 par 3/22/77
Under plan of reorganization each share Common $7.25 par automatically became (1) share TrustCompany Bancorporation Common $7.25 par 11/1/85
TrustCompany Bancorporation name changed to Trust Co. of New Jersey (New) (Jersey City, NJ) 12/28/93 which merged into North Fork Bancorporation, Inc. 5/17/2004 which merged into Capital One Financial Corp. 12/1/2006

TRUST CO NATL BK (MORRISTOWN, NJ)
Common $10 par changed to $4 par and (2) additional shares issued 09/17/1969
Merged into American National Bank & Trust (Montclair, NJ) 07/10/1970
Each share Common $4 par exchanged for (1) share Common $4 par
American National Bank & Trust (Montclair, NJ) reorganized as Princeton American Bancorp 01/01/1972 which name changed to Horizon Bancorp 12/31/1973
(See Horizon Bancorp)

TRUST CO OCEAN CNTY (LAKEWOOD, NJ)
Merged into First National State Bancorporation 11/10/1972
Each share Common $10 par exchanged for (1.55) shares Common $6.25 par
First National State Bancorporation name changed to First Fidelity Bancorporation (Old) 05/01/1985 which merged into First Fidelity Bancorporation (New) 02/29/1988 which merged into First Union Corp. 01/01/1996 which name changed to Wachovia Corp. (Ctfs. dated after 09/01/2001) 09/01/2001 which merged into Wells Fargo & Co. (New) 12/31/2008

TRUST ENDOWMENT SHARES
Trust terminated in 1947
Details not available

TRUST FOR CASH RESVS (MA)
Trust terminated 01/24/1989
Details not available

TRUST FOR EQUITABLE INTERESTS IN ANHEUSER-BUSCH, INC. SHARES
Trust terminated 00/00/1946
Details not available

TRUST FOR FED SECS (PA)
Name changed 03/02/1987
Name changed from Trust For Short-Term Federal Securities to Trust For Federal Securities 03/02/1987
Under plan of reorganization each FedFund Fund Class Share of Bene. Int., FedFund Dollar Share of Bene. Int., Federal Fund Class Share of Bene. Int., Federal Fund Dollar Share of Bene. Int., T-Fund Fund Class Share of Bene. Int., T-Fund Dollar Share of Bene. Int., and Treasury Trust Fund Share of Bene. Int. automatically became Provident Institutional Funds FedFund Shares of Bene. Int., FedFund Dollar Shares of Bene. Int., Federal Trust Fund Shares of Bene. Int., Federal Trust Dollar Shares of Bene. Int., T-Fund Shares of Bene. Int., T-Fund Dollar Shares of Bene. Int., or Treasury Trust Fund Shares of Bene. Int. on a net asset value basis respectively 02/10/1999
Provident Institutional Funds name changed to BlackRock Provident Institutional Funds 01/29/2001 which name changed to BlackRock Liquidity Funds 11/19/2003

TRUST FOR SHORT TERM U S GOVT SECS (MA)
Merged into Money Market Obligations Trust 04/26/1999
Details not available

TR INC (UT)
Proclaimed dissolved for failure to file annual report 02/01/1992

TRUST LICENSING INC (DE)
Name changed to Connected Media Technologies, Inc. 05/23/2005

TR MINERALS LTD (ON)
Recapitalized as Pangea Goldfields Inc. 01/11/1994
Each share Common no par exchanged for (0.22222222) share Common no par
(See Pangea Goldfields Inc.)

TRUST SHARES OF AMERICA
Trust terminated 00/00/1940
Details not available

COPYRIGHTED MATERIAL   NO UNAUTHORIZED REPRODUCTION

TRUST SHARES STANDARD OILSTOCKS
Trust terminated 00/00/1949
Details not available

TRUSTBANK FED SVGS BK (TYSONS CORNER, VA)
Reorganized 01/29/1991
Name and location changed from Trustbank Savings, F.S.B. (McLean, VA) to Trustbank Federal Savings Bank (Tysons Corner, VA) 01/29/1991
Bank failed 03/21/1992
No stockholders' equity

TRUSTCO GEN CDA INC (QC)
Common no par split (2) for (1) by issuance of (1) additional share 06/18/1987
Name changed to Genecan Financial Corp. 01/14/1994
(See Genecan Financial Corp.)

TRUSTCOMPANY BANCORPORATION (NJ)
Common $7.25 par split (2) for (1) by issuance of (1) additional share 08/06/1990
Name changed to Trust Co. of New Jersey (New) (Jersey City, NJ) 12/28/1993
Trust Co. of New Jersey (New) (Jersey City, NJ) merged into North Fork Bancorporation, Inc. 05/17/2004 which merged into Capital One Financial Corp. 12/01/2006

TRUSTCOR INTERNATIONAL BOND FUND (LUXEMBOURG)
Name changed to RoyWest U.S. Dollar Income Fund 07/31/1986
RoyWest U.S. Dollar Income Fund name changed to TrustCor U.S. Dollar Income Fund 09/14/1988

TRUSTCOR INTERNATIONAL FUND (BAHAMAS)
Completely liquidated 01/09/1986
Each Unit no par exchanged for first and final distribution of $11.30 cash

TRUSTCORP INC (DE)
$2.90 Conv. Preferred Ser. A no par called for redemption 10/24/1988
Stock Dividend - 25% 12/19/1986
Acquired by Society Corp. 01/05/1990
Each share Common $20 par exchanged for (0.75) share Common $1 par
Society Corp. merged into KeyCorp (New) 03/01/1994

TRUSTED INFORMATION SYS INC (DE)
Merged into Network Associates, Inc. 04/28/1998
Each share Common 1¢ par exchanged for (0.323) share Common 1¢ par
Network Associates, Inc. name changed to McAfee, Inc. 06/30/2004
(See McAfee, Inc.)

TRUSTEE STANDARD INVESTMENT SHARES SERIES C & D
Trusts terminated 00/00/1949
Details not available

TRUSTEE STANDARD OILSHARES SERIES A
Trust terminated 00/00/1948
Details not available

TRUSTEE STANDARD OILSHARES SERIES B
Trust terminated 00/00/1947
Details not available

TRUSTEE STANDARD UTILITY SHARES
Liquidated 00/00/1937
Details not available

TRUSTEED AMERICAN BANK SHARES, SERIES A
Trust agreement terminated 00/00/1941
Details not available

TRUSTEED AMERICAN BANK SHARES, SERIES B
Trust agreement terminated 00/00/1943
Details not available

TRUSTEED DIVERSIFIED ROYALTY TRUST
Liquidated 00/00/1953
Details not available

TRUSTEED INDUSTRY SHARES
Name changed to Aberdeen Fund 00/00/1951
Aberdeen Fund merged into Steadman Investment Fund, Inc. (New) 01/25/1973 which name changed to Ameritor Investment Fund 09/23/1998
(See Ameritor Investment Fund)

TRUSTEED NEW YORK BANK SHARES
Trust terminated 00/00/1948
Details not available

TRUSTEED NEW YORK CITY BANK STOCKS
Trust terminated 00/00/1933
Details not available

TRUSTEED OIL PROPERTIES
Trust terminated 07/22/1955
Details not available

TRUSTEED PROPERTIES
Liquidated 00/00/1953
Details not available

TRUSTEES EQUITY FD INC (MD)
Acquired by Windsor Fund, Inc. (MD) 09/29/1978
Each share Capital Stock $1 par exchanged for (0.91169) share Capital Stock $1 par
Windsor Fund, Inc. (MD) reincorporated in Pennsylvania 01/02/1985 which reincorporated in Maryland as Windsor Funds, Inc. 12/30/1985 which name changed to Vanguard/Windsor Funds, Inc. (MD) 04/30/1993 which reincorporated in Delaware as Vanguard Windsor Funds 05/29/1998

TRUSTEES SYSTEM DISCOUNT CO., OF CHICAGO
Reorganized as Trustee System Discount Corp. of Chicago 00/00/1936
Each share Preferred exchanged for (1) share Class B no par
No other stockholders' equity
Trustees System Discount Corp. of Chicago name changed to Associated Plastic Companies, Inc. 00/00/1949 which reorganized as Commercial Plastics Co. 10/03/1955

TRUSTEES SYSTEM DISCOUNT CORP. OF CHICAGO
Name changed to Associated Plastic Companies, Inc. 00/00/1949
Associated Plastic Companies, Inc. reorganized as Commercial Plastics Co. 10/03/1955

TRUSTEES SYSTEM SERVICE CORP.
Bankrupt 00/00/1937
Stockholders' equity unlikely

TRUSTEES' COMMINGLED EQUITY FUND, INC. (MD)
Reincorporated under the laws of Pennsylvania as Trustees' Commingled Fund and Common 10¢ par reclassified as U.S. Portfolio Shares of Bene. Int. no par 11/12/84

TRUSTMARK AUTO GROUP INC (BC)
Recapitalized as Keymark Resources Inc. 06/28/2011
Each share Common no par exchanged for (0.1) share Common no par
Keymark Resources Inc. name changed to Alabama Graphite Corp. 08/31/2012 which merged into Westwater Resources, Inc. 04/23/2018

TRUSTREET PPTYS INC (MD)
Merged into GE Capital Solutions 2/26/2007
Each share $1.93 Preferred Ser. A $0.001 par exchanged for $25 cash
Each share Common $0.001 par exchanged for $17.05 cash

TRUVEL CORP (CA)
Plan of reorganization under Chapter 11 Federal Bankruptcy proceedings confirmed 09/04/1990
No stockholders' equity

TRVLSYS INC (NV)
Reincorporated 09/00/1994
State of incorporation changed from (NM) to (NV) 09/00/1994
Name changed to Triden Telecom, Inc. 11/23/1994
Triden Telecom, Inc. name changed to Permanent Technologies, Inc. 12/07/2007

TRW AUTOMOTIVE HLDGS CORP (DE)
Acquired by ZF Friedrichshafen AG 05/15/2015
Each share Common 1¢ par exchanged for $105.60 cash

TRW INC (OH)
Common $2.50 par changed to $1.25 par and (1) additional share issued 05/27/1968
4% Preferred $100 par called for redemption 06/15/1979
$4.25 Conv. Preference Ser. A no par called for redemption 06/15/1979
$5 Conv. Preference Ser. B no par called for redemption 06/15/1979
Common $1.25 par changed to $0.625 par and (1) additional share issued 06/01/1987
Preferred Stock Purchase Rights declared for Common stockholders of record 01/02/1986 were redeemed at $0.01 per right 06/15/1996 for holders of record 05/17/1996
$4.40 Conv. Preference Ser. 1 no par called for redemption at $104 plus $1.10 accrued dividend on 08/30/2002
$4.50 Conv. Preference Ser. 3 no par called for redemption at $100 plus $1.125 accrued dividend 08/30/2002
Common $0.625 par split (2) for (1) by issuance of (1) additional share payable 12/09/1996 to holders of record 11/08/1996 Ex date - 12/10/1996
Merged into Northrop Grumman Corp. 12/11/2002
Each share Common $0.625 par exchanged for (0.5357) share Common $1 par

TRX INC (GA)
Acquired by Concur Technologies, Inc. 07/16/2013
Each share Common 1¢ par exchanged for $2.285913 cash
Note: Each share Common 1¢ par received an initial additional distribution of $0.128759 cash 02/05/2014
Each share Common 1¢ par received a second additional distribution of $0.150338 cash 03/25/2015
Each share Common 1¢ par received a third additional distribution of $0.024505 cash 07/27/2015

TRYALAX MANUFACTURING CO. (DE)
Charter cancelled and declared void for non-payment of taxes 04/01/1930

TRYGON ELECTRS INC (NY)
Merged into Excaliber Enterprises, Inc. 04/30/1971
Each share Common 25¢ par exchanged for $0.80 cash

TRYGVESTA AS (DENMARK)
Name changed to Tryg A/S 03/19/2012

TRYLON CHEMS INC (PA)
Common no par split (3) for (1) by issuance of (2) additional shares 02/27/1963
Common no par split (2) for (1) by issuance of (1) additional share 11/10/1966
Common no par split (2) for (1) by issuance of (1) additional share 12/02/1968
Completely liquidated 05/25/1970
Each share Common no par exchanged for first and final distribution of (1.1) shares Emery Industries, Inc. Common no par
Emery Industries, Inc. merged into National Distillers & Chemical Corp. 05/19/1978 which name changed to Quantum Chemical Corp. 01/04/1988 which merged into Hanson PLC (Old) 10/01/1993 which reorganized as Hanson PLC (New) 10/15/2003
(See Hanson PLC (New))

TRYLOX ENVIRONMENTAL CORP (WY)
Reincorporated 09/14/1990
Place of incorporation changed from (BC) to (WY) 09/14/1990
Charter revoked for failure to pay taxes 03/15/1994

TRYX VENTURES CORP (BC)
Reorganized as MGN Technologies, Inc. 12/06/2005
Each share Common no par exchanged for (5.5) shares Common no par
(See MGN Technologies, Inc.)

TS ELEC INC (DE)
Name changed to China Pharma Holdings, Inc. (DE) 05/04/2006
China Pharma Holdings, Inc. (DE) reincorporated in Nevada 12/27/2012

TS INDS INC (NV)
Common 2¢ par split (3) for (2) by issuance of (0.5) additional share 04/13/1987
Plan of reorganization under Chapter 11 Federal Bankruptcy proceedings confirmed 10/18/1991
No stockholders' equity

TS&B HLDGS INC (UT)
Each share old Common $0.001 par exchanged for (0.025) share new Common $0.001 par 08/16/2004
Recapitalized as CALI Holdings Inc. 04/08/2008
Each share new Common $0.001 par exchanged for (0.01) share Common $0.001 par
CALI Holdings Inc. name changed to Sovereign Exploration Associates International, Inc. 10/27/2005

TS&W / CLAYMORE TAX ADVANTAGED BALANCED FD (DE)
Auction Market Preferred Ser. M7 1¢ par called for redemption at $25,000 on 01/10/2012
Auction Market Preferred Ser. T28 1¢ par called for redemption at $25,000 on 01/11/2012
(Additional Information in Active)

TSA EXPLS LTD (BC)
Name changed to Boron Chemicals International Ltd. 07/06/1992
Boron Chemicals International Ltd. name changed to Atacama Minerals Corp. 08/08/1997 which name changed to Sirocco Mining Inc. 01/30/2012 which merged into RB Energy Inc. 02/05/2014

TSB BKG GROUP PLC (UNITED KINGDOM)
ADR agreement terminated 09/28/2015
Each ADR for Ordinary exchanged for $10.38936 cash

TSB FINL CORP (NC)
Stock Dividend - 10% payable

05/15/2007 to holders of record 04/15/2007 Ex date - 05/22/2007
Merged into SCBT Financial Corp. 11/30/2007
Each share Common 1¢ par exchanged for (0.993) share Common $2.50 par
SCBT Financial Corp. name changed to First Financial Holdings, Inc. 07/30/2013 which name changed to South State Corp. 06/30/2014

TSB INTL INC (CANADA)
Each share Common no par received distribution of (1) share Contour Telecom Management Services Inc. Common no par payable 07/16/1996 to holders of record 07/15/1996
Name changed to Telco Research Corp. 10/20/1999
Telco Research Corp. merged into Peregrine Systems, Inc. 03/30/2000
(See Peregrine Systems, Inc.)

TSC CORP (MA)
Liquidation completed
Each share Common $1 par received initial distribution of $2.10 cash 10/14/1985
Each share Common $1 par received second and final distribution of $0.47 cash 09/15/1986
Note: Certificates were not required to be surrendered and are without value

TSC INC (OH)
Acquired by Westinghouse Electric Corp. 08/16/1985
Each share Common no par exchanged for $12.875 cash
Note: An additional $0.625 cash per share was placed in escrow for possible future distribution

TSC INDS INC (DE)
Acquired by National Industries, Inc. (KY) 12/06/1969
Each share 70¢ Conv. Preferred Ser. 1 $1 par exchanged for (0.6) share $1.25 Conv. Preferred Ser. B $1 par and (1) Common Stock Purchase Warrant
Each share Common $1 par exchanged for (0.5) share $1.25 Conv. Preferred Ser. B $1 par and (1.5) Common Stock Purchase Warrants
National Industries, Inc. (KY) merged into Fuqua Industries, Inc. 01/03/1978 which name changed to Actava Group Inc. 07/21/1993 which name changed to Metromedia International Group, Inc. 11/01/1995
(See Metromedia International Group, Inc.)

TSC SHANNOCK CORP (CANADA)
Acquired by Video One Canada Ltd. 11/04/1998
Each share Class A Common no par exchanged for $1.10 cash

TSENG LABS INC (UT)
Merged into Cell Pathways, Inc. (New) 11/04/1998
Each share Common no par exchanged for (0.3631326) share Common 1¢ par
Cell Pathways, Inc. (New) merged into OSI Pharmaceuticals, Inc. 06/12/2003
(See OSI Pharmaceuticals, Inc.)

TSET INC (NV)
Name changed to Kronos Advanced Technologies Inc. 01/18/2002
(See Kronos Advanced Technologies Inc.)

TSI CAP CORP (NV)
Name changed to Chasseur Holdings, Inc. 06/15/2000

TSI CORP (DE)
Acquired by Genzyme Transgenics Corp. 09/30/1994
Each share Common 2¢ par exchanged for (0.2) share Common 1¢ par
Genzyme Transgenics Corp. name changed to GTC Biotherapeutics, Inc. 06/03/2002
(See GTC Biotherapeutics, Inc.)

TSI HANDLING INC (NV)
Name changed to Dyna-Cam Engine Corp. 03/31/2000
Dyna-Cam Engine Corp. recapitalized as Chiste Corp. 05/14/2004 which recapitalized as HydroGen Corp. 08/19/2005
(See HydroGen Corp.)

TSI INC (KY)
Merged into American Consolidated Corp. 02/28/1977
Each share Common $2 par exchanged for (0.16666666) share Common no par
American Consolidated Corp. merged into I.C.H. Corp. 04/18/1985 which name changed to Southwestern Life Corp. (New) 06/15/1994 which name changed to I.C.H. Corp. (New) 10/10/1995
(See I.C.H. Corp. (New))

TSI INC (MN)
Merged into JJF Group, Inc. 05/04/2000
Each share Common 10¢ par exchanged for $15.25 cash

TSI INC (MT)
Involuntarily dissolved 12/04/2006

TSI INTL SOFTWARE LTD (DE)
Common 1¢ par split (2) for (1) by issuance of (1) additional share payable 04/01/1999 to holders of record 03/15/1999
Name changed to Mercator Software Inc. 04/03/2000
(See Mercator Software Inc.)

TSI LASER INC (NV)
Each share old Common $0.001 par exchanged for (0.25) share new Common $0.001 par 08/24/2005
Note: Holders of between (100) and (399) shares will receive (100) shares
Holders of (99) or fewer shares were not affected by the reverse split
Name changed to TSI Emery Inc. 04/27/2009

TSI TELSYS CORP (DE)
Reincorporated 04/01/1996
Reincorporated 10/20/2003
Class A Subordinate no par reclassified as Common no par 03/22/1996
Place of incorporation changed from (BC) to (NB) 04/01/1996
Each share old Common no par exchanged for (0.2) share new Common no par 08/31/1998
Place of incorporation changed from (NB) to (DE) and Common no par changed to 1¢ par 10/20/2003
Ceased operations 00/00/2006
Attorney opined no stockholders' equity

TSIC INC (DE)
Chapter 11 bankruptcy proceedings terminated 01/11/2013
Stockholders' equity unlikely

TSINGYUAN BREWERY LTD (DE)
SEC revoked common stock registration 10/17/2013

TSL HLDGS INC (DE)
Charter cancelled and declared inoperative and void for non-payment of taxes 03/01/1994

TSL INC (CO)
Each share Common $0.000333 par exchanged for (0.06666666) share Common $0.005 par 12/03/1991
Name changed to Optical Security Group, Inc. 12/15/1994
(See Optical Security Group, Inc.)

TSN LIQUIDATING, INC. (TX)
Liquidation completed
Each share Common no par stamped to indicate initial distribution of $3.80 cash 01/12/1973
Each share Stamped Common no par exchanged for second distribution of $0.039674 cash 07/31/1975
Each share Stamped Common no par received third distribution of $0.147628 cash 08/26/1977
Each share Stamped Common no par received fourth distribution of $0.137803957 cash 09/07/1979
Each share Stamped Common no par received fifth and final distribution of $1.380530 cash 02/02/1982

TSO FINL CORP (DE)
Name changed to Advanta Corp. 01/28/1988
(See Advanta Corp.)

TSS LTD (DE)
Each share old Common $0.00297 par exchanged for (0.1) share new Common $0.00297 par 02/24/1993
Charter cancelled and declared inoperative and void for non-payment of taxes 03/01/1995

TST COMMUNICATIONS INC (DE)
Charter cancelled and declared inoperative and void for non-payment of taxes 04/15/1973

TST/IMPRESO INC (DE)
Under plan of reorganization each share Common 1¢ par automatically became (1) share Impreso.com, Inc. Common 1¢ par 03/08/2000
Impreso.com, Inc. name changed to Impreso, Inc. 04/18/2001

TST INDS INC (DE)
Merged into Elgin National Industries, Inc. 02/28/1969
Each share Common 10¢ par exchanged for (0.4) share Common $5 par
(See Elgin National Industries, Inc.)

TSUBAKI NAKASHIMA CO LTD (JAPAN)
Name changed 04/01/1996
Name changed from Tsubakimoto Precision Products Co. Ltd. to Tsubaki Nakashima Co. Ltd. 04/01/1996
Acquired by Nomura Holdings, Inc. 02/22/2007
Details not available

TSV CORP (DE)
Charter cancelled and declared inoperative and void for non-payment of taxes 03/01/1989

TSX CORP (NV)
Common 1¢ par split (2) for (1) by issuance of (1) additional share 11/04/1994
Common 1¢ par split (3) for (2) by issuance of (0.5) additional share payable 07/18/1996 to holders of record 06/28/1996
Merged into ANTEC Corp. 02/07/1997
Each share Common 1¢ par exchanged for (1) share Common 1¢ par
ANTEC Corp. name changed to Arris Group, Inc. (Old) 08/03/2001 which reorganized as ARRIS Group, Inc. (New) 04/16/2013 which merged into ARRIS International PLC 01/05/2016

TSX GROUP INC (ON)
Issue Information - 18,978,238 shares COM offered at $18 per share on 11/05/2002
Common no par split (2) for (1) by issuance of (1) additional share payable 05/20/2005 to holders of record 05/17/2005 Ex date - 05/13/2005
Name changed to TMX Group Inc. 06/18/2008

TMX Group Inc. merged into TMX Group Ltd. 09/14/2012

TT & T REALTY EQUITIES, INC. (DE)
Charter cancelled and declared inoperative and void for non-payment of taxes 03/01/1986

TT&T PUB CO LTD (THAILAND)
GDR agreement terminated 03/31/2016
Each 144A GDR for Ordinary exchanged for (3) shares Ordinary
Note: Unexchanged GDR's will be sold and the proceeds, if any, held for claim after 04/03/2017

TTC TECHNOLOGY CORP (BC)
SEC revoked common stock registration 03/12/2012

TTC/TRUCK TECH CORP (BC)
Name changed to Unicomm Signal Inc. 04/13/1994
Unicomm Signal Inc. recapitalized as SmarTire Systems Inc. (BC) 12/24/1997 which reincorporated in Yukon 02/06/2003 which reincorporated back under the laws of British Columbia 12/20/2006 which name changed to TTC Technology Corp. 04/14/2010
(See TTC Technology Corp.)

TTCM CHINA INC (DE)
Each share old Common $0.000009 par exchanged for (0.001) share new Common $0.000009 par 09/27/2011
Reincorporated under the laws of Delaware as VaporBrands International, Inc. and New Common $0.000009 par changed to $0.001 par 10/19/2012

TTE PETE LTD (AUSTRALIA)
ADR agreement terminated 08/08/2016
Each Sponsored ADR for Ordinary exchanged for $0.672854 cash

TTI HLDGS AMER CORP (DE)
Each share Common $0.0001 par received distribution of (1/3) share Panama Industries, Ltd. Common $0.001 par payable 07/02/2001 to holders of record 06/22/2001
Recapitalized as Steam Cleaning USA, Inc. 09/03/2002
Each share Common $0.0001 par exchanged for (0.2) share Common $0.0001 par
Steam Cleaning USA, Inc. recapitalized as Humana Trans Services Holding Corp. 08/11/2003 which name changed to Accountabilities, Inc. 12/06/2005 which name changed to Corporate Resource Services, Inc. 04/21/2010

TTI INDS INC (NY)
Merged into Peoples Telephone Co., Inc. 07/00/1987
Each share Common 1¢ par exchanged for (0.1) share Common 1¢ par
Peoples Telephone Co., Inc. merged into Davel Communications, Inc. 12/23/1998
(See Davel Communications, Inc.)

TTI INDS INC (TX)
Chapter 7 bankruptcy proceedings terminated 04/16/2004
No stockholders' equity

TTI TEAM TELECOM INTERNATIONAL LTD (ISRAEL)
Acquired by TEOCO Corp. 08/23/2010
Each share Ordinary ILS 0.5 par exchanged for $3 cash

TTI TELEPHONE TECHNOLOGIES INC (BC)
Struck off register and declared dissolved for failure to file returns 8/13/93

TTM TECHNOLOGIES INC (WA)
Reincorporated under the laws of

Delaware and Common no par changed to $0.001 par 08/29/2005

TTR TECHNOLOGIES INC (DE)
Name changed 01/30/1999
Name changed from TTR Inc. to TTR Technologies, Corp. 01/30/1999
Name changed to Amedia Networks, Inc. 05/26/2004
(See Amedia Networks, Inc.)

TTTICKETS HLDG CORP (DE)
Name changed to Shelron Group, Inc. 12/04/2002

T2 MED INC (DE)
Common 1¢ par split (2) for (1) by issuance of (1) additional share 8/30/91
Merged into Coram Healthcare Corp. 7/8/94
Each share Common 1¢ par exchanged for (0.63) share Common $0.001 par
(See Coram Healthcare Corp.)

TU ELEC CAP I (DE)
Name changed to TXU Electric Capital I 6/14/99
(See TXU Electric Capital I)

TU ELEC CAP II (DE)
9% Trust Originated Preferred Securities called for redemption at $25 on 1/1/98

TU INTL INC (UT)
Each share Common 5¢ par exchanged for (0.5) share Common 10¢ par 10/10/1983
Filed a petition under Chapter 11 Federal Bankruptcy Code 09/05/1985
Stockholders' equity unlikely

TU TAHL PETRO INC (BC)
Name changed to Creator Capital Inc. (BC) 5/10/90
Creator Capital Inc. (BC) reincorporated in Bermuda as SkyGames International Ltd. 1/26/95 which name changed to Interactive Entertainment Ltd. 5/13/97 which name changed to Creator Capital Ltd. 5/16/200

TUALATIN VALLEY BANK (HILLSBORO, OR)
Acquired by United Savings Bank (Salem, OR) 04/16/1988
Details not available

TUBAC HLDGS INC (WY)
Common $0.0001 par split (10) for (1) by issuance of (9) additional shares payable 09/10/2004 to holders of record 09/07/2004 Ex date - 09/13/2004
Reorganized under the laws of Nevada as China Vitup Health Care Holdings, Inc. 10/13/2006
Each share Common $0.0001 par exchanged for (0.005) share Common $0.0001 par
China Vitup Health Care Holdings, Inc. recapitalized as Emergency Pest Services, Inc. 05/28/2015

TUBBYS INC (NJ)
Merged into R Corp. 5/23/2000
Each share Common $0.001 par exchanged for $1.10 cash

TUBBYS SUB SHOPS INC (MI)
Merged into Tubby's Inc. 4/2/90
Each share Common $0.001 par exchanged for (1) share Common $0.001 par
(See Tubby's Inc.)

TUBE INVTS LTD (ENGLAND)
Name changed to TI Group PLC 05/24/1982
(See TI Group PLC)

TUBE MEDIA CORP (DE)
SEC revoked common stock registration 07/06/2011

TUBE REDUCING CORP. (DE)
Common no par changed to $5 par in 1941
Each share Common $5 par exchanged for (5) shares Common $1 par in 1947
Merged into American Metal Products Co. (Mich.) in 1954
Each share Common $1 par exchanged for (63/250) share 5-1/2% Preferred $20 par
(See American Metal Products Co. (Mich.))

TUBEAROO INC (FL)
Recapitalized as Emerging World Pharma, Inc. 11/24/2009
Each share Common no par exchanged for (0.04) share Common no par

TUBEMOGUL INC (DE)
Acquired by Adobe Systems Inc. 12/19/2016
Each share Common $0.001 par exchanged for $14 cash

TUBIZE ARTIFICIAL SILK CO. OF AMERICA
Merged into Tubize Chatillon Corp. 00/00/1930
Details not available

TUBIZE CHATILLON CORP.
Recapitalized as Tubize Rayon Corp. 12/12/1943
Each share Class A exchanged for (4) shares Common $1 par
Each share Common exchanged for (0.5) share Common $1 par
Tubize Rayon Corp. merged into Celanese Corp. of America 02/07/1946 which name changed to Celanese Corp. 04/13/1966
(See Celanese Corp.)

TUBIZE RAYON CORP.
7% Preferred $100 par called for redemption 04/01/1944
Merged into Celanese Corp. of America 02/07/1946
Each share 4-3/4% Preferred $100 par exchanged for (1) share $4.75 Preferred no par
Each share Common $1 par exchanged for (0.66666666) share Common no par
Celanese Corp. of America name changed to Celanese Corp. 04/13/1966
(See Celanese Corp.)

TUBOS DE ACERO DE MEXICO S A (MEXICO)
Each ADR for (1) share Bearer Ser. A $50 par or Ser. B P$50 par exchanged for (1.09) ADR's for Common P50 par 6/26/67
ADR's for Common P50 par split (7) for (5) by issuance of (0.4) additional share 8/7/81
Each (20) ADR's for Common P50 par exchanged for (6) ADR's for Common P1000 par 9/21/83
ADR's for Common P1000 par changed to no par 7/10/84
Stock Dividends - 300% 9/17/79; 25% 9/22/80
Acquired by Tenaris S.A. 9/12/2003
Each ADR for Ordinary no par exchanged for (0.528988) Sponsored ADR's for Ordinary

TUBOSCOPE CO. (DE)
Common $2 par split (5) for (4) by issuance of (0.25) additional share 10/24/62
Acquired by American Machine & Foundry Co. 10/8/63
Each share Common $2 par exchanged for (0.9) share Common $1.75 par
American Machine & Foundry Co. name changed to AMF Inc. 4/30/70
(See AMF Inc.)

TUBOSCOPE CORP (DE)
Name changed to Tuboscope Vetco International Corp. 5/15/92
Tuboscope Vetco International Corp. name changed to Tuboscope Inc.
5/19/97 which name changed to Varco International, Inc. 5/31/2000

TUBOSCOPE INC (DE)
Name changed 5/19/97
Name changed from Tuboscope Vetco International Corp. to Tuboscope Inc. 5/19/97
Under plan of merger name changed to Varco International, Inc. (DE) 5/31/2000
Varco International, Inc. (DE) merged into National Oilwell Varco, Inc. 3/11/2005

TUC METALS MINES LTD. (ON)
Charter cancelled for failure to pay taxes and file returns 12/2/59

TUCAN VENTURES INC (BC)
Name changed to Sandhurst Resource Ltd. 10/15/1996
(See Sandhurst Resource Ltd.)

TUCANA LITHIUM CORP (NV)
Recapitalized as Rimrock Gold Corp. 02/08/2013
Each share Common $0.001 par exchanged for (0.125) share Common $0.001 par

TUCKAHOE FINL CORP (ON)
Name changed to Merchant Private Ltd. 10/6/92
Merchant Private Ltd. name changed to Connor Clark Ltd. 5/26/97
(See Connor Clark Ltd.)

TUCKAHOE GOLD MINES, LTD. (ON)
Charter cancelled for failure to file reports and pay taxes 2/1/58

TUCKAMORE CAP MGMT INC (ON)
Name changed to ClearStream Energy Services Inc. 10/18/2016

TUCKER ANTHONY GROUP TAX EXEMPT FDS (MA)
Name changed to Freedom Group of Tax Exempt Funds 05/31/1993
(See Freedom Group of Tax Exempt Funds)

TUCKER ANTHONY SUTRO (DE)
Merged into Royal Bank of Canada (Montreal, QUE) 10/31/2001
Each share Common 1¢ par exchanged for $24 cash

TUCKER CORP. (DE)
Charter cancelled and declared inoperative and void for non-payment of taxes 4/1/51

TUCKER DRILLING INC (DE)
Stock Dividend - 25% 4/10/81
Merged into Patterson Energy Inc. 7/30/96
Each share Common 1¢ par exchanged for (0.74) share Common 1¢ par

TUCKER HLDG INC (FL)
Proclaimed dissolved for failure to file reports and pay fees 10/20/92

TUCKER PPTYS CORP (MD)
Merged into Bradley Real Estate, Inc. 03/15/1996
Each share Common $0.001 par exchanged for (0.686) share Common 1¢ par
(See Bradley Real Estate, Inc.)

TUCKER STEEL CO., INC. (MS)
Stock Dividend - 10% 10/15/67
Acquired by U.S. Industries, Inc. 12/5/67
(See U.S. Industries, Inc.)

TUCKER STEEL CORP. (TN)
Acquired by U.S. Industries, Inc. 12/05/1967
Details not available

TUCKERTON RAILROAD CO.
Dissolved in 1937
No stockholders' equity

TUCO ENERGY CORP (BC)
Struck off register and declared dissolved for failure to file reports 01/07/1994

TUCSON ACQUISITION CORP (AB)
Name changed to Nouveau Monde Mining Enterprises Inc. 01/15/2013
Nouveau Monde Mining Enterprises Inc. name changed to Nouveau Monde Graphite Inc. 02/10/2017

TUCSON-ARIZONA COPPER CO. (AZ)
Charter revoked for failure to file reports and pay fees 7/5/27

TUCSON CAP CORP (AB)
Name changed to First Step Inc. 08/12/1997
First Step Inc. name changed to Footsource Inc. 08/29/2001
(See Footsource Inc.)

TUCSON ELEC PWR CO (AZ)
Reincorporated 02/20/1964
Name changed 05/10/1979
Each share Common no par exchanged for (2) shares Common $10 par 05/12/1948
Each share Common $10 par exchanged for (2) shares Common $5 par 10/30/1953
Common $5 par split (2) for (1) by issuance of (1) additional share 01/23/1959
Common $5 par changed to $2.50 par and (1) additional share issued 04/27/1962
Name and place of incorporation changed from Tucson Gas, Electric Light & Power Co. (CO) to Tucson Gas & Electric Co. (AZ) 02/20/1964
5% Preferred $100 par called for redemption 07/31/1965
Name changed from Tucson Gas & Electric Co. to Tucson Electric Power Co. 05/10/1979
$2.89 Preferred $25 par called for redemption 09/15/1986
7.50% Preferred $100 par called for redemption 09/29/1986
8.25% Preferred $100 par called for redemption 09/29/1986
8.50% Preferred $100 par called for redemption 09/29/1986
Auction Preferred Ser. A no par called for redemption 00/00/1988
Common $2.50 par changed to no par 05/00/1988
Each share old Common no par exchanged for (0.2) share new Common no par 05/17/1996
Under plan of reorganization each share new Common no par automatically became (1) share UniSource Energy Corp. Common no par 01/01/1998
UniSource Energy Corp. name changed to UNS Energy Corp. 05/14/2012
(See UNS Energy Corp.)

TUCSON TURF CLUB (AZ)
Charter revoked for failure to file reports and pay taxes 1971

TUCSON URANIUM CO. (AZ)
Charter revoked for failure to file reports and pay fees 11/15/60

TUDEX PETES LTD (AB)
Merged into Tudor Energy Corp. Ltd. 07/20/1983
Each share Common no par exchanged for (1) share Common no par
Tudor Energy Corp. Ltd. name changed to Tudor Corp. Ltd. 11/14/1986
(See Tudor Corp. Ltd.)

TUDOR CAP FD (DE)
Liquidation completed
Each share Common $1 par exchanged for initial distribution of $8.07 cash 02/06/1974
Each share Common $1 par received second and final distribution of $0.042 cash 12/18/1974

TUDOR CITY SECOND UNIT INC. (NY)
Preferred $100 par changed to $50 par 3/15/62
Merged into French (Fred F.) Investing Co., Inc. 9/30/66
Each share Preferred $50 par exchanged for (4) shares Common no par and $13 cash
Each share Common no par exchanged for $2 cash
Each Unit consisting of (1) share Preferred $50 par and (1) share Common no par exchanged for (4.75) shares Common no par
(See French (Fred F.) Investing Co., Inc.)

TUDOR CITY FOURTH UNIT INC. (NY)
Preferred $100 par changed to $1 par in 1946
Merged into French (Fred F.) Investing Co., Inc. 5/31/67
Each share Preferred $1 par exchanged for (8) shares Common no par
Each share Common no par exchanged for $2 cash
Each Unit consisting of (1) share Preferred $1 par and (1) share Common no par exchanged for (8.1) shares Common no par
(See French (Fred F.) Investing Co., Inc.)

TUDOR CITY FIFTH UNIT INC. (NY)
Dissolved 7/31/59

TUDOR CITY SIXTH UNIT INC. (NY)
Merged into French (Fred F.) Investing Co., Inc. 5/31/67
Each share Preferred $100 par exchanged for (2) shares Common no par and $18 cash
Each share Common no par exchanged for $2 cash
Each Unit consisting of (1) share Preferred $100 par and (1) share Common no par exchanged for (3) shares Common no par
(See (French (Fred F.) Investing Co., Inc.)

TUDOR CITY SEVENTH UNIT INC. (NY)
Preferred $100 par changed to $1 par in 1942
Merged into French (Fred F.) Investing Co., Inc. 5/31/67
Each share Preferred $1 par exchanged for (6) shares Common no par and $4 cash
Each share Common no par exchanged for $2 cash
Each Unit consisting of (1) share Preferred $1 par and (1) share Common no par exchanged for (6.3) shares Common no par
(See French (Fred F.) Investing Co., Inc.)

TUDOR CITY EIGHTH UNIT INC. (NY)
Merged into French (Fred F.) Investing Co., Inc. 5/31/67
Each share Preferred $100 par exchanged for (2) shares Common no par and $10 cash
Each share Common no par exchanged for $2 cash
Each Unit consisting of (1) share Preferred $100 par and (1) share Common no par exchanged for (2.6) shares Common no par
(See French (Fred F.) Investing Co., Inc.)

TUDOR CITY NINTH UNIT INC. (NY)
Merged into French (Fred F.) Investing Co., Inc. 9/30/66
Each share Preferred $1 par exchanged for (7) shares Common no par and $8 cash
Each share Common no par exchanged for $2 cash
Each Unit consisting of (1) share Preferred $1 par and (1) share Common no par exchanged for (7.5) shares Common no par
(See French (Fred F.) Investing Co., Inc.)

TUDOR CITY TENTH UNIT INC. (NY)
Merged into French (Fred F.) Investing Co., Inc. 5/31/67
Each share Preferred $100 par exchanged for (2) shares Common no par and $3 cash
Each share Common no par exchanged for $2 cash
Each Unit consisting of (1) share Preferred $100 par and (1) share Common no par exchanged for (2.25) shares Common no par
(See French (Fred F.) Investing Co., Inc.)

TUDOR CITY TWELFTH UNIT INC. (NY)
Merged into French (Fred F.) Investing Co., Inc. 12/31/59
Each share Preferred $100 par exchanged for (1) share Common no par and $110 principal amount of 6% Ser. B Debentures
Each share Common no par exchanged for (1) share Common no par
(See French (Fred F.) Investing Co., Inc.)

TUDOR CORP. (DE)
Charter cancelled and declared inoperative and void for non-payment of taxes 4/15/72

TUDOR FD (DE)
Name changed to WPG Tudor Fund 12/29/1989
(See WPG Tudor Fund)

TUDOR HEDGE FD (DE)
Common $1 par split (3) for (1) by issuance of (2) additional shares 06/29/1979
Name changed to Tudor Fund 06/18/1980
Tudor Fund name changed to WPG Tudor Fund 12/29/1989
(See WPG Tudor Fund)

TUDOR HYDROCARBONS LTD (AB)
Merged into Tudor Energy Corp. Ltd. 07/20/1983
Each share Common no par exchanged for (1) share Common no par
Tudor Energy Corp. Ltd. name changed to Tudor Corp. Ltd. 11/14/1986
(See Tudor Corp. Ltd.)

TUDOR INDS CORP (DE)
Charter forfeited for failure to maintain a registered agent 06/03/1978

TUDOR LTD (AB)
Name changed 11/14/1986
Name changed from Tudor Energy Corp. Ltd. to Tudor Corp. Ltd. 11/14/1986
Ceased operations 09/15/2016
Stockholders' equity unlikely

TUDOR MINING CORP. LTD. (ON)
Merged into Dynacore Enterprises Ltd. 07/15/1967
Each share Capital Stock $1 par exchanged for (0.04) share Common no par
Dynacore Enterprises Ltd. recapitalized as Dynaco Resources Ltd. 05/09/1971
(See Dynaco Resources Ltd.)

TUDOR SELECT FUTURES FUND, L.P. (DE)
Ceased operations 11/00/1991
Details not available

TUDOU HLDGS LTD (CAYMAN ISLANDS)
Merged into Youku Inc. 08/23/2012
Each Sponsored ADS for Class B Ordinary exchanged for (1.595) Sponsored ADR's for Class A Ordinary
Youku Inc. name changed to Youku Tudou Inc. 08/27/2012
(See Youku Tudou Inc.)

TUESDAY MORNING CORP (DE)
Common 1¢ par split (2) for (1) by issuance of (1) additional share 11/19/91
Common 1¢ par split (3) for (2) by issuance of (0.5) additional share payable 6/17/97 to holders of record 6/3/97
Acquired by Madison Dearborn Partners II 12/29/97
Each share Common 1¢ par exchanged for $25 cash
13.25% Sr. Exchangeable Preferred 1¢ par called for redemption at $113.25 plus $2.17 accrued dividends on 5/14/99
13.25% Sr. Exchangeable Preferred 144A 1¢ par called for redemption at $113.25 plus $2.17 accrued dividends on 5/14/99

TUFCO TECHNOLOGIES INC (DE)
Merged into Griffin Holdings, LLC 02/25/2014
Each share Common 1¢ par exchanged for $6.07 cash

TUFFNELL LTD (NV)
Common $0.001 par split (4) for (1) by issuance of (3) additional shares payable 03/25/2011 to holders of record 03/24/2011 Ex date - 03/28/2011
SEC revoked common stock registration 12/21/2015

TUFTCO CORP (TN)
Acquired by Delton Industries, Inc. 09/30/1977
Each share Common $1 par exchanged for $11.50 cash

TUGBOAT INTL INC (DE)
Name changed to MidNet, Inc. 03/25/2004
(See MidNet, Inc.)

TUGOLD RES INC (BC)
Recapitalized as Gold Power Resources Corp. 12/28/1988
Each share Ser. A Common no par exchanged for (0.33333333) share Ser. A Common no par
Gold Power Resources Corp. recapitalized as Triple Force Industries Inc. 12/06/1991 which recapitalized as Petrock Ventures Inc. 01/08/1997 which recapitalized as Croydon Mercantile Corp. 12/31/2002 which name changed to World Mahjong Ltd. 12/01/2015

TUJAX INDS INC (DE)
Merged into Babbitt (B.T.), Inc. 12/4/68
Each share Common no par exchanged for (0.2) share Common $1 par
Babbitt (B.T.), Inc. name changed to B.T.B. Corp. 12/5/69 which name changed to International Banknote Co., Inc. 1/2/73 which merged into United States Banknote Corp. (NY) 7/25/90 which reincorporated in (DE) 9/21/93 which name changed to American Banknote Corp. 7/3/95

TULANE CAP CORP (BC)
Name changed to Fibre-Crown Manufacturing Inc. 6/2/2003

TULARIK INC (DE)
Issue Information - 6,950,000 shares COM offered at $14 per share on 12/09/1999
Merged into Amgen Inc. 8/13/2004
Each share Common $0.001 par exchanged for (0.451) share Common $0.0001 par

TULBANCORP INC (OK)
Merged into Liberty Bancorp Inc. 12/31/93
Details not available

TULIP BIOMED INC (NV)
Each share old Common $0.001 par exchanged for (0.1) share new Common $0.001 par 10/03/2007
Reorganized under the laws of Florida as Bitcoin Services, Inc. 03/21/2016
Each share new Common $0.001 par exchanged for (5) shares Common $0.0001 par

TULIP CUP CORP.
Acquired by Lily-Tulip Cup Corp. 00/00/1929
Details not available

TULL J M INDS INC (GA)
Common $1 par split (2) for (1) by issuance of (1) additional share 6/10/76
Common $1 par split (8) for (5) by issuance of (0.6) additional share 11/10/83
Stock Dividends - 20% 1/25/79; 80% 1/19/81
Merged into Bethlehem Steel Corp. 6/20/85
Each share Common $1 par exchanged for $22 cash

TULL (J.M.) METAL & SUPPLY CO., INC. (GA)
Name changed to Tull (J.M.) Metals Co., Inc. in December 1962
Tull (J.M.) Metals Co., Inc. name changed to Tull (J.M.) Industries, Inc. 1/19/67
(See Tull (J.M.) Industries, Inc.)

TULL (J.M.) METALS CO., INC. (GA)
Name changed to Tull (J.M.) Industries, Inc. 1/19/67
(See Tull (J.M.) Industries, Inc.)

TULLAREE CAP INC (YT)
Recapitalized as Valucap Investments Inc. (Yukon) 12/02/2003
Each (15) shares Common no par exchanged for (1) share Common no par
Valucap Investments Inc. (Yukon) reincorporated in Ontario 12/15/2008

TULLAREE RES LTD (BC)
Reincorporated under the laws of Yukon as Tullaree Capital Inc. 11/09/2000
Tullaree Capital Inc. recapitalized as Valucap Investments Inc. (Yukon) 12/02/2003 which reincorporated in Ontario 12/15/2008

TULLOCH RES INC (BC)
Name changed to Eyetel Technologies Inc. (BC) 10/1/92
Eyetel Technologies Inc. (BC) reincorporated in Wyoming 6/23/94
(See Eyetel Technologies Inc.)

TULLOCH RES LTD (BC)
Recapitalized as Tidal Royalty Corp. 07/18/2017
Each share Common no par exchanged for (0.33333333) share Common no par

TULLOS CORP (DE)
Name changed to Teletimer International Inc. 08/20/1986
(See Teletimer International Inc.)

TULLOW OIL PLC (ENGLAND AND WALES)
ADR agreement terminated 11/23/2009
Each Sponsored ADR for Ordinary exchanged for $160.319063 cash (Additional Information in Active)

TULLY CORP VA (VA)
Common $1 par split (3) for (2) by issuance of (0.5) additional share 4/2/73
Stock Dividend - 25% 12/16/75
Name changed to Tultex Corp. 2/27/76
(See Tultex Corp.)

TULOMA ENERGIES, INC. (UT)
Name changed to Tuloma Corp. and

Common $0.005 par changed to $0.001 par 7/28/83

TULOX HR ONLINE MGMT INC (BC)
Reorganized under the laws of Ontario as Hotline to HR Inc. 05/11/2011
Each share Common no par exchanged for (0.5) share Common no par

TULOX REAL ESTATE DEVS INC (BC)
Reorganized under the laws of Ontario as Organic Potash Corp. 08/15/2011
Each share Common no par exchanged for (0.4) share Common no par

TULOX RES INC (BC)
Each share Common no par received distribution of (1) share Canadian Data Preserve Inc. Common no par, (1) share Greenfab Build Systems Inc. Common no par, (1) share Manuweb Software Systems Inc. Common no par, (1) share Media Script Marketing Inc. Common no par, (1) share Tulox HR Online Management Inc. Common no par and (1) share Tulox Real Estate Developments Inc. Common no par payable 01/12/2011 to holders of record 08/09/2010
Plan of arrangement effective 09/09/2011
Each share Common no par exchanged for (0.16666666) share Argentium Resources Inc. Common no par, (1) share Newlox Gold Ventures Corp. Common no par and (1) share Silicon Processing Corp. Common no par
Argentium Resources Inc. recapitalized as Northern Sphere Mining Corp. 08/24/2015

TULSA COMMERCE BANCSHARES, INC. (OK)
Taken over by FDIC 05/08/1986
No stockholders' equity

TULSA CRUDE OIL CORP. (BC)
Name changed to Perkins Oil Ltd. 03/26/1982
(See Perkins Oil Ltd.)

TULTEX CORP (VA)
Common $1 par split (2) for (1) by issuance of (1) additional share 10/01/1980
Common $1 par split (2) for (1) by issuance of (1) additional share 06/30/1983
Common $1 par split (2) for (1) by issuance of (1) additional share 07/31/1986
Common $1 par split (3) for (2) by issuance of (0.5) additional share 07/31/1987
Stock Dividend - 50% 05/31/1977
Plan of reorganization under Chapter 11 Federal Bankruptcy Code effective 11/26/2001
No stockholders' equity

TUMA CORP NEV (NV)
Common $1 par changed to 2¢ par 09/18/1969
Charter revoked 12/31/2003

TUMBLEWEED COMMUNICATIONS CORP (DE)
Merged into Sopra Group SA 09/04/2008
Each share Common $0.001 par exchanged for $2.70 cash

TUMBLEWEED INC (DE)
Each share old Common 1¢ par exchanged for (1) share new Common 1¢ par to reflect a (1) for (5,000) reverse split followed by a (5,000) for (1) forward split 11/24/2003
Note: Holders of (4,999) or fewer pre-split shares received $1.10 cash per share

Chapter 11 bankruptcy proceedings terminated 03/31/2010
No stockholders' equity

TUMI HLDGS INC (DE)
Acquired by Samsonite International S.A. 08/01/2016
Each share Common 1¢ par exchanged for $26.75 cash

TUMI RES LTD (BC)
Each share old Common no par exchanged for (0.25) share new Common no par 02/25/2013
Name changed to Kingsmen Resources Ltd. 07/07/2015

TUNDRA ENVIRONMENTAL LTD (ON)
Reincorporated 12/16/1994
Place of incorporation changed from (AB) to (ON) 12/16/1994
Delisted from Alberta Stock Exchange 12/23/1996

TUNDRA GOLD MINES LTD (BC)
Reincorporated 02/05/1982
Common $1 par changed to no par 09/24/1975
Place of incorporation changed from (ON) to (BC) 02/05/1982
Delisted from Vancouver Stock Exchange 05/04/1994

TUNDRA MINES LTD. (ON)
Charter cancelled for failure to file reports and pay taxes 00/00/1956

TUNDRA SEMICONDUCTOR CORP (CANADA)
Merged into Integrated Device Technology, Inc. 06/29/2009
Each share Common no par exchanged for $6.25 cash

TUNEX INTL INC (UT)
Each share Common 10¢ par exchanged for (0.5) share old Common $0.001 par 01/01/1986
Each share old Common $0.001 par exchanged for (0.25) share new Common $0.001 par 09/19/1986
Reorganized under Chapter 11 Federal Bankruptcy Code 05/22/1990
Each share new Common $0.001 par exchanged for (0.4) share Common $0.001 par, (1) Class A Common Stock Purchase Warrant expiring 07/01/1991, (1) Class B Common Stock Purchase Warrant expiring 07/01/1992 and (1) Class C Common Stock Purchase Warrant expiring 07/01/1993
Note: No holder will receive fewer than (50) shares
Recapitalized as Aone Dental International Group, Inc. 03/15/2011
Each share Common $0.001 par exchanged for (0.5) share Common $0.001 par
(See Aone Dental International Group, Inc.)

TUNG DING RES INC (FL)
SEC revoked common stock registration 12/11/2007

TUNG FONG HUNG HLDGS LTD (CAYMAN ISLANDS)
Name changed to Hansom Eastern Holdings Ltd. 07/25/2001
Hansom Eastern Holdings Ltd. name changed Inner Mongolia Development (Holdings) Ltd. 09/15/2005 which name changed to Freeman Corp., Ltd. 07/06/2006 which name changed to Freeman Financial Corp. Ltd. 05/14/2012
(See Freeman Financial Corp. Ltd.)

TUNG-SOL ELECTRIC INC. (DE)
4.3% Preferred Ser. 1954 $50 par called for redemption 06/18/1957
5% Preferred Ser. 1957 $50 par called for redemption 03/07/1966
Merged into Wagner Electric Corp. (Old) 09/30/1966
Each share Common $1 par exchanged for (1) share Common $1 par

Wagner Electric Corp. (Old) acquired by Studebaker Corp. (MI) 05/19/1967 which merged into Studebaker-Worthington, Inc. 11/27/1967
(See Studebaker-Worthington, Inc.)

TUNG-SOL LAMP WORKS, INC.
Name changed to Tung-Sol Electric Inc. 00/00/1951
Tung-Sol Electric Inc. merged into Wagner Electric Corp. (Old) 09/30/1966 which was acquired by Studebaker Corp. (MI) 05/19/1967 which merged into Studebaker-Worthington, Inc. 11/27/1967
(See Studebaker-Worthington, Inc.)

TUNGCO RES CORP (BC)
Recapitalized as Royal Bay Gold Corp. 08/29/1990
Each share Common no par exchanged for (0.25) share Common no par
Royal Bay Gold Corp. recapitalized as Featherstone Resources Ltd. 07/08/1998 which recapitalized as Newcastle Minerals Ltd. 05/03/2002 which recapitalized as GoldON Resources Ltd. 03/07/2013

TUNGSTEN COMET MINING CO. (NV)
Charter revoked for failure to file reports and pay fees 03/01/1924

TUNGSTEN CORP. OF CANADA LTD. (ON)
Recapitalized as Consolidated Tungsten Mining Corp. of Canada Ltd. 04/01/1955
Each share Common no par exchanged for (0.25) share Common no par
Consolidated Tungsten Mining Corp. of Canada Ltd. recapitalized as Mount Wright Iron Mines Co. Ltd. 04/18/1958 which name changed to Mantaur Goldfields Corp. 04/30/1996 which name changed to Mantaur Petroleum Corp. 06/25/1997 which merged into Videoflicks.com Inc. 03/24/1999
(See Videoflicks.com Inc.)

TUNGSTEN CORP AMER (DE)
Charter revoked and declared inoperative and void for non-payment of taxes 04/15/1972

TUNGSTEN MINERALS INC (UT)
Recapitalized as Lucky Custer Gold, Inc. 08/06/1980
Each share Common 25¢ par exchanged for (10) shares Common 1¢ par

TUNGSTEN MOUNTAIN MINING CO. (NV)
Charter revoked for failure to file reports and pay fees 03/06/1967

TUNGSTEN OF BRITISH COLUMBIA LTD. (BC)
Dissolved 02/12/1959
Details not available

TUNGSTEN PRODUCTION CO., INC. (CO)
Name changed to Gold, Silver & Tungsten, Inc. 11/30/1934
(See Gold, Silver & Tungsten, Inc.)

TUNKWA COPPER MINES LTD (BC)
Merged into United Gold Corp. 11/20/1984
Each share Common no par exchanged for (0.2) share Common no par
United Gold Corp. merged into ABM Gold Corp. 11/17/1989 which reorganized as NorthWest Gold Corp. 06/01/1990 which merged into Northgate Exploration Ltd. (ON) 06/08/1993 which reincorporated in British Columbia 07/01/2001 which name changed to Northgate Minerals Corp. 05/20/2004 which merged into AuRico Gold Inc. 10/26/2011

TUNNEL STREET GARAGE, INC. (PA)
Name changed to Midtown Motors, Inc. 05/14/1945
(See Midtown Motors, Inc.)

TUNSTALL RES INC (BC)
Name changed to Ray-Net Communication Systems Inc. 02/24/1986
Ray-Net Communication Systems Inc. name changed to Ixora Communication Systems Inc. 12/21/1988
(See Ixora Communication Systems Inc.)

TUNTEX DISTINCT CORP (TAIWAN)
Each old GDR for Ordinary exchanged for (0.7) new GDR for Ordinary 03/18/2003
Each new GDR for Ordinary exchanged again for (0.55) new GDR for Ordinary 09/26/2003
Each new GDR for Ordinary exchanged again for (0.5) GDR for Ordinary 03/07/2005
Stock Dividends - 6.96% payable 10/14/1997 to holders of record 08/12/1997; 3.98465% payable 10/09/1998 to holders of record 08/03/1998
GDR agreement terminated 01/23/2006
Each 144A GDR for Ordinary exchanged for $0.03733 cash

TUPPER LAKE NATL BK (TUPPER LAKE, NY)
Under plan of reorganization each share Common $10 par automatically became (1) share TLNB Financial Corp. Common 40¢ par 05/24/2000
(See TLNB Financial Corp.)

TUPPERWARE CORP (DE)
Name changed to Tupperware Brands Corp. 12/05/2005

TUPRAS TURKIYE PETROL RAFINERILERI A S (TURKEY)
Name changed 07/17/2000
Name changed from Turkiye Petrol Rafinerileri A.S. to Tupras-Turkiye Petrol Rafinerileri A.S. 07/17/2000
Stock Dividend - 235% payable 11/01/2001 to holders of record 09/21/2001 Ex date - 09/24/2001
Basis changed from (1:200) to (1:0.2) 01/05/2005
GDR agreement terminated 07/20/2016
Each 144A GDR for Class A exchanged for $4.103191 cash
Each Reg. S GDR for Class A exchanged for $4.103191 cash

TURBINE TRUCK ENGINES INC (NV)
Reincorporated 02/20/2008
State of incorporation changed from (DE) to (NV) 02/20/2008
Each share old Common $0.001 par exchanged for (0.05) share new Common $0.001 par 05/05/2015
Name changed to Novo Integrated Sciences, Inc. 07/12/2017

TURBO CAP INC (BC)
Recapitalized as Cruz Capital Corp. 04/12/2016
Each share Common no par exchanged for (0.05) share Common no par
Cruz Capital Corp. name changed to Cruz Cobalt Corp. 02/23/2017

TURBO CAST INDS INC (DE)
Adjudicated bankrupt 07/24/1970
No stockholders' equity

TURBO DYNAMICS CORP. (NV)
Merged into Gold Check System, Inc. 08/07/1972
Each share Common 1¢ par exchanged for (0.1) share Capital Stock 10¢ par
(See Gold Check Systems, Inc.)

TURBO ENERGY SYSTEMS, INC. (WA)
Charter cancelled and proclaimed dissolved for failure to pay fees 07/01/1975

TURBO GENSET INC (AB)
Each share Class A Common no par exchanged for (4) shares Common no par 01/30/2001
Reincorporated under the laws of Yukon as Turbo Power Systems Inc. 07/19/2006

TURBO INC (AZ)
Recapitalized as A Priori AG 12/22/2000
Each share Common 1¢ par exchanged for (1/6) share Common 1¢ par

TURBO RES LTD (AB)
Each share Capital Stock no par exchanged for (0.5) share Conv. Class A Common no par and (0.5) share Class B Common no par 05/16/1978
Conv. Class A no par reclassified as Common no par 05/20/1980
8.25% Conv. Second Preferred 1979 Ser. $20 par called for redemption 12/19/1980
Special Stock no par split (3) for (1) by issuance of (2) additional shares 06/02/1981
Common no par split (3) for (1) by issuance of (2) additional shares 06/02/1981
Plan of Arrangement effective 07/05/1985
Each share 8.75% First Preferred Ser. A $20 par exchanged for (8) shares Common no par
Each share 10.5% Second Preferred 1980 Ser. $20 par exchanged for (7) shares Common no par
Each share Special Stock no par exchanged for (1.2) shares Common no par
Recapitalized as Canadian Turbo Inc. 11/08/1990
Each share Common no par exchanged for (0.1) share Common no par
(See Canadian Turbo Inc.)

TURBOCHEF TECHNOLOGIES INC (DE)
Name changed 06/30/1998
Common 1¢ par split (2) for (1) by issuance of (1) additional share payable 01/11/1996 to holders of record 12/29/1995
Name changed from Turbochef, Inc. to to Turbochef Technologies, Inc. 06/30/1998
Each share old Common 1¢ par exchanged for (1/3) share new Common 1¢ par 12/27/2004
Acquired by Middleby Corp. 01/05/2009
Each share Common 1¢ par exchanged for (0.0486) share Common 1¢ par and $3.67 cash

TURBODYNE CORP (DE)
Merged into Studebaker-Worthington, Inc. 08/05/1976
Each share Common $1 par exchanged for $19.50 cash

TURBODYNE TECHNOLOGIES INC (DE)
Reincorporated 12/03/1996
Reincorporated 07/24/1998
Place of incorporation changed from (BC) to Canada 12/03/1996
Place of incorporation changed from Canada to (DE) and Common no par changed to $0.001 par 07/24/1998
Reincorporated under the laws of Nevada 09/12/2002

TURBOMATIC, INC. (MN)
Recapitalized as Mobility, Inc. 9/20/72
Each share Common 10¢ par exchanged for (0.1) share Common 1¢ par
(See Mobility, Inc.)

TURBOSONIC TECHNOLOGIES INC (DE)
Common 10¢ par split (5) for (4) by issuance of (0.25) additional share payable 07/22/2005 to holders of record 07/15/2005 Ex date - 07/25/2005
Acquired by MEGTEC Systems, Inc. 01/31/2013
Each share Common 10¢ par exchanged for $0.21 cash

TURF & PADDOCK, INC. (DE)
Name changed to Kaiser Produce, Inc. 1/9/67
Kaiser Produce, Inc. name changed to Kaiser Diversified Enterprises, Inc. 12/6/68
(See Kaiser Diversified Enterprises, Inc.)

TURF IRR CORP (NY)
In process of liquidation
Each share Common 10¢ par exchanged for initial distribution of 50¢ cash 12/17/70
Each share Common 10¢ par received second distribution of $1.44 cash 2/1/71
Each share Common 10¢ par received third distribution of $0.0505 cash 6/27/72
Note: Details on subsequent distributions, if any, are not available

TURF OIL CO (CA)
Charter cancelled for failure to file reports and pay taxes 12/1/76

TURF PARADISE INC (AZ)
Common $10 par changed to no par and (3) additional shares issued 7/11/72
5% Preferred $20 par called for redemption 5/25/94
Merged into Hollywood Park, Inc. (New) 8/11/94
Each share Common no par exchanged for (0.577) share Common 10¢ par
Hollywood Park, Inc. (New) name changed to Pinnacle Entertainment, Inc. 2/23/2000

TURFSKI INC (MA)
Proclaimed dissolved for failure to file reports and pay taxes 10/19/1983

TURINCO INC (NV)
Each share old Common $0.001 par exchanged for (9) shares new Common $0.001 par 3/28/2005
Name changed to Arvana, Inc. 8/9/2006

TURISMO INDS LTD (BC)
Recapitalized as General Energy Corp. (BC) 07/31/1978
Each share Capital Stock no par exchanged for (0.25) share Common no par
(See General Energy Corp.)

TURK CORP (UT)
Proclaimed dissolved for failure to file annual reports 08/01/1988

TURK EKONOMI BANKASI AS (TURKEY)
Sponsored Reg. S GDR's for Ordinary split (2.25) for (1) by issuance of (1.25) additional GDR's payable 09/01/2000 to holders of record 08/17/2000 Ex date - 08/18/2000
Sponsored 144A GDR's for Ordinary split (2.25) for (1) by issuance of (1.25) additional GDR's payable 09/01/2000 to holders of record 08/17/2000 Ex date - 08/18/2000
Basis changed from (1:2,000) to (1:1) 01/03/2005
Sponsored Reg. S GDR's for Ordinary split (5.45) for (1) by issuance of (4.45) additional GDR's payable 10/02/2007 to holders of record 09/20/2007
Sponsored 144A GDR's for Ordinary split (5.45) for (1) by issuance of (4.45) additional GDR's payable 10/02/2007 to holders of record 09/20/2007
Stock Dividends - 4.8526% payable 03/17/2004 to holders of record 03/10/2004; in Sponsored Reg. S GDR's to holders of Sponsored Reg. S GDR's 30.71895% payable 06/26/2007 to holders of record 06/13/2007 Ex date - 06/27/2007
ADR agreement terminated 06/03/2015
Each Sponsored Reg. S GDR for Ordinary exchanged for $0.667334 cash
Each Sponsored 144A GDR for Ordinary exchanged for $0.667334 cash

TURK OTOMOBIL FABRIKASI A S (TURKEY)
Name changed 02/19/2009
Each old GDR for Class E exchanged for (0.002) new GDR for Class E 06/23/1999
Each old 144A Sponsored ADR for Class E exchanged for (0.002) new 144A Sponsored ADR for Class E 06/23/1999
Basis changed from (1:1) to (1:500) 06/23/1999
Basis changed from (1:500) to (1:2.5) 01/03/2005
Stock Dividends - 40% payable 12/18/1998 to holders of record 12/11/1998; 75% payable 07/26/1999 to holders of record 06/24/1999; 150% payable 12/21/2001 to holders of record 12/11/2001; 1.6406% payable 06/05/2003 to holders of record 05/23/2003; 11.11% payable 07/25/2005 to holders of record 07/15/2005
Name changed from Tofas Turk Otomobil Fabrikasi A.S to Turk Otomobil Fabrikasi A.S. 02/19/2009
GDR agreement terminated 10/24/2018
Each new GDR for Class E exchanged for (2.5) shares Class E
ADR agreement terminated 10/24/2018
Each new ADR for Class E exchanged for (2.5) shares Class E
Note: Unexchanged GDR/ADR's will be sold and the proceeds, if any, held for claim after 10/26/2020

TURKEY DELITE INTL INC (NV)
Each share old Common $0.001 par exchanged for (0.25) share new Common $0.001 par 11/01/1995
Name changed to Barrier International Corp. 04/00/1998
Barrier International Corp. recapitalized as MATCO Enterprises Inc. 07/30/1998 which recapitalized as PetroQuest Resources, Inc. 11/30/2005

TURKEY GAP COAL & COKE CO.
Liquidated in 1952

TURKEY JERKY INC (UT)
Name changed to Flavor Brands, Inc. 02/12/1992
(See Flavor Brands, Inc.)

TURKISH INVT FD INC (MD)
Completely liquidated
Each share Common 1¢ par received first and final distribution of $9.1469 cash payable 12/29/2017 to holders of record 12/22/2017

TURKPOWER CORP (DE)
Recapitalized as Zinco do Brasil, Inc. 12/28/2012
Each (15) shares Common $0.0001 par exchanged for (1) share Common $0.0001 par

TURN TECHNOLOGY INC (NV)
Charter revoked for failure to file reports and pay fees 8/1/95

TURNAROUND PARTNERS INC (NV)
Recapitalized as Advanced Clean Technologies, Inc. 01/12/2009
Each (300) shares Common $0.001 par exchanged for (1) share Common $0.001 par
Advanced Clean Technologies, Inc. name changed to Act Clean Technologies, Inc. 12/09/2009

TURNBERRY GOURMET MEATS CORP (FL)
Recapitalized as Krypton Distribution Corp. 11/27/1996
Each share Common $0.001 par exchanged for (0.5) share Common $0.001 par
Krypton Distribution Corp. recapitalized as Sobik's International Franchising, Inc. 02/02/2001 which name changed to Quality Restaurant Ventures, Inc. 01/12/2004 which name changed to Airborne Security & Protective Services, Inc. (Ctfs. dated after 09/30/2009) 05/25/2010

TURNBERRY RES LTD (BC)
Common no par split (3) for (1) by issuance of (2) additional shares payable 03/26/2012 to holders of record 02/15/2012
Name changed to Anthem United Inc. 04/22/2014
Anthem United Inc. merged into JDL Gold Corp. 10/07/2016 which name changed to Trek Mining Inc. 03/31/2017 which name changed to Equinox Gold Corp. 12/22/2017

TURNBULL ELEVATOR LTD. (CANADA)
Name changed to Combined Engineered Products Ltd. 6/8/66
Combined Engineered Products Ltd. name changed to Compro Ltd.-Compro Ltee. 2/12/75
(See Compro Ltd.-Compro Ltee.)

TURNER & NEWALL PLC (ENGLAND)
Stock Dividend - 33-1/3% 03/26/1965
Name changed to T&N PLC 09/01/1987
(See T&N PLC)

TURNER & SEYMOUR MFG CO (CT)
Merged into T & S Inc. 05/16/1984
Each share Capital Stock no par exchanged for $70 cash

TURNER ADVERTISING CO (GA)
Completely liquidated 07/08/1977
Each share Common no par exchanged for first and final distribution of $12 cash

TURNER AIRLINES, INC. (DE)
Name changed to Lake Central Airlines, Inc. in 1950
Lake Central Airlines, Inc. merged into Allegheny Airlines, Inc. 7/1/68 which name changed to U S Air, Inc. 10/29/79 which reorganized as USAir Group, Inc. 2/1/83 which name changed to US Airways Group, Inc. 2/21/97
(See US Airways Group, Inc.)

TURNER BROADCASTING SYS INC (GA)
Name changed 08/16/1979
Each share Common $1 par exchanged for (4) shares Common 25¢ par 05/12/1978
Stock Dividend - 160% 05/07/1979
Name changed from Turner Communications Corp. to Turner Broadcasting System, Inc. 08/16/1979
Common 25¢ par changed to $0.125 par and (1) additional share issued 07/10/1981
Preferred Ser. A 10¢ par called for redemption 06/18/1987
Common $0.125 par reclassified as

Class A Common $0.0625 par 08/25/1987
Each share Class A Common $0.0625 par received distribution of (1) share Class B Common $0.0625 par 09/02/1987
Class A Common $0.0625 par split (3) for (1) by issuance of (2) additional shares 09/04/1990
Class B Common $0.0625 par split (3) for (1) by issuance of (2) additional shares 09/04/1990
Merged into Time Warner Inc. (Old) 10/10/1996
Each share Conv. Class C Preferred $0.125 par exchanged for (4.8) shares Common 1¢ par
Each share Class A Common $0.0625 par exchanged for (0.75) share Common 1¢ par
Each share Class B Common $0.0625 par exchanged for (0.75) share Common 1¢ par
Time Warner Inc. (Old) merged into AOL Time Warner Inc. 01/11/2001 which name changed to Time Warner Inc. (New) 10/16/2003 which merged into AT&T Inc. 06/15/2018

TURNER CONSTR CO (NY)
Each share Common $5 par exchanged for (10) shares Common no par in 1945
Common no par split (4) for (1) by issuance of (3) additional shares 4/14/64
Common no par changed to $1 par and (2) additional shares issued 8/18/69
Each share 7% Preferred $100 par exchanged for (4.25) shares Common $1 par 5/10/73
Common $1 par split (2) for (1) by issuance of (1) additional share 3/13/84
Stock Dividend - 100% 12/12/80
Reorganized under the laws of Delaware as Turner Corp. 6/1/84
(See Turner Corp.)

TURNER CORP (DE)
Common $1 par split (3) for (2) by issuance (0.5) additional share payable 8/14/98 to holders of record 8/3/98 Ex date - 8/17/98
Merged into Hochtief AG 9/22/99
Each share Common $1 par exchanged for $28.625 cash

TURNER DAY & WOOLWORTH HANDLE CO.
Acquired by American Fork & Hoe Co. 00/00/1947
Details not available

TURNER ENERGY & RES LTD (BC)
Recapitalized as Golden Arch Resources Ltd. 08/16/1989
Each share Common no par exchanged for (0.2) share Common no par

TURNER EQUITY INVS INC (MD)
Acquired by MGI Properties 12/22/1988
Each (2.8) shares Common 1¢ par exchanged for (1) share Common $1 par
(See MGI Properties)

TURNER GROUP INC (NV)
Recapitalized as AutoAuction.com, Inc. (NV) 05/04/1999
Each share Common $0.000001 par exchanged for (0.01) share Common $0.000001 par
AutoAuction.com, Inc. (NV) reorganized in Wyoming as HLV Trading Corp. 02/08/2005 which name changed to X-tra Petroleum 08/30/2006 which recapitalized as Xtra Energy Corp. 11/05/2010

TURNER VALLEY FINL LTD (AB)
Conv. Jr. Preferred $1 par called for redemption 06/03/1983
Name changed to Financial Trustco Capital Ltd. 07/05/1983

Financial Trustco Capital Ltd. name changed to FT Capital Ltd. 07/25/1989
(See FT Capital Ltd.)

TURNER VALLEY HOLDINGS LTD. NEW (AB)
Name changed to Turner Valley Financial Ltd. 01/28/1982
Turner Valley Financial Ltd. name changed to Financial Trustco Capital Ltd. 07/05/1983 which name changed to FT Capital Ltd. 07/25/1989
(See FT Capital Ltd.)

TURNER VALLEY HOLDINGS LTD. OLD (AB)
Merged into Turner Valley Holdings Ltd. (ALTA) (New) 07/10/1980
Each share Common no par exchanged for (0.5) Conv. Jr. Preferred $1 par or (1) share Common no par
Note: Option to receive Common Stock expired 12/24/1980
Turner Valley Holdings Ltd. (New) name changed to Turner Valley Financial Ltd. 01/28/1982 which name changed to Financial Trustco Capital Ltd. 07/05/1983 which name changed to FT Capital Ltd. 07/25/1989
(See FT Capital Ltd.)

TURNER VALLEY OIL CO. LTD. (AB)
Capital Stock no par reclassified as Common no par 00/00/1964
Name changed to Turner Valley Holdings Ltd. (ALTA) (Old) 03/05/1973
Turner Valley Holdings Ltd. (ALTA) (Old) merged into Turner Valley Holdings Ltd. (ALTA) (New) 07/10/1980 which name changed to Turner Valley Financial Ltd. 01/28/1982 which name changed to Financial Trustco Capital Ltd. 07/05/1983 which name changed to FT Capital Ltd. 07/25/1989
(See FT Capital Ltd.)

TURNING BASIN INC (NY)
Charter cancelled and proclaimed dissolved for failure to pay taxes 12/29/1982

TURNKEY E&P INC (AB)
Company's prinicpal asset's Chapter 11 bankruptcy proceedings converted to Chapter 7 on 06/07/2010
Stockholders' equity unlikely

TURNO CADILLAC GOLD MINES, LTD. (ON)
Charter cancelled for failure to file reports and pay taxes in 1953

TURNSTONE SYS INC (DE)
Common $0.001 par split (2) for (1) by issuance of (1) additional share payable 08/23/2000 to holders of record 08/09/2000
Each share Common $0.001 par received distribution of $2.77 cash payable 11/28/2003 to holders of record 11/21/2003
Liquidation completed
Each share Common $0.001 par received initial distribution of $0.17 cash payable 07/08/2004 to holders of record 12/04/2003 Ex date - 07/09/2004
Each share Common $0.001 par received second and final distribution of $0.014711 cash payable 11/11/2009 to holders of record 12/04/2003
Note: Certificates were not required to be surrendered and are without value

TURQUOISE CAP CORP (BC)
Name changed to Five Star Diamonds Ltd. 04/25/2017

TURTLEBACK MTN GOLD INC (AZ)
Name changed to Windstar Resources Inc. 12/31/97
Windstar Resources Inc. name changed to Nexland Inc. (AZ) 12/8/99 which reincorporated in Delaware 9/13/2000
(See Nexland Inc.)

TURZONE EXPLORATIONS LTD. (ON)
Merged into Junction Explorations Ltd. 12/12/78
Each share Capital Stock $1 par exchanged for (1/6) share Common no par
(See Junction Explorations Ltd.)

TUSCALOOSA OIL & GAS INC (BC)
Merged into Aurex Resources Inc. 7/11/85
Each (3.5) shares Common no par exchanged for (1) share Common no par
Aurex Resources Inc. merged into Galveston Resources Ltd. 7/29/86 which merged into Corona Corp. 7/1/88 which recapitalized as International Corona Corp. 6/1/91
(See International Corona Corp.)

TUSCAN INDS INC (FL)
Recapitalized as Apache Group Inc. 12/31/95
Each share Common $0.001 par exchanged for (0.02) share Common $0.001 par

TUSCANY ENERGY LTD NEW (AB)
Common no par split (2) for (1) by issuance of (1) additional share payable 05/07/2014 to holders of record 05/02/2014 Ex date - 05/08/2014
Discharged from receivership 03/07/2017
No stockholders' equity

TUSCANY ENERGY LTD OLD (AB)
Reorganized as Tuscany Energy Ltd. (New) 07/19/2013
Each share Common no par exchanged for (0.125) share Common no par
(See Tuscany Energy Ltd. (New))

TUSCANY INTL DRILLING INC (AB)
Plan of reorgnization under Chapter 11 Federal Bankruptcy proceedings effective 06/09/2014
No stockholders' equity

TUSCANY MINERALS LTD (WY)
Reincorporated 06/26/2006
Reincorporated 07/07/2009
State of incorporation changed from (NV) to (WA) 06/26/2006
State of incorporation changed from (WA) to (WY) 07/07/2009
Reincorporated under the laws of Cayman Islands 10/06/2009
Tuscany Minerals, Ltd. (Cayman Islands) name changed to Qwick Media Inc. 07/15/2010

TUSCANY RES LTD (AB)
Recapitalized as Tuscany Energy Ltd. (Old) 08/13/1998
Each share Common no par exchanged for (0.2) share Common no par
Tuscany Energy Ltd. (Old) reorganized as Tuscany Energy Ltd. (New) 07/19/2013
(See Tuscany Energy Ltd. (New))

TUSCARORA INC (PA)
Name changed 7/20/92
Common no par split (2) for (1) by issuance of (1) additional share 4/14/92
Name changed from Tuscorora Plastics, Inc. to Tuscarora Inc. 7/20/92
Common no par split (3) for (2) by issuance of (0.5) additional share payable 1/11/97 to holders of record 12/27/96

Merged into Svenska Cellulosa Aktiebolaget SCA 3/12/2001
Each share Common no par exchanged for $21.50 cash

TUSK ENERGY CORP (AB)
Merged into Polar Star Canadian Oil & Gas, Inc. 04/15/2009
Each share Common no par exchanged for $2.15 cash

TUSK ENERGY INC (AB)
Recapitalized 11/22/1991
Recapitalized 09/08/1995
Recapitalized from Tusk Minerals Inc. to Tusk Resources Inc. 11/22/1991
Each share Common no par exchanged for (0.2) share Common no par
Recapitalized from Tusk Resources Inc. to Tusk Energy Inc. 09/08/1995
Each share Common no par exchanged for (0.1) share Common no par
Plan of arrangement effective 11/02/2004
Each share Common no par exchanged for (0.5) TKE Energy Trust Trust Units no par and (0.5) share Tusk Energy Corp. Common no par
(See each company's listing)

TUSSIK INC (DE)
Charter cancelled and declared inoperative and void for non-payment of taxes 3/1/91

TUSSING BUILDING CORP. (MI)
Liquidation completed
Each share Common $1 par exchanged for initial distribution of $200 cash 6/23/69
Each share Common $1 par received second distribution of $80 cash 8/12/69
Each share Common $1 par received third distribution of $6.03 cash 9/29/69
Each share Common $1 par received fourth and final distribution of $3.727 cash 6/29/70

TUT ENTERPRISES INC (BC)
Recapitalized as Simmonds Communications Ltd. 05/31/1991
Each share Common no par exchanged for (0.1) share Common no par
Simmonds Communications Ltd. recapitalized as Simmonds Capital Ltd. 10/06/1995

TUT EXPLORATIONS INC. (BC)
Name changed to Tut Enterprises Inc. 10/8/82
Tut Enterprises Inc. recapitalized as Simmonds Communications Ltd. 5/31/91 which recapitalized as Simmonds Capital Ltd. 10/6/95

TUT SYS INC (DE)
Merged into Motorola, Inc. 03/30/2007
Each share Common $0.001 par exchanged for $1.15 cash

TUTAG S J & CO (MI)
Common $1 par split (2) for (1) by issuance of (1) additional share 7/21/75
Acquired by Ciga-Geigy S.A. 8/31/79
Each share Common $1 par exchanged for $7.40 cash

TUTOGEN MED INC (FL)
Merged into RTI Biologics, Inc. 02/27/2008
Each share Common 1¢ par exchanged for (1.22) shares Common $0.001 par
RTI Biologics, Inc. name changed to RTI Surgical, Inc. 07/18/2013

TUTORNET COM GROUP INC (DE)
Recapitalized as Sunmark International Industries, Inc. (DE) 02/07/2005
Each share Common $0.00001 par exchanged for (0.001) share Common $0.001 par

Sunmark International Industries, Inc. (DE) reorganized in Washington as Royal Sunmark Energy Corp. 08/22/2005 which name changed to Detex Security Systems, Inc. 10/19/2005 which name changed to Detection Security Systems, Inc. 05/15/2006 which recapitalized as Nexis International Industries, Inc. 08/30/2007
(See Nexis International Industries, Inc.)

TUTTLE & BAILEY MANUFACTURING CO. (NY)
Acquired by Hart & Cooley, Inc. 00/00/1933
Details not available

TUXEDO RES LTD (BC)
Issue Information - 3,259,000 shares COM offered at $0.25 per share on 02/07/2003
Recapitalized as Signature Resources Ltd. 04/21/2004
Each share Common no par exchanged for (0.5) share Common no par
Signature Resources Ltd. name changed to UrAsia Energy Ltd. 11/07/2005 which merged into sxr Uranium One Inc. 04/20/2007 which name changed to Uranium One Inc. 06/18/2007
(See Uranium One Inc.)

TUXPAM STAR OIL CORP. (DE)
Charter cancelled and declared inoperative and void for non-payment of taxes in 1925

TV AZTECA S A DE C V (MEXICO)
Issue Information - 17,007,816 ADR'S offered at $18.25 per ADR on 08/14/1997
ADR agreement terminated 7/17/2005
Each Sponsored ADR for Participation Certificates no par exchanged for $9.29389 cash

TV COMMUNICATIONS NETWORK INC (CO)
Each share Common $0.0001 par exchanged for (0.2) share Common $0.0005 par 12/23/1991
Company went private through purchase offer which expired 08/10/2001

TV FILME INC (DE)
Reorganized under the laws of the Cayman Islands as ITSA Ltd. 07/21/2000
Each share Common 1¢ par exchanged for (0.46) share Ordinary 1¢ par
(See ITSA Ltd.)

TV GUIDE INC (DE)
Class A Common 1¢ par split (2) for (1) by issuance of (1) additional share payable 12/17/1999 to holders of record 12/03/1999
Merged into Gemstar-TV Guide International, Inc. 07/12/2000
Each share Class A Common 1¢ par exchanged for (0.6573) share Common 1¢ par
Gemstar-TV Guide International, Inc. merged into Macrovision Solutions Corp. 05/05/2008 which name changed to Rovi Corp. 07/16/2009

TV JUNIOR PUBLICATIONS INC. (NY)
Dissolved by proclamation 12/15/65

TV R INC (NY)
Plan of Arrangement under Chapter XI Federal Bankruptcy Act confirmed 02/09/1977
No stockholders' equity

TV 3 ENTMT CORP (FL)
Administratively dissolved 09/22/2000

TV TOKYO CORP (JAPAN)
ADR agreement terminated 01/28/2009
No ADR's remain outstanding

TVC IMAGE TECHNOLOGY INC (DE)
Charter cancelled and declared inoperative and void for non-payment of taxes 03/01/1992

TVE CORP (DE)
Name changed to Echo Resources, Inc. and (1) additional share issued 08/13/2004
Echo Resources, Inc. name changed to Fortress Exploration, Inc. (DE) 09/30/2009 which reincorporated in Nevada 06/04/2010 which name changed to Greenworld Development, Inc. 08/20/2010

TVE HLDGS LTD (HONG KONG)
Acquired by Self China Morning Post 07/26/1996
Each ADR for Ordinary HKD $0.50 par exchanged for $1.62 cash

TVI COPPER INC (AB)
Name changed to TVI Pacific Inc. 7/11/94

TVI CORP NEW (MD)
Each share 10% Preferred 1¢ par exchanged for (2) shares Common 1¢ par 01/13/1995
Chapter 11 bankruptcy proceedings terminated 02/29/2012
No stockholders' equity

TVI CORP OLD (MD)
Name changed 06/27/1985
Name changed from TVI Energy Corp. to TVI Corp. (Old) 06/27/1985
Reorganized as TVI Corp. (New) 03/21/1993
Each share Common 1¢ par exchanged for (0.1) share Common 1¢ par
(See TVI Corp. (New))

TVIA INC (DE)
Issue Information - 5,000,000 shares COM offered at $11 per share on 08/14/2000
Plan of reorganization under Chapter 11 Federal Bankruptcy proceedings effective 12/28/2009
Each share Common $0.001 par held by holders of (15,000) shares or more exchanged for (1) share new Common $0.001 par
Each share Common $0.001 par held by holders of (14,999) shares or fewer exchanged for $0.0747 cash
Note: Company is now privately held

TVNET INC (DE)
Name changed to Vegas Chips Inc. 02/10/1989
Vegas Chips Inc. name changed to Skydoor Media & Entertainment Inc. 12/15/1995 which name changed to Ice Holdings, Inc. (DE) 10/09/1996 which reorganized in Nevada as Gaia Resources, Inc. 10/20/2006 which recapitalized as Ram Gold & Exploration, Inc. 02/08/2008 which name changed to DPollution International Inc. 08/31/2010 which recapitalized as Ecrid, Inc. 10/16/2017

TVTRAVEL COM INC (FL)
Name changed to Emailthatpays.com, Inc. (FL) 12/21/1999
Emailthatpays.com, Inc. (FL) reorganized in Delaware as Forge, Inc. 05/13/2002 which name changed to Encore Clean Energy, Inc. (DE) 12/19/2003 which reincorporated in Nevada 10/21/2005
(See Encore Clean Energy, Inc.)

TVX BROADCAST GROUP INC (VA)
Acquired by Paramount Communications Inc. 02/26/1991
Each share Common 1¢ par exchanged for $9.50 cash

TVX GOLD INC (CANADA)
Additional Offering - 71,500,000 shares COM offered at $1.05 per share on 04/05/2002
Each share old Common no par exchanged for (0.2) share new Common no par 7/31/2000
Each share new Common no par exchanged again for (0.1) share new Common no par 6/30/2002
Merged into Kinross Gold Corp. 1/31/2003
Each share new Common no par exchanged for (2.1667) shares new Common no par

TVX MNG CORP (ON)
Recapitalized as Consolidated TVX Mining Corp. 12/1/86
Each share Common no par exchanged for (1/3) share Common no par
Consolidated TVX Mining Corp. reincorporated in Canada as TVX Gold Inc. which merged into Kinross Gold Corp. 1/31/2003

TW HLDGS INC (DE)
Recapitalized as Flagstar Companies, Inc. 06/16/1993
Each share Common 10¢ par exchanged for (0.2) share Common 10¢ par $2.25 Conv. Preferred Ser. A 10¢ par not affected except for change of name
(See Flagstar Companies, Inc.)

TW SVCS INC (DE)
Merged into TW Holdings Inc. 12/6/89
Each share Common 1¢ par exchanged for $34 cash

TW TELECOM INC (DE)
Merged into Level 3 Communications, Inc. 10/31/2014
Each share Class A Common 1¢ par exchanged for (0.7) share new Common 1¢ par and $10 cash
Level 3 Communications, Inc. merged into CenturyLink, Inc. 11/01/2017

TWEED MARIJUANA INC (CANADA)
Name changed to Canopy Growth Corp. 09/22/2015

TWEEN BRANDS INC (DE)
Merged into Dress Barn, Inc. (CT) 11/25/2009
Each share Common 1¢ par exchanged for (0.47) share Common 5¢ par
Dress Barn, Inc. (CT) reincorporated in Delaware as Ascena Retail Group, Inc. 01/03/2011

TWEETER HOME ENTMT GROUP INC (DE)
Common 1¢ par split (2) for (1) by issuance of (1) additional share payable 12/02/1999 to holders of record 11/18/1999
Plan of reorganization under Chapter 11 Federal Bankruptcy proceedings effective 10/31/2014
Stockholders' equity unlikely

12TH STREET STORE CORP. (IL)
Adjudicated bankrupt 3/2/65
No stockholders' equity

1257 LUNT AVENUE BLDG. CORP. (IL)
Liquidation completed 8/21/62

12 NORTH CLINTON, INC.
Trust terminated in 1948
Details not available

1263 PRATT BUILDING CORP.
Liquidated in 1949

12 TO 20 PLUS INC (NV)
Old Common $0.001 par split (6) for (1) by issuance of (5) additional shares payable 11/04/2004 to holders of record 10/30/2004
Ex date - 11/14/2002
Each share old Common $0.001 par exchanged for (0.01754385) share new Common $0.001 par 11/05/2004
Name changed to Secured Financial Network, Inc. 01/18/2005
Secured Financial Network, Inc. name changed to Redfin Network, Inc. 04/28/2011

(See Redfin Network, Inc.)

1225 MAPLE CORP (DE)
In process of liquidation
Each share Common $1 par exchanged for initial distribution of $6 cash 1/8/79
Each share Class B $1 par exchanged for initial distribution of $6 cash 1/8/79
Each share Common $1 par received second distribution of $2.50 cash 6/27/80
Each share Class B $1 par received second distribution of $2.50 cash 6/27/80
Details on subsequent distributions, if any, are not available

TWENTIETH BANCORP INC (WV)
Merged into Horizon Bancorp Inc. 09/01/1996
Each share Common $10 par exchanged for (1.01) shares Common $1 par
Horizon Bancorp Inc. merged into City Holding Co. 12/31/1998

20TH CENTURY CORP. (PA)
Name changed to Consumers Financial Corp. (PA) 05/30/1980
Consumers Financial Corp. (PA) reincorporated in Nevada 02/26/2008
(See Consumers Financial Corp.)

20TH CENTY ENERGY CORP (BC)
Each share old Common no par exchanged for (2) shares new Common no par 05/17/1979
New Common no par split (2) for (1) by issuance of (1) additional share 12/29/1979
New Common no par split (2) for (1) by issuance of (1) additional share 03/06/1981
Cease trade order 04/12/1991

TWENTIETH CENTURY FIXED TRUST SHARES
Original Series and Series B trusts Terminated in 1936
Details not available

TWENTIETH CENTURY FOODS CORP. (MO)
Petition in bankruptcy approved 11/9/61
Court order confirmed plan of reorganization 8/30/67
No stockholders' equity

TWENTIETH CENTURY-FOX FILM CORP. (NY)
Reorganized 9/27/52
Each share Common no par exchanged for (1) share Twentieth Century-Fox Film Corp. (Del.) Common $1 par and (1) share National Theatres, Inc. Common $1 par
(See each company's listing)

TWENTIETH CENTURY FUELS, INC. (NV)
Common 20¢ par changed to 5¢ par 4/17/62
Recapitalized as Twentieth Century Engineering Corp. 8/30/63
Each share Common 5¢ par exchanged for (0.02) share Common 50¢ par
Twentieth Century Engineering Corp. merged into Radiant Industries, Inc. 12/29/69 which name changed to Caltem Liquidating, Inc. 6/30/80
(See Caltem Liquidating, Inc.)

20TH CENTY GUARDIAN LIFE INS CO (MI)
Each share Common $1 par exchanged for (0.00001) share Common $1 par 05/13/1980
Note: In effect holders received $2.55 cash per share and public interest was eliminated

20TH CENTY INDS (CA)
Each share Common $1 par

exchanged for (0.1) share Common $10 par 05/03/1972
Common $10 par changed to no par and (14) additional shares issued 12/05/1977
Common no par split (3) for (1) by issuance of (2) additional shares 04/10/1979
Common no par split (2) for (1) by issuance of (1) additional share 05/15/1981
Common no par split (2) for (1) by issuance of (1) additional share 01/17/1983
Common no par split (2) for (1) by issuance of (1) additional share 02/15/1985
Common no par split (2) for (1) by issuance of (1) additional share 04/04/1986
Common no par split (2) for (1) by issuance of (1) additional share 07/15/1991
Stock Dividend - 100% 02/03/1983
Name changed to 21st Century Insurance Group (CA) 01/01/2000
21st Century Insurance Group (CA) reincorporated in Delaware 12/04/2003
(See 21st Century Insurance Group (DE))

20TH CENTY INDS INC (DE)
Charter cancelled and declared inoperative and void for non-payment of taxes 3/1/77

TWENTIETH CENTURY INTERNATIONAL, INC. (NV)
Name changed to Stallone (Jacqueline), Inc. 02/13/1984 which name changed back to Twentieth Century International, Inc. 09/27/1985
Charter revoked for failure to file reports and pay fees 02/01/1988

TWENTIETH CENTURY MINING CO. (UT)
Merged into North Lily Mining Co. 12/1/76
Each share Common 10¢ par exchanged for (0.0126) share Capital Stock 10¢ par
(See North Lily Mining Co.)

TWENTIETH CENTURY MINING CO. LTD. (ON)
Merged into Twentieth Century Explorations Ltd. (QC) 09/12/1969
Each share Capital Stock $1 par exchanged for (0.2) share Capital Stock no par
Twentieth Century Explorations Ltd. (QC) reincorporated in Ontario as Twentieth Century Explorations Inc. 03/01/1975 which recapitalized as Minefinders Corp. Ltd. 04/26/1979 which merged into Pan American Silver Corp. 04/02/2012

20TH CENTURY PICTURES CORP.
Merged into Twentieth Century-Fox Film Corp. (N.Y.) in 1935 which reorganized as Twentieth Century-Fox Film Corp. (Del.) and National Theatres, Inc. 9/27/52
(See each company's listing)

TWENTIETH CENTY ENGR CORP (NV)
Merged into Radiant Industries, Inc. 12/29/1969
Each share Common 50¢ par exchanged for (1.5) shares Common 10¢ par
Radiant Industries, Inc. name changed to Caltem Liquidating, Inc. 06/30/1980
(See Caltem Liquidating, Inc.)

TWENTIETH CENTY EXPLS LTD (ON)
Name changed 03/01/1975
Name and place of incorporation changed from Twentieth Century Explorations Ltd. (QC) to Twentieth Century Exploration Inc. (ON) 03/01/1975

Recapitalized as Minefinders Corp. Ltd. 04/26/1979
Each share Capital Stock no par exchanged for (0.2) share Capital Stock no par
Minefinders Corp. Ltd. merged into Pan American Silver Corp. 04/02/2012

TWENTIETH CENTY FOX FILM CORP (DE)
Common $1 par split (2) for (1) by issuance of (1) additional share 11/10/67
Common $1 par split (4) for (3) by issuance of (1/3) additional share 5/30/80
Merged into TCF Holdings, Inc. 6/12/81
Each share $3 Conv. Preferred Ser. A no par exchanged for $80 cash
Each share Common $1 par exchanged for $60 cash

TWENTIETH CENTY INVS INC (MD)
Reincorporated 02/22/1991
Income Investors Shares $1 par reclassified as Select Investors Shares $1 par 07/17/1979
Stock Dividends - Income Investors Shares - 25% 01/31/1962; Growth Investors Shares - 100% 06/01/1962; 42.5% 01/10/1973
State of incorporation changed from (DE) to (MD) 02/22/1991
Name changed to American Century Mutual Funds, Inc. and Growth Investors Shares $1 par, Select Investors Shares $1 par, Ultra Investors Shares $1 par and Vista Investors Shares $1 par reclassified as Twentieth Century Select Fund Investor Class 1¢ par, Twentieth Century Select Fund Investor Class 1¢ par, Ultra Fund Investor Class 1¢ par and Twentieth Century Vista Fund Investor Class 1¢ par respectively 12/11/1996

TWENTIETH CENTY INVTS INC (DE)
Name changed to Polymerix Inc. 01/05/1988
(See Polymerix Inc.)

TWENTIETH CENTY OIL CO (NV)
Name changed to Twentieth Century International, Inc. 11/21/72
Twentieth Century International, Inc. name changed to Stallone (Jacqueline), Inc. 2/13/84 which name changed back to Twentieth Century International, Inc. 9/27/85
(See Twentieth Century International, Inc.)

TWENTIETH CENTY UNDERWRITERS INC (CA)
Name changed to 20th Century Industries 12/31/1968
20th Century Industries name changed to 21st Century Insurance Group (CA) 01/01/2000 which reincorporated in Delaware 12/04/2003
(See 21st Century Insurance Group (DE))

TWENTIETH STR BK (HUNTINGTON, WV)
Each share Capital Stock $50 par exchanged for (3) shares Capital Stock $25 par 01/26/1943
Capital Stock $25 par changed to $10 par 01/11/1973
Stock Dividends - 100% 06/30/1945; 33.33333333% 06/26/1950; 10% 12/29/1955; 33.33333333% 12/31/1963; 50% 02/01/1973
Reorganized as Twentieth Bancorp Inc. 09/30/1983
Each share Capital Stock $10 par exchanged for (1) share Common $10 par
Twentieth Bancorp Inc. merged into Horizon Bancorp Inc. 09/01/1996 which merged into City Holding Co. 12/31/1998

2847 WASHINGTON BOULEVARD CORP.
Liquidation completed in 1946

2800 BELMONT CORP. (IL)
Liquidation completed
Each share Common $3 par stamped to indicate initial distribution of (0.069065) share Corn Products Co. Common 50¢ par 09/22/1967
Each share Stamped Common $3 par exchanged for second and final distribution of (0.019229) share Corn Products Co. Common 50¢ par 11/22/1968
Corn Products Co. name changed to CPC International Inc. 04/23/1969 which name changed to BestFoods 01/01/1998
(See BestFoods)

2860 EAST 76TH CORP. (IL)
Dissolved 00/00/1952
Details not available

25TH STREET CORP. (MD)
In process of liquidation
Each share Common 10¢ par exchanged for initial distribution of $13.50 cash 01/15/1980
Each share Common 10¢ par received second distribution of $0.20 cash 09/22/1980
Each share Common 10¢ par received third distribution of $0.51 cash 10/21/1981
Each share Common 10¢ par received fourth distribution of $0.35 cash 09/09/1983
Note: Details on subsequent distributions, if any, are not available

21ST CENTY AMERN TECHNOLOGY DEV CORP (FL)
Proclaimed dissolved for failure to file reports and pay fees 08/13/1993

21ST CENTY DISTR CORP (NY)
Each share old Common 1¢ par exchanged for (0.2) share new Common 1¢ par 08/11/1988
Stock Dividend - 25% 04/16/1982
Reincorporated under the laws of Delaware as Cannon Pictures, Inc. 12/22/1989
(See Cannon Pictures, Inc.)

21ST CENTY ELECTRS INC (DE)
Adjudicated bankrupt 09/06/1977
No stockholders' equity

21ST CENTY FILMS CORP (DE)
Charter cancelled and declared inoperative and void for non-payment of taxes 03/01/1995

21ST CENTY FRONTIER GROUP INC (NV)
Each share old Common $0.0001 par exchanged for (0.1) share new Common $0.0001 par 09/20/1997
Recapitalized as Goldplate Holdings Enterprises Inc. 02/10/1999
Each share new Common $0.0001 par exchanged for (0.1) share Common $0.001 par
Goldplate Holdings Enterprises Inc. name changed to Eagletech Communications, Inc. 03/17/1999
(See Eagletech Communications, Inc.)

21ST CENTY GROUP INC (DE)
Name changed 07/07/1988
Name changed from 21st Century Envelope Co., Inc. to 21st Century Group, Inc. 07/07/1988
Charter cancelled and declared inoperative and void for non-payment of taxes 06/26/1990

21ST CENTY HLDG CO (FL)
Common 1¢ par split (3) for (2) by issuance of (0.5) additional share payable 09/07/2004 to holders of record 08/23/2004 Ex date - 09/08/2004
Name changed to Federated National Holding Co. 09/12/2012
Federated National Holding Co. name changed to FedNat Holding Co. 06/07/2018

21ST CENTY HLDGS INC (NV)
Each share Common $0.001 par exchanged for (0.01) share Common 1¢ par 08/20/1991
Recapitalized as AFGL International, Inc. (NV) 08/24/1993
Each share Common 1¢ par exchanged for (0.125) share Common 1¢ par
AFGL International, Inc. (NV) reincorporated in Delaware as Headway Corporate Resources, Inc. 11/14/1996
(See Headway Corporate Resources, Inc.)

21ST CENTY INS GROUP (DE)
Reincorporated 12/04/2003
State of incorporation changed from (CA) to (DE) and Common no par changed to $0.001 par 12/04/2003
Merged into American International Group, Inc. 09/27/2007
Each share Common $0.001 par exchanged for $22 cash

21ST CENTY ROBOTICS INC (GA)
Recapitalized as TFC Teleservices Corp. 12/31/1985
Each share Common 1¢ par exchanged for (0.25) share Common 1¢ par
TFC Teleservices Corp. name changed to Central Corp. 03/31/1987 which reorganized as Resurgens Communications Group, Inc. 05/16/1989 which name changed to LDDS Communications, Inc. 09/15/1993 which name changed to WorldCom, Inc. 05/26/1995 which name changed to MCI WorldCom, Inc. 09/14/1998 which name changed to WorldCom Inc. (New) 05/01/2000
(See WorldCom Inc. (New))

21ST CENTY TECHNOLOGIES INC (NV)
Each share old Common $0.001 par exchanged for (0.01) share new Common $0.001 par 02/20/2003
Each share new Common $0.001 par exchanged again for (0.03333333) share new Common $0.001 par 01/07/2005
Plan of reorganization under Chapter 11 Federal Bankruptcy proceedings effective 06/29/2007
No stockholders' equity

21ST CENTY TELECOM GROUP INC (IL)
Stock Dividends - 3.4375% payable 08/16/1999 to holders of record 08/02/1999; 3.4375% payable 11/15/1999 to holders of record 11/01/1999; 3.4375% payable 02/15/2000 to holders of record 02/01/2000
Each share 13.75% Sr. Exchangeable Preferred 1¢ par exchanged for $100 principal amount of 13.75% Exchangeable Subordinated Debentures due 02/15/2010 on 02/15/2000
Merged into RCN Corp. 04/28/2000
Each share Common 1¢ par exchanged for (0.3620) share Common $1 par
Note: 10% of exchange amount was placed in escrow. Subsequent litigation resulted in holders receiving an undetermined amount of Common Stock Purchase Warrants expiring 12/21/2006.

21ST CENTY VISION INC (NV)
Name changed to Eyemakers, Inc. 08/26/1996
Eyemakers, Inc. name changed to Homeland Security Technology, Inc. 06/30/2004 which merged into Amnis Energy Inc. 03/15/2005 which name changed to Homeland

Security Group International, Inc. 10/10/2005 which recapitalized as Domestic Energy Corp. 04/07/2008
(See Domestic Energy Corp.)

TWENTY FIRST CENTY COMMUNICATIONS INC (NY)
Stock Dividend - 100% 06/28/1974
Name changed to National Lampoon, Inc. (NY) 08/27/1979
National Lampoon, Inc. (NY) acquired by J2 Communications (CA) 10/24/1990 which reincorporated in Delaware as National Lampoon, Inc. 11/05/2002
(See National Lampoon, Inc. (DE))

TWENTY FIRST CENTY HEALTH INC (UT)
Name changed to Bio-Tech Industries Inc. 05/21/1997
(See Bio-Tech Industries Inc.)

21ST SENTRY CORP (NV)
Name changed to Bullzi Security, Inc. 01/16/2007
Bullzi Security, Inc. name changed to Bullzi Holdings, Inc. 02/11/2014

TWENTY FIVE FD INC (MD)
Completely liquidated 06/30/1975
Details not available

2545-16TH STREET CORP. (DE)
In process of liquidation
Each share Common $1 par exchanged for initial distribution of (0.3063) share Consolidated Foods Corp. Common $1.33-1/3 par 01/16/1967
Each share Common $1 par received second distribution of (0.046682) share Consolidated Foods Corp. Common $1.33-1/3 par 10/14/1967
Each share Common $1 par received third distribution of (0.0172693) share Consolidated Foods, Corp. Common $1.33-1/3 par 12/21/1967
Each share Common $1 par received fourth distribution of (0.046686) share Consolidated Foods Corp. Common $1.33-1/3 par 10/16/1968
Each share Common $1 par received fifth distribution of (0.077808) share Consolidated Foods Corp. Common $1.33-1/3 par 10/29/1969
Note: Details on subsequent distribution(s), if any, are not available

247 MEDIA GROUP INC (FL)
Recapitalized as Fantastic Fun, Inc. 09/22/2006
Each share Common 1¢ par exchanged for (0.1) share Common 1¢ par
Fantastic Fun, Inc. name changed to Global Profit Technologies, Inc. 02/13/2008

24 / 7 REAL MEDIA INC (DE)
Name changed 12/10/2001
Name changed from 24/7 Media, Inc. to 24/7 Real Media Inc. 12/10/2001
Each share old Common 1¢ par exchanged for (0.2) share new Common 1¢ par 02/27/2004
Merged into WPP Group PLC (Old) 07/13/2007
Each share Common 1¢ par exchanged for $11.75 cash

TWENTY GRAND MARINE SERVICE, INC. (LA)
Merged into Tidewater Marine Service, Inc. 03/01/1968
Each share Common no par exchanged for (0.5) share $1.50 Conv. Preferred Ser. A no par
(See Tidewater Marine Service, Inc.)

29 SOUTH LA SALLE, INC.
Liquidated 00/00/1939
Details not available

2930 BRISTOL STREET CORP. (CA)
Completely liquidated 10/08/1962
Details not available

29TH STREET TOWERS CORP. (NY)
Liquidation completed 04/01/1957
Details not available

21 C CORP (DE)
Charter cancelled and declared inoperative and void for non-payment of taxes 03/15/1975

TWENTY ONE HUNDRED THIRTY LINCOLN PARK WEST BLDG. CORP. (DE)
Liquidation completed 00/00/1956
Details not available

22ND & ARCH STREETS, INC.
Liquidation completed 00/00/1948
Details not available

TWENTY SVCS INC (AL)
Acquired by Twenty Services Holding, Inc. 03/17/2014
Each share 7% Preferred Ser. A-1980 $1 par exchanged for $1.05 cash
Each share 7% Preferred Ser. A-1982 $1 par exchanged for $1.05 cash
Each share Common $1 par exchanged for $3.75 cash

TWENTY-SEVEN CAP CORP (CANADA)
Acquired by Mega Uranium Ltd. 02/13/2007
Each share Common no par exchanged for 0.33333333) share Common no par and (0.16666666) Common Stock Purchase Warrant expiring 02/15/2012

26 JOURNAL SQUARE CORP.
In process of liquidation 00/00/1946
Details not available

20/10 PRODS INC (OR)
Merged into CP Merger Co. 05/17/1985
Each share Common no par exchanged for $2 cash

TWENTY THIRD STREET RAILWAY CO.
Dissolved 00/00/1937
Details not available

2361 WEHRLE DRIVE LIQUIDATING CORP. (NY)
Liquidation completed
Each share Common 10¢ par exchanged for initial distribution of (0.125925) share Singer Co. Common $10 par 12/17/1969
Certificates of Assignment distributed 06/05/1970
Each Certificate of Assignment received first and final distribution of (0.022222) share Singer Co. Common $10 par 03/31/1971
Note: Certificates of Assignment were not required to be surrendered and are without value
(See Singer Co.)

20/20 FINL CORP (ON)
Merged into AGF Management Ltd. 12/21/1995
Each share Common no par exchanged for either (0.225) shares Class B Preferred no par and $11.25 cash or $14.25 cash
Note: Option to receive stock and cash expired 01/17/1996

20/20 NETWORKS INC (NV)
Common $0.001 par split (20) for (1) by issuance of (19) additional shares payable 12/30/2003 to holders of record 12/22/2003 Ex date - 12/31/2003
Name changed to Micro Bio-Medical Waste Systems, Inc. 01/02/2004
Micro Bio-Medical Waste Systems, Inc. name changed to Crown Equity Holdings Inc. 10/05/2006

20-20 TECHNOLOGIES INC (QC)
Acquired by Vector Capital Corp. 09/13/2012
Each share Common no par exchanged for $4 cash
Note: Unexchanged certificates were cancelled and became without value 09/13/2018

20 / 20 WEB DESIGN INC (NV)
Name changed to Bentleytel.com Inc. 04/16/2001 which name changed back to 20 / 20 Web Design Inc. 07/12/2001
Recapitalized as 20/20 Networks Inc. 02/14/2003
Each share Common $0.001 par exchanged for (0.01) share Common $0.001 par
20/20 Networks Inc. name changed to Micro Bio-Medical Waste Systems, Inc. 01/02/2004 which name changed to Crown Equity Holdings Inc. 10/05/2006

20 WACKER DRIVE BUILDING CORP.
Merged into Wacker Corp. 00/00/1944
Each share Preferred exchanged for (1) share Class A Preferred
Each share Common exchanged for (1) share new Common
Wacker Corp. name changed to G.F.C. Corp.
(See G.F.C. Corp.)

20 WACKER DRIVE TRUST
Liquidated 00/00/1949
Details not available

TWENTYFOUR/SEVEN VENTURES INC (CO)
Common $0.001 par split (8) for (1) by issuance of (7) additional shares payable 07/21/2014 to holders of record 07/15/2014 Ex date - 07/22/2014
Recapitalized as EFH Group, Inc. 11/20/2014
Each share Common $0.001 par exchanged for (0.01) share Common $0.001 par
EFH Group, Inc. name changed to EF Hutton America, Inc. 05/21/2015 which name changed to HUTN, Inc. 10/17/2017

21 BRANDS INC (NY)
Merged into Foremost-McKesson, Inc. 01/30/1970
Each share Common $1 par exchanged for (0.375) share Common $2 par
Foremost-McKesson, Inc. name changed to McKesson Corp. (MD) 07/27/1983 which reincorporated in Delaware 07/31/1987
(See McKesson Corp. (Old) (DE))

2020 CHINACAP ACQUIRCO INC (DE)
Issue Information - 7,500,000 UNITS consisting of (1) share COM and (1) WT offered at $8 per Unit on 11/08/2007
Reincorporated under the laws of British Virgin Islands as Exceed Co. Ltd. and Common $0.0001 par reclassified as Ordinary $0.0001 par 10/21/2009

TWILIGHT PRODUCTIONS LTD (DE)
Name changed to Advant-E Corp. 9/18/2020

TWIN ARROW PETROLEUM CORP. (DE)
Merged into Little Star Uranium Co., Inc. in 1956
Each share Class A Common 10¢ par exchanged for (2.25) shares Common 10¢ par
Each share Class B Common 10¢ par exchanged for (1.125) shares Common 10¢ par
Little Star Uranium Co., Inc. merged into Anschutz Drilling Co., Inc. 7/27/56 which recapitalized as Webb Resources, Inc. 10/17/61 which merged into Standard Oil Co. (OH) 12/11/79
(See Standard Oil Co. (OH))

TWIN BAY MINING & EXPLORATION LTD. (AB)
Struck off register by Province of Alberta for default 12/15/61

TWIN BAY URANIUM LTD. (AB)
Name changed to Twin Bay Mining & Exploration Ltd. in 1956
(See Twin Bay Mining & Exploration Ltd.)

TWIN BUTTES EXPL INC (CANADA)
Name changed to Transglobal Business News Network Inc. 06/28/1988
Transglobal Business News Network Inc. recapitalized as Megasol Corp. 04/05/1993 which recapitalized as Clonus Corp. 09/17/1996 which name changed to San-Mar Environmental Corp. 09/22/1997 which recapitalized as Pure Zinc Technologies, Inc. 08/21/1998 which name changed to Charityville.com International Inc. 08/27/1999 which name changed to eNblast productions inc. 06/14/2000
(See eNblast productions inc.)

TWIN CITY BANCORP INC (TN)
Common $1 par split (3) for (2) by issuance of (0.5) additional share payable 9/8/97 to holders of record 8/25/97
Merged into Citco Community Bancshares, Inc. 11/20/2000
Each share Common $1 par exchanged for $17.15 cash

TWIN CITY BARGE & TOWING CO. (DE)
Stock Dividends - 10% 6/9/75; 10% 6/13/80
Name changed to Twin City Barge, Inc. 1/1/81
Twin City Barge, Inc. name changed to Brix Maritime Co. 8/11/88
(See Brix Maritime Co.)

TWIN CITY BARGE INC (DE)
Each share old Common $1 par exchanged for (0.2) share new Common $1 par 4/13/88
Stock Dividend - 50% 1/30/81
Name changed to Brix Maritime Co. 8/11/88
(See Brix Maritime Co.)

TWIN-CITY DISPOSAL CO. (IL)
Proclaimed dissolved for failure to pay taxes and file reports 10/27/37

TWIN CITY GAS LTD (ON)
Merged into Northern & Central Gas Corp. Ltd. 1/1/68
Each share Capital Stock no par exchanged for (1.2) shares Common no par
(See Northern & Central Gas Corp. Ltd.)

TWIN CITY RAPID TRANSIT CO. (MN)
Reincorporated 12/7/39
Common $100 par changed to no par in December 1932
State of incorporation changed from (NJ) to (MN) 12/7/39
Name changed to Minnesota Enterprises Inc. (MN) 6/15/62
Minnesota Enterprises Inc. (MN) reincorporated in Delaware as MEI Corp. 2/20/70
(See MEI Corp.)

TWIN COACH CO. (DE)
Common no par changed to $1 par in 1935
Name changed to Twin Industries Corp. 4/9/62
Twin Industries Corp. name changed to Wheelabrator Corp. 12/31/63 which merged into Wheelabrator-Frye Inc. 11/4/71 which merged into Signal Companies, Inc. 2/1/83 which merged into Allied-Signal Inc. 9/19/85 which name changed to AlliedSignal Inc. 4/26/93 which

name changed to Honeywell International Inc. 12/1/99

TWIN CREEK EXPL INC (UT)
Recapitalized as Inland Casino Corp. 05/23/1995
Each share Common $0.001 par exchanged for (0.01) share Common $0.001 par
Inland Casino Corp. name changed to Inland Entertainment Corp. 12/11/1997 which name changed to Venture Catalyst Inc. 12/10/1999
(See Venture Catalyst Inc.)

TWIN DISC CLUTCH CO. (WI)
Common no par split (4) for (1) by issuance of (3) additional shares 10/10/62
Common no par split (3) for (2) by issuance of (0.5) additional share 12/30/63
Stock Dividend - 100% 12/26/44
Name changed to Twin Disc, Inc. 10/23/67

TWIN EAGLE RES INC (BC)
Recapitalized as Cordal Resources Ltd. 05/17/1993
Each share Common no par exchanged for (0.25) share Common no par
Cordal Resources Ltd. recapitalized as Skyharbour Developments Ltd. 11/04/1999 which name changed to Skyharbour Resources Ltd. 10/25/2002

TWIN ENERGY LTD (AB)
Merged into Pinnacle Resources Ltd. (New) 11/17/1988
Each share Ser. A Preferred no par exchanged for (1) share Class B Preferred no par
Each share Common no par exchanged for (0.86206896) share Common no par
Pinnacle Resources Ltd. (New) merged into Renaissance Energy Ltd. 07/16/1998 which merged into Husky Energy Inc. 08/25/2000

TWIN FACES EAST ENTMT CORP (NV)
SEC revoked common stock registration 02/24/2012

TWIN FAIR INC (NY)
Merged into Simplicity Pattern Co., Inc. 03/23/1984
Each share Common $1 par exchanged for $6 cash

TWIN FALLS BK & TR CO (TWIN FALLS, ID)
Merged into First Security Bank of Idaho, N.A. (Boise, ID) 01/12/1990
Each share Capital Stock $100 par exchanged for $1,737.098 cash

TWIN FALLS NORTH SIDE LAND & WATER CO.
Reorganized as Idaho Farms Co. in December 1936
Idaho Farms Co. completely liquidated 9/7/73

TWIN FALLS OAKLEY LAND & WATER CO.
Dissolved in 1930

TWIN FAULT MINES, LTD. (ON)
Charter surrendered 12/20/1956

TWIN GLACIER RES LTD (BC)
Merged into Dolly Varden Silver Corp. 01/30/2012
Each share Common no par exchanged for (1) share Common no par

TWIN GOLD CORP (BC)
Name changed to Twin Mining Corp. 3/15/2000
Twin Mining Corp. recapitalized as Atlanta Gold Inc. 3/28/2007

TWIN GOLD MINES LTD (ON)
Capital Stock no par split (2) for (1) by issuance of (1) additional share 03/06/1981

Delisted from Alberta Stock Exchange 02/28/1992

TWIN INDUSTRIES CORP. (DE)
Name changed to Wheelabrator Corp. 12/31/63
Wheelabrator Corp. merged into Wheelabrator-Frye Inc. 11/4/71 which merged into Signal Companies, Inc. 2/1/83 which merged into Allied-Signal Inc. 9/19/85 which name changed to AlliedSignal Inc. 4/26/93 which name changed to Honeywell International Inc. 12/1/99

TWIN J MINES LTD.
Liquidated in 1951

TWIN MNG CORP (BC)
Recapitalized as Atlanta Gold Inc. 3/28/2007
Each (15) shares Common no par exchanged for (1) share Common no par

TWIN PEAK RESOURCES LTD. (BC)
Cease trade order effective 12/24/1976

TWIN PEAKS LAND & CATTLE CO. (TX)
Proclaimed dissolved by Court order 2/24/67

TWIN RICHFIELD OILS LTD (CANADA)
Each (2) shares Common no par exchanged for (1) share Conv. Class A Common no par and (1) share Class B Common no par 09/04/1980
Note: Each remaining share Common no par exchanged for (1) share Conv. Class A Common no par
Dissolved 05/02/2002
Details not available

TWIN RIV RES LTD (BC)
Recapitalized as T.R.V. Minerals Corp. 11/18/1974
Each share Common no par exchanged for (1/3) share Common no par
(See T.R.V. Minerals Corp.)

TWIN RIVER PETROLEUMS (ALBERTA) LTD. (AB)
Name changed 00/00/1952
Name changed from Twin River Petroleums to Ltd. Twin River Petroleums (Alberta) Ltd. 00/00/1952
Struck from the register 00/00/1958

TWIN STAR ENERGY CORP (ON)
Merged into Blue Power Energy Corp. 11/14/1995
Each share Common no par exchanged for (0.25) share Common no par
Blue Power Energy Corp. recapitalized as Cadillac Ventures Inc. 04/20/2006

TWIN STAR MINERALS LTD (BC)
Reincorporated under the laws of Yukon as American Copper Corp. 8/7/98
American Copper Corp. name changed to E-Phoria Online Systems Inc. 7/29/99
(See E-Phoria Online Systems Inc.)

TWIN STATES NATURAL GAS CO.
Reorganized as Hillcrest Natural Gas Co. in 1932 which merged into Northeastern Oil & Gas Co. in 1936 which was liquidated in 1942

TWIN TIRES SYS INC (BC)
Struck off register and declared dissolved for failure to file returns 11/3/95

TWIN TUBE & RUBBER CO. (DE)
No longer in existence having become inoperative and void for non-payment of taxes 3/22/22

TWIN VENTURES LTD (DE)
Name changed to Rincon Resources,

Inc. and (9) additional shares issued 7/23/2004
Rincon Resources, Inc. name changed to Caliber Energy, Inc. 3/17/2005

TWIND ENERGY CORP (DE)
Charter cancelled and declared inoperative and void for non-payment of taxes 10/29/91

TWINDYKE MINES LTD. (ON)
Dissolved 5/19/58

TWINLAB CORP (DE)
Issue Information - 8,500,000 shares COM offered at $12 per share on 11/15/1996
Name changed to TL Administration Corp. 12/23/2003
(See TL Administration Corp.)

TWISCO CORP. (NJ)
Liquidation completed 10/19/1956
Details not available

TWISTEE FREEZ CORP. (CO)
Name changed to Twistee Treat Corp. 07/26/1984
Twistee Treat Corp. recapitalized as INAV Travel Corp. 02/15/1991 which name changed to MB Software Corp. (CO) 06/18/1996 which reorganized in Texas 06/24/2002 which name changed to Wound Management Technologies, Inc. 06/12/2008

TWISTEE TREAT CORP (CO)
Recapitalized as INAV Travel Corp. 02/15/1991
Each share Common $0.001 par exchanged for (1/6) share Common $0.001 par
INAV Travel Corp. name changed to MB Software Corp. (CO) 06/18/1996 which reorganized in Texas 06/24/2002 which name changed to Wound Management Technologies, Inc. 06/12/2008

TWISTEE TREAT CORP (DE)
Each share old Common $0.0001 par exchanged for (0.1) share new Common $0.0001 par 11/11/2002
Reorganized under the laws of Oklahoma as V Group, Inc. 03/13/2014
Each share Common $0.0001 par exchanged for (0.0117647) share Common $0.0001 par

TWISTER NETWORKS INC (NV)
Reorganized as Reynaldos Mexican Food Co., Inc. 3/4/2005
Each share Common $0.001 par exchanged for (0.025) share Common $0.001 par

TWL CORP (UT)
Reorganized 12/12/2007
Reorganized from Utah to under the laws of Nevada 12/12/2007
Each share Common no par exchanged for (0.05) share Common no par
Chapter 7 bankruptcy proceedings terminated 12/17/2015
No stockholders' equity

2 BI 2 INC (CO)
Name changed to USA Health Technologies Inc. (CO) 10/22/1993
USA Health Technologies Inc. (CO) reorganized under the laws of Nevada 03/15/1995 which name changed to to Healthtech International, Inc. 10/27/1995
(See Healthtech International, Inc.)

2 BIRCH STREET CORP. (NY)
Proclaimed dissolved 09/17/1987

TWO BROTHERS VALLEY GOLD MINES, LTD. (CANADA)
Deemed not to be a subsisting company for failure to comply with corporate laws of the Dominion of Canada 02/27/1944

2CONNECT EXPRESS INC (FL)
Plan of reorganization under Chapter 11 Federal Bankruptcy proceedings effective 12/10/1998
No stockholders' equity

TWO COUNT HLDG CO (CO)
Merged into BBRT, Inc. 12/18/1992
Each share Common $0.0001 par exchanged for $0.16 cash

TWO DOG NET INC (UT)
Proclaimed dissolved for failure to pay taxes 10/23/2002

2 EAST 61ST STREET CORP.
Bankrupt 00/00/1939
Stockholders' equity unlikely

280 BROADWAY HLDG CORP (MB)
Merged into Power Financial Corp.- Corporation Financiere Power 12/04/1986
Each share Preference 1978 Ser. no par exchanged for (1) share 1st Preferred 1978 Ser. no par
Each share 5% Preferred 1969 Ser. $25 par exchanged for (1) share 1st Preferred 1969 Ser. $25 par
Each share Common 5¢ par exchanged for (6.5) shares Common no par
Each share Class A Non-Vtg. 5¢ par exchanged for (6.5) shares Common no par

245 FIFTH AVENUE CORP. (DE)
Liquidated 00/00/1953
Details not available

TWO-FORTY FOUR NORTH BAY SHORE DRIVE, INC. (NY)
Dissolved 00/00/1957
Preferred Stockholders received $12.93 per share Common stockholders had no equity

247MGI INC (FL)
Name changed to Baron Capital Enterprise, Inc. 12/16/2011

TWO GUYS FROM HARRISON, INC. (NY)
Merged into Vornado, Inc. (KS) 11/05/1959
Each share Class A Common 10¢ par exchanged for (1) share Common 10¢ par
Vornado, Inc. (KS) reincorporated in Delaware 06/30/1965 which reorganized as Vornado Realty Trust (MD) 05/06/1993

TWO HUNDRED & FIFTY EAST MAIN STREET CORP. (NJ)
Liquidation completed
Each share Common $12.50 par exchanged for initial distribution of $35 cash 01/07/1965
Each share Common $12.50 par received second and final distribution of $0.37 cash 08/22/1966

200 EAST OCEAN BOULEVARD CO.
Dissolved 00/00/1939
Details not available

208 LIQUIDATING CO. STOCKHOLDERS TRUST (DE)
Liquidation completed
Each share Common no par received second distribution of $4.50 cash 03/31/1982
Each share Common no par received third distribution of $1 cash 02/28/1983
Each share Common no par received fourth distribution of $0.70 cash 01/25/1984
Each share Common no par received fifth distribution of $0.75 cash 01/29/1985
Each share Common no par received sixth and final distribution of $4.87 cash 04/12/1985
Note: Certificates were not required to be surrendered and are without value
(See 208 South La Salle Corp. for

208 SOUTH LA SALLE STREET CORP. (DE)
Common no par split (3) for (1) by issuance of (2) additional shares 05/15/1964
Liquidation completed
Each share Common no par received initial distribution of $90 cash 07/07/1981
Name changed to 208 Liquidating Co. Stockholders Trust 05/27/1981
(See 208 Liquidating Co. Stockholders Trust)

200 OFFICE PARK DRIVE, INC. (AL)
In process of liquidation
Each share Common $0.33333333 par exchanged for initial distribution of $3.55 cash 04/20/1977
Note: An additional cash distribution may have been made from escrow account

277 PARK AVENUE CORP. (NY)
Name changed to Chilton Properties, Inc. 06/18/1963
Chilton Properties, Inc. recapitalized as HSC Services, Inc. 02/01/1971
(See HSC Services, Inc.)

267 WEST 39TH STREET CORP.
Liquidated 00/00/1945
Details not available

236-40 WEST 27TH STREET CORP. (NY)
Liquidation completed
Each share Capital Stock no par stamped to indicate initial distribution of $100 cash 05/21/1974
Each share stamped Capital Stock no par exchanged for second and final distribution of $56.10 cash 01/14/1975

202 DATA SYS INC (PA)
Under plan of liquidation each share Common 10¢ par received distribution of $3 cash 10/11/1988
Each share old Common 10¢ par exchanged for (0.0005) share new Common 10¢ par 12/23/1997
Note: In effect holders received $0.24 cash per share and public interest was eliminated

2 I INC (WA)
SEC revoked common stock registration 12/23/2008

2-INFINITY INC (CO)
Name changed 08/25/2000
Name changed from 2-Infinity.com, Inc. to 2-Infinity, Inc. 08/25/2000
SEC revoked common stock registration 12/23/2008

2KSOUNDS CORP (NV)
Common $0.001 par split (20) for (1) by issuance of (19) additional shares payable 05/21/2002 to holders of record 05/20/2002
SEC revoked common stock registration 12/07/2004

TWO MOONS KACHINAS CORP (DE)
Each share Common $0.001 par exchanged for (8.3) shares Common $0.001 par 11/09/2004
Name changed to A.C.T. Holdings, Inc. 01/06/2005
A.C.T. Holdings, Inc. name changed to Advanced Cell Technology, Inc. 06/23/2005 which name changed to Ocata Therapeutics, Inc. 11/14/2014
(See Ocata Therapeutics, Inc.)

II MORROW INC (OR)
Acquired by United Parcel Service of America, Inc. 12/29/1986
Each share Common 1¢ par exchanged for $9 cash

TWO PESOS INC (TX)
Assets transferred to TPI Dissolution Corp. 06/30/1993
(See TPI Dissolution Corp.)

TWO RIV CMNTY BK (MIDDLETOWN, NJ)
Common $5 par changed to $2 par and (1.5) additional shares issued payable 12/29/2003 to holders of record 12/10/2003 Ex date - 12/30/2003
Stock Dividends - 3% payable 02/22/2002 to holders of record 02/08/2002; 3% payable 08/23/2002 to holders of record 08/09/2002 Ex date - 08/15/2002; 3% payable 02/21/2003 to holders of record 02/07/2003 Ex date - 02/06/2003
Merged into Community Partners Bancorp 04/03/2006
Each share Common $2 par exchanged for (1) share Common no par
Community Partners Bancorp name changed to Two River Bancorp 06/28/2013

TWO RIVS WTR CO (CO)
Name changed to Two Rivers Water & Farming Co. 03/19/2013

2001 INC (DE)
Charter cancelled and declared inoperative and void for non-payment of taxes 03/01/1976

2001 RESOURCE INDS LTD (BC)
Struck off register and declared dissolved for failure to file returns 07/22/1994

2002 TARGET TERM TR INC (MD)
Trust terminated 11/29/2002
Each share Common $10 par exchanged for $0.61 cash

TWO TOP GAS & OIL CO. (SD)
Charter cancelled for failure to file annual reports 07/01/1970

2-TRACK GLOBAL INC (NV)
Each share old Common $0.001 par exchanged for (0.01428571) share new Common $0.001 par 10/26/2011
Name changed to Organic Farm Group, Corp. 11/14/2013

220 BAGLEY CORP (MI)
Liquidation completed
Each share Common $1 par exchanged for initial distribution of $45 cash 03/06/1967
Each share Common $1 par received second and final distribution of $6.94 cash 07/25/1968

226 MUSIC GROUP INC (TX)
Reorganized under the laws of Nevada as Hear AtLast Holdings, Inc. 08/08/2007
Each share Common $0.0001 par exchanged for (0.001) share Common $0.001 par

226 RECORDS INC (TX)
Name changed to 226 Music Group, Inc. (TX) 05/31/2005
226 Music Group, Inc. (TX) reorganized in Nevada as Hear AtLast Holdings, Inc. 08/08/2007

222 PIZZA EXPRESS CORP (BC)
Name changed to Kadywood Capital Corp. 05/01/2008
Kadywood Capital Corp. name changed to Gold Wheaton Gold Corp. 07/16/2008
(See Gold Wheaton Gold Corp.)

TWO WAY TV US INC (DE)
SEC revoked common stock registration 03/01/2012

TWO YEAR TRUST SHARES, SERIES B
Trust terminated 00/00/1932
Details not available

2B SYS INC (DE)
Liquidation completed
Each share Common 10¢ par exchanged for initial distribution of $2 cash 02/11/1992
Each share Common 10¢ par received second and final distribution of $1.85 cash 07/31/1992

TWOCO PETE LTD (AB)
Discharged from receivership 02/10/2014
Stockholders' equity unlikely

2DOBIZ COM INC (NV)
Name changed to New York International Commerce Group, Inc. 01/09/2002
(See New York International Commerce Group, Inc.)

2ENERGIA INC (NV)
Stock Dividend - 5% payable 03/17/2003 to holders of record 03/10/2003
Name changed to Coastal Holdings, Inc. 07/02/2003
Coastal Holdings, Inc. name changed to Canadian Blue Gold, Inc. 10/18/2007 which recapitalized as Boreal Water Collection, Inc. 03/19/2008
(See Boreal Water Collection, Inc.)

2M ENERGY CORP (ON)
Acquired by Middlefield Bancorp Ltd. 01/30/2001
Each share Common no par exchanged for $1.15 cash

2980304 CANADA INC. (CANADA)
Delisted from NEX 01/12/2009

2THEMART COM INC (OK)
SEC revoked common stock registration 12/23/2008

2U ONLINE COM INC (DE)
Each share old Common $0.0001 par exchanged for (0.1) share new Common $0.0001 par 01/09/2003
Name changed to Golden Spirit Minerals Ltd. and (3) additional shares issued 10/08/2003
Golden Spirit Minerals Ltd. name changed to Golden Spirit Mining Ltd. 10/18/2004 which name changed to Golden Spirit Gaming Ltd. 07/18/2005 which recapitalized as Golden Spirit Enterprises Ltd. 06/30/2006 which name changed to Terralene Fuels Corp. 11/29/2011 which recapitalized as Golden Star Enterprises Ltd. 07/16/2013

TX INDS INC (NJ)
Charter revoked for failure to file reports and pay fees 08/31/1994

TX RES LTD (BC)
Delisted from Vancouver Stock Exchange 04/02/1984

TXCO RES INC (DE)
Plan of reorganization under Chapter 11 Federal Bankruptcy Code effective 02/11/2010
Holders may receive an undetermined amount of cash

TXF FDS INC (MD)
Completely liquidated
Each share Large Companies ETF $0.001 par received first and final distribution of $38.17265 cash payable 09/30/2010 to holders of record 09/24/2010

TXI CAP TR I (DE)
5.5% Trust Preferred Securities called for redemption at $50 plus $0.6494 accrued dividends on 3/26/2007

TXL OIL CORP. (DE)
Acquired by Texaco Inc. on a (7/11) for (1) basis 4/19/62
Texaco Inc. merged into ChevronTexaco Corp. 10/9/2001 which name changed to Chevron Corp. 5/9/2005

TXON INTL DEV CORP (NV)
Each share old Common $0.001 par exchanged for (0.1) share new Common new $0.001 par 06/16/2000
New Common $0.001 par split (8) for (1) by issuance of (7) additional shares payable 09/13/2000 to holders of record 09/05/2000 Ex date - 09/14/2000
Name changed to China World Trade Corp. 09/15/2000
China World Trade Corp. name changed to Uonlive Corp. 09/05/2008

TXP CORP (NV)
Chapter 11 bankruptcy proceedings dismissed 05/20/2010
No stockholders' equity

TXU CAP I (DE)
7.25% Trust Preferred Capital Securities called for redemption at $25 on 4/24/2004

TXU CAP II (DE)
8.70% Trust Originated Preferred Securities called for redemption at $25 on 12/31/2004

TXU CORP (TX)
Each Income Preferred Redeemable Increased Dividend Equity Security received (0.5997) share Common no par 08/16/2002
Each Growth Preferred Redeemable Increased Dividend Equity Security received (0.5997) share Common no par 08/16/2002
Each Corporate Unit received (0.449) share Common no par 11/16/2005
Common no par split (2) for (1) by issuance of (1) additional share payable 12/08/2005 to holders of record 11/18/2005 Ex date - 12/09/2005
Each 8.125% Preferred Redeemable Increased Dividend Equity Security received (1.5894) shares Common no par 05/16/2006
Merged into Kohlberg, Kravis, Roberts & Co. 10/10/2007
Each share Common no par exchanged for $69.25 cash

TXU ELEC CO (TX)
Name changed to TXU US Holdings Co. 1/1/2002
(See TXU US Holdings Co.)

TXU ELEC CAP I (DE)
8.25% Trust Originated Preferred Securities called for redemption at $25 plus $0.4526 accrued dividend on 12/20/2001

TXU ELEC CAP III (DE)
8% Guaranteed Quarterly Income Preferred Securities called for redemption at $25 plus $0.4389 accrued dividend on 12/20/2001

TXU EUROPE CAP I (DE)
9.75% Trust Originated Preferred Securities called for redemption at $6.503483 on 11/22/2005

TXU GAS CO (TX)
Depositary Preferred Ser. F called for redemption at $25 on 11/5/2004

TXU US HLDGS CO (TX)
Depositary Preferred Ser. A called for redemption at $25 on 7/1/2003
Depositary Preferred Ser. B called for redemption at $25 on 7/1/2003
$6.98 Preferred called for redemption at $100 on 7/1/2003
$7.22 Preferred called for redemption 7/1/2003
$7.50 Preferred called for redemption 7/1/2003
$7.98 Preferred called for redemption at $103.99 on 7/1/2003
$6.375 Preferred called for redemption at $100 on 10/1/2003
$4 Dallas Power Preferred called for redemption at $103.56 on 8/25/2005
$4 Texas Electric Preferred called for redemption at $102 on 8/25/2005
$4 Texas Power Preferred called for redemption at $102 on 8/25/2005
$4.24 Preferred called for redemption at $103.50 on 8/25/2005

$4.44 Preferred called for redemption at $102.61 on 8/25/2005
$4.50 Preferred called for redemption at $110 on 8/25/2005
$4.56 Texas Electric Preferred called for redemption at $112 on 8/25/2005
$4.56 Texas Power Preferred called for redemption at $112 on 8/25/2005
$4.64 Preferred called for redemption at $103.25 on 8/25/2005
$4.76 Preferred called for redemption at $102 on 8/25/2005
$4.80 Preferred called for redemption at $102.79 on 8/25/2005
$4.84 Preferred called for redemption at $101.79 on 8/25/2005
$5.08 Preferred called for redemption at $103.60 on 8/25/2005

TYBOR STORES, INC.
Name changed to Caribe Stores, Inc. in 1951

TYCE ENGINEERING CORP. (CA)
Adjudicated bankrupt 12/28/65
No stockholders' equity

TYCHE ENERGY INC (NV)
Common $0.001 par split (6) for (1) by issuance of (5) additional shares payable 03/13/2007 to holders of record 03/07/2007 Ex date - 03/14/2007
Recapitalized as Timberlake Energy Solutions, Inc. 04/13/2009
Each share Common $0.001 par exchanged for (0.00033333) share Common $0.001 par
(See Timberlake Energy Solutions, Inc.)

TYCHE LONGLAC GOLD MINES, LTD. (CANADA)
Charter surrendered 11/25/1948

TYCO, INC. (DE)
Name changed to Vestar, Inc. 10/19/64
Vestar, Inc. merged into Nexstar Pharmacueticals Inc. 2/21/95 which merged into Gilead Sciences, Inc. 7/29/99

TYCO ELECTRONICS LTD (BERMUDA)
Reincorporated under the laws of Switzerland and Common 20¢ par reclassified as Registered Shares CHF 2.60 par 06/26/2009

TYCO ELECTRONICS LTD (SWITZERLAND)
Registered Shares CHF 2.60 par changed to CHF 2.43 par 09/25/2009
Registered Shares CHF 2.43 par changed to CHF 2.09 par 03/26/2010
Registered Shares CHF 2.09 par changed to CHF 1.73 par 09/24/2010
Name changed to TE Connectivity Ltd. 03/17/2011

TYCO INTERNATIONAL, INC. (UT)
Name changed to Stinson & Farr Thoroughbred Management Co. 10/01/1984
(See Stinson & Farr Thoroughbred Management Co.)

TYCO INTERNATIONAL LTD. (SWITZERLAND)
Common CHF 8.53 par changed to CHF 8.30 par 05/27/2009
Common CHF 8.30 par changed to CHF 8.07 par 08/26/2009
Common CHF 8.07 par changed to CHF 7.84 par 11/24/2009
Common CHF 7.84 par changed to CHF 7.60 par 02/24/2010
Common CHF 7.60 par changed to CHF 7.38 par 05/26/2010
Common CHF 7.38 par changed to CHF 7.16 par 08/25/2010
Common CHF 7.16 par changed to CHF 6.93 par 11/23/2010
Common CHF 6.93 par changed to CHF 6.70 par 02/23/2011

Each share Common CHF 6.70 par received distribution of (0.5) share ADT Corp. Common 1¢ par and (0.239943) Pentair Ltd. Registered Share CHF 0.5 par payable 09/28/2012 to holders of record 09/17/2012 Ex date - 10/01/2012
Reorganized under the laws of Ireland as Tyco International PLC 11/17/2014
Each share Common CHF 6.70 par exchanged for (1) share Ordinary USD $0.01 par
Tyco International PLC merged into Johnson Controls International PLC 09/06/2016

TYCO INTL LTD (MA)
Name changed 11/09/1993
Common $1 par split (2) for (1) by issuance of (1) additional share 09/30/1968
Common $1 par changed to 50¢ par and (1) additional share issued 12/04/1981
Common 50¢ par split (2) for (1) by issuance of (1) additional share 03/27/1986
Common 50¢ par split (2) for (1) by issuance of (1) additional share 09/25/1987
Name changed from Tyco Laboratories, Inc. to Tyco International Ltd. 11/09/1993
Common 1¢ par split (2) for (1) by issuance of (1) additional share 11/14/1995
Merged into Tyco International Ltd. (Bermuda) 07/02/1997
Each share Common 50¢ par exchanged for (1) share Common 20¢ par
Tyco International Ltd. (Bermuda) reincorporated in Switzerland 03/17/2009

TYCO INTL LTD NEW (BERMUDA)
Common 20¢ par split (2) for (1) by issuance of (1) additional share payable 10/22/1997 to holders of record 10/01/1997 Ex date - 10/23/1997
Common 20¢ par split (2) for (1) by issuance of (1) additional share payable 10/21/1999 to holders of record 10/01/1999 Ex date - 10/22/1999
Each share Common 20¢ par received distribution of (0.25) share Covidien Ltd. Common 20¢ par payable 06/29/2007 to holders of record 06/18/2007
Each share Common 20¢ par received distribution of (0.25) share Tyco Electronics Ltd. Common 20¢ par payable 06/29/2007 to holders of record 06/18/2007
Each share Common 20¢ par exchanged for (0.25) share Common 80¢ par 07/02/2007
Reincorporated under the laws of Switzerland and Common 80¢ par changed to CHF 8.53 par 03/17/2009

TYCO INTL PLC (IRELAND)
Merged into Johnson Controls International PLC 09/06/2016
Each share Ordinary USD $0.01 par exchanged for (0.955) share Ordinary USD $0.01 par

TYCO TOYS INC (DE)
Common 1¢ par split (2) for (1) by issuance of (1) additional share 06/10/1992
Merged into Mattel, Inc. 03/27/1997
Each Depositary Preferred Ser. C exchanged for (1) Depositary Preferred Ser. C
Each share 8.25% Conv. Preferred Ser. C 1¢ par exchanged for (1) share 8.25% Conv. Preferred Ser. C 1¢ par
Each share Common 1¢ par exchanged for (0.48876) share Common 1¢ par

TYCODYNE INDS CORP (DE)
Charter cancelled and declared inoperative and void for non-payment of taxes 4/15/72

TYCOM CORP (DE)
Charter cancelled and declared inoperative and void for non-payment of taxes 3/1/78

TYCOM LTD (BERMUDA)
Merged into Tyco International Ltd. (Bermuda) 12/18/2001
Each share Common 25¢ par exchanged for (0.3133) share Common 20¢ par
Tyco International Ltd. (Bermuda) reincorporated in Switzerland 03/17/2009 which merged into Johnson Controls International PLC 09/06/2016

TYCONDA MINERALS CORP. (DE)
Recapitalized as Hy-Poll Technology, Inc. 11/02/1983
Each share Common 1¢ par exchanged for (10) shares Common $0.0001 par
Hy-Poll Technology, Inc. recapitalized as Universal Turf Inc. 09/22/1995 which name changed to Universal Media Holdings, Inc. 12/03/1999 which recapitalized as National Management Consulting Inc. 11/12/2002 which name changed to Genio Group, Inc. 09/11/2003 which recapitalized as Millennium Prime, Inc. 10/29/2009

TYCONDA MINERALS CORP. (NV)
Charter revoked for failure to file reports and pay fees 3/7/66

TYCOON VENTURES INC (BC)
Recapitalized as Paloma Ventures Inc. 6/14/95
Each share Common no par exchanged for (1/3) share Common no par
Paloma Ventures Inc. recapitalized as Paloma Resources Inc. 2/25/2004

TYCORE VENTURES INC (NV)
Name changed to Hondo Minerals Corp. 03/07/2011

TYE EXPLS INC (BC)
Delisted from Vancouver Stock Exchange 10/11/1985

TYEE LAKE RES LTD (BC)
Recapitalized as New Tyee Resources Ltd. 05/14/1980
Each share Capital Stock no par exchanged for (1/3) share Capital Stock no par
New Tyee Resources Ltd. recapitalized as Alban Explorations Ltd. 01/24/1985 which recapitalized as Pacific Amber Resources Ltd. (BC) 05/19/1994 which reincorporated in Alberta 07/25/2002 which recapitalized as Grand Banks Energy Corp. 05/14/2003
(See Grand Banks Energy Corp.)

TYEE PETROLEUMS LTD. (BC)
Dissolved 9/29/59

TYER RUBBER CO. (MA)
Common no par changed to $10 par and (2) additional shares issued in 1954
Name changed to Ryte Investors Co., Inc. 2/27/61 which completed liquidation 11/29/63

TYGARTS VALLEY NATIONAL BANK (ELKINS, WV)
Acquired by CB&T Financial Corp. 9/1/91
Each share Common $10 par exchanged for (2.3) shares Common $1 par
CB&T Financial Corp. acquired by Huntington Bancshares Inc. 6/25/93

TYGAS ENERGY INC (AB)
Merged into Tygas Resource Corp. 1/4/89
Each share Class A Common no par exchanged for (4.536) shares Common no par
Tygas Resource Corp. merged into Alberta Oil & Gas Ltd. 8/2/90 which recapitalized as Alberta Oil & Gas Petroleum Corp. 11/19/97 which recapitalized as Edge Energy Inc. 4/14/98 which merged into Ventus Energy Ltd. 8/11/2000 which name changed to Navigo Energy Inc. 5/24/2002
(See Navigo Energy Inc.)

TYGAS INDS LTD (AB)
Recapitalized as Tygas Energy Inc. 7/5/88
Each share Class A Common no par exchanged for (0.4) share Class A Common no par
Tygas Energy Inc. merged into Tygas Resource Corp. 1/4/89 which merged into Alberta Oil & Gas Ltd. 8/2/90 which recapitalized as Alberta Oil & Gas Petroleum Corp. 11/19/97 which recapitalized as Edge Energy Inc. 4/14/98 which merged into Ventus Energy Ltd. 8/11/2000 which name changed to Navigo Energy Inc. 5/24/2002
(See Navigo Energy Inc.)

TYGAS RESOURCE CORP (AB)
Merged into Alberta Oil & Gas Ltd. 08/02/1990
Each share Common no par exchanged for (6) shares Common no par
Alberta Oil & Gas Ltd. recapitalized as Alberta Oil & Gas Petroleum Corp. 11/19/1997 which recapitalized as Edge Energy Inc. 04/14/1998 which merged into Ventus Energy Ltd. 08/11/2000 which name changed to Navigo Energy Inc. 05/24/2002
(See Navigo Energy Inc.)

TYHEE DEV CORP (BC)
Name changed to Tyhee Gold Corp. 02/01/2011

TYLAN CORP (CA)
Acquired by Vacuum General Inc. 10/05/1989
Each share Common no par exchanged for $4.25 cash

TYLAN GEN INC (DE)
Merged into Millipore Corp. 1/27/97
Each share Common no par exchanged for $16 cash

TYLER BK & TR CO (TYLER, TX)
Each share Capital Stock $100 par exchanged for (5) shares Capital Stock $20 par 00/00/1947
Each share Capital Stock $20 par exchanged for (2) shares Capital Stock $10 par 02/04/1964
Stock Dividends - 50% 00/00/1948; 12.5% 00/00/1955; 11.1% 00/00/1959; 25% 01/00/1966; 20% 01/00/1970; 23.27% 02/04/1974
Merged into RepublicBank Corp. 10/01/1982
Each share Capital Stock $10 par exchanged for (2.4) shares Common $5 par
RepublicBank Corp. name changed to First RepublicBank Corp. 06/06/1987
(See First RepublicBank Corp.)

TYLER BUILDING CORP. (NY)
In process of liquidation since 1952

TYLER CABOT MTG SECS FD (MD)
Acquired by Capstead Mortgage Corp. 12/2/92
Each share Common 1¢ par exchanged for (1) share $1.26 Conv. Preferred Ser. B 10¢ par

TYLER CORP (DE)
Name changed to Tyler Technologies Inc. 5/20/99

TYLER CORP NEW (DE)
Reorganized as Tyler Corp. 5/21/90
Each share Common 1¢ par exchanged for (1) share Common 1¢ par
Tyler Corp. name changed to Tyler Technologies Inc. 5/20/99

TYLER CORP OLD (DE)
Common 10¢ par split (2) for (1) by issuance of (1) additional share 5/26/76
Common 10¢ par split (2) for (1) by issuance of (1) additional share 8/29/78
Common 10¢ par split (2) for (1) by issuance of (1) additional share 4/11/85
Merged into Akzo N.V. 8/24/89
Each share Common 10¢ par exchanged for (0.145569) Sponsored ADR for American shares 50 Gldrs. par
AKZO N.V. name changed to AKZO Nobel N.V. 2/25/94

TYLER FIXTURE CORP. (MI)
Name changed to Tyler Refrigeration Corp. in 1953
Tyler Refrigeration Corp. acquired by Clark Equipment Co. (MI) 9/30/63 which reincorporated under the laws of Delaware 7/1/68
(See Clark Equipment Co. (DE))

TYLER PIPE & FOUNDRY CO. (TX)
Name changed to Tyler Pipe Industries, Inc. 3/7/67

TYLER PIPE INDS INC (TX)
100% acquired by Saturn Industries, Inc. through purchase offer which expired 07/03/1973
Public interest eliminated

TYLER REFRIGERATION CORP. (MI)
Acquired by Clark Equipment Co. (MI) on a (4/7) for (1) basis 9/30/63
Clark Equipment Co. (MI) reincorporated under the laws of Delaware 7/1/68
(See Clark Equipment Co. (DE))

TYLER RES INC (AB)
Reincorporated 04/27/1995
Place of incorporation changed from (BC) to (AB) 04/27/1995
Acquired by Jinchuan Group Ltd. 03/13/2008
Each share Common no par exchanged for $1.60 cash

TYLERSTONE VENTURES CORP (DE)
Reorganized as nCoat, Inc. 02/20/2007
Each share Common $0.001 par exchanged for (20) shares Common $0.001 par
(See nCoat, Inc.)

TYLOX RESOURCE CORP (BC)
Name changed to Tracer Petroleum Corp. 12/2/91
Tracer Petroleum Corp. name changed to Forum Energy Corp. 7/21/2003 which name changed to FEC Resources Inc. 6/9/2005

TYMAN PLC (UNITED KINGDOM)
ADR agreement terminated 07/24/2017
No ADR's remain outstanding

TYMAR RES INC (BC)
Recapitalized as Baja Gold, Inc. 01/25/1993
Each share Common no par exchanged for (0.1) share Common no par
Baja Gold, Inc. merged into Viceroy Resource Corp. 05/30/1996 which merged into Quest Capital Corp. (BC) 06/30/2003 which reincorporated in Canada 05/27/2008 which name changed to Sprott Resource Lending Corp. 09/10/2010 which merged into Sprott Inc. 07/24/2013

TYME RES LTD (BC)
Recapitalized as North American Tire Recycling Ltd. 11/04/1991
Each share Common no par exchanged for (0.25) share Common no par
North American Tire Recycling Ltd. merged into Omnicorp Ltd. 04/08/1993
(See Omnicorp Ltd.)

TYMSHARE INC (CA)
Common no par split (2) for (1) by issuance of (1) additional share 12/19/80
Merged into McDonnell Douglas Corp. 5/18/84
Each share Common no par exchanged for $25 cash

TYNDALL EXPLORATIONS LTD. (ON)
Charter cancelled in March 1967

TYNER MNG CORP (AB)
Recapitalized as Delmay Mining Corp. 11/4/87
Each share Common no par exchanged for (0.5) share Common no par
Delmay Mining Corp. name changed to Delmay Energy Corp. 7/16/93

TYON GOLD MINES, LTD. (ON)
Charter cancelled for failure to file reports and pay taxes 11/19/56

TYPE BY WIRE CORP. (DE)
Charter cancelled and declared inoperative and void for non-payment of taxes 4/1/29

TYPE 1 MEDIA INC (DE)
Name changed to Diego Pellicer Worldwide, Inc. 03/13/2015

TYPHOON ENTERPRISES INC (NV)
Name changed to Typhoon Touch Technologies, Inc. 10/10/2007

TYPHOON TUNES INC (NV)
Reorganized as Typhoon Enterprises Inc. 08/13/2007
Each share Common $0.001 par exchanged for (4) shares Common $0.001 par
Typhoon Enterprises Inc. name changed to Typhoon Touch Technologies, Inc. 10/10/2007

TYPHOON VENTURE CAP CORP (CANADA)
Name changed to Typhoon Exploration Inc. 02/06/2003

TYPHOON YELLOWKNIFE MINES, LTD. (ON)
Charter cancelled and declared dissolved for default in filing returns in 1968

TYR-MAC GOLDS, LTD. (ON)
Charter cancelled for failure to file reports and pay taxes in 1957

TYRAE RES INC (AB)
Name changed to North American Gold Corp. 09/04/1990
North American Gold Corp. name changed to North American Technologies Inc. 11/26/1991 which merged into North American Technologies Group, Inc. 11/25/1993
(See North American Technologies Group, Inc.)

TYRANEX GOLD INC (ON)
Recapitalized as Dotcom 2000 Inc. 08/24/1999
Each share Common no par exchanged for (0.2) share Common no par
Dotcom 2000 Inc. name changed to Konexus Ltd. 01/10/2002
(See Konexus Technologies Ltd.)

TYRANITE GRANITE & MARBLE INC (ON)
Recapitalized 09/17/1992
Recapitalized from Tyranite Mines Ltd. to Tyranite Granite & Marble Inc. 09/17/1992
Each share Common $1 par exchanged for (0.1) share Common no par
Name changed to Footmaxx Holdings Inc. 11/17/1994
Footmaxx Holdings Inc. name changed to FMX Ventures Inc. 12/07/2007 which recapitalized as Tolima Gold Inc. 12/12/2011

TYREX OIL CO (WY)
Name changed to 3SI Holdings, Inc. (WY) 06/18/1998
3SI Holdings, Inc. (WY) reorganized in Florida as Bulova Technologies Group, Inc. 02/25/2009

TYRON INC (DE)
Charter cancelled and declared inoperative and void for non-payment of taxes 3/1/90

TYRONA RES LTD (BC)
Merged into Signal Hill Energy Corp. 12/20/82
Each share Common no par exchanged for (0.25) share Common no par
Signal Hill Energy Corp. recapitalized as Texas Petroleum Corp. (B.C.) 6/13/85 which recapitalized as North American Equity Corp. 3/7/89
(See North American Equity Corp.)

TYRONE HYDRAULICS INC (DE)
Merged into Dana Corp. 06/16/1980
Each share Common $1 par exchanged for (1.13) shares Common $1 par
(See Dana Corp.)

TYRONE MINES LTD. (QC)
Charter cancelled for failure to file reports and pay fees in 1970

TYSON BEARING CORP. (DE)
Common $5 par changed to $1 par in 1949
Acquired by SKF Industries, Inc. through payment of $3 per share 7/1/57

TYSON FINL CORP (BC)
Recapitalized as Midd Financial Corp. 6/1/92
Each share Common no par exchanged for (0.2) share Common no par
(See Midd Financial Corp.)

TYSON FOODS INC (DE)
Name changed 03/31/1971
Reincorporated 02/28/1986
Common $2 par changed to $1 par and (1) additional share issued 10/07/1968
Name changed from Tyson's Foods, Inc. to Tyson Foods, Inc. 03/31/1971
Common $1 par split (4) for (1) by issuance of (3) additional shares 11/15/1978
Common $1 par split (5) for (2) by issuance of (1.5) additional shares 04/15/1985
Stock Dividend - 100% 04/15/1983
Reincorporated under the laws of Delaware and Common $1 par changed to 10¢ par 02/28/1986
Each 4.75% Tangible Equity Unit automatically became (1.0738) shares Class A Common 10¢ par 07/17/2017

TYSON ROLLER BEARING CORP.
Name changed to Tyson Bearing Corp. in 1943
Tyson Bearing Corp. was acquired by SKF Industries, Inc. for cash 7/1/57

TYSONS FINL CORP (VA)
Merged into Mainstreet BankGroup Inc. 2/28/98
Each share Common $5 par exchanged for (0.527) share Common $5 par
MainStreet BankGroup Inc. name changed to MainStreet Financial Corp. 6/1/98 which merged into BB&T Corp. 3/8/99

TYTAN RES INC (UT)
Name changed to Sterling Continental Corp. 3/10/88
(See Sterling Continental Corp.)

TYUMENAVIATRANS A O (RUSSIA)
Name changed to UTair Aviation JSC 10/01/2002
(See UTair Aviation JSC)

TYUMENTELECOM (RUSSIA)
ADR agreement terminated 12/19/2002
Each Sponsored ADR for Preferred exchanged for $2.70219 cash
Each Sponsored ADR for Ordinary exchanged for $2.24476 cash

TZAAR CORP (NV)
Recapitalized as Gencell Inc. 12/27/96
Each share Common $0.001 par exchanged for (0.1) share Common $0.001 par
Gencell Inc. name changed to Gene-Cell, Inc. 10/8/97

U

U & I INC (UT)
Name changed to UI Group, Inc. 08/22/1983
(See UI Group, Inc.)

U & W URANIUM, INC. (WA)
Out of existence and automatically dissolved for non-payment of corporate license fees 7/1/62

U A P INC (QC)
Each share old Class A Common no par exchanged for (2) shares new Class A Common no par 12/10/1968
New Class A Common no par split (2) for (1) by issuance of (1) additional share 12/07/1984
New Class A Common no par split (2) for (1) by issuance of (1) additional share 07/06/1987
New Class A Common no par split (3) for (2) by issuance of (0.5) additional share 05/20/1994
Merged into Genuine Parts Acquisition Inc. 12/02/1998
Each share new Class A Common no par exchanged for $28.50 cash

U B BANCSHARES INC (OH)
Merged into Park National Corp. 4/30/2000
Each share Common no par exchanged for (0.577209) share Common no par

U B S CHEMICAL CORP. (MA)
Merged into Staley (A.E.) Manufacturing Co. 6/30/59
Each (1.75) shares Common $1 par exchanged for (1) share Common $10 par
Staley (A.E.) Manufacturing Co. reorganized as Staley Continental, Inc. 2/12/85

U B S FUND OF CANADA, LTD. (CANADA)
Merged into Canada General Fund, Inc. (MA) 12/28/1964
Each share Common $1 par exchanged for (0.54982) share Common $1 par
Canada General Fund, Inc. (MA) name changed to Boston Common Stock Fund, Inc. 09/17/1968 which name changed to Vance, Sanders Common Stock Fund, Inc. 12/29/1972 which name changed to Eaton Vance Growth Fund, Inc. 11/16/1981 which reorganized as Eaton Vance Growth Trust 07/01/2007

U-BAKE GOURMET PIZZA INC (NV)
Name changed to Oregon Outerwear Inc. 3/20/98
Oregon Outerwear Inc. name changed to Pacific Sports Holdings, Inc. 6/18/98 which recapitalized as Tahoe Pacific Corp. 8/30/99 which name changed to Ameri-First Financial Group Inc. (NV) 1/6/2000 which reincorporated in Delaware 3/22/2000

U-BEVA URANIUM CO. (UT)
Recapitalized as U-Beva Mines 3/4/68
Each share Capital Stock 5¢ par exchanged for (0.04) share Capital Stock 5¢ par
U-Beva Mines name changed to Newport International Companies, Inc. 9/30/70

U C INVTS LTD (SOUTH AFRICA)
Under plan of merger name changed to Gencor Investments Corp. Ltd. 11/4/83
Gencor Investments Corp. Ltd. name changed to Genbel Investments Ltd. 8/13/84 which name changed to Genbel South Africa Ltd. 11/24/95
(See Genbel South Africa Ltd.)

U C VALVE CORP (BC)
Reorganized as Blackbridge Capital Corp. 12/1/89
Each share Common no par exchanged for (1) share Common no par
Blackbridge Capital Corp. name changed to Rupert Resources Ltd. 11/1/94

U-CAN-BREW CORP (ON)
Name changed to Brew Kettle Corp. 10/21/1993
Brew Kettle Corp. recapitalized as Lago Resources Ltd. 10/13/1995 which recapitalized as RUX Resources Inc. 01/16/1997 which name changed to Galaxy Online Inc. 12/08/1999
(See Galaxy Online Inc.)

U CAN RES INC (UT)
Each share old Common 1¢ par exchanged for (0.5) share new Common 1¢ par 11/30/84
Merged into Trinity Gas Corp. 5/26/93
Each share new Common 1¢ par exchanged for (0.04) share Common $0.001 par
Trinity Gas Corp. name changed to Petro-Sers Corp. 7/8/93 which name changed to Mid-Atlantic Home Health Network Inc. 12/9/94

U-FINISH HOMES, INC. (TN)
Name changed to Kemwall Financial Corp. 1/7/63
Kemwall Financial Corp. name changed to Allied Mortgage & Development Co., Inc. 6/10/63 which name changed to Alodex Corp. 4/18/69
(See Alodex Corp.)

U G M CORP (PA)
Adjudicated bankrupt 02/18/1975
Stockholders' equity unlikely

U I P CORP (DE)
Common $2.60 par changed to $1 par 05/01/1973
Merged into Eastmet Corp. 12/20/1979
Each share Common $1 par exchanged for (0.5264) share Common $1 par
(See Eastmet Corp.)

U K CAP INC
Money Market Preferred called for redemption at $1,000,000 on 5/26/98

U-KAN MINERALS, INC. (KS)
Name changed to Shawnee Oil Corp., Inc. 1/13/58
(See Shawnee Oil Corp., Inc.)

U.N. BERYLLIUM CORP. (UT)
Name changed to U.N. Oil & Exploration Co. 00/00/1958
U.N. Oil & Exploration Co. recapitalized as U.N. Industries Inc. 02/12/1968
(See U.N. Industries Inc.)

U.N. OIL & EXPLORATION CO. (UT)
Recapitalized as U.N. Industries Inc. 02/12/1968
Each share Capital Stock 1¢ par exchanged for (0.1) share Capital Stock no par
(See U.N. Industries Inc.)

U N A CORP (DE)
Plan of reorganization under Chapter 11 Federal Bankruptcy proceedings confirmed 05/06/1988
No old Common stockholders' equity
Merged into Okura Acquisition Corp. 09/28/1990
Each share new Common 10¢ par exchanged for $0.20 cash
Each share new Common 10¢ par received escrow payment of $0.003 cash 11/08/1991

U N ALLOY STL CORP (DE)
Name changed to U.N.A. Corp. 03/20/1969
(See U.N.A. Corp.)

U N BANCSHARES INC (MO)
Merged into Boatmen's Bancshares, Inc. 8/8/74
Each share Common $5 par exchanged for (1.0484) shares Common $10 par
Boatmen's Bancshares, Inc. merged into NationsBank Corp. 1/7/97 which reincorporated in Delaware as BankAmerica Corp. (Old) 9/25/98 which merged into BankAmerica Corp. (New) 9/30/98 which name changed to Bank of America Corp. 4/28/99

U N DLRS (CO)
Each share old Common 1¢ par exchanged for (0.001) share new Common 1¢ par 09/07/2000
Reincorporated under the laws of Nevada as Slateco International Group Inc. 01/29/2002
Slateco International Group Inc. (NV) reincorporated in Wyoming as Terrablock Development, Inc. 02/21/2006 which name changed to Linked Media Group, Inc. 12/30/2008
(See Linked Media Group, Inc.)

U N INDS INC (UT)
Proclaimed dissolved for failure to file annual reports 12/31/1985

U NEVA INDS INC (NV)
Recapitalized as Silvex Industries, Inc. 8/22/69
Each share Common $1 par exchanged for (1) share Common 10¢ par
Silvex Industries, Inc. reorganized as Silvex Corp. 12/9/71
(See Silvex Corp.)

U-NEVA URANIUM CORP. (NV)
Recapitalized as U-Neva Industries, Inc. 5/12/59
Each share Common 2¢ par exchanged for (0.02) share Common $1 par
U-Neva Industries, Inc. name changed to Silvex Industries, Inc. 8/22/69 which reorganized as Silvex Corp. 12/9/71
(See Silvex Corp.)

U-PAK SHIPPING CONTAINERS INC (AB)
Recapitalized 04/18/1991
Recapitalized from U-Pak Shipping Systems Inc. to U-Pak Shipping Containers Inc. 04/18/1991
Each share Common no par exchanged for (1/3) share Common no par
Reincorporated under the laws of British Columbia as Citation Resources Inc. 11/29/1996
Citation Resources Inc. recapitalized as Macarthur Diamonds Ltd. (BC) 10/24/2002 which reincorporated in Australia 12/02/2002 which recapitalized as Macarthur Minerals Ltd. 07/07/2005

U R FLOWERS CORP (BC)
Recapitalized as Redstar Resources Corp. 4/19/96
Each share Common no par exchanged for (1/3) share Common no par
Redstar Resources Corp. recapitalized as Redstar Gold Corp. 4/26/2002

U.S. AIRLINES, INC. (FL)
Adjudicated bankrupt 09/00/1953
No stockholders' equity

U.S. ASSURANCE CO. (OH)
Name changed to Mansfield Insurance Corp. 12/19/72
(See Mansfield Insurance Corp.)

U.S. BEARING CORP. (CA)
Stock Dividend - 10% 01/28/1960
Merged into Networks Electronic Corp. on a (0.8) for (1) basis 10/31/1962
(See Networks Electronic Corp.)

U.S. BOBBIN & SHUTTLE CO. (RI)
Common $100 par changed to $50 par in 1928
Common $50 par changed to $10 par in 1939
Merged into Baker Industries, Inc. 10/18/60
Each share Preferred $100 par exchanged for (8) shares Common $1 par
Each share Common $10 par exchanged for (0.5) share Common $1 par
(See Baker Industries, Inc.)

U.S. CAPITAL CORP. (OH)
Charter cancelled for failure to file reports 4/3/75

U.S. CHICLE & CONFECTION CO. (DE)
Charter cancelled for non-payment of taxes in 1922

U.S. CITIES CORP. (DE)
Charter forfeited in 1929

U.S. CONSOLIDATED MINES, INC. (NV)
Charter revoked for failure to file reports and pay fees 03/05/1962

U.S. CONTROLS, INC. (NY)
Charter cancelled and proclaimed dissolved for failure to pay taxes and file reports 12/16/68

U.S. DISCOUNT CORP. (FL)
Voluntarily dissolved 6/25/65
Details not available

U.S. EAGLE FUND, INC. (MD)
Merged into Fidelity & Guaranty Life Insurance Co. 05/31/1991
Details not available

U.S. ELECTRONICS DEVELOPMENT CORP. (CA)
Charter revoked for failure to file reports and pay fees 3/1/60

U.S. EXPORT CHEMICAL CORP. (DE)
Charter cancelled and declared inoperative and void for non-payment of taxes 04/01/1934

U.S. FIBER GLASS INDUSTRIAL PLASTICS, INC. (NY)
Recapitalized 5/15/56
Each (10) shares Class A 10¢ par exchanged for (13) shares Common 10¢ par
Each (10) shares Class B 10¢ par exchanged for (12) shares Common 10¢ par
Adjudicated bankrupt 1/14/57

U.S. FIBERGLASS PRODUCTS CO. (TX)
Merged into Red Fish Boat Co. 4/9/62
Each share Common $1 par exchanged for (1.5) shares Class A Common 10¢ par
Red Fish Boat Co. was adjudicated bankrupt 1/11/63

U.S. FOOD PRODUCTS CORP. (NJ)
Assets purchased by National Distillers Products Corp. in 1924
No stockholders' equity

U.S. GOLD CORP. (WA)
Automatically dissolved for non-payment of corporate license fees 7/1/59

U.S. GRANT MINING CO. (MT)
Charter suspended for failure to file returns and pay taxes 01/21/1954

U.S. HOME & DEVELOPMENT CORP. (DE)
Class A Capital Stock 10¢ par reclassified as Common 10¢ par 8/13/68
Name changed to U.S. Home Corp. (Old) 6/22/71
U.S. Home Corp. (Old) reorganized as U.S. Home Corp. (New) 6/21/93 which merged into Lennar Corp. 5/2/2000

U.S. LABORATORIES (CA)
Charter revoked for failure to file reports and pay fees 12/1/69

U.S. LAND & UTILITIES CO. (DE)
Name changed to Dynastar Corp. 4/19/74
Dynastar Corp. charter cancelled 3/1/84

U.S. LAND DEVELOPMENT CORP. (FL)
Common $1 par changed to 10¢ par 2/27/62
Liquidated for benefit of creditors 3/16/66
No stockholders' equity

U.S. LEASING REAL ESTATE INVESTORS (CA)
Name changed to San Francisco Real Estate Investors 7/1/76
San Francisco Real Estate Investors reorganized in Delaware as San Francisco Real Estate Investors, Inc. 6/30/83 which merged into REIT of America, Inc. 10/4/83 which merged into Unicorp American Corp. (New) 12/13/84
(See Unicorp American Corp. (New))

U.S. MACHINE CORP. (IN)
Acquired by Stewart-Warner Corp. in 1953
Each (9.428) shares Common $1 par exchanged for (1) share Capital Stock $5 par
(See Stewart-Warner Corp.)

U.S. MANGANESE CORP. (AZ)
Each share Common $1 par exchanged for (4) shares Common 25¢ par 3/19/52
Name changed to National Resources Corp. 9/25/62
Each share Common 25¢ par exchanged for (0.033333) share Common no par
(See National Resources Corp.)

U.S. MARKETS, INC. (CA)
Merged into P&X Markets, Inc. for cash 2/11/64

U.S. MERCURY CORP. (DE)
Merged into Shawano Development Corp. 4/20/55
Each (4.65) shares Common 1¢ par exchanged for (1) share Common $1 par
Shawno Development Corp. proclaimed dissolved 6/7/66

U.S. NO-JOINT CONCRETE PIPE CO. (CO)
Merged into Mancos Corp. 7/10/70

Each share Common $1 par exchanged for (0.1) share Capital Stock 1¢ par
Mancos Corp. acquired by Union Oil Co. of California 11/27/78 which reorganized as Unocal Corp. 4/25/83 which merged into Chevron Corp. 8/10/2005

U.S. OIL & GAS CORP. (DE)
Merged into TM Industries, Inc. 10/31/69
Each share Common 10¢ par exchanged for (0.1) share Common 1¢ par
TM Industries, Inc. adjudicated bankrupt 4/9/73

U.S. PHOTO SUPPLY CO., INC. (DE)
Common 50¢ par changed to 10¢ par and (4) additional shares issued 4/21/61
No longer in existence having become inoperative and void for non-payment of taxes 4/1/65

U.S. PLASTIC & CHEMICAL CORP.
Name changed to USPAC Corp. 4/1/65
(See USPAC Corp.)

U.S. POLYMERIC CHEMICALS, INC. (DE)
Stock Dividend - 10% 4/1/64
Name changed to U.S. Polymeric, Inc. 3/25/65
U.S. Polymeric, Inc. acquired by Hitco 1/6/69 which merged into Armco Steel Corp. 12/31/69 which name changed to Armco Inc. 7/1/78 which merged into AK Steel Holding Corp. 9/30/99

U.S. RAILROAD SECURITIES FUND, INC. (OH)
Completely liquidated 04/27/1964
Each share Common $2 par exchanged for first and final distribution of $1.80 cash

U.S. REALTY INVESTMENTS LIQUIDATING TRUST (OH)
In process of liquidation
Each Ctf. of Bene. Int. no par received third distribution of $1 cash 7/29/83
Each Ctf. of Bene. Int. no par received fourth distribution of $0.50 cash 12/5/83
Each Ctf. of Bene. Int. no par received fifth distribution of $0.75 cash 7/30/86
Each Ctf. of Bene. Int. no par received sixth distribution of $0.25 cash 12/1/86
Each Ctf. of Bene. Int. no par received seventh and final distribution of $0.035 cash 9/30/87
Note: Certificates were not required to be surrendered and are now valueless
(See U.S. Realty Investments for previous distributions)

U.S. SEMICONDUCTOR PRODUCTS, INC. NEW (AZ)
Ctfs. dated after 6/11/59
Acquired by Nuclear Corp. of America (DE) on a (0.8) for (1) basis 4/30/62
Nuclear Corp. of America (DE) recapitalized as Nucor Corp. 12/29/71

U.S. SEMICONDUCTOR PRODUCTS, INC. OLD (AZ)
Assets sold to Topp Industries, Inc. (CA) on a (0.15311) for (1) basis 06/11/1959
Topp Industries, Inc. (CA) reincorporated in Delaware as Topp Industries Corp. 12/31/1959 which merged into United Industrial Corp. (DE) 12/31/1959
(See United Industrial Corp.)

U.S. SONICS CORP. (MA)
Adjudicated bankrupt in January 1964
No stockholders' equity

U.S. SYSTEMS, INC. (DE)
No longer in existence having become inoperative and void for non-payment of taxes 4/1/63

U.S. THERMO CONTROL CO. (MN)
Name changed to Thermo King Corp. 6/4/56, which was acquired by Westinghouse Electric Corp. 8/12/61

U.S. TRANSISTOR CORP. (NY)
Adjudicated bankrupt 10/22/62
No stockholders' equity

U.S. URANIUM CORP. (UT)
Name changed to Anglo Oil & Exploration Co. in 1958
(See Anglo Oil & Exploration Co.)

U.S. VITAMIN & PHARMACEUTICAL CORP. (DE)
Each share Common $1 par or VTC for Common $1 par split (2) for (1) respectively by issuance of (1) additional share 12/19/58
Merged into Revlon, Inc. 1/4/66
Each share Common $1 par or VTC for Common $1 par exchanged for (1) share $1 Conv. Preferred $1 par
(See Revlon, Inc.)

U.S. VITAMIN CORP. (DE)
Name changed to U.S. Vitamin & Pharmaceutical Corp. 12/18/58
U.S. Vitamin & Pharmaceutical Corp. merged into Revlon, Inc. 1/4/66
(See Revlon, Inc.)

U S A FLORAL PRODS INC (DE)
Plan of reorganization under Chapter 11 Federal Bankruptcy Code effective 07/18/2002
No stockholders' equity

U S A GROWTH INC (DE)
Name changed to World Shopping Network Inc. (DE) 10/04/1999
World Shopping Network Inc. (DE) reincorporated in Nevada as WSN Group, Inc. 06/01/2001 which recapitalized as Niteagle Systems, Inc. 04/11/2006 which recapitalized as Alternative Green Technologies Inc. 12/12/2008

U S A LD CORP (NY)
Dissolved by proclamation 12/17/2000

U S A MED CORP (WY)
Common $0.001 par split (10) for (1) by issuance of (9) additional shares 01/23/1989
Name changed to Life Concepts, Inc. 03/01/1991
Life Concepts, Inc. name changed to World Vision Holding Inc. 11/26/1997
(See Vision Holding Inc.)

USA URANIUM CORP (NV)
SEC revoked common stock registration 06/21/2010

U S AGGREGATES INC (DE)
Issue Information - 5,000,000 shares COM offered at $15 per share on 08/12/1999
Plan of reorganization under Chapter 11 Federal Bankruptcy Code effective 10/6/2003
No stockholders' equity

U S AGY MTG BKD REIT ADVANTAGED FD (ON)
Trust terminated 07/06/2016
Each Class A Unit received net asset value

U S AIR INC (DE)
$3 Conv. Preferred Ser. A no par called for redemption 03/27/1981
$1.875 Conv. Sr. Preferred Ser. B no par called for redemption 06/05/1981
$3 Conv. Preferred Ser. A no par called for redemption 02/26/1982
Under plan of reorganization each share Conv. Preferred Ser. C no par and Common $1 par automatically became (1) share USAir Group, Inc. Conv. Preferred Ser. C no par and Common $1 par respectively 02/01/1983
USAir Group, Inc. name changed to US Airways Group, Inc. 02/21/1997
(See US Airways Group, Inc.)

U S AIRWAYS GROUP INC (DE)
Name changed 02/21/1997
Conv. Preferred Ser. C no par called for redemption 11/02/1987
Name changed from USAir Group, Inc. to US Airways Group, Inc. 02/21/1997
Depositary Conv. Preferred Ser. B called for redemption 09/15/1997
Conv. Preferred Ser. B no par called for redemption 09/15/1997
Plan of reorganization under Chapter 11 Federal Bankruptcy Code effective 03/31/2003
No Common stockholders' equity
Plan of reorganization under Chapter 11 Federal Bankruptcy Code effective 09/27/2005
No stockholders' equity

U S ALCOHOL TESTING AMER INC (DE)
Common 1¢ par split (3) for (2) by issuance of (0.5) additional share 11/12/91
Common 1¢ par split (3) for (2) for issuance of (0.5) additional share 2/24/92
$0.40 Conv. Preferred Class B 1¢ par called for redemption 11/1/94
Name changed to Substance Abuse Technologies Inc. 10/25/96
(See Substance Abuse Technologies Inc.)

U S AMATEUR SPORTS INC (FL)
Name changed to eCom eCom.com, Inc. 01/29/1999
(See eCom eCom.com, Inc.)

U S AMMUNITION LTD (BC)
Recapitalized as Keynote Resources Inc. 11/21/1990
Each share Common no par exchanged for (0.2) share Common no par
(See Keynote Resources Inc.)

U S ASSET CORP (DE)
Each share old Common $0.001 par exchanged for (0.2) share new Common $0.001 par 03/07/1996
Name changed to Securitek International Corp. 07/02/1996
(See Securitek International Corp.)

U S ASSURN CORP (NV)
Name changed to U.S. General Corp. 09/25/1989
(See U.S. General Corp.)

U S AUTOMOTIVE MFG INC (DE)
Each (15) shares old Common $0.001 par exchanged for (1) share new Common $0.001 par 2/12/99
Assets sold for the benefit of creditors 3/15/2001
No stockholders' equity

U S AWYS GROUP INC (DE)
Ctfs. dated after 09/27/2005
Merged into American Airlines Group Inc. 12/09/2013
Each share Common 1¢ par exchanged for (1) share Common 1¢ par

U.S.B. & M. LIQUIDATION CORP.
Dissolved in 1945

U S B HLDG INC (DE)
Common $10 par changed to $5 par and (1) additional share issued 08/21/1991
Common $5 par split (2) for (1) by issuance of (1) additional share payable 12/30/1996 to holders of record 12/13/1996
Common $5 par split (2) for (1) by issuance of (1) additional share payable 12/24/1997 to holders of record 12/15/1997 Ex date - 12/26/1997
Common $5 par changed to 1¢ par 05/20/1998
Stock Dividends - 10% payable 06/14/1996 to holders of record 05/31/1996; 10% payable 12/21/1998 to holders of record 12/07/1998; 5% payable 05/15/2000 to holders of record 05/01/2000; 10% payable 01/22/2002 to holders of record 01/08/2002; 5% payable 09/26/2003 to holders of record 09/12/2003; 5% payable 09/24/2004 to holders of record 09/10/2004; 5% payable 09/23/2005 to holders of record 09/09/2005 Ex date - 09/07/2005
Merged into KeyCorp (New) 01/01/2008
Each share Common 1¢ par exchanged for (0.455) share Common $1 par and $8.925 cash

U S BANCORP (DE)
8.125% Preferred Ser. A no par called for redemption at $25 on 11/14/1997
Common $1.25 par split (3) for (1) by issuance of (2) additional shares payable 05/18/1998 to holders of record 05/04/1998 Ex date - 05/19/1998
Under plan of merger each share Common $1.25 par exchanged for (1.265) shares Common 1¢ par 02/27/2001
Depositary Preferred Ser. D called for redemption at $25 plus $0.26797 accrued dividends on 06/03/2013
6% Depositary Preferred Ser. G called for redemption at $25 on 04/15/2017
(Additional Information in Active)

U S BANCORP (OR)
Common $10 par changed to $5 par and (1) additional share issued 05/28/1973
Common $5 par split (5) for (4) by issuance of (0.25) additional share 03/01/1982
Common $5 par split (3) for (2) by issuance of (0.5) additional share 09/02/1986
Common $5 par split (6) for (5) by issuance of (0.2) additional share 09/14/1990
Common $5 par split (3) for (2) by issuance of (0.5) additional share 08/12/1991
Stock Dividends - 10% 04/15/1969; 10% 05/03/1976; 10% 03/01/1978; 20% 05/30/1979; 10% 02/29/1980; 10% 10/01/1984; 20% 09/15/1989
Merged into U.S. Bancorp (DE) 08/01/1997
Each share 8.125% Preferred Ser. A no par exchanged for (1) share 8.125% Preferred Ser. A no par
Each share Common $5 par exchanged for (0.755) share Common $1.25 par

U S BANCORP RLTY & MTG TR (OR)
Name changed to Pacific Realty Trust 03/01/1979
(See Pacific Realty Trust)

U S BERYLLIUM CORP (CO)
Charter suspended for failure to maintain a resident agent 03/16/1987

U S BIODEFENSE INC (UT)
Each share old Common $0.001 par exchanged for (3) shares new Common $0.001 par 01/31/2005
Each share new Common $0.001 par received distribution of (0.01) share Emergency Disaster Systems, Inc. Restricted Common $0.001 par payable 09/07/2007 to holders of record 09/07/2007
Each share new Common $0.001 par exchanged again for (0.001) share new Common $0.001 par 01/10/2008
Name changed to Elysium Internet, Inc. 07/28/2008

U S-U S

FINANCIAL INFORMATION, INC.

Elysium Internet, Inc. name changed to TheDirectory.com, Inc. 08/17/2011

U S BIOMEDICAL CORP (DE)
Ceased operations 04/00/1998
Stockholders' equity unlikely

U S BIOSCIENCE INC (DE)
Common $0.005 par split (2) for (1) by issuance of (1) additional share 01/16/1992
Each share Common $0.005 par exchanged for (0.5) share Common 1¢ par 04/22/1996
Merged into MedImmune, Inc. 11/23/1999
Each share Common 1¢ par exchanged for (0.15) share Common 1¢ par
(See MedImmune, Inc.)

U S BRDG CORP (DE)
Name changed to USABG Corp. 01/13/1998
(See USABG Corp.)

U S BRDG N Y INC (NY)
Name changed to USA Bridge Construction of N.Y., Inc. 1/12/98
(See USA Bridge Construction of N.Y., Inc.)

U S CAN CORP (DE)
Merged into Pac Packaging Acquisition Corp. 10/4/2000
Each share Common 1¢ par exchanged for $20 cash

U S CDN MINERALS INC (NV)
Each share old Common $0.001 par exchanged for (3) shares new Common $0.001 par 10/27/2004
Each share new Common $0.001 par exchanged again for (0.02) share new Common $0.001 par 10/09/2007
Name changed to Noble Consolidated Industries Corp. 01/15/2010
(See Noble Consolidated Industries Corp.)

U S CAP CORP (DE)
Under plan of reorganization each share Common 10¢ par automatically became (1) share American Capital Holdings, Inc. Common 10¢ par 2/4/89
(See American Capital Holdings, Inc.)

U S CARD INVS INC (UT)
Involuntarily dissolved 07/01/1994

U S CAST PRODS INC (NV)
Charter permanently revoked 11/30/2001

U S CELLULAR TEL CO (CO)
Merged into Sequel Corp. (CO) 02/12/1986
Each share Common $0.001 par exchanged for (0.01) share Common 1¢ par
Sequel Corp. (CO) reincorporated in Delaware 04/22/1988 which name changed to Hanger Orthopedic Group, Inc. 08/14/1989 which name changed to Hanger, Inc. 06/11/2012

U S-CHINA INDL EXCHANGE INC (NY)
Each share old Common 1¢ par exchanged for (0.125) share new Common 1¢ par 02/26/1999
Stock Dividends - 10% payable 09/27/2000 to holders of record 09/13/2000; 10% payable 07/15/2002 to holders of record 06/19/2002 Ex date - 06/17/2002
Reincorporated under the laws of Delaware as Chindex International, Inc. 07/16/2002
(See Chindex International, Inc.)

U S COAL CORP (MN)
Statutorily dissolved 11/12/91

U S COBALT INC (DE)
Recapitalized as U.S. Geothermal Inc. 12/22/2003
Each share Common $0.001 par exchanged for (0.2) share Common $0.001 par
(See U.S. Geothermal Inc.)

U S COML CORP S A DE CV (MEXICO)
ADR agreement terminated 09/21/2007
Each Sponsored ADR for B-1 shares exchanged for $0.18941 cash
Each 144A Sponsored ADR for B-1 shares exchanged for $0.18941 cash

U S COMTRAC CORP (DE)
Charter cancelled and declared inoperative and void for non-payment of taxes 3/1/91

U S CONCRETE INC (DE)
Plan of reorganization under Chapter 11 Federal Bankruptcy proceedings effective 08/31/2010
Each share Common $0.001 par received (0.04046233) Common Stock Purchase Warrant Class A expiring 08/31/2017 and (0.04046233) Common Stock Purchase Warrant Class B expiring 08/31/2017
Note: Certificates were not required to be surrendered and are without value
(Additional Information in Active)

U S CONNECT 1995 INC (NV)
Recapitalized as Technology Guardian Inc. 08/24/1998
Each share Common $0.001 par exchanged for (0.02) share Common $0.001 par
Technology Guardian Inc. name changed to eSAT, Inc. 02/04/1999
(See eSAT, Inc.)

U S CRUDE LTD (NV)
Name changed to United States Crude International Inc. 6/7/2002
(See United States Crude International Inc.)

U S DELIVERY SYS INC (DE)
Merged into Corporate Express, Inc. 03/01/1996
Each share Common 1¢ par exchanged for (1.2) shares Common $0.0002 par
(See Corporate Express, Inc.)

U S DESIGN CORP (MD)
Merged into Maxtor Corp. 5/22/87
Each share Common 3¢ par exchanged for (0.06931) share Common no par
(See Maxtor Corp.)

U S DEVELOPMENT CORP (OK)
Recapitalized as Gulf Ethanol Corp. 07/31/2006
Each share Common $0.001 par exchanged for (0.05) share Common $0.0001 par
Gulf Ethanol Corp. recapitalized as Gulf Alternative Energy Corp. 03/24/2009

U S DIAGNOSTIC INC (DE)
Name changed 09/24/1996
Name changed from U.S. Diagnostic Labs Inc. to U.S. Diagnostic Inc. 09/24/1996
Plan of reorganization under Chapter 11 Federal Bankruptcy Code effective 01/29/2003
No stockholders' equity

U S DIAMOND CORP (BC)
Cease trade order effective 01/04/2002
Stockholders' equity unlikely

U S DIELECTRIC INC (DE)
Name changed to Golden Viking Industries, Inc. 07/10/1970
(See Golden Viking Industries, Inc.)

U S DIGITAL COMMUNICATIONS INC (NV)
SEC revoked preferred and common stock registration 10/30/2006

U S DIVID GROWERS INCOME CORP (ON)
Under plan of reorganization each Equity Share automatically became (0.78975513) share Middlefield Mutual Funds Ltd. U.S. Dividend Growers Class Ser. F 07/06/2017

U S DRUG TESTING INC (DE)
Name changed to Lifepoint, Inc. 02/27/1998
(See Lifepoint, Inc.)

U S DRY CLEANING CORP (DE)
Plan of reorganization under Chapter 11 Federal Bankruptcy proceedings effective 09/23/2011
Each share Common $0.001 par became entitled to receive (0.025) share U.S. Dry Cleaning Corp. (New) Common
Company is now privately held

U S DYNAMICS INC (DE)
Charter cancelled and declared inoperative and void for non-payment of taxes 04/15/1972

U S ELECTRICAR CORP (DE)
Charter cancelled and declared inoperative and void for non-payment of taxes 3/1/84

U S ELECTRICAR INC (CA)
Recapitalized as Enova Systems, Inc. 11/17/99
Each share Common no par exchanged for (0.05) share Common no par

U S ELECTRS GROUP INC (CO)
Chapter 11 Federal Bankruptcy Code converted to Chapter 7 and proceedings subsequently dismissed 11/21/88
Stockholders' equity unlikely

U S ENER MARK CORP (UT)
Involuntarily dissolved 12/31/1985

U S ENERGY SEARCH INC (DE)
Common 1¢ par changed to $0.005 par and (1) additional share issued 5/27/83
Name changed to Espero Energy Corp. 5/15/89
(See Espero Energy Corp.)

U S ENERGY SYS INC (DE)
Plan of reorganization under Chapter 11 Federal Bankruptcy proceedings effective 12/10/2010
No stockholders' equity

U S ENVIRONMENTAL INC (DE)
Each share old Common $0.0001 par exchanged for (0.01) share new Common $0.0001 par 03/24/1999
Name changed to FreeHand Systems International, Inc. 09/30/2005
(See FreeHand Systems International, Inc.)

U S ENVIRONMENTAL SOLUTIONS INC (DE)
Recapitalized as EnviroResolutions, Inc. 07/23/2007
Each share Common $0.001 par exchanged for (0.001) share Common $0.001 par
(See EnviroResolutions, Inc.)

U S ENVIROSYSTEMS INC (DE)
Each share old Common 1¢ par exchanged for (0.025) share new Common 1¢ par 05/10/1996
Name changed to U.S. Energy Systems, Inc. 06/27/1996
(See U.S. Energy Systems, Inc.)

U S EXPL CORP (TX)
Charter forfeited for failure to pay taxes 05/20/1985

U S FED FINL CORP (NV)
Name changed to Vibe Records Inc. 04/23/2002
Vibe Records Inc. name changed to Great Entertainment & Sports Inc. 03/07/2003 which name changed to Rockit!, Inc. 06/11/2007
(See Rockit!, Inc.)

U S FINL INC (DE)
Name changed 08/11/1972
Common $5 par changed to $2.50 par and (1) additional share issued 01/06/1969
Stock Dividend - 50% 10/30/1969
Name and state of incorporation changed from U.S. Financial (CA) to U.S. Financial Inc. (DE) 08/11/1972
Reorganized under Chapter X bankruptcy proceedings as USF Liquidating Corp. 11/02/1977
Only holders of U.S. Financial Overseas, N.V. 9% Debentures due 04/01/1982 participated.
No Common stockholders' equity

U S FLYWHEEL SYS INC (NV)
Recapitalized as Famous Sams Group Inc. 03/31/1996
Each share Common $0.001 par exchanged for (0.001) share Common $0.001 par
Famous Sams Group Inc. name changed to BioProgress Technology International, Inc. (NV) 12/22/1997 which reincorporated in England & Wales as BioProgress PLC 05/21/2003 which name changed to Meldex International PLC 09/28/2007

U S FOODSERVICE (DE)
Common 1¢ par split (2) for (1) by issuance of (1) additional share payable 08/04/1999 to holders of record 07/20/2000 Ex date - 08/05/1999
Merged into Koninklijke Ahold N.V. 04/12/2000
Each share Common 1¢ par exchanged for $26 cash

U S FRANCHISE SYS INC NEW (DE)
Name changed 03/12/1998
Name changed from U.S. Franchise Systems, Inc. (Old) to U.S. Franchise Systems, Inc. (New) 03/12/1998
Merged into Pritzer Family Business Interest 11/17/2000
Each share new Class A Common 1¢ par exchanged for $5 cash

U S FUEL CORP (NV)
Chapter 7 bankruptcy proceedings terminated 06/15/2016
Stockholders' equity unlikely

U S GEN CORP (NV)
Charter revoked for failure to file reports and pay fees 12/01/1990

U S GEOTHERMAL INC (DE)
Each share old Common $0.001 par exchanged for (0.16666666) share new Common $0.001 par 11/10/2016
Acquired by Ormat Technologies, Inc. 04/24/2018
Each share new Common $0.001 par exchanged for $5.45 cash

U S GNT GOLD MNG LTD (BC)
Recapitalized as Atrium Resources Ltd. 08/13/1990
Each share Common no par exchanged for (0.14285714) share Common no par
Atrium Resources Ltd. name changed to McCulloch's Canadian Beverages Ltd. 07/08/1992 which recapitalized as MCB Investments Corp. 10/06/1994
(See MCB Investments Corp.)

U S GOLD COIN VENTURES LTD (NY)
Recapitalized as Columbine Telenet Inc. 05/20/1987
Each share Common $0.00001 par exchanged for (0.01) share Common 1¢ par
Columbine Telenet Inc. name changed to Metrolink Group, Inc. 08/25/1989
(See Metrolink Group, Inc.)

U S GOLD CORP (CO)
Each share Common 1¢ par
exchanged for (0.1) share Common
10¢ par 12/24/1991
Common 10¢ par changed to no par
11/14/2005
Name changed to McEwen Mining
Inc. 01/27/2012

U S HEALTH & REC INC (DE)
Name changed to U.S. Health Inc.
12/23/1981
(See U.S. Health Inc.)

U S HEALTH INC (DE)
Common 25¢ par split (3) for (1) by
issuance of (2) additional shares
07/17/1986
Merged into Bally Manufacturing
Corp. 01/13/1989
Each share Common 25¢ par
exchanged for $5.34 cash

U S HEALTH RES INC (DE)
Charter cancelled and declared
inoperative and void for
non-payment of taxes 03/01/1988

U S HEALTH SVCS INC (NY)
Name changed to Diamond Trade
Center, Inc. 10/30/1990
(See Diamond Trade Center, Inc.)

U S HEALTHCARE INC (PA)
Common $0.005 par split (3) for (2)
by issuance of (0.5) additional share
05/10/1991
Class B Common $0.005 par split (3)
for (2) by issuance of (0.5)
additional share 05/10/1991
Common $0.005 par split (3) for (2)
by issuance of (0.5) additional share
09/28/1992
Class B Common $0.005 par split (3)
for (2) by issuance of (0.5)
additional share 09/28/1992
Common $0.005 par split (3) for (2)
by issuance of (0.5) additional share
03/29/1994
Class B Common $0.005 par split (3)
for (2) by issuance of (0.5)
additional share 03/29/1994
Merged into Aetna Inc. (Old)
07/19/1996
Each share Common $0.005 par
exchanged for (0.0749) share Conv.
Class C Preferred 1¢ par, (0.2246)
share Common 1¢ par and $34.20
cash
Each share Class B Common $0.005
par exchanged for (0.0749) share
Conv. Class C Preferred 1¢ par,
(0.2246) share Common 1¢ par and
$34.20 cash
Aetna, Inc. (CT) merged into ING
Groep N.V. 12/13/2000

U S HOME & GARDEN INC (DE)
Name changed to Ionatron, Inc.
04/30/2004
Ionatron, Inc. name changed to
Applied Energetics, Inc. 02/20/2008

U S HOME & GARDEN TR I (DE)
Name changed to Easy Gardener
Products Trust I 11/01/2003
(See Easy Gardener Products Trust I)

U S HOME CORP (DE)
Common 10¢ par split (2) for (1) by
issuance of (1) additional share
07/30/1971
Common 10¢ par split (2) for (1) by
issuance of (1) additional share
04/15/1983
Stock Dividends - 10% 05/30/1980;
10% 11/28/1980
Reorganized as U.S. Home Corp.
(New) 06/21/1993
Each share Common 10¢ par
exchanged for (0.077480) share
Common 1¢ par and Common Stock
Purchase Warrants Class B expiring
06/21/1998
U.S. Home Corp. (New) merged into
Lennar Corp. 05/02/2000

U S HOME CORP NEW (DE)
Preferred no par called for
redemption 03/18/1997
Merged into Lennar Corp. 05/02/2000
Each share Common 10¢ par
exchanged for (0.96) share Common
10¢ par and $18 cash

U S HOME SYS INC (DE)
Acquired by The Home Depot, Inc.
10/29/2012
Each share Common $0.001 par
exchanged for $12.50 cash

U S HOMECARE CORP (NY)
Common 1¢ par split (3) for (2) by
issuance of (0.5) additional share
03/05/1992
Assets foreclosed upon and company
ceased operations 04/28/2000
No stockholders' equity

U S HOMES & PPTYS INC (NV)
SEC revoked common stock
registration 07/30/2004

U S HOMES INC (IA)
Charter cancelled for failure to file
annual reports 11/25/1985

U S HSG RECOVERY FD (ON)
Trust terminated 10/31/2017
Each Class A Unit received $10.1078
cash

U S HYDROFOILS LEHIGH DISTR SVCS INC (NY)
Name changed to Hydroplex Corp.
11/21/1969
(See Hydroplex Corp.)

U S I NETWORK LTD (DE)
Charter cancelled and declared
inoperative and void for
non-payment of taxes 03/01/1984

U S INDL SVCS INC (DE)
Name changed to Nextgen
Communications Corp. and
Common 1¢ par changed to $0.001
par 08/07/2001
Nextgen Communications Corp. name
changed to Home Solutions of
America, Inc. 12/23/2002
(See Home Solutions of America, Inc.)

U S INDS INC (DE)
4.25% Preferred Ser. A $50 par called
redemption 07/01/1967
Each Ctf. of Participation received
initial distribution of (0.0108853)
share Special Conv. Preference Ser.
A $2.50 par 05/10/1968
Common $1 par split (2) for (1) by
issuance of (1) additional share
05/22/1968
Each Ctf. of Participation received
second distribution of (0.0194) share
Special Conv. Preference Ser. A
$2.50 par 05/10/1969
Each Ctf. of Participation received
third distribution of (0.0209) share
Special Conv. Preference Ser. A
$2.50 par 05/10/1970
Each Ctf. of Participation received
fourth and final distribution of
$0.0241 cash 05/30/1971
Note: Certificates of Participation
were not required to be surrendered
and are without value
Special Conv. Preference Ser. I $2.50
par called for redemption 12/11/1978
Special Preference Ser. N $2.50 par
called for redemption 06/30/1979
Merged into HMAC Industries Inc.
07/18/1984
Each share Special Conv. Preference
Ser. A $2.50 par exchanged for
$94.285 cash
Each share Special Conv. Preference
Ser. J $2.50 par exchanged for
$69.9319 cash
Each share Special Preference Ser. L
$2.50 par exchanged for $74.3211
cash
Each share Special Conv. Preference
Ser. M $2.50 par exchanged for
$72.5324 cash
Each share Special Preference Ser. O
$2.50 par exchanged for $69.57
cash
Each share Special Preference Ser. P
$2.50 par exchanged for $66.1821
cash
Each share Special Preference Ser. Q
$2.50 par exchanged for $83.1055
cash
Each share Common $1 par
exchanged for $22.81 cash

U S INDS INC NEW (DE)
Common 1¢ par split (3) for (2) by
issuance of (0.5) additional share
payable 09/23/1997 to holders of
record 09/02/1997 Ex date -
09/24/1997
Name changed to Jacuzzi Brands,
Inc. 06/05/2003
(See Jacuzzi Brands, Inc.)

U S INTEC INC (TX)
Merged into G-I Holdings Inc.
10/24/1995
Each share Common 2¢ par
exchanged for $9.05 cash

U S INTERACTIVE INC (DE)
Plan of reorganization under Chapter
11 Federal Bankruptcy Code
effective 09/21/2001
No stockholders' equity

U.S.L. BATTERY CORP.
Acquired by Electric Auto-Lite Co.
05/00/1928
Details not available

U S LABORATORIES INC (DE)
Merged into Bureau Veritas, S.A.
11/11/2002
Each share Common 1¢ par
exchanged for $14.50 cash

U S LD RES INC (DE)
Each share Conv. Preferred 1¢ par
exchanged for (2.0223) shares
Common 1¢ par 06/30/1978
Stock Dividend - 100% 07/30/1976
Merged into United States Merger
Corp. 12/20/1985
Each share Common 1¢ par
exchanged for $3.75 cash

U S LEASING CORP (CA)
Name changed to United States
Leasing International, Inc. (CA)
01/02/1968
United States Leasing International,
Inc. (CA) reincorporated in Delaware
10/27/1986
(See United States Leasing International, Inc. (DE))

U S LIQUIDS INC (DE)
Assets sold and SEC registration
subsequently terminated 03/30/2004
Stockholders' equity unlikely

U S LONG DISTANCE CORP (DE)
Each share old Common 1¢ par
exchanged for (0.33333333) share
new Common 1¢ par 02/15/1991
Each share new Common 1¢ par
received distribution of (1) share
Billing Information Concepts Corp.
Common 1¢ par payable 08/02/1996
to holders of record 07/29/1996
Name changed to USLD
Communications Corp. 08/19/1997
USLD Communications Corp. merged
into LCI International Inc.
12/22/1997 which merged into
Qwest Communications International
Inc. 06/05/1998 which merged into
CenturyLink, Inc. 04/01/2011

U S MAGNET & ALLOY CORP (DE)
Assets transferred to U.S. Magnet &
Alloy Corp. Liquidating Trust and
Common 10¢ par reclassified as
Shares of Bene. Int. no par
12/30/1988
(See U.S. Magnet & Alloy Corp. Liquidating Trust)

U S MAGNET & ALLOY CORP LIQ TR (DE)
Filed a petition under Chapter 11
Federal Bankruptcy Code
04/10/1990
Details not available

U S MFG & GALVANIZING CORP (FL)
Proclaimed dissolved for failure to file
reports and pay fees 08/25/1995

U S MED ALLIANCE INC (DE)
Name changed to I-Trax.com Inc.
08/19/1999
I-Trax.com Inc. reorganized as I-Trax,
Inc. 02/05/2001
(See I-Trax, Inc.)

U S MED ENTERPRISES INC (DE)
Merged into InterCare, Inc.
01/07/1987
Each share Common 10¢ par
exchanged for (0.44444444) share
Common 1¢ par
(See InterCare, Inc.)

U S MED GROUP INC (NV)
Name changed to North American
Industries Inc. 06/13/2002
(See North American Industries Inc.)

U S MED PRODS INC (TX)
Assets sold 11/01/1997
Stockholders' equity unlikely

U S MED SYS INC (DE)
Recapitalized as Sharps Compliance
Corp. 07/23/1998
Each share Common 1¢ par
exchanged for (0.1986999) share
Common 1¢ par

U S MEDSYS CORP (CO)
Reincorporated under the laws of
Delaware as InternetArray, Inc. and
Common no par changed to $0.0001
par 09/12/2008

U S MINE MAKERS INC (NV)
Each share old Common $0.001 par
exchanged for (0.04) share new
Common $0.001 par 03/09/2009
Each share new Common $0.001 par
exchanged again for (0.01428571)
share new Common $0.001 par
07/21/2010
Each share new Common $0.001 par
received distribution of (1) share
Intelligent Inventions International
Inc. Restricted Common payable
04/30/2013 to holders of record
10/16/2012
Reincorporated under the laws of
Wyoming as Vid3G, Inc. and
Common $0.001 par changed to
$0.0001 par 02/13/2014
Vid3G, Inc. recapitalized as Argus
Worldwide Corp. 11/14/2016

U S MINERAL & RTY CORP (OK)
Each share Common $0.002 par
exchanged for (0.00014285) share
Common 10¢ par 06/29/1988
Common 10¢ par split (70) for (1) by
issuance of (70) additional shares
06/30/1988
Name changed to Habersham Energy
Co. 02/28/1989
Habersham Energy Co. recapitalized
as Trinity Companies Inc. (OK)
03/15/2002 which reincorporated in
Utah 05/07/2002 which name
changed to Trinity Learning Corp.
03/31/2003 which name changed to
TWL Corp. (UT) 10/13/2006 which
reorganized in Nevada 12/12/2007
(See TWL Corp.)

U S MINERALS EXPL CO (CO)
Each share old Common no par
exchanged for (0.2) share new
Common no par 11/24/1986
Reincorporated under the laws of
Delaware as USMX Inc. and new
Common no par changed to $0.001
par 02/04/1988
USMX Inc. merged into Dakota
Mining Corp. 05/29/1997
(See Dakota Mining Corp.)

U S MINT INC (CO)
Each shares old Common $0.0001
par exchanged for (0.03333333)

U S-U S   FINANCIAL INFORMATION, INC.

share new Common $0.0001 par 11/18/1989
Reported out of business 09/00/1990
Details not available

U S MOBILE DENTAL CORP (NV)
Name changed to Ingenex Corp. 07/29/2005
(See Ingenex Corp.)

U S MOBILE SVCS INC (DE)
Charter forfeited for failure to maintain a registered agent 11/19/1999

U S MUT FINL CORPORATION (MI)
Reorganized 08/01/1983
Reorganized from United States Mutual Real Estate Investment Trust to U.S. Mutual Financial Corp. 08/01/1983
Name changed to Jove Corp. 05/28/2004
(See Jove Corp.)

U S NAT GAS CORP (DE)
Name changed to U.S. Natural Resources, Inc. 11/01/1968
(See U.S. Natural Resources, Inc.)

U S NAT NUTRIENTS & MINERALS INC (NV)
Reorganized as U.S. Rare Earth Minerals, Inc. 05/02/2011
Each share Common $0.001 par exchanged for (3) shares Common $0.001 par

U S NAT RES INC (DE)
Merged into Resource Acquisition Corp. 11/30/1977
Each share Common $1 par exchanged for $8.25 cash

U S NATL CML PARTNERS INC (NV)
Recapitalized as Data-Fit, Inc. 09/10/2003
Each share Common $0.001 par exchanged for (0.02) share Common $0.001 par
Data-Fit, Inc. recapitalized as Real Security Co., Inc. 12/12/2005
(See Real Security Co., Inc.)

U S NETWORK FDG INC (NV)
Name changed to Apple Ventures Inc. 03/23/1995
Apple Ventures Inc. recapitalized as Kelcord International Inc. 10/26/1997
(See Kelcord International Inc.)

U S NEUROSURGICAL INC (DE)
Name changed to U.S. NeuroSurgical Holdings, Inc. 10/08/2015

U S OFFICE PRODS CO (DE)
Old Common $0.001 par split (3) for (2) by issuance of (0.5) additional share payable 11/06/1997 to holders of record 10/23/1997
Each share old Common $0.001 par exchanged for (0.25) share new Common $0.001 par 06/09/1998
Each share new Common $0.001 par received distribution of (0.2) share Aztec Technology Partners, Inc. Common $0.001 par, (0.1) share Navigant International Inc. Common $0.001 par, (0.111111) share School Specialty, Inc. Common $0.001 par and (0.1333333) share Workflow Management, Inc. Common $0.001 par payable 06/10/1998 to holders of record 06/09/1998
Plan of reorganization under Chapter 11 Federal Bankruptcy Code effective 12/28/2001
No stockholders' equity

U S OIL & GAS INC (BC)
Merged into U.S. Oil & Gas Resources Inc. 11/13/1997
Each share Common no par exchanged for (1) share Common no par
U.S. Oil & Gas Resources Inc. reorganized as Odyssey Petroleum Corp. 08/25/2005 which recapitalized as Petrichor Energy Inc. 03/03/2011

U S OIL & GAS RES INC (BC)
Reorganized as Odyssey Petroleum Corp. 08/25/2005
Each share Common no par exchanged for (0.5) share Common no par
Note: Holders entitled to (499) or fewer shares had the option to receive $0.26 cash per share in lieu of stock Option expired 09/25/2005
Note: Unexchanged certificates were cancelled and became without value 08/25/2011
Odyssey Petroleum Corp. recapitalized as Petrichor Energy Inc. 03/03/2011

U S OPPORTUNITY SEARCH INC (DE)
Name changed to Milestone Scientific Inc. 12/06/1996

U S PAWN INC (CO)
Each share old Common no par exchanged for (0.25) share new Common no par 09/24/1993
Reorganized under the laws of Delaware as U.S. Home Systems, Inc. 02/15/2001
Each share new Common no par exchanged for (0.25) share Common $0.001 par
(See U.S. Home Systems, Inc.)

U S PAY TEL INC (BC)
Reincorporated under the laws of Delaware as U.S. Long Distance Corp. and Common no par changed to 1¢ par 09/29/1987
U.S. Long Distance Corp. name changed to USLD Communications Corp. 08/19/1997 which merged into LCI International Inc. 12/22/1997 which merged into Qwest Communications International Inc. 06/05/1998 which merged into CenturyLink, Inc. 04/01/2011

U S PETE CORP (NV)
Common $0.001 par split (25) for (1) by issuance of (24) additional shares payable 03/07/2003 to holders of record 02/28/2003 Ex date - 03/10/2003
Recapitalized as Emergent Energy Corp. 07/29/2008
Each share Common $0.001 par exchanged for (0.25) share Common $0.001 par

U S PLASTIC LMBR CORP (NV)
Plan of reorganization under Chapter 11 Federal Bankruptcy Code effective 11/30/2006
No stockholders' equity

U S PLATINUM INC (BC)
Name changed to Universal Energy Corp. 01/10/2006
Universal Energy Corp. name changed to Supreme Resources Ltd. 02/09/2007 which name changed to Supreme Pharmaceuticals Inc. (BC) 03/14/2014 which reincorporated in Canada 12/21/2015 which name changed to Supreme Cannabis Co. Inc. 12/29/2017

U S PLAYING CARD CORP (DE)
Common 10¢ par split (3) for (2) by issuance of (0.5) additional share 03/15/1983
Stock Dividend - 100% 10/04/1982
Merged into Jesup Group, Inc. 12/24/1987
Each share Common 10¢ par exchanged for (1.2) shares Common 1¢ par
(See Jesup Group, Inc.)

U S PLYWOOD CHAMPION PAPERS INC (NY)
4.75% Preferred Ser. A $100 called for redemption 03/06/1968
Common $1 par changed to 50¢ par and (1) additional share issued 06/03/1969
Name changed to Champion International Corp. 05/12/1972
Champion International Corp. merged into International Paper Co. 06/20/2000

U S POLYMERIC INC (DE)
Stock Dividend - 10% 06/01/1966
Completely liquidated 01/06/1969
Each share Common 50¢ par exchanged for first and final distribution of (0.85) share Hitco Common no par
Hitco merged into Armco Steel Corp. 12/31/1969 which name changed to Armco Inc. 07/01/1978 which merged into AK Steel Holding Corp. 09/30/1999

U S PWR SYS INC (NV)
Each share old Common $0.001 par exchanged for (0.005) share new Common $0.001 par 04/11/2006
Name changed to Premier Organic Farms Group, Inc. 06/15/2006
Premier Organic Farms Group, Inc. recapitalized as Amstar Financial Holdings, Inc. 12/19/2006 which recapitalized as China Du Kang Co. Ltd. 03/19/2008

U S PRECIOUS METALS INC (BC)
Merged into Siskon Gold Corp. 08/23/1991
Each share Common no par exchanged for (0.5) share Common no par
(See Siskon Gold Corp.)

U S REALTEL INC (DE)
Reincorporated 05/09/2000
State of incorporation changed from (IL) to (DE) 05/09/2000
Name changed to Cypress Communications Holding Co., Inc. 06/16/2004
(See Cypress Communications Holding Co., Inc.)

U S RLTY INVTS (OH)
Ctfs. of Bene. Int. no par split (5) for (4) by issuance of (0.25) additional share 07/01/1972
In process of liquidation
Each Ctf. of Bene. Int. no par received initial distribution of $3 cash 06/15/1982
Each Ctf. of Bene. Int. no par received second distribution of $10 cash 01/04/1983
Under plan of reorganization each Ctf. of Bene. Int. no par automatically became (1) U.S. Realty Investments Liquidating Trust Ctf. of Bene. Int. no par 01/05/1983
(See U.S. Realty Investments Liquidating Trust)

U S RLTY PARTNERS LTD PARTNERSHIP (DE)
Merged into AIMCO Properties, L.P. 02/11/2011
Each Depositary Unit Certificate exchanged for either (0.11) Common Unit or $2.76 cash
Note: Option to receive Common Units expired 03/14/2011

U S REDUCTION CO (DE)
Common $1 par split (2) for (1) by issuance of (1) additional share 08/14/1975
Merged into American Can Co. 06/17/1976
Each share Common $1 par exchanged for (0.7) share Common $12.50 par
American Can Co. name changed to Primerica Corp. (NJ) 04/28/1987 which was acquired by Primerica Corp. (DE) 12/15/1988 which name changed to Travelers Inc. 12/31/1993 which name changed to Travelers Group Inc. 04/16/1995 which name changed to Citigroup Inc. 10/08/1998

U S RENTALS INC (DE)
Merged into United Rentals Inc. 09/29/1998
Each share Common 1¢ par exchanged for (0.9625) share Common 1¢ par

U S RES INC (DE)
Charter cancelled and declared inoperative and void for non-payment of taxes 06/25/1987

U S RESTAURANT PPTYS INC (MD)
Common no par split (3) for (2) by issuance of (0.5) additional share payable 10/30/1997 to holders of record 10/20/1997 Ex date - 10/31/1997
Under plan of merger name changed to Trustreet Properties, Inc. 02/25/2005
(See Trustreet Properties, Inc.)

U S RESTAURANT PPTYS MASTER L P (DE)
Reorganized as U.S. Restaurants Properties, Inc. (MD) 10/15/1997
Each Depositary Receipt exchanged for (1) share Common $0.001 par
U.S. Restaurant Properties, Inc. (MD) name changed to Trustreet Properties, Inc. 02/25/2005
(See Trustreet Properties, Inc.)

U S RICH HILL MINERALS INC (UT)
Name changed to Kelwynn Inc. (UT) 03/18/1983
Kelwynn Inc. (UT) reincorporated in Delaware 12/16/1983

U S ROBOTICS CORP (DE)
Common 1¢ par split (2) for (1) by issuance of (1) additional share payable 09/08/1995 to holders of record 08/25/1995
Common 1¢ par split (2) for (1) by issuance of (1) additional share payable 05/10/1996 to holders of record 04/25/1996
Merged into 3Com Corp. 06/12/1997
Each share Common 1¢ par exchanged for (1.75) shares Common no par
(See 3Com Corp.)

U S ROBOTICS INC (DE)
Under plan of merger name changed to U.S. Robotics Corp. 02/22/1995
U.S. Robotics Corp. merged into 3Com Corp. 06/12/1997
(See 3Com Corp.)

U S RTY OIL CORP (CA)
In process of liquidation
Each share Capital Stock $1 par received initial distribution of (0.5) share Consolidated Royalties, Inc. Common $1 par 7/2/74
Each share Capital Stock $1 par received second distribution of (0.125) share Clark Oil Co. Common $1 par 7/22/74
Each share Capital Stock $1 par received third distribution of $5 cash 1/6/75
Each share Capital Stock $1 par received fourth distribution of $2.10 cash 6/24/75
Each share Capital Stock $1 par received fifth distribution of $0.85 cash 1/21/77
Note: Details on subsequent distributions, if any, are not available

U S RUBR RECLAIMING INC (NY)
Each share 8% Prior Preferred $25 par exchanged for (1.46) unstamped shares $1.40 Preferred no par 00/00/1947
Each share $1.50 Class A Preferred no par exchanged for (0.1) unstamped share $1.40 Preferred no par and (2) shares old Common $1 par 00/00/1947
Each share Common no par exchanged for (2/3) share old Common $1 par 00/00/1947
Each stamped share $1.40 Preferred no par exchanged for (3.2) shares new Common $1 par 07/01/1959
Each unstamped share $1.40 Preferred no par exchanged for (3.5)

shares new Common $1 par 07/01/1959
Each share old Common $1 par exchanged for (0.5) share new Common $1 par 07/01/1959
Merged into Genstar Ltd. 01/10/1980
Each share new Common $1 par exchanged for (1) share $1.68 Conv. 2nd Preferred Ser. B no par
Genstar Ltd. name changed to Genstar Corp. 06/15/1981
(See Genstar Corp.)

U S S E CORP (NV)
Reincorporated under the laws of Delaware as Quick Start Holdings, Inc. 10/12/2018

U S SERVICATOR CORP (DE)
Charter cancelled and became inoperative and void for non-payment of taxes 04/15/1969

U S SHANGHAI CHEM CORP (NJ)
Name changed to AmeriWorks Financial Services, Inc. 12/16/2010
AmeriWorks Financial Services, Inc. recapitalized as AmeriWorks, Inc. 01/29/2014

U S SHELTER (MA)
Under plan of merger each Share of Bene. Int. no par automatically became (1) share U.S. Shelter Corp. (DE) Common $1 par 5/31/84
(See U.S. Shelter Corp. (DE))

U S SHELTER CORP (DE)
Liquidation completed
Each share Common $1 par exchanged for initial distribution of (0.011428490) share Apartment Investment & Management Co. Class A Common 1¢ par and (0.031836094) share Insignia Financial Group, Inc. (New) Common 1¢ par 9/30/99
Each share Common $1 par received second and final distribution of approximately $0.02 cash in October 2001

U S SHELTER CORP (SC)
Under plan of merger each share Common 25¢ par automatically became (1) share U.S. Shelter Corp. (DE) Common $1 par 5/31/84
(See U.S. Shelter Corp. (DE))

U S SHIPPING PARTNERS L P (DE)
Plan of reorganization under Chapter 11 Federal Bankruptcy proceedings effective 11/12/2009
No stockholders' equity

U S SILVER & GOLD INC (ON)
Merged into Scorpio Mining Corp. 12/31/2014
Each share Common no par exchanged for (1.68) shares Common no par
Note: Unexchanged certificates will be cancelled and become without value 12/31/2019
Scorpio Mining Corp. name changed to Americas Silver Corp. 05/27/2015

U S SILVER CORP (CANADA)
Each share old Common no par exchanged for (0.2) share new Common no par 01/30/2012
Merged into U.S. Silver & Gold Inc. 08/13/2012
Each share new Common no par exchanged for (0.67) share Common no par
Note: Unexchanged certificates were cancelled and became without value 08/13/2018
U.S. Silver & Gold Inc: merged into Scorpio Mining Corp. 12/31/2014 which name changed to Americas Silver Corp. 05/27/2015

U S STL CDA INC (CANADA)
9% Retractable Preferred Ser. 1 no par called for redemption 04/30/1990
Public interest eliminated

U S SUSTAINABLE ENERGY CORP (NV)
Common $0.001 par split (2) for (1) by issuance of (1) additional share payable 05/03/2007 to holders of record 12/01/2006 Ex date - 05/04/2007
Recapitalized as Zeons Corp. 02/26/2010
Each (5,200) shares Common $0.001 par exchanged for (1) share Common $0.001 par

U S SYS & SOFTWARE INC (CA)
Charter suspended for failure to file reports and pay taxes 08/01/1975

U S T MASTER FDS INC (MD)
Reorganized as Excelsior Funds, Inc. 01/01/1996
Details not available

U S TECHNOLOGIES INC (DE)
Each share Common $1 par exchanged for (0.2) share Common 2¢ par 02/09/1993
SEC revoked common stock registration 08/26/2004

U S TEL INC (TX)
Merged into United Telecommunications, Inc. 06/20/1984
Each share Common no par exchanged for (0.25) share Common $2.50 par
United Telecommunications, Inc. name changed to Sprint Corp. (KS) 02/26/1992 which name changed to Sprint Nextel Corp. 08/12/2005 which merged into Sprint Corp. (DE) 07/10/2013

U S TELESIS HLDGS INC (DE)
Recapitalized as Catcher Holdings, Inc. 06/23/2005
Each (7.2) shares Common $0.001 par exchanged for (1) share Common $0.001 par
(See Catcher Holdings, Inc.)

U S TIMBERLANDS CO L P (DE)
Issue Information - 7,458,684 COM UNITS offered at $21 per Unit on 11/13/1997
Merged into U.S. Timberlands Holdings Group, LLC 6/26/2003
Each Common Unit no par exchanged for $3 cash

U S TIME SHARING INC (DC)
Name changed to USTS, Inc. 5/17/72
(See USTS, Inc.)

U S TRANSN SYS INC (NV)
Each share old Common 1¢ par exchanged for (0.2) share new Common 1¢ par 01/26/1994
Each share new Common 1¢ par exchanged again for (1/6) share new Common 1¢ par 08/26/1996
Name changed to Transportation Equities, Inc. 03/31/1998
(See Transportation Equities, Inc.)

U S TREND FD INC (PA)
Reincorporated under the laws of Maryland as Capstone U.S. Trend Fund, Inc. and Common 1¢ par changed to $0.001 par 05/11/1992
Capstone U.S. Trend Fund, Inc. name changed to Capstone Growth Fund, Inc. 08/26/1994 which name changed to Capstone Series Fund, Inc. 01/22/2002

U S TRUCK LINES INC DEL (DE)
Capital Stock $1 par split (2) for (1) by issuance of (1) additional share 06/15/1971
Capital Stock $1 par split (2) for (1) by issuance of (1) additional share 06/15/1972
Stock Dividends - 50% 11/10/1959; 10% 03/16/1964; 20% 05/02/1967
Acquired by ADM Acquisition Corp. 05/27/1988
Each share Capital Stock $1 par exchanged for $6.75 cash

U S TRUCKING INC (CO)
Recapitalized as Logistics Management Resources Inc. 2/12/2001
Each share Common no par exchanged for (0.01) share Common no par
Logistics Management Resources Inc. name changed to American Business Corp. 6/28/2004

U S TR CORP NEW (NY)
Common $1 par split (2) for (1) by issuance of (1) additional share payable 2/21/97 to holders of record 2/7/97
Merged into Schwab (Charles) Corp. 5/31/2000
Each share Common $1 par exchanged for (5.1405) shares Common 1¢ par

U S TR CORP OLD (NY)
Common $5 par split (3) for (2) by issuance of (0.5) additional share 02/19/1985
Common $5 par split (3) for (2) by issuance of (0.5) additional share 12/01/1986
Common $5 par changed to $1 par 00/00/1993
Stock Dividend - 50% 03/01/1983
Merged into Chase Manhattan Corp. (Old) 09/02/1995
Each share Common $1 par exchanged for (0.68) share Common $2 par
Chase Manhattan Corp. (Old) merged into Chase Manhattan Corp (New) 03/31/1996 which name changed to J.P. Morgan Chase & Co. 12/31/2000 which name changed to JPMorgan Chase & Co. 07/20/2004

U S VACATION RESORTS INC (CA)
Each share old Common no par exchanged for (0.1) share new Common no par 12/28/1988
Charter suspended 06/17/1997

U S VISION INC (DE)
Merged into Kayak Acquisition Corp. 10/31/2002
Each share Common 1¢ par exchanged for $4.25 cash

U S WASTE GROUP (NV)
Recapitalized 08/30/1988
Recapitalized from U.S. Waste Management to U.S. Waste Group 08/30/1988
Each share Common $0.00001 par exchanged for (0.025) share Common $0.0001 par
Each share new Common $0.0001 par exchanged for (0.1) share Common $0.001 par 05/13/1994
Name changed to Genco Corp. 02/21/2008

U S WEST FING I (DE)
7.96% Trust Originated Preferred Securities called for redemption at $25 plus $0.353777 accrued dividend on 03/04/2002

U S WEST HOMES INC (NV)
Recapitalized as Investco Corp. 05/30/2003
Each share Common $0.001 par exchanged for (0.01) share Common $0.001 par

U S WEST INC NEW (DE)
Merged into Qwest Communications International Inc. 06/30/2000
Each share Common 10¢ par exchanged for (1.72932) shares Common 1¢ par
Qwest Communications International Inc. merged into CenturyLink, Inc. 04/01/2011

U S WEST INC OLD (DE)
Reincorporated 10/31/95
Common no par split (2) for (1) by issuance of (1) additional share 05/28/1986
Common no par split (2) for (1) by issuance of (1) additional share 05/02/1990
State of incorporation changed from (CO) to (DE) and Common no par reclassified to Common-Communications Group 1¢ par 10/31/1995
Each share Common-Communications Group 1¢ par received distribution of (1) share Common-Media Group 1¢ par 11/01/1995
Plan of separation effective 06/12/1998
Each share Conv. Preferred Ser. D 1¢ par exchanged for (1) share MediaOne Group, Inc. Conv. Preferred Ser. D 1¢ par
Each share Common-Communications Group 1¢ par exchanged for (1) share U.S. West Inc. (New) Common 1¢ par
Each share Common-Media Group 1¢ par exchanged for (1) share MediaOne Group, Inc. Common 1¢ par
Each 7.625% Debt Exchangeable for Common Stock exchanged for (1) MediaOne Group, Inc. 7.625% Debt Exchangeable for Common Stock
(See each company's listing)

U S WEST INVTS INC (DE)
Common 10¢ par changed to 1¢ par in November 1973
Charter cancelled and declared inoperative and void for non-payment of taxes 6/29/78

U S WEST NEWVECTOR GROUP INC (CO)
Merged into U.S. West, Inc. (Old) 7/11/91
Each share Common no par exchanged for (1.14) shares Common no par
(See U.S. West, Inc. (Old))

U S WIRELESS CORP (DE)
Plan of reorganization under Chapter 11 Federal Bankruptcy proceedings confirmed 06/09/2003
Stockholders' equity unlikely

U S WIRELESS DATA INC (DE)
Reorganized 10/17/2000
Reorganized from under the laws of (CO) to (DE) 10/17/2000
Each share Class A Common no par exchanged for (0.25) share Class A Common no par
Conv. Preferred Ser. B no par called for redemption on 05/03/2000
Under plan of reorganization each share Conv. Preferred Ser. C no par received (0.043341) share Class A Common 1¢ par and each share new Class A Common no par received (0.007709) share Class A Common 1¢ par payable 05/24/2005 to holders of record 02/07/2005
Note: Certificates were not required to be surrendered and are without value
Recapitalized as StarVox Communications, Inc. 10/03/2007
Each share Class A Common 1¢ par exchanged for (0.4) share Class A Common 1¢ par
(See StarVox Communications, Inc.)

U S WTR INC (NV)
Name changed to Ajax Resources, Inc. 07/02/1979
Ajax Resources, Inc. name changed to Min-Tex Energy, Corp. 07/30/1981
(See Min-Tex Energy, Corp.)

U S XPRESS ENTERPRISES INC (NV)
Merged into New Mountain Lake Holdings, LLC 10/12/2007
Each share Class A Common 1¢ par exchanged for $20.10 cash
(Additional Information in Active)

U SAVE FOODS LTD (BC)
Reorganized as USV International Investment Corp. 04/25/1989
Each share Common no par exchanged for (4) shares Common no par
(See USV International Investment Corp.)

U-SHIP INC (UT)
Each share old Common 1¢ par exchanged for (0.25) share Common $0.004 par 02/26/1996
Name changed to United Shipping & Technology Inc. (UT) 05/03/1999
United Shipping & Technology Inc. (UT) reincorporated in Delaware as Velocity Express Corp. 01/14/2002
(See Velocity Express Corp.)

U-STORE-IT TR (MD)
Name changed to CubeSmart 09/19/2011

U-SUMAC CORP. (UT)
Name changed to I.I.S. Ltd. 4/14/86

U T I CHEMS INC (NV)
Recapitalized as Urethane Technologies, Inc. 11/25/1991
Each share Common $0.001 par exchanged for (0.1) share Common 1¢ par
(See Urethane Technologies, Inc.)

U T TECHNOLOGIES LTD (BC)
Delisted from Vancouver Stock Exchange 01/10/1990

U-TOTE'M, INC. (TX)
Common $2 par changed to $1 par and (1) additional share issued 08/19/1966
5.5% Preferred $10 par called for redemption 03/10/1967
Merged into Fairmont Foods Co. 07/31/1967
Each share Common $1 par exchanged for (1) share $1 Conv. Preferred no par
Fairmont Foods Co. merged into American Financial Corp. 07/24/1980
(See American Financial Corp.)

U-VEND INC (DE)
Name changed to BoxScore Brands, Inc. 03/01/2018

UA CABLEVISION INC (DE)
Merged into UA-Columbia Cablevision, Inc. 12/29/1972
Each share Common 10¢ par exchanged for (1.0667) shares Common 5¢ par
(See UA-Columbia Cablevision, Inc.)

UA COLUMBIA CABLEVISION INC (DE)
Stock Dividend - 100% 07/06/1979
Under plan of merger each share Common 5¢ par exchanged for $90 cash 11/19/1981

UA GRANITE CORP (NV)
Name changed to Vortex Blockchain Technologies Inc. 05/31/2018

UA INTL GROUP LTD (NV)
Each share old Common $0.001 par exchanged for (0.002) share new Common $0.001 par 01/09/2006
Name changed to Ukraine Energy Acquisition Corp. 04/17/2007
Ukraine Energy Acquisition Corp. recapitalized as Alter Energy Group, N.A., Inc. 04/28/2011

UAL CORP (DE)
Issue Information - 14,416,000 DEPOSITARY SH REPSTG 1/1000 PFD B 12.25% offered at $25 per share on 06/30/1994
Recapitalized 07/12/1994
Each share Common $5 par exchanged for (0.5) share old Common 1¢ par and $84.81 cash
Old Common 1¢ par split (4) for (1) by issuance of (3) additional shares payable 05/20/1996 to holders of record 05/06/1996 Ex date - 05/21/1996
Plan of reorganization under Chapter 11 Federal Bankruptcy Code effective 02/01/2006
No old Common stockholders' equity
Under plan of merger name changed to United Continental Holdings, Inc. 10/01/2010

UAL CORP CAP TR I (DE)
Plan of reorganization under Chapter 11 Federal Bankruptcy Code effective 02/01/2006
No stockholders' equity

UAL INC (DE)
40¢ Conv. Preferred Ser. A no par called for redemption 03/30/1984
$2.40 Conv. Preferred Ser. B no par called for redemption 01/16/1986
Name changed to Allegis Corp. 04/30/1987
Allegis Corp. name changed to UAL Corp. 05/27/1988
(See UAL Corp.)

UAM FDS TR (MA)
Completely liquidated 02/11/2002
Each TJ Core Equity Portfolio received first and final distribution of $11.98 cash

UAP HLDG CORP (DE)
Merged into Agrium Inc. 05/07/2008
Each share Common $0.001 par exchanged for $39 cash

UARCO INC (DE)
Reincorporated 02/27/1970
Each share Common no par exchanged for (1.333333) shares Common $10 par 00/00/1951
Common $10 par changed to $2.50 par and (3) additional shares issued 12/28/1961
State of incorporation changed from (IL) to (DE) 02/27/1970
Merged into City Investing Co. 02/01/1979
Each share Common $2.50 par exchanged for $52 cash

UAS AUTOMATION SYS INC (DE)
Each share old Common 1¢ par exchanged for (0.002) share new Common 1¢ par 04/05/1991
Note: Option for holders of (499) shares or fewer to elect to receive stock expired 08/30/1991
Non-electing holders received $0.05 cash per share and public interest was eliminated

UAUTHORIZE CORP (NV)
Name changed to Ablaze Technologies, Inc. 04/04/2005

UAXS GLOBAL HLDGS CORP (DE)
Name changed to Universal Access Global Holdings Inc. 11/01/2001
(See Universal Access Global Holdings Inc.)

UB FINL CORP (DE)
Common $5 par split (3) for (2) by issuance of (0.5) additional share 11/30/1972
Name changed to United Bancorp of Arizona 10/17/1978
(See United Bancorp of Arizona)

UB&T FINL SVCS CORP (GA)
Merged into GB&T Bancshares, Inc. 03/01/2000
Each share Common exchanged for (1.517) shares Common $5 par
GB&T Bancshares, Inc. merged into SunTrust Banks, Inc. 05/01/2008

UBANCO INC (WA)
Stock Dividend - 10% 04/09/1984
Merged into Washington Community Bancshares, Inc. 09/29/1987
Each share Capital Stock $10 par exchanged for (0.66666666) share Common $10 par
Washington Community Bancshares, Inc. merged into KeyCorp (NY) 01/25/1990 which merged into KeyCorp (New) (OH) 03/01/1994

UBANTCO CORP (IN)
Name changed to Union Banc Corp. 04/30/1984
(See Union Banc Corp.)

UBARTER COM INC (NV)
Merged into Network Commerce Inc. 06/01/2000
Each share Common $0.001 par exchanged for (0.366) share Common $0.001 par
(See Network Commerce Inc.)

UBETIGOLF INC (UT)
Name changed to NECO Energy Corp. 05/17/2002
(See NECO Energy Corp.)

UBIC INC (JAPAN)
Basis changed from (1:0.2) to (1:2) 04/01/2014
Name changed to FRONTEO, Inc. 07/01/2016

UBICS INC (DE)
Acquired by UB Special Transaction Corp. 06/15/2012
Each share Common 1¢ par exchanged for $0.75 cash

UBID COM HLDGS INC (DE)
Name changed to Enable Holdings, Inc. 08/04/2008
(See Enable Holdings, Inc.)

UBID INC (DE)
Merged into CMGI, Inc. 05/01/2000
Each share Common $0.001 par exchanged for (0.2628) share Common 1¢ par
CMGI, Inc. name changed to ModusLink Global Solutions, Inc. 09/30/2008 which name changed to Steel Connect, Inc. 02/27/2018

UBIQUITEL INC (DE)
Merged into Sprint Nextel Corp. 07/01/2006
Each share Common $0.0005 par exchanged for $10.35 cash

UBIQUITY BROADCASTING CORP (NV)
Common $0.001 par split (3) for (1) by issuance of (2) additional shares payable 03/22/2013 to holders of record 03/22/2013
Common $0.001 par split (4) for (1) by issuance of (3) additional shares payable 12/06/2013 to holders of record 12/06/2013
Recapitalized as Ubiquity, Inc. 04/24/2014
Each share Common $0.001 par exchanged for (0.28571428) share Common no par

UBM PLC (JERSEY)
Each old Sponsored ADR for Ordinary exchanged for (0.88888888) new Sponsored ADR for Ordinary 07/05/2016
ADR agreement terminated 07/18/2016
Each new Sponsored ADR for Ordinary exchanged for $13.817183 cash

UBRANDIT COM (NV)
Recapitalized as China Green Material Technologies, Inc. 01/14/2008
Each share Common $0.001 par exchanged for (0.00666666) share Common $0.001 par
Note: No holder will receive fewer than (100) shares

UBROADCAST INC (DE)
Name changed to Santeon Group Inc. 06/11/2010

UBS AG (SWITZERLAND)
Sponsored ADR's for Ordinary split (2) for (1) by issuance of (1) additional ADR payable 05/08/2000 to holders of record 05/05/2000 Ex date - 05/08/2000
ADR agreement terminated 05/17/2001
Each Sponsored ADR for Ordinary exchanged for $7.5398 cash
(Additional Information in Active)

UBS GLOBAL ALLOCATION TR (ON)
Issue Information - 20,000,000 UNITS offered at $10 per Unit on 03/16/2004
Name changed to UBS (Canada) Global Tactical Allocation ETF Fund and Units reclassified as Ser. A Units 01/31/2014

UBS INC (DE)
Auction Market Preferred Ser. C called for redemption at $100,000 on 01/13/1999
Auction Market Preferred Ser. D called for redemption at $100,000 on 01/20/1999
Auction Market Preferred Ser. F called for redemption at $100,000 on 01/27/1999
Auction Market Preferred Ser. E called for redemption at $100,000 on 02/24/1999

UBS PAINEWEBBER CASHFUND, INC. (MD)
Name changed to UBS Cashfund, Inc. 06/09/2003

UBS PATHFINDERS TR (DE)
Treasury & Growth Stock Units Ser. 20 called for redemption at $1.89437 on 08/29/2007

UBS PFD FDG TR III (DE)
7.25% Guaranteed Trust Preferred Securities called for redemption at $25 plus $0.055381 accrued dividends on 06/26/2006

UBS PFD FDG TR IV (DE)
Non-Cum Floating Rate Trust Preferred Securities called for redemption at $25 on 06/15/2016

UBS TOTAL RETURN TR (ON)
Merged into UBS Global Allocation Trust 06/10/2008
Each Unit no par received (1.0246995) Units no par
UBS Global Allocation Trust name changed to UBS (Canada) Global Tactical Allocation ETF Fund 01/31/2014

UBUYHOLDINGS INC (NV)
Charter permanently revoked 11/30/2004

UBUYNETWORK COM INC (NV)
Recapitalized as Elm Technologies, Inc. 06/21/2007
Each share Common 1¢ par exchanged for (0.1) share Common 1¢ par
Elm Technologies, Inc. name changed to Perla Group International, Inc. 12/10/2010

UBZ CORP (DE)
Voluntarily dissolved 09/16/1987
Details not available

UC CORP (VA)
Liquidation completed
Each share Common 34¢ par received initial distribution of $2.60 cash 12/30/1987
Each share Common 34¢ par received second distribution of $1.90 cash 11/01/1988
Each share Common 34¢ par received third distribution of $1.90 cash 11/09/1989
Each share Common 34¢ par received fourth distribution of $1.95 cash 11/08/1990
Note: Details on number or amount of subsequent distributions are available through Trustee

UC HUB GROUP INC (NV)
SEC revoked common stock registration 05/07/2013

UC NWIN SYS CORP (DE)
Recapitalized as Winner's Edge.com, Inc. 10/29/1999
Each share Common no par exchanged for (0.25) share Common 1¢ par
Winner's Edge.com, Inc. name changed to Sealant Solutions Inc. 08/06/2001 which name changed to PowerChannel, Inc. 07/28/2003 which recapitalized as Qualibou Energy Inc. 02/05/2008

UC NWIN SYS LTD (CANADA)
Reincorporated under the laws of Delaware as UC'NWIN Systems Corp. 12/11/1995
UC'NWIN Systems Corp. recapitalized as Winner's Edge.com, Inc. 10/29/1999 which name changed to Sealant Solutions Inc. 08/06/2001 which name changed to PowerChannel, Inc. 07/28/2003 which recapitalized as Qualibou Energy Inc. 02/05/2008

UC TELEVISION NETWORK CORP (DE)
Recapitalized as College Television Network, Inc. 11/12/97
Each share Common $0.001 par exchanged for (0.2) share Common $0.005 par
College Television Network, Inc. name changed to CTN Media Group Inc. 11/18/99

UCAN CORP (UT)
Reincorporated under the laws of Florida as Madison Systems, Inc. 10/28/1997

UCAP INC (CO)
SEC revoked common stock registration 08/23/2005

UCAP INC (NV)
Reincorporated 02/25/1991
State of incorporation changed from (UT) to (NV) 02/25/1991
Each share old Common $0.001 par exchanged for (0.2) share new Common $0.001 par 06/27/1991
Each share new Common $0.001 par exchanged again for (0.1) share new Common $0.001 par 12/01/1994
Recapitalized as Medical Resources Technologies Ltd. 06/01/1998
Each share new Common $0.001 par exchanged for (0.14285714) share Common $0.001 par
Medical Resources Technologies Ltd. name changed to Coinless Systems Inc. 08/12/1999 which recapitalized as NHS Health Solutions, Inc. (NV) 07/11/2007 which reincorporated in Florida 02/28/2012
(See NHS Health Solutions, Inc.)

UCAR INTL INC (DE)
Name changed to GrafTech International Ltd. 05/07/2002
(See GrafTech International Ltd.)

UCBH HLDGS INC (DE)
Common 1¢ par split (2) for (1) by issuance of (1) additional share payable 04/10/2001 to holders of record 03/31/2001 Ex date - 04/11/2001
Common 1¢ par split (2) for (1) by issuance of (1) additional share payable 04/08/2003 to holders of record 03/31/2003 Ex date - 04/09/2003
Common 1¢ par split (2) for (1) by issuance of (1) additional share payable 04/12/2005 to holders of record 03/31/2005 Ex date - 04/13/2005
Chapter 7 bankruptcy proceedings terminated 01/05/2017
Stockholders' equity unlikely

UCCEL CORP (DE)
Merged into Computer Associates International, Inc. 08/19/1987
Each share Capital Stock 10¢ par exchanged for (1.6964) shares Common 10¢ par
Computer Associates International, Inc. name changed to CA, Inc. 02/01/2006

UCF INDS INC (DE)
Charter cancelled and declared inoperative and void for non-payment of taxes 3/1/76

UCHI GOLD MINES LTD. (ON)
Bankrupt in 1943

UCI MED AFFILIATES INC (DE)
Each share Common 1¢ par exchanged for (0.2) share Common 5¢ par 06/03/1994
Acquired by BlueChoice HealthPlan of South Carolina, Inc. 05/06/2011
Each share Common 5¢ par exchanged for $6.50 cash

UCLUELET EXPL CORP (NV)
Name changed to California Oil & Gas Corp. 02/07/2006
(See California Oil & Gas Corp.)

UCN INC (DE)
Name changed to inContact, Inc. 01/01/2009
(See inContact, Inc.)

UCOLO URANIUM CO. (UT)
Recapitalized as American Host 3/7/69
Each share Common 1¢ par exchanged for (0.1) share Common 10¢ par
(See American Host)

UCORE URANIUM INC (AB)
Common no par split (2) for (1) by issuance of (1) additional share payable 10/12/2006 to holders of record 10/12/2006 Ex date - 10/10/2006
Name changed to Ucore Rare Metals Inc. 06/29/2010

UCP INC (DE)
Merged into Century Communities, Inc. 08/04/2017
Each share Class A Common 1¢ par exchanged for (0.2309) share Common 1¢ par and $5.32 cash

UDATE COM INC (DE)
Reincorporated 3/29/2001
State of incorporation changed from (CA) to (DE) 3/29/2001
Merged into USA Interactive 4/7/2003
Each share Common $0.001 par exchanged (0.18956) share Common 1¢ par
USA Interactive name changed to InterActiveCorp 6/23/2003 which name changed to IAC/InterActiveCorp 7/14/2004

UDC HOMES INC (DE)
Plan of reorganization under Chapter 11 Federal Bankruptcy Code effective 11/14/95
Holders of Exchangeable Prime Preferred 1¢ par received trust certificates representing pro rata interest in $3,000,000 principal amount of Ser. C Subordinate Notes
No stockholders' equity for holders of Ser. A Preferred, Ser. B Preferred or Common

UDC UNVL DEV L P (DE)
Depositary Receipts split (3) for (2) by issuance of (0.5) additional Depositary Receipt 7/31/86
$15 Exchangeable Preferred Units of Ltd. Partnership changed to $3.75 and (3) additional Units issued 7/5/88
Merged into UDC Homes, Inc. 9/30/92
Each Series B Preferred Unit exchanged for (1) share Preferred Ser. B 1¢ par
Each $3.75 Exchangeable Preferred Unit of Ltd. Partnership exchanged for (1) share Preferred Ser. A 1¢ par
Each Depositary Receipt exchanged for (1) share Common 1¢ par
(See UDC Homes, Inc.)

UDDLEN MINES LTD. (ON)
Name changed to Aull Metal Mines Ltd. 3/27/56
(See Aull Metal Mines Ltd.)

UDICO CORP (CA)
Name changed to UDO Pacific Corp. 02/16/1972
UDO Pacific Corp. reorganized as Winkler/Scheid Corp. 08/30/1972 which name changed to Winkler Scheid Vineyards Inc. 07/29/1974 which name changed to Winkler Scheid Inc. 05/19/1977 which name changed to HS Group Inc. 05/28/1980 which assets were transferred to HS Group Inc. Liquidating Trust 08/23/1985
(See HS Group Inc. Liquidating Trust)

UDICO ELECTRIC CO. (CA)
Name changed to Udico Corp. 8/17/66
Udico Corp. name changed to UDO Pacific Corp. 2/16/72 which reorganized as Winkler/Scheid Corp. 8/30/72 which name changed to Winkler Scheid Vineyards Inc. 7/29/74 which name changed to Winkler Scheid Inc. 5/19/77 which name changed to HS Group Inc. 5/28/80 which assets were transferred to HS Group Inc. Liquidating Trust 8/23/85
(See HS Group Inc. Liquidating Trust)

UDL HLDGS LTD (BERMUDA)
ADR agreement terminated 04/27/2015
No ADR's remain outstanding

UDO PAC CORP (CA)
Reorganized under the laws of Delaware as Winkler/Scheid Corp. 08/30/1972
Each share Common no par exchanged for (1) share Common 10¢ par
Winkler/Scheid Corp. name changed to Winkler Scheid Vineyards Inc. 07/29/1974 which name changed to Winkler Scheid Inc. 05/19/1977 which name changed to HS Group Inc. 05/28/1980 which assets were transferred to HS Group Inc. Liquidating Trust 08/23/1985
(See HS Group Inc. Liquidating Trust)

UDR INC (MD)
8.60% Preferred Ser. B $1 par called for redemption at $25 plus $0.525553 accrued dividends on 05/29/2007
6.75% Preferred Ser. G no par called for redemption at $25 on 05/31/2012
(Additional Information in Active)

UDS CAP I (DE)
Issue Information - $200,000,000 TR ORIGINATED PFD SECS 8.32% offered at $25 per share on 07/16/1997
8.32% Trust Originated Preferred Securities called for redemption at $25 on 6/30/2003

UDS INC (AR)
Merged into Artex Investors, Inc. 02/01/1985
Each share Common $1 par exchanged for $0.25 principal amount of UDS, Inc. 10% Promissory Notes due 11/01/1985

UDYCO INDS INC (MI)
Common $5 par changed to $1 par 07/14/1970
Assets sold for benefit of creditors 10/25/1974
No stockholders' equity

UDYLITE CORP. (DE)
Stock Dividend - 10% 12/29/55
Merged into Hooker Chemical Corp. 1/2/68
Each share Common $1 par exchanged for (0.6) share $2.16 Conv. Preference $1 par and (0.333333) share Common $5 par
Hooker Chemical Corp. acquired by Occidental Petroleum Corp. (Calif.) 7/24/68
(See Occidental Petroleum Corp. (Calif.))

UE WATERHEATER INCOME FD (ON)
Units called for redemption at $23 on 06/29/2007

UF BANCORP INC (DE)
Merged into CNB Bancshares Inc. 8/4/95
Each share Common 1¢ par exchanged for (1.366) shares Common $5 par
CNB Bancshares Inc. merged into Fifth Third Bancorp 10/29/99

UF INDS INC (NY)
Name changed to RDA Industries, Inc. 05/03/1976
(See RDA Industries, Inc.)

UFH CAP TR I (DE)
9.4% Trust Preferred Securities called for redemption at $5 on 12/19/2003

UFLEX LTD (INDIA)
GDR agreement terminated 04/13/2016
Each 144A GDR for Ordinary exchanged for (2) shares Ordinary
Each Reg. S GDR for Ordinary exchanged for (2) shares Ordinary

UFM VENTURES LTD (BC)
Name changed to Uracan Resources Ltd. 08/03/2006
Uracan Resources Ltd. recapitalized as Vanadian Energy Corp. 10/05/2018

UFOOD RESTAURANT GROUP INC (NV)
Name changed 10/04/2007
Common $0.001 par split (3) for (2) by issuance of (0.5) additional share payable 09/07/2007 to holders of record 09/04/2007 Ex date - 09/10/2007
Name changed from UFood Franchise Co. to UFood Restaurant Group, Inc. 10/04/2007
Plan of reorganization under Chapter 11 Federal Bankruptcy proceedings effective 04/23/2014
No stockholders' equity

UGANDA GOLD LTD (AB)
Name changed to CanAfrican Metals & Mining Corp. 07/10/2006
CanAfrican Metals & Mining Corp. name changed to Canaf Group Inc. 06/01/2007 which name changed to Canaf Investments Inc. 07/27/2018

UGC EUROPE INC (DE)
Merged into Unitedglobalcom, Inc. 12/22/2003
Each share Common 1¢ par exchanged for (10.3) shares Class A Common 1¢ par
Unitedglobalcom, Inc. merged into Liberty Global, Inc. (DE) 06/15/2005 which reorganized in England & Wales as Liberty Global PLC 06/10/2013

UGI CORP OLD (PA)
$2.75 Preferred no par called for redemption 6/20/86
Common $4.50 par changed to $2.25 par and (1) additional share issued 6/29/90
Each share $9 Preferred no par converted into (6) shares Common $2.25 par 4/1/91
Under plan of reorganization each share Common $2.25 par automatically became (1) share UGI Corp. (New) Common no par 4/10/92
$8.50 Preferred no par called for redemption 11/5/93
$1.80 Conv. Preferred no par called for redemption at $23.50 on 4/1/98

UGI UTILS INC (PA)
$7.75 Preferred no par called for redemption at $100 on 10/1/2004

UGL ENTERPRISES LTD (BC)
Name changed to Red Hill Energy Inc. 05/31/2006
(See Red Hill Energy Inc.)

UGLY DUCKLING CORP (DE)
Merged into UDC Acquisition Corp. 3/5/2002
Each share Common $0.001 par exchanged for $3.53 cash

UGOMEDIA INTERACTIVE CORP (NV)
Name changed to Sciax Corp. 7/28/2004
Sciax Corp. recapitalized as RMD Entertainment Group 10/21/2005

UGTC HLDG CORP (DE)
Merged into Tire Holding 2, Inc. 05/02/1990
Each share Class A Common 1¢ par exchanged for $5.17745445 cash

UHF INC (DE)
Reincorporated under the laws of Nevada as Adamant DRI Processing & Minerals Group 08/29/2014

UHF INC (MI)
Reorganized under the laws of Delaware 01/13/2012
Each share Common $0.001 par exchanged for (0.2) share Common $0.001 par
Note: Holders of between (250) to (499) pre-split shares received (100) shares
UHF Inc. (DE) reincorporated in Nevada as Adamant DRI Processing & Minerals Group 08/29/2014

UHLMANN CO (DE)
Merged into Valley Grain Co. 12/20/1985
Each share Class A Common $1 par exchanged for $20.25 cash
Each share Class B Common $1 par exchanged for $20.25 cash

UI CAP INC (CANADA)
Name changed to Urbanimmersive Technologies Inc. 10/15/2012
Urbanimmersive Technologies Inc. name changed to Urbanimmersive Inc. 10/13/2015

UI GROUP INC (UT)
Acquired by the Mormon Church 04/24/1984
Each share Common $5 par exchanged for $14.50 cash

UICI (DE)
Merged into Blackstone Group 04/05/2006
Each share Common 1¢ par exchanged for $37 cash

UIL HLDG CORP (CT)
Common no par split (5) for (3) by issuance of (0.66666666) additional share payable 07/03/2006 to holders of record 06/06/2006 Ex date - 07/05/2006
Merged into Avangrid, Inc. 12/16/2015
Each share Common no par exchanged for (1) share Common 1¢ par and $10.50 cash

UINTA FINANCE CO. (UT)
Name changed to Sentry Finance Co. 03/18/1963

UINTA OIL & EXPLORATION CO. (CO)
Declared defunct and inoperative for failure to pay taxes and file annual reports 10/12/1931

UINTAH BASIN MINERALS INC (UT)
Involuntarily dissolved 03/01/1993

UINTAH MTN COPPER CO (NV)
Reorganized 01/31/2005
Reorganized from under the laws of (UT) to (NV) 01/31/2005
Each share Common 10¢ par exchanged for (0.01) share Common 10¢ par
Note: Holders of (99) or fewer shares were not affected by the reverse split
No holder of (100) or more shares will receive fewer than (100) shares
Each share old Common $0.001 par exchanged for (0.5) share new Common $0.001 par 07/13/2005
Note: Holders of (99) or fewer shares were not affected by the reverse split
No holder of (100) or more shares will receive fewer than (100) shares
Name changed to Voxpath Holdings Inc. 12/29/2005
Voxpath Holdings Inc. name changed to TheRetirementsoultion.com, Inc. 09/18/2006 which name changed to Global Investor Services, Inc. 10/01/2008 which recapitalized as Investview, Inc. 04/09/2012

UINTAH WYO OIL & GAS CO (UT)
Merged into Utah Resources International, Inc. 10/31/1972
Each share Capital Stock 1¢ par exchanged for (0.2) share Capital Stock 10¢ par

UJB FINL CORP (NJ)
Name changed to Summit Bancorp 03/01/1996
Summit Bancorp merged into FleetBoston Financial Corp. 03/01/2001 which merged into Bank of America Corp. 04/01/2004

UKARMA CORP (NV)
Recapitalized as Innolog Holdings Corp. 08/18/2010
Each share Common $0.001 par exchanged for (0.08992075) share Common $0.001 par
(See Innolog Holdings Corp.)

UKE RES LTD (BC)
Name changed to Hews Star Resources Ltd. 11/04/1986
Hews Star Resources Ltd. name changed to Arch Global Technologies Inc. 04/26/1989
(See Arch Global Technologies Inc.)

UKRAGRO CORP (NV)
Name changed to Amarok Resources, Inc. and Common $0.00001 par changed to $0.001 par 02/17/2010
Amarok Resources, Inc. recapitalized as 3DX Industries, Inc. 11/22/2013

UKRAINE ENERGY ACQUISITION CORP (NV)
Recapitalized as Alter Energy Group, N.A., Inc. 04/28/2011
Each share Common $0.001 par exchanged for (0.1) share Common $0.001 par

UKRAINE ENTERPRISE CORP (ON)
Merged into Softchoice Corp. (New) 05/15/2002
Each share Common no par exchanged for (0.1) share Common no par
(See Softchoice Corp. (New))

UKRAINE FINL SVCS INC (NV)
Name changed to National Investment Corporation, Real Estate Holdings 06/23/2008
(See National Investment Corporation, Real Estate Holdings)

UKRNAFTA OPEN JT STK CO (UKRAINE)
ADR agreement terminated 12/27/2016
Each Sponsored ADR for Ordinary exchanged for (6) shares Ordinary
Note: Unexchanged ADR's will be sold and the proceeds, if any, held for claim after 01/02/2018

UKT RECYCLING TECHNOLOGIES INC (BC)
Reorganized under the laws of Canada as Cogent Integrated Solutions Corp. 12/04/2003
Each share Common no par exchanged for (0.33333333) share Common no par
Cogent Integrated Solutions Corp. recapitalized as Cogent Integrated Healthcare Solutions Corp. 11/28/2005 which name changed to Silver Recycling Co., Inc. 01/17/2007
(See Silver Recycling Co., Inc.)

ULA MNG CORP (CO)
Declared defunct and inoperative for failure to file reports and pay taxes 10/16/1971

ULA URANIUM, INC. (CO)
Recapitalized as Ula Mining Corp. 09/12/1957
Each share Common 1¢ par exchanged for (0.05) share Common 20¢ par
(See Ula Mining Corp.)

ULDAMAN CAP CORP (BC)
Recapitalized as Dawson Gold Corp. 08/10/2010
Each share Common no par exchanged for (0.5) share Common no par

ULEN & CO.
Reorganized as Ulen Realization Corp. 00/00/1942
No stockholders' equity

ULEN MANAGEMENT CO. (DE)
Name changed to Development Corp. of America and Common 10¢ par changed to $1 par 02/19/1957
(See Development Corp. of America)

ULEN REALIZATION CORP. (DE)
Merged into Ulen Management Co. 04/07/1955
Each share Common 10¢ par exchanged for (1) share Common 10¢ par
Ulen Management Co. name changed to Development Corp. of America 02/19/1957
(See Development Corp. of America)

ULH CORP (DE)
SEC revoked common stock registration 05/27/2010
Stockholders' equity unlikely

ULRICH MFG CO (DE)
Adjudicated bankrupt 06/20/1969
No stockholders' equity

ULS CAP CORP (ON)
Floating Rate Retractable 1st Preferred Ser. A no par called for redemption 01/15/1992

ULSTER & DELAWARE RAILROAD CO.
Purchased by New York Central Railroad Co. (NY, OH, IL, IN, PA & MI) 00/00/1932
Details not available

ULSTER PETES LTD (AB)
Each share old Common no par exchanged for (0.5) share new Common no par 06/05/1996
Merged into Anderson Exploration Ltd. 05/23/2000
Each share new Common no par exchanged for (0.09655) share Common no par and $11 cash
(See Anderson Exploration Ltd.)

ULT-I-MED HEALTH CTRS INC (UT)
Each share old Common $0.001 par exchanged for (0.001) share new Common $0.001 par 04/06/1999
Reincorporated under the laws of Delaware as Youthline USA, Inc. and Common $0.001 par changed to $0.0001 par 08/17/1999
(See Youthline USA, Inc.)

ULTA SALON COSMETICS & FRAGRANCE INC (DE)
Name changed to Ulta Beauty, Inc. 01/30/2017

ULTEK CORP. (CA)
Completely liquidated 03/31/1967

Each share Capital Stock 50¢ par exchanged for (0.36) share Perkin-Elmer Corp. Common $1 par
Perkin-Elmer Corp. name changed to PE Corp. 05/05/1999 which name changed to Applera Corp. 11/30/2000
(See Applera Corp.)

ULTICOM INC (NJ)
Each share old Common no par exchanged for (0.25) share new Common no par 11/18/2009
Acquired by Utah Intermediate Holding Corp. 12/03/2010
Each share new Common no par exchanged for $2.33 cash

ULTIMA ENERGY TR (AB)
Merged into Petrofund Energy Trust 06/16/2004
Each Trust Unit exchanged for (0.442) Trust Unit
Petrofund Energy Trust merged into Penn West Energy Trust 07/04/2006 which reorganized as Penn West Petroleum Ltd. (New) 01/03/2011 which name changed to Obsidian Energy Ltd. 06/29/2017

ULTIMACC SYS INC (DE)
Acquired by Storage Technology Corp. 08/28/1975
Each share Common 2¢ par exchanged for (0.5) share Common 10¢ par
(See Storage Technology Corp.)

ULTIMAP CORP (MN)
Reorganized 07/08/1991
Reorganized from Ultiman International Corp. to Ultimap Corp. 07/08/1991
Each share Class A Common 1¢ par exchanged for (0.1) share Common 1¢ par
Each share Class B Common 1¢ par exchanged for (0.1) share Common 1¢ par
Each share old Common 1¢ par exchanged for (0.5) share new Common 1¢ par 04/09/1992
Filed a petition under Chapter 11 Federal Bankruptcy Code 09/01/1993
Stockholders' equity unlikely

ULTIMATE CORP (NJ)
Common no par split (3) for (2) by issuance of (0.5) additional share 09/15/1983
Name changed to Allerion, Inc. 09/22/1993
(See Allerion, Inc.)

ULTIMATE DIRECT INC (NV)
Name changed 07/22/1999
Each share old Common $0.001 par exchanged for (0.1) share Common $0.001 par 06/01/1998
Name changed from Ultimate Cigar Inc. to Ultimate Direct, Inc. 07/22/1999
Recapitalized as Altadyne, Inc. 04/14/2005
Each share new Common $0.001 par exchanged for (0.0025) share Common $0.001 par
Altadyne, Inc. name changed to Stem Cell International, Inc. 10/14/2005 which name changed to Stem Cell Therapy International, Inc. 10/18/2005 which name changed to AmStem Corp. 02/23/2010

ULTIMATE ELECTRS INC (DE)
Plan of reorganization under Chapter 11 Federal Bankruptcy Code effective 01/11/2006
No stockholders' equity

ULTIMATE ESCAPES INC (DE)
Plan of reorganization under Chapter 11 Federal Bankruptcy proceedings effective 01/03/2012
No stockholders' equity

ULTIMATE FRANCHISE SYS INC (CO)
Each share old Common no par exchanged for (0.1) share new Common no par 08/17/2001
Reincorporated under the laws of Nevada and Common no par changed to $0.001 par 04/25/2002

ULTIMATE JUKEBOX INC (DE)
Merged into NetMusic Entertainment Corp. 11/03/2004
Each share Common exchanged for (1) share Common
NetMusic Entertainment Corp. recapitalized as Enterayon, Inc. 03/22/2006 which recapitalized as North Bay Resources Inc. 02/07/2008

ULTIMATE NOVELTY SPORTS INC (NV)
Name changed to Earth Science Tech, Inc. 05/28/2014

ULTIMISTICS INC (DE)
Common $0.00001 par split (2) for (1) by issuance of (1) additional share 09/14/1989
Each share old Common $0.00001 par exchanged for (0.1) share new Common $0.00001 par 08/16/1994
Each share new Common $0.00001 par exchanged again for (0.5) share new Common $0.00001 par 08/11/1995
Name changed to Continental Holdings International, Inc. 03/31/1997

ULTRA BANCORP (OH)
Merged into Mid Am, Inc. 12/31/1992
Each share Common 1¢ par exchanged for (1.0923) shares Common no par
Mid Am, Inc. merged into Sky Financial Group, Inc. 10/02/1998 which merged into Huntington Bancshares Inc. 07/02/2007

ULTRA BANCORPORATION (NJ)
Common $5 par split (2) for (1) by issuance of (1) additional share 12/09/1985
Acquired by National Westminster Bank PLC 08/18/1989
Each share Common $5 par exchanged for $50 cash

ULTRA CAP CORP (NV)
Each share old Common $0.001 par exchanged for (1.3) shares new Common $0.001 par 9/17/92
Reincorporated under the laws of Delaware Tracker Corp. of America 7/12/94

ULTRA CAP INC (AB)
Issue Information - 1,000,000 shares COM offered at $0.25 per share on 04/30/1997
Name changed to AG Growth Industries Inc. 1/30/98

ULTRA CARE INC (NV)
Name changed to TechMedia Advertising, Inc. and (21) additional shares issued 02/17/2009
(See TechMedia Advertising, Inc.)

ULTRA DYNAMICS CORP (DE)
Name changed to Puroflow Inc. 06/01/1983
Puroflow Inc. name changed to Argan, Inc. 10/29/2003

ULTRA ELECTR HLDGS LTD (ENGLAND)
Name changed 07/21/1969
Name changed from Ultra Electric Holdings Ltd. to Ultra Electronic Holdings Ltd. 07/21/1969
ADR's for Ordinary Reg. 5s par changed to 25p par per currency change 02/15/1971
Liquidation completed
Each ADR for Ordinary Reg. 5s par exchanged for $12.79 cash 11/02/1978

Note: Details on subsequent distributions, if any, are not available

ULTRA GLOW COSMETICS LTD (BC)
Class A Common no par split (2) for (1) by issuance of (1) additional share 07/03/1984
Reorganized under the laws of Nevada as E-International Fund Management Inc. 08/20/1999
Each share Class A Common no par exchanged for (0.1) share Common $0.001 par
E-International Fund Management Inc. name changed to Mobile Self Storage, Inc. 04/10/2001
(See Mobile Self Storage, Inc.)

ULTRA HLDGS INC (BC)
Acquired by Cubix Investments Ltd. 10/23/2001
Each share Common no par exchanged for $4 principal amount of Cubix Acquisitionco Inc. Exchangeable Note due 3/31/2002 and $3 cash

ULTRA JET INDS INC (FL)
Charter cancelled and proclaimed dissolved for non-payment of taxes 06/28/1971

ULTRA-MECHANISMS, INC.
Assets acquired by Ultrasonic Corp. 00/00/1953
Details not available

ULTRA MED DEVICES INC (CA)
Charter cancelled for failure to file reports and pay taxes 7/2/84

ULTRA MOTORCYCLE CO (CA)
Reincorporated under the laws of Delaware as New Dover Capital Corp. 08/02/2007

ULTRA PAC INC (MN)
Merged into Ivex Packaging Corp. 04/23/1998
Each share Common 1¢ par exchanged for $15.50 cash

ULTRA PETE CORP (BC)
Reincorporated under the laws of Yukon 03/01/2000

ULTRA PLASTICS, INC. (PA)
Adjudicated bankrupt in July 1964
Stock declared worthless

ULTRA PURE WTR SYS INC (AB)
Delisted from Alberta Stock Exchange 06/19/1996

ULTRA RES CORP (BC)
Recapitalized as Empire Rock Minerals Inc. 10/22/2015
Each share Common no par exchanged for (0.33333333) share Common no par
Empire Rock Minerals Inc. name changed to Empire Metals Corp. 02/02/2017

ULTRA SHAWKEY MINES LTD. (ON)
Recapitalized as Con-Shawkey Gold Mines Ltd. on a (1) for (3) basis 10/01/1962
Con-Shawkey Gold Mines Ltd. name changed to Kenn Holdings & Mining Ltd. 09/15/1969
(See Kenn Holdings & Mining Ltd.)

ULTRA-SONIC PRECISION CO. INC. (NY)
Assets sold for the benefit of creditors in 1964
No stockholders' equity

ULTRA SUN CORP (NV)
Name changed to Cannabis Sativa, Inc. 11/18/2013

ULTRA URANIUM CORP (BC)
Recapitalized as Ultra Resources Corp. 11/14/2012
Each share Common no par exchanged for (0.33333333) share Common no par
Ultra Resources Corp. recapitalized as Empire Rock Minerals Inc. 10/22/2015 which name changed to Empire Metals Corp. 02/02/2017

ULTRACELL MED TECHNOLOGIES LTD (ON)
Recapitalized as AMT Fine Foods Ltd. 08/12/1997
Each share Common no par exchanged for (0.1) share Common no par
AMT Fine Foods Ltd. recapitalized as Skor Food Group Inc. 06/27/2002
(See Skor Food Group Inc.)

ULTRACIRCUITS INC (DE)
Charter cancelled and declared inoperative and void for non-payment of taxes 06/26/1985

ULTRADATA CORP (DE)
Issue Information - 350,000 shares COM offered at $5 per share on 01/31/1995
Merged into Concentrex Inc. 8/16/99
Each share Common $0.001 par exchanged for $7.50 cash

ULTRADATA SYS INC (DE)
Recapitalized as China Huaren Organic Products, Inc. 01/17/2007
Each share Common 1¢ par exchanged for (0.02564102) share Common 1¢ par
(See China Huaren Organic Products, Inc.)

ULTRAFEM INC (DE)
Plan of reorganization under Chapter 11 Federal Bankruptcy Code effective 08/31/2000
No stockholders' equity

ULTRAFIT CTRS INC (CO)
Name changed to FDN, Inc. 2/18/99

ULTRAGUARD WTR SYS CORP (NV)
Recapitalized as Creative Eateries Corp. 07/08/2005
Each share Common $0.001 par exchanged for (0.01) share Common $0.001 par
Creative Eateries Corp. recapitalized as Diners Acquisition Corp. 10/20/2006 which recapitalized as LaSalle Brands Corp. 07/10/2007
(See LaSalle Brands Corp.)

ULTRAK INC (DE)
Reincorporated 12/22/1995
Each share old Common no par exchanged for (0.2) share new Common no par 12/22/1986
Each share new Common no par exchanged again for (1/6) share Common no par 12/28/1993
State of incorporation changed from (CO) to (DE) and Common no par changed to 1¢ par 12/22/1995
Secondary Offering - 2,800,000 shares COM offered at $26 per share on 11/18/1996
Name changed to American Building Control, Inc. 12/20/2002
American Building Control, Inc. name changed to MDI, Inc. 09/24/2004
(See MDI, Inc.)

ULTRALIFE BATTERIES INC (DE)
Name changed to Ultralife Corp. 06/05/2008

ULTRAMAR CAP CORP (ON)
8.75% Retractable 1st Preferred Ser. 1 $25 par called for redemption 09/25/1990
Public interest eliminated

ULTRAMAR CORP (DE)
Name changed to Ultramar Diamond Shamrock Corp. 12/3/96
Ultra Diamond Shamrock Corp. merged into Valero Energy Corp. (New) 12/31/2001

ULTRAMAR DIAMOND SHAMROCK CORP (DE)
5% Conv. Preferred 1¢ par called for redemption at $50 on 3/18/98
Merged into Valero Energy Corp. (New) 12/31/2001
Each share Common 1¢ par exchanged for $49.4683 cash

ULTRAMAR MINERALS CORP (DE)
Charter forfeited for failure to maintain a registered agent 02/17/1975

ULTRAMAR PLC (ENGLAND)
Name changed 01/08/1982
Each share Ordinary Reg. 50p exchanged for (2) shares Ordinary Reg. 25p par 05/27/1971
ADR's for Ordinary Reg. 50p par changed to 25p par and (1) additional share issued 06/18/1971
Each old ADR for Ordinary Reg. 25p par exchanged for (1) new ADR for Ordinary Reg. 25p par 11/28/1977
Stock Dividend - 100% 06/06/1980
Name changed from Ultramar Co. Ltd. to Ultramar PLC 01/08/1982
Ordinary Reg. 25p par split (2) for (1) by issuance of (1) additional share 06/12/1984
ADR's for Ordinary Reg. 25p par split (2) for (1) by issuance of (1) additional share 06/12/1984
Acquired by Lasmo PLC 04/10/1992
Each share Ordinary Reg. 25p par exchanged for (0.8695652) share Ordinary Stock 25p par
Each ADR for Ordinary Reg. 25p par exchanged for (0.38333) Sponsored ADR for Ordinary 25p par
Lasmo PLC acquired by Eni S.p.A. 04/17/2001

ULTRAMAX INC (ID)
Charter forfeited for failure to file reports 12/3/90

ULTRAPHONICS-USA INC (GA)
Each old share Common $0.001 par exchanged for (0.001) share new Common $0.001 par 11/17/1999
Name changed to PediaNet.com, Inc. 12/27/1999
PediaNet.com, Inc. recapitalized as Morgan Equities Group, Inc. 09/19/2005 which name changed to Deaf-Talk, Inc. 09/14/2010
(See Deaf-Talk, Inc.)

ULTRAQUEST INC (FL)
Name changed to Leviathan International Ltd. 6/6/91
(See Leviathan International Ltd.)

ULTRASCIENCES, INC. (PA)
Reincorporated under the laws of Florida as Florida Medical Plan, Inc. 11/15/71
(See Florida Medical Plan, Inc.)

ULTRASONIC CORP. (MA)
Common $5 par changed to $1 par 01/21/1955
Name changed to Advance Industries, Inc. 01/18/1957
Advance Industries, Inc. acquired by Wilson Brothers 01/22/1964 which name changed to Wilson Brothers USA, Inc. 08/20/1997
(See Wilson Brothers USA, Inc.)

ULTRASONIC INDS INC (NY)
Proclaimed dissolved for failure to file reports and pay fees 12/15/1969

ULTRASONIC SYS INC (DE)
Incorporated 10/03/1986
Recapitalized as E.T. Canada Inc. 07/11/1990
Each share Common 1¢ par exchanged for (0.5) share Common 2¢ par
(See E.T. Canada Inc.)

ULTRASONIC SYSTEMS, INC. (DE)
Adjudicated bankrupt 03/25/1976
Details not available

ULTRASTRIP SYS INC (FL)
Reincorporated under the laws of Delaware as Ecosphere Technologies, Inc. 8/22/2006

ULTRASYSTEMS INC (DE)
Reincorporated 10/31/86
Common no par split (5) for (3) by issuance of (2/3) additional share 2/9/83
State of incorporation changed from

(CA) to (DE) and Common no par changed to 1¢ par 10/31/86
Acquired by Hadson Corp. (Old) 4/15/88
Each share Common 1¢ par exchanged for (2) shares Common 10¢ par and $1.50 cash
Hadson Corp. (Old) merged into Hadson Corp. (New) 12/14/93

ULTRATECH CEMCO LTD (INDIA)
Name changed to UltraTech Cement Ltd. 11/10/2004

ULTRATECH INC (DE)
Name changed 06/05/2003
Common $0.001 par split (2) for (1) by issuance of (1) additional share 05/10/1995
Name changed from Ultratech Stepper, Inc. to Ultratech, Inc. 06/05/2003
Merged into Veeco Instruments Inc. 05/26/2017
Each share Common $0.001 par exchanged for (0.2675) share Common 1¢ par and $21.75 cash

ULTRATECH INDS CORP (NV)
Recapitalized as Teledata World Services, Inc. 1/6/97
Each share old Common $0.001 par exchanged for (1/27) share new Common $0.001 par

ULTRATECH KNOWLEDGE SYS INC (CO)
Common $0.001 par split (3) for (1) by issuance of (2) additional shares 09/25/1990
Each share old Common $0.001 par exchanged for (0.1) share new Common $0.001 par 05/15/1993
Name changed to AGTsports Inc. (CO) 06/17/1993
AGTsports Inc. (CO) reorganized in Nevada as HealthRenu Medical, Inc. 09/19/2003
(See HealthRenu Medical, Inc.)

ULTRAVISION CORP (AB)
Recapitalized 05/12/1999
Recapitalized from UltraVision, Inc. to UltraVision Corp. 05/12/1999
Each share Common no par exchanged for (0.25) share Common no par
Filed an assignment in bankruptcy 09/12/2002
Stockholders' equity unlikely

ULTREXX CORP (UT)
Each share old Common $0.001 par exchanged for (0.14285714) share new Common $0.001 par 05/31/2001
Reorganized under the laws of Nevada as IP Matrix Corp. 06/30/2004
Each share Common $0.001 par exchanged for (0.25) share Common $0.001 par
IP Matrix Corp. name changed to Airprotek International, Inc. (NV) 03/24/2005 which reorganized in Wyoming as Rafarma Pharmaceuticals, Inc. 11/20/2012

ULTRONIC SYSTEMS CORP. (DE)
Completely liquidated 6/15/67
Each share Common 1¢ par exchanged for first and final distribution of (0.2) share General Telephone & Electronics Corp. 5% Conv. Preferred $50 par
General Telephone & Electronics Corp. name changed to GTE Corp. 7/1/82 which merged into Verizon Communications Inc. 6/30/2000

ULTRONICS INC (NV)
Name changed to General Environmental Management, Inc. 03/21/2005
(See General Environmental Management, Inc.)

ULYSSES DIVERSIFIED HLDG CORP. (DE)
Name changed to JNS Holdings Corp. 02/16/2012

ULYSSES GROUP LTD (AB)
Name changed to Semper Energy Ltd. 10/29/2002
Semper Energy Ltd. acquired by Val Vista Energy Ltd. 08/21/2003 which was acquired by Avenir Diversified Income Trust 04/18/2005 which reorganized as AvenEx Energy Corp. 01/07/2011 which merged into Spyglass Resources Corp. 04/04/2013

ULYSSES HLDG CORP (DE)
Common $0.0001 par split (2) for (1) by issuance of (1) additional share payable 02/29/2008 to holders of record 02/11/2008 Ex date - 03/03/2008
Name changed to Ulysses Diversified Holdings Corp. 05/08/2008
Ulysses Diversified Holdings Corp. name changed to JNS Holdings Corp. 02/16/2012

ULYSSES INTL RES LTD (BAHAMAS)
Recapitalized as Auric Resources Ltd. (Bahamas) 03/05/1999
Each share Common no exchanged for (0.5) share Common no par
Auric Resources Ltd. (Bahamas) reorganized in Yukon as Lalo Ventures Ltd. 11/02/2001 which reincorporated in British Columbia 07/29/2005 which name changed to Sunrise Minerals Inc. 12/20/2005 which recapitalized as Cronus Resources Ltd. (BC) 03/10/2008 which reincorporated in Ontario 06/25/2009 which merged into Continental Gold Ltd. (New) (Bermuda) 03/30/2010 which reorganized in Ontario as Continental Gold Inc. 06/12/2015

UMAIRCO INC (CO)
Name changed to Digital Arts Media Network, Inc. 03/10/2015

UMATILLA TONOPAH MINING CO. (NV)
Capital Stock $1 par changed to 25¢ par 6/14/34
Recapitalized as Rich Minerals & Oil, Inc. 9/11/57
Each share Capital Stock 25¢ par exchanged for (2) shares Capital Stock 50¢ par
Rich Minerals & Oil, Inc. recapitalized as Rich International, Inc. 6/23/71 which recapitalized as Rich International Energies, Inc. 1/24/74
(See Rich International Energies, Inc.)

UMB EQUITIES INC (DE)
Charter cancelled and declared inoperative and void for non-payment of taxes 5/30/96

UMBERTINOS RESTAURANTS INC (BC)
Name changed 11/10/87
Name changed from Umberto's Pasta Enterprises Inc. to Umbertino's Restaurants Inc. 11/10/87
Struck off register and declared dissolved for failure to file returns 5/28/93

UMBRA INC (UT)
Proclaimed dissolved for failure to file reports 10/1/96

UMBRAL ENERGY CORP (BC)
Name changed to Heritage Cannabis Holdings Corp. 01/10/2018

UMBRELLA BANCORP INC (MD)
Reincorporated 5/28/2002
State of incorporation changed from (DE) to (MD) 5/28/2002
Goodwill Conv. Preferred called for redemption at $0.005 on 8/1/2003
Name changed to Terme Bancorp, Inc. 2/1/2007

UMC ELECTRS CO (DE)
Capital Stock $1 par changed to no par 02/02/1982
Capital Stock no par split (5) for (4) by issuance of (0.25) additional share 04/15/1982
Capital Stock no par changed to 1¢ par 02/13/1990
Stock Dividends - 10% 04/15/1977; 10% 11/15/1978; 15% 04/15/1980; 10% 04/15/1981; 10% 05/27/1983
Chapter 11 bankruptcy proceedings dismissed 12/28/2004
Stockholders' equity unlikely

UMC INDS INC (DE)
Name changed to Unidynamics Corp. 04/19/1984
(See Unidynamics Corp.)

UMED HLDGS INC (TX)
Name changed to Greenway Technologies, Inc. 01/18/2018

UMET PPTYS CORP (DE)
Reorganized 08/31/1982
Under plan of reorganization each Umet Trust Conv. Preferred Share of Bene. Int. $9.50 par and Share of Bene. Int. $1 par automatically became (1) share Umet Properties Corp. Conv. Preferred $9.50 par and Common $1 par respectively 08/31/1982
Merged into Hallwood Group Inc. 04/30/1984
Each share Conv. Preferred $9.50 par exchanged for (1.3) shares 7% Participating Conv. Preferred $8 par
Each share Common $1 par exchanged for (0.5) share 7% Participating Conv. Preferred $8 par
(See Hallwood Group Inc.)

UMF SYS INC (CA)
Name changed to Sierra Monitor Corp. 09/13/1989

UMINING RES INC (NY)
Recapitalized as Stargaze Entertainment Group Inc. 03/12/2015
Each share Common 1¢ par exchanged for (0.008) share Common 1¢ par

UNAC INTL CORP (IN)
Common $1 par split (5) for (4) by issuance of (0.25) additional share 7/1/72
Acquired in 1987
Each share Common $1 par exchanged for approximately $0.15 cash

UNAGUSTA CORP (NC)
Name changed 04/27/1972
Name changed from Unagusta Manufacturing Corp. to Unagusta Corp. 04/27/1972
Charter suspended for failure to pay taxes 09/30/1977

UNAPIX ENTMT INC (DE)
Stock Dividend - 5% payable 05/06/1996 to holders of record 04/22/1996
Petition filed under Chapter 11 Bankruptcy Code dismissed 12/23/2002
No stockholders' equity

UNARCO INDS INC (DE)
Reincorporated 05/22/1970
Common $5 par changed to $2.50 par and (1) additional share issued 01/28/1965
State of incorporation changed from (IL) to (DE) 05/22/1970
Common $2.50 par split (5) for (4) by issuance of (0.25) additional share 02/14/1975
Under plan of reorganization each share Common $2.50 par automatically became (1) share UNR Industries, Inc. Common $2.50 par 09/30/1980
UNR Industries, Inc. name changed to ROHN Industries, Inc. 12/17/1997

which name changed to Frankfort Tower Industries, Inc. 02/17/2004
(See Frankfort Tower Industries, Inc.)

UNAS INVTS LTD (CANADA)
Merged into Slater, Walker of Canada Ltd. 7/7/72
Each share Common no par exchanged for (2-2/3) shares Common no par
Slater, Walker of Canada Ltd. name changed to Talcorp Associates Ltd. 3/10/76 which name changed to Talcorp Ltd. 9/14/82 which reorganized as Consolidated Talcorp Ltd. 8/7/86 which name changed to Sound Insight Enterprises Ltd. 12/7/90 which merged into CamVec Corp. 9/11/92 which name changed to AMJ Campbell Inc. 8/14/2001
(See AMJ Campbell Inc.)

UNAVEST CAP CORP (CANADA)
Merged into Genterra Investment Corp. 04/30/1999
Each share Class A Common no par exchanged for (0.07142) share Class A Subordinate no par
Each share Class B Common no par exchanged for (0.07142) share Class B Multiple no par
Genterra Investment Corp. merged into Genterra Inc. 12/31/2003 which merged into Genterra Capital Inc. (New) 05/10/2010 which merged into Gencan Capital Inc. 10/30/2015

UNB BANCSHARES INC (DE)
Merged into James Madison Ltd. 10/22/86
Each share Common $5 par exchanged for (1) share Common $1 par and (1) share Class A Common $1 par
(See James Madison Ltd.)

UNB CORP (OH)
Common $5 par changed to $3.33 par and (0.5) additional share issued 3/31/87
Common $3.33 par split (3) for (2) by issuance of (0.5) additional share 5/8/87
Common $3.33 par changed to no par and (1) additional share issued 4/20/93
Common no par split (2) for (1) by issuance of (1) additional share payable 10/15/98 to holders of record 10/1/98
Under plan of merger name changed to Unizan Financial Corp. 3/8/2002
Unizan Financial Corp. merged into Huntington Bancshares Inc. 3/1/2006

UNBRIDLED ENERGY CORP (BC)
Merged into Altima Resources Ltd. 02/11/2010
Each share Common no par exchanged for (1) share Common no par

UNC INC (DE)
Name changed 06/03/1986
Reincorporated 04/30/1987
Name changed from UNC Resources, Inc. to UNC Inc. (VA) 06/03/1986
State of incorporation changed from (VA) to (DE) 04/30/1987
Acquired by Greenwich Air Services, Inc. 09/17/1997
Each share Common 20¢ par exchanged for $15 cash

UNCAS POWER CO.
Merged into Connecticut Light & Power Co. 00/00/1929
Details not available

UNCLE B S BAKERY INC (IA)
Reorganized under the laws of Nevada as NetCert, Inc. 03/04/2005
Each share Common 1¢ par exchanged for (0.005) share Common $0.001 par
NetCert, Inc. name changed to Ise Blu Equity Corp. 07/24/2006
(See Ise Blu Equity Corp.)

UNCLE BENS INDS LTD (BC)
Placed in receivership 01/29/1976
No stockholders' equity

UNCLE GEORGES PIZZA & SUBS INC (CO)
Reorganized under the laws of Delaware as Massimo da Milano, Inc. 1/18/95
Each share Common $0.00001 par exchanged for (0.00076923) share Common $0.001 par
Massimo da Milano, Inc. recapitalized as Uptrend Corp. 3/22/2004

UNCLE JOHNS RESTAURANTS INC (DE)
Name changed to Envirofood, Inc. 09/29/1969
(See Envirofood, Inc.)

UNCLE SAM OIL CO. (AZ)
Charter revoked for failure to file reports and pay fees 3/23/26

UNCOMMON MEDIA GROUP INC (FL)
SEC revoked common stock registration 06/03/2004
No stockholders' equity

UNCOMPAHGRE URANIUM, INC. (ID)
Charter forfeited for failure to pay taxes 12/1/58

UNDER SEA INDS INC (CA)
Completely liquidated 04/16/1974
Each share Common 50¢ par exchanged for first and final distribution of $11.15 cash

UNDERBALANCED DRILLING SYS INC (AB)
Merged into Precision Drilling Corp. 7/30/99
Each share Common no par exchanged for (0.02308) share Common no par
(See Precision Drilling Corp.)

UNDERGROUND ATLANTA INC (GA)
Administratively dissolved 1/9/92

UNDERGROUND SOLUTIONS INC (NV)
Acquired by Aegion Corp. 02/18/2016
Each share Common $0.001 par exchanged for $0.101 cash

UNDERGROUND SURVEYS CORP (CA)
Charter suspended for failure to file reports and pay fees 03/01/1983

UNDERSEA RECOVERY CORP (NV)
Charter revoked for failure to file reports and pay taxes 07/31/2013

UNDERWATER STORAGE INC (MD)
Charter annulled for failure to file reports 01/28/1975

UNDERWATER TECHNOLOGY CORP (NY)
Charter cancelled and proclaimed dissolved for failure to pay taxes 09/26/1979

UNDERWATER TECHNOLOGY CORP AMER INC (NV)
Company believed out of business 00/00/1987
Details not available

UNDERWEAR CORP. OF AMERICA (DE)
Charter cancelled and declared inoperative and void for non-payment of taxes 4/1/32

UNDERWOOD COMPUTING MACHINE CO.
Acquired by Underwood Elliott Fisher Co. in 1928
Details not available

UNDERWOOD CORP. (DE)
Acquired by Olivetti-Underwood, Inc. for cash 10/23/63

UNDERWOOD ELLIOTT FISHER CO.
Name changed to Underwood Corp. 3/23/45
(See Underwood Corp.)

UNDERWOOD TYPEWRITER CO.
Name changed to Underwood Elliott Fisher Co. 12/29/27
Underwood Elliott Fisher Co. name changed to Underwood Corp. 3/23/45
(See Underwood Corp.)

UNDERWORLD RES INC (BC)
Merged into Kinross Gold Corp. 07/06/2010
Each share Common no par exchanged for (0.141) share Common no par and $0.01 cash
Note: Unexchanged certificates were cancelled and became without value 06/30/2016

UNDERWRITERS BK & TR CO (NEW YORK, NY)
Capital Stock $40 par changed to $4 par and (9) additional shares issued plus a 2-1/2% stock dividend paid 11/12/1969
Name changed to United Americas Bank (New York, NY) 01/17/1974
United Americas Bank (New York, NY) name changed to Banco Central of New York (New York, NY) 12/19/1980 which name changed to Banco Central Hispano - USA (New York, NY) 10/01/1992 which name changed to BCH - USA (New York, NY) 12/04/1998
(See BCH - USA (New York, NY))

UNDERWRITERS CASUALTY CO.
Merged into Independence Indemnity Co. 00/00/1931
Details not available

UNDERWRITERS FACTORS CORP. (DE)
No longer in existence having become inoperative and void for non-payment of taxes 04/01/1959

UNDERWRITERS FINANCE CO., INC.
Liquidated 00/00/1936
Details not available

UNDERWRITERS FINANCE CORP. (LA)
Adjudicated bankrupt 03/15/1965
No stockholders' equity

UNDERWRITERS FINL GROUP INC (CO)
Plan of reorganization under Chapter 11 Federal Bankruptcy proceedings confirmed 05/24/2000
No stockholders' equity

UNDERWRITERS GROUP DIVERSIFIED ROYALTY TRUST
Completely liquidated 12/30/1980
Each Series H Trust Certificate exchanged for first and final distribution of 20% of the face value

UNDERWRITERS GROUP INC.
Liquidated 00/00/1953
Details not available

UNDERWRITERS INVESTMENT CO. (OK)
Merged into Underwriters Life Insurance Co. 04/13/1965
Each share Common 10¢ par exchanged for (1) share Common 20¢ par
(See Underwriters Life Insurance Co.)

UNDERWRITERS INVT CORP (OH)
Merged into Pan-Western Corp. 07/29/1980
Each share Class A Common $1 par exchanged for (1) share Common $1 par
Each share Class B Common no par exchanged for (1) share Common $1 par
Pan-Western Corp. merged into North American National Corp. 08/30/1984
(See North American National Corp.)

UNDERWRITERS LAND CO.
Merged into Consolidated Lead & Zinc Co. 00/00/1926
Details not available

UNDERWRITERS LIFE INS CO (OK)
Common 20¢ par changed to 11¢ par 04/09/1974
Liquidation completed
Each share Common 11¢ par exchanged for initial distribution of $0.75 cash 12/19/1975
Each share Common 11¢ par received second distribution of $0.05 cash 12/17/1976
Each share Common 11¢ par received third and final distribution of $0.093699 cash 12/20/1978

UNDERWRITERS NATL ASSURN CO (IN)
Capital Stock $2.50 par changed to $1.50 par 07/19/1966
Capital Stock $1.50 par split (4) for (3) by issuance of (0.33333333) additional share 07/01/1969
Capital Stock $1.50 par split (5) for (4) by issuance of (0.25) additional share 07/01/1970
Under plan of reorganization each share Capital Stock $1.50 par automatically became (1) share UNAC International Corp. Common $1 par 12/21/1970
(See UNAC International Corp.)

UNDERWRITERS TR CO (NEW YORK, NY)
Each share Capital Stock $20 par exchanged for (0.119402) share Capital Stock $100 par 10/11/1932
Capital Stock $100 par changed to $40 par and (4) additional shares issued 02/08/1961
Stock Dividend - 20% 03/02/1964
Name changed to Underwriters Bank & Trust Co. (New York, NY) 11/10/1969
Underwriters Bank & Trust Co. (New York, NY) name changed to United Americas Bank (New York, NY) 01/17/1974 which name changed to Banco Central of New York (New York, NY) 12/19/1980 which name changed to Banco Central Hispano - USA (New York, NY) 10/01/1992 which name changed to BCH - USA (New York, NY) 12/04/1998
(See BCH - USA (New York, NY))

UNDUR TOLGOI MINERALS INC (BC)
Reincorporated under the laws of British Virgin Islands as Khot Infrastructure Holdings, Ltd. 01/15/2014
Khot Infrastructure Holdings, Ltd. name changed to Blockchain Holdings Ltd. 10/12/2018

UNERGIE INC (QC)
Merged into Atlas Yellowknife Resources Ltd. 12/31/1985
Each share Common $1 par exchanged for (0.36363636) share Common no par and (2) Common Stock Purchase Warrants expiring 12/31/1987
Atlas Yellowknife Resources Ltd. recapitalized as Panatlas Energy Inc. 02/08/1988 which was acquired by Velvet Exploration Ltd. 07/17/2000
(See Velvet Exploration Ltd.)

UNEXCELLED CHEMICAL CORP. (NY)
Common $5 par changed to $1 par 03/16/1964
Stock Dividend - 10% 09/15/1952
Name changed to Unexcelled, Inc. 07/13/1966
Unexcelled, Inc. name changed to Twin Fair, Inc. 07/05/1972
(See Twin Fair, Inc.)

UNEXCELLED INC (NY)
Common $1 par split (2) for (1) by issuance of (1) additional share 08/15/1967
Name changed to Twin Fair, Inc. 07/05/1972
(See Twin Fair, Inc.)

UNEXCELLED MANUFACTURING CO., INC.
Name changed to Unexcelled Chemical Corp. 00/00/1946
Unexcelled Chemical Corp. name changed to Unexcelled, Inc. 07/13/1966 which name changed to Twin Fair, Inc. 07/05/1972
(See Twin Fair, Inc.)

UNGAVA BAY MINES LTD. (ON)
Charter surrendered 04/00/1962
No stockholders' equity

UNGAVA COPPER LTD (QC)
Recapitalized as New Ungava Copper Corp. Ltd. 06/23/1971
Each share Capital Stock $1 par exchanged for (0.25) share Capital Stock $1 par
New Ungava Copper Corp. Ltd. name changed to Unergie Inc. 11/18/1982 which merged into Atlas Yellowknife Resources Ltd. 12/31/1985 which recapitalized as Panatlas Energy Inc. 02/08/1988 which was acquired by Velvet Exploration Ltd. 07/17/2000
(See Velvet Exploration Ltd.)

UNGAVA MINERALS CORP (CANADA)
Name changed to Nearctic Nickel Mines Inc. 09/07/2007

UNGERLEIDER FINANCIAL CORP.
Name changed to Financial Corp. 00/00/1933
(See Financial Corp.)

UNGERMANN BASS INC (DE)
Reincorporated 03/31/1987
State of incorporation changed from (CA) to (DE) and Common 1¢ par changed to $0.001 par 03/31/1987
Merged into Tandem Computers Inc. 06/15/1988
Each share Common $0.001 par exchanged for $12.50 cash

UNI-FOAM CORP. (TN)
Became defunct 12/31/1971
No stockholders' equity

UNI-INVEST LTD (AB)
Name changed to Homburg Invest Inc. 01/11/2001
(See Homburg Invest Inc.)

UNI INVEST U S A LTD (MD)
Name changed to Cedar Income Fund Ltd. (New) 08/03/2000
Cedar Income Fund Ltd. name changed to Cedar Shopping Centers Inc. 08/05/2003 which name changed to Cedar Realty Trust, Inc. 11/10/2011

UNI LINE CORP (NV)
Name changed to Porter Holding International, Inc. 05/15/2017

UNI MARTS INC (DE)
Class A Common 10¢ par reclassified as Common 10¢ par 02/25/1993
Class B Common 10¢ par reclassified as Common 10¢ par 02/25/1993
Stock Dividends - 10% 03/25/1988; In Class A Common 10% 09/05/1990
Merged into Green Valley Acquisition Co., LLC 06/30/2004
Each share Common 10¢ par exchanged for $2.25 cash

UNI-PRESIDENT ENTERPRISES CORP (TAIWAN)
Stock Dividends - 10% payable 10/08/1999 to holders of record 08/03/1999; 8% payable 09/26/2000 to holders of record 08/03/2000; 6% payable 10/16/2001 to holders of record 08/02/2001 Ex date - 07/31/2001; 3% payable 10/17/2002 to holders of record 08/15/2002
ADR agreement terminated 12/01/2003
Each 144A GDR for Common NT$10 par exchanged for $4.21 cash

UNI-RAIL INTERNATIONAL, INC. (KS)
Charter cancelled for failure to file reports 08/26/1968

UNI SHIELD INTL CORP (DE)
Charter cancelled and declared inoperative and void for non-payment of taxes 03/01/1976

UNI TRADE MARKETING INC (UT)
Recapitalized as Golden Gate Safety Products, Inc. 07/29/1985
Each share Common 1¢ par exchanged for (0.1) share Common 1¢ par

UNI-VITE INC (NV)
Name changed to Lifeworks Holdings Inc. 03/29/1994
(See Lifeworks Holdings Inc.)

UNI-WAY CORP. (NV)
Charter revoked for failure to file reports and pay fees 12/01/1990

UNI-WAY PAC HLDGS LTD (BC)
Recapitalized as New Uni-Way Holdings Ltd. 09/16/1993
Each share Common no par exchanged for (0.2) share Common no par
New Uni-Way Holdings Ltd. name changed to Full Riches Investments Ltd. 02/26/1998 which was acquired by Medoro Resources Ltd. 03/02/2004 which merged into Gran Colombia Gold Corp. 06/14/2011

UNIBAIL-RODAMCO SE (FRANCE)
ADR agreement terminated 06/29/2018
Each ADR for Ordinary issued by Citibank exchanged for $22.183091 cash

UNIBANCO-UNIAO DE BANCOS BRASILEIROS S A (BRAZIL)
GDR basis changed from (1:500) to (1:5) 08/30/2004
GDR basis changed from (1:5) to (1:10) 07/15/2006
Merged into Itau Unibanco Banco Multiplo S.A. 03/30/2009
Each GDR for Preferred Units exchanged for (5.75010062) Sponsored ADR's for Preferred
Itau Unibanco Banco Multiplo S.A. name changed to Itau Unibanco Holding S.A. 08/31/2009

UNIBANCORP INC (DE)
$1.53 Conv. Preferred Ser. A no par called for redemption 04/17/1987
Common $5 par split (3) for (2) by issuance of (0.5) additional share 08/12/1987
Acquired by Old Kent Financial Corp. 10/18/1988
Each share Common $5 par exchanged for (1.32) shares Common $1 par
Old Kent Financial Corp. merged into Fifth Third Bancorp 04/02/2001

UNIBANK (BROOKVILLE, PA)
Merged into Savings & Trust Co. of Pennsylvania (Indiana, PA) 03/31/1983
Each share Common $2.50 par exchanged for (1) share Common $2.50 par and $25 cash

UNIBANK (STEUBENVILLE, OH)
Merged into Citizens Bancshares, Inc. 03/06/1998
Each share Common no par exchanged for (13.25) shares Common no par
Citizens Bancshares, Inc. name changed to Sky Financial Group Inc. 10/02/1998 which merged into Huntington Bancshares Inc. 07/02/2007

UNIBRAZE CORP (DE)
Common 10¢ par split (3) for (2) by issuance of (0.5) additional share 08/29/1969
Name changed to UBZ Corp. 01/26/1981

(See UBZ Corp.)

UNIBROUE INC (CANADA)
Acquired by Sleeman Breweries Ltd. 06/30/2004
Each share Subordinate no par exchanged for $5.25 cash

UNICA CORP (DE)
Acquired by International Business Machines Corp. 10/05/2010
Each share Common 1¢ par exchanged for $21 cash

UNICACHE INC (NV)
Name changed 07/26/2001
Name changed from Unicache.com, Inc. to Unicache Inc. 07/26/2001
Merged out of existence 04/01/2003
Details not available

UNICAL CORP. OF AMERICA (DE)
Charter cancelled and declared inoperative and void for non-payment of taxes 4/15/70

UNICAN SEC SYS LTD (CANADA)
Common no par split (2) for (1) by issuance of (1) additional share 12/20/85
Common no par reclassified as Class A no par 11/14/86
Each share Class A no par received distribution of (1) share Class B Subordinate no par 11/19/86
Acquired by Kaba Holding AG 4/12/2001
Each share Class A no par exchanged for $36 cash
Each share Class B Subordinate no par exchanged for $36 cash

UNICAP COML CORP (CANADA)
Recapitalized as Unavest Capital Corp. 08/19/1998
Each share Class A Common no par exchanged for (0.14285714) share Class A Common no par
Each share Class B Common no par exchanged for (0.14285714) share Class B Common no par
Unavest Capital Corp. merged into Genterra Investment Corp. 04/30/1999 which merged into Genterra Inc. 12/31/2003 which merged into Genterra Capital Inc. (New) 05/10/2010 which merged into Gencan Capital Inc. 10/30/2015

UNICAP INTL INC (DE)
Charter cancelled and declared inoperative and void for non-payment of taxes 3/1/85

UNICAPITAL CORP (DE)
Ctfs. dated prior to 12/08/1980
Stock Dividend - 150% 07/30/1971
Name changed to Production Operators Corp. 12/08/1980
Production Operators Corp. merged into Camco International Inc. 06/13/1997 which merged into Schlumberger Ltd. 08/31/1998

UNICAPITAL CORP (DE)
Ctfs. dated after 05/14/1998
Issue Information - 28,000,000 shares COM offered at $19 per share on 05/14/1998
Plan of reorganization under Chapter 11 Federal Banruptcy Code effective 01/31/2002
Stockholders' equity unlikely

UNICARE FINL CORP (CA)
Common no par split (5) for (4) by issuance of (0.25) additional share 04/11/1990
Stock Dividend - 10% 10/14/1988
Merged into Wellpoint Health Networks Inc. (Old) 01/20/1994
Each share Common no par exchanged for $29 cash

UNICARE SVCS INC (DE)
Name changed 11/15/1973
Common 10¢ par split (4) for (1) by issuance of (3) additional shares 12/15/1968
Name changed from Unicare Health Services, Inc. to Unicare Services, Inc. 11/15/1973
Merged into Extendicare Ltd. 07/01/1983
Each share Common 10¢ par exchanged for $5.8914 cash

UNICEPT INC (UT)
Each share Common Capital Stock 1¢ par exchanged for (0.1) share Common Capital Stock $0.001 par 09/24/1976
Name changed to Power-Train, Inc. 11/29/1976
Power-Train, Inc. name changed to Scanner Energy Exploration Corp. 08/28/1980 which name changed to Odin-Phoenix, Ltd. 10/18/1982

UNICLUB INC (NY)
Dissolved by proclamation 3/23/93

UNICO ENVIRONMENTAL INSTRS INC (NY)
Merged into Gelman Instrument Co. (DE) 03/11/1970
Each share Common 2¢ par exchanged for (0.2) share Common no par
Gelman Instrument Co. (DE) name changed to Gelman Sciences, Inc. (DE) 01/05/1979 which reincorporated in Michigan 01/30/1981 which merged into Pall Corp. 02/03/1997
(See Pall Corp.)

UNICO INC (DE)
Each share old Common 1¢ par exchanged for (0.25) share new Common 1¢ par 12/30/1997
Each share new Common 1¢ par exchanged again for (1/3) share new Common 1¢ par 09/07/1999
Each share new Common 1¢ par exchanged again for (0.1) share new Common 1¢ par 09/10/2001
Recapitalized as ABSS Corp. (DE) 04/25/2002
Each (30) shares new Common 1¢ par exchanged for (1) share Common 1¢ par
ABSS Corp. (DE) reorganized in Nevada as NT Holding Corp. 08/04/2004 which recapitalized as HST Global, Inc. 07/07/2008

UNICO INC (NM)
Each share old Common 1¢ par exchanged for (0.05) share new Common 20¢ par 07/28/1994
Each share new Common 20¢ par received distribution of (1) share Intermountain Refining Inc. Common no par payable 05/31/2001 to holders of record 07/12/1999
Recapitalized as MorNorth Mortgage Holdings, Inc. 07/17/2003
Each share new Common 20¢ par exchanged for (0.02) share Common 20¢ par
MorNorth Mortgage Holdings, Inc. recapitalized as Westlake Canyon International, Inc. 09/09/2005 which name changed to Vision International, Inc. 04/26/2006 which name changed to Exlites Holdings International, Inc. 09/19/2008

UNICOA CORP (NV)
Name changed to United Insurance Co. of America (NV) 11/02/1987
(See United Insurance Co. of America (NV))

UNICOL COLLECTION AGYS LTD CDS- (CANADA)
Declared bankrupt 4/26/83
Details not available

UNICOM CORP (IL)
Merged into Exelon Corp. 10/20/2000
Each share Common no par exchanged for (0.875) share Common no par and $3 cash

UNICOM INC (DE)
Recapitalized as Unistone Inc. 01/11/2000
Each share Common $0.001 par exchanged for (0.025) share Common $0.001 par
Unistone Inc. name changed to Cash Systems Inc. 10/17/2001
(See Cash Systems Inc.)

UNICOM INDS (UT)
Name changed to Universal Metals, Inc. 03/03/1975
(See Universal Metals, Inc.)

UNICOM INS GROUP INC (PA)
Name changed to Academy Insurance Group, Inc. (PA) 05/22/1974
Academy Insurance Group, Inc. (PA) reincorporated in Delaware 06/17/1988
(See Academy Insurance Group, Inc. (DE))

UNICOMM SIGNAL INC (BC)
Recapitalized as SmarTire Systems Inc. (BC) 12/24/1997
Each share Common no par exchanged for (0.125) share Common no par
SmarTire Systems Inc. (BC) reincorporated in Yukon 02/06/2003 which reincorporated back under the laws of British Columbia 12/20/2006 which name changed to TTC Technology Corp. 04/14/2010
(See TTC Technology Corp.)

UNICOMP INC (CO)
Secondary Offering - 1,500,000 shares COM offered at $5 per share on 11/12/1996
Each share Common $0.001 par exchanged for (0.125) share Common 1¢ par 05/09/1998
Each share old Common 1¢ par exchanged for (0.05) share new Common 1¢ par 08/17/1992
Chapter 11 bankruptcy proceedings converted to Chapter 7 on 12/26/2006
No stockholders' equity

UNICORN AMER LTD (NY)
Name changed to Motivision America Inc. 06/04/1996
(See Motivision America Inc.)

UNICORN CORP (ON)
Delisted from Alberta Stock Exchange 03/26/1992

UNICORN ELECTRICAL PRODS (CA)
Merged into 1511 Corp. 02/28/1982
Each share Common 10¢ par exchanged for $3 cash

UNICORN INDUSTRIES (CA)
Name changed to Unicorn Electrical Products 5/15/79
(See Unicorn Electrical Products)

UNICORN RESOURCES INC. (CA)
Completely liquidated 9/1/83
Each share Common 10¢ par exchanged for first and final distribution of $0.29 cash

UNICORN RES LTD (BC)
Reorganized as Pacific Unicorn Resources Ltd. 11/22/1988
Each share Common no par exchanged for (0.2) share Common no par
Pacific Unicorn Resources Ltd. recapitalized as Biopac Industries Inc. 08/21/1992 which recapitalized as BPI Industries Inc. 01/18/1995 which name changed to BPI Energy Holdings, Inc. 02/09/2006
(See BPI Energy Holdings, Inc.)

UNICORN RESTAURANTS INC (NV)
Recapitalized as 1st Texas Natural Gas Co., Inc. 06/14/2007
Each share Common $0.001 par exchanged for (0.005) share Common $0.001 par
1st Texas Natural Gas Co., Inc. recapitalized as Riverdale Capital Ltd. 08/25/2009 which name changed to Diversified Energy & Fuel International, Inc. 04/30/2012

which name changed to Zyrox Mining International, Inc. 08/21/2012

UNICORN SVCS PLC (UNITED KINGDOM)
Sponsored ADR's for Ordinary no par split (4) for (1) by issuance of (3) additional ADR's payable 5/8/96 to holders of record 5/6/96
ADR agreement terminated 11/1/2005
Each Sponsored ADR for Ordinary no par exchanged for (10) Ordinary Shares
Note: Unexchanged ADR's will be sold and proceeds, if any, held for claim after 11/1/2006

UNICORP AMERN CORP NEW (DE)
Each share old Common 1¢ par exchanged for (1) share new Common 1¢ par or $12.125 cash
Note: For holdings of (14) shares or fewer each share old Common 1¢ par exchanged for $12.125 cash
For holdings between (15) shares and (1,499) shares option to receive stock expired 7/12/85
Conv. Preferred Ser. Ba 1¢ par called for redemption 12/15/86
Recapitalized as Lincorp Holdings Inc. 9/15/92
Each share new Common 1¢ par exchanged for (0.1) share Common 1¢ par
(See Lincorp Holdings Inc.)

UNICORP AMERN CORP OLD (PA)
Merged into Unicorp American Corp. (New) 2/15/84
Each share Common 10¢ par exchanged for (26.75) shares Common 1¢ par
Unicorp American Corp. (New) recapitalized as Lincorp Holdings Inc. 9/15/92
(See Lincorp Holdings Inc.)

UNICORP CDA CORP (ON)
Name changed 07/11/1974
Name changed 07/13/1982
Under plan of merger name changed from Unicorp Financial Inc. to Unicorp Financial Corp. and each share Common $1 par exchanged for (1) share Common no par 07/11/1974
Each share Common no par exchanged for (0.5) share Class A Common no par and (0.5) share Class B Common no par 07/19/1979
Name changed from Unicorp Financial Corp. to Unicorp Canada Corp. 07/13/1982
9% Conv. Preference Ser. B $20 par called for redemption 05/27/1983
Each share 80¢ Conv. Class II Preference Ser. A no par exchanged for (1) share Class A Common no par 12/31/1985
Under plan of reorganization name changed to Unicorp Energy Corp. and each share $1.17 Retractable Class II Preference Ser. B no par automatically became (1) share $1.17 Retractable Class II Preference Ser. B par, each share 10% Class I Preference Ser. C $20 par automatically became (1) share 10% Class I Preference Ser. C $20 par, each share Class A Common no par exchanged for (1/3) share Class A Common no par and each share Class B Common no par exchanged for (1/3) share Class B Common no par 06/25/1991
Unicorp Energy Corp. name changed to Unicorp Inc. 05/28/1999 which name changed to Wilmington Capital Management Inc. 03/08/2002

UNICORP INC (ON)
Name changed 05/28/1999
$1.17 Retractable Class II Preference Ser. B no par called for redemption 04/30/1992
10% Class I Preference Ser. C $20 par called for redemption 04/30/1992
Name changed from Unicorp Energy Corp. to Unicorp Inc. 05/28/1999
Name changed to Wilmington Capital Management Inc. 03/08/2002

UNICORP INC NEW (NV)
Name changed 03/03/2000
Each shares old Common 1¢ par exchanged for (0.003663) share new Common 1¢ par 01/20/1998
Each share new Common 1¢ par exchanged again for (0.2) share new Common 1¢ par 02/11/1999
Note: Name change to Auto Axzpt.com, Inc. reported 03/01/1999 was never legally transacted
Name changed from Unicorp, Inc. (Old) to Unicorp, Inc. (New) 03/03/2000
Common 1¢ par reclassified as Class A Common 1¢ par 03/06/2000
Each share Class A Common 1¢ par received distribution of (1) share AZ Capital, Inc. Common payable 12/31/2001 to holders of record 07/01/2001
Each share Class A Common 1¢ par received distribution of (1) share Laissez-Faire Group, Inc. Common payable 12/31/2001 to holders of record 07/01/2001
Each share Class A Common 1¢ par received distribution of (1) share Marcap International, Inc. Common payable 12/31/2001 to holders of record 07/01/2001
Each share Class A Common 1¢ par received distribution of (1) share Med-X Systems, Inc. Common payable 12/31/2001 to holders of record 07/01/2001
Each share Class A Common 1¢ par received distribution of (1) share Texas Nevada Oil & Gas Co. Common no par payable 12/31/2001 to holders of record 07/01/2001
Each share Class A Common 1¢ par exchanged for (0.04992511) share Common $0.001 par to reflect a (100) for (1) forward split followed by a (1) for (2,003) reverse split 01/03/2002
Note: No holder will receive fewer than (100) shares
Recapitalized as Striker Oil & Gas, Inc. 04/24/2008
Each share Common $0.001 par exchanged for (0.2) share Common $0.001 par
(See Striker Oil & Gas, Inc.)

UNICORP RLTY INVS INC (MD)
Each share Common 10¢ par exchanged for (0.0001) share Common $1000 par 10/31/1983
Note: In effect holders received $8.60 cash per share and public interest was eliminated

UNICORP RES LTD (AB)
Acquired by Asamera Inc. 5/1/86
Each share Conv. Class A no par exchanged for (0.1) share 7% Non-Vtg. Conv. 2nd Preferred Ser. D no par and (0.1) Common Stock Purchase Warrant expiring 3/7/89
Each share Class B no par exchanged for (0.1) share 7% Non-Vtg. Conv. 2nd Preferred Ser. D no par and (0.1) Common Stock Purchase Warrant expiring 3/7/89
Asamera Inc. acquired by Gulf Canada Resources Ltd. 8/4/88
(See Gulf Canada Resources Ltd.)

UNICREDIT SPA (ITALY)
Basis changed from (1:15) to (1:1.5) 02/23/2017
ADR agreement terminated 06/15/2017
Each ADR for Ordinary exchanged for $25.354483 cash
(Additional Information in Obsolete)

UNICREDITO ITALIANO S P A (ITALY)
Stock Dividend - 18.23899% payable 05/28/2009 to holders of record 05/18/2009 Ex date - 05/20/2009
Recapitalized as UniCredit S.p.A. 01/20/2012
Each Sponsored ADR for Ordinary exchanged for (0.1) Sponsored ADR for Ordinary
(See UniCredit S.p.A.)

UNICYCLE CORP. OF AMERICA (NM)
Merged into Push Button Container Corp. on a (0.5) for (1) basis 07/25/1962
(See Push Button Container Corp.)

UNIDANMARK A/S (DENMARK)
ADR agreement terminated 05/08/2000
Each 144A Sponsored ADR for Class A exchanged for $79.2079 cash

UNIDAT CORP (DE)
Name changed to Americas Corp. 09/27/1972
(See Americas Corp.)

UNIDATA SYS INC (DE)
Name changed to Systems Assurance Inc. 03/09/1984
Systems Assurance Inc. name changed to Digital Commerce International, Inc. 06/11/1999 which name changed to NetCare Health Group, Inc. 04/05/2002
(See NetCare Health Group, Inc.)

UNIDEX COMMUNICATIONS CORP (WY)
Reincorporated 4/25/96
Place of incorporation changed from (BC) to (WY) 4/25/96
Recapitalized as United Digital Network, Inc. 7/9/96
Each share Common no par exchanged for (0.25) share Common no par
United Digital Network, Inc. merged into Star Telecommunications, Inc. 3/24/99
(See Star Telecommunications, Inc.)

UNIDIGITAL INC (DE)
Recapitalized as Better Environment Concepts, Inc. 08/27/2009
Each (60) shares Common $0.01 par exchanged for (1) share Common $0.01 par

UNIDYN CORP (NV)
Charter revoked for failure to file reports and pay fees 04/30/2010

UNIDYNAMICS CORP (DE)
Merged into Crane Co. 03/28/1985
Each share Common $2.50 par exchanged for $29 cash

UNIDYNE (NV)
Name changed to National Video Corp. 9/21/81
National Video Corp. name changed to Unidyne Corp. 1/14/83
(See Unidyne Corp.)

UNIDYNE CORP (DE)
Charter cancelled and declared void for failure to pay franchise taxes 03/01/2001

UNIDYNE CORP (NV)
Each share old Common 10¢ par exchanged for (0.05) share new Common 10¢ par 1/12/87
Charter permanently revoked 4/1/2004

UNIFAB INTL INC (LA)
Issue Information - 2,815,000 shares COM offered at $18 per share on 09/18/1997
Each share old Common 1¢ par exchanged for (0.1) share new Common 1¢ par 8/4/2003
Merged into Midland Fabricators & Process Systems, LLC 3/31/2005
Each share new Common 1¢ par exchanged for $0.20 cash

UNIFAST INDS INC (NY)
Common 1¢ par split (3) for (2) by issuance of (0.5) additional share 12/15/83
Stock Dividends - 10% 7/28/83; 10% 12/27/85
Charter cancelled and declared inoperative and void for non-payment of taxes 9/29/93

UNIFIED ACCUMULATION FD INC (IN)
Recapitalized 12/30/1977
Recapitalized from Unified Funds, Inc. to Unified Accumulation Fund, Inc. 12/30/1977
Each share Common $2 par exchanged for (0.04) share Common no par
Name changed to Unified Municipal Fund Inc. and Common no par reclassified as Indiana Series Common no par 04/16/1985
(See Unified Municipal Fund Inc.)

UNIFIED CAP INC (DE)
Each share old Common $0.001 par exchanged for (0.04) share new Common $0.001 par 2/22/91
Name changed to Sanyo Industries Inc. 7/7/92
Sanyo Industries Inc. recapitalized as Brake Headquarters U.S.A., Inc. 8/8/95
(See Brake Headquarters U.S.A., Inc.)

UNIFIED ENERGY SYS RUSSIA (RUSSIA)
Each Sponsored ADR for Class A Preferred received distribution of $1.225 cash payable 12/05/2007 to holders of record 09/03/2007
Each Sponsored ADR for Ordinary received distribution of $1.3394 cash payable 12/05/2007 to holders of record 09/03/2007
Merged into Federal Grid Co. of Unified Energy System JSC 06/06/2008
Each Sponsored ADR for Class A Preferred exchanged for (0.415042) Sponsored 144A GDR for Ordinary and $0.6883 cash
Each Sponsored ADR for Ordinary exchanged for (0.453201) Sponsored 144A GDR for Ordinary and $0.7544 cash
Federal Grid Co. of Unified Energy System JSC name changed to Federal Grid Co. of Unified Energy System PJSC 10/30/2015

UNIFIED GROWTH FD INC (IN)
Voluntarily dissolved 03/28/1991
Details not available

UNIFIED INCOME FD INC (IN)
Voluntarily dissolved 12/31/1990
Details not available

UNIFIED INDS INC (CO)
Name changed to Nite-Lite USA, Ltd. 05/15/1989
Nite-Lite USA, Ltd. name changed to Concorde Strategies Group Inc. 11/11/1996 which recapitalized as W3 Group, Inc. (CO) 10/01/1999 which reincorporated in Delaware 05/07/2003 which name changed to Aftersoft Group, Inc. 01/19/2006 which name changed to MAM Software Group, Inc. 05/27/2010

UNIFIED MGMT CORP (IN)
Merged into Mutual of New York Co., Inc. 07/18/1986
Each share Common no par exchanged for $14.25 cash

UNIFIED MUN FD INC (IN)
Voluntarily dissolved 12/31/1990
Details not available

UNIFIED MUT SHS INC (IN)
Voluntarily dissolved 12/31/1990
Details not available

UNIFIED RESERVE LIFE INSURANCE CO. (IN)
Capital Stock $2 par changed to $1.25 par 5/29/61
Merged into Wabash Life Insurance Co. 5/14/64
Each share Capital Stock $1.25 par exchanged for (0.349127) share Common $1 par
Wabash Life Insurance Co. name changed to Wabash International Corp. 12/28/67
(See Wabash International Corp.)

UNIFIED RES INC (NV)
Name changed to Odyssey Filmpartners Ltd. 04/28/1986
Odyssey Filmpartners Ltd. name changed to Odyssey Entertainment Ltd. 10/30/1987 which merged into Communications & Entertainment Corp. 09/06/1990 which name changed to Odyssey Pictures Corp. 01/21/1997
(See Odyssey Pictures Corp.)

UNIFIED TELECOMMUNICATIONS CORP. (UT)
Proclaimed dissolved for failure to pay taxes 12/31/1986

UNIFIED UNDERWRITERS INC (IN)
Name changed to Unified Management Corp. 02/25/1976
(See Unified Management Corp.)

UNIFIED URANIUM & OIL INC (NV)
Completely liquidated 12/30/69
Each share Common 25¢ par exchanged for first and final distribution of (1) share Beef Industries, Inc. Common 5¢ par
Beef Industries, Inc. merged into Cyclone Entertainment Ltd., Inc. 2/27/87
(See Cyclone Entertainment Ltd., Inc.)

UNIFIED VENTURES INC (UT)
Proclaimed dissolved for failure to pay taxes 5/1/94

UNIFIRST FED SVGS BK (HOLLYWOOD, FL)
Merged into Republic Security Financial Corp. 07/06/1998
Each share Common no par exchanged for (1.017) shares Common 1¢ par
Republic Security Financial Corp. merged into Wachovia Corp. (New) (Ctfs. dated between 05/20/1991 and 09/01/2001) 03/01/2001 which merged into Wachovia Corp. (Ctfs. dated after 09/01/2001) 09/01/2001 which merged into Wells Fargo & Co. (New) 12/31/2008

UNIFLEX INC (DE)
Reincorporated 7/1/73
State of incorporation changed from (NY) to (DE) 7/1/73
Common 10¢ par split (2) for (1) by issuance of (1) additional share 10/30/92
Common 10¢ par split (2) for (1) by issuance of (1) additional share 12/17/93
Common 10¢ par split (3) for (2) by issuance of (0.5) additional share payable 10/15/96 to holders of record 9/25/96 Ex date - 10/16/96
Merged into Uniflex Acquisition Corp. 6/30/99
Each share Common 10¢ par exchanged for $7.57 cash

UNIFLIGHT INC (DE)
Charter cancelled and declared inoperative and void for non-payment of taxes 3/1/75

UNIFLITE INC (WA)
Common $2 par changed to 66-2/3¢ par and (2) additional shares issued 03/20/1968
Merged into Murray Industries, Inc. 03/30/1984
Each share Common 66-2/3¢ par exchanged for $10 cash

UNIFORCE SVCS INC (NY)
Name changed 10/10/1995
Common 1¢ par split (3) for (2) by issuance of (0.5) additional share 09/17/1984
Common 1¢ par split (3) for (2) by issuance of (0.5) additional share 06/30/1986
Common 1¢ par split (3) for (2) by issuance of (0.5) additional share 05/15/1987
Name changed from Uniforce Temporary Personnel, Inc. to Uniforce Services Inc. 10/10/1995
Merged into COMFORCE Corp. 12/03/1997
Each share Common 1¢ par exchanged for (0.5217) share Common 1¢ par and $28 cash
(See COMFORCE Corp.)

UNIFORET INC (CANADA)
Name changed to Arbec Forest Products Inc. 05/10/2005
Each share Class A Subordinate no par exchanged for (1) share Class A Subordinate no par
(See Arbec Forest Products Inc.)

UNIFORMS FOR AMER (NV)
Each share old Common $0.001 par exchanged for (0.01) share new Common $0.001 par 05/15/1996
Recapitalized as HomeFoodClub.com Inc. (NV) 07/12/1999
Each share new Common $0.001 par exchanged for (0.05) share Common $0.001 par
HomeFoodClub.com Inc. (NV) reincorporated in Delaware as iKarma Inc. 02/02/2006 which recapitalized as Medtino, Inc. 10/12/2010 which name changed to IntelaKare Marketing, Inc. 03/01/2011

UNIFUND INC (CA)
Merged into Paramount Mutual Fund, Inc. 02/01/1977
Each share Common $1 par exchanged for (1.103329) shares Capital Stock 25¢ par
Paramount Mutual Fund, Inc. name changed to FPA Paramount Fund, Inc. 06/01/1984

UNIFUND LEASING INC (DE)
Charter cancelled and declared inoperative and void for non-payment of taxes 03/01/1981

UNIFY CORP (DE)
Old Common $0.001 par split (2) for (1) by issuance of (1) additional share payable 12/21/1999 to holders of record 12/02/1999
Each share old Common $0.001 par exchanged for (0.2) share new Common $0.001 par 06/25/2007
Name changed to Daegis Inc. 07/07/2011
(See Daegis Inc.)

UNIGARD OLYMPIC LIFE INS CO (WA)
100% owned by holding co. as of 07/21/1981
Public interest eliminated

UNIGATE PLC (ENGLAND)
ADR agreement terminated 07/12/2000
Each ADR for Ordinary exchanged for $4.128 cash

UNIGENE LABS INC (DE)
Filed a petition under Chapter 7 Federal Bankruptcy Code 07/02/2013
Stockholders' equity unlikely

UNIGESCO INC (QC)
Reorganized on a proportional basis 02/11/1982
95% of Class A $1 par and Class B $1 par exchanged for $1 cash per share respectively
Remaining 5% of Class A $1 par and Class B $1 par changed to no par and (19) additional shares issued per share respectively
Class B no par reclassified as Class B Subordinate no par 03/26/1987
Name changed to Sodisco-Howden Group, Inc., new Class A no par and new Class B no par reclassified as Common no par 09/23/1994

UNIGLOBE COM INC (CANADA)
Name changed 07/02/1999
Common no par reclassified as Class B Common no par 05/04/1999
Name changed from Uniglobe Travel Online Inc. to Uniglobe.com Inc. 07/02/1999
Cease trade order effective 06/18/2004
Stockholders' equity unlikely

UNIGLOBE INTL ENERGY CORP (BC)
Declared bankrupt 05/18/1989
No stockholders' equity

UNIGLOBE VENTURES LTD (AB)
Merged into Diaz Resources Ltd. 06/08/1999
Each share Common no par exchanged for (0.85) share Class A Subordinate no par
Diaz Resources Ltd. merged into Tuscany Energy Ltd. (Old) 07/18/2013 which reorganized as Tuscany Energy Ltd. (New) 07/19/2013
(See Tuscany Energy Ltd. (New))

UNIGOLD RES INC (CANADA)
Merged into Unigold Inc. 12/30/2002
Each share Common no par exchanged for (0.5) share Common no par

UNIGRAPHICS SOLUTIONS INC (DE)
Merged into Electronic Data Systems Corp. (DE) 09/28/2001
Each share Class A Common 1¢ par exchanged for $32.50 cash

UNIHOLDING CORP (DE)
Each share old Common 1¢ par exchanged for (0.25) share new Common 1¢ par 01/05/1996
Each share new Common 1¢ par received distribution of (1) share Global Unilabs Clinical Trials Ltd. Common 15¢ par payable 02/27/1998 to holders of record 02/19/1998
Name changed to ULH Corp. 11/21/2000
(See ULH Corp.)

UNIHOST CORP (ON)
Subordinate no par reclassified as Common no par 09/18/1998
Merged into W-Westmont Corp. 05/27/1999
Each share Common no par exchanged for $7 cash

UNILAB CORP (CO)
Merged into Unilab Corp. (New) (DE) 11/10/1993
Each share Common 1¢ par exchanged for (1) share Common 1¢ par
(See Unilab Corp. (New) (DE))

UNILAB CORP NEW (DE)
Merged into Kelso Investment Associates VI, L.P. 11/24/1999
Each share Common 1¢ par exchanged for $5.85 cash
Merged into Quest Diagnostics, Inc. 03/03/2003
Each share new Common 1¢ par exchanged for (0.3424) share Common 1¢ par

UNILAND INVESTMENTS LTD. (ON)
Charter cancelled for default in filing returns or pay fees 03/27/1967

UNILENS VISION INC (DE)
Recapitalized 03/16/1992
Reincorporated 04/01/2010
Recapitalized from Unilens Optical Corp. to Unilens Vision Inc. 03/16/1992
Each share Common no par exchanged for (0.1) share Common no par
Place of incorporation changed from (BC) to (DE) and Common no par changed to $0.001 par 04/01/2010
Acquired by Valeant Pharmaceuticals International, Inc. 09/02/2015
Each share Common $0.001 par exchanged for $12.75 cash

UNILIFE CORP (DE)
Each share old Common 1¢ par exchanged for (0.1) share new Common 1¢ par 05/13/2016
Plan of reorganization under Chapter 11 Federal Bankruptcy proceedings effective 12/29/2017
No stockholders' equity

UNILIFE CORP (DE)
Merged into Unilife Acquisition Co. 09/02/1988
Each share Common 50¢ par exchanged for $1.35 cash

UNILIFE INS CO (AZ)
Reincorporated under the laws of Delaware as Unilife Corp. 09/30/1982
(See Unilife Corp. (DE))

UNILINK TELE COM INC (BC)
Cease trade order effective 08/06/2003

UNIMAR CO (TX)
Note: Each Indonesian Participation Unit entitled holder to 1/14,077,747 of 32% net positive cash flow paid quarterly
Indonesian Participation Units expired with no residual value 09/25/1999

UNIMART, INC. (CA)
Merged into Food Giant Markets, Inc. 06/14/1961
Each share Common exchanged for (15.73357) shares Common $1 par
Food Giant Markets, Inc. merged into Vornado, Inc. (DE) 09/29/1967 which reorganized as Vornado Realty Trust (MD) 05/06/1993

UNIMATION INC (DE)
Merged into Westinghouse Electric Corp. 02/15/1983
Each share Common 10¢ par exchanged for $21 cash

UNIMAX CORP (DE)
Each share Common 75¢ par exchanged for (0.5) share Common $1.50 par 02/01/1982
Merged into Unimax Holdings Corp. 07/06/1984
Each share Special Conv. Preference Ser. A Class A $3 par exchanged for $9.50 principal amount of Unimax Corp. 9% Subordinated Debentures due 07/06/1993 and $1 cash
Each share Common $1.50 par exchanged for $12 principal amount of Unimax Holdings Corp. 9% Subordinated Income Debentures due 07/06/1999

UNIMAX GROUP, INC. (DE)
Name changed to Unimax Corp. 09/11/1980
(See Unimax Corp.)

UNIMAX INC (UT)
Involuntarily dissolved 05/16/1991

UNIMED PHARMACEUTICALS INC (DE)
Name changed 05/02/1994
Common $1 par changed to 25¢ par and (2) additional shares issued 02/27/1981
Name changed from Unimed, Inc. to Unimed Pharmaceuticals Inc. 05/02/1994

Merged into Solvay S.A. 07/21/1999
Each share Common 25¢ par exchanged for $12 cash

UNIMET CORP (DE)
Merged into Azcon Corp. 10/31/1973
Each share Common 1¢ par exchanged for $10.125 cash

UNIMET CORP (OH)
Plan of reorganization under Chapter 11 Federal proceedings confirmed 11/24/1986
No stockholders' equity

UNIMEX TRANSNATIONAL CONSULTANTS INC (TX)
Name changed to Canadian Northern Lites, Inc. (TX) 04/26/1996
Canadian Northern Lites, Inc. (TX) reorganized in Nevada as Leopard Capital, Inc. 12/01/2000 which name changed to China Expert Technology, Inc. 03/29/2004
(See China Expert Technology, Inc.)

UNIOIL (NV)
Each share Common $0.001 par exchanged for (0.1) share old Common 1¢ par 07/26/1983
Each share old Common 1¢ par exchanged for (0.1) share new Common 1¢ par 02/08/2006
Merged into Petroleum Development Corp. 12/08/2006
Each share new Common 1¢ par exchanged for $1.91 cash

UNION & NEW HAVEN TR CO. (NEW HAVEN, CT)
Each share Capital Stock $100 par exchanged for (4) shares Capital Stock $25 par 00/00/1952
Capital Stock $25 par changed to $10 par and (1.5) additional shares issued 06/25/1956
Merged into Union Trust Co. (New Haven, CT) 10/01/1969
Each share Capital Stock $10 par exchanged for (1.3) shares Capital Stock $5 par
Union Trust Co. (New Haven, CT) reorganized as Northeast Bancorp, Inc. 12/29/1972 which merged into First Fidelity Bancorporation (New) 05/03/1993 which merged into First Union Corp. 01/01/1996 which name changed to Wachovia Corp. (Ctfs. dated after 09/01/2001) 09/01/2001 which merged into Wells Fargo & Co. (New) 12/31/2008

UNION ACCEP CORP (IN)
Class A Common no par reclassified as Common no par 11/16/2001
Recapitalized as White River Capital, Inc. 08/11/2005
Each share Common no par exchanged for (0.01) share Common no par
(See White River Capital, Inc.)

UNION ACCEP LTD (ON)
Each share old Common no par exchanged for (1) share Part. 2nd Preference no par and (1) share new Common no par 02/28/1955
6% 1st Preference called for redemption 08/04/1959
Under plan of merger each share Part. 2nd Preference no par exchanged for (1) share $1.60 Conv. Jr. Preference no par 12/30/1977
Under plan of merger each share new Common no par exchanged for (1) share $1.60 Conv. Jr. Preference no par 12/30/1977
$1.60 Conv. Jr. Preference no par called for redemption 02/20/1978
6% 1st Preference Ser. C $50 par called for redemption 08/31/1978
6.25% 1st Preference Ser. A $50 par called for redemption 08/31/1978
6.25% 1st Preference Ser. B $50 par called for redemption 08/31/1978
Public interest eliminated

UNION AMERICAN INVESTING CORP.
Dissolved 00/00/1936
Details not available

UNION ANDINA DE CEMENTOS S A A (PERU)
ADR agreement terminated 11/27/2017
Each Sponsored ADR for Ordinary exchanged for (10) shares Ordinary
Each 144A Sponsored ADR for Ordinary exchanged for (10) shares Ordinary
Note: Unexchanged ADR's will be sold and the proceeds, if any, held for claim after 11/30/2018

UNION APPLE CO., INC. (VA)
Automatically dissolved for failure to pay franchise taxes 06/01/1961

UNION ASBESTOS & RUBBER CO. (IL)
Name changed to Unarco Industries, Inc. (IL) 04/17/1963
Unarco Industries, Inc. (IL) reincorporated in Delaware 05/22/1970 which reorganized as UNR Industries, Inc. 09/30/1980 which name changed to ROHN Industries, Inc. 12/17/1997 which name changed to Frankfort Tower Industries, Inc. 02/17/2004
(See Frankfort Tower Industries, Inc.)

UNION BAG & PAPER CORP. (NJ)
Capital Stock $100 par changed to no par in 1930
Capital Stock no par exchanged (4) for (1) in 1937
Capital Stock no par changed to $20 par in 1952
Capital Stock $20 par changed to $6-2/3 par and (2) additional shares issued 2/23/56
Under plan of merger name changed to Union Bag-Camp Paper Corp. 7/12/56
Union Bag-Camp Paper Corp. name changed to Union Camp Corp. 4/27/66 which merged into International Paper Co. 4/30/99

UNION BAG-CAMP PAPER CORP. (VA)
Name changed to Union Camp Corp. 4/27/66
Union Camp Corp. merged into International Paper Co. 4/30/99

UNION BANC CORP (IN)
Merged into AmeriTrust Corp. 11/18/1986
Each share Capital Stock no par exchanged for $51.35 cash

UNION BANCORP (CA)
Name changed to Unionamerica, Inc. (CA) and Common $10 par changed to no par 05/09/1969
(See Unionamerica, Inc. (CA))

UNION BANCORP INC (DE)
Ctfs. dated prior to 04/17/1979
Merged into Standard Chartered Bank Ltd. 04/17/1979
Each share Common $1 par exchanged for $33 cash

UNION BANCORP INC (MI)
Reincorporated 10/1/82
State of incorporation changed from (DE) to (MI) 10/1/82
Common $1 par split (3) for (2) by issuance of (0.5) additional share 2/24/84
Common $1 par split (2) for (1) by issuance of (1) additional share 11/22/85
Merged into NBD Bancorp, Inc. 6/30/86
Each share Common $1 par exchanged for $38 cash

UNION BANCORP INC (PA)
Stock Dividend - 5% payable 02/28/2007 to holders of record 12/22/2006 Ex date - 03/19/2007
Merged into Riverview Financial Corp. (New) 11/01/2013
Each share Common 50¢ par exchanged for (1.95) shares Common no par

UNION BANCORP LOS ANGELES CALIF (CA)
Merged into Union Bank (San Francisco, CA) 11/01/1998
Each share Auction Market Preferred no par exchanged for (1) share Auction Market Preferred no par
Each share Money Market Preferred no par exchanged for (1) share Money Market Preferred no par
(See Union Bank (San Francisco, CA))

UNION BANCORP W VA INC (WV)
Merged into Key Centurion Bancshares, Inc. 3/13/87
Each share Common $6.25 par exchanged for (2.86) shares Common $3 par
Key Centurion Bancshares, Inc. merged into Banc One Corp. 5/3/93 which merged into Bank One Corp. 10/2/98 which merged into J.P. Morgan Chase & Co. 12/31/2000 which name changed to JPMorgan Chase & Co. 7/20/2004

UNION BANCSHARES CO (OH)
Under plan of merger name changed to Peoples Bancshares Inc. 10/01/1973
(See Peoples Bancshares Inc.)

UNION BANCSHARES INC (KS)
Acquired by Commerce Bancshares Inc. 04/17/1995
Each share Class A Common $10 par exchanged for $242 cash

UNION BK & TR (DENVER, CO)
Under plan of reorganization each share Common $10 par automatically became (1) share Union Bankshares, Ltd. (DE) Common $0.001 par 2/15/85
(See Union Bankshares, Ltd. (DE))

UNION BANK & TRUST CO. (BETHLEHEM, PA)
Name changed to Union Bank & Trust Co. of Eastern Pennsylvania (Bethlehem, PA) 01/14/1963
Union Bank & Trust Co. of Eastern Pennsylvania (Bethlehem, PA) merged into Independence Bancorp, Inc. (PA) 08/31/1983 which merged into CoreStates Financial Corp 06/27/1994 which merged into First Union Corp. 04/28/1998 which name changed to Wachovia Corp. (Ctfs. dated after 09/01/2001) 09/01/2001 which merged into Wells Fargo & Co. (New) 12/31/2008

UNION BANK & TRUST CO. (GRAND RAPIDS, MI)
Stock Dividend - 20% 4/2/62
Name changed to Union Bank & Trust Co. (N.A.) (Grand Rapids, MI) 2/1/66
Union Bank & Trust Co. (N.A.) (Grand Rapids, MI) merged into Great Lakes Financial Corp. 3/30/73 which name changed to Union Bancorp, Inc. (DE) 5/18/81 which reincorporated in Michigan 10/1/82
(See Union Bancorp, Inc. (MI))

UNION BANK & TRUST CO. (LOS ANGELES, CA)
Each share Capital Stock $50 par exchanged for (5) shares Capital Stock par 07/07/1955
Name changed to Union Bank (Los Angeles, CA) 01/17/1958
(See Union Bank (Los Angeles, CA))

UNION BK & TR CO (ERIE, PA)
Capital Stock $12.50 par changed to $6.25 par and (1) additional share issued 02/28/1973
Merged into Northwest Pennsylvania Corp. 03/31/1983

Each share Capital Stock $6.25 par exchanged for (1.08) shares Common $5 par
Northwest Pennsylvania Corp. merged into Mellon National Corp. 04/12/1984 which name changed to Mellon Bank Corp. 09/30/1984 which name changed to Mellon Financial Corp. 10/17/1999 which merged into Bank of New York Mellon Corp. 07/01/2007

UNION BK & TR CO (KOKOMO, IN)
Each share Capital Stock $100 par exchanged for (10) shares Capital Stock $10 par 01/22/1945
Stock Dividends - 25% 00/00/1950; 20% 00/00/1955; 25% 00/00/1957; 33-1/3% 01/21/1963; 25% 02/01/1967; 20% 02/02/1970; 33-1/3% 02/01/1972
Under plan of reorganization each share Capital Stock $10 par automatically became (1) share Ubantco Corp. Capital Stock no par 04/25/1973
Ubantco Corp. name changed to Union Banc Corp. 04/30/1984
(See Union Banc Corp.)

UNION BK & TR CO (MONTGOMERY, AL)
Each share Common $10 par exchanged for (2) shares Common $5 par 10/3/60
Common $5 par split (4) for (3) by issuance of (1/3) additional share 3/30/73
Common $5 par split (2) for (1) by issuance of (1) additional share 9/26/83
Common $5 par changed to $1 par and (1) additional share issued 5/3/85
Common $1 par changed to 50¢ par and (1) additional share issued 5/1/87
Stock Dividends - 100% 4/1/41; 100% 1/27/48; 14.3% 4/20/64; 10% 1/10/67; 20% 3/31/80
Merged into Regions Financial Corp. (Old) 12/30/94
Each share Common 50¢ par exchanged for (0.5261) share Common $0.625 par
Note: Each share Common 50¢ par received additional payment of $0.0172512 cash 10/31/96
Regions Financial Corp. (Old) merged into Regions Financial Corp. (New) 7/1/2004

UNION BK & TR CO (OKLAHOMA CITY, OK)
Reorganized as Union Bancorporation, Inc. 10/22/1979
Each share Capital Stock $5 par exchanged for (1) share Common Capital Stock $5 par

UNION BK & TR CO (POTTSVILLE, PA)
Under plan of reorganization each share Common $1 par automatically became (1) share Union Bancorp Inc. Common $1 par 07/01/1987
Union Bancorp Inc. merged into Riverview Financial Corp. (New) 11/01/2013

UNION BK & TR CO EASTN PA (BETHLEHEM, PA)
Common $10 par changed to $5 par and (1) additional share issued 05/11/1978
Stock Dividend - 100% 11/22/1966
Merged into Independence Bancorp, Inc. (PA) 08/31/1983
Each share Common $5 par exchanged for (1.7) shares Common $2.50 par
Independence Bancorp, Inc. (PA) merged into CoreStates Financial Corp 06/27/1994 which merged into First Union Corp. 04/28/1998 which name changed to Wachovia Corp. (Ctfs. dated after 09/01/2001)

09/01/2001 which merged into Wells Fargo & Co. (New) 12/31/2008

UNION BK & TR CO N A (GRAND RAPIDS, MI)
Stock Dividends - 33-1/3% 01/16/1967; 50% 04/18/1969
Merged into Great Lakes Financial Corp. 03/30/1973
Each share Common $10 par exchanged for (2) shares Common $1 par
Great Lakes Financial Corp. name changed to Union Bancorp, Inc. (DE) 05/18/1981 which reincorporated in Michigan 10/01/1982
(See Union Bancorp, Inc. (MI))

UNION BANK (ERIE, PA)
Name changed to Union Bank & Trust Co. (Erie, PA) 02/08/1962
Union Bank & Trust Co. (Erie, PA) merged into Northwest Pennsylvania Corp. 03/31/1983 which merged into Mellon National Corp. 04/12/1984 which name changed to Mellon Bank Corp. 09/30/1984 which name changed to Mellon Financial Corp. 10/17/1999 which merged into Bank of New York Mellon Corp. 07/01/2007

UNION BK (HOUSTON, TX)
Common $10 par changed to $1 par and (9) additional shares issued plus a 16.279% stock dividend paid 2/18/70
Stock Dividends - 10% 4/1/71; 10% 3/1/72; 10% 3/1/73; 12.69722% 3/7/74
Merged into Union Texas Bancshares, Inc. 7/28/83
Each share Common $1 par exchanged for (1) share Common $1 par
(See Union Texas Bancshares, Inc.)

UNION BK (LOS ANGELES, CA)
Capital Stock $10 par changed to $7.50 par and (1) additional share issued 09/26/1959
Stock Dividend - 20% 02/07/1964
Each share Capital Stock $7.50 par exchanged for (0.001) share Capital Stock $7,500 par 11/19/1969
Note: In effect holders received $49.24 cash per share and public interest was eliminated

UNION BK (MORRISVILLE, VT)
Each share Capital Stock $10 par exchanged for (5) shares Capital Stock $2 par 06/30/1977
Reorganized as Union Bankshares, Inc. 01/05/1983
Each share Capital Stock $2 par exchanged for (1) share Common $2 par

UNION BK (SAN FRANCISCO, CA)
Auction Market Preferred completely liquidated 11/30/1992
Details not available
Money Market Preferred completely liquidated 11/30/1992
Details not available
Merged into UnionBanCal Corp. (CA) 04/01/1996
Each share 8.375% Depositary Preferred Ser. A $100 par exchanged for (1) share 8.375% Depositary Preferred Ser. A $100 par
Each share Common $5 par exchanged for (1) share Common no par
UnionBanCal Corp. (CA) reincorporated in Delaware 09/30/2003
(See UnionBanCal Corp. (DE))

UNION BANK (TACOMA, WA)
Stock Dividends - 10% 06/26/1979; 10% 05/16/1980; 10% 05/26/1981; 20% 05/25/1982; 10% 04/11/1983; 10% 04/09/1984

Reorganized as Ubanco Inc. 03/12/1984
Each share Capital Stock $10 par exchanged for (1) share Capital Stock $10 par
Ubanco Inc. merged into Washington Community Bancshares, Inc. 09/29/1987 which merged into KeyCorp (NY) 01/25/1990 which merged into KeyCorp (New) (OH) 03/01/1994

UNION BK (TUCSON, AZ)
Common $10 par changed to $5 par and (1) additional share issued 03/00/1972
Name changed to Interwest Bank of Arizona (Tucson, AZ) 11/12/1984
Interwest Bank of Arizona (Tucson, AZ) name changed to Arizon Bank (Tucson, AZ) 07/20/1992 which merged into Compass Bancshares, Inc. 12/15/1998 which merged into Banco Bilbao Vizcaya Argentaria, S.A. 09/07/2007

UNION BK FLA (LAUDERHILL, FL)
Acquired by Colonial BancGroup, Inc. 02/11/2005
Details not available

UNION BANK OF COMMERCE (CLEVELAND, OH)
Each share Common $100 par exchanged for (10) shares Common $10 par 05/27/1946
Stock Dividend - 100% 02/20/1951
Name changed to Union Commerce Bank (Cleveland, OH) 01/10/1957
(See Union Commerce Bank (Cleveland, OH))

UNION BK SWITZ (SWITZERLAND)
ADR agreement terminated 5/26/98
Each Sponsored ADR for Ordinary 100 Fr. par exchanged for approximately $36.79 cash

UNION BANKERS INS CO (TX)
75¢ Class A Conv. Preferred $1 par called for redemption 07/01/1970
60¢ Class B Conv. Preferred $1 par called for redemption 07/01/1970
Each share Common $1 par exchanged for (1/90,000) share Common no par 10/30/1985
Note: In effect holders received $72.50 cash per share and public interest was eliminated

UNION BANKSHARES CAP TR I (DE)
9% Guaranteed Trust Preferred Securities called for redemption at $7.60 on 12/17/2003

UNION BANKSHARES CO (ME)
Common $25 par split (4) for (3) by issuance of (1/3) additional share 05/17/1995
Stock Dividends - 25% 10/15/1986; 25% 05/20/1989; 33-1/3% 04/23/1993; 20% payable 08/14/1997 to holders of record 06/27/1997; 20% payable 05/28/1999 to holders of record 04/23/1999
Merged into Camden National Corp. 01/03/2008
Each share Common $25 par exchanged for (1.9106) shares Common no par

UNION BANKSHARES CORP (VA)
Common $4 par changed to $2 par and (1) additional share issued payable 06/01/1998 to holders of record 05/21/1998
Common $2 par changed to $1.33 par and (0.5) additional share issued payable 10/13/2006 to holders of record 10/02/2006 Ex date - 10/16/2006
Name changed to Union First Market Bankshares Corp. 02/01/2010
Union First Market Bankshares Corp. name changed to Union Bankshares Corp. 04/28/2014

UNION BANKSHARES LTD (DE)
Common $0.001 par split (2) for (1) by issuance of (1) additional share payable 05/28/1998 to holders of record 05/27/1998
Merged into KeyCorp. (New) 12/12/2002
Each share Common $0.001 par exchanged for $22.63 cash

UNION BAY STATE CHEMICAL CO., INC. (MA)
Name changed to U B S Chemical Corp. in 1956
U B S Chemical Corp. merged into Staley (A.E.) Manufacturing Co. 6/30/59 which reorganized as Staley Continental, Inc. 2/12/85

UNION BKG & TR CO (DU BOIS, PA)
Under plan of reorganization each share Capital Stock $2.50 par automatically became (1) share Union Bancorp of Du Bois, Pennsylvania, Inc. Common $2.50 par 04/10/1983

UNION BLEACHERY CO.
Acquired by Aspinook (The) Corp. in 1947
Details not available

UNION BREWING CO.
Bankrupt in 1949

UNION CAMP CORP (VA)
Capital Stock $6-2/3 par reclassified as Common $1 par 4/30/68
Common $1 par split (2) for (1) by issuance of (1) additional share 5/20/69
Common $1 par split (3) for (2) by issuance of (0.5) additional share 5/18/76
Common $1 par split (2) for (1) by issuance of (1) additional share 5/15/84
Common $1 par split (3) for (2) by issuance of (0.5) additional share 6/15/87
Merged into International Paper Co. 4/30/99
Each share Common $1 par exchanged for (1.4852) shares Common $1 par

UNION CAP FD INC (MD)
Capital Stock $1 par split (2) for (1) by issuance of (1) additional share 02/14/1981
Name changed to Seligman Capital Fund, Inc. 05/01/1982

UNION CARBIDE & CARBON CORP. (NY)
Each share Capital Stock no par exchanged for (3) shares Capital Stock no par 00/00/1929
Capital Stock no par split (3) for (1) by issuance of (2) additional shares 00/00/1948
Name changed to Union Carbide Corp. (Old) 05/01/1957
Union Carbide Corp. (Old) reorganized as Union Carbide Corp. (New) 07/01/1989 which merged into Dow Chemical Co. 02/06/2001 which merged into DowDuPont Inc. 09/01/2017

UNION CARBIDE AUSTRALIA & NEW ZEALAND LTD (AUSTRALIA)
Stock Dividends - 20% 04/29/1971; 75% 01/11/1974; 25% 05/07/1975
Acquired by Acmex Investments (No. 1) pty. Ltd. 03/15/1988
Each ADR for Ordinary Reg. AUD $1 par exchanged for $5.20 cash

UNION CARBIDE AUSTRALIA LTD (AUSTRALIA)
Each ADR for Ordinary Reg. A£1 par exchanged for (2) ADR's for Ordinary Reg. A$1 par 02/14/1966
Stock Dividend - 20% 04/29/1968
Name changed to Union Carbide Australia & New Zealand Ltd. 11/28/1969

(See Union Carbide Australia & New Zealand Ltd.)

UNION CARBIDE CDA LTD (CANADA)
Common no par split (2) for (1) by issuance of (1) additional share 05/25/1981
Acquired by Union Carbide Corp. 04/08/1991
Each share Common no par exchanged for $19 cash

UNION CARBIDE CORP NEW (NY)
Reorganized 07/01/1989
Capital Stock no par changed to $4 par and (1) additional share issued 06/15/1965
Capital Stock $4 par reclassified as Common $1 par 04/29/1969
Common $1 par split (3) for (1) by issuance of (2) additional shares 03/03/1986
Reorganized from Union Carbide Corp. (Old) to Union Carbide Corp. (New) 07/01/1989
Each share Common $1 par exchanged for (1) share Common $1 par
Merged into Dow Chemical Co. 02/06/2001
Each share Common $1 par exchanged for (1.611) shares Common $2.50 par
Dow Chemical Co. merged into DowDuPont Inc. 09/01/2017

UNION CARBIDE FIN CORP (DE)
Asset Backed Short Term Auction Preferred Ser. B no par called for redemption 05/03/1990
Asset Backed Short Term Auction Preferred Ser. C no par called for redemption 05/17/1990
Asset Backed Short Term Auction Preferred Ser. A no par called for redemption 06/07/1990
Public interest eliminated

UNION CAS UNDERWRITERS INC (NE)
Merged out of existence 01/29/1987
Details not available

UNION CASH MGMT FD INC (MD)
Name changed to Seligman Cash Management Fund, Inc. 05/01/1982

UNION CENTRAL LIFE INSURANCE CO.
Mutualized in 1947

UNION CHEM CORP (NV)
Name changed to Hotyellow98.com Inc. 06/15/1999
Hotyellow98.com Inc. recapitalized as Azur International, Inc. 02/09/2004
(See Azur International, Inc.)

UNION CHEMICAL & MATERIALS CORP. (DE)
Merged into Vulcan Materials Co. 12/31/57
Each share 5% Preferred $5 par exchanged for (0.05) share 5-3/4% Preferred $100 par
Each share Common $10 par exchanged for (0.1) share 6-1/4% Preferred $100 par and (1.25) shares Common $1 par

UNION CHIEF MINING CO.
Name changed to Trans-Union Oil & Mining Co. 00/00/1952
Trans-Union Oil & Mining Co. name changed to Water Wonderland Corp. 12/15/1960 which name changed to Progressive National Industries Inc. 08/17/1972
(See Progressive National Industries, Inc.)

UNION CIGAR CO. (MD)
Charter revoked for failure to file reports and pay fees 2/10/33

UNION COMM BK (CLEVELAND, OH)
Stock Dividend - 100% 02/15/1962 Through exchange offer 98%

acquired by Union Commerce Corp. as of 03/19/1974
Public interest eliminated

UNION COMM CORP (DE)
Common 10¢ par split (3) for (2) by issuance of (0.5) additional share 5/10/72
Merged into Huntington Bancshares Inc. 3/31/83
Each share $2.25 Preferred no par exchanged for (1) share $2.25 Preferred no par
Each share Common 10¢ par exchanged for (0.77) share Common no par

UNION CMNTY BANCORP (IN)
Merged into MainSource Financial Group, Inc. 03/20/2006
Each share Common no par exchanged for either (1.4791) shares Common no par or $27.33 cash
MainSource Financial Group, Inc. merged into First Financial Bancorp 04/02/2018

UNION COMPRESS & WHSE CO (DE)
Each share Common no par exchanged for (4) shares Common $1 par 00/00/1954
Name changed to Union Service Industries, Inc. 08/15/1969
(See Union Service Industries, Inc.)

UNION CONNECTION INC (NV)
Name changed to Orbit Petroleum, Inc. and (4) additional shares issued 09/08/2004
(See Orbit Petroleum, Inc.)

UNION CORP. OF AMERICA (MO)
Common no par changed to $3 par 10/4/56
Charter cancelled for failure to file reports and pay fees 1/1/71

UNION CORP (DE)
Reincorporated 07/24/1987
State of incorporation changed from (NJ) to (DE) 07/24/1987
Merged into Outsourcing Solutions Inc. 03/31/1998
Each share Common 50¢ par exchanged for $31.50 cash

UNION CORP LTD (SOUTH AFRICA)
ADR's for Ordinary splitt (4) for (1) by issuance of (3) additional shares 11/19/1970
Merged into General Mining & Finance Corp. Ltd. 04/11/1980
Each ADR for Ordinary exchanged for (0.8) ADR for Ordinary
General Mining & Finance Corp. Ltd. name changed to General Mining Union Corp. Ltd. 07/09/1980 which reorganized as Gencor Ltd. 09/25/1989
(See Gencor Ltd.)

UNION COTTON MANUFACTURING CO.
Liquidation completed in 1932

UNION COUNTY CORP.
Liquidated in 1942

UNION CNTY TR CO (ELIZABETH, NJ)
Common $1 par changed to $2.50 par 01/00/1945
Common $2.50 par changed to $2.75 par 03/00/1945
Common $2.75 par changed to $3 par 07/00/1945
Common $3 par changed to $3.25 par 05/00/1946
Common $3.25 par changed to $3.50 par 09/00/1946
Common $3.50 par changed to $4 par 01/00/1949
Common $4 par changed to $5 par 01/00/1952
Common $5 par changed to $9.60 par 10/00/1952
Common $9.60 par changed to $10 par 00/00/1954
Common $10 par changed to $5 par and (2) additional shares issued 12/13/1968
Stock Dividend - 14-2/7% 08/01/1967
Under plan of merger name changed to United Counties Trust Co. (Elizabeth, NJ) 04/03/1972
United Counties Trust Co. (Elizabeth, NJ) reorganized as United Counties Bancorporation 10/01/83 which merged into Meridian Bancorp, Inc. 02/23/1996 which merged into CoreStates Financial Corp 04/09/1996 which merged into First Union Corp. 04/28/1998 which name changed to Wachovia Corp. (Ctfs. dated after 09/01/2001) 09/01/2001 which merged into Wells Fargo & Co. (New) 12/31/2008

UNION CTR NATL BK (UNION, NJ)
Common $100 par changed to $25 par and (3) additional shares issued 08/08/1946
Each share Common $25 par exchanged for (2.5) shares Common $10 par 01/20/1959
Common $10 par changed to $5 par and (1) additional share issued 01/27/1969
Stock Dividends - 25% 02/13/1952; 20% 01/24/1966; 20% 01/23/1967; 11-1/9% 01/22/1968; 14.29% 04/06/1976
Reorganized as Center Bancorp Inc. 05/01/1983
Each share Common $5 par exchanged for (1) share Common $5 par
Center Bancorp Inc. name changed to ConnectOne Bancorp, Inc. (New) 07/01/2014

UNION DRILLING INC (DE)
Acquired by Sidewinder Drilling Inc. 11/06/2012
Each share Common 1¢ par exchanged for $6.50 cash

UNION ELEC CO (MO)
Common $10 par changed to $5 par and (1) additional share issued 04/29/1963
$4 Preferred 1982 Ser. no par called for redemption 02/15/1987
$2.72 Preferred no par called for redemption 05/15/1987
$2.98 Preferred no par called for redemption 08/15/1988
$2.125 Preferred no par called for redemption 02/15/1989
$4.60 Preferred no par called for redemption 08/15/1989
$8 Preferred Ser. 69 no par called for redemption 02/22/1993
$8 Preferred Ser. 71 no par called for redemption 09/17/1993
$5.50B Preferred no par called for redemption 01/21/1997
$6.30 Preferred no par called for redemption 01/21/1997
$6.40 Preferred no par called for redemption 01/21/1997
$7.44 Preferred no par called for redemption 01/21/1997
Merged into Ameren Corp. 12/31/1997
Each share Common $5 par exchanged for (1) share Common 1¢ par
$1.735 Preferred no par called for redemption at $25 on 09/23/2002
$7.64 Preferred no par called for redemption at $100.85 on 08/20/2010
(Additional Information in Active)

UNION ELEC STL CORP (PA)
Each share Common $10 par exchanged for (4) shares Common $5 par 00/00/1955
Common $5 par changed to $2.50 par and (1) additional share issued 04/05/1960
Common $2.50 par changed to $1.25 par and (1) additional share issued 05/28/1971
Merged into Ampco-Pittsburgh Corp. 12/14/1984
Each share Common $1.25 par exchanged for $40 cash

UNION ELECTRIC & GAS CO.
Merged into Consolidated Gas Utilities Co. in 1927
(See Consolidated Gas Utilities Co.)

UNION ELECTRIC CO. OF MISSOURI (MO)
Name changed to Union Electric Co. 4/24/56

UNION ELECTRIC LIGHT & POWER CO. (CT)
Merged into Connecticut Power Co. 00/00/1936
Details not available

UNION ELECTRIC LIGHT & POWER CO. (MO)
Name changed to Union Electric Co. of Missouri in 1937 which name was changed to Union Electric Co. 4/24/56

UNION ELECTRIC RAILWAY CO.
Dissolved 3/18/54

UNION ENERGY INC (ON)
Name changed 6/27/90
Name changed from Union Enterprises Ltd. to Union Energy Inc. 6/27/90
Acquired by Westcoast Energy Inc. 12/15/92
Each share Common no par exchanged for (1) share Common no par
(See Westcoast Energy Inc.)

UNION EQUITY INC (DE)
Old Common $0.0000001 par split (7) for (1) by issuance of (6) additional shares payable 05/16/2005 to holders of record 04/27/2005
Ex date - 05/17/2005
Each share old Common $0.0000001 par exchanged for (0.0001) share new Common $0.0000001 par 09/22/2010
Recapitalized as Kona Gold Solutions, Inc. 08/13/2015
Each share new Common $0.0000001 par exchanged for (0.00066666) share Common $0.0000001 par

UNION EXPL PARTNERS LTD (TX)
Reorganized under the laws of Delaware as Unocal Exploration Corp. 8/2/90
Each Depositary Receipt exchanged for (1) share Common 10¢ par
Unocal Exploration Corp. merged into Unocal Corp. 5/2/92 which merged into Chevron Corp. 8/10/2005

UNION FD INC (DE)
Name changed to ICM Equity Fund, Inc. 02/24/1970
ICM Equity Fund, Inc. acquired by MagnaCap Fund, Inc. 12/21/1971 which name changed to Pilgrim Magnacap Fund, Inc. 06/20/1985

UNION FED SVGS & LN ASSN (FL)
Name changed to Miami Federal Savings & Loan Association 04/30/1982

UNION FED SVGS & LN ASSN LOS ANGELES CALIF (USA)
Under plan of reorganization each share Common no par automatically became (1) share UnionFed Financial Corp. (DE) Common 1¢ par 06/09/1987

UNION FID CORP (PA)
Reincorporated 06/12/1970
Common $1 par changed to 66-2/3¢ par and (0.5) additional share issued 01/15/1969
Common 66-2/3¢ par changed to 10¢ par and (1) additional share issued 05/07/1970
Stock Dividend - 10% 05/29/1968
State of incorporation changed from (DE) to (PA) 06/12/1970
Common 10¢ par split (3) for (2) by issusuance of (0.5) additional share 04/13/1971
Common 10¢ par split (4) for (3) by issuance of (1/3) additional share 04/18/1972
Merged into Filmways, Inc. 02/03/1978
Each share Common 10¢ par exchanged for (1.18) shares Common 25¢ par
Filmways, Inc. name changed to Orion Pictures Corp. 07/30/1982 which merged into Metromedia International Group, Inc. 11/01/1995
(See Metromedia International Group, Inc.)

UNION FID TRUSTEE CO AUSTRALIA LTD (AUSTRALIA)
Name changed to Trust Co. of Australia Ltd. 07/04/1988
(See Trust Co. of Australia Ltd.0

UNION FINANCE CORP. (FL)
Acquired by Seaboard Finance Co. 9/30/64
Each share 6% Non-Cum. Preferred $20 par exchanged for (0.2) share $5 Preferred no par
Each share Common $1 par or Class A Common $1 par exchanged for (0.5) share $2.75 Conv. Preferred no par which was called for redemption 12/8/69
(See listing for Seaboard Finance Co.)

UNION FINL BANCSHARES INC (DE)
Common 1¢ par split (2) for (1) by issuance of (1) additional share payable 07/30/1996 to holders of record 07/09/1996
Common 1¢ par split (3) for (2) by issuance of (0.5) additional share payable 02/19/1998 to holders of record 01/29/1998
Stock Dividend - 5% payable 02/19/1999 to holders of record 01/31/1999
Name changed to Provident Community Bancshares, Inc. 04/20/2006
(See Provident Community Bancshares, Inc.)

UNION FINANCIAL CORP. OF AMERICA (DE)
No longer in existence having become inoperative and void for non-payment of taxes 4/1/34

UNION FINL CORP (OH)
Merged into Transohio Financial Corp. 06/11/1974
Each share Common $1 par exchanged for (1.03) shares Common $1 par
Transohio Financial Corp. name changed to Transcapital Financial Corp. 04/29/1986
(See Transcapital Financial Corp.)

UNION FIRE INSURANCE CO.
Merged into New York State Fire Insurance Co. of Albany in 1931
New York State Fire Insurance Co. of Albany merged into Richmond Insurance Co. of New York in 1932 which merged into Westchester Fire Insurance Co. in 1948 which was acquired by Crum & Forster 11/7/69
(See Crum & Forster)

UNION FIRST MKT BANKSHARES CORP (VA)
Name changed to Union Bankshares Corp. 04/28/2014

UNION FIRST NATL BK (WASHINGTON, DC)
Name changed to First American Bank, N.A. (Washington, DC) 03/17/1980
(See First American Bank, N.A. (Washington, DC))

UNION GAS & ELECTRIC CO. (DE)
Liquidated in 1937

UNION GAS CO. OF CANADA, LTD. (ON)
Capital Stock no par split (5) for (1) by issuance of (4) additional shares 8/15/58
Capital Stock no par reclassified as Common no par 1/27/59
Common no par split (3) for (1) by issuance of (2) additional shares 6/30/66
Name changed to Union Gas Ltd. 10/11/72

UNION GAS CORP.
Property acquired by Union Gas System, Inc. in 1933
(See Union Gas System, Inc.)

UNION GAS LTD (ON)
Common no par reclassified as Conv. Class A Common no par 08/07/1975
8-3/4% Class B Conv. Preference Ser. 1 $20 par called for redemption 02/21/1981
Conv. Class A Common no par reclassified as Common no par 09/15/1981
Conv. Class B Common no par reclassified as Common no par 09/15/1981
Under plan of reorganization each share Common no par automatically became (1) share Union Enterprises Ltd. Common no par 01/02/1985
(See Union Enterprises Ltd.)
14.38% Class B Preference Ser. 5 $20 par called for redemption 10/01/1987
6.74% Class B Retractable Preference Ser. Ser. 9 $25 par called for redemption at $25 on 01/31/1998
(Additional Information in Active)

UNION GAS SYS INC (KS)
Each share old Common no par exchanged for (10) shares new Common no par 00/00/1949
New Common no par changed to $10 par 12/31/1956
5% Preferred $10 par called for redemption 12/01/1962
Common $10 par changed to $3.33-1/3 par and (2) additional shares issued 07/30/1963
Common $3.33-1/3 par changed to $1 par and (1) additional share issued 03/01/1974
Stock Dividends - 10% 04/02/1962; 100% 03/25/1965
Merged into ZG Transitory Corp. 08/01/1984
Each share Common $1 par exchanged for $20 cash

UNION GAS UTILITIES, INC.
Company insolvent Properties sold in 1933

UNION GOLD INC (AB)
Each share old Common no par exchanged for (2.5) shares new Common no par 08/27/2008
Merged into Jubilee Gold Inc. 01/01/2010
Each share new Common no par exchanged for (0.557) share Common no par
Jubilee Gold Inc. merged into Jubilee Gold Exploration Ltd. 01/25/2013

UNION GUARANTEE & MORTGAGE CO.
Liquidation completed in 1942

UNION-GULF OIL & MINING CORP. (CO)
Reported out of business 00/00/1957
Charter revoked for failure to pay taxes 09/29/1958

UNION HARDWARE CO. (CT)
Each share Common $100 par exchanged for (10) shares Common no par 00/00/1940
Liquidation completed 12/07/1964

Each share 7% Preferred $100 par exchanged for (1.96214) shares Brunswick Corp. Common no par 06/15/1960; shares not presented for exchange were called for redemption 06/15/1960 On 12/23/1960 distribution paid to Common holders of record 12/16/1960 in Brunswick Corp. Common on (0.285) for (1) basis
Each share Common no par exchanged for final distribution of (0.224) share Brunswick Corp. Common no par 12/07/1964

UNION ICE CO (CA)
Merged into UI Acquisition Corp. 06/26/1981
Each share Capital Stock $100 par exchanged for $440 cash

UNION INCOME FD INC (MD)
Name changed to Seligman Income Fund, Inc. 05/01/1982
Seligman Income Fund, Inc. name changed to Seligman Income & Growth Fund, Inc. 11/06/2002

UNION INVT CO (MI)
Each share $3 Preferred no par exchanged for (1) share 1st Preferred $50 par in 1934
Each share old Common no par exchanged for (2) shares new Common no par in 1936
New Common no par changed to $4 par in 1948
Common $4 par split (5) for (4) by issuance of (0.25) additional share 12/18/68
Common $4 par split (5) for (4) by issuance of (0.25) additional share 8/9/71
Common $4 par split (5) for (4) by issuance of (0.25) additional share 12/15/72
Stock Dividends - 20% 1/2/51; 10% 1/30/56
Acquired by Orbanco Inc. 7/10/78
Each share Common $4 par exchanged for (0.38948) share Common no par
Orbanco, Inc. name changed to Orbanco Financial Services Corp. 5/9/80 which was acquired by Security Pacific Corp. 4/15/87 which merged into BankAmerica Corp. (Old) 4/22/92 which merged into BankAmerica Corp. (New) 9/30/98 which name changed to Bank of America Corp. 4/28/99

UNION INVESTORS, INC.
Liquidated in 1931

UNION LIBERTY CO. (IL)
Proclaimed dissolved for failure to pay taxes and file reports 7/1/21

UNION LMBR CO (CA)
Each share 7% Preferred $100 par exchanged for (19) shares 5% Preferred $10 par 00/00/1943
Each share Common $100 par exchanged for (10) shares Common $10 par 00/00/1943
Acquired by Boise Cascade Corp. 01/16/1969
Each share Common $10 par exchanged for (2.355) shares Common $2.50 par
Boise Cascade Corp. name changed to OfficeMax Inc. 11/01/2004 which merged into Office Depot, Inc. 11/05/2013

UNION MFG CO (CT)
COM ($25) 907022 10 7
Stock Dividends - 50% 10/15/1948; 20% 03/31/1965; 25% 08/29/1966
Dissolved 01/16/1987
Details not available

UNION METAL MFG CO (OH)
Each share 8% Preferred $100 par exchanged for (1) share 6% Prior Preferred $100 par, (1) share Common no par and $7 cash 00/00/1937
6% Prior Preferred $100 par changed to 6% Preferred $100 par 00/00/1944
Each share Common no par exchanged for (2) shares Common $1 par 00/00/1944
6% Preferred $100 par called for redemption 00/00/1948
Stock Dividends - 20% 03/30/1950; 10% 02/28/1952; 10% 05/18/1955; 200% 12/30/1964; 10% 03/03/1967; 10% 01/24/1968; 10% 06/30/1975; 10% 03/19/1981
Name changed to UNIMET Corp. 06/15/1984
(See UNIMET Corp.)

UNION MILLS, INC.
Liquidation completed in 1940

UNION MINES, INC. (DE)
Declared inoperative and void for non-payment of taxes 04/01/1958

UNION MNG CORP (AB)
Name changed to Union Gold Inc. 03/05/1993
Union Gold Inc. merged into Jubilee Gold Inc. 01/01/2010 which merged into Jubilee Gold Exploration Ltd. 01/25/2013

UNION MKT NATL BK (WATERTOWN, MA)
Stock Dividends - 20% 01/16/1946; 25% 01/17/1950; 20% 05/26/1955; 11-1/9% 01/22/1959; 25% 01/31/1967
Merged into BayBank Newton-Waltham Trust Co. (Waltham, MA) 07/06/1976
Each share Capital Stock $10 par exchanged for (1) share Capital Stock $10 par
BayBank Newton-Waltham Trust Co. (Waltham, MA) merged into BayBank Middlesex (Burlington, MA) 11/09/1979 which name changed to BayBank Trust Co. (Burlington, MA) 06/30/1983 which name changed back to BayBank Middlesex (Burlington, MA) 12/08/1983

UNION MORTGAGE CO. (NY)
Name changed to Consolidated Assets Corp. in 1949
Consolidated Assets Corp. dissolved 10/31/68

UNION MORTGAGE CO. (OH)
Liquidated in 1928

UNION MORTGAGE CO. OF DETROIT (DE)
Charter cancelled and declared inoperative and void for non-payment of taxes 4/1/30

UNION NATL BANCORP INC (MD)
Stock Dividend - 10% payable 10/22/1998 to holders of record 10/15/1998
Merged into Mercantile Bankshares Corp. 07/14/2000
Each share Common 1¢ par exchanged for (1.15) shares Common $2 par
Mercantile Bankshares Corp. merged into PNC Financial Services Group, Inc. 03/02/2007

UNION NATIONAL BANK & TRUST CO. (MOUNT HOLLY, NJ)
Merged into South Jersey National Bank (Camden, N.J.) 5/1/70
Each share Common $10 par exchanged for (1) share Common $5.625 par
South Jersey National Bank (Camden, N.J.) reorganized as Heritage Bancorporation 11/1/71
(See Heritage Bancorporation)

UNION NATL BK & TR CO (ELGIN, IL)
Common $20 par split (2) for (1) by issuance of (1) additional share 02/13/1979
Acquired by Elgin Bancshares, Inc. 02/09/1981

Details not available

UNION NATL BK & TR CO (HUNTINGDON, PA)
Under plan of reorganization each share Common $2.50 par automatically became (1) share United National Bancorporation Common $2.50 par 1/4/82
United National Bancorporation merged into First Commonwealth Financial Corp. 9/27/94

UNION NATL BK & TR CO (JOLIET, IL)
Capital Stock $100 par changed to $10 par 00/00/1963
Stock Dividends - 150% 12/21/1949; 100% 04/01/1963; 25% 12/24/1970; 10% 07/10/1977; 20% 03/01/1981
Merged into First Midwest Bancorp, Inc. (MO) 10/21/1985
Each share Capital Stock $1 par exchanged for $18 cash

UNION NATIONAL BANK (CHARLOTTE, NC)
Capital Stock $100 par changed to $10 par and (9) additional shares issued 2/10/49
Merged into First Union National Bank of North Carolina (Charlotte, NC) 7/18/58
Each share Capital Stock $10 par exchanged for (2.5) shares Capital Stock $5 par
First Union National Bank of North Carolina (Charlotte, NC) merged into First Union National Bancorp, Inc. 4/4/68 which name changed to Cameron Financial Corp. 5/19/72 which name changed to First Union Corp. 4/23/75 which name changed to Wachovia Corp. (Ctfs. dated after 9/1/2001) 9/1/2001

UNION NATL BK (CLARKSBURG, WV)
Common $50 par changed to $12.50 par and (5) additional shares issued to effect a (4) for (1) split and a 50% stock dividend 3/13/73
Common $12.50 par changed to $6.25 par and (1) additional share 5/5/80
Stock Dividends - 100% 1/20/61; 100% 2/16/70
Reorganized as Union Bancorp of West Virginia, Inc. 10/1/82
Each share Common $6.25 par exchanged for (1) share Common $6.25 par
Union Bancorp of West Virginia, Inc. merged into Key Centurion Bancshares, Inc. 3/13/87 which merged into Banc One Corp. 5/3/93 which merged into Bank One Corp. 10/2/98 which merged into J.P. Morgan Chase & Co. 12/31/2000 which name changed to JPMorgan Chase & Co. 7/20/2004

UNION NATL BK (DENVER, CO)
Name changed to Union Bank & Trust (Denver, CO) 1/7/72
Union Bank & Trust (Denver, CO) reorganized as Union Bankshares, Ltd. (DE) 2/15/85
(See Union Bankshares, Ltd. (DE))

UNION NATL BK (FRANKINVILLE, NY)
Merged into First Trust Union Bank (Wellsville, NY) 12/3/68
Each share Common $10 par exchanged for (3.5) shares Common $10 par
First Trust Union Bank (Wellsville, NY) acquired by Security New York State Corp. 7/31/73 which merged into Norstar Bancorp Inc. 5/1/84 which merged into Fleet/Norstar Financial Group, Inc. 1/1/88 which name changed to Fleet Financial Group, Inc. (New) 4/15/92 which name changed to Fleet Boston Corp. 10/1/99 which name changed

to FleetBoston Financial Corp. 4/18/2000 which merged into Bank of America Corp. 4/1/2004

UNION NATL BK (HOUSTON, TX)
Name changed to Union Bank (Houston, TX) 08/11/1969
Union Bank (Houston, TX) merged into Union Texas Bancshares, Inc. 07/28/1983
(See Union Texas Bancshares, Inc.)

UNION NATL BK (KANSAS CITY, MO)
Stock Dividends - 11-1/9% 01/20/1938; 33-1/3% 03/15/1961; 25% 04/14/1964
Merged into Columbia Union National Bank & Trust Co. (Kansas City, MO) 09/12/1969
Each share Common $10 par exchanged for (1) share Common $10 par
(See Columbia Union National Bank & Trust Co. (Kansas City, MO))

UNION NATL BK (LITTLE ROCK, AR)
Common $20 par changed to $10 par and (1) additional share issued 04/21/1972
Stock Dividends - 66-2/3% 09/30/1946; 25% 06/30/1950; 20% 06/30/1952; 16-2/3% 06/30/1954; 14.2% 06/30/1956; 12-1/2% 06/30/1958; 11-1/9% 01/29/1960; 20% 01/26/1962; 16-2/3% 06/30/1964; 14-2/7% 06/30/1966
Merged into Union National Bank (Jacksonville, AR) 10/31/1990
Each share Common $10 par exchanged for $73.06 cash

UNION NATL BK (LOWELL, MA)
Each share Capital Stock $25 par exchanged for (2) shares Capital Stock $12.50 par 9/9/57
Stock Dividend - 10% 7/19/56
Acquired by State Street Boston Financial Corp. 8/9/73
Each share Capital Stock $12.50 par exchanged for (1.6) shares Common $10 par
State Street Boston Financial Corp. name changed to State Street Boston Corp. 5/3/77 which name changed to State Street Corp. 4/16/97

UNION NATIONAL BANK (PASADENA, CA)
Each share Capital Stock $100 par exchanged for (10) shares Capital Stock $10 par in 1954
Merged into California Bank (Los Angeles, CA) 8/19/55
Each share Capital Stock $10 par exchanged for (0.477272) share Common $12.50 par
California Bank (Los Angeles, CA) merged into United California Bank (Los Angeles, CA) 2/24/61 which merged into Western Bancorporation 1/16/78 which name changed to First Interstate Bancorp 6/1/81 which merged into Wells Fargo & Co. (Old) 4/1/96 which merged into Wells Fargo & Co. (New) 11/2/98

UNION NATL BK (PITTSBURGH, PA)
Each share Common $100 par exchanged for (10) shares Common $10 par 00/00/1954
Under plan of merger each share Common $10 par received (0.39054) additional share Common $10 par 02/28/1964
Under plan of merger each share Common $10 par received (0.27455) additional share Common $10 par 12/31/1969
Common $10 par changed to $8-1/3 par and (0.2) additional share issued 10/22/1974
Stock Dividend - 25% 04/12/1971
Reorganized as Union National Corp. 02/08/1982
Each share Common $8-1/3 par exchanged for (1) share Common $1 par

Union National Corp. merged into Integra Financial Corp. 01/26/1989 which merged into National City Corp. 05/03/1996 which was acquired by PNC Financial Services Group, Inc. 12/31/2008

UNION NATL BK (SHENANDOAH, PA)
Acquired by Keystone Financial Inc. 01/01/1987
Details not available

UNION NATL BK (SISTERSVILLE, WV)
Acquired by Union Bank of Tyler County (Middlebourne, WV) 01/03/1984
Details not available

UNION NATIONAL BANK (SPRINGFIELD, MO)
Common $100 par changed to $20 par and (4) additional shares issued plus a 33-1/3% stock dividend paid 10/20/65
Stock Dividends - 100% 12/8/44; 66-2/3% 8/1/51; 50% 11/22/61
Thru purchase offer 99.25% acquired by U.N. Bancshares, Inc. as of 5/24/71
Public interest eliminated

UNION NATL BK (STREATOR, IL)
Reorganized as First Union Bancorporation, Inc. 08/20/1982
Details not available

UNION NATL BK (TROY, NY)
Common $16-2/3 par changed to $20 par 08/26/1960
Common $20 par changed to $25 par 01/19/1965
Common $25 par changed to $30 par 01/11/1966
Common $30 par changed to $10 par and (2) additional shares issued 01/18/1968
Merged into Charter New York Corp. 01/18/1972
Each share Common $10 par exchanged for (2) shares Common $10 par
Charter New York Corp. name changed to Irving Bank Corp. 10/17/1979 which merged into Bank of New York Co., Inc. 12/30/1988 which merged into Bank of New York Mellon Corp. 07/01/2007

UNION NATIONAL BANK (TULSA, OK)
Name changed to First City Bank N.A., (Tulsa, Okla.) 4/15/85

UNION NATL BK (WICHITA, KS)
Common $62.50 par changed to $50 par and (0.25) additional share issued 01/01/1946
Common $50 par changed to $10 par and (4) additional shares issued 03/19/1957
Common $10 par changed to $5 par and (1) additional share issued 01/12/1965
4.60% Preferred $100 par called for redemption 12/31/1965
Common $5 par changed to $10 par 04/01/1979
Stock Dividends - 50% 01/25/1950; 66-2/3% 03/19/1957; 40% 08/29/1958; 25% 05/01/1964; 42.68% 12/24/1965
Reorganized as Union Bancshares, Inc. 07/01/1982
Each share Common $10 par exchanged for (1) share Common $10 par
(See Union Bancshares, Inc.)

UNION NATL BK (YOUNGSTOWN, OH)
Each share Capital Stock $100 par exchanged for (5) shares Capital Stock $20 par 00/00/1944
Each share Capital Stock $20 par exchanged for (2.4) shares Capital Stock $1 par to effect a (2) for (1)

split and 20% stock dividend 02/08/1960
Stock Dividend - 100% 07/20/1954
Merged into Banc One Corp. (DE) 03/01/1982
Each share Capital Stock $10 par exchanged for (2.09524) shares Common no par
Banc One Corp. (DE) reincorporated in Ohio 05/01/1989 which merged into Bank One Corp. 10/02/1998 which merged into J.P. Morgan Chase & Co. 12/31/2000 which name changed to JPMorgan Chase & Co. 07/20/2004

UNION NATL CORP (PA)
Common $1 par split (4) for (3) by issuance of (1/3) additional share 05/10/1982
Common $1 par split (2) for (1) by issuance of (1) additional share 05/10/1985
Merged into Integra Financial Corp. 01/26/1989
Each share Common $1 par exchanged for (1.24) shares Common $1 par
Integra Financial Corp. merged into National City Corp. 05/03/1996 which was acquired by PNC Financial Services Group, Inc. 12/31/2008

UNION NATL FINL CORP (PA)
Common 50¢ par changed to 25¢ par and (1) additional share issued 06/01/1995
Stock Dividends - 5% payable 05/14/1999 to holders of record 04/26/1999; 5% payable 05/19/2000 to holders of record 05/02/2000; 5% payable 05/20/2005 to holders of record 05/05/2005 Ex date - 05/03/2005
Merged into Donegal Group Inc. 05/06/2011
Each share Common 25¢ par exchanged for (0.2134) share Class A Common 1¢ par and $5.45 cash

UNION NATIONAL INVESTMENT CO. (SC)
Merged into Domestic Finance Group, Inc. on a (1.1) for (1) basis 12/10/57
Domestic Finance Group, Inc. name changed to First Southern Co. 9/18/58 which liquidated for Liberty Loan Corp. 6/8/65 which name changed to LLC Corp. 3/14/80 which name changed to Valhi, Inc. 3/10/87

UNION NATL MOUNT JOY BK (MOUNT JOY, PA)
Reorganized as Union National Financial Corp. 01/02/1987
Each share Common $1 par exchanged for (4) shares Common 50¢ par
Union National Financial Corp. merged into Donegal Group Inc. 05/06/2011

UNION NATURAL GAS CO. OF CANADA, LTD.
Name changed to Union Gas Co. of Canada Ltd. in 1931
Union Gas Co. of Canada Ltd. name changed to Union Gas Ltd. 10/11/72

UNION OF TEXAS OIL CO. (TX)
Common no par changed to 10¢ par 10/17/55
Charter revoked for failure to file reports and pay fees 5/3/65

UNION OIL & GAS CORP. OF LOUISIANA (DE)
Class A & B $1 par split (5) for (2) by issuance of (1.5) additional shares 3/2/59
Under plan of merger name changed to Union Texas Natural Gas Corp. 3/3/60
Union Texas Natural Gas Corp. merged into Allied Chemical Corp. 2/20/62 which name changed to Allied Corp. 4/27/81 which merged

into Allied-Signal Inc. 9/19/85 which name changed to AlliedSignal Inc. 4/26/93 which name changed to Honeywell International Inc. 12/1/99

UNION OIL ASSOCIATES
Merged into Union Oil Co. of California in 1932
Details not available

UNION OIL CO CALIF (CA)
$3.75 Preferred Ser. A called for redemption 4/8/55
Common $25 par changed to $8-1/3 par and (2) additional shares issued 12/4/64
$2.50 Conv. Preferred no par called for redemption 3/10/78
Common $8-1/3 par changed to $4-1/6 par and (1) additional share issued 6/1/79
Common $4-1/6 par changed to $2-1/12 par and (1) additional share issued 8/8/80
Stock Dividends - 10% 12/10/53; 10% 1/14/56
Reorganized under the laws of Delaware as Unocal Corp. and Common $2-1/12 par changed to $1 par 4/25/83
Unocal Corp. merged into Chevron Corp. 8/10/2005

UNION OIL CO CDA LTD (CANADA)
Common $1 par changed to no par and (2) additional shares issued 11/20/1972
Acquired by Union Oil Co. of California 08/17/1981
Each share Common no par exchanged for $65 cash

UNION PAC CAP TR (DE)
6.25% Conv. Preferred 144A Term Income Deferrable Equity Securities called for redemption at $50.52 on 12/5/2003
6.25% Conv. Preferred Term Income Deferrable Equity Securities called for redemption at $50.52 on 12/5/2003

UNION PAC CORP (UT)
4-3/4% Conv. Preferred Ser. A called for redemption 4/12/80
$7.25 Conv. Preferred Ser. A no par called for redemption 3/1/88
(Additional Information in Active)

UNION PAC RES GROUP INC (UT)
Merged into Anadarko Petroleum Corp. 7/14/2000
Each share Common no par exchanged for (0.455) share Common 1¢ par

UNION PAC RR CO (UT)
Recapitalized 00/00/1948
Each share Preferred $100 par exchanged for (2) shares Preferred $50 par
Each share Common $100 par exchanged for (2) shares Common $50 par
Preferred $50 par and Common $50 par changed to $10 par and (4) additional shares issued respectively 07/30/1956
Merged into Union Pacific Corp. 06/25/1971
Each share Preferred $10 par exchanged for (1) share 4-3/4% Conv. Preferred Ser. A no par and $0.093333 cash
Each share Common $10 par exchanged for (1) share Common $10 par

UNION PASSENGER RAILWAY CO. OF PHILADELPHIA
Acquired by Philadelphia Transportation Co. in 1940
Each share Common exchanged for $59.15 principal amount of 3%-6% Consolidated Mortgage Bonds and (0.495) share $1 Part. Preferred $20 par
Philadelphia Transportation Co. completed liquidation 11/20/73

UNION PETROCHEMICAL CORP NEV (NV)
Capital Stock 10¢ par changed to 1¢ par 00/00/1977
Charter revoked for failure to file a list of officers 08/01/1991

UNION PLANTERS CORP (TN)
Common $5 par split (2) for (1) by issuance of (1) additional share 03/03/1989
Increasing Rate Preferred Ser. C no par called for redemption 10/31/1994
Common $5 par split (2) for (1) by issuance of (1) additional share 03/03/1989
Common $5 par split (3) for (2) by issuance of (0.5) additional share payable 06/06/2002 to holders of record 05/22/2002 Ex date - 06/07/2002
Conv. Preferred Ser. E no par called for redemption at $25 plus $0.34 accrued dividend on 03/31/2004
Merged into Regions Financial Corp. (New) 07/01/2004
Each share Common $5 par exchanged for (1) share Common 1¢ par

UNION PLANTERS NATL BK (MEMPHIS, TN)
Stock Dividends - 14-2/7% 1/18/46; 25% 6/30/51; 15% 2/6/56; 20% 2/9/68
Reorganized as Union Planters Corp. 7/1/72
Each share Common $10 par exchanged for (2) shares Common $5 par
Union Planters Corp. merged into Regions Financial Corp. (New) 7/1/2004

UNION PLATINUM MNG CO (SOUTH AFRICA)
Under plan of merger name changed to Rustenburg Platinum Holdings Ltd. 09/13/1976
Rustenburg Platinum Holdings Ltd. name changed to Anglo American Platinum Corp. Ltd. (New) 09/02/1997 which name changed to Anglo Platinum Ltd. 05/30/2005 which name changed to Anglo American Platinum Ltd. 05/25/2011

UNION POTASH & CHEMICAL CO.
Merged into International Minerals & Chemical Corp. 00/00/1942
Each share Preferred no par exchanged for (0.8) share Common $5 par and $25 cash
Each share Common $1 par exchanged for (0.8) share Common $5 par
International Minerals & Chemical Corp. name changed to Imcera Group Inc. 06/14/1990 which name changed to Mallinckrodt Group Inc. 03/15/1994 which name changed to Mallinckrodt Inc. 10/16/1996 which merged into Tyco International Ltd. (Bermuda) 10/17/2000 which reincorporated in Switzerland 03/17/2009 which merged into Johnson Controls International PLC 09/06/2016

UNION POWER CORP.
Bankrupt in 1934

UNION PREMIER FOOD STORES, INC.
Name changed to Food Fair Stores, Inc. in 1942
Food Fair Stores, Inc. name changed to Food Fair, Inc. 12/1/76 which reorganized in Delaware as Pantry Pride, Inc. (Old) 7/6/81 which merged into Pantry Pride, Inc. (New) 1/20/83 which name changed to Revlon Group Inc. 4/7/86
(See Revlon Group Inc.)

UNION PPTY INVS INC (DE)
Merged into Kranzco Realty Trust 2/27/97
Each share Common 1¢ par exchanged for (0.3125) share Conv. Preferred Shares of Bene. Int. Ser. B-1 1¢ par
Kranzco Realty Trust merged into Kramont Realty Trust 6/16/2000
(See Kramont Realty Trust)

UNION PUBLIC SERVICE CO. (MN)
Merged into Otter Tail Power Co. in 1941
(See Otter Tail Power Co.)

UNION REALTY & MANAGEMENT CO. (OH)
Liquidation completed
Each share Common $1 par exchanged for initial distribution of $5 cash 4/5/61
Each share Common $1 par received second and final distribution of $0.64 cash 9/19/63

UNION REFINING CO. (DE)
Charter cancelled for non-payment of taxes 1/19/25

UNION RESERVE LIFE INSURANCE CO. (ND)
Merged into National Western Life Insurance Co. (CO) 09/28/1965
Each share Class A 20¢ par exchanged for (0.11534025) share Class A Common $1 par
Each share Class B 20¢ par exchanged for (0.13333333) shares Class B 20¢ par
National Western Life Insurance Co. (CO) reincorporated in Delaware as National Western Life Group, Inc. 10/02/2015

UNION RES INC (DE)
Name changed to Miraplast, Inc. 10/24/1983
(See Miraplast, Inc.)

UNION RESVS INC (CA)
Charter cancelled for failure to file reports and pay taxes 08/01/1988

UNION ROCHESTER SHARE CORP.
Acquired by Niagara Share Corp. of Maryland in August, 1930
(See Niagara Share Corp. of Maryland)

UNION ROCK & MATLS CORP (AZ)
Company went private 8/26/87
Details not available

UNION ROCK CO.
Merged into Consolidated Rock Products Co. in 1929
(See Consolidated Rock Products Co.)

UNION SAFE DEP BK (STOCKTON, CA)
Under plan of reorganization each share Common $6.75 par automatically became (1) share USDB Bancorp Common $6.75 par 6/19/98

UNION SAVINGS & LOAN CO. (OH)
Capital Stock $100 par changed to $25 par in 1942
Acquired for cash by Union Financial Corp. in January 1960

UNION SVGS & TR CO (WARREN, OH)
Stock Dividends - 50% 01/17/1940; 11-1/9% 02/02/1942; 20% 02/01/1950; 33-1/3% 02/01/1951; 25% 02/01/1957; 20% 05/01/1961; 33-1/3% 05/05/1965; 25% 04/11/1968; 100% 05/31/1972; 20% 05/21/1976; 33-1/3% 05/23/1978
Merged into Banc One Corp. (DE) 05/01/1984
Each share Capital Stock $20 par exchanged for (3.2928) shares Common no par
Banc One Corp. (DE) reincorporated in Ohio 05/01/1989 which merged into Bank One Corp. 10/02/1998
which merged into J.P. Morgan Chase & Co. 12/31/2000 which name changed to JPMorgan Chase & Co. 07/20/2004

UNION SVGS BK & TR CO (MORRISVILLE, VT)
Name changed to Union Bank (Morrisville, VT) 06/14/1974
Union Bank (Morrisville, Vt.) reorganized as Union Bankshares, Inc. 01/05/1983

UNION SECURITIES CORP.
Dissolved in 1945

UNION SECURITY & INVESTMENT CO. (FL)
Merged into First Florida Banks, Inc. 3/31/77
Each share Common $2.50 par exchanged for $13.12 cash

UNION SVC INDS INC (DE)
Stock Dividends - 200% 08/29/1969; 25% 07/01/1971
Under plan of merger each share Common $1 par exchanged for $3.50 cash 06/22/1979

UNION 69 LTD (DE)
Each share old Common $0.001 par exchanged for (0.005) share new Common $0.001 par 5/13/97
Name changed to Save on Meds.Com, Inc. 3/2/2000
Save on Meds.Com, Inc. name changed to My Meds Express.Com, Inc. 7/26/2000
(See My Meds Express.Com, Inc.)

UNION SOLVENTS CORP.
Liquidated in 1934

UNION SPECIAL MACHINE CO. (DE)
Name changed to Union Special Corp. 6/18/73
(See Union Special Corp.)

UNION SPL CORP (DE)
Acquired by Industrial Equity (Pacific) Ltd. 05/11/1988
Each share Common $1 par exchanged for $26 cash

UNION SPRING & MANUFACTURING CO. (NJ)
Each share Common 10¢ par exchanged for (0.2) share Common 50¢ par 00/00/1954
Each share 4% Preferred 50¢ par exchanged for (4) shares Common 50¢ par 11/02/1955
Name changed to Union Corp. (NJ) 01/19/1966
Union Corp. (NJ) reincorporated in Delaware 07/24/1987
(See Union Corp. (DE))

UNION ST BK (EAST BERNARD, TX)
Merged into First Prosperity Bank (El Campo, TX) 10/1/98
Each share Common $10 par exchanged for $251.43 cash

UNION ST BK (PAYNE, OH)
Merged into First Financial Bancorp (OH) 4/1/98
Each share Common $8 par exchanged for $355.52 cash

UNION STATE BANK (CARMEL, IN)
Merged into National City Bank (Cleveland, OH) 2/28/93
Details not available

UNION STATE BANK (MONSEY, NY)
Under plan of reorganization each share Common $10 par automatically became (1) share U.S.B. Holding Co., Inc. Common $10 par 01/11/1983
U.S.B. Holding Co., Inc. merged into KeyCorp (New) 01/01/2008

UNION STEEL CASTING CO.
Acquired by Blaw-Knox Co. (N.J.) in 1929
(See Blaw-Knox Co. (N.J.))

UNION STEEL PRODUCTS CO. (MI)
Acquired by Eagle-Picher Industries, Inc. 12/01/1968
Each share Capital Stock $10 par exchanged for $10 cash or equivalent dollar amount in 1.40 Conv. Preferred Ser. C no par
(See Eagle-Picher Industries, Inc.)

UNION STK YDS CO OMAHA LTD (NE)
Common $100 par changed to $20 par and (4) additional shares issued 2/11/56
Merged into Kay Corp. 3/1/73
Each share Common $20 par exchanged for (1.5) shares Common $1 par or $14 cash
Note: Option to receive cash expired 4/12/73
Kay Corp. name changed to Balfour Maclaine Corp. 5/26/88 which recapitalized as Anti Aging Medical Group Corp. 1/23/2006 which changed to Innolife Pharma, Inc. 5/2/2007

UNION STORAGE CO.
Liquidated in 1950

UNION STR ACQUISITION CORP (DE)
Units separated 11/20/2008
Completely liquidated 11/20/2008
Each share Common $0.0001 par exchanged for first and final distribution of $8.0900358 cash

UNION STR INC (DE)
Liquidation completed
Each share Common $1 par received initial distribution of $1 cash 05/15/1975
Each share Common $1 par received second distribution of $0.50 cash 05/31/1978
Each share Common $1 par received third distribution of $1 cash 03/31/1979
Each share Common $1 par received fourth distribution of $1 cash 10/12/1979
Each share Common $1 par received fifth distribution of $0.50 cash 05/27/1980
Each share Common $1 par exchanged for sixth and final distribution of $0.40 cash 11/30/1981

UNION STREET RAILWAY CO. (MA)
Each share Capital Stock $100 par exchanged for (1) share Capital Stock $50 par and $50 cash 4/4/56
Acquired by Eastern Massachusetts Street Railway Co. in July 1962
Each share Capital Stock $50 par exchanged for $85 cash

UNION SUGAR CO (CA)
Each share Common $25 par exchanged for (2) shares Common $12.50 par 00/00/1945
Common $12.50 par changed to $5 par and (1.5) additional shares issued 07/30/1959
Common $5 par changed to no par 10/18/1967
Stock Dividend - 50% 12/05/1955
Liquidation completed
Each share Common no par exchanged for initial distribution of (1.15) shares Consolidated Foods Corp. Common $1.33333333 par and $21 cash 06/10/1974
(See Consolidated Foods Corp.)
Each share Common no par received second distribution of $1.45 cash 02/21/1975
Each share Common no par received third and final distribution of $0.16 cash 04/09/1976

UNION SULPHUR & OIL CORP (DE)
Each share Capital Stock $1 par exchanged for (2) shares Class A $1 par and (1) share Class B $1 par in 1952
Recapitalized as Union Oil & Gas Corp. of Louisiana and Class A & B

$1 par split (2) for (1) by issuance of (1) additional share 5/10/55
Union Oil & Gas Corp. of Louisiana name changed to Union Texas Natural Gas Corp. 3/3/60 which merged into Allied Chemical Corp. 2/20/62 which name changed to Allied Corp. 4/27/81 which merged into Allied-Signal Inc. 9/19/85 which name changed to AlliedSignal Inc. 4/26/93 which name changed to Honeywell International Inc. 12/1/99

UNION SULPHUR CO., INC. (DE)
Name changed to Union Sulphur & Oil Corp. in 1950
Union Sulphur & Oil Corp. recapitalized as Union Oil & Gas Corp. of Louisiana 5/10/55 which name changed to Union Texas Natural Gas Corp. 3/3/60 which merged into Allied Chemical Corp. 2/20/62 which name changed to Allied Corp. 4/27/81 which merged into Allied-Signal Inc. 9/19/85 which name changed to AlliedSignal Inc. 4/26/93 which name changed to Honeywell International Inc. 12/1/99

UNION SWITCH & SIGNAL INC (DE)
Merged into Ansaldo Signal N.V. 12/11/96
Each share Common 1¢ par exchanged for (1) share Common NLG 0.01 par
(See Ansaldo Signal N.V.)

UNION TANK CAR CO (DE)
Reincorporated 4/30/68
Each share Capital Stock $100 par exchanged for (4) shares Capital Stock no par in 1930
Stock Dividend - 100% 6/1/54
State of incorporation changed from (NJ) to (DE) and Capital Stock no par reclassified as Common $1 par 4/30/68
Common $1 par split (5) for (2) by issuance of (1.5) additional shares 9/3/68
Reorganized as Trans Union Corp. 6/1/69
Each share Common $1 par exchanged for (1) share Common $1 par
(See Trans Union Corp.)

UNION TELEPHONE CO. (MI)
Merged into General Telephone Co. of Michigan 2/28/57
Each share $1.35 Preferred $25 par exchanged for $26.5925 cash
Each share $1.44 Preferred $25 par exchanged for $26.61 cash
Each share $2.70 Preferred $50 par exchanged for $52.675 cash
Each share $2.75 Preferred $50 par exchanged for $52.6875 cash
Public interest eliminated

UNION TELEPHONE CORP. (DE)
Assets acquired by General Telephone Co. in 1941
No stockholders' equity

UNION TERM COLD STORAGE INC (DE)
4% Preferred called for redemption 12/26/1969
Public interest eliminated

UNION TEX BANCSHARES INC (TX)
Assets sold 12/1/88
No stockholders' equity

UNION TEX PETE HLDGS INC (DE)
Merged into Atlantic Richfield Co. 6/29/98
Each share Common 5¢ par exchanged for $29 cash

UNION TEXAS NATURAL GAS CORP. (DE)
Merged into Allied Chemical Corp. 2/20/62
Each share Class A $1 par or Class B $1 par exchanged for (7/8) share Common $9 par
Allied Chemical Corp. name changed to Allied Corp. 4/27/81 which merged into Allied-Signal Inc. 9/19/85 which name changed to AlliedSignal Inc. 4/26/93 which name changed to Honeywell International Inc. 12/1/99

UNION TITLE CO. (AZ)
Under plan of merger name changed to Financial Corp. of Arizona (Ariz.) 10/17/62
Financial Corp. of Arizona (Ariz.) reincorporated under the laws of Delaware 6/1/70 which name changed to FCA Industries, Inc. 4/24/75
(See FCA Industries, Inc.)

UNION TOBACCO CO.
Dissolved in 1936

UNION TRACTION CO.
Acquired by Philadelphia Transportation Co. in 1940
Each share Common exchanged for $4.02 principal amount of 3%-6% Consolidated Mortgage Bonds and (0.287) share $1 Part. Preferred $20 par
Philadelphia Transportation Co. completed liquidation 11/20/73

UNION TRACTION CO. OF INDIANA
Sold to Indiana Railroad in 1930

UNION TRANSPORTATION LINES (DE)
Charter cancelled and declared inoperative and void for non-payment of taxes 03/18/1925

UNION TR & DEP CO (PARKERSBURG, WV)
Each share Common $100 par exchanged for (10) shares Common $10 par 11/01/1967
Stock Dividends - 20% 10/30/1968; 10% 02/02/1970; 10% 05/27/1971
Name changed to Union Trust National Bank (Parkersburg, WV) 01/03/1972
Union Trust National Bank (Parkersburg, WV) merged into Parkersburg National Bank (Parkersburg, WV) 12/13/1982 which reorganized as United Bankshares, Inc. 05/01/1984

UNION TR & SVGS BK (FORT DODGE, IA)
Through purchase offer over 99% acquired by Central National Bancshares, Inc. as of 06/15/1978
Public interest eliminated

UNION TR BANCORP (MD)
Common $5 par changed to $2.50 par 04/22/1985
Common $2.50 par split (2) for (1) by issuance of (1) additional share 08/14/1985
Acquired by Bank of Virginia Co. 12/31/1985
Each share Common $2.50 par exchanged for (2.05) shares Common $5 par
Bank of Virginia Co. name changed to Signet Banking Corp. 07/14/1986 which merged into First Union Corp. 11/28/1997 which name changed to Wachovia Corp. (Ctfs. dated after 09/01/2001) 09/01/2001 which merged into Wells Fargo & Co. (New) 12/31/2008

UNION TRUST CO. (PITTSBURGH, PA)
Each share Capital Stock $100 par exchanged for (5) shares Capital Stock $20 par 00/00/1942
Merged into Mellon National Bank & Trust Co. (Pittsburgh, PA) 09/23/1946
Each share Capital Stock $20 par exchanged for (8) shares Capital Stock $100 par
Mellon National Bank & Trust Co. (Pittsburgh, PA) reorganized as Mellon National Corp. 11/28/1972 which name changed to Mellon Bank Corp. 09/30/1984 which name changed to Mellon Financial Corp. 10/17/1999 which merged into Bank of New York Mellon Corp. 07/01/2007

UNION TRUST CO. (ST. PETERSBURG, FL)
Each share Common $100 par exchanged for (4) shares Common $25 par in 1948
Each share Common $25 par exchanged for (2) shares Common $12.50 par 6/12/57
Stock Dividends - 50% 9/21/48; 33-1/3% 10/11/48; 50% 9/20/54; 60% 6/11/57
Name changed to Union Trust National Bank (St. Petersburg, FL) 4/29/65
Union Trust National Bank (St. Petersburg, FL) name changed to Landmark Union Trust Bank of St. Petersburg, N.A. (St. Petersburg, FL) 10/1/74
(See Landmark Union Trust Bank of St. Petersburg, FL))

UNION TR CO (ELLSWORTH, ME)
Stock Dividends - 20% 05/12/1971; 25% 05/10/1974
Reorganized as Union Bankshares Co. 07/00/1984
Each share Common $25 par exchanged for (1.2) shares Common $25 par
Union Bankshares Co. merged into Camden National Corp. 01/03/2008

UNION TR CO (NEW HAVEN, CT)
Reorganized as Northeast Bancorp, Inc. 12/29/1972
Each share Capital Stock $5 par exchanged for (1) share Common $5 par
Northeast Bancorp, Inc. merged into First Fidelity Bancorporation (New) 05/03/1993 which merged into First Union Corp. 01/01/1996 which name changed to Wachovia Corp. (Ctfs. dated after 09/01/2001) 09/01/2001 which merged into Wells Fargo & Co. (New) 12/31/2008

UNION TR CO (SHELBY, NC)
Merged into Independence National Bank (Gastonia, NC) 6/1/76
Each share Common $5 par exchanged for (1.75) shares Common $2.50 par
Independence National Bank (Gastonia, NC) merged into Branch Corp. 10/5/81 which name changed to BB&T Financial Corp. 5/10/88 which merged into Southern National Corp. 2/28/95 which name changed to BB&T Corp. 5/19/97

UNION TR CO D C (WASHINGTON, DC)
Each share Capital Stock $50 par exchanged for (5) shares Capital Stock $10 par 00/00/1947
Stock Dividends - 100% 04/06/1955; 10% 12/05/1966; 21.2121% 12/04/1970; 25% 12/06/1972
Merged into Union First National Bank (Washington, DC) 01/01/1976
Each share Capital Stock $10 par exchanged for (2.8525) shares Common $10 par
Union First National Bank (Washington, DC) name changed to First American Bank, N.A. (Washington, DC) 03/17/1980
(See First American Bank, N.A. (Washington, DC))

UNION TR CO MD (BALTIMORE, MD)
Each share Capital Stock $50 par exchanged for (5) shares Capital Stock $10 par 07/00/1929
Stock Dividend - 100% 04/14/1969
Reorganized as Union Trust Bancorp 07/03/1972
Each share Capital Stock $10 par exchanged for (2) shares Common $5 par
Union Trust Bancorp acquired by Bank of Virginia Co. 12/31/1985 which name changed to Signet Banking Corp. 07/14/1986 which merged into First Union Corp. 11/28/1997 which name changed to Wachovia Corp. (Ctfs. dated after 09/01/2001) 09/01/2001 which merged into Wells Fargo & Co. (New) 12/31/2008

UNION TR INC LOUISVILLE (KY)
Through purchase offer 99.5% acquired by Commercial Credit Co. as of 03/31/1978
Public interest eliminated

UNION TRUST LIFE INSURANCE CO. (MN)
Voting Trust Agreement terminated 12/15/1961
Each VTC for Common $1 par exchanged for (1) share Common $1 par
Merged into Missouri Fidelity/Union Trust Life Insurance Co. 12/31/1965
Each share Common $1 par exchanged for (1) share Common $1 par
Missouri Fidelity/Union Trust Life Insurance Co. merged into National Western Life Insurance Co. (CO) 10/15/1970 which reincorporated in Delaware as National Western Life Group, Inc. 10/02/2015

UNION TR NATL BK (PARKERSBURG, WV)
Merged into Parkersburg National Bank (Parkersburg, WV) 12/13/1982
Each share Common $10 par exchanged for (0.976) share Common $2.50 par
Parkersburg National Bank (Parkersburg, WV) reorganized as United Bankshares, Inc. 05/01/1984

UNION TR NATL BK (ST. PETERSBURG, FL)
Common $12.50 par changed to $5 par and (1.5) additional share issued plus a 20% stock dividend paid 09/19/1969
Name changed to Landmark Union Trust Bank of St. Petersburg, N.A. (St. Petersburg, FL) 10/01/1974
(See Landmark Union Trust Bank of St. Petersburg, N.A. (St. Petersburg, FL))

UNION TRUSTEED FUNDS, INC. (DE)
Acquired by American Business Shares, Inc. 00/00/1952
Details not available

UNION TWIST DRILL CO. (MA)
Common $5 par split (3) for (1) by issuance of (2) additional shares in 1953
Stock Dividends - 10% 12/20/54; 10% 3/30/62; 10% 6/28/63
Name changed to UTD Corp. 2/12/64
UTD Corp. acquired by Litton Industries, Inc. 9/11/68
(See Litton Industries, Inc.)

UNION URANIUM CO. (CO)
Recapitalized as Polytechnic Industries, Inc. 2/17/72
Each share Common 1¢ par exchanged for (0.1) share Common 10¢ par
Polytechnic Industries, Inc. declared defunct 1/31/77

UNION UTILITIES, INC.
Liquidated in 1931

UNION VY CORP (NJ)
Plan of reorganization under Chapter 11 Federal Bankruptcy proceedings confirmed 06/18/1993
No stockholders' equity

UNION WARREN SVGS BK (BOSTON, MA)
Acquired by Home Owners Federal Savings & Loan Association 10/7/87

Each share Common $1 par exchanged for $50 cash

UNION WIRE ROPE CORP. (DE)
Each share Common no par exchanged for (2) shares Common $5 par in 1953
Stock Dividends - 100% 1/15/46; 10% 6/17/57
Merged into Armco Steel Corp. on a (1) for (2.5) basis in 1958
Armco Steel Corp. name changed to Armco Inc. 7/1/78 which merged into AK Steel Holding Corp. 9/30/99

UNIONAMERICA HLDGS PLC (ENGLAND)
Merged into MMI Companies, Inc. 12/11/1997
Each Sponsored ADR for Ordinary exchanged for (0.836) share Common 10¢ par

UNIONAMERICA INC (CA)
Common no par split (2) for (1) by issuance of (1) additional share 4/30/71
Under plan of reorganization each share Common no par exchanged for (1) share Union Bancorp, Inc. Common $1 par and (0.5) share Unionamerica, Inc. (DE) Common $1 par 12/31/73
(See each company's listing)

UNIONAMERICA INC (DE)
Name changed to Westmor Corp. 01/28/1977
(See Westmor Corp.)

UNIONAMERICA MTG & EQUITY TR (CA)
Name changed to Umet Trust 09/03/1974
Umet Trust reorganized as Umet Properties Corp. 08/31/1982 which merged into Hallwood Group Inc. 04/30/1984
(See Hallwood Group Inc.)

UNIONBANCAL CORP (DE)
Reincorporated 09/30/2003
8.375% Depositary Preferred Ser. A called for redemption at $25 on 09/03/1997
Common no par split (3) for (1) by issuance of (2) additional shares payable 12/21/1998 to holders of record 12/07/1998
Secondary Offering - 25,000,000 shares COM offered at $30 per share on 02/25/1999
State of incorporation changed from (CA) to (DE) and Common no par changed to $1 par 09/30/2003
Merged into Mitsubishi UFJ Financial Group, Inc. 11/04/2008
Each share Common $1 par exchanged for $73.50 cash

UNIONBANCAL FIN TR I (DE)
7.375% Capital Securities called for redemption $25 on 2/19/2004

UNIONBANCORP INC (DE)
Under plan of merger name changed to Centrue Finanical Corp. (New) 11/13/2006
Centrue Financial Corp. (New) merged into Midland States Bancorp, Inc. 06/09/2017

UNIONFED FINL CORP (DE)
Common 1¢ par split (3) for (2) by issuance of (0.5) additional share 9/29/87
Each share old Common 1¢ par exchanged for (0.1) share new Common 1¢ par 8/18/93
Dissolved in 1996
No stockholders' equity

UNIONTOWN WATER CO.
All owned by Pennsylvania State Water Corp. a subsidiary of American Water Works Co., Inc. as of 1964

UNIPAC CORP (DE)
Name changed to Hansen Natural Corp. 10/27/1992
Hansen Natural Corp. name changed to Monster Beverage Corp. (Old) 01/09/2012 which reorganized as Monster Beverage Corp. (New) 06/15/2015

UNIPAK INC (DE)
Recapitalized as Uni-Shield International Corp. 8/17/72
Each share Common 10¢ par exchanged for (0.375) share Common 26-2/3¢ par
(See Uni-Shield International Corp.)

UNIPHASE CORP (DE)
Common $0.001 par split (2) for (1) by issuance of (1) additional share payable 06/03/1996 to holders of record 05/20/1996
Common $0.001 par split (2) for (1) by issuance of (1) additional share payable 11/12/1997 to holders of record 11/03/1997
Under plan of merger name changed to JDS Uniphase Corp. 07/06/1999
JDS Uniphase Corp. name changed to Viavi Solutions Inc. 08/04/2015

UNIPOL GRUPPO FINANZIARIO SPA (ITALY)
Each old ADR for Ordinary exchanged for (0.01) new ADR for Ordinary 04/13/2012
ADR agreement terminated 07/27/2015
No ADR's for Preference remain outstanding
Name changed to Unipol Gruppo S.p.A. 10/06/2017

UNIPOLD INC (DE)
Liquidation completed
Each share Common 1¢ par exchanged for initial distribution of $2 cash 04/15/1976
Each share Common 1¢ par received second distribution of $1.05 cash 08/25/1976
Each share Common 1¢ par received third and final distribution of (1) share United Pool & Products Corp. Common 1¢ par 12/06/1976

UNIPRIME CAP ACCEP INC NEW (NV)
Name changed to Deep Blue Marine, Inc. 12/16/2005

UNIPRIME CAP ACCEP INC OLD (NV)
Each share old Common $0.001 par exchanged for (0.05) share new Common $0.001 par 10/16/2001
Recapitalized as Flash Automotive Acceptance Corp. 2/25/2004
Each share new Common $0.001 par exchanged for (0.01) share Common $0.001 par
Flash Automotive Acceptance Corp. name changed to Uniprime Capital Acceptance, Inc. (New) 12/22/2004 which name changed to Deep Blue Marine, Inc. 12/16/2005

UNIPRO FINL SVCS INC (FL)
Each share old Common $0.001 par exchanged for (0.2) share new Common $0.001 par 09/14/2006
Name changed to China Fire & Security Group, Inc. 02/09/2007
(See China Fire & Security Group, Inc.)

UNIPROOF INC (NY)
Out of business 12/00/1988
No stockholders' equity

UNIQUAD RESOURCE CO (DE)
Charter cancelled and declared inoperative and void for non-payment of taxes 3/1/88

UNIQUE BAGEL INC (DE)
Each share old Common $0.0001 par exchanged for (5.25) shares new Common $0.0001 par 12/14/2000

Name changed to CTI Diversified Holdings, Inc. 01/12/2001
CTI Diversified Holdings, Inc. name changed to Wescorp Energy Inc. 12/17/2003
(See Wescorp Energy Inc.)

UNIQUE BROADBAND SYS INC (ON)
Recapitalized as Kure Technologies Inc. 03/20/2017
Each share Common no par exchanged for (0.001) share Common no par
Note: Holders of (999) or fewer pre-split shares received $0.0075 cash per share
Unexchanged certificates entitled to cash will be cancelled and become without value 03/20/2019

UNIQUE CAP CORP (ON)
Recapitalized as Pele Mountain Resources Inc. 9/30/97
Each (11.7) shares Common no par exchanged for (1) share Common no par

UNIQUE CASUAL RESTAURANTS INC (DE)
Name changed to Champps Entertainment Inc. (DE) 07/28/1999
(See Champps Entertainment Inc. (DE))

UNIQUE FASHIONS INC (NV)
Recapitalized as Rhino Enterprises Group, Inc. 04/30/1999
Each share Common no par exchanged for (0.05) share Common no par
Rhino Enterprises Group, Inc. recapitalized as Physicians Adult Daycare, Inc. 07/25/2006
(See Physicians Adult Daycare, Inc.)

UNIQUE FORCE ENTMT INC (BC)
Name changed 12/13/89
Name changed from Unique Resources Ltd. to Unique Force Ent. Inc. 12/13/89
Recapitalized as Greenswan Ventures Inc. 12/2/93
Each share Common no par exchanged for (0.25) share Common no par
Greenswan Ventures Inc. name changed to Canbras Communications Corp. 2/23/95
(See Canbras Communications Corp.)

UNIQUE MOBILITY INC (CO)
Name changed to UQM Technologies, Inc. 1/25/2001

UNIQUE PIZZA & SUBS CORP (DE)
Each share old Common $0.0001 par exchanged for (0.0004) share new Common $0.0001 par 05/20/2010
Each share new Common $0.0001 par exchanged again for (0.004) share new Common $0.0001 par 03/06/2014
Name changed to Unique Foods Corp. 06/28/2018

UNIQUE PRODUCTS, INC. (NV)
Charter revoked for failure to file reports and pay fees 3/3/58

UNIQUE PROSPECTS (UT)
Each (15) shares old Common $0.001 par exchanged for (1) share new Common $0.001 par 6/15/89
Charter expired 11/18/91

UNIQUE RES CORP (BC)
Recapitalized as Bee Vectoring Technologies International Inc. (BC) 07/07/2015
Each share Common no par exchanged for (0.41666666) share Common no par
Bee Vectoring Technologies International Inc. (BC) reincorporated in Ontario 08/25/2016

UNIQUE TIRE RECYCLING INC (BC)
Recapitalized as UKT Recycling Technologies Inc. (BC) 01/19/1998

Each share Common no par exchanged for (0.33333333) share Common no par
UKT Recycling Technologies Inc. (BC) reorganized in Canada as Cogent Integrated Solutions Corp. 12/04/2003 which recapitalized as Cogent Integrated Healthcare Solutions Inc. 11/28/2005 which name changed to Silver Recycling Co., Inc. 01/17/2007
(See Silver Recycling Co., Inc.)

UNIQUE TRANSN SOLUTIONS INC (NV)
Charter revoked for failure to file reports and pay fees 11/20/2012

UNIQUE UNDERWRITERS INC (TX)
Reorganized under the laws of Nevada as JunkieDog.com, Inc. 07/29/2014
Each share Common $0.001 par exchanged for (0.01) share Common $0.001 par
JunkieDog.com, Inc. name changed to Grand Havana, Inc. 07/24/2017

UNIQUE ZIPPER DISTRIBUTING CO. (WA)
Completely liquidated 08/29/1969
Each share Capital Stock 33-1/3¢ par exchanged for first and final distribution of (1/6) share American Can Co. Common $12.50 par
American Can Co. name changed to Primerica Corp. (NJ) 04/28/1987 which was acquired by Primerica Corp. (DE) 12/15/1988 which name changed to Travelers Inc. 12/31/1993 which name changed to Travelers Group Inc. 04/26/1995 which name changed to Citigroup Inc. 10/08/1998

UNIQUEST INC (FL)
SEC revoked common stock registration 07/10/2001

UNIREX CORP (WY)
Recapitalized 07/19/2001
Recapitalized from UNIREX Technologies Inc. to UNIREX Corp. 07/19/2001
Each share Common no par exchanged for (0.2) share Common no par
Administratively dissolved for failure to pay taxes 05/28/2007

UNIREX INC (CO)
Company believed out of business 00/00/1975
Details not available

UNIROM TECHNOLOGIES INC (CANADA)
Delisted from Toronto Venture Stock Exchange 06/20/2005

UNIROYAL CHEM CORP (DE)
Merged into Crompton & Knowles Corp. 08/21/1996
Each share Common 1¢ par exchanged for (0.9577) share Common 10¢ par
Crompton & Knowles Corp. name changed to CK Witco Corp. 09/01/1999 which name changed to Crompton Corp. 04/27/2000 which name changed to Chemtura Corp. 07/01/2005
(See Chemtura Corp.)

UNIROYAL INC (NJ)
Common $2.50 par changed to $1.25 par and (1) additional share issued 02/10/1969
Merged into Clayton & Dubilier, Inc. 09/24/1985
Each share Common $1.25 par exchanged for $22 cash
8% 1st Non-Cum. Preferred $100 par reclassified as 8% 1st Preferred $100 par 10/10/1985
Completely liquidated 12/05/1986
Each share 8% 1st Preferred $100 par exchanged for first and final distribution of $108 cash

Public interest eliminated

UNIROYAL TECHNOLOGY CORP (DE)
Common 1¢ par split (2) for (1) by issuance of (1) additional share payable 4/5/2000 to holders of record 3/20/2000
Plan of reorganization under Chapter 11 Federal Bankruptcy Code converted to Chapter 7 on 10/30/2003
No stockholders' equity

UNISAT INC (NV)
Name changed to Blagman Media International Inc. 5/6/99
Blagman Media International Inc. recapitalized as Innovation Holdings, Inc. 3/5/2003 which name changed to Marketing Concepts International 10/20/2006

UNISAVE ENERGY LTD (BC)
Recapitalized as U.C. Valve Corp. 4/26/89
Each share Common no par exchanged for (0.2) share Common no par
U.C. Valve Corp. reorganized as Blackbridge Capital Corp. 12/1/89 which name changed to Rupert Resources Ltd. 11/1/94

UNISEL GOLD MINES LTD (SOUTH AFRICA)
Merged into Harmony Gold Mining Ltd. 9/9/96
Each ADR for Ordinary no par exchanged for (0.4) Sponsored ADR for Ordinary Rand-50 par

UNISERVICE CORP (FL)
Issue Information - 1,400,000 shares CL A offered at $5 per share on 08/03/1998
Name changed to Associated Automotive Group Inc. 01/04/2002
Associated Automotive Group Inc. name changed to Motor Cars Auto Group, Inc. 12/30/2002
(See Motor Cars Auto Group, Inc.)

UNISERVICE CORP (OR)
Merged into SCI Oregon Funeral Services, Inc. 3/1/95
Each share Common $1 par exchanged for $140 cash

UNISERVICES INC (DE)
Adjudicated bankrupt 7/16/75
Stockholders' equity unlikely

UNISHELTER INC (WI)
Each share Common 1¢ par exchanged for (0.2) share Common 5¢ par 01/31/1977
Reorganized under Chapter 11 bankruptcy proceedings 11/30/1982
No stockholders' equity

UNISHOPS INC (NY)
Common 10¢ par split (2) for (1) by issuance of (1) additional share 6/14/68
Common 10¢ par split (2) for (1) by issuance of (1) additional share 6/16/69
Name changed to Marcade Group, Inc. 6/25/81
Marcade Group, Inc. reorganized as Aris Industries, Inc. 6/30/93
(See Aris Industries, Inc.)

UNISIL INC (DE)
Charter cancelled and declared inoperative and void for non-payment of taxes 3/1/99

UNISON ELECTRONICS CORP. (DE)
Name changed to International Lumber Corp. 10/16/64
(See International Lumber Corp.)

UNISON HEALTHCARE CORP (DE)
Plan of reorganization under Chapter 11 Federal Bankruptcy Code effective 1/31/99
No stockholders' equity

UNISON MEDIA INC (UT)
Proclaimed dissolved for failure to file reports 6/30/88

UNISON SOFTWARE INC (DE)
Issue Information - 2,316,550 shares COM offered at $9 per share on 07/20/1995
Common $0.001 par split (3) for (2) by issuance of (0.5) additional share payable 1/31/97 to holders of record 1/2/97
Merged into International Business Machines Corp. 12/9/97
Each share Common $0.001 par exchanged for $15 cash

UNISORB INC (MA)
Involuntarily dissolved 8/31/98

UNISOURCE ENERGY CORP (AZ)
Name changed to UNS Energy Corp. 05/14/2012
(See UNS Energy Corp.)

UNISOURCE WORLDWIDE INC (DE)
Merged into Georgia-Pacific Corp. 07/06/1999
Each share Common no par exchanged for $12 cash

UNISPHERE COMMUNICATIONS, INC. (NV)
Name changed to Viral Research Technologies, Inc. 1/26/87
Viral Research Technologies, Inc. charter revoked 4/1/91

UNISPHERE EXPLORERS LTD (AB)
Recapitalized as New Unisphere Resources Ltd. 10/6/69
Each share Common no par exchanged for (0.1) share Common no par
(See New Unisphere Resources Ltd.)

UNISPHERE SATELLITE CORP (ON)
Delisted from Canadian Dealer Network 01/03/1995

UNISPHERE WASTE CONVERSION LTD (ON)
Filed a Notice of Intention to Make a Proposal under the Bankruptcy and Insolvency Act 02/09/2005
Stockholders' equity unlikely

UNISTAR FINL SVC CORP (DE)
Common $0.001 par split (2) for (1) by issuance of (1) additional share payable 08/31/1999 to holders of record 07/30/1999
SEC filed a civil lawsuit against the company 08/07/2003
No stockholders' equity

UNISTONE INC (DE)
Each share old Common $0.001 par exchanged for (0.5) share new Common $0.001 par 07/16/2001
Name changed to Cash Systems Inc. 10/17/2001
(See Cash Systems Inc.)

UNISYS CORP (DE)
$3.75 Conv. Preferrred Ser. A $1 par called for redemption at $50 plus $0.1849 accrued dividends on 08/02/1999
Issue Information - 2,250,000 shares 6.25% PFD SER A MANDATORY CONV offered at $100 per share on 02/22/2011
Each share 6.25% Mandatory Conv. Preferred Ser. A $1 par exchanged for (2.6717) shares new Common 1¢ par 03/03/2014
(Additional Information in Active)

UNISYSTEMS INC (DE)
Merged into UI Merger Corp. 5/31/2000
Each share Common 1¢ par exchanged for $35 cash

UNIT CORP. OF AMERICA
Reorganized as Unit Holding Corp. 00/00/1935
Details not available

UNIT DRILLING & EXPL CO (DE)
Stock Dividend - 100% 12/15/1980
Merged into Unit Corp. 09/15/1986
Each share Common 20¢ par exchanged for (1) share Common 20¢ par

UNIT HOLDING CORP.
Name changed to Fuller Manufacturing Co. 00/00/1936
Fuller Manufacturing Co. acquired by Eaton Manufacturing Co. 08/15/1958 which name changed to Eaton Yale & Towne Inc. 12/31/1965 which name changed to Eaton Corp. (OH) 04/21/1971 which reincorporated in Ireland as Eaton Corp. PLC 11/30/2012

UNIT INSTRS INC (CA)
Merged into United States Filter Corp. (New) 01/22/1999
Each share Common 15¢ par exchanged for (0.43609) share Common 1¢ par
(See United States Filter Corp. (New))

UNIT OPTION CORP. OF AMERICA (CA)
Name changed to Securities Clearing Corp. of America 7/28/72
(See Securities Clearing Corp. of America)

UNIT RAIL ANCHOR CORP. (NJ)
Merged into Dyson-Kissner Corp. 5/15/64
Each share $5.50 Preferred $100 par exchanged for (1) share $5.50 Preferred $100 par
(See Dyson-Kissner Corp.)

UNITAS JOHNNY QUARTERBACK CLUBS INC (DE)
Name changed to Energy Recycling Corp. and Common 10¢ par changed to $0.001 par 8/11/89
(See Energy Recycling Corp.)

UNITAX INC (CA)
Stock Dividend - 75% 01/02/1974
Merged into Tymshare, Inc. 09/02/1976
Each share Common 10¢ par exchanged for (0.25) share Common no par
(See Tymshare, Inc.)

UNITCAST CORP (OH)
Merged into Midland-Ross Corp. 01/31/1968
Each share Common $5 par exchanged for (0.225) share $5 Conv. Preferred Ser. B no par
(See Midland-Ross Corp.)

UNITE CAP CORP (ON)
Merged into Lakeside Minerals Inc. 06/27/2014
Each share Common no par exchanged for (0.4884) share new Common no par and (0.2442) Common Stock Purchase Warrant expiring 06/24/2017
Lakeside Minerals Inc. name changed to Lineage Grow Co. Ltd. 07/25/2017

UNITEC INDS INC (DE)
Reincorporated 12/31/1968
State of incorporation changed from (MD) to (DE) 12/31/1968
Name changed to Campbell Chain Co. 11/20/1972
(See Campbell Chain Co.)

UNITEC INTL CTLS CORP (BC)
Delisted from Toronto Venture Stock Exchange 03/30/2005

UNITECH ENERGY CORP (AB)
Merged into Unitech Energy Resources Inc. 07/07/2006
Each share Common no par exchanged for (0.4603343) share Common no par
Unitech Energy Resources Inc. recapitalized as Jadela Oil Corp. 07/21/2011 which recapitalized as Tenth Avenue Petroleum Corp. 05/19/2015

UNITECH ENERGY RES INC (AB)
Recapitalized as Jadela Oil Corp. 07/21/2011
Each share Common no par exchanged for (0.1) share Common no par
Jadela Oil Corp. recapitalized as Tenth Avenue Petroleum Corp. 05/19/2015

UNITECH INDS INC NEW (DE)
Name changed to UTTI Corp. 01/14/1999
UTTI Corp. recapitalized as Vianet Technology Group, Ltd. 02/05/2007 which name changed to Oncology Med, Inc. 04/12/2007 which recapitalized as Bellatora Inc. 09/28/2016

UNITECH INDS INC OLD (CA)
Reorganized under the laws of Delaware as Unitech Industries Inc. (New) 12/23/1996
Each share Common no par exchanged for (0.4) share Common $0.001 par
Unitech Industries Inc. (New) name changed to UTTI Corp. 01/14/1999 which recapitalized as Vianet Technology Group, Ltd. 02/05/2007 which name changed to Oncology Med, Inc. 04/12/2007 which recapitalized as Bellatora Inc. 09/28/2016

UNITECH PLC (UNITED KINGDOM)
Merged into Siebe PLC 10/23/1996
Each Sponsored ADR for Ordinary exchanged for $48.37 cash

UNITECH WTR & RENEWABLE ENERGY INC (NV)
Charter revoked 02/02/2015

UNITED ACCOUNTING MACHINE CO.
Acquired by Remington Rand, Inc. 00/00/1934
Details not available

UNITED ACQUISITION II CORP (DE)
Recapitalized as U S Mobile Services Inc. 05/01/1998
Each share Common $0.001 par exchanged for (0.04) share Common $0.001 par
(See U S Mobile Services Inc.)

UNITED AERO PRODUCTS CORP. (NJ)
Merged into Aero-Chatillon Corp. 12/03/1962
Each share Common 10¢ par exchanged for (1) share Common 10¢ par
Aero-Chatillon Corp. merged into Macrodyne-Chatillon Corp. 04/01/1969 which merged into Macrodyne Industries, Inc. 01/01/1974
(See Macrodyne Industries, Inc.)

UNITED AEROTEST LABORATORIES INC. (NY)
Completely liquidated 12/13/1966
Each share Common 10¢ par exchanged for first and distribution of (0.1708) share Ogden Corp. Common 50¢ par
Ogden Corp. name changed to Covanta Energy Corp. 03/14/2001
(See Covanta Energy Corp.)

UNITED AIR LINES INC (DE)
4.50% Preferred $100 par called for redemption 04/01/1948
4.50% Preferred 1952 Ser. $100 par called for redemption 10/10/1955
Common 10 par changed to $5 par and (1) additional share issued 05/09/1966
Under plan of reorganization each share 5.50% Preferred 1960 Ser. $100 par and Common $5 par automatically became (1) share UAL, Inc. 5.50% Prior Preferred $100 par and Common $5 par respectively 08/01/1969

UAL, Inc. name changed to Allegis Corp. 04/30/1987 which name changed to UAL Corp. 05/27/1988
(See UAL Corp.)

UNITED AIR LINES TRANSPORT CORP.
Name changed to United Air Lines, Inc. and Capital Stock $5 par changed to Common $10 par 00/00/1943
United Air Lines, Inc. reorganized as UAL, Inc. 08/01/1969 which name changed to Allegis Corp. 04/30/1987 which name changed to UAL Corp. 05/27/1988
(See UAL Corp.)

UNITED AIR SPECIALISTS INC (OH)
Each share old Common no par exchanged (0.5) share new Common no par 02/05/1973
New Common no par split (3) for (1) by issuance of (2) additional shares 06/02/1994
New Common no par split (5) for (4) by issuance of (0.25) additional share payable 02/02/1996 to holders of record 01/19/1996
Merged into Clarcor 02/28/1997
Each share new Common no par exchanged for (0.3702116) share Common $1 par
(See Clarcor)

UNITED AIRCRAFT & TRANSPORT CORP.
Reorganized as United Aircraft Corp., Boeing Airplane Co. and United Air Lines Transport Corp. 00/00/1934
(See each company's listing)

UNITED AIRCRAFT CORP (DE)
4% Preference 1955 Ser. $100 par called for redemption 10/05/1965
4% Preference 1956 Ser. $100 par called for redemption 10/05/1965
Common $5 par split (3) for (2) by issuance of (0.5) additional share 10/29/1965
Stock Dividends - 20% 05/25/1951; 50% 09/26/1955; 20% 12/12/1957
Name changed to United Technologies Corp. 04/30/1975

UNITED AIRCRAFT MANUFACTURING CORP.
Dissolved 00/00/1936
Details not available

UNITED AIRCRAFT PRODS INC (OH)
5.50% Preferred $20 par called for redemption 01/10/1946
Each share Common $1 par exchanged for (2) shares Common 50¢ par 10/11/1946
Common 50¢ par split (5) for (4) by issuance of (0.25) additional share 12/08/1976
Common 50¢ par split (4) for (3) by issuance of (1/3) additional share 01/25/1983
Stock Dividends - 10% 01/18/1978; 10% 01/26/1979; 10% 01/15/1980; 10% 01/18/1981; 10% 01/24/1986
Acquired by Parker-Hannifin Corp. 09/15/1986
Each share Common 50¢ par exchanged for $26 cash

UNITED ALA BANCSHARES INC (AL)
Merged into First Bancgroup-Alabama, Inc. 09/02/1975
Each share Common $1 par exchanged for (0.1304087) share Common $4 par
First Bancgroup-Alabama, Inc. name changed to Firstgulf Bancorp 03/30/1984
(See Firstgulf Bancorp)

UNITED AMER BK (CHICAGO IL)
Common $10 par changed to $5 par and (1) additional share issued 03/21/1968
Common $5 par changed to $3 par and (0.25) additional shares issued 12/23/1982

Declared insolvent by FDIC 04/26/1984
No stockholders' equity

UNITED AMER EHEALTH TECH INC (BC)
Name changed 06/01/2000
Name changed from United America Enterprises Ltd. to United America eHealth Technologies Inc. 06/01/2000
Delisted from Toronto Venture Stock Exchange 06/05/2002

UNITED AMER GROUP INC (IA)
Placed in receivership 10/18/1974
No stockholders' equity

UNITED AMER INDTY LTD (CAYMAN ISLANDS)
Reorganized under the laws of Ireland as Global Indemnity PLC 07/02/2010
Each share Class A Common $0.0001 par exchanged for (0.5) share Class A Ordinary $0.0001 par
Global Indemnity PLC (Ireland) reincorporated in Cayman Islands as Global Indemnity Ltd. 11/07/2016

UNITED AMERICAN BANK (JOHNSON CITY, TN)
Name changed to City & County Bank of Washington County (Johnson City, TN) 09/14/1982
City & County Bank of Washington County (Johnson City, TN) name changed to First Peoples Bank of Washington County (Johnson City, TN) 07/25/1983
(See First Peoples Bank of Washington County (Johnson City, TN))

UNITED AMERN BK (KNOXVILLE, TN)
Name changed 11/01/1976
Name changed from United American Bank, N.A. (Knoxville, TN) to United American Bank in Knoxville (Knoxville, TN) 11/01/1976
Common $5 par changed to $2.50 par and (1.2) shares issued to effect a (2) for (1) split and a 10% stock dividend 09/15/1977
Declared insolvent and ordered closed by state banking authorities 02/14/1983
No stockholders' equity

UNITED AMERN BK (SAN MATEO, CA)
Each share old Common no par exchanged for (0.02) share new Common no par 03/24/2017
Merged into Heritage Commerce Corp. 05/04/2018
Each share new Common no par exchanged for (2.1644) shares Common no par

UNITED AMERICAN BANK (WESTMINSTER, CA)
Merged into Guaranty Bank (Los Angeles, CA) 10/14/1994
Each share Common no par exchanged for $5.77 cash

UNITED AMERICAN BOSCH CORP. (NY)
Name changed to American Bosch Corp. and Capital Stock no par changed to $1 par 09/27/1938
American Bosch Corp. name changed to American Bosch Arma Corp. 07/21/1954 which name changed to Ambac Industries, Inc. 04/30/1968 which merged into United Technologies Corp. 07/14/1978

UNITED AMERN ENERGY INC (TN)
Administratively dissolved for non-payment of taxes 09/03/1984

UNITED AMERN HEALTHCARE CORP (MI)
Common no par split (5) for (4) by issuance of (0.25) additional share 03/25/1993
Reincorporated under the laws of

Nevada and Common no par changed to $0.001 par 08/01/2014

UNITED AMERN INC (CO)
Name changed to Cardiff International Inc. (CO) 12/04/1989
Cardiff International Inc. (CO) reorganized in Florida 09/12/2014 which name changed to Cardiff Lexington Corp. 02/07/2018

UNITED AMERN INDS INC (DE)
Charter cancelled and declared inoperative and void for non-payment of taxes 04/15/1971

UNITED AMERICAN INSURANCE CO. OF PENNSYLVANIA (PA)
Merged into Allemannia Fire Insurance Co. of Pittsburgh 09/30/1931
Each share Capital Stock $50 par exchanged for (3.2) shares Common $10 par
Allemannia Fire Insurance Co. of Pittsburgh merged into United States Fire Insurance Co. 05/31/1951
(See United States Fire Insurance Co.)

UNITED AMERN INS CO (TX)
Merged into Liberty National Insurance Holding Co. 12/31/1981
Each share Class A Common $1 par exchanged for $120 principal amount of NU Life Insurance Co. 4-yr. 11% Restricted Surplus Installment Notes due 01/18/1986
Each share Class B Common $1 par exchanged for $120 principal amount of NU Life Insurance Co. 4-yr. 11% Restricted Surplus Installment Notes due 01/18/1986

UNITED AMERICAN INVESTMENT CO. (GA)
Common no par changed to 1¢ par 06/18/1956
Merged into United American Life Insurance Co. (GA) 03/14/1961
Each share Common 1¢ par exchanged for (1.1) shares Common 50¢ par
United American Life Insurance Co. (GA) merged into United Family Life Insurance Co. 04/09/1962 which reorganized as Interfinancial Inc. 07/01/1969
(See Interfinancial Inc.)

UNITED AMERICAN LIFE INSURANCE CO. (GA)
Merged into United Family Life Insurance Co. 04/09/1962
Each share Common 50¢ par exchanged for (0.5) share Common $1 par
United Family Life Insurance Co. reorganized as Interfinancial Inc. 07/01/1969
(See Interfinancial Inc.)

UNITED AMERN LIFE INS CO (CO)
Stock Dividends - 15% 00/00/1950; 20% 06/30/1960; 10% 05/01/1961; 10% 05/15/1962; 10% 05/15/1963; 10% 05/15/1964; 10% 05/15/1965; 10% 06/15/1966; 50% 04/14/1967; 10% 05/10/1968; 10% 05/15/1970; 10% 05/14/1971
Under plan of merger name changed to World Service Life Insurance Co. (CO) 07/31/1978
World Service Life Insurance Co. (CO) merged into Western Preferred Corp. 02/21/1979
(See Western Preferred Corp.)

UNITED AMERICAN PUBLISHING CO. INC. (NY)
Charter revoked for failure to file reports and pay fees 12/15/1933

UNITED-AMERICAN SVGS BK (PITTSBURGH, PA)
Acquired by Emclaire Financial Corp. 04/29/2016

Each share Common 1¢ par exchanged for $42.67 cash

UNITED AMERICAN SHARE CORP.
Name changed to United American Utilities, Inc. 00/00/1930
United American Utilities, Inc. reorganized as Community Gas & Power Co. 00/00/1933 which reorganized as Minneapolis Gas Co. 07/30/1948 which name changed to Minnesota Gas Co. 05/10/1974
(See Minnesota Gas Co.)

UNITED AMERICAN UTILITIES, INC.
Reorganized as Community Gas & Power Co. 00/00/1933
Details not available

UNITED AMERS BK (NEW YORK, NY)
Par value changed from $4 par to 40¢ par 08/22/1980
Name changed to Banco Central of New York (New York, NY) 12/19/1980
Banco Central of New York (New York, NY) name changed to Banco Central Hispano - USA (New York, NY) 10/01/1992 which name changed to BCH - USA (New York, NY) 12/04/1998
(See BCH - USA (New York, NY))

UNITED AMUSEMENT CORP. LTD. (QC)
Each share Class A $100 par exchanged for (4) shares old Class A no par in 1928
Recapitalized in 1951
Each share old Class A no par exchanged for (4) shares new Class A no par
Each share 1931 VTC for old Class A no par exchanged for (4) 1931 VTC's for new Class A no par
Each share 1948 VTC for old Class A no par exchanged for (4) 1948 VTC's for new Class A no par
Each share old Class B no par exchanged for (4) shares new Class B no par
1931 Voting Trust Agreement terminated 1/1/57
Each VTC for new Class A no par exchanged for (1) share new Class A no par
1948 Voting Trust Agreement terminated 8/31/60
Each VTC for new Class A no par exchanged for (1) share new Class A no par
Name changed to United Theatres Ltd. - Cinemas Unis Ltee. 10/31/70
United Theatres Ltd. - Cinemas Unis Ltee. name changed to Cinemas Unis Ltee. in 1979
(See Cinemas Unis Ltee.)

UNITED ARIZONA COPPER MINING & SMELTING CO. (AZ)
Charter revoked for failure to file reports and pay fees 8/21/27

UNITED ARK CORP (AR)
Merged into BNL Financial Corp. 11/1/94
Each share Common no par exchanged for (0.9) share Common no par

UNITED ARTISTS COMMUNICATIONS INC (MD)
Common $1 par split (2) for (1) by issuance of (1) additional share 2/28/85
Common $1 par reclassified as Class A Common $1 par 3/10/86
Class A Common $1 par split (2) for (1) by issuance of (1) additional share 5/28/86
Class A Common 1¢ par reclassified as Common 1¢ par 6/18/87
Stock Dividend - 100% 2/28/83
Merged into United Artists Entertainment Co. 5/25/89
Each share Common 1¢ par exchanged for (1) share Class A

Common $0.001 par and (1) share Conv. Class B Common $0.001 par
United Artists Entertainment Co. merged into Tele-Communications, Inc. (Old) 12/2/91 which merged into Tele-Communications, Inc. (New) 8/5/94 which merged into AT&T Corp. 3/9/99 which merged into AT&T Inc. 11/18/2005

UNITED ARTISTS CORP (DE)
Incorporated 04/17/1917
Common $1 par and Class B Common $1 par split (2) for (1) respectively by issuance of (1) additional share 03/30/1966
Merged into Transamerica Corp. 01/16/1970
Each share Common $1 par exchanged for $35 cash

UNITED ARTISTS CORP NEW (DE)
Incorporated 6/1/81
Name changed to MGM/UA Communications Co. 9/2/86
(See MGM/UA Communications Co.)

UNITED ARTISTS ENTMT CO (DE)
Merged into Tele-Communications, Inc. (Old) 12/2/91
Each share 12.875% Compounding Preferred 1¢ par exchanged for (1) share 12-7/8% Compounding Preferred Ser. A $1 par
Each share Class A Common $0.001 par exchanged for (1.02) shares Class A $1 par
Each share Conv. Class B Common $0.001 par exchanged for (1.02) shares Class A $1 par
Tele-Communications, Inc. (Old) merged into Tele-Communications, Inc. (New) 8/5/94 which merged into AT&T Corp. 3/9/99 which merged into AT&T Inc. 11/18/2005

UNITED ARTISTS THEATRE CIRCUIT, INC. (MD)
Each share 7% Preferred $100 par exchanged for (1) share 5% Preferred $100 par, (3-1/3) shares Common no par and $15 cash in 1937
Common no par changed to $1 par in 1955
5% Preferred $100 par called for redemption 3/15/62
Stock Dividends - 25% 7/10/72; 25% 3/2/76; 25% 5/31/78; 200% 7/20/81
Name changed to United Artists Communications, Inc. 1/19/82
United Artists Communications, Inc. merged into United Artists Entertainment Co. 5/25/89 which merged into Tele-Communications, Inc. (Old) 12/2/91 which merged into Tele-Communications, Inc. (New) 8/5/94 which merged into AT&T Corp. 3/9/99 which merged into AT&T Inc. 11/18/2005

UNITED ASBESTOS INC (QC)
Merged into Campbell Resources Inc. (New) 06/08/1983
Each share Capital Stock no par exchanged for (1) share Preference Ser. 1 no par and (0.3) share Common no par
(See Campbell Resources Inc. (New))

UNITED ASBESTOS LTD (QC)
Merged into United Asbestos Inc. 06/29/1973
Each share Capital Stock $1 par exchanged for (1) share Common no par
United Asbestos Inc. merged into Campbell Resources Inc. (New) 06/08/1983
(See Campbell Resources Inc. (New))

UNITED ASSET MGMT CORP (DE)
Common 1¢ par split (2) for (1) by issuance of (1) additional share payable 6/21/96 to holders of record 6/7/96 Ex date - 6/24/96
Merged into Old Mutual plc 10/6/2000

Each share Common 1¢ par exchanged for $25 cash

UNITED ATHLETES INC (NV)
Name changed to S2C Global Systems, Inc. 02/04/2005
S2C Global Systems, Inc. name changed to VIPR Corp. 08/06/2014

UNITED AUSTRALIAN OIL INC (DE)
Common 56¢ par changed to 10¢ par 10/20/67
Charter proclaimed inoperative and void for non-payment of taxes 4/15/70

UNITED AUTO GROUP INC (DE)
Issue Information - 6,250,000 shares COM offered at $30 per share on 10/23/1996
Common $0.0001 par split (2) for (1) by issuance of (1) additional share payable 06/01/2006 to holders of record 05/11/2006 Ex date - 06/02/2006
Name changed to Penske Automotive Group, Inc. 07/02/2007

UNITED AUTO PARTS INC. (QC)
Name changed to UAP Inc. 10/26/67
(See UAP Inc.)

UNITED AUTOGRAPHIC REGISTER CO. (IL)
Name changed to Uarco, Inc. (IL) 00/00/1946
Uarco, Inc. (IL) reincorporated in Delaware 02/27/1970
(See Uarco, Inc. (DE))

UNITED AUTOMOBILE INSURANCE CO.
Succeeded by Hawkeye Casualty Co. in 1939
Hawkeye Casualty Co. name changed to Hawkeye-Security Insurance Co. in 1950
(See Hawkeye-Security Insurance Co.)

UNITED AUTOMOTIVE INDUSTRIES, INC. (CA)
Merged into Interdyne Co. 12/11/1968
Each share Common $1 par exchanged for (0.0965) share Common 25¢ par

UNITED BANCORP (DE)
Each share Common 1¢ par exchanged for (0.125) share Common $0.0125 par 04/01/1991
Name changed to United London Group, Inc. 09/05/1991

UNITED BANCORP (OR)
Each share old Common $2.50 par exchanged for (1/60) share new Common $2.50 par 08/28/1996
Merged into PremierWest Bancorp 05/08/2000
Each share new Common $2.50 par exchanged for (1.971) shares Common no par
(See PremierWest Bancorp)

UNITED BANCORP ARIZ (DE)
Common $5 par split (4) for (3) by issuance of (1/3) additional share 3/3/80
Common $5 par split (3) for (2) by issuance of (0.5) additional share 6/1/82
Common $5 par split (3) for (2) by issuance of (0.5) additional share 2/24/84
Common $5 par split (3) for (2) by issuance of (0.5) additional share 5/17/85
Acquired by Union Bancorp 1/8/87
Each share Common $5 par exchanged for $33 cash

UNITED BANCORP INC (MI)
Common no par split (2) for (1) by issuance of (1) additional share payable 05/31/2007 to holders of record 05/11/2007 Ex date - 06/01/2007
Stock Dividends - 50% 06/15/1988; 5% payable 05/30/1999 to holders of record 05/01/1999; 5% payable 05/30/2000 to holders of record 05/01/2000; 5% payable 05/30/2001 to holders of record 05/01/2001 Ex date - 04/27/2001; 5% payable 05/30/2002 to holders of record 05/01/2002 Ex date - 04/29/2002; 5% payable 05/30/2003 to holders of record 05/01/2003 Ex date - 04/29/2003; 5% payable 05/28/2004 to holders of record 05/03/2004 Ex date - 04/29/2004; 5% payable 05/31/2006 to holders of record 05/05/2006 Ex date - 05/03/2006
Fixed Rate Perpetual Preferred Ser. A no par called for redemption at $1,000 on 12/27/2013
Merged into Old National Bancorp 07/31/2014
Each share Common no par exchanged for (0.7) share Common no par and $2.66 cash

UNITED BANCORP MD INC (MD)
Stock Dividend - 100% 5/2/86
Merged into First Virginia Banks, Inc. 8/26/87
Each share Common $10 par exchanged for (2.5) shares Common $1 par
First Virginia Banks, Inc. merged into BB&T Corp. 7/1/2003

UNITED BANCORP ME (ME)
Stock Dividend - 11-1/9% 3/27/70
Name changed to Canal Corp. 4/1/76
Canal Corp. merged into Depositors Corp. 8/31/83 which merged into Key Banks Inc. 2/29/84 which name changed to KeyCorp (NY) 8/28/85 which merged into KeyCorp (New) (OH) 3/1/94

UNITED BANCORP OF KENTUCKY INC. (KY)
Merged into National City Corp. 07/01/1995
Each share Common 10¢ par exchanged for (2.35) shares Common $4 par
National City Corp. acquired by PNC Financial Services Group, Inc. 12/31/2008

UNITED BANCORPORATION ALASKA INC (AK)
Stock Dividends - 10% 4/16/85; 10% 5/8/86
Merged into Alliance Bancorporation 12/29/87
Each share Common 20¢ par exchanged for (0.05) share Common $5 par
(See Alliance Bancorporation)

UNITED BANCSHARES FLA INC (FL)
Common $1 par split (2) for (1) by issuance of (1) additional share 06/30/1969
Merged into United First Florida Banks, Inc. 06/29/1973
Each share Common $1 par exchanged for (1.2) shares Common $1 par
United First Florida Banks, Inc. name changed to Flagship Banks, Inc. 06/30/1974 which merged into Sun Banks, Inc. 01/01/1984 which merged into SunTrust Banks, Inc. 07/01/1985

UNITED BANK & TRUST (MADISON, WI)
Preferred $100 par called for redemption 10/1/76
99% held by United Banks of Wisconsin, Inc. as of 1979
Public interest eliminated

UNITED BK & TR CO (BROOKLYN, NY)
Merged into Royal National Bank (New York, NY) 2/28/69
Each share Common $100 par exchanged for (0.9) share Capital Stock $5 par
Royal National Bank (New York, NY) merged into Security National Bank (Hempstead, NY) 5/8/72
(See Security National Bank (Hempstead, NY))

UNITED BK & TR CO (HARTFORD, CT)
Common $10 par changed to $5 par and (1) additional share issued 10/15/1968
Under plan of reorganization each share Common $5 par exchanged for (1) share First Connecticut Bancorp, Inc. Common $10 par 11/12/1970
First Connecticut Bancorp, Inc. merged into Fleet Financial Group, Inc. (Old) 03/17/1986 which merged into Fleet/Norstar Financial Group, Inc. 01/01/1988 which name changed to Fleet Financial Group, Inc. (New) 04/15/1992 which name changed to Fleet Boston Corp. 10/01/1999 which name changed to FleetBoston Financial Corp. 04/18/2000 which merged into Bank of America Corp. 04/01/2004

UNITED BK & TR CO MD (OXEN HILL, MD)
Reorganized as United Bancorp of Maryland, Inc. 7/30/82
Each share Common $10 par exchanged for (1) share Common $10 par
United Bancorp of Maryland, Inc. merged into First Virginia Banks, Inc. 8/26/87 which merged into BB&T Corp. 7/1/2003

UNITED BK (BANGOR, ME)
Acquired by UnitedKingfield Bank (Bangor, ME) 02/07/2000
Details not available

UNITED BK (CHATTANOOGA, TN)
Each share Common $10 par exchanged for (4) shares Common $2.50 par 04/01/1972
Acquired by United American Bank (Knoxville, TN) 00/00/1981
Details not available

UNITED BK (STAR LAKE, NY)
Acquired by St. Lawrence County National Bank (Canton, NY) 09/11/1971
Details not available

UNITED BK (TACOMA, WA)
Common $5 par split (3) for (2) by issuance of (0.5) additional share 12/18/85
Acquired by Rainier Bancorporation 3/15/87
Each share Common $5 par exchanged for (0.843) share Common $2.50 par
Rainier Bancorporation acquired by Security Pacific Corp. 8/31/87 which merged into BankAmerica Corp. (Old) 4/22/92 which merged into BankAmerica Corp. (New) 9/30/98 which name changed to Bank of America Corp. 4/28/99

UNITED BK (UHRICHSVILLE, OH)
Acquired by Banc One Corp. 10/01/1986
Details not available

UNITED BK ARIZ (PHOENIX, AZ)
Reorganized as UB Financial Corp. 4/30/70
Each share Common $5 par exchanged for (1) share Common $5 par
UB Financial Corp. name changed to United Bancorp of Arizona 10/17/78
(See United Bancorp of Arizona)

UNITED BK CORP N Y (NY)
Conv. Preferred Ser. A $20 par called for redemption 03/10/1981
Conv. Preferred Ser. B $20 par called for redemption 05/15/1981
Name changed to Norstar Bancorp Inc. 01/04/1982
Norstar Bancorp Inc. merged into

Fleet/Norstar Financial Group, Inc. 01/01/1988 which name changed to Fleet Financial Group, Inc. (New) 04/15/1992 which name changed to Fleet Boston Corp. 10/01/1999 which name changed to FleetBoston Financial Corp. 04/18/2000 which merged into Bank of America Corp. 04/01/2004

UNITED BK CORP N Y (NY)
Each share old Common exchanged for (0.01) share new Common 12/24/1994
Note: Holders of (99) or fewer shares received $4.85 cash per share
Holders of (100) or more shares also received an undetermined amount of IFS Catskill L.L.C. Shares of Bene. Int.
(See IFS Catskill L.L.C.)
Liquidation completed
Each share new Common received initial distribution of $100 cash payable 04/07/1996 to holders of record 03/31/1996
Each share new Common received second distribution of $25 cash payable 08/22/1996 to holders of record 06/30/1996
Each share new Common received third distribution of $98 cash payable 10/11/1996 to holders of record 09/30/1996
Each share new Common received fourth and final distribution of $150 cash payable 01/20/1997
Note: Certificates were not required to be exchanged and are without value

UNITED BK DENVER N A (DENVER, CO)
Acquired by United Banks of Colorado, Inc. 09/01/1970
Details not available

UNITED BK F S B (SAN FRANCISCO, CA)
Capital Stock no par split (6) for (5) by issuance of (0.2) additional share 1/31/84
Reorganized as United Bank, S.S.B. (San Francisco, CA) 5/23/84
(See United Bank, S.S.B. (San Francisco, CA))

UNITED BK ORE (OAK GROVE, OR)
Bank closed by State Banking Commissioner 3/2/84
Stockholders' equity undetermined

UNITED BK S S B (SAN FRANCISCO, CA)
Stock Dividend - 10% 05/31/1984
Declared insolvent by Federal Home Loan Bank Board 03/28/1986
No stockholders' equity

UNITED BANKERS INC (DE)
Stock Dividends - 10% 10/11/1983; 10% 11/30/1984; 10% 01/24/1986
Filed a petition under Chapter 7 Federal Bankruptcy Code 03/09/1990
No stockholders' equity

UNITED BANKERS LIFE INS CO (TX)
Placed in receivership 10/28/1982
No stockholders' equity

UNITED BKS COLO INC (CO)
Common $5 par changed to $2.50 par and (1) additional share issued 05/15/1981
Merged into Norwest Corp. 04/19/1991
Each share Adjustable Rate Preferred Ser. A $10 par exchanged for $51.50 cash
Each share Common $2.50 par exchanged for (1.22) shares Common $1-2/3 par
Norwest Corp. name changed to Wells Fargo & Co. (New) 11/02/1998

UNITED BKS CORP (NH)
Merged into BankEast Corp. 2/27/87
Each share Common $2 par exchanged for (1.86) shares Common $1 par
(See BankEast Corp.)

UNITED BKS WIS INC (WI)
Each share Common $10 par exchanged for (2) shares Common $5 par 03/23/1973
Stock Dividends - 10% 07/14/1978; 10% 07/20/1979; 10% 04/20/1981; 10% 01/20/1982
Merged into Valley Bancorporation 08/16/1985
Each share Common $5 par exchanged for $29.25 cash

UNITED BATA RES LTD (BC)
Completely liquidated 02/05/1971
Each share Common 50¢ par exchanged for first and final distribution of (1/3) share Pan Ocean Oil Corp. Common 1¢ par
(See Pan Ocean Oil Corp.)

UNITED BENEFIT FIRE INSURANCE CO. (NE)
Capital Stock $10 par changed to $7 par in 1954
Capital Stock $7 par changed to $6 par in 1956
Capital Stock $6 par changed to $5 par 1/30/61
Assets sold for benefit of creditors 11/24/65
No stockholders' equity

UNITED BENEFIT LIFE INS CO (NE)
Stock Dividends - 400% 03/10/1965; 20% 06/10/1969; 20% 06/01/1972; 25% 06/01/1976
Majority acquired by Mutual of Omaha Insurance Co. through voluntary purchase offer which expired 05/05/1980
Public interest eliminated

UNITED BEVERAGES LTD (BC)
Struck off register and declared dissolved for failure to file returns 7/28/95

UNITED BISCUIT CO.
Dissolved in 1929

UNITED BISCUIT CO AMER (DE)
Stock Dividend - 100% 5/23/47
Name changed to Keebler Co. 6/8/66
Keebler Co. merged into United Biscuits (Holdings) Ltd. 4/24/74

UNITED BISCUITS GROUP (UNITED KINGDOM)
Each Sponsored ADR for Ordinary 25p par exchanged for (0.888888) Sponsored ADR for Ordinary 29p par and $0.4528 cash 7/20/98
Acquired by Rothchild 8/17/2000
Each Sponsored ADR for Ordinary 29p par exchanged for $3.9384 cash

UNITED BISON RES LTD (ON)
Merged into Nalcap Holdings Inc. 04/25/1991
Each share Class A no par exchanged for (0.12987012) share new Common no par
Nalcap Holdings Inc. recapitalized as Arbatax International Inc. (Canada) 03/28/1996 which reincorporated in Yukon 08/06/1996 which name changed to MFC Bancorp Ltd. (YT) 03/03/1997 which reincorporated in British Columbia 11/03/2004 which name changed to KHD Humboldt Wedag International Ltd. 11/01/2005 which reorganized as Terra Nova Royalty Corp. 03/30/2010 which name changed to MFC Industrial Ltd. 09/30/2011 which name changed to MFC Bancorp Ltd. (BC) 02/16/2016
(See MFC Bancorp Ltd. (BC))

UNITED BLDG SVCS CORP (DE)
Charter cancelled and declared inoperative and void for non-payment of taxes 3/1/90

UNITED BOATBUILDERS, INC. (WA)
Name changed to Uniflite, Inc. 10/19/67
(See Uniflite, Inc.)

UNITED BOLERO DEV CORP (BC)
Reincorporated under the laws of Ontario as Bolero Resources Corp. 09/18/2007
Canada Carbon Inc. 10/05/2012

UNITED BOND & SHARE CORP.
Reorganized as United Bond & Share, Ltd. in 1931 which was completely liquidated 4/25/56

UNITED BOND & SHARE LTD. (QC)
Completely liquidated 4/25/56
Each share Common no par exchanged for first and final distribution of $29.21 cash

UNITED BONDING INS CO (IN)
Name changed to United International Inc. 11/10/1967
(See United International Inc.)

UNITED BOWLING CTRS INC (DE)
Common $1 par changed to 1¢ par 01/25/1971
Merged into Treadway Companies, Inc. 09/18/1973
Each share Common 1¢ par exchanged for (1/3) share Common $1 par
(See Treadway Companies, Inc.)

UNITED BRANDS CO (NJ)
$3 Conv. Preferred no par called for redemption 03/27/1986
$1.20 Conv. Preference Ser. A no par called for redemption 09/19/1986
$3.20 Conv. Preference Ser. B no par called for redemption 09/19/1986
Common $1 par changed to 33¢ par and (2) additional shares issued 05/31/1988
Name changed to Chiquita Brands International, Inc. 03/20/1990
(See Chiquita Brands International, Inc.)

UNITED BRD & CARTON CORP (NJ)
6% Preferred called for redemption 04/15/1955
Common $10 par split (5) for (4) by issuance of (0.25) additional share 02/27/1963
Common $10 par changed to $5 par and (1) additional share issued 01/14/1966
Name changed to Garber (A.L.) Co., Inc. (NJ) 12/31/1971
Garber (A.L.) Co., Inc. (NJ) reincorporated in Delaware 05/31/1972 which merged into Wheelabrator-Frye Inc. 09/18/1973

UNITED BRICK & TILE CO. (DE)
Liquidation completed in 1954

UNITED BUCKINGHAM FGHT LINES INC (SD)
Completely liquidated 01/06/1975
Each share Class A Common $1 par exchanged for first and final distribution of $9.40 cash
Each share Class B Common $1 par exchanged for first and final distribution of $9.40 cash

UNITED-BUCKINGHAM FREIGHT LINES (SD)
Name changed to United-Buckingham Freight Lines, Inc. 6/24/67
(See United-Buckingham Freight Lines, Inc.)

UNITED BUFFADISON MINES LTD (ON)
Acquired by Western-Buff Mines & Oils Ltd. 5/20/69
Each share Common $1 par exchanged for (1) share Common 50¢ par
(See Western-Buff Mines & Oils Ltd.)

UNITED BUSINESS MEDIA PLC (UNITED KINGDOM)
Each Sponsored ADR for Ordinary 25p par received distribution of (0.31818) additional ADR for Ordinary and $7.01 $7.01 cash payable 04/30/2001 to holders of record 04/20/2001
Basis changed from (1:2) to (1:1) 04/23/2001
ADR agreement terminated 03/22/2005
Each ADR for Ordinary exchanged for $8.8916 cash

UNITED BUSINESS PUBLISHERS, INC.
Liquidated in 1934

UNITED BUYING SVC INTL INC (DE)
Charter cancelled and declared inoperative and void for non-payment of taxes 3/1/91

UNITED CABLE TELEVISION CORP (DE)
Common 10¢ par split (2) for (1) by issuance of (1) additional share 10/15/79
Common 10¢ par split (3) for (2) by issuance of (0.5) additional share 7/15/85
Common 10¢ par split (3) for (2) by issuance of (0.5) additional share 3/17/86
Common 10¢ par split (3) for (2) by issuance of (0.5) additional share 8/31/87
Stock Dividend - 100% 12/23/80
Merged into United Artists Entertainment Co. 5/25/89
Each share Common 10¢ par exchanged for $38.50 cash

UNITED CABLE TELEVISION DENVER INC (DE)
Through purchase offer 99.5% acquired by United Cable Television Corp. as of 05/26/1983
Public interest eliminated

UNITED CALIF BK (LOS ANGELES, CA)
Merged into Western Bancorporation 1/16/78
Each share Capital Stock $12.50 par exchanged for (1.667) shares Capital Stock $2 par
Western Bancorporation name changed to First Interstate Bancorp 6/1/81 which merged into Wells Fargo & Co. (Old) 4/1/96 which merged into Wells Fargo & Co. (New) 11/2/98

UNITED CAMBRIDGE MINES LTD (BC)
Recapitalized as Consolidated Cambridge Mines Ltd. 12/27/1989
Each share Capital Stock no par exchanged for (0.2) share Common no par
Consolidated Cambridge Mines Ltd. name changed to Cambridge Environmental Systems Inc. (BC) 07/20/1993 which reincorporated in Alberta 12/09/1993
(See Cambridge Environmental Systems Inc.)

UNITED CAN & GLASS CO. (DE)
Merged into Hunt Foods & Industries, Inc. 12/05/1958
Each share Preferred Ser. A $50 par exchanged for (0.5) share 5% Preferred Ser. A $100 par
Each share Common $2.50 par exchanged for (1.25) shares Common $5 par
Hunt Foods & Industries, Inc. merged into Simon (Norton), Inc. 07/17/1968 which merged into Esmark, Inc. (Inc. 03/14/1969) 09/09/1983
(See Esmark, Inc. (Inc. 03/14/1969))

UNITED-CANADIAN OIL CORP. (DE)
No longer in existence having become inoperative and void for non-payment of taxes 04/01/1958

UNITED CDN SHS LTD (CANADA)
Merged 12/31/1979
Capital Stock no par split (4) for (1)

by issuance of (3) additional shares 12/15/1972
Merged from United Canadian Shares Ltd. (MB) to United Canadian Shares, Ltd. (Canada) 12/31/1979
Each share Capital Stock no par exchanged for (1) share Common no par
Merged into Tanbridge Corp. 04/30/1999
Each share Common no par exchanged for (2) shares Common no par
(See Tanbridge Corp.)

UNITED CANSO OIL & GAS LTD (NS)
Reincorporated 06/06/1980
Voting Trust Agreement terminated 04/20/1964
Each VTC for Capital Stock $1 par exchanged for (1) share Capital Stock $1 par
Place of incorporation changed from (Canada) to (NS) 06/06/1980
Stock Dividend - 10% 08/18/1980
Placed in Receivership by Court Order 04/13/1988
No stockholders' equity

UNITED CAP CORP (DE)
Common 10¢ par split (2) for (1) by issuance of (1) additional share payable 08/29/2003 to holders of record 08/15/2003 Ex date - 09/02/2003
Shares reacquired 10/06/2015
Each share Common 10¢ par exchanged for $32 cash

UNITED CAP FDG PARTNERSHIP L P
9.625% Guaranteed Capital Preferred Securities called for redemption at $25 on 09/25/2000

UNITED CAP HLDGS INC (CO)
Administratively dissolved 02/01/2001

UNITED CAP INVT CORP (MN)
Acquired by Analysts International Corp. 02/15/1969
Each share Common 10¢ par exchanged for (0.083333) share Common 10¢ par
(See Analysts International Corp.)

UNITED CAP LIFE INVS CORP (MN)
Name changed to United Capital Investors Corp. 08/25/1968
United Capital Investors Corp. acquired by Analysts International Corp. 02/15/1969
(See Analysts International Corp.)

UNITED CAPE COD CRANBERRY CO (MA)
Voluntarily dissolved 11/16/1977
Details not available

UNITED CAP TR I
Trust Preferred Securities called for redemption at $25 on 06/20/2002

UNITED CARBON CO. (DE)
Common no par split (3) for (2) by issuance of (0.5) additional share 12/27/1954
Stock Dividend - 100% 05/14/1947
Liquidation completed
Each share Common no par stamped to indicate initial distribution of $100 cash 03/04/1963
Each share Stamped Common no par exchanged for second distribution of $7.26 cash 06/21/1963
Each share Stamped Common no par received third distribution of $0.45 cash 02/14/1964
Each share Stamped Common no par received fourth and final distribution of $0.047 cash 03/15/1968

UNITED CARDIGAN DEV LTD (BC)
Struck off register and declared dissolved for failure to file returns 07/28/1980

UNITED CARINA RES CORP (CANADA)
Name changed to United Uranium Corp. (Canada) 07/25/2007
United Uranium Corp. (Canada) reincorporated in Saskatchewan 11/05/2008 which reorganized in British Columbia as Karoo Exploration Corp. 09/15/2013 which recapitalized as Bruin Point Helium Corp. 12/11/2017 which name changed to American Helium Inc. 05/11/2018

UNITED CAROLINA BANCSHARES CORP (NC)
Common $5 par changed to $4 par and (0.25) share issued 12/14/1972
Common $4 par split (2) for (1) by issuance of (1) additional share 09/14/1987
Common $4 par split (3) for (2) by issuance of (0.5) additional share payable 02/07/1996 to holders of record 01/31/1996
Stock Dividends - 10% 01/11/1971; 10% 10/29/1976; 10% 07/10/1981; 50% 07/18/1982; 10% 07/19/1984
Merged into BB&T Corp. 07/01/1997
Each share Common $4 par exchanged for (1.135) shares Common $5 par

UNITED-CARR FASTENER CORP. (DE)
Reincoporated 12/31/1954
State of incorporation changed from (MA) to (DE) and Common no par changed to $5 par 12/31/1954
Common $5 par changed to $2.50 par and (1) additional share issued 09/04/1959
Stock Dividend - 100% 03/30/1950
Name changed to United-Carr Inc. 04/28/1964
United-Carr Inc. merged into TRW Inc.
(See TRW Inc.)

UNITED-CARR INC. (DE)
Common $2.50 par split (2) for (1) by issuance of (1) additional share 01/31/1966
Merged into TRW Inc. 02/19/1968
Each share Common $2.50 par exchanged for (0.5) share $4.40 Conv. Preference Ser. 1 no par
(See TRW Inc.)

UNITED CASH MGMT INC (MD)
Capital Stock 1¢ par reclassified as Common $0.001 par 06/22/1999
Under plan of reorganization each share Class A $0.001 par automatically became (1) share Waddell & Reed Advisors Funds Inc. Cash Management Fund Class A $0.001 par 10/01/2000
(See Waddell & Reed Advisors Funds Inc.)

UNITED CASH MGMT II INC (MD)
Dissolved 10/00/1981
Each share Capital Stock 1¢ par exchanged for (1) share United Cash Management, Inc. Capital Stock 1¢ par
United Cash Management, Inc. reorganized as Waddell & Reed Advisors Funds Inc. 10/01/2000
(See Waddell & Reed Advisors Funds Inc.)

UNITED CASINO CORP (NV)
Each share old Common $1 par exchanged for (0.02) share new Common $1 par 11/04/1999
Name changed to United Trading.com 08/03/2000
United Trading.com name changed to Global Links Corp. (Old) 02/04/2003 which name changed to Global Links Corp. (New) 08/04/2003

UNITED CENT BANCSHARES INC (IA)
Name changed to First Interstate of Iowa, Inc. 06/24/1985
First Interstate of Iowa, Inc. merged into Boatmen's Bancshares, Inc. 04/01/1992 which merged into NationsBank Corp. (NC) 01/07/1997 which reincorporated in Delaware as BankAmerica Corp. (Old) 09/25/1998 which merged into BankAmerica Corp. (New) 09/30/1999 which name changed to Bank of America Corp. 04/28/1999

UNITED CENTRAL BANK OF DES MOINES N.A. (DES MOINES, IA)
Acquired by NationsBank Corp. 08/16/1997
Details not available

UNITED CHEM CO (TX)
Name changed to United Scientific Inc. 12/18/1969

UNITED CHEMICALS, INC.
Dissolved 00/00/1950
Details not available

UNITED CHIEFTAIN RES LTD (BC)
Struck off register and declared dissolved for failure to file returns 06/09/1995

UNITED CHINA INTERNATIONAL ENTERPRISES GROUP LTD (CANADA)
Reincorporated under the laws of Bermuda 10/31/1995

UNITED CIGAR STORES CO. OF AMERICA
Reorganized as United Cigar-Whelan Stores Corp. 00/00/1937
Each share Preferred exchanged for (20) shares Common 10¢ par
Each share Common exchanged for (0.075) share Common 10¢ par
United Cigar-Whelan Stores Corp. name changed to United Whelan Corp. 07/01/1957 which name changed to Perfect Film & Chemical Corp. 05/31/1967 which name changed to Cadence Industries Corp. 10/22/1970
(See Cadence Industries Corp.)

UNITED CIGAR-WHELAN STORES CORP. (DE)
Each share Common 10¢ par exchanged for (0.33333333) share Common 30¢ par 00/00/1945
$5 Preferred $100 par called for redemption 01/04/1946
$1.25 Prior Preferred $20 par called for redemption 08/15/1946
Name changed to United Whelan Corp. 07/01/1957
United Whelan Corp. name changed to Perfect Film & Chemical Corp. 05/31/1967 which name changed to Cadence Industries Corp. 10/22/1970
(See Cadence Industries Corp.)

UNITED CITIES GAS CO (IL & VA)
6% Preferred $10 par called for redemption 11/24/1958
Preferred $10 par called for redemption 08/06/1962
Common $1 par changed to $5 par 07/15/1963
Common $5 par changed to $3.33333333 par and (0.2) additional share issued 08/25/1967
Common $3.33333333 par changed to no par and (1) additional share issued 11/13/1987
11.50% Conv. Preference $100 par called for redemption 06/15/1993
Merged into Atmos Energy Corp. 07/31/1997
Each share Common no par exchanged for (1) share Common no par

UNITED CITIES REALTY CORP. (NY)
Liquidation completed 07/30/1956
Details not available

UNITED CITIES UTILITIES CO. (DE)
Recapitalized 00/00/1947
Each share Class A Common no par exchanged for (25) shares Class A Common $1 par
Each share Class B Common no par exchanged for (26.67736) shares Class B Common $1 par
Merged into United Cities Gas Co. 07/01/1957
Each share 6% Preferred $10 par exchanged for (1) share new 6% Preferred $10 par
Each share old 5.5% Preferred $10 par exchanged for (1) share new 5.5% Preferred $10 par
Each share Class A or B Common $1 par exchanged for (1) share Common $1 par
United Cities Gas Co. merged into Atmos Energy Corp. 07/31/1997

UNITED CITIZENS NATIONAL BANK (LOS ANGELES, CA)
Name changed to Nara Bank N.A. (Los Angeles, CA) 02/07/1994
Nara Bank N.A. (Los Angeles, CA) reorganized as Nara Bancorp, Inc. 02/05/2001 which name changed to BBCN Bancorp, Inc. 12/01/2011 which name changed to Hope Bancorp, Inc. 08/01/2016

UNITED CITY CORP (TX)
Charter forfeited for failure to pay taxes 08/17/1993

UNITED CLAY PIPE CO. (OK)
Charter suspended for failure to pay taxes 04/13/1978

UNITED CLAY PRODUCTS CORP.
Property sold at public auction 00/001928
Details not available

UNITED CMNTYS CORP (FL)
Stock Dividend - 10% 05/07/1973
Name changed to Southward Ventures Inc. 05/08/1978
Southward Ventures Inc. assets transferred to Southward Ventures Depositary Trust 05/13/1982
(See Southward Ventures Depositary Trust)

UNITED CO RUSAL PLC (RUSSIA)
Name changed 02/24/2010
Name changed from United Company RUSAL Ltd. to United Company RUSAL PLC 02/24/2010
GDR agreement terminated 07/05/2018
Each Reg. S Sponsored GDR for Ordinary exchanged for $5.22884 cash
Each 144A Sponsored GDR for Ordinary exchanged for $5.22884 cash

UNITED COASTS CORP (DE)
Merged into Acmat Corp. 09/16/1996
Each share Common 1¢ par exchanged for (0.66666666) share Common no par

UNITED COBALT MINES LTD (ON)
Merged into Langis Silver & Cobalt Mining Co. Ltd. 04/30/1980
Each share Capital Stock $1 par exchanged for (0.45) share Capital Stock no par
Langis Silver & Cobalt Mining Co. name changed to Aranka Gold Inc. 07/27/2005 which merged into Guyana Goldfields Inc. 01/28/2009

UNITED COIN MINES LTD (ON)
Name changed to Winstaff Ventures Ltd. 06/25/1993
Winstaff Ventures Ltd. merged into Romarco Minerals Inc. (ON) 07/11/1995 which reincorporated in British Columbia 06/16/2006 which merged into OceanaGold Corp. 10/01/2015

UNITED COIN SVCS INC (DE)
Merged into Solon Automated Services, Inc. 12/08/1975
Each share Common 50¢ par exchanged for $5 principal amount

of 8-1/2% Conv. Subord. Debentures due 12/31/1985

UNITED COLLISION CENTRES AMER INC (BC)
Struck off register and declared dissolved for failure to file returns 04/29/1994

UNITED COMM BANCORP (IN)
Merged into German American Bancorp, Inc. 10/01/2013
Each share Common no par exchanged for (0.5456) share Common no par and $1.51 cash

UNITED CMNTY BANCORP (IN)
Merged into Civista Bancshares, Inc. 09/17/2018
Each share Common 1¢ par exchanged for (1.027) shares Common no par and $2.54 cash

UNITED CMNTY BANCORP (NC)
Name changed to Integrity Financial Corp. 05/30/2003
Integrity Financial Corp. merged into FNB United Corp. 04/28/2006 which name changed to CommunityOne Bancorp 07/01/2013

UNITED CMNTY BANCORP (USA)
Reorganized under the laws of Indiana 01/10/2013
Each share Common 1¢ par exchanged for (0.6573) share Common 1¢ par
United Community Bancorp (IN) merged into Civista Bancshares, Inc. 09/17/2018

UNITED COMMUNITY BANK (WESTLAKE VILLAGE, CA)
Declared insolvent and taken over by FDIC 12/20/89
Stockholders' equity unlikely

UNITED CMNTY BANKSHARES INC (VA)
Merged into Atlantic Financial Corp. 12/01/1998
Each share Common $1 par exchanged for (1.075) shares Common $5 par
Atlantic Financial Corp. merged into F & M National Corp. 02/26/2001 which merged into BB&T Corp. 08/09/2001

UNITED CMNTY NATL BK (WASHINGTON, DC)
Name changed to United National Bank (Washington, DC) 2/14/73
United National Bank (Washington, DC) reorganized as UNB Bancshares, Inc. 6/30/82 which merged into James Madison Ltd. 10/22/86
(See James Madison Ltd.)

UNITED COMPANIES LIFE INSURANCE OF AMERICA (LA)
Name changed to United Companies Life Insurance Co. 2/21/66
United Companies Life Insurance Co. reorganized as United Companies Financial Corp. 6/19/72
(See United Companies Financial Corp.)

UNITED COMPASS RES LTD (BC)
Recapitalized as Tartan Energy Inc. (BC) 10/2/98
Each share Common no par exchanged for (0.25) share Common no par
Tartan Energy Inc. (BC) reincorporated in Alberta 8/1/2001
(See Tartan Energy Inc.)

UNITED COMPONENTS INC (NJ)
Charter revoked for failure to file reports and pay fees 01/03/1967

UNITED COMPUTING CORP (CA)
Completely liquidated 05/03/1976
Each share Common 5¢ par exchanged for first and final distribution of $2.87 cash

UNITED COMSTOCK LODE MINES LTD (ON)
Charter cancelled and proclaimed dissolved for failure to file returns and pay taxes 02/14/1973

UNITED CONS INDS INC (DE)
Merged into Uconind, Inc. 02/19/1982
Each share Common 10¢ par exchanged for $2 cash

UNITED CONSORTIUM LTD OLD (NV)
Each share old Common $0.0001 par exchanged for (0.000625) share new Common $0.0001 par 04/11/2008
Reorganized as United Consortium, Ltd. (New) 05/05/2010
Each share new Common $0.0001 par exchanged for (0.001) share Common $0.0001 par

UNITED CONTL ENERGY CORP (BC)
Name changed to Hilton Resource Corp. 12/5/83
Hilton Resource Corp. recapitalized as North Slope Minerals Inc. 6/13/91 which recapitalized as Sino Pacific Development Ltd. 1/18/95 which name changed to Prominex Resource Corp. 11/17/2005

UNITED CONTL GROWTH FD INC (MD)
Reincorporated 12/31/74
State of incorporation changed from (DE) to (MD) 12/31/74
Name changed to United International Growth Fund, Inc. 9/10/81
United International Growth Fund, Inc. reorganized as Waddell & Reed Advisors Funds Inc. 10/1/2000

UNITED CONTL INCOME FD INC (MD)
Reincorporated 12/31/74
State of incorporation changed from (DE) to (MD) 12/31/74
Common $1 par reclassified as Class A $1 par 8/29/95
Class A $1 par changed to $0.001 par 6/22/99
Under plan of reorganization each share Class A $0.001 par automatically became (1) share Waddell & Reed Advisors Funds Inc. Continental Income Fund Class A $0.001 par 10/1/2000

UNITED CONVALESCENT HOSPS INC (CA)
Merged into Hillhaven Inc. (WA) 01/05/1972
Each share Common $1 par exchanged for (0.38) share Common $16-2/3¢ par
Hillhaven Inc. (WA) reincorporated in Delaware 10/07/1974 which name changed to Hillhaven Corp. 03/31/1978
(See Hillhaven Corp.)

UNITED COPPER & MINING LTD. (AB)
Struck from Alberta register and involuntarily dissolved for failure to file reports 9/30/70

UNITED COPPER LTD (BC)
Recapitalized as Medallion Explorations Ltd. 1/18/74
Each share Common 50¢ par exchanged for (1/3) share Common no par
Medallion Explorations Ltd. recapitalized as Compass Resources Ltd. 7/14/87 which recapitalized as United Compass Resources Ltd. 6/9/93 which recapitalized as Tartan Energy Inc. (BC) 10/2/98 which reincorporated in Alberta 8/1/2001
(See Tartan Energy Inc.)

UTD CORP. (MA)
Common $5 par split (2) for (1) by issuance of (1) additional share 8/6/65

Completely liquidated 9/11/68
Each share Common $5 par exchanged for first and final distribution of (0.75) share Litton Industries, Inc. $2 Conv. Preferred Ser. B $5 par
(See Litton Industries, Inc.)

UNITED CORP (DE)
$3 Preference no par changed to $5 par 00/00/1946
Common no par changed to $1 par 00/00/1946
Each share $3 Preference $5 par exchanged for (1) share Public Service Electric & Gas Co. Common no par, (1) share Columbia Gas System, Inc. Common no par, (0.3) share Cincinnati Gas & Electric Co. Common $8.50 par and $6 cash 04/29/1949
(See each company's listing)
Merged into Baldwin-United Corp. 01/27/1978
Each share Common $1 par exchanged for (0.23) share $2.06 Class A Conv. Preferred $25 par and (0.362) share $2.06 Conv. Class U Preferred $25 par
Baldwin-United Corp. reorganized as PHLCorp., Inc. (DE) 11/13/1986 which merged into PHLCorp, Inc. (PA) 04/22/1987 which merged into Leucadia National Corp. 12/31/1992

UNITED CORP AMER (VA)
Completely liquidated 11/22/1974
No stockholders' equity

UNITED COS CORP (NV)
Recapitalized as Brownie's Marine Group, Inc. (NV) 08/22/2007
Each share Common $0.001 par exchanged for (0.01) share Common $0.001 par
Brownie's Marine Group, Inc. (NV) reincorporated in Florida 12/07/2015

UNITED COS FINL CORP (LA)
Common $2 par split (2) for (1) by issuance of (1) additional share 4/1/85
Common $2 par split (2) for (1) by issuance of (1) additional share 10/18/93
Issue Information - 1,000,000 shares COM offered at $32 per share on 12/14/1993
Issue Information - 1,700,000 shares PFD CONV 6.75% offered at $44 per share on 06/12/1995
Common $2 par split (2) for (1) by issuance of (1) additional share 10/20/95
Stock Dividends - 10% 7/12/89; 15% 9/9/91; 10% 1/10/95
Plan of reorganization under Chapter 11 Federal Bankruptcy Code effective 11/9/2000
Each share 6.75% Conv. Preferred $2 par received initial distribution of $0.60298126 cash payable 6/25/2004 to holders of record 11/1/2000
Each share 6.75% Conv. Preferred $2 par received second distribution of $0.01067077 cash payable 11/8/2005 to holders of record 11/1/2000
Each share 6.75% Conv. Preferred $2 par received third and final distribution of $0.01274656 cash payable 11/10/2006 to holders of record 11/1/2000
Each share Common $2 par received initial distribution of $0.30149048 cash payable 6/25/2004 to holders of record 11/1/2000
Each share Common $2 par received second distribution of $0.00671345 cash payable 11/8/2005 to holders of record 11/1/2000
Each share Common $2 par received third and final distribution of $0.00641536 cash payable

11/10/2006 to holders of record 11/1/2000
Note: Certificates were not required to be surrendered and are without value

UNITED COS LIFE INS CO (LA)
Common $2.50 par changed to $2 par and (1) additional share issued 09/15/1969
Reorganized as United Companies Financial Corp. 06/19/1972
Each share Common $2 par exchanged for (1) share Common $2 par
(See United Companies Financial Corp.)

UNITED CNTYS BANCORPORATION (NJ)
Merged into Meridian Bancorp, Inc. 02/23/1996
Each share Common no par exchanged for (5) shares Common $5 par
Meridian Bancorp, Inc. merged into CoreStates Financial Corp 04/09/1996 which merged into First Union Corp. 04/28/1998 which name changed to Wachovia Corp. (Ctfs. dated after 09/01/2001) 09/01/2001 which merged into Wells Fargo & Co. (New) 12/31/2008

UNITED CNTYS TR CO (ELIZABETH, NJ)
Reorganized as United Counties Bancorporation 10/01/1983
Each share Common $5 par exchanged for (1) share Common no par
United Counties Bancorporation merged into Meridian Bancorp, Inc. 02/23/1996 which merged into CoreStates Financial Corp 04/09/1996 which merged into First Union Corp. 04/28/1998 which name changed to Wachovia Corp. (Ctfs. dated after 09/01/2001) 09/01/2001 which merged into Wells Fargo & Co. (New) 12/31/2008

UNITED CTL CORP (WA)
Completely liquidated 6/7/67
Each share Common $1 par exchanged for first and final distribution of (0.5) share Sundstrand Corp. (DE.) Common $1 par
Sundstrand Corp. (DE) merged into United Technologies Corp. 6/10/99

UNITED CUBAN OIL INC (DE)
Charter cancelled and declared inoperative and void for non-payment of taxes 6/29/83

UNITED DAIRIES LTD. (CANADA)
5% Non-Cumulative Class B Preferred 25¢ par called for redemption 03/10/1965
5% Preferred $100 par called for redemption 01/15/1967
5% Class A Preferred $100 par called for redemption 01/15/1967
Acquired by Silverwood Dairies Ltd. 10/13/1968
Each share Common no par exchanged for $50 cash

UNITED DATA CTRS INC (NY)
Merged into Tymshare, Inc. 12/10/1974
Each share Common 10¢ par exchanged for (0.45173) share Common no par
(See Tymshare, Inc.)

UNITED DATA PROCESSING, INC. (OR)
Completely liquidated 5/18/67
Each share Common 3-1/3¢ par exchanged for first and final distribution of (0.725391) share Randolph Computer Corp. Common $1 par
Randolph Computer Corp. merged into Travelers Corp. 11/7/69 which merged into Travelers Inc. 12/31/93

which name changed to Travelers Group Inc. 4/16/95 which name changed to Citigroup Inc. 10/8/98

UNITED DATACOPY INC (UT)
Recapitalized as Pen International Inc. 03/21/1994
Each share Common $1 par exchanged for (0.214286) share Common $1 par
Pen International Inc. recapitalized as Telnet World Communications, Inc. (UT) 03/02/1998 which reincorporated in Nevada as Givemepower Corp. 07/05/2001

UNITED DEFENSE INDS INC (DE)
Merged into BAE Systems PLC 06/24/2005
Each share Common 1¢ par exchanged for $75 cash

UNITED DENTAL CARE INC (DE)
Merged into Protective Life Corp. 09/11/1998
Each share Common 10¢ par exchanged for (0.2893) share Common 50¢ par
(See Protective Life Corp.)

UNITED DEV INTL (OR)
Recapitalized as Mindenao Gold Mining Corp. 07/01/2005
Each share Common no par exchanged for (0.0001) share Common no par
Note: Holders of between (101) and (999,999) shares received (100) shares
Holders of (100) shares or fewer were not affected
Mindenao Gold Mining Corp. name changed to Grand Pacaraima Gold Corp. 03/13/2006 which name changed to First Bitcoin Capital Corp. 08/15/2016

UNITED DIAGNOSTIC INC (DE)
Each share old Common 1¢ par exchanged for (0.05) share new Common 1¢ par 03/09/2005
Name changed to SPO Medical Inc. 04/21/2005
SPO Medical Inc. recapitalized as SPO Global Inc. 10/07/2013

UNITED DIGITAL NETWORK INC (WY)
Merged into Star Telecommunications, Inc. 3/24/99
Each share Common no par exchanged for (0.146428) share Common $0.001 par
(See Star Telecommunications, Inc.)

UNITED DISCOUNT CORP. (VA)
Name changed to United Corp. of America and Common $1 par changed to 10¢ par 2/27/68
United Corp. of America completely liquidated 11/22/74

UNITED DISTILLERS OF CANADA, LTD. (CANADA)
Liquidation completed 6/12/62

UNITED DIVERSIFIED CORP (DE)
Merged into United Diversified Corp. (IL) 01/01/1985
Details not available

UNITED DIXIE RES INC (ON)
Each share Common no par exchanged for (1) share Class B Common no par 01/13/1997
Merged into United Pacific Capital Resources Corp. 03/12/1998
Each share Class B Common no par exchanged for (5.4) shares Class B Common no par
(See United Pacific Capital Resources Corp.)

UNITED DLR STORES INC (AR)
Stock Dividend - 33-1/3% 12/28/1969
Name changed to UDS, Inc. 06/24/1976
(See UDS, Inc.)

UNITED DOMINION INDS LTD (ON)
9.25% Retractable Preferred Ser. 3 no par called for redemption 09/01/1990
9.5% Conv. Preferred Ser. 2 no par called for redemption 08/25/1995
Acquired by SPX Corp. 05/24/2001
Each share Common no par exchanged for (0.2353) share Common $10 par

UNITED DOMINION MINING CO., LTD. (CANADA)
Charter surrendered 12/31/1949

UNITED DOMINION RLTY TR INC (MD)
Reincorporated 06/11/2003
Common $1 par split (2) for (1) by issuance of (1) additional share 05/05/1993
9.250% Preferred Ser. A no par called for redemption at $25 on 06/15/2001
State of incorporation changed from (VA) to (MD) 06/11/2003
Common $1 par changed to 1¢ par 07/27/2005
Name changed to UDR, Inc. 03/14/2007

UNITED DRILL & TOOL CORP. (MI)
Recapitalized in 1941
Class A no par changed to $10 par
Class B no par changed to $1 par
Class B $1 par changed to $10 par in 1949
Recapitalized 4/12/55
Class A $10 par reclassified as Preferred $10 par
Class B $10 par reclassified as Common $10 par
Stock Dividend - 100% 8/15/57
Merged into United-Greenfield Corp. 2/14/58
Each share Common $10 par exchanged for (1) share Common $10 par
Each share Preferred $10 par exchanged for (1) share 6% Preferred $10 par
United-Greenfield Corp. merged into TRW Inc. 9/20/68 which merged into Northrop Grumman Corp. 12/11/2002

UNITED DRUG, INC.
Name changed to United-Rexall Drug, Inc. in 1946
United-Rexall Drug, Inc. name changed to Rexall Drug, Inc. in 1947 which merged into Rexall Drug Co. 5/6/55 which name changed to Rexall Drug & Chemical Co. 4/24/59 which name changed to Dart Industries, Inc. 4/22/69 which reorganized as Dart & Kraft, Inc. 9/25/80 which name changed to Kraft, Inc. (New) 11/21/86
(See Kraft, Inc. (New))

UNITED DRUG CO. (MA)
Acquired by Drug, Inc. in 1928 for which stock of five new companies was issued in exchange in accordance with the plan of segregation in 1933

UNITED DRUG PLC (IRELAND)
Name changed to UDG Healthcare PLC 10/24/2013

UNITED DRY DOCKS, INC.
Reorganized as United Shipyards, Inc. in 1936 which was completely liquidated in 1947

UNITED DUVEX OILS & MINES LTD (ON)
Cease trade order issued 07/12/1978

UNITED DYE & CHEMICAL CORP. (DE)
Each share 7% Preferred $100 par exchanged for (10) shares Common $1 par 00/00/1958
Name changed to Chemoil Industries, Inc. 06/30/1958
Chemoil Industries, Inc. merged into Szabo Food Service, Inc. 02/27/1962 which name changed to Oakbrook Consolidated, Inc. 08/19/1975
(See Oakbrook Consolidated, Inc.)

UNITED DYEWOOD CORP. (DE)
Name changed to United Dye & Chemical Corp. in 1950
United Dye & Chemical Corp. name changed to Chemoil Industries, Inc. 6/30/58 which merged into Szabo Food Service, Inc. 2/27/62 which name changed to Oakbrook Consolidated, Inc. 8/19/75
(See Oakbrook Consolidated, Inc.)

UNITED E&P INC (NV)
Charter revoked for failure to file reports and pay fees 06/20/2010

UNITED ECOENERGY CORP (NV)
Name changed to United Health Products, Inc. 09/30/2010

UNITED ED & SOFTWARE INC (DE)
Name changed 10/08/1987
Common no par split (3) for (2) by issuance of (0.5) additional share 10/08/1985
Name and state of incorporation changed from United Education & Software (CA) to United Education & Software, Inc. (DE) and Common no par changed to 1¢ par 10/08/1987
Common 1¢ par split (3) for (2) by issuance of (0.5) additional share 04/14/1988
Charter cancelled and declared inoperative and void for non-payment of taxes 03/01/1995

UNITED EDUCATORS INC (MA)
Involuntarily dissolved for failure to file reports and pay taxes 12/31/1990

UNITED EDUCATORS LIFE INSURANCE CO. OF FLORIDA (FL)
Acquired by Windsor Life Insurance Co. of America 7/21/66
Each share Common $1 par exchanged for (0.363636) share Capital Stock $2 par
Windsor Life Insurance Co. of America name changed to Empire State Life Insurance Co. 6/10/88
(See Empire State Life Insurance Co.)

UNITED EDUCATORS UTAH INC (UT)
Proclaimed dissolved for failure to pay taxes 5/1/95

UNITED ELASTIC CORP. (MA)
Common no par changed to $20 par in 1951
Common $20 par changed to $10 par and (1) additional share issued 10/30/64
Stock Dividends - 50% 11/1/50; 10% 12/26/51; 10% 12/17/52; 50% 12/10/55; 25% 2/10/59; 10% 2/10/60; 33-1/3% 2/13/62
Merged into Stevens (J.P.) & Co., Inc. 6/14/68
Each share Common $10 par exchanged for (0.495) share Capital Stock $15 par
(See Stevens (J.P.) & Co., Inc.)

UNITED ELECTRIC COAL COMPANIES (DE)
Common no par changed to $5 par in 1937
Stock Dividend - 20% 12/20/50
Merged into General Dynamics Corp. 11/7/66
Each share Common $5 par exchanged for $50 cash

UNITED ELECTRIC LIGHT CO.
Acquired by Duquesne Light Co. (PA) in 1927
Details not available

UNITED ELECTRIC RAILWAYS CO. (RI)
Name changed to United Transit Co. 4/29/52

UNITED ELECTRODYNAMICS, INC. (CA)
Acquired by Teledyne, Inc. 11/13/1964
Each share Common $1 par exchanged for (0.08333333) share Common $1 par
Teledyne, Inc. merged into Allegheny Teledyne, Inc. 08/15/1996 which name changed to Allegheny Technologies Inc. 11/29/1999

UNITED EMPIRE INDUSTRIES, INC. (UT)
Recapitalized as Fli-Co. Corp. 07/17/1969
Each share Common $1 par exchanged for (100) shares Common 1¢ par
Fli-Co. Corp. recapitalized as AutoBale America Corp. 01/18/1972
(See AutoBale America Corp.)

UNITED ENERGY CORP (NV)
Each share old Common 1¢ par exchanged for (0.03333333) share new Common 1¢ par 04/11/1994
Charter revoked 07/31/2018

UNITED ENERGY RES INC (DE)
Common $1 par split (2) for (1) by issuance of (1) additional share 4/1/80
Merged into MidCon Corp. 12/11/85
Each share Common $1 par exchanged for (0.904) share Common no par
MidCon Corp. merged into Occidental Petroleum Corp. (CA) 4/1/86 which reincorporated in Delaware 5/21/86

UNITED ENERGY TECHNOLOGIES INC (FL)
Proclaimed dissolved for failure to file reports and pay fees 10/13/1989

UNITED ENGR & FDRY CO (PA)
Each share Common $100 par exchanged for (6) shares Common no par in 1927
Each share Common no par exchanged for (2) shares Common $5 par in 1935
Stock Dividend - 200% 5/19/52
Merged into Wean United, Inc. (OH) 12/31/68
Each share Preferred $100 par exchanged for $150 principal amount of 5-1/2% Conv. Subord. Debentures due 3/1/93
Each share Common $5 par exchanged for $30 principal amount of 5-1/2% Conv. Subord. Debentures due 3/1/93

UNITED ENVIRONMENTAL CORP (NV)
Name changed to International Safety Inc. 7/1/91
(See International Safety Inc.)

UNITED EQUITABLE CORP (DE)
In process of liquidation and trust created
Each share Common 25¢ par exchanged for initial distribution of (1) United Equitable Corp. Liquidating Trust Unit of Bene. Int. 4/10/87
(See United Equitable Corp. Liquidating Trust)

UNITED EQUITABLE CORP STOCKHOLDERS LIQ TR (DE)
In process of liquidation
Each Unit of Bene. Int. exchanged for initial distribution of $2 cash 5/22/87
Each Unit of Bene. Int. received second distribution of $2 cash 12/30/87
Note: Details on subsequent distributions, if any, are not available

UNITED EQUITIES, INC.
Merged into Incorporated Investors Equities in 1930
Details not available

UNITED EQUITIES CORP.
Succeeded by International Equities Corp. in 1927
Details not available

UNITED EQUITIES INC (DE)
Charter cancelled and declared inoperative and void for non-payment of taxes 1/25/72

UNITED EQUITY LIFE INSURANCE CO. (IL)
Merged into Insurance City Life Co. on a (0.5) for (1) basis 06/28/1963
(See Insurance City Life Co.)

UNITED ESTELLA MINES LTD. (BC)
Charter revoked for failure to file reports and pay fees 3/26/64

UNITED EUROPEAN HLDGS LTD (NV)
Name changed to Innovative Beverage Group, Inc. 03/03/2005
(See Innovative Beverage Group, Inc.)

UNITED EXCHANGE BUILDING CORP. (WA)
Name changed to Northwest Building Corp. in 1958

UNITED EXPLORATION CO. (NV)
Charter revoked for failure to file reports and pay fees 3/2/64

UNITED EXPLORATIONS & MINING CORP. LTD. (QC)
Acquired by Reactor Uranium Mines Ltd. 05/14/1969
Each share Common $1 par exchanged for (1) share Common no par
Reactor Uranium Mines Ltd. name changed to Reactor Industries Ltd. 12/16/1971 which recapitalized as Consolidated Reactor Uranium Mines Ltd. 02/05/1979 which name changed to Canaustra Gold Explorations Ltd. 10/23/1987 which merged into Cliff Resources Corp. 01/09/1989 which name changed to Mineral Resources Corp. 09/13/1995 which name changed to Minroc Mines Inc. 06/10/1998 which name changed to Cassiar Mines & Metals, Inc. 06/10/1999 which name changed to Cassiar Magnesium Inc. 04/25/2000 which name changed to Cassiar Resources Inc. 07/25/2001 which name changed to Troutline Investments Inc. (ONT) 06/30/2003 which reorganized in Alberta as Innova Exploration Ltd. 04/16/2004
(See Innova Exploration Ltd.)

UNITED EXPOSITION SERVICE CO. (NJ)
Common 10¢ par split (11) for (10) by issuance of (0.1) additional share 5/15/63
Common 10¢ par split (11) for (10) by issuance of (0.1) additional share 8/15/64
Completely liquidated 9/9/66
Each share Common 10¢ par exchanged for first and final distribution of (0.42442) share Hertz Corp. $2 Conv. Part. Preferred Ser. B no par
Hertz Corp. merged into Radio Corp. of America 5/11/67 which name changed to RCA Corp. 5/9/69
(See RCA Corp.)

UNITED FABRICATORS & ELECTRS INC (MN)
Name changed to Kroy Industries Inc. and Common 50¢ par reclassified as Capital Stock 50¢ par 06/26/1969
Kroy Industries Inc. name changed to Kroy Inc. 07/23/1981
(See Kroy Inc.)

UNITED FABRICATORS INC (SC)
Involuntarily dissolved for failure to pay taxes 04/21/1986

UNITED FAMILY LIFE INS CO (GA)
Under plan of merger Common $1 par changed to 50¢ par 12/31/1963
Reorganized as Interfinancial Inc. 07/01/1969
Each share Common 50¢ par exchanged for (0.25) share Common $1 par
(See Interfinancial Inc.)

UNITED FARMERS OF NEW ENGLAND, INC. (VT)
Called for redemption 1/1/73
Public interest eliminated

UNITED FASHIONS INC (GA)
Reorganized under the laws of Delaware as UniHolding Corp. 08/30/1993
Each share Common 50¢ par exchanged for (0.1) share Common 1¢ par
UniHolding Corp. name changed to ULH Corp. 11/21/2000
(See ULH Corp.)

UNITED FDS CDA INTL LTD (CANADA)
Merged into United Continental Growth Fund, Inc. (DE) 10/13/72
Each share Common $1 par exchanged for (0.459584) share Capital Stock $1 par
United Continental Growth Fund, Inc. (DE) reincorporated in Maryland 12/31/74 which name changed to United International Growth Fund Inc. 9/10/81

UNITED FDS MGMT LTD (CANADA)
Name changed to United Financial Management Ltd. 5/22/73
United Financial Management Ltd. acquired by Central Capital Corp. 10/23/86 which recapitalized as YMG Capital Management Inc. 2/20/98
(See YMG Capital Management Inc.)

UNITED FED BANCORP INC (PA)
Reincorporated 6/15/90
State of incorporation changed from (DE) to (PA) 6/15/90
Merged into PNC Bank Corp. 1/21/94
Each share Common 1¢ par exchanged for $32.50 cash

UNITED FED BK FSB (MANCHESTER, NH)
Merged into United Saver's Bancorp, Inc. 06/20/1986
Each share Common $1 par exchanged for (1) share Common $1 par
United Saver's Bancorp, Inc. name changed to Dartmouth Bancorp, Inc. 04/12/1990
(See Dartmouth Bancorp, Inc.)

UNITED FED SVGS & LN ASSN (USA)
Name changed to United Bank, F.S.B. (San Francisco, CA) 05/31/1983
United Bank, F.S.B. (San Francisco, CA) reorganized as United Bank, S.S.B. (San Francisco, CA) 05/23/1984
(See United Bank, S.S.B. (San Francisco, CA))

UNITED FED SVGS BK (ROCKY MOUNT, NC)
Name changed 6/14/90
Common 1¢ par split (2) for (1) by issuance of (1) additional share 12/17/84
Common 1¢ par split (2) for (1) by issuance of (1) additional share 7/1/87
Name changed from United Federal Savings & Loan Association of Rocky Mount, North Carolina to United Federal Savings Bank (Rocky Mount, NC) 6/14/90
Merged into Triangle Bancorp Inc. 9/17/98
Each share Common 1¢ par exchanged for (1.098) shares Common no par
Triangle Bancorp, Inc. merged into Centura Banks, Inc. 2/18/2000 which merged into Bank of Canada (Montreal, QC) 6/5/2001

UNITED FELDSPAR & MINERALS CORP. (DE)
Name changed to Carolina Pyrophyllite Co. in 1954

UNITED FID LIFE INS CO (TX)
Common $10 par changed to $5 par and (1) additional share issued 11/24/1964
Stock Dividends - 50% 02/11/1948; 100% 07/12/1956
Merged into MM Life Insurance Co. 12/31/1977
Each share Common $5 par exchanged for $50 cash

UNITED FIDELITY HOSPITAL ASSURANCE CO. (OR)
Involuntarily dissolved 4/10/72
No stockholders' equity

UNITED FIDUCIARY SHS INC (MD)
Name changed to United Retirement Shares, Inc. 9/28/83
United Retirement Shares, Inc. reorganized as Waddell & Reed Advisors Funds Inc. 10/1/2000

UNITED FILM & VIDEO HLDGS LTD (BRITISH VIRGIN ISLANDS)
Reincorporated under the laws of Cayman Islands as United Media Holdings Ltd. 06/24/1998
United Media Holdings Ltd. name changed to United Media Ltd. 12/20/1999
(See United Media Ltd.)

UNITED FINANCE CORP. (MI)
Merged into Palace Corp. 08/31/1968
Each share Preferred $1 par exchanged for (0.1) share Common no par
Unexchanged certificates were cancelled and became without value 12/24/1968

UNITED FINL BANCORP INC (DE)
Merged into National City Bancshares, Inc. 08/31/1995
Each share Common 1¢ par exchanged for (1.063503) shares Common $3.33-1/3 par
National City Bancshares, Inc. name changed to Integra Bank Corp. 05/22/2000
(See Integra Bank Corp.)

UNITED FINL BANCORP INC (MD)
Merged into United Financial Bancorp, Inc. (CT) 05/01/2014
Each share Common 1¢ par exchanged for (1.3472) shares Common no par

UNITED FINL BANCORP INC (USA)
Reorganized under the laws of Maryland 12/03/2007
Each share Common 1¢ par exchanged for (1.04079) shares Common 1¢ par
United Financial Bancorp, Inc. (MD) merged into United Financial Bancorp, Inc. (CT) 05/01/2014

UNITED FINL BKG COS INC (VA)
Each share old Common $1 par exchanged for (0.2) share new Common $1 par 12/31/1997
Stock Dividends - 10% 08/24/1988; 10% 08/30/1990
Merged into Cardinal Financial Corp. 01/16/2014
Each share new Common $1 par exchanged for (1.154) shares Common $1 par and $19.13 cash
Cardinal Financial Corp. merged into United Bankshares, Inc. 04/24/2017

UNITED FINL CORP (KS)
Name changed to Polaris Financial Corp. 03/13/1973
(See Polaris Financial Corp.)

UNITED FINL CORP (MN)
Common $1 par split (5) for (4) by issuance of (0.25) additional share payable 12/28/2005 to holders of record 12/14/2005 Ex date - 12/29/2005
Stock Dividends - 10% payable 06/28/2002 to holders of record 06/24/2002 Ex date - 06/20/2002; 50% payable 06/30/2003 to holders of record 06/23/2003 Ex date - 07/01/2003
Merged into U.S. Bancorp 02/06/2007
Each share Common $1 par exchanged for (0.6825) share Common 1¢ par

UNITED FINL CORP CALIF (DE)
Capital Stock $1 par split (5) for (4) by issuance of (0.25) additional share 03/15/1979
Merged into National Steel Corp. 01/04/1980
Each share Capital Stock $1 par exchanged for $33.60 cash

UNITED FINL CORP S C INC (DE)
Common $1 par split (3) for (2) by issuance of (0.5) additional share 07/02/1993
Common $1 par split (2) for (1) by issuance of (1) additional share 05/31/1994
Merged into First Union Corp. 10/04/1995
Each share Common $1 par exchanged for (0.423) share Common $3.33-1/3 par
First Union Corp. name changed to Wachovia Corp. (Ctfs. dated after 09/01/2001) 09/01/2001 which merged into Wells Fargo & Co. (New) 12/31/2008

UNITED FINL CORP VA (VA)
Merged into International Bank (Washington, DC) 6/30/81
Each share Common 10¢ par exchanged for (0.8) share Class A Common $1 par
International Bank (Washington, DC) merged into USLICO Corp. 12/31/85 which merged into NWNL Companies, Inc. 1/17/95 which name changed to ReliaStar Financial Corp. 2/13/95
(See ReliaStar Financial Corp.)

UNITED FINL DATA CTRS INC (MI)
Name changed to Universal Computer Techniques, Inc. 06/24/1970
(See Universal Computer Techniques, Inc.)

UNITED FINL GROUP INC (DE)
Plan of reorganization under Chapter 11 Federal Bankruptcy Code effective 9/25/97
No stockholders' equity

UNITED FINL GROUP INC (MN)
Statutorily dissolved 07/29/1996

UNITED FINL HLDGS INC (FL)
Common no par split (3) for (1) by issuance of (2) additional shares payable 7/31/98 to holders of record 7/1/98
Merged into Synovus Financial Corp. 3/3/2003
Each share Common no par exchanged for $16.47 cash

UNITED FINL INC (NC)
Common $1 par split (5) for (4) by issuance of (0.25) additional share payable 02/17/2003 to holders of record 01/31/2003 Ex date - 02/18/2003
Merged into FNB Corp. 11/04/2005
Each share Common $1 par exchanged for (0.4093) share Common $2.50 par and $5.71 cash
FNB Corp. name changed to FNB United Corp. 04/28/2006 which name changed to CommunityOne Bancorp 07/01/2013 which merged into Capital Bank Financial Corp. 10/26/2016

UNITED FINL MGMT LTD (CANADA)
Acquired by Central Capital Corp. 10/23/86
Each share Common no par

exchanged for (3.2) shares Common no par
Central Capital Corp. recapitalized as YMG Capital Management Inc. 2/20/98
(See YMG Capital Management Inc.)

UNITED FINL MTG CORP (IL)
Each share old Common no par exchanged for (2/3) share new Common no par 5/22/95
Merged into ARH Mortgage Inc. 11/30/2005
Each share new Common no par exchanged for $5.64 cash

UNITED FINL OPERATIONS INC (CO)
Charter cancelled and proclaimed dissolved for failure to pay fees 1/1/98

UNITED FIRE & CAS CO (IA)
6% Preferred $10 par called for redemption 04/01/1958
6% Class B Preferred $100 par called for redemption 06/15/1968
$1.60 Class C Preferred $10 par changed to $15 par 12/27/1968
Common $10 par changed to $5 par and (1) additional share issued 12/27/1968
Common $5 par changed to $3.33-1/3 par and (0.5) additional share issued 03/05/1971
$1.60 Class C Preferred $15 par called for redemption 00/00/1973
Common $3.33-1/3 par split (5) for (4) by issuance of (0.25) additional share 01/05/1982
Common $3.33-1/3 par split (3) for (2) by issuance of (0.5) additional share 03/17/1986
Common $3.33-1/3 par split (3) for (2) by issuance of (0.5) additional share 06/15/1992
Common $3.33-1/3 par split (3) for (2) by issuance of (0.5) additional share 01/05/1995
Common $3.33-1/3 par split (3) for (2) by issuance of (0.5) additional share payable 01/05/1996 to holders of record 12/18/1995
Common $3.33-1/3 par split (2) for (1) by issuance of (1) additional share payable 12/15/2004 to holders of record 12/02/2004 Ex date - 12/16/2004
6.375% Conv. Preferred Ser. A no par called for redemption at $26.02 plus $0.27 accrued dividends on 05/15/2005
Stock Dividends - 50% 09/15/1976; 50% 12/15/1977; 50% 06/15/1979
Name changed to United Fire Group, Inc. and Common $3.33-1/3 par changed to $0.001 par 02/02/2012

UNITED FIRE INS CO (NY)
Common $5 par changed to $2.50 par and (1) additional share issued plus a 25% Stock Dividend paid 04/01/1965
Stock Dividends - 20% 05/01/1964; 20% 05/16/1966
Under plan of reorganization each share Common $2.50 par automatically became (1) share United Diversified Corp. Common $2.50 par 07/01/1976
(See United Diversified Corp.)

UNITED FIRST FED SVGS & LN ASSN SARASOTA FLA (USA)
Merged into Barnett Banks of Florida, Inc. 12/22/1986
Each share Common 1¢ par exchanged for (1.082) shares Common $2 par
Barnett Banks of Florida, Inc. name changed to Barnett Banks, Inc. 04/24/1987 which merged into NationsBank Corp. 01/09/1998 which reincorporated in Delaware as BankAmerica Corp. (Old) 09/25/1998 which merged into BankAmerica Corp. (New)

09/30/1998 which name changed to Bank of America Corp. 04/28/1999

UNITED FIRST FLA BKS INC (FL)
Name changed to Flagship Banks, Inc. 06/30/1974
Flagship Banks, Inc. merged into Sun Banks, Inc. 01/01/1984 which merged into SunTrust Banks, Inc. 07/01/1985

UNITED FIXED SHARES
Series Y Trust Agreement terminated 00/00/1950 and completely liquidated 00/00/1952
Details not available

UNITED FLEX CORP. (NY)
Assets sold for benefit of creditors and ceased business 3/25/72
No stockholders' equity

UNITED FOODS INC (DE)
Reincorporated 9/30/83
60¢ Conv. Preferred $8.50 par called for redemption 12/1/67
State of incorporation changed from (TX) to (DE) and Common $1 par reclassified as Conv. Class B $1 par 9/30/83
Each share Conv. Class B $1 par received distribution of (1) share Class A $1 par 12/1/83
Merged into Pictsweet LLC 9/24/99
Each share Class A Common $1 par exchanged for $3.50 cash
Each share Conv. Class B Common $1 par exchanged for $3.50 cash

UNITED FORTUNE CHANNEL MINES LTD (BC)
Recapitalized as Surewin Resources Corp. 02/07/1984
Each share Capital Stock no par exchanged for (0.2) share Common no par
(See Surewin Resources Corp.)

UNITED FOUNDERS CORP. (MD)
Common no par changed to $1 par 3/13/33
Merged into American General Corp. on a (0.1) for (1) basis 11/23/35
American General Corp. merged into Equity Corp. 10/17/50 which name changed to Wheelabrator-Frye Inc. 11/4/71 which merged into Signal Companies, Inc. 2/1/83 which merged into Allied-Signal Inc. 9/19/85 which name changed to AlliedSignal Inc. 4/26/93 which name changed to Honeywell International Inc. 12/1/99

UNITED FOUNDERS CORP (OK)
Each share Common $1 par exchanged for (0.1) share Common $10 par 07/01/1963
Acquired by United Founders Life Insurance Co. 11/28/1969
Each share Common $10 par exchanged for (1) share Common $1 par
(See United Founders Life Insurance Co.)

UNITED FOUNDERS LIFE INS CO (OK)
Old Common $1 par changed to 10¢ par and (1) additional share issued 12/18/1957
Each share Common 10¢ par exchanged for (0.1) share new Common $1 par 05/18/1967
New Common $1 par changed to 25¢ par 06/24/1971
Common 25¢ par changed to 10¢ par 10/28/1974
Stock Dividend - 10% 01/31/1970
Merged into Protective Corp. 12/31/1982
Each share Common 10¢ par exchanged for $2.60 cash

UNITED FRUIT CO (NJ)
Each share Capital Stock $100 par exchanged for (2.5) shares Capital Stock no par 00/00/1926

Capital Stock no par reclassified as Common $1 par 04/20/1966
Stock Dividend - 200% 06/24/1946
Merged into United Brands Co. 06/30/1970
Each share $2 Conv. Preferred Ser. A no par exchanged for (1.4) shares $1.20 Conv. Preference Ser. A no par and (2.38) shares Capital Stock $1 par
Each share Common $1 par exchanged for (1) share $1.20 Conv. Preference Ser. A no par and (1.7) shares Capital Stock $1 par
United Brands Co. name changed to Chiquita Brands International, Inc. 03/20/1990
(See Chiquita Brands International, Inc.)

UNITED FUEL & ENERGY CORP (NV)
Merged into Southern Counties Oil Co. 02/10/2010
Each share Common $0.001 par exchanged for $0.30 cash

UNITED FUEL & SUPPLY CO.
Liquidated in 1929

UNITED FUNDS CANADA LTD. (ON)
Stock Dividend - 300% 12/31/64
Name changed to United Funds Canada- International Ltd. 1/5/65
United Funds Canada-International Ltd. merged into United Continental Growth Fund, Inc. (Del.) 10/13/72 which reincorporated in Maryland 12/31/74 which name changed to United International Growth Fund Inc. 9/10/81

UNITED GAMING INC (NV)
Name changed to Alliance Gaming Corp. 12/19/1994
Alliance Gaming Corp. name changed to Bally Technologies, Inc. 03/08/2006
(See Bally Technologies, Inc.)

UNITED GAS & ELECTRIC CO.
Liquidated in 1941

UNITED GAS & ELECTRIC CORP.
Dissolved in 1943

UNITED GAS CO.
Acquired by United Gas Corp. 00/00/1930
Details not available

UNITED GAS CORP (DE)
Common no par changed to $1 par 00/00/1932
Each share Common $1 par exchanged for (0.16666666) share Common $10 par 11/28/1944
7% Preferred $100 par called for redemption 12/29/1944
Merged into Pennzoil United, Inc. 04/01/1968
Each share Common $10 par exchanged for (0.5) share $4 Conv. Preference Common $2.50 par
Pennzoil United, Inc. name changed to Pennzoil Co. (DE) 06/01/1972 which name changed to PennzEnergy Co. 12/30/1998 which merged into Devon Energy Corp. (New) 08/17/1999

UNITED GAS IMPT CO (PA)
Each share Common $50 par exchanged for (0.125) share Preferred no par and (5) shares Common no par 00/00/1929
Common no par reclassified as Capital Stock no par 00/00/1943
Each share Capital Stock no par exchanged for (0.1) share Capital Stock $13.50 par 00/00/1944
Under plan of merger Capital Stock $13.50 par reclassified as Common $13.50 par 00/00/1952
Common $13.50 par changed to $4.50 par and (2) additional shares issued 05/25/1962
4-1/4% Preferred $100 par called for redemption 04/01/1965

Name changed to UGI Corp. (Old) 07/01/1968
UGI Corp. (Old) reorganized as UGI Corp. (New) 04/10/1992

UNITED GAS INC (TX)
Name changed to Entex, Inc. 4/5/74
Entex, Inc. acquired by Arkla, Inc. 2/2/88 which name changed to NorAm Energy Corp. 5/11/94 which merged into Houston Industries Inc. 8/6/97 which name changed to Reliant Energy Inc. 2/8/99 which reorganized as CenterPoint Energy, Inc. 8/31/2002

UNITED GAS PIPE LINE CO (DE)
Name changed to United Energy Resources, Inc. 08/27/1976
United Energy Resources, Inc. merged into MidCon Corp. 12/11/1985 which merged into Occidental Petroleum Corp. (CA) 04/01/1986 which reincorporated in Delaware 05/21/1986

UNITED GEN CORP (NV)
Charter revoked for failure to file reports and pay fees 03/03/1980

UNITED GEN CORP (TX)
Charter forfeited for failure to pay taxes 1/18/88

UNITED GEN INS CO (TX)
Stock Dividend - 15% 12/28/1979
Under plan of reorganization each share Common $1 par automatically became (1) share United General Corp. Common $1 par 06/30/1981
(See United General Corp.)

UNITED GEN LIFE INS CO (TX)
Each (12) shares Common $1 par exchanged for (1) share Common $10 par 04/21/1975
Each share Common $10 par exchanged for (0.1) share Common $100 par 10/04/1979
Merged into National Health Agency Associates, Inc. 04/00/1981
Each share Common $100 par exchanged for $232 cash

UNITED GIBRALTER CORPORATION DELAWARE, INC. (DE)
Reorganized 8/25/86
Reorganized from United Gibralter Corp. (FL) to United Gibralter Corporation Delaware, Inc. (DE) and Common 10¢ par changed to $0.001 par 8/25/86
Charter cancelled and declared inoperative and void for non-payment of taxes 3/1/92

UNITED GLOBAL GROWTH FUND LTD. (CANADA)
Voluntarily dissolved 01/02/1998
Details not available

UNITED GLOBAL PETE INC (BC)
Struck off register and declared dissolved for failure to file returns 4/19/91

UNITED GOLD & GOVT FD INC (MD)
Common 1¢ par reclassified as Class A 1¢ par 2/19/96
Class A 1¢ par changed to $0.001 par 6/22/99
Under plan of reorganization each share Class A $0.001 par or Class Y $0.001 par automatically became (1) share Waddell & Reed Advisors Funds Inc. Asset Strategy Fund Class A $0.001 par or Class Y $0.001 par respectively 10/1/2000

UNITED GOLD & SILVER CO (WA)
Recapitalized as Auto America Inc. 11/22/1999
Each share Common no par exchanged for (0.18118019) share Common no par
Auto America Inc. reorganized as Charter Equities, Inc. (WA) 06/04/2007 which reincorporated in Arizona 01/23/2008 which reorganized in Nevada as Global

Recycle Energy, Inc. 04/15/2008 which name changed to ATI Modular Technology Corp. 06/13/2017 which recapitalized as AmericaTowne Holdings, Inc. 03/08/2018

UNITED GOLD CORP (BC)
Merged into ABM Gold Corp. 11/17/1989
Each share Common no par exchanged for (1/6) share Common no par
ABM Gold Corp. reorganized as NorthWest Gold Corp. 06/01/1990 which merged into Northgate Exploration Ltd. (ON) 06/08/1993 which reincorporated in British Columbia 07/01/2001 which name changed to Northgate Minerals Corp. 05/20/2004 which merged into AuRico Gold Inc. 10/26/2011

UNITED GOLD EQUITIES OF CANADA, LTD.
Acquired by Commonwealth International Corp., Ltd. 00/00/1947
Each share Common $1 par exchanged for (0.6) share Common $1 par
Commonwealth International Corp., Ltd. name changed to Eaton Commonwealth Fund Ltd. 04/15/1974 which name changed to Eaton/Bay Commonwealth Fund Ltd. 04/12/1978 which name changed back to Eaton Commonwealth Fund Ltd. 04/16/1986 which name changed to Viking Commonwealth Fund Ltd. 04/16/1987 which name changed to Laurentian Commonwealth Fund Ltd. 05/31/1993 which name changed to Strategic Value Commonwealth Fund Ltd. 06/05/1997 which name changed to StrategicNova Commonwealth Fund Ltd. 09/26/2000
(See StrategicNova Commonwealth Fund Ltd.)

UNITED GOLD MINES CO (CO)
Administratively dissolved 3/1/99

UNITED GOLD MINES CORP. (DE)
No longer in existence having become inoperative and void for non-payment of taxes 4/1/40

UNITED GOLD RANGE CORP. (AZ)
Charter cancelled for failure to pay fees in 1924

UNITED GOLF PRODS INC (DE)
Recapitalized as Order Logistics, Inc. 12/13/2005
Each share Common $0.001 par exchanged for (0.01) share Common $0.001 par
Order Logistics, Inc. name changed to World Logistics Services, Inc. 12/21/2007

UNITED GOVT SECS FD INC (MD)
Name changed 4/9/84
Name changed from United Government Cash Fund, Inc. to United Government Securities Fund, Inc. 4/9/84
New Common $1 par reclassified as Class A $1 par 7/31/95
Class A $1 par changed to $0.001 par 6/22/99
Under plan of reorganization each share Class A $0.001 par automatically became (1) share Waddell & Reed Advisors Funds Inc. Government Securities Fund Class A $0.001 par 10/1/2000

UNITED GRAIN GROWERS LTD (CANADA)
Each share new Ltd. Vtg. Common no par exchanged for (1) share Common no par to reflect a (1) for (100) reverse split followed by a (100) for (1) forward split 02/22/2004
Note: Holders of (99) or fewer pre-split shares received $9.63 cash per share
Acquired by Saskatchewan Wheat Pool Inc. 06/19/2007
Each share Conv. Preferred Ser. A no par exchanged for $24 cash
Each share new Ltd. Vtg. Common no par exchanged for $20.50 cash

UNITED GRAPE PRODUCTS, INC.
Bankrupt in 1934

UNITED-GREENFIELD CORP. (DE)
Common $10 par changed to $5 par and (1) additional share issued 05/05/1967
Merged into TRW Inc. 09/20/1968
Each share Common $5 par exchanged for (0.41) share $4.50 Conv. Preference II Ser. 3 no par and (0.2) share Common $1.25 par
TRW Inc. merged into Northrop Grumman Corp. 12/11/2002

UNITED GREENWATER COPPER CO (SD)
Charter cancelled for failure to file annual reports 7/1/77

UNITED GREENWOOD EXPLS LTD (BC)
Name changed to Elektra Power Inc. 3/15/85
(See Elektra Power Inc.)

UNITED GROUP INC (NC)
Each share Common $1 par exchanged for (0.1) share Common no par 08/01/1984
Merged into Norwest Corp. 03/21/1997
Each share Common no par exchanged for (0.32935) share Common $1-2/3 par
Norwest Corp. name changed to Wells Fargo & Co. (New) 11/02/1998

UNITED GTY CORP (NC)
Common no par split (5) for (4) by issuance of (0.25) additional share 5/26/78
Merged into American International Group, Inc. 10/1/81
Each share Common no par exchanged for (0.4) share $5.85 Conv. Preferred Ser. B $5 par
(See American International Group, Inc.)

UNITED GTY LIFE INS CO (TX)
Completely liquidated 12/03/1968
Each share Capital Stock $1 par exchanged for first and final distribution of (0.350877) share Silco, Inc. Common $1 par
(See Silco, Inc.)

UNITED GUNN RES LTD (BC)
Delisted from Toronto Venture Stock Exchange 06/20/2003

UNITED GYPSUM CORP. LTD. (BC)
Ceased operations 12/10/1973
Stockholders' equity unlikely

UNITED HAWAIIAN INVT CORP (HI)
Each share Common $1 par exchanged for (0.25) share Common $4 par 11/28/1967
Involuntarily dissolved for failure to file annual reports 11/09/1984

UNITED HEALTHCARE CORP (MN)
Common 1¢ par split (2) for (1) by issuance of (1) additional share 09/15/1992
Common 1¢ par split (2) for (1) by issuance of (1) additional share 03/10/1994
Name changed to UnitedHealth Group Inc. (MN) 03/01/2000
UnitedHealth Group Inc. (MN) reincorporated in Delaware 07/01/2015

UNITED HEARNE RES LTD (CANADA)
Reincorporated 11/17/86
Place of incorporation changed from (BC) to Canada 11/17/86
Delisted from Vancouver Stock Exchange 2/27/87

UNITED HEAVY MACHY URALMASH-IZHORA GROUP (RUSSIA)
Name changed to Omz OJSC Uralmash-Izhora Group 04/03/2009
(See Omz OJSC Uralmash-Izhora Group)

UNITED HELICOPTERS, INC. (CA)
Recapitalized as Hiller Helicopters, Inc. and Capital Stock no par changed to $1 par 3/9/51
Hiller Helicopters, Inc. name changed to Hiller Aircraft Corp. 7/11/58 which name was changed to Hiller Realization Corp. 11/30/60 which was liquidated 1/25/61
(See Hiller Realization Corp.)

UNITED HERITAGE BANKSHARES FLA INC (FL)
Merged into Marshall & Ilsley Corp. (Old) 04/02/2007
Each share Common 1¢ par exchanged for (0.874) share Common $1 par
(See Marshall & Ilsley Corp. (Old))

UNITED HERITAGE CORP (UT)
Each share old Common $0.001 par exchanged for (0.1) share new Common $0.001 par 11/01/1999
Each share new Common $0.001 par exchanged again for (1/3) share new Common $0.001 par 12/22/2005
Reincorporated under the laws of Delaware as Glen Rose Petroleum Corp. 06/05/2008

UNITED HIGH INCOME FD II INC (MD)
Common $1 par reclassified as Class A $1 par 1/12/96
Class A $1 par changed to $0.001 par 6/22/99
Under plan of reorganization each share Class A $0.001 par, Class B $0.001 par, Class C $0.001 par, or Class Y $0.001 par automatically became (1) share Waddell & Reed Advisors Funds Inc. High Income Fund Class A $0.001 par, Class B $0.001 par, Class C $0.001 par, or Class Y $0.001 par respectively 10/1/2000

UNITED HIGH INCOME FD INC (MD)
Common $1 par reclassified as Class A $1 par 7/31/95
Class A $1 par changed to $0.001 par 6/22/99
Under plan of reorganization each share Class A $0.001 par, Class B $0.001 par, Class C $0.001 par, or Class Y $0.001 par automatically became (1) share Waddell & Reed Advisors Funds Inc. High Income Fund Class A $0.001 par, Class B $0.001 par, Class C $0.001 par, or Class Y $0.001 par respectively 10/1/2000

UNITED HOLDING CORP.
Dissolved in 1936

UNITED HOME LIFE INS CO (IN)
Common $1 par split (5) for (4) by issuance of (0.25) additional share 10/5/95
Stock Dividend - 10% 10/6/65
Merged into United Farm Family 11/14/97
Each share Common $1 par exchanged for $8.75 cash

UNITED HOMES INC (BC)
Name changed to Great Icelandic Water Corp. (BC) 5/14/92
Great Icelandic Water Corp. (BC) reincorporated in Canada 10/28/92
(See Great Icelandic Water Corp.)

UNITED HORIZON FD LTD (CANADA)
Merged into United Global Growth Fund 02/17/1983
Each Mutual Fund Share no par exchanged for (0.7514451) Mutual Fund Share no par
(See United Global Growth Fund)

UNITED HOTELS CORP. (DE)
Merged into United Resort Hotels, Inc. for cash 11/27/59
Holders of fewer than (100) shares Common 10¢ par received $1 cash per share without presentation of certificates
Holders of (100) shares or more Common 10¢ par were required to exchange certificates in order to receive payment of $1 per share

UNITED HUDSON RES INC (BC)
Recapitalized as Northrich Pacific Ventures Inc. 02/17/1993
Each share Common no par exchanged for (0.33333333) share Common no par
(See Northrich Pacific Ventures Inc.)

UNITED ICE & COAL CO.
Liquidation completed in 1951

UNITED ICE SERVICE CO.
Name changed to Southern Ice Co. (Del.) in 1928
Southern Ice Co. (Del.) name changed to Southern-Piedmont Ice Co. 4/10/79

UNITED IDAHO MINING CO. (ME)
Liquidated 4/30/70
No equity for holders of Preferred $10 par or Common no par

UNITED ILLUM CO (CT)
Each share old Capital Stock no par exchanged for (6) shares new Capital Stock no par 00/00/1926
New Capital Stock no par changed to Common no par and (1) additional share issued 07/31/1956
Stock Dividend - 100% 01/24/1942
15.88% Preference 1980 Ser. $25 par called for redemption 11/21/1986
16% Preferred 1981 Ser. $25 par called for redemption 01/15/1987
19% Depositary Preferred 1984 Ser. $10 par called for redemption 07/15/1989
19% Preferred 1984 Ser. $100 par called for redemption 07/15/1989
8.8% Preferred Ser. 1976 $25 par called for redemption 04/15/1994
7.6% CMT Preferred Ser. E $100 par called for redemption 05/10/1995
7.6% CDT Preferred Ser. F $100 par called for redemption 05/10/1995
4.35% Preferred Ser. A $100 par called for redemption at $102 on 05/14/1999
4.64% Preferred Ser. C $100 par called for redemption at $101 on 05/14/1999
4.72% Preferred Ser. B $100 par called for redemption at $101 on 05/14/1999
5.625% Preferred Ser. D $100 par called for redemption at $101 on 05/14/1999
Under plan of reorganization each share Common no par automatically became (1) share UIL Holdings Corp. Common no par 07/20/2000
UIL Holdings Corp. merged into Avangrid, Inc. 12/16/2015

UNITED IMPT & INVESTING CORP (DE)
Name changed to U.I.P. Corp. 5/7/68
U.I.P. Corp. merged into Eastmet Corp. 12/20/79
(See Eastmet Corp.)

UNITED INC (AB)
Company went private 10/25/2001
Each share Common no par exchanged for $1.50 cash

UNITED INCOME INC (OH)
Each share old Common $1 par exchanged for (0.07000002) share new Common $1 par 5/13/97
Merged into United Trust Group, Inc. (IL) 7/26/99
Each share new Common $1 par exchanged for (1) share Common no par
United Trust Group, Inc. (IL)

reincorporated in Delaware as UTG Inc. 7/6/2005

UNITED INDUSTRIAL BANK (BROOKLYN, NY)
Name changed to United Bank & Trust Co. (Brooklyn, N.Y.) 12/22/67
United Bank & Trust Co. (Brooklyn, N.Y.) merged into Royal National Bank (New York, N.Y.) 2/28/69 which merged into Security National Bank (Hempstead, N.Y.) 5/8/72
(See Security National Bank (Hempstead, N.Y.))

UNITED INDL CORP (DE)
Reincorporated 12/31/1959
Under plan of merger state of incorporation changed from (MI) to (DE) and each share Common $2 par exchanged for (1) share Ser. A Preferred $8.50 par and (1) share Common $1 par 12/31/1959
Conv. Preferred Ser. A $8.50 par called for redemption 11/28/1980
Common $1 par split (3) for (2) by issuance of (0.5) additional share 10/28/1982
Common $1 par split (2) for (1) by issuance of (1) additional share 09/30/1983
Stock Dividends - 10% 02/14/1975; 10% 02/17/1976; 10% 02/17/1977; 10% 02/17/1978; 10% 02/16/1979; 10% 02/15/1980; 10% 02/16/1981; 10% 02/15/1982; 10% 02/15/1983; 10% 02/28/1985; 10% 02/28/1986; 10% 02/27/1987
Merged into Textron Inc. 12/18/2007
Each share Common $1 par exchanged for $81 cash

UNITED INDUSTRIES CO., INC. (TX)
Name changed to United Foods, Inc. (TX) 4/24/61
United Foods, Inc. (TX) reincorporated in Delaware 9/30/83
(See United Foods, Inc. (DE))

UNITED INFORMATION SYS INC (DE)
Charter cancelled and declared inoperative and void for non-payment of taxes 3/1/99

UNITED INNS INC (DE)
Reincorporated 4/1/71
Common Capital Stock no par changed to $1 par and (1) additional share issued 12/16/68
Common Capital Stock $1 par split (3) for (2) by issuance of (0.5) additional share 9/30/69
State of incorporation changed from (TN) to (DE) 4/1/71
Merged into United/Harvey Hotels Co. 1/27/95
Each share Common $1 par exchanged for $25 cash

UNITED INSURANCE CO. OF ILLINOIS (IL)
Name changed to United Insurance Co. of America (IL) 07/01/1955
United Insurance Co. of America (IL) reincorporated in Nevada as Unicoa Corp. 08/09/1969 which name changed to United Insurance Co. of America (NV) 11/02/1987
(See United Insurance Co. of America (NV))

UNITED INS CO AMER (IL)
Each share Common $25 par exchanged for (10) shares Common $2.50 par and a 200% stock dividend distributed 09/20/1955
Stock Dividends - 50% 03/02/1959; 28% 08/01/1960; 25% 03/01/1962; 20% 03/15/1963; 10% 06/20/1966
Reincorporated under the laws of Nevada as Unicoa Corp. 08/09/1968
Unicoa Corp. name changed to United Insurance Co. of America (NV) 11/02/1987
(See United Insurance Co. of America (NV))

UNITED INS CO AMER NEW (NV)
Merged into United Transition Co. 12/28/89
Each share Common $2.50 par exchanged for $321.19 cash

UNITED INS COS INC (DE)
Common 1¢ par split (2) for (1) by issuance of (1) additional share 8/31/92
Common 1¢ par split (4) for (1) by issuance of (3) additional shares 5/31/95
Name changed to UICI 7/1/96
(See UICI)

UNITED INSURANCE FUND, INC. (WA)
Common $1 par changed to 50¢ par and (1) additional share issued 1/14/64
Liquidation completed
Each share Common 50¢ par exchanged for initial distribution of $1.25 cash 7/9/68
Each share Common 50¢ par received second and final distribution of $0.1142 cash 12/3/68

UNITED INSURANCE TRUST SHARES
Trust terminated 00/00/1949 and completely liquidated 00/00/1952
Details not available

UNITED INTERNATIONAL CORP. (AZ)
Charter revoked for failure to file reports and pay fees 12/26/72

UNITED INTL CORP (NV)
Completely liquidated 06/30/1971
Each share Common $1 par exchanged for first and final distribution of (1) share Transport Life Insurance Co. Common $1 par
(See Transport Life Insurance Co.)

UNITED INTL DEV ENTERPRISES (CA)
Name changed to Monterey Enterprises, Inc. 12/30/1970
(See Monterey Enterprises, Inc.)

UNITED INTERNATIONAL FUND LTD. (BERMUDA)
Acquired by United Funds Canada-International Ltd. 1/5/65
Each share Common £1 par exchanged for (1.75359) shares Common $1 par
United Funds Canada-International Ltd. merged into United Continental Growth Fund, Inc. (DE) 10/13/72 which reincorporated in Maryland 12/31/74 which name changed to United International Growth Fund Inc. 9/10/81 which reorganized as Waddell & Reed Advisors Funds Inc. 10/1/2000

UNITED INTL GOLD INC (UT)
Proclaimed dissolved for failure to pay taxes 5/1/89

UNITED INTL GROWTH FD INC (MD)
Common $1 par reclassified as Class A $1 par 7/4/95
Class A $1 par changed to $0.001 par 6/22/99
Under plan of reorganization each share Class A $0.001 par, Class B $0.001 par, Class C $0.001 par, or Class Y $0.001 par automatically became (1) share Waddell & Reed Advisors Funds Inc. International Growth Fund Class A $0.001 par, Class B $0.001 par, Class C $0.001 par, or Class Y $0.001 par respectively 10/1/2000

UNITED INTL HLDGS INC (DE)
Class A Common 1¢ par split (2) for (1) by issuance of (1) additional share 04/15/1994
Name changed to Unitedglobalcom, Inc. 07/23/1999
Unitedglobalcom, Inc. merged into Liberty Global, Inc. (DE) 06/15/2005 which reorganized in England & Wales as Liberty Global PLC 06/10/2013

UNITED INTERNATIONAL INC. (IN)
Charter revoked for failure to file annual reports 6/30/78

UNITED INTL RESH INC (NY)
Name changed to United-Guardian, Inc. 02/16/1982

UNITED INVESTMENT SHARES, INC.
Series A terminated in 1946
Series B & C terminated in 1947

UNITED INVESTORS CORP. (DE)
Class B 1964 Ser. $1 par reclassified as Class A $1 par 12/31/64
Class B 1965 Ser. $1 par reclassified as Class A $1 par 12/31/65
Class B 1966 Ser. $1 par reclassified as Class A $1 par 12/31/66
Class B 1967 Ser. $1 par reclassified as Class A $1 par 12/31/67
Under plan of merger name changed to United National Investors Corp. and Class A $1 par and Class B 1968 Ser. $1 par reclassified as Common $1 par 10/10/68
United National Investors Corp. name changed to United National Corp. (Del.) 7/15/70 which merged into Goldome National Corp. 5/13/83
(See Goldome National Corp.)

UNITED INVESTORS CORP. (IA)
Dissolved 6/26/36

UNITED INVESTORS CORP. (MN)
Name changed to United Capital Life Investors Corp. 04/15/1965
United Capital Life Investors Corp. name changed to United Capital Investors Corp. 04/25/1968 which was acquired by Analysts International Corp. 02/15/1969
(See Analysts International Corp.)

UNITED INVESTORS CORP. OF DELAWARE (DE)
Name changed to United Investors Corp. (Del.) 6/22/62
United Investors Corp. (Del.) merged into United National Investors Corp. 10/10/68 which name changed to United National Corp. (Del.) 7/15/70 which merged into Goldome National Corp. 5/13/83
(See Goldome National Corp.)

UNITED INVS INC (OK)
Completely liquidated 12/05/1980
Each share 6% Class A Preferential Common 50¢ par received first and final distribution of (2) shares Liberty Investors Life Insurance Co. Common Capital Stock 2¢ par
Note: Certificates were not required to be surrendered and are without value
(See Liberty Investors Life Insurance Co.)

UNITED INVS MGMT CO (DE)
Merged into Torchmark Corp. 10/1/93
Each share Common $1 par exchanged for $31.25 cash

UNITED INVS RLTY TR (TX)
Merged into Equity One, Inc. 09/21/2001
Each share Common no par exchanged for (0.14) share Common 1¢ par and $5.71 cash
Equity One, Inc. merged into Regency Centers Corp. 03/01/2017

UNITED IOWA CORP (IA)
Name changed to BNL Financial Corp. 02/28/1994
(See BNL Financial Corp.)

UNITED JERSEY BKS (NJ)
Common $5 par changed to $2.50 par and (1) additional share issued 02/28/1973
Common $2.50 par changed to $1.11111111 par and (0.5) additional share issued 09/24/1985
Common $1.11111111 par changed to $1.20 par and (0.5) additional share issued 09/24/1986
Adjustable Rate Preferred Ser. A no par called for redemption 05/01/1988
Name changed to UJB Financial Corp. 06/30/1989
UJB Financial Corp. name changed to Summit Bancorp 03/01/1996 which merged into FleetBoston Financial Corp. 03/01/2001 which merged into Bank of America Corp. 04/01/2004

UNITED KENO HILL MINES LTD (CANADA)
Plan of Arrangement under Companies' Creditors Agreement Act effective 01/03/2002
Stockholders' equity unlikely

UNITED KIEV RES INC (AB)
Name changed to Carpatsky Petroleum Inc. 7/21/97
(See Carpatsky Petroleum Inc.)

UNITED KINGDOM ENERGY INC (BC)
Struck off register and declared dissolved for failure to file returns 3/20/92

UNITED KINGDOM FD INC (MD)
Completely liquidated 6/18/99
Each share Common 1¢ par exchanged for first and final distribution of $16.04 cash

UNITED KIRKLAND GOLD MINES LTD.
Succeeded by Macassa Mines Ltd. on a (1) for (10) basis in 1934
Macassa Mines Ltd. merged into Macassa Gold Mines Ltd. 11/1/61 which merged into Willroy Mines Ltd. 1/8/71 which merged into Lac Minerals Ltd. (Old) 12/31/82 which merged into LAC Minerals Ltd. (New) 7/29/85 which was acquired by American Barrick Resources Corp. 10/17/94 which name changed to Barrick Gold Corp. 1/18/95

UNITED KY INC (KY)
Merged into Liberty United Bancorp, Inc. 12/23/82
Each share Common $10 par exchanged for (0.7273) share Common $8.333333 par
Liberty United Bancorp, Inc. name changed back to Liberty National Bancorp, Inc. 4/17/86 which merged into Banc One Corp. 8/15/94 which merged into Bank One Corp. 10/2/98 which merged into J.P. Morgan Chase & Co. 12/31/2000 which name changed to JPMorgan Chase & Co. 7/20/2004

UNITED LANDS CORP. LTD. OLD (ON)
Merged into United Lands Corp. Ltd. (New) 11/1/78
Each (10,000) shares Capital Stock no par exchanged for (1) share Class A Special no par

UNITED LEAD & ZINC MINES LTD. (QC)
Acquired by United Montauban Mines Ltd. on a (1) for (2) basis in 1953
United Montauban Mines Ltd. recapitalized as Satellite Metal Mines Ltd. 7/30/58 which recapitalized as Satellite Consolidated Metals Ltd. 6/23/83 which name changed to Phoenix Gold Mines Ltd. 6/30/86
(See Phoenix Gold Mines Ltd.)

UNITED LEAD ZINC MINES CO (ID)
Completely liquidated 11/04/1970
Each share Common 5¢ par exchanged for first and final distribution of (0.937) share Alice Consolidated Mines, Inc. Common 10¢ par

UNITED LEADER RES INC (BC)
Name changed to Vertica Systems Corp. 4/13/87
Vertica Systems Corp. recapitalized as Siscoe Callahan Mining Corp. 8/3/88
(See Siscoe Callahan Mining Corp.)

UNITED LEISURE CORP (DE)
Charter cancelled and declared inoperative and void for non-payment of taxes 03/01/2004

UNITED LEISURE GOLD LTD (BC)
Recapitalized as Forum Resources Ltd. 04/17/1978
Each share Capital Stock no par exchanged for (0.5) share Capital Stock no par
Forum Resources Ltd. name changed to Forum Beverages Inc. 02/16/1989
(See Forum Beverages Inc.)

UNITED LIBERTY LIFE INS CO (OH)
Reincorporated 11/10/1974
Common no par split (5) for (4) by issuance of (0.25) additional share 08/13/1971
State of incorporation changed from (TX) to (OH) 11/10/1974
Merged into American Financial Corp. 08/08/1980
Each share Common no par exchanged for (0.534521) share Common no par
(See American Financial Corp.)

UNITED LIBERTY RES LTD (BC)
Name changed to United Liberty Financial Corp. 04/28/1988

UNITED LIFE & ACC INS CO (NH)
Capital Stock $25 par changed to $20 par 00/00/1933
Each share Capital Stock $20 par exchanged for (56) shares Capital Stock $1 par 09/09/1963
Capital Stock $1 par split (5) for (4) by issuance of (0.25) additional share 06/16/1969
Merged into Chubb Corp. 07/16/1971
Each share Capital Stock $1 par exchanged for (0.4) share Common $1 par
Chubb Corp. merged into Chubb Ltd. 01/15/2016

UNITED LIFE INSURANCE CO. (IA)
Common $2 par changed to $3 par 4/17/74
Each share Common $3 par exchanged for (0.001) share Common $4,000 par 5/16/84
Note: In effect holders received $19.63 cash per share and public interest was eliminated

UNITED LIGHT & POWER CO.
Liquidated in 1945

UNITED LIGHT & RAILWAYS CO.
Liquidated in 1950

UNITED LINCOLN RES INC (BC)
Merged into Continental Gold Corp. (New) 03/15/1989
Each share Common no par exchanged for (1) share Common no par
(See Continental Gold Corp. (New))

UNITED LITHIUM CORP (BC)
Name changed to United Battery Metals Corp. 08/20/2018

UNITED LOAN CORP. (QC)
Operations ceased 7/25/60
Reported assets sold for benefit of creditors with nothing for stockholders and affairs wound up in 1969

UNITED MACFIE MINES LTD (ON)
Capital Stock $1 par changed to no par 6/4/74
Name changed to Macfie Resources Inc. 6/12/80
(See Macfie Resources Inc.)

UNITED MAGAZINE CO (OH)
Each share old Common no par exchanged for (0.1) share new Common no par 10/8/97
Company went out of business 9/20/99
Details not available

UNITED MGMT INC (NV)
Name changed to Rrun Ventures Network Inc. 12/29/2000
Rrun Ventures Network Inc. name changed to Livestar Entertainment Group Inc. 7/10/2003 which name changed to Jupiter Global Holdings Corp. 12/22/2004 which merged into Paivis, Corp. 5/19/2006

UNITED MANUFACTURING & ENGINEERING CORP. (DE)
Merged into General United Corp., Inc. on a (1) for (3) basis 4/26/63
(See General United Corp., Inc.)

UNITED MARINE, INC. (DE)
Name changed to Richardson Boat Co. and Common $1 par changed to no par 3/7/61
Richardson Boat Co. adjudicated bankrupt 6/1/62

UNITED MARINE INDS INC (DE)
Charter cancelled and declared inoperative and void for non-payment of taxes 4/15/71

UNITED MED CORP (NJ)
Stock Dividends - 10% 6/2/82; 10% 6/2/86
Acquired by UMC Acquisition Corp. 5/13/93
Each share Common no par exchanged for $9.50 cash

UNITED MEDIA GROUP INC (FL)
Reincorporated under the laws of Nevada as 21st Century Frontier Group, Inc. 08/04/1997
21st Century Frontier Group, Inc. recapitalized as Goldplate Holdings Enterprises Inc. 02/10/1999 which recapitalized as Eagletech Communications, Inc. 03/17/1999
(See Eagletech Communications, Inc.)

UNITED MEDIA LTD (CAYMAN ISLANDS)
Name changed 12/20/1999
Name changed from United Media Holdings Ltd. to United Media Ltd. 12/20/1999
Delisted from Toronto Venture Stock Exchange 11/06/2002

UNITED MEDICAL PRODUCTS CO., INC. (MN)
Merged into Unimed, Inc. 9/6/62
Each share Common 25¢ par exchanged for (1) share Common 25¢ par
Unimed, Inc. name changed to Unimed Pharmaceuticals Inc. 5/2/94
(See Unimed Pharmaceuticals Inc.)

UNITED MEDICAL PROPERTIES ADVISOR, INC. (TX)
Charter forfeited for failure to pay taxes 2/22/82

UNITED MEDICORP INC (DE)
Each share old Common 1¢ par exchanged exchanged for (0.5) share new Common 1¢ par 06/21/1990
Name changed to UMC, Inc. 09/10/2007

UNITED MERCANTILE BANK & TRUST CO., N.A. (PASADENA, CA)
Closed by the Comptroller of Currency and the FDIC was named receiver 3/20/92
Stockholders' equity unlikely

UNITED MERCHANTS & MFRS INC (DE)
Each share 6% Preferred $100 par exchanged for (3) shares old Common $1 par 00/00/1933
Each share 6% Preferred Series A $100 par exchanged for (3) shares old Common $1 par 00/00/1933
Each share 6% Preference A $50 par exchanged for (1.3) shares old Common $1 par 00/00/1933
Each share Common no par exchanged for (0.5) share old Common $1 par 00/00/1933
Stock Dividends - 10% 05/15/1944; 100% 03/07/1945; 200% 08/14/1946; 10% 07/30/1948; 10% 07/31/1951
Plan of reorganization under Federal Bankruptcy proceedings confirmed 04/10/1997
No stockholders' equity

UNITED MERCURY CORP. (DE)
Name changed to Mercury Electronics Corp. (Del.) 5/19/58
Mercury Electronics Corp. (Del.) recapitalized as Mercury Industries, Inc. 4/25/74

UNITED MERIDIAN CORP (DE)
Secondary Offering - 5,750,000 shares COM offered at $46.50 per share on 11/01/1996
Merged into Ocean Energy Inc. (Old) 3/27/98
Each share Common 1¢ par exchanged for (1.3) shares Common 1¢ par
Ocean Energy Inc. (Old) merged into Ocean Energy, Inc. (TX) 3/30/99 which reincorporated in Delaware 5/9/2001 which merged into Devon Energy Corp. 4/25/2003

UNITED METAL CRAFT CO. (MI)
Merged into Gar Wood Industries, Inc. on a (1/3) for (1) basis 10/31/58
Gar Wood Industries, Inc. acquired by Sargent Industries, Inc. (Del.) 4/2/70
(See Sargent Industries, Inc. (Del.))

UNITED MIC MAC MINES LTD. (ON)
Merged into Indian Lake Mines Ltd. share for share 00/00/1956
Indian Lake Mines Ltd. merged into Hydra Explorations Ltd. 11/16/1959 which name changed to Hydra Capital Corp. 12/30/1992 which name changed to Waterford Capital Management Inc. 11/12/1996 which merged into CPI Plastics Group Ltd. 09/21/1998
(See CPI Plastics Group Ltd.)

UNITED MICH CORP (MI)
Reincorporated 8/1/81
Stock Dividend - 10% 1/18/74
State of incorporation changed from (DE) to (MI) 8/1/81
Acquired by NBD Bancorp, Inc. 3/28/85
Each share Common $5 par exchanged for $56.10 cash

UNITED MILK CRATE CORP.
Dissolved in 1937
Details not available

UNITED MILK PRODS CO (DE)
Each share Preferred no par exchanged for (4) shares 5¢ Preferred no par 02/27/1947
Each share old Common no par exchanged for (4) shares new Common no par 02/27/1947
New Common no par changed to $5 par 03/01/1957
Plan of arrangement under Chapter XI bankruptcy proceedings confirmed 11/11/1965
Assets sold for benefit of creditors
No stockholders' equity

UNITED MILK PRODUCTS CORP.
Reorganized as United Milk Products Co. in 1933
Details not available

UNITED MINDAMAR METALS LTD (ON)
Name changed to Mindamar Energy Resources Ltd. 07/13/1973
(See Mindamar Energy Resources Ltd.)

UNITED MINERALS CORP. (NV)
Name changed to United Minerals Resources, Inc. 12/06/1965
United Minerals Resources, Inc. recapitalized as Galaxy Oil Co. 01/28/1969
(See Galaxy Oil Co.)

UNITED MINERALS LAND CORP.
Merged into Paymaster Consolidated Mines Ltd. on a (1) for (5) or (1) for (15) basis, depending on assessments 00/00/1930
Paymaster Consolidated Mines Ltd. recapitalized as Porcupine Paymaster Ltd. 04/10/1964 which merged into Associated Porcupine Mines Ltd. 11/05/1968 which merged into American Reserve Mining Corp. 02/27/1989 which recapitalized as AMI Resources Inc. 12/21/1994 which name changed to Ashanti Sankofa Inc. 01/19/2017

UNITED MINERALS RESERVE CORP. (NV)
Name changed to United Minerals Corp. in 1951
United Minerals Corp. name changed to United Minerals Resources, Inc. 12/6/65 which recapitalized as Galaxy Oil Co. 1/28/69
(See Galaxy Oil Co.)

UNITED MINERALS RESOURCES, INC. (NV)
Recapitalized as Galaxy Oil Co. 01/28/1969
Each share Common 10¢ par exchanged for (0.1) share Common 10¢ par
(See Galaxy Oil Co.)

UNITED MINERALS UNLIMITED, INC. (NV)
Merged into Copper Lode Mines, Inc. 6/15/70
Each share Common 2¢ par exchanged for (1) share Common no par
Copper Lode Mines, Inc. name changed to Trade Industries, Inc. 2/11/71 which recapitalized as Traco Corp. 3/21/72 which name changed to Energy International, Inc. 3/1/74
(See Energy International, Inc.)

UNITED MINES INC (AZ)
Stock Dividends - 1.5% payable 04/05/2010 to holders of record 03/31/2010 Ex date - 03/29/2010; 1.5% payable 07/16/2010 to holders of record 06/30/2010 Ex date - 06/28/2010; 1.5% payable 10/18/2010 to holders of record 09/30/2010 Ex date - 09/28/2010; 1.5% payable 03/10/2011 to holders of record 12/31/2010 Ex date - 12/29/2010
Name changed to WEED, Inc. 02/02/2015

UNITED MINES INC (ID)
Charter forfeited for failure to file reports 12/1/93

UNITED MINES OF HONDURAS, INC. (DE)
No longer in existence having become inoperative and void for non-payment of taxes 10/1/53

UNITED MINING & LEASING CORP. (CO)
Declared defunct and inoperative for failure to pay taxes and file annual reports 10/30/59

UNITED MNG GROUP INC (BC)
Name changed to United Silver Corp. 06/08/2011
(See United Silver Corp.)

UNITED MO BANCSHARES INC (MO)
Common $12.50 par split (3) for (2) by issuance of (0.5) additional share 5/11/73
Common $12.50 par split (3) for (2) by issuance of (0.5) additional share 3/8/77

Common $12.50 par split (3) for (2) by issuance of (0.5) additional share 1/2/87
Stock Dividends - 10% 1/3/79; 10% 1/3/80; 10% 1/6/81; 15% 1/5/82; 10% 1/4/83; 10% 1/3/84; 10% 1/2/85; 10% 1/2/86; 10% 1/2/92
Name changed to UMB Financial Corp. 4/22/94

UNITED MOBILE HOMES INC (MD)
Reincorporated 9/29/2003
State of incorporation changed from (NJ) to (MD) 9/29/2003
Name changed to UMH Properties, Inc. 4/1/2006

UNITED MOLASSES LTD (ENGLAND)
Ordinary Reg. 6s8d par changed to 10s par 00/00/1951
Stock Dividend - 50% 10/19/1956
Acquired by Tate & Lyle Ltd. 09/06/1965
Each share Ordinary Reg. 10s par or ADR for Ordinary Reg. 10s par exchanged for (0.4) share Ordinary Reg. £1 par, 12s principal amount of 6-3/4% Convertible Unsecured Loan Stock 1985/90 and 9s3d in cash

UNITED MONTAUBAN MINES LTD. (ON)
Recapitalized as Satellite Metal Mines Ltd. 7/30/58
Each share Capital Stock $1 par exchanged for (0.25) share Capital Stock $1 par
Satellite Metal Mines Ltd. recapitalized as Satellite Consolidated Metals Ltd. 6/23/83 which name changed to Phoenix Gold Mines Ltd. 6/30/86
(See Phoenix Gold Mines Ltd.)

UNITED MORTGAGE CORP. (MD)
Name changed to Atlantic Investment & Development Corp. 12/31/75

UNITED MUN BD FD INC (MD)
Common $1 par reclassified as Class A $0.001 par 1/21/96
Under plan of reorganization each share Class A $0.001 par automatically became (1) share Waddell & Reed Advisors Funds Inc. Municipal Bond Fund Class A $0.001 par 10/1/2000

UNITED MUN HIGH INCOME FD INC (MD)
Common $1 par reclassified as Class A $1 par 01/30/1996
Class A $1 par changed to $0.001 par 06/22/1999
Under plan of reorganization each share Class A $0.001 par, Class B $0.001 par, Class C $0.001 par, or Class Y $0.001 par automatically became (1) share Waddell & Reed Advisors Funds Inc. Municipal High Income Fund Class A $0.001 par, Class B $0.001 par, Class C $0.001 par, or Class Y $0.001 par respectively 10/01/2000

UNITED MUNICIPAL INCINERATOR CORP. (PA)
Name changed to Scienscope, Inc. 9/15/69
(See Scienscope, Inc.)

UNITED MUSIC & MEDIA GROUP INC (DE)
Common $0.0001 par split (10) for (1) by issuance of (9) additional shares payable 08/09/2010 to holders of record 08/02/2010 Ex date - 08/10/2010
Recapitalized as New Generation Consumer Group, Inc. 10/07/2014
Each share Common $0.0001 par exchanged for (0.001) share Common $0.0001 par

UNITED MUTUAL AGENCY, INC. (IN)
Charter revoked for failure to file reports and pay fees 9/20/65

UNITED N J RR & CANAL CO (NJ)
Merged into Penn Central Corp. 10/24/78
Each share Capital Stock $100 par exchanged for (2.63) shares Conv. Preference Ser. B $20 par, (1.18) shares Common $1 par, $52.50 principal amount of 7% General Mortgage Bonds Ser. B due 12/31/87 and $18.50 cash
Note: a) Distribution is certain only for certificates surrendered prior to 5/1/85 b) Distribution may also be made for certificates surrendered between 5/1/85 and 12/31/86 c) No distribution will be made for certificates surrendered after 12/31/86
Penn Central Corp. name changed to American Premier Underwriters, Inc. 3/25/94 which merged into American Premier Group, Inc. 4/3/95 which name changed to American Financial Group, Inc. 6/9/95 which merged into American Financial Group, Inc. (Holding Co.) 12/2/97

UNITED N MEX FINL CORP (NM)
Merged into First United Bank Group, Inc. 03/26/1993
Each share $2.125 Preferred Stock Ser. A $1 par exchanged for (1) share Conv. Exchangeable Preferred Ser. A $1 par
Each share Common $5 par exchanged for (1) share Common $1 par
First United Bank Group, Inc. merged into Norwest Corp. 01/14/1994 which name changed to Wells Fargo & Co. (New) 11/02/1998

UNITED NATL BANCORP (NJ)
Common $2.50 par split (2) for (1) by issuance of (1) additional share payable 07/01/1997 to holders of record 06/13/1997
Stock Dividends - 6% payable 11/01/1996 to holders of record 10/15/1996; 6% payable 11/03/1997 to holders of record 10/15/1997; 10% payable 10/22/1998 to holders of record 10/15/1998; 6% payable 11/01/1999 to holders of record 10/15/1999
Merged into PNC Financial Services Group, Inc. 01/01/2004
Each share Common $2.50 par exchanged for $35.83 cash

UNITED NATL BANCORPORATION (PA)
Common $2.50 par split (5) for (3) by issuance of (2/3) additional share 1/20/87
Stock Dividends - 10% 1/15/92; 10% 1/18/94
Merged into First Commonwealth Financial Corp. 9/27/94
Each share Common $2.50 par exchanged for (2) shares Common $1 par

UNITED NATL BK & TR CO (CANTON, OH)
Common $20 par changed to $13-1/3 par and (0.5) additional share 5/20/77
Reorganized as UNB Corp. 10/1/84
Each share Common $13-1/3 par exchanged for (2) shares Common $5 par
UNB Corp. name changed to Unizan Financial Corp. 3/8/2002 which merged into Huntington Bancshares Inc. 3/1/2006

UNITED NATL BK (COCOA BEACH, FL)
Merged into First American Bank & Trust of Palm Beach County (North Palm Beach, FL) 3/21/83
Each share Common $12.50 par exchanged for shares of Class A Common $1 par, Class B Common $1 par and $43 cash
(See First American Bank & Trust of Palm Beach (North Palm Beach, FL))

UNITED NATIONAL BANK (DALLAS, TX)
Merged into First City Bancorporation of Texas, Inc. (TX) 06/01/1979
Each share Common $4 par exchanged for (0.420975) share Common $6.50 par
(See First City Bancorporation of Texas, Inc. (TX))

UNITED NATL BK (MIAMI, FL)
Common $10 par changed to $7.50 par 03/27/1969
Name changed to Flagship National Bank (Miami, FL) 11/08/1974
Flagship National Bank (Miami, FL) merged into Flagship National Bank of Miami (Miami Beach, FL) 05/01/1978 which location was changed to (Miami, FL) 03/18/1980 which name changed to Sun Bank/Miami, N.A. (Miami, FL) 04/01/1985 which name changed to SunTrust Bank, Miami, N.A. (Miami, FL) 10/06/1995
(See SunTrust Bank, Miami, N.A. (Miami, FL))

UNITED NATL BK (PLAINFIELD, NJ)
Common $5 par changed to $2.50 par and (1) additional share issued 5/16/86
Reorganized as United National Bancorp 8/1/88
Each share Common $2.50 par exchanged for (1) share Common $2.50 par
(See United National Bancorp)

UNITED NATL BK (WASHINGTON, DC)
Stock Dividend - 10% 2/28/75
Reorganized as UNB Bancshares, Inc. 6/30/82
Each share Common $5 par exchanged for (1) share Common $5 par
UNB Bancshares, Inc. merged into James Madison Ltd. 10/22/86
(See James Madison Ltd.)

UNITED NATL BK BERGEN CNTY (CLIFFSIDE PARK, NJ)
Merged into Hudson United Bank (Union City, NJ) 6/30/72
Each share Common $25 par exchanged for (6.5) shares Common $8 par
Hudson United Bank (Union City, NJ) reorganized as HUBCO, Inc. 10/1/82 which name changed to Hudson United Bancorp 4/21/99 which merged into TD Banknorth Inc. 1/31/2006
(See TD Banknorth Inc.)

UNITED NATL BK CENT JERSEY (PLAINFIELD, NJ)
Name changed to United National Bank (Plainfield, NJ) 1/1/73
United National Bank (Plainfield, NJ) reorganized as United National Bancorp 8/1/88
(See United National Bancorp)

UNITED NATL BK LONG ISLAND NEW YORK (FOREST HILLS, NY)
Merged into Valley Bank of New York (Valley Stream, NY) 4/1/74
Each share Common Capital Stock $10 par exchanged to $165 cash

UNITED NATIONAL CORP. (WA)
$1 Preferred no par and Common no par changed to $1 par respectively in 1935
Name changed to United Pacific Corp. in 1954
United Pacific Corp. merged into VWR United Corp. 11/30/66 which name changed to Univar Corp. (DE) 3/1/74 which reincorporated in Washington 3/1/96
(See Univar Corp. (WA))

UNITED NATL CORP (DE)
Merged into Goldome National Corp. 05/13/1983
Each share 70¢ Conv. Preferred $1 par exchanged for (0.5) share Preferred $1 par
Each share Common $1 par exchanged for (1) share Preferred $1 par
(See Goldome National Corp.)

UNITED NATL FILM CORP (NV)
Reincorporated 10/20/2006
Each share Common no par exchanged for (0.001) share Common $0.001 par 02/05/1998
State of incorporation changed from (CO) to (NV) 10/20/2006
Each share old Common $0.001 par exchanged for (0.0005) share new Common $0.001 par 12/28/2006
Note: No holder will receive fewer than (100) post-split shares
Name changed to Wuhan General Group (China), Inc. 03/16/2007

UNITED NATL FINL CORP (IL)
Involuntarily dissolved 08/01/1994

UNITED NATL GROUP LTD (CAYMAN ISLANDS)
Under plan of merger name changed to United America Indemnity, Ltd. (Cayman Islands) 01/25/2005
United America Indemnity, Ltd. (Cayman Islands) reorganized in Ireland as Global Indemnity PLC 07/02/2010 which reincorporated in Cayman Islands as Global Indemnity Ltd. 11/07/2016

UNITED NATL INVS CORP (DE)
Name changed to United National Corp. (DE) 07/15/1970
United National Corp. (DE) merged into Goldome National Corp. 05/13/1983
(See Goldome National Corp.)

UNITED NATL LIFE INS CO (IL)
Each share Common 50¢ par exchanged for (0.5) share Common $1 par 05/28/1969
Through voluntary exchange offer 100% acquired by First United National Corp. as of 08/27/1975
Public interest eliminated

UNITED NATIONS INS CO (CO)
Common 50¢ par changed to 25¢ par 8/15/63
Merged into Western Preferred Corp. 8/12/75
Each share Common 25¢ par exchanged for (0.001216) share 8% Conv. Preferred Ser. A $5 par
(See Western Preferred Corp.)

UNITED NETWORK MARKETING SVCS INC (DE)
Name changed to Knockout Holdings, Inc. 01/12/2005
(See Knockout Holdings, Inc.)

UNITED NETWORK TECHNOLOGIES INC (NY)
Name changed to Panagra International Corp. 10/01/1998
Panagra International Corp. name changed to Minghua Group International Holdings Ltd. 08/02/2001 which recapitalized as China Longyi Group International Holdings Ltd. 12/12/2007

UNITED NEW CONCEPTS FD INC (MD)
Common $1 par reclassified as Class A $1 par 7/18/95
Class A $1 par changed to $0.001 par 6/22/99
Under plan of reorganization each share Class A $0.001 par automatically became (1) share Waddell & Reed Advisors Funds Inc. New Concepts Fund Class A $0.001 par 10/1/2000

UNITED NEW FORTUNE MINES LTD (ON)
Charter cancelled for failure to pay taxes and file returns 6/23/80

UNITED NEW YORK BANK TRUST SHARES
Trust terminated 00/00/1949 and liquidation completed 00/00/1952
Details not available

UNITED NEWS & MEDIA PLC (UNITED KINGDOM)
Name changed 6/1/95
Name changed from United Newspapers PLC to United News & Media PLC 6/1/95
Each Sponsored ADR for Ordinary 25p par received distribution of (0.6485) Garban Group Holdings Ltd. Sponsored ADR for Ordinary 50p par payable 11/30/98 to holders of record 11/24/98
Name changed to United Business Media PLC 12/18/2000
(See United Business Media PLC)

UNITED NORTH AMERN RES INC (QC)
Reorganized under the laws of the United Kingdom as Alliance Resources PLC and Common no par reclassified as Ordinary 10p par 02/11/191
Alliance Resources plc merged into AROC Inc. 12/08/1999
(See AROC Inc.)

UNITED NORTH ATLANTIC SECURITIES LTD. (CANADA)
Reorganized as Unas Investments Ltd. 12/29/64
Each share Class A $10 par exchanged for (1) share Common no par
Each share Class B $1 par exchanged for (0.1) share Common no par
Unas Investments Ltd. merged into Slater, Walker of Canada Ltd. 7/7/72 which name changed to Talcorp Associates Ltd. which name changed to Talcorp Ltd. 9/14/82 which reorganized as Consolidated Talcorp Ltd. 8/7/86 which name changed to Sound Insight Enterprises Ltd. 12/7/90 which merged into CamVec Corp. 9/11/92 name changed to AMJ Campbell Inc. 8/14/2001
(See AMJ Campbell Inc.)

UNITED NORTH CAROLINA INDS INC (NC)
Name changed to United Group, Inc. 04/27/1976
United Group, Inc. merged into Norwest Corp. 03/21/1997 which name changed to Wells Fargo & Co. (New) 11/02/1998

UNITED NORTHN PETE CORP (BC)
Name changed to UNP Industries Ltd. 11/06/1989
UNP Industries Ltd. recapitalized as International UNP Holdings Ltd. (BC) 11/29/1990 which reincorporated in Canada 08/04/1993
(See International UNP Holdings Ltd.)

UNITED NUCLEAR CORP (DE)
Under plan of merger each share Common $1 par exchanged for (1-7/17) shares Common 20¢ par 4/4/62
Common 20¢ par split (3) for (2) by issuance of (0.5) additional share 4/21/78
Reincorporated under the laws of Virginia as UNC Resources, Inc. 8/31/78
UNC Resources, Inc. name changed to UNC Inc. (VA) 6/3/86 which reincorporated in Delaware 4/30/87
(See UNC Inc.)

UNITED OBALSKI MNG LTD (QC)
Merged into Allied Mining Corp. 09/22/1969
Each share Capital Stock $1 par exchanged for (0.272479) share Common no par
Allied Mining Corp. merged into United Asbestos Inc. 06/29/1973 which merged into Campbell Resources Inc. (New) 06/08/1983
(See Campbell Resources Inc. (New))

UNITED OHIO INSURANCE CO. (OH)
Merged into Centurion Financial, Inc. 01/10/1973
Each share Common $4 par exchanged for (1) share Common $1 par
(See Centurion Financial, Inc.)

UNITED OIL CO.
Acquired by Richfield Oil Co. of California 00/00/1927
Details not available

UNITED OIL CORP. (DE)
Incorporated 00/00/1928
No longer in existence having become inoperative and void for non-payment of taxes 04/01/1944

UNITED OIL CORP. (DE)
Incorporated 00/00/1948
No longer in existence having become inoperative and void for non-payment of taxes 04/01/1964

UNITED OIL CORP. (OK)
Charter suspended for failure to file reports and pay fees 03/08/1974

UNITED OIL INC (MD)
6% Preferred called for redemption at $11 on 07/01/1999

UNITED OIL PRODUCERS CORP.
Reorganized as Middle States Petroleum Corp. 00/00/1930
Details not available

UNITED OIL TRUST SHARES, SERIES H
Trust terminated and dissolved 00/00/1938
Details not available

UNITED OILS LTD (CANADA)
Each share Capital Stock $1 par exchanged for (10) shares Capital Stock no par 00/00/1929
Each share Capital Stock no par stamped to indicate distribution of (0.1) share Class A no par and (0.3) share Class B no par of Cygnus Corp. Ltd. 06/01/1964
(See Cygnus Corp. Ltd.)
Majority of shares acquired through purchase offer which expired 00/00/1965
Public interest eliminated

UNITED OKLA BANKSHARES INC (OK)
Merged into Ameribank Corp. 07/11/1997
Each share 9% Preferred $30 par exchanged for $58.35 cash
Each share Common $1 par exchanged for $0.776901 cash

UNITED ONLINE INC (DE)
Old Common $0.001 par split (3) for (2) by issuance of (0.5) additional share payable 10/31/2003 to holders of record 10/14/2003 Ex date - 11/03/2003
Each share old Common $0.001 par received distribution of (0.2) share FTD Companies, Inc. Common $0.0001 par payable 11/01/2013 to holders of record 10/10/2013 Ex date - 11/01/2013
Each share old Common $0.001 par exchanged for (0.14285714) share new Common $0.001 par 11/01/2013
Acquired by B. Riley Financial, Inc. 07/01/2016
Each share new Common $0.001 par exchanged for $11 cash

UNITED OVERSEAS LD LTD (SINGAPORE)
Each Unsponsored ADR for Ordinary S$1 par exchanged for (0.25) Sponsored ADR for Ordinary S$1 par 10/24/1997
Name changed to UOL Group Ltd. 05/09/2006

UNITED OVERTON CORP (DE)
Under plan of partial liquidation each share Common $1 par received distribution of $4.86 cash 02/27/1984
Merged into Enticements, Ltd. 11/13/1986
Each share Common $1 par exchanged for $0.90 cash
Note: An additional distribution of $0.07160 cash per share was paid 08/21/1987

UNITED PAC CAP RES CORP (ON)
Cease trade order effective 10/01/2001

UNITED PAC CORP (WA)
Recapitalized 03/16/1959
Each share $1 Preference $1 par exchanged for (1) share new Common $1 par
Each share old Common $1 par exchanged for (1) share new Common $1 par
Stock Dividend - 200% 11/13/1959
Merged into VWR United Corp. 11/30/1966
Each share new Common $1 par exchanged for (1) share Common $1 par
VWR United Corp. name changed to Univar Corp. (DE) 03/01/1974 which reincorporated in Washington 03/01/1996
(See Univar Corp. (WA))

UNITED PAC GOLD LTD (BC)
Struck off register and declared dissolved for failure to file returns 11/12/1993

UNITED PACIFIC ALUMINUM CORP. (CA)
Acquired by Cerro Corp. 02/21/1961
Each share Common $1 par exchanged for (0.2096436) share Common $5 par
Cerro Corp. merged into Cerro-Marmon Corp. 02/24/1976 which name changed to Marmon Group, Inc. 06/03/1977
(See Marmon Group, Inc.)

UNITED PAN-EUROPE COMMUNICATIONS N V (NETHERLANDS)
Each Unsponsored ADR for Ordinary EUR 0.30 par exchanged for (1) Sponsored ADR for Class A Ordinary EUR 2 par 07/23/1999
Sponsored ADR's for Class A Ordinary EUR 2 par split (3) for (1) by issuance of (2) additional ADR's payable 03/23/2000 to holders of record 03/17/2000
Plan of reorganization under Chapter 11 Federal Bankruptcy Code effective 09/03/2003
Each Sponsored ADR for Class A Ordinary EUR 2 par exchanged for (0.0018) share UGC Europe, Inc. Common 1¢ par
Note: Unexchanged certificates were cancelled and became without value 03/03/2004
UGC Europe, Inc. merged into Unitedglobalcom, Inc. 12/22/2003 which merged into Liberty Global, Inc. (DE) 06/15/2005 which reorganized in England & Wales as Liberty Global PLC 06/10/2013

UNITED PANAM FINL CORP (CA)
Acquired by Pan American Financial, L.P. 03/01/2011
Each share Common no par exchanged for $7.05 cash

UNITED PAPERBOARD CO. (NJ)
Name changed to United Board & Carton Corp. 00/00/1947
United Board & Carton Corp. name changed to Garber (A.L.) Co., Inc. (NJ) 12/31/1971 which reincorporated in Delaware 05/31/1972 which merged into Wheelabrator-Frye Inc. 09/18/1973 which merged into Signal Companies, Inc. 02/01/1983 which merged into Allied-Signal Inc. 09/19/1985 which name changed to AlliedSignal Inc. 04/26/1993 which name changed to Honeywell International Inc. 12/01/1999

UNITED PARAGON MNG CORP (PHILIPPINES)
ADR agreement terminated 02/25/2013
No ADR's remain outstanding

UNITED PARAMOUNT THEATRES, INC. (NY)
Under plan of merger name changed to American Broadcasting-Paramount Theatres, Inc. 02/09/1953
American Broadcasting-Paramount Theatres, Inc. name changed to American Broadcasting Companies, Inc. 07/02/1965
(See American Broadcasting Companies, Inc.)

UNITED PARCEL SVC AMER INC (DE)
Common $5 par changed to $3 par 05/08/1964
Common $3 par changed to $1.50 par 05/25/1971
Under plan of merger each share Common 10¢ par automatically became (0.66666666) share United Parcel Service, Inc. Class A-1, Class A-2, and Class A-3 Restricted 1¢ par 10/25/1999

UNITED PARK CITY MINES CO (DE)
Capital Stock $1 par changed to 1¢ par 01/30/1987
Each share old Common 1¢ par exchanged for (0.05) share new Common 1¢ par 08/25/1995
Merged into Capital Growth Partners, LLC 07/18/2003
Each share new Common 1¢ par exchanged for $20.51 cash

UNITED PAYORS & UTD PROVIDERS INC (DE)
Merged into BCE Emergis Inc. 03/28/2000
Eash share Common 1¢ par exchanged for $27 cash

UNITED PAYPHONE SVCS INC (NV)
Each share old Common $0.001 par exchanged for (0.2) share new Common $0.001 par 05/08/1992
Name changed to Diamond Equities, Inc. 06/20/1997
(See Diamond Equities, Inc.)

UNITED PENN CORP (PA)
Common no par split (2) for (1) by issuance of (1) additional share 12/28/1973
Merged into Continental Bancorp Inc. 08/17/1984
Each share Common no par exchanged for (0.7733) share Common no par
Continental Bancorp, Inc. merged into Midlantic Corp. 01/30/1987 which merged into PNC Bank Corp. 12/31/1995 which name changed to PNC Financial Services Group, Inc. 03/15/2000

UNITED PERFORMANCE INDS INC (MN)
Merged into United Financial Group, Inc. (MN) 05/07/1982
Each share Common 1¢ par exchanged for (2) shares Common 1¢ par

(See United Financial Group, Inc. (MN))

UNITED PERLITE CORP. (DE)
Common 10¢ par changed to 1¢ par 02/01/1961
Proclaimed inoperative and void for non-payment of taxes 12/15/1969

UNITED PETE CORP (DE)
Each share Common $0.001 par exchanged for (0.1) share old Common 1¢ par 03/13/1986
Each share old Common 1¢ par exchanged for (0.75) share new Common 1¢ par 04/26/1993
Each share new Common 1¢ par exchanged again for (0.33333333) share new Common 1¢ par 06/14/1995
Each share new Common 1¢ par exchanged again for (0.00654) share new Common 1¢ par 12/13/1999
SEC revoked common stock registration 06/07/2010

UNITED PETROLEUM & MINING CORP. (ND)
Merged into Keldon Oil Co. 10/24/1977
Each share Class A Common $1 par exchanged for (4.7105) shares Common no par
Each share 4% Class B Common Preference $1 par exchanged for (4.7105) shares Common no par
(See Keldon Oil Co.)

UNITED PETROSEARCH INC (TX)
Acquired by Pollock Petroleum Inc. 12/30/1981
Each share Common no par exchanged for (0.4696) share Common no par
Pollock Petroleum Inc. name changed to Pangea Petroleum Co. (CA) 05/29/1984 which reincorporated in Delaware 05/26/1987 which name changed to Harcor Energy, Inc. 01/06/1988
(See Harcor Energy, Inc.)

UNITED PHOSPHORUS LTD NEW (INDIA)
Sponsored Reg. S GDR's for Equity Shares split (5) for (1) by issuance of (4) additional GDR's payable 10/12/2005 to holders of record 10/04/2005
Sponsored Reg. S GDR's for Equity Shares split (2) for (1) by issuance of (1) additional GDR payable 12/18/2008 to holders of record 10/30/2008
Name changed to UPL Ltd. 11/19/2013

UNITED PHOSPHORUS LTD OLD (INDIA)
Name changed to Uniphos Enterprises Ltd. 01/16/2004

UNITED PIECE DYE WKS (NJ)
Each share old Common no par exchanged for (2) shares new Common no par 00/00/1929
Each share 6.5% Preferred $100 par exchanged for (1) share $4.25 Preferred $75 par and (9) shares Common 10¢ par 00/00/1948
Each share new Common no par exchanged for (0.33333333) share Common 10¢ par 00/00/1948
Each share $4.25 Preferred $75 par exchanged for (1) share $5.50 Preferred $75 par 07/17/1963
Each share $5.50 Preferred $75 par exchanged for (5) shares Common 10¢ par 10/16/1968
Merged into UPDW, Inc. 01/26/1979
Each share Common 10¢ par exchanged for $8 cash

UNITED PLAINS OIL CO. (OK)
Charter cancelled for failure to file reports and pay fees 03/16/1973

UNITED PLASTIC PRODUCTS, INC.
Out of business 00/00/1941
No stockholders' equity

UNITED PORCUPINE MINES LTD. (ON)
Merged into Dynacore Enterprises Ltd. 07/15/1967
Each share Common $1 par exchanged for (0.16) share Common no par
Dynacore Enterprises Ltd. recapitalized as Dynaco Resources Ltd. 02/09/1971
(See Dynaco Resources Ltd.)

UNITED PORTO RICAN SUGAR CO. (MD)
Reorganized as East Porto Rican Sugar Co. 06/29/1934
Each share Preferred exchanged for (1) share Common $1 par
Each share Common exchanged for (0.3125) share Common $1 par
East Porto Rican Sugar Co. name changed to Eastern Sugar Associates 04/16/1935 which name changed to Fajardo Eastern Sugar Associates 05/02/1958
(See Fajardo Eastern Sugar Associates)

UNITED POST OFFICES CORP.
Bankrupt 00/00/1948
No stockholders' equity

UNITED POSTAL BANCORP INC (DE)
Common 1¢ par split (2) for (1) by issuance of (1) additional share 04/26/1993
Merged into Mercantile Bancorporation, Inc. 02/01/1994
Each share Common 1¢ par exchanged for (0.6154) share Common $5 par
Mercantile Bancorporation, Inc. merged into Firstar Corp. (New) 09/20/1999 which merged into U.S. Bancorp (DE) 02/27/2001

UNITED POWER, GAS & WATER CORP.
Name changed to Tri-Utilities Corp. 00/00/1928
(See Tri-Utilities Corp.)

UNITED POWER & LIGHT CORP.
Acquired by Kansas Power & Light Co. 00/00/1935
Details not available

UNITED PREMIUM FINANCE CORP. (OK)
Charter cancelled for failure to pay taxes 03/09/1979

UNITED PRESIDENTIAL CORP (IN)
Common 50¢ par split (3) for (2) by issuance of (0.5) additional share 09/15/1983
Acquired by Washington National Insurance Co. 03/06/1987
Each share Common 50¢ par exchanged for $19 cash

UNITED PRESIDENTIAL LIFE INS CO (IN)
Stock Dividends - 10% 06/30/1978; 10% 05/18/1979
Under plan of merger each share Common $1 par automatically became (1) share United Presidential Corp. Common 50¢ par 10/24/1980
(See United Presidential Corp.)

UNITED PRINCIPAL PROPERTIES LTD. (ON)
Recapitalized as Canadian Interurban Properties Ltd. 8/28/63
Each share Capital Stock no par exchanged for (0.1) share Common no par
Canadian Interurban Properties Ltd. merged into Campeau Corp. 10/9/73
(See Campeau Corp.)

UNITED PRINTERS & PUBLISHERS, INC. (DE)
Each share Preference no par exchanged for (1) share Preference $10 par, (2) shares Common $1 par and $1.25 in cash 00/00/1937
Each share Common no par exchanged for (1) share Common $1 par 00/00/1937
Name changed to Rust Craft Greeting Cards, Inc. 07/13/1962
(See Rust Craft Greeting Cards, Inc.)

UNITED PRODS INTL INC (DE)
Reorganized under the laws of Florida as Environmental Digital Services Inc. 12/30/1996
Each share Class A Common 5¢ par exchanged for (0.05) share Common no par
Environmental Digital Services Inc. (FL) reincorporated in Delaware 07/01/2008 which recapitalized as Sabre Industrial, Inc. 04/12/2010 which name changed to Tsingyuan Brewery Inc. 01/19/2011
(See Tsingyuan Brewery Ltd.)

UNITED PRODUCTION CO., INC. (DE)
Declared inoperative and void for non-payment of taxes 04/01/1956

UNITED PROFESSIONAL DATA PROCESSING CORP (DE)
Charter cancelled and declared inoperative and void for non-payment of taxes 04/15/1972

UNITED PROFIT-SHARING CORP. (DE)
Common no par changed to 25¢ par in 1938
Recapitalized as Highway Trailer Industries, Inc. 9/3/58
Each share Preferred $10 par exchanged for (4) shares Common 25¢ par and either $15.50 in cash or (8) shares Common in lieu of cash
Common 25¢ par exchanged for new Common 25¢ par
Highway Trailer Industries, Inc. merged into Highway Industries Inc. for cash 12/31/69

UNITED PROPERTIES CO. OF CALIFORNIA (DE)
Charter cancelled and declared inoperative and void for non-payment of taxes 03/19/1919

UNITED PROTN SEC GROUP INC (AB)
Declared bankrupt 06/10/2013
Stockholders' equity unlikely

UNITED PROVINCIAL INVT LTD (BC)
Name changed to Dunhill Development Corp. Ltd. 4/18/72
(See Dunhill Development Corp. Ltd.)

UNITED PUBG CORP (DC)
Voluntarily dissolved 12/28/76
No stockholders' equity

UNITED PUBLIC MARKETS, INC. (RI)
Completely liquidated 2/2/65
Each share Common $1 par exchanged for first and final distribution of $9.17 cash

UNITED PUBLIC SERVICE CO.
Reorganized as United Public Service Corp. in 1935 which was liquidated in 1952

UNITED PUBLIC SERVICE CORP. (DE)
Liquidated 00/00/1952
Details not available

UNITED PUBLIC UTILITIES CO.
Reorganized as United Public Utilities Corp. in 1935 which was completely liquidated in 1954

UNITED PUBLIC UTILITIES CORP.
Liquidation completed in 1954

UNITED PUBLISHERS CORP. (DE)
Name changed to Chilton Co. in 1934
(See Chilton Co.)

UNITED RACEWAYS INC (DE)
Name changed to Square Shooter International Ltd. 11/05/1999
(See Square Shooter International Ltd.)

UNITED RAILWAYS & ELECTRIC CO. OF BALTIMORE
Reorganized as Baltimore Transit Co. in 1935
(See Baltimore Transit Co.)

UNITED RAILWAYS CO. OF ST. LOUIS
Acquired by St. Louis Public Service Co. in 1927 liquidation of which was completed 11/12/63

UNITED RAILWAYS INVESTMENT CO.
Dissolved in 1926

UNITED RAYORE GAS LTD (BC)
Merged into StarTech Energy Inc. 8/1/97
Each share Common no par exchanged for (0.1) share Common no par
StarTech Energy Inc. merged into Impact Energy Inc. (Canada) 1/31/2001 which merged into Thunder Energy Inc. 4/30/2004
(See Thunder Energy Inc.)

UNITED RD SVCS INC (DE)
Each share old Common $0.001 par exchanged for (0.1) share new Common $0.001 par 05/05/2000
Merged into United Road Merger Corp. 12/06/2004
Each share Common $0.001 par exchanged for $0.04 cash

UNITED RLTY GROUP L P (DE)
Completely liquidated 07/31/2000
Each Unit of Ltd. Partnership Int. no par exchanged for first and final distribution of $0.174 cash

UNITED RLTY INVS INC (DE)
Name changed 7/11/80
Name changed from United Realty Trust (CA) to United Realty Investors, Inc. (DE) and Shares of Bene. Int. $1 par reclassified as Common $1 par 7/11/80
Merged into Butterfield Equities Corp. 10/27/83
Each share Common $1 par exchanged for (2.3) shares Common no par
(See Butterfield Equities Corp.)

UNITED REALTY SERVICE CO.
Liquidated in 1942

UNITED RECORD & TAPE INDS INC (FL)
Name changed to URT Industries, Inc. 01/02/1975
(See URT Industries, Inc.)

UNITED REDFORD RES INC (BC)
Delisted from Vancouver Stock Exchange 08/31/1992

UNITED REEF LTD (ON)
Name changed 09/01/1993
Name changed from United Reef Petroleums Ltd. to United Reef Ltd. 09/01/1993
Recapitalized as New Klondike Exploration Ltd. 08/17/2012
Each share Common no par exchanged for (0.125) share Common no par
(See New Klondike Exploration Ltd.)

UNITED REFNG CO (PA)
Common $1 par split (3) for (2) by issuance of (0.5) additional share 9/10/79
Merged into Coral Petroleum Inc. 2/26/81
Each share Common $1 par exchanged for $50 cash

UNITED REFNG ENERGY CORP (DE)
Completely liquidated 12/16/2009
Each Unit exchanged for first and final distribution of $10.04062876 cash
Each share Common $0.0001 par

exchanged for first and final distribution of $10.04062876 cash

UNITED RENTALS TR I (DE)
144A 6.5% Conv. Quarterly Income Preferred Securities called for redemption at $50 plus $0.388194 accrued dividends on 06/13/2013
6.5% Conv. Quarterly Income Preferred Securities called for redemption at $50 plus $0.388194 accrued dividends on 06/13/2013

UNITED REP INVT CO (PA)
Stock Dividend - 20% 4/23/79
Merged into Monumental Corp. 7/16/81
Each share Class A $1 par exchanged for cash

UNITED REP LIFE INVT CO (PA)
Name changed to United Republic Investment Co. 5/7/70
(See United Republic Investment Co.)

UNITED REPRODUCERS CORP.
Out of business in 1930

UNITED RESEARCH, INC. (MA)
Each share Class A Common $10 par or Class B Common $10 par exchanged for (5) shares Common $2 par respectively 06/16/1960
Merged into URS Systems Corp. 11/26/1968
Each share Common $2 par exchanged for (1.448) shares Common no par
URS Systems Corp. name changed to URS Corp. (CA) 03/28/1974 which reincorporated in Delaware 05/18/1976 which name changed to Thortec International Inc. 11/18/1987 which name changed back to URS Corp. 02/21/1990

UNITED RESEARCH & DEVELOPMENT CO. (CO)
Completely liquidated 9/20/65
Each share Common 10¢ par exchanged for first and final distribution of $0.089 cash

UNITED RESERVE LIFE INSURANCE CO. (NE)
Under plan of merger name changed to Lincoln Life & Casualty Co. 12/30/65
(See Lincoln Life & Casualty Co.)

UNITED RESERVE UNDERWRITING CORP. (MT)
Voluntarily dissolved 2/16/78
Details not available

UNITED RESH HOMES INC (DE)
Completely liquidated 12/15/70
Each share Common 10¢ par exchanged for first and final distribution of (0.09) share Starrett Brothers & Eken, Inc. Common $1 par
Starrett Brothers & Eken, Inc. name changed to Starrett Housing Corp. 5/26/71 which name changed to Starrett Corp. 6/23/95
(See Starrett Corp.)

UNITED RESOURCES, INC. (NV)
Charter revoked for failure to file reports and pay fees 03/05/1962

UNITED RESOURCES, INC. (UT)
Name changed to Pacific Air Transport Inc. 01/31/1968
Pacific Air Transport Inc. name changed to Pacific Air Transport International Inc. 09/28/1970 which recapitalized as Chase Hanover Corp. 09/17/1983
(See Chase Hanover Corp.)

UNITED RES INC (FL)
SEC revoked common stock registration 06/07/2010

UNITED RESTAURANT MGMT INC (DE)
Each share old Common $0.001 par exchanged for (1/9) share new Common $0.001 par 05/01/2009

Name changed to Optimized Transportation Management, Inc. 07/31/2009
(See Optimized Transportation Management, Inc.)

UNITED RESTAURANTS INC (DE)
Name changed to Grand Havana Enterprises, Inc. 2/25/97
(See Grand Havana Enterprises, Inc.)

UNITED RETAIL GROUP INC (DE)
Merged into Redcats USA, Inc. 11/02/2007
Each share Common $0.001 exchanged for $13.70 cash

UNITED RETIREMENT SHS INC (MD)
Common $1 par changed to $0.001 par 6/22/99
Under plan of reorganization each share Common $0.001 par automatically became (1) share Waddell & Reed Advisors Fund Inc. Retirement Fund Class A $0.001 par 10/1/2000

UNITED-REXALL DRUG, INC.
Name changed to Rexall Drug, Inc. in 1947
Rexall Drug, Inc. merged into Rexall Drug Co. 5/6/55 which name changed to Rexall Drug & Chemical Co. 4/24/59 which name changed to Dart Industries, Inc. 4/22/69 which reorganized as Dart & Kraft, Inc. 9/25/80 which name changed to Kraft, Inc. (New) 11/21/86
(See Kraft, Inc. (New))

UNITED RIVER PLATTE TELEPHONE CO.
Acquired by International Telephone & Telegraph Corp. (Md.) in 1929
(See International Telephone & Telegraph Corp. (Md.))

UNITED ROYALTIES CO., INC. (DE)
Charter cancelled and declared inoperative and void for non-payment of taxes 4/1/30

UNITED SAFETY TECHNOLOGY INC (BC)
Recapitalized as Consolidated United Safety Technology Inc. 01/03/1990
Each share Common no par exchanged for (0.2) share Common no par
Consolidated United Safety Technology Inc. recapitalized as Genetronics Biomedical Ltd. (BC) 10/04/1994 which reincorporated in Delaware as Genetronics Biomedical Corp. 06/21/2001 which name changed to Inovio Biomedical Corp. 03/31/2005 which name changed to Inovio Pharmaceuticals, Inc. 05/14/2010

UNITED SALT CORP (TX)
Name changed to Houston Salt Corp. 10/02/1978
(See Houston Salt Corp.)

UNITED SARTIS ENTERPRISES INC (BC)
Name changed to Wellco Energy Services Inc. (BC) 02/11/1999
Wellco Energy Services Inc. (BC) reorganized in Alberta as Wellco Energy Services Trust 08/06/2002 which merged into Peak Energy Services Trust 03/12/2008 which reorganized as Peak Energy Services Ltd. (New) 01/06/2011
(See Peak Energy Services Ltd. (New))

UNITED SATELLITE AMER INC (DE)
Name changed 2/8/88
Name changed 6/23/89
Name changed from United Satellite Associates, Inc. to United Satellite America, Inc. 2/8/88
Name changed from United Satellite America, Inc. to United Satellite/ America, Inc. 6/23/89
Charter cancelled and declared

inoperative and void for non-payment of taxes 5/25/94

UNITED SAVERS BANCORP INC (NH)
Name changed to Dartmouth Bancorp, Inc. 04/12/1990
(See Dartmouth Bancorp, Inc.)

UNITED SAVINGS & LOAN ASSOCIATION (VA)
Capital Stock $10 par reclassified as Common $10 par 08/06/1970
Common $10 par changed to $5 par and (1) additional share issued 12/18/1982
Name changed to United Savings Bank (Vienna, VA) 05/01/1984
(See United Savings Bank (Vienna, VA))

UNITED SVGS & LN ASSN GREENWOOD (SC)
Under plan of reorganization each share Common $1 par automatically became (1) share United Financial Corp. of South Carolina, Inc. (DE) Common $1 par 07/18/1988
United Financial Corp. of South Carolina, Inc. merged into First Union Corp. 10/04/1995 which name changed to Wachovia Corp. (Ctfs. dated after 09/01/2001) 09/01/2001 which merged into Wells Fargo & Co. (New) 12/31/2008

UNITED SVGS & LN ASSN INC MT AIRY (NC)
Merged into First Financial Savings & Loan Association, Inc. 05/15/1984
Each share Common $1 par exchanged for $25 cash

UNITED SVGS ASSN (MIAMI, FL)
Name changed to BankUnited, A Savings Bank (Miami, FL) 09/30/1989
BankUnited, A Savings Bank (Miami, FL) reorganized as BankUnited Financial Corp. 03/05/1993
(See BankUnited Financial Corp.)

UNITED SVGS BK (SALEM, OR)
Merged into First Security Corp. 03/02/1990
Each share Common $1 par exchanged for (0.7083) share Common $1.25 par
First Security Corp. merged into Wells Fargo & Co. (New) 10/26/2000

UNITED SVGS BK (VIENNA, VA)
Placed in receivership 08/01/1990
No stockholders' equity

UNITED SVGS BK F A (GREAT FALLS, MT)
Under plan of reorganization each share Common $1 par automatically became (1) share United Financial Corp. Common $1 par 05/01/1996
United Financial Corp. merged into U.S. Bancorp 02/06/2007

UNITED SAVINGS LIFE INSURANCE CO. (TX)
Name changed to Detinu Liquidating Life Insurance Co. 9/30/70
Detinu Liquidating Life Insurance Co. acquired by United International Corp. (NV) 11/24/70 which completely liquidated for Transport Life Insurance Co. 6/30/71
(See Transport Life Insurance Co.)

UNITED SAVINGS LIFE INSURANCE CO. OF ILLINOIS (IL)
Name changed to United Savings Life Insurance Co. 7/17/72
(See United Savings Life Insurance Co.)

UNITED SVGS LIFE INS CO (IL)
Common $1.50 par changed to $1 par 5/15/79
Order of Liquidation with a Finding of Insolvency entered 8/27/86
Stockholders' equity unlikely

UNITED SCIENTIFIC CORP (CA)
Merged into Data-Design Laboratories (CA) 12/21/1979
Each share Common 10¢ par exchanged for (0.18181818) share Capital Stock $0.33333333 par
Data-Design Laboratories (CA) reincorporated in Delaware as Data-Design Laboratories, Inc. 12/01/1986 which name changed to DDL Electronics, Inc. 12/17/1993 which name changed to SMTEK International, Inc. 10/09/1998 which merged into CTS Corp. 02/01/2005

UNITED SCIENTIFIC LABORATORIES, INC. (NY)
Acquired by Vernitron Corp. (Old) (NY) on a (1) for (5) basis 10/09/1963
Vernitron Corp. (Old) (NY) reincorporated in Delaware 06/28/1968 which reorganized as Vernitron Corp. (New) 08/28/1987 which name changed to Axsys Technologies, Inc. 12/04/1996
(See Axsys Technologies, Inc.)

UNITED SCREW & BOLT CORP (OH)
Class B no par reclassified as Common no par 4/26/65
Stock Dividends - 100% 5/23/66; 150% 6/8/76; 200% 5/28/93
Merged into Plastech Engineered Products, Inc. 5/23/97
Each share Common no par exchanged for $130.21 cash
Note: An additional distribution of $3.12633898 cash per share was made from escrow 11/12/98

UNITED SEC BANCORPORATION (WA)
Stock Dividends - 10% 08/23/1995; 10% payable 02/05/1996 to holders of record 01/29/1996; 10% payable 02/25/1997 to holders of record 02/10/1997; 10% payable 02/26/1999 to holders of record 02/12/1999; 10% payable 02/15/2001 to holders of record 01/30/2001 Ex date - 02/01/2001
Name changed to AmericanWest Bancorporation 03/05/2001
(See AmericanWest Bancorporation)

UNITED SEC BANCSHARES INC (DE)
Reincorporated 08/04/1999
State of incorporation changed from (AL) to (DE) 08/04/1999
Common 1¢ par split (2) for (1) by issuance of (1) additional share payable 07/22/2003 to holders of record 06/30/2003 Ex date - 07/23/2003
Name changed to First US Bancshares, Inc. 10/11/2016

UNITED SEC BK (FRESNO, CA)
Name changed 02/00/1999
Name changed from United Security Bank, N.A. (Fresno, CA) to United Security Bank (Fresno, CA) 02/00/1999
Common no par split (3) for (1) by issuance of (2) additional shares payable 10/01/1999 to holders of record 09/15/1999
Under plan of reorganization each share Common no par automatically became (1) share United Security Bancshares Common no par 06/12/2001

UNITED SEC FINL CORP ILL (IL)
Voluntarily dissolved 11/13/92
Details not available

UNITED SEC HLDG CO (DE)
Completely liquidated 02/22/1978
Each share Common 10¢ par exchanged for first and final distribution of (0.09) share National Producers Life Insurance Co. Common 50¢ par
National Producers Life Insurance Co.

name changed to NPL Corp. 03/27/1981
(See NPL Corp.)

UNITED SEC LIFE CO (IA)
Merged into All American Life & Casualty Co. 05/31/1973
Each share Common 25¢ par exchanged for $6.35 cash

UNITED SEC LIFE INS CO (AL)
Reorganized as United Security Holding Co. 01/20/1970
Each share Common $1 par exchanged for (1) share Common 10¢ par
United Security Holding Co. liquidated for National Producers Life Insurance Co. 02/22/1978 which name changed to NPL Corp. 03/27/1981
(See NPL Corp.)

UNITED SECS FINL CORP (WA)
Charter cancelled and proclaimed dissolved for failure to pay fees 07/02/1981

UNITED SECURITIES CORP. (RI)
Dissolved in 1936

UNITED SECURITIES LTD. (QC)
Liquidation completed 12/13/57

UNITED SECURITIES TRUST ASSOCIATES
Merged into Massachusetts Investors Trust in 1931

UNITED SECURITY LIFE INSURANCE CO. (LA)
Name changed to United Companies Life Insurance of America 3/1/65
United Companies Life Insurance of America name changed to United Companies Life Insurance Co. 2/21/66 which reorganized as United Companies Financial Corp. 6/19/72
(See United Companies Financial Corp.)

UNITED SERVICE CORP., LTD. (NS)
Acquired by Canadian Petrofina Ltd. for cash in 1955

UNITED SVC SOURCE INC (DE)
Name changed to UNSI Corp. 05/14/1991
(See UNSI Corp.)

UNITED SVCS ADVISORS INC (TX)
Name changed to U.S. Global Investors, Inc. and Non-Dividend Preferred 5¢ par reclassified as Class A Common 5¢ par 06/01/1996

UNITED SERVICES GENERAL LIFE CO. (OK)
Each share Capital Stock $4.60 par exchanged for (0.0021786) share Capital Stock $3,000 par 10/22/81
Note: In effect holders received $15.50 cash per share and public interest was eliminated

UNITED SVCS LIFE INS CO (DC)
Common $2.50 par changed to $1 par and (2) additional shares issued 6/30/59
Stock Dividends - 33-1/3% 5/26/61; 25% 12/31/62; 25% 10/30/64; 20% 12/21/65; 20% 5/21/70; 20% 2/26/71; 10% 5/15/72; 10% 2/27/76; 10% 2/27/81; 10% 2/25/83
Reorganized under the laws of Delaware as USLICO Corp. 8/15/84
Each share Common $1 par exchanged for (1) share Common $1 par
USLICO Corp. merged into NWNL Companies, Inc. 1/17/95 which name changed to ReliaStar Financial Corp. 2/13/95
(See ReliaStar Financial Corp.)

UNITED SERVOMATION CORP. (DE)
Name changed to Servomation Corp. 7/1/63
(See Servomation Corp.)

UNITED SHIELDS CORP (CO)
SEC revoked common stock registration 09/09/2010

UNITED SHIPPING & TECHNOLOGY INC (UT)
Reincorporated under the laws of Delaware as Velocity Express Corp. 01/14/2002
(See Velocity Express Corp.)

UNITED SHIPYARDS, INC.
Liquidation completed in 1947

UNITED SHIRT DISTRS INC (DE)
Common no par changed to $1 par in 1947
Common $1 par split (3) for (1) by issuance of (2) additional shares 1/5/70
Merged into Interco Inc. (Old) 1/31/74
Each share Common $1 par exchanged for (0.491836) share Common no par
(See Interco Inc. (Old))

UNITED SHOE MACHY CORP (NJ)
Name changed to USM Corp. 7/26/68
(See USM Corp.)

UNITED SHOPPERS AMER INC (NV)
Recapitalized as MPTV, Inc. 06/04/1992
Each share Common $0.005 par exchanged for (0.1) share Common 5¢ par
(See MPTV, Inc.)

UNITED SILVER CORP (BC)
Discharged from receivership 04/17/2014
No stockholders' equity

UNITED SISCOE MINES INC (QC)
Name changed 2/11/81
Name changed from United Siscoe Mines Ltd. to United Siscoe Mines Inc.-Les Mines United Siscoe Inc. 02/11/1981
Recapitalized as Horsham Corp.-Corporation Horsham (QC) 07/08/1987
Each share Capital Stock no par exchanged (0.33333333) share Subordinate no par
Horsham Corp. - Corporation Horsham (QC) reincorporated in Ontario as Trizec Hahn Corp. 11/01/1996 which was acquired by Trizec Canada Inc. 05/08/2002
(See Trizec Canada Inc.)

UNITED SMELTERS, RAILWAY & COPPER CO. (WY)
Charter revoked for failure to file reports and pay fees 07/19/1927

UNITED SOFTWARE ASSOC INC (WA)
Name changed to Diadus Inc. 12/02/1985
(See Diadus Inc.)

UNITED SOFTWARE SEC INC (VA)
Charter cancelled and proclaimed dissolved for failure to file reports 09/01/1995

UNITED SOLAR ASSOC INC (CO)
Charter suspended for failure to file annual reports 09/30/1989

UNITED SOUTHERN BANK (CLARKSDALE, MS)
Common $10 par changed to $5 par and (1) additional share issued 04/16/1981
Stock Dividend - 10% 04/25/1981
Reorganized as United Southern Corp. 01/30/1984
Each share Common $5 par exchanged for (1) share Common $5 par
United Southern Corp. acquired by Union Planters Corp. 02/28/1989 which merged into Regions Financial Corp. (New) 07/01/2004

UNITED SOUTHERN CORP. (MS)
Acquired by Union Planters Corp. 02/28/1989
Each share Common $5 par exchanged for (0.73256) share Common $5 par
Union Planters Corp. merged into Regions Financial Corp. (New) 07/01/2004

UNITED SOUTHFORK ENERGY INC (CANADA)
Company dissolved 00/00/1987
Details not available

UNITED SOUTHLAND CORP (CO)
Recapitalized as Shecom Corp. 11/30/1990
Each share Common no par exchanged for (0.1) share Common no par
(See Shecom Corp.)

UNITED SOUTHN MINERALS CORP (BC)
Struck off register and declared dissolved for failure to file returns 10/30/1992

UNITED SOUTHWEST INDUSTRIES, INC. (DE)
Charter cancelled and declared inoperative and void for non-payment of taxes 03/01/1975

UNITED SPECIALTIES CO. (DE)
Merged into Industrial Enterprises, Inc. 09/12/1957
Each share Common $1 par exchanged for (0.75) share Common $1 par
Industrial Enterprises, Inc. (NY) name changed to Novo Industrial Corp. 04/28/1960 which name changed to Novo Corp. 05/05/1969
(See Novo Corp.)

UNITED SPECIALTIES INC (CO)
Name changed to WaterColor Holdings Corp. 04/10/2006
(See WaterColor Holdings Corp.)

UNITED SPORTS INTL INC (WY)
Recapitalized as Tour Design International, Inc. 04/12/2000
Each share Common no par exchanged for (0.02857142) share Common no par
Tour Design International, Inc. name changed to Carolina Co. At Pinehurst 10/31/2001
(See Carolina Co. At Pinehurst Inc.)

UNITED SPORTS TECHNOLOGIES, INC. (NY)
Dissolved by proclamation 06/26/1996

UNITED STAR COMPANIES, INC. (FL)
Adjudicated bankrupt 09/05/1963
No stockholders' equity

UNITED STATES & BRITISH INTERNATIONAL CO., LTD. (MD)
Class A Common no par changed to $1 par 03/13/1933
Merged into American General Corp. 11/23/1935
Each share $3 Preferred no par exchanged for (0.4) share $2 Series Preferred $1 par
Each share Class A Common $1 par exchanged for (0.1) share Common 10¢ par
Each share Class B Common exchanged for (0.05) share Class B Common 10¢ par
American General Corp. merged into Equity Corp. 10/17/1950 which name changed to Wheelabrator-Frye Inc. 11/04/1971 which merged into Signal Companies, Inc. 02/01/1983 which merged into Allied-Signal Inc. 09/19/1985 which name changed to AlliedSignal Inc. 04/26/1993 which name changed to Honeywell International Inc. 12/01/1999

UNITED STATES & FGN SECS CORP (MD)
Common no par changed to $1 par and (2) additional shares issued 07/08/1955
Liquidation completed

Each share Common $1 par received initial distribution of $19.50 cash 05/03/1984
Each share Common $1 par received second distribution of $2.30 cash 06/15/1984
Each share Common $1 par exchanged for third and final distribution of $1.09 cash 12/20/1984

UNITED STATES & INTERNATIONAL SECURITIES CORP. (MD)
Merged into United States & Foreign Securities Corp. 06/30/1955
Each share Common no par exchanged for (0.5) share Common no par
(See Unites States & Foreign Securities Corp.)

UNITED STATES & OVERSEAS CORP.
Acquired by Public Utility Holding Corp. of America 00/00/1930
Details not available

UNITED STATES AIR CONDITIONING CORP. (DE)
Plan of merger effective 06/16/1957
Each share $7 Preferred A no par exchanged for (165) shares Capital Stock 10¢ par
Common 10¢ par changed to Capital Stock 10¢ par
Each share Capital Stock 10¢ par exchanged for (0.2) share Capital Stock 50¢ par 04/07/1958
Name changed to Transairco, Inc. 04/05/1966
(See Transairco, Inc.)

UNITED STATES AIRCRAFT CORP (DE)
Name changed to Neo Vision Corp. 09/27/1999
Neo Vision Corp. recapitalized as Storage Suites America, Inc. 11/07/2002 which recapitalized as Bio-Matrix Scientific Group, Inc. 12/20/2004 which name changed to BMXP Holdings, Inc. 08/28/2006 which recapitalized as Freedom Environmental Services, Inc. 06/11/2008

UNITED STATES ALTERNATE ENERGY CORP (NV)
Name changed to Capital Assurance Corp. 04/30/1994
Capital Assurance Corp. name changed to Phelps Engineered Plastics Corp. 05/17/1999 which name changed to Clayton, Dunning Group Inc. 07/29/2005 which recapitalized as Carlton Companies, Inc. 07/09/2008

UNITED STATES ASBESTOS CO.
Merged into Raybestos-Manhattan, Inc. (NJ) 00/00/1929
Details not available

UNITED STATES AUTOMATIC MERCHANDISING CO (CA)
Each share Capital Stock $1 par exchanged for (0.1) share Capital Stock 10¢ par 03/23/1971
Name changed to Wilshire General Corp. 08/31/1972
(See Wilshire General Corp.)

UNITED STATES AUTOMOTIVE CORP. (DE)
Charter cancelled and declared inoperative and void for non-payment of taxes 03/18/1925

UNITED STATES BAKING CO., INC. (DE)
Name changed to Mareight Corp. and Class A Common 1¢ par reclassified as Common 1¢ par 12/27/1967
(See Mareight Corp.)

UNITED STATES BANKING CORP. (DE)
Recapitalized as National Consumer Finance Corp. 09/05/1955
Each share Common no par

exchanged for (17.75) share Common no par
National Consumer Finance Corp. name changed to Guardian Consumer Finance Corp. 11/21/1955 which merged into Liberty Loan Corp. 04/04/1960 which name changed to LLC Corp. 03/14/1980 which name changed to Valhi, Inc. 03/10/1987

UNITED STATES BANKNOTE CORP (DE)
Reincorporated 09/21/1993
15% Preferred 1¢ par called for redemption 06/25/1992
$0.40 Conv. Preference 1¢ par called for redemption 04/23/1993
State of incorporation changed from (NY) to (DE) 09/21/1993
Name changed to American Banknote Corp. 07/03/1995

UNITED STATES BANKNOTE CORP (VA)
Merged into Midwest Rubber Reclaiming Co. (DE) 07/28/1976
Each share Common $1 par exchanged for $8 cash

UNITED STATES BOND & MORTGAGE CORP. (NY)
Succeeded by U.S.B. & M. Liquidation Corp. 00/00/1936
No stockholders' equity

UNITED STATES BOND & SHARE CO.
Dissolved 00/00/1935
Details not available

UNITED STATES BORAX & CHEM CORP (NV)
4.5% Preferred $100 par called for redemption 09/01/1964
Under plan of merger each share Common $1 par exchanged for $34 cash 12/02/1969
$1.25 Preferred $1 par called for redemption 01/04/1971
Public interest eliminated

UNITED STATES BRASS CORP. (MN)
Completely liquidated 12/07/1967
Each share Common 10¢ par exchanged for first and final distribution of (0.2) share Hydrometals, Inc. 60¢ Conv. Preferred no par
(See Hydrometals, Inc.)

UNITED STATES CAN CO.
Acquired by Continental Can Co., Inc. 00/00/1928
Details not available

UNITED STATES CAST IRON PIPE & FOUNDRY CO.
Name changed to United States Pipe & Foundry Co. 00/00/1929
United States Pipe & Foundry Co. merged into Walter (Jim) Corp. 08/30/1969
(See Walter (Jim) Corp.)

UNITED STATES CASUALTY CO. (NY)
Conv. Preferred $2 par changed to $4 par 04/30/1947
Common $2 par changed to $4 par 04/30/1957
Conv. Preferred $4 par called for redemption 04/06/1962
Merged into Security Insurance Co. of Hartford 06/30/1966
Each share Common $4 par exchanged for (0.65625) share Common $10 par
Security Insurance Co. of Hartford name changed to Security Corp. 06/30/1968 which was acquired by Textron Inc. 06/29/1973

UNITED STATES CERAMIC TILE CO (DE)
Name changed to Spartek Inc. 02/19/1974
(See Spartek Inc.)

UNITED STATES CHEMICAL MILLING CORP. (CA)
Stock Dividends - 20% 01/06/1958; 20% 07/07/1958; 100% 09/15/1958; 20% 04/15/1959; 100% 11/17/1959
Bankrupt 09/18/1963
No stockholders' equity

UNITED STATES COLD STORAGE CORP (DE)
Each share 7% Preferred $100 par exchanged for (2) shares 4% Prior Preference $50 par, (1) share 4% Jr. Preference $15 par and (1) share Common no par 00/00/1941
Common no par split (2) for (1) by issuance of (1) additional share 06/16/1959
Stock Dividend - 20% 11/10/1950
Merged into American Consumer Industries, Inc. 10/15/1972
Each share Common no par exchanged for (3) shares Common no par
(See American Consumer Industries, Inc.)

UNITED STATES COMMUNICATIONS, INC. (NY)
Merged into Schaffer (S.) Grocery Corp. 05/15/1964
Each share Common exchanged for (0.1) share Common 1¢ par
Schaffer (S.) Grocery Corp. name changed to Schaffer Food Service Corp. 04/18/1995
(See Schaffer Food Service Corp.)

UNITED STATES CONSUMER PRODUCTS (CA)
Merged into APL Corp. 05/20/1966
Each share Common $1 par exchanged for (1) share Class B Conv. Preferred Ser. B $1 par
(See APL Corp.)

UNITED STATES CROWN CORP (DE)
Charter cancelled and declared inoperative and void for non-payment of taxes 04/15/1971

UNITED STATES DAILY PUBLISHING CORP.
Discontinued business 00/00/1933
Details not available

UNITED STATES DAIRY PRODUCTS CORP.
Reorganized as Philadelphia Dairy Products Co., Inc. 00/00/1936
Each share $7 1st Preferred exchanged for (1) share $4 Preferred
Each share 2nd Preferred exchanged for (2) shares new Common
Common had only the right to purchase new Common
Philadelphia Dairy Products Co., Inc. merged into Foremost Dairies, Inc. (NY) 06/30/1956 which merged into Foremost-McKesson, Inc. 07/19/1967 which name changed to McKesson Corp. (MD) 07/27/1983 which reincorporated in Delaware 07/31/1987
(See McKesson Corp. (Old) (DE))

UNITED STATES DISTRIBUTING CORP.
Merged into Pittston Co. (DE & VA) in 1943
Each share 7% Preferred $100 par exchanged for (1) share Class A Preference $100 par and (1) share Common $1 par
Each share Common $5 par exchanged for (0.05) share Common $1 par
Pittston Co. (DE & VA) Delaware incorporation rescinded 5/14/86
Pittston Co. (VA) name changed to Brink's Co. 5/5/2003

UNITED STATES ELECTRIC LIGHT & POWER SHARES, INC. (DE)
Liquidation completed
Each Ser. A Trust Share stamped to indicate initial distribution of $20 cash 6/6/47
Each Stamped Ser. A Trust Share exchanged for second and final distribution of $3.026 cash 9/17/47
Each Ser. B Trust Share exchanged for first and final distribution of $3.1556 cash 5/15/50

UNITED STATES ELECTRIC LIGHT & POWER SHARES, INC. (MD)
Each share Capital Stock $1 par exchanged for (8) shares Capital Stock 25¢ par in 1933
Liquidation completed
Each share Capital Stock 25¢ par received initial distribution of $0.60 cash 9/4/41
Each share Capital Stock 25¢ par exchanged for second and final distribution of $0.19 cash 12/14/42

UNITED STATES ELECTRIC POWER CORP. (MD)
Dissolved 11/5/36
No stockholders' equity

UNITED STATES ENVELOPE CO (ME)
Each share Preferred or Common $100 par exchanged for (2) shares Preferred or Common $50 par 00/00/1950
Preferred or Common $50 par changed to $10 par and (4) additional shares issued 03/16/1956
Stock Dividends - 50% 03/17/1949; 25% 11/29/1954
Merged into Westvaco Corp. 10/31/1977
Each share Preferred $10 par exchanged for $19.50 cash
Each share Common $10 par exchanged for $33 cash

UNITED STATES EQUITY & MTG TR (WA)
Merged into Hotel Investors Trust 03/29/1993
Each Share of Bene. Int. $1 par exchanged for $28.20 cash

UNITED STATES EXPL INC (CO)
Each share old Common $0.0001 par exchanged for (0.2) share new Common $0.0001 par 3/16/93
Merged into U.S. Exploration Holdings, Inc. 1/29/2004
Each share new Common $0.0001 par exchanged for $2.82 cash

UNITED STATES EXPRESS CO.
Liquidated in 1930

UNITED STATES FGHT CO (DE)
Capital Stock no par split (3) for (1) by issuance of (2) additional shares 05/29/1956
Capital Stock no par split (2) for (1) by issuance of (1) additional share 01/16/1968
Stock Dividend - 100% 01/17/1962
Name changed to Transway International Corp. 06/03/1974
(See Transway International Corp.)

UNITED STATES FID & GTY CO (MD)
Each share Common $50 par exchanged for (5) shares Common $10 par 00/00/1929
Common $10 par changed to $2 par 00/00/1932
Common $2 par changed to $10 par 00/00/1943
Common $10 par changed to $5 par and (1) additional share issued 09/30/1959
Common $5 par changed to $2.50 par and (1) additional share issued 04/30/1970
Common $2.50 par split (3) for (2) by issuance of (0.5) additional share 04/30/1977
Stock Dividends - 10% 01/23/1950; 10% 04/15/1953; 10% 04/15/1954; 20% 04/15/1955; 10% 09/30/1959; 10% 10% 04/16/1962; 10% 04/30/1966; 10% 04/29/1978
Under plan of reorganization each share Common $2.50 par automatically became (1) share USF&G Corp. Common $2.50 par 10/01/1981
USF&G Corp. merged into St. Paul Companies, Inc. 04/24/1998 which name changed to St. Paul Travelers Companies, Inc. 04/01/2004 which name changed to Travelers Companies, Inc. 02/27/2007

UNITED STATES FIDELITY FIRE CORP.
Name changed to Fidelity & Guaranty Fire Corp. in 1929
Fidelity & Guaranty Fire Corp. name changed to Fidelity & Guaranty Insurance Corp. in 1947 which merged into United States Fidelity & Guaranty Co. in 1952 which reorganized as USF&G Corp. 10/1/81 which merged into St. Paul Companies, Inc. 4/24/98 which name changed to St. Paul Travelers Companies, Inc. 4/1/2004 which name changed to Travelers Companies, Inc. 2/27/2007

UNITED STATES FILTER CORP NEW (DE)
Each share old Common $0.001 par exchanged for (0.01333333) share new Common 1¢ par 02/25/1991
New Common 1¢ par split (3) for (2) by issuance of (0.5) additional share 12/05/1994
New Common 1¢ par split (3) for (2) by issuance of (0.5) additional share payable 07/15/1996 to holders of record 06/14/1996 Ex date - 07/16/1996
Merged into Vivendi S.A. 04/29/1999
Each share new Common 1¢ par exchanged for $31.50 cash

UNITED STATES FILTER CORP OLD (DE)
Each share old Common no par exchanged for (0.1) share new Common no par 3/18/66
5% Preferred $10 par called for redemption 3/1/81
Merged into Ashland Oil, Inc. (Old) 3/31/81
Each share new Common no par exchanged for $33 cash

UNITED STATES FIN CO (FL)
Stock Dividend - 100% 09/03/1968
Reincorporated under the laws of Delaware as Unicapital Corp. (Ctfs. dated prior to 12/08/1980) 07/01/1969
Unicapital Corp. name changed to Production Operators Corp. 12/08/1980 which merged into Camco International Inc. 06/13/1997 which merged into Schlumberger Ltd. 08/31/1998

UNITED STATES FINANCIAL HOLDING CORP.
Dissolved 00/00/1936
Details not available

UNITED STATES FINISHING CO. (CT)
Each share Common $100 par exchanged for (3) shares Common no par 00/00/1929
Common no par changed to $1 par 00/00/1954
Assets sold to Gera Corp. (NJ) 03/01/1955
Each share $4 Preferred no par received $50 principal amount of 6% Debentures and $52.50 cash
Each share Common $1 par received $18 principal amount of 6% Debentures and $12 cash

UNITED STATES FIRE INS CO (NY)
Each share Capital Stock $20 par exchanged for (2) shares Capital Stock $10 par 00/00/1928
Capital Stock $10 par changed to $4 par 00/00/1932
Under plan of merger each share Capital Stock $4 par exchanged for

(1.76) shares Capital Stock $3 par 00/00/1951
Stock Dividend - 100% 07/28/1955
Acquired by Crum & Forster 11/07/1969
Each share Capital Stock $3 par exchanged for $54.41 cash

UNITED STATES FOIL CO. (DE)
Recapitalized 00/00/1928
Each share Class A Common $100 par exchanged for (40) shares Class B Common no par
Each share Class B Common $10 par exchanged for (4) shares Class B Common no par
Class A Common no par and Class B Common no par changed to $1 par 00/00/1933
Class A Common $1 par and Class B Common $1 par split (6) for (1) by issuance of (5) additional shares respectively 11/10/1955
Class A Common $1 par and Class B Common $1 par changed to no par and (0.5) additional share issued respectively 11/04/1959
Recapitalized 04/10/1961
Each share Class A Common no par exchanged for (3) shares Common no par
Each share Class B Common no par exchanged for (1) share Common no par
Class B Common Stock Dividend - 20% 02/01/1952
Merged into Reynolds Metals Co. 04/10/1961
Each share Common no par exchanged for (0.85) share Common no par
Reynolds Metals Co. merged into Alcoa Inc. 05/03/2000 which name changed to Arconic Inc. (PA) 11/01/2016 which reincorporated in Delaware 12/31/2017

UNITED STATES FUEL OIL CO. (TX)
Charter forfeited for failure to pay taxes 5/19/50

UNITED STATES GAUGE CO.
Merged into American Machine & Metals, Inc. 00/00/1945
Details not available

UNITED STATES GENERAL INVESTING CO.
Merged into Finance Co. of America at Baltimore in 1929 which name was changed to Finance Co. of America 12/1/61

UNITED STATES GLASS & CHEMICAL CORP. (PA)
Stock Dividend - 200% 11/28/1958
Name changed to United States Diversified Industries Corp. 04/20/1961

UNITED STATES GLASS CO. (PA)
Common $25 par changed to $1 par 00/00/1937
Name changed to United States Glass & Chemical Corp. 10/15/1958
United States Glass & Chemical Corp. name changed to United States Diversified Industries Corp. 04/20/1961

UNITED STATES GRAPHITE CO.
Merged into Wickes Corp. (MI) on a (3) for (1) basis in 1948
Wickes Corp. (MI) reincorporated under the laws of Delaware 7/2/71 which merged into Wickes Companies, Inc. 8/13/80 which name changed to Collins & Aikman Group Inc. 7/17/92
(See Collins & Aikman Group Inc.)

UNITED STATES GUANO CO. (NY)
Charter cancelled and proclaimed dissolved for failure to pay taxes 4/2/24

UNITED STATES GUARANTEE CO. (NY)
Each share Capital Stock $100 par exchanged for (10) shares Capital Stock $10 par 00/00/1934
Merged into Federal Insurance Co. 00/00/1953
Each share Capital Stock $10 par exchanged for (5.5) shares Capital Stock $4 par
Federal Insurance Co. acquired by Chubb Corp. 12/29/1967 which merged into ACE Ltd. 01/14/2016

UNITED STATES GUARANTY LIFE INSURANCE CO. (GA)
Common $5 par changed to $2.50 par and (1) additional share issued 05/29/1957
Merged into Piedmont Life Insurance Co. 11/01/1957
Each share Common exchanged for (0.5) share Capital Stock $10 par
Piedmont Life Insurance Co. merged into Piedmont Southern Life Insurance Co. 07/11/1960 which was acquired by Piedmont Management Co. Inc. 07/11/1968 which merged into Chartwell RE Corp. 12/13/1995 which merged into Trenwick Group Inc. 10/27/1999 which merged into Trenwick Group Ltd. 09/27/2000
(See Trenwick Group Ltd.)

UNITED STATES GYPSUM CO (DE)
Reincorporated 06/30/1966
Common $20 par changed to $4 par and (4) additional shares issued 01/27/1956
State of incorporation changed from (IL) to (DE) and each share Preferred $100 par exchanged for $175 principal amount of 4-7/8% Subord. Debentures due 1991 on 06/30/1966
Common $4 par split (2) for (1) by issuance of (1) additional share 12/29/1971
Under plan of reorganization each share $1.80 Conv. Preferred and Common $4 par automatically became (1) share USG Corp. $1.80 Conv. Preferred $1 par and Common $4 par respectively 01/01/1985

UNITED STATES HAMMERED PISTON RING CO. (NJ)
Insolvent and dissolved 6/28/61
No Common stockholders' equity

UNITED STATES HEALTH CARE SYS INC (PA)
Common $0.005 par split (3) for (2) by issuance of (0.5) additional share 9/15/83
Common $0.005 par split (3) for (2) by issuance of (0.5) additional share 8/15/84
Common $0.005 par split (3) for (2) by issuance of (0.5) additional share 1/30/85
Common $0.005 par split (3) for (2) by issuance of (0.5) additional share 6/28/85
Stock Dividends - 50% 5/31/83; 50% 11/22/85
Name changed to U.S. Healthcare, Inc. 4/22/86
U.S Healthcare, Inc. merged into Aetna Inc. (CT) 7/19/96 which merged into ING Groep N.V. 12/13/2000

UNITED STATES HOFFMAN MACHY CORP (DE)
Common no par changed to $5 par 00/00/1933
Common $5 par changed to $1.65 par and (2) additional shares issued 05/17/1955
Each share 4-1/4% Preferred $100 par exchanged for (2) shares 5% Class A Preference, Ser. 1 $50 par and (0.2) share Common 82-1/2¢ par 05/10/1956
Common $1.65 par changed to 82-1/2¢ par and (1) additional share issued 05/18/1956
Out of business 06/00/1965

No stockholders' equity

UNITED STATES HOLDING CO.
Liquidated in 1944

UNITED STATES HYDROFOILS CORP. (NY)
Name changed to U.S. Hydrofoils-Lehigh Distribution Services, Inc. 4/11/69
U.S. Hydrofoils-Lehigh Distribution Services, Inc. name changed to Hydroplex Corp. 11/21/69
(See Hydroplex Corp.)

UNITED STS INDEMNITY & CAS INC (NV)
Each share old Common $0.001 par exchanged for (0.001) share new Common $0.001 par 12/15/99
Note: No holder will receive fewer than (1) post split share
Each share new Common $0.001 par exchanged for (100) shares Common 1¢ par 12/17/99
Name changed to Birch Financial, Inc. 1/20/2000

UNITED STATES INDUSTRIAL ALCOHOL CO. (WV)
Merged into United States Industrial Chemicals, Inc. on a share for share basis 7/16/43
United States Industrial Chemicals, Inc. merged into National Distillers Products Corp. in 1951 which name was changed to National Distillers & Chemical Corp. 5/1/57 which name changed to Quantum Chemical Corp. 1/4/88 which merged into Hanson PLC (Old) 10/1/93 which reorganized as Hanson PLC (New) 10/15/2003

UNITED STATES INDUSTRIAL CHEMICALS, INC. (DE)
Merged into National Distillers Products Corp. in 1951
Each share Common no par exchanged for (2) shares new Common $5 par
National Distillers Products Corp. name changed to National Distillers & Chemical Corp. 5/1/57 which name changed to Quantum Chemical Corp. 1/4/88 which merged into Hanson PLC (Old) 10/1/93 which reorganized as Hanson PLC (New) 10/15/2003

UNITED STATES KINGS COUNTY BOND & MORTGAGE CORP. (NY)
Voluntarily dissolved 12/2/76
Details not available

UNITED STATES LEASING INTL INC (DE)
Reincorporated 10/27/1986
Capital Stock $1 par reclassified as Common $1 par 03/03/1970
Common $1 par split (3) for (2) by issuance of (0.5) additional share 06/15/1972
State of incorporation changed from (CA) to (DE) 10/27/1986
Merged into Ford Motor Co. 11/19/1987
Each share Common $1 par exchanged for $68 cash

UNITED STATES LEATHER INC (WI)
Plan of reorganization under Chapter 11 Federal Bankruptcy Code effective 3/28/2002
Stockholders' equity unlikely

UNITED STATES LIFE INSURANCE CO.
Merged into United States Life Insurance Co. in the City of New York 00/00/1935
Details not available

UNITED STATES LIFE INS CO CITY N Y (NY)
Capital Stock $10 par changed to $5 par 00/00/1938
Capital Stock $5 par changed to $4 par 00/00/1940
Each share Capital Stock $4 par exchanged for (2) shares Capital Stock $2 par 05/16/1956
Stock Dividends - 100% 06/05/1956; 25% 12/26/1958; 20% 06/21/1961; 20% 02/14/1964
Merged into USLIFE Holding Corp. 10/10/1969
Each share Capital Stock $2 par exchanged for $33.50 cash

UNITED STATES LIGHT & HEAT CORP.
Merged into U. S. L. Battery Corp. in 1927
Details not available

UNITED STATES LINES CO. (NV)
Merged into United States Lines Co. (NJ) and Preferred exchanged share for share in 1943
United States Lines Co. (NJ) merged into Kidde (Walter) & Co., Inc. (DE) 1/10/69 which name changed to Kidde, Inc. 4/18/80 which merged into Hanson Trust p.l.c. 12/31/87 which name changed to Hanson PLC (Old) 1/29/88 which reorganized as Hanson PLC (New) 11/15/2003

UNITED STATES LINES CO (NJ)
Stock Dividend - 10% 1/15/47
4-1/2% Preferred $10 par called for redemption 5/28/68
Merged into Kidde (Walter) & Co., Inc. (DE) 1/10/69
Each share Common $1 par exchanged for (0.25) share $4 Conv. Preference Ser. B $1 par and (0.423351) share Common $2.50 par
Kidde (Walter) & Co., Inc. (DE) name changed to Kidde, Inc. 4/18/80 which merged into Hanson Trust p.l.c. 12/31/87 which name changed to Hanson PLC (Old) 1/29/88 which reorganized as Hanson PLC (New) 10/15/2003

UNITED STATES LINES INC (DE)
Merged into United States Lines Co. (NV) in 1941
Each share Preference exchanged for (0.85) share Preferred
Common received nothing
(See United States Lines Co. (NV))

UNITED STATES LITHIUM CORP (UT)
Charter revoked for failure to file reports and pay fees 09/30/1966

UNITED STATES LOAN SOCIETY (DE)
Recapitalized as Commercial Investment Corp. 10/16/58
Each share Common $10 par exchanged for (2) shares 6% Preferred $10 par, (4) shares Common $1 par and warrants to purchase (2) additional shares
Commercial Investment Corp. recapitalized as Spiegl Farms, Inc. 10/27/60 which recapitalized as Spiegl Foods, Inc. 1/2/66
(See Spiegl Foods, Inc.)

UNITED STATES LUMBER CO. (PA)
Reincorporated in 1948
State of incorporation changed from (DE) to (PA) and each share Capital Stock no par exchanged for (1) share Common no par 8/25/67
Common $1 par changed to 10¢ par 8/25/67
Stock Dividend - 300% 6/30/52
Merged into City Investing Co. (DE) 3/10/72
Each share Common 10¢ par exchanged for (0.42954) share Common $1.25 par
(See City Investing Co. (DE))

UNITED STATES MARITIME CORP. (DE)
No longer in existence having become inoperative and void for non-payment of taxes 3/19/24

UNITED STATES MERCHANTS & SHIPPERS INSURANCE CO.
Merged into Westchester Fire Insurance Co. 00/00/1932
Details not available

UNITED STATES MILLING & MINERALS CORP. (DE)
Bankrupt in 1963
Assets sold in 1964 with no equity for stockholders

UNITED STATES MINERAL PRODS CO (NJ)
Stock Dividends - 25% 6/30/72; 15% 3/25/77
Filed a petition under Chapter 11 Federal Bankruptcy Code 7/23/2001
Stockholders' equity unlikely

UNITED STATES MINERAL WOOL CO. (NJ)
Stock Dividend - 25% 3/25/60
Name changed to United States Mineral Products Co. 12/24/64
(See United States Mineral Products Co.)

UNITED STATES MNG & EXPL INC (UT)
Each share old Common $0.001 par exchanged for (0.01158457) share new Common $0.001 par 06/04/1997
Name changed to Global Digital Information, Inc. 01/23/1998
Global Digital Information, Inc. name changed to Masterpiece Technology Group, Inc. 06/15/1999
(See Masterpiece Technology Group, Inc.)

UNITED STATES MINING & MILLING CORP. (CO)
Charter revoked for failure to file reports and pay fees 10/24/60

UNITED STATES MINING & MILLING CORP. (DE)
Name changed to United States Milling & Minerals Corp. in 1958 which became bankrupt in 1963

UNITED STATES MNG CORP (NV)
Name changed to 1st American Rent-A-Car Corp. and Capital Stock 20¢ par changed to 10¢ par 1/10/69
1st American Rent-A-Car Corp. name changed to 1st American Capital Corp. 6/18/71
(See 1st American Capital Corp.)

UNITED STATES MOLYBDENUM CORP. (CO)
Merged into United States Mining & Milling Corp. (CO) in 1940
(See United States Mining & Milling Corp. (CO))

UNITED STATES MORTGAGE BOND CO.
Dissolved in 1941

UNITED STATES NATL BANCSHARES INC (DE)
$3.50 Preferred $10 par called for redemption 04/30/1982
Acquired by Cullen/Frost Bankers, Inc. 05/03/1982
Each share Common $1 par exchanged for (1.026667) shares Common $5 par

UNITED STATES NATL BK (GALVESTON, TX)
Capital Stock $50 par changed to $20 par and a 100% stock dividend paid 02/01/1962
Reorganized as United States National Bancshares, Inc. 07/01/1971
Each share Capital Stock $20 par exchanged for (1) share $3.50 Preferred $10 par and (1) share Common $1 par
United States National Bancshares, Inc. acquired by Cullen/Frost Bankers, Inc. 05/03/1982

UNITED STATES NATL BK (JOHNSTOWN, PA)
Capital Stock $20 par changed to $5 par and (3) additional shares issued 02/26/1965
Capital Stock $5 par changed to $2.50 par and (1) additional share issued 10/28/1971
Stock Dividends - 10% 01/17/1968; 10% 02/10/1975
Reorganized as USBANCORP, Inc. 01/05/1983
Each share Capital Stock $2.50 par exchanged for (1) share Common $2.50 par
USBANCORP, Inc. name changed to AmeriServ Financial, Inc. 05/07/2001

UNITED STATES NATIONAL BANK (PORTLAND, OR)
Common $100 par changed to $20 par and (4) additional shares issued 6/21/29
Stock Dividends - 25% 3/1/47; 20% 9/15/50; 14-2/7% 2/15/54; 10% 2/16/59
Name changed to United States National Bank of Oregon (Portland, OR) 2/3/64
United States National Bank of Oregon (Portland, OR) reorganized in Oregon as U.S. Bancorp 12/31/68 which merged into U.S. Bancorp (Old) (DE) 8/1/97 which merged into U.S. Bancorp (New) 2/27/2001

UNITED STATES NATL BK (SAN DIEGO, CA)
Each share Capital Stock $100 par exchanged for (5) shares Capital Stock $20 par 02/15/1950
Each share Capital Stock $20 par exchanged for (2) shares Capital Stock $10 par 08/18/1953
Declared insolvent and placed in receivership 10/18/1973

UNITED STATES NATL BK ORE (PORTLAND, OR)
Name changed 02/03/1964
Common $100 par changed to $20 par and (4) additional shares issued 06/21/1929
Name changed from United States National Bank of Oregon 02/03/1964
Common Capital Stock $20 par changed to $10 par and (1) additional share issued 04/01/1965
Stock Dividends - 25% 03/01/1947; 20% 09/15/1950; 14-2/7% 02/15/1954; 10% 02/16/1959; 10% 08/10/1966; 10% 04/19/1968
Reorganized as U.S. Bancorp (OR) 12/31/1968
Each share Common Capital Stock $10 par exchanged for (1) share Common $10 par
U.S. Bancorp (OR) merged into U.S. Bancorp (Old) (DE) 08/01/1997 which merged into U.S. Bancorp 02/27/2001

UNITED STATES OIL & ROYALTIES CO.
Liquidation completed in 1948

UNITED STATES OIL CO (DE)
Each share Common 1¢ par exchanged for (0.1) share Common 10¢ par 6/16/88
Charter cancelled and declared inoperative and void for non-payment of taxes 3/1/91

UNITED STATES PAGING CORP (DE)
Acquired by Mobile Telecommunication Technologies Corp. 2/17/95
Each share Common 1¢ par exchanged for (0.415) share Common 1¢ par
Mobile Telecommunication Technologies Corp. name changed to Skytel Communications Inc. 5/22/98 which merged into MCI Worldcom, Inc. 10/1/99 which name changed to WorldCom Inc. (New) 5/1/2000
(See WorldCom Inc. (New))

UNITED STATES PATENTS CORP. (DE)
No longer in existence having become inoperative and void for non-payment of taxes 4/1/53

UNITED STATES PETROLEUM CO.
Liquidated 00/00/1943
Details not available

UNITED STATES PIPE & FDRY CO (NJ)
Common $20 par changed to $5 par and (3) additional shares issued 10/10/1955
Merged into Walter (Jim) Corp. 08/30/1969
Each share Common $5 par exchanged for (1) share $1.60 4th Conv. Preferred no par
(See Walter (Jim) Corp.)

UNITED STATES PLASTICS, INC. (FL)
Common 10¢ par split (3) for (1) by issuance of (2) additional shares 06/29/1965
Name changed to Panelfab, Inc. 02/01/1968
Panelfab, Inc. merged into Panelfab International Corp. 03/10/1970
(See Panelfab International Corp.)

UNITED STATES PLAYING CARD CO (OH)
Each share Common $20 par exchanged for (2) shares Common $10 par 00/00/1927
Common $10 par changed to $5 par and (3) additional shares issued 11/24/1959
Merged into Diamond International Corp. 07/08/1969
Each share Common $5 par exchanged for (1) share Common 50¢ par
(See Diamond International Corp.)

UNITED STATES PLYWOOD CORP (NY)
3.75% Preferred Ser. B called for redemption 04/01/1960
$4.50 2nd Preferred called for redemption 04/01/1962
Common $1 par split (2) for (1) by issuance of (1) additional share 06/05/1964
Stock Dividends - 100% 05/01/1945; 100% 12/23/1946; 10% 04/12/1951
Merged into U.S. Plywood-Champion Papers Inc. 02/28/1967
Each share 3.75% Preferred Ser. A $100 par exchanged for (1) share 4.75% Preferred $100 par
Each share Common $1 par exchanged for (1) share Common $1 par
U.S. Plywood-Champion Papers Inc. name changed to Champion International Corp. 05/12/1972 which merged into International Paper Co. 06/20/2000

UNITED STATES POOL CORP. (NJ)
Declared insolvent 07/20/1961
No stockholders' equity

UNITED STATES POSTAL METER CORP.
Name changed to Continental Corp. 00/00/1945
Continental Corp. name changed to Continental Eastern Corp. 05/14/1968
(See Continental Eastern Corp.)

UNITED STATES POTASH CO., INC. (NM)
Merged into United States Borax & Chemical Corp. 07/02/1956
Each share Common no par exchanged for (0.2) share 4.5% Preferred $100 par and (1) share Common $1 par
(See United States Borax & Chemical Corp.)

UNITED STATES PRINTING & LITHOGRAPH CO. (OH)
Each share Preferred $100 par exchanged for (2) shares $3 Preferred $50 par 00/00/1929
Each share Common $100 par exchanged for (3) shares Common no par 00/00/1929
Each share $3 Preferred $50 par exchanged for (1.5) shares 5% Preference Ser. A $50 par 00/00/1944
5% Preference Ser. A $50 par called for redemption 10/01/1959
Stock Dividend - 100% 03/01/1952
Merged into Diamond National Corp. 09/28/1959
Each share Common no par exchanged for (2.7) shares Common $1 par
Diamond National Corp. name changed to Diamond International Corp. 10/29/1964
(See Diamond International Corp.)

UNITED STATES RADIATOR CORP. (NY)
Each share Common $100 par exchanged for (5) shares Common no par 00/00/1926
Reorganized 00/00/1937
Each share 7% Preferred $100 par exchanged for (1) share 6% Preferred $50 par and (2.5) shares Common $1 par
Each share Common no par exchanged for (0.5) share Common $1 par
Recapitalized 00/00/1948
Each share 6% Old Preferred $50 par exchanged for (1.5) shares new 6% Preferred $50 par
Stock Dividend - 100% 09/01/1948
Merged into National-U.S. Radiator Corp. 04/01/1955
Each share 6% Preferred $50 par exchanged for $50 principal amount of 4.5% Debentures due 05/01/1975
Each share Common $1 par exchanged for (0.5) share Common $1 par
National-U.S. Radiator Corp. name changed for Natus Corp. 02/01/1960 which name changed to Kirkeby-Natus Corp. 06/30/1961 which name changed to United Ventures, Inc. 06/24/1966 which merged into Federated Development Co. 07/31/1970
(See Federated Development Co.)

UNITED STATES RADIO & TELEVISION CORP.
Name changed to General Household Utilities Co. 00/00/1933
(See General Household Utilities Co.)

UNITED STATES RADIUM CORP (DE)
Common $2 par split (3) for (1) by issuance of (2) additional shares 01/05/1960
Common $2 par changed to $1 par and (1) additional share issued 05/06/1966
Common $1 par split (2) for (1) by issuance of (1) additional share 05/06/1968
Under plan of reorganization each share Common $1 par automatically became (1) share USR Industries, Inc. Common $1 par 08/27/1980
(See USR Industries, Inc.)

UNITED STATES REALTY & IMPROVEMENT CO. (NJ)
Merged into United States Realty-Sheraton Corp. 05/17/1946
Each (3) shares Common exchanged for (1.15) shares Common $1 par and (1) Ctf. of Bene. Int.
United States Realty-Sheraton Corp. name changed to Sheraton Corp. of America 08/19/1946 which was acquired by International Telephone

& Telegraph Corp. (DE) 02/29/1968 which name changed to ITT Corp. 12/31/1983 which reorganized in Indiana as ITT Industries Inc. 12/19/1995 which name changed to ITT Corp. 07/01/2006

UNITED STATES RLTY & INVT CO N J (NJ)
Capital Stock no par changed to $1.50 par and (9) additional shares issued 04/03/1962
Merged into DID Realty Corp. 03/31/1989
Each share Capital Stock $1.50 par exchanged for $16.9528 cash

UNITED STATES REALTY-SHERATON CORP. (NJ)
Name changed to Sheraton Corp. of America 08/19/1946
Sheraton Corp. of America acquired by International Telephone & Telegraph Corp. (DE) 02/29/1968 which name changed to ITT Corp. 12/31/1983 which reorganized in Indiana as ITT Industries Inc. 12/19/1995 which name changed to ITT Corp. 07/01/2006

UNITED STATES RES CORP (CA)
Out of business 11/23/1971
Company's former president opined that stock is worthless

UNITED STATES RUBR CO (NJ)
Common $100 par changed to no par 00/00/1928
Common no par changed to $10 par 00/00/1938
Common $10 par changed to $5 par and (2) additional shares issued 00/00/1952
Common $5 par changed to $2.50 par and (1) additional share issued 02/15/1966
Name changed to Uniroyal, Inc. 02/28/1967
(See Uniroyal, Inc.)

UNITED STATES SECURITIES INVESTMENT CO.
Dissolved 00/00/1930
Details not available

UNITED STATES SERVATERIA CORP. (CA)
Name changed to United States Consumer Products 11/02/1964
United States Consumer Products acquired by APL Corp. 05/20/1966
(See APL Corp.)

UNITED STATES SHARES CORP. (MD)
Dissolution approved 00/00/1935
Details not available

UNITED STATES SHARES FINANCIAL CORP.
Name changed to United States Financial Holding Corp. 00/00/1930
(See United States Financial Holding Corp.)

UNITED STATES SHEET & WINDOW GLASS CO.
Merged into Libbey-Owens Sheet Glass Co. 00/00/1928
Details not available

UNITED STATES SHELL HOMES, INC. (FL)
Name changed to United States Finance Co., Inc. 07/13/1962
United States Finance Co., Inc. reincorporated in Delaware as Unicapital Corp. (Ctfs. dated prior to 12/08/1980) 07/01/1969 which name changed to Production Operators Corp. 12/08/1980 which merged into Camco International Inc. 06/13/1997 which merged into Schlumberger Ltd. 08/31/1998

UNITED STATES SHOE CORP (OH)
Each share Common $4 par exchanged for (2) shares Common $2 par 00/00/1952
Common $2 par changed to $1 par and (1) additional share issued 06/01/1956
Common $1 par changed to no par and (1) additional share issued 03/16/1962
Common no par split (3) for (2) by issuance of (0.5) additional share 09/30/1968
Common no par split (3) for (2) by issuance of (0.5) additional share 07/13/1981
Common no par split (2) for (1) by issuance of (1) additional share 06/17/1983
Common no par split (2) for (1) by issuance of (1) additional share 06/13/1986
Stock Dividend - 10% 02/15/1955
Merged into Luxottica Group S.P.A. 05/24/1995
Each share Common no par exchanged for $28 cash

UNITED STATES SILVER & MNG CORP (NV)
Recapitalized as Diversified Resources Corp. 09/01/1972
Each share Common 1¢ par exchanged for (0.25) share Common 4¢ par
(See Diversified Resources Corp.)

UNITED STATES SMELTING REFINING & MINING CO. OLD (ME)
Merged into United States Smelting Refining & Mining Co. (ME) (New) 09/24/1965
Each share 7% Preferred $50 par exchanged for $50 principal amount of 5.375% Debentures due 11/15/1995, (0.25) share $5.50 Preferred $5 par and $10 cash
Each share Common $50 par exchanged for (4) shares Common $1 par
United States Smelting Refining & Mining Co. (ME) (New) name changed to UV Industries, Inc. 06/09/1972 which name changed to UV Industries, Inc. Liquidating Trust 03/25/1980
(See UV Industries, Inc. Liquidating Trust)

UNITED STATES SMLT REFNG & MNG CO NEW (ME)
Name changed to UV Industries, Inc. 06/09/1972
UV Industries, Inc. name changed to UV Industries, Inc. Liquidating Trust 03/25/1980
(See UV Industries, Inc. Liquidating Trust)

UNITED STATES SPRING & BUMPER CO. (CA)
Acquired by Rheem Manufacturing Co. 00/00/1954
Each share Common $1 par exchanged for (0.44) share Common $1 par
(See Rheem Manufacturing Co.)

UNITED STATES STEEL CORP. (NJ)
Common $100 par changed to no par 00/00/1938
Common no par split (3) for (1) by issuance of (2) additional shares 00/00/1949
Common no par changed to $16.66666666 par and (1) additional share issued 06/02/1955
Merged into United States Steel Corp. (Old) (DE) 01/01/1966
Each share 7% Preferred $100 par exchanged for $175 principal amount of 4.625% 30-year Subord. Debentures due 01/01/1996
Each share Common $16.66666666 par exchanged for (1) share Common $30 par
United States Steel Corp. (DE) name changed to USX Corp. 07/08/1986 which reorganized as USX-Marathon Group Inc. 05/06/1991 which name changed to Marathon Oil Corp. 12/31/2001

UNITED STATES STL CORP OLD (DE)
Common $30 par changed to $1 par and (0.5) additional share issued 06/01/1976
$12.75 Conv. Preference no par called for redemption 09/16/1985
Name changed to USX Corp. 07/08/1986
USX Corp. reorganized into USX-Marathon Group Inc. 05/06/1991 which name changed to Marathon Oil Corp. 12/31/2001

UNITED STATES STORES CORP.
Recapitalized as Butler (P.H.) Co. 00/00/1942
Each share $7 1st Preferred exchanged for (1) share 5% Preferred and (5) shares Common
Each share $2.50 Preference exchanged for (3) shares Common
Each share Common exchanged for (0.05) share new Common
Each share Class A Common exchanged for (0.01666666) share new Common
Each share Class B Common exchanged for (0.005) shares new Common
Butler (P.H.) Co. name changed to Thorofare Markets, Inc. 00/00/1949 which name changed to Thorofare Corp. 05/21/1982 which name changed to Casablanca Industries Inc. 01/31/1983
(See Casablanca Industries Inc.)

UNITED STATES SUGAR CO. (CT)
Charter revoked for failure to file reports and pay fees 06/30/1932

UNITED STATES SUGAR CORP (DE)
Stock Dividends - 10% 04/17/1964; 40% 07/18/1973; 100% 07/16/1980
Acquired by Sugar Acquisition Corp. 12/29/1987
Each share Common $1 par exchanged for $80 cash

UNITED STATES SULPHUR & CHEMICAL CORP. (NV)
Acquired by Minerals Corp. of America on a (3) for (1) basis 2/14/55
Minerals Corp. of America charter revoked 4/1/64

UNITED STATES SURGICAL CORP (DE)
Reincorporated 10/01/1975
Reincorporated 05/01/1990
State of incorporation changed from (MD) to (NY) 10/01/1975
Common 10¢ par split (2) for (1) by issuance of (1) additional share 12/08/1980
State of incorporation changed from (NY) to (DE) 05/01/1990
Common 10¢ par split (2) for (1) by issuance of (1) additional share 05/31/1990
Common 10¢ par split (2) for (1) by issuance of (1) additional share 06/07/1991
Depositary Preferred called for redemption 04/01/1997
$2.20 144A Dividend Enhanced Conv. Stock called for redemption 04/01/1997
Depositary Preferred called for redemption 04/01/1997
$2.20 Dividend Enhanced Conv. Stock called for redemption 04/01/1997
Merged into Tyco International Ltd. (Bermuda) 10/01/1998
Each share Common 10¢ par exchanged for (0.7606) share Common 20¢ par
Tyco International Ltd. (Bermuda) reincorporated in Switzerland 03/17/2009 which merged into Johnson Controls International PLC 09/06/2016

UNITED STATES SWITCH CO. (DE)
Charter cancelled and declared inoperative and void for non-payment of taxes 3/16/21

UNITED STATES TELEVISION MANUFACTURING CORP.
Bankrupt in 1952

UNITED STATES TESTING INC (NY)
Each share Capital Stock $25 par exchanged for (10) shares Capital Stock $5 par 02/01/1957
Merged into USTESCO, Inc. 10/12/1982
Each share Capital Stock $5 par exchanged for $200 cash

UNITED STATES TIME CORP (CT)
Name changed to Timex Corp. (CT) 07/01/1969
Timex Corp. (CT) reincorporated in Delaware 01/01/1970
(See Timex Corp. (DE))

UNITED STATES TITLE GUARANTY CO.
Merged into New York Title & Mortgage Co. in 1929
New York Title & Mortgage Co. liquidation for cash completed 9/16/57

UNITED STATES TOB CO (DE)
Reincorporated 05/06/1986
Each share 7% Preferred $100 par exchanged for (4) shares 7% Preferred $25 par 00/00/1938
Each share old Common no par exchanged for (4) shares new Common no par 00/00/1938
New Common no par changed to $1 par and (1) additional share issued 05/01/1968
Each share 7% Preferred $25 par exchanged for (2.2142) shares Common $1 par 04/08/1970
Common $1 par changed to 50¢ par and (1) additional share issued 05/01/1972
Common 50¢ par split (3) for (1) by issuance of (2) additional shares 01/24/1983
State of incorporation changed from (NJ) to (DE) 05/06/1986
Common 50¢ par split (2) for (1) by issuance of (1) additional share 01/27/1987
Under plan of reorganization each share Common 50¢ par automatically became (1) share UST Inc. Common 50¢ par 05/05/1987
(See UST Inc.)

UNITED STATES TRUCKING CORP.
Reorganized as United States Distributing Corp. in 1927
(See United States Distributing Corp.)

UNITED STATES TR CO (BOSTON, MA)
Each share Capital Stock $100 par exchanged for (4) shares Capital Stock $25 par 07/00/1929
Capital Stock $25 par changed to $10 par 01/00/1932
Each share old Capital Stock $10 par exchanged for (0.5) share new Capital Stock $10 par 01/00/1934
8% Conv. Preferred called for redemption 07/01/1946
Stock Dividend - 100% 05/03/1968
Under plan of merger each share Capital Stock $10 par exchanged for $47 cash 12/31/1971

UNITED STATES TR CO (NEW YORK, NY)
Capital Stock $100 par changed to $20 par and (4) additional shares issued 1/12/56
Capital Stock $20 par changed to $10 par and (1) additional share issued 4/12/63
Capital Stock $10 par changed to $5 par and (1) additional share issued 9/16/68

Stock Dividends - 100% 12/27/45; 150% 12/27/50; 42.857% 10/18/73
Under plan of reorganization each share Capital Stock $5 par automatically became (1) share U.S. Trust Corp. Capital Stock $5 par 6/2/78
U.S. Trust Corp. merged into Chase Manhattan Corp. (Old) 9/2/95 which merged into Chase Manhattan Corp. (New) 3/31/96 which name changed to J.P. Morgan Chase & Co. 12/31/2000 which name changed to JPMorgan Chase & Co. 7/20/2004

UNITED STATES UNIVERSAL JOINTS CO. (MI)
Name changed to Shelby Universal Corp. (MI) 4/15/65
Shelby Universal Corp. (MI) merged into Shelby Universal Corp. (DE) 12/1/83 which recapitalized as NA American Technologies, Inc. 4/3/2006 which name changed to JSX Energy, Inc. 8/30/2006

UNITED STATES VIDEO VENDING CORP (VT)
Charter revoked for failure to file annual reports 01/19/1988

UNITED STATES WINDOW CORP. (IN)
Charter revoked for failure to file reports and pay fees 10/28/66

UNITED STATES WINDOW GLASS CO.
Property sold in 1927

UNITED STATES WORSTED CORP.
Liquidated in 1931

UNITED STATIONERS INC (DE)
Common 10¢ par split (2) for (1) by issuance of (1) additional share 03/03/1983
Common 10¢ par split (2) for (1) by issuance of (1) additional share 05/15/1984
Common 10¢ par split (2) for (1) by issuance of (1) additional share 11/09/1995
Common 10¢ par split (2) for (1) by issuance of (1) additional share payable 09/28/1998 to holders of record 09/14/1998
Common 10¢ par split (2) for (1) by issuance of (1) additional share payable 05/31/2011 to holders of record 05/16/2011 Ex date - 06/01/2011
Name changed to Essendant Inc. 06/01/2015

UNITED STD ASSET GROWTH CORP (IN)
Merged into Life Investors Inc. 09/01/1983
Each share Common no par exchanged for $1.50 principal amount of United Standard Asset Growth Corp. 9% Promissory Notes due 03/01/1986 and $1.45 cash

UNITED STEEL & WIRE CO., INC. (MI)
Each share Common no par exchanged for (2) shares Common $2.50 par in 1937
Acquired by Roblin Industries, Inc. in a cash transaction 10/10/68

UNITED STEEL CORP. LTD. (CANADA)
Recapitalized as James United Steel Ltd. 06/28/1965
Each share Common no par exchanged for (0.1) share Common no par
James United Steel Ltd. name changed to James United Industries, Ltd. 09/25/1969
(See James United Industries, Ltd.)

UNITED STL COS LTD (ENGLAND)
Stock Dividend - 25% 08/03/1961
Nationalized by the United Kingdom 08/08/1967
Each ADR for Ordinary £1 par exchanged for £1-12s-0.1056d principal amount of 6-1/2% Treasury Stock due 01/28/1971

UNITED STOCKYARDS CORP. (DE)
Ctfs. dated prior to 11/1/64
70¢ Conv. Preferred no par called for redemption 10/15/59
Common $1 par changed to 25¢ par and (3) additional shares issued 4/6/62
Merged into Canal-Randolph Corp. 11/1/64
Each share Common 25¢ par exchanged for (0.4) share Common $1 par
(See Canal-Randolph Corp.)

UNITED STOCKYARDS CORP (DE)
Ctfs. dated after 06/01/1984
Stock Dividend - 10% 01/24/1986
Name changed to Canal Capital Corp. 10/03/1988

UNITED STORES CORP. (DE)
Class A no par changed to $5 par 06/01/1939
Common Voting Trust expired and each VTC for Common no par exchanged for (1) share Common 50¢ par 06/01/1939
Recapitalized 03/20/1946
Class A $5 par reclassified as $4.20 2nd Preferred $5 par
Each share $6 Preferred no par received (1) share $4.20 2nd Preferred $5 par
Each share Common 50¢ par received (0.04) share $4.20 2nd Preferred $5 par
Merged into McCrory Corp. 07/16/1960
Each share $6 Preferred no par exchanged for (1) share $6 Conv. Preferred $100 par
Each share $4.20 2nd Preferred $5 par exchanged for (0.75) share Common 50¢ par
Each share Common 50¢ par exchanged for (3/14) share Common 50¢ par
(See McCrory Corp.)

UNITED STOVE CO. (MI)
Each share Common no par exchanged for (4) shares Common $1 par 00/00/1936
Name changed to United Metal Craft Co. 00/00/1953
United Metal Craft Co. merged into Gar Wood Industries, Inc. 10/31/1958 which was acquired by Sargent Industries, Inc. (DE) 04/02/1970
(See Sargent Industries, Inc. (DE))

UNITED STS COMMODITY INDEX FDS TR (DE)
Trust terminated 03/25/2015
Each United States Metals Index Fund Common Share of Bene. Int. received $18.722639 cash
Trust terminated 09/12/2018
Each share United States Agriculture Index Fund received $15.794616 cash
(Additional Information in Active)

UNITED STS CRUDE INTL INC (NV)
Each share old Common $0.001 par exchanged for (0.001) share new Common $0.001 par 08/05/2003
SEC revoked common stock registration 04/12/2005

UNITED STS DIESEL HEATING OIL FD LP (DE)
Trust terminated 09/12/2018
Each Unit received $20.005151 cash

UNITED STS EXPL CORP (AB)
Name changed to Triangulum Corp. 11/18/1999
(See Triangulum Corp.)

UNITED STS HEATING OIL FD LP (DE)
Name changed to United States Diesel-Heating Oil Fund, L.P. 08/07/2012
(See United States Diesel-Heating Oil Fund, L.P.)

UNITED STS SATELLITE BROADCASTING INC (MN)
Merged into General Motors Corp. 05/18/1999
Each share Class A Common $0.0001 par exchanged for either (0.3199) share new Class H Common 1¢ par or $18 cash
Each share Common $0.0001 par exchanged for either (0.3199) share new Class H Common 1¢ par or $18 cash
Note: Option to receive stock expired 06/28/1999
(See General Motors Corp.)

UNITED STS SHORT OIL FD LP (DE)
Trust terminated 09/12/2018
Each Unit received $46.53836 cash

UNITED SULPHUR & CHEMICAL CO., INC. (NV)
Name changed to Kar-N Corp. 1/5/70

UNITED SURGICAL PARTNERS INTL INC (DE)
Issue Information - 9,000,000 shares COM offered at $14 per share on 6/7/2001
Common 1¢ par split (3) for (2) by issuance of (0.5) additional share payable 7/15/2005 to holders of record 6/30/2005 Ex date - 7/18/2005
Merged into Welsh, Carson, Anderson & Stowe 4/19/2007
Each share Common 1¢ par exchanged for $31.05 cash

UNITED SYS TECHNOLOGY INC (IA)
Common 10¢ par changed to 1¢ par 06/30/2004
Each share old Common 1¢ par exchanged for (0.0001) share new Common 1¢ par to reflect a (1) for (10,000) reverse split immediately followed by a (10,000) for (1) forward split 09/22/2005
Note: Holders of (9,999) or fewer pre-split shares received for $0.08 cash per share
Acquired by USTI Holdings, Inc. 10/19/2010
Each share new Common 1¢ par exchanged for $0.10 cash

UNITED TECHNICAL INDUSTRIES, INC. (DE)
Liquidated 12/02/1964
Each share Common $1 par exchanged for first and final distribution of (0.1017087) share Stickelber & Sons, Inc. Common no par
Stickelber & Sons, Inc. merged into Marion Corp. 02/01/1965
(See Marion Corp.)

UNITED TECHNICAL INDUSTRIES CORP. (IN)
Dissolved 12/31/67
No stockholders' equity

UNITED TECHNOLOGIES CORP (DE)
$2.84 Conv. Prior Preferred $1 par called for redemption 05/15/1979
$7.32 Conv. Preferred $1 par called for redemption 08/10/1981
$3.875 Conv. Preferred $1 par called for redemption 12/15/1983
$8 Conv. Preferred $1 par called for redemption 04/02/1984
$2.55 Conv. Preferred $1 par called for redemption 09/02/1986
$4.50 Preferred $1 par called for redemption 05/11/1990
Common Stock Purchase Rights declared for Common stockholders were redeemed at $0.10 per right 03/10/1992 for holders of record 02/28/1992
Each 7.5% Corporate Unit automatically became (0.513) share Common $1 par 08/03/2015
(Additional Information in Active)

UNITED TECHNOLOGY LABS INC (DE)
Name changed to UTL Corp. 06/30/1975
(See UTL Corp.)

UNITED TEL CO IND INC (IN)
Name changed 00/00/1953
Name changed from United Telephone Co. to United Telephone Co. of Indiana, Inc. 00/00/1953
$5 Preferred $100 par called for redemption 07/31/1992
Public interest eliminated

UNITED TEL CO OHIO (OH)
8.40% Preferred $100 par called for redemption 01/01/1987
Public interest eliminated

UNITED TEL CO PA (PA)
6% Preferred called for redemption 09/16/1940
4.50% Preferred $100 par called for redemption 12/01/1993

UNITED TELE-TRONICS, INC. (UT)
Name changed to United Resources Inc. (UT) 04/24/1967
United Resources Inc. (UT) name changed to Pacific Air Transport Inc. 01/31/1968 which name changed to Pacific Air Transport International Inc. 09/28/1970 which recapitalized as Chase Hanover Corp. 09/17/1983
(See Chase Hanover Corp.)

UNITED TELECOMMUNICATIONS CORP (NY)
Stock Dividend - 50% 10/26/1979
Name changed to UTC Group Inc. 05/29/1980
UTC Group Inc. name changed to Coradian Corp. 01/02/1981
(See Coradian Corp.)

UNITED TELECOMMUNICATIONS INC (KS)
Common $2.50 par split (2) for (1) by issuance of (1) additional share 12/28/1989
Name changed to Sprint Corp. 02/26/1992
Sprint Corp. name changed to Sprint Nextel Corp. 08/12/2005 which merged into Sprint Corp. (DE) 07/10/2013

UNITED TELECONTROL ELECTRS INC (NJ)
Common 10¢ par split (5) for (2) by issuance of (1.5) additional shares 06/10/1968
Common 10¢ par split (4) for (1) by issuance of (3) additional shares 12/22/1983
Merged into Mechanical Technology Inc. 06/30/1987
Each share Common 10¢ par exchanged for $10.50 cash

UNITED TELEFILMS LTD. (ON)
Recapitalized as Creative Telefilms & Artists Ltd. 01/26/1960
Each share Common no par exchanged for (0.25) share Common no par
Creative Telefilms & Artists Ltd. name changed to Seven Arts Productions Ltd. 08/12/1960 which name changed to Warner Bros.-Seven Arts Ltd. 07/15/1967 which was acquired by Kinney National Service, Inc. 07/08/1969 which name changed to Kinney Services, Inc. (NY) 02/17/1971 which reincorporated in Delaware as Warner Communications Inc. 02/11/1972
(See Warner Communications Inc.)

UNITED TELEGROUP INTL INC (DE)
Name changed to UTG Communications International, Inc. 08/15/1996

UNITED TELEPHONE & ELECTRIC CO. (DE)
Reorganized as United Utilities, Inc. 11/15/1938
Each share 7% Preferred exchanged for (7.3) shares Common $10 par
Each share 6% Preferred exchanged for (0.1666666) share Common $10 par
Each share Common exchanged for (0.75) share Common $10 par
United Utilities, Inc. name changed to United Telecommunications, Inc. 06/02/1972 which name changed to Sprint Corp. (KS) 02/26/1992 which name changed to Sprint Nextel Corp. 08/12/2005 which merged into Sprint Corp. (DE) 07/10/2013

UNITED TELEVISION INC (DE)
Merged into News Corp., Ltd. 07/31/2001
Each share Common 10¢ par exchanged for either (2.0253) ADR's for Limited Voting Preferred and $60 cash (Mixed election) or (0.9378) ADR for Limited Voting Preferred and $93.18 cash (Cash election)
Note: All Stock or Non-electors received (3.9919) ADR's per share
News Corp., Ltd. reorganized as News Corp. 11/03/2004

UNITED TENN BANCSHARES CORP (TN)
Common $5 par changed to $2 par 10/12/1971
Name changed to National Commerce Bancorporation 04/27/1978
National Commerce Bancorporation name changed to National Commerce Financial Corp. 04/25/2001 which merged into SunTrust Banks, Inc. 10/01/2004

UNITED TERREX CORP (AB)
Name changed to Siberian Pacific Resources Inc. 12/21/1994
(See Siberian Pacific Resources Inc.)

UNITED TEX-SOL MINES INC (AB)
Acquired by St. Andrew Goldfields Ltd. 06/23/2002
Each share Common no par exchanged for (1) share Common no par

UNITED TEXTILES & TOYS CORP (DE)
Each share old Common 1¢ par exchanged for (0.1) share new Common 1¢ par 03/26/1997
Name changed to U.S. Biomedical Corp. 05/23/2002
(See U.S. Biomedical Corp.)

UNITED THACKER COAL CO.
Acquired by Island Creek Coal Co. (ME) 00/00/1941
Details not available

UNITED THEATRES LTD.-CINEMAS UNIS LTEE. (QC)
Name changed to Cinemas Unis Ltee. 00/00/1979
(See Cinemas Unis Ltee.)

UNITED THERMAL CORP (DE)
Merged into Trigen Acquisition Inc. 12/10/1993
Each share Common 10¢ par exchanged for $4.50 cash

UNITED THRIFT PLAN, INC.
Liquidation ordered by Court 00/00/1935
Details not available

UNITED TIRE & RUBR LTD (ON)
Common no par reclassified as Conv. Class A Special Common no par 07/21/1975
Conv. Class B Special Common no par reclassified as Common no par 07/15/1980
Conv. Preferred Ser. A $2.25 par called for redemption 05/17/1995
Merged into a private company 08/28/1996

Each share Common no par exchanged for $2.825 cash

UNITED TOTE INC (DE)
Common 1¢ par split (3) for (2) by issuance of (0.5) additional share 05/22/1989
Name changed to Autotote Corp. 02/28/1992
Autotote Corp. name changed to Scientific Games Corp. (DE) 04/27/2001 which reincorporated in Nevada 01/10/2018

UNITED TOWNS ELECTRIC CO. LTD. (NL)
Merged into Newfoundland Light & Power Co. Ltd. 09/08/1966
Each share 5.50% Preference $10 par exchanged for (1) share 5.50% Preference Ser. A $10 par
Each share 5.25% Preference $10 par exchanged for (1) share 5.25% Preference Ser. B $10 par
Each share Ordinary $10 par exchanged for (1.5) shares Common no par
Newfoundland Light & Power Co. Ltd. name changed to Fortis Inc. 12/29/1987

UNITED TRACTION CO. OF PITTSBURGH
Merged into Pittsburgh Railways Co. 09/30/1950
Each share Preferred $50 par exchanged for (4.2) shares Common no par and $5 cash
Pittsburgh Railways Co. name changed to Pittway Corp. (PA) 11/28/1967 which merged into Pittway Corp. (DE) 12/28/1989
(See Pittway Corp. (DE))

UNITED TRACTION CO. OLD (NY)
Reorganized as United Traction Co. (New) 00/00/1943
No stockholders' equity

UNITED TRACTION CO NEW (NY)
Completely liquidated 04/01/1971
Each share Common no par exchanged for first and final distribution of $24.50 cash

UNITED TRADING COM (NV)
Each share old Common $1 par exchanged for (3) shares new Common $1 par 10/06/2000
Each share new Common $1 par exchanged for (0.125) share Common $0.001 par 12/21/2001
Name changed to Global Links Corp. (Old) 02/04/2003
Global Links Corp. (Old) name changed to Global Links Corp. (New) 08/04/2003

UNITED TRAFFIC SYS INC (BC)
Recapitalized as Corpus Resources Corp. 12/14/2007
Each share Common no par exchanged for (0.1) share Common no par
Corpus Resources Corp. name changed to NeoMedyx Medical Corp. 08/04/2009 which name changed to Blue Marble Media Corp. 03/30/2010 which name changed to KBridge Energy Corp. 01/31/2012

UNITED TRANS WESTN INC (DE)
Reincorporated 07/26/1989
State of incorporation changed from (TX) to (DE) and Ser. A Common no par changed to 1¢ par 07/26/1989
SEC revoked common stock registration 05/03/2010

UNITED TRANSNET INC (DE)
Merged into Corporate Express, Inc. 11/08/1996
Each share Common $0.001 par exchanged for (0.45) share Common $0.0002 par
(See Corporate Express, Inc.)

UNITED TREATMENT CTRS INC (WY)
Common $0.0001 par changed to $0.00001 par 08/06/2012

Name changed to PotNetwork Holdings, Inc. (WY) 07/24/2015
PotNetwork Holdings, Inc. (WY) reincorporated in Colorado 03/03/2017

UNITED TRI STAR RES LTD (CANADA)
Reincorporated 10/27/1994
Place of incorporation changed from (BC) to (Canada) 10/27/1994
Under plan of merger name changed to UTS Energy Corp. 06/30/1998
UTS Energy Corp. merged into SilverBirch Energy Corp. 10/01/2010 which merged into SilverWillow Energy Corp. 04/04/2012
(See SilverWillow Energy Corp.)

UNITED TRINITY MINES (CA)
Charter forfeited for failure to pay taxes 00/00/1929

UNITED TRUCK LEASING INC (MN)
99.8% held by National Presto Industries, Inc. as of 09/15/1976
Public interest eliminated

UNITED TR CO (TORONTO, ON)
Shares $5 par changed to no par 08/01/1974
Through voluntary exchange offer 99% acquired by Royal Trust Co. (Montreal, QC) as of 03/10/1977
Public interest eliminated

UNITED TRUST CORP.
Dissolved 00/00/1944
Details not available

UNITED TR GROUP INC (IL)
Reincorporated under the laws of Delaware as UTG Inc. 07/06/2005

UNITED TR INC (IL)
Each share old Common no par exchanged for (0.1) share new Common no par 05/12/1997
Under plan of merger name changed to United Trust Group, Inc. (IL) 07/26/1999
United Trust Group, Inc. (IL) reincorporated in Delaware as UTG Inc. 07/06/2005

UNITED TRUST LIFE INSURANCE CO. (GA)
Completely liquidated 09/30/1968
Each share Common $1 par exchanged for first and final distribution of (0.625) share Georgia International Corp. Common $1 par
Georgia International Corp. acquired by Capital Holding Corp. 12/31/1972 which name changed to Providian Corp. 05/12/1994 which merged into Aegon N.V. 06/10/1997

UNITED UNIFORM SVCS PLC (UNITED KINGDOM)
Name changed to Horace Small Apparel PLC 05/07/1993
Horace Small Apparel PLC name changed to Redbus Interhouse PLC 04/05/2000
(See Redbus Interhouse PLC)

UNITED UNITS CORP. (CO)
Declared defunct and inoperative for failure to pay taxes and file annual reports 10/10/1941

UNITED URANIUM & OIL CORP. (DE)
Name changed to United Mercury Corp. (DE) 04/29/1955
United Mercury Corp. name changed to Mercury Electronics Corp. (DE) 05/19/1958 which recapitalized as Mercury Industries, Inc. 04/25/1974
(See Mercury Industries, Inc.)

UNITED URANIUM CORP. (CO)
Proclaimed defunct and inoperative for non-payment of taxes 10/11/1961

UNITED URANIUM CORP (SK)
Place of incorporation changed from (Canada) to (SK) 11/05/2008
Reorganized under the laws of British Columbia as Karoo Exploration Corp. 09/15/2013

Each share Common no par exchanged for (0.2) share Common no par
Karoo Exploration Corp. recapitalized as Bruin Point Helium Corp. 12/11/2017 which name changed to American Helium Inc. 05/11/2018

UNITED UTILITIES & SPECIALTY CORP. (DE)
Adjudicated bankrupt 5/26/58
No stockholders' equity

UNITED UTILS CORP FLA (FL)
Name changed to United Communities Corp. 7/16/70
United Communities Corp. name changed to Southward Ventures Inc. 5/8/78 which assets were transferred to Southward Ventures Depositary Trust 5/13/82
(See Southward Ventures Depositary Trust)

UNITED UTILS INC (KS)
Common $10 par changed to $5 par and (1) additional share issued 04/05/1961
Common $5 par changed to $2.50 par and (1) additional share issued 02/11/1965
Name changed to United Telecommunications, Inc. 06/02/1972
United Telecommunications, Inc. name changed to Sprint Corp. (KS) 02/26/1992 which name changed to Sprint Nextel Corp. 08/12/2005 which merged into Sprint Corp. (DE) 07/10/2013

UNITED UTILS PLC (UNITED KINGDOM)
Reorganized as United Utilities Group PLC 07/28/2008
Each Sponsored ADR for Ordinary exchanged for (0.77272727) Sponsored ADR for Ordinary and approximately $6.26414 cash

UNITED VA BK ST PLANTERS (RICHMOND, VA)
Name changed to United Virginia Bank (Richmond, VA) 12/15/71
(See United Virginia Bank (Richmond, VA))

UNITED VA BANKSHARES INC (VA)
Common $10 par split (2) for (1) by issuance of (1) additional share 05/20/1970
Common $10 par changed to $5 par and (1) additional share issued 06/17/1983
Common $5 par split (2) for (1) by issuance of (1) additional share 05/23/1986
Name changed to Crestar Financial Corp. 09/01/1987
Crestar Financial Corp. merged into SunTrust Banks Inc. 12/31/1998

UNITED VY BANCORP INC (PA)
Merged into JeffBanks, Inc. 01/21/1997
Each share Class A Common no par exchanged for (0.339) share Common no par
JeffBanks, Inc. merged into Hudson United Bancorp 11/30/1999 which merged into TD Banknorth Inc. 01/31/2006
(See TD Banknorth Inc.)

UNITED VY BK (FARMERSVILLE, CA)
Merged into Stockmans Bancorp 2/3/97
Each share Common $6.25 par exchanged for $0.8526 cash

UNITED VY BK (PHILADELPHIA, PA)
Merged into United Valley Bancorp Inc. 03/31/1995
Each share Class A Common no par exchanged for (1) share Class A Common no par
United Valley Bancorp Inc. merged into JeffBanks, Inc. 01/19/1997

which merged into Hudson United Bancorp 11/30/1999 which merged into TD Banknorth Inc. 01/31/2006
(See TD Banknorth Inc.)

UNITED VANGUARD FD INC (MD)
Reincorporated 12/31/74
State of incorporation changed from (DE) to (MD) 12/31/74
Capital Stock $1 par split (3) for (1) by issuance of (2) additional shares 12/2/83
Capital Stock $1 par reclassified as Class A $1 par 8/15/95
Class A $1 par changed to $0.001 par 6/22/99
Under plan of reorganization each share Class A $0.001 par automatically became (1) share Waddell & Reed Advisors Funds Inc. Vanguard Fund Class A $0.001 par 10/1/2000

UNITED VANGUARD HOMES INC (DE)
Each share old Common 1¢ par exchanged for (0.599988) share new Common 1¢ par 03/31/1996
81% owned by Vanguard Ventures, Inc. as of 12/18/2001
Public interest eliminated

UNITED VENTURE FD LTD (CANADA)
Merged into United Global Growth Fund 02/17/1983
Details not available

UNITED VENTURES GROUP INC (DE)
Name changed to American Jewelry Corp. (DE) 10/13/2000
American Jewelry Corp. (DE) reincorporated in Nevada 01/31/2002 which name changed to MSM Jewelry Corp. 06/24/2002 which name changed to GEMZ Corp. 10/27/2003

UNITED VENTURES INC (MD)
Merged into Federated Development Co. 07/31/1970
Each share Common $1 par exchanged for (0.1) Share of Bene. Int. no par and (1/3) Purchase Warrant which expired expired 12/31/1975
(See Federated Development Co.)

UNITED VERDE COPPER CO.
Acquired by Phelps Dodge Corp. 00/00/1934
Details not available

UNITED VERDE EXTENSION MINING CO.
Dissolved in 1940

UNITED VIDEO SATELLITE GROUP INC (DE)
Class A Common 1¢ par split (2) for (1) by issuance of (1) additional share payable 03/12/1996 to holders of record 02/22/1996
Class A Common 1¢ par split (2) for (1) by issuance of (1) additional share payable 08/20/1998 to holders of record 08/10/1998
Name changed to TV Guide Inc. 03/02/1999
TV Guide Inc. merged into Gemstar-TV Guide International, Inc. 07/12/2000 which merged into Macrovision Solutions Corp. 05/05/2008 which name changed to Rovi Corp. 07/16/2009

UNITED VIRGINIA BANK (RICHMOND, VA)
100% held by United Virginia Bancshares Inc. as of 00/00/1980
Public interest eliminated

UNITED VIRGINIA BANK/FIRST & CITIZENS NATIONAL (ALEXANDRIA, VA)
Merged into United Virginia Bank/National (Vienna, Va.) 1/2/74
Each share Common $10 par exchanged for $146.85 cash

UNITED VISION GROUP INC (DE)
Recapitalized as Apollo Eye Group Inc. 11/1/96
Each share Common $0.001 par exchanged for (0.2) share Common $0.001 par
(See Apollo Eye Group Inc.)

UNITED VT BANCORPORATION (VT)
Common $1 par changed to 50¢ par and (1) additional share issued 12/30/83
Common 50¢ par split (5) for (3) by issuance of (2/3) additional share 4/4/89
Merged into Arrow Financial Corp. 7/2/90
Each share Common 50¢ par exchanged for (1.13) shares Common $1 par

UNITED WALL PAPER FACTORIES, INC. (DE)
Name changed to United Wallpaper, Inc. 00/00/1944
United Wallpaper, Inc. name changed to DeSoto Chemical Coatings, Inc. 10/28/1959 which name changed to DeSoto, Inc. 05/09/1967 which merged into Keystone Consolidated Industries, Inc. 09/26/1996
(See Keystone Consolidated Industries, Inc.)

UNITED WALLPAPER, INC. (DE)
Each share 4% Preferred $50 par exchanged for (1) share 5% 2nd Preferred B $14 par and (0.5) share Common $1 par 08/01/1956
Each share Common $2 par exchanged for (0.2) share Common $1 par 08/01/1956
Name changed to DeSoto Chemical Coatings, Inc. 10/28/1959
DeSoto Chemical Coatings, Inc. name changed to DeSoto, Inc. 05/09/1967 which merged into Keystone Consolidated Industries, Inc. 09/26/1996
(See Keystone Consolidated Industries, Inc.)

UNITED WASTE SYS INC (DE)
Common $0.001 par split (2) for (1) by issuance of (1) additional share payable 6/18/96 to holders of record 6/7/96
Merged into USA Waste Services, Inc. 8/26/97
Each share Common $0.001 par exchanged (1.075) shares Common 1¢ par
USA Waste Services, Inc. merged into Waste Management, Inc. 7/16/98

UNITED WESTBURNE INDS LTD (AB)
Common $2.50 par changed to no par 00/00/1978
Common no par split (5) for (1) by issuance of (4) additional shares 10/19/1981
Merged into Dumez Investments I Inc. 08/18/1987
Each share Common no par exchanged for $25 cash
6-1/4% 1st Preferred Ser. A $50 par called for redemption 08/20/1987
Public interest eliminated

UNITED WESTERN BANCORP INC (CO)
SEC revoked common stock registration 10/07/2014

UNITED WESTERN CONSOLIDATED OIL CO. (WY)
Charter revoked for failure to file reports and pay fees 7/19/27

UNITED WESTERN LIFE INSURANCE CO. (TX)
Merged into Western Republic Life Insurance Co. 4/30/67
Each share Common no par exchanged for (1) share Common no par
Western Republic Life Insurance Co. merged into First National Life Insurance Co. (AL) 12/31/67 which reorganized as First National Corp. (NV) 12/31/69 which recapitalized as Seal Fleet, Inc. (NV) 8/9/79 which reorganized in Delaware as Seal Holdings Corp. 6/30/97 which name changed to Le@p Technology, Inc. 7/6/2000

UNITED WESTERN MINERALS CO. (DE)
Acquired by Sabre-Pinon Corp. 10/16/61
Each share Common received (1/17) share Sabre-Pinon Common and (1) Unit of Beneficial Interest in United Western Trust
(See listings for Sabre-Pinon Corp. and United Western Trust)

UNITED WESTERN MINES, INC. (WA)
Charter cancelled and proclaimed dissolved for failure to pay fees 12/18/77

UNITED WESTERN SALES DIVISION, INC. (CO)
Declared defunct and inoperative for failure to pay taxes and file annual reports 10/16/71

UNITED WESTLAND RES LTD (BC)
Recapitalized as Daleco Resources Corp. (DE) 5/2/86
Each share Common no par exchanged for (0.2) share Common no par 5/2/86
Daleco Resources Corp. (BC) reincorporated in Delaware 10/1/96 which reincorporated in Nevada 4/1/2002

UNITED WESTN CORP (OH)
Liquidation completed
Each share Common no par received initial distribution of $2 cash 07/16/1984
Each share Common no par received second distribution of $1 cash 01/15/1985
Each share Common no par received third distribution of $2.04 cash 05/31/1985
Each share Common no par received fourth and final distribution of $0.515 cash 12/29/1986
Note: Certificates were not required to be surrendered and are without value

UNITED WESTN ENERGY CORP (AZ)
Charter revoked for failure to file reports and pay fees 8/10/87

UNITED WESTN OIL & GAS LTD (AB)
Merged into Trans-Canada Resources Ltd. (New) 11/01/1982
Each (2.7) shares no par exchanged for (1) share Class A Common no par
Trans-Canada Resources Ltd. (New) recapitalized as Consolidated Trans-Canada Resources Ltd. 09/22/1988 which merged into Ranchmen's Resources Ltd. 09/30/1989 which name changed to Ranchmen's Resources (1975) Ltd. 08/28/1975 which merged into Ranchmen's Resources (1976) Ltd. 01/31/1977 which name changed to Ranchmen's Resources Ltd. 05/31/1985 which merged into Crestar Energy Inc. 10/11/1995 which was acquired by Gulf Canada Resources Ltd. 11/13/2000
(See Gulf Canada Resources Ltd.)

UNITED WESTN TR
Trust terminated 1/17/74
No stockholders' equity

UNITED WHELAN CORP. (DE)
Each share Common 30¢ par exchanged for (0.25) share Common $1.20 par 6/30/67
Name changed to Perfect Film & Chemical Corp. 5/31/67
Perfect Film & Chemical Corp. name changed to Cadence Industries Corp. 10/22/70
(See Cadence Industries Corp.)

UNITED WHOLESALE BUILDING SUPPLY CO. (NJ)
Adjudicated bankrupt 9/10/64
No stockholders' equity

UNITED WINE TRADERS LTD. (ENGLAND)
Name changed to International Distillers & Vintners Ltd. 5/14/62
(See International Distillers & Vintners Ltd.)

UNITED WIS SVCS INC NEW (WI)
Name changed to Cobalt Corp. 03/23/2001
Cobalt Corp. merged into WellPoint Health Networks Inc. 09/24/2003 which merged into WellPoint, Inc. 12/01/2004 which name changed to Anthem, Inc. (New) 12/03/2014

UNITED WIS SVCS INC OLD (WI)
Common no par split (3) for (2) by issuance of (0.5) additional share 09/30/1992
Common no par split (2) for (1) by issuance of (1) additional share payable 10/14/1997 to holders of record 10/06/1997
Each share Common no par received distribution of (1) share United Wisconsin Services, Inc. (New) Common no par payable 09/25/1998 to holders of record 09/11/1998
Ex date - 09/29/1998
Name changed to American Medical Security Group, Inc. 09/11/1998
(See American Medical Security Group, Inc.)

UNITED WORTH HYDROCHEM CORP (TX)
Each share Part. Preferred 25¢ par exchanged for (1) share Common 25¢ par 7/3/72
Each share old Common 25¢ par exchanged for (0.001) share new Common 25¢ par 7/22/2006
Note: In effect holders received $1.50 cash per share and public interest was eliminated

UNITED WTR IDAHO INC (ID)
5% Preferred $100 par called for redemption at $102 on 3/17/2006

UNITED WTR NEW JERSEY INC (NJ)
4.5% Preferred $100 par called for redemption at $100.50 plus $0.38 accrued dividends on 01/31/2011
4.55% Preferred $100 par called for redemption at $100.50 plus $0.38 accrued dividends on 01/31/2011

UNITED WTR RES (NJ)
7.625% Preferred Ser. no par called for redemption at $104.58 on 1/8/99
Acquired by Suez Lyonnaise des Eaux 7/27/2000
Each share 5% Conv. Preferred Ser. A no par exchanged for $29.2218 cash
Each share Common no par exchanged for $35.4905 cash

UNITED ZINC SMELTING CORP.
Property sold under foreclosure in 1950
No stockholders' equity

UNITEDCORP (ME)
Merged into Camden National Corp. 12/29/1995
Each share Common $6.25 par exchanged for (0.85076) share Common no par

UNITEDGLOBALCOM INC (DE)
Class A Common 1¢ par split (2) for (1) by issuance of (1) additional share payable 11/30/1999 to holders of record 11/22/1999
Class B Common 1¢ par split (2) for (1) by issuance of (1) additional share payable 11/30/1999 to holders of record 11/22/1999

UNI-UNI

Merged into Liberty Global, Inc. (DE) 06/15/2005
Each share Class A Common 1¢ par exchanged for (0.2155) share Class A Common 1¢ par
Each share Class B Common 1¢ par exchanged for (0.2155) share Class B Common 1¢ par
Liberty Global, Inc. (DE) reorganized in England & Wales as Liberty Global PLC 06/10/2013

UNITEDHEALTH GROUP INC (MN)
Common 1¢ par split (2) for (1) by issuance of (1) additional share payable 12/22/2000 to holders of record 12/01/2000 Ex date - 12/26/2000
Common 1¢ par split (2) for (1) by issuance of (1) additional share payable 06/18/2003 to holders of record 06/02/2003 Ex date - 06/19/2003
Common 1¢ par split (2) for (1) by issuance of (1) additional share payable 05/27/2005 to holders of record 05/20/2005 Ex date - 05/31/2005
Reincorporated under the laws of Delaware 07/01/2015

UNITEK CORP (CA)
Common no par split (2) for (1) by issuance of (1) additional share 06/13/1969
Merged into Bristol-Myers Co. 04/06/1978
Each share Common no par exchanged for (1.733) shares Common $1 par
Bristol-Myers Co. name changed to Bristol-Myers Squibb Co. 10/04/1989

UNITEK GLOBAL SVCS INC (DE)
Each share old Common $0.00002 par exchanged for (0.03571428) share new Common $0.00002 par 11/10/2010
Each share new Common $0.00002 par exchanged again for (0.5) share new Common $0.00002 par 12/22/2010
Plan of reorganization under Chapter 11 Federal Bankruptcy proceedings effective 01/13/2015
No stockholders' equity

UNITEK INC (UT)
Involuntarily dissolved 06/01/1987

UNITEL VIDEO INC (DE)
Reincorporated 1/16/84
Stock Dividends - 10% 3/1/82; 10% 3/1/83; 10% 3/1/84
Reincorporated from under the laws of (PA) to (DE) on 1/16/84
Plan of reorganization under chapter 11 Federal Bankruptcy Code effective 10/22/2001
No stockholders' equity

UNITERRE RES LTD (BC)
Name changed to NaiKun Wind Energy Group Inc. 11/3/2006

UNITEX, INC. (UT)
Involuntarily dissolved 02/01/1992

UNITEX INDUSTRIES, INC. (TX)
Recapitalized 12/28/59
Each share 72¢ Preferred no par exchanged for $10 principal amount of 5% Debentures and $2 cash
Common no par changed to $1 par
Completely liquidated 12/19/66
Each share Common $1 par exchanged for first and final distribution of (0.525) share Texstar Corp. 6% Preferred $5 par and (0.2) share Common $1 par
(See Texstar Corp.)

UNITI BK (BUENA PARK, CA)
Under plan of reorganization each share Common no par automatically became (1) share Uniti Financial Corp. Common no par 7/8/2005

UNITOG CO. (MO)
Reincorporated under the laws of Delaware 5/26/69
(See Unitog Co. (Del.))

UNITOG CO NEW (DE)
Common 1¢ par split (3) for (2) by issuance of (0.5) additional share 9/23/94
Merged into Cintas Corp. 3/24/99
Each share Common 1¢ par exchanged for (0.5518) share Common no par

UNITOG CO OLD (DE)
Common $2 par split (3) for (2) by issuance of (0.5) additional share 6/2/82
Stock Dividend - 25% 5/26/69
Merged into UTOG, Inc. 5/1/84
Each share Common $2 par exchanged for $37 cash

UNITOR ASA (NORWAY)
Name changed 3/1/95
Name changed from Unitor Ships Service A.S. to Unitor ASA 3/1/95
ADR agreement terminated 11/26/2001
Each Sponsored ADR for Ordinary Kr.12-1/2 par exchanged for $4.563116 cash

UNITRANSACT BUSINESS SOLUTIONS INC (FL)
Each share old Common $0.001 par exchanged for (0.01) share new Common $0.001 par 02/11/2000
Name changed to MoneyFocus USA.com Inc. 04/03/2000
MoneyFocus USA.com Inc. name changed to Amnis Energy Inc. 03/22/2002 which name changed to Homeland Security Group International, Inc. 10/10/2005 which recapitalized as Domestic Energy Corp. 04/07/2008
(See Domestic Energy Corp.)

UNITRIN INC (DE)
Common 10¢ par split (2) for (1) by issuance of (1) additional share payable 03/26/1999 to holders of record 03/05/1999
Each share Common 10¢ par received distribution of (0.06494753) share Curtiss Wright Corp. Class B Common $1 par payable 11/29/2001 to holders of record 11/12/2001 Ex date - 11/07/2001
Name changed to Kemper Corp. (New) 08/25/2011

UNITRODE CORP (MD)
Common 20¢ par split (2) for (1) by issuance of (1) additional share 07/17/1981
Common 20¢ par split (2) for (1) by issuance of (1) additional share 07/29/1983
Common 20¢ par changed to 1¢ par 09/29/1997
Common 20¢ par split (2) for (1) by issuance of (1) additional share payable 10/14/1997 to holders of record 10/06/1997 Ex date - 10/15/1997
Stock Dividend - 100% 07/21/1969
Merged into Texas Instruments Inc. 10/15/1999
Each share Common 1¢ par exchanged for (0.5023) share Common $1 par

UNITROL DATA PROTN SYS INC (BC)
Name changed to Radical Advanced Technologies Corp. 04/12/1994
(See Radical Advanced Technologies Corp.)

UNITRONICS CORP. (NY)
Merged into Siegler Corp. 9/13/57
Each share Common $1 par exchanged for (0.5) share Common no par
Siegler Corp. name changed to Lear Siegler, Inc. 6/5/62
(See Lear Siegler, Inc.)

UNITS SERVICE, INC.
Trust terminated in 1935
Details not available

UNITY AUTO PTS INC (NV)
Name changed to Unity Management Group, Inc. 01/08/2010
Unity Management Group, Inc. name changed to Petrotech Oil & Gas, Inc. 03/26/2013

UNITY BANCORP, INC. (OH)
Merged into Citizens Bancshares, Inc. 12/16/1994
Each share Common exchanged for (1.09) shares Common no par
Citizens Bancshares, Inc. name changed to Sky Financial Group, Inc. 10/02/1998 which merged into Huntington Bancshares Inc. 07/02/2007

UNITY BANCORP INC (DE)
Common no par split (3) for (2) by issuance of (0.5) additional share payable 06/01/1998 to holders of record 05/15/1998 Ex date - 06/02/1998
Stock Dividends - 5% payable 01/15/1996 to holders of record 12/31/1995; 5% payable 01/08/1999 to holders of record 12/21/1998
Reincorporated under the laws of New Jersey 07/17/2002

UNITY BK & TR CO (ROXBURY, MA)
Taken over by the Commissioner of Banking of the State and FDIC appointed liquidating agent 07/30/1982
Stockholders' equity unlikely

UNITY BK CDA (TORONTO, ON)
Merged into Banque Provinciale du Canada (Montreal, QC) (New) 06/16/1977
Each Share $5 par exchanged for (0.25) share Common $2 par
Banque Provinciale du Canada (Montreal, QC) (New) merged into National Bank of Canada (Montreal, QC) 11/01/1979

UNITY BUYING SVC INC (DE)
In process of liquidation
Each share Common 10¢ par received initial distribution of $10 cash 3/13/85
Each share Common 10¢ par exchanged for second distribution of $8 cash 4/24/85
Assets transferred to Unity Liquidating Trust 4/24/85
(See Unity Liquidating Trust)

UNITY CAP CORP AMER (CA)
Adjudicated bankrupt 10/02/1974

UNITY COTTON MILLS
Merged into Callaway Mills in 1932 which was completely liquidated in 1947

UNITY FIRST ACQUISITION CORP (DE)
Name changed to GraphOn Corp. 07/12/1999
GraphOn Corp. name changed to hopTo Inc. 09/10/2013

UNITY GOLD PRODUCTION CO.
Bankrupt in 1945

UNITY HEALTHCARE HLDG INC (NY)
Common 1¢ par split (2) for (1) by issuance of (1) additional share 10/10/1989
Plan of reorganization under Chapter 11 Federal Bankruptcy proceedings confirmed 07/27/1993
No stockholders' equity

UNITY HLDGS INC (GA)
Company's sole asset closed and placed in receivership 03/26/2010
Stockholders' equity unlikely

UNITY LIQUIDATING TRUST (DE)
In process of liquidation
Each Share of Bene. Int. received initial distribution of $2.75 cash 7/10/86
Note: Details on subsequent distributions, if any, are not available

UNITY MANAGEMENT GROUP INC (NV)
Old Common $0.001 par split (20) for (1) by issuance of (19) additional shares payable 01/11/2010 to holders of record 01/11/2010 Ex date - 01/12/2010
Each share old Common $0.001 par exchanged for (0.00044782) share new Common $0.001 par 01/30/2013
Name changed to Petrotech Oil & Gas, Inc. 03/26/2013

UNITY SVGS & LN ASSN BEVERLY HILLS (CA)
Assets seized by the Resolution Trust Corp. 08/02/1991
No stockholders' equity

UNITY WIRELESS CORP (DE)
SEC revoked common stock registration 03/21/2014

UNIVA INC (QC)
Name changed to Provigo Inc. (New) 5/25/94
Provigo Inc. (New) acquired by Loblaw Companies Ltd. 12/10/98

UNIVAR CORP (WA)
Reincorporated 03/01/1996
Conv. Preferred Ser. A no par called for redemption 09/08/1975
Common $1 par changed to $0.33333333 par and (2) additional shares issued 03/10/1976
Common $0.33333333 par split (2) for (1) by issuance of (1) additional share 11/03/1989
State of incorporation changed from (DE) to (WA) 03/01/1996
Merged into Royal Pakhoed N.V. 09/30/1996
Each share Common $0.33333333 par exchanged for $19.45 cash

UNIVATION INC (CA)
Charter cancelled for failure to file reports and pay taxes 3/15/94

UNIVAX BIOLOGICS INC (DE)
Merged into North American Biologicals, Inc. 11/29/1995
Each share Common 1¢ par exchanged for (0.79) share Common 10¢ par
North American Biologicals, Inc. name changed to Nabi 01/18/1996 which name changed to Nabi Biopharmaceuticals 03/05/2002 which recapitalized as Biota Pharmaceuticals, Inc. 11/09/2012 which name changed to Aviragen Therapeutics, Inc. 04/13/2016 which recapitalized as Vaxart, Inc. 02/14/2018

UNIVENTURE CAP CORP (UT)
Name changed to Health & Leisure, Inc. 12/16/1986
Health & Leisure, Inc. recapitalized as Marketshare Recovery, Inc. 08/22/2003 which name changed to bioMETRX, Inc. 10/10/2005
(See bioMETRX, Inc.)

UNIVERAL DISC INC (MN)
Name changed to Universal International, Inc. 06/03/1977
(See Universal International, Inc.)

UNIVERCELL HLDGS INC (CA)
Administratively dissolved for failure to file annual report 09/24/2010

UNIVERSAL ABBEY CORP (DE)
Name changed to Video Enterprises, Inc. 8/2/79
(See Video Enterprises, Inc.)

UNIVERSAL ACCEP CORP (CO)
Each share old Common 1¢ par exchanged for (0.1) share new Common 1¢ par 09/17/1968

Merged into Universal Acceptance Corp. International Ltd. 11/22/1971
Each share new Common 1¢ par exchanged for (1) share Common 1¢ par
(See Universal Acceptance Corp. International Ltd.)

UNIVERSAL ACCEP CORP (OR)
Name changed to Universal Financial Services, Inc. 04/20/1972
(See Universal Financial Services, Inc.)

UNIVERSAL ACCEP CORP INTL LTD (NV)
Charter revoked for failure to file reports and pay fees 03/05/1973

UNIVERSAL ACCESS GLOBAL HLDGS INC (DE)
Each share old Common 1¢ par exchanged for (0.05) share new Common 1¢ par 8/11/2003
Plan of reorganization under Chapter 11 Federal Bankruptcy Code effective 2/17/2006
No stockholders' equity

UNIVERSAL ACCESS INC (DE)
Name changed to UAXS Global Holdings Inc. 07/20/2001
UAXS Global Holdings Inc. name changed to Universal Access Global Holdings Inc. 11/01/2001
(See Universal Access Global Holdings Inc.)

UNIVERSAL AIR LINES
Acquired by Universal Aviation Corp. in 1928
(See Universal Aviation Corp.)

UNIVERSAL AIRLS CO (DE)
Charter cancelled and declared inoperative and void for non-payment of taxes 4/15/73

UNIVERSAL AMERICAN CORP. (HI)
Involuntarily dissolved 11/15/1991

UNIVERSAL AMERN CORP (DE)
Ctfs. dtd. after 04/29/2011
8.5% Mandatorily Redeemable Preferred Ser. A 1¢ par called for redemption at $25 plus $0.614 accrued dividends on 04/28/2017
Acquired by WellCare Health Plans, Inc. 04/28/2017
Each share Common 1¢ par exchanged for $10 cash

UNIVERSAL AMERN CORP (DE)
Ctfs. dated prior to 01/12/1968
Common $1 par changed to 25¢ par 00/00/1954
Conv. Preferred $5 par called for redemption 12/26/1967
Merged into Gulf & Western Industries, Inc. (DE) 01/12/1968
Each share 2nd Conv. Preferred 1st Ser. $35 par exchanged for (0.625) share $3.875 Conv. Preferred Ser. C. $2.50 par
Each share Common 25¢ par exchanged for (0.163265) share $1.75 Conv. Preferred Ser. A $2.50 par
(See Gulf & Western Industries, Inc. (DE))

UNIVERSAL AMERN CORP (NY)
Name changed 11/30/2007
Name changed from Universal American Financial Corp. to Universal American Corp. 11/30/2007
Merged into Universal American Corp. (DE) (Ctfs. dtd. after 04/29/2011) 04/29/2011
Each share Common 1¢ par exchanged for (1) share Common 1¢ par and $14 cash
(See Universal American Corp. (DE) (Ctfs. dtd. after 04/29/2011))

UNIVERSAL AMERICAN EXPORT CORP. (HI)
Name changed to Universal American Corp. (Hawaii) 3/18/70

UNIVERSAL AMERICAN LIFE INSURANCE CO. (AR)
Merged into Investors Preferred Life Insurance Co. (Ark.) 12/31/68
Each share 6% Preferred $1 par exchanged for (3.125) shares Common 12¢ par
Each share Common no par exchanged for (0.625) share Common 12¢ par
(See Investors Preferred Life Insurance Co. (Ark.))

UNIVERSAL AUTOMATED INDUSTRIES, INC. (NY)
Completely liquidated 10/11/67
Each share Common 10¢ par exchanged for first and final distribution of (1) share Castleton Industries, Inc. Common $1 par
(See Castleton Industries, Inc.)

UNIVERSAL AUTOMOBILE INSURANCE CO. (IN)
Declared insolvent 8/6/62
No stockholders' equity

UNIVERSAL AVIATION CORP.
Acquired by Aviation Corp. in 1929
(See Aviation Corp.)

UNIVERSAL BANCORP INC (FL)
Merged into Totalbank (Miami, FL) 6/20/97
Each share Common $1 par exchanged for $54.647 cash

UNIVERSAL BEVERAGE INC (ON)
Reorganized under the laws of Wyoming as Global X-Ray Exchange, Inc. 05/10/2005
Each share Common no par exchanged for (0.001) share Common no par
Global X-Ray Exchange, Inc. recapitalized as Air to Water Co. 08/15/2007 which name changed to New Horizon Group, Inc. 10/15/2008
(See New Horizon Group, Inc.)

UNIVERSAL BEVERAGES HLDGS CORP (FL)
SEC revoked common stock registration 04/22/2010

UNIVERSAL BIOTECHNOLOGIES INC (DE)
Recapitalized as Queen Sand Resources, Inc. 3/3/95
Each share Common $0.0015 par exchanged for (0.25) share Common $0.0015 par
Queen Sand Resources, Inc. name changed to Devx Energy Inc. 9/19/2000
(See Devx Energy Inc.)

UNIVERSAL BROADBAND NETWORKS INC (DE)
Plan of reorganization under Chapter 11 Federal Bankruptcy Code effective 11/20/2002
No stockholders' equity

UNIVERSAL BROADCASTING SYSTEM, INC. (MI)
Charter voided for failure to file reports and pay fees 5/15/56

UNIVERSAL BUSINESS MACHINES CORP. (CT)
Dissolved 9/24/66

UNIVERSAL BUSINESS MACHS INC (SC)
Common $1 par changed to 50¢ par and (1) additional share issued 12/9/68
Name changed to Percival Corp. 12/12/77
Percival Corp. liquidated for Recognition Equipment Inc. 1/30/79 which name changed to Recognition International Inc. 3/12/93

UNIVERSAL BUSINESS PMT SOLUTIONS ACQUISITION CORP (DE)
Issue Information - 12,000,000 UNITS consisting of (1) share COM and (1) WT offered at $6 per Unit on 05/09/2011
Each Unit exchanged for (1.1333) shares Common $0.001 par 12/28/2012
Name changed to JetPay Corp. 08/12/2013

UNIVERSAL BY PRODS INC (CA)
Common $1 par split (2) for (1) by issuance of (1) additional share 3/28/69
Merged into Waste Management, Inc. 9/19/72
Each share Common $1 par exchanged for (0.2452) share Common $1 par
Waste Management, Inc. name changed to WMX Technologies Inc. 5/14/93 which name changed to Waste Management, Inc. (New) 5/12/97 which merged into Waste Management, Inc. 7/16/98

UNIVERSAL CAMERA CORP.
Bankrupt in 1952

UNIVERSAL CAP CORP (CO)
Each share old Common no par exchanged for (0.01) share new Common no par 6/12/95
Reorganized under the laws of Nevada as Odyssey Marine Exploration, Inc. 9/9/97
Each share new Common no par exchanged for (0.2) share Common $0.0001 par

UNIVERSAL CAP MGMT INC (DE)
Each share old Common $0.001 par received distribution of (0.055) share Theater Xtreme Entertainment Group, Inc. Common $0.001 par payable 08/11/2006 to holders of record 07/31/2006 Ex date - 07/27/2006
Each share old Common $0.001 par exchanged for (0.2) share new Common $0.001 par 06/19/2014
Name changed to Major League Football, Inc. 11/24/2014

UNIVERSAL CAP MTG CO (DE)
Reincorporated under the laws of Texas as MortgageBanque Inc. 04/01/1975
(See MortgageBanque Inc.)

UNIVERSAL CAPITAL CORP. (DE)
Completely liquidated 3/15/67
Each share Common 50¢ par exchanged for first and final distribution of (0.056818) share State Security Life Insurance Co. Common $1 par

UNIVERSAL CHAIN THEATRES CORP.
Liquidation completed in 1936

UNIVERSAL CHEMS INC (OH)
Reverted to a private company through purchase offer 11/30/1981
Public interest eliminated

UNIVERSAL CIGAR CORP (NY)
5% Preferred $25 par called for redemption 01/31/1984
Merged into a private company 08/28/1984
Each share Common 10¢ par exchanged for $15 cash

UNIVERSAL COMMODITY CORP. (NY)
Charter revoked for failure to file reports and pay fees 12/15/49

UNIVERSAL COMMUNICATION SYS INC (NV)
Each share old Common $0.001 par exchanged for (0.001) share new Common $0.001 par 08/22/2002
Recapitalized as Air Water International Corp. 10/02/2007
Each share new Common $0.001 par exchanged for (0.004) share Common $0.001 par
(See Air Water International Corp.)

UNIVERSAL COMMUNICATION SYS INC (VA)
Common 50¢ par changed to 34¢ par and (0.5) additional share issued 12/31/1982
Name changed to UC Corp. 10/01/1987

UNIVERSAL COMMUNICATIONS INC (NY)
Out of business and declared insolvent 05/31/1974
No stockholders' equity

UNIVERSAL COMPOSITES INC (WY)
Reincorporated under the laws of British Columbia as Ravencrest Resources Inc. 10/25/2004
Ravencrest Resources Inc. name changed to RavenQuest Biomed Inc. 10/04/2017

UNIVERSAL COMPRESSION HLDGS INC (DE)
Under plan of merger name changed to Exterran Holdings, Inc. 08/20/2007
Exterran Holdings, Inc. name changed to Archrock, Inc. 11/04/2015

UNIVERSAL COMPRESSION PARTNERS L P (DE)
Name changed to Exterran Partners, L.P. 08/20/2007
Exterran Partners, L.P. name changed to Archrock Partners, L.P. 11/04/2015 which merged into Archrock, Inc. 04/26/2018

UNIVERSAL COMPUTA DATA CORP (DE)
Each share old Common 10¢ par exchanged for (0.1) share new Common 10¢ par 12/01/1970
Note: Old certificates were not actually exchanged but were stamped "each Common share held prior to 12/01/1970 has been changed into (1/10) of (1) share"
Name changed to Leisure Inns & Resorts, Inc. 05/10/1971
(See Leisure Inns & Resorts, Inc.)

UNIVERSAL COMPUTER TECHNIQUES, INC. (MI)
Adjudicated bankrupt in September 1971

UNIVERSAL CONSOLIDATED OIL CO. (CA)
Each (10) shares Capital Stock $1 par exchanged for (1) share Capital Stock $10 par in 1930
Stock Dividends - 50% 7/48; 100% 8/1/52; 50% 1/25/56
Liquidation completed 4/17/62

UNIVERSAL CONTAINER CORP (KY)
Class A Common 10¢ par reclassified as Common 10¢ par 05/23/1969
Charter revoked for failure to file annual reports 01/30/1986

UNIVERSAL CONTROLS, INC. (MD)
Common $1 par changed to 25¢ par and (3) additional shares issued 06/17/1959
Stock Dividend - 10% 04/30/1959
Merged into General Instruments Corp. (Incorporated 06/12/1967) 08/31/1967
Each share Common 25¢ par exchanged for (1/15) share $3 Conv. Preferred Ser. A no par and (0.08) share Common $1 par
(See General Instrument Corp. (Incorporated 06/12/1967))

UNIVERSAL COOLER CO. LTD. (ON)
Each share old Common no par exchanged for (0.5) share 50¢ Preference B no par and (1) share new Common no par 07/06/1956
Adjudicated bankrupt 11/21/1963

No stockholders' equity

UNIVERSAL COOLER CORP.
Merged into International Detrola Corp. 00/00/1945
Each share Class A exchanged for (1) share Common
Each share Class B exchanged for (0.25) share Common
International Detrola Corp. name changed to Newport Steel Corp. 03/04/1949 which name changed to Newcorp, Inc. 09/18/1956
(See Newcorp, Inc.)

UNIVERSAL CORP. (DC)
Capital Stock $19.50 par changed to $14 par 11/09/1956
Name changed to Universal Marion Corp. (DC) 04/10/1957
Universal Marion Corp. (DC) reincorporated in Florida 05/29/1959
(See Universal Marion Corp. (FL))

UNIVERSAL CORP. (DE)
Under plan of merger name changed to Universal Pictures Co. Inc. 00/00/1943
(See Universal Pictures Co. Inc.)

UNIVERSAL CORP (MI)
Merged into Banc One Corp. (DE) 04/01/1988
Each share Common $5 par exchanged for (2.2) shares Common no par
Banc One Corp. (DE) reincorporated in Ohio 05/01/1989 which merged into Bank One Corp. 10/02/1998 which merged into J.P. Morgan Chase & Co. 12/31/2000 which name changed to JPMorgan Chase & Co. 07/20/2004

UNIVERSAL CORP (VA)
Each share 6.75% Conv. Perpetual Preferred Ser. B no par automatically became (22.4306) shares Common no par 01/13/2017
(Additional Information in Active)

UNIVERSAL COVERAGE CORP (NV)
Recapitalized as Unico American Corp. 08/01/1973
Each share Common $0.13333333 par exchanged for (0.02) share Common no par

UNIVERSAL-CYCLOPS STEEL CORP. (PA)
Common $1 par split (2) for (1) by issuance of (1) additional share 07/16/1957
Name changed to Cyclops Corp. 04/30/1965
(See Cyclops Corp.)

UNIVERSAL DATA PROCESSING CORP. (CA)
Completely liquidated 11/27/1967
Each share Common no par exchanged for first and final distribution of (0.256377) share Rucker Co. Common no par
Rucker Co. merged into N L Industries, Inc. 01/21/1977

UNIVERSAL DEV CORP (MD)
Completely liquidated 07/01/1985
Each share Common 1¢ par exchanged for first and final distribution of (1) UDC-Universal Development L.P. Depositary Receipt UDC-Universal Development L.P. merged into UDS Homes, Inc. 09/30/1992
(See UDC Homes, Inc.)

UNIVERSAL DISCOUNT STORES, INC. (MN)
Name changed to Universal Discount, Inc. 04/08/1969
Universal Discount, Inc. name changed to Universal International, Inc. 06/03/1977
(See Universal International, Inc.)

UNIVERSAL DOMAINS INC (CANADA)
Recapitalized as Pure Capital Inc. 10/11/2004
Each share Common no par exchanged for (0.025) share Common no par
Pure Capital Inc. name changed to Tombstone Exploration Corp. 02/12/2007

UNIVERSAL DRILLING CO., INC. (DE)
Reincorporated 09/22/1965
State of incorporation changed from (LA) to (DE) 09/22/1965
Merged into Empire Land Corp. 08/29/1977
Each share Class A Common $1 par exchanged for $3.25 cash
Each share Class B Common $1 par exchanged for $3.25 cash

UNIVERSAL DYNAMIC SCIENTIFIC & ENGINEERING CONSULTING, INC. (OK)
Charter suspended for failure to file reports and pay taxes 02/06/1976

UNIVERSAL DYNAMICS INC (MN)
Merged into Mann & Hummel Acquisition Corp. 01/11/1995
Each share Common 1¢ par exchanged for $7.55 cash

UNIVERSAL ELECTRS CORP (DE)
Name changed to Tran-Aire Systems, Inc. 09/29/1969
Tran-Aire Systems, Inc. name changed to United Southwest Industries, Inc. 12/03/1973
(See United Southwest Industries, Inc.)

UNIVERSAL ELECTRS LABS CORP (DE)
Common 10¢ par changed to 1¢ par 12/17/1968
Name changed to Universal Electronics Corp. 12/30/1968
Universal Electronics Corp. name changed to Tran-Aire Systems, Inc. 09/29/1969 which name changed to United Southwest Industries, Inc. 12/03/1973
(See United Southwest Industries, Inc.)

UNIVERSAL EMPIRE CAP CORP (AB)
Name changed to Bromley Marr Ecos Inc. 09/24/1996
(See Bromley Marr Ecos Inc.)

UNIVERSAL ENERGIES, INC. (MN)
Name changed to Empire Associates, Inc. 12/29/1972
Empire Associates, Inc. name changed to Empire-Crown Auto, Inc. 05/26/1976 which name changed to Crown Auto Inc. 05/18/1984
(See Crown Auto Inc.)

UNIVERSAL ENERGY CORP (BC)
Name changed to Supreme Resources Ltd. 02/09/2007
Supreme Resources Ltd. name changed to Supreme Pharmaceuticals Inc. (BC) 03/14/2014 which reincorporated in Canada 12/21/2015 which name changed to Supreme Cannabis Co. Inc. 12/29/2017

UNIVERSAL ENERGY CORP (OK)
Reincorporated 04/30/1981
State of incorporation changed from (WA) to (OK) 04/30/1981
Name changed to ORS Corp. 05/23/1986
ORS Corp. name changed to Electromagnetic Oil Recovery, Inc. 04/22/1991 which reorganized in Delaware as Fountain Oil Inc. 12/16/1994 which merged into CanArgo Energy Corp. 07/15/1998
(See CanArgo Energy Corp.)

UNIVERSAL ENERGY GROUP LTD (CANADA)
Reorganized as Just Energy Exchange Corp. 07/03/2009
Each share Common no par exchanged for (0.58) Exchangeable Share Ser. 1 no par
Just Energy Exchange Corp. reorganized as Just Energy Group Inc. 01/04/2011

UNIVERSAL ENERGY HLDGS INC (NV)
Charter revoked for failure to file reports and pay fees 12/31/2009

UNIVERSAL ENERGY INC (UT)
Proclaimed dissolved for failure to file annual reports 05/01/1990

UNIVERSAL EXPL CORP (BC)
Reorganized as Universal Power Corp. (BC) 10/05/2007
Each share Common no par exchanged for (3) shares Common no par
Universal Power Corp. (BC) reincorporated in Alberta as UNX Energy Corp. 09/20/2010 which merged into HRT Participacoes em Petroleo S.A 04/29/2011 which name changed to Petro Rio S.A. 07/07/2015
(See Petro Rio S.A.)

UNIVERSAL EXPLORATIONS (83) LTD. (AB)
Name changed to Universal Explorations Ltd. (New) 12/08/1986
Universal Explorations Ltd. (New) merged into Canadian Conquest Exploration Inc. 04/17/1989 which merged into Cypress Energy Inc. 05/10/1999 which merged into PrimeWest Energy Trust 05/29/2001
(See PrimeWest Energy Trust)

UNIVERSAL EXPLS LTD NEW (AB)
Merged into Canadian Conquest Exploration Inc. 04/17/1989
Each share Common no par exchanged for (0.3734) share Common no par
Note: Upon exchange for each full share received distribution of (0.3125) Series I Common Stock Purchase Warrant expiring 04/30/1993, (0.3125) Series II Common Stock Purchase Warrant expiring 04/30/1993 and (0.6250) Series III Common Stock Purchase Warrant expiring 04/30/1993
Canadian Conquest Exploration Inc. merged into Cypress Energy Inc. 05/10/1999 which merged into PrimeWest Energy Trust 05/29/2001
(See PrimeWest Energy Trust)

UNIVERSAL EXPLS LTD OLD (AB)
Merged into Universal Explorations (83) Ltd. 11/01/1983
Each share Common no par exchanged for (0.16666666) share Common no par
Universal Explorations (83) Ltd. name changed to Universal Explorations Ltd. (New) 12/08/1986 which merged into Canadian Conquest Exploration Inc. 04/17/1989 which merged into Cypress Energy Inc. 05/10/1999 which merged into PrimeWest Energy Trust 05/29/2001
(See PrimeWest Energy Trust)

UNIVERSAL EXPRESS INC (NV)
Each share Common $0.005 par received distribution of (0.04) Restricted Class A Common Stock Purchase Warrant expiring 11/01/2003 payable 12/20/2002 to holders of record 11/01/2002
Each share Common $0.005 par received distribution of (0.04) Restricted Class B Common Stock Purchase Warrant expiring 11/01/2003 payable 12/20/2002 to holders of record 11/01/2002
Each share Common $0.005 par received distribution of (0.04) Restricted Class C Common Stock Purchase Warrant expiring 05/01/2004 payable 12/20/2002 to holders of record 11/01/2002
Each share Common $0.005 par received distribution of (0.04) Restricted Class D Common Stock Purchase Warrant expiring 05/01/2004 payable 12/20/2002 to holders of record 11/01/2002
Stock Dividends - 4% payable 04/30/1999 to holders of record 04/30/1999; 4% payable 07/20/2000 to holders of record 07/20/2000; 8% payable 10/16/2001 to holders of record 09/21/2001 Ex date - 09/19/2001
SEC revoked common stock registration 09/03/2009
Stockholders' equity unlikely

UNIVERSAL FABRICATORS, INC. (NY)
Out of business 08/19/1964
No stockholders' equity

UNIVERSAL FID LIFE INS CO (OK)
Merged into Pioneer Financial Services Inc. 03/12/1996
Each share Common $1 par exchanged for $28 cash

UNIVERSAL FINANCE CORP. (DE)
Reincorporated 10/15/1952
State of incorporation changed from (NE) to (DE) 10/15/1952
5.50% Preferred $100 par called for redemption 10/15/1952
Acquired by General Acceptance Corp. (New) 12/31/1953
Each share 6% Preferred $10 par exchanged for (0.4) share $1.50 Preferred no par
General Acceptance Corp. (New) name changed to GAC Corp. (PA) 07/01/1968 which reincorporated in Delaware 12/20/1973
(See GAC Corp. (DE))

UNIVERSAL FINANCE CORP. (TX)
70¢ Preferred no par changed to $5 par 08/18/1956
In process of liquidation
Each share 70¢ Preferred $5 par exchanged for initial distribution of (0.06451612903) share Liberty Loan Corp. Common $1 par 08/04/1966
Note: Details on subsequent distributions, if any, are not available

UNIVERSAL FINL CAP CORP (NV)
Name changed to International Sensor Technologies, Inc. 10/18/1985
International Sensor Technologies, Inc. recapitalized as BioPulse International, Inc. 03/17/1999 which recapitalized as Only You, Inc. 01/17/2006

UNIVERSAL FINL SVCS INC (OR)
Involuntarily dissolved for failure to file reports and pay fees 06/05/1987

UNIVERSAL FLIRTS CORP (DE)
Common $0.001 par split (4) for (1) by issuance of (3) additional shares payable 03/31/2005 to holders of record 03/28/2005 Ex date - 04/01/2005
Name changed to Orsus Xelent Technologies, Inc. 04/18/2005

UNIVERSAL FLUID DYNAMICS CO (MI)
Name changed to Udyco Industries, Inc. 02/10/1970
(See Udyco Industries, Inc.)

UNIVERSAL FOG INC (DE)
Each share old Common $0.0001 par exchanged for (0.05) share new Common $0.0001 par 11/13/2008
Name changed to China Health Industries Holdings, Inc. 02/19/2009

UNIVERSAL FOOD & BEVERAGE CO (NV)
Chapter 11 bankruptcy proceedings dismissed 12/16/2008
No stockholders' equity

UNIVERSAL FOOD PRODS INC (DE)
Each share Common 1¢ par exchanged for (0.1) share Common 10¢ par 08/14/1964
Recapitalized as Orange Blossom Products, Inc. 02/04/1972
Each share Common 10¢ par exchanged for (0.2) share Common 10¢ par
(See Orange Blossom Products, Inc.)

UNIVERSAL FOODS CORP (WI)
$4.40 Conv. Preferred Ser. B no par called for redemption 09/08/1978
Preferred Stock Purchase Rights declared for Common stockholders of record 09/11/1989 were redeemed at $0.005 per right 09/01/1998 for holders of record 08/06/1998
Common $1 par split (3) for (2) by issuance of (0.5) additional share 08/16/1976
Common $1 par changed to 10¢ par 01/17/1978
Common 10¢ par split (3) for (2) by issuance of (0.5) additional share 11/16/1978
Common 10¢ par split (3) for (2) by issuance of (0.5) additional share 08/17/1986
Common 10¢ par split (3) for (2) by issuance of (0.5) additional share 10/07/1988
Common 10¢ par split (3) for (2) by issuance of (0.5) additional share 10/13/1989
Common 10¢ par split (2) for (1) by issuance of (1) additional share payable 05/22/1998 to holders of record 05/06/1998 Ex date - 05/26/1998
Stock Dividends - 10% 01/08/1968; 10% 09/29/1970
Name changed to Sensient Technologies Corp. 11/06/2000

UNIVERSAL FRANCHISE OPPORTUNITIES CORP (DE)
Name changed to Innovative Materials Inc. 11/19/1997
(See Innovative Materials Inc.)

UNIVERSAL FUEL & CHEM CORP (PA)
Out of business 00/00/1961
No stockholders' equity

UNIVERSAL FUELS CO (CO)
Recapitalized as Remington-Hall Capital Corp. 02/06/1998
Each share Common 1¢ par exchanged for (0.1) share Common 1¢ par
Remington-Hall Capital Corp. name changed to Ault Glazer & Co., Inc. 03/12/2008 which name changed to Tytan Holdings Inc. 10/02/2009

UNIVERSAL FURNITURE LTD (BRITISH VIRGIN ISLANDS)
Ordinary Stock 1¢ par split (2) for (1) by issuance of (1) additional share 04/24/1987
Merged into Masco Corp. 05/30/1989
Each share Ordinary Stock 1¢ par exchanged for (0.95) share Common $1 par

UNIVERSAL GAS & OIL CORP (NM)
Recapitalized as Transcontinental Video Corp. Ltd. 08/09/1973
Each share Common 10¢ par exchanged for (2/3) share Common 10¢ par
(See Transcontinental Video Corp. Ltd.)

UNIVERSAL GAS & POWER CORP.
Dissolved in 1938

UNIVERSAL GAS LTD (AB)
Merged into Acquitaine Co. of Canada Ltd. 04/10/1979
Each share Capital Stock no par exchanged for $12 cash

UNIVERSAL GENETICS LTD (ON)
Merged into Starbright Venture Capital Inc. 11/18/1997
Each share Common no par exchanged for (1) share Common no par
Starbright Venture Capital Inc. merged into Grasslands Entertainment Inc. (AB) 07/11/2001 which reorganized in Ontario as Lakeside Minerals Inc. 01/04/2012 which name changed to Lineage Grow Co. Ltd. 07/25/2017

UNIVERSAL GLASS CO. (DE)
No longer in existence having become inoperative and void for non-payment of taxes 3/16/27

UNIVERSAL GRAPHICS CORP (NJ)
Name changed to Video Music Productions, Inc. 04/04/1985
Video Music Productions, Inc. name changed to Direct Medical Equipment & Supplies Inc. 03/20/1989

UNIVERSAL GTY INVT CO (DE)
Each share Class A Common $1 par exchanged for (0.2) share Common $1 par 06/17/1991
Voluntarily dissolved 03/12/1996
Details not available

UNIVERSAL GUARANTY LIFE INSURANCE CO. (LA)
Each share Common $1 par exchanged for (0.5) share Common $1.10 par 12/22/64
Merged into State Security Life Insurance Co. 6/30/66
Each share Common $1.10 par exchanged for (0.5) share Common $1 par

UNIVERSAL GUARANTY LIFE INSURANCE CO. (TX)
Reincorporated under the laws of Louisiana and Common $1 par exchanged share for share 6/30/63
Universal Guaranty Life Insurance Co. (LA) merged into State Security Life Insurance Co. 6/30/66

UNIVERSAL GUARANTY LIFE INSURANCE CO. OF OHIO (OH)
Common $2 par changed to 25¢ par and (7) additional shares issued 3/31/64
Merged into Coastal States Life Insurance Co. 12/31/66
Each share Common 25¢ par exchanged for (0.2444) share Common $1 par
Coastal States Life Insurance Co. reorganized as Coastal States Corp. 10/5/72

UNIVERSAL GUARDIAN HLDGS INC (DE)
SEC revoked common stock registration 04/19/2012

UNIVERSAL GUN-LOC INDUSTRIES LTD (BC)
Recapitalized as UGL Enterprises Ltd. 04/25/2002
Each share Common no par exchanged for (0.5) share Common no par
UGL Enterprises Ltd. name changed to Red Hill Energy Inc. 05/31/2006
(See Red Hill Energy Inc.)

UNIVERSAL GYPSUM & LIME CO.
Acquired by National Gypsum Co. in 1935
(See National Gypsum Co.)

UNIVERSAL HEALTH INC (DE)
Charter revoked and proclaimed inoperative and void for non-payment of taxes 4/1/64

UNIVERSAL HEALTHCARE MGMT SYS INC (FL)
Name changed to In Touch Media Group, Inc. 06/06/2005
(See In Touch Media Group, Inc.)

UNIVERSAL HEIGHTS INC (DE)
Each share old Common 1¢ par exchanged for (0.25) share new Common 1¢ par 12/2/94
Name changed to Universal Insurance Holdings, Inc. 2/27/2001

UNIVERSAL HLDGS INC (NV)
Name changed to Recovery Energy, Inc. 10/20/2009
Recovery Energy, Inc. name changed to Lilis Energy, Inc. 12/02/2013

UNIVERSAL HLDGS LTD (CAYMAN ISLANDS)
Name changed to Asian Union New Media (Group) Ltd. 07/31/2007
Asian Union New Media (Group) Ltd. name changed to China Jiuhao Health Industry Corp. Ltd. 05/30/2014
(See China Jiuhao Health Industry Corp. Ltd.)

UNIVERSAL HLDG CORP (NY)
Name changed to Universal American Financial Corp. 07/23/1996
Universal American Financial Corp. name changed to Universal American Corp. (NY) 11/30/2007 which merged into Universal American Corp. (DE) (Ctfs. dtd. after 04/29/2011) 04/29/2011
(See Universal American Corp. (DE) (Ctfs. dtd. after 04/29/2011))

UNIVERSAL HOSP SVCS INC (MN)
Merged into J.W. Childs Equity Partners, L.P. 2/25/98
Each share Common 1¢ par exchanged for $15.50 cash

UNIVERSAL HSG & DEV CO (MA)
Merged into Security Management Corp. 02/10/1984
Each Share of Bene. Int. $1 par exchanged for $1.25 cash

UNIVERSAL ICE BLAST INC (NV)
Each share old Common $0.001 par exchanged for (0.025) share new Common $0.001 par 02/15/2005
SEC revoked common stock registration 02/17/2012

UNIVERSAL INFRASTRUCTURE CORP (AB)
Completely liquidated
Each share Common no par received first and final distribution of $0.0374 cash payable 10/15/2010 to holders of record 09/30/2010
Note: Certificates were not required to be surrendered and are without value

UNIVERSAL INSTRS CORP (NY)
Common $2.50 par changed to $1.25 par and (1) additional share issued 04/17/1974
Merged into Dover Corp. 07/10/1979
Each share Common $1.25 par exchanged for $36 cash

UNIVERSAL INSURANCE CO. (NJ)
Capital Stock $20 par changed to $8 par 00/00/1933
Capital Stock $8 par changed to $10 par 00/00/1944
Capital Stock $10 par changed to $15 par 00/00/1954
Capital Stock $15 par changed to $17.78 par and a 50% stock dividend paid 06/30/1960
Stock Dividend - 50% 04/30/1952
Name changed to Universal Reinsurance Corp. 03/25/1971
(See Universal Reinsurance Corp.)

UNIVERSAL INTL INC (MN)
Under plan of recapitalization each share Common 10¢ par exchanged for (0.1) share Class A Common 10¢ par and (0.5) share Non-Voting Class B Common 10¢ par 03/27/1989
Each share Class A Common 10¢ par exchanged for (4) shares Common 5¢ par 10/11/1990
Each share Non-Voting Class B Common 10¢ par exchanged for (4) shares Common 5¢ par 10/11/1990
94% acquired by 99¢ Only Stores on a (0.0625) for (1) share basis through voluntary exchange offer which expired 09/16/1998
Merged into 99¢ Only Stores 01/25/2000
Each share Common 5¢ exchanged for $2.32 cash

UNIVERSAL INVT PPTYS INC (CO)
Reported out of business 00/00/2000
Details not available

UNIVERSAL INVESTORS, INC. (LA)
Completely liquidated 04/17/1958
Each share Common no par exchanged for (1.2) shares Universal Guaranty Life Insurance Co. (TX) Common 50¢ par
Universal Guaranty Life Insurance Co. (TX) reincorporated in Louisiana 06/30/1963 which merged into State Security Life Insurance Co. 06/30/1966

UNIVERSAL INVS TR (MA)
Name changed to Universal Housing & Development Co. 03/17/1971
(See Universal Housing & Development Co.)

UNIVERSAL INVTS INC (WA)
Name changed to Universal Energy Corp. (WA) 11/28/1975
Universal Energy Corp. (WA) reincorporated in Oklahoma 04/31/1981 which name changed to ORS Corp. 05/23/1986 which name changed to Electromagnetic Oil Recovery, Inc. 04/22/1991 which reorganized in Delaware as Fountain Oil Inc. 12/16/1994 which merged into CanArgo Energy Corp. 07/15/1998
(See CanArgo Energy Corp.)

UNIVERSAL JET INDS INC (FL)
Proclaimed dissolved for failure to file reports and pay fees 09/21/2001

UNIVERSAL KNICKERBOCKER CORP. (NY)
Charter cancelled and proclaimed dissolved for failure to pay taxes and file reports 12/16/74

UNIVERSAL LABORATORIES, INC.
Name changed to Universal American Corp. (DE) in 1952
Universal American Corp. (DE) merged into Gulf & Western Industries, Inc. (DE) 1/12/68
(See Gulf & Western Industries, Inc. (DE))

UNIVERSAL LEAF TOB INC (VA)
Each share Common $100 par exchanged for (2) shares Common no par 00/00/1926
Common no par split (2) for (1) by issuance of (1) additional share 11/07/1960
Common no par split (2) for (1) by issuance of (1) additional share 11/10/1965
Common no par split (2) for (1) by issuance of (1) additional share 11/11/1975
Common no par split (2) for (1) by issuance of (1) additional share 03/03/1978
Common no par split (2) for (1) by issuance of (1) additional share 03/01/1984
Stock Dividends - 35% 00/00/1930; 300% 12/11/1947
Under plan of reorganization each share 8% Preferred $100 par or Common no par automatically became (1) share Universal Corp.

8% Preferred $100 par or Common no par respectively 12/31/1987

UNIVERSAL LEARNING CORP (NY)
Charter cancelled and proclaimed dissolved for failure to pay taxes and file reports 12/20/1977

UNIVERSAL LICENSING CORP (DE)
Name changed to Discovery Studio, Inc. 06/04/1996
(See Discovery Studio, Inc.)

UNIVERSAL LIFE & ACCIDENT INSURANCE CO. (TX)
Capital Stock $10 par changed to $5 par and (1) additional share issued 09/08/1961
Stock Dividends - 100% 03/13/1945; 100% 03/11/1947; 100% 11/16/1949; 25% 03/00/1953
Completely liquidated 01/28/1969
Each share Capital Stock $5 par exchanged for first and final distribution of (0.966667) share Southwestern Life Insurance Co. Capital Stock $2.50 par
Southwestern Life Insurance Co. reorganized as Southwestern Life Corp. 12/28/1972 which liquidated for Tenneco Inc. 05/01/1980 which merged into El Paso Natural Gas Co. 12/12/1996 which reorganized as El Paso Energy Corp. 08/01/1998 which name changed to El Paso Corp. 02/05/2001

UNIVERSAL LIFE HLDG CORP (IL)
Involuntarily dissolved for failure to pay taxes and file reports 01/22/1999

UNIVERSAL LITHIUM CORP. (DE)
Each share Common 2¢ par exchanged for (0.05) share Common 40¢ par 10/15/1959
No longer in existence having become inoperative and void for non-payment of taxes 04/01/1963

UNIVERSAL LOCK-TIP CO. (MA)
Dissolved 01/01/1936
Details not available

UNIVERSAL LOGISTICS LTD. (DE)
Charter cancelled and declared inoperative and void for non-payment of taxes 03/01/1974

UNIVERSAL LTG PRODS INC (DE)
Merged into Vernusal Lighting Products, Inc. 06/30/1967
Each share Common 1¢ par exchanged for $2 cash

UNIVERSAL MACHINE & TOOL CORP. (DE)
Charter revoked for failure to pay taxes and file reports 01/23/1922

UNIVERSAL MAJOR CORP. (NV)
Name changed to Universal Major Industries Corp. 12/19/1966
(See Universal Major Industries Corp.)

UNIVERSAL MAJOR ELEC APPLIANCES, INC. (DE)
Merged into Birdsboro Steel Foundry & Machine Co. (DE) on a (0.1) for (1) basis 7/2/56
Birdsboro Steel Foundry & Machine Co. (DE) merged into Birdsboro Corp. 12/31/59
(See Birdsboro Corp.)

UNIVERSAL MAJOR INDS CORP (NV)
Charter revoked for failure to file reports and pay taxes 03/03/1975

UNIVERSAL MFG CO (MN)
Each share Common 10¢ par exchanged for (0.5) share Common 20¢ par 08/29/1963
Recapitalized as Fiberite Corp. 10/15/1964
Each share Common 20¢ par exchanged for (0.66666666) share Common 30¢ par
(See Fiberite Corp.)

UNIVERSAL MARINE & SHARK PRODS INC (DE)
Charter cancelled and declared inoperative and void for non-payment of taxes 03/01/1988

UNIVERSAL MARION CORP (FL)
Reincorporated 05/29/1959
Place of incorporation changed from (DC) to (FL) 05/29/1959
Common $14 par changed to no par 04/12/1960
Common no par changed to 1¢ par 02/04/1971
4.5% Preferred $100 par called for redemption 02/26/1971
Liquidation completed
Each share Common 1¢ par received initial distribution of $5 cash 03/26/1971 and (0.175438) share Daitch Crystal Dairies, Inc. Common 50¢ par 04/12/1971
Each share Common 1¢ par received second distribution of $4 cash 05/29/1973
Each share Common 1¢ par received third distribution of $5 cash 01/30/1974
Each share Common 1¢ par received fourth distribution of $3 cash 01/14/1975
Each share Common 1¢ par received fifth distribution of $2 cash 01/21/1976
Each share Common 1¢ par received sixth distribution of $1 cash 01/25/1977
Each share Common 1¢ par received seventh distribution of $1 cash 01/25/1978
Each share Common 1¢ par received eighth distribution of $1 cash 01/09/1979
Each share Common 1¢ par received ninth distribution of $1 cash 01/16/1980
Each share Common 1¢ par received tenth distribution of $0.75 cash 02/16/1981
Each share Common $10 par exchanged for (0.001) share Common $10 par 12/28/1981
Each share Common $10 par received eleventh distribution of $500 cash 05/21/1982
Each share Common $10 par received twelfth distribution of $250 cash 02/21/1983
Each share Common $10 par received thirteenth and final distribution of $500 cash 12/22/1986
Note: Certificates were not required to be exchanged and are without value

UNIVERSAL MARKETING & ENTMT INC (NV)
Each share old Common $0.001 par exchanged for (0.05) share new Common $0.001 par 03/11/1998
Recapitalized as Odyssey Capital Group Ltd. 05/11/2001
Each share new Common $0.001 par exchanged for (0.2) share Common $0.001 par 05/11/2001
Odyssey Capital Group Ltd. name changed to Print Data Corp. (NV) 08/13/2001 which reorganized in Delaware 10/11/2002 which name changed to ACL Semiconductors Inc. 12/16/2003 which name changed to USmart Mobile Device Inc. 04/17/2013 which name changed to Eagle Mountain Corp. 05/06/2015

UNIVERSAL MARKING SYS INC (MN)
Name changed to North Star Universal Inc. 03/03/1981
North Star Universal Inc. merged into Michael Foods, Inc. (New) 02/28/1997
(See Michael Foods, Inc. (New))

UNIVERSAL MATCH CORP. (DE)
Each share Common $25 par exchanged for (2) shares Common $12.50 par 00/00/1951
Common $12.50 par changed to $6.25 par and (1) additional share issued 07/10/1959
Common $6.25 par changed to $2.50 par and (1.5) additional shares issued 06/15/1960
5.5% Preferred A called for redemption 05/10/1962
Stock Dividend - 25% 12/22/1955
Name changed to UMC Industries, Inc. 05/17/1966
UMC Industries, Inc. name changed to Unidynamics Corp. 04/19/1984
(See Unidynamics Corp.)

UNIVERSAL MATCHBOX GROUP LTD (BERMUDA)
Acquired by Tyco Toys, Inc. 10/05/1992
Each share Common 10¢ par exchanged for (0.236242) share Common 1¢ par and $4.25 cash

UNIVERSAL MED BLDGS INC (DE)
Under plan of reorganization each share Common 1¢ par automatically became (1) Universal Medical Buildings, Limited Partnership Common Unit of Ltd. Partnership 12/08/1986
Universal Medical Buildings, Limited Partnership name changed to Integrated Healthcare Facilities, L.P. 06/10/1994
(See Integrated Healtcare Faciliites, L.P.)

UNIVERSAL MED BLDGS LTD PARTNERSHIP (DE)
Each old Common Unit of Ltd. Partnership exchanged for (0.33333333) new Common Unit of Ltd. Partnership 05/01/1990
Recapitalized as Integrated Healthcare Facilities, L.P. 12/06/1994
Each Ser. A Preferred Unit exchanged for (4.67) Common Units
Each Ser. B Preferred Unit exchanged for (2.96) Common Units
Each new Common Unit exchanged for (0.08333333) Common Unit
(See Integrated Healthcare Facilities, L.P.)

UNIVERSAL MED SYS INC (NV)
SEC revoked common stock registration 06/21/2006

UNIVERSAL MEDIA CORP (TX)
Name changed to UMED Holdings Inc. 04/14/2011
UMED Holdings Inc. name changed to Greenway Technologies, Inc. 01/18/2018

UNIVERSAL MEDIA HLDGS INC (DE)
Each share old Common $0.001 par exchanged for (0.03333333) share new Common $0.001 par 04/12/2002
Recapitalized as National Management Consulting Inc. 11/12/2002
Each share new Common $0.001 par exchanged for (0.08333333) share Common $0.001 par
National Management Consulting Inc. name changed to Genio Group, Inc. 09/11/2003 which recapitalized as Millennium Prime, Inc. 10/29/2009

UNIVERSAL MEDIA HLDGS INC (FL)
Each share old Common no par exchanged for (0.005) share new Common no par 02/14/2005
Each share new Common no par exchanged again for (0.00333333) share new Common no par 02/15/2006
Name changed to Lyric Jeans, Inc. 03/08/2006

UNIVERSAL MEDICAL EQUIPMENT CORP. (NY)
Dissolved by proclamation 12/24/1991

UNIVERSAL MEDTECH INC (DE)
Recapitalized as Consolidated Travel Systems, Inc. 11/30/1987
Each share Class A 1¢ par exchanged for (0.25) share Class A 1¢ par
Consolidated Travel Systems, Inc. recapitalized as Knobias, Inc. 11/17/2004
(See Knobias, Inc.)

UNIVERSAL METALS & MACHY INC (TX)
Stock Dividend - 25% 04/17/1972
Voluntarily dissolved 12/31/2008
Details not available

UNIVERSAL METALS INC (UT)
Charter suspended for failure to pay taxes 09/30/1975

UNIVERSAL MINERAL RES INC (NY)
Charter cancelled and proclaimed dissolved for non-payment of taxes 12/15/1970

UNIVERSAL MINERALS & METALS, INC. (DE)
Adjudicated bankrupt 02/04/1970
Stockholders' equity unlikely

UNIVERSAL MINERALS CORP (QC)
Name changed to Laurier Resources Ltd. 03/07/1981
Laurier Resources Ltd. was acquired by Humboldt Energy Corp. 00/00/1982 which recapitalized as HEC Investments Ltd. 08/04/1989 which name changed to Humboldt Capital Corp. 08/29/1994
(See Humboldt Capital Corp.)

UNIVERSAL MINING & MILLING CO. (NM)
Charter forfeited for failure to pay taxes 12/11/1956

UNIVERSAL MOBILE SVCS CORP (DE)
Acquired by Wickes Corp. 11/02/1973
Each share Common 10¢ par exchanged for (0.43347) share Common $2.50 par
Wickes Corp. merged into Wickes Companies, Inc. 08/13/1980 which name changed to Collins & Aikman Group Inc. 07/17/1992
(See Collins & Aikman Group Inc.)

UNIVERSAL MONEY CTRS PLC (ENGLAND)
Name changed to Financial Systems Technology PLC 09/02/1986
(See Financial Systems Technology PLC)

UNIVERSAL MTG & INVT CORP (DE)
Name changed to Delphi Group Inc. 03/03/1972
Delphi Group Inc. name changed to Sutton Corp. 07/15/1974
(See Sutton Corp.)

UNIVERSAL MTG & RLTY TR (MA)
Merged into Lee National Corp. 01/03/1978
Each Share of Bene. Int. $1 par exchanged for $3 cash

UNIVERSAL MOULDED FIBER GLASS CORP. (DE)
Merged into Koppers Co., Inc. 11/15/1967
Each share Common 10¢ par exchanged for $1.25 cash

UNIVERSAL MOULDED PRODUCTS CORP. (DE)
Merged into American Moulding Corp. 06/30/1960
Details not available

UNIVERSAL MOVIE BUTLER INC (BC)
Name changed to Pacific Vending Technology Ltd. 04/15/1986
Pacific Vending Technology Ltd. name changed to Nelson Vending Technology Ltd. (BC) 07/10/1987 which reincorporated in Canada 07/23/1987 which was acquired by

Cinram Ltd. 07/31/1993 which name changed to Cinram International Inc. 06/12/1997 which reorganized as Cinram International Income Fund 05/08/2006

UNIVERSAL OIL & URANIUM CORP. (CO)
Merged into Lisbon Valley Uranium Co. 00/00/1957
Details not available

UNIVERSAL OIL PRODS CO (DE)
Capital Stock $1 par split (2) for (1) by issuance of (1) additional share 06/03/1968
Capital Stock $1 par reclassified as Common $1 par 05/19/1969
Name changed to UOP Inc. 07/15/1975
(See UOP Inc.)

UNIVERSAL OUTDOOR HLDGS INC (DE)
Merged into Clear Channel Communications, Inc. 04/01/1998
Each share Common 1¢ par exchanged for (0.67) share Common 10¢ par
(See Clear Channel Communications, Inc.)

UNIVERSAL PATENT & DEV LTD (BC)
Recapitalized as Trans-America Industries Ltd. 04/20/1972
Each share Common no par and VTC for Common no par exchanged for (0.2) share Common no par or (0.2) VTC for Common no par respectively
Trans-America Industries Ltd. merged into Primary Corp. 08/05/2008 which name changed to Marret Resource Corp. 07/06/2012

UNIVERSAL PETROLEUM EXPLORATIONS & DRILLING CO. (NV)
Charter revoked for failure to file reports and pay fees 03/03/1958

UNIVERSAL PICTURES CO., INC. (DE)
Under plan of merger each share Common exchanged for (3) shares new Common $1 par 00/00/1943
4.25% Preferred $100 par called for redemption 08/30/1963
Merged into Universal City Studios, Inc. 03/25/1966
Each share Common $1 par exchanged for $75 cash

UNIVERSAL PIPE & RADIATOR CO.
Reorganized as Central Foundry Co. 00/00/1936
Each share Preferred exchanged for (2.5) shares Common
Each share old Common exchanged for (0.05) share new Common
Central Foundry Co. name changed to Gable Industries, Inc. 06/30/1971 which name changed to Hajoca Corp. 12/29/1978
(See Hajoca Corp.)

UNIVERSAL PWR CORP (BC)
Reincorporated under the laws of Alberta as UNX Energy Corp. 09/20/2010
UNX Energy Corp. merged into HRT Participacoes em Petroleo S.A 04/29/2011 which name changed to Petro Rio S.A. 07/07/2015
(See Petro Rio S.A.)

UNIVERSAL PWR GROUP INC (TX)
Acquired by UPGI Holdings, Inc. 06/14/2018
Each share Common 1¢ par exchanged for $2.24 cash

UNIVERSAL PRE VENT INC (BC)
Struck off register and declared dissolved for failure to file returns 04/16/1993

UNIVERSAL PRODUCTS CO., INC. (DE)
Each share Common no par exchanged for (2) shares Common $10 par 00/00/1946
Common $10 par changed to $2 par and (2) additional shares issued 07/31/1956
Merged into Universal Controls, Inc. 10/01/1958
Each share Common $2 par exchanged for (2) shares Common $1 par
Universal Controls, Inc. merged into General Instrument Corp. (Incorporated 06/12/1967) 08/31/1967
(See General Instrument Corp. (Incorporated 06/12/1967))

UNIVERSAL PPTY DEV & ACQUISITION CORP (NV)
Each share old Common $0.001 par received distribution of (0.02) share Continental Fuels Inc. Restricted Common $0.001 par payable 08/01/2007 to holders of record 07/11/2007
Each share old Common $0.001 par exchanged for (0.1) share new Common $0.001 par 05/12/2008
SEC revoked common stock registration 06/09/2010
Stockholders' equity unlikely

UNIVERSAL PUBG & DISTRG CORP (NY)
Dissolved by proclamation 03/25/1992

UNIVERSAL RECTIFIER CORP. (DE)
Name changed to Eastern Railroad Industries, Inc. 06/01/1967
Eastern Railroad Industries, Inc. name changed to Computers & Railroads Inc. 11/29/1968

UNIVERSAL REDUCTION MELTING TECHNOLOGIES INC (NV)
Name changed 06/30/1998
Name changed from Universal Funding Services, Inc. to Universal Reduction Melting Technologies, Inc. 06/30/1998
Name changed to Internet Solutions For Business, Inc. 03/09/1999
Internet Solutions For Business, Inc. recapitalized as GlobalOne Real Estate, Inc. 05/16/2005 which name changed to Glow Holdings, Inc. 10/07/2011

UNIVERSAL REHABILITATION CTRS AMER INC (FL)
Name changed to Universal Medical Concepts Inc. 12/28/1999

UNIVERSAL REINSURANCE CORP. (NJ)
Each share Capital Stock $17.78 par exchanged for (1/281) share Capital Stock $5,000 par 07/24/1975
Note: In effect holders received $109.59 cash per share and public interest was eliminated

UNIVERSAL RES CORP (TX)
Common 50¢ par split (3) for (2) by issuance of (0.5) additional share 10/10/1980
Common 50¢ par split (3) for (2) by issuance of (0.5) additional share 01/27/1981
Merged into Questar Corp. 03/20/1987
Each share Common 50¢ par exchanged for $3 cash

UNIVERSAL ROCKWELL CORP (UT)
Each share old Common 1¢ par exchanged for (0.1) share new Common 1¢ par 03/26/1980
Proclaimed dissolved for failure to pay taxes 09/30/1986

UNIVERSAL ROLLER COTTON GIN CO. (NY)
Dissolved 01/05/1911
Details not available

UNIVERSAL RUNDLE CORP (DE)
Acquired by Nortek, Inc. 05/27/1986
Each share Common $1 par exchanged for $27 cash

UNIVERSAL SA (POLAND)
ADR agreement terminated 01/12/2005
Company declared bankruptcy ADR holders' equity unlikely

UNIVERSAL SATELLITE CORP (NY)
Reorganized under the laws of Delaware as USATCO, Inc. 08/07/2007
Each share Common 1¢ par exchanged for (0.1) share Common 1¢ par
Note: No holder will receive fewer than (100) shares

UNIVERSAL SVGS EQUITY FD LTD (ON)
Common $1 par changed to no par 04/21/1983
Name changed to Universal Canadian Equity Fund Ltd. 00/00/1990

UNIVERSAL SVGS INCOME FD (ON)
Name changed to Universal Canadian Bond Fund 04/06/1990

UNIVERSAL SVGS NAT RES & ENERGY FD (ON)
Name changed to Universal Canadian Resources Fund 03/26/1990

UNIVERSAL SEC LIFE INS CO (WA)
Each share Common $10 par exchanged for (6) shares Common $1 par 09/09/1975
Each share old Common $1 par exchanged for (0.4) share new Common $1 par 12/31/1985
Placed into liquidation 05/20/1988
No stockholders' equity

UNIVERSAL SECTS LTD NEW (ON)
Name changed 05/30/1979
Under plan of merger name changed from Universal Sections Ltd. (Old) to Universal Sections Ltd. (New) and each share Capital Stock no par exchanged for (1) share $0.90 Sinking Fund Preference no par 05/30/1979
Adjudicated bankrupt 12/17/1981
Stockholders' equity unlikely

UNIVERSAL SEISMIC ASSOC INC (DE)
Name changed to Pocketop Corp. 03/07/2007

UNIVERSAL SELF CARE INC (DE)
Name changed to Tadeo Holdings Inc. 02/23/1998
Tadeo Holdings Inc. name changed to TekInsight.com Inc. 12/03/1999 which name changed to DynTek Inc. 12/31/2001

UNIVERSAL SVCS ALLIANCE INC (NV)
Charter revoked for failure to file reports and pay fees 12/1/98

UNIVERSAL SVCS GROUP INC (DE)
Ceased operations 08/30/1993

UNIVERSAL SHELTER CORP (WI)
Name changed to Unishelter, Inc. 10/15/1976
(See Unishelter, Inc.)

UNIVERSAL SILVER/GOLD/ENERGY CO. (NV)
Name changed to Capital Funding & Development Corp. 08/26/1982
Capital Funding & Development Corp. name changed to International Property Exchange, Inc. 05/03/1983
(See International Property Exchange, Inc.)

UNIVERSAL SILVERS CO. (NV)
Recapitalized as Universal Silver/Gold/ Energy Co. 05/02/1980
Each share Capital Stock 25¢ par exchanged for (0.1) share Capital Stock 5¢ par
Universal Silver/Gold/Energy Co. name changed to Capital Funding & Development Corp. 08/26/1982 which name changed to International Property Exchange, Inc. 05/03/1983
(See International Property Exchange, Inc.)

UNIVERSAL STAMPING & MANUFACTURING CO.
Name changed to Ampro Corp. in 1940
(See Ampro Corp.)

UNIVERSAL STAR VENTURES CORP (AB)
Recapitalized as Global Express Energy Inc. (AB) 06/22/2005
Each share Common no par exchanged for (0.2) share Common no par
Global Express Energy Inc. (AB) reincorporated in Canada as Challenger Energy Corp. 12/12/2005 which merged into Canadian Superior Energy Inc. 09/24/2009 which recapitalized as Sonde Resources Corp. 06/08/2010
(See Sonde Resources Corp.)

UNIVERSAL STD HEALTHCARE INC (MI)
Name changed 08/25/1997
Name changed from Universal Standard Medical Laboratories, Inc. to Universal Standard Healthcare, Inc. 08/25/1997
Chapter 7 bankruptcy proceedings terminated 04/22/2008
No stockholders' equity

UNIVERSAL STEEL CO.
Merged into Universal-Cyclops Steel Corp. in 1936
(See Universal-Cyclops Steel Corp.)

UNIVERSAL SURGICAL SUPPLY INC (CA)
Name changed to Greater Energy Corp. 11/16/81
(See Greater Energy Corp.)

UNIVERSAL SYS INC (DC)
Adjudicated bankrupt 07/06/1970
Stockholders' equity unlikely

UNIVERSAL TAPE DEX CORP. (DE)
Charter cancelled and declared inoperative and void for non-payment of taxes 4/15/70

UNIVERSAL TAX SYS INC (NY)
Recapitalized as Vent-Air Optics, Inc. 9/6/73
Each share Common 1¢ par exchanged for (0.4) share Common 5¢ par
(See Vent-Air Optics, Inc.)

UNIVERSAL TECH CORP (DE)
Name changed to Sanborn Resources, Ltd. 04/02/2013
Sanborn Resources, Ltd. recapitalized as Bay Stakes Corp. 11/30/2016 which name changed to Chill N Out Cryotherapy, Inc. 01/25/2018

UNIVERSAL TECHNOLOGY SYS CORP (FL)
Reorganized as NanoFlex Power Corp. 11/25/2013
Each share Common $0.0001 par exchanged for (1.2) shares Common $0.0001 par

UNIVERSAL TEL INC (DE)
Common $1 par split (5) for (4) by issuance of (0.25) additional share 6/30/68
Each (2,000) shares Common $1 par exchanged for (1) share Common $2,000 par 1/28/87
Each (2,000) shares Class A Special $1 par exchanged for (1) share Class A Special $2,000 par 1/28/87
Note: In effect each share Common $1 par and Class A Special $1 par received $10 cash per share respectively and public interest was eliminated

UNIVERSAL TELEVISION CORP. (DE)
Out of existence in 1952

UNIVERSAL THEATRES CONCESSION CO.
Under plan of merger name changed to General Candy Corp. 2/19/29
General Candy Corp. acquired by Warner-Lambert Pharmaceutical Co. 3/25/66 which name changed to Warner-Lambert Co. 11/13/70 which merged into Pfizer Co. 6/19/2000

UNIVERSAL TRADING EXCHANGE INC (NY)
Class A Common 1¢ par split (3) for (2) by issuance of (0.5) additional share 11/05/1984
Reincorporated under the laws of Delaware as Minority Business Enterprises Inc. 10/04/1988
(See Minority Business Enterprises Inc.)

UNIVERSAL TRANSISTOR PRODUCTS CORP. (DE)
Each share Common 10¢ par exchanged for (0.285714) share VTC for Class B Common 10¢ par 5/2/60
Assets sold for benefit of creditors 7/11/63
No stockholders' equity

UNIVERSAL TRIDENT INDS LTD (BC)
Recapitalized as Poseidon Minerals Ltd. (BC) 08/29/1994
Each share Common no par exchanged for (1/3) share Common no par
Poseidon Minerals Ltd. (BC) reorganized in Canada as Stingray Resources Inc. 07/22/2003 which name changed to Stingray Copper Inc. 07/18/2007 which merged into Mercator Minerals Ltd. 12/21/2009

UNIVERSAL TRUCKLOAD SVCS INC (MI)
Name changed to Universal Logistics Holdings, Inc. 05/02/2016

UNIVERSAL TRUST SHARES
Trust terminated in 1948
Details not available

UNIVERSAL TURF INC (DE)
Each share old Common $0.001 par exchanged for (0.005) share new Common $0.001 par 11/03/1999
Name changed to Universal Media Holdings, Inc. 12/03/1999
Universal Media Holdings, Inc. recapitalized as National Management Consulting Inc. 11/12/2002 which name changed to Genio Group, Inc. 09/11/2003 which recapitalized as Millennium Prime, Inc. 10/29/2009

UNIVERSAL URANIUM & MILLING CORP. (NV)
Merged into Little Star Uranium Co. in March 1956
(See Little Star Uranium Co.)

UNIVERSAL URANIUM CO (CO)
Name changed to Universal Fuels Co. 11/05/1979
Universal Fuels Co. recapitalized as Remington-Hall Capital Corp. 02/06/1998 which name changed to Ault Glazer & Co., Inc. 03/12/2008 which name changed to Tytan Holdings Inc. 10/02/2009

UNIVERSAL URANIUM CORP. (UT)
Involuntarily dissolved 6/27/58

UNIVERSAL URANIUM LTD (BC)
Name changed to Expedition Mining Inc. 07/07/2010
Expedition Mining Inc. name changed to Imagin Medical Inc. 02/24/2016

UNIVERSAL UTILITIES CORP. (MI)
Company went into receivership in December 1921 and assets were sold for the benefit of creditors
No stockholders' equity

UNIVERSAL VENTURES INC (BC)
Recapitalized as Universal mCloud Corp. 10/18/2017
Each share Common no par exchanged for (0.5) share Common no par

UNIVERSAL VOLTRONICS CORP (DE)
Common 10¢ par changed to 5¢ par and (1) additional share issued 12/14/76
Common 10¢ par split (2) for (1) by issuance of (1) additional share 8/7/81
Recapitalized as Thermo Voltek Corp. 11/13/92
Each share Common 5¢ par exchanged for (1/3) share Common 5¢ par
(See Thermo Voltek Corp.)

UNIVERSAL WATERPROOFING CORP (NY)
Charter revoked for failure to file reports and pay fees 12/16/1968

UNIVERSAL WINDING CO. (MA)
Each share Common $100 par exchanged for (15) shares Common $5 par in 1946
Stock Distribution - 100% 6/30/59
Name changed to Leesona Corp. 9/28/59
(See Leesona Corp.)

UNIVERSAL WING TECHNOLOGIES INC (BC)
Recapitalized as Red Oak Mining Corp. 03/21/2014
Each share Common no par exchanged for (0.5) share Common no par

UNIVERSAL ZONOLITE INSULATION CO. (MT)
Name changed to Zonolite Co. 00/00/1948
Zonolite Co. merged into Grace (W.R.) & Co. (CT) 04/16/1963 which reincorporated in New York 05/19/1988
(See Grace (W.R.) & Co.)

UNIVERSE2U INC (NV)
Common $0.00001 par split (20) for (1) by issuance of (19) additional shares payable 06/01/2000 to holders of record 05/25/2000
Charter revoked for failure to file reports and pay fees 06/30/2004

UNIVERSITY ASSOCIATES TRUSTEES
Liquidation completed 4/1/60

UNIVERSITY AVE FINL CORP (ON)
Name changed to Blue Heron Financial Corp. 10/18/2001
Blue Heron Financial Corp. recapitalized as Avenue Financial Corp. 05/21/2002 which name changed to Mantis Mineral Corp. 06/20/2007 which name changed to Gondwana Oil Corp. 02/26/2014 which name changed to European Metals Corp. 11/07/2014

UNIVERSITY BANCORPORATION, INC. (IL)
Company reported out of business 04/05/2006
Details not available

UNIVERSITY BANK & TRUST CO. (CHESTNUT HILL, MA)
Par value changed from $10 par to $5 par in 1979
Each share Common $5 par exchanged for (0.001) share Common $5,015.04 par 6/15/85
In effect holders received $26.50 cash per share and public interest was eliminated

UNIVERSITY BK & TR CO (NEWTON, MA)
Common 30¢ par split (3) for (2) by issuance of (0.5) additional share 1/15/88
Name changed to University Bank, N.A. (Newton, MA) 6/2/88
(See University Bank, N.A. (Newton, MA))

UNIVERSITY BK & TR CO (PALO ALTO, CA)
Merged into Comerica Inc. 3/31/95
Each Common $2.50 par exchanged for (1.748) share Common $2.50 par

UNIVERSITY BK (GREEN BAY, WI)
Reorganized as Financial Concepts Bancorp Inc. 02/28/1983
Each share Common $10 par exchanged for (1) share Common $10 par
(See Financial Concepts Bancorp Inc.)

UNIVERSITY BK NATL ASSN (NEWTON, MA)
Declared insolvent and closed 05/31/1991
No stockholders' equity

UNIVERSITY COMPUTING CO (DE)
Reincorporated 06/30/1972
Common no par split (3) for (1) by issuance of (2) additional shares 01/31/1968
State of incorporation changed from (TX) to (DE) and Common no par changed to 10¢ par 06/30/1972
Name changed to Wyly Corp. 05/25/1973
Wyly Corp. name changed to Uccel Corp. 05/22/1984 which merged into Computer Associates International, Inc. 08/19/1987 which name changed to CA, Inc. 02/01/2006

UNIVERSITY COURT, INC. (NJ)
Charter revoked for failure to file annual reports 10/16/1997

UNIVERSITY DINING SVCS INC (DE)
Recapitalized as Host America Corp. (DE) 02/15/1998
Each share Common $0.001 par exchanged for (0.01) share Common $0.001 par
Host America Corp. (DE) reincorporated in Colorado 04/30/1999 which name changed to EnerLume Energy Management Corp. 11/01/2007

UNIVERSITY FEDERAL SAVINGS & LOAN ASSOCIATION (USA)
Name changed to University Federal Savings Bank (Seattle, WA) 04/25/1983
University Federal Savings Bank (Seattle, WA) name changed to University Savings Bank (Seattle, WA) 09/28/1987
(See University Savings Bank (Seattle, WA))

UNIVERSITY FED SVGS BK (SEATTLE, WA)
Common 1¢ par split (2) for (1) by issuance of (1) additional share 5/6/83
Name changed to University Savings Bank (Seattle, WA) 9/28/87
(See University Savings Bank (Seattle, WA))

UNIVERSITY GEN HEALTH SYS INC (NV)
Plan of reorganization under Chapter 11 Federal Bankruptcy proceedings effective 02/04/2016
No stockholders' equity

UNIVERSITY GENETICS CO (DE)
Charter cancelled and declared inoperative and void for non-payment of taxes 03/01/1991

UNIVERSITY GIRLS CALENDAR LTD (DE)
Name changed to Towerstream Corp. 01/24/2007

UNIVERSITY GRAPHICS INC (NJ)
Reorganized 12/14/92
Each share Common 10¢ par exchanged for (1.2212875) shares Common 1¢ par 12/14/92
Recapitalized as Dr. Christopher's Original Formulas, Inc. 4/24/2000
Each share Common 1¢ par exchanged for (1/3) share Common $0.001 par
Dr. Christopher's Original Formulas, Inc. recapitalized as NFI Holdings Inc. 12/11/2001 which name changed to ICR Systems, Inc. 11/18/2002 which name changed to Redux Holdings, Inc. 5/30/2006

UNIVERSITY GROUP INC (DE)
Each share Common 25¢ par exchanged for (0.2) share Common $1.25 par 07/01/1976
Merged into Southmark Corp. 02/08/1984
Each share Common $1.25 par exchanged for (0.3341645) share Common $1 par
(See Southmark Corp.)

UNIVERSITY HEALTH INDS INC (FL)
Name changed to Cognitiv, Inc. 09/19/2012

UNIVERSITY NATL BK & TR CO (PALO ALTO, CA)
Common $5 par changed to $2.50 par and (1) additional share issued 11/13/89
Under plan of reorganization each share Common $2.50 par automatically became (1) share University Bank & Trust Co. (Palo Alto, CA) Common $2.50 par 6/17/94
University Bank & Trust Co. (Palo Alto, CA) merged into Comerica Inc. 3/31/95

UNIVERSITY NATIONAL BANK (COLLEGE PARK, MD)
Principal location changed to University National Bank (Rockville, Md.) 5/1/70
(See University National Bank (Rockville, Md.))

UNIVERSITY NATIONAL BANK (FULLERTON, CA)
Merged into Newport National Bank (Newport Beach, CA) 12/31/67
Each share Capital Stock $10 par exchanged for (0.666666) share Common $10 par
Newport National Bank (Newport Beach, CA) reorganized as Newport National Corp. 6/2/69 which merged into Southern California First National Corp. 9/23/71
(See Southern California First National Corp.)

UNIVERSITY NATL BK (PEORIA, IL)
Merged into Commercial National Corp. (DE) 04/20/1982
Each share Common Capital Stock $20 par exchanged for (1.41) shares Common $10 par
Commercial National Corp. (DE) merged into Midwest Fianancial Group, Inc. 02/08/1983 which merged into First of America Bank Corp. 11/01/1989 which merged into National City Corp. 03/31/1998 which was acquired by PNC Financial Services Group, Inc. 12/31/2008

UNIVERSITY NATL BK (ROCKVILLE, MD)
Merged into Equitable Bancorporation 10/17/1977
Each share Capital Stock $8 par exchanged for $22 cash

UNIVERSITY NATIONAL LIFE INSURANCE CO. (OK)
Stock Dividend - 25% 7/10/60
Merged into University National Life Insurance Co. (TN) on a (9/22) for (1) basis 8/16/61
University National Life Insurance Co. (TN) merged into South Coast Life Insurance Co. 9/30/63 which was

acquired by USLIFE Holding Corp. 7/25/67 which name changed to USLIFE Corp. 5/22/70 which merged into American General Corp. 6/17/97 which merged into American International Group, Inc. 8/29/2001

UNIVERSITY NATIONAL LIFE INSURANCE CO. (TN)
Merged into South Coast Life Insurance Co. on a (0.5) for (1) basis 9/30/63
South Coast Life Insurance Co. acquired by USLIFE Holding Corp. 7/25/67 which name changed to USLIFE Corp. 5/22/70 which merged into American General Corp. 6/17/97 which merged into American International Group, Inc. 8/29/2001

UNIVERSITY PATENTS INC (DE)
Common $1 par changed to no par 01/03/1973
Common no par split (3) for (2) by issuance of (0.5) additional share 03/16/1981
Common no par changed to 1¢ par 00/00/1982
Name changed to Competitive Technologies, Inc. 12/20/1994
Competitive Technologies, Inc. name changed to Calmare Therapeutics Inc. 06/04/2015

UNIVERSITY PPTYS INVT CORP (FL)
Name changed to John Phillip Tuba Corp. 4/22/83
(See John Phillip Tuba Corp.)

UNIVERSITY REAL ESTATE TR (CA)
Name changed to National Capital Real Estate Trust 8/10/84
National Capital Real Estate Trust reorganized as National Capital Management Corp. 2/25/88 which name changed to Fragrancenet.Com, Inc. 7/28/99

UNIVERSITY SAVINGS & LOAN ASSOCIATION (CA)
In process of liquidation
Each share Capital Stock $10 par exchanged for initial distribution of $15 cash 3/24/69
Note: Details on subsequent distributions, if any, are not available

UNIVERSITY SVGS ASSN (TX)
Merged into Center Savings Association 09/15/1978
Each share Perm. Reserve Fund Stock $1 par exchanged for $24 cash

UNIVERSITY SVGS BK (SEATTLE, WA)
Acquired by GLENFED, Inc. 3/31/89
Each share Common 1¢ par exchanged for $25.09 cash

UNIVERSITY SCIENCE PARTNERS INC (DE)
Name changed to Wavemat Inc. 05/05/1989
(See Wavemat Inc.)

UNIVERSITY ST BK (GREEN BAY, WI)
Name changed to University Bank (Green Bay, WI) 10/25/1974
University Bank (Green Bay, WI) reorganized as Financial Concepts Bancorp Inc. 02/28/1983
(See Financial Concepts Bancorp Inc.)

UNIVEST CORP (WI)
Stock Dividends - 150% 06/18/1971; 50% 02/25/1972
Through purchase offer 100% acquired by two individuals as of 05/21/1982
Public interest eliminated

UNIVEST LIFE INS CO (TX)
Merged into Transport Life Insurance Co. 07/01/1971
Each share Common no par exchanged for (0.666666) share Common $1 par
(See Transport Life Insurance Co.)

UNIVEST TECH INC (CO)
Common $0.001 par split (9) for (1) by issuance of (8) additional shares payable 05/20/2014 to holders of record 05/20/2014
Name changed to High Desert Assets, Inc. 10/22/2014
High Desert Assets, Inc. name changed to New Asia Energy, Inc. 08/12/2015 which recapitalized as LNPR Group Inc. 01/17/2018

UNIVEST TECHNOLOGIES, INC. (ID)
Name changed to Outpatient Treatment Centers, Inc. 12/22/1986
(See Outpatient Treatment Centers, Inc.)

UNIVEX MNG LTD (BC)
Recapitalized as Copperstone Resources Corp. 09/18/1991
Each share Common no par exchanged for (0.25) share Common no par
Copperstone Resources Corp. recapitalized as Consolidated Copperstone Resources Corp. 12/10/1998 which name changed to Bonanza Silver Corp. 03/14/2000 which recapitalized as Bonanza Explorations Inc. 09/07/2001 which recapitalized as Bonanza Resources Corp. 05/29/2002 which name changed to BRS Resources Ltd. 02/18/2011

UNIVIEW TECHNOLOGIES CORP (TX)
Each share old Common 10¢ par exchanged for (0.1) share new Common 10¢ par 04/24/1998
Each share new Common 10¢ par exchanged for (0.125) share Common 80¢ par 09/10/2001
Name changed to VPGI Corp. and Common 80¢ par changed to $0.001 par 08/14/2003
(See VPGI Corp.)

UNIVIS INC (OH)
Common 50¢ par split (3) for (2) by issuance of (0.5) additional share 8/31/64
Common 50¢ par split (3) for (2) by issuance of (0.5) additional share 8/31/65
Common 50¢ par split (3) for (2) by issuance of (0.5) additional share 8/31/67
Merged into Itek Corp. (DE) 5/11/70
Each share Common 50¢ par exchanged for (0.22262) share Common no par
(See Itek Corp. (DE))

UNIVIS LENS CO. (OH)
Name changed to Univis, Inc. 12/1/60
Univis, Inc. merged into Itek Corp. (Del.) 5/11/70
(See Itek Corp. (Del.))

UNIVISION COMMUNICATIONS INC (DE)
Class A Common 1¢ par split (2) for (1) by issuance of (1) additional share payable 1/12/98 to holders of record 12/17/97 Ex date - 1/13/98
Class A Common 1¢ par split (2) for (1) by issuance of (1) additional share payable 8/11/2000 to holders of record 7/28/2000 Ex date - 8/14/2000
Merged into Umbrella Holdings, LLC 3/29/2007
Each share Class A Common 1¢ par exchanged for $36.25 cash

UNIWAT CAP CORP (AB)
Name changed to Waterfront Capital Corp. 7/28/94

UNIWELL ELECTR CORP (DE)
Name changed to Analytica Bio-Energy Corp. 09/19/2013

UNIZAN FINL CORP (OH)
Merged into Huntington Bancshares Inc. 3/1/2006

Each share Common no par exchanged for (1.1424) shares Common no par

UNLIMITED COATINGS CORP (NV)
Each share old Common $0.001 par exchanged for (0.03546099) share new Common $0.001 par 10/01/2003
New Common $0.001 par split (20) for (1) by issuance of (19) additional shares payable 08/25/2004 to holders of record 08/20/2004 Ex date - 08/26/2004
Name changed to International American Technologies, Inc. 03/22/2005
International American Technologies, Inc. name changed to Hammonds Industries, Inc. 05/14/2007 which recapitalized as Delta Seaboard International, Inc. 06/10/2010 which recapitalized as American International Holdings Corp. 08/13/2012

UNLISTED MKT SVC CORP (NY)
Name changed to Market Guide Inc. 9/3/86
Market Guide Inc. merged into Multex.com, Inc. 9/24/99
(See Multex.com, Inc.)

UNO INC (MN)
Statutorily dissolved 12/30/94

UNO RESTAURANT CORP (DE)
Common 1¢ par split (5) for (4) by issuance of (0.25) additional share 6/5/89
Common 1¢ par split (5) for (4) by issuance of (0.25) additional share 9/10/90
Common 1¢ par split (5) for (4) by issuance of (0.25) additional share 2/28/95
Stock Dividends - 10% 9/23/88; 10% payable 12/23/99 to holders of record 12/13/99
Merged into Uno Restaurant Holdings Corp. 7/31/2001
Each share Common 1¢ par exchanged for $9.75 cash

UNOCAL CAP TR (DE)
6.25% Conv. Trust Preferred Securities called for redemption at $101.25 on 1/19/2005

UNOCAL CORP (DE)
Common $1 par split (2) for (1) by issuance of (1) additional share 11/13/89
$3.50 Conv. Preferred $1 par called for redemption 10/11/96
Merged into Chevron Corp. 8/10/2005
Each share Common $1 par exchanged for (0.618) share Common 75¢ par and $27.60 cash

UNOCAL EXPL CORP (DE)
Merged into Unocal Corp. 5/2/92
Each share Common 10¢ par exchanged for (0.54) share Common $1 par
Unocal Corp. merged into Chevron Corp. 8/10/2005

UNOR INC (ON)
Recapitalized as Hornby Bay Mineral Exploration Ltd. 04/12/2010
Each share Common no par exchanged for (1/3) share Common no par

UNOVA INC (DE)
Name changed to Intermec Inc. 01/01/2006
(See Intermec Inc.)

UNP INDS LTD (BC)
Recapitalized as International UNP Holdings Ltd. (BC) 11/29/1990
Each share Common no par exchanged for (0.16666666) share Class A Subordinate no par and (1) share Class B Multiple no par
International UNP Holdings Ltd. (BC) reincorporated in Canada 08/04/1993
(See International UNP Holdings Ltd.)

UNR INDS INC (DE)
Name changed to ROHN Industries, Inc. 12/17/1997
ROHN Industries, Inc. name changed to Frankfort Tower Industries, Inc. 02/17/2004
(See Frankfort Tower Industries, Inc.)

UNS ENERGY CORP (AZ)
Acquired by FortisUS Inc. 08/15/2014
Each share Common no par exchanged for $60.25 cash

UNSEEN SOLAR INC (DE)
Common $0.0001 par split (40) for (1) by issuance of (39) additional shares payable 12/06/2012 to holders of record 12/05/2012 Ex date - 12/07/2012
Name changed to Pacific Clean Water Technologies, Inc. 12/12/2012

UNSI CORP (DE)
Charter cancelled and declared inoperative and void for non-payment of taxes 03/01/1998

UNSL FINL CORP (DE)
Merged into Mercantile Bancorporation, Inc. 01/03/1995
Each share Common $1 par exchanged for (1.0604) shares Common $5 par
Mercantile Bancorporation, Inc. merged into Firstar Corp. (New) 09/20/1999 which merged into U.S. Bancorp (DE) 02/27/2001

UNUK GOLD CORP (BC)
Name changed to Auterra Ventures Inc. 10/1/98
Auterra Ventures Inc. name changed to Global Hunter Corp. 2/24/2005

UNUM CORP (DE)
Common 10¢ par split (2) for (1) by issuance of (1) additional share 03/09/1992
Preferred Stock Purchase Rights declared for Common stockholders of record 03/21/1988 were redeemed at $0.025 per right 04/02/1992 for holders of record 03/23/1992
Common 10¢ par split (2) for (1) by issuance of (1) additional share payable 06/02/1997 to holders of record 05/19/1997 Ex date - 06/03/1997
Under plan of merger name changed to UNUMProvident Corp. 06/30/1999
UNUMProvident Corp. name changed to Unum Group 03/02/2007

UNUMPROVIDENT CORP (DE)
Each 8.25% Adjustable Conversion Rate Equity Security Unit received (1.8843) shares UNUMProvident Corp. Common 10¢ par 5/15/2006
Name changed to Unum Group 3/2/2007

UNWALL INTL INC (NV)
Name changed to 3 Shine Technologies Inc. 08/20/2015
3 Shine Technologies Inc. name changed to Rorine International Holding Corp. 10/07/2015

UNWIRED PLANET INC (DE)
Each share old Common $0.001 par exchanged for (0.08333333) share new Common $0.001 par 01/06/2016
Name changed to Great Elm Capital Group, Inc. 06/17/2016

UNX ENERGY CORP (AB)
Merged into HRT Participacoes em Petroleo S.A. 04/29/2011
Each share Common no par exchanged for (0.5495) Sponsored GDR for Common
HRT Participacoes em Petroleo S.A. name changed to Petro Rio S.A. 07/07/2015
(See Petro Rio S.A.)

UOL PUBG INC (DE)
Issue Information - 1,430,000 shares COM offered at $13 per share on 11/26/1996
Name changed to VCampus Corp. 09/10/1999
(See VCampus Corp.)

UOP INC (DE)
Merged into Signal Companies, Inc. 05/26/1978
Each share Common $1 par exchanged for $21 cash

UP RIGHT INC (CA)
Acquired by Chatswood, Inc. 02/09/1988
Each share Common no par exchanged for $14.80 cash

UPBANCORP INC (DE)
Common $10 par changed to $1 par 10/20/98
Common $1 par split (4) for (1) by issuance of (3) additional shares payable 12/15/98 to holders of record 9/7/98
Merged into Bridgeview Bancorp, Inc. 6/12/2003
Each share Common $1 par exchanged for $69.097 cash

UPEX, INC. (CO)
Charter revoked for failure to file reports and pay fees 10/13/66

UPGRADE INTL CORP (WA)
Reincorporated 08/21/2000
Each share old Common $0.0001 par exchanged for (0.5) share new Common $0.0001 par 11/14/1997
State of incorporation changed from (FL) to (WA) 08/21/2000
SEC revoked common stock registration 06/02/2005

UPHONIA INC (DE)
SEC revoked common stock registration 10/01/2013

UPJOHN CO (DE)
Reincorporated 11/26/1958
State of incorporation changed from (MI) to (DE) and each share Common $10 par exchanged for (25) shares Common $1 par 11/26/58
Common $1 par split (2) for (1) by issuance of (1) additional share 06/22/1973
Common $1 par split (2) for (1) by issuance of (1) additional share 05/01/1986
Common $1 par split (3) for (1) by issuance of (2) additional shares 05/01/1987
Preferred Stock Purchase Rights declared for Common stockholders of record 06/17/1986 were redeemed at $0.05 per right 11/20/1995 for holders of record 11/01/1995
Merged into Pharmacia & Upjohn Inc. 11/02/1995
Each share Common $1 par exchanged for (1.45) shares Common 1¢ par
Pharmacia & Upjohn Inc. merged into Pharmacia Corp. 03/31/2000 which merged into Pfizer Inc. 04/16/2003

UPLAND BK (UPLAND, CA)
Merged into First Community Bancorp 08/22/2002
Each share Common no par exchanged for $11.73 cash

UPLAND CORP (PA)
Common 10¢ par split (3) for (2) by issuance of (0.5) additional share 5/5/70
Acquired by Emerson Electric Co. 2/18/76
Each share Common 10¢ par exchanged for (1) Non-Transferable Ctf. of Equity Participation and $4.41 cash

UPLAND ENERGY CORP (UT)
Each share old Common $0.001 par exchanged for (0.05) share new Common $0.001 par 03/20/1995
Recapitalized as LifeSmart Nutrition Technologies Inc. 02/19/2002
Each share new Common $0.001 par exchanged for (0.5) share Common $0.001 par
(See LifeSmart Nutrition Technologies Inc.)

UPLAND GLOBAL CORP (AB)
Assets reported seized by tax authorities 10/25/2005
Stockholders' equity unlikely

UPLAND INVT CORP (UT)
Recapitalized as Upland Energy Corp. 11/12/1993
Each share Common $0.001 par exchanged for (0.5) share Common $0.001 par
Upland Energy Corp. recapitalized as LifeSmart Nutrition Technologies, Inc. 02/19/2002
(See LifeSmart Nutrition Technologies, Inc.)

UPLAND MINERALS & CHEMS CORP (DE)
Each share old Common $0.001 par exchanged for (0.1) share new Common $0.001 par 1/20/89
Charter cancelled and declared inoperative and void for non-payment of taxes 3/1/90

UPLAND PPTYS INC (NV)
Name changed to World Wide Wireless Communications, Inc. 07/27/1998
World Wide Wireless Communications, Inc. name changed to Universal Communication Systems, Inc. 04/02/2002 which recapitalized as Air Water International Corp. 10/02/2007
(See Air Water International Corp.)

UPLAND RESOURCE CORP (BC)
Reorganized under the laws of Canada as New Sleeper Gold Corp. 3/25/2004
Each share Common no par exchanged for (0.4) share Common no par
New Sleeper Gold Corp. name changed to Reunion Gold Corp. 6/6/2006

UPPER AVE NATL BK (CHICAGO, IL)
Each share Capital Stock $100 par exchanged for (3.333334) shares Capital Stock $50 par to effect a (2) for (1) split and a 66-2/3% stock dividend 00/00/1943
Stock Dividends - 20% 11/23/1949; 33-1/3% 05/20/1954; 50% 01/13/1961; 20% 02/02/1967; 25% 02/10/1971
Reorganized as Dearborn Financial Corp. 06/30/1973
Each share Capital Stock $50 par exchanged for (1) share Common $10 par
(See Dearborn Financial Corp.)

UPPER CDA BREWING LTD (ON)
Merged into Sleeman Breweries Ltd. 3/11/98
Each share Common no par exchanged for (0.433) share Common no par and $2.75 cash
(See Sleeman Breweries Ltd.)

UPPER CDA GAMING CORP (AB)
Name changed to Q-Tel Wireless Inc. 09/11/2000
(See Q-Tel Wireless Inc.)

UPPER CDA GOLD CORP (AB)
Name changed to California Gold Mining Inc. (AB) 04/15/2013
California Gold Mining Inc. (AB) reorganized in Ontario 06/07/2016

UPPER CANADA MINES LTD. (ON)
Name changed to Upper Canada Resources Ltd. 10/5/72
Upper Canada Resources Ltd. reorganized as Challenger International Services Ltd. 7/7/78
(See Challenger International Services Ltd.)

UPPER CDA RES LTD (ON)
Reorganized as Challenger International Services Ltd. 07/07/1978
Each share Common $1 par exchanged for (0.1) share $2.50 Special Conv. Class A no par
(See Challenger International Services Ltd.)

UPPER COOS RAILROAD CO.
Merged into Maine Central Railroad Co. in 1932
Maine Central Railroad Co. merged into United States Filter Corp. 12/10/80
(See Maine Central Railroad Co.)

UPPER KIRKLAND MINES LTD (ON)
Assets sold 07/00/1978
Each share Capital Stock $1 par received first and final distribution of $0.024 cash
Note: Certificates were not required to be surrendered and are without value

UPPER LAKE OIL & GAS LTD (AB)
Merged into Monterey Exploration Ltd. 09/03/2008
Each share Common no par exchanged for (0.28) share Common no par
(See Monterey Exploration Ltd.)

UPPER PENINSULA ENERGY CORP (MI)
Reorganized 12/31/1988
Common $9 par split (3) for (2) by issuance of (0.5) additional share 05/01/1963
5.5% Preferred $100 par called for redemption 06/16/1963
Common $9 par changed to no par 06/30/1982
8% Preferred $100 par called for redemption 09/01/1988
Under plan of reorganization each share Upper Peninsula Power Co. Common no par automatically became (1) share Upper Peninsula Energy Corp. Common 1¢ par 12/31/1988
11% Preferred $100 par called for redemption 07/01/1991
Common 1¢ par split (2) for (1) by issuance of (1) additional share 09/01/1992
Merged into WPS Resources Corp. 09/29/1998
Each share Common 1¢ par exchanged for (0.9) share Common $1 par
5.25% Preferred $100 par called for redemption at $105 on 12/31/1998
WPS Resources Corp. name changed to Integrys Energy Group, Inc. 02/21/2007 which merged into WEC Energy Group, Inc. 06/30/2015

UPPER SEINE GOLD MINES LTD.
Bankrupt in 1943

UPPER UNGAVA MINING CORP. LTD. (QC)
Declared dissolved for failure to file reports or pay fees 12/10/74

UPPER VY BANCORP INC (PA)
Merged into First Liberty Bank Corp. 6/26/98
Each share Common $20 par exchanged for (0.689) share Common $1.25 par
First Liberty Bank Corp. merged into Community Bank System, Inc. 5/14/2001

UPPER VALLEY FARM & LAND CO. (CO)
Declared defunct and inoperative for failure to pay taxes and file annual reports 10/14/65

UPPSTER CORP (DE)
Common 1¢ par split (2) for (1) by issuance of (1) additional share 7/15/76
Charter cancelled and declared inoperative and void for non-payment of taxes 3/1/90

UPRESSIT METAL CAP CORP. (DE)
Name changed to Danbury Products, Inc. 1/16/59 which completely liquidated 7/20/61

UPROAR INC (DE)
Merged into Flipside, Inc. 03/21/2001
Each share Common 1¢ par exchanged for $3 cash

UPS N DOWNS INC (NY)
Merged into Tootal Ltd. 01/12/1979
Each share Common $0.025 par exchanged for $13 cash

UPSCALE TRENDS INC (NV)
Name changed to Electric Entertainment International Inc. 03/07/1997
Electric Entertainment International Inc. recapitalized as Private Media Group Ltd. 12/16/1997
(See Private Media Group Ltd.)

UPSIDE DEV INC (DE)
Recapitalized as AmoroCorp, Inc. 05/25/2006
Each (300) shares Common 1¢ par exchanged for (1) share Common 1¢ par
(See AmoroCorp, Inc.)

UPSON BANCSHARES INC (GA)
Stock Dividend - 4.2% payable 1/30/2004 to holders of record 12/9/2003 Ex date - 3/4/2004
Merged into SouthCrest Financial Group, Inc. 9/30/2004
Each share Common no par exchanged for either (1) share Common no par or $16 cash

UPSON CO (NY)
Common $12.50 par changed to $10 par 00/00/1937
Common $10 par changed to $5 par and (1) additional share issued 11/06/1972
Stock Dividends - 20% 02/21/1952; 100% 12/27/1968
Plan of reorganization under Chapter 11 Federal Bankruptcy Act confirmed 04/14/1984
No stockholders' equity

UPSON WALTON CO (OH)
Each share Common no par exchanged for (4) shares Common $1 par 00/00/1936
Name changed to Anvil Equipment Co. 11/09/1978
(See Anvil Equipment Co.)

UPSTATE CAPITAL CORP.
Name changed to Equitable Credit Corp. in 1940
Equitable Credit Corp. merged into State Loan & Finance Corp. 9/30/59 which name changed to American Finance System Inc. 5/1/68 which merged into Security Pacific Corp. 12/15/78 which merged into BankAmerica Corp. (Old) 4/22/92 which merged into BankAmerica Corp. (New) 9/30/98 which name changed to Bank of America Corp. 4/28/99

UPSTREAM BIOSCIENCES INC (NV)
Each share old Common $0.001 par exchanged for (0.02857142) share new Common $0.001 par 12/07/2012
Name changed to RealSource Residential, Inc. 08/06/2013

UPSTREAM WORLDWIDE INC (DE)
Each share old Common $0.0001 par exchanged for (0.0190532) share new Common $0.0001 par 06/19/2012

UPT-URA

UPTICK VENTURES INC (CO)
Name changed to usell.com, Inc. 07/27/2012
Recapitalized as Alpha Bytes, Inc. 12/30/94
Each share Common $0.0001 par exchanged for (0.02) share Common $0.0001 par
Alpha Bytes, Inc. name changed to H-Net.com, Inc. 12/15/99 which name changed to H-Net.Net Inc. 8/1/2000

UPTIME CORP. (WY)
Liquidated for cash in March 1971
Surrender of certificates was not required and are now valueless

UPTON COPPER LTD (QC)
Merged into Central Canada Foods Corp. 9/4/98
Each share Common no par exchanged for (0.2) share Class A Common no par
Central Canada Foods Corp. name changed to Central Industries Corp. Inc. 6/5/2007

UPTON RES INC (SK)
Class A no par reclassified as Common no par 09/28/1994
Merged into StarPoint Energy Ltd. 01/27/2004
Each share Common no par exchanged for (1.1) shares Common no par
(See StarPoint Energy Ltd.)

UPTOWN INDS CORP (BC)
Name changed to North American Scientific, Inc. (BC) 09/05/1990
North American Scientific, Inc. reincorporated in Canada 05/03/1994 which reincorporated in Delaware 04/20/1995
(See North American Scientific, Inc.)

UPTOWN NATL BK (CHICAGO, IL)
Each share Capital Stock $100 par exchanged for (4) shares Capital Stock $25 par in 1943
Capital Stock $25 par changed to $10 par and (1.5) additional shares issued 2/19/76
Stock Dividends - 20% 3/10/59; 14.28% 3/5/63; 12-1/2% 10/3/67; 11-1/9% 8/4/69
Reorganized under the laws of Delaware as Upbancorp, Inc. 6/1/83
Each share Capital Stock $10 par exchanged for (1) share Common $10 par
(See Upbancorp, Inc.)

UPTOWN RESTAURANT GROUP INC (CO)
Each share old Common no par exchanged for (0.25) share new Common no par 10/15/2001
Name changed to FransAction, Inc. 11/24/2003
Each share new Common no par exchanged for (1) share Common no par 11/24/2003
FransAction, Inc. name changed to H3 Enterprises, Inc. 5/13/2005

UPTOWNER INNS INC (WV)
Each (25,000) shares old Common 50¢ par exchanged for (1) share new Common 50¢ par 6/22/2004
Note: In effect holders received $1.07 cash per share and public interest was eliminated

UPTURN INC (NV)
Recapitalized as Cityside Tickets Inc. 12/10/2009
Each (45) shares Common $0.001 par exchanged for (1) share Common $0.001 par
Cityside Tickets Inc. name changed to Causeway Entertainment Co. 10/11/2010 which recapitalized as United Bullion Exchange Inc. 05/10/2011

UPWARD TECHNOLOGY CORP (NY)
Dissolved by proclamation 10/26/2011

URACAN RES LTD (BC)
Each share old Common no par exchanged for (0.2) share new Common no par 12/07/2012
Recapitalized as Vanadian Energy Corp. 10/05/2018
Each share new Common no par exchanged for (0.25) share Common no par

URAGOLD BAY RES INC (CANADA)
Each share old Common no par exchanged for (0.25) share new Common no par 08/03/2012
Name changed to HPQ-Silicon Resources Inc. 07/25/2016

URALKALI PJSC (RUSSIA)
Name changed 01/22/2015
Name changed from Uralkali JSC to Uralkali PJSC 01/22/2015
GDR agreement terminated 01/11/2016
Each 144A Sponsored GDR for Ordinary exchanged for $10.207957 cash
(Additional Information in Active)

URALMASH ZAVODY (RUSSIA)
Name changed to United Heavy Machinery Uralmash-Izhora Group 07/07/2000
United Heavy Machinery Uralmash-Izhora Group name changed to Omz OJSC Uralmash-Izhora Group 04/03/2009
(See Omz OJSC Uralmash-Izhora Group)

URALSVYASINFORM JSC (RUSSIA)
Merged into Rostelecom OJSC 04/13/2011
Each Sponsored ADR for Preferred exchanged for $9.93782 cash
Each Sponsored ADR for Ordinary RUB 1,000 par exchanged for $12.712158 cash

URAMIN INC (BRITISH VIRGIN ISLANDS)
Acquired by Compagnie Francaise de Mines et Metaux S.A. 08/20/2007
Each share Common no par exchanged for $7.75 cash

URANERZ ENERGY CORP (NV)
Merged into Energy Fuels, Inc. 06/19/2015
Each share Common $0.001 par exchanged for (0.255) share new Common $0.001 par

URANINITE CORP (NV)
Name changed to Albro Industries Corp. 03/01/1972
Each share Common $1 par exchanged for (1) share Common $1 par
Albro Industries Corp. name changed to Energy Resources of America, Inc. 07/28/1977

URANIUM, INC. (CO)
Declared defunct and inoperative for failure to pay taxes and file annual reports 10/19/1964

URANIUM, INC. (UT)
Merged into Utida Uranium Co. share for share 00/00/1955
Utida Uranium merged into Federal Uranium Corp. (NV) 04/28/1955 which merged into Federal Resources Corp. 05/02/1960
(See Federal Resources Corp.)

URANIUM BAY RES INC (CANADA)
Name changed to Uragold Bay Resources Inc. 07/15/2009
Uragold Bay Resources Inc. name changed to HPQ-Silicon Resources Inc. 07/25/2016

URANIUM CHIEF, INC. (UT)
Merged into International Oil & Metals Corp. 02/28/1956
Each share Common 1¢ par exchanged for (0.01) share Common 1¢ par
International Oil & Metals Corp.

liquidated by exchange for Perfect Photo, Inc. 03/24/1965 which was acquired by United Whelan Corp. 06/30/1966 which name changed to Perfect Film & Chemical Corp. 05/31/1967 which name changed to Cadence Industries Corp. 10/22/1970
(See Cadence Industries Corp.)

URANIUM CITY MNG CORP (NV)
Name changed to U.S. Mine Makers, Inc. (NV) 01/28/2008
U.S. Mine Makers, Inc. (NV) reincorporated in Wyoming as Vid3G, Inc. 02/13/2014 which recapitalized as Argus Worldwide Corp. 11/14/2016

URANIUM CITY RES INC (ON)
Name changed to Strategic Resources Inc. (ON) 03/09/2009
Strategic Resources Inc. (ON) reincorporated in British Columbia 06/07/2016

URANIUM CORP. OF AMERICA (MT)
Name changed to Oremont, Inc. 05/27/1959
(See Oremont, Inc.)

URANIUM CORP. OF AMERICA (UT)
Each share Capital Stock 1¢ par exchanged for (0.05) share Capital Stock 20¢ par 04/05/1955
Merged into Chemical & Metallurgical Enterprises, Inc. 11/05/1956
Each share Capital Stock 20¢ par exchanged for (0.1) share Capital Stock
(See Chemical & Metallurgical Enterprises, Inc.)

URANIUM DISCOVERY & DEVELOPMENT CO. (ID)
Name changed to Keystone Silver Mines, Inc. 02/05/1962
Keystone Silver Mines, Inc. name changed to Scope Industries, Inc. 12/01/2000 which name changed to American Motorcycle Corp. 12/23/2002
(See American Motorcycle Corp.)

URANIUM DRILLING & EXPLORATION, INC. (CO)
Dissolved 10/23/1962
Details not available

URANIUM EXPL CORP (CO)
Merged into National Energy Corp. (CO) 08/31/1968
Each share Common 10¢ par exchanged for (0.33333333) share Common 20¢ par
National Energy Corp. (CO) reincorporated in Tennessee as Aaminex Gold Corp. 04/01/1975 which reincorporated in Nevada 01/29/1981 which name changed to Aaminex Capital Corp. 12/23/1986
(See Aaminex Capital Corp.)

URANIUM FOCUSED ENERGY FD (ON)
Under plan of merger each Unit automatically became (0.3271222) share MBN Corp. Common no par 08/28/2013

URANIUM HOLDINGS, INC. (ID)
Under plan of merger name changed to Idaho-Montana Silver, Inc. 10/23/1963
Idaho-Montana Silver, Inc. recapitalized as Grant Douglas Acquisition Inc. 03/09/2001 which recapitalized as Pediatric Prosthetics, Inc. 11/10/2003 which recapitalized as Marathon Group Corp. (ID) 08/03/2010 which reincorporated in Wyoming 06/02/2011

URANIUM HUNTER CORP (NV)
Recapitalized as Resgreen Group International Inc. 09/15/2016
Each share Common $0.001 par exchanged for (0.0001) share Common $0.001 par

URANIUM INDUSTRIES, INC. (OK)
Merged into Ampet Corp. 11/17/1956
Each share Common 1¢ par exchanged for (0.5) share Common 1¢ par
(See Ampet Corp.)

URANIUM INTL (UT)
Proclaimed dissolved for failure to pay taxes 12/01/1988

URANIUM INTL CORP (NV)
Common $0.001 par split (3) for (2) by issuance of (0.5) additional share payable 03/10/2008 to holders of record 02/25/2008 Ex date - 03/11/2008
Name changed to Mercer Gold Corp. 06/09/2010
Mercer Gold Corp. name changed to Tresoro Mining Corp. 11/04/2011
(See Tresoro Mining Corp.)

URANIUM KING CORP. (QC)
Acquired by International Mining & Development Corp. 07/01/1955
Each share Capital Stock $11 par exchanged for (0.2) share Common 1¢ par
(See International Mining & Development Corp.)

URANIUM KING CORP (NM)
Reincorporated 05/01/1969
Each share old Common 1¢ par exchanged for (0.1) share new Common 1¢ par 04/09/1969
State of incorporation changed from (UT) to (NM) 05/01/1969
Charter revoked for failure to file reports and pay fees 06/30/1990

URANIUM LTD (GUERNSEY)
Merged into Uranium Participation Corp. 03/30/2010
Each share Ordinary no par automatically became (0.5) share Common no par

URANIUM MINES, INC. (ID)
Name changed to Idaho-Montana Silver, Inc. 10/15/1963
Idaho-Montana Silver, Inc. recapitalized as Grant Douglas Acquisition Inc. 03/09/2001 which recapitalized as Pediatric Prosthetics, Inc. 11/10/2003 which recapitalized as Marathon Group Corp. (ID) 08/03/2010 which reincorporated in Wyoming 06/02/2011

URANIUM MINES, INC. (NV)
Merged into Apex Uranium, Inc. (NV) 11/01/1955
Each share Capital Stock 25¢ par exchanged for (1) share Capital Stock 10¢ par
Apex Uranium, Inc. (NV) name changed to Apex Minerals Corp. 08/23/1956 which recapitalized as Limotran Corp. 08/01/1972

URANIUM MINES OF AMERICA, INC.
Merged into Consolidated Uranium Mines, Inc. 11/30/1954
Each share Common 1¢ par exchanged for (0.25) share Common 1¢ par
(See Consolidated Uranium Mines, Inc.)

URANIUM NORTH RES CORP (BC)
Merged into Adamera Minerals Corp. 02/19/2013
Each share Common no par exchanged for (0.2) share Common no par

URANIUM OF UTAH, INC. (OK)
Recapitalized as Chase Oils & Minerals Corp. 11/10/1959
Each share Common 1¢ par exchanged for (0.5) share Common 2¢ par
Chase Oils & Minerals Corp. recapitalized as Hemisphere Minerals Inc. 06/05/1969
(See Hemisphere Minerals Inc.)

URANIUM OIL & TRADING CO. (UT)
Merged into Elaterite Basin Uranium Co. 07/15/1954
Each share Common 1¢ par exchanged for (0.1) share Capital Stock $2.50 par
Elaterite Basin Uranium Co. merged into Sun Tide Corp. 11/15/1957 which name changed to Maxa Corp. 04/13/1974
(See Maxa Corp.)

URANIUM ONE INC (CANADA)
Acquired by Effective Energy N.V. 10/21/2013
Each share Common no par exchanged for $2.86 cash
Note: Unexchanged certificates will be cancelled and become without value 10/21/2019

URANIUM-PETROLEUM CO. (NV)
Merged into General Contracting Corp. 02/28/1961
Each share Common 5¢ par exchanged for (0.01) share Common 5¢ par
General Contracting Corp. name changed to General International, Inc. 08/04/1969
(See General International, Inc.)

URANIUM PLUS RESOURCE CORP (NV)
Common $0.001 par split (6.8) for (1) by issuance of (5.8) additional shares payable 04/24/2008 to holders of record 04/21/2008
Ex date - 04/25/2008
Reorganized as Artventive Medical Group, Inc. 02/16/2010
Each share Common $0.001 par exchanged for (1.65) shares Common $0.001 par

URANIUM PWR CORP (BC)
Merged into Titan Uranium Inc. 07/31/2009
Each share Common no par exchanged for (0.5393) share Common no par
Note: Unexchanged certificates were cancelled and became without value 07/31/2015
Titan Uranium Inc. merged into Energy Fuels Inc. 02/24/2012

URANIUM PWR CORP (CO)
Name changed to Canwest Petroleum Corp. 11/26/2004
Canwest Petroleum Corp. name changed to Oilsands Quest Inc. 11/01/2006
(See Oilsands Quest Inc.)

URANIUM QUEEN EXPLORATION CO. (CO)
Incorporated 03/03/1955
Charter revoked for failure to file reports and pay fees 09/29/1958

URANIUM REDUCTION CO. (NV)
Merged into Atlas Corp. 08/17/1962
Details not available

URANIUM RESEARCH & DEVELOPMENT CO. (CO)
Recapitalized as United Research & Development Co. 08/19/1960
Each share Common 10¢ par exchanged for (0.25) share Common 10¢ par
(See United Research & Development Co.)

URANIUM RES INC (DE)
Each share old Common $0.001 par exchanged for (0.25) share new Common $0.001 par 08/01/1990
Each share new Common $0.001 par exchanged again for (0.25) share new Common $0.001 par 04/11/2006
Each share new Common $0.001 par exchanged again for (0.1) share new Common $0.001 par 01/23/2013
Each share new Common $0.001 par exchanged again for (0.08333333) share new Common $0.001 par 03/08/2016
Name changed to Westwater Resources, Inc.

URANIUM RIDGE MINES LTD (ON)
Charter cancelled for failure to pay taxes and file returns 01/26/1977

URANIUM ROYALTIES, INC. (NV)
Charter revoked for failure to file reports and pay fees 03/03/1958

URANIUM SHARES, INC. (CO)
Recapitalized as Space Data Industries, Inc. 05/09/1969
Each share Common 1¢ par exchanged for (0.01) share Common 1¢ par
Space Data Industries, Inc. recapitalized as Golden Spike Petroleum Inc. 02/10/1981
(See Golden Spike Petroleum Inc.)

URANIUM STAR CORP (MN)
Name changed to Energizer Resources Inc. 04/29/2010
Energizer Resources Inc. name changed to NextSource Materials Inc. (MN) 04/24/2017 which reincorporated in Canada 12/27/2017

URANIUM STD RES LTD (BC)
Recapitalized as Palisades Ventures Inc. 12/01/2015
Each share Common no par exchanged for (0.5) share Common no par
Palisades Ventures Inc. recapitalized as Fremont Gold Ltd. 07/07/2017

URANIUM STRATEGIES INC (NV)
Name changed to Leisure Direct, Inc. 06/07/2004
Leisure Direct, Inc. name changed to LD Holdings, Inc. 10/27/2008

URANIUM 308 CORP (NV)
SEC revoked common stock registration 05/28/2014

URANIUM VALLEY AIRLINES (MT)
Charter suspended for non-compliance with corporation laws 03/09/1955

URANIUM VY MINES LTD (BC)
Name changed to International Prospect Ventures Ltd. 10/27/2017

URANIUM VY MINES LTD (ON)
Name changed to Superstar Petroleums Ltd. 11/19/1973
Each share Capital Stock no par exchanged for (1) share Capital Stock no par
(See Superstar Petroleums Ltd.)

URANIUM VENTURES CORP. (NV)
Name changed to Mineral Ventures Co. 12/14/1955
Mineral Ventures Co. merged into Globe Minerals, Inc. 03/07/1969 which recapitalized as Globe Inc. 10/16/1970
(See Globe Inc.)

URANIUMCORE CO (DE)
Each share old Common 1¢ par exchanged for (4) shares new Common 1¢ par 12/12/2006
Name changed to Horizon Health International Corp. 10/09/2009
Horizon Health International Corp. name changed to Horizons Holdings International, Corp. 04/16/2015

URASIA ENERGY LTD (BC)
Merged into sxr Uranium One Inc. 04/20/2007
Each share Common no par exchanged for (0.45) share Common no par
sxr Uranium One Inc. name changed to Uranium One Inc. 06/18/2007
(See Uranium One Inc.)

URASTAR ENERGY INC (BC)
Name changed to Urastar Gold Corp. 08/03/2011
(See Urastar Gold Corp.)

URASTAR GOLD CORP (BC)
Acquired by Agnico Eagle Mines Ltd. 05/16/2013
Each share Common no par exchanged for $0.25 cash

URAVAN URANIUM & OIL, INC. (CO)
Charter dissolved for failure to file annual reports 01/01/1963

URBAN AG CORP (DE)
SEC revoked common stock registration 06/19/2015

URBAN COMMUNICATIONS INC (BC)
Each share old Common no par exchanged for (0.1) share new Common no par 09/18/2012
Acquired by ACME Communications Canada, Inc. 11/20/2017
Each share new Common no par exchanged for $0.07 cash
Note: Unexchanged certificates will be cancelled and become without value 11/20/2023

URBAN CMNTY ENHANCEMENT CORP (NV)
Name changed to Vision Digital Multimedia Corp. 12/22/2005
Vision Digital Multimedia Corp. name changed to Clinicares, Inc. 03/08/2007 which recapitalized as Catch By Gene, Inc. 04/09/2010
(See Catch By Gene, Inc.)

URBAN COMPUTER SYS INC (MA)
Stock Dividend - 200% 06/14/1972
Proclaimed dissolved for failure to file reports and pay taxes 01/10/1979

URBAN JUICE & SODA LTD (WY)
Reincorporated 12/31/1999
Place of incorporation changed from (BC) to (WY) 12/31/1999
Reincorporated under the laws of Washington as Jones Soda Co. 08/03/2000

URBAN (GEORGE) MILLING CO. (NY)
Capital Stock $10 par changed to $5 par 06/30/1961
Merged into Seaboard Allied Milling Corp. 06/01/1965
Details not available

URBAN MOTION PICTURE INDUSTRIES, INC. (NY)
Charter revoked for failure to file reports and pay fees 12/15/1930

URBAN NATL BK (FRANKLIN LAKES, NJ)
Merged into HUBCO, Inc. 06/30/1995
Each share Common $5 par exchanged for (2.17) shares Common no par
HUBCO, Inc. name changed to Hudson United Bancorp 04/21/1999 which merged TD Banknorth Inc. 01/31/2006
(See TD Banknorth Inc.)

URBAN RESOURCE TECHNOLOGIES INC (AB)
Struck off register for failure to file annual returns 03/13/1999

URBAN RES LTD (ON)
Name changed 05/18/1982
Name changed from Urban Quebec Mines Ltd. to Urban Resources Ltd. 05/18/1982
Recapitalized as Urbana Corp. 06/06/1985
Each share Capital Stock no par exchanged for (0.2) share Common no par

URBAN SELECT EXPL INC (BC)
Name changed to Cascadia Consumer Electronic Corp. 11/23/2012
Cascadia Consumer Electronics Corp. name changed to Cascadia Blockchain Group Corp. 09/10/2018

URBAN SHOPPING CTRS INC (MD)
Merged into Rodamco North American N.V. 11/08/2000
Each share Conv. Preferred Ser. A 1¢ par exchanged for $48 cash
Each share Conv. Preferred Ser. B 1¢ par exchanged for $48 cash
Each share Common 1¢ par exchanged for $48 cash

URBANA CA INC (NV)
Recapitalized as Pitts & Spitts, Inc. 07/17/2002
Each share Common no par exchanged for (0.00125) share Common no par
Pitts & Spitts, Inc. name changed to PSPP Holdings, Inc. 06/17/2004 which recapitalized as Mod Hospitality, Inc. 09/22/2008 which recapitalized as Stakool, Inc. 12/16/2009 which name changed to Fresh Promise Foods, Inc. 11/12/2013

URBANALIEN CORP (NV)
Recapitalized as Favored, Inc. 07/25/2006
Each share Common $0.001 par exchanged for (0.01) share Common $0.001 par

URBANFIND INC (DE)
Each share old Common $0.0001 par exchanged for (1.5) shares new Common $0.0001 par 07/29/2003
Name changed to Klondike Star Mineral Corp. 01/21/2004
(See Klondike Star Mineral Corp.)

URBANFUND CORP (AB)
Reincorporated under the laws of Ontario 12/01/2003

URBANI HLDGS INC (CO)
Name changed to United Specialties, Inc. 07/28/2003
United Specialties, Inc. name changed to WaterColor Holdings Corp. 04/10/2006
(See WaterColor Holdings Corp.)

URBANIMMERSIVE TECHNOLOGIES INC (CANADA)
Name changed to Urbanimmersive Inc. 10/13/2015

URBCO INC (AB)
Plan of arrangement effective 05/30/2002
Each share Common no par exchanged for (0.2781) Northern Property Real Estate Investment Trust, Trust Unit no par, (1) share NewNorth Projects Ltd. Common no par, $0.57 principal amount of NewNorth Projects Ltd. 10% Debentures due 05/30/2012 and $1.29 cash
(See each company's listing)

URBI DESARROLLOS URBANOS S A B DE C V (MEXICO)
Sponsored Reg. S ADR's for Ordinary split (3) for (1) by issuance of (2) additional ADR's payable 05/18/2006 to holders of record 05/15/2006
Sponsored 144A ADR's for Ordinary split (3) for (1) by issuance of (2) additional ADR's payable 05/18/2006 to holders of record 05/15/2006
ADR agreement terminated 07/31/2014
Each Sponsored Reg. S ADR for Ordinary exchanged for $0.007542 cash
Each Sponsored 144A ADR for Ordinary exchanged for $0.007542 cash

URCAN MINES LTD. (BC)
Capital Stock 50¢ par changed to no par 02/05/1969
Name changed to Spectrum Resources Ltd. 02/07/1969
Spectrum Resources Ltd. recapitalized as Spectrum Industrial Resources Ltd. 01/09/1970 which recapitalized as International Data Service Corp. 11/26/1987

(See International Data Service Corp.)

URCARCO INC (TX)
Common 1¢ par split (3) for (2) by issuance of (0.5) additional share 05/04/1990
Name changed to AmeriCredit Corp. 11/13/1992
(See AmeriCredit Corp.)

URCO MINES LTD. (ON)
Charter revoked for failure to file reports and pay fees 05/13/1965

URECOATS INDS INC (DE)
Each share old Common 1¢ par exchanged for (0.1) share new Common 1¢ par 05/31/2002
Name changed to IFT Corp. 12/31/2004
IFT Corp. name changed to Lapolla Industries, Inc. 11/08/2005
(See Lapolla Industries, Inc.)

URETHANE CORP. OF CALIFORNIA (CA)
Merged into Califoam Corp. of America 10/09/1963
Details not available

URETHANE INDUSTRIES INTERNATIONAL, INC. (CA)
Name changed to American Urethane, Inc. 09/20/1962
(See American Urethane, Inc.)

URETHANE TECHNOLOGIES INC (NV)
Each share old Common 1¢ par exchanged for (0.72) share new Common 1¢ par 06/25/1992
Charter revoked for failure to file reports and pay fees 12/01/1997

UREX ENERGY CORP (NV)
Recapitalized as Mustang Geothermal Corp. 07/22/2010
Each share Common $0.001 par exchanged for (0.005) share Common $0.001 par
Mustang Geothermal Corp. recapitalized as Dakota Territory Resource Corp. 09/26/2012

URGENT CARE CTRS AMER INC (CA)
Common no par split (3) for (1) by issuance of (2) additional shares 06/06/1983
Name changed to ReadiCare, Inc. 07/12/1985
ReadiCare, Inc. merged into HealthSouth Corp. 12/02/1996 which name changed to Encompass Health Corp. 01/02/2018

URI THERM X INC (NY)
Dissolved by proclamation 12/23/1992

URIS BLDGS CORP (NY)
Common 10¢ par split (2) for (1) by issuance of (1) additional share 02/28/1969
Acquired by National Kinney Corp. 06/24/1974
Each share Common 10¢ par exchanged for $15 cash

UROCOR INC (DE)
Merged into DIANON Systems, Inc. 11/09/2001
Each share Common 1¢ par exchanged for (0.3843) share Common 1¢ par
(See DIANON Systems, Inc.)

URODYNAMIX TECHNOLOGIES LTD (BC)
Recapitalized as Venturi Ventures Inc. 08/29/2011
Each share Common no par exchanged for (0.05) share Common no par
(See Venturi Ventures Inc.)

UROGEN CORP (DE)
Name changed to Genstar Therapeutics Corp. 03/22/2000
Genstar Therapeutics Corp. name changed to CorAutus Genetics, Inc.

02/05/2003 which recapitalized as VIA Pharmaceuticals, Inc. 06/06/2007
(See VIA Pharmaceuticals, Inc.)

UROHEALTH SYS INC (DE)
Each share old Class A Common no par exchanged for (0.33333333) share new Class A Common no par 12/29/1995
Under plan of merger name changed to Imagyn Medical Technologies, Inc. 09/29/1997
(See Imagyn Medical Technologies, Inc.)

UROLOGIX INC (MN)
Assets sold for the benefit of creditors 02/02/2016
No stockholders' equity

UROMED CORP (DE)
Reincorporated 03/01/2005
Each share old Common no par exchanged for (0.2) share new Common no par 05/19/1998
State of incorporation changed from (MA) to (DE) 03/01/2005
Common no par changed to $0.0001 par 05/20/2005
Each share old Common $0.0001 par exchanged for (0.03333333) share new Common $0.0001 par 02/02/2007
Name changed to St. Lawrence Energy Corp. 01/02/2008
(See St. Lawrence Energy Corp.)

URON INC (MN)
Each share old Common no par exchanged for (0.1) share new Common no par 12/31/2007
Name changed to Western Capital Resources, Inc. (MN) 08/08/2008
Western Capital Resources, Inc. (MN) reincorporated in Delaware 05/11/2016

UROPLASTY INC (MN)
Each share old Common 1¢ par exchanged for (0.33333333) share new Common 1¢ par 04/03/2002
Merged into Cogentix Medical, Inc. 04/01/2015
Each share new Common 1¢ par exchanged for (0.72662) share Common 1¢ par
(See Cogentix Medical, Inc.)

UROQUEST MED CORP (DE)
Acquired by Chemfab Corp. 12/28/1999
Each share Common $0.001 par exchanged for $2.2665 cash

URREA ENTERPRISES INC (NV)
Reorganized as Edulink, Inc. 11/10/1999
Each share Common $0.001 par exchanged for (50) shares Common $0.001 par
Edulink, Inc. recapitalized as Learning Priority, Inc. 01/25/2008
(See Learning Priority, Inc.)

URS CORP (CA)
Class A $1 par changed to 25¢ par and (3) additional shares issued 04/29/1968
Name changed to URS Systems Corp. and Class A 25¢ par reclassified as Common no par 05/22/1968 which name changed back to URS Corp. and Common no par changed to 25¢ par 03/28/1974
Reincorporated under the laws of Delaware 05/18/1976
URS Corp. (DE) name changed to Thortec International Inc. 11/18/1987 which name changed back to URS Corp. (DE) 02/21/1990 which merged into AECOM Technology Corp. 10/17/2014 which name changed to AECOM 01/06/2015

URS CORP (DE)
Name changed to Thortec International Inc. 11/18/1987 which

name changed back to URS Corp. (DE) 02/21/1990
Merged into AECOM Technology Corp. 10/17/2014
Each share Common 1¢ par exchanged for (0.3856) share Common 1¢ par and $42.9632 cash
AECOM Technology Corp. name changed to AECOM 01/06/2015

URS SYSTEMS CORP. (CA)
Name changed to URS Corp. (CA) and Common no par changed to 25¢ par 03/28/1974
URS Corp. (CA) reincorporated in Delaware 05/18/1976 which name changed to Thortec International Inc. 11/18/1987 which name changed back to URS Corp. 02/21/1990

URSA MAJOR INTERNATIONAL INC (BARBADOS)
Reorganized under the laws of Ontario as Auriga Gold Corp. 04/26/2010
Each share Common no par exchanged for (0.25) share Common no par
Auriga Gold Corp. name changed to Minnova Corp. 06/27/2014

URSA MAJOR MINERALS INC (ON)
Merged into Prophecy Platinum Corp. 07/16/2012
Each share Common no par exchanged for (0.04) share Common no par
Prophecy Platinum Corp. name changed to Wellgreen Platinum Ltd. 12/19/2013 which name changed to Nickel Creek Platinum Corp. 01/11/2018

URSTADT BIDDLE PPTYS INC (MD)
8.5% Preferred Ser. C 1¢ par called for redemption at $100 plus $0.684722 accrued dividends on 05/29/2013
7.5% Sr. Preferred Ser. D 1¢ par called for redemption at $25 plus $0.109375 accrued dividends on 11/21/2014
7.125% Preferred Ser. F 1¢ par called for redemption at $25 plus $0.410677 accrued dividends on 10/24/2017
(Additional Information in Active)

URSUS TELECOM CORP (FL)
Chapter 11 bankruptcy proceedings converted to Chapter 7 on 02/20/2002
Stockholders' equity unlikely

URT INDS INC (FL)
Common 1¢ par reclassified as Class A Common 1¢ par 12/20/1976
Stock Dividends - 200% 05/12/1975; 20% 01/13/1976; 20% 02/17/1978; 100% 11/27/1978
Voluntarily dissolved 06/23/2003
Details not available

URUGUAY MINERAL EXPL INC (YT)
Reincorporated 02/11/2002
Name and place of incorporation changed from Uruguay Goldfields Inc. (AB) to Uruguay Mineral Exploration Inc. (YT) 02/11/2002
Under plan of merger name changed to Orosur Mining Inc. 01/08/2010

URZ ENERGY CORP (BC)
Merged into Azarga Uranium Corp. 07/06/2018
Each share Common no par exchanged for (2) shares Common no par
Note: Unexchanged certificates will be cancelled and become without value 07/06/2024

US BANCORP (IN)
Merged into Merchants National Corp. 11/28/1986
Each share Common $10 par exchanged for (5.4380) shares Common no par
Merchants National Corp. merged into

National City Corp. 05/02/1992 which was acquired by PNC Financial Services Group, Inc. 12/31/2008

US BIOENERGY CORP (SD)
Merged into VeraSun Energy Corp. 04/01/2008
Each share Common 1¢ par exchanged for (0.81) share Common 1¢ par
(See VeraSun Energy Corp.)

US BUYBACK LEADERS ETF (ON)
Name changed to US Equity Plus Income ETF 06/22/2017
US Equity Plus Income ETF name changed to Harvest US Equity Plus Income ETF 06/19/2018

US BUYBACK LEADERS FD (ON)
Under plan of reorganization each Class A Unit automatically became (1) US Buyback Leaders ETF Class A Unit 10/24/2016
US Buyback Leaders ETF name changed to US Equity Plus Income ETF 06/22/2017 which name changed to Harvest US Equity Plus Income ETF 06/19/2018

US CA MEX EXPLS LTD (ON)
Recapitalized as Tri-Coast Resource Corp. 01/05/1984
Each share Common no par exchanged for (0.1) share Common no par
Tri-Coast Resource Corp. reorganized as Tri-Coast Finanical Corp. 12/07/1984 which recapitalized as Gold Medal Group Inc. 08/19/1987
(See Gold Medal Group Inc.)

US COBALT INC (BC)
Merged into First Cobalt Corp. (BC) 06/05/2018
Each share Common no par exchanged for (1.5) shares Common no par
Note: Unexchanged certificates will be cancelled and become without value 06/05/2024
First Cobalt Corp. (BC) reincorporated in Canada 09/04/2018

US CMNTY BANCORP (CA)
Merged into Los Padres Savings Bank of Solvang (Solvang, CA) 5/30/97
Each share Common no par exchanged for $2.20 cash

US DATA AUTH INC (FL)
SEC revoked common stock registration 09/26/2005

US DATAWORKS INC (NV)
Each share old Common $0.0001 par exchanged for (0.2) share new Common $0.0001 par 09/29/2003
Each share new Common $0.0001 par exchanged again for (0.01) share new Common $0.0001 par 07/01/2013
Note: Holders of (99) or fewer pre-split shares received $0.12 cash per share
Plan of reorganization under Chapter 11 Federal Bankrutpcy proceedings effective 12/13/2017
No stockholders' equity

US ENERGY HLDGS INC (NV)
Name changed to Lonestar Group Holdings, Co. 01/10/2007
Lonestar Group Holdings, Co. recapitalized as Guardian Angel Group, Inc. 12/14/2007 which recapitalized as Ree International, Inc. 06/29/2011

US ENERGY INITIATIVES CORP (DE)
Reincorporated 05/26/2008
State of incorporation changed from (GA) to (DE) 05/26/2008
Reincorporated under the laws of Nevada as U.S. Energy Initiatives Corporation Inc. and Common 1¢ par changed to $0.001 par 04/03/2013

US EQUITY PLUS INCOME ETF (ON)
Name changed to Harvest US Equity Plus Income ETF 06/19/2018

US FACS CORP (DE)
Name changed to Centris Group, Inc. 05/14/1997
(See Centris Group, Inc.)

US GLOBAL AEROSPACE INC (DE)
Common 1¢ par split (3) for (1) by issuance of (2) additional shares payable 3/5/2003 to holders of record 2/24/2003 Ex date - 3/6/2003
Name changed to US Global Nanospace, Inc. 7/24/2003

US GOLD CDN ACQUISITION CORP (AB)
Each Exchangeable Share no par exchanged for (1) share McEwen Mining Inc. Common no par 05/29/2012

US HIGHLAND INC (OK)
Old Common 1¢ par split (7) for (1) by issuance of (6) additional shares payable 04/07/2010 to holders of record 04/06/2010 Ex date - 04/08/2010
Each share old Common 1¢ par exchanged for (0.03333333) share new Common 1¢ par 04/13/2012
Reincorporated under the laws of Nevada as Cruzani, Inc. and new Common 1¢ par changed to $0.00001 par 10/02/2018

US JET INC (NV)
Recapitalized as American Coal Corp. (New) 10/29/1999
Each share Common $0.001 par exchanged for (0.002) share Common $0.001 par
Note: No holder will receive fewer than (100) shares
American Coal Corp. (New) name changed to Kevcorp Services, Inc. 06/22/2004 which recapitalized as Center For Wound Healing, Inc. 02/15/2006
(See Center For Wound Healing, Inc.)

US LAN SYS CORP (VA)
Charter cancelled and proclaimed dissolved for failure to file reports 11/30/98

US LEC CORP (DE)
Issue Information - 5,500,000 shares CL A offered at $15 per share on 04/23/1998
Name changed to PAETEC Holding Corp. and Class A Common 1¢ par reclassified as Common 1¢ par 02/28/2007
PAETEC Holding Corp. merged into Windstream Corp. 12/01/2011 which name changed to Windstream Holdings, Inc. 09/03/2013

US NAT GAS CORP (FL)
Each share old Common $0.001 par exchanged for (0.00333333) share new Common $0.001 par 08/12/2013
Name changed to Sylios Corp. 06/20/2014

US OIL SANDS INC (BC)
Reincorporated under the laws of Alberta 05/09/2011

US ONCOLOGY INC (DE)
Merged into US Oncology Holdings, Inc. 8/20/2004
Each share Common 1¢ par exchanged for $15.05 cash

US 1 INDS INC (IN)
Reincorporated 02/00/1995
State of incorporation changed from (CA) to (IN) 02/00/1995
Acquired by Trucking Investment Co., Inc. 08/12/2011
Each share Common no par exchanged for $1.43 cash

US ONE TR (DE)
Name changed to Russell Exchange Traded Funds Trust and One Fund reclassified as Equity ETF 04/15/2011
(See Russell Exchange Traded Funds Trust)

US ORDER INC (DE)
Merged into InteliData Technologies Corp. 11/07/1996
Each share Common $0.001 par exchanged for (1) share Common $0.001 par
InteliData Technologies Corp. merged into Corillian Corp. 10/06/2005
(See Corillian Corp.)

US PATRIOT INC (SC)
Common $0.0001 par split (14) for (1) by issuance of (13) additional shares payable 10/08/2002 to holders of record 10/07/2002 Ex date - 10/09/2002
Reincorporated under the laws of Delaware as TriMedia Entertainment Group, Inc. 11/27/2002
(See TriMedia Entertainment Group, Inc.)

US PTS ONLINE (NV)
Name changed to One 4 Art Ltd. 04/01/2015

US SEARCH CORP COM (DE)
Issue Information - 6,000,000 shares COM offered at $9 per share on 06/25/1999
Merged into First Advantage Corp. 06/05/2003
Each share Common $0.001 par exchanged (0.04) share Class A Common $0.001 par
First Advantage Corp. acquired by First American Corp. (CA) 11/18/2009 which reincorporated in Delaware as CoreLogic, Inc. 06/01/2010

US SERVIS INC (DE)
Merged into HBO & Co. 10/01/1998
Each share Common 1¢ par exchanged for (0.16265) share Common 5¢ par
HBO & Co. merged into McKesson HBOC Inc. 01/12/1999 which name changed to McKesson Corp. 07/30/2001

US-SINO GATEWAY INC (CA)
Name changed to ClickPay Solutions, Inc. (CA) 7/28/2005
ClickPay Solutions, Inc. (CA) reincorporated in Nevada 4/6/2006

US TRAILS INC (NV)
Merged into Thousand Trails Inc. (DE) 11/20/96
Each share Common no par exchanged for (1) share Common no par
(See Thousand Trails Inc. (DE))

US TUNGSTEN CORP (NV)
Recapitalized as Aziel Corp. 01/23/2018
Each share Common $0.001 par exchanged for (0.001) share Common $0.001 par

US UNWIRED INC (LA)
Issue Information - 8,000,000 shares CL A offered at $11 per share on 05/17/2000
Class A Common 1¢ par reclassified as Common 1¢ par 3/29/2002
Merged into Sprint Corp. 8/12/2005
Each share Common 1¢ par exchanged for $6.25 cash
Sprint Corp. name changed to Sprint Nextel Corp. 8/12/2005

US URANIUM INC (NV)
Name changed to California Gold Corp. 03/30/2009
California Gold Corp. recapitalized as MV Portfolios, Inc. 09/08/2014

US WATS INC (NY)
Reincorporated under the laws of Delaware as Capsule Communications Inc. 05/02/2000
Capsule Communications Inc. merged into Covista Communications, Inc. 02/08/2002

US WEST FING II (DE)
Issue Information - 19,200,000 TR ORIGINATED PFD SECS 8.25% offered at $25 per share on 10/24/1996
Name changed to MediaOne Financing B 6/12/98
(See MediaOne Financing B)

USA BANCORP INC (MA)
Closed by FDIC 06/26/1992
No stockholders' equity

USA BK (PORT CHESTER, NY)
Bank closed and FDIC appointed receiver 07/09/2010
Stockholders' equity unlikely

USA BIOMASS CORP (DE)
Each share Common $0.002 par received distribution of (0.1) share Amcor Financial Corp. Common no par payable 01/15/2000 to holders of record 12/30/1999
Plan of reorganization under Chapter 11 Federal Bankruptcy Code effective 02/10/2003
Each share 9% Conv. Preferred Ser. A no par exchanged for (4) shares Common $0.002 par
SEC revoked common stock registration 12/28/2009

USA BRDG CONSTR N Y INC (NY)
Petition filed under Chapter 11 Federal Bankruptcy Code dismissed 7/15/2004
No stockholders' equity

USA CLASSIC INC (DE)
Charter cancelled and declared inoperative and void for non-payment of taxes 05/30/1996

USA DEALERS AUCTION COM INC (NV)
Each share old Common $0.001 par exchanged for (0.125) share new Common $0.001 par 01/07/2002
Name changed to Brands Shopping Network, Inc. 01/15/2002
Brands Shopping Network, Inc. recapitalized as United Fuel & Energy Corp. 01/31/2005
(See United Fuel & Energy Corp.)

USA DETERGENTS INC (DE)
Common 1¢ par split (3) for (2) by issuance of (0.5) additional share payable 2/9/96 to holders of record 1/30/96
Merged into Church & Dwight Co., Inc. 5/29/2001
Each share Common 1¢ par exchanged for $7 cash

USA DIGITAL INC (NV)
Common no par split (2) for (1) by issuance of (1) additional share payable 3/3/2000 to holders of record 2/25/2000
Name changed to Avix Technologies, Inc. 1/2/2002
(See Avix Technologies, Inc.)

USA ED INC (DE)
Name changed to SLM Corp. 5/17/2002

USA ENTMT CTR INC (PA)
Name changed to USA Technologies, Inc. 05/12/1995

USA FAST LUBE SYS INC (CO)
Company became private 10/00/1988
Details not available

USA FINL SVCS INC (DE)
Charter cancelled and declared inoperative and void for non-payment of taxes 3/27/95

USA GRAPHITE INC (NV)
Common $0.001 par split (3.5) for (1) by issuance of (2.5) additional shares payable 04/17/2012 to holders of record 04/17/2012
SEC revoked common stock registration 04/08/2016

USA HEALTH TECHNOLOGIES INC (NV)
Reorganized 03/15/1995
Reorganized from (CO) to under the laws of Nevada 03/15/1995
Each share Common 1¢ par exchanged for (0.02) share Common $0.001 par 03/15/1995
Name changed to Healthtech International, Inc. 10/27/1995
(See Healthtech International, Inc.)

USA INTERACTIVE (DE)
Name changed 05/09/2002
Common 1¢ par split (2) for (1) by issuance of (1) additional share payable 03/26/1998 to holders of record 03/12/1998
Common 1¢ par split (2) for (1) by issuance of (1) additional share payable 02/24/2000 to holders of record 02/10/2000
Name changed from USA Networks, Inc. to USA Interactive 05/09/2002
Name changed to InterActiveCorp 06/23/2003
InterActiveCorp name changed to IAC/InterActiveCorp 07/14/2004

USA INTL CHEM INC (DE)
Each share old Common no par exchanged for (0.01) share new Common no par
Stock Dividend - 11.29% payable 4/28/2000 to holders of record 4/17/2000 Ex date - 4/13/2000
Under plan of merger name changed to Aspac Communications, Inc. (New) 6/20/2000

USA MOBILE COMMUNICATIONS HLDGS INC (DE)
Merged into Arch Communications Group, Inc. 09/07/1995
Each share Common 1¢ par exchanged for (0.802) share Common 1¢ par
Arch Communications Group, Inc. name changed to Arch Wireless, Inc. 09/25/2000
(See Arch Wireless, Inc.)

USA MOBILITY INC (DE)
Name changed to Spok Holdings, Inc. 07/09/2014

USA NETWORK (UT)
Recapitalized as Madison Sports & Entertainment Group, Inc. 5/13/92
Each share Common $0.001 par exchanged for (0.5) share Common $0.001 par

USA PROMOTIONS, INC. (UT)
Name changed to Prime Resources, Inc. 06/01/1990
Prime Resources, Inc. name changed to IPCOR, Ltd. 09/11/1990 which name changed to Luxury Seaside Resorts, Inc. (UT) 12/20/1991 which reincorporated in Nevada as RE/COMM Corp. 03/22/1992 which name changed to Metro Wireless Interactive Corp. 12/27/1993 which name changed to Red Rock International Corp. (NV) 04/01/1996 which reorganized in Kentucky as Page International Inc. 11/05/1997 which reincorporated in Nevada 12/31/1997 which name changed to China TianRen Organic Food, Inc. 06/14/2007

USA REAL ESTATE INVT TR (CA)
Each old Share of Bene. Int. $1 par exchanged for (0.03333333) new Share of Bene. Int. $1 par 07/01/1998
Each new Share of Bene. Int. $1 par exchanged again for (0.25) new Share of Bene. Int. $1 par 10/10/2000
Liquidation completed
Each new Share of Bene. Int. $1 par received initial distribution of $38 cash payable 12/30/2013 to holders of record 12/16/2013 Ex date - 12/31/2013

USA-USD

Each new Share of Bene. Int. $1 par received second and final distribution of $13 cash payable 03/02/2015 to holders of record 12/30/2014 Ex date - 04/22/2015

USA RESTAURANT FDG INC (NV)
Name changed to Chron Organization, Inc. and Common $0.001 par reclassified as Class A Common $0.001 par 03/24/2016
Chron Organization, Inc. name changed to Zenergy Brands, Inc. 12/01/2017

USA SIGNAL TECHNOLOGY INC (NV)
Each share old Common $0.0004 par exchanged for (0.01) share new Common $0.0004 par 04/18/2007
Name changed to Icon Media Holdings, Inc. 06/10/2011

USA SPORTS GROUP INC (DE)
Name changed to Collectible Concepts Group Inc. 06/29/1999
(See Collectible Concepts Group Inc.)

USA SUNRISE BEVERAGES INC (SD)
Name changed to Advanced ID Corp. (SD) 11/26/2002
Advanced ID Corp. (SD) reincorporated in Nevada 05/26/2006
(See Advanced ID Corp.)

USA SUPERIOR ENERGY HLDGS INC (NV)
Recapitalized as Xsilent Solutions Inc. 06/23/2014
Each share Common $0.001 par exchanged (0.004) share Common $0.0001 par
Xsilent Solutions Inc. name changed to Saxon Capital Group Inc. 06/05/2015

USA SYNTHETIC FUEL CORP (DE)
Chapter 11 bankruptcy proceedings converted to Chapter 7 on 09/25/2015
Stockholders' equity unlikely

USA TALKS COM INC (NV)
Old Common $0.001 par split (4) for (1) by issuance of (3) additional shares payable 02/05/1999 to holders of record 02/01/1999
Each share old Common $0.001 par exchanged for (0.000025) share new Common $0.001 par 10/7/2002
Charter permanently revoked 12/31/2009

USA TELCOM INTERNATIONALE (NV)
Name changed to ZannWell, Inc. 06/30/2004
ZannWell, Inc. recapitalized as BlackHawk Fund 01/03/2005 which recapitalized as Vidable, Inc. 07/01/2011 which recapitalized as Vibe I, Inc. 08/03/2015 which name changed to Coresource Strategies, Inc. (NV) 10/26/2015 which reincorporated in Oklahoma as NUGL, Inc. 12/11/2017

USA THERAPY INC (NV)
Name changed to China Printing & Packaging, Inc. 11/30/2010
(See China Printing & Packaging, Inc.)

USA VIDEO INTERACTIVE CORP (WY)
Reorganized 02/23/1995
Reorganized from USA Video Corp. (AB) to under the laws of Wyoming as USA Video Interactive Corp. 02/23/1995
Each share Common no par exchanged for (0.2) share Common no par
Recapitalized as Oculus VisionTech Inc. 01/26/2012
Each (15) shares Common no par exchanged for (1) share Common no par

USA WASTE SVCS INC (DE)
Reincorporated 6/30/95
State of incorporation changed from (OK) to (DE) 6/30/95
Merged into Waste Management, Inc. 7/16/98
Each share Common 1¢ par exchanged for (1) share Common $1 par

USAA CAP GROWTH FD INC (TX)
Reorganized under the laws of Maryland as USAA Mutual Fund, Inc., Growth Fund 02/02/1981
(See USAA Mutual Fund, Inc.)

USAA INCOME FD INC (TX)
Reorganized under the laws of Maryland as USAA Mutual Fund, Inc., Income Fund 02/02/1981
(See USAA Mutual Fund, Inc.)

USAA INCOME PPTYS PARTNERSHIP (DE)
Merged into American Industrial Properties REIT 1/20/98
Each Unit of Ltd. Partnership Int. III exchanged for (16.6) new Shares of Bene. Int. 10¢ par
Each Unit of Ltd. Partnership Int. IV exchanged for (15.14) new Shares of Bene. Int. 10¢ par
(See American Industrial Properties REIT)

USAA INVT TR (MA)
Merged into USAA Mutual Funds Trust 07/31/2006
Details not available

USAA MUT FD INC (MD)
Sunbelt Era Fund name changed to Aggressive Growth Fund 01/31/1989
Merged into USAA Mutual Funds Trust 07/31/2006
Details not available

USAA REAL ESTATE INCOME INVTS LTD (TX)
Merged into American Industrial Properties REIT 1/20/98
Each Unit of Ltd. Partnership Int. 1 exchanged for (15.9) new Shares of Bene. Int. 10¢ par
Each Unit of Ltd. Partnership Int. 2 exchanged for (28.63) new Shares of Bene. Int. 10¢ par
(See American Industrial Properties REIT)

USAA ST TAX FREE TR (DE)
Merged into USAA Mutual Funds Trust 07/31/2006
Details not available

USAA TAX EXEMPT FD INC (MD)
Merged into USAA Mutual Funds Trust 07/31/2006
Details not available

USABANCSHARES COM INC (PA)
Name changed 5/13/99
Name changed 9/17/99
Common $1 par split (4) for (3) by issuance of (1/3) additional share payable 7/18/97 to holders of record 7/1/97
Common $1 par split (4) for (3) by issuance of (1/3) additional share payable 8/17/98 to holders of record 8/3/98
Name changed from USABancshares, Inc. to USABANC.Com 5/13/99
Common $1 par split (2) for (1) by issuance of (1) additional share payable 6/15/99 to holders of record 6/1/99
Name changed from USABANC.COM to USABancShares.com Inc. 9/17/99
Merged into Berkshire Financial Holdings, Inc. 11/1/2002
Each share Common 1¢ par exchanged for $0.60 cash

USABG CORP (DE)
Each share old Common $0.001 par exchanged for (0.25) share new Common $0.001 par 08/03/1998
Charter cancelled and declared inoperative and void for non-payment of taxes 03/01/2000

USACAFES (NV)
Assets transferred to USACafes, L.P. 12/31/86
Each share Common 10¢ par exchanged for (1) Unit of Ltd. Partnership
USACafes, L.P. name changed to Cafes One, L.P. 10/25/89
(See Cafes One L.P.)

USACAFES L P (DE)
Name changed to Cafes One, L.P. 10/25/89
(See Cafes One, L.P.)

USAMERIBANCORP INC (FL)
Merged into Valley National Bancorp 01/01/2018
Each share Common 1¢ par exchanged for (6.1) shares Common no par

USANA INC (UT)
Common no par split (2) for (1) by issuance of (1) additional share payable 08/03/1998 to holders of record 07/31/1998
Name changed to USANA Health Sciences, Inc. and Common no par changed to $0.001 par 06/28/2000

USAONESTAR NET INC (NV)
Name changed to Palladium Communications, Inc. 12/25/2001
Palladium Communications, Inc. name changed to Peak Entertainment Holdings, Inc. 05/20/2003 which name changed to Encore Energy Systems, Inc. 08/20/2007
(See Encore Energy Systems, Inc.)

USASIA INTL PUBNS INC (DE)
Name changed to NJS Acquisition Corp. 12/07/1995
NJS Acquisition Corp. name changed to KIWI Holdings Inc. 11/21/1997 name changed to Chariot International Holdings Inc. 04/30/1999
(See Chariot International Holdings Inc.)

USASURANCE GROUP INC (CO)
Settled lawsuit with Federal Trade Commission 01/29/2001
Stockholders' equity unlikely

USAT FIN II INC (DE)
Auction Market Preferred no par called for redemption 10/05/1988
Public interest eliminated

USAT FIN III INC (DE)
Auction Market Preferred no par called for redemption 08/31/1988
Public interest eliminated

USB CAP II (DE)
Issue Information - 14,000,000 TR ORIGINATED PFD SECS 7.20% offered at $25 per share on 02/17/1998
7.20% Trust Originated Preferred Securities called for redemption at $25 on 4/1/2003

USB CAP III (DE)
Issue Information - $700,000,000 TR PFD SECS 7.75% offered at $25 per share on 08/10/1999
7.75% Trust Preferred Securities called for redemption at $25 on 5/4/2006

USB CAP IV (DE)
7.35% Guaranteed Trust Preferred Securities called for redemption at $25 on 12/28/2006

USB CAP V (DE)
7.25% Guaranteed Trust Preferred Securities called for redemption at $25 on 12/28/2006

USB CAP VI (DE)
5.75% Trust Preferred Securities called for redemption at $25 on 09/08/2011

USB CAP VII (DE)
5.875% Trust Preferred Securities called for redemption at $25 on 09/08/2011

USB CAP VIII (DE)
6.35% Trust Preferred Securities called for redemption at $25 on 02/22/2012

USB CAP X (DE)
6.50% Trust Preferred Securities called for redemption at $25 on 02/22/2012

USB CAP XI (DE)
6.60% Guaranteed Trust Preferred Securities called for redemption at $25 on 05/18/2012

USB CAP XII (DE)
6.30% Guaranteed Trust Preferred Securities called for redemption at $25 on 05/18/2012

USBANCORP CAP TR I (DE)
Name changed to Ameriserv Financial Capital Trust I 05/07/2001

USBANCORP INC (PA)
$2.125 Preferred Ser. A no par called for redemption 04/07/1993
Common $2.50 par split (3) for (1) by issuance of (2) additional shares payable 07/31/1998 to holders of record 07/16/1998
Each share Common $2.50 par received distribution of (0.5) share Three Rivers Bancorp Common 1¢ par payable 04/01/2000 to holders of record 03/24/2000
Stock Dividend - 100% 05/15/1986
Name changed to AmeriServ Financial, Inc. 05/07/2001

USC INC (NJ)
Name changed to Asset Growth Partners Inc. 8/14/87
Asset Growth Partners Inc. name changed to AGP & Co. Inc. 12/10/90
(See AGP & Co. Inc.)

USCANA OILS LTD. (BC)
Acquired by Prosper Oils Ltd. on a (1) for (5) basis 00/00/1955
Prosper Oils Ltd. name changed to Prosper Oils & Mines Ltd. 11/29/1965 which name changed to Southern Pacific Petroleum Ltd. 08/11/1969 which recapitalized as Sonic-Ray Resources Ltd. 05/01/1972 which recapitalized as Stryker Resources Ltd. 09/25/1979 which recapitalized as Stryker Ventures Corp. 08/25/1997
(See Stryker Ventures Corp.)

USCF ETF TR (DE)
Trust terminated 10/20/2017
Each share Restaurant Leaders Fund no par received $1.68792994 cash
Each share Stock Split Index Fund no par received $1.28370105 cash

USCHINA CHANNEL INC (NV)
Name changed to China Education International, Inc. 06/01/2011

USCHINA TAIWAN INC (NV)
Name changed to RadTek, Inc. 04/10/2013

USCI INC (DE)
SEC revoked common stock registration 06/18/2008

USCS INTL INC (DE)
Merged into DST Systems, Inc. 12/21/1998
Each share Common 5¢ par exchanged for (0.62) share Common 1¢ par
(See DST Systems, Inc.)

USD ENERGY CORP (NV)
Name changed to Casablanca Mining Ltd. 02/17/2011

USDATA CORP (DE)
Each share old Common 1¢ par exchanged for (0.2) share new Common 1¢ par 08/21/2001
Company terminated registration of

common stock and is no longer public as of 06/18/2003

USEC INC (DE)
Each share old Common 10¢ par exchanged for (0.04) share new Common 10¢ par 07/02/2013
Reorganized as Centrus Energy Corp. 09/30/2014
Each share new Common 10¢ par exchanged for approximately (0.0917) share Class A Common 10¢ par

USED KAR PTS INC (FL)
Common $0.001 par changed to $0.0001 par and (110) additional shares issued payable 07/26/2004 to holders of record 07/23/2004
Ex date - 07/27/2004
Name changed to Xenomics, Inc. (FL) 07/27/2004
Xenomics, Inc. (FL) reincorporated in Delaware as TrovaGene, Inc. 03/01/2010

USENCO INC (NV)
Name changed to Arch Petroleum, Inc. (NV) 06/01/1988
Arch Petroleum, Inc. (NV) reincorporated initial distribution 12/31/1991 which merged into Pogo Producing Co. 08/14/1998 which merged into Plains Exploration & Production Co. 11/06/2007 which merged into Freeport-McMoRan Copper & Gold Inc. 05/31/2013

USER FRIENDLY MEDIA INC (BC)
Name changed to UFM Ventures Ltd. 03/04/2004
UFM Ventures Ltd. name changed to Uracan Resources Ltd. 08/03/2006 which recapitalized as Vanadian Energy Corp. 10/05/2018

USF CORP (DE)
Merged into Yellow Roadway Corp. 5/24/2005
Each share Common 1¢ par exchanged for (0.31584) share Common 1¢ par and $29.25 cash
Yellow Roadway Corp. name changed to YRC Worldwide Inc. 1/4/2006

USF INVS (GA)
Name changed to Independence Mortgage Trust 09/28/1973
Independence Mortgage Trust reorganized as Independence Holding Co. (Old) 12/31/1980 which name changed to Stamford Capital Group, Inc. 11/04/1987 which name changed to Independence Holding Co. (New) 09/10/1990

USF LIQUIDATING CORP. (DE)
Liquidation completed
Each share Common 10¢ par received initial distribution of $5.382 cash 1/4/78
Each share Common 10¢ par received second distribution of $2.75 cash 5/15/78
Each share Common 10¢ par received third distribution of $1.75 cash 8/14/78
Each share Common 10¢ par received fourth distribution of $3.75 cash 11/20/78
Each share Common 10¢ par received fifth distribution of $4 cash 2/14/79
Each share Common 10¢ par received sixth distribution of $1.50 cash 8/14/79
Each share Common 10¢ par received seventh distribution of $1.55 cash 2/14/80
Each share Common 10¢ par received eighth distribution of $0.75 cash 8/14/80
Each share Common 10¢ par received ninth distribution of $0.70 cash 2/15/81
Each share Common 10¢ par received tenth distribution of $4 cash 8/14/81

Each share Common 10¢ par received eleventh distribution of $0.60 cash 2/16/82
Each share Common 10¢ par received twelfth distribution of $0.40 cash 8/16/82
Each share Common 10¢ par received thirteenth distribution of $0.35 cash 11/15/82
Assets transferred to USF Liquidating Trust 12/31/82
(See USF Liqudating Trust)

USF LIQUIDATING TRUST (DE)
Liquidation completed
Each Share of Bene. Int. 10¢ par received initial distribution of $1.50 cash 4/30/85
Each Share of Bene. Int. 10¢ par received second and final distribution of $0.375 cash 9/15/85
Note: Certificates were not required to be surrendered and are now valueless

USF&G CORP (MD)
Common $2.50 par split (2) for (1) by issuance of (1) additional share 06/12/1984
$5 Conv. Preferred Ser. C $50 par called for redemption 02/24/1995
$10.25 Conv. Preferred Ser. B $50 par called for redemption 11/10/1995
$4.10 Conv. Exchangeable Preferred Ser. A $50 par called for redemption 04/14/1997
Merged into St. Paul Companies, Inc. 04/24/1998
Each share Common $2.50 par exchanged for (0.2821) share Common no par
St. Paul Companies, Inc. name changed to St. Paul Travelers Companies, Inc. 04/01/2004 which name changed to Travelers Companies, Inc. 02/27/2007

USF&G MONEY MKT FDS INC (MD)
Dissolved 00/00/1997
Details not available

USF&G PACHOLDER FD INC (MD)
Name changed to Pacholder Fund, Inc. 08/24/1998
Pacholder Fund, Inc. name changed to Pacholder High Yield Fund, Inc. 11/18/1999
(See Pacholder High Yield Fund, Inc.)

USF&G TAX EXEMPT MONEY MKT FDS INC (MD)
Dissolved 00/00/1997
Details not available

USFREIGHTWAYS CORP (DE)
Name changed to USF Corp. 5/2/2003
USF Corp. merged into Yellow Roadway Corp. 5/24/2005 which name changed to YRC Worldwide Inc. 1/4/2006

USG CORP (DE)
Common $4 par split (2) for (1) by issuance of (1) additional share 03/18/1985
Common $4 par split (2) for (1) by issuance of (1) additional share 06/23/1986
$1.80 Conv. Preferred $1 par called for redemption 06/23/1988
Each share Common $4 par exchanged for $5 principal amount of 16% 5-year Jr. Subordinated Debentures due 07/15/2008, (1) share Common 10¢ par and $37 cash 07/13/1988
Preferred Stock Purchase Rights declared for Common stockholders of record 05/00/1993 were redeemed at $0.01 per right 05/01/1998 to holders of record 04/15/1998
(Additional Information in Active)

USHA BELTRON LTD (INDIA)
Name changed to Usha Martin, Ltd. 7/22/2003

USHA MARTIN ED & SOLUTIONS LTD (INDIA)
Name changed 07/14/2010
Name changed from Usha Martin Infotech Ltd. to Usha Martin Education & Solutions Ltd. 07/14/2010
GDR agreement terminated 10/17/2017
Each Reg. S GDR for Ordinary exchanged for (1) share Ordinary
Note: Unexchanged GDR's will be sold and the proceeds, if any, held for claim after 10/21/2017

USHEALTH GROUP INC (DE)
Merged into CAA Acquisition Corp. 10/18/2005
Each share Common 1¢ par exchanged for $0.31 cash

USI COMMUNICATIONS INC (NV)
Each share old Common $0.001 par exchanged for (0.01) share new Common $0.001 par 09/22/1999
Recapitalized as Square Shooter Inc. 06/12/2002
Each share new Common $0.001 par exchanged for (0.22222222) share Common $0.001 par
Square Shooter Inc. recapitalized as VisiTrade, Inc. 12/07/2006 which recapitalized as BlackBox SemiConductor, Inc. 01/19/2011 which name changed to Vision Dynamics Corp. 01/16/2013 which recapitalized as Secured Technology Innovations Corp. 02/14/2014

USI HLDGS CORP (DE)
Name changed 5/26/2005
Issue Information - 9,000,000 shares COM offered at $10 per share on 10/21/2002
Name changed from U.S.I. Holdings Corp. to USI Holdings Corp. 5/26/2005
Merged into Compass Acquisition Holdings Corp. 5/4/2007
Each share Common 1¢ par exchanged for $17 cash

USINTERNETWORKING INC (DE)
Issue Information - 6,000,000 shares COM offered at $21 per share on 04/08/1999
Common $0.001 par split (3) for (2) by issuance of (0.5) additional share payable 12/17/99 to holders of record 12/3/99
Common $0.001 par split (3) for (2) by issuance of (0.5) additional share payable 3/28/2000 to holders of record 3/14/2000
Plan of reorganization under Chapter 11 Federal Bankruptcy Code effective 5/22/2002
No stockholders' equity

USIP COM INC (NV)
Reincorporated 09/09/2005
State of incorporation changed from (UT) to (NV) and Common 1¢ par changed to $0.0001 par 09/09/2005
Recapitalized as Eastern Environment Solutions, Corp. 12/28/2006
Each share Common $0.0001 par exchanged for (0.00605657) share Common $0.0001 par
Eastern Environment Solutions, Corp. recapitalized as Precicion Trim, Inc. 09/20/2016

USL SVGS INSTNS INS GROUP LTD (DE)
Name changed to Financial Institutions Insurance Group Ltd. in June 1990
(See Financial Institutions Insurance Group Ltd.)

USLAB COM INC (NV)
Name changed to Fly Networks Inc. 09/15/2000
Fly Networks Inc. name changed to InterCommerceCorp 12/15/2003 which recapitalized as CipherPass Corp. 06/06/2005 which recapitalized as Javalon Technology Group, Inc. (NV) 09/06/2007 which reincorporated in British Virgin Islands as WorldVest Equity, Inc. 11/13/2008

USLD COMMUNICATIONS CORP (DE)
Merged into LCI International Inc. 12/22/1997
Each share Common 1¢ par exchanged for (0.7576) share Common 1¢ par
LCI International Inc. merged into Qwest Communications International Inc. 06/05/1998 which merged into CenturyLink, Inc. 04/01/2011

USLICO CORP (DC)
Common $1 par split (3) for (2) by issuance of (0.5) additional share 3/15/85
Merged into NWNL Companies, Inc. 1/17/95
Each share Common $1 par exchanged for (0.69) share Common no par
NWNL Companies, Inc. name changed to ReliaStar Financial Corp. 2/13/95
(See ReliaStar Financial Corp.)

USLIFE CORP (NY)
Common $2 par changed to $1 par and (1) additional share issued 06/19/1973
$2.25 Conv. Preferred Ser. D $1 par called for redemption 03/28/1985
$3.33 Preferred Ser. C $1 par called for redemption 09/01/1992
Common $1 par split (3) for (2) by issuance of (0.5) additional share 12/22/1992
Common $1 par split (3) for (2) by issuance of (0.5) additional share 09/22/1995
$4.50 Conv. Preferred Ser. A $1 par called for redemption at $100 plus $0.87 accrued dividends on 05/09/1997
$5 Conv. Preferred Ser. A $1 par called for redemption at $100 plus $0.96 accrued dividends on 05/09/1997
Merged into American General Corp. 06/17/1997
Each share Common $1 par exchanged for (1.1069) shares Common 50¢ par
American General Corp. merged into American International Group, Inc. 08/29/2001

USLIFE HLDG CORP (NY)
Capital Stock $2 par reclassified as Common $2 par 11/24/1967
Name changed to USLIFE Corp. and $4.50 Conv. Preferred Ser. A no par and $5 Conv. Preferred Ser. B no par changed to $1 par 05/22/1970
USLIFE Corp. merged into American General Corp. 06/17/1997 which merged into American International Group, Inc. 08/29/2001

USLIFE INCOME FD INC (MD)
Name changed to Boulder Growth & Income Fund, Inc. 4/29/2002

USLIFE SAVINGS & LOAN ASSOCIATION (CA)
Each share old Guarantee Stock $1 par exchanged for (0.0005) share new Guarantee Stock $1 par 09/01/1976
Note: In effect holders received $16 cash per share and public interest was eliminated

USM CORP (NJ)
Common $25 par changed to $12.50 par and (1) additional share issued 08/23/1968
Recapitalized 02/02/1971
Each share Common $12.50 par stamped to indicate reduction in amount to (0.84) share Common $12.50 par and distribution of (1)

share Transamerican Shoe Machinery Corp. Common 75¢ par Holder had option to advise exchange agent not to release Transamerican Shoe Machinery Corp. shares but to wait until merger into Katy Industries, Inc. was effective and then issue proportionate number of Katy Industries, Inc. shares
(See Transamerican Shoe Machinery Corp.)
Merged into Emhart Corp. (VA) 05/04/1976
Each share $2.10 Conv. Preference no par exchanged for (1) share $2.10 Conv. Preference no par
Each share 6% Preferred $25 par exchanged for (1.15) shares Common $1 par
Each share stamped Common $12.50 par exchanged for (1.125) shares Common $1 par
(See Emhart Corp. (VA))

USM OIL CO (TX)
Common $10 par changed to no par and (9) additional shares issued 2/15/66
Name changed to Olix Industries Inc. 4/21/71
Olix Industries Inc. merged into Adobe Oil & Gas Corp. 7/22/81 which merged into Adobe Resources Corp. 10/31/85 which merged into Santa Fe Energy Resources, Inc. 5/19/92 which name changed to Santa Fe Snyder Corp. 5/5/99 which merged into Devon Energy Corp. (New) 8/29/2000

USMART MOBILE DEVICE INC (DE)
Name changed to Eagle Mountain Corp. 05/06/2015

USMD HLDGS INC (DE)
Acquired by WellMed Medical Management, Inc. 09/30/2016
Each share Common 1¢ par exchanged for $22.34 cash

USMX INC (DE)
Merged into Dakota Mining Corp. 05/29/1997
Each share Common $0.001 par exchanged for (0.90909090) share Common no par
(See Dakota Mining Corp.)

USN COMMUNICATIONS INC (DE)
Plan of reorganization under Chapter 11 Federal Bankruptcy Code effective 04/04/2000
No stockholders' equity

USN CORP (CO)
Class A Common $0.002 par reclassified as Common $0.0001 par 03/15/2006
Reorganized under the laws of Delaware as Holdings US, Inc. 03/30/2012
Each share Common $0.0001 par exchanged for (0.02857142) share Common $0.0001 par
Holdings US, Inc. name changed to California Style Palms, Inc. 09/25/2013

USOL HLDGS INC (OR)
Administratively dissolved 02/24/2006

USP REAL ESTATE INVT TR (IA)
Liquidation completed
Each Share of Bene. Int. $1 par received initial distribution of $6.83 cash payable 6/15/2000 to holders of record 6/15/2000
Each Share of Bene. Int. $1 par received second and final distribution of $0.06816 cash payable 8/31/2001 to holders of record 8/31/2001

USPAC CORP. (DE)
Liquidation completed
Each share Common 10¢ par exchanged for initial distribution of (0.0208333) share Koppers Co., Inc. Common $10 par 04/15/1965
Each share Common 10¢ par received second distribution of (0.0208333) share Koppers Co., Inc. Common $10 par 06/07/1965
Each share Common 10¢ par received third distribution of (0.041666) share Koppers Co., Inc. Common $10 par 09/01/1965
Each share Common 10¢ par received fourth and final distribution of (0.0256272) share Koppers Co., Inc. Common $10 par 03/15/1966

USPCI INC (DE)
Common 10¢ par split (3) for (2) by issuance of (0.5) additional share 02/28/1985
Common 10¢ par split (3) for (2) by issuance of (0.5) additional share 12/19/1986
Common 10¢ par split (3) for (2) by issuance of (0.5) additional share 07/15/1987
Merged into Union Pacific Corp. 06/30/1988
Each share Common 10¢ par exchanged for $28 cash

USR HLDGS CO (CO)
Each share old Common $0.001 par exchanged for (0.0025) share new Common $0.001 par 12/19/2001
Name changed to Technol Fuel Conditioners Inc. (CO) 01/31/2002
Technol Fuel Conditioners Inc. (CO) reorganized in Florida as Allied Energy Group, Inc. 08/18/2006 which name changed to Allied Energy, Inc. 04/22/2010

USR INDS INC (DE)
SEC revoked common stock registration 08/19/2010

USR TECHNOLOGY INC (NV)
Each share old Common $0.001 par exchanged for (0.33333333) share new Common $0.001 par 09/17/2008
Recapitalized as Ecologic Transportation, Inc. 06/11/2009
Each share Common $0.001 par exchanged for (0.5) share Common $0.001 par
Ecologic Transportation, Inc. recapitalized as Peartrack Security Systems, Inc. 10/17/2014

USSPI MEDIA INC (DE)
Completely liquidated 01/04/2016
Each share Common 1¢ par exchanged for first and final distribution of $0.3055 cash

UST CORP (MA)
Common $1.25 par changed to $0.625 par and (1) additional share issued 05/19/1983
Common $0.625 par split (3) for (2) by issuance of (0.5) additional share 01/15/1986
Common $0.625 par split (2) for (1) by issuance of (1) additional share 01/15/1987
Merged into Citizens Acquisition Corp. 01/11/2000
Each share Common $0.625 par exchanged for $32 cash

UST INC (DE)
Common 50¢ par split (2) for (1) by issuance of (1) additional share 01/27/1989
Common 50¢ par split (2) for (1) by issuance of (1) additional share 01/27/1992
Merged into Altria Group, Inc. 01/06/2009
Each share Common 50¢ par exchanged for $69.50 cash

USTEL INC (MN)
Chapter 11 bankruptcy proceedings converted to Chapter 7 on 11/22/2002
No stockholders' equity

USTELEMATICS INC (DE)
SEC revoked common stock registration 03/01/2012

USTMAN TECHNOLOGIES INC (CA)
Plan of liquidation approved 09/21/2000
No stockholders' equity

USTS, INC. (DC)
Assets sold for benefit of creditors 12/14/1973
No stockholders' equity

USURF AMER INC (NV)
Name changed to Cardinal Communications, Inc. 06/24/2005
(See Cardinal Communications, Inc.)

USV INTL INVT CORP (BC)
Struck off register and declared dissolved for failure to file returns 11/13/1992

USV TELEMANAGEMENT INC (BC)
Reorganized under the laws of Canada as E*Comnetrix Inc. 06/19/2000
Each share Common no par exchanged for (1) share Common no par
E*Comnetrix Inc. name changed to Moving Bytes Inc. 07/29/2002 which recapitalized as China International Enterprises Inc. (Canada) 03/23/2006 which reincorporated in Delaware as China Software Technology Group Co., Ltd. 11/16/2006 which recapitalized as American Wenshen Steel Group, Inc. 10/12/2007
(See American Wenshen Steel Group, Inc.)

USWEB CORP (DE)
Merged into Whittman-Hart, Inc. 03/01/2000
Each share Common $0.001 par exchanged for (0.865) share Common $0.001 par
Whittman-Hart, Inc. name changed to Marchfirst Inc. 03/23/2000
(See Marchfirst Inc.)

USX CAP TR I (DE)
6.75% Conv. Quarterly Income Preferred Securities called for redemption at $50 plus $0.01875 accrued dividends on 01/02/2002

USX CAPITAL LLC (TURKS & CAICOS ISLANDS)
8.75% Monthly Income Preferred Ser. A $1 par called for redemption at $25 plus $0.18 accrued dividends on 12/31/2001

USX-DELHI GROUP (DE)
Common $1 par called for redemption at $20.60 on 01/26/1998
Public interest eliminated

USX MARATHON GROUP (DE)
Reorganized 05/06/1991
Money Market Preferred Ser. A no par called for redemption 05/28/1987
$2.25 Conv. Exchangeable Preferred no par called for redemption 07/15/1987
$10.75 Preferred no par called for redemption 09/15/1988
Each share $3.50 Conv. Exchangeable Preference no par exchanged for $50 principal amount of 7% Conv. Subordinated Debentures due 06/15/2017 on 12/15/1989
Reorganized from USX Corp to USX-Marathon Group Inc. 05/06/1991
Common $1 par automatically became (1) share USX-Marathon Group Inc. Common $1 par 05/06/1991
Each share Common $1 par received distribution of (0.2) share USX-U.S. Steel Group Common $1 par 05/06/1991
6.5% Conv. Preferred no par called for redemption at $50 on 12/31/2001

USX-MARATHON GROUP INC.
Adjustable Rate Preferred no par called for redemption 09/29/1995
Each Debt Equity Convertible Security exchanged for (1) share RTI International Metals, Inc. Common 1¢ par 02/01/2000
(See RTI International Metals, Inc.)
Name changed to Marathon Oil Corp. 12/31/2001

USX-U S STL GROUP (DE)
Reorganized as United States Steel Corp. (New) 12/31/2001
Each share Common $1 par exchanged for (1) share Common $1 par

UTACO URANIUM, INC. (UT)
Charter suspended for failure to pay taxes 10/15/1958

UTACO URANIUM INC. (NV)
Charter revoked for failure to file reports and pay fees 03/03/1958

UTAH APEX MINING CO.
Merged into National Tunnel & Mines Co. 00/00/1937
Details not available

UTAH APEX URANIUM CO. (UT)
Name changed to Apex Mining & Industrial Co. 01/22/1969
Apex Mining & Industrial Co. merged into Conix Western, Inc. 12/27/1972
(See Conix Western, Inc.)

UTAH ARTIST GUILD, INC. (UT)
Recapitalized as Organized Producing Energy Corp. 07/15/1983
Each share Capital Stock $0.001 par exchanged for (0.33333333) share Capital Stock $0.001 par
(See Organized Producing Energy Corp.)

UTAH BANCORPORATION (UT)
Common no par split (3) for (2) by issuance of (0.5) additional share 07/15/1978
Name changed to Valley Utah Bancorporation 05/14/1985
Valley Utah Bancorporation acquired by Valley National Corp. 05/18/1987 which merged into Banc One Corp. 03/31/1993 which merged into Bank One Corp. 10/02/1998 which merged into J.P. Morgan Chase & Co. 12/31/2000 which name changed to JPMorgan Chase & Co. 07/20/2004

UTAH CLAY TECHNOLOGY, INC. (UT)
Recapitalized as NeWave, Inc. 02/09/2004
Each share Common $0.001 par exchanged for (344.33) shares Common $0.001 par
NeWave, Inc. name changed to Commerce Planet, Inc. 06/22/2006

UTAH COAL & CHEMS CORP (NV)
Reincorporated 04/16/1979
State of incorporation changed from (CO) to (NV) 04/16/1979
Each share Common 5¢ par exchanged for (0.1) share new Common 10¢ par 11/11/1987
Recapitalized as Lifestream Technologies Inc. 02/11/1994
Each share new Common 10¢ par exchanged for (0.25) share Common 10¢ par
(See Lifestream Technologies Inc.)

UTAH CONCRETE PIPE CO (UT)
Name changed to Amcor, Inc. and Common $1 par changed to 50¢ par 10/31/1970
Amcor, Inc. merged into Diversified Earth Sciences, Inc. 12/27/1972
(See Diversified Earth Sciences, Inc.)

UTAH CONS MNG & MLG CO (UT)
Reincorporated under the laws of Delaware as Copley Power, Inc. and Capital Stock 10¢ par reclassified as Common 10¢ par 09/07/1984

UTAH CONSTR & MNG CO (DE)
Stock Dividends - 100% 05/03/1963; 200% 02/14/1969
Name changed to Utah International Inc. 10/18/1971
Utah International Inc. merged into General Electric Co. 12/20/1976

UTAH CONSTRUCTION CO. (DE)
Stock Dividend - 100% 05/15/1957
Name changed to Utah Construction & Mining Co. 08/10/1959
Utah Construction & Mining Co. name changed to Utah International Inc. 10/18/1971 which merged into General Electric Co. 12/20/1976

UTAH CONSTRUCTION CO. (UT)
Each share Common $10 par exchanged for (5) shares Common $2 par 01/22/1954
Reincorporated under the laws of Delaware 01/31/1957
Utah Construction Co. (DE) name changed to Utah Construction & Mining Co. 08/10/1959 which name changed to Utah International Inc. 10/18/1971 which merged into General Electric Co. 12/20/1976

UTAH CORP. (UT)
Name changed to Utah Shale Land Corp. 10/18/1965
Utah Shale Land Corp. name changed to Industrial Resources, Inc. 11/09/1972 which name changed to NaTec Resources, Inc. 10/31/1989
(See NaTec Resources, Inc.)

UTAH DELAWARE MINING CO.
Merged into National Tunnel & Mines Co. 00/00/1937
Details not available

UTAH ELECTRONICS (CANADA) LTD.
Bankrupt 00/00/1951
Stockholders' equity unlikely

UTAH EQUITIES, INC. (UT)
Name changed to Chandler Oil & Gas Co. 08/29/1980
Chandler Oil & Gas Co. recapitalized as Pana Petrol Corp. 12/30/1985

UTAH FIRE CLAY CO. (UT)
Merged into Gladding, McBean & Co. 04/24/1961
Each share Common $10 par exchanged for (0.615) share Common $10 par
Gladding, McBean & Co. merged into International Pipe & Ceramics Corp. 09/27/1962 which name changed to Interpace Corp. 04/25/1968 which merged into Clevepak Corp. 08/15/1983
(See Clevepak Corp.)

UTAH FORTUNA GOLD CO. (UT)
Name changed to North American Research & Development Corp. 06/20/1967
(See North American Research & Development Corp.)

UTAH GAS & COKE CO.
Merged into Mountain Fuel Supply Co. (UT) 00/00/1935
Details not available

UTAH GAS & OIL CORP (UT)
Charter expired 12/31/1983

UTAH GAS SVC CO (UT)
Merged into Questar Corp. 07/12/2001
Details not available

UTAH HOME FIRE INS CO (UT)
Each share Capital Stock $100 par exchanged for (10) shares Capital Stock $10 par 00/00/1950
Stock Dividend - 25% 12/15/1952
99.07% owned as of 00/00/1982
Public interest eliminated

UTAH HYDRO CORP. (UT)
Name changed to Hydro Flame Corp. 6/5/65
(See Hydro Flame Corp.)

UTAH IDAHO CONS URANIUM INC (ID)
Each share old Common 10¢ par exchanged for (0.1) share new Common 10¢ par 11/18/2002
Reorganized under the laws of Nevada as IDGlobal Corp. 05/05/2006
Each share new Common 10¢ par exchanged for (0.1) share Common $0.001 par

UTAH-IDAHO EXPLORATION CO. (UT)
Recapitalized as Sitka Oil & Gas Exploration, Inc. (UT) 9/11/69
Each share Common 2¢ par exchanged for (0.166666) share Common no par
Sitka Oil & Gas Exploration, Inc. (UT) reincorporated in Texas as First Texas Financial, Inc. 9/28/70 which name changed to Triland, Inc. 7/18/72
(See Triland, Inc.)

UTAH-IDAHO PETROLEUM & MANUFACTURING CO.
Name changed to Odor-Ridd Corp. of America, Inc. 00/00/1953
Odor-Ridd Corp. of America, Inc. recapitalized as O & R Corp. 07/07/1972 which recapitalized as General Financial Industries, Inc. 12/29/1972 which name changed to Monarch Molybdenum & Resources, Inc. (Ctfs. dated prior to 03/07/1988) 09/14/1978 which recapitalized as Mediacom Communications, Inc. 03/07/1988 which name changed to Duraco Industries, Inc. 09/15/1990

UTAH IDAHO SUGAR CO (UT)
Recapitalized 00/00/1935
Each share 7% Preferred $10 par exchanged for (1.45) shares Preferred Ser. A no par
Preferred Ser. A no par called for redemption 04/01/1958
Common $6 par changed to $5 par
Name changed to U & I Inc. 09/17/1975
U & I Inc. name changed to UI Group, Inc. 08/22/1983
(See UI Group, Inc.)

UTAH INTL INC (DE)
Common $2 par split (2) for (1) by issuance of (1) additional share 05/07/1973
Merged into General Electric Co. 12/20/1976
Each share Common $2 par exchanged for (1.3) shares Common $2.50 par

UTAH LD & PPTY INC (UT)
Name changed to Allergy Control Inc. 02/14/1978

UTAH LIBRA CORP (UT)
Involuntarily dissolved 09/30/1980

UTAH METAL & TUNNEL CO.
Merged into National Tunnel & Mines Co. in 1944 which became bankrupt in 1948

UTAH MINING, MILLING & TRANSPORTATION CO. (ME)
Charter suspended for non-payment of taxes 00/00/1915

UTAH MOAB URANIUM CORP. (UT)
Charter suspended for failure to pay taxes 03/31/1958

UTAH NATIONAL URANIUM MINING CORP. (UT)
Merged into Sterling Uranium Corp. share for share 03/01/1955
Sterling Uranium Corp. recapitalized as Sterling Beryllium & Oil Co. 02/04/1958 which merged into Elgin Gas & Oil Co. 06/12/1959
(See Elgin Gas & Oil Co.)

UTAH NETWORKING SVCS INC. (NV)
Name changed to White Mountain Titanium Corp. 2/26/2004
Each share Common $0.001 par exchanged for (1) share Common $0.001 par

UTAH-NEW MEXICO GAS CO. (UT)
Merged into Diversified Minerals, Inc. on a (0.5) for (1) basis in March 1961
(See Diversified Minerals, Inc.)

UTAH OIL REFINING CO. (UT)
Acquired by Standard Oil Co. (Ind.) 8/8/56
Each share Common $5 par exchanged for (0.5) share Capital Stock $25 par
Standard Oil Co. (Ind.) name changed to Amoco Corp. 4/23/85

UTAH PA OIL CO (UT)
Common 25¢ par changed to 1¢ par 3/14/81
Involuntarily dissolved 7/1/89

UTAH PETROCHEMICAL CORP (UT)
Reincorporated under the laws of Delaware as Premier Technology, Inc. 1/28/85
Premier Technology, Inc. name changed to Premier Technology Holdings, Inc. 5/5/86
(See Premier Technology Holdings, Inc.)

UTAH PLATEAU URANIUM CORP. (UT)
Name changed to Wyoming Southern Resources 02/21/1969
(See Wyoming Southern Resources)

UTAH PWR & LT CO (UT)
Reincorporated 08/31/1976
$7 Preferred $100 par and $6 Preferred $100 par changed to no par 00/00/1927
Each share Common $100 par exchanged for (10) shares Common no par 00/00/1927
Each share $6 Preferred no par exchanged for (4.375) shares Common no par 00/00/1946
Each share $7 Preferred no par exchanged for (4.875) shares Common no par 00/00/1946
Common no par changed to $12.80 par and (1) additional share issued 10/18/1956
State of incorporation changed from (ME) to (UT) 08/31/1976
Common $12.80 par changed to $6.40 par and (1) additional share issued 06/20/1977
$2.80 Preferred Ser. G $25 par called for redemption 10/22/1986
$2.90 Preferred Ser. J $25 par called for redemption 10/22/1986
$2.04 Preferred Ser. H $25 par called for redemption 05/26/1987
$2.34 Preferred Ser. F $25 par called for redemption 05/26/1987
$2.36 Preferred Ser. I $25 par called for redemption 05/26/1987
Merged into PacifiCorp 01/09/1989
Each share $1.16 Preferred Ser. C $25 par exchanged for (1) share $1.16 Preferred Ser. C no par
Each share $1.18 Preferred Ser. B $25 par exchanged for (1) share $1.18 Preferred Ser. B no par
Each share $1.28 Preferred Ser. A $25 par exchanged for (1) share $1.28 Preferred Ser. A no par
Each share $1.76 Preferred Ser. D $25 par exchanged for (1) share $1.76 Preferred Ser. D no par
Each share $1.98 Preferred Ser. E $25 par exchanged for (1) share $1.98 Preferred Ser. E no par
Each share Common $6.40 par exchanged for (0.909) share Common $3.25 par
(See PacifiCorp)

UTAH PREMIER URANIUM CO. (UT)
Merged into Resource Ventures Corp. 2/28/56
Each share Common 1¢ par exchanged for (0.1) share Common $1 par
Resource Ventures Corp. merged into Petroleum Resources Corp. 6/30/65 which name changed to PRC Corp. 11/9/70 which name changed to CorTerra Corp. 11/28/72 which assets were transferred to CorTerra Corp. Liquidating Corp. 10/8/80
(See CorTerra Corp. Liquidating Corp.)

UTAH RADIO PRODUCTS CO.
Merged into International Detrola Corp. on a (0.6) for (1) basis in 1945
Name changed to Newport Steel Corp. in 1949

UTAH RES INTL INC (UT)
Each share old Common 10¢ par exchanged for (0.001) share new Common 10¢ par 03/17/1999
Each share new Common 10¢ par exchanged again for (0.002) share new Common 10¢ par 06/15/2004
Note: In effect holders received $10.50 cash per share and public interest was eliminated

UTAH SHALE LD & MINERALS CORP (DE)
Name changed to Geowaste Inc. 11/25/91
Geowaste Inc. merged into Superior Services Inc. 11/2/98

UTAH SHALE LD CORP (UT)
Name changed to Industrial Resources, Inc. 11/9/72
Industrial Resources, Inc. name changed to NaTec Resources, Inc. 10/31/89
(See NaTec Resources, Inc.)

UTAH SOUTHERN OIL CO. (UT)
Common $5 par changed to $2.50 par and $2.50 principal amount of 4% Notes paid 00/00/1948
Stock Dividend - 100% 12/30/1955
Liquidation completed
Each share Common $2.50 par exchanged for initial distribution of $15.50 cash 03/10/1960
Each share Common $2.50 par received second and final distribution of $0.50 cash 07/21/1960

UTAH STARTER MINING CO. (UT)
Merged into Durst (S.F.) & Co., Inc. 12/31/68
Each share Capital Stock 25¢ par exchanged for (1) share Common 25¢ par

UTAH URANIUM COALITION MINES CO (UT)
Recapitalized as Anderson Industries, Inc. (UT) 9/15/72
Each share Common 2¢ par exchanged for (0.1) share Common 2¢ par
Anderson Industries, Inc. (UT) name changed to Environ Corp. 12/14/74
(See Environ Corp.)

UTAH URANIUM CORP. (DE)
Acquired by Consolidated Uranium Mines, Inc. on a share for share basis in 1952
(See Consolidated Uranium Mines, Inc.)

UTAH URANIUM CORP (NV)
Name changed to Universal Potash Corp. 06/16/2008

UTAH VALLEY GAS & COKE CO.
Property sold in 1927

UTAH-VERNAL OIL & URANIUM CO. (UT)
Merged into Unified Uranium & Oil, Inc. 6/6/55
Each share Common 10¢ par

UTA-UTI

exchanged for (0.1) share Common 25¢ par
Unified Uranium & Oil, Inc. liquidated by exchange for Beef Industries, Inc. Common $1 par 12/30/69 which merged into Cyclone Entertainment, Ltd. 2/27/87
(See Cyclone Entertainment Ltd., Inc.)

UTAH-VERNAL OIL CO.
Name changed to Utah-Vernal Oil & Uranium Co. in 1953
Utah-Vernal Oil & Uranium Co. merged into Unified Uranium & Oil, Inc. 6/6/55 which liquidated by exchange for Beef Industries, Inc. Common $1 par 12/30/69 which merged into Cyclone Entertainment Ltd., Inc. 2/27/87
(See Cyclone Entertainment Ltd., Inc.)

UTAH WYO CONS OIL CO (UT)
Common $1 par changed to 10¢ par in 1945
Charter expired 8/26/87

UTAHCAN, INC. (WA)
Automatically dissolved for non-payment of license fees 7/1/63

UTAIR (RUSSIA)
ADR agreement terminated 04/20/2015
Each Sponsored ADR for Ordinary exchanged for $14.361885 cash

UTALK COMMUNICATIONS INC (NV)
Name changed to Lithium Corp. 10/01/2009

UTANA BASINS OIL CO. (UT)
Merged into Seneca Oil Co. 00/00/1954
Each (15) shares Common 1¢ par exchanged for (1) share Class A 50¢ par
(See Seneca Oil Co.)

UTC GROUP INC (NY)
Stock Dividend - 50% 09/05/1980
Name changed to Coradian Corp. 01/02/1981
(See Coradian Corp.)

UTCO URANIUM CORP. (CO)
Recapitalized as Delta Corp. 10/23/61
Each share Common 1¢ par exchanged for (0.05) share Common 20¢ par
Delta Corp. name changed to A.I.D. Inc. (CO) 12/29/72
(See A.I.D. Inc.)

UTE GOLD MINING CO. (CO)
Declared defunct and inoperative for failure to file reports and pay taxes 10/10/35

UTE MTN CORP (CO)
Name changed to Utex, Inc. 11/09/1973
(See Utex, Inc.)

UTE PRODTN CO (UT)
Proclaimed dissolved for failure to pay taxes 12/31/1986

UTE ROYALTY CORP. (UT)
Merged into Texota Oil Co. share for share 10/31/1955
Texota Oil Co. name changed to North America Resources Corp. 12/15/1968

UTE URANIUM INC (CO)
Recapitalized as Geonics, Inc. 02/24/1969
Each share Common 1¢ par exchanged for (0.01) share Capital Stock 1¢ par
Geonics, Inc. name changed to Variegate Properties, Inc. 02/13/1979 which name changed to Applied Solar Technologies, Inc. 09/21/1981
(See Applied Solar Technologies, Inc.)

UTEC INC (NV)
Name changed to Tiger Oil & Energy, Inc. 09/23/2010

UTEK CORP (DE)
Name changed to Innovaro Inc. 03/16/2010

UTEX, INC. (CO)
Merged into U, Inc. in December 1975
Each share Capital Stock $1 par exchanged for $0.001 cash

UTI BANK LTD (INDIA)
Name changed to Axis Bank Ltd. 07/30/2007

UTI ENERGY CORP (DE)
Common $0.001 par split (3) for (1) by issuance of (2) additional shares payable 09/05/1997 to holders of record 08/25/1997 Ex date - 09/08/1997
Common $0.001 par split (2) for (1) by issuance of (1) additional share payable 10/03/2000 to holders of record 09/25/2000 Ex date - 10/04/2000
Merged into Patterson-UTI Energy, Inc. 05/09/2001
Each share Common $0.001 par exchanged for (1) share Common 1¢ par

UTI WORLDWIDE INC (BRITISH VIRGIN ISLANDS)
Ordinary no par split (3) for (1) by issuance of (2) additional shares payable 03/27/2006 to holders of record 03/17/2006 Ex date - 03/28/2006
Acquired by DSV A/S 01/22/2016
Each share Ordinary no par exchanged for $7.10 cash

UTICA, CHENANGO & SUSQUEHANNA VALLEY RAILWAY CO.
Merged into Delaware, Lackawanna & Western Railroad Co. through an exchange of $100 of bonds for each share Common in 1945

UTICA, CLINTON & BINGHAMTON RAILROAD CO.
Liquidation completed in 1943

UTICA & MOHAWK COTTON MILLS, INC.
Acquired by Stevens (J.P.) & Co., Inc. in 1952
Each share Common no par exchanged for (1) share Capital Stock $15 par
(See Stevens (J.P.) & Co., Inc.)

UTICA B.M.C., INC. (NY)
Merged into Dunham-Bush, Inc. 4/15/57
Each share Common $1 par exchanged for (0.25) share Common $2 par and $6 principal amount of 6% Debentures
Dunham-Bush, Inc. merged into Signal Oil & Gas Co. 12/29/67 which name changed to Signal Companies, Inc. 5/1/68 which merged into Allied-Signal Inc. 9/19/85 which name changed to AlliedSignal Inc. 4/26/93 which name changed to Honeywell International Inc. 12/1/99

UTICA BANKSHARES CORP (NV)
Each share Common $5.20833 par exchanged for (0.0025) share Common $2,083.332 par 9/3/86
Stock Dividend - 50% 5/2/78
Placed in receivership 7/20/89
No stockholders' equity

UTICA GAS & ELECTRIC CO.
Merged into Niagara Hudson Public Service Corp. and name changed to Central New York Power Corp. 7/31/37
Each share 7% and/or $6 Preferred exchanged for (1.05) shares 5% Preferred $100 par

Central New York Power Corp. merged into Niagara Mohawk Power Corp. 1/5/50

UTICA KNITTING CO. (NY)
Name changed to Flagg-Utica Corp. in 1952
Flagg-Utica Corp. merged into Genesco Inc. 1/2/65

UTICA MINES (1937) LTD. (BC)
Recapitalized as Utica Mines Ltd. (New) 12/23/60
Each share Capital Stock 50¢ par exchanged for (0.05) share Capital Stock $10 par

UTICA MINES LTD. OLD (BC)
Suceeded by Utica Mines (1937) Ltd. on a (1) for (3) basis in 1937
Utica Mines (1937) Ltd. recapitalized as Utica Mines Ltd. (New) 12/23/60 which recapitalized as Dankoe Mines Ltd. 9/25/71 which recapitalized as Emerald Dragon Mines Inc. 10/30/96
(See Emerald Dragon Mines Inc.)

UTICA MINES LTD NEW (BC)
Common $10 par changed to $1 par in February 1962
Common $1 par changed to no par in May 1964
Recapitalized as Dankoe Mines Ltd. 9/25/71
Each share Common no par exchanged for (0.2) share Common no par
Dankoe Mines Ltd. recapitalized as Emerald Dragon Mines Inc. 10/30/96
(See Emerald Dragon Mines Inc.)

UTICA NATL BK & TR (TULSA, OK)
Capital Stock $6.25 par changed to $5.208 par and (0.2) additional share issued 03/04/1975
Reorganized as Utica Bankshares Corp. 10/14/1975
Each share Capital Stock $5.208 par exchanged for (1) share Common $5.20833 par
(See Utica Bankshares Corp.)

UTICA SQUARE NATL BK (TULSA, OK)
Capital Stock $15 par changed to $10 par and (0.5) additional share issued 01/09/1962
Capital Stock $10 par changed to $6.25 par and (0.6) additional share issued 03/09/1965
Stock Dividend - 25% 01/20/1961
Name changed to Utica National Bank & Trust Co. (Tulsa, OK) 06/10/1971
Utica National Bank & Trust Co. (Tulsa, OK) reorganized as Utica Bankshares Corp. 10/14/1975
(See Utica Bankshares Corp.)

UTICA STEAM & MOHAWK VALLEY COTTON MILLS
Name changed to Utica & Mohawk Cotton Mills, Inc. in 1932
Utica & Mohawk Cotton Mills, Inc. acquired by Stevens (J.P.) & Co., Inc. in 1952
(See Stevens (J.P.) & Co., Inc.)

UTICA TRAN CORP (NY)
Liquidation completed
Each share Common no par exchanged for initial distribution of $10 cash 08/08/1967
Each share Common no par received second distribution of $2.50 cash 12/22/1967
Each share Common no par received third and final distribution of $2.25 cash 05/03/1968

UTICS CORP (NV)
Charter permanently revoked 12/31/2001

UTIDA URANIUM CO., INC. (ID)
Merged into Federal Uranium Corp. (NV) on a (1) for (13-1/3) basis 04/28/1955
Federal Uranium Corp. merged into

Federal Resources Corp. 05/02/1960

UTILICORE CORP (DE)
Name changed to Bezenet Inc. 02/08/2001
Bezenet Inc. recapitalized as Allarae Healthcare, Inc. 11/15/2007 which recapitalized as MP2 Technologies, Inc. 09/12/2008 which recapitalized as The Kiley Group, Inc. 11/03/2009

UTILICORP CAP L P (DE)
8.875% Monthly Income Preferred Securities Ser. A called for redemption at $25 on 6/18/2001

UTILICORP UTD INC (DE)
Reincorporated 04/01/1987
4.30% Preferred $100 par called for redemption 06/19/1986
5.52% Preferred $100 par called for redemption 06/19/1986
6.70% Preferred $100 par called for redemption 06/19/1986
State of incorporation changed from (MO) to (DE) 04/01/1987
$4.125 Preference no par called for redemption 06/01/1987
Common $1 par split (3) for (2) by issuance of (0.5) additional share 07/08/1987
$2.4375 Preference no par called for redemption 03/16/1992
$2.6125 Preference no par called for redemption 03/16/1992
$1.775 Conv. Preference no par called for redemption 05/26/1994
$2.05 Preferred no par called for redemption 03/01/1997
Common $1 par split (3) for (2) by issuance of (0.5) additional share payable 03/12/1999 to holders of record 02/22/1999 Ex date - 03/15/1999
Name changed to Aquila, Inc. (New) 03/15/2002
Aquila, Inc. (New) acquired by Great Plains Energy Inc. 07/14/2008 which merged into Evergy, Inc. 06/05/2018

UTILISOURCE INTL CORP (FL)
Name changed 08/29/2007
Name changed from Utilisource Corp. to Utilisource International Corp. 08/29/2007
Each share old Common $0.0001 par exchanged for (0.01) share new Common $0.0001 par 02/05/2009
Name changed to Whole In One Organics Corp., Inc. 08/19/2009
Whole In One Organics Corp., Inc. name changed to Liberty International Holding Corp. 05/02/2012

UTILITECH INC (CA)
Reincorporated under the laws of Delaware as Decora Industries, Inc. and Common no par changed to 1¢ par 04/08/1992
(See Decora Industries Inc.)

UTILITIES & FDG LTD (ON)
Name changed to Glenayr Kitten Ltd. (ONT) 2/15/84
Glenayr Kitten Ltd. (ONT) reincorporated in Canada 7/10/89

UTILITIES & INDS CORP (DE)
Common 10¢ par split (1.333) for (1) by issuance of (0.333) additional share 01/24/1975
Under plan of merger each share Common 10¢ par exchanged for $14.50 cash 09/17/1979

UTILITIES & INDS CORP (NY)
Merged into Carter Group Inc. 11/19/1974
Each share Common $2 par exchanged for $35 cash

UTILITIES ASSOCIATES, INC.
Liquidation completed in 1941

UTILITIES BUILDING CORP. (IL)
Liquidation completed
Each share Common $1 par

exchanged for initial distribution of $28.30 cash 8/5/56
Each share Common $1 par received second distribution of $1 cash 12/23/57
Each share Common $1 par received third and final distribution of $0.49 cash 4/15/60

UTILITIES GAS & ELECTRIC CO.
Bankrupt in 1931

UTILITIES HOLDRS TR (DE)
Trust terminated
Each Depositary Receipt received first and final distribution of $105.962159 cash payable 01/08/2013 to holders of record 12/24/2012

UTILITIES HYDRO & RAILS SHARES CORP.
Liquidated in 1943

UTILITIES INC (DE)
Common 10¢ par split (2) for (1) by issuance of (1) additional share payable 12/2/99 to holders of record 12/1/99
Acquired by Nuon NV 3/18/2002
Each share Common 10¢ par exchanged for $42 cash

UTILITIES LEASING CORP (PA)
Out of existence 11/17/1971
Details not available

UTILITIES POWER & LIGHT CORP. (VA)
Reorganized as Ogden Corp. 4/15/40
Each share 7% Preferred exchanged for (5) shares Common $4 par
Class A, Class B and Common had no equity
Ogden Corp. name changed to Covanta Energy Corp. 3/14/2001
(See Covanta Energy Corp.)

UTILITIES POWER & LIGHT REALTY TRUST
Assets acquired by Utilities Realty Liquidation Trust in 1935
Utilities Realty Liquidation Trust completed liquidation in 1956

UTILITIES POWER CO.
Acquired by Public Service Co. of New Hampshire 00/00/1928
Details not available

UTILITIES PUBLIC SERVICE CO.
Reorganized in 1938
No stockholders' equity

UTILITIES PUBLIC SERVICE SHARES
Dissolved in 1933

UTILITIES REALTY LIQUIDATION TRUST (IL)
Completely liquidated in 1956
Each Ctf. of Bene. Int. no par exchanged for first and final distribution on (1) share Utilities Building Corp. Common $1 par
Utilities Building Corp. liquidation completed 4/15/60

UTILITIES STOCK & BOND CORP.
Liquidation completed in 1945

UTILITY & INDUSTRIAL CORP. (DE)
Merged into General Finance Corp. (Mich.) in 1941
Each (100) shares Preferred exchanged for (30.45) shares 5% Preferred Ser. A $10 par plus a purchase warrant for (30.45) shares Common $1 par
Each (113) shares Common exchanged for (1) share 5% Preferred Ser. A $10 par plus a purchase warrant for (1) share Common $1 par
General Finance Corp. (Mich.) reincorporated under the laws of Delaware in 1954 which merged into General Finance Discount Corp. for cash 12/12/69

UTILITY APPLIANCE CORP. (CA)
Under plan of merger name changed to Gaffers & Sattler Corp. 5/31/63
(See Gaffers & Sattler Corp.)

UTILITY CABLE PLC (UNITED KINGDOM)
Placed in administrative receivership 09/14/1998
ADR holders' equity unlikely

UTILITY COMMUNICATIONS INTL INC (UT)
Reorganized as Intermost Corp. (UT) 11/10/1998
Each share Common $0.001 par exchanged (2) shares Common $0.001 par
Intermost Corp. (UT) reincorporated in Wyoming 02/25/2003 which name changed to Uni Core Holdings Corp. 01/29/2010

UTILITY CORP (ON)
Class A Shares called for redemption 05/19/1998
Class C Shares split (3) for (1) by issuance of (2) additional shares payable 05/22/2008 to holders of record 05/21/2008 Ex date - 05/16/2008
Completely liquidated 05/22/2018
Each Class C Share exchanged for first and final distribution of $25.4757 cash

UTILITY EQUITIES CORP.
Merged into First York Corp. 00/00/1946
Each share $5.50 Priority Stock exchanged for (1.5) shares $2 Preferred $1 par, (7.625) shares Common 10¢ par and $11.50 cash
Each share Common exchanged for (1) share Common 10¢ par
First York Corp. merged into Equity Corp. 11/03/1952 which name changed to Wheelabrator-Frye Inc. 11/04/1971 which merged into Signal Companies, Inc. 02/01/1983 which merged into Allied-Signal Inc. 09/19/1985 which name changed to AlliedSignal Inc. 04/26/1993 which name changed to Honeywell International Inc. 12/01/1999

UTILITY INVT RECOVERY INC (NV)
Name changed to General Automotive Co. 03/07/2008
General Automotive Co. name changed to MDCorp 05/26/2017 which name changed to Qian Yuan Baixing Inc. 05/01/2018

UTILITY NETWORK OF AMERICA, INC. (DE)
Merged into Itel Corp. (Old) 10/7/76
Each share Class A Common 10¢ par exchanged for (0.85) share Common $1 par
Itel Corp. (Old) reorganized as Itel Corp. (New) 9/19/83 which name changed to Anixter International Inc. 9/1/95

UTILITY SHARES CORP.
Merged into American Superpower Corp. in 1929
Details not available

UTILITY SPLIT TR (ON)
Preferred Securities called for redemption at $10 plus $0.15 accrued dividends on 01/03/2012
Trust terminated 01/03/2017
Each Class B Preferred Security received $10.1313 cash
Each Capital Unit received $16.8393 cash

UTILITY VERIFICATION CORP (DE)
Charter cancelled and declared inoperative and void for non-payment of taxes 3/1/84

UTILX CORP (DE)
Merged into Puget Sound Energy, Inc. 9/15/2000
Each share Common 1¢ par exchanged for $6.125 cash

UTIX GROUP INC (DE)
Each share old Common $0.001 par exchanged for (0.01) share new Common $0.001 par 04/11/2006
Filed a petition under Chapter 7 Federal Bankruptcy Code 05/20/2008
No stockholders' equity

UTL CORP (DE)
Common 50¢ par changed to 25¢ par and (1) additional share issued 08/19/1983
Merged into ARGO Systems Holding Co. 09/17/1990
Each share Common 25¢ par exchanged for $4.75 cash

UTOPIA MARKETING INC (FL)
Reincorporated 08/03/1998
State of incorporation changed from (CA) to (FL) 08/03/1998
Recapitalized as Daytonabrands Inc. 09/19/2006
Each share Common $0.001 par exchanged for (0.03333333) share Common $0.001 par
(See Daytonabrands Inc.)

UTOPIA MINING CO. (OK)
Charter cancelled for failure to pay taxes 12/15/30

UTRONICS CORP. (PA)
Acquired by Defiance Industries, Inc. 07/10/1963
Each share Common 50¢ par exchanged for (0.073633) share Class B Common $1 par
Defiance Industries, Inc. merged into El-Tronics, Inc. 10/03/1969 which name changed to ELT, Inc. 01/04/1974 which name changed to Dutch Boy, Inc. 02/23/1977 which name changed to Artra Group Inc. 12/31/1980 which merged into Entrade Inc. 09/23/1999
(See Entrade Inc.)

UTRONICS INC (NY)
Charter cancelled and proclaimed dissolved for failure to pay taxes and file reports 12/20/1977

UTS ENERGY CORP (CANADA)
Merged into SilverBirch Energy Corp. 10/01/2010
Each share Common no par exchanged for (0.1) share Common no par and $3.08 cash
SilverBirch Energy Corp. merged into SilverWillow Energy Corp. 04/04/2012
(See SilverWillow Energy Corp.)

UTSTARCOM INC (DE)
Each share Preferred Ser. E exchanged for (2) shares Common $0.00125 par 03/08/2000
Reorganized under the laws of Cayman Islands as UTStarcom Holdings Corp. 06/24/2011
Each share Common $0.00125 par exchanged for (1) share Ordinary USD $0.00125 par

UTTI CORP (DE)
Recapitalized as Vianet Technology Group, Ltd. 02/05/2007
Each share Common $0.001 par exchanged for (0.00285714) share Common $0.001 par
Vianet Technology Group, Ltd. name changed to Oncology Med, Inc. 04/12/2007 which recapitalized as Bellatora Inc. 09/28/2016

UTZ TECHNOLOGIES INC (NJ)
Name changed 4/3/91
Name changed 1/17/2002
Name changed from UTZ (Donald) Engineering Inc. to UTZ Engineering Inc. 4/3/91
Name changed from UTZ Engineering Inc. to UTZ Technologies, Inc. 1/17/2002
Name changed to PhoneBrasil International, Inc. 5/30/2007

UUNET TECHNOLOGIES INC (DE)
Issue Information - 4,725,000 shares COM offered at $14 per share on 05/25/1995
Merged into MFS Communications Inc. 8/12/96
Each share Common $0.001 par exchanged for (1.777776) shares Common 1¢ par
MFS Communications Inc. merged into WorldCom, Inc. 12/31/96 which name changed MCI WorldCom, Inc. 9/14/98 which name changed to WorldCom Inc. (New) 5/1/2000
(See WorldCom Inc. (New))

UV COATING SYSTEMS, INC. (DE)
Charter cancelled and declared inoperative and void for non-payment of taxes 3/1/84

UV INDUSTRIES, INC. LIQUIDATING TRUST (ME)
Liquidation completed
Each Share of Bene. Int. $1 par exchanged for initial distribution of $8 cash 7/24/81
Each Share of Bene. Int. $1 par received second distribution of $2 cash 9/4/81
Each Share of Bene. Int. $1 par received third distribution of $3 cash 7/28/82
Each Share of Bene. Int. $1 par received fourth distribution of $2 cash 10/5/82
Each Share of Bene. Int. $1 par received fifth distribution of $1.86 cash 3/7/83
Each Share of Bene. Int. $1 par received sixth distribution of $0.50 cash 4/5/83
Each Share of Bene. Int. $1 par received seventh distribution of $1.82 cash 3/8/84
Each Share of Bene. Int. $1 par received eighth distribution of $1.83 cash 9/12/84
Each Share of Bene. Int. $1 par received ninth distribution of $28 principal amount of Sharon Steel Corp. 13-1/2% Subord. S.F. Debentures due 1/1/2000 on 3/19/85
Each Share of Bene. Int. $1 par received tenth distribution of $0.50 cash 5/20/85
Each Share of Bene. Int. $1 par received eleventh distribution of $0.68 cash 1/14/91
Each Share of Bene. Int. $1 par received twelfth distribution of $0.22 cash 3/22/91
Each Share of Bene. Int. $1 par received thirteenth distribution of $0.06 cash 3/2/92
Each Share of Bene. Int. $1 par received fourteenth and final distribution of $0.02 cash 8/20/92

UV INDS INC (ME)
Common $1 par split (3) for (2) by issuance of (0.5) additional share 4/30/74
Common $1 par split (2) for (1) by issuance of (1) additional share 6/14/77
$1.265 Conv. Preferred $5 par called for redemption 2/28/79
$5.50 Preferred $5 par called for redemption 5/21/79
Under plan of liquidation each share Common $1 par received initial distribution of $18 cash 4/30/79
Under plan of liquidation each share Common $1 par automatically became (1) Share of Bene. Int. $1 par of UV Industries, Inc. Liquidating Trust 3/25/80
(See UV Industries, Inc. Liquidating Trust)

UVALDE ROCK ASPHALT CO (TX)
Voluntarily dissolved 11/17/1993
Details not available

UVENTUS TECHNOLOGIES CORP (NV)
Name changed to Sara Creek Gold Corp. 09/24/2009
Sara Creek Gold Corp. name changed to Hawker Energy, Inc. 09/26/2014

UVIC INC (NV)
Name changed to Zoompass Holdings, Inc. 01/26/2017

UVUMOBILE INC (DE)
SEC revoked common stock registration 05/15/2014

UWHARRIE RIVER GOLD MINING & DREDGING CO. (CO)
Declared defunct and inoperative for failure to pay taxes and file annual reports 09/16/1913

UWINK INC (UT)
Reorganized under the laws of Delaware as uWink, Inc. 07/26/2007
Each share Common $0.001 par exchanged for (0.25) share Common $0.001 par

UXBRIDGE DEVELOPMENT CO. LTD. (ON)
All but (6) shares Common $10 par acquired by an individual through purchase offer in 1963

UXC LTD (AUSTRALIA)
ADR agreement terminated 05/05/2016
No ADR's remain outstanding

UZEL MAKINA SANAYI A S (TURKEY)
Sponsored 144A ADR's for Ordinary split (4.5) for (1) by issuance of (3.5) additional ADR's payable 01/13/2000 to holders of record 12/09/1999
Sponsored Reg. S ADR's for Ordinary split (4.5) for (1) by issuance of (3.5) additional ADR's payable 01/13/2000 to holders of record 12/09/1999
Stock Dividends - 50% payable 06/07/2002 to holders of record 05/23/2002; 188% payable 11/02/2004 to holders of record 09/03/2004; 10% payable 03/28/2008 to holders of record 03/21/2008
ADR agreement terminated 04/30/2009
Each Sponsored 144A ADR for Ordinary exchanged for (0.25) Ordinary share Each Sponsored Reg. S ADR's for Ordinary exchanged for (0.25) Ordinary share
Note: Unexchanged ADR's will be sold and the proceeds, if any, held for claim after 04/30/2010

V

V. G. A. CO. (MI)
Liquidation completed
Each share Common no par exchanged for initial distribution of $9 cash 7/5/66
Each share Common no par received second distribution of $0.613 cash 7/22/71
Each share Common no par received third and final distribution of $0.15 cash 10/8/71

V BAND CORP (NY)
Name changed 5/18/87
Common 1¢ par split (3) for (2) by issuance of (0.5) additional share 2/28/86
Name changed from V Band Systems, Inc. to V Band Corp. 5/18/87
Merged into IPC Merger Sub 6/21/99
Each share Common 1¢ par exchanged for $0.27 cash

V.F. LIQUIDATING CO. (MO)
Liquidation completed 1/10/64

V G TECH INC (NV)
Each share old Common $0.001 par exchanged for (4) shares new Common $0.001 par 08/24/2004
Name changed to Aqua Society, Inc. 12/27/2004
(See Aqua Society, Inc.)

V-GPO INC (FL)
SEC revoked common stock registration 06/09/2010
Stockholders' equity unlikely

V I P LEASING SYS INC (NY)
Charter cancelled and proclaimed dissolved for failure to pay taxes 12/15/1970

V I TECHNOLOGIES INC (DE)
Issue Information - 3,000,000 shares COM offered at $12 per share on 06/10/1998
Each share old Common $0.001 par exchanged for (0.1) share new Common $0.001 par 03/15/2005
Name changed to Panacos Pharmaceuticals, Inc. 08/18/2005
(See Panacos Pharmaceuticals, Inc.)

V-LOAN FINL SVCS INC (ANTIGUA)
Recapitalized as Biotelemetric Signaling Inc. 01/07/2005
Each share Ordinary $0.0001 par exchanged for (0.005) share Ordinary $0.0001 par
Biotelemetric Signaling Inc. name changed to Flirty Girl International Inc. 12/27/2005 which name changed to PlayStar Corp. (Antigua) (New) 07/27/2006
(See PlayStar Corp. (Antigua) (New))

V MEDIA CORP (DE)
Acquired by Eastern Jin Kai International Ltd. 04/22/2015
Each share Common $0.0001 par exchanged for $0.60 cash

V-NET BEVERAGE INC (NV)
Name changed to RushNet, Inc. 07/08/2005
Each share Common $0.001 par exchanged for (1) share Common $0.001 par
(See RushNet, Inc.)

V O C ANALYTICAL LABORATORIES INC (FL)
Charter dissolved for failure to file annual reports 9/24/99

V-ONE CORP (DE)
Each share old Common $0.001 par exchanged for (0.5) share new Common $0.001 par 05/14/2004
Plan of reorganization under Chapter 11 Federal Bankruptcy Code effective 09/04/2007
No stockholders' equity

V TECH DIAGNOSTICS CDA INC (BC)
Delisted from Vancouver Stock Exchange 10/31/1994

V-TWIN HLDGS INC (DC)
Name changed 12/00/1999
Name changed from V-Twin Acquisitions, Inc. to V-Twin Holdings, Inc. 12/00/1999
Reorganized as Tobacco One, Inc. 02/15/2008
Each (45) shares Class A Common $0.001 par exchanged for (1) share Common $0.001 par
(See Tobacco One, Inc.)

VA SOFTWARE CORP (DE)
Name changed 12/06/2001
Name changed from VA Linux Systems, Inc. to VA Software Corp. 12/06/2001
Name changed to SourceForge, Inc. 05/24/2007
SourceForge, Inc. name changed to Geeknet, Inc. 11/04/2009
(See Geeknet, Inc.)

VA TECHNOLOGIE AG (AUSTRIA)
Acquired by Siemens AG 7/15/2005
Each Sponsored ADR for Ordinary exchanged for $7.464 cash
Note: Holders may also receive an additional cash distribution upon the sale of a private company

VAAL REEFS EXPL & MNG LTD (SOUTH AFRICA)
Each old ADR for Ordinary Reg. Rand-50 par exchanged for (10) new ADR's for Ordinary Reg. Rand-50 par 9/4/84
Name changed to Anglogold Ltd. 3/30/98
AngloGold Ltd. name changed to AngloGold Ashanti Ltd. 4/26/2004

VAALCO ENERGY INC (DE)
Preferred Stock Purchase Rights declared for Common stockholders of record 09/28/2007 were redeemed at $0.001 per right 08/01/2009 for holders of record 07/24/2009
(Additional Information in Active)

VAALDIAM MNG INC (CANADA)
Acquired by BCKP Ltd. 06/29/2012
Each shares Common no par exchanged for $0.2649292 cash

VAALDIAM RES LTD (CANADA)
Each share old Common no par exchanged for (0.25) share new Common no par 11/07/2003
Merged into Vaaldiam Mining Inc. 03/26/2010
Each share new Common no par exchanged for (0.08) share Common no par
Note: Option for holders entitled to receive (499) or fewer shares in lieu of $0.30 cash expired 04/22/2010
Unexchanged certificates were cancelled and became without value 03/26/2016
(See Vaaldiam Mining Inc.)

VAC TEC SYS INC (CO)
Each share old Common 1¢ par exchanged for (0.02) share new Common 1¢ par 07/30/1997
Name changed to Recycling Centers of America, Inc. 01/08/1999
Recycling Centers of America, Inc. name changed to Reclamation Consulting & Applications Inc. 02/27/2002 which recapitalized as Alderox, Inc. 05/20/2008
(See Alderox, Inc.)

VAC VACATION AMER INC (NY)
Dissolved by proclamation 6/23/93

VACA OIL EXPLORATION CO., INC. (DE)
Recapitalized as Vaca Oil Co., Inc. 6/19/53
Each share Common $1 par exchanged for (4) shares Common 25¢ par
Vaca Oil Co., Inc. completely liquidated 3/11/74
(See Vaca Oil Co., Inc.)

VACA OIL INC (DE)
Completely liquidated 3/11/74
Each share Common 25¢ par received first and final distribution of (0.166666) share Exeter Oil Co., Ltd. (CA) Class A 25¢ par
Note: Certificates were not surrendered and are now valueless

VACATION BREAK U S A INC (FL)
Merged into Fairfield Communities Inc. 12/19/97
Each share Common 1¢ par exchanged for (0.6075) share Common 1¢ par

VACATION HOME SWAP INC (NV)
Common $0.001 par split (92) for (1) by issuance of (91) additional shares payable 01/18/2013 to holders of record 01/18/2013
Recapitalized as R-Three Technologies, Inc. 10/06/2015
Each share Common $0.001 par exchanged for (0.002) share Common $0.001 par

VACATION MOTELS OF FLORIDA, INC. (FL)
Charter cancelled and proclaimed dissolved for failure to file reports and pay fees 9/3/76

VACATION OWNERSHIP MARKETING INC (DE)
Each share old Common $0.001 par exchanged for (0.05) share new Common $0.001 par 08/23/2001
Recapitalized as Capital Solutions I, Inc. 05/11/2004
Each share new Common $0.001 par exchanged for (0.02) share Common $0.0000001 par
Capital Solutions I, Inc. name changed to Fuda Faucet Works, Inc. 01/03/2008

VACATION SPA RESORTS INC (TN)
Merged into Mego Financial Corp. 03/11/1993
Each share Common 10¢ par exchanged for (0.25) share Common 1¢ par
(See Mego Financial Corp.)

VACATIONS TO GO INC (DE)
Name changed to Vacation Publications, Inc. 08/16/1989

VACCO INDS (CA)
Each share old Common no par exchanged for (0.1) share new Common no par 04/14/1975
Merged into Emerson Electric Co. 10/03/1983
Each share new Common no par exchanged for $27.81 cash

VACCO VALVE CO. (CA)
Common no par split (2) for (1) by issuance of (1) additional share 3/8/65
Name changed to Vacco Industries 4/18/66
(See Vacco Industries)

VACHON-CONTEL INC (NV)
Name changed to Computer Giftware Co. 07/07/1989
(See Computer Giftware Co.)

VACTORY INC (FL)
Name changed 08/20/2000
Name changed from Vactory.com, Inc. to Vactory Inc. 08/20/2000
Name changed to Her Personal Feminine Care Products, Inc. 08/06/2001
Her Personal Feminine Care Products, Inc. recapitalized as OJsys, Inc. 11/07/2006

VACTRON CORP. (TX)
Charter forfeited for failure to pay taxes 3/12/63

VACTRONIC LAB EQUIP INC (NY)
Completely liquidated 6/18/69
Each share Common 10¢ par exchanged for first and final distribution of (1) share Luna Industries, Inc. Common 10¢ par
(See Luna Industries, Inc.)

VACU BLAST CORP (CA)
Capital Stock no par reclassified as Common no par 08/23/1972
Merged into BTR International Ltd. 12/02/1980
Each share Common no par exchanged for $3.95 cash

VACU DRY CO (CA)
6% Conv. Class A $10 par called for redemption 06/23/1967
Name changed to SonomaWest Holdings, Inc. (CA) 12/10/1999
SonomaWest Holdings, Inc. (CA) reincorporated in Delaware 11/15/2004
(See SonomaWest Holdings, Inc. (DE))

VACUDYNE ASSOCIATES, INC. (NY)
Name changed to K. A. Electronics Corp. 6/27/62
K. A. Electronics Corp. proclaimed dissolved 12/15/75

VACUUM CONCRETE CORP. (DE)
Merged into Vacuum Concrete Corp. of America on a share for share basis 5/27/60
Vacuum Concrete Corp. of America name changed to Aerovac Corp. 5/21/70

VACUUM CONCRETE CORP AMER (PA)
Name changed to Aerovac Corp. 5/21/70

VACUUM-ELECTRONICS CORP. (NY)
Name changed to Veeco Instruments, Inc. 01/22/1965
(See Veeco Instruments, Inc.)

VACUUM FOODS CORP.
Name changed to Minute Maid Corp. in 1949 which was merged into Coca Cola Co. 12/30/60

VACUUM GAS & OIL CO. LTD. (ON)
Charter cancelled for failure to file reports and pay fees 4/18/60

VACUUM OIL CO.
Merged into Socony-Vacuum Corp. on a (2.5) for (1) basis in 1931
Socony-Vacuum Corp. name changed to Socony-Vacuum Oil Co., Inc. in 1934 which name was changed to Socony Mobil Oil Co. Inc. 4/29/55 which name changed to Mobil Oil Corp. 5/18/66 which reorganized as Mobil Corp. 6/21/76 which merged into Exxon Mobil Corp. 11/30/99

VADA URANIUM CORP. (DE)
No longer in existence having become inoperative and void for non-payment of taxes 4/1/59

VADDA ENERGY CORP (FL)
SEC revoked common stock registration 04/21/2016

VADER GROUP INC (NY)
Name changed to SoftNet Systems, Inc. (NY) and Common 10¢ par changed to 1¢ par 06/29/1993
SoftNet Systems, Inc. (NY) reincorporated in Delaware 04/13/1999 which name changed to American Independence Corp. 11/14/2002

VADSCO SALES CORP.
Merged into Universal Laboratories, Inc. in 1943
Each share Preferred exchanged for (1) share Preferred $50 par and (5) shares Common $1 par
Each share Common exchanged for (0.1) share Common $1 par
Universal Laboratories, Inc. name changed to Universal American Corp. (DE) in 1952
(See Universal American Corp. (DE))

VAGABOND COACH MANUFACTURING CO. (MI)
Name changed to Vagabond Corp. 12/19/62
Vagabond Corp. acquired by Guerdon Industries, Inc. for cash 1/31/64

VAGABOND CORP. (MI)
Acquired by Guerdon Industries, Inc. for cash 1/31/64

VAGABOND HOTELS INC (CA)
Capital Stock no par split (2) for (1) by issuance of (1) additional share 5/17/76
Capital Stock no par split (2) for (1) by issuance of (1) additional share 12/22/83
Name changed to Northview Corp. (CA) 6/21/84
Northview Corp. (CA) reincorporated in Delaware 6/14/85
(See Northview COrp. (DE))

VAGABOND INVT PPTYS (CA)
Merged into Real Estate Investment Properties 10/01/1977
Each Share of Bene. Int. $1 par exchanged for (1.17) Shares of Bene. Int. $1 par
Real Estate Investment Properties reorganized as Hotel Properties, Inc. 12/31/1984 which merged into Hotel Investors Trust 09/16/1986 which recapitalized as Starwood Lodging Trust 02/01/1995 which name changed to Starwood Hotels & Resorts Trust 01/02/1998 which name changed to Starwood Hotels & Resorts 02/24/1998 which reorganized as Starwood Hotels & Resorts Worldwide, Inc. 01/06/1999 which merged into Marriott International, Inc. (New) 09/23/2016

VAGABOND MOTOR HOTELS, INC. (CA)
Name changed to Vagabond Hotels, Inc. 10/17/75
Vagabond Hotels, Inc. name changed to Northview Corp. (CA) 6/21/84 which reincorporated in Delaware 6/14/85
(See Northview Corp. (DE))

VAGABOND REAL ESTATE EQUITIES (CA)
Shares of Bene. Int. $1 par split (50) for (1) by issuance of (49) additional Shares 04/10/1976
Under plan of merger name changed to Real Estate Investment Properties 10/01/1977
Real Estate Investment Properties reorganized as Hotel Properties, Inc. 12/31/1984 which merged into Hotel Investors Trust 09/16/1986 which recapitalized as Starwood Lodging Trust 02/01/1995 which name changed to Starwood Hotels & Resorts Trust 01/02/1998 which name changed to Starwood Hotels & Resorts 02/24/1998 which reorganized as Starwood Hotels & Resorts Worldwide, Inc. 01/06/1999 which merged into Marriott International, Inc. (New) 09/23/2016

VAGIM PACKING CO. (CA)
Charter revoked for failure to file reports and pay fees 1/3/61

VAHLSING INC (DE)
Common 10¢ par changed to 3-1/3¢ par and (2) additional shares issued 7/15/69
Charter cancelled and declared inoperative and void for non-payment of taxes 5/30/96

VAIBHAV GEMS LTD (INDIA)
Name changed to Vaibhav Global Ltd. 12/10/2012

VAIL ASSOC INC (CO)
Merged into Gillett Productions, Inc. 10/31/1985
Each share Capital Stock no par exchanged for $35 cash

VAIL BKS INC (CO)
Merged into U.S. Bancorp 08/31/2006
Each share Common $1 par exchanged for $17 cash

VAILLANCOURT (JOS.) INC. (QC)
Name changed to Vaillancourt Inc. 4/8/64

VAL D OR EXPLS LTD (BC)
Merged into Meridor Resources Ltd. 04/01/1985
Each share Common no par exchanged for (1/3) share Common no par
Meridor Resources Ltd. merged into Hughes Lang Corp. 08/01/1989 which merged into CanGold Resources Inc. (BC) 01/31/1994 which reorganized in Ontario as Amalgamated CanGold Inc. 07/31/1995 which merged into Central Asia Goldfields Corp. 01/08/1996
(See Central Asia Goldfields Corp.)

VAL D OR INDS INC (NY)
Merged into Consolidated Foods Corp. 03/29/1974
Each share Common 10¢ par exchanged for (0.19701) share Common $1.33333333 par
Consolidated Foods Corp. name changed to Sara Lee Corp. 04/02/1985 which recapitalized as Hillshire Brands Co. 06/29/2012
(See Hillshire Brands Co.)

VAL D'OR CONSOLIDATED MINES LTD. (QC)
Out of business in 1955

VAL D'OR MINERAL HOLDINGS LTD. (ON)
Merged into Little Long Lac Gold Mines Ltd. (The) 4/27/67
Each share Capital Stock $1 par exchanged for (0.2) share Capital Stock no par
Little Long Lac Gold Mines Ltd. (The) merged into Little Long Lac Mines Ltd. 1/8/71 which name changed to Little Long Lac Gold Mines Ltd. (New) 7/3/75 which merged into LAC Minerals Ltd. (New) 7/29/85 which was acquired by American Barrick Resources Corp. 10/17/94 which name changed to Barrick Gold Corp. 1/18/95

VAL MAR SWIMMING POOLS LTD (QC)
Each share Class A $1 par exchanged for (3) shares Class A 33-1/3¢ par 3/26/69
Acquired by KLK, Inc. 3/31/80
Each share Class A 33-1/3¢ par exchanged for $1.35 cash

VAL VISTA ENERGY LTD (AB)
Each share old Common no par exchanged for (1/6) share new Common no par 06/25/2004
Acquired by Avenir Diversified Income Trust 04/18/2005
Each share new Common no par exchanged for either (0.13364) Trust Unit, $4.43 cash or a combination thereof
Avenir Diversified Income Trust reorganized as AvenEx Energy Corp. 01/07/2011 which merged into Spyglass Resources Corp. 04/04/2013

VALAR RES LTD (BC)
Struck off register and declared dissolved for failure to file returns 11/12/93

VALASSIS COMMUNICATIONS INC (DE)
Common 1¢ par split (3) for (2) by issuance of (0.5) additional share payable 05/12/1999 to holders of record 04/16/1999 Ex date - 05/13/1999
Acquired by Harland Clarke Holdings Corp. 02/04/2014
Each share Common 1¢ par exchanged for $34.04 cash

VALAVAARA ENVIRONMENTAL TECHNOLOGIES LTD (ON)
Recapitalized as Kenridge Investment Corp. (ONT) 4/12/96
Each share Common no par exchanged for (0.1) share Common no par
Kenridge Investment Corp. (ONT) reorganized in Yukon Territory as Exploro Minerals Corp. Ltd. 3/6/97
(See Exploro Minerals Corp. Ltd.)

VALCENT PRODS INC (AB)
Each share old Common no par exchanged for (0.05555555) share new Common no par 07/16/2009
Name changed to Alterrus Systems Inc. 06/12/2012

VALCLAIR RES LTD (BC)
Name changed to SCI Satellite Conferencing International Corp. 12/2/85
(See SCI Satellite Conferencing International Corp.)

VALCO COMMUNICATIONS INC (FL)
Each (30) shares old Common $0.0002 par exchanged for (1) share new Common $0.0002 par 3/15/90
Proclaimed dissolved for failure to file reports and pay fees 10/11/91

VALCO MINES CO. (QC)
Declared dissolved for failure to file reports and pay fees 3/7/89

VALCOM INC (DE)
Each share old Common $0.001 par exchanged for (0.1) share new Common $0.001 par 09/27/2001
Each share new Common $0.001 par exchanged again for (0.05) share new Common $0.001 par 12/11/2006
SEC revoked common stock registraton 07/29/2013

VALCOM INC (VA)
Under plan of merger name changed to InaCom Corp. 8/6/91
(See InaCom Corp.)

VALDE CONNECTIONS INC (CO)
Name changed to Signature Leisure, Inc. 8/18/2003

VALDERA RES LTD (AUSTRALIA)
Under plan of merger name changed to Golden Gate Petroleum Ltd. 06/30/2003

VALDESE MFG INC (NC)
Merged into Valdese Holding Corp. 3/10/83
Each share Capital Stock $10 par exchanged for $10 cash

VALDESTOR MINES, LTD. (ON)
Charter cancelled by the Province of Ontario 6/12/52

VALDEX MINES INC (QC)
Merged into Brominco Inc. 06/01/1976
Each share Capital Stock no par exchanged for (0.025) share Capital Stock no par
Brominco Inc. merged into Aur Resources Inc. 05/16/1985 which was acquired by Teck Cominco Ltd. 09/28/2007 which name changed to Teck Resources Ltd. 04/27/2009

VALDEZ GOLD INC (ON)
Recapitalized as Ryan Gold Corp. 12/24/2010
Each share Common no par exchanged for (0.28571428) share Common no par
Ryan Gold Corp. merged into Oban Mining Corp. 08/27/2015 which name changed to Osisko Mining Inc. 06/21/2016

VALDEZ RESOURCE INDS LTD (BC)
Recapitalized as Goldera Resources Inc. 5/5/80
Each share Capital Stock no par exchanged for (1/3) share Capital Stock no par
(See Goldera Resources Inc.)

VALDINA GOLD MINES, LTD. (ON)
Charter surrendered 00/00/1957

VALDOR FIBER OPTICS INC (BC)
Recapitalized as Valdor Technology International Inc. 07/21/2008
Each share Common no par exchanged for (0.15384615) share Common no par

VALDOR GOLD CORP (UT)
Involuntarily dissolved for failure to file annual reports 7/1/90

VALDOR LTD (DE)
Each share old Common $0.0001 par exchanged for (0.002) share new Common $0.0001 par 04/06/1998

Name changed to Pear Technologies, Inc. 06/12/1998
Pear Technologies, Inc. recapitalized as Sanswire Technologies Inc. 05/20/2002 which name changed to Wireless Holdings Group, Inc. 03/30/2005 which recapitalized as Vega Promotional Systems, Inc. (DE) 12/26/2006 which reorganized in Wyoming as Vega Biofuels, Inc. 07/29/2010

VALDORA MINES, LTD. (ON)
Charter cancelled by the Province of Ontario in 1962

VALE S A (BRAZIL)
Each ADR for Class A Preferred exchanged for (0.9342) Sponsored ADR for Common 11/27/2017
(Additional Information in Active)

VALEANT PHARMACEUTICALS INTL (DE)
Merged into Valeant Pharmaceuticals International, Inc. (Canada) 09/28/2010
Each share Common 1¢ par exchanged for (1.7809) shares Common no par
Valeant Pharmaceuticals International, Inc. (Canada) reincorporated in British Columbia 08/09/2013

VALEANT PHARMACEUTICALS INTL INC (CANADA)
Reincorporated 08/09/2013
Place of incorporation changed from (Canada) to (BC) 08/09/2013
Name changed to Bausch Health Companies Inc. 07/16/2018

VALENCE CORP (AR)
Charter revoked for failure to file reports or pay fees 12/31/2009

VALENCE 9 DEV INC (NV)
Each share old Common $0.001 par exchanged for (0.00125) share new Common $0.001 par 06/22/1999
Name changed to New Cinema Partners Inc. 07/31/1999
New Cinema Partners Inc. name changed to Witnet International, Inc. 08/28/2002 which recapitalized as KSign International, Inc. 02/25/2004 which name changed to Columbus Geographic Systems (GIS) Ltd. 09/06/2007
(See Columbus Geographic Systems (GIS) Ltd.)

VALENCE TECHNOLOGY INC (DE)
Plan of reorganization under Chapter 11 Federal Bankruptcy proceedings effective 12/04/2013
No stockholders' equity

VALENCIA BANCORP (CA)
Charter cancelled for failure to file reports and pay taxes 6/1/87

VALENCIA BK & TR (NEWHALL, CA)
Stock Dividends - 5% payable 04/21/1999 to holders of record 03/31/1999; 5% payable 06/19/2000 to holders of record 05/22/2000
Merged into UnionBanCal Corp. (CA) 11/01/2002
Each share Common $5 par exchanged for either (0.437629) share Common no par and $15.6050618 cash, (0.734665) share Common no par and $3.032687 cash, or $34.12813 cash
Note: Option to elect stock or cash only expired 12/06/2002
UnionBanCal Corp. (CA) reincorporated in Delaware 09/30/2003
(See UnionBanCal Corp. (DE))

VALENCIA BK (FULLERTON, CA)
Capital Stock $5 par changed to $2.50 par and (1) additional share issued 8/30/79
Stock Dividend - 20% 1/2/79; 10% 1/15/81
Under plan of reorganization each share Capital Stock $2.50 par automatically became (1) share Valencia Bancorp Capital Stock $2.50 par 2/25/83
(See Valencia Bancorp)

VALENCIA CAP INC (CO)
Each share old Common no par exchanged for (0.25) share new Common no par 10/4/90
Name changed to Jones Naughton Entertainment Inc. (CO) 1/3/91
Jones Naughton Entertainment Inc. (CO) reincorporated in Delaware as Go Online Networks Corp. 9/23/99
(See Go Online Networks Corp.)

VALENCIA ENTERPRISES INC (UT)
Name changed to Viral Control Technology Inc. (UT) 08/30/1989
Viral Control Technology Inc. (UT) reincorporated in Delaware 12/00/1990 which reorganized as Veridien Corp. 11/08/1991
(See Veridien Corp.)

VALENCIA NATL BK (VALENCIA, CA)
Common $5 par split (2) for (1) by issuance of (1) additional share payable 06/15/1998 to holders of record 05/28/1998
Name changed to Valencia Bank & Trust (Newhall, CA) 09/01/1998
Valencia Bank & Trust (Newhall, CA) merged into UnionBanCal Corp. (CA) 11/01/2002 which reincorporated in Delaware 09/30/2003
(See UnionBanCal Corp. (DE))

VALENCIA VENTURES INC (QC)
Each share old Common no par exchanged for (0.1) share new Common no par 07/16/2012
Reincorporated under the laws of Ontario 06/02/2014

VALENTEC SYS INC (DE)
SEC revoked common stock registration 03/12/2012

VALENTINE & CO.
Acquired by Valspar Corp. 00/00/1930
Details not available

VALENTINE GOLD CORP (BC)
Recapitalized as Point Resources Ltd. 1/11/90
Each share Common no par exchanged for (0.1) share Common no par
(See Point Resources Ltd.)

VALENTINE SHERMAN & ASSOC INC (MN)
Out of business 06/00/1975
Details not available

VALENTINE VENTURES CORP (AB)
Merged into Cumberland Oil & Gas Ltd. 02/26/2010
Each share Common no par exchanged for (0.3474) share Common no par
Note: Unexchanged certificates were cancelled and became without value 02/26/2015
Cumberland Oil & Gas Ltd. merged into Kallisto Energy Corp. 10/15/2012 which name changed to Toro Oil & Gas Ltd. 11/25/2014
(See Toro Oil & Gas Ltd.)

VALENTIS INC (DE)
Each share old Common $0.001 par exchanged for (0.03333333) share new Common $0.001 par 01/27/2003
Name changed to Urigen Pharmaceuticals, Inc. 07/30/2007

VALERA PHARMACEUTICALS INC (DE)
Issue Information - 3,750,000 shares COM offered at $9 per share on 02/01/2006
Merged into Indevus Pharmaceuticals, Inc. 04/18/2007
Each share Common $0.001 par exchanged for (1.1337) shares Common $0.001 par and (3) Contingent Stock Rights
(See Indevus Pharmaceuticals, Inc.)

VALERE INC (CO)
Charter proclaimed dissolved for failure to file reports 1/1/92

VALERIE GOLD RES LTD (BC)
Name changed to ValGold Resources Ltd. 03/27/2003
ValGold Resources Ltd. merged into Metalla Royalty & Streaming Ltd. 08/01/2018

VALERO ENERGY CORP NEW (DE)
Name changed 7/31/97
Name changed from Valero Refining & Marketing Co. to Valero Energy Corp. (New) 7/31/97
Each share 2% Conv. Preferred exchanged for (1.981992981) shares Common 1¢ par 7/1/2006
(Additional Information in Active)

VALERO ENERGY CORP OLD (DE)
$2.0625 Conv. Serial Preference $1 par called for redemption 10/2/89
Conv. Preferred $1 par called for redemption at $52.188 plus $0.0086 accrued dividend on 6/2/97
Each share Common $1 par received distribution of (1) share Valero Refining & Marketing Co. Common 1¢ par payable 8/11/97 to holders of record 7/31/97
Merged into PG&E Corp. 7/31/97
Each share Common $1 par exchanged for (0.554) share Common no par

VALERO GP HLDGS LLC (DE)
Name changed to NuStar GP Holdings, LLC 04/01/2007
NuStar GP Holdings, LLC merged into NuStar Energy L.P. 07/20/2018

VALERO L P (DE)
Name changed to NuStar Energy L.P. 4/1/2007

VALERO NAT GAS PARTNERS L P (DE)
Preference Units converted to Common Units 5/29/92
Merged into Valero Energy Corp. 5/31/94
Each Common Unit exchanged for $12.10 cash

VALERON CORP (MI)
Merged into GTE Corp. 2/29/84
Each share Common $1 par exchanged for (1) share $2 Conv. Preferred no par
GTE Corp. merged into Verizon Communications Inc. 6/30/2000

VALESC HLDGS INC (DE)
SEC revoked common stock registration 05/25/2010

VALESC INC (DE)
Name changed to Valesc Holdings Inc. 04/29/2003
Each share Common $0.0001 par exchanged for (1) share Common $0.0001 par
(See Valesc Holdings Inc.)

VALEX PETE INC (DE)
Each share old Common 1¢ par exchanged for (0.1) share new Common 1¢ par 09/17/1987
Each share new Common 1¢ par exchanged again for (0.0000001) share new Common 1¢ par 09/08/1989
Note: In effect holders received $0.09 cash per share and public interest was eliminated

VALFOUR CORP. (DE)
Liquidation completed 05/02/1960
Details not available

VALGOLD RES LTD (BC)
Each share old Common no par exchanged for (0.2) share new Common no par 03/01/2010
Merged into Metalla Royalty & Streaming Ltd. 08/01/2018
Each share new Common no par exchanged for (0.1667) share Common no par
Note: Unexchanged certificates will be cancelled and become without value 08/01/2024

VALHALLA GOLD GROUP CORP (BC)
Name changed 02/26/1988
Name changed from Valhalla Energy Corp. to Valhalla Gold Group Corp. 02/26/1988
Merged into Solomon Resources Ltd. 08/01/1989
Each share Common no par exchanged for (1) share Common no par
Solomon Resources Ltd. recapitalized as Damara Gold Corp. 10/01/2014

VALHALLA MINERALS INC. (BC)
Name changed to Valhalla Energy Corp. 01/08/1985
Valhalla Energy Corp. name changed to Valhalla Gold Group Corp. 02/26/1988 which merged into Solomon Resources Ltd. 08/01/1989 which recapitalized as Damara Gold Corp. 10/01/2014

VALHALLA MINES LTD. (ON)
Charter cancelled and declared dissolved for default in filing returns 3/25/70

VALHI INC (DE)
Ctfs. dated prior to 06/06/1981
Under plan of merger each share Common $1 par exchanged for (1.5) shares $2 Preferred Ser. A $10 par or $33.87 cash 06/06/1978
Note: Option to receive Preferred expired 08/05/1978
Unexchanged certificates were cancelled and became without value 06/06/1981
$2 Preferred Ser. A $10 par called for redemption 02/01/1982
Public interest eliminated

VALIANT CORP (CO)
Name changed to Media U S A Inc. 02/27/1990
Media U S A Inc. recapitalized as Life Medical Technologies Inc. (CO) 02/21/1994 which reincorporated in Delaware 08/29/1994 which recapitalized as I-Sim International Inc. 06/04/1999 which name changed back to Life Medical Technologies Inc. 1/26/2000 which name changed to iBonZai.com, Inc. 05/12/2000 which name changed to IbonZi.com, Inc. (DE) 01/10/2002 which reorganized in Nevada as China Global Development, Inc. 01/23/2002 which recapitalized as Arizona Ventures, Inc. 11/18/2002 which name changed to Fox River Holdings, Inc. 10/13/2003 which name changed to Zynex Medical Holdings, Inc. 12/23/2003 which name changed to Zynex, Inc. 07/08/2008

VALIANT ENERGY INC (AB)
Merged into Peerless Energy Inc. 09/19/2006
Each share Common no par exchanged for (1.06) shares Class A Common no par
Peerless Energy Inc. merged into Petrobank Energy & Resources Ltd. (Old) 01/28/2008 which reorganized as Petrobank Energy & Resources Ltd. (New) 01/07/2013 which recapitalized as Touchstone Exploration Inc. 05/20/2014

VALIANT ENTERPRISES LTD (AB)
Delisted from Canadian Venture Exchange 05/31/2000

VALIANT HEALTH CARE INC (FL)
Plan of reorganization under Chapter

11 Federal Bankruptcy proceedings confirmed 10/20/2014
Stockholders' equity unlikely

VALIANT INTL INC (DE)
Name changed to Techno Dynamics Inc. 11/22/93
(See Techno Dynamics Inc.)

VALIANT MINERALS LTD (BC)
Recapitalized as Convalo Health International, Corp. 02/12/2015
Each share Common no par exchanged for (0.5) share Common no par
Convalo Health International, Corp. name changed to BLVD Centers Corp. 06/13/2017

VALICERT INC (DE)
Issue Information - 4,000,000 shares COM offered at $10 per share on 07/27/2000
Merged into Tumbleweed Communications Corp. 06/23/2003
Each share Common $0.001 par exchanged for (0.385) share Common $0.001 par
(See Tumbleweed Communications Corp.)

VALID LOGIC SYS INC (DE)
Reincorporated 02/03/1987
State of incorporation changed from (CA) to (DE) and Common no par changed to $0.001 par 02/03/1987
Merged into Cadence Design Systems, Inc. 12/31/1991
Each share Common $0.001 par exchanged for (0.323) share Common 1¢ par

VALID SOLUCOES E SERVICOS DE SEGURANCA EM MEIOS DE PAGAMENTO E IDENTIFICACAO S A (BRAZIL)
Name changed to Valid Solucoes S.A. 08/10/2018

VALIDUS HOLDINGS LTD (BERMUDA)
Acquired by American International Group, Inc. 07/18/2018
Each share Common $0.175 par exchanged for $68 cash
(Additional Information in Active)

VALIER CO. (MT)
Liquidation completed 12/31/54

VALKYRIES PETE CORP (CANADA)
Acquired by Lundin Petroleum AB 07/31/2006
Each share Common no par exchanged for (1) share Common no par
Note: Unexchanged certificates were cancelled and became without value 07/31/2012

VALLE DE ORO BK N A (SPRING VALLEY, CA)
Common $5 par changed to $3.33 par and (0.5) additional share issued 5/12/87
Stock Dividends - 5% payable 4/6/95 to holders of record 3/27/95; 5% payable 4/30/98 to holders of record 4/3/98
Reorganized under the laws of Delaware as Valley National Corp. 4/1/99
Each share Common $3.33 par exchanged for (2) shares Common $3.33 par
Valley National Corp. merged into Community First Bankshares, Inc. 10/8/99
(See Community First Bankshares, Inc.)

VALLECITO WATER CO. (CA)
Merged into San Gabriel Valley Water Co. 12/20/74
Each share Capital Stock $10 par exchanged for $16.10 cash

VALLEE LITHIUM MINING CORP. LTD. (ON)
Charter cancelled and declared dissolved for failure to file returns and pay fees 5/9/77

VALLEN CORP (TX)
Common 50¢ par split (3) for (1) by issuance of (2) additional shares 1/17/90
Common 50¢ par split (3) for (2) by issuance of (0.5) additional share 1/17/91
Merged into Hagemeyer N.V. 12/22/99
Each share Common 50¢ par exchanged for $25 cash

VALLES STEAK HOUSE (ME)
Common $1 par split (4) for (3) by issuance of (1/3) additional share 3/27/69
Stock Dividends - 10% 8/10/73; 10% 2/28/74; 10% 4/3/75; 10% 6/16/76; 10% 11/29/78
Merged into VSH Acquisition Corp. 10/12/82
Each share Common $1 par exchanged for $7 cash

VALLEY AIRLS INC (UT)
Name changed to Pacific Airlines, Inc. (UT) 6/9/75
(See Pacific Airlines, Inc. (UT))

VALLEY BANCORP (NV)
Issue Information - 925,000 shares COM offered at $18 per share on 09/23/2004
Merged into Community Bancorp 10/13/2006
Each share Common 73¢ par exchanged for (1.4516) shares Common $0.001 par
(See Community Bancorp)

VALLEY BANCORP INC (AZ)
Acquired by Marquette Financial Companies 08/01/2003
Details not available

VALLEY BANCORP INC (MD)
Merged into Bradford Bancorp, Inc. 01/19/2007
Each share Common exchanged for $71 cash

VALLEY BANCORP INC (PA)
Common $5 par split (2) for (1) by issuance of (1) additional share 10/04/1985
Common $5 par split (2) for (1) by issuance of (1) additional share 10/01/1990
Acquired by Dauphin Deposit Corp. 01/01/1994
Each share Common $5 par exchanged for (2.1401) shares Common $5 par
Dauphin Deposit Corp. merged into Allied Irish Banks, PLC 07/08/1997
(See Allied Irish Banks, PLC)

VALLEY BANCORPORATION (WI)
Common $20 par changed to $5 par and (1.5) additional shares issued 05/20/1970
Common $5 par split (3) for (2) by issuance of (0.5) additional share 08/13/1979
Common $5 par split (3) for (2) by issuance of (0.5) additional share 09/12/1983
Common $5 par changed to $2.50 par 10/07/1983
Common $2.50 par changed to $1.50 par 06/04/1985
Common $1.50 par changed to $1 par and (0.5) additional share issued 05/30/1986
Common $1 par split (3) for (2) by issuance of (0.5) additional share 08/27/1993
Stock Dividends - 10% 05/26/1978; 10% 05/27/1988
Merged into Marshall & Ilsley Corp. (Old) 05/31/1994
Each share Common $1 par exchanged for (1.72) shares Common $1 par
(See Marshall & Ilsley Corp. (Old))

VALLEY BANK & TRUST CO. (DES MOINES, IA)
Stock Dividends - 33-1/3% 09/12/1941; 200% 02/13/1948; 66-2/3% 02/28/1949; 25% 01/28/1959
100% held by Banks of Iowa, Inc. as of 11/30/1971
Public interest eliminated

VALLEY BK & TR CO (GRAND FORKS, ND)
Stock Dividends - 33-1/3% 4/1/70; 25% 4/2/73
Acquired by Bremer Financial Corp. 9/27/93
Details not available

VALLEY BK & TR CO (SALT LAKE CITY, UT)
Reorganized as Utah Bancorporation 3/8/73
Each share Common $5 par exchanged for (2) shares Common no par
Utah Bancorporation name changed to Valley Utah Bancorporation 5/14/85 which was acquired by Valley National Corp. 5/18/87 which merged into Banc One Corp. 3/31/93 which merged into Bank One Corp. 10/2/98 which merged into J.P. Morgan Chase & Co. 12/31/2000 which name changed to JPMorgan Chase & Co. 7/20/2004

VALLEY BK & TR CO (SHELTON, CT)
Stock Dividends - 10% 1/25/80; 10% 2/20/81; 10% 1/29/82
Acquired by UST Corp. 4/2/87
Each share Common $5 par exchanged for (2.118) shares Common $0.625 par
An initial additional distribution of (0.0105) share Common $0.625 par was made 10/2/87
A second and final additional distribution of (0.0417) share Common $0.625 par was made 4/2/88
(See UST Corp.)

VALLEY BK (BRISTOL, CT)
Stock Dividend - 10% payable 01/30/2005 to holders of record 11/15/2004 Ex date - 02/15/2005
Under plan of reorganization each share Common no par automatically became (1) share First Valley Bancorp, Inc. Common no par 07/01/2005
First Valley Bancorp, Inc. merged into New England Bancshares, Inc. 07/13/2007 which merged into United Financial Bancorp, Inc. (MD) 11/19/2012 which merged into United Financial Bancorp, Inc. (CT) 05/01/2014

VALLEY BK (MORENO VALLEY, CA)
Merged into BBVA Bancomer Financial Holdings Inc. 10/13/2004
Each share Common $5 par exchanged for $5.48 cash

VALLEY BK (WHITE RIVER JUNCTION, VT)
Bank failed 09/14/1991
No stockholders' equity

VALLEY BK N Y (VALLEY STREAM, NY)
Acquired by Bank of New York Co., Inc. 04/28/1972
Each share Common $5 par exchanged for (0.85) share Common $7.50 par
Bank of New York Co., Inc. merged into Bank of New York Mellon Corp. 07/01/2007

VALLEY BK NEV (LAS VEGAS, NV)
Common $2 par changed to $8 par 05/01/1979
Stock Dividends - 100% 05/15/1979; 20% 09/08/1980; 50% 07/31/1981
Under plan of reorganization each share Common $8 par automatically became (1) share Valley Capital Corp. Common $1 par 07/29/1982
Valley Capital Corp. merged into BankAmerica Corp. (Old) 03/13/1992 which merged into BankAmerica Corp. (New) 09/30/1998 which name changed to Bank of America Corp. 04/28/1999

VALLEY BANK OF NEVADA (RENO, NV)
Merged into Valley Bank of Nevada (Las Vegas, NV) 7/1/69
Each share Capital Stock $25 par exchanged for (10) shares Common $2 par
Valley Bank of Nevada (Las Vegas, NV) reorganized as Valley Capital Corp. 7/29/82 which merged into BankAmerica Corp. (Old) 3/13/92 which merged into BankAmerica Corp. (New) 9/30/98 which name changed to Bank of America Corp. 4/28/99

VALLEY BUSINESS BK (SALEM OR)
Name changed to Willamette Valley Bank (Salem, OR) 04/18/2002
Williamette Valley Bank (Salem, OR) reorganized as Oregon Bancorp, Inc. 03/05/2009

VALLEY CAMP COAL CO (DE)
Acquired by Quaker State Oil Refining Corp. 5/14/76
Each share Common $1 par exchanged for (3.625) shares Capital Stock $1.25 par
Quaker State Oil Refining Corp. name changed to Quaker State Corp. 7/1/87 which merged into Pennzoil-Quaker State Co. 12/30/98
(See Pennzoil-Quaker State Co.)

VALLEY CAP CORP (NV)
Common $1 par split (4) for (3) by issuance of (0.33333333) additional share 08/05/1988
Common $1 par split (4) for (3) by issuance of (0.33333333) additional share 08/29/1989
Merged into BankAmerica Corp. (Old) 03/13/1992
Each share Common $1 par exchanged for (0.926944) share Common $1.5625 par
BankAmerica Corp. (Old) merged into BankAmerica Corp. (New) 09/30/1998 which name changed to Bank of America Corp. 04/28/1999

VALLEY CAP GROUP INC (NV)
Name changed to Executive Office Group, Inc. 5/27/88
Executive Office Group, Inc. name changed to Alliance National Inc. 4/24/96 which name changed to Vantas Inc. 7/23/99
(See Vantas Inc.)

VALLEY CEMENT INDS INC (MS)
In process of liquidation
Each share Capital Stock no par received initial distribution of $1.75 cash 9/25/78
Each share Capital Stock no par received second distribution of $0.50 cash 12/31/79
Each share Capital Stock no par received third and final distribution of $0.09 cash 10/15/84
Note: No information regarding surrender of certificates available

VALLEY COMM BANCORP (CA)
Common no par split (3) for (2) by issuance of (0.5) additional share payable 09/03/2004 to holders of record 08/20/2004 Ex date - 09/07/2004
Stock Dividends - 5% payable 05/09/2003 to holders of record 04/22/2003 Ex date - 05/09/2003; 5% payable 05/16/2004 to holders of record 04/27/2004 Ex date - 04/23/2004; 5% payable 05/16/2006 to holders of record 04/28/2006 Ex date - 04/26/2006; 5% payable

VAL-VAL

FINANCIAL INFORMATION, INC.

06/20/2007 to holders of record 06/06/2007 Ex date - 06/04/2007; 5% payable 06/25/2008 to holders of record 06/11/2008 Ex date - 06/09/2008; 5% payable 06/25/2009 to holders of record 06/10/2009 Ex date - 06/08/2009; 5% payable 06/28/2011 to holders of record 06/14/2011 Ex date - 06/10/2011; 5% payable 06/26/2014 to holders of record 06/05/2014 Ex date - 06/03/2014
Merged into CVB Financial Corp. 03/10/2017
Each share Common no par exchanged for (0.5442) share Common no par and $7.73 cash

VALLEY COMM BANCORP LTD (DE)
Merged into BOK Financial Corp. 04/06/2005
Each share Common $5 par exchanged for $20.07 cash
Note: Each share Common $5 par received a distribution of approximately $0.34 cash from escrow 04/06/2006

VALLEY COMM BK (PHOENIX, AZ)
Common $5 par split (2) for (1) by issuance of (1) additional share payable 12/21/1998 to holders of record 11/30/1998
Stock Dividends - 5% payable 05/14/1999 to holders of record 04/30/1999; 5% payable 05/12/2000 to holders of record 04/28/2000 Ex date - 05/01/2000; 5% payable 05/15/2001 to holders of record 04/30/2001 Ex date - 04/30/2001; 5% payable 05/15/2002 to holders of record 04/30/2002 Ex date - 04/30/2002; 5% payable 05/15/2003 to holders of record 04/30/2003 Ex date - 04/29/2003; 5% payable 05/20/2004 to holders of record 05/10/2004 Ex date - 05/06/2004
Under plan of reorganization each share Common $5 par automatically became (1) share Valley Commerce Bancorp, Ltd. Common $5 par 10/13/2003
(See Valley Commerce Bancorp, Ltd.)

VALLEY CMNTY BANCSHARES INC (WA)
Each (600) shares old Common $1 par exchanged for (1) share new Common $1 par 12/16/2004
Note: In effect holders received $35 cash per share and public interest was eliminated

VALLEY CMNTY BK (MC MINNVILLE, OR)
Merged into Columbia Bancorp (OR) 11/30/1998
Each share Common no par exchanged for $16.30 cash

VALLEY CMNTY BK (PLEASANTON, CA)
Stock Dividends - 5% payable 11/15/2004 to holders of record 11/01/2004 Ex date - 10/28/2004; 5% payable 07/19/2006 to holders of record 07/05/2006 Ex date - 06/30/2006; 5% payable 06/12/2007 to holders of record 05/29/2007 Ex date - 05/24/2007
Common no par split (3) for (2) by issuance of (0.5) additional share payable 08/01/2005 to holders of record 07/18/2005 Ex date - 08/02/2005
Merged into Bay Commercial Bank (Walnut Creek, CA) 02/13/2015
Each share Common no par exchanged for (0.345) share Common no par
Bay Commercial Bank (Walnut Creek, CA) reorganized as BayCom Corp 01/27/2017

VALLEY COPPER CO (NV)
Name changed to Valley Energy Ltd. 7/24/81

VALLEY COPPER MINES LTD (BC)
Merged into Cominco Ltd. 8/17/81
Each share Common no par exchanged for $33 cash

VALLEY EXCAVATION & TRUCKING INC (NV)
Name changed to RX Technology Holdings, Inc. 02/16/2000
RX Technology Holdings, Inc. name changed to Crosspoint Group, Inc. 08/23/2005 which recapitalized as The Employer Inc. 03/08/2007 which recapitalized as Vana Blue, Inc. 02/21/2008 which name changed to Osyka Corp. 05/19/2010

VALLEY EXPLORATIONS LTD. (BC)
Dissolved 7/13/61

VALLEY FAIR CORP (DE)
Each (30) shares Common 1¢ par exchanged for (1) share Common 30¢ par 05/07/1984
Merged into Little Ferry Corp. 05/09/1997
Each share Common 30¢ par exchanged for $30 cash

VALLEY FALLS CO.
Merged into Berkshire Fine Spinning Associates, Inc. 00/00/1929
Details not available

VALLEY FASHIONS CORP (DE)
Name changed to Westpoint Stevens, Inc. 12/10/93
(See Westpoint Stevens, Inc.)

VALLEY FED SVGS & LN ASSN EASTON PA (USA)
Common $1 par split (5) for (4) by issuance of (0.25) additional share 08/26/1986
Common $1 par split (4) for (3) by issuance of (1/3) additional share 05/29/1987
Common $1 par split (6) for (5) by issuance of (0.2) additional share 02/20/1992
Common $1 par split (5) for (4) by issuance of (0.25) additional share 09/04/1992
Stock Dividend - 10% 12/31/1985
Merged into Sovereign Bancorp, Inc. 11/05/1993
Each share Common $1 par exchanged for (3.2) shares Common no par
Sovereign Bancorp, Inc. merged into Banco Santander, S.A. 01/30/2009

VALLEY FED SVGS & LN ASSN VAN NUYS CALIF (USA)
Common no par split (2) for (1) by issuance of (1) additional share 4/30/87
Stock Dividend - 10% 3/20/86
Placed in receivership 4/10/92
Stockholders' equity unlikely

VALLEY FED SVGS BK (SHEFFIELD, AL)
Merged into Union Planters Corp. 10/1/96
Each share Common 1¢ par exchanged for (1.0976) shares Common $5 par
Union Planters Corp. merged into Regions Financial Corp. (New) 7/1/2004

VALLEY FED SVGS BK (TERRE HAUTE, IN)
Acquired by CNB Bancshares Inc. 10/31/90
Each share Common 1¢ par exchanged for (0.525) share Common no par
CNB Bancshares Inc. merged into Fifth Third Bancorp 10/29/99

VALLEY FID BK & TR CO (KNOXVILLE, TN)
5% Preferred $100 par called for redemption 10/15/1986
Each share Common $16 par exchanged for (4) shares Common $5 par 02/16/1971
Stock Dividend - 25% 03/09/1973

Acquired by First Tennessee National Corp. 09/01/1991
Details not available

VALLEY FINL CORP (VA)
Stock Dividend - 5% payable 02/15/2000 to holders of record 01/31/2000
Common no par split (2) for (1) by issuance of (1) additional share payable 05/31/2004 to holders of record 05/14/2004 Ex date - 06/01/2004
Merged into BNC Bancorp 07/01/2015
Each share Common no par exchanged for (1.1081) shares Common no par
BNC Bancorp merged into Pinnacle Partners, Inc. 06/16/2017

VALLEY FINANCIAL SERVICES, INC. (IN)
Merged into Fort Wayne National Corp. 06/01/1996
Details not available

VALLEY FINL SVCS INC (IL)
Merged into First Illinois Corp. 06/29/1990
Each share Common no par exchanged for (1.36) shares Common $1 par
First Illinois Corp. acquired by Banc One Corp. 03/02/1992 which merged into Bank One Corp. 10/02/1998 which merged into J.P. Morgan Chase & Co. 12/31/2000 which name changed to JPMorgan Chase & Co. 07/20/2004

VALLEY FORGE CORP (DE)
Reincorporated 06/12/1997
Common 50¢ par split (3) for (2) by issuance of (0.5) additional share payable 03/12/1996 to holders of record 03/01/1996 Ex date - 03/13/1996
State of incorporation changed from (GA) to (DE) 06/12/1997
Common 50¢ par split (3) for (2) by issuance of (0.5) additional share payable 09/16/1997 to holders of record 09/05/1997 Ex date - 09/17/1997
Merged into Key Components, LLC 01/19/1999
Each share Common 50¢ par exchanged for $19 cash

VALLEY FORGE FD INC (PA)
Reincorporated 08/01/1988
State of incorporation changed from (DE) to (PA) 08/01/1988
Completely liquidated 05/27/2016
Each share Common $0.001 par received first and final distribution of $7.11 cash

VALLEY FORGE PRODUCTS, INC. (NY)
Completely liquidated 9/15/64
Each share Class A Capital Stock 25¢ par exchanged for $6.53 cash
Each share Class B Capital Stock 25¢ par exchanged for $6.11-1/3 cash

VALLEY FORGE SCIENTIFIC CORP (PA)
Reincorporated under the laws of Delaware as Synergetics USA, Inc. and Common no par changed to $0.001 par 09/21/2005
(See Synergetics USA, Inc.)

VALLEY GAS CO (RI)
Under plan of reorganization each share Common $10 par automatically became (1) share Valley Resources, Inc. Common $10 par 12/14/79
6-1/4% Preferred Ser. A $100 par called for redemption in 1990
9-1/4% Preferred Ser. B $100 par called for redemption in 1990
(See Valley Resources Inc.)

VALLEY GAS PRODUCTION, INC. (TX)
Merged into Houston Natural Gas Corp. (Tex.) 11/1/63
Each share Common $1 par exchanged for (1/3) share Class B Common $5 par
(See Houston Natural Gas Corp. (Tex.))

VALLEY HIGH MNG CO (WY)
Reincorporated 07/13/2004
Reincorporated 02/03/2016
State of incorporation changed from (UT) to (NV) 07/13/2004
State of incorporation changed from (NV) to (WY) and Common $0.001 par changed to $0.00001 par 02/03/2016
Name changed to Premier Products Group, Inc. 06/30/2016

VALLEY HIGH OIL GAS & MINERALS (UT)
Each share old Common $0.001 par exchanged for (0.1) share new Common $0.001 par 01/10/1985
Reorganized under the laws of Nevada as Valley High Mining Co. 07/13/2004
Each share Common $0.001 par exchanged for (0.02857142) share Common $0.001 par
Valley High Mining Co. (NV) reincorporated in Wyoming 02/03/2016 which name changed to Premier Products Group, Inc. 06/30/2016

VALLEY HIGH VENTURES LTD (BC)
Merged into Levon Resources Ltd. (Old) 03/25/2011
Each share Common no par exchanged for (1) share Common no par and (0.125) share Bearing Resources Ltd. (Old) Common no par
(See each company's listing)

VALLEY INDPT BK (EL CENTRO, CA)
Common no par split (3) for (2) by issuance of (0.5) additional share payable 11/15/95 to holders of record 10/20/95
Stock Dividends - 4% payable 6/3/96 to holders of record 5/16/96; 2% payable 1/16/98 to holders of record 12/26/97
Under plan of reorganization each share Common no par automatically became (1) share VIB Corp. Common no par 3/23/98
(See VIB Corp.)

VALLEY INDUSTRIES CO. (OH)
Liquidation completed
Each share Common no par exchanged for initial distribution of (17) shares Vulcan Corp. (OH) Common no par 8/5/69
Each share Common no par received second distribution of $25 cash 10/3/69
Each share Common no par received third distribution of $185 cash 12/26/69
Each share Common no par received fourth distribution of $34.50 cash 6/12/70
Each share Common no par received fifth distribution of $18.20 cash 3/31/71
Each share Common no par received sixth and final distribution of $17.0236 cash 6/27/75
Vulcan Corp. (OH) reincorporated in Delaware as Vulcan International Corp. 12/14/88

VALLEY INDS INC (NJ)
Common 1¢ par split (2) for (1) by issuance of (1) additional share 05/14/1976
Liquidating Plan of Reorganization under Chapter 11 Federal Bankruptcy proceedings confirmed 03/19/1993

No stockholders' equity

VALLEY LIFE & CASUALTY INSURANCE CO. (AZ)
Dissolved 05/16/2007
No stockholders' equity

VALLEY MEDIA INC (DE)
Issue Information - 3,500,000 shares COM offered at $16 per share on 03/26/1999
Plan of reorganization under Chapter 11 Federal Bankruptcy Code effective 5/25/2005
No stockholders' equity

VALLEY MERCHANTS BK N A (HEMET, CA)
Merged into Business Bancorp (New) 8/31/2000
Each share Common no par exchanged for $22.69 cash

VALLEY METALLURGICAL PROCESSING INC (CT)
Common no par split (2) for (1) by issuance of (1) additional share 03/01/1966
Name changed to Gram Industries, Inc. 12/19/1978
Gram Industries, Inc. name changed to Transact International Inc. 10/13/1982
(See Transact International Inc.)

VALLEY MOULD & IRON CORP. (NY)
Each share 7% Preferred $100 par exchanged for $5 cash and (1.3) shares $5.50 Prior Preference no par in 1936 which was called for redemption 3/1/64
Each share Common $1 par exchanged for (4) shares Common $5 par in 1951
Common $5 par split (2) for (1) by issuance of (1) additional share 10/20/55
Common $5 par changed to $2.50 par and (1) additional share issued 12/30/65
Under plan of merger name changed to Vare Corp. 12/4/67
Vare Corp. merged into Microdot Inc. (CA) 1/31/69 which reincorporated under the laws of Delaware 7/2/71
(See Microdot Inc. (DE))

VALLEY MUSIC HALL, INC. (UT)
Name changed to Family Achievement Institute, Inc. 10/28/68
Family Achievement Institute, Inc. name changed to Intermountain Industries, Inc. 12/3/70 which recapitalized as Dynapac, Inc. 9/22/71
(See Dynapac, Inc.)

VALLEY NATL BK (GLENDALE, CA)
Common $5 par split (2) for (1) by issuance of (1) additional share 4/15/84
Common $5 par split (3) for (2) by issuance of (0.5) additional share 4/15/87
Stock Dividends - 100% 4/15/79; 10% 4/15/80
Merged into Wells Fargo & Co. 1/1/90
Each share Common $5 par exchanged for $30 cash

VALLEY NATL BK (PASSAIC, NJ)
Under plan of reorganization each share Common $5 par automatically became (1) share Valley National Bancorp Common no par 5/2/83

VALLEY NATIONAL BANK (PHOENIX, AZ)
Stock Dividend - 66-2/3% 6/25/41; 50% 4/29/44; 25% 1/17/46; 23.07692% 5/18/51; 10% 2/10/58; 25% 2/16/60
Name changed to Valley National Bank of Arizona (Phoenix, AZ) 6/1/61
Valley National Bank of Arizona (Phoenix, AZ) reorganized as Valley National Corp. 7/1/81 which merged into Banc One Corp. 3/31/93 which merged into Bank One Corp. 10/2/98 which merged into J.P. Morgan Chase & Co. 12/31/2000 which name changed to JPMorgan Chase & Co. 7/20/2004

VALLEY NATL BK (SALINAS, CA)
Common $5 par split (2) for (1) by issuance of (1) additional share 01/29/1971
Common $5 par changed to $8 par 02/28/1974
Through purchase offer all but (200) shares acquired by Household Finance International, Inc. as of 09/00/1981
Public interest eliminated

VALLEY NATL BK ARIZ (PHOENIX, AZ)
Common $5 par changed to $2.50 par and (1) additional share issued plus a 10% stock dividend paid 3/19/65
Stock Dividends - 10% 2/26/64; 10% 3/15/66; 10% 3/15/67; 10% 3/20/68
Under plan of reorganization each share Common $2.50 par automatically became (1) share Valley National Corp. Common $2.50 par and (1) additional share distributed 7/1/81
Valley National Corp. merged into Banc One Corp. 3/31/93 which merged into Bank One Corp. 10/2/98 which merged into J.P. Morgan Chase & Co. 12/31/2000 which name changed to JPMorgan Chase & Co. 7/20/2004

VALLEY NATL BK LONG ISLAND (VALLEY STREAM, NY)
Under plan of conversion name changed to Valley Bank of New York (Valley Stream, NY) 04/06/1972
Valley Bank of New York (Valley Stream, NY) acquired by Bank of New York Co., Inc. 04/28/1972 which merged into Bank of New York Mellon Corp. 07/01/2007

VALLEY NATIONAL CORP. (OR)
Acquired by U.S. Bancorp (OR) 06/01/1987
Each share Common $1 par exchanged for (0.5) share Common $5 par
U.S. Bancorp (OR) merged into U.S. Bancorp (Old) (DE) 08/01/1997 which merged into U.S. Bancorp 02/27/2001

VALLEY NATL CORP (AZ)
Merged into Banc One Corp. 3/31/93
Each share Common $2.50 par exchanged for (1.2) shares Common no par
Banc One Corp. merged into Bank One Corp. 10/2/98 which merged into J.P. Morgan Chase & Co. 12/31/2000 which name changed to JPMorgan Chase & Co. 7/20/2004

VALLEY NATL CORP (DE)
Stock Dividend - 5% payable 5/28/99 to holders of record 5/3/99
Merged into Community First Bankshares, Inc. 10/8/99
Each share Common $3.33 par exchanged for (1.0862) shares Common 1¢ par
(See Community First Bankshares, Inc.)

VALLEY NATL GASES INC (PA)
Issue Information - 2,000,000 shares COM offered at $8 per share on 04/10/1997
Merged into VNG Acquisition, LLC 2/28/2007
Each share Common $0.001 par exchanged for $27 cash

VALLEY OAKS NATL BK (SOLVANG, CA)
Stock Dividends - 5% payable 4/1/99 to holders of record 2/1/99; 5% payable 4/1/2000 to holders of record 3/1/2000; 5% payable 4/1/2001 to holders of record 3/1/2001 Ex date - 2/27/2001
Merged into Montecito Bancorp 10/1/2001
Each share Common $10 par exchanged for $34.60 cash

VALLEY OF THE ROGUE BANK (ROGUE RIVER, OR)
Under plan of reorganization each share Capital Stock $10 par automatically became (1) share VRB Bancorp Common no par in December 1983
VRB Bancorp merged into Umpqua Holdings Corp. 12/1/2000

VALLEY OIL & GAS CORP (BC)
Recapitalized as Consolidated Valley Ventures Ltd. 01/25/1994
Each share Common no par exchanged for (0.25) share Common no par
Consolidated Valley Ventures Ltd. name changed to CVL Resources Ltd. 03/12/1997 which recapitalized as Newport Exploration Ltd. 02/04/2002

VALLEY RAILROAD CO.
Acquired by Delaware, Lackawanna & Western Railroad Co. by payment of $79 per share in 1944

VALLEY REP BK (BAKERSFIELD, CA)
Under plan of reorganization each share Common no par automatically became (1) share Valley Republic Bancorp Common no par 07/05/2016

VALLEY RES INC (RI)
Merged into Southern Union Co. (New) 09/21/2000
Each share Common $1 par exchanged for $25 cash

VALLEY RIDGE FINL CORP (MI)
Old Common $10 par split (3) for (2) by issuance of (0.5) additional share payable 4/26/2000 to holders of record 3/31/2000
Each share old Common $10 par exchanged for (0.002) share new Common $10 par 11/26/2003
New Common $10 par split (5) for (1) by issuance of (4) additional shares payable 6/24/2005 to holders of record 6/1/2005 Ex date - 6/30/2005
Merged into ChoiceOne Financial Services, Inc. 11/1/2006
Each share new Common $10 par exchanged for (8.5) shares Common no par

VALLEY ST BK (VAN NUYS, CA)
Common $6.25 par changed to $3.125 par and (1) additional share issued 12/15/80
Bank closed by FDIC 9/28/87
No stockholders' equity

VALLEY STREAM NATIONAL BANK & TRUST CO. (VALLEY STREAM, NY)
Under plan of merger name changed to Valley National Bank of Long Island (Valley Stream, NY) 07/11/1960
Valley National Bank of Long Island (Valley Stream, NY) name changed to Valley Bank of New York (Valley Stream, NY) 04/06/1972 which was acquired by Bank of New York Co., Inc. 04/28/1972 which merged into Bank of New York Mellon Corp. 07/01/2007

VALLEY SYS INC (DE)
Name changed to VSI Liquidation Corp. 1/5/99
(See VSI Liquidation Corp.)

VALLEY TECH INDS INC (NV)
Recapitalized as National Superstars, Inc. (NV) 02/05/1986
Each share Common $0.001 par exchanged for (0.2) share Common $0.005 par

National Superstars, Inc. (NV) reorganized in Delaware as MSO Holdings, Inc. 06/01/2005

VALLEY TELEPHONE CO. (OR)
Acquired by Sunnyside Telephone Co. 8/1/66
Each share Common $10 par exchanged for (6) shares Common $1 par
Sunnyside Telephone Co. acquired by Continental Telephone Corp. 10/15/69 which name changed to Continental Telecom Inc. 5/6/82 which name changed to Contel Corp. 5/1/86 which merged into GTE Corp. 3/14/91 which merged into Verizon Communications Inc. 6/30/2000

VALLEY TR CO (PALMYRA, PA)
Common $10 par changed to $5 par and (1) additional share issued 03/01/1979
Merged into American Bancorp, Inc. 12/10/1982
Each share Common $5 par exchanged for (3) shares Capital Stock $5 par and $85 cash
American Bancorp, Inc. merged into Meridian Bancorp, Inc. 06/30/1983 which merged into CoreStates Financial Corp 04/09/1996 which merged into First Union Corp. 04/28/1998 which name changed to Wachovia Corp. (Ctfs. dated after 09/01/2001) 09/01/2001 which merged into Wells Fargo & Co. (New) 12/31/2008

VALLEY UTAH BANCORPORATION (UT)
Common no par split (3) for (2) by issuance of (0.5) additional share 7/22/85
Acquired by Valley National Corp. 5/18/87
Each share Common no par exchanged for (0.8232) share Common $2.50 par
Valley National Corp. merged into Banc One Corp. 3/31/93 which merged into Bank One Corp. 10/2/98 which merged into J.P. Morgan Chase & Co. 12/31/2000 which name changed to JPMorgan Chase & Co. 7/20/2004

VALLEY VA BANKSHARES INC (VA)
Merged into Dominion Bankshares Corp. 09/01/1980
Each share Common Capital Stock $5 par exchanged for (1.0232) shares Common $5 par
Dominion Bankshares Corp. merged into First Union Corp. 03/01/1993 which name changed to Wachovia Corp. (Ctfs. dated after 09/01/2001) 09/01/2001 which merged into Wells Fargo & Co. (New) 12/31/2008

VALLEY VIEW GOLD MINES LTD (UT)
Recapitalized as Jefferson Valley Gold Mines Inc. 06/01/1988
Each share Common $0.001 par exchanged for (0.4) share Common $0.001 par
(See Jefferson Valley Gold Mines Inc.)

VALLEY VIEW VENTURES INC (CO)
Name changed to Regional Air Group Corp. 9/20/88
Regional Air Group Corp. recapitalized as Environmental Remediation Holding Corp. 9/2/96 which name changed to ERHC Energy Inc. 2/15/2005

VALLEY WEST BANCORP (OR)
Stock Dividend - 10% 4/6/90
Name changed to Centennial Bancorp 5/25/90
Centennial Bancorp merged into Umpqua Holdings Corp. 11/18/2002

VALLEY WEST DEV CORP (UT)
Each share old Common 5¢ par

VAL-VAL

VALLEYLAB INC (CO)
exchanged for (2.5) shares new Common 5¢ par 09/23/1996
Name changed to Credit Store, Inc. 10/11/1996
(See Credit Store, Inc.)

VALLEYLAB INC (CO)
Common no par split (3) for (2) by issuance of (0.5) additional share 12/27/76
Common no par split (3) for (2) by issuance of (0.5) additional share 9/29/78
Common no par split (3) for (2) by issuance of (0.5) additional share 6/30/82
Merged into Pfizer Inc. 1/28/83
Each share Common no par exchanged for (0.448) share Common 11-1/9¢ par

VALLEYLAND & SECURITIES CO. (AZ)
Charter revoked 6/7/27
No stockholders' equity

VALLICORP HLDGS INC (DE)
Merged into Westamerica Bancorporation 4/12/97
Each share Common 1¢ par exchanged for (0.3479) share Common no par

VALLOC GOLD MINES, LTD. (ON)
Charter cancelled by the province of Ontario in 1958

VALMAC INDS INC (DE)
Common $3 par changed to $2 par and (0.5) additional share issued 01/09/1976
Merged into Tyson Foods, Inc. 07/01/1987
Each share Common $2 par exchanged for $30 cash

VALMET CORP/RAUMA CORP (FINLAND)
Name changed to Metso Corp. 8/24/99

VALMET OY (FINLAND)
Sponsored ADR's for Ordinary FIM10 par split (2) for (1) by issuance of (1) additional ADR payable 4/18/96 to holders of record 4/17/96
Each old Sponsored ADR for Ordinary FIM10 par exchanged for (0.5) new Sponsored ADR for Ordinary FIM10 par 5/30/96
Merged into Valmet-Rauma Corp. 7/1/99
Each new Sponsored ADR for Ordinary FIM10 par exchanged for (2) Sponsored ADR's for Ordinary FIM10 par
Valmet-Rauma Corp. name changed to Metso Corp. 8/24/99

VALMONT INDS INC (NE)
Reincorporated under the laws of Delaware 12/28/1974

VALMONT MINING EXPLORATION LTD. (QC)
Merged into Resource Exploration & Development Co. Ltd. 6/11/68
Each share Capital Stock $1 par exchanged for (0.33448) share Capital Stock no par
(See Resource Exploration & Development Ltd.)

VALMORIS CAP INC (CANADA)
Name changed to Biotonix (2010) Inc. 03/24/2010
Biotonix (2010) Inc. recapitalized as AtmanCo Inc. 12/11/2012 which name changed to ATW Tech Inc. 06/12/2018

VALNICLA COPPER MINE LTD. (BC)
Completely liquidated 3/6/70
Each share Common 50¢ par exchanged for first and final distribution of (0.184526) share National Nickel Ltd. Common no par
National Nickel Ltd. recapitalized as Aberdeen Minerals Ltd. 2/9/73
(See Aberdeen Minerals Ltd.)

VALOR COMMUNICATIONS GROUP INC (DE)
Issue Information - 29,375,000 shares COM offered at $15 per share on 02/08/2005
Name changed to Windstream Corp. 07/17/2006
Windstream Corp. name changed to Windstream Holdings, Inc. 09/03/2013

VALOR ENERGY CORP (NV)
Each share old Common $0.001 par exchanged for (0.0002) share new Common $0.001 par 10/01/2009
SEC revoked common stock registration 07/11/2012

VALOR GOLD CORP (DE)
Name changed to Vaporin, Inc. 02/07/2014
Vaporin, Inc. merged into Vapor Corp. 03/05/2015

VALOR INTERNATIONAL INC. (DE)
Charter cancelled and declared inoperative and void for non-payment of taxes 3/1/90

VALOR INVT FD INC (MI)
Reincorporated 10/08/1979
State of incorporation changed from (DE) to (MI) 10/08/1979
Completely liquidated
Each share Common $1 par received first and final distribution of approximately $15.57 cash payable 08/24/2005 to holders of record 07/31/2005
Note: Certificates were not required to be surrendered and are without value

VALOR LITHIUM MINES LTD. (QC)
Name changed 02/02/1955
Name changed from Valor Mines Ltd. to Valor Lithium Mines Ltd. 02/02/1955
Merged into Massval Resources Inc. 11/10/1959
Each share Capital Stock $1 par exchanged for (0.25) share Common $1 par
Massval Resources Inc. recapitalized as MSV Resources Inc. 10/10/1986 which merged into Campbell Resources Inc. (New) 06/03/2001
(See Campbell Resources Inc. (New))

VALOR VENTURES INC (BC)
Each share old Common no par exchanged for (0.33333333) share new Common no par 04/18/2011
Each share new Common no par exchanged again for (0.2) share new Common no par 03/23/2015
Name changed to North South Petroleum Corp. 05/19/2015
North South Petroleum Corp. name changed to Advantage Lithium Corp. 07/05/2016

VALORA EXPLORATIONS & DEVELOPMENTS LTD. (ON)
Merged into Xtra Developments Inc. 5/25/72
Each share Capital Stock no par exchanged for (0.058824) share Capital Stock no par
Xtra Developments Inc. merged into Sumtra Diversified Inc. 8/30/78

VALORA GOLD EXPLORATION CO., LTD. (ON)
Charter cancelled by the Province of Ontario 11/15/60

VALPAR RES INC (BC)
Recapitalized as Carnival Resources Ltd. 11/14/1995
Each (12) shares Common no par exchanged for (1) share Common no par
(See Carnival Resources Ltd.)

VALPARAISO ENERGY INC (AB)
Each share old Common no par exchanged for (0.25) share new Common no par 09/23/2015
Reincorporated under the laws of British Columbia as Catalina Gold Corp. 02/06/2017

VALPARAISO INC (DE)
Recapitalized as Merlin Mining Co. 07/27/1988
Each share Common $0.0001 par exchanged for (0.2) share Common $0.0001 par
Merlin Mining Co. name changed to European American Resources Inc. 01/19/1996
(See European American Resources Inc.)

VALPEY-FISHER CORP (MD)
Acquired by CTS Corp. 01/25/2012
Each share Common 5¢ par exchanged for $4.15 cash

VALRAY EXPLS LTD (ON)
Charter cancelled for failure to file reports and pay taxes 7/27/76

VALREX GOLD MINES LTD. (ON)
Charter revoked for failure to file reports and pay fees 5/13/65

VALRICO BANCORP INC (FL)
Under plan of merger each share Common no par exchanged for $53 cash 11/9/2004
Note: Holders of (101) or more shares retained their interests

VALRICO ST BK (VALRICO, FL)
Reorganized as Valrico Bancorp Inc. 5/31/95
Each share Common no par exchanged for (1) share Common no par
(See Valrico Bancorp Inc.)

VALRITA MINES, LTD. (ON)
Dissolved 9/21/59

VALSPAR CORP (DE)
Each share $6 Preferred $5 par exchanged for (1) share $4 Preferred $5 par and (5) shares Common $1 par 00/00/1938
$4 Preferred $5 par called for redemption 03/20/1959
100% of 4% Preferred acquired at $65 per share through purchase offer which expired 01/15/1971
Common $1 par split (2) for (1) by issuance of (1) additional share 04/02/1984
Common $1 par changed to 50¢ par 02/28/1986
Common 50¢ par split (2) for (1) by issuance of (1) additional share 03/23/1987
Common 50¢ par split (2) for (1) by issuance of (1) additional share 03/27/1992
Common 50¢ par split (2) for (1) by issuance of (1) additional share payable 03/21/1997 to holders of record 03/07/1997 Ex date - 03/24/1997
Common 50¢ par split (2) for (1) by issuance of (1) additional share payable 09/23/2005 to holders of record 09/02/2005 Ex date - 09/26/2005
Stock Dividend - 10% 09/04/1959
Acquired by Sherwin-Williams Co. 06/01/2017
Each share Common 50¢ par exchanged for $113 cash

VALTEC CORP (MA)
Acquired by M/A-Com, Inc. 09/24/1980
Each share Common 1¢ par exchanged for (1) share Common $1 par
M/A-Com, Inc. merged into AMP Inc. 06/30/1995 which merged into Tyco International Ltd. (Bermuda) 04/01/1999 which reincorporated in Switzerland 03/17/2009 which merged into Johnson Controls International PLC 09/06/2016

VALTEK INC (UT)
Each share Common $1 par exchanged for (5) shares Common 20¢ par 5/18/70
Merged into Duriron Co., Inc. 3/24/87
Each share Common 20¢ par exchanged for $11.75 cash

VALTERRA RESOURCE CORP (YT)
Reincorporated under the laws of British Columbia 02/22/2008

VALTERRA WINES LTD (YT)
Name changed to Valterra Resource Corp. (Yukon) 01/22/2007
Valterra Resource Corp. (Yukon) reincorporated in British Columbia 02/22/2008

VALU CONCEPTS INTL CORP (BC)
Reorganized under the laws of Canada as Double Impact Communications Corp. 09/08/1994
Each share Common no par exchanged for (0.33333333) share Common no par
Double Impact Communications Corp. recapitalized as Next Millennium Commercial Corp. 08/20/1998 which name changed to Roadrunner Oil & Gas Inc. 07/17/2008 which name changed to Bowood Energy Inc. 06/21/2010 which recapitalized as LGX Oil + Gas Inc. (Canada) 08/22/2012 which reincorporated in Alberta 06/27/2013

VALU-NET CORP (AB)
Name changed to BSM Technologies Inc. 7/12/2001

VALUCAP INVTS INC (YT)
Reincorporated under the laws of Ontario 12/15/2008

VALUDYNE INC (NV)
Name changed to Prosperity Software Inc. 9/21/2001
Prosperity Software Inc. name changed to Polarwearz Inc. 6/25/2003 which name changed to Risingtide, Inc. 6/2/2004 which name changed to Equiline Corp. 4/8/2005 which recapitalized as Chelsea Collection, Inc. 6/15/2005 which recapitalized as G-H-3 International, Inc. 10/30/2006

VALUE-ADDED COMMUNICATIONS INC (DE)
Plan of reorganization under Chapter 11 Federal Bankruptcy proceedings confirmed 08/21/1996
No stockholders' equity

VALUE ADDED INC (NV)
Name changed to Advanced Video Robotics Corp. 11/14/1987
(See Advanced Video Robotics Corp.)

VALUE AMER INC (VA)
Issue Information - 5,500,000 shares COM offered at $23 per share on 04/08/1999
Plan of reorganization under Chapter 11 Federal Bankruptcy proceedings confirmed 03/12/2001
No stockholders' equity

VALUE CAPITAL LTD. (BAHAMAS)
In process of liquidation
Each Share 1¢ par exchanged for initial distribution of $1.80 cash 09/00/1982
Each Share 1¢ par received second distribution of $0.35 cash 08/00/1984
Each Share 1¢ par received third distribution of $0.47 cash 12/17/1986
Each Share 1¢ par received fourth distribution of $0.15 cash 05/20/1988
Note: Details on subsequent distributions, if any, are not available

VALUE CITY DEPT STORES INC (OH)
Common no par split (2) for (1) by issuance of (1) additional share 12/02/1991
Reorganized as Retail Ventures, Inc. 10/08/2003

Each share Common no par exchanged for (1) share Common no par
Retail Ventures, Inc. merged into DSW Inc. 05/26/2011

VALUE COMPUTING, INC. (DE)
Merged into VCI Acquisition Co., Inc. 11/15/84
Details not available

VALUE CONSULTING INC (NV)
Name changed to Smarts Oil & Gas, Inc. 08/25/2006
Smarts Oil & Gas, Inc. name changed to Dynamic Natural Resources, Inc. 08/27/2007 which name changed to Universal Tracking Solutions, Inc. 10/31/2008

VALUE ENGR CO (DE)
Each share Common 10¢ par exchanged for (0.5) share Common 20¢ par 04/18/1964
Common 20¢ par changed to 5¢ par and (3) additional shares issued 04/22/1968
Name changed to VSE Corp. 05/25/1979

VALUE FINL SVCS INC (FL)
Acquired by EZCORP, Inc. 12/31/2008
Each share Common 1¢ par exchanged for either (0.75) share Common 1¢ par or $11 cash

VALUE HEALTH INC (DE)
Common no par split (3) for (2) by issuance of (0.5) additional share 09/21/1992
Merged into Columbia/HCA Healthcare Corp. 08/06/1997
Each share Common no par exchanged for $20.50 cash

VALUE HLDGS INC (FL)
Recapitalized as Galea Life Sciences Inc. 07/24/2007
Each share Common $0.0001 par exchanged for (0.04) share Common $0.0001 par
(See Galea Life Sciences Inc.)

VALUE INVT CORP (BC)
Part. Preferred $25 par called for redemption 11/20/89
Liquidation completed
Each share Common 1¢ par received initial distribution of $5.25 cash 9/28/90
Each share Common 1¢ par received second distribution of $3.62 cash 6/17/91
Each share Common 1¢ par received third distribution of $0.165 cash 12/30/91
Each share Common 1¢ par received fourth and final distribution of $0.0426 cash 1/6/93
Note: Certificates were not required to be exchanged and are without value

VALUE LINE AGGRESSIVE INCOME TR (MA)
Name changed to Value Line Core Bond Fund 12/10/2012

VALUE LINE BD FD INC (MD)
Name changed to Value Line U.S. Government Securities Fund, Inc. 04/10/1986
Value Line U.S. Government Securities Fund, Inc. reorganized as Value Line Core Bond Fund 03/22/2013

VALUE LINE CASH FD INC (MD)
Name changed to Value Line U.S. Government Money Market Fund, Inc. 08/19/2009
(See Value Line U.S. Government Money Market Fund, Inc.)

VALUE LINE CONV FD INC (MD)
Under plan of reorganization each Share of Bene. Int. $1 par automatically became Value Line Income & Growth Fund, Inc. Common $1 par on a net asset basis 12/11/2011 Value Line Income & Growth Fund, Inc. name changed to Value Line Capital Appreciation Fund, Inc. 02/09/2018

VALUE LINE DEV CAP CORP (NY)
Name changed to Sterling Capital Corp. 10/28/80
Sterling Capital Corp. merged into Gabelli Equity Trust, Inc. 9/12/2005

VALUE LINE FD INC (MD)
Reincorporated 04/03/1972
Stock Dividend - 10% 03/04/1955
State of incoporation changed from (DE) to (MD) 04/03/1972
Name changed to Value Line Mid Cap Focused Fund, Inc. and Common $1 par reclassified as Investor Class $0.001 par 03/27/2015

VALUE LINE INCOME & GROWTH FD INC (MD)
Reincorporated 04/03/1972
Name changed 05/01/1999
State of incorporation changed from (DE) to (MD) 04/03/1972
Name changed from Value Line Income Fund, Inc. to Value Line Income & Growth Fund, Inc. 05/01/1999
Common $1 par reclassified as Investor Class $0.001 par 08/18/2015
Name changed to Value Line Capital Appreciation Fund, Inc. 02/09/2018

VALUE LINE LARGER COS FD INC (MD)
Name changed 06/01/2006
Name changed from Value Line Leveraged Growth Investors, Inc. to Value Line Larger Companies Fund, Inc. 06/01/2006
Name changed to Value Line Larger Companies Focused Fund, Inc. and Common $1 par reclassified as Investor Class $0.001 par 03/27/2015

VALUE LINE SPL SITUATIONS FD INC (MD)
Reincorporated 04/03/1972
State of incorporation changed from (DE) to (MD) and Capital Stock 10¢ par changed to $1 par 04/03/1972
Name changed to Value Line Premier Growth Fund, Inc. 10/05/2005

VALUE LINE U S GOVT SECS FD INC (MD)
Under plan of reorganization each share Common $1 par automatically became (2.289) Value Line Core Bond Fund Shares of Bene. Int. 1¢ par 03/22/2013

VALUE LINE U S GOVT SECS MONEY MKT FD INC (MD)
Under plan of reorganization each share Common 10¢ par automatically became Daily Income Fund U.S. Government Income Portfolio on a net asset basis 10/12/2012

VALUE MERCHANTS INC (OLD) (WI)
Plan of reorganization under Chapter 11 Bankruptcy Code effective 6/27/95
Each share Common 1¢ par exchanged for (0.05) share Value Merchants, Inc. (New) Common 1¢ par
(See Value Merchants, Inc. (New))

VALUE MERCHANTS INC NEW (WI)
SEC revoked common stock registration 10/15/2009
Stockholders' equity unlikely

VALUE PPTY TR (MD)
Merged into Wellsford Real Properties, Inc. 02/23/1998
Each share Common $1 par exchanged for (0.2984) share Common $1 par and $11.58 cash
Note: Option to increase either the amount of stock or cash to be received expired 03/06/1998
Wellsford Real Properties, Inc. name changed to Reis, Inc. 06/01/2007
(See Reis, Inc.)

VALUE SOFTWARE CORP (NV)
Recapitalized as Technology Enterprises, Inc. 1/26/2005
Each share Common $0.001 par exchanged for (0.001) share Common $0.001 par
Technology Enterprises, Inc. reorganized as Life Exchange, Inc. 1/20/2006

VALUE TRADING INDS INC (CA)
Charter suspended for failure to file reports and pay fees 07/01/1992

VALUECLICK INC (DE)
Name changed to Conversant, Inc. 02/05/2014
Conversant, Inc. merged into Alliance Data Systems Corp. 12/11/2014

VALUERICH INC (DE)
Name changed to Twin Vee Powercats, Inc. 04/22/2016

VALUESTAR CORP (CO)
Assets assigned for the benefit of creditors 10/26/2001
Stockholders' equity unlikely

VALUEVISION MEDIA INC (MN)
Name changed 05/16/2002
Name changed from ValueVision International, Inc. to ValueVision Media, Inc. 05/16/2002
Name changed to EVINE Live Inc. 11/20/2014

VALUJET AIRLS INC (NV)
Issue Information - 2,817,200 shares COM offered at $12.50 per share on 06/28/1994
Common 1¢ par split (2) for (1) by issuance of (1) additional share 04/10/1995
Under plan of reorganization each share Common 1¢ par automatically became (1) share Valujet Inc. Common $0.001 par 10/20/1995
Valujet Inc. name changed to AirTran Holdings Inc. 11/18/1997 which merged into Southwest Airlines Co. 05/02/2011

VALUJET INC (NV)
Common $0.001 par split (2) for (1) by issuance of (1) additional share 11/21/1995
Name changed to AirTran Holdings Inc. 11/18/1997
AirTran Holdings Inc. merged into Southwest Airlines Co. 05/02/2011

VALUSALES INC (FL)
Recapitalized as Video Without Boundaries Inc. 11/19/2001
Each share Common $0.001 par exchanged for (0.05) share Common $0.001 par
Video Without Boundaries Inc. name changed to MediaREADY, Inc. 09/22/2006 which recapitalized as China Logistics Group, Inc. 03/12/2008

VALUSHIP LTD (BAHAMAS)
Reincorporated 01/04/2002
Each share old Common no par exchanged for (1) share new Common no par 09/04/2001
Place of incorporation changed from (CO) to (Bahamas) 01/04/2002
Reorganized under the laws of Delaware as Vorsatech Ventures Inc. 03/03/2004
Each share Common no par exchanged for (0.005) share Common $0.0001 par
Vorsatech Ventures Inc. name changed to Synutra International, Inc. 09/12/2005
(See Synutra International, Inc.)

VALUTRON DISTRIBUTION TRUST (DE)
In process of liquidation
Details not available

VALVE CORP AMER (DE)
Common 25¢ par split (3) for (2) by issuance of (0.5) additional share 7/28/65
Common 25¢ par split (3) for (2) by issuance of (0.5) additional share 1/26/68
Name changed to VCA Corp. 2/27/70
VCA Corp. merged into Ethyl Corp. 10/30/74

VALVERDE CAP CORP (AB)
Recapitalized as Americas Petrogas Inc. 10/17/2008
Each share Common no par exchanged for (0.5) share Common no par
Americas Petrogas Inc. name changed to GrowMax Resources Corp. 08/09/2016

VALVOLINE OIL CO.
Merged into Freedom-Valvoline Oil Co. on a (6) for (1) basis 12/31/45
Freedom-Valvoline Oil Co. acquired by Ashland Oil & Refining Co: 1/31/50 which name changed to Ashland Oil, Inc. 2/2/70 which name changed to Ashland Inc. (Old) 1/27/95
(See Ashland Inc. (Old))

VAM LTD (AUSTRALIA)
ADR's for Ordinary Reg. AUD $0.50 par changed to AUD $0.20 par 07/17/1989
ADR agreement terminated 06/16/1995
Each ADR for Ordinary Reg. AUD $0.20 par exchanged for (0.1) share Hillgrove Gold Ordinary
Note: Unexchanged ADR's will be sold and the proceeds, if any, held for claim after 12/18/1995

VAMCO CORP (NY)
Proclaimed dissolved for failure to file reports and pay fees 12/15/1969

VAN AMERN CAP LTD (NV)
Name changed to Salesrepcentral.com, Inc. 11/9/99
(See Salesrepcentral.com, Inc.)

VAN BRIGGLE ART POTTERY CO (CO)
Each (450) shares old Common $1 par exchanged for (1) share new Common $1 par 07/11/2008
Note: Holders of (449) or fewer pre-split shares received $109.56 cash per share
$10 Preferred $10 par called for redemption at $10 plus $4.90 accrued dividends on 07/12/2008
Public interest eliminated

VAN BUREN STATE BANK (HARTFORD, MI)
Stock Dividend - 20% 03/05/1971
Merged into First American Bank Corp. 12/30/1978
Each share Common $20 par exchanged for (4) to (5) shares Common $10 par or $72.50 cash
Note: Option to receive cash expired 01/16/1976
First American Bank Corp. name changed to First of America Bank Corp. 01/14/1983 which merged into National City Corp. 03/31/1998 which was acquired by PNC Financial Services Group, Inc. 12/31/2008

VAN CAMP MILK CO.
Each share Preferred $100 par exchanged for (1) share $4 Preferred no par and (2) shares Common $1 par in 1936
Merged into Pet Milk Co. 4/1/44
Each share $4 Preferred no par exchanged for (1) share 4-1/4% 2nd Preferred $100 par
Each share Common $1 par exchanged for (0.213221) share 4-1/4% 2nd Preferred $100 par
(See Pet Milk Co.)

VAN-VAN FINANCIAL INFORMATION, INC.

VAN CAMP PACKING CO., INC.
Bankrupt in 1932; stock worthless

VAN CAMP PRODUCTS CO.
Receiver appointed in 1932
Part of assets sold in 1933

VAN CAMP SEA FOOD CO. (CA)
Common $2 par changed to $1 par and (1) additional share issued 12/15/61
Stock Dividends - 100% 9/9/60; 100% 3/1/61
Merged into Ralston Purina Co. 6/28/63
Each share Common and/or VTC for Common $1 par exchanged for (0.53) share Common $2.50 par
7% Preferred $100 par called for redemption 7/1/63
(See Ralston Purina Co.)

VAN CAMP'S, INC.
Acquired by Stokely Brothers & Co., Inc. on a (6) for (1) basis in 1937
Stokely Brothers & Co., Inc. name changed to Stokely-Van Camp, Inc. in 1944
(See Stokely-Van Camp, Inc.)

VAN-CITY CULTURED MARBLE PRODS LTD (BC)
Recapitalized as Consolidated Van-City Marble Ltd. 10/03/1995
Each share Common no par exchanged for (0.2) share Common no par
(See Consolidated Van-City Marble Ltd.)

VAN CLEVE HOTEL CO. (OH)
Liquidation completed
Each share Common no par exchanged for initial distribution of $150 cash 1/10/68
Each share Common no par received second distribution of $25 cash 3/1/68
Each share Common no par received third and final distribution of $5.29 cash 11/6/69

VAN (JOHN) CO.
Liquidated in 1935
Details not available

VAN DE KAMP'S HOLLAND DUTCH BAKERS, INC. (DE)
Merged into General Baking Co. 04/01/1957
Each share Common no par exchanged for (4) shares Common $5 par
General Baking Co. name changed to General Host Corp. 04/20/1967
(See General Host Corp.)

VAN DER HOUT ASSOC LTD (ON)
Merged into Maremont Corp. 11/17/1987
Each share Common no par exchanged for $7.25 cash

VAN DER MOOLEN HLDG NV (NETHERLANDS)
ADR agreement terminated 12/28/2007
Each Sponsored ADR for Ordinary exchanged for $3.90302 cash

VAN DIEMENS COMPANY LTD (BERMUDA)
Recapitalized as VDC Corp. Ltd. 07/17/1995
Each share Common 10¢ par exchanged for (0.05) share Common 10¢ par
VDC Corp. Ltd. merged into VDC Communications, Inc. 11/06/1998
(See VDC Communications, Inc.)

VAN DORN CO (OH)
Common no par split (2) for (1) by issuance of (1) additional share 07/15/1964
Common no par split (5) for (4) by issuance of (4) additional shares 07/30/1965
Common no par split (2) for (1) by issuance of (1) additional share 01/30/1970
Common no par split (5) for (4) by issuance of (0.25) additional share 04/28/1972
Common no par split (3) for (2) by issuance of (0.5) additional share 06/26/1984
Common no par split (2) for (1) by issuance of (1) additional share 06/30/1988
Stock Dividends - 10% 01/26/1968; 10% 10/25/1968
Merged into Crown Cork & Seal Co., Inc 04/16/1993
Each share Common no par exchanged for (0.542) share Common $5 par
Crown Cork & Seal Co., Inc. reorganized as Crown Holdings, Inc. 02/25/2003

VAN DORN IRON WORKS CO. (OH)
Stock Dividend - 10% 04/21/1953
Name changed to Van Dorn Co. 06/30/1964
Van Dorn Co. merged into Crown Cork & Seal Co., Inc. 04/16/1993 which reorganized as Crown Holdings, Inc. 02/25/2003

VAN DUSEN AIR INC (MN)
Stock Dividends - 20% 07/28/1977; 20% 07/31/1978; 50% 07/27/1979
Acquired by APL Limited Partnership 01/24/1986
Each share Common $1 par exchanged for $21 cash

VAN DUSEN AIRCRAFT SUPPLIES INC (MN)
Name changed to Van Dusen Air Inc. 07/14/1969
(See Van Dusen Air Inc.)

VAN DYK RESH CORP (NJ)
Name changed to Precision Resources, Inc. (NJ) 11/13/1986
Precision Resources, Inc. (NJ) reincorporated in Delaware as Kemp Industries Inc. 07/01/1991
(See Kemp Industries Inc.)

VAN DYKE SNOW LAKE GOLD MINES LTD. (ON)
Succeeded by Lynnita Consolidated Gold Mines Ltd. on a (1) for (3) basis in 1948
(See Lynnita Consolidated Gold Mines Ltd.)

VAN ECK FDS INC (MD)
Name changed 01/01/2002
Government Securities Fund completely liquidated 05/26/1999
Details not available
Money Market Fund completely liquidated 05/26/1999
Details not available
Tax Exempt Fund completely liquidated 05/26/1999
Details not available
Total Return Fund Class A completely liquidated 05/26/1999
Details not available
Name changed from Van Eck/Chubb Funds, Inc. to Van Eck Funds, Inc. and Growth & Income Fund Class A 1¢ par reclassified as Mid Cap Value Fund Class A $0.001 par 01/01/2002
Completely liquidated 12/13/2007
Each share Mid Cap Value Fund Class A $0.001 par received first and final distribution of $25.65 cash

VAN ECK MERK GOLD TR (NY)
Name changed to VanEck Merk Gold Trust 04/29/2016

VAN ESS LABORATORIES, INC.
Acquired by American Home Products Corp. 00/00/1930
Details not available

VAN GOLD RES INC (NV)
Recapitalized as Zhuding International Ltd. 08/01/2016
Each share Common $0.001 par exchanged for (0.01) share Common $0.001 par

VAN HORN BUTANE SERVICE (CA)
Each share Common $5 par exchanged for (2) shares Common $2.50 par in 1954
Name changed to Vangas, Inc. 11/12/57
(See Vangas, Inc.)

VAN HORNE GOLD EXPL INC (ON)
Merged into Moss Resources Ltd. (ONT) 4/22/88
Each share Common no par exchanged for (1.1) shares Common no par
Moss Resources Ltd. (ONT) merged into Moss-Power Resources Inc. 2/28/90 which recapitalized as WisCan Resources Ltd. 2/14/91
(See WisCan Resources Ltd.)

VAN HOUTEN GOLD MINES, LTD. (ON)
Charter cancelled by the Province of Ontario 12/21/59

VAN HOUTTE INC (CANADA)
Name changed 09/13/2000
Subordinate no par split (2) for (1) by issuance of (1) additional share payable 09/23/1997 to holders of record 09/22/1997
Name changed from Van Houtte (A.L.) Ltee. to Van Houtte Inc. 09/13/2000
Merged into Littlejohn & Co., LLC 07/19/2007
Each share Subordinate no par exchanged for $25 cash

VAN KAMPEN ADVANTAGE MUN INCOME TR (MA)
Name changed 12/29/1995
Name changed 08/28/1998
Name changed from Van Kampen Merritt Advantage Municipal Income Trust to Van Kampen American Capital Advantage Municipal Income Trust 12/29/1995
Name changed from Van Kampen American Capital Advantage Municipal Income Trust to Van Kampen Advantage Municipal Income Trust 08/28/1998
Merged into Van Kampen Municipal Opportunity Trust 01/27/2006
Each share Auction Preferred Ser. A 1¢ par exchanged for (1) share Auction Preferred Ser. C 1¢ par
Each share Auction Preferred Ser. B 1¢ par exchanged for (1) share Auction Preferred Ser. D 1¢ par
Each share Auction Preferred Ser. C 1¢ par exchanged for (1) share Auction Preferred Ser. E 1¢ par
Each share Auction Preferred Ser. D 1¢ par exchanged for (1) share Auction Preferred Ser. F 1¢ par
Each share Common 1¢ par exchanged for (0.984721) Common Share of Bene. Int. 1¢ par
Van Kampen Municipal Opportunity Trust name changed to Invesco Van Kampen Municipal Opportunity Trust (MA) 06/01/2010 which reincorporated in Delaware 10/15/2012 which name changed to Invesco Municipal Opportunity Trust 12/03/2012

VAN KAMPEN ADVANTAGE MUN INCOME TR II (MA)
Name changed 08/28/1998
Name changed from Van Kampen American Capital Advantage Municipal Income Trust to Van Kampen Advantage Municipal Income Trust II 08/28/1998
Name changed to Invesco Van Kampen Advantage Municipal Income Trust II (MA) 06/01/2010
Invesco Van Kampen Advantage Municipal Income Trust II (MA) reincorporated in Delaware 08/27/2012 which name changed to Invesco Advantage Municipal Income Trust II 12/03/2012

VAN KAMPEN ADVANTAGE PA MUN INCOME TR (PA)
Name changed 12/29/1995
Name changed 08/28/1998
Name changed from Van Kampen Merritt Advantage Pennsylvania Municipal Income Trust to Van Kampen American Capital Advantage Pennsylvania Municipal Income Trust 12/29/1995
Name changed from Van Kampen American Capital Advantage Pennsylvania Municipal Income Trust to Van Kampen Advantage Pennsylvania Muncipal Income Trust 08/28/1998
Merged into Van Kampen Pennsylvania Value Municipal Income Trust 12/02/2005
Each share Auction Preferred 1¢ par exchanged for (1) share Auction Preferred Ser. B share 1¢ par
Each share Share of Bene. Int. 1¢ par exchanged for (1.005624) shares Common 1¢ par
Van Kampen Pennsylvania Value Municipal Income Trust name changed to Invesco Van Kampen Pennsylvania Value Municipal Income Trust (PA) 06/01/2010 which reincorporated in Delaware 08/27/2012 which name changed to Invesco Pennsylvania Value Municipal Income Trust 12/03/2012

VAN KAMPEN AMERN CAP CORPORATE BD FD (DE)
Name changed to Van Kampen Corporate Bond Fund 07/14/1998

VAN KAMPEN AMERN CAP ENTERPRISE FD (DE)
Name changed to Van Kampen Enterprise Fund 08/31/1998

VAN KAMPEN AMERN CAP GROWTH & INCOME FD (DE)
Name changed to Van Kampen Growth & Income Fund 7/14/98

VAN KAMPEN AMERN CAP HBR FD (DE)
Name changed to Van Kampen Harbor Fund 07/14/1998

VAN KAMPEN AMERN CAP SR FLTG RATE FD (MA)
Name changed to Van Kampen Senior Floating Rate Fund 8/28/98

VAN KAMPEN BD FD (DE)
Reincorporated 10/31/1996
Name changed 08/28/1998
State of incorporation changed from (MD) to (DE) and Common Shares of Bene. Int. $1 par changed to 1¢ par 10/31/1996
Name changed from Van Kampen American Capital Bond Fund, Inc. to Van Kampen Bond Fund 08/28/1998
Name changed to Invesco Van Kampen Bond Fund 06/01/2010
Invesco Van Kampen Bond Fund name changed to Invesco Bond Fund 12/03/2012

VAN KAMPEN CALIF MUN TR (MA)
Name changed 08/28/1998
Name changed from Van Kampen American Capital California Municipal Trust to Van Kampen California Municipal Trust 08/28/1998
Merged into Van Kampen California Value Municipal Income Trust 12/02/2005
Each share Remarketed Preferred 1¢ par exchanged for (2) shares Auction Preferred Ser. A 1¢ par
Each Common Share of Bene. Int. 1¢ par exchanged for (0.591825) Common Share of Bene. Int. 1¢ par
Van Kampen California Value Municipal Income Trust name changed to Invesco Van Kampen

California Value Municipal Income Trust (MA) 06/01/2010 which reincorporated in Delaware 08/27/2012
Which name changed to Invesco California Value Municipal Income Trust 12/03/2012

VAN KAMPEN CALIF QUALITY MUN TR (MA)
Name changed 12/29/1995
Name changed 08/28/1998
Name changed from Van Kampen Merritt California Quality Municipal Trust to Van Kampen American Capital California Quality Municipal Trust 12/29/1995
Name changed from Van Kampen American Capital California Quality Municipal Trust to Van Kampen California Quality Municipal Trust 08/28/1998
Merged into Van Kampen California Value Municipal Income Trust 07/29/2005
Each share Common 1¢ par exchanged for (0.9764) share Common Shares of Bene. Int. 1¢ par
Van Kampen California Value Municipal Income Trust name changed to Invesco Van Kampen California Value Municipal Income Trust (MA) 06/01/2010 which reincorporated in Delaware 08/27/2012 which name changed to Invesco California Value Municipal Income Trust 12/03/2012

VAN KAMPEN CALIF VALUE MUN INCOME TR (MA)
Name changed 12/29/1995
Name changed 08/28/1998
Name changed from Van Kampen Merritt California Value Municipal Income Trust to Van Kampen American Capital California Value Municipal Income Trust 12/29/1995
Name changed from Van Kampen American Capital California Value Municipal Income Trust to Van Kampen California Value Municipal Income Trust 08/28/1998
Name changed to Invesco Van Kampen California Value Municipal Income Trust (MA) 06/01/2010
Invesco Van Kampen California Value Municipal Income Trust (MA) reincorporated in Delaware 08/27/2012 which name changed to Invesco California Value Municipal Income Trust 12/03/2012

VAN KAMPEN CONV SECS INC (DE)
Reincorporated 10/16/96
Name changed 8/28/98
State of incorporation changed from (MD) to (DE) and Common $1 par changed to 1¢ par 10/29/96
Name changed from Van Kampen American Capital Convertible Securities Inc. to Van Kampen Convertible Securities Inc. 8/28/98
Under plan of reorganization each share Common 1¢ par automatically became (1) share Van Kampen American Capital Harbor Fund Class A Common 1¢ par 8/15/2000

VAN KAMPEN DYNAMIC CR OPPORTUNITIES FD (DE)
Issue Information - 71,000,000 shares COM SHS BEN INT offered at $20 per share on 06/26/2007
Name changed to Invesco Van Kampen Dynamic Credit Opportunities Fund 06/01/2010
Invesco Van Kampen Dynamic Credit Opportunities Fund name changed to Invesco Dynamic Credit Opportunities Fund 12/03/2012

VAN KAMPEN FLA MUN OPPORTUNITY TR (MA)
Name changed 08/28/1998
Name changed from Van Kampen American Capital Florida Municipal Opportunity Trust to Van Kampen Florida Municipal Opportunity Trust 08/28/1998
Under plan of reorganization each share Auction Preferred Shares 1¢ par and Common 1¢ par automatically became (1) share Van Kampen Trust for Investment Grade Florida Municipals Auction Preferred 1¢ par or Common 1¢ par respectively 05/18/2001
Van Kampen Trust for Investment Grade Florida Municipals merged into Van Kampen Trust for Investment Grade Municipals 06/08/2007 which name changed to Invesco Van Kampen Trust for Investment Grade Municipals (MA) 06/01/2010 which reincorporated in Delaware 08/27/2012 which name changed to Invesco Trust for Investment Grade Municipals 12/03/2012

VAN KAMPEN FLA QUALITY MUN TR (MA)
Name changed 12/29/1995
Name changed 08/28/1998
Name changed from Van Kampen Merritt Florida Quality Municipal Trust to Van Kampen American Capital Florida Quality Municipal Trust 12/29/1995
Name changed from Van Kampen American Capital Florida Quality Municipal Trust to Van Kampen Florida Quality Municipal Trust 08/28/1998
Merged into Van Kampen Trust for Investment Grade Florida Municipals 10/28/2005
Each share Auction Preferred 1¢ par exchanged for (1) share Auction Preferred Ser. B 1¢ par
Each share Common 1¢ par exchanged for (0.943077) Common Share of Bene. Int. 1¢ par
Note: Holders also received a final dividend of $0.0295 cash payable 10/28/2005 to holders of record 10/27/2005
Van Kampen Trust for Investment Grade Florida Municipals merged into Van Kampen Trust for Investment Grade Municipals 06/08/2007 which name changed to Invesco Van Kampen Trust for Investment Grade Municipals (MA) 06/01/2010 which reincorporated in Delaware 08/27/2012 which name changed to Invesco Trust for Investment Grade Municipals 12/03/2012

VAN KAMPEN HIGH INCOME TR (MA)
Name changed 12/29/1995
Name changed 03/07/1997
Name changed 08/28/1998
Name changed from Van Kampen Merritt Intermediate Term High Income Trust to Van Kampen American Capital Intermediate Term High Income Trust 12/29/1995
Name changed from Van Kampen American Capital Intermediate Term High Income Trust to Van Kampen American Capital High Income Trust 03/07/1997
Name changed from Van Kampen American Capital High Income Trust to Van Kampen High Income Trust 08/28/1998
Merged into Van Kampen High Income Trust II 07/29/2005
Each share Auction Market Preferred 1¢ par exchanged for (4) shares Auction Preferred Ser. B 1¢ par
Each Common Share of Bene. Int. 1¢ par exchanged for (0.786581) Common Share of Bene. Int. 1¢ par
Van Kampen High Income Trust II name changed to Invesco Van Kampen High Income Trust II (MA) 06/01/2010 which reincorporated in Delaware 08/27/2012 which name changed to Invesco High Income Trust II 12/03/2012

VAN KAMPEN HIGH INCOME TR II (MA)
Name changed 12/29/1995
Name changed 08/01/1997
Name changed 08/28/1998
9.50% Preferred 1¢ par called for redemption 11/18/1992
Name changed from Van Kampen Merritt Limited Term High Income Trust to Van Kampen American Capital Limited Term High Income Trust 12/29/1995
Name changed from Van Kampen American Capital Limited Term High Income Trust to Van Kampen American Capital High Income Trust II 08/01/1997
Name changed from Van Kampen American Capital High Income Trust II to Van Van Kampen High Income Trust II 08/28/1998
Each share old Common 1¢ par exchanged for (0.2) share new Common 1¢ par 05/26/2009
Auction Preferred Ser. A 1¢ par called for redemption at $25,000 on 01/19/2010
Auction Preferred Ser. B 1¢ par called for redemption at $25,000 on 02/01/2010
Name changed to Invesco Van Kampen High Income Trust II (MA) 06/01/2010
Invesco Van Kampen High Income Trust II (MA) reincorporated in Delaware 08/27/2012 which name changed to Invesco High Income Trust II 12/03/2012

VAN KAMPEN INCOME TRUST (MA)
Name changed 08/28/1998
Name changed from Van Kampen American Capital Income Trust to Van Kampen Income Trust 08/28/1998
Liquidation completed
Each Share of Bene. Int. 1¢ par received initial distribution of $6.08 cash payable 05/29/2007 to holders of record 04/30/2007
Each Share of Bene. Int. 1¢ par received second and final distribution of $0.3239 cash payable 06/25/2007 to holders of record 04/30/2007
Note: Certificates were not required to be surrendered and are without value

VAN KAMPEN INVT GRADE MUN TR (MA)
Name changed 12/29/1995
Name changed 08/28/1998
Name changed from Van Kampen Merritt Investment Grade Municipal Trust to Van Kampen American Capital Investment Grade Municipal Trust 12/29/1995
Name changed from Van Kampen American Capital Investment Grade Municipal Trust to Van Kampen Investment Grade Municipal Trust 08/28/1998
Merged into Van Kampen Municipal Trust 08/26/2005
Each Remarketed Preferred 1¢ par exchanged for (4) shares Auction Preferred Ser. E 1¢ par
Each share Common 1¢ par exchanged for (0.622886) Common Share of Bene. Int. 1¢ par
Van Kampen Municipal Trust name changed to Invesco Van Kampen Municipal Trust (MA) 06/01/2010 which reincorporated in Delaware 10/15/2012

VAN KAMPEN MASS VALUE MUN INCOME TR (MA)
Name changed 08/28/1998
Name changed from Van Kampen American Capital Massachusetts Value Municipal Income Trust to Van Kampen Massachusetts Value Municipal Income Trust 08/28/1998
Name changed to Invesco Van Kampen Massachusetts Value Municipal Income Trust 06/01/2010
Invesco Van Kampen Massachusetts Value Municipal Income Trust merged into Invesco Van Kampen Municipal Trust 10/15/2012 which name changed to Invesco Municipal Trust 12/03/2012

VAN KAMPEN MERRITT GROWTH & INCOME FD (MA)
Name changed to Van Kampen American Capital Growth & Income Fund 12/29/95

VAN KAMPEN MERRITT HIGH YIELD FD (MA)
Name changed to Van Kampen American Capital High Yield Fund 12/29/95

VAN KAMPEN MERRITT INSD TAX FREE INCOME FD INC (MD)
Name changed to Van Kampen American Capital Insured Tax Free Income Fund Inc. 12/29/95

VAN KAMPEN MERRITT MONEY MKT TR (MA)
Name changed Van Kampen American Capital Money Market Trust 12/29/95

VAN KAMPEN MERRITT PA TAX FREE INCOME FD (PA)
Name changed to Van Kampen American Capital Pennsylvania Tax Free Income Fund 12/29/95

VAN KAMPEN MERRITT TAX FREE HIGH INCOME FD INC (MD)
Name changed to Van Kampen American Capital Tax Free High Income Fund Inc. 12/29/95

VAN KAMPEN MERRITT U S GOVT FD INC (MD)
Name changed to Van Kampen American Capital U.S. Government Fund Inc. 12/29/95

VAN KAMPEN MUN INCOME TR (MA)
Name changed 12/29/1995
Name changed 08/28/1998
Name changed from Van Kampen Merritt Municipal Income Trust to Van Kampen American Capital Municipal Income Trust 12/29/1995
Name changed from Van Kampen American Capital Municipal Income Trust to Van Kampen Municipal Income Trust 08/28/1998
Merged into Van Kampen Trust for Investment Grade Municipals 10/07/2005
Each share Adjustable Rate Tax-Exempt Preferred Ser. A 1¢ par exchanged for (20) shares Auction Preferred Ser. E 1¢ par
Each share Adjustable Rate Tax-Exempt Preferred Ser. B 1¢ par exchanged for (20) shares Auction Preferred Ser. F 1¢ par
Each share Adjustable Rate Tax-Exempt Preferred Ser. C 1¢ par exchanged for (20) shares Auction Preferred Ser. G 1¢ par
Each share Common 1¢ par exchanged for (0.585182) Common Share of Bene. Int. 1¢ par
Van Kampen Trust for Investment Grade Municipals name changed to Invesco Van Kampen Trust for Investment Grade Municipals (MA) 06/01/2010 which reincorporated in Delaware 08/27/2012 which name changed to Invesco Trust for Investment Grade Municipals 12/03/2012

VAN KAMPEN MUN OPPORTUNITY TR (MA)
Name changed 12/29/1995
Name changed 08/28/1998
Name changed from Van Kampen

VAN-VAN

Merritt Municipal Opportunity Trust to Van Kampen American Capital Municipal Opportunity Trust 12/29/1995
Name changed from Van Kampen American Capital Municipal Opportunity Trust to Van Kampen Municipal Opportunity Trust 08/28/1998
Name changed to Invesco Van Kampen Municipal Opportunity Trust (MA) 06/01/2010
Invesco Van Kampen Municipal Opportunity Trust (MA) reincorporated in Delaware 10/15/2012 which name changed to Invesco Municipal Opportunity Trust 12/03/2012

VAN KAMPEN MUN TR (MA)
Name changed 12/29/1995
Name changed 08/28/1998
Name changed from Van Kampen Merritt Municipal Trust to Van Kampen American Capital Municipal Trust 12/29/1995
Name changed from Van Kampen American Capital Municipal Trust to Van Kampen Municipal Trust 08/28/1998
Name changed to Invesco Van Kampen Municipal Trust (MA) 06/01/2010 Invesco Van Kampen Municipal Trust (MA) reincorporated in Delaware 10/15/2012

VAN KAMPEN MUN OPPORTUNITY TR II (MA)
Name changed 12/29/1995
Name changed 08/28/1998
Name changed from Van Kampen Merritt Municipal Opportunity Trust II to Van Kampen American Capital Municipal Opportunity Trust II 12/29/1995
Name changed from Van Kampen American Capital Municipal Opportunity Trust II to Van Kampen Municipal Opportunity Trust II 08/28/1998
Merged into Van Kampen Advantage Municipal Income Trust II 01/27/2006
Each share Auction Preferred Ser. A 1¢ par exchanged for (1) share Auction Preferred Ser. C 1¢ par
Each share Auction Preferred Ser. B 1¢ par exchanged for (1) share Auction Preferred Ser. D 1¢ par
Each share Auction Preferred Ser. C 1¢ par exchanged for (1) share Auction Preferred Ser. E 1¢ par
Each share Common 1¢ par exchanged for (1.025341) Common Shares of Bene. Int. 1¢ par
Van Kampen Advantage Municipal Income Trust II name changed to Invesco Van Kampen Advantage Municipal Income Trust II (MA) 06/01/2010 which reincorporated in Delaware 08/27/2012 which name changed to Invesco Advantage Municipal Income Trust II 12/03/2012

VAN KAMPEN N J VALUE MUN INCOME TRUST (MA)
Name changed 08/28/1998
Name changed from Van Kampen American Capital New Jersey Value Municipal Income Trust to Van Kampen New Jersey Value Municipal Income Trust 08/28/1998
Reorganized as Van Kampen Trust for Investment Grade New Jersey Municipals 05/18/2001
Each share Auction Preferred 1¢ par exchanged for (1) share Auction Preferred 1¢ par
Each share Common 1¢ par exchanged for (0.86686) share Common 1¢ par
Van Kampen Trust for Investment Grade New Jersey Municipals name changed to Invesco Van Kampen Trust for Investment Grade New Jersey Municipals 06/01/2010 which merged into Invesco Van Kampen Municipal Trust 10/15/2012 which name changed to Invesco Municipal Trust 12/03/2012

VAN KAMPEN N Y QUALITY MUN TR (MA)
Name changed 12/29/1995
Name changed 08/28/1998
Name changed from Van Kampen Merritt New York Quality Municipal Trust to Van Kampen American Capital New York Quality Municipal Trust 12/29/1995
Name changed from Van Kampen American Capital New York Quality Municipal Trust to Van Kampen New York Quality Municipal Trust 08/28/1998
Merged into Van Kampen Trust for Investment Grade New York Municipals 10/28/2005
Each share Auction Preferred 1¢ par exchanged for (1) share Auction Preferred Ser. B 1¢ par
Each share Common 1¢ par exchanged for (0.928864) Common Share of Bene. Int. 1¢ par
Note: Holders also received a final dividend of $0.2004 cash payable 10/28/2005 to holders of record 10/27/2005
Van Kampen Trust for Investment Grade New York Municipals name changed to Invesco Van Kampen Trust for Investment Grade New York Municipals (MA) 06/01/2010 which reincorporated in Delaware 08/27/2012 which name changed to Invesco Trust for Investment Grade New York Municipals 12/03/2012

VAN KAMPEN N Y VALUE MUN INCOME TR (MA)
Name changed 12/29/1995
Name changed 08/28/1998
Name changed from Van Kampen Merritt New York Value Municipal Income Trust to Van Kampen American Capital New York Value Municipal Income Trust 12/29/1995
Name changed from Van Kampen American Capital New York Value Municipal Income Trust to Van Kampen New York Value Municipal Income Trust 08/28/1998
Merged into Van Kampen Trust for Investment Grade New York Municipals 10/28/2005
Each share Auction Preferred 1¢ par exchanged for (1) share Auction Preferred Ser. C 1¢ par
Each share Common 1¢ par exchanged for (0.936312) Common Share of Bene. Int. 1¢ par
Note: Holders also received a final dividend of $0.1439 cash payable 10/28/2005 to holders of record 10/27/2005
Van Kampen Trust for Investment Grade New York Municipals name changed to Invesco Van Kampen Trust for Investment Grade New York Municipals (MA) 06/01/2010 which reincorporated in Delaware 08/27/2012 which name changed to Invesco Trust for Investment Grade New York Municipals 12/03/2012

VAN KAMPEN OHIO QUALITY MUN TR (MA)
Name changed 12/29/1995
Name changed 08/28/1998
Name changed from Van Kampen Merritt Ohio Quality Municipal Trust to Van Kampen American Capital Ohio Quality Municipal Trust 12/29/1995
Name changed from Van Kampen American Capital Ohio Quality Municipal Trust to Van Kampen Ohio Quality Municipal Trust 08/28/1998
Name changed to Invesco Van Kampen Ohio Quality Municipal Trust 06/01/2010 Invesco Van Kampen Ohio Quality Municipal Trust merged into Invesco Van Kampen Municipal Trust 10/15/2012 which name changed to Invesco Municipal Trust 12/03/2012

VAN KAMPEN OHIO VALUE MUN INCOME TR (MA)
Name changed 08/28/1998
Name changed from Van Kampen American Capital Ohio Value Municipal Income Trust to Van Kampen Ohio Value Municipal Income Trust 08/28/1998
Merged into Van Kampen Ohio Quality Municipal Trust 10/07/2005
Each share Auction Preferred 1¢ par exchanged for (1) share Auction Preferred Ser. B 1¢ par
Each Share of Bene. Int. 1¢ par exchanged for (0.894103) Common Share of Bene. Int. 1¢ par
Van Kampen Ohio Quality Municipal Trust name changed to Invesco Van Kampen Ohio Quality Municipal Trust 06/01/2010 which merged into Invesco Van Kampen Municipal Trust 10/15/2012 which name changed to Invesco Municipal Trust 12/03/2012

VAN KAMPEN PA QUALITY MUN TR (PA)
Name changed 12/29/1995
Name changed 08/28/1998
Name changed from Van Kampen Merritt Pennsylvania Quality Municipal Trust to Van Kampen American Capital Pennsylvania Quality Municipal Trust 12/29/1995
Name changed from Van Kampen American Capital Pennsylvania Quality Municipal Trust to Van Kampen Pennsylvania Quality Municipal Trust 08/28/1998
Merged into Van Kampen Pennsylvania Value Municipal Income Trust 12/02/2005
Each share Auction Preferred 1¢ par exchanged for (1) share Auction Preferred Ser. C 1¢ par
Each share Common 1¢ par exchanged for (1.00266) Common Shares of Bene. Int. 1¢ par
Van Kampen Pennsylvania Value Municipal Income Trust name changed to Invesco Van Kampen Pennsylvania Value Municipal Income Trust (PA) 06/01/2010 which reincorporated in Delaware 08/27/2012 which name changed to Invesco Pennsylvania Value Municipal Income Trust 12/03/2012

VAN KAMPEN PA VALUE MUN INCOME TR (PA)
Name changed 12/29/1995
Name changed 08/28/1998
Name changed from Van Kampen Merritt Pennsylvania Value Municipal Income Trust to Van Kampen American Capital Pennsylvania Value Municipal Income Trust 12/29/1995
Name changed from Van Kampen American Capital Pennsylvania Value Municipal Income Trust to Van Kampen Pennsylvania Value Municipal Income Trust 08/28/1998
Name changed to Invesco Van Kampen Pennsylvania Value Municipal Income Trust (PA) 06/01/2010
Invesco Van Kampen Pennsylvania Value Municipal Income Trust (PA) reincorporated in Delaware 08/27/2012 which name changed to Invesco Pennsylvania Value Municipal Income Trust 12/03/2012

VAN KAMPEN SELECT SECTOR MUN TR (MA)
Name changed 12/29/1995
Name changed 08/28/1998
Name changed from Van Kampen Merritt Select Sector Municipal Trust to Van Kampen American Capital Select Sector Municipal Trust 12/29/1995
Name changed from Van Kampen American Capital Select Sector Municipal Trust to Van Kampen Select Sector Municipal Trust 08/28/1998
Name changed to Invesco Van Kampen Select Sector Municipal Trust 06/01/2010
Invesco Van Kampen Select Sector Municipal Trust merged into Invesco Van Kampen Municipal Opportunity Trust 10/15/2012 which name changed to Invesco Municipal Opportunity Trust 12/03/2012

VAN KAMPEN SR INCOME TR (MA)
Name changed 08/28/1998
Name changed from Van Kampen American Capital Senior Income Trust to Van Kampen Senior Income Trust 08/28/1998
Name changed to Invesco Van Kampen Senior Income Trust (MA) 06/01/2010
Invesco Van Kampen Senior Income Trust (MA) reincorporated in Delaware 08/27/2012 which name changed to Invesco Senior Income Trust 12/03/2012

VAN KAMPEN SR LN FD (MA)
Name changed 12/29/1995
Name changed 08/28/1998
Name changed 06/16/2003
Name changed from Van Kampen Merritt Prime Rate Income Trust to Van Kampen American Capital Prime Rate Income Trust 12/29/1995
Name changed from Van Kampen American Capital Prime Rate Income Trust to Van Kampen Prime Rate Income Trust 08/28/1998
Name changed from Van Kampen Prime Rate Income Trust to Van Kampen Senior Loan Fund 06/16/2003
Class B Shares reclassified as Class IB shares 02/18/2005
Class C Shares reclassified as Class IC shares 02/18/2005
Name changed to Invesco Van Kampen Senior Loan Fund 06/01/2010
Invesco Van Kampen Senior Loan Fund name changed to Invesco Senior Loan Fund 09/24/2012

VAN KAMPEN STRATEGIC SECTOR MUN TR (MA)
Name changed 12/29/1995
Name changed 08/28/1998
Issue Information - 9,500,000 COM SHS BEN INT offered at $15 per share on 01/22/1993
Name changed from Van Kampen Merritt Strategic Sector Municipal Trust to Van Kampen American Capital Strategic Sector Municipal Trust 12/29/1995
Name changed from Van Kampen American Capital Strategic Sector Municipal Trust to Van Kampen Strategic Sector Municipal Trust 08/28/1998
Merged into Van Kampen Select Sector Municipal Trust 10/07/2005
Each share Auction Preferred Ser. A 1¢ par exchanged for (1) share Remarketed Preferred Ser. C 1¢ par
Each share Auction Preferred Ser. B 1¢ par exchanged for (1) share Remarketed Preferred Ser. D 1¢ par
Each Common Share of Bene. Int. 1¢ par exchanged for (1.001654) Common Shares of Bene. Int. 1¢ par
Van Kampen Select Sector Municipal Trust name changed to Invesco Van Kampen Select Sector Municipal Trust 06/01/2010 which merged into Invesco Van Kampen Municipal Opportunity Trust 10/15/2012 which

name changed to Invesco Municipal Opportunity Trust 12/03/2012

VAN KAMPEN TAX FREE MONEY FD (MA)
Reorganized 07/31/1995
Name changed 09/29/1998
Reorganized from Van Kampen Merritt Tax Free Money Fund (MA) to Van Kampen American Capital Tax Free Money Fund (DE) and Shares of Bene. Int. no par changed to 1¢ par 07/31/1995
Name changed from Van Kampen American Capital Tax Free Money Fund to Van Kampen Tax Free Money Fund 09/29/1998
Under plan of reorganization each Share of Bene. Int. 1¢ par automatically became (1) AIM Tax-Exempt Funds Invesco Tax-Exempt Cash Fund Class A $0.001 par 06/07/2010

VAN KAMPEN TR INSD MUNS (MA)
Name changed 12/29/1995
Name changed 08/28/1998
Name changed from Van Kampen Merritt Trust for Insured Municipals to Van Kampen American Capital Trust for Insured Municipals 12/29/1995
Name changed from Van Kampen American Capital Trust for Insured Municipals to Van Kampen Trust for Insured Municipals 08/28/1998
Name changed to Invesco Van Kampen Trust for Insured Municipals 06/01/2010
Invesco Van Kampen Trust for Insured Municipals name changed to Invesco Van Kampen Trust for Value Municipals 01/23/2012 which merged into Invesco Van Kampen Municipal Opportunity Trust 10/15/2012 which name changed to Invesco Municipal Opportunity Trust 12/03/2012

VAN KAMPEN TR INVT GRADE CALIF MUNS (MA)
Name changed 12/29/1995
Name changed 08/28/1998
Name changed from Van Kampen Merritt Trust Investment Grade California Municipals to Van Kampen American Capital Trust for Investment Grade California Municipals 12/29/1995
Name changed from Van Kampen American Capital Trust for Investment Grade California Municipals to Van Kampen Trust for Investment Grade California Municipals 08/28/1998
Merged into Van Kampen California Value Municipal Income Trust 07/29/2005
Each share Auction Preferred 1¢ par exchanged for (4) shares Auction Preferred Ser. B 1¢ par
Each share Common 1¢ par exchanged for (0.958305) Common Share of Bene. Int. 1¢ par
Van Kampen California Value Municipal Income Trust name changed to Invesco Van Kampen California Value Municipal Income Trust (MA) 06/01/2010 which reincorporated in Delaware 08/27/2012 which name changed to Invesco California Value Municipal Income Trust 12/03/2012

VAN KAMPEN TR INVT GRADE FLA MUNS (MA)
Name changed 12/29/1995
Name changed 08/28/1998
Name changed from Van Kampen Merritt Trust for Investment Grade Florida Municipals to Van Kampen American Capital Trust for Investment Grade Florida Municipals 12/29/1995
Name changed from Van Kampen American Capital Trust for Investment Grade Florida Municipals to Van Kampen Trust for Investment Grade Florida Municipals 08/28/1998
Merged into Van Kampen Trust for Investment Grade Municipals 06/08/2007
Each share Auction Preferred Ser. A 1¢ exchanged for (1) share Auction Preferred Ser. I 1¢ par
Each share Auction Preferred Ser. B 1¢ exchanged for (1) share Auction Preferred Ser. I 1¢ par
Each share Common 1¢ par exchanged for (0.996574) share Common 1¢ par
Van Kampen Trust for Investment Grade Municipals name changed to Invesco Van Kampen Trust for Investment Grade Municipals (MA) 06/01/2010 which reincorporated in Delaware 08/27/2012 which name changed to Invesco Trust for Investment Grade Municipals 12/03/2012

VAN KAMPEN TR INVT GRADE MUNS (MA)
Name changed 12/29/1995
Name changed 08/28/1998
Name changed from Van Kampen Merritt Trust for Investment Grade Municipals to Van Kampen American Capital Trust for Investment Grade Municipals 12/29/1995
Name changed from Van Kampen American Capital Trust for Investment Grade Municipals to Van Kampen Trust for Investment Grade Municipals 08/28/1998
Name changed to Invesco Van Kampen Trust for Investment Grade Municipals (MA) 06/01/2010
Invesco Van Kampen Trust for Investment Grade Municipals (MA) reincorporated in Delaware 08/27/2012 which name changed to Invesco Trust for Investment Grade Municipals 12/03/2012

VAN KAMPEN TR INVT GRADE N J MUNS (MA)
Name changed 12/29/1995
Name changed 08/28/1998
Name changed from Van Kampen Merritt Trust for Investment Grade New Jersey Municipals to Van Kampen American Capital Trust for Investment Grade New Jersey Municipals 12/29/1995
Name changed from Van Kampen American Capital Trust for Investment Grade New Jersey Municipals to Van Kampen Trust for Investment Grade New Jersey Municipals 08/28/1998
Name changed to Invesco Van Kampen Trust for Investment Grade New Jersey Municipals 06/01/2010
Invesco Van Kampen Trust for Investment Grade New Jersey Municipals merged into Invesco Van Kampen Municipal Trust 10/15/2012 which name changed to Invesco Municipal Trust 12/03/2012

VAN KAMPEN TR INVT GRADE N Y MUNS (MA)
Name changed 12/29/1995
Name changed 08/28/1998
Name changed from Van Kampen Merrit Trust for Investment Grade New York Municipals to Van Kampen American Capital Trust for Investment Grade New York Municipals 12/29/1995
Name changed from Van Kampen American Capital Trust for Investment Grade New York Municipals to Van Kampen Trust for Investment Grade New York Municipals 08/28/1998
Name changed to Invesco Van Kampen Trust for Investment Grade New York Municipals (MA) 06/01/2010
Invesco Van Kampen Trust for Investment Grade New York Municipals (MA) reincorporated in Delaware 08/27/2012 which name changed to Invesco Trust for Investment Grade New York Municipals 12/03/2012

VAN KAMPEN TR INVT GRADE PENN MUNS (PA)
Name changed 12/29/1995
Name changed 08/28/1998
Name changed from Van Kampen Merritt Trust Investment Grade Pennsylvania Municipals to Van Kampen American Capital Trust Investment Grade Pennsylvania Municipals 12/29/1995
Name changed from Van Kampen American Capital Trust Investment Grade Pennsylvania Municipals to Van Kampen Trust Investment Grade Pennsylvania Municipals 08/28/1998
Merged into Van Kampen Pennsylvania Value Municipal Income Trust 12/02/2005
Each share Auction Preferred 1¢ par exchanged for (1) share Auction Preferred Ser. D 1¢ par
Each share Common 1¢ par exchanged for (1.0021) Common Share of Bene. Int. 1¢ par
Van Kampen Pennsylvania Value Municipal Income Trust name changed to Invesco Van Kampen Pennsylvania Value Municipal Income Trust (PA) 06/01/2010 which reincorporated in Delaware 08/27/2012 which name changed to Invesco Pennsylvania Value Municipal Income Trust 12/03/2012

VAN KAMPEN VALUE MUN INCOME TR (MA)
Name changed 12/29/1995
Name changed 08/28/1998
Name changed from Van Kampen Merritt Value Municipal Income Trust to Van Kampen American Capital Value Municipal Income Trust 12/29/1995
Name changed from Van Kampen American Capital Value Municipal Income Trust to Van Kampen Value Municipal Income Trust 08/28/1998
Merged into Van Kampen Advantage Municipal Income Trust II 01/27/2006
Each share Auction Preferred Ser. A 1¢ par exchanged for (1) share Auction Preferred Ser. F 1¢ par
Each share Auction Preferred Ser. B 1¢ par exchanged for (1) share Auction Preferred Ser. G 1¢ par
Each share Auction Preferred Ser. C 1¢ par exchanged for (1) share Auction Preferred Ser. H 1¢ par
Each share Auction Preferred Ser. D 1¢ par exchanged for (1) share Auction Preferred Ser. I 1¢ par
Each share Auction Preferred Ser. E 1¢ par exchanged for (1) share Auction Preferred Ser. J 1¢ par
Each share Common 1¢ par exchanged for (1.05929) Common Shares of Bene. Int. 1¢ par
Van Kampen Advantage Municipal Income Trust II name changed to Invesco Van Kampen Advantage Municipal Income Trust II (MA) 06/01/2010 which reincorporated in Delaware 08/27/2012 which name changed to Invesco Advantage Municipal Income Trust II 12/03/2012

VAN NESS FDS (DE)
Completely liquidated 01/31/2002
Each share Extended Market Index Fund received net asset value
Each share International Index Fund received net asset value
Each share Money Market Fund received net asset value
Each share S&P 500 Index Fund received net asset value
Each share Total Bond Index Fund received net asset value

VAN NESS INDS LTD (AB)
Name changed to Claiborne Industries Ltd. 6/4/75
(See Claiborne Industries Ltd.)

VAN NORMAN CO. (MA)
Name changed to Van Norman Industries, Inc. 12/13/1955
Van Norman Industries, Inc. merged into Universal American Corp. (DE) (Ctfs. dtd. prior to 01/12/1968) 01/31/1962 which merged into Gulf & Western Industries, Inc. (DE) 01/12/1968
(See Gulf & Western Industries, Inc. (DE))

VAN NORMAN INDUSTRIES, INC. (MA)
Merged into Universal American Corp. (DE) (Ctfs. dtd. prior to 01/12/1968) 01/31/1962
Each share Preferred $5 par exchanged for (1) share $2.50 Preferred $5 par
Each share Common $2.50 par exchanged for (1) share Common 25¢ par plus (1) Common Stock Purchase Warrant
Universal American Corp. (DE) (Ctfs. dtd. prior to 01/12/1968) merged into Gulf & Western Industries, Inc. (DE) 01/12/1968
(See Gulf & Western Industries, Inc. (DE))

VAN NORMAN MACHINE TOOL CO. (MA)
Name changed to Van Norman Co. 00/00/1943
Van Norman Co. name changed to Van Norman Industries, Inc. 12/31/1955 which merged into Universal American Corp. (DE) (Ctfs. dtd. prior to 01/12/1968) 01/31/1962 which merged into Gulf & Western Industries, Inc. (DE) 01/12/1968
(See Gulf & Western Industries, Inc. (DE))

VAN OLLIE EXPLS LTD (ON)
Recapitalized as Engineering Power Systems Group Inc. 05/07/1996
Each share Common no par exchanged for (1/30) share Common no par
Engineering Power Systems Group Inc. recapitalized as Engineering Power Systems Ltd. 01/29/1999 which recapitalized as Energy Power Systems Ltd. 02/06/2001 which recapitalized as EnerNorth Industries, Inc. 02/12/2003
(See EnerNorth Industries, Inc.)

VAN OMMEREN CETECO N V (NETHERLANDS)
Name changed to Royal Vopak N.V. 12/17/99
(See Royal Vopak N.V.)

VAN PAK INC (IA)
Common no par changed to 20¢ par 04/03/1969
Name changed to Manley Industries, Inc. 07/29/1969
(See Manley Industries, Inc.)

VAN RAALTE CO., INC. (NY)
Common no par changed to $5 par in 1933
Common $5 par changed to $10 par in 1944
Common $10 par changed to $6.66-2/3 par and (0.5) additional share issued 1/15/65
Stock Dividends - 50% 1/23/48; 20% 10/16/50; 80% 11/3/60
Acquired by Cluett, Peabody & Co., Inc. 7/31/68
Each share Common $6.66-2/3 par exchanged for (0.85) share $1 Conv.

Preferred $1 par and (0.95) share Common $1.08-1/3 par
Cluett, Peabody & Co., Inc. merged into West Point-Pepperell, Inc. 1/15/86
(See West Point-Pepperell, Inc.)

VAN ROI CONSOLIDATED MINES LTD. (BC)
Recapitalized as Slocan Van Roi Mines Ltd. on a (1) for (3) basis 9/6/55
Slocan Van Roi Mines Ltd. recapitalized as Kopan Developments Ltd. 5/19/60 which recapitalized as Jordesco Resources Ltd. 8/14/72
(See Jordesco Resources Ltd.)

VAN ROI MINES (1947) LTD. (BC)
Name changed to Van Roi Consolidated Mines Ltd. in 1950
Van Roi Consolidated Mines Ltd. recapitalized as Slocan Van Roi Consolidated Mines Ltd. 9/6/55 which recapitalized as Kopan Developments Ltd. 5/19/60 which recapitalized as Jordesco Resources Ltd. 8/14/72
(See Jordesco Resources Ltd.)

VAN SCHAACK & CO (CO)
Stock Dividend - 100% 08/11/1972
Acquired by Austin Capital Corp. 12/24/1985
Each share Common $1 par exchanged for $12 cash

VAN SICKLEN CORP.
Out of business in 1935
No stockholders' equity

VAN SILVER EXPLS LTD (BC)
Name changed to Van Silver Mines Ltd. and Common 50¢ par changed to no par 01/03/1977
Van Silver Mines Ltd. recapitalized as Silver Tusk Mines Ltd. 05/04/1979 which recapitalized as Consolidated Silver Tusk Mines Ltd. (BC) 03/07/1994 which reincorporated in Yukon 00/00/2000
(See Consolidated Silver Tusk Mines Ltd.)

VAN SILVER MINES LTD (BC)
Recapitalized as Silver Tusk Mines Ltd. 05/04/1979
Each share Common no par exchanged for (1/3) share Common no par
Silver Tusk Mines Ltd. recapitalized as Consolidated Silver Tusk Mines Ltd. (BC) 03/07/1994 which reincorporated in Yukon 00/00/2000
(See Consolidated Silver Tusk Mines Ltd.)

VAN STRUM & TOWNE STOCK FUND, INC. (DE)
Acquired by Institutional Shares, Ltd. 11/07/1957
Each share Common $1 par exchanged for (1) Growth Fund Share 1¢ par
Institutional Shares, Ltd. name changed to Channing Shares, Inc. (DE) 04/01/1964 which reincorporated in Maryland 10/09/1973 which merged into American General Shares, Inc. 09/02/1975 which merged into American General Enterprise Fund, Inc. 08/31/1979 which name changed to American Capital Enterprise Fund, Inc. (MD) 09/09/1983 which reincorporated in Delaware as Van Kampen American Capital Enterprise Fund 08/03/1995 which name changed to Van Kampen Enterprise Fund 08/31/1998

VAN SWERINGEN CO. (OH)
Liquidation completed 12/26/62

VAN SWERINGEN CORP. (DE)
Reorganized under laws of Maryland in 1950 which was liquidated in 1951

VAN SWERINGEN CORP. (MD)
Liquidated in 1951

VAN-TOR OILS & EXPLORATIONS LTD. (BC)
Recapitalized as Consolidated Van-Tor Resources Ltd. 4/12/66
Each share Common 50¢ par exchanged for (0.2) share Common no par
Consolidated Van-Tor Resources Ltd. merged into International Mariner Resources Ltd. 2/9/71 which was struck
(See International Mariner Resources Ltd.)

VAN WATERS & ROGERS, INC. (WA)
Merged into VWR United Corp. 11/30/66
Each share Capital Stock $1 par exchanged for (2.9) shares Common $1 par
VWR United Corp. name changed to Univar Corp. (DE) 3/1/74 which reincorporated in Washington 3/1/96
(See Univar Corp. (WA))

VAN WYCK INTL CORP (NY)
Common 10¢ par split (3) for (2) by issuance of (0.5) additional share 05/19/1972
Name changed to Robeson Industries Corp. (NY) 07/26/1982
Robeson Industries Corp. (NY) reincorporated in Delaware 10/23/1984
(See Robeson Industries Corp.)

VANA BLUE INC (NV)
Name changed to Osyka Corp. 05/19/2010

VANACOR GOLD MINES, LTD. (ON)
Dissolved 12/22/58

VANADIUM-ALLOYS STEEL CANADA LTD. (ON)
Name changed to Vascan Ltd. 11/08/1966
Vascan Ltd. name changed to Teledyne Canada, Ltd. 11/20/1969
(See Teledyne Canada, Ltd.)

VANADIUM-ALLOYS STEEL CO. (PA)
Capital Stock no par changed to $5 par 06/03/1957
Stock Dividend - 100% 06/01/1951
Name changed to Vasco Metals Corp. 06/08/1965
Vasco Metals Corp. acquired by Teledyne, Inc. 06/30/1966 which merged into Allegheny Teledyne Inc. 08/15/1996 which name changed to Allegheny Technologies Inc. 11/29/1999

VANADIUM CORP AMER (DE)
Common no par changed to $1 par and (1) additional share issued 00/00/1954
4.5% Conv. Preferred $100 par called for redemption 06/15/1967
Merged into Foote Mineral Co. 08/31/1967
Each share Common $1 par exchanged for (1) share $2.20 Conv. Preferred $1 par
(See Foote Mineral Co.)

VANADIUM INTL INC (NV)
Name changed to Vectoria, Inc. 11/19/2001
Vectoria, Inc. recapitalized as Satelinx International, Inc. 10/21/2004 which recapitalized as Affinity Networks, Inc. 08/13/2007

VANADIUM QUEEN URANIUM CORP. (NV)
Name changed to Queen Corp. 7/1/58
(See Queen Corp.)

VANALTA, LTD. (CANADA)
Merged into Sarcee Petroleums Ltd. on a (4) for (15) basis 4/15/59 which was acquired by Husky Oil Canada Ltd. for cash 12/14/64

VANALTA OILS, LTD.
Name changed to Vanalta, Ltd. in 1934 which merged into Sarcee Petroleums Ltd. 4/15/59 which was acquired by Husky Oil Canada Ltd. for cash 12/14/64

VANALTA RES LTD (BC)
Merged into Canadian Hidrogas Resources Ltd. 09/14/1981
Each share Common no par exchanged for $0.97 cash

VANANDA EXPLS LTD (BC)
Recapitalized as Ramco Industries Ltd. 2/1/73
Each share Capital Stock no par exchanged for (0.2) share Capital Stock no par
Ramco Industries Ltd. recapitalized as Black Diamond Resources Ltd. 11/15/79 which name changed to Com-Air Containers (Canada) Inc. 1/14/87
(See Com-Air Containers (Canada) Inc.)

VANANDA GOLD LTD (BC)
Recapitalized as Consolidated Van Anda Gold Ltd. 02/28/1995
Each share Common no par exchanged for (0.2) share Common no par
(See Consolidated Van Anda Gold Ltd.)

VANANDA MINES (1948) LTD. (BC)
Recapitalized as Vananda Explorations Ltd. 9/7/62
Each share Capital Stock $1 par exchanged for (1/3) share Capital Stock no par
Vananda Explorations Ltd. recapitalized as Ramco Industries Ltd. 2/1/73 which recapitalized as Black Diamond Resources Ltd. 11/15/79 which name changed to Com-Air Containers (Canada) Inc. 1/14/87
(See Com-Air Containers (Canada) Inc.)

VANANDA MINING CO. LTD.
Acquired by Vananda Mines (1948) Ltd. in 1948
Each share Capital Stock $1 par exchanged for (0.5) share Capital Stock $1 par
Vananda Mines (1948) Ltd. recapitalized as Vananda Explorations Ltd. 9/7/62 which recapitalized as Ramco Industries Ltd. 2/1/73 which recapitalized as Black Diamond Resources Ltd. 11/15/79 which name changed to Com-Air Containers (Canada) Inc. 1/14/87
(See Com-Air Containers (Canada) Inc.)

VANCAN CAP CORP (AB)
Name changed to Max Resource Corp. 5/14/2004

VANCE SANDERS & CO INC (MD)
Name changed to Eaton & Howard, Vance, Sanders, Inc. 06/01/1979
Eaton & Howard, Vance, Sanders, Inc. name changed to Eaton Vance Corp. 02/20/1981

VANCE SANDERS COM STK FD INC (MA)
Name changed to Eaton Vance Growth Fund, Inc. 11/16/1981
Eaton Vance Growth Fund, Inc. name changed to Eaton Vance Growth Trust 08/18/1992

VANCE SANDERS INCOME FD INC (MA)
Merged into Eaton Vance Income Fund of Boston, Inc. 7/5/83
Each share Common $1 par exchanged for (1.24890729) shares Capital Stock $1 par
Eaton Vance Income Fund of Boston, Inc. name changed to Eaton Vance Series Trust II 10/3/2003

VANCE SANDERS INVS FD INC (MA)
Name changed to Eaton Vance Investors Fund, Inc. 09/24/1982
Eaton Vance Investors Fund, Inc. name changed to Eaton Vance Investors Trust 09/29/1993
(See Eaton Vance Investors Trust)

VANCE SANDERS SPL FD INC (MA)
Merged into Eaton Vance Growth Fund 6/21/91
Details not available

VANCEINFO TECHNOLOGIES INC (CAYMAN ISLANDS)
Merged into Pactera Technology International Ltd. 11/13/2012
Each ADR for Ordinary exchanged for (1) Sponsored ADR for Common
(See Pactera Technology International Ltd.)

VANCOUVER AMERICAN TIMBER CO.
In process of liquidation in 1940

VANCOUVER BANCORP (WA)
Merged into West Coast Bancorp (New) 04/08/1996
Each share Common $1 par exchanged for (3.5974) shares Common no par
(See West Coast Bancorp (New))

VANCOUVER BARGE TRANSPORTATION LTD. (BC)
6% Preference $10 par called 1/17/63

VANCOUVER FINANCE CO. LTD. (BC)
Name changed to Credit Acceptance Corp. Ltd. in 1955
Credit Acceptance Corp. Ltd. name changed to Commonwealth Acceptance Corp. Ltd. 3/26/65 which was adjudicated bankrupt 2/28/69

VANCOUVER KRAFT CORP. LTD.
Liquidation completed in 1951

VANCOUVER VENTURE CORP (BC)
Name changed to Jackson Hole Holdings Corp. 8/23/93
(See Jackson Hole Holdings Corp.)

VANCOUVERS FINEST COFFEE CO (NV)
Name changed to China NetTV Holdings, Inc. 05/30/2000
China NetTV Holdings, Inc. name changed to Great China Mining, Inc. 01/20/2006 which merged into Continental Minerals Corp. (Incorporated 02/07/1962) 12/15/2006
(See Continental Minerals Corp. (Incorporated 02/07/1962))

VANDALIA NATL CORP (DE)
Merged into Wesbanco, Inc. 12/30/96
Each share Common $1 par exchanged for (1.2718) shares Common $2.0833 par

VANDEN CAP GROUP INC (CO)
Recapitalized as Entropin Inc. (CO) 01/16/1998
Each (300) shares Common $0.0001 par exchanged for (1) share Common $0.001 par
Entropin Inc. (CO) reincorporated in Delaware 06/14/2002
(See Entropin Inc.)

VANDENBERG INN & HOTEL INC (CA)
Charter revoked for failure to file reports and pay fees 10/03/1966

VANDERBILT ENERGY CORP (TX)
Common 10¢ par split (5) for (4) by issuance of (0.25) additional share 10/31/77
Stock Dividends - 15% 10/15/76; 50% 4/20/81
Merged into Madison Fund, Inc. 1/11/84

Each share Common 10¢ par exchanged for $7.14 cash

VANDERBILT GOLD CORP (DE)
Reincorporated 04/24/1987
State of incorporation changed from (CA) to (DE) 04/24/1987
Charter cancelled and declared inoperative and void for non-payment of taxes 03/01/2008

VANDERBILT GROWTH FD INC (MD)
Merged into St. Paul Capital Fund, Inc. 06/14/1977
Each share Capital Stock $1 par exchanged for (0.457497) share Common 1¢ par
St. Paul Capital Fund, Inc. name changed to AMEV Capital Fund, Inc. 05/01/1985 which reorganized as Fortis Equity Portfolios Inc. 02/22/1992
(See Fortis Equity Portfolios Inc.)

VANDERBILT INCOME FD INC (DE)
Merged into St. Paul Capital Fund, Inc. 06/14/1977
Each share Capital Stock $1 par exchanged for (0.485774) share Common 1¢ par
St. Paul Capital Fund, Inc. name changed to AMEV Capital Fund, Inc. 05/01/1985 which reorganized as Fortis Equity Portfolios Inc. 02/22/1992
(See Fortis Equity Portfolios Inc.)

VANDERBILT MUT FD INC (DE)
Name changed to Vanderbilt Income Fund, Inc. 07/01/1975
Vanderbilt Income Fund, Inc. merged into St. Paul Capital Fund, Inc. 06/14/1977 which name changed to AMEV Capital Fund, Inc. 05/01/1985 which reorganized as Fortis Equity Portfolios Inc. 02/22/1992
(See Fortis Equity Portfolios Inc.)

VANDERBILT SQUARE CORP (FL)
Stock Dividend - 10% payable 9/24/96 to holders of record 8/23/96
Name changed to Treasure & Exhibits International Inc. 9/26/2000
Treasure & Exhibits International Inc. name changed to Affinity International Marketing, Inc. 3/28/2001 which name changed to Global Security & Intelligence Group Inc. 1/3/2003

VANDERBILT TIRE & RUBBER CORP. (NY)
Name changed to VTR, Inc. 1/3/62
VTR, Inc. proclaimed dissolved 6/24/81

VANDERGRIFT LAND & IMPROVEMENT CO. (PA)
Liquidated 11/10/54

VANDERGRIFT WATER CO.
Dissolved in 1950

VANDERVOORTS INC (MO)
Adjudicated bankrupt 06/08/1971
No stockholders' equity

VANDEVENTER LEAD & ZINC MINING CO. (WI)
Involuntarily dissolved 7/7/19

VANDOO CONS EXPLS LTD (ON)
Charter cancelled and declared dissolved for failure to file returns and pay fees 11/09/1976

VANDOO COPPER MINING CORP. LTD. (ON)
Merged into Vandoo Consolidated Explorations Ltd. share for share 3/16/56
(See Vandoo Consolidated Explorations Ltd.)

VANDOREX ENERGY CORP (BC)
Name changed to Bentech Industries Inc. 03/07/1990
(See Bentech Industries Inc.)

VANDUZEN OIL CO. (WY)
Charter forfeited for failure to pay taxes 7/19/27

VANECK VECTORS ETF TR (DE)
Trust terminated 10/14/2016
Each share Gulf States Index ETF no par received $22.94001 cash
Each share Indonesia Small-Cap ETF no par received $8.62266 cash
Trust terminated 10/06/2017
Each share AMT-Free 6-8 Year Municipal Index ETF no par received $24.516 cash
Each share AMT-Free 12-17 Year Municipal Index ETF no par received $24.5198 cash
Each share Solar Energy ETF no par received $43.3701 cash
Each share Treasury-Hedged High Yield Bond ETF no par received $23.7875 cash
Global Spin-Off ETF no par reclassified as Spin-Off ETF no par 02/01/2018
Trust terminated 08/07/2018
Each share EM Investment Grade + BB Rated USD Sovereign Bond ETF no par received $23.5165 cash
Each share Spin-Off ETF no par received $20.0398 cash
 (Additional Information in Active)

VANELL CORP (NV)
Common $0.001 par split (5) for (1) by issuance of (4) additional shares payable 04/03/2014 to holders of record 03/31/2014 Ex date - 04/04/2014
Name changed to Train Travel Holdings, Inc. 04/11/2014
Train Travel Holdings, Inc. name changed to Turnkey Capital, Inc. 02/04/2016

VANETTE HOSIERY MLS (TX)
Stock Dividend - 100% 05/22/1946
Name changed to VHM Liquidating Corp. 01/03/1966
VHM Liquidating Corp. in process of liquidation 01/03/1966

VANEX MINERALS LTD. (BC)
Acquired by Alscope Consolidated Ltd. on a share for share basis 8/28/62
Alscope Consolidated Ltd. recapitalized as Almarco Industries Ltd. 8/3/76
(See Almarco Industries Ltd.)

VANEX RES LTD (BC)
Recapitalized as Poplar Resources Ltd. 07/15/1991
Each share Common no par exchanged for (0.25) share Common no par
Poplar Resources Ltd. merged into Nordic Diamonds Ltd. 11/24/2003 which recapitalized as Western Standard Metals Ltd. 06/12/2009 which merged into Terraco Gold Corp. (AB) 01/25/2011 which reincorporated in British Columbia 06/08/2011

VANEXX INC (DE)
Recapitalized as Infotag Corp. 12/13/95
Each share Common $0.001 par exchanged for (0.25) share Class A Common $0.001 par

VANFED BANCORP (WA)
Acquired by Washington Mutual Savings Bank (Seattle, WA) 07/31/1991
Each share Common $1 par exchanged for $19 cash

VANGAS INC (CA)
$1.50 Preferred Ser. A $25 par called for redemption 12/01/1961
Through purchase offer 99% acquired by Suburban Propane Gas Corp. as of 11/08/1971
Public interest eliminated

VANGOLD RES INC (BC)
Recapitalized as Pacific Vangold Mines Ltd. 03/04/1994
Each share Common no par exchanged for (0.33333333) share Common no par
Pacific Vangold Mines Ltd. recapitalized as Paccom Ventures Inc. 04/18/2000 which name changed to Vangold Resources Ltd. 08/29/2003 which name changed to Vangold Mining Corp. 05/10/2017

VANGOLD RES LTD (BC)
Each share old Common no par received distribution of (0.1175) share Vanoil Energy Ltd. Common no par and (0.1175) Common Stock Right that expired 02/04/2010 and was payable 01/04/2010 to holders of record 12/31/2009
Each share old Common no par exchanged for (0.33333333) share new Common no par 01/04/2010
Each share new Common no par exchanged again for (0.1) share new Common no par 10/09/2012
Each share new Common no par exchanged again for (0.33333333) share new Common no par 11/07/2016
Name changed to Vangold Mining Corp. 05/10/2017

VANGUARD / WELLINGTON FD INC (MD)
Under plan of reorganization each share Common $1 par automatically became (1) share Vanguard Wellington Fund (DE) Investor Share $0.001 par 05/29/1998

VANGUARD / WINDSOR FDS INC (MD)
Reincorporated under the laws of Delaware as Vanguard Windsor Funds and Common 1¢ par changed to $0.001 par 05/29/1998

VANGUARD AIR & MARINE CORP. (PA)
Under plan of merger each share Common $1 par changed to (2) shares Common 50¢ par 8/1/60
Adjudicated bankrupt 12/6/63
No stockholders' equity

VANGUARD AIRLS INC (DE)
Each share old Common $0.001 par exchanged for (0.2) share new Common $0.001 par 5/20/99
Each share new Common $0.001 par exchanged for (0.2) share Common $0.005 par 5/31/2002
Plan of reorganization under Chapter 11 Federal Bankruptcy Code effective 12/31/2003
No stockholders' equity

VANGUARD AVIATION CORP (AB)
Placed in receivership and assets liquidated 06/01/2004
No stockholders' equity

VANGUARD BD INDEX FD INC (MD)
Reorganized under the laws of Delaware as Vanguard Bond Index Funds 05/29/1998

VANGUARD CELLULAR SYS INC (NC)
Common 1¢ par split (3) for (2) by issuance of (0.5) additional share 03/15/1989
Common 1¢ par reclassified as Class A Common 1¢ par 05/12/1989
Class A Common 1¢ par split (3) for (2) by issuance of (0.5) additional share 08/24/1994
Merged into AT&T Corp. 05/03/1999
Each share Class A Common 1¢ par exchanged for either (0.59805) share Common $1 par, $23 cash, or a combination thereof
AT&T Corp. merged into AT&T Inc. 11/18/2005

VANGUARD DATA SYS (CA)
Charter suspended for failure to file reports and pay taxes 02/01/1974

VANGUARD ENERGY CORP (CO)
Units separated 12/19/2011
Each share old Common $0.00001 par exchanged for (0.01) share new Common $0.00001 par 08/19/2014
Name changed to Solar Quartz Technology Corp. 08/15/2017

VANGUARD ENTERPRISES INC (DE)
Recapitalized as Activeworlds.com, Inc. 01/21/1999
Each share Common $0.001 par exchanged for (0.5) share Common $0.001 par
Activeworlds.com, Inc. name changed to Activeworlds Corp. 06/27/2001 which name changed to Kingold Jewelry Inc. 02/18/2010

VANGUARD EXPLORATIONS LTD. (BC)
Recapitalized as Newvan Resources Ltd. 11/24/1971
Each share Capital Stock 50¢ par exchanged for (0.2) share Capital Stock no par
Newvan Resources Ltd. recapitalized as Tricor Resources Ltd. 06/02/1977
(See Tricor Resources Ltd.)

VANGUARD EXPLORATIONS LTD. (QC)
Recapitalized as Guardian Mines Ltd. 09/20/1965
Each share Capital Stock $1 par exchanged for (0.25) share Capital Stock no par
Guardian Mines Ltd. recapitalized as Green Coast Resources Ltd. 07/20/1971 which recapitalized as Ridgepoint Resources Ltd. 06/15/1988 which recapitalized as Ridgepoint Mineral Corp. 10/31/1997 which name changed to Jet Drill Canada Inc. 09/15/2000
(See Jet Drill Canada Inc.)

VANGUARD EXPLORER FD INC (MD)
Under plan of reorganization each Share of Bene. Int. $0.001 par automatically became (1) Vanguard Explorer Fund (DE) Share of Bene. Int. $0.001 par 06/30/1998

VANGUARD FD INC (DE)
Merged into Pilgrim Fund, Inc. 6/24/74
Each share Capital Stock $1 par exchanged for (0.1650) share Common $1 par
Pilgrim Fund, Inc. merged into Pilgrim Magnacap Fund, Inc. 6/20/85

VANGUARD FINL INC (FL)
Involuntarily dissolved for failure to maintain a resident agent 05/03/1988

VANGUARD FTSE ALL-WORLD EX CDA INDEX ETF (ON)
Name changed to Vanguard FTSE Global All Cap ex Canada Index ETF 10/05/2015

VANGUARD FTSE DEVELOPED ASIA PAC INDEX ETF (ON)
Name changed to Vanguard FTSE Developed Asia Pacific All Cap Index ETF 10/05/2015

VANGUARD FTSE DEVELOPED EUROPE INDEX ETF (ON)
Name changed to Vanguard FTSE Developed Europe All Cap Index ETF 10/05/2015

VANGUARD FTSE DEVELOPED EX NORTH AMER INDEX ETF (ON)
Name changed to Vanguard FTSE Developed All Cap Ex U.S. Index ETF 12/23/2015

VANGUARD FTSE DEVELOPED EX NORTH AMER INDEX ETF CAD HEDGED (ON)
Name changed to Vanguard FTSE Developed All Cap Ex U.S. Index ETF (CAD-Hedged) 12/23/2015

VANGUARD FTSE EMERGING MKTS INDEX ETF (ON)
Name changed to Vanguard FTSE Emerging Markets All Cap Index ETF 11/04/2015

VAN-VAN

VANGUARD HEALTH SYS INC (DE)
Issue Information - 25,000,000 shares COM offered at $18 per share on 06/22/2011
Acquired by Tenet Healthcare Corp. 10/01/2013
Each share Common 1¢ par exchanged for $21 cash

VANGUARD INDEX BD FD INC (MD)
Name changed to Vanguard Bond Index Fund, Inc. (MD) and Common $0.001 par reclassified as Total Bond Market Index Investor Class $0.001 par 05/03/1993
Vanguard Bond Index Fund, Inc. (MD) reorganized in Delaware as Vanguard Bond Index Funds 05/29/1998

VANGUARD INTL INC (MD)
Recapitalized as C L Financial Corp. 07/14/1972
Each share Common $1 par exchanged for (0.2) share Common $1 par
C L Financial Corp. name changed to California Life Corp. 05/20/1974
(See California Life Corp.)

VANGUARD INVTS CORP (AB)
Name changed to Vinergy Resources Ltd. 06/20/2011

VANGUARD LIFE INS CO (AZ)
Charter withdrawn by reversion 01/20/1992
Stockholders' equity unlikely

VANGUARD LONG LAC GOLD MINES, LTD. (ON)
Charter cancelled by the Province of Ontario in 1949

VANGUARD MINERALS CORP (NV)
Each share old Common $0.001 par exchanged for (0.00333333) share new Common $0.001 par 04/16/2010
Name changed to Zoned Properties, Inc. 10/25/2013

VANGUARD MNG CORP (NV)
Each share old Common $0.001 par exchanged for (4) shares new Common $0.001 par 11/17/2014
Name changed to Myson Group, Inc. 06/08/2015

VANGUARD MONEY MARKET TRUST (PA)
Reincorporated under the laws of Maryland as Vanguard Money Market Trust, Inc. and Shares of Bene. Int. no par reclassified as Common $0.001 par 12/31/85
Vanguard Money Market Trust, Inc. name changed to Vanguard Money Market Reserves, Inc. 3/13/89

VANGUARD MONEY MKT TR (MD)
Name changed to Vanguard Money Market Reserves, Inc. and Insured Portfolio reclassified as U.S. Treasury Portfolio 3/13/89

VANGUARD MORGAN GROWTH FD INC (MD)
Under plan of reorganization each share Common 10¢ par automatically became (1) share Vanguard Morgan Growth Fund (DE) Common $0.001 par 06/30/1998

VANGUARD MSCI CDA INDEX ETF (ON)
Name changed to Vanguard FTSE Canada Index ETF 04/02/2013

VANGUARD MSCI EAFE INDEX ETF CAD HEDGED (ON)
Name changed to Vanguard FTSE Developed ex North America Index ETF (CAD-Hedged) 05/31/2013
Vanguard FTSE Developed ex North America Index ETF (CAD-Hedged) name changed to Vanguard FTSE Developed All Cap Ex U.S. Index ETF (CAD-Hedged) 12/23/2015

VANGUARD MSCI EMERGING MKTS INDEX ETF (ON)
Name changed to Vanguard FTSE Emerging Markets Index ETF 01/14/2013
Vanguard FTSE Emerging Markets Index ETF name changed to Vanguard FTSE Emerging Markets All Cap Index ETF 11/04/2015

VANGUARD MSCI US BROAD MKT INDEX ETF CAD HEDGED (ON)
Name changed to Vanguard U.S. Total Market Index ETF (CAD-hedged) 06/05/2013

VANGUARD MUN BD FD INC (PA)
Reincorporated back in Maryland as Vanguard Municipal Bond Fund, Inc. and each Portfolio 10¢ par reclassified as Common $0.001 par 12/31/85

VANGUARD NAT RES LLC (DE)
Plan of reorganization under Chapter 11 Federal Bankruptcy proceedings effective 08/01/2017
Holders accepting the Plan received equity interest in Vanguard Natural Resources, Inc.
Each share 7.625% Perpetual Preferred Unit Ser. B received (0.00003776) share Common $0.001 par and (0.00011187) Common Stock Purchase Warrant expiring 02/01/2021
Each share 7.75% Perpetual Preferred Unit Ser. C received (0.0000378) share Common $0.001 par and (0.0011199) Common Stock Purchase Warrant expiring 02/01/2021
Each share 7.875% Perpetual Preferred Unit Ser. A received (0.00003784) share Common $0.001 par and (0.00112106) Common Stock Purchase Warrant expiring 02/01/2021
Each Common Unit received (0.004892) Common Stock Purchase Warrant expiring 02/01/2021

VANGUARD NATL BK (HEMPSTEAD, NY)
Name changed to Guardian Bank, N.A. (Hempstead, NY) 06/16/1980
(See Guardian Bank, N.A. (Hempstead, NY))

VANGUARD OIL CORP (AB)
Acquired by Bitech Petroleum Corp. 5/24/2001
Each share Common no par exchanged for (0.1) share Common no par
(See Bitech Petroleum Corp.)

VANGUARD PETE LTD (AUSTRALIA)
ADR agreement terminated 02/09/1998
No stockholders' equity

VANGUARD REAL ESTATE FD 1 (MA)
Liquidation completed
Each Share of Bene. Int. no par received initial distribution of $3.15 cash 4/30/96
Each Share of Bene. Int. no par received second and final distribution of $0.1202 cash payable 5/31/96 to holders of record 4/22/96

VANGUARD REAL ESTATE FD II (MA)
Liquidation completed
Each Share of Bene. Int. no par received initial distribution of $1.20 cash payable 9/30/96 to holders of record 9/23/96
Each Share of Bene. Int. no par received second and final distribution of $0.10017 cash 10/31/96

VANGUARD RESPONSE SYS INC (ON)
Name changed to Allen-Vanguard Corp. 03/25/2005
(See Allen-Vanguard Corp.)

VANGUARD SVGS BK (HOLYOKE, MA)
Common 10¢ par split (2) for (1) by issuance of (1) additional share 2/27/87
Under plan of reorganization each share Common 10¢ par automatically became (1) share Affiliated Banc Corp. Common 10¢ par 8/1/88
(See Affiliated Banc Corp.)

VANGUARD STUDIOS INC (CA)
Stock Dividend - 10% 01/29/1973
Name changed to VSI Liquidating Corp. 12/12/1974
(See VSI Liquidating Corp.)

VANGUARD TECHNOLOGIES INC (CANADA)
Name changed to Eloda 2006 Corp. 12/13/2006
Eloda 2006 Corp. name changed to Eloda Corp. 01/12/2007
(See Eloda Corp.)

VANGUARD TECHNOLOGIES INTL INC (DE)
Merged into Cincinnati Bell Inc. (New) 8/8/88
Each share Class A Common 1¢ par exchanged for $19 cash
Each share Class B Common 1¢ par exchanged for $19 cash

VANGUARD U S A CORP (UT)
Recapitalized as Norton-BSA Inc. 1/28/94
Each share Common $0.001 par exchanged for (0.02) share Common $0.0005 par
Norton-BSA Inc. name changed to Brooklyn Drink Co. Inc. 2/20/95 which name changed to Net Tel International, Inc. 5/28/96
(See Net Tel International, Inc.)

VANGUARD VENTURE CORP (BC)
Struck off register and declared dissolved for failure to file returns 4/8/94

VANGUARD WELLESLEY INCOME FD (MD)
Reincorporated under the laws of Delaware as Vanguard Wellesley Income Fund and Common 10¢ par changed to Common Shares of Bene. Int. $0.001 par 05/29/1998

VANGUARD WORLD FD (MA)
Under plan of reorganization each share International Growth Fund and U.S. Growth Portfolio $1 par automatically became (1) share Vanguard World Fund (DE) International Growth Fund or U.S. Growth Fund $0.001 par respectively 06/30/1998

VANGUARDA AGRO S A (BRAZIL)
Each old Sponsored 144A ADR for Ordinary exchanged for (0.11111111) new Sponsored 144A ADR for Ordinary 05/22/2013
Each old Sponsored Reg. S ADR for Ordinary exchanged for (0.11111111) new Sponsored Reg. S ADR for Ordinary 05/22/2013
Each new Sponsored 144A ADR for Ordinary exchanged again for (0.03333333) new Sponsored 144A ADR for Ordinary 10/26/2015
Each new Sponsored Reg. S ADR for Ordinary exchanged again for (0.03333333) new Sponsored Reg. S ADR for Ordinary 10/26/2015
Name changed to Terra Santa Agro S.A. 12/22/2016
(See Terra Santa Agro S.A.)

VANHARBOUR INTL INC (DE)
Name changed to Jackson Tech Inc. 10/14/1996
Jackson Tech Inc. name changed to Electronic Kourseware International Inc. 08/28/1997
(See Electronic Kourseware International Inc.)

VANIER GRAPHICS CORP (CA)
Stock Dividend - 50% 7/31/75
Merged into American Business Products, Inc. (DE) 7/1/76
Each share Common $1 par exchanged for (0.9) share Common $2 par
American Business Products, Inc. (DE) reincorporated in Georgia 4/30/86
(See American Business Products, Inc. (GA))

VANITY EVENTS HLDG INC (DE)
Each share old Common $0.001 par exchanged for (0.00333333) share new Common $0.001 par 02/10/2012
Name changed to Thinspace Technology, Inc. 02/26/2014

VANITY FAIR MLS INC (PA)
Common $5 par changed to $2.50 par and (1) additional share issued 01/20/1964
Common $2.50 par changed to $1.66-2/3 par and (0.5) additional share issued 01/17/1966
Common $1.66-2/3 par changed to no par and (0.5) additional share issued 01/19/1968
Name changed to V.F. Corp. 04/16/1969

VANMAR, INC. (NC)
Name changed to Wellington-Hall Vanmar, Inc. 12/06/1968
Wellington-Hall Vanmar, Inc. name changed to Wellington Hall, Ltd. 04/30/1970
(See Wellington Hall, Ltd.)

VANMETALS EXPL LTD (BC)
Recapitalized as Rand Resources Ltd. 10/05/1970
Each share Capital Stock no par exchanged for (1/3) share Capital Stock no par
(See Rand Resources Ltd.)

VANNESSA VENTURES LTD (BC)
Name changed to Infinito Gold Ltd. 05/28/2008

VANS INC (DE)
Merged into V.F. Corp. 6/30/2004
Each share Common $0.001 par exchanged for $20.55 cash

VANSEA RES LTD (BC)
Dissolved 07/28/1981

VANSON MANITOBA GOLD MINES (CANADA)
Charter cancelled for failure to file reports and pay taxes 8/8/49

VANSTAR CORP (DE)
Merged into Inacom Corp. 2/17/99
Each share Common $0.001 par exchanged for (0.64) share Common 10¢ par
(See InaCom Corp.)

VANSTAR FILMS INC (NV)
Recapitalized as Garuda Capital Corp. 2/20/2002
Each share Common $0.001 par exchanged for (0.05) share Common $0.001 par

VANSTATES RES LTD (BC)
Recapitalized as Southport Resources Inc. 07/16/1990
Each share Capital Stock no par exchanged for (0.33333333) share Common no par
Southport Resources Inc. recapitalized as Olds Industries Inc. 06/03/1992
(See Olds Industries Inc.)

VANTAGE DRILLING CO (CAYMAN ISLANDS)
Placed in Official Liquidation 02/09/2016
Stockholders' equity unlikely

VANTAGE ENERGY SVCS INC (DE)
Reincorporated under the laws of Cayman Islands as Vantage Drilling Co. and Common $0.001 par reclassified as Ordinary $0.001 par 06/13/2008
(See Vantage Drilling Co.)

VANTAGE ENTERPRISES CORP (BC)
Name changed to African Gemstones Ltd. 07/14/1998
(See African Gemstones Ltd.)

VANTAGE GROUP LTD (BC)
Name changed to Barron Hunter Hargrave Strategic Resources Inc. 3/14/85
(See Barron Hunter Hargrave Strategic Resources Inc.)

VANTAGE INC (NV)
Name changed to Cofitras Entertainment, Inc. 00/00/1995
Cofitras Entertainment Inc. name changed to BingoGold.com Inc. 10/27/1999 which name changed to Gameweaver.com Inc. 11/26/1999 which name changed to Inform Media Group, Inc. 03/15/2002 which name changed to Acquisition Media, Inc. 08/12/2002 which name changed to Actionview International, Inc. 08/20/2003 which recapitalized as AVEW Holdings, Inc. 07/31/2015

VANTAGE MHEALTHCARE INC (DE)
Reincorporated 01/15/2015
Name and state of incorporation changed from Vantage Health (NV) to Vantage mHealthcare, Inc. (DE) 01/15/2015
Name changed to Nano Mobile Healthcare, Inc. 09/10/2015

VANTAGE POINT ENERGY INC (OK)
Merged into Convest Energy Corp. 08/19/1992
Each share 5% Conv. Preferred Ser. A $1 par exchanged for $70 cash
Each share Common 15¢ par converted into (1) Vantage Point Liquidating Trust Share of Bene. Int.
(See Vantage Point Liquidating Trust)
Convest Energy Corp. merged into Forcenergy Inc. 10/22/1997 which merged into Forest Oil Corp. 12/07/2000 which name changed to Sabine Oil & Gas Corp. 01/13/2015
(See Sabine Oil & Gas Corp.)

VANTAGE POINT LIQUIDATING TRUST (OK)
Liquidation completed
Each share of Bene. Int. exchanged for for initial distribution of $6.25 cash
Each share of Bene. Int. received second and final distribution of $0.20 cash 10/31/92

VANTAGE RES LTD (BC)
Name changed to Vat Petroleum Ltd. 10/17/79
(See Vat Petroleum Ltd.)

VANTAGEMED CORP (DE)
Merged into Nightingale Informatix Corp. 04/20/2007
Each share Common $0.001 par exchanged for $0.75 cash

VANTAGEPOINT SYS INC (BC)
Acquired by Solarsoft Business Systems 03/19/2008
Each share Common no par exchanged for USD $0.70 cash

VANTAGESOUTH BANCSHARES INC (DE)
Merged into Yadkin Financial Corp. 07/04/2014
Each share Common $1 par exchanged for (0.3125) share Common $1 par

Yadkin Financial Corp. merged into F.N.B. Corp. 03/11/2017

VANTAS INC (NV)
Merged into HQ Global Workplaces 6/1/2000
Each share Common 1¢ par exchanged for $8 cash

VANTEC VENTURES CORP (AB)
Struck off register and declared dissolved for failure to file returns 1/1/97

VANTECK VRB TECHNOLOGY CORP (CANADA)
Name changed to VRB Power Systems Inc. 01/17/2003
VRB Power Systems Inc. name changed to Nevaro Capital Corp. (Old) 08/24/2009
(See Nevaro Capital Corp. (Old))

VANTERRA RES LTD (BC)
Assets sold for the benefit of creditors 00/00/1987
No stockholders' equity

VANTEX CORP (DE)
Each share Common 10¢ par exchanged for (0.1) share Common 1¢ par 9/15/74
Merged into Vitamat, Inc. 12/31/81
Each share Common 1¢ par exchanged for $0.022 cash

VANTEX OIL GAS & MINERALS LTD (CANADA)
Reincorporated 06/19/1998
Place of incorporation changed from (BC) to (Canada) 06/19/1998
Name changed to Vantex Resources Ltd. 05/20/2004

VANTEX RES INC (BC)
Name changed to General Cybernetics Corp. 3/12/86
(See General Cybernetics Corp.)

VANTIV INC (DE)
Name changed to Worldpay, Inc. 01/16/2018

VANTIVE CORP (DE)
Common $0.001 par split (2) for (1) by issuance of (1) additional share payable 10/14/1996 to holders of record 09/30/1996
Merged into PeopleSoft Inc. 12/31/1999
Each share Common $0.001 par exchanged for (0.825) share Common 1¢ par
(See PeopleSoft, Inc.)

VANTREAL RES LTD (BC)
Recapitalized as Caspian Resources Ltd. 04/11/1978
Each share Capital Stock no par exchanged for (0.2) share Capital Stock no par
(See Caspian Resources Ltd.)

VANURA URANIUM, INC. (NV)
Merged into Micro Copper Corp. (Del.) 11/5/58
Each (20) shares Common 1¢ par exchanged for (1) share Common 4¢ par
Micro Copper Corp. (Del.) reincorporated in Nevada 6/6/84

VANWIN RES CORP (BC)
Delisted from Vancouver Stock Exchange 10/06/1989

VANZETTI SYS INC (MA)
Name changed 5/17/82
Name changed from Vanzetti Infrared & Computer Systems, Inc. to Vanzetti Systems, Inc. 5/17/82
Proclaimed dissolved for failure to file reports and pay fees 8/31/98

VAPETEK INC (DE)
Name changed to Nodechain, Inc. 03/01/2018

VAPIR ENTERPRISES INC (NV)
Name changed to Gratitude Health, Inc. 03/23/2018

VAPOR CAR HEATING CO., INC.
Recapitalized as Vapor Heating Corp. in 1947
Each share Preferred exchanged for (1) share 5% Preferred $100 par and (1.5) share Common $1 par
Each share Common exchanged for (3) shares Common $1 par
Vapor Heating Corp. name changed to Vapor Corp. 9/29/61 which merged into Amercon Corp. 3/17/66 which was acquired by General Precision Equipment Corp. 3/27/67 which merged into Singer Co. (NJ) 7/11/68 which reorganized in Delaware in 1988 which name changed to Bicoastal Corp. 10/16/89
(See Bicoastal Corp.)

VAPOR CAR HEATING CO. OF CANADA, LTD. (CANADA)
Name changed to Vapor Heating (Canada) Ltd. 10/1/58
Vapor Heating (Canada) Ltd. name changed to Vapor Heating Ltd. 12/22/61 which was acquired by Vapor Corp. for cash 12/21/65
(See listing for Vapor Corp.)

VAPOR CORP. (DE)
Ctfs. dated prior to 3/17/66
Merged into Amercon Corp. 3/17/66
Each share Common $1 par exchanged for (1) share Capital Stock no par
Amercon Corp. acquired by General Precision Equipment Corp. 3/27/67 which merged into Singer Co. (NJ) 7/11/68 which reincorporated in Delaware in 1988 which name changed to Bicoastal Corp. 10/16/89
(See Bicoastal Corp.)

VAPOR CORP (DE)
Reorganized 12/27/2013
State of incorporation changed from (NV) to (DE) 12/27/2013
Each share old Common $0.001 par exchanged for (0.2) share new Common $0.001 par 07/09/2015
Units separated 01/25/2016
Each Unit automatically became (0.25) share Ser. A Conv. Preferred $0.001 par and (20) Common Stock Purchase Warrants Ser. A expiring 07/23/2020
Each share new Common $0.001 par exchanged for (0.01428571) share old Common $0.0001 par 03/09/2016
Each share old Common $0.0001 par exchanged for (0.00005) share new Common $0.0001 par 06/02/2016
Name changed to Healthier Choices Management Corp. 03/06/2017

VAPOR CORP (DE)
Common $1 par split (5) for (4) by issuance of (0.25) additional share 09/23/1977
Acquired by Brunswick Corp. 09/15/1978
Each share Common $1 par exchanged for (1) share $2.40 Conv. Preferred Ser. A no par

VAPOR HEATING (CANADA) LTD. (CANADA)
Name changed to Vapor Heating Ltd. 12/22/61
Vapor Heating Ltd. acquired by Vapor Corp. for cash 12/21/65
(See listing for Vapor Corp.)

VAPOR HEATING CORP. (DE)
Each share 5% Preferred $100 par exchanged for (4) shares Common $1 par 8/5/59
Common $1 par split (2) for (1) by issuance of (1) additional share 8/5/59
Name changed to Vapor Corp. 9/29/61
Vapor Corp. merged into Amercon Corp. 3/17/66 which was acquired by General Precision Equipment Corp. 3/27/67 which merged into Singer Co. (NJ) 7/11/68 which reincorporated in Delaware in 1988 which name changed to Bicoastal Corp. 10/16/89
(See Bicoastal Corp.)

VAPOR HEATING LTD (CANADA)
Acquired by Vapor Corp. 12/21/1965
Each share Preferred $100 par exchanged for $110 cash
Each share Common no par exchanged for $36 cash

VAPORIN INC (DE)
Each share old Common $0.0001 par exchanged for (0.02) share new Common $0.0001 par 09/10/2014
Merged into Vapor Corp. 03/05/2015
Each share new Common $0.0001 par exchanged for (2.077183) shares Common $0.001 par

VAQCOURT GOLD MINES, LTD. (ON)
Charter cancelled by the Province of Ontario in 1953

VAQUERO ENERGY LTD (AB)
Merged into Highpine Oil & Gas Ltd. 05/31/2005
Each share Common no par exchanged for (0.391) share Common no par
Highpine Oil & Gas Ltd. merged into Daylight Resources Trust 10/08/2009 which reorganized as Daylight Energy Ltd. 05/12/2010
(See Daylight Energy Ltd.)

VAR-ACA, INC. (DE)
Charter cancelled and declared inoperative and void for non-payment of taxes 12/31/87

VAR COMPUTER SOLUTIONS CORP (BC)
Name changed to Econ Ventures Ltd. 06/05/1995
Econ Ventures Ltd. recapitalized as Richcor Ventures Ltd. (BC) 09/12/2000 which reincorporated in Canada 07/24/2001 which name changed to Bioxel Pharma Inc. 08/13/2001
(See Bioxel Pharma Inc.)

VAR-JAZZ ENTMT INC (NV)
Common $0.001 par split (3) for (1) by issuance of (2) additional shares payable 3/13/2001 to holders of record 3/8/2001
Name changed to Cal-Bay International Inc. 3/13/2001

VARAC INDS INC (PA)
Name changed to Epidyne Inc. (PA) 6/29/73
Epidyne Inc. (PA) reincorporated in Delaware 9/27/74 which name changed to Brady Energy Corp. 10/29/79
(See Brady Energy Corp.)

VARADYNE INDS INC (CA)
Ceased operations 2/13/81

VARAH L A LTD (BC)
Name changed to Saynor Varah Inc. 07/30/1986
(See Saynor Varah Inc.)

VARCO INDUSTRIES, INC. (DE)
Bankrupt in 1963; stock valueless

VARCO INTL INC (CA)
Common no par split (2) for (1) by issuance of (1) additional share 3/21/80
Common no par split (2) for (1) by issuance of (1) additional share 12/12/80
$2 Conv. Preferred Ser. A no par called for redemption 10/1/92
Common no par split (2) for (1) by issuance of (1) additional share payable 12/4/97 to holders of record 11/20/97 Ex date - 12/5/97
Merged into Varco International, Inc. (DE) 5/31/2000
Each share Common no par exchanged for (0.7125) share Common 1¢ par

Varco International, Inc. (DE) merged into National Oilwell Varco, Inc. 3/11/2005

VARCO INTL INC (DE)
Merged into National Oilwell Varco, Inc. 3/11/2005
Each share Common 1¢ par exchanged for (0.8363) share Common 1¢ par

VARCO STEEL, INC. (AR)
Acquired by Fuqua Industries, Inc. (PA) 11/01/1967
Each share Common $1 par exchanged for (0.2) share Common $5 par
Fuqua Industries, Inc. (PA) reincorporated in Delaware 05/06/1968 which name changed to Actava Group Inc. 07/21/1993 which name changed to Metromedia International Group, Inc. 11/01/1995
(See Metromedia International Group, Inc.)

VARD A S (NORWAY)
Sponsored ADR's for Class B Kr 5 par changed to Kr 2.50 par and (1) additional ADR issued 06/19/1989
Each Sponsored ADR for Class B Ordinary Kr 2.50 par exchanged for (2) Sponsored ADR's for Class A Ordinary Kr 2.50 par 03/03/1992
ADR agreement terminated 05/11/1995
Details not available

VARDAMAN SHOE CO.
Out of business in 1944

VARE CORP (NY)
Merged into Microdot Inc. (CA) 01/31/1969
Each share Common $2.50 par exchanged for (0.8) share Common no par
Microdot Inc. (CA) reincorporated in Delaware 07/02/1971
(See Microdot Inc. (DE))

VARENNA HLDGS LTD (AB)
9-1/4% Preferred $25 par called for redemption 12/31/1990
Public interest eliminated

VARGAS MINES LTD (BC)
Recapitalized as Charleston Resources Ltd. 08/15/1974
Each share Common 50¢ par exchanged for (0.2) share Common no par
Charleston Resources Ltd. recapitalized as Envipco Canada Western Inc. 01/06/1988 which name changed to Automated Recycling Inc. 08/20/1999 which name changed to Oceanlake Commerce Inc. 03/01/2001

VARI CARE INC (DE)
Common 1¢ par split (2) for (1) by issuance of (1) additional share 8/22/83
Common 1¢ par split (4) for (3) by issuance of (1/3) additional share 4/24/85
Common 1¢ par split (4) for (3) by issuance of (1/3) additional share 9/30/86
Stock Dividends - 100% 1/15/82; 100% 11/4/82
Merged into Living Centers of America, Inc. 10/1/93
Each share Common 1¢ par exchanged for (0.2239) share Common 1¢ par and $3.3653 cash
Living Centers of America, Inc. merged into Paragon Health Network, Inc. 11/4/97 which name changed to Mariner Post-Acute Network, Inc. 7/31/98
(See Mariner Post-Acute Network, Inc.)

VARI-L INC (CO)
Name changed to VL Dissolution Corp. 5/5/2003
(See VL Dissolution Corp.)

VARI-LITE INTL INC (DE)
Issue Information - 2,000,000 shares COM offered at $12 per share on 10/16/1997
Name changed to VLPS Lighting Services International, Inc. 3/7/2003
(See VLPS Lighting Services International, Inc.)

VARI PAC CORP (NJ)
Adjudicated bankrupt 05/12/1967

VARIABLE ANNUITY LIFE INS CO (TX)
Merged into American General Insurance Co. 1/20/77
Each share Capital Stock $1 par exchanged for (0.75) share Common $1.50 par or $11.50 cash
Note: Option to receive cash or stock or both expired 1/18/77 after which holders received cash only
American General Insurance Co. reorganized as American General Corp. 7/1/80 which merged into American International Group, Inc. 8/29/2001

VARIABLE ANNUITY LIFE INS CO AMER (DC)
Reincorporated under the laws of Texas as Variable Annuity Life Insurance Co. 5/1/69
Variable Annuity Life Insurance Co. merged into American General Insurance Co. 1/20/77 which reorganized as American General Corp. 7/1/80 which merged into American International Group, Inc. 8/29/2001

VARIABLE STK FD INC (MD)
Under plan of reorganization each share Common $1 par automatically became (1) share Price (T. Rowe) Growth Stock Fund, Inc. Common $1 par 01/27/1992

VARIAGENICS INC (DE)
Issue Information - 5,000,000 shares COM offered at $14 per share on 07/21/2000
Merged into Nuvelo, Inc. (NV) 01/31/2003
Each share Common 1¢ par exchanged for (1.6451) shares Common $0.001 par
Nuvelo, Inc. (NV) reorganized in Delaware 02/23/2004 which recapitalized as ARCA biopharma, Inc. 01/28/2009

VARIAN ASSOC INC (DE)
Reincorporated 10/07/1976
6% Preferred Ser. A called for redemption 09/30/1957
Capital Stock $1 par reclassified as Common $1 par 02/21/1966
Stock Dividend - 100% 06/01/1959
Name and state of incorporation changed from Varian Associates (CA) to Varian Associates, Inc. (DE) 10/07/1976
Common $1 par split (2) for (1) by issuance of (1) additional share 02/28/1983
Common $1 par split (2) for (1) by issuance of (1) additional share 03/17/1994
Each share Common $1 par received distribution of (1) share Varian, Inc. Common 1¢ par and (1) share Varian Semiconductor Equipment Associates, Inc. Common 1¢ par payable 04/02/1999 to holders of record 03/24/1999 Ex date - 04/08/1999
Name changed to Varian Medical Systems, Inc. 04/03/1999

VARIAN INC (DE)
Merged into Agilent Technologies, Inc. 05/14/2010
Each share Common 1¢ par exchanged for $52 cash

VARIAN SEMICONDUCTOR EQUIPMENT ASSOCS INC (DE)
Common 1¢ par split (3) for (2) by issuance of (0.5) additional share payable 02/28/2006 to holders of record 02/13/2006 Ex date - 03/01/2006
Common 1¢ par split (3) for (2) by issuance of (0.5) additional share payable 05/30/2007 to holders of record 05/15/2007 Ex date - 05/31/2007
Acquired by Applied Materials, Inc. 11/10/2011
Each share Common 1¢ par exchanged for $63 cash

VARIANT CORP (KS)
Reincorporated 12/24/1974
State of incorporation changed from (DE) to (KS) 12/24/1974
Each share Common 25¢ par exchanged for (0.25) share Common $1 par 02/13/1978
Charter forfeited 06/15/1989

VARIED IND PLAN INC (MD)
Merged into Pilgrim Fund, Inc. 10/24/1980
Each share Capital Stock $1 par exchanged for (0.346) share Common $1 par
Pilgrim Fund, Inc. merged into Pilgrim Magnacap Fund, Inc. 06/20/1985

VARIEGATE PROPERTIES INC (CO)
Name changed to Applied Solar Technologies, Inc. 09/21/1981
(See Applied Solar Technologies, Inc.)

VARIETY VIDEO ENTERPRISES INC (ON)
Charter cancelled for failure to pay taxes and file returns 7/29/91

VARIFAB INC (NY)
Filed Certificate of dissolution 10/30/1974
Assets subsequently sold for benefit of creditors; no stockholders' equity

VARIFLEX INC (DE)
Merged into Bravo Sports 10/26/2004
Each share Common $0.001 par exchanged for $7.60 cash

VARIGRAPHICS, INC. (CA)
Charter revoked for failure to file reports and pay fees 1/4/65

VARISYSTEMS CORP (DE)
Name changed to PLA Standard Corp. 11/22/1978
(See PLA Standard Corp.)

VARITECH INVS CORP (ON)
Each share Retractable Floating Rate Preferred $25 par exchanged for (3.333) shares GLP NT Corp. Non-Vtg. Class A no par 01/19/1996
(See GLP NT Corp.)

VARITECH RES LTD (BC)
Name changed to Prime Spot Media Inc. 02/10/1993
Prime Spot Media Inc. recapitalized as New Media Systems Inc. (BC) 08/11/2000 which reorganized in Canada as Wavefront Energy & Environmental Services Inc. 10/01/2003 which name changed to Wavefront Technology Solutions Inc. 03/27/2009

VARITEK INDS INC (TX)
Each share old Common no par exchanged for (0.125) share new Common no par 12/28/2001
Reincorporated under the laws of Delaware as Remote Knowldege Inc. 09/15/2003
(See Remote Knowldege Inc.)

VARITRONIC SYS INC (MN)
Merged into W.H. Brady Co. 4/8/96
Each share Common 1¢ par exchanged for $17.50 cash
(See Brady (W.H.) Co.)

VARITRONIX INTL LTD (HONG KONG)
ADR agreement terminated 01/12/2017
Each Sponsored ADR for Ordinary exchanged for $3.441197 cash

VARITY CORP (DE)
Reorganized 8/1/91
Reorganized from Varity Corp. (Canada) to under the laws of (DE) as Varity Corp. 8/1/91
Each share U.S. $1.30 Sr. Conv. Preferred Class 1 Ser. A no par exchanged for (1) share U.S. $1.30 Sr. Conv. Preferred Class 1 Ser. A no par
Each share old Common no par exchanged for (0.1) share new Common no par
U.S. $1.30 Sr. Conv. Preferred Class 1 Ser. A no par called for redemption 10/27/93
Preference Class II no par called for redemption 8/12/96
Merged into LucasVarity PLC 9/6/96
Each share new Common no par exchanged for (1.38) Sponsored ADR's for Ordinary 25p par
(See LucasVarity PLC)

VARLEN CORP (DE)
Common 10¢ par split (3) for (2) by issuance of (0.5) additional share 10/14/93
Common 10¢ par split (3) for (2) by issuance of (0.5) additional share payable 11/18/97 to holders of record 10/31/97
Common 10¢ par split (5) for (4) by issuance of (0.25) additional share payable 11/17/98 to holders of record 10/30/98
Stock Dividends - 25% 7/22/81; 10% 7/10/95; 10% payable 7/15/96 to holders of record 7/1/96
Merged into Amsted Industries Inc. 8/16/99
Each share Common 10¢ par exchanged for $42 cash

VARNA GOLD INC (AB)
Name changed to New Island Minerals Ltd. 01/18/1993
New Island Minerals Ltd. name changed to New Island Resources Inc. 04/22/1997

VARNER (R.G.) STEEL PRODUCTS, INC. (AR)
Each share Common no par exchanged for (5) shares Common $1 par 10/01/1961
Name changed to Varco Steel, Inc. 07/31/1962
Varco Steel, Inc. acquired by Fuqua Industries, Inc. (PA) 11/01/1967 which reincorporated in Delaware 05/06/1968 which name changed to Actava Group Inc. 07/21/1993 which name changed to Metromedia International Group, Inc. 11/01/1995
(See Metromedia International Group, Inc.)

VARNER TECHNOLOGIES INC (NV)
Common $0.001 par split (5) for (1) by issuance of (4) additional shares payable 08/22/2001 to holders of record 08/22/2001
SEC revoked common stock registration 10/15/2009

VARNER WARD LEASING CO (CA)
Common $1.25 par changed to 45¢ par and (2) additional shares issued 12/29/1972
Merged into Varner-Ward Inc. 05/31/1978

VARNEY AIR LINES, INC.
Acquired by United Aircraft & Transport Corp. in 1930
Details not available

VARNISHES & PAINTS, INC.
Name changed to Truscon Laboratories, Inc. in 1936
Truscon Laboratories, Inc. acquired by Devoe & Raynolds Co., Inc. in 1945 which name changed to Revday Industries, Inc. 8/28/64 which completely liquidated 7/15/68

VARO INC (TX)
Common no par split (2) for (1) by issuance of (1) additional share 7/11/69
Common no par changed to 10¢ par 1/23/74
Merged into Imo Delaval Inc. 11/21/88
Each share Common 10¢ par exchanged for $25 cash

VARO MFG. CO., INC. (TX)
Recapitalized as Varo, Inc. 1/31/61
Each share Common $5 par exchanged for (3) shares Common no par
(See Varo, Inc.)

VARSITY BRANDS INC (DE)
Merged into VBR Holding Corp. 9/24/2003
Each share Common 1¢ par exchanged for $6.57 cash

VARSITY GROUP INC (DE)
Merged into Follett Corp. 04/16/2008
Each share Common $0.0001 par exchanged for $0.20 cash

VARSITY HOUSE INC (DE)
Completely liquidated 11/14/1969
Each share Common 5¢ par exchanged for first and final distribution of (0.31424) share National Student Marketing Corp. (DC) Common 1¢ par
National Student Marketing Corp. (DC) reincorporated in Delaware 04/01/1970
(See National Student Marketing Corp. (DE))

VARSITY SPIRIT CORP (TN)
Common 1¢ par split (3) for (2) by issuance of (0.5) additional share 2/24/95
Merged into Riddell Sports Inc. 7/25/97
Each share Common 1¢ par exchanged for $18.90 cash

VARSITYBOOKS COM INC (DE)
Issue Information - 4,075,000 shares COM offered at $10 per share on 02/15/2000
Name changed to Varsity Group Inc. 06/26/2000
(See Varsity Group Inc.)

VASCAN LTD (ON)
Name changed to Teledyne Canada, Ltd. 11/20/1969
(See Teledyne Canada, Ltd.)

VASCO CORP (DE)
Merged into VASCO Data Security International Inc. 10/28/1998
Each share Common $0.001 par exchanged for (1) share Common $0.001 par
VASCO Data Security International, Inc. name changed to OneSpan Inc. 06/04/2018

VASCO DATA SECURITY INTL INC (DE)
Name changed to OneSpan Inc. 06/04/2018

VASCO METALS CORP. (PA)
Capital Stock $5 par changed to $2.50 par and (1) additional share issued 11/17/1965
Acquired by Teledyne, Inc. 06/30/1966
Each share Capital Stock $2.50 par exchanged for (0.33333333) share $3.50 Conv. Preferred $1 par
(See Teledyne, Inc.)

VASCULAR INTL INC (UT)
Reincorporated under the laws of Delaware as Rascals of Delaware Inc. 3/29/99

VASCULAR INTL NEV INC (NV)
Recapitalized as Rose Group Corp. Nevada 3/26/98
Each share Common $0.001 par exchanged for (0.02) share Common $0.001 par
Rose Group Corp. Nevada name changed to IDVIEWS, Inc. 1/25/2006

VASCULAR SOLUTIONS INC (MN)
Acquired by Teleflex Inc. 02/17/2017
Each share Common 1¢ par exchanged for $56 cash

VASO ACTIVE PHARMACEUTICALS INC (DE)
Class A Common $0.0001 par split (3) for (1) by issuance of (2) additional shares payable 03/05/2004 to holders of record 02/23/2004
Ex date - 03/08/2004
Chapter 11 bankruptcy proceedings converted to Chapter 7 on 07/11/2016
Stockholders' equity unlikely

VASOGEN INC (CANADA)
Reincorporated 08/09/1999
Place of incorporation changed from (ON) to (Canada) 08/09/1999
Each share old Common no par exchanged for (0.1) share new Common no par 04/17/2007
Merged into IntelliPharmaCeutics International Inc. 10/22/2009
Each share new Common no par exchanged for (0.06596306) share Common no par

VASOMEDICAL INC (DE)
Name changed to Vaso Corp. 01/26/2017

VASSAN RES INC (QC)
Recapitalized as Savanor Resources Inc. 12/18/89
Each share Common no par exchanged for (0.1) share Common no par
(See Savanor Resources Inc.)

VASSAR CO.
Merged into Munsingwear, Inc. in 1951
Each share Common $5 par exchanged for (0.5) share 5-1/4% Preferred $20 par and (0.375) share new Common $5 par
Munsingwear, Inc. name changed to PremiumWear, Inc. 9/6/96
(See PremiumWear, Inc.)

VASSAR CORP (NY)
Adjudicated bankrupt 03/05/1975
Stockholders' equity unlikely

VAST CAP POOL LTD (BC)
Name changed to User Friendly Media Inc. 03/26/2001
User Friendly Media Inc. name changed to UFM Ventures Ltd. 03/04/2004 which name changed to Uracan Resources Ltd. 08/03/2006 which recapitalized as Vanadian Energy Corp. 10/05/2018

VAST EXPL INC (ON)
Each share old Common no par exchanged for (0.02) share new Common no par 08/09/2013
Name changed to ARHT Media Inc. 10/17/2014

VAST INC (DE)
Name changed to TRC Companies, Inc. 11/03/1976
(See TRC Companies, Inc.)

VAST INC (MN)
Statutorily dissolved 10/17/91

VAST SOLUTIONS INC (DE)
Charter cancelled and declared inoperative and void for non-payment of taxes 03/01/2002

VAST TECHNOLOGIES HLDG CORP (DE)
Name changed to Accelerated Learning Languages Inc. 11/13/2000
Accelerated Learning Languages Inc. recapitalized as Integrated Enterprises Inc. 06/20/2001 which recapitalized as SeaLife Corp. (DE) 12/20/2002 which reincorporated in Nevada 10/06/2016

VASTAR RES INC (DE)
Merged into BP Amoco PLC 09/15/2000
Each share Common 1¢ par exchanged for $83 cash

VASTERA INC (DE)
Merged into JPMorgan Chase & Co. 04/01/2005
Each share Common 1¢ par exchanged for $3 cash

VASTLODE MINING CO. LTD. (BC)
Recapitalized as Ashcroft Resources Ltd. 05/29/1972
Each share Common 50¢ par exchanged for (0.2) share Common no par
Ashcroft Resources Ltd. recapitalized as Tchaikazan Enterprises Ltd. 12/05/1986
(See Tchaikazan Enterprises Ltd.)

VAT PETE LTD (BC)
Delisted from Vancouver Stock Exchange 11/11/87

VAUGHAN E. FARRIE, INC. (NY)
See - Farrie (Vaughan E.), Inc.

VAUGHAN FOODS INC (OK)
Acquired by Reser's Fine Foods, Inc. 09/15/2011
Each share Common $0.001 par exchanged for approximately $1.58 cash

VAUGHAN JACKLIN CORP (DE)
Reacquired 11/16/1983
Each share Common 10¢ par exchanged for $0.75 principal amount of 13.50% Subordinated Debentures due 11/16/1985, $0.75 principal amount of 13.50% Subordinated Debentures due 11/16/1986 and $11.50 cash

VAUGHNS COMMUNICATIONS INC (MN)
Name changed 6/30/87
Common $1 par changed to 10¢ par 10/29/82
Stock Dividends - 50% 11/15/77; 50% 11/22/78
Name changed from Vaughns Inc. to Vaughns Communications, Inc. 6/30/87
Merged into Allied Digital, Inc. 3/4/99
Each share Common 10¢ par exchanged for $10 cash

VAULT AMER INC (NV)
Name changed to Green PolkaDot Box Inc. 04/23/2012

VAULT ENERGY TR (AB)
Merged into Penn West Energy Trust 01/10/2008
Each Trust Unit exchanged for (0.14) Trust Unit
Penn West Energy Trust reorganized as Penn West Petroleum Ltd. (New) 01/03/2011 which name changed to Obsidian Energy Ltd. 06/29/2017

VAULT EXPLS INC (BC)
Name changed to Sun Entertainment Holding Corp. 07/07/1987
(See Sun Entertainment Holding Corp.)

VAULT FINL SVCS INC (NV)
Each share old Common $0.001 par exchanged for (0.016) share new Common $0.001 par 05/30/2005
Each share new Common $0.001 par exchanged again for (0.05) share new Common $0.001 par 03/24/2006
Name changed to Prime Restaurants, Inc. 04/18/2007
Prime Restaurants, Inc. name changed to BIH Corp. 03/19/2008
(See BIH Corp.)

VAULT INDS INC (UT)
Involuntarily dissolved 01/01/1997

VAULT MINERALS INC (ON)
Reincorporated 07/25/2005
Place of incorporation changed from (BC) to (ON) 07/25/2005
Merged into Queenston Mining Inc. 04/23/2010
Each share Common no par exchanged for (0.1) share Common no par
Queenston Mining Inc. merged into Osisko Mining Corp. 01/02/2013
(See Osisko Mining Corp.)

VAULT SYS INC (BC)
Recapitalized as Vault Minerals Inc. (BC) 06/18/2003
Each share Common no par exchanged for (0.16666666) share Common no par
Vault Minerals Inc. (BC) reincorporated in Ontario 07/25/2005 which merged into Queenston Mining Inc. 04/23/2010 which merged into Osisko Mining Corp. 01/02/2013
(See Osisko Mining Corp.)

VAULT TECHNOLOGY INC (NV)
Recapitalized as Modern Renewable Technologies, Inc. 09/17/2009
Each share Common $0.001 par exchanged for (0.01428571) share Common $0.001 par
Modern Renewable Technologies, Inc. name changed to Eco Ventures Group, Inc. 05/16/2011 which recapitalized as Petlife Pharmaceuticals, Inc. (Old) 08/12/2014 which reorganized as Petlife Pharmaceuticals, Inc. (New) 09/12/2016

VAUMONT MINES LTD. (ON)
Charter cancelled for failure to file reports and pay taxes in 1950

VAUPEL'S OF WHITWOOD (CA)
Voluntarily dissolved 8/5/82
No stockholders' equity

VAUQUELIN IRON MINES LTD. (QC)
Name changed to Vauquelin Mines Ltd. in 1964
Vauquelin Mines Ltd. name changed to Bridgepoint International Inc. 12/2/99 which was acquired by Afcan Mining Corp. 11/3/2003 which merged into Eldorado Gold Corp. (New) 9/13/2005

VAUQUELIN MINES LTD (QC)
Name changed to Bridgepoint International Inc. 12/02/1999
Bridgepoint International Inc. acquired by Afcan Mining Corp. 11/03/2003 which merged into Eldorado Gold Corp. (New) 09/13/2005

VAUZE DUFAULT MINES LTD. (ON)
Recapitalized as Consolidated Vauze Mines Ltd. 00/00/1956
Each share Capital Stock $1 par exchanged for (0.33333333) share Capital Stock $1 par
Consolidated Vauze Mines Ltd. acquired by Vauze Mines Ltd. 06/23/1961 which name changed to North American Gas Ltd. 05/27/1965
(See North American Gas Ltd.)

VAUZE MINES LTD. (QC)
Name changed to North American Gas Ltd. 5/27/65
North American Gas Ltd. charter cancelled 8/18/73

VAWTPOWER INC (DE)
Each share old Common 1¢ par exchanged exchanged for (0.25) share new Common 1¢ par 12/23/1986
Company reported out of business 10/31/1999
Stockholders' equity unlikely

VAXCEL INC (DE)
Name changed to Chattown.com Network Inc. 03/02/2000
Chattown.com Network Inc. name changed to eLocity Networks Corp.

12/19/2000 which name changed to Diversified Financial Resources Corp. (DE) 08/23/2002 which reincorporated in Nevada 05/12/2006 which name changed to China Fruits Corp. 09/08/2006

VAXGEN INC (DE)
Issue Information - 3,100,000 shares COM NEW offered at $13 per share on 06/29/1999
Each share old Common 1¢ par exchanged for (0.5) share new Common 1¢ par 04/01/1999
Name changed to diaDexus, Inc. 11/01/2010

VB CLOTHING INC (NV)
Common $0.001 par split (4) for (1) by issuance of (3) additional shares payable 02/26/2013 to holders of record 02/25/2013 Ex date - 02/27/2013
Name changed to VizConnect, Inc. 05/24/2013

VB TRADE INC (NV)
Name changed to Endeavor Uranium, Inc. 10/05/2007
Endeavor Uranium, Inc. name changed to Endeavor Power Corp. 01/23/2009 which name changed to Parallax Health Sciences, Inc. 01/29/2014

VB&T BANCSHARES CORP. (GA)
Acquired by Regions Financial Corp. (Old) 01/01/1999
Each share Common $5 par exchanged for (0.7202) share Common $0.625 par
Regions Financial Corp. (Old) merged into Regions Financial Corp. (New) 07/01/2004

VBC CAP I (DE)
Captial Securities called for redemption at $25 on 4/30/2002

VBI VACCINES INC (DE)
Merged into VBI Vaccines Inc. (BC) 05/09/2016
Each share Common $0.0001 par exchanged for (0.520208) share Common no par

VCA ANTECH INC (DE)
Common $0.001 par split (2) for (1) by issuance of (1) additional share payable 08/25/2004 to holders of record 08/11/2004 Ex date - 08/26/2004
Name changed to VCA Inc. 06/03/2014
(See VCA Inc.)

VCA CORP (DE)
Merged into Ethyl Corp. 10/30/74
Each share 80¢ Conv. Preferred 1970 Ser. no par exchanged for $19 cash
Each share Common 25¢ par exchanged for $18.50 cash

VCA INC (DE)
Acquired by Mars, Inc. 09/12/2017
Each share Common $0.001 par exchanged for $93 cash

VCAMPUS CORP (DE)
Each share old Common 1¢ par exchanged for (0.1) share new Common 1¢ par 07/08/2002
Company terminated common stock registration and is no longer public as of 06/11/2008

VCG HLDG CORP (CO)
Acquired by Family Dog, L.L.C. 04/18/2011
Each share Common $0.0001 par exchanged for $2.25 cash

VCI INC (NY)
Dissolved by proclamation 12/24/91

VCOM INC (CANADA)
Name changed to Vecima Networks Inc. 11/13/2006

VCS INC (DE)
Common $1 par split (2) for (1) by issuance of (1) additional share 7/15/88
Common $1 par split (5) for (1) by issuance of (4) additional shares 8/31/88
Common $1 par changed to 10¢ par 10/11/88
Name changed to American Video Imaging, Inc. 5/9/90
(See American Video Imaging, Inc.)

VDC COMMUNICATIONS INC (DE)
SEC revoked common stock registration 11/16/2005

VDC CORP LTD (BERMUDA)
Merged into VDC Communications, Inc. 11/06/1998
Each share Common 10¢ par exchanged for (1) share Common $0.0001 par
(See VDC Communications, Inc.)

VDG CAP CORP (CO)
Recapitalized as Vinculum Inc. (CO) 12/23/1994
Each share Class A Common $0.001 par exchanged for (0.2) share Class A Common $0.001 par
Vinculum Inc. (CO) reorganized in Nevada 06/08/1998 which name changed to CPU Micromart, Inc. 06/30/1998 which name changed to Ebiz Enterprises, Inc. 05/06/1999
(See Ebiz Enterprises, Inc.)

VDI MULTIMEDIA (CA)
Name changed 08/16/1999
Name changed from VDI Media to VDI Multimedia 08/16/1999
Name changed to Point.360 (Old) 06/04/2001
Point.360 (Old) merged into DG FastChannel, Inc. 08/14/2007 which name changed to Digital Generation, Inc. 11/07/2011 which merged into Sizmek Inc. 02/07/2014
(See Sizmek Inc.)

VDO COM INC (FL)
Name changed to Hundred Mile Plus, Ltd. 09/19/2001
Hundred Mile Plus, Ltd. recapitalized as Ultra Pure Water Technologies, Inc. 05/24/2004

VEBA AG (GERMANY)
Sponsored ADR's for Ordinary DM5 par changed to no par 10/04/1999
Name changed to E.ON AG 06/19/2000
E.ON AG name changed to E. ON SE 01/04/2013

VECTOLL INVESTMENTS LTD. (BC)
Liquidation completed
Each share Common no par received initial distribution of $0.20 cash 9/10/64
Each share Common no par received second and final distribution of $0.414953 cash 11/19/65
Note: Certificates were not required to be surrendered and are without value

VECTOR AEROMOTIVE CORP (NV)
Each share Common $0.001 par exchanged for (0.02) share Common 1¢ par 07/09/1990
Each share old Common 1¢ par exchanged for (0.2) share new Common 1¢ par 11/25/1998
Recapitalized as Vector Holdings Corp. 07/10/2000
Each share new Common 1¢ par exchanged for (0.01) share Common 1¢ par
Vector Holdings Corp. name changed to NCI Holdings, Inc. 06/17/2003 which name changed to Dark Dynamite, Inc. 05/07/2004 which name changed to China International Tourism Holdings, Ltd. 10/26/2007 which name changed to China Logistics, Inc. (NV) 08/10/2009 which reorganized in British Virgin Islands as Hutech21 Co., Ltd. 03/21/2011

VECTOR AEROSPACE CORP (CANADA)
Acquired by Eurocopter Holdings SAS 07/26/2011
Each share Common no par exchanged for $13 cash

VECTOR AUTOMATION INC (MD)
Charter forfeited for failure to file reports 10/8/93

VECTOR DIAMOND CORP (BC)
Name changed 06/28/1994
Name changed from Vector Industries International Inc. to Vector Diamond Corp. 06/28/1994
Name changed to Canabrava Diamond Corp. 11/01/1994
Canabrava Diamond Corp. merged into Superior Diamonds Inc. (Yukon) 11/27/2003 which reincorporated in British Columbia 06/30/2004 name changed to Northland Resources Inc. 04/15/2008

VECTOR ELECTRIC LTD. (ON)
Charter revoked for failure to file reports and pay fees 1/5/67

VECTOR ENERGY CORP (OK)
Merged into Fossil Oil & Gas, Inc. 8/25/83
Each share Common 1¢ par exchanged for (1/6) share Common 10¢ par
Fossil Oil & Gas, Inc. merged into Premier Technology Holding, Inc. 5/12/86
(See Premier Technology Holding, Inc.)

VECTOR ENERGY CORP NEW (TX)
Reorganized under the laws of Nevada as VTEX Energy, Inc. 11/15/2002
Each share 10% Conv. Preferred Ser. A no par exchanged for (1) share 10% Conv. Preferred Ser. A $0.001 par
Each (30) shares Common no par exchanged for (1) share Common $0.001 par
(See VTEX Energy, Inc.)

VECTOR ENERGY FD (ON)
Merged into ACTIVEnergy Income Fund 04/27/2016
Each Trust Unit exchanged for (0.9598691) Trust Unit
ACTIVEnergy Income Fund reorganized as Middlefield Mutual Funds Ltd. 06/05/2017

VECTOR ENVIRONMENTAL TECHNOLOGIES INC (DE)
Name changed to WaterPur International, Inc. 07/07/1997
WaterPur International, Inc. recapitalized as Aquentium, Inc. 05/22/2002

VECTOR GRAPHIC INC (CA)
Chapter 11 Federal Bankruptcy Code converted to Chapter 7 on 9/30/87
Stockholders' equity unlikely

VECTOR HLDGS CORP (NV)
Each share old Common 1¢ par exchanged for (0.04) share new Common 1¢ par 01/18/2002
Each share new Common 1¢ par exchanged for (0.005) share Common $0.001 par 05/05/2003
Name changed to NCI Holdings, Inc. 06/17/2003
NCI Holdings, Inc. name changed to Dark Dynamite, Inc. 05/07/2004 which name changed to China International Tourism Holdings, Ltd. 10/26/2007 which name changed to China Logistics, Inc. (NV) 08/10/2009 which reorganized in British Virgin Islands as Hutech21 Co., Ltd. 03/21/2011

VECTOR INTERMEDIARIES INC (AB)
Placed in receivership 06/00/2004
Stockholders' equity unlikely

VECTOR INTERSECT SEC ACQUISITION CORP (DE)
Name changed to Cyalume Technologies Holdings, Inc. 12/19/2008
(See Cyalume Technologies Holdings, Inc.)

VECTOR MGMT CORP (OR)
Name changed to Hinkle Northwest, Inc. 6/25/73
Hinkle Northwest, Inc. name changed to Hinkle & Lamear, Inc. 5/27/83 which name changed to L & H Capital Services Corp. 6/18/84
(See L & H Capital Services Corp.)

VECTOR MANUFACTURING CO., INC. (PA)
Acquired by United Aircraft Corp. 2/14/64
Each share Common no par exchanged for (1/9) share Common $5 par
United Aircraft Corp. name changed to United Technologies Corp. 4/30/75

VECTOR RES INC (ON)
Reorganized under the laws of Alberta as Razor Energy Corp. 02/13/2017
Each share Common no par exchanged for (0.05) share Common no par

VECTOR VENTURE CORP (BC)
Acquired by Vector Environmental Technologies, Inc. 08/29/1995
Each share Common no par exchanged for (1) share Common $0.005 par
Vector Environmental Technologies, Inc. name changed to WaterPur International, Inc. 07/07/1997 which recapitalized as Aquentium, Inc. 05/22/2002

VECTOR VENTURES CORP (NV)
Reorganized as Celsius Holdings, Inc. 12/26/2006
Each share Common $0.001 par exchanged for (4) shares Common $0.001 par

VECTOR WIND ENERGY INC (CANADA)
Merged into Canadian Hydro Developers, Inc. 1/5/2007
Each share Common no par exchanged for $0.30 cash

VECTORIA INC (NV)
Each share old Common $0.001 par exchanged for (1/6) share new Common $0.001 par 08/23/2004
Recapitalized as Satelinx International, Inc. 10/21/2004
Each share Common $0.001 par exchanged for (0.1) share Common 1¢ par
Satelinx International, Inc. recapitalized as Affinity Networks, Inc. 08/13/2007

VECTORVISION CORP (MN)
Merged into Realty Sales Network Corp. 4/21/2000
Each share Preferred exchanged for (0.4) share Common 1¢ par

VECTR SYS INC (NV)
Charter revoked 08/01/2011

VECTRA BKG CORP (CO)
$0.95 Preferred Ser. A 10¢ par called for redemption at $10.30 on 05/23/1997
Common 1¢ par split (3) for (2) by issuance of (0.5) additional share payable 05/30/1997 to holders of record 05/15/1997
Merged into Zions Bancorporation 01/06/1998
Each share Conv. Preferred Ser. A 1¢ par exchanged for (7.755) shares Common no par
Each share Common 1¢ par exchanged for (0.685) share Common no par

Zions Bancorporation merged into Zions Bancorporation, N.A. (Salt Lake City, UT) 10/01/2018

VECTRA TECHNOLOGIES INC (WA)
Plan of reorganization under Chapter 11 Federal Bankruptcy proceedings confirmed 09/23/1998
No stockholders' equity

VECTRON, INC. (MA)
Merged into Itek Corp. (MA) 05/20/1958
Each share Common exchanged for (0.15835313) share Common $1 par Itek Corp. (MA) reincorporated in Delaware 02/10/1960
(See Itek Corp.)

VEDCO WAH WAH MINES INC (UT)
Each share Common 20¢ par exchanged for (20) shares Common 1¢ par 07/01/1970
Each share Common 1¢ par exchanged for (0.01) share Common $1 par 05/22/1974
Proclaimed dissolved for failure to pay taxes 09/30/1975

VEDRON GOLD INC (ON)
Recapitalized 01/04/1995
Recapitalized from Vedron Ltd. to Vedron Gold Inc. 01/04/1995
Each share Common no par exchanged for (0.1) share Common no par
Name changed to VG Gold Corp. 08/07/2007
VG Gold Corp. merged into Lexam VG Gold Inc. 01/04/2011 which merged into McEwen Mining Inc. 05/01/2017

VEECO INSTRS INC (NY)
Common $1 par split (3) for (2) by issuance of (0.5) additional share 12/07/1973
Common $1 par split (3) for (2) by issuance of (0.5) additional share 10/07/1977
Common $1 par split (3) for (2) by issuance of (0.5) additional share 12/21/1978
Common $1 par split (2) for (1) by issuance of (1) additional share 03/10/1980
Common $1 par split (3) for (2) by issuance of (0.5) additional share 01/22/1981
Merged into Unitech plc 02/22/1989
Each share Common $1 par exchanged for $26.50 cash

VEEDER INDS INC (CT)
Stock Dividends - 10% 09/27/1968; 20% 11/15/1974
Merged into Western Pacific Industries Inc. 06/15/1976
Each share Common $6.25 par exchanged for $28 principal amount of 10% Subord. Debentures due 07/01/2001

VEEDER ROOT INC. (CT)
Common no par changed to $12.50 par 00/00/1954
Common $12.50 par changed to $6.25 par and (1) additional share issued 12/31/1964
Stock Dividends - 100% 04/00/1947; 20% 12/23/1955; 10% 10/20/1964
Name changed to Veeder Industries Inc. 04/19/1966
(See Veeder Industries Inc.)

VEGA AIRPLANE CO.
Acquired by Lockheed Aircraft Corp. (CA) 00/00/1942
Each share Capital Stock exchanged for (0.33333333) share Common $1 par 00/00/1942
Lockheed Aircraft Corp. (CA) name changed to Lockheed Corp. (CA) 09/30/1977 which reincorporated in Delaware 06/30/1986 which merged into Lockheed Martin Corp. 03/15/1995

VEGA ATLANTIC CORP (CO)
Each share old Common $0.00001 par exchanged for (0.25) share new Common $0.00001 par 12/22/2000
Each share new Common $0.00001 par exchanged again for (0.05) share new Common $0.00001 par 03/31/2003
Name changed to Transax International Ltd. 08/14/2003
Transax International Ltd. recapitalized as Big Tree Group, Inc. 12/11/2012

VEGA BIOTECHNOLOGIES INC (DE)
Charter cancelled and declared inoperative and void for non-payment of taxes 3/1/95

VEGA CAP CORP (NY)
Placed in receivership by U.S. District Court Southern District of New York 02/24/2000
No stockholders' equity

VEGA EXPLS LTD (ON)
Recapitalized as Verena Minerals Corp. 07/01/1996
Each share Common no par exchanged for (0.2) share Common no par
Verena Minerals Corp. name changed to Belo Sun Mining Corp. 07/14/2010

VEGA GOLD LTD (BC)
Recapitalized as Vega Resources Inc. 09/10/2010
Each share Common no par exchanged for (0.5) share Common no par
Vega Resources Inc. recapitalized as Pacific Coal Resources Ltd. 03/14/2011 which name changed to Caribbean Resources Corp. 02/10/2016
(See Caribbean Resources Corp.)

VEGA PRECISION LABS INC (VA)
Merged into VPL, Inc. 03/28/1979
Each share Common $1 par exchanged for $10.50 cash

VEGA PROMOTIONAL SYS INC (DE)
Each share old Common $0.0001 par exchanged for (2) shares new Common $0.0001 par 03/09/2007
Each share new Common $0.0001 par exchanged again for (0.01) share new Common $0.0001 par 04/16/2008
Reorganized under the laws Wyoming as Vega Biofuels, Inc. 07/29/2010
Each shares new Common $0.0001 par exchanged for (0.00333333) share Common $0.001 par

VEGA RES INC (BC)
Recapitalized as Pacific Coal Resources Ltd. 03/14/2011
Each share Common no par exchanged for (0.6) share Common no par
Pacific Coal Resources Ltd. name changed to Caribbean Resources Corp. 02/10/2016
(See Caribbean Resources Corp.)

VEGAN LITHIUM MINES LTD. (ON)
Charter cancelled and declared dissolved for failure to file reports 11/18/70

VEGAS CHIPS INC (DE)
Each share Common $0.0001 par exchanged for (0.05) share Common $0.002 par 12/07/1989
Each share Common $0.002 par exchanged for (0.06666666) share Common 3¢ par 08/18/1992
Name changed to Skydoor Media & Entertainment Inc. 12/15/1995
Skydoor Media & Entertainment Inc. name changed to Ice Holdings, Inc. (DE) 10/09/1996 which reorganized in Nevada as Gaia Resources, Inc. 10/20/2006 which recapitalized as Ram Gold & Exploration, Inc. 02/08/2008 which name changed to DPollution International Inc. 08/31/2010 which recapitalized as Ecrid, Inc. 10/16/2017

VEGAS EQUITY INTL CORP (NV)
Each share old Common $0.0001 par exchanged for (0.0005) share new Common $0.0001 par 11/13/2007
Each share new Common $0.0001 par exchanged again for (0.16666666) share Common $0.0001 par 04/25/2008
SEC revoked common stock registration 08/05/2010

VEGAS VENTURES INC (NV)
Recapitalized as Telemall Communications, Inc. 06/03/1996
Each share Common $0.001 par exchanged for (0.1) share Common $0.001 par
Telemall Communications, Inc. recapitalized as Stein's Holdings, Inc. 04/22/1999 which name changed to Crown Partners Inc. 01/22/2002 which recapitalized as TaxMasters, Inc. 08/12/2009
(See TaxMasters, Inc.)

VEGETABLE OIL PRODUCTS CO., INC. (DE)
Acquired by Drew Food Corp. for cash 5/22/63

VEGEX INC. (DE)
Name changed to Vitamin Food Co., Inc. 12/17/41

VEHICLE PROTN CORP (NV)
Name changed to Point of Care Technologies Inc. 10/15/96
(See Point of Care Technologies Inc.)

VEHICLE RECYCLING TECHNOLOGIES INC (AB)
Name changed to AADCO Industries.com Inc. 08/11/1999
AADCO Industries.com Inc. name changed to AADCO Automotive Inc. 02/18/2002 which recapitalized as Royce Resources Corp. (AB) 01/02/2008 which reincorporated in British Columbia 05/11/2011 which name changed to Lithium X Energy Corp. 11/30/2015
(See Lithium X Energy Corp.)

VEIN VENTURES LTD (BC)
Name changed to HMR World Enterprises Inc. 04/13/1987
(See HMR World Enterprises Inc.)

VEITSCH-RADEX AG (AUSTRIA)
Name changed 4/30/93
Name changed from Veitscher Magnesitwerke A.G. to Veitsch-Radex A.G. 4/30/93
Merged into Radex Heraklith AG 12/13/95
Each ADR for Ordinary 100 Schillings par exchanged for $5.105 cash

VELATEL GLOBAL COMMUNICATIONS INC (NV)
Each share old Ser. A Common $0.001 par exchanged for (0.01) share new Ser. A Common $0.001 par 07/24/2012
SEC revoked common stock registration 10/04/2017

VELCO RESEARCH & DEVELOPMENT, INC. (UT)
Name changed to Ion Laser Technology, Inc. (Old) in August 1984
Ion Laser Technology, Inc. (Old) merged into Laser Holding, Inc. 8/28/87 which name changed to Ion Laser Technology, Inc. (New) 8/22/88 which name changed to Britesmile, Inc. 8/24/98 which name changed to BSML, Inc. 11/1/2006

VELCRO INDS LTD (CANADA)
Completely liquidated 06/30/1972
Each share Common no par exchanged for first and final distribution of (1) share Velcro Industries N.V. Common $1 par

(See Velcro Industries N.V.)

VELCRO INDS N V (NETHERLANDS ANTILLES)
Common $1 par split (10) for (1) by issuance of (9) additional shares payable 02/19/1999 to holders of record 02/09/1999
Acquired by Cohere Ltd. 04/06/2009
Each share Common $1 par exchanged for $21 cash

VELIE MOTORS CORP.
Dissolved in 1929

VELLA PRODUCTIONS INC (NV)
Name changed to Jade Art Group Inc. 12/05/2007

VELO-BIND, INC. (CA)
Common $1 par changed to 50¢ par and (1) additional share issued 5/1/85
Name changed to VeloBind, Inc. (CA) 6/19/86
VeloBind, Inc. (CA) reincorporated in Delaware 9/22/88
(See VeloBind, Inc. (DE))

VELO ENERGY INC (CANADA)
Recapitalized as Canadian Overseas Petroleum Ltd. 08/03/2010
Each share Common no par exchanged for (0.25) share Common no par

VELOBIND INC (DE)
Reincorporated 9/22/88
State of incorporation changed from (CA) to (DE) 9/22/88
Merged into General Binding Corp. 11/1/91
Each share Common 50¢ par exchanged for $9.77 cash

VELOCITY AEROSPACE INC (FL)
Name changed to Critical Power Solutions International, Inc. (FL) 08/08/2007
Critical Power Solutions International, Inc. (FL) reincorporated in Delaware as Critical Solutions, Inc. 03/03/2008

VELOCITY COMPUTER SOLUTIONS LTD (BERMUDA)
Name changed to Voyus Ltd. 06/09/2000
(See Voyus Ltd.)

VELOCITY EXPRESS CORP (DE)
Each share old Common $0.004 par exchanged for (0.2) share new Common $0.004 par 04/25/2002
Each share new Common $0.004 par exchanged again for (0.02) share new Common $0.004 par 02/16/2005
Each share new Common $0.004 par exchanged again for (0.06666666) share new Common $0.004 par 12/07/2007
Assets sold under Section 363 of the Bankruptcy Code 11/25/2009
Stockholders' equity unlikely

VELOCITY INTL CORP (CO)
Each share old Common $0.001 par exchanged for (0.01) share new Common $0.001 par 11/10/2005
Reincorporated under the laws of Nevada as Deep Blue, Inc. 03/13/2006
Deep Blue, Inc. recapitalized as Bell Rose Capital, Inc. 03/05/2014

VELOCITY OIL & GAS INC (NV)
Recapitalized as Generation Zero Group, Inc. 03/08/2010
Each share Common $0.001 par exchanged for (0.01) share Common $0.001 par

VELOCITY PORTFOLIO GROUP INC (DE)
Recapitalized 11/17/2008
Recapitalized from Velocity Asset Management, Inc. to Velocity Portfolio Group, Inc. 11/17/2008
Each share Conv. Preferred Ser. A $0.001 par exchanged for (0.05)

share Conv. Preferred Ser. A $0.001 par
Each share Common $0.001 par exchanged for (0.05) share Common $0.001 par
Each share Conv. Preferred Ser. A $0.001 par exchanged for (6) shares Common $0.001 par 09/19/2016
(Additional Information in Active)

VELOCITYHSI INC (DE)
Filed a petition under Chapter 7 Federal Bankruptcy Code 08/14/2001
Stockholders' equity unlikely

VELOK LTD. (CANADA)
Common no par split (10) for (1) by issuance of (9) additional shares 10/07/1966
5% Conv. Preferred $20 par called for redemption 11/15/1966
Name changed to Velcro Industries Ltd. 02/01/1967
Velcro Industries Ltd. liquidated for Velcro Industries N.V. 06/30/1972
(See Velcro Industries N.V.)

VELTEX INDS INC (CA)
Stock Dividend - 10% payable 9/25/98 to holders of record 6/30/98
Charter forfeited for failure to file reports and pay fees 12/1/99

VELVET EXPL LTD (AB)
Reincorporated 5/26/98
Reincorporated from Velvet Exploration Co., Ltd. (BC) to Velvet Exploration Ltd. (ALTA) 5/26/98
Acquired by El Paso Corp. 8/2/2001
Each share Common no par exchanged for $8.15 cash

VELVET LARDER MINES, LTD. (ON)
Dissolved 3/24/58

VELVET O DONNELL CORP (MI)
Common $1 par split (2) for (1) by issuance of (1) additional share 4/30/73
Name changed to VOD Corp. 2/13/85

VENA RES INC (ON)
Each share old Common no par exchanged for (0.5) share new Common no par 10/15/2012
Name changed to Forrester Metals Inc. 10/06/2016
Forrester Metals Inc. merged into Zinc One Resources Inc. 06/02/2017

VENATOR GROUP INC (NY)
Name changed to Foot Locker, Inc. 11/02/2001

VENATOR PETE LTD (AB)
Acquired by Primewest Resources Ltd. 04/18/2000
Each share Common no par exchanged for (0.657)
Exchangeable Share no par
Primewest Resources Ltd. name changed to PrimeWest Energy Inc. 01/01/2002

VENAXIS INC (CO)
Each share old Common no par exchanged for (0.125) share new Common no par 03/31/2016
Name changed to Bioptix, Inc. (CO) 12/12/2016
Bioptix, Inc. (CO) reincorporated in Nevada 09/28/2017 which name changed to Riot Blockchain, Inc. 10/19/2017

VENCAN GOLD CORP (ON)
Name changed to Red Pine Exploration Inc. 03/02/2009

VENCAP CAP CORP (NV)
Common $0.001 par split (15) for (1) by issuance of (14) additional shares payable 03/08/2000 to holders of record 02/10/2000
Recapitalized as American Scientific Resources, Inc. 01/08/2004
Each share Common $0.001 par exchanged for (0.005) share Common $0.0001 par

VENCAP EQUITIES ALTA LTD (AB)
Acquired by Onex Corp. 01/03/1996
Each share Common no par exchanged for $8.50 cash

VENCAP HLDGS INC (NV)
Each share old Common $0.001 par exchanged for (0.1) share new Common $0.001 par 2/16/2001
Name changed to Blue Planet Research & Technology, Inc. 4/22/2004

VENCAP INVTS LTD (ON)
Placed in receivership 11/05/1975
No stockholders' equity

VENCOR INC NEW (DE)
Plan of reorganization under Chapter 11 Federal Bankruptcy Code effective 04/20/2001
No stockholders' equity

VENCOR INC OLD (DE)
Name changed 09/03/1993
Common 25¢ par split (3) for (2) by issuance of (0.5) additional share 06/17/1991
Common 25¢ par split (5) for (4) by issuance of (0.25) additional share 01/15/1992
Name changed from Vencor, Inc. to Vencor Inc. (Old) 09/03/1993
Common 25¢ par split (3) for (2) by issuance of (0.5) additional share 10/25/1994
Each share Common 25¢ par received distribution of (1) share Vencor, Inc. (New) Common 25¢ par payable 04/30/1998 to holders of record 04/27/1998 Ex date - 05/04/1998
Name changed to Ventas, Inc. 05/01/1998

VENCOR INTL INC (UT)
Each share old Common $0.001 par exchanged for (0.5) share new Common $0.001 par 12/23/1997
Recapitalized as PLAD, Inc. 11/06/2015
Each share new Common $0.001 par exchanged for (0.005) share Common $0.001 par
PLAD, Inc. name changed to Elev8 Brands, Inc. 12/28/2016

VEND A PHONE INC (NY)
Dissolved by proclamation 3/25/92

VENDALL, INC. (NY)
Charter cancelled and proclaimed dissolved for failure to pay taxes 12/15/67

VENDALUX CORP (DE)
SEC revoked common stock registration 03/01/2012

VENDAVERSAL MANUFACTURING CORP. (CO)
Bankrupt 8/12/63; stock valueless

VENDELCO INC (RI)
Charter forfeited for non-payment of taxes 12/31/1976

VENDELL HEALTHCARE INC (DE)
Plan of reorganization under Chapter 11 Federal Bankruptcy proceedings confirmed 10/10/1997
No stockholders' equity

VENDEX KBB N V (NETHERLANDS)
Name changed 7/16/99
Name changed from Vendex International N.V. to Vendex KBB N.V. 7/16/99
Name changed to Koninklijke Vendex KBB N.V. 5/17/2000
(See Koninklijke Vendex KBB N.V.)

VENDIN ONE CAP CORP (YUKON)
Recapitalized as Dynasty Metals & Mining Inc. (Yukon) 09/26/2003
Each share Common no par exchanged for (0.5) share Common no par
Dynasty Metals & Mining Inc. (Yukon) reincorporated in British Columbia as Core Gold Inc. 09/28/2017

VENDING INTERNATIONAL, INC. (DE)
Completely liquidated 5/16/65
Each share Common 10¢ par exchanged for (0.018530795) share 3-3/4% Preferred Series A $100 par and (0.060070341) share Common $5 par of Standard Oil Co. (Ohio)
(See Standard Oil Co. (Ohio))

VENDINGDATA CORP (NV)
Each share old Common $0.001 par exchanged for (0.33333333) share new Common $0.001 par 01/03/2003
Name changed to Elixir Gaming Technologies, Inc. 09/12/2007
Elixir Gaming Technologies, Inc. name changed to Entertainment Gaming Asia Inc. 07/26/2010
(See Entertainment Gaming Asia Inc.)

VENDO CO (MO)
Common $2.50 par changed to $1.25 par and (1) additional share issued 08/16/1960
$2.25 Preferred Ser. 1 $50 par called for redemption 02/28/1966
Acquired by Sanden Corp. 05/27/1988
Each share Common $1.25 par exchanged for $9 cash

VENDOMATIC SERVICES LTD. (CANADA)
Name changed to Versafood Services Ltd. 5/19/64
Versafood Services Ltd. name changed to VS Services Ltd.-VS Services Ltee. 7/12/72 which name changed to Versa Services Ltd./Versa Services Ltee. 11/27/91
(See Versa Services Ltd./Versa Services Ltee.)

VENDOME CAP CORP (ON)
Recapitalized as Axiotron Corp. 08/27/2007
Each share Common no par exchanged for (0.25) share Common no par

VENDOME CAP II CORP (ON)
Name changed to Vendome Resources Corp. 05/26/2010
Vendome Resources Corp. name changed to Vanadium One Energy Corp. 01/16/2017

VENDOME FINL & MGMT CORP (MN)
Name changed to Nutrition Marketing Inc. 3/20/97

VENDOME RES CORP (ON)
Each share old Common no par exchanged for (0.1) share new Common no par 09/28/2016
Name changed to Vanadium One Energy Corp. 01/16/2017

VENDORLATOR MANUFACTURING CO. (CA)
Stock Dividend - 20% 6/1/56
In process of liquidation 9/18/56

VENDOTRONICS CORP (DE)
Charter cancelled and declared inoperative and void for non-payment of 4/1/66

VENDRON CORP. LTD. (CANADA)
Dissolved in April 1971
Only debentureholders participated in distribution of assets
No stockholders' equity

VENDTEK SYS INC (BC)
Each share old Common no par exchanged for (0.1) share new Common no par 04/24/2015
Assets voluntarily foreclosed upon 10/30/2015
Stockholders' equity unlikely

VENDUM BATTERIES INC (NV)
Common $0.001 par split (2.79792806) for (1) by issuance of (1.79792806) additional shares payable 06/04/2010 to holders of record 06/04/2010
Common $0.001 par split (5) for (1) by issuance of (4) additional shares payable 12/06/2010 to holders of record 12/06/2010
Common $0.001 par changed to $0.00001 par 11/15/2012
Recapitalized as Link Reservations Inc. 05/15/2015
Each share Common $0.00001 par exchanged for (0.000025) share Common $0.00001 par

VENEPAL S A C A (VENEZUELA)
Stock Dividend - 5% payable 04/02/1998 to holders of record 03/31/1998
ADR agreement terminated 04/25/2007
No ADR holders' equity

VENEZOLANA DE PRERREDUCIDOS CARONI VENPRECAR C A (VENEZUELA)
GDR agreement terminated 06/30/2002
Each 144A Sponsored GDR for Ordinary exchanged for (9) Ordinary shares
Note: Unexchanged GDR's will be sold and proceeds held for claim after 06/30/2003

VENEZUELA MAXUDIAN OIL CO.
Succeeded by Venezuela Syndicate, Inc. 00/00/1930
Details not available

VENEZUELA SYNDICATE, INC. (DE)
Capital Stock $2 par changed to 20¢ par in 1939
Merged into Kirby Vensyn Petroleum Co. share for share 2/15/57
Kirby Vensyn Petroleum Co. name changed to Kirby Petroleum Co. (NV) 1/3/58 which name changed to Kirby Industries, Inc. 11/13/67
(See Kirby Industries, Inc.)

VENEZUELAN GOLDFIELDS LTD (BC)
Reincorporated under the laws of Canada as Vengold Inc. 05/13/1994
Vengold Inc. name changed to itemus inc. 04/26/2000
(See itemus inc.)

VENEZUELAN HOLDING CORP. (DE)
Common no par changed to $1 par in 1935
Charter cancelled and company declared inoperative and void for non-payment of taxes 4/1/65

VENEZUELAN LEASEHOLDS INC. (LIBERIA)
Dissolved 00/00/1959
No stockholders' equity

VENEZUELAN-MEXICAN OIL CORP.
Name changed to Wichita River Oil Corp. (VA) (Old) 00/00/1939
Wichita River Oil Corp. (VA) (Old) name changed to Wichita Industries, Inc. (VA) (New) 01/08/1969 which merged into Wichita River Oil Corp. (VA) (New) 11/04/1987 which reincorporated in Delaware 03/30/1990
(See Wichita River Oil Corp. (DE))

VENEZUELAN OIL CONCESSIONS, LTD.
Acquired by Shell Transport & Trading Co. Ltd. 00/00/1949
Details not available

VENEZUELAN OIL CONCESSIONS HOLDING, LTD.
Acquired by Venezuelan Oil Concessions, Ltd. share for share in 1930
Venezuelan Oil Concessions Ltd. was acquired by Shell Transport & Trading Co. Ltd. in 1949

VENEZUELAN PETROLEUM CO. (DE)
Common $5 par changed to $1 par in 1936
Name changed to Sinclair Venezuelan Oil Co. 2/6/58

(See Sinclair Venezuelan Oil Co.)

VENEZUELAN PWR LTD (CANADA)
Recapitalized as Venpower Ltd. 01/14/1969
Each share 6% Preferred $10 par exchanged for (2.5) shares Common no par
Each share Common no par exchanged for (0.5) share Common no par
(See Venpower Ltd.)

VENEZUELAN SULPHUR CORP. OF AMERICA (DE)
Name changed to Chemical Natural Resources, Inc. 2/4/59
Chemical Natural Resources, Inc. charter cancelled 3/1/79

VENFIN LTD (SOUTH AFRICA)
Acquired by Vodafone Group PLC 5/19/2006
Each Sponsored ADR for Ordinary Rand-10 par exchanged for $7.74065 cash

VENGOLD INC (CANADA)
Name changed to itemus inc. 04/26/2000
(See itemus inc.)

VENICE INDS INC (DE)
Common 10¢ par split (4) for (3) by issuance of (1/3) additional share 12/18/69
Common 10¢ par split (4) for (3) by issuance of (1/3) additional share 3/22/71
Merged into Logan (Jonathan), Inc. 5/31/79
Each share Common 10¢ par exchanged for $3.50 cash

VENICE-NOKOMIS BANK & TRUST CO. (VENICE, FL)
Common $10 par changed to $7.50 par 4/5/71
Common $7.50 par changed to $5 par and (0.5) additional share issued 12/28/73
Stock Dividend - 10% 1/26/70
Merged into First National Bank of Florida (Tampa, Fla.) 11/1/82
Each share Common $5 par exchanged for (1.263) shares Capital Stock $5 par

VENICE-NOKOMIS BANK (VENICE, FL)
Name changed to Venice-Nokomis Bank & Trust Co. (Venice, Fla.) 8/27/69
Venice-Nokomis Bank & Trust Co. (Venice, Fla.) merged into First National Bank of Florida (Tampa, Fla.) 11/1/82

VENICE WEST, INC. (FL)
Proclaimed dissolved for failure to file reports and pay fees 9/3/76

VENKOREN INTERNATIONAL INC. (NV)
Name changed to Vivante Internationale Inc. 1/14/94
Vivante Internationale Inc. name changed Viva Pharmaceutical Inc. 5/16/95
(See Viva Pharmaceutical Inc.)

VENMARK INC (NV)
Charter revoked for failure to file reports and pay fees 7/1/88

VENNING GROUP INC (DE)
Name changed to ComTech Consolidation Group, Inc. 07/00/1997
ComTech Consolidation Group, Inc. recapitalized as Summit National Consolidation Group Inc. 11/05/2001 which name changed to Superwipes, Inc. 10/12/2004
(See Superwipes, Inc.)

VENOCO INC (DE)
Issue Information - 12,500,000 shares COM offered at $17 per share on 11/16/2006

Acquired by Denver Parent Corp. 10/03/2012
Each share Common 1¢ par exchanged for $12.50 cash

VENORO GOLD CORP (CANADA)
Recapitalized as New Venoro Gold Corp. 10/30/1997
Each share Class A Common no par exchanged for (0.125) share Class A Common no par
New Venoro Gold Corp. name changed to Vanteck (VRB) Technology Corp. 06/20/2000 which name changed to VRB Power Systems Inc. 01/17/2003 which name changed to Nevaro Capital Corp. (Old) 08/24/2009
(See Nevaro Capital Corp. (Old))

VENPATH INVTS INC (AB)
Name changed to OPE Holdings Ltd. 11/09/2007
OPE Holdings Ltd. name changed to SSP Offshore Inc. 05/21/2009
(See SSP Offshore Inc.)

VENPOWER LTD (CANADA)
Acquired by Phi International Inc. 8/18/82
Each share Common no par exchanged for $0.90 cash

VENQUEST CAP LTD (AB)
Name changed to Nightingale Informatix Corp. 09/12/2005
Nightingale Informatix Corp. name changed to Nexia Health Technologies Inc. 09/28/2016

VENSEARCH CAP CORP (CANADA)
Name changed to Genetic Diagnostics Technologies Corp. 08/12/2005
Genetic Diagnostics Technologies Corp. recapitalized as Polar Star Mining Corp. 08/15/2007 which merged into Revelo Resources Corp. 12/17/2014

VENSTAR INC (AB)
Placed in receivership 10/19/2004
Stockholders' equity unlikely

VENSTONE ONE CAP CORP (BC)
Reincorporated under the laws of Alberta as Shift Networks Inc. 10/09/2002
(See Shift Networks Inc.)

VENSTONE VENTURES CORP (CANADA)
Recapitalized as iWave.com, Inc. 02/02/1999
Each share Common no par exchanged for (0.25) share Common no par
iWave.com, Inc. recapitalized as iWave Information Systems Inc. 06/28/2002 which name changed to First Factor Developments Inc. 07/22/2005 which name changed to Millrock Resources Inc. (Canada) 08/14/2007 which reincorporated in British Columbia 07/24/2008

VENT AIR OPTICS INC (NY)
Dissolved by proclamation 12/30/81

VENTANA BIOTECH INC (NV)
Common $0.001 par split (92) for (1) by issuance of (91) additional shares payable 11/20/2008 to holders of record 11/20/2008
Charter revoked 02/28/2012

VENTANA EQUITIES INC (AB)
Name changed to Steeplejack Industrial Group Inc. 01/05/1993
(See Steeplejack Industrial Group Inc.)

VENTANA GOLD CORP (BC)
Acquired by AUX Canada Acquisition Inc. 03/25/2011
Each share Common no par exchanged for $13.06 cash

VENTANA MED SYS INC (DE)
Common $0.001 par split (2) for (1) by issuance of (1) additional share payable 03/14/2005 to holders of record 03/04/2005 Ex date - 03/15/2005
Merged into Roche Holding Ltd. 02/19/2008
Each share Common $0.001 par exchanged for $89.50 cash

VENTAS DEV INC (UT)
Name changed to Read Industries, Inc. 10/07/1988
(See Read Industries, Inc.)

VENTAS INC (DE)
Sr. Preferred Ser. A $1 par called for redemption at $1,000 on 05/23/2007 (Additional Information in Active)

VENTAUR CAP CORP (ON)
Name changed to Goldcrest Resources Ltd. 10/23/2003
Goldcrest Resources Ltd. merged into Volta Resources Inc. 03/31/2008 which merged into B2Gold Corp. 12/27/2013

VENTEC INC (LA)
Charter revoked for failure to file annual reports 11/19/1990

VENTEC RES INC (BC)
Dissolved 07/26/1991
Details not available

VENTECH CAP CORP (AB)
Name changed to Walker's Capital Corp. 1/28/88
(See Walker's Capital Corp.)

VENTECH HEALTHCARE CORP INC (ON)
Name changed to NWE Capital Corp. 01/28/1992
NWE Capital Corp. name changed to Petersburg Long Distance Inc. 12/31/1992 which name changed to PLD Telekom, Inc. (ON) 08/01/1996 which reincorporated in Delaware 02/28/1997 which merged into Metromedia International Group, Inc. 09/30/1999
(See Metromedia International Group, Inc.)

VENTECH HEALTHCARE INC (CANADA)
Recapitalized as Ventech Healthcare International Inc. 07/02/1987
Each share Common no par exchanged for (0.4) share Common no par
Ventech Healthcare International Inc. (Canada) reincorporated in Ontario 08/11/1987 which name changed to Ventech Healthcare Corp. Inc. 09/10/1987 which name changed to NWE Capital Corp. 01/28/1992 which name changed to Petersburg Long Distance Inc. 12/31/1992 which name changed to PLD Telekom, Inc. (ON) 08/01/1996 which reincorporated in Delaware 02/28/1997 which merged into Metromedia International Group, Inc. 09/30/1999
(See Metromedia International Group, Inc.)

VENTECH HEALTHCARE INTL INC (ON)
Reincorporated 08/11/1987
Place of incorporation changed from (Canada) to (ON) 08/11/1987
Name changed to Ventech Healthcare Corp. Inc. 09/10/1987
Ventech Healthcare Corp. Inc. name changed to NWE Capital Corp. 01/28/1992 which name changed to Petersburg Long Distance Inc. 12/31/1992 which name changed to PLD Telekom, Inc. (ON) 08/01/1996 which reincorporated in Delaware 02/28/1997 which merged into Metromedia International Group, Inc. 09/30/1999
(See Metromedia International Group, Inc.)

VENTECH INDUSTRIALS LTD (AB)
Issue Information - 3,000,000 shares

COM offered at $0.10 per share on 09/22/1997
Name changed to Alta Terra Ventures Corp. 07/09/1998
(See Alta Terra Ventures Corp.)

VENTECH INTL CORP (FL)
Name changed to VDO.com, Inc. 06/15/1999
VDO.com, Inc. name changed to Hundred Mile Plus, Ltd. 09/19/2001 which recapitalized as Ultra Pure Water Technologies, Inc. 05/24/2004

VENTECH TECHNOLOGY INC (NY)
Name changed to United Sports Technologies, Inc. 11/19/87
(See United Sports Technologies, Inc.)

VENTEL INC (CANADA)
Recapitalized as Fifty-Plus.Net International Inc. 07/09/1999
Each share Common no par exchanged for (0.2) share Common no par
Fifty-Plus.Net International Inc. name changed to ZoomerMedia Ltd. 07/02/2008

VENTERSPOST GOLD MNG LTD (SOUTH AFRICA)
Each ADR for Ordinary Reg. Rand 1 par exchanged for (4) ADR's for Ordinary Reg. Rand 0.25 par 11/20/1987
Merged into Kloof Gold Mining Co. Ltd. 09/18/1992
Each ADR for Ordinary Reg. Rand-0.25 par exchanged for (0.06) ADR for Ordinary Reg. Rand-0.25 par
Kloof Gold Mining Co. Ltd. merged into Gold Fields Ltd. (Old) 02/02/1998 which merged into Gold Fields Ltd. (New) 05/10/1999

VENTEX CORP (NY)
Charter cancelled and proclaimed dissolved for failure to pay taxes and file reports 12/15/1972

VENTEX ENERGY LTD (BC)
Struck off register and declared dissolved for failure to file returns 10/30/1992

VENTEX TECHNOLOGIES CORP (AB)
Name changed 09/10/1993
Name changed from Ventex Resources Corp. to Ventex Technologies Corp. 09/10/1993
Delisted from Alberta Stock Exchange 06/26/1997

VENTIC CORP. (CA)
Charter suspended for failure to file reports and pay fees 11/1/77

VENTIR CHALLENGE ENTERPRISES LTD (BC)
Recapitalized as Whistler Gold Corp. 02/03/2006
Each share Common no par exchanged for (0.2) share Common no par
Whistler Gold Corp. name changed to Svit Gold Corp. 08/11/2008 which name changed to Catalyst Copper Corp. 02/02/2010 which merged into NewCastle Gold Ltd. 05/27/2016 which merged into Equinox Gold Corp. 12/22/2017

VENTIV HEALTH INC (DE)
Name changed to inVentiv Health, Inc. 06/16/2006
(See inVentiv Health, Inc.)

VENTNOR BOAT CORP.
Bankrupt in 1948

VENTNOR CORP (DE)
Name changed to Topox, Inc. 10/19/1990
Topox, Inc. name changed to Supra Medical Corp. 10/26/1992

VENTORA RES LTD (BC)
Recapitalized as Torrent Resources Ltd. 1/11/85
Each share Capital Stock no par exchanged for (0.2) share Common no par
Torrent Resources Ltd. merged into Galveston Resources Ltd. 7/29/86 which merged into Corona Corp. 7/1/88 which recapitalized as International Corona Corp. 6/11/91
(See International Corona Corp.)

VENTRA GROUP INC (ON)
Each share Non-Cum. Conv. 2nd Preference Ser. 1 no par exchanged for (12) shares Common no par 9/10/91
Conv. 1st Preference Ser. 1 no par called for redemption at $10 on 9/28/98
Acquired by Flex-N-Gate Corp. 10/1/2001
Each share Common no par exchanged for $1.65 cash

VENTRA MGMT INC (DE)
Recapitalized as Advanced Plant Pharmaceuticals Inc. 06/30/1994
Each (30) shares Common $0.0001 par exchanged for (1) share Common $0.0001 par
Advanced Plant Pharmaceuticals Inc. name changed to World Health Energy Holdings, Inc. 06/09/2010

VENTRACOR LTD (AUSTRALIA)
ADR agreement terminated 05/04/2011
No ADR holders' equity

VENTREX LABS INC (DE)
Merged into Hycor Biomedical Inc. 8/6/91
Each share Common 1¢ par exchanged for (0.21425) share Common 1¢ par and (0.04463) Common Stock Purchase Warrant expiring 8/6/98
Hycor Biomedical Inc. merged into Stratagene Corp. 6/2/2004
(See Stratagene Corp.)

VENTRITEX INC (DE)
Reincorporated 12/28/1994
State of incorporation changed from (CA) to (DE) 12/28/1994
Merged into St. Jude Medical, Inc. 05/15/1997
Each share Common no par exchanged for (0.5) share Common 10¢ par
St. Jude Medical, Inc. merged into Abbott Laboratories 01/04/2017

VENTRO CORP (DE)
Name changed to NexPrise, Inc. 01/15/2002

VENTRON CORP (MA)
Merged into Thiokol Corp. (DE) (Old) 12/31/78
Each share Common $5 par exchanged for $44 cash

VENTRUS BIOSCIENCES INC (DE)
Recapitalized as Assembly Biosciences, Inc. 07/14/2014
Each share Common $0.001 par exchanged for (0.2) share Common $0.001 par

VENTURA ACQUISITIONS INC (CO)
Name changed to Pace Group International, Inc. 10/05/1987
Pace Group International, Inc. recapitalized as Riley Investments Inc. 01/31/1996 which name changed to Grand Adventures Tour & Travel Publishing Corp. (OR) 10/07/1996 which reincorporated in Delaware 06/05/2000
(See Grand Adventures Tour & Travel Publishing Corp. (DE))

VENTURA ASSETS LTD (CO)
Common no par split (133) for (1) by issuance of (132) additional shares payable 03/10/2011 to holders of record 03/10/2011 Ex date - 03/11/2011
Name changed to Bonamour, Inc. 12/06/2011

VENTURA ASSOC INC (CA)
Each share old Common $0.001 par exchanged for (0.05) share new Common $0.001 par 11/21/92
Recapitalized as Victory Waste Inc. 2/2/94
Each share new Common $0.001 par exchanged for (1/9) share Common $0.001 par
Victory Waste Inc. merged into Continental Waste Industries, Inc. in June 1995 which merged into Republic Industries Inc 12/30/96 which name changed to AutoNation, Inc. 4/6/99

VENTURA CONSOLIDATED OIL FIELDS
Dissolved and assets acquired by California Petroleum Corp. in 1927 which was dissolved in 1938

VENTURA CNTY BUSINESS BK (OXNARD, CA)
Common no par split (3) for (2) by issuance of (0.5) additional share payable 07/31/2006 to holders of record 07/12/2006 Ex date - 08/01/2006
Acquired by Royal Business Bank (Los Angeles, CA) 09/28/2011
Each share Common no par exchanged for $0.011015 cash

VENTURA CNTY NATL BANCORP (CA)
Common no par split (3) for (2) by issuance of (0.5) additional share 10/29/1984
Common no par split (2) for (1) by issuance of (1) additional share 03/07/1986
Common no par split (3) for (2) by issuance of (0.5) additional share 01/30/1989
Stock Dividends - 10% 02/22/1990; 10% 03/27/1991
Merged into City National Corp. 01/17/1997
Each share Common no par exchanged for $5.03 cash

VENTURA CNTY NATL BK (OXNARD, CA)
Under plan of reorganization each share Common $5 par automatically became (1) share Ventura County National Bancorp Common no par 9/12/84
(See Ventura County National Bancorp)

VENTURA ENTMT GROUP LTD (DE)
Common $0.001 par split (2) for (1) by issuance of (1) additional share 08/15/1990
Recapitalized 07/26/1994
Each share old Common $0.001 par exchanged for (0.06666666) Unit consisting of (3.5) shares new Common $0.001 par, (1) Common Stock Purchase Warrant, Class C expiring 07/26/1998, (1) Common Stock Purchase Warrant Class D expiring 07/26/1996 and (1) Right to receive (5) shares Producers Entertainment Group Ltd. Common $0.001 par
Name changed to Insight Entertainment Corp. 09/20/1995
(See Insight Entertainment Corp.)

VENTURA GOLD CORP (BC)
Reincorporated 10/07/2004
Place of incorporation changed from (YT) to (BC) 10/07/2004
Merged into International Minerals Corp. 01/20/2010
Each share Common no par exchanged for (0.1) share Common no par
(See International Minerals Corp.)

VENTURA INTL INC (NV)
Liquidation completed
Each share Capital Stock $1 par received initial distribution of $2.50 cash 12/27/1973
Each share Capital Stock $1 par received second distribution of $5.50 cash 01/11/1974
Each share Capital Stock $1 par received third distribution of $2.50 cash 12/26/1974
Each share Capital Stock $1 par exchanged for fourth and final distribution of $1.11 cash 12/23/1975

VENTURA MOTION PICTURE GROUP LTD (DE)
Name changed to Producers Entertainment Group Ltd. 12/00/1991
Producers Entertainment Group Ltd. name changed to IAT Resources Corp. 05/26/1999 which name changed to NetCurrents, Inc. 01/04/2000 which reorganized as NetCurrents Information Services, Inc. 08/30/2001
(See NetCurrents Information Services, Inc.)

VENTURA OIL CO. (NV)
Name changed to Ventura Resources, Inc. 11/30/71
(See Ventura Resources, Inc.)

VENTURA PROMOTIONS GROUP INC (FL)
Name changed to American Surface Technologies International, Inc. (FL) 11/17/1998
American Surface Technologies International, Inc. (FL) name changed to Global Environmental, Inc. 06/22/2006 which name changed back to American Surface Technologies International, Inc. (FL) 10/18/2007 which reorganized in Delaware as Ravenwood Bourne, Ltd. 10/30/2008 which name changed to PopBig, Inc. 11/07/2011 which name changed to EMAV Holdings, Inc. 01/03/2014

VENTURA RES INC (NV)
Merged into Gayno, Inc. 12/31/1973
Each share Common 10¢ par exchanged for $2.30 cash

VENTURBON ENTERPRISES INC (QC)
Recapitalized as Java Joe's International Corp. 10/08/1997
Each share Common no par exchanged for (0.2) share Common no par
(See Java Joe's International Corp.)

VENTURE ACQUISITIONS CORP (CO)
Each share old Common $0.001 par exchanged for (0.05) share new Common $0.001 par 12/28/1985
Administratively dissolved 01/01/1994

VENTURE CAPITAL CORP. OF AMERICA (NY)
Under plan of merger name changed to Royal Business Funds Corp. 12/31/65

VENTURE CATALYST INC (UT)
Merged into International Game Technology 12/21/2006
Each share Common $0.001 par exchanged for $2.58 cash

VENTURE CONCEPTS INC (NY)
Dissolved by proclamation 6/26/96

VENTURE CONS INC (NV)
Recapitalized as Tires, Inc. 10/5/84
Each share Common $0.0001 par exchanged for (0.05) share Common 2¢ par
Tires, Inc. name changed to Big O Tires, Inc. 12/26/86
(See Big O Tires, Inc.)

VENTURE CORP AMER (DE)
Charter forfeited for failure to maintain a registered agent 02/05/1979

VENTURE ENTERPRISES INC (DE)
Each share old Common $0.0001 par exchanged for (0.05) share new Common $0.0001 par 12/31/1990
Name changed to Hanover Gold Co., Inc. 01/02/1991
Hanover Gold Co., Inc. recapitalized as Rock Energy Resources, Inc. 02/19/2008

VENTURE FDG CORP (CO)
Each share old Common $0.0001 par exchanged for (0.05) share new Common $0.0001 par 10/31/1991
Name changed to Global Venture Funding Inc. 06/29/1993
Global Venture Funding Inc. name changed to U.S. Microbics, Inc. 04/24/1998

VENTURE FINL GROUP INC (WA)
Company's sole asset placed in receivership 09/11/2009
Stockholders' equity unlikely

VENTURE GOLD CORP (BC)
Struck off register and declared dissolved for failure to file returns 6/19/92

VENTURE GROUP INC (NV)
Name changed to Asdar Corp. 02/13/1986
Asdar Corp. name changed to Asdar Group, Inc. 12/10/1987 which name changed to Precise Life Sciences Ltd. 05/02/2002 which name changed to Iceberg Brands Corp. 03/03/2003 which recapitalized as Avalon Gold Corp. 09/08/2003 which name changed to Avalon Energy Corp. 03/22/2005 which recapitalized as Shotgun Energy Corp. 09/25/2007 which name changed to Organa Gardens International Inc. 04/07/2009 which recapitalized as Bravo Enterprises Ltd. 06/08/2012

VENTURE INCOME PLUS INC (MD)
Name changed to Davis High Income Fund Inc. 10/01/1995
Davis High Income Fund Inc. name changed to Davis Intermediate Investment Grade Bond Fund, Inc. 08/02/1999 which reorganized as Evergreen Intermediate Term Bond Fund 03/17/2000
(See Evergreen Intermediate Term Bond Fund)

VENTURE INVTS PLUS CORP (CO)
Recapitalized as Triumph Group, Inc. 8/31/89
Each share Common no par exchanged for (0.1) share Common no par
Triumph Group, Inc. name changed to Novatek International, Inc. 12/28/90 which name changed to Medical Diagnostic Products, Inc. 11/1/98
(See Medical Diagnostic Products, Inc.)

VENTURE MEDIA COMMUNICATIONS INC (NV)
Name changed to Global Debit Cash Card, Inc. 12/26/2003
Global Debit Cash Card, Inc. name changed to 1st Global Financial Corp. 03/27/2006 which recapitalized as Incorporated Productions 08/01/2013

VENTURE MUNI PLUS INC (MD)
Name changed to Davis Tax-Free High Income Fund Inc. 10/1/95
Davis Tax-Free High Income Fund Inc. reorganized as Evergreen Municipal Trust 3/17/2000

VENTURE MUSIC GROUP INTL LTD (DE)
Each share old Common $0.0001 par exchanged for (0.00396825) share

new Common $0.0001 par 12/31/2004
Name changed to Standard Holdings Group, Ltd. 02/02/2005

VENTURE NEXUS INC (NV)
Name changed to Custom Arrays Corp. 10/23/1987
(See Custom Arrays Corp.)

VENTURE ONE CAP CORP (AB)
Reincorporated under the laws of British Columbia as NMC Resource Corp. 02/26/2010
(See NMC Resource Corp.)

VENTURE OPTIONS, INC. (DE)
Name changed to Aidco Corp. and Common no par changed to 1¢ par 1/17/68
Aidco Corp. name changed to Fedonics, Inc. 4/28/69
(See Fedonics, Inc.)

VENTURE PAC DEV CORP (BC)
Recapitalized as Pacific Harbour Capital Ltd. 10/21/2002
Each share Common no par exchanged for (0.5) share Common no par
Pacific Harbour Capital Ltd. name changed to Oceanic Iron Ore Corp. 12/06/2010

VENTURE PPTYS LTD (AB)
Recapitalized as Allied Venture Properties Ltd. 9/2/75
Each share Common $1 par exchanged for (0.1) share Common no par
Allied Venture Properties Ltd. recapitalized as Buckingham International Holdings Ltd. 3/22/79
(See Buckingham International Holdings Ltd.)

VENTURE QUEST INC (UT)
Proclaimed dissolved for failure to file reports 4/1/88

VENTURE SECS FD INC (DE)
Capital Stock $1 par split (3) for (1) by issuance of (2) additional shares 04/28/1961
Acquired by Stratton Growth Fund, Inc. (DE) 11/19/1974
Each share Capital Stock $1 par exchanged for (0.0901) share Common 10¢ par
Stratton Growth Fund, Inc. (DE) reincorporated in Maryland 06/21/1985 which name changed to Stratton Multi-Cap Fund, Inc. 05/01/2006

VENTURE SEISMIC LTD (AB)
Discharged from receivership 06/30/2005
No stockholders' equity

VENTURE SER INC (MD)
Name changed to Davis International Series Inc. 10/2/95
(See Davis International Series Inc.)

VENTURE STORES INC (DE)
Plan of reorganization under Chapter 11 Federal Bankruptcy proceedings confirmed 11/23/1998
No stockholders' equity

VENTURE TECH CORP (NY)
Recapitalized as U.S.A. Land Corp. 1/21/88
Each share Common $0.0001 par exchanged for (0.08) share Common $0.0001 par
(See U.S.A. Land Corp.)

VENTURE TECH INC (ID)
Reincorporated under the laws of Nevada as VentureQuest Group, Inc. 05/10/2001
VentureQuest Group, Inc. name changed to Northwater Resources, Inc. 02/15/2006 which name changed to Dex-Ray Resources, Inc. 03/27/2008
(See Dex-Ray Resources, Inc.)

VENTURE TR MONEY MKT FD (MA)
Reorganized under the laws of Maryland as Retirement Planning Funds of America, Inc. 12/31/1989
Each share General Purpose Portfolio $0.001 par received Money Market Shares on a net asset basis
Each share Government Portfolio $0.001 par received Government Money Market Fund Class A shares on a net asset basis
Retirement Planning Funds of America, Inc. name changed to Davis Series, Inc. 10/01/1995

VENTURE TR TAX FREE MONEY MKT FD (MA)
Under plan of reorganization each share Money Market Portfolio automatically became (1) share Retirement Planning Funds of America, Inc. Tax Free Money Market Fund 12/31/89
Retirement Planning Funds of America, Inc. name changed to Davis Series, Inc. 10/1/95

VENTURE WORLD LTD (DE)
Each share old Common $0.0001 par exchanged for (0.004) share new Common $0.0001 par 06/08/1998
Name changed to NetAmerica Corp. 10/06/1998
NetAmerica Corp. name changed to NetAmerica.com Corp. 06/18/1999 which name changed to RateXchange Corp. 04/20/2000 which name changed to MCF Corp. 07/22/2003 which name changed to Merriman Curhan Ford Group, Inc. 05/20/2008 which recapitalized as Merriman Holdings, Inc. 08/16/2010

VENTURECAP INC (NV)
Recapitalized as Fibercore, Inc. 07/10/1995
Each share Common $0.001 par exchanged for (0.7849696) share Common 1¢ par
(See Fibercore, Inc.)

VENTURECORP CAP INC (BC)
Name changed to BioteQ Environmental Technologies Inc. 12/18/2000
BioteQ Environmental Technologies Inc. name changed to BQE Water Inc. 03/01/2017

VENTURELIST COM INC (NV)
Each share old Common $0.001 par exchanged for (0.01) share new Common $0.001 par 05/16/2002
Name changed to Hartville Group Inc. 09/13/2002
(See Hartville Group Inc.)

VENTURENET CAP GROUP INC (DE)
Name changed 11/06/2001
Name changed from VentureNet, Inc. to VentureNet Capital Group, Inc. 11/06/2001
Reincorporated under the laws of Nevada 03/14/2003

VENTURENET COM INC (NV)
Name changed to Venture Media Communications Inc. 06/21/2000
Venture Media Communications Inc. name changed to Global Debit Cash Card, Inc. 12/26/2003 which name changed to 1st Global Financial Corp. 03/27/2006 which recapitalized as Incorporated Productions 08/01/2013

VENTUREQUEST GROUP INC (NV)
Each share old Common $0.001 par exchanged for (0.1) share new Common $0.001 par 09/13/2002
Each share new Common $0.001 par exchanged again for (0.04) share new Common $0.001 par 06/16/2003
Name changed to Northwater Resources, Inc. 02/15/2006
Northwater Resources, Inc. name changed to Dex-Ray Resources, Inc. 03/27/2008

(See Dex-Ray Resources, Inc.)

VENTURES, LTD. (CANADA)
Capital Stock no par exchanged (1) for (5) in 1937
Merged into Falconbridge Nickel Mines Ltd. 5/23/62
Each share Capital Stock no par exchanged for (1.04) shares Capital Stock no par
Falconbridge Nickel Mines Ltd. name changed to Falconbridge Nickel Mines Ltd.-Les Mines Falconbridge Nickel Ltee. 4/29/80 which name changed to Falconbridge Ltd. 2/10/83
(See Falconbridge Ltd.)

VENTURES GAINED INC (AB)
Recapitalized as Tomahawk Corp. 6/18/93
Each share Common no par exchanged for (0.5) share Common no par
(See Tomahawk Corp.)

VENTURES MNG LTD (BC)
Recapitalized as Giant Ventures Development Co. Ltd. 06/21/1972
Each share Capital Stock $1 par exchanged for (0.2) share Capital Stock no par
Giant Ventures Development Co. Ltd. recapitalized as Nor-Quest Resources Ltd. 08/10/1977 which recapitalized as Western & Pacific Resources Corp. 04/22/1991 which recapitalized as Consolidated Western & Pacific Resources Corp. 07/05/1994 which name changed to Synergy Resource Technologies Inc. 07/02/1996 which recapitalized as Synergy Renewable Resources Inc. 01/09/1997
(See Synergy Renewable Resources Inc.)

VENTURES NATL INC (UT)
Each (6,000) shares old Common $0.001 par exchanged for (1) share new Common $0.001 par 2/22/2002
Name changed to Titan General Holdings Inc. 8/31/2002
Titan General Holdings Inc. name changed to Titan Global Holdings, Inc. 11/14/2005

VENTURES RESH & DEV GROUP (NJ)
Voluntarily dissolved in 1989
No stockholders' equity

VENTURES RES CORP (BARBADOS)
Each share old Common no par exchanged for (0.1) share new Common no par 11/15/2002
Merged into BrazMin Corp. 04/06/2005
Each share new Common no par exchanged for (0.02) share Common
BrazMin Corp. name changed to Talon Metals Corp. 07/09/2007

VENTURES UTD INC (NV)
Reorganized 09/27/2006
Reorganized from under the laws of (UT) to (NV) 09/27/2006
Each share Common $0.001 par exchanged for (0.025) share Common $0.001 par
Name changed to Avasoft, Inc. 03/05/2007
(See Avasoft, Inc.)

VENTUREVEST CORP (DE)
Voluntarily dissolved 10/06/1993
Details not available

VENTUREX CORP (CO)
Recapitalized as Ricksha, Inc. 07/21/1986
Each share Common $0.0001 par exchanged for (0.1) share Common $0.0001 par
(See Ricksha, Inc.)

VENTUREX EXPLORATIONS INC (BC)
Recapitalized as Black Panther Mining Corp. 06/17/2008
Each share Common no par exchanged for (0.1) share Common no par
Black Panther Mining Corp. name changed to Canadian International Pharma Corp. 06/22/2015

VENTUREX RES LTD (BC)
Recapitalized as Consolidated Venturex Holdings Ltd. 09/24/1992
Each share Common no par exchanged for (0.2) share Common no par
Consolidated Venturex Holdings Ltd. name changed to Venturex Explorations Inc. 05/24/2007 which recapitalized as Black Panther Mining Corp. 06/17/2008 which name changed to Canadian International Pharma Corp. 06/22/2015

VENTURI PARTNERS INC (DE)
Name changed to COMSYS IT Partners, Inc. 09/30/2004
COMSYS IT Partners, Inc. merged into Manpower Inc. 04/05/2010 which name changed to ManpowerGroup 04/18/2011

VENTURI TECHNOLOGIES INC (NV)
Name changed 7/29/98
Name changed from Venturi Technology Enterprises Inc. to Venturi Technologies, Inc. 7/29/98
Plan of reorganization under Chapter 11 Federal Bankruptcy Code effective 10/25/2001
No stockholders' equity

VENTURI VENTURES INC (BC)
Voluntarily dissolved 04/29/2016
Details not available

VENTURIAN CORP (MN)
Common $1 par split (3) for (2) by issuance of (0.5) additional share payable 4/30/98 to holders of record 4/15/98
Stock Dividend - 10% payable 10/15/99 to holders of record 9/30/99
Merged into Venturian Holdings LLC 10/23/2001
Each share Common $1 par exchanged for $5 cash

VENTUS ENERGY LTD (AB)
Name changed to Navigo Energy Inc. 05/24/2002
(See Navigo Energy Inc.)

VENUS CRUISE LINE INC (FL)
Proclaimed dissolved for failure to file reports and pay fees 11/4/88

VENUS DRUG DISTRS INC (CA)
Stock Dividends - 25% 08/09/1965; 25% 08/15/1966; 25% 09/15/1967
Adjudicated bankrupt 05/02/1975
No stockholders' equity

VENUS ESTERBROOK CORP (NY)
Each share $1.50 Conv. Preferred $40 par exchanged for (1.85) shares Common $1 par and $11 cash 12/22/1972
Each share 5% Preferred $100 par exchanged for (2.2) shares Common $1 par 12/22/1972
Name changed to Domac Enterprises Inc. (NY) 10/05/1973
Domac Enterprises Inc. (NY) reincorporated in Delaware 10/01/1975
(See Domac Enterprises Inc.)

VENUS EXPL INC (CO)
Plan of reorganization under Chapter 11 Federal Bankruptcy Code effective 8/9/2004
In the event that all creditors are paid in full, a distribution is expected to be made to holders of record 8/9/2004

VENUS GAS & OIL, INC. (UT)
Name changed to Arcana Corp. 11/04/1982
(See Arcana Corp.)

VENUS MINES LTD (BC)
Struck off register and declared dissolved for failure to file returns 10/06/1980

VENUS PEN & PENCIL CORP. (NY)
Under plan of merger name changed to Venus Esterbrook Corp. 11/29/1967
Venus Esterbrook Corp. name changed to Domac Enterprises Inc. (NY) 10/05/1973 which reincorporated in Delaware 10/01/1975
(See Domac Enterprises Inc.)

VENUS VENTURES LTD (DE)
Name changed to Health Technologies International, Inc. 04/04/1988
(See Health Technologies International, Inc.)

VENZA GOLD CORP (BC)
Name changed to CoreComm Solutions Inc. 01/08/2014
CoreComm Solutions Inc. name changed to VGrab Communications Inc. 02/13/2015

VEOS PLC (UNITED KINGDOM)
ADR agreement terminated 2/12/2007
No ADR holders' equity

VER-MILLION GOLD PLACER MINING LTD. (ON)
Charter cancelled and company declared dissolved for failure to file reports and pay fees 08/24/1964

VERA CRUZ MINERALS CORP (BC)
Recapitalized as Copper Creek Ventures Ltd. (BC) 08/20/1996
Each share Common no par exchanged for (0.2) share Common no par
Copper Creek Ventures Ltd. (BC) reincorporated in Canada 08/13/1997 which reincorporated in British Columbia 11/06/2017 which reorganized as Surge Exploration Inc. 05/01/2018

VERADO HLDS INC (DE)
Plan of liquidation under Chapter 11 Federal Bankruptcy Code effective 06/07/2002
Each share Accredited Investors Common Ser. B $0.0001 par received $0.00686 cash payable 12/02/2013 to holders of record 06/07/2002
Each share 144A Common Ser. B $0.0001 par received $0.00686 cash payable 12/02/2013 to holders of record 06/07/2002
Each share Common Ser. B $0.0001 par received $0.00686 cash payable 12/02/2013 to holders of record 06/07/2002

VERAMARK TECHNOLOGIES INC (DE)
Acquired by Hubspoke Holdings, Inc. 07/22/2013
Each share Common 10¢ par exchanged for $1.18 cash

VERASUN ENERGY CORP (SD)
Plan of reorganization under Chapter 11 Federal Bankrutpcy Code effective 12/17/2009
No stockholders' equity

VERAZ NETWORKS INC (DE)
Recapitalized as Dialogic Inc. 10/04/2010
Each share Common $0.001 par exchanged for (0.2) share Common $0.001 par
(See Dialogic Inc.)

VERAZ PETE LTD (AB)
Reincorporated 01/24/2008
Place of incorporation changed from (BC) to (AB) 01/24/2008
Each share Common no par received distribution of (0.00588) share Petrominerales Ltd. Common no par payable 07/27/2012 to holders of record 07/27/2012
Name changed to AlkaLi3 Resources Inc. 08/16/2016

VERAZZANA VENTURES LTD (NV)
Recapitalized as PCT Holdings Inc. (NV) 2/15/95
Each share Common $0.001 par exchanged for (0.005) share Common $0.001 par
PCT Holdings Inc. (NV) reincorporated in Washington as Pacific Aerospace & Electronics Inc. 11/30/96
(See Pacific Aerospace & Electronics, Inc.)

VERB EXCHANGE INC (CANADA)
Each share old Common no par exchanged for (0.05) share new Common no par 05/17/2005
Recapitalized as Seymour Ventures Corp. 07/05/2010
Each share new Common no par exchanged for (0.04) share Common no par
Seymour Ventures Corp. name changed to Rare Earth Industries Ltd. 07/13/2011 which recapitalized as Ackroo Inc. 10/10/2012

VERBANC FINL CORP (VT)
Acquired by Chittenden Corp. 04/28/1993
Each share Common $1 par exchanged for (1.32) shares Common $1 par
(See Chittenden Corp.)

VERBATIM CORP (CA)
Common no par split (2) for (1) by issuance of (1) additional share 03/04/1982
Common no par split (2) for (1) by issuance of (1) additional share 12/20/1982
Common no par split (2) for (1) by issuance of (1) additional share 08/29/1983
Merged into Eastman Kodak Co. 06/14/1985
Each share Common no par exchanged for $7.55 cash

VERBINA RES INC (ON)
Name changed to Buccaneer Gold Corp. 04/19/2011

VERCAN INVTS INC (BC)
Name changed to WaterSave Logic Corp. 01/26/1998
WaterSave Logic Corp. name changed to Abode Mortgage Holdings Corp. 08/15/2006 which recapitalized as Ayubowan Capital Ltd. 08/19/2013 which name changed to Discovery Metals Corp. 06/13/2017

VERCHERES ORE-OIL CORP. (QC)
Charter cancelled in May 1974

VERCO ENERGY CORP (DE)
Charter cancelled and declared inoperative and void for non-payment of taxes 3/1/77

VERDANT AUTOMOTIVE CORP (DE)
Name changed to VRDT Corp. 02/09/2012
(See VRDT Corp.)

VERDANT BRANDS INC (MN)
Each share old Common 1¢ par exchanged for (0.2) share new Common 1¢ par 08/24/1999
Assets sold for the benefit of creditors 07/17/2001
No stockholders' equity

VERDANT FINL PARTNERS I INC (CANADA)
Recapitalized as Axis Auto Finance Inc. 08/04/2016
Each share Common no par exchanged for (0.16666666) share Common no par

VERDANT TECHNOLOGY CORP (DE)
SEC revoked common stock registration 03/12/2012

VERDANT VALLEY VENTURES INC. (AB)
Name changed to Biotechna Environmental Ltd. 05/25/1990
Biotechna Environmental Ltd. name changed to Biotechna Environmental Technologies Corp. (AB) 09/13/1996 which reincorporated in British West Indies 05/08/1998 which recapitalized as Biotechna Environmental (2000) Corp. 05/12/2000
(See Biotechna Environmental (2000) Corp.)

VERDE-MAY MINING CO., LTD. (ID)
Name changed to Silver Verde May Mining Co., Inc. 7/31/67

VERDE POTASH PLC (ENGLAND & WALES)
Name changed to Verde Agritech PLC 07/28/2016

VERDE VENTURES INC (MN)
Merged into Angeion Corp. 07/01/1988
Each share Common 1¢ par exchanged for (1.9) shares Common 1¢ par
Angeion Corp. name changed to MGC Diagnostics Corp. 08/21/2012
(See MGC Diagnostics Corp.)

VERDI DEVELOPMENT CO. (NV)
Recapitalized as United Resources Corp. 1/27/70
Each share Capital Stock 10¢ par exchanged for (0.05) share Capital Stock 10¢ par

VERDI MINING CO.
Name changed to Verdi Development Co. in 1942
Verdi Development Co. was recapitalized as United Resources Corp. 1/27/70

VERDISYS INC (CA)
Name changed to Blast Energy Services, Inc. (CA) 06/06/2005
Blast Energy Services, Inc. (CA) reincorporated in Texas 02/27/2008 which recapitalized as PEDEVCO Corp. 08/03/2012

VERDIX CORP (DE)
Name changed to Rational Software Corp. 3/31/94
(See Rational Software Corp.)

VERDSTONE GOLD CORP (BC)
Recapitalized as Goldrea Resources Corp. 4/17/2002
Each share Common no par exchanged for (0.1) share Common no par

VERDUGO BKG CO (CA)
Common no par split (3) for (1) by issuance of (2) additional shares payable 09/14/2001 to holders of record 08/20/2001 Ex date - 09/17/2001
Stock Dividend - 5% payable 04/20/2000 to holders of record 03/31/2000
Merged into First Community Bancorp 08/22/2003
Each share Common no par exchanged for $17.75 cash

VERDURIN CO. (MI)
Liquidation completed 12/17/58

VERDX MINERALS CORP (AB)
Delisted from Toronto Venture Stock Exchange 06/05/2002

VERENA MINERALS CORP (ON)
Name changed to Belo Sun Mining Corp. 07/14/2010

VERENEX ENERGY INC (AB)
Merged into Libyan Investment Authority 12/21/2009
Each share Common no par exchanged for $7.2882 cash

VERENIUM CORP (DE)
Each share old Common $0.001 par exchanged for (0.08333333) share new Common $0.001 par 09/10/2009
Acquired by BASF Corp. 10/31/2013
Each share new Common $0.001 par exchanged for $4 cash

VERESEN INC (AB)
Merged into Pembina Pipeline Corp. 10/02/2017
Each share Preferred Ser. A no par exchanged for (1) share Rate Reset Class A Preferred Ser. 15 no par
Each share Preferred Ser. C no par exchanged for (1) share Rate Reset Class A Preferred Ser. 17 no par
Each share Preferred Ser. E no par exchanged for (1) share Rate Reset Class A Preferred Ser. 19 no par
Each share Common no par exchanged for (0.4287) share Common no par

VEREX CORP (DE)
Merged into Greyhound Corp. 1/5/79
Each share Common $2.50 par exchanged for $30 cash

VEREX LABS INC (CO)
Each share old Common no par exchanged for (0.1) share new Common no par 05/05/1993
SEC revoked common stock registration 09/18/2009
Stockholders' equity unlikely

VERGENE CAP CORP (ON)
Name changed to Greencastle Resources Ltd. 5/17/2004

VERI-TEK INTL CORP (MI)
Issue Information - 2,500,000 shares COM offered at $6 per share on 02/14/2005
Name changed to Manitex International, Inc. 05/28/2008

VERICHIP CORP (DE)
Issue Information - 3,100,000 shares COM offered at $6.50 per share on 02/09/2007
Under plan of merger name changed to PositiveID Corp. 11/10/2009

VERIDA INTERNET CORP (NV)
SEC revoked common stock registration 11/23/2009
Stockholders' equity unlikely

VERIDIAN CORP (DE)
Issue Information - 13,500,000 shares COM offered at $16 per share on 06/04/2002
Merged into General Dynamics Corp. 08/11/2003
Each share Common $0.0001 par exchanged for $35 cash

VERIDICOM INTL INC (DE)
SEC revoked common stock registration 07/16/2012

VERIDIEN CORP (DE)
SEC revoked common stock registration 01/30/2014

VERIDIGM INC (DE)
Each (809) shares old Common $0.0001 par exchanged for (1) share new Common $0.0001 par 01/09/2008
Stock Dividend - 18.5% payable 05/27/2008 to holders of record 05/22/2008 Ex date - 05/20/2008
Recapitalized as Mobile Media Unlimited Holdings Inc. 02/02/2009
Each share Common $0.0001 par exchanged for (0.002) share Common $0.0001 par
Mobile Media Unlimited Holdings Inc. recapitalized as EnableTS, Inc. 04/18/2011

VERIDIUM CORP (DE)
Name changed to GS CleanTech Corp. 07/19/2006
GS CleanTech Corp. name changed to GreenShift Corp. 02/13/2008

VERIFONE INC (DE)
Merged into Hewlett-Packard Co. (CA) 06/25/1997
Each share Common 1¢ par exchanged for (1) share Common $1 par
Hewlett-Packard Co. (CA) reincorporated in Delaware 05/20/1998 which name changed to HP Inc. 11/02/2015

VERIFONE SYS INC (DE)
Name changed 05/18/2010
Name changed from VeriFone Holdings, Inc. to VeriFone Systems, Inc. 05/18/2010
Acquired by Vertex Holdco LLC 08/20/2018
Each share Common 1¢ par exchanged for $23.04 cash

VERIGY LTD (SINGAPORE)
Issue Information - 8,500,000 ORD SHS offered at $15 per share on 06/12/2006
Acquired by Advantest Corp. 06/30/2011
Each share Ordinary exchanged for USD $15 cash

VERILINK CORP (DE)
Each share old Common 1¢ par exchanged for (0.00038744) share new Common 1¢ par 06/30/2008
New Common 1¢ par split (3) for (1) by issuance of (2) additional shares payable 08/20/2012 to holders of record 07/27/2012 Ex date - 08/21/2012
Name changed to LMK Global Resources, Inc. 08/29/2012
LMK Global Resources, Inc. name changed to Alas Aviation Corp. 07/23/2013 which name changed to Energie Holdings, Inc. 02/13/2014 which name changed to ExeLED Holdings Inc. 12/30/2015

VERIO INC (DE)
Merged into Nippon Telegraph & Telephone Corp. 9/8/2000
Each share 6.75% Conv. Preferred Ser. A $0.001 par exchanged for $62.136 cash
Each share Common $0.001 par exchanged for $60 cash

VERIS BIOTECHNOLOGY CORP (ON)
Recapitalized as Capital Diagnostic Corp. 5/5/2004
Each share Common no par exchanged for (0.2) share Common no par

VERISITY LTD (ISRAEL)
Issue Information - 3,335,000 ORD shs. offered at $7 per share on 03/20/2001
Merged into Cadence Design Systems, Inc. 04/07/2005
Each Ordinary share NIS 0.01 par exchanged for $12 cash

VERIT INDS (DE)
Reincorporated 01/02/1992
Each share Common $1 par exchanged for (0.5) share Common $2 par 11/13/1974
Name and state of incorporation changed from Verit Industries (CA) to Verit Industries, Inc. (DE) 01/02/1992
Charter cancelled and declared inoperative and void for non-payment of taxes 03/01/1995

VERITAS DGC INC (DE)
Merged into Compagnie Generale de Geophysique-Veritas 01/12/2007
Each share Common 1¢ par exchanged for (2.0097) Sponsored ADR's for Ordinary
Compagnie Generale de Geophysique-Veritas name changed to CGG 05/29/2013

VERITAS ENERGY SVCS INC NEW (AB)
Each Class A Exchangeable Share Ser. 1 exchanged for (1) share Veritas DGC Inc. Common 1¢ par 5/16/2006
Each Exchangeable Share exchanged for (1) share Veritas DGC Inc. Common 1¢ par 5/16/2006
Veritas DGC Inc. merged into Compagnie Generale de Geophysique-Veritas 1/12/2007

VERITAS ENERGY SVCS INC OLD (AB)
Merged into Veritas DGC Inc. 08/30/1996
Each share Common no par exchanged for (0.8) share Common 1¢ par
Veritas DGC Inc. merged into Compagnie Generale de Geophysique-Veritas 01/12/2007 which name changed to CGG 05/29/2013

VERITAS MUSIC ENTMT INC (TN)
Name changed to Imprint Records Inc. 8/5/96
(See Imprint Records Inc.)

VERITAS SOFTWARE CORP (DE)
Reincorporated 4/25/97
Common no par split (2) for (1) by issuance of (1) additional share 5/19/95
Common no par split (3) for (2) by issuance of (1) additional share payable 9/30/96 to holders of record 9/17/96
State of incorporation changed from (CA) to (DE) and Common no par changed to $0.001 par 4/25/97
Common $0.001 par split (3) for (2) by issuance of (0.5) additional share payable 9/12/97 to holders of record 8/28/97
Common $0.001 par split (3) for (2) by issuance of (0.5) additional share payable 5/20/98 to holders of record 5/4/98
Common $0.001 par split (2) for (1) by issuance of (1) additional share payable 7/8/99 to holders of record 6/18/99
Common $0.001 par split (3) for (2) by issuance of (0.5) additional share payable 11/19/99 to holders of record 11/2/99
Common $0.001 par split (3) for (2) by issuance of (0.5) additional share payable 3/3/2000 to holders of record 2/18/2000
Merged into Symantec Corp. 7/2/2005
Each share Common $0.001 par exchanged for (1.1242) shares Common 1¢ par

VERITEC INC (NV)
Each share old Common 1¢ par exchanged for (0.1) share new Common 1¢ par 05/05/1994
Plan of reorganization under Chapter 11 Federal Bankruptcy Code effective 08/05/1997
Each share new Common 1¢ par exchanged for (0.1) share Common 1¢ par and (0.3) Common Stock Purchase Warrant expiring 05/15/1998
(Additional Information in Active)

VERITEK TECHNOLOGIES INC (AB)
Name changed to California Nanotechnologies Corp. 2/12/2007

VERITY INC (DE)
Common $0.001 par split (2) for (1) by issuance of (1) additional share payable 12/03/1999 to holders of record 11/17/1999
Merged into Autonomy Corp. PLC 12/29/2005
Each share Common $0.001 par exchanged for $13.50 cash

VERLAC GOLD MINES, LTD. (ON)
Dissolved in 1959

VERMILATA OILS, LTD.
Acquired by Apex Consolidated Resources Ltd. 00/00/1946
Each share Capital Stock $1 par exchanged for (0.5) share Capital Stock no par
Apex Consolidated Resources Ltd. recapitalized as Abacus Mines Ltd. 06/01/1959 which name changed to Abacus Mines & Realty Ltd. 00/00/1962 which recapitalized as Abacon Developments Ltd. 03/21/1963
(See Abacon Developments Ltd.)

VERMILION BANCORP INC (DE)
Merged into Founders Group 8/23/2005
Each share Common 1¢ par exchanged for $38.02 cash

VERMILION BAY LD CO (DE)
Common $1 par changed to 10¢ par 03/17/1962
Merged into Crystal Oil Co. 12/04/1989
Each share Common 10¢ par exchanged for $93 cash

VERMILION BAYLAND LLC (DE)
Charter cancelled for failure to pay franchise taxes 6/1/2002

VERMILION CONSOLIDATED OILS LTD. (AB)
Completely liquidated 07/31/1977
Each share Capital Stock no par exchanged for first and final distribution of $0.05 cash

VERMILION ENERGY TR (AB)
Reorganized as Vermilion Energy Inc. 09/07/2010
Each Trust Unit exchanged for (1) share Common no par
Note: Unexchanged certificates were cancelled and became without value 09/07/2015

VERMILION RES INC (BC)
Name changed to Island Technologies Corp. 09/13/1985
Island Technologies Corp. name changed to Hiburd Properties Inc. 02/11/1987
(See Hiburd Properties Inc.)

VERMILION RES LTD (AB)
Plan of arrangement effective 1/22/2003
Each share Common no par exchanged for (1) share Clear Energy Inc. Common no par and (1) share Vermilion Energy Trust Trust Unit no par
(See each company's listing)

VERMILLION VENTURES INC (NV)
Each share old Common $0.001 par exchanged for (0.00033333) share new Common $0.001 par 05/19/2000
Name changed to CirTran Corp. 07/11/2000

VERMONT AMERN CORP (DE)
Class A Common $1 par split (3) for (2) by issuance of (0.5) additional share 5/11/73
Class B Common $1 par split (3) for (2) by issuance of (0.5) additional share 5/11/73
Class A Common $1 par split (3) for (2) by issuance of (0.5) additional share 12/31/76
Class B Common $1 par split (3) for (2) by issuance of (0.5) additional share 12/31/76
Class A Common $1 par split (5) for (4) by issuance of (0.25) additional share 8/28/87
Class B Common $1 par split (5) for (4) by issuance of (0.25) additional share 8/28/87
Stock Dividends - 10% 11/28/75; 12% 11/30/77; 12% 11/30/78; 15% 11/30/79; 15% 12/5/80; 15% 1/4/82; 10% 2/25/83; 10% 11/30/83; 10% 11/28/84; 10% 8/29/86; 10% 5/31/89
Merged into Maple Acquisition Corp. 1/4/90
Each share Class A Common $1 par exchanged for $41 cash
Each share Non-Vtg. Class B $1 par exchanged for $41 cash

VERMONT BK & TR CO (BRATTLEBORO, VT)
Capital Stock $12 par changed to $6 par and (1) additional share issued 10/10/69
Name changed to First Vermont Bank & Trust Co. (Brattleboro, VT) 7/1/72
First Vermont Bank & Trust Co. (Brattleboro, VT) reorganized as First Vermont Financial Corp. 8/31/82 which name changed to BankNorth Group, Inc. (VT) 5/13/86 which merged into BankNorth Group, Inc. (DE) 12/1/89 which merged into Banknorth Group, Inc. (ME) 5/10/2000 which merged into TD Banknorth Inc. 3/1/2005
(See TD Banknorth Inc.)

VERMONT FED BK FSB (BURLINGTON, VT)
Common 1¢ par split (3) for (2) by issuance of (0.5) additional share 04/14/1986
Under plan of reorganization each share Common 1¢ par automatically became (1) share Eastern Bancorp, Inc. 1¢ par 07/30/1986
Eastern Bancorp, Inc. merged into Vermont Financial Services Corp. 06/26/1997 which merged into Chittenden Corp. 05/28/1999
(See Chittenden Corp.)

VERMONT FINL SVCS CORP (DE)
Reincorporated 04/17/1990
Common $1 par split (2) for (1) by issuance of (1) additional share 10/25/1986
State of incorporation changed from (VT) to (DE) 04/17/1990
Common $1 par split (2) for (1) by issuance of (1) additional share payable 10/10/1997 to holders of record 09/12/1997
Merged into Chittenden Corp. 05/28/1999
Each share Common $1 par exchanged for (1.07) shares Common $1 par
(See Chittenden Corp.)

VERMONT HYDRO-ELECTRIC CORP.
Acquired by Central Vermont Public Service Corp. 00/00/1929
Details not available

VERMONT INDUSTRIES, INC. (VT)
Charter revoked 6/30/54

VERMONT LIGHTING CORP. (VT)
Name changed to Gas Co. of Vermont, Inc. 10/05/1956
(See Gas Co. of Vermont, Inc.)

VERMONT MINES LTD. (ON)
Charter cancelled and declared dissolved for failure to file returns and pay fees 5/9/77

VERMONT NATIONAL & SAVINGS BANK (BRATTLEBORO, VT)
Common $25 par changed to $10 par and (1.5) additional shares issued plus a 50% stock dividend paid 06/30/1958
Under plan of merger name changed to Vermont National Bank (Brattleboro, VT) 12/31/1964
Vermont National Bank (Brattleboro, VT) reorganized as Vermont Financial Services Corp. (VT) 02/28/1983 which reincorporated in Delaware 04/17/1990 which merged into Chittenden Corp. 05/28/1999
(See Chittenden Corp.)

VERMONT NATL BK (BRATTLEBORO, VT)
Common $10 par changed to $5 par and (1) additional share issued 11/30/1973
5-1/4% Preferred $50 par called for redemption 07/01/1975

VER-VER

Reorganized as Vermont Financial Services Corp. (VT) 02/28/1983
Each share Common $5 par exchanged for (1) share Common $1 par
Vermont Financial Services Corp. (VT) reincorporated in Delaware 04/17/1990 which merged into Chittenden Corp. 05/28/1999
(See Chittenden Corp.)

VERMONT-PEOPLES NATIONAL BANK (BRATTLEBORO, VT)
Name changed to Vermont National & Savings Bank (Brattleboro, VT) 06/30/1958
Vermont National & Savings Bank (Brattleboro, VT) name changed to Vermont National Bank (Brattleboro, VT) 12/31/1964 which reorganized as Vermont Financial Services Corp. (VT) 02/28/1983 which reincorporated in Delaware 04/17/1990 which merged into Chittenden Corp. 05/28/1999
(See Chittenden Corp.)

VERMONT PURE HLDGS LTD NEW (DE)
Name changed to Crystal Rock Holdings, Inc. 05/03/2010
(See Crystal Rock Holdings, Inc.)

VERMONT PURE HLDGS LTD OLD (DE)
Class A Common $0.001 par reclassified as Common $0.001 par 11/09/2000
Under plan of reorganization each share Common $0.001 par automatically became (1) share Vermont Pure Holdings, Ltd. (New) Common $0.001 par 11/09/2000
Vermont Pure Holdings, Ltd. (New) name changed to Crystal Rock Holdings, Inc. 05/03/2010
(See Crystal Rock Holdings, Inc.)

VERMONT RESH INC (VT)
Common $5 par changed to 50¢ par and (9) additional shares issued 02/06/1970
Common 50¢ par split (2) for (1) by issuance of (1) additional share 05/15/1980
Stock Dividend - 25% 11/01/1979
Acquired by Storage Computer Corp. 03/06/1995
Each share Common 50¢ par exchanged for (0.28) share Common $0.001 par
(See Storage Computer Corp.)

VERMONT TEDDY BEAR INC (NY)
Merged into Hibernation Holding Co., Inc. 9/30/2005
Each share Common 5¢ par exchanged for $6.50 cash

VERMONT WITCH HAZEL CO (VT)
Reincorporated 10/8/2002
Each share Common no par received distribution of (1) share Vermont Witch Hazel Co. LLC Common no par payable 12/31/2001 to holders of record 12/10/2001
State of incorporation changed from (VT) to (NV) 10/8/2002
Name changed to Soyo Group, Inc. 12/6/2002

VERMONT YANKEE NUCLEAR PWR CORP (VT)
7.48% Preferred $100 par called for redemption in 1989
Public interest eliminated

VERMONT ZINC MINES LTD. (ON)
Name changed to Vermont Mines Ltd. in April 1960
Vermont Mines Ltd. charter cancelled 5/9/77

VERNA CORP (DE)
Stock Dividend - 10% 01/29/1982
Charter cancelled and declared inoperative and void for non-payment of taxes 03/01/1988

VERNAL OIL & GAS CO. (UT)
Name changed to Loring Industries, Inc. 06/13/1969
(See Loring Industries, Inc.)

VERNEY CORP. (NH)
Acquired by Gera Corp. (NJ) 11/18/1955
Each share $5 Preferred no par exchanged for (1.0875) shares $6 Preferred no par
Each share $5 Non-Vtg. Preferred no par exchanged for (1.05) shares $6 Preferred no par
Each share Common $2.50 par exchanged for (0.03) share $6 Preferred no par
Gera Corp. (NJ) merged into Gera Corp. (DE) 07/28/1964
(See Gera Corp.)

VERNEY CORP. OF CANADA, LTD. (CANADA)
Bankrupt 8/1/54

VERNEY MILLS OF CANADA, LTD.
Name changed to Verney Corp. of Canada, Ltd. 00/00/1948
(See Verney Corp. of Canada, Ltd.)

VERNEY SHAWMUT MILLS, INC.
Merged into Verney Corp. 00/00/1946
Details not available

VERNITRON CORP NEW (DE)
Reincorporated 06/28/1968
Reorganized 08/28/1987
Stock Dividend - 50% 08/31/1961
State of incorporation changed from (NY) to (DE) 06/28/1968
Common 10¢ par split (5) for (4) by issuance of (0.25) additional share 07/19/1968
Common 10¢ par split (4) for (3) by issuance of (1/3) additional share 01/24/1969
Common 10¢ par split (5) for (4) by issuance of (0.25) additional share 01/02/1981
Reorganized from Vernitron Corp. (Old) to Vernitron Corp. (New) 08/28/1987
Each share Common 10¢ par exchanged for (0.5) share $3.75 Exchangeable Preferred 1¢ par and $1 cash
Each share new Common 1¢ par exchanged again for (0.2) share new Common 1¢ par 07/25/1996
Stock Dividend - in Preferred to holders of Preferred 3.75% payable 02/22/1996 to holders of record 02/12/1996
Name changed to Axsys Technologies, Inc. 12/04/1996
(See Axsys Technologies, Inc.)

VERNON BK CORP (NY)
Merged into Oneida Financial Corp. 04/02/2007
Each share Common $5 par exchanged for $54 cash

VERNON CO (IA)
Common $7.50 par changed to $3.75 par and (1) additional share issued 08/29/1968
Stock Dividends - 25% 09/01/1972; 25% 09/01/1973
Merged into Vernon Acquisition Co. 08/26/1986
Each share Common $3.75 par exchanged for $34.75 cash

VERNON COPPER LTD. (BC)
Struck off register and declared dissolved for failure to file returns 2/25/83

VERNON FINL CORP (IN)
Preferred Class A $1 par called for redemption 04/20/1972
General Series Conv. Preferred called for redemption 10/31/1972
Acquired by Meridian Acquisition Corp. 10/01/1987
Each share Common $1 par exchanged for $5.72 cash

VERNON FIRE & CASUALTY INSURANCE CO. (IN)
Preferred $2 par changed to $1 par 12/12/62
Name changed to Vernon Financial Corp. 7/19/68
(See Vernon Financial Corp.)

VERNON NATL BK (VERNON, CT)
Common $10 par changed to $2 par and (4) additional shares issued 01/00/1965
Stock Dividend - 10% 05/00/1967
Merged into United Bank & Trust Co. (Hartford, CT) 08/14/1981
Each share Common $2 par exchanged for $23.50 cash

VERNON VY REC ASSN INC (NJ)
Common 5¢ par changed to 1¢ par 10/31/1972
Name changed to Great American Recreation, Inc. 11/02/1981
(See Great American Recreation, Inc.)

VERNORS, INC. (MI)
Name changed to V. G. A. Co. 6/21/66
V. G. A. Co. completed liquidation 10/8/71

VERNORS GINGER ALE INC (MI)
Name changed to Vernors, Inc. (Mich.) 2/6/64
Vernors, Inc. (Mich.) name changed to V. G. A. Co. 6/21/66 which completed liquidation 10/8/71

VERO ENERGY INC (AB)
Name changed to TORC Oil & Gas Ltd. 11/21/2012

VERO RESOURCE MANAGEMENT LTD. (AB)
Name changed to Vero Resources Ltd. 10/6/87
Vero Resources Ltd. merged into Excel Energy Inc. 2/1/94 which merged into Ranchmen's Resources Ltd. 7/25/95

VERO RES LTD (AB)
Merged into Excel Energy Inc. 2/1/94
Each share Common no par exchanged for (0.35087666) share Common no par
Excel Energy Inc. merged into Ranchmen's Resources Ltd. 7/25/95

VERO SOFTWARE PLC (UNITED KINGDOM)
Acquired by BV Acquisitions SARL 07/15/2010
Each Sponsored ADR for Ordinary exchanged for $5.41455 cash

VERONA BANKSHARES LTD. (WI)
Merged into S.B.C.P. Bancorp, Inc. 12/4/2006
Each share Common $25 par exchanged for approximately $138 cash

VERONA DEV CORP (BC)
Each share old Common no par exchanged for (0.03333333) share new Common no par 05/18/2016
Name changed to SVT Capital Corp. 08/19/2016
SVT Capital Corp. name changed to Delta 9 Cannabis Inc. 11/06/2017

VERONEX RESOURCES LTD (BC)
Recapitalized as International Veronex Resources Ltd. 10/20/1992
Each share Common no par exchanged for (1/7) share Common no par
International Veronex Resources Ltd. name changed to Veronex Technologies Inc. 12/04/1997
(See Veronex Technologies Inc.)

VERONEX TECHNOLOGIES INC (BC)
SEC revoked common stock registration 10/15/2009

VERONIQUE INC (DE)
Name changed to Digital Launch Inc. 04/13/1999
Digital Launch Inc. name changed to Global e Tutor, Inc. 02/03/2000 which recapitalized as Winning Brands Corp. 11/09/2005

VERPLANCK & TOMPKINS COVE FERRY CO., INC. (NY)
Charter cancelled and proclaimed dissolved for failure to pay taxes 12/15/33

VERREAUX CORP (DE)
Charter cancelled and declared inoperative and void for non-payment of taxes 03/01/1986

VERSA SVCS LTD (CANADA)
Acquired by ARAMARK Corp. 11/18/94
Each share Common no par exchanged for $11.125 cash

VERSA TECHNOLOGIES INC (WI)
Reincorporated 7/14/86
Each share Conv. Preferred Ser. A no par exchanged for (1.35) shares Common 10¢ par 3/31/75
Common 10¢ par split (5) for (4) by isssuance of (0.25) additional share 8/10/81
Common 10¢ par split (5) for (4) by issuance of (0.25) additional share 8/31/82
Common 10¢ par split (3) for (2) by issuance of (0.5) additional share 11/10/83
Common 10¢ par split (3) for (2) by issuance of (0.5) additional share 6/16/86
State of incorporation changed from (WI) to (DE) and Common 10¢ par changed to 1¢ par 7/14/86
Common 1¢ par split (5) for (4) by issuance of (0.25) additional share 8/10/87
Stock Dividends - 25% 12/1/72; 25% 5/10/78; 25% 8/10/88; 20% 8/10/89
Merged into Applied Power Inc. 10/9/97
Each share Common 1¢ par exchanged for $24.625 cash

VERSABANK OLD (LONDON, ON)
Under plan of merger name changed to Versabank (New) (London, ON) 02/02/2017

VERSACOLD CORP (BC)
Recapitalized as Versacold Income Fund 02/12/2002
Each share Common no par exchanged for (1) Unit no par
(See Versacold Income Fund)

VERSACOLD INCOME FD (BC)
Acquired by HF. Eimskipafelag Islands 08/02/2007
Each share Common no par exchanged for $12.25 cash

VERSACOM INTL INC (UT)
Each share old Common $0.001 par exchanged for (0.2) share new Common $0.001 par 08/20/2001
Charter expired 09/16/2002

VERSAFOOD SVCS LTD (CANADA)
Name changed to VS Services Ltd.-VS Services Ltee. 7/12/72
VS Services Ltd.-VS Services Ltee. name changed to Versa Services Ltd./Versa Services Ltee. 11/27/91
(See Versa Services Ltd./Versa Services Ltee.)

VERSAILLES APARTMENTS, INC. (MO)
Capital Stock $5 par changed to $1 par in 1941
Liquidated in 1954

VERSAILLES CAP CORP (CO)
Name changed to Amerimmune Pharmaceuticals Inc. 08/06/1999
(See Amerimmune Pharmaceuticals Inc.)

VERSANT CORP (CA)
Name changed 07/22/1998
Name changed from Versant Object

Technology Corp. to Versant Corp. 07/22/1998
Each share old Common no par exchanged for (0.1) share new Common no par 08/23/2005
Acquired by Actian Corp. 12/24/2012
Each share new Common no par exchanged for $13 cash

VERSANT INTL INC (NV)
Name changed to Global Vision Holdings, Inc. 01/11/2013

VERSAPAK FILM & PACKAGING MACHY CORP (NY)
Name changed to Coventry Energy Corp. 04/18/1978

VERSAR INC (DE)
Each share Common 1¢ par received distribution of (1) share Sarnia Corp. Common 1¢ par 06/27/1994
Acquired by KW Genesis Merger Sub, Inc. 11/13/2017
Each share Common 1¢ par exchanged for $0.15 cash

VERSARTIS INC (DE)
Recapitalized as Aravive, Inc. 10/16/2018
Each share Common $0.0001 par exchanged for (0.16666666) share Common $0.0001 par

VERSATA INC (CA)
Issue Information - 3,850,000 shares COM offered at $24 per share on 03/03/2000
Each share old Common $0.001 par exchanged for (1/6) share new Common $0.001 par 05/24/2002
Merged into Trilogy, Inc. 01/31/2006
Each share new Common $0.001 par exchanged for $0.40 cash

VERSATECH GROUP INC (CANADA)
Company placed in receivership 10/13/2000
Stockholders' equity unlikely

VERSATECH INC (NV)
Name changed to VersaTech USA 05/13/2013

VERSATECH INDS INC (ID)
Merged into Versatech Group Inc. 06/30/1998
Each share Common 1¢ par exchanged for (1) share Common no par
(See Versatech Group Inc.)

VERSATEL TELECOM INTL N V (NETHERLANDS)
Issue Information - 21,250,000 SPONSORED ADR'S offered at $10.51 per ADR on 07/23/1999
Each (12) Sponsored ADR's for Ordinary NLG 0.05 par exchanged for (1) Sponsored ADR for Ordinary Euro 0.02 par 5/15/2002
Each Sponsored ADR for Ordinary Euro 0.02 par received (1) ADR Euro Warrant expiring 10/4/2004 on 10/8/2002
ADR agreement terminated 2/10/2003
Each Sponsored ADR for Ordinary Euro 0.02 par exchanged for $10.6921 cash

VERSATILE CORP (CANADA)
Reincorporated 2/9/81
Common no par split (2) for (1) by issuance of (1) additional share 6/7/80
Reincorporated from Versatile Cornat Corp. (BC) to Versatile Corp. (Canada) and Common no par reclassified as Class B Common no par 2/9/81
Each share Class B Common no par received distribution of (1) share Class A Common no par 2/23/81
Class A Common no par reclassified as Class A Subordinate no par in 1983
Reorganized under the laws of British Columbia as B.C. Pacific Capital Corp. 5/16/88
Each share $1.40 Preferred Ser. A no par exchanged for (1.25) shares Class A Subordinate no par
Each share $2.625 Conv. Jr. Preferred Ser. 1 no par exchanged for (1.75) shares Class A Subordinate no par
Each share Class A Subordinate no par exchanged for (0.1) share Class A Subordinate no par
Each share Class B Common no par exchanged for (0.1) share Class B Common no par
(See B.C. Pacific Capital Corp.)

VERSATILE MFG LTD (BC)
Reincorporated 5/25/78
Under plan of recapitalization each share Common no par received (2) shares Class A Common no par
Place of incorporation changed from (MAN) to (BC) 5/25/78
Merged into Versatile Cornat Corp. (BC) 7/1/78
Each share Common no par exchanged for (1) share $1.40 Preferred Ser. A no par
Each share Class A Common no par exchanged for (1) share $1.40 Preferred Ser. A no par
Versatile Cornat Corp. (BC) reincorporated in Canada as Versatile Corp. 2/9/81 which reorganized in British Columbia as B.C. Pacific Capital Corp. 5/16/88
(See B.C. Pacific Capital Corp.)

VERSATILE MOBILE SYS (CANADA) INC (YT)
Reincorporated 02/23/2004
Place of incorporation changed from (BC) to (Yukon) 02/23/2004
Reincorporated under the laws of British Columbia as Versatile Systems Inc. 11/16/2005

VERSATILITY INC (DE)
Merged into Oracle Corp. 12/04/1998
Each share Common 1¢ par exchanged for $1.50 cash

VERSENT CORP (ON)
Merged into Buckingham Technology Acquisition Group Inc. 10/17/2000
Each share Common no par exchanged for $1.75 cash

VERSICOR INC (DE)
Name changed to Vicuron Pharmaceuticals Inc. 3/24/2003
(See Vicuron Pharmaceuticals Inc.)

VERSO CORP (DE)
Name changed 01/08/2015
Name changed from Verso Paper Corp. to Verso Corp. 01/08/2015
Plan of reorganization under Chapter 11 Federal Bankruptcy proceedings effective 07/15/2016
No stockholders' equity

VERSO TECHNOLOGIES INC (MN)
Each share old Common 1¢ par exchanged for (0.2) share new Common 1¢ par 10/11/2005
Plan of reorganization under Chapter 11 Federal Bankruptcy proceedings confirmed 06/04/2009
No stockholders' equity

VERSUS TECHNOLOGIES INC (CANADA)
Merged into E*Trade Group, Inc. 08/28/2000
Each share Common no par exchanged for either (0.724757) share Common 1¢ par or (0.724757) EGI Canada Corp. Exchangeable Share no par
(See each company's listing)

VERSUS TECHNOLOGY INC (DE)
Acquired by Midmark Corp. 05/04/2016
Each share Common 1¢ par exchanged for $0.35716182 cash

VERTEC CORP. (MN)
Name changed to Corporate Recruiters, Inc. (MN) 04/27/1971
Corporate Recruiters, Inc. (MN) reincorporated in Nevada as Connection China Trading Corp. 09/00/1989 which name changed to Asian Pacific Co., Ltd. 09/09/1992
(See Asian Pacific Co., Ltd.)

VERTEC HELICOPTERS INC (MN)
Name changed to National Mobile Health Care, Inc. 05/30/1972
(See National Mobile Health Care, Inc.)

VERTECH SYS CORP (BC)
Recapitalized as Vercan Investments Inc. 07/12/1989
Each share Common no par exchanged for (0.33333333) share Common no par
Vercan Investments Inc. name changed to WaterSave Logic Corp. 01/26/1998 which name changed to Abode Mortgage Holdings Corp. 08/15/2006 which recapitalized as Ayubowan Capital Ltd. 08/19/2013 which name changed to Discovery Metals Corp. 06/13/2017

VERTEL CORP (CA)
Reorganized under the laws of Delaware as Hayden Hall, Inc. 01/05/2009
Each share Common 1¢ par exchanged for (0.001) share Common 1¢ par

VERTEX COMMUNICATIONS CORP (TX)
Merged into TriPoint Global Communications Inc. 2/9/2000
Each share Common 10¢ par exchanged for $22 cash

VERTEX COMPUTER CABLE & PRODS INC (DE)
Name changed to DataWorld Solutions Inc. 04/30/1999
DataWorld Solutions Inc. name changed to Defense Technology Systems, Inc. 07/08/2004
(See Defense Technology Systems, Inc.)

VERTEX INTERACTIVE INC (NJ)
Name changed 02/14/2000
Common 1¢ par split (2) for (1) by issuance of (1) additional share 04/26/1993
Name changed from Vertex Industries, Inc. to Vertex Interactive, Inc. 02/14/2000
Name changed to Cape Systems Group, Inc. 04/08/2005
(See Cape Systems Group, Inc.)

VERTEX PPTYS INC (AB)
Delisted from Canadian Venture Stock Exchange 8/22/2001

VERTEX RES LTD (BC)
Struck off register and declared dissolved for failure to file returns 07/05/1991

VERTEX VENTURES INC (ON)
Name changed to First Strike Diamonds Inc. 02/23/2000
(See First Strike Diamonds Inc.)

VERTICA SOFTWARE INC (CO)
Each share old Common $0.0001 par exchanged for (0.01) share new Common $0.0001 par 9/30/2004
Name changed to New Century Energy Corp. 11/1/2004
Each share Common $0.0001 par exchanged for (1) share Common $0.0001 par

VERTICA SYS CORP (BC)
Recapitalized as Siscoe Callahan Mining Corp. 8/3/88
Each share Common no par exchanged for (0.5) share Common no par
(See Siscoe Callahan Mining Corp.)

VERTICAL BRANDING INC (DE)
SEC revoked common stock registration 06/11/2014

VERTICAL COMMUNICATIONS INC (DE)
Company terminated common stock registration and is no longer public as of 07/29/2008
Note: Company effected (1) for (100) reverse splits 06/00/2009 and 12/07/2011
Each share new Common 1¢ par received $0.00001 cash 10/02/2015

VERTICAL HEALTH SOLUTIONS INC (FL)
Each share old Common $0.001 par exchanged for (0.66666666) share new Common $0.001 par 02/28/2002
Each share new Common $0.001 par exchanged again for (0.85714285) share new Common $0.001 par 06/10/2002
New Common $0.001 par split (5) for (1) by issuance of (4) additional shares payable 11/20/2003 to holders of record 11/10/2003 Ex date - 11/21/2003
Each share new Common $0.001 par exchanged again for (0.00609756) share new Common $0.001 par 04/11/2011
Plan of reorganization under Chapter 11 Federal Bankruptcy proceedings effective 10/17/2014
No stockholders' equity

VERTICALBUYER INC (DE)
Recapitalized as Computer Software Innovations, Inc. 02/10/2005
Each share Common $0.001 par exchanged for (0.025) share Common $0.001 par
(See Computer Software Innovations, Inc.)

VERTICALNET INC (PA)
Issue Information - 3,500,000 shares OC-COM offered at $16 per share on 02/10/1999
Old Common 1¢ par split (2) for (1) by issuance of (1) additional share payable 08/20/1999 to holders of record 08/09/1999
Old Common 1¢ par split (2) for (1) by issuance of (1) additional share payable 03/31/2000 to holders of record 03/17/2000
Each share old Common 1¢ par exchanged for (0.1) share new Common 1¢ par 07/15/2002
Each share new Common 1¢ par exchanged again for (1/7) share new Common 1¢ par 06/12/2006
Each share new Common 1¢ par exchanged again for (0.125) share new Common 1¢ par 08/16/2007
Merged into BravoSolution, S.p.A. 01/25/2008
Each share Common 1¢ par exchanged for $2.56 cash

VERTICOM INC (CA)
Acquired by Western Digital Corp. 8/31/88
Each share Common no par exchanged for (0.24) share Common 10¢ par
Note: An additional (0.06) share per share has been placed in an escrow fund for future distribution

VERTIENTES-CAMAGUEY SUGAR CO.
Reorganized as Vertientes-Camaguey Sugar Co. of Cuba share for share in 1942

VERTIENTES SUGAR CO.
Reorganized as Vertientes-Camaguey Sugar Co. in 1937
No stockholders' equity

VERTIGO 3D INC (ON)
Common no par reclassified as Class A Common no par 7/25/96
Recapitalized as Vertigo Software Corp. 10/27/98
Each share Class A Common no par

exchanged for (1/7) share Class A
Common no par
Vertigo Software Corp. name
changed to Even Technologies Inc.
6/22/2004

VERTIGO SOFTWARE CORP (ON)
Name changed to Even Technologies
Inc. 6/22/2004

VERTIGO THEME PKS INC (NV)
SEC revoked common stock
registration 05/05/2010

VERTIGO VISUAL SYS HLDGS INC (NV)
Recapitalized as World Poker Store,
Inc. 10/18/2005
Each share Common $0.001 par
exchanged for (0.001) share
Common $0.001 par

VERTIMAC DEV INC (AB)
Name changed to Copper States
Resources Inc. 12/15/95
Copper States Resources Inc.
recapitalized as American
Coppermine Resources Ltd. 8/26/96
which recapitalized as Carleton
Resources Corp. 2/4/97
(See Carleton Resources Corp.)

VERTIPILE INC (NY)
Stock Dividend - 50% 05/26/1972
Reincorporated under the laws of
Delaware as Quaker Fabric Corp.
08/03/1987
(See Quaker Fabric Corp. (DE))

VERTOL AIRCRAFT CORP. (PA)
Stock Dividends - 15% 10/29/56; 10%
10/21/57
Acquired by Boeing Airplane Co. on a
(2/3) for (1) basis 4/1/60 which
name was changed to Boeing Co.
5/4/61

VERTRO INC (DE)
Each share Common $0.001 par
exchanged for (0.2) share Common
$0.005 par 08/18/2010
Merged into Inuvo, Inc. 03/01/2012
Each share Common $0.005 par
exchanged for (1.546) shares
Common $0.001 par

VERTRUE INC (DE)
Merged into Velo Holdings Inc.
08/16/2007
Each share Common 1¢ par
exchanged for $50 cash

VERTX CORP (NV)
Charter revoked for failure to file
reports and pay fees 05/01/2008

VERUTEK TECHNOLOGIES INC (DE)
Reincorporated 05/26/2009
State of incorporation changed from
(NV) to (DE) 05/26/2009
Assets sold 08/27/2014
Details not available

VERVE VENTURES INC (NV)
Name changed to American Strategic
Minerals Corp. and Common $0.001
par changed to $0.0001 par
12/13/2011
American Strategic Minerals Corp.
name changed to Marathon Patent
Group, Inc. 02/21/2013

VERYBESTOFTHEINTERNET COM INC (DE)
Name changed to Refocus Group Inc.
2/25/2003

VESCAN EQUITIES INC (CANADA)
Recapitalized as Inouye Technologies
(Canada) Inc. 01/26/2000
Each share Common no par
exchanged for (0.0090909) share
Common no par
(See Inouye Technologies (Canada) Inc.)

VESCO CORP (PA)
Name changed to Allister Corp.
02/21/1978
(See Allister Corp.)

VESELY CO (MI)
Charter declared inoperative and void
for failure to file reports 5/15/84

VESPAR MINES LTD (ON)
Capital Stock $1 par changed to no
par 07/21/1971
Merged into Parlake Resources Ltd.
06/18/1979
Each share Capital Stock no par
exchanged for (0.2) share Common
no par
Parlake Resources Ltd. name
changed to Concord Capital Corp.
07/23/1991
(See Concord Capital Corp.)

VESPER CORP (PA)
Merged into Arrowhead Holdings
11/29/93
Each share Common $5 par
exchanged for $3.25 cash
5% Preferred $100 par called for
redemption at $105 on 4/24/2001
Public interest eliminated

VESTA CAP CORP (ON)
Name changed to United Hunter Oil &
Gas Corp. 09/16/2010

VESTA INC (CO)
Recapitalized as Bonita Corp.
07/16/1991
Each share Common no par
exchanged for (0.05) share Common
no par
Bonita Corp. recapitalized as
European Securities & Trading
Group, Inc. 07/05/1994
(See European Securities & Trading Group, Inc.)

VESTA INS GROUP INC (DE)
Common 1¢ par split (3) for (2) by
issuance of (0.5) additional share
01/22/1996
Plan of reorganization under Chapter
11 Federal Bankruptcy Code
effective 12/26/2006
No stockholders' equity

VESTA INTL CORP (NV)
Common $0.001 par split (2.44) for
(1) by issuance of (1.44) additional
shares payable 01/26/2015 to
holders of record 01/20/2015
Ex date - 01/27/2015
Name changed to Content Checked
Holdings, Inc. 02/03/2015

VESTA YELLOWKNIFE MINES, LTD. (ON)
Charter cancelled by the Province of
Ontario 10/21/57

VESTABURG OIL & GAS DEVELOPMENT CO. (MI)
Charter revoked for failure to file
reports and pay fees 5/15/37

VESTALEE CORP. (NV)
Name changed to Computer Parking
Systems, Inc. 9/29/69

VESTALEE URANIUM & THORIUM CORP. (NV)
Name changed to Vestalee Corp.
6/20/69
Vestalee Corp. name changed to
Computer Parking Systems, Inc.
9/29/69

VESTAR INC (DE)
Merged into Nexstar Pharmaceuticals
Inc. 2/21/95
Each share Common 1¢ par
exchanged for (0.88) share Common
1¢ par
Nexstar Pharmaceuticals Inc. merged
into Gilead Sciences, Inc. 7/29/99

VESTART INC (OH)
Charter cancelled for non-payment of
taxes 10/30/1980

VESTAUR SECS FD (DE)
Name changed 5/26/2004
Name changed from Vestaur
Securities, Inc. to Vestaur Securities
Fund 5/26/2004

Merged into Evergreen Fixed Income
Trust 5/20/2005
Each share Common 1¢ par
exchanged for (1.0792143)
Diversified Bond Fund Class A
shares

VESTCOM INTL INC (NJ)
Issue Information - 3,850,000 shares
COM offered at $13 per share on
07/30/1997
Merged into Cornerstone Equity
Investors LLC 11/18/2002
Each share Common no par
exchanged for $6.25 cash

VESTEC CORP (NY)
Charter cancelled and proclaimed
dissolved for failure to pay taxes
09/25/1991

VESTEL ELEKTRONIK SANAYI VE TICARET A S (TURKEY)
Old 144A Sponsored GDR's for
Ordinary split (35) for (1) by
issuance of (34) additional GDR's
payable 01/10/2001 to holders of
record 12/19/2000 Ex date -
12/20/2000
Old Reg. S Sponsored GDR's for
Ordinary split (35) for (1) by
issuance of (34) additional GDR's
payable 01/10/2001 to holders of
record 12/19/2000 Ex date -
12/20/2000
Each old 144A Sponsored GDR for
Ordinary exchanged for (0.05) new
144A Sponsored GDR for Ordinary
01/29/2001
Each old Reg. S Sponsored GDR for
Ordinary exchanged for (0.05) new
Reg. S Sponsored GDR for Ordinary
01/29/2001
Basis changed from (1:1,000) to (1:1)
01/03/2005
Stock Dividend - In Reg. S Sponsored
GDR's for Ordinary to holders of
Reg. S Sponsored GDR's for
Ordinary 10.2806% payable
01/02/2009 to holders of record
12/31/2008
GDR agreement terminated
09/15/2017
Each new 144A Sponsored GDR for
Ordinary exchanged for $2.13 cash
Each new Reg. S Sponsored GDR for
Ordinary exchanged for $2.13 cash

VESTEX INC (NY)
Reorganized under the laws of
Nevada as CyberOpticLabs, Inc.
5/9/2000
Each share Common $0.001 par
exchanged for (0.025) share
Common $0.001 par
CyberOpticLabs, Inc. name changed
to Cordia Corp. 5/25/2001

VESTGRON MINES LTD (CANADA)
Recapitalized as VGM Capital Corp.
07/28/1987
Each share Capital Stock no par
exchanged for (0.2) share Common
no par
(See VGM Capital Corp.)

VESTIGE INC (DE)
Name changed to Liberty Alliance,
Inc. (New) 02/28/2007
Liberty Alliance, Inc. (New) name
changed to SinoHub, Inc.
07/18/2008

VESTIN GROUP INC (DE)
Each share old Common $0.0001 par
exchanged for (0.5) share new
Common $0.0001 par 7/20/2004
Merged into Vestin Holdings, Inc.
5/26/2005
Each share new Common $0.0001
par for $2.85 cash

VESTOR EXPLS LTD (AB)
Recapitalized as International Vestor
Resources Ltd. 09/30/1988
Each share Common no par
exchanged for (0.5) share Common
no par
International Vestor Resources Ltd.

name changed to EuroZinc Mining
Corp. 04/21/1999 which merged into
Lundin Mining Corp. 11/01/2006

VESTRO NATURAL FOODS INC (DE)
Name changed 7/12/94
Each share Common 1¢ par
exchanged for (0.1) share new
Common 1¢ par 2/7/94
Name changed from Vestro Foods
Inc. to Vestro Natural Foods Inc.
7/12/94
Name changed to Westbrae Natural
Inc. 7/7/97
(See Westbrae Natural Inc.)

VESTRON INC (DE)
Completely liquidated 10/7/94
Each share Common 1¢ par
exchanged for first and final
distribution of $2.50 cash
Note: Certificates were required to be
surrendered by 11/9/94 to receive
distribution

VESUVIUS INC (DE)
Name changed to GSB Financial
Services, Inc. 11/30/2001
GSB Financial Services, Inc.
recapitalized as Nationwide Delivery
Inc. 07/29/2008

VETA GRANDE COS INC NEW (NV)
Name changed to Forum Re Group
Inc. 07/29/1988
Forum Re Group Inc. name changed
to THE Group, Inc. 02/05/1990
(See THE Group, Inc.)

VETA GRANDE COS INC OLD (NV)
Recapitalized as Veta Grande
Companies, Inc. (New) 07/28/1986
Each share Common Capital Stock
1¢ par exchanged for (0.05) share
Common 1¢ par
Veta Grande Companies, Inc. (New)
name changed to Forum Re Group
Inc. 07/29/1988 which name
changed to THE Group, Inc.
02/05/1990
(See THE Group, Inc.)

VETCO INC (CA)
Merged into Combustion Engineering,
Inc. 04/20/1978
Each share Common 50¢ par
exchanged for $23 cash

VETCO OFFSHORE INDUSTRIES, INC. (CA)
Common 50¢ par split (3) for (2) by
issuance of (0.5) additional share
4/27/71
Common 50¢ par split (3) for (2) by
issuance of (0.5) additional share
3/24/72
Common 50¢ par split (2) for (1) by
issuance of (1) additional share
12/28/72
Name changed to Vetco Inc. 9/14/76
(See Vetco Inc.)

VETERAN RES INC (AB)
Merged into Bear Ridge Resources
Ltd. 01/19/2006
Each share Common no par
exchanged for (0.2358) share
Common no par and $0.48 cash
Bear Ridge Resources Ltd. merged
into Sabretooth Energy Ltd.
08/21/2007 which name changed to
Cequence Energy Ltd. 08/17/2009

VETERANS BROADCASTING CO., INC. (NY)
Common $5 par changed to no par
04/18/1962
Through purchase offer of $85 per
share all Common no par was
acquired by Rust Craft Broadcasting
of New York, Inc. as 03/16/1965
Public interest eliminated

VETERANS IN PACKAGING INC (NV)
Name changed to Ehouse Global, Inc.
02/12/2013

VETERINARY CTRS AMER INC (DE)
Merged into Green Equity Investors
III, L.P. 9/20/2000

VETLINE INC (CO)
Common $0.001 par split (4) for (1) by issuance of (3) additional shares 2/25/88
Each share old Common $0.001 par exchanged for (0.05) share new Common $0.001 par 12/2/91
Recapitalized as DK Industries Inc. 5/23/96
Each share new Common $0.001 par exchanged for (0.05) share Common $0.001 par
DK Industries Inc. name changed to GDC Group, Inc. 11/14/96
(See GDC Group, Inc.)

VETO RES LTD (BC)
Name changed to Baron Gold Corp. 01/24/1997
Baron Gold Corp. name changed to BG Baron Group Inc. 03/20/1998 which recapitalized as Consolidated BG Baron Group Inc. 10/25/1999 which name changed to In.Sync Industries Inc. 04/03/2000 which name changed to Jet Gold Corp. 05/27/2003 which recapitalized as Deep-South Resources Inc. 11/16/2016

VETRO INC (NV)
Name changed to Anvi Global Holdings, Inc. 10/25/2017

VEVAY DEPOSIT BANK (VEVAY, IN)
Reorganized as Southeastern Indiana Bancorp 1/11/82
Each share Capital Stock $20 par exchanged for (1) share Common no par
(See Southeastern Indiana Bancorp)

VEXCO HEALTHCARE INC (AB)
Name changed 4/18/96
Name changed from Vexco Laboratories Inc. to Vexco Healthcare Inc. 4/18/96
Recapitalized as Ceapro Inc. (ALTA) 12/31/96
Each (4.5) shares Common no par exchanged for (1) share Common no par
Ceapro Inc. (ALTA) reincorporated in Canada 8/28/2002

VEXILAR ENGINEERING, INC. (MN)
Name changed to Vexilar, Inc. 7/29/70
Vexilar, Inc. name changed to Aptek Technologies, Inc. 1/10/86
(See Aptek Technologies, Inc.)

VEXILAR INC (MN)
Name changed to Aptek Technologies, Inc. 01/10/1986
(See Aptek Technologies, Inc.)

VF CAP LTD (AB)
Name changed to Canadian Dental Partners Inc. 10/12/1999
Canadian Dental Partners Inc. name changed to International Health Partners Inc. 12/19/2000 which name changed to Patient Home Monitoring Corp. (AB) 06/08/2010 which reincorporated in British Columbia 12/30/2013
(See Patient Home Monitoring Corp.)

VFC INC (CANADA)
Merged into Toronto-Dominion Bank (Toronto, ONT) 4/21/2006
Each share Common no par exchanged for $19.50 cash

VFINANCE INC (DE)
Name changed 11/28/2001
Name changed from vFinance.com, Inc. to vFinance, Inc. 11/28/2001
Merged into National Holdings Corp. 07/01/2008
Each share Common 1¢ par exchanged for (0.14) share Common 2¢ par

VFP LIQUIDATING CORP (NY)
Liquidation completed

Each share Common 25¢ par stamped to indicate initial distribution of $26 cash 04/01/1969
Each share Stamped Common 25¢ par exchanged for second and final distribution of $1.14 cash 05/01/1970

VG GOLD CORP (ON)
Merged into Lexam VG Gold Inc. 01/04/2011
Each share Common no par exchanged for (1) share Common no par
Lexam VG Gold Inc. merged into McEwen Mining Inc. 05/01/2017

VGAMBLING INC (NV)
Name changed to Esports Entertainment Group, Inc. 05/25/2017

VGC CORP (DE)
Merged into VRG-Groep N.V. 06/16/1989
Each share Class A Common 10¢ par exchanged for $12 cash
Each share Conv. Class B Common 10¢ exchanged for $12 cash

VGM CAP CORP (CANADA)
Each share old Common no par exchanged for (0.001) share new Common no par 02/15/1993
Note: In effect holders received $0.15 cash per share and public interest was eliminated
Shareholders of (999) shares or fewer received script certificates to exchange for cash. Unexchanged certificates were declared null and void 01/22/1994

VGM TRUSTCO LTD (ON)
Name changed to Victoria & Grey Trustco Ltd. 03/17/1981
Victoria & Grey Trustco Ltd. name changed to National Victoria & Grey Trustco Ltd. 08/31/1984 which name changed to National Trustco Inc.-Trustco National Inc. 03/22/1989 which merged into Bank of Nova Scotia (Halifax, NS) 08/15/1997

VGS SEISMIC CANADA INC (CANADA)
Merged into Plainfield Luxembourg S.a.r.l. 09/25/2009
Each share Common no par exchanged for $0.06 cash

VH DEVELOPMENT CO. (MI)
Voluntarily dissolved 2/13/74
Details not available

VHC LTD (MI)
Acquired by a private co. 10/3/90
Each share Common 3¢ par exchanged for $5.75 cash
Note: An additional consideration may be paid contingent on disposition of assets

VHGI HLDGS INC (DE)
SEC revoked common stock registration 01/14/2015

VHQ ENTMT INC (CANADA)
Merged into Movie Gallery, Inc. 6/29/2005
Each share Common no par exchanged for $1.15 cash

VHS NETWORK INC (FL)
Each share old Common $0.001 par exchanged for (0.05) share new Common $0.001 par 12/1/97
Recapitalized as Dialex Minerals, Inc. 9/22/2003
Each share Common $0.001 par exchanged for (0.1) share Common $0.001 par
Dialex Minerals, Inc. recapitalized as Reliant Home Warranty Corp. 3/16/2005 which name changed to Reliant Financial Service Corp. 6/14/2007

VI GROUP PLC (UNITED KINGDOM)
Name changed to Vero Software PLC 10/25/2007
(See Vero Software PLC)

VIA NET WKS INC (DE)
Issue Information - 14,300,000 shares COM offered at $21 per share on 02/11/2000
Completely liquidated
Each share Common $0.001 par received first and final distribution of $0.0283 cash payable 10/29/2012 to holders of record 11/04/2005
Note: Certificates were not required to be surrendered and are without value

VIA PHARMACEUTICALS INC (DE)
Company terminated common stock registration and is no longer public as of 03/25/2011

VIA TV MARKETING CORP (DE)
Recapitalized as Marketvision Direct, Inc. 07/22/1998
Each share Common no par exchanged for (0.1) share Common no par
Marketvision Direct, Inc. name changed to APIC Petroleum Corp. (DE) 05/24/2011 which reincorporated in Canada 06/08/2012 which merged into Longreach Oil & Gas Ltd. 12/20/2012 which name changed to PetroMaroc Corp. PLC 07/14/2014

VIABLE RES INC (NV)
Recapitalized as Statmon Technologies Corp. 6/13/2002
Each share Common 1¢ par exchanged for (0.0625) share Common 1¢ par

VIACELL INC (DE)
Issue Information - 7,500,000 shares COM offered at $7 per share on 01/20/2005
Merged into PerkinElmer, Inc. 11/15/2007
Each share Common 1¢ par exchanged for $7.25 cash

VIACOM INC OLD (DE)
Recapitalized 03/31/1989
Each share 15.50% Exchangeable Preferred 1¢ par exchanged for $25.96875 principal amount of 15.50% Jr. Subordinated Exchangeable Debentures due 12/31/2006
Each share Common 1¢ par received distribution of (1) share Non-Vtg. Common 1¢ par 06/13/1990
Common 1¢ par reclassified as Class A Common 1¢ par 05/21/1992
Non-Vtg. Common 1¢ par reclassified as Class B Common 1¢ par 05/21/1992
Contingent Value Rights called for redemption 07/07/1995
Class A Common 1¢ par split (2) for (1) by issuance of (1) additional share payable 03/31/1999 to holders of record 03/15/1999 Ex date - 04/01/1999
Class B Common 1¢ par split (2) for (1) by issuance of (1) additional share payable 03/31/1999 to holders of record 03/15/1999 Ex date - 04/01/1999
Under plan of merger each share Class A Common 1¢ par exchanged for (0.5) share CBS Corp. Class A Common $0.001 par and (0.5) share Viacom Inc. (New) Class A Common $0.001 par 12/31/2005
Each share Class B Common 1¢ par exchanged for (0.5) share CBS Corp. Class B Common $0.001 par and (0.5) share Viacom Inc. (New) Class B Common $0.001 par 12/31/2005

VIACOM INTL INC (OH)
Reincorporated 04/17/1975
State of incorporation changed from (DE) to (OH) 04/17/1975
Common $1 par split (2) for (1) by issuance of (1) additional share 05/11/1981
$2.10 Conv. Preferred no par called for redemption 03/09/1984
Common $1 par split (2) for (1) by issuance of (1) additional share 05/23/1986
Merged into Viacom Inc. (Old) 06/09/1987
Each share Common $1 par exchanged for (0.30097) share 15.50% Exchangeable Preferred 1¢ par, (0.2) share Common 1¢ par and $43.20 cash
(See Viacom Inc. (Old))

VIAD CORP (DE)
$4.75 Preferred $100 par called for redemption at $101 plus $1.1875 accrued dividends on 07/16/2004 (Additional Information in Active)

VIADOR INC (DE)
Merged into MASBC, Inc. 3/19/2003
Each share Common $0.001 par exchanged for $0.075 cash

VIADUCT CORP (UT)
Name changed to Scilife, Inc. 04/02/1987
(See Scilife, Inc.)

VIADUX HEALTH INC (NV)
Name changed to Solos Endoscopy, Inc. 3/14/2006

VIAG AKTIENGESELLSCHAFT (GERMANY)
ADR agreement terminated 4/2/99
Each Sponsored ADR for Bearer Shares exchanged for $153.545 cash

VIAGENE INC (DE)
Merged into Chiron Corp. 9/19/95
Each share Common $0.001 par exchanged for $9 cash

VIAGRAFIX CORP (DE)
Issue Information - 2,200,000 shares COM offered at $13 per share on 03/04/1998
Merged into Learn2.com Inc. 08/23/1999
Each share Common 1¢ par exchanged for (1.846) shares Common 1¢ par
Learn2.com Inc. merged into Learn2 Corp. 09/26/2001 which name changed to LTWC Corp. 09/06/2002
(See LTWC Corp.)

VIALINK CO (DE)
Reincorporated 11/16/1999
State of incorporation changed from (OK) to (DE) 11/16/1999
Common $0.001 par split (2) for (1) by issuance of (1) additional share payable 12/20/1999 to holders of record 12/15/1999
Stock Dividend - 100% payable 03/27/2000 to holders of record 03/17/2000
Recapitalized as Prescient Applied Intelligence, Inc. 01/03/2005
Each share Common $0.001 par exchanged for (0.05) share Common $0.001 par
(See Prescient Applied Intelligence, Inc.)

VIALOG CORP (MA)
Merged into Genesys S.A. 04/25/2001
Each share Common 1¢ par exchanged for (0.6703) Sponsored ADR for Ordinary
(See Genesys S.A.)

VIALTA INC (DE)
Class A Common $0.001 par reclassified as Common $0.001 par 7/1/2002
Class B Common $0.001 par

reclassified as Common $0.001 par 7/1/2002
Merged into Victory Acquisition Corp. 10/7/2005
Each share Common $0.001 par exchanged for $0.36 cash

VIANET TECHNOLOGIES INC (DE)
Reincorporated 06/02/2000
State of incorporation changed from (NV) to (DE) 06/02/2000
SEC revoked common stock registration 11/18/2005

VIANET TECHNOLOGY GROUP LTD (DE)
Name changed to Oncology Med, Inc. 04/12/2007
Oncology Med, Inc. recapitalized as Bellatora Inc. 09/28/2016

VIANET TECHNOLOGY GROUP LTD (DE)
Name changed to Tradestream Global Corp. 07/27/2005
Tradestream Global Corp. recapitalized as Empire Global Corp. 09/30/2005 which name changed to Newgioco Group, Inc. 02/16/2017

VIANOR MALARTIC MINES LTD. (ON)
Charter cancelled for failure to pay taxes and file returns 11/8/77

VIANT CORP (DE)
Issue Information - 3,000,000 shares COM offered at $16 per share on 06/17/1999
Common $0.001 par split (2) for (1) by issuance of (1) additional share payable 2/23/2000 to holders of record 2/8/2000
Acquired by divine, Inc. 9/30/2002
Each share Common $0.001 par exchanged for (0.0725) share Class A Common $0.001 par
(See divine, inc.)

VIAPAY LTD (NV)
SEC revoked common stock registration 10/15/2009

VIASOFT INC (DE)
Issue Information - 2,500,000 shares COM offered at $8 per share on 03/01/1995
Merged into Allen Systems Group, Inc. 8/31/2000
Each share Common $0.001 par exchanged for $8.40 cash

VIASOURCE COMMUNICATIONS INC (NJ)
Issue Information - 5,000,000 shares COM offered at $8 per share on 08/18/2000
Plan of reorganization under Chapter 11 Federal Bankruptcy proceedings confirmed 09/02/2003
No stockholders' equity

VIASTAR MEDIA CORP (NV)
Name changed 01/23/2004
Each share old Common $0.001 par exchanged for (0.1) share new Common $0.001 par 07/22/2001
Name changed from ViaStar Holdings, Inc. to ViaStar Media Corp. 01/23/2004
Name changed to Pop3 Media Corp. 01/21/2005
(See Pop3 Media Corp.)

VIASYS HEALTHCARE INC (DE)
Each (1.5384615) share old Common 1¢ par exchanged for (1) share new Common 1¢ par 10/19/2001
Merged into Cardinal Health, Inc. 06/28/2007
Each share new Common 1¢ par exchanged for $42.75 cash

VIASYSTEMS GROUP INC (DE)
Plan of reorganization under Chapter 11 Federal Bankruptcy Code effective 01/31/2003
No old Common stockholders' equity
Each share new Common 1¢ par exchanged for (0.083647) share new Common 1¢ par 02/16/2010
Merged into TTM Technologies, Inc. 05/31/2015
Each share new Common 1¢ par exchanged for (0.706) share Common $0.001 par and $11.33 cash

VIATECH COMMUNICATIONS GROUP INC (DE)
SEC revoked common stock registration 11/09/2009

VIATECH CORP (NV)
Name changed to Gray Fox Petroleum Corp. 06/20/2013
Gray Fox Petroleum Corp. name changed to Grey Fox Holdings Corp. 06/23/2016

VIATECH INC (DE)
Common 25¢ par split (2) for (1) by issuance of (1) additional share 10/30/1987
Name changed to Continental Can Co., Inc. 10/21/1992
Continental Can Co., Inc. merged into Suiza Foods Corp. 05/29/1998 which name changed to Dean Foods Co. (New) 12/21/2001

VIATEL FING TR I (DE)
Plan of reorganization under Chapter 11 Federal Bankruptcy Code effective 6/7/2002
Each share 7.75% Conv. Trust Preferred received approximately (0.2) share Vitel Holding (Bermuda) Ltd. Common U.S.$0.01 par in June 2003
Each share 7.75% 144A Conv. Trust Preferred received approximately (0.2) share Vitel Holding (Bermuda) Ltd. Common U.S.$0.01 par in June 2003
Each share 7.75% Conv. Trust Preferred received an additional distribution of (0.02985) share Common U.S.$0.01 par 4/30/2004
Each share 7.75% 144A Conv. Trust Preferred received an additional distribution of (0.02985) share Common U.S.$0.01 par 4/30/2004

VIATEL HLDG BERMUDA LTD (BERMUDA)
Each share Common 1¢ par exchanged for (0.00333333) share Common $3 par 04/09/2008
Note: Holders of (299) or fewer pre-split shares received $0.44 cash per share
Acquired by Digiweb Holdings Ltd. 06/06/2013
Each share Common $3 par exchanged for $1 cash

VIATEL INC (DE)
Issue Information - 8,667,000 shares COM offered at $12 per share on 10/17/1996
Plan of reorganization under Chapter 11 Federal Bankruptcy Code effective 06/07/2002
No stockholders' equity

VIATRON COMPUTER SYS CORP (MA)
Reorganized under Chapter X Bankruptcy proceedings 10/27/1977
No stockholders' equity

VIAU BISCUIT CORP. LTD.
Reorganized as Viau Ltd. 00/00/1936
Each share 1st Preferred received distribution of (2) shares Common no par
Each share 2nd Preferred exchanged for (5) shares Common no par
Each (10) shares Common exchanged for (1) share new Common no par
(See Viau Ltd.)

VIAU LTD (QC)
Each share Common no par exchanged for (4) shares Common $2.40 par 3/30/60
90% of 1% Preferred and 99% of Common held by Grissol Foods Ltd. as of 5/22/73
Public interest eliminated

VIB CORP (CA)
Common no par split (5) for (4) by issuance of (0.25) additional share payable 6/12/98 to holders of record 5/29/98
Stock Dividends - 3% payable 12/12/98 to holders of record 11/20/98; 3% payable 6/4/99 to holders of record 5/14/99; 3% payable 12/29/99 to holders of record 12/8/99; 3% payable 6/9/2000 to holders of record 5/26/2000; 3% payable 1/17/2001 to holders of record 12/29/2000
Ex date - 12/27/2000; 3% payable 6/15/2001 to holders of record 5/25/2001; 3% payable 1/14/2002 to holders of record 12/26/2001
Ex date - 12/21/2001; 3% payable 6/14/2002 to holders of record 5/24/2002 Ex date - 5/22/2002
Merged into Rabobank Netherland 12/27/2002
Each share Common no par exchanged for $15.10 cash

VIBE I INC (NV)
Name changed to Coresource Strategies, Inc. (NV) and Common $0.0001 par changed to $0.001 par 10/26/2015
Coresource Strategies, Inc. (NV) reincorporated in Oklahoma as NUGL, Inc. 12/11/2017

VIBE RECORDS INC (NV)
Name changed to Great Entertainment & Sports Inc. 03/07/2003
Great Entertainment & Sports Inc. name changed to Rockit!, Inc. 06/11/2007
(See Rockit!, Inc.)

VIBE WIRELESS CORP (NV)
Name changed to Green Vision Biotechnology Corp. 10/24/2016

VIBRA SPA PRODS INC (NY)
Charter cancelled and proclaimed dissolved for failure to pay taxes 06/27/1979

VIBRATION MOUNTINGS & CTLS INC (NY)
Merged into Aeroflex Laboratories Inc. 3/7/84
Each share Common 10¢ par exchanged for $25 cash

VIBROSAUN INTL INC (NV)
Each share old Common $0.001 par exchanged for (0.004) share new Common $0.001 par 03/06/1997
Name changed to Cleopatra International Group, Inc. 02/04/2011

VICAN RES INC (NV)
Each share old Common $0.001 par exchanged for (0.001) share new Common $0.001 par 03/08/2017
Name changed to Frelii, Inc. 03/09/2018

VICANA RIDGE RES INC (AB)
Acquired by Startech Energy Inc. 09/28/1995
Each share Common no par exchanged for $0.37 cash

VICEROY EXPL LTD (BC)
Acquired by Yamana Gold Inc. 10/31/2006
Each share Common no par exchanged for (0.97) share Common no par

VICEROY HOMES LTD (ON)
Acquired by Joint Stock Company Open Investments 02/28/2008
Each share Class A Subordinate no par exchanged for $5 cash

VICEROY PETES LTD (BC)
Merged into Viceroy Resource Corp. 04/06/1984
Each share Common no par exchanged for (1) share Common no par
Viceroy Resource Corp. merged into Quest Capital Corp. (BC) 06/30/2003 which reincorporated in Canada 05/27/2008 which name changed to Sprott Resource Lending Corp. 09/10/2010 which merged into Sprott Inc. 07/24/2013

VICEROY RESOURCE CORP (BC)
Each share Common no par received distribution of (0.1) share Viceroy Exploration Ltd. Common no par and (0.03333333) share SpectrumGold Inc. Common no par payable 06/30/2003 to holders of record 05/13/2003
Note: Holders entitled to fewer than (500) shares of either distribution and non-electing holders received $0.50 cash per Viceroy share and $0.25 cash per SpectrumGold share
No payment of less than $10 cash will be made
Merged into Quest Capital Corp. (BC) 06/30/2003
Each share Common no par exchanged for (0.33333333) share Class A Subordinate no par
Note: Non-electing holders and holders of (299) shares or fewer received $0.36-2/3 cash per share
No payment of less than $10 cash will be made
Quest Capital Corp. (BC) reincorporated in Canada 05/27/2008 which name changed to Sprott Resource Lending Corp. 09/10/2010 which merged into Sprott Inc. 07/24/2013

VICEROY VENTURES LTD (CO)
Name changed to DMI, Inc. 11/25/87
DMI, Inc. recapitalized as Dega Technology Inc. 12/26/97

VICINITY CORP (DE)
Merged into Microsoft Corp. 12/12/2002
Each share Common $0.001 par exchanged for $3.33 cash

VICK CHEMICAL, INC.
Name changed to Vick Chemical Co. 00/00/1936
Vick Chemical Co. name changed to Richardson-Merrell Inc. 10/21/1960 which merged into Dow Chemical Co. 03/10/1981 which merged into DowDuPont Inc. 09/01/2017

VICK CHEMICAL CO. (DE)
Each share Capital Stock $5 par exchanged for (2) shares Capital Stock $2.50 par 00/00/1946
Capital Stock $2.50 par split (5) for (4) by issuance of (0.25) additional share 10/22/1957
Capital Stock $2.50 par changed to $1.25 par and (1) additional share issued 11/09/1959
Name changed to Richardson-Merrell Inc. and (0.33333333) additional share issued 10/21/1960
Richardson-Merrell Inc. merged into Dow Chemical Co. 03/10/1981 which merged into DowDuPont Inc. 09/01/2017

VICK FINANCIAL CORP.
Reorganized as Reinsurance Corp. of New York on a share for share basis in 1936
Reinsurance Corp. of New York acquired by Piedmont Management Co. Inc. 7/11/68 which merged into Chartwell RE Corp. 12/13/95 which merged into Trenwick Group Inc. 10/27/99 which merged into Trenwick Group Ltd. 9/27/2000
(See Trenwick Group Ltd.)

VICKERS CDA INC (CANADA)
Acquired by Canvick Industries Inc. 01/12/1979
Each share Common no par

exchanged for $50 cash

VICKERS-CROW MINES, INC. (DE)
Charter revoked for non-payment of taxes 4/1/63

VICKERS PLC (UNITED KINGDOM)
Each old ADR for Ordinary exchanged for (1) new ADR for Ordinary 7/6/98
Acquired by Rolls-Royce PLC 11/18/99
Each new ADR for Ordinary exchanged for $3.161 cash

VICKSBURG SHREVEPORT & PAC RY CO (LA)
Merged into Illinois Central Railroad Co. 05/29/1959
Each share Common exchanged for (2.474) shares Common no par
Illinois Central Railroad Co. merged into Illinois Central Industries, Inc. 08/10/1972 which name changed to IC Industries, Inc. 05/21/1975 which name changed to Whitman Corp. (Old) 12/01/1988 which name changed to Whitman Corp. (New) 11/30/2000 which name changed to PepsiAmericas, Inc. (DE) 01/24/2001 which merged into PepsiCo, Inc. 02/26/2010

VICO CORP (DE)
Liquidation completed
Each share Common $1 par received initial distribution of $3 cash 02/15/1978
Each share Common $1 par exchanged for second and final distribution of $1.12 cash 01/02/1979

VICO EXPLORATIONS LTD. (ON)
Charter cancelled 12/12/60

VICOM INC (MN)
Common no par split (5) for (4) by issuance of (0.25) additional share 01/15/1985
Name changed to Multiband Corp. 07/16/2004
(See Multiband Corp.)

VICOM MULTIMEDIA INC (AB)
Recapitalized as Brooklyn Energy Corp. 1/14/2002
Each share Common no par exchanged for (0.2) share Common no par
(See Brooklyn Energy Corp.)

VICON FIBER OPTICS CORP (DE)
Common 10¢ par split (2) for (1) by issuance of (1) additional share 05/18/1981
Charter cancelled and declared inoperative and void for non-payment of taxes 03/01/2004

VICON INC. (CO)
Liquidation completed
Each share Common $1 par exchanged for initial distribution of $0.08 cash and (1) Ctf. of Bene. Int. 9/16/63
Each Ctf. of Bene. Int. received second distribution of $0.04 cash 7/24/64
Each Ctf. of Bene. Int. received third distribution of $0.06 cash 9/15/64
Each Ctf. of Bene. Int. received fourth distribution of $0.10 cash 12/15/64
Each Ctf. of Bene. Int. received fifth distribution of $0.06 cash 3/15/65
Each Ctf. of Bene. Int. received sixth distribution of $0.08 cash 6/15/65
Each Ctf. of Bene. Int. received seventh distribution of $0.07 cash 9/15/65
Each Ctf. of Bene. Int. received eighth distribution of $0.08 cash 12/15/65
Each Ctf. of Bene. Int. received ninth distribution of $0.07 cash 3/25/66
Each Ctf. of Bene. Int. received tenth distribution of $0.12 cash 10/21/66
Each Ctf. of Bene. Int. received eleventh distribution of $0.05 cash 1/20/67
Each Ctf. of Bene. Int. received twelfth distribution of $0.09 cash 10/9/67
Each Ctf. of Bene. Int. received thirteenth distribution of $0.30 cash 1/20/69
Each Ctf. of Bene Int. received fourteenth distribution of $0.06 cash 2/12/71
Each Ctf. of Bene. Int. received fifteenth distribution of $0.20 cash 5/24/71
Each Ctf. of Bene. Int. received sixteenth distribution of $0.35 cash 11/30/71
Each Ctf. of Bene. Int. received seventeenth distribution of $0.65 cash 1/31/72
Each Ctf. of Bene. Int. received eighteenth and final distribution of $0.192 cash 7/5/72
Note: Certificates were not required to be surrendered and are without value

VICON PRODS CORP (DE)
Common 10¢ par split (3) for (2) by issuance of (0.5) additional share 03/26/1980
Name changed to Vicon Fiber Optics Corp. 04/24/1981
(See Vicon Fiber Optics Corp.)

VICOR INC (CA)
Adjudicated bankrupt 07/11/1974
Stockholders' equity unlikely

VICOR RES LTD (BC)
Merged into Tay River Petroleum Ltd. 01/30/1981
Each share Common no par exchanged for (1) share Common 50¢ par
Tay River Petroleum Ltd. name changed to Butec International Chemical Corp. 11/27/1985 which recapitalized as International Butec Industries Corp. 05/05/1988 which recapitalized as WebSmart.com Communications, Inc. 10/17/2000 which name changed to Gold Reach Resources Ltd. 10/13/2004 which name changed to Surge Copper Corp. 02/21/2018

VICOR TECHNOLOGIES INC (DE)
Chapter 7 bankruptcy proceedings terminated 04/18/2018
No stockholders' equity

VICORP RESTAURANTS INC (CO)
Each share Conv. Preferred Ser. A 10¢ par exchanged for (1.13636) shares Common 5¢ par 7/16/91
Common 5¢ par split (2) for (1) by issuance of (1) additional share 8/26/83
Merged into Midway Investors 5/14/2001
Each share Common 5¢ par exchanged for $25.65 cash

VICOUR MINES LTD. (ON)
Recapitalized as Vico Explorations Ltd. on a (0.2) for (1) basis 4/13/56
(See Vico Explorations Ltd.)

VICTHOM HUMAN BIONICS INC (CANADA)
Each share old Common no par exchanged for (0.1) share new Common no par 06/23/2009
Acquired by Ergoresearch Ltd. 04/29/2013
Each share new Common no par exchanged for $0.08 cash

VICTOR ADDING MACHINE CO. (IL)
Each share Common $5 par exchanged for (5) shares Common $1 par and 300% stock dividend paid in 1949
Merged into Victor Comptometer Corp. 10/30/61
Preferred exchanged share for share
Each share Common $1 par exchanged for (3.6) shares Common $1 par
Victor Comptometer Corp. merged into Kidde (Walter) & Co., Inc. (DE) 7/15/77 which name changed to Kidde, Inc. 4/18/80 which merged into Hanson p.l.c. 12/31/87 which name changed to Hanson PLC (Old) 1/29/88 which reorganized as Hanson PLC (New) 10/15/2003

VICTOR AMERN FUEL CO (ME)
Administratively dissolved for failure to file annual reports 10/25/2005

VICTOR BREWING CO. (PA)
Assets acquired by Fort Pitt Brewing Co. 00/00/1941
Details not available

VICTOR CAP CORP (CO)
Each (16.5) shares old Common $0.0001 par exchanged for (1) share new Common $0.0001 par 3/27/92
Name changed to Haas Neveux & Co. 6/11/92
Haas Neveux & Co. recapitalized as Century Milestone S & T Co. Ltd. 7/24/2000 which recapitalized as Sino Real Property Development Corp. 10/21/2003

VICTOR CHEMICAL WORKS (IL)
Each share Common no par exchanged for (4) shares Common $5 par in 1937
Stock Dividend - 100% 6/20/51
Merged into Stauffer Chemical Co. 10/30/59
Each share 3-1/2% Preferred $100 par exchanged for (1) share new 3-1/2% Preferred $100 par
Each share Common $5 par exchanged for (1) share new Common $5 par
(See Stauffer Chemical Co.)

VICTOR CO JAPAN LTD (JAPAN)
Stock Dividend - 10% 06/14/1984
Merged into JVC Kenwood Holdings, Inc. 10/01/2008
Each ADR for Common 50 Yen par exchanged for $1.8948 cash
Note: Due to ADR's being unsponsored exchange rate may vary dependent upon depositary agent

VICTOR COMPTOMETER CORP (IL)
Merged into Kidde (Walter) & Co., Inc. (DE) 7/15/77
Each share $4 Conv. Preferred Ser. A $1 par exchanged for (1) share $4 Conv. Preference Ser. C $1 par
Each share Common $1 par exchanged for (0.5) share $1.64 Conv. Preference Ser. D $1 par
Kidde (Walter) & Co., Inc. (DE) name changed to Kidde, Inc. 4/18/80 which merged into Hanson Trust p.l.c. 12/31/87 which name changed to Hanson PLC (Old) 1/29/88 which reorganized as Hanson PLC (New) 10/15/2003

VICTOR CONS MNG CO (UT)
Merged into North Lily Mining Co. 12/1/76
Each share Capital Stock 50¢ par exchanged for (0.002) share Capital Stock 10¢ par
(See North Lily Mining Co.)

VICTOR EBNER ENTERPRISES INC (FL)
Proclaimed dissolved for failure to file reports and pay fees 09/16/2005

VICTOR EQUIP CO (DE)
Each share $1.50 Preferred no par exchanged for (1) share $1 Conv. Preferred $5 par and dividend of 25% in same Preferred paid 00/00/1935
Capital Stock no par changed to $1 par 00/00/1936
$1 Conv. Preferred $5 par called for redemption 07/31/1946
Capital Stock $1 par split (2) for (1) by issuance of (1) additional share 09/11/1967
Stock Dividend - 100% 02/10/1969
Merged into Pacific Lumber Co. 03/16/1970
Each share Capital Stock $1 par exchanged for (0.5) share Capital Stock $3-1/3 par
(See Pacific Lumber Co.)

VICTOR GRAPHIC SYS INC (NY)
Liquidation completed
Each share Common 10¢ par exchanged for initial distribution of $1.43 cash 08/31/1976
Each share Common 10¢ par received second and final distribution of $0.16888575 cash 11/04/1976

VICTOR INDS INC (ID)
Common 5¢ par changed to $0.0001 par 04/15/2002
Reorganized under the laws of Nevada as Ethos Environmental, Inc. 11/16/2006
Each share Common $0.0001 par exchanged for (0.00083333) share Common $0.0001 par
Ethos Environmental, Inc. name changed to Regeneca, Inc. 06/14/2011
(See Regeneca, Inc.)

VICTOR INSULATORS, INC. (NY)
Acquired by I-T-E Circuit Breaker Co. on a (0.7) for (1) basis in 1954
I-T-E Circuit Breaker Co. merged into I-T-E Imperial Corp. 4/30/68
(See I-T-E Imperial Corp.)

VICTOR-MONAGHAN CO.
Merged into Stevens (J.P.) & Co., Inc. in 1946
Each share Common $100 par exchanged for (10.17759) shares new Capital Stock $15 par
(See Stevens (J.P.) & Co., Inc.)

VICTOR OIL CO.
Assets sold in 1940
In process of liquidation

VICTOR PAGE MOTORS CORP. (DE)
No longer in existence having become inoperative and void for non-payment of taxes 4/1/28

VICTOR PAINT CO. (MI)
Merged into Carter (Mary) Paint Co. 4/9/62
Each share Common $1 par exchanged for (0.625) share Class A Common $1 par
Carter (Mary) Paint Co. name changed to Resorts International, Inc. 6/28/68
(See Resorts International, Inc.)

VICTOR PETROLEUMS LTD. (ON)
Name changed to Jodee Explorations Ltd. in 1955
Jodee Explorations Ltd. charter cancelled in August 1972

VICTOR PRODS CORP (DE)
Reincorporated 11/22/1971
Class A Common no par and Class B Common no par reclassified as Capital Stock $5 par 00/00/1940
Each share Capital Stock $5 par exchanged for (5) shares Capital Stock $1 par 00/00/1947
Stock Dividends - 20% 07/01/1953; 10% 01/12/1954
State of incorporation changed from (MD) to (DE) 11/22/1971
Name changed to Reed Industries, Inc. (Old) 08/07/1972
Reed Industries, Inc. (Old) merged into Reed Industries, Inc. (New) 09/30/1974
(See Reed Industries, Inc. (New))

VICTOR REITER CORP. (FL)
See - Reiter (Victor) Corp.

VICTOR TALKING MACHINE CO.
Acquired by Radio Corp. of America 00/00/1929
Details not available

VICTOR TECHNOLOGIES INC (DE)
Reorganized under Chapter 11

VIC-VIC

Federal Bankruptcy Code
10/26/1987
Each (16.28) shares Common 10¢
par exchanged for (1) share
Common 1¢ par
Merged into VT Acquisition Inc.
02/06/1991
Each share Common 1¢ par
exchanged for $0.33 cash

VICTOR VALUE HLDGS LTD (ENGLAND)
Acquired by Tesco Stores (Holdings) Ltd. 11/08/1968
Each ADR for A Ordinary Reg. 1s par exchanged for (0.33333333) ADR for Ordinary Reg. 1s par
Tesco Stores (Holdings) PLC name changed to Tesco PLC 07/29/1983

VICTOR WELDING EQUIPMENT CO.
Merged into Victor Equipment Co.
00/00/1931
Details not available

VICTOREEN INC (OH)
Under plan of merger name changed to Victoreen Leece Neville, Inc. 02/01/1969
Victoreen Leece Neville, Inc. name changed to VLN Corp. 04/29/1970 which merged into Sheller-Globe Corp. 09/30/1974
(See Sheller-Globe Corp.)

VICTOREEN INSTRUMENT CO. (OH)
Stock Dividend - 25% 6/16/59
Name changed to Victoreen Inc. 5/5/67
Victoreen Inc. name changed to Victoreen Leece Neville, Inc. 2/1/69 which name changed to VLN Corp. 4/29/70 which merged into Sheller-Globe Corp. 9/30/74
(See Sheller-Globe Corp.)

VICTOREEN LEECE NEVILLE INC (OH)
Name changed to VLN Corp. 04/29/1970
VLN Corp. merged into Sheller-Globe Corp. 09/30/1974
(See Sheller-Globe Corp.)

VICTORIA, INC.
Liquidation completed in 1944

VICTORIA & GREY TRUST CO. (LINDSAY, ONT)
Each share Capital Stock $10 par exchanged for (5) shares Capital Stock $2 par 03/21/1963
Under plan of merger each share Capital Stock $2 par exchanged for (1) share Common $2 par 09/30/1965
Common $2 par changed to $1 par and (1) additional share issued 02/21/1972
Common $1 par reclassified as Conv. Class A Common $1 par 02/28/1977
Name changed to Victoria & Grey Trust Co./La Compagnie de Fiducie Victoria et Grey (Lindsay, ONT) 10/31/1978
Victoria & Grey Trust Co./La Compagnie de Fiducie Victoria et Grey (Lindsay, ONT) merged into Victoria Grey Metro Trust Co. (Stratford, ONT) 10/31/1979 which name changed to Victoria & Grey Trust Co. (Stratford, ONT) 04/07/1980 which merged into National Victoria & Grey Trust Co. (Toronto, ONT) 08/31/1984 which name changed to National Trust Co. (Toronto, ONT) 10/28/1985
(See National Trust Co. (Toronto, ONT))

VICTORIA & GREY TR CO (LINDSAY, ONT)
Conv. Class A Common $1 par changed to no par and (1) additional share issued 11/21/1978
Conv. Class B Common $1 par changed to no par and (1) additional share issued 11/21/1978
Merged into Victoria Grey Metro Trust Co. (Stratford, ONT) 10/31/1979
Each share 5.35% Preference Ser. A $50 par exchanged for (1) share 5.35% Preference Ser. A $50 par
Each share Conv. Class A Common no par exchanged for (1) share Common $3 par
Each share Conv. Class B Common no par exchanged for (1) share Common $3 par
Victoria Grey Metro Trust Co. (Stratford, ONT) name changed to Victoria & Grey Trust Co. (Stratford, ONT) 04/07/1980 which merged into National Victoria & Grey Trust Co. (Toronto, ONT) 08/31/1984 which name changed to National Trust Co. (Toronto, ONT) 10/28/1985
(See National Trust Co. (Toronto, ONT))

VICTORIA & GREY TR CO (STRATFORD, ONT)
Merged into National Victoria & Grey Trust Co. (Toronto, ONT) 08/31/1984
Each share 5.35% Preference Ser. A $50 par exchanged for (1) share 5.35% Preference Ser. A $50 par
Each share Common $3 par exchanged for (1) share Common no par
National Victoria & Grey Trust Co. (Toronto, ONT) name changed to National Trust Co. (Toronto, ONT) 10/28/1985
(See National Trust Co. (Toronto, ONT))

VICTORIA & GREY TRUSTCO LTD (ON)
Name changed to National Victoria & Grey Trustco Ltd. 08/31/1984
National Victoria & Grey Trustco Ltd. name changed to National Trustco Inc.- Trustco National Inc. 03/22/1989 which merged into Bank of Nova Scotia (Halifax, NS) 08/15/1997

VICTORIA ALGOMA MINERAL LTD (ON)
Charter cancelled for failure to pay taxes and file returns 03/16/1976

VICTORIA BK & TR CO (VICTORIA, TX)
Each share Capital Stock $20 par exchanged for (2.2) shares Capital Stock $10 par to effect a (2) for (1) split and a 10% stock dividend 12/10/1963
Stock Dividends - 75% 09/01/1945; 100% 01/10/1950; 30% 01/20/1956; 25% 01/01/1959; 16-2/3% 02/15/1971
Reorganized as Victoria Bankshares, Inc. 04/01/1974
Each share Capital Stock $10 par exchanged for (2) shares Common $10 par
Victoria Bankshares, Inc. merged into Norwest Corp. 04/11/1996 which name changed to Wells Fargo & Co. (New) 11/02/1998

VICTORIA BANKSHARES INC (TX)
Common $10 par changed to $1 par 09/13/1994
Stock Dividends - 20% 12/29/1978; 25% 02/07/1979; 10% 02/02/1981; 20% 12/18/1981
Merged into Norwest Corp. 04/11/1996
Each share Common $1 par exchanged for (1.05) shares Common $1-2/3 par
Norwest Corp. name changed to Wells Fargo & Co. (New) 11/02/1998

VICTORIA BONDHOLDERS CORP. (NY)
Liquidation completed
Each share Common no par exchanged for initial distribution of $1,570 cash 2/5/63
Each share Common no par received second distribution of $574.28 cash 12/31/63
Each share Common no par received third distribution of $106.93 cash 1/17/64
Each share Common no par received fourth and final distribution of $35.65 cash 6/20/66

VICTORIA COPPER MINING CO.
Liquidation completed in 1933

VICTORIA CREATIONS INC (RI)
Name changed to Reunited Holdings Inc. 07/01/1996
(See Reunited Holdings Inc.)

VICTORIA DIEGO RES CORP (BC)
Struck off register and declared dissolved for failure to file returns 8/14/92

VICTORIA EXPL N L (AUSTRALIA)
Name changed to Victoria Petroleum N.L. 02/09/1989
Victoria Petroleum N.L. name changed to Senex Energy Ltd. 05/07/2012

VICTORIA FINL CORP (DE)
Each share old Common 1¢ par exchanged for (0.4) share new Common 1¢ par 07/30/1993
Merged into USF&G Corp. 05/22/1995
Each share new Common 1¢ par exchanged for (0.91572) share Common $2.50 par
USF&G Corp. merged into St. Paul Companies, Inc. 04/24/1998 which name changed to St. Paul Travelers Companies, Inc. 04/01/2004 which name changed to Travelers Companies, Inc. 02/27/2007

VICTORIA GREY METRO TR CO (STRATFORD, ON)
Name changed to Victoria & Grey Trust Co. (Stratford, ON) 04/07/1980
Victoria & Grey Trust Co. (Stratford, ON) merged into National Victoria & Grey Trust Co. (Toronto, ON) 08/31/1984 which name changed to National Trust Co. (Toronto, ON) 10/28/1985
(See National Trust Co. (Toronto, ON))

VICTORIA GYPSUM CO., LTD. (NS)
Common no par changed to $1 par in 1952
Name changed to Victoria Investment Co. Ltd. 6/21/55

VICTORIA INDS INC (NV)
Name changed to Motor Sport Country Club Holdings, Inc. 10/21/2010

VICTORIA INTERNET SVCS INC (NV)
Common $0.0000001 par split (50) for (1) by issuance of (49) additional shares payable 01/11/2012 to holders of record 11/14/2011
Ex date - 01/12/2012
Name changed to Earn-A-Car Inc. 03/09/2012

VICTORIA INVT LTD (NS)
7% Preference $100 par called for redemption 7/29/60
5-1/2% Preferred $10 par called for redemption 12/3/68
(Additional Information in Active)

VICTORIA LAND & MINERALS LTD. (AB)
Completely liquidated 07/22/1966
Each share Capital Stock $1 par exchanged for first and final distribution of (2) shares Plains Petroleums Ltd. Common no par
(See Plains Petroleums Ltd.)

VICTORIA NATIONAL BANK (VICTORIA, TX)
Each share Capital Stock $100 par exchanged for (5) shares Capital Stock $20 par in 1952
Stock Dividend - 100% 7/5/55
Name changed to First Victoria National Bank (Old) (Victoria, TX) 3/1/63
First Victoria National Bank (Old) (Victoria, TX) reorganized as First Victoria Corp. 5/31/85 which merged into First Victoria National Bank (New) (Victoria, TX) 6/17/91 which reorganized as FVNB Corp. 9/17/98
(See FVNB Corp.)

VICTORIA OIL CO. (WV)
Dissolved for non-payment of corporate taxes 6/3/27

VICTORIA PETE N L (AUSTRALIA)
Each Unsponsored ADR for Ordinary AUD $0.20 par exchanged for (0.05) Sponsored ADR for Ordinary AUD $0.20 par 07/27/1990
Each old Sponsored ADR for Ordinary exchanged for (0.1) new Sponsored ADR for Ordinary 12/14/2006
Name changed to Senex Energy Ltd. 05/07/2012

VICTORIA RESOURCE CORP (BC)
Name changed to Victoria Gold Corp. 08/06/2008

VICTORIA STA ACQUISITION CORP (DE)
Charter cancelled and declared inoperative and void for non-payment of taxes 03/01/1990

VICTORIA STA INC (DE)
Reincorporated 10/16/1976
State of incorporation changed from (CA) to (DE) 10/16/1976
Reorganized under Chapter 11 Federal Bankruptcy Code as Victoria Station Acquisition Corp. 12/03/1987
Each share Common no par exchanged for (0.22) share Common 1¢ par
(See Victoria Station Acquisition Corp.)

VICTORIA WOOD DEV INC (ON)
7-1/2% Sr. Preference A $10 par called for redemption 07/09/1973
Public interest eliminated

VICTORIA WOOD DEV LTD (ON)
Merged into Victoria Wood Development Corp. Inc. 12/20/1971
Each share 7-1/2% Sr. Preference Ser. A $10 par exchanged for (1) share 7-1/2% Sr. Preference Ser. A $10 par
Each share Common no par exchanged for (5) shares Jr. Preference $2.50 par
(See Victoria Wood Development Corp. Inc.)

VICTORIAN ENURETIC SVCS LTD (BC)
Dissolved and struck from the register 8/22/94

VICTORMAXX TECHNOLOGIES INC (IL)
Name changed to SHC Corp. 09/18/2000
(See SHC Corp.)

VICTORS L G GOLD & CO INC (AZ)
Name changed to First Great Western Investment Corp. 6/5/73
First Great Western Investment Corp. name changed to Miller Medical Electronics, Inc. 8/19/76
(See Miller Medical Electronics, Inc.)

VICTORY ACQUISITION CORP (DE)
Issue Information - 30,000,000 UNITS consisting of (1) share COM and (1) WT offered at $10 per Unit on 04/24/2007
Completely liquidated 04/30/2009
Each Unit exchanged for first and final distribution of $10 cash
Each share Common $0.0001 par exchanged for first and final distribution of $10 cash

VICTORY BANCSHARES INC (TN)
Merged into Deposit Guaranty Corp. 03/23/1998
Each share Common $1 par

exchanged for (0.90425) share Common no par
Deposit Guaranty Corp. merged into First American Corp. (TN) 05/01/1998 which merged into AmSouth Bancorporation 10/01/1999 which merged into Regions Financial Corp. (New) 11/04/2006

VICTORY CAP HLDGS CORP (NV)
Name changed to Victory Energy Corp. 05/11/2006
Victory Energy Corp. name changed to Victory Oilfield Tech, Inc. 05/31/2018

VICTORY DEV CORP (NV)
Name changed to Seven Ventures, Inc. 09/14/1988
Seven Ventures, Inc. name changed to FastFunds Financial Corp. 07/08/2004

VICTORY DIVIDE MNG CO (NV)
Each share old Common $0.001 par exchanged for (0.000005) share new Common $0.001 par 04/24/2007
New Common $0.001 par split (100) for (1) by issuance of (99) additional shares payable 09/14/2007 to holders of record 09/04/2007
Ex date - 09/17/2007
Name changed to Yanglin Soybean, Inc. 01/25/2008

VICTORY ELECTR CIGS CORP (NV)
Name changed to Electronic Cigarettes International Group, Ltd. 07/11/2014

VICTORY ELECTRONICS, INC. (NY)
Adjudicated bankrupt 3/14/66
No stockholders' equity

VICTORY ENERGY CORP (NV)
Each share old Common $0.001 par exchanged for (0.04) share new Common $0.001 par 11/10/2006
New Common $0.001 par split (5) for (4) by issuance of (0.25) additional share payable 07/01/2008 to holders of record 05/02/2008
Each share new Common $0.001 par exchanged again for (0.02) share new Common $0.001 par 01/13/2012
Each share new Common $0.001 par exchanged again for (0.02631578) share new Common $0.001 par 12/19/2017
Name changed to Victory Oilfield Tech, Inc. 05/31/2018

VICTORY GOLD MINES, LTD. (ON)
Charter cancelled and proclaimed dissolved for failure to pay taxes and file returns 7/2/53

VICTORY GOLD MINES, LTD. (QC)
Charter cancelled for failure to file reports 8/12/78

VICTORY GOLD MINES INC (ON)
Merged into Northern Gold Mining Inc. 02/06/2013
Each share Common no par exchanged for (0.5) share Common no par
Northern Gold Mining Inc. merged into Oban Mining Corp. 12/24/2015 which name changed to Osisko Mining Inc. 06/21/2016

VICTORY INSURANCE CO.
Merged into Reliance Insurance Co. of Philadelphia 00/00/1934
Details not available

VICTORY LAKE MINES LTD. (MB)
Charter cancelled and declared dissolved for failure to file returns 3/9/72

VICTORY LG INC (NV)
Name changed to Soul & Vibe Interactive Inc. 10/25/2012

VICTORY LIFE INS CO (KS)
Stock Dividends - 100% 12/15/1964; 100% 05/03/1967; 25% 05/15/1968
Each share Capital Stock $5 par exchanged for (0.01) share Capital Stock $500 par 05/21/1975
Note: In effect holders received $100 cash per share and public interest was eliminated

VICTORY MAJORS INVTS CORP (CANADA)
Acquired by 3925241 Canada Inc. 12/26/2001
Each share Common no par exchanged for $0.15 cash

VICTORY MINES CORP. (WA)
Completely liquidated 4/16/64
Each share Common 10¢ par received (4) shares Kromona Consolidated Mines, Inc. Common 10¢ par and 40¢ cash
Certificates were not required to be surrendered and are now valueless

VICTORY MKTS INC (NY)
Class A and B Common $2 par reclassified as Common $2 par 05/06/1963
Common $2 par changed to $1 par and (1) additional share issued 11/30/1964
Common $1 par changed to 50¢ par and (1) additional share issued 10/08/1965
Common 50¢ par changed to $0.33333333 par and (0.5) additional share issued 06/13/1986
Stock Dividend - 10% 12/16/1985
Merged into LNC Industries Pty. Ltd. 09/22/1986
Each share Common $0.33333333 par exchanged for $24.67 cash

VICTORY OIL SHALE CO. (CO)
Charter dissolved for failure to file annual reports 1/1/26

VICTORY SILVER MINES LTD.
Property sold in 1927

VICTORY ST BK (COLUMBIA, SC)
Name changed 11/18/1997
Name changed from Victory Savings Bank (Columbia, SC) to Victory State Bank (Columbia, SC) 11/18/1997
Placed in receivership with FDIC 03/29/1999
No stockholders' equity

VICTORY ST BK (STATEN ISLAND, NY)
Reorganized as VSB Bancorp, Inc. 5/30/2003
Each share Common $5 par exchanged for (1.5) shares Common $5 par

VICTORY VENTURES INC (BC)
Incorporated 11/08/2009
Name changed to Power Americas Minerals Corp. 02/17/2017
Power Americas Minerals Corp. name changed to Edison Cobalt Corp. 09/05/2018

VICTORY VENTURES INC (BC)
Incorporated 12/12/1977
Name changed to Global Investment.com Financial Inc. 07/28/1999
Global Investment.com Financial Inc. name changed to Global Investment Financial Group Inc. 04/04/2001 which recapitalized as Global Financial Group Inc. 03/04/2002 which name changed to egX Group Inc. 04/17/2007

VICTORY WASTE INC (CA)
Merged into Continental Waste Industries, Inc. 06/00/1995
Each share Common $0.001 par exchanged for (0.02963841) share Common $0.001 par
Continental Waste Industries, Inc. merged into Republic Industries Inc.
12/30/1996 which name changed to AutoNation, Inc. 04/06/1999

VICTORY WASTE INC (CO)
Recapitalized as Econometrics, Inc. (CO) 11/21/1997
Each share Common no par exchanged for (1.6666) shares Common no par
Econometrics, Inc. (CO) reorganized in Delaware 06/20/2008 which name changed to JinZangHuang Tibet Pharmaceuticals, Inc. 02/27/2009
(See JinZangHuang Tibet Pharmaceuticals, Inc.)

VICTORY YARN MILLS
Merged into Textiles, Inc. 00/00/1931
Details not available

VICUNA INC (NV)
Recapitalized as Seair Group, Inc. 5/27/98
Each share Class A Common $0.001 par exchanged for (2) shares Class A Common $0.001 par
Seair Group, Inc. name changed to Gourmet Group, Inc. (NV) 9/18/2000 which reorganized in Delaware as Drinks Americas Holdings, Ltd. 6/2/2005

VICURON PHARMACEUTICALS INC (DE)
Merged into Pfizer Inc. 9/14/2005
Each share Common $0.001 par exchanged for $29.10 cash

VICWEST CORP (ON)
Reorganized as Vicwest Income Fund 07/01/2005
Each share Common no par exchanged for (1) Trust Unit no par
Vicwest Income Fund reorganized as Vicwest Inc. 01/04/2011
(See Vicwest Inc.)

VICWEST INC (ON)
Acquired by Ag Growth International Inc. 05/26/2015
Each share Common no par exchanged for $12.70 cash
Note: Unexchanged certificates will be cancelled and become without value 05/26/2021

VICWEST INCOME FD (ON)
Under plan of reorganization each Trust Unit no par automatically became (1) share Vicwest Inc. Common no par 01/04/2011
(See Vicwest Inc.)

VIDA MED SYS INC (NV)
Recapitalized as Oasis Oil Corp. 10/06/1997
Each (13.2054541) shares Common 5¢ par exchanged for (1) share Common 5¢ par
Oasis Oil Corp. name changed to MVP Network, Inc. 09/07/2005
(See MVP Network, Inc.)

VIDA VENTURES LTD (BC)
Name changed to First Growth Holdings Ltd. 11/25/2013
(See First Growth Holdings Ltd.)

VIDA VENTURES LTD (MN)
Merged into MacGregor Sports & Fitness, Inc. 12/30/1993
Each share Common 1¢ par exchanged for (0.5) share Common 1¢ par
MacGregor Sports & Fitness, Inc. name changed to Intranet Solutions, Inc. 07/31/1996 which name changed to Stellent, Inc. 08/29/2001

VIDABLE INC (NV)
Recapitalized as Vibe I, Inc. 08/03/2015
Each share Common $0.0001 par exchanged (0.0005) share Common $0.0001 par
Vibe I, Inc. name changed to Coresource Strategies, Inc. (NV) 10/26/2015 which reincorporated in Oklahoma as NUGL, Inc. 12/11/2017

VIDAMED INC (DE)
Merged into Medtronic, Inc. 04/15/2002
Each share Common $0.001 par exchanged for $7.91 cash

VIDAR SYSTEMS CORP. (VA)
Charter cancelled and proclaimed dissolved for failure to file reports 9/1/93

VIDATRON ENTMT GROUP INC (BC)
Recapitalized 02/17/1992
Recapitalized 02/05/1997
Recapitalized from Vidatron Enterprises Ltd. to Vidatron Group 02/17/1992
Each share old Common no par exchanged for (0.2) share new Common no par
Recapitalized from Vidatron Group to Vidatron Entertainment Group Inc. 02/05/1997
Each share new Common no par exchanged for (0.25) share Common no par
Recapitalized as Peace Arch Entertainment Group Inc. (BC) 07/19/1999
Each share Common no par exchanged for (0.2) share Class A Multiple no par and (0.2) share Class B Subordinate no par
Peace Arch Entertainment Group Inc. (BC) reincorporated in Ontario 09/01/2004
(See Peace Arch Entertainment Group Inc.)

VIDATRON INDS INC (BC)
Name changed to VTI Industries Inc. 04/03/1987
VTI Industries Inc. recapitalized as Emerald Ventures Inc. (BC) 11/23/1990 which reincorporated in Yukon as Spatializer Audio Laboratories, Inc. 12/27/1991 which reincorporated in Delaware 07/27/1994 which recapitalized as AMERI Holdings, Inc. 05/26/2015

VIDCOM POST INC (NV)
Plan of reorganization under Chapter 11 Federal Bankruptcy Code effective 3/28/94
Each (100) shares Common $0.0001 par exchanged for (1) Unit of TeleLink Corp. consisting of (1) share Common, (1) Common Stock Purchase Warrant, Class A expiring 3/28/96 and (1) Common Stock Purchase Warrant, Class B expiring 3/28/97

VIDEO AD NETWORK INC (CO)
Charter suspended for failure to file annual reports 09/30/1990

VIDEO CITY INC (DE)
Each share old Common 1¢ par exchanged for (0.04249893) share new Common 1¢ par 08/29/2001
Filed a petition under Chapter 7 Federal Bankruptcy Code 03/24/2004
Stockholders' equity unlikely

VIDEO COLOR CORP. (MN)
Name changed to Electro Vision Industries, Inc. 2/20/69

VIDEO COMMUNICATIONS & RADIO INC (CO)
Name changed to First Entertainment Inc. (CO) 06/01/1993
First Entertainment Inc. (CO) reincorporated in Nevada as First Entertainment Holding Corp. 12/15/1997 which name changed to F2 Broadcast Networks Inc. 01/04/2001 which name changed to Strat Petroleum, Ltd. 07/08/2004
(See Strat Petroleum, Ltd.)

VIDEO CONFERENCE TECHNOLOGY GROUP INC (DE)
Charter cancelled and declared inoperative and void for non-payment of taxes 03/01/2000

VIDEO CONNECTION AMER INC (NY)
Dissolved by proclamation 12/23/92

VIDEO CORP. OF AMERICA (DE)
Ctfs. prior to 1953
Name changed to Radar-Electronics, Inc. and each share Common 10¢ par exchanged for (2) shares Common 1¢ par in 1953
Radar-Electronics, Inc. out of business in 1956 and charter cancelled 4/1/58

VIDEO CORP (CA)
Each share old Common no par exchanged for (0.2) share new Common no par 5/16/69
Name changed to Parker Resources, Inc. 9/16/69
Parker Resources, Inc. name changed to Pacific Bancorporation 1/24/72 which merged into ValliCorp Holdings, Inc. 11/15/93 which merged into Westamerica Bancorporation 4/12/97

VIDEO CORP AMER (DE)
Incorporated 10/22/1970
Stock Dividend - 10% 03/02/1979
Acquired by MacAndrews & Forbes Holdings, Inc. 02/13/1985
Each share Common 1¢ par exchanged for $20 cash

VIDEO DELIVERY INC (DE)
Name changed to Global Alternatives Corp. 05/10/1995
Global Alternatives Corp. name changed to Environmental Alternatives Corp. 02/01/1996 which name changed to Healthspan Inc. 03/04/1997 which recapitalized as Riverside Information Technologies, Inc. (DE) 10/10/2006 which reincorporated in Nevada as Clean Coal Technologies, Inc. 10/12/2007

VIDEO ENTERPRISES INC (DE)
Charter cancelled and declared inoperative and void for non-payment of taxes 3/1/83

VIDEO GRAPHICS CORP (UT)
Name changed to Inovion Corp. 10/1/84
(See Inovion Corp.)

VIDEO HEADQUARTERS INC (AB)
Each share old Common no par exchanged for (0.5) share new Common no par 10/2/98
Reincorporated under the laws of Canada as VHQ Entertainment Inc. 12/7/2000
(See VHQ Entertainment Inc.)

VIDEO IMAGE INC (DE)
Name changed to TM Communications, Inc. 10/31/85
TM Communications, Inc. name changed to TM Century, Inc. 10/1/90
(See TM Century, Inc.)

VIDEO INC. (PA)
Bankrupt 2/4/55
Stockholders' equity unlikely

VIDEO INSTR CORP (NY)
Recapitalized as Storybook Village, Inc. 4/2/73
Each share Capital Stock 10¢ par exchanged for (0.5) share Common 1¢ par

VIDEO JUKEBOX NETWORK INC (FL)
Name changed to Box Worldwide, Inc. 02/21/1997
Box Worldwide, Inc. merged into TCI Music, Inc. 12/17/1997 which name changed to Liberty Digital Inc. 09/10/1999 which merged into Liberty Media Corp. (New) 03/14/2002 which reorganized as Liberty Media Corp. (Incorporated 02/28/2006) 05/10/2006 which name changed to Liberty Interactive Corp. 09/26/2011 which name changed to Qurate Retail, Inc. 04/10/2018

VIDEO LEARNING SYS INC (MN)
Merged into Cardia Inc. 10/06/1999
Each share Common no par exchanged for (0.188) share Common 1¢ par

VIDEO LIBR INC (CA)
Merged into Blockbuster Entertainment Corp. 5/4/88
Each share Common no par exchanged for $4.75 cash

VIDEO LOTTERY TECHNOLOGIES INC (DE)
Name changed to Powerhouse Technologies, Inc. 01/01/1998
(See Powerhouse Technologies, Inc.)

VIDEO MUSIC PRODTNS INC (NJ)
Each share old Common no par exchanged for (0.25) share new Common no par 3/6/89
Name changed to Direct Medical Equipment & Supplies Inc. 3/20/89

VIDEO NETWORK COMMUNICATIONS INC (DE)
Each share old Common 1¢ par exchanged for (0.2) share new Common 1¢ par 02/07/2002
Name changed to TalkPoint Communications, Inc. 08/14/2003
(See TalkPoint Communications, Inc.)

VIDEO PREMIERE INTL CORP (ON)
Each share old Common no par exchanged for (1/6) share new Common no par 08/14/1986
Recapitalized as S.T.I. Industries Inc. 06/12/1990
Each share new Common no par exchanged for (0.1) share Common no par
(See S.T.I. Industries Inc.)

VIDEO PROFESSOR INDS INC (LA)
Under plan of merger each share Common $0.001 par exchanged for $0.05 cash 9/30/95

VIDEO SCIENCE TECHNOLOGY INC (TX)
Reincorporated under the laws of Delaware as Latex Resources, Inc. 5/28/92
Latex Resources, Inc. merged into Alliance Resources plc (United Kingdom) 4/30/97 which merged into AROC Inc. 12/8/99
(See AROC Inc.)

VIDEO SENTRY CORP (MN)
Merged into Sentry Technology Corp. 02/12/1997
Each share Common 1¢ par exchanged for (1) share Common $0.001 par

VIDEO SVCS CORP (DE)
Merged into AT&T Corp. 12/21/2000
Each share Common 1¢ par exchanged for (0.104) share Common Liberty Media Group Class A $1 par and $2.75 cash
AT&T Corp. merged into AT&T Inc. 11/18/2005

VIDEO STA INC NEW (CA)
Each share old Common no par exchanged for (0.1) share new Common no par 08/01/1985
Charter suspended for failure to file reports and pay fees 10/01/1986

VIDEO STREAM INTL INC (WY)
Name changed to TeraGlobal Communications Corp. (WY) 09/29/1998
TeraGlobal Communications Corp. (WY) reincorporated in Delaware 08/26/1999
(See TeraGlobal Communications Corp. (DE))

VIDEO SUPERSTORES AMER INC (CO)
Each share old Common no par exchanged for (0.02) share new Common no par 10/03/1988
Charter suspended for failure to file annual reports 02/01/1993

VIDEO SYS CORP (DE)
Charter cancelled and declared inoperative and void for non-payment of taxes 3/1/83

VIDEO TECHNIQUES INC (NY)
Charter cancelled and declared inoperative and void for non-payment of taxes 12/24/91

VIDEO TIME CAPSULE INC (NV)
Name changed to Zippi Networks Inc. 10/16/2006
Zippi Networks Inc. recapitalized as Mobile Matchmaking Inc. 05/02/2013

VIDEO TO GO INC (NY)
Reorganized under Chapter 11 Federal Bankruptcy Code 11/5/85
Each share Common 1¢ par exchanged for (1/3) share Vision Communications Corp. Common 1¢ par
(See Vision Communications Corp.)

VIDEO U S A INC (UT)
Each share Common $0.001 par exchanged for (0.25) share Common 1¢ par 11/7/85
Liquidating Plan of Reorganization under Chapter 11 Federal Bankruptcy Code effective 1/7/94
No stockholders' equity

VIDEO UPDATE INC (DE)
Plan of reorganization under Chapter 11 Federal Bankruptcy Code effective 12/21/2001
No stockholders' equity

VIDEO WEST DISTR LTD (BC)
Struck off register and declared dissolved for failure to file returns 10/22/93

VIDEO WITHOUT BOUNDARIES INC (FL)
Each (300) shares old Common $0.001 par exchanged for (1) share new Common $0.001 par 09/13/2002
Each share new Common $0.001 par received distribution of (0.00666666) share Cornerstone Entertainment Inc. Restricted Common payable 09/30/2002 to holders of record 08/23/2002
Name changed to MediaREADY, Inc. 09/22/2006
MediaREADY, Inc. recapitalized as China Logistics Group, Inc. 03/12/2008

VIDEOCART INC (DE)
Acquired by Klever Marketing Inc. 06/07/1996
Each share Common 1¢ par exchanged for (0.008189) share Common 1¢ par
Klever Marketing Inc. name changed to DarkPulse, Inc. 09/04/2018

VIDEOCOM INTL INC (NV)
Name changed to Canadian Tasty Fries, Inc. 2/1/95
Canadian Tasty Fries, Inc. name changed to International Tasty Fries Inc. 4/13/95 which recapitalized as Filtered Souls Entertainment Inc. 11/25/98 which name changed to Skyline Entertainment, Inc. 3/31/99 which name changed to Quotemedia.Com Inc. 8/19/99 which name changed to Quotemedia, Inc. 3/11/2003

VIDEOCOMM INC (CO)
Each share old Common $0.00001 par exchanged for (0.001) share new Common $0.00001 par 6/4/93
Name changed to Vanguard Environmental Solutions, Inc. 9/28/93

VIDEOCON D2H LTD (INDIA)
Scheme of Arrangement effective 04/12/2018
Each ADR for Equity Shares exchanged for (8.07331699) Sponsored GDR's for Equity Shares

VIDEOCON INTL LTD (INDIA)
Merged into Videocon Industries Ltd. 04/04/2006
Each 144A GDR for Ordinary exchanged for $1.596 cash

VIDEOFLICKS COM INC (ON)
Merged into 2053938 Ontario Ltd. 1/7/2005
Each share Common no par exchanged for $0.02 cash

VIDEOGRAM INTL CORP (BC)
Recapitalized as Interactive Video Systems Inc. 10/08/1992
Each share Common no par exchanged for (0.1) share Common no par
Interactive Video Systems Inc. name changed to Interactive VideoSystems Inc. 07/19/1994 which name changed to NCC Mining Corp. 08/16/1995 which recapitalized as BMA Mining Corp. 07/11/1997 which recapitalized as Dasher Energy Corp. 05/26/1999 which name changed to Dasher Resources Corp. 10/03/2002 which recapitalized as Dasher Exploration Ltd. 04/16/2003 which name changed to New World Resource Corp. 06/27/2005

VIDEOLABS INC (DE)
Name changed to e.mergent Inc. 07/03/2000
e.mergent Inc. merged into ClearOne Communications, Inc. 05/31/2002 which which name changed to ClearOne, Inc. 12/13/2012

VIDEOLAN TECHNOLOGIES INC (DE)
Each share old Common 1¢ par exchanged for (0.125) share new Common 1¢ par 09/26/1997
Filed a petition under Chapter 11 Federal Bankruptcy Code 02/17/1998
Stockholders' equity unlikely

VIDEONICS INC (CA)
Issue Information - 2,000,000 shares COM offered at $11 per share on 12/15/1994
Merged into FOCUS Enhancements, Inc. 01/16/2001
Each share Common no par exchanged for (0.87) share Common $0.01 par
(See FOCUS Enhancements, Inc.)

VIDEOPLEX INC (NJ)
Reincorporated under the laws of Nevada as MTN Holdings Inc. 12/15/2000
MTN Holdings Inc. recapitalized as Nextronics II Inc. 02/18/2005 which name changed to National Investment Corporation, Real Estate Holdings 06/23/2008
(See National Investment Corporation, Real Estate Holdings)

VIDEORATED INC (NV)
Ceased operations 6/19/90
Note: Stockholders were given the opportunity to exchange their certificates for shares of Phoenix Pacific Properties Trust, a private company seeking to go public, on a share-for-share basis between 3/15/94 to 4/15/94
Note: Certificates are valueless if not exchanged by 4/15/94
Each (10) shares Phoenix Pacific Properties Trust Common $0.001 par was subsequently exchanged for (1.5) shares BioTherapeutics Corp. Common $0.001 par 8/25/94 which name changed to Granite Development Corp. 1/14/97 which recapitalized as Technology Logistics Systems Inc. 4/15/99 which recapitalized as Interactive Business Development, Inc. (New) 1/3/2006 which name changed to American BioDiesel Fuels Corp.

2/2/2007 which name changed to Planet Resource Recovery, Inc. 3/9/2007

VIDEOSERVER INC (DE)
Issue Information - 2,625,000 shares COM offered at $17 per share on 05/24/1995
Name changed to Ezenia! Inc. 11/4/99

VIDEOSPECTION INC (UT)
Name changed to VyStar Group, Inc. 06/04/1990
VyStar Group, Inc. name changed to Megahertz Corp. 06/25/1993 which merged into U.S. Robotics Corp. 02/22/1995 which merged into 3Com Corp. 06/12/1997
(See 3Com Corp.)

VIDEOTELECOM CORP (DE)
Name changed to VTEL Corp. 06/22/1993
VTEL Corp. name changed to Forgent Networks, Inc. 01/18/2002 which recapitalized as Asure Software, Inc. 12/29/2009

VIDEOTRIP CORP (CO)
Recapitalized as Video Communications & Radio, Inc. 10/15/1988
Each share Common no par exchanged for (0.005) share Common $0.008 par
Video Communications & Radio, Inc. name changed to First Entertainment Inc. 06/01/1993 which name changed to First Entertainment Holding Corp. 12/15/1997 which name changed to F2 Broadcast Networks Inc. 01/04/2001 which name changed to Strat Petroleum, Ltd. 07/08/2004
(See Strat Petroleum, Ltd.)

VIDEOTRON GROUP LTD (QC)
Subordinate no par split (2) for (1) by issuance of (1) additional share 03/18/1994
Subordinate no par reclassified as Multiple no par 10/18/2000
Acquired by Quebecor Inc. 12/01/2000
Each share Multiple no par exchanged for $45 cash

VIDEOTRON HLDGS PLC (ENGLAND)
ADR agreement terminated 09/10/1997
Each Sponsored ADR for Ordinary 5p par exchanged for $20.1094 cash

VIDEOTRON INC (DE)
Name changed to Suprema International, Inc. 04/25/1984
(See Suprema International, Inc.)

VIDEOVISION INC (NY)
Name changed to Vision Communications Corp. 5/25/84
(See Vision Communications Corp.)

VIDESH SANCHAR NIGAM LTD (INDIA)
Each 144A GDR for Equity Shares exchanged for (1) old Sponsored ADR for Equity Shares 08/18/2000
Each old Sponsored ADR for Equity Shares exchanged for (0.75) new Sponsored ADR for Equity Shares 12/11/2000
Each Sponsored ADR for Equity Shares exchanged for (1) new 144A ADR for Equity Shares 12/11/2000
ADR basis changed from (1:0.5) to (1:2) 12/11/2000
Each new 144A Sponsored ADR for Equity Shares exchanged for (1) new Sponsored ADR for Equity Shares 02/22/2001
Name changed to Tata Communications Ltd. 01/28/2008

VIDETICS INTL CORP (BC)
Struck off register and declared dissolved for failure to file returns 2/21/92

VIDICOM CORP. OF AMERICA (WY)
Recapitalized as Computer Measurements, Inc. (II) 8/15/70
Each share Common 2-1/2¢ par exchanged for (0.1) share Common 2-1/2¢ par
(See Computer Measurements, Inc. (II))

VIDIKRON TECHNOLOGIES GROUP INC (DE)
SEC revoked preferred and common stock registration 09/18/2009

VIDIONICS DIGITAL LABS INC (UT)
Involuntarily dissolved 02/01/1989

VIDKID DISTRIBUTIONS INC (FL)
Recapitalized as IBX Group, Inc. 10/02/2001
Each share Common $0.005 par exchanged for (0.5) share Common $0.005 par
(See IBX Group, Inc.)

VIDMAR ACQUISITIONS INC (NV)
Recapitalized as Online Transaction Systems, Inc. 08/05/2003
Each share Common $0.001 par exchanged for (0.01) share Common $0.001 par
Online Transaction Systems, Inc. name changed to Delta Mining & Exploration Corp. 01/28/2004
(See Delta Mining & Exploration Corp.)

VIDMARK INC (DE)
Name changed to Trimark Holdings, Inc. 6/1/92
Trimark Holdings, Inc. recapitalized as Lions Gate Entertainment Corp. 10/13/2000

VIDSHADOW COM INC (DE)
Name changed to DME Interactive Holdings, Inc. (New) 05/13/2008
(See DME Interactive Holdings, Inc. (New))

VIDSHADOW INC (DE)
Each share old Common $0.001 par exchanged for (0.87267649) share new Common $0.001 par 05/28/2008
Recapitalized as OneScreen Inc. 03/06/2009
Each share Common $0.001 par exchanged for (0.1) share Common $0.001 par

VID3G INC (WY)
Recapitalized as Argus Worldwide Corp. 11/14/2016
Each share Common $0.0001 par exchanged for (0.00028571) share Common $0.0001 par 11/14/2016

VIDTOR COMMUNICATIONS INC (CO)
Recapitalized as American Financial Holding, Inc. (CO) 07/11/1988
Each share Common 5¢ par exchanged for (0.1) share Common $0.001 par
American Financial Holding, Inc. (CO) reorganized in Delaware 10/12/1992 which name changed to Isolagen, Inc. 11/13/2001
(See Isolagen, Inc.)

VIE DE FRANCE CORP (DE)
Name changed to Cuisine Solutions Inc. 11/7/97

VIE FINL GROUP INC (DE)
Each share old Common 1¢ par exchanged for (0.01) share new Common 1¢ par 4/20/2004
In process of liquidation
Each share new Common 1¢ par received initial distribution of $0.37 cash payable 12/7/2004 to holders of record 12/6/2004 Ex date - 12/8/2004
Each share new Common 1¢ par received second distribution of $0.15 cash payable 9/26/2005 to holders of record 12/6/2004 Ex date - 9/29/2005

VIECO RES LTD (BC)
Struck off register and declared dissolved for failure to file returns 02/25/1983

VIEH CO.
Name changed to Brodhead-Garrett Co. in 1950
(See Brodhead-Garrett Co.)

VIEJO BANCORP (CA)
Common no par split (5) for (4) by issuance of (0.25) additional share 9/21/89
Receiver appointed over assets 2/28/92
Stockholders' equity unlikely

VIENNA CORP (UT)
Completely liquidated
Each share Common 1¢ par received first and final distribution of approximately $0.17 cash payable 11/09/2009 to holders of record 08/10/2009
Note: Certificates were not required to be surrendered and are without value

VIENNA INS GROUP AG OLD (AUSTRIA)
Each Unsponsored ADR for Ordinary exchanged for (1) Vienna Insurance Group AG (New) Sponsored ADR for Ordinary 04/27/2011

VIENNA SILVER MINES CO (UT)
Name changed to Vienna Corp. 08/22/1991
(See Vienna Corp.)

VIER CAP CORP (AB)
Recapitalized as Vertex Resource Group Ltd. 10/18/2017
Each share Common no par exchanged for (0.1) share Common no par

VIETNAM MNG CORP (NV)
Name changed to Vanguard Mining Corp. 06/03/2014
Vanguard Mining Corp. name changed to Myson Group, Inc. 06/08/2015

VIETNAM UTD STL CORP (NV)
Recapitalized as Vietnam Mining Corp. 07/12/2010
Each share Common $0.001 par exchanged for (0.05) share Common $0.001 par
Vietnam Mining Corp. name changed to Vanguard Mining Corp. 06/03/2014 which name changed to Myson Group, Inc. 06/08/2015

VIEW MASTER IDEAL GROUP INC (DE)
Common 1¢ par split (3) for (2) by issuance of (0.5) additional share 4/25/86
Common 1¢ par split (3) for (2) by issuance of (0.5) additional share 3/9/87
Merged into Tyco Toys, Inc. 9/11/89
Each share Common 1¢ par exchanged for (0.373) share Common 1¢ par and (0.225) Common Stock Purchase Warrant expiring 6/7/93
Tyco Toys, Inc. merged into Mattel Inc. 3/27/97

VIEW-MASTER INTERNATIONAL GROUP, INC. (DE)
Name changed to View-Master Ideal Group, Inc. 04/24/1986
View-Master Ideal Group, Inc. merged into Tyco Toys, Inc. 09/11/1989 which merged into Mattel, Inc. 03/27/1997

VIEW SYS INC (FL)
Common $0.001 par split (2) for (1) by issuance of (1) additional share payable 10/07/1998 to holders of record 09/30/1998
Reincorporated under the laws of Nevada 07/31/2003

VIEW TECH INC (DE)
State of incorporation changed from (CA) to (DE) 11/26/96
Recapitalized as Wire One Technologies, Inc. 5/18/2000
Each share Common 1¢ par exchanged for (0.5) share Common no par
Wire One Technologies, Inc. name changed to Glowpoint, Inc. 9/24/2003

VIEW TECHNOLOGIES INC (CO)
Name changed to Geoscopix, Inc. 10/02/2006
Geoscopix, Inc. recapitalized as Fight Zone, Inc. 03/03/2008

VIEW X INC (CA)
Company believed out of business 00/00/1972
Details not available

VIEWCAST COM INC (DE)
Each share 8.5% Conv. Preferred Ser. A $0.0001 par exchanged for (2.759) shares Common $0.0001 par 08/00/1999
(Additional Information in Active)

VIEWLEX INC (NY)
Class A Common 25¢ par and Class B Common 25¢ par split (3) for (1) respectively by issuance of (2) additional shares 10/16/1961
Class B Common 25¢ par reclassified as Class A Common 25¢ par 04/17/1968
Class A Common 25¢ par reclassified as Common 25¢ par 10/16/1968
Recapitalized as Electrosound Group, Inc. 11/29/1977
Each share Common 25¢ par exchanged for (0.2) share Common 1¢ par
(See Electrosound Group, Inc.)

VIEWLOCITY INC (GA)
Merged into Viesta Corp. 12/31/2003
Each share Common 1¢ par exchanged for $0.000014 cash

VIEWLOGIC SYS INC (DE)
Merged into Synopsys Inc. 12/4/97
Each share Common 1¢ par exchanged for (0.6521) share Common 1¢ par

VIEWPOINT CORP (DE)
Name changed to Enliven Marketing Technologies Corp. 01/01/2008
Enliven Marketing Technologies Corp. merged into DG FastChannel, Inc. 10/02/2008 which name changed to Digital Generation, Inc. 11/07/2011 which merged into Sizmek Inc. 02/07/2014
(See Sizmek Inc.)

VIEWPOINT EXPLS LTD (ON)
Merged into Lumsden Building Corp. Inc. (New) 08/15/1978
Each (29) shares Capital Stock no par exchanged for (1) share Common no par
(See Lumsden Building Corp. Inc. (New))

VIEWPOINT FINL GROUP (USA)
Reorganized under the laws of Maryland as ViewPoint Financial Group, Inc. 07/07/2010
Each share Common 1¢ par exchanged for (1.4) shares Common 1¢ par
ViewPoint Financial Group, Inc. name changed to LegacyTexas Financial Group, Inc. 01/02/2015

VIEWPOINT FINL GROUP INC (MD)
Name changed to LegacyTexas Financial Group, Inc. 01/02/2015

VIEWRAY INC (NV)
Reincorporated under the laws of Delaware and Common $0.001 par changed to 1¢ par 07/21/2015

VIEWTONE TELEVISION & RADIO CORP.
Bankrupt in 1948

VIE-VIK — FINANCIAL INFORMATION, INC.

Stockholders' equity unlikely

VIGGLE INC (DE)
Each share old Common $0.001 par exchanged for (0.0125) share new Common $0.001 par 03/19/2014
Name changed to DraftDay Fantasy Sports, Inc. 01/28/2016
DraftDay Fantasy Sports, Inc. name changed to Function(x) Inc. 06/13/2016

VIGIL LOCATING SYS CORP (CANADA)
Dissolved for non-compliance 06/16/2009

VIGILANCE SYS CORP (DE)
Recapitalized as Western Transmedia Inc. 1/2/92
Each share Common 1¢ par exchanged for (0.0333) share Common 30¢ par
Western Transmedia Inc. name changed to Western Systems Corp. 1/3/97 which name changed to American Country Holdings Inc. 7/29/97
(See American Country Holdings Inc.)

VIGNETTE CORP (DE)
Issue Information - 4,000,000 shares COM offered at $19 per share on 02/18/1999
Old Common 1¢ par split (2) for (1) by issuance of (1) additional share payable 12/01/1999 to holders of record 11/15/1999
Old Common 1¢ par split (3) for (1) by issuance of (2) additional shares payable 04/13/2000 to holders of record 03/27/2000
Each share old Common 1¢ par exchanged for (0.1) share new Common 1¢ par 06/11/2005
Merged into Open Text Corp. 07/22/2009
Each share Common 1¢ par exchanged for (0.1447) share Common no par and $8 cash

VIGOR RES LTD (BC)
Merged into Biomax Technologies Inc. 03/25/1999
Each share Common no par exchanged for (4.31081) shares Common no par
(See Biomax Technologies Inc.)

VIGORO CORP (DE)
Merged into IMC Global Inc. 03/01/1996
Each share Common no par exchanged for (1.6) shares Common $1 par
IMC Global Inc. merged into Mosaic Co. (Old) 10/22/2004 which merged into Mosaic Co. (New) 05/25/2011

VIISAGE TECHNOLOGY INC (DE)
Each share old Common $0.001 par exchanged for (0.4) share new Common $0.001 par 12/19/2005
Under plan of merger name changed to L-1 Identity Solutions, Inc. 08/30/2006
(See L-1 Identity Solutions, Inc.)

VIKA CORP. (AZ)
99% privately held as of 1980
Public interest eliminated

VIKA CORP (NV)
Reincorporated under the laws of Delaware as Handheld Entertainment, Inc. and Common $0.001 par changed to $0.0001 par 02/22/2006
Handheld Entertainment, Inc. name changed to ZVUE Corp. 11/02/2007
(See ZVUE Corp.)

VIKING AWYS INC (DE)
Placed in receivership 07/00/1970
No stockholders' equity

VIKING BROADCASTING CORP (UT)
Recapitalized as Meditecnic Inc. 4/18/98
Each share Common $0.001 par exchanged for (0.001) share Common $0.001 par

VIKING CANADIAN FUND LTD. (CANADA)
Name changed to Laurentian Canadian Equity Fund Ltd. 05/31/1993
Laurentian Canadian Equity Fund Ltd. name changed to Strategic Value Canadian Equity Fund Ltd. 06/05/1997 which name changed to StrategicNova Canadian Large Cap Value Fund Ltd. 09/26/2000
(See StrategicNova Canadian Large Cap Value Fund Ltd.)

VIKING CAP GROUP INC (UT)
Each share old Common $0.001 par exchanged for (0.2) share new Common $0.001 par 11/11/1991
Each (300) shares new Common $0.001 par exchanged again for (1) share new Common $0.001 par 12/22/2009
Recapitalized as Arizona Gold & Onyx Mining Co. 06/25/2010
Each share new Common $0.001 par exchanged for (0.1) share Common $0.001 par

VIKING COMMONWEALTH FUND LTD. (CANADA)
Name changed to Laurentian Commonwealth Fund Ltd. 05/31/1993
Laurentian Commonwealth Fund Ltd. name changed to Strategic Value Commonwealth Fund Ltd. 06/05/1997 which name changed to StrategicNova Commonwealth Fund Ltd. 09/26/2000
(See StrategicNova Commonwealth Fund Ltd.)

VIKING COMMUNICATIONS LTD (NY)
Name changed to Dalt Brands Inc. 07/28/1976
(See Dalt Brands Inc.)

VIKING CONS INC (DE)
Common $0.005 par split (3) for (1) by issuance of (2) additional shares payable 08/15/2006 to holders of record 08/09/2006 Ex date - 08/16/2006
Reincorporated under the laws of Nevada as Tailor Aquaponics World Wide, Inc. and Common $0.005 par changed to $0.001 par 08/15/2006
Tailor Aquaponics World Wide, Inc. recapitalized as Diversified Acquisitions, Inc. 08/20/2007 which recapitalized as Vitalcare Diabetes Treatment Centers, Inc. 03/24/2008 which recapitalized as China Advanced Technology 06/23/2010 which name changed to Goliath Film & Media Holdings 01/20/2012

VIKING CORPORATE DIVID FD INC (MD)
Ceased operations 06/11/1986
Details not available

VIKING DIVIDEND FUND LTD. (CANADA)
Name changed to Laurentian Dividend Fund Ltd. 05/31/1993
Laurentian Dividend Fund Ltd. name changed to Strategic Value Dividend Fund Ltd. 06/05/1997 which name changed to StrategicNova Canadian Dividend Fund Ltd. 09/26/2000
(See StrategicNova Canadian Dividend Fund Ltd.)

VIKING ENERGY RTY TR (AB)
Additional Offering - 2,950,000 TR UNITS offered at $6.85 per Trust Unit on 03/12/2002
Merged into Harvest Energy Trust 02/07/2006
Each Trust Unit no par exchanged for (0.25) Trust Unit no par
Note: Unexchanged Units were cancelled and became without value 02/07/2012
(See Harvest Energy Trust)

VIKING EQUITY INDEX FD INC (MD)
Voluntarily dissolved 02/03/1992
Details not available

VIKING EXPL INC (NV)
Recapitalized as Sierra Gold Corp. (New) 8/11/2006
Each share Common $0.00001 par exchanged for (0.2) share Common $0.00001 par

VIKING FGHT INC (CA)
Merged into Roadway Services, Inc. 10/28/88
Each share Common no par exchanged for $35.50 cash

VIKING FREIGHT CO. (MO)
Completely liquidated 6/17/68
Each share 6% Preferred $20 par exchanged for first and final distribution of $23.36 cash
Each share Class A Common $1 par or Class B Common $1 par exchanged for first and final distribution of $10.90 cash

VIKING FREIGHT SYSTEM, INC. (CA)
Each share old Common no par exchanged for (0.8) share new Common no par 12/23/81
New Common no par split (3) for (2) by issuance of (0.5) additional share 6/6/83
Under plan of reorganization each share new common no par automatically became (1) share Viking Freight Inc. Common no par 6/29/86
(See Viking Freight, Inc.)

VIKING GEN CORP (FL)
Name changed to American Capital Corp. 05/18/1977
American Capital Corp. name changed to America Capital Corp. 05/30/1996

VIKING GOLD CORP (ON)
Merged into Dragon Mining NL 12/30/99
Each share Common no par exchanged for (3.33) shares Common no par

VIKING GROWTH FD INC (MN)
Merged into Industries Trend Fund Inc. 09/29/1975
Each share Common 1¢ par exchanged for (0.45165) share Common $1 par
Industries Trend Fund Inc. merged into Pilot Fund, Inc. 05/01/1981 which name changed to Transamerica Technology Fund 06/23/1989 which name changed to Transamerica Capital Appreciation Fund 04/19/1991 which merged into Hancock (John) Capital Growth Fund 12/22/1994
(See Hancock (John) Capital Growth Fund)

VIKING GROWTH FUND LTD. (CANADA)
Name changed to Laurentian American Equity Fund Ltd. 05/31/1993
Laurentian American Equity Fund Ltd. name changed to Strategic Value American Equity Fund Ltd. 06/05/1997 which name changed to StrategicNova U.S. Large Cap Growth Fund Ltd. 09/26/2000
(See StrategicNova U.S. Large Cap Growth Fund Ltd.)

VIKING INCOME FUND (ON)
Name changed to StrategicNova Income Fund 09/26/2000
StrategicNova Income Fund name changed to StrategicNova Canadian Bond Fund 12/00/2001
(See StrategicNova Canadian Bond Fund)

VIKING INDUSTRIES, INC. (DE)
Common 10¢ par changed to 6-2/3¢ par and (0.5) additional share issued 05/27/1966
Name changed to Vikoa, Inc. 05/11/1967
Vikoa, Inc. name changed to Acton Corp. 08/13/1976 which name changed to Sunstates Corp. (New) 01/03/1994
(See Sunstates Corp. (New))

VIKING INDS INC (CA)
Merged into Heath Tecna Corp. 01/05/1979
Each share Common $1 par exchanged for $16 cash

VIKING INTERNATIONAL FUND LTD. (CANADA)
Name changed to Laurentian International Fund Ltd. 05/31/1993
Laurentian International Fund Ltd. name changed to Strategic Value International Fund Ltd. 06/05/1997 which name changed to StrategicNova World Large Cap Fund Ltd. 09/26/2000
(See StrategicNova World Large Cap Fund Ltd.)

VIKING INVS FD INC (MN)
Merged into Industries Trend Fund Inc. 09/29/1975
Each share Common 1¢ par exchanged for (0.6992) share Common $1 par
Industries Trend Fund Inc. merged into Pilot Fund, Inc. 05/01/1981 which name changed to Transamerica Technology Fund 06/23/1989 which name changed to Transamerica Capital Appreciation Fund 04/19/1991 which merged into Hancock (John) Capital Growth Fund 12/22/1994
(See Hancock (John) Capital Growth Fund)

VIKING INVTS GROUP INC (NV)
Name changed to Viking Energy Group, Inc. 05/08/2017

VIKING LITHOGRAPHERS INC (FL)
Name changed to Viking General Corp. 04/10/1969
Viking General Corp. name changed to American Capital Corp. 05/18/1977 which name changed to America Capital Corp. 05/30/1996

VIKING MGMT GROUP INC (DE)
Name changed to Viking Resources International Inc. 10/09/1995
(See Viking Resources International Inc.)

VIKING MEDIA A S (NORWAY)
ADR agreement terminated 00/00/1991
Details not available

VIKING MINERALS INC (NV)
Old Common $0.001 par split (35) for (1) by issuance of (34) additional shares payable 02/03/2011 to holders of record 01/27/2011 Ex date - 02/04/2011
Each share old Common $0.001 par exchanged for (0.001) share new Common $0.001 par 07/05/2012
Recapitalized as Indie Growers Association 04/15/2014
Each share new Common $0.001 par exchanged for (0.005) share Common $0.001 par
Indie Growers Association recapitalized as Nexgen Applied Solutions Inc. 04/04/2016 which name changed to Bingo Nation, Inc. 11/08/2016

VIKING MINES & PETES LTD (BC)
Recapitalized 10/02/1972
Recapitalized from Viking Mines Ltd. to Viking Mines & Petroleums Ltd. 10/02/1972
Each share Capital Stock no par exchanged for (1/3) share Capital Stock no par
Struck off register and declared dissolved for failure to file returns 05/28/1979

FINANCIAL INFORMATION, INC. VIK-VIL

VIKING MONEY MKT FD INC (MD)
Voluntarily dissolved 02/03/1992
Details not available

VIKING OFFICE PRODS INC (CA)
Common no par split (2) for (1) by issuance of (1) additional share 2/13/92
Common no par split (2) for (1) by issuance of (1) additional share 6/14/94
Common no par split (2) for (1) by issuance of (1) additional share payable 5/15/96 to holders of record 5/1/96
Merged into Office Depot, Inc. 8/26/98
Each share Common no par exchanged for (1) share Common 1¢ par

VIKING OIL RES INC (QC)
Reincorporated under the laws of British Columbia as Pacific Viking Resources Inc. 03/23/1987
Pacific Viking Resources Inc. name changed to International Viking Resources Inc. 02/18/1988 which recapitalized as Saxony Explorations Ltd. (BC) 11/13/1992 which reorganized in Yukon as Century Mining Corp. 09/24/2003 which reincorporated in Canada 07/22/2004 which merged into White Tiger Gold Ltd. 10/20/2011 which name changed to Mangazeya Mining Ltd. 09/23/2013

VIKING PUMP CO (IA)
Common no par changed to $5 par 00/00/1943
Stock Dividends - 100% 03/31/1950; 10% 02/01/1965; 10% 05/02/1966; 25% 03/25/1968
Merged into Houdaille Industries, Inc. (DE) 10/01/1968
Each share Common $5 par exchanged for (2.44276) shares Common 75¢ par
(See Houdaille Industries, Inc. (DE))

VIKING RES INTL INC (DE)
SEC revoked registration of securities 10/29/2004

VIKING SAVINGS & LOAN ASSOCIATION (CA)
Merged into Westside Savings & Loan Association 4/10/89
Each share Common $8 par exchanged for either (0.0302) share Common $8 par or $0.532 cash
Westside Savings & Loan Association name changed to Westside Bank of Southern California (Los Angeles, CA) 7/16/90 which was placed in conservatorship 9/24/93

VIKING SNOWMOBILES INC (MN)
Common $1 par changed to 10¢ par 4/9/70
Adjudicated bankrupt 1/6/77
Stockholders' equity unlikely

VIKING SYS INC (DE)
Reincorporated 07/25/2006
State of incorporation changed from (NV) to (DE) 07/25/2006
Each share old Common $0.001 par exchanged for (0.02) share new Common $0.001 par 01/07/2008
Acquired by CONMED Corp. 09/26/2012
Each share new Common $0.001 par exchanged for $0.27 cash

VIKOA INC (DE)
Name changed to Acton Corp. 08/13/1976
Acton Corp. name changed to Sunstates Corp. (New) 01/03/1994
(See Sunstates Corp. (New))

VIKON INC (TX)
Each share old Common 1¢ par exchanged for (0.2) share new Common 1¢ par 04/23/1974
Charter forfeited for failure to pay taxes 03/13/1978

VIKON INTL RES INC (BC)
Recapitalized as Covik Development Corp. 04/17/1998
Each share Common no par exchanged for (0.2) share Common no par
Covik Development Corp. name changed to Monarch Energy Ltd. (BC) 10/23/2006 which reincorporated in Ontario as ChroMedX Corp. 09/18/2014 which name changed to Relay Medical Corp. 07/09/2018

VIKONICS INC (NY)
Common 2¢ par split (6) for (5) by issuance of (0.2) additional share 5/3/91
Chapter 11 bankruptcy proceedings converted to Chapter 7 on 3/1/2005
Stockholders' equity unlikely

VILAROI GOLD MINES, LTD. (ON)
Dissolved in 1958

VILLA CARE INC (WA)
Merged into Emeritus Ltd. 07/01/1980
Each share Common no par exchanged for $6 cash

VILLA LEAD MINING CORP. LTD. (ON)
Reorganized 2/1/52
Each (3) shares old Capital Stock $1 par exchanged for (2) shares new Capital Stock $1 par and (1) share Capital Stock $1 par of Cobalt Badger Silver Mines Ltd.
(See Cobalt Badger Silver Mines Ltd.)

VILLA MFG INC (NY)
Dissolved by proclamation 3/31/82

VILLACENTRES LTD (AB)
Common no par split (2) for (1) by issuance of (1) additional share 10/31/1972
Common no par split (3) for (1) by issuance of (2) additional shares 09/23/1981
Merged into Crownx Inc. 03/21/1984
Each share Common no par exchanged for (0.2) share Class A Non-Vtg. no par, (0.5) Class A Non-Vtg. Stock Purchase Warrant expiring 01/12/1989 and $3.50 cash
Crownx Inc. name changed to Extendicare Inc. 11/17/1994
(See Extendicare Inc.)

VILLAGE BANC (NAPLES, FL)
Merged into Bank of Montreal (Montreal, Que) 7/1/2000
Each share Common no par exchanged for $21 cash

VILLAGE BANCORP INC (CT)
Common $3.33 par split (2) for (1) by issuance of (1) additional share payable 12/1/97 to holders of record 11/28/97
Merged into Webster Financial Corp. 5/20/99
Each share Common $3.33 par exchanged for (0.8545) share Common 1¢ par

VILLAGE BANK & TRUST CO. (RIDGEFIELD, CT)
Reorganized as Village Bancorp Inc. 7/19/83
Each share Common $10 par exchanged for (1) share Common $3.33 par
Village Bancorp Inc. merged into Webster Financial Corp. 5/19/99

VILLAGE BK (CHAPEL HILL, NC)
Merged into Triangle Bancorp Inc. 11/1/95
Each share Common $5 par exchanged for (1.3) shares Common no par
Triangle Bancorp Inc. merged into Centura Banks, Inc. 2/18/2000 which merged into Royal Bank of Canada (Montreal, QC) 6/5/2001

VILLAGE BANK N.A. (DALLAS, TX)
Merged into Texas Commerce Bancshares, Inc. 10/01/1975
Each share Common $20 par exchanged for (3.4163) shares Common $4 par
Texas Commerce Bancshares, Inc. acquired by Chemical New York Corp. 05/01/1987 which name changed to Chemical Banking Corp. 04/29/1988 which name changed to Chase Manhattan Corp. (New) 03/31/1996 which name changed to J.P. Morgan Chase & Co. 12/31/2000 which name changed to JPMorgan Chase & Co. 07/20/2004

VILLAGE BANKSHARES INC (FL)
Merged into Regions Financial Corp. (Old) 8/31/98
Each share Common $10 par exchanged for (1.34) shares Common $0.625 par
Regions Financial Corp. (Old) merged into Regions Financial Corp. (New) 7/1/2004

VILLAGE ENTERPRISES, INC. (GA)
Acquired by Daniel Village Inc. 1/15/69
Each share Common $2 par exchanged for $11.10 cash

VILLAGE FARMS INCOME FD (CANADA)
Under plan or reorganization each Trust Unit no par automatically became (1) share Village Farms International, Inc. Common no par 12/31/2009

VILLAGE FINL SVCS LTD (DE)
Merged into First Fidelity Bancorporation (New) 08/11/1993
Each share Common 1¢ par exchanged for (0.235) share Common $1 par and $17.01 cash
First Fidelity Bancorporation (New) merged into First Union Corp. 01/01/1996 which name changed to Wachovia Corp. (Ctfs. dated after 09/01/2001) 09/01/2001 which merged into Wells Fargo & Co. (New) 12/31/2008

VILLAGE GREEN BOOKSTORE INC (NY)
Each share Common $0.0001 par exchanged for (0.1) share Common $0.001 par 06/15/1992
Charter cancelled and proclaimed dissolved for failure to pay taxes 06/30/2004

VILLAGE HOMES CO. OF GROSSE POINTE (MI)
Name changed to VH Development Co. 7/2/69
(See VH Development Co.)

VILLAGE SVGS BK (GREENVILLE, NH)
Merged into Cheshire Financial Corp. 06/22/1990
Each share Common $1 par exchanged for $22 cash

VILLAGE VENTURES INC (AB)
Recapitalized as Sunventures Corp. 09/01/1992
Each share Common no par exchanged for (0.5) share Common no par
Sunventures Corp. name changed to Sunventures Resources Inc. 12/02/1993 which recapitalized as Commonwealth Energy Inc. 01/13/1995 which name changed to Scimitar Hydrocarbons Corp. 02/08/1996 which was acquired by Rally Energy Corp. 07/10/2002
(See Rally Energy Corp.)

VILLAGE WTR CO SIMSBURY (CT)
Merged into Aquarion Co. 5/18/2000
Each share Common no par exchanged for $150 cash

VILLAGEEDOCS INC (DE)
Reincorporated 09/07/2007
State of incorporation changed from (CA) to (DE) and Common no par changed to to $0.0001 par 09/07/2007
Each share old Common $0.0001 par exchanged for (1) share new Common $0.0001 par to reflect a (1) for (10,000) reverse split followed by a (10,000) for (1) forward split 08/20/2010
Note: Holders of (9,999) or fewer pre-split shares received $0.015 cash per share
Name changed to Holiday Island Holdings, Inc. 02/13/2014

VILLAGER, INC. (DE)
Common $1 par split (5) for (4) by issuance of (0.25) additional share 06/01/1966
Common $1 par split (5) for (4) by issuance of (0.25) additional share 05/17/1976
Name changed to Villager Industries, Inc. 11/14/1968
(See Villager Industries, Inc.)

VILLAGER INDS INC (DE)
Merged into Logan (Jonathan), Inc. 05/30/1973
Each share Common $1 par exchanged for $0.50 cash

VILLAGER SHOE SHOPPES CDA LTD (CANADA)
Acquired by VWV Enterprises Ltd. in 1981
Details not available

VILLAGEWORLD COM INC (NY)
Name changed to Biometrics 2000 Corp. 03/04/2004
(See Biometrics 2000 Corp.)

VILLANOVA CAP CORP (BC)
Name changed to Africa West Minerals Corp. 01/31/2008
Africa West Minerals Corp. recapitalized as Advance Gold Corp. 05/03/2010

VILLANOVA NAT GAS LTD (AB)
Merged into Evergreen International Corp. 03/29/1985
Each share Common no par exchanged for (0.5) share Common no par
(See Evergreen International Corp.)

VILLARET RES LTD (CANADA)
Recapitalized as Kast Telecom Inc. (Canada) 05/23/2000
Each share Common no par exchanged for (0.33333333) share Common no par
Kast Telecom Inc. (Canada) reincorporated in Luxembourg as Kast Telecom Europe S.A. 04/25/2001

VILLBONA GOLD MINES LTD. (ON)
Recapitalized as Avillabona Mines Ltd. 00/00/1953
Each share Capital Stock $1 par exchanged for (0.5) share Capital Stock $1 par
Avillabona Mines Ltd. merged into Hydra Explorations Ltd. 11/16/1959 which name changed to Hydra Capital Corp. 12/30/1992 which name changed to Waterford Capital Management Inc. 11/12/1996 which merged into CPI Plastics Group Ltd. 09/21/1998
(See CPI Plastics Group Ltd.)

VILLEBON RES LTD (BC)
Recapitalized as Victoria Diego Resource Corp. 5/24/85
Each share Common no par exchanged for (1/3) share Common no par
(See Victoria Diego Resource Corp.)

VILLEMAQUE GOLD MINES LTD. (ON)
Charter cancelled for failure to file returns and pay fees 3/7/77

VILLENEUVE RES LTD (BC)
Delisted from Vancouver Stock Exchange 03/04/1992

VILNIAUS BANKAS AB (LITHUANIA)
Stock Dividend - 400% payable 06/19/1998 to holders of record 06/18/1998
ADR agreement terminated 03/22/2001
Each 144A GDR for Ordinary exchanged for approximately $12.418 cash
Each Reg. S GDR for Ordinary exchanged for approximately $12.418 cash

VILTER MFG CO (WI)
Voting Trust Agreement terminated and each VTC for Common $5 par exchanged for (1) share Common $5 par 08/17/1971
Stock Dividends - 10% 01/15/1963; 100% 12/15/1965; 50% 11/27/1972
Merged into VMC Corp. (WI) 12/15/1988
Each share Common $5 par exchanged for $175 cash

VIM LABORATORIES CO., INC. (MD)
Charter revoked for failure to file reports and pay fees 11/9/65

VIMETCO N V (NETHERLANDS)
GDR agreement terminated 07/12/2017
Each Reg. S GDR for Ordinary exchanged for (1) share Ordinary
Each 144A GDR for Ordinary exchanged for (1) share Ordinary
Note: Unexchanged GDR's will be sold and the proceeds, if any, held for claim after 01/12/2018

VIMICRO INTL CORP (CAYMAN ISLANDS)
ADR agreement terminated 01/22/2016
Each ADR for Ordinary exchanged for $13.45 cash

VIMPELCOM LTD (BERMUDA)
Name changed to VEON Ltd. 03/31/2017

VIMRX PHARMACEUTICALS INC (DE)
Name changed to Nexell Therapeutics Inc. 5/26/99
(See Nexell Therapeutics Inc.)

VINA CONCHA Y TORO S A (CHILE)
Sponsored ADR's for Ordinary split (5) for (2) by issuance of (1.5) additional ADR's payable 09/30/2005 to holders of record 09/29/2005 Ex date - 10/03/2005
Basis changed from (1:50) to (1:20) 09/30/2005
ADR agreement terminated 09/27/2018
Each Sponsored ADR for Ordinary exchanged for (20) shares Ordinary
Note: Unexchanged ADR's will be sold and the proceeds, if any, held for claim after 09/30/2019

VINA TECHNOLOGIES INC (DE)
Issue Information - 3,000,000 shares COM offered at $12 per share on 08/10/2000
Merged into Larscom Inc. 6/5/2003
Each share Common $0.0001 par exchanged for (0.03799) share new Common 1¢ par

VINCAM GROUP INC (FL)
Common $0.001 par split (3) for (2) by issuance of (0.5) additional share payable 12/10/97 to holders of record 11/21/97
Merged into Automatic Data Processing Inc. 3/11/99
Each share Common $0.001 par exchanged (0.458) share Common 10¢ par

VINCENNES ELECTRIC RAILWAY CO.
Dissolved in 1938

VINCENT MINING CORP. LTD.
Name changed to Mindus Corp. Ltd. 00/00/1948
(See Mindus Corp. Ltd.)

VINCENT RES LTD (BC)
Name changed to Latin American Telecommunications Corp. 09/09/1993
Latin American Telecommunications Corp. name changed to Latelco International, Inc. (BC) 10/17/1997 which reincorporated in Wyoming 12/01/2000
(See Latelco International, Inc.)

VINCO CORP (MI)
5% Preferred called for redemption 12/01/1961
Dissolved 05/09/1969
No stockholders' equity

VINCO TOOL CO.
Name changed to Vinco Corp. 00/00/1940
(See Vinco Corp.)

VINCOMPASS CORP (DE)
Name changed to Enterra Corp. (New) 11/13/2015

VINCOR INTL INC (CANADA)
Class A Preferred no par called for redemption 06/06/1996
Merged into Constellation Brands, Inc. 06/08/2006
Each share Common no par exchanged for $36.50 cash

VINCULUM INC (NV)
Reorganized 06/08/1998
Under plan of reorganization state of incorporation changed from (CO) to (NV) 06/08/1998
Each share Class A Common $0.001 par exchanged for (0.1) share Common no par
Name changed to CPU Micromart, Inc. 06/30/1998
CPU Micromart, Inc. name changed to Ebiz Enterprises, Inc. 05/06/1999
(See Ebiz Enterprises, Inc.)

VINDALE CORP (OH)
Stock Dividend - 50% 07/28/1972
Merged into Vinco, Inc. 12/03/1981
Each share Common no par exchanged for $0.70 cash

VINDICATOR INC (FL)
Name changed 07/22/1992
Name changed from Vindicator of Florida, Inc. to Vindicator Inc. 07/22/1992
Name changed to Food Technology Service, Inc. 07/13/1994
(See Food Technology Service, Inc.)

VINE PERSHING MINES, LTD. (ON)
Charter cancelled for failure to file reports and pay taxes 3/4/57

VINELAND NATL BK & TR CO (VINELAND, NJ)
Merged into Peoples National Bank of New Jersey (Westmont, NJ) 05/22/1970
Each share Capital Stock $10 par exchanged for (3.25) shares Common Capital Stock $6.75 par
Peoples National Bank of New Jersey (Westmont, NJ) name changed to First Peoples National Bank of New Jersey (Westmont, NJ) 06/30/1974 which name changed to First Peoples Bank of New Jersey (Westmont, NJ) 04/20/1978 which reorganized as First Peoples Financial Corp. 03/03/1987 which merged into CoreStates Financial Corp 09/03/1992 which merged into First Union Corp. 04/28/1998 which name changed to Wachovia Corp. (Ctfs. dated after 09/01/2001) 09/01/2001 which merged into Wells Fargo & Co. (New) 12/31/2008

VINER E A HLDGS LTD (ON)
Name changed to Fahnestock Viner Holdings Inc. 06/28/1988

Fahnestock Viner Holdings Inc. name changed to Oppenheimer Holdings Inc. (ONT) 09/02/2003 which reincorporated in Canada 05/11/2005 which reincorporated in Delaware 05/11/2009

VINEX WINES INC (NV)
SEC revoked common stock registration 10/20/2005

VINEYARD NATL BANCORP (CA)
Common no par split (2) for (1) by issuance of (1) additional share payable 08/30/2004 to holders of record 08/20/2004 Ex date - 08/31/2004
Stock Dividends - 20% payable 08/31/1995 to holders of record 08/15/1995; 5% payable 01/15/2003 to holders of record 12/23/2002 Ex date - 12/24/2002; 5% payable 01/26/2004 to holders of record 01/12/2004 Ex date - 01/08/2004; 5% payable 06/22/2007 to holders of record 06/08/2007 Ex date - 06/06/2007
Plan of reorganization under Chapter 11 Federal Bankruptcy proceedings effective 08/26/2010
No stockholders' equity

VINEYARD NATL BK (RANCHO CUCAMONGA, CA)
5.60% Conv. Preferred Ser. B called for redemption at $25 plus $0.24888 accrued dividend on 6/3/2004

VINEYARD OIL & GAS CO (PA)
Each share old Common no par exchanged for (1) share new Common no par to reflect a (1) for (1,875) reverse split followed by a (1,875) for (1) forward split 3/31/2006
Note: In effect holders received $0.5695 cash per share and public interest was eliminated

VININGS INVT PPTYS TR (MA)
Each share old Common no par exchanged for (0.125) share new Common no par 7/1/96
Each (1,000) shares new Common no par exchanged again for (1) share new Common no par 9/17/2001
Note: In effect holders received $3.20 cash per share and public interest was eliminated

VINLAND PPTY TR (CA)
Each old Share of Bene. Int. no par exchanged for (0.2) new Share of Bene. Int. no par 12/01/1995
Reincorporated under the laws of Nevada as Tarragon Realty Investors Inc. and new Shares of Bene. Int. no par reclassified as Common 1¢ par 07/25/1997
Tarragon Realty Investors Inc. name changed to Tarragon Corp. 07/01/2004
(See Tarragon Corp.)

VINOBLE INC (DE)
Name changed to Matrixx Resource Holdings, Inc. 07/14/2006
(See Matrixx Resource Holdings, Inc.)

VINRAY MALARTIC MINES LTD. (ON)
Recapitalized as New Vinray Mines Ltd. in 1954
Each share Capital Stock $1 par exchanged for (0.5) share Capital Stock $1 par
New Vinray Mines Ltd. recapitalized as Atlas Telefilm Ltd. 3/11/60 which recapitalized as Allied Telemedia Ltd. 1/24/64
(See Allied Telemedia Ltd.)

VINSON BIOTECH INC (MB)
Issue Information - 2,944,270 shares COM offered at $0.30 per share on 03/20/2003
Name changed to Kane Biotech Inc. 10/1/2003

VINSOR CORP (NY)
Name changed to AB Holding Group, Inc. 1/31/90
AB Holding Group, Inc. name changed to AG-Bag International Ltd. (NY) 10/12/90 which reincorporated in Delaware in January 1995 which name changed to AB Holding Group, Inc. 1/24/2005
(See AB Holding Group, Inc.)

VINTA EXPLS LTD (BC)
Recapitalized as Progressive Technologies Inc. 08/11/1992
Each share Common no par exchanged for (0.25) share Common no par
Progressive Technologies Inc. recapitalized as Progressive Applied Technologies Inc. 08/12/1999 which recapitalized as Pacific Vegas Global Strategies Inc. (BC) 07/23/2002 which reorganized in Canada as Cathay Forest Products Corp. 09/30/2004
(See Cathay Forest Products Corp.)

VINTAGE BK (NAPA, CA)
Common no par split (2) for (1) by issuance of (1) additional share payable 11/4/97 to holders of record 10/1/97
Stock Dividends - 5% payable 3/20/98 to holders of record 2/27/98; 5% payable 3/22/99 to holders of record 3/1/99
Under plan of reorganization each share Common no par automatically became (1) share North Bay Bancorp Common no par 6/11/99
North Bay Bancorp merged into Umpqua Holdings Corp. 4/26/2007

VINTAGE ENERGY & EXPL INC (NV)
SEC revoked common stock registration 03/02/2010

VINTAGE ENTERPRISES INC (GA)
Chapter 11 proceedings converted to Chapter 7 on 08/28/1990
No stockholders' equity

VINTAGE PETE INC (DE)
Common $0.005 par split (2) for (1) by issuance of (1) additional share payable 10/7/97 to holders of record 9/26/97 Ex date - 10/8/97
Merged into Occidental Petroleum Corp. 1/30/2006
Each share Common $0.005 exchanged for (0.42) share Common 20¢ par and $20 cash

VINTAGE PPTYS INC (NV)
Name changed to Xecom Corp. 10/24/1995
Xecom Corp. name changed to AirStar Technologies, Inc. 04/28/1998
(See AirStar Technologies, Inc.)

VINTAGE RESOURCE CORP (AB)
Acquired by Acclaim Energy Inc. 7/23/2001
Each share Common no par exchanged for $0.292 cash

VINTAGE WINES OF CANADA (CANADA)
Name changed to Andres Wines (Canada) Ltd. 3/13/69
Andres Wines (Canada) Ltd. name changed to Andres Wines Ltd. 10/23/70 which name changed to Andrew Peller Ltd. 10/27/2006

VINTNER INC (UT)
Name changed to West Coast Vineyards, Inc. 12/5/73
(See West Coast Vineyards, Inc.)

VINTON MILLING CO., INC. (VA)
Charter cancelled and proclaimed dissolved for failure to file reports 4/22/38

VINYL PLASTICS INC (WI)
Each share Class A Common 5¢ par exchanged for (0.001) share Common $50 par 4/7/78

Each share Common $50 par exchanged for (0.0117647) share Common no par 5/2/91
Note: In effect holders received $0.19 cash per share and public interest was eliminated

VINYL PRODS INC (NV)
Name changed to Crowd Shares Aftermarket, Inc. 02/13/2014
Crowd Shares Aftermarket, Inc. name changed to AAA Century Group USA, Inc. 12/09/2016

VIOCLONE BIOLOGICALS INC (BC)
Struck off register and declared dissolved for failure to file returns 4/22/94

VIOLA GROUP INC (NY)
Name changed to Datameg Corp. (NY) 09/07/2000
Datameg Corp. (NY) reincorporated in Delaware 04/27/2005 which recapitalized as Natural Blue Resources, Inc. 07/24/2009

VIOLAMAC MINES LTD. (ON)
Name changed to Kam-Kotia Mines Ltd. 3/11/66
(See Kam-Kotia Mines Ltd.)

VIOLIN MEMORY INC (DE)
Each share old Common $0.0001 par exchanged for (0.25) share new Common $0.0001 par 07/06/2016
Plan of reorganization under Chapter 11 Federal Bankruptcy proceedings effective 04/21/2017
No stockholders' equity

VION PHARMACEUTICALS INC (DE)
Each share old Common 1¢ par exchanged for (0.1) share new Common 1¢ par 02/21/2008
Plan of reorganization under Chapter 11 Federal Bankruptcy proceedings effective 04/08/2010
No stockholders' equity

VIOQUEST PHARMACEUTICALS INC (MN)
Reincorporated under the laws of Delaware and Common 1¢ par changed to $0.001 par 10/06/2005

VIP, INC. (NH)
Dissolved 12/26/67
No stockholders' equity

VIP DYNASTY INTL MARKETING CORP (BC)
Struck off register and declared dissolved for failure to file returns 12/11/87

VIP GLOBAL CAP INC (CO)
Each share old Common no par exchanged for (0.1) share new Common no par 01/05/1993
Each share new Common no par exchanged for (0.33333333) share Common $0.001 par 02/14/1994
SEC revoked common stock registration 10/07/2010

VIP SCANDINAVIA A S (NORWAY)
Stock Dividend - 50% 03/18/1987
Name changed to Viking Media A/S 06/29/1990

VIP WORLDNET INC (NV)
Charter delinquent for failure to file annual reports 06/01/2001

VIP'S RESTAURANTS, INC. (OR)
Name changed to VIP'S Industries, Inc. 1/1/87

VIPAR INC (UT)
Name changed to Umbra, Inc. 2/12/93
(See Umbra, Inc.)

VIPC COMMUNICATIONS INC (DE)
SEC revoked common stock registration 01/12/2011

VIPER GOLD LTD (AB)
Each share old Common no par exchanged for (0.1) share new Common no par 02/18/2015

Name changed to QuikFlo Health Inc. 11/30/2015
QuikFlo Health Inc. recapitalized as Friday Night Inc. (AB) 06/16/2017 which reincorporated in British Columbia as 1933 Industries Inc. 10/01/2018

VIPER INTL HLDGS LTD (NV)
Name changed to 50on.com, Inc. 06/13/2000
50on.com, Inc. reorganized as Design Marketing Concepts Inc. 10/31/2000 which name changed to WEB Pay-Per-View Inc. 05/30/2001 which name changed to U.S Federal Financial Corp. 09/25/2001 which name changed to Vibe Records Inc. 04/23/2002 which name changed to Great Entertainment & Sports Inc. 03/07/2003 which name changed to Rockit!, Inc. 06/11/2007
(See Rockit!, Inc.)

VIPER NETWORKS INC (UT)
Common $0.001 par split (11) for (10) by issuance of (0.1) additional share payable 10/17/2004 to holders of record 09/17/2004 Ex date - 09/15/2004
Reincorporated under the laws of Nevada 05/18/2005

VIPER POWERSPORTS INC (NV)
Each share old Common $0.001 par exchanged for (0.25) share new Common $0.001 par 09/28/2009
SEC revoked common stock registration 04/05/2016

VIPER RES INC (AZ)
Reorganized under the laws of Bermuda as ImuMed International, Ltd. 01/05/2000
Each share Common $0.001 par exchanged for (0.5) share Common $0.001 par
ImuMed International, Ltd. name changed to Ashby Corp. Ltd. 05/13/2002

VIPER RES INC (NV)
Recapitalized as Rambo Medical Group, Inc. 08/09/2013
Each share Common $0.00001 par exchanged for (0.01) share Common $0.00001 par
Rambo Medical Group, Inc. name changed to HK eBus Corp. 09/15/2015

VIPOND CONSOLIDATED MINES LTD.
Merged into Anglo-Huronian Ltd. on a (1) for (5) basis in 1933
Anglo-Huronian Ltd. merged into Kerr Addison Mines Ltd. 11/18/63 which merged into Noranda Inc. 4/11/96 which name changed to Falconbridge Ltd. (New) 2005 on 7/1/2005
(See Falconbridge Ltd. (New) 2005)

VIPONT MNG CO (WY)
Name changed to Lander Energy Co. (WY) 1/11/80
Lander Energy Co. (WY) reincorporated in Colorado 7/8/86 which recapitalized as Voice It Worldwide Inc. 12/29/94
(See Voice It Worldwide Inc.)

VIPONT PHARMACEUTICAL INC (DE)
Name changed 12/22/1980
Reorganized 06/04/1982
Name changed 04/24/1987
Name changed from Vipont Chemical to Vipont Laboratories, Inc. (WY) 12/22/1980
Reorganized from (WY) to under the laws of Delaware 06/04/1982
Each share Common 10¢ par exchanged for (0.2) share Common $0.001 par
Name changed from Vipont Laboratories, Inc. to Vipont Pharmaceutical, Inc. 04/24/1987

Merged into Colgate-Palmolive Co. 03/02/1990
Each share Common $0.001 par exchanged for $14 cash

VIQ SOLUTIONS INC (AB)
Reincorporated under the laws of Ontario 08/14/2017

VIRACOCHA ENERGY INC (AB)
Plan of arrangement effective 6/7/2004
Each share Common no par exchanged for (0.1) share Chamaelo Energy Inc. Common no par and (0.248) Provident Energy Trust Trust Unit no par
(See each company's lising)

VIRAGE INC (DE)
Merged into Autonomy Corp. PLC 09/02/2003
Each share Common $0.001 par exchanged for $1.10 cash

VIRAGE LOGIC CORP (DE)
Issue Information - 3,750,000 shares COM offered at $12 per share on 07/31/2000
Acquired by Synopsys, Inc. 09/03/2010
Each share Common $0.001 par exchanged for $12 cash

VIRAGEN INC (DE)
Each share old Common 1¢ par exchanged for (0.1) share new Common 1¢ par 06/15/2004
Executed an Assignment for the Benefit of Creditors 10/18/2007
Stockholders' equity unlikely

VIRAGEN INTL INC (DE)
Name changed 03/27/2002
Name changed from Viragen (Europe) Ltd. to Viragen International, Inc. 03/27/2002
Each share Common 1¢ par exchanged for (1) share Common 1¢ par
Each share old Common 1¢ par exchanged for (0.025) share new Common 1¢ par 09/05/2007
Executed an Assignment for the Benefit of Creditors 10/18/2007
Stockholders' equity unlikely

VIRAL CTL TECHNOLOGY INC NEW (DE)
Reincorporated 12/00/1990
State of incorporation changed from (UT) to (DE) 12/00/1990
Reorganized as Veridien Corp. 11/08/1991
Each share Common $0.001 par exchanged for (1) share Common $0.001 par
(See Veridien Corp.)

VIRAL GENETICS INC (DE)
Recapitalized as VG Life Sciences Inc. 11/27/2012
Each (600) shares Common $0.0001 par exchanged for (1) share Common $0.0001 par

VIRAL RESH TECHNOLOGIES INC (NV)
Charter revoked for failure to file reports and pay fees 4/1/91

VIRAL TESTING SYS CORP (DE)
Charter cancelled and declared inoperative and void for non-payment of taxes 3/1/91

VIRALYTICS LTD (AUSTRALIA)
Basis changed from (1:30) to (1:3) 08/23/2011
ADR agreement terminated 06/29/2018
Each Sponsored ADR for Ordinary exchanged for $3.814 cash

VIRANY CREATIONS LTD (NY)
Each share Common 1¢ par exchanged for (0.4) share Common 10¢ par 07/06/1972
Charter cancelled and proclaimed dissolved for failure to pay taxes 09/30/1981

VIRATA CORP (DE)
Common $0.001 par split (2) for (1) by issuance of (1) additional share payable 5/18/2000 to holders of record 5/4/2000 Ex date - 5/19/2000
Merged into GlobeSpan Virata, Inc. 12/14/2001
Each share Common $0.001 par exchanged for (1.02) shares Common $0.001 par
GlobeSpan Virata, Inc. merged into Conexant Systems, Inc. 2/27/2004

VIRATEK INC (DE)
Common 10¢ par split (2) for (1) by issuance of (1) additional share 08/18/1986
Merged into ICN Pharmaceuticals, Inc. (New) 11/10/1994
Each share Common 10¢ par exchanged for (0.499) share Common 1¢ par
ICN Pharmaceuticals, Inc. (New) name changed to Valeant Pharmaceuticals International 11/12/2003 which merged into Valeant Pharmaceuticals International, Inc. (Canada) 09/28/2010 which reincorporated in British Columbia 08/09/2014

VIRBAC CORP (DE)
Merged into Virbac S.A. 11/13/2006
Each share Common 1¢ par exchanged for $5.75 cash

VIRCO MFG CO (CA)
Stock Dividends - 10% 6/1/82; 10% 6/1/83; 10% 4/23/84
Reincorporated under the laws of Delaware and Common $1 par changed to 1¢ par 7/13/84

VIRDEN PACKING CO. (CA)
Name changed to Vica Co. 6/7/35

VIREXX MED CORP (AB)
Plan of reorganization under Bankruptcy and Insolvency Act effective 12/23/2008
No stockholders' equity

VIREXX RESH INC (AB)
Merged into ViRexx Medical Corp. 12/23/2003
Each share Common no par exchanged for (0.5285974) share Common no par
(See ViRexx Medical Corp.)

VIRGIN AMER INC (DE)
Merged into Alaska Air Group, Inc. 12/14/2016
Each share Common 1¢ par exchanged for $57 cash

VIRGIN AUSTRALIA HLDGS LTD (AUSTRALIA)
Name changed 04/09/2012
Name changed from Virgin Blue Holdings Ltd. to Virgin Australia Holdings Ltd. 04/09/2012
ADR agreement terminated 12/26/2017
No ADR's remain outstanding

VIRGIN ENERGY INC (AB)
Name changed to NTI Newmerical Inc. 10/29/2001
(See NTI Newmerical Inc.)

VIRGIN EXPRESS HLDGS PLC (ENGLAND & WALES)
Each old Sponsored ADR for Ordinary exchanged for (0.33333333) new Sponsored ADR for Ordinary 05/28/2002
ADR basis changed from (1:1/3) to (1:1) 05/28/2002
ADR agreement terminated 07/17/2005
Each new Sponsored ADR for Ordinary exchanged for $1.1521 cash

VIRGIN MEDIA INC (DE)
Merged into Liberty Global PLC 06/10/2013
Each share Common 1¢ par exchanged for (0.2582) share Class

A Ordinary 1¢ par, (0.1928) share Class C Ordinary 1¢ par and $17.50 cash

VIRGIN METALS INC (ON)
Each share old Common no par exchanged for (0.2) share new Common no par 09/17/2010
Recapitalized as Minera Alamos Inc. 05/15/2014
Each share new Common no par exchanged for (0.1) share Common no par

VIRGIN MOBILE USA INC (DE)
Issue Information - 27,500,000 shares CL A offered at $15 per share on 10/10/2007
Merged into Sprint Nextel Corp. 11/24/2009
Each share Class A Common 1¢ par exchanged for (1.3668) shares Ser. 1 Common $2 par
Sprint Nextel Corp. merged into Sprint Corp. (DE) 07/10/2013

VIRGIN VENTURES INC (NV)
Name changed to Dial Food, Inc. 06/29/1988
(See Dial Food, Inc.)

VIRGINIA ALBERENE CORP.
Reorganized as Alberene Stone Corp. of Virginia in 1935
Details not available

VIRGINIA BANCORP INC (VA)
Merged into Bay Banks of Virginia, Inc. 04/01/2017
Each share Common no par exchanged for (1.178) shares Common $5 par

VIRGINIA BK & TR CO (DANVILLE, VA)
Under plan of reorganization each share Common $5 par automatically became (1) share Virginia Bank Bankshares, Inc. Common $5 par 01/01/1998

VIRGINIA BEACH FED FINL CORP (VA)
Name changed to First Coastal Bankshares, Inc. 5/20/98
First Coastal Bankshares, Inc. merged into Centura Banks, Inc. 3/26/99 which merged into Royal Bank of Canada (Montreal, QC) 6/5/2001

VIRGINIA BEACH FED SVGS BK (VIRGINIA BEACH, VA)
Name changed 1/14/88
Stock Dividend - 10% 2/15/85
Common 1¢ par split (3) for (2) by issuance of (0.5) additional share 4/15/86
Name changed from Virginia Beach Federal Savings & Loan Association (U.S.A.) to Virginia Beach Federal Savings Bank (Virginia Beach, VA) 1/14/88
Common 1¢ par split (3) for (2) by issuance of (0.5) additional share 10/24/89
Under plan of reorganization each share Common 1¢ par automatically became (1) share Virginia Beach Federal Financial Corp. Common 1¢ par 6/28/91
Virginia Beach Federal Financial Corp. name changed to First Coastal Bankshares, Inc. 5/20/98 which merged into Centura Banks, Inc. 3/26/99 which merged into Royal Bank of Canada (Montreal, QC) 6/5/2001

VIRGINIA BEACH FESTIVAL PARK, LTD. (VA)
Charter cancelled and proclaimed dissolved for failure to file reports 6/1/76

VIRGINIA BRIDGE & IRON CO.
Assets sold in 1936

VIRGINIA CAP BANCSHARES INC (VA)
Merged into BB&T Corp. 6/28/2001
Each share Common 1¢ par exchanged for (0.5109) shares Common $5 par

VIRGINIA CAP CORP (VA)
Liquidation completed
Each share Common $1 par received initial distribution of (0.47) share Atlantic Research Corp. Common $1 par 09/30/1982
Each share Common $1 par received second distribution of (0.33) share Gulf Energy & Development Corp. Common 10¢ par, (0.58) share Pandick Press, Inc. Common 10¢ par and $12 cash 01/19/1983
(See each company's listing)
Each share Common $1 par received third distribution of $16 cash 05/02/1983
Each share Common $1 par received fourth and final distribution of $3.43 cash 06/07/1983
Note: Certificates were not required to be surrendered and are without value

VIRGINIA-CAROLINA CHEMICAL CORP. (VA)
Common no par changed to $1 par 10/14/60
Recapitalized 9/28/62
Each share 6% Preferred $100 par exchanged for (1.3) shares 5% Prior Preferred $50 par, (1) share 5% Conv. Preferred $50 par and (1) share Common $1 par
5% Prior Preferred $50 par called for redemption 10/16/63
Merged into Socony Mobil Oil Co., Inc. 11/29/63
Each share 5% Conv. Preferred $50 par exchanged for (1.32) shares Capital Stock $15 par
Each share Common $1 par exchanged for (1.2) shares Capital Stock $15 par
Socony Mobil Oil Co., Inc. name changed to Mobil Oil Corp. 5/18/66 which reorganized as Mobil Corp. 6/21/76 which merged into Exxon Mobil Corp. 11/30/99

VIRGINIA CHEMICALS & SMELTING CO. (ME)
5% 1st Preferred called for redemption 01/01/1963
Common no par changed to $2 par 04/18/1963
Name changed to Virginia Chemicals, Inc. 03/22/1965
Virginia Chemicals, Inc. merged into Celanese Corp. 01/19/1981
(See Celanese Corp.)

VIRGINIA CHEMS INC (ME)
Common $2 par split (3) for (2) by issuance of (0.5) additional share 04/15/1969
Common $2 par split (3) for (2) by issuance of (0.5) additional share 08/27/1976
Common $2 par split (3) for (2) by issuance of (0.5) additional share 05/25/1979
Merged into Celanese Corp. 01/19/1981
Each share Common $2 par exchanged for (0.475) share Common no par
(See Celanese Corp.)

VIRGINIA CITY GOLD MINES INC (ID)
Recapitalized as NEW AGE CITIES.com, Inc. (ID) 03/29/1999
Each share Common 2¢ par exchanged for (0.0125) share Common 2¢ par
NEW AGE CITIES.com, Inc. (ID) reincorporated in Florida as Genesis Technology Group, Inc. 10/15/2001 which name changed to Genesis Pharmaceuticals Enterprises, Inc. 10/26/2007 which name changed to Jiangbo Pharmaceuticals, Inc. 05/12/2009
(See Jiangbo Pharmaceuticals, Inc.)

VIRGINIA CO BK (NEWPORT NEWS, VA)
Merged into Eastern Virginia Bankshares, Inc. 11/14/2014
Each share Common $5 par exchanged for (0.9259) share Common $2 par
Eastern Virginia Bankshares, Inc. merged into Southern National Bancorp of Virginia, Inc. 06/23/2017

VIRGINIA COAL & IRON CO. (VA)
Capital Stock $100 par changed to $25 par and (3) additional shares issued 10/25/1963
Name changed to Penn Virginia Corp. (Old) 04/19/1967
(See Penn Virginia Corp. (Old))

VIRGINIA COMM BANCORP INC (VA)
Common $1 par split (5) for (4) by issuance of (0.25) additional share payable 04/12/2002 to holders of record 03/15/2002 Ex date - 04/15/2002
Common $1 par split (2) for (1) by issuance of (1) additional share payable 05/30/2003 to holders of record 05/05/2003 Ex date - 06/02/2003
Common $1 par split (5) for (4) by issuance of (0.25) additional share payable 07/15/2004 to holders of record 06/15/2004 Ex date - 07/16/2004
Common $1 par split (5) for (4) by issuance of (0.25) additional share payable 05/09/2005 to holders of record 04/15/2005 Ex date - 05/10/2005
Common $1 par split (3) for (2) by issuance of (0.5) additional share payable 05/12/2006 to holders of record 04/28/2006 Ex date - 05/15/2006
Stock Dividends - 10% payable 05/26/2000 to holders of record 05/12/2000; 25% payable 05/11/2001 to holders of record 04/16/2001 Ex date - 05/14/2001; 10% payable 05/01/2007 to holders of record 04/16/2007 Ex date - 04/12/2007; 10% payable 05/07/2008 to holders of record 04/14/2008 Ex date - 04/10/2008
Merged into United Bankshares, Inc. 01/31/2014
Each share Common $1 par exchanged for (0.5442) share Common $2.50 par

VIRGINIA COMM BK (ARLINGTON, VA)
Stock Dividends - 35% payable 06/26/1997 to holders of record 06/16/1997; 10% payable 06/10/1999 to holders of record 05/31/1999
Under plan of reorganization each share Common $1 par automatically became (1) share Virginia Commerce Bancorp, Inc. Common $1 par 12/22/1999
Virginia Commerce Bancorp, Inc. merged into United Bankshares, Inc. 01/31/2014

VIRGINIA COMWLTH BANKSHARES INC (VA)
Common $5 par split (3) for (2) by issuance of (0.5) additional share 11/20/1969
Name changed to Bank of Virginia Co. 07/17/1972
Bank of Virginia Co. name changed to Signet Banking Corp. 07/14/1986 which merged into First Union Corp. 11/28/1997 which name changed to Wachovia Corp. (Ctfs. dated after 09/01/2001) 09/01/2001 which merged into Wells Fargo & Co. (New) 12/31/2008

VIRGINIA COMMONWEALTH CORP. (VA)
Common $10 par changed to $5 par and (1) additional share issued 03/29/1965
Name changed to Virginia Commonwealth Bankshares, Inc. 10/10/1966
Virginia Commonwealth Bankshares, Inc. name changed to Bank of Virginia Co. 07/17/1972 which name changed to Signet Banking Corp. 07/14/1986 which merged into First Union Corp. 11/28/1997 which name changed to Wachovia Corp. (Ctfs. dated after 09/01/2001) 09/01/2001 which merged into Wells Fargo & Co. (New) 12/31/2008

VIRGINIA COMMONWEALTH FINL CORP (VA)
Merged into Virginia Financial Group, Inc. 01/22/2002
Each share Common $2.50 par exchanged for (1.4391) shares Common $5 par
Virginia Financial Group, Inc. name changed to StellarOne Corp. 02/28/2008 which merged into Union First Market Bankshares Corp. 01/02/2014 which name changed to Union Bankshares Corp. 04/28/2014

VIRGINIA COMPUTER COLLEGE, INC. (VA)
Assets sold for benefit of creditors 3/14/74
No stockholders' equity

VIRGINIA DARE, LTD. (ON)
Adjudicated bankrupt 10/24/67
No stockholders' equity

VIRGINIA DARE STORES CORP. (DE)
Common $1 par reclassified as Class A $1 par in 1947
Class A $1 par reclassified as Common $1 par in 1950
Common $1 par split (3) for (1) by issuance of (2) additional shares 11/30/61
Name changed to Atlantic Thrift Centers, Inc. 11/29/63
(See Atlantic Thrift Centers, Inc.)

VIRGINIA DATA CTR INC (VA)
Each share Common 10¢ par exchanged for (0.004) share $25 par 09/10/1979
Stock Dividend - 10% 10/31/1975
Merged into E.D.S. Corp. of Virginia, Inc. 10/05/1982
Each share Common $5 par exchanged for $450 cash

VIRGINIA ELEC & PWR CO (VA)
Each share $6 Preferred no par exchanged for (1) share $5 Preferred $100 par 00/00/1944
Common no par changed to $10 par 00/00/1948
Common $10 par changed to $8 par and (1) additional share issued 05/04/1957
Common $8 par changed to no par and (0.5) additional share issued 05/24/1963
Common no par split (4) for (3) by issuance of (0.33333333) additional share 05/11/1968
Reorganized as Dominion Resources, Inc. (Old) 05/19/1983
Each share Common no par exchanged for (0.66666666) share Common no par
(See Dominion Resources, Inc. (Old))
$2.90 Preference no par called for redemption 02/02/1984
$9.75 Preferred $100 par called for redemption 06/30/1986
$8.84 Preferred $100 par called for redemption 09/30/1986
$8.20 Preferred $100 par called for redemption 08/07/1992
$8.40 Preferred $100 par called for redemption 08/07/1992
$8.60 Preferred Old Money Stamped

$100 par called for redemption 08/07/1992
$8.625 Preferred $100 par called for redemption 08/07/1992
$8.925 Preferred $100 par called for redemption 08/07/1992
$8.60 Preferred $100 par called for redemption 09/08/1992
$7.325 Preferred $100 par called for redemption 03/11/1993
$7.72 Preferred $100 par called for redemption 08/02/1993
$7.72 Preferred 1972 Ser. $100 par called for redemption 09/14/1993
$7.58 Preferred $100 par called for redemption 09/14/1993
$7.20 Preferred $100 par called for redemption 10/02/1995
$7.30 Preferred Dividend $100 par called for redemption 10/02/1995
$7.45 Preferred $100 par called for redemption 10/02/1995
$5.58 Preferred $100 par called for redemption at $100 on 03/01/2000
$6.35 Preferred $100 par called for redemption at $100 on 09/01/2000
Money Market Preferred called for redemption at $100 on 12/20/2001
Money Market Preferred June 1987 Ser. called for redemption at $100 on 12/27/2001
Auction Market Preferred Ser. 1992A $100 par called for redemption at $100 on 09/05/2002
Auction Market Preferred Ser. 1992 B called for redemption at $100 on 09/05/2002
Auction Market Preferred Ser. 1992 A called for redemption at $100 on 09/12/2002
Money Market Preferred October 1988 Ser. $100 par called for redemption at $100 on 09/26/2002
Auction Market Preferred Ser. 1992B $100 par called for redemption at $100 on 09/12/2002
Money Market Preferred October 1988 Ser. called for redemption at $100,000 on 09/26/2002
Money Market Preferred June 1989 Ser. $100 par called for redemption at $100 on 10/03/2002
Flexible Money Market Preferred Ser. A $100 par called for redemption at $100 on 03/20/2014
$4.04 Preferred $100 par called for redemption at $102.27 plus $0.3321 accrued dividends on 10/20/2014
$4.12 Preferred $100 par called for redemption at $103.73 plus $0.3386 accrued dividends on 10/20/2014
$4.20 Preferred $100 par called for redemption at $102.50 plus $0.3452 accrued dividends on 10/20/2014
$4.80 Preferred $100 par called for redemption at $101 plus $0.3945 accrued dividends on 10/20/2014
$5 Preferred $100 par called for redemption at $112.50 plus $0.411 accrued dividends on 10/20/2014
$6.98 Preferred $100 par called for redemption at $100 plus $0.5737 accrued dividends on 10/20/2014
$7.05 Preferred $100 par called for redemption at $100 plus $0.5795 accrued dividends on 10/20/2014

VIRGINIA ENERGY CORP (AB)
Name changed to Winstar Resources Ltd. (Old) and (4) additional shares issued 08/01/2000
Winstar Resources Ltd. (Old) recapitalized as Winstar Resources Ltd. (New) 10/25/2005 which merged into Serinus Energy Inc. (AB) 06/27/2013 which reincorporated in Jersey as Serinus Energy PLC 05/15/2018
(See Serinus Energy PLC)

VIRGINIA ENERGY RES INC OLD (BC)
Reorganized as Anthem Resources Inc. 09/28/2012
Each share Common no par exchanged for (0.33333333) share Common no par and (0.1) share Virginia Energy Resources Inc. (New) Common no par
Note: Unexchanged certificates were cancelled and became without value 09/28/2018
Anthem Resources Inc. merged into Boss Power Corp. 07/23/2015 which name changed to Eros Resources Corp. 07/29/2015

VIRGINIA FERRY CORP. (VA)
Liquidation completed 1/28/65

VIRGINIA FINL GROUP INC (VA)
Name changed 01/22/2002
Common $5 par split (2) for (1) by issuance of (1) additional share payable 12/30/1997 to holders of record 12/10/1997
Under plan of merger name changed from Virginia Financial Corp. to Virginia Financial Group, Inc. 01/22/2002
Common $5 par changed to $1 par 08/24/2006
Common $1 par split (3) for (2) by issuance of (0.5) additional share payable 09/06/2006 to holders of record 08/14/2006 Ex date - 09/07/2006
Under plan of merger name changed to StellarOne Corp. 02/28/2008
StellarOne Corp. merged into Union First Market Bankshares Corp. 01/02/2014 which name changed to Union Bankshares Corp. 04/28/2014

VIRGINIA FIRST FINL CORP (VA)
Name changed 7/31/84
Reorganized 1/18/94
Common $8 par changed to $4 par and (1) additional share issued in November 1979
Name changed from Virginia First Savings & Loan Association (Petersburg, VA) to Virginia First Savings, F.S.B. (Petersburg, VA) 7/31/84
Each share Common $4 par exchanged for (1) share Common $4 par
Common $4 par split (2) for (1) by issuance of (1) additional share 8/1/86
Stock Dividend - 10% 1/10/86
Under plan of reorganization each share Virginia First Savings, F.S.B. (Petersburg, VA) Common $4 par automatically became (1) share Virginia First Financial Corp. Common $1 par 1/18/94
Merged into BB&T Corp. 12/1/97
Each share Common $1 par exchanged for (0.326455) share Common $5 par and $7.50 cash

VIRGINIA GAS CO (DE)
Merged into NUI Corp. (New) 3/28/2001
Each share Common no par exchanged for (0.144) share Common no par
(See NUI Corp. (New))

VIRGINIA HEARTLAND BK (FREDERICKSBURG, VA)
Merged into Virginia Commonwealth Financial Corp. 10/08/1998
Each share Common no par exchanged for (1.15) shares Common $2.50 par
Virginia Commonwealth Financial Corp. merged into Virginia Financial Group, Inc. 01/22/2002 which name changed to StellarOne Corp. 02/28/2008 which merged into Union First Market Bankshares Corp. 01/02/2014 which name changed to Union Bankshares Corp. 04/28/2014

VIRGINIA HERITAGE BK (FAIRFAX, VA)
Merged into Eagle Bancorp, Inc. 10/31/2014
Each share Common $4 par exchanged for (0.6632) share Common 1¢ par and $7.50 cash

VIRGINIA HILLS OIL CORP (AB)
Adjudged bankrupt 05/03/2017
No stockholders' equity

VIRGINIA HOME LOAN CORP. (VA)
Charter revoked for failure to file reports 6/1/75

VIRGINIA HOT SPRINGS INC (VA)
Each share 7% Preferred $100 par exchanged for (1) share 5% Preferred $100 par in 1940
Each share 5% Preferred $100 par exchanged for (5) shares Common $25 par in 1948
Each share Common $100 par exchanged for (1) share Common $1 par in 1940
Each share Common $1 par exchanged for (1) share Common $25 par in 1948
Common $25 par changed to no par and (9) additional shares issued 11/2/92
Merged into Celebration Associates LLC 3/8/2002
Each share Common no par exchanged for $27.50 cash

VIRGINIA INTERNATIONAL CO. (VA)
Merged into Alaska Interstate Co. (Alaska) 7/28/77
Each share Common 50¢ par exchanged for (1.325) shares Common $1 par and (1) share Virginia International Co. (Del.) Special Stock $1 par
(See each company's listing)

VIRGINIA INTL CO (DE)
Special Shares 1¢ par called for redemption 12/24/1985
Public interest eliminated

VIRGINIA IRON COAL & COKE CO (VA)
Recapitalized 00/00/1947
Each share 5% Preferred $100 par exchanged for (7) shares 4% Preferred $25 par
Each share Common $100 par exchanged for (1) share Common $10 par
Each share Common $10 par exchanged for (5) shares Common $2 par 06/01/1956
Stock Dividend - 10% 12/09/1960
Merged into Bates Manufacturing Co., Inc. 10/31/1969
Each share Common $2 par exchanged for (1) share $1 Conv. Preferred Ser. A $7.50 par
(See Bates Manufacturing Co., Inc.)

VIRGINIA LIFE & CASUALTY CO.
Acquired by United Insurance Co. 00/00/1949
Details not available

VIRGINIA MINES INC (CANADA)
Merged into Osisko Gold Royalties Ltd. 02/18/2015
Each share Common no par exchanged for (0.92) share Common no par
Note: Unexchanged certificates will be cancelled and become without value 02/18/2021

VIRGINIA MINING CORP. (QC)
Recapitalized as Consolidated Virginia Mining Corp. 2/24/64
Each share Capital Stock $1 par exchanged for (0.2) share Capital Stock $1 par
(See Consolidated Virginia Mining Corp.)

VIRGINIA NATL BK (CHARLOTTESVILLE, VA)
Stock Dividend - 15% payable 06/30/2011 to holders of record 06/15/2011 Ex date - 06/13/2011
Under plan of reorganization each share Common $2.50 par automatically became (1) share Virginia National Bankshares Corp. Common $2.50 par 12/18/2013

VIRGINIA NATL BK (CHARLOTTESVILLE, VA)
Each share Conv. Preferred Ser. A exchanged for (1) share Common $2.50 par 02/10/2006
(Additional Information in Active)

VIRGINIA NATL BK (NORFOLK, VA)
Stock Dividend - 50% 3/24/69
Under plan of reorganization each share Common $5 par automatically became (1) share of Virginia National Bankshares, Inc. Common $5 par 7/10/72
Virginia National Bankshares, Inc. merged into Sovran Financial Corp. 12/31/83 which merged into C&S/Sovran Corp. 9/1/90 which merged into NationsBank Corp. 12/31/91 which reincorporated in Delaware as BankAmerica Corp. (Old) 9/25/98 which merged into BankAmerica Corp. (New) 9/30/98 which name changed to Bank of America Corp. 4/28/99

VIRGINIA NATL BANKSHARES INC (VA)
Common $5 par split (3) for (2) by issuance of (0.5) additional share 8/31/78
Merged into Sovran Financial Corp. 12/31/83
Each share Common $5 par exchanged for (1.15) shares Common $5 par
Sovran Financial Corp. merged into C&S/Sovran Corp. 9/1/90 which merged into NationsBank Corp. 12/31/91 which reincorporated in Delaware as BankAmerica Corp. (Old) 9/25/98 which merged into BankAmerica Corp. (New) 9/30/98 which name changed to Bank of America Corp. 4/28/99

VIRGINIA ORANGE FREE ST GOLD MNG LTD (SOUTH AFRICA)
Merged into Harmony Gold Mining Co. Ltd. 06/15/1973
Each ADR for Ordinary ZAR 50 par exchanged for (0.72) Unsponsored ADR for Ordinary ZAR 50 par

VIRGINIA PWR CAP TR I (DE)
8.05% Trust Preferred Securities called for redemption at $25 on 09/30/2002

VIRGINIA PWR CAP TR II (DE)
7.375% Guaranteed Trust Preferred Securities called for redemption at $25 on 05/19/2008

VIRGINIA PUBLIC SERVICE CO.
Merged into Virginia Electric & Power Co. 00/00/1944
Each share 7% Preferred exchanged for (1) share $5 Preferred and $24.50 cash plus accrued dividends from 03/31/1944
Each share 6% Preferred exchanged for (1) share $5 Preferred and $19 cash plus accrued dividends from 03/31/1944
Virginia Electric & Power Co. reorganized as Dominion Resources, Inc. (Old) 05/19/1983
(See Dominion Resources Inc. (Old))

VIRGINIA REAL ESTATE INVT TR (VA)
Merged into VREI Corp. 01/30/1981
Each Share of Bene. Int. no par exchanged for $21.25 cash

VIRGINIA RED LAKE MINES LTD. (ON)
Charter cancelled for failure to file reports and pay taxes in 1957

VIRGINIA SAVSHARES INC (VA)
Charter revoked for failure to file reports and pay taxes 06/01/1979

VIRGINIA SKY LINE INC (VA)
$6 Preferred $50 par changed to $100 par 10/25/1960
$6 Preferred $100 par called for redemption 10/25/1971
Merged into ARA Services, Inc. 09/22/1971
Each share Common $1 par exchanged for (0.42871) share Common 50¢ par
(See ARA Services, Inc.)

VIRGINIA STAGE LINES, INC. (VA)
Merged into Transcontinental Bus System, Inc. 9/17/68
Each share Common $1 par exchanged for (0.85) share Common $1 par
Transcontinental Bus System, Inc. name changed to TCO Industries, Inc. 4/29/68 which merged into Holiday Inns of America, Inc. 2/27/69 which name changed to Holiday Inns, Inc. 5/22/69 which reorganized in Delaware as Holiday Corp. 5/15/85 which merged into Bass PLC 2/7/90 which name changed to Six Continents PLC 7/31/2001

VIRGINIA TEL & TELEG CO (VA)
5-1/2% Preferred $50 par called for redemption 3/31/59
Common $10 par split (4) for (3) by issuance of (1/3) additional share 1/5/62
Merged into Central Telephone Co. (New) 12/1/71
Each share Common $10 par exchanged for (0.82) share Conv. Jr. Preferred no par
(See Central Telephone Co. (New))

VIRGINIA TR CO (RICHMOND, VA)
Stock Dividend - 100% 12/14/43
Each share Capital Stock $50 par exchanged for (2.5) shares Capital Stock $20 par 1/17/57
Capital Stock $20 par changed to $10 par and (1) additional share issued plus a 20% stock dividend paid 3/30/64
Acquired by Virginia National Bankshares, Inc. 5/31/73
Each share Capital Stock $10 par exchanged for (3.75) shares Common $5 par
Virginia National Bankshares, Inc. merged into Sovran Financial Corp. 12/31/83 which merged into C&S/Sovran Corp. 9/1/90 which merged into NationsBank Corp. 12/31/91 which reincorporated in Delaware as BankAmerica Corp. (Old) 9/25/98 which merged into BankAmerica Corp. (New) 9/30/98 which name changed to Bank of America Corp. 4/28/99

VIRGINIAN POWER CO.
Acquired by Appalachian Electric Power Co. in 1931 which name changed to Appalachian Power Co. (Va.) (New) 4/17/58

VIRGINIAN RY CO (VA)
Each share Preferred $100 par exchanged for (4) shares Preferred $25 par 00/00/1939
Each share Common $100 par exchanged for (4) shares Common $25 par 00/00/1939
Preferred and Common $25 par changed to $10 par and (1.5) additional shares issued respectively 08/20/1957
Merged into Norfolk & Western Railway Co. 12/01/1959
Each share Preferred $10 par exchanged for (1) share 6% Preferred $10 par
Each share Common $10 par exchanged for (0.55) share Common $25 par
Norfolk & Western Railway Co. merged into Norfolk Southern Corp. 06/01/1982

VIRGO LARDER MINES, LTD. (ON)
Merged into Pardee Amalgamated Mines Ltd. in December 1954
Each share Capital Stock $1 par exchanged for (0.025) share Common $1 par
Pardee Amalgamated Mines Ltd. liquidated for Rio Algom Mines Ltd. 11/9/61 which name changed to Rio Algom Ltd. 4/30/75
(See Rio Algom Ltd.)

VIRIDIAN INC (CANADA)
Each share Common no par received distribution of (0.33333333) share Westaim Corp. Common no par payable 07/11/1996 to holders of record 07/08/1996 Ex date - 07/04/1996
Each share Common no par received distribution of (0.64) share Westaim Corp. Common no par payable 09/16/1996 to holders of record 09/09/1996 Ex date - 09/05/1996
Merged into Agrium Inc. 12/10/1996
Each share Common no par exchanged for (0.975) share Common no par
Agrium Inc. merged into Nutrien Ltd. 01/02/2018

VIRIDIS ENERGY INC (BC)
Each share old Common no par exchanged for (0.1) share new Common no par 06/16/2014
Name changed to Viridis Holdings Corp. 08/14/2018

VIRILITEC INDS INC (DE)
Name changed to ROO Group, Inc. 03/08/2004
ROO Group, Inc. name changed to KIT digital, Inc. 05/29/2008

VIRITA PORCUPINE GOLD MINES, LTD. (ON)
Charter cancelled by the Province of Ontario 11/5/53

VIROGEN INC (ID)
Charter forfeited for failure to file reports 12/01/1988

VIROGEN INC (TX)
Each share old Common $0.0001 par exchanged for (0.05) share new Common $0.0001 par 01/08/2009
Each share new Common $0.0001 par exchanged again for (0.001) share new Common $0.0001 par 12/03/2009
Each share new Common $0.0001 par exchanged again for (0.005) share new Common $0.0001 par 02/05/2010
Each share new Common $0.0001 par exchanged again for (0.001) share new Common $0.0001 par 02/04/2011
Recapitalized as Small Business Development Group, Inc. 09/05/2013
Each share new Common $0.0001 par exchanged for (0.00002) share Common $0.0001 par

VIROGROUP INC (FL)
Each share old Common 1¢ par exchanged for (0.125) share new Common 1¢ par 1/28/97
Merged into Safety-Kleen Corp. (New) 10/30/98
Each share new Common 1¢ par exchanged for $0.75 cash

VIROLOGIC INC (DE)
Name changed to Monogram Biosciences, Inc. 09/07/2005
(See Monogram Biosciences, Inc.)

VIROLOGY TESTING SCIENCES INC (DE)
Name changed to Viral Testing Systems Corp. 12/31/1992
(See Viral Testing Systems Corp.)

VIRONIC SYS INC (DE)
Charter cancelled and declared inoperative and void for non-payment of taxes 03/01/1986

VIROPHARMA INC (DE)
Acquired by Shire PLC 01/24/2014
Each share Common $0.002 par exchanged for $50 cash

VIROTEC INTL PLC (AUSTRALIA)
Name changed 06/26/2007
Name changed from Virotec International Ltd. to Virotec International PLC 06/26/2007
ADR agreement terminated 09/29/2008
No ADR's remain outstanding

VIRTEK VISION INTL INC (ON)
Acquired by Gerber Scientific, Inc. 11/10/2008
Each share Common no par exchanged for $1.05 cash

VIRTGAME CORP (DE)
Name changed 02/25/2002
Name changed from VirtGame.com Corp. to VirtGame Corp. 02/25/2002
Merged into Mikohn Gaming Corp. 10/07/2005
Each share Common $0.0001 par exchanged for (0.028489) share Common 10¢ par
Mikohn Gaming Corp. name changed to Progressive Gaming International Corp. 04/03/2006
(See Progressive Gaming International Corp.)

VIRTRA SYS INC (TX)
Reincorporated under the laws of Nevada as VirTra, Inc. and Common $0.005 par changed to $0.0001 par 10/07/2016

VIRTUAL ACADEMICS COM INC (DE)
Name changed to Cenuco, Inc. 12/16/2002
Cenuco, Inc. name changed to Ascendia Brands, Inc. 05/12/2006
(See Ascendia Brands, Inc.)

VIRTUAL CHINA TRAVEL SVCS CO LTD (AB)
Reorganized under the laws of British Columbia as Melco China Resorts (Holding) Ltd. 05/27/2008
Each share Common no par exchanged for (0.05) share Common no par
Melco China Resorts (Holding) Ltd. name changed to Mountain China Resorts (Holding) Ltd. 10/22/2010

VIRTUAL CLOSET INC (NV)
Reorganized as DK Sinopharma, Inc. 06/30/2010
Each share Common $0.001 par exchanged for (13.75) shares Common $0.001 par
DK Sinopharma, Inc. name changed to VGambling, Inc. 08/14/2014 which name changed to Esports Entertainment Group, Inc. 05/25/2017

VIRTUAL COMMUNITIES INC (DE)
SEC revoked common stock registration 12/14/2009

VIRTUAL CURRICULA CORP (NV)
Name changed to Scout Exploration, Inc. 04/10/2006

VIRTUAL DYNAMICS CORP (AB)
Recapitalized as Las Western Entertainment Inc. 10/28/97
Each share Common no par exchanged for (0.5) share Common no par
Las Western Entertainment Inc. name changed to mBase.com Inc. 10/26/99 which name changed to mBase Commerce Inc. 7/5/2002 which recapitalized as Bri-Chem Corp. 1/11/2007

VIRTUAL ENTERPRISES INC (NV)
Name changed to NetCommerce Inc. 09/08/1999
(See NetCommerce Inc.)

VIRTUAL GAMES INC (NV)
Recapitalized as MidAmerica Oil & Gas Inc. 08/13/2002
Each share Common exchanged for (0.005) share Common $0.001 par
MidAmerica Oil & Gas Inc. name changed to Sounds 24-7, Inc. 01/15/2004 which recapitalized as Allied Energy Corp. 01/26/2006

VIRTUAL GAMING ENTERPRISES INC (NV)
Each share old Common $0.001 par exchanged for (0.02) share new Common $0.001 par 02/23/1999
Each share new Common $0.001 par exchanged again for (0.02) share new Common $0.001 par 12/20/2001
Each share new Common $0.001 par exchanged again for (0.02) new Common $0.001 par 08/13/2002
Name changed to Asgard Holdings, Inc. 08/25/2004
Asgard Holdings, Inc. recapitalized as Principal Capital Group, Inc. (Old) 02/26/2008
(See Principal Capital Group, Inc. (Old))

VIRTUAL GAMING TECHNOLOGIES INC (DE)
Name changed to VirtGame.com Corp. 09/28/1999
VirtGame.com Corp. name changed to VirtGame Corp. 02/25/2002 which merged into Mikohn Gaming Corp. 10/07/2005 which name changed to Progressive Gaming International Corp. 04/03/2006
(See Progressive Gaming International Corp.)

VIRTUAL INNOVATIONS INC (FL)
Name changed to University Health Industries, Inc. 05/09/2008
University Health Industries, Inc. name changed to Cognitiv, Inc. 09/19/2012

VIRTUAL LEARNING CO INC (NV)
Name changed to Dream Homes & Development Corp. 05/02/2017

VIRTUAL LENDER COM INC (CO)
Each share Common $0.001 par received distribution of (1) share Homesmart.com, Inc. Common no par payable 08/02/1999 to holders of record 07/23/1999
Name changed to VLDC Technologies, Inc. 10/29/1999
VLDC Technologies, Inc. name changed to JTS International, Inc. 01/24/2006 which recapitalized as Fuji Construction Company International, Inc. 02/08/2008 which name changed to Hokutou Holdings International, Inc. (CO) 11/06/2008 which reincorporated in Nevada 05/23/2014 which name changed to Platinum Pari-Mutuel Holdings, Inc. 12/09/2014 which name changed to Point to Point Methodics, Inc. 04/27/2017

VIRTUAL MEDIA HLDGS INC (BC)
Name changed to Biomass Secure Power Inc. 03/12/2009

VIRTUAL OPEN NETWORK ENVIRONMENT CORP (DE)
Issue Information - 3,000,000 shares COM offered at $5 per share on 10/24/1996
Name changed to V-One Corp. 07/02/1996
(See V-One Corp.)

VIRTUAL PIGGY INC (DE)
Name changed to Rego Payment Architectures, Inc. 03/16/2017

VIRTUAL PROTOTYPES INC (CANADA)
Name changed to eNGENUITY Technologies Inc. 3/28/2001
(See eNGENUITY Technologies Inc.)

VIRTUAL RADIOLOGIC CORP (DE)
Issue Information - 4,000,000 shares COM offered at $17 per share on 11/14/2007

Acquired by Viking Holdings L.L.C. 07/12/2010
Each share Common $0.001 par exchanged for $17.25 cash

VIRTUAL REALITY INC (NV)
Each share old Common 15¢ par exchanged for (0.2) share new Common 15¢ par 3/18/92
Each share new Common 15¢ par exchanged again for (0.1) share Common 15¢ par 1/3/2001
Name changed to Sterling Business Solutions Inc. 2/1/2001

VIRTUAL TECHNOLOGIES INC (NV)
Reincorporated 07/00/1996
Each share old Common 1¢ par exchanged for (0.33333333) share new Common 1¢ par 02/29/1996
State of incorporation changed from (UT) to (NV) 07/00/1996
Each share new Common 1¢ par exchanged for (0.2) share Common $0.001 par 10/30/1996
Name changed to Solpower Corp. 01/06/1998
Solpower Corp. name changed to Bitcoin Collect, Inc. 06/10/2014 which name changed to Good Vibrations Shoes Inc. 09/09/2014

VIRTUAL TECHNOLOGY CORP (MN)
Name changed to Graphics Technologies Inc. 12/20/2000

VIRTUAL TELECOM INC (DE)
Name changed to Firstquote, Inc. 4/29/99

VIRTUAL UNIVERSE CORP (AB)
Acquired by Man Prince Holdings Ltd. 04/18/2013
Each share Common no par exchanged for $0.02 cash

VIRTUAL WORLD SPORTS INC (NV)
Charter revoked for failure to file reports and pay fees 09/30/2005

VIRTUALARMOR INTL INC (BC)
Name changed to VirtualArmour International Inc. 11/01/2016

VIRTUALFUND COM INC (MN)
Recapitalized as ASFG, Inc. 08/11/2004
Each (15) shares Common 1¢ par exchanged for (1) share Common 1¢ par

VIRTUALHEALTH TECHNOLOGIES INC (DE)
Name changed to VHGI Holdings, Inc. 05/25/2010
(See VHGI Holdings, Inc.)

VIRTUALISTICS INC (DE)
Name changed to Consolidated American Industries Inc. 06/09/1989
Consolidated American Industries Inc. name changed to Quality Products, Inc. 12/11/1991
(See Quality Products, Inc.)

VIRTUALITY GROUP PLC (UNITED KINGDOM)
Each old Sponsored ADR for Ordinary 5p par exchanged for (0.5) new Sponsored ADR for Ordinary 5p par 12/30/1994
Placed in bankruptcy 00/00/1997
No ADR holders' equity

VIRTUALSCOPICS INC (DE)
Each share old Common $0.001 par exchanged for (0.1) share new Common $0.001 par 08/22/2013
Acquired by BioTelemetry, Inc. 05/11/2016
Each share new Common $0.001 par exchanged for $4.05 cash

VIRTUALSELLERS COM INC (CANADA)
Name changed to Healthtrac, Inc. 03/25/2002
(See Healthtrac, Inc.)

VIRTUS ENERGY LTD (AB)
Merged into Titan Exploration Ltd. 06/23/2005
Each share Common no par exchanged for (0.18) share Class A Common no par
Titan Exploration Ltd. acquired by Penn West Energy Trust 01/11/2008 which reorganized as Penn West Petroleum Ltd. (New) 01/03/2011 which name changed to Obsidian Energy Ltd. 06/29/2017

VIRTUS TOTAL RETURN FD (DE)
Merged into Virtus Total Return Fund Inc. 04/03/2017
Each share Common $0.001 par exchanged for (0.391206) share Common 40¢ par

VIRTUSONICS CORP (DE)
Charter cancelled and declared inoperative and void for non-payment of taxes 06/17/1993

VIRUS RESH INST INC (DE)
Issue Information - 2,300,000 shares COM offered at $12 per share on 06/05/1996
Merged into AVANT Immunotherapeutics, Inc. 08/21/1998
Each share Common $0.001 par exchanged for (1.55) shares Common $0.001 par and (0.2) Common Stock Purchase Warrant expiring 08/21/2003
AVANT Immunotherapeutics, Inc. name changed to Celldex Therapeutics, Inc. 10/01/2008

VIRYANET LTD (ISRAEL)
Each share Ordinary ILS 0.1 par exchanged for (0.1) share Ordinary ILS 1 par 05/01/2002
Each share Ordinary ILS 1 par exchanged for (0.2) share Ordinary ILS 5 par 01/17/2007
Acquired by Verisae, Inc. 08/26/2014
Each share Ordinary ILS 5 par exchanged for $3.186677 cash

VIS OPPS MARKETING INC (NV)
SEC revoked common stock registration 01/18/2008

VIS VIVA CORP (NV)
Reincorporated 06/30/1995
State of incorporation changed from (UT) to (NV) 06/30/1995
Recapitalized as WideBand Corp. 02/29/2000
Each share Common 1¢ par exchanged for (0.14285714) share Common 1¢ par
WideBand Corp. name changed to GoldKey Corp. 12/30/2014

VISA ENERGY CORP (DE)
Reorganized under the laws of Arizona as Visa Industries of Arizona, Inc. 04/01/1985
Each share Common 1¢ par exchanged for (0.1) share Common 1¢ par

VISA EXPL CORP (CO)
Merged into Visa Energy Corp. 03/31/1982
Each share Capital Stock no par exchanged for (0.45) share Common 1¢ par
Visa Energy Corp. reorganized in Arizona as Visa Industries of Arizona, Inc. 04/01/1985

VISA GOLD EXPLORATIONS INC (ON)
Delisted from Toronto Venture Stock Exchange 05/27/2004

VISALIA CMNTY BK (VISALIA, CA)
8% Conv. Perpetual Preferred called for redemption at $20 on 05/16/2002
Merged into Central Valley Community Bancorp 07/01/2013
Each share Common no par exchanged for (2.971) shares Common no par and $26 cash

VISATOR INC (FL)
Name changed to GoldSpring, Inc. (FL) 03/18/2003
GoldSpring, Inc. (FL) reincorporated in Nevada 11/12/2008 which name changed to Comstock Mining Inc. 07/21/2010

VISCO-METER CORP. (NY)
Dissolved 6/6/63
No stockholders' equity

VISCORP (NV)
Name changed to U.S. Digital Communications, Inc. 10/29/1997
(See U.S. Digital Communications, Inc.)

VISCORP INC (DE)
Name changed to Tianyin Pharmaceutical Co., Inc. 03/11/2008

VISCOSE CO. (DE)
Name changed to American Viscose Corp. in 1937
American Viscose Corp. name changed to A.V.C. Corp. 8/6/63 which merged into Raybestos-Manhattan, Inc. (CT) 4/30/81 which name changed to Raymark Corp. 6/28/82 which reorganized in Delaware as Raytech Corp. 10/15/86
(See Raytech Corp.)

VISCOUNT INC (UT)
Name changed to Sigma Medical Associates, Inc. 4/28/88
(See Sigma Medical Associates, Inc.)

VISCOUNT OIL & GAS LTD. (SK)
Acquired by Bison Petroleum & Minerals Ltd. 09/15/1960
Each share Common no par exchanged for (0.11111111) share Capital Stock $1 par
Bison Petroleum & Minerals Ltd. recapitalized as United Bison Resources Ltd. 12/22/1987 which merged into Nalcap Holdings Inc. 04/25/1991 which recapitalized as Arbatax International Inc. (Canada) 03/28/1996 which reincorporated in Yukon 08/06/1996 which name changed to MFC Bancorp Ltd. (YT) 03/03/1997 which reincorporated in British Columbia 11/03/2004 which name changed to KHD Humboldt Wedag International Ltd. 11/01/2005 which reorganized as Terra Nova Royalty Corp. 03/30/2010 which name changed to MFC Industrial Ltd. 09/30/2011 which name changed to MFC Bancorp Ltd. (BC) 02/16/2016
(See MFC Bancorp Ltd. (BC))

VISCOUNT RES LTD (BC)
Recapitalized as Consolidated Viscount Resources Ltd. 11/05/1993
Each share Common no par exchanged for (0.2) share Common no par
Consolidated Viscount Resources Ltd. recapitalized as Choice Resources Corp. (BC) 02/20/2001 which reincorporated in Alberta 09/29/2004 which merged into Buffalo Resources Corp. 08/03/2007 which merged into Twin Butte Energy Ltd. 10/15/2009

VISEON INC (NV)
SEC revoked common stock registration 06/19/2013

VISHAL INFORMATION TECHNOLOGIES LTD (INDIA)
Name changed to Coral Hub Ltd. 07/09/2010

VISHNU RES INC (BC)
Name changed to Club Mate Holdings Ltd. 10/25/89
Club Mate Holdings Ltd. recapitalized as International Millennium Mining Corp. 7/4/97

VISI TOUR VISION INC (MN)
Name changed to Circuit Board One, Inc. 05/29/1990
(See Circuit Board One, Inc.)

VISIBLE GENETICS INC (ON)
Merged into Bayer Corp. 10/14/2002
Each share Common no par exchanged for $1.50 (U.S.) cash

VISIBLE GOLD INC (BC)
Recapitalized as Lansing Enterprises Inc. 11/9/90
Each share Common no par exchanged for (1/3) share Common no par
Lansing Enterprises Inc. recapitalized as White Hawk Ventures Inc. 1/19/93 which recapitalized as E-Energy Ventures Inc. 1/9/2001

VISICU INC (DE)
Issue Information - 6,000,000 shares COM offered at $16 per share on 04/04/2006
Merged into Philips Holding USA Inc. 02/20/2008
Each share Common $0.0001 par exchanged for $12 cash

VISIGENIC SOFTWARE INC (DE)
Merged into Borland International, Inc. 02/27/1998
Each share Common $0.001 par exchanged for (0.81988) share Common $0.001 par
Borland International, Inc. name changed to Inprise Corp. 06/05/1998 which name changed to Borland Software Corp. 01/22/2001
(See Borland Software Corp.)

VISIJET INC (DE)
Name changed to Advanced Refractive Technologies, Inc. 07/28/2005
(See Advanced Refractive Technologies, Inc.)

VISIO CORP (WA)
Common 1¢ par split (2) for (1) by issuance of (1) additional share payable 8/8/97 to holders of record 8/8/97
Merged into Microsoft Corp. 1/7/2000
Each share Common 1¢ par exchanged for (0.45) share Common $0.0000125 par

VISION AEROSPACE INC (NV)
Charter revoked for failure to file reports and pay fees 5/1/2001

VISION BANCSHARES INC (AL)
Merged into Park National Corp. 3/9/2007
Each share Common $1 par exchanged for (0.2475) share Common no par

VISION CABLE COMMUNICATIONS INC (DE)
Each share Class A Common 10¢ par exchanged for (0.001) shares Class A Common $100 par 11/7/77
Public interest eliminated

VISION CAP INC (DE)
Name changed to Diversified Photographic Industries, Inc. 12/01/1990
Diversified Photographic Industries, Inc. name changed to Spectrum Equities Inc. 02/26/1996 which recapitalized as Imtek Office Solutions Inc. 04/22/1997
(See Imtek Office Solutions Inc.)

VISION COATINGS GROUP LTD (BC)
Delisted from Toronto Venture Stock Exchange 06/23/2006

VISION COMMUNICATIONS CORP (NY)
Chapter 11 bankruptcy proceedings converted to Chapter 7 in 1994
No stockholders' equity

VISION DIGITAL MULTIMEDIA CORP (NV)
Name changed to Clinicares, Inc. 03/08/2007
Clinicares, Inc. recapitalized as Catch By Gene, Inc. 04/09/2010
(See Catch By Gene, Inc.)

VISION DYNAMICS CORP (NV)
Recapitalized as Secured Technology Innovations Corp. 02/14/2014
Each share Common $0.001 par exchanged for (0.1) share Common $0.001 par

VISION ENERGY GROUP INC (NV)
Each share old Common $0.001 par exchanged for (2) shares new Common $0.001 par 07/19/2006
Name changed to Advanced Mineral Technologies, Inc. 04/30/2007
(See Advanced Mineral Technologies, Inc.)

VISION FINL SVCS CORP (DE)
Charter cancelled and declared inoperative and void for non-payment of taxes 3/1/91

VISION GATE VENTURES LTD. (BC)
Name changed to Northern Lion Gold Corp. 7/10/2003

VISION GLOBAL SOLUTIONS INC (ON)
Reincorporated 01/07/2005
Place of incorporation changed from (ON) to (NV) and Common no par changed to $0.001 par 01/07/2005
Each share old Common $0.001 par exchanged for (0.01) share new Common $0.001 par 01/18/2005
Recapitalized as Eco-Stim Energy Solutions, Inc. 12/11/2013
Each share new Common $0.001 par exchanged for (0.00208333) share Common $0.001 par

VISION HRM SOFTWARE INC (AB)
Name changed to Serenic Corp. 01/13/2005
Serenic Corp. name changed to OneSoft Solutions Inc. 08/01/2014

VISION INC (AB)
Delisted from Alberta Stock Exchange 05/14/1998

VISION INDS CORP (FL)
Chapter 7 bankruptcy proceedings terminated 09/08/2017
Stockholders' equity unlikely

VISION INTL INC (NM)
Name changed to Exlites Holdings International, Inc. 09/19/2008

VISION MEDIA TECHNOLOGIES INC (FL)
Recapitalized as ASF Group, Inc. (FL) 08/01/2008
Each share Common 1¢ par exchanged for (0.2) share Common 1¢ par
ASF Group, Inc. (FL) reincorporated in Georgia as American Seniors Association Holding Group, Inc. 04/28/2010

VISION REAL ESTATE MGMT & DEV INC (FL)
Each share old Common $0.001 par exchanged for (0.0025) share new Common $0.001 par 07/26/2004
Stock Dividend - 40% payable 01/14/2004 to holders of record 12/31/2003 Ex date - 01/15/2004
Name changed to MEM Financial Solutions, Inc. 11/23/2004
MEM Financial Solutions, Inc. recapitalized as Sebastian River Holdings, Inc. 04/05/2006 which recapitalized as Novacab International Inc. 11/12/2013 which name changed to Global Pole Trusion Group Corp. 07/24/2017

VISION SCIENCES INC (CA)
Charter suspended for failure to file reports and pay fees 08/01/1994

VISION-SCIENCES INC (DE)
Recapitalized as Cogentix Medical, Inc. 04/01/2015
Each share Common 1¢ par exchanged for (0.2) share Common 1¢ par
(See Cogentix Medical, Inc.)

VISION SCMS INC (AB)
Delisted from NEX 06/25/2004

VISION TECHNOLOGIES INTL INC (DE)
Each share old Common $0.001 par exchanged for (0.1) share new Common $0.001 par 02/12/1992
Name changed to Medplus Corp. 01/23/1993
Medplus Corp. recapitalized as Atlantis Business Development Corp. 08/25/2003 which reorganized as Atlantis Technology Group 10/11/2007

VISION TECHNOLOGY CORP (NV)
Charter permanently revoked 09/30/2008

VISION TWENTY-ONE INC (FL)
Issue Information - 2,100,000 shares COM offered at $10 per share on 08/18/1997
Assets sold for the benefit of creditors 08/12/2002
Stockholders' equity unlikely

VISION 2000 EXPLORATION LTD (AB)
Issue Information - 1,500,000 UNITS consisting of (1) share Cl A and (1) WT offered at $0.50 per Unit on 08/08/1997
Merged into Yoho Resources Inc. 06/04/2008
Each share Class A Common no par exchanged for (0.24) share Common no par

VISION WKS MEDIA GROUP INC (DE)
Each share old Common $0.001 par exchanged for (0.001) share new Common $0.001 par 06/21/2005
Each share new Common $0.001 par exchanged again for (2) shares new Common $0.001 par 08/31/2005
Each share new Common $0.001 par exchanged again for (0.0001) share new Common $0.001 par 07/27/2007
Stock Dividend - 15% payable 06/15/2006 to holders of record 06/01/2006 Ex date - 05/30/2006
Name changed to Perihelion Global, Inc. (DE) 10/25/2006
Perihelion Global, Inc. (DE) reincorporated in Nevada 04/01/2008 which recapitalized as Nymet Holdings Inc. 04/21/2009

VISIONAMERICA INC (DE)
Chapter 11 bankruptcy proceedings converted to Chapter 7 on 12/19/2001
Stockholders' equity unlikely

VISIONARY MNG CORP (BC)
Name changed 07/25/1996
Name changed from Visionary Industries Ltd. to Visionary Mining Corp. 07/25/1996
Recapitalized as Nu-Vision Resource Corp. 07/11/2001
Each (12) shares Common no par exchanged for (1) share Common no par
Nu-Vision Resource Corp. name changed to Vision Coatings Group Ltd. 02/16/2004
(See Vision Coatings Group Ltd.)

VISIONARY SOLUTIONS CORP (AB)
Merged into 813495 Alberta Ltd. 3/3/99
Each share Common no par exchanged for $0.85 cash

VISIONCHINA MEDIA INC (CAYMAN ISLANDS)
Each old Sponsored ADR for Ordinary (92833U 10 3) exchanged for (0.05) new Sponsored ADR's for Ordinary 12/12/2012
Basis changed from (1:1) to (1:20) 12/12/2012
ADR agreement terminated 12/15/2017

ADR holders' equity unlikely due to company being in Official Liquidation

VISIONCORP INC (FL)
Each share old Common $0.001 par exchanged for (1/15) share new Common $0.001 par 3/12/98
Name changed to Sagamore Trading Group Inc. 10/7/98

VISIONEER INC (DE)
Merged into ScanSoft, Inc. 3/2/99
Each share Common $0.001 par exchanged for (1) share Common $0.001 par
ScanSoft, Inc. name changed to Nuance Communications, Inc. (New) 11/21/2005

VISIONGATEWAY INC (NV)
SEC revoked common stock registration 05/25/2010
Stockholders' equity unlikely

VISIONICS CORP (DE)
Merged into Identix Inc. 06/25/2002
Each share Common 1¢ par exchanged for (1.3436) shares Common 1¢ par
Identix Inc. merged into L-1 Identify Solutions, Inc. 08/30/2006
(See L-1 Identify Solutions, Inc.)

VISIONQUEST ENTERPRISE GROUP INC (BC)
Name changed to VisionQuest Energy Group Inc. 11/03/2006

VISIONQUEST WORLDWIDE HLDGS CORP (DE)
SEC revoked common stock registration 05/27/2011

VISIONS IN GLASS INC (DE)
Name changed to China Automotive Systems, Inc. 5/19/2003

VISIONSKY CORP (AB)
Each (15) shares old Common no par exchanged for (1) share new Common no par 12/23/2010
Reorganized as Dixie Energy Trust 03/01/2013
Each share new Common no par exchanged for (0.125) Trust Unit

VISIONSKY CORP (CANADA)
Reincorporated under the laws of Alberta as VisionSky Corp. 02/16/2006
VisionSky Corp. reorganized as Dixie Energy Trust 03/01/2013

VISIONTECH INC (DE)
Plan of reorganization under Chapter 11 Federal Bankruptcy proceedings confirmed 03/01/1990
No stockholders' equity

VISITEL NETWORK INC (NV)
Recapitalized as PRG Group, Inc. 08/11/2006
Each share Common $0.002 par exchanged for (0.001) share Common $0.002 par
(See PRG Group, Inc.)

VISITORS SVCS INTL CORP (FL)
Name changed to Teleservices International Group, Inc. 03/10/1997
Teleservices International Group, Inc. name changed to Teleservices Internet Group, Inc. 07/12/1999 which recapitalized as Opus Magnum Ameris, Inc. 02/16/2012
(See Opus Magnum Ameris, Inc.)

VISITRADE INC (NV)
Recapitalized as BlackBox SemiConductor, Inc. 01/19/2011
Each share Common $0.001 par exchanged for (0.0037037) share Common $0.001 par
Note: Holders of (100) or fewer pre-split shares are not affected
Holders of between (101) and (27,000) pre-split shares received (100) shares
BlackBox SemiConductor, Inc. name changed to Vision Dynamics Corp. 01/16/2013 which recapitalized as

Secured Technology Innovations Corp. 02/14/2014

VISKASE COS INC (DE)
Plan of reorganization under Chapter 11 Federal Bankruptcy Code effective 04/03/2003
Each share old Common 1¢ par exchanged for (0.02) Common Stock Purchase Warrant expiring 04/02/2010
(Additional Information in Active)

VISKING CORP. (VA)
Class A Common $5 par changed to Common $5 par 00/00/1947
Common $5 par split (3) for (1) by issuance of (2) additional shares 02/10/1956
Stock Dividend - 10% 12/30/1953
Merged into Union Carbide & Carbon Corp. 12/31/1956
Each share Common $5 par exchanged for (0.4) share Common $5 par
Union Carbide & Carbon Corp. name changed to Union Carbide Corp. (Old) 05/01/1957 which reorganized as Union Carbide Corp. (New) 07/01/1989 which merged into Dow Chemical Co. 02/06/2001 which merged into DowDuPont Inc. 09/01/2017

VISKON-AIRE CORP (NJ)
Each share old Common 10¢ par exchanged for (0.0000487) share new Common 10¢ par 01/15/2010
Note: In effect holders received $8.25 cash per share and public interest was eliminated

VISOR MINES LTD. (ON)
Charter cancelled by the Province of Ontario 1/2/56

VISSAT FROG & SWITCH CO. (DE)
Incorporated 3/3/15
Charter cancelled and declared inoperative and void for non-payment of taxes 3/18/25

VISSAT FROG & SWITCH CO. (DE)
Incorporated 11/9/26
Charter cancelled and declared inoperative and void for non-payment of taxes 4/1/34

VIST FINL CORP (PA)
Merged into Tompkins Financial Corp. 08/01/2012
Each share Common $5 par exchanged for (0.3127) share Common 10¢ par

VISTA BANCORP INC (NJ)
Common $1.50 par changed to 50¢ par and (2) additional shares issued 5/27/94
Stock Dividends - 10% payable 6/10/98 to holders of record 6/1/98; 5% payable 5/21/99 to holders of record 5/3/99; 5% payable 5/26/2000 to holders of record 5/12/2000; 5% payable 5/25/2001 to holders of record 5/11/2001
Merged into United National Bancorp 8/21/2002
Each share Common 50¢ par exchanged for (1.0319) shares Common $2.50 par and $3.8858 cash
(See United National Bancorp)

VISTA BANKS INC. (FL)
Merged into South-Trust of Central Florida, Inc. 12/14/87
Each share Common 1¢ par exchanged for $10.7529 cash

VISTA CAPITAL CORP (DE)
Name changed to Bima Entertainment Ltd. 9/9/88
(See Bima Entertainment Ltd.)

VISTA CHEM CO (DE)
Acquired by Alpha Acquisition Corp. 7/15/91
Each share Common 1¢ par exchanged for $55 cash

VISTA CONTL CORP (DE)
Name changed to Wolverine Holding Corp. 11/06/2009

VISTA CORP (UT)
Involuntarily dissolved 3/1/91

VISTA DORADA CORP (NV)
Old Common $0.001 par split (30) for (1) by issuance of (29) additional shares payable 03/03/2008 to holders of record 02/08/2008
Ex date - 03/04/2008
Each share old Common $0.001 par exchanged for (0.5) share new Common $0.001 par 05/20/2009
Name changed to Nordic Turbines, Inc. 06/15/2009
Nordic Turbines, Inc. name changed to GC China Turbine Corp. 09/14/2009

VISTA ENERGY INC (NV)
Recapitalized as On Queue, Inc. (Old) 05/09/1990
Each share Common $0.001 par exchanged for (0.02) share Common $0.001 par
On Queue, Inc. (Old) name changed to Mactavish International, Inc. 01/24/1992 which name changed to On Queue, Inc. (New) 08/10/1992 which name changed to Sunlogic, Inc. 07/01/1994 which name changed to Dawson Science Corp. (NV) 03/17/1995 which reorganized in Delaware as Integrated Transportation Network Group Inc. 06/30/1998
(See Integrated Transportation Network Group Inc.)

VISTA ENERGY RES INC (DE)
Recapitalized as Prize Energy Corp. 2/9/2000
Each share Common 1¢ par exchanged for (1/7) share Common 1¢ par
Prize Energy Corp. merged into Magnum Hunter Resources, Inc. 3/15/2002 which merged into Cimarex Energy Co. 6/7/2005

VISTA EXPL CORP (CO)
Name changed to ICOP Digital, Inc. 11/12/2004
(See ICOP Digital, Inc.)

VISTA EYECARE INC (GA)
Plan of reorganization under Chapter 11 Federal Bankruptcy Code effective 5/31/2001
No stockholders' equity

VISTA FILMS CORP (DE)
Name changed to Vistar Films Corp. 6/20/85
Vistar Films Corp. name changed to Vista Organization Ltd. 4/8/86
(See Vista Organization Ltd.)

VISTA GOLD CORP (YT)
Reincorporated 12/27/1997
Place of incorporation changed from (BC) to (YT) 12/27/1997
Each share old Common no par exchanged for (0.05) share new Common no par 06/19/2002
Plan of arrangement effective 05/10/2007
Each share new Common no par exchanged again for (1) share new Common no par and (0.794) share Allied Nevada Gold Corp. Common no par
(See Allied Nevada Gold Corp.)
Reincorporated back under the laws of British Columbia 06/12/2013

VISTA HLDG GROUP CORP (NV)
Name changed to That Marketing Solution, Inc. 09/17/2014

VISTA INDS CORP (DE)
Each (3) shares Common 1¢ par exchanged for (1) share Class A Common 3¢ par 11/7/80
Charter cancelled and declared inoperative and void for non-payment of taxes 3/1/85

VISTA INFORMATION SOLUTIONS INC (DE)
Reorganized 03/27/1998
Reorganized from under the laws of (MN) to (DE) 03/27/1998
Each share Common 1¢ par exchanged for (0.5) share Common 1¢ par
Recapitalized as Fidelity National Information Solutions, Inc. 08/01/2001
Each share Common 1¢ par exchanged for (1/7) share Common 1¢ par
Fidelity National Information Solutions, Inc. merged into Fidelity National Financial, Inc. 09/30/2003 which merged into Fidelity National Information Services, Inc. 11/09/2006

VISTA INTL CORP (UT)
Charter suspended for failure to file reports 12/31/1974

VISTA INTL PETES LTD (SK)
Acquired by Paladrom Energy 10/19/95
Each share Class A no par exchanged for $2.20 cash

VISTA INVTS INC (AB)
Recapitalized as Rifco Inc. 4/1/2003
Each share Common no par exchanged for (0.5) share Common no par

VISTA MGMT INC (DE)
Recapitalized as Meditech Management Inc. 10/16/90
Each share Common $0.001 par exchanged for (0.1) share Common $0.001 par
(See Meditech Management Inc.)

VISTA MED TECHNOLOGIES INC (DE)
Each share old Common 1¢ par exchanged for (0.25) share new Common 1¢ par 08/17/2001
Name changed to iVOW, Inc. 02/23/2005
iVOW, Inc. name changed to Sound Health Solutions, Inc. 10/29/2007

VISTA MINES INC (SK)
Class B Subordinate no par reclassified as Class A Common no par 7/31/87
Delisted from Toronto Stock Exchange 12/7/90

VISTA MINES LTD. (ON)
Merged into Great Eagle Explorations & Holdings Ltd. 7/7/69
Each share Capital Stock $1 par exchanged for (0.25) share Common no par
Great Eagle Explorations & Holdings Ltd. merged into Belle Aire Resource Explorations Ltd. 8/29/78 which merged into Sprint Resources Ltd. 9/23/82 which name changed to Meacon Bay Resources Inc. 3/9/87 which recapitalized as Advantex Marketing International Inc. 9/16/91

VISTA MTG & RLTY INC (DE)
Merged into Lomas & Nettleton Financial Corp. 3/29/82
Each share Common 10¢ par exchanged for $9.75 cash

VISTA NATIONAL BANK (VISTA, CA)
Merged into La Jolla Bank & Trust Co. (La Jolla, CA) 7/16/81
Each share Common $5 par exchanged for (1/3) share Capital Stock $2 par
La Jolla Bank & Trust Co. (La Jolla, CA) reorganized as La Jolla Bancorp 7/31/82 which merged into Security Pacific Corp. 8/23/90 which merged into BankAmerica Corp. (Old) 4/22/92 which merged into BankAmerica Corp. (New) 9/30/98 which name changed to Bank of America Corp. 4/28/99

VISTA ORGANIZATION LTD (DE)
Merged into Carolco Pictures Inc. 10/20/93
Each share Common $0.001 par exchanged for $0.75 cash

VISTA ORGANIZATION PARTNERSHIP L P (DE)
Plan of reorganization under Chapter 11 Federal Bankruptcy Code effective 6/2/97
Each Depositary Unit exchanged for initial distribution of approximately $3.23 cash in June 1997
Each Depositary Unit received second distribution of approximately $1.75 cash in December 1997
Each Depositary Unit received third distribution of approximately $0.54 cash in April 1998

VISTA PETE CORP (NV)
Charter cancelled for failure to file reports and pay fees 3/5/73

VISTA PPTYS INC (NV)
Acquired by Centex Corp. as a result of Chapter 11 Federal Bankruptcy Code settlement
Each share Class A Common $1 par received approximately $2.50 cash 9/27/95 and $0.04 cash in October 1997
Note: Certificates were not required to be surrendered and are without value

VISTA RES INC (DE)
Common $2.50 par split (5) for (1) by issuance of (4) additional shares 8/4/89
Name changed to Fuqua Enterprises, Inc. 9/8/95
Fuqua Enterprises, Inc. merged into Graham-Field Health Products Inc. 12/30/97
(See Graham-Field Health Products Inc.)

VISTA RES LTD (BC)
Name changed to Brenzac Development Corp. 09/04/1992
Brenzac Development Corp. recapitalized as Consolidated Brenzac Development Corp. 04/20/1993 which name changed to Borneo Gold Corp. 04/16/1996 which name changed to Nexttrip.com Travel Inc. 01/04/2000 which recapitalized as WorldPlus Ventures Ltd. 05/26/2003 which recapitalized as New Global Ventures Ltd. 06/07/2007 which recapitalized as New Global Ventures International Ltd. 03/14/2008 which name changed to Auro Resources Corp. 10/15/2010 which recapitalized as Tesoro Minerals Corp. 08/26/2013

VISTA TECHNOLOGIES INC (NV)
Each share Common no par exchanged for (0.2) share Common $0.005 par 03/15/1996
Charter permanently revoked 04/01/2003

VISTA 2000 INC (DE)
Recapitalized as Boss Holdings, Inc. 12/07/1998
Each share Common 1¢ par exchanged for (0.04) share Common 25¢ par

VISTACARE INC (DE)
Merged into Odyssey HealthCare, Inc. 03/06/2008
Each share Class A Common 1¢ par exchanged for $8.60 cash

VISTANA INC (FL)
Merged into Starwood Hotels & Resorts Worldwide, Inc. 10/01/1999
Each share Common 1¢ par exchanged for (0.4667) Combined Ctf. and $5 cash
Starwood Hotels & Resorts Worldwide, Inc. merged into Marriott International, Inc. (New) 09/23/2016

VISTAPRINT LTD (BERMUDA)
Reorganized under the laws of Netherlands as Vistaprint N.V. 08/31/2009
Each share Common $0.001 par exchanged for (1) share Ordinary EUR 0.01 par
Vistaprint N.V. name changed to Cimpress N.V. 11/17/2014

VISTAPRINT N V (NETHERLANDS)
Name changed to Cimpress N.V. 11/17/2014

VISTAR FILMS CORP (DE)
Name changed to Vista Organization Ltd. 04/08/1986
(See Vista Organization Ltd.)

VISTATECH CORP (AB)
Name changed to VR Interactive Corp. 10/24/2007
VR Interactive Corp. recapitalized as Muskrat Minerals Inc. 03/29/2012 which name changed to Metalo Manufacturing Inc. 12/16/2015

VISTATRONICS INC (MN)
Liquidation completed 00/00/2005
Each share Common received an undetermined amount of cash
Note: Certificates were not required to be surrendered and are without value

VISTECH CAP CORP (BC)
Name changed to Cayden Resources Inc. 09/24/2010
Cayden Resources Inc. merged into Agnico Eagle Mines Ltd. 11/28/2014

VISTEON CORP (DE)
Plan of reorganzation under Chapter 11 Federal Bankruptcy Code effective 10/01/2010
Each share Common $1 par exchanged for (0.007834) share Common 1¢ par and (0.012115) Common Stock Purchase Warrant expiring 10/15/2015
Note: Unexchanged certificates were cancelled and became without value 10/01/2011
(Additional Information in Active)

VISTULA COMMUNICATIONS SVCS INC (DE)
SEC revoked common stock registration 07/08/2013

VISUAL ART INDS INC (DE)
Charter cancelled and declared inoperative and void for non-payment of taxes 3/1/81

VISUAL BIBLE INTL INC (FL)
Each share old Common $0.0001 par exchanged for (0.5) share new Common $0.0001 par 04/03/2001
Each share new Common $0.0001 par exchanged for (0.33333333) share old Common $0.001 par 09/25/2001
Each share old Common $0.0001 par exchanged for (0.1) share new Common $0.001 par 02/19/2002
Recapitalized as Secure Luggage USA, Inc. 06/09/2008
Each share new Common $0.001 par exchanged for (0.001) share new Common $0.001 par
Secure Luggage USA, Inc. reorganized as Ambush Media, Inc. 09/16/2009 which name changed to Azia Corp. 03/19/2010 which name changed to Axxess Unlimited Inc. 03/20/2013 which name changed to Encompass Compliance Corp. 06/22/2015

VISUAL CYBERNETICS CORP (NY)
Reorganized under Chapter 11 Federal Bankruptcy proceedings 02/05/1997
Each (28.345) shares old Common 1¢ par exchanged for (1) share new Common 1¢ par 02/05/1997
Dissolved by proclamation 03/26/1997

VIS-VIT

VISUAL DATA CORP (FL)
Each share old Common $0.0001 par exchanged for (0.06666666) share new Common $0.0001 par 06/24/2003
Name changed to Onstream Media Corp. 01/01/2005

VISUAL DYNAMICS CORP. (NJ)
Charter void for non-payment of taxes 4/12/73

VISUAL EDGE SYS INC (DE)
Issue Information - 1,300,000 shares COM offered at $5 per share on 07/24/1996
Recapitalized as Edge Technology Group Inc. 8/9/2000
Each share Common 1¢ par exchanged for (0.25) share Common 1¢ par
Edge Technology Group Inc. name changed to Axtive Corp. 11/4/2002

VISUAL ELECTRS CORP (NY)
Reincorporated under the laws of Delaware as Visual Industries, Inc. 04/08/1987
(See Visual Industries, Inc.)

VISUAL ENVIRONMENTS INC (DE)
Adjudicated bankrupt 7/29/71
Stockholders' equity unlikely

VISUAL EQUITIES INC (NV)
Each (13,000) shares old Common 1¢ par exchanged for (1) share new Common 1¢ par 7/30/2002
Note: In effect holders received $0.37 cash per share and public interest was eliminated

VISUAL FRONTIER INC (DE)
SEC revoked common stock registration 03/30/2012

VISUAL GRAPHICS CORP (DE)
Common 10¢ par reclassified as Conv. Class B Common 10¢ par 01/09/1987
Stock Dividends - 10% 08/10/1973; 10% 01/31/1975; 10% 02/10/1976
Name changed to VGC Corp. 04/07/1989
(See VGC Corp.)

VISUAL INDS CORP (DE)
Name changed to Southeast Equity Management, Inc. 3/21/79
Southeast Equity Management, Inc. name changed to Nationwide Power Corp. 9/7/82 which merged into Brooks Satellite Inc. 5/29/86
(See Brooks Satellite Inc.)

VISUAL INDS INC (DE)
Charter cancelled and declared inoperative and void for non-payment of taxes 03/01/1994

VISUAL INDS INC (NV)
Charter revoked for failure to file reports and pay fees 11/30/2010

VISUAL MGMT SCIENCES INC (NV)
Merged into Datascoops, Inc. 11/23/2014
Each share Common $0.001 par exchanged for (0.2) share Common
Note: Company is now private

VISUAL MGMT SYS INC (NV)
Chapter 11 bankruptcy proceedings converted to Chapter 7 on 11/21/2011
Stockholders' equity unlikely

VISUAL NETWORK DESIGN INC (NV)
Name changed to Rackwise, Inc. 10/27/2011

VISUAL NETWORKS INC (DE)
Merged into Danaher Corp. 01/20/2006
Each share Common 1¢ par exchanged for $1.83 cash

VISUAL SCIENCES INC (DE)
Merged into Omniture, Inc. 01/17/2008
Each share Common $0.001 par exchanged for (0.49) share Common $0.001 par and $2.39 cash

(See Omniture, Inc.)

VISUAL SCIENCES INC (NY)
Liquidation completed
Each share Common 1¢ par received initial distribution of $12.75 cash 07/26/1983
Each share Common 1¢ par received second and final distribution of $0.2954 cash 10/18/1985

VISUAL SKILLS INC (NV)
Company believed to be out of business in 1994

VISUAL SOUNDS INC (DE)
Charter cancelled and declared inoperative and void for non-payment of taxes 3/1/76

VISUAL TECHNOLOGY INC (MA)
Each share Common 10¢ par exchanged for (0.1) share Common 1¢ par 03/31/1987
Plan of reorganization under Chapter 11 bankruptcy proceedings effective 10/30/1989
No stockholders' equity

VISUAL TEL INTL INC (DE)
Name changed 1/2/97
Name changed from Visual Telephone of New Jersey Inc. to Visual Telephone International, Inc. 1/2/97
Name changed to Ivoice.Com Inc. 5/15/99
Ivoice.Com Inc. name changed to iVoice, Inc. (DE) 8/18/2001 which reincorporated in New Jersey 5/5/2003

VISUALABS INC (AB)
Name changed to Pretium Industries Inc. 12/04/2002
Pretium Industries Inc. name changed to PetroFalcon Corp. (AB) 06/24/2003 which reincorporated in British Columbia as Etrion Corp. 09/16/2009

VISUALANT INC (NV)
Each share old Common $0.001 par exchanged for (0.00666666) share new Common $0.001 par 06/17/2015
Name changed to Know Labs, Inc. 05/25/2018

VISUALMED CLINICAL SYS CORP (NV)
Name changed to Visual Healthcare Corp. 12/20/2004

VISUALVAULT CORP (BC)
Recapitalized as Certive Solutions Inc. 10/07/2013
Each share Common no par exchanged for (0.5) share Common no par

VISWAY TRANS INC (CANADA)
Merged into Intercan Leasing Inc. 4/11/88
Each share Common no par exchanged for $5.75 cash

VISX INC (CA)
Merged into VISX, Inc. (DE) 11/28/1990
Each (1.3597) shares Common no par exchanged for (1) share Common 1¢ par
VISX, Inc. (DE) merged into Advanced Medical Optics, Inc. 05/27/2005
(See Advanced Medical Optics, Inc.)

VISX INC (DE)
Common 1¢ par split (2) for (1) by issuance of (1) additional share payable 01/13/1999 to holders of record 12/28/1998
Common 1¢ par split (2) for (1) by issuance of (1) additional share payable 05/12/1999 to holders of record 04/27/1999
Merged into Advanced Medical Optics, Inc. 05/27/2005
Each share Common 1¢ par exchanged for (0.552) share Common 1¢ par and $3.50 cash

(See Advanced Medical Optics, Inc.)

VITA BIOTECH CORP (DE)
Name changed to August Energy Corp. 07/02/2004
August Energy Corp. recapitalized as Canyon Gold Corp. 05/02/2011 which name changed to Defense Technologies International Corp. 06/15/2016

VITA EQUITY INC (NV)
Each share Common $0.001 par exchanged for (2.6) shares Common $0.001 par 03/22/2007
Name changed to Euoko, Inc. 05/25/2007
Euoko, Inc. name changed to Euoko Group Inc. 01/10/2008 which recapitalized as Dermaxar Inc. 12/31/2010
(See Dermaxar Inc.)

VITA FOOD PRODS INC (NV)
Acquired by VFP Merger Co. 04/23/2009
Each share Common 1¢ par exchanged for $1.05 cash

VITA FOOD PRODS INC (NY)
Name changed to VFP Liquidating Corp. 01/29/1969
(See VFP Liquidating Corp.)

VITA GLASS CORP.
Dissolved in 1950

VITA-HEALTH INC (DE)
Name changed to VitaWarehouse.com, Inc. 11/1/99
VitaWarehouse.com, Inc. recapitalized as Texas Diversified Distributions, Inc. 8/17/2001 which name changed to Black Dragon Resources, Inc. 3/10/2004 which recapitalized as Black Dragon Resource Companies, Inc. 1/5/2005

VITA PLUS INDS INC (NV)
Name changed to Prevention Insurance.Com 3/10/99

VITA SPIRITS CORP (NV)
Name changed to Gold Dynamics Corp. 03/05/2010

VITA VENTURES INC (UT)
Name changed to Pegasus Gymnastics Equipment, Inc. 3/1/88
(See Pegasus Gymnastics Equipment, Inc.)

VITABATH INC (NY)
Common $1 par split (3) for (2) by issuance of (0.5) additional share 03/31/1970
Merged into Remwell Investment Co. 10/31/1972
Each share Common $1 par exchanged for $3.75 cash

VITACHLOR CORP (IN)
Each (50,000) shares old Common 1¢ par exchanged for (1) share new Common 1¢ par 11/22/99
Note: In effect holders received $3 cash per share and public interest was eliminated

VITACIG INC (NV)
Name changed to Omni Health, Inc. 11/21/2016

VITACOST COM INC (DE)
Acquired by Kroger Co. 08/18/2014
Each share Common $0.00001 par exchanged for $8 cash

VITACUBE SYS HLDGS INC (NV)
Each share old Common $0.001 par exchanged for (0.2) share new Common $0.001 par 12/08/2004
Name changed to XELR8 Holdings, Inc. 03/19/2007
XELR8 Holdings, Inc. name changed to Bazi International, Inc. 10/01/2010 which recapitalized as True Drinks Holdings, Inc. 01/22/2013

VITAE PHARMACEUTICALS INC (DE)
Acquired by Allergan PLC 10/25/2016

(See Advanced Medical Optics, Inc.)

VITA BIOTECH CORP (DE)
(continued above)

Each share Common $0.0001 par exchanged for $21 cash

VITAFORT INTL CORP (DE)
Each share old Common $0.0001 par exchanged for (0.05) share new Common $0.0001 par 10/05/1996
Charter cancelled and declared inoperative and void for non-payment of taxes 03/01/2002

VITAL DEVELOPMENT, INC. (UT)
Name changed to Mitek Systems, Inc. (Utah) 4/19/85
Mytek Systems, Inc. (Utah) reincorporated in Delaware in September, 1987

VITAL HEALTH TECHNOLOGIES INC (MN)
Recapitalized 10/02/2000
Recapitalized from Vital Heart Systems, Inc. to Vital Health Technologies, Inc. 10/02/2000
Each (60) shares Common no par exchanged for (1) share Common 1¢ par
Each share old Common 1¢ par exchanged for (0.1) share new Common 1¢ par 01/08/2002
Name changed to Caribbean American Health Resorts, Inc. 03/31/2003
(See Caribbean American Health Resorts, Inc.)

VITAL IMAGES INC (MN)
Acquired by Toshiba Corp. 06/17/2011
Each share Common 1¢ par exchanged for $18.75 cash

VITAL LIVING INC (NV)
SEC revoked common stock registration 02/06/2014

VITAL LIVING PRODS INC (DE)
Recapitalized as Bounce Mobile Systems, Inc. 10/16/2006
Each share Common 1¢ par exchanged for (0.01) share Common 1¢ par

VITAL MINERALS, INC. (TX)
Bankrupt in 1963
No stockholders' equity

VITAL PAC RES LTD (BAHAMAS)
Reincorporated 05/26/1987
Reincorporated 08/21/1998
Place of incorporation changed from (BC) to (Canada) 05/26/1987
Place of incorporation changed from (Canada) to (Bahamas) 08/21/1998
Reorganized under the laws of Yukon as First Majestic Resource Corp. 01/03/2002
Each share Common no par exchanged for (0.1) share Common no par
First Majestic Resource Corp. (YT) reincorporated in British Columbia 01/17/2005 which name changed to First Majestic Silver Corp. 11/22/2006

VITAL PRODS INC (DE)
Each share old Common $0.0001 par exchanged for (0.01) share new Common $0.0001 par 07/06/2009
Each share new Common $0.0001 par exchanged again for (0.001) share new Common $0.0001 par 08/27/2010
Each share new Common $0.0001 par exchanged again for (0.001) share new Common $0.0001 par 03/05/2012
Each share new Common $0.0001 par exchanged for (0.0002) share new Common $0.0001 par 05/02/2017
Name changed to XCPCNL Business Services Corp. 07/12/2017

VITAL RES CORP (CANADA)
Recapitalized as Fulcrum Resources Inc. 01/15/2009
Each share Common no par exchanged for (0.1) share Common no par

VITAL SIGNS INC (NJ)
Merged into General Electric Co. 10/30/2008
Each share Common no par exchanged for $74.50 cash

VITALCARE DIABETES TREATMENT CTRS INC (NV)
Recapitalized as China Advanced Technology 06/23/2010
Each share Common $0.001 par exchanged for (0.001) share Common $0.001 par
China Advanced Technology name changed to Goliath Film & Media Holdings 01/20/2012

VITALCOM INC (DE)
Merged into Data Critical Corp. 6/8/2001
Each share Common $0.0001 par exchanged for (0.62) share Common $0.001 par
(See Data Critical Corp.)

VITALINK COMMUNICATIONS CORP (DE)
Merged into NSC Acquisition Corp. 07/01/1991
Each share Common 1¢ par exchanged for $10.50 cash

VITALINK PHARMACY SVCS INC (DE)
Merged into Genesis Health Ventures, Inc. 8/28/98
Each share Common 1¢ par exchanged for either (0.045) share Conv. Preferred Ser. G 1¢ par, $22.50 cash, or a combination thereof
Note: Option to receive stock or combination of stock and cash expired 8/25/98

VITALITY UNLIMITED INC (MI)
Name changed to VHC, Ltd. 07/16/1986
(See VHC, Ltd.)

VITALLABS INC (NV)
Each (17) shares old Common $0.001 par exchanged for (1) share new Common $0.001 par 06/11/2002
Name changed to America Asia Corp. (NV) 10/19/2004
America Asia Corp. (NV) reincorporated in Washington as America Asia Energy Corp. 11/08/2005 which name changed to Renegade Energy Corp. 09/14/2006 which recapitalized as Carson Development Corp. 10/20/2008
(See Carson Development Corp.)

VITALMETRICS INC (CA)
Common no par split (2) for (1) by issuance of (1) additional share 08/06/1982
Recapitalized as AutoFinance Group Inc. 08/23/1990
Each share Common no par exchanged for (0.2) share Common no par
AutoFinance Group Inc. acquired by KeyCorp (New) 09/27/1995

VITALSTREAM HLDGS INC (NV)
Each share old Common $0.001 par exchanged for (0.25) share new Common $0.001 par 04/05/2006
Merged into Internap Network Services Corp. 02/20/2007
Each share new Common $0.001 par exchanged for (0.5132) share Common $0.001 par
Internap Network Services Corp. name changed to Internap Corp. 12/04/2014

VITALTRUST BUSINESS DEV CORP (NV)
Name changed to Renew Energy Resources, Inc. 05/27/2008
(See Renew Energy Resources, Inc.)

VITALWORKS INC (DE)
Name changed to AMICAS, Inc. 01/03/2005
(See AMICAS, Inc.)

VITAMED BIOPHARMACEUTICALS LTD (CANADA)
Name changed to Receptagen Ltd. (Canada) and Class A Common no par reclassified as Common no par 07/12/1993
Receptagen Ltd. (Canada) reorganized in Florida as Spantel Communications Inc. 10/16/2001 which recapitalized as Systems America, Inc. 05/27/2010
(See Systems America, Inc.)

VITAMIN FOOD INC (DE)
Each share Preferred $10 par exchanged for (0.1) share Preferred $10 par 7/6/34
(Additional Information in Active)

VITAMIN INC (UT)
Recapitalized as Caltag, Inc. 11/14/85
Each share Common $0.001 par exchanged for (0.125) share Common $0.008 par
(See Caltag, Inc.)

VITAMIN SPECIALTIES CORP (DE)
Issue Information - 900,000 shares COM offered at $4.50 per share on 12/30/1993
Name changed to Healthrite, Inc. 07/17/1995
Healthrite, Inc. name changed to Medifast, Inc. 02/05/2001

VITAMIN SPICE (WY)
SEC revoked common stock registration 12/10/2014

VITAMINSHOPPE COM INC (DE)
Issue Information - 4,545,455 shares CL A offered at $11 per share on 10/08/1999
Merged into Vitamin Shoppe Industries 4/16/2001
Each share Class A Common 1¢ par exchanged for $1 cash

VITAMIX PHARMACEUTICALS, INC. (PA)
Name changed to Wynn Pharmaceuticals, Inc. 10/31/66
Wynn Pharmaceuticals, Inc. merged into Cooper Laboratories, Inc. 2/29/68
(See Cooper Laboratories, Inc.)

VITAS GROUP INC (NV)
Name changed to Sealand Natural Resources Inc. 02/26/2013

VITASTI INC (DE)
Name changed to Welwind Energy International Corp. 10/31/2006
(See Welwind Energy International Corp.)

VITATONICS CORP (NV)
Recapitalized as Rapid Bio Tests Corp. 06/16/2003
Each share Common $0.001 par exchanged for (0.004) share Common $0.001 par
Rapid Bio Tests Corp. name changed to Bio-Warm Corp. 12/15/2004 which recapitalized as DDC Industries, Inc. 04/23/2007 which name changed to PHI Mining Group, Inc. 12/19/2008 which name changed to PHI Gold Corp. 01/28/2011

VITAWAREHOUSE COM INC (DE)
Recapitalized as Texas Diversified Distributions, Inc. 8/17/2001
Each share Common $0.001 par exchanged for (0.2) share Common $0.001 par
Texas Diversified Distributions, Inc. name changed to Black Dragon Resources, Inc. 3/10/2004 which recapitalized as Black Dragon Resource Companies, Inc. 1/5/2005

VITEBSKER CREDIT ASSOCIATION, INC.
Dissolved in 1930

VITECH AMER INC (FL)
Issue Information - 2,000,000 shares COM offered at $10 per share on 11/01/1996
Stock Dividend - 10% payable 07/27/1998 to holders of record 07/13/1998
Reincorporated under the laws of Delaware as Darwin Resources, Inc. and Common no par changed to $0.000001 par 01/31/2008
Darwin Resources, Inc. recapitalized as A Clean Slate, Inc. 12/10/2010

VITEL FIBER OPTICS CORP (DE)
Company believed out of business 00/00/1990
Details not available

VITERBO CORP AMER (DE)
Charter cancelled and declared inoperative and void for non-payment of taxes 03/01/1991

VITERRA INC (CANADA)
Acquired by Glencore International PLC 12/18/2012
Each share Common no par exchanged for $16.25 cash

VITESSE SEMICONDUCTOR CORP (DE)
Old Common 1¢ par split (3) for (2) by issuance of (0.5) additional share payable 02/28/1997 to holders of record 02/12/1997
Old Common 1¢ par split (2) for (1) by issuance of (1) additional share payable 05/26/1998 to holders of record 05/04/1998
Old Common 1¢ par split (2) for (1) by issuance of (1) additional share payable 10/21/1999 to holders of record 09/30/1999
Each share old Common 1¢ par exchanged for (0.05) share new Common 1¢ par 07/02/2010
Acquired by Microsemi Corp. 04/28/2015
Each share new Common 1¢ par exchanged for $5.28 cash

VITRAMON INC (DE)
Stock Dividends - 10% 09/15/1966; 10% 09/15/1972; 10% 02/16/1981
Merged into Thomas & Betts Corp. (NJ) 07/17/1987
Each share Common 10¢ par exchanged for (0.6) share Common 50¢ par
Thomas & Betts Corp. (NJ) reincorporated in Tennessee 05/03/1996
(See Thomas & Betts Corp.)

VITRAN INC (ON)
Class A no par reclassified as Common no par 04/29/2004
Acquired by TransForce Inc. 03/28/2014
Each share Common no par exchanged for USD$6.50 cash

VITREOUS CAP INC (AB)
Recapitalized 3/6/98
Recapitalized from Vitreous Environmental Group Inc. to Vitreous Capital Inc. 3/6/98
Each share Common no par exchanged for (0.1) share Common no par
Name changed to Vitreous Glass Inc. 2/15/2007

VITRIA TECHNOLOGY INC (DE)
Old Common $0.001 par split (2) for (1) by issuance of (1) additional share payable 1/17/2000 to holders of record 12/28/99
Old Common $0.001 par split (2) for (1) by issuance of (1) additional share payable 4/5/2000 to holders of record 3/22/2000
Each share old Common $0.001 par exchanged for (0.25) share new Common $0.001 par 5/28/2003
Merged into Innovation Technology Group, Inc. 3/7/2007
Each share new Common $0.001 par exchanged for $2.75 cash

VITRIFIED WHEEL CO. (MA)
Acquired by Waltham Grinding Wheel Co:, Inc. on a (0.068) for (1) basis 1/31/63

VITRISEAL INC (NV)
Name changed to Liquitek Enterprises Inc. 07/31/2000
(See Liquitek Enterprises Inc.)

VITRIX INC (NV)
Each share old Common $0.005 par exchanged for (0.1) share new Common $0.005 par 04/04/2001
Name changed to Time America, Inc. 12/09/2003
Time America, Inc. name changed to NETtime Solutions, Inc. 05/11/2007 which name changed to Tempco, Inc. 10/14/2008 which name changed to Esio Water & Beverage Development Corp. 01/18/2013 which name changed to UPD Holding Corp. 03/01/2017

VITRO CORP. OF AMERICA (DE)
Merged into Automation Industries, Inc. (CA) 12/20/68
Each share Common 50¢ par exchanged for (0.725) share Common $1 par
(See Automation Industries, Inc. (CA))

VITRO MANUFACTURING CO. (PA)
Each share Preferred and Common $100 par exchanged for (100) shares Common $1 par 00/00/1948
Each share Common $1 par exchanged for (2) shares Common 50¢ par 00/00/1951
Reincorporated under the laws of Delaware as Vitro Corp. of America 00/00/1953
Vitro Corp. of America merged into Automation Industries, Inc. (CA) 12/20/1968
(See Automation Industries, Inc. (CA))

VITRO SOCIEDAD ANONIMA (MEXICO)
Sponsored ADR's for Ordinary no par split (6) for (5) by issuance of (0.2) additional ADR 05/18/1995
ADR agreement terminated 08/24/2009
Each Sponsored ADR for Ordinary Participation Certificates no par exchanged for $1.539791 cash

VITRONICS CORP (MA)
Merged into Dover Corp. 12/02/1997
Each share Common 1¢ par exchanged for $1.50 cash

VITROSEAL INC (NV)
Name changed to VitriSeal Inc. 02/18/1999
VitriSeal Inc. name changed to Liquitek Enterprises Inc. 07/31/2000
(See Liquitek Enterprises Inc.)

VITROTECH CORP (NV)
Charter permanently revoked 07/31/2006

VITTFORGE INC (CANADA)
Placed in bankruptcy and assets subsequently liquidated by May 1990
No stockholders' equity

VIVA ASSOC INC (DE)
Charter cancelled and declared inoperative and void for non-payment of taxes 3/1/89

VIVA GAMING & RESORTS INC (FL)
Name changed 09/30/1999
Name changed from Viva Gaming & Resorts.com Inc. to Viva Gaming & Resorts Inc. 09/30/1999
SEC revoked common stock registration 10/07/2010

VIVA GOLF MFG INC (FL)
Name changed to Connect One Telcom Corp. 5/25/99
Connect One Telcom Corp. name changed to Green Machine Development Corp. 7/1/99

VIVA GOLF U S A CORP (FL)
Each share old Common no par exchanged for (0.2) share new Common no par 10/22/98
Name changed to Lifekeepers International, Inc. (FL) 11/5/98
Lifekeepers International, Inc. (FL) reorganized in Nevada as East Coast Diversified Corp. 10/23/2003

VIVA GOLF USA CORP (DE)
Name changed to Advanced Environmental Solutions Inc. 4/28/97
Advanced Environmental Solutions Inc. name changed to Viva Holdings, Inc. 7/1/98 which name changed to Chemicorp International, Inc. 12/23/98

VIVA HLDGS INC (DE)
Name changed to Chemicorp International, Inc. 12/23/98

VIVA INTL INC (NV)
Reincorporated 03/14/2005
Each share Common $0.001 par received distribution of (1) share Harvey-Westbury Corp. Common $0.001 par payable 04/18/2005 to holders of record 01/09/2003
State of incorporation changed from (DE) to (NV) 03/14/2005
Recapitalized as River Hawk Aviation, Inc. 02/27/2007
Each share Common $0.001 par exchanged for (0.025) share Common $0.001 par

VIVA MED SCIENCES CORP (DE)
Name changed to American Stone Industries, Inc. 07/31/1995
American Stone Industries, Inc. name changed to ASI Liquidating Corp. 01/31/2008
(See ASI Liquidating Corp.)

VIVA PHARMACEUTICAL INC. (NV)
Charter revoked for failure to file reports and pay fees 3/1/2000

VIVANT GROUP INC (AB)
Delisted from Canadian Venture Stock Exchange 05/31/2000

VIVANT NAT SPRING WTR INC (AB)
Name changed to Vivant Group Inc. 09/28/1993
(See Vivant Group Inc.)

VIVANTE INTERNATIONALE INC (NV)
Name changed to Viva Pharmaceutical Inc. 5/16/95
(See Viva Pharmaceutical Inc.)

VIVATAE INC (CO)
Recapitalized as Eagle Entertainment, Inc. 11/20/1986
Each share Common no par exchanged for (0.005) share Common $0.00001 par
Eagle Entertainment, Inc. name changed to Eagle Holdings Inc. (CO) 01/17/1992 which reincorporated in Nevada 10/21/1993 which name changed to Eagle Automotive Enterprises, Inc. 12/01/1993 which name changed to Chariot Entertainment Inc. 04/13/1994 which name changed to AutoCorp Equities, Inc. 09/23/1994 which name changed to Homeland Security Network, Inc. 03/16/2005 which name changed to Global Ecology Corp. 01/05/2010

VIVAUDOU (V.) INC.
Merged into Vadsco Sales Corp. 00/00/1929
Details not available

VIVAX MED CORP (DE)
Plan of reorganization under Chapter 11 Federal Bankruptcy Code effective 5/1/2002
Each share old Common 1¢ par exchanged for (0.002) share new Common 1¢ par
(Additional Information in Active)

VIVE YELLOWKNIFE GOLD MINES, LTD. (ON)
Charter cancelled for failure to file reports and pay taxes 2/10/58

VIVENDI (FRANCE)
Merged 12/08/2000
Name changed 04/24/2006
Old Sponsored ADR's for Ordinary split (3) for (1) by issuance of (2) additional ADR's payable 05/19/1999 to holders of record 05/18/1999
Merged from Vivendi S.A. to Vivendi Universal 12/08/2000
Each old Sponsored ADR for Ordinary exchanged for (0.2) new Sponsored ADR for Ordinary
Name changed from Vivendi Universal to Vivendi 04/24/2006
ADR agreement terminated 08/03/2006
Each new Sponsored ADR for Ordinary exchanged for $34.23288 cash

VIVENDI ENVIRONNEMENT (FRANCE)
Name changed to Veolia Environnement 05/02/2003

VIVENDI EXCHANGECO INC (CANADA)
Each Exchangeable Share no par exchanged for (1) Ser. A Exchangeable Share no par 11/06/2006
Each Ser. A Exchangeable Share no par exchanged for (1) share Vivendi S.A. (Old) Ordinary and $1.42 cash 11/27/2006

VIVENDI S A OLD (FRANCE)
Reorganized as Vivendi S.A. (New) 12/30/2008
Each ADR for Ordinary exchanged for (0.2) Sponsored ADR for Ordinary
(See Vivendi S.A. (New))

VIVENDI SA NEW (FRANCE)
ADR agreement terminated 01/10/2011
Each Sponsored ADR for Ordinary exchanged for $23.9324 cash
(Additional Information in Active)

VIVENDI UNVL EXCHANGECO INC (CANADA)
Name changed to Vivendi Exchangeco Inc. 05/18/2006
(See Vivendi Exchangeco Inc.)

VIVENTIA BIOTECH INC (BC)
Each share old Common no par exchanged for (0.1) share new Common no par 5/12/2004
Merged into Dan Group 12/28/2005
Each share new Common no par exchanged for $2.50 cash

VIVER INCORPORADORA E CONSTRUTORA S A (BRAZIL)
GDR agreement terminated 08/04/2017
No GDR's remain outstanding

VIVEVE MED INC (YT)
Each share old Common no par exchanged for (0.125) share new Common no par 04/18/2016
Reincorporated under the laws of Delaware and Common no par changed to $0.0001 par 05/10/2016

VIVIAN CONSOLIDATED LTD. (NV)
Merged into Entrada Corp. on a (1) for (10) basis 5/14/57
Entrada Corp. recapitalized as Pacific Energy Corp. 1/14/76 which name changed to Aimco, Inc. 9/1/77 which recapitalized as Colt Technology, Inc. 3/31/83

VIVIAN MINING CO., INC. (CA)
Reincorporated under laws of Nevada 3/15/56
Vivian Mining Co., Inc. (NV) name changed to Vivian Consolidated Ltd. 5/26/56 which merged into Entrada Corp. 5/14/57 which recapitalized as Pacific Energy Corp. 1/14/76 which name changed to Aimco, Inc. 9/1/77 which recapitalized as Colt Technology, Inc. 3/31/83

VIVIAN MINING CO., INC. (NV)
Name changed to Vivian Consolidated Ltd. 5/26/56
Vivian Consolidated Ltd. merged into Entrada Corp. 5/14/57 which recapitalized as Pacific Energy Co. 1/14/76 which name changed to Aimco, Inc. 9/1/77 which recapitalized as Colt Technology, Inc. 3/31/83

VIVIANE WOODARD CORP (CA)
Completely liquidated 12/22/1969
Each share Common no par exchanged for first and final distribution of $30 cash

VIVID CAP CORP (AB)
Name changed to Divcom Technologies Inc. (ALTA) 10/20/2000
Divcom Technologies Inc. (ALTA) reincorporated in Canada as Divcom Lighting Inc. 11/27/2003

VIVID LEARNING SYS INC (WA)
Reincorporated 03/15/2009
State of incorporation changed from (DE) to (WA) 03/15/2009
Each share old Common $0.0001 par exchanged for (1) share new Common $0.0001 par to reflect a (1) for (1,000) reverse split followed by a (1,000) for (1) forward split 01/12/2010
Note: Holders of (999) or fewer pre-split shares received $0.60 cash per share
Acquired by Health & Safety Institute 03/07/2018
Each share new Common $0.0001 par exchanged for $1.94 cash

VIVID TECHNOLOGIES INC (DE)
Issue Information - 2,000,000 shares Common offered at $12 per share on 12/11/1996
Merged into PerkinElmer, Inc. 1/14/2000
Each share Common 1¢ par exchanged for (0.1613) share Common 1¢ par

VIVIGEN INC (NM)
Acquired by Genzyme Corp. 10/29/1992
Each share Common 1¢ par exchanged for (0.3741) share Common 1¢ par
(See Genzyme Corp.)

VIVO PARTICIPACOES S A (BRAZIL)
Each old Sponsored ADR for Preferred exchanged for (0.25) new Sponsored ADR for Preferred 10/17/2008
Merged into Telecomunicacoes de Sao Paulo S.A. - Telesp 06/07/2011
Each new Sponsored ADR for Preferred exchanged for (1.55) Sponsored ADR's for Preferred Telecomunicacoes de Sao Paulo S.A. name changed to Telefonica Brasil, S.A. 10/11/2011

VIVRA INC (DE)
Common 1¢ par split (3) for (2) by issuance of (0.5) additional share 8/10/90
Common 1¢ par split (3) for (2) by issuance of (0.5) additional share 5/31/91
Common 1¢ par split (3) for (2) by issuance of (0.5) additional share 11/29/93
Common 1¢ par split (3) for (2) by issuance of (0.5) additional share 11/22/95
Merged into Incentive AB 6/12/97
Each share Common 1¢ par exchanged for $35.62 cash

VIVUS INC (CA)
Reincorporated under the laws of Delaware 05/24/1996

VIXEL CORP (DE)
Merged into Emulex Corp. 11/17/2003
Each share Common $0.0015 par exchanged for $10 cash

VIXS SYS INC (CANADA)
Merged into Pixelworks, Inc. 08/03/2017
Each share Common no par exchanged for (0.04836) share new Common $0.001 par
Note: Unexchanged certificates will be cancelled and become without value 08/03/2023

VIYON CORP (DE)
Name changed to First Guardian Financial Corp. 07/22/2005
First Guardian Financial Corp. name changed to New Capital Funding Corp. 05/07/2007 which recapitalized as Ulysses Holding Corp. 10/29/2007 which name changed to Ulysses Diversified Holdings Corp. 05/08/2008 which name changed to JNS Holdings Corp. 02/16/2012

VIYYA TECHNOLOGIES INC (NV)
Name changed 08/09/2004
Name changed from Viyon Technologies, Inc. to Viyya Technologies, Inc. 08/09/2004
Charter permanently revoked 06/30/2008

VIZACOM INC (DE)
Each share old Common $0.0001 par exchanged for (0.1) share new Common $0.0001 par 05/23/2001
Charter cancelled and declared inoperative and void for non-payment of taxes 03/01/2005

VIZARIO INC (NV)
SEC revoked common stock registration 01/12/2011
Stockholders' equity unlikely

VIZSTAR INC (NV)
Old Common $0.0001 par split (16) for (1) by issuance of (15) additional shares payable 03/30/2010 to holders of record 03/30/2010
Each share old Common $0.0001 par exchanged for (0.04) share new Common $0.0001 par 01/22/2013
Recapitalized as Kimberly Parry Organics Corp. 04/03/2014
Each share new Common $0.0001 par exchanged for (0.000125) share Common $0.0001 par

VL DISSOLUTION CORP (CO)
Liquidation completed
Each share Common 1¢ par received initial distribution of (0.15) share Sirenza Microdevices, Inc. Common $0.001 par payable 10/31/2003 to holders of record 10/6/2003 Ex date - 11/3/2003
Each share Common 1¢ par received second and final distribution of (0.137072) share Sirenza Microdevices, Inc. Common $0.001 par and $0.159 cash payable 6/28/2004 to holders of record 6/18/2004 Ex date - 6/29/2004
Note: Certificates were not required to be surrendered and are without value

VLASIC FOODS INTL INC (NJ)
Plan of reorganization under Chapter 11 Federal Bankruptcy Code effective 12/5/2001
No stockholders' equity

VLCHEK TOOL CO. (OH)
Liquidation completed 1/15/63

VLDC TECHNOLOGIES INC (CO)
Each share old Common $0.001 par exchanged for (0.005) share new Common $0.001 par 09/09/2005
Name changed to JTS International, Inc. 01/24/2006
JTS International, Inc. recapitalized as Fuji Construction Company International, Inc. 02/08/2008 which

name changed to Hokutou Holdings International, Inc. (CO) 11/06/2008 which reincorporated in Nevada 05/23/2014 which name changed to Platinum Pari-Mutuel Holdings, Inc. 12/09/2014 which name changed to Point to Point Methodics, Inc. 04/27/2017

VLI CORP (DE)
Acquired by American Home Products Corp. 12/31/87
Each share Common 1¢ par exchanged for $6.25 cash

VLINX TECHNOLOGY INC (NV)
Name changed to Vision Plasma Systems, Inc. 04/03/2012

VLM VENTURES LTD (BC)
Recapitalized as Altan Nevada Minerals Ltd. 12/20/2011
Each share Common no par exchanged for (0.4) share Common no par

VLN CORP (OH)
Merged into Sheller-Globe Corp. 9/30/74
Each share $3 Conv. Preferred Ser. A no par exchanged for (1) share $3 Conv. Preferred no par
Each share Common $1 par exchanged for (0.6) share Common no par
(See Sheller-Globe Corp.)

VLOV INC (NV)
Each share old Common $0.00001 par exchanged for (0.4) share new Common $0.00001 par 12/12/2011
Each share new Common $0.00001 par exchanged again for (0.33333333) share new Common $0.00001 par 09/24/2012
Name changed to Kali, Inc. 02/23/2016

VLPS LTG SVCS INTL INC (DE)
Merged into Production Resource Group, LLC 07/09/2004
Each share Common 10¢ par exchanged for $8.3184 cash
Note: Each share Common 10¢ par received an additional distribution of approximately $0.4747 cash from escrow 05/00/2005

VLSI TECHNOLOGY INC (CA)
Merged into Koninklijke Philips Electronics N.V. 06/23/1999
Each share Common no par exchanged for $21 cash

VM SOFTWARE INC (DE)
Common 1¢ par split (3) for (2) by issuance of (0.5) additional share 12/19/1986
Name changed to Systems Center, Inc. 02/27/1989
Systems Center, Inc. merged into Sterling Software, Inc. 07/01/1993 which merged into Computer Associates International, Inc. 04/07/2000 which name changed to CA, Inc. 02/01/2006

VMAILER.COM INC. (NY)
Dissolved by proclamation 6/27/2001

VMARK SOFTWARE INC (DE)
Name changed to ARDENT Software, Inc. 2/10/98
ARDENT Software, Inc. merged into Informix Corp. 3/1/2000 which name changed to Ascential Software Corp. 7/3/2001

VMH VIDEOMOVIEHOUSE COM INC (BC)
Name changed to Virtual Media Holdings, Inc. 05/18/2006
Virtual Media Holdings, Inc. name changed to Biomass Secure Power Inc. 03/12/2009

VMIC INC (DE)
Merged into GE Fanuc 9/10/2001
Each share Common 10¢ par exchanged for $13.3524 cash
Note: Approximately $1.51 cash per share is being held in escrow for possible future distribution

VMS HOTEL INVT FD (DE)
Reorganized 07/20/1987
Under plan of reorganization each VMS Hotel Investment Trust (MA) Share of Bene. Int. no par automatically became (1) share VMS Hotel Investment Fund (DE) Common 1¢ par 07/20/1987
Name changed to Banyan Hotel Investment Fund 03/21/1991
Banyan Hotel Investment Fund name changed to B.H.I.T. Inc. 01/04/2008 which name changed to Banyan Rail Services Inc. 01/29/2010

VMS INVESTORS FIRST-STAGED EQUITY L.P. II (DE)
In process of liquidation
Each Unit of Undivided Int. received initial distribution of $19.85 cash 06/00/1997
Note: Details on subsequent distributions, if any, are not available
Partnership terminated registration 05/14/1999

VMS MTG INVT FD (DE)
Name changed to Banyan Mortgage Investment Fund 6/20/91
Banyan Mortgage Investment Fund recapitalized as Legend Properties, Inc. 12/31/96

VMS MTG INVS L P (DE)
Name changed to Banyan Mortgage Investors L.P. I 03/01/1991
(See Banyan Mortgage Investors L.P. I)

VMS MTG INVS L P II (DE)
Name changed to Banyan Mortgage Investors L.P. II 3/1/91
(See Banyan Mortgage Investors L.P. II)

VMS MTG INVS L P III (DE)
Name changed to Banyan Mortgage Investors L.P. III 03/01/1991
(See Banyan Mortgage Investors L.P. III)

VMS SHORT TERM INCOME TR (MA)
Name changed to Banyan Short Term Income Trust 3/11/91
(See Banyan Short Term Income Trust)

VMS STRATEGIC LD FD II (DE)
Name changed to Banyan Strategic Land Fund II 6/20/91
Banyan Strategic Land Fund II name changed to Semele Group Inc. 11/14/97
(See Semele Group Inc.)

VMS STRATEGIC LD TR (MA)
Name changed to Banyan Strategic Land Trust 3/13/91
Banyan Strategic Land Trust name changed to Banyan Strategic Realty Trust 5/1/93
(See Banyan Strategic Realty Trust)

VMS VENTURES INC (BC)
Merged into Royal Nickel Corp. 04/28/2016
Each share Common no par exchanged for (0.245765) share Common no par and $0.023942 cash
Each share Common no par received distribution of (0.2047) share North American Nickel Inc. Common no par payable 05/06/2016 to holders of record 04/26/2016
Note: Unexchanged certificates will be cancelled and become without value 04/28/2022

VMX INC (DE)
Merged into Octel Communications Corp. 3/31/94
Each share Common 5¢ par exchanged for (0.2) share Common $0.001 par
Octel Communications Corp. merged into Lucent Technologies Inc. 9/29/97 which merged into Alcatel-Lucent S.A. 11/30/2006

VMX RES INC (BC)
Name changed to Monster Uranium Corp. 09/07/2007

VNB CAP TR I (DE)
7.75% Guaranteed Trust Preferred Securities called for redemption at $25 plus $0.215278 accrued dividends on 10/25/2013

VNC VIDEO NETWORK CORP (BC)
Name changed to Westpost Capital Inc. 01/23/1990
Westpost Capital Inc. recapitalized as Telepost Communications Inc. 12/11/1990
(See Telepost Communications Inc.)

VNI COMMUNICATIONS INC (FL)
Proclaimed dissolved for failure to file reports and pay fees 08/13/1993

VNU N V (NETHERLANDS)
ADR agreement terminated 04/05/2007
Each Sponsored ADR for Ordinary 5 Gldrs. par exchanged for $46.58949 cash

VNUS MED TECHNOLOGIES INC (DE)
Issue Information - 5,375,995 shares COM offered at $15 per share on 10/20/2004
Acquired by Covidien PLC 06/17/2009
Each share Common $0.001 par exchanged for $29 cash

VOCALINE CO AMER INC (CT)
Stock Dividends - 10% 04/25/1966; 10% 04/21/1967
Name changed to Pratt-Read Corp. 10/22/1970
(See Pratt-Read Corp.)

VOCALSCAPE INC (DE)
Old Common $0.00001 par split (10) for (1) by issuance of (9) additional shares payable 05/11/2004 to holders of record 05/07/2004 Ex date - 05/12/2004
Each share Common $0.00001 par exchanged for (0.004) share Common $0.0001 par 10/28/2005
Name changed to Nevstar Precious Metals, Inc. 11/07/2005
Nevstar Precious Metals, Inc. recapitalized as Deploy Technologies Inc. (DE) 11/06/2008 which reincorporated in Nevada 09/15/2010 which recapitalized as Body & Mind Inc. 12/07/2017

VOCALSCAPE NETWORKS INC (NV)
Recapitalized as Kaleidoscope Venture Capital Inc. 07/14/2008
Each share Common $0.001 par exchanged for (0.005) share Common $0.001 par

VOCALTEC COMMUNICATIONS LTD (ISRAEL)
Name changed 04/00/1997
Name changed from VocalTec Ltd. to VocalTec Communications Ltd. 04/00/1997
Each (13) shares Ordinary ILS 0.01 par exchanged for (1) share Ordinary ILS 0.13 par 11/25/2005
Each share Ordinary ILS 0.13 par exchanged for (0.2) share Ordinary ILS 0.65 par 07/19/2010
Ordinary ILS 0.65 par changed to no par 12/17/2010
Name changed to magicJack VocalTec Ltd. 05/23/2011

VOCALTECH INC (DE)
Each share Common 1¢ par exchanged for (0.15873015) share Common 5¢ par 02/03/1992
Name changed to Innotek Inc. 01/07/1993
Innotek Inc. name changed to Dermarx Corp. 12/15/1994 which recapitalized as GoPublicNow.com, Inc. 04/07/2000 which name changed to GPN Network Inc. 11/08/2000 which name changed to IR Biosciences Holdings, Inc. 08/28/2003

VOCAM SYS INC (MN)
Liquidation completed
Each share Common $0.001 par received initial distribution of (0.02) share Pitney Bowes Inc. Common $2 par 04/19/1990
Each share Common $0.001 par received second and final distribution of (0.024128) share Pitney Bowes Inc. Common $2 par and $0.009 cash 08/17/1990
Note: Certificates were not required to be surrendered and are without value

VOCATIONAL ADVANCEMENT SVCS INC (DE)
Merged into NuCorp, Inc. (DE) 04/15/1976
Each share Common 10¢ par exchanged for $0.10 cash

VOCUS INC (DE)
Acquired by GTCR Valor Companies, Inc. 05/30/2014
Each share Common 1¢ par exchanged for $18 cash

VODAFONE AG (GERMANY)
ADR agreement terminated 04/25/2002
Each Sponsored ADR for Ordinary exchanged for $223.387 cash

VODAFONE AIRTOUCH PLC (ENGLAND & WALES)
Name changed 06/30/1999
Sponsored ADR's for Ordinary split (3) for (1) by issuance of (2) additional ADR's 07/22/1994
Name changed from Vodafone Group PLC (Old) to Vodafone AirTouch PLC 06/30/1999
Sponsored ADR's for Ordinary split (5) for (1) by issuance of (4) additional ADR's payable 10/01/1999 to holders of record 09/30/1999 Ex date - 10/04/1999
Name changed to Vodafone Group PLC (New) 06/28/2000

VODAFONE HLDGS K K (JAPAN)
ADR agreement terminated 11/24/2004
Each ADR for Common exchanged for $2.146 cash

VODAFONE LIBERTEL N V (NETHERLANDS)
ADR agreement terminated 09/15/2003
Each ADR for Ordinary exchanged for $21.552189 cash
Each 144A ADR for Ordinary exchanged for $21.552189 cash

VODAFONE-PANAFON HELLENIC TELECOMMUNICATIONS CO S A (GREECE)
GDR agreement terminated 5/30/2005
Each 144A Sponsored GDR for Ordinary exchanged for $8.1874 cash
Each Reg. S Sponsored GDR for Ordinary exchanged for $8.1874 cash

VODAFONE-TELECEL COMUNICACOES PESSOAIS S A (PORTUGAL)
Acquired by Vodafone Group PLC 7/7/2003
Each Sponsored ADR for Ordinary exchanged for $9.8423 cash

VODATEL NETWORKS HLDGS LTD (HONG KONG)
ADR agreement terminated 04/27/2015
No ADR's remain outstanding

VOD-VOL   FINANCIAL INFORMATION, INC.

VODAVI TECHNOLOGY CORP (DE)
Reincorporated 05/07/1985
State of incorporation changed from (CA) to (DE) 05/07/1985
Under plan of merger name changed to Executone Information Systems, Inc. (DE) 07/08/1988
Executone Information Systems, Inc. (DE) reincorporated in Virginia 06/00/1989 which name changed to eLOT, Inc. (VA) which reorganized in Delaware 12/31/2002
(See eLOT, Inc. (DE))

VODAVI TECHNOLOGY INC (DE)
Merged into Vertical Communications, Inc. 12/01/2006
Each share Common $0.001 par exchanged for $7.50 cash

VODCO OIL INC (UT)
Reorganized under the laws of Nevada as Granite Golf Group Inc. 06/27/1996
Each share Common $0.001 par exchanged for (0.02) share Common $0.001 par
Granite Golf Group Inc. (NV) reincorporated in Delaware as Granite Golf Corp. 07/24/1998 which recapitalized as Beverage Creations, Inc. 01/24/2008

VODEL CORP (NY)
Charter cancelled and proclaimed dissolved for failure to pay taxes and file reports 12/15/1972

VOGART CRAFTS CORP (NY)
Chapter 11 bankruptcy proceedings converted to Chapter 7 on 3/2/93
No stockholders' equity

VOGT MFG CORP (NY)
Capital Stock no par changed to $1 par 04/01/1969
Stock Dividends - 10% 12/01/1964; 100% 02/27/1970
Name changed to Voplex Corp. 05/04/1970
(See Voplex Corp.)

VOGUE FASHIONS INC (BC)
Delisted from Vancouver Stock Exchange 08/03/1983

VOGUE INSTR CORP (NY)
Plan of reorganization under Chapter 11 bankruptcy proceedings confirmed 12/21/1976
Details not available

VOGUE INTERNATIONALE INC (MA)
Placed in receivership 00/00/1972
Attorney opined no stockholders' equity

VOGUE INVTS 1987 LTD (AB)
Delisted from Alberta Stock Exchange 09/24/1990

VOGUE RECORDINGS, INC.
Out of existence in 1950

VOGUE RES INC (CANADA)
Name changed to Gearunlimited.com Inc. 12/02/1999
(See Gearunlimited.com Inc.)

VOGUE SHOES, INC. (TX)
5-1/2% Conv. Preferred $25 par called for redemption 07/15/1968
Acquired by Craddock-Terry Shoe Corp. 04/00/1969
Details not available

VOGUE TRAVEL SVCS INC (NV)
Name changed to 31E Cellular Corp. 06/10/2005
31E Cellular Corp. recapitalized as Capital Acquisitions Holdings Ltd. 12/05/2005 which name changed to Sun Peaks Energy, Inc. 02/13/2007
(See Sun Peaks Energy, Inc.)

VOI-SHAN INDUSTRIES, INC. (IL)
Stock Dividend - 100% 6/15/61
Name changed to VSI Corp. (Ill.) 10/22/62
VSI Corp. (Ill.) reincorporated under the laws of Delaware 11/1/67
(See VSI Corp. (Del.))

VOICE & WIRELESS CORP (MN)
Recapitalized as MIXED Entertainment Inc. 08/25/2004
Each share Common no par exchanged for (0.01) share Common no par
MIXED Entertainment Inc. name changed to Conscious Co. 08/30/2006 which name changed to American Environmental Energy, Inc. 05/06/2008

VOICE CTL SYS INC (DE)
Merged into Koninklijke Philips Electronics N.V. 06/28/1999
Each share Common 1¢ par exchanged for $4 cash

VOICE DIARY INC (DE)
Each (11.1) shares old Class A Common 1¢ par exchanged for (1) share new Class A Common 1¢ par 01/26/2007
Name changed to China Health Resource, Inc. 06/07/2007

VOICE IT SOLUTIONS INC (CANADA)
Recapitalized 04/11/1996
Recapitalized from Voice-It Technologies Inc. to Voice-It Solutions Inc. 04/11/1996
Each share old Common no par exchanged for (0.1) share Common no par
Dissolved 07/12/2004
Details not available

VOICE IT WORLDWIDE INC (CO)
Plan of reorganization under Chapter 11 Federal Bankruptcy proceedings confirmed 01/19/2000
No stockholders' equity

VOICE POWERED TECHNOLOGY INTL INC (CA)
Recapitalized as World Waste Technologies, Inc. 08/30/2004
Each (60) shares Common $0.001 par exchanged for (1) share Common $0.001 par
World Waste Technologies, Inc. merged into Vertex Energy, Inc. 05/04/2009

VOICECALL LTD (AUSTRALIA)
Name changed to Matrix Telecommunications Ltd. 04/27/1989
(See Matrix Telecommunications Ltd.)

VOICEFLASH NETWORKS INC (FL)
Assets assigned for the benefit of creditors 1/24/2003
Stockholders' equity unlikely

VOICEIQ INC (ON)
Reorganized under the laws of Alberta as Yoho Resources Inc. (Old) 12/23/2004
Each share Common no par exchanged for (0.012877) share Common no par and distribution of (1) share VIQ Solutions Inc. Common no par
Yoho Resources Inc. (Old) reorganized as Yoho Resources Inc. (New) 03/21/2014
(See Yoho Resources Inc. (New))

VOICEMAIL INTL INC (CA)
Chapter 7 bankruptcy proceedings terminated 02/05/1996
Stockholders' equity unlikely

VOICENET INC (DE)
Common 1¢ par split (2) for (1) by issuance of (1) additional share payable 04/07/2000 to holders of record 03/17/2000
Charter cancelled and declared inoperative and void for non-payment of taxes 03/01/2007

VOICENETWORKX INC (DE)
Recapitalized as Greenway Design Group, Inc. 04/07/2010
Each share Common $0.001 par exchanged for (0.00148148) share Common $0.001 par
Greenway Design Group, Inc.

recapitalized as Redwood Scientific Technologies, Inc. 02/14/2018

VOICESTREAM WIRELESS CORP (DE)
Reincorporated 02/25/2000
State of incorporation changed from (WA) to (DE) 02/25/2000
Stock Dividend - 0.75% payable 04/06/2001 to holders of record 03/23/2001 Ex date - 03/21/2001
Merged into Deutsche Telekom AG 05/31/2001
Each share Common no par exchanged for (3.6693) Sponsored ADR's for Ordinary and $15.7262 cash

VOIGT BREWING CO.
Merged into Voigt-Pros't Brewing Co. in 1936 whose assets were sold in 1937

VOIGT (ALBERT) INDUSTRIES, INC. (NY)
Adjudicated bankrupt 09/08/1967
No stockholders' equity

VOIGT-PROS'T BREWING CO.
Assets sold in 1937

VOILA FOODS FOR PETS INC (NY)
Name changed to Combined Media, Inc. (NY) 02/26/1970
Combined Media, Inc. (NY) reincorporated in Florida as Combined Financial Services, Inc. 05/24/1973
(See Combined Financial Services, Inc.)

VOIP 5000 INC (DE)
Each share old Common $0.001 par exchanged for (0.02) share new Common $0.001 par 10/10/2006
Name changed to Target Development Group, Inc. (DE) 04/30/2007
Target Development Group, Inc. (DE) reincorporated in Wyoming 04/13/2009 which name changed to Hannover House, Inc. 04/03/2012

VOIP INC (TX)
Each share old Common $0.001 par exchanged for (0.05) share new Common $0.001 par 08/16/2007
SEC revoked common stock registration 07/14/2009

VOIP MDU COM (NV)
Name changed to VoIP-PAL.com Inc. 09/21/2006

VOIP TECHNOLOGIES INC (NV)
Charter revoked for failure to file reports and pay taxes 03/01/2013

VOIP TECHNOLOGY INC (NV)
Recapitalized as Oxford Ventures Inc. 1/30/2002
Each share Common $0.001 par exchanged for (0.005) share Common $0.001 par
Oxford Ventures Inc. recapitalized as Uluru Inc. 4/5/2006

VOIP TELECOM INC (NV)
Each share old Common $0.001 par exchanged for (1.2) shares new Common $0.001 par 09/11/2000
Each share new Common $0.001 par exchanged for (0.05) share Common $0.0001 par 02/25/2002
Name changed to Diversified Thermal Solutions Inc. 07/01/2002
(See Diversified Thermal Solutions Inc.)

VOIPCOM USA INC (DE)
Each share old Common 1¢ par exchanged for (0.005) share new Common 1¢ par 06/11/2008
Name changed to Maplex Alliance Ltd. 01/26/2011

VOIPLABS HLDGS INC (NV)
Common $0.001 par split (3) for (1) by issuance of (2) additional shares payable 11/08/2004 to holders of record 11/08/2004

Name changed to Concorde Resources Corp. 10/04/2005
Concorde Resources Corp. recapitalized as Real Hip Hop Matrix Corp. 11/03/2006 which name changed to RHNMedia 01/12/2007 which name changed to Massive G Media Corp. 03/16/2007 which name changed to International Minerals Mining Group, Inc. 06/21/2007 which name changed to Advanced Content Services, Inc. 02/05/2008 which recapitalized as New Wave Holdings, Inc. 12/08/2014 which name changed to PAO Group, Inc. 06/29/2017

VOIR ENERGY CORP (BC)
Merged into Zone Petroleum Corp. 5/28/82
Each share Common no par exchanged for (1/3) share Common no par
(See Zone Petroleum Corp.)

VOIS INC (FL)
Reincorporated 03/18/2009
State of incorporation changed from (DE) to (FL) 03/18/2009
Common $0.001 par split (100) for (1) by issuance of (99) additional shares payable 07/08/2009 to holders of record 07/06/2009 Ex date - 07/09/2009
Common $0.001 par changed to $0.00001 par 10/29/2009
Each share Common $0.00001 par exchanged for (0.005) share Common $0.001 par 11/23/2010
Reorganized under the laws of Nevada as Mind Solutions, Inc. 10/31/2013
Each share Common $0.001 par exchanged for (0.0005) share Common $0.001 par

VOISEY BAY RES INC (BC)
Merged into Twin Gold Corp. 4/4/97
Each share Common no par exchanged for (1.5) shares Common no par
Twin Gold Corp. name changed to Twin Mining Corp. 3/15/2000 which recapitalized as Atlanta Gold Inc. 3/28/2007

VOIT CORP (NY)
Merged into Voit Acquisition Corp. 8/17/93
Each share Common $0.005 par exchanged for $4.50 cash

VOKAR CORP. (MI)
Each (10) shares Common no par exchanged for (1) share Common $1 par in 1949
Voluntarily dissolved 5/13/64
Details not available

VOL AIR INC (NY)
Name changed to 89 East Fulton Corp. 11/27/64
89 East Fulton Corp. reorganized under the laws of Delaware as YGAC Corp. 4/18/69 which name changed to Hargrom Services Corp. 5/19/69
(See Hargrom Services Corp.)

VOLCANIC CAP CORP (BC)
Name changed to Volcanic Metals Corp. 02/19/2010
Volcanic Metals Corp. name changed to Volcanic Gold Mines Inc. 01/19/2017

VOLCANIC GOLD INC (NV)
Recapitalized as A Power Agro Agriculture Development, Inc. 08/24/2007
Each (71) shares Common 2¢ par exchanged for (1) share Common $0.001 par
A Power Agro Agriculture Development, Inc. name changed to Sino Agro Food Inc. 12/04/2007

VOLCANIC METALS CORP (BC)
Each share old Common no par

COPYRIGHTED MATERIAL   2790   NO UNAUTHORIZED REPRODUCTION

exchanged for (0.1) share new
Common no par 05/06/2013
Name changed to Volcanic Gold
Mines Inc. 01/19/2017

VOLCANIC METALS EXPL INC (AB)
Reincorporated 5/17/2005
Place of incorporation changed from
(ALTA) to (ONT) 5/17/2005
Name changed to Energy Fuels Inc.
6/27/2006

VOLCANIC OIL & GAS CO. LTD.
Dissolved in 1929

VOLCANO CORP (DE)
Acquired by Koninklijke Philips N.V.
02/17/2015
Each share Common $0.001 par
exchanged for $18 cash

VOLCANO RES CORP (BC)
Delisted from Vancouver Stock
Exchange 11/16/1990

VOLCOM INC (DE)
Issue Information - 4,687,500 shares
COM offered at $19 per share on
06/29/2005
Acquired by PPR S.A. 06/24/2011
Each share Common $0.001 par
exchanged for $24.50 cash

VOLGATELECOM PUB JT STK CO (RUSSIA)
Merged into Rostelecom OJSC
04/13/2011
Each Sponsored ADR for Registered
Shares exchanged for $12.460225
cash

VOLKSWAGEN INS CO (AR)
Each share Common $1 par
exchanged for (0.0001) share
Common $10,000 par 08/01/1974
Note: In effect holders received $4.50
cash per share and public interest
was eliminated

VOLKSWAGENWERK A G (GERMANY)
Stock Dividend - 20% 08/03/1970
Name changed to Volkswagen AG
07/04/1985

VOLT INC (NV)
Name changed to Kore Holdings, Inc.
10/20/2004
(See Kore Holdings, Inc.)

VOLT RESEARCH, INC. (UT)
Reincorporated under the laws of
Delaware as Age Research, Inc.
05/12/1987
Age Research, Inc. name changed to
SalesTactix, Inc. 08/02/2004 which
name changed to Strativation, Inc.
10/14/2005 which name changed to
CNS Response, Inc. 03/09/2007
which name changed to MYnd
Analytics, Inc. 01/12/2016

VOLT SOLAR SYS INC (FL)
Administratively dissolved 09/25/2015

VOLT TECHNICAL CORP. (NY)
Class A 50¢ par reclassified as
Common 50¢ par 12/29/67
Name changed to Volt Information
Sciences, Inc. 7/17/68

VOLTA RES INC (ON)
Merged into B2Gold Corp. 12/27/2013
Each share Common no par
exchanged for (0.15) share Common
no par

VOLTAIRE LTD (ISRAEL)
Issue Information - 5,770,000 ORD
shs. offered at $9 per share on
07/25/2007
Acquired by Mellanox Technologies,
Ltd. 02/07/2011
Each share Ordinary ILS 0.01 par
exchanged for $8.75 cash

VOLTAR ELECTRONICS, INC. (DE)
No longer in existence having
become inoperative and void for
non-payment of taxes 4/1/60

VOLTERRA RES INC (AB)
Merged into Edge Energy Inc.
05/27/1999
Each share Common no par
exchanged for (0.227) share
Common no par
Edge Energy Inc. merged into Ventus
Energy Ltd. 08/11/2000 which name
changed to Navigo Energy Inc.
05/24/2002
(See Navigo Energy Inc.)

VOLTERRA SEMICONDUCTOR CORP (DE)
Issue Information - 4,500,000 shares
COM offered at $8 per share on
07/28/2004
Acquired by Maxim Integrated
Products, Inc. 10/01/2013
Each share Common $0.001 par
exchanged for $23 cash

VOLU-SOL INC (UT)
Each share old Common $0.0001 par
exchanged for (0.2) share new
Common $0.0001 par 04/29/2000
Name changed to RemoteMDx, Inc.
05/04/2002
RemoteMDx, Inc. name changed to
SecureAlert, Inc. 02/22/2010 which
name changed to Track Group, Inc.
(UT) 05/26/2015 which
reincorporated in Delaware
08/05/2016

VOLU SOL MED INDS INC (NV)
Merged into Logos Scientific, Inc.
11/29/84
Each share Common 10¢ par
exchanged for (0.3937) share
Common $0.001 par
Logos Scientific, Inc. recapitalized as
Logos International Inc. 5/15/92
which recapitalized as China Food &
Beverage Co. 4/10/97

VOLU SOL REAGENTS CORP (UT)
Reincorporated under the laws of
Delaware as ActiveCare, Inc.
07/15/2009

VOLUME DISTRIBUTORS, INC. (MO)
Name changed to Volume Shoe Corp.
Inc. 11/29/66
Volume Shoe Corp. Inc. name
changed to Volume Shoe Corp.
1/11/68 which merged into May
Department Stores Co. 11/16/79
which merged into Federated
Department Stores, Inc. 8/30/2005
which name changed to Macy's, Inc.
6/1/2007

VOLUME MERCHANDISE INC (NY)
Common 10¢ par split (8) for (5) by
issuance of (0.6) additional share
12/10/65
Common 10¢ par split (5) for (4) by
issuance of (0.25) additional share
12/15/67
Acquired by VM Acquisition Corp.
9/24/84
Each share Common 10¢ par
exchanged for $7.50 cash

VOLUME SVCS AMER HLDGS INC (DE)
Issue Information - 16,785,450
INCOME DEP SECS IDS consisting
of (1) share COM and $5.70
principal amount of 13.5%
Subordinated Notes offered at $15
per security on 12/10/2003
Name changed to Centerplate, Inc.
10/13/2004
(See Centerplate, Inc.)

VOLUME SHOE CORP (MO)
Name changed 1/11/68
Class B Common $1 par reclassified
as Common $1 par 9/1/67
Name changed from Volume Shoe
Corp. Inc. to Volume Shoe Corp.
1/11/68
Common $1 par changed to 50¢ par
and (1) additional share issued
12/26/69
Common 50¢ par split (3) for (2) by
issuance of (0.5) additional share
9/30/71
Common 50¢ par split (3) for (2) by
issuance of (0.5) additional share
12/29/77
Common 50¢ par split (3) for (2) by
issuance of (0.5) additional share
10/6/78
Stock Dividends - 25% 9/29/67; 25%
9/27/68
Merged into May Department Stores
Co. 11/16/79
Each share Common 50¢ par
exchanged for (1.35) shares
Common $1.66-2/3 par
May Department Stores Co. merged
into Federated Department Stores,
Inc. 8/30/2005 which name changed
to Macy's, Inc. 6/1/2007

VOLUNTEER BANCSHARES INC (TN)
Common $1 par split (2) for (1) by
issuance of (1) additional share
06/04/1984
Common $1 par split (2) for (1) by
issuance of (1) additional share
08/10/1986
Acquired by Bancorp of Mississippi
08/03/1992
Each share Common $1 par
exchanged for (0.7769) share
Common $2.50 par
Bancorp of Mississippi name changed
to BancorpSouth, Inc. 10/06/1992
which reorganized as BancorpSouth
Bank (Tupelo, MS) 11/01/2017

VOLUNTEER CAP CORP NEW (TN)
Name changed to Winners Corp.
05/06/1982 which name changed
back to Volunteer Capital Corp.
08/24/1989
Common 5¢ par split (2) for (1) by
issuance of (1) additional share
06/19/1978
Stock Dividend - 100% 06/01/1976
Name changed to J. Alexander's
Corp. 02/07/1997
(See J. Alexander's Corp.)

VOLUNTEER FD INC (TN)
Completely liquidated 9/2/71
Each share Common $5 par
exchanged for first and final
distribution of (1) share Volunteer
Capital Corp. Common 5¢ par
Volunteer Capital Corp. name
changed to J. Alexander's Corp.
2/7/97

VOLUNTEER NAT GAS CO (TN)
Stock Dividends - 25% 07/30/1971;
25% 05/31/1979; 10% 10/09/1980
Reincorporated under the laws of
Tennessee and Virginia as
Tennessee-Virginia Energy Corp.
12/05/1980
Tennessee-Virginia Energy Corp.
acquired by United Cities Gas Co.
12/04/1986 which merged into
Atmos Energy Corp. 07/31/1997

VOLUNTEER PORTLAND CEMENT CO. (DE)
Merged into Ideal Cement Co.
12/31/59
Each share Common $1 par
exchanged for (3-3/8) shares Capital
Stock $5 par
Ideal Cement Co. merged into Ideal
Basic Industries, Inc. (CO) 12/31/67
which reincorporated in Delaware
5/15/87 which merged into Holnam
Inc. 3/8/90
(See Holnam Inc.)

VOLUNTEER ST LIFE INS CO (TN)
Capital Stock $25 par changed to $10
par 00/00/1933
Each share Capital Stock $10 par
exchanged for (2) shares Capital
Stock $5 par 11/30/1964
Stock Dividends - 20% 12/00/1943;
33-1/3% 12/00/1947; 25%
02/00/1952; 100% 12/03/1956; 20%
12/11/1961
Acquired by Monumental Corp.
03/21/1969
Each share Capital Stock $5 par
exchanged for (1.85) shares
Common $5 par
(See Monumental Corp.)

VOLVO AKTIEBOLAGET (SWEDEN)
ADR's for Class B split (5) for (1) by
issuance of (4) additional ADR's
08/15/1994
Each ADR for Ordinary Class B
received distribution of (0.1)
Swedish Match AB Sponsored ADR
payable 05/15/1996 to holders of
record 05/13/1996
ADR's for Ordinary Class B split (5)
for (1) by issuance of (4) additional
ADR's additional ADR's payable
05/09/2007 to holders of record
04/30/2007 Ex date - 05/10/2007
Each ADR for Ordinary Class B
received distribution of $3.038518
cash payable 06/07/2007 to holders
of record 04/30/2007
ADR agreement terminated
01/07/2016
Each ADR for Ordinary Class B
exchanged for $10.272784 cash

VOLZHSKOYE OIL TANKER SHIPPING VOLGATANKER OPEN JT STK CO (RUSSIA)
GDR agreement terminated
11/06/2013
No GDR's remain outstanding
Note: Company declared bankrupt
03/00/2008

VON HAMM-YOUNG CO., INC. (HI)
Name changed to Hawaii Corp.
7/9/64
(See Hawaii Corp.)

VON HAMM-YOUNG CO., LTD. (HI)
Each share Common $20 par
exchanged for (2) shares Common
no par 3/21/60
Common no par split (2) for (1) by
issuance of (1) additional share
10/31/61
Stock Dividend - 25% 9/29/59
Name changed to Von Hamm-Young
Co., Inc. 7/11/61
Von Hamm-Young Co., Inc. name
changed to Hawaii Corp. 7/9/64
(See Hawaii Corp.)

VONS, INC.
Dissolved 00/00/1930
Details not available

VONS COS INC (MI)
Merged into Safeway Inc. 04/08/1997
Each share Common 10¢ par
exchanged for (1.425) shares
Common 1¢ par
(See Safeway Inc.)

VONS GROCERY CO (DE)
Merged into Household Finance Corp.
12/15/1969
Each share Common $1 par
exchanged for (0.74) share $2.50
Conv. Preferred no par
Household Finance Corp. reorganized
as Household International, Inc.
06/26/1981
(See Household International, Inc.)

VOODOO VENTURES LTD (BC)
Recapitalized as Pacific Royal
Ventures Ltd. 03/01/1996
Each share Common no par
exchanged for (1/3) share Common
no par
Pacific Royal Ventures Ltd. merged
into Pacific Rodera Ventures Inc.
03/01/1999 which name changed to
Pacific Rodera Energy Inc. (BC)
06/22/2004 which reincorporated in
Alberta 06/14/2006 which name
changed to PRD Energy Inc.
08/12/2010

VOODOOVOX INC (AB)
Each share old Common no par
exchanged for (0.02) share new
Common no par 09/04/2013

Name changed to UpSnap, Inc. 07/25/2014

VOORHEES P W INC (CA)
Recapitalized as Capital Planning Resources 08/02/1972
Each share Common no par exchanged for (0.2) share Common 5¢ par
Capital Planning Resources name changed to Carlsberg Capital Corp. (CA) 08/21/1975 which reincorporated in Delaware as Carlsberg Corp. 07/01/1980 which merged into Southmark Corp. 02/25/1986

VOPIA INC (NV)
Common $0.001 par split (20) for (1) by issuance of (19) additional shares payable 09/09/2014 to holders of record 09/09/2014
Name changed to Drone Guarder, Inc. 03/24/2017

VOPLEX CORP (NY)
Common $1 par split (2) for (1) by issuance of (1) additional share 06/15/1977
Common $1 par split (2) for (1) by issuance of (1) additional share 08/29/1983
Filed a petition under Chapter 11 Federal Bankruptcy Code 12/04/1991
Stockholders' equity unlikely

VORCLONE CORP.
Name changed to Vorsec Co. in 1931 which was liquidated in 1934

VORNADO INC (DE)
Reincorporated 6/30/65
State of incorporation changed from (KS) to (DE) 6/30/65
Common 10¢ par changed to 4¢ par and (1.5) additional shares issued 4/15/66
Common 4¢ par split (5) for (1) by issuance of (4) additional shares 5/31/91
Common 4¢ par split (3) for (2) by issuance of (0.5) additional share 3/25/93
Reorganized under the laws of Maryland as Vornado Realty Trust 5/6/93
Each share Common 4¢ par exchanged for (1) share Common 4¢ par

VORNADO OPER CO (MD)
Liquidation completed
Each share Common 4¢ par exchanged for initial distribution of $2 cash and (1) Contingent Right 01/05/2005
Each share Common 4¢ par received second and final distribution of $0.882 cash payable 04/29/2005 to holders of record 12/29/2004

VORNADO RLTY TR (MD)
8.5% Preferred Shares of Bene. Int. Ser. B no par called for redemption at $25 on 03/17/2004
8.5% Preferred Shares of Bene. Int. Ser. C no par called for redemption at $25 on 01/19/2005
7% Preferred Shares of Bene. Int. Ser. E no par called for redemption at $25 plus $0.2236 accrued dividends on 08/16/2012
6.75% Preferred Shares of Bene. Int. Ser. F no par called for redemption at $25 plus $0.2297 accrued dividends on 02/19/2013
6.75% Preferred Shares of Bene. Int. Ser. H no par called for redemption at $25 plus $0.296007 accrued dividends on 02/19/2013
6.875% Preferred Shares of Bene. Int. Ser. J no par called for redemption at $25 plus $0.2297 accrued dividends on 09/01/2016
6.625% Preferred Shares of Bene. Int. Ser. G no par called for redemption at $25 plus $0.009201 accrued dividends on 01/04/2018
6.625% Preferred Shares of Bene. Int. Ser. I no par called for redemption at $25 plus $0.041406 accrued dividends on 01/11/2018
(Additional Information in Active)

VORSATECH VENTURES INC (DE)
Name changed to Synutra International, Inc. 09/12/2005
(See Synutra International, Inc.)

VORSEC CO.
Liquidated in 1934

VORTAC INC (SD)
Each share old Common 1¢ par exchanged for (1/6) share new Common 1¢ par 8/12/91
Each share new Common 1¢ par exchanged for (0.5) share Common no par 9/14/92
Merged into Care-Tran Inc. 11/19/93
Each share Common no par exchanged for (1) share Common no par
Care-Tran Inc. name changed to Claims Direct, Inc. 4/12/96

VORTEC CORP (OH)
Acquired by Chicago West Pullman Corp. 07/08/1988
Each share Common no par exchanged for $5 cash

VORTEC ELECTRONICS INC (NV)
Name changed to Well Power, Inc. 01/06/2014

VORTEX CORP (VA)
Each share Common 10¢ par exchanged for (0.02857142) share Common 20¢ par 09/05/1973
Each share old Common 20¢ par exchanged for (0.00083333) share new Common 20¢ par 00/00/1983
Public interest eliminated

VORTEX CUP CO.
Name changed to Dixie-Vortex Co. in 1936
Dixie-Vortex Co. name changed to Dixie Cup Co. in 1943 which merged into American Can Co. 6/26/57 which name changed to Primerica Corp. (NJ) 4/28/87 which was acquired by Primerica Corp. (DE) 12/15/88 which name changed to Travelers Inc. 12/31/93 which name changed to Travelers Group Inc. 4/16/95 which name changed to Citigroup Inc. 10/8/98

VORTEX ENERGY & MINERALS LTD (AB)
Recapitalized as Vortex Integrated Industrial Corp. 05/02/2001
Each share Common no par exchanged for (0.2) share Common no par
Vortex Integrated Industrial Corp. name changed to Sienna Gold Inc. (AB) 04/15/2005 which reincorporated in British Columbia as Peruvian Precious Metals Corp. 07/02/2013 which name changed to PPX Mining Corp. 08/05/2016

VORTEX ENERGY SYS INC (BC)
Recapitalized as Autumn Industries Inc. 09/16/1994
Each share Common no par exchanged for (0.2) share Common no par
Autumn Industries Inc. name changed to Altex Power Corp. 03/07/2001

VORTEX INTEGRATED INDL CORP (AB)
Name changed to Sienna Gold Inc. (AB) 04/14/2005
Each share Common no par exchanged for (1) share Common no par
Sienna Gold Inc. (AB) reincorporated in British Columbia as Peruvian Precious Metals Corp. 07/02/2013 which name changed to PPX Mining Corp. 08/05/2016

VORTEX MANUFACTURING CO.
Name changed to Vortex Cup Co. in 1929
Vortex Cup Co. name changed to Dixie-Vortex Co. in 1936 which name changed to Dixie Cup Co. in 1943 which merged into American Can Co. 6/26/57 which name changed to Primerica Corp. (NJ) 4/28/87 which was acquired by Primerica Corp. (DE) 12/15/88 which name changed to Travelers Inc. 12/31/93 which name changed to Travelers Group Inc. 4/16/95 which name changed to Citigroup Inc. 10/8/98

VORTEX RES CORP (DE)
Each share old Common $0.001 par exchanged for (0.01) share new Common $0.001 par 02/24/2009
Name changed to Yasheng Eco-Trade Corp. 07/15/2009
Yasheng Eco-Trade Corp. recapitalized as Eco-Trade Corp. 12/09/2010

VORTICES INC (NV)
Each share old Common $0.001 par exchanged for (0.00095238) share new Common $0.001 par 3/5/98
Under plan of merger name changed to Simulator Systems, Inc. 4/21/98
Simulator Systems, Inc. name changed to Casino Pirata.Com Ltd. 5/5/99 which name changed to Advantage Technologies Inc. 11/30/99 which recapitalized as Expo Holdings Inc. 5/30/2006

VOS INTL INC (CO)
Recapitalized as IdeaEdge, Inc. 10/18/2007
Each share Common $0.001 par exchanged for (0.04) share Common $0.001 par
IdeaEdge, Inc. name changed to Socialwise, Inc. 05/13/2009 which name changed to BillMyParents, Inc. 06/13/2011 which name changed to SpendSmart Payments Co. (CO) 02/28/2013 which reincorporated in Delaware as SpendSmart Networks, Inc. 06/20/2014

VOSS CORP. (CA)
Charter suspended for failure to file reports or pay taxes 11/01/1973

VOSS ENGR CO (PA)
Merged into STV, Inc. 10/15/1969
Each share Common $1 par exchanged for (0.75) share Common $1 par
STV, Inc. name changed to STV Engineers, Inc. 02/05/1979 which name changed to STV Group, Inc. 06/25/1991
(See STV Group, Inc.)

VOSS OIL CO. (DE)
Each share Common $1 par exchanged for (1/6) share Class B Common no par 05/22/1959
In process of liquidation 12/14/1964
Holders of Class A Common no par may receive a distribution of less than $0.01 cash per share but payment will not be paid for a period of approximately three years
No Class B Common stockholders' equity

VOTING INSTRS & PRODS CORP (IL)
Proclaimed dissolved 00/00/1973
No stockholders' equity

VOTORANTIM CELULOSE E PAPEL S A (BRAZIL)
ADR basis changed from (1:500) to (1:2.5) 12/01/2004
Sponsored ADR's for Preferred no par split (5) for (2) by issuance of (1.5) additional ADR's payable 12/07/2004 to holders of record 12/06/2004 Ex date - 12/08/2004
ADR basis changed from (1:2.5) to (1:1) 12/08/2004
Each Sponsored ADR for Preferred no par exchanged for (0.91) Sponsored ADR for Common no par 08/17/2009
Under plan of merger name changed to Fibria Celulose S.A. 11/18/2009

VOTRAX INC (DE)
Reincorporated 11/1/85
Recapitalized 11/5/87
State of incorporation changed from (WA) to (DE) 11/1/85
Recapitalized from Votrax International, Inc. to Votrax, Inc. 11/5/87
Each share Common 1¢ par exchanged for (0.25) share Common 1¢ par
Charter forfeited for failure to maintain a registered agent 1/11/93

VOUGHT DEFENSE SYS CORP (NV)
Name changed to Alas Defense Systems, Inc. 06/29/2010
Alas Defense Systems, Inc. name changed to ALAS International Holdings, Inc. 07/11/2011 which name changed to PV Enterprises International, Inc. 08/19/2013 which recapitalized as Drone Services USA, Inc. 04/29/2015

VOX POP WORLDWIDE INC (NV)
Common 1¢ par changed to $0.0001 par 12/13/2013
Name changed to Renovate Neighborhoods, Inc. 01/06/2014

VOXBOX WORLD TELECOM INC (NV)
Name changed to Internet Media Technologies, Inc. 11/21/2007
Internet Media Technologies, Inc. name changed to Star Entertainment Group, Inc. 01/19/2010

VOXCOM HLDGS INC (NV)
Name changed to Max Internet Communications, Inc. 11/15/1999
Max Internet Communications, Inc. recapitalized as China Health Management Corp. 08/04/2006
(See China Health Management Corp.)

VOXCOM INC (CANADA)
Each share old Common no par exchanged for (0.2) share new Common no par 9/14/99
New Common no par called for redemption at $1.03 on 5/10/2004

VOXCOM INCOME FD (AB)
Acquired by UE Waterheater Income Fund 06/25/2007
Each Unit no par received $13.25 cash

VOXEL (CA)
Reorganized under the laws of Delaware as Dover Glen, Inc. 09/24/2008
Each share Common no par exchanged for (0.0117647) share Common $0.001 par
Dover Glen, Inc. name changed to PetroAlgae Inc. 01/16/2009 which name changed to Parabel Inc. 04/03/2012
(See Parabel Inc.)

VOXPATH HLDGS INC (NV)
Each share old Common $0.001 par exchanged for (7) shares new Common $0.001 par 07/24/2006
Name changed to TheRetirementSolution.com, Inc. 09/18/2006
TheRetirementSolution.com, Inc. name changed to Global Investor Services, Inc. 10/01/2008 which recapitalized as Investview, Inc. 04/09/2012

VOXWARE INC (DE)
Each share old Common $0.001 par exchanged for (0.00666666) share new Common $0.001 par 12/12/2005
Each share new Common $0.001 par

exchanged for (0.0002) share
Restricted Common $0.001 par
01/07/2011
Note: In effect holders received $1 cash per share and public interest was eliminated

VOYA DIVERSIFIED FLOATING RATE SR LN FD (ON)
Name changed to Redwood Floating Rate Bond Fund 12/20/2017
Redwood Floating Rate Income Fund name changed to Purpose Floating Rate Income Fund 06/18/2018

VOYA FLOATING RATE SR LN FD (ON)
Name changed to Redwood Floating Rate Income Fund 12/20/2017
Redwood Floating Rate Income Fund name changed to Purpose Floating Rate Income Fund 06/18/2018

VOYA GLOBAL INCOME SOLUTIONS FD (ON)
Trust terminated 12/05/2016
Each Class A Unit received $8.872978 cash

VOYA HIGH INCOME FLOATING RATE FD (ON)
Merged into Voya Floating Rate Senior Loan Fund 07/21/2017
Each Class A Unit automatically became (0.8572) Class A Unit
Each Class U Unit automatically became (0.96336) Class U Unit
Voya Floating Rate Senior Loan Fund name changed to Redwood Floating Rate Income Fund 12/20/2017 which name changed to Purpose Floating Rate Income Fund 06/18/2018

VOYAGER ENERGY INC (AB)
Merged into Poco Petroleums Ltd. 06/01/1991
Each share Common no par exchanged for (0.85) share Common no par
Poco Petroleums Ltd. merged into Burlington Resources Inc. 11/18/1999 which merged into ConocoPhillips 03/31/2006

VOYAGER ENTMT INTL INC (ND)
Reincorporated under the laws of Nevada 6/23/2003

VOYAGER EXPLS LTD (ON)
Acquired by Gold Summit Mines Ltd. (BC) 07/13/2001
Each share Common no par exchanged for (0.37) share Common no par
Gold Summit Mines Ltd. (BC) reincorporated in Ontario 09/05/2002
(See Gold Summit Mines Ltd.)

VOYAGER FINL NEWS COM PLC (UNITED KINGDOM)
Name changed to Griffin Group PLC 02/17/2004
(See Griffin Group PLC)

VOYAGER GROUP INC (DE)
Each share old Common $0.001 par exchanged for (0.1) share new Common $0.001 par 10/16/2000
New Common $0.001 par split (2) for (1) by issuance of (1) additional share payable 08/29/2001 to holders of record 08/23/2001 Ex date - 08/30/2001
Charter cancelled and declared inoperative and void for non-payment of taxes 03/01/2003

VOYAGER GROUP INC (FL)
Merged into American Can Co. 10/17/1983
Each share Common $1 par exchanged for $15 cash

VOYAGER GROUP INC (NV)
Name changed to Band, Ltd. 03/26/1996
(See Band, Ltd.)

VOYAGER GROUP INC NEW (NV)
Common $0.001 par split (3) for (1) by issuance of (2) additional shares payable 08/29/2001 to holders of record 08/23/2001 Ex date - 08/30/2001
Recapitalized as Neoteric Group Inc. 06/17/2002
Each share Common $0.001 par exchanged for (0.00001) share Common $0.001 par
(See Neoteric Group Inc.)

VOYAGER INTERNET GROUP COM (NV)
Name changed 7/21/99
Recapitalized 1/31/2000
Name changed from Voyager Group USA-Brazil Ltd. to Voyager Group Ltd. 7/21/99
Recapitalized from Voyager Group Ltd. to Voyager Internet Group.com 1/31/2000
Each share Common $0.001 par exchanged for (1/6) share Common $0.001 par
Each share Common $0.001 par received distribution of (1) share Voyager Group Inc. Common $0.001 par payable 5/1/2000 to holders of record 3/31/2000
Name changed to Save On Meds.Net 7/31/2000
Save On Meds.Net recapitalized as Voyager Group Inc. (New) 5/31/2001

VOYAGER LEARNING CO (DE)
Merged into Cambium Learning Group, Inc. 12/09/2009
Each share Common $0.001 par exchanged for (1) share Common $0.001 par
Note: An additional initial distribution of $0.037 cash was made from escrow 11/23/2010
A second additional distribution of $0.06663411 cash was made from escrow 07/11/2011
A third and final additional distribution of $0.25658627 cash was made from escrow 06/26/2013

VOYAGER NET INC (DE)
Issue Information - 9,000,000 shares COM offered at $15 per share on 07/20/1999
Merged into CoreComm Ltd. (New) (DE) 9/29/2000
Each share Common $0.0001 par exchanged for (0.614) share Common 1¢ par and $1.14 cash
CoreComm Ltd. (New) (DE) merged into CoreComm Holdco, Inc. 7/1/2002 which name changed to ATX Communications, Inc. 7/15/2002

VOYAGER OIL & GAS INC (MT)
Reincorporated 06/03/2011
Each share Common $0.001 par received distribution of (1) share ante5, Inc. Common $0.001 par payable 06/14/2010 to holders of record 04/15/2010 Ex date - 06/24/2010
State of incorporation changed from (DE) to (MT) 06/03/2011
Name changed to Emerald Oil, Inc. (MT) 09/04/2012
Emerald Oil, Inc. (MT) reincorporated in Delaware 06/11/2014
(See Emerald Oil, Inc.)

VOYAGER PETE INC (NV)
Name changed 12/08/2006
Name changed from Voyager One, Inc. to Voyager Petroleum, Inc. 12/08/2006
Recapitalized as USA Recycling Industries, Inc. 03/14/2011
Each share Common $0.001 par exchanged for (0.005) share Common $0.001 par

VOYAGER PETES LTD (AB)
Common no par split (2) for (1) by issuance of (1) additional share 02/18/1977
Acquired by Nu-West Development Ltd. 06/05/1979
Each share Common no par exchanged for $25 cash

VOYAGERIT COM PLC (UNITED KINGDOM)
Name changed to Cater Barnard PLC 5/3/2001

VOYAGEUR ARIZ MUN INCOME FD (MN)
Name changed to Delaware Investments Arizona Municipal Income Fund Inc. 12/01/2001
Delaware Investments Arizona Municipal Income Fund Inc. merged into Delaware Investments National Municipal Income Fund 06/17/2011

VOYAGEUR COLO INSD MUN INCOME FD INC (MN)
Name changed to Delaware Investments Colorado Insured Municipal Income Fund Inc. 12/01/2001
Delaware Investments Colorado Insured Municipal Income Fund Inc. name changed to Delaware Investments Colorado Municipal Income Fund, Inc. 01/02/2008

VOYAGEUR FDS (DE)
Reorganized 02/12/1989
Reorganized 11/23/1999
Under plan of reorganization each share Common 1¢ par automatically became (1) share Voyageur Funds, Inc. (MD) U.S. Government Securities Class A 1¢ par 02/12/1989
U.S. Government Securities Class A, B and C 1¢ par reclassified as Delaware U.S. Government Securities Class A, B or C 1¢ par respectively 06/10/1997
Reorganized from Voyageur Funds, Inc. (MD) to under the laws of Delaware as Voyageur Funds and Delaware U.S. Government Securities Class A, B and C 1¢ par changed to no par 11/23/1999
Completely liquidated 08/24/2001
Details not available

VOYAGEUR FILM CAP CORP (AB)
Name changed to Highwire Entertainment Group Inc. 12/06/2000
Highwire Entertainment Group Inc. recapitalized as Creation Ventures Inc. 05/21/2002 which name changed to Creation Casinos Inc. (AB) 11/28/2003 which reincorporated in British Columbia 12/16/2004 which recapitalized as Orca Power Corp. (BC) 07/22/2008 which reorganized in Canada as AFG Flameguard Ltd. 04/11/2012

VOYAGEUR FIRST INC (CO)
Name changed to North American Resorts Inc. 03/30/1995
North American Resorts Inc. name changed to Immulabs Corp. 09/15/2000 which name changed to Xerion EcoSolutions Group, Inc. (CO) 04/07/2003 which reorganized in Nevada as SINO-American Development Corp. 06/19/2006 which recapitalized as Harvest Bio-Organic International Co., Ltd. 12/07/2010
(See Harvest Bio-Organic International Co., Ltd.)

VOYAGEUR FLA INSD MUN INCOME FD (MA)
Name changed to Delaware Investments Florida Insured Municipal Income Fund 12/01/2001
Delaware Investments Florida Insured Municipal Income Fund name changed to Delaware Investments National Municipal Income Fund 10/16/2007

VOYAGEUR MINN MUN INCOME FD INC (MN)
Name changed to Delaware Investments Minnesota Municipal Income Fund Inc. 12/1/2001
Delaware Investments Minnesota Municipal Income Fund Inc. merged into Delaware Investments Minnesota Municipal Income Fund II Inc. 2/24/2006

VOYAGEUR MINN MUN INCOME FD II INC (MN)
Name changed to Delaware Investments Minnesota Municipal Income Fund II Inc. 12/1/2001

VOYAGEUR MINN MUN INCOME FUND III INC (MN)
Name changed to Delaware Investments Minnesota Municipal Income Fund III Inc. 12/1/2001
Delaware Investments Minnesota Municipal Income Fund III Inc. merged into Delaware Investments Minnesota Municipal Income Fund II Inc. 2/24/2006

VOYANT INTL CORP (NV)
Charter revoked for failure to file reports and pay taxes 10/31/2010

VOYUS LTD (BERMUDA)
Cease trade order effective 10/15/2004
Stockholders' equity unlikely

VP GROUP MEDIA LTD (ON)
Reincorporated 01/06/2005
Place of incorporation changed from (BC) to (ON) 01/06/2005
Recapitalized as DVD Investments Ltd. 02/03/2006
Each share Common no par exchanged for (0.2) share Common no par
DVD Investments Ltd. name changed to Mooncor Oil & Gas Corp. 10/22/2007 which recapitalized as Sensor Technologies Inc. 10/24/2018

VPGI CORP (TX)
SEC revoked common stock registration 03/12/2012

VPI (NV)
Recapitalized as Pathfinder Holding Inc. 5/25/94
Each share Common $0.001 par exchanged for (0.1) share Common $0.001 par

VPN COMMUNICATIONS CORP (NV)
Each share old Common $0.001 par exchanged for (0.11111111) share new Common $0.001 par 09/14/2001
Name changed to Resource Asset Management Corp. 04/16/2002

VR BUSINESS BROKERS INC (DE)
Each (17) shares old Common 10¢ par exchanged for (1) share new Common 10¢ par 7/21/88
Charter cancelled and declared void for failure to pay franchise taxes 3/1/93

VR INTERACTIVE CORP (AB)
Recapitalized as Muskrat Minerals Inc. 03/29/2012
Each share Common no par exchanged for (0.125) share Common no par
Muskrat Minerals Inc. name changed to Metalo Manufacturing Inc. 12/16/2015

VR SYS INC (NV)
Each share old Common $0.001 par exchanged for (0.25) share new Common $0.001 par 01/26/2004
Name changed to Hansen Gray & Co., Inc. 03/29/2004
Hansen Gray & Co., Inc. recapitalized as AMF Capital, Inc. 06/22/2007 which name changed to Pro Motors Group Corp. 10/29/2007 which recapitalized as Hydrogen Hybrid

VRB BANCORP (OR)
Corp. 11/25/2008 which name changed to Get Real USA Inc. 01/12/2011

VRB BANCORP (OR)
Common no par split (3) for (2) by issuance of (0.5) additional share 10/15/94
Common no par split (3) for (2) by issuance of (0.5) additional share payable 11/20/96 to holders of record 10/20/96
Common no par split (2) for (1) by issuance of (1) additional share payable 9/17/97 to holders of record 9/10/97
Stock Dividend - 4% payable 10/1/98 to holders of record 9/10/98
Merged into Umpqua Holdings Corp. 12/1/2000
Each share Common no par exchanged for (0.8135) share Common 83-1/3¢ par

VRB PWR SYS INC (CANADA)
Name changed to Nevaro Capital Corp. (Old) 08/24/2009
(See Nevaro Capital Corp. (Old))

VRDT CORP (DE)
SEC revoked common stock registration 12/02/2015

VRI BIOMEDICAL LTD (AUSTRALIA)
Name changed to Probiomics Ltd. 05/10/2005
(See Probiomics Ltd.)

VRINGO INC (DE)
Units separated 07/27/2010
Each share old Common 1¢ par exchanged for (0.1) share new Common 1¢ par 11/30/2015
Name changed to FORM Holdings Corp. 05/09/2016
FORM Holdings Corp. name changed to XpresSpa Group, Inc. 01/08/2018

VRX WORLDWIDE INC (AB)
Name changed to MediaValet Inc. 10/06/2014

VS SVCS LTD (CANADA)
Each share Class A Common no par exchanged for (1.35) shares Common no par 03/01/1979
Common no par split (2) for (1) by issuance of (1) additional share 02/20/1986
Common no par split (2) for (1) by issuance of (1) additional share 03/16/1990
Name changed to Versa Services Ltd./Versa Services Ltee. 11/27/1991
(See Versa Services Ltd./Versa Services Ltee.)

VSB BANCORP INC (DE)
Common 1¢ par split (6) for (5) by issuance of (0.2) additional share 01/21/1992
Common 1¢ par split (6) for (5) by issuance of (0.2) additional share 12/18/1992
Stock Dividend - 20% 11/10/1993
Merged into UJB Financial Corp. 07/01/1994
Each share Common 1¢ par exchanged for (0.7727) share Common $1.20 par
UJB Financial Corp name changed to Summit Bancorp 03/01/1996 which merged into FleetBoston Financial Corp. 03/01/2001 which merged into Bank of America Corp. 04/01/2004

VSC TECHNOLOGY INC (BC)
Cease trade order effective 4/27/93
Stockholders' equity unlikely

VSI CORP (DE)
Reincorporated 11/1/67
Stock Dividend - 100% 8/15/63
State of incorporation changed from (IL) to (DE) 11/1/67
Common $4 par changed to $2 par and (1) additional share issued 11/15/67
Common $2 par split (2) for (1) by issuance of (1) additional share 12/2/77
Merged into Fairchild Industries, Inc. 11/7/80
Each share Common $2 par exchanged for (1) share $3.60 Conv. Preferred Ser. A no par or $45 cash
Note: Option to receive stock expired 11/7/80
(See Fairchild Industries, Inc.)

VSI ENTERPRISES INC (DE)
Each share Common $0.00001 par exchanged for (0.04) share Common $0.00025 par 8/19/91
Each share Common $0.00025 par exchanged for (0.25) share Common $0.001 par 1/15/99
Name changed to Simtrol, Inc. 10/1/2001

VSI HLDGS INC (GA)
Plan of reorganization under Chapter 11 Federal Bankruptcy Code effective 9/5/2003
No stockholders' equity

VSI LIQ CORP (DE)
In process of liquidation
Each share Common 1¢ par received initial distribution of $2.13 cash payable 01/29/1999 to holders of record 01/22/1999
Each share Common 1¢ par received second distribution of $0.15 cash payable 02/12/2000 to holders of record 01/31/2000
Each share Common 1¢ par received third distribution of $0.10 cash payable 02/11/2001 to holders of record 01/31/2001
Each share Common 1¢ par received fourth distribution of $0.12 cash payable 02/11/2002 to holders of record 01/31/2002
Each share Common 1¢ par received fifth distribution of approximately $0.004 cash payable 03/28/2007 to holders of record 03/28/2007

VSI LIQUIDATING CORP. (CA)
Liquidation completed
Each share Common 50¢ par exchanged for initial distribution of $6.02 cash 1/1/75
Each share Common 50¢ par received second and final distribution of $0.44638 cash 7/1/77

VSM EXPL INC (QC)
Merged into Cambior Inc. 1/24/93
Each share Common no par exchanged for (0.06060606) share Common no par
Cambior Inc. acquired by Iamgold Corp. 11/8/2006

VSM MEDTECH LTD (AB)
Reincorporated under the laws of British Columbia as VSM MedTech Ltd. 6/19/2006

VSOURCE INC (DE)
Reincorporated 11/08/2000
State of incorporation changed from (NV) to (DE) 11/08/2000
Each share old Common $0.028 par exchanged for (0.05) share new Common $0.028 par 11/20/2002
Name changed to Tri-Isthmus Group, Inc. 12/30/2005
Tri-Isthmus Group, Inc. name changed to First Physicians Capital Group, Inc. 01/08/2010

VST HLDGS LTD (CAYMAN ISLANDS)
Name changed to VSTECS Holdings Ltd. 08/21/2017

VS2 INC (DE)
Recapitalized as EuroWork Global, Ltd. 11/08/2004
Each share Common $0.001 par exchanged for (0.01) share Common $0.001 par
EuroWork Global, Ltd. name changed to Quintessence Holdings, Inc.

07/25/2007 which name changed to Terminus Energy, Inc. 12/04/2009

VSURANCE INC (NV)
Each share old Common $0.001 par exchanged for (0.0125) share new Common $0.001 par 08/14/2007
Each (65) shares Class A Preferred $0.001 par exchanged for (1) share new Common $0.001 par 08/14/2007
Each (65) shares Class B Preferred $0.001 par exchanged for (1) share new Common $0.001 par 08/14/2007
Each share Class C Preferred $0.001 par exchanged for (0.2) share new Common $0.001 par 08/14/2007
Recapitalized as Ensurapet, Inc. 02/19/2008
Each share Common $0.001 par exchanged for (0.001) Common $0.001 par

VSUS TECHNOLOGIES INC (DE)
Each (1,500) shares old Common $0.001 par exchanged for (1) share new Common $0.001 par 01/20/2009
Name changed to New Colombia Resources, Inc. 01/24/2013

VTEC CAP CORP (BC)
Name changed to Coast Mountain Power Corp. 12/17/2001
Coast Mountain Power Corp. acquired by NovaGold Resources Inc. (NS) 08/03/2006 which reincorporated in British Columbia 06/12/2013

VTEC INC (NV)
Name changed to United Consortium, Ltd. (Old) 03/10/2008
United Consortium, Ltd. (Old) reorganized as United Consortium, Ltd. (New) 05/05/2010

VTECH HLDGS LTD (BERMUDA)
Sponsored ADR's for Ordinary $0.005 par split (6) for (5) by issuance of (0.2) additional ADR payable 10/28/1996 to holders of record 09/27/1996
ADR agreement terminated 01/21/2011
Each Sponsored ADR for Ordinary $0.005 par exchanged for $101.838832 cash
(Additional Information in Active)

VTEL CORP (DE)
Name changed to Forgent Networks, Inc. 01/18/2002
Forgent Networks, Inc. recapitalized as Asure Software, Inc. 12/29/2009

VTEX ENERGY INC (NV)
SEC revoked preferred and common stock registration 06/21/2012

V3 SEMICONDUCTOR INC (NV)
Name changed 6/12/96
Name changed from V3 Inc. to V3 Semiconductor Inc. 6/12/96
Under plan of reorganization under Chapter 11 Federal Bankruptcy Code each share Common 1¢ par received distribution of (0.056156) share Quicklogic Corp. Common $0.001 par payable 1/23/2004 to holders of record 7/2/2002 Ex date - 1/26/2004
Note: Certificates were not required to surrendered and are without value

VTI INDS INC (BC)
Recapitalized as Emerald Ventures Inc. 11/23/1990
Each share Common no par exchanged for (0.5) share Common no par
Emerald Ventures Inc. (BC) reincorporated in Yukon as Spatializer Audio Laboratories, Inc. 12/27/1991 which reincorporated in Delaware 07/27/1994 which recapitalized as AMERI Holdings, Inc. 05/26/2015

VTL VENTURE CORP (ON)
Each share Common no par received distribution of (1) share Class A no par and (1) share Conv. Class C Special no par 08/01/1986
Name changed to Allcorp United Inc. 07/06/1994
Allcorp United Inc. recapitalized as Ntex Inc. 11/07/1997
(See Ntex Inc.)

VTL VENTURE EQUITIES LTD. (ON)
Name changed to VTL Venture Corp. 07/07/1986
VTL Venture Corp. name changed to Allcorp United Inc. 07/06/1994 which recapitalized as NTEX Inc. 11/07/1997
(See NTEX Inc.)

VTN CORP (DE)
Charter forfeited for failure to maintain a registered agent 6/23/95

VTR INC (NY)
Charter cancelled and proclaimed dissolved for failure to pay taxes 06/24/1981

VTTI ENERGY PARTNERS L P (MARSHALL ISLANDS)
Acquired by VTTI B.V. 09/15/2017
Each Common Unit exchanged for $19.50 cash

V2K INTL INC (CO)
Each share old Common $0.001 par exchanged for (0.008) share new Common $0.001 par 12/17/2009
Name changed to AgriSolar Solutions, Inc. 02/25/2010

VTX ELECTRS CORP (DE)
Common 10¢ par split (5) for (4) by issuance of (0.25) additional share 04/09/1987
Reorganized as Vertex Computer Cable & Products Inc. 12/29/1997
Each share Common 10¢ par exchanged for (0.2) share Common 10¢ par
Vertex Computer Cable & Products Inc. name changed to DataWorld Solutions Inc. 04/30/1999 which name changed to Defense Technology Systems, Inc. 07/08/2004
(See Defense Technology Systems, Inc.)

VU-DATA CORP (NV)
SEC revoked common stock registration 10/07/2010

VUANCE LTD (ISRAEL)
Name changed to SuperCom, Ltd. 03/15/2013

VUBOTICS INC (GA)
Reincorporated 01/31/2007
State of incorporation changed from (NV) to (GA) 01/31/2007
Chapter 11 bankruptcy proceedings dismissed 01/24/2011
No stockholders' equity

VUEBOTICS CORP (CA)
Chapter 11 Federal Bankruptcy Code converted to Chapter 7 on 10/6/86
Stockholders' equity unlikely

VULCAN CONTAINERS CDA LTD (CANADA)
Name changed to Vulcan Industrial Packaging Ltd. 10/1/70
Vulcan Industrial Packaging Ltd. name changed to Vulcan Industrial Packaging Ltd.-Emballages Industriels Vulcan Ltee. 6/28/83 which name changed to Vulcan Packaging Inc.-Vulcan, Emballages Inc. 5/30/86
(See Vulcan Packaging Inc.- Vulcan, Emballages Inc.)

VULCAN CORP (OH)
Each share $6 Preferred no par exchanged for (1) share $4.50 Preferred no par, (0.5) share $3 Prior Preferred no par and $1 cash 00/00/1938

Each share Common no par exchanged for (1) share Common $1 par 00/00/1938
Common $1 par changed to 50¢ par and (1) additional share issued 05/15/1961
Common 50¢ par changed to 25¢ par and (1) additional share issued 06/16/1967
Common 25¢ par changed to no par and (1) additional share issued 05/15/1969
Reincorporated under the laws of Delaware as Vulcan International Corp. 12/14/1988

VULCAN DETINNING CO. (NJ)
Each share $7 Preferred or Common $100 par exchanged for (5) shares $7 Preferred or Common $20 par in 1947
Each share Common $20 par exchanged for (2) shares Common $10 par in 1950
Merged into Vulcan Materials Co. 12/31/56
Each share $7 Preferred $20 par exchanged for (2) shares 5% Preferred $16 par
Each share Common $10 par exchanged for (1) share 5% Preferred $16 par and (1.125) shares Common $1 par

VULCAN EXTENSION, INC. (ID)
Merged into Vulcan Silver-Lead Corp. 04/27/1956
Each share Capital Stock 20¢ par exchanged for (0.5) share Common $1 par
Vulcan Silver-Lead Corp. merged into Callahan Mining Corp. 04/30/1958 which merged into Coeur D'Alene Mines Corp. (ID) 12/31/1991 which reincorporated in Delaware as Coeur Mining, Inc. 05/17/2013

VULCAN HART CORP (IN)
Stock Dividend - 10% 11/15/59
Acquired by Heller (Walter E.) & Co. 12/2/63
Each share Common $5 par exchanged for (1.5) shares Common 25¢ par
Heller (Walter E.) & Co. reorganized as Heller (Walter E.) International Corp. 7/28/69 which name changed to Amerifin Corp. 1/26/84
(See Amerifin Corp.)

VULCAN INC (PA)
Common $1 par changed to 50¢ par and (1) additional share issued 05/20/1968
Common 50¢ par changed to 12-1/2¢ par 06/00/1969
Common 12-1/2¢ par changed to no par 04/12/1977
$1 Conv. Preferred Ser. AA $1 par called for redemption 12/15/1978
Acquired by Ampco-Pittsburgh Corp. 06/14/1984
Each share Common no par exchanged for $13 cash

VULCAN INDL PACKAGING LTD (CANADA)
Name changed 6/28/83
Common no par split (2) for (1) by issuance of (1) additional share 1/31/73
Common no par split (2) for (1) by issuance of (1) additional share 6/29/77
Common no par split (3) for (2) by issuance of (0.5) additional share 1/6/81
Common no par split (3) for (1) by issuance of (2) additional shares 5/13/81
Name changed from Vulcan Industrial Packaging Ltd. to Vulcan Industrial Packaging Ltd.-Emballages Industriels Vulcan Ltee. 6/28/83
Name changed to Vulcan Packaging Inc.- Vulcan, Emballages Inc. 5/30/86
(See Vulcan Packaging Inc.-Vulcan, Emballages Inc.)

VULCAN INTL CORP (DE)
$3 Senior Preferred no par called for redemption at $100 on 6/30/97
$4.50 Preferred no par called for redemption at $100 on 6/30/97
(Additional Information in Active)

VULCAN IRON WORKS (PA)
Common $50 par changed to no par 00/00/1941
Each share Common no par exchanged for (10) shares Common 50¢ par 00/00/1944
Name changed to Hardie Manufacturing Co. 11/11/1959
(See Hardie Manufacturing Co.)

VULCAN LIFE INS CO (AL)
Name changed 04/21/1971
Name changed from Vulcan Life & Accident Insurance Co. to Vulcan Life Insurance Co. and Capital Stock $2.50 par changed to $1 par 04/21/1971
Stock Dividends - 10% 03/29/1954; 10% 03/29/1955; 10% 03/29/1956; 10% 03/29/1957; 10% 04/30/1958; 10% 04/30/1959; 10% 04/15/1960; 10% 04/15/1961; 10% 04/01/1962; 10% 04/15/1963; 10% 03/10/1964; 10% 03/15/1965; 20% 07/30/1966; 10% 06/01/1967; 10% 06/10/1968; 10% 05/26/1972; 10% 05/18/1974
Acquired by Conseco, Inc. 05/24/2001
Each share Capital Stock $1 par exchanged for $19.23 cash

VULCAN MATLS CO (NJ)
5% Conv. Preferred $16 par called for redemption 02/08/1963
5-3/4% Preferred $100 par called for redemption 02/08/1963
6-1/4% Preferred $100 par called for redemption 11/02/1970
$5 Preference Ser. C no par called for redemption 02/19/1974
(Additional Information in Active)

VULCAN MINES LTD. (ON)
Merged into Little Long Lac Gold Mines Ltd. (The) 4/27/67
Each share Capital Stock $1 par exchanged for (0.2) share Capital Stock no par
Little Long Lac Gold Mines Ltd. (The) merged into Little Long Lac Mines Ltd. 1/8/71 which name changed to Little Long Las Gold Mines Ltd. (New) 7/3/75 which merged into LAC Minerals Ltd. (New) 7/29/85 which was acquired by American Barrick Resources Corp. 10/17/94 which name changed to Barrick Gold Corp. 1/18/95

VULCAN MOLD & IRON CO (PA)
Each share Capital Stock $5 par exchanged for (5) shares Capital Stock $1 par in 1946
Capital Stock $1 par reclassified as Common $1 par 8/25/61
Name changed to Vulcan, Inc. 4/17/67
(See Vulcan, Inc.)

VULCAN OILS LTD. (AB)
Capital Stock $1 par changed to no par in 1949 and to $1 par in 1952
Recapitalized as Siscalta Oils Ltd. on a (0.5) for (1) basis 8/15/58
(See Siscalta Oils Ltd.)

VULCAN PACKAGING INC (CANADA)
Merged into RMV Acquisition Inc. 11/21/88
Each share Common no par exchanged for $3.70 cash

VULCAN RES LTD (BC)
Recapitalized as Overlord Resources Ltd. 10/30/1984
Each share Common no par exchanged for (0.2) share Common no par
Overlord Resources Ltd. name changed to Devran Petroleum Ltd. (BC) 05/07/1986 which reincorporated in Canada 09/24/1986 which name changed to Reserve Royalty Corp. 11/16/1995 which merged into PrimeWest Energy Trust 07/27/2000
(See PrimeWest Energy Trust)

VULCAN SILVER-LEAD CORP. (ID)
Merged into Callahan Mining Corp. 04/30/1958
Each share Common $1 par exchanged for (1) share Common $1 par
Callahan Mining Corp. merged into Coeur D'Alene Mines Corp. (ID) 12/31/1991 which reincorporated in Delaware as Coeur Mining, Inc. 05/17/2013

VULCAN VENTURES CORP (BC)
Name changed to VVC Exploration Corp. (BC) 10/1/2001
VVC Exploration Corp. (BC) reincorporated in Canada 9/25/2003

VULCANIZED RUBBER CO. (ME)
Name changed to Vulcanized Rubber & Plastics Co. 00/00/1945
(See Vulcanized Rubber & Plastics Co.)

VULCANIZED RUBR & PLASTICS CO (ME)
Common $100 par changed to no par 00/00/1954
Charter suspended for failure to maintain a registered agent 03/31/1981

VULCATRON CORP. (NH)
Dissolved for non-payment of state fees 7/3/67

VULTEE AIRCRAFT, INC.
Merged into Consolidated Vultee Aircraft Corp. 00/00/1943
$1.25 Preferred no par exchanged for new $1.25 Preferred no par
Each share Common $1 par exchanged for (45/100) share new Common $1 par
Consolidated Vultee Aircraft Corp. merged into General Dynamics Corp. 00/00/1954

VUQO HLDGS CORP (NY)
Name changed to WMAC Holdings Corp. (NY) 07/08/2013
WMAC Holdings Corp. (NY) reincorporated in Nevada as Lighthouse Global Holdings Inc. 05/03/2018

VUTEK SYS INC (DE)
Each share old Common $0.001 par exchanged for (0.01) share new Common $0.001 par 6/21/99
Reorganized as Three Shades for Everybody Inc. 7/16/99
Each share new Common $0.001 par exchanged for (2.8) shares Common $0.001 par

VVC EXPL CORP (BC)
Reincorporated under the laws of Canada 9/25/2003

VWAY INTL (NV)
Name changed to WorldWide Cannery & Distribution, Inc. 2/8/2006

VWR CORP (DE)
Acquired by Avantor, Inc. 11/21/2017
Each share Common 1¢ par exchanged for $33.25 cash

VWR SCIENTIFIC PRODS CORP (DE)
Name changed 9/15/95
Common $1 par split (2) for (1) by issuance of (1) additional share 6/3/92
Name changed from VWR Corp. to VWR Scientific Products Corp. 9/15/95
Merged into EM Laboratories, Inc. 7/27/99
Each share Common $1 par exchanged for $37 cash

VWR UTD CORP (DE)
Name changed to Univar Corp. 3/1/74
Univar Corp. (DE) reincorporated in Washinton 3/1/96
(See Univar Corp. (WA))

VYAPAR INDS LTD (INDIA)
Each old Sponsored Reg. S GDR for Equity exchanged for (0.125) new Sponsored Reg. S GDR for Equity 02/25/2011
GDR basis changed from (1:0.25) to (1:2) 02/25/2011
GDR agreement terminated 05/24/2013
Each new Sponsored Reg. S GDR for Equity exchanged for (2) Equity Shares

VYNAMICS CORP (NY)
Merged into HF Acquisition Corp. 9/24/92
Each share Common 10¢ par exchanged for $2.50 cash

VYQUEST INC (NJ)
Reorganized 07/01/1981
Under plan of reorganization each Vyquest Trust (MA) Share of Bene. Int. no par automatically became (1) share Vyquest Inc. (NJ) Common 1¢ par 07/01/1981
Filed petition under Chapter 7 Federal Bankruptcy Code 09/20/1990
No stockholders' equity

VYQUEST INTL CAP INC (FL)
Each share Common 2¢ par exchanged for (0.05) share Common 2¢ par 2/9/87
Name changed to Triton Asset Management, Inc. (FL) 2/17/87
Triton Asset Management, Inc. (FL) reorganized under the laws of Nevada as Triton Acquisition Corp. 12/28/98 which name changed to Light Management Group, Inc. 5/20/99

VYREX CORP (DE)
Name changed to PowerVerde, Inc. 10/01/2008

VYREX CORP (NV)
Reorganized under the laws of Delaware 06/30/2006
Each share Common $0.001 par exchanged for (0.12) share Common $0.0001 par
Vyrex Corp.(DE) name changed to PowerVerde, Inc. 10/01/2008

VYSIS INC (DE)
Issue Information - 3,000,000 shares COM offered at $12 per share on 02/04/1998
Merged into Abbott Laboratories Inc. 12/5/2001
Each share Common $0.001 par exchanged for $30.50 cash

VYSTAR GROUP INC (UT)
Each share old Common $0.001 par exchanged for (0.25) share new Common $0.001 par 06/28/1991
New Common $0.001 par split (2) for (1) by issuance of (1) additional share 04/25/1993
Name changed to Megahertz Corp. 06/25/1993
Megahertz Corp. merged into U.S. Robotics Corp. 02/22/1995 which merged into 3Com Corp. 06/12/1997
(See 3Com Corp.)

VYTA CORP (DE)
Reincorporated 08/20/2010
State of incorporation changed from (NV) to (DE) 08/20/2010
Recapitalized as Bio Lab Naturals, Inc. 11/05/2010
Each share Common $0.0001 par exchanged for (0.0025) share Common $0.0001 par

VYTERIS HLDGS NEV INC (NV)
Name changed to Vyteris, Inc. 07/02/2007
(See Vyteris, Inc.)

VYTERIS INC (NV)
Each share old Common $0.001 par exchanged for (0.06666666) share new Common $0.001 par 06/17/2008
Chapter 7 bankruptcy proceedings terminated 08/17/2015
Stockholders' equity unlikely

VYYO INC (DE)
Secondary Offering - 4,000,000 shares COM offered at $31.5625 per share on 09/14/2000
Each share old Common $0.0001 par exchanged for (1/3) share new Common $0.0001 par 08/01/2002
Acquired by Vision Acquisition Corp. 01/07/2009
Each share Common $0.0001 par exchanged for $0.17 cash

VZILLION INC (DE)
Reincorporated under the laws of Nevada 08/25/2008

W

W. H. S., INC. (IL)
Liquidation completed
Each share Common $10 par received initial distribution of $21.81 cash 10/25/62
Each share Common $10 par exchanged for second and final distribution of $0.6288038 cash 9/11/63

W & B LIQUIDATING CORP. (NY)
Liquidation completed
Each share Common no par received initial distribution of $35 cash 7/24/72
Each share Common no par exchanged for second distribution of $22 cash 3/15/73
Each share Common no par exchanged for third and final distribution of $2.115 cash 4/15/75

W & J SLOANE CORP (DE)
Plan of liquidation under Chapter 11 Federal Bankruptcy proceedings confirmed 11/05/1987
No stockholders' equity

W & M OIL CO. (NE)
Merged into Wyoming Oil Co. (Del.) on a (1.5) for (1) basis 6/30/56
Wyoming Oil Co. (Del.) became bankrupt in 1962

W A I CORP (TX)
Charter forfeited for failure to pay taxes 03/16/1981

W.B. LIQUIDATING CORP. (DE)
Completely liquidated 6/1/70
Each share Capital Stock $1 par exchanged for first and final distribution of (1) share West Bay Financial Corp. (CA) Common 5¢ par
(See West Bay Financial Corp. (CA))

W.C.C., INC. (PA)
Liquidation completed
Each share Common $5 par stamped to indicate initial distribution of $37 cash 2/4/66
Each share Stamped Common $5 par exchanged for second and final distribution of $4.58 cash 11/15/66

W-C INDUSTRIES, INC. (DE)
Charter cancelled and declared inoperative and void for non-payment of taxes 3/1/75

W C N INVT CORP (BC)
Each share old Common no par exchanged for (2) shares new Common no par 01/16/1989
Each share new Common no par exchanged again for (2) shares new Common no par 11/14/1989
Struck off register and declared dissolved for failure to file returns 06/24/1994

W C W WESTN CDA WTR ENTERPRISES INC (BC)
Name changed to Western Canada Beverage Corp. 3/31/92
(See Western Canada Beverage Corp.)

W COLLECT COM INC (FL)
Recapitalized as Granite Energy Inc. (FL) 12/23/2005
Each share Common no par exchanged for (0.02) share Common no par
Granite Energy Inc. (FL) reincorporated in Nevada 04/11/2006 which name changed to Refill Energy, Inc. 11/19/2009 which name changed to Medical Cannabis Payment Solutions 12/05/2013

W D M ENERGY INC (UT)
Name changed to Stellar Petroleum, Inc. 03/25/1987

W.E.B. CAPITAL, INC. (NY)
Dissolved 09/06/1996
Details not available

W.F.P. CO., INC. (MD)
Liquidation completed
Each share Common $10 par exchanged for initial distribution of (0.827) share Harper & Row, Publishers, Inc. (IL) Common no par 01/31/1967
Each share Common $10 par received second and final distribution of (0.183760) share Harper & Row, Publishers, Inc. (IL) Common no par 10/09/1970
Harper & Row, Publishers, Inc. (IL) reincorporated in Delaware 09/05/1969
(See Harper & Row, Publishers, Inc.)

W H ENERGY SVCS INC (TX)
Issue Information - 10,000,000 shares COM offered at $16.50 per share on 10/10/2000
Merged into Smith International, Inc. 08/29/2008
Each share Common $0.0001 par exchanged for (0.48) share Common $1 par and $56.10 cash
Smith International, Inc. merged into Schlumberger Ltd. 08/27/2010

W.I.D.E., INC. (NV)
Charter revoked for failure to file reports and pay fees 3/6/78

W I G CORP (UT)
Name changed to Messina Meat Products, Inc. 9/18/74
(See Messina Meat Products, Inc.)

W I N GAMING CORP (ON)
Name changed to Funtime Hospitality Corp. 02/01/2000
(See Funtime Hospitality Corp.)

W I WHEELS INTL LTD (BC)
Recapitalized as Annisquam Art Co., Ltd. 6/8/90
Each share Common no par exchanged for (1/3) share Common no par
Annisquam Art Co., Ltd. name changed to PHL Pinnacle Holdings Ltd. 7/18/94 which recapitalized as Citrine Holdings Ltd. 1/9/97

W-J INTL LTD (NV)
Reincorporated 10/24/2003
State of incorporation changed from (DE) to (NV) and Common 1¢ par changed to $0.001 par 10/24/2003
Recapitalized as InZon Corp. 09/22/2004
Each share Common $0.001 par exchanged for (0.16666666) share Common $0.001 par
(See InZon Corp.)

W M HELIJET AWYS INC (BC)
Name changed to Helijet International Inc. 02/14/2000
Each share Common no par exchanged for (2) shares Common no par

W M S DEV CORP (NV)
Name changed to Immune America, Inc. 9/18/87
Immune America, Inc. name changed to King Power International Group Ltd. 6/13/97
(See King Power International Group Ltd.)

W P CAREY & CO LLC (DE)
Under plan of reorganization each share Common no par automatically became (1) share W.P. Carey Inc. (MD) Common $0.001 par 09/28/2012

W P I PHARMACEUTICAL INC (UT)
Recapitalized as Medical Discoveries Inc. 08/12/1992
Each share Common $0.0001 par exchanged for (0.5) share Common $0.0001 par
Medical Discoveries Inc. name changed to Global Clean Energy Holdings, Inc. (UT) 02/29/2008 which reincorporated in Delaware 07/19/2010

W R PARTNERS LTD (BC)
Name changed to bioAsis Technologies Inc. 04/03/2008

W.S. LIQUIDATING CORP. (PA)
Liquidation completed
Each share Capital Stock $10 par exchanged for initial distribution of $18 cash 1/15/65
Each share Capital Stock $10 par received second and final distribution of $3.50 cash 12/17/65

W S & W FD INC (NY)
Completely liquidated 10/25/1972
Each share Common $1 par received first and final distribution of $7.3174 cash
Note: Certificates were not required to be surrendered and are without value

W S & W SPL FD INC (NY)
Merged into W, S & W Fund, Inc. 03/10/1971
Each share Common $1 par exchanged for (1.07495) shares Common $1 par
(See W, S & W Fund, Inc.)

W S INDS INC (NV)
Name changed to Silver Stream Mining Corp. 08/08/2013
Silver Stream Mining Corp. merged into Stratabound Minerals Corp. 05/17/2016

W S LIQUIDATING CORP. (WA)
Completely liquidated 11/13/68
Each share Common no par exchanged for first and final distribution of (0.81336) share Simon (Norton), Inc. $1.60 Conv. Preferred Ser. A $5 par
(See Simon (Norton), Inc.)

W 7 ACQUISITION CORP (CANADA)
Merged into ViXS Systems Inc. 07/12/2013
Each share Common no par exchanged for (0.02571427) share Common no par
ViXS Systems Inc. merged into Pixelworks, Inc. 08/03/2017

W.T., INC. (OR)
Name changed to West-Tech Group, Inc. 07/22/1985
West-Tech Group, Inc. name changed to American Aircraft Corp. (OR) 10/28/1985 which reincorporated in Nevada as Hunter Aircraft Corp. 09/27/1996 which recapitalized as Prepaid Depot Inc. 08/18/2001 which recapitalized as Reed Holdings Corp. 07/30/2002 which name changed to Ostara Corp., Inc. 03/12/2004 which name changed to Rheologics Technologies, Inc. 10/18/2005 which name changed to KKS Venture Management, Inc. 07/24/2007 which recapitalized as Codima, Inc. 06/09/2008
(See Codima, Inc.)

W T C AIR FGHT (CA)
Common no par split (3) for (2) by issuance of (0.5) additional share 5/7/69
Name changed to WTC, Inc. 7/1/76
WTC, Inc. reorganized as WTC International N.V. 3/1/84 which was acquired by Pittson Co. 7/1/87 which name changed to Brink's Co. 5/5/2003

W T C INC (CA)
Under plan of reorganization each share Common no par automatically became (1) share WTC International N.V. Common 1¢ par 03/01/1984
WTC International N.V. acquired by Pittson Co. 07/01/1987

W-WAVES USA INC (NV)
Recapitalized as China Titanium & Chemical Corp. 09/07/2004
Each share Class A Common $0.001 par exchanged for (0.01) share Class A Common $0.001 par
China Titanium & Chemical Corp. name changed to Far Vista Interactive Corp. 09/19/2008 which name changed to Far Vista Petroleum Corp. 05/30/2013

WABAN INC (DE)
Each share Common 1¢ par received distribution of (1) share BJ's Wholesale Club, Inc. Common 1¢ par payable 7/28/97 to holders of record 7/28/97 Ex date - 7/29/97
Name changed to HomeBase, Inc. 7/28/97
HomeBase, Inc. name changed to House2Home, Inc. 9/8/2001
(See House2Home, Inc.)

WABANC INC. (IN)
Acquired by Lincoln Financial Corp. 05/19/1988
Each share Capital Stock $10 par exchanged for (4) shares Common no par
Lincoln Financial Corp. acquired by Norwest Corp. 02/09/1993 which name changed to Wells Fargo & Co. (New) 11/02/1998

WABANSIA APARTMENTS, INC.
Liquidated in 1940

WABASH AVENUE & MONROE STREET (IL)
Merged into Bradley Real Estate Trust (MA) 03/31/1970
Each $100 of Trust Receipts exchanged for (20) Trust Shares $1 par
Bradley Real Estate Trust (MA) reorganized in Maryland as Bradley Real Estate, Inc. 10/17/1994
(See Bradley Real Estate, Inc.)

WABASH CONS CORP (IN)
Name changed to Warner National Corp. 01/01/1972
(See Warner National Corp.)

WABASH FIRE & CASUALTY INSURANCE CO. (IN)
Old Capital Stock $1 par changed to 50¢ par 12/21/64
Each share Capital Stock 50¢ par exchanged for (0.5) share new Capital Stock $1 par 4/20/67
Acquired by Wabash Consolidated Corp. 2/29/68
Each share new Capital Stock $1 par exchanged for (1) share Common $1 par
Wabash Consolidated Corp. name changed to Warner National Corp. 1/1/72

(See Warner National Corp.)

WABASH-HARRISON CORP. (IL)
Liquidated in 1950

WABASH INC (IN)
Merged into Kearney-Wabash, Inc. 06/26/1981
Each share Common no par exchanged for $30.50 cash

WABASH INTL CORP (IN)
Liquidation completed
Each share Common no par exchanged for initial distribution of $7.90 cash 02/13/1981
Each share Common no par received second and final distribution of $0.1845 cash 11/19/1981

WABASH-LAKE CO. (IL)
Assets sold and liquidation completed 7/21/59

WABASH LIFE INSURANCE CO. (IN)
Stock Dividends - 10% 3/1/60; 10% 5/15/61
Name changed to Wabash International Corp. and Common $1 par changed to no par 12/28/67
(See Wabash International Corp.)

WABASH MAGNETICS INC (IN)
Name changed to Wabash, Inc. 05/24/1976
(See Wabash, Inc.)

WABASH PORTLAND CEMENT CO.
Liquidated in 1947

WABASH RAILROAD CO. (MI, IN, IL, MO & IA)
Incorporated 00/00/1889
Placed in receivership 12/26/1911
No stockholders' equity

WABASH RAILWAY CO.
Reorganized as Wabash Railroad Co. in 1942
No stockholders' equity

WABASH RR CO (OH)
Incorporated 09/02/1937
Acquired by Norfolk Southern Corp. 11/12/1991
Each share 4-1/2% Preferred $100 par exchanged for $78.90 cash
Each share Common no par exchanged for $649.97 cash

WABASH TELEPHONE SECURITIES CO.
Dissolved in 1935

WABASSO COTTON CO., LTD. (CANADA)
Each share old Common no par exchanged for (5) shares new Common no par in 1948
Name changed to Wabasso Ltd. 12/29/67
Wabasso Ltd. name changed to Wabasso Inc. 6/29/79
(See Wabasso Inc.)

WABICO MINES LTD. (ON)
Assets liquidated for benefit of creditors 4/27/67
No stockholders' equity

WABSSSO INC (CANADA)
Name changed 6/29/79
4% Non-Cum. Class B Preferred $1 par called for redemption 10/15/70
Name changed from Wabasso Ltd. to Wabasso Inc. 6/29/79
Completely liquidated in 1985
Details not available

WACCAMAW BK & TR CO (WHITEVILLE, NC)
Reorganized as Waccamaw Corp. 1/1/70
Each share Capital Stock $5 par exchanged for (1.3) shares Common $5 par
Waccamaw Corp. name changed to United Carolina Bancshares Corp. 7/31/70 which merged into BB&T Corp. 7/1/97

WACCAMAW BK (WHITEVILLE, NC)
Common $5 par split (6) for (5) by issuance of (0.2) additional share payable 02/28/2000 to holders of record 01/31/2000
Reorganized as Waccamaw Bankshares, Inc. 06/30/2001
Each share Common $5 par exchanged for (1.2) shares Common no par
(See Waccamaw Bankshares, Inc.)

WACCAMAW BANKSHARES INC (NC)
Common no par split (6) for (5) by issuance of (0.2) additional share payable 08/15/2003 to holders of record 08/05/2003 Ex date - 08/18/2003
Common no par split (6) for (5) by issuance of (0.2) additional share payable 05/14/2004 to holders of record 04/30/2004
Common no par split (2) for (1) by issuance of (1) additional share payable 09/30/2004 to holders of record 09/15/2004 Ex date - 10/01/2004
Stock Dividend - 10% payable 09/18/2007 to holders of record 09/02/2007 Ex date - 09/06/2007
Company's principal asset placed in receivership 06/08/2012
Stockholders' equity unlikely

WACCAMAW CORP (NC)
Under plan of merger name changed to United Carolina Bancshares Corp. 7/31/70
United Carolina Bancshares Corp. merged into BB&T Corp. 7/1/97

WACE GROUP PLC (UNITED KINGDOM)
Acquired by Graphics Technologies Inc. 11/1/99
Each Sponsored ADR for Ordinary £0.20 par exchanged for $4.38 cash

WACHOVIA BK & TR CO (WINSTON SALEM, NC)
Each share Common $100 par exchanged for (4) shares Common $25 par 00/00/1941
Each share Common $25 par exchanged for (5) shares Common $5 par 00/00/1953
Stock Dividends - 200% 09/05/1957; 10% 05/29/1964
Reorganized as Wachovia Corp. (Old) 01/01/1969
Each share Common $5 par exchanged for (1) share Common $5 par
Wachovia Corp. (Old) merged into First Wachovia Corp. 12/05/1985 which name changed to Wachovia Corp. (New) (Ctfs. dated between 05/20/1991 and 09/01/2001) 05/20/1991 which merged into Wachovia Corp. (Ctfs. dated after 09/01/2001) 09/01/2001 which merged into Wells Fargo & Co. (New) 12/31/2008

WACHOVIA CAP TR IV (DE)
6.375% Trust Preferred Securities called for redemption at $25 plus $0.132813 accrued dividends on 04/13/2012

WACHOVIA CAP TR IX (DE)
6.375% Trust Preferred Securities called for redemption at $25 plus $0.402865 accrued dividends on 06/15/2012

WACHOVIA CAP TR X (DE)
7.85% Trust Preferred Securities called for redemption at $25 plus $0.103576 accrued dividends on 10/03/2011

WACHOVIA CORP 2ND NEW (NC)
Ctfs. dated after 09/01/2001
Merged into Wells Fargo & Co. (New) 12/31/2008
Each share 7.5% Non-Cumulative Perpetual Conv. Preferred Class A Ser. L exchanged for (1) share 7.5% Perpetual Conv. Preferred Class A
Each share 8% Depositary Perpetual Preferred Class A Ser. J exchanged for (1) share 8% Depositary Preferred Ser. J
Each share Common $3.33333333 par exchanged for (0.1991) share Common $1.66666666 par

WACHOVIA CORP NEW (NC)
Ctfs. dated between 05/20/1991 and 09/01/2001
Common $5 par split (2) for (1) by issuance of (1) additional share 03/31/1993
Merged into Wachovia Corp. (Ctfs. dated after 09/01/2001) 09/01/2001
Each share Common $5 par exchanged for (2) shares Common $3.33-1/3 par
Note: Holders had the option to receive either (2) shares Dividend Equalization Preferred or $0.48 cash
Option to receive cash expired 11/30/2001
Wachovia Corp. (Ctfs. dated after 09/01/2001) merged into Wells Fargo & Co. (New) 12/31/2008

WACHOVIA CORP OLD (NC)
Ctfs. dated prior to 12/05/1985
Common $5 par split (2) for (1) by issuance of (1) additional share 06/01/1972
Common $5 par split (2) for (1) by issuance of (1) additional share 08/30/1984
$2.20 Conv. Preferred Ser. A $5 par called for redemption 09/14/1984
Merged into First Wachovia Corp. 12/05/1985
Each share Common $5 par exchanged for (1) share Common $5 par
First Wachovia Corp. name changed to Wachovia Corp. (New) (Ctfs. dated between 05/20/1991 and 09/01/2001) 05/20/1991 which merged into Wachovia Corp. (Ctfs. dated after 09/01/2001) 09/01/2001 which merged into Wells Fargo & Co. (New) 12/31/2008

WACHOVIA PFD FDG CORP (DE)
7.25% Non-Cum. Perpetual Preferred Securities Ser. A 1¢ par called for redemption at $25 plus $0.010069 accrued dividends on 01/02/2014

WACHOVIA RLTY INVTS (SC)
Acquired by Old Stone Corp. 03/19/1982
Each share of Bene. Int. $1 par exchanged for (0.5) share $2.60 Conv. Preferred Ser. C $1 par
(See Old Stone Corp.)

WACKENHUT CORP (FL)
Common 10¢ par split (4) for (3) by issuance of (1/3) additional share 3/9/70
Common 10¢ par reclassified as Ser. A Common 10¢ par 1/4/93
Each share Ser. A Common 10¢ par received distribution of (1) share Non-Vtg. Ser. B Common 10¢ par 1/4/93
Each share Ser. A Common 10¢ par received distribution of (0.25) share Non-Vtg. Ser. B Common 10¢ par 1/9/95
Each share Non-Vtg. Ser. B Common 10¢ par received distribution of (0.25) additional share 1/9/95
Each share Ser. A Common 10¢ par received distribution of (0.25) share Non-Vtg. Ser. B Common 10¢ par 1/9/96
Stock Dividends - 50% 3/29/68; 10% 6/1/78; 10% 3/1/79; 10% 6/2/80; 10% 3/2/81; 10% 3/2/82; 10% 3/1/83
Merged into Group 4 Falck 5/8/2002
Each share Ser. A Common 10¢ par exchanged for $33 cash
Each share Non-Vtg. Ser. B Common 10¢ par exchanged for $33 cash

WACKENHUT CORRECTIONS CORP (FL)
Common 1¢ par split (2) for (1) by issuance of (1) additional share payable 06/03/1996 to holders of record 05/15/1996
Name changed to GEO Group, Inc. (Old) 11/25/2003
GEO Group, Inc. (Old) reorganized as GEO Group, Inc. (New) 06/27/2014

WACKER CORP. (IL)
Name changed to G.F.C. Corp. 9/29/49
G.F.C. Corp. filed Articles of Dissolution 5/5/61

WACKER WABASH CORP (DE)
Liquidation completed
Each share Capital Stock $1 par stamped to indicate initial distribution of $16 cash 05/15/1973
Each share Stamped Capital Stock $1 par exchanged for second and final distribution of $2.056 cash 02/04/1974

WACO AIRCRAFT CO. (OH)
Merged into Aero Industries, Inc. 5/3/63
Each share Common no par exchanged for (1.625) shares Common 25¢ par
Aero Industries, Inc. name changed to Allied Aero Industries, Inc. 4/22/64
(See Allied Aero Industries, Inc.)

WACO CLASSIC AIRCRAFT CORP (DE)
Name changed to Centennial Aviation Inc. 10/22/97
(See Centennial Aviation Inc.)

WACO HLDG CO (NV)
Name changed to Millenia Corp. 10/31/1994
Millenia Corp. name changed to Internet Multi-Media Corp. 01/25/2000 which recapitalized as AmEurotech Corp. (NV) 12/18/2000 which reincorporated in Florida 04/18/2007 which recapitalized as Scott Contracting Holdings, Inc. 07/11/2007 which name changed to Liverpool Group, Inc. 04/29/2008

WACO PETE LTD (ON)
Charter cancelled for failure to pay taxes and file returns 04/00/1975

WACO-PORTER CORP. (MN)
Class B Common $1.25 par reclassified as Common $1.25 par 12/1/64
Completely liquidated 1/6/66
Each share Common $1.25 par exchanged for first and final distribution of (0.4) share of Bliss & Laughlin Industries Inc. (Old) Common $2.50 par
Bliss & Laughlin Industries Inc. (Old) name changed to Axia Inc. 5/6/82
(See Axia Inc.)

WACOAL CORP (JAPAN)
Name changed to Wacoal Holdings Corp. 10/3/2005

WADASA GOLD MINES LTD. (ON)
Proclaimed dissolved 11/29/72

WADDELL & REED INC (NY)
Merged into CWR Corp. 12/31/1969
Each share Class A Common $1 par exchanged for $80 cash

WADDELL RANCH CO (AZ)
Liquidated 5/5/79
Details not available

WADDINGHAM GOLD & SILVER MINING CO. (NY)
Charter cancelled and proclaimed dissolved for failure to pay taxes 4/2/24

WADDINGTON MINING CORP. LTD. (CANADA)
Name changed to Cop-Ex-Mining Corp. Ltd. 3/28/68

WAD-WAI

WADDY LAKE RES INC (CANADA)
Merged into Golden Rule Resources Ltd. 10/12/95
Each share Common no par exchanged for (0.53) share Common no par

WADE, WENGER, SERVICEMASTER CO. (IL)
Name changed to Servicemaster Industries, Inc. (IL) and Capital Stock no par and Class B no par reclassified as Common no par 05/11/1967
Servicemaster Industries, Inc. (IL) reincorporated under the laws of Delaware 06/30/1969 which reorganized as ServiceMaster Limited Partnership 12/30/1986 which name changed to ServiceMaster Co. 12/29/1997
(See ServiceMaster Co.)

WADE & BUTCHER CORP.
Liquidated in 1938
No stockholders' equity

WADE COOK FINL CORP (NV)
Each share old Common 1¢ par exchanged for (0.1) share new Common 1¢ par 9/3/2002
Assets sold for the benefit of creditors 10/13/2005
No stockholders' equity

WADE (DAVID) INDUSTRIES, INC. (DE)
See - David Wade Industries Inc.

WADEL-CONNALLY HARDWARE CO. (TX)
Name changed to Wadel-Connally Co. 8/9/60

WADEL-DICKIE HARDWARE CO. (TX)
Name changed to Wadel-Connally Hardware Co. in 1915 which name changed to Wadel-Connally Co. 8/9/60

WADELL EQUIP INC (NJ)
Stock Dividend - 25% 05/17/1968
Name changed to Wedco Technology, Inc. 03/15/1984
Wedco Technology, Inc. acquired by ICO, Inc. (Old) 04/30/1996 which reorganized as ICO, Inc. (New) 04/01/1998 which merged into Schulman (A.), Inc. 04/30/2010
(See Schulman (A.), Inc.)

WADHAMS OIL CORP.
Acquired by Vacuum Oil Co. 00/00/1930
Details not available

WADSWORTH & WOODMAN CO.
Acquired by Interchemical Corp. 00/00/1946
Details not available

WADSWORTH ELEC MFG CO (KY)
Company liquidated in September 1990
Details not available

WADSWORTH PUBG INC (DE)
Common $1 par changed to 50¢ par and (1) additional share issued 05/31/1969
Stock Dividend - 10% 08/10/1977
Merged into Thomson Equitable Corp. Ltd. 03/15/1978
Each share Common 50¢ par exchanged for $31.50 cash

WAFERBOARD LTD (ON)
Common $1 par reclassified as Subordinate $1 par 05/00/1984
Name changed to Malette Inc. 02/15/1989
Malette Inc. acquired by Tembec Inc. (QC) 07/25/1995 which reorganized in Canada 02/29/2008 which merged into Rayonier Advanced Materials Inc. 11/21/2017

WAFERGEN BIO-SYSTEMS INC (NV)
Old Common $0.001 par split (3.8888889) for (1) by issuance of (2.8888889) additional shares payable 03/02/2007 to holders of record 02/23/2007 Ex date - 03/06/2007
Each share old Common $0.001 par exchanged for (0.01006137) share new Common $0.001 par 08/28/2013
Each share new Common $0.001 par exchanged again for (0.1) share new Common $0.001 par 07/01/2014
Each share new Common $0.001 par exchanged again for (0.2) share new Common $0.001 par 11/29/2016
Acquired by Takara Bio USA Holdings, Inc. 02/28/2017
Each share new Common $0.001 par exchanged for $7.3471 cash

WAFFLE WAGON INC (DE)
Recapitalized as New-Breed, Inc. 08/06/1981
Each share Common 1¢ par exchanged for (1/6) share Common 1¢ par
New-Breed, Inc. recapitalized as Genetic Research Laboratories, Inc. 11/25/1985 which merged into Organo Med Products, Ltd. 05/28/1987
(See Organo Med Products, Ltd.)

WAGENER MATERIALS CORP. (NV)
Charter revoked for failure to file reports and pay fees 03/03/1958

WAGGONER NATL BANCSHARES INC (TX)
Reorganized 7/1/97
Reorganized from Waggoner National Bank (Vernon, TX) to Waggoner National Bancshares Inc. 7/1/97
Under plan of merger each share Common $10 par exchanged for $450 cash 12/21/2005

WAGNER BAKING CORP. (DE)
Stock Dividend - 100% 6/10/46
Common Voting Trust terminated and VTC's exchanged for Common share for share 9/10/61
Adjudicated bankrupt 7/22/66
No stockholders' equity

WAGNER E R MFG CO (WI)
Common $1 par changed to 66-2/3¢ par and (0.5) additional share issued 05/24/1979
Acquired by Wagner Acquisition Corp. 10/15/1988
Each share 6% Preferred 2nd Issue $100 par exchanged for $100 cash
Each share Common 66-2/3¢ par exchanged for $39.19 cash

WAGNER ELEC CORP NEW (DE)
Ctfs. dated after 3/29/71
Merged into Studebaker-Worthington, Inc. 8/6/76
Each share Common $1 par exchanged for $15 cash

WAGNER ELECTRIC CORP. OLD (DE)
Ctfs. dated prior to 05/19/1967
Each share Common no par exchanged for (4) shares Common $15 par 00/00/1929
Common $15 par split (2) for (1) by issuance of (1) additional share 12/16/1959
Under plan of merger each share Common $15 par exchanged for $17.50 principal amount of 6-7/8% Subord. Debentures due 10/01/1986 and (0.5) share $1.6625 Conv. Preferred Ser. A $10 par 09/30/1966
Stock Dividend - 50% 02/17/1954
Completely liquidated 05/19/1967
Each share $1.6625 Conv. Preferred Ser. A $10 par exchanged for first and final distribution of (1) share $2.50 2nd Preferred Ser. A $10 par and (0.2) share Common $5 par of Studebaker Corp. (MI)
Each share Common $1 par exchanged for first and final distribution of (1.3) shares Common $5 par of Studebaker Corp. (MI)
Studebaker Corp. (MI) merged into Studebaker-Worthington, Inc. 11/27/1967
(See Studebaker-Worthington, Inc.)

WAGNER INDS INC (DE)
Merged into Staley (A.E.) Manufacturing Co. 05/29/1968
Each share Common 50¢ par exchanged for (0.5) share Common $10 par
Staley (A.E.) Manufacturing Co. reorganized as Staley Continental, Inc. 02/12/1985
(See Staley Continental, Inc.)

WAGNER MNG EQUIP INC (OR)
Common 10¢ par split (3) for (2) by issuance of (0.5) additional share 02/22/1971
Merged into PACCAR Inc 11/01/1973
Each share Common 10¢ par exchanged for $10 cash

WAGNER OILS, LTD. (AB)
Recapitalized as Blue Crown Petroleums Ltd. on a (1) for (3) basis in 1952
Blue Crown Petroleums Ltd. acquired by Blue Crown, Inc. 9/14/70
(See Blue Crown, Inc.)

WAH KING INVEST CORP (DE)
Each share Common $0.001 par received distribution of (1.75862105) shares Puritan Financial Group Inc. Common 1¢ par payable 3/17/2006 to holders of record 11/21/2005
Name changed to Royal Invest International Corp. 3/1/2007

WAH KWONG SHIPPING HLDGS LTD (HONG KONG)
Name changed 02/13/1987
Name changed 07/11/1991
Name changed from Wah Kwong Shipping & Investment Co. (Hong Kong) Ltd. to Wah Kwong Shipping Group Ltd. 2/13/87
Each ADR for Ordinary HKD $1.50 par exchanged for (0.02) ADR for B Ordinary HKD $0.10 par 05/20/1988
ADR's for B Ordinary HKD $0.10 par reclassified as ADR's for Ordinary HKD $0.10 par 5/20/88
Name changed from Wah Kwong Shipping Group Ltd. to Wah Kwong Shipping Holdings Ltd. 07/11/1991
ADR agreement terminated 09/07/2000
Each ADR for Ordinary HKD $0.10 par exchanged for $3.592 cash

WAHL CO.
Recapitalized as Eversharp, Inc. in 1940
Each share 7% Preferred $100 par exchanged for (6) shares 5% Preferred $20 par and (5) shares Common $1 par
Each share Common no par exchanged for (0.4) share Common $1 par
(See listing for Eversharp, Inc.)

WAHLCO ENVIRONMENTAL SYS INC (DE)
Each share old Common 1¢ par exchanged for (0.1) share new Common 1¢ par 05/15/1998
Merged into Thermatrix, Inc. 01/13/1999
Each share new Common 1¢ par exchanged for $0.0969 cash
Note: A portion of the merger consideration will be held in escrow for possible future distribution

WAHLSON PRODS INC (NY)
Charter cancelled and proclaimed dissolved for failure to file reports and pay taxes 01/00/1974

WAIALUA AGRIC LTD (HI)
Each share Capital Stock $20 par exchanged for (1) share Capital Stock $10 and (1) share Helemano Co. Ltd. Capital Stock $10 par 00/00/1948
(See Helemano Co. Ltd.)
Merged into Castle & Cooke, Inc. (Old) 05/21/1968
Each share Capital Stock $10 par exchanged for (0.67) share Common $10 par
Castle & Cooke, Inc. (Old) name changed to Dole Food Co., Inc. (HI) 07/30/1991 which reincorporated in Delaware 07/01/2001
(See Dole Food Co., Inc. (Old) (DE))

WAILUKU AGRIBUSINESS CO (HI)
Name changed 04/24/1985
Name changed from Wailuku Sugar Co. to Wailuku Agribusiness Co., Inc. 04/24/1985
Each share Common $20 par received distribution of (1) share Wailuku Water Co., LLC Common payable 10/03/2005 to holders of record 09/21/2005
Merged into Brewer (C.) & Co., Ltd. 01/31/2006
Each share Common $20 par exchanged for $497.45 cash

WAIMANALO SUGAR CO.
Liquidated in 1950

WAIN-CON OILS LTD. (AB)
Acquired by Western Allenbee Oil & Gas Co. Ltd. 00/00/1960
Each share Capital Stock $1 par exchanged for (6) shares Capital Stock no par
Western Allenbee Oil & Gas Co. Ltd. name changed to Convoy Capital Corp. 04/28/1989 which recapitalized as Hariston Corp. 09/25/1992 which recapitalized as Midland Holland Inc. (Canada) 02/10/1999 which reincorporated in Yukon 03/11/1999 which name changed to Mercury Partners & Co. Inc. 02/22/2000 which name changed to Black Mountain Capital Corp. 05/02/2005 which recapitalized as Grand Peak Capital Corp. (YT) 11/20/2007 which reincorporated in British Columbia 04/27/2010

WAIN RES INC (DE)
Charter cancelled and declared inoperative and void for non-payment of taxes 04/15/1973

WAINOCO OIL CORP (WY)
Name changed 10/13/1971
Reincorporated 10/02/1973
Name changed 10/31/1976
Common $1 par changed to 25¢ par 10/11/1968
Stock Dividend - 10% 04/20/1971
Name changed from Wainoco Oil & Chemicals Ltd. to Wainoco Oil Ltd. and Common 25¢ par changed to no par 10/13/1971
Place of incorporation changed from (ON) to (AB) 10/02/1973
Name and place of incorporation changed from Wainoco Ltd. (AB) to Wainoco Oil Corp. (WY) 12/31/1976
Common no par split (2) for (1) by issuance of (1) additional share 10/31/1979
Name changed to Frontier Oil Corp. 04/28/1998
Frontier Oil Corp. merged into HollyFrontier Corp. 07/01/2011

WAINRITE GROUP INC (NY)
Name changed 12/08/1981
Stock Dividends - 10% 07/08/1971; 10% 08/14/1972; 10% 08/06/1973
Name changed from Wainrite Stores, Inc. to Wainrite Group, Inc. 12/08/1981
Dissolved by proclamation 10/26/2011

WAINSCOTT CAP CORP (DE)
Name changed to Enzymes of America Holding Corp. 7/31/87
(See Enzymes of America Holding Corp.)

WAINWRIGHT BK & TR CO (BOSTON, MA)
Stock Dividends - 10% payable 08/10/2001 to holders of record 07/25/2001 Ex date - 07/23/2001; 10% payable 06/28/2002 to holders of record 06/21/2002; 10% payable 06/23/2003 to holders of record 06/03/2003 Ex date - 05/30/2003; 10% payable 06/30/2004 to holders of record 06/21/2004 Ex date - 06/17/2004; 5% payable 06/20/2005 to holders of record 05/27/2005 Ex date - 05/25/2005; 5% payable 06/19/2006 to holders of record 05/26/2006 Ex date - 05/24/2006; 5% payable 06/18/2007 to holders of record 05/25/2007 Ex date - 05/23/2007
Acquired by Eastern Bank Corp. 11/18/2010
Each share Common $1 par exchanged for $19 cash

WAINWRIGHT PRODUCERS & REFINERS LTD. (ON)
Name changed to Wainoco Oil & Chemicals Ltd. 06/21/1966
Wainoco Oil & Chemicals Ltd. name changed to Wainoco Oil Ltd. (ON) 10/13/1971 which reincorporated in Alberta 10/02/1973 which reincorporated in Wyoming as Wainoco Oil Corp. 12/31/1976 which name changed to Frontier Oil Corp. 04/28/1998 which merged into HollyFrontier Corp. 07/01/2011

WAIRIRI GOLD MINES, LTD. (ON)
Charter cancelled for failure to file reports and pay taxes in 1952

WAITE-ACKERMAN-MONTGOMERY MINES LTD.
Merged into Waite Amulet Mines Ltd. share for share in 1933
Waite Amulet Mines Ltd. was acquired by Noranda Mines Ltd. 5/11/62 which name changed to Noranda Inc. 5/28/84 which name changed to Falconbridge Ltd. (New) 2005 on 7/1/2005
(See Falconbridge Ltd. (New) 2005)

WAITE AMULET MINES LTD. (CANADA)
Acquired by Noranda Mines Ltd. on a (1/7) for (1) basis 5/11/62
Noranda Mines Ltd. name changed to Noranda Inc. 5/28/84 which name changed to Falconbridge Ltd. (New) 2005 on 7/1/2005
(See Falconbridge Ltd. (New) 2005)

WAITE (JACK) CONSOLIDATED MINING CO.
Reorganized as Waite (Jack) Mining Co. in 1930
Details not available

WAITE DUFAULT MINES LTD (QC)
Recapitalized as KPI International Inc. 05/28/1996
Each share Common $1 par exchanged for (0.1) share Common $1 par
(See KPI International Inc.)

WAITE (JACK) MINING CO. (AZ)
See - Jack Waite Mining Co.

WAITE (JACK) MINING CO., LTD.
Merged into Waite (Jack) Consolidated Mining Co. in 1928
Details not available

WAITSFIELD CAP INC (QC)
Completely liquidated 10/22/2013
Each share Conv. Class A no par exchanged for first and final distribution of $2.84 cash
Each share Class B no par exchanged for first and final distribution of $2.84 cash

WAJAX INCOME FD (CANADA)
Reorganized as Wajax Corp. 01/04/2011
Each Unit no par exchanged for (1) share Common no par

Note: Unexchanged certificates were cancelled and became without value 06/15/2011

WAJAX LTD (CANADA)
Old Common no par split (2) for (1) by issuance of (1) additional share 01/15/1969
Old Common no par split (2) for (1) by issuance of (1) additional share 06/05/1972
Old Common no par reclassified as Conv. Class A Common no par 09/20/1973
Conv. Class A Common no par split (2) for (1) by issuance of (1) additional share 10/27/1977
Conv. Class B Common no par split (2) for (1) by issuance of (1) additional share 10/27/1977
Conv. Class A Common no par split (2) for (1) by issuance of (1) additional share 05/15/1981
Conv. Class B Common no par split (2) for (1) by issuance of (1) additional share 05/15/1981
$1.86 Conv. Preferred Ser. A no par called for redemption 04/07/1986
Conv. Class A Common no par reclassified as new Common no par 05/09/1996
Conv. Class B Common no par reclassified as new Common no par 05/09/1996
Reorganized as Wajax Income Fund 06/15/2005
Each share new Common no par exchanged for (1) Fund Unit
Wajax Income Fund reorganized as Wajax Corp. 01/04/2011

WAKE FST FED SVGS & LN ASSN (USA)
Under plan of reorganization each share Common 1¢ par automatically became (1) share Wake Forest Bancshares, Inc. Common 1¢ par 05/07/1999

WAKEFIELD CO. (OH)
Merged into Wakefield Corp. on a (2.6) for (1) basis 4/28/61
Wakefield Corp. name changed to 729 Meldrum Corp. 2/24/66
(See 729 Meldrum Corp.)

WAKEFIELD CORP. (MI)
5% Preferred called for redemption 2/28/65
Name changed to 729 Meldrum Corp. 2/24/66
(See 729 Meldrum Corp.)

WAKEFIELD ENGR INC (MA)
Stock Dividends - 10% 5/31/72; 10% 6/29/73
Merged into EG&G, Inc. 7/1/74
Each share Common no par exchanged for (0.75) share Common $1 par
EG&G, Inc. name changed to PerkinElmer, Inc. 10/25/99

WAKEFIELD SEAFOODS, INC. (WA)
Name changed to W S Liquidating Corp. (WA) 10/29/68
(See W S Liquidating Corp. (WA))

WAKEKO MINES, LTD. (ON)
Charter surrendered 8/2/62
No stockholders' equity

WAKEMAC DENTON GOLD MINES, LTD. (ON)
Charter cancelled for failure to file reports and pay taxes 4/3/61

WAKITA QUEBEC GOLD MINES LTD.
Acquired by Lynnita Consolidated Gold Mines Ltd. in 1947
Each share Common exchanged for (1/3) share Common
(See Lynnita Consolidated Gold Mines Ltd.)

WAKO LOGISTICS GROUP INC (DE)
Name changed to WLG Inc. 12/31/2007
(See WLG Inc.)

WAKOTA ARENA, INC. (MN)
Dissolved by Court Order 10/12/77
Each share Common $1 par received first and final distribution of $0.65 cash

WAKULLA BANCORP (FL)
Company's principal asset placed in receivership 10/01/2010
Stockholders' equity unlikely

WAL-MART DE MEXICO S A DE C V (MEXICO)
ADR agreement terminated 09/13/2002
Each ADR for Ordinary exchanged for $2.5832 cash
ADR agreement terminated 03/02/2004
Each ADR for Ordinary C Shares exchanged for $3.058 cash
Note: Due to ADR's being unsponsored exchange rate may vary dependent upon depositary agent
Sponsored ADR's for Ser. V split (2) for (1) by issuance of (1) additional ADR payable 02/17/2006 to holders of record 02/15/2006 Ex date - 02/21/2006
(Additional Information in Active)

WAL MART STORES INC (DE)
Common 10¢ par split (2) for (1) by issuance of (1) additional share 04/07/1972
Common 10¢ par split (2) for (1) by issuance of (1) additional share 08/22/1975
Common 10¢ par split (2) for (1) by issuance of (1) additional share 07/09/1982
Common 10¢ par split (2) for (1) by issuance of (1) additional share 07/08/1983
Common 10¢ par split (2) for (1) by issuance of (1) additional share 10/04/1985
8% Conv. Preferred Ser. A 10¢ par called for redemption 10/01/1986
Common 10¢ par split (2) for (1) by issuance of (1) additional share 07/10/1987
Common 10¢ par split (2) for (1) by issuance of (1) additional share 07/06/1990
Common 10¢ par split (2) for (1) by issuance of (1) additional share 02/25/1993
Common 10¢ par split (2) for (1) by issuance of (1) additional share payable 04/19/1999 to holders of record 03/19/1999 Ex date - 04/20/1999
Stock Dividends - 100% 06/11/1971; 100% 12/16/1980
Name changed to Walmart Inc. 02/01/2018

WALBAR INC (MA)
Common 1¢ par split (2) for (1) by issuance of (1) additional share 7/19/83
Merged into Colt Industries Inc. 12/17/85
Each share Common 1¢ par exchanged for $37 cash

WALBRIDGE OPERATING CO., INC.
Reorganized in 1950
No stockholders' equity

WALBRO CAP TR (DE)
Issue Information - 2,400,000 shares CONV TR PFD SECS 8% offered at $25 per share on 01/29/1997
Conv. Trust Preferred Securities called for redemption 2/2/2000

WALBRO CORP (DE)
Common $1 par split (3) for (2) by issuance of (0.5) additional share 08/31/1983
Common $1 par changed to 50¢ par and (1) additional share issued 05/27/1985
Common 50¢ par split (3) for (2) by issuance of (0.5) additional share 08/26/1988
Merged into TI Group PLC 06/16/1999
Each share Common 50¢ par exchanged for $20 cash

WALBURT OILS LTD. (CANADA)
Charter surrendered 11/18/1959

WALCO NATL CORP (NY)
Stock Dividends - 10% 07/18/1973; 10% 07/19/1974; 10% 07/16/1975; 20% 07/13/1976; 20% 07/15/1977; 20% 07/07/1978; 20% 07/12/1979; 20% 06/16/1980; 20% 06/18/1981; 25% 06/18/1982
Acquired by Newgen Sub Inc. 08/30/1985
Each share Common $5 par exchanged for $16.50 cash

WALD RESEARCH, INC. (NJ)
Bankrupt 7/23/63
No stockholders' equity

WALDAG MINING CO., LTD. (ON)
Charter cancelled for failure to file reports and pay taxes in 1971

WALDBAUM INC (NY)
Common $1 par split (3) for (2) by issuance of (0.5) additional share 7/31/69
Common $1 par split (2) for (1) by issuance of (1) additional share 5/27/83
Common $1 par reclassified as Class A $1 par 6/18/85
Merged into APW Merger Corp. 3/20/87
Each share Class A $1 par exchanged for $50 cash
Each share Class B Common $1 par exchanged for $50 cash

WALDEC CDA LTD (ON)
Capital Stock 50¢ par reclassified as Common no par 12/01/1965
Common no par reclassified as Conv. Participating Class A Common no par 05/30/1974
Company advised private 00/00/1976
Details not available

WALDEN BANCORP INC (MA)
Merged into UST Corp. 1/3/97
Each share Common $1 par exchanged for (1.9) shares Common $0.625 par
(See UST Corp.)

WALDEN RESIDENTIAL PPTYS INC (MD)
Issue Information - 6,842,000 shares COM offered at $19.25 per share on 02/02/1994
Merged into Olympus Real Estate 2/29/2000
Each share Sr. Preferred 1¢ par exchanged for $22 cash
Each share 9% Preferred 1¢ par exchanged for $19.50 cash
Each share 9.16% Conv. Preferred Ser. A 1¢ par exchanged for $26.39 cash
Each share 9.16% Conv. Preferred Ser. B 1¢ par exchanged for $26.39 cash
Each share Common 1¢ par exchanged for $23.14 cash

WALDEN TEL CO (NY)
Merged into Highland Telephone Co. 2/1/72
Each share 4-1/2% Preferred Ser. B $50 par or 5-1/2% Preferred Ser. C $50 par exchanged for (0.5) share 5-7/8% Preferred Ser. A $100 par
Each share Common no par exchanged for (2.6) shares Common $4.50 par
(See Highland Telephone Co.)

WALDORF AUTO LEASING INC (NY)
Name changed to Waldorf Group, Inc. and Common 10¢ par reclassified as Class A Common 1¢ par 08/18/1983
Waldorf Group, Inc. recapitalized as Ascot Solutions Inc. 03/24/1998

(See Ascot Solutions Inc.)

WALDORF GROUP INC (NY)
Stock Dividend - 200% 10/01/1984
Recapitalized as Ascot Solutions Inc. 03/24/1998
Each share Class A Common 1¢ par exchanged for (0.05) share Class A Common 4¢ par
(See Ascot Solutions Inc.)

WALDORF PAPER PRODUCTS CO. (MN)
Merged into Hoerner Waldorf Corp. 5/17/66
Each share Common $1 par exchanged for (0.024572) share $4 Conv. Preferred Ser. A $1.50 par and (1.4672) shares Common 50¢ par
Hoerner Waldorf Corp. merged into Champion International Corp. 2/24/77 which merged into International Paper Co. 6/20/2000

WALDORF SYSTEM, INC. (MA)
Under plan of merger name changed to Restaurant & Waldorf Associates, Inc. 1/14/66
Restaurant & Waldorf Associates, Inc. name changed to Restaurant Associates Industries, Inc. (Mass.) 5/17/68 which reincorporated under the laws of Delaware 7/15/68
(See Restaurant Associates Industries, Inc. (Del.))

WALDORF VENTURES INC (AB)
Issue Information - 2,000,000 shares COM offered at $0.10 per share on 06/13/1997
Recapitalized as Hospital Greetings Corp. 10/10/2001
Each share Common no par exchanged for (0.25) share Common no par
Hospital Greetings Corp. recapitalized as Culane Energy Corp. 05/14/2003
(See Culane Energy Corp.)

WALDRON (JOHN) CORP. (NJ)
Dissolved 12/30/59

WALGREEN CO (IL)
Common no par changed to $10 par 00/00/1952
Common $10 par changed to $5 par and (1) additional share issued 09/27/1963
Common $5 par changed to $2.50 par and (1) additional share issued 10/06/1967
Common $2.50 par changed to $1.25 par and (1) additional share issued 02/12/1982
Common $1.25 par split (2) for (1) by issuance of (1) additional share 02/11/1983
Common $1.25 par split (2) for (1) by issuance of (1) additional share 05/08/1985
Common $1.25 par changed to $0.625 par and (1) additional share issued 02/01/1991
Common $0.625 par changed to $0.3125 par and (1) additional share issued 08/08/1995
Common $0.3125 par changed to $0.15625 par and (1) additional share issued payable 08/08/1997 to holders of record 07/22/1997
Ex date - 08/11/1997
Common $0.15625 par changed to $0.078125 par and (1) additional share issued payable 02/12/1999 to holders of record 01/27/1999
Ex date - 02/16/1999
Reincorporated under the laws of Delaware as Walgreens Boots Alliance, Inc. and Common $0.078125 par changed to 1¢ par 12/31/2014

WALHALLA COM LTD (AUSTRALIA)
Name changed 6/2/99
Each ADR for Ordinary AUD $0.20 par exchanged for (1) ADR for Ordinary AUD $2 par 06/01/1987
Each ADR for Ordinary AUD$2 par exchanged for (0.05) ADR for Ordinary AUD $0.20 par 10/10/1990
Each ADR for Ordinary AUD $0.20 par exchanged for (0.2) ADR for Ordinary AUD $1 par 10/05/1995
Name changed from Walhall Mining Co. N.L. to Walhalla.Com Ltd. 06/02/1999
ADR agreement terminated 01/24/2000
Each ADR for Ordinary AUD $1 par exchanged for $0.116 cash

WALHART GOLD MINES LTD. (ON)
Charter cancelled for failure to file reports and pay taxes 2/1/61

WALK THRU ENTMT INC (CO)
Proclaimed dissolved for failure to maintain a registered agent 1/1/90

WALKER & PRATT MANUFACTURING CO.
Acquired by Kalamazoo Stove & Furnace Co. in 1939
Details not available

WALKER (H.W.) & CO. (DE)
Adjudicated bankrupt 9/7/72

WALKER B B CO (NC)
Class B Common $1 par reclassified as Common $1 par 02/14/1978
Chapter 11 bankruptcy proceedings terminated 11/28/2006
Stockholders' equity unlikely

WALKER B B SHOE CO (NC)
Common $1 par and Class B Common $1 par split (2) for (1) by issuance of (1) additional share respectively 12/13/1971
Name changed to Walker (B.B.) Co. 05/12/1972
(See Walker (B.B.) Co.)

WALKER BK & TR CO (SALT LAKE CITY, UT)
Each share Capital Stock $100 par exchanged for (4) shares Capital Stock $25 par in 1949
Capital Stock $25 par changed to $12.50 par and (1) additional share issued 12/18/56
Capital Stock $12.50 par changed to $6.25 par and (1) additional share issued plus 100% stock dividend paid 3/9/62
Stock Dividends - 10% 2/3/64; 10% 2/14/66; 10% 12/10/69; 10% 7/26/74
Merged into Western Bancorporation 1/16/78
Each share Capital Stock $6.25 par exchanged for (1) share Capital Stock $2 par
Western Bancorporation name changed to First Interstate Bancorp 6/1/81 which merged into Wells Fargo & Co. (Old) 4/1/96 which merged into Wells Fargo & Co. (New) 11/2/98

WALKER COAL & ICE CO. (MA)
Completely liquidated
Each share 8% Preferred $100 par exchanged for first and final distribution of $32.21 cash 6/30/65

WALKER COLOR INC (DE)
Name changed to Walker International Industries, Inc. 7/18/85
Walker International Industries, Inc. name changed to Walker Financial Corp. 12/13/2002

WALKER ENERGY PARTNERS (TX)
Name changed to Texas Meridian Resources, Ltd. 08/23/1988
Texas Meridian Resources, Ltd. merged into Texas Meridian Resources Corp. 12/18/1990 which name changed to Meridian Resources Corp. 06/19/1997
(See Meridian Resource Corp.)

WALKER FINL CORP (DE)
Common 10¢ par changed to $0.0001 par 05/23/2006
Stock Dividend - 900% payable 12/20/2002 to holders of record 12/15/2002 Ex date - 12/23/2002
Company terminated common stock registration and is no longer public as of 02/01/2010

WALKER HIRAM CONSUMERS HOME LTD (ON)
Under plan of reorganization each share 5% Preference Group 1, Ser. C $100 par, 5-1/2% Preference Group 1, Ser. A $100 par and 5-1/2% Preference Group 1, Ser. B $100 par automatically became (1) share Consumers' Gas Co. Ltd. 5% Preference Group 1, Ser. C $100 par, 5-1/2% Preference Group 1, Ser. A $100 par and 5-1/2% Preference Group 1, Ser. B $100 par respectively and each share 7-1/2% Conv. Preference Group 5, 1st Ser. $25 par, 9% Conv. Preference Group 3, 1st Ser. no par and Common no par automatically became (1) share Walker (Hiram) Resources Ltd. 7-1/2% Conv. Class D Preference 1st Ser. $25 par, 9% Conv. Class C Preference 1st Ser. $20 par and Common no par respectively 06/01/1981
(See each company's listing)

WALKER HIRAM GOODERHAM & WORTS LTD (CANADA)
Each share Common no par exchanged for (0.25) share new Common no par and (0.25) share Preference no par in 1932
Common no par exchanged (4) for (1) in 1946
Common no par split (3) for (1) by issuance of (2) additional shares 2/7/58
Common no par split (2) for (1) by issuance of (1) additional share 3/19/64
Common no par reclassified as Conv. Class A Common no par 7/18/73
Conv. Class A Common no par and Conv. Class B Common no par reclassified as Common no par 1/8/80
Common no par split (2) for (1) by issuance of (1) additional share 1/22/80
Merged into Walker (Hiram)-Consumers Home Ltd. 4/14/80
Each share Common no par exchanged for (1.375) shares Common no par
(See - Walker (Hiram)-Consumers Home Ltd.)

WALKER HIRAM RES LTD (ON)
9% Conv. Class C Preference 1st Ser. $20 par called for redemption 11/2/84
7-1/2% Conv. Class D Preference 1st Ser. $25 par called for redemption 7/18/86
9-1/2% Conv. Class B Preference 1st Ser. $25 par called for redemption 9/12/86
14.16% Class A Preference 1st Ser. $25 par called for redemption 9/12/86
Merged into Gulf Canada Corp. 10/24/86
Each share Common no par exchanged for (2.6) shares Common no par
Gulf Canada Corp. reorganized as Gulf Canada Resources Ltd. 7/1/87
(See Gulf Canada Resources Ltd.)

WALKER INTERACTIVE SYS INC (DE)
Name changed to Elevon, Inc. 7/15/2002
(See Elevon, Inc.)

WALKER INTL INDS INC (DE)
Name changed to Walker Financial Corp. 12/13/2002

WALKER LABORATORIES, INC. (NY)
Acquired by Vick Chemical Co. and each share Class A or B Common 25¢ par exchanged for (0.09) share Capital Stock $2.50 par 7/2/58
Vick Chemical Co. name changed to Richardson-Merrell, Inc. 10/21/60

WALKER MANUFACTURING CO. OF WISCONSIN (WI)
Name changed in 1939
Name changed from Walker Manufacturing Co. to Walker Manufacturing Co. of Wisconsin in 1939
Each share Common no par exchanged for (3) shares Common $4 par in 1950
Stock Dividend - 10% 12/20/57
Acquired by Kern County Land Co. on a (20) for (21) basis 6/30/59
Kern County Land Co. acquired by Tenneco Inc. 8/30/67 which was merged into El Paso Natural Gas Co. 12/12/96 which reorganized as El Paso Energy Corp. 8/1/98 which name changed to El Paso Corp. 2/5/2001

WALKER MCNEIL MARKETING INC (CT)
Name changed to Oxford Capital Corp. 4/19/88
Oxford Capital Corp. name changed to Americas Gaming International Inc. 11/27/95

WALKER MINING CO.
Assets sold in 1945
No stockholders' equity

WALKER PWR INC (NH)
Name changed to WPI Group, Inc. 2/12/93
WPI Group, Inc. name changed to Nexiq Technologies Inc. 11/13/2000
(See Nexiq Technologies Inc.)

WALKER SCOTT CORP (CA)
Each share Class A Common no par exchanged for (4) shares Class A Common $1 par 02/20/1957
Each share Class B Common no par exchanged for (4) shares Class B Common $1 par 02/20/1957
Class A Common $1 par and Class B Common $1 par reclassified as Common $1 par 04/24/1958
Preferred $100 par called for redemption 07/11/1958
Merged into Desmond's & Associates 08/09/1985
Each share Common $1 par exchanged for $12 cash

WALKER TELECOMMUNICATIONS CORP (NY)
Charter cancelled and proclaimed dissolved for failure to pay taxes 5/18/98

WALKER VITAMIN PRODUCTS, INC.
Each share Class A and Class B 50¢ par exchanged for (2) shares Class A or Class B 25¢ par 01/00/1951
Name changed to Walker Laboratories, Inc. 07/24/1951
Walker Laboratories, Inc. was acquired by Vick Chemical Co. 07/02/1958 which name changed to Richardson-Merrell, Inc. 10/21/1960 which merged into Dow Chemical Co. 03/10/1981

WALKER WELL HEADS, INC. (OK)
Liquidated in December 1966
No stockholders' equity

WALKER'S (HIRAM), LTD.
Merged into Walker (Hiram)-Gooderham & Worts Ltd. 00/00/1927
Details not available

WALKERS CAP CORP (AB)
Struck off register and declared dissolved for failure to file returns 2/1/94

WALKERS HOOK INTL LTD (DE)
Name changed to Quadrant Resources Corp. 11/08/1999
Quadrant Resources Corp. recapitalized as Pinnacle Transportation Corp. 05/27/2003 which name changed to ZYTO Corp. 09/19/2006 which name changed to Global Unicorn Holdings, Inc. 05/02/2018

WALKING CO HLDGS INC (DE)
Plan of reorganization under Chapter 11 Federal Bankruptcy proceedings effective 06/29/2018
No stockholders' equity

WALKING STICK OIL & GAS CORP (BC)
Merged into Ascentex Energy Inc. 2/25/94
Each share Common no par exchanged for (0.28571428) share Common no par
Ascentex Energy Inc. recapitalized as Bonavista Petroleum Ltd. 3/3/97
(See Bonavista Petroleum Ltd.)

WALL & BEAVER STREET CORP. (NY)
Liquidation for cash completed 8/28/59

WALL & REDEKOP CORP. LTD. (BC)
Name changed to Wall & Redekop Corp. 6/25/74
Wall & Redekop Corp. name changed to Wall Financial Corp. 8/8/88

WALL & REDEKOP CORP (BC)
Common no par split (3) for (1) by issuance of (2) additional shares 7/3/81
Name changed to Wall Financial Corp. 8/8/88

WALL DATA INC (WA)
Merged into NetManage, Inc. 12/29/99
Each share Common no par exchanged for $9 cash

WALL INDUSTRIES, INC. (NJ)
Assets sold and each share Common $5 par exchanged for (0.74884) share Phillips Petroleums Co. Common $5 par effective 8/1/63
Note: 90% of Phillips Common shares distributed 8/1/64 and final 10% of escrowed Phillips Common shares distributed 8/20/68

WALL MANUFACTURING CO. OF KINSTON (NC)
Name changed to Wall-Lenk Manufacturing Co. 8/14/73

WALL (P.) MANUFACTURING CO. (PA)
Recapitalized 12/27/61
Each share 6% Preferred 1937 Ser. $10 par exchanged for (8.4907) shares Common 50¢ par
Each share 6% Preferred 1949 Ser. $10 par exchanged for (7.7355) shares Common 50¢ par
Each share 6% Preferred 1954 Ser. $10 par exchanged for (7.3675) shares Common 50¢ par
Each share Common no par exchanged for (0.5942) share Common 50¢ par
Last date to exchange old stock was 2/10/64, after which date cash only will be distributed
Merged into Wall Manufacturing Co. of Kinston 1/1/68
Each share Common 50¢ par exchanged for (1) share Common 50¢ par
Wall Manufacturing Co. of Kinston name changed to Wall-Lenk Manufacturing Co. 8/14/73

WALL ROPE WORKS, INC. (NJ)
Name changed to Wall Industries, Inc. 4/13/60
Wall Industries, Inc. was acquired by Phillips Petroleum Co. 8/1/63 which name changed to ConocoPhilllips 8/30/2002

WALL STR CAP CORP NEW (UT)
Proclaimed dissolved for failure to file reports 8/1/96

WALL STR CAP CORP OLD (UT)
Name changed to Silk Parade Inc. 4/8/93
Silk Parade Inc. name changed to Wall Street Capital Corp. (New) 4/8/94
(See Wall Street Capital Corp. (New))

WALL STR COMPUTER CORP (DE)
Name changed to Marketime Corp. 10/07/1974
(See Marketime Corp.)

WALL STR COTTON CLUB INC (DE)
Sale of assets and dissolution of company approved 10/26/93
No stockholders' equity

WALL STR DELI INC (DE)
Common 5¢ par split (3) for (2) by issuance of (0.5) additional share 03/03/1993
Plan of reorganization under Chapter 11 Federal Bankruptcy proceedings confirmed 11/24/2003
No stockholders' equity

WALL STR FD INC (MD)
Name changed 06/12/1978
Name changed from Wall Street Growth Fund, Inc. to Wall Street Fund, Inc. 06/12/1978
Reorganized as Wall Street EWM Funds Trust 10/01/2014
Each share Common $1 par exchanged for (1) share Wall Street Fund no par

WALL STR FINL CORP (DE)
Each share old Common 1¢ par exchanged for (0.25) share new Common 1¢ par 12/13/93
Name changed to WSF Corp. 7/9/98
(See WSF Corp.)

WALL STR INFORMATION SVCS HLDG INC (ID)
Name changed to American Image Motor Co., Inc. 09/16/1998
(See American Image Motor Co., Inc.)

WALL STR RECORDS INC (UT)
Name changed to ANTRA Holdings Group, Inc. 04/16/1996
ANTRA Holdings Group, Inc. recapitalized as Peku Manufacturing, Inc. 11/15/2005 which name changed to GHL Technologies, Inc. 03/03/2006 which recapitalized as NXGen Holdings, Inc. 09/07/2007 which name changed to Green Bridge Industries, Inc. 08/20/2009

WALL STR STRATEGIES CORP (NV)
Each share old Common $0.001 par exchanged for (0.01) share new Common $0.001 par 09/11/2002
Chapter 11 bankruptcy petition dismissed 09/29/2006
No stockholders' equity

WALL STREET INVESTING CORP. (MD)
Stock Dividend - 200% 11/30/1955
Name changed to Wall Street Growth Fund, Inc. 04/19/1971
Wall Street Growth Fund, Inc. name changed to Wall Street Fund, Inc. 06/12/1978 which reorganized as Wall Street EWM Funds Trust 10/01/2014

WALL STREET VENTURES INC (BC)
Recapitalized as Bionic Enterprises, Inc. 3/23/93
Each share Common no par exchanged for (0.25) share Common no par
Bionic Enterprises, Inc. name changed to Hymex Diamond Corp. (BC) 10/18/94 which reincorporated in Yukon 9/4/96
(See Hymex Diamond Corp. (Yukon))

WALL TO WALL SOUND & VIDEO INC (PA)
Reorganized under Chapter 11 Federal Bankruptcy Code 5/23/91
Each share Common 1¢ par exchanged for initial distribution of $0.41509433962 cash 7/1/91
Each share Common 1¢ par received second and final distribution of $0.0016 cash 8/20/92

WALLAC YELLOWKNIFE GOLD MINES LTD. (ON)
Name changed to Valray Explorations Ltd. 7/31/56
(See Valray Explorations Ltd.)

WALLACE & TIERNAN INC (DE)
Common $1 par changed to 50¢ par and (1) additional share issued 12/16/1960
Stock Dividend - 10% 02/26/1954
Merged into Pennwalt Corp. 03/31/1969
Each share Common 50¢ par exchanged for (0.5) share Conv. Preference 2nd Ser. $1 par and (0.5) share Common $1 par
(See Pennwalt Corp.)

WALLACE BUSINESS FORMS, INC. (DE)
Common $10 par changed to $5 par and (1) additional share issued 8/6/65
Common $5 par changed to $2.50 par and (1) additional share issued 11/23/70
Common $2.50 par changed to no par and (1) additional share issued 11/28/80
Name changed to Wallace Computer Services, Inc. 11/4/81
Wallace Computer Services, Inc. merged into Moore Wallace Inc. 5/15/2003 which was acquired by Donnelley (R.R.) & Sons Co. 2/27/2004

WALLACE (WILLIAM) CO. (CA)
Stock Dividends - 10% 11/28/58; 10% 12/22/59; 10% 12/22/61
Liquidation completed 8/24/62

WALLACE COMPUTER SVCS INC (DE)
Common no par changed to $1 par and (1) additional share issued 5/9/83
Common $1 par split (2) for (1) by issuance of (1) additional share 8/1/89
Common $1 par split (2) for (1) by issuance of (1) additional share payable 7/26/96 to holders of record 7/15/96 Ex date - 7/29/96
Merged into Moore Wallace Inc. 5/15/2003
Each share Common $1 par exchanged for (0.36) share Common no par and $22.53 cash
Moore Wallace Inc. acquired by Donnelley (R.R.) & Sons Co. 2/27/2004

WALLACE CONTAINER CO. (CA)
Dissolved 10/23/58

WALLACE INVESTMENTS, INC. (DE)
Name changed to Lomas & Nettleton Financial Corp. 07/26/1965
Lomas & Nettleton Financial Corp. name changed to Lomas Financial Corp. (Old) 10/28/1988 which reorganized as Lomas Financial Corp. (New) 01/31/1992
(See Lomas Financial Corp. (New))

WALLACE MANUFACTURING CO.
Merged into Stevens (J.P.) & Co., Inc. in 1946
Each old share exchanged for (7.69333) shares new Capital Stock $15 par
(See Stevens (J.P.) & Co., Inc.)

WALLACE MTN RES CORP (NV)
Name changed to AgFeed Industries, Inc. 11/22/2006
(See AgFeed Industries, Inc.)

WALLACE MURRAY CORP (DE)
Common $7.50 par changed to $3.75 par and (1) additional share issued 05/13/1966
$1.70 Conv. Preference no par called for redemption 07/28/1978
$1.10 Preferred no par called for redemption 04/20/1981
Stock Dividends - 20% 05/31/1978; 10% 05/30/1980
Merged into Household International, Inc. 06/29/1981
Each share Common $3.75 par exchanged for (1) share $6.25 Conv. Preferred no par
(See Household International, Inc.)

WALLACE PRESS, INC. (IL)
Merged into Wallace Business Forms, Inc. on a share for share basis 8/30/63
Wallace Business Forms, Inc. name changed to Wallace Computer Services, Inc. 11/4/81 which merged into Moore Wallace Inc. 5/15/2003 which was acquired by Donnelley (R.R.) & Sons Co. 2/27/2004

WALLACE PROPERTIES, INC. (DE)
Name changed to Wallace Investments, Inc. 09/22/1961
Wallace Investments, Inc. name changed to Lomas & Nettleton Financial Corp. 07/26/1965 which name changed to Lomas Financial Corp. (Old) 10/28/1988 which reorganized as Lomas Financial Corp. (New) 01/31/1992
(See Lomas Financial Corp. (New))

WALLACE RES INC (ID)
Name changed 07/01/2002
Name changed from Wallace Silver, Inc. to Wallace Resources, Inc. and Common 5¢ par changed to no par 07/01/2002
Each share old Common no par exchanged for (0.2) share new Common no par 09/09/2003
Name changed to Systems Evolution, Inc. 10/24/2003
Systems Evolution, Inc. name changed to Highline Technical Innovations, Inc. 04/19/2010 which name changed to SPO Networks, Inc. 01/12/2017

WALLACE SAM P INC (TX)
Common $1 par changed to 66-2/3¢ and (0.5) additional share issued 07/18/1969
Reorganized as SPW Corp. 11/08/1983
Each share Common 66-2/3¢ par exchanged for (1) share Common $1 par
(See SPW Corp.)

WALLACE WILLIAM CORP (DE)
Merged into Wallace-Murray Corp. 9/1/65
Each share $1.10 Preferred Series A no par exchanged for (1) share $1.10 Preferred no par
Each share Common 50¢ par exchanged for (1) share Common $7.50 par or (1) share $1.70 Convertible Preference no par
Option to receive Preference expired 9/29/65
Wallace-Murray Corp. merged into Household International, Inc. 6/29/81

WALLACE'S BOOKSTORES, INC. (KY)
Administratively dissolved 11/01/2001

WALLEN MANOR APARTMENTS LIQUIDATING TRUST
Trust liquidated in 1951

WALLFRIN INDS INC (NV)
Filed a petition under Chapter 7 Federal Bankruptcy Code 07/03/1989
Stockholders' equity unlikely

WALLICHS MUSIC & ENTMT INC (DE)
Name changed to National Industrial Security Corp. 11/01/1983
National Industrial Security Corp. recapitalized as NPS International Corp. 11/06/1998 which name changed to OneClass Synergy Corp. 12/21/2000 which recapitalized as ABCI Holdings Inc. (DE) 08/13/2001 which reorganized in Nevada as Metaphor Corp. 01/06/2005 which name changed to Medical Solutions Management Inc. 08/04/2006
(See Medical Solutions Management Inc.)

WALLOPER GOLD RES LTD (BC)
Name changed to East Asia Minerals Corp. 4/25/2005

WALLS INDS INC (TX)
Stock Dividend - 50% 04/28/1972
Name changed to Samarnan Investment Corp. 04/25/1978
(See Samarnan Investment Corp.)

WALLSON ASSOCIATES, INC. (NJ)
Adjudicated bankrupt 5/15/63
Common Stock worthless

WALLSTREET RACING STABLES INC (CO)
Name changed to Pipeline Technologies, Inc. 10/27/2000
(See Pipeline Technologies, Inc.)

WALLSTREET-REVIEW FINL SVCS INC (FL)
Name changed to 247 Media Group, Inc. and Class A Common 1¢ par reclassified as Common 1¢ par 03/10/2006
247 Media Group, Inc. recapitalized as Fantastic Fun, Inc. 09/22/2006 which name changed to Global Profit Technologies, Inc. 02/13/2008

WALLSTREET-REVIEW INC (FL)
Recapitalized as Champion American Energy Reserves, Inc. 10/15/2004
Each share Common 1¢ par exchanged for (0.01) share Common 1¢ par
(See Champion American Energy Reserves, Inc.)

WALLY F FINDLAY GALLERIES INTERNATIONAL, INC. (DE)
See - Findlay Wally F Galleries Intl Inc

WALMER CAP CORP (AB)
Name changed to EnerSpar Corp. 04/03/2017

WALMONT PRECIOUS METALS CORP (CANADA)
Recapitalized as IGF Metals Inc. 08/01/1986
Each share Common no par exchanged for (0.1) share Common no par
IGF Metals Inc. name changed to Independent Growth Finders Inc. 07/10/1998
(See Independent Growth Finders Inc.)

WALNUT APARTMENTS CORP. (PA)
Liquidation completed
Each share Capital Stock no par exchanged for initial distribution of $102 cash 07/23/1965
Each share Capital Stock no par received second distribution of $10 cash 09/29/1965
Each share Capital Stock no par received third and final distribution of $1.70 cash 03/29/1967

WALNUT CAP INC (NVV)
Name changed to Enter Tech Corp. 5/21/98
(See Enter Tech Corp.)

WALNUT CREEK MINING & MILLING CO. (CA)
Charter suspended for failure to file reports and pay fees 03/05/1921

WALNUT EQUIP LEASING INC (PA)
Filed a petition under Chapter 11 Federal Bankruptcy Code 8/8/97
Stockholders' equity unlikely

WALNUT FINL SVCS INC (UT)
Each share old Common $0.002 par exchanged for (1/6) share new Common $0.002 par 01/22/1999
Name changed to THCG, Inc. (UT) 11/01/1999
THCG, Inc. (UT) reincorporated in Delaware 05/16/2000 which name changed to THCG Liquidating Trust 07/16/2001
(See THCG Liquidating Trust)

WALNUT GROVE PRODUCTS CO., INC. (IA)
Each share Class A Common $2 par exchanged for (1.2) shares new Common $2 par 11/21/1961
Each share Class B Common $2 par exchanged for (0.5) share new Common $2 par 11/21/1961
Acquired by Grace (W.R.) & Co. (CT) 10/01/1964
Each share Common $2 par exchanged for (1/3) share Common $1 par
Grace (W.R.) & Co. (CT) reincorporated in New York 05/19/1988
(See Grace (W.R.) & Co.)

WALRON MINERALS CORP (CANADA)
Dissolved 5/6/2004
Details not available

WALSH COMMUNICATIONS GROUP INC (NV)
Name changed to AVE, Inc. 01/05/1990
AVE, Inc. recapitalized as Cyco.net, Inc. 08/12/1999 which name changed to Nexicon, Inc. 01/25/2005
(See Nexicon, Inc.)

WALSH INDUSTRIES, INC. (MN)
Ceased operations 6/18/73
No stockholders' equity

WALSH INTL INC (DE)
Merged into Cognizant Corp. 06/24/1998
Each share Common 1¢ par exchanged for (1) share Common 1¢ par
Cognizant Corp. name changed to Nielsen Media Research Inc. 07/01/1998
(See Nielsen Media Research Inc.)

WALSHIRE ASSURN CO (PA)
Stock Dividends - 10% 10/30/89; 10% 12/27/95; 10% payable 12/26/96 to holders of record 12/11/96
Merged into Kingsway Financial Services Inc. 12/14/98
Each share 6.50% Conv. Preferred 1¢ par exchanged for $50 cash
Each share Common 1¢ par exchanged for $8.25 cash

WALSTON AVIATION INC (DE)
Name changed to Walston Enterprises, Inc. 11/14/1973
(See Walston Enterprises, Inc.)

WALSTON ENTERPRISES, INC. (DE)
Completely liquidated 3/20/76
Each share Common $1 par exchanged for first and final distribution of $8.22 cash

WALTER AMUSEMENTS INC (DE)
Name changed to Energy Systems United Corp. 11/06/1980
(See Energy Systems United Corp.)

WALTER E. HELLER & CO. (DE)
See - Heller (Walter E.) & Co.

WALTER E. HELLER INTERNATIONAL CORP. (DE)
See - Heller (Walter E.) International Corp.

WALTER E. SELCK & CO. (DE)
See - Selck (Walter E.) & Co.

WALTER ENTERPRISES INC (DE)
Charter cancelled and declared inoperative and void for non-payment of taxes 03/01/1982

WALTER HARVEY CORP. (FL)
See - Harvey (Walter) Corp.

WALTER INDS INC (DE)
Secondary Offering - 10,040,408 shares COM offered at $17.50 per share on 02/11/1998
Each share Common 1¢ par received distribution of (1.6524432) shares Mueller Water Products, Inc. Ser. B Common 1¢ par payable 12/14/2006 to holders of record 12/06/2006
Ex date - 12/15/2006
Each share Common 1¢ par received distribution of (0.39) share Walter Investment Management Corp. Common 1¢ par payable 04/17/2009 to holders of record 02/27/2009
Name changed to Walter Energy, Inc. 04/27/2009

WALTER INVT MGMT CORP (MD)
Each share Common 1¢ par received distribution of (0.00850322) additional share payable 11/15/2011 to holders of record 09/22/2011
Ex date - 09/20/2011
Plan of reorganization under Chapter 11 Federal Bankruptcy proceedings effective 02/09/2018
Each share Common 1¢ par automatically became (0.05689208) share Ditech Holding Corp. Common 1¢ par, (0.09692659) Common Stock Purchase Warrant Ser. A expiring 02/09/2028 and (0.0769092) Common Stock Purchase Warrant Ser. B expiring 02/09/2028

WALTER JIM CORP (FL)
Common 16-2/3¢ par split (3) for (1) by issuance of (2) additional shares 1/1/69
$1.20 Preferred no par conversion privilege expired 1/31/71
$1.20 Preferred no par called for redemption 6/1/71
3rd Preferred Ser. 4 no par called for redemption 4/1/74
5-3/4% 5th Conv. Preferred $100 par called for redemption 4/1/75
$2 3rd Conv. Preferred Ser. 1 no par called for redemption 5/1/76
3rd Conv. Preferred Ser. 3 no par called for redemption 5/1/78
Common 16-2/3¢ par split (5) for (4) by issuance of (0.25) additional share 4/11/84
Common 16-2/3¢ par split (5) for (4) by issuance of (0.25) additional share 4/11/86
Common 16-2/3¢ par split (5) for (4) by issuance of (0.25) additional share 7/10/87
5% Preferred $20 par called for redemption 8/31/87
$1.60 4th Conv. Preferred no par called for redemption 10/1/87
Merged into Hillsborough Holdings Corp. 1/7/88
Each share Common 16-2/3¢ par exchanged for $60 cash

WALTER JIM INVS (FL)
Name changed to Walter Realty Investors (FL) 12/1/75
Walter Realty Investors (FL) reorganized in Maryland as Walter Realty Investors, Inc. 4/30/80 which name changed to Unicorp Realty Investors, Inc. 4/1/82
(See Unicorp Realty Investors, Inc.)

WALTER KIDDE & CO., INC. (DE)
See - Kidde (Walter) & Co., Inc.

WALTER KIDDE & CO., INC. (NY)
See - Kidde (Walter) & Co., Inc.

WALTER M. LOWNEY CO., LTD. (CANADA)
See - Lowney (Walter M.) Co., Ltd.

WALTER READE ORGANIZATION INC (DE)
Reorganized under Chapter XI Federal Bankruptcy Code 5/15/81
Each share $4.55 Preferred $1 par exchanged for (60) shares new Common 25¢ par
Each share old Common 25¢ par exchanged for (0.6) share new Common 25¢ par
Acquired by Columbia Pictures Industries, Inc. 1/23/86
Each share new Common 25¢ par exchanged for $5.25 cash

WALTER READE/STERLING, INC. (DE)
Name changed to Reade (Walter) Organization, Inc. 9/8/66
(See Reade (Walter) Organization, Inc.)

WALTER RLTY INVS INC (MD)
Name changed 4/30/80
Name changed from Walter Realty Investors (FL) to Walter Realty Investors, Inc. (MD) and Shares of Bene. Int. 10¢ par changed to Common 10¢ par 4/30/80
Name changed to Unicorp Realty Investors, Inc. 4/1/82
(See Unicorp Realty Investors, Inc.)

WALTERRA GOLD MINES, LTD. (ON)
Charter cancelled for failure to file reports and pay taxes in 1952

WALTERS CONSULTING CORP (ON)
Name changed to YWL Corp. 05/14/2003
YML Corp. merged into Icefloe Technologies Inc. 04/01/2004
(See Icefloe Technologies Inc.)

WALTERS URANIUM CORP. (UT)
Merged into Sun Tide Corp. 11/15/1957
Each share Capital Stock 1¢ par exchanged for (0.4) share Capital Stock 10¢ par
Sun Tide Corp. name changed to Maxa Corp. 04/13/1974
(See Maxa Corp.)

WALTHALL NATURAL GAS CO., INC. (MS)
5% Preferred $25 par called for redemption 12/31/65
(Additional Information in Active)

WALTHAM CTZNS NATL BK (WALTHAM, MA)
Merged into Community National Bank (Framingham, MA) 12/31/1971
Each share Capital Stock $10 par exchanged for (3.4) shares Common $5 par
Community National Bank (Framingham, MA) name changed to Shawmut Community Bank, N.A. (Framingham, MA) 04/01/1975
(See Shawmut Community Bank N.A. (Framington, MA))

WALTHAM CORP (DE)
Name changed to Sterling Bancshares Corp. 5/13/91
Sterling Bancshares Corp. merged into Fleet Financial Group, Inc. (New) 8/15/94 which name changed to Fleet Boston Corp. 10/1/99 which name changed to FleetBoston Financial Corp. 4/18/2000 which merged into Bank of America Corp. 4/1/2004

WALTHAM INDS CORP (DE)
Reorganized in December 1973
No stockholders' equity

WALTHAM PRECISION INSTRS INC (MA)
Reincorporated under the laws of Delaware as Waltham Industries Corp. 1/17/69
(See Waltham Industries Corp.)

WALTHAM PRECISION INSTRUMENT CO., INC. (MA)
Name changed to Newal, Inc. 4/28/64

Newal, Inc. reorganized as Waltham Precision Instruments, Inc. (MA) 12/6/66 which reincorporated in Delaware as Waltham Industries Corp. 1/17/69
(See Waltham Industries Corp.)

WALTHAM SVGS BK (WALTHAM, MA)
Reorganized under the laws of Delaware as Waltham Corp. 10/1/87
Waltham Corp. name changed to Sterling Bancshares Corp. 5/13/91 which merged into Fleet Financial Group, Inc. (New) 8/15/94 which name changed to Fleet Boston Corp. 10/1/99 which name changed to FleetBoston Financial Corp. 4/18/2000 which merged into Bank of America Corp. 4/1/2004

WALTHAM WATCH CO. (DE)
Common $1 par changed to 50¢ par 4/20/59
Each share Common 50¢ par exchanged for (0.2) share Common $2.50 par 4/3/61
Stock Dividend - 10% 5/6/63
Merged into Iseca Inc. 5/1/69
Each share Common $2.50 par exchanged for $16 cash

WALTHAM WATCH CO (MA)
Each share Class B Common no par exchanged for (1) share Common $1 par in 1945
Each share Common $1 par exchanged for (0.1) VTC for Common $1 par in 1949
Voting Trust Agreement terminated 5/12/53
Each VTC for Common $1 par exchanged for (1) share Common $1 par
Name changed to Waltham Precision Instrument Co., Inc. 7/17/57 and (0.2) share Waltham Watch Co., (DE) Common $1 par distributed 8/23/57
Waltham Precision Instrument Co., Inc. name changed to Newal, Inc. 4/28/64 which reorganized as Waltham Precision Instruments, Inc. 12/6/66 which reincorporated in Delaware as Waltham Industries Corp. 1/17/69
(See Waltham Industries Corp.)

WALTKE (WM.) & CO.
Acquired by Procter & Gamble Co. in 1927
Details not available

WALTON BK & TR CO (GA)
Merged into Main Street Banks, Inc. (GA) 1/25/2001
Each share Common exchanged for (2.752) shares Common no par Main Street Banks, Inc. (GA) merged into BB&T Corp. 6/1/2006

WALTON OIL CO (CO)
Merged into October Oil Co. (New) 10/18/82
Each share Common no par exchanged for (0.125) share Common $0.001 par
(See October Oil Co. (New))

WALTON PLACE BUILDING CORP.
Liquidation completed in 1950

WALTON VAIREX CORP (DE)
Name changed to M.S.E. Cable Systems, Inc. 11/7/84
(See M.S.E. Cable Systems, Inc.)

WALTON YELLOWHEAD DEV CORP (AB)
Voluntarily dissolved 03/30/2015
Each share Non-Vtg. Class B Common no par exchanged for $0.14 cash

WALWORTH CO (MA)
Each share old 6% Preferred $50 par exchanged for (8) shares Common no par 00/00/1936
Common no par changed to $2.50 par 00/00/1950
Merged into International Utilities Corp. 01/01/1972
Each share 6% Conv. Preferred Ser. A $25 par exchanged for $34.75 cash
Each share Common $2.50 par exchanged for $6.85 cash

WALWYN INC (NS)
Merged into Midland Walwyn Inc. 06/01/1990
Each (3.5) shares Common no par exchanged for (1) share Common no par
Midland Walwyn Inc. merged into Merrill Lynch & Co., Inc. 08/27/1998 which was acquired by Bank of America Corp. 01/02/2009

WAMAD ASSOCIATES
Succeeded by Boston Fund, Inc. in 1936
Details not available

WAMCO TECHNOLOGY GROUP LTD (ON)
Name changed 12/14/2000
Reincorporated 09/01/2011
Name changed from Wamco Resources Ltd. to Wamco Technology Group Ltd. 12/14/2000
Place of incorporation changed from (BC) to (ON) 09/01/2011
Each share old Common no par exchanged for (0.33333333) share new Common no par 12/09/2011
Each share new Common no par exchanged again for (0.2) share new Common no par 01/24/2017
Recapitalized as Generic Gold Corp. 03/01/2018
Each share new Common no par exchanged for (0.45454545) share Common no par

WAMEX HLDGS INC (NY)
Common $0.0001 par split (4) for (1) by issuance of (3) additional shares payable 04/06/2000 to holders of record 03/17/2000
SEC revoked common stock registration 09/19/2008

WAMPUM OILS LTD. (AB)
Struck from Alberta Registrar of Companies and declared dissolved 9/15/64

WAMPUM RES INC (AB)
Name changed to Prostar Group Inc. 11/15/1990

WAMSUTTA MILLS (MA)
Common $100 par changed to no par in 1941
Each share Common no par exchanged for (2) shares Common $5 par in 1951
Stock Dividends - 200% 11/20/50; 10% 3/15/51
Completely liquidated 12/30/58
Each share Common $5 par exchanged for first and final distribution of $10.34 cash

WANAKIRK-ROUYN MINES LTD.
Bankrupt in 1945

WANAMAX VENTURES INC (DE)
Filed Petition under Chapter 7 Federal Bankruptcy Code 3/2/92
No stockholders' equity

WANAPITEI BASIN MINES LTD.
Acquired by Sudore Gold Mines Ltd. in 1946
Details not available

WANBURY LTD (INDIA)
GDR agreement terminated 06/12/2015
Each Sponsored GDR for Reg. S exchanged for $1.361507 cash

WAND CAP CORP (ON)
Recapitalized as True North Apartment Real Estate Investment Trust 06/11/2012
Each share Common no par exchanged for (0.125) Unit
Note: Unexchanged certificates were cancelled and became without value 06/11/2018
True North Apartment Real Estate Investment Trust merged into Northview Apartment Real Estate Investment Trust 11/05/2015

WANDEL & GOLTERMANN TECHNOLOGIES INC (NC)
Issue Information - 2,000,000 shares COM offered at $11 per share on 04/07/1994
Merged into Wandel & Goltermann Management Holding GmbH 9/18/98
Each share Common 1¢ par exchanged for $15.90 cash

WANDERLUST INTERACTIVE INC (DE)
Name changed to Adrenalin Interactive Inc. 06/15/1998
Adrenalin Interactive Inc. name changed to McGlen Internet Group, Inc. 12/03/1999 which recapitalized as Northgate Innovations, Inc. 03/20/2002 which name changed to Digital Lifestyles Group, Inc. 06/25/2004 which name changed to TN-K Energy Group Inc. 10/29/2009

WANG LABS INC (MA)
Common 50¢ par split (2) for (1) by issuance of (1) additional share 11/24/69
Each share Common 50¢ par received distribution of (1) share Class B Common 50¢ par 7/30/77
Class B Common 50¢ par split (2) for (1) by issuance of (1) additional share 7/30/77
Each share Common 50¢ par received distribution of (1) share Class B Common 50¢ par 6/12/79
Class B Common 50¢ par split (2) for (1) by issuance of (1) additional share 6/12/79
Common 50¢ par reclassified as Class C Common 50¢ par 6/13/79
Class B Common 50¢ par split (2) for (1) by issuance of (1) additional share 10/31/80
Each share Class C Common 50¢ par received distribution of (1) share Class B Common 50¢ par 10/31/80
Class C Common 50¢ par reclassified as Conv. Class C Common 50¢ par 10/26/82
Class B Common 50¢ par split (2) for (1) by issuance of (1) additional share 12/30/82
Stock Dividend - Class B Common - 25% 4/29/76
Plan of reorganization under Chapter 11 Federal Bankruptcy Code effective 12/18/93
Each share Class B Common 50¢ par exchanged for (0.04347826) Wang Laboratories, Inc. (DE) Common Stock Purchase Warrant expiring 7/20/2001
Each share Conv. Class C Common 50¢ par exchanged for (0.04347826) Wang Laboratories, Inc. (DE) Common Stock Purchase Warrant expiring 7/20/2001
(See Wang Laboratories, Inc. (DE))

WANG LABS INC NEW (DE)
Merged into Getronics NV 6/24/99
Each 6.50% Depositary Conv. Preferred Ser. B exchanged for $55.05 cash
Each 6.50% Conv. Preferred Ser. B 1¢ par exchanged for $1,101.17 cash
Each share Common 50¢ par exchanged for $29.25 cash

WANGCO INC (CA)
Merged into Perkin-Elmer Corp. 06/29/1976
Each share Common 10¢ par exchanged for (0.9) share Common $1 par
Perkin-Elmer Corp. name changed to PE Corp. 05/05/1999 which name changed to Applera Corp. 11/30/2000
(See Applera Corp.)

WANGTON CAP CORP (AB)
Each share old Common no par exchanged for (0.2) share new Common no par 01/14/2013
Each share new Common no par exchanged again for (0.5) share new Common no par 12/12/2014
Reincorporated under the laws of British Columbia 03/19/2018

WANNIGAN CAP CORP (CO)
SEC revoked common stock registration 05/31/2007

WANT WANT HLDGS LTD (SINGAPORE)
ADR agreement terminated 07/10/2006
Each Sponsored ADR for Ordinary exchanged for $4.41175 cash

WANTED TECHNOLOGIES CORP (CANADA)
Acquired by CEB Inc. 11/06/2015
Each share Class A Common no par exchanged for $1.79 cash
Note: Unexchanged certificates will be cancelled and become without value 11/06/2021

WAPORA INC (DE)
Merged into Kemron Environmental Services, Inc. 4/27/93
Details not available

WAPRO GROUP INC (NV)
Recapitalized as Royal Waterlily, Inc. 07/20/2000
Each share Common $0.001 par exchanged for (0.04) share Common $0.001 par
Royal Waterlily, Inc. name changed to Royal Acquisitions & Development, Inc. 03/28/2005 which recapitalized as Innovative Health Sciences, Inc. (NV) 06/11/2008 which reincorporated in Delaware 02/24/2011 which name changed to Innovative Holdings Alliance, Inc. 05/27/2011

WAR EAGLE MINING CO., INC. (ID)
Administratively dissolved 07/07/2003

WAR EAGLE MNG INC (BC)
Each share old Common no par exchanged for (0.16666666) share new Common no par 12/31/2003
Each share new Common no par exchanged again for (0.05) share new Common no par 07/22/2011
Name changed to Warrior Gold Inc. 10/01/2018

WAR EAGLE RESOURCES LTD. (BC)
Name changed to Admiral Mines Ltd. 10/03/1966
Admiral Mines Ltd. recapitalized as Camino Resources Ltd. 09/17/1986 which recapitalized as Advanced Projects Ltd. 03/08/1991 which recapitalized as Skye Resources Inc. 05/23/2001 which was acquired by HudBay Minerals Inc. 08/26/2008

WAR VETERANS OIL & GAS CO., INC. (MT)
Charter expired by time limitation 11/29/61

WARATAH COAL INC (BC)
Acquired by Mineralogy Pty Ltd. 04/03/2009
Each share Common no par exchanged for $1.60 cash

WARATAH PHARMACEUTICALS INC (CANADA)
Acquired by Transition Therapeutics Inc. 01/15/2002
Each share Common no par exchanged for (0.83333) share Common no par
Transition Therapeutics Inc. merged into OPKO Health, Inc. 08/31/2016

WARBERN PACKAGING INDS INC (NY)
Through purchase offer 100% acquired by A&E Plastik Pak Co., Inc. 01/16/1976
Public interest eliminated

WARBURG PINCUS CAP APPRECIATION FD (MA)
Name changed to Credit Suisse Warburg Pincus Capital Appreciation Fund 03/16/2001
Credit Suisse Warburg Pincus Capital Appreciation Fund name changed to Credit Suisse Capital Appreciation Fund 12/12/2001 which name changed to Credit Suisse Large Cap Growth Fund 11/27/2006
(See Credit Suisse Large Cap Growth Fund)

WARBURG PINCUS CASH RESV FD (MD)
Name changed to Credit Suisse Warburg Pincus Cash Reserve Fund, Inc. 03/26/2001
Credit Suisse Warburg Pincus Cash Reserve Fund, Inc. name changed to Credit Suisse Cash Reserve Fund, Inc. 12/12/2001
(See Credit Suisse Cash Reserve Fund, Inc.)

WARBURG PINCUS EMERGING GROWTH FD (MD)
Name changed to Credit Suisse Emerging Growth Fund, Inc. 12/12/2001
Credit Suisse Emerging Growth Fund, Inc. name changed to Credit Suisse Mid-Cap Growth Fund, Inc. 05/01/2004 which name changed to Credit Suisse Mid-Cap Core Fund, Inc. 11/27/2006
(See Credit Suisse Mid-Cap Core Fund, Inc.)

WARBURG PINCUS EMERGING MKTS FD INC (MD)
Name changed to Credit Suisse Warburg Pincus Emerging Markets Fund, Inc. 03/26/2001
Credit Suisse Warburg Pincus Emerging Markets Fund, Inc. name changed to Credit Suisse Emerging Markets Fund, Inc. 12/12/2001
(See Credit Suisse Emerging Markets Fund, Inc.)

WARBURG PINCUS FIXED INCOME FD (MA)
Name changed to Credit Suisse Warburg Pincus Fixed Income Fund 03/26/2001
Credit Suisse Warburg Pincus Fixed Income Fund name changed to Credit Suisse Fixed Income Fund 12/12/2001
(See Credit Suisse Fixed Income Fund)

WARBURG PINCUS FOCUS FD INC (MD)
Name changed 01/01/2000
Name changed from Warburg, Pincus Select Economic Value Equity Fund, Inc. to Warburg, Pincus Focus Fund, Inc. 01/01/2000
Name changed to Credit Suisse Warburg Pincus Focus Fund, Inc. 03/26/2001
Credit Suisse Warburg Pincus Focus Fund, Inc. name changed to Credit Suisse Select Equity Fund, Inc. 12/12/2001 which name changed to Credit Suisse Large Cap Blend Fund 08/08/2005
(See Credit Suisse Large Cap Blend Fund, Inc.)

WARBURG PINCUS GLOBAL FIXED INCOME FD (MD)
Name changed to Credit Suisse Warburg Pincus Global Fixed Income Fund, Inc. 03/26/2001
Credit Suisse Warburg Pincus Global Fixed Income Fund, Inc. name changed to Credit Suisse Global Fixed Income Fund, Inc. 12/12/2001
(See Credit Suisse Global Fixed Income Fund, Inc.)

WARBURG PINCUS GLOBAL POST VENTURE CAP FD (MD)
Name changed to Credit Suisse Warburg Pincus Global Post-Venture Capital Fund, Inc. 3/26/2001
Credit Suisse Warburg Pincus Global Post-Venture Capital Fund, Inc. name changed to Credit Suisse Global Post-Venture Capital Fund, Inc. 12/12/2001 which name changed to Credit Suisse Global Small Cap Fund 2/21/2005

WARBURG PINCUS HIGH YIELD FD INC (MD)
Name changed to Credit Suisse Institutional High Yield Fund Inc. 3/26/2001
Credit Suisse Institutional High Yield Fund Inc. name changed to Credit Suisse Global High Yield Fund Inc. 2/21/2005

WARBURG PINCUS INTER MAT GOVT FD (MD)
Common Ser. 2 $0.001 par reclassified as Advisor Share $0.001 par 11/20/1996
Name changed to Credit Suisse Warburg Pincus Intermediate Maturity Government Fund, Inc. 03/06/2001
Credit Suisse Warburg Pincus Intermediate Maturity Government Fund, Inc. name changed to Credit Suisse Investment Grade Bond Fund, Inc. 11/15/2001 which merged into Credit Suisse Fixed Income Fund 10/10/2003
(See Credit Suisse Fixed Income Fund)

WARBURG PINCUS INTL EQUITY FD (MD)
Name changed to Credit Suisse Warburg Pincus International Equity Fund, Inc. and Common Ser. 2 $0.001 par reclassified as Advisor Class $0.001 par 03/06/2001
Credit Suisse Warburg Pincus International Equity Fund, Inc. name changed to Credit Suisse International Equity Fund, Inc. 12/12/2001 which merged into Credit Suisse International Focus Fund, Inc. 04/26/2002

WARBURG PINCUS JAPAN GROWTH FD INC (MD)
Name changed to Credit Suisse Warburg Pincus Japan Growth Fund, Inc. 03/26/2001
Credit Suisse Warburg Pincus Japan Growth Fund, Inc. name changed to Credit Suisse Japan Growth Fund, Inc. 12/12/2001 which name changed to Credit Suisse Japan Equity Fund, Inc. 05/27/2003
(See Credit Suisse Japan Equity Fund, Inc.)

WARBURG PINCUS MAJOR FOREIGN MKTS FD INC (MD)
Name changed 2/9/98
Name changed from Warburg, Pincus Managed EAFE Countries Fund, Inc. to Warburg, Pincus Major Foreign Markets Fund, Inc. 2/9/98
Name changed to Credit Suisse Warburg Pincus Major Foreign Markets Fund, Inc. 3/26/2001
Credit Suisse Warburg Pincus Major Foreign Markets Fund, Inc. name changed to Credit Suisse International Focus Fund, Inc. 12/12/2001

WARBURG PINCUS N Y MUN BD FD (MA)
Name changed to Credit Suisse Warburg Pincus New York Intermediate Municipal Fund 02/28/1995
Credit Suisse Warburg Pincus New York Intermediate Municipal Fund name changed to Credit Suisse New York Municipal Fund 12/12/2001
(See Credit Suisse New York Municipal Fund)

WARBURG PINCUS SMALL CO GROWTH FD INC (MD)
Name changed to Credit Suisse Warburg Pincus Small Company Growth Fund, Inc. 3/26/2001
Credit Suisse Warburg Pincus Small Company Growth Fund, Inc. name changed to Credit Suisse Small Cap Growth Fund, Inc. 12/12/2001

WARBURG PINCUS TR II (MD)
Name changed to Credit Suisse Warburg Pincus Trust II 3/26/2001

WARBURTON MINERALS INC (BC)
Reincorporated under the laws of Canada as APP Applied Polymer Products Inc. 02/23/1987
(See APP Applied Polymer Products Inc.)

WARCHEL CORP.
Recapitalized as Automatic Products Corp. (IL) 00/00/1933
Details not available

WARD BAKING CO (NY)
Preferred $100 par changed to $50 par in 1942
Recapitalized in 1945
Each share $7 Preferred $50 par exchanged for (0.25) share 5-1/2% Preferred $100 par, (2.5) shares Common $1 par and $25 in debentures
Each share Class A no par exchanged for (1) share Common $1 par and (1) Common Stock Purchase Warrant
Each share Class B no par received (1) Common Stock Purchase Warrant
Under plan of merger name changed to Ward Foods, Inc. 5/22/64
(See Ward Foods, Inc.)

WARD BAKING CORP.
Merged into Ward Baking Co. in 1938
Details not available

WARD CUT RATE DRUG CO (DE)
Merged into Eckerd (Jack) Corp. 09/01/1973
Each share Common $1 par exchanged for (0.5) share Common 10¢ par
(See Eckerd (Jack) Corp.)

WARD ELECTRIC REFRIGERATOR CORP.
Liquidated in 1928

WARD FOODS INC (NY)
5-1/2% Preferred $100 par called for redemption 11/16/1967
Acquired by Terson Co. 12/31/1980
Each share Common $1 par exchanged for $13 cash

WARD INDUSTRIES CORP. (DE)
Name changed to Dragor Shipping Corp. 8/14/64
Dragor Shipping Corp. merged into American Export Industries, Inc. 10/17/67 which name changed to Aeicor, Inc. 3/31/78 which name changed to Doskocil Companies Inc. 9/30/83 which name changed to Foodbrands America Inc. 5/15/95 which merged into IBP, Inc. 5/7/97 which merged into Tyson Foods, Inc. 9/28/2001

WARD LA FRANCE TRUCK CORP.
Liquidated in 1942

WARD LAKE GOLD MINES LTD. (ON)
Charter cancelled by Province of Ontario by default in 1948

WARD-LEE CHEMICAL CORP. (CA)
Declared defunct and inoperative for failure to pay taxes and file annual reports 7/1/60

WARD LEONARD ELEC CO (NY)
Each share Capital Stock no par exchanged for (10) shares Capital Stock $4 par 00/00/1944
Stock Dividend - 10% 04/15/1957
Merged into Riker-Maxson Corp. 02/13/1970
Each share Capital Stock $4 par exchanged for (1.2) shares Common 25¢ par
Riker-Maxson Corp. recapitalized as Unimax Group, Inc. 09/02/1975 which name changed to Unimax Corp. 09/11/1980
(See Unimax Corp.)

WARD MOTOR VEHICLE CO. (NY)
Dissolved 6/30/65

WARD SAMUEL MFG INC (MA)
Proclaimed dissolved for failure to file reports and pay taxes 10/19/1983

WARD TOM ENTERPRISES INC (NY)
Charter cancelled and proclaimed dissolved for failure to file reports and pay fees 12/15/1973

WARD WHITE GROUP PLC (ENGLAND)
Acquired by Boots Co. PLC 12/11/1989
Each ADR for Ordinary 25p par exchanged for $21.80395 cash
Each ADR for Ordinary 25p par received late payment compensation of approximately $0.20 cash 03/12/1990

WARDAIR CANADA LTD. (AB)
Name changed to Wardair Intenational Ltd. 6/10/76
Wardair International Ltd. merged into Wardair Inc. 9/4/87 which was acquired by PWA Corp. 5/30/89 which recapitalized as Canadian Airlines Corp. 5/11/95
(See Canadian Airlines Corp.)

WARDAIR INC (CANADA)
Acquired by PWA Corp. 5/30/89
Each share Conv. Class A Subordinate no par exchanged for (0.42323) share Common no par and $10 cash
Each share Conv. Class B no par exchanged for (0.42323) share Common no par and $10 cash
PWA Corp. recapitalized as Canadian Airlines Corp. 5/11/95
(See Canadian Airlines Corp.)

WARDAIR INTL LTD (AB)
Each share old Common no par exchanged for (0.5) share Class A no par and (0.5) share Conv. Class B no par 12/22/83
Class A no par reclassified as new Common no par 7/13/84
Conv. Class B no par reclassified as new Common no par 7/13/84
Merged into Wardair Inc. 9/4/87
Each share Common no par exchanged for (2) shares Conv. Class B no par
Wardair Inc. acquired by PWA Corp. 5/30/89 which recapitalized as Canadian Airlines Corp. 5/11/95
(See Canadian Airlines Corp.)

WARDEAN DRILLING CO. LTD. (ON)
Completely liquidated 5/4/89
Each share Common no par exchanged for first and final distribution of $0.4686 cash

WARDELL CORP. (MI)
Common $5 par changed to $1 par in 1954
Merged into Amerace Corp. 5/29/57
Each share Common $1 par exchanged for (0.275) share Common $12.50 par
Amerace Corp. name changed to Amerace Esna Corp. 8/30/68 which name changed back to Amerace Corp. 4/27/73
(See Amerace Corp.)

WARDLEE GOLD MINES LTD. (ON)
Charter cancelled for failure to file reports and pay taxes 5/26/58

WARDLEY CHINA INVT TR (BC)
Liquidation completed
Each Trust Unit no par received initial distribution of $4 cash payable 01/29/1999 to holders of record 01/05/1999
Each Trust Unit no par received second distribution of $1 cash payable 11/30/1999 to holders of record 11/15/1999
Each Trust Unit no par received third distribution of $1 cash payable 03/15/2000 to holders of record 12/31/1999
Each Trust Unit no par received fourth distribution of $1.16 cash 09/27/2000
Each Trust Unit no par received fifth distribution of $0.169 cash payable 03/15/2001 to holders of record 12/31/2000
Each Trust Unit received sixth distribution of $0.50 cash payable 08/24/2001 to holders of record 08/10/2001
Each Trust Unit received seventh and final distribution of $0.35230474 cash payable 08/26/2005 to holders of record 08/10/2005
Note: Certificates were not required to be exchanged and are without value

WARDS INC (VA)
Common $1 par split (3) for (2) by issuance of (1) additional share 02/28/1966
5-1/2% Conv. Preferred $20 par called for redemption 05/19/1978
Common $1 par split (2) for (1) by issuance of (1) additional share 08/14/1981
Common $1 par split (3) for (2) by issuance of (0.5) additional share 02/28/1983
Common $1 par split (3) for (1) by issuance of (2) additional shares 11/14/1983
Stock Dividend - 10% 11/05/1964
Name changed to Circuit City Stores, Inc. 06/21/1984
(See Circuit City Stores, Inc.)

WARE RES LTD (BC)
Recapitalized as World Enzymes Ltd. 06/20/1988
Each share Capital Stock no par exchanged for (1) share Capital Stock no par
(See World Enzymes Ltd.)

WARE RIVER RAILROAD CO. (MA)
Merged into New York Central Railroad Co. (DE) 4/3/61
Each share Capital Stock $100 par exchanged for $125 principal amount of 5-3/4% Coll. Trust Bonds due 1/1/80

WARE SHOALS MANUFACTURING CO.
Merged into Riegel Textile Corp. on a (4.2) for (1) basis in 1946
(See Riegel Textile Corp.)

WARE SOLUTIONS CORP (AB)
Merged into BCE Emergis Inc. 01/16/2004
Each share Common no par exchanged for $0.2848 cash

WARE TR CO (WARE, MA)
Acquired by T.N.B. Financial Corp. 5/31/75
Each share Common $100 par exchanged for (27) shares Common $1 par 5/31/75
T.N.B. Financial Corp. merged into New England Merchants Co., Inc. 9/30/81 which name changed to Bank of New England Corp. 5/1/82
(See Bank of New England Corp.)

WAREFORCE COM INC (NV)
Name changed 1/26/99
Name changed from Wareforce One Inc. to Wareforce.Com Inc. 1/26/99
Plan of reorganization under Chapter 11 Federal Bankruptcy Code effective 10/27/2003
No stockholders' equity

WAREHOUSE & TERMS CORP (MI)
Acquired by Central Detroit Warehouse Co. 06/11/1970
Each share Common $1 par exchanged for (1) share Common $1 par
(See Central Detroit Warehouse Co.)

WAREHOUSE AUTO CTRS INC (DE)
Recapitalized as Newgold, Inc. 11/21/1996
Each (65) shares Common $0.005 par exchanged for (1) share Common $0.005 par
Newgold, Inc. name changed to Firstgold Corp. 12/08/2006
(See Firstgold Corp.)

WAREHOUSE CLUB INC (DE)
SEC revoked common stock registration 07/30/2009

WARKA CAP CORP (AB)
Recapitalized as Nevada Bob's Canada Inc. 9/12/97
Each share Common no par exchanged for (0.4) share Common no par
Nevada Bob's Canada Inc. name changed to Nevada Bob's Golf Inc. 10/5/99
(See Nevada Bob's Golf Inc.)

WARLOCK COMPUTER CORP (DE)
Name changed to W-C Industries, Inc. 10/1/73
(See W-C Industries, Inc.)

WARLOCK HLDGS INC (ON)
Reincorporated under the laws of Nevada as Professional Services Network, Inc. and Preferred no par and Common no par changed to $0.001 par 09/24/2003
(See Professional Services Network, Inc.)

WARLUND MINES LTD. (ON)
Liquidation completed
Each share Capital Stock no par received initial distribution of $0.14 cash in 1950
Each share Capital Stock no par exchanged for second and final distribution of $0.0125 cash in September 1960

WARNACO CDA LTD (CANADA)
Acquired by C.F. Hathaway Co. and Warnaco Men's Sportwear Inc. 05/03/1985
Each share Common no par exchanged for $30 cash

WARNACO GROUP INC (DE)
Class A Common 1¢ par split (2) for (1) by issuance of (1) additional share 10/03/1994
Plan of reorganization under Chapter 11 Federal Bankruptcy Code effective 02/04/2003
No Class A Common stockholders' equity
Merged into PVH Corp. 02/13/2013
Each share Common 1¢ par exchanged for (0.1822) share Common $1 par and $51.75 cash

WARNACO INC (CT)
$1.225 Conv. Preferred no par called for redemption 01/02/1969
Common no par split (3) for (2) by issuance of (0.5) additional share 05/28/1969
$1.50 Conv. Preferred no par called for redemption 12/20/1982
$1.10 Conv. Preferred Ser. A no par called for redemption 01/17/1983
Common no par split (2) for (1) by issuance of (1) additional share 06/02/1983
$3 Non-Cum. Preferred no par called for redemption 01/20/1986
Merged into W Acquisition Corp. 05/22/1986
Each share Common no par exchanged for $46.50 cash

WARNER (WILLIAM R.) & CO., INC.
Name changed to Warner-Hudnut, Inc. in 1950
Warner-Hudnut, Inc. name changed to Warner-Lambert Pharmaceutical Co. 3/31/55 which name changed to Warner-Lambert Co. 11/13/70 which merged into Pfizer Co. 6/19/2000

WARNER & SWASEY CO (OH)
Each share Common $5 par exchanged for (3) shares Common no par 08/20/1940
Common no par changed to $1 par 04/07/1954
Common $1 par split (2) for (1) by issuance of (1) additional share 12/18/1963
Common $1 par split (5) for (4) by issuance of (0.25) additional share 10/13/1965
Common $1 par split (5) for (4) by issuance of (0.25) additional share 07/13/1967
Merged into Bendix Corp. 03/31/1980
Each share Common $1 par exchanged for (2) shares 9.75% Conv. Preferred Ser. B no par

WARNER AIRCRAFT CORP.
Acquired by Clinton Machine Co. in 1950
Each share Capital Stock $1 par exchanged for (2) shares Common $1 par
Clinton Machine Co. name changed to Clinton Engines Corp. 2/28/58
(See Clinton Engines Corp.)

WARNER BROS SEVEN ARTS LTD (ON)
Acquired by Kinney National Service, Inc. 07/08/1969
Each share Common no par exchanged for (0.81) share $1.25 Conv. Preferred Ser. D $1 par and (0.8) share 5¢ Conv. Preferred Ser. C $1 par
Kinney National Service, Inc. name changed to Kinney Services, Inc. 02/17/1971 which reincorporated in Delaware as Warner Communications Inc. 02/11/1972
(See Warner Communications Inc.)

WARNER BROTHERS CO. (CT)
6% Preferred no par called for redemption 7/1/65
Name changed to Warnaco Inc. 1/9/68
(See Warnaco Inc.)

WARNER BROTHERS PICTURES, INC. (DE)
Common no par changed to old Common $5 par 00/00/1932
Each share old Common $5 par exchanged for (0.5) share new Common $5 par and (0.5) share Warner (Stanley) Corp. Common $5 par 00/00/1953
(See Warner (Stanley) Corp.)
New Common $5 par changed to $1.25 par and (3) additional shares issued 03/02/1962
Stock Dividend - 100% 08/26/1946
Merged into Warner-Bros.-Seven Arts Ltd. 07/15/1967
Each share Common $1.25 par exchanged for $10 principal amount of 5% Subord. Conv. Debentures due 07/14/1988, (0.333333) share Common no par and $5 cash
Warner-Bros.-Seven Arts Ltd. acquired by Kinney National Service, Inc. 07/08/1969 which name changed to Kinney Services, Inc. (NY) 02/17/1971 which reincorporated in Delaware as Warner Communications Inc. 02/11/1972
(See Warner Communications Inc.)

WARNER CENTER BANK (WOODLAND HILLS, CA)
Merged into City National Corp. 06/29/1990
Each share Common no par exchanged for (0.66666666) share Common $1 par
City National Corp. merged into Royal Bank of Canada (Montreal, QC) 11/02/2015

WARNER CHILCOTT LTD (BERMUDA)
Issue Information - 70,600,000 shares CL A COM offered at $15 per share on 09/20/2006
Reincorporated under the laws of Ireland as Warner Chilcott PLC (New) and Class A Common 1¢ par reclassified as Ordinary 1¢ par 08/20/2009
Warner Chilcott PLC (New) merged into Actavis PLC 10/01/2013

WARNER CHILCOTT PLC (IRELAND)
Ctfs. dated prior to 09/29/2000
Issue Information - 3,500,000 ADR'S offered at $17.50 per ADR on 08/08/1997
Merged into Galen Holdings PLC 09/29/2000
Each Sponsored ADR 5¢ par exchanged for (0.625) Sponsored ADR no par
Galen Holdings PLC name changed to Warner Chilcott PLC (Old) 06/28/2004
(See Warner Chilcott PLC (Old))

WARNER CHILCOTT PLC NEW (IRELAND)
Merged into Actavis PLC 10/01/2013
Each share Ordinary 1¢ par exchanged for (0.16) share Ordinary EUR $0.0001 par

WARNER CHILCOTT PLC OLD (IRELAND)
Merged into Waren Acquisition Ltd. 01/05/2005
Each Sponsored ADR for Ordinary exchanged for $64.55 cash

WARNER CO (DE)
Each share $7 1st Preferred no par exchanged for (1) share 7% 1st Preferred $50 par and (2) shares Common $1 par 00/00/1934
Each share Common no par exchanged for (0.2) share Common $1 par 00/00/1934
Common $1 par changed to $10 par and (1) additional share issued 12/31/1958
Common $10 par changed to $3.33-1/3 par and (2) additional shares issued 05/15/1972
Stock Dividend - 10% 12/27/1961
Merged into EMW Corp. 01/23/1978
Each share Common $3.33-1/3 par exchanged for $15.75 cash

WARNER COLLIERIES CO. (DE)
Each share Common no par exchanged for (5) shares Common $10 par 3/10/49
Merged into North American Coal Corp. 6/1/59
Each share Common $10 par exchanged for (0.75) share Common $1 par
North American Coal Corp. reorganized in Delaware as NACCO Industries, Inc. 6/6/86

WARNER COMMUNICATIONS INC (DE)
$4.25 Conv. Preferred Ser. B $1 par called for redemption 05/22/1978
Common $1 par split (4) for (3) by issuance of (0.33333333) additional share 03/30/1979
7% Conv. Preferred Ser. C $1 par called for redemption 08/03/1979

$1.25 Conv. Preferred Ser. D $1 par called for redemption 01/07/1980
Common $1 par split (4) for (3) by issuance of (0.33333333) additional share 03/28/1980
Common $1 par split (2) for (1) by issuance of (1) additional share 01/09/1981
Common $1 par split (2) for (1) by issuance of (1) additional share 08/22/1986
$3.625 Conv. Exchangeable Preferred Ser. A $1 par called for redemption 04/26/1989
Conv. Preferred Ser. C $1 par called for redemption 05/31/1989
Merged into Time Warner Inc. 01/10/1990
Each share Common $1 par exchanged for (0.7188774) share 8.75% Conv. Exchangeable Depositary Preferred Ser. C, (0.5421044) share 11% Conv. Exchangeable Depositary Preferred Ser. D and (0.15166) share BHC Communications, Inc. Class A Common 1¢ par
Time Warner Inc. (Old) merged into AOL Time Warner Inc. 01/11/2001 which name changed to Time Warner Inc. (New) 10/16/2003 which merged into AT&T Inc. 06/15/2018

WARNER COMPUTER SYS INC (DE)
Reincorporated 04/22/1985
State of incorporation changed from (NY) to (DE) 04/22/1985
Name changed to Warner Insurance Services, Inc. 03/19/1992
Warner Insurance Services, Inc. name changed to Cover-All Technologies Inc. 06/21/1996 which merged into Majesco 06/26/2015

WARNER (STANLEY) CORP. (DE)
Common $5 par split (2) for (1) by issuance of (1) additional share 3/10/67
Merged into Glen Alden Corp. (DE) 12/22/67
Each share Common $5 par exchanged for (0.55) share $3 Class B Conv. Preferred no par
Glen Alden Corp. (DE) merged into Rapid-American Corp. (DE) 11/6/72
(See Rapid-American Corp. (DE))

WARNER E C INVTS LTD (BC)
Each share Class A Common no par or Class B Common no par exchanged for (5) shares Common no par 10/2/73
Merged into Ardiem Industrial Corp. 1/2/76
Each share Common no par exchanged for (1) share Class A no par
(See Ardiem Industrial Corp.)

WARNER ELEC BRAKE & CLUTCH CO (DE)
Common $1 par split (5) for (4) by issuance of (0.25) additional share 6/30/64
Common $1 par split (3) for (2) by issuance of (0.5) additional share 3/31/65
Common $1 par split (3) for (2) by issuance of (0.5) additional share 3/31/66
Stock Dividends - 25% 6/30/65; 50% 1/2/78; 100% 6/1/81
Merged into Dana Corp. 1/25/85
Each share Common $1 par exchanged for $30 cash

WARNER ELECTRIC BRAKE & CLUTCH CO. (IL)
Common no par changed to $1 par 7/29/60
Stock Dividend - 25% 6/30/62
Reincorporated under the laws of Delaware 2/11/63
(See Warner Electric Brake & Clutch Co. (Del.))

WARNER ELECTRIC BRAKE MANUFACTURING CO.
Name changed to Warner Electric Brake & Clutch Co. (Ill.) in 1950
Warner Electric Brake & Clutch Co. (Ill.) reincorporated in Delaware 2/11/63
(See Warner Electric Brake & Clutch Co. (Del.))

WARNER GEAR CO.
Merged into Borg-Warner Corp. (IL) 00/00/1928
Details not available

WARNER-HUDNUT, INC. (DE)
Each share Class A Common or Class B Common no par exchanged for (3) shares Common $1 par in 1951 6% 1st Preferred called for redemption 12/31/54
Under plan of merger name changed to Warner-Lambert Pharmaceutical Co. 3/31/55
Warner-Lambert Pharmaceutical Co. name changed to Warner-Lambert Co. 11/13/70 which merged into Pfizer Co. 6/19/2000

WARNER INS SVCS INC (DE)
Common 1¢ par split (5) for (4) by issuance of (0.25) additional share 05/05/1993
Name changed to Cover-All Technologies Inc. 06/21/1996
Cover-All Technologies Inc. merged into Majesco 06/26/2015

WARNER LAKE MINES LTD. (CANADA)
Charter cancelled for failure to file returns 2/26/37

WARNER LAMBERT CO (DE)
Common $1 par split (2) for (1) by issuance of (1) additional share 6/8/73
Common $1 par split (2) for (1) by issuance of (1) additional share 5/16/90
Common $1 par split (2) for (1) by issuance of (1) additional share payable 5/17/96 to holders of record 5/3/96 Ex date - 5/20/96
Common $1 par split (3) for (1) by issuance of (2) additional shares payable 5/22/98 to holders of record 5/8/98 Ex date - 5/26/98
Merged into Pfizer Inc. 6/19/2000
Each share Common $1 par exchanged for (2.75) shares Common 5¢ par

WARNER LAMBERT PHARMACEUTICAL CO (DE)
Common $1 par split (2) for (1) by issuance of (1) additional share 6/10/59
Common $1 par split (3) for (1) by issuance of (2) additional shares 6/12/62
$4 Conv. Preferred $100 par called for redemption 12/30/68
Under plan of merger name changed to Warner-Lambert Co. 11/13/70
Warner-Lambert Co. merged into Pfizer Inc. 6/19/2000

WARNER-LONDON, INC. (SC)
Involuntarily dissolved for failure to file reports and pay taxes 10/10/86

WARNER MUSIC GROUP CORP (DE)
Issue Information - 32,600,000 shares COM offered at $17 per share on 05/10/2005
Acquired by Airplanes Music L.L.C. 07/20/2011
Each share Common $0.001 par exchanged for $8.25 cash

WARNER NATL CORP (IN)
Each share Common $1 par exchanged for (0.008) share Common $125 par 12/24/1976
Note: In effect holders received $4.50 cash per share and public interest was eliminated

WARNER OILS LTD. (CANADA)
Recapitalized as Western Warner Oils Ltd. 1/25/54
Each share Common no par exchanged for (0.5) share Capital Stock no par

WARNER-QUINLAN CO. (ME)
Reorganized as Cities Service Asphalt Products Co. in 1937
No stockholders' equity

WARNER RANCH CO., INC. (CA)
Dissolved 5/7/64

WARNER TECHNOLOGIES INC (NV)
Each share Common $0.001 par exchanged for (0.025) share Common 4¢ par 8/24/90
Name changed to MGPX Ventures Inc. 4/22/98
MGPX Ventures Inc. name changed to Contango Oil & Gas Co. (NV) 10/7/99 which reorganized in Delaware 12/1/2000

WARNER VENTURES LTD (BC)
Recapitalized as Copper Ridge Explorations Inc. 10/06/1998
Each share Common no par exchanged for (0.25) share Common no par
Copper Ridge Explorations Inc. name changed to Redtail Metals Corp. 05/31/2011 which merged into Golden Predator Mining Corp. (AB) 04/22/2014 which reincorporated in British Columbia 10/21/2015

WARNEX INC (CANADA)
Each share old Common no par exchanged for (0.25) share new Common no par 12/27/2012
Merged into Diagnos Inc. 07/11/2014
Each share new Common no par exchanged for (1) share Common no par and (0.5) Common Stock Purchase Warrant expiring 07/21/2015

WARNEX PHARMA INC (CANADA)
Name changed to Warnex Inc. 07/24/2001
Warnex Inc. merged into Diagnos Inc. 07/11/2014

WARNIC 1 ENTERPRISES LTD (BC)
Merged into Cumberland Oil & Gas Ltd. 02/26/2010
Each share Common no par exchanged for (0.3032) share Common no par
Note: Unexchanged certificates were cancelled and became without value 02/26/2015
Cumberland Oil & Gas Ltd. merged into Kallisto Energy Corp. 10/15/2012 which name changed to Toro Oil & Gas Ltd. 11/25/2014
(See Toro Oil & Gas Ltd.)

WARNING MGMT SVCS INC (NY)
Name changed 09/27/2004
Name changed from Warning Model Management, Inc. to Warning Management Services, Inc. 09/27/2004
SEC revoked common stock registration 05/22/2009
Stockholders' equity unlikely

WARNOCK HERSEY INTL LTD (CANADA)
Under plan of merger each share Common no par exchanged for (1) share Common no par 07/02/1968
Under plan of merger name changed to TIW Industries Ltd.-Les Industries TIW Ltee. 12/31/1977
(See TIW Industries Ltd.-Les Industries TIW Ltee.)

WARP 9 INC (NV)
Each share old Common $0.001 par exchanged for (0.5) share new Common $0.001 par 07/07/2011
Name changed to CloudCommerce, Inc. 09/30/2015

WARP TECHNOLOGY HLDGS INC (NV)
Old Common $0.00001 par split (4) for (1) by issuance of (3) additional shares payable 10/02/2002 to holders of record 09/24/2002 Ex date - 10/03/2002
Each share old Common $0.00001 par exchanged for (0.01) share new Common $0.00001 par 11/18/2004
Name changed to Halo Technology Holdings, Inc. 04/03/2006
(See Halo Technology Holdings, Inc.)

WARP 10 TECHNOLOGIES INC (ON)
Name changed to Brandera.Com Inc. 01/19/2000
Brandera.Com Inc. recapitalized as BrandEra Inc. 04/23/2001 which name changed to National Construction Inc. 05/16/2002 which name changed to E.G. Capital Inc. 03/16/2005 which recapitalized as Quantum International Income Corp. 03/14/2014

WARPRADIO COM INC (NV)
SEC revoked common stock registration 07/25/2008

WARRANT CORP.
Merged into Equity Corp. 00/00/1931
Details not available

WARRANTECH CORP (NV)
Reincorporated 6/15/2005
Each share Common $0.0007 par exchanged exchanged for (0.1) share Common $0.007 par 8/3/90
State of incorporation changed from (DE) to (NV) 6/15/2005
Merged into WT Acquisition Holdings, LLC 1/31/2007
Each share Common $0.007 par exchanged for $0.75 cash

WARREN AXE & TOOL CO.
Sold to Collins Co. in 1950
(See listing for Collins Co.)

WARREN BANCORP INC (MA)
Reincorporated 05/10/1995
State of incorporation changed from (DE) to (MA) 05/10/1995
Common 10¢ par split (2) for (1) by issuance of (1) additional share payable 05/12/1998 to holders of record 04/27/1998
Merged into Banknorth Group, Inc. (ME) 12/31/2002
Each share Common 10¢ par exchanged for either (0.7012) share Common 1¢ par or $15.75 cash
Note: Option to receive stock expired 01/27/2003
Banknorth Group, Inc. (ME) merged into TD Banknorth Inc. 03/01/2005
(See TD Banknorth Inc.)

WARREN BANCORP INC (MI)
Company's sole asset placed in receivership 10/02/2009
Stockholders' equity unlikely

WARREN BANK & TRUST CO. (WARREN, PA)
Stock Dividend - 66-2/3% 2/27/52
Merged into Pennsylvania Bank & Trust Co. (Titusville, Pa.) for cash 5/3/63

WARREN BK (WARREN, MI)
Reorganized as Kasco Financial Corp. 12/31/81
Each share Common $5 par exchanged for (1) share Common $10 par
Kasco Financial Corp. merged into Huntington Bancshares Inc. 11/28/86
Preferred $50 par called for redemption 6/15/87

WARREN BRADSHAW EXPLORATION CO. (OK)
Assets sold and each share Common $1 par received (0.3421053) share of Sunset International Petroleum Corp. Common $1 par and cash 5/1/59

WARREN BROTHERS CO. (DE)
Common $10 par changed to $5 par and (1) additional share issued 8/12/65
Completely liquidated 8/25/66
Each share Common $5 par exchanged for first and final distribution of (0.54) share Ashland Oil & Refining Co. $2.40 Conv. Preferred 1966 Ser. no par
Ashland Oil & Refining Co. name changed to Ashland Oil, Inc. 2/2/70 which name changed to Ashland Inc. (Old) 1/27/95
(See Ashland Inc. (Old))

WARREN BROTHERS CO. (WV)
Each share 1st Preferred $50 par exchanged for (3) shares 1st Preferred no par in 1930
Each share 2nd Preferred $50 par exchanged for (3) shares 2nd Preferred no par in 1930
Common no par exchanged (3) for (1) in 1930
Each share 1st Preferred no par exchanged for (1) share Class A no par in 1942
Each share 2nd Preferred no par exchanged for (1) share Class A no par in 1942
Each share $3 Preferred no par exchanged for (1) share Class B no par and (2.9) shares Class C no par in 1942
Each share Common no par exchanged for (0.25) share Class C no par in 1942
Class B no par reclassified as Preferred $50 par in 1949
Class C no par reclassified as Common $5 par in 1949
Common $5 par changed to $10 par and (1) additional share issued 5/27/60
Under plan of merger reincorporated under the laws of Delaware 3/31/64
Warren Brothers Co. (DE) acquired by Ashland Oil & Refining Co. 8/25/66 which name changed to Ashland Oil, Inc. 2/2/70 which name changed to Ashland Inc. (Old) 1/27/95
(See Ashland Inc. (Old))

WARREN (S.D.) CO. (MA)
Common no par split (2) for (1) by issuance of (1) additional share 3/9/60
$4.50 Preferred no par called for redemption 4/27/67
Stock Dividends - 300% 2/28/47; 100% 4/20/51; 10% 12/1/56; 10% 11/3/66
Merged into Scott Paper Co. 5/17/67
Each share Common no par exchanged for (2.05) shares Common no par
Scott Paper Co. merged into Kimberly Clark Corp. 12/12/95

WARREN (J.C.) CORP. (NY)
Charter revoked for failure to file reports and pay fees 12/15/65

WARREN EXPLS LTD (ON)
Recapitalized as Paragon Petroleum Ltd. 06/30/1988
Each share Common no par exchanged for (0.125) share Common no par
Paragon Petroleum Ltd. merged into Paragon Petroleum Corp. 01/01/1991
(See Paragon Petroleum Corp.)

WARREN FIVE CENTS SVGS BK (PEABODY, MA)
Under plan of reorganization each share Common 10¢ par automatically became (1) share Warren Bancorp, Inc. Common 10¢ par 08/01/1988
Warren Bancorp, Inc. reincorporated under the laws of Massachusetts 05/10/1995

WARREN FOUNDRY & PIPE CORP. (DE)
Common no par changed to $2.50 par and (3) additional shares issued 02/27/1956
Name changed to Shahmoon Industries, Inc. 05/15/1956
Shahmoon Industries, Inc. name changed to Shire National Corp. 01/02/1973 which name changed to Stacy Industries, Inc. 06/20/1985
(See Stacy Industries, Inc.)

WARREN GORHAM & LAMONT INC (GA)
Each share Common 1¢ par exchanged for (0.05) share Common 20¢ par 07/31/1974
Merged into General Publishing Co. 08/14/1975
Each share Common 20¢ par exchanged for $17 cash

WARREN JOHNSON'S, INC. (MN)
See - Johnson's (Warren), Inc.

WARREN NATL BK (WARREN, PA)
Each share Common $100 par exchanged for (4) shares Common $25 par 02/26/1954
Common $25 par changed to $12.50 par and (1) additional share issued 03/15/1972
Common $12.50 par changed to $6.25 par and (1) additional share issued 04/12/1977
Stock Dividends - 20% 12/01/1958; 10% 11/15/1962; 10% 03/01/1966; 10% 03/02/1970
Merged into Marine Bancorp, Inc. 07/01/1982
Each share Common $6.25 par exchanged for (3) shares $2.20 Conv. Preferred Ser. A no par
Marine Bancorp, Inc. (PA) merged into PNC Financial Corp. 01/23/1984 which name changed to PNC Bank Corp. 02/08/1993 which name changed to PNC Financial Services Group, Inc. 03/15/2000

WARREN OHIO TELEPHONE CO.
Liquidated in 1938

WARREN PETROLEUM CORP. (DE)
Each share Common no par exchanged for (1.5) shares Common $5 par in 1945
Each share Common $5 par exchanged for (2) shares Common $3 par in 1947
3-3/4% Preferred called for redemption 2/9/48
Acquired by Gulf Oil Corp. 10/30/56
Each share Common $3 par exchanged for (0.8) share Capital Stock $25 par
Gulf Oil Co. reorganized in Delaware as Gulf Corp. 1/18/84
(See Gulf Corp.)

WARREN PUMPS INC (MA)
Under plan of merger each share old Common $5 par exchanged for (0.9848) share new Common $5 par 01/31/1969
98% held by Houdaille Industries, Inc. and 2% by individual as of 07/20/1973
Public interest eliminated

WARREN RAILROAD CO.
Merged into Delaware, Lackawanna & Western Railroad Co. and each share Capital Stock $50 par exchanged for $50 principal amount of 4%-6% bonds in 1946

WARREN-RANDALL CORP (UT)
Reorganized under the laws of Nevada as Pacific Snax Corp. 06/23/1994
Each (3.5) shares Common $0.001 par exchanged for (1) share Class A Common $0.0035 par
(See Pacific Snax Corp.)

WARREN REFNG & CHEM CO (OH)
Name changed to 5151 Corp. 9/6/67

(See 5151 Corp.)

WARREN RES INC (MD)
Reincorporated 09/05/2002
Reincorporated 07/07/2004
State of incorporation changed from (NY) to (DE) 9/5/2002
State of incorporation changed from (DE) to (MD) 07/07/2004
Plan of reorganization under Chapter 11 Federal Bankruptcy proceedings effective 10/05/2016
No stockholders' equity

WARREN STEAM PUMP INC (MA)
Merged into Warren Pumps, Inc. 01/31/1969
Each share Common no par exchanged for (1) share Common $5 par
(See Warren Pumps, Inc)

WARREN TED FD (CA)
Name changed back to California Mutual Fund 5/9/73
(See California Mutual Fund)

WARREN TELEPHONE CO. (OH)
$5 Preferred no par called for redemption 07/01/1967
Acquired by United Utilities, Inc. 07/03/1967
Each share Common no par exchanged for (0.2) share Common $2.50 par
United Utilities, Inc. name changed to United Telecommunications, Inc. 06/02/1972 which name changed to Spint Corp. (KS) 02/26/1992 which name changed to Sprint Nextel Corp. 08/12/2005 which merged into Sprint Corp. (DE) 07/10/2013

WARREN TOOL & FORGE CO.
Property sold to Warren Tool Corp. in 1932
(See Warren Tool Corp.)

WARREN TOOL CORP (OH)
Preferred no par called for redemption 06/30/1978
Public interest eliminated

WARREN TOWNSHIP, ST. JOSEPH COUNTY, SCHOOL BUILDING CORP. (IN)
Completely liquidated for cash in April, 1963

WARRINGTON INC (CANADA)
Recapitalized as Canstar Sports Inc. 9/12/88
Each share Common no par exchanged for (0.05) share Common no par
(See Canstar Sports Inc.)

WARRINGTON PRODUCTS LTD. (ON)
8% Non-Cum. Conv. Preference $4.50 par called for redemption 9/1/71
Reincorporated under the laws of Canada as Warrington Inc. 5/22/81
Warrington Inc. recapitalized as Canstar Sports Inc. 9/12/88
(See Canstar Sports Inc.)

WARRIOR ENERGY N V (NETHERLANDS)
Each share old Common EUR 0.15 par exchanged for (0.2) share new Common EUR 0.15 par 01/20/2012
Name changed to Summus Solutions N.V. 11/16/2012

WARRIOR ENERGY SVCS CORP (DE)
Merged into Superior Energy Services, Inc. 12/12/2006
Each share Common $0.005 par exchanged for (0.452) share Common $0.001 par and $14.50 cash

WARRIOR INDS LTD (BC)
Struck off register and declared dissolved for failure to file returns 09/09/1994

WARRIOR RES LTD (BC)
Name changed to Warrior Industries Ltd. 12/19/1986
(See Warrior Industries Ltd.)

WARSAW BREWING CORP (IL)
Common no par changed to $1 par 04/21/1954
Involuntarily dissolved 10/01/1973

WARSHOW H & SONS INC (DE)
Reincorporated 11/12/1975
Class A $1 par reclassified as Common $1 par 10/23/1968
State of incorporation changed from (NY) to (DE) 11/12/1975
Merged into HW&S, Inc. 05/16/1977
Each share Common $1 par exchanged for $5 cash

WARSTAR RES INC (BC)
Struck off register and declared dissolved for failure to file returns 5/14/92

WARWICK CMNTY BANCORP INC (DE)
Merged into Provident Bancorp, Inc. 10/4/2004
Each share Common 1¢ par exchanged for either (2.7779409) shares Common 1¢ par and $0.035486 cash or $32.26 cash
Note: Option to receive cash and stock expired 9/22/2004

WARWICK ELECTRS INC (DE)
Common 50¢ par changed to 5¢ par 12/29/1976
Name changed to Thomas International Corp. 03/01/1977
(See Thomas International Corp.)

WARWICK HOTEL, INC. (TX)
Liquidation completed 6/25/62

WARWICK INS MGRS INC (NJ)
Each share old Common no par exchanged for (0.5) share new Common no par 11/01/1985
Conv. Preferred Ser. B $10 par called for redemption 09/03/1986
SEC revoked common stock registration 10/15/2009
Stockholders' equity unlikely

WARWICK MUN BD FD INC (MD)
Name changed to Vanguard Municipal Bond Fund, Inc. (MD) 5/1/80
Vanguard Municipal Bond Fund, Inc. (MD) reincorporated in Pennsylvania as Vanguard Municipal Bond Fund 1/3/84 which reincorporated back in Maryland as Vanguard Municipal Bond Fund, Inc. 12/31/85

WARWICK PETE LTD (BC)
Merged into Europa Petroleum Ltd. 2/22/83
Each share Common no par exchanged for (0.26) share Common no par
Europa Petroleum Ltd. merged into Orbit Oil & Gas Ltd. 11/8/84
(See Orbit Oil & Gas Ltd.)

WARWICK VALLEY TEL CO (NY)
Common no par split (3) for (1) by issuance of (2) additional shares payable 11/20/1997 to holders of record 11/10/1997
Common no par changed to 1¢ par and (2) additional shares issued payable 10/13/2003 to holders of record 10/06/2003 Ex date - 10/14/2003
Name changed to Alteva, Inc. 05/16/2013
(See Alteva, Inc.)

WASA LAKE GOLD MINES LTD.
Recapitalized as Lake Wasa Mining Corp. 01/00/1947
Each share Capital Stock $1 par exchanged for (0.5) share Capital Stock $1 par
Lake Wasa Mining Corp. recapitalized as Wasamac Mines Ltd. 10/07/1960 which was acquired by Wright-Hargreaves Mines, Ltd.

01/03/1969 which merged into LAC Minerals Ltd. (New) 07/29/1985 which was acquired by American Barrick Resources Corp. 10/17/1994 which name changed to Barrick Gold Corp. 01/18/1995

WASABI ENERGY LTD (AUSTRALIA)
Each old Sponsored ADR for Ordinary exchanged for (0.00130718) new Sponsored ADR for Ordinary 06/09/2014
Name changed to Enhanced Systems Technologies Ltd. 06/20/2014
(See Enhanced Systems Technologies Ltd.)

WASABI RES LTD (CANADA)
Reincorporated 5/20/86
Reincorporated from under the laws of Brisith Columbia to Canada 5/20/86
Struck off register and dissolved for failure to file returns 2/7/96

WASAGA CAP CORP (AB)
Reorganized as RepeatSeat Ltd. 08/02/2005
Each share Common no par exchanged for (0.13157894) share Common no par and (0.06578947) Common Stock Purchase Warrant, Class B expiring 12/31/2006
(See RepeatSeat Ltd.)

WASAMAC MINES LTD (QC)
Completely liquidated 01/03/1969
Each share Capital Stock $1 par exchanged for first and final distribution of (0.5) share Wright-Hargreaves Mines, Ltd. Capital Stock no par
Wright-Hargreaves Mines, Ltd. merged into LAC Minerals Ltd. (New) 07/29/1985 which wasacquired by American Barrick Resources Resources Corp. 10/17/1994 which name changed to Barrick Gold Corp. 01/18/1995

WASATCH CORP. (DE)
Common no par changed to 40¢ par 06/01/1954
Merged into Atlas Corp. 05/31/1956
Each share $6 Preferred no par exchanged for (13) shares Common $1 par
Each share Common 40¢ par exchanged for (1.3) shares Common $1 par
(See Atlas Corp.)

WASATCH ED SYS CORP (UT)
Each share old Common no par exchanged for (0.1) share new Common no par 01/29/1990
Each share new Common no par exchanged again for (1/6) share new Common no par 02/28/1992
Charter expired 12/04/2002

WASATCH FOOD SVCS INC (NV)
Name changed to Xinde Technology Co. 06/03/2010
(See Xinde Technology Co.)

WASATCH INTERACTIVE LEARNING CORP (WA)
Merged into Plato Learning, Inc. 04/05/2001
Each share Common $0.0001 par exchanged for (0.07092346) share Common 1¢ par
(See Plato Learning, Inc.)

WASATCH INTL CORP (NV)
Name changed to E-Pawn.com Inc. 02/29/2000
E-Pawn.com Inc. name changed to UbuyHoldings Inc. 06/01/2001
(See UbuyHoldings Inc.)

WASATCH IRON & GOLD CO. (UT)
Recapitalized as W.I.G. Corp. 4/14/72
Each share Common $1 par exchanged for (1) share Common 5¢ par
W.I.G. Corp. name changed to Messina Meat Products, Inc. 9/18/74
(See Messina Meat Products, Inc.)

WASATCH MINES CO (UT)
Company no longer operating as of 00/00/1980 but will repurchase stock at $0.16 cash per share...Contact Lee Herins at (801) 742-2222

WASATCH PHARMACEUTICAL INC (UT)
Each share old Common 1¢ par exchanged for (0.25) share new Common 1¢ par 09/16/1996
Each share new Common 1¢ par exchanged for (0.5) share Common $0.001 par 06/22/2000
Each share old Common $0.001 par exchanged for (0.02) share new Common $0.001 par 09/11/2001
Each share new Common $0.001 par exchanged again for (0.00004) share new Common $0.001 par 12/03/2002
Charter expired 07/15/2003

WASATCH WEB ADVISORS INC (UT)
Each share old Common 1¢ par exchanged for (2) shares new Common 1¢ par 09/22/2003
Name changed to Raser Technologies Inc. (UT) 10/14/2003
Raser Technologies Inc. (UT) reincorporated in Delaware 06/12/2007
(See Raser Technologies Inc.)

WASCANA ENERGY INC (SK)
Conv. Participating Preferred Ser. 1 no par called for redemption 12/14/94
Merged into CXY Holdings 6/30/97
Each share Common no par exchanged for $20.50 cash

WASECOWL CO. (DE)
Liquidation completed
Each share Preferred $50 par exchanged for (1) share Chas. Pfizer & Co., Inc. Common 33-1/3¢ par 8/31/62
Each share Common no par stamped to show initial distribution of (0.33) share Chas. Pfizer & Co., Inc. Common 33-1/3¢ par 8/20/64
Each share stamped Common no par exchanged for 2nd and final distribution of (0.075) share Chas. Pfizer & Co., Inc. Common 33-1/3¢ par 8/20/64

WASHBURN CO. (MA)
Name changed to Washburn Investment Co. 03/11/1968
Washburn Investment Co. acquired by State Street Investment Corp. 08/24/1970 which name changed to State Street Investment Trust 05/01/1989 which name changed to State Street Master Investment Trust 12/14/1989 which name changed to State Street Research Master Investment Trust 05/25/1995
(See State Street Research Master Investment Trust)

WASHBURN GRAPHICS INC
Merged into Cadmus Communications Corp. 6/30/84
Each share Common $1 par exchanged for (1.04795) shares Common 50¢ par
(See Cadmus Communications Corp.)

WASHBURN INVESTMENT CO. (MA)
Acquired by State Street Investment Corp. 08/24/1970
Each share Common $20 par exchanged for (2.125135) shares Common $10 par
State Street Investment Corp. name changed to State Street Investment Trust 05/01/1989 which name changed to State Street Master Investment Trust 12/14/1989 which name changed to State Street Research Master Investment Trust 05/25/1995
(See State Street Research Master Investment Trust)

WASHBURN WIRE CO (DE)
Each share Common $100 par exchanged for (4) shares Common no par in 1930
Each share Common no par exchanged for (2) shares Common $12.50 par in 1948
Common $12.50 par changed to $1 par 6/6/78
Merged into Brenco, Inc. 12/31/80
Each share Common $1 par exchanged for (0.096) share Common $1 par
(See Brenco, Inc.)

WASHINGTON, BALTIMORE & ANNAPOLIS ELECTRIC RAILROAD
Property acquired by Bondholders Committee in 1936
No stockholders' equity

WASHINGTON, BALTIMORE & ANNAPOLIS REALTY CORP.
Liquidated in 1946

WASHINGTON & LINCOLNTON R.R. CO.
Line abandoned in 1932

WASHINGTON & OLD DOMINION RWY.
Dissolved in 1935

WASHINGTON & SUBURBAN COMPANIES
Liquidated in 1940

WASHINGTON (G.) COFFEE REFINING CO.
Acquired by American Home Products Corp. 05/14/1943
Details not available

WASHINGTON ALUM INC (DE)
Each share Common no par exchanged for (5) shares Common $2 par 07/20/1955
Merged into Eastern Stainless Steel Corp. 03/27/1969
Each share Common $2 par exchanged for (1) share $2.25 Conv. Preferred 1968 Ser. B $1 par
Eastern Stainless Steel Corp. name changed to Easco Corp. 04/29/1969
(See Easco Corp.)

WASHINGTON AUDITORIUM CORP. (VA)
Liquidation completed 6/21/61

WASHINGTON BANCORP (IA)
Acquired by Washington Merger Co. 01/11/2013
Each share Common 1¢ par exchanged for $28.25 cash

WASHINGTON BANCORP INC (DE)
Merged into HUBCO, Inc. 07/01/1994
Each share Common 10¢ par exchanged for either (0.6708) share Ser. A Preferred no par, $16.10 cash, or a combination thereof
HUBCO, Inc. name changed to Hudson United Bancorp 04/21/1999 which merged into TD Banknorth Inc. 01/31/2006
(See TD Banknorth Inc.)

WASHINGTON BANCORPORATION (DE)
Each share Common $10 par exchanged for (4) shares Common $2.50 par 12/31/86
Charter cancelled and declared inoperative and void for non-payment of taxes 6/24/92

WASHINGTON BANCSHARES INC (IL)
Principal asset placed in receivership 12/15/2017
Stockholders' equity unlikely

WASHINGTON BANCSHARES INC (WA)
Stock Dividend - 10% 06/07/1974
Name changed to Old National Bancorporation (WA) 06/21/1976
Old National Bancorporation (WA) reincorporated in Delaware 07/01/1977

(See Old National Bancorporation (DE))

WASHINGTON BANK, N.A. (WASHINGTON, DC)
Merged into Security National Bank (Washington, DC) 01/01/1982
Each share Common $12.50 par exchanged for (0.09736) share Capital Stock $5 par
Security National Bank (Washington, DC) reorganized as Security National Corp. (DE) 06/01/1982
(See Security National Corp. (DE))

WASHINGTON BK & TR CO (FRANKLINTON, LA)
Merged into Hancock Holding Co. 01/31/1995
Each share Common $10 par exchanged for (6.7138) shares Common $3.33 par
Hancock Holding Co. name changed to Hancock Whitney Corp. 05/25/2018

WASHINGTON BK (WASHINGTON TOWNSHIP, NJ)
Merged into First Jersey National Corp. 07/00/1982
Each share Common $10 par exchanged for (1.85) shares Common $5 par
(See First Jersey National Corp.)

WASHINGTON BKG CO (WA)
Common no par split (4) for (3) by issuance of (0.33333333) additional share payable 05/17/2005 to holders of record 05/02/2005 Ex date - 05/18/2005
Common no par split (5) for (4) by issuance of (0.25) additional share payable 09/06/2006 to holders of record 08/21/2006 Ex date - 09/07/2006
Stock Dividends - 10% payable 10/24/2002 to holders of record 10/08/2002 Ex date - 10/04/2002; 15% payable 02/26/2004 to holders of record 02/10/2004 Ex date - 02/06/2004
Merged into Heritage Financial Corp. 05/01/2014
Each share Common no par exchanged for (0.89) share Common no par and $2.75 cash

WASHINGTON BLVD BLDGS INC (MI)
Each share old Class A Common no par exchanged for (0.1) share new Class A Common no par 06/30/1981
Each share old Class B Common no par exchanged for (0.1) share new Class B Common no par 06/30/1981
Charter declared inoperative and void for failure to file reports 06/12/1985

WASHINGTON BUILDING TRUST (MA)
Liquidation completed
Each share Capital Stock $100 par exchanged for initial distribution of $36.50 cash 1/14/63
Each share Capital Stock $100 par received second and final distribution of $1.66 cash 1/19/65

WASHINGTON CAREY TRUST
Acquired by Prugh Petroleum Co. 12/31/53
Each Ctf. of Bene. Int. no par exchanged for (2) shares Common $5 par
Prugh Petroleum Co. merged into Livingston Oil Co. 9/1/56 which name changed to LVO Corp. 9/24/69 which merged with Utah International Inc. 10/31/74 which merged into General Electric Co. 12/20/76

WASHINGTON COML BANCORP (WA)
Common no par split (3) for (1) by issuance of (2) additional shares payable 4/1/2000 to holders of record 3/17/2000
Stock Dividends - 5% payable 4/1/98 to holders of record 3/13/98; 5%

payable 4/1/99 to holders of record 3/12/99; 8% payable 4/2/2001 to holders of record 3/15/2001 Ex date - 3/13/2001; 10% payable 4/1/2002 to holders of record 3/15/2002 Ex date - 3/13/2002; 5% payable 4/1/2003 to holders of record 3/17/2003 Ex date - 5/1/2003
Merged into Venture Financial Group, Inc. 9/2/2005
Each share Common no par exchanged for either (2.0739) shares Common no par or $43.43 cash

WASHINGTON COMMUNITY BANCSHARES, INC. (WA)
Merged into KeyCorp (NY) 01/25/1990
For holdings of (52) shares or fewer each share Common $10 par exchanged for $69.21 cash
For holdings of (53) shares or more each share Common $10 par exchanged for (1.8994) shares Common $5 par and $19.54 cash
KeyCorp (NY) merged into KeyCorp (New) (OH) 03/01/1994

WASHINGTON CONSOLIDATED TITLE CO.
Reorganized as Consolidated Title Corp. in 1935 which name was changed to Realty Title Insurance Co., Inc. 12/31/62
(See Realty Title Insurance Co., Inc.)

WASHINGTON CONSTR GROUP INC (DE)
Under plan of reorganization name changed to Morrison Knudsen Corp. (New) 9/11/96
Morrison Knudsen Corp. (New) name changed to Washington Group International, Inc. 9/15/2000
(See Washington Group International, Inc.)

WASHINGTON CORP. (NY)
Merged into Marcellus Corp. for cash 8/14/63
Details not available

WASHINGTON CORP (MD)
Plan of reorganization under Chapter 11 Federal Bankruptcy proceedings confirmed 07/14/1992
Each share Common $1 par exchanged for (0.04) share Class B Common $1 par
Completely liquidated
Each share Class A Common $1 par received first and final distribution of $1.08 cash payable 04/27/2004 to holders of record 04/22/2004 Ex date - 04/28/2004
No stockholders' equity for Class B and Class C Common
Note: Certificates were not required to be surrendered and are without value

WASHINGTON CNTY BANCSHARES INC (TX)
Taken over by FDIC 12/14/90
No stockholders' equity

WASHINGTON CNTY NATL SVGS BK (WILLIAMSPORT, MD)
Merged into Financial Trust Corp. 9/30/95
Each share Common $10 par exchanged for (2.25) shares Common $5 par
Financial Trust Corp. merged into Keystone Financial, Inc. 5/30/97 which merged into M&T Bank Corp. 10/6/2000

WASHINGTON DEHYDRATED FOOD CO. (WA)
Charter cancelled and proclaimed dissolved for failure to pay fees 7/1/76

WASHINGTON DIVERSIFIED INVT CORP (WA)
Charter cancelled and proclaimed dissolved for failure to pay taxes 11/19/2001

WASHINGTON ENERGY CO (WA)
Common $5 par split (3) for (2) by issuance of (0.5) additional share 04/13/1987
5% Preferred Ser. A $100 par called for redemption 04/01/1993
6% Preferred Ser. B $100 par called for redemption 04/01/1993
8.875% Preferred Ser. C $100 par called for redemption 04/01/1993
Merged into Puget Sound Energy, Inc. 02/10/1997
Each share Common $5 par exchanged for (0.86) share Common no par
Puget Sound Energy, Inc. reorganized as Puget Energy, Inc. 01/01/2001

WASHINGTON ENGR SVCS INC (MD)
Charter annulled for failure to file annual reports 12/15/1971

WASHINGTON FED BK SVGS (CHICAGO, IL)
Under plan of reorganization each share Common 10¢ par automatically became (1) share Washington Bancshares, Inc. Common 10¢ par 11/30/1998
(See Washington Bancshares, Inc.)

WASHINGTON FED SVGS & LN ASSN SEATTLE (WA)
Common $1 par split (3) for (2) by issuance of (0.5) additional share 02/15/1984
Common $1 par split (3) for (2) by issuance of (0.5) additional share 06/21/1985
Common $1 par split (3) for (2) by issuance of (0.5) additional share 03/19/1987
Common $1 par split (3) for (2) by issuance of (0.5) additional share 03/09/1990
Common $1 par split (3) for (2) by issuance of (0.5) additional share 02/28/1992
Stock Dividends - 10% 02/15/1985; 10% 02/14/1986; 10% 03/11/1988; 10% 03/30/1989; 10% 02/25/1993; 10% 02/18/1994
Under plan of reorganization each share Common $1 par automatically became (1) share Washington Federal, Inc. Common $1 par 02/06/1995

WASHINGTON FED SVGS BK (HILLSBORO, OR)
Merged into West One Bancorp 12/02/1991
Each share Common $1 par exchanged for (0.614) share Common $1 par
West One Bancorp merged into U.S. Bancorp (OR) 12/26/1995 which merged into U.S. Bancorp (DE) 08/01/1997

WASHINGTON FED SVGS BK (WASHINGTON, DC)
Merged into 1st Washington Bancorp Inc. 6/22/95
Each share Common 1¢ par exchanged for (1) share Common 1¢ par
(See 1st Washington Bancorp Inc.)

WASHINGTON FIRST FINL GROUP INC (WA)
Stock Dividends - 20% payable 07/23/2001 to holders of record 06/29/2001 Ex date - 08/22/2001; 20% payable 05/28/2002 to holders of record 05/15/2002; 20% payable 04/18/2003 to holders of record 04/18/2003; 20% payable 05/07/2004 to holders of record 04/30/2004; 20% payable 05/16/2005 to holders of record 04/30/2005 Ex date - 05/17/2005; 20% payable 04/18/2006 to holders of record 03/31/2006 Ex date - 03/29/2006; 20% payable 04/18/2007 to holders of record 03/31/2007 Ex date - 03/28/2007
Chapter 11 bankruptcy proceedings terminated 07/20/2017
No stockholders' equity

WASHINGTON FIRST INTL BK (SEATTLE, WA)
Stock Dividends - 20% payable 05/03/1999 to holders of record 05/03/1999; 20% payable 05/31/2000 to holders of record 04/26/2000
Under plan of reorganization each share Common automatically became (1) share Washington First Financial Group, Inc. Common 07/13/2001
(See Washington First Financial Group, Inc.)

WASHINGTON GAS & ELECTRIC CO. NEW (DE)
Ctfs. dated after 05/07/1950
Common no par changed to $10 par 00/00/1953
Name changed to Washington Natural Gas Co. (DE) 07/29/1955
Washington Natural Gas Co. (DE) reorganized in Washington as Washington Energy Co. 08/09/1978 which merged into Puget Sound Energy, Inc. 02/10/1997 which reorganized as Puget Energy, Inc. 01/01/2001

WASHINGTON GAS & ELECTRIC CO. OLD (DE)
Ctfs. dated prior to 5/8/50
Reorganized as Washington Gas & Electric Co. (New) in 1950
No stockholders' equity

WASHINGTON GAS LT CO (VA)
Reincorporated 11/01/2000
Each share Common $20 par exchanged for (3) shares Common no par 00/00/1937
$5 Preferred no par called for redemption 01/19/1946
$4.50 Preferred no par called for redemption 05/23/1958
$4.25 Preferred no par reclassified as $4.25 Ser. Preferred no par 05/27/1958
Common no par split (2) for (1) by issuance of (1) additional share 11/20/1961
Common no par changed to $1 par and (1) additional share issued 11/08/1984
$2.55 Ser. Preferred no par called for redemption 11/01/1985
Common $1 par split (2) for (1) by issuance of (1) additional share 05/01/1995
$4.36 Conv. Preferred no par called for redemption at $100 on 02/01/2000
$4.60 Conv. Preferred no par called for redemption at $100 on 02/01/2000
Under plan of reorganization each share Common $1 par automatically became (1) share WGL Holdings, Inc. Common $1 par 11/01/2000
(See WGL Holdings, Inc.)
State of incorporation changed from (DC & VA) to (VA) 11/01/2000
(Additional Information in Active)

WASHINGTON GROUP INC (NC)
Common $1 par changed to 50¢ par and (1) additional share issued 02/07/1973
Common 50¢ par changed to 25¢ par and (1) additional share issued 06/21/1974
Each share Common 25¢ par exchanged for (0.005) share Common $50 par 03/18/1983
Stock Dividend - 10% 11/15/1974
Name changed to Syntek Finance Corp. 07/12/1984

WASHINGTON GROUP INTL INC (DE)
Plan of reorganization under Chapter 11 Federal Bankruptcy proceedings confirmed 01/25/2002
No old Common stockholders' equity
Preferred Stock Purchase Rights declared for Common stockholders of record 07/15/2002 were redeemed at $0.01 per share 12/31/2005 for holders of record 12/02/2005
Merged into URS Corp. (DE) 11/15/2007
Each share new Common 1¢ par exchanged for (0.9) share Common 1¢ par and $43.80 cash
URS Corp. (DE) merged into AECOM Technology Corp. 10/17/2014 which name changed to AECOM 01/06/2015

WASHINGTON HOMES INC NEW (MD)
Merged into Hovnanian Enterprises, Inc. 1/23/2001
Each share Common 1¢ par exchanged for $10.08 cash

WASHINGTON HOMES INC OLD (MD)
Common no par split (3) for (2) by issuance of (0.5) additional share 01/18/1985
Common no par split (3) for (2) by issuance of (0.5) additional share 01/17/1986
Common no par split (3) for (2) by issuance of (0.5) additional share 02/13/1987
Stock Dividend - 100% 05/01/1972
Merged into SDS Acquisition Corp. 08/02/1988
Each share Common no par exchanged for (0.1906) share Washington Savings Bank, F.S.B. (Waldorf, MD) Common $1 par and $14.25 cash
Washington Savings Bank, F.S.B. (Waldorf, MD) reorganized as WSB Holdings, Inc. 01/03/2008
(See WSB Holdings, Inc.)

WASHINGTON-ILLINOIS, INC. (IN)
Voluntarily dissolved 6/15/65
Details not available

WASHINGTON INDPT BANCSHARES INC (WA)
Merged into Heritage Financial Corp. 3/5/99
Each share Common $5 par exchanged for (0.5934) share Common no par

WASHINGTON INVS NETWORK INC (DE)
Liquidation completed
Each share Common $1 par received initial distribution of $0.73 cash 11/1/74
Each share Common $1 par received second and final distribution of $0.07451 cash 8/25/75
Note: Certificates were not required to surrendered and are without value

WASHINGTON IRVING TRUST CO. (TARRYTOWN, NY)
Each share Common $10 par exchanged for (2) shares Common $20 par 00/00/1943
Merged into County Trust Co. (White Plains, NY) 07/30/1947
Each share Common $20 par exchanged for (1.5) shares Capital Stock $16 par
County Trust Co. (White Plains, NY) merged into Bank of New York Co., Inc. 05/29/1969 which merged into Bank of New York Mellon Corp. 07/01/2007

WASHINGTON-JEFFERSON REALTY CORP.
Liquidated in 1946

WASHINGTON LEE SVGS & LN ASSN (VA)
Ser. A Common $10 par changed to

WAS-WAS

$5 par and (1) additional share issued 02/15/1973
Reorganized as First Financial of Virginia Corp. 01/31/1974
Each share Ser. A Common $5 par exchanged for (1) share Common $5 par
(See First Financial of Virginia Corp.)

WASHINGTON LIFE INS CO AMER (LA)
Common $1 par split (3) for (2) by issuance of (0.5) additional share 05/01/1993
Merged into Vesta Insurance Group, Inc. 08/14/2001
Each share Common $1 par exchanged for $3.588345 cash

WASHINGTON MACHINE & TOOL WORKS, INC. (MN)
Name changed to Washington Scientific Industries, Inc. 8/5/60
Washington Scientific Industries, Inc. name changed to WSI Industries, Inc. 11/22/98

WASHINGTON MEDICAL CENTER, INC. (VA)
Common $100 par changed to $10 par and (9) additional shares issued 07/15/1967
Charter cancelled and proclaimed dissolved for failure to file reports 06/01/1985

WASHINGTON MINERALS INC (MT)
Involuntarily dissolved 12/3/90

WASHINGTON MINING & MILLING CO. (WA)
Charter revoked for failure to file reports and pay fees 7/1/35

WASHINGTON MLS CO (NC)
Each share Common $100 par exchanged for (4) shares Common $25 par 01/31/1956
Common $25 par changed to $1 par 06/29/1972
Name changed to Washington Group, Inc. 01/18/1973
Washington Group, Inc. name changed to Syntek Finance Corp. 07/12/1984

WASHINGTON MORTGAGE & DEVELOPMENT INC. (DE)
Name changed to Universal Mortgage & Investment Corp. 5/24/60
Universal Mortgage & Investment Corp. name changed to Delphi Group Inc. 3/3/72 which name changed to Sutton Corp. 7/15/74
(See Sutton Corp.)

WASHINGTON MOTOR COACH CO.
Acquired by Greyhound Corp. at $30 a share in 1947

WASHINGTON MUT INC (WA)
Conv. Preferred Ser. D no par called for redemption 12/31/1996
Secondary Offering - 14,589,649 shares COM offered at $47.50 per share on 01/22/1997
Depositary Share Ser. F no par called for redemption at $25 on 11/01/1997
Perpetual Preferred Ser. C $1 par called for redemption at $25 on 01/01/1998
Perpetual Preferred Ser. E no par called for redemption at $25 on 09/16/1998
Common no par split (3) for (2) by issuance of (0.5) additional share payable 06/01/1998 to holders of record 05/18/1998 Ex date - 06/02/1998
Common no par split (3) for (2) by issuance of (0.5) additional share payable 05/15/2001 to holders of record 04/30/2001 Ex date - 05/16/2001
Each Premium Income Equity Security exchanged for (2.1704) shares Common no par and (1.113) Bank United Corp. Litigation Contingent Payment Rights Trust Contingent Payment Right 08/16/2002
(See Bank United Corp. Litigation Contingent Payment Rights Trust)
7.25% Preferred Ser. H repurchased at $50.25 per share 08/16/2002
Plan of reorganization under Chapter 11 Federal Bankruptcy proceedings effective 03/19/2012
Each share Common no par exchanged for initial distribution of (0.03349842) share WMI Holdings Corp. (WA) Common $0.00001 par 03/19/2012
Each share Common no par received second distribution of (0.00076346) share WMI Holdings Corp. (WA) Common $0.00001 par payable 08/01/2012 to holders of record 09/25/2008
Note: Distributions to holders of Preferred to be determined
WMI Holdings Corp. (WA) reincorporated in Delaware as WMIH Corp. 05/14/2015

WASHINGTON MUT SVGS BK (SEATTLE, WA)
Common $1 par split (3) for (2) by issuance of (0.5) additional share 08/15/1986
Common $1 par split (3) for (2) by issuance of (0.5) additional share 08/14/1987
Common $1 par split (3) for (2) by issuance of (0.5) additional share 02/14/1992
$3.75 Non-Cum. Conv. Preferred Ser. A $1 par called for redemption 02/12/1993
Common $1 par split (3) for (2) by issuance of (0.5) additional share 08/13/1993
Under plan of reorganization each share Preferred Ser. C $1 par, Conv. Perpetual Preferred Ser. D, Perpetual Preferred Ser. E and Common $1 par automatically became (1) share Washington Mutual, Inc. Preferred Ser. C $1 par, Conv Perpetual Preferred Ser. D no par, Perpetual Preferred Ser. E no par and Common $1 par respectively 11/29/1994
(See Washington Mutual, Inc.)

WASHINGTON NAT GAS CO (DE)
Common $10 par changed to $5 par and (1) additional share issued 05/22/1964
Stock Dividend - 125% 09/15/1955
Reincorporated under the laws of Washington as Washington Energy Co. 08/09/1978
Washington Energy Co. merged into Puget Sound Energy, Inc. 02/10/1997 which reorganized as Puget Energy, Inc. 01/01/2001

WASHINGTON NAT GAS CO (WA)
Issue Information - 2,400,000 shares PFD SER II 7.45% offered at $25 per share on 11/18/1993
Merged into Puget Sound Energy, Inc. 02/10/1997
Each share 7.45% Preferred Ser. II $25 par exchanged for (1) share 7.45% Preferred Ser. II $25 par
Each share 8.50% Preferred Ser. III $25 par exchanged for (1) share 8.50% Preferred Ser. III $25 par
(See Puget Sound Energy, Inc.)

WASHINGTON NATL CORP (DE)
Common $5 par split (3) for (2) by issuance of (0.5) additional share 4/16/81
Stock Dividend - 25% 5/7/73
$2.50 Conv. Preferred $5 par called for redemption at $55 plus $0.4315 accrued dividend on 6/2/97
Stock Dividend - 25% 5/7/73
Merged into Conseco Inc. 12/5/97
Each share Common $5 par exchanged for $33.25 cash

WASHINGTON NATIONAL DEVELOPMENT CORP. (DC)
Completely liquidated 12/31/68
Each share Common $1 par exchanged for first and final distribution of approximately $1.06 cash

WASHINGTON NATL FD INC (DE)
Merged into Fundamental Investors, Inc. (DE) 07/21/1978
Each share Common $1 par exchanged for (1.552706) shares Capital Stock $1 par
Fundamental Investors, Inc. (DE) reincorporated in Maryland 02/01/1990 which reorganized in Delaware as Fundamental Investors 09/01/2010

WASHINGTON NATL INS CO (IL)
Common $10 par changed to $5 par and (1) additional share issued 05/29/1964
Stock Dividends - 60% 12/31/1940; 100% 10/28/1943; 25% 12/04/1946; 50% 12/11/1950; 33.33333333% 09/02/1952; 50% 05/18/1955; 33.33333333% 10/31/1958; 25% 08/15/1961
Reorganized under the laws of Delaware as Washington National Corp. 10/02/1968
Each share Common $5 par exchanged for (1) share Common $5 par
(See Washington National Corp.)

WASHINGTON OIL CO (PA)
Each share Capital Stock $10 par exchanged for (1.6) shares Capital Stock $25 par 00/00/1926
Name changed to Lacock Jolly Oil Co. 01/30/1975
(See Lacock Jolly Oil Co.)

WASHINGTON PFD LIFE INS CO (WA)
Merged into Northern National Life Insurance Co. 09/07/1971
Each share Common $1 par exchanged for (0.526315) share Conv. Preferred $1 par
Northern National Life Insurance Co. name changed to Manhattan National Life Insurance Co. 01/01/1982
(See Manhattan National Life Insurance Co.)

WASHINGTON PLANNING CORP. OF MARYLAND (MD)
Each share Preferred $1 par exchanged for (1) share Common 1¢ par 3/12/63
Each share Class A Common 50¢ par exchanged for (0.5) share Common 1¢ par 3/12/63
Name changed to Combined Enterprises, Inc. (MD) 10/30/68
Combined Enterprises, Inc. (MD) merged into Doric Distributors, Inc. 3/5/69
(See Doric Distributors, Inc.)

WASHINGTON PLANNING CORP (NY)
Each share Preferred $5 par exchanged for (2) shares Common 1¢ par 10/18/1961
Each share Class A 10¢ par exchanged for (0.1) share Common 1¢ par 10/18/1961
Ceased operations 00/00/1974
No stockholders' equity

WASHINGTON POST CO (DE)
Class A Common $1 par and Class B Common $1 par split (2) for (1) by issuance of (1) additional share respectively 12/17/1976
Class A Common $1 par and Class B Common $1 par split (2) for (1) by issuance of (1) additional share respectively 01/05/1979
Name changed to Graham Holdings Co. 11/29/2013

WASHINGTON PRIME GROUP INC OLD (IN)
Name changed to WP Glimcher Inc. 05/21/2015
WP Glimcher Inc. name changed to Washington Prime Group Inc. (New) 08/31/2016

WASHINGTON PROPERTIES, INC. (DE)
Liquidated in 1954

WASHINGTON PULP & PAPER CORP.
Merged into Crown Zellerbach Corp. 00/00/1936
Details not available

WASHINGTON RAILWAY & ELECTRIC CO. CO.
Plan of simplification effective 00/00/1947
Each share 5% Preferred $100 par exchanged for (1) share Potomac Electric Power Co. 3.6% Preferred $50 par, (4.25) shares Common $10 par and $41.66666666 cash
Each share Common $100 par exchanged for (40) shares Common $10 par
Each Participation Unit for (0.025) share Common exchanged for (1) share Common $10 par
Potomac Electric Power Co. merged into Pepco Holdings, Inc. 08/01/2002
(See Pepco Holdings, Inc.)

WASHINGTON RAPID TRANSIT CO.
Merged into Capital Transit Co. (DC) 00/00/1936
Details not available

WASHINGTON REAL ESTATE INVT TR (DC)
Each Share of Bene. Int. $1 par exchanged for (0.5) Share of Bene. Int. $2 par 11/18/1968
Shares of Bene. Int. $2 par split (3) for (1) by issuance of (2) additional shares 03/31/1981
Shares of Bene. Int. $2 par changed to no par 06/23/1982
Shares of Bene. Int. no par split (3) for (2) by issuance of (0.5) additional share 07/12/1985
Shares of Bene. Int. no par split (3) for (2) by issuance of (0.5) additional share 12/16/1988
Shares of Bene. Int. no par split (3) for (2) by issuance of (0.5) additional share 05/29/1992
Reincorporated under the laws of Maryland and Shares of Bene. Int. no par changed to 1¢ par 07/01/1996

WASHINGTON RTYS CO (DE)
Merged into Fabco Oil Co., Inc. 7/1/86
Details not available

WASHINGTON SANITARY IMPROVEMENT CO.
In process of liquidation in 1950

WASHINGTON SVGS & LN ASSN STOCKTON CALIF (CA)
Placed in conservatorship in April 1989
Stockholders' equity unlikely

WASHINGTON SVGS (MS)
Charter suspended 03/09/1964

WASHINGTON SVGS BK F S B (BOWIE, MD)
Common $1 par split (3) for (2) by issuance of (0.5) additional share 12/16/1991
Common $1 par split (3) for (2) by issuance of (0.5) additional share 12/17/1993
Common $1 par split (3) for (2) by issuance of (0.5) additional share payable 04/23/2003 to holders of record 04/10/2003 Ex date - 04/24/2003
Under plan of reorganization each share Common $1 par automatically

became (1) share WSB Holdings, Inc. Common $0.0001 par 01/03/2008
(See WSB Holdings, Inc.)

WASHINGTON SCIENTIFIC INDS INC (MN)
Common 10¢ par split (3) for (2) by issuance of (0.5) additional share 09/24/1984
Common 10¢ par split (3) for (2) by issuance of (0.5) additional share 07/05/1985
Name changed to WSI Industries, Inc. 01/08/1999

WASHINGTON STANDARD LIFE INSURANCE CO. (AR)
Name changed to Washington Independent Life Insurance Co. 6/28/60

WASHINGTON STL CORP (PA)
Common $1 par split (2) for (1) by issuance of (1) additional share 1/12/56
4.80% Conv. Preferred $50 par called for redemption 1/14/65
Common $1 par split (2) for (1) by issuance of (1) additional share 1/12/68
Merged into WS-B Subsidiary, Inc. 6/16/79
Each share Common $1 par exchanged for $40 cash

WASHINGTON TECHNOLOGICAL ASSOC INC (DE)
Under plan of merger each share Common no par exchanged for (1) share Quanta Systems Corp. Common 10¢ par 11/27/1968
(See Quanta Systems Corp.)

WASHINGTON TIN PLATE CO.
In process of liquidation in 1943

WASHINGTON TROTTING ASSN INC (PA)
Acquired by Global Development, Inc. (PA) 01/31/1971
Each share Common $1 par exchanged for (1) share Class A Common $1 par and $5 cash
Each share Class B Common $5 par exchanged for (1) share Class B Common no par and $5 cash
Global Development, Inc. (PA) reorganized as Global Real Estate Investment Trust 07/01/1975 which reorganized in Delaware as Global Development, Inc. 10/25/1979 which reincorporated in Pennsylvania 06/30/1982
(See Global Development, Inc.)

WASHINGTON TRUST BANK (SPOKANE, WA)
Each share Capital Stock $100 par exchanged for (5) shares Capital Stock $100 par 9/16/48
Reorganized as W.T.B. Financial Corp. (DE) 4/30/82
Each share Capital Stock $100 par exchanged for (1) share Class A Common $20 par

WASHINGTON TRUST CO. (WASHINGTON, PA)
Taken over by State Banking Commission in October, 1931
No stockholders' equity

WASHINGTON TR CO (WESTERLY, RI)
Each share Capital Stock $100 par exchanged for (4) shares Capital Stock $25 par 00/00/1946
Stock Dividends - 20% 10/01/1953; 66-2/3% 02/24/1959; 50% 02/22/1967; 100% 03/15/1973
Reorganized as Washington Trust Bancorp, Inc. 07/01/1984
Each share Capital Stock $25 par exchanged for (1) share Common $1 par

WASHINGTON TRUST INSURANCE CO. (AL)
Name changed to National Capitol Life Insurance Co. (AL) 04/15/1968
(See National Capitol Life Insurance Co. (AL))

WASHINGTON TRUST LIFE INSURANCE CO. (AL)
Name changed to Washington Trust Insurance Co. 08/18/1967
Washington Trust Insurance Co. name changed to National Capitol Life Insurance Co. (AL) 04/15/1968
(See National Capitol Life Insurance Co. (AL))

WASHINGTON WTR PWR CAP I (DE)
Issue Information - 2,400,000 TR ORIGINATED PFD SECS A 7.875% offered at $25 per share on 01/17/1997
Name changed to Avista Capital I 1/1/99
(See Avista Capital I)

WASHINGTON WTR PWR CO (WA)
Common no par split (2) for (1) by issuance of (1) additional share 6/15/64
$12.96 Preferred Ser. B no par called for redemption 5/15/86
$9 Preferred Ser. A no par called for redemption 3/12/92
Common no par split (2) for (1) by issuance of (1) additional share 11/9/93
Flexible Auction Rate Preferred Ser. J no par called for redemption at $100 on 8/7/97
$8.625 Preferred Ser. I no par called for redemption at $100 on 6/15/98
Name changed to Avista Corp. 12/2/98

WASHINGTONFIRST BK (RESTON, VA)
Location changed 05/01/2008
Location changed from (Washington, DC) to (Reston, VA) 05/01/2008
Under plan of reorganization each share Common $5 par automatically became (1) share WashingtonFirst Bankshares, Inc. Common 1¢ par 09/10/2009
WashingtonFirst Bankshares, Inc. merged into Sandy Spring Bancorp, Inc. 01/01/2018

WASHINGTONFIRST BANKSHARES INC (VA)
Stock Dividends - 5% payable 02/29/2012 to holders of record 02/15/2012 Ex date - 02/13/2012; 5% payable 05/17/2013 to holders of record 04/26/2013 Ex date - 04/24/2013; 5% payable 09/02/2014 to holders of record 08/12/2014 Ex date - 08/08/2014; 5% payable 12/28/2016 to holders of record 12/13/2016 Ex date - 12/09/2016
Merged into Sandy Spring Bancorp, Inc. 01/01/2018
Each share Common 1¢ par exchanged for (0.8713) share Common $1 par

WASHMAX CORP (AB)
Recapitalized as Upper Canada Gold Corp. 02/09/2010
Each share Common no par exchanged for (0.25) share Common no par
Upper Canada Gold Corp. name changed to California Gold Mining Inc. (AB) 04/15/2013 which reorganized in Ontario 06/07/2016

WASHTEC AG (GERMANY)
ADR agreement terminated 05/05/2005
Details not available

WASHTENAW GROUP INC (MI)
Charter declared inoperative and void for failure to file reports 12/26/2007

WASP INTL RES INC (BC)
Name changed to Plexus Resources Corp. 2/1/82
Plexus Resources Corp. merged into Kinross Gold Corp. 5/31/93

WASSANOR GOLD MINES, LTD. (ON)
Charter cancelled for failure to file reports and pay taxes 1/16/56

WASTE COMBUSTION CORP (VA)
Common $10 par changed to $2.50 par and (3) additional shares issued 9/11/69
Name changed to Consumat Systems, Inc. and Common $2.50 par changed to $1 par 10/22/73
Consumat Systems, Inc. reorganized as Reorganized Consumat Systems, Inc. 3/12/96 which name changed to Consumat Environmental Systems, Inc. 12/12/96
(See Consumat Environmental Systems, Inc.)

WASTE CONNECTIONS INC (DE)
Common 1¢ par split (3) for (2) by issuance of (0.5) additional share payable 06/24/2004 to holders of record 06/10/2004 Ex date - 06/25/2004
Common 1¢ par split (3) for (2) by issuance of (0.5) additional share payable 03/13/2007 to holders of record 02/27/2007 Ex date - 03/14/2007
Common 1¢ par split (3) for (2) by issuance of (0.5) additional share payable 11/12/2010 to holders of record 10/29/2010 Ex date - 11/15/2010
Merged into Waste Connections, Inc. (ON) 06/01/2016
Each share Common 1¢ par exchanged for (1) share Common no par

WASTE CONVERSION SYS INC (NV)
Each share old Common 1¢ par exchanged for (0.1) share new Common 1¢ par 3/15/93
Name changed to Urban Television Network Corp. 6/10/2002

WASTE INDS INC (NC)
Issue Information - 2,150,000 shares COM offered at $13.50 per share on 06/13/1997
Under plan of reorganization each share Common no par automatically became (1) share Waste Holdings, Inc. Common no par 04/02/2001
Waste Holdings, Inc. name changed to Waste Industries USA, Inc. 06/17/2002
(See Waste Industries USA, Inc.)

WASTE INDS USA INC (NC)
Name changed 06/17/2002
Name changed from Waste Holdings, Inc. to Waste Industries USA, Inc. 06/17/2002
Merged into Marlin HoldCo LP 05/09/2008
Each share Common no par exchanged for $38 cash

WASTE KING CORP (CA)
6% Preferred Ser. B $10 par called for redemption 05/08/1959
6% Conv. Preferred Ser. C $17.50 par called for redemption 05/15/1970
Completely liquidated 12/20/1973
Each share Common $1 par exchanged for first and final distribution of $20 cash

WASTE MGMT INC NEW (DE)
Incorporated 5/12/97
Merged into Waste Management, Inc. 7/16/98
Each share Common $1 par exchanged for (0.725) share Common $1 par

WASTE MGMT INC OLD (DE)
Common $1 par split (2) for (1) by issuance of (1) additional share 5/26/72
Common $1 par split (3) for (2) by issuance of (0.5) additional share 6/11/73
Common $1 par split (3) for (1) by issuance of (2) additional shares 6/29/81
Common $1 par split (2) for (1) by issuance of (1) additional share 12/3/85
Common $1 par split (2) for (1) by issuance of (1) additional share 4/21/87
Common $1 par split (2) for (1) by issuance of (1) additional share 12/8/89
Name changed to WMX Technologies Inc. 5/14/93
WMX Technologies Inc. name changed to Waste Manangement, Inc. (New) 5/12/97

WASTE MGMT INTL PLC (ENGLAND & WALES)
Merged into Waste Management Holdings, Inc. 11/03/1998
Each ADR for Ordinary 10p par exchanged for $11.382 cash

WASTE PROCESSOR INDS INC (UT)
Merged into American Ecology Corp. 03/09/1993
Each share Common $0.001 par exchanged for (0.07) share Common no par and $0.675 cash
American Ecology Corp. name changed to US Ecology, Inc. 02/22/2010

WASTE RECOVERY INC (TX)
Recapitalized as GreenGold Ray Energies, Inc. (TX) 07/31/2008
Each share Common 10¢ par exchanged for (0.0001) share Common 10¢ par
Note: No holder will receive fewer than (100) shares
GreenGold Ray Energies, Inc. (TX) reincorporated in Tennessee 12/17/2013 which reorganized in South Africa as Au Min Africa Pty Ltd. 08/27/2014

WASTE RES CORP (TX)
Merged into Warner Co. 07/06/1977
Each share Common 10¢ par exchanged for (0.65) share Common $3.33-1/3 par
(See Warner Co.)

WASTE SVC TECHNOLOGIES INC (NV)
Each share Common $0.001 par exchanged for (0.25) share Common $0.004 par 06/19/1989
Each share Common $0.004 par exchanged for (0.2) share Common $0.001 par 01/15/1993
Name changed to Largo Vista Group Ltd. 04/15/1994
(See Largo Vista Group, Ltd.)

WASTE SVCS INC (DE)
Each share old Common 1¢ par exchanged for (0.33333333) share new Common 1¢ par 06/30/2006
Merged into IESI-BFC Ltd. 07/02/2010
Each share new Common 1¢ par exchanged for (0.5833) share Common no par
IESI-BFC Ltd. name changed to Progressive Waste Solutions Ltd. 05/11/2011 which recapitalized as Waste Connections, Inc. 06/01/2016

WASTE SYS INTL INC (DE)
Each share Common $0.001 par exchanged for (0.2) share Common 1¢ par 02/18/1998
Plan of reorganization under Chapter 11 Federal Bankruptcy Code effective 06/28/2002
No stockholders' equity

WASTE TECHNOLOGY CORP (DE)
Each share old Common 1¢ par exchanged for (0.25) share new Common 1¢ par 11/13/1991
New Common no par split (2) for (1)

WAS-WAT

by issuance of (1) additional share payable 06/16/1997 to holders of record 06/02/1997
Name changed to International Baler Corp. (New) 03/16/2009

WASTE TO ENERGY GROUP INC (NV)
Name changed to Abakan, Inc. 12/08/2009

WASTE WTR TREATMENT CORP (NY)
Dissolved by proclamation 12/15/75

WASTEC INC (DE)
Name changed to Environmental Services Group Inc. 1/10/94
(See Environmental Services Group Inc.)

WASTECH INC (NV)
Charter revoked for failure to file reports and pay fees 06/01/1990

WASTECH INC (OK)
SEC revoked registration of securities 03/06/2007

WASTECO INC (OR)
Charter dissolved for failure to file reports and pay fees 12/11/1975

WASTECORP INTL INVTS INC (ON)
Chapter 7 bankruptcy proceedings terminated 06/24/2010
No stockholders' equity

WASTEMASTERS INC (MD)
Reincorporated under the laws of Delaware as Environmental Energy Services Inc. 06/29/2001
(See Environmental Energy Services Inc.)

WASTEMATE CORP (CA)
Charter cancelled for failure to file reports and pay taxes 11/1/93

WASTE2ENERGY HLDGS INC (DE)
Plan of reorganization under Chapter 11 Federal Bankruptcy proceedings effective 09/04/2013
No stockholders' equity

WASU PORCUPINE MINES LTD. (ON)
Charter cancelled for default in filing annual returns 4/18/60

WATAB PAPER CO.
Assets acquired by St. Regis Paper Co. and dissolved in 1947
(See St. Regis Paper Co.)

WATAIR INC (WA)
Recapitalized as Cabo Verde Capital Inc. (WA) 05/22/2014
Each share Common $0.0001 par exchanged for (0.01) share Common $0.0001 par
Cabo Verde Capital Inc. (WA) reincorporated in Delaware 07/23/2014 which reincorporated in Nevada 11/05/2015

WATAIRE ECOSAFE TECHNOLOGIES INC (NV)
Reincorporated 08/18/2004
Name changed 02/14/2007
Reincorporated from Wataire Industries Inc. (Canada) to under the laws of Nevada as Wataire Industries Inc. 08/18/2004
Common no par split (2) for (1) by issuance of (1) additional share payable 04/14/2006 to holders of record 03/24/2006 Ex date - 04/17/2006
Name changed from Wataire Industries Inc. to Wataire Ecosafe Technologies Inc. 02/14/2007
Name changed to Ecosafe Innotech, Inc. 03/11/2008
(See Ecosafe Innotech, Inc.)

WATAIRE INTL INC (WA)
Name changed to Watair Inc. 10/08/2010
Watair Inc. recapitalized as Cabo Verde Capital Inc. (WA) 05/22/2014 which reincorporated in Delaware 07/23/2014 which reincorporated in Nevada 11/05/2015

WATASH COBALT MINES LTD.
Liquidated in 1936

WATCH RES LTD NEW (AB)
Merged into Pearl Exploration & Production Ltd. 10/21/2007
Each share Common no par exchanged for (0.23) share Common no par
Pearl Exploration & Production Ltd. name changed to BlackPearl Resources Inc. 05/14/2009

WATCH RES LTD OLD (AB)
Reincorporated 07/20/2006
Place of incorporation changed from (BC) to (AB) 07/20/2006
Recapitalized as Watch Resources Ltd. (New) 01/17/2007
Each share Common no par exchanged for (0.2) share Common no par
Watch Resources Ltd. (New) merged into Pearl Exploration & Production Ltd. 10/21/2007 which name changed to BlackPearl Resources Inc. 05/14/2009

WATCHDOG PATROLS INC (NY)
Common 1¢ par changed to $0.0033 par and (2) additional shares issued 03/21/1986
Stock Dividends - 20% 12/17/1975; 20% 06/22/1977
Name changed to Netwolves Corp. 11/22/1998
(See Netwolves Corp.)

WATCHGUARD TECHNOLOGIES INC (DE)
Issue Information - 3,500,000 shares COM offered at $13 per share on 07/30/1999
Merged into Gladiator Corp. 10/5/2006
Each share Common $0.001 par exchanged for $4.25 cash

WATCHIT MEDIA INC (DE)
Assets sold for the benefit of creditiors 10/19/2007
Stockholders' equity unlikely

WATCHIT TECHNOLOGIES INC (NV)
Reincorporated 09/05/2007
State of incorporation changed from (TX) to (NV) 09/05/2007
SEC revoked common stock registration 05/28/2014

WATCHOUT INC (UT)
Each share old Common $0.001 par exchanged for (0.1) share new Common $0.001 par 10/12/2000
Name changed to Cormax Business Solutions Inc. 4/2/2001
Cormax Business Solutions Inc. recapitalized as Sure Trace Security Corp. 2/4/2003

WATCOR PURIFICATION SYS INC (BC)
Struck off register and declared dissolved for failure to file returns 6/26/92

WATER APPARATUS & VEHICULAR ENGR INC (CA)
Charter suspended for failure to file reports and pay fees 07/01/1976

WATER CHEF INC (DE)
Name changed to PureSafe Water Systems, Inc. 06/16/2009

WATER INDUSTRIES CAPITAL CORP. (NY)
Liquidation completed
Each share Common $1 par received initial distribution of $8.35 cash 5/17/63
Each share Common $1 par received second and final distribution of $1.615 cash 8/10/64
Note: Certificates were not required to be surrendered and are now without value

WATER-JEL TECHNOLOGIES INC (NY)
Each share Common 1¢ par exchanged for (0.125) share Common 8¢ par 11/25/1994
Recapitalized under the laws of Delaware as Xceed Inc. and Common 8¢ par changed to 1¢ par 02/24/1998
Xceed Inc. name changed to Worldwide Xceed Group, Inc. 11/29/2000
(See Worldwide Xceed Group, Inc.)

WATER PETE & ENVIRONMENTAL TECHNOLOGIES CO (NV)
Each share old Common $0.0001 par exchanged for (0.02) share new Common $0.0001 par 12/21/1999
Each share new Common $0.0001 par exchanged again for (4) shares new Common $0.0001 par 07/15/2000
Reorganized as Skygivers, Inc. 12/15/2000
Each share new Common $0.0001 par exchanged for (47.214457) shares Common $0.0001 par
(See Skygivers, Inc.)

WATER PIK TECHNOLOGIES INC (DE)
Merged into Coast Acquisition Corp. 04/12/2006
Each share Common 1¢ par exchanged for $27.75 cash

WATER POLLUTION RESH & APPLICATIONS INC (DE)
Name changed to Wapora, Inc. 10/19/70
(See Wapora, Inc.)

WATER PT SYS INC (TX)
Filed a petition under Chapter 11 Federal Bankruptcy Code 3/10/95
No stockholders' equity

WATER PURIFICATION INDS INC (FL)
Recapitalized as Marsan Capital Corp. 03/19/1982
Each share Common $0.0001 par exchanged for (0.1) share Common $0.001 par
(See Marsan Capital Corp.)

WATER PURIFICATION SYS INC (DE)
Charter cancelled and declared inoperative and void for non-payment of taxes 04/15/1973

WATER RES GROUP LTD (AUSTRALIA)
ADR agreement terminated 05/12/2017
Each Sponsored ADR for Ordinary exchanged for (20) shares Ordinary
Note: Unexchanged ADR's will be sold and the proceeds, if any, held for claim after 09/14/2017

WATER TECHNOLOGIES CORP (DE)
Name changed to WTC Industries Inc. 06/30/1992
(See WTC Industries Inc.)

WATER TOWER BK (CHICAGO, IL)
Merged into Popular North America, Inc. 12/17/98
Each share Common no par exchanged for $103.21 cash

WATER TREATMENT CORP (DE)
Merged into Chromalloy American Corp. (DE) 06/01/1971
Each share Common 10¢ par exchanged for (0.5) share Common $1 par
Chromalloy American Corp. (DE) merged into Sun Chemical Corp. 12/23/1986 which name changed to Sequa Corp. 05/08/1987
(See Sequa Corp.)

WATER U S A INC (NV)
Charter revoked for failure to file reports and pay fees 6/1/99

WATER WITCH CONSOLIDATED MINES INC. (NV)
Charter revoked for failure to file reports and pay fees 3/1/37

WATER WONDERLAND CORP (UT)
Each share Capital Stock 50¢ par exchanged for (0.2) share Capital Stock no par 06/20/1966
Name changed to Progressive National Industries, Inc. 08/17/1972
(See Progressive National Industries, Inc.)

WATERBANK AMER USA INC (UT)
Recapitalized as Global Water Asset Corp. (UT) 01/14/2010
Each (45) shares Common $0.001 par exchanged for (1) share Common $0.001 par
Global Water Asset Corp. (UT) reincorporated in Delaware 10/26/2010

WATERBURY BUCKLE CO (CT)
Merged into Illinois Tool Works Inc. 4/28/88
Each share Common $25 par exchanged for (4.2683) shares Common no par
Note: 5% of the above ratio will be held in escrow for approximately one year to cover pending claims

WATERBURY CLOCK CO.
Name changed to United States Time Corp. in 1944
United States Time Corp. name changed to Timex Corp. (CT) 7/1/69 which reincorporated in Delaware 1/1/70
(See Timex Corp. (DE))

WATERBURY FARREL FOUNDRY & MACHINE CO. (CT)
Common $100 par changed to $25 par in 1935
Stock Dividend - 50% 4/20/50
Liquidation approved and $50 per share distributed 8/21/58

WATERBURY GAS LIGHT CO.
Merged into Connecticut Light & Power Co. 00/00/1931
Details not available

WATERBURY HYDRAULIC & POLLUTION SCIENCES INC (DE)
Adjudicated bankrupt 10/18/1974
No stockholders' equity

WATERBURY NATL BK (WATERBURY, CT)
Each share Capital Stock $25 par exchanged for (2) shares Capital Stock $12.50 par 3/13/56
Stock Dividends - 20% 2/1/40; 33-1/3% 6/1/43; 25% 11/23/54; 12-1/2% 2/15/62
Merged into City National Bank of Connecticut (Waterbury, CT) 6/30/71
Each share Capital Stock $12.50 par exchanged for (3) shares Connecticut Financial Services Corp. Common $5 par
Connecticut Financial Services Corp. name changed to Citytrust Bancorp, Inc. 4/12/78
(See Citytrust Bancorp, Inc.)

WATERCOLOR HLDGS CORP (CO)
SEC revoked common stock registration 09/07/2007

WATERFIELD MORTGAGE CO., INC. (IN)
Called for redemption 06/01/1971
Public interest eliminated

WATERFORD CAP MGMT INC (ON)
Merged into CPI Plastics Group Ltd. 09/21/1998
Each share Common no par exchanged for either (0.1) Multiple Share no par and (0.1) Subordinate Share no par or (0.205) Subordinate Share no par
Note: Option to receive Multiple and Subordinate shares expired 09/08/1998

(See CPI Plastics Group Ltd.)

WATERFORD COPPER MINES LTD. (ON)
Charter revoked for failure to file reports and pay fees 4/1/65

WATERFORD GLASS GROUP PLC (IRELAND)
Name changed to Waterford Wedgewood PLC 07/25/1989
(See Waterford Wedgewood PLC)

WATERFORD INTL INC (CO)
Name changed to ATI Networks, Inc. 6/18/98
(See ATI Networks, Inc.)

WATERFORD RES INC (BC)
Recapitalized as Premier Minerals Ltd. 06/01/1993
Each share Common no par exchanged for (0.25) share Common no par
Premier Minerals Ltd. recapitalized as Premier Diamond Corp. (BC) 03/05/2001 which reincorporated in Alberta as Mexican Silver Mines Ltd. 05/07/2007 which name changed to Rio Alto Mining Ltd. 07/24/2009 which merged into Tahoe Resources Inc. 04/01/2015

WATERFORD STERLING CORP (NV)
Recapitalized as Eternal Technologies Group, Inc. 12/13/2002
Each share Common $0.001 par exchanged for (1/6) share Common $0.001 par
(See Eternal Technologies Group, Inc.)

WATERFORD VLG BK (WILLIAMSVILLE, NY)
Discharged from receivership 11/01/2013
Stockholders' equity unlikely

WATERFORD WEDGEWOOD PUB LTD CO (IRELAND)
ADR agreement terminated 02/15/2006
Each ADR for Units exchanged for $0.58594 cash

WATERFURNACE RENEWABLE ENERGY INC (CANADA)
Acquired by NIBE Industrier AB 08/27/2014
Each share Common no par exchanged for $30.60 cash

WATERHOUSE INV SVCS INC (DE)
Common 1¢ par split (5) for (4) by issuance of (0.25) additional share 6/5/91
Common 1¢ par split (3) for (2) by issuance of (0.5) additional share 2/26/92
Common 1¢ par split (5) for (4) by issuance of (0.25) additional share 3/3/93
Common 1¢ par split (3) for (2) by issuance of (0.5) additional share 11/8/93
Common 1¢ par split (5) for (4) by issuance of (0.25) additional share 9/14/95
Merged into Toronto-Dominion Bank (Toronto, Ont) 10/15/96
Each share Common 1¢ par exchanged for (0.6146029) share Common no par and $25.5138153 cash

WATERLINK INC (DE)
Issue Information - 4,500,000 shares COM offered at $11 per share on 06/24/1997
Plan of reorganization under Chapter 11 Federal Bankruptcy Code effective 8/18/2004
No stockholders' equity

WATERLOO, CEDAR FALLS & NORTHERN RAILROAD (IA)
Each share Common no par exchanged for (3) shares Common $10 par in 1948
Liquidation completed 9/6/57

WATERLOO, CEDAR FALLS & NORTHERN RAILWAY CO.
Reorganized as Waterloo, Cedar Falls & Northern Railroad in 1944
No stockholders' equity

WATERLOO GOLD MINES LTD.
Liquidated in 1938

WATERLOO MFG LTD (CANADA)
Reorganized in 1939
Each (3) shares Class A no par exchanged for (1) share Common no par
Class B no par had no equity
Assets sold to a group of employees in 1985
Details not available

WATERLOO MILK CO., INC. (DE)
Charter cancelled and declared inoperative and void for non-payment of taxes 4/15/71

WATERLOO RES INC (BC)
Recapitalized as Burcon Developments Ltd. 2/28/92
Each share Common no par exchanged for (1/3) share Common no par
Burcon Developments Ltd. recapitalized as Burcon International Developments Ltd. 6/26/95 which name changed to Burcon Properties Ltd. 7/11/97 which merged into Oxford Properties Group Inc. 5/29/98
(See Oxford Properties Group Inc.)

WATERLOO RES LTD (BC)
Recapitalized as Lowell Copper Ltd. 07/15/2013
Each share Common no par exchanged for (0.5) share Common no par
Lowell Copper Ltd. recapitalized as JDL Gold Corp. 10/07/2016 which name changed to Trek Mining Inc. 03/31/2017 which name changed to Equinox Gold Corp. 12/22/2017

WATERLOO SAVINGS BANK (WATERLOO, IA)
Reorganized as Metro Bancorporation 6/6/83
Each share Capital Stock $20 par exchanged for (1) share Capital Stock $5 par
Metro Bancorporation merged into Mercantile Bancorporation Inc. 1/3/94 which merged into Firstar Corp. (New) 9/20/99 which merged into U.S. Bancorp (New) 2/27/2001

WATERLOO VENTURES INC (NV)
Common $0.001 par split (22) for (1) by issuance of (21) additional shares payable 06/25/2004 to holders of record 06/24/2004 Ex date - 06/28/2004
Name changed to Maverick Oil & Gas, Inc. 06/28/2004
(See Maverick Oil & Gas, Inc.)

WATERMAN MARINE CORP (DE)
Merged into International Shipholding Corp. 03/30/1989
Each share Preferred Ser. A $1 par exchanged for $7.65 cash
Each share Preferred Ser. B $1 par exchanged for $4.25 cash
Each share Common $1 par exchanged for $19.8712 cash

WATERMAN (L.E.) PEN CO. LTD. (QC)
Adjudicated bankrupt 1/7/64
No stockholders' equity

WATERMAN PRODUCTS CO., INC. (PA)
Chapter X bankruptcy proceedings filed in 1962 and closed 12/31/68
Nathan Lavine, Attorney for the company opined Common stock is worthless

WATERMARC FOOD MGMT CO (TX)
Plan of reorganization under Chapter 11 Federal Bankruptcy Code effective 9/13/99
No stockholders' equity

WATEROUS GM DIESEL LTD (AB)
Name changed 05/16/1967
Name changed from Waterous Equipment Ltd. to Waterous GM. Diesel Ltd. 05/16/1967
Acquired by Wajax Ltd. 10/00/1968
Each share Common exchanged for (0.5) share Conv. Class A Common no par
Wajax Ltd. reorganized as Wajax Income Fund 06/15/2005 which reorganized as Wajax Corp. 01/04/2011

WATERPUR INTL INC (DE)
Recapitalized as Aquentium, Inc. 05/22/2002
Each share Common $0.005 par exchanged for (0.005) share Common $0.005 par

WATERS ASSOC INC (DE)
Stock Dividend - 100% 10/24/1977
Merged into Millipore Corp. 05/09/1980
Each share Common 8-1/3¢ par exchanged for (1) share Common 8-1/3¢ par
(See Millipore Corp.)

WATERS ELECTRONICS CO. (DE)
Liquidated in 1967

WATERS EQUIPMENT, INC. (CT)
Each (4,000) shares Common no par exchanged for (1) share Common no par 10/26/78
Note: In effect holders received $4 cash per share and public interest eliminated

WATERS INSTRS INC (MN)
Common 10¢ par split (3) for (2) by issuance of (0.5) additional share 08/29/1986
Common 10¢ par split (3) for (2) by issuance of (0.5) additional share payable 06/14/2002 to holders of record 05/31/2002 Ex date - 06/17/2002
Common 10¢ par changed to 1¢ par 11/03/2004
Name changed to Zareba Systems, Inc. 11/01/2005
(See Zareba Systems, Inc.)

WATERS MFG INC (MA)
Stock Dividends - 50% 3/15/62; 10% 1/11/63; 10% 7/24/64; 10% 7/30/65
Merged into Talley Industries, Inc. 10/29/85
Each share Common $1 par exchanged for $7.01 cash
Each share Common $1 par received additional and final payment of $0.6604 cash from escrow 3/27/90

WATERSAVE LOGIC CORP (BC)
Name changed to Abode Mortgage Holdings Corp. 08/15/2006
Abode Mortgage Holdings Corp. recapitalized as Ayubowan Capital Ltd. 08/19/2013 which name changed to Discovery Metals Corp. 06/13/2017

WATERSTONE FINL INC (USA)
Reorganized under the laws of Maryland 01/23/2014
Each share Common 1¢ par exchanged for (1.0973) shares Common 1¢ par

WATERTOWN NATIONAL BANK (WATERTOWN, NY)
Common $35 par changed to $40 par in 1943
Each share Common $40 par exchanged for (4) shares Common $10 par 11/21/57
Stock Dividends - (3) for (22) 1955; 30% 4/17/58
Name changed to National Bank of Northern New York (Watertown, NY) 10/1/63
National Bank of Northern New York (Watertown, NY) merged into Key Banks Inc. 11/28/80 which name changed to KeyCorp (NY) 8/28/85 which merged into KeyCorp (New) (OH) 3/1/94

WATERTOWNE INTL INC (CANADA)
Recapitalized as Sightus Inc. 03/15/2006
Each share Common no par exchanged for (0.125) share Common no par
(See Sightus Inc.)

WATERVAL PLATINUM MNG LTD (SOUTH AFRICA)
Merged into Rustenburg Platinum Holdings Ltd. 09/13/1976
Each ADR for Ordinary ZAR 5 par exchanged for (1.055) ADR's for Ordinary ZAR 10 par
Rustenburg Platinum Holdings Ltd. name changed to Anglo American Platinum Corp. Ltd. (New) 09/02/1997 which name changed to Anglo Platinum Ltd. 05/30/2005 which name changed to Anglo American Platinum Ltd. 05/25/2011

WATERWAYS COPPER MINES LTD. (ON)
Charter cancelled for failure to file reports and pay taxes in 1952

WATKINS JOHNSON CO (CA)
Common no par split (3) for (1) by issuance of (2) additional shares 2/3/84
Stock Dividend - 100% 9/8/67
Merged into Fox Paine Capital Fund, L.P. 1/31/2000
Each share Common no par exchanged for $41.125 cash

WATLING INDS INC (ID)
Name changed to Watronics, Inc. 06/30/1981
Watronics, Inc. name changed to Measurements Game Technology, Inc. 08/30/1982
(See Measurements Game Technology, Inc.)

WATLING LARDER MINES LTD. (ON)
Name changed to Hearst Larder Mines Ltd. in 1952
(See Hearst Larder Mines Ltd.)

WATROLA MANUFACTURING CO.
Liquidation approved in 1939

WATRONICS INC (ID)
Name changed to Measurements Game Technology, Inc. 08/30/1982
(See Measurements Game Technology, Inc.)

WATSON BELL COMMUNICATIONS INC (BC)
Recapitalized as Cosworth Ventures Ltd. (BC) 11/22/1995
Each share Common no par exchanged for (0.2) share Common no par
Cosworth Ventures Ltd. (BC) reincorporated in Yukon as Cosworth Minerals Ltd. 03/30/1998 which name changed to Palcan Fuel Cells Ltd. 02/13/2002 which name changed to Palcan Power Systems Inc. 08/10/2004

WATSON BROS. TRANSPORTATION CO., INC. (NE)
Name changed to Watson-Wilson Transportation System, Inc. 6/18/62
Watson-Wilson Transportation System, Inc. merged into Yellow Freight System, Inc. 12/9/68 which reorganized as Yellow Freight System, Inc. of Delaware 6/1/83 which name changed to Yellow Corp. 4/22/93 which name changed to Yellow Roadway Corp. 12/12/2003 which name changed to YRC Worldwide Inc. 1/4/2006

WATSON ELECTRS & ENGR INC (VA)
Charter cancelled and proclaimed

dissolved for failure to file reports 6/1/70

WATSON GEN CORP (CA)
Name changed 04/24/1987
Name changed 03/04/1991
Name changed from Watson General Corp. to Watson General Pictures Inc. 04/24/1987
Name changed from Watson General Pictures Inc. to Watson General Corp. 03/04/1991
Name changed to USTMAN Technologies, Inc. 02/12/1998
(See USTMAN Technologies, Inc.)

WATSON INDS INC (PA)
5% Preferred $100 par called for redemption at $102.50 on 01/01/2005
Each share old Common no par exchanged for (0.002) share new Common no par 09/28/2011
Note: In effect holders received $132,500 cash per post-split share and public interest was eliminated

WATSON INTL RES LTD (BC)
Recapitalized as Watson Resources Corp. 10/18/1982
Each share Common no par exchanged for (0.25) share Common no par
(See Watson Resources Corp.)

WATSON LAKE MINES LTD (QC)
Delisted from Alberta Stock Exchange 03/31/1992

WATSON PHARMACEUTICALS INC (NV)
Common $0.0033 par split (2) for (1) by issuance of (1) additional share payable 10/29/1997 to holders of record 10/22/1997 Ex date - 10/30/1997
Name changed to Actavis, Inc. (NV) 01/20/2013
Actavis, Inc. (NV) reorganized in Ireland as Actavis PLC 10/01/2013 which name changed to Allergan PLC 06/15/2015

WATSON RES CORP (BC)
Struck off register and declared dissolved for failure to file returns 08/22/1986

WATSON STD CO (PA)
Merged into Watson Industries Inc. 05/31/1994
Each share 5% Preferred $100 par exchanged for (1) share 5% Preferred $100 par
Each share Common no par exchanged for (1) share Common no par
(See Watson Industries Inc.)

WATSON-WILSON TRANSPORTATION SYSTEM, INC. (NE)
Merged into Yellow Freight System, Inc. 12/9/68
Each share Class A Common $1 par exchanged for (0.15) share Common $1 par
Yellow Freight System, Inc. reorganized as Yellow Freight System, Inc. of Delaware 6/1/83 which name changed to Yellow Corp. 4/22/93 which name changed to Yellow Roadway Corp. 12/12/2003 which name changed to YRC Worldwide Inc. 1/4/2006

WATSON WYATT WORLDWIDE INC (DE)
Name changed 01/01/2006
Name changed from Watson Wyatt & Company Holdings to Watson Wyatt Worldwide, Inc. 01/01/2006
Merged into Towers Watson & Co. 01/04/2010
Each share Class A Common 1¢ par exchanged for (1) share Class A Common 1¢ par
Towers Watson & Co. merged into Willis Towers Watson PLC 01/05/2016

WATT COMM INTL INC (FL)
Name changed to Viva Gaming & Resorts.com Inc. 05/11/1999
Viva Gaming & Resorts.com Inc. name changed to Viva Gaming & Resorts Inc. 09/30/1999
(See Viva Gaming & Resorts Inc.)

WATTACHAK PUB LTD (THAILAND)
ADR agreement terminated 12/19/2006
No ADR holders' equity

WATTAGE MONITOR INC (NV)
Ceased operations 06/30/2002
Stockholders' equity unlikely

WATTMONITOR INC (TX)
Each share old Common $0.001 par exchanged for (0.1) share new Common $0.001 par 11/09/1998
Name changed to Healthbridge Inc. 05/28/1999
Healthbridge, Inc. name changed to Providence Resources, Inc. 10/09/2006

WATTS INDS INC (DE)
Class A Common 10¢ par split (2) for (1) by issuance of (1) additional share 03/15/1994
Each share Class A Common 10¢ par received distribution of (0.5) share CIRCOR International, Inc. Common 1¢ par payable 10/18/1999 to holders of record 10/06/1999 Ex date - 10/19/1999
Name changed to Watts Water Technologies, Inc. 10/15/2003

WATTS MILLS
Merged into Stevens (J.P.) & Co., Inc. in 1946
Each old share exchanged for (15.36912) shares new Capital Stock $15 par
(See Stevens (J.P.) & Co., Inc.)

WATUSI CAP CORP (AB)
Recapitalized as Aethon Minerals Corp. 05/03/2018
Each share Common no par exchanged for (0.33333333) share Common no par

WAUKESHA MINERAL WATER CO.
Property acquired by bondholders in 1935

WAUKESHA MOTOR CO. (WI)
Each share Common no par exchanged for (4) shares Common $5 par in 1935
Merged into Bangor Punta Corp. 7/30/68
Each share Common $5 par exchanged for (1.2) shares $2 Conv. Preference Ser. C $1 par and (0.25) share Common $1 par
(See Bangor Punta Corp.)

WAUREGAN CO.
Merged into Wauregan-Quinnebaug Mills, Inc. 00/00/1932
Details not available

WAUREGAN MLS INC (CT)
Charter forfeited for failure to file reports 03/30/1990

WAUREGAN-QUINNEBAUG MILLS, INC.
Reorganized as Wauregan Mills, Inc. 00/00/1943

WAUSAU PAPER CORP (WI)
Name changed 05/12/2005
Name changed from Wausau-Mosinee Paper Corp. to Wausau Paper Corp. 05/12/2005
Acquired by SCA Americas Inc. 01/21/2016
Each share Common no par exchanged for $10.25 cash

WAUSAU PAPER MLS CO (WI)
Common $1 par split (5) for (4) by issuance of (0.25) additional share 01/19/1973
Common $1 par changed to $0.6667 par and (0.5) additional share issued 03/01/1974
Common $0.6667 par changed to 50¢ par and (0.33333333) additional share issued 01/17/1975
Common 50¢ par split (5) for (4) by issuance of (0.25) additional share 01/11/1991
Common 50¢ par changed to no par and (1) additional share issued 01/16/1992
Common no par split (4) for (3) by issuance of (0.33333333) additional share 01/13/1993
Common no par split (4) for (3) by issuance of (0.33333333) additional share 01/07/1994
Common no par split (5) for (4) by issuance of (0.25) additional share payable 01/17/1996 to holders of record 01/02/1996
Stock Dividends - 100% 04/02/1979; 100% 04/02/1980; 10% 01/06/1986; 10% 01/09/1987; 10% 01/14/1988; 10% 01/13/1989; 10% 01/12/1990; 10% 01/17/1995
Under plan of merger name changed to Wausau-Mosinee Paper Corp. 12/17/1997
Wausau-Mosinee Paper Corp name changed to Wausau Paper Corp. 05/12/2005
(See Wausau Paper Corp.)

WAUWATOSA BANCORP INC (WI)
Merged into Marshall & Ilsley Corp. (Old) 10/01/1984
Each share Common $1 par exchanged for (1) share Common $1 par
(See Marshall & Ilsley Corp. (Old))

WAUWATOSA HLDGS INC (USA)
Reincorporated 09/28/2007
Place of incorporation changed from (WI) to (USA) 09/28/2007
Name changed to Waterstone Financial, Inc. 08/01/2008
Waterstone Financial, Inc. (USA) reorganized in Maryland 01/23/2014

WAUWATOSA ST BK (WAUWATOSA, WI)
Capital Stock $50 par changed to $10 par and (4) additional shares issued plus a 33-1/3% stock dividend paid 02/03/1965
Stock Dividends - 100% 06/26/1951; 33-1/3% 02/01/1956; 25% 04/05/1957; 25% 08/11/1960; 100% 03/10/1970; 100% 02/07/1980
Reorganized as Wauwatosa Bancorp, Inc. 11/14/1983
Each share Capital Stock $10 par exchanged for (1) share Common $1 par
Wauwatosa Bancorp, Inc. merged into Marshall & Ilsley Corp. (Old) 10/01/1984
(See Marshall & Ilsley Corp. (Old))

WAVE EXPL CORP (BC)
Recapitalized as Roxgold Inc. 1/16/2007
Each share Common no par exchanged for (0.5) share Common no par

WAVE PWR NET INC (DE)
Recapitalized as telcoBlue, Inc. (DE) 08/29/2002
Each share Common $0.001 par exchanged for (0.2) share Common $0.001 par telcoBlue, Inc. (DE) reincorporated in Wyoming 12/23/2004
(See telcoBlue, Inc.)

WAVE SYS CORP (DE)
Each share old Class A Common 1¢ par exchanged for (0.33333333) share new Class A Common 1¢ par 07/26/2006
Each share old Class B Common 1¢ par exchanged for (0.33333333) share new Class B Common 1¢ par 07/26/2006
Each share new Class A Common 1¢ par exchanged again for (0.25) share new Class A Common 1¢ par 07/01/2013
Each share new Class B Common 1¢ par exchanged again for (0.25) share new Class B Common 1¢ par 07/01/2013
Each share new Class A Common 1¢ par exchanged again for (0.1) share new Class A Common 1¢ par 12/31/2015
Each share new Class B Common 1¢ par exchanged again for (0.1) share new Class B Common 1¢ par 12/31/2015
Plan of reorganization under Chapter 11 Federal Bankruptcy proceedings effective 08/29/2016
No stockholders' equity

WAVE TECHNOLOGIES INTL INC (MO)
Issue Information - 1,200,000 shares COM offered at $7 per share on 08/10/1994
Merged into Thomson Corp. 4/25/2000
Each share Common 50¢ par exchanged for $9.75 cash

WAVE TECHNOLOGY GROUP INC (NV)
Name changed to eMamba International Corp. 07/27/2011

WAVE URANIUM HLDG (NV)
Old Common $0.001 par split (15) for (1) by issuance of (14) additional shares payable 08/06/2007 to holders of record 07/30/2007
Ex date - 08/07/2007
Each (300) shares old Common $0.001 par exchanged for (1) share new Common $0.001 par 11/20/2008
Name changed to FBC Holding, Inc. 10/26/2009

WAVE WIRELESS CORP (DE)
Plan of reorganization under Chapter 11 Federal Bankruptcy Code effective 06/28/2007
No stockholders' equity

WAVECOM DEV LTD (BC)
Recapitalized as Neptune Resources Corp. 06/21/1979
Each share Capital Stock no par exchanged for (1/3) share Capital Stock no par
Neptune Resources Corp. merged into ABM Gold Corp. 12/05/1989 which reorganized as NorthWest Gold Corp. 06/01/1990 which merged into Northgate Exploration Ltd. (ON) 06/08/1993 which reincorporated in British Columbia 07/01/2001 which name changed to Northgate Minerals Corp. 05/20/2004 which merged into AuRico Gold Inc. 10/26/2011

WAVECOM INDS (CA)
Merged into Frequency Sources, Inc. 6/1/78
Each share Common 30¢ par exchanged for (0.109224) share Common 10¢ par
Note: An additional distribution of escrowed shares was made at a later date
Frequency Sources, Inc. merged into Loral Corp. 8/15/80
(See Loral Corp.)

WAVECOM S A (FRANCE)
Issue Information - 3,300,000 SPONSORED ADR'S offered at $13.50 per ADR on 06/09/1999
Acquired by Sierra Wireless, Inc. 04/29/2009
Each Sponsored ADR for Ordinary Euro 1 par exchanged for $11.48875 cash

WAVECREST RES LTD (BC)
Recapitalized as Quartz Mountain Gold Corp. 6/18/86
Each share Common no par exchanged for (3) shares Common no par
Quartz Mountain Gold Corp. recapitalized as Quartz Mountain Resources Ltd. 11/5/97

WAVEFIRE COM INC (AB)
Name changed to Butte Energy Inc. (AB) 06/14/2011
Butte Energy Inc. (AB) reincorporated in British Columbia 06/19/2018

WAVEFORM ENERGY LTD (AB)
Name changed to Second Wave Petroleum Ltd. 10/11/2007
Second Wave Petroleum Ltd. recapitalized as Second Wave Petroleum Inc. 06/27/2008
(See Second Wave Petroleum Inc.)

WAVEFRONT ENERGY & ENVIRONMENTAL SVCS INC (CANADA)
Name changed to Wavefront Technology Solutions Inc. 03/27/2009

WAVEFRONT TECHNOLOGIES INC (CA)
Issue Information - 2,000,000 shares COM offered at $5.75 per share on 06/02/1994
Merged into Silicon Graphics, Inc. 6/15/95
Each share Common no par exchanged for (0.49) share Common $0.001 par
(See Silicon Graphics, Inc.)

WAVEHILL INTL VENTURES INC (NY)
Name changed to PCR International, Inc. 1/4/88
(See PCR International, Inc.)

WAVELIT INC (NV)
Recapitalized as CN Dragon Corp. 01/11/2010
Each share Common $0.001 par exchanged for (0.01) share Common $0.001 par

WAVEMAT INC (DE)
SEC revoked common stock registration 07/30/2009
Stockholders' equity unlikely

WAVENETWORX INC (NV)
Recapitalized as Clear Peak Energy, Inc. 03/15/2010
Each share Common $0.001 par exchanged for (0.1) share Common $0.001 par

WAVEPHORE INC (IN)
Name changed to WAVO Corp. 05/27/1999
(See WAVO Corp.)

WAVEPOWER SYS INTL INC (ON)
Name changed to Delta Uranium Inc. 06/06/2007

WAVERIDER COMMUNICATIONS INC (NV)
Each share old Common $0.001 par exchanged for (0.1) share new Common $0.001 par 07/01/2004
Merged into Wave Wireless Corp. 03/30/2006
Each share new Common $0.001 par exchanged for (1.4323) shares Common $0.0001 par
(See Wave Wireless Corp.)

WAVERLEY BIOTECH INC (CANADA)
Name changed to Fox Resources Ltd. (Canada) 08/12/2008
Fox Resources Ltd. (Canada) reincorporated in British Columbia 07/06/2009 which name changed to Big Sky Petroleum Ltd. 12/01/2011

WAVERLY GROUP INC (OR)
Recapitalized as MetalTech Corp. 06/04/2001
Each (150) shares Common $0.0001 par exchanged for (1) share Common $0.0001 par
MetalTech Corp. name changed to Enerphaze Corp. 12/13/2001
(See Enerphaze Corp.)

WAVERLY INC (MD)
Common $2 par split (2) for (1) by issuance of (1) additional share payable 6/12/96 to holders of record 5/28/96
Merged into Wolters Kluwer U.S. Corp. 5/20/98
Each share Common $2 par exchanged for $39 cash

WAVERLY OIL WKS CO (THE) (PA)
Merged into Witco Chemical Corp. 2/28/75
Each share Common $1 par exchanged for (1.61) shares Common $5 par
Witco Chemical Corp. name changed to Witco Corp. 10/1/85 which name changed to CK Witco Corp. 9/1/99 which name changed to Crompton Corp. 4/27/2000 which name changed to Chemtura Corp. 7/1/2005

WAVERLY OIL WORKS CO.
Reorganized as Waverly Oil Works Co. (The) 05/01/1941
Each share Class A no par exchanged for (2) shares Common $1 par
Waverly Oil Works Co. (The) merged into Witco Chemical Corp. 02/28/1975 which name changed to Witco Corp. 10/01/1985 which merged into CK Witco Corp. 09/01/1999 which name changed to Crompton Corp. 04/27/2000 which name changed to Chemtura Corp. 07/01/2005
(See Chemtura Corp.)

WAVERLY PRESS INC (MD)
Common $2 par split (3) for (1) by issuance of (2) additional shares 9/12/83
Common $2 par split (3) for (2) by issuance of (0.5) additional share 9/19/86
Stock Dividends - 10% 9/12/79; 10% 6/12/81
Name changed to Waverly, Inc. 5/2/88
(See Waverly, Inc.)

WAVESCRIBE INTL CORP (FL)
Each share old Common $0.0001 par exchanged for (0.005) share new Common $0.0001 par 12/31/2004
Recapitalized as Security Financing Services, Inc. 09/29/2006
Each share Common $0.0001 par exchanged for (0.00625) share Common $0.0001 par
Security Financing Services, Inc. recapitalized as Echo Satellite Communications, Inc. 02/11/2008 which recapitalized as SatMAX Corp. 05/05/2009 which name changed to Green Energy Solution Industries, Inc. 03/02/2012

WAVETECH INC (NJ)
Each share old Common $0.001 par exchanged for (0.05) share new Common $0.001 par 3/21/94
Reincorporated under the laws of Nevada as Wavetech International Inc. 2/20/98
Wavetech International Inc. name changed to BestNet Communications Corp. 10/12/2000 which name changed to Oncologix Tech, Inc. 2/7/2007

WAVETECH INTL INC (NV)
Each share old Common $0.001 par exchanged for (1/6) share new Common $0.001 par 12/18/98
Name changed to BestNet Communications Corp. 10/12/2000
BestNet Communications Corp. name changed to Oncologix Tech, Inc. 2/7/2007

WAVETEK CORP (DE)
Name changed 2/24/82
Common 40¢ par changed to no par and (0.5) additional share issued 10/23/78
Common no par split (3) for (2) by issuance of (0.5) additional share 10/20/80
Name changed from Wavetek (CA) to Wavetek Corp. (DE) and Common no par changed to $1 par 2/24/82
Stock Dividend - 50% 3/24/83
Acquired by Torrey Investments Inc. 6/28/91
Each share Common $1 par exchanged for $3.15 cash

WAVETRONICS INC. (NJ)
Completely liquidated 1/25/72
Each share Common 10¢ par exchanged for first and final distribution of (0.5) share Capital Resources Industries, Inc. Common 1¢ par
Capital Resources Industries, Inc. merged into Health Corp. of America 10/3/72

WAVO CORP (IN)
Filed a petition under Chapter 7 Federal Bankruptcy Code 10/01/2001
Stockholders' equity unlikely

WAVVE TELECOMMUNICATIONS INC (YUKON)
Delisted from Toronto Venture Stock Exchange 06/05/2002

WAWASET SECURITIES CO.
Merged into Warner Co. on a (1.9) for (1) basis in 1947
(See Warner Co.)

WAWEL SVGS BK (WALLINGTON, NJ)
Acquired by Spencer Savings Bank (Elmwood Park, NJ) 03/26/2018
Each share Common 1¢ par exchanged for $3.92 cash

WAX MAN INC (MD)
Charter forfeited for failure to file annual reports 10/1/87

WAXESS HLDGS INC (DE)
Name changed to AirTouch Communications, Inc. 08/18/2011

WAXIE MAXIE QUALITY MUSIC CO (DC)
Each share Common 10¢ par received distribution of (2) shares Common Ser. B 10¢ par 12/11/1987
Acquired by W.M. Acquisition Corp. 03/02/1990
Each share Common 10¢ par exchanged for $21.07 cash
Each share Common Ser. B 10¢ par exchanged for $21.07 cash

WAXMAN INDS INC (OH)
Common no par split (2) for (1) by issuance of (1) additional share 01/22/1972
Common no par split (3) for (2) by issuance of (0.5) additional share 04/05/1985
Class B Common no par split (3) for (2) by issuance of (0.5) additional share 07/01/1988
Common no par split (3) for (2) by issuance of (0.5) additional share 07/01/1988
Reincorporated under the laws of Delaware 11/29/1989

WAY COOL IMPORTS INC (NV)
Name changed to QuantumSphere, Inc. 04/25/2014

WAY VENTURES INC (ON)
Recapitalized as UGE International Ltd. 08/13/2014
Each share Common no par exchanged for (0.2) share Common no par

WAYAGAMACK PULP & PAPER CO. LTD.
Acquired by Canada Power & Paper Corp. 00/00/1929
Details not available

WAYBO RES INC (BC)
Struck off register and declared dissolved for failure to file returns 8/28/92

WAYBURN RES INC (AB)
Name changed 3/7/97
Name changed from Wayburn Oil & Natural Gas Corp. to Wayburn Resources Inc. 3/7/97
Recapitalized as Hellix Ventures Inc. 6/20/2009
Each share Common no par exchanged for (1/9) share Common no par

WAYFAIR EXPLS LTD (ON)
Cease trade order effective 10/16/84
Stockholders' equity unlikely

WAYMAR RES LTD (BC)
Reincorporated 02/28/2006
Reincorporated 07/21/2006
Place of incorporation changed from (BC) to (YT) 02/28/2006
Place of incorporation changed from (YT) back to (BC) 07/21/2006
Merged into Orosur Mining Inc. 07/10/2014
Each share Common no par exchanged for (0.375) share Common no par
Note: Unexchanged certificates will be cancelled and become without value 07/10/2020

WAYMORE HLDGS LTD (UKRAINE)
Name changed to TKS Real Estate Public Co. Ltd. 05/29/2009
(See TKS Real Estate Public Co. Ltd.)

WAYNE APPLIANCE CORP (NY)
Merged into Centaur Sciences, Inc. 08/25/1983
Each share Common 1¢ par exchanged for (4) shares Common 10¢ par
(See Centaur Sciences, Inc.)

WAYNE BANCORP, INC. (WV)
Merged into Key Centurion Bancshares, Inc. 3/13/87
Each share Common $10 par exchanged for (5.5) shares Common $3 par
Key Centurion Bancshares, Inc. merged into Banc One Corp. 5/3/93 which merged into Bank One Corp. 10/2/98 which merged into J.P. Morgan Chase & Co. 12/31/2000 which name changed to JPMorgan Chase & Co. 7/20/2004

WAYNE BANCORP INC (DE)
Merged into Valley National Bancorp 10/16/98
Each share Common 1¢ par exchanged for (1.1) shares Common no par

WAYNE BANCORP INC (GA)
Merged into First Banking Co. of Southeast Georgia 4/2/99
Each share Common $1 par exchanged for (1.57024) shares Common $1 par
First Banking Co. of Southeast Georgia merged into BB&T Corp. 6/15/2000

WAYNE BANCORP INC (OH)
Common $2 par changed to $1 par and (1) additional share issued 05/01/1988
Common $1 par split (2) for (1) by issuance of (1) additional share 06/15/1993
Stock Dividends - 5% payable 12/31/1996 to holders of record 12/06/1996; 5% payable 12/28/2001 to holders of record 12/03/2001
Ex date - 11/29/2001; 5% payable 12/27/2002 to holders of record

12/06/2002 Ex date - 12/04/2002; 5% payable 12/26/2003 to holders of record 12/05/2003 Ex date - 12/03/2003
Merged into National City Corp. 10/05/2004
Each share Common $1 par exchanged for $28.50 cash

WAYNE BK (HONESDALE, PA)
Name changed 11/15/1993
Name changed from Wayne County Bank & Trust Co. (Honesdale, PA) to Wayne Bank (Honesdale, PA) 11/15/1993
Under plan of reorganization each share Common $1 par automatically became (1) share Norwood Financial Corp. Common 10¢ par 03/29/1996

WAYNE CANDIES, INC. (IN)
Preferred $100 par called 9/1/61

WAYNE COUNTY BANK (ECORSE, MI)
Stock Dividend - 50% 6/5/44
Name changed to Ecorse-Lincoln Park Bank (Lincoln Park, MI) 6/13/44
Ecorse-Lincoln Park Bank (Lincoln, MI) name changed to Security Bank (Lincoln Park, MI) which name changed to Security Bank & Trust Co. (Southgate, MI) 2/4/65
(See Security Bank & Trust Co. (Southgate, MI))

WAYNE CNTY NATL BK (WOOSTER, OH)
Common $50 par changed to $10 par and (4) additional shares issued 2/8/54
Common $10 par split (2) for (1) by issuance of (1) additional share 1/28/64
Common $10 par changed to $5 par and (1) additional shares issued 1/31/68
Common $5 par changed to $2.50 par and (1) additional shares issued 1/28/71
Common $2.50 par split (2) for (1) by issuance of (1) additional share 9/18/73
Reorganized as Wayne Bancorp, Inc. (OH) 4/30/86
Each share Common $2.50 par exchanged for (1.25) shares Common $2 par

WAYNE ELECTRONIC PRODUCTS CO. (OK)
Charter suspended for failure to pay taxes 2/28/75

WAYNE-GEORGE CORP. (MA)
Completely liquidated 4/25/67
Each share Common no par exchanged for first and final distribution of (0.090909) share Itek Corp. (Del.) Common no par
(See Itek Corp. (Del.))

WAYNE GOSSARD CORP (IN)
Common $3.33333333 par split (2) for (1) by issuance of (1) additional share 07/16/1969
Name changed to Signal Apparel Co., Inc. 02/12/1987
(See Signal Apparel Co., Inc.)

WAYNE KNITTING MILLS (IN)
Common $5 par changed to $3.33-1/3 par and (0.5) additional shares issued 3/22/65
Under plan of merger name changed to Wayne-Gossard Corp. 1/31/67
Wayne-Gossard Corp. name changed to Signal Apparel Co., Inc. 2/12/87
(See Signal Apparel Co., Inc.)

WAYNE LOCK CO.
Dissolved in 1939

WAYNE MFG CO (CA)
Capital Stock $1 par split (3) for (2) by issuance of (0.5) additional share 10/20/1961
Capital Stock $1 par split (3) for (2) by issuance of (0.5) additional share 03/26/1968
Merged into FMC Corp. 10/19/1972
Each share Capital Stock $1 par exchanged for (0.7778) share Common $5 par

WAYNE NATIONAL LIFE INSURANCE CO. (MI)
Each share Conv. Class A $1 par exchanged for (3) shares Common $1 par 11/9/65
Merged into Hamilton (Alexander) Life Insurance Co. of America 11/6/67
Each share Common $1 par or VTC for Common $1 par exchanged for (0.350877) share Common $1 par
Hamilton (Alexander) Life Insurance Co. of America merged into Hamilton International Corp. 8/15/69
(See Hamilton International Corp.)

WAYNE OAKLAND BK (ROYAL OAK, MI)
Capital Stock $20 par changed to $10 par and (1) additional share issued 06/09/1972
Stock Dividends - 10% 02/10/1950; 25% 03/25/1952; 10% 03/02/1953; 50% 02/03/1955; 11-1/9% 01/31/1956; 10% 01/24/1957; 10% 02/14/1966
Merged into First American Bank Corp. 07/01/1980
Each share Capital Stock $10 par exchanged for (0.25) share Common $10 par plus $46.72 principal amount 9-1/2% Subordinated Installment Notes due 07/01/1995 or $50.31 cash
Note: Holdings of (100) shares or fewer received cash only
Holdings of (101) shares or more received stock and notes only
First American Bank Corp. name changed to First of America Bank Corp. 01/14/1983 which merged into National City Corp. 03/31/1998 which was acquired by PNC Financial Services Group, Inc. 12/31/2008

WAYNE PETROLEUMS LTD. (ON)
Name changed to Anglo United Development Corp. Ltd. 3/19/62
(See Anglo United Development Corp. Ltd.)

WAYNE PUMP CO. (MD)
Reorganized in 1935
Each share Preferred no par exchanged for (5) shares Common $1 par
Each share Common no par exchanged for (0.25) share Common $1 par
Merged into Symington Wayne Corp. 3/12/58
Each share Common $1 par exchanged for (2.25) shares Common $1 par
Symington Wayne Corp. merged into Dresser Industries, Inc. (New) 4/30/68 which merged into Halliburton Co. 9/29/98

WAYNE SVGS & LN CO (OH)
Common no par split (3) for (2) by issuance of (0.5) additional share payable 6/12/97 to holders of record 5/23/97
Stock Dividends - 10% 6/29/94; 5% payable 6/11/96 to holders of record 5/21/96
Name changed to Wayne Savings Community Bank (Wooster, OH) 10/10/97
Wayne Savings Community Bank (Wooster, OH) reorganized as Wayne Savings Bancshares, Inc. (OH) 11/25/97 which reorganized in Delaware as Wayne Savings Bancshares, Inc. 1/8/2003

WAYNE SVGS BANCSHARES INC (OH)
Stock Dividends - 10% payable 6/10/98 to holders of record 5/20/98; 5% payable 6/10/99 to holders of record 5/27/99
Reorganized under the laws of Delaware 1/8/2003
Each share Common $1 par exchanged for (1.5109) shares Common 10¢ par

WAYNE SVGS CMNTY BK (WOOSTER, OH)
Under plan of reorganization each share Common $1 par automatically became (1) share Wayne Savings Bancshares, Inc. (OH) Common $1 par 11/25/97
Wayne Savings Bancshares, Inc. (OH) reorganized in Delaware as Wayne Savings Bancshares, Inc. 1/8/2003

WAYNE SCREW PRODUCTS CO. (MI)
Each share Common $4 par exchanged for (4) shares Common $1 par in 1946
Liquidation completed 12/19/58

WAYNE SECURITIES CO.
Liquidated in 1945

WAYNE SOAP CO. (MI)
Acquired by Associated Brewing Co. for cash in September 1969

WAYNE UNITED GAS CO.
Properties acquired by Bondholders Committee in 1938

WAYNES PHOTO FINISHING INC (WA)
Common $1 par changed to no par and (4) additional shares issued 07/09/1969
Name changed to Photoway Corp. 12/04/1978
(See Photoway Corp.)

WAYPOINT FINL CORP (PA)
Stock Dividend - 5% payable 08/15/2003 to holders of record 08/01/2003 Ex date - 07/30/2003
Merged into Sovereign Bancorp, Inc. 01/21/2005
Each share Common 1¢ par exchanged for $28 cash

WAYPOYSET MANUFACTURING CO.
Property sold in 1938
No stockholders' equity

WAYSIDE CONSOLIDATED GOLD MINES, LTD.
In liquidation in 1945

WAYSIDE GOLD MINES LTD (BC)
Recapitalized as International Wayside Gold Mines Ltd. 02/08/1994
Each (3.7) shares Common no par exchanged for (1) share Common no par
International Wayside Gold Mines Ltd. name changed to Barkerville Gold Mines Ltd. 01/21/2010

WAYTRONX INC (CO)
Name changed to CUI Global, Inc. 01/04/2011

WB III ACQUISITION CORP (ON)
Recapitalized as Frankly Inc. (ON) 01/05/2015
Each share Common no par exchanged for (0.04918113) share Common no par
Frankly Inc. (ON) reincorporated in British Columbia 07/11/2016

WB II ACQUISITION CORP (ON)
Reorganized under the laws of Saskatchewan as Input Capital Corp. 07/22/2013
Each share Common no par exchanged for (0.0625) share Common no par

WBK STRYPES TR (DE)
Issue Information - 29,000,000 STRUCTURED YIELD PROD offered at $31.35 per share on 09/30/1997
Each Structured Yield Product exchanged for (3.75) shares Westpac Banking Corp. Ltd. Ordinary and $5.31796875 cash or (0.75) Sponsored ADR for Ordinary 11/15/2000
Note: Option to receive ADR's expired 10/16/2000

WBNI INC (DE)
Name changed to Segmentz Inc. 11/08/2001
Segmentz Inc. name changed to Express-1 Expedited Solutions, Inc. 06/06/2006 which recapitalized as XPO Logistics, Inc. 09/02/2011

WCA INTL INC (FL)
Proclaimed dissolved for failure to file reports and pay fees 11/21/84

WCA WASTE CORP (DE)
Issue Information - 9,000,000 shares COM offered at $9.50 per share on 06/22/2004
Acquired by Cod Intermediate, L.L.C. 03/23/2012
Each share Common 1¢ par exchanged for $6.50 cash

WCB CAP LTD (BC)
Name changed to WCB Resources Ltd. 04/14/2010
(See WCB Resources Ltd.)

WCB RES LTD (BC)
Under plan of merger each share Common no par automatically became (4.5) shares Kingston Resources Ltd. Ordinary 11/21/2017
Note: Kingston Resources Ltd. trades on the Australian Stock Exchange

WCC SVCS INC (AB)
Completely liquidated
Each share Common no par received first and final distribution of approximately (0.399) share Greenshield Resources Ltd. Common no par and (0.199) Common Stock Purchase Warrant expiring 06/09/2005 payable 06/16/2004 to holders of record 06/16/2004
Note: Certificates were not required to be surrendered and are without value
Greenshield Resources Ltd. recapitalized as Greenshield Explorations Ltd. (ON) 06/13/2006 which reincorporated in British Columbia 10/19/2007

WCI CDA LTD (CANADA)
Merged into White Consolidated Industries, Inc. 08/16/1984
Each share Common no par exchanged for $33.50 cash

WCI CMNTYS INC (DE)
Plan of reorganization under Chapter 11 Federal Bankruptcy proceedings effective 09/03/2009
No old Common stockholders' equity
Issue Information - 6,819,091 shares COM NEW offered at $15 per share on 07/24/2013
Acquired by Lennar Corp. 02/10/2017
Each share new Common 1¢ par exchanged for $23.50 cash

WCI HLDGS CORP (DE)
Name changed to Collins & Aikman Holdings Corp. 07/17/1992
(See Collins & Aikman Holdings Corp.)

WCI STL ACQUISITION INC (DE)
Each share Preferred exchanged for (3.5) shares Common $0.0001 par 05/01/2008
Acquired by OAO Severstal 07/07/2008
Each share Common $0.0001 par exchanged for $3.293033 cash

WCI STL INC (OH)
Issue Information - 5,000,000 shares COM offered at $10 per share on 07/13/1994

Merged into Renco Group, Inc. 11/27/96
Each share Common no par exchanged for $10 cash

WCM CAP INC (DE)
Each share old Common 1¢ par exchanged for (0.33333333) share new Common 1¢ par 12/20/1999
Reincorporated under the laws of Nevada as Franklin Mining, Inc. and Common 1¢ par changed to $0.001 par 02/09/2004

WCN BANCORP INC (WI)
Each share old Common no par exchanged for (0.002) share new Common no par 2/19/97
Note: In effect holders received $435 cash per share and public interest was eliminated

WCS INTL (CA)
Recapitalized as Adams International Metals Corp. 02/10/1987
Each share Common 2¢ par exchanged for (0.4) share Common 5¢ par
(See Adams International Metals Corp.)

WCSB GORR OIL & GAS INCOME PARTN 2008-I LTD PARTNERSHIP (BC)
Merged into CRC Royalty Corp. 10/28/2011
Each Unit of Ltd. Partnership exchanged for (1.811) shares Common no par

WCSB OIL & GAS RTY INCOME 2008-II LTD PARTNERSHIP (BC)
Merged into CRC Royalty Corp. 10/28/2011
Each Unit of Ltd. Partnership exchanged for (4.513) shares Common no par

WCSB OIL & GAS RTY INCOME 2010 LTD PARTNERSHIP (BC)
Completely liquidated
Each Unit of Ltd. Partnership received first and final distribution of (1.83714) shares Toscana Energy Income Corp. Common no par payable 09/12/2013 to holders of record 09/04/2013

WCSB OIL & GAS RTY INCOME 2010-II LTD PARTNERSHIP (BC)
Completely liquidated
Each Unit of Ltd. Partnership received first and final distribution of (2.77046) shares Toscana Energy Income Corp. Common no par payable 09/12/2013 to holders of record 09/04/2013

WCSB OIL & GAS RTY INCOME 2009 LTD PARTNERSHIP (BC)
Merged into CRC Royalty Corp. 10/28/2011
Each Unit of Ltd. Partnership exchanged for (5.534) shares Common no par

WCT COMMUNICATIONS INC (WA)
Acquired by Frontier Corp. 5/18/95
Each share Common no par exchanged for $5.875 cash

WD 40 CO (CA)
Common no par split (2) for (1) by issuance of (1) additional share 10/30/1978
Common no par split (3) for (1) by issuance of (2) additional shares 04/29/1983
Common no par split (2) for (1) by issuance of (1) additional share payable 07/31/1997 to holders of record 07/11/1997
Reincorporated under the laws of Delaware and Common no par changed to $0.001 par 12/15/1999

WDC DEV INC (DE)
Name changed to Predict It, Inc. 05/10/1999
(See Predict It, Inc.)

WDC SVCS INC (DE)
Merged into AID, Inc. (DE) 06/25/1971
Each share Class A Common 5¢ par exchanged for (1) share Class A Common 5¢ par
AID, Inc. (DE) merged into INA Corp. 06/16/1978 which merged into Cigna Corp. 04/01/1982

WDF CAP CORP (BC)
Name changed to Soligen Technologies, Inc. (BC) 03/29/1993
Soligen Technologies, Inc. (BC) reincorporated in Wyoming 04/13/1993
(See Soligen Technologies, Inc.)

WE SAVE HOMES INC (NV)
SEC revoked common stock registration 08/07/2014

WE SELL FOR U CORP (FL)
Common $0.0001 par split (6) for (1) by issuance of (5) additional shares payable 03/03/2009 to holders of record 02/14/2009 Ex date - 03/04/2009
Common $0.0001 par split (2) for (1) by issuance of (1) additional share payable 08/31/2009 to holders of record 08/12/2009 Ex date - 08/31/2009
Reincorporated under the laws of Delaware as ProIndia International Inc. 08/31/2009
ProIndia International Inc. name changed to Electrum International, Inc. 11/19/2010 which name changed to Consolidated Gems, Inc. 10/01/2012

WEACO RES LTD (BC)
Recapitalized as Hayden Resources Ltd. 08/25/1993
Each share Common no par exchanged for (0.33333333) share Common no par
Hayden Resources Ltd. recapitalized as Austin Developments Corp. 03/14/2000 which recapitalized as Universal Wing Technologies Inc. 12/11/2009 which recapitalized as Red Oak Mining Corp. 03/21/2014

WEALDEN CO (DE)
4-1/4% Preferred called for redemption 10/01/1951
Common $5 par changed to 10¢ par 07/26/1955
Voluntarily dissolved 06/07/2005
Details not available

WEALTH INTL INC (NV)
Each share old Common $0.001 par exchanged for (4) shares new Common $0.001 par 10/25/96
Name changed to World Internetworks Inc. 4/13/98
World Internetworks Inc. name changed to GTDATA Corp. 12/3/2001 which recapitalized as Frontier Energy Corp. 9/28/2005

WEALTH OF THE EARTH LTD (NY)
Charter cancelled and proclaimed dissolved for failure to pay taxes 12/16/1974

WEALTH RES LTD (BC)
Recapitalized as Sterlingmarc Mining Ltd. 2/28/96
Each share Common no par exchanged for (0.1) share Common no par

WEALTHCRAFT SYSTEMS INC (NV)
Name changed to Wealthcraft Capital, Inc. 02/01/2017

WEALTHHOUND COM INC (DE)
Recapitalized as Eurosport Active World Corp. 04/07/2008
Each share Common $0.001 par exchanged for (0.001) share Common $0.001 par

WEAN INC (DE)
Liquidating plan of reorganization under Chapter 11 Federal Bankruptcy proceedings confirmed 05/31/1996
Each share 5.25% Preferred Ser. A $24 par exchanged for first and final distribution of $0.93319919 cash
Each share Common $1 par exchanged for first and final distribution of $0.17728791 cash

WEAN INDS INC (OH)
Name changed to Wean United, Inc. (OH) 5/1/68
Wean United, Inc. (OH) reincorporated in Delaware as Wean Inc. 9/16/87
(See Wean Inc.)

WEAN UNITED, INC. (OH)
Reincorporated under the laws of Delaware as Wean Inc. 09/16/1987
(See Wean Inc.)

WEAR WELD ENGR & MFG CO (OR)
Dissolved 11/13/1967
No stockholders' equity

WEAREVER PROCTORSILEX INC (DE)
Merged into NACCO Industries, Inc. 04/12/1988
Each share Common 1¢ par exchanged for $17.50 cash

WEATHER ALL MFG USA INC (FL)
Recapitalized as Cerro Dorado, Inc. (FL) 03/29/1999
Each share Common $0.001 par exchanged for (0.06666666) share Common $0.001 par
Cerro Dorado, Inc. (FL) reincorporated in Nevada 07/14/1999 which recapitalized as AURYN Mining Corp. 08/14/2018

WEATHER RITE INC (MN)
Placed in permanent receivership 07/19/1974
No stockholders' equity

WEATHER-SEAL, INC. (OH)
Acquired by Georgia-Pacific Corp. 6/10/68
Each share 6% Preferred $50 par exchanged for (1.5) shares $1.40 Conv. Preferred no par
Each share Common $1 par exchanged for (0.6) share $1.40 Conv. Preferred no par
(See Georgia-Pacific Corp.)

WEATHERBY NASCO INC (WI)
Common 33-1/3¢ par changed to 25¢ par and (0.25) additional share issued 04/30/1972
Name changed to Nasco International, Inc. 08/08/1974
(See Nasco International, Inc.)

WEATHERFORD & CO (MO)
Charter forfeited for failure to file reports 11/2/87

WEATHERFORD BANCSHARES INC
8% Preferred called for redemption at $104 on 1/7/2002

WEATHERFORD ENTERRA INC (DE)
Merged into EVI Weatherford, Inc. 05/27/1998
Each share Common 10¢ par exchanged for (0.95) share Common $1 par
EVI Weatherford, Inc. name changed to Weatherford International Inc. (New) (DE) 09/21/1998 which reincorporated in Bermuda as Weatherford International Ltd. 06/26/2002 which reincorporated in Switzerland 02/25/2009 which reincorporated in Ireland as Weatherford International PLC 06/18/2014

WEATHERFORD INTL INC NEW (DE)
Each share Common $1 par received distribution of (1) share Grant Prideco, Inc. Common 1¢ par payable 04/14/2000 to holders of record 03/23/2000 Ex date - 04/17/2000
Reincorporated under the laws of Bermuda as Weatherford International Ltd. 06/26/2002
Weatherford International Ltd. (Bermuda) reincorporated in Switzerland 02/25/2009 which reincorporated in Ireland as Weatherford International PLC 06/18/2014

WEATHERFORD INTL INC OLD (DE)
Common 10¢ par split (3) for (2) by issuance of (0.5) additional share 04/30/1981
$2.625 Conv. Exchangeable Preferred $1 par called for redemption 11/30/1993
Recapitalized as Weatherford Enterra, Inc. 10/05/1995
Each share Common 10¢ par exchanged for (0.5) share Common 10¢ par
Weatherford Enterra, Inc. merged into EVI Weatherford, Inc. 05/27/1998 which name changed to Weatherford International Inc. (New) (DE) 09/21/1998 which reincorporated in Bermuda as Weatherford International Ltd. 06/26/2002 which reincorporated in Switzerland 02/25/2009 which reincorporated in Ireland as Weatherford International PLC 06/18/2014

WEATHERFORD INTL LTD (BERMUDA)
Common $1 par split (2) for (1) by issuance of (1) additional share payable 11/30/2005 to holders of record 11/14/2005 Ex date - 12/01/2005
Common $1 par split (2) for (1) by issuance of (1) additional share payable 05/23/2008 to holders of record 05/09/2008 Ex date - 05/27/2008
Reincorporated under the laws of Switzerland and Common $1 par reclassified as Registered Shares CHF 1.16 par 02/25/2009
Weatherford International Inc. (Switzerland) reincorporated in Ireland as Weatherford International PLC 06/18/2014

WEATHERFORD INTL LTD (SWITZERLAND)
Reincorporated under the laws of Ireland as Weatherford International PLC and Registered Shares CHF 1.16 par reclassified as Ordinary 06/18/2014

WEATHERFORD NATIONAL BANCSHARES INC. (TX)
Merged into First Financial Bankshares, Inc. 1/17/96
Each share Common $5 par exchanged for (1.5) shares Common $10 par

WEATHERFORD OIL SVCS INC (AB)
Each Exchangeable share Ser. 1 no par exchanged for (1) share Weatherford International Inc. (New) (DE) Common $1 par 04/20/2001
Weatherford International Inc. (New) (DE) reincorporated in Bermuda 06/26/2002 which reincorporated in Switzerland 02/25/2009 which reincorporated in Ireland as Weatherford International PLC 06/18/2014

WEATHERFORD R V CO (CA)
Stock Dividend - 10% 02/16/1972
Capital Stock no par split (3) for (2) by issuance of (0.5) additional share 09/16/1983
Capital Stock no par split (2) for (1) by issuance of (1) additional share 12/27/1983
Charter suspended for failure to file reports and pay fees 05/01/1992

WEATHERHEAD CO (OH)
Merged into Dana Corp. 09/19/1977
Each share Common no par

exchanged for (0.6) share Common $1 par or $14 cash
Note: Option to receive $14 cash or a combination of cash and stock expired 10/03/1977
(See Dana Corp.)

WEATHERMATIC CORP (DE)
Name changed to Mebco Industries, Inc. 08/21/1970
(See Mebco Industries, Inc.)

WEATHERS CORP. (DE)
Charter cancelled and declared inoperative and void for non-payment of taxes 3/1/74

WEAVER (L.F.) CO.
Acquired by Commercial Investment Trust Corp. 00/00/1927
Details not available

WEAVER ARMS CORP (CA)
Reorganized under the laws of Nevada as Madera International Inc. 02/01/1994
Each share Common 1¢ par exchanged for (0.01) share Common 1¢ par

WEAVER LAKE EXPLS LTD (ON)
Recapitalized as Edifice Explorations Ltd. 12/06/1995
Each share Common no par exchanged for (0.1) share Common no par
Edifice Explorations Ltd. recapitalized as Goldmint Explorations Ltd. 06/14/1996 which name changed to AXcension Capital Corp. (ONT) 11/06/1998 which reorganized in Bermuda as Caspian Oil Tools Ltd. 08/30/1999
(See Caspian Oil Tools Ltd.)

WEB CAP GROUP INC (NV)
Merged into Web Capital Ventures, Inc. 03/31/2000
Each share Common 1¢ par exchanged for (1.5) shares Common 1¢ par
Web Capital Ventures, Inc. recapitalized as Troy Gold & Mineral Corp. 10/09/2007

WEB CAP VENTURES INC (NV)
Recapitalized as Troy Gold & Mineral Corp. 10/09/2007
Each share Common 1¢ par exchanged for (0.1) share Common 1¢ par
Note: Holders of (99) or fewer pre-split shares received $0.005 cash per share

WEB COM GROUP INC (DE)
Acquired by Siris Capital Group, LLC 10/11/2018
Each share Common $0.001 par exchanged for $28 cash

WEB COM INC (MN)
Merged into Website Pros, Inc. 10/01/2007
Each share Common 1¢ par exchanged for (0.6875) share Common $0.001 par
Website Pros, Inc. name changed to Web.com Group, Inc. 10/27/2008
(See Web.com Group, Inc.)

WEB HOLDING CORP.
Bankrupt in 1931

WEB PAY-PER-VIEW INC (NV)
Name changed to U.S. Federal Financial Corp. 09/25/2001
U.S. Federal Financial Corp. name changed to Vibe Records Inc. 04/23/2002 which name changed to Great Entertainment & Sports Inc. 03/07/2003 which name changed to Rockit!, Inc. 06/11/2007
(See Rockit!, Inc.)

WEB PRESS CORP (WA)
Chapter 11 bankruptcy proceedings dismissed 11/08/2012
No stockholders' equity

WEB SVCS INTL INC (RI)
Name changed to Cytation Corp. (RI) 12/14/1998
(See Cytation Corp. (RI))

WEB STR INC (DE)
Merged into E*Trade Group, Inc. 8/6/2001
Each share Common 1¢ par exchanged for (0.1864) share Common 1¢ par
E*Trade Group, Inc. name changed to E*Trade Financial Corp. 10/1/2003

WEB TECH INC (NV)
Name changed to Cynergy Inc. 04/16/1997
Cynergy Inc. recapitalized as Mercantile Factoring Credit Online Corp. 09/29/1999 which name changed to Incitations Inc. 10/03/2000 which recapitalized as Osprey Gold Corp. 05/16/2003 which recapitalized as Gilla Inc. 03/30/2007

WEB VIEWS CORP (NV)
Name changed to Cascade Mountain Mining Co., Inc. and (60) additional shares issued 06/24/2003
Cascade Mountain Mining Co., Inc. recapitalized as National Parking Systems, Inc. 01/07/2005 which name changed to BioStem, Inc. 11/18/2005 which recapitalized as Joytoto USA, Inc. 10/31/2007 which recapitalized as Pollex, Inc. 10/24/2008 which name changed to eMARINE Global Inc. 09/12/2017

WEB WIZARD INC (NV)
Name changed to Psychic Friends Network Inc. 02/24/2012
Psychic Friends Network Inc. name changed to Peer to Peer Network 09/30/2014

WEB4BOATS COM INC (DE)
Recapitalized as Federal Security Protection Services, Inc. 03/25/2002
Each share Common $0.001 par exchanged for (0.1) share Common $0.001 par
Federal Security Protection Services, Inc. name changed to Platina Energy Group, Inc. 06/17/2005

WEBB & KNAPP CDA LTD (CANADA)
5% Preferred Ser. A $5 par called for redemption 02/29/1980
Common no par called for redemption 04/18/1989
Public interest eliminated

WEBB & KNAPP INC (DE)
Plan of reorganization under bankruptcy proceedings confirmed 09/26/1972
No stockholders' equity

WEBB BAY RESOURCES LTD (AB)
Name changed to National Gold Corp. (AB) 02/16/2000
National Gold Corp. (AB) reincorporated in British Columbia 01/24/2003 which merged into Alamos Gold Corp. (Old) 02/20/2003 which merged into Alamos Gold Inc. (New) 07/06/2015

WEBB CO (DE)
Common no par split (4) for (3) by issuance of (1/3) additional share 8/19/83
Common no par split (3) for (2) by issuance of (0.5) additional share 8/20/84
Stock Dividends - 100% 8/20/76; 50% 8/20/80; 50% 8/20/82
Merged into BPCC (US) Acquisition Corp. 11/1/86
Each share Common no par exchanged for $16.75 cash

WEBB DEL CORP (DE)
Name changed 05/19/1988
Reincorporated 11/03/1994
Name changed from Webb (Del E.)

Corp. to Webb (Del) Corp. (AZ) 05/19/1988
Reincorporated from Arizona to under the laws of Delaware and Common no par changed to $0.001 par 11/03/1994
Merged into Pulte Homes, Inc. 07/31/2001
Each share Common $0.001 par exchanged for (0.894) share Common 1¢ par
Pulte Homes, Inc. name changed to PulteGroup, Inc. 03/22/2010

WEBB DEL E INVT PPTYS INC (DE)
Name changed to B.B. Real Estate Investment Corp. 07/18/1988
B.B. Real Estate Investment Corp. acquired by California Real Estate Investment Trust 07/18/1989 which name changed to Capital Trust (CA) 07/15/1997 which reorganized as Capital Trust, Inc. (MD) which recapitalized as Blackstone Mortgage Trust, Inc. 05/07/2013

WEBB INTERACTIVE SVCS INC (CO)
Common no par changed to $0.0001 par 10/30/2017
Name changed to Web Global Holdings, Inc. 06/01/2018

WEBB PUBG CO (DE)
Name changed to Webb Co. 05/09/1973
(See Webb Co.)

WEBB RES INC (CO)
Merged into Standard Oil Co. (OH) 12/11/1979
Each share Common 10¢ par exchanged for (0.5) share Common no par
(See Standard Oil Co. (OH))

WEBB'S CUT RATE DRUG CO., INC. (FL)
Name changed to Webb's City, Inc. 11/02/1945
(See Webb's City, Inc.)

WEBBOAT COM INC (DE)
Name changed to Web4boats.Com Inc. 05/04/1999
Web4boats.Com Inc. recapitalized as Federal Security Protection Services, Inc. 03/25/2002 which name changed to Platina Energy Group, Inc. 06/17/2005
(See Platina Energy Group, Inc.)

WEBBS CITY INC (FL)
Proclaimed dissolved for failure to file reports and pay fees 12/08/1980

WEBBS STORES LTD (WA)
Charter cancelled and proclaimed dissolved for failure to pay fees 00/00/1986

WEBBWOOD EXPLORATION CO. LTD. (ON)
Charter cancelled for failure to pay taxes and file returns 8/9/72

WEBCATALYST INC (GA)
SEC revoked common stock registration 10/04/2006

WEBCOR, INC. (IL)
Adjudicated bankrupt 10/25/67
No stockholders' equity

WEBCOR ELECTRS INC (DE)
Common 1¢ par split (2) for (1) by issuance of (1) additional share 10/16/81
Common 1¢ par split (3) for (2) by issuance of (0.5) additional share 8/25/83
Stock Dividend - 100% 4/22/82
Recapitalized as eNote.Com Inc. 3/31/99
Each (6.75) shares Common 1¢ par exchanged for (1) share Common 1¢ par
(See eNote.Com Inc.)

WEBDIGS INC (DE)
Each share old Common $0.001 par exchanged for (0.005) share new Common $0.001 par 05/17/2012
Name changed to RealBiz Media Group, Inc. 10/05/2012
RealBiz Media Group, Inc. name changed to Verus International, Inc. 10/16/2018

WEBENGINE CORP (ON)
Reorganized under the laws of Canada as Foccini International Inc. 11/13/2003
Each share Common no par exchanged for (1/3) share Common no par
Foccini International Inc. name changed to Arch Biopartners Inc. 05/07/2010

WEBER & HEILBRONER
Merged into Fashion Park Associates, Inc. in 1929 whose assets were sold at bankruptcy sale in 1933

WEBER SHOWCASE & FIXTURE CO., INC. (DE)
Each share 1st Preferred no par exchanged for (6) shares Common $5 par in 1947
Each share 2nd Preferred no par exchanged for (5) shares Common $5 par in 1947
Each share Common no par exchanged for (2) shares Common $5 par in 1947
Acquired by Kidde (Walter) & Co., Inc. (NY) 7/31/65
Each share Common $5 par exchanged for (0.8) share Common $2.50 par
4% Preferred $25 par called for redemption 8/31/65
Kidde (Walter) & Co., Inc. (NY) reincorporated in Delaware 7/2/68 which name changed to Kidde, Inc. 4/18/80 which merged into Hanson Trust p.l.c. 12/31/87 which name changed to Hanson PLC (Old) 1/29/88 which name changed to Hanson PLC (New) 10/15/2003

WEBEX COMMUNICATIONS INC (DE)
Issue Information - 3,500,000 shares COM offered at $14 per share on 07/27/2000
Merged into Cisco Systems, Inc. 5/25/2007
Each share Common $0.001 par exchanged for $57 cash

WEBEX RES LTD (AB)
Recapitalized 7/15/92
Recapitalized from Webex Oil & Gas Ltd. to Webex Resources Ltd. 7/15/92
Each share Common no par exchanged for (0.1) share new Common no par
Merged into Courage Energy Inc. 9/1/95
Each share new Common no par exchanged for (1) share Common no par
(See Courage Energy Inc.)

WEBFINANCIAL CORP (DE)
Each share old Common $0.001 par exchanged for (0.25) share new Common $0.001 par 04/05/2005
Merged into WebFinancial L.P. 12/31/2008
Each share Common $0.001 par exchanged for (1) Unit of Ltd. Partnership Int.
WebFinancial L.P. name changed to Steel Partners Holdings L.P. 04/08/2009

WEBFINANCIAL L P (DE)
Name changed to Steel Partners Holdings L.P. 04/08/2009

WEBGALAXY INC (NV)
Recapitalized as Nanoforce, Inc. 4/11/2005
Each share Common 1¢ par exchanged for (0.001) share Common 1¢ par

WEBHIRE INC (DE)
Each share old Common 1¢ par exchanged for (0.2) share new Common 1¢ par 06/18/2001
Merged into Kenexa Corp. 01/13/2006
Each share new Common 1¢ par exchanged for $5.8836 cash
Note: An additional $1.0346 cash per share was paid from escrow 07/27/2007

WEBLINK WIRELESS INC (DE)
Plan of reorganization under Chapter 11 Federal Bankruptcy Code effective 09/09/2002
No Class A Common stockholders' equity
Liquidation completed
Each share Common $0.0001 par received initial distribution of $2 cash payable 04/26/2006 to holders of record 04/06/2006
Each share Common $0.0001 par received second distribution of $1.25 cash payable 04/23/2007 to holders of record 04/16/2007
Each share Common $0.0001 par received third distribution of $0.28 cash payable 05/16/2008 to holders of record 05/09/2008
Each share Common $0.0001 par received fourth and final distribution of $0.0765 cash payable 11/23/2011 to holders of record 11/02/2011
Note: Certificates were not required to be surrendered and are without value

WEBMD CORP (DE)
Name changed to Emdeon Corp. 10/17/2005
Emdeon Corp. name changed to HLTH Corp. 05/21/2007 which merged into WebMD Health Corp. 10/23/2009
(See WebMD Health Corp.)

WEBMD HEALTH CORP (DE)
Class A Common 1¢ par reclassified as Common 1¢ par 10/23/2009
Acquired by MH Sub I, LLC 09/15/2017
Each share Common 1¢ par exchanged for $66.50 cash

WEBMD INC (DE)
Merged into Healtheon/WebMD Corp. 11/11/99
Each share Common exchanged for (1.796) shares Common $0.0001 par
Healtheon/WebMD Corp. name changed to WebMD Corp. 9/12/2000 which name changed to Emdeon Corp. 10/17/2005 which name changed to HLTH Corp. 5/21/2007

WEBMEDIABRANDS INC (DE)
Each share old Common 1¢ par exchanged for (0.14285714) share new Common 1¢ par 08/17/2012
Name changed to Mediabistro Inc. 06/13/2013
Mediabistro Inc. name changed to Mecklermedia Corp. (New) 08/25/2014
(See Mecklermedia Corp. (New))

WEBMETHODS INC (DE)
Issue Information - 4,100,000 shares COM offered at $35 per share on 02/10/2000
Merged into Software AG 06/01/2007
Each share Common 1¢ par exchanged for $9.15 cash

WEBQUEST INTL INC (NV)
Reincorporated 04/18/1998
State of incorporation changed from (UT) to (NV) 04/18/1998
SEC revoked preferred and common stock registration 10/24/2008
Stockholders' equity unlikely

WEBRIB STEEL CORP. (NY)
Name changed to Hico Corp. of America, May, 1957

WEBS INDEX FD INC (MD)
Name changed to iShares Inc. 5/12/2000

WEBSENSE INC (DE)
Common 1¢ par split (2) for (1) by issuance of (1) additional share payable 03/17/2006 to holders of record 02/13/2006 Ex date - 03/20/2006
Acquired by Tomahawk Acquisition, LLC 06/25/2013
Each share Common 1¢ par exchanged for $24.75 cash

WEBSIDESTORY INC (DE)
Issue Information - 5,000,000 shares COM offered at $8.50 per share on 09/27/2004
Name changed to Visual Sciences, Inc. 05/11/2007
Visual Sciences, Inc. merged into Omniture, Inc. 01/17/2008
(See Omniture, Inc.)

WEBSITE PROS INC (DE)
Name changed to Web.com Group, Inc. 10/27/2008
(See Web.com Group, Inc.)

WEBSMART COM COMMUNICATIONS INC (BC)
Name changed to Gold Reach Resources Ltd. 10/13/2004
Gold Reach Resources Ltd. name changed to Surge Copper Corp. 02/21/2018

WEBSTAKES COM INC (DE)
Name changed to Promotions.com Inc. 1/31/2000
Promotions.com Inc. merged into iVillage Inc. 5/24/2002
(See iVillage Inc.)

WEBSTATION COM INC (FL)
Name changed to Cor Equity Holdings Inc. 11/12/2003
Cor Equity Holdings Inc. name changed to 727 Communications, Inc. 2/13/2006

WEBSTER CASH RESV FD INC (MD)
Name changed to Kidder, Peabody Cash Reserve Fund, Inc. 04/27/1992
(See Kidder, Peabody Cash Reserve Fund, Inc.)

WEBSTER-CHICAGO CORP. (IL)
Stock Dividends - 20% 12/20/50; 10% 12/21/53
Name changed to Webcor, Inc. 5/1/56
Webcor, Inc. adjudicated bankrupt 10/25/67

WEBSTER CITY FED BANCORP (USA)
Common 10¢ par split (2) for (1) by issuance of (1) additional share payable 09/24/2003 to holders of record 09/09/2003 Ex date - 09/25/2003
Reorganized under the laws of Iowa as WCF Bancorp, Inc. 07/14/2016
Each share Common 10¢ par exchanged for (0.8115) share Common 1¢ par

WEBSTER CITY FED SVGS BK (WEBSTER CITY, IA)
Under plan of reorganization each share Common 10¢ par automatically became (1) share Webster City Federal Bancorp (USA) Common 10¢ par 07/01/1999
Webster City Federal Bancorp (USA) reorganized as WCF Bancorp, Inc. (IA) 07/14/2016

WEBSTER CLOTHES INC (DE)
Merged into Edison Brothers Stores, Inc. 10/04/1994
Each share Common 1¢ par exchanged for $5.50 cash

WEBSTER COMPUTER CORP (NY)
Dissolved by proclamation 12/15/75

WEBSTER-EISENLOHR, INC.
Name changed to Webster Tobacco Co., Inc. in 1945
Webster Tobacco Co., Inc. name changed to Webster Investment Co., Inc. in 1953 which reincorporated as Webster Investors, Inc. (Del.) 4/30/56 which merged into American Manufacturing Co., Inc. 12/20/60 which assets were transferred to American Manufacturing Co., Inc. Liquidating Trust 5/20/80
(See American Manufacturing Co., Inc. Liquidating Trust)

WEBSTER ELECTRIC CO. (DE)
Each share Common no par exchanged for (5) shares Common $1 par in 1946
Stock Dividends - 10% 12/31/64; 33-1/3% 6/30/65
Merged into Sta-Rite Industries, Inc. 5/31/66
Each share Common $1 par exchanged for (0.4) share 5% Conv. Preferred Ser. A $25 par and (0.5) share Common $2 par
Sta-Rite Industries, Inc. merged into Wicor, Inc. 8/31/82

WEBSTER FINL CORP (DE)
7.5% Conv. Preferred Ser. B no par called for redemption 01/15/1997
Each share 8.5% Non-Cum Conv. Perpetual Preferred Ser. A 1¢ par automatically became (36.8046) shares Common 1¢ par 06/01/2015
6.4% Depositary Preferred Ser. E called for redemption at $25.40 on 12/15/2017
(Additional Information in Active)

WEBSTER HALL HOTEL, INC. (PA)
Liquidation completed 9/1/62

WEBSTER INVESTMENT CO., INC. (PA)
Reincorporated under the laws of Delaware as Webster Investors, Inc. 04/30/1956
Webster Investors, Inc. merged into American Manufacturing Co., Inc. 12/20/1960 which assets were transferred to American Manufacturing Co., Inc. Liquidating Trust 05/20/1980
(See American Manufacturing Co., Inc. Liquidating Trust)

WEBSTER INVESTORS, INC. (DE)
Merged into American Manufacturing Co., Inc. 12/20/60
Each share Common $5 par exchanged for (1.25) share Common $12.50 par and (0.04570) share Common represented by an Interim Certificate
American Manufacturing Co., Inc. assets transferred to American Manufacturing Co., Inc. Liquidating Trust 5/20/80
(See American Manufacturing Co., Inc. Liquidating Trust)

WEBSTER MONEY MKT FD INC (MD)
Voluntarily dissolved 00/00/1992
Details not available

WEBSTER (C.J.) OIL & GAS CO. (OK)
Charter cancelled for failure to pay taxes 3/25/39

WEBSTER PFD CAP CORP
7.375% Preferred Ser. A $1 par called for redemption at $1,000 on 01/15/2001
8.625% Preferred Ser. B $1 par called for redemption at $10 on 12/15/2011

WEBSTER PUBLISHING CO., INC. (MO)
Merged into McGraw-Hill Publishing Co., Inc. 04/30/1963
Each share Common 50¢ par exchanged for (0.5) share Class A $1 par
(See McGraw-Hill Publishing Co., Inc.)

WEBSTER TOBACCO CO., INC. (PA)
Stock Dividend - 10% 1/47
Name changed to Webster Investment Co. Inc. in 1953
Webster Investment Co. Inc. reincorporated as Webster Investors, Inc. 4/30/56 which merged into American Manufacturing Co., Inc. 12/20/60 which assets were transferred to American Manufacturing Co., Inc. Liquidating Trust 5/20/80
(See American Manufacturing Co., Inc. Liquidating Trust)

WEBSTERS EDDIE INC (MN)
Statutorily dissolved 8/1/97

WEBTECH WIRELESS INC (BC)
Reincorporated 08/01/2006
Place of incorporation changed from (AB) to (BC) 08/01/2006
Each share old Common no par exchanged for (0.2) share new Common no par 07/29/2014
Merged into BSM Technologies Inc. 10/05/2015
Each share new Common no par exchanged for (2.136) shares Common no par and $0.52 cash
Note: Unexchanged certificates will be cancelled and become without value 10/05/2021

WEBTRADEX INTL CORP (NV)
Common $0.001 par split (2) for (1) by issuance of (1) additional share payable 07/23/2010 to holders of record 07/23/2010
Name changed to ZD Ventures Corp. 09/11/2013
ZD Ventures Corp. name changed to Plyzer Technologies Inc. 05/01/2017

WEBTRENDS CORP (OR)
Issue Information - 3,500,000 shares COM offered at $13 per share on 02/19/1999
Common no par split (2) for (1) by issuance of (1) additional share payable 2/29/2000 to holders of record 2/8/2000
Merged into NetIQ Corp. 3/30/2001
Each share Common no par exchanged for (0.48) share Common $0.001 par
(See NetIQ Corp.)

WEBTRONICS INC (FL)
Each share Common $0.001 par exchanged for (475) shares Common $0.0001 par 04/03/2003
Reincorporated under the laws of Delaware as Callisto Pharmaceuticals, Inc. 05/20/2003
Callisto Pharmaceuticals, Inc. merged into Synergy Pharmaceuticals, Inc. 01/18/2013

WEB2 CORP (DE)
Recapitalized as Full Motion Beverage, Inc. 12/08/2008
Each (300) shares Common $0.001 par exchanged for (1) share Common $0.001 par

WEBVAN GROUP INC (DE)
Each share Preferred Ser. A $0.0001 par exchanged for (1) share Common $0.0001 par 11/10/1999
Each share Preferred Ser. B $0.0001 par exchanged for (1) share Common $0.0001 par 11/10/1999
Each share Preferred Ser. C $0.0001 par exchanged for (1) share Common $0.0001 par 11/10/1999
Each share Preferred Ser. D-2 $0.0001 par exchanged for (1) share Common $0.0001 par 11/10/1999
Plan of reorganization under Chapter 11 Federal Bankruptcy proceedings effective 03/07/2002
No stockholders' equity

WEBWORX INC (DE)
Name changed to Transoft Technologies, Inc. 12/26/2006
Transoft Technologies, Inc. name

changed to Quri Resources Inc. 02/05/2009

WEC, INC. (DE)
Dissolved 9/15/67

WEC CAP TR I (DE)
Issue Information - 8,000,000 TR PFD SECS offered at $25 per share on 03/16/1999
6.85% Guaranteed Trust Preferred called for redemption at $25 plus $0.040909 accrued dividend on 3/26/2004

WECAST NETWORK INC (NV)
Name changed to Seven Stars Cloud Group, Inc. 07/17/2017

WECK EDWARD & CO INC (DE)
Acquired by Squibb Corp. 05/27/1971
Each share Common 10¢ par exchanged for (0.252) share Common $1 par
Squibb Corp. merged into Bristol-Myers Squibb Co. 10/04/1989

WECO DEV CORP (DE)
Name changed to Worldwide Energy Corp. 06/14/1977
Worldwide Energy Corp. merged into Triton Energy Corp. (TX) 11/18/1986 which reincorporated in Delaware 05/12/1995 which merged into Triton Energy Ltd. 03/25/1996
(See Triton Energy Ltd.)

WECO PRODUCTS CO. (IL)
Capital Stock $1 par split (4) for (1) by issuance of (3) additional shares 2/26/54
Merged into Chemway Corp. 1/29/62
Each share Capital Stock $1 par exchanged for (2) shares Capital Stock $1 par
Chemway Corp. completely liquidated for Cooper Laboratories, Inc. 4/30/71
(See Cooper Laboratories, Inc.)

WEDA BAY MINERALS INC (AB)
Merged into Eramet S.A. 8/1/2006
Each share Common no par exchanged for $2.70 cash

WEDCO TECHNOLOGY INC (NJ)
Stock Dividend - 10% 03/24/1994
Acquired by ICO, Inc. (Old) 04/30/1996
Each share Common 10¢ par exchanged for either (2.2) shares Common no par and $3.50 cash or (2.84) shares Common no par
Note: Option to receive stock and cash expired 06/10/1996
ICO, Inc. (Old) reorganized as ICO, Inc. (New) 04/01/1998 which merged into Schulman (A.), Inc. 04/30/2010
(See Schulman (A.), Inc.)

WEDDING RIVER GOLD MINES, LTD. (ON)
Charter surrendered in May 1963
No stockholders' equity

WEDDINGPAGES INC (DE)
Name changed 9/19/97
Name changed from Wedding Information Network, Inc. to Weddingpages Inc. 9/19/97
Merged into Knot Acquisition Corp. 3/30/2000
Each share Common 1¢ par exchanged for $1.68 cash
Note: Each share Common 1¢ par received an additional distribution of $0.0777217 cash from escrow 5/4/2001

WEDEN ELECTRS INC (NY)
Name changed to New-Tek-Nic Industries Ltd. 11/16/1970
(See New-Tek-Nic Industries Ltd.)

WEDGE ENERGY INTL INC (ON)
Reorganized under the laws of British Columbia as Undur Tolgoi Minerals Inc. 11/14/2011
Each share Common no par exchanged for (0.05) share Common no par
Undur Tolgoi Minerals Inc. (BC) reincorporated in British Virgin Islands as Khot Infrastructure Holdings, Ltd. 01/15/2014 which name changed to Blockchain Holdings Ltd. 10/2018

WEDGE NET EXPERTS INC (CA)
Name changed to Sequiam Corp. 05/01/2002
(See Sequiam Corp.)

WEDGESTONE FINL (MA)
Name changed 12/17/87
Name changed from Wedgestone Realty Investors Trust to Wedgestone Financial 12/17/87
Merged into Wedgestone Acquisition LLC 7/6/98
Each Share of Bene. Int. $1 par exchanged for $0.67 cash

WEDGESTONE PART MTG TR (MA)
Merged into Wedgestone Realty Investors Trust 8/22/85
Each Share of Bene. Int. $1 par exchanged for (1.05) Shares of Bene. Int. $1 par and (1) Special Income Share no par
Wedgestone Realty Investors Trust name changed to Wedgestone Financial 12/17/87
(See Wedgestone Financial)

WEDGEWOOD INVESTING CORP.
Acquired by Tri-Continental Corp. in 1931
Details not available

WEDGEWOOD RES LTD (BC)
Recapitalized as Clan Resources Ltd. 12/23/1998
Each share Common no par exchanged for (0.1) share Common no par
Clan Resources Ltd. name changed to Energy Metals Corp. 12/20/2004 which merged into Uranium One Inc. 08/10/2007
(See Uranium One Inc.)

WEDTECH CORP (NY)
Common 1¢ par split (3) for (2) by issuance of (0.5) additional share 09/18/1985
Plan of reorganization under Chapter 11 Federal Bankruptcy proceedings confirmed 11/10/1990
No stockholders' equity

WEE GEE URANIUM MINES LTD (ON)
Charter cancelled for failure to pay taxes and file returns 12/19/73

WEE WEES INC (NV)
Name changed to Financial Intranet, Inc. 12/17/1996
Financial Intranet, Inc. name changed to Technest Holdings, Inc. (NV) 07/12/2001 which reincorporated in Delaware as AccelPath, Inc. 05/09/2012

WEED GROWTH FD INC (NV)
Company terminated registration and is no longer public as of 11/30/2017

WEEDEN & CO (DE)
4% Preferred $50 par called for redemption 04/01/1959
Stock Dividends - 25% 03/01/1955; 100% 04/15/1959; 200% 02/03/1969
Under plan of merger each share Common no par automatically became (1) share Weeden Holding Corp. (DE) Common $1 par 06/02/1975
Weeden Holding Corp. (DE) reincorporated in Nevada 06/02/1975 which merged into Moseley, Hallgarten, Estabrook & Weeden Holding Corp. 02/16/1979 which name changed to Moseley Holding Corp. 05/01/1986
(See Moseley Holding Corp.)

WEEDEN HLDG CORP
Reincorporated 06/02/1975
State of incorporation changed from (DE) to (NV) 06/02/1975
Under plan of merger each share Common $1 par automatically became (1) share Moseley, Hallgarten, Estabrook & Weeden Holding Corp. Common $1 par 02/16/1979
Moseley, Hallgarten, Estabrook & Weeden Holding Corp. name changed to Moseley Holding Corp. 05/01/1986
(See Moseley Holding Corp.)

WEEDON, PYRITE & COPPER CORP. LTD. (QC)
Name changed to Weedon Mining Corp. Ltd. 6/8/59
Weedon Mining Corp. Ltd. recapitalized as Wisconsin Mining Co., Ltd. 11/12/64 which recapitalized as Joubi Mining Corp. Ltd. 3/9/73
(See Joubi Mining Corp.)

WEEDON MINING CORP. LTD. (QC)
Recapitalized as Wisconsin Mining Co., Ltd. 11/12/64
Each share Capital Stock $1 par exchanged for (0.25) share Capital Stock $1 par
Wisconsin Mining Co., Ltd. recapitalized as Joubi Mining Corp. Ltd. 3/9/73
(See Joubi Mining Corp. Ltd.)

WEEKS CORP (GA)
Issue Information - 6,000,000 shares COM offered at $19.25 per share on 08/17/1994
Merged into Duke-Weeks Realty Corp. 7/2/99
Each share 8% Preferred Ser. A 1¢ par exchanged for (0.5) share 8% Depositary Preferred Ser. F 1¢ par
Each share Common 1¢ par exchanged for (1.38) shares Common 1¢ par

WEETAMOE BANCORP (MA)
Name changed to Slade's Ferry Bancorp 01/02/1997
Slade's Ferry Bancorp merged into Independent Bank Corp. 03/01/2008

WEGER ENGINE CO. (OH)
Charter cancelled for failure to file reports and pay taxes 11/15/32

WEHLE BREWING CO. (CT)
Inoperative in 1942

WEHR CORP (WI)
Stock Dividend - 25% 05/28/1965
Each (220) shares old Common $1 par exchanged for (1) share new Common $1 par 11/19/1986
Note: In effect holders received $150 cash per share and public interest was eliminated

WEIDA COMMUNICATIONS INC (NJ)
Filed a petition under Chapter 7 Federal Bankruptcy Code 03/29/2006
No stockholders' equity

WEIDER NUTRITION INTL INC (DE)
Issue Information - 5,600,000 shares CL A offered at $11 per share on 04/30/1997
Name changed to Schiff Nutrition International, Inc. 10/25/2005
(See Schiff Nutrition International, Inc.)

WEIFEI CAP INC (BC)
Issue Information - 4,000,000 shares COM offered at $0.10 per share on 10/13/2010
Recapitalized as Angkor Gold Corp. 10/19/2011
Each share Common no par exchanged for (0.57142857) share Common no par

WEIGH TRONIX INC (DE)
Reincorporated 09/01/1988
State of incorporation changed from (IA) to (DE) and Common no par changed to 1¢ par 09/01/1988
Merged into WTI Acquisition Corp. 08/23/1991
Each share Common 1¢ par exchanged for $22 cash

WEIGHT LOSS FOREVER INTL INC (NV)
Name changed to Beverly Hills Weight Loss & Wellness, Inc. (NV) 7/8/2004
Beverly Hills Weight Loss & Wellness, Inc. (NV) reincorporated in Delaware as Cardiovascular Sciences, Inc. 5/30/2006

WEIGHT WATCHERS INTL INC (NY)
Common 25¢ par split (3) for (2) by issuance of (0.5) additional share 2/16/73
Stock Dividend - 100% 6/16/69
Merged into Heinz (H.J.) Co. 9/25/78
Each share Common 25¢ par exchanged for $24 cash

WEIL-MC LAIN CO., INC. (IN)
Class A Common 50¢ par and Class B Common 3rd thru 5th Ser. 50¢ par changed to 25¢ par respectively and (1) additional share issued 03/07/1969
5% Preferred $100 par called for redemption 02/14/1972
Stock Dividend - Class A & B Common 50% 10/06/1967
Reincorporated under the laws of Delaware, Class A Common 25¢ par reclassified as Common 25¢ par and Conv. 2nd Ser. A Preferred $10 par reclassified as Conv. Ser. A Preferred $10 par 05/01/1972
Weil-McLain Co., Inc. (DE) name changed to Wylain, Inc. 04/26/1976 which merged into Marley Co. 05/06/1980
(See Marley Co.)

WEIL MCLAIN INC (DE)
$1 Preferred Ser. A called for redemption 05/01/1972
Conv. Preferred Ser. A $10 par called for redemption 01/08/1974
Name changed to Wylain, Inc. 04/26/1976
Wylain, Inc. merged into Marley Co. 05/06/1980
(See Marley Co.)

WEILL (RAPHAEL) & CO. (NV)
Common $100 par changed to no par and (4) additional shares issued 5/1/57
Stock Dividend - 50% 10/48
Adjudicated bankrupt 2/3/65
No stockholders' equity

WEIMAN INC (DE)
Reincorporated 04/30/1969
State of incorporation changed from (NY) to (DE) 04/30/1969
Merged into Weico Holdings, Inc. 09/11/1990
Each share Common $1 par exchanged for $4.75 cash

WEINBERGER DRUG STORES, INC.
Name changed to Gray Drug Stores, Inc. in 1945
(See Gray Drug Stores, Inc.)

WEINERS STORES INC (DE)
Plan of reorganization under Chapter 11 Federal Bankruptcy Code effective 6/7/2002
No stockholders' equity

WEINGARTEN J INC (TX)
4-1/2% Preferred Ser. 1945 $50 par called for redemption 5/23/55
Class A no par reclassified as Common no par which was split (5) for (1) by issuance of (4) additional shares 9/30/68
Merged into Cavenham Ltd. 3/28/80

Each share Common no par exchanged for $12 cash

WEINGARTEN MARKETS REALTY CO. (TX)
Each share Common no par exchanged for (8) shares Common $1 par 9/29/58
Name changed to Weingarten Realty, Inc. 3/29/74
Weingarten Realty, Inc. reorganized as Weingarten Realty Investors 4/5/88

WEINGARTEN RLTY INC (TX)
Each share Common $1 par exchanged for (35) shares Common 3¢ par 08/23/1985
Reorganized as Weingarten Realty Investors 04/05/1988
Each share Common 3¢ par exchanged for (1) Share of Bene. Int. 3¢ par

WEINGARTEN RLTY INVS (TX)
7.44% Preferred Ser. A 3¢ par called for redemption at $25 plus $0.18 accrued dividends on 05/05/2003
7.125% Preferred Ser. B called for redemption at $25 plus $0.02 accrued dividends on 12/19/2003
7% Preferred Ser C 3¢ par called for redemption at $50 plus $0.01556 accrued dividends on 04/01/2004
6.95% Depositary Preferred Ser. E called for redemption at $25 plus $0.3185 accrued dividends on 11/21/2012
6.75% Depositary Preferred Ser. D called for redemption at $25 plus $0.0141 accrued dividends on 03/18/2013
6.5% Depositary Preferred Ser. F called for redemption at $25 plus $0.2392 accrued dividends on 05/08/2015
(Additional Information in Active)

WEINKLES LIQUOR STORES INC (FL)
Name changed to Shell's City Inc. 10/11/1968
Shell's City Inc. merged into Hill Bros., Inc. 08/27/1971
(See Hill Bros., Inc.)

WEINSCHEL ENGR INC (DE)
Capital Stock $1 par changed to 50¢ par and (1) additional share issued 06/07/1971
Merged into Lucas Industries, Inc. 09/24/1986
Each share Capital Stock 50¢ par exchanged for $17.0633 cash

WEINSTOCK-LUBIN & CO.
Acquired by Hale Brothers Stores, Inc. on a (0.85) for (1) basis 00/00/1949
Hale Brothers Stores, Inc. merged into Broadway Department Stores, Inc. 04/20/1951 which name changed to Broadway-Hale Stores, Inc. (DE) 05/15/1951 which merged into Broadway-Hale Stores, Inc. (CA) 08/27/1970 which name changed to Carter Hawley Hale Stores Inc. (CA) 05/30/1974 which reincorporated in Delaware 07/26/1984 which name changed to Broadway Stores, Inc. 06/17/1994 which merged into Federated Department Stores, Inc. 10/11/1995 which name changed to Macy's, Inc. 06/01/2007

WEIRTON STEEL CORP.
Merged into National Steel Corp. 00/00/1929
Details not available

WEIRTON STL CORP (DE)
Plan of reorganization under Chapter 11 Federal Bankruptcy Code effective 9/9/2004
No stockholders' equity

WEISBAUM BROTHERS-BROWER CO.
Name changed to Beau Brummell, Inc. in 1939
Beau Brummell, Inc. name changed to Beau Brummell Ties, Inc. in 1940 which merged into B.V.D. Co., Inc. 2/28/62 which was acquired by Glen Alden Corp. (Del.) 5/19/67 which merged into Rapid- American Corp. (Del.) 11/6/72
(See Rapid-American Corp. (Del.))

WEISFIELDS INC (DE)
Common $2 par split (2) for (1) by issuance of (1) additional share 4/20/84
Merged into Ratners Group plc 12/6/89
Each share Common $2 par exchanged for $57.50 cash

WEISS BROS. STORES, INC. (DE)
Name changed to Mayer (Gus) Stores, Inc. 11/25/68
Mayer (Gus) Stores, Inc. acquired by Warnaco Inc. 9/30/69
(See Warnaco Inc.)

WEISS ENGINEERING CORP. (NJ)
Liquidation completed 6/21/51
Common had no equity

WEISS POLLUTION CTL CORP (MI)
Merged into Weiss Investment Co. 06/30/1980
Details not available

WEISSBERG H R CORP (DE)
Adjudicated bankrupt 04/01/1968
No stockholders' equity

WEISSMULLERS JOHNNY AMERN NAT FOODS INC (MN)
Statutorily dissolved 10/4/91

WEISSNER BREWING CO., INC. (MD)
Dissolved 6/18/53
No stockholders' equity

WEITEK CORP (CA)
In process of liquidation
Each share Common no par received initial distribution of $0.73 cash payable 9/29/97 to holders of record 9/15/97
Note: Details on subsequent distributions, if any, are not available

WEITZ VALUE FD INC (NE)
Reorganized as Weitz Series Fund 02/07/1990
Details not available

WEITZER HOMEBUILDERS INC (FL)
Name changed to Century Builders Group, Inc. and Class A Common 1¢ par reclassified as Common $0.001 par 4/20/2000
Century Builders Group, Inc. merged into New Century Homebuilders, Inc. 5/7/2002

WEJ IT CORP (DE)
Name changed 09/15/1972
Name changed from Wej-It Expansion Products, Inc. to Wej-It Corp. 09/15/1972
Each share Common 10¢ par exchanged for (0.2) share Common 50¢ par 07/01/1977
Merged into WI Products Inc. 03/28/1980
Each share Common 50¢ par exchanged for $11.50 cash

WEKSLER INSTRS CORP (NY)
Merged into WIC Newco, Inc. 05/10/1978
Each share Common 30¢ par exchanged for $8 cash

WEKUSKO CONSOLIDATED LTD. (MB)
Recapitalized as Amanda Mines Ltd. on a (0.2) for (1) basis 6/29/55
Amanda Mines Ltd. name changed to Explorers Alliance Ltd. 7/9/56
(See Explorers Alliance Ltd.)

WELAND MINING LTD. (BC)
Recapitalized as Welland Consolidated Mining Ltd. 10/15/70
Each share Common $1 par exchanged for (0.25) share Common $1 par

WELBACK HLDGS LTD (HONG KONG)
Name changed to Terabit Access Technology International Ltd. 04/26/2002
Terabit Access Technology International Ltd. name changed to Ruili Holdings Ltd. 01/06/2005 which name changed to See Corp. Ltd. 11/07/2005
(See See Corp. Ltd.)

WELBILT CORP (MI)
Each share old Common $1 par exchanged for (0.1) share new Common $1 par 09/08/1977
5% Conv. Preferred $10 par called for redemption 08/23/1982
New Common $1 par split (3) for (1) by issuance of (2) additional shares 08/08/1983
New Common $1 par split (3) for (2) by issuance of (0.5) additional share 07/12/1984
New Common $1 par split (2) for (1) by issuance of (1) additional share 08/05/1985
New Common $1 par split (3) for (2) by issuance of (0.5) additional share 07/24/1987
Merged into CA Holdings Corp. 09/09/1988
Each share new Common $1 par exchanged for $26.50 cash

WELBILT CORP NEW (DE)
Acquired by Berisford International plc 01/24/1995
Each share Common 1¢ par exchanged for $33.75 cash

WELCH GRAPE JUICE CO. (NY)
Name changed to Old Welch Co., Inc. in 1952 which was in liquidation in 1956

WELCH INDUSTRIES, INC. (DE)
Assets acquired by Texas Gulf Industries, Inc. 5/29/56

WELCH SCIENTIFIC CO. (IL)
Under plan of merger name changed to Sargent-Welch Scientific Co. 05/31/1968
(See Sargent-Welch Scientific Co.)

WELCH-WILMARTH CORP.
Succeeded by Grand Rapids Store Equipment Corp. in 1927
Details not available

WELCOM CAP INC (CO)
Each share old Common $0.001 par exchanged for (0.1) share new Common $0.001 par 05/14/1992
Recapitalized as Great Earth Vitamin Group Inc. 01/10/1994
Each share new Common $0.001 par exchanged for (0.05) share Common $0.001 par
Great Earth Vitamin Group Inc. name changed to Kelly's Coffee Group, Inc. (CO) 04/22/1994 which reincorporated in Nevada 10/10/2000 which name changed to Nexia Holdings Inc. (NV) 03/21/2002 which reincorporated in Utah as Sack Lunch Productions, Inc. 04/20/2015

WELCOME ABOARD VACATION CTRS INC (NY)
Completely liquidated 10/15/71
Each share Common 5¢ par exchanged for (0.5) share Equitable Development Corp. (FL) Common 1¢ par
Equitable Development Corp. (FL) name changed to Solar Industries, Inc. (FL) 2/23/77 which name changed to Pan American Gold, Inc. 4/10/87

(See Pan American Gold, Inc.)

WELCOME HOME INC (DE)
Issue Information - 2,500,000 shares COM offered at $11 per share on 09/22/1994
Reorganized under Chapter 11 Federal Bankruptcy Code 5/19/99
Each share old Common 1¢ par exchanged for (0.20291384) share new Common 1¢ par
Merged into a private co. 6/2/2000
Each share new Common 1¢ par exchanged for $2.25 cash

WELCOME NORTH RES INC (BC)
Name changed 06/20/1990
Common 50¢ par changed to no par 05/14/1979
Name changed from Welcome North Mines Ltd. to Welcome North Resources, Inc. 06/20/1990
Each share old Common no par exchanged for (1) share new Common no par
Recapitalized as Welcome Opportunities Ltd. 07/07/1995
Each share new Common no par exchanged for (0.125) share Common no par
Welcome Opportunities Ltd. reorganized as Endeavour Mining Capital Corp. (Cayman Islands) 09/10/2002 which name changed to Endeavour Financial Corp. 07/16/2008 which name changed to Endeavour Mining Corp. 09/20/2010

WELCOME OPPORTUNITIES LTD (BC)
Plan of Arrangement effective 09/10/2002
Each share Common no par exchanged for (1) share Endeavour Mining Capital Corp. (Cayman Islands) Ordinary USD $0.01 par and (1) Contingent Value Right
Endeavour Mining Capital Corp. name changed to Endeavour Financial Corp. 07/16/2008 which name changed to Endeavour Mining Corp. 09/20/2010

WELCOME SEARCH ENGINE INC (FL)
Name changed to CityXpress.com Corp. 10/21/1999
CityXpress.com Corp. name changed to CityXpress Corp. (FL) 06/17/2002 which reincorporated in Oklahoma as Cigars MFOV, Inc. 07/09/2015 which name changed to Fernhill Beverage, Inc. 12/09/2015

WELDED TUBE CO AMER (PA)
Class B Common $1 par reclassified as Class A Common $1 par 9/30/65
Class A Common $1 par reclassified as Common $1 par 6/1/66
Common $1 par split (3) for (2) by issuance of (0.5) additional share 2/15/80
Stock Dividends - 100% 6/17/66; 10% 1/5/79
Merged into Palmer Tube Mills Ltd. 9/30/87
Each share Common $1 par exchanged for $15.25 cash

WELDING ENGINEERS INC (PA)
Merged out of existence 06/30/1981
Details not available

WELDOTRON CORP (NJ)
Common 10¢ par changed to 5¢ par and (1) additional share issued plus a 50% stock dividend paid 07/05/1961
Common 5¢ par split (3) for (2) by issuance of (0.5) additional share 12/10/1982
Assets sold for the benefit of creditors 11/18/1998
No stockholders' equity

WELDWOOD CDA LTD (BC)
Common no par split (2) for (1) by issuance of (1) additional share 05/25/1984

Common no par split (2) for (1) by issuance of (1) additional share 06/01/1987
Merged into Champion International Corp. 07/03/1996
Each share Common no par exchanged for $40.50 cash

WELEX JET SERVICES, INC. (DE)
Common $1 par split (2) for (1) by issuance of (1) additional share 09/07/1956
Assets acquired by Halliburton Oil Well Cementing Co. on a (1) for (2.4) basis 10/15/1957
Halliburton Oil Well Cementing Co. name changed to Halliburton Co. 07/05/1960

WELEX JET SERVICES, INC. (TX)
Reorganized under the laws of Delaware 00/00/1954
Each share Common no par exchanged for (2) shares Common $1 par
Welex Jet Services, Inc. (DE) acquired by Halliburton Oil Well Cementing Co. 10/15/1957 which name changed to Halliburton Co. 07/05/1960

WELICHEM BIOTECH INC (BC)
Each share old Common no par exchanged for (0.1) share new Common no par 09/03/2009
94.1% acquired through purchase offer which expired 06/19/2014
Public interest eliminated

WELKOM GOLD HLDGS LTD (SOUTH AFRICA)
Plan of arrangement effective 04/19/1994
Each ADR for Ordinary ZAR 50 par exchanged for (0.6786) FreeState Consolidated Gold Mines Ltd. ADR for Ordinary ZAR 50 par
FreeState Consolidated Gold Mines Ltd. merged into AngloGold Ltd. 06/29/1998 which name changed to AngloGold Ashanti Ltd. 04/26/2004

WELKOM GOLD MINING CO. LTD. (SOUTH AFRICA)
Name changed to Welkom Gold Holdings Ltd. 2/24/86
Welkom Gold Holdings Ltd. reorganized into FreeState Consolidated Gold Mines Ltd. 4/19/94 which merged into AngloGold Ltd. 6/29/98 which name changed to AngloGold Ashanti Ltd. 4/26/2004

WELL RENEWAL INC (DE)
Recapitalized as Lighthouse Petroleum, Inc. 10/15/2008
Each share Common $0.001 par exchanged for (0.001) share Common $0.001 par
Lighthouse Petroleum, Inc. name changed to Supurva Healthcare Group, Inc. 06/30/2015

WELL SUPERVISION, INC. (UT)
Name changed to Titan Wells, Inc. 05/31/1968
(See Titan Wells, Inc.)

WELLCARE MGMT GROUP INC (NY)
Merged into Wellcare Acquisition Co. 8/1/2002
Each share Common 1¢ par exchanged for $0.24838 cash

WELLCHOICE INC (DE)
Merged into WellPoint, Inc. 12/28/2005
Each share Common 1¢ par exchanged for (0.5191) share Common 1¢ par and $38.25 cash
WellPoint, Inc. name changed to Anthem, Inc. (New) 12/03/2014

WELLCO ENERGY SVCS INC (BC)
Reorganized under the laws of Alberta as Wellco Energy Services Trust 08/06/2002
Each share Common no par exchanged for (0.1) Trust Unit no par
Wellco Energy Services Trust merged into Peak Energy Services Trust 03/12/2008 which reorganized as Peak Energy Services Ltd. (New) 01/06/2011
(See Peak Energy Services Ltd. (New))

WELLCO ENERGY SVCS TR (AB)
Merged into Peak Energy Services Trust 03/12/2008
Each Trust Unit no par exchanged for (0.9) Trust Unit no par
Peak Energy Services Trust reorganized as Peak Energy Services Ltd. (New) 01/06/2011
(See Peak Energy Services Ltd. (New))

WELLCO ENTERPRISES INC (NC)
Common $1 par split (2) for (1) by issuance of (1) additional share 5/9/86
Common $1 par split (3) for (1) by issuance of (2) additional shares payable 1/3/97 holders of record 12/6/96 Ex date - 1/6/97
Merged into Wasatch Boot Holdings, Inc. 5/9/2007
Each share Common $1 par exchanged for $14 cash

WELLCO RO-SEARCH INDUSTRIES, INC. (NC)
Name changed to Wellco Enterprises, Inc. 11/24/67
(See Wellco Enterprises, Inc.)

WELLCOME PLC (ENGLAND)
Merged into Glaxo Wellcome PLC 06/21/1995
Each Sponsored ADR for Ordinary exchanged for (0.47) share Ordinary and approximately $11.50 cash
Glaxo Wellcome PLC name changed to GlaxoSmithKline PLC 12/27/2000

WELLCORP INTL INC (DE)
Involuntary bankruptcy filed 12/00/1988
Stockholders' equity unlikely

WELLENTECH SVCS INC (NV)
Common $0.001 par split (2) for (1) by issuance of (1) additional share payable 09/02/2008 to holders of record 08/28/2008 Ex date - 09/03/2008
Name changed to Implex Corp. 10/01/2008
Implex Corp. name changed to Consorteum Holdings, Inc. 06/09/2009

WELLESLEY INCOME FD (MD)
Reincorporated 04/01/1973
State of incorporation changed from (DE) to (MD) 04/01/1973
Name changed to Vanguard/Wellesley Income Fund, Inc. (MD) 04/30/1993
Vanguard/Wellesley Income Fund, Inc. (MD) reincorporated in Delaware as Vanguard Wellesley Income Fund 05/29/1998

WELLFLEET COMMUNICATIONS INC (DE)
Common 1¢ par split (2) for (1) by issuance of (1) additional share 12/31/1992
Common 1¢ par split (2) for (1) by issuance of (1) additional share 05/13/1994
Name changed to Bay Networks, Inc. 10/20/1994
Bay Networks, Inc. merged into Northern Telecom Ltd.-Northern Telecom Ltee. 08/31/1998 which name changed to Nortel Networks Corp. (Old) 04/30/1999 which reorganized as Nortel Networks Corp. (New) 05/01/2000
(See Nortel Networks Corp. (New))

WELLGREEN PLATINUM LTD (BC)
Name changed to Nickel Creek Platinum Corp. 01/11/2018

WELLING HLDG LTD (HONG KONG)
ADR agreement terminated 09/23/2016
No ADR's remain outstanding

WELLINGTON BK INTL LTD (NASSAU, BAHAMAS)
Name changed to Wellington Corp. Ltd. 12/06/1972
Wellington Corp. Ltd. acquired by York Lambton Corp. Ltd. 09/15/1975 which name changed to York Lambton Inc. 05/29/1979
(See York Lambton Inc.)

WELLINGTON BANK OF CANADA INTERNATIONAL LTD. (NASSAU, BAHAMAS)
Name changed to Wellington Bank International Ltd. (Nassau) 4/22/66
Wellington Bank International Ltd. (Nassau) name changed to Wellington Corp. Ltd. 12/6/72 which was acquired by York Lambton Corp. Ltd. 9/15/75 which name changed to York Lambton Inc. 5/29/79

WELLINGTON COMMUNICATIONS INTL LTD (NY)
Charter cancelled and proclaimed dissolved for failure to pay taxes 06/26/1996

WELLINGTON COMPUTER GRAPHICS INC (DE)
Each share Common $1 par exchanged for (0.005) share Common $200 par 11/29/1974
Under plan of merger name changed to Wellington Industries, Inc. 04/30/1982
(See Wellington Industries, Inc.)

WELLINGTON CORP. LTD. (BAHAMAS)
Acquired by York Lambton Corp. Ltd. 9/15/75
Each share Class A £1 par exchanged for (1.17) shares Class B no par
Each share Class B £1 par exchanged for (1.17) shares Class B no par
York Lambton Corp. Ltd. name changed to York Lambton Inc. 5/29/79

WELLINGTON COVE EXPLORATIONS LTD (ON)
Reincorporated under the laws of Canada as GoldQuest Mining Corp. 7/7/2004

WELLINGTON 8 INDS INC (NJ)
Adjudicated bankrupt 02/14/1973
Stockholders' equity unlikely

WELLINGTON ELECTRONICS, INC. (NY)
Name changed to Wellington Technical Industries Inc. 3/18/68
Wellington Technical Industries, Inc. merged into Wellington Industries, Inc. 4/30/82

WELLINGTON EQUITY FUND, INC. (DE)
Name changed to Windsor Fund, Inc. (DE) 08/16/1963
Windsor Fund, Inc. (DE) reincorporated in Maryland 04/01/1973 which reincorporated in Pennsylvania 01/02/1985 which reincorporated in Maryland as Windsor Funds, Inc. 12/30/1985 which name changed to Vanguard/Windsor Funds, Inc. (MD) 04/30/1993 which reincorporated in Delaware as Vanguard Windsor Funds 05/29/1998

WELLINGTON FD INC (MD)
Reincorporated 04/01/1973
Common $1 par split (2) for (1) by issuance of (1) additional share 04/23/1956
State of incorporation changed from (DE) to (MD) 04/01/1973

Name changed to Vanguard/Wellington Fund, Inc. (MD) 03/17/1993
Vanguard/Wellington Fund, Inc. (MD) reorganized in Delaware as Vanguard Wellington Fund 05/29/1998

WELLINGTON FINANCIAL CORP., LTD. (CANADA)
Common no par reclassified as Class B no par 11/4/64
Name changed to York Lambton Corp. Ltd. 12/27/66
York Lambton Corp. Ltd. name changed to York Lambton Inc. 5/29/79
(See York Lambton Inc.)

WELLINGTON FINL SVCS INC (CO)
Each share old Common $0.025 par exchanged for (0.1) share new Common $0.025 par 07/12/1991
Name changed to Fajita Junction, Inc. 03/30/1993
Fajita Junction, Inc. name changed to Tostel Corp. 03/23/1995 which merged into Polus, Inc. 06/22/1998
(See Polus, Inc.)

WELLINGTON GROUP, LTD. (NV)
Name changed to Heartland Financial Inc. 09/20/1989
(See Heartland Financial Inc.)

WELLINGTON GROUP I INC (DE)
Name changed to American Spirit Corp. 01/22/1990
(See American Spirit Corp.)

WELLINGTON HALL LTD (NC)
Each share Common no par exchanged for (0.25) share old Common $4 par 05/17/1989
Each share old Common $4 par exchanged for (0.005) share new Common $4 par 04/27/2001
Note: Holders of (199) or fewer pre-split shares received $0.30 per share
Administratively dissolved 05/05/2005

WELLINGTON HALL VANMAR INC (NC)
Name changed to Wellington Hall, Ltd. 04/30/1970
(See Wellington Hall, Ltd.)

WELLINGTON INDS INC (DE)
Each share Common $200 par exchanged for (0.0625) share new Common $3,200 par 05/24/1988
Each share Common $3,200 par exchanged for (0.14545454) share Common $70,400 par 06/27/1989
Note: In effect holders received an undetermined amount of cash and public interest was eliminated

WELLINGTON LEISURE PRODS INC (DE)
Acquired by Standard Industries Inc. 1/12/94
Each share Common 1¢ par exchanged for $7.625 cash

WELLINGTON MGMT CO (DE)
Under plan of merger each share Class A Common 10¢ par exchanged for $11 cash 10/30/1979

WELLINGTON MILLS, INC. (DE)
Merged into West Point Manufacturing Co. 12/31/55
Each share Common no par exchanged for (16) shares Capital Stock $5 par
West Point Manufacturing Co. name was changed to West Point-Pepperell, Inc. 3/29/65
(See West Point-Pepperell, Inc.)

WELLINGTON MINES, LTD. (BC)
Recapitalized as New Wellington Mines Ltd. on a (1) for (10) basis 00/00/1953
New Wellington Mines Ltd. name changed to New Wellington Resources Ltd. 09/01/1970 which recapitalized as International

Wellington Resources Ltd.
03/25/1976 which recapitalized as Consolidated Wellington Resources Ltd. 12/12/1983 which name changed to First Hospitality (Canada) Corp. 09/24/1987 which recapitalized as Southern Pacific Development Corp. 11/05/1991 which recapitalized as Southern Pacific Resource Corp. (BC) 03/03/2006 which reincorporated in Alberta 11/17/2006

WELLINGTON MINES CO.
Liquidated in 1928

WELLINGTON OIL CO. LTD.
Merged into Wellington Oil Co. of Delaware share for share in 1937 Wellington Oil Co. of Delaware merged into Seaboard Oil Co. (DE) in 1942 which merged into Texas Co. (New) 6/2/58 which name changed to Texaco Inc. 5/1/59 which merged into ChevronTexaco Corp. 10/9/2001 which name changed to Chevron Corp. 5/9/2005

WELLINGTON OIL CO. OF DELAWARE (CO)
Merged into Seaboard Oil Co. (DE) on a (1) for (4) basis 00/00/1942 Seaboard Oil Co. (DE) merged into Texas Co. (New) 06/02/1958 which name changed to Texaco Inc. 05/01/1959 which merged into ChevronTexaco Corp. 10/09/2001 which name changed to Chevron Corp. 05/09/2005

WELLINGTON PPTYS TR (MD)
Shares of Bene. Int. 1¢ par split (4.75) for (3) by issuance of (0.5833333) additional share payable 03/24/1999 to holders of record 03/22/1999
Name changed to Stonehaven Realty Trust 01/19/2000
Stonehaven Realty Trust name changed to Paragon Real Estate Equity & Investment Trust 07/01/2003 which name changed to Pillarstone Capital REIT 06/20/2016

WELLINGTON TECHNICAL INDS INC (NY)
Common 75¢ par split (3) for (2) by issuance of (0.5) additional share 8/15/68
Merged into Wellington Industries, Inc. 4/30/82
Each (78) shares Common 75¢ par exchanged for (1) share Common $200 par
(See Wellington Industries, Inc.)

WELLINGTON UNDERWRITING PLC (UNITED KINGDOM)
Merged into Catlin Group Ltd. 12/18/2006
Each 144A Sponsored ADR for Ordinary exchanged for $24.6783 cash

WELLINGTON VENTURE CORP (CO)
Recapitalized as Nulon of America, Inc. 05/20/1988
Each share Common $0.0001 par exchanged for (0.05) share Common $0.0001 par

WELLMAN ENGINEERING CO. (OH)
Recapitalized 00/00/1939
Each share Preferred $100 par exchanged for (20) shares Common no par
Each share Common no par exchanged for (1) share new Common no par
Common no par changed to $5 par 00/00/1942
Merged into McDowell-Wellman Engineering Co. 05/31/1963
Each share Common $5 par exchanged for (1) share Class A Common $5 par
(See McDowell-Wellman Engineering Co.)

WELLMAN HLDGS INC (DE)
Acquired by Grupo Petromex, S.A. de C.V. 08/31/2011
Each share Common 1¢ par exchanged for $4.44848 cash

WELLMAN INC (DE)
Common $0.001 par split (2) for (1) by issuance of (1) additional share 06/15/1989
Plan of reorganization under Chapter 11 Federal Bankruptcy Code effective 01/30/2009
No stockholders' equity

WELLMAN INDS INC (TX)
Merged into Eckton Corp. 10/15/1984
Each share Common 10¢ par exchanged for $1.75 cash

WELLMAN OPERATING CORP. (DE)
Company advised private 00/00/1979
Details not available

WELLMAN-SEAVER-MORGAN CO. (OH)
Name changed to Wellman Engineering Co. 02/24/1930
Wellman Engineering Co. merged into McDowell-Wellman Engineering Co. 05/31/1963
(See McDowell-Wellman Engineering Co.)

WELLNESS AMER ONLINE INC (NV)
Name changed to General Ventures, Inc. 04/01/2005
(See General Ventures, Inc.)

WELLNESS INTL INC (DE)
Charter cancelled and declared inoperative and void for non-payment of taxes 03/01/1989

WELLNESS LIFESTYLES INC (BC)
Name changed to WELL Health Technologies Corp. 07/13/2018

WELLNESS UNIVERSE CORP (MN)
SEC halted trading and filed a complaint 02/16/2009. Company subsequently settled 09/00/2006 and is no longer active. Stockholders' equity unlikely

WELLORE ENERGY INC (CANADA)
Merged into Cabre Exploration Ltd. 09/04/1990
Each share Class A Common no par exchanged for (0.405) share Common no par
Cabre Exploration Ltd. acquired by EnerMark Income Fund 01/10/2001 which merged into Enerplus Resources Fund 06/22/2001 which reorganized as Enerplus Corp. 01/03/2011

WELLORE RES LTD (CANADA)
Recapitalized as Wellore Energy Inc. 10/14/1987
Each share Class A Common no par exchanged for (0.25) share Class A Common no par
Wellore Energy Inc. merged into Cabre Exploration Ltd. 09/04/1990 which was acquired by EnerMark Income Fund 01/10/2001 which merged into Enerplus Resources Fund 06/22/2001 which reorganized as Enerplus Corp. 01/03/2011

WELLPOINT HEALTH NETWORKS INC (DE)
Reincorporated 08/04/1997
State of incorporation changed from (CA) to (DE) 08/04/1997
Common 1¢ par split (2) for (1) by issuance of (1) additional share payable 03/15/2002 to holders of record 03/05/2002 Ex date - 03/18/2002
Merged into WellPoint, Inc. 12/01/2004
Each share Common 1¢ par exchanged for (1) share Common 1¢ par and $23.80 cash
WellPoint, Inc. name changed to Anthem, Inc. (New) 12/03/2014

WELLPOINT HEALTH NETWORKS INC OLD (DE)
Merged into Wellpoint Health Networks Inc. (CA) 05/20/1996
Each share Class A Common 1¢ par exchanged for (0.667) share Common 1¢ par
Each share Class B Common 1¢ par exchanged for (0.667) share Common 1¢ par
Wellpoint Health Networks Inc. (CA) reincorporated in Delaware 08/04/1997 which merged into WellPoint, Inc. 12/01/2004 which name changed to Anthem, Inc. (New) 12/03/2014

WELLPOINT INC (IN)
Common 1¢ par split (2) for (1) by issuance of (1) additional share payable 05/31/2005 to holders of record 05/13/2005 Ex date - 06/01/2005
Name changed to Anthem, Inc. (New) 12/03/2014

WELLPOINT SYS INC (AB)
Placed in receivership 01/31/2011
Stockholders' equity unlikely

WELLS AMERN CORP (MD)
Filed a petition under Chapter 7 Federal Bankruptcy Code 03/09/1990
Stockholders' equity unlikely

WELLS BENRUS CORP (DE)
Plan of reorganization under Chapter 11 Federal Bankruptcy proceedings confirmed 06/10/1986
No stockholders' equity

WELLS FARGO & CO. (CO)
Each share Capital Stock $1 par exchanged for (0.2) share 4-1/2% Preferred $10 par, (0.1) share Common no par and (1) right to receive shares of 4-1/2% Prior Preference $10 par in 1945
Under plan of merger all Preferred and Common stocks redeemed for cash 11/25/63

WELLS FARGO & CO NEW (DE)
Adjustable Fixed Rate Preferred Ser. H no par called for redemption at $50 on 10/01/2001
Adjustable Rate Preferred Ser. B no par called for redemption at $50 on 11/15/2003
8% Depositary Preferred Class A Ser. J called for redemption at $25 on 09/17/2018
(Additional Information in Active)

WELLS FARGO & CO OLD (DE)
Reincorporated 6/30/87
Common $10 par changed to $5 par and (1) additional share issued 12/6/72
Common $5 par split (2) for (1) by issuance of (1) additional share 1/20/87
State of incorporation changed from (CA) to (DE) 6/30/87
Market Auction Preferred Ser. I no par called for redemption 1/15/91
Market Auction Preferred Ser. II no par called for redemption 1/23/91
Market Auction Preferred Ser. III no par called for redemption 1/29/91
Adjustable Rate Preferred Ser. A no par called for redemption 3/21/94
9.875% Depositary Preferred Ser. F called for redemption 11/15/96
9.875% Preferred Ser. F no par called for redemption 11/15/96
9% Depositary Preferred Ser. C called for redemption 12/31/96
Depositary Preferred Ser. D called for redemption 3/5/97
Preferred Ser. D $5 par called for redemption 3/5/97
9% Depositary Preferred Ser. G called for redemption at $25 on 5/29/97
Merged into Wells Fargo & Co. (New) 11/2/98
Each share Adjustable Rate Preferred Ser. B no par exchanged for (1) share Adjustable Rate Preferred Ser. B no par
Each share Fixed/Adjustable Rate Preferred Ser. H $5 par exchanged for (1) share Fixed/Adjustable Rate Preferred Ser. H no par
Each share Common $5 par exchanged for (10) shares Common $1-2/3 par

WELLS FARGO ADVANTAGE GLOBAL DIVID OPPORTUNITY FD (DE)
Name changed to Wells Fargo Global Dividend Opportunity Fund 12/15/2015

WELLS FARGO ADVANTAGE INCOME OPPORTUNITIES FD (DE)
Name changed to Wells Fargo Income Opportunities Fund 12/15/2015

WELLS FARGO ADVANTAGE MULTI SECTOR INCOME FD (DE)
Name changed to Wells Fargo Multi-Sector Income Fund 12/15/2015

WELLS FARGO ADVANTAGE UTILS & HIGH INCOME FD (DE)
Name changed to Wells Fargo Utilities & High Income Fund 12/15/2015

WELLS FARGO BANK (SAN FRANCISCO, CA)
Stock Dividends - 10% 8/20/59; 75% 3/13/64
Capital Stock $20 par changed to $10 par and (1) additional share issued 7/30/59
Merged into Wells Fargo Bank American Trust Co. (San Francisco, CA) 3/25/60
Each share Capital Stock $10 par exchanged for (1) share Capital Stock $10 par
Wells Fargo Bank American Trust Co. (San Francisco, CA) name changed to Wells Fargo Bank (San Francisco, CA) 1/31/62 which name changed to Wells Fargo Bank N.A. (San Francisco, CA) 8/15/68 which reorganized as Wells Fargo & Co. (Old) (CA) 2/28/69 which reincorporated in Delaware 6/30/87 which merged into Wells Fargo & Co. (New) 11/2/98

WELLS FARGO BANK AMERICAN TRUST CO. (SAN FRANCISCO, CA)
Stock Dividend - 10% 1/16/61
Name changed to Wells Fargo Bank (San Francisco, CA) 1/31/62
Wells Fargo Bank (San Francisco, CA) name changed to Wells Fargo Bank N.A. (San Francisco, CA) 8/15/68 which reorganized as in California as Wells Fargo & Co. (Old) (CA) 2/28/69 which reincorporated in Delaware 6/30/87 which merged into Wells Fargo & Co. (New) 11/2/98

WELLS FARGO BK N A (SAN FRANCISCO, CA)
Reorganized under the laws of California as Wells Fargo & Co. 2/28/69
Each share Capital Stock $10 par exchanged for (1) share Common $10 par
Wells Fargo & Co. (Old) (CA) reincorporated in Delaware 6/30/87 which merged into Wells Fargo & Co. (New) 11/2/98

WELLS FARGO CAP IV (DE)
Issue Information - 52,000,000 GTD CAP SECS 7% offered at $25 per share on 08/22/2001
7% Guaranteed Capital Securities called for redemption at $25 plus $0.2625 accrued dividends on 04/25/2011

WELLS FARGO CAP V (DE)
Issue Information - 8,000,000 QUARTERLY INCOME PFD SECS 7% offered at $25 per share on 11/28/2001
7% Quarterly Income Preferred Securities called for redemption at $25 on 04/19/2007

WELLS FARGO CAP VI (DE)
6.95% Guaranteed Capital Securities called for redemption at $25 on 04/19/2007

WELLS FARGO CAP VII (DE)
5.85% Guaranteed Trust Preferred Securities called for redemption at $25 plus $0.012188 accrued dividends on 02/04/2013

WELLS FARGO CAP VIII (DE)
Issue Information - 8,000,000 GTD TR PFD SECS TRUPS 5.625% offered at $25 per share on 07/21/2003
5.625% Guaranteed Trust Preferred Securities called for redemption at $25 plus $0.011719 accrued dividends on 02/04/2013

WELLS FARGO CAP IX (DE)
Issue Information - 20,000,000 TR ORIGINATED PFD SECS 5.625% offered at $25 per share on 04/01/2004
5.625% Trust Originated Preferred Securities called for redemption at $25 plus $0.128906 accrued dividends on 02/04/2013

WELLS FARGO CAP XI (DE)
6.25% Enhanced Trust Preferred Securities called for redemption at $25 plus $0.390625 accrued dividends on 06/15/2012

WELLS FARGO CAP XII (DE)
7.875% Enhanced Trust Preferred Securities called for redemption at $25 plus $0.492188 accrued dividends on 03/15/2013

WELLS FARGO CAP XIV (DE)
8.625% Enhanced Trust Preferred Securities called for redemption at $25 plus $0.107813 accrued dividends on 10/03/2011

WELLS FARGO MTG & EQUITY TR (MA)
Liquidation completed
Each Common Share of Bene. Int. no par received initial distribution of $19.50 cash 8/28/89
Each Common Share of Bene. Int. no par exchanged for second and final distribution of $1.43 cash 12/22/89

WELLS FARGO MORTGAGE INVESTORS (MA)
Name changed to Wells Fargo Mortgage & Equity Trust and Shares of Bene. Int. no par reclassified as Common Shares of Bene. Int. no par 12/14/1977
(See Wells Fargo Mortgage & Equity Trust)

WELLS FINL CORP (MN)
Each share old Common 10¢ par exchanged for (0.01) share new Common 10¢ par 02/22/2005
Note: Holders of (99) or fewer pre-split shares received $31.50 cash per share
Merged into Citizens Community Bancorp, Inc. 08/18/2017
Each share new Common 10¢ par exchanged for (0.7598982) share Common 1¢ par and $41.31 cash

WELLS GARDNER ELECTRS CORP (IL)
Name changed 04/21/1960
Name changed from Wells-Gardner & Co. to Wells-Gardner Electronics Corp. 04/21/1960
Common $1 par split (2) for (1) by issuance of (1) additional share 12/17/1980
Common $1 par split (2) for (1) by issuance of (1) additional share 06/03/1981
Common $1 par split (2) for (1) by issuance of (1) additional share 12/15/1981
Stock Dividends - 5% payable 04/22/1999 to holders of record 04/13/1999; 5% payable 04/14/2000 to holders of record 04/07/2000; 5% payable 04/13/2001 to holders of record 04/06/2001 Ex date - 04/04/2001; 5% payable 04/12/2002 to holders of record 04/05/2002 Ex date - 04/03/2002; 5% payable 04/11/2003 to holders of record 04/04/2003 Ex date - 04/02/2003; 5% payable 03/26/2004 to holders of record 03/19/2004; 5% payable 03/25/2005 to holders of record 03/18/2005 Ex date - 03/16/2005; 5% payable 03/30/2006 to holders of record 03/16/2006 Ex date - 03/14/2006; 5% payable 03/30/2007 to holders of record 03/09/2007 Ex date - 03/07/2007; 5% payable 04/18/2008 to holders of record 03/28/2008 Ex date - 03/26/2008; 5% payable 04/09/2010 to holders of record 03/19/2010 Ex date - 03/17/2010; 5% payable 03/31/2011 to holders of record 03/15/2011 Ex date - 03/14/2011
Name changed to AG&E Holdings, Inc. 10/30/2014

WELLS GOLD LTD (BC)
Name changed to Astridon Development Corp. 11/23/89
(See Astridon Development Corp.)

WELLS INDS CORP (CA)
Recapitalized as Continental Transportation Systems, Inc. 7/13/70
Each share Common 50¢ par exchanged for (0.4) share Common $1.25 par
(See Continental Transportation Systems, Inc.)

WELLS LONGLAC MINES LTD.
Liquidated in 1938

WELLS NATL SVCS CORP (NY)
Acquired by American Hospital Supply Corp. 08/31/1973
Each share Common $1 par exchanged for (0.66279) share Common no par
American Hospital Supply Corp. merged into Baxter Travenol Laboratories, Inc. 11/25/1985 which name changed to Baxter International Inc. 05/18/1988

WELLS OIL CO. OF DECATUR
Name changed to Owens-Wells Oil Co. in 1948
Owens-Wells Oil Co. completely liquidated 12/2/68

WELLS REAL ESTATE FD LTD PARTNERSHIP (GA)
Completely liquidated
Each Class A Unit of Ltd. Partnership I received first and final distribution of approximately $16.208162 cash payable 08/01/2009 to holders of record 08/01/2009
(See Note for Class B Units)
Completely liquidated
Each Class A Unit of Ltd. Partnership II received first and final distribution of approximately $5.1716833 cash payable 11/02/2009 to holders of record 10/01/2009
(See Note for Class B Units)
Each Class A Unit of Ltd. Partnership II-OW received first and final distribution of approximately $9.2543714 cash payable 11/02/2009 to holders of record 10/01/2009
(See Note for Class B Units)
Each Class A Unit of Ltd. Partnership III received first and final distribution of approximately $0.01841 cash payable 11/02/2009 to holders of record 11/02/2009
(See Note for Class B Units)
Note: All Class B Units were structured to benefit from passive losses only and will not receive any distribution

WELLS REAL ESTATE INVT TR INC (MD)
Name changed to Piedmont Office Realty Trust, Inc. 08/08/2007

WELLS RICH GREENE INC (NY)
Under plan of merger each share Common $1 par exchanged for $22 cash 11/03/1977

WELLS TELEVISION INC (NY)
Stock Dividend - 100% 08/20/1971
Name changed to Wells National Services Corp. 12/09/1971
Wells National Services Corp. acquired by American Hospital Supply Corp. 08/31/1973 which merged into Baxter Travenol Laboratories, Inc. 11/25/1985 which name changed to Baxter International Inc. 05/18/1988

WELLS TP SCIENCES INC (NY)
Merged into Graphic Scanning Corp. 09/07/1972
Each share Common 1¢ par exchanged for (0.141817) share Common 1¢ par
(See Graphic Scanning Corp.)

WELLSBURG BKG & TR CO (WV)
Acquired by First West Virginia Bancorp, Inc. 01/04/1993
Each share Common $10 par exchanged for (86) shares Common $10 par and $300 cash
First West Virginia Bancorp, Inc. merged into CB Financial Services Inc. 05/01/2018

WELLSFORD REAL PPTYS INC (MD)
Each share Common 1¢ par exchanged for (0.5) share Common 2¢ par 06/12/2000
Under plan of partial liquidation each share Common 2¢ par received distribution of $14 cash payable 12/14/2005 to holders of record 12/02/2005 Ex date - 12/15/2005
Name changed to Reis, Inc. 06/01/2007
(See Reis, Inc.)

WELLSFORD RESIDENTIAL PPTY TR (MD)
Each Common Share of Bene. Int. 1¢ par received distribution of (0.25) share Wellsford Real Properties, Inc. Common 1¢ par payable 6/5/97 to holders of record 5/30/97
Merged into Equity Residential Properties Trust 5/30/97
Each share 7% Conv. Preferred Ser. A 1¢ par exchanged for (1) 7% Preferred Share of Bene. Int. Ser. F 1¢ par
Each 9.65% Preferred Share of Bene. Int. 1¢ par exchanged for (1) 9.65% Preferred Share of Bene. Int. Ser. F 1¢ par
Each Common Share of Bene. Int. 1¢ par exchanged for (0.625) Common Share of Bene. Int. 1¢ par
Equity Residential Properties Trust name changed to Equity Residential 5/15/2002

WELLSHIRE EQUITIES INC (CO)
Recapitalized as Feather Industries, Inc. 12/30/1986
Each share Common $0.00001 par exchanged for (1) share Common $0.00001 par
(See Feather Industries, Inc.)

WELLSTAR INTL INC (NV)
Each share old Common $0.001 par exchanged for (0.01) share new Common $0.00001 par 01/15/2010
Ceased operations 04/06/2011
Stockholders' equity unlikely

WELLSTEAD INDS INC (DE)
Company liquidated assets in 1996
No stockholders' equity

WELLSTONE FILTER SCIENCES INC (DE)
Name changed 09/30/2009
Old Common $0.001 par split (5) for (1) by issuance of (4) additional shares payable 07/19/2003 to holders of record 07/09/2003 Ex date - 07/21/2003
Old Common $0.001 par split (1.4) for (1) by issuance of (0.4) additional share payable 09/30/2003 to holders of record 09/25/2003 Ex date - 10/01/2003
Old Common $0.001 par split (3) for (1) by issuance of (2) additional shares payable 10/05/2004 to holders of record 09/27/2004 Ex date - 10/06/2004
Each share old Common $0.001 par exchanged for (0.04) share new Common $0.001 par 06/29/2006
Each share new Common $0.001 par exchanged again for (0.01) share new Common $0.001 par 06/07/2007
Name changed from Wellstone Filters, Inc. to Wellstone Filter Sciences, Inc. 09/30/2009
Each share Common $0.001 par received distribution of (1) share Wellstone Tobacco Co. Restricted Common $0.001 par payable 08/09/2010 to holders of record 07/27/2010
Name changed to Auri, Inc. 04/14/2011

WELLSTREAM HLDGS PLC (UNITED KINGDOM)
Merged into General Electric Co. 02/03/2011
Each ADR for Ordinary exchanged for $63.403973 cash

WELLSWAY VENTURES INC (DE)
Name changed to IFS International Inc. 06/19/1989
IFS International Inc. name changed to IFS Holdings, Inc. 07/03/1992 which name changed to IFS International, Inc. 03/17/1999 which name changed to IFS International Holdings, Inc. 11/16/2000
(See IFS International Holdings, Inc.)

WELLTECH INC (DE)
Acquired by Bechtel Corp. and Hanna Mining Co. 06/06/1979
Each share Class A Common 10¢ par exchanged for $39 cash

WELLTEK INC (NV)
Ctfs. dated prior to 11/05/2009
Name changed to Nashville Records, Inc. (New) 11/05/2009

WELLTOWER INC (DE)
6.5% Preferred Ser. J $1 par called for redemption at $25 plus $0.234722 accrued dividends on 03/07/2017
(Additional Information in Active)

WELLUX INTL INC (NV)
Name changed to Readen Holding Corp. 08/22/2011

WELSBACH CO. (NJ)
Dissolved in 1944
No stockholders' equity

WELSBACH CORP (DE)
Each share Class B Common $1 par exchanged for (2) shares Class B Common 50¢ par 12/12/57
Each share Class A Common $10 par or Class B Common 50¢ par exchanged for (1) share Common $5 par in 1958
Common $5 par changed to $2.50 par and (1) additional share issued 9/12/61
Stock Dividends - 10% 11/16/59; 10% 11/15/60; 10% 11/15/61

Merged into Jamaica Water & Utilities, Inc. 11/23/70
Each share Common $2.50 par exchanged for (0.066666) share $15 Preferred Ser. B $100 par and (1) share Common 10¢ par
Jamaica Water & Utilities, Inc. name changed to Welsbach Corp. (NY) 11/1/74 which name changed to Jamaica Water Properties, Inc. 10/21/76 which name changed to JWP Inc. (NY) 5/12/86 which reincorporated in Delaware 8/4/87
(See JWP Inc.)

WELSBACH CORP (NY)
Name changed to Jamaica Water Properties, Inc. 10/21/76
Jamaica Water Properties, Inc. name changed to JWP Inc. (NY) 5/12/86 which reincorporated in Delaware 8/4/87
(See JWP Inc.)

WELSBACH ENGINEERING & MANAGEMENT CORP. (DE)
Name changed to Welsbach Corp. (DE) 4/24/47
Welsbach Corp. (DE) merged into Jamaica Water & Utilities, Inc. 11/23/70 which name changed to Welsbach Corp. (NY) 11/1/74 which name changed to Jamaica Water Properties, Inc. 10/21/76 which name changed to JWP Inc. 5/12/86
(See JWP Inc.)

WELSH CORP (WA)
Plan of Arrangement under Chapter XI bankruptcy proceedings confirmed 12/09/1975
Attorney opined no stockholders' equity

WELSH PANEL CO (WA)
Name changed to Welsh Corp. 04/17/1969
(See Welsh Corp.)

WELSPUN CORP LTD (INDIA)
GDR agreement terminated 09/05/2017
No GDR's remain outstanding

WELSPUN GUJARAT STAHL ROHREN LTD (INDIA)
Name changed to Welspun Corp. Ltd. 04/30/2010
(See Welspun Corp. Ltd.)

WELTE CO., INC.
Acquired by Welte-Mignon Corp. in 1928 which liquidated in 1930

WELTE-MIGNON CORP.
Liquidated in 1930

WELTON ENERGY CORP NEW (ON)
Merged into Churchill Energy Inc. 02/13/2009
Each share Common no par exchanged for (0.0199255) share Common no par
Churchill Energy Inc. merged into Zargon Energy Trust 09/23/2009 which reorganized as Zargon Oil & Gas Ltd. (New) 01/07/2011

WELTON ENERGY CORP OLD (ON)
Each share old Common no par exchanged for (0.1) share new Common no par 12/30/2004
Reorganized as Welton Energy Corp. (New) 08/04/2005
Each share Common no par exchanged for (1) share Common no par
Welton Energy Corp. (New) merged into Churchill Energy Inc. 02/13/2009 which merged into Zargon Energy Trust 09/23/2009 which reorganized as Zargon Oil & Gas Ltd. (New) 01/07/2011

WELWIND ENERGY INTL CORP (DE)
SEC revoked common stock registration 06/17/2013

WELWYN ENERGY LTD (AB)
Recapitalized as Welwyn Resources Ltd. 7/18/2003
Each share Common no par exchanged for (0.2) share Common no par
Welwyn Resources Ltd. name changed to Pan Orient Energy Corp. 7/27/2005

WELWYN RES LTD (AB)
Name changed to Pan Orient Energy Corp. 7/27/2005

WEMBLEY PLC (UNITED KINGDOM)
Liquidation completed
Each Sponsored ADR for Ordinary exchanged for initial distribution of $24.50889 cash 12/15/2005
Each Sponsored ADR for Ordinary received second distribution of $14.696 cash payable 06/27/2006 to holders of record 12/15/2005
Each Sponsored ADR for Ordinary received third distribution of $0.39379 cash payable 01/25/2008 to holders of record 12/15/2005
Each Sponsored ADR for Ordinary received fourth distribution of $0.710144 cash payable 09/20/2010 to holders of record 12/15/2005
Each Sponsored ADR for Ordinary received fifth distribution of $1.260318 cash payable 02/04/2013 to holders of record 12/15/2005
Each Sponsored ADR for Ordinary received sixth and final distribution of $0.56549 cash payable 07/17/2014 to holders of record 12/15/2005

WEMS INC (CA)
Completely liquidated 12/05/1967
Each share Common $1 par exchanged for first and final distribution of (0.5) share Electronic Memories, Inc. Common $1 par
Electronic Memories, Inc. merged into Electronic Memories & Magnetics Corp. 07/11/1969 which name changed to Titan Corp. 05/30/1985
(See Titan Corp.)

WEN LI INC (NV)
Recapitalized as Sentry Entertainment Group Ltd. 10/11/1985
Each share Common $0.0001 par exchanged for (0.05) share Common $0.002 par
Sentry Entertainment Group Ltd. name changed to International Message Switching Inc. 08/07/1986

WENATCHEE RES LTD (BC)
Reincorporated under the laws of Canada as Compleat Health Corp. 08/14/1978
(See Compleat Health Corp.)

WENCARRO RES LTD (BC)
Delisted from Vancouver Stock Exchange 05/01/1990

WENDELL FEDERAL SAVINGS & LOAN ASSOCIATION (USA)
Merged into Pioneer Savings Bank, Inc. 12/21/1987
Each share Common $1 par exchanged for (2.5) shares Common $1 par
Pioneer Savings Bank, Inc. reorganized as Pioneer Bancorp, Inc. 12/28/1988
(See Pioneer Bancorp, Inc.)

WENDELL MINERAL PRODUCTS LTD. (QC)
Name changed 00/00/1949
Name changed from Wendell Gold Mines Ltd. to Wendell Mineral Products Ltd. 00/00/1949
Recapitalized as Black River Mining Ltd. 05/18/1961
Each share Capital Stock no par exchanged for (0.2) share Capital Stock no par
Black River Mining Ltd. recapitalized as Menorah Mines Ltd. 03/04/1968 which name changed to Menora Resources Inc. 04/28/1983 which recapitalized as Mengold Resources Inc. 12/04/2003 which recapitalized as MGold Resources Inc. (QC) 09/22/2010 which reincorporated in Alberta 07/25/2013 which name changed to Tanager Energy Inc. 09/23/2013

WENDELL PHILLIPS CO.
Liquidated in 1945

WENDEN COPPER MINING CO.
Dissolved in 1936

WENDIGO GOLD MINES LTD.
Liquidation completed in 1945

WENDOVER BUILDING CORP. (CA)
Completely liquidated for cash 9/1/63

WENDT BRISTOL CO (DE)
Merged into Temco National Corp. 03/02/1989
Each share Common 1¢ par exchanged for (2.5) shares Common 1¢ par
Temco National Corp. name changed to Wendt-Bristol Health Services Corp. 10/26/1992
(See Wendt-Bristol Health Services Corp.)

WENDT-BRISTOL DIAGNOSTICS L P (DE)
86% owned by Temco National Corp. as of 07/26/1999
Public interest eliminated

WENDT-BRISTOL HEALTH SVCS CORP (DE)
SEC revoked common stock registration 10/28/2008

WENDY JEWELRY ENTERPRISES INC (NY)
Common 1¢ par split (5) for (1) by issuance of (4) additional shares 5/15/86
Common 1¢ par split (2) for (1) by issuance of (1) additional share 3/18/87
Name changed to Goldtech Corp. 8/5/87
(See Goldtech Corp.)

WENDY'S OF WEST MICHIGAN LIMITED PARTNERSHIP (MI)
Certificate of cancellation issued 1/30/98

WENDYS / ARBYS GROUP INC (DE)
Name changed to Wendy's Co. 07/11/2011

WENDYS FING I
$2.50 Guaranteed Term Conv. Securities Ser. A called for redemption at $51.25 on 6/10/2002

WENDYS INTL INC (OH)
Common no par split (4) for (3) by issuance of (1/3) additional share 09/15/1977
Common no par split (2) for (1) by issuance of (1) additional share 06/02/1978
Common no par split (3) for (2) by issuance of (0.5) additional share 03/20/1981
Common no par split (3) for (2) by issuance of (0.5) additional share 11/24/1982
Common no par split (4) for (3) by issuance of (1/3) additional share 03/13/1984
Common no par split (4) for (3) by issuance of (1/3) additional share 03/13/1985
Common no par split (5) for (4) by issuance of (0.25) additional share 05/14/1986
Each share Common no par received distribution of (1.3542759) shares Tim Hortons, Inc. Common $0.001 par payable 09/29/2006 to holders of record 09/15/2006 Ex date - 10/02/2006
Merged into Wendy's/Arby's Group, Inc. 09/29/2008
Each share Common no par exchanged for (4.25) shares Class A Common 10¢ par
Wendy's/Arby's Group, Inc. name changed to Wendy's Co. 07/11/2011

WENGA COPPER MINES, INC. (DE)
Merged into Milburn Mining Co., Inc. 9/10/64
Each share Capital Stock 5¢ par exchanged for (0.2) share Common 2¢ par
Milburn Mining Co., Inc. merged into Milburn Industries, Inc. 7/22/70
(See Milburn Industries, Inc.)

WENGA GOLD MINES, LTD. (ON)
Charter revoked for failure to file reports and pay fees 3/25/65

WENGRACE EXPLORATIONS LTD. (ON)
Went out of business 00/00/1967
No stockholders' equity

WENR CORP (UT)
Each share old Common no par exchanged for (0.02) share new Common no par 11/04/2002
Charter expired 10/23/2002

WENTWORTH MFG CO (DE)
Each share Common $5 par exchanged for (4) shares Common $1.25 par 00/00/1937
Liquidation completed
Each share Common $1.25 par exchanged for initial distribution of $0.85 cash 10/26/1979
Each share Common $1.25 par received second and final distribution of $0.03 cash 01/04/1982

WENTWORTH III INC (DE)
Name changed to Catalyst Lighting Group, Inc. 09/03/2003
Catalyst Lighting Group, Inc. name changed to Phototron Holdings, Inc. 03/09/2011 which name changed to Growlife, Inc. 08/08/2012

WENWOOD ORGANIZATIONS, INC. (DE)
Reorganized as Holiday Park Properties, Inc. 6/21/62
Each share Capital Stock 25¢ par exchanged for (0.06) share Common no par and a stock purchase warrant

WENZEL DOWNHOLE TOOLS LTD (AB)
Acquired by Basin Tools, L.P. 08/07/2013
Each share Common no par exchanged for $2.25 cash

WEPCO ENERGY CO (DE)
Each (150) shares old Common 1¢ par exchanged for (1) share new Common 1¢ par 12/17/1991
New Common 1¢ par split (150) for (1) by issuance of (149) additional shares 12/18/1991
Recapitalized as American Atlas Resources Corp. 08/09/1993
Each share new Common 1¢ par exchanged for (0.01) share Common 1¢ par
(See American Atlas Resources Corp.)

WERNER CONTL INC (MN)
4-3/4% Conv. Preferred $17 par called for redemption 12/23/1977
Merged into Hall's Motor Transit Co. 12/30/1978
Each (3) shares Common 50¢ par exchanged for (2) shares Common no par
Hall's Motor Transit Co. merged into Tiger International, Inc. 01/24/1980
(See Tiger International, Inc.)

WERNER DAHNZ LTD (ON)
Filed an assignment in bankruptcy under the Canada Federal Bankruptcy Statute 08/03/1989
No stockholders' equity

WERNER LAKE NICKEL MINES LTD (ON)
Completely liquidated 00/00/1975
No stockholders' equity

WERNER OIL & GAS CORP (BC)
Recapitalized as International Werner Technologies Inc. 10/14/87
Each share Common no par exchanged for (0.5) share Common no par
(See International Werner Technologies Inc.)

WERNER TRANSPORTATION CO. (MN)
Common $1 par and Class B Common $1 par changed to 50¢ par respectively and (1) additional share issued 4/29/65
Common 50¢ par and Class B Common 50¢ split (3) for (2) respectively by issuance of (0.5) additional share 4/29/66
Under plan of merger name changed to Werner Continental, Inc. 3/1/68
Werner Continental, Inc. merged into Hall's Transit Co. 12/30/78 which merged into Tiger International, Inc. 1/24/80
(See Tiger International, Inc.)

WERSHOW (MILTON J.) ENTERPRISES (CA)
Name changed to Jilco Industries, Inc. 7/26/72

WES CONSULTING INC (FL)
Name changed to Liberator, Inc. 03/04/2011
Liberator, Inc. name changed to Luvu Brands, Inc. 11/05/2015

WES-TENN BANCORP, INC. (TN)
Name changed to Telecom Technologies Inc. 04/24/2002
Telecom Technologies Inc. name changed to Precise Positioning Products Inc. 08/02/2002 which recapitalized as Free DA Connection Services, Inc. 02/14/2005 which recapitalized as Earthshine International Ltd. 09/11/2007

WESCAL RES INC (BC)
Recapitalized as CCC Coded Communications Corp. 11/26/87
Each share Common no par exchanged for (1) share Common no par
CCC Coded Communications Corp. recapitalized as CCI Coded Communications Inc. 10/21/92 which reincorporated in Delaware as Coded Communications Corp. 8/27/93

WESCAM INC (ON)
Acquired by L-3 Communications Corp. 12/6/2002
Each share Common no par exchanged for $9.50 cash

WESCAN ENERGY LTD (BC)
Struck off register and declared dissolved for failure to file returns 8/20/93

WESCAP ENTERPRISES LTD (BC)
Name changed 12/2/86
Name changed from Wescap Energy Corp. to Wescap Enterprises Ltd. 12/2/86
Struck from the register and dissolved 4/13/95

WESCAST INDS INC (ON)
Acquired by Sichuan Bohong Industry Co., Ltd. 03/27/2013
Each share Class A Subordinate no par exchanged for $11 cash

WESCO AUTO PTS CORP (NV)
Name changed to Reddi Brake Supply Corp. 05/09/1994
Reddi Brake Supply Corp. name changed to America West Resources, Inc. 03/05/2008

WESCO FINL CORP (DE)
Capital Stock $1 par split (3) for (1) by issuance of (2) additional shares 04/04/1977
Merged into Berkshire Hathaway Inc. 06/24/2011

Each share Capital Stock $1 par exchanged for $385 cash

WESCO GEN CORP (NV)
Name changed to International Leisure Time & Development Corp. 12/20/71
International Leisure Time & Development Corp. recapitalized as G & F T Mfg. Corp. 8/25/75 which name changed to G & FT Oil & Gas Corp. 4/30/80 which name changed to Yankee Energy Group 1/13/81
(See Yankee Energy Group)

WESCO INDUSTRIES, INC. (DE)
Completely liquidated 1/5/68
Each share Common 10¢ par exchanged for first and final distribution of (0.13023) share Whittaker Corp. (CA) Common $1 par
Whittaker Corp. (CA) reincorporated in Delaware 6/16/86
(See Whittaker Corp. (DE))

WESCORP ENERGY INC (DE)
Company announced they are without assets or ability to fund operations and all directors have resigned 04/26/2013
Stockholders' equity unlikely

WESCORP INDS LTD (BC)
Through purchase offer reverted to private company status 00/00/1980
Public interest eliminated

WESDEL PORCUPINE GOLD MINES LTD. (ON)
Name changed to Huston Red Lake Resources Ltd. 1/29/82
(See Huston Red Lake Resources Ltd.)

WESDOME GOLD MINES INC (QC)
Merged into Wesdome Gold Mines Ltd. 2/1/2006
Each share Common no par exchanged for (1) share Common no par

WESGOLD MINERALS INC (BC)
Issue Information - 1,200,000 shares COM offered at $0.30 per share on 09/21/2010
Name changed to Cordoba Minerals Corp. 04/30/2012

WESGOLD RES INC (BC)
Name changed to Terra Nova Energy Inc. 05/31/1983
Terra Nova Energy Inc. recapitalized as Sato Stevia International Inc. 12/08/1987
(See Sato Stevia International Inc.)

WESIX, INC.
Name changed to Wesix Electric Heater Co. in 1935
(See Wesix Electric Heater Co.)

WESIX ELEC HEATER CO (CA)
Thru 1967 purchase offer of $45 cash for each share Capital Stock $10 par, Federal Pacific Electric Co. has acquired 100% as of January 1968
Public interest eliminated

WESKENSON CORP. (RI)
Charter forfeited for non-payment of taxes 12/31/75

WESKO MINES LTD. (BC)
Acquired by Vectoll Investments Ltd. on a (0.1) for (1) basis 6/24/58
Vectoll Investments Ltd. completed liquidation 11/19/65

WESLEY JESSEN VISIONCARE INC (DE)
Merged into Novartis AG 10/04/2000
Each share Common 1¢ par exchanged for $38.50 cash

WESLEY MASON MILLS LTD. (CANADA)
See - Mason (Wesley) Mills Ltd.

WESLEY MINES LTD. (ON)
Name changed 9/7/56
Name changed from Wesley Gold Mines Ltd. to Wesley Mines Ltd. 9/7/56
Charter cancelled for failure to pay taxes and file returns 3/16/76

WESPAC INVS TR (CA)
Each Share of Bene. Int. $1 par received initial liquidation distribution of $0.18 cash 07/15/1985
Each Share of Bene. Int. $1 par received second liquidation distribution of $0.18 cash 09/16/1985
Each Share of Bene. Int. $1 par received third liquidation distribution of $0.19 cash 06/24/1986
Plan of liquidation revoked in April 1987
Recapitalized as Medical Resource Companies of America 04/04/1990
Each Share of Bene. Int. $1 par exchanged for (0.1) Share of Bene. Int. no par
Medical Resource Companies of America name changed to Greenbriar Corp. 03/27/1996 which name changed to CabelTel International Corp. 02/10/2005 which name changed to New Concept Energy, Inc. 06/03/2008

WESPAC INVS TR II (CA)
Chapter 11 bankruptcy proceedings converted to Chapter 7 on 04/29/1993
No stockholders' equity

WESPAC INVS TR III (CA)
Reincorporated under the laws of Nevada as First Equity Properties, Inc. and Shares of Bene. Int. no par reclassified as Common 1¢ par 02/11/1997

WESPAC MNG CORP (BC)
Name changed to Genesis II Enterprises Ltd. 11/19/1998
(See Genesis II Enterprises Ltd.)

WESPAC PETES LTD (ON)
Recapitalized as Canada Geothermal Oil Ltd. 09/07/1971
Each share Capital Stock no par exchanged for (0.2) share Capital Stock no par
(See Canada Geothermal Oil Ltd.)

WESPAC TECHNOLOGIES CORP (NV)
Reincorporated 08/21/2001
Old Common 1¢ par split (4) for (3) by issuance of (0.33333333) additional share 09/14/1987
State of incorporation changed from (MN) to (NV) 08/21/2001
Each share old Common 1¢ par received distribution of (0.00333333) share Olympic Oil & Gas Inc. Common $0.0001 par payable 02/01/2002 to holders of record 12/07/2001 Ex date - 12/05/2001
Each share old Common 1¢ par exchanged for (0.008) share new Common 1¢ par 03/14/2002
Name changed to Strata Coal Co. 09/27/2002
Strata Coal Co. name changed to Delmar Management Inc. 11/26/2002 which name changed to 2energia Inc. 01/31/2003 which name changed to Coastal Holdings, Inc. 07/02/2003 which name changed to Canadian Blue Gold, Inc. 10/18/2007 which recapitalized as Boreal Water Collection, Inc. 03/19/2008
(See Boreal Water Collection, Inc.)

WESPAK INC (NJ)
Merged into Packaging Systems Corp. 06/11/1971
Each share Common 10¢ par exchanged for (1/3) share 6% 2nd Conv. Preferred $1 par
(See Packaging Systems Corp.)

WESPERCORP (CA)
Name changed to Alton Group Inc. 11/11/1991

Alton Group Inc. name changed to Source Scientific, Inc. 02/03/1995
(See Source Scientific, Inc.)

WESRESERVE OIL CO. LTD. (ON)
Declared dissolved 4/7/55
No stockholders' equity

WESSEX CORP (DE)
Name changed to Diversicare Corp. of America 05/01/1989
(See Diversicare Corp. of America)

WESSEX INTL INC (ID)
Name changed to Ocean Express Lines, Inc. (ID) 05/00/1991
Ocean Express Lines, Inc. (ID) reincorporated in Nevada 03/02/2000 which name changed to American Thorium Inc. 07/29/2003 which recapitalized as Cementitious Materials, Inc. 10/21/2003 which name changed to NaturalNano, Inc. 12/02/2005 which name changed to Omni Shrimp, Inc. 05/03/2017

WESSON METAL CORP. (PA)
Became a division of Fansteel Metallurgical Corp. in 1961
Details not available

WESSON OIL & SNOWDRIFT CO., INC. (LA)
Each share Common no par exchanged for (2) shares Common $2.50 par 00/00/1948
Merged into Hunt Foods & Industries, Inc. 06/30/1960
Each share 4.8% Preferred $50 par exchanged for (0.5) share 5% Preferred Ser. A $100 par
Each share Common $2.50 par exchanged for (1.75) shares Common $5 par
Hunt Foods & Industries, Inc. merged into Simon (Norton), Inc. 07/17/1968 which merged into Esmark, Inc. (Inc. 03/14/1969) 09/09/1983
(See Esmark, Inc. (Inc. 03/14/1969))

WEST AFRICA ENERGY INC (BC)
Name changed to Centric Energy Corp. 08/20/2007
Centric Energy Corp. merged into Africa Oil Corp. 02/22/2011

WEST AFRICA GOLD INC (WY)
Common $0.0001 par split (10) for (1) by issuance of (9) additional shares payable 05/13/2004 to holders of record 05/10/2004 Ex date - 05/14/2004
Stock Dividend - 20% payable 11/12/2004 to holders of record 11/08/2004 Ex date - 11/04/2004
Name changed to Great West Gold, Inc. 10/29/2004
Great West Gold, Inc. name changed to Fortress Financial Group, Inc. 10/08/2007
(See Fortress Financial Group, Inc.)

WEST AFRICA MINERALS CORP (CO)
Name changed to Foothills Capital, Inc. (CO) 12/24/1996
Foothills Capital, Inc. (CO) reorganized in Nevada as Allied Matrix Corp. 08/21/1997
(See Allied Matrix Corp.)

WEST AFRICA MNG EXPL INC (QC)
Name changed to Semafo Inc. 05/13/1997

WEST AFRICAN GOLD CORP (YT)
Recapitalized as First AU Strategies Corp. 04/28/1999
Each share Common no par exchanged for (0.08333333) share Common no par
First AU Strategies Corp. name changed to Cangold Ltd. (YT) 06/04/2003 which reincorporated in British Columbia 12/22/2004 which merged into Great Panther Silver Ltd. 05/27/2015

WEST AFRICAN IRON ORE CORP (BC)
Recapitalized as WAI Capital Investments Corp. 03/31/2015
Each share Common no par exchanged for (0.1) share Common no par

WEST AFRICAN VENTURE EXCHANGE CORP (BC)
Recapitalized as Wave Exploration Corp. 9/17/2002
Each share Common no par exchanged for (0.1) share Common no par
Wave Exploration Corp. recapitalized as Roxgold Inc. 1/16/2007

WEST ALLIS ST BK (WEST ALLIS, WI)
Capital Stock $10 par changed to $5 par and (1) additional share issued 02/10/1971
Stock Dividend - 20% 10/20/1961
99% held by Bancorporation of Wisconsin, Inc. as of 09/00/1977
Public interest eliminated

WEST AMERICA ENERGY, INC. (UT)
Proclaimed dissolved for failure to pay taxes 4/1/89

WEST AMERN FIN CO (DE)
Class A Common $10 par changed to no par 00/00/1930
Class A Common no par and Class B Common no par changed to $1 par 00/00/1934
Liquidation completed
Each share Preferred $10 par exchanged for first and final distribution of $25.40 cash 05/24/1971
Each share Class A Common $1 par exchanged for initial distribution of $10 cash 09/28/1971
Each share Class A Common $1 par received second distribution of $5.69125 cash 12/21/1971
Each share Class A Common $1 par received third distribution of $16.80 cash 03/06/1972
Each share Class A Common $1 par received fourth and final distribution of $1.417 cash 01/13/1977
Holders of Class B Common Stock did not participate in the liquidation and their shares are deemed to be valueless as of 05/21/1971

WEST AMERN INDS INC (TX)
Each share Common 50¢ par exchanged for (0.2) share Common 1¢ par 02/02/1963
Name changed to W.A.I. Corp. 05/09/1974
(See W.A.I. Corp.)

WEST AMULET MINES LTD. (QC)
Recapitalized as New West Amulet Mines Ltd. on a (1) for (3) basis 00/00/1955
New West Amulet Mines Ltd. recapitalized as Waite Dufault Mines Ltd. 09/13/1966 which recapitalized as KPI International Inc. 05/28/1996
(See KPI International Inc.)

WEST AUSTRALIAN NEWSPAPER HLDG LTD (AUSTRALIA)
Name changed to Seven West Media Ltd. 10/02/2012

WEST BATON ROUGE BANCSHARES INC (LA)
Name changed to American Gateway Financial Corp. 11/18/2004
American Gateway Financial Corp. merged into Business First Bancshares, Inc. 03/31/2015

WEST BAY FINL CORP (CA)
Voluntarily dissolved 2/1/96
Details not available

WEST BAY FINL CORP (DE)
Name changed to W.B. Liquidating Corp. 05/07/1970
(See W.B. Liquidating Corp.)

WEST-BAY YELLOWKNIFE MINES LTD. (ON)
Charter revoked for failure to file reports and pay fees 1/26/67

WEST BOSTON GAS CO.
Dissolved in 1931

WEST BOYLSTON MANUFACTURING CO. (MA)
Succeeded by West Boylston Manufacturing Co. of Alabama in 1932
Details not available

WEST BOYLSTON MANUFACTURING CO. OF ALABAMA
Liquidation completed in 1946

WEST-CAN PLASTIC INDUSTRIES LTD. (SK)
Operations ceased in 1967
Struck off register for failure to file reports and pay fees in December 1968
Former transfer agent opined that the shares are worthless

WEST CANADIAN HYDRO ELECTRIC CORP.
Liquidation completed 00/00/1952
Details not available

WEST CDN MINERAL HLDGS LTD (AB)
Merged into Resource Service Group Ltd. 11/24/1972
Each share Capital Stock 10¢ par exchanged for (1) share Common 10¢ par
(See Resource Service Group Ltd.)

WEST CANADIAN OIL & GAS LTD. (CANADA)
Merged into Canadian Delhi Oil Ltd. 01/01/1962
Each share Capital Stock $1.25 par exchanged for (0.26666666) share Capital Stock 10¢ par
Canadian Delhi Oil Ltd. recapitalized as CanDel Oil Ltd. 01/10/1972
(See CanDel Oil Ltd.)

WEST CENTRAL ILLINOIS BANCORP, INC. (DE)
Acquired by First Midwest Corp. of Delaware 01/04/1993
Each share Common $20 par exchanged for $130 cash

WEST CHEM PRODS INC (NY)
$5 Preferred no par called for redemption 3/1/62
Common 50¢ par split (4) for (3) by issuance of (1/3) additional share 9/15/62
Common 50¢ par split (3) for (2) by issuance of (0.5) additional share 7/1/65
Common 50¢ par split (3) for (2) by issuance of (0.5) additional share 7/15/71
Merged into Wechco, Inc. 10/15/85
Each share Common 50¢ par exchanged for $11 cash

WEST CIRQUE RES LTD (BC)
Merged into Kaizen Discovery Inc. 07/08/2014
Each share Common no par exchanged for (0.5) share Common no par
Note: Unexchanged certificates will be cancelled and become without value 07/08/2020

WEST COAST AIRLS INC (WA)
Stock Dividends - 200% 7/5/63; 10% 2/20/67
Merged into Air West, Inc. 4/17/68
Each share Common $1 par exchanged for (1) share Common $1 par
Air West, Inc. name changed to AW Liquidating Co. 4/1/70
(See AW Liquidating Co.)

WEST COAST BANCORP (CA)
Incorporated 09/23/1980
Stock Dividend - 20% 06/15/1983
Reorganized as Genesis Learning Systems, Inc. 05/22/1986
Each (5) shares Common no par exchanged for (1) share Common no par, (1) Class A Common Stock Purchase Warrant expiring 05/19/1987 and (1) Class B Common Stock Purchase Warrant expiring 05/19/1989
(See Genesis Learning Systems, Inc.)

WEST COAST BANCORP (CA)
Incorporated 02/10/1981
Merged into Sunwest Bank (New) (Tustin, CA) 02/04/2002
Each share Common no par exchanged for (0.03304) share Common no par
(See Sunwest Bank (New) (Tustin, CA))

WEST COAST BANCORP INC (FL)
Merged into F.N.B. Corp. (PA) 4/18/97
Each share Common $1 par exchanged for (0.794) share Common $2 par
F.N.B. Corp. (PA) reincorporated in Florida 6/13/2001

WEST COAST BANCORP NEW (OR)
Old Common no par split (5) for (4) by issuance of (0.25) additional share payable 10/30/1996 to holders of record 10/07/1996
Old Common no par split (3) for (2) by issuance of (0.5) additional share payable 11/10/1997 to holders of record 10/06/1997
Each share old Common no par exchanged for (0.2) share new Common no par 05/20/2011
Stock Dividends - 10% 10/31/1995; 10% payable 10/20/1998 to holders of record 10/06/1998; 10% payable 10/20/1999 to holders of record 10/06/1999; 10% payable 10/23/2000 to holders of record 10/09/2000 Ex date - 10/04/2000
Merged into Columbia Banking System, Inc. 04/01/2013
Each share new Common no par exchanged for $24.11 cash

WEST COAST BANCORP OLD (OR)
Stock Dividends - 10% 08/27/1993; 10% 04/08/1994; 100% 06/08/1994
Merged into West Coast Bancorp (New) 03/01/1995
Each share Common $2 par exchanged for (0.6) share Common no par
(See West Coast Bancorp (New))

WEST COAST BANCORPORATION
Liquidated in 1930

WEST COAST BK (ENCINO, CA)
Stock Dividends - 125% 7/29/81; 33-1/3% 5/21/82
Under plan of reorganization each share Common no par automatically became (1) share West Coast Bancorp Common no par 12/16/81
West Coast Bancorp reorganized as Genesis Learning Systems, Inc. 5/22/86
(See Genesis Learning Systems, Inc.)

WEST COAST BK (SARASOTA, FL)
Merged into F.N.B. Corp. (PA) 1/20/98
Each share Common no par exchanged for (1) share Common $2 par
F.N.B. Corp. (PA) reincorporated in Florida 6/13/2001

WEST COAST CAR CO (DE)
Name changed to Shengtai Pharmaceutical, Inc. 07/31/2007

WEST COAST ENGR CO (WA)
Completely liquidated 04/15/1965
Each share Common no par exchanged for (2.5) shares Silver Buckle Mines, Inc. Common 10¢ par

WEST COAST ENTMT CORP (DE)
Filed plan of liquidation under Chapter 7 Federal Bankruptcy Code 7/30/2001
No stockholders' equity

WEST COAST FINANCIAL (CA)
Name changed to U.S. Financial (CA) 09/01/1964
U.S. Financial (CA) reincorporated in Delaware as U.S. Financial Inc. 08/11/1972
(See U.S. Financial Inc.)

WEST COAST LIFE INS CO (CA)
Capital Stock $10 par changed to $5 par 00/00/1935
Voting Trust Agreement terminated 07/15/1964
Each VTC for Capital Stock $5 par exchanged for (1) share Capital Stock $5 par
Stock Dividends - 33-1/3% 11/00/1946; 100% 03/00/1950; 50% 09/04/1953; 33-1/3% 03/13/1956; 25% 03/10/1958; 20% 03/07/1960; 33-1/3% 03/07/1962; 25% 12/31/1963
Merged into Nationwide Corp. 12/24/1973
Each share Capital Stock $5 par exchanged for $18 cash

WEST COAST MINES INC (CA)
Each share old Common 1¢ par exchanged for (0.25) share new Common 1¢ par 01/31/1997
Reincorporated under the laws of Delaware as DynaResource, Inc. 11/02/1998

WEST COAST OIL CO.
Liquidated in 1940

WEST COAST ORES, INC. (OR)
Involuntarily dissolved for failure to file reports and pay taxes 1/12/65

WEST COAST RLTY INVS INC (DE)
Each share old Common 1¢ par exchanged for (0.33333333) share new Common 1¢ par 11/15/2002
Name changed to Meredith Enterprises, Inc. 03/24/2003
(See Meredith Enterprises, Inc.)

WEST COAST RES LTD (BC)
Struck off register and declared dissolved for failure to file returns 5/25/76

WEST COAST TELEPHONE CO. (WA)
Common $12.50 par changed to $20 par 2/25/49
Common $20 par changed to $10 par and (1) additional share issued 9/23/53
Common $10 par changed to $5 par and (1) additional share issued 6/15/62
$1.44 Jr. Conv. Preferred $25 par called for redemption 6/29/64
Merged into General Telephone & Electronics Corp. 6/30/64
Each share Common $5 par exchanged for (1) share Common $3.33-1/3 par
$1.44 Preferred 1960 Ser. $25 par called for redemption 7/25/64
$1.18 Preferred $25 par called for redemption 7/25/64
$1.20 Preferred $25 par called for redemption 7/25/64
$1.24 Preferred $25 par called for redemption 7/25/64
$1.28 Preferred $25 par called for redemption 7/25/64
General Telephone & Electronics Corp. name changed to GTE Corp. 7/1/82 which merged into Verizon Communications Inc. 6/30/2000

WEST COAST TRADERS INC (WA)
Charter expired 9/30/2004

WEST COAST VINEYARDS INC (UT)
Involuntarily dissolved 12/31/82
No stockholders' equity

WEST COLUMBIA NATL BK (WEST COLUMBIA, TX)
Merged into Norwest Corp. 12/27/1996

Each share Common no par exchanged for $335 cash

WEST CORP (DE)
Acquired by Omaha Acquisition Corp. 10/25/2006
Each share Common 1¢ par exchanged for $48.75 cash
Issue Information - 21,275,000 shares COM offered at $20 per share on 03/21/2013
Acquired by Mount Olympus Holdings, Inc. 10/10/2017
Each share Common $0.001 par exchanged for $23.50 cash

WEST DELTA RES LTD (CANADA)
Recapitalized as International Delta Resources Ltd. 05/18/1988
Each share Common no par exchanged for (0.33333333) share Common no par
International Delta Resources Ltd. recapitalized as Delpet Resources Ltd. 11/13/1992 which name changed to HTI Ventures Corp. (Canada) 06/06/2000 which reincorporated in British Columbia as Leagold Mining Corp. 08/31/2016

WEST DEPTFORD BK (WEST DEPTFORD, NJ)
Name changed to Lenape State Bank (West Deptford, NJ) 3/1/77
Lenape State Bank (West Deptford, NJ) acquired by Commercial Bancshares, Inc. (NJ) 11/27/85 which merged into United Jersey Banks 12/1/86 which name changed to UJB Financial Corp. 6/30/89 which name changed to Summit Bancorp 3/1/96 which merged into FleetBoston Financial Corp. 3/1/2001 which merged into Bank of America Corp. 4/1/2004

WEST DISINFECTING CO. (NY)
Each (11) shares Common no par exchanged for (1) share 5% Preferred $100 par and (5) shares Common $2 par in 1943
Each share 5% Preferred $100 par exchanged for (1) share $5 Preferred no par in 1947
Each share Common $2 par exchanged for (4) shares Common 50¢ par in 1947
Stock Dividend - 50% 11/1/55
Name changed to West Chemical Products, Inc. 3/12/57
(See West Chemical Products, Inc.)

WEST DOME LAKE MINES LTD.
Merged into Paymaster Consolidated Mines Ltd. 00/00/1930
Each share Capital Stock $1 par exchanged for (0.1) share Capital Stock $1 par
Paymaster Consolidated Mines Ltd. recapitalized as Porcupine Paymaster Ltd. 04/10/1964 which merged into Associated Porcupine Mines Ltd. 11/05/1968 which merged into American Reserve Mining Corp. 02/27/1989 which recapitalized as AMI Resources Inc. 12/21/1994 which name changed to Ashanti Sankofa Inc. 01/19/2017

WEST DRIEFONTEIN GOLD MNG LTD (SOUTH AFRICA)
Merged into Driefontein Consolidated Ltd. 7/1/81
Each ADR for Ordinary Reg. Rand-1 par exchanged for (2.85) ADR's for Ordinary Rand-1 par
Driefontein Consolidated Ltd. name changed to Gold Fields Ltd. (New) 5/10/99

WEST DYNAMIC TOLL RD LTD (BERMUDA)
Reincorporated 04/04/1997
Place of incorporation changed from (BC) to (Bermuda) 04/04/1997
Cease trade order effective 10/26/2001
Stockholders' equity unlikely

WEST END BREWING CO (NY)
Name changed to W.E.B. Capital, Inc. 07/07/1989
(See W.E.B. Capital, Inc.)

WEST END CHEMICAL CO. (CA)
Merged into Stauffer Chemical Co. 10/1/56
Each (60) shares Preferred $1 par exchanged for (1) share Common $10 par
Each (5.6) shares Common $1 par exchanged for (1) share Common $10 par
(See Stauffer Chemical Co.)

WEST END CONS MINES CORP (NV)
Liquidation completed
Each share Common $1 par stamped to indicate initial distribution of $0.35 cash 10/06/1969
Each share Stamped Common $1 par exchanged for second and final distribution of $0.05 cash 06/09/1970

WEST END OPOTECA MINES CO. (CA)
Charter revoked for failure to file reports and pay fees 1/4/60

WEST ENERGY LTD (AB)
Merged into Daylight Energy Ltd. 05/14/2010
Each share Common no par exchanged for (0.465) share Common no par
Note: Unexchanged certificates were cancelled and became without value 05/13/2015
(See Daylight Energy Ltd.)

WEST ESSEX BANCORP INC (USA)
Common 1¢ par split (5) for (4) by issuance of (0.25) additional share payable 10/22/2001 to holders of record 10/8/2001 Ex date - 10/25/2001
Merged into Kearny Financial Corp. 7/1/2003
Each share Common 1¢ par exchanged for $35.10 cash

WEST EXCELSIOR ENTERPRISES INC (NV)
Common $0.001 par split (10) for (1) by issuance of (9) additional shares payable 10/23/2006 to holders of record 10/23/2006 Ex date - 10/24/2006
Name changed to Trend Exploration, Inc. 3/15/2007

WEST FC FIN CO (BC)
Merged into MFC Bancorp Ltd. 04/03/1997
Each share Common no par exchanged for $0.10 cash

WEST FELICIANA OIL & DRILLING CO. (LA)
Charter revoked for failure to file annual reports and pay fees 5/13/82

WEST FLA NAT GAS CO (FL)
Stock Dividends - to holders of Class A Common - 10% 10/31/1969
Paid in Common Non-Vtg. to holders of Class A Common - 10% 03/04/1977; 10% 10/01/1978
Merged into Martin Gas Florida 07/01/1984
Each share Class A Common $1 par exchanged for $55 cash
Each share Non-Vtg. Common $1 par exchanged for $30 cash
7-1/2% Preferred $5 par called for redemption 01/31/1986
Public interest eliminated

WEST 49 INC (ON)
Acquired by Billabong International Ltd. 09/01/2010
Each share Common no par exchanged for $1.30 cash

WEST FOURTH CAP INC (CANADA)
Recapitalized as Conifex Timber Inc. 06/08/2010
Each share Common no par exchanged for (0.03636364) share Common no par

WEST HILL COPPER MINES LTD (ON)
Name changed to West Hill Enterprises & Mining Ltd. and Capital Stock $1 par changed to no par 10/30/1969
West Hill Enterprises & Mining Ltd. name changed to West Hill Energy Inc. 08/06/1981 which recapitalized as Consolidated West Hill Energy, Inc. 07/02/1996 which merged into African Selection Mining Corp. (ON) 11/21/1997 which reincorporated in Yukon 04/23/1998
(See African Selection Mining Corp.)

WEST HILL ENERGY INC (ON)
Name changed 08/06/1981
Name changed from West Hill Enterprises & Mining Ltd. to West Hill Energy Inc. 08/06/1981
Recapitalized as Consolidated West Hill Energy, Inc. 07/02/1996
Each share Common no par exchanged for (0.2) share Common no par
Consolidated West Hill Energy, Inc. merged into African Selection Mining Corp. (ON) 11/21/1997 which reincorporated in Yukon 04/23/1998
(See African Selection Mining Corp.)

WEST INC (PA)
Common 50¢ par changed to 25¢ par and (1) additional share issued 10/09/1972
Common 25¢ par split (2) for (1) by issuance of (1) additional share 05/05/1982
Common 25¢ par split (2) for (1) by issuance of (1) additional share 06/01/1987
Name changed to West Pharmaceutical Services, Inc. 01/04/1999

WEST INDIES BANK & TRUST CO. (ST. THOMAS, VIRGIN ISLANDS)
Acquired by Chase Manhattan Bank (New York, NY) 9/15/59
Each share Capital Stock $1 par exchanged for (0.0632911) share Capital Stock $12.50 par
Chase Manhattan Bank (New York, NY) name changed to Chase Manhattan Bank (N.A.) (New York, NY) 9/23/65 which reorganized as Chase Manhattan Corp. (Old) 6/4/69 which merged into Chase Manhattan Corp. (New) 3/31/96 which name changed to J.P. Morgan Chase & Co. 12/31/2000 which name changed to JPMorgan Chase & Co. 7/20/2004

WEST INDIES ENTERPRISES INC (VIRGIN ISLANDS)
Name changed to Co-Build Companies, Inc. 8/19/70
(See Co-Build Companies, Inc.)

WEST INDIES INSURANCE CO. (VIRGIN ISLANDS)
Declared bankrupt 05/03/1963
No stockholders' equity

WEST INDIES PLANTATIONS LTD (ON)
Name changed to Caruscan Corp. 06/15/1977
Caruscan Corp. merged into Crownx Inc. 01/31/1986 which name changed to Extendicare Inc. 11/17/1994
(See Extendicare Inc.)

WEST INDIES SUGAR LTD (DE)
In process of liquidation
Each share Common $1 par exchanged for initial distribution of (0.535) share Stamped Common $1 par and $34.34 cash 2/28/58
Each share Stamped Common $1 par received second distribution of $14.54 cash 2/12/60

Note: Details on subsequent distributions, if any, are not available

WEST JAY PETES LTD (BC)
Merged into Carlyle Energy Ltd. 10/28/83
Each share Common no par exchanged for (0.564) share Common no par
(See Carlyle Energy Ltd.)

WEST JERSEY & SEASHORE RR CO (NJ)
Liquidation completed
Each share Special Guaranteed Stock $50 par received initial distribution of $15.09 cash 09/30/1980
Each share Common 50¢ par received initial distribution of $12.09 cash 09/30/1980
Each share Special Guaranteed Stock $50 par received second distribution of $5 cash 12/10/1980
Each share Common $50 par received second distribution of $5 cash 12/10/1980
Each share Special Guaranteed Stock $50 par received third distribution of $33 cash 06/19/1981
Each share Common $50 par received third distribution of $33 cash 06/19/1981
Each share Special Guaranteed Stock $50 par exchanged for fourth and final distribution of $10 cash 06/18/1982
Each share Common $50 par exchanged for fourth and final distribution of $10 cash 06/18/1982
Note: a) Distribution is certain only for certificates surrendered prior to 05/01/1985 b) Distribution may also be made for certificates surrendered between 05/01/1985 and 12/31/1986 c) No distribution will be made for certificates surrendered after 12/31/1986

WEST JERSEY BANCSHARES INC (NJ)
Acquired by Sovereign Bancorp, Inc. 05/31/1996
Each share Common no par exchanged for (0.8335) share Common no par
Sovereign Bancorp, Inc. merged into Banco Santander, S.A. 01/30/2009

WEST JERSEY TITLE & GTY CO (NJ)
Each share Common $50 par exchanged for (10) shares Common $10 par 00/00/1941
Common $10 par changed to $5 par 00/00/1951
Common $5 par changed to $10 par 01/09/1956
Through various purchase offers over 99% reacquired by the company as of 01/15/1971
Public interest eliminated

WEST KENTUCKY COAL CO. (NJ)
Merged into Island Creek Coal Co. (Del.) 12/31/64
Each share Common $4 par exchanged for (0.375) share Common 50¢ par
Island Creek Coal Co. (Del.) merged into Occidental Petroleum Corp. (Calif.) 1/29/68 which reincorporated in Delaware 5/21/86

WEST KNITTING CORP (NC)
Name changed to WKC Liquidating Corp. 03/08/1977
(See WKC Liquidating Corp.)

WEST KOOTENAY PWR LTD (BC)
$1.975 Retractable Preferred Ser. 2 $25 par called for redemption 12/1/93
Public interest eliminated

WEST MACANDA RES LTD (ON)
Merged into Nuinsco Resources Ltd. (BC) 9/21/81
Each share Capital Stock no par exchanged for (0.25) share Common no par

Nuinsco Resources Ltd. (BC) reincorporated in Ontario 7/26/89

WEST MALARTIC MINES LTD (QC)
Charter surrendered 02/28/1969
No stockholders' equity

WEST MAR RES LTD (BC)
Recapitalized as Mar-West Resources Ltd. 6/2/93
Each share Common no par exchanged for (1/3) share Common no par
Mar-West Resources Ltd. merged into Glamis Gold Ltd. 10/19/98 which merged into Goldcorp Inc. (New) 11/4/2006

WEST MARINE INC (DE)
Common $0.001 par split (2) for (1) by issuance of (1) additional share payable 07/31/1996 to holders of record 07/08/1996
Merged into Rising Tide Parent Inc. 09/14/2017
Each share Common $0.001 par exchanged for $12.97 cash

WEST MASS BANKSHARES INC (MA)
Merged into Vermont Financial Services Corp. 06/14/1994
Each share Common 10¢ par exchanged for (0.9861) share Common $1 par
Vermont Financial Services Corp. merged into Chittenden Corp. 05/28/1999
(See Chittenden Corp.)

WEST MAYGILL GAS & OIL LTD. (ON)
Name changed to Ranger Oil (Canada) Ltd. (Ont) 9/9/58
Ranger Oil (Canada) Ltd. (Ont) reincorporated in Canada as Ranger Oil Ltd. 6/30/80 which merged into Canadian Natural Resources Ltd. 7/28/2000

WEST MELVILLE METALS INC (BC)
Each share old Common no par exchanged for (0.1) share new Common no par 05/25/2015
Each share new Common no par exchanged again for (0.25) share new Common no par 03/02/2016
Name changed to K2 Gold Corp. 11/02/2016

WEST MICH FINL CORP (MI)
Merged into National Detroit Corp. 8/1/80
Each share Common $1 par exchanged for $12.50 principal amount of 9% Installment Notes due 8/1/87 or $12.50 cash
Note: Option to receive $12.50 cash expired 8/1/80

WEST MICH NATL BK (FRANKFORT, MI)
Name changed to West Michigan National Bank & Trust (Frankfort, MI) 4/9/97

WEST MICHIGAN STEEL FOUNDRY CO. (MI)
Each share old Common no par exchanged for (3) shares new Common no par 00/00/1936
New Common no par changed to $1 par 00/00/1941
Each share old Common $1 par exchanged for (2) shares new Common $1 par 00/00/1950
$1.75 Preferred $10 par called for redemption 08/01/1956
7% Preferred $10 par called for redemption 08/01/1956
Name changed to Westran Corp. 02/12/1962
(See Westran Corp.)

WEST MILTON BANCORP INC (PA)
Common $1 par split (3) for (1) by issuance of (2) additional shares payable 01/15/1999 to holders of record 12/17/1998
Name changed to Susquehanna Community Financial, Inc. 02/24/2016

WEST MILTON ST BK (WEST MILTON, PA)
Common $50 par changed to $10 par and (4) additional shares issued 12/10/1976
Reorganized as West Milton Bancorp Inc. 07/01/1992
Each share Common $10 par exchanged for (10) shares Common $1 par
West Milton Bancorp Inc. name changed to Susquehanna Community Financial, Inc. 02/24/2016

WEST MTN CAP CORP (AB)
Name changed to West Mountain Environmental Corp. 07/02/2014
(See West Mountain Environmental Corp.)

WEST MTN ENVIRONMENTAL CORP (AB)
Placed in receivership 07/04/2017
Stockholders' equity unlikely

WEST NEWTON SVGS BK (WEST NEWTON, MA)
Acquired by Shawmut National Corp. 9/30/94
Each share Common 10¢ par exchanged for $25 cash

WEST NORSE RES LTD (BC)
Name changed to Absorptive Technology Inc. 07/30/1986
Absorptive Technology Inc. recapitalized as International Absorbents Inc. 12/18/1990
(See International Absorbents Inc.)

WEST OAK RES CORP (BC)
Name changed to Telesis North Communications Inc. 03/06/2001
(See Telesis North Communications Inc.)

WEST OHIO GAS CO (OH)
Reorganized 00/00/1940
Each share Preferred $100 par exchanged for (1) share Common $2 par
Common no par declared to be without value
Common $2 par changed to $4 par 00/00/1944
Common $4 par changed to $5 par 00/00/1950
Common $5 par split (3) for (2) by issuance of (0.5) additional share 07/20/1961
Common $5 par split (5) for (4) by issuance of (0.25) additional share 11/15/1967
Stock Dividend - 20% 09/20/1950
Merged into Consolidated Natural Gas Co. 04/16/1969
Each share Common $5 par exchanged for (0.8) share Capital Stock $8 par
Consolidated Natural Gas Co. merged into Dominion Resources Inc. (New) 01/28/2000 which name changed to Dominion Energy, Inc. 05/11/2017

WEST OMAHA NATL BK (OMAHA, NE)
Stock Dividends - 20% 02/12/1970; 11.11% 02/22/1972
Name changed to American National Bank (Omaha, NE) 03/03/1975
American National Bank (Omaha, NE) reorganized as American National Corp. (NE) 09/30/1980
(See American National Corp. (NE))

WEST ONE BANCORP (ID)
Common $1 par split (2) for (1) by issuance of (1) additional share 08/13/1993
Merged into U.S. Bancorp (OR) 12/26/1995
Each share Common $1 par exchanged for (1.47) shares Common $5 par

U.S. Bancorp (OR) merged into U.S. Bancorp (DE) 08/01/1997

WEST PACIFIC VENTURES INC (AB)
Struck off register and declared dissolved for failure to file returns 1/1/92

WEST PARK INTL INC (UT)
Name changed to International Energy Development Corp. 08/10/1979

WEST PENN CEMENT CO.
Acquired by Pennsylvania-Dixie Cement Corp. 00/00/1948
Details not available

WEST PENN CO.
Dissolved in 1926

WEST PENN ELEC CO (MD)
Common no par changed to $5 par and (1) additional share issued 02/17/1955
Name changed to Allegheny Power System, Inc. 11/10/1960
Allegheny Power System, Inc. name changed to Allegheny Energy, Inc. 09/16/1997 which merged into FirstEnergy Corp. 02/25/2011

WEST PENN GAS CORP.
Dissolved in 1933

WEST PENN PWR CO (PA)
Merged into Allegheny Power System, Inc. 04/16/1965
Each share Common no par exchanged for (3.4) shares Common $2.50 par
$9.40 Preferred Ser. K $100 par called for redemption 07/15/1986
$9.88 Preferred Ser. F $100 par called for redemption 07/15/1986
$7 Preferred Ser. D $100 par called for redemption 07/10/1995
$7.12 Preferred Ser. E $100 par called for redemption 07/10/1995
$7.60 Preferred Ser. H $100 par called for redemption 07/10/1995
$7.64 Preferred Ser. I $100 par called for redemption 07/10/1995
$8.08 Preferred Ser. G $100 par called for redemption 07/10/1995
$8.20 Preferred Ser. J $100 par called for redemption 07/10/1995
4.10% Preferred Ser. C $100 called for redemption at $103.50 on 07/15/1999
4.20% Preferred Ser. B $100 called for redemption at $102.205 on 07/15/1999
4.50% Preferred $100 called for redemption at $110 on 07/15/1999
Market Auction Preferred Units called for redemption at $100,000 plus $922.64 accrued dividends on 07/15/1999
Allegheny Power System, Inc. name changed to Allegheny Energy, Inc. 09/16/1997 which merged into FirstEnergy Corp. 02/25/2011

WEST PENN STEEL CO. (PA)
Merged into Allegheny Steel Co. 05/06/1929
Details not available

WEST PETROLEUM LTD.
Name changed to Consolidated West Petroleum, Ltd. in 1950
(See Consolidated West Petroleum, Ltd.)

WEST PHILADELPHIA PASSENGER RAILWAY CO.
Acquired by Philadelphia Transportation Co. in 1940
Each share Common exchanged for $62.32 principal amount of 3%-6% Consolidated Mortgage Bonds and (0.5215) share $1 Part. Preferred $20 par
Philadelphia Transportation Co. completed liquidation 11/20/73

WEST PK RES INC (BC)
Reincorporated under the laws of Ontario as DXStorm.com Inc. 06/20/2000

WEST PLAINS OIL RESOURCES LTD. (ON)
Charter revoked for failure to file reports and pay fees 01/05/1967

WEST POINT MANUFACTURING CO. (AL)
Each share Capital Stock $100 par exchanged for (5) shares Capital Stock $20 par in 1937
Each share Capital Stock $20 par exchanged for (4) shares Capital Stock $5 par in 1946
Stock Dividend - 100% 12/11/50
Reincorporated under the laws of Georgia 8/29/55
West Point Manufacturing Co. (GA) name was changed to West Point-Pepperell, Inc. 3/29/65
(See West Point-Pepperell, Inc.)

WEST POINT MANUFACTURING CO. (GA)
Under plan of merger name changed to West Point-Pepperell, Inc. and Capital Stock $5 par reclassified as Common $5 3/29/65
(See West Point-Pepperell, Inc.)

WEST POINT PEPPERELL INC (GA)
Common $5 par split (2) for (1) by issuance of (1) additional share 8/14/81
Common $5 par split (2) for (1) by issuance of (1) additional share 9/15/87
Merged into Valley Fashions Tender Corp. 12/10/93
Each share Common $5 par exchanged for $46 cash

WEST POINTE BANCORP INC (IL)
Common $1 par split (2) for (1) by issuance of (1) additional share payable 07/02/2001 to holders of record 06/14/2001 Ex date - 07/17/2001
Merged into Commerce Bancshares, Inc. 09/01/2006
Each share Common $1 par exchanged for (1.422028) shares Common $5 par

WEST POINTE BK & TR CO (BELLVILLE, IL)
Under plan of reorganization each share Common $1 par automatically became (1) share West Pointe Bancorp Inc. Common $1 par 04/08/1997
West Pointe Bancorp Inc. merged into Commerce Bancshares, Inc. 09/01/2006

WEST PRIDE INDS CORP (CANADA)
Recapitalized as Big Horn Resources Ltd. 09/07/1993
Each share Common no par exchanged for (0.14285714) share Common no par
Big Horn Resources Ltd. merged into Westlinks Resources Ltd. 08/16/2001 which name changed to Enterra Energy Corp. 12/18/2001
(See Enterra Energy Corp.)

WEST PROVIDENT RES LTD (BC)
Name changed to Argyll Resources Ltd. (BC) 6/21/79
Argyll Resources Ltd. (BC) reincorporated in Canada 9/2/82 which merged into Argyll Energy Corp. 8/16/83
(See Argyll Energy Corp.)

WEST PT CAP INC (NV)
Name changed to Intelective Communications, Inc. 10/02/2007
Intelective Communications, Inc. name changed to Beacon Redevelopment Industrial Corp. 07/09/2008

WEST PT RES INC (BC)
Name changed to Cannabix Technologies Inc. 08/13/2014

WEST RANCHERIA MINING CO. LTD. (ON)
Charter cancelled and company declared dissolved for default in filing returns 1/13/71

WEST RAND CONS MINES LTD (SOUTH AFRICA)
Acquired by Harmony Gold Mining Co. Ltd. 10/8/99
Each ADR for Ordinary Rand-1 par exchanged for $1.95 cash

WEST RAND INVT TR LTD (SOUTH AFRICA)
Under plan of merger each ADR for Ordinary Rand-1 par automatically became (1) Anglo American Gold Investment Co. Ltd. ADR for Ordinary Rand-1 par 6/12/72
Anglo American Gold Investment Co. Ltd. merged into Anglo American plc 5/24/99

WEST RANGE IRON MINES LTD. (ON)
Name changed to Great West Mining & Smelting Corp. Ltd. 07/31/1963
(See Great West Mining & Smelting Corp. Ltd.)

WEST RES LTD (UT)
Involuntarily dissolved for failure to pay taxes 10/01/1996

WEST RIM RES INC (BC)
Name changed to Cimtek Integrated Manufacturing Technologies Inc. 08/11/1989
Cimtek Integrated Manufacturing Technologies Inc. recapitalized as Jakarta Development Corp. 01/17/1997 which name changed to P.P.M. Development Corp. 07/10/1998 which name changed to Consolidated P.P.M. Development Corp. 04/27/1999 which name changed to Consolidated Global Diamond Corp. 04/23/2004 which name changed to Gem International Resources Inc. 10/30/2009

WEST SEA DEV CORP (BC)
Recapitalized as Seawest Resources Ltd. 9/14/92
Each share Common no par exchanged for (0.25) share Common no par
Seawest Resources Ltd. recapitalized as Starfire Minerals Inc. 5/2/96

WEST SEA MARKETING CORP. (BC)
Name changed to West Sea Development Corp. 8/31/88
West Sea Development Corp. recapitalized as Seawest Resources Ltd. 9/14/92 which recapitalized as Starfire Minerals Inc. 5/2/96

WEST SHORE GOLD MINES, LTD. (QC)
Acquired by West Shore Malartic Gold Mines Ltd. 02/06/1936
Details not available

WEST SHORE MALARTIC GOLD MINES LTD. (QC)
Charter revoked for failure to file reports and pay fees in 1951

WEST SIDE BANK (MILWAUKEE, WI)
Name changed to Continental Bank & Trust Co. (Old) (Milwaukee, WI) 11/15/67
Continental Bank & Trust Co. (Old) (Milwaukee, WI) merged into Continental Bank & Trust Co. (New) (Milwaukee, WI) 12/31/83
(See Continental Bank & Trust Co. (New) (Milwaukee, WI))

WEST SIDE BK (SCRANTON, PA)
Common $25 par changed to $5 par and (4) additional shares issued 03/15/1971
Name changed and location changed to First State Bank (Hawley, PA) 10/01/1978
First State Bank (Hawley, PA) reorganized as Number One Bancorp, Inc. 07/28/1983 which merged into Merchants Bancorp, Inc. (PA) 03/01/1985 which was acquired by Fidelcor, Inc. 12/31/1986 which merged into First Fidelity Bancorporation (New) 02/29/1988 which merged into First Union Corp. 01/01/1996 which name changed to Wachovia Corp. (Ctfs. dated after 09/01/2001) 09/01/2001 which merged into Wells Fargo & Co. (New) 12/31/2008

WEST SIDE SECURITIES CO.
Name changed to Wayne Securities Co. which was liquidated in 1945

WEST SIDE TRUST CO. (NEWARK, NJ)
Under plan of merger name changed to Bank of Commerce (Newark, N.J.) 11/21/56
Bank of Commerce (Newark, N.J.) merged into First Jersey National Corp. 12/29/69
(See First Jersey National Corp.)

WEST SISCOE GOLD MINES, LTD. (CANADA)
Charter surrendered 07/15/1949

WEST STEEL CASTING CO. (OH)
Bankrupt in 1961; no stockholders' equity

WEST STR CAP CORP (ON)
Acquired by Brookfield Asset Management Inc. 10/01/2009
Each 7% Conv. Class E Preferred Ser. 1 no par exchanged for $37.50 cash
Acquired by Brookfield Asset Management Inc. 11/29/2013
Each share Common no par exchanged for $0.32 cash

WEST-TECH GROUP, INC. (OR)
Name changed to American Aircraft Corp. (OR) 10/28/1985
American Aircraft Corp. (OR) reincorporated in Nevada as Hunter Aircraft Corp. 09/27/1996 which recapitalized as Prepaid Depot Inc. 08/18/2001 which recapitalized as Reed Holdings Corp. 07/30/2002 which name changed to Ostara Corp., Inc. 03/12/2004 which name changed to Rheologics Technologies, Inc. 10/18/2005 which name changed to KKS Venture Management, Inc. 07/24/2007 which recapitalized as Codima, Inc. 06/09/2008
(See Codima, Inc.)

WEST TELESERVICES CORP (DE)
Name changed to West Corp. 12/29/2000
(See West Corp.)

WEST TENNESSEE FINANCIAL CORP. (DE)
Acquired by Wes-Tenn Bancorp, Inc. 04/03/1995
Details not available

WEST TERRITORIES OIL LTD. (AB)
Acquired by Canadian Homestead Oils Ltd. on a (0.1) for (1) basis 2/21/55
Canadian Homestead Oils Ltd. merged into Inter-City Gas Corp. (Man.) 4/14/80 which reorganized as Inter-City Products Corp. 4/18/90

WEST TEX UTILS CO (TX)
6% Preferred called for redemption 05/25/1954
10.16% Preferred called for redemption 05/28/1987
7.25% Preferred $100 par called for redemption 07/20/1994
Name changed to AEP Texas North Co. 12/23/2002
(See AEP Texas North Co.)

WEST TEXAS SULPHUR CO. (DE)
Charter cancelled and declared inoperative and void for non-payment of taxes 3/18/25

WEST TIMMINS GOLD CORP (BC)
Merged into Lake Shore Gold Corp. 11/05/2009
Each share Common no par exchanged for (0.73) share Common no par
Lake Shore Gold Corp. merged into Tahoe Resources Inc. 04/07/2016

WEST TOLEDO MINES CO (UT)
Merged into Toledo Mining Co. 09/16/1968
Each share Common 10¢ par exchanged for (1) share Common 10¢ par
Toledo Mining Co. name changed to Toledo Technology, Inc. 03/26/1984 which recapitalized as HIPP International Inc. 08/31/1994 which name changed to Assembly & Manufacturing Systems Corp. 04/12/1995 which recapitalized as American Ship Inc. 09/05/1997 which name changed to Petshealth, Inc. 05/20/1998
(See Petshealth, Inc.)

WEST TREND RES LTD (BC)
Merged into Canadian Continental Oil Corp. 4/19/84
Each share Common no par exchanged for (1) share Common no par
Canadian Continental Oil Corp. recapitalized as CBO Resources Corp. 3/25/87
(See CBO Resources Corp.)

WEST TURNER PETROLEUMS LTD.
Acquired by Pacific Petroleums Ltd. 00/00/1939
Details not available

WEST VALLEY BANK (TARZANA, CA)
Dissolved 6/2/89
No stockholders' equity

WEST VIRGINIA ACCEP CORP (WV)
Stock Dividend - 100% 07/01/1972
Through purchase offer 98% reacquired as of 11/30/1983
Public interest eliminated

WEST VIRGINIA-AMERICAN WTR CO (WV)
99.97% owned by American Water Works Co. Inc. (Old) as of 00/00/2000
Public interest eliminated

WEST VIRGINIA COAL & COKE CO.
Sold at receiver's sale in 1929
No stockholders' equity

WEST VIRGINIA COAL & COKE CORP. (WV)
Common no par changed to $5 par in 1941
Name changed to Midland Enterprises, Inc. (WV) 4/19/56
Midland Enterprises, Inc. (WV) reincorporated in New York 11/28/56 which was acquired by Eastern Gas & Fuel Associates 8/22/61 which name changed to Eastern Enterprises 4/28/89
(See Eastern Enterprises)

WEST VIRGINIA GAS CORP. (WV)
Merged into Commonwealth Gas Corp. share for share 12/31/55
(See Commonwealth Gas Corp.)

WEST VIRGINIA INSURANCE MANAGEMENT CORP. (WV)
Merged into North Central Co. 5/1/64
Each share Common 10¢ par exchanged for (0.111111) share Common $1 par
North Central Co. name changed to North Central Companies, Inc. 7/25/72

WEST VIRGINIA MIDLAND RWY. CO.
Road abandoned in 1931

WEST VIRGINIA-OHIO RIVER BRIDGE CO.
Reorganized as West Virginia-Ohio River Bridge Corp. in 1935
(See West Virginia-Ohio River Bridge Corp.)

WEST VIRGINIA-OHIO RIVER BRIDGE CORP.
In process of liquidation in 1942

WEST VIRGINIA-PITTSBURGH COAL CO. (WV)
Liquidation completed in 1955

WEST VIRGINIA PULP & PAPER CO (DE)
Common no par changed to $5 par and (3) additional shares issued 00/00/1953
Common $5 par split (2) for (1) by issuance of (1) additional share 08/23/1968
Name changed to Westvaco Corp. 03/03/1969
Westvaco Corp. merged into MeadWestvaco Corp. 01/29/2002 which merged into WestRock Co. 07/01/2015

WEST VIRGINIA WATER SERVICE CO. (WV)
Stock Dividend - 100% 03/00/1946
Name changed to Southern Gas & Water Co. 06/01/1960
Southern Gas & Water Co. name changed to West Virginia Water Co. 05/19/1965 which name changed to West Virginia-American Water Co. 01/01/1987
(See West Virginia-American Water Co.)

WEST VIRGINIA WTR CO (WV)
Name changed to West Virginia-American Water Co. 01/01/1987
(See West Virginia-American Water Co.)

WEST WASA MINES LTD (ON)
Recapitalized as West Macanda Resources Ltd. 4/1/77
Each share Capital Stock no par exchanged for (0.25) share Capital Stock no par
West Macanda Resources Ltd. merged into Nuinsco Resources Ltd. (BC) 9/21/81 which reincorporated in Ontario 7/26/89

WEST WITWATERSRAND AREAS LTD (SOUTH AFRICA)
Name changed to Gold Fields of South Africa Ltd. 11/29/1971

WESTAB INC. (DE)
Merged into Mead Corp. 05/31/1966
Each share 5% Preferred $100 par exchanged for (1) share 5% Preferred $100 par
Each share Common no par exchanged for (1) share $2.80 Conv. Preferred no par
(See Mead Corp.)

WESTAFF INC (DE)
Acquired by Koosharem Corp. 03/19/2009
Each share Common 1¢ par exchanged for $1.25 cash

WESTAG CORP. (DE)
Merged into Zapata Petroleum Corp. 12/13/56
Each share Capital Stock 10¢ par exchanged for (0.285716) share Common 10¢ par
Zapata Petroleum Corp. merged into Pennzoil Co. (PA) (New) 7/3/63 which merged into Pennzoil United, Inc. 4/1/68 which name changed to Pennzoil Co. (DE) 6/1/72 which name changed to PennzEnergy Co. 12/30/98

WESTAIR, INC. (NY)
Proclaimed dissolved for failure to file reports and pay fees 12/15/59

WESTAIR HLDG INC (CA)
Merged into Mesa Airlines, Inc. (NM) 05/29/1992
Each share Common 1¢ par

exchanged for (0.31) share Common no par
Mesa Airlines, Inc. (NM) reincorporated in Nevada as Mesa Air Group, Inc. 09/27/1996
(See Mesa Air Group, Inc.)

WESTALL RES LTD (BC)
Reported out of business 00/00/1988
Details not available

WESTAM CORP (UT)
Name changed to Holiday Industries 07/19/1976
(See Holiday Industries)

WESTAM OIL LTD (CANADA)
Reincorporated 12/10/1981
Place of incorporation changed from (BC) to (Canada) 12/10/1981
Name changed to BayWest Capital Equities Corp. 05/04/1987
Baywest Capital Equities Corp. recapitalized as Diversified Baywest Capital Corp. 06/25/1990 which name changed to Nextwave Software Corp. 11/01/1991 which recapitalized as Stox Infolink Systems Inc. 07/21/1994 which name changed to stox.com Inc. 02/24/1999
(See stox.com Inc.)

WESTAMERICA AUTOMOTIVE CORP (CA)
Charter suspended for failure to file reports and pay fees 05/01/1981

WESTAMERICA INC (MN)
Statutorily dissolved 12/30/94

WESTAR CORP (ID)
Name changed to Pan American Corp. 9/29/95
(See Pan American Corp.)

WESTAR ENERGY INC (KS)
$4.25 Preferred $100 par called for redemption at $101.50 on 07/01/2012
$4.50 Preferred $100 par called for redemption at $108 on 07/01/2012
$5 Preferred $100 par called for redemption at $102 on 07/01/2012
Merged into Evergy, Inc. 06/05/2018
Each share Common $5 par exchanged for (1) share Common no par

WESTAR FINL SVCS INC (WA)
Common no par split (2) for (1) by issuance of (1) additional share payable 06/14/1996 to holders of record 05/31/1996
Plan of reorganization under Chapter 11 Federal Bankruptcy proceedings effective 08/07/2004
No stockholders' equity

WESTAR GROUP LTD (BC)
$2.6875 Exchangeable Preferred no par called for redemption 09/25/1989
Each share old Common no par exchanged for (0.008) share new Common no par 04/28/1995
Merged into Great Pacific Capital Corp. 07/02/1997
Each share Common no par exchanged for C$70 cash

WESTAR INDS INTL INC (CO)
Administratively dissolved 09/01/2000

WESTAR MNG LTD (BC)
Discharged from bankruptcy 02/04/2002
Stockholders' equity unlikely

WESTATE ENERGY INC (BC)
Delisted from Vancouver Stock Exchange 03/04/1994

WESTATE RES INC (BC)
Name changed to LifeTrends Behavorial Systems Inc. 05/06/1985
Each share Common no par exchanged for (1) share Common no par
(See LifeTrends Behavorial Systems Inc.)

WESTATES ITALO CO (CAYMAN ISLANDS)
Acquired by Petrex S.p.A. 12/10/1985
Each share Ordinary Stock $1 par exchanged for $21 cash

WESTATES ITALO CO (DE)
Reorganized under the laws of Cayman Islands 07/23/1979
Each share Common $1 par exchanged for (1) share Ordinary Stock $1 par
(See Westates-Italo Co. (Cayman Islands))

WESTATES PETE CO (DE)
Each share Common $1 par exchanged for (0.1) share Common $2 par 10/27/1958
Each share 70¢ Preferred $1 par exchanged for (1) share 5% Preferred $10 par and (2) shares Common $1 par 12/24/1959
Each share Common $2 par exchanged for (2) shares Common $1 par 12/24/1959
5% Preferred $10 par called for redemption 02/28/1977
In process of liquidation
Each share Common $1 par exchanged for initial distribution of $8.50 cash 02/02/1977
Assets transferred to Westates Petroleum Co. Liquidating Trust 05/02/1977
(See Westates Petroleum Co. Liquidating Trust)

WESTATES PETROLEUM CO. LIQUIDATING TRUST (DE)
Liquidation completed
Each share Common $1 par received second distribution of $0.50 cash 8/8/77
Each share Common $1 par received third distribution of $0.39 cash 3/30/78
Each share Common $1 par received fourth distribution of $0.05 cash 3/29/79
Each share Common $1 par received fifth distribution of $0.12906 cash 3/11/80
Each share Common $1 par received sixth distribution of $0.18 cash 3/17/81
Each share Common $1 par received seventh distribution of $0.16 cash 3/9/82
Each share Common $1 par received eighth distribution of $0.64 cash 3/14/83
Each share Common $1 par received ninth distribution of $0.03 cash 3/9/84
Each share Common $1 par received tenth and final distribution of $0.55427 cash 1/17/86

WESTAURUM INDS INC (CANADA)
Recapitalized as Opal Energy Inc. 10/14/1993
Each share Common no par exchanged for (0.25) share Common no par
Opal Energy Inc. acquired by Founders Energy Ltd. 01/12/1999 which reorganized as Provident Energy Trust 03/06/2001 which reorganized as Provident Energy Ltd. (New) 01/03/2011 which merged into Pembina Pipeline Corp. 04/02/2012

WESTBANK CAP TR I (DE)
9.60% Capital Securities called for redemption at $10 on 9/30/2004

WESTBANK CORP (MA)
Common $5 par changed to $2 par and (1.5) additional shares issued 01/30/1986
Common $2 par split (3) for (1) by issuance of (2) additional shares 12/31/1987
Stock Dividends - 5% payable 01/14/2003 to holders of record 01/14/2003 Ex date - 01/10/2003; 5% payable 05/18/2004 to holders of record 05/12/2004
Merged into NewAlliance Bancshares, Inc. 01/02/2007
Each share Common $2 par exchanged for either (1.08515696) shares Common 1¢ par and $7.0479291 cash or $23 cash
Note: Option to receive stock and cash expired 01/03/2007
NewAlliance Bancshares, Inc. merged into First Niagara Financial Group, Inc. (New) 04/15/2011 which merged into KeyCorp (New) 08/01/2016

WESTBANK DEV CORP (UT)
Name changed to Valley Airlines, Inc. 2/7/75
Valley Airlines, Inc. name changed to Pacific Airlines, Inc. (UT) 6/9/75
(See Pacific Airlines, Inc. (UT))

WESTBANK RES INC (BC)
Delisted from Vancouver Stock Exchange 03/02/1990

WESTBAY VENTURES INC (BC)
Name changed to Cryptanite Blockchain Technologies Corp. 03/12/2018

WESTBOROUGH FINL SVCS INC (MA)
Merged into Assabet Valley Bancorp 08/27/2007
Each share Common 1¢ par exchanged for $35 cash

WESTBOUND BK (KATY, TX)
Merged into Guaranty Bancshares, Inc. 06/01/2018
Each share Common $5 par exchanged for (0.38928) share Common $1 par and $1.54 cash
Note: An additional $0.76 cash per share is being held in escrow

WESTBOW ENERGY INC (CANADA)
Under plan of merger name changed to Western Canada Energy Ltd. 04/07/2008
(See Western Canada Energy Ltd.)

WESTBRAE NAT INC (DE)
Merged into Hain Food Group, Inc. 10/14/97
Each share Common 1¢ par exchanged for $3.625 cash

WESTBRIDGE CAP CORP (DE)
Common 10¢ par split (2) for (1) by issuance of (1) additional share 08/24/1983
Stock Dividend - 20% 01/28/1983
Plan of reorganization under Chapter 11 Federal Bankruptcy proceedings effective 03/24/1999
Each share Conv. Preferred Ser. A exchanged for (21.78467) shares Ascent Assurance, Inc. Common 1¢ par and (23.25136647) Common Stock Purchase Warrants expiring 03/24/2004
Each share Common 10¢ par exchanged for (0.0184769) share Ascent Assurance, Inc. Common 1¢ par and (0.09860419) Common Stock Purchase Warrant expiring 03/24/2004
Ascent Assurance, Inc. name changed to USHEALTH Group, Inc. 03/03/2005
(See USHEALTH Group, Inc.)

WESTBRIDGE COMPUTER CORP (SASK)
Name changed to ISM Information Systems Management Corp. 12/19/1991
(See ISM Information Systems Management Corp.)

WESTBRIDGE LD DEVS CORP (AB)
Delisted from Toronto Venture Stock Exchange 06/18/2002

WESTBRIDGE RES LTD (BC)
Name changed to American Pacific Mining Co. (BC) 10/27/1987

American Pacific Mining Co. Inc. (BC) reincorporated in Canada 11/14/1988 which merged into Breakwater Resources Ltd. (BC) 03/15/1990 which reincorporated in Canada 05/11/1992
(See Breakwater Resources Ltd.)

WESTBROOK OIL CORP. (TX)
Liquidation completed
Each share Capital Stock $1 par exchanged for initial distribution of a Trust Receipt representing (1) deposited share of Westbrook Oil Corp., (1) share Westbrook-Thompson Holding Corp. Capital Stock $0.07264 par and $11 cash 10/13/65
Each share Capital Stock $1 par received second distribution of $1.50 cash 1/15/66
Each share Capital Stock $1 par received third distribution of (1/14) share Westbrook-Thompson Holding Corp. Capital Stock $0.07264 par and $1 cash 3/15/66
Each Trust Receipt for Capital Stock $1 par exchanged for fourth and final distribution of $1 cash 5/27/66
(See Westbrook-Thompson Holding Corp.)

WESTBROOK THOMPSON HLDG CORP (DE)
Capital Stock no par changed to $0.07264 par in 1942
Liquidation completed
Each share Capital Stock $0.07264 par received initial distribution of $0.30 cash 7/1/66
Each share Capital Stock $0.07264 par exchanged for second distribution of (0.1) Overriding Royalty Units no par 7/15/66
Each share Capital Stock $0.07264 par received third distribution of $0.05 cash 6/24/67
Each share Capital Stock $0.07264 par received fourth and final distribution of $0.09 cash 4/15/68

WESTBROOK-WINKLER COUNTY CORP. (TX)
Name changed to Westbrook Oil Corp. 10/12/26 which completed liquidation 5/27/66

WESTBURNE INC (QC)
Merged into Rexel S.A. 9/25/2000
Each share Common no par exchanged for $22.75 cash

WESTBURNE INDUSTRIES LTD. (AB)
Recapitalized as United Westburne Industries Ltd. 3/28/67
Each share Capital Stock no par exchanged for (13) share Common $2.50 par
(See United Westburne Industries Ltd.)

WESTBURNE INTL INDS LTD (CANADA)
Reincorporated 10/18/1977
8% Conv. Preferred Ser. A $25 par called for redemption 10/01/1975
Place of incorporation changed from (AB) to (Canada) and Common $1 par changed to no par 10/18/1977
Common no par split (2) for (1) by issuance of (1) additional share 09/10/1979
Merged into Dumez Investments I Inc. 07/07/1987
Each share Common no par exchanged for $22.50 cash

WESTBURNE OIL CO. LTD. (AB)
Name changed to Westburne Industries Ltd. 12/20/65
Westburne Industries Ltd. recapitalized as United Westburne Industries Ltd. 3/28/67
(See United Westburne Industries Ltd.)

WESTBURNE PETROLEUM & MINERALS LTD. (AB)
Under plan of merger each share

Ordinary no par automatically became (1) share 7% Preferred Ser. B $5.16 par 04/28/1970
7% Preferred Ser. A $11.77 par called for redemption 03/30/1971
7% Preferred Ser. B $5.16 par called for redemption 03/30/1971
Public interest eliminated

WESTBURY FASHIONS INC (NY)
Common 25¢ par changed to 10¢ par and (1.5) additional shares issued 04/23/1962
Out of business 04/01/1976
No stockholders' equity

WESTBURY METALS GROUP INC (NY)
Ceased operations and began process of liquidating assets 11/21/2002
Stockholders' equity unlikely

WESTBURY RES INC (DE)
Charter cancelled and declared inoperative and void for non-payment of taxes 3/1/81

WESTCALIND CORP (DE)
Merged into EB Merger Corp. 06/15/1988
Each share Common $1 par exchanged for $0.20 cash

WESTCAN PPTY DEV CORP (AB)
Name changed to Clay-Tech Industries Inc. 2/1/94
(See Clay-Tech Industries Inc.)

WESTCASTLE ENERGY TR (CANADA)
Merged into OPTUS Natural Gas Distribution Income Fund 10/28/98
Each Trust Unit no par exchanged for $5.70 cash

WESTCHESTER BOND & MORTGAGE CORP.
Taken over for liquidation by New York State Superintendent of Insurance in 1934

WESTCHESTER CORP (TX)
Stock Dividend - 50% 05/20/1972
Merged into Unaco, Inc. 05/11/1978
Each share Common 10¢ par exchanged for $0.50 cash

WESTCHESTER FINL SVCS CORP (DE)
Acquired by Marine Midland Banks, Inc. 9/28/86
Each share Common 1¢ par exchanged for $53.05 cash

WESTCHESTER FIRE INS CO (NY)
Each share Capital Stock $10 par exchanged for (1.24) shares Capital Stock $2.50 par 00/00/1932
Under plan of merger each share Capital Stock $2.50 par exchanged for (1.95) shares Capital Stock $2 par 00/00/1948
Acquired by Crum & Forster 11/07/1969
Each share Capital Stock $2 par exchanged for $67.58 cash

WESTCHESTER NATL BK DADE CNTY (MIAMI, FL)
Name changed to Barnett Bank at Westchester, N.A. (Miami, FL) 12/13/1972
(See Barnett Bank at Westchester, N.A. (Miami, FL))

WESTCHESTER NEWSPAPERS, INC. (NY)
$6 1st Preferred $100 par called for redemption 5/16/64
Public interest eliminated

WESTCHESTER PORCUPINE GOLD MINES LTD. (ON)
Bankrupt in 1949

WESTCHESTER PREMIER THEATRE INC (NY)
Adjudicated bankrupt 04/10/1978
Stockholders' equity unlikely

WESTCHESTER TITLE & TRUST CO.
Liquidation ordered by Court in 1935

WESTCLIFF INC (CO)
Name changed to Master Systems Computer Corp. 02/12/1988

WESTCO BANCORP INC (DE)
Common 1¢ par split (3) for (2) by issuance of (0.5) additional share payable 05/17/1996 to holders of record 04/30/1996
Merged into MAF Bancorp, Inc. 12/31/1998
Each share Common 1¢ par exchanged for (1.395) shares Common 1¢ par
MAF Bancorp, Inc. merged into National City Corp. 09/01/2007 which was acquired by PNC Financial Services Group, Inc. 12/31/2008

WESTCO INTERNATIONAL, INC. (UT)
Name changed to TR Inc. 10/24/88
(See TR Inc.)

WESTCOAST ENERGY INC (CANADA)
8.25% Conv. 2nd Preferred Ser. A no par called for redemption 9/1/93
7.68% Retractable 1st Preferred Ser. 1 no par called for redemption 12/12/96
6.90% 1st Preferred Ser. 4 no par called for redemption at $25 on 10/12/99
Each share 8.08% 1st Preferred Ser. 2 no par exchanged for (0.63751595) share Common no par 10/29/2001
4.90% Preferred Ser. 5 no par called for redemption at $25 plus $0.269332 accrued dividend on 12/21/2001
Merged into Duke Energy Corp. (NC) 3/14/2002
Each share Common no par exchanged for either (0.7711) share Common no par or (0.7711) Duke Energy Canada Exchangeco Inc. Exchangeable Share no par
(See each company's listing)
1st Preferred Ser. 6 called for redemption at $25 plus $0.152753 accrued dividend on 6/1/2004
5% 1st Preferred Ser. 9 called for redemption at $25 on 10/15/2004

WESTCOAST GOLF EXPERIENCES INC (NV)
Common $0.001 par split (13) for (1) by issuance of (12) additional shares payable 03/26/2008 to holders of record 03/25/2008 Ex date - 03/27/2008
Name changed to CrowdGather, Inc. 04/08/2008

WESTCOAST HOSPITALITY CAP TR (DE)
Name changed to Red Lion Hotels Capital Trust 09/19/2005
(See Red Lion Hotels Capital Trust)

WESTCOAST HOSPITALITY CORP (WA)
Name changed to Red Lion Hotels Corp. 9/19/2005

WESTCOAST LEASING LTD. (BC)
Name changed to Inland Empire Resource Ltd. 7/14/69

WESTCOAST PETE LTD (BC)
$1.50 Exchangeable Preferred $25 par called for redemption 7/6/82
Acquired by Westcoast Transmission Holdings Ltd. 9/8/82
Each share Common $2 par exchanged for $29 cash

WESTCOAST PRODTN LTD (BC)
Merged into Westcoast Petroleum Ltd. 9/21/71
Each share Common $2 par exchanged for (1) share Common $2 par
(See Westcoast Petroleum Ltd.)

WESTCOAST TRANSMISSION LTD (CANADA)
Voting Trust Agreement terminated 10/28/63
Each VTC for Capital Stock no par exchanged for (1) share Capital Stock no par
Capital Stock no par reclassified as Common no par 8/16/71
8-1/2% Preferred Ser. A $50 par changed to no par 5/5/76
Common no par split (3) for (1) by issuance of (2) additional shares 5/26/78
8-1/2% Preferred Ser. A no par called for redemption 4/15/85
Name changed to Westcoast Energy Inc. 6/1/88

WESTCORP (CA)
Reincorporated 05/14/1987
Name changed 04/08/1988
Name changed 09/28/1990
State of incorporation changed from (CA) to (DE) 05/14/1987
Name changed from Westcorp to Westcorp, Inc. 04/08/1988
Name changed from Westcorp, Inc. back to Wescorp and state of incorporation changed from (DE) back to (CA) 09/28/1990
Stock Dividend - 5% payable 06/17/1996 to holders of record 05/20/1996
Merged into Wachovia Corp. (Ctfs. dated after 09/01/2001) 03/01/2006
Each share Common $1 par exchanged for (1.2749) shares Common $3.33-1/3 par
Wachovia Corp. (Ctfs. dated after 09/01/2001) merged into Wells Fargo & Co. (New) 12/31/2008

WESTCOTT COMMUNICATIONS INC (TX)
Common 1¢ par split (2) for (1) by issuance of (1) additional share 12/6/93
Merged into K-III Communications Corp. 5/31/96
Each share Common 1¢ par exchanged for $21.50 cash

WESTCOTT FINL CORP (DE)
Name changed to Entertainment Technologies & Programs Inc. 05/11/1995
(See Entertainment Technologies & Programs Inc.)

WESTCOTT PRODS CORP (DE)
Each share old Common $0.001 par exchanged for (0.0008) share new Common $0.001 par to reflect a (1) for (250,000) reverse split followed by a (200) for (1) forward split 12/20/2006
Note: No holder will receive fewer than (200) shares
Name changed to Dala Petroleum Corp. 09/18/2014
Dala Petroleum Corp. name changed to KonaTel, Inc. 02/16/2018

WESTDALE OIL & GAS LTD (BC)
Acquired by Canusa Energy Ltd. 07/05/1983
Each share Common no par exchanged for (0.5) share Common no par
Canusa Energy Ltd. merged into Bonanza Resources Ltd. 10/07/1983 which recapitalized as CanCapital Corp. (ALTA) 02/09/1987 which reincorporated in British Columbia 05/12/1993 which recapitalized as Prada Holdings Ltd. (BC) 07/14/1994 which reincorporated in Yukon 07/26/1996
(See Prada Holdings Ltd.)

WESTDALE SVG & LN ASSN (CA)
Over 99% held by Mr. D.K. Ludwig as of 08/22/1980
Public interest eliminated

WESTEC CORP (NV)
Each share assented Common 10¢ par exchanged for (1) share Validated Common 10¢ par 03/17/1969
Note: Unexchanged certificates were cancelled and became without value 07/16/1985
Name changed to Tech-Sym Corp. 05/25/1970
(See Tech-Sym Corp.)

WESTECH CAP CORP (DE)
Reincorporated 04/30/2001
Common $0.001 par split (3.28767) for (1) by issuance of (2.28767) additional shares payable 11/01/1999 to holders of record 08/13/1999
State of incorporation changed from (NY) to (DE) 04/30/2001
Each share old Common $0.001 par exchanged for (0.1) share new Common $0.001 par 06/29/2001
New Common $0.001 par split (2) for (1) by issuance of (1) additional share payable 11/22/2004 to holders of record 11/21/2004 Ex date - 11/23/2004
Name changed to Tejas Inc. 12/13/2004
Tejas Inc. name changed to Westech Capital Corp. 08/05/2010

WESTECH RES LTD (BC)
Reincorporated under the laws of Canada as Butte Resources Ltd. 9/14/87
Butte Resources Ltd. recapitalized as Kingtron International Inc. 9/22/89
(See Kingtron International Inc.)

WESTECHESTER RES INC (ON)
Name changed to WSR Gold Inc 02/16/2007
WSR Gold Inc. recapitalized as White Pine Resources Inc. 12/18/2008 which name changed to SBD Capital Corp. 09/15/2017

WESTEEL PRODUCTS, LTD. (CANADA)
Each share old Common no par exchanged for (4) shares new Common no par 00/00/1950
Name changed to Westeel-Rosco Ltd. 12/31/1965
(See Westeel-Rosco Ltd.)

WESTEEL ROSCO LTD (CANADA)
Common no par split (2) for (1) by issuance of (1) additional share 05/18/1973
Common no par split (2) for (1) by issuance of (1) additional share 03/31/1975
Through purchase offer 100% acquired by Jannock Ltd. as of 08/20/1980
Public interest eliminated

WESTEK COMMUNICATIONS INC (BC)
Struck off register and declared dissolved for failure to file returns 12/9/94

WESTERBEKE CORP (DE)
Merged into Westerbeke Acquisition Corp. 3/2/2004
Each share Common 1¢ par exchanged for $3.26 cash

WESTERFED FINL CORP (DE)
Merged into Glacier Bancorp, Inc. (New) (DE) 2/28/2001
Each share Common 1¢ par exchanged for $23.47 cash

WESTERGAARD ONLINE SYS INC (DE)
Name changed to Westergaard.com, Inc. 02/18/1999

WESTERN & PAC RES CORP (BC)
Recapitalized as Consolidated Western & Pacific Resources Corp. 07/05/1994
Each share Common no par exchanged for (0.05) share Common no par
Consolidated Western & Pacific

Resources Corp. name changed to Synergy Resource Technologies Inc. 07/02/1996 which recapitalized as Synergy Renewable Resources Inc. 01/09/1997
(See Synergy Renewable Resources Inc.)

WESTERN & TEXAS OIL CO. LTD. (ON)
Each share Preference Stock 20¢ par exchanged for $0.95 cash 8/15/77
Each share Common $1 par exchanged for $1.75 cash 8/15/77
Public interest eliminated

WESTERN ACCEPTANCE CORP. (MN)
Placed in bankruptcy 3/13/68
Stock declared worthless 3/3/70

WESTERN ADERA LTD (CO)
Reincorporated 10/17/75
Place of incorporation changed from (BC) to (CO) 10/17/75
Name changed to Aerolift, Inc. 3/7/84
Each share Common no par exchanged for (1) share Common no par
(See Aerolift, Inc.)

WESTERN AERO SUPPLY CORP. (TX)
Charter forfeited for failure to pay taxes 12/13/1996

WESTERN AERONAUTICAL & ENGR CORP (UT)
Involuntarily dissolved for failure to pay taxes 11/09/1974

WESTERN AIR EXPRESS CORP. (DE)
Name changed to Western Air Lines, Inc. 3/11/41
Western Air Lines, Inc. acquired by Delta Air Lines, Inc. 12/18/86
(See Delta Air Lines, Inc.)

WESTERN AIR LINES INC (DE)
Capital Stock $1 par split (3) for (1) by issuance of (2) additional shares 6/1/64
Capital Stock $1 par split (5) for (2) by issuance of (1.5) additional shares 10/31/72
Capital Stock $1 par reclassified as Common $1 par 5/1/73
$2.1375 Conv. Preferred Ser. B no par called for redemption 9/18/85
$2.40 Conv. Preferred Ser. D no par called for redemption 6/16/86
$2 Conv. Preferred Ser. A no par called for redemption 6/30/86
Stock Dividend - 10% 3/5/71
Acquired by Delta Air Lines, Inc. 12/18/86
Each share Common $1 par exchanged for (0.1349) shares Common $3 par and $6.25 cash

WESTERN ALBERTA OIL CO. LTD. (MB)
Charter cancelled and declared dissolved for failure to file returns 10/13/34

WESTERN ALLENBEE OIL & GAS LTD (CANADA)
Name changed to Convoy Capital Corp. 04/28/1989
Convoy Capital Corp. recapitalized as Hariston Corp. 09/25/1992 which recapitalized as Midland Holland Inc. (Canada) 02/10/1999 which reincorporated in Yukon 03/11/1999 which name changed to Mercury Partners & Co. Inc. 02/22/2000 which name changed to Black Mountain Capital Corp. 05/02/2005 which recapitalized as Grand Peak Capital Corp. (YT) 11/20/2007 which reincorporated in British Columbia 04/27/2010

WESTERN ALLIANCE BANCORPORATION (NV)
Reincorporated under the laws of Delaware 06/02/2014

WESTERN ALLOYS, INC. (NV)
Recapitalized as Western Gold Reserves, Inc. in December 1962
Each share Common 10¢ par exchanged for (0.01) share Common $10 par
(See Western Gold Reserves, Inc.)

WESTERN AMER ENERGY CORP (NY)
Charter cancelled and proclaimed dissolved for failure to pay taxes 06/30/1982

WESTERN AMER RES INC (AB)
Name changed to CFE Industries Inc. 10/21/1998
CFE Industries Inc. recapitalized as Commercial Solutions Inc. 10/01/2002
(See Commercial Solutions Inc.)

WESTERN AMERN FD INC (WA)
Voluntarily dissolved 4/4/75
Details not available

WESTERN AMERICAN INDUSTRIES, INC. (NV)
Name changed to Cardiodynamics, Inc. 9/29/69
Cardiodynamics, Inc. name changed to Vida Medical Systems, Inc. 10/16/74 which recapitalized as Oasis Oil Corp. 10/6/97 which name changed to MVP Network, Inc. 9/7/2005

WESTERN AMERN INDS INC (AZ)
Merged into Great Western Corp. (DE) 12/31/1969
Each share Common $10 par exchanged for (1) share Common $1 par and $27.24 cash
Great Western Corp. (DE) name changed to Patagonia Corp. 06/09/1970
(See Patagonia Corp.)

WESTERN AMERICAN INVESTMENT CORP. (TX)
Completely liquidated in 1968

WESTERN AMERICAN LIFE INSURANCE CO. (NM)
Under plan of merger each share Capital Stock 25¢ par exchanged for (0.095462) share Capital Stock $1 par 6/10/71
Placed in Receivership 5/14/75
No stockholders' equity

WESTERN AMERICAN LIFE INSURANCE CO. (NV)
Merged into Continental Life Insurance Co. for cash 6/2/54

WESTERN ANTENNA CORP. (UT)
Name changed to Hortitech, Inc. 03/05/1990
Hortitech, Inc. name changed to Microaccel, Inc. 02/02/2000 which name changed to Health Anti-Aging Lifestyle Options, Inc. 03/18/2002 which name changed to Previsto International Holdings, Inc. 12/07/2010

WESTERN AREAS LTD (SOUTH AFRICA)
Name changed 10/19/98
Stock Dividends - 0.67469% payable 3/1/96 to holders of record 1/5/96; 0.993% payable 8/29/96 to holders of record 7/5/96; 0.00749% payable 2/21/97 to holders of record 12/27/96
Name changed from Western Areas Gold Mining Co. Ltd. to Western Areas Ltd. 10/19/98
Stock Dividend - 12.36005% payable 11/15/2002 to holders of record 11/4/2002 Ex date - 10/31/2002
Each ADR for Ordinary Rand-1 received distribution of approximately $0.07 cash payable 1/16/2003 to holders of record 11/14/2002 Ex date - 11/12/2002
Each Unsponsored ADR for Ordinary Rand-1 par exchanged for (1) Sponsored ADR for Ordinary Rand-1 par 2/7/2005
Acquired by Gold Fields Ltd. (New) 3/27/2007
Each Sponsored ADR for Ordinary Rand-1 exchanged for $6.6004 cash

WESTERN ARKANSAS TELEPHONE CO. (AR)
6% Preferred 1964 Ser. $100 par called for redemption 6/1/66
Public interest eliminated

WESTERN ARLINGTON RES LTD (BC)
Recapitalized as Lightning Creek Mines Ltd. 12/19/86
Each share Common no par exchanged for (1) share Common no par
(See Lightning Creek Mines Ltd.)

WESTERN ASBESTOS & DEVELOPMENT LTD. (BC)
Merged into Castle Oil & Gas Ltd. in 1955
Each share Capital Stock 50¢ par exchanged for (1) share Capital Stock no par
(See Castle Oil & Gas Ltd.)

WESTERN ASHLEY MINERALS LTD. (ON)
Recapitalized as Consolidated Ashley Minerals Ltd. 03/29/1956
Each share Capital Stock $1 par exchanged for (0.25) share Capital Stock $1 par
Consolidated Ashley Minerals Ltd. name changed to Daering Explorers Corp. Ltd. 08/20/1956 which recapitalized as Consolidated Daering Enterprises & Mining Inc. 08/20/1971 which recapitalized as Sim-Tek Enterprises & Exploration Inc. 12/11/1981 which name changed to Bonaventure Technologies Inc. 09/14/1983
(See Bonaventure Technologies Inc.)

WESTERN ASSET / CLAYMORE INFLATION - LKD OPPORTUNITIES & INCOME FD (MA)
Name changed 08/13/2007
Name changed from Western Asset/Claymore U.S. Treasury Inflation Protected Securities Fund 2 to Western Asset/ Claymore Inflation-Linked Opportunities & Income Fund 08/13/2007
Name changed to Western Asset Inflation-Linked Opportunities & Income Fund 04/27/2018

WESTERN ASSET / CLAYMORE INFLATION - LKD SECS & INCOME FD (MA)
Name changed 08/13/2007
Taxable Preferred Ser. W called for redemption at $25,000 on 11/09/2006
Taxable Preferred Ser. TH called for redemption at $25,000 on 11/10/2006
Taxable Preferred Ser. F called for redemption at $25,000 on 11/13/2006
Taxable Preferred Ser. M called for redemption at $25,000 on 11/14/2006
Taxable Preferred Ser. T called for redemption at $25,000 on 11/15/2006
Name changed from Western Asset/ Claymore U.S. Treasury Inflation Protected Securities Fund to Western Asset/Claymore Inflation Linked Securities & Income Fund 08/13/2007
Name changed to Western Asset Inflation-Linked Income Fund 04/27/2018

WESTERN ASSET EMERGING MKTS FLOATING RATE FD INC (MD)
Merged into Western Asset Emerging Markets Debt Fund Inc. 09/14/2009
Each share Common $0.001 par exchanged for (0.63291) share Common $0.001 par

WESTERN ASSET EMERGING MKTS INCOME FD INC NEW (MD)
Name changed 11/03/2008
Under plan of merger name changed from Western Asset Emerging Markets Income Fund II, Inc. to Western Asset Emerging Markets Income Fund Inc. (New) 11/03/2008
Merged into Western Asset Emerging Markets Debt Fund Inc. 12/19/2016
Each share Common $0.001 par exchanged for (0.715479) share Common $0.001 par

WESTERN ASSET EMERGING MKTS INCOME FD INC OLD (MD)
Merged into Western Asset Emerging Markets Income Fund Inc. (New) 11/03/2008
Each share Common $0.001 par exchanged for (0.992105) share Common $0.001 par
Western Asset Emerging Markets Income Fund Inc. (New) merged into Western Asset Emerging Markets Debt Fund Inc. 12/19/2016

WESTERN ASSET GLOBAL PARTNERS INCOME FD INC (MD)
Merged into Western Asset Global High Income Fund Inc. 08/29/2016
Each share Common $0.001 par exchanged for (0.910322) share Common $0.001 par

WESTERN ASSET HIGH INCOME FD INC (MD)
Merged into Western Asset High Income Opportunity Fund, Inc. 06/24/2013
Each share Common $0.001 par exchanged for (1.50724) shares Common $0.001 par

WESTERN ASSET INCOME FD (DE)
Name changed to Western Asset Investment Grade Income Fund Inc. 03/29/2018

WESTERN ASSET MANAGED HIGH INCOME FD INC (MD)
Merged into Western Asset High Income Opportunity Fund, Inc. 08/29/2016
Each share Common $0.001 par exchanged for (0.964839) share Common $0.001 par

WESTERN ASSET MUN PARTNERS FD II INC (MD)
Merged into Western Asset Municipal Partners Fund, Inc. 07/23/2007
Each share Auction Rate Preferred Ser. M $0.001 par exchanged for (1) share Auction Rate Preferred Ser. M $0.001 par
Each share Common $0.001 par exchanged for (0.973323) share Common $0.001 par

WESTERN ASSET PREMIER BD FD (MA)
Taxable Auction Market Preferred Ser. M no par called for redemption at $25,000 on 09/26/2014
Taxable Auction Market Preferred Ser. W no par called for redemption at $25,000 on 09/30/2014
(Additional Information in Active)

WESTERN ASSET 2008 WORLDWIDE DLR GOVT TR INC (MD)
Trust terminated 12/01/2008
Each share Common $0.001 par received $10.1597 cash
Note: Certificates were not required to be surrendered and are without value

WESTERN ASSET WORLDWIDE INCOME FD INC (MD)
Merged into Western Asset Emerging Markets Debt Fund Inc. 12/19/2016
Each share Common $0.001 par

exchanged for (0.727316) share Common $0.001 par

WESTERN ASSET ZENIX INCOME FD INC (MD)
Merged into Western Asset High Income Fund II Inc. 09/24/2008
Each share Auction Rate Preferred 1¢ par exchanged for $25,000 cash
Each share Common 1¢ par exchanged for (0.22624) share Common $0.001 par

WESTERN ASSOCIATED ENTERPRISES, INC. (UT)
Name changed to WestAm Corp. 4/24/72
WestAm Corp. name changed to Holiday Industries 7/19/76 which charter was suspended 9/30/77

WESTERN ATLAS INC (DE)
Each share Common $1 par received distribution of (1) share UNOVA, Inc. Common $1 par payable 10/31/1997 to holders of record 10/24/1997 Ex date - 11/03/1997
Merged into Baker Hughes Inc. 08/10/1998
Each share Common $1 par exchanged for (2.7) shares Common $1 par
Baker Hughes Inc. merged into Baker Hughes, a GE company 07/05/2017

WESTERN AUTO PARTS CO.
Merged into Western Auto Supply Co. (California) in 1929
(See Western Auto Supply Co. (Calif.))

WESTERN AUTO SUPPLY AGENCY OF LOS ANGELES
Merged into Western Auto Supply Co. (California) in 1929
Details not available

WESTERN AUTO SUPPLY CO. (CA)
Merged into Gamble-Skogmo, Inc. share for share in 1946

WESTERN AUTO SUPPLY CO. (MO)
Each share Class A Common no par and Class B Common no par exchanged for (3) shares Common $10 par in 1937
Common $10 par changed to $5 par and (1) additional share issued 12/10/56
4.80% Preferred $100 par called for redemption 10/2/61
Stock Dividend - 100% 4/1/55
Merged into Beneficial Finance Co. 10/27/61
Each share Common $5 par exchanged for (0.2) share $4.50 Preferred $100 par and (0.55) share Common $1 par
Beneficial Finance Co. name changed to Beneficial Corp. (New) 5/1/70

WESTERN AUTO SUPPLY CO. OF KANSAS CITY
Merged into Western Auto Supply Co. (MO) in 1929
Details not available

WESTERN AUTO SUPPLY CO (DE)
Merged into Sears, Roebuck & Co. 04/25/1988
Each share Common 1¢ par exchanged for $19 cash

WESTERN BANCORP (CA)
Merged into U.S. Bancorp 11/15/1999
Each share Common no par exchanged for (1.2915) shares Common $1.25 par

WESTERN BANCORPORATION (DE)
Capital Stock $2 par split (3) for (2) by issuance of (0.5) additional share 09/29/1978
Capital Stock $2 par reclassified as Common $2 par 04/18/1979
Name changed to First Interstate Bancorp 06/01/1981
First Interstate Bancorp merged into Wells Fargo & Co. (Old) 04/01/1996 which merged into Wells Fargo & Co. (New) 11/02/1998

WESTERN BANCSHARES INC (NM)
Acquired by Compass Bancshares, Inc. 01/14/2000
Each share Common exchanged for (24.78) shares Common $2 par Compass Bancshares, Inc. merged into Banco Bilbao Vizcaya Argentaria, S.A. 09/07/2007

WESTERN BK & TR CO (WEST SPRINGFIELD, MA)
Common $10 par changed to $5 par and (1) additional share issued 08/25/1971
Stock Dividends - 10% 03/15/1970; 15% 03/15/1971
Under plan of merger name changed to Park West Bank & Trust Co. (West Springfield, MA) 07/16/1976
Park West Bank & Trust Co. (West Springfield, MA) reorganized as Westbank Corp. 07/01/1984 which merged into NewAlliance Bancshares, Inc. 01/02/2007 which merged into First Niagara Financial Group, Inc. (New) 04/15/2011 which merged into KeyCorp (New) 08/01/2016

WESTERN BK (COOS BAY, OR)
Each share Common $100 par exchanged for (0.05) share Common $5 par 01/23/1965
Each share Common $5 par exchanged for (2) shares Common $2.50 par 05/01/1977
Class A Conv. Preferred $20 par called for redemption 09/30/1988
Common $2.50 par split (2) for (1) by issuance of (1) additional share 08/05/1993
Stock Dividends - 100% 10/25/1955; 66.66666666% 10/01/1959; 20% 01/01/1964; 10% 04/03/1979; 10% 03/31/1988; 10% 03/15/1989; 10% 04/30/1991; 10% 05/15/1992; 10% 04/15/1993
Merged into Washington Mutual, Inc. 01/31/1996
Each share Common $2.50 par exchanged for (0.69126) share Common $1 par
(See Washington Mutual, Inc.)

WESTERN BK (LAS CRUCES, NM)
Acquired by Bank of the West (San Francisco, CA) 08/29/2000
Details not available

WESTERN BK (LOS ANGELES, CA)
Common no par split (5) for (4) by issuance of (0.25) additional share 02/15/1994
Stock Dividends - 25% 05/13/1988; 10% 06/11/1989; 10% 05/15/1990; 10% 05/15/1991; 10% 05/15/1992; 10% 05/15/1993; 10% 03/31/1995
Merged into Monarch Bancorp 09/30/1996
Each share Common no par exchanged for $17.25 cash

WESTERN BANK HOLDING CO. (WA)
Acquired by Moore Financial Group Inc. 9/26/88
Each share Common no par exchanged for $36.197018 cash

WESTERN BANK OF COMMERCE (LOS ANGELES, CA)
Name changed to Western Bank (Los Angeles, CA) 9/21/81
(See Western Bank (Los Angeles, CA))

WESTERN BARIUM CORP (CA)
Liquidation completed
Each share Preferred $1 par received initial distribution of $0.07 cash 2/10/65
Each share Preferred $1 par received second and final distribution of $0.10 cash 3/15/71
Note: Certificates were not required to be surrendered and are without value
No Common stockholders' equity

WESTERN BEAVER LODGE MINES LTD (BC)
Recapitalized as Portcomm Communications Corp. Ltd. 08/19/1969
Each share Capital Stock no par exchanged for (0.2) share Class A Common no par
Portcomm Communications Corp. Ltd. name changed to Roach (Hal) Studios Corp. 11/01/1977 which merged into H.R.S. Industries, Inc. 05/21/1982 which merged into International H.R.S. Industries Inc. 05/15/1984 which name changed to Glenex Industries Inc. 05/25/1987 which merged into Quest Investment Corp. 07/04/2002 which merged into Quest Capital Corp. (BC) 06/30/2003 which reincorporated in Canada 05/27/2008 which name changed to Sprott Resource Lending Corp. 09/10/2010 which merged into Sprott Inc. 07/24/2013

WESTERN BEEF INC (DE)
Merged into Cactus Acquisition Inc. 12/22/99
Each share Common 5¢ par exchanged for $8.75 cash

WESTERN BEEF INC (TX)
Merged into Century Cattle Corp. 04/30/1985
Each share Common no par exchanged for $2.25 cash

WESTERN BELL COMMUNICATIONS INC (UT)
Each share old Capital Stock $0.005 par exchanged for (0.25) share new Capital Stock $0.005 par 12/16/1985
Charter suspended for failure to pay taxes 05/01/1989

WESTERN BREWERIES LTD.
Stock purchased at $31.50 a share by Brewers & Distillers of Vancouver Ltd. in 1950

WESTERN BROADCASTING LTD (BC)
Common no par split (2) for (1) by issuance of (1) additional share 08/03/1967
Common no par split (3) for (1) by issuance of (2) additional shares 09/10/1971
Common no par reclassified as Conv. Class A no par 08/31/1973
5-3/4% Conv. Preferred $25 par called for redemption offer 12/31/1976
Through exchange offer 100% acquired by North Continent Holdings Ltd. 06/22/1981
Public interest eliminated

WESTERN BUFF MINES & OILS LTD (BC)
Struck off register and declared dissolved for failure to file returns 06/27/1977

WESTERN BUR INVESTIGATION (CA)
Charter suspended for failure to file reports and pay taxes 10/01/1975

WESTERN CALIFORNIA DEVELOPMENT CO. (NV)
Dissolved 4/25/58

WESTERN CDA BEVERAGE CORP (BC)
Trustee discharged 3/25/2003
No stockholders' equity

WESTERN CANADA BREWERIES, LTD. (CANADA)
Acquired by Canadian Breweries Ltd. 1/14/63
Each share Capital Stock $5 par exchanged for $36 cash

WESTERN CDA ENERGY LTD (AB)
Assets sold for the benefit of creditors 03/31/2010
No stockholders' equity

WESTERN CANADA FLOUR MILLS CO., LTD.
Recapitalized as Purity Flour Mills, Ltd. 00/00/1945
Each share 6-1/2% Preference $100 par exchanged for (2) shares new Preference $40 par and (2) shares Common $10 par
Each share Common no par exchanged for (1) share Common $10 par
Purity Flour Mills Ltd. merged into Maple Leaf Mills Ltd. 03/31/1961
(See Maple Leaf Mills Ltd.)

WESTERN CANADA STEEL LTD. (BC)
Name changed to Western Canada Steel (1952) Ltd. 08/05/1964
Western Canada Steel (1952) Ltd. liquidated for Consolidated Mining & Smelting Co. of Canada Ltd. 04/01/1966 which name changed to Cominco Ltd. 05/16/1966 which merged into Teck Corp. 07/20/2001 which name changed to Teck Cominco Ltd. 09/12/2001 which name changed to Teck Resources Ltd. 04/27/2009

WESTERN CANADA STEEL (1952) LTD. (BC)
Liquidation completed
Each share Capital Stock no par received initial distribution of (0.4) share Consolidated Mining & Smelting Co. of Canada Ltd. Capital Stock no par 08/05/1964
Each share Capital Stock no par exchanged for second distribution of $2 cash 04/14/1965
Each share Capital Stock no par received third and final distribution of $0.026 cash 04/01/1966
Consolidated Mining & Smelting Co. of Canada Ltd. name changed to Cominco Ltd. 05/16/1966 which merged into Teck Corp. 07/20/2001 which name changed to Teck Cominco Ltd. 09/12/2001 which name changed to Teck Resources Ltd. 04/27/2009

WESTERN CANADA VEGETABLE OIL PRODUCTS LTD. (SK)
Assets liquidated for benefit of creditors in 1964
No stockholders' equity

WESTERN CDN COAL CORP (BC)
Name changed to Western Coal Corp. 10/07/2009
Western Coal Corp. merged into Walter Energy, Inc. 04/06/2011

WESTERN CDN ENTMT CORP (AB)
Issue Information - 3,950,000 shares COM offered at $0.10 per share on 04/13/1995
Recapitalized as PowerTel Communications Inc. 12/31/1996
Each share Common no par exchanged for (0.5) share Common no par
PowerTel Communications Inc. name changed to Equess Communications Inc. 08/10/1998
(See Equess Communications Inc.)

WESTERN CDN LD CORP (BC)
Recapitalized as King George Development Corp. (BC) 11/29/1996
Each share Common no par exchanged for (0.2) share Common no par
King George Development Corp. (BC) reincorporated in Canada as Allied Hotel Properties Inc. 10/21/1999 which reincorporated in British Columbia 06/22/2009

WESTERN CDN MNG CORP (BC)
Merged into Consolidated Brinco Ltd. 12/31/1990
Each (4.25) shares Common no par exchanged for (1) share Common no par
Consolidated Brinco Ltd. merged into

Hillsborough Resources Ltd. (ON) 02/06/1992 which reincorporated in Canada 11/05/1997
(See Hillsborough Resources Ltd. (Canada))

WESTERN CANADIAN OIL SYNDICATE
Acquired by Lindale Petroleums Ltd. 9/30/60
Each Unit for Capital Stock $100 par exchanged for (10) shares Capital Stock

WESTERN CDN RES FD LTD (MB)
Liquidation completed
Each share Special Capital Stock $1 par exchanged for initial distribution of $55 cash 2/17/81
Each share Special Capital Stock $1 par received second and final distribution of $10.38 cash 11/20/81

WESTERN CDN SEED PROCESSORS LTD (AB)
Name changed to Canbra Foods Ltd. 5/17/74
(See Canbra Foods Ltd.)

WESTERN CAP FINL CORP (NV)
Recapitalized as Global Diamond Resources, Inc. 07/17/1995
Each share Common $0.001 par exchanged for (0.03466685) share Common $0.005 par
(See Global Diamond Resources, Inc.)

WESTERN CAP INVT CORP (DE)
Acquired by First Bank System, Inc. 12/18/1992
Each share Common $1 par exchanged for (0.565) share Common $1.25 par
First Bank System, Inc. name changed to U.S. Bancorp 08/01/1997

WESTERN CAP RES INC (MN)
Each share old Common no par exchanged for (0.05) share new Common no par 06/24/2014
Reincorporated under the laws of Delaware and Common no par changed to $0.0001 par 05/11/2016

WESTERN CARLYLE CONCEPTS INC (BC)
Struck off register and declared dissolved for failure to file returns 11/20/92

WESTERN CAROLINA SVGS & LN ASSN VALDESE (NC)
Merged into Southern National Corp. 8/31/90
Each share Common $1 par exchanged for (1.91724) shares Common $5 par
Southern National Corp. name changed to BB&T Corp. 5/19/97

WESTERN CAROLINA TEL CO (CA)
Acquired by General Telephone & Electronics Corp. 5/29/64
Each share Common $10 par exchanged for (2.2) shares Common $3.33-1/3 par
General Telephone & Electronics Corp. name changed to GTE Corp. 7/1/82 which merged into Verizon Communications Inc. 6/30/2000

WESTERN CAROLINA TELEPHONE CO. (NC)
Under plan of merger each share Capital Stock $50 par exchanged for (5.8137370) shares Common $10 par in 1952
Common $10 par changed to $5 par 9/17/56
Merged into Continental Telephone Corp. 5/19/78
Each share Common $5 par exchanged for $20 cash

WESTERN CARTRIDGE CO.
Merged into Olin Industries, Inc. in 1945

Preferred $100 par exchanged share for share
Each share Common exchanged for (75) shares Common $1 par
Olin Industries, Inc. merged into Olin Mathieson Chemical Corp. in 1954 which name changed to Olin Corp. 9/1/69

WESTERN CAS & SURETY CO (KS)
Each share Capital Stock $100 par exchanged for (10) shares Capital Stock $10 par 09/08/1928
Each share Capital Stock $10 par exchanged for (2) shares Capital Stock $5 par 00/00/1953
Capital Stock $5 par changed to $1.25 par and (3) additional shares issued 06/15/1972
Stock Dividends - 25% 11/21/1945; 15% 12/05/1950; 25% 12/31/1952; 11-1/9% 04/14/1956; 25% 01/19/1962
Acquired by Lincoln National Corp. 04/16/1985
Each share Capital Stock $1.25 par exchanged for $67.50 cash

WESTERN CENTRAL PETROLEUMS, INC. (DE)
Merged into Consolidated Rimrock Oil Corp. on a (1) for (3) basis 10/01/1956
Consolidated Rimrock Oil Corp. merged into Consolidated Oil & Gas, Inc. (CO) 04/30/1958 which was acquired by Hugoton Energy Corp. 09/07/1995 which merged into Chesapeake Energy Corp. 03/10/1998

WESTERN CLAY PRODUCTS LTD. (SK)
Name changed to Ceramics Holdings Ltd. 6/18/65

WESTERN CLOCK CO.
Merged into General Time Instruments Corp. 00/00/1930
Details not available

WESTERN CO NORTH AMER (DE)
Common 30¢ par split (2) for (1) by issuance of (1) additional share 05/17/1974
Common 30¢ par split (5) for (4) by issuance of (0.25) additional share 10/25/1978
Common 30¢ par split (3) for (2) by issuance of (0.5) additional share 10/26/1979
Common 30¢ par split (2) for (1) by issuance of (1) additional share 09/11/1980
$2.125 Conv. Preferred Ser. A no par called for redemption 12/31/1980
Common 30¢ par split (2) for (1) by issuance of (1) additional share 06/12/1981
Reorganized under Chapter 11 Federal Bankruptcy Code 04/25/1989
Each share $7.25 Preferred Ser. A no par exchanged for (0.5625) share Common 10¢ par
Each share Common 30¢ par exchanged for (0.008736) share Common 10¢ par
Stock Dividends - 10% 10/23/1975; 10% 10/22/1976
Merged into BJ Services Co. 04/13/1995
Each share Common 10¢ par exchanged for (1.0028) shares Common 10¢ par and (0.2) Common Stock Purchase Warrant expiring 04/13/2000
BJ Services Co. merged into Baker Hughes Inc. 04/28/2010 which merged into Baker Hughes, a GE company 07/05/2017

WESTERN COAL CORP (BC)
Merged into Walter Energy, Inc. 04/06/2011
Each share Common no par exchanged for approximately

(0.0114) share Common 1¢ par and $10.35 cash
Note: Unexchanged certificates were cancelled and became without value 04/06/2016

WESTERN COATINGS & CHEMICAL CO. (DE)
Each share old Common 1¢ par exchanged for (0.1) share new Common 1¢ par 09/17/1962
Name changed to Valley Fair Corp. 01/13/1964
(See Valley Fair Corp.)

WESTERN COML BK (WOODLAND HILLS, CA)
Under plan of reorganization each share Common no par automatically became (1) share WCB Holdings, Inc. Common no par 09/21/2007

WESTERN COML INC (DE)
Name changed 7/27/87
Name changed from Western Commercial (CA) to Western Commercial, Inc. (DE) 7/27/87
Merged into ValliCorp Holdings, Inc. 11/30/89
Each share Common no par exchanged for (0.5) share Common no par
ValliCorp Holdings, Inc. merged into Westamerica Bancorporation 4/12/97

WESTERN COMWLTH DEVS INC (BC)
Delisted from Vancouver Stock Exchange 03/15/1991

WESTERN COMMUNITY BANCORP (CA)
Closed by the California State Banking Superintendent and FDIC was appointed receiver 7/29/94
Stockholders' equity unlikely

WESTERN CONCRETE PRODUCTS CORP. (MN)
Adjudicated bankrupt 7/10/73
Stockholders' equity unlikely

WESTERN CONSOLIDATED MINES LTD. (BC)
Struck off register and declared dissolved for failure to file returns 9/12/35

WESTERN CONSORTIUM INC (UT)
Proclaimed dissolved for failure to file annual reports 05/01/1990

WESTERN CONTL INC (ID)
Administratively dissolved 12/09/2005

WESTERN CONTL INC (NV)
Charter revoked for failure to file reports and pay fees 03/04/1974

WESTERN COPPER CORP (BC)
Reorganized as Western Copper & Gold Corp. 10/17/2011
Each share Common no par exchanged for (1) share Common no par, (0.5) share Copper North Mining Corp. Common no par and (0.5) share NorthIsle Copper & Gold Inc. Common no par

WESTERN COPPER HLDGS LTD (BC)
Name changed to Western Silver Corp. 3/25/2003
(See Western Silver Corp.)

WESTERN COPPER MILLS LTD. (BC)
Acquired by Northwood Mills Ltd. for cash 10/18/63

WESTERN COPPER MINING CO. (ME)
Charter revoked for failure to file reports and pay fees in 1922

WESTERN CORN DOG FACTORIES (UT)
Merged into Resources West, Inc. 7/27/81
Each share Common 1¢ par exchanged for (5) shares Common $0.005 par

Resources West, Inc. recapitalized as Magma Resources 1/27/89 which name changed to Cellular Telecommunications & Technologies Inc. 7/15/93 which recapitalized as China Biomedical Group Inc. 4/3/95 which name changed to Internet Holdings Ltd. 6/30/96 which name changed to HTTP Technology, Inc. (UT) 11/28/2000 which reincorporated in Delaware which name changed Medicsight, Inc. 10/28/2002 which name changed to MGT Capital Investments, Inc. 1/24/2007

WESTERN CORP (UT)
Recapitalized as Spring Kist Corp. on a (0.05) for (1) basis 1/3/62
(See Spring Kist Corp.)

WESTERN CORPORATE ENTERPRISES INC (BC)
Plan of Arrangement effective 11/1/94
Each share Common no par exchanged for $7.53 cash

WESTERN CORPORATE FARM LTD (AB)
Recapitalized as Sound Communication Corp. 7/12/90
Each share Common no par exchanged for (0.5) share Common no par
(See Sound Communication Corp.)

WESTERN CRUDE OIL INC (DE)
Merged into Reserve Oil & Gas Co. 04/17/1973
Each share Capital Stock 10¢ par exchanged for ((0.5733) share Common $1 par
(See Reserve Oil & Gas Co.)

WESTERN CTRY CLUBS INC (CO)
Reincorporated under the laws of Oklahoma as Atomic Burrito, Inc. and Common 1¢ par changed to $0.001 par 09/07/1999
(See Atomic Burrito, Inc.)

WESTERN D ELDONA RES LTD (ON)
Merged into Paramount Resources Ltd. 1/1/92
Each share Common no par exchanged for $3.25 cash

WESTERN DAIRIES, INC. (DE)
Under plan of merger name changed to Arden Farms Co. (New) 08/01/1940
Arden Farms Co. (New) name changed to Arden-Mayfair, Inc. 04/24/1965 which reorganized as Arden Group, Inc. 12/19/1978
(See Arden Group, Inc.)

WESTERN DAIRY PRODUCTS, INC. (MD)
Name changed to Arden Farms, Inc. 06/09/1936
Arden Farms, Inc. merged into Arden Farms Co. (New) 08/01/1940 which name changed to Arden-Mayfair, Inc. 04/24/1965 which reorganized as Arden Group, Inc. 12/19/1978
(See Arden Group, Inc.)

WESTERN DAIRY PRODUCTS CO. (DE)
Name changed to Arden Farms Co. (Old) 05/02/1936
Arden Farms Co. (Old) merged into Arden Farms Co. (New) 08/01/1940 which name changed to Arden-Mayfair, Inc. 04/24/1965 which reorganized as Arden Group, Inc. 12/19/1978
(See Arden Group, Inc.)

WESTERN DECALTA PETE LTD (CANADA)
Acquired by Wesdec Petroleum Ltd. 03/11/1977
Each share Capital Stock $1 par exchanged for $8 cash

WESTERN DECOR & FURNISHINGS INDS (CA)
Charter suspended for failure to file reports and pay taxes 05/01/1975

WESTERN DEEP LEVELS LTD (SOUTH AFRICA)
Each ADR for A Ordinary Reg. Rand-2 par or ADR for B Ordinary Reg. Rand-2 par exchanged for (1) ADR for Ordinary Reg. Rand-2 par 8/5/66
Merged into Anglogold Ltd. 6/29/98
Each ADR for Ordinary Rand-2 par exchanged for (1.06) Sponsored ADR's for Ordinary Rand-50 par AngloGold Ltd. name changed to AngloGold Ashanti Ltd. 4/26/2004

WESTERN DEPARTMENT STORES (CA)
Each share 7% Preferred $25 par exchanged for (1) share 6% Special Preferred $25 par and holders had the option of exchanging each share for (1.5) shares 6% Preferred $25 par or (1) share 6% Preferred $25 par and (1) share Common $1 par in 1944
Common no par changed to $1 par in 1944
Each share Common $1 par exchanged for (2) shares Common 50¢ par in 1946
Each share Common 50¢ par exchanged for (2) shares Common 25¢ par in 1951
Name changed to Rhodes Western 8/2/60
Rhodes Western was acquired by Amfac, Inc. 12/2/69
(See Amfac, Inc.)

WESTERN DEV CORP (CO)
Completely liquidated 11/01/1984
Each share Common 1¢ par exchanged for first and final distribution of $2.85 cash

WESTERN DEV CORP (DE)
Name changed to WDC Services, Inc. 09/29/1970
WDC Services, Inc. merged into AID, Inc. (DE) 06/25/1971 which merged into INA Corp. 06/16/1978 which merged into Cigna Corp. 04/01/1982

WESTERN DEVELOPMENT CO. OF DELAWARE (DE)
Name changed to International Oil & Gas Corp. 12/31/62 which completed liquidation 1/9/67

WESTERN DIE CASTING CO (CA)
Name changed to Western Safety Devices, Inc. 12/12/1985
(See Western Safety Devices, Inc.)

WESTERN DIGITAL CORP (CA)
Reincorporated under the laws of Delaware 01/09/1987

WESTERN DIST WAREHOUSING CORP (KY)
Acquired by Clear Creek Capital, LLC 09/26/2012
Each share Non-Vtg. Capital Stock $1 par exchanged for $5.115 cash

WESTERN DOMINION INVT LTD (BC)
Merged into WDI Investments Ltd. 6/6/96
Each share Common no par exchanged for $1.50 cash

WESTERN E-COM INC (MB)
Name changed to OMT Inc. (MB) 10/04/2001
OMT Inc. (MB) reorganized in British Columbia as AnalytixInsight Inc. 07/11/2013

WESTERN ELEC INC (NY)
Each share Common no par exchanged for (5) shares Common no par in 1927
Acquired by American Telephone & Telegraph Co. 10/14/66
Each share Common no par exchanged for (6) shares Capital Stock $16-2/3 par

WESTERN ELECTRS & ENGR LTD (AB)
Name changed to Pancana Industries Ltd. 06/11/1971
Pancana Industries Ltd. name changed to Pan Cana Resources Ltd. 03/06/1980 which merged into Geocrude Energy Inc. 02/04/1983
(See Geocrude Energy, Inc.)

WESTERN EMPIRE CORP (UT)
Recapitalized 04/18/1978
Each share Common 10¢ par exchanged for (0.02) share Common $5 par 04/17/1973
Recapitalized from Western Empire Petroleum Co. to Western Empire Corp. 04/18/1978
Each share Common $5 par exchanged for (0.04) share Common no par
Completely liquidated 03/29/1984
Each share Common no par exchanged for first and final distribution of (2) shares Continental Industries Inc. (UT) Common 1¢ par

WESTERN EMPIRE FINL INC (DE)
Charter cancelled and declared inoperative and void for non-payment of taxes 06/27/1980

WESTERN EMPIRE LIFE INS CO (CO)
Under plan of merger each share Common 25¢ par exchanged for (0.125) share Common $1.35 par 9/24/63
Merged into Bankers Union Life Insurance Co. 3/12/73
Each share Common $1.35 par exchanged for (0.1) share Common $5 par
Bankers Union Life Insurance Co. merged into I.C.H. Corp. 10/14/82 which name changed to Southwestern Life Corp. (New) 6/15/94 which name changed to I.C.H. Corp. (New) 10/10/95
(See I.C.H. Corp. (New))

WESTERN EMPIRE OIL CO. (CO)
Merged into Empire Petroleum Co. on a (1) for (4) basis in 1955
Empire Petroleum Co. name changed to Empire International Inc. 7/15/70 which was adjudicated bankrupt 5/9/73

WESTERN EMPIRE SVGS & LN ASSN (CA)
Merged into WESL Merger Corp. 12/30/1988
Each share Guarantee Stock $8 par exchanged for $0.21 cash

WESTERN ENERGIES INC (WA)
Recapitalized as Ametex, Inc. 6/19/84
Each share Common no par exchanged for (1/3) share Common no par
(See Ametex, Inc.)

WESTERN ENERGY CORP (AZ)
Recapitalized as United Western Energy Corp. 11/29/78
Each share Capital Stock 50¢ par exchanged for (0.2) share Common 10¢ par
(See United Western Energy Corp.)

WESTERN ENERGY DEV INC (CO)
Merged into Oxford Consolidated, Inc. 02/01/1988
Each share Common $0.001 par exchanged for (0.0146) Common 10¢ par and (0.00887) Common Stock Purchase Warrant expiring 02/01/1990
(See Oxford Consolidated, Inc.)

WESTERN ENERGY EMPIRE INC. (DE)
Name changed to Accurate Business Systems, Inc. 04/20/1987
(See Accurate Business Systems, Inc.)

WESTERN ENERGY INC (UT)
Name changed to WENR Corp. 04/14/2000
(See WENR Corp.)

WESTERN ENERGY MGMT INC (DE)
Merged into Onsite Energy Corp. 2/1/94
Each share Common 1¢ par exchanged for (0.2) share Class A Common $0.001 par

WESTERN ENERGY RES INC (CA)
Recapitalized as Omnipower Inc. 8/23/95
Each (15) shares Common no par exchanged for (1) share Common no par
(See Omnipower Inc.)

WESTERN ENVIROTECH INC (AB)
Name changed to Aquasol International Group Inc. 10/31/1995
(See Aquasol International Group Inc.)

WESTERN EQUITIES, INC. (NV)
Name changed to Westec Corp. 5/20/66
Westec Corp. name changed to Tech-Sym Corp. 5/25/70

WESTERN EXPLORATION CO.
Merged into Consolidated Royalty Oil Co. in 1930
Consolidated Royalty Oil Co. completed liquidation 6/29/70

WESTERN EXPL INC (DE)
Each share old Common $0.001 par exchanged for (0.5) share new Common $0.001 par 10/11/2005
Name changed to MDWerks, Inc. 10/25/2005

WESTERN EXPL LTD (BC)
Common 50¢ par changed to no par 12/15/67
Merged into Tacoma Resources Ltd. 10/31/74
Each share Common no par exchanged for (0.2) share Common no par
(See Tacoma Resources Ltd.)

WESTERN FACS FD (AB)
Recapitalized as Acclaim Energy Trust 04/20/2001
Each (14) Trust Units exchanged for (1) Trust Unit and $0.807 principal amount of 6% Debentures expiring 12/31/2003
(See Acclaim Energy Trust)

WESTERN FACTORS, INC. (UT)
Adjudicated bankrupt 11/25/66
No stockholders' equity

WESTERN FD (AZ)
Name changed to Dayton Industries, Inc. 05/21/1969
Dayton Industries, Inc. merged into Galaxie National Corp. 12/24/1969 which reorganized as Marathon Office Supply, Inc. 05/12/1982
(See Marathon Office Supply, Inc.)

WESTERN FDG INC (FL)
Administratively dissolved 09/24/1999

WESTERN FED SVGS & LN ASSN MARINA DEL REY CALIF (USA)
Acquired by WestFed Holdings, Inc. 09/23/1988
Each share Common $1 par exchanged for $41.83 cash

WESTERN FED SVGS BK (MAYAGUEZ, PR)
Stock Dividend - 10% 7/15/86
Name changed to WesternBank Puerto Rico (Mayaguez, PR) 11/30/94

WESTERN FID FDG INC (CO)
Chapter 11 bankruptcy proceedings converted to Chapter 7 on 7/14/99
Stockholders' equity unlikely

WESTERN FIDELITY CORP. (KS)
Merged into Gibraltar Life Insurance Co. of America 1/9/80
Each share Common 75¢ par exchanged for $4.50 cash

WESTERN FINL CORP (DE)
Common $1 par split (3) for (2) by issuance of (0.5) additional share 12/29/72
Common $1 par split (3) for (2) by issuance of (0.5) additional share 2/16/73
Reorganized under the laws of Arizona as Western Savings & Loan Association and Common $1 par reclassified as Permanent Reserve Guarantee $1 par 12/28/82
(See Western Savings & Loan Association)

WESTERN FINL CORP (KS)
Merged into Metropolitan Financial Corp. 6/11/93
Each share Common $1 par exchanged for (0.55) share Common 1¢ par
Metropolitan Financial Corp. merged into First Bank System, Inc. 1/24/95 which name changed to U.S. Bancorp (Old) 8/1/97 which merged into U.S. Bancorp (New) 2/27/2001

WESTERN FINL CORP (TX)
Name changed back to First Continental Corp. 10/27/71
(See First Continental Corp.)

WESTERN FINL GROUP INC NEW (AB)
1st Preferred Ser. 3 no par called for redemption at $100 plus $1.13 accrued dividends on 08/01/2012
1st Preferred Ser. 5 no par called for redemption at $100 plus $4.50 accrued dividends on 09/30/2012
1st Preferred Ser. 4 no par called for redemption at $100 plus $0.56 accrued dividends on 12/31/2012
Public interest eliminated

WESTERN FINL GROUP INC OLD (AB)
Conv. 1st Preferred Ser. 2 no par called for redemption at $100 on 06/30/2011
Merged into Desjardins Financial Corp. Inc. 07/12/2011
Each 1st Preferred Series 3 no par exchanged for (1) share Western Financial Group Inc. (New) 1st Preferred Series 3 no par
Each 1st Preferred Series 4 no par exchanged for (1) share Western Financial Group Inc. (New) 1st Preferred Series 4 no par
Each 1st Preferred Series 5 no par exchanged for (1) share Western Financial Group Inc. (New) 1st Preferred Series 5 no par
(See Western Financial Group Inc. (New))
Each share Common no par exchanged for $4.15 cash
Note: Unexchanged certificates were cancelled and became without value 07/12/2016

WESTERN FIRE & INDEMNITY CO. (TX)
Common $10 par changed to $5 par in 1958
Name changed to Trans Plains Insurance Co. 1/25/67
Trans Plains Insurance Co. charter cancelled 6/4/71

WESTERN FOOD DISTRS INC (NV)
Reorganized as Blue Zone Inc. 10/04/1999
Each share Common $0.001 par exchanged for (1.125) shares Common $0.001 par
(See Blue Zone Inc.)

WESTERN FROZEN FOODS CO., INC. (CA)
Dissolved 07/10/1964
Each share 5% Conv. Preferred $10 par exchanged for 13¢ cash
No equity for holders of Common $1 par

WESTERN FROZEN PRODUCTS CO., INC. (UT)
Proclaimed dissolved for failure to pay taxes 11/9/74

WESTERN GAMING CORP (NV)
Recapitalized as InRob Tech, Ltd. 09/01/2005
Each (10.98) shares Common $0.001 par exchanged for (1) share Common $0.001 par

WESTERN GARNET INTL LTD (BC)
Name changed 07/05/1996
Name changed from Western Garnet Co., Ltd. to Western Garnet International Ltd. 07/05/1996
Name changed to WGI Heavy Minerals, Inc. 11/27/2002
(See WGI Heavy Minerals, Inc.)

WESTERN GAS PROCESSORS LTD (CO)
Merged into Western Gas Resources, Inc. 5/1/91
Each share $1.80 Part. Preference Units exchanged for (1) share Common 10¢ par
(See Western Gas Resources, Inc.)

WESTERN GAS RES INC (DE)
7.25% Sr. Conv. Perpetual Preferred called for redemption 5/31/95
$2.28 Preferred 10¢ par called for redemption at $25 plus $5.56398 accrued dividends on 12/27/2002
$2.625 Conv. Preferred 10¢ par called for redemption at $50 plus $0.467 accrued dividends on 4/20/2004
Common 10¢ par split (2) for (1) by issuance of (1) additional share payable 6/18/2004 to holders of record 6/4/2004 Ex date - 6/21/2004
Merged into Anadarko Petroleum Corp. 8/23/2006
Each share Common 10¢ par exchanged for $61 cash

WESTERN GAS SERVICE CO. (DE)
Merged into Southern Union Gas Co. (Del.) (New) 1/19/68
Each share Common $2 par exchanged for (1) share Jr. Conv. Preferred $7.50 par
Southern Union Gas Co. (Del.) (New) name changed to Southern Union Co. (Old) 5/7/76
(See Southern Union Co. (Old))

WESTERN GEAR CORP (WA)
Stock Dividend - 50% 6/15/81
Merged into Bucyrus-Erie Co. 12/31/81
Each share Common $1 par exchanged for $28 cash

WESTERN GEOPOWER CORP (BC)
Merged into Ram Power, Corp. 10/20/2009
Each share Common no par exchanged for (0.0622) share Common no par
Ram Power, Corp. recapitalized as Polaris Infrastructure Inc. 05/19/2015

WESTERN GEOTHERMAL & PWR CORP (MT)
Each share Common 1¢ par exchanged for (0.25) share Common 4¢ par 07/01/1977
Involuntarily dissolved for failure to file annual reports and pay taxes 12/15/1982

WESTERN GLORY HOLE INC (NV)
Each share old Common $0.001 par exchanged for (2) shares new Common $0.001 par 11/12/2003
Name changed to Health Enhancement Products, Inc. 12/12/2003
Health Enhancement Products, Inc. name changed to Zivo Bioscience, Inc. 11/10/2014

WESTERN GOLD & URANIUM, INC. (NV)
Name changed to Western Equities, Inc. 12/14/61

Western Equities, Inc. name changed to Westec Corp. 5/20/66 which name changed to Tech-Sym Corp. 5/25/70

WESTERN GOLD MINES INC. (NV)
Name changed to Western Gold & Uranium, Inc. 7/20/53
Western Gold & Uranium, Inc. name changed to Western Equities, Inc. 12/14/61 which name changed to Westec Corp. 5/20/66 which name changed to Tech-Sym Corp. 5/25/70

WESTERN GOLD MNG INC (WA)
Recapitalized as Lundell Technologies, Inc. 07/26/1996
Each share Common 5¢ par exchanged for (0.08) share Common $0.001 par
Lundell Technologies, Inc. name changed to Worldtek Corp. 12/17/2003
(See Worldtek Corp.)

WESTERN GOLD N GAS CO (NV)
Name changed to Amtech Resources, Inc. (NV) 3/9/84
Amtech Resources, Inc. (NV) reincorporated in Colorado 12/15/2003 which recapitalized as Hat Trick Beverage, Inc. 12/10/2004

WESTERN GOLD RESERVES, INC. (NV)
Charter revoked for failure to file documents and pay fees 3/4/63

WESTERN GOLDFIELDS INC (ON)
Incorporated 00/00/1982
Merged into WMC Acquisition Inc. 03/24/1988
Each share Common no par exchanged for $11.25 cash

WESTERN GOLDFIELDS INC CDA (ON)
Incorporated 03/08/2007
Reincorporated 06/29/2007
Place of incorporation changed from (ID) to (ONT) 06/29/2007
Merged into New Gold Inc. 06/04/2009
Each share Common 1¢ par exchanged for (1) share Common no par and $0.0001 cash

WESTERN GRAIN CO. LTD. (CANADA)
Liquidation completed in 1954

WESTERN GRAIN INTL INC (FL)
Name changed back to Riverside Group, Inc. 06/12/1984
(See Riverside Group, Inc.)

WESTERN GREYHOUND RACING, INC. (DE)
Name changed to Western Racing, Inc. in 1957
Western Racing, Inc. name changed to WRI Liquidating Co., Inc. 12/22/80
(See WRI Liquidating Co., Inc.)

WESTERN GROCER CO. (IA)
Acquired by Consolidated Grocers Corp. for cash in 1946

WESTERN GROCERS LTD. (CANADA)
Recapitalized in 1926
Each share Preferred $100 par exchanged for (0.5) share new Preferred $100 par, (0.5) share Common no par and $2.50 cash
Each share Common $100 par exchanged for (1/6) share Common no par
Recapitalized in 1946
Each share 7% Preferred $100 par exchanged for (5) shares 7% Preferred $20 par and (3) shares Common no par
Each share Common no par exchanged for (4) shares Class A no par and (3) shares new Common no par
Name changed to Westfair Foods Ltd. 1/3/61

(See Westfair Foods Ltd.)

WESTERN GROWTH CORP (NV)
Recapitalized as CVF Corp. 09/13/1995
Each share Common $0.001 par exchanged for (0.5) share Common $0.001 par
CVF Corp. name changed to CVF Technologies Corp. 09/22/1998

WESTERN HARNESS RACING ASSOCIATION (CA)
Recapitalized 04/29/1960
Each share Capital Stock $1,000 par exchanged for (20) shares Capital Stock $50 par
Each share Capital Stock $100 par exchanged for (2) shares Capital Stock $50 par
Capital Stock $50 par changed to $25 par and (1) additional share issued 02/08/1967
Stock Dividends - 10% 01/29/1962; 14% 01/18/1963; 14% 02/28/1964; 20% 02/28/1968
Name changed to Western Harness Racing, Inc. 11/12/1968
Western Harness Racing, Inc. name changed to Wincorp (CA) 10/01/1974 which reincorporated in Delaware as Wincorp Industries Inc. 11/18/1977
(See Wincorp Industries Inc.)

WESTERN HARNESS RACING INC (CA)
Capital Stock $25 par changed to no par and (9) additional shares issued 08/24/1972
Name changed to Wincorp 10/01/1974
Wincorp reincorporated in Delaware as Wincorp Industries Inc. 11/18/1977 which reorganized as Wincorp Realty Investments Inc. 12/01/1981
(See Wincorp Realty Investments Inc.)

WESTERN HARNESS RACING INC (DE)
(Issued only in Non-Seperable Units of (1) share of Wincorp Realty Investments Inc. Capital Stock $1 par and (1) share Western Harness Racing Inc. Capital Stock $1 par)
Liquidation completed
Each share Capital Stock $1 par received initial distribution of $1.65 cash 12/18/1984
Each share Capital Stock $1 par exchanged for second distribution of $0.42 cash 07/19/1985
Each share Capital Stock $1 par received third distribution of $0.302162 cash 03/14/1986
Each share Capital Stock $1 par received fourth and final distribution of $1.2719 cash 10/06/1989

WESTERN HARVEST SEAFARMS LTD (BC)
Struck off register and declared dissolved for failure to file returns 12/30/94

WESTERN HEALTH PLANS INC (CA)
Common no par split (3) for (2) by issuance of (0.5) additional share 12/30/1985
Plan of reorganization under Chapter 11 Federal Bankruptcy proceedings confirmed 03/01/1991
No stockholders' equity

WESTERN HELIUM LTD. (ON)
Name changed to Western Tin Mines Ltd. 04/00/1965
(See Western Tin Mines Ltd.)

WESTERN HEMISPHERE PETROLEUM CORP. (DE)
Merged into Wabash Magnetics, Inc. 3/30/61
Each share Common 50¢ par exchanged for (1) share Common no par

Wabash Magnetics, Inc. name changed to Wabash, Inc. 5/24/76
(See Wabash, Inc.)

WESTERN HERITAGE PPTYS LTD (ON)
Name changed to Home Smith International Ltd. 01/01/1971
(See Home Smith International Ltd.)

WESTERN HLDGS BANCORP
Merged into Heritage Commerce Corp. 10/1/2000
Each share Common exchanged for (1.2264) shares Common no par

WESTERN HLDGS LTD (SOUTH AFRICA)
Merged into Orange Free State Investments Ltd. 3/4/86
Each ADR for Ordinary Reg. Rand-50¢ par exchanged for (1) ADR for Ordinary Reg. Rand-50¢ par
Orange Free State Investments Ltd. reorganized into FreeState Consolidated Gold Mines Ltd. 4/19/94 which merged into AngloGold Ltd. 6/29/98 which name changed to AngloGold Ashanti Ltd. 4/26/2004

WESTERN HLDG CORP IOWA (IA)
Recapitalized as Continental Western Industries, Inc. 1/3/72
Each share Common 50¢ par exchanged for (0.1) share Common $5 par
Continental Western Industries, Inc. merged into NN Corp. 2/10/78 which merged into Armco Inc. 12/1/80 which merged into AK Steel Holding Corp. 9/30/99

WESTERN HOME FINANCIAL CORP. (UT)
Ceased operations 01/24/1986
Stockholders' equity unlikely

WESTERN HOMES LTD (MB)
Merged into Summit Resources Ltd. 10/2/72
Each share Capital Stock $35 par exchanged for (32.72) shares Common no par
(See Summit Resources Ltd.)

WESTERN HOMESTEAD OILS LTD. (AB)
Recapitalized as Canadian Homestead Oils Ltd. on a (0.25) for (1) basis 3/1/54
Canadian Homestead Oils Ltd. merged into Inter-City Gas Corp. (Man.) 4/14/80 which reorganized as Inter-City Products Corp. 4/18/90

WESTERN HOTELS CO. (WA)
Name changed to Western International Hotels Co. (WA) 6/14/63
Western International Hotels Co. (WA) acquired by Western International Hotels Co. (CA) 9/11/65 which reincorporated under the laws of Delaware 6/13/66 which merged into UAL, Inc. 8/1/70 which name changed to Allegis Corp. 4/30/87 which name changed to UAL Corp. 5/27/88
(See UAL Corp.)

WESTERN INDPT CORP (NV)
Capital Stock $1 par changed to no par and (0.25) additional share issued 06/20/1969
Each share old Capital Stock no par exchanged for (0.005) share new Capital Stock no par 04/15/1975
Name changed to Financial Group of America 08/14/1975
Financial Group of America merged into Financial Group of America, Inc. 08/05/1980

WESTERN INDL SHS INC (NV)
Acquired by Foursquare Fund, Inc. 04/13/1976
Each share Common 25¢ par

exchanged for (0.336) share Common $1 par
Foursquare Fund, Inc. merged into Eaton Vance Investors Fund, Inc. 09/12/1983 which name changed to Eaton Vance Investors Trust 09/29/1993
(See Eaton Vance Investors Trust)

WESTERN INDUSTRIES, INC. (NV)
Name changed to Torginol Industries, Inc. 9/11/64
Torginol Industries, Inc. charter revoked 3/1/81

WESTERN INSTL PPTYS TR (CA)
Reorganized under the laws of Delaware as Western Real Estate Fund, Inc. 09/30/1987
Each Share of Bene. Int. $10 par exchanged for (0.2) share Common no par
(See Western Real Estate Fund Inc.)

WESTERN INS SECS CO (DE)
Common no par changed to $1 par and (9) additional shares issued 08/12/1964
Merged into Lincoln National Corp. 04/16/1985
Each share 6% Preferred $100 par exchanged for $100 cash
Each share $2.50 Class A Part. Preference no par exchanged for $60 cash
Each share Common $1 par exchanged for $220 cash

WESTERN INTL GOLD & SILVER INC (CO)
Proclaimed dissolved for failure to file annual reports 1/1/91

WESTERN INTERNATIONAL HOTELS CO. (WA)
Acquired by Western International Hotels Co. (CA) 9/11/65
Each share Common $2.50 par exchanged for (2.74) shares Common $2.50 par
Western International Hotels Co. (CA) reincorporated in Delaware 6/13/66 which name changed to Allegis Corp. 4/30/87 which name changed to UAL Corp. 5/27/88
(See UAL Corp.)

WESTERN INTL HOTELS CO (DE)
Reincorporated 6/13/66
State of incorporation changed from (CA) to (DE) 6/13/66
Merged into UAL, Inc. 8/1/70
Each share Common $2.50 par exchanged for (1.3) shares 40¢ Conv. Preferred Ser. A no par
(See UAL, Inc.)

WESTERN INTL INDS (AZ)
Charter revoked for failure to file reports and pay fees 12/26/1972

WESTERN INTL PIZZA CORP (NV)
Each share old Common $0.001 par exchanged for (0.0005) share new Common $0.001 par 05/06/2002
Recapitalized as AccuPoll Holding Corp. 05/28/2002
Each share new Common $0.001 par exchanged for (0.2) share Common $0.001 par
AccuPoll Holding Corp. recapitalized as Rudy Nutrition 02/08/2008
(See Rudy Nutrition)

WESTERN INTERPROVINCIAL PETROLEUM PRODUCERS LTD. (AB)
Acquired by Canadian Pipelines & Petroleums Ltd. 00/00/1954
Details not available

WESTERN INTST BANCORP (CA)
Merged into FirstPlus Financial Group, Inc. 08/09/1997
Each share Common no par exchanged for (0.472) share Common $0.001 par
(See FirstPlus Financial Group, Inc.)

WESTERN INVT REAL ESTATE TR (CA)
Shares of Bene. Int. no par split (4) for (3) by issuance of (1/3) additional share 12/15/78
Shares of Bene. Int. no par split (6) for (5) by issuance of (0.2) additional share 5/17/82
Shares of Bene. Int. no par split (3) for (2) by issuance of (0.5) additional share 3/6/87
Name changed to Western Properties Trust 8/19/99
Western Properties Trust merged into Pan Pacific Retail Properties, Inc. 11/13/2000 which merged into Kimco Realty Corp. 10/31/2006

WESTERN IOWA PORK CO. (IA)
Merged into American Beef Packers, Inc. (IA) 2/8/68
Each share Common no par exchanged for (0.75) share Common $1 par
American Beef Packers, Inc. (IA) reincorporated under the laws of Delaware 12/30/69 which name changed to Sudbury Holdings, Inc. 8/18/83 which reorganized as Sudbury, Inc. 5/27/87
(See Sudbury, Inc.)

WESTERN KELTIC MINES INC (BC)
Acquired by Sherwood Copper Corp. 05/27/2008
Each share Common no par exchanged for (0.08) share Common no par
Sherwood Copper Corp. merged into Capstone Mining Corp. 11/25/2008

WESTERN KY GAS CO (DE)
Common $5 par split (3) for (2) by issuance of (0.5) additional share 03/01/1954
Common $5 par split (4) for (3) by issuance of (1/3) additional share 05/16/1956
Stock Dividend - 12-1/2% 10/07/1960
Merged into Texas American Energy Corp. 11/28/1980
Each share 7-1/2% Conv. Preferred $25 par exchanged for $28 cash
Each share Common $5 par exchanged for $28 cash

WESTERN LAKOTA ENERGY SVCS INC (AB)
Acquired by Savanna Energy Services Corp. 08/25/2006
Each share Common no par exchanged for (0.64) share Common no par
Savanna Energy Services Corp. merged into Total Energy Services Inc. 06/23/2017

WESTERN LD & RES INC (NV)
Charter revoked for failure to file reports and pay fees 06/01/2004

WESTERN LD CORP (DE)
Charter cancelled and declared inoperative and void for non-payment of taxes 3/1/76

WESTERN LEAD PRODS CO (CA)
Name changed to Quemetco, Inc. 05/18/1970
(See Quemetco, Inc.)

WESTERN LEASEHOLDS LTD. (AB)
Completely liquidated for cash 1/4/62

WESTERN LIBERTY BANCORP (DE)
Units separated 10/28/2010
Merged into Western Alliance Bancorporation 10/17/2012
Each share Common $0.0001 par exchanged for $4.02 cash

WESTERN LIGHT & TELEPHONE CO.
Merged into Western Light & Telephone Co., Inc. 00/00/1945
Each share 7% Preferred $25 par exchanged for (1) share 5% Preferred $25 par and $1 cash
Each share Common $1 par exchanged for (0.2) share Common $10 par
Western Light & Telephone Co., Inc. name changed to Western Power & Gas Co., Inc. 07/01/1965 which name changed to Central Telephone & Utilities Corp. 06/05/1968 which name changed to Centel Corp. 04/30/1982 which was acquired by Sprint Corp. (KS) 03/09/1993 which name changed to Sprint Nextel Corp. 08/12/2005 which merged into Sprint Corp. (DE) 07/10/2013

WESTERN LITHIUM CDA CORP (BC)
Name changed to Western Lithium USA Corp. 05/31/2010
Western Lithium USA Corp. name changed to Lithium Americas Corp. (New) 03/30/2016

WESTERN LITHIUM USA CORP (BC)
Name changed to Lithium Americas Corp. (New) 03/30/2016

WESTERN LOGIC RES INC (BC)
Name changed 9/18/96
Name changed from Western Logic Technologies Inc. to Western Logic Resources Inc. 9/18/96
Delisted from Canadian Dealer Network 5/31/2001

WESTERN LT & TEL INC (KS)
Common $10 par changed to $5 par and (1) additional share issued 5/5/61
5-1/2% Preferred $25 par called for redemption 2/1/57
5.20% Conv. Preferred $25 par called for redemption 10/22/64
Under plan of merger name changed to Western Power & Gas Co., Inc. 7/1/65
Western Power & Gas Co., Inc. name changed to Central Telephone & Utilities Corp. 6/5/68 which name changed to Centel Corp. 4/30/82

WESTERN LUCRATIVE ENTERPRISES INC (NV)
Recapitalized as Zhong Ya International Ltd. 09/28/2018
Each share Common $0.001 par exchanged for (0.01) share Common $0.001 par

WESTERN LUMBER CO.
Succeeded by Wesfir Lumber Co. in 1936 which was acquired by Hines (Edward) Lumber Co. in 1945
(See Hines (Edward) Lumber Co.)

WESTERN MAINE POWER CO.
Purchased by Central Maine Power Co. in 1927

WESTERN MARBLE INC (NV)
Charter revoked for failure to file reports and pay fees 5/1/98

WESTERN MARINE ELECTRS CO (WA)
Common no par split (3) for (1) by issuance of (2) additional shares 2/28/77
Common no par changed to 1¢ par and (1) additional share issued 9/10/82
Acquired by a group of investors 2/8/85
Each share Common 1¢ par exchanged for $5 cash

WESTERN MASS ELEC CO (MA)
Adjustable Rate Preferred Ser. D $100 par called for redemption 08/23/1988
Depository Preferred Shares for Ser. D $100 par called for redemption 08/23/1988
9.60% Preferred Ser. A $100 par called for redemption 12/01/1992
Dutch Auction Rate Preferred Class A 1988 Unit 4000 called for redemption 12/19/1996
7.60% Class A Preferred $25 par called for redemption at $25.13 on 04/30/2001
7.72% Preferred Ser. B $100 par called for redemption at $103.51 plus $0.621888 accrued dividend on 04/30/2001

WESTERN MASSACHUSETTS COMPANIES (MA)
Common no par changed to $1 par 02/25/1955
Common $1 par changed to 50¢ par and (1) additional share issued 03/09/1959
Name changed to Northeast Utilities and Common 50¢ par changed to $5 par 11/22/1965
Northeast Utilities name changed to Eversource Energy 02/19/2015

WESTERN MD CO (MD)
Merged into CSX Corp. 04/15/1983
Each share Common $1 par exchanged for $33 cash

WESTERN MD RY CO (MD & PA)
Common $100 par changed to no par 11/23/1955
7% 1st Preferred $100 par changed to $40 par and (1.5) additional shares issued 11/23/1959
5% 1st Preferred $30 par changed to $12 par and (1.5) additional shares issued 11/23/1959
4% 2nd Preferred $100 par changed to $40 par and (1.5) additional shares issued 11/23/1959
Common no par split (5) for (2) by issuance of (1.5) additional shares 11/23/1959
4% Conv. Non-Cum. 2nd Preferred $40 par called for redemption 08/14/1964
5% 1st Preferred $12 par called for redemption 03/11/1983
Merged into CSX Corp. 04/15/1983
Each share 7% 1st Preferred $40 par exchanged for $40.39 cash
Each share Common no par exchanged for $55 cash

WESTERN MED INC (MN)
Name changed to Chemgraphics Inc. (MN) 5/18/98
Chemgraphics Inc. (MN) reincorporated in Nevada as Flagship International Holding, Ltd. 11/22/99

WESTERN MED INDS (CA)
Name changed to Western Decor & Furnishings Industries 11/26/69
(See Western Decor & Furnishings Industries)

WESTERN MED INDS INC (NV)
Name changed to Ameracol Technology, Inc. and Common 2¢ par changed to $0.004 par 11/04/1980
Ameracol Technology, Inc. name changed to Chiropractic 21 International, Inc. 05/31/1983 which name changed to visionGATEWAY, Inc. 03/10/2004
(See visionGATEWAY, Inc.)

WESTERN MEDIA GROUP CORP (MN)
Each share old Common $0.001 par exchanged for (0.1) share new Common $0.001 par 10/18/2000
Reorganized under the laws of Delaware as MedLink International, Inc. 11/22/2005
Each share new Common $0.001 par exchanged for (0.2) share Class A Common $0.001 par

WESTERN METALCRAFT, INC. (WA)
Merged into General Metalcraft, Inc. on a share for share basis in 1952
(See General Metalcraft, Inc.)

WESTERN METALS LTD (AUSTRALIA)
Name changed to Indago Resources Ltd. 05/05/2009

WESTERN MICH CORP (MI)
Merged into Pacesetter Financial Corp. (DE) 02/01/1978
Each share Capital Stock $5 par

exchanged for (1.153) shares Common $10 par
Pacesetter Financial Corp. (DE) reincorporated in Michigan 03/10/1980
(See Paceseter Financial Corp. (MI))

WESTERN MICRO TECHNOLOGY INC (DE)
Reincorporated in August 1997
State of incorporation changed from (CA) to (DE) and Common no par changed to 1¢ par in August 1997
Name changed to Savoir Technology Group Inc. 11/24/97
Savoir Technology Group Inc. merged into Avnet, Inc. 7/3/2000

WESTERN MICROWAVE INC (VA)
Name changed 02/19/1981
Name changed from Western Microwave Laboratories, Inc. to Western Microwave, Inc. 02/19/1981
In process of liquidation
Each share Common 10¢ par received initial distribution of $2.36 cash payable 11/28/1997 to holders of record 11/14/1997 Ex date - 12/01/1997
Note: Number or amount of subsequent distributions, if any, are not available

WESTERN MILLING CO. (UT)
Name changed to Basic Resources Corp. 9/21/59
(See Basic Resources Corp.)

WESTERN MINES LTD (BC)
Each share Capital Stock $1 par exchanged for (0.5) share Common $2 par 02/04/1957
Common $2 par changed to no par 09/17/1975
Reincorporated under the laws of Canada as Westmin Resources Ltd. 04/02/1981
Westmin Resources Ltd. (Canada) merged into Boliden Ltd. 02/12/1998 which reorganized in Sweden as Boliden AB 12/07/2001

WESTERN MNG HLDGS LTD (AUSTRALIA)
Name changed 11/16/1979
Name changed from Western Mining Corp. to Western Mining Corp. Holdings Ltd. 11/16/1979
Each Unsponsored ADR for Ordinary AUD $0.50 par exchanged for (0.25) Sponsored ADR for Ordinary AUD $0.50 par 11/06/1989
Stock Dividend - 62-1/2% 06/19/1987
Name changed to WMC Ltd. 01/18/1996
WMC Ltd. name changed to Alumina Ltd. 12/02/2002

WESTERN MTG INVS (MA)
Name changed to WMI Equity Investors 12/17/1982
(See WMI Equity Investors)

WESTERN MOTO-CADDY, INC. (CA)
Merged into Western Fund on a (1) for (18.75) basis 03/15/1963
Western Fund name changed to Dayton Industries, Inc. 05/21/1969 which merged into Galaxie National Corp. 12/24/1969 which reorganized as Marathon Office Supply, Inc. 05/12/1982
(See Marathon Office Supply, Inc.)

WESTERN MOTOR ASSOCIATION, INC. (WA)
Proclaimed dissolved for non-payment of fees 7/1/69

WESTERN MOTOR UNDERWRITERS, INC. (WA)
Proclaimed dissolved 1/15/73
No stockholders' equity

WESTERN MULTIPLEX CORP (DE)
Issue Information - 7,500,000 shares CL A offered at $12 per share on 07/31/2000
Under plan of merger name changed to Proxim Corp. 3/26/2002

(See Proxim Corp.)

WESTERN NACO PETROLEUMS LTD. (AB)
Merged into Provo Gas Producers Ltd. 03/02/1961
Each share Capital Stock no par exchanged for (0.166666) share Capital Stock no par
Provo Gas Producers Ltd. acquired by Dome Petroleum Ltd. 06/28/1967
(See Dome Petroleum Ltd.)

WESTERN NAT GAS CO (DE)
Certificates dated prior to 12/26/1963
5% Conv. Preferred 1952 Ser. $30 par called for redemption 12/30/1963
5% Conv. Preferred 1955 Ser. $30 par called for redemption 12/30/1963
5% Conv. Preferred 1961 Ser. $30 par called for redemption 12/30/1963
Stock Dividend - 200% 09/10/1952
Liquidation completed
Each share Common $1 par stamped to indicate initial distribution of (0.2105263) share Pacific Petroleums Ltd. Common $1 par and $9.50 cash 12/26/1963
Each share Stamped Common $1 par received second distribution of $0.40 cash 11/20/1964
Each share Stamped Common $1 par received third distribution of $0.25 cash 10/27/1965
Each share Stamped Common $1 par received fourth distribution of $0.26 cash 03/17/1967
Each share Stamped Common $1 par received fifth distribution of $0.09 cash 06/30/1972
Each share Stamped Common $1 par received sixth distribution of $0.90 cash 12/21/1973
Each share Stamped Common $1 par exchanged for seventh distribution of $1 cash 07/19/1976
Each share Stamped Common $1 par received eighth and final distribution of $0.1419 cash 07/19/1977
(See Pacific Petroleums Ltd.)

WESTERN NAT GAS CO (DE)
Certificates dated after 12/13/1979
Each share Common 10¢ par exchanged for (0.02) share Common 1¢ par 08/20/1985
Recapitalized as North American Gaming & Entertainment Corp. (DE) 10/17/1994
Each share new Common 1¢ par exchanged for (0.33333333) share Common 1¢ par
North American Gaming & Entertainment Corp. (DE) reorganized in Nevada as China Changjiang Mining & New Energy Co., Ltd. 08/02/2010

WESTERN NAT GASOLINE CORP (NV)
Completely liquidated 01/15/1975
Each share Class A Common no par exchanged for first and final distribution of $7 cash

WESTERN NATIONAL BANK (YORK, PA)
Each share Capital Stock $100 par exchanged for (10) shares Capital Stock $10 par 00/00/1945
Stock Dividends - 100% 02/17/1947; 11-1/9% 01/20/1956
Merged into National Bank of York County (York, PA) 02/28/1959
Each share Capital Stock $10 par exchanged for (1.37) shares Capital Stock $10 par
National Bank of York County (York, PA) merged into National Bank & Trust Co. of Central Pennsylvania (York, PA) 10/13/1961 which merged into National Central Bank (Lancaster, PA) 12/07/1970 which reorganized as National Central

Financial Corp. 12/31/1972 which merged into CoreStates Financial Corp 05/02/1983 which merged into First Union Corp. 04/28/1998 which name changed to Wachovia Corp. (Ctfs. dated after 09/01/2001) 09/01/2001 which merged into Wells Fargo & Co. (New) 12/31/2008

WESTERN NATIONAL CORP. (WA)
Merged into Hy-Lond Enterprises 6/20/69
Each share Common $1 par exchanged for (0.454545) share Common $1 par
Hy-Lond Enterprises name changed to Consolidated Liberty Inc. 1/30/79 which merged into Beverly Enterprises (CA) 3/12/81 which reorganized in Delaware as Beverly Enterprises, Inc. 7/31/87
(See Beverly Enterprises, Inc.)

WESTERN NATL CORP (DE)
Issue Information - 32,350,000 shares COM offered at $12 per share on 02/08/1994
Merged into American General Corp. 2/25/98
Each share Common $0.001 par exchanged for either (0.5413) share Common 50¢ par or $30.8951 cash
Note: Option to receive stock expired 2/23/98
American General Corp. merged into American International Group, Inc. 8/29/2001

WESTERN NEBRASKA OIL & URANIUM CO., INC. (DE)
Name changed to Havana Racing Co., Inc. 9/6/57
Havana Racing Co., Inc. charter revoked 4/1/60

WESTERN NEW YORK FUND, INC.
Liquidation completed in 1946
Details not available

WESTERN NEW YORK GAS & ELECTRIC CORP.
Purchased by New York State Electric & Gas Corp. in 1929
Details not available

WESTERN NEW YORK INVESTORS, INC.
Acquired by M. & T. Securities Corp. in 1929
Details not available

WESTERN NEW YORK SECURITIES CORP.
Merged into Western New York Fund, Inc. share for share in 1941
(See Western New York Fund, Inc.)

WESTERN NUCLEAR CORP. (WY)
Merged into Western Nuclear, Inc. 12/23/1959
Each share Common 1¢ par exchanged for (0.2) share Common 5¢ par
Western Nuclear, Inc. merged into Phelps Dodge Corp. 05/07/1971 which merged into Freeport-McMoRan Copper & Gold Inc. 03/19/2007 which name changed to Freeport-McMoRan Inc. 07/14/2014

WESTERN NUCLEAR INC (DE)
Merged into Phelps Dodge Corp. 05/07/1971
Each share Common 5¢ par exchanged for (0.16666666) share Capital Stock $6.25 par
Phelps Dodge Corp. merged into Freeport-McMoRan Copper & Gold Inc. 03/19/2007 which name changed to Freeport-McMoRan Inc. 07/14/2014

WESTERN OHIO FINL CORP (DE)
Merged into WesBanco, Inc. 8/31/2004
Each share Common 1¢ par exchanged for either (1.18) shares Common $2.0833 par or $35 cash

WESTERN OIL & REFINING CO.
Liquidated in 1936

WESTERN OIL & TIRE DISTRS INC (NV)
Name changed to Saratoga International Holdings Corp. 3/24/99
Saratoga International Holdings Corp. name changed to Fortune Credit & Insurance Services, Inc. 9/27/2001

WESTERN OIL CORP. (NV)
Charter revoked for failure to file reports and pay fees 3/4/63
Company was subsequently adjudicated bankrupt 5/11/64

WESTERN OIL DEVELOPMENT CORP. (UT)
Name changed to Artists & Producers International 06/18/1973
(See Artists & Producers International)

WESTERN OIL FIELDS INC (CO)
Each share Common 1¢ par exchanged for (0.25) share Common $1.25 par 00/00/1953
Reorganized under the laws of Nevada as Summit Energy, Inc. 08/01/1970
Each share Common $1.25 par exchanged for (1) share Common 10¢ par
Summit Energy, Inc. name changed to Caspen Oil, Inc. 09/13/1988
(See Caspen Oil, Inc.)

WESTERN OIL SANDS INC (AB)
Common no par split (3) for (1) by issuance of (2) additional shares payable 06/06/2005 to holders of record 06/01/2005 Ex date - 05/30/2005
Acquired by Marathon Oil Corp. 10/18/2007
Each share Common no par exchanged for (0.5932) share Common $1 par, (1) share WesternZagros Resources Ltd. Common no par and (0.1) Common Stock Purchase Warrant expiring 01/18/2008
(See each company's listing)

WESTERN OIL SHALE CORP (UT)
Common $1 par changed to 40¢ par and (1.5) additional shares issued 11/21/1966
Common 40¢ par changed to 16¢ par and (1.5) additional shares issued 10/02/1978
Reorganized under the laws of Oklahoma as Magic Circle Energy Corp. 08/01/1980
Each share Common 16¢ par exchanged for (0.5) share Common 10¢ par
(See Magic Circle Energy Corp.)

WESTERN ONTARIO RESOURCES LTD. (ON)
Merged into Lumsden Building Corp. Inc. 8/15/78
Each (150) shares Common no par exchanged for (1) share Common no par

WESTERN ORBIS CO (DE)
Class A Common 10¢ par reclassified as Common 10¢ par 01/16/1969
Each share Class B Common 10¢ par exchanged for (1/3) share Common 10¢ par 01/16/1969
Adjudicated bankrupt 06/11/1976
No stockholders' equity

WESTERN PA NATL BK (PITTSBURGH, PA)
Capital Stock $10 par changed to $5 par and (1) additional share issued 10/08/1965
Under plan of merger Capital Stock $5 par reclassified as Common $5 par 02/09/1968
Reorganized as WPNB Corp. 04/01/1969
Each share $2.10 Conv. Preferred

$35 par exchanged for (1) share $2.10 Conv. Preferred $35 par
Each share Common $5 par exchanged for (1) share Common $5 par
WPNB Corp. name changed to Equimark Corp. (PA) 05/10/1971 which reorganized in Delaware 03/24/1988 which merged into Integra Financial Corp. 01/15/1993 which merged into National City Corp. 05/03/1996 which was acquired by PNC Financial Services Group, Inc. 12/31/2008

WESTERN PA WTR CO (PA)
Name changed to Pennsylvania-American Water Co. 02/01/1989
(See Pennsylvania-American Water Co.)

WESTERN PAC AIRLS INC (DE)
Filed petition under Chapter 11 Federal Bankruptcy Code 10/5/97
Stockholders' equity unlikely

WESTERN PAC ENERGY CORP (BC)
Recapitalized as Durham Resources Ltd. 08/18/1989
Each share Common no par exchanged for (0.5) share Common no par
Durham Resources Ltd. merged into Gothic Resources Inc. (BC) 07/09/1991 which reincorporated in Canada 08/01/1991 which reincorporated in Oklahoma as American Natural Energy Corp. (Ctfs. dtd. after 02/12/2002) 02/12/2002
(See American Natural Energy Corp. (Ctfs. dtd. after 02/12/2002)

WESTERN PAC ENERGY LTD (UT)
Name changed to Technedyne, Inc. and Capital Stock 1¢ par changed to no par 04/19/1980
(See Technedyne, Inc.)

WESTERN PAC FINL CORP (CA)
Merged into Shearson Hayden Stone Inc. 07/02/1979
Each share Common no par exchanged for $16.25 cash

WESTERN PAC GOLD INC (AB)
Recapitalized as WPI Gold Ltd. (AB) 03/17/2004
Each share Common no par exchanged for (0.2) share Common no par
WPI Gold Ltd. (AB) reincorporated in British Columbia as Salmon River Resources Ltd. 07/13/2005
(See Salmon River Resources Ltd.)

WESTERN PAC INDS INC (DE)
Each share Common $1 par received extraordinary distribution of $23 cash 12/31/1979
Merged into Danaher Corp. 12/31/1986
Each share Common $1 par exchanged for $163 cash

WESTERN PAC INDS INC (WA)
Name changed to Pacific Western Industries Inc. 04/05/1972
Pacific Western Industries Inc. name changed to Timberland Industries, Inc. 05/24/1977
(See Timberland Industries, Inc.)

WESTERN PAC INS CO (WA)
Through voluntary purchase offer American States Insurance Co. acquired 100% as of 09/18/1969
Public interest eliminated

WESTERN PAC MNG EXPL INC (QC)
Recapitalized as Sierra Minerals Inc. 12/05/2002
Each share Common no par exchanged for (0.1) share Common no par
Sierra Minerals Inc. recapitalized as Goldgroup Mining Inc. 05/07/2010

WESTERN PAC OILS LTD (AB)
Cease trade order effective 09/27/1989

WESTERN PAC PRODS & CRUDE OIL PIPE LINES LTD (BC)
Capital Stock $5 par changed to $1.25 par and (3) additional shares issued 12/07/1966
Merged into Westcoast Petroleum Ltd. 09/21/1971
Each share Capital Stock $1.25 par exchanged for (0.2) share $1.50 Exchangeable Preferred $25 par
(See Westcoast Petroleum Ltd.)

WESTERN PAC RR CO (CA)
Common no par split (3) for (1) by issuance of (2) additional shares 03/03/1960
Merged into Western Pacific Industries Inc. (DE) 05/11/1972
Each share Common no par exchanged for (1) share Common $1 par
(See Western Pacific Industries Inc. (DE))

WESTERN PAC RR CO (DE)
Merged into Union Pacific Corp. 05/24/1983
Each share Class A Common $5 par exchanged for $20 cash

WESTERN PACIFIC INDUSTRIES, INC. (NV)
Charter permanently revoked 4/1/2003

WESTERN PACIFIC OIL CO., LTD. (AB)
Struck off register for failure to file reports 4/15/40

WESTERN PACIFIC RAILROAD CORP. (DE)
Receiver appointed for purpose of liquidation in October 1949
No Preferred or Common stockholders' equity

WESTERN PETE CORP (CO)
Filed a petition under Chapter 7 Federal Bankruptcy Code in 1989
Stockholders' equity unlikely

WESTERN PETROCHEMICAL CORP. LTD. (AB)
No longer in existence; struck from register and shares apparently worthless 6/15/64

WESTERN PFD CORP (CO)
Each share Common 20¢ par exchanged for (0.025) share Common $1 par 06/18/1982
Chapter 11 bankruptcy proceedings converted to Chapter 7 on 07/24/1986
No stockholders' equity

WESTERN PFD LIFE INS CO (CO)
Merged into Western Preferred Corp. 08/23/1973
Each share Common 20¢ par exchanged for (1) share Common 20¢ par
(See Western Preferred Corp.)

WESTERN PINNACLE LTD (YT)
Reincorporated 05/15/1997
Place of incorporation changed from (BC) to (YT) 05/15/1997
Recapitalized as WPN Resources Ltd. 01/08/2002
Each share Common no par exchanged for (0.25) share Common no par
WPN Resources Ltd. name changed to Grove Energy Ltd. (YT) 06/01/2004 which reincorporated in British Columbia 06/02/2005 which was acquired by Stratic Energy Corp. 04/24/2007
(See Stratic Energy Corp.)

WESTERN PIONEER INS CO (CA)
Common $10 par changed to $15 par 06/30/1967
Acquired by Trivest Holdings Ltd. 03/01/1984
Each share Common $15 par exchanged for $315 cash

WESTERN PIONEER LIFE INS CO (KY)
Under plan of merger each share old Common $1 par exchanged for (0.5) share new Common $1 par 11/16/1972
Merged into I.C.H. Corp. (Old) 04/18/1985
Each share new Common $1 par exchanged for (1.25) shares Common $1 par
I.C.H. Corp. (Old) name changed to Southwestern Life Corp. (New) 06/15/1994 which name changed to I.C.H. Corp. (New) 10/10/1995
(See I.C.H. Corp. (New))

WESTERN PIPE & STEEL CO.
Dissolved 00/00/1946
Details not available

WESTERN PLAINS PETE LTD (AB)
Assets sold for the benefit of creditors 04/01/2014
Stockholders' equity unlikely

WESTERN PLASTICS CORP (WA)
Common 25¢ par changed to 8-1/3¢ par and (2) additional shares issued 11/20/1972
Through purchase offer over 99% acquired by Hepworth Ceramic Holdings Ltd. as of 10/10/1980
Public interest eliminated

WESTERN PLATINUM HLDGS LTD (YT)
Recapitalized as Orsa Ventures Corp. (YT) 07/23/2002
Each share Common no par exchanged for (0.2) share Common no par
Orsa Ventures Corp. (YT) reincorporated in British Columbia 12/31/2007
(See Orsa Ventures Corp.)

WESTERN PLYWOOD CO. LTD. (CANADA)
Class B no par split (2) for (1) by issuance of (1) additional share in 1953
All Class A no par and Class B no par acquired thru purchase and exchange offers by United States Plywood Co. Ltd. as of 3/17/64
Public interest eliminated

WESTERN POTASH CORP. LTD. (ON)
Name changed to Continental Potash Corp. Ltd. and stock exchanged (1) for (5) 12/30/55
Continental Potash Corp. Ltd. charter cancelled 3/16/76

WESTERN POTASH CORP (BC)
Reorganized as Western Resources Corp. 04/05/2017
Each share Common no par exchanged for (0.2) share Common no par
Note: Unexchanged certificates will be cancelled and become without value 04/05/2023

WESTERN POWER, LIGHT & TELEPHONE CO.
Reorganized as Western Light & Telephone Co. in 1935
Details not available

WESTERN POWER & GAS CO., INC. (KS)
Common $5 par split (4) for (3) by issuance of (0.33333333) additional share 07/23/1965
Common $5 par changed to $2.50 par and (1) additional share issued 07/15/1967
Name changed to Central Telephone & Utilities Corp. 06/05/1968
Central Telephone & Utilities Corp. name changed to Centel Corp. 04/30/1982 which was acquired by Sprint Corp. (KS) 03/09/1993 which name changed to Sprint Nextel Corp. 08/12/2005 which merged into Sprint Corp. (DE) 07/10/2013

WESTERN PWR & GAS INC (DE)
Common $5 par split (6) for (5) by issuance of (0.2) additional share 05/19/1961
5.44% Preferred 3rd Ser. $50 par called for redemption 12/06/1963
$2.75 Preferred no par called for redemption 01/01/1965
Merged into Western Power & Gas Co., Inc. 07/01/1965
All Preferreds and Common became like shares of new company
Western Power & Gas Co., Inc. name changed to Central Telephone & Utilities Corp. 06/05/1968 which name changed to Centel Corp. 04/30/1982 which was acquired by Sprint Corp. (KS) 03/09/1993 which name changed to Sprint Nextel Corp. 08/12/2005 which merged into Sprint Corp. (DE) 07/10/2013

WESTERN POWER CORP.
Dissolved in 1936

WESTERN PPTYS TR (CA)
Merged into Pan Pacific Retail Properties, Inc. 11/13/2000
Each Share of Bene. Int. no par exchanged for (0.62) share Common 1¢ par
Pan Pacific Retail Properties, Inc. merged into Kimco Realty Corp. 10/31/2006

WESTERN PRECIPITATION CORP. (CA)
Acquired by Joy Manufacturing Co. 11/02/1959
Each share Common $1 par exchanged for (0.44444444) share Common $1 par
Joy Manufacturing Co. merged into Joy Technologies Inc. 06/24/1987
(See Joy Technologies Inc.)

WESTERN PREM RESOURCE CORP (BC)
Name changed to Zodiac Exploration Corp. 08/29/1997
Zodiac Exploration Corp. recapitalized as Donnybrook Resources Inc. 12/21/1998 which recapitalized as Rodinia Minerals Inc. (BC) 08/13/2003 which reincorporated in Ontario 11/03/2009 which name changed to Rodinia Lithium Inc. 06/30/2010 which recapitalized as Routemaster Capital Inc. 09/20/2016

WESTERN PROGRESS CORP (DE)
Charter cancelled and declared inoperative and void for non-payment of taxes 3/1/78

WESTERN PROSPECTOR GROUP LTD (BC)
Acquired by CNNC International Ltd. 08/14/2009
Each share Common no par exchanged for $0.56 cash

WESTERN PUBG GROUP INC (DE)
Name changed to Golden Books Family Entertainment, Inc. 5/9/96
(See Golden Books Family Entertainment, Inc.)

WESTERN PUBG INC (WI)
Old Common $1 par reclassified as new Common $1 par 04/24/1973
Class B Common $1 par reclassified as new Common $1 par 04/24/1973
Merged into Mattel, Inc. 06/15/1979
Each share new Common $1 par exchanged for (1.134) shares $25 Conv. Preferred Ser. A $1 par

WESTERN PUBLIC SERVICE CORP.
Reorganized as Mountain Fuel Supply Co. 00/00/1935
Details not available

WESTERN QUE MINES INC (QC)
Name changed 06/00/1986
Name changed from Western Quebec

Mines Co. Ltd. to Western Quebec Mines Inc. 06/00/1986
Merged into Wesdome Gold Mines Ltd. 07/18/2007
Each share Common $1 par exchanged for (1.45) shares Common no par

WESTERN RACING INC (DE)
Name changed to WRI Liquidating Co., Inc. 12/22/1980
(See WRI Liquidating Co., Inc.)

WESTERN RAILWAY OF ALABAMA (AL)
Acquired by Seaboard System Railroad, Inc. 9/28/83
Each share Common $100 par exchanged for $180 cash

WESTERN REAL ESTATE FD INC (DE)
Plan of liquidation approved 12/31/93
No stockholders' equity

WESTERN REAL ESTATE TRUSTEES (MA)
Merged into Real Estate Investment Trust of America on a (8) for (1) basis 6/1/56
(See Real Estate Investment Trust of America)

WESTERN RLTY PROJS LTD (AB)
Merged into Abbey Glen Property Corp. 05/08/1974
Each share Common no par exchanged for (1) share Common no par
(See Abbey Glen Property Corp.)

WESTERN REC INC (OR)
Name changed to Charvet/Jackson & Co., Inc. 9/20/72
Each share Common 1¢ par exchanged for (1) share Common 1¢ par
(See Charvet/Jackson & Co., Inc.)

WESTERN REFNG INC (DE)
Merged into Tesoro Corp. 06/01/2017
Each share Common 1¢ par exchanged for (0.435) share Common $0.16666666 par
Tesoro Corp. name changed to Andeavor 08/01/2017 which merged into Marathon Petroleum Corp. 10/01/2018

WESTERN REFNG LOGISTICS LP (DE)
Merged into Andeavor Logistics L.P. 10/30/2017
Each Common Unit exchanged for (0.5233) Common Unit

WESTERN REFUSE HAULING INC (CA)
Name changed to WRH Industries 6/19/79
WRH Industries name changed to Western Waste Industries 11/8/82 which name changed to USA Waste Services Inc. 5/7/96 which merged into Waste Management, Inc. 7/16/98

WESTERN REPUBLIC LIFE INSURANCE CO. (TX)
Merged into First National Life Insurance Co. (AL) 12/31/67
Each share Common no par exchanged for (0.25) share Class A Common $1 par
First National Life Insurance Co. (AL) reorganized as First National Co. (NV) 12/31/69 which recapitalized as Seal Fleet, Inc. (NV) 8/9/79 which reorganized in Delaware as Seal Holdings Corp. 6/30/97 which name changed to Le@p Technology, Inc. 7/6/2000

WESTERN RESERVE LIFE INSURANCE CO. (WY)
Name changed to Pacific Western Life Insurance Co. 8/31/67
Pacific Western Life Insurance Co. reorganized as Pacific Western Corp. 12/31/69
(See Pacific Western Corp.)

WESTERN RESH & DEV INC (CA)
Charter cancelled for failure to file reports and pay taxes 11/1/77

WESTERN RESH & MFG CO (UT)
Name changed to Tierra Energy Corp. 04/17/1980
Tierra Energy Corp. name changed to Tradestar Corp. (UT) 08/19/1985 which reorganized in Nevada as Tradestar Resources Corp. 06/29/2006
(See Tradestar Resources Corp.)

WESTERN RESOURCE TECHNOLOGIES INC (BC)
Reorganized under the laws of Texas as WRT Energy Corp. 10/12/92
Each share Common no par exchanged for (0.2) share Common 1¢ par and (0.2) Common Stock Purchase Warrant expiring 3/31/93
WRT Energy Corp. name changed to Gulfport Energy Corp. 3/30/98

WESTERN RESOURCES, INC. (WA)
Common 10¢ par changed to 25¢ par 04/25/1958
Charter automatically dissolved for non-payment of license fees 07/01/1961

WESTERN RES CAP I (DE)
7-7/8% Guaranteed Quarterly Income Preferred Securities called for redemption at $25 plus $0.082031 accrued dividend on 4/16/2004

WESTERN RES CAP II (DE)
8.50% Quarterly Income Preferred Securities Ser. B called for redemption at $25 plus $0.484027 accrued dividend on 9/22/2003

WESTERN RES CORP (NV)
Stock Dividend - 10% 06/30/1972
Name changed to Western Resources Life Insurance Co. 01/08/1980
Western Resources Life Insurance Co. merged into Tidelands Capital Corp. 06/06/1980 which merged into Western Preferred Corp. 03/06/1981
(See Western Preferred Corp.)

WESTERN RES INC (KS)
8.5% Preference no par called for redemption 07/01/1996
7.58% Preference $100 par called for redemption at $103.03 on 04/01/1998
Name changed to Westar Energy, Inc. 06/19/2002
Westar Energy, Inc. merged into Evergy, Inc. 06/05/2018

WESTERN RESOURCES LIFE INSURANCE CO. (NV)
Merged into Tidelands Capital Corp. 06/06/1980
Each share Common $1 par exchanged for (3) shares Common no par
Tidelands Capital Corp. merged into Western Preferred Corp. 03/06/1981
(See Western Preferred Corp.)

WESTERN RESV BANCORP INC (OH)
Common no par split (5) for (4) by issuance of (0.25) additional share payable 09/22/2006 to holders of record 09/05/2006 Ex date - 09/25/2006
Acquired by Westfield Bancorp Inc. 11/30/2012
Each share Common no par exchanged for $29 cash

WESTERN RESV BK OF OHIO (YOUNGSTOWN, OH)
Merged into Citizens Bancshares, Inc. (OH) 12/31/1995
Each share Common $5 par exchanged for (2.625) shares Common no par
Citizens Bancshares, Inc. name changed to Sky Financial Group, Inc. 10/02/1998 which merged into Huntington Bancshares Inc. 07/02/2007

WESTERN RESV CORP (TX)
Name changed to Computronic Industries Corp. (TX) 04/19/1968
Computronic Industries Corp. (TX) reincorporated in Delaware 10/30/1968
(See Computronic Industries Corp. (DE))

WESTERN RESV ELECTRS INC (OH)
Voluntarily dissolved 06/05/2000
Details not available

WESTERN RESV HLDG CORP (OH)
Reincorporated under the laws of Delaware as Pioneer Western Corp. 05/01/1969
(See Pioneer Western Corp.)

WESTERN RESV LIFE ASSURN CO OHIO (OH)
Merged into Western Reserve Holding Corp. (OH) 12/31/1968
Each share Common $1 par exchanged for (1) share Common $1 par
Western Reserve Holding Corp. (OH) reincorporated in Delaware as Pioneer Western Corp. 05/01/1969
(See Pioneer Western Corp.)

WESTERN RESV TEL CO (OH)
5.85% Preferred 1956 Ser. $20 par called for redemption 12/31/93
5.85% Preferred 1957 Ser. $20 par called for redemption 12/31/93
5.50% Preferred 1958 Ser. $20 par called for redemption 12/31/93
Public interest eliminated

WESTERN RESVS INC (NV)
Recapitalized as Great Western Equities Group, Inc. 06/10/1986
Each share Common 1¢ par exchanged for (0.05) share Common 1¢ par
Great Western Equities Group, Inc. name changed to American International Marketing, Inc. 09/21/1989

WESTERN RIDGE MINERALS INC (NV)
Name changed to Sunvalley Solar, Inc. 07/15/2010

WESTERN ROLLING HILLS MINES & OILS LTD (BC)
Merged into Invex Resources Ltd. 9/29/80
Each share Common no par exchanged for (1.5) shares Common Stock no par
Invex Resources Ltd. merged into Imperial Metals Corp. (Old) 12/1/81 which reorganized as Imperial Metals Corp. (New) 4/30/2002

WESTERN ROLLING MILLS LTD. (AB)
Liquidation completed
Each share Common no par received initial distribution of $0.10 cash 11/7/67
Each share Common no par received second distribution of $0.15 cash 7/13/70
Each share Common no par received third distribution of $0.15 cash 8/20/71
Each share Common no par received fourth distribution of $0.40 cash 8/29/73
Each share Common no par exchanged for fifth and final distribution of $1.02 cash 11/22/74

WESTERN SAFETY DEVICES, INC. (CA)
Charter suspended for not complying with statutory requirements 07/01/1987

WESTERN SALES LTD (BAHAMAS)
Reorganized under the laws of Luxembourg as Overseas Industries, S.A. 09/29/1969
Each ADR for Class A 11s par or ADR for Class B 11s par exchanged for (1) share Common $2 par
Overseas Industries, S.A. name changed to Overseas Inns, S.A. 05/12/1971
(See Overseas Inns, S.A.)

WESTERN SVGS & LN ASSN PHOENIX (AZ)
Permanent Reserve Guarantee Stock $1 par split (2) for (1) by issuance of (1) additional share 11/15/1983
Permanent Reserve Guarantee Stock $1 par split (3) for (1) by issuance of (2) additional shares 07/12/1985
Placed in receivership 06/14/1989
No stockholders' equity

WESTERN SEC BK (SANDUSKY, OH)
Acquired by BancOhio Corp. 02/21/1973
Each share Common $10 par exchanged for (3.536) shares Capital Stock $6.66-2/3 par
(See BancOhio Corp.)

WESTERN SEC FINL CORP (OR)
Acquired by KeyCorp (NY) 12/31/1987
Each share Common $2 par exchanged for (0.8712) share Common $5 par
KeyCorp (NY) merged into KeyCorp (New) (OH) 03/01/1994

WESTERN SECURITY BANK N.A. (BURBANK, CA)
Reorganized as Western Security Bancorp 11/19/87
Each share Common $5 par exchanged for (1) share Common no par

WESTERN SEMICONDUCTORS INC (CA)
Recapitalized as Western Research & Development, Inc. 1/2/70
Each share Capital Stock no par exchanged for (0.1) share Common no par
(See Western Research & Development, Inc.)

WESTERN SHELL HOMES CORP (OR)
Name changed to American Maid Products Corp. 6/1/68
(See American Maid Products Corp.)

WESTERN SHOPPING CENTRES (BC)
Shares reverted to company by Court Order 3/31/83
Each share Common no par exchanged for $0.05 cash

WESTERN SIERRA BANCORP (CA)
Common no par split (3) for (2) by issuance of (0.5) additional share payable 5/21/2004 to holders of record 5/7/2004 Ex date - 5/24/2004
Stock Dividends - 10% payable 11/14/97 to holders of record 10/20/97; 5% payable 11/1/99 to holders of record 10/22/99; 5% payable 11/13/2000 to holders of record 11/1/2000 Ex date - 10/30/2000; 5% payable 11/26/2001 to holders of record 11/15/2001 Ex date - 11/13/2001; 5% payable 6/14/2002 to holders of record 6/3/2002 Ex date - 5/30/2002; 5% payable 8/14/2003 to holders of record 7/21/2003 Ex date - 7/17/2003
Merged into Umpqua Holdings Corp. 6/5/2006
Each share Common 1¢ par exchanged for (1.61) shares Common no par

WESTERN SIERRA NATL BK (CAMERON PARK, CA)
Merged into Western Sierra Bancorp 12/31/96
Each share Common $2.50 par exchanged for (1) share Common no par

Western Sierra Bancorp merged into Umpqua Holdings Corp. 6/5/2006

WESTERN SILICA PRODUCTS LTD. (BC)
Name changed to Javelin Mines Ltd. 7/14/69
Javelin Mines Ltd. name changed to Javelin Enterprises Ltd. 1/8/71 which name changed to Canterra Development Corp. Ltd. 6/1/71
(See Canterra Development Corp. Ltd.)

WESTERN SILVER CORP (BC)
Merged into Glamis Gold Ltd. 05/04/2006
Each share Common no par exchanged for (0.688) share Common no par and (1) share Western Copper Corp. Common no par
Note: Unexchanged certificates were cancelled and became without value 05/04/2012
(See each company's listing)

WESTERN SILVER LEAD CORP (ID)
Reorganized under the laws of Florida as Lexor Holdings, Inc. 10/13/2003
Each share Class A Common 5¢ par exchanged for (0.1) share Common $0.001 par
Each share Class B Common 5¢ par exchanged for (0.002) share Class B Common $0.001 par
Lexor Holdings, Inc. name changed to Jeantex Group, Inc. 07/25/2005 which name changed to Catalyst Resource Group, Inc. 05/24/2010
(See Catalyst Resource Group, Inc.)

WESTERN SIZZLIN CORP (DE)
Each share old Common 1¢ par exchanged for (0.1) share new Common 1¢ par 08/10/2006
Merged into The Steak n Shake Co. 03/30/2010
Each share new Common 1¢ par exchanged for $8.071644 principal amount of 14% Subordinated Debentures due 03/30/2015
Note: Debentures will only be issued in integral multiples of $1,000

WESTERN SLOPE OIL & REFINING CO. (WY)
Name changed to Vidicom Corp. of America 7/15/69
Vidicom Corp. of America recapitalized as Computer Measurements, Inc. (II) 8/15/70
(See Computer Measurements, Inc. (II))

WESTERN SMELTING & REFINING INC. (NV)
Charter revoked for failure to file reports and pay fees 3/2/81

WESTERN SPIRIT INVTS LTD (AB)
Merged into Avenir Diversified Income Trust 03/31/2004
Each share Class A Common no par exchanged for (0.95) Trust Unit and (1) Performance Right
Avenir Diversified Income Trust reorganized as AvenEx Energy Corp. 01/07/2011 which merged into Spyglass Resources Corp. 04/04/2013

WESTERN STAFF SVCS INC (DE)
Common 1¢ par split (3) for (2) by issuance of (0.5) additional share payable 05/29/1998 to holders of record 05/18/1998
Name changed to Westaff, Inc. 09/24/1998
(See Westaff, Inc.)

WESTERN STANDARD SILVER MINES LTD. (BC)
Name changed to Western Standard Industries Ltd. 10/9/75
Western Standard Industries Ltd. name changed to Alkey Industries Ltd. 5/25/81 which name changed to American Volcano Minerals Corp.

10/24/83 which name changed to Genco Industries Inc. 2/24/87 which recapitalized as Consolidated Genco Industries Inc. 5/8/90
(See Consolidated Genco Industries Inc.)

WESTERN STAR EXPL LTD (AB)
Recapitalized 08/30/1994
Recapitalized from Western Star Energy Corp. to Western Star Exploration Ltd. 08/30/1994
Each share Common no par exchanged for (0.1) share Common no par
Merged into EnerMark Income Fund 01/25/2000
Each share Common no par held by Canadian residents exchanged for either (0.48) Trust Unit and (0.75) Common Stock Purchase Warrant expiring 12/31/2000, or $1.80 cash
Each share Common no par held by Non-Canadian residents exchanged for $1.80 cash
Note: Option for Canadian residents to receive cash expired 02/09/2000
EnerMark Income Fund merged into Enerplus Resources Fund 06/22/2001 which reorganized as Enerplus Corp. 01/03/2011

WESTERN STAR INC (OR)
Name changed 05/20/1988
Each share old Common 1¢ par exchanged for (1/3) share new Common 1¢ par 05/29/1986
Name changed from Western Star Business Systems, Inc. to Western Star, Inc. 05/20/1988
Name changed to Informedics Inc. 01/04/1994
Informedics Inc. merged into Mediware Information Systems, Inc. 09/24/1998
(See Mediware Information Systems, Inc.)

WESTERN STAR TRUCKS HLDGS LTD (BC)
Acquired by DaimlerChrysler AG 09/26/2000
Each share Common no par exchanged for $42 cash

WESTERN STATES GAS & ELECTRIC CO.
Merged into Pacific Gas & Electric Co. in 1928

WESTERN STATES LIFE INSURANCE CO. (CA)
Merged into California-Western States Life Insurance Co. in 1931
(See California-Western States Life Insurance Co.)

WESTERN STATES LIFE INSURANCE CO. (TX)
Name changed to Western States Life Insurance Co. of Texas 05/24/1966
Western States Life Insurance Co. of Texas merged into Western Preferred Life Insurance Co. 01/01/1963 which merged into Western Preferred Corp. 08/23/1973
(See Western Preferred Corp.)

WESTERN STATES LIFE INSURANCE CO. OF TEXAS (TX)
Merged into Western Preferred Life Insurance Co. 01/01/1968
Each share Common no par exchanged for (0.33333333) share Common 20¢ par
Western Preferred Life Insurance Co. merged into Western Preferred Corp. 08/23/1973
(See Western Preferred Corp.)

WESTERN STS LIFE INS CO (ND)
1955 Voting Trust Agreement expired 8/1/65
Holders had option to exchange each Ser. 1965 VTC for Common $1 par for Ser. 1975 VTC for Common $1 par or Common $1 par on a share for share basis

1975 Voting Trust Agreement expired 8/1/75
Holders had option to exchange each Ser. 1975 VTC for Common $1 par for Ser. 1985 VTC for Common $1 par or Common $1 par on a share for share basis
Common $1 par split (6) for (5) by issuance of (0.2) additional share 3/31/83
Common $1 par split (3) for (2) by issuance of (0.5) additional share 3/30/84
Stock Dividends - 40% 5/1/59; 33-1/3% 5/1/61; 25% 3/25/64; 20% 3/30/79; 25% 3/31/80
Acquired by Association of Life Insurance Co. 3/25/86
Each share Common $1 par exchanged for $16.25 cash
Each 1985 Ser. VTC's for Common $1 par exchanged for $16.25 cash

WESTERN STS MNG INC (WY)
Name changed to U.S. Energy Corp. 2/22/73

WESTERN STATES OIL & LAND CO.
Acquired by Argo Oil Co. 00/00/1928
Details not available

WESTERN STATES OIL & METALS CO. (UT)
Name changed to Three M's West 3/14/72
Three M's West name changed to Modern Mining & Milling Co., Inc. 2/28/73 which recapitalized as Copper Mountain Energy, Inc. 12/1/78
(See Copper Mountain Energy, Inc.)

WESTERN STATES OIL CORP. (DE)
Charter cancelled and declared inoperative and void for non-payment of taxes 4/1/33

WESTERN STATES PROPERTIES, INC. (UT)
Name changed to Newport Pharmaceuticals International, Inc. (UT) 3/2/70
Newport Pharmaceuticals International, Inc. (UT) recapitalized under the laws of California 7/15/70 which reincorporated in Delaware 11/30/87 which name changed to Systemed Inc. (DE) 10/1/91
(See Systemed Inc. (DE))

WESTERN STATES REFINING CO. (UT)
Dissolved 8/18/60
6% 1st Preferred $5 par and Common 25¢ par exchanged for cash

WESTERN STATES THRIFT & LOAN CO. (UT)
Assets taken over by the Commissioner of Financial Institutions for the State of Utah 6/7/72
No stockholders' equity

WESTERN STATES THRIFT (UT)
Name changed to Western States Thrift & Loan Co. 07/06/1966
(See Western States Thrift & Loan Co.)

WESTERN STATES URANIUM, INC. (UT)
Merged into Federal Uranium Corp. (NV) on a (1) for (400) basis 04/28/1955
Federal Uranium Corp. merged into Federal Resources Corp. 05/02/1960
(See Federal Resources Corp.)

WESTERN STD CORP (WY)
Name changed 07/27/1971
Each share Common 1¢ par exchanged for (0.2) share Common 5¢ par 09/09/1968
Name changed from Western Standard Uranium, Inc. to Western Standard Corp. 07/27/1971
Merged into Snow King Interests LLC 03/28/2005

Each share Common 5¢ par exchanged for $0.32 cash

WESTERN STD ENERGY CORP (NV)
Common $0.001 par split (5) for (2) by issuance of (1.5) additional shares payable 09/07/2007 to holders of record 09/07/2007
Name changed to Dominovas Energy Corp. 04/24/2014

WESTERN STD INDS LTD (BC)
Name changed to Alkey Industries Ltd. 5/25/81
Alkey Industries Ltd. name changed to American Volcano Minerals Corp. 10/24/83 which name changed Genco Industries Inc. 2/24/87 which recapitalized as Consolidated Genco Industries Inc. 5/8/90
(See Consolidated Genco Industries Inc.)

WESTERN STD METALS LTD (BC)
Merged into Terraco Gold Corp. (AB) 01/25/2011
Each share Common no par exchanged for (0.75) share Common no par
Terraco Gold Corp. (AB) reincorporated in British Columbia 06/08/2011

WESTERN STEEL PRODUCTS CORP. LTD.
Name changed to Westeel Products Ltd. 00/00/1945
Westeel Products Ltd. name changed to Westeel-Rosco Ltd. 12/31/1965
(See Westeel-Rosco Ltd.)

WESTERN STEEL PRODUCTS LTD.
Reorganized as Western Steel Products Corp. Ltd. 00/00/1937
Each share Preferred exchanged for (1) share Common
Each (80) shares Common exchanged for (1) share new Common
Western Steel Products Corp. Ltd. name changed to Westeel Products Ltd. 00/00/1945 which name changed to Westeel-Rosco Ltd. 12/31/1965
(See Westeel-Rosco Ltd.)

WESTERN STEER-MOM N POPS INC (NC)
Stock Dividend - 25% 2/20/86
Common $1 par split (5) for (4) by issuance of (0.25) additional share 7/15/87
Name changed to WSMP Inc. 7/6/88
WSMP Inc. name changed to Fresh Foods Inc. 5/7/98 which name changed to Pierre Foods Inc. 7/27/2000
(See Pierre Foods Inc.)

WESTERN STOCKHOLDERS INVT TR LTD (ENGLAND)
Ordinary Reg. 1s par and ADR's for Ordinary Reg. 1s par changed to 5p par per currency change 02/15/1971
Merged into Border & Southern Stockholders Trust p.l.c. 08/08/1972
Each share Ordinary Reg. 5p exchanged for (0.16666666) share Ordinary Reg. 50p par
Each ADR for Ordinary Reg. 5p par exchanged for (0.16666666) ADR for Ordinary Reg. 50p par
Note: the above basis of exchange applied to holders of (200) or more shares
Holders of less than (200) shares exchanged each share or ADR for 57 pence cash if surrendered prior to 08/07/1972 and for the above ratio of Border & Southern Stockholders Trust Ltd. if surrendered on and after 08/07/1972
Border & Southern Stockholders Trust p.l.c. name changed to Govett Strategic Investment Trust P.L.C. 01/29/1986
(See Govett Strategic Investment Trust P.L.C.)

WESTERN STOCKYARDS LTD. (ON)
Class A Common no par reclassified as Preferred no par in October 1972
Old Common no par reclassified as Conv. Class B Common no par in October 1972
Preferred no par reclassified as new Common no par 9/30/80
Each share Conv. Class A Common no par and Conv. Class B Common no par exchanged for (2) shares new Common no par respectively 9/30/80
Shares reacquired in 1982
Details not available

WESTERN STS EXPL INC (UT)
Name changed to Intercontinental Minerals & Petroleum, Inc. 6/27/82
Intercontinental Minerals & Petroleum, Inc. reorganized in Florida as American Fuel & Power Corp. 2/16/83
(See American Fuel & Power Corp.)

WESTERN SULPHUR INDUSTRIES, INC.
Operations discontinued in 1936

WESTERN SUPPLIES LTD OLD (AB)
Each share Class A no par exchanged for (2.2) shares Common no par 11/18/76
Merged into Western Supplies Ltd. (New) 3/28/79
Each share Common no par exchanged for $18.50 cash

WESTERN SURF INLET MINES LTD. (BC)
Acquired by Matachewan Consolidated Mines, Ltd. 04/26/1966
Each share Class A Common 50¢ par exchanged for (1.25) shares Capital Stock no par

WESTERN SYS CORP (DE)
Name changed to American Country Holdings Inc. 7/29/97
(See American Country Holdings Inc.)

WESTERN TABLET & STATIONERY CORP. (DE)
Each share 7% Preferred $100 par exchanged for (1) share 5% Preferred $100 par and (0.5) share Common no par 00/00/1936
Stock Dividends - 25% 01/30/1950; 200% 04/30/1958
Name changed to Westab Inc. 03/04/1964
Westab Inc. merged into Mead Corp. 05/31/1966
(See Mead Corp.)

WESTERN TAR SANDS INC (CO)
Declared defunct and inoperative for failure to pay taxes and file annual reports 01/01/1991

WESTERN TECHNOLOGY & RESH INC (WY)
Reincorporated under the laws of Delaware as Cimnet, Inc. 07/02/1999
(See Cimnet, Inc.)

WESTERN TELE COMMUNICATIONS INC (NV)
Class A Common 1¢ par split (2) for (1) by issuance of (1) additional share 9/4/84
Class B Common 1¢ par split (2) for (1) by issuance of (1) additional share 9/4/84
Class A Common 1¢ par split (2) for (1) by issuance of (1) additional share 6/24/85
Class B Common 1¢ par split (2) for (1) by issuance of (1) additional share 6/24/85
Name changed to WestMarc Communications, Inc. 6/24/88
(See WestMarc Communications, Inc.)

WESTERN TELEPHONE CO. (CA)
Merged into Golden West Telephone Co. 12/30/66
Each share 5-1/2% Preferred $25 par exchanged for (1) share 5-1/2% Preference $25 par
Each share 5% Preferred $25 par exchanged for (1) share 5% Preference $25 par
Each share Common $25 par exchanged for (10.8) shares Common $1 par
Golden West Telephone Co. liquidated for Continental Telephone Co. of California 8/27/71 which name changed to Contel of California, Inc. 2/19/88
(See Contel of California, Inc.)

WESTERN TELEVISION CORP. (DE)
No longer in existence having become inoperative and void for non-payment of taxes 4/1/35

WESTERN TIN MINES LTD (ON)
Charter cancelled for failure to pay taxes and file returns 03/00/1976

WESTERN TOOL & STAMPING CO. (IA)
Acquired by American Machine & Foundry Co. on a share for share basis 7/27/63
American Machine & Foundry Co. name changed to AMF Inc. 4/30/70
(See AMF Inc.)

WESTERN TRADE CORP (FL)
Name changed to Western Trade Holdings Corp. 4/25/2000

WESTERN TRAILS, INC. (OR)
Name changed to W.T., Inc. and Common no par changed to $0.001 par 03/27/1985
W.T., Inc. name changed to West-Tech Group, Inc. 07/22/1985 which name changed to American Aircraft Corp. (OR) 10/28/1985 which reincorporated in Nevada as Hunter Aircraft Corp. 09/27/1996 which recapitalized as Prepaid Depot Inc. 08/18/2001 which recapitalized as Reed Holdings Corp. 07/30/2002 which name changed to Ostara Corp., Inc. 03/12/2004 which name changed to Rheologics Technologies, Inc. 10/18/2005 which name changed to KKS Venture Management, Inc. 07/24/2007 which recapitalized as Codima, Inc. 06/09/2008
(See Codima, Inc.)

WESTERN TRANSISTOR CORP. (CA)
Adjudicated bankrupt 8/7/62

WESTERN TRANSITIONS INC (NV)
Each (24) shares old Common $0.001 par exchanged for (1) share new Common $0.001 par 02/26/2009
Name changed to KAT Exploration, Inc. 05/15/2009

WESTERN TRANSMEDIA INC (DE)
Each (60) shares Common 1¢ par exchanged for (1) share Common 60¢ par 5/11/92
Name changed to Western Systems Corp. 1/3/97
Western Systems Corp. name changed to American Country Holdings Inc. 7/29/97
(See American Country Holdings Inc.)

WESTERN TRANSMISSION CORP (DE)
Capital Stock $1 par reclassified as Common $1 par 10/18/1967
Name changed to Westrans Industries, Inc. 10/31/1969
Westrans Industries, Inc. merged into Aquitaine Pennsylvania, Inc. 04/30/1975

WESTERN TRAVEL, INC. (NV)
Name changed to Royal Executive Inns of America, Inc. 08/11/1966
Royal Executive Inns of America, Inc. name changed to Rinn Corp. 03/01/1972 which recapitalized as Sun Fruit, Ltd. 05/09/1974
(See Sun Fruit, Ltd.)

WESTERN TRAVELERS LIFE INS CO (CA)
Acquired by Marlennan Corp. 01/01/1972
Each share Common 60¢ par exchanged for (0.0625) share Common $1 par
Marlennan Corp. name changed to Marsh & McLennan Companies, Inc. 05/21/1975

WESTERN TUNGSTEN COPPER MINES LTD. (BC)
Recapitalized as Farwest Tungsten Copper Mines Ltd. 08/16/1955
Each share Capital Stock $1 par exchanged for (0.1) share Capital Stock $1 par
Farwest Tungsten Copper Mines Ltd. name changed to Farwest Mining Ltd. 00/00/1959
(See Farwest Mining Ltd.)

WESTERN UN CAP CORP (NV)
Recapitalized as Lionshead Entertainment Corp. 5/15/97
Each share Common $0.001 par exchanged for (0.2) share Common $0.005 par
Lionshead Entertainment name changed to Trans-Global Holdings Inc. 3/17/99 which name changed to Clear Cut Film Technology Studios, Inc. 4/17/2006 which recapitalized as Trans-Global Capital Management, Inc. 2/13/2007

WESTERN UN COMPUTER UTILS INC (DE)
Merged into Western Union Corp. (Old) 06/12/1975
Each share Common 15¢ par exchanged for $0.05 cash

WESTERN UN CORP NEW (DE)
Name changed to New Valley Corp. (NY) 04/22/1991
New Valley Corp. (NY) reorganized in Delaware 07/29/1996 which was acquired by Vector Group Ltd. 12/13/2005

WESTERN UN CORP OLD (DE)
4.90% Conv. 2nd Preferred $100 par reclassified as 4.90% Conv. Preferred $100 par 05/18/1984
Merged into Western Union Corp. (New) 12/31/1987
Each share 4.60% Conv. Preferred $100 par exchanged for (0.12) share Class A Increasing Rate Sr. Preferred 1¢ par and (0.72) share Class B Conv. Preferred 10¢ par
Each share 4.90% Conv. Preferred $100 par exchanged for (0.12) share Class A Increasing Rate Sr. Preferred 1¢ par and (0.72) share Class B Conv. Preferred 10¢ par
Each share 9.50% Depositary Preferred $100 par exchanged for (0.015) share Class A Increasing Rate Sr. Preferred 1¢ par and (0.09) share Class B Conv. Preferred 10¢ par
Each share 14% Depositary Preferred $100 par exchanged for (0.018) share Class A Increasing Rate Sr. Preferred 1¢ par and (0.108) share Class B Conv. Preferred 10¢ par
Under plan of merger each share Common $2.50 par automatically became (1) share Western Union Corp. (New) Common $2.50 par
Western Union Corp. (New) name changed to New Valley Corp. (NY) 04/22/1991 which reorganized in Delaware 07/29/1996 which was acquired by Vector Group Ltd. 12/13/2005

WESTERN UN INTL INC (DE)
Common $1 par changed to no par and (2) additional shares issued 08/10/1967
Under plan of reorganization each share Common no par automatically became (1) share WUI, Inc. Common no par 12/29/1972
WUI, Inc. merged into Xerox Corp. 11/21/1979

WESTERN UN TELEG CO (NY)
Each share Capital Stock $100 par exchanged for (1) share Class A no par 00/00/1943
Each share Class B no par exchanged for (0.6) share Class A no par 00/00/1947
Class A no par reclassified as Common $10 par 00/00/1952
Common $10 par changed to $2.50 par and (3) additional shares issued 05/23/1955
Under plan of reorganization each share 4.60% Conv. Preferred $100 par, 4.90% Conv. 2nd Preferred $100 par and Common $2.50 par automatically became (1) share Western Union Corp. (Old) 4.60% Conv. Preferred $100 par, 4.90% Conv. 2nd Preferred $100 par and Common $2.50 par respectively 01/30/1970
Merged into Western Union Corp. (New) 12/31/1987
Each share 5.20% Preferred $100 par exchanged for (0.26) share Class A Increasing Rate Sr. Preferred 1¢ par and (1.56) shares Class B Conv. Preferred 10¢ par
Each share 6% Preferred $100 par exchanged for (0.26) share Class A Increasing Rate Sr. Preferred 1¢ par and (1.56) shares Class B Conv. Preferred 10¢ par
Each share 9.5% Preferred $100 par exchanged for (0.26) share Class A Increasing Rate Sr. Preferred 1¢ par and (1.56) shares Class B Conv. Preferred 10¢ par
Each share 10.25% Class A Preferred $1 par exchanged for (0.065) share Class A Increasing Rate Sr. Preferred 1¢ par and (0.39) share Class B Conv. Preferred 10¢ par
Western Union Corp. (New) name changed to New Valley Corp. (NY) 04/22/1991 which reorganized in Delaware 07/29/1996 which was acquired by Vector Group Ltd. 12/13/2005

WESTERN UNDERWRITERS CORP. (NM)
Charter expired by time limitation in December, 1982

WESTERN UNITED CORP.
Dissolved in 1935

WESTERN UTD HLDG CO (WA)
Completely liquidated 04/20/2011
Each share Variable Rate Preferred Ser. A $2.50 par received first and final distribution of $0.89 cash

WESTERN UNITED NATIONAL BANK (LOS ANGELES, CA)
Common $6.25 par changed to $5 par and (0.25) additional share issued 2/4/85
Closed by the FDIC 9/24/93
Stockholders' equity unlikely

WESTERN UTD RES INC (NV)
Adjudicated bankrupt 02/09/1978
Stockholders' equity unlikely

WESTERN URANIUM COBALT MINES LTD. (BC)
Name changed to Western Tungsten Copper Mines Ltd. in 1952
Western Tungsten Copper Mines Ltd. reorganized as Farwest Tungsten Copper Mines Ltd. 8/16/55 which name was changed to Farwest Mining Ltd. in 1959
(See Farwest Mining Ltd.)

WESTERN URANIUM CORP. (NV)
Charter revoked for failure to file reports and pay fees 3/2/59

WESTERN URANIUM CORP (BC)
Name changed to Concordia Resource Corp. 04/05/2011
Concordia Resource Corp. recapitalized as Kaizen Discovery Inc. 12/06/2013

WESTERN URANIUM CORP (ON)
Name changed to Western Uranium & Vanadium Corp. 10/04/2018

WESTERN UTAH EXTENSION COPPER CO. (DE)
Charter cancelled and declared inoperative and void for non-payment of taxes 3/21/23

WESTERN UTILITIES CORP. (DE)
Merged into General Telephone & Electronics Corp. on a (0.8) for (1) basis 6/30/64
General Telephone & Electronics Corp. name changed to GTE Corp. 7/1/82 which merged into Verizon Communications Inc. 6/30/2000

WESTERN VENDING MACHINE CO. (AR)
Voluntarily dissolved 6/22/11
Details not available

WESTERN VENTURES, INC. (NV)
Charter revoked for failure to file reports and pay fees 3/2/53

WESTERN WARRIOR RES INC (AB)
Recapitalized as Whetstone Minerals Inc. (AB) 10/29/2008
Each share Common no par exchanged for (0.25) share Common no par
Whetstone Minerals Inc. (AB) reincorporated in Channel Islands as Whetstone Minerals Ltd. 11/20/2009

WESTERN WASH BANCORP INC (WA)
Merged into Heritage Financial Corp. 6/1/2006
Each share Common $1 par exchanged for (1.2653) shares Common no par and $20.56 cash

WESTERN WASTE INDS (CA)
Each share Common 10¢ par exchanged for (4) shares Common no par 4/8/83
Common no par split (2) for (1) by issuance of (1) additional share 7/31/90
Merged into USA Waste Services Inc. 5/7/96
Each share Common no par exchanged for (1.5) shares Common 1¢ par
USA Waste Services Inc. merged into Waste Management, Inc. 7/16/98

WESTERN WIND ENERGY CORP (BC)
Acquired by Brookfield Renewable Energy Partners L.P. 05/24/2013
Each share Common $0.001 par exchanged for $2.60 cash

WESTERN WINE & LIQUOR CO. (NE)
Voluntarily dissolved 12/6/78
Details not available

WESTERN WIRELESS CORP (WA)
Each share Class A Common no par received distribution of (1) share VoiceStream Wireless Corp. Common no par payable 05/03/1999 to holders of record 04/30/1999
Each share Class B Common no par received distribution of (1) share VoiceStream Wireless Corp. Common no par payable 05/03/1999 to holders of record 04/30/1999
Merged into Alltel Corp. 08/01/2005
Each share Class A Common no par exchanged for (0.535) share Common no par and $9.25 cash
Each share Class B Common no par exchanged for (0.535) share Common no par and $9.25 cash
(See Alltel Corp.)

WESTERN WOMENS BK (SAN FRANCISCO, CA)
Name changed to Golden Gate Bank (San Francisco, CA) 09/05/1980
(See Golden Gate Bank (San Francisco, CA))

WESTERN WOOL PROCESSORS, INC. (CO)
Charter revoked for failure to file reports and pay fees 10/14/65

WESTERN WORLD TELEVISION INC (CA)
Name changed to Westernworld-Samuel Communications, Inc. (CA) 7/30/86
Westernworld-Samuel Communications, Inc. (CA) reincorporated in Delaware as Westernworld Inc. 3/30/90
(See Westernworld Inc.)

WESTERN WTR CO (DE)
Reincorporated 03/23/1994
State of incorporation changed from (CA) to (DE) and Common no par changed to $0.001 par 03/23/1994
Common $0.001 par split (2) for (1) by issuance of (1) additional share payable 03/28/1996 to holders of record 03/18/1996
Plan of reorganization under Chapter 11 Federal Bankruptcy Code effective 02/17/2006
No stockholders' equity

WESTERNBANK P R (MAYAGUEZ, PR)
Common $1 par split (3) for (1) by issuance of (2) additional shares payable 10/18/95 to holders of record 10/2/95
Common $1 par split (2) for (1) by issuance of (1) additional share payable 6/3/96 to holders of record 5/24/96
Common $1 par split (2) for (1) by issuance of (1) additional share payable 3/3/97 to holders of record 2/21/97
Common $1 par split (2) for (1) by issuance of (1) additional share payable 3/2/98 to holders of record 2/20/98
Stock Dividend - 15% payable 3/3/97 to holders of record 3/3/97
Reorganized as W Holding Co., Inc. 11/30/99
Each share 7.125% Conv. Preferred 1998 Ser. A $1 par exchanged for (1) share 7.125% Conv. Preferred Ser. A $1 par
Each share 7.25% Preferred Ser. B $1 par exchanged for (1) share 7.25% Preferred Ser. B $1 par
Each share Common $1 par exchanged for (1) share Common $1 par

WESTERNONE EQUITY INCOME FD (BC)
Plan of arrangement effective 12/31/2012
Each Unit automatically became (1) share WesternOne Inc. (Canada) Common no par

WESTERNWORLD INC. (DE)
Charter cancelled and declared inoperative and void for non-payment of taxes 3/1/96

WESTERNWORLD SAMUEL COMMUNICATIONS INC (CA)
Reincorporated under the laws of Delaware as Westernworld Inc. 3/30/90
(See Westernworld Inc.)

WESTERNZAGROS RES LTD (AB)
Acquired by Crest Energy International LLC 07/28/2017
Each share Common no par exchanged for $0.28 cash
Note: Unexchanged certificates will be cancelled and become without value 07/27/2020

WESTERRA RES LTD (BC)
Name changed to HSI Hydrosystems International Inc. 03/13/1990
HSI Hydrosystems International Inc. recapitalized as R.W. Gas Group Inc. 05/09/1994 which recapitalized as Anglo-Canadian Gas Corp. 10/28/1996 which recapitalized as Jager Metal Corp. 01/20/2011 which name changed to Jagercor Energy Corp. 01/27/2014

WESTFAIR FOODS LTD (CANADA)
7% Preferred $1.40 Ser. $20 par called for redemption 6/30/86
Class A no par called for redemption at $350 on 1/19/2004

WESTFIELD AMER INC (MO)
Issue Information - 18,000,000 shares COM offered at $15 per share on 05/15/1997
Merged into Westfield America Trust 10/1/2001
Each share Common 1¢ par exchanged for $16.25 cash

WESTFIELD CORP (AUSTRALIA)
Name changed 06/30/2014
Each Sponsored ADR for Ordinary received distribution of $5.292205 cash payable 01/20/2011 to holders of record 01/10/2011 Ex date - 01/21/2011
Name changed from Westfield Group to Westfield Corp. 06/30/2014
ADR agreement terminated 07/02/2018
Each Sponsored ADR for Stapled Securities exchanged for $13.336537 cash
Note: Each Stapled Security consists of (1) Westfield America Trust Unit, (1) share Westfield Holdings Ltd. Ordinary and (1) Westfield Trust Unit

WESTFIELD FIN INC (DE)
Asset Backed Short Term Auction Rate Preferred Ser. A no par called for redemption 06/17/1992
Asset Backed Short Term Auction Rate Preferred Ser. B no par called for redemption 06/24/1992
Asset Backed Short Term Auction Rate Preferred Ser. C no par called for redemption 07/01/1992
Asset Backed Short Term Auction Rate Preferred Ser. D no par called for redemption 07/15/1992
Public interest eliminated

WESTFIELD FINL INC NEW (MA)
Under plan of merger name changed to Western New England Bancorp, Inc. 10/24/2016

WESTFIELD FINL INC OLD (MA)
Merged into Westfield Financial, Inc. (New) 01/03/2007
Each share Common 1¢ par exchanged for (3.28138) shares Common 1¢ par
Westfield Financial, Inc. (New) name changed to Western New England Bancorp, Inc. 10/24/2016

WESTFIELD GROWTH FD INC (OH)
Merged into Investment Co. of America 02/21/1978
Each share Common $1 par exchanged for (0.510894) share Common $1 par

WESTFIELD INCOME FUND, INC. (OH)
Name changed to Westfield Investment Fund, Inc. 02/19/1974
Westfield Investment Fund, Inc. merged into American Mutaul Fund, Inc. (DE) 02/21/1978 which reincorporated in Maryland 09/20/1983

WESTFIELD INVT FD INC (OH)
Merged into American Mutual Fund, Inc. (DE) 02/21/1978
Each share Common $1 par exchanged for (0.926471) share Capital Stock $1 par

American Mutual Fund, Inc. (DE) reincorporated in Maryland 09/20/1983

WESTFIELD MINERALS LTD (CANADA)
5% Conv. Preferred $7.50 par called for redemption 4/5/71
Common 10¢ par changed to no par 7/23/79
Merged into B.C. Pacific Capital Corp. 2/28/2000
Each share Common no par exchanged for $2.35 cash

WESTFIELD PPTYS LTD (CANADA)
Name changed to Westfield Real Estate Investment Trust and Common no par reclassified as Trust Units no par 12/22/2004
Westfield Real Estate Investment Trust name changed to Artis Real Estate Investment Trust 2/15/2007

WESTFIELD REAL ESTATE INVT TR (CANADA)
Each (15) old Trust Units no par exchanged for (1) new Trust Unit no par 2/1/2006
Name changed to Artis Real Estate Investment Trust 2/15/2007

WESTFIR LUMBER CO.
Acquired by Hines (Edward) Lumber Co. in 1945
(See Hines (Edward) Lumber Co.)

WESTFIRE ENERGY LIMITED (AB)
Under plan of merger name changed to Long Run Exploration Ltd. 10/29/2012
(See Long Run Exploration Ltd.)

WESTFLANK OIL CO., LTD.
Merged into Amalgamated Oils, Ltd. in 1941 liquidation of which was completed 10/15/58

WESTFORD GROUP INC (OH)
Merged into Bancinsurance Corp. 2/29/2000
Each share Common no par exchanged for $0.70 cash

WESTFORT ENERGY LTD (AB)
Reorganized 11/23/1993
Common no par split (3) for (1) by issuance of (2) additional shares 05/19/1981
Reorganized from Westfort Petroleums Ltd. (BC) to Westfort Energy Ltd. (ALTA) 11/23/1993
Each (15) shares Common no par exchanged for (1) share Common no par
Delisted from Toronto Stock Exchange 03/29/2004

WESTGAGE-GREENLAND OIL CO. (NV)
Merged into National Gas & Oil Corp. in 1953
Each share Capital Stock $1 par exchanged for (0.5) share Common $5 par
National Gas & Oil Corp. reorganized as National Gas & Oil Co. 9/1/81
(See National Gas & Oil Co.)

WESTGATE-CAREY TRUST
Acquired by Prugh Petroleum Co. 12/31/53
Each Unit of Bene. Int. no par exchanged for (1.35) shares Common $5 par
Prugh Petroleum Co. merged into Livingston Oil Co. 9/1/56 which name changed to LVO Corp. 9/24/69 which merged into Utah International Inc. 10/31/74 which merged into General Electric Co. 12/20/76

WESTGATE ENERGY INC (NV)
Name changed to Taco, Inc. 12/16/96
Taco, Inc. name changed to Communique Wireless Corp. 4/10/97 which name changed to Communique Corp. 10/10/97 which name changed to Formal Systems America Inc. 12/17/98

(See Formal Systems America Inc.)

WESTGATE LIQUIDATING TR (CA)
Assets transferred 04/16/1982
Each share Class A Common $10 par exchanged for (2) shares Class A Common $5 par 11/31/1961
Reorganized under Chapter X Bankruptcy Act 05/26/1981
Each share 5% Preferred $70 par, 6% Preferred $10 par and Class A Common $5 par exchanged an undetermined amount of Common no par
Each Non-Transferable Common Equivalent Certificate (issued per merger of Air California) received an undetermined amount of Common no par
Note: Non-Transferable Common Equivalent Certificates were not required to be surrendered and are without value
Assets transferred from Westgate-California Corp. to Westgate Liquidating Trust 04/16/1982
Liquidation completed
Each Unit of Bene. Int. received initial distribution of $28.25 cash 05/03/1982
Each Unit of Bene. Int. received second distribution of $0.50 cash 06/10/1983
Each Unit of Bene. Int. received third distribution of $2 cash 12/18/1984
Each Unit of Bene. Int. received fourth distribution of $2 cash 12/20/1985
Each Unit of Bene. Int. received fifth distribution of $3.90 cash 03/21/1988
Each Unit of Bene. Int. received sixth and final distribution of $0.46 cash 12/28/1988
Note: Certificates were not required to be surrendered and are without value

WESTGROUP CORPS INC (AB)
Recapitalized as Beaumont Select Corporations Inc. 02/28/1995
Each Class A Common no par exchanged for (0.14285714) share Class A Common no par
(See Beaumont Select Corporations Inc.)

WESTGROWTH PETES LTD (AB)
Reincorporated 6/6/80
Place of incorporation changed from (BC) to (ALTA) 6/6/80
12% Conv. 1st Preferred Ser. C $5 par reclassified as 12% Conv. 1st Preferred Ser. B $5 par 5/11/84
Recapitalized as Canadian Westgrowth Ltd. 10/14/86
Each share Common no par exchanged for (0.05) share Common no par
Canadian Westgrowth Ltd. merged into Ulster Petroleums Ltd. 10/27/87 which merged into Anderson Exploration Ltd. 5/23/2000
(See Anderson Exploration Ltd.)

WESTHAM RES CORP (BC)
Name changed to Roughrider Exploration Ltd. 07/18/2014

WESTHILL RES LTD (BC)
Recapitalized as Breckenridge Resources Ltd. 03/03/1992
Each share Common no par exchanged for (0.2) share Common no par
Breckenridge Resources Ltd. recapitalized as GTO Resources Inc. 08/07/2003 which recapitalized as Ram Power, Corp. 10/20/2009 which recapitalized as Polaris Infrastructure Inc. 05/19/2015

WESTHOPE CAP CORP (ON)
Recapitalized as EPM Mining Ventures Inc. (ON) 03/12/2010
Each share Common no par exchanged for (0.1) share Common no par
EPM Mining Ventures Inc. (ON) reincorporated in Yukon 05/20/2011 which name changed to Crystal Peak Minerals Inc. 06/26/2015

WESTIN HOTELS LTD PARTNERSHIP (DE)
In process of liquidation
Each Unit of Limited Partnership Int. received initial distribution of $800 cash payable 02/25/2005 to holders of record 02/25/2005
Note: Number or amount of subsequent distributions, if any, are not available

WESTINGHOUSE AIR BRAKE CO (PA)
Each share Capital Stock $50 par exchanged for (4) shares Capital Stock no par in 1927
Each share Capital Stock no par exchanged for (1.3) shares Common $10 par 7/1/51
Merged into American Standard Inc. 6/7/68
Each share Common $10 par exchanged for (0.5) share $4.75 Conv. Preference Ser. A no par
(See American Standard Inc.)

WESTINGHOUSE AIR BRAKE TECHNOLOGIES CORP (DE)
Name changed 12/27/99
Issue Information - 7,000,000 shares COM offered at $14 per share on 06/15/1995
Name changed from Westinghouse Air Brake Co. (New) to Westinghouse Air Brake Technologies Corp. 12/27/99
Name changed to Wabtec Corp. 5/1/2000

WESTINGHOUSE CDA INC (CANADA)
Name changed 5/15/80
Name changed from Westinghouse Canada Ltd.-Westinghouse Canada Ltee. to Westinghouse Canada Inc. 5/15/80
Each share old Capital Stock no par exchanged for (1/127,660) share new Capital Stock no par 1/20/87
Note: In effect holders received $105 cash per share and public interest was eliminated

WESTINGHOUSE CR CORP (DE)
Variable Term Preferred Class A $1 par called for redemption 12/15/1992
Each share Variable Term Preferred Class B $1 par exchanged for (4) shares Westinghouse Electric Corp. Common $1 par 09/01/1995
Each share Variable Term Preferred Class C $1 par exchanged for (8) shares Westinghouse Electric Corp. Common $1 par 05/30/1997
Westinghouse Electric Corp. name changed to CBS Corp. 12/01/1997 which merged into Viacom Inc. (Old) 05/04/2000
(See Viacom Inc. (Old))

WESTINGHOUSE ELEC CORP (PA)
Each share 7% Preferred $12.50 par exchanged for (0.25) share 3-1/2% Preferred Ser. A $100 par and (0.5) share Common $12.50 par 12/10/1946
3-1/2% Preferred Ser. A $100 par called for redemption 02/01/1950
Common $12.50 par changed to $6.25 par and (1) additional share issued 02/01/1960
Common $6.25 par changed to $3.12-1/2 par and (1) additional share issued 12/15/1971
Each Interim Ctf. surrendered by 12/18/1975 received (0.8898) share Common $3.12-1/2 par after which date unsurrendered certificates became worthless

3.80% Preferred Ser. B $100 par called for redemption 06/27/1983
Common $3.12-1/2 par changed to $1 par and (1) additional share issued 05/29/1984
Common $1 par split (2) for (1) by issuance of (1) additional share 05/21/1990
Preferred Stock Purchase Rights declared for Common stockholders of record 12/17/1989 were redeemed at $0.005 per right 12/02/1992
Each share Conv. Depositary Preferred Ser. B exchanged for (1) share Common $1 par 09/01/1995
Each share Conv. Preferred Ser. B $1 par exchanged for (4) shares Common $1 par 09/01/1995
144A Conv. Depositary Preferred Ser. C called for redemption 05/30/1997
Name changed to CBS Corp. 12/01/1997
CBS Corp. merged into Viacom Inc. (Old) 05/04/2000
(See Viacom Inc. (Old))

WESTINGHOUSE ELECTRIC & MANUFACTURING CO. (PA)
Recapitalized as Westinghouse Electric Corp. 5/10/45
Each share 7% Preferred exchanged for (4) shares 7% Preferred
Each share Common $50 par exchanged for (4) shares Common $12.50 par
Westinghouse Electric Corp. name changed to CBS Corp. 12/1/97 which merged into Viacom Inc. (Old) 5/4/2000
(See Viacom Inc. (Old))

WESTINGHOUSE SOLAR (DE)
Name changed to Andalay Solar, Inc. 09/27/2013

WESTLAKE CANYON INTL INC (NM)
Name changed to Vision International, Inc. 04/26/2006
Vision International, Inc. name changed to Exlites Holdings International, Inc. 09/19/2008

WESTLAKE CAP LTD (BC)
Completely liquidated
Each share Common no par received first and final distribution of (0.704545) share RockBridge Resources Inc. Restricted Common no par and (0.704545) Common Stock Purchase Warrant expiring 00/00/2014 payable 10/23/2013 to holders of record 09/09/2013

WESTLAKE INDS LTD (BC)
Merged into Minera Rayrock Inc. 10/31/90
Each share Common no par exchanged for (0.55) share Common no par
Minera Rayrock Inc. merged into Rayrock Yellowknife Resources Inc. 5/27/98 which name changed to Rayrock Resources Inc. 11/27/98
(See Rayrock Resources Inc.)

WESTLAKE RES INC (BC)
Name changed to Westlake Industries Ltd. 3/5/87
Westlake Industries Ltd. merged into Minera Rayrock Inc. 10/31/90 which merged into Rayrock Yellowknife Resources Inc. 5/27/98 which named changed to Rayrock Resources Inc. 11/27/98
(See Rayrock Resources Inc.)

WESTLAND CAP CORP (CA)
Under plan of dissolution liquidating distributions of $6.50 cash 01/17/1964; (1) share General Television, Inc. Common 10¢ par plus $1.60 cash 02/15/1965 and $0.15 cash 06/14/1965 were paid
Plan of dissolution abandoned, company reactivated and each share Common $1 par exchanged for (0.2) Common $5 par 10/01/1965

Common $5 par changed to $1 par 09/30/1974
Charter cancelled for failure to file reports and pay fees 05/21/1985

WESTLAND INVT CORP (YT)
Reincorporated 11/27/96
Place of incorporation changed from (ALTA) to (Yukon) 11/27/96
Name changed to Sepik Gold Corp. 8/15/97
(See Sepik Gold Corp.)

WESTLAND MINERALS CORP (UT)
Each share Common 1¢ par exchanged for (0.1) share Common 10¢ par 06/12/1972
Charter dissolved for failure to pay taxes 09/28/1973

WESTLAND MINES LTD (BC)
Recapitalized as United Westland Resources Ltd. 8/16/74
Each share Common no par exchanged for (0.5) share Common no par
United Westland Resources Ltd. name changed to Daleco Resources Corp. (BC) 5/2/86 which reincorporated in Delaware 10/1/96 which reincorporated in Nevada 4/1/2002

WESTLAND OIL CORP. (DE)
Name changed to Gray Wolfe Co. in 1945
(See Gray Wolfe Co.)

WESTLAND PLATING CO (MN)
Adjudicated bankrupt 11/6/70
Stockholders' equity unlikely

WESTLAND RES INC (UT)
Charter expired 09/27/1995

WESTLANDS BK (SANTA ANA, CA)
Common $5 par changed to $1.25 par and (3) additional shares issued 03/24/1972
Stock Dividends - 10% 05/16/1979; 10% 04/23/1980
Under plan of reorganization each share Common $1.25 par automatically became (1) share Westlands Diversified Bancorp, Inc. Common $1.25 par 05/24/1982
(See Westlands Diversified Bancorp, Inc.)

WESTLANDS CORP. (LA)
Charter revoked for failure to file annual reports 11/17/98

WESTLANDS DIVERSIFIED BANCORP INC (DE)
Merged into Canadian Commercial Bank (Edmonton, AB) 06/27/1984
Each share Common $1.25 par exchanged for $2 cash

WESTLEY MINES INTERNATIONAL INC (ON)
Name changed 10/28/1992
Name changed 04/17/1997
Reincorporated 12/09/1998
Name changed from Westley Mines Ltd. to Westley Technologies Ltd. 10/28/1992
Name changed from Westley Technologies Ltd. to Westley Mines International Inc. 04/17/1997
Place of incorporation changed from (BC) to (ON) 12/09/1998
Recapitalized as Moydow Mines International Inc. (ON) 12/16/1998
Each (12) shares Common no par exchanged for (1) share Common no par
Moydow Mines International Inc. (ON) reincorporated in British Columbia 12/18/2006 which merged into Franco-Nevada Corp. 01/27/2010

WESTLINKS RES LTD (AB)
Name changed to Enterra Energy Corp. 12/18/2001
Enterra Energy Corp. recapitalized as Enterra Energy Trust 11/25/2003 which reorganized as Equal Energy Ltd. 06/03/2010

(See Equal Energy Ltd.)

WESTLOCK PETROLEUMS LTD. (ON)
Merged into Wespac Petroleums Ltd. on a (1) for (4.1) basis 7/11/55
Wespac Petroleums Ltd. recapitalized as Canada Geothermal Oil Ltd. 9/7/71

WESTMARC COMMUNICATIONS INC (NV)
Merged into Tele-Communications, Inc. (Old) 1/3/90
Each share Class A Common 1¢ par exchanged for $32.25 cash
Each share Class B Common 1¢ par exchanged for $32.25 cash

WESTMARK GROUP HLDGS INC (DE)
Reincorporated 06/00/1996
Each (30) shares old Common no par exchanged for (1) share new Common no par 07/11/1995
State of incorporation changed from (CO) to (DE) and Common no par changed to $0.001 par 06/00/1996
Each share Common $0.001 par exchanged for (0.2) share Common $0.005 par 09/02/1997
Recapitalized as Viking Consolidated, Inc. (DE) 05/15/2006
Each share Common $0.005 par exchanged for (0.01) share Common $0.005 par
Viking Consolidated, Inc. (DE) reincorporated in Nevada as Tailor Aquaponics World Wide, Inc. 08/15/2006 which recapitalized as Diversified Acquisitions, Inc. 08/20/2007 which recapitalized as Vitalcare Diabetes Treatment Centers, Inc. 03/24/2008 which recapitalized as China Advanced Technology 06/23/2010 which name changed to Goliath Film & Media Holdings 01/20/2012

WESTMARK INTL INC (DE)
Name changed to Advanced Technology Laboratories, Inc. (DE) 6/26/92
Advanced Technology Laboratories, Inc. (DE) reincorporated in (WA) 5/11/95 which name changed to ATL Ultrasound, Inc. 7/1/97
(See ATL Ultrasound, Inc.)

WESTMED VENTURE PARTNERS L P (DE)
Liquidation completed
Each Unit of Ltd. Partnership Int. 2 received initial distribution of $7 cash 00/00/1990
Each Unit of Ltd. Partnership Int. 1 received initial distribution of $85 cash 00/00/1992
Each Unit of Ltd. Partnership Int. 2 received second distribution of $77 cash payable 01/21/1997 to holders of record 12/31/1996
Each Unit of Ltd. Partnership Int. 1 received second distribution of $67 cash payable 01/30/1997 to holders of record 12/31/1996
Each Unit of Ltd. Partnership Int. 1 received third distribution of $82 cash payable 10/21/1997 to holders of record 09/30/1997
Each Unit of Ltd. Partnership Int. 1 received fourth distribution of $45 cash payable 01/22/1999 to holders of record 12/31/1998
Each Unit of Ltd. Partnership Int. 1 received fifth and final distribution of $15.40 cash payable 09/30/1999 to holders of record 06/30/1999
Each Unit of Ltd. Partnership Int. 2 received third distribution of $111 cash payable 01/28/2000 to holders of record 12/31/1999
Each Unit of Ltd. Partnership Int. 2 received fourth and final distribution of $32.57 cash payable 07/31/2000 to holders of record 07/31/2000

WESTMILLS CANADA INC (BC)
Name changed 1/1/84
Name changed from Westmills Carpets Ltd. to Westmills Canada Inc. 1/1/84
Wound up in 1993
No stockholders' equity

WESTMIN RES LTD (CANADA)
Common no par split (2) for (1) by issuance of (1) additional share 04/22/1981
Merged into Boliden Ltd. (Canada) 02/12/1998
For Canadian Residents: Each share Common no par exchanged for either (0.5329) share Common no par or C$5.40 cash
Note: Option to receive stock expired 03/09/1998
For Non-Canadian Residents: Each share Common no par exchanged for U.S. dollar equivalent of C$5.40 cash
$2.125 Conv. Preferred Class B Ser. 1 no par called for redemption 05/19/1998
Boliden Ltd. (Canada) reorganized in Sweden as Boliden AB 12/07/2001

WESTMINISTER BD FD INC (MD)
Common 10¢ par reclassified as Investment Grade Portfolio 10¢ par 08/15/1978
Name changed to Vanguard Fixed Income Securities Fund, Inc. 05/20/1980

WESTMINSTER CAP INC (DE)
Merged into Westminster Acquisition Corp. 8/29/2003
Each share Common $1 par exchanged for $2.95665 cash

WESTMINSTER CORP. (CO)
Charter revoked for failure to file reports and pay fees 10/28/59

WESTMINSTER CORP (MD)
Liquidation completed
Each share Common 33-1/3¢ par received initial distribution of $1.50 cash 10/17/1975
Each share Common 33-1/3¢ par received second distribution of $1 cash 01/21/1976
Each share Common 33-1/3¢ par received third distribution of $0.30 cash 08/13/1976
Each share Common 33-1/3¢ par exchanged for fourth and final distribution of $0.68 cash 07/19/1977

WESTMINSTER FD INC (MD)
Acquired by Anchor Growth Fund, Inc. 05/03/1971
Each share Capital Stock $1 par exchanged for (1.42199) shares Capital Stock $1 par
Anchor Growth Fund, Inc. merged into Amcap Fund, Inc. 08/31/1981

WESTMINSTER PAPER CO., LTD. (BC)
Common $10 par changed to no par in May 1948
Each share Common no par exchanged for (1) share Class A no par and (3) shares Class B no par in December 1948
Class A and B no par reclassified as Common no par 5/12/59
Name changed to Scott Paper Ltd. 6/1/64
Scott Paper Ltd. name changed to Scott Paper Ltd./Les Papiers Scott Ltee. 12/4/78
(See Scott Paper Ltd./Les Papiers Scott Ltee.)

WESTMINSTER RES LTD (AB)
Name changed to Vaquero Energy Ltd. 06/19/2002
Vaquero Energy Ltd. merged into Highpine Oil & Gas Ltd. 05/31/2005 which merged into Daylight Resources Trust 10/08/2009 which reorganized as Daylight Energy Ltd. 05/12/2010
(See Daylight Energy Ltd.)

WESTMONT CAP RES LTD (BC)
Name changed to Wescap Energy Corp. 4/1/79
Wescap Energy Corp. name changed to Wescap Enterprises Ltd. 11/29/86
(See Wescap Enterprises Ltd.)

WESTMONT RES INC (NV)
Each share old Common $0.001 par exchanged for (0.02) share new Common $0.001 par 11/18/2009
Each shares new Common $0.001 par exchanged again for (0.00333333) share share new Common $0.001 par 01/05/2011
SEC revoked common stock registration 07/29/2014

WESTMOORE HLDGS INC (NV)
Name changed to Rockwall Holdings, Inc. 04/22/2010
(See Rockwall Holdings, Inc.)

WESTMOR CORP (DE)
Merged into Genstar Ltd. 01/30/1979
Each share Common $1 par exchanged for $2.50 cash

WESTMORE, INC. (NJ)
Adjudicated bankrupt 12/12/63; no stockholders' equity

WESTMORELAND, INC. (DE)
Capital Stock no par changed to $10 par 00/00/1940
Merged into Virginia Coal & Iron Co. 10/31/1963
Each share Capital Stock $10 par exchanged for (0.66666666) share Capital Stock $25 par
Virginia Coal & Iron Co. name changed to Penn Virginia Corp. (Old) 04/19/1967
(See Penn Virginia Corp. (Old))

WESTMORELAND COAL CO. NEW (PA)
Capital Stock no par changed to $20 par in 1940
Merged into Westmoreland Coal Co. (DE) on a (2.85) for (1) basis 4/30/64

WESTMORELAND COAL CO. OLD (PA)
Each share Capital Stock $50 par exchanged for (1) share Westmoreland Coal Co. (New) Capital Stock no par and (1) share Westmoreland, Inc. Capital Stock no par 00/00/1929
(See each company's listing)

WESTMORELAND COAL CO (DE)
Depositary Preferred Ser. A called for redemption at $25 plus $0.2066 accrued dividends on 02/04/2015 (Additional Information in Active)

WESTMORELAND WATER CO.
Liquidated in 1950

WESTMOUNT FINANCIAL HOLDINGS LTD. (AB)
Completely liquidated 9/24/75
Ordinary Stock $1 par exchanged for first and final distribution of Westmount Life Insurance Co. Capital Stock $10 par
Westmount Life Insurance Co. merged into Family Life Assurance Co.-La Familiale Compagnie D'Assurance-Vie 12/31/78

WESTMOUNT LIFE INS CO (CANADA)
Merged into Family Life Assurance Co.-La Familiale Compagnie D'Assurance-Vie 12/31/1978
Each share Capital Stock $10 par exchanged for either (55) shares Preferred $1 par or (10) shares Common $1 par
(See Family Life Assurance Co.-La Familiale Compagnie D'Assurance-Vie)

WESTMOUNT MEMORIAL PARK, LTD. (ON)
Dissolved 7/17/50

WESTMOUNT RES LTD (BC)
Liquidation completed
Each share Capital Stock no par received initial distribution of $0.25 cash 03/27/1990
Each share Capital Stock no par received second and final distribution of $11.978 cash 12/11/1990

WESTMOUNT RES LTD NEW (BC)
Recapitalized as Mt. Tom Minerals Corp. 05/20/1998
Each share Common no par exchanged for (0.5) share Common no par
Mt. Tom Minerals Corp. name changed to Global Net Entertainment Corp. 10/14/1999 which recapitalized as Guildhall Minerals Ltd. 02/21/2006 which name changed to Edge Resources Inc. 07/28/2009
(See Edge Resources Inc.)

WESTMOUNTAIN ALTERNATIVE ENERGY INC (CO)
Name changed to C-Bond Systems Inc. 07/25/2018

WESTMOUNTAIN ASSET MGMT INC (CO)
Name changed to WestMountain Co. 02/28/2014

WESTMOUNTAIN INDEX ADVISOR INC (CO)
Each share old Common $0.001 par exchanged for (0.25) share new Common $0.001 par 10/12/2010
Name changed to WestMountain Gold, Inc. 03/08/2013

WESTON ART CORP (NY)
Name changed to Weston Group Corp. 8/30/72
(See Weston Group Corp.)

WESTON ELECTRICAL INSTRUMENT CORP. (NJ)
Capital Stock no par changed to $12.50 par in 1940
Capital Stock $12.50 par split (2) for (1) by issuance of (1) additional share in 1953
Merged into Daystrom, Inc. 5/16/55
Each share Capital Stock $12.50 par exchanged for (1) share Common $10 par
Daystrom, Inc. acquired by Schlumberger, Ltd. 2/1/62

WESTON GEORGE LTD (CANADA)
Each share Common no par exchanged for (2) shares Common no par 00/00/1935
Each share Common no par exchanged for (1-1/3) shares Common no par 00/00/1951
Each share Common no par exchanged for (2) shares Class A Common no par and (2) shares Class B Common no par 11/01/1955
4-1/2% Preferred $100 par reclassified as 4-1/2% Preferred 1st Ser. $100 par 09/18/1957
Class A Common no par and Class B Common no par split (3) for (1) respectively by issuance of (2) additional shares 06/02/1961
Class A Common no par and Class B Common no par reclassified as Common no par 06/14/1968
6% Preferred 2nd Ser. $100 par reclassified as 6% Sr. Preferred 2nd Ser. $100 par 07/03/1980
4-1/2% Preferred 1st Ser. $100 par reclassified as 4-1/2% Sr. Preferred 1st Ser. $100 par 07/03/1980
4-1/2% Sr. Preferred 1st Ser. $100 par called for redemption 06/08/1987
Floating Rate Preferred Ser. A no par called for redemption 12/30/1992

6% Sr. Preferred 2nd Ser. $100 par called for redemption 10/31/1996
5.15% Preferred Ser. II no par called for redemption at $25 plus $0.321875 accrued dividends on 04/01/2009
(Additional Information in Active)

WESTON GROUP CORP (NY)
Dissolved by proclamation 6/23/93

WESTON HOTELS & PPYTS INC (CO)
Recapitalized as Irvine Pacific Corp. (CO) 08/30/2002
Each share Common $0.00001 par exchanged for (0.01) share Common $0.001 par
Irvine Pacific Corp. (CO) reincorporated in Delaware as iMedia International, Inc. 11/26/2003

WESTON INTL CORP (MD)
Acquired by Faraday Leasing Corp. 7/30/80
Each share Common 1¢ par exchanged for $0.05 cash

WESTON LEASING CO. (MD)
Name changed to Weston International Corp. 12/20/71
(See Weston International Corp.)

WESTON ROY F INC NEW (PA)
Each share old Common 10¢ par exchanged for (0.04) share new Common 10¢ par 12/3/79
Each share Class A Common 10¢ par exchanged for (130) shares Ser. A Common 10¢ par 6/19/86
New Common 10¢ par split (130) for (1) by issuance of (129) additional shares 6/19/86
Ser. A Common 10¢ par split (3) for (2) by issuance of (0.5) additional share 3/2/87
New Common 10¢ par split (3) for (2) by issuance of (0.5) additional share 3/2/87
Merged into American Capital Strategies, Ltd. 6/4/2001
Each share Class A Common 10¢ par exchanged for $5.02 cash

WESTONE VENTURES INC (AB)
Name changed to Secure One, Inc. 04/02/2004
Secure One, Inc. name changed to United Protection Security Group Inc. 11/28/2005
(See United Protection Security Group Inc.)

WESTONKA TELEPHONE CO. (MN)
Called for redemption 07/01/1970
Public interest eliminated

WESTONS SHOPPERS CITY INC (DE)
Merged into Weston Equities Inc. 12/19/1980
Each share Common $1 par exchanged for $6 cash

WESTORE MINES LTD. (ON)
Acquired by Bison Petroleum & Minerals Ltd. 09/15/1960
Each share Capital Stock $1 par exchanged for (0.07692308) share Capital Stock $1 par
Bison Petroleum & Minerals Ltd. recapitalized as United Bison Resources Ltd. 12/22/1987 which merged into Nalcap Holdings Inc. 04/25/1991 which recapitalized as Arbatax International (Canada) 03/28/1996 which reincorporated in Yukon 08/06/1996 which name changed to MFC Bancorp Ltd. (YT) 03/03/1997 which reincorporated in British Columbia 11/03/2004 which name changed to KHD Humboldt Wedag International Ltd. 11/01/2005 which reorganized as Terra Nova Royalty Corp. 03/30/2010 which name changed to MFC Industrial Ltd. 09/30/2011 which name changed to MFC Bancorp Ltd. (BC) 02/16/2016
(See MFC Bancorp Ltd. (BC))

WESTOURS INC (WA)
Merged into Westours Interim Corp. 07/21/1977
Each share Common no par exchanged for $12.50 cash

WESTOWER CORP (WA)
Common 1¢ par split (3) for (2) by issuance of (0.5) additional share payable 06/08/1998 to holders of record 06/01/1998 Ex date - 06/09/1998
Merged into SpectraSite Holdings, Inc. 09/03/1999
Each share Common 1¢ par exchanged for (1.81) shares Common $0.001 par
(See SpectraSite Holdings, Inc.)

WESTPAC BKG CORP (AUSTRALIA)
Sponsored ADR's for Preference called for redemption 10/17/1994
(Additional Information in Active)

WESTPAC CAP TR I (DE)
8% Trust Originated Preferred Securities called for redemption at $25 plus $0.09 accrued dividend on 7/16/2004

WESTPAN HYDROCARBON CO. (DE)
Liquidation completed 4/28/61

WESTPAR CORP (NV)
Each share old Common $0.001 par exchanged for (0.01) share new Common $0.001 par 05/01/1988
Recapitalized as Air-O Industries, Inc. 10/21/1991
Each share new Common $0.001 par exchanged for (0.0004) share Common $0.001 par

WESTPINE METALS LTD (BC)
Recapitalized as Great Quest Metals Ltd. 07/08/1998
Each share Common no par exchanged for (0.25) share Common no par
Great Quest Metals Ltd. name changed to Great Quest Fertilizer Ltd. 06/09/2014

WESTPOINT ENERGY INC (AB)
Acquired by Alberta Energy Co. Ltd. 05/30/2000
Each share Common no par exchanged for $8 cash

WESTPOINT STEVENS INC (DE)
Class A Plan Shares 1¢ par reclassified as Common 1¢ par 05/10/1994
Common 1¢ par split (2) for (1) by issuance of (1) additional share payable 03/02/1998 to holders of record 02/16/1998
Assets sold for the benefit of creditors 07/08/2005
No stockholders' equity

WESTPORT BANCORP INC (DE)
Common $2.50 par split (2) for (1) by issuance of (1) additional share 10/30/1984
Common $2.50 par split (2) for (1) by issuance of (1) additional share 07/06/1987
Common $2.50 par changed to 1¢ par 05/16/1990
Merged into HUBCO, Inc. 12/13/1996
Each share Common 1¢ par exchanged for (0.332175) share Common no par
HUBCO, Inc. name changed to Hudson United Bancorp 04/21/1999 which merged into TD Banknorth Inc. 01/31/2006
(See TD Banknorth Inc.)

WESTPORT BK & TR CO (WESTPORT, CT)
Capital Stock $100 par changed to $50 par and (1) additional share issued 04/24/1934
Capital Stock $50 par changed to $10 par and (4) additional shares issued plus 100% stock dividend 02/22/1972
Capital Stock $10 par changed to $5 par and (1) additional share issued plus 50% stock dividend 10/01/1978
Stock Dividend - 100% 11/15/1946
Under plan of reorganization each share Capital Stock $5 par automatically became (1) share Westport Bancorp, Inc. Common $2.50 par 09/28/1984
Westport Bancorp, Inc. merged into HUBCO, Inc. 12/13/1996 which name changed to Hudson United Bancorp 04/21/1999 which merged into TD Banknorth Inc. 01/31/2006
(See TD Banknorth Inc.)

WESTPORT CO (MA)
Name changed to CenTrust Trust 7/17/84
(See CenTrust Trust)

WESTPORT INNOVATIONS INC (AB)
Each share old Common no par exchanged for (0.28571428) share new Common no par 07/24/2008
Under plan of merger name changed to Westport Fuel Systems Inc. 06/08/2016

WESTPORT NATL BK (WESTPORT, CT)
Acquired by State National Bancorp Inc. (DE) 11/23/81
Each share Common $4 par exchanged for $53.30 cash

WESTPORT NATL BK NEW (WESTPORT, CT)
Reorganized as Associated Community Bancorp, Inc. 2/25/2000
Each share Common exchanged for (1.275) shares Common 1¢ par

WESTPORT PROPERTIES CORP. (DE)
Stock Dividend - 10% 12/20/55
Name changed to Tri-State Motor Transit Co. 4/21/60
Tri-State Motor Transit Co. reorganized as Tri-State Motor Transit Co. of Delaware 7/2/84
(See Tri-State Motor Transit Co. of Delaware)

WESTPORT RES CORP (DE)
Merged into Westport Resources Corp. (NV) 8/21/2001
Each share Common $0.001 par exchanged for (1) share Common $0.001 par
Westport Resources Corp. (NV) merged into Kerr-McGee Corp. 6/25/2004

WESTPORT RES CORP (NV)
6.50% Conv. Preferred 1¢ par called for redemption at $25.65 plus $0.03 accrued dividend on 12/21/2004
Merged into Kerr-McGee Corp. 6/25/2004
Each share Common 1¢ par exchanged for (0.71) share Common $1 par

WESTPOST CAP INC (BC)
Recapitalized as Telepost Communications Inc. 12/11/1990
Each share Common no par exchanged for (0.25) share Common no par
(See Telepost Communications Inc.)

WESTRALIAN GAS & PWR LTD (AUSTRALIA)
Name changed to Titan Energy Ltd. 11/21/2011
Titan Energy Ltd. name changed to TTE Petroleum Ltd. 09/25/2015
(See TTE Petroleum Ltd.)

WESTRAN CORP (MI)
Merged into KZ Co. 08/14/1985
Each share Common $1 par exchanged for $70 cash

WESTRANGE CORP (AB)
Name changed to HTC Hydrogen Technologies Corp. 01/25/2005
HTC Hydrogen Technologies Corp. name changed to HTC Purenergy Inc. 02/21/2008

WESTRANS INDUSTRIES, INC. (DE)
Merged into Aquitaine Pennsylvania, Inc. 04/30/1975
Each share Common $1 par exchanged for $36 cash

WESTREND NAT GAS INC (BC)
Recapitalized as Westrend Oil & Gas Technologies Corp. 08/12/1999
Each (15) shares Common no par exchanged for (1) share Common no par
(See Westrend Oil & Gas Technologies Corp.)

WESTREND OIL & GAS TECHNOLOGIES CORP (BC)
Cease trade order effective 08/18/1999
Stockholders' equity unlikely

WESTREX DEV CORP (BC)
Recapitalized as Consolidated Westrex Development Corp. 02/01/1988
Each (2.7) shares Common no par exchanged for (1) share Common no par
Consolidated Westrex Development Corp. name changed to Westrex Energy Corp. (BC) 07/25/1991 which reincorporated in Alberta 05/12/1994 which recapitalized as Search Energy Corp. 01/09/1997 which merged into Advantage Energy Income Fund 05/24/2001 which reorganized as Advantage Oil & Gas Ltd. 07/09/2009

WESTREX ENERGY CORP (AB)
Reincorporated 05/12/1994
Place of incorporation changed from (BC) to (AB) 05/12/1994
Recapitalized as Search Energy Corp. 01/09/1997
Each share Common no par exchanged for (0.2) share Common no par
Search Energy Corp. merged into Advantage Energy Income Fund 05/24/2001 which reorganized as Advantage Oil & Gas Ltd. 07/09/2009

WESTRIDGE RES INC (BC)
Each share old Common no par exchanged for (0.5) share new Common no par 03/03/2014
Name changed to Harrys Manufacturing Inc. 10/22/2018

WESTRIDGE RES INC (DE)
Charter forfeited for failure to maintain a registered agent 06/12/1992

WESTROCK ENERGY INCOME FD I (AB)
Merged into Enerplus Resources Fund 06/08/2000
Each Trust Unit Ser. A exchanged for (0.447) new Trust Unit no par
Enerplus Resources Fund reorganized as Enerplus Corp. 01/03/2011

WESTROCK ENERGY INCOME FD II (AB)
Merged into Enerplus Resources Fund 06/08/2000
Each Trust Unit exchanged for (0.445) new Trust Unit no par
Enerplus Resources Fund reorganized as Enerplus Corp. 01/03/2011

WESTROK CAP INC (AB)
Reincorporated 01/25/1988
Place of incorporation changed from (BC) to (ALTA) 01/25/1988
Recapitalized as Merit Energy Ltd. 01/08/1996
Each share Common no par exchanged for (0.25) share Common no par
(See Merit Energy Ltd.)

WES-WES   FINANCIAL INFORMATION, INC.

WESTRON DIVERSIFIED INDUSTRIES, INC. (FL)
Proclaimed dissolved for failure to file reports and pay fees 6/28/71

WESTRON VENTURE LTD (BC)
Name changed to JefJen Capital Corp. 06/27/1988

WESTRONIX INC (DE)
Name changed to Flagship Express, Inc. 07/12/1990
(See Flagship Express, Inc.)

WESTSHIRE CAP CORP (AB)
Each share old Common no par exchanged for (0.4) share new Common no par 12/05/2013
Name changed to Avagenesis Corp. (AB) 12/16/2013
Avagenesis Corp. (AB) reincorporated in British Columbia as Liberty Biopharma Inc. 01/06/2017 which name changed to HooXi Network Inc. 10/11/2018

WESTSHIRE CAP II CORP (BC)
Recapitalized as Wonderfilm Media Corp. 04/02/2018
Each share Common no par exchanged for (0.25) share Common no par

WESTSHORE TERMS INCOME FD (BC)
Reorganized as Westshore Terminals Investment Corp. 01/07/2011
Each Trust Unit no par exchanged for (1) Stapled Unit

WESTSIDE ATLANTIC BANK (DAYTONA BEACH, FL)
99.71% acquired by Atlantic Bancorporation through exchange offer which expired 10/22/1973
Public interest eliminated

WESTSIDE ATLANTIC BANK (JACKSONVILLE, FL)
100% acquired thru voluntary exchange offer by Atlantic Bancorporation as of 10/1/73

WESTSIDE BANCORPORATION INC (DE)
Placed in receivership by FSLIC 08/30/1985
No stockholders' equity

WESTSIDE BANK OF SOUTHERN CALIFORNIA (LOS ANGELES, CA)
Placed in conservatorship 9/24/93
Stockholders' equity undetermined

WESTSIDE CMNTY BK (TACOMA, WA)
Under plan of reorganization each share Common $1 par automatically became (1) share Westside Banking Co. Common $1 par 1/1/2006

WESTSIDE ENERGY CORP (NV)
Common 10¢ par changed to 1¢ par 07/02/2004
Name changed to Crusader Energy Group Inc. 06/27/2008
(See Crusader Energy Group Inc.)

WESTSIDE FED SVGS & LN ASSN SEATTLE (WA)
Common 1¢ par split (2) for (1) by issuance of (1) additional share 7/21/83
Reorganized under the laws of Delaware as Westside Bancorporation, Inc. 4/1/84
(See Westside Bancorporation, Inc.)

WESTSIDE FINANCIAL CORP (GA)
Reorganized 08/31/1994
Under plan of reorganization each share Westside Bank & Trust Co. (Marietta, GA) Common no par automatically became (1) share Westside Financial Corp. Common no par 08/31/1994
Stock Dividend - 23% payable 07/30/1996 holders of record 07/30/1996
Under plan of merger name changed to First Sterling Banks, Inc. (Old) 07/31/1996
First Sterling Banks, Inc. (Old) name changed to First Sterling Banks, Inc. (New) 05/24/2000 which name changed to Main Street Banks, Inc. (New) 01/02/2001

WESTSIDE SAVINGS & LOAN ASSOCIATION (CA)
Name changed to Westside Bank of Southern California (Los Angeles, CA) 7/16/90
Westside Bank of Southern California (Los Angeles, CA) was placed in conservatorship 9/24/93

WESTSPHERE ASSET CORP INC (CO)
Each share old Common no par exchanged for (0.05) share new Common no par 04/01/2005
Name changed to E-Debit Global Corp. 06/17/2010
E-Debit Global Corp. name changed to GreenLink International Inc. 07/30/2018

WESTSTAR FINL SVCS CORP (NC)
Common $1 par split (6) for (5) by issuance of (0.2) additional share payable 09/30/2003 to holders of record 09/19/2003 Ex date - 09/17/2003
Common $1 par split (5) for (4) by issuance of (0.25) additional share payable 06/19/2007 to holders of record 06/05/2007 Ex date - 06/20/2007
Stock Dividends - 10% payable 11/13/2001 to holders of record 10/30/2001 Ex date - 10/26/2001; 10% payable 12/13/2002 to holders of record 11/30/2002 Ex date - 11/26/2002; 20% payable 01/31/2005 to holders of record 01/11/2005 Ex date - 01/07/2005; 20% payable 05/02/2006 to holders of record 04/18/2006 Ex date - 04/13/2006
SEC revoked common stock registration 05/28/2014

WESTSTAR GROUP INC (NV)
Recapitalized as Arena Group Inc. 08/15/1997
Each share Common $0.001 par exchanged (0.14285714) share Common $0.001 par
Arena Group Inc. name changed to Elligent Consulting Group, Inc. 08/13/1998 which name changed to E-Vantage Solutions, Inc. 07/16/2000
(See E-Vantage Solutions, Inc.)

WESTSTAR RES CORP (BC)
Each share old Common no par exchanged for (2) shares new Common no par 05/29/2007
Each share new Common no par exchanged again for (0.08333333) share new Common no par 09/28/2010
Each share new Common no par exchanged again for (0.5) share new Common no par 06/09/2014
Name changed to Liberty Leaf Holdings Ltd. 10/21/2016

WESTSUN PETES & MINERALS LTD (BC)
Reincorporated under the laws of Canada as Telepanel, Inc. 10/29/1986
Telepanel, Inc. recapitalized as Telepanel Systems Inc. 07/12/1989
(See Telepanel Systems Inc.)

WESTUNIT RES CORP (BC)
Name changed to Avanti Productions Inc. 4/4/86
(See Avanti Productions Inc.)

WESTVACO CHEMICAL CORP.
Merged into Food Machinery & Chemical Corp. 9/10/48
Each share $3.75 Preferred no par exchanged for (1) share 3-3/4% Preferred $100 par
Each share Common no par exchanged for (1.25) shares Common $10 par
Food Machinery & Chemical Corp. name changed to FMC Corp. 6/30/61

WESTVACO CHLORINE PRODUCTS CORP.
Common no par split (3) for (2) by issuance of (0.5) additional share 5/12/47
Name changed to Westvaco Chemical Corp. 5/1/48
Westvaco Chemical Corp. merged into Food Machinery & Chemical Corp. 9/10/48 which name changed to FMC Corp. 6/30/61

WESTVACO CORP (DE)
4.5% Preferred $100 par called for redemption 02/15/1984
Common $5 par split (3) for (2) by issuance of (0.5) additional share 10/01/1976
Common $5 par split (3) for (2) by issuance of (0.5) additional share 04/30/1981
Common $5 par split (3) for (2) by issuance of (0.5) additional share 10/01/1986
Common $5 par split (3) for (2) by issuance of (0.5) additional share 09/30/1987
Common $5 par split (3) for (2) by issuance of (0.5) additional share 10/02/1995
Merged into MeadWestvaco Corp. 01/29/2002
Each share Common $5 par exchanged for (0.97) share Common 1¢ par
MeadWestvaco Corp. merged into WestRock Co. 07/01/2015

WESTVIEW COML INC (AB)
Reincorporated under the laws of British Columbia as Mega Moly Inc. 11/29/2007
Mega Moly Inc. recapitalized as Terreno Resources Corp. 08/23/2010

WESTVIEW INVT LTD (BC)
Dissolved 04/30/1979
No stockholders' equity

WESTVIEW LIFECARE CENTRES INC (AB)
Recapitalized as Westview Commercial Inc. (AB) 01/24/2003
Each share Class A Common no par exchanged for (0.1) share Common no par
Westview Commercial Inc. (AB) reincorporated in British Columbia as Mega Moly Inc. 11/29/2007 which recapitalized as Terreno Resources Corp. 08/23/2010

WESTVIEW MNG LTD (BC)
Merged into Charta Mines Ltd. (New) 01/31/1972
Each share Capital Stock 50¢ par exchanged for (1) share Common 50¢ par
Charta Mines Ltd. (New) recapitalized as Windmill Enterprises Ltd. 05/30/1977 which recapitalized as Todwind Development Corp. 07/20/1984
(See Todwind Development Corp.)

WESTVIEW RES INC (BC)
Recapitalized as Consolidated Westview Resources Corp. 09/20/1996
Each share Common no par exchanged for (0.33333333) share Common no par
Consolidated Westview Resources Corp. name changed to Lithoquest Diamonds Inc. 11/29/2017

WESTVILLE MINES LTD (ON)
Charter cancelled for failure to file reports and pay fees 11/08/1973

WESTVILLE OIL & MANUFACTURING, INC. (IN)
Name changed to Cam-or, Inc. 07/30/1968
(See Cam-or, Inc.)

WESTWARD ENERGY & RES CORP (BC)
Recapitalized as International Westward Development Corp. 11/04/1982
Each share Common no par exchanged for (0.25) share Common no par
International Westwood Development Corp. recapitalized as J.R. Energy Ltd. 04/23/1986
(See J.R. Energy Ltd.)

WESTWARD ENERGY LTD (AB)
Each share Non-Vtg. Class B Common no par exchanged for (1) share Class A Common no par 7/14/97
Merged into Seventh Energy Ltd. (NV) 8/1/97
Each share Class A Common no par exchanged for (0.6) share Class A Common no par
(See Seventh Energy Ltd. (NV))

WESTWARD EXPLS LTD (BC)
Name changed to West African Iron Ore Corp. 04/01/2011
West African Iron Ore Corp. recapitalized as WAI Capital Investments Corp. 03/31/2015

WESTWARD LEISURE CONCEPTS LTD (BC)
Name changed to Keg Restaurants Ltd. 08/18/1973
(See Keg Restaurants Ltd.)

WESTWATER CORP. (DE)
Under plan of merger name changed to North Star Oil Corp. 05/12/1961
North Star Oil Corp. was acquired by Texam Oil Corp. 04/22/1964 which name changed to Energy Resources Corp. 10/23/1967 which merged into ENERTEC Corp. 05/04/1984
(See ENERTEC Corp.)

WESTWATER INDS LTD (BC)
Cease trade order effective 1/9/92
Stockholders' equity unlikely

WESTWATER RES LTD (BC)
Name changed to American Westwater Technology Group Ltd. 03/25/1986
(See American Westwater Technology Group Ltd.)

WESTWAY GROUP INC (DE)
Units separated 05/24/2011
Each share Common $0.0001 par received distribution of (0.01002805) additional share payable 10/24/2011 to holders of record 09/09/2011
Each share Common $0.0001 par received distribution of (0.00697216) additional share payable 04/23/2012 to holders of record 02/27/2012 Ex date - 02/23/2012
Each share Common $0.0001 par received distribution of (0.00654043) additional share payable 07/23/2012 to holders of record 05/23/2012 Ex date - 05/21/2012
Acquired by EQT Infrastructure II Ltd. 02/01/2013
Each share Common $0.0001 par exchanged for $6.70 cash

WESTWEGO RES LTD (BC)
Name changed to Corum Resource Corp. 10/3/95
Corum Resource Corp. recapitalized as El Nino Ventures Inc. 8/19/99

WESTWELLS CORP (DE)
Charter cancelled and declared inoperative and void for non-payment of taxes 3/1/82

WESTWIN VENTURES INC (BC)
Recapitalized as New Westwin Ventures Inc. 01/06/1995

Each share Common no par exchanged for (1/3) share Common no par
New Westwin Ventures Inc. name changed to Arimex Mining Corp. 07/29/1997 which recapitalized as International Arimex Resources Inc. 02/22/1999 which name changed to WestCan Uranium Corp. 09/10/2007

WESTWIND ENERGY LTD (AB)
Delisted from Alberta Stock Exchange 04/30/1990

WESTWIND GROUP INC (DE)
Each share Common $0.001 par exchanged for (0.025) share Common $0.004 par 02/23/1990
Recapitalized as CTC Cosmetics Holding Inc. 03/21/1997
Each share Common $0.004 par exchanged for (0.07733952) share Common $0.004 par
CTC Cosmetics Holding Inc. name changed to Combine Corp. 11/02/2000
(See Combine Corp.)

WESTWIND MINES LTD (BC)
Name changed to Territorial Petroleum Ventures Ltd. 4/24/80
Territorial Petroleum Ventures Ltd. recapitalized as First Medical Management Ltd. 10/16/87
(See First Medical Management Ltd.)

WESTWOOD CAP INC (DE)
Recapitalized as Cruise of a Lifetime USA, Inc. 11/24/1987
Each (6.67) shares Common $0.001 par exchanged for (1) share Common $0.001 par
(See Cruise of a Lifetime USA, Inc.)

WESTWOOD CORP (NV)
Each share Common $0.001 par exchanged (0.33333333) share Common $0.003 par 02/04/1992
Stock Dividends - 10% 12/22/1993; 10% 12/22/1994; 10% 03/22/1995; 10% 12/22/1995; 10% payable 12/22/1996 to holders of record 12/01/1996; 10% payable 12/22/1997 to holders of record 12/01/1997
Merged into L-3 Communications Corp. 11/13/2002
Each share Common $0.003 par exchanged for $2.30 cash

WESTWOOD FD INC (CA)
Name changed to East/West Growth Stock Fund, Inc. 1/11/74
(See East/West Growth Stock Fund, Inc.)

WESTWOOD FINL CORP (NJ)
Merged into Lakeview Financial Corp. 2/27/98
Each share Common 10¢ par exchanged for either (1.1646) shares Common $2 par or $29.25 cash
Note: Non-electing holders received combination of cash and stock at the rate of 49.9% in stock and 51.1% in cash

WESTWOOD GROUP INC (MA)
Reincorporated 07/11/1984
State of incorporation changed from (MA) to (DE) and Common no par changed to 1¢ par 07/11/1984
Each share old Common 1¢ par exchanged for (0.002) share new Common 1¢ par 11/09/2004
Note: In effect holders received $4 cash per share and public interest was eliminated

WESTWOOD HOMESTEAD FINL CORP (IN)
Merged into Camco Financial Corp. 01/06/2000
Each share Common 1¢ par exchanged for (0.611) share Common $1 par
(See Camco Financial Corp.)

WESTWOOD INC (DE)
Name changed to Wyntex Mill Inc. 02/08/1999
Wyntex Mill Inc. name changed to Wintex Mill Inc. 06/18/1999
(See Wintex Mill Inc.)

WESTWOOD NATL BK (LOS ANGELES, CA)
Name changed to Metrobank, N.A. (Los Angeles, CA) 07/01/1980
Metrobank, N.A. (Los Angeles, CA) reorganized as Metrobank (Los Angeles, CA) 11/01/1988 which merged into Comerica Inc. 01/17/1996

WESTWOOD ONE INC NEW (DE)
Acquired by Cumulus Media Holdings Inc. 12/12/2013
Each share Class A Common 1¢ par exchanged for $0.155 cash

WESTWOOD ONE INC OLD (DE)
Reincorporated 07/10/1985
State of incorporation changed from (CA) to (DE) and Common no par changed to 1¢ par 07/10/1985
Old Common 1¢ par split (2) for (1) by issuance of (1) additional share 03/12/1986
Old Common 1¢ par split (3) for (2) by issuance of (0.5) additional share 04/06/1987
Old Common 1¢ par split (2) for (1) by issuance of (1) additional share payable 03/22/2000 to holders of record 03/08/2000 Ex date - 03/23/2000
Each share old Common 1¢ par exchanged for (0.005) share new Common 1¢ par 08/05/2009
New Common 1¢ par reclassified as Class A Common 1¢ par 10/21/2011
Name changed to Dial Global, Inc. 12/12/2011
Dial Global, Inc. name changed to Westwood One, Inc. (New) 11/25/2013
(See Westwood One, Inc. (New))

WESTWORLD, INC. (DE)
Name changed to Westworld Resources, Inc. 7/25/88
Westworld Resources, Inc. merged into Battle Mountain Gold Co. 5/28/91 which merged into Newmont Mining Corp. 1/10/2001

WESTWORLD CMNTY HEALTHCARE INC (DE)
Plan of reorganization under Chapter 11 Federal Bankruptcy proceedings confirmed 03/12/1992
No stockholders' equity

WESTWORLD RES INC (DE)
Merged into Battle Mountain Gold Co. 5/28/91
Each share Common $1 par exchanged for (0.2779033) share Common 10¢ par
Battle Mountain Gold Co. merged into Newmont Mining Corp. 1/10/2001

WESUMAT HLDG AKTIENGESELLSCHAFT (GERMANY)
Name changed to Washtec AG 05/17/2000
(See Washtec AG)

WET SEAL INC (DE)
Class A Common 10¢ par split (3) for (2) by issuance of (0.5) additional share payable 07/24/2001 to holders of record 07/16/2001 Ex date - 07/25/2001
Class A Common 10¢ par split (3) for (2) by issuance of (0.5) additional share payable 05/09/2002 to holders of record 04/25/2002 Ex date - 05/10/2002
Plan of reorganization under Chapter 11 Federal Bankruptcy proceedings effective 12/31/2015
No stockholders' equity

WETHERILL GEO D & CO INC (PA)
Preferred called for redemption 06/01/1947
Common $100 par changed to $25 par and (3) additional shares issued 07/12/1963
Name changed to G.D.W. Corp. 05/06/1968
(See G.D.W. Corp.)

WETHERLY VENTURE ASSOC INC (DE)
Name changed to Magic Restaurants, Inc. 09/30/1988
Magic Restaurants, Inc. name changed to Redheads, Inc. 03/00/1997
(See Redheads, Inc.)

WETHERSFIELD CO.
Dissolved in 1940

WETJET INTL LTD (DE)
Name changed to W-J International Ltd. (DE) 04/01/1993
W-J International Ltd. (DE) reincorporated in Nevada 10/24/2003 which recapitalized as InZon Corp. 09/22/2004
(See InZon Corp.)

WETSONS CORP (NY)
Merged into Nathan's Famous, Inc. 04/17/1978
Each share Common 10¢ par exchanged for (1/6) share Common 10¢ par
(See Nathan's Famous, Inc.)

WETTERAU INC (MO)
Name changed 09/04/1973
Name changed from Wetterau Foods, Inc. to Wetterau Inc. 09/04/1973
Common $1 par split (2) for (1) by issuance of (1) additional share 10/08/1987
Stock Dividends - 100% 12/31/1964; 50% 09/13/1968; 50% 09/15/1969; 25% 08/22/1972; 10% 08/06/1976
Merged into Supervalu Inc. 10/29/1992
Each share Common $1 par exchanged for $30.25 cash

WETTERAU MARKETING, INC. (PA)
Preferred Ser. A $10 par called for redemption 2/29/88
Public interest eliminated

WETTERAU PPTYS INC (MO)
Merged into Supervalu Inc. 06/01/1994
Each share Common 1¢ par exchanged for $22 cash

WEW VENTURES INC (BC)
Name changed to Independence Resources Inc. 05/11/1994
Independence Resources Inc. name changed to iLoveTV Entertainment Inc. 01/15/2002
(See iLoveTV Entertainment Inc.)

WEWEARABLES INC (NV)
Name changed to Asia Training Institute, Inc. 02/29/2016
Asia Training Institute, Inc. name changed to Po Yuen Cultural Holdings (Hong Kong) Co., Ltd. 12/06/2017

WEWOKA PETROLEUM CORP. (OK)
Dissolved 12/9/53

WEX PHARMACEUTICALS INC (CANADA)
Common no par reclassified as Restricted Vtg. Shares no par 10/23/2007
Acquired by Pharmagesic (Holdings) Inc. 05/05/2011
Each Restricted Vtg. Share no par exchanged for $0.14 cash
Note: Unexchanged certificates were cancelled and became without value 05/05/2017

WEX TECHNOLOGIES INC (CANADA)
Recapitalized as International Wex Technologies Inc. 08/28/1996

Each share Common no par exchanged for (0.14285714) share Common no par
International Wex Technologies Inc. name changed to WEX Pharmaceuticals Inc. 10/22/2004
(See WEX Pharmaceuticals Inc.)

WEXFORD MINES LTD. (ON)
Completely liquidated 08/28/1968
Each share Capital Stock $1 par received first and final distribution of (1) share Madeleine Mines Ltd. Common no par
Note: Certificates were not required to be surrendered and are without value
Madeleine Mines Ltd. name changed to North American Palladium Ltd. (Old) 07/07/1993 which reorganized as North American Palladium Ltd. (New) 08/10/2015

WEXFORD TECHNOLOGY INC (UT)
Each (2.7) shares old Common $0.001 par exchanged for (1) share new Common $0.001 par 05/23/1994
Each share new Common $0.001 par exchanged again for (0.2) share new Common $0.001 par 12/15/1997
Each share new Common $0.001 par exchanged again for (1/6) share new Common $0.001 par 05/25/1999
Name changed to sureBET Casinos, Inc. 06/24/1999
(See sureBET Casinos, Inc.)

WEYENBERG SHOE MFG CO (WI)
Each share Common no par exchanged for (3) shares Common $1 par in 1937
Common $1 par split (3) for (2) by issuance of (0.5) additional share 7/1/77
Stock Dividend - In Conv. Class B Common to holders of Common - 100% 6/5/87
Name changed to Weyco Group, Inc. 4/25/90

WEYERHAEUSER CO (WA)
$6.75 Conv. Preferred Ser. A no par called for redemption 09/25/1972
$2.75 Conv. 2nd Preferred 1st Ser. no par called for redemption 09/24/1973
$4.50 Conv. Preference Ser. A $1 par called for redemption 07/11/1986
$2.80 Conv. Preferred 1st Ser. $1 par called for redemption 03/13/1987
Market Auction Preferred Ser. B called for redemption 07/31/1990
$2.625 Conv. Exchangeable Preference $1 par called for redemption 09/15/1990
Each share 6.375% Mandatory Conv. Preference Ser. A $1 par automatically became (1.6929) shares Common $1.25 par 07/01/2016
(Additional Information in Active)

WEYERHAEUSER LTD (CANADA)
Each Non-Vtg. Exchangeable Share no par exchanged for (1) share Weyerhaeuser Co. Common $1.25 par 04/29/2008

WEYERHAEUSER TIMBER CO. (WA)
Each share Capital Stock no par exchanged for (2) shares Capital Stock $25 par 00/00/1950
Capital Stock $25 par changed to $7.50 par and (3) additional shares issued 01/10/1956
Name changed to Weyerhaeuser Co. 09/01/1959

WEYMIN MNG CORP (BC)
Recapitalized as GCP Mining Corp. 09/10/2002
Each (15) shares Common no par exchanged for (1) share Common no par
GCP Mining Corp. name changed to Kodiak Exploration Ltd. 09/08/2003

WEY-WHE

WEYMOUTH LIGHT & POWER CO. (MA) (continued from previous)
which name changed to Prodigy Gold Inc. 01/04/2011

WEYMOUTH LIGHT & POWER CO. (MA)
Merged into New England Electric System on a (2.8) for (1) basis 6/30/59
(See New England Electric System)

WFI INDS LTD (CANADA)
Reincorporated 08/28/1997
Reincorporated 09/13/2004
Place of incorporation changed from (BC) to (ON) 08/28/1997
Place of incorporation changed from (ON) to (Canada) 09/13/2004
Name changed to WaterFurnace Renewable Energy, Inc. 06/16/2008
(See WaterFurnace Renewable Energy, Inc.)

WFS BANCORP INC (DE)
Merged into Emprise Bank (Wichita, KS) 09/18/1996
Each share Common 1¢ par exchanged for $23.25 cash

WFS FINL INC (CA)
Stock Dividend - 10% payable 08/09/1996 to holders of record 07/19/1996
Merged into Wachovia Corp. (Ctfs. dated after 09/01/2001) 03/01/2006
Each share Common no par exchanged for (1.4661) shares Common $3.33-1/3 par
Wachovia Corp. (Ctfs. dated after 09/01/2001) merged into Wells Fargo & Co. (New) 12/31/2008

WGI HEAVY MINERALS (BC)
Acquired by Opta Minerals Inc. 11/14/2012
Each share Common no par exchanged for $0.60 cash

WGL ENTMT HLDGS INC (DE)
Each share old Common $0.001 par exchanged for (0.01) share new Common $0.001 par 02/20/2007
Each share new Common $0.001 par exchanged again for (0.005) share new Common $0.001 par 02/25/2008
Recapitalized as Heathrow Natural Food & Beverage Inc. 03/09/2009
Each (300) shares Common $0.001 par exchanged for (1) share Common $0.001 par

WGL HLDGS INC (VA)
Acquired by AltaGas Ltd. 07/06/2018
Each share Common $1 par exchanged for $88.25 cash

WGNB CORP (GA)
Common $2.50 par changed to $1.25 par and (1) additional share issued payable 04/15/1999 to holders of record 02/22/1999
Common $1.25 par split (3) for (2) by issuance of (0.5) additional share payable 11/15/2006 to holders of record 10/16/2006
Principal asset placed in receivership 01/29/2010
Stockholders' equity unlikely

WHALE ELECTRS INC (TN)
Name changed to Whale, Inc. 1/31/69
(See Whale, Inc.)

WHALE INC (TN)
Adjudicated bankrupt 5/20/70
No stockholders' equity

WHALEN FULLERTON CORP (IL)
Completely liquidated
Each share Capital Stock $2.50 par exchanged for first and final distribution of $140 cash 01/17/1985

WHALEY CO., INC. (TX)
Liquidation for cash completed 4/30/65

WHAM INC (FL)
Recapitalized as Berith Holdings Corp. 06/12/2017
Each share Common no par exchanged for (0.00333333) share Common no par
Berith Holdings Corp. name changed to Syntrol Corp. 11/29/2017

WHAM O MFG CO (CA)
Merged into Kransco 10/15/1982
Each share Common 5¢ par exchanged for $16 cash

WHARF HLDGS LTD (HONG KONG)
Each Unsponsored ADR for Ordinary HKD $10 par exchanged for (1) Sponsored ADR for Ordinary HKD $10 par 09/16/1992
Stock Dividends - 10% 10/15/1986; 10% 10/26/1989
ADR agreement terminated 06/19/1997
Each Sponsored ADR for Ordinary HKD $10 par exchanged for (0.2) share Ordinary HKD $10 par
(Additional Information in Active)

WHARF RES LTD (BC)
Merged into Goldcorp Inc. 12/11/1996
Each share Common no par exchanged for $9 cash
Adjustable Rate Exchangeable Preferred
$25 par called for redemption 12/30/1996
Public interest eliminated

WHARTON BK & TR CO (WHARTON, TX)
Name changed to Heritage Bank (Wharton, TX) 12/14/1992
(See Heritage Bank (Wharton, TX))

WHAT A WORLD INC (DE)
Name changed to TeleHubLink Corp. 02/04/1999
(See TeleHubLink Corp.)

WHATIFI FDS (DE)
Name changed to Van Ness Funds 05/01/2001
(See Van Ness Funds)

WHATS-ONLINE COM INC (AB)
Recapitalized as Great Pacific International Inc. 10/16/2001
Each share Common no par exchanged for (0.1) share Common no par
Great Pacific International Inc. recapitalized as WesCan Energy Corp. 10/04/2012

WHATSFORFREE TECHNOLOGIES INC (NV)
Stock Dividend - 10% payable 03/30/2000 to holders of record 01/31/2000
Recapitalized as Krifter Holdings Inc. 04/18/2005
Each (15) shares Common $0.001 par exchanged for (1) share Common $0.001 par
(See Krifter Holdings Inc.)

WHATSONLINE COM INC (NV)
Name changed to Entheos Technologies Inc. and (1) additional share issued 07/31/2000
Entheos Technologies Inc. name changed to Janus Resources, Inc. 02/14/2011 which name changed to RenovaCare, Inc. 01/09/2014

WHATSUPMUSIC COM INC (NV)
Name changed to New Millennium Development Group 05/14/2001
New Millennium Development Group name changed to Millennium National Events, Inc. 10/05/2004 which recapitalized as Extensions, Inc. 08/24/2007
(See Extensions, Inc.)

WHATTOZEE NETWORKS INC (BC)
Name changed to Chemistree Technology Inc. 08/04/2017

WHDH CORP (MA)
Merged into Blair (John) & Co. 01/18/1974
Each share Common no par or VTC's for Common no par exchanged for $33 cash

WHEATENA CORP (DE)
Preferred $100 par called for redemption 11/30/65
In process of liquidation
Each share Common no par exchanged for initial distribution of $2 cash 12/21/66
Each share Common no par received second distribution of $2 cash 12/11/67
Each share Common no par received third distribution of $2 cash 12/3/68
Each share Common no par received fourth distribution of $1.50 cash 12/2/69
Note: Details on subsequent distributions, if any, are not available

WHEATLAND BK (DAVENPORT, WA)
Stock Dividend - 8% payable 03/03/1998 to holders of record 02/05/1998
Under plan of reorganization each share Common $30 par automatically became (1) share Community Financial Group, Inc. Common no par 12/31/1998

WHEATLEY FOODS, INC.
Name changed to Shedd-Bartush Foods, Inc. in 1949
Shedd-Bartush Foods, Inc. merged into Beatrice Foods Co. 5/26/59 which name changed to Beatrice Companies, Inc. 6/5/84
(See Beatrice Companies, Inc.)

WHEATLEY MAYONNAISE CO.
Name changed to Wheatley Foods, Inc. in 1947
Wheatley Foods, Inc. name changed to Shedd-Bartush Foods, Inc. in 1949 which merged into Beatrice Foods Co. 5/26/59 which name changed to Beatrice Companies, Inc. 6/5/84
(See Beatrice Companies, Inc.)

WHEATLEY TXT CORP (DE)
Merged into Dresser Industries, Inc. (New) 8/5/94
Each share Common 1¢ par exchanged for (0.7) share Common 25¢ par
Dresser Industries, Inc. (New) merged into Halliburton Co. 9/29/98

WHEATMAN PETROLEUM, LTD. (AB)
Struck off the register and deemed to have been dissolved 3/31/55

WHEATON INDUSTRIES, INC. (DE)
Completely liquidated 8/27/64
Each share Common 10¢ par exchanged for (0.5) share Lowell Toy Manufacturing Corp. Common 50¢ par
Lowell Toy Manufacturing Corp. name changed to Lowell Corp. 11/25/64 which charter cancelled 12/15/69

WHEATON RIV MINERALS LTD (ON)
Merged into Goldcorp Inc. 04/15/2005
Each share Common no par exchanged for (0.25) share Common no par

WHEATSWORTH, INC.
Acquired by National Biscuit Co. 00/00/1931
Details not available

WHEEL GOODS CORP (DE)
Adjudicated bankrupt 12/09/1975
Stockholders' equity unlikely

WHEEL OF BARGAINS INC (AZ)
Name changed to Envira Minerals, Inc. (AZ) 05/20/1997
Envira Minerals, Inc. (AZ) reorganized in Nevada as KoreaStation Inc. 05/01/2000 which name changed to E4World Corp. 01/01/2001 which name changed to Xcelplus Global Holdings, Inc. 08/18/2006 which name changed to Clean Energy Pathways, Inc. 02/04/2011

WHEELABRATOR CORP (DE)
$1.50 Conv. Preferred $35 par called for redemption 7/26/71
Merged into Wheelabrator-Frye Inc. 11/4/71
Each share Common $1 par exchanged for (5.5) shares Common 10¢ par
Wheelabrator-Frye Inc. merged into Signal Companies, Inc. 2/1/83 which merged into Allied-Signal Inc. 9/19/85 which name changed to AlliedSignal Inc. 4/26/93 which name changed to Honeywell International Inc. 12/1/99

WHEELABRATOR FRYE INC (DE)
Each share Common 10¢ par exchanged for (0.33333333) share Common 30¢ par 08/01/1972
Merged into Signal Companies, Inc. 02/01/1983
Each share 8.25% Conv. Preferred Ser. A $1 par exchanged for (1) share 8.25% Conv. Preferred Ser. A $1 par
Each share Conv. Preferred Ser. B $1 par exchanged for (1) share Conv. Preferred Ser. B $1 par
Each share Common 30¢ par exchanged for (2) shares Common $2 par
Signal Companies, Inc. merged into Allied-Signal, Inc. 09/19/1985 which name changed to AlliedSignal Inc. 04/26/1993 which name changed to Honeywell International Inc. 12/01/1999

WHEELABRATOR TECHNOLOGIES INC NEW (DE)
Recapitalized 8/24/89
Recapitalized from Wheelabrator Group Inc. to Wheelabrator Technologies Inc. (New) 8/24/89
Each share Common 1¢ par exchanged for (0.25) share Common 1¢ par
Under plan of merger each share old Common 1¢ par exchanged for (0.574) share new Common 1¢ par and (0.469) share Waste Management, Inc. Common $1 par 9/7/90
New Common 1¢ par split (2) for (1) by issuance of (1) additional share 4/8/91
New Common 1¢ par split (2) for (1) by issuance of (1) additional share 1/7/93
Merged into Waste Management, Inc. (New) 3/30/98
Each share new Common 1¢ par exchanged for $16.50 cash

WHEELABRATOR TECHNOLOGIES INC OLD (DE)
Merged into Wheelabrator Technologies Inc. (New) 8/24/89
Each share Common 1¢ par exchanged for (0.845) share Common 1¢ par
(See Wheelabrator Technologies Inc. (New))

WHEELED COACH INDS INC (FL)
Merged into Collins Industries, Inc. 06/01/1985
Each share Common 50¢ par exchanged for $3 cash

WHEELER, OSGOOD CO. (WA)
Liquidation approved 4/4/52

WHEELER FIBRE GLASS BOAT CORP. (DE)
Reported out of business 00/00/1961
Charter revoked for non-payment of taxes 04/01/1963

WHEELER METAL PRODUCTS CORP.
Bankrupt in 1932

WHEELING & LAKE ERIE RY CO (OH)
Merged into Norfolk Southern Corp. 09/20/1988

Each share 4% Prior Lien $100 par exchanged for $100 cash
Each share Common $100 par exchanged for $110 cash

WHEELING DLR SVGS & TR CO (WHEELING, WV)
Each share Capital Stock $100 par exchanged for (4) shares Capital Stock $25 par 00/00/1945
Stock Dividend - 100% 07/01/1965
Reorganized as Wesbanco, Inc. 01/01/1977
Each share Capital Stock $25 par exchanged for (1) share Common $25 par

WHEELING FIRE INSURANCE CO. OF WHEELING (WV)
Acquired by Southern Fire Insurance Co. (Durham, NC) 00/00/1933
Details not available

WHEELING MACH PRODS CO (WV)
Stock Dividends - 100% 07/01/1970; 100% 07/21/1976
Merged into Joy Manufacturing Co. 07/29/1977
Each share Capital Stock $10 par exchanged for (0.86) share Common $1 par
Joy Manufacturing Co. merged into Joy Technologies Inc. 06/24/1987
(See Joy Technologies Inc.)

WHEELING MOULD & FOUNDRY CO.
Merged into Continental Roll & Steel Foundry Co. in 1930 which name was changed to Continental Foundry & Machine Co. in 1944 which completed liquidation 11/25/58
(See Continental Foundry & Machine Co.)

WHEELING PITTSBURGH CORP (DE)
Under plan of reorganization each share Conv. Preferred Ser. A 10¢ par and Common 1¢ par automatically became (1) share WHX Corp. Conv. Preferred Ser. A 10¢ par or Common 1¢ par respectively 07/26/1994
(See WHX Corp.)
Merged into Esmark, Inc. (Inc. 02/24/1986) 11/27/2007
Each share new Common 1¢ par exchanged for (1) share Common 1¢ par
(See Esmark, Inc. (Inc. 02/24/1986))

WHEELING PITTSBURGH STL CORP (DE)
Reorganized under Chapter 11 Federal Bankruptcy Code as Wheeling-Pittsburgh Corp. 01/03/1991
Each share Preferred Ser. A $25 par exchanged for (0.2808) share Common 1¢ par
Each share $5 Preferred no par exchanged for (2.3136) shares Common 1¢ par
Each share 6% Prior Preferred $100 par exchanged for (3.1108) shares Common 1¢ par
Each share Common $10 par exchanged for (0.3402) share Common 1¢ par and (0.391) Common Stock Purchase Warrant expiring 01/03/1996
Wheeling-Pittsburgh Corp. reorganized as WHX Corp. 07/26/1994
(See WHX Corp.)

WHEELING ROOFING & CORNICE CO. (WV)
Proclaimed dissolved for non-payment of taxes 3/6/09

WHEELING STL CORP (DE)
Each share 8% Preferred $100 par exchanged for (1.333334) shares 6% Preferred $100 par 00/00/1931
Each share 10% Preferred $100 par exchanged for (1.404) shares 6% Preferred $100 par 00/00/1931
Each share Common $100 par exchanged for (1) share Common no par 00/00/1931
Each share 6% Preferred $100 par exchanged for (1) share $5 Conv. Preferred no par and (0.5) share Common no par 08/31/1937
Common no par changed to $10 par 04/27/1955
Stock Dividends - 100% 05/15/1950; 25% 10/25/1950; 10% 10/14/1955
Under plan of merger name changed to Wheeling-Pittsburgh Steel Corp. 12/05/1968
Wheeling-Pittsburgh Steel Corp. reorganized as Wheeling-Pittsburgh Corp. 01/03/1991 which reorganized as WHX Corp. 07/26/1994
(See WHX Corp.)

WHEELING TILE CO. (WV)
Adjudicated bankrupt 3/4/65
No stockholders' equity

WHEELING WHSL GROCERY CO (WV)
Charter revoked 12/07/2001

WHEELOCK & CO LTD (HONG KONG)
ADR agreement terminated 06/16/1997
Each Sponsored ADR for Ordinary HK$0.50 par exchanged for (0.1) share Ordinary HK$0.50 par
(Additional Information in Active)

WHEELOCK MARDEN & CO LTD (HONG KONG)
Stock Dividend - 10% 08/15/1981
Merged into HongKong & Kowloon Wharf & Godown Co., Ltd. 09/18/1985
Each ADR for A Ordinary HKD $1 par exchanged for $4.70 cash

WHEELS, INC. (NY)
Capital Stock no par changed to $1 par and (9) additional shares issued 4/9/64
Acquired by Gulf & Western Industries, Inc. (Del.) 5/17/68
(See Gulf & Western Industries, Inc. (Del.))

WHEELS GROUP INC (ON)
Merged into Radiant Logistics, Inc. 04/08/2015
Each share Common no par exchanged for (0.151384) share Common $0.001 par
Note: Unexchanged certificates will be cancelled and become without value 04/08/2021

WHEELS SPORTS GROUP INC (NC)
Merged into Racing Champions Corp. 06/12/1998
Each share Common 1¢ par exchanged for (0.51) share Common 1¢ par
Racing Champions Corp. name changed to Racing Champions Ertl Corp. 04/03/2002 which name changed to RC2 Corp. 04/09/2003
(See RC2 Corp.)

WHELCHEL MINES CO. (ID)
Charter revoked for failure to file reports and pay fees 11/30/64

WHEREHOUSE ENTMT INC NEW (DE)
Plan of reorganization under Chapter 11 Federal Bankruptcy Code effective 6/1/2004
No stockholders' equity

WHEREHOUSE ENTMT INC OLD (DE)
Common 1¢ par split (5) for (4) by issuance of (0.25) additional share 8/15/86
Stock Dividends - 25% 10/15/84; 25% 11/13/85
Merged into Adler & Shaykin 2/23/88
Each share Common 1¢ par exchanged for $14 cash

WHEREVER NET HLDG CORP (CAYMAN ISLANDS)
Issue Information - 4,500,000 ADR'S offered at $9 per ADR on 05/02/2000
ADR agreement terminated 04/25/2011
No ADR holders' equity

WHERIFY WIRELESS INC (DE)
SEC revoked common stock registration 06/27/2012

WHETSTONE MINERALS INC (AB)
Reincorporated under the laws of Channel Islands as Whetstone Minerals Ltd. 11/20/2009

WHETSTONE MINERALS LTD (JERSEY)
Voluntarily dissolved 11/21/2014
Details not available

WHG BANCSHARES CORP (MD)
Merged into Baltimore County Savings Bank, F.S.B. (Baltimore, MD) 7/24/2002
Each share Common 10¢ par exchanged for $14.25 cash

WHG RESORTS & CASINOS INC (DE)
Merged into Patriot American Hospitality Inc. 1/16/98
Each share Common 50¢ par exchanged for (0.784) Paired Certificate
Patriot American Hospitality Inc. merged into Wyndham International, Inc. 6/29/99
(See Wyndham International, Inc.)

WHIDBEY IS BK (COUPEVILLE, WA)
Under plan of reorganization each share Common $20 par automatically became (1) share Washington Banking Co. Common no par 04/30/1996
Washington Banking Co. merged into Heritage Financial Corp. 05/01/2014

WHIPOORWILL CORP.
Bankrupt in 1934

WHIPPANY ELECTRS INC (NJ)
Name changed to Technology General Corp. 07/22/1981

WHIPPANY PAPER BRD INC (NJ)
Merged into Neu (Hugo) & Co. 12/24/1986
Each share Common 10¢ par exchanged for $2.50 cash
Each share Class B 10¢ par exchanged for $2.50 cash

WHIPPLE (J.R.) CORP.
Liquidated in 1933

WHIPSAW MINES LTD. (BC)
Name changed to Whipsaw Resources Ltd. 3/27/74

WHIPSAW RES LTD (BC)
Struck off register and declared dissolved for failure to file returns 2/25/83

WHIRLDWIND VENTURES INC (DE)
Name changed to Direct III Marketing, Inc. 4/24/99
Direct III Marketing, Inc. name changed to Education Lending Group, Inc. 5/21/2002

WHIRLPOOL CORP. (NY)
Under plan of merger each share Common $5 par exchanged (2) for (1) in 1952
Stock Dividend - 100% 12/31/54
Merged into Whirlpool-Seeger Corp. share for share 9/15/55 which name was changed to Whirlpool Corp. (Del.) 4/1/57

WHIRLPOOL CORP (DE)
4.25% Conv. Preferred $80 par called for redemption 04/01/1965
(Additional Information in Active)

WHIRLPOOL FINL CORP (DE)
144A Preferred Ser. A called for redemption at $100 on 09/01/1998
6.09% 144A Preferred Ser. C called for redemption at $100 on 02/01/2002
144A Preferred Ser. B called for redemption at $100 on 09/02/2008

WHIRLPOOL SEEGER CORP (DE)
Under plan of merger name changed to Whirlpool Corp. (Del.) 4/1/57

WHIRLY BALL INTL INC (NV)
Name changed to National Entertainment Corp. 12/4/84
National Entertainment Corp. recapitalized as Major Video Corp. 3/16/87 which merged into Blockbuster Entertainment Corp. 1/17/89 which merged into Viacom Inc. (Old) 9/30/94
(See Viacom Inc. (Old))

WHISKEY CREEK RES INC (BC)
Recapitalized as ARC Pacific Metals Ltd. 03/02/1998
Each share Common no par exchanged for (0.25) share Common no par
ARC Pacific Metals Ltd. recapitalized as Rampart Ventures Ltd. 03/06/2000 which name changed to RPT Uranium Corp. 02/23/2007 which name changed to RPT Resources Ltd. (BC) 06/05/2009 which reincorporated in Alberta as ArPetrol Ltd. 04/08/2011

WHISPERING OAKS INTL INC (TX)
Reincorporated under the laws of Nevada as BioCurex Inc. 03/16/2001

WHISTLER BLACKCOMB HLDGS INC OLD (BC)
Merged into Vail Resorts, Inc. 10/17/2016
Each share Common no par exchanged for (0.097294) share Common 1¢ par and $17.50 cash
Note: Opiton to receive 1068877 B.C. Ltd. Exchangeable Shares in lieu of Common expired 10/12/2016
Unexchanged certificates will be cancelled and become without value 10/17/2022
1068877 B.C. Ltd. name changed to Whistler Blackcomb Holdings Inc. (New) 10/20/2016

WHISTLER GOLD CORP (BC)
Name changed to Svit Gold Corp. 08/11/2008
Svit Gold Corp. name changed to Catalyst Copper Corp. 02/02/2010 which merged into NewCastle Gold Ltd. 05/27/2016 which merged into Equinox Gold Corp. 12/22/2017

WHISTLER INVTS INC (NV)
Each share old Common $0.001 par exchanged for (0.1) share new Common $0.001 par 07/11/2003
Each share new Common $0.001 par exchanged again for (3) shares Common $0.001 par 03/10/2004
Each share new Common $0.001 par exchanged again for (3) shares new Common $0.001 par 11/19/2004
Stock Dividend - 10% payable 03/04/2005 to holders of record 02/28/2005 Ex date - 02/24/2005
Recapitalized as Hybrid Technologies, Inc. 03/09/2005
Each share new Common $0.001 par exchanged for (0.1) share Common $0.001 par
Hybrid Technologies, Inc. recapitalized as EV Innovations, Inc. 02/19/2009 which recapitalized as Li-ion Motors Corp. 02/01/2010 which recapitalized as Terra Inventions Corp. 12/21/2012
(See Terra Inventions Corp.)

WHISTLER PETES LTD (AB)
Acquired by Ratel Resources Ltd. 00/00/1976
Each share Capital Stock exchanged for $0.74 cash

WHITACRE-GREER CO (OH)
Name changed 05/03/2006
Name changed from Whitacre-Greer Fireproofing Co. to Whitacre-Greer Co. 05/03/2006
Class A Preferred $1 par called for redemption at $4.395 on 04/16/2012
Class A Preferred $1 par called for redemption at $3.93 on 04/16/2012

WHITAKER BATTERY SUPPLY CO.
Name changed to Whitaker Cable Corp. 00/00/1944
Whitaker Cable Corp. name changed to Murphy Industries Inc. 02/21/1984
(See Murphy Industries Inc.)

WHITAKER CABLE CORP (DE)
Each share Common no par exchanged for (4) shares Common $1 par in 1947
Common $1 par split (2) for (1) by issuance of (1) additional share 3/15/67
Common $1 par split (3) for (2) by issuance of (0.5) additional share 12/6/72
Stock Dividend - 100% 9/16/63
Name changed to Murphy Industries Inc. 2/21/84
(See Murphy Industries Inc.)

WHITAKER METALS CORP. (MO)
Merged into Universal Minerals & Metals, Inc. on a (0.2) for (1) basis 4/6/62
Universal Minerals & Metals, Inc. adjudicated bankrupt 2/4/70

WHITAKER OIL CO (TX)
Charter forfeited for failure to pay taxes 03/16/1981

WHITAKER PAPER CO. (OH)
Each share old Common no par exchanged for (4) shares new Common no par 1/24/48
Acquired by Champion Papers Inc. on a (2.5) for (1) basis 2/28/62
Champion Papers Inc. merged into U.S. Plywood-Champion Papers Inc. 2/28/67 which name changed to Champion International Corp. 5/12/72 which merged into International Paper Co. 6/20/2000

WHITALL TATUM CO.
Acquired by Armstrong Cork Co. in 1938
Details not available

WHITCOMB (GEORGE D.) CO.
Sold at foreclosure sale in 1930

WHITE & WYCKOFF MANUFACTURING CO. (MA)
Recapitalized 00/00/1935
Each share Preferred $100 par exchanged for (1) share Preferred $75 par and (2) shares Common no par
Each share Class A Common $5 par exchanged for (1) share Common no par
Class B Common $5 par cancelled
Acquired by Western Tablet & Stationery Corp. 02/27/1961
Each share Common no par exchanged for (1) share Common no par
Western Tablet & Stationery Corp. name changed to Westab Inc. 03/04/1964 which merged into Mead Corp. 05/31/1966
(See Mead Corp.)

WHITE ACCEPTANCE CORP. (DE)
Liquidation completed 3/23/51

WHITE ACQUISITION GROUP INC (NM)
Recapitalized as Nattem USA Inc. 1/4/93
Each share Common no par exchanged for (0.5) share Common no par
Nattem USA Inc. name changed to Comtec International, Inc. 10/26/95

WHITE AIRCRAFT (CANADA) LTD.
Name changed to White-Bellanca Aircraft (Canada) Ltd. which was changed back to original name and then changed to White Canadian Aircraft Ltd. in 1940 which was liquidated in 1950

WHITE AVIONICS CORP. (DE)
Common 10¢ par reclassified as Class A Common 10¢ par 4/13/61
Assets sold 1/13/65
No equity for holders of Class A Common 10¢ par

WHITE BEAR RES INC (BC)
Each share old Common no par exchanged for (0.5) share new Common no par 10/15/2010
Each share new Common no par exchanged again for (0.1) share new Common no par 09/20/2013
Name changed to Tinkerine Studios Ltd. 04/14/2014

WHITE-BELLANCA AIRCRAFT (CANADA) LTD.
Name changed to White Aircraft (Canada) Ltd. and then to White Canadian Aircraft Ltd. in 1940 which was liquidated in 1950

WHITE CANADIAN AIRCRAFT LTD.
Liquidated in 1950

WHITE CANYON MINING CO. (CO)
Acquired by Yuba Consolidated Industries, Inc. 01/29/1960
Each share Common 33-1/3¢ par exchanged for (0.03) share Common $1 par and $0.09 cash
Yuba Consolidated Industries, Inc. reorganized as Yuba Industries, Inc. (DE) 12/06/1965
(See Yuba Industries, Inc. (DE))

WHITE CANYON URANIUM LTD (AUSTRALIA)
Acquired by Denison Mines Corp. 07/12/2011
Each share Ordinary exchanged for AUD $0.24 cash

WHITE CAP INDS INC (DE)
Merged into Leonard Green & Partners, L.P. 3/10/2000
Each share Common 1¢ par exchanged for $16.50 cash

WHITE CAPS EXTENSION MINES CO. (NV)
Name changed to Silver Empire, Inc. 9/13/68
Silver Empire, Inc. name changed to Du Pont Energy Control Corp. 12/1/78
(See Du Pont Energy Control Corp.)

WHITE CAPS GOLD MNG CO (NV)
Common 10¢ par changed to 4¢ par 1/29/67
Recapitalized as Transworld Energy Corp. 5/7/76
Each share Common 4¢ par exchanged for (0.02) share Common 10¢ par
(See Transworld Energy Corp.)

WHITE CLOUD EXPL INC (UT)
Each (173) shares old Common $0.001 par exchanged for (1) share new Common $0.001 par 6/30/97
Name changed to Watchout Inc. 11/23/98
Watchout Inc. name changed to Cormax Business Solutions Inc. 4/2/2001 which recapitalized as Sure Trace Security Corp. 2/4/2003

WHITE (DAVID) CO. (WI)
Reincorporated under the laws of Delaware as Realist, Inc. 00/00/1950
Realist, Inc. name changed to White (David), Inc. (DE) 12/15/1989 which reincorporated in (WI) 05/05/1992
(See David White Inc. (WI))

WHITE (S.S.) CO. (PA)
Merged into Pennsalt Chemicals Corp. 7/1/66
Each share Capital Stock $10 par exchanged for (0.5) share $2.50 Conv. Preference $1 par
Pennsalt Chemicals Corp. merged into Pennwalt Corp. 3/31/69
(See Pennwalt Corp.)

WHITE CONS INDS INC (DE)
$3 Conv. Preferred $50 par called for redemption 11/15/65
Common $1 par split (2) for (1) by issuance of (1) additional share 7/11/66
$2 Prior Preference $50 par called for redemption 2/1/68
Recapitalized under plan of merger 3/27/68
Each share 5-1/2% Preferred $50 par exchanged for (1) share $3 Preferred Ser. A $50 par
Each share $2.75 Class B Preferred $50 par exchanged for (1) share $3 Preferred Ser. B $50 par
Common $1 par split (2) for (1) by issuance of (1) additional share 7/23/68
Merged into AB Electrolux 4/30/86
Each share Common $1 par exchanged for $47 cash
$3 Preferred Ser. A $50 par called for redemption 5/12/86
$3 Preferred Ser. B $50 par called for redemption 5/12/86
$3 Preferred Ser. C $50 par called for redemption 5/12/86
Public interest eliminated

WHITE CNTY BANCSHARES INC (GA)
Acquired by United Community Banks, Inc. 09/01/1995
Details not available

WHITE CNTY BK (CLEVELAND, GA)
Reorganized as White County Bancshares, Inc. 08/23/1984
Each share Common $10 par exchanged for (1) share Common $10 par
(See White County Bancshares, Inc.)

WHITE CROSS DISC CTRS (CA)
Charter suspended for failure to file reports and pay fees 05/01/1978

WHITE CROSS STORES INC (PA)
Common $1 par changed to 50¢ par and (1) additional share issued 07/06/1967
Merged into Revco D.S., Inc. 07/06/1972
Each share Common 50¢ par exchanged for (0.75) share Common $1 par
(See Revco D.S., Inc.)

WHITE, (S.S.) DENTAL MANUFACTURING CO. (PA)
Each share Capital Stock $100 par exchanged for (5) shares Capital Stock $20 par in 1929
Capital Stock $20 par changed to $10 par and (1) additional share issued 4/21/64
Name changed to White (S.S.) Co. 4/12/65
White (S.S.) Co. merged into Pennsalt Chemicals Corp. 7/1/66 which merged into Pennwalt Corp. 3/31/69
(See Pennwalt Corp.)

WHITE DENTAL SUPPLY INC (NV)
Common $0.001 par split (9) for (1) by issuance of (8) additional shares payable 07/17/2008 to holders of record 06/18/2008 Ex date - 07/18/2008
Name changed to Pitooey!, Inc. 02/07/2013
Pitooey!, Inc. name changed to Raadr, Inc. 10/13/2015

WHITE DEVELOPMENT CO. (MT)
Bankrupt in 1960

WHITE DRUG ENTERPRISES, INC. (ND)
Merged into Farm House Foods Corp. 3/8/76
Each share Common $1 par exchanged for (1) share Conv. Preferred Ser. A $1 par
(See Farm House Foods Corp.)

WHITE EAGLE INTL INC (DE)
Each share Common 10¢ par exchanged for (0.1) share Common $1 par 5/6/64
Common $1 par changed to 10¢ par 7/10/75
Charter cancelled and declared inoperative and void for non-payment of taxes 3/1/83

WHITE EAGLE INTERNATIONAL OIL CO. (DE)
Name changed to White Eagle International, Inc. 5/23/60
(See White Eagle International, Inc.)

WHITE EAGLE OIL & REFINING CO. OF KANSAS CITY
Acquired by Standard Oil Co. of New York in 1930
(See Standard Oil Co. of New York)

WHITE EAGLE OIL CO. (DE)
Under plan of merger each share Capital Stock 10¢ par exchanged for (2.191) shares Common 10¢ par 00/00/1952
Stock Dividends - 10% 12/18/1952; 10% 01/04/1954; 10% 01/03/1955; 10% 12/15/1955; 10% 12/17/1956
Name changed to Helmerich & Payne, Inc. 08/01/1959

WHITE EAGLE URANIUM CO. (UT)
Name changed to Dax Corp. 4/15/71
(See Dax Corp.)

WHITE ELECTR DESIGNS CORP (IN)
$3 Sr. Conv. Preferred $1 par called for redemption at $25 on 02/07/2000
Merged into Microsemi Corp. 04/30/2010
Each share Common no par exchanged for $7 cash

WHITE ELECTROMAGNETICS INC (MD)
Adjudicated bankrupt 10/01/1970
Stockholders' equity unlikely

WHITE FIRE ENERGY LTD (AB)
Merged into Highpine Oil & Gas Ltd. 02/21/2006
Each share Common no par exchanged for (0.132) share Common no par
Highpine Oil & Gas Ltd. merged into Daylight Resources Trust 10/08/2009 which reorganized as Daylight Energy Ltd. 05/12/2010

WHITE (MARTHA) FOODS, INC. (TN)
See - Martha White Foods Inc.

WHITE GOLD VENTURES LTD (AB)
Name changed to Cash Canada Pawn Corp. 09/25/1992
Cash Canada Pawn Corp. recapitalized as Cash Canada Group Ltd. 01/05/1996
(See Cash Canada Group Ltd.)

WHITE GUYATT MINING CO., LTD. (ON)
Charter cancelled for failure to pay taxes and file returns 8/20/77

WHITE HAINES OPTICAL CO (OH)
4-3/4% Preferred $100 par called for redemption 12/00/1974
Public interest eliminated

WHITE HALL INVESTMENTS, INC. (DE)
Charter cancelled and declared inoperative and void for non-payment of taxes 3/1/92

WHITE HARDWARE LTD. (ON)
Name changed to Handy Andy Merchandising Corp. (Eastern) Ltd. 2/24/66

(See Handy Andy Merchandising Corp. (Eastern) Ltd.)

WHITE HAWK VENTURES INC (BC)
Recapitalized as E-Energy Ventures Inc. 01/09/2001
Each share Common no par exchanged for (0.2) share Common no par

WHITE HORSE GOLD MINES LTD.
Acquired by Jellicoe Mines (1939) Ltd. 00/00/1939
Details not available

WHITE HORSE URANIUM, INC. (NV)
Name changed to Ranrex Oil & Mining Co. 11/24/56
Ranrex Oil & Mining Co. recapitalized as Ranrex Beryllium, Inc. 4/29/60 which merged into Ranrex, Inc. 8/16/71 which merged into Argus Resources, Inc. (NV) 12/27/72 which reincorporated in Delaware as 1st Global Petroleum Group, Inc. 3/31/2005 which name changed to Commonwealth American Financial Group, Inc. 5/13/2005 which name changed to James Monroe Capital Corp. 5/30/2006

WHITE (DAVID), INC. (DE)
See - David White Inc.

WHITE (MARTHA), INC. (TN)
Name changed to White (Martha) Foods, Inc. 9/29/67
White (Martha) Foods, Inc. merged into Beatrice Foods Co. 11/18/75 which name changed to Beatrice Companies, Inc. 6/5/84
(See Beatrice Companies, Inc.)

WHITE K M CO (KY)
Merged into Armor Elevator Co., Inc. 04/14/1969
Each share Common no par exchanged for (0.256923) share Common $1 par
(See Armor Elevator Co., Inc.)

WHITE KNIGHT RES LTD (BC)
Acquired by US Gold Canadian Acquisition Corp. 07/09/2007
Each share Common no par exchanged for (0.35) Exchangeable Share no par
US Gold Canadian Acquisition Corp. exchanged for McEwen Mining Inc. 05/29/2012

WHITE KNIGHT SST INC (FL)
Name changed to Online Sales Strategies, Inc. 09/12/2005
Online Sales Strategies, Inc. recapitalized as Growth Technologies International, Inc. 12/20/2007 which recapitalized as Alternafuels, Inc. 03/18/2011
(See Alternafuels, Inc.)

WHITE KNOB COPPER & DEVELOPMENT CO. LTD.
Liquidated in 1941

WHITE LTG CO (CA)
Completely liquidated 05/31/1968
Each share Class A 25¢ par exchanged for first and final distribution of $0.50 cash

WHITE (MARTHA) MILLS, INC. (TN)
Name changed to White (Martha), Inc. 9/22/65
White (Martha), Inc. name changed to White (Martha) Foods, Inc. 9/29/67 which merged into Beatrice Foods Co. 11/18/75 which name changed to Beatrice Companies, Inc. 6/5/84
(See Beatrice Companies, Inc.)

WHITE MOTOR CO. (OH)
Capital Stock $50 par changed to $1 par in 1937
Capital Stock $50 par reclassified as Common $10 par in 1948
Common $10 par split (2) for (1) by issuance of (1) additional share 3/24/59
Common $10 par split (2) for (1) by issuance of (1) additional share 7/17/63
5-1/4% Preferred $100 par called for redemption 12/31/64
Stock Dividends - 10% 2/4/46; 15% 10/25/55
Name changed to White Motor Corp. 4/26/65
White Motor Corp. reorganized as Northeast Ohio Axle, Inc. 11/15/83 which name changed to NEOAX, Inc. (OH) 5/13/86 which reincorporated in Delaware 5/21/87 which name changed to EnviroSource, Inc. 11/14/89 which recapitalized as Envirosource, Inc. 6/22/98
(See Envirosource, Inc.)

WHITE MOTOR SECURITIES CORP.
Dissolved in 1932

WHITE MOUNTAIN TELEPHONE & TELEGRAPH CO.
Merged into New England Telephone & Telegraph Co. in 1930
(See New England Telephone & Telephone Co.)

WHITE MOUNTAIN VINEYARDS, INC. (NH)
Charter dissolved for failure to file reports and pay fees 10/31/1984

WHITE MTN INC (NV)
Name changed to Cyanotech Corp. 09/30/1983
Each share Common $0.001 par exchanged for (1) share Common $0.001 par

WHITE MTNS INS GROUP INC (DE)
Reincorporated under the laws of Bermuda as White Mountains Insurance Group, Ltd. 10/25/1999

WHITE MTR CORP (OH)
Stock Dividend - 10% 8/30/67
Reorganized as Northeast Ohio Axle, Inc. 11/15/83
Each share Common $1 par exchanged for (0.1) share Common 5¢ par
Northeast Ohio Axle, Inc. name changed to NEOAX, Inc. (OH) 5/13/86 which reincorporated in Delaware 5/21/87 which name changed to EnviroSource, Inc. 11/14/89 which recapitalized as Envirosource, Inc. 6/22/98
(See Envirosource, Inc.)

WHITE MULE GOLD PPTYS INC (DE)
Charter cancelled and declared inoperative and void for non-payment of taxes 3/1/85

WHITE OIL CO., INC. (UT)
Involuntarily dissolved 05/22/1989

WHITE PASS & YUKON LTD (CANADA)
Capital Stock no par reclassified as Common no par 10/31/68
Common no par split (2) for (1) by issuance of (1) additional share 11/29/68
Acquired by Federal Industries Ltd. 4/22/76
Each share Common no par exchanged for $9.50 cash
6-3/4% Preferred Ser. A $25 par called for redemption 5/31/88
Public interest eliminated

WHITE PINE INC (UT)
Name changed to Symphony Holding Co. 11/4/86
Symphony Holding Co. reorganized under the laws of Nevada as Symphony Ventures Inc. 3/23/94 which recapitalized as Micro-ASI International Inc. 9/6/96 which name changed to McHenry Metals Golf Corp. 4/1/97

WHITE PINE RES INC (ON)
Each share old Common no par exchanged for (0.02) share new Common no par 01/25/2017
Name changed to SBD Capital Corp. 09/15/2017

WHITE PINE SOFTWARE INC (DE)
Name changed to CUseeMe Networks Inc. 5/15/2000
CUseeMe Networks Inc. merged into First Virtual Communications, Inc. 6/19/2001
(See First Virtual Communications, Inc.)

WHITE PLAINS RES CORP (BC)
Recapitalized as American Wollastonite Mining Corp. 07/26/1994
Each share Common no par exchanged for (0.5) share Common no par
American Wollastonite Mining Corp. recapitalized as Previa Resources Ltd. 04/25/1997 which recapitalized as Rose Marie Resources Ltd. 10/18/2006 which recapitalized as Cheetah Ventures Ltd. 07/17/2008 which name changed to Emperor Minerals Ltd. 10/21/2010 which name changed to Emperor Oil Ltd. 08/24/2012

WHITE PROVISION CO.
Acquired by Swift & Co. (Ill.) in 1930
(See Swift & Co. (Ill.))

WHITE RIV CORP (DE)
Merged into WRC Merger Corp. 6/30/98
Each share Common 1¢ par exchanged for $90.85 cash

WHITE RIV MINES LTD (BC)
Recapitalized as Ventora Resources Ltd. 10/28/74
Each share Capital Stock no par exchanged for (0.2) share Capital Stock no par
Ventora Resources Ltd. recapitalized as Torrent Resources Ltd. 1/11/85 which merged into Galveston Resources Ltd. 7/29/86 which merged into Corona Corp. 7/1/88 which recapitalized as International Corona Corp. 6/11/91
(See International Corona Corp.)

WHITE RIV PETE CORP (NY)
Dissolved by proclamation 12/24/91

WHITE RIVER CAPITAL INC (IN)
Acquired by Coastal Credit Holdings, Inc. 02/14/2013
Each share Common no par exchanged for $21.93 cash

WHITE RIVER LUMBER CO.
Merged into Weyerhaeuser Timber Co. on a (3) for (1) basis in 1949 which name was changed to Weyerhaeuser Co. 9/1/59

WHITE RIVER PROPANE GAS CO., INC. (AR)
Completely liquidated for cash 11/2/64

WHITE RIVER RAILROAD, INC.
Road abandoned in 1934

WHITE ROCK ENERGY INC (AB)
Name changed to Darford International Inc. 02/04/2010
(See Darford International Inc.)

WHITE ROCK ENTERPRISES LTD (NV)
Name changed to SNAP2 Corp. 07/10/2000
SNAP2 Corp. recapitalized as Vertigo Theme Parks, Inc. 02/16/2007
(See Vertigo Theme Parks, Inc.)

WHITE ROCK MINERAL SPRINGS CO.
Assets acquired by National Distillers Products Corp. in 1944
Preferred Stock redeemed
Common stock exchanged (2) for (7) National Distillers Products Corp. name changed to National Distillers & Chemical Corp. 5/1/57 which name changed to Quantum Chemical Corp. 1/4/88 which merged into Hanson PLC (Old) 10/1/93 which reorganized as Hanson PLC (New) 10/15/2003

WHITE ROCK MINES LTD. (ON)
Merged into Drope Lake Explorations Ltd. 2/10/67
Each share Capital Stock $1 par exchanged for (0.1) share Common no par
Drope Lake Explorations Ltd. name changed to Drope Lake Metals & Holdings Ltd. 12/22/70
(See Drope Lake Metals & Holdings Ltd.)

WHITE ROCK WATER WORKS CO., LTD. (BC)
Liquidation completed in August, 1979
Holders received total distribution of $72.87 cash per share

WHITE-RODGERS CO. (DE)
Stock Dividend - 10% 7/29/60
Acquired by Emerson Electric Manufacturing Co. on a (1.05311) for (1) basis 2/28/62
Emerson Electric Manufacturing Co. name changed to Emerson Electric Co. 2/6/64

WHITE ROSE CRAFTS & NURSERY SALES LTD (ON)
Each share old Common no par exchanged for (0.05) share new Common no par 3/26/2000
Dissolved 10/16/2002
No stockholders' equity

WHITE ROSE FOOD CORP (NY)
Merged into Di Giorgio Corp. 06/27/1986
Details not available

WHITE SAGE URANIUM CORP. (UT)
Name changed to Hidden Splendor Mining Co. (Utah) 7/19/67
Hidden Splendor Mining Co. (Utah) merged into Trans Pacific Enterprises Inc. 1/29/69

WHITE SAND OIL CO. (DE)
Charter cancelled for failure to pay taxes 1/24/24

WHITE SEWING MACHINE CORP. (DE)
Each share Common no par exchanged for (0.4) share Common $1 par 00/00/1939
$4 Conv. Preferred no par called for redemption 08/01/1949
Stock Dividend - 100% 11/16/1950
Name changed to White Consolidated Industries, Inc. 05/15/1964
(See White Consolidated Industries, Inc.)

WHITE SHIELD CORP (NY)
Each share Common 10¢ par exchanged for (0.1) share Common 5¢ par 3/9/66
Common 5¢ par split (2) for (1) by issuance of (1) additional share 8/15/69
Name changed to Basic Resources Corp. (NY) 10/17/77
Basic Resources Corp. (NY) name changed to Basix Corp. 1/3/84

WHITE SHIELD EXPL CORP (MD)
Category B Common 1¢ par reclassified as Category A Common 1¢ par 08/12/1971
Merged into Basic Resources Corp. (NY) 08/01/1979
Each share Category A Common 1¢ par exchanged for (0.67) share Common 5¢ par
Basic Resources Corp. (NY) name changed to Basix Corp. 01/03/1984

WHITE SHIELD INDONESIA OIL CORP (DE)
Preferred 5¢ par conversion privilege expired 4/30/76
Charter cancelled and declared inoperative and void for non-payment of taxes 3/1/91

WHITE SHIELD OIL & GAS (CANADA) LTD. (ON)
Completely liquidated 1/15/76
Each share Capital Stock no par exchanged for first and final distribution of $0.07 cash

WHITE SHIELD OIL & GAS CDA LTD (MD)
Name changed to White Shield Exploration Corp. 07/20/1970
White Shield Exploration Corp. merged into Basic Resources Corp. (NY) 08/01/1979 which name changed to Basix Corp. 01/03/1984

WHITE SMILE GLOBAL INC (NV)
Common $0.001 par split (20) for (1) by issuance of (19) additional shares payable 08/08/2011 to holders of record 08/08/2011
Common $0.001 par split (2) for (1) by issuance of (1) additional share payable 03/22/2012 to holders of record 03/22/2012
Reincorporated under the laws of Florida as Williamsville Sears Management, Inc. 04/03/2018

WHITE STAG MANUFACTURING CO. (OR)
Each share Common $10 par exchanged for (1) share Class A Common $1 par and (5) shares Class B Common $1 par 3/4/59
Class A Common $1 par split (3) for (2) by issuance of (0.5) additional share 4/1/63
4-1/2% Preferred $100 par called for redemption 12/1/65
Merged into Warner Brothers Co. 1/28/66
Each share Class A Common $1 par exchanged for (5/7) share $1.50 Conv. Preferred no par
Warner Brothers Co. name changed to Warnaco Inc. 1/9/68
(See Warnaco Inc.)

WHITE STAR COPPER MINES LTD (ON)
Capital Stock $1 par changed to 95¢ par 03/04/1966
Capital Stock 95¢ par changed to no par 02/14/1974
Delisted from Canadian Dealer Network 10/13/2000

WHITE STAR OIL CO. (DE)
Charter revoked for non-payment of taxes 4/1/60

WHITE STAR REFINING CO.
Acquired by Vacuum Oil Co. in 1930
(See Vacuum Oil Co.)

WHITE STORES, INC. (DE)
5-1/2% Preferred $25 par called for redemption 12/1/58
Stock Dividend - 10% 6/1/66
Acquired by Household Finance Corp. 11/15/66
Each share Common no par received (1) share Common no par
Certificates were not retired and are now without value
Household Finance Corp. reorganized as Household International, Inc. 6/26/81

WHITE SWAN RES INC (AB)
Recapitalized as Africa Diamond Holdings Ltd. (ALTA) 01/19/1999
Each share Common no par exchanged for (0.2) share Common no par
Africa Diamond Holdings Ltd. (ALTA) reincorporated in Bermuda as Sierra Leone Diamond Co. Ltd. 01/06/2004 which name changed to African Minerals Ltd. 08/15/2007

WHITE TIGER GOLD LTD (BRITISH VIRGIN ISLANDS)
Name changed to Mangazeya Mining Ltd. 09/23/2013

WHITE TIGER MNG CORP (BC)
Name changed to Copper Lake Resources Ltd. 09/24/2014

WHITE VILLA GROCERS INC (OH)
Voluntarily dissolved 12/23/93
Details not available

WHITE WELD MONEY MKT FD INC (MD)
Name changed to Merrill Lynch Institutional Fund Inc. 07/31/1978

WHITE WTR RES LTD (SOUTH AFRICA)
Name changed to Goliath Gold Mining Ltd. 05/26/2011
(See Goliath Gold Mining Ltd.)

WHITE'S AUTO STORES, INC. (DE)
Name changed to White Stores, Inc. 4/30/56
White Stores, Inc. acquired by Household Finance Corp. 11/15/66 which reorganized as Household International, Inc. 6/26/81

WHITEBURN GOLD MNG CORP (DE)
Charter cancelled and declared inoperative and void for non-payment of taxes 3/1/77

WHITECAP ENERGY RES LTD (BC)
Name changed back to Copper Lake Explorations Ltd. 05/28/1980
(See Copper Lake Explorations Ltd.)

WHITECAT ENERGY VENTURES LTD (AB)
Name changed to North Eastern Energy Group Inc. 10/24/1988
North Eastern Energy Group Inc. recapitalized as Ensign Resource Service Group Inc. 01/28/1991 which name changed to Ensign Energy Services Inc. 06/07/2005

WHITECRAFT INDS INC (FL)
Merged into Southern Cross Industries, Inc. 02/06/1979
Each share Common 10¢ par exchanged for $5 cash

WHITEDELF MNG & DEV CO (DE)
Charter cancelled and declared inoperative and void for non-payment of taxes 4/1/61

WHITEFISH BAY BK & TR CO (MILWAUKEE, WI)
Name changed to Heritage Bank of Whitefish Bay (Milwaukee, WI) 04/29/1971
(See Heritage Bank of Whitefish Bay (Milwaukee, WI))

WHITEFISH BAY STATE BANK (WHITEFISH BAY, WI)
Name changed to Whitefish Bay Bank & Trust Co. (Milwaukee, Wisc.) 1/17/67
Whitefish Bay Bank & Trust Co. (Milwaukee, Wisc.) name changed to Heritage Bank of Whitefish Bay (Milwaukee, Wisc.) 4/29/71
(See Heritage Bank of Whitefish Bay (Milwaukee, Wisc.))

WHITEGATE MINING CO. LTD. (ON)
Charter cancelled for failure to pay taxes and file returns 8/2/72

WHITEGOLD NAT RES CORP (BC)
Recapitalized as Spirit Energy Corp. 05/28/2002
Each share Common no par exchanged for (1/3) share Common no par
Spirit Energy Corp. name changed to Canadian Spirit Resources Inc. (BC) 06/23/2004 which reincorporated in Alberta 05/25/2012

WHITEGOLD RES CORP (BC)
Recapitalized as Whitegold Natural Resource Corp. 04/09/2001
Each share Common no par exchanged for (1/3) share Common no par
Whitegold Natural Resource Corp. recapitalized as Spirit Energy Corp. 05/28/2002 which name changed to Canadian Spirit Resources Inc. (BC) 06/23/2004 which reincorporated in Alberta 05/25/2012

WHITEHALL CEM MFG CO (PA)
Each share Common $50 par exchanged for (2) shares Common $25 par 00/00/1951
Each share Common $25 par exchanged for (2.5) shares Common $10 par 04/00/1955
Merged into General Portland Inc. 06/02/1981
Each share Common $10 par exchanged for $70 cash

WHITEHALL CORP (DE)
Common 10¢ par split (2) for (1) by issuance of (1) additional share 2/9/82
Common 10¢ par split (2) for (1) by issuance of (1) additional share payable 4/15/97 to holders of record 3/25/97 Ex date - 4/16/97
Merged into Aviation Sales Co. 7/31/98
Each share Common 10¢ par exchanged for (0.5143) share Common $0.001 par
Aviation Sales Co. recapitalized as TIMCO Aviation Services, Inc. 2/28/2002
(See TIMCO Aviation Services, Inc.)

WHITEHALL ELECTRS CORP (DE)
Reincorporated 11/6/63
State of incorporation changed from (MN) to (DE) 11/6/63
Name changed to Whitehall Corp. 4/23/73
Whitehall Corp. merged into Aviation Sales Co. 7/31/98 which recapitalized as TIMCO Aviation Services, Inc. 2/28/2002
(See TIMCO Aviation Services, Inc.)

WHITEHALL ENTERPRISES INC (DE)
SEC revoked common stock registration 03/10/2005
Stockholders' equity unlikely

WHITEHALL FD INC (MD)
Capital Stock $1 par split (2) for (1) by issuance of (1) additional share 03/31/1956
Name changed to Union Income Fund, Inc. 05/01/1974
Union Income Fund, Inc. name changed to Seligman Income Fund, Inc. 05/01/1982 which name changed to Seligman Income & Growth Fund, Inc. 11/06/2002

WHITEHALL JEWELERS HLDGS INC (DE)
Chapter 11 bankruptcy proceedings dismissed 08/16/2010
No stockholders' equity

WHITEHALL JEWELLERS INC (DE)
Common 1¢ par split (3) for (2) by issuance of (1) additional share payable 1/4/2000 to holders of record 12/24/99
Merged into WJ Acquisition Corp. 6/8/2006
Each share Common 1¢ par exchanged for $1.60 cash

WHITEHALL LTD INC (FL)
SEC revoked common stock registration 10/15/2009

WHITEHALL MONEY MKT TR (PA)
Name changed to Vanguard Money Market Trust (PA) 05/01/1980
Vanguard Money Market Trust (PA) reincorporated in Maryland as Vanguard Money Market Trust, Inc. 12/31/1985 which name changed to Vanguard Money Market Reserves, Inc. 03/13/1989

WHITEHALL PLASTICS INC. (FL)
Administratively dissolved 09/26/1997

WHITEHALL TELEVISION CORP. (DE)
No longer in existence having become inoperative and void for non-payment of taxes 10/1/53

WHITEHEAD BROS. RUBBER CO. (NJ)
Merged into Goodall Rubber Co. (N.J.) in 1954
Each (7) shares Capital Stock $10 par exchanged for (8) shares Class A Common $5 par
(See Goodall Rubber Co. (N.J.))

WHITEHORSE COPPER MINES LTD (AB)
Merged into Hudson Bay Mining & Smelting Co., Ltd. 10/31/1978
Each share Capital Stock no par exchanged for $4 cash

WHITEHORSE OIL & GAS INC (DE)
Charter cancelled and declared inoperative and void for non-payment of taxes 03/01/1989

WHITEHOUSE PLASTIC CORP. (TX)
Name changed to West American Industries, Inc. 12/14/62
West American Industries, Inc. name changed to W.A.I. Corp. 5/9/74
(See W.A.I. Corp.)

WHITEKNIGHT ACQUISITIONS INC (ON)
Issue Information - 3,000,000 shares COM offered at $0.20 per share on 03/22/2011
Name changed to Smart Employee Benefits Inc. 08/28/2012

WHITEKNIGHT ACQUISITIONS II INC (ON)
Name changed to Diamond Estates Wines & Spirits Inc. 10/03/2013

WHITEKNIGHT ACQUISITIONS III INC (ON)
Recapitalized as Delivra Corp. 01/05/2016
Each share Common no par exchanged for (0.26666666) share Common no par

WHITELEY INDS INC (MA)
Adjudicated bankrupt 04/10/1974
Stockholders' equity unlikely

WHITELOCK CORP (UT)
Proclaimed dissolved for failure to pay taxes 9/30/80

WHITELOCK URANIUM CO. (UT)
Name changed to Whitelock Corp. and Common 3¢ par changed to 1¢ par 5/5/72
Whitelock Corp. proclaimed dissolved 9/30/80

WHITENIGHTS, INC.
Bankrupt in 1929

WHITEPINE RES INC (UT)
Involuntarily dissolved for failure to pay taxes 4/30/87

WHITEROCK INDS LTD (QC)
Name changed 2/25/72
Name changed from Whiterock Estates Development Corp. Ltd. to Whiterock Industries Ltd. 2/25/72
Each share Common no par exchanged for (3) shares Common no par
Declared dissolved for failure to file reports and pay fees 11/15/89

WHITEROCK REAL ESTATE INVT TR (MB)
Each old Trust Unit exchanged for (0.25) new Trust Unit no par 08/21/2006
Each new Trust Unit exchanged again for (0.33333333) new Trust Unit no par 12/22/2008
New Trust Units split (2) for (1) by issuance of (1) additional Trust Unit payable 11/13/2009 to holders of record 11/11/2009 Ex date - 11/06/2009
New Trust Units split (3) for (2) by issuance of (0.5) additional Trust Unit payable 01/28/2011 to holders of record 01/27/2011 Ex date - 01/25/2011

Merged into Dundee Real Estate Investment Trust 03/02/2012
Each new Trust Unit exchanged for either (0.4729) Ser. A Unit or $16.25 cash
Note: Non-Canadian redidents received cash
Dundee Real Estate Investment Trust name changed to Dream Office Real Estate Investment Trust 05/08/2014

WHITESAIL MINES LTD (BC)
Merged into Twin Peak Resources Ltd. 12/11/1972
Each share Common 50¢ par exchanged for (1) share Common no par
(See Twin Peak Resources Ltd.)

WHITESTAR RES INC (UT)
Recapitalized as Charista Global Corp. 02/24/2009
Each share Common $0.001 par exchanged for (0.001) share Common $0.001 par
Charista Global Corp. name changed to UBK Resources Co. 09/12/2011

WHITESTOCK CORP (NC)
Completely liquidated 1/3/85
Each (14) shares Common $1 par exchanged for first and final distribution of (1) share First Citizens Corp. (NC) Common $100 par
First Citizens Corp. (NC) reorganized in Delaware as First Citizens BancShares, Inc. 10/20/86

WHITESTONE INDS INC NEW (DE)
Each share Common $0.00001 par exchanged for (0.1) share Common $0.0001 par 02/01/1996
Recapitalized as Proformix Systems Inc. 07/15/1997
Each share old Common $0.0001 par exchanged for (0.00729927) share Common $0.0001 par
Proformix Systems Inc. name changed to Magnitude Information Systems, Inc. 12/03/1998 which name changed to Kiwibox.Com, Inc. 03/02/2010

WHITESTONE INDS INC OLD (DE)
Name changed to Entertainment & Gaming International, Inc. 08/03/1994
Entertainment & Gaming International, Inc. name changed to Whitestone Industries Inc. (New) 06/16/1995 which recapitalized as Proformix Systems Inc. 07/15/1997 which name changed to Magnitude Information Systems, Inc. 12/03/1998 which name changed to Kiwibox.Com, Inc. 03/02/2010

WHITESTONE MANAGEMENT CO.
Bankrupt in 1933

WHITETAIL INC (OK)
Liquidated and dissolved 11/26/1990
No stockholders' equity

WHITEWATER CAP CORP (BC)
Name changed to Preferred Dental Technologies Inc. 06/09/2017

WHITEWATER GOLD MINES LTD. (ON)
Merged into Berkwater Explorations Ltd. 07/28/1976
Each share Capital Stock no par exchanged for (1.1) shares Capital Stock no par
Berkwater Explorations Ltd. merged into Branly Enterprises Inc. 12/09/1976 which recapitalized as Consolidated Branly Resources Inc. 02/27/1984 which name changed to CBR Holdings Inc. 06/20/1985

WHITEWATER MINES, LTD. (BC)
Charter revoked for failure to file reports and pay fees 7/2/54

WHITEWATER PRODS LTD (UT)
Recapitalized as Medisys Technologies, Inc. 8/6/92
Each share Common $0.0005 par exchanged for (0.5) share Common $0.0005 par

WHITEWAVE FOODS CO (DE)
Class B Common 1¢ par reclassified as Class A Common 1¢ par 09/24/2013
Class A Common 1¢ par reclassified as Common 1¢ par 06/18/2014
Acquired by Danone S.A. 04/12/2017
Each share Common 1¢ par exchanged for $56.25 cash

WHITEWING ENVIRONMENTAL CORP (DE)
Name changed 05/21/2002
Name changed from Whitewing Labs, Inc. to Whitewing Environmental Corp. 05/21/2002
Recapitalized as Princeton Consulting & Services Corp. 09/27/2007
Each share Common $0.001 par exchanged for (0.1) share Common $0.001 par
Princeton Consulting & Services Corp. recapitalized as Andes Gold Corp. 09/22/2009

WHITIN MACHINE WORKS (MA)
Each share Common $100 par exchanged for (4) shares Common $25 par 00/00/1945
Each share Common $25 par exchanged for (2) shares Common $12.50 par 00/00/1951
Merged into White Consolidated Industries, Inc. 01/14/1966
Each share Common $12.50 par exchanged for (0.52) share 5-1/2% Preferred $50 par and (0.5) share Common $1 par
(See White Consolidated Industries, Inc.)

WHITING CORP (IL)
Common $25 par changed to $20 par in 1934
Each share Common $20 par exchanged for (4) shares Common $5 par in 1945
6% Preferred Ser. A $25 par called for redemption 3/15/57
Common $5 par split (2) for (1) by issuance of (1) additional share 10/25/74
Stock Dividends - 20% 4/28/65; 20% 4/28/67; 25% 11/14/75; 25% 11/19/76
Merged into Wheelabrator-Frye Inc. 4/10/78
Each share Common $5 par exchanged for (1) share Conv. Preferred Ser. B $1 par
Wheelabrator-Frye Inc. merged into Signal Companies, Inc. 2/1/83 which merged into Allied-Signal Inc. 9/19/85 which name changed to AlliedSignal Inc. 4/26/93 which name changed to Honeywell International Inc. 12/1/99

WHITING PETE CORP (DE)
Issue Information - 3,000,000 shares PERP PFD CONV offered at $100 per share on 06/17/2009
Each share 6.25% Conv. Perpetual Preferred $0.001 par exchanged for (4.60656481) shares Common $0.001 par 06/27/2013
(Additional Information in Active)

WHITING PETE CORP (DE)
Acquired by IES Industries Inc. 2/18/92
Each share Common 1¢ par exchanged for (0.1) share Common no par
IES Industries Inc. merged into Interstate Energy Corp. 4/21/98 which name changed to Alliant Energy Corp. 5/19/99

WHITING USA TR I (DE)
Completely liquidated
Each Trust Unit received first and final distribution of $0.061505 cash payable 09/08/2015 to holders of record 03/19/2015 Ex date - 09/09/2015

WHITLAUR CAP CORP (AB)
Name changed to Petro Field Industries Inc. 09/15/1997
Petro Field Industries Inc. name changed to Tornado Technologies Inc. 05/02/2007 which merged into Empire Industries Ltd. (Old) 12/03/2007 which reorganized as Empire Industries Ltd. (New) 06/30/2016

WHITLOCK COIL PIPE CO.
Name changed to Whitlock Manufacturing Co. in 1950
(See Whitlock Manufacturing Co.)

WHITLOCK CORP (MN)
Merged into Whitlock Holdings, Inc. 06/04/1981
Each share Common 10¢ par exchanged for $14 cash

WHITLOCK MFG CO (CT)
Merged into Schutte & Koerting Co. 11/17/1971
Each share Common $25 par exchanged for $28 cash

WHITMAN & BARNES, INC.
Name changed to United Drill & Tool Corp. in 1937
United Drill & Tool Corp. merged into United-Greenfield Corp. 2/14/58 which merged into TRW Inc. 9/20/68 which merged into Northrop Grumman Corp. 12/11/2002

WHITMAN & BARNES MANUFACTURING CO.
Liquidated in 1944

WHITMAN (STEPHEN F.) & SON, INC.
Recapitalized 9/12/56
Each share Class A Common no par exchanged for (2) shares Class A Common $5 par
Each share Class B Common no par exchanged for (2) shares Class B Common $5 par
Acquired by Pet Milk Co. 12/31/62
Each share Class A Common $5 par or Class B Common $5 par exchanged for (1.5) shares Common no par
Pet Milk Co. name changed to Pet Inc. 9/1/66
(See Pet Inc.)

WHITMAN (CLARENCE) & SONS, INC. (PA)
Capital Stock $25 par changed to $10 par 00/00/1952
Name changed to Prince Gardner Co., Inc. 10/31/1956
Prince Gardner Co., Inc. name changed to Settlement Corp. 10/28/1966
(See Settlement Corp.)

WHITMAN (WILLIAM) CO., INC. (MA)
Common no par split (10) for (1) by issuance of (9) additional shares 00/00/1948
Common no par changed to $1 par 00/00/1952
Initial liquidating distribution in cash was paid to Common holders of record 11/25/1952 with no presentation of certificates necessary
Name changed to Carolet Corp. 12/28/1952
Four (4) subsequent distributions of cash and/or other securities were paid to Carolet Corp. Common holders of record on various dates from 1952 to 1955, the final distribution paid 02/14/1955
Note: Certificates were not required to be surrendered and are without value

WHITMAN (WILLIAM) CO., INC. (OH)
Liquidation completed 08/19/1955
Liquidation commenced 00/00/1946 and (5) liquidating distributions in cash and/or other securities were paid to holders of record on various dates from 00/00/1946 to 00/00/1952 with no presentation of certificates necessary
The sixth and final distribution of $2.27 per share of Common stock was paid upon surrender of certificates 08/19/1955

WHITMAN CORP NEW (DE)
Name changed to PepsiAmericas, Inc. (DE) 01/24/2001
PepsiAmericas, Inc. (DE) merged into PepsiCo, Inc. 02/26/2010

WHITMAN CORP OLD (DE)
Each share Common no par received distribution of (0.5) share Hussmann International, Inc. Common $0.001 par and (0.1666) share Midas, Inc. Common $0.001 par payable 01/30/1998 to holders of record 01/16/1998 Ex date - 01/30/1998
Common no par changed to 1¢ par 05/20/1999
Under plan of merger name changed to Whitman Corp. (New) 11/30/2000
Whitman Corp. (New) name changed to PepsiAmericas, Inc. (DE) 01/24/2001 which merged into PepsiCo, Inc. 02/26/2010

WHITMAN ED GROUP INC (FL)
Reincorporated 11/21/97
Common no par split (2) for (1) by issuance of (1) additional share payable 5/13/96 to holders of record 4/29/96
State of incorporation changed from (NJ) to (FL) 11/21/97
Merged into Career Education Corp. 7/1/2003
Each share Common no par exchanged for (0.138) share Common 1¢ par and $6 cash

WHITMAN INDS INC (MI)
Filed for bankruptcy 06/00/1982
No stockholders' equity

WHITMAN MED CORP (NJ)
Name changed to Whitman Education Group, Inc. (NJ) 3/19/96
Whitman Education Group, Inc. (NJ) reincorporated in Florida 11/21/97 which name changed to Career Education Corp. 7/1/2003

WHITMAN MILLS
Bankrupt in 1932

WHITMER PARSONS PULP & PAPER CO.
Property sold in 1930

WHITMORE RESOURCE CORP (CANADA)
Name changed to Minera Delta Inc. (New) 10/15/2001
Minera Delta Inc. (New) name changed to Vector Wind Energy Inc. 11/26/2004
(See Vector Wind Energy Inc.)

WHITMOYER LABORATORIES, INC. (DE)
Acquired by Rohm & Haas Co. on a (0.125) for (1) basis 06/23/1964
(See Rohm & Haas Co.)

WHITNEY AMERN CORP NEW (DE)
Each share old Common $0.00001 par exchanged for (0.00006622) share new Common $0.00001 par 01/31/2003
Note: In effect holders received $0.50 cash per share and public interest was eliminated

WHITNEY AMERN CORP OLD (DE)
Name changed to Industrial Waste Processing, Inc. 10/31/1988
Industrial Waste Processing, Inc. recapitalized as Whitney American Corp. (New) 02/20/1997
(See Whitney American Corp. (New))

WHITNEY BLAKE CO (CT)
Stock Dividend - 100% 7/21/47
Merged into Continental Telephone Corp. 6/30/71

Each share Common $5 par exchanged for (1.6) shares Common $1 par
Continental Telephone Corp. name changed to Continental Telecom Inc. 5/6/82 which name changed to Contel Corp. 5/1/86 which merged into GTE Corp. 3/14/91 which merged into Verizon Communications Inc. 6/30/2000

WHITNEY CORP. (NE)
Recapitalized under the laws of Iowa 12/30/66
Each share Common $1 par exchanged for (1) share Common $1 par

WHITNEY (BC) ENTERPRISES, INC.
Out of business in 1930

WHITNEY FIDALGO SEAFOODS INC (ME)
Through voluntary purchase offer over 99% acquired by Kyokuyo Co. Ltd. as of 03/31/1978
Public interest eliminated

WHITNEY HLDG CORP (LA)
Common no par split (2) for (1) by issuance of (1) additional share 04/28/1978
Common no par split (2) for (1) by issuance of (1) additional share 02/27/1984
Common no par split (3) for (2) by issuance of (0.5) additional share 01/21/1987
Common no par split (3) for (2) by issuance of (0.5) additional share 02/22/1993
Common no par split (3) for (2) by issuance of (0.5) additional share 11/29/1993
Common no par split (3) for (2) by issuance of (0.5) additional share payable 04/09/2002 to holders of record 03/20/2002 Ex date - 04/10/2002
Common no par split (3) for (2) by issuance of (0.5) additional share payable 05/25/2005 to holders of record 05/11/2005 Ex date - 05/26/2005
Merged into Hancock Holding Co. 06/04/2011
Each share Common no par exchanged for (0.418) share Common $3.33 par
Hancock Holding Co. name changed to Hancock Whitney Corp. 05/25/2018

WHITNEY INFORMATION NETWORK INC (CO)
Name changed to Tigrent Inc. 10/29/2009

WHITNEY NATL BK (NEW ORLEANS, LA)
Reorganized as Whitney Holding Corp. 05/24/1962
Each share Common $25 par exchanged for (10) shares Common no par
Whitney Holding Corp. merged into Hancock Holding Co. 06/04/2011 which name changed to Hancock Whitney Corp. 05/25/2018

WHITNEY SCREW CORP. (NH)
Involuntarily dissolved 11/03/1997

WHITTAKER (WM. R.) CO. LTD. (CA)
Merged into Telecomputing Corp. 10/31/57
Each share Common $1 par exchanged for (4) shares Common $1 par
Telecomputing Corp. name changed to Whittaker Corp. (CA) 5/4/64 which reincorporated in Delaware 6/16/86
(See Whittaker Corp. (DE))

WHITTAKER CORP (DE)
Reincorporated 6/16/86
$1.25 Conv. Preferred no par changed to $1 par 4/15/68

Common $1 par split (2) for (1) by issuance of (1) additional share plus a 3% stock dividend paid 3/10/69
$1.25 Conv. Preferred $1 par called for redemption 5/2/86
State of incorporation changed from (CA) to (DE) 6/16/86
Under plan of recapitalization each share Common $1 par exchanged for (1) share Common 1¢ par and $40 cash 6/29/89
Merged into Meggitt PLC 7/19/99
Each share Common 1¢ par exchanged for $28 cash

WHITTALL (M.J.) ASSOCIATES, LTD.
Acquired by Whittall (M.J.) Associates, Inc. in 1939

WHITTELSEY MANUFACTURING CO., INC.
Liquidated in 1933

WHITTIER CORP. (MI)
Liquidation completed 12/30/60

WHITTIER ENERGY CORP (NV)
Each share old Common no par exchanged for (0.33333333) share new Common no par 07/01/2005
Merged into Sterling Energy PLC 03/28/2007
Each share new Common no par exchanged for $11 cash

WHITTINGTON OIL INC (UT)
Name changed to Louisiana-Pacific Resources, Inc. 10/04/1971
(See Louisiana-Pacific Resources, Inc.)

WHITTMAN-HART INC (DE)
Common $0.001 par split (2) for (1) by issuance of (1) additional share payable 12/10/1996 to holders of record 12/03/1996
Common $0.001 par split (2) for (1) by issuance of (1) additional share payable 07/31/1998 to holders of record 07/12/1998
Name changed to Marchfirst Inc. 03/23/2000
(See Marchfirst Inc.)

WHOLE EARTH MKTS INC (NV)
Each share old Common $0.001 par exchanged for (0.01) share new Common $0.001 par 7/31/95
Charter revoked for failure to file reports and pay fees 12/1/95

WHOLE FOODS MKT INC (TX)
Common no par split (2) for (1) by issuance of (1) additional share 11/29/1993
Common no par split (2) for (1) by issuance of (1) additional share payable 06/04/2001 to holders of record 05/21/2001 Ex date - 06/05/2001
Common no par split (2) for (1) by issuance of (1) additional share payable 12/27/2005 to holders of record 12/12/2005 Ex date - 12/28/2005
Common no par split (2) for (1) by issuance of (1) additional share payable 05/29/2013 to holders of record 05/17/2013 Ex date - 05/30/2013
Acquired by Amazon.com, Inc. 08/28/2017
Each share Common no par exchanged for $42 cash

WHOLE GRAIN WHEAT CO. (AZ)
Charter expired by time limitation 2/6/42

WHOLE IN ONE ORGANICS INC (FL)
Name changed to Liberty International Holding Corp. 05/02/2012

WHOLE LIVING INC (NV)
Each (15) shares old Common $0.001 par exchanged for (1) share new Common $0.001 par 2/24/2006
Name changed to ForeverGreen Worldwide Corp. 12/29/2006

WHOLEFOOD FARMACY CORP (FL)
Name changed to Wham Inc. 02/21/2012
Wham Inc. recapitalized as Berith Holdings Corp. 06/12/2017 which name changed to Syntrol Corp. 11/29/2017

WHOLESALE CELLULAR USA INC (DE)
Issue Information - 2,000,000 shares COM offered at $6.25 per share on 04/07/1994
Name changed to Brightpoint, Inc. (DE) 09/15/1995
Brightpoint, Inc. (DE) reincorporated in Delaware 06/03/2004
(See Brightpoint, Inc.)

WHOLESALE CLUB INC (IN)
$2.125 Conv. Exchangeable Preferred $1 par called for redemption 09/19/1989
Merged into Wal-Mart Stores, Inc. 02/02/1991
Each share Common $1 par exchanged for either (0.672) share Common 10¢ par or $21 cash
Note: Option to receive cash expired 03/06/1991
Wal-Mart Stores, Inc. name changed to Walmart Inc. 02/01/2018

WHOLESALE COMMUNICATIONS NETWORK INC (NV)
Charter revoked for failure to file reports and pay fees 10/01/2012

WHOLESALE ON THE NET INC (NV)
Recapitalized as Wickliffe International Corp. 4/5/2001
Each share Common $0.001 par exchanged for (0.5) share Common $0.001 par
Wickliffe International Corp. name changed to Axiom Pharmaceuticals Inc. 3/27/2003 which name changed to AXM Pharma, Inc. 10/3/2003

WHOLESALE OPTL CLUB INTL INC (FL)
Recapitalized as Nu-Vision International, Inc. 12/14/1990
Each share Common $0.001 par exchanged for (0.2) share Common $0.001 par
Nu-Vision International, Inc. name changed to Highland Healthcare Corp. 05/31/1991 which recapitalized as Systems Communications Inc. 09/09/1994 which recapitalized as Hitsgalore.com, Inc. 03/19/1999 which name changed to Diamond Hitts Production, Inc. (FL) 05/01/2001 which reincorporated in Nevada 09/04/2001
(See Diamond Hitts Production, Inc.)

WHOLESOME AND HEARTY FOODS INC (OR)
Common no par split (2) for (1) by issuance of (1) additional share 7/8/93
Common no par split (3) for (2) by issuance of (0.5) additional share 2/22/94
Name changed to Gardenburger, Inc. 10/17/97
(See Gardenburger, Inc.)

WHONNOCK INDS LTD NEW (BC)
Reorganized 12/07/1979
Class A Common no par and Class B Common no par split (2) for (1) by issuance of (1) additional share respectively 04/02/1973
Class A Common no par split (3) for (2) by issuance of (0.5) additional share 07/26/1978
Class B Common no par split (3) for (2) by issuance of (0.5) additional share 07/26/1978
Reorganized from Whonnock Industries Ltd. (Old) to Whonnock Industries Ltd. (New) 12/07/1979
Each share Class A Common no par exchanged for (2) shares Class A Common no par
Each share Class B Common no par exchanged for (2) shares Class B Common no par
Name changed to International Forest Products Ltd. 01/13/1988
International Forest Products Ltd. name changed to Interfor Corp. 05/12/2014

WHONNOCK LUMBER CO. (BC)
Common no par reclassified as Class B Common no par 11/12/1970
Name changed to Whonnock Industries Ltd. (Old) 07/23/1971
Whonnock Industries Ltd. (Old) merged into Whonnock Industries Ltd. (New) 12/07/1979 which name changed to International Forest Products Ltd. 01/13/1988 which name changed to Interfor Corp. 05/12/2014

WHOODOO COM INC (DE)
Name changed to Ballistic Ventures, Inc. 07/14/2000
Ballistic Ventures, Inc. name changed to River Capital Group, Inc. 06/07/2004 which recapitalized as Sonterra Resources, Inc. 02/14/2008 which name changed to Velocity Energy Inc. 04/14/2009

WHOS YOUR DADDY INC (NV)
Each share old Common $0.001 par exchanged for (0.16666666) share new Common $0.001 par 10/30/2007
Name changed to FITT Highway Products, Inc. 07/19/2010
FITT Highway Products, Inc. name changed to Global Future City Holding Inc. 10/29/2014

WHX CORP (DE)
Each share old Common 1¢ par exchanged for (0.33333333) share new Common 1¢ par 08/22/2002
Plan of reorganization under Chapter 11 Federal Bankruptcy Code effective 07/29/2005
Each share 6.5% Conv. Preferred Ser. A 1¢ par exchanged for (0.1423203) share old Common 1¢ par and (0.1339036) Common Stock Purchase Warrant expiring 02/28/2008
Each share $3.75 Conv. Preferred Ser. B 1¢ par exchanged for (0.1470593) share old Common 1¢ par and (0.1383622) Common Stock Purchase Warrant expiring 02/28/2008
No Common stockholders' equity for certificates dated prior to 07/29/2005
Each share old Common 1¢ par exchanged for (0.1) share new Common 1¢ par 11/25/2008
Name changed to Handy & Harman Ltd. 01/03/2011
Handy & Harman Ltd. merged into Steel Partners Holdings L.P. 10/12/2017

WHY NOT INC (NV)
Reorganized as Light Energy Management Co. 12/30/1998
Each share Common $0.001 par exchanged for (5) shares Common $0.001 par
Light Energy Management Co. name changed to Forlink Software Corp. Inc. 12/15/1999
(See Forlink Software Corp. Inc.)

WHY U S A FINL GROUP INC (NV)
SEC revoked common stock registration 06/11/2014

WI-LAN INC (CANADA)
Reincorporated 08/02/2007
Place of incorporation changed from (AB) to (Canada) 08/02/2007
Name changed to Quarterhill Inc. 06/05/2017

WI2WI CORP (CANADA)
Each share Preferred no par

exchanged for (0.000001) share Common no par 11/28/2014
(Additional Information in Active)

WIARD PLOW CO. (NY)
Bankrupt in 1954

WIATT NORMAN CO (CA)
Adjudicated bankrupt 07/07/1975
Stockholders' equity unlikely

WIC WESTN INTL COMMUNICATIONS LTD (CANADA)
Acquired by CanWest Global Communications Corp. 04/13/2000
Each share Class A Common no par exchanged for $43.50 cash
Each share Conv. Class B Common no par exchanged for $43.50 cash

WICAT SYS INC (DE)
Merged into Jostens, Inc. 8/24/92
Each share Common 1¢ par exchanged for (0.1859) share Common 33-1/3¢ par
(See Jostens, Inc.)

WICHITA BUILDING MATERIAL CO., INC. (KS)
Each share 6% Preferred $100 par exchanged for (0.1448571) share Common $20 par 5/1/65
Common $20 par changed to $10 par 9/26/66
Charter forfeited for failure to file annual reports 1/15/98

WICHITA DEV CORP (NV)
Charter revoked for failure to file reports and pay fees 3/1/2006

WICHITA INDS INC (VA)
Common $1 par split (5) for (4) by issuance of (0.25) additional share 11/2/81
Merged into Wichita River Oil Corp. (VA) (New) 11/4/87
Each share Common $1 par exchanged for (0.166667) share Common no par
Wichita River Oil Corp. (VA) (New) reincorporated in Delaware 3/30/90

WICHITA PETROLEUM CORP. (UT)
Proclaimed dissolved for failure to pay taxes 4/1/88

WICHITA RIV OIL CORP (DE)
Chapter 7 bankruptcy proceedings terminated 06/15/2011
No stockholders' equity

WICHITA RIV OIL CORP NEW (VA)
Each (100) shares old Common no par exchanged for (20) shares new Common no par 03/21/1988
Note: Holdings of (99) shares or fewer exchanged for $1.50 cash per share
Reincorporated under the laws of Delaware 03/30/1990
(See Wichita River Oil Corp. (DE))

WICHITA RIVER OIL CORP OLD (VA)
Each share Common $10 par exchanged for (3) shares Common $1 par 00/00/1952
Name changed to Wichita Industries, Inc. 01/08/1969
Wichita Industries, Inc. merged into Wichita River Oil Corp. (VA) (New) 11/04/1987 which reincorporated in Delaware 03/30/1990
(See Wichita River Oil Corp. (DE))

WICHITA TELEVISION CORP., INC. (KS)
Name changed to Kansas State Network, Inc. 1/4/66
(See Kansas State Network, Inc.)

WICHITA UN STK YDS CO (KS)
84% of 4% Preferred and 94.8% of Common acquired by Sierra Petroleum Co., Inc. through exchange offer which expired 09/29/1971
Public interest eliminated

WICK INVESTING CORP. OF DELAWARE (DE)
Class A Deferred $1 par reclassified as Class A $1 par in May 1964
Name changed to Mountain Equities, Inc. 9/22/65
Mountain Equities, Inc. adjudicated bankrupt 1/30/75

WICKED WINGS BUFFALO INC (FL)
Name changed to Welcome To Search Engine Inc. 10/28/1998
Welcome To Search Engine Inc. name changed to CityXpress.com Corp. 10/21/1999 which name changed to CityXpress Corp. (FL) 06/17/2002 which reorganized in Oklahoma as Cigars MFOV, Inc. 07/09/2015 which name changed to Fernhill Beverage, Inc. 12/09/2015

WICKER BALDWIN CORP (DE)
Charter cancelled and declared inoperative and void for non-payment of taxes 4/15/72

WICKER-BALDWIN URANIUM MINING CO. (SD)
Merged into Wicker-Baldwin Corp. 7/27/70
Each share Common 25¢ par exchanged for (1/3) share Common 10¢ par
(See Wicker-Baldwin Corp.)

WICKER WORLD INC (FL)
Name changed to Dimensional Entertainment Corp. 07/15/1976
(See Dimensional Entertainment Corp.)

WICKES CORP (DE)
Reincorporated 07/02/1971
Common $5 par split (3) for (2) by issuance of (0.5) additional share 11/17/1959
Common $5 par changed to $2.50 par and (1) additional share issued 11/15/1963
Stock Dividend - 33-1/3% 11/22/1955
State of incorporation changed from (MI) to (DE) 07/02/1971
Merged into Wickes Companies, Inc. 08/13/1980
Each share Common $2.50 par exchanged for (1) share Common $2.50 par
Wickes Companies, Inc. name changed to WCI Holdings Corp. 04/13/1989 which name changed to Collins & Aikman Group Inc. 07/17/1992
(See Collins & Aikman Group Inc.)

WICKES COS INC NEW (DE)
Under plan of reorganization each (5) shares Common $2.50 par exchanged for (1) share Common 10¢ par and (1) Common Stock Purchase Warrant expiring 01/26/1992 on 01/26/1985
$2.50 Conv. Exchangeable Preferred 10¢ par called for redemption 05/30/1986
Each share old Common 10¢ par exchanged for (0.2) share new Common 10¢ par 08/11/1987
Merged into WCI Holdings Corp. 04/13/1989
Each share new Common 10¢ par exchanged for (0.45) share 15-1/2% Exchangeable Preferred 10¢ par
WCI Holdings Corp. name changed to Collins & Aikman Group Inc. 07/17/1992
(See Collins & Aikman Group Inc.)

WICKES INC (DE)
Name changed 06/10/1997
Name changed from Wickes Lumber Co. to Wickes Inc. 06/10/1997
Plan of reorganization under Chapter 11 Federal Bankruptcy Code effective 12/18/2007
No stockholders' equity

WICKLIFFE INTL CORP (NV)
Name changed to Axiom Pharmaceuticals Inc. 3/27/2003

Axiom Pharmaceuticals Inc. name changed to AXM Pharma, Inc. 10/3/2003

WICKLOW MINING CO. (CANADA) LTD. (ON)
Charter cancelled by the Province of Ontario 3/25/65

WICKLUND (J.V.) DEVELOPMENT CO. (MI)
Name changed to Peninsular Oil Co. 7/18/52
(See Peninsular Oil Co.)

WICKLUND HLDG CO (WY)
Reorganized 01/28/1987
Reincorporated 01/22/2004
Under plan of reorganization each share Wicklund Petroleum Corp. Common 1¢ par automatically became (1) share Wicklund Holding Co. Common 1¢ par 01/28/1987
State of incorporation changed from (DE) to (WY) and Common 1¢ par changed to 5¢ par 01/22/2004
Common 5¢ par split (8) for (1) by issuance of (7) additional shares payable 02/10/2004 to holders of record 01/30/2004 Ex date - 02/11/2004
Note: CUSIP® number changed from (967535 10 5) 03/19/2004 with no certificate exchange
Name changed to Plasticon International, Inc. 09/19/2004
Each share new Common 5¢ par exchanged for (1) share Common 5¢ par
(See Plasticon International, Inc.)

WICKWIRE SPENCER STEEL CO.
Merged into Colorado Fuel & Iron Corp. and each share Common exchanged for (1.1) shares 5% Preferred $20 par in 1945
Colorado Fuel & Iron Corp. name changed to CF&I Steel Corp. 8/1/66
(See CF&I Steel Corp.)

WICO ELECTRIC CO. (MA)
Common no par changed to $10 par 00/00/1949
Each share Common $10 par exchanged for (5) shares Common $5 par 00/00/1952
Merged into Globe-Union Inc. 06/11/1956
Each share Common $5 par exchanged for (1) share Capital Stock $5 par
6% Preference called for redemption 10/01/1956
Globe-Union Inc. merged into Johnson Controls, Inc. 10/10/1978 which merged into Johnson Controls International PLC 09/06/2016

WICOR INC (WI)
Merged into Wisconsin Energy Corp. 4/26/2000
Each share Common $1 par exchanged for $31.50 cash

WIDCOM INC (NV)
Chapter 11 Federal Bankruptcy Code converted to Chapter 7 on 8/10/87
Stockholders' equity undetermined

WIDE E-CONVERGENCE TECHNOLOGIES AMERS CORP (NV)
Recapitalized as All World Resources Corp. 10/13/2006
Each share Common $0.001 par exchanged for (0.01) share Common $0.001 par

WIDE ENTMT INC (WA)
Name changed to Omega Mining & Exploration Corp. (WA) 09/12/2005
Omega Mining & Exploration Corp. (WA) reincorporated in Nevada as Cardio Infrared Technologies, Inc. 08/06/2007 which reorganized in Wyoming 07/15/2010 which recapitalized as Enchanted World, Inc. 12/08/2014

WIDE WEST ENERGY INC (UT)
Involuntarily dissolved 03/31/1985

WIDEBAND CORP (NV)
Name changed to GoldKey Corp. 12/30/2014

WIDECOM GROUP INC (ON)
Each share old Common no par exchanged for (0.25) share new Common no par 1/29/99
Placed in receivership 7/8/2004
Stockholders' equity unlikely

WIDENER PL FD INC (NY)
In process of liquidation
Each share Common 1¢ par exchanged for initial distribution of (0.83) share Dreyfus Tax Exempt Bond Fund, Inc. Common 1¢ par 7/16/81
Note: Details not available on number or amount of subsequent distribution(s) made, if any
Dreyfus Tax Exempt Bond Fund, Inc. name changed to Dreyfus Municipal Bond Fund Inc. 2/9/93

WIDERGREN COMMUNICATIONS INC (NV)
Name changed to Widcom, Inc. 12/23/1983
(See Widcom, Inc.)

WIDERTHAN CO LTD (KOREA)
ADR agreement terminated 11/27/2006
Each Sponsored ADR for Common exchanged for $17 cash

WIDESCOPE RES INC (BC)
Recapitalized as North American Nickel Inc. 07/07/2010
Each share Common no par exchanged for (0.5) share Common no par

WIDESCOPE RES LTD (BC)
Name changed to Gemini Technology Inc. 09/17/1985
Gemini Technology Inc. recapitalized as International Gemini Technology Inc. 09/23/1993 which name changed to Widescope Resources Inc. 07/12/2006 which recapitalized as North American Nickel Inc. 07/07/2010

WIDLAR FOOD PRODUCTS CO.
Acquired by Standard Brands, Inc. 00/00/1929
Details not available

WIDMANN L F INC (PA)
Each (4,243) shares old Common 50¢ par exchanged for (1) share new Common 50¢ par 08/29/1983
Note: In effect holders received $9 cash per share and public interest was eliminated

WIDS FILMS & FILM FOLK INC (NY)
Name changed to Langdon Group, Inc. 10/30/70
(See Langdon Group, Inc.)

WIEBOLDT STORES INC (IL)
$5 Prior Preferred no par called for redemption 1/1/46
Common no par split (3) for (1) by issuance of (2) additional shares 6/25/65
6% Conv. Preferred $50 par called for redemption 1/1/68
Common no par split (2) for (1) by issuance of (1) additional share 7/1/68
3-1/4% Jr. Preferred $100 par called for redemption 8/1/72
Acquired by WSI Acquisition Corp. 5/2/86
Each share $4.25 Preferred no par exchanged for $104.0625 cash
Each share Common no par exchanged for $13.50 cash

WIEGAND (EDWIN L.) CO. (PA)
Merged into Emerson Electric Co. 2/29/68
Each share Common $5 par

WIEN AIR ALASKA INC (AK)
exchanged for (1) share $1.80 Conv. Preferred Ser. B $5 par
Merged into Household Finance Corp. 12/16/1980
Each share Common $1 par exchanged for $6 cash

WIEN ALASKA AIRLINES, INC. (AK)
Merged into Northern Consolidated Airlines, Inc. 04/01/1968
Each share Common $1 par exchanged for (1) share Common $1 par
Northern Consolidated Airlines, Inc. name changed to Wien Consolidated Airlines, Inc. 07/17/1968 which name changed to Wien Air Alaska, Inc. 07/16/1973
(See Wien Air Alaska, Inc.)

WIEN CONSOLIDATED AIRLINES, INC. (AK)
Non-Vtg. Common $1 par reclassified as Common $1 par 05/03/1969
Name changed to Wien Air Alaska, Inc. 07/16/1973
(See Wien Air Alaska, Inc.)

WIEN GROUP INC (NY)
Common 1¢ par split (2) for (1) by issuance of (1) additional share payable 07/29/2005 to holders of record 07/11/2005 Ex date - 08/01/2005
Reincorporated under the laws of New Jersey as MM2 Group, Inc. and Common 1¢ par reclassified as Class A Common no par 10/27/2005
(See MM2 Group, Inc.)

WIENER CORP (LA)
Common $1 par split (4) for (3) by issuance of (1/3) additional share 10/21/76
Stock Dividends - 50% 8/27/71; 10% 1/24/78
Under plan of reorganization each share Common $1 par automatically became (1) share Wiener Enterprises Inc. Common $1 par 12/1/80
(See Wiener Enterprises Inc.)

WIENER ENTERPRISES INC (LA)
Common $1 par split (2) for (1) by issuance of (1) additional share 7/1/83
Chapter 11 bankruptcy proceesings converted to Chapter 7 on 7/20/93
No stockholders' equity

WIENER SHOES INC. (LA)
Name changed to Wiener Corp. 05/21/1971
Wiener Corp. reorganized as Wiener Enterprises Inc. 12/01/1980
(See Wiener Enterprises Inc.)

WIERIG INTL INC (CANADA)
Recapitalized as SpecOpS Labs Inc. 3/5/2004
Each share Common no par exchanged for (0.2) share Common no par
SpecOpS Labs Inc. recapitalized as Link Linux Inc. 3/10/2006

WIESSNER BREWING CO., INC. (MD)
Charter annulled for failure to file annual reports 10/31/56

WIFI WIRELESS INC (OR)
Each share old Common no par exchanged for (0.1) share new Common no par 06/12/2006
Name changed to World of Wireless International Telecom, Inc. 11/09/2017

WIG CORP AMER (FL)
Common 1¢ par changed to 1/3¢ par and (2) additional shares issued 08/06/1971
Name changed to WCA International, Inc. 01/01/1972
(See WCA International, Inc.)

WIGGIN TERMS INC (MA)
Common $100 par changed to $10 par 00/00/1933
Reorganized 00/00/1937
Each (5) shares 7% Preferred $100 par exchanged for (1) share Common $10 par Old Common $10 par had no equity
Liquidation completed
Each share Common $10 par exchanged for initial distribution of $125 cash 11/00/1972
Each share Common $10 par received second distribution of $155 cash 01/00/1973
Each share Common $10 par received third distribution of $17.19 cash 02/00/1973
Each share Common $10 par received fourth distribution of $5.684416 cash 12/20/1974
Each share Common $10 par received fifth and final distribution of $1.8264275 cash 02/03/1975

WIGGINS BERRY & CO LTD (UNITED KINGDOM)
Name changed to KCA International, Ltd. 12/20/1977
KCA International, Ltd. name changed to Bristol Oil & Minerals PLC 12/05/1983 which name changed to BOM Holdings PLC 11/06/1986
(See BOM Holdings PLC)

WIGGINS GROUP PLC (UNITED KINGDOM)
Name changed to Planestation Group PLC 1/9/2004

WIGI4YOU INC (NV)
Name changed to Ajia Innogroup Holdings Ltd. 03/05/2018

WIGWAM DEV INC (DE)
Name changed to Nano Superlattice Technology, Inc. 05/19/2004
(See Nano Superlattice Technology, Inc.)

WIGWAM STORES LTD (WA)
Name changed to Webb's Stores Ltd. 04/09/1974
(See Webb's Stores Ltd.)

WIJIM CORP (NY)
Charter cancelled and proclaimed dissolved for failure to pay taxes 8/29/96

WIKE CORP (NV)
Name changed to GSG Group Inc. 09/18/2017

WIKI GROUP INC (DE)
Recapitalized as Source Financial, Inc. 03/21/2013
Each share Common $0.001 par exchanged for (0.01) share Common $0.001 par
Source Financial, Inc. name changed to Alltemp, Inc. 04/27/2017

WIKIFAMILIES INC (NV)
Name changed to Gepco, Ltd. 10/08/2013

WIKILOAN INC (DE)
Old Common $0.001 par split (10) for (1) by issuance of (9) additional shares payable 06/01/2011 to holders of record 06/01/2011
Each share old Common $0.001 par exchanged for (0.1) share new Common $0.001 par 08/30/2011
Name changed to Wiki Group, Inc. 03/26/2012
Wiki Group, Inc. recapitalized as Source Financial, Inc. 03/21/2013 which name changed to Alltemp, Inc. 04/27/2017

WIL-LOW CAFETERIAS, INC.
Liquidated in 1938
No stockholders' equity

WIL-MAR EXPLORATION & MINING, LTD. (NV)
Merged into National Energy Corp. (NV) 2/9/72
Each share Common 1¢ par exchanged for (0.01) share Common $1 par
(See National Energy Corp. (NV))

WIL WRIGHTS ICE CREAM INC (DE)
Each share Common 1¢ par exchanged for (1/3) share Common 3¢ par 01/05/1987
Dissolved 02/11/1985
Details not available

WILAND SVCS INC (VA)
Merged into Neodate Services 09/30/1992
Each share Common 10¢ par exchanged for (0.25) share Concepts Direct, Inc. Common 10¢ par and $6.87 cash
(See Concepts Direct, Inc.)

WILANOUR RES LTD (ON)
Merged into Goldcorp Inc. 2/20/98
Each share Common no par exchanged for (1/6) Unit consisting of (1) share Class A Subordinate no par and (1) Class A Purchase Warrant expiring 6/30/99

WILBER CORP (NY)
Common no par split (4) for (1) by issuance of (3) additional shares 02/15/1990
Common no par split (4) for (1) by issuance of (3) additional shares payable 02/15/1998 to holders of record 02/01/1998
Common no par changed to 1¢ par and (3) additional shares issued payable 09/18/2003 to holders of record 07/31/2003 Ex date - 09/19/2003
Merged into Community Bank System, Inc. 04/08/2011
Each share Common 1¢ par exchanged for (0.3131438) share Common $1 par and $1.90 cash

WILBER NATL BK (ONEONTA, NY)
Stock Dividends - 10% 04/15/1974; 10% 04/15/1976; 10% 04/30/1979; 10% 05/01/1981
Under plan of reorganization each share Capital Stock $10 par automatically became (1) share Wilber Corp. Common no par 04/28/1983
Wilber Corp. merged into Community Bank System, Inc. 04/08/2011

WILBERT MINING CO. LTD. (UT)
Charter revoked for failure to file reports and pay fees 4/1/63

WILBRAHAM MFG CORP (DE)
Charter cancelled and declared inoperative and void for non-payment of taxes 04/15/1969

WILBUR (H.O.) & SONS, INC.
Merged into Wilbur-Suchard Chocolate Co., Inc. in 1932 which name changed to Wilbur Chocolate Co. 12/31/58
Wilbur Chocolate Co. name changed to W.C.C., Inc. 1/3/66 which completed liquidation 11/15/66

WILBUR B. DRIVER CO. (NJ)
See - Driver (Wilbur B.) Co.

WILBUR CHOCOLATE CO. (PA)
Recapitalized 04/30/1962
Each share $5 Preferred no par exchanged for (2.75) shares Common $5 par
Name changed to W.C.C., Inc. 01/03/1966
(See W.C.C., Inc.)

WILBUR-SUCHARD CHOCOLATE CO., INC. (PA)
Reorganized 00/00/1937
Each share Class A no par exchanged for (0.5) share Common 50¢ par
Each share Class B no par exchanged for (0.2) share Common 50¢ par
Recapitalized 00/00/1945
Each share 5% Preferred $50 par exchanged for (0.5) share $5 Preferred no par
Common 50¢ par changed to $5 par
Stock Dividends - 100% 12/09/1946; 100% 06/26/1947; 10% 07/17/1958
Name changed to Wilbur Chocolate Co. 12/31/1958
Wilbur Chocolate Co. name changed to W.C.C., Inc. 01/03/1966
(See W.C.C., Inc.)

WILCARR MINES, LTD. (ON)
Charter surrendered 00/00/1952

WILCO COML CORP (NY)
Charter cancelled and proclaimed dissolved for failure to pay taxes 12/16/1968

WILCO MNG LTD (ON)
Merged into Deak International Resources Corp. 12/30/88
Each share Capital Stock $1 par exchanged for (0.8) share Common no par
Deak International Resources Corp. name changed to Deak Resources Corp. 3/27/89 which name changed to AJ Perron Gold Corp. 10/7/94
(See AJ Perron Gold Corp.)

WILCO OIL & MINERALS CORP. (DE)
Name changed to Microbiological Sciences, Inc. 12/11/1968
Microbiological Sciences, Inc. name changed to Microbiological Research Corp. 11/16/1970 which recapitalized as General Biometrics Inc. 08/01/1987 which recapitalized as Syntello, Inc. 08/10/1993 which reorganized as Maxim Pharmaceuticals, Inc. 10/09/1996 which merged into EpiCept Inc. 01/05/2006 which recapitalized as Immume Pharmaceuticals Inc. 08/21/2013

WILCOX FORGING CORP
Merged into WFC Acquisition Corp. 3/14/2000
Each share Common exchanged for $34 cash

WILCOX GAY CORP. (MI)
Each (4) shares Common $1 par exchanged for (1) share Common $4 par 9/1/60
Adjudicated bankrupt 11/16/64
No stockholders' equity

WILCOX (H.F.) OIL & GAS CO. (DE)
Name changed to Wilcox Oil Co. 8/11/44
Wilcox Oil Co. was acquired by Tennessee Gas Transmission Co. 7/21/64 which name changed to Tenneco Inc. 4/11/66 which merged into El Paso Natural Gas Co. 12/12/96 which reorganized as El Paso Energy Corp. 8/1/98 which name changed to El Paso Corp. 2/5/2001

WILCOX OIL CO. (DE)
Common $5 par split (2) for (1) by issuance of (1) additional share 1/19/62
Acquired by Tennessee Gas Transmission Co. on a (1.6) for (1) basis 7/21/64
Tennessee Gas Transmission Co. name changed to Tenneco Inc. 4/11/66 which merged into El Paso Natural Gas Co. 12/12/96 which reorganized as El Paso Energy Corp. 8/1/98 which name changed to El Paso Corp. 2/5/2001

WILCOX PRODUCTS CORP.
Merged into Wilcox-Rich Corp. in 1928 which was dissolved in 1936

WILCOX-RICH CORP.
Dissolved in 1936

WILD HORSE INDS INC (BC)
Recapitalized as International Hi-Tech Industries, Inc. (BC) 12/11/92
Each share Common no par

exchanged for (1/7) share Common no par
International Hi-Tech Industries, Inc. (BC) reincorporated in Canada 5/31/96

WILD HORSE RES LTD (AB)
Recapitalized as Azure Dynamics Corp. 04/27/2001
Each share Common no par exchanged for (0.1) share Common no par
(See Azure Dynamics Corp.)

WILD OATS MKTS INC (DE)
Common $0.001 par split (3) for (2) by issuance of (0.5) additional share payable 01/07/1998 to holders of record 12/22/1997
Common $0.001 par split (3) for (2) by issuance of (0.5) additional share payable 12/01/1999 to holders of record 11/17/1999
Merged into Whole Foods Market, Inc. 08/31/2007
Each share Common $0.001 par exchanged for $18.50 cash

WILD RIV RES INC (ON)
Recapitalized as Oil Springs Energy Corp. 02/19/1996
Each share Common no par exchanged for (0.2) share Common no par
Oil Springs Energy Corp. recapitalized as OSE Corp. 08/07/2002 which recapitalized as Petro Basin Energy Corp. (ON) 09/19/2011 which reincorporated in British Columbia as Peace River Capital Corp. 09/16/2016 which name changed to Liberty One Lithium Corp. 12/02/2016

WILD ROSE RES LTD (BC)
Name changed to China Cellular Communications Corp. 12/18/1991
China Cellular Communications Corp. name changed to China Jinrong Corp. 12/09/1993 which recapitalized as Rystar Development Ltd. (BC) 06/25/1996 which reincorporated in Canada as Rystar Communications Ltd. 03/31/1998
(See Rystar Communications Ltd.)

WILD ROVER CORP (NJ)
Acquired by Refac Technology Development Corp. 8/28/74
Each share Common no par exchanged for $0.05 cash

WILD STREAM EXPL INC (AB)
Merged into Crescent Point Energy Corp. 03/15/2012
Each share Common no par exchanged for (0.17) share Common no par, (1) share Raging River Exploration Inc. Common no par and (0.2) Common Stock Purchase Warrant expiring 04/16/2012
(See each company's listing)

WILD WINGS INC (NV)
Name changed to Red Oak Hereford Farms Inc. 3/14/97

WILDCARD WIRELESS SOLUTIONS INC (AB)
Reincorporated 06/30/2001
Place of incorporation changed from (BC) to (AB) 06/30/2001
Name changed to TransAKT Corp. 07/02/2003
TransAKT Corp. recapitalized as TransAKT Ltd. (AB) 08/04/2006 which reincorporated in Nevada 12/15/2010

WILDCAT ACQUISITIONS INC (CANADA)
Name changed to Condor Gold Fields Inc. 04/08/1997
Condor Gold Fields Inc. recapitalized as Cloudbreak Resources Ltd. (Canada) 11/08/2002 which reorganized in British Columbia 04/26/2010 which name changed to Petro One Energy Corp. 12/14/2010

which merged into Goldstrike Resources Ltd. 02/29/2016

WILDCAT EXPL CO (UT)
Name changed to S.H. Resources & Development Corp. 06/30/1981

WILDCAT EXPL LTD (BC)
Reincorporated 05/31/2016
Each share old Common no par exchanged for (0.05) share new Common no par 12/07/2012
Place of incorporation changed from (MB) to (BC) 05/31/2016
Name changed to LiCo Energy Metals Inc. 10/04/2016

WILDCAT MTN CORP (NH)
Liquidated in 1991
Details not available

WILDCAT PETE LTD (BC)
Recapitalized as International Wildcat Resources Ltd. 07/24/1984
Each share Common no par exchanged for (1/3) share Common no par
International Wildcat Resources Ltd. recapitalized as Wildcat Trading Corp. 10/02/1991 which name changed to Pacific Wildcat Resources Corp. 04/21/1994

WILDCAT SILVER CORP (BC)
Each share Common no par received distribution of (1) share Ventana Gold Corp. Common no par payable 12/14/2006 to holders of record 12/14/2006
Note: Non-Canadian residents who did not obtain a clearance certificate will receive cash from the sale of stock
Each share Common no par received distribution of (0.098318) share Riva Gold Corp. Common no par payable 07/19/2010 to holders of record 07/19/2010
Name changed to AZ Mining Inc. 06/05/2015
AZ Mining Inc. name changed to Arizona Mining Inc. 10/28/2015
(See Arizona Mining Inc.)

WILDCAT TRADING CORP (BC)
Name changed to Pacific Wildcat Resources Corp. 4/21/94

WILDCAT U S A INC (FL)
Proclaimed dissolved for failure to file reports and pay fees 8/13/93

WILDCAT URANIUM CORP. (UT)
Merged into Midwest Consolidated Uranium Corp. on a (0.04) for (1) basis 6/10/55
Midwest Consolidated Uranium Corp. merged into COG Minerals Corp. 5/1/56 which was acquired by Colorado Oil & Gas Corp. for cash 12/31/60

WILDER TRANSN INC (NY)
Adjudicated bankrupt 01/29/1973
Stockholders' equity unlikely

WILDERNESS EXPERIENCE INC (CA)
Chapter 11 Federal Bankruptcy Code converted to Chapter 7 on 9/26/89
Stockholders' equity unlikely

WILDEY INC (DE)
Charter cancelled and declared inoperative and void for non-payment of taxes 03/01/1991

WILDFIRE CAP CORP (NV)
Recapitalized as Pacific Magtron International Corp. 8/3/98
Each share Common $0.001 par exchanged for (2/3) share Common $0.001 par
Pacfic Magtron International Corp. reorganized as Herborium Group, Inc. 12/14/2006

WILDFIRE RES LTD (BC)
Recapitalized as Crusader Gold Corp. 10/26/1989
Each share Common no par

exchanged for (0.2) share Common no par
Crusader Gold Corp. recapitalized as Shorewood Explorations Ltd. 11/13/1992 which merged into International Broadlands Resources Ltd. 04/06/1995 which recapitalized as Broadlands Resources Ltd. (New) 03/15/1999 which recapitalized as Pinnacle Mines Ltd. (Ctfs. dated after 07/16/2003) 07/16/2003 which name changed to Jayden Resources Inc. (BC) 06/29/2010 which reincorporated in Cayman Islands 10/03/2012

WILDFLOWER MARIJUANA INC (BC)
Name changed to Wildflower Brands Inc. 05/03/2018

WILDING INC. (DE)
Completely liquidated 8/29/67
Each share Common $1 par exchanged for (0.27027) share Bell & Howell Co. (III.) Common no par
Bell & Howell Co. (III.) reincorporated in Delaware 5/6/77
(See Bell & Howell Co. (Del.))

WILDLAW CAP CPC 2 INC (CANADA)
Recapitalized as AcuityAds Holdings Inc. 07/22/2014
Each share Common no par exchanged for (0.03144654) share Common no par

WILDLIFE VACCINES INC (CO)
Reincorporated under the laws of Delaware as Techniquest International, Inc. 06/26/1986
(See Techniquest International, Inc.)

WILDNEST MINES LTD. (ON)
Charter cancelled by the Province of Ontario 6/12/61

WILDON PRODUCTIONS INC (NV)
Reorganized as Visual Management Systems, Inc. 07/09/2007
Each share Common $0.001 par exchanged for (1/7) share Common $0.001 par
(See Visual Management Systems, Inc.)

WILDOR GOLD MINES LTD. (ON)
Charter cancelled and declared dissolved for failure to file reports in 1969

WILDROSE PETE LTD (BC)
Recapitalized as International Wildrose Resources Ltd. 9/11/84
Each share Common no par exchanged for (0.25) share Common no par
International Wildrose Resources Ltd. merged into Colossus Resource Equities Inc. 12/8/87 which merged into Prime Resources Corp. (BC) 2/1/89 which recapitalized as Prime Resources Group Inc. 1/26/90 which merged into HomeStake Mining Co. 12/3/98 which merged into Barrick Gold Corp. 12/14/2001

WILDROSE RES LTD (BC)
Each share Common no par received distribution of (1) share Cariboo Rose Resources Ltd. no par payable 12/13/2006 to holders of record 12/05/2006
Merged into Skygold Ventures Ltd. 06/27/2008
Each share Common no par exchanged for (0.82) share Common no par
Skygold Ventures Ltd. name changed to Spanish Mountain Gold Ltd. 01/14/2010

WILDROSE VENTURES INC (AB)
Delisted from Alberta Stock Exchange 04/19/1994

WILDSIDE CORP (FL)
Name changed to Houstron Corp. 04/20/1972
(See Houstron Corp.)

WILDWOOD PETE LTD (BC)
Name changed to Frobisher Resources Ltd. 10/19/81
Frobisher Resources Ltd. merged into Canadian Frobisher Resources Ltd. 11/21/91 which merged into Orbit Oil & Gas Ltd. 8/26/94
(See Orbit Oil & Gas Ltd.)

WILESS CTLS INC (NV)
Name changed to Next Galaxy Corp. 08/19/2014

WILEY-BICKFORD-SWEET CO.
Acquired by Wiley-Bickford-Sweet Corp. in 1931 which completed liquidation 9/19/55

WILEY-BICKFORD-SWEET CORP. (MA)
Liquidation completed 9/19/55

WILEY JOHN & SONS INC (NY)
Each share Capital Stock $1 par exchanged for (1.5) shares Class A Common $1 par and (1) share Class B Common $1 par 09/13/1982
(Additional Information in Active)

WILEY OILFIELD HAULING LTD (AB)
Capital Stock no par split (2) for (1) by issuance of (1) additional share 3/23/73
Merged into Majestic Wiley Contractors Ltd. (Alta.) 5/17/74
Each share Capital Stock no par exchanged for (1) share Capital Stock no par
Majestic Wiley Contractors Ltd. (Alta.) reincorporated in Ontario 12/17/77 which name changed to Majestic Contractors Ltd. 5/6/83
(See Majestic Contractors Ltd.)

WILFRED AMERN EDL CORP (NY)
Petition filed under Chapter 11 Federal Bankruptcy Code dismissed 6/2/94
No stockholders' equity

WILHELM ENTERPRISES CORP. (DE)
Called for redemption 1/11/77
Public interest eliminated

WILHITE INSTRS INC (MN)
Merged into Johnson & Johnson 06/28/1979
Each share Common 10¢ par exchanged for $2.15 cash

WILKES-BARRE & HAZELTON TERMINAL CORP. (DE)
Charter cancelled and declared inoperative and void for non-payment of taxes 4/1/33

WILKES-BARRE DEPOSIT & SAVINGS BANK (WILKES-BARRE, PA)
Merged into Northeastern Pennsylvania National Bank & Trust Co. (Scranton, PA) 08/01/1958
Each share Capital Stock $25 par exchanged for (2.65) shares Capital Stock $18 par
Northeastern Pennsylvania National Bank & Trust Co. (Scranton, PA) name changed to Northeastern National Bank of Pennsylvania (Scranton, PA) 04/02/1971 which name changed to Northeastern Bank of Pennsylvania (Scranton, PA) 01/02/1974 which reorganized as Northeastern Bancorp, Inc. 08/12/1981 which merged into PNC Financial Corp 01/30/1985 which name changed to PNC Bank Corp. 02/08/1993 which name changed to PNC Financial Services Group, Inc. 03/15/2000

WILKES-BARRE LACE MANUFACTURING CO. (PA)
Name changed to Whitman (Clarence) & Sons, Inc. 00/00/1952
Whitman (Clarence) & Sons, Inc. name changed to Prince Gardner Co., Inc. 10/31/1956 which name changed to Settlement Corp. 10/28/1966

(See Settlement Corp.)

WILL & BAUMER CANDLE INC (NY)
Name changed to W & B Liquidating Corp. 06/01/1972
(See W & B Liquidating Corp.)

WILL ROSS INC (WI)
Common $2.50 par changed to $1.25 par and (2) additional shares issued 06/30/1961
Common $1.25 par changed to $1 par and (1) additional share issued 08/06/1968
Stock Dividend - 50% 08/06/1964
Merged into Searle (G.D.) & Co. (DE) 12/31/1973
Each share Common $1 par exchanged for (1.2) shares Common 33-1/3¢ par
(See Searle (G.D.) & Co. (DE))

WILLAMETTE INDS INC (OR)
Common $1 par changed to 50¢ par and (1) additional share issued 03/10/1969
Common 50¢ par split (5) for (3) by issuance of (2/3) additional share 05/13/1986
Common 50¢ par split (2) for (1) by issuance of (1) additional share 05/22/1992
Common 50¢ par split (2) for (1) by issuance of (1) additional share payable 09/12/1997 to holders of record 08/25/1997 Ex date - 09/15/1997
Merged into Weyerhaeuser Co. 03/14/2002
Each share Common 50¢ par exchanged for $55.50 cash

WILLAMETTE VY BK (SALEM, OR)
Stock Dividend - 5% payable 05/01/2007 to holders of record 04/02/2007 Ex date - 04/03/2007
Reorganized as Oregon Bancorp, Inc. 03/05/2009
Each share Common no par exchanged for (1) share Common no par

WILLAPA HARBOR LUMBER MILLS
Merged into Weyerhaeuser Timber Co. on a (1) for (5) basis in 1949 which name was changed to Weyerhaeuser Co. 9/1/59

WILLARD BOAT WORKS (CA)
Name changed to Willard Co. Inc. 07/02/1975
(See Willard Co.)

WILLARD CO (CA)
Assets foreclosed upon 10/29/1990
No stockholders' equity

WILLBROS GROUP INC (DE)
Acquired by Primoris Services Corp. 06/01/2018
Each share Common 5¢ par exchanged for $0.60 cash

WILLBROS GROUP INC (PANAMA)
Reincorporated under the laws of Delaware 03/03/2009
(See Willbros Group, Inc. (DE))

WILLCOX & GIBBS INC (DE)
Chapter 11 bankruptcy proceedings converted to Chapter 7 on 4/9/2002
Stockholders' equity unlikely

WILLCOX & GIBBS INC (NY)
Class A Conv. $1.50 par called for redemption 6/17/83
Common $1 par split (4) for (3) by issuance of (1/3) additional share 6/30/87
Common $1 par split (4) for (3) by issuance of (1/3) additional share 6/30/88
Common $1 par split (4) for (3) by issuance of (1/3) additional share 6/30/89
Name changed to Rexel Inc. 5/12/95
(See Rexel Inc.)

WILLCOX & GIBBS SEWING MACHINE CO. (NY)
Each share Common $50 par exchanged for (5) shares Common $5 par in 1948
Common $5 par changed to $1 par and (4) additional shares issued 11/22/60
Name changed to Willcox & Gibbs, Inc. 3/31/67
Willcox & Gibbs, Inc. name changed to Rexel Inc. 5/12/95
(See Rexel Inc.)

WILLCREST RES LTD (BC)
Recapitalized as Trincana Resources Ltd. 11/8/94
Each share Common no par exchanged for (1/3) share Common no par
Trincana Resources Ltd. name changed to Bevo Agro Inc. 7/11/2000

WILLEMS INDUSTRIES, INC. (NY)
Charter revoked for failure to file reports and pay fees 12/15/60

WILLER COLOR TELEVISION SYSTEM, INC. (NY)
Charter cancelled and proclaimed dissolved for failure to pay taxes 12/15/70

WILLETT (CONSIDER H.), INC. (KY)
Each share Capital Stock $10 par exchanged for (3) shares Capital Stock $5 par 00/00/1946
Stock Dividend - 100% 07/14/1950
Name changed to C.H.W. Co. 06/29/1963
(See C.H.W. Co.)

WILLIAM & CLARISSA INC (DE)
Name changed to Finet Holdings Corp. 03/00/1992
Finet Holdings Corp. name changed to FiNet.com, Inc. 05/28/1999
(See FiNet.com, Inc.)

WILLIAM BRADLEY & SON
See - Bradley (William) & Son

WILLIAM BYRD PRESS INC (VA)
Merged into Cadmus Communications Corp. 6/30/84
Each share Common 50¢ par exchanged for (1) share Common 50¢ par
(See Cadmus Communications Corp.)

WILLIAM CARTER CO. (MA)
See - Carter (William) Co.

WM. CRAMP & SONS SHIP & ENGINE BUILDING CO.
See - Cramp (Wm.) & Sons Ship & Engine Building Co.

WILLIAM DAVIES CO., INC.
See - Davies (William) Co., Inc.

WM. E. WRIGHT CO. (DE)
See - Wright (Wm. E.) Co.

WILLIAM FREIHOFER BAKING CO. (DE)
See - Freihofer (William) Baking Co.

WILLIAM GANSCHOW CO.
See - Ganschow (William) Co.

WILLIAM H. HASKELL MANUFACTURING CO. (RI)
See - Haskell (William H.) Manufacturing Co.

WILLIAM HODGES & CO., INC. (PA)
See - Hodges (William) & Co., Inc.

WILLIAM HOLDEN IRON MINES LTD. (ON)
Charter surrendered 00/00/1962

WILLIAM L. GILBERT CLOCK CORP. (CT)
See - Gilbert (William L.) Clock Corp.

WILLIAM MULTI-TECH INC (QC)
Recapitalized as Valencia Ventures Inc. (QC) 01/17/2003
Each share Common no par exchanged for (0.01) share Common no par
Valencia Ventures Inc. (QC) reincorporated in Ontario 06/02/2014

WILLIAM O. GOODRICH CO.
See - Goodrich (William O.) Co.

WILLIAM PENN RACING ASSN (PA)
Merged into WPR, Inc. 12/20/77
Each share Class A Common $1 par exchanged for $5 cash
Each share Class B Common $1 par exchanged for $5 cash

WILLIAM R. WARNER & CO., INC.
See - Warner (William R.) & Co., Inc.

WILLIAM S. MORRIS INC. (NY)
See - Morris (William S.) Inc.

WM. WALTKE & CO.
See - Waltke (Wm.) & Co.

WILLIAM WALLACE CO. (CA)
See - Wallace (William) Co.

WILLIAM WALLACE CORP. (DE)
See - Wallace (William) Corp.

WILLIAM WHITMAN CO., INC. (MA)
See - Whitman (William) Co., Inc.

WILLIAM WHITMAN CO., INC. (OH)
See - Whitman (William) Co., Inc.

WM. R. WHITTAKER CO. LTD. (CA)
See - Whittaker (Wm. R.) Co. Ltd.

WM. WRIGLEY, JR., CO. (WV)
See - Wrigley (Wm.), Jr., Co.

WM. ZOLLER CO.
See - Zoller (Wm.) Co.

WILLIAMHOUSE, INC. (NY)
Stock Dividend - 25% 3/19/62
Name changed to Williamhouse-Regency Inc. 11/1/67
(See Williamhouse-Regency Inc.)

WILLIAMHOUSE REGENCY INC (NY)
Common 10¢ par split (3) for (2) by issuance of (0.5) additional share 12/5/68
Common 10¢ par split (4) for (3) by issuance of (1/3) additional share 12/1/69
Common 10¢ par split (3) for (2) by issuance of (0.5) additional share 3/28/81
Stock Dividend - 33-1/3% 11/17/67
Merged into W.R. Holdings 12/23/82
Each share Common 10¢ par exchanged for $30 cash

WILLIAMS & CO INC (PA)
Each share Common $5 par exchanged for (2) shares Common $2.50 par 00/00/1947
Common $2.50 par changed to $1 par and (1.5) additional shares issued 10/03/1963
Merged into Superior Tube Co. 04/10/1980
Each share Common $1 par exchanged for $27.75 cash

WILLIAMS A L CORP (DE)
Common 10¢ par split (5) for (2) by issuance of (1.5) additional shares 4/21/83
Common 10¢ par split (5) for (4) by issuance of (0.25) additional share 9/15/83
Merged into Primerica Corp. (DE) 11/1/89
Each share Common 10¢ par exchanged for (0.82) share Common 1¢ par
Primerica Corp. (DE) name changed to Travelers Inc. 12/31/93 which name changed to Travelers Group Inc. 4/16/95 which name changed to Citigroup Inc. 10/8/98

WILLIAMS BROS CO (NV)
Common $1 par split (2) for (1) by issuance of (1) additional share 3/30/67
Common $1 par split (2) for (1) by issuance of (1) additional share 6/30/69
Name changed to Williams Companies (NV) 5/11/71
Williams Companies (NV) reincorporated in Delaware as Williams Companies Inc. 6/1/87

WILLIAMS CLAYTON ENERGY INC (DE)
Merged into Noble Energy, Inc. 04/24/2017
Each share Common 10¢ par exchanged for (3.7222) shares Common 1¢ par

WILLIAMS COAL SEAM GAS RTY TR (DE)
Liquidation completed
Each Trust Unit received initial distribution of $2.381443 cash payable 11/29/2010 to holders of record 11/15/2010
Each Trust Unit received second and final distribution of $0.043749 cash payable 12/31/2010 to holders of record 11/15/2010
Note: Certificates were not required to be surrendered and are without value

WILLIAMS COMMUNICATIONS GROUP INC (DE)
Issue Information - 29,600,000 shares COM offered at $23 per share on 09/30/1999
Plan of reorganization under Chapter 11 Federal Bankruptcy Code effective 10/15/2002
No stockholders' equity

WILLIAMS (J.B.) CO. (CT)
Each share Common $10 par exchanged for (1) share Preferred $5 par and (1) share Common $5 par 00/00/1937
Stock Dividend - 100% 04/15/1948
Merged into Pharmaceuticals, Inc. 06/02/1959
Details not available

WILLIAMS COS INC (DE)
Name changed 06/01/1987
Common $1 par split (2) for (1) by issuance of (1) additional share 02/28/1975
80¢ Conv. Preferred Ser. A no par changed to $1 par on 05/23/1975
80¢ Conv. Preferred Ser. A $1 par called for redemption 12/28/1979
Name and state of incorporation changed from Williams Companies (NV) to Williams Companies, Inc. (DE) 06/01/1987
$3.875 Conv. Exchangeable Preferred $1 par called for redemption 06/10/1993
$2.21 Preferred $1 par called for redemption at $25 on 09/01/1997
9.6% Quarterly Income Capital Securities called for redemption 09/30/1997
$3.50 Conv. Preferred $1 par called for redemption at $51.40 plus $0.875 accrued dividend on 11/01/1999
Issue Information - 44,000,000 INCOME PACS offered at $24 per Income Pacs on 01/07/2002
Each Income PACS exchanged for (1) share Common $1 par 02/16/2005
(Additional Information in Active)

WILLIAMS CRAFT INC (TX)
Merged into Avtek Corp. 03/17/1972
Each share Common no par exchanged for (1) share Common 4¢ par
(See Avtek Corp.)

WILLIAMS CREEK EXPLS LTD (BC)
Recapitalized 08/19/1988
Reincorporated 07/05/1990
Recapitalized from Williams Creek Gold Quartz Mining Co. to Williams Creek Explorations Ltd. 08/18/1988
Each share Common no par exchanged for (0.25) share Common no par
Place of incorporation changed from (ON) to (BC) 07/05/1990
Name changed to Williams Creek Gold Ltd. 06/14/2011
Williams Creek Gold Ltd. merged into

Barkerville Gold Mines Ltd. 08/16/2016

WILLIAMS CREEK GOLD LTD (BC)
Merged into Barkerville Gold Mines Ltd. 08/16/2016
Each share Common no par exchanged for (0.06235257) share Common no par
Note: Unexchanged certificates were cancelled and became without value 08/16/2018

WILLIAMS CTLS INC (DE)
Each share old Common 1¢ par exchanged for (1/6) share new Common 1¢ par 03/20/2006
Acquired by Curtiss-Wright Corp. 12/17/2012
Each share new Common 1¢ par exchanged for $15.42 cash

WILLIAMS ELECTRS INC (DE)
Common 50¢ par split (3) for (2) by issuance of (0.5) additional share 01/05/1982
Name changed to WMS Industries Inc. 02/20/1987
(See WMS Industries Inc.)

WILLIAMS ENERGY PARTNERS L P (DE)
Issue Information - 4,000,000 COM UNITS REPSTG LTD PARTNER INT offered at $21.50 per Unit on 02/05/2001
Name changed to Magellan Midstream Partners, L.P. 9/1/2003

WILLIAMS FOUNDRY & MACHINE CO.
Acquired by National Erie Co. in 1929 which was reorganized as National Erie Corp. in 1935 which was dissolved in 1954

WILLIAMS HYDRAULICS, INC. (CA)
Charter revoked for failure to file reports and pay fees in March 1943

WILLIAMS MFG CO (OH)
Reincorporated under the laws of Delaware as Escalade, Inc. and Common no par changed to $1 par 03/23/1973
Escalade, Inc. (DE) reincorporated in Indiana 07/23/1987

WILLIAMS-MCWILLIAMS INDUSTRIES, INC. (DE)
Merged into Zapata Off-Shore Co. 04/12/1968
Each share Common $10 par exchanged for (0.72) share Common 25¢ par
Zapata Off-Shore Co. name changed to Zapata Norness Inc. 11/25/1968 which name changed to Zapata Corp. (DE) 02/15/1972 which reincorporated in Nevada 04/30/1999 which reincorporated in Delaware as Harbinger Group Inc. 12/23/2009 which name changed to HRG Group, Inc. 03/11/2015 which recapitalized as Spectrum Brands Holdings, Inc. (New) 07/16/2018

WILLIAMS NAT GAS CO (DE)
Company advised Adjustable Rate Preferred Ser. A $1 par no longer public 08/17/2005
Details not available

WILLIAMS OIL-O-MATIC HEATING CORP.
Acquired by Eureka Vacuum Cleaner Co. in 1945
Each share Common exchanged for either (0.5) share Common or $5.16 cash
Eureka Vacuum Cleaner Co. name changed to Eureka Williams Corp. in 1946 which name changed to Wardell Corp. in 1954 which merged into Amerace Corp. 5/29/57 which name changed to Amerace Esna Corp. 8/30/68 which name changed back to Amerace Corp. 4/27/73
(See Amerace Corp.)

WILLIAMS PARTNERS L P NEW (DE)
Merged into Williams Companies, Inc. 08/10/2018
Each Common Unit exchanged for (1.494) shares Common $1 par

WILLIAMS PARTNERS L P OLD (DE)
Merged into Williams Partners L.P. (New) 02/02/2015
Each Common Unit exchanged for (0.86672) Common Unit
Williams Partners L.P. (New) merged into Williams Companies, Inc. 08/10/2018

WILLIAMS PIPELINE PARTNERS L P (DE)
Merged into Williams Partners L.P. (Old) 08/31/2010
Each Common Unit exchanged for (0.7584) Common Unit
Williams Partners L.P. (Old) merged into Williams Partners L.P. (New) 02/02/2015 which merged into Williams Companies, Inc. 08/10/2018

WILLIAMS PLC (UNITED KINGDOM)
Name changed 5/28/97
Name changed from Williams Holdings PLC to Williams PLC 5/28/97
Each old Sponsored ADR for Ordinary exchanged for approximately (0.9) new Sponsored ADR for Ordinary 7/10/98
Plan of demerger effective 11/8/2000
Each new Sponsored ADR for Ordinary exchanged for approximately $12.2341 cash

WILLIAMS R C & CO (NY)
Capital Stock no par changed to $1 par 07/31/1956
Capital Stock $1 par reclassified as Common $1 par 03/25/1957
Charter cancelled and proclaimed dissolved for failure to file reports and pay taxes 12/15/1971

WILLIAMS RALPH ENTERPRISES INC (CA)
Adjudicated bankrupt 06/06/1974
Stockholders' equity unlikely

WILLIAMS ROGER MUSIC LTD (ON)
Name changed to RWMC Productions Ltd. 8/8/74
RWMC Productions Ltd. name changed to International Phoenix Capital Corp. 1/18/77 which name changed to Fairway Automotive Industries Ltd. 9/25/86 which recapitalized as Fairway Industries Ltd. 2/26/88 which recapitalized as Pharmaglobe Inc. (ONT) 3/14/94 which reincorporated in Delaware 3/1/2001 which name changed to Pharmaglobe America Group, Inc. 5/12/2004

WILLIAMS SCOTSMAN INTL INC (DE)
Merged into Ristretto Group S.a.r.l. 10/31/2007
Each share Common 1¢ par exchanged for $28.25 cash

WILLIAMS SONOMA INC (CA)
Common split (3) for (2) by issuance of (0.5) additional share 06/26/1986
Common split (3) for (2) by issuance of (0.5) additional share 06/28/1989
Common split (3) for (2) by issuance of (0.5) additional share 06/29/1990
Common split (3) for (2) by issuance of (0.5) additional share 02/18/1994
Common split (3) for (2) by issuance of (0.5) additional share 09/26/1994
Common 1¢ par split (2) for (1) by issuance of (1) additional share payable 05/15/1998 to holders of record 05/04/1998
Common 1¢ par split (2) for (1) by issuance of (1) additional share payable 05/09/2002 to holders of record 04/29/2002 Ex date - 05/10/2002

Reincorporated under the laws of Delaware 05/26/2011

WILLIAMS STORES CO. (DE)
Name changed to Mac (W.W.) Co. in 1936
(See Mac (W.W.) Co.)

WILLIAMS T E PHARMACEUTICALS INC (OK)
Charter suspended for failure to pay taxes 06/05/1989

WILLIAMS VALLEY RAILROAD CO.
Merged into Reading Co. on a (0.04) for (1) basis 12/31/47
Reading Co. merged into Reading Entertainment Inc. (DE) 10/15/96 which reincorporated in Nevada 12/29/99 which merged into Reading International, Inc. 12/31/2001

WILLIAMS W W CO (OH)
Each share Class A Common $1 par or Class B Common $1 par exchanged for (1) share Common $1 par 7/12/66
Common $1 par split (4) for (3) by issuance of (1/3) additional share 8/2/71
Common $1 par split (2) for (1) by issuance of (1) additional share 8/25/78
Stock Dividends - 25% 2/15/68; 20% 8/5/74; 20% 11/3/76; 10% 5/16/86
Each share Common $1 par exchanged for (0.001) share Common $1,000 par 10/19/93
Note: In effect holders received $19 cash per share and public interest was eliminated

WILLIAMSBURG CORP (DE)
Charter cancelled and declared inoperative and void for non-payment of taxes 3/1/77

WILLIAMSBURG DATA PROCESSING CORP (DE)
Name changed to Williamsburg Corp. 4/5/74
(See Williamsburg Corp.)

WILLIAMSBURG GREETINGS CORP. (DE)
Common 25¢ par changed to 20¢ par 3/20/63
No longer in existence having become inoperative and void for non-payment of taxes 4/1/67

WILLIAMSBURG LIFE INSURANCE CO. (MD)
Merged into Independent Liberty Life Insurance Co. 12/30/1967
Each share Capital Stock $1 par exchanged for (0.47619) share Common $1 par
(See Independent Liberty Life Insurance Co.)

WILLIAMSBURG LIFE INSURANCE CO. (VA)
Merged into Williamsburg Life Insurance Co. (MD) 09/14/1966
Each share Capital Stock $2 par exchanged for (1.7) shares Capital Stock $1 par
Williamsburg Life Insurance Co. (MD) merged into Independent Liberty Life Insurance Co. 12/30/1967
(See Independent Liberty Life Insurance Co.)

WILLIAMSBURG NATL BK (WILLIAMSBURG, VA)
Acquired by Southern Bankshares, Inc. 3/31/71
Each share Capital Stock $10 par exchanged for (1) share $3.50 Conv. Preferred $10 par

WILLIAMSON CO (OH)
Merged into Carroll Acquisition Co. 03/07/1988
Each share Common Capital Stock no par exchanged for $92.50 cash

WILLIAMSON COUNTY BANCORP, INC. (TN)
Under plan of merger name changed to Central South Bancorp, Inc. 1/31/86
Central South Bancorp, Inc. merged into Commerce Union Corp. 9/22/86 which merged into Sovran Financial Corp. 11/1/87 which merged into C&S/Sovran Corp. 9/1/90 which merged into NationsBank Corp. 12/31/91 which reincorporated in Delaware as BankAmerica Corp. (Old) 9/25/98 which merged into BankAmerica Corp. (New) 9/30/98 which name changed to Bank of America Corp. 4/28/99

WILLIAMSON E B & CO INC (CO)
Charter suspended for failure to maintain a resident agent 09/02/1989

WILLIAMSON GOLD MINES, LTD. (ON)
Dissolved 5/26/58

WILLIAMSON PAR THREE INC (FL)
Voluntarily dissolved 09/23/1983
Details not available

WILLIAMSPORT & NORTH BRANCH RAILWAY CO.
Property sold in 1937
No stockholders' equity

WILLIAMSPORT NATL BK (WILLIAMSPORT, PA)
Common $20 par changed to $10 par and (1) additional share issued plus a 4% stock dividend paid 08/30/1968
Common $10 par changed to $2.50 par and (3) additional shares issued 07/01/1976
Stock Dividend - 100% 06/30/1963
Merged into Susquehanna Bancshares, Inc. 07/01/1986
Each share Common $2.50 par exchanged for (5.25) shares Common $2 par
Susquehanna Bancshares, Inc. merged into BB&T Corp. 08/01/2015

WILLIAMSPORT WATER CO. (PA)
Acquired by Williamsport Municipal Water Authority in 1947

WILLIAMSPORT WIRE ROPE CO.
Sold to Bethlehem Steel Corp. (Del.) in 1937

WILLIAMSVILLE SHARE CORP.
Acquired by Iroquois Share Corp. 00/00/1930
Details not available

WILLIE C S CAFE & BAR KAW VY INC (KS)
Plan of reorganization under Chapter 11 Federal Bankruptcy Code effective 11/5/2002
No Limited Partnership holders' equity

WILLIMANTIC TR CO (WILLIMANTIC, CT)
Common $10 par changed to $5 par and (1) additional share issued 3/1/74
Name changed to Independent Bank & Trust Co. (Willimantic, CT) 7/1/81
Independent Bank & Trust Co. (Willimantic, CT) merged into First Connecticut Bancorp, Inc. 10/31/83 which merged into Fleet Financial Group, Inc. (Old) 3/17/86 which merged into Fleet/Norstar Financial Group, Inc. 1/1/88 which name changed to Fleet Financial Group, Inc. (New) 4/15/92 which name changed to Fleet Boston Corp. 10/1/99 which name changed to FleetBoston Financial Corp. 4/18/2000 which merged into Bank of America Corp. 4/1/2004

WILLING HLDG INC (FL)
Name changed to Valiant Health Care, Inc. 08/10/2010
(See Valiant Health Care, Inc.)

WILLIS CORROON GROUP PLC (ENGLAND)
Name changed 01/22/1992
Name changed from Willis Corroon PLC to to Willis Corroon Group PLC 01/22/1992
Acquired by Trinity Acquisition PLC 11/09/1998
Each Sponsored ADR for Ordinary 12-1/2p par exchanged for £10 cash

WILLIS GROUP HOLDINGS LTD (BERMUDA)
Reincorporated under the laws of Ireland as Willis Group Holdings PLC and Common $0.000115 par reclassified as Ordinary $0.000115 par 12/31/2009
Willis Group Holdings PLC (Ireland) reorganized in Bermuda as Willis Towers Watson PLC 01/05/2016

WILLIS GROUP HOLDINGS PLC (IRELAND)
Reorganized under the laws of Bermuda as Willis Towers Watson PLC 01/05/2016
Each share Ordinary $0.000115 par exchanged for (0.37750094) share Ordinary $0.000304635 par

WILLIS LEASE FIN CORP (DE)
Reincorporated 06/08/1998
State of incorporation changed from (CA) to (DE) and Common no par changed to 1¢ par 06/08/1998
9% Preferred Ser. A 1¢ par called for redemption at $10 plus $0.0425 accrued dividends on 11/02/2012
(Additional Information in Active)

WILLIS-WAY CORP. (OR)
Charter revoked for failure to file reports and pay fees 7/20/72

WILLISTON BASIN OIL & EXPLORATION CO. (UT)
Capital Stock 5¢ par changed to 10¢ par in 1953
Each share Capital Stock 10¢ par exchanged for (0.1) share Capital Stock $1 par 10/1/62
Recapitalized as Whittington Oil Co., Inc. 9/5/67
Each share Capital Stock $1 par exchanged for (1) share Capital Stock 20¢ par
Whittington Oil Co., Inc. name changed to Louisiana-Pacific Resources, Inc. 10/4/71

WILLISTON BASIN OIL & GAS LANDS LTD. (CANADA)
Liquidated 00/00/1952
Details not available

WILLISTON BASIN OIL VENTURES, INC. (DE)
Charter cancelled for non-payment of taxes 4/1/58

WILLISTON INTERNATIONAL CORP. (DE)
Name changed to Allstate Investment Corp. 8/16/67
Allstate Investment Corp. charter cancelled 4/15/75

WILLISTON OIL & DEVELOPMENT CORP. (NV)
Each share old Common $0.001 par exchanged for (0.02) share new Common $0.001 par 10/14/73
Name changed to Williston Oil Corp. and new Common $0.001 par reclassified as Class A Common no par 7/9/79
Williston Oil Corp. name changed to Medco Health Corp. 12/12/95
(See Medco Health Corp.)

WILLISTON OIL CORP (NV)
Stock Dividends - 10% 7/30/79; 150% 5/29/80
Name changed to Medco Health Corp. 12/12/95
(See Medco Health Corp.)

WILLISTON PIONEER OIL CORP. (DE)
Name changed to Williston International Corp. 2/18/66
Williston International Corp. name changed to Allstate Investment Corp. 8/16/67
(See Allstate Investment Corp.)

WILLISTON WILDCATTERS OIL CORP (AB)
Cease trade order effective 12/21/95
Stockholders' equity unlikely

WILLITS SHOPPING CENTER, INC. (CA)
Name changed to McFarland Logging Co. 8/7/68

WILLNER INDS (NJ)
Through indefinitely open purchase offer majority shares reacquired 00/00/1982
Public interest eliminated

WILLNER'S LIQUORS (NJ)
Name changed to Willner Industries 5/14/71
(See Willner Industries)

WILLOUGHBY TOWER BUILDING CORP. (IL)
Voting Trust Agreement terminated 4/15/66
Each VTC for Common $1 par exchanged for $1 cash

WILLOW CREEK ENTERPRISES INC (DE)
Common $0.001 par split (21) for (1) by issuance of (20) additional shares payable 02/23/2010 to holders of record 02/23/2010
Common $0.001 par split (4) for (1) by issuance of (3) additional shares payable 01/14/2011 to holders of record 01/14/2011
Recapitalized as Shale Oil International Inc. 10/27/2014
Each share Common $0.001 par exchanged for (0.001) share Common $0.001 par

WILLOW CREEK EXPL LTD (AB)
Reorganized as Promotional Products International, Ltd. (AB) 01/29/2002
Each share Common no par exchanged for (2) shares Common no par
Promotional Products International, Ltd. (AB) reorganized in British Columbia as Ava Resources Corp. 11/20/2009
(See Ava Resources Corp.)

WILLOW FD INC (DE)
Name changed to Sigma Special Fund, Inc. 05/01/1980
Sigma Special Fund, Inc. name changed to ProvidentMutual Special Fund, Inc. 03/01/1990
(See ProvidentMutual Special Fund, Inc.)

WILLOW FINL BANCORP INC (PA)
Name changed 09/22/2006
Name changed from Willow Grove Bancorp, Inc. (New) to Willow Financial Bancorp, Inc. 09/22/2006
Stock Dividend - 5% payable 02/23/2007 to holders of record 02/09/2007 Ex date - 02/07/2007
Merged into Harleysville National Corp. 12/08/2008
Each share Common 1¢ par exchanged for (0.73) share Common $1 par
Harleysville National Corp. merged into First Niagara Financial Group, Inc. (New) 04/09/2010 which merged into KeyCorp (New) 08/01/2016

WILLOW GROVE BANCORP INC OLD (PA)
Reorganized as Willow Grove Bancorp, Inc. (New) 04/03/2002
Each share Common 1¢ par exchanged for (2.28019) shares Common 1¢ par
Willow Grove Bancorp, Inc. (New) name changed to Willow Financial Bancorp, Inc. 09/22/2006 which merged into Harleysville National Corp. 12/08/2008 which merged into First Niagara Financial Group, Inc. (New) 04/09/2010 which merged into KeyCorp (New) 08/01/2016

WILLOW INDS INC (NY)
Adjudicated bankrupt 03/24/1977
Stockholders' equity unlikely

WILLOW INVTS INC (NV)
Charter revoked for failure to file reports and pay fees 4/1/93

WILLOW LAKE MINES LTD (ON)
Merged into Branly Enterprises Inc. 12/09/1976
Each (25) shares Capital Stock no par exchanged for (12) shares Capital Stock no par
Branly Enterprises Inc. recapitalized as Consolidated Branly Resources Inc. 02/27/1984 which name changed to CBR Holdings Inc. 06/20/1985

WILLOW RES LTD (BC)
Delisted from Vancouver Stock Exchange 03/16/1998

WILLOW RUN INC (WY)
Name changed to Action Sports Ltd. 05/01/1998
Action Sports Ltd. recapitalized as Action Sports International, Inc. 01/15/1999 which recapitalized as United Sports International, Inc. 07/15/1999 which recapitalized as Tour Design International, Inc. 04/12/2000 which name changed to Carolina Co. At Pinehurst Inc. 10/31/2001
(See Carolina Co. At Pinehurst Inc.)

WILLOW VALLEY MINES, INC. (NV)
Charter revoked for failure to file reports and pay fees 3/6/61

WILLOW VALLEY MINES OF CALIFORNIA (CA)
Charter suspended for failure to pay franchise taxes 01/03/1961

WILLOW WOOD HOUSING CREDIT FUND 88 LIMITED PARTNERSHIP (TN)
Charter revoked for non-payment of taxes 08/29/2005

WILLOWCREST ENTERPRISES LTD (AB)
Recapitalized as World Environmental Inc. 04/14/1993
Each share Common no par exchanged for (0.25) share Common no par
(See World Environmental Inc.)

WILLOWSTAR CAP INC (ON)
Name changed to Creso Exploration Inc. (ON) 06/10/2010
Creso Exploration Inc. (ON) reincorporated in Canada 09/29/2010 which merged into Dundee Sustainable Technologies Inc. 04/08/2014

WILLOWTREE ADVISOR INC (NV)
Name changed to OmniReliant Holdings, Inc. 12/29/2006
OmniReliant Holdings, Inc. name changed to Infusion Brands International, Inc. 01/07/2011

WILLROY MINES LTD (ON)
Under plan of merger each share Capital Stock $1 par exchanged for (1) share Capital Stock no par 05/31/1966
Merged into Lac Minerals Ltd. (Old) 12/31/1982
Each share Capital Stock no par exchanged for (1.24) shares Common no par
Lac Minerals Ltd. (Old) merged into LAC Minerals Ltd. (New) 07/29/1985 which was acquired by American Barrick Resources Corp. 10/17/1994 which name changed to Barrick Gold Corp. 01/18/1995

WILLSON PRODUCTS, INC. (PA)
Stock Dividend - 20% 04/25/1946
Merged into Ray-O-Vac Co. on a (2) for (3) basis 03/31/1956
Ray-O-Vac Co. merged into Electric Storage Battery Co. 11/20/1957 which reincorporated in Delaware as ESB Inc. 06/30/1967
(See ESB Inc.)

WILLYS-OVERLAND CO. (OH)
Reorganized as Willys-Overland Motors, Inc. in September 1936.
Preferred and Common stockholders received nothing but Rights

WILLYS-OVERLAND MOTORS, INC. (DE)
Name changed to Overland Corp. 5/1/54
Overland Corp. completed liquidation for cash 4/15/65

WILMA K URANIUM MINING CORP. (CO)
Merged into Commonwealth Oil & Gas Co. on a (0.01) for (1) basis in 1956
(See Commonwealth Oil & Gas Co.)

WILMAR INDS INC (NJ)
Merged into WM Acquisition Inc. 5/16/2000
Each share Common no par exchanged for $18.25 cash

WILMAR MINES LTD. (ON)
Capital Stock $1 par changed to 95¢ par 12/5/63
Merged into Wilanour Resources Ltd. 12/28/88
Each share Capital Stock 95¢ par exchanged for (0.41666666) share Capital Stock no par
Wilanour Resources Ltd. merged into Goldcorp Inc. 2/20/98

WILMETTE BK (WILMETTE, IL)
Acquired by First Illinois Corp. 8/11/83
Each share Capital Stock $10 par exchanged for (1.5) shares Common $5 par
First Illinois Corp. acquired by Banc One Corp. 3/2/92 which merged into Bank One Corp. 10/2/98 which merged into J.P. Morgan Chase & Co. 12/31/2000 which name changed to JPMorgan Chase & Co. 7/20/2004

WILMINGTON CHEMICAL CORP.
Bankrupt in 1949

WILMINGTON GAS CO.
Acquired by United Gas Improvement Co. 00/00/1930
Details not available

WILMINGTON REXFORD INC (DE)
Recapitalized as China Pharmaceuticals Corp. (DE) 03/25/2004
Each share Common no par exchanged for (0.05) share Common no par
China Pharmaceuticals Corp. (DE) reincorporated in British Virgin Islands as China Pharmaceuticals International Corp. 08/26/2004 which recapitalized as China Heli Resource Renewable Inc. 11/07/2008
(See China Heli Resource Renewable Inc.)

WILMINGTON SVGS FD SOC FSB (WILMINGTON, DE)
Reorganized as Star States Corp. 12/1/88
Each share Common 1¢ par exchanged for (1) share Common 1¢ par
Star States Corp. name changed to WSFS Financial Corp. 6/1/93

WILMINGTON STEAMBOAT CO.
Acquired by Wilson Line, Inc. in 1929

liquidation of which was completed 10/8/60

WILMINGTON SUBURBAN WATER CO.
Merged into General Waterworks Corp. 00/00/1948
Each share Preferred exchanged for (0.1) share 5% Preferred $100 par
No Common stockholders' equity
General Waterworks Corp. merged into International Utilities Corp. 03/01/1968 which name changed to IU International Corp. 04/27/1973
(See IU International Corp.)

WILMINGTON TR CO (WILMINGTON, DE)
Each share Common $50 par exchanged for (2) shares Common $25 par 00/00/1945
Each share Common $25 par exchanged for (4) shares Common $6.25 par 02/01/1959
Common $6.25 par split (2) for (1) by issuance of (1) additional share 11/15/1983
Common $6.25 par changed to $1 par 05/31/1985
Common $1 par split (2) for (1) by issuance of (1) additional share 08/15/1985
Common $1 par split (2) for (1) by issuance of (1) additional share 11/14/1986
Stock Dividends - 20% 09/13/1954; 100% 04/15/1966
Under plan of reorganization each share Common $1 par automatically became (1) share Wilmington Trust Corp. Common 1¢ par 08/23/1991
Wilmington Trust Corp. merged into M&T Bank Corp. 05/16/2011

WILMINGTON TR CORP (DE)
Common $1 par split (2) for (1) by issuance of (1) additional share 05/15/1992
Common $1 par split (2) for (1) by issuance of (1) additional share payable 06/17/2002 to holders of record 06/03/2002 Ex date - 05/18/2002
Merged into M&T Bank Corp. 05/16/2011
Each share Common $1 par exchanged for (0.051372) share Common 50¢ par

WILPORT GOLD MINES LTD. (ON)
Charter cancelled for failure to file reports and pay taxes November 1959

WILRICH PETROLEUMS LTD. (ON)
Recapitalized as Richwell Petroleums Ltd. 01/09/1957
Each share Capital Stock no par exchanged for (0.125) share Capital Stock no par
Richwell Petroleums Ltd. merged into North West Pacific Developments Ltd. 06/25/1962 which recapitalized as N.W.P. Developments Ltd. 02/28/1966 which recapitalized as N.W.P. Resources Ltd. 06/17/1981 which merged into Golden North Resource Corp. 09/11/1984 which merged into Caledonia Mining Corp. (BC) 02/04/1992 which reincorporated in Canada 03/29/1995 which reincorporated in Jersey as Caledonia Mining Corp. PLC 03/24/2016

WILSHIRE BANCORP INC (CA)
Common no par split (2) for (1) by issuance of (1) additional share payable 12/14/2004 to holders of record 12/03/2004 Ex date - 12/15/2004
Merged into Hope Bancorp, Inc. 08/01/2016
Each share Common no par exchanged for (0.7034) share Common $0.001 par

WILSHIRE BANCORPORATION (CA)
Reported out of business 05/31/1990
Details not available

WILSHIRE ENERGY RES INC (ON)
Cease trade order effective 3/27/90
Stockholders' equity unlikely

WILSHIRE ENTERPRISES INC (DE)
Name changed 07/01/2003
Stock Dividend - 3% payable 02/20/1998 to holders of record 01/16/1998
Name changed from Wilshire Oil Co. of Texas to Wilshire Enterprises, Inc. 07/01/2003
Each share old Common $1 par exchanged for (1) share new Common $1 par to reflect a (1) for (500) reverse split followed by a (500) for (1) forward split 03/02/2011
Note: Holders of (499) or fewer pre-split share received $1 cash per share
Acquired by J&J Brothers Holdings Inc. 02/19/2016
Each share new Common $1 par exchanged for $3.38 cash

WILSHIRE FD INC (MD)
Name changed to Aid Investment Fund, Inc. 02/28/1972
(See Aid Investment Fund, Inc.)

WILSHIRE FIGUEROA SEVENTH BLDG. CORP.
Liquidation completed in 1948

WILSHIRE FINL SVCS GROUP INC (DE)
Each share old Common 1¢ par exchanged for (0.012933) share new Common 1¢ par 06/10/1999
Name changed to Beverly Hills Bancorp Inc. 08/18/2004
(See Beverly Hills Bancorp Inc.)

WILSHIRE GENERAL CORP. (CA)
Charter suspended for failure to file reports and pay fees 11/01/1974

WILSHIRE INS CO (CA)
Reorganized as Wilshire Resources Corp. 07/28/1969
Each share Common $2 par exchanged for (1) share Common $2 par
(See Wilshire Resources Corp.)

WILSHIRE NATIONAL BANK (LOS ANGELES, CA)
Merged into Heritage-Wilshire National Bank (Los Angeles, CA) 10/15/1965
Each share Common $7.50 par exchanged for (1.4) shares Capital Stock $10 par or $19.50 cash at election of holders
Note: Option to receive stock expired 09/30/1965
(See Heritage-Wilshire National Bank (Los Angeles, CA))

WILSHIRE REAL ESTATE INVT INC (MD)
Name changed 9/13/99
Name changed from Wilshire Real Estate Investment Trust Inc. to Wilshire Real Estate Investment Inc. 9/13/99
Name changed to Fog Cutter Capital Group Inc. 2/1/2001

WILSHIRE RES CORP (CA)
Liquidation completed
Each share Common $2 par received initial distribution of (0.4) share General United Group, Inc. Common 25¢ par 1/30/70
Each share Common $2 par exchanged for second and final distribution of (0.28) share General United Group, Inc. Common 25¢ par 11/19/70
(See General United Group, Inc.)

WILSHIRE SAVINGS & LOAN ASSOCIATION (CA)
Charter suspended for failure to pay taxes 06/01/1992

WILSHIRE ST BK (LOS ANGELES, CA)
Common no par split (2) for (1) by issuance of (1) additional share payable 01/15/1998 to holders of record 12/30/1997
Common no par split (2) for (1) by issuance of (1) additional share payable 08/15/2002 to holders of record 07/31/2002
Common no par split (2) for (1) by issuance of (1) additional share payable 12/17/2003 to holders of record 11/30/2003 Ex date - 12/18/2003
Stock Dividends - 10% payable 03/31/2000 to holders of record 03/15/2000 Ex date - 08/16/2002; 10% payable 05/15/2003 to holders of record 04/30/2003 Ex date - 04/28/2003
Under plan of reorganization each share Common no par automatically became (1) share Wilshire Bancorp, Inc. Common no par 08/30/2004
Wilshire Bancorp, Inc. merged into Hope Bancorp, Inc. 08/01/2016

WILSHIRE TECHNOLOGIES INC (CA)
Merged into Wiltec Acquisition Corp. 3/31/2003
Each share Common no par exchanged for $0.18 cash

WILSON & CO. INC. OLD (DE)
Ctfs. dated prior to 6/19/67
Recapitalized in 1934
Each share 7% Preferred $100 par exchanged for (1.4292) shares $6 Preferred no par which was subsequently called
Each share Class A no par exchanged for (5) shares Common no par
Common no par split (3) for (2) by issuance of (0.5) additional share 2/1/67
$4.25 Preferred no par called for redemption 5/1/67
Merged into Ling-Temco-Vought, Inc. 6/19/67
Each share Common no par exchanged for (0.666666) share $5 Conv. Preferred Ser. A $5 par
Ling-Temco-Vought, Inc. name changed to LTV Corp. (Old) 5/5/72 which reorganized as LTV Corp. (New) 6/28/93
(See LTV Corp. (New))

WILSON & CO INC DEL 1967 (DE)
Ctfs. dated between 6/19/67 and 8/18/72
Common 50¢ par split (2) for (1) by issuance of (1) additional share 9/15/71
Merged into LTV Corp. 8/18/72
Each share Common 50¢ par exchanged for $12.50 cash

WILSON & CO INC DEL 1972 (DE)
Ctfs. dated between 01/01/1973 and 01/07/1974
Merged into Wilson & Co., Inc. (New) 01/07/1974
Each share Common 50¢ par exchanged for $13 principal amount of 9-1/2% S.F. Debentures due 01/01/1984

WILSON BEEF & LAMB CO (DE)
Merged into Wilson & Co., Inc. (Ctfs. dated between 01/01/1973 and 01/07/1974) 01/02/1973
Each share Common 50¢ par exchanged for (0.125) share Common 50¢ par
(See Wilson & Co., Inc. (Ctfs. dated dated between 01/01/1973 and 01/07/1974))

WILSON BROS USA INC (IL)
Name changed 08/20/1997
5% Preferred $25 par called for redemption 01/10/1966
Common $1 par split (2) for (1) by issuance of (1) additional share 07/16/1971
Common $1 par split (4) for (3) by issuance of (0.33333333) additional share 02/22/1972
Name changed from Wilson Brothers to Wilson Brothers USA, Inc. 08/20/1997
Common $1 par changed to 1¢ par 10/04/2001
Proclaimed dissolved for failure to pay taxes and file reports 06/08/2007

WILSON CAP INC (NV)
Name changed to SVI Holdings, Inc. (NV) 03/24/1994
SVI Holdings, Inc. (NV) reincorporated in Delaware as SVI Solutions Inc. 03/26/2001 which name changed to Island Pacific Inc. 07/11/2003 which name changed to Retail Pro, Inc. 01/29/2008
(See Retail Pro, Inc.)

WILSON CERTIFIED FOODS INC (DE)
Common 50¢ par split (3) for (2) by issuance of (0.5) additional share 11/19/1970
Merged into Wilson & Co., Inc. (Ctfs. dated between 01/01/1973 and 01/02/1973
Each share Common 50¢ par exchanged for (0.363636) share Common 50¢ par
(See Wilson & Co., Inc. (Ctfs. dated between 01/01/1973 and 01/07/1974))

WILSON CYPRESS CO. (FL)
Proclaimed dissolved for failure to file reports and pay fees 6/2/83

WILSON DOUG STUDIOS INC (DE)
Name changed to Wall Street Cotton Club Inc. 06/26/1990
(See Wall Street Cotton Club Inc.)

WILSON FGHT CO (OH)
Common no par split (2) for (1) by issuance of (1) additional share 6/22/72
Filed Chapter 11 bankruptcy 7/23/80
Assets liquidated and case dismissed 5/24/89
No stockholders' equity

WILSON FOODS CORP (DE)
Merged into Doskocil Companies Inc. 2/7/89
Each share Common 50¢ par exchanged for $14.50 cash

WILSON FUND, LTD. (TN)
Name changed to Patriot Futures Fund L.P. 05/01/1991
(See Patriot Futures Fund L.P.)

WILSON GREATBATCH TECHNOLOGIES INC (DE)
Name changed to Greatbatch, Inc. 05/24/2005
Greatbatch, Inc. name changed to Integer Holdings Corp. 07/01/2016

WILSON H J INC (LA)
Common no par split (2) for (1) by issuance of (1) additional share 4/24/72
Common no par split (5) for (4) by issuance of (0.25) additional share 12/29/75
Stock Dividends - 50% 6/23/78; 10% 8/1/80; 10% 7/24/81; 10% 5/4/82
Merged into Service Merchandise Co., Inc. 5/8/85
Each share Common no par exchanged for $20 cash

WILSON HLDGS INC (NV)
Secondary Offering - 5,000,000 shares COM offered at $3.25 per share on 05/14/2007
Reincorporated under the laws of Texas as Green Builders, Inc. 04/08/2008
(See Green Builders, Inc.)

WIL-WIN

WILSON (H. & H.), INC. (CA)
Completely liquidated 10/2/64
Each share Class A Common no par or Class B Common no par exchanged for first and final distribution of (0.3555536) share Colt Industries, Inc. (Pa) Common $3 par
Colt Industries, Inc. (PA) reincorporated in Delaware 10/17/68 then reincorporated in Pennsylvania 5/6/76
(See Colt Industries Inc. (PA))

WILSON INDS INC (TX)
Merged into Smith International, Inc. 04/30/1998
Each share Common $25 par exchanged for (21.2633) shares Common $1 par
Smith International, Inc. merged into Schlumberger Ltd. 08/27/2010

WILSON JERRY C ENTMT CORP (DE)
Name changed to Transamerica Entertainment Corp. 6/14/96
(See Transamerica Entertainment Corp.)

WILSON-JONES CO. (MA)
Common no par changed to $10 par in 1942
Stock Dividend - 10% 12/28/51
Merged into Swingline, Inc. 3/29/63
Each share Common $10 par exchanged for (1) share Class A $1 par
Swingline, Inc. merged into American Brands, Inc. for cash 9/1/70

WILSON LAUREL FARMS INC (DE)
Merged into Wilson & Co., Inc. (Ctfs. dated between 01/01/1973 and 01/07/1974) 01/02/1973
Each share Common 50¢ par exchanged for (0.083333) share Common 50¢ par
(See Wilson & Co., Inc. (Ctfs. dated between 01/01/1973 and 01/07/1974))

WILSON LEASING CO (IL)
Merged into Wilson Delaware, Inc. 11/12/1975
Each share Class A Common no par exchanged for $2.50 principal amount of Non-Transferable Note Paticipating Unit

WILSON (J.C.) LTD. (CANADA)
Merged into Price Brothers & Co., Ltd. for cash in 1959

WILSON LINE, INC. (DE)
Liquidation completed 10/8/60

WILSON MARINE TRANSIT CO. (DE)
Name changed to First Grant Corp. 3/21/67
First Grant Corp. merged into Pittsburgh Coke & Chemical Co. for cash 2/19/71

WILSON NATIONAL LIFE INSURANCE CO. (FL)
Merged into Gulf Life Insurance Co. 8/18/74
Each share Common $1 par exchanged for $10.81 cash

WILSON ORGANIC CHEMICALS, INC. (NJ)
Charter declared void for non-payment of taxes 2/5/63

WILSON PHARMACEUTICAL & CHEM CORP (DE)
Common 50¢ par split (2) for (1) by issuance of (1) additional share 5/10/68
Name changed to Inolex Corp. 4/24/74
(See Inolex Corp.)

WILSON (RALPH) PLASTICS, INC. (TX)
Liquidation completed
Each share Common $1 par exchanged for initial distribution of (0.666055) share Rexall Drug & Chemical Co. Common $1.25 par 1/25/66
Each share Common $1 par received second and final distribution of (0.01998165) share Rexall Drug & Chemical Co. Common $1.25 par 3/4/66
Rexall Drug & Chemical Co. name changed to Dart Industries, Inc. 4/22/69 which reorganized as Dart & Kraft, Inc. 9/25/80 which name changed to Kraft, Inc. (New) 11/21/86
(See Kraft, Inc. (New))

WILSON SINCLAIR CO (DE)
Common 50¢ par split (3) for (2) by issuance of (0.5) additional share 11/19/1970
Merged into Wilson & Co., Inc. (Ctfs. dated between 01/01/1973 and 01/07/1974) 01/02/1973
Each share Common 50¢ par exchanged for (0.5) share Common 50¢ par
(See Wilson & Co., Inc. (Ctfs. dated between 01/01/1973 and 01/07/1974))

WILSON SPORTING GOODS CO (DE)
Common 50¢ par split (2) for (1) by issuance of (1) additional share 7/31/68
Merged into PepsiCo, Inc. 12/22/72
Each share Common 50¢ par exchanged for $17.50 cash

WILSON TRANSIT CO. (DE)
Name changed to Wilson Marine Transit Co. 4/9/57
Wilson Marine Transit Co. name changed to First Grant Corp. 3/21/67
(See First Grant Corp.)

WILSON'S (AL) POWER-FUL DISPLAYS (FL)
Proclaimed dissolved for non-payment of taxes 6/28/71

WILSONITE CORP.
Reorganized as Wilsonite Products Corp. Inc. in 1939 which was in process of liquidation in 1946

WILSONITE PRODUCTS CORP., INC.
In process of dissolution in 1946

WILSONS THE LEATHER EXPERTS INC (MN)
Issue Information - 1,100,000 UNITS consisting of (1) share COM and (1) WT offered at $9 per Unit on 05/27/1997
Common 1¢ par split (3) for (2) by issuance of (0.5) additional share payable 03/15/2000 to holders of record 02/29/2000
Name changed to PreVu, Inc. 07/08/2008

WILTEK INC (CT)
Common $1 par changed to no par and (2) additional shares issued 03/17/1972
Reincorporated under the laws of Delaware as E-Sync Networks Inc. 07/28/1999
(See E-Sync Networks Inc.)

WILTEL COMMUNICATIONS GROUP INC (NV)
Merged into Leucadia National Corp. 11/07/2003
Each share Common 1¢ par exchanged for (0.4242) share Common 1¢ par and (1) Contingent Sale Right expiring 10/15/2004
Leucadia National Corp. name changed to Jefferies Financial Group Inc. 05/24/2018

WILTON APARTMENTS TRUST
Trust terminated and liquidated 00/00/1948
Details not available

WILTON BK (WILTON, CT)
Acquired by Bankwell Financial Group, Inc. 11/05/2013
Each share Common $5 par exchanged for $13.50 cash

WILTON ENTERPRISES INC (DE)
Acquired by a management group 12/29/1988
Each share Common 10¢ par exchanged for $7.375 cash

WILTON RAILROAD CO.
Property acquired by Boston & Maine Railroad (Me., N.H., Mass., N.Y.) in 1944
(See Boston & Maine Railroad)

WILTON WOOLEN CO. (MI)
Liquidation completed 8/7/56

WILTS VENEER CO.
Name changed to Plymouth Box & Panel Co. in 1937
(See Plymouth Box & Panel Co.)

WILTSEY-COGHLAN MINES, LTD. (ON)
Recapitalized as Wilco Mining Co. Ltd. 12/30/64
Each share Capital Stock $1 par exchanged for (0.2) share Capital Stock $1 par
Wilco Mining Co. Ltd. merged into Deak International Resources Corp. 12/30/88 which name changed to Deak Resources Corp. 3/27/89 which name changed to AJ Perron Gold Corp. 10/7/94
(See AJ Perron Gold Corp.)

WILWOOD GOLD MINES LTD. (ON)
Charter cancelled in March 1971
No stockholders' equity

WIMBERLEY RES LTD (ON)
Delisted from Vancouver Stock Exchange 04/14/1986

WIMM-BILL-DANN FOODS OJSC (RUSSIA)
Sponsored 144A ADR's for Common split (4) for (1) by issuance of (3) additional ADR's payable 11/16/2009 to holders of record 11/13/2009
Ex date - 11/17/2009
ADR basis changed from (1:1) to (1:0.25) on 11/17/2009
Acquired by PepsiCo, Inc. 09/09/2011
Each Sponsored 144A ADR for Common exchanged for $32.67897 cash

WIMPYS USA INC (IL)
Proclaimed dissolved for failure to pay taxes and file reports 11/1/84

WIN-CHEK INDUSTRIES, INC. (NJ)
Reincorporated under the laws of Delaware as International Aluminum Ltd. and Class A 10¢ par reclassified as Common no par 7/28/67
(See International Aluminum Ltd.)

WIN GAMING MEDIA INC (NV)
Name changed to Win Global Markets, Inc. 11/09/2011
Win Global Markets, Inc. name changed to EZTrader, Inc. (NV) 10/09/2014 which reincorporated in Delaware as EZTD Inc. 12/29/2015

WIN-GATE EQUITY GROUP INC (FL)
Name changed to Globaltron Corp. (FL) 12/18/2000
Globaltron Corp. (FL) reincorporated under the laws of Delaware as Phone1 Globalwide Corp. 09/26/2001 which name changed to Celexpress Inc. 12/10/2007

WIN GLOBAL MKTS INC (NV)
Name changed to EZTrader, Inc. (NV) 10/09/2014
EZTrader, Inc. (NV) reincorporated in Delaware as EZTD Inc. 12/29/2015

WIN INC (DE)
Recapitalized as Avon Rent-A-Car & Truck Corp. 10/28/1988
Each (70) shares Common $0.0001 par exchanged for (1) share Common 1¢ par
(See Avon Rent-A-Car & Truck Corp.)

WIN STEPHENS COMPANIES, INC. (MN)
See - Stephens (Win) Companies, Inc.

WIN STEPHENS LEASING CO. (MN)
See - Stephens (Win) Leasing Co.

WIN SYS INTL INC (CO)
Name changed to Whitney Information Network, Inc. 06/03/1999
Whitney Information Network, Inc. name changed to Tigrent Inc. 10/29/2009

WINALTA INC (AB)
Name changed 05/13/1999
Name changed from Winalta Shelters Inc. to Winalta Inc. 05/13/1999
Merged into CERF Inc. 09/05/2014
Each share Class A no par exchanged for (0.3352) share Common no par
Note: Unexchanged certificates were cancelled and became without value 09/05/2017
CERF Inc. name changed to Canadian Equipment Rentals Corp. 06/27/2016 which name changed to Zedcor Energy Inc. 06/30/2017

WINBOND ELECTRS CORP (TAIWAN)
Each 1999 144A Temporary Sponsored GDR for Ordinary exchanged for (1) Sponsored GDR for Ordinary 02/18/2000
(Additional Information in Active)

WINCANTON CORP (WA)
Recapitalized as Parks America! Inc. (WA) 12/16/1999
Each share Common $0.0001 par exchanged for (0.01) share Common $0.0001 par
Parks America! Inc. (WA) reincorporated in Nevada as Grand Slam Treasures Inc. 06/20/2000 which recapitalized as Asconi Corp. 04/16/2001
(See Asconi Corp.)

WINCAP FD (CA)
Name changed to Research Capital Fund, 2/26/73
Research Capital Fund, Inc. name changed to Franklin Gold Fund (CA) 10/26/83 which reincorporated in Delaware as Franklin Gold & Precious Metals Fund 4/10/2000

WINCASH APOLO GOLD & ENERGY INC (NV)
Name changed to Banny Cosmic International Holdings, Inc. 07/27/2018

WINCASH RES INC (NV)
Name changed to Fovea Jewelry Holdings, Ltd. 02/06/2018

WINCHELL DONUT HOUSE, INC. (CA)
Capital Stock no par split (5) for (4) by issuance of (0.25) additional share 3/31/65
Capital Stock no par split (3) for (2) by issuance of (0.5) additional share 7/29/66
Capital Stock no par split (3) for (2) by issuance of (0.5) additional share 11/30/67
Merged into Denny's Restaurants, Inc. 4/30/68
Each share Capital Stock no par exchanged for (0.4363) share $1 Conv. Preferred no par and (0.1667) share Common $1 par
Denny's Restaurants, Inc. name changed to Denny's, Inc. 12/8/72
(See Denny's, Inc.)

WINCHELLS DONUT HOUSES L P (DE)
Completely liquidated 12/15/89
Each Class A Depositary Unit exchanged for first and final distribution of $3.80 cash

WINCHESTER CORP.
Acquired by Winchester Repeating Arms Co. in 1929
Winchester Repeating Arms Co. acquired by Western Cartridge Co. in 1931 which merged into Olin Industries, Inc. in 1945 which merged into Olin Mathieson Chemical Corp. in 1954 which name changed to Olin Corp. 9/1/69

WINCHESTER DIVERSIFIED LTD (BERMUDA)
Acquired by Winchester Futures Ltd. 9/19/88
Each share Common B$1 par exchanged for (1) share Diversified Series Common $1 par
(See Winchester Futures Ltd.)

WINCHESTER FINL LTD (BERMUDA)
Acquired by Winchester Futures Ltd. 9/19/88
Each share Common $1 par exchanged for (1) share Orion Series Common $1 par
(See Winchester Futures Ltd.)

WINCHESTER FUTURES LTD (BERMUDA)
Company delisted registration in Canada 3/4/92
Details not available

WINCHESTER LARDER MINES LTD. (ON)
Name changed to Winchester Exploration Ltd. 2/11/64

WINCHESTER MANOR
Trust terminated 00/00/1950
Details not available

WINCHESTER MNG CORP (DE)
Name changed to PNW Capital, Inc. 07/14/2000
PNW Capital, Inc. name changed to Industrial Minerals, Inc. 05/01/2002 which recapitalized as Mindesta Inc. 07/26/2011 which recapitalized as CTT Pharmaceutical Holdings, Inc. 08/28/2015

WINCHESTER NATL BK (WINCHESTER, MA)
Name changed to Shawmut Winchester Bank, N.A. (Winchester, MA) 03/31/1975
Shawmut Winchester Bank, N.A. (Winchester, MA) merged into Shawmut County Bank, N.A. (Cambridge, MA) 06/26/1975
(See Shawmut County Bank, N.A. (Cambridge, MA))

WINCHESTER NORTH INC (PA)
Name changed to Radice Realty & Construction Corp. 04/13/1972
Radice Realty & Construction Corp. name changed to Radice Corp. (PA) 11/27/1978 which reincorporated in Florida 02/15/1985 which name changed to Major Group, Inc. 05/29/1990 which merged into Stoneridge Resources, Inc. 09/25/1992 which recapitalized as Acceptance Insurance Companies Inc. 12/22/1992
(See Acceptance Insurance Companies Inc.)

WINCHESTER OVERSEAS LTD (BERMUDA)
Name changed to Winchester Financial Ltd. 3/13/84
Winchester Financial Ltd. acquired by Winchester Futures Ltd. 9/19/88
(See Winchester Futures Ltd.)

WINCHESTER REPEATING ARMS CO.
Acquired by Western Cartridge Co. in 1931
Western Cartridge Co. merged into Olin Industries, Inc. in 1945 which merged into Olin Mathieson Chemical Corp. in 1954 which name changed to Olin Corp. 9/1/69

WINCHESTER SECS CORP (PA)
Name changed to Winchester Corp. 06/02/1972

WINCHESTER SPINNING CORP. (CT)
100% acquired by Fieldcrest Mills, Inc. thru voluntary exchange offer in 1967

WINCO MNG & EXPL LTD (BC)
Struck off register and declared dissolved for failure to file returns 04/04/1977

WINCO PETE CORP (CO)
Recapitalized as RCS Holdings Inc. 06/25/2001
Each share Common no par exchanged for (0.025) share Common no par
(See RCS Holdings Inc.)

WINCO STEAK N BURGER RESTAURANTS LTD (ON)
Capital Stock no par reclassified as Conv. Class A Capital Stock no par 7/30/75
Conv. Class A Capital Stock no par and Conv. Class B Capital Stock no par reclassified as 8% Preference $7.50 par respectively 2/6/78
8% Preference $7.50 par called for redemption 2/28/78
Public interest eliminated

WINCOM CORP (MA)
Each share old Common 1¢ par exchanged for (0.1) share new Common 1¢ par 10/29/87
Involuntarily dissolved 12/31/90

WINCOR NIXDORF AG (GERMANY)
Name changed to Diebold Nixdorf AG 12/08/2016

WINCORP INDS INC (DE)
Name changed 11/18/1977
Name changed from Wincorp (CA) to Wincorp Industries Inc. (DE) and Capital Stock no par changed to $1 par 11/18/1977
Under plan of reorganization each share Capital Stock no par exchanged for (1) Non-Separable Unit consisting of (1) share Wincorp Realty Investments Inc. Capital Stock $1 par and (1) share Western Harness Racing Inc. Capital Stock $1 par 12/01/1981
(See each company's listing)

WINCORP RLTY INVTS INC (DE)
(Issued only in Non-Seperable Units of (1) share of Wincorp Realty Investments Inc. Capital Stock $1 par and (1) share Western Harness Racing Inc. Capital Stock $1 par)
(See each company's listing)
Acquired by Copzel Inc. 12/11/1984
Each share Capital Stock $1 par exchanged for $46.85 cash
Note: An additional final payment of $1.3969 cash per share was made 12/22/1986

WINCROFT INC (CO)
Reorganized under the laws of Nevada 02/12/2008
Each share Common no par exchanged for (0.125) share Common $0.001 par
Wincroft, Inc. (NV) name changed to Apollo Solar Energy, Inc. 11/03/2008

WINCROFT INC (NV)
Name changed to Apollo Solar Energy, Inc. 11/03/2008

WIND BARON CORP (DE)
Each share old Common 1¢ par exchanged for (0.2) share new Common 1¢ par 9/4/90
Charter cancelled and declared inoperative and void for non-payment of taxes 3/1/95

WIND ENERGY AMER INC (MN)
Each share Common 5¢ par received distribution of (0.2) share PuraMed BioScience, Inc. Common no par payable 02/22/2008 to holders of record 04/12/2007 Ex date - 03/10/2008
SEC revoked common stock registration 05/14/2015

WIND RIV RES LTD (BC)
Incorporated 06/18/1987
Recapitalized as Teslin River Resources Corp. 01/03/2008
Each share Common no par exchanged for (0.2) share Common no par
Teslin River Resources Corp. recapitalized as Siyata Mobile Inc. 07/29/2015

WIND RIV SYS INC (DE)
Common $0.001 par split (3) for (2) by issuance of (0.5) additional share payable 05/24/1996 to holders of record 05/10/1996
Common $0.001 par split (3) for (2) by issuance of (0.5) additional share payable 03/10/1997 to holders of record 02/24/1997
Common $0.001 par split (3) for (2) by issuance of (0.5) additional share payable 02/04/1999 to holders of record 01/19/1999
Merged into Intel Corp. 07/17/2009
Each share Common $0.001 par exchanged for $11.50 cash

WIND RIVER PRODUCING & REFINING CO. (ME)
Charter suspended for non-payment of taxes 00/00/1921

WIND RIVER RES LTD (BC)
Incorporated 03/22/1983
Recapitalized as Richlode Investments Corp. 05/03/1993
Each share Common no par exchanged for (1/3) share Common no par
Richlode Investments Corp. recapitalized as Thundelarra Exploration Ltd. (BC) 07/30/1998 which reincorporated in Yukon 01/23/2001 which reincorporated in Western Australia 09/08/2003 which name changed to Thundelarra Ltd. 03/21/2013

WIND RIVER URANIUM CO. (UT)
Charter suspended for non-payment of taxes 10/15/1958

WINDAMERE VENTURES LTD (BC)
Reincorporated under the laws of Ontario as Antofagasta Gold Inc. 02/12/2013
Antofagasta Gold Inc. name changed to Arena Minerals Inc. 12/06/2013

WINDARRA MINERALS LTD (BC)
Merged into Wesdome Gold Mines Ltd. 10/03/2013
Each share Common no par exchanged for (0.1) share Common no par
Note: Unexchanged certificates will be cancelled and become without value 10/03/2019

WINDAUS GLOBAL ENERGY INC (WY)
Name changed to WindStream Technologies, Inc. 03/27/2014

WINDE GROUP INC (DE)
Ceased operations and went out of business 04/23/1976
No stockholders' equity

WINDECKER INDS INC (TX)
Charter forfeited for failure to pay taxes 03/16/1981

WINDECKER RESH INC (TX)
Name changed to Windecker Industries, Inc. 12/07/1970
(See Windecker Industries, Inc.)

WINDERMERE EXPLORATION LTD. (BC)
Recapitalized as Barrier Reef Resources Ltd. 05/31/1972
Each share Capital Stock 50¢ par exchanged for (0.5) share Capital Stock 50¢ par
Barrier Reef Resources Ltd. recapitalized as Consolidated Barrier Reef Resources Ltd. 10/01/1984 which name changed to M F C Mining Finance Corp. 05/05/1986 which merged into Minven Gold Corp. 08/12/1988 which reorganized as Dakota Mining Corp. 09/15/1993
(See Dakota Mining Corp.)

WINDERMERE HOTEL CO. (IL)
Reorganized 5/15/62
No stockholders' equity

WINDFALL ENTMT INC (NY)
Name changed to Blueberry Holdings, Inc. (NY) 06/29/2005
Blueberry Holdings, Inc. (NY) reincorporated in Nevada as Alentus Corp. 03/25/2008 which recapitalized as Areti Web Innovations, Inc. 07/05/2012

WINDFALL OILS & MINES LTD (ON)
Capital Stock $1 par changed to no par 05/29/1974
Name changed to Camreco Inc. 07/10/1981
Camreco Inc. merged into Environmental Technologies International Inc. 11/29/1991 which recapitalized as Eco Technologies International Inc. 04/24/1998
(See Eco Technologies International Inc.)

WINDFALL VENTURES NEVIS INC (FL)
Common $0.001 par split (3) for (1) by issuance of (2) additional shares payable 08/27/2002 to holders of record 07/25/2002 Ex date - 08/28/2002
Voluntarily dissolved 04/13/2005
Details not available

WINDFIRE CAP CORP (AB)
Each share old Common no par exchanged for (0.33333333) share new Common no par 04/10/2015
Each share new Common no par exchanged again for (0.2) share new Common no par 06/28/2017
Name changed to Global Vanadium Corp. 10/19/2018

WINDFLOW TECHNOLOGY LTD (NEW ZEALAND)
ADR agreement terminated 09/28/2018
Each Sponsored ADR for Ordinary exchanged for (4) shares Ordinary
Note: Unexchanged ADR's will be sold and the proceeds, if any, held for claim after 01/31/2019

WINDFLOWER MNG LTD (BC)
Recapitalized as Energold Mining Ltd. 8/16/94
Each share Common no par exchanged for (1/3) share Common no par
Energold Mining Ltd. name changed to Energold Drilling Corp. 10/3/2005

WINDJAMMER INTL CORP (MD)
Charter annulled for failure to file annual reports 04/18/1973

WINDJAMMER SOFTWARE INC (NJ)
Charter declared void for non-payment of taxes 7/30/93

WINDMERE-DURABLE HLDGS INC (FL)
Name changed 06/21/1996
Common 10¢ par split (2) for (1) by issuance of (1) additional share 09/01/1983
Common 10¢ par split (3) for (2) by issuance of (0.5) additional share 06/10/1988
Name changed from Windmere Corp. to Windmere-Durable Holdings, Inc. 06/21/1996
Name changed to Applica, Inc. 05/10/2000
(See Applica, Inc.)

WIN-WIN

WINDMILL ENTERPRISES LTD (BC)
Recapitalized as Todwind Development Corp. 07/20/1984
Each share Common no par exchanged for (0.1) share Common no par
(See Todwind Development Corp.)

WINDOW GLASS MACHINE CO. (NJ)
Voluntarily dissolved 2/3/78
Details not available

WINDOW INTERIOR MARKETING CO (NV)
Name changed to ERICA 09/08/1999
ERICA recapitalized as NPOWR Digital Media, Inc. 06/30/2005 which name changed to NPW Development, Inc. 07/28/2005 which name changed to GreenZap, Inc. 11/07/2005 which name changed to Blue Star Opportunities Corp. 07/28/2008

WINDOW ROCK CAP HLDGS INC (NV)
Charter revoked for failure to file reports and pay fees 05/31/2008

WINDPOWER INNOVATIONS INC (WY)
Name changed to NexGen Holdings Corp. 01/10/2014

WINDRIDGE TECHNOLOGY CORP (BC)
Name changed to Dajin Resources Corp. 01/19/2005

WINDRIFT STABLES INC (DE)
Charter cancelled and declared inoperative and void for non-payment of taxes 3/1/86

WINDROSE MED PPTYS TR (MD)
Merged into Health Care REIT, Inc. 12/20/2006
Each Conv. Preferred Share of Bene. Int. Ser. A 1¢ par exchanged for (1) share 7.5% Conv. Preferred Ser. G $1 par
Each share Common 1¢ par exchanged for (0.4509) share Common $1 par
Health Care REIT, Inc. name changed to Welltower Inc. 09/30/2015

WINDSOR BANK & TRUST CO. (WINDSOR, CT)
Reorganized under the laws of Delaware as Olde Windsor Bancorp, Inc. 6/3/85
Each share Common 10¢ par exchanged for (1) share Common 10¢ par
Olde Windsor Bancorp, Inc. name changed to New England Community Bancorp, Inc. 9/27/94 which merged into Webster Financial Corp. 12/1/99

WINDSOR CAP CORP (DE)
Name changed to Innovative Health Systems, Inc. 07/11/1995 which name changed back to Windsor Capital Corp. 07/17/1995
Recapitalized as Energy Control Technology Inc. 02/12/2001
Each (3.85704) shares Common $0.001 par exchanged for (1) share Common $0.001 par
Energy Control Technology Inc. name changed to 5Fifty5.com, Inc. 09/26/2005 which recapitalized as Swap-A-Debt, Inc. 02/26/2008 which name changed to WikiLoan Inc. 06/26/2009 which name changed to Wiki Group, Inc. 03/26/2012 which recapitalized as Source Financial, Inc. 03/21/2013 which name changed to Alltemp, Inc. 04/27/2017

WINDSOR-COBALT SILVERS LTD. (ON)
Charter revoked for failure to file reports and pay fees 10/21/63

WINDSOR COUNTY NATIONAL BANK (WINDSOR, VT)
Merged into Vermont National Bank (Brattleboro, VT) 12/31/1964
Each share Common $100 par exchanged for (23) shares Common $10 par
Vermont National Bank (Brattleboro, VT) reorganized as Vermont Financial Services Corp. (VT) 02/28/1983 which reincorporated in Delaware 04/17/1990 which merged into Chittenden Corp. 05/28/1999
(See Chittenden Corp.)

WINDSOR COURT APARTMENTS, LTD. (ON)
Liquidation completed
Each share Common no par exchanged for initial distribution of $11 cash 1/7/69
Each share Common no par received second distribution of $1.25 cash 5/27/69
Each share Common no par received third and final distribution of $0.46 cash 1/25/71

WINDSOR COURT APARTMENTS LIQUIDATION TRUST
Liquidated in 1951

WINDSOR COURT HLDGS INC (BC)
Recapitalized as Teledata Ventures Corp. (BC) 10/01/1996
Each (4.7) shares Common no par exchanged for (1) share Common no par
Teledata Ventures Corp. (BC) reincorporated in Yukon as CTF Technologies Inc. 04/06/1998 which reincorporated in British Columbia 08/11/2008
(See CTF Technologies Inc.)

WINDSOR ENERGY CORP (AB)
Delisted from Canadian Dealer Network 10/13/2000

WINDSOR FDS INC (MD)
Reincorporated 04/01/1973
Reincorporated 01/02/1985
Name changed 12/30/1985
Stock Dividend - 100% 05/31/1969
State of incorporation changed from (DE) to (MD) 04/01/1973
State of incorporation changed from (MD) (PA) 01/02/1985
Name and state of incorporation changed from Windsor Fund, Inc. (PA) to Windsor Funds, Inc. (MD) and Capital Stock $1 par reclassified as Common 1¢ par 12/30/1985
Name changed to Vanguard/Windsor Funds, Inc. (MD) 04/30/1993
Vanguard/Windsor Funds, Inc. (MD) reincorporated in Delaware as Vanguard Windsor Funds 05/29/1998

WINDSOR HLDG CORP (DE)
Charter forfeited for failure to maintain a registered agent 10/29/91

WINDSOR HOTEL LTD (QC)
Each share Preferred $100 par exchanged for (1.25) shares Capital Stock no par in 1938
(Additional Information in Active)

WINDSOR INDUSTRIES, INC. (DE)
Certificates dated prior to 05/15/1965
Merged into Bates Manufacturing Co., Inc. 05/15/1965
Each share Common 10¢ par exchanged for (1) share Common $10 par
(See Bates Manufacturing Co., Inc.)

WINDSOR INDS INC (DE)
Certificates dated after 09/13/1982
Each share Common 1¢ par exchanged for (0.5) share Common 10¢ par 06/01/1983
Name changed to Windsor Holding Corp. 12/16/1985
(See Windsor Holding Corp.)

WINDSOR INSURANCE CO. (IL)
Merged into State Fire & Casualty Co. 12/31/1965
Each share Common $10 par exchanged for (1.2) shares Common $5 par
(See State Fire & Casualty Co.)

WINDSOR LIFE INS CO AMER (NY)
Capital Stock $2 par changed to $1 par 5/28/68
Name changed to Empire State Life Insurance Co. 6/10/88
(See Empire State Life Insurance Co.)

WINDSOR MANUFACTURING CO. (UT)
Name changed to Charneka Mining Co. Inc. 07/18/1984

WINDSOR NUCLEAR INC (CT)
Name changed to Surgicot, Inc. 08/29/1974
Surgicot, Inc. merged into Squibb Corp. 06/22/1979 which merged into Bristol-Myers Squibb Co. 10/04/1989

WINDSOR OAKS NATL BK (WINDSOR, CA)
Name changed to North Coast Bank N.A. (Windsor, CA) 1/8/97
North Coast Bank N.A. (Windsor, CA) merged into American River Holdings 10/25/2000 which name changed to American River Bankshares 6/2/2004

WINDSOR PK BK N A (SAN ANTONIO, TX)
Merged into First City Bancorporation of Texas, Inc. (TX) 5/1/81
Each share Common $1.25 par exchanged for (0.4) share $3.83 Conv. Preferred $10 par
(See First City Bancorporation of Texas, Inc. (TX))

WINDSOR PK PPTYS LTD PARTNERSHIP (CA)
Units of Ltd. Partnership Int. 2 completely liquidated 12/31/1996
Details not available
Completely liquidated 03/12/1997
Each Unit of Ltd. Partnership Int. 1 received first and final distribution of $12.37 cash
Units of Ltd. Partnership Int. 3 completely liquidated 08/01/2000
Details not available
Units of Ltd. Partnership Int. 4 completely liquidated 08/01/2000
Details not available
Units of Ltd. Partnership Int. 6 completely liquidated 08/01/2000
Details not available
Units of Ltd. Partnership Int. 5 completely liquidated 02/12/2001
Details not available
Units of Ltd. Partnership Int. 7 completely liquidated 02/12/2001
Details not available

WINDSOR RACEWAY HOLDINGS LTD. (ON)
Class B $1 par called for redemption 11/15/77
Recapitalized as Windsor Raceway Inc. 6/7/84
Each share Class A $9 par exchanged for (0.001) share Class A no par

WINDSOR REAL ESTATE INVT TR 8 (CA)
Name changed to N'Tandem Trust, Preferred no par and Common no par changed to 1¢ par 10/23/1998
(See N'Tandem Trust)

WINDSOR RESOURCE CORP (DE)
Each share old Common $0.000001 par exchanged for (0.0005) share new Common $0.000001 par 08/28/2008
Name changed to Kleangas Energy Technologies, Inc. 02/25/2013

WINDSOR RES INC (BC)
Struck off register and declared dissolved for failure to file returns 1/5/90

WINDSOR YELLOWKNIFE GOLD MINES LTD. (ON)
Charter cancelled for failure to file reports and pay taxes October 1960

WINDSORTECH INC (DE)
Name changed to QSGI, Inc. 10/18/2005
(See QSGI, Inc.)

WINDSTAR ENERGY LTD (AB)
Merged into BelAir Energy Corp. 01/28/1998
Each share Common no par exchanged for (0.6) share Common no par
BelAir Energy Corp. merged into Purcell Energy Ltd. (New) 09/04/2003
(See Purcell Energy Ltd. (New))

WINDSTAR INC (NV)
Reorganized as Regenicin, Inc. 08/02/2010
Each share Common $0.001 par exchanged for (34) shares Common $0.001 par

WINDSTAR RES INC (AZ)
Each share old Common $0.0001 par exchanged for (0.004) share new Common $0.0001 par 7/13/98
Name changed to Nexland Inc. (AZ) 12/8/99
Nexland Inc. (AZ) reincorporated in Delaware 9/13/2000
(See Nexland Inc.)

WINDSTORM RES INC (BC)
Merged into Blue Sky Uranium Corp. 07/05/2012
Each share Common no par exchanged for (0.38868) share Common no par
Note: Unexchanged certificates were cancelled and became without value 07/05/2015

WINDSTREAM CORP (DE)
Name changed to Windstream Holdings, Inc. 09/03/2013

WINDSWEPT ENVIRONMENTAL GROUP INC (DE)
SEC revoked common stock registration 07/16/2012

WINDTAMER CORP (NY)
Name changed to Arista Power, Inc. 05/20/2011

WINDWARD GOLD MINES LTD. (ON)
Recapitalized as Windfall Oils & Mines Ltd. on a (1) for (3.5) basis 07/10/1957
Windfall Oils & Mines Ltd. name changed to Camreco Inc. 07/10/1981 which merged into Environmental Technologies International Inc. 11/29/1991 which recapitalized as Eco Technologies International Inc. 04/24/1998
(See Eco Technologies International Inc.)

WINDY CITY CAP CORP (IL)
Recapitalized as Innovative Tech Systems Inc. 1/31/90
Each share Common $0.0001 par exchanged for (0.1) share Common $0.0001 par
Innovative Tech Systems Inc. merged into Peregrine Systems, Inc. 7/30/98
(See Peregrine Systems, Inc.)

WINDY CREEK DEVS INC (NV)
Each share old Common $0.0001 par exchanged for (6.09756) shares new Common $0.0001 par 09/28/2006
Reincorporated under the laws of Delaware as Surfect Holdings, Inc. 10/06/2006
(See Surfect Holdings, Inc.)

WINDY HILL MINING CORP. LTD. (ON)
Charter cancelled for failure to pay taxes and file returns 4/9/75

WINDY MTN EXPLS LTD (ON)
Assets sold for the benefit of creditors 1/5/2004
No stockholders' equity

WINDYS NATL FRANCHISE SYS INC (NJ)
Name changed to Tri-Way Leisure Industries, Inc. 03/06/1973
(See Tri-Way Leisure Industries, Inc.)

WINE-BERRE DISTRIBUTING CO. (MO)
Charter forfeited for failure to file annual reports 1/1/41

WINE SOC AMER INC (DE)
Each share old Common $0.001 par exchanged for (0.01) share new Common $0.001 par 4/30/90
Charter cancelled and declared inoperative and void for non-payment of taxes 3/1/92

WINE SYS DESIGN INC (NV)
Reorganized as Janel World Trade Ltd. 07/10/2002
Each share Common $0.001 par exchanged for (19.2307693) shares Common $0.001 par
Janel World Trade Ltd. recapitalized as Janel Corp. 04/21/2015

WINECOM INC (NV)
Reorganized as Green Innovations Ltd. 10/01/2012
Each share Common $0.0001 par exchanged for (20) shares Common $0.0001 par

WINEX RES INC (BC)
Recapitalized as Workhorse Manufacturing Inc. 1/8/91
Each share Common no par exchanged for (0.4) share Common no par
Workhorse Manufacturing Inc. recapitalized as Koala Beverages Ltd. 9/4/92 which name changed to Tribridge Enterprises Corp. 7/21/97 which recapitalized as Vision Gate Ventures Ltd. 3/16/99

WINFIELD CAP CORP (NY)
Discharged from receivership 10/14/2015
No stockholders' equity

WINFIELD CORP. (PA)
Marked off Pennsylvania active records 6/20/66
Former transfer agent advised defunct for several years as of 1970

WINFIELD ENERGY LTD (AB)
Acquired by Ballistic Energy Corp. 1/13/95
Each share Common no par exchanged for (0.235) share Common no par
(See Ballistic Energy Corp.)

WINFIELD FINL GROUP INC (NV)
Name changed to Healthcare Business Services Groups, Inc. 01/13/2005
Healthcare Business Services Groups, Inc. recapitalized as PPJ Enterprise (NV) 04/24/2008 witch reorganized in Florida as PPJ Healthcare Enterprises, Inc. 12/01/2014

WINFIELD GROWTH FD INC (DE)
Stock Dividend - 100% 05/09/1969
Name changed to Research Equity Fund, Inc. (DE) 01/26/1973
Research Equity Fund, Inc. (DE) reincorporated in Maryland 09/09/1973 which reincorporated in California as Franklin Equity Fund 10/10/1984

WINFIELD GROWTH INDUSTRIES FUND, INC. (DE)
Stock Dividend - 100% 11/24/61
Name changed to Winfield Growth Fund, Inc. 9/21/66
Winfield Growth Fund, Inc. name changed to Research Equity Fund, Inc. (Del.) 1/26/73 which reincorporated in Maryland 9/9/73 which reincorporated in California as Franklin Equity Fund 10/10/84

WING AIRCRAFT CO (CA)
Dissolved 12/26/1973
No stockholders' equity

WING HANG BK LTD (HONG KONG)
ADR agreement terminated 12/05/2014
Each Sponsored ADR for Ordinary exchanged for $32.155187 cash

WINGAIT DIVERSIFIED LTD (ON)
Name changed to Aquablast Inc. 07/29/1971
(See Aquablast Inc.)

WINGAIT GOLD MINES LTD. (ON)
Recapitalized as Gaitwin Explorations Ltd. 00/00/1952
Each share Common no par exchanged for (0.2) share Common no par
Gaitwin Explorations Ltd. recapitalized as Wingait Diversified Ltd. 02/06/1970 which name changed to Aquablast Inc. 07/29/1971
(See Aquablast Inc.)

WINGATE CORP. (RI)
Reorganized under Chapter X of the Bankruptcy Act 4/13/64
No stockholders' equity

WINGBACK, INC. (NY)
Voluntarily dissolved 1/30/73
No stockholders' equity

WINGDAM & LIGHTNING CREEK MINING CO. LTD. (BC)
Merged into Consolidated Vigor Mines Ltd. 1/28/69
Each share Common no par exchanged for (0.066666) share Capital Stock no par
Consolidated Vigor Mines Ltd. struck off register 3/22/73

WINGET YARN MILLS
Merged into Textiles, Inc. in 1931
Textiles, Inc. name changed to Ti-Caro Inc. 9/30/78
(See Ti-Caro Inc.)

WINGOLD MINES LTD.
Liquidation completed in 1946

WINGS & WHEELS EXPRESS INC (IL)
Common 1¢ par split (2) for (1) by issuance of (1) additional share 5/1/67
Stock Dividend - 10% 3/30/64
Name changed to Air Express International Corp. (IL) 10/18/72
Air Express International Corp. (IL) reincorporated in Delaware 12/31/81
(See Air Express International Corp.)

WINGS LTD.
Dissolved in 1948

WINGS OF ISRAEL, INC. (LA)
Charter revoked for failure to file annual reports 8/18/98

WINGS WEST AIRLS INC (CA)
Common no par split (8) for (5) by issuance of (0.6) additional share 08/12/1985
Acquired by AMR Corp. 08/09/1988
Each share Common no par exchanged for $10.50 cash

WINJAK INC (DE)
Reorganized under Chapter 11 Federal Bankruptcy Code 5/9/89
Each (15) shares Class A Common $1 par exchanged for (1) share Class A Common 15¢ par
Each share Class B Common $1 par exchanged for (1) share Class A Common 15¢ par
Charter cancelled and declared inoperative and void for non-payment of taxes 3/1/95

WINK COMMUNICATIONS INC (DE)
Merged into Liberty Broadband Interactive Television, Inc. 08/23/2002
Each share Common $0.001 par exchanged for $3 cash

WINKELHAAK MINES LTD (SOUTH AFRICA)
Merged into Evander Gold Mines Ltd. 11/18/96
Each ADR for Ordinary Rand-1 par exchanged for (0.78125) ADR for Ordinary Rand-1 par
Evander Gold Mines Ltd. merged into Harmony Gold Mining Co. Ltd. 8/28/98

WINKELMAN BROTHERS APPAREL, INC. (MI)
Name changed to Winkelman Stores, Inc. and Class A Common $3 par reclassified as Common $3 par 5/18/66
Winkelman Stores, Inc. merged into Petrie Stores Corp. 2/15/85 which assets were transferred to Petrie Stores Liquidating Trust 1/22/96
(See Petrie Stores Liquidating Trust)

WINKELMAN STORES INC (MI)
Common $3 par split (2) for (1) by issuance of (1) additional share 6/2/66
Common $3 par split (3) for (2) by issuance of (0.5) additional share 6/1/76
Merged into Petrie Stores Corp. 2/15/85
Each share Common $3 par exchanged for (0.4054) share Common $1 par
Petrie Stores Corp. assets were transferred to Petrie Stores Liquidating Trust 1/22/96
(See Petrie Stores Liquidating Trust)

WINKELMANN COUNTERMEASURES INC (BC)
Dissolved 2/10/89

WINKLER/SCHEID CORP. (DE)
Name changed to Winkler Scheid Vineyards Inc. 7/29/74
Winkler Scheid Vineyards Inc. name changed to Winkler Scheid Inc. 5/19/77 which name changed to HS Group Inc. 5/28/80 which assets were transferred to HS Group Inc. Liquidating Trust 8/23/85
(See HS Group Inc. Liquidating Trust)

WINKLER SCHEID INC (DE)
Each share Common 10¢ par exchanged for (0.2) share Common 50¢ par 6/8/78
Common 50¢ par split (4) for (3) by issuance of (1/3) additional share 3/30/79
Name changed to HS Group Inc. 5/28/80
HS Group Inc. assets transferred to HS Group Inc. Liquidating Trust 8/23/85
(See HS Group Inc. Liquidating Trust)

WINKLER SCHEID VINEYARDS INC. (DE)
Name changed to Winkler Scheid Inc. 5/19/77
Winkler Scheid Inc. name changed to HS Group Inc. 5/28/80 which assets were transferred to HS Group Inc. Liquidating Trust 8/23/85
(See HS Group Inc. Liquidating Trust)

WINLAND ELECTRS INC (MN)
Stock Dividend - 10% payable 12/31/2003 to holders of record 12/19/2003
Name changed to Winland Holdings Corp. 02/06/2018

WINLAND ONLINE SHIPPING HLDGS CORP (TX)
Name changed to Winland Ocean Shipping Corp. 03/22/2011

WINMAX TRADING GROUP INC (FL)
Each share old Common $0.001 par exchanged for (0.04) share new Common $0.001 par 03/19/2001
Each share new Common $0.001 par exchanged again for (0.05) share new Common $0.001 par 03/14/2002
Each share new Common $0.001 par exchanged again for (0.05) share new Common $0.001 par 06/07/2007
Common $0.001 par changed to no par 04/09/2008
Name changed to Eastern Asteria, Inc. 05/21/2010

WINN & LOVETT GROCERY CO (FL)
Recapitalized in 1944
Each share 7% Preferred $100 par exchanged for $100 principal amount of Debentures
Each (3-2/3) shares Class A no par exchanged for $100 principal amount of Debentures
Each share Class B no par exchanged for (1) share Common no par
Recapitalized in 1950
Each share Common no par exchanged for (3) shares Common $1 par
Common $1 par split (3) for (1) by issuance of (2) additional shares in 1954
Under plan of merger name changed to Winn-Dixie Stores, Inc. 11/14/55
(See Winn-Dixie Stores, Inc.)

WINN DIXIE STORES INC (FL)
Common $1 par split (2) for (1) by issuance of (1) additional share 10/28/1960
Common $1 par and Conv. Class B Common $1 par split (3) for (2) by issuance of (0.5) additional share respectively 10/31/1972
Conv. Class B Common $1 par split (4) for (3) by issuance of (0.33333333) additional share 10/31/1978
Common $1 par split (4) for (3) by issuance of (0.33333333) additional share 10/31/1978
Conv. Class B Common $1 par split (5) for (3) by issuance of (0.66666666) additional share 10/31/1983
Common $1 par split (5) for (3) by issuance of (0.66666666) additional share 10/31/1983
Conv. Class B Common $1 par split (2) for (1) by issuance of (1) additional share 10/31/1990
Common $1 par split (2) for (1) by issuance of (1) additional share 10/31/1990
Common $1 par split (2) for (1) by issuance of (1) additional share 11/30/1995
Plan of reorganization under Chapter 11 Federal Bankruptcy Code effective 11/21/2006
No Common $1 par stockholders' equity
Acquired by Opal Holdings, L.L.C. 03/09/2012
Each share Common $0.001 par exchanged for $9.50 cash

WINN ENTERPRISES (FL)
Proclaimed dissolved for failure to file reports and pay fees 10/13/89

WINNEMUCCA MOUNTAIN MINES CO. (NV)
Charter revoked for failure to file reports and pay fees 3/4/57

WINNER BOATS, INC. (TN)
Each share Common 1¢ par exchanged for (0.33333333) share Common 3¢ par 08/01/1968
Name changed to Winner Corp. 10/01/1971
(See Winner Corp.)

WINNER CORP (TN)
Charter revoked for non-payment of taxes 04/09/1985

WINNER INDS INC (NV)
Name changed to Kiva Corp. 10/28/1981
(See Kiva Corp.)

WINNER MED GROUP INC (NV)
Each share old Common $0.001 par exchanged for (0.5) share new Common $0.001 par 10/06/2009
Acquired by Winner Holding Ltd. 12/12/2012
Each share new Common $0.001 par exchanged for $4.50 cash

WINNERNET INDS INC (NV)
Name changed to Pacific Vision Group, Inc. 07/18/2000
(See Pacific Vision Group, Inc.)

WINNERS ALL INTL INC (DE)
Each share Common $0.005 par exchanged for (0.5) share Common 1¢ par 06/10/1994
Name changed to Urecoats Industries, Inc. 02/12/1999
Urecoats Industries, Inc. name changed to IFT Corp. 12/31/2004 which name changed to Lapolla Industries, Inc. 11/08/2005
(See Lapolla Industries, Inc.)

WINNERS CIRCLE INC (CA)
Common no par split (16) for (15) by issuance of (0.06) additional share 8/16/93
Name changed to Sky Scientific Inc. 11/1/93
(See Sky Scientific Inc.)

WINNERS CIRCLE MGMT INC (DE)
Out of business 04/30/1991
No stockholders' equity

WINNERS CORP (TN)
Stock Dividend - 33-1/3% 3/9/83
Name changed back to Volunteer Capital Corp. 8/24/89
Volunteer Capital Corp. name changed to J. Alexander's Corp. 2/7/97

WINNERS EDGE COM INC (DE)
Name changed to Sealant Solutions Inc. 08/06/2001
Sealant Solutions Inc. name changed to PowerChannel, Inc. 07/28/2003 which recapitalized as Qualibou Energy Inc. 02/05/2008

WINNERS ENTMT INC (DE)
Name changed to MTR Gaming Group, Inc. 10/18/1996
MTR Gaming Group, Inc. merged into Eldorado Resorts, Inc. 09/19/2014

WINNERS INTERNET NETWORK INC (NV)
Recapitalized as American Television & Film Co. 2/17/2004
Each share Common $0.001 par exchanged for (0.01) share Common $0.001 par
American Television & Film Co. name changed to Spotlight Homes, Inc. 4/6/2004

WINNETKA BK (WINNETKA, IL)
Merged into First Chicago Corp. 11/30/89
Each share Common $100 par exchanged for (89.823) shares Common $5 par
First Chicago Corp. merged into First Chicago NBD Corp. 12/1/95

WINNING EDGE INTL INC (DE)
Assets transferred to W Technologies, Inc. 10/20/2007

WINNIPEG & CENTRAL GAS CO. (MB)
Recapitalized as Greater Winnipeg Gas Co. 10/09/1958
Each share Common no par exchanged for (0.5) share Common no par
Greater Winnipeg Gas Co. name changed to ICG Utilities (Manitoba) Ltd. 11/30/1989 which name changed to Centra Gas Manitoba Inc. 01/21/1991
(See Centra Gas Manitoba Inc.)

WINNIPEG CENTRAL HEATING CO. LTD. (MB)
Completely liquidated in June 1966
Details available at Canada Permanent Trust Co., Winnipeg

WINNIPEG GOLD LTD (MB)
Charter cancelled and declared dissolved for failure to file returns 03/31/1976

WINNIPEG RIVER TIN MINES LTD. (CANADA)
Name changed to Spacemaster Minerals Ltd. 03/28/1967
Spacemaster Minerals Ltd. recapitalized as Spacemaster Resources Ltd. 11/04/1977 which name changed to Exmoor Oil & Gas Corp. 09/26/1988 which recapitalized as Koala Kreme Inc. 02/16/1990 which recapitalized as Sur American Gold Corp. (Canada) 06/15/1995 which reincorporated in British Columbia as Cadan Resources Corp. 08/28/2007 which name changed to Rizal Resources Corp. 10/07/2016

WINNIPEG SUPPLY & FUEL LTD (MB)
Through purchase offer 97.31% acquired by Bakham Holdings Ltd. 00/00/1973
Public interest eliminated

WINNIPEG SYMPHONY ORCHESTRA (MB)
Each share Capital Stock $5 par exchanged for $0.01 cash 7/1/81
Public interest eliminated

WINNS STORES INC (TX)
Common $2.50 par changed to $1.25 par and (1) additional share issued 05/17/1971
Common Stock $1.25 par split (2) for (1) by issuance of (1) additional share 05/25/1979
Stock Dividends - 15% 05/27/1977; 10% 05/26/1978
Merged into Heinrich Bauer Verlag 12/27/1979
Each share Common $1.25 par exchanged for $19.80 cash

WINOGA PATRICIA GOLD MINES LTD. (ON)
Charter cancelled for failure to file reports and pay taxes 9/9/58

WINONA COPPER CO.
Properties sold in 1933

WINONA MINES INC (DE)
Charter forfeited for failure to maintain a registered agent 10/21/77

WINORA GOLD MINES LTD. (ON)
Recapitalized as Rockwin Mines Ltd. on a (1) for (3.5) basis 5/30/55
Rockwin Mines Ltd. merged into Roman Corp. Ltd. 11/21/66
(See Roman Corp. Ltd.)

WINPORT MFG INC (NY)
Each share old Common 10¢ par exchanged for (0.2) share new Common 10¢ par 12/2/71
Merged into Electric Avenue, Inc. 12/14/88
Each share new Common 10¢ par exchanged for (1) share Common $0.001 par
(See Electric Avenue, Inc.)

WINROCK RES INC (BC)
Name changed to Newnote Financial Corp. 04/09/2014

WINS SATELLITE INC (DE)
Charter cancelled and declared inoperative and void for non-payment of taxes 3/1/91

WINSCON ELECTRONICS CO LTD (DE)
Name changed to Uniwell Electronic Corp. 09/16/2010
Uniwell Electronic Corp. name changed to Analytica Bio-Energy Corp. 09/19/2013

WINSLOEW FURNITURE INC (DE)
Merged into Trivest Furniture Corp. 8/27/99
Each share Common 1¢ par exchanged for $34.75 cash

WINSLOW GOLD CORP (BC)
Recapitalized as Winslow Resources Inc. 12/21/2000
Each share Common no par exchanged for (0.2) share Common no par
Winslow Resources Inc. was acquired by DualEx Energy International Inc. 08/30/2007 which recapitalized as Return Energy Inc. 12/20/2016

WINSLOW LANIER INTERNATIONAL CORP.
Liquidation approved in 1930

WINSLOW RES INC (BC)
Acquired by DualEx Energy International Inc. 08/30/2007
Each share Common no par exchanged for (0.44) Unit consisting of (1) share Common no par and (0.5) Common Stock Purchase Warrant expiring 02/28/2009
DualEx Energy International Inc. recapitalized as Return Energy Inc. 12/20/2016

WINSLOW TELE TRONICS INC (PA)
Name changed to Winslow Technology, Inc. 05/20/1970

WINSOME TEXTILES INDS LTD (INDIA)
ADR basis changed from (1:50) to (1:5) 07/20/2011
GDR agreement terminated 06/15/2015
Each Sponsored Reg. S GDR for Equity Shares exchanged for (5) Equity Shares
Note: Unexchanged GDR's will be sold and the proceeds, if any, held for claim after 06/18/2015

WINSOR INDL LTD (HONG KONG)
Stock Dividend - 25% 10/22/1987
Acquired by a private investor group 12/20/2006
Each ADR for Ordinary HKD $0.50 par exchanged for $3.50016 cash

WINSPEAR DIAMONDS INC (BC)
Name changed 6/13/2000
Name changed from Winspear Resources Ltd. (New) to Winspear Diamonds, Inc. 6/13/2000
Merged into De Beers Consolidated Mines Ltd. 9/8/2000
Each share Common no par exchanged for $5 cash

WINSPEAR RES LTD (BC)
Merged into Winspear Resources Ltd. (New) 1/13/97
Each share Common no par exchanged for (1) share Common no par
Winspear Resources Ltd. (New) name changed to Winspear Diamonds Inc. 6/13/2000

WINSTAFF VENTURES LTD (ON)
Merged into Romarco Minerals Inc. (ON) 07/11/1995
Each share Common no par exchanged for (0.04) share Common no par
Romarco Minerals Inc. (ON) reincorporated in British Columbia 06/16/2006 which merged into OceanaGold Corp. 10/01/2015

WINSTAR COMMUNICATIONS INC (DE)
Common 1¢ par split (3) for (2) by issuance of (0.5) additional share payable 03/02/2000 to holders of record 02/16/2000
Each share Sr. Exchangeable Preferred Ser. C exchanged for $1,000 principal amount of 14.25% Sr. Subordinated Exchangeable Debentures due 12/15/2007 on 06/15/2000
Chapter 7 bankruptcy proceedings terminated 04/02/2013
No stockholders' equity

WINSTAR NATL CORP (NY)
Class A Common 10¢ par changed to 4¢ par and (2) additional shares issued 11/8/68
Merged into Alderson Research Industries, Inc. 12/30/68
Each share Class A Common 4¢ par exchanged for (5) shares Conv. Preferred Ser. A. 1¢ par
Alderson Research Industries, Inc. reorganized as Stebar National Corp. 6/20/73 which reincorporated in Oklahoma as Tetra International Corp. 3/7/83
(See Tetra International Corp.)

WINSTAR RES LTD NEW (AB)
Merged into Serinus Energy Inc. (AB) 06/27/2013
Each share Common no par exchanged for (0.7555) share Common no par
Serinus Energy Inc. (AB) reincorporated in Jersey as Serinus Energy PLC 05/15/2018
(See Serinus Energy PLC)

WINSTAR RES LTD OLD (AB)
Recapitalized as Winstar Resources Ltd. (New) 10/25/2005
Each share Common no par exchanged for (0.2) share Common no par
Winstar Resources Ltd. (New) merged into Serinus Energy Inc. (AB) 06/27/2013 which reincorporated in Jersey as Serinus Energy PLC 05/15/2018
(See Serinus Energy PLC)

WINSTED HLDGS INC (FL)
Each shares old Common no par exchanged for (0.00066666) share new Common no par 06/23/2005
Each shares new Common no par exchanged again for (0.0008) share new Common no par 01/26/2006
Recapitalized as Aventura Equities, Inc. 11/03/2008
Each share Common no par exchanged for (0.00013333) share Common no par
Note: No holder will receive fewer than (100) shares

WINSTED HOSIERY CO (CT)
Name changed to Winchester Spinning Corp. in November 1963
(See Winchester Spinning Corp.)

WINSTON & NEWELL CO. (DE)
Recapitalized as Super Valu Stores, Inc. 00/00/1954
Each share 4% Preferred $50 par exchanged for (1) share 5% Preferred 1948 Ser. $50 par
Each share Common $5 par or VTC for Common $5 par exchanged for (1) share Common $5 par or (1) VTC for Common $5 par
Super Valu Stores, Inc. name changed to Supervalu Inc. 06/30/1992
(See Supervalu Inc.)

WINSTON (N.K.) CORP. LIQUIDATING TRUST (DE)
In process of liquidation
Each share Common no par received initial distribution of $1.06 cash 10/17/1975
Each share Common no par received second distribution of $0.40 cash 02/23/1976
Each share Common no par received third distribution of $1 cash 04/11/1979
Each share Common no par received fourth distribution of $0.32 cash 06/29/1979
Each share Common no par received

fifth distribution of $0.44 cash 07/02/1981
Each share Common no par received sixth distribution of $0.22 cash 10/01/1981
Each share Common no par received seventh distribution of $0.22 cash 03/10/1982
Details on subsequent distributions, if any, are not available
(See Winston (N.K.) Corp. for previous distribution)

WINSTON FDG LTD (CAYMAN ISLANDS)
144A 3C7 Preferred called for redemption at $1 on 04/24/2006

WINSTON FURNITURE INC (DE)
Merged into WF Holdings, Inc. 12/29/88
Each share Common 10¢ par exchanged for $16.875 cash

WINSTON FURNITURE INC (DE)
Merged into WinsLoew Furniture, Inc. 12/19/94
Each share Common 1¢ par exchanged for (1) share Common 1¢ par
(See WinsLoew Furniture, Inc.)

WINSTON GOLD MNG CORP (MB)
Reincorporated under the laws of British Columbia as Winston Gold Corp. and Class A Common no par reclassified as Common no par 09/01/2017

WINSTON HOTELS INC (NC)
Issue Information - 5,540,000 shares COM offered at $10 per share on 05/25/1994
9.25% Preferred Ser. A 1¢ par called for redemption at $25 on 02/24/2004
Merged into Inland American Real Estate Trust, Inc. 07/01/2007
Each share 8% Preferred Ser. B $0.001 par exchanged for $25.38 cash
Each share Common 1¢ par exchanged for $15 cash

WINSTON MLS INC (DE)
Acquired by McGregor Corp. 06/11/1987
Each share Common 10¢ par exchanged for $4 cash

WINSTON MUSS CORP (DE)
Name changed to Winston (N.K.) Corp. 12/26/1968
(See Winston (N.K.) Corp.)

WINSTON N K CORP (DE)
Completely liquidated 04/04/1975
Each share Common no par exchanged for first and final distribution of (0.4362278) share Centex Corp. Common 25¢ par
(See Centex Corp.)
Assets transferred to Winston (N.K.) Corp. Liquidating Trust 04/14/1975
(See Winston (N.K.) Corp. Liquidating Trust)

WINSTON NETWORK INC (DE)
Common 10¢ par split (3) for (1) by issuance of (2) additional shares 3/15/79
Merged into WNI Acquisition Corp. 8/16/85
Each share Common 10¢ par exchanged for $14 cash

WINSTON PHARMACAL CORP. (NY)
Charter cancelled and proclaimed dissolved for failure to pay taxes 3/25/81

WINSTON RES INC (DE)
Merged into Winston Resources Acquisition Corp. 11/09/1999
Each share Common 1¢ par exchanged for $4.625 cash

WINSTON RES LTD (BC)
Name changed to Sandpiper Oil & Gas Ltd. 11/19/1987
Sandpiper Oil & Gas Ltd.

recapitalized as Pax Petroleum Ltd. 09/11/1990
(See Pax Petroleum Ltd.)

WINSTON-SALEM HOTEL CO. (NC)
Completely liquidated 12/28/72
Each share Common $50 par received first and final distribution of $11.59 cash
Note: Certificates were not required to be surrendered and are now valueless

WINTEC CORP (NV)
Recapitalized as Syntron Communications, Inc. 12/28/89
Each share Common $0.001 par exchanged for (0.04) share Common $0.001 par
(See Syntron Communications, Inc.)

WINTEK CORP (TAIWAN)
Stock Dividends - in 144A GDR's to holders of 144A GDR's 12% payable 09/17/2003 to holders of record 07/25/2003; 18.22% payable 09/10/2004 to holders of record 07/15/2004; 20.12% payable 09/14/2005 to holders of record 07/26/2005; 10.02% payable 07/28/2006 to holders of record 06/21/2006; 9.99246% payable 09/02/2011 to holdrs of record 08/02/2011 Ex date - 07/29/2011 in Reg. S GDR's to holders of Reg. S GDR's 12% payable 09/17/2003 to holders of record 07/25/2003; 18.22% payable 09/10/2004 to holders of record 07/15/2004; 20.12% payable 09/14/2005 to holders of record 07/26/2005; 10.02% payable 07/28/2006 to holders of record 06/21/2006; 9.99246% payable 09/02/2011 to holdrs of record 08/02/2011 Ex date - 07/29/2011
GDR agreement terminated 09/14/2015
GDR holders' equity unlikely

WINTER & HIRSCH INC (IL)
Completely liquidated in 1970
Each share 7% Preferred Stock exchanged for first and final cash distribution
Details not available
No Common stockholders' equity

WINTER GARDEN HARVESTING CORP. (FL)
Acquired by Safety Suspension Systems Corp. 11/1/69
Each share Common 1¢ par exchanged for (1) share Common 1¢ par
(See Safety Suspension Systems Corp.)

WINTER (BENJAMIN), INC. (DE)
Charter cancelled and declared inoperative and void for non-payment of taxes 04/01/1942

WINTER JACK INC (DE)
Reincorporated 12/23/75
5% Preferred $100 par conversion privilege expired 10/31/73
Common $1 par split (2) for (1) by issuance of (1) additional share 7/31/74
Stock Dividend - 25% 1/31/74
State of incorporation changed from (WI) to (DE) 12/23/75
5% Preferred $100 par called for redemption 12/31/75
Common $1 par split (3) for (2) by issuance of (0.5) additional share 4/30/76
Common $1 par reclassified as Class A Common $1 par 6/25/86
Note: Option to exchange Class A Common for Class B Common expired 8/27/86
Name changed to Winjak Inc. 7/2/87
(See Winjak Inc.)

WINTER PARK HARVESTING CORP.
Charter cancelled and proclaimed

dissolved for non-payment of taxes 7/11/72

WINTER PARK TEL CO (FL)
Common $10 par changed to $5 par and (1) additional share issued 03/26/1962
Common $5 par changed to $2.50 par and (1) additional share issued 05/14/1965
Common $2.50 par changed to $1.25 par and (1) additional share issued 06/01/1972
5% Preferred $100 par called for redemption 02/01/1977
5-1/2% Preferred $100 par called for redemption 02/01/1977
Stock Dividends - 20% 04/01/1963; 20% 08/01/1967; 100% 07/01/1973
Merged into United Telecommunications, Inc. 06/21/1979
Each share Common $1.25 par exchanged for (0.7) share Common $2.50 par
United Telecommunications, Inc. name changed to Sprint Corp. (KS) 02/26/1992 which name changed to Sprint Nextel Corp. 08/12/2005 which merged into Sprint Corp. (DE) 07/10/2013

WINTER SPORTS INC (MT)
Stock Dividend - 4% payable 12/27/96 to holders of record 12/3/96
Each (150) shares old Common no par exchanged for (1) share new Common no par 5/7/2004
Note: Holders of (149) or fewer pre-split shares received $17.50 cash per share
Each (15) shares new Common no par exchanged again for (1) share new Common no par 12/5/2006
Note: Holders of (14) or fewer pre-split shares received $3,000 cash per share

WINTERCREST RES LTD (AB)
Recapitalized as Mahdia Gold Corp. (AB) 12/02/2009
Each share Common no par exchanged for (0.5) share Common no par
Mahdia Gold Corp. (AB) reincorporated in Ontario 03/25/2013

WINTERHALTER INC (MI)
Merged into Interface Systems, Inc. 4/9/87
Each share Common $0.002 par exchanged for $0.15 cash

WINTERS & CRAMPTON CORP. (MI)
Name changed to Jervis Corp. in 1952
Jervis Corp. name changed to Harman International Industries, Inc. 1/25/74 which merged into Beatrice Foods Co. 8/1/77 which name changed to Beatrice Companies, Inc. 6/5/84
(See Beatrice Companies, Inc.)

WINTERS & CRAMPTON MANUFACTURING CO.
Reorganized as Winters & Crampton Corp. in 1934
(See Winters & Crampton Corp.)

WINTERS GOLD HEDLEY LTD (BC)
Recapitalized as Regal Gold Corp. 08/26/1993
Each share Common no par exchanged for (0.4) share Common no par
Regal Gold Corp. name changed to International Thunderbird Gaming Corp. (BC) 06/23/1994 which reincorporated in Yukon 02/05/1999 which name changed to Thunderbird Resorts, Inc. (Yukon) 10/05/2005 which reorganized in British Virgin Islands 11/20/2007

WINTERS NATL BK & TR CO (DAYTON, OH)
Each share Common $100 par exchanged for (5) shares Common $20 par 00/00/1944
Common $20 par changed to $10 par and (1) additional share issued 00/00/1954
Stock Dividends - 14-2/7% 01/30/1962; 10% 02/15/1965
Merged into Winters National Corp. 07/09/1973
Each share Common $10 par exchanged for (1) share Common $10 par
Winters National Bank merged into Banc One Corp. (DE) 06/01/1983 which reincorporated in Ohio 05/01/1989 which merged into Bank One Corp. 10/02/1998 which merged into J.P. Morgan Chase & Co. 12/31/2000 which name changed to JPMorgan Chase & Co. 07/20/2004

WINTERS NATL CORP (OH)
Stock Dividend - 10% 02/11/1980
Merged into Banc One Corp. (DE) 06/01/1983
Each share Conv. Preferred Ser. A $10 par exchanged for $36.225 cash
Each share Common $10 par exchanged for (0.43) share Conv. Preferred Ser. A no par and (0.9947) share Common no par
Banc One Corp. (DE) reincorporated in Ohio 05/01/1989 which merged into Bank One Corp. 10/02/1998 which merged into J.P. Morgan Chase & Co. 12/31/2000 which name changed to JPMorgan Chase & Co. 07/20/2004

WINTERTHERM CORP (AB)
Recapitalized as Wintercrest Resources Ltd. 08/20/1997
Each share Common no par exchanged for (0.125) share Common no par
Wintercrest Resources Ltd. recapitalized as Mahdia Gold Corp. (AB) 12/02/2009 which reincorporated in Ontario 03/25/2013

WINTEX ML INC (DE)
Liquidation completed
Each share Common $1 par received initial distribution of $7.65590166 cash 12/04/2009
Each share Common $1 par received second and final distribution of $0.0947 cash 02/08/2011
Note: Certificates were not required to be surrendered and are without value

WINTHROP (LAWRENCE) BUILDING (IL)
Merged into Trianon Commercial Properties, Inc. 4/1/46
Each share Common $25 par exchanged for $76 principal amount of 5% Debentures due 4/1/56

WINTHROP FOCUS FDS (MA)
Aggressive Growth Fund reclassified as Aggressive Growth Fund Class A 02/28/1996
Fixed Income Fund 1¢ par reclassified as Fixed Income Class A 02/28/1996
Growth Fund 1¢ par reclassified as Growth Fund Class A 02/28/1996
Growth & Income Fund reclassified as Growth & Income Fund Class A 02/28/1996
Municipal Trust Fund reclassified as Municipal Trust Fund Class A 02/28/1996
Aggressive Growth Fund Class A reclassified as Small Co. Value Class A 02/20/1997
Aggressive Growth Fund Class B reclassified as Small Co. Value Fund Class B 02/20/1997

Name changed to DLJ Winthrop Focus Funds 01/29/1999
DLJ Winthrop Focus Funds name changed to DLJ Focus Funds 08/01/2000 which reorganized as Credit Suisse Warburg Pincus Capital Funds 01/18/2001

WINTHROP INDS INC (NV)
Recapitalized as Compass Knowledge Holdings Inc. 11/16/1999
Each (3.33) shares Common $0.001 par exchanged for (1) share Common $0.001 par
(See Compass Knowledge Holdings Inc.)

WINTHROP INSD MTG INVS II (MD)
Liquidation completed
Each Unit of Ltd. Partnership received initial distribution of $12.58 cash 3/15/91
Each Unit of Ltd. Partnership received second and final distribution of $0.32 cash 4/15/91
Note: Certificates were not required to be surrendered and are without value

WINTHROP RLTY TR (OH)
Each Conv. Preferred Share of Bene. Int. Ser. A $1 par exchanged for (4.92) old Common Shares of Bene. Int. $1 par 02/07/2006
Each old Common Share of Bene. Int. $1 par exchanged for (0.2) new Common Share of Bene. Int. $1 par 12/01/2008
Completely liquidated 09/12/2014
Each share 9.25% Preferred Share of Bene. Int. Ser. D $1 par exchanged for $25.4815 cash
In process of liquidation
Each new Common Share of Bene. Int. $1 par received initial distribution of $1.25 cash payable 06/16/2015 to holders of record 06/09/2015 Ex date - 06/05/2015
Each new Common Share of Bene. Int. $1 par received second distribution of $1 cash payable 12/03/2015 to holders of record 11/25/2015 Ex date - 11/23/2015
Each new Common Share of Bene. Int. $1 par received third distribution of $2 cash payable 05/17/2016 to holders of record 05/10/2016 Ex date - 05/06/2016
Each new Common Share of Bene. Int. $1 par received fourth distribution of $1.25 cash payable 07/01/2016 to holders of record 06/24/2016 Ex date - 06/22/2016
Assets transferred to Winthrop Realty Liquidating Trust and Common Shares of Bene. Int. $1 par reclassified as Units of Bene. Int. 08/05/2016

WINTHROP RES CORP (MN)
Merged into TCF Financial Corp. 6/24/97
Each share Common 1¢ par exchanged for (0.7766) share Common 1¢ par

WINTHROP SCOTT CORP (CO)
Completely liquidated 06/27/1980
Each share Common 15¢ par received first and final distribution of $0.2604 cash
Note: Certificates were not required to be surrendered and are without value

WINTHROP TOWERS HOTEL CORP.
Liquidated in 1943

WINTON ENGINE CO.
Acquired by General Motors Corp. 00/00/1930
Details not available

WINTON FINL CORP (OH)
Common $1 par split (2) for (1) by issuance of (1) additional share 2/28/94
Common $1 par split (2) for (1) by issuance of (1) additional share payable 3/31/98 to holders of record 3/6/98 Ex date - 4/1/98
Merged into WesBanco, Inc. 1/3/2005
Each share Common $1 par exchanged for $20.75 cash

WINTON OIL N L (AUSTRALIA)
Struck off register 10/03/1990
No stockholders' equity

WINTON SVGS & LN CO (CINCINNATI, OH)
Under plan of reorganization each share Common $1 par automatically became (1) share Winton Financial Corp. Common $1 par 7/2/90
(See Winton Financial Corp.)

WINTRAYSAN CAP CORP (AB)
Recapitalized as Orion Oil & Gas Corp. 01/11/2010
Each share Common no par exchanged for (0.5) share Common no par
Orion Oil & Gas Corp. merged into WestFire Energy Ltd. 06/30/2011 which changed to Long Run Exploration Ltd. 10/29/2012
(See Long Run Exploration Ltd.)

WINTRUST CAP TR I (DE)
9% Guaranteed Trust Preferred Securities called for redemption at $25 on 09/05/2006

WINTRUST CAP TR II (DE)
10.5% Guaranteed Trust Preferred Securities called for redemption at $10 on 08/16/2005

WINTRUST FINL CORP (IL)
Each share 5% Non-Cum. Conv. Perpetual Preferred Ser. C no par automatically became (24.72) shares Common no par 04/27/2017
(Additional Information in Active)

WINWELL VENTURES INC (BC)
Each share old Common no par exchanged for (0.1) share new Common no par 12/07/2010
Reorganized under the laws of Nevada as Contact Gold Corp. 06/15/2017
Each share new Common no par exchanged for (0.125) share Common $0.001 par
Note: Unexchanged certificates will be cancelled and become without value 06/07/2023

WINWEST OIL & MNG LTD (ON)
Charter cancelled for failure to pay taxes and file returns 03/13/1979

WINWHEEL BULLION INC (DE)
Name changed to Verdant Automotive Corp. 06/09/2011
Verdant Automotive Corp. name changed to VRDT Corp. 02/09/2012
(See VRDT Corp.)

WINWIN GAMING INC (DE)
SEC revoked common stock registration 06/27/2012

WINZEN PPTYS INC (BC)
Name changed 01/02/2003
Name changed from Winzen International Inc. to Winzen Properties Inc. 01/02/2003
Ceased to be a reporting issuer 08/14/2013
Company will repurchase shares upon request

WIRBAC RES INC (AB)
Recapitalized as Virtus Energy Ltd. 09/12/2001
Each share Common no par exchanged for (0.25) share Common no par
Virtus Energy Ltd. merged into Titan Exploration Ltd. 06/23/2005 which was acquired by Penn West Energy Trust 01/11/2008 which reorganized as Penn West Petroleum Ltd. (New) 01/03/2011 which name changed to Obsidian Energy Ltd. 06/29/2017

WIRE GRAPHICS INC (NV)
Charter revoked for failure to file reports and pay fees 10/1/2006

WIRE ONE TECHNOLOGIES INC (DE)
Name changed to Glowpoint, Inc. 9/24/2003

WIRE WHEEL CORP. OF AMERICA
Merged into Kelsey-Hayes Wheel Corp. 00/00/1929
Details not available

WIRED ASSOCS SOLUTIONS INC (NV)
Name changed to Wild Craze, Inc. 05/16/2012

WIRELESS ATTACHMENTS INC (CO)
Name changed to Mountain High Acquisitions Corp. 03/12/2014

WIRELESS CABLE ATLANTA INC (GA)
Merged into BellSouth Corp. 5/28/97
Each share Common $1 par exchanged for (0.483) share Common $1 par
BellSouth Corp. merged into AT&T Inc. 12/29/2006

WIRELESS CAP CORP (AB)
Name changed to Elkwater Resources Ltd. 07/15/2003
Elkwater Resources Ltd. recapitalized as Striker Exploration Corp. 03/02/2015 which merged into Gear Energy Ltd. 07/29/2016

WIRELESS DATA SOLUTIONS INC (UT)
Reorganized under the laws of Nevada 08/09/2007
Each share Common $0.001 par exchanged for (0.01) share Common $0.001 par

WIRELESS DEV CORP (NV)
Name changed to Harris Exploration Inc. 08/21/1995
(See Harris Exploration Inc.)

WIRELESS FACS INC (DE)
Issue Information - 4,000,000 shares COM offered at $15 per share on 11/04/1999
Name changed to Kratos Defense & Security Solutions, Inc. 09/17/2007

WIRELESS FRONTIER INTERNET INC (DE)
Common no par split (2) for (1) by issuance of (1) additional share payable 03/31/2004 to holders of record 03/20/2004 Ex date - 04/01/2004
SEC revoked common stock registration 08/08/2008
Stockholders' equity unlikely

WIRELESS HLDGS GROUP INC (DE)
Recapitalized as Vega Promotional Systems, Inc. (DE) 12/26/2006
Each (150) shares Common $0.0001 par exchanged for (1) share Common $0.0001 par
Vega Promotional Systems, Inc. (DE) reorganized in Wyoming as Vega Biofuels, Inc. 07/29/2010

WIRELESS HLDGS INC (FL)
Name changed to H2Diesel Holdings, Inc. 11/29/2006
H2Diesel Holdings, Inc. name changed to New Generation Biofuels Holdings, Inc. 04/16/2008
(See New Generation Holdings, Inc.)

WIRELESS HOLDRS TR (DE)
Trust terminated
Each Depositary Receipt received first and final distribution of $43.795312 cash payable 01/08/2013 to holders of record 12/24/2012

WIRELESS MATRIX CORP (AB)
Liquidation completed
Each share Common no par received initial distribution of USD $0.56 cash payable 04/18/2013 to holders of record 04/16/2013 Ex date - 04/19/2013
Each share Common no par received second and final distribution of USD $0.03723 cash payable 12/06/2013 to holders of record 12/04/2013 Ex date - 12/09/2013

WIRELESS NETCOM INC (NV)
Recapitalized as eCommercial.com Inc. (NV) 04/29/1999
Each share Common $0.001 par exchanged for (0.1) share Common $0.001 par
eCommercial.com Inc. (NV) reincorporated in Delaware as MindArrow Systems, Inc. 04/03/2000 which merged into Avalon Digital Marketing Systems, Inc. 10/01/2002

WIRELESS ONE INC (DE)
Plan of reorganization under Chapter 11 Federal Bankruptcy Code effective 12/10/99
Each share Common 1¢ par exchanged for $1.319248 cash

WIRELESS ONE INC CDA (MB)
Under plan of arrangement each share Common no par automatically became (0.1) Lanesborough Real Estate Investment Trust Trust Unit 08/30/2002

WIRELESS RONIN TECHNOLOGIES INC (MN)
Each share old Common 1¢ par exchanged for (0.2) share new Common 1¢ par 12/17/2012
Name changed to Creative Realities, Inc. 09/17/2014

WIRELESS SYNERGIES INC (NV)
Name changed to 2KSounds Corp. 05/21/2002
(See 2KSounds Corp.)

WIRELESS TECHNOLOGIES INC (NV)
Name changed to Mattman Specialty Vehicles, Inc. 12/14/2005
Mattman Specialty Vehicles, Inc. name changed to Remote Surveillance Technologies, Inc. 01/11/2007 which name changed to Stratera, Inc. 07/15/2008 which recapitalized as Gulf West Investment Properties, Inc. 12/16/2009

WIRELESS VENTURES INC (DE)
Name changed to Pivotal Self-Service Technologies Inc. 10/02/2001
Pivotal Self-Service Technologies Inc. name changed to Phantom Fiber Corp. 07/21/2004 which recapitalized as Accelerated Technologies Holding Corp. 09/18/2017

WIRELESS WEBCONNECT INC (DE)
SEC revoked common stock registration 10/03/2008

WIRELESS2 TECHNOLOGIES INC (BC)
Name changed to Nanotech Security Corp. 04/15/2010

WIREMASTER CORP AMER (NY)
Reincorporated under the laws of Delaware as Ampower Instrument Co. Inc. 4/4/78
Ampower Instrument Co. Inc. name changed to Ampower Technologies, Inc. 11/29/83
(See Ampower Technologies, Inc.)

WIREMEDIA COM INC (FL)
Reincorporated 3/11/2005
Place of incorporation changed from (FL) to (NV) 3/11/2005
Name changed to Wiremedia, Inc. 3/28/2005

WIREMOLD CO. (CT)
5% Preferred Ser. A $25 par called for redemption 07/01/1971
Public interest eliminated

WIRESAT CORP (FL)
Proclaimed dissolved for failure to file reports and pay fees 11/04/1988

WIRLWIND RES LTD (BC)
Recapitalized as Spirit Resources Ltd. (BC) 12/13/1991
Each share Common no par exchanged for (0.33333333) share Common no par
Spirit Resources Ltd. (BC) reincorporated in Delaware as Hygeia Holdings Ltd. 03/03/1993 which name changed to Novopharm Biotech Inc. (DE) 07/28/1995 which merged into Novopharm Biotech Inc. (BC) 08/25/1997 which name changed to Viventia Biotech Inc. 09/11/2000
(See Viventia Biotech Inc.)

WIRTZ PRODTNS LTD (MN)
Merged into A.M.W., Inc. 08/02/1978
Each share Common $1 par exchanged for $7.10 cash

WISCAN RES LTD (ON)
Under plan of reorganization each share Common no par exchanged for (1) share Moss Resources Inc. Common no par and (1/15) share Yamana Resources Inc. Common no par 02/09/1995
(See each company's listing)

WISCASSET, WATERVILLE & FARMINGTON RAILWAY CO.
Road sold in 1932

WISCASSETT MLS CO (NC)
98% acquired by Cannon Mills Co. 07/00/1978
Public interest eliminated

WISCO CDA LTD (BC)
Name changed to Teleguard Systems International Inc. 10/20/1987
(See Teleguard Systems International Inc.)

WISCONSIN BANKSHARES CORP. (WI)
Each share Capital Stock $10 par exchanged for (0.2) share Capital Stock no par 00/00/1933
Name changed to First Wisconsin Bankshares Corp. and Capital Stock no par changed to Common $5 par 01/15/1960
First Wisconsin Bankshares Corp. name changed to First Wisconsin Corp. 03/30/1974 which name changed to Firstar Corp. (Old) 01/01/1989 which merged into Firstar Corp. (New) 11/20/1998 which merged into U.S. Bancorp (DE) 02/27/2001

WISCONSIN CENT RR CO (MN)
Merged into Soo Line Railroad Co. 12/30/60
Each (2.05) shares Common no par exchanged for (1) share Common no par
Soo Line Railroad Co. reorganized as Soo Line Corp. 12/31/84
(See Soo Line Corp.)

WISCONSIN CENT TRANSN CORP (DE)
Common 1¢ par split (2) for (1) by issuance of (1) additional share 7/5/94
Common 1¢ par split (3) for (1) by issuance of (2) additional shares payable 5/31/96 to holders of record 5/17/96
Merged into Canadian National Railway Co. 10/9/2001
Each share Common 1¢ par exchanged for $17.15 cash

WISCONSIN CENTRAL AIRLINES
Name changed to Wisconsin Central Airlines, Inc. in 1947
Wisconsin Central Airlines, Inc. name changed to North Central Airlines, Inc. in 1952 which merged into Republic Airlines, Inc. 7/1/79
(See Republic Airlines, Inc.)

WISCONSIN CENTRAL AIRLINES, INC. (WI)
Name changed to North Central Airlines Inc. in 1952
North Central Airlines Inc. merged into Republic Airlines, Inc. 7/1/79
(See Republic Airlines, Inc.)

WISCONSIN CENTRAL RAILWAY CO. (WI)
Reorganized as Wisconsin Central Railroad Co. (Minn.) in 1954
No stockholders' equity

WISCONSIN CENTRIFUGAL INC (WI)
Stock Dividends - 10% 7/12/74; 10% 7/17/75; 10% 7/15/76; 10% 7/14/77; 10% 7/10/78
Merged into Atlantic Richfield Co. (PA) 8/13/80
Each share Common $1 par exchanged for (0.6682) share Common $2.50 par
Atlantic Richfield Co. (PA) reincorporated in Delaware 5/7/85 which merged into BP Amoco p.l.c 4/18/2000

WISCONSIN ELEC PWR CO (WI)
Common $20 par changed to $1 par 00/00/1940
Common $10 par split (2) for (1) by issuance of (1) additional share 05/16/1963
Common $10 par split (3) for (2) by issuance of (0.5) additional share 07/27/1982
Under plan of reorganization each share Common $10 par automatically became (1) share Wisconsin Energy Corp. Common 1¢ par 01/01/1987
7.75% Preferred $100 par called for redemption 04/14/1987
8.8% Preferred $100 par called for redemption 04/14/1987
8.9% Preferred $100 par called for redemption 04/14/1987
6.75% Preferred $100 par called for redemption 06/01/1994
Wisconsin Energy Corp. name changed to WEC Energy Group, Inc. 06/30/2015
(Additional Information in Active)

WISCONSIN ENERGY CORP (WI)
Common 1¢ par split (2) for (1) by issuance of (1) additional share 06/30/1987
Common 1¢ par split (3) for (2) by issuance of (0.5) additional share 06/30/1992
Common 1¢ par split (2) for (1) by issuance of (1) additional share payable 03/01/2011 to holders of record 02/14/2011 Ex date - 03/02/2011
Under plan of merger name changed to WEC Energy Group, Inc. 06/30/2015

WISCONSIN FD INC (DE)
Name changed to Wisconsin Income Fund, Inc. 4/6/76
Wisconsin Income Fund, Inc. name changed to Nicholas Income Fund, Inc. (DE) 9/9/83 which reincorporated in Maryland in 1986 which name changed to Nicholas High Income Fund, Inc. 2/7/2005

WISCONSIN FUEL & LT CO (WI)
Common $100 par changed to $10 par and (9) additional shares issued 05/20/1955
Common $10 par split (2) for (1) by issuance of (1) additional share 09/10/1984
Common $10 par split (2) for (1) by issuance of (1) additional share payable 12/01/1999 to holders of record 11/15/1999
Stock Dividends - 25% 07/12/1954; 20% 05/04/1955; 100% 06/17/1960; 50% 05/28/1964; 50% 07/13/1973; 10% 06/26/1978
Merged into WPS Resources Corp. 04/01/2001
Each share Common $10 par exchanged for (1.73) shares Common $1 par
WPS Resources Corp. name changed to Integrys Energy Group, Inc. 02/21/2007 which merged into WEC Energy Group, Inc. 06/30/2015

WISCONSIN GAS CO (WI)
Under plan of reorganization each share Common $8 par automatically became (1) share Wicor, Inc. Common $1 par 04/30/1980
(See Wicor, Inc.)
$2.55 Preferred called for redemption 10/31/1988
Public interest eliminated

WISCONSIN HYDRO ELECTRIC CO. (WI)
Each share 6% Preferred $100 par exchanged for (10) shares Common $12 par in 1948
Stock Dividends - 10% 12/28/49; 10% 6/20/55
Assets sold and each share Common $12 par exchanged for (1.1) shares Common $5 par of Northern States Power Co. (MN) 11/1/57
Northern States Power Co. name changed to Xcel Energy Inc. 8/18/2000

WISCONSIN INCOME FD INC (DE)
Name changed to Nicholas Income Fund, Inc. (DE) 9/9/83
Nicholas Income Fund, Inc. (DE) reincorporated in Maryland in 1986 which name changed to Nicholas High Income Fund, Inc. 2/17/2005

WISCONSIN INSURANCE CORP. OF AMERICA (WI)
Common $1 par changed to 25¢ par 12/10/1965
Merged into Wayne National Life Insurance Co. 12/31/1966
Each share Common 25¢ par exchanged for (0.25) share Common $1 par
Wayne National Life Insurance Co. merged into Hamilton (Alexander) Life Insurance Co. of America 11/6/1967 which merged into Hamilton International Corp. 08/15/1969
(See Hamilton International Corp.)

WISCONSIN INVESTMENT CO. (DE)
Each share Preferred $25 par exchanged for (1) share Preferred $10 par and (3) shares Common $1 par in 1933
Each share Class A or B no par exchanged for (1) share Common $1 par in 1933
Name changed to Wisconsin Fund, Inc. in April 1955
Wisconsin Fund, Inc. name changed to Wisconsin Income Fund, Inc. 4/6/76 which name changed to Nicholas Income Fund, Inc. (DE) 9/9/83 which reincorporated in Maryland in 1986 which name changed to Nicholas High Income Fund, Inc. 2/7/2005

WISCONSIN MICH PWR CO (WI)
4-1/2% Preferred $100 par called for redemption 06/30/1977
Public interest eliminated

WISCONSIN MNG LTD (QC)
Recapitalized as Joubi Mining Corp. Ltd. 3/9/73
Each share Capital Stock $1 par exchanged for (0.285714) share Capital Stock $1 par
(See Joubi Mining Corp. Ltd.)

WISCONSIN MOTOR CORP.
Acquired by Wisconsin Motor Corp. in 1933
Details not available

WISCONSIN MTR CORP (WI)
Merged into Continental Motors Corp. 03/19/1969
Each share Common $1 par exchanged for $25 principal amount of Promissory Notes

WISCONSIN NATL LIFE INS CO (WI)
Common $10 par changed to $5 par and (1) additional share issued plus a 50% stock dividend paid 05/01/1965
Common $5 par changed to $2.50 par and (1) additional share issued 05/11/1973
Stock Dividends - 150% 05/01/1951; 100% 05/01/1959
Each share Common $2.50 par exchanged for (0.0001) share Common $25,000 par 04/29/1976
Note: In effect holders received $24 cash per share and public interest was eliminated

WISCONSIN OIL REFINING CO., INC. (WI)
Merged into Empire Petroleum Co. 1/3/56
Each (4) shares Class A Common $1 par exchanged for (1) share Common $1 par
Each (2) shares Class B Common $1 par exchanged for (1) share Common $1 par
Empire Petroleum Co. name changed to Empire International, Inc. 7/15/70 which was adjudicated bankrupt 5/9/73

WISCONSIN PARTS CO.
Acquired by Timken-Detroit Axle Co. in 1929
Details not available

WISCONSIN PHARMACAL INC (WI)
Name changed to Female Health Co. 02/08/1996
Female Health Co. name changed to Veru Inc. 08/07/2017

WISCONSIN PWR & LT CO (WI)
Common $100 par changed to $50 par 00/00/1933
Each share Common $50 par exchanged for (5) shares Common $10 par 00/00/1945
6% Preferred $100 par called for redemption 12/17/1945
7% Preferred $100 par called for redemption 12/17/1945
Common $10 par changed to $5 par and (1) additional share issued 05/15/1962
12% Preferred $100 par called for redemption 09/30/1985
Under plan of reorganization each share Common $5 par automatically became (1) share WPL Holdings, Inc. Common 1¢ par 04/01/1988
7.56% Preferred $100 par called for redemption 11/30/1993
8.48% Preferred $100 par called for redemption 11/30/1993
WPL Holdings, Inc. merged into Interstate Energy Corp. 04/21/1998 which name changed to Alliant Energy Corp. 05/19/1999
4.40% Preferred $100 par called for redemption at $104.5611 plus $0.048219 accrued dividends on 03/20/2013
4.50% Preferred $100 par called for redemption at $107.5611 plus $0.049315 accrued dividends on 03/20/2013
4.76% Preferred $100 par called for redemption at $101.0661 plus $0.052164 accrued dividends on 03/20/2013
4.80% Preferred $100 par called for redemption at $101.0667 plus $0.052603 accrued dividends on 03/20/2013
4.96% Preferred $100 par called for redemption at $101.0689 plus $0.054356 accrued dividends on 03/20/2013

6.20% Preferred $100 par called for redemption at $100.3961 plus $0.067945 accrued dividends on 03/20/2013
6.50% Preferred $100 par called for redemption at $25.0226 plus $0.017808 accrued dividends on 03/20/2013

WISCONSIN PROPANE GAS CORP. (WI)
Merged into Wisconsin Southern Gas Co. Inc. on a (1.5) for (1) basis 6/1/64
Wisconsin Southern Gas Co., Inc. merged into Wisconsin Energy Corp. 1/1/94

WISCONSIN PUB SVC CORP (WI)
Common $10 par changed to $8 par and (1) additional share issued 07/14/1964
10.75% Preferred $100 par called for redemption 05/01/1986
Common $8 par changed to $4 par and (1) additional share issued 07/15/1987
10.5% Preferred $100 par called for redemption 11/01/1990
7.72% Preferred $100 par called for redemption 08/01/1993
Under plan of reorganization each share Common $4 par automatically became (1) share WPS Resources Corp. Common $1 par 09/01/1994
WPS Resources Corp. name changed to Integrys Energy Group, Inc. 02/21/2007 which merged into WEC Energy Group, Inc. 06/30/2015
5% Preferred $100 par called for redemption at $107.50 plus $0.166666 accrued dividends on 11/13/2015
5.04% Preferred $100 par called for redemption at $102.81 plus $0.167999 accrued dividends on 11/13/2015
5.08% Preferred $100 par called for redemption at $101 plus $0.169333 accrued dividends on 11/13/2015
6.76% Preferred $100 par called for redemption at $103.35 plus $0.225333 accrued dividends on 11/13/2015
6.88% Preferred $100 par called for redemption at $100 plus $0.229333 accrued dividends on 11/13/2015

WISCONSIN REAL ESTATE INVT TR (WI)
Name changed 12/07/1970
Shares of Bene. Int. no par changed to $1 par 02/29/1968
Name changed from Wisconsin Real Estate Investment Fund to Wisconsin Real Estate Investment Trust 12/07/1970
Assets sold for the benefit of creditors 04/01/1996
No stockholders' equity

WISCONSIN SVGS ASSN TOMAH (WI)
Merged into Heritage Mutual Insurance Co. 01/31/1991
Each share Common $1 par exchanged for $20 cash

WISCONSIN SECS CO DEL (DE)
Ceased operations 07/09/1990
Details not available

WISCONSIN SOUTHERN GAS & APPLIANCE CORP. (WI)
Name changed to Wisconsin Southern Gas Co., Inc. 00/00/1954
Wisconsin Southern Gas Co., Inc. merged into Wisconsin Energy Corp. 01/01/1994 which name changed to WEC Energy Group, Inc. 06/30/2015

WISCONSIN SOUTHN GAS CO (WI)
Common $10 par changed to $5 par and (1) additional share issued 12/1/64
Common $5 par split (3) for (2) by issuance of (0.5) additional share 9/9/85
Stock Dividend - 10% 6/1/55
Merged into Wisconsin Energy Corp. 1/1/94
Each share Common $5 par exchanged for (1.633) shares Common 1¢ par

WISCONSIN TOY INC (WI)
Name changed to Value Merchants, Inc. (Old) 3/13/90
Value Merchants, Inc. (Old) reorganized as Value Merchants, Inc. (New) 6/27/95
(See Value Merchants, Inc. (New))

WISDOM INTL CORP (NV)
Each share old Common no par exchanged for (0.005) share new Common no par 03/14/2005
Charter revoked for failure to file reports and pay taxes 08/31/2007

WISDOMTREE COAL FD (DE)
Trust terminated 09/29/2016
Each Share of Bene. Int. no par received $45.942927 cash

WISDOMTREE INTL QUALITY DIVID GROWTH DYNAMIC HEDGED INDEX ETF (ON)
Name changed to WisdomTree International Quality Dividend Growth Variably Hedged Index ETF 01/13/2017

WISDOMTREE TR (DE)
U.S. Cash Fund $0.001 par reclassified as U.S. Current Income Fund $0.001 par 05/20/2008
International Consumer Cyclical Sector Fund $0.001 par reclassified as International Consumer Discretionary Sector Fund $0.001 par 06/20/2008
International Consumer Non-Cyclical Sector Fund $0.001 par reclassified as International Consumer Staples Sector Fund $0.001 par 06/20/2008
U.S. Current Income Fund $0.001 par reclassified as U.S. Short-Term Government Income Fund $0.001 par 05/25/2009
Trust terminated 03/30/2010
Each share Earnings Top 100 Fund $0.001 par received $40.35254 cash
Each share Europe Total Dividend Fund $0.001 par received $42.278 cash
Each share International Communications Sector Fund $0.001 par received $22.53 cash
Each share International Consumer Discretionary Sector Fund $0.001 par received $19.99944 cash
Each share International Consumer Staples Sector Fund $0.001 par received $24.93447 cash
Each share International Financial Sector Fund $0.001 par received $15.2741 cash
Each share International Health Care Sector Fund $0.001 par received $23.70624 cash
Each share International Industrial Sector Fund $0.001 par received $22.19619 cash
Each share International Technology Sector Fund $0.001 par received $19.64539 cash
Each share U.S. Short-Term Government Income Fund $0.001 par received $24.99375 cash
International Energy Sector Fund $0.001 par reclassified as Global Natural Resources Fund $0.001 par 06/20/2011
International Utilities Sector Fund $0.001 par reclassified as Global ex-U.S. Utilities Fund $0.001 par 06/20/2011
International Basic Materials Sector Fund $0.001 par reclassified as Commodity Country Equity Fund $0.001 par 06/20/2011
New Zealand Dollar Fund $0.001 par reclassified as Australia & New Zealand Debt Fund $0.001 par 10/25/2011
Dreyfus Euro Fund $0.001 par reclassified as Euro Debt Fund $0.001 par 12/19/2011
Trust terminated 12/10/2012
Each share Dreyfus Japanese Yen Fund $0.001 par received $31.54 cash
Each share LargeCap Growth Fund $0.001 par received $34.06 cash
Each share South African Rand Fund $0.001 par received $31.56 cash
Dreyfus Commodity Currency Fund $0.001 par reclassified as Commodity Currency Fund $0.001 par 01/14/2013
Dreyfus Indian Rupee Fund $0.001 par reclassified as Indian Rupee Fund $0.001 par 01/14/2013
Commodity Currency Fund $0.001 par reclassified as Commodity Currency Strategy Fund $0.001 par 01/07/2014
Indian Rupee Fund $0.001 par reclassified as Indian Rupee Strategy Fund $0.001 par 01/07/2014
Trust terminated 02/18/2015
Each share Euro Debt Fund $0.001 par received $20.420175 cash
Japan Dividend Growth Fund $0.001 par reclassified as Japan Quality Dividend Growth Fund $0.001 par 08/31/2015
Trust terminated 09/29/2016
Each share Commodity Country Equity Fund $0.001 par received $24.28429 cash
Each share Commodity Currency Strategy Fund $0.001 par received $17.264304 cash
Each share Global ex-U.S. Utilities Fund $0.001 par received $16.254533 cash
Each share Global Natural Resources Fund $0.001 par received $13.346265 cash
Each share Japan Interest Rate Strategy Fund $0.001 par received $43.88654 cash
Strong Dollar U.S. Equity Fund $0.001 par reclassified as U.S. Domestic Economy Fund $0.001 par 03/17/2017
Weak Dollar U.S. Equity Fund $0.001 par reclassified as U.S. Export & Multinational Fund $0.001 par 03/17/2017
Trust terminated 03/29/2017
Each share Australia & New Zealand Debt Fund $0.001 par received $18.215649 cash
Each share Indian Rupee Strategy Fund $0.001 par received $22.707032 cash
Each share Japan Hedged Tech, Media & Telecom Fund $0.001 par received $27.823891 cash
Each share International Hedged Equity Fund $0.001 par received $26.316394 cash
Each share International Hedged SmallCap Dividend Fund $0.001 par received $25.800097 cash
Each share Japan Quality Dividend Growth Fund $0.001 par received $25.739812 cash
Each share Korea Hedged Equity Fund $0.001 par received $23.311628 cash
Trust terminated 08/17/2017
Each share Global Real Return Fund $0.001 par received $40.35 cash
Each share Strategic Corporate Bond Fund $0.001 par received $76.049353 cash
Each share Western Asset Unconstrained Bond Fund $0.001 par received $51.275295 cash
Trust terminated 03/23/2018
Each share Global ex-U.S. Hedged Dividend Fund $0.001 par received $25.996477 cash
Each share Global ex-U.S. Hedged Real Estate Fund $0.001 par received $27.602883 cash
Each share Japan Hedged Capital Goods Fund $0.001 par received $26.775929 cash
Each share Japan Hedged Health Care Fund $0.001 par received $37.710922 cash
Each share Japan Hedged Real Estate Fund $0.001 par received $14.308472 cash
Each share Strong Dollar Emerging Markets Equity Fund $0.001 par received $28.393839 cash
Each share United Kingdom Hedged Equity Fund $0.001 par received $23.119627 cash
Each share U.S. Domestic Economy Fund $0.001 par received $30.895603 cash
Each share U.S. Export & Multinational Fund $0.001 par received $32.166118 cash
(Additional Information in Active)

WISDOMTREE U S QUALITY DIVID GROWTH DYNAMIC HEDGED INDEX ETF (ON)
Name changed to WisdomTree U.S. Quality Dividend Growth Variably Hedged Index ETF 01/13/2017

WISE BOY RES INC (BC)
Recapitalized as Hatthaway-Matheson Enterprises Inc. 4/20/92
Each share Common no par exchanged for (1/7) share Common no par
Hatthaway-Matheson Enterprises Inc. name changed to Innovis Corp. (BC) 10/8/93 which reincorporated in Wyoming 10/15/93
(See Innovis Corp. (WY))

WISE CARD CONS INC (AB)
Recapitalized 12/31/90
Recapitalized from Wise Card Holdings Inc. to Wise Card Consolidated Inc. 12/30/90
Each share Common no par exchanged for (0.5) share Common no par
Struck off register and declared dissolved for failure to file returns 6/1/93

WISE HOMES INC (DE)
Voluntarily dissolved 07/17/1967
No stockholders' equity

WISE INDS INC (PA)
Each share Common 50¢ par exchanged for (0.5) share Common $1 par 05/06/1964
Assets sold for benefit of creditors 00/00/1968
No stockholders' equity

WISE LAND CO. (MI)
Charter dissolved 1/15/55

WISE OAKWOOD VENTURES INC (AB)
Recapitalized as Zomedica Pharmaceuticals Corp. 05/02/2016
Each share Common no par exchanged for (0.4) share Common no par

WISE VENTURES INC (DE)
Name changed to Bio-Imaging Technologies, Inc. 10/07/1991
Bio-Imaging Technologies, Inc. name changed to BioClinica, Inc. 07/13/2009
(See BioClinica, Inc.)

WISE WOOD CORP (AB)
Name changed 07/09/2003
Name changed from Wise Wood Energy Ltd. to Wise Wood Corp. 07/09/2003
Recapitalized as Diamond Tree Energy Ltd. 12/31/2004
Each share Common no par exchanged for (0.1) share Common no par

(See Diamond Tree Energy Ltd.)

WISEBUYS INC (FL)
Name changed to Empire Pizza Holdings, Inc. 04/20/2011
Empire Pizza Holdings, Inc. recapitalized as Vestiage, Inc. 03/22/2013

WISEMOBI INC (NV)
Common $0.001 par split (5) for (2) by issuance of (1.5) additional shares payable 06/03/2008 to holders of record 05/21/2008
Ex date - 06/04/2008
Recapitalized as New Infinity Holdings, Ltd. 02/23/2015
Each share Common $0.001 par exchanged for (0.001) share Common $0.001 par

WISER OIL CO (DE)
Common $10 par split (2) for (1) by issuance of (1) additional share 03/10/1977
Common $10 par split (2) for (1) by issuance of (1) additional share 06/03/1980
Common $10 par changed to $3 par and (2) additional shares issued 01/18/1982
Merged into Forest Oil Corp. 07/01/2004
Each share Common $3 par exchanged for $10.60 cash

WISER OIL CO (OK)
Merged into Wiser Oil Co. (DE) 12/31/1970
Each share Capital Stock $25 par exchanged for (2.2) shares Common $10 par
(See Wiser Oil Co. (DE))

WISHART ENTERPRISES LTD (NV)
Name changed to Vendum Batteries Inc. 06/04/2010
Vendum Batteries Inc. recapitalized as Link Reservations Inc. 05/05/2015

WISHBONE GOLD PLC (GIBRALTAR)
ADR agreement terminated 04/24/2015
Each Sponsored ADR for Ordinary exchanged for $0.2414 cash

WISHBONE PET PRODS INC (NV)
Name changed to Blue Eagle Lithium, Inc. 07/26/2018

WISIK GOLD MINES LTD. (ON)
Merged into Kiena Gold Mines Ltd. 11/16/1959
Each share Capital Stock no par exchanged for (0.2) share Common no par
Kiena Gold Mines, Ltd. merged into Placer Dome Inc. 06/17/1988 which merged into Barrick Gold Corp. 03/08/2006

WISMER MARTIN INC (WA)
Merged into Physician Computer Network, Inc. 09/10/1996
Each share Common $0.001 par exchanged for (0.05692) share Common 1¢ par and $0.12054 cash
(See Physician Computer Network, Inc.)

WISPER INC (ON)
Recapitalized as Eclips Inc. 03/29/2004
Each share Common no par exchanged for (0.1) share Common no par
Eclips Inc. recapitalized as Cadillac Mining Corp. (ON) 07/10/2006 which reincorporated in British Columbia 05/22/2007 which merged into Pilot Gold Inc. 08/29/2014 which name changed to Liberty Gold Corp. 05/12/2017

WISPY INTERNATIONAL, INC. (FL)
Administratively dissolved for failure to file annual reports 8/13/93

WISSAHICKON CO., INC.
Liquidated in 1946

WIT CAP GROUP INC (DE)
Issue Information - 7,600,000 shares COM offered at $9 per share on 06/04/1999
Name changed to Wit SoundView Group, Inc. 06/12/2000
Wit SoundView Group, Inc. name changed to SoundView Technology Group, Inc. 08/20/2001
(See SoundView Technology Group, Inc.)

WIT SOUNDVIEW GROUP INC (DE)
Name changed to SoundView Technology Group Inc. 08/20/2001
(See SoundView Technology Group Inc.)

WITCO CHEMICAL CO., INC. (DE)
Common $5 par split (3) for (2) by issuance of (0.5) additional share 4/17/64
Stock Dividend - 50% 6/15/60
Name changed to Witco Chemical Corp. 4/25/68
Witco Chemical Corp. name changed to Witco Corp. 10/1/85 which merged into CK Witco Corp. 9/1/99 which name changed to Crompton Corp. 4/27/2000 which name changed to Chemtura Corp. 7/1/2005

WITCO CORP (DE)
Name changed 10/01/1985
Common $5 par split (3) for (2) by issuance of (0.5) additional share 05/22/1968
Common $5 par split (3) for (2) by issuance of (0.5) additional share 07/13/1978
Common $5 par split (3) for (2) by issuance of (0.5) additional share 07/07/1983
Name changed from Witco Chemical Corp. to Witco Corp. 10/1/1985
Common $5 par split (3) for (2) by issuance of (0.5) additional share 07/15/1986
Common $5 par split (2) for (1) by issuance of (1) additional share 10/05/1993
$2.65 Preferred $1 par called for redemption at $66 on 09/01/1999
Merged into CK Witco Corp. 09/01/1999
Each share Common $5 par exchanged for (0.9242) share Common 1¢ par
CK Witco Corp. name changed to Crompton Corp. 04/27/2000 which name changed to Chemtura Corp. 07/01/2005
(See Chemtura Corp.)

WITH DESIGN IN MIND INTL INC (CO)
Each (352) shares old Common no par exchanged for (1) share new Common no par 6/11/90
Name changed to Janex International, Inc. 8/16/94
(See Janex International, Inc.)

WITHERBEE CO., INC.
Dissolved in 1940

WITHERBEE SHERMAN & CO.
Reorganized as Witherbee-Sherman Corp. 00/00/1933
Details not available

WITHEROW STEEL CORP.
Merged into Donner Steel Co., Inc. 00/00/1929
Details not available

WITNESS SYS INC (DE)
Merged into Verint Systems Inc. 5/29/2007
Each share Common 1¢ par exchanged for $27.50 cash

WITNET INTL INC (NV)
Recapitalized as KSign International, Inc. 02/25/2014
Each share Common $0.001 par exchanged for (0.1) share Common $0.001 par

KSign International, Inc. name changed to Columbus Geographic Systems (GIS) Ltd. 09/06/2007
(See Columbus Geographic Systems (GIS) Ltd.)

WITT TAX CTRS INC (NY)
Common 1¢ par split (2) for (1) by issuance of (1) additional share 5/9/69
Charter cancelled and proclaimed dissolved for failure to pay taxes 12/15/75

WITTCOMM INC (DE)
Charter cancelled and declared inoperative and void for non-payment of taxes 03/01/2000

WITTER DEAN & CO INC (DE)
Under plan of reorganization each share Common $1 par automatically became (1) share Witter (Dean) Organization Inc. Common $1 par 2/28/74
Witter (Dean) Organization Inc. name changed to Witter (Dean) Reynolds Organization Inc. 1/3/78 which merged into Sears, Roebuck & Co. 12/31/81 which merged into Sears Holdings Corp. 3/24/2005

WITTER DEAN ORGANIZATION INC (DE)
Under plan of merger name changed to Witter (Dean) Reynolds Organization Inc. 1/3/78
Witter (Dean) Reynolds Organization Inc. merged into Sears, Roebuck & Co. 12/31/81 which merged into Sears Holdings Corp. 3/24/2005

WITTER DEAN REYNOLDS ORGANIZATION INC (DE)
Common $1 par split (5) for (4) by issuance of (0.25) additional share 12/2/80
$2.50 Ser. A Conv. Preferred $1 par called for redemption 7/31/81
Merged into Sears, Roebuck & Co. 12/31/81
Each share Common $1 par exchanged for (3.11) shares Common 75¢ par
Sears, Roebuck & Co. merged into Sears Holdings Corp. 3/24/2005

WITTKE INC (AB)
Merged into Federal Signal Corp. 10/3/2002
Each share Common no par exchanged for (0.2005) share Common $1 par and $6.25 cash

WITWATERSRAND CONS GOLD RES LTD (SOUTH AFRICA)
Acquired by Sibanye Gold Ltd. 04/14/2014
Each share Ordinary no par exchanged for CAD$1.204665 cash
ADR agreement terminated 04/14/2014
Each Sponsored ADR for Ordinary exchanged for USD$1.04346 cash
Note: Unexchanged certificates were cancelled and became without value 04/14/2017

WITWATERSRAND NIGEL LTD (SOUTH AFRICA)
Name changed to New Mining Corp. Ltd. 02/01/1999
New Mining Corp. Ltd. name changed to Matodzi Resources Ltd. 12/06/2002 which name changed to White Water Resources Ltd. 03/02/2009 which name changed to Goliath Gold Mining Ltd. 05/26/2011
(See Goliath Gold Mining Ltd.)

WIX ACCESSORIES CORP. (NC)
Name changed to Wix Corp. 00/00/1955
Wix Corp. merged into Dana Corp. 07/02/1979
(See Dana Corp.)

WIX CORP. LTD. (ON)
Name changed to Wix Inc. 12/1/81
(See Wix Inc.)

WIX CORP (NC)
5-1/2% Conv. Preferred Ser. B $25 par called for redemption 01/01/1967
Common $1 par split (3) for (1) by issuance of (2) additional shares 05/25/1968
6% Preferred $100 par called for redemption 10/01/1971
Common $1 par split (3) for (1) by issuance of (2) additional shares 10/15/1971
Merged into Dana Corp. 07/02/1979
Each share Common $1 par exchanged for (1.44) shares Common $1 par
(See Dana Corp.)

WIX INC (ON)
Merged into Hayes-Dana Inc. 11/22/1984
Each share Common no par exchanged for $10.50 cash

WIZ TECHNOLOGY INC (NV)
Recapitalized as Wireless Technologies Inc. 07/21/2005
Each share Common $0.001 par exchanged for (0.001) share Common $0.001 par
Wireless Technologies Inc. name changed to Mattman Specialty Vehicles, Inc. 12/14/2005 which name changed to Remote Surveillance Technologies, Inc. 01/11/2007 which name changed to Stratera, Inc. 07/15/2008 which recapitalized as Gulf West Investment Properties, Inc. 12/16/2009

WIZAN PRODTNS INC (DE)
Charter cancelled and declared inoperative and void for non-payment of taxes 03/01/1991

WIZARD BOATS, INC. (CA)
Adjudicated a bankrupt in December 1961
Capital Stock is valueless

WIZARD BOATS OF TENNESSEE, INC. (TN)
Name changed to Winner Boats, Inc. 9/1/60
Winner Boats, Inc. name changed to Winner Corp. 10/1/71
(See Winner Corp.)

WIZARD INC. (UT)
Name changed to Micronetics, Inc. 04/00/1985
Micronetics, Inc. recapitalized as Praxis Pharmaceuticals, Inc. (UT) 07/08/1998 which reincorporated in Nevada as Patch International Inc. 06/15/2004 which reincorporated in Alberta 08/29/2008
(See Patch International Inc.)

WIZBANG TECHNOLOGIES INC (WA)
Common $0.0001 par changed to $0.00005 par and (1) additional share issued payable 08/12/2003 to holders of record 08/11/2003
Ex date - 08/13/2003
Name changed to Golden Hand Resources, Inc. 08/27/2003
Golden Hand Resources, Inc. name changed to BrainStorm Cell Therapeutics Inc. (WA) 11/18/2004 which reincorporated in Delaware 12/21/2006

WIZEWOOD LTD. (SK)
All Preferred $10 par and Common $1 par were redeemed by company prior to acquisition by the Province of Saskatchewan (which had held majority interest) 00/00/1965

WIZTEC SOLUTIONS LTD (ISRAEL)
Acquired by Convergys Corp. 11/22/1999
Each share Ordinary ILS 1 par exchanged for $25 cash

WIZZARD SOFTWARE CORP (CO)
Each (12) shares old Common $0.001

par exchanged for (1) share new Common $0.001 par 02/23/2012
Each share new Common $0.001 par received distribution of (1) share Future Healthcare of America Common $0.001 par payable 10/01/2012 to holders of record 09/05/2012
Stock Dividend - 10% payable 10/30/2006 to holders of record 10/15/2006 Ex date - 10/11/2006
Name changed to FAB Universal Corp. 10/09/2012

WJ COMMUNICATIONS INC (DE)
Merged into TriQuint Semiconductor, Inc. 05/22/2008
Each share Common 1¢ par exchanged for $1 cash

WJDX INC (DE)
Liquidation completed
Each share Common 1¢ par received initial distribution of $6.50 cash 01/25/1982
Each share Common 1¢ par exchanged for second and final distribution of $0.7319 cash 09/24/1982

WJR GOODWILL STATION (MI)
Each share Common $10 par exchanged for (2) shares Common $5 par 00/00/1935
Each share Common $5 par exchanged for (2) shares Common $2.50 par 00/00/1945
Each share Common $2.50 par exchanged for (2) shares Common $1.25 par 00/00/1946
Name changed to Goodwill Stations, Inc. 05/03/1961
(See Goodwill Stations, Inc.)

WKAY RES INC (BC)
Name changed to Magnatron International Corp. 10/18/90
Magnatron International Corp. recapitalized as QI Technologies Corp. 3/17/94 which name changed to QI Systems Inc. (BC) 5/25/2001 which reincorporated in Delaware 7/1/2006

WKC LIQUIDATING CORP. (NC)
Liquidation completed
Each share Common $3.33-1/3 par exchanged for initial distribution of $12.75 cash 2/25/77
Each share Common $3.33-1/3 par received second distribution of $1.25 cash 3/20/78
Each share Common $3.33-1/3 par received third distribution of $0.35 cash 5/26/78
Each share Common $3.33-1/3 par received fourth and final distribution of $0.21 cash 1/29/79

WL ROSS HLDG CORP (DE)
Name changed to Nexeo Solutions, Inc. 06/10/2016

WLD INC (ON)
Name changed to Astris Energi Inc. 07/12/1995
Astris Energi Inc. name changed to Carthew Bay Technologies Inc. 08/22/2007

WLG INC (DE)
Acquired by WLG Merger Sub, Inc. 10/27/2011
Each share Common $0.001 par exchanged for $0.34 cash

WLR FOODS INC (VA)
Common no par split (3) for (2) by issuance of (0.5) additional share 05/09/1990
Common no par split (3) for (2) by issuance of (0.5) additional share 05/12/1995
Stock Dividends - 0.00525% payable 05/02/1997 to holders of record 04/11/1997; 0.0064% payable 08/01/1997 to holders of record 07/11/1997

Merged into Pilgrim's Pride Corp. (Old) 01/29/2001
Each share Common no par exchanged for $14.25 cash

WM BANCORP (MD)
Stock Dividend - 10% 1/29/88
Acquired by Keystone Financial, Inc. 1/7/94
Each share Common $2.50 par exchanged for (1.67) shares Common $2 par
Keystone Financial, Inc. merged into M&T Bank Corp. 10/6/2000

WMA CORP (DE)
Name changed to Global Preferred Holdings, Inc. 08/15/2001
(See Global Preferred Holdings, Inc.)

WMA INTL CORP (DE)
Name changed to WMA Corp. 07/07/1995
WMA Corp. name changed to Global Preferred Holdings, Inc. 08/15/2001
(See Global Preferred Holdings, Inc.)

WMAC HLDGS CORP (NY)
Each share new Common $0.001 par received distribution of (1) share El Coco Wines & Spirits Inc. Restricted Common and (1) share Vu Qo International Beverages, Inc. Restricted Common payable 07/16/2013 to holders of record 07/15/2013
Reincorporated under the laws of Nevada as Lighthouse Global Holdings Inc. 05/03/2018

WMC LTD (AUSTRALIA)
Name changed to Alumina Ltd. 12/02/2002

WMC RES LTD (AUSTRALIA)
Merged into BHP Billiton Ltd. 08/02/2005
Each Sponsored ADR for Ordinary exchanged for $23.89 cash

WMD MICRO DISTRS INC (CA)
Recapitalized as PCC Group Inc. 10/03/1989
Each share Common no par exchanged for (0.00133333) share Common 1¢ par
PCC Group Inc. recapitalized as Non-Lethal Weapons, Inc. (CA) 10/17/2005 which reorganized in Nevada as Advanced Growing Systems, Inc. 06/22/2006
(See Advanced Growing Systems, Inc.)

WMF GROUP LTD (DE)
Merged into Prudential Mortgage Capital LLC 6/26/2000
Each share Common 1¢ par exchanged for $8.90 cash

WMI EQUITY INVS (MA)
Merged into Eaton Vance Corp. 10/17/1983
Each Share of Bene. Int. $1 par exchanged for $7 principal amount of 9% 10-yr. Conv. Debentures due 10/17/1993

WMIH CORP (DE)
Name changed 05/14/2015
Name and state of incorporation changed from WMI Holdings Corp. (WA) to WMIH Corp. (DE) 05/14/2015
Recapitalized as Mr. Cooper Group Inc. 10/11/2018
Each share Common $0.00001 par exchanged for (0.08333333) share Common 1¢ par

WMP BK AG AUSTRIA (AUSTRIA)
ADR agreement terminated 7/13/2004
Each Sponsored ADR for Ordinary exchanged for (1) Ordinary Share

WMS INDS INC (DE)
Common 50¢ par split (2) for (1) by issuance of (1) additional share 02/28/1992
Each share Common 50¢ par received distribution of (0.25) share

WHG Resorts & Casinos Inc. Common 50¢ par payable 04/21/1997 to holders of record 03/31/1997 Ex date - 04/22/1997
Each share Common 50¢ par received distribution of (1.19773) shares Midway Games Inc. Common 50¢ par payable 04/06/1998 to holders of record 03/31/1998 Ex date - 04/07/1998
Common 50¢ par split (3) for (2) by issuance of (0.5) additional share payable 06/14/2007 to holders of record 05/29/2007 Ex date - 06/15/2007
Acquired by Scientific Games Corp. 10/18/2013
Each share Common 50¢ par exchanged for for $26 cash

WMX GROUP HLDGS INC (FL)
Each share old Common $0.0001 par exchanged for (0.00025) share new Common $0.0001 par 04/24/2013
Name changed to Oxford City Football Club, Inc. 08/05/2013
(See Oxford City Football Club, Inc.)

WMX TECHNOLOGIES INC (DE)
Name changed to Waste Management, Inc. (New) 5/12/97
Waste Management, Inc. (New) merged into Waste Management, Inc. 7/16/98

WNS EMERGENT INC (AB)
Name changed 05/01/2002
Name changed from WNS Inc. to WNS Emergent Inc. 05/01/2002
Name changed to CriticalControl Solutions Corp. 06/14/2004
CriticalControl Solutions Corp. name changed to Critical Control Energy Services Corp. 07/03/2015

WNS INC (TX)
Plan of reorganization under Chapter 11 Federal Bankruptcy proceedings confirmed 11/05/1992
Company was acquired by a private investment company
Details not available

WNS STUDIOS INC (NV)
Name changed to Watermark Group, Inc. 08/31/2015

WO KEE HONG HLDGS LTD (BERMUDA)
Sponsored ADR's for Ordinary split (5) for (1) by issuance of (4) additional ADR's payable 02/23/2010 to holders of record 02/22/2010 Ex date - 02/24/2010
Stock Dividend - 20% payable 05/09/2008 to holders of record 04/23/2008 Ex date - 04/21/2008
Name changed to Auto Italia Holdings Ltd. 10/16/2012
(See Auto Italia Holdings Ltd.)

WOBURN FIVE CENTS SVGS BK (WOBURN, MA)
Reorganized under the laws of Delaware as First Woburn Bancorp, Inc. 3/7/88
(See First Woburn Bancorp, Inc.)

WOBURN NATL BK (WOBURN, MA)
Capital Stock $25 par changed to $6.25 par and (4) additional shares issued to provide for a (4) for (1) stock split and a 25% stock dividend 2/14/74
Merged into Citizens National Bank (Riverside, RI) 8/13/98
Each share Common $6.25 par exchanged for $300 cash

WOCO GOLD DEVELOPMENT, LTD. (ON)
Charter surrendered 00/00/1955

WOIZE INTL LTD (NV)
Name changed to Smart Comm International Ltd. 10/17/2008
(See Smart Comm International Ltd.)

WOKINGHAM CAP CORP (CANADA)
Name changed to Coniston Capital Corp. 07/18/1994
Coniston Capital Corp. name changed to CPL Ventures Ltd. 08/08/1996 which recapitalized as Manfrey Capital Corp. 11/11/1996
(See Manfrey Capital Corp.)

WOLEKO INDS INC (NV)
Charter permanently revoked for failure to file reports and pay fees 06/30/1999

WOLF & DESSAUER CO. (IN)
Name changed to D.N.W. Inc. 8/11/66
D.N.W., Inc. liquidated 9/30/71

WOLF CAP CORP (AB)
Name changed to Mirage Energy Ltd. 08/31/2006
Mirage Energy Ltd. merged into Sahara Energy Ltd. 03/31/2008

WOLF CORP (DE)
Charter cancelled and declared inoperative and void for non-payment of taxes 3/1/83

WOLF FINL GROUP INC (NY)
Plan of reorganization under Chapter 11 Federal Bankruptcy Code effective 01/16/1997
No stockholders' equity

WOLF HOWARD B INC (TX)
Common $1 par changed to 50¢ par and (1) additional share issued 11/27/1969
Common 50¢ par changed to 33-1/3¢ par and (0.5) additional share issued 05/25/1971
In process of liquidation
Each share Common 33-1/3¢ par received initial distribution of $4 cash payable 11/23/1999 to holders of record 10/08/1999 Ex date - 10/12/1999
Note: Details on subsequent distributions, if any, are not available

WOLF INDUSTRIES INC (NV)
Each share old Common $0.001 par exchanged for (1/3) share new Common $0.001 par 7/27/98
Name changed to Travelport Systems, Inc. 12/1/2000
Travelport Systems, Inc. name changed to American Petro-Hunter Inc. 9/7/2001

WOLF RESOURCE DEV CORP (ON)
Name changed to Fura Emeralds Inc. 03/09/2015
Fura Emeralds Inc. name changed to Fura Gems Inc. 04/11/2017

WOLF RES INC (NV)
Common $0.001 par split (8.612) for (1) by issuance of (7.612) additional shares payable 02/18/2010 to holders of record 02/18/2010
Name changed to AISystems, Inc. 05/13/2010
(See AISystems, Inc.)

WOLF RIV RES LTD (BC)
Name changed to Interchem (N.A.) Industries Inc. 6/8/89

WOLF'S HEAD OIL REFINING CO. (DE)
Acquired by South Penn Oil Co. for cash in 1963

WOLFDEN RES INC (ON)
Plan of arrangement effective 08/18/2006
Each share old Common no par exchanged for (1) share new Common no par and (0.7) share Premier Gold Mines Ltd. Common no par
(See Premier Gold Mines Ltd.)
Note: Unexchanged certificates were cancelled and became without value 08/17/2012
Merged into Zinifex Ltd. 06/18/2007
Each share new Common no par exchanged for $3.81 cash

WOLFE CREEK MNG INC (DE)
Common $0.001 par split (15) for (1) by issuance of (14) additional shares payable 03/11/2010 to holders of record 03/11/2010 Ex date - 03/12/2010
Name changed to Green EnviroTech Holdings Corp. 08/03/2010

WOLFE OIL CORP.
Acquired by Barnsdall Corp. in 1928 which name changed to Barnsdall Oil Co. in 1936
(See Barnsdall Oil Co.)

WOLFEYE RESOURCE CORP (BC)
Each share old Common no par exchanged for (0.1) share new Common no par 02/28/2014
Name changed to Lexagene Holdings Inc. 10/19/2016

WOLFF & MARX, INC. (TX)
Merged into Joske Bros. Co. 2/15/65
Each share Common $5 par exchanged for $11 in cash

WOLFPACK CAP CORP (AB)
Name changed to Pulse Oil Corp. 12/01/2016

WOLFPACK CORP (DE)
Each share old Common $0.001 par exchanged for (0.5) share new Common $0.001 par 09/19/2001
Name changed to equitel, inc. 05/01/2002
(See equitel, inc.)

WOLFPACK GOLD CORP (BC)
Plan of arrangement effective 08/20/2014
Each share Common no par exchanged for (1) share enCore Energy Corp. Common no par and (0.75) share Timberline Resources Corp. Common $0.001 par
Note: Unexchanged certificates will be cancelled and become without value 08/20/2020

WOLFPACK YELLOWKNIFE MINES, LTD. (ON)
Charter revoked for failure to file reports and pay fees 12/23/65

WOLFSTONE CORP (NV)
Each share old Common $0.001 par exchanged for (0.05) share new Common $0.001 par 02/24/1999
Each share new Common $0.001 par exchanged again for (1/6) share new Common $0.001 par 02/21/2002
Recapitalized as FreeGolfStats.com 09/12/2002
Each share new Common $0.001 par exchanged for (0.04) share Common $0.001 par
FreeGolfStats.com recapitalized as Mobile Nation, Inc. 08/19/2003 which name changed to AuraSource, Inc. 09/09/2008

WOLINS PHARMACAL CORP (NY)
Merged into Generics Corp. of America 7/26/71
Each share Common 20¢ par exchanged for (1) share Common 10¢ par
(See Generics Corp. of America)

WOLLARD AIRCRAFT SERVICE EQUIPMENT, INC. (FL)
Merged into Heath Tecna Corp. 04/30/1968
Each share Common 10¢ par exchanged for (0.36363636) share Common no par
Heath Tecna Corp. name changed to Criton Corp. 07/01/1980
(See Criton Corp.)

WOLLASCO MINERALS INC (ON)
Recapitalized as Gold Port Resources Ltd. (ON) 12/16/2004
Each share Common no par exchanged for (0.125) share Common no par
Gold Port Resources Ltd. (ON) reincorporated in British Columbia 01/15/2007 which recapitalized as Codrington Resource Corp. 10/28/2013 which name changed to NRG Metals Inc. 11/23/2015

WOLLASTON LAKE MINES LTD. (BC)
Recapitalized as Comaplex Resources International Ltd. (BC) 09/08/1971
Each share Common 50¢ par exchanged for (0.25) share Common no par
Comaplex Resources International Ltd. (BC) reincorporated in Alberta 00/00/1987
(See Comaplex Resources International Ltd.)

WOLLASTON PORCUPINE GOLD MINES, LTD. (ON)
Charter cancelled for failure to file reports and pay taxes 1/2/56

WOLLEMI MNG CORP (DE)
Common $0.0001 par split (3) for (2) by issuance of (0.5) additional share payable 10/29/2009 to holders of record 10/28/2009 Ex date - 10/30/2009
Name changed to Pacific Bepure Industry Inc. 12/17/2009

WOLLENBERGER & CO. (DE)
No longer in existence having become inoperative and void for non-payment of taxes 4/1/34

WOLOHAN LMBR CO (MI)
Common $1 par split (3) for (2) by issuance of (0.5) additional share 2/21/78
Common $1 par split (3) for (2) by issuance of (0.5) additional share 9/1/78
Stock Dividends - 25% 8/1/77; 10% 12/11/89; 10% 12/11/91
Merged into Wolohan Acquisition Co. 11/5/2003
Each share Common $1 par exchanged for $25.76 cash

WOLSELEY PLC (ENGLAND & WALES)
Sponsored ADR's for Ordinary split (5) for (2) by issuance of (1.5) additional ADR's payable 02/02/2004 to holders of record 01/30/2004 Ex date - 02/03/2004
Sponsored ADR's for Ordinary split (2) for (1) by issuance of (1) additional ADR payable 07/06/2006 to holders of record 06/30/3006 Ex date - 07/07/2006
Basis changed from (1:2) to (1:1) 07/07/2006
Basis changed from (1:1) to (1:0.1) 04/02/2009
Reorganized under the laws of Jersey 11/23/2010
Each Sponsored ADR for Ordinary exchanged for (1) Sponsored ADR for Ordinary
Note: Unexchanged ADR's will be sold and the proceeds held for claim after 01/24/2012
Wolseley PLC (Jersey) name changed to Ferguson PLC 07/31/2017

WOLSELEY PLC (JERSEY)
Each old Sponsored ADR for Ordinary exchanged for (0.95652173) new Sponsored ADR for Ordinary 12/10/2012
Each new Sponsored ADR for Ordinary exchanged again for (0.96774193) new Sponsored ADR for Ordinary 12/02/2013
Name changed to Ferguson PLC 07/31/2017

WOLTA INDS INC (NY)
Charter cancelled and proclaimed dissolved for failure to pay taxes and file reports 12/16/1974

WOLVERINE ALUM CORP (MI)
Under plan of merger name changed to Wolverine-Pentronix, Inc. 4/30/69 which name changed back to Wolverine Aluminum Corp. 5/10/76
Common $1 par split (2) for (1) by issuance of (1) additional share 6/14/84
Stock Dividend - 25% 2/28/69
Name changed to Wolverine Technologies Inc. 10/1/84
(See Wolverine Technologies Inc.)

WOLVERINE BANCORP INC (MD)
Merged into Horizon Bancorp 10/17/2017
Each share Common 1¢ par exchanged for (1.0152) shares Common no par and $14 cash
Horizon Bancorp name changed to Horizon Bancorp, Inc. 05/08/2018

WOLVERINE BRASS WORKS (MI)
Each share Common $100 par exchanged for (10) shares Common $10 par in 1938
Common $10 par split (2) for (1) by issuance of (1) additional share 10/10/67
Stock Dividends - 10% 2/1/60; 10% 2/1/62; 10% 3/1/67
Completely liquidated 2/1/68
Each share Common $10 par exchanged for first and final distribution of (1) share Wolverine Industries, Inc. Common $1 par
Wolverine Industries, Inc. name changed to Citation Companies, Inc. (DE) 5/1/74 which reincorporated in Michigan 5/31/77
(See Citation Companies, Inc. (MI))

WOLVERINE BREWING CO.
In process of dissolution in 1943

WOLVERINE DEVS INC (ON)
Merged into Lumsden Building Corp. Inc. (New) 08/15/1978
Each share Common no par exchanged for (0.45454545) share Common no par
(See Lumsden Building Corp. Inc. (New))

WOLVERINE-EMPIRE REFINING CO.
Name changed to Wolf's Head Oil Refining Co. in 1940
(See Wolf's Head Oil Refining Co.)

WOLVERINE ENERGY CORP (AB)
Merged into Atlas Energy Ltd. 11/29/2000
Each share Common no par exchanged for (0.125) share Common no par
Atlas Energy Ltd. merged into Pearl Exploration & Production Ltd. 12/26/2006 which name changed to BlackPearl Resources Inc. 05/14/2009

WOLVERINE EXPL CO (DE)
Name changed to Amerac Energy Corp. 03/17/1995
Amerac Energy Corp. merged into Southern Mineral Corp. 01/28/1998
(See Southern Mineral Corp.)

WOLVERINE EXPL INC (NV)
Name changed to Wolverine Technologies Corp. 08/12/2015

WOLVERINE FABRICATING & MFG INC (MI)
Merged into Eagle-Picher Industries, Inc. 04/01/1967
Details not available

WOLVERINE HLDGS INC (DE)
Name changed to New World Power Corp. 10/16/1991
New World Power Corp. recapitalized as Distributed Power Inc. 10/24/2003 which name changed to Global Pay Solutions, Inc. 04/23/2007 which recapitalized as China National Appliance of North America Corp. 03/26/2009

WOLVERINE INDS INC (DE)
Common $1 par split (2) for (1) by issuance of (1) additional share 4/17/68
Name changed to Citation Companies, Inc. (DE) 5/1/74
Citation Companies, Inc. (DE) reincorporated in Michigan 5/31/77
(See Citation Companies, Inc. (MI))

WOLVERINE INSURANCE CO. (MI)
Stock Dividends - 150% 12/20/1950; 100% 02/16/1953; 50% 04/12/1960
Through purchase offer Transamerica Insurance Co. has acquired all but (168) shares as of 01/17/1970
Public interest eliminated

WOLVERINE MINERALS CORP (BC)
Each share old Common no par exchanged for (0.25) share new Common no par 01/21/2013
Each share new Common no par exchanged again for (0.2) share new Common no par 05/24/2016
Name changed to Aloro Mining Corp. 02/21/2018

WOLVERINE MINES LTD.
Out of business in 1947
No stockholders' equity

WOLVERINE MOULDINGS, INC. (MI)
Each share Common no par exchanged for (0.2) share Common $1 par 7/8/58
Name changed to Wolverine Aluminum Corp. 8/18/61
Wolverine Aluminum Corp. name changed to Wolverine-Pentronix, Inc. 4/30/69 which name changed back to Wolverine Aluminum Corp. 5/10/76 which name changed to Wolverine Technologies Inc. 10/1/84
(See Wolverine Technologies Inc.)

WOLVERINE NATURAL GAS CORP.
Liquidated in 1946

WOLVERINE OFFICE BUILDING CORP.
Dissolved in 1947

WOLVERINE PENTRONIX INC (MI)
Name changed back to Wolverine Aluminum Corp. 5/10/76
Wolverine Aluminum Corp. name changed to Wolverine Technologies Inc. 10/1/84
(See Wolverine Technologies Inc.)

WOLVERINE PORTLAND CEMENT CO.
Liquidation completed in 1948

WOLVERINE POWER CO.
Reorganized as Wolverine Power Corp. 00/00/1934
Details not available

WOLVERINE PWR CORP (MI)
Voting Trust Agreement terminated 12/24/1976
Each VTC for Capital Stock $5 par exchanged for (1) share Capital Stock $5 par
Acquired by Wolverine Holdings Inc. 11/26/1986
Details not available

WOLVERINE SHOE & TANNING CORP. (MI)
Common $5 par changed to $2.50 par and (1) additional share issued 6/1/62
Common $2.50 par changed to $2 par and (0.25) additional share issued 6/19/64
Common $2 par changed to $1 par and (1) additional share issued 3/15/65
Stock Dividend - 10% 9/1/61
Name changed to Wolverine World Wide, Inc. (MI) 4/29/66
Wolverine World Wide, Inc. (MI) reincorporated in Delaware 5/14/69

WOLVERINE TECHNOLOGIES INC (MI)
Common $1 par split (3) for (2) by issuance of (0.5) additional share 6/27/86

Merged into SG Acquisition Corp. 6/6/88
Each share Common $1 par exchanged for $23 cash

WOLVERINE TUBE CO.
Liquidated 00/00/1942
Details not available

WOLVERINE TUBE INC (DE)
Plan of reorganization under Chapter 11 Federal Bankruptcy proceedings effective 06/28/2011
No stockholders' equity

WOLVERINE WORLD WIDE INC (MI)
Reincorporated under the laws of Delaware 5/14/69

WOLVERTON LAKE GOLD MINES LTD. (ON)
Name changed to Nearctic Resources Inc. and Common $1 par changed to no par 01/13/1981
(See Nearctic Resources Inc.)

WOM CORP (NY)
Voluntarily dissolved 12/18/2007
Stockholders' equity unlikely

WOMAN RIVER GOLD MINES, LTD. (ON)
Charter cancelled for failure to file reports and pay taxes in 1951

WOMANS LIFE INS CO AMER INC (MD)
Class B Common $1 par reclassified as Common $1 par 03/19/1963
Common $1 par changed to 80¢ par 04/01/1968
Name changed to Atlantic National Life Insurance Co. 03/03/1972
Atlantic National Life Insurance Co. name changed to American Centennial Life Insurance Co. 12/31/1978
(See American Centennial Life Insurance Co.)

WOMBAT PRODTNS INC (NY)
Name changed to CorTech Inc. 07/08/1983
Cortech Inc. name changed to Cortech Communications Inc. 02/24/1988 which name changed to CineMasters Group Inc. (NY) 03/17/1995 which reincorporated in Delaware as Avenue Entertainment Group, Inc. 04/14/1997 which name changed to alpha-En Corp. 07/22/2008

WOMEN COM NETWORKS INC (DE)
Issue Information - 3,750,000 shares COM offered at $10 per share on 10/14/1999
Merged into iVillage Inc. 6/18/2001
Each share Common $0.001 par exchanged for (0.322) share Common 1¢ par and $0.0046207 cash
(See iVillage Inc.)

WOMEN FIRST HEALTHCARE INC (DE)
Issue Information - 4,500,000 shares COM offered at $11 per share on 06/28/1999
Plan of reorganization under Chapter 11 Federal Bankruptcy Code effective 01/18/2005
No stockholders' equity

WOMEN IN MOTION INC (NV)
Reorganized as Accsys Global Network Inc. 12/27/96
Each share Common $0.001 par exchanged for (2) shares Common $0.001 par
Accsys Global Network Inc. name changed to Classic Golf Corp. 1/30/98 which recapitalized as Indexonly Technologies Inc. 9/14/99 which name changed to Nutrifeeds Technologies Inc. 5/5/2003 which name changed to Advanced Solutions & Technologies, Inc. 1/16/2004

(See Advanced Solutions & Technologies, Inc.)

WOMEN'S BANK (SAN DIEGO, CA)
Name changed to California Coastal Bank (San Diego, CA) 08/14/1978
California Coastal Bank (San Diego, CA) merged into Heritage Bank (Anaheim, CA) 06/30/1981 which reorganized as Heritage Bancorp 12/28/1981
(See Heritage Bancorp)

WOMEN'S NATIONAL BANK (WASHINGTON, DC)
Under plan of reorganization each share Capital Stock $10 par automatically became (1) share First WNB Corp. Common $10 par 04/01/1982
First WNB Corp. name changed to Abigail Adams National Bancorp, Inc. 06/19/1986 which merged into Premier Financial Bancorp, Inc. 10/01/2009

WOMENS GOLF UNLIMITED INC (NJ)
Company terminated registration of common stock and is no longer public as of 09/29/2003
Details not available

WOMENS HEALTH CTRS AMER INC (CA)
Name changed to Chemical Dependency Healthcare Inc. 02/08/1990
Chemical Dependency Healthcare Inc. recapitalized as La Jolla Diagnostics, Inc. 04/17/1995 which name changed to NatureWell, Inc. (CA) 01/04/2001 which reincorporated in Delaware 10/25/2001 which recapitalized as Brazil Interactive Media, Inc. 05/30/2013 which name changed to American Cannabis Co., Inc. 10/10/2014

WOMETCO CABLE TV INC (DE)
Acquired by a group of investors 04/12/1984
Each share Common $1 par exchanged for $29.50 cash

WOMETCO COMMONWEALTH CORP. (PR)
Preferred 10¢ par called for redemption 11/12/1968
Public interest eliminated

WOMETCO ENTERPRISES INC (FL)
Class A Common $1 par and Class B Common $1 par split (3) for (2) by issuance of (0.5) additional share respectively 01/16/1968
Class A Common $1 par and Class B Common $1 par split (3) for (2) by issuance of (0.5) additional share respectively 03/26/1969
Class A Common $1 par and Class B Common $1 par split (3) for (2) by issuance of (0.5) additional share respectively 06/30/1976
Class A Common $1 par and Class B Common $1 par split (5) for (4) by issuance of (0.25) additional share respectively 12/06/1982
Stock Dividends - 10% 01/15/1962; 30% 12/21/1962; 20% 12/23/1963; 25% 12/22/1964; 50% 12/09/1980
Acquired by a group of investors 04/12/1984
Each share Class A Common $1 par exchanged for $46.50 cash

WONDER AUTO TECHNOLOGY INC (NV)
In process of liquidation
Each share Common $0.0001 par received initial distribution of $1.05 cash payable 12/27/2013 to holders of record 12/27/2013
Note: Details on additional distribution(s), if any, are not available

WONDER CAP INC (UT)
Each share old Common $0.001 par exchanged for (0.05) share new Common $0.001 par 10/25/93
Name changed to Dry Dairy International Inc. 2/3/95
Dry Dairy International Inc. name changed to Dryden Industries, Inc. 10/1/99 which recapitalized as E Resources Inc. 3/31/2000 which name changed to Central Wireless Inc. 8/27/2002

WONDER INTL ED & INVT GROUP CORP (AZ)
Company terminated common stock registration and is no longer public as of 01/05/2016

WONDER MARINE RES LTD (BC)
Struck off register and declared dissolved for failure to file returns 12/22/95

WONDER MODULAR SYS INC (NV)
Charter revoked for failure to file reports and pay fees 3/2/81

WONDER RAINSTORM MINING CO. OF NEVADA (NV)
Charter revoked for failure to file reports and pay fees 3/3/24

WONDER WORLD INDS INC (NV)
Name changed to Chanin Development Corp. 3/31/71
Chanin Development Corp. name changed to Regency Development Corp. 2/5/74
(See Regency Development Corp.)

WONDERBOWL, INC. (CA)
Reorganization proceedings in United States Bankruptcy Court finalized in 1982
No details on equity

WONDERBOWL-DOWNEY, INC. (CA)
Charter suspended for failure to file reports and pay taxes 00/00/1967

WONDERSIGNS CORP. (DE)
No longer in existence having become inoperative and void for non-payment of taxes 4/1/32

WONDERWARE CORP (DE)
Merged into Siebe plc 4/14/98
Each share Common $0.001 par exchanged for $24 cash

WOOD, ALEXANDER & JAMES LTD.
Acquired by Wood Alexander Ltd. in 1951
(See Wood Alexander Ltd.)

WOOD, GUNDY & CO. LTD. (CANADA)
Name changed to Wood Gundy Holdings Ltd. 4/18/66

WOOD (ARTHUR W.) CO. (MA)
Involuntarily dissolved 12/31/1990

WOOD ALEXANDER LTD (ON)
Merged into Macleod Steadman Ltd. 08/17/1978
Each share 6% Preference $100 par exchanged for $25 cash
Each share Common no par exchanged for $2.50 cash

WOOD BANCORP INC (DE)
Common 1¢ par split (3) for (2) by issuance of (0.5) additional share payable 07/29/1996 to holders of record 07/15/1996
Common 1¢ par split (3) for (2) by issuance of (0.5) additional share payable 07/29/1997 to holders of record 07/15/1997
Common 1¢ par split (5) for (4) by issuance of (0.25) additional share payable 01/29/1998 to holders of record 01/15/1998
Merged into Sky Financial Group, Inc. 07/19/1999
Each share Common 1¢ par exchanged for (0.7315) share Common no par
Sky Financial Group, Inc. merged into Huntington Banchshares Inc. 07/02/2007

WOOD BROS HOMES INC (DE)
Merged into M.D.C. Holdings, Inc. 01/23/1986
Each share Common 1¢ par exchanged for $5.50 cash

WOOD BROS MFG CO (IL)
Acquired by Hesston Corp. 05/23/1969
Each share Class A Common $10 par and Common $10 par exchanged for (1.595) shares Common $2 par
(See Hesston Corp.)

WOOD CADILLAC MINES LTD.
Assets sold in 1943
No stockholders' equity

WOOD CHEMICAL PRODUCTS CO.
Name changed to Southern Pine Chemical Co. in 1934
(See Southern Pine Chemical Co.)

WOOD (JOHN) CO. (DE)
Acquired by Anthes Imperial Ltd. in March 1964
Each share Common no par exchanged for $14 (Canadian) cash

WOOD (T.H.) CO., INC. (CT)
Liquidation completed 12/21/61

WOOD COMPOSITE TECHNOLOGIES INC (AB)
Each share old Common no par exchanged for (0.06666666) share new Common no par 02/16/2005
Each share new Common no par received distribution of $0.0445 cash payable 10/16/2012 to holders of record 10/09/2012
Reorganized under the laws of British Columbia as Boardwalktech Software Corp. 06/06/2018
Each share new Common no par exchanged for (0.00243902) share Common no par

WOOD CONVERSION CO. (DE)
Common no par split (8) for (1) by issuance of (7) additional shares 11/29/50
Under plan of merger each share Common no par exchanged for (4.151) shares Capital Stock $5 par 11/30/55
Name changed to Conwed Corp. 8/1/67
(See Conwed Corp.)

WOOD CNTY BK (PARKERSBURG, WV)
Merged into National Banc of Commerce Co. 11/04/1991
Each share Common $5 par exchanged for $10.38 cash

WOOD CROESUS GOLD MINES LTD (ON)
Merged into Jubilee Gold Inc. 01/01/2010
Each share new Common $1 par exchanged for (0.367) share Common no par
Jubilee Gold Inc. merged into Jubilee Gold Exploration Ltd. 01/25/2013

WOOD FIBRE BOARD CORP.
Out of business in 1934

WOOD FLONG CORP.
Liquidation completed in 1950

WOOD G H & CO LTD (CANADA)
5-1/2% Preferred $100 par called for redemption 09/01/1965
Acquired by Ecolab Ltd. 01/01/1981
Details not available

WOOD HARMON CORP. (NY)
Completely liquidated 9/21/74
Each share Common $1 par exchanged for (0.000555) BIM Associates Ctf. of Bene. Int.

WOOD INDS INC (VA)
Merged into M.A.N. Finance Corp. 02/09/1979
Each share Common $1 par exchanged for $10.625 cash

WOOD (JOHN) INDUSTRIES LTD. (CANADA)
Class A Common no par and Class B Common no par reclassified as Common no par 12/3/62
Acquired by Wood (John) Co. on a (4) for (1) basis 12/3/62
4-1/2% 1st Preferred $100 par called for redemption 12/24/62
Wood (John) Co. acquired by Anthes Imperial Ltd. in March 1964
(See Anthes Imperial Ltd.)

WOOD J R & SONS INC (NY)
Merged into Lenox, Inc. 06/01/1970
Each share Common $2.50 par exchanged for (1/3) share Common $2.50 par
(See Lenox, Inc.)

WOOD MOSAIC CORP (KY)
Each share Class B Common $1 par exchanged for (1) share Class A Common $1 par 10/01/1966
Class A Common $1 par reclassified as Common $1 par 03/07/1967
Acquired by Olin Mathieson Chemical Corp. 08/11/1969
Each share 4% Preferred $100 par exchanged for (3.333333) shares Common $5 par
Each share Common $1 par exchanged for (0.9066) share Common $5 par
Olin Mathieson Chemical Corp. name changed to Olin Corp. 09/01/1969

WOOD NEWSPAPER MACHINERY CORP. (VA)
Each share $7 Prior Preference no par exchanged for (4) shares 5% Preferred $25 par and (6) shares Common $1 par in 1946
Each share $7 Preferred no par exchanged for (1) share 5% Preferred $25 par and (3) shares Common $1 par in 1946
Each share Common no par exchanged for (1/3) share Common $1 par in 1946
Common $1 par split (2) for (1) by issuance of (1) additional share 11/15/55
Common $1 par split (1.5) for (1) by issuance of (0.5) additional share 12/27/62
Name changed to Wood Industries, Inc. 11/2/67
(See Wood Industries, Inc.)

WOOD PRESERVING CORP.
Preferred liquidated for cash in 1940

WOOD PRODUCTS INC (NV)
Each share old Common $0.001 par exchanged for (10) shares new Common $0.001 par 4/21/2004
Recapitalized as Dixie Lee International Industries, Inc. 6/13/2007
Each share new Common $0.001 par exchanged for (0.001) share Common $0.001 par

WOOD (ALAN) STEEL CO. (PA)
See - Alan Wood Steel Co.

WOODALL INDS INC (DE)
Reincorporated 8/31/68
Common no par changed to $2 par in 1936
5% Preferred $25 par called for redemption 12/1/58
Stock Dividends - 33-1/3% 11/8/45; 25% 2/15/60
State of incorporation changed from (MI) to (DE) 8/31/68
Merged into Libbey-Owens-Ford Co. 2/2/70
Each share Common $2 par exchanged for (1/3) share $4.75 Conv. Preferred Ser. A no par
Libbey-Owens-Ford Co. name changed to Trinova Corp. 8/1/86
(See Trinova Corp.)

WOODARD RESH CORP (VA)
Stock Dividends - 20% 1/14/65; 10% 3/1/66
Voluntarily dissolved 2/3/82
Details not available

WOODBINE GOLD MINING CO. LTD.
Bankrupt in 1932

WOODBINE INDS INC (FL)
Name changed to Rose International, Inc. 03/31/1975
(See Rose International, Inc.)

WOODBINE PETE INC (CO)
Plan of reorganization under the laws of Delaware 12/4/85
Each share Common no par exchanged for (1/7) share Common 1¢ par

WOODBINE PETE INC (DE)
Merged into Sunlite Resources 9/23/92
Each share Common 1¢ par exchanged for $0.20 cash

WOODBRIDGE ENERGY LTD (BC)
Merged into Terrace Resources Inc. (New) 06/02/2009
Each share Common no par exchanged for (0.43152709) share Common no par
Terrace Resources Inc. (New) name changed to Terrace Energy Corp. 06/24/2011

WOODBRIDGE HLDGS CORP (FL)
Each share old Class A Common 1¢ par exchanged for (0.2) share new Class A Common 1¢ par 09/29/2008
Merged into BFC Financial Corp. 09/22/2009
Each share new Class A Common 1¢ par exchanged for (3.47) shares Class A Common 1¢ par
BFC Financial Corp. name changed to BBX Capital Corp. (New) 02/03/2017

WOODBURN OIL CORP.
Dissolved in 1935

WOODBURY COUNTY SAVINGS BANK (SIOUX CITY, IA)
Merged into First National Bank (Sioux City, IA) 00/00/1963
Details not available

WOODBURY INC (NV)
Name changed to N.U. Pizza Holding Corp. 04/19/1994
(See N.U. Pizza Holding Corp.)

WOODBURY MINES LTD. (BC)
Dissolved by Province of British Columbia for default of taxes 12/1/60

WOODBURY TEL CO (CT)
Capital Stock $25 par changed to $12.50 par and (1) additional share issued 9/1/75
Capital Stock $12.50 par split (5) for (1) by issuance of (4) additional shares 10/14/88
Merged into Southern New England Telecommunications Corp. 7/31/97
Each share Common $12.50 par exchanged for (1.0814) shares Common $1 par
Southern New England Telecommunications Corp. merged into SBC Communications Inc. 10/26/98 which name changed to AT&T Inc. 11/18/2005

WOODCLIFF CAP CORP (DE)
Name changed to International Gaming Management, Inc. 8/18/87
(See International Gaming Management, Inc.)

WOODCO RES INC (AB)
Issue Information - 1,500,000 shares COM offered at $0.15 per share on 11/05/1993
Reincorporated under the laws of Yukon as Anatolia Minerals Development Ltd. 02/20/1998
Anatolia Minerals Development Ltd. name changed to Alacer Gold Corp. 02/23/2011

WOODFORD CORP (TX)
Each share Common 1¢ par exchanged for (0.000025) share Common $400 par 03/07/1975
Note: In effect holders received $0.044 cash per share and public interest was eliminated

WOODFORD INVTS LTD (CANADA)
Name changed 4/12/77
Name changed from Woodford Investments Ltd. to Woodford Investments Ltd.- Investissements Woodford Ltee. and Class A $10 par changed to no par 4/12/77
Class A no par called for redemption 7/31/78
Acquired by Brameda Resources Ltd. in 1978
Each share Class B no par exchanged for $15 cash

WOODFORD ROYALTY CORP. LTD. (CANADA)
Name changed to Woodford Investments Ltd. 11/14/67
Woodford Investments Ltd. name changed to Woodford Investments Ltd.-Investissements Woodford Ltee. 4/12/77
(See Woodford Investments Ltd.-Investissements Woodford Ltee.)

WOODGREEN COPPER MINES LTD. (ON)
Recapitalized as Consolidated Woodgreen Mines Ltd. on a (0.125) for (1) basis in February 1959
Consolidated Woodgreen Mines Ltd. recapitalized as Cumberland Mining Co. Ltd. 4/20/64
(See Cumberland Mining Co.)

WOODHEAD INDS INC (DE)
Name changed 10/01/1970
Reincorporated 01/26/1978
Name changed 02/14/1985
Common $1 par split (3) for (2) by issuance of (0.5) additional share 07/18/1969
Name changed from Woodhead (Daniel) Co. to Woodhead (Daniel), Inc. 10/01/1970
State of incorporation changed from (IL) to (DE) 01/26/1978
Stock Dividends - 25% 07/07/1971; 33-1/3% 08/18/1972; 25% 02/20/1973; 25% 02/20/1974; 25% 08/20/1977; 25% 05/19/1978; 25% 05/18/1979
Name changed from Woodhead (Daniel), Inc. to Woodhead Industries, Inc. 02/14/1985
Common $1 par split (2) for (1) by issuance of (1) additional share 03/01/1993
Common $1 par split (3) for (2) by issuance of (0.5) additional share 05/22/1995
Acquired by Molex Inc. 08/10/2006
Each share Common $1 par exchanged for $19.25 cash

WOODIE 1 INC (NV)
Common $0.001 par split (2) for (1) by issuance of (1) additional share payable 07/16/1997 to holders of record 06/01/1997
Recapitalized as Vencap Capital Corp. 05/12/1999
Each share Common $0.001 par exchanged for (0.01) share Common $0.001 par
Vencap Capital Corp. recapitalized as American Scientific Resources, Inc. 01/08/2004

WOODINGTON GROUP INC (NV)
Each share old Common 1¢ par exchanged for (0.1) share new Common 1¢ par 11/28/1989
Charter revoked for failure to file reports and pay fees 05/10/1992

WOODLAND COMMUNICATIONS GROUP INC (DE)
Each (1.333) shares old Common $0.001 par exchanged for (1) share new Common $0.001 par 06/01/1999
Name changed to U.S. Telesis Holdings Inc. 06/03/1999
(See U.S. Telesis Holdings Inc.)

WOODLAND CORP (IA)
Charter cancelled for failure to file reports 11/21/1972

WOODLAND ELECTRONICS CO., INC. (DE)
Name changed to Electronic Transmission Systems, Inc. 7/12/66
(See Electronic Transmission Systems, Inc.)

WOODLAND HATCHERY INC (NV)
Recapitalized as Dwango North America Corp. 9/29/2003
Each (4.5) shares Common $0.001 par exchanged for (1) share Common $0.001 par
Dwango North America Corp. name changed to Dijji Corp. 12/13/2005

WOODLAND OIL & GAS CO., INC. (DE)
Name changed to Woodland Electronics Co., Inc. 1/9/61
Woodland Electronics Co., Inc. name changed to Electronic Transmission Systems, Inc. 7/12/66
(See Electronic Transmission Systems, Inc.)

WOODLANDS BK (WILLIAMSPORT, PA)
Reorganized as Woodlands Financial Services Co. 7/1/2001
Each share Common $10 par exchanged for (2) shares Common $5 par

WOODLAWN MEM PK INC (LA)
Merged into Alderwoods (Louisiana), Inc. 01/03/2002
Details not available

WOODLAWN NATL BK VA ALEXANDRIA (ALEXANDRIA, VA)
Merged into Clarendon Bank & Trust (Arlington, VA) 02/12/1973
Each share Common $10 par exchanged for (1) share Capital Stock $10 par
Clarendon Bank & Trust (Arlington, VA) merged into First American Bank of Virginia (McLean, VA) 03/31/1978
(See First American Bank of Virginia (McLean, VA))

WOODLEY PETROLEUM CO. (DE)
Common $10 par changed to $1 par in 1926
Common $1 par changed to $8 par and 50% Stock Dividend paid in 1948
Common $8 par split (3) for (2) by issuance of (1) additional share in 1953
Assets sold to Pure Oil Co. on a (1.4) for (1) basis plus a distribution of (0.428) share of Seven J Stock Farm, Inc. Common 4/1/60
(See each company's listing)

WOODLIKE INDS INC (CA)
Under plan of merger name changed to French Bar Industries, Inc. in April 1984
French Bar Industries, Inc. merged into Paradigm Medical Industries, Inc. (CA) 5/9/93 which reincorporated in Delaware in February 1996

WOODMAN INC (GA)
Merged into Kliklok Corp. 12/31/1968
Each share Common 10¢ par exchanged for (0.4) share Common $1 par
(See Kliklok Corp.)

WOODMERE CEMETERY ASSN (MI)
Voluntarily dissolved 05/05/1982
Details not available

WOODMONT CORP (MI)
Each share $3 Preferred no par

exchanged for (15) shares Common $1 par 3/19/69
(Additional Information in Active)

WOODMOOR CORP (DE)
Reincorporated 10/12/1987
State of incorporation changed from (CO) to (DE) 10/12/1987
Name changed to Phoenix Group International, Inc. 12/05/1988
Phoenix Group International, Inc. recapitalized as Canam Energy Inc. 09/27/2006 which recapitalized as Registered Express Corp. 06/29/2009 which name changed to Proactive Pet Products, Inc. 02/20/2015 which recapitalized as GVCL Ventures, Inc. 11/02/2016 which recapitalized as Rain Forest International, Inc. 05/22/2018

WOODRIDGE BUILDING CORP. (IL)
Liquidation completed 1/31/58

WOODRIDGE RES INC (BC)
Name changed to Telemac Cellular International Inc. 10/13/1993
Telemac Cellular International Inc. name changed to Cancall Cellular Communications Inc. 12/06/1994
(See Cancell Cellular Communications Inc.)

WOODROAST SYS INC (MN)
Each share old Common $0.005 par exchanged for (1/3) share new Common $0.005 par 5/25/95
Common $0.005 par split (3) for (1) by issuance of (2) additional shares payable 1/18/96 to holders of record 1/4/96
Statutorily dissolved 6/3/2002

WOODROSE CORP (AB)
Each share old Common no par exchanged for (0.5) share new Common no par 07/16/2012
Reincorporated under the laws of British Columbia as Woodrose Ventures Corp. 11/07/2016
Woodrose Ventures Corp. recapitalized as Novoheart Holdings Inc. 10/03/2017

WOODROSE VENTURES CORP (BC)
Recapitalized as Novoheart Holdings Inc. 10/03/2017
Each share Common no par exchanged for (0.28020744) share Common no par

WOODROW DOUGLAS OIL CO (TX)
Name changed 12/5/69
Name changed from Woodrow Douglas Oil Co. to Woodrow-Douglas Oil Co. and Common $1 par changed to 1¢ par 12/5/69
Name changed to Chado Oil & Gas Co., Inc. 12/18/73
Chado Oil & Gas Co., Inc. name changed to Mineral Development, Inc. 12/12/77 which recapitalized as Exco Resources Inc. 7/18/96
(See Exco Resources Inc.)

WOODRUFF & EDWARDS, INC. (DE)
Common no par changed to $8 par in 1950
Name changed to Ruffwards, Inc. 1/5/61
(See Ruffwards, Inc.)

WOODRUFF CAP MGMT INC (ON)
Name changed to Cogitore Resources Inc. 07/11/2006
Cogitore Resources Inc. recapitalized as CR Capital Corp. 03/26/2015

WOODS (FRANK H.) & CO., INC.
Acquired by Sahara Coal Co., Inc. 00/00/1950
Details not available

WOODS COMMUNICATION CORP (NY)
Charter cancelled and proclaimed dissolved for failure to pay taxes 12/29/82

WOODS CORP (DE)
Common $1 par split (3) for (2) by issuance of (0.5) additional share 3/1/68
Stock Dividend - 10% 6/15/67
Name changed to Woods Investment Co. 12/13/78
(See Woods Investment Co.)

WOOD'S 5 & 10¢ STORES, INC. (NC)
Name changed to Debtor Corp. 09/01/1981
(See Debtor Corp.)

WOODS (S.E.)-HOLDEN LTD.- WOODS (S.E.)- HOLDEN LTEE. (ON)
Name changed to Cantrend Industries Ltd.-Les Industries Cantrend Ltee. 05/28/1968
(See Cantrend Industries Ltd.-Les Industries Cantrend Ltee.)

WOODS INVT CO (DE)
In process of liquidation
Each share Common $1 par exchanged for initial distribution of $9.42 cash 6/6/91
Each share Common $1 par received second distribution of $0.08 cash 12/24/92
Note: Details on subsequent distributions, if any, are not available

WOODS (HARVEY) LTD. (ON)
See - Harvey Woods Ltd.

WOODS MANUFACTURING CO. LTD. (CANADA)
Common $100 par changed to no par in 1932
Each share 7% Preferred $100 par exchanged for (4) shares new Common no par in 1944
Each share old Common no par exchanged for (0.2) share new Common no par in 1944
Completely liquidated 4/17/63
Each share new Common no par exchanged for (32) shares 4% Non-Cum. Class B Preferred $1 par and (3) shares Common no par of Wabasso Cotton Co., Ltd. plus 50¢ cash
Wabasso Cotton Co., Ltd. name changed to Wabasso Ltd. 12/29/67 which name changed to Wabasso Inc. 6/29/79
(See Wabasso Inc.)

WOODS PETE CORP (DE)
Common $1 par split (2) for (1) by issuance of (1) additional share 09/22/1976
Common $1 par split (2) for (1) by issuance of (1) additional share 03/17/1980
Merged into Sunshine Mining Co. 07/31/1985
Each share Common $1 par exchanged for (1) share $11.94 Preferred $1 par, (1.5) shares Common 50¢ par and $5 cash
Sunshine Mining Co. name changed to Sunshine Mining & Refining Co. 06/20/1994
(See Sunshine Mining & Refining Co.)

WOODSBORO SVGS BK (FREDERICK CNTY, MD)
Reorganized as Woodsboro Bancshares Inc. 6/9/97
Each share Common $10 par exchanged for (0.25) share Common $10 par

WOODSIDE BURMAH OIL N L (AUSTRALIA)
Name changed to Woodside Petroleum Ltd. 04/26/1977

WOODSIDE COTTON MILLS CO.
Name changed to Woodside Mills in 1948
Woodside Mills merged into Dan River Mills, Inc. 1/5/70 which name changed to Dan River Inc. 7/1/70
(See Dan River Inc.)

WOODSIDE MILLS (SC)
Merged into Dan River Mills, Inc. 1/5/70
Details not available

WOODSREEF MINERALS LTD (AB)
Recapitalized as Transpacific Asbestos, Inc. 04/30/1981
Each share Capital Stock no par exchanged for (0.2) share Capital Stock no par
Transpacific Asbestos, Inc. name changed Transpacific Resources Inc. 09/06/1984
(See Transpacific Resources Inc.)

WOODSTOCK FINL GROUP INC (GA)
Name changed to Woodstock Holdings, Inc. 01/10/2011

WOODSTOCK INVT CO (DE)
Name changed to Lamar Auto Parts, Inc. 11/25/85
(See Lamar Auto Parts, Inc.)

WOODSTOCK RAILWAY CO.
Road abandoned in 1933

WOODSTOCK STATE BANCORP., INC. (DE)
Acquired by Suburban Bancorp, Inc. 9/30/87
Each share Common $10 par exchanged for $128 cash

WOODSTOWN NATL BK & TR CO (WOODSTOWN, NJ)
Merged into Fulton Financial Corp. 2/28/97
Each share Common $5 par exchanged for (1.6) shares Common $2.50 par

WOODSTREAM CORP (PA)
Common no par split (3) for (2) by issuance of (0.5) additional share 04/15/1987
Stock Dividends - 20% 11/25/1968; 100% 09/01/1969; 10% 09/22/1978
Acquired by Ekco Corp., Inc. 01/23/1989
Each share Common no par exchanged for $17.12 cash
5% Preferred called for redemption at $52 plus $0.625 accrued dividends on 08/10/2015
Public interest eliminated

WOODTEK INC (OR)
Adjudicated bankrupt 06/02/1972
Stockholders' equity unlikely

WOODUSE INC. (CA)
Name changed to Fersolin Corp. 05/29/1958
(See Fersolin Corp.)

WOODVIEW CORP (ON)
Each share old Common no par exchanged for (0.1) share new Common no par 8/16/99
Merged into Woodview Acquisition Corp. 8/1/2002
Each share new Common no par exchanged for $0.15 cash

WOODWARD & LOTHROP (DC)
Name changed to Woodward & Lothrop, Inc. 2/3/55
(See Woodward & Lothrop, Inc.)

WOODWARD & LOTHROP INC (DC)
Common $10 par split (3) for (1) by issuance of (2) additional shares 11/16/1962
Common $10 par split (3) for (2) by issuance of (0.5) additional share 07/29/1983
5% Preferred $100 par called for redemption 06/01/1984
Stock Dividends - 100% 11/27/1964; 10% 12/29/1975
Merged into Taubman Holdings, Inc. 09/18/1984
Each share Common $10 par exchanged for $60.50 cash

WOODWARD CORP. (DE)
Merged into Mead Corp. 11/30/1968
Each share 6% Preferred $100 par exchanged for (1) share 6% Preferred $100 par
Each share Common $10 par exchanged for (0.9) share $2.80 Conv. Preferred 1968 Ser. no par
(See Mead Corp.)

WOODWARD GOVERNOR CO (DE)
Reincorporated 01/10/1977
State of incorporation changed from (IL) to (DE) 01/10/1977
Common $1 par changed to 25¢ par and (3) additional shares issued 01/28/1981
Common 25¢ par changed to $0.125 par and (1) additional share issued 02/03/1984
Common $0.125 par changed to $0.0625 par and (1) additional share issued 02/08/1988
Common $0.0625 par changed to $0.00875 par and (3) additional shares issued payable 02/07/1997 to holders of record 01/23/1997
Common $0.00875 par changed to $0.00291 par and (2) additional shares issued payable 02/14/2006 to holders of record 02/01/2006
Ex date - 02/15/2006
Common $0.00291 par changed to $0.001455 par and (1) additional share issued payable 02/14/2008 to holders of record 02/01/2008
Ex date - 02/15/2008
Name changed to Woodward, Inc. 01/26/2011

WOODWARD IRON CO. (DE)
Reorganized 00/00/1937
Each share old 6% Preferred $100 par exchanged for (3.5) shares Common $10 par
Each share 7% Preferred $100 par exchanged for (3.5) shares Common $10 par and $2.81 cash
Each share Common $100 par exchanged for (1) share Common $10 par
Common $10 par split (3) for (1) by issuance of (2) additional shares 12/15/1955
Stock Dividend - 100% 11/10/1947
Name changed to Woodward Corp 04/19/1968
Woodward Corp. merged into Mead Corp. 11/30/1968
(See Mead Corp.)

WOODWARD OIL INC (CO)
Reorganized under the laws of Nevada 11/5/69
Each share Common Capital Stock 5¢ par exchanged for (0.066666) share Common Capital Stock $0.001 par
(See Woodward Oil Inc. (NV))

WOODWARD OIL INC (NV)
Charter revoked for failure to file reports and pay fees 03/01/1971

WOODWARD STORES (1947) LTD. (BC)
Each share 4-1/2% Preferred $100 par exchanged for (1) share 4-1/2% Preferred $5 par 5/7/58
Name changed to Woodward Stores Ltd. 4/27/64
Woodward Stores Ltd. name changed to Woodward's Ltd. 6/13/84
(See Woodward's Ltd.)

WOODWARDS LTD (BC)
Name changed 06/13/1984
Each share Class A $5 par exchanged for (2) shares Class A no par 06/30/1967
Each share Class B $5 par exchanged for (2) shares Class B no par 06/30/1967
Class E no par called for redemption 05/01/1981
Class A no par split (2) for (1) by issuance of (1) additional share 06/29/1981
Class B no par split (2) for (1) by

issuance of (1) additional share 06/29/1981
Class C no par split (2) for (1) by issuance of (1) additional share 06/29/1981
Name changed from Woodward Stores Ltd. to Woodward's Ltd. 06/13/1984
Under plan of reorganization each share Class A no par, Class B no par and Class C no par received distribution of $13.75 cash 10/17/1985
Each share Class A no par exchanged for (1) share Class A 1985 no par 10/15/1985
Each share Class B no par exchanged for (1) share Class B 1985 no par 10/15/1985
Each share Class C no par exchanged for (1) share Class C 1985 no par 10/15/1985
Each share Class A 1985 no par exchanged for (1) share Common no par 06/30/1991
Each share Class B 1985 no par exchanged for (1) share Common no par 06/30/1991
Each share Class C 1985 no par exchanged for (1) share Common no par 06/30/1991
Plan of Arangement under Companies Creditors Arrangement Act effective 06/09/1993
Each share Common no par received $0.35 cash

WOODWORKERS WHSE INC (DE)
Plan of reorganization under Chapter 11 Federal Bankruptcy Code effective 8/10/2004
No stockholders' equity

WOODWORTH, INC.
Merged into International Perfume Co., Inc. in 1929
International Perfume Co., Inc. name changed to Bourjois, Inc. in 1930 which merged into Chanel, Inc. 6/7/74

WOODY'S INC. (MN)
Adjudicated bankrupt 7/29/74

WOOL COMBING CORP. OF CANADA, LTD. (CANADA)
Liquidation completed 12/21/1962
Details not available

WOOLF BROS INC (MO)
7% Preferred $100 par called for redemption 03/01/1946
$1 Class B Preferred no par called for redemption 04/29/1946

WOOLSON SPICE CO (OH)
Placed in receivership 07/20/1966
Common no par declared worthless
Each share Preferred $100 par received initial distribution of $5 cash 09/20/1968
Each share Preferred $100 par received second and final distribution of $5.38 12/28/1968

WOOLTRU LTD (SOUTH AFRICA)
Each Sponsored ADR for Ordinary Rand-5 par received distribution of $0.8437 cash payable 07/31/2002 to holders of record 07/17/2002
ADR agreement terminated 05/19/2006
Each Sponsored ADR for Ordinary exchanged for $0.04009 cash
Each Sponsored ADR for Ser. A exchanged for $0.04009 cash

WOOLWORTH CORP (NY)
Common 1¢ par split (2) for (1) by issuance of (1) additional share 05/31/1990
$2.20 Conv. Preferred Ser. A $1 par called for redemption 10/23/1996
Name changed to Venator Group Inc. 06/12/1998
Venator Group Inc. name changed to Foot Locker, Inc. 11/02/2001

WOOLWORTH F W CO (NY)
Each share Common $25 par exchanged for (2.5) shares Common $10 par in 1929
Common $10 par changed to $3-1/3 par and (2) additional shares issued 6/17/64
Common $3-1/3 par split (2) for (1) by issuance of (1) additional share 5/30/86
Under plan of reorganization each share $2.20 Conv. Preferred Ser. A $1 par and Common $3-1/3 par automatically became (1) share Woolworth Corp. $2.20 Conv. Preferred Ser. A $1 par and Common 1¢ par respectively 8/7/89
Woolworth Corp. name changed to Venator Group Inc. 6/12/98 which name changed to Foot Locker, Inc. 11/2/2001

WOOLWORTH F W PLC (ENGLAND)
ADR's for 6% Preference $1 par called for redemption 03/21/1967
ADR's for Ordinary Reg. 5s par changed to 25p par per currency change 02/15/1971
Stock Dividends - 50% 11/02/1954; 50% 03/28/1957; 40% 11/10/1960; 100% 03/31/1964
Note: Common Market regulation required all publicly held British companies to replace LTD with PLC 00/00/1982
Acquired by Paternoster Stores PLC 10/19/1982
Each ADR for Ordinary Reg. 25p par exchanged for $1.225 cash

WOOLWORTH HLDGS PLC (UNITED KINGDOM)
ADR's for Ordinary 25p par split (2) for (1) by issuance of (1) additional ADR 7/17/87
Name changed to Kingfisher PLC 3/16/89
(See Kingfisher PLC)

WOOLWORTHS LTD (AUSTRALIA)
Each Unsponsored ADR for Ordinary exchanged for (1) 144A Sponsored ADR for Ordinary 07/10/1993
Name changed to Woolworths Group Ltd. 01/02/2018

WOONGJIN COWAY CO LTD (KOREA)
GDR agreement terminated 02/29/2016

WOORI FIN HLDGS (KOREA)
Each old ADR for Common exchanged for (0.83903908) new ADR for Common and $6.049904 cash 05/22/2014
Merged into Woori Bank 11/19/2014
Each new ADR for Common exchanged for (1) ADR for Common

WOOSTER RUBBER CO. (OH)
Stock Dividend - 300% 05/16/1955
Name changed to Rubbermaid, Inc. 12/12/1957
Rubbermaid, Inc. merged into Newell Rubbermaid Inc. 03/24/1999 which name changed to Newell Brands Inc. 04/18/2016

WOOZYFLY INC (NV)
Plan of reorganization under Chapter 11 Federal Bankruptcy Code effective 02/22/2010
No old Common stockholders' equity
Name changed to STW Resources Holding Corp. and Common $0.00001 par changed to $0.001 par 03/03/2010

WORCESTER BANCORP INC (MA)
Acquired by Shawmut Corp. 5/3/82
Each share Common $1 par exchanged for (1.113) shares Common $5 par
Shawmut Corp. merged into Shawmut National Corp. 2/29/88 which merged into Fleet Financial Group Inc. (New) 11/30/95 which name changed to Fleet Boston Corp.

10/1/99 which name changed to FleetBoston Financial Corp. 4/18/2000 which merged into Bank of America Corp. 4/1/2004

WORCESTER CNTY ELEC CO (MA)
Merged into New England Electric System on a (4.2) for (1) basis 6/30/59
(See New England Electric System)

WORCESTER CNTY INSTN FOR SVGS (WORCESTER, MA)
Under plan of reorganization each share Common 10¢ par automatically became (1) share BankWorcester Corp. (DE) Common 10¢ par 12/14/1987
(See BankWorcester Corp.)

WORCESTER CNTY NATL BK (WORCESTER, MA)
Common $25 par changed to $10 par and (1.5) additional shares issued 7/15/60
Stock Dividend - 10% 1/22/65
Reorganized as Worcester Bancorp, Inc. 3/21/69
Each share Common $10 par exchanged for (2) shares Common $1 par
Worcester Bancorp, Inc. acquired by Shawmut Corp. 5/3/82 which merged into Shawmut National Corp. 2/29/88 which merged into Fleet Financial Group, Inc. (New) 11/30/95 which name changed to Fleet Boston Corp. 10/1/99 which name changed to FleetBoston Financial Corp. 4/18/2000 which merged into Bank of America Corp. 4/1/2004

WORCESTER CTLS CORP (MA)
Common $1 par split (3) for (2) by issuance of (0.5) additional share 08/01/1975
Merged into BTR, Inc. 08/28/1978
Each share Common $1 par exchanged for $30 cash

WORCESTER ELECTRIC LIGHT CO.
Acquired by New England Power Association in 1929
(See New England Power Association)

WORCESTER INVT ASSOC (MA)
Completely liquidated 12/31/1976
Each share Common no par exchanged for first and final distribution of $331.9374 cash

WORCESTER SALT CO.
Liquidated in 1943

WORCESTER SUBURBAN ELECTRIC CO.
Merged into Worcester County Electric Co. share for share or $75 in cash in 1951
Worcester County Electric Co. merged into New England Electric System 6/30/59
(See New England Electric System)

WORCESTER TRANSPORTATION ASSOCIATES (MA)
Recapitalized as Worcester Investment Associates on a (1) for (10) basis 5/15/54
(See Worcester Investment Associates)

WORD MAKING PRODTNS INC (UT)
Name changed to Molecular Technology, Inc. 7/5/72
(See Molecular Technology, Inc.)

WORD TRONICS CORP (NY)
SEC revoked common stock registration 10/15/2009
Stockholders' equity unlikely

WORDCRAFT SYS INC (CA)
Reorganized under the laws of Delaware as Wake Up Now, Inc. 12/01/2010
Each share Common 5¢ par exchanged for (0.004) share Common 5¢ par

WORDCRUNCHER INTERNET TECHNOLOGIES INC (NV)
Name changed to Logio Inc. 06/21/2000
Logio Inc. merged into Pacific WebWorks, Inc. 01/31/2001 which name changed to Heyu Biological Technology Corp. 06/28/2018

WORDSTAR INTL INC (CA)
Name changed SoftKey International Inc. 02/04/1994
Each share Common no par exchanged for (0.1) share Common 1¢ par
SoftKey International Inc. name changed to Learning Co. Inc. 10/24/1996 which merged into Mattel, Inc. 05/13/1999

WORDTRONIX INC (MN)
Name changed to Remington Rand Corp. (MN) 12/1/83
Remington Rand Corp. (MN) reincorporated in Georgia as Dominion Cable Corp. 7/1/88
(See Dominion Cable Corp.)

WORIC CORP (NY)
Merged into Hillsboro Acquisition Corp. 07/29/1988
Each share Common 2¢ par exchanged for $2.15 cash

WORK HORSE CAP & STRATEGIC ACQUISITIONS LTD (ON)
Name changed to LeoNovus Inc. 03/07/2011

WORK MINING & MILLING CO. (CO)
Declared defunct and inoperative for failure to pay taxes and file annual reports 10/30/1916

WORK RECOVERY INC (DE)
Reorganized 02/11/1997
Reorganized from (CO) to under the laws of Delaware 02/01/1997
Each share old Common $0.004 par exchanged for (0.1) share new Common $0.004 par and (0.1) share Common Stock Purchase Warrant expiring 07/31/1997
Recapitalized as Jinhua Marine Biological (USA), Inc. 08/31/2005
Each (300) shares new Common $0.004 par exchanged for (1) share Common $0.004 par

WORK WEAR CORP (OH)
Common $1 par split (2) for (1) by issuance of (1) additional share 06/01/1965
Class B Common $1 par split (2) for (1) by issuance of (1) additional share 06/01/1965
Merged into ARA Services, Inc. 07/26/1977
Each share Common $1 par exchanged for (0.17) share Common 50¢ par
(See ARA Services, Inc.)

WORK WEAR INC (OH)
Acquired by an investor group 06/19/1986
Each share Common $1 par exchanged for $28 cash

WORKBRAIN CORP (ON)
Merged into Infor Global Solutions European Finance, S.a.R.L. 06/01/2007
Each share Common no par exchanged for $12.50 cash

WORKERS COMPENSATION MED CTRS INC (FL)
Name changed to Spectrum Health Solutions Inc. 9/29/97

WORKERS LOAN CO. (PA)
Merged into Lincoln Service Corp. 2/4/57
Each share Class A Common 25¢ par exchanged for (0.05) share $1.50 Preferred 2nd Ser. no par and (0.05) share Common $1 par
Lincoln Service Corp. merged into State Loan & Finance Corp. 3/16/59

which name changed to American Finance System Inc. 5/1/68 which merged into Security Pacific Corp. 12/15/78 which merged into BankAmerica Corp. (Old) 4/22/92 which merged into BankAmerica Corp. (New) 9/30/98 which name changed to Bank of America Corp. 4/28/99

WORKFIRE COM INC (CO)
Name changed to BCS Investment Corp. 2/14/2000
BCS Investment Corp. recapitalized as Crossnet Communications Inc. 12/18/2000 which recapitalized as Cirond Technologies Inc. 7/1/2002 which name changed to Seaside Holdings Inc. 3/17/2003

WORKFLOW MGMT INC (DE)
Merged into WF Holdings, Inc. 4/26/2004
Each share Common $0.001 par exchanged for $5.56 cash

WORKFORCE SYS CORP (FL)
Each share old Common $0.001 par exchanged for (0.25) share new Common $0.001 par 04/04/1997
Name changed to Coventry Industries Corp. 10/29/1997
Coventry Industries Corp. name changed to American Risk Management Group, Inc. 09/07/1999 which name changed to Comprehensive Medical Diagnostics Group Inc. 07/21/2000 which recapitalized as My Vintage Baby, Inc. 06/01/2007
(See My Vintage Baby, Inc.)

WORKGROUP TECHNOLOGY CORP (DE)
Each share old Common 1¢ par exchanged for (0.25) share new Common 1¢ par 12/21/2000
Merged into SofTech, Inc. 6/18/2003
Each share new Common 1¢ par exchanged for $2 cash

WORKHORSE MFG INC (BC)
Recapitalized as Koala Beverages Ltd. 9/4/92
Each share Common no par exchanged for (1/3) share Common no par
Koala Beverages Ltd. name changed to Tribridge Enterprises Corp. 7/21/97 which recapitalized as Vision Gate Ventures Ltd. 3/16/99 which name changed to Northern Lion Gold Corp. 7/10/2003

WORKING GIRL INC (NJ)
Name changed to New Dimensions Learning Corp. 08/09/1972
(See New Dimensions Learning Corp.)

WORKINGMENS CAP HLDGS INC (IN)
Common no par split (2) for (1) by issuance of (1) additional share 10/14/94
Merged into Old National Bancorp 10/19/96
Each share Common no par exchanged for (0.6123) share Common no par

WORKINGMENS CORP (MA)
Involuntarily dissolved 8/31/98

WORKMENS BANCORP INC (DE)
Merged into Southern National Corp. 3/20/92
Each share Common $1 par exchanged for (1.5) shares Common $5 par
Southern National Corp. name changed to BB&T Corp. 5/19/97

WORKSAFE INDS INC (NY)
Ceased operations 01/05/2001
Stockholders' equity unlikely

WORKSHOP LTD (NV)
Name changed to Children's Creative Workshop, Ltd. 08/30/1989

Children's Creative Workshop, Ltd. name changed to Kent Holdings Ltd. 06/20/1991
(See Kent Holdings Ltd.)

WORKSTREAM INC (CANADA)
Each share old Common no par exchanged for (0.0025) share new Common no par 05/10/2011
Recapitalized as HR Soft Inc. 03/11/2014
Each share new Common no par exchanged for (1) share Common no par
Note: Holders of (1,499) or fewer pre-split shares received $0.60 cash per share

WORLCO INC (DE)
Class A Common 10¢ par changed to 5¢ par and (1) additional share issued in February 1971
Charter cancelled and declared void for failure to pay franchise taxes 3/1/91

WORLD ACCEP CORP (SC)
Ctfs. dated prior to 10/31/1973
Common 50¢ par split (3) for (2) by issuance of (0.5) additional share 10/22/1972
Stock Dividend - 10% 05/20/1971
Merged into Southern Bancorporation, Inc. 10/31/1973
Each share Common 50¢ par exchanged for (0.634921) share Common $2.50 par
(See Southern Bancorporation, Inc.)

WORLD ACCEPTANCE CORP. (DE)
Charter cancelled and declared inoperative and void for non-payment of taxes 04/15/1973

WORLD ACCESS INC (DE)
Plan of reorganization under Chapter 11 Federal Bankruptcy Code effective 10/12/2004
No stockholders' equity

WORLD ACCESS TELEVISION INC (DE)
Charter cancelled and declared inoperative and void for non-payment of taxes 3/1/90

WORLD AIR HLDGS INC (DE)
Merged into Global Aero Logistics Inc. 08/14/2007
Each share Common $0.001 par exchanged for $12.50 cash

WORLD-AM COMMUNICATIONS INC (NV)
Reincorporated 12/19/2002
State of incorporation changed from (FL) to (NV) 12/19/2002
Each share old Common $0.001 par exchanged for (0.25) share new Common $0.001 par 2/10/2000
Each (30) shares new Common $0.001 par exchanged again for (1) share new Common $0.001 par 12/1/2000
Name changed to World Am, Inc. 8/2/2004

WORLD AQUATHEMES LTD (AB)
Name changed to Telesis Corp. Inc. 09/02/1986
Telesis Corp. Inc. recapitalized as P.C. Ventures Ltd. 02/23/1989
(See P.C. Ventures Ltd.)

WORLD ASSETS GROUP INC (ON)
Reincorporated under the laws of Nevada as Mobile Assets Corp. and Common no par changed to $0.001 par 01/14/2005
Mobile Assets Corp. recapitalized as Sunland Media Group 07/09/2008 which name changed to Homestead Gold & Silver Ltd. 09/09/2011

WORLD ASSURN GROUP INC (NV)
Each share old Common $0.001 par exchanged for (0.02) share new Common $0.001 par 06/16/2014
Name changed to Power Clouds Inc. 04/24/2015

WORLD AWYS INC NEW (DE)
Under plan of reorganization each share Common $0.001 par automatically became (1) share World Air Holdings, Inc. Common $0.001 par 01/10/2005
(See World Air Holdings, Inc.)

WORLD AWYS INC OLD (DE)
Common $1 par split (2) for (1) by issuance of (1) additional share 7/28/67
Name changed to WorldCorp, Inc. 6/23/87
(See WorldCorp, Inc.)

WORLD BINGO LEAGUE CO INC (NV)
Common $0.001 par split (3) for (1) by issuance of (2) additional shares payable 01/19/2005 to holders of record 01/19/2005
Name changed to World Entertainment Corp. 07/14/2005
World Entertainment Corp. name changed to World Mobile Network Corp. 03/16/2006 which recapitalized as Guyana Gold Corp. 02/07/2008

WORLD BOOK CO. (DE)
Common no par split (4) for (1) by issuance of (3) additional shares 4/25/53
Common no par split (3) for (1) by issuance of (2) additional shares 5/7/58
Merged into Harcourt, Brace & World, Inc. 12/13/60
Each share Common no par exchanged for (5.77722) shares Common $1 par
Harcourt, Brace & World, Inc. name changed to Harcourt Brace Jovanovich, Inc. 6/2/70 which merged into General Cinema Corp. 11/25/91 which name changed to Harcourt General, Inc. 3/15/93
(See Harcourt General, Inc.)

WORLD CALLNET INC (DE)
SEC revoked common stock registration 09/04/2008

WORLD CAP INVT CORP (UT)
Charter suspended for failure to pay taxes 03/31/1976

WORLD CEM INDS INC (BC)
Recapitalized as Topper Gold Corp. 07/05/1989
Each share Capital Stock no par exchanged for (0.25) share Common no par
Topper Gold Corp. recapitalized as Consolidated Topper Gold Corp. 04/13/2000 which name changed to Topper Resources Inc. (BC) 02/06/2002 which reincorporated in Alberta 05/03/2006 which name changed to Century Energy Ltd. (AB) 05/19/2006 which reincorporated in British Columbia 10/20/2016

WORLD COLLECTIBLES INC (DE)
Name changed to Designer & Decorator House Holdings, Inc. 11/24/2000
(See Designer & Decorator House Holdings, Inc.)

WORLD COLOR PRESS INC (CANADA)
Merged into Quad/Graphics, Inc. 07/02/2010
Each share Common no par exchanged for (0.2154) share Class A Common $0.025 par and USD $0.556558 cash

WORLD COLOR PRESS INC (DE)
Merged into Quebecor Printing Inc. 10/08/1999
Each share Common no par exchanged for (1.2685) shares Subordinate no par and $8.18 cash
Quebecor Printing Inc. name changed to Quebecor World Inc. 04/25/2000

(See Quebecor World Inc.)

WORLD COLOR PRESS INC (MO)
Completely liquidated 6/25/68
Each share Common $1 par exchanged for first and final distribution of (0.612) share City Investing Co. (DE) $1.31 Conv. Preference Ser. A $1 par
(See City Investing Co. (DE))

WORLD COMM ONLINE INC (DE)
Petition filed under Chapter 11 Federal Bankruptcy Code dismissed 5/8/2002
No stockholders' equity

WORLD COMM ONLINE INC (NV)
Reincorporated under the laws of Delaware 10/15/99
(See World Commerce Online, Inc. (DE))

WORLD COMPUTER CORP (TX)
Adjudicated bankrupt 02/08/1972
No stockholders' equity

WORLD CONTAINER CORP (MN)
SEC revoked common stock registration 09/15/2008

WORLD CORP (DE)
Charter cancelled and declared inoperative and void for non-payment of taxes 3/1/91

WORLD CREDIT CORP. (LA)
Liquidation completed 5/9/62

WORLD CURRENCY GOLD TR (DE)
Name changed to World Gold Trust 04/25/2018

WORLD CYBERLINKS CORP (NY)
SEC revoked common stock registration 06/04/2007

WORLD DIAGNOSTICS INC (DE)
Name changed to EGM International, Inc. 4/28/2006

WORLD ECOLOGY RES INC (NV)
Charter revoked for failure to file reports and pay fees 03/01/1976

WORLD ENERGY SOLUTIONS INC (DE)
Each share old Common $0.0001 par exchanged for (0.1) share new Common $0.0001 par 04/02/2009
Acquired by EnerNOC, Inc. 01/05/2015
Each share new Common $0.0001 par exchanged for $5.50 cash

WORLD ENERGY SOLUTIONS INC (FL)
Name changed to EClips Energy Technologies, Inc. (FL) 03/26/2009
EClips Energy Technologies, Inc. (FL) reincorporated in Delaware as EClips Media Technologies, Inc. 05/13/2010 which name changed to Silver Horn Mining Ltd. (DE) 04/27/2011 which reorganized in Nevada as Great West Resources, Inc. 04/21/2014 which name changed to Orbital Tracking Corp. 02/20/2015

WORLD ENTMT CONCEPTS INC (NY)
Dissolved by proclamation 09/28/1994

WORLD ENTMT CORP (NV)
Name changed to World Mobile Network Corp. 03/16/2006
World Mobile Network Corp. recapitalized as Guyana Gold Corp. 02/07/2008

WORLD ENVIRONMENTAL INC (AB)
Cease trade order effective 11/28/1996

WORLD ENVIROTECH INC (CO)
Recapitalized as Link Group Inc. 2/28/2002
Each share Common $0.001 par exchanged for (0.25) share Common $0.001 par

WORLD ENZYMES LTD (BC)
Delisted from Vancouver Stock Exchange 07/07/1989

WORLD EXPLORATION CO. (DE)
No longer in existence having become inoperative and void for non-payment of taxes 4/1/32

WORLD EXPLORERS SPORTSMENS CLUB INC (NY)
Dissolved by proclamation 12/15/72

WORLD FIDELITY LIFE INSURANCE CO. (CO)
Proclaimed defunct and inoperative by Governor of Colorado for failure to pay taxes 11/28/62

WORLD FINANCE INVESTMENT TRUST CO. (MA)
Name changed to World Investment Trust 00/00/1934
World Investment Trust name changed to Investment Trust of Boston 00/00/1948 which name changed to TNE Funds Trust 04/01/1992 which name changed to New England Funds Trust II 04/18/1994 which name changed to Nvest Funds Trust II 02/01/2000 which name changed to CDC Nvest Funds Trust II 05/01/2001
(See CDC Nvest Funds Trust II)

WORLD FOODS CORP (CO)
Adjudicated bankrupt 02/02/1971
Assets sold for benefit of creditors
No stockholders' equity

WORLD GAMING PLC (ENGLAND & WALES)
Company placed in liquidation 03/23/2009
ADR holders' equity unlikely

WORLD GOLF LEAGUE INC (DE)
Each share old Common $0.001 par exchanged for (10) shares new Common $0.001 par 03/21/2003
Name changed to WGL Entertainment Holdings, Inc. 08/29/2006
WGL Entertainment Holdings, Inc. recapitalized as Heathrow Natural Food & Beverage Inc. 03/09/2009

WORLD HEALTH ALTERNATIVES INC (FL)
Common $0.0001 par split (2) for (1) by issuance of (1) additional share payable 10/08/2002 to holders of record 10/07/2002 Ex date - 10/09/2002
Chapter 11 bankruptcy proceedings converted to Chapter 7 on 10/31/2006
No stockholders' equity

WORLD HEART CORP (DE)
Reincorporated 12/14/2005
Reincorporated 01/01/2010
Each share old Common no par exchanged for (0.14285714) share new Common no par 12/04/2003
Place of incorporation changed from (ON) to (Canada) 12/14/2005
Each share old Common no par exchanged for (0.1) share new Common no par 05/31/2007
Each share new Common no par exchanged again for (0.03333333) share new Common no par 10/28/2008
Place of incorporation changed from (Canada) to (DE) and Common no par changed to $0.001 par 01/01/2010
Merged into HeartWare International, Inc. 08/02/2012
Each share Common $0.001 par exchanged for (0.003) share Common $0.001 par
(See HeartWare International, Inc.)

WORLD HERITAGE LIFE INSURANCE CO. (TN)
Merged into World Service Life Insurance Co. (TX) 04/28/1967
Each share Common $1 par exchanged for (0.5) share Common $1 par
World Service Life Insurance Co. (TX) merged into World Service Life Insurance Co. (CO) 07/31/1978 which merged into Western Preferred Corp. 02/21/1979
(See Western Preferred Corp.)

WORLD HOMES INC (NV)
Name changed to Composite Industries of America, Inc. 8/23/2001
Composite Industries of America, Inc. recapitalized as Composite Holdings, Inc. 5/8/2002 which name changed to Gold Rock Holdings, Inc. 1/7/2005

WORLD IMPORTS, INC. (MN)
Name changed to Progressive Distributing, Inc. 11/13/72
Progressive Distributing, Inc. name changed to Progressive Companies, Inc. 11/12/73

WORLD IMPORTS U S A INC (DE)
Recapitalized as Seiler Pollution Control Systems Inc. 07/08/1993
Each share Common $0.0001 par exchanged for (0.01) share Common $0.0001 par
(See Seiler Pollution Control Systems Inc.)

WORLD INCOME FD INC (MD)
Name changed to Merrill Lynch World Income Fund, Inc. and Common 10¢ par reclassified as Class A Common 10¢ par 11/15/1991
Merrill Lynch World Income Fund, Inc. name changed to BlackRock World Income Fund, Inc. 09/26/2006

WORLD INDS INC (DE)
Recapitalized as World Corp. 03/31/1976
Each share Common 1¢ par exchanged for (0.1) share Common 1¢ par
(See World Corp.)

WORLD INDS INC (NV)
Charter revoked for failure to file reports and pay fees 03/05/1973

WORLD INFORMATION NETWORK CORP (UT)
Name changed to Quest Entertainment Corp. 02/28/1992

WORLD INFORMATION TECHNOLOGY INC (NV)
Each share old Common $0.001 par exchanged for (2) shares new Common $0.001 par 08/15/2003
SEC revoked common stock registration 11/08/2006

WORLD INSTS TECHNOLOGY INC (NY)
Recapitalized as Investors General Realty Corp. 3/30/73
Each share Common 1¢ par exchanged for (0.5) share Common 1¢ par
(See Investors General Realty Corp.)

WORLD INTERNET TECHNOLOGIES INC (DE)
Recapitalized as Soundworks Entertainment Inc. 6/11/2002
Each share Common $0.001 par exchanged for (0.05) share Common $0.001 par
Soundworks Entertainment Inc. recapitalized as Data Evolution Holdings, Inc. 4/12/2004

WORLD INTERNETWORKS INC (NV)
Each share old Common $0.001 par exchanged for (0.25) share new Common $0.001 par 9/4/98
Each share new Common $0.001 par exchanged again for (0.5) share new Common $0.001 par 3/21/2001
Name changed to GTDATA Corp. 12/3/2001
GTDATA Corp. recapitalized as Frontier Energy Corp. 9/28/2005

WORLD INVESTMENT CORP. (UT)
Name changed to Energy Stock Exchange 03/06/1978
Energy Stock Exchange name changed to Burke Oil Co. (UT) 04/20/1981 which reincorporated in Nevada as Centre Capital Corp. 09/06/1988 which name changed to Golden Health Holdings, Inc. 04/15/2004
(See Golden Health Holdings, Inc.)

WORLD INVESTMENT TRUST (MA)
Name changed to Investment Trust of Boston 00/00/1948
Investment Trust of Boston name changed to TNE Funds Trust 04/01/1992 which name changed to New England Funds Trust II 04/18/1994 which name changed to Nvest Funds Trust II 02/01/2000 which name changed to CDC Nvest Funds Trust II 05/01/2001
(See CDC Nvest Funds Trust II)

WORLD JAI ALAI INC (DE)
Merged into WJA Realty 11/22/1978
Each share Common 10¢ par exchanged for $5 principal amount of 10% Subord. Debentures due 07/03/1988 and $10 cash

WORLD LAND CO. (CO)
Bankrupt in 1963; no stockholders' equity

WORLD MAIL CTR INC (CA)
Petition under Chapter 7 Federal Bankruptcy Code filed 6/30/86
No stockholders' equity

WORLD MARKETING & TRAVEL INC (DE)
Recapitalized as Savant Biotechnology Inc. 2/10/97
Each share Common $0.001 par exchanged for (0.001) share Common $0.001 par
Savant Biotechnology Inc. name changed to Children's Beverage Group, Inc. 5/13/97
(See Children's Beverage Group, Inc.)

WORLD MARKETING INC (DE)
Name changed to Royal Energy Resources, Inc. 12/14/2007

WORLD MED MFG CORP (FL)
Merged into Arterial Vascular Engineering, Inc. 12/15/1998
Each share Common exchanged for (0.6813) share Common $0.001 par
Arterial Vascular Engineering, Inc. merged into Medtronic, Inc. (MN) 01/28/1999 which reincorporated in Ireland as Medtronic PLC 01/27/2015

WORLD MEDIA & TECHNOLOGY CORP (NV)
Name changed to World Technology Corp. 12/04/2017

WORLD MINT INC (NV)
Recapitalized as NCP Industries, Inc. 05/28/1974
Each share Common 10¢ par exchanged for (0.5) share Common no par
(See NCP Industries, Inc.)

WORLD MKTG CORP (BC)
Delisted from Vancouver Stock Exchange 05/04/1994

WORLD MOBILE NETWORK CORP (NV)
Recapitalized as Guyana Gold Corp. 02/07/2008
Each share Common $0.001 par exchanged for (0.002) share Common $0.001 par

WORLD NET HLDGS INC (FL)
Each share old Common $0.001 par exchanged for (0.25) share new Common $0.001 par 11/09/1998
Reincorporated under the laws of Georgia as StupidPC, Inc. 12/08/1998
StupidPC, Inc. name changed to Webcatalyst, Inc. 10/20/2000
(See Webcatalyst, Inc.)

WORLD OF SCIENCE INC (NY)
Issue Information - 2,450,000 shares COM offered at $6 per share on 07/08/1997
Merged into Natural Wonders, Inc. 9/11/2000
Each share Common 1¢ par exchanged for $1.15 cash

WORLD OF TECHNOLOGY INC (CO)
Merged into Financial Strategic Portfolios, Inc. 05/12/1988
Each share Common 1¢ par exchanged for (1) share Technology Portfolio Capital Stock 1¢ par
Financial Strategic Portfolios, Inc. name changed to INVESCO Strategic Portfolios Inc. 12/01/1994 which name changed to INVESCO Sector Funds, Inc. 10/29/1998
(See INVESCO Sector Funds, Inc.)

WORLD PATENT DEV CORP (DE)
Charter cancelled and declared inoperative and void for non-payment of taxes 03/01/1978

WORLD PWR BIKE INC (BC)
Recapitalized as Parkside 2000 Resources Corp. 3/13/2000
Each share Common no par exchanged for (1/7) share Common no par
Parkside 2000 Resources Corp. name changed to Amador Gold Corp. 5/16/2003

WORLD PT TERMS INC (CANADA)
Each share old Common no par exchanged for (0.2) share new Common no par 02/14/2000
Merged into World Point Inc. 07/05/2010
Each share new Common no par exchanged for $12.90 cash
Note: Unexchanged certificates were cancelled and became without value 06/29/2016

WORLD PT TERMS LP (DE)
Acquired by World Point Terminals, Inc. 07/10/2017
Each Common Unit exchanged for $17.30 cash

WORLD PUBLISHING CO. (OH)
Common no par changed to $1 par and (2) additional shares issued 08/29/1956
Common $1 par split (3) for (1) by issuance of (2) additional shares 11/04/1959
Acquired by Times Mirror Co. (Old) 12/12/1963
Each share Common $1 par exchanged for (0.525) share Common no par
Times Mirror Co. (Old) merged into Times Mirror Co. (New) 02/01/1995 which merged into Tribune Co. 06/12/2000
(See Tribune Co.)

WORLD RACING GROUP INC (DE)
Each (101) shares old Common $0.0001 par exchanged for (1) share new Common $0.0001 par 09/11/2009
Note: Holders of (100) or fewer pre-split shares received $0.10 cash per share
Each share new Common $0.0001 par exchanged again for (0.00002) share new Common $0.0001 par 05/12/2011
Note: Holders of (49,999) or fewer pre-split shares received $0.10 cash per share
Each share new Common $0.0001 par exchanged again for (0.1) share new Common $0.0001 par 01/30/2013

WORLD RES INTL INC (DE)
Reorganized as Vision Financial Services Corp. 8/14/89
Each share Common 1¢ par exchanged for (1) share Common 1¢ par

(See Vision Financial Services Corp.)

WORLD SALES & MERCHANDISING INC (ON)
Name changed from World Sports Merchandising Inc. to World Sales & Merchandising Inc. 02/22/2000
Cease trade order effective 02/08/2002

WORLD SATELLITE NETWORK INC (MN)
Each share old Common no par exchanged for (0.1) share new Common no par 8/23/87
Merged into WSN Acquisition Corp. 2/8/99
Each share new Common no par exchanged for $3.50 cash
Note: Holders may also be entitled to a contingent payment subject to achievement of certain conditions

WORLD SERVICE & INVESTMENT CORP. (UT)
Involuntarily dissolved for failure to pay taxes 9/30/78

WORLD SVC LIFE INS CO (CO)
Merged into Western Preferred Corp. 2/21/79
Each share Common $1 par exchanged for (2.25) shares Common 20¢ par
(See Western Preferred Corp.)

WORLD SVC LIFE INS CO (TX)
Stock Dividends - 21.95% 6/15/70; 25% 6/15/73
Merged into World Service Life Insurance Co. (CO) 7/31/78
Each share Common $1 par exchanged for (1.5) shares Common $1 par
World Service Life Insurance Co. (CO) merged into Western Preferred Corp. 2/21/79
(See Western Preferred Corp.)

WORLD SHOPPING NETWORK INC (DE)
Each (12) shares old Common $0.001 par exchanged for (1) share new Common $0.001 par 10/06/1999
Reincorporated under the laws of Nevada as WSN Group, Inc. 06/01/2001
WSN Group, Inc. recapitalized as Niteagle Systems, Inc. 04/11/2006 which recapitalized as Alternative Green Technologies Inc. 12/12/2008

WORLD SPORTS LICENSING CORP (DE)
Reorganized as Choice Sports Network, Inc. 3/14/2000
Each share Common $0.00001 par exchanged for (1.5) shares Common $0.00001 par
Choice Sports Network, Inc. name changed to Sports Entertainment & Learning Network Inc. 9/15/2000

WORLD STAFFING II INC (TX)
Name changed to Wattmonitor Inc. 11/4/98
Wattmonitor Inc. name changed to Healthbridge, Inc. 5/28/99 which name changed to Providence Resources, Inc. 10/9/2006

WORLD STAR ASIA INC (NV)
Each share old Common $0.001 par exchanged for (3) shares new Common $0.001 par 11/11/1998
Name changed to Comgen Corp. 11/16/1998
Comgen Corp. name changed to Planet 411.com Corp. (NV) 02/11/1999 which reincorporated in Delaware as Planet411.com Inc. 10/07/1999 which name changed to Ivany Mining, Inc. 07/27/2007 which name changed to Ivany Nguyen, Inc. 02/16/2010 which name changed to Myriad Interactive Media, Inc. 07/25/2011

WORLD STEVIA CORP (NV)
Common $0.001 par split (5) for (1) by issuance of (4) additional shares payable 08/15/2013 to holders of record 08/15/2013
Name changed to Cannabis Capital Corp. 03/04/2014
Cannabis Capital Corp. name changed to Crown Baus Capital Corp. 07/25/2014

WORLD STRATEGIC YIELD FD (ON)
Each Instalment Receipt plus payment of $10 cash received (1) Trust Unit 11/10/1998
Completely liquidated 08/14/2002
Each Trust Unit received first and final distribution of $13.664 cash
Note: Certificates were not required to be surrendered and are without value

WORLD TEA INC (NV)
Name changed to BroadWebAsia, Inc. 02/29/2008

WORLD TEC INDS INC (BC)
Name changed to Solucorp Industries Inc. (BC) 08/19/1994
Solucorp Industries Inc. (BC) reincorporated in Yukon 04/04/1997

WORLD TECHNOLOGIES & TRADING CO (NV)
Recapitalized as Gaensel Gold Mines Inc. 08/06/1984
Each share Common $0.0001 par exchanged for (0.1) share Common $0.0001 par
Gaensel Gold Mines Inc. name changed to Best Medical Treatment Group Inc. 12/19/1997 which name changed to Jenson International Inc. 06/12/1998
(See Jenson International Inc.)

WORLD TELEVISION INC (DE)
Each share old Common $0.001 par exchanged for (0.1) share new Common $0.001 par 1/19/88
Charter cancelled and declared inoperative and void for non-payment of taxes 3/1/89

WORLD TOURNAMENT INTL INC (UT)
Proclaimed dissolved for failure to pay taxes 6/1/90

WORLD TOY HOUSE, INC. (MN)
Name changed to Telmont Corp. 10/9/68
Telmont Corp. merged into Cosmetex Industries, Inc. (Del.) 12/30/75

WORLD TRADE ENTERPRISES INC (DE)
Recapitalized as International Medical Science, Inc. 11/4/85
Each share Common 1¢ par exchanged for (0.1) share Common 1¢ par
International Medical Science, Inc. recapitalized as International Investment Group, Ltd. 7/26/88 which name changed to Intermedia Net Inc. 6/1/96 which name changed to Fortune Media, Inc. 5/21/99 which name changed to Cyberedge Enterprises, Inc. 11/10/2000 which name changed to Wayne's Famous Phillies Inc. 3/10/2003

WORLD TRADE RECORDS INC (DE)
Name changed to Rainbow Media Corp. 7/3/85
(See Rainbow Media Corp.)

WORLD TROPHY OUTFITTERS INC (NV)
Name changed to Chisen Electric Corp. 04/30/2009
Chisen Electric Corp. recapitalized as Digital Day Agency, Inc. 09/26/2017

WORLD URANIUM CORP. (UT)
Merged into Midwest Consolidated Uranium Corp. on a (0.04) for (1) basis 6/10/55
Midwest Consolidated Uranium Corp. merged into COG Minerals Corp. 5/1/56 which was acquired by Colorado Oil & Gas Corp. for cash 12/31/60

WORLD VIDEO ARTS (AZ)
Charter revoked for failure to file reports or pay fees 9/12/78

WORLD VIDEOPHONE TELECONFERENCING TECHNOLOGIES (BC)
Cease trade order effective 07/13/1990

WORLD VISION HLDG INC. (WY)
Administratively dissolved for failure to pay taxes 06/25/1999

WORLD WASTE TECHNOLOGIES INC (CA)
Merged into Vertex Energy, Inc. 05/04/2009
Each share 8% Conv. Preferred Ser. B $0.001 par exchanged for (11.651) shares Conv. Preferred Ser. A $0.001 par
Each share Common $0.001 par exchanged for (0.1) share Common $0.001 par

WORLD WHSL INC (UT)
Name changed to Omicron Industries, Inc. and Common 1¢ par changed to $0.001 par 01/29/1982
Omicron Industries, Inc. name changed to Supermail International, Inc. 07/20/1987 which name changed to First Automated, Inc. 10/27/2003 which recapitalized as PBHG, Inc. 07/19/2004
(See PBHG, Inc.)

WORLD-WIDE ARTISTS INC. (DE)
No longer in existence having become inoperative and void for non-payment of taxes 04/01/1962

WORLD WIDE BINGO INC (CO)
Proclaimed dissolved for failure to file reports and pay fees 4/3/95

WORLD WIDE CO-GENERATION INC (ON)
Recapitalized as World Wide Inc. 07/17/2007
Each share Common no par exchanged for (0.05) share Common no par

WORLD WIDE COIN INVTS LTD (DE)
Charter cancelled and declared inoperative and void for non-payment of taxes 3/1/84

WORLD WIDE CONNECT INC (NV)
Reincorporated under the laws of Utah as International Card Services, Inc. 10/26/2007
Each share old Common no par exchanged for (1) share new Common no par 04/05/2004

WORLD WIDE ENERGY CORP (NV)
Recapitalized as Czech Republic Resource Corp. 10/30/2007
Each share Common $0.001 par exchanged for (0.00000013) share Common $0.001 par
Czech Republic Resource Corp. name changed to Global Senior Enterprises Inc. 04/26/2013 which recapitalized as World Financial Holding Group 05/01/2018

WORLD WIDE HELICOPTERS LTD (BAHAMAS)
Name changed to World Wide Ltd. 12/7/81
(See World Wide Ltd.)

WORLD WIDE INDS INC (MN)
In process of liquidation
Each share Common 10¢ par exchanged for initial distribution of $0.35 cash 4/15/79
Note: Details on subsequent distributions, if any, are not available

WORLD WIDE INTERACTIVE DISCS INC (ON)
Name changed to World Wide Co-Generation Inc. 02/13/2004
World Wide Co-Generation Inc. recapitalized as World Wide Inc. 07/17/2007

WORLD WIDE LTD (BAHAMAS)
Liquidation completed
Each ADR for Ordinary $2.86 par received initial distribution of $31 cash payable 01/28/2005 to holders of record 01/20/2005
Each ADR for Ordinary $2.86 par received second distribution of $3.50 cash payable 01/19/2007 to holders of record 12/29/2006 Ex date - 01/22/2007
Each ADR for Ordinary $2.86 par received third and final distribution of $5.16 cash payable 11/02/2007 to holders of record 10/04/2007
Note: Certificates were not required to be surrendered and are without value

WORLD WIDE MEATS, INC. (IA)
Liquidation completed
Each share Common $1 par exchanged for initial distribution of $0.50 cash 1/27/75
Each share Common $1 par received second distribution of $0.10 cash 6/26/75
Each share Common $1 par received third distribution of $0.20 cash 11/15/75
Each share Common $1 par received fourth distribution of $0.07 cash in June, 1976
Each share Common $1 par received fifth and final distribution of $0.09 cash in August, 1982

WORLD WIDE MINERALS LTD (BC)
Reincorporated under the laws of Ontario 02/22/1995

WORLD WIDE MOTION PICTURES CORP (MI)
Each share old Common $0.001 par exchanged for (0.2) share new Common $0.001 par 12/18/2001
Name changed to Buckeye Ventures, Inc. (MI) 04/27/2006
Buckeye Ventures, Inc. (MI) reincorporated in Nevada 10/29/2007 which name changed to Energy King, Inc. 02/26/2008 which name changed to Godfather Media, Inc. 10/18/2011 which name changed to Embark Holdings, Inc. 08/20/2012 which name changed to Muscle Warfare International, Inc. 06/28/2013 which name changed to Cannabusiness Group, Inc. 02/18/2019

WORLD WIDE NET INC (NV)
Name changed to Unlimited Coatings Corp. 05/14/2001
Unlimited Coatings Corp. name changed to International American Technologies, Inc. 03/22/2005 which name changed to Hammonds Industries, Inc. 05/14/2007 which recapitalized as Delta Seaboard International, Inc. 06/10/2010 which recapitalized as American International Holdings Corp. 08/13/2012

WORLD WIDE OIL & GAS INC (BC)
Delisted from Vancouver Stock Exchange 3/2/98

WORLD WIDE OUTFITTERS, INC. (CA)
Charter suspended for failure to file reports and pay fees 01/02/1990

WORLD WIDE PETROLEUM CORP. (MN)
Name changed to World Wide Industries, Inc. 10/8/68
(See World Wide Industries, Inc.)

WORLD WIDE RLTY & INVESTING CORP (DE)
Charter cancelled and declared inoperative and void for non-payment of taxes 3/1/76

WORLD WIDE RELICS INC (NV)
Name changed to China PharmaHub Corp. 09/07/2010

WORLD WIDE STONE CORP (DE)
Reincorporated under the laws of Nevada 11/30/89

WORLD-WIDE TECHNOLOGY INC (DE)
Name changed to Computone Corp. 05/03/1991
Computone Corp. name changed to Symbiat, Inc. 07/01/2002
(See Symbiat, Inc.)

WORLD WIDE VENTURE CAP CORP (CO)
Name changed to AOE Ventures, Inc. 12/16/88
(See AOE Ventures, Inc.)

WORLD WIDE VIDEO INC (CO)
Recapitalized as Reva, Inc. (CO) 05/05/2003
Each share Common $0.0001 par exchanged for (0.01) share Common 1¢ par
Reva, Inc. (CO) reincorporated in Delaware as Blue Wireless & Data, Inc. 11/15/2004 which name changed to Big Star Media Group, Inc. 10/02/2009 which name changed to Pharmstar Pharmaceuticals, Inc. (DE) 04/08/2011 which reorganized in Nevada as Nexus Energy Services, Inc. 10/15/2013 which name changed to Illegal Restaurant Group, Inc. 06/02/2015 which name changed back to Nexus Energy Services, Inc. 08/13/2015

WORLD WIDE WARRANTY INC (AB)
Name changed to W3 Solutions, Inc. 08/30/2004
W3 Solutions, Inc. name changed to WWI Resources Ltd. (AB) 11/09/2006 which reincorporated in British Columbia 07/11/2007 which name changed to Petromanas Energy Inc. 02/25/2010 which recapitalized as PMI Resources Ltd. 06/14/2016 which name changed to PentaNova Energy Corp. 06/05/2017 which recapitalized as CruzSur Energy Corp. 09/04/2018

WORLD WIDE WEALTH AGENCIES, INC. (DE)
Name changed to National Leisure Corp. 08/14/1979
(See National Leisure Corp.)

WORLD WIDE WEB INC (NV)
Each share old Common $0.001 par exchanged for (0.5) share new Common $0.001 par 3/10/2004
Name changed to Navitone Technologies, Inc. 3/7/2005

WORLD WIDE WIRELESS COMMUNICATIONS INC (NV)
Name changed to Universal Communication Systems, Inc. 04/02/2002
Universal Communication Systems, Inc. recapitalized as Air Water International Corp. 10/02/2007
(See Air Water International Corp.)

WORLD WISE TECHNOLOGIES INC (NV)
Name changed 09/14/1994
Reincorporated 11/01/2004
Name changed from World Wise Resources Inc. to World Wise Technologies Inc. 09/14/1994
Place of incorporation changed from (BC) to (NV) 11/01/2004
Recapitalized as W2 Energy, Inc. 12/15/2004
Each share Common no par exchanged for (0.1) share Common no par
W2 Energy, Inc. recapitalized as Converde Energy USA, Inc. (NV) 01/20/2015 which reorganized in Colorado as American Energy Partners, Inc. 08/17/2017

WORLD WRESTLING FEDN ENTMT INC (DE)
Issue Information - 10,000,000 shares CL A offered at $17 per share on 10/18/1999
Name changed to World Wrestling Entertainment, Inc. 6/13/2002

WORLDBID CORP (NV)
Old Common $0.001 par split (2) for (1) by issuance of (1) additional share payable 6/26/2000 to holders of record 6/26/2000 Ex date - 6/27/2000
Each share old Common $0.001 par exchanged for (0.04) share new Common $0.001 par 9/19/2005
Name changed to Royalite Petroleum Co., Inc. 3/5/2007

WORLDCALL CORP (DE)
SEC revoked common stock registration 07/30/2009

WORLDCAST INTERACTIVE INC (FL)
Reorganized under the laws of Delaware as Andorra Capital Corp. 05/28/2008
Each share Common $0.001 par exchanged for (0.1) share Common $0.001 par
Andorra Capital Corp. recapitalized as Savenergy Holdings, Inc. 08/04/2010

WORLDCOM INC (DE)
Name changed to Charter West Corp. 06/28/1982
Charter West Corp. name changed to Sellinger Pharmaceuticals Inc. 06/22/1983 which name changed to Promedica Inc. 06/28/1988 which name changed to Zhou Lin International Inc. 11/28/1994 which name changed to Renu-U-International Inc. 12/24/1996 which name changed to Colormax Technologies, Inc. 09/07/1999
(See Colormax Technologies, Inc.)

WORLDCOM INC (GA)
6.5% Conv. Sr. Preferred Ser. 2 called for redemption 06/05/1996
Common 1¢ par split (2) for (1) by issuance of (1) additional share payable 07/03/1996 to holders of record 06/06/1996
Depositary Dividend Enhanced Conv. Ser. A $1 par called for redemption 05/31/1998
Under plan of merger name changed to MCI WorldCom, Inc. 09/14/1998 which name changed to WorldCom Inc. (New) 05/01/2000
Conv. Preferred Ser. B 1¢ par called for redemption at $1 plus $0.465 accrued dividends on 10/01/2001
(See WorldCom Inc. (New))

WORLDCOM INC NEW (GA)
Common 1¢ par reclassified as WorldCom Group Common 1¢ par 06/07/2001
Each share WorldCom Group Common 1¢ par received distribution of (0.04) share MCI Group Common 1¢ par payable 06/15/2001 to holders of record 06/08/2000
Plan of reorganization under Chapter 11 Federal Bankruptcy Code effective 04/20/2004
No stockholders' equity

WORLDCORP INC (DE)
Plan of reorganization under Chapter 11 Federal Bankruptcy Code effective 5/24/2000
No stockholders' equity

WORLDGATE COMMUNICATIONS INC (DE)
SEC revoked common stock registration 07/08/2014

WORLDMARK PRESS, INC. (NY)
Recapitalized as Photosystems Corp. 03/25/1966
Each share Common 10¢ par exchanged for (0.25) share Common 10¢ par
(See Photosystems Corp.)

WORLDMASTERS CORP (DE)
Charter cancelled and declared inoperative and void for non-payment of taxes 6/25/87

WORLDMODAL NETWORK SVCS INC (DE)
Charter cancelled and declared inoperative and void for non-payment of franchise taxes 3/1/2003

WORLDNET RESOURCES GROUP INC (UT)
Recapitalized as Asset Equity Group, Inc. 12/12/2001
Each share Common $0.001 par exchanged for (0.05) share Common $0.001 par
(See Asset Equity Group, Inc.)

WORLDPAGES COM INC (DE)
Merged into TransWestern Publishing Co. LLC 6/28/2001
Each share Common $0.0001 par exchanged for $3 cash

WORLDPLUS VENTURES LTD (BC)
Recapitalized as New Global Ventures Ltd. 06/07/2007
Each share Common no par exchanged for (0.33333333) share Common no par
New Global Ventures Ltd. recapitalized as New Global Ventures International Ltd. 03/14/2008 which name changed to Auro Resources Corp. 10/15/2010 which recapitalized as Tesoro Minerals Corp. 08/26/2013

WORLDPORT COMMUNICATIONS INC (DE)
Merged into W.C.I. Acquisition Corp. 11/9/2004
Each share Common $0.0001 par exchanged for $0.95 cash

WORLDQUEST NETWORKS INC (DE)
Issue Information - 2,750,000 shares COM offered at $13 per share on 02/04/2000
Name changed to WQN, Inc. 11/9/2004

WORLDS COM INC (NJ)
Reincorporated under the laws of Delaware as Worlds Inc. 02/14/2011

WORLDS FARE INC (NV)
Name changed to Futureone Inc. 8/28/98
(See Futureone Inc.)

WORLDS INC (NJ)
Name changed to Worlds.com Inc. (NJ) 12/15/1999
Worlds.com Inc. (NJ) reincorporated in Delaware as Worlds Inc. 02/14/2011

WORLDS OF WONDER INC (CA)
Plan of reorganization under Chapter 11 Federal Bankruptcy proceedings confirmed 05/03/1989
No stockholders' equity

WORLDS ONLINE INC (DE)
Name changed to MariMed Inc. 05/10/2017

WORLDSAGE INC (DE)
Name changed to Career College Holding Co. Inc. 10/29/2008

WORLDSAGE INC (NV)
Reincorporated under the laws of Delaware 04/11/2008
Worldsage, Inc. (DE) name changed to Career College Holding Co. Inc. 10/29/2008

WORLDSOURCE INC (DE)
SEC revoked common stock registration 05/31/2011

WORLDSPACE INC (DE)
Chapter 11 bankruptcy proceedings converted to Chapter 7 on 06/12/2012
Stockholders' equity unlikely

WORLDTALK COMMUNICATIONS CORP (DE)
Merged into Tumbleweed Communications Corp. 01/31/2000
Each share Common 1¢ par exchanged for (0.26) share Common $0.001 par
(See Tumbleweed Communications Corp.)

WORLDTEK CDA LTD (ON)
Cease trade order effective 07/20/2000
Stockholders' equity unlikely

WORLDTEK CORP (WA)
Charter expired 03/31/2008

WORLDTEQ GROUP INTL INC (NV)
Name changed to China Printing, Inc. 4/19/2005
China Printing, Inc. name changed to CYIOS Corp. 11/7/2005

WORLDTEX INC (DE)
Reorganized under Chapter 11 Federal Bankruptcy proceedings 03/06/2002
Each share old Common 1¢ par exchanged for approximately (0.0029) share new Common 1¢ par and (0.0182) Common Stock Purchase Warrant expiring 03/07/2007
Note: Company is now private

WORLDTRADESHOW COM INC (NV)
Common $0.001 par split (20) for (1) by issuance of (19) additional shares payable 03/27/2000 to holders of record 03/24/2000
Name changed to Business.vn, Inc. 06/25/2007
Business.vn, Inc. recapitalized as Omni Global Technologies, Inc. 11/18/2016 which name changed to Blockchain Industries, Inc. 01/10/2018

WORLDTRON INTERNATIONAL, INC. (UT)
Recapitalized as POS Systems Inc. 12/10/85
Each share Common $0.001 par exchanged for (1/3) share Common $0.001 par

WORLDVEST INC (FL)
Name changed to Iron Mining Group, Inc. 11/10/2010
(See Iron Mining Group, Inc.)

WORLDWATER & SOLAR TECHNOLOGIES CORP (DE)
Reincorporated 05/01/2001
Name changed 08/04/2005
Name changed 10/12/2007
State of incorporation changed from (NV) to (DE) 05/01/2001
Name changed from WorldWater Corp. to WorldWater & Power Corp. 08/04/2005
Name changed from WorldWater & Power Corp. to WorldWater & Solar Technologies Corp. 10/12/2007
Name changed to Entech Solar, Inc. 01/12/2009
(See Entech Solar, Inc.)

WORLDWAY CORP (NC)
Merged into Arkansas Best Corp. 08/10/1995
Each share Common 50¢ par exchanged for $11 cash

WORLDWIDE BIOTECH & PHARMACEUTICAL CO (DE)
SEC revoked common stock registration 08/28/2015

WORLDWIDE CANNERY & DISTR INC (NV)
Name changed to Global Diamond Exchange Inc. 9/22/2006

WORLDWIDE COLLECTIBLES INC (NV)
Recapitalized as World Wide Net Inc. 07/30/1999
Each share Common $0.001 par exchanged for (0.2) share Common $0.001 par
World Wide Net Inc. name changed to Unlimited Coatings Corp. 05/14/2001 which name changed to International American Technologies, Inc. 03/22/2005 which name changed to Hammonds Industries, Inc. 05/14/2007 which recapitalized as Delta Seaboard International, Inc. 06/10/2010 which recapitalized as American International Holdings Corp. 08/13/2012

WORLDWIDE COLLECTIONS FD INC (NJ)
Completely liquidated 05/00/1993
Each share Common no par received first and final distribution of approximately (1.73036) share Plaza Investments Ltd. Common
Note: Certificates were not required to be surrendered and are without value

WORLDWIDE COMM INC (NY)
Dissolved by proclamation 09/30/1981

WORLDWIDE COMPUTER SERVICES INC. (NY)
Name changed to Worldwide Commerce Inc. 02/24/1972
(See Worldwide Commerce Inc.)

WORLDWIDE COMPUTER SVCS INC (NJ)
Merged into Computer Horizons Corp. 08/04/1992
Each share Common 1¢ par exchanged for (0.172421) share Common 10¢ par
(See Computer Horizons Corp.)

WORLDWIDE DATA CORP (FL)
Reincorporated 06/06/1974
State of incorporation changed from (NY) to (FL) and Common 10¢ par changed to 1¢ par 06/06/1974
Name changed to Engel Industries Corp. 08/26/1974
(See Engel Industries Corp.)

WORLDWIDE DATA INC (DE)
Each share old Common $0.0001 par exchanged for (0.1) share new Common $0.0001 par 02/12/1998
Charter cancelled and declared inoperative and void for non-payment of taxes 03/01/1998

WORLDWIDE DENTAL DISTR CORP (FL)
Name changed to Full Power Group, Inc. 9/17/98

WORLDWIDE DLRVEST FD INC (MD)
Reorganized as Merrill Lynch Emerging Markets Debt Fund Inc. 11/06/2000
Each share Common 1¢ par exchanged for (0.981415) share Class A Common 10¢ par
Merrill Lynch Emerging Markets Debt Fund Inc. merged into Merrill Lynch World Income Fund, Inc. 02/24/2003 which name changed to BlackRock World Income Fund, Inc. 09/26/2006

WORLDWIDE ENERGY & MFG USA INC (CO)
Plan of reorganization under Chapter 11 Federal Bankruptcy proceedings effective 06/26/2014
No stockholders' equity

WORLDWIDE ENERGY CORP (DE)
Common 20¢ par split (4) for (3) by issuance of (1/3) additional share 1/26/81
Merged into Triton Energy Corp. (TX) 11/18/86
Each share $1.80 Conv. Preferred Ser. A $1 par exchanged for (0.45) share Common Capital Stock $1 par
Each share Common 20¢ par exchanged for (0.1) share Common Capital Stock $1 par
Triton Energy Corp. (TX) reincorporated in Delaware 5/12/95

WORLDWIDE ENERGY INC (OK)
Name changed to Worldwide E Commerce Inc. 12/16/99

WORLDWIDE ENERGY LTD (AB)
Reorganized under the laws of Delaware as Weco Development Corp. 07/17/1972
Each share Common no par exchanged for (1) share Common 20¢ par
Weco Development Corp. name changed to Worldwide Energy Corp. 06/14/1977 which merged into Triton Energy Corp. (TX) 11/18/1986 which reincorporated in Delaware 05/12/1995 which merged into Triton Energy Ltd. 03/25/1996
(See Triton Energy Ltd.)

WORLDWIDE ENTMT & SPORTS CORP (DE)
Recapitalized as Magnum Sports & Entertainment Inc. 10/19/2000
Each share Common no par exchanged for (0.2) share Common no par

WORLDWIDE ENTMT INC (ID)
Reorganized under the laws of Nevada as EJH Entertainment, Inc. 11/12/1997
Each share Common $0.0001 par exchanged for (0.02) share Common $0.001 par
EJH Entertainment, Inc. name changed to Findex.com, Inc. 05/10/1999

WORLDWIDE EQUIP CORP (FL)
Each share old Common $0.001 par exchanged for (0.02) share new Common $0.001 par 11/19/2000
Name changed to OnCure Technologies Corp. (FL) 3/19/2001
OnCure Technologies Corp. (FL) reincorporated in Delaware as Oncure Medical Corp. 4/21/2003
(See Oncure Medical Corp.)

WORLDWIDE FAMILY RESTAURANTS INC (NY)
Recapitalized as Worldwide Ventures Corp. 10/3/80
Each share Common 1¢ par exchanged for (0.05) share Common 1¢ par
(See Worldwide Ventures Corp.)

WORLDWIDE FILM FDG INC (FL)
SEC revoked common stock registration 10/15/2009
Stockholders' equity unlikely

WORLDWIDE FINL HLDGS INC (NV)
Each share old Common no par exchanged for (0.5) share new Common no par 01/05/2000
Recapitalized as Integrated Software Development Inc. 03/31/2003
Each (15) shares new Common no par exchanged for (1) share Common no par
Integrated Software Development Inc. name changed to BSK & Tech, Inc. 05/29/2008

WORLDWIDE FOOD SVCS INC (UT)
Each share old Common $0.001 par exchanged for (0.01333333) share new Common $0.001 par 03/24/2010
Name changed to Global Holdings, Inc. 10/29/2013
Global Holdings, Inc. name changed to Element Global, Inc. 08/06/2015

WORLDWIDE GINSENG CORP (CANADA)
Dissolved 6/10/2004
Details not available

WORLDWIDE GOLF RES INC (NV)
Charter revoked for failure to file reports and pay fees 04/30/2010

WORLDWIDE INDOOR KARTING INC (NV)
Name changed to Vault Financial Services Inc. 10/08/2003
Vault Financial Services Inc. name changed to Prime Restaurants, Inc. 04/18/2007 which name changed to BIH Corp. 03/19/2008
(See BIH Corp.)

WORLDWIDE INTERNET INC (NV)
Name changed to Worldwide Diversified Holdings, Inc. 01/05/2014

WORLDWIDE INTERNET MARKETING INC (CO)
Proclaimed dissolved for failure to file reports and pay fees 07/01/2003

WORLDWIDE LEISURE CORP (MN)
Name changed to Wellness Universe Corp. 06/04/1999
(See Wellness Universe Corp.)

WORLDWIDE MFG USA INC (CO)
Each share old Common no par exchanged for (0.06666666) share new Common no par 04/21/2006
Name changed to Worldwide Energy & Manufacturing USA, Inc. 02/25/2008
(See Worldwide Energy & Manufacturing USA, Inc.)

WORLDWIDE MED CORP (DE)
SEC revoked common stock registration 01/18/2008
Stockholders' equity unlikely

WORLDWIDE MOBILE MARKETING CORP (FL)
Name changed to Worldwide Media Technologies Inc. 07/03/2007

WORLDWIDE MONITORING CORP (DE)
Voluntarily dissolved 01/22/1996
Details not available

WORLDWIDE PETROMOLY INC (CO)
Reorganized under the laws of Nevada as Small Town Radio, Inc. 5/29/2002
Each (18) shares Common no par exchanged for (1) share Common no par
Small Town Radio, Inc. recapitalized as Tombstone Western Resources, Inc. 5/12/2006 which name changed to Dutch Gold Resources, Inc. 12/12/2006

WORLDWIDE PROMOTIONAL MGMT INC (BC)
Name changed to Black Smoker Ventures Inc. 10/19/2011
Black Smoker Ventures Inc. recapitalized as Jager Resources Inc. 11/28/2012 which recapitalized as Sora Capital Corp. 02/20/2014 which name changed to ProSmart Enterprises Inc. 07/12/2017

WORLDWIDE RESCUE SYS LTD (UT)
Involuntarily dissolved for failure to file reports and pay fees 12/31/1986

WORLDWIDE RESTAURANT CONCEPTS INC (DE)
Merged into Pacific Equity Partners PTY Ltd. 9/22/2005
Each share Common 1¢ par exchanged for $6.92 cash

WORLDWIDE TECHNOLOGIES INC (BC)
Delisted from Vancouver Stock Exchange 06/04/1999

WORLDWIDE VALUE FD INC (MD)
Reorganized under the laws of Massachusetts as Bartlett Capital Trust 07/18/1997
Each share Common $0.001 par exchanged for (1) share Europe Fund Class A $0.001 par
(See Bartlett Capital Trust)

WORLDWIDE VENTURES CORP (NY)
Each share Common 1¢ par exchanged for (0.05) share old Common $0.0001 par 8/22/81
Each share old Common $0.0001 par exchanged for (0.1) share new Common $0.0001 par 9/10/84
Dissolved by proclamation 3/25/92

WORLDWIDE WEB NETWORX CORP (DE)
SEC revoked common stock registration 10/15/2009
Stockholders' equity unlikely

WORLDWIDE WIRELESS NETWORKS INC (NV)
Each share old Common $0.001 par exchanged for (4) shares new Common $0.001 par 3/31/99
Reorganized as eChex Worldwide Corp. 3/4/2004
Each share new Common $0.001 par exchanged for (0.0002) share Common $0.001 par
eChex Worldwide Corp. name changed to BBMF Corp. 4/9/2004

WORLDWIDE XCEED GROUP INC (DE)
Each share old Common 1¢ par exchanged for (0.1) share new Common 1¢ par 3/21/2001
Plan of reorganization under Chapter 11 Federal Bankruptcy Code effective 6/3/2002
No stockholders' equity

WORLDWISE TRAVEL INC (NV)
Name changed to North American Building Inc. 4/23/2002

WORONOCO BANCORP INC (DE)
Issue Information - 3,570,000 shares COM minimum; 4,830,000 shares maximum offered at $10 per share on 01/13/1999
Merged into Berkshire Hills Bancorp, Inc. 6/1/2005
Each share Common $1 par exchanged for (0.5624619) share Common 1¢ par and $15.75137156 cash

WORTH CHEM PRODS CO (TX)
Common $1 par changed to 25¢ par 7/9/64
Name changed to Worth Hydrochem Corp. 7/12/68
Worth Hydrochem Corp. recapitalized as United Worth Hydrochem Corp. 9/1/71
(See United Worth Hydrochem Corp.)

WORTH CORP (DE)
Reincorporated 7/31/92
State of incorporation changed from (NV) to (DE) 7/31/92
Name changed to Krauses Furniture Inc. 12/8/94
(See Krauses Furniture Inc.)

WORTH FD INC (DE)
Stock Dividend - 200% 05/15/1962
Name changed to E & E Mutual Fund, Inc. 06/20/1972
E & E Mutual Fund, Inc. merged into Drexel Burnham Fund 12/29/1975

WORTH FINANCIAL CORP. (NY)
Acquired by WFC Equity Corp. for cash in January 1964

WORTH HYDROCHEM CORP (TX)
Recapitalized as United Worth Hydrochem Corp. 9/1/71
Each share Common 25¢ par exchanged for (0.25) share Preferred 25¢ par or Common 25¢ par or a combination thereof
(See United Worth Hydrochem Corp.)

WORTH MILLS
Liquidation completed in 1945
No Common stockholders' equity

WORTHCORP INC (DE)
Charter cancelled and declared inoperative and void for non-payment of taxes 3/1/89

WORTHEN AGENCY, INC. (AR)
Name changed to Cobb, Atkins, Boyd & Eggleston, Inc. 6/14/66
(See Cobb, Atkins, Boyd & Eggleston, Inc.)

WORTHEN BK & TR CO (LITTLE ROCK, AR)
Name changed 09/20/1972
Common $50 par changed to $25 par and (1) additional share issued 06/01/1959
Name changed from Worthen Bank & Trust Co., N.A. (Little Rock, AR) to Worthen Bank & Trust Co. (Little Rock, AR) 09/20/1972
99.34% held by First Arkansas Bankstock Corp. as of 10/06/1970
Public interest eliminated

WORTHEN BKG CORP (AR)
Common $6.25 par changed to $1 par 06/22/1985
Merged into Boatmen's Bancshares, Inc. 02/28/1995
Each share Common $1 par exchanged for (1) share Common $1 par
Boatmen's Bancshares, Inc. merged into NationsBank Corp. (NC) 01/07/1997 which reincorporated in Delaware as BankAmerica Corp. (Old) 09/25/1998 which name changed to Bank of America Corp. 04/28/1999

WORTHING INDS INC (AB)
Recapitalized as United Tex-Sol Mines Inc. 12/12/96
Each share Class A Common no par exchanged for (0.25) share Common no par
United Tex-Sol Mines Inc. acquired by St. Andrew Goldfields Ltd. 6/23/2003

WORTHINGTON (GEORGE) CO. (OH)
4% Preferred $25 par called for redemption 03/31/1965
Common $25 par changed to no par 02/27/1962
Company completely liquidated 00/00/1991
Details not available

WORTHINGTON BALL CO. (OH)
Class B no par reclassified as Common no par 8/15/47
Liquidation completed
Each share Common no par exchanged for initial distribution of $70 cash 3/21/61
Each share Common no par received second and final distribution of $2.90 cash 9/21/61

WORTHINGTON BIOCHEMICAL CORP (DE)
Merged into Millipore Corp. 12/17/1975
Each share Common 10¢ par exchanged for (1/3) share Common 16-2/3¢ par
(See Millipore Corp.)

WORTHINGTON CORP. (DE)
Common no par changed to $10 par 3/22/55
Common $10 par changed to $5 par and (1) additional share issued 8/12/65
Merged into Studebaker-Worthington, Inc. 11/27/67
Each share 4-1/2% Preferred $100 par exchanged for (1) share $5 Conv. Preferred Ser. B no par
Each share Common $5 par exchanged for (1) share $1.40 Conv. Preferred Ser. A no par and (0.4) share Common $1 par

WORTHINGTON FOODS INC (OH)
Common no par split (5) for (4) by issuance of (0.25) additional share 12/26/95
Common no par split (4) for (3) by issuance of (1/3) additional share payable 12/6/96 to holders of record 11/15/96
Common no par split (4) for (3) by issuance of (1/3) additional share payable 12/5/97 to holders of record 11/14/97
Merged into WF Acquisition Inc. 11/29/99
Each share Common no par exchanged for $24 cash

WORTHINGTON INDS INC (DE)
Reincorporated 10/13/98
Common no par split (2) for (1) by issuance of (1) additional share 11/1/74
Common no par split (3) for (2) by issuance of (0.5) additional share 6/25/76
Common no par split (3) for (2) by issuance of (0.5) additional share 11/18/77
Common no par split (3) for (2) by issuance of (0.5) additional share 6/23/78
Common no par split (3) for (2) by issuance of (0.5) additional share 5/18/79
Common no par split (4) for (3) by issuance of (1/3) additional share 3/31/83
Common no par split (3) for (2) by issuance of (0.5) additional share 10/25/85
Common no par split (3) for (2) by issuance of (0.5) additional share 10/31/86
Common no par changed to 1¢ par and (0.5) additional share issued 10/25/91
Common 1¢ par split (3) for (2) by issuance of (0.5) additional share 10/22/93
State of incorporation changed from (OH) to (DE) 10/13/98
Each Debt Exchangeable Convertible Security exchanged for (1) share Rouge Industries, Inc. Class A Common 1¢ par 3/1/2000
(Additional Information in Active)

WORTHINGTON MINES LTD. (ON)
Charter cancelled for failure to pay taxes and file returns 8/9/72

WORTHINGTON PUMP & MACHINERY CORP.
Name changed to Worthington Corp. in 1952
Worthington Corp. merged into Studebaker- Worthington, Inc. 11/27/67

WORTHINGTON RES CORP (BC)
Name changed to Canadian Imperial Ginseng Products Ltd. 10/18/93

WORTHINGTON STL CO (OH)
Reincorporated under the laws of Delaware as Worthington Industries, Inc. 10/26/71
Worthington Industries, Inc. (DE) reincorporated in Ohio 10/13/98

WORTHINGTON VENTURE FD INC (DE)
Reincorporated 06/03/1998
State of incorporation changed from (UT) to (DE) 06/03/1998
Name changed to Admax Technology Inc. 08/16/1998
Admax Technology Inc. name changed to Aamaxan Transport Group, Inc. 08/28/1998

WORUMBO MANUFACTURING CO. (DE)
Merged into Stevens (J.P.) & Co., Inc. upon payment of $15 per share in cash 1/8/59

WORUMBO MANUFACTURING CO. (ME)
7% Preferred $100 par changed to 5% Prior Preference $100 par in 1935
Each share Common $100 par exchanged for (10) shares Common $10 par in 1946
Merged into Worumbo Manufacturing Co. (Del.) share for share 11/1/58
(See Worumbo Manufacturing Co. (Del.))

WOTAN CAP INC (CANADA)
Recapitalized as International Technologies Corp. 01/25/2002
Each share Common no par exchanged for (0.5) share Common no par
(See International Technologies Corp.)

WOTIF COM HLDGS LTD (AUSTRALIA)
ADR agreement terminated 08/22/2016
No ADR's remain outstanding

WOULFE MNG CORP (BC)
Merged into Almonty Industries Inc. 09/14/2015
Each share Common no par exchanged for (0.1029) share Common no par
Note: Unexchanged certificates will be cancelled and become without value 09/14/2021

WOW ENTMT INC (DE)
Name changed to Fortune Diversified Industries, Inc. (DE) 08/16/2001
Fortune Diversified Industries, Inc. (DE) reorganized in Indiana 06/02/2005 which name changed to Fortune Industries, Inc. 04/17/2006
(See Fortune Industries, Inc.)

WOW HLDGS INC (WY)
SEC revoked common stock registration 06/26/2008
Stockholders' equity unlikely

WOWO LTD (CAYMAN ISLANDS)
Name changed to JMU Ltd. 01/06/2017

WOWSTORES COM INC (CO)
Common $0.001 par split (25) for (1) by issuance of (24) additional shares payable 05/19/1999 to holders of record 05/12/1999
Name changed to USR Holdings Co. 02/02/2001
USR Holdings Co. name changed to Technol Fuel Conditioners Inc. (CO) 01/31/2002 which reorganized in Florida as Allied Energy Group, Inc. 08/18/2006 which name changed to Allied Energy, Inc. 04/22/2010

WOWTOWN COM INC (DE)
Recapitalized as Phoenix Star Ventures, Inc. 04/12/2001
Each share Common $0.0001 par exchanged for (0.2) share Common $0.0001 par
Phoenix Star Ventures, Inc. name changed to WPCS International Inc. 05/29/2002 which recapitalized as DropCar, Inc. 01/31/2018

WP GLIMCHER INC (IN)
8.125% Preferred Ser. G $0.0001 par called for redemption at $25 plus $0.5868 accrued dividends on 04/15/2015
Name changed to Washington Prime Group Inc. (New) 08/31/2016

WPCS INTL INC (DE)
Each share old Common $0.0001 par exchanged for (0.08333333) share new Common $0.0001 par 01/10/2005
Each share new Common $0.0001 par exchanged again for (0.14285714) share new Common $0.0001 par 05/28/2013
Each share new Common $0.0001 par exchanged again for (0.04545454) share new Common $0.0001 par 04/20/2015
Recapitalized as DropCar, Inc. 01/31/2018
Each share new Common $0.0001 par exchanged for (0.25) share Common $0.0001 par

WPFH BROADCASTING CO. (DE)
Liquidation completed 10/6/58

WPG GROWTH & INCOME FD (MA)
Reincorporated 04/29/1988
Name changed 12/29/1989
State of incorporation changed from (DE) to (MA) 04/29/1988
Name changed from WPG Fund, Inc. to WPG Growth & Income Fund 12/29/1989
Name changed to WPG Large Cap Growth Fund 10/18/2000
(See WPG Large Cap Growth Fund)

WPG LARGE CAP GROWTH FD (MA)
Merged into RBB Fund, Inc. 04/29/2005
Details not available

WPG TUDOR FD (DE)
Merged into RBB Fund, Inc. 04/29/2005
Details not available

WPI GOLD LTD (AB)
Reincorporated under the laws of British Columbia as Salmon River Resources Ltd. 07/13/2005
(See Salmon River Resources Ltd.)

WPI GROUP INC (NH)
Name changed to Nexiq Technologies Inc. 11/13/2000
(See Nexiq Technologies Inc.)

WPL HLDGS INC (WI)
Common 1¢ par split (2) for (1) by issuance of (1) additional share 9/23/88
Under plan of merger name changed to Interstate Energy Corp. 4/21/98
Interstate Energy Corp. name changed to Alliant Energy Corp. 5/19/99

WPN RES LTD (YT)
Name changed to Grove Energy Ltd. (YT) 06/01/2004
Grove Energy Ltd. (YT) reincorporated in British Columbia 06/02/2005 which was acquired by Stratic Energy Corp. 04/24/2007
(See Stratic Energy Corp.)

WPNB CORP (PA)
Name changed to Equimark Corp. (PA) 05/10/1971
Equimark Corp. (PA) reorganized in Delaware 03/24/1988 which merged into Integra Financial Corp. 01/15/1993 which merged into National City Corp. 05/03/1996 which was acquired by PNC Financial Services Group, Inc. 12/31/2008

WPP GROUP PLC (UNITED KINGDOM)
Each old ADR for Ordinary 10p par exchanged for (0.2) new Sponsored ADR for Ordinary 10p par 11/13/1995
New Sponsored ADR's for Ordinary 10p par split (2) for (1) by issuance of (1) additional ADR payable 11/18/1999 to holders of record 11/15/1999
Each new Sponsored ADR for Ordinary 10p par exchanged again for (1) new Sponsored ADR for Ordinary 10p par 10/25/2005
Reorganized under the laws of Jersey as WPP PLC (Old) 11/20/2008
Each Sponsored ADR for Ordinary 10p par exchanged for (1) Sponsored ADR for Ordinary 10p par
WPP PLC (Old) reorganized as WPP PLC (New) 01/02/2013

WPP PLC OLD (JERSEY)
Under plan of reorganization each ADR for Ordinary automatically became (1) WPP PLC (New) ADR for Ordinary 01/02/2013

WPS RES CORP (WI)
Under plan of merger name changed to Integrys Energy Group, Inc. 02/21/2007
Integrys Energy Group, Inc. merged into WEC Energy Group, Inc. 06/30/2015

WPSR CAP TR I (DE)
7% Trust Preferred Securities called for redemption at $25 plus $0.038889 accrued dividend on 1/8/2004

WPT ENTERPRISES INC (DE)
Name changed to ante4, Inc. 11/04/2009
ante4, Inc. name changed to Voyager Oil & Gas, Inc. (DE) 05/25/2010 which reincorporated in Montana 06/03/2011 which name changed to Emerald Oil, Inc. (MT) 09/04/2012 which reincorporated in Delaware 06/11/2014
(See Emerald Oil, Inc.)

WPVC INC (MB)
Recapitalized as Huntingdon Real Estate Investment Trust (MB) 02/25/2005
Each share Common no par exchanged for (0.2) Trust Unit Huntingdon Real Estate Investment Trust (MB) reorganized in British Columbia as Huntingdon Capital Corp. 01/05/2012
(See Huntingdon Capital Corp.)

WPX ENERGY INC (DE)
Each share 6.25% Mandatory Conv. Preferred Ser. A 1¢ par automatically became (4.1254) shares Common 1¢ par 07/30/2018
(Additional Information in Active)

WR CAP GROUP INC (DE)
Recapitalized as Future Information Systems Inc. 06/28/1994
Each share Common $0.0001 par exchanged for (0.02) share Common $0.0001 par
Future Information Systems Inc. name changed to Globalnet Systems Ltd. 04/18/1996

WRANGLER WEST CAP CORP (AB)
Recapitalized as Wrangler West Energy Corp. 01/20/2003
Each share Common no par exchanged for (0.14285714) share Common no par
(See Wrangler West Energy Corp.)

WRANGLER WEST ENERGY CORP (AB)
Acquired by Trident Exploration Corp. 03/14/2014
Each share Common no par exchanged for $0.2552 cash
Note: Unexchanged certificates were cancelled and became without value 03/14/2017

WRAPMAIL INC (FL)
Each share old Common no par exchanged for (0.1) share new Common no par 06/04/2013
Name changed to Canbiola, Inc. 05/15/2017

WRAPSTERS INC (CO)
Name changed to Uptown Restaurant Group, Inc. 1/3/2000
Uptown Restaurant Group, Inc. name changed to FransAction, Inc. 11/24/2003 which name changed to H3 Enterprises, Inc. 5/13/2005

WRAPTURE LTD (AB)
Name changed to Tallagium Corp. 03/01/2002
(See Tallagium Corp.)

WRATHER CORP (DE)
Reincorporated 12/1/83
Capital Stock no par reclassified as Common no par 4/28/69
State of incorporation changed from (CA) to (DE) 12/1/83
Common no par split (3) for (1) by issuance of (2) additional shares 6/8/84
Merged into Wrather Acquisition Corp. 1/21/88
Each share Common no par exchanged for $21 cash

WREAD, INC. (CA)
Liquidation completed
Each share Capital Stock $1 par exchanged for initial distribution of $2 cash 09/21/1965
Each share Capital Stock $1 par received second distribution of $0.80 cash 10/25/1966
Each share Capital Stock $1 par received third and final distribution of $0.415 cash 04/10/1967

WREN AIRCRAFT CORP (TX)
Adjudicated bankrupt 10/15/1969
No stockholders' equity

WREN INC (NV)
Name changed to NextFit, Inc. 06/18/2009
(See NextFit, Inc.)

WREN RES LTD (BC)
Reincorporated under the laws of Canada as Control Science Corp. 10/21/87
Control Science Corp. (Canada) reincorporated under the laws of Yukon as Steppe Gold International Inc. 8/29/96 which name changed to Steppe Gold Resources Ltd. 6/7/96
(See Steppe Gold Resources Ltd.)

WRESTLE-PLEX SPORTS ENTMT GROUP LTD (NV)
Name changed to Cirmaker Technology Corp. 3/21/2003

WRH INDS (CA)
Name changed to Western Waste Industries 11/8/82
Western Waste Industries name changed to USA Waste Services Inc. 5/7/96 which merged into Waste Management, Inc. 7/16/98

WRI LIQUIDATING CO., INC. (DE)
In process of liquidation
Each share Common 1¢ par exchanged for initial distribution of $1.05 cash 2/21/81
Each share Common 1¢ par received second distribution of $0.10 cash 2/18/82
Note: Details on subsequent distributions, if any, are not available

WRIGHT AERONAUTICAL CORP.
Merged into Curtiss-Wright Corp. by payment of $115 a share in 1951

WRIGHT AIR LINES INC (OH)
Chapter 11 bankruptcy proceedings converted to Chapter 7 on 3/12/86
Stockholders' equity unlikely

WRIGHT BROS ENERGY INC (TX)
Plan of reorganization under Chapter 11 Federal Bankruptcy Code effective 7/13/2004
Stockholders' equity unlikely

WRIGHT ENERGY CORP (NY)
Plan of reorganization under Chapter 11 Federal Bankruptcy Code dismissed 1/30/87
No stockholders' equity

WRIGHT EQUIFUND EQUITY TR (MA)
Italian Fund trust terminated 12/31/1995
Details not available
Spanish Fund trust terminated 05/01/1997
Details not available
Merged into Netherlands Fund 12/18/1998
Details not available for Belgian/Luxembourg Fund
Nordic Fund trust terminated 12/18/1998
Details not available
Netherlands Fund trust terminated 12/22/2000
Details not available

WRIGHT EXPRESS CORP (DE)
Issue Information - 40,000,000 shares COM offered at $18 per share on 02/15/2005
Name changed to WEX Inc. 10/29/2012

WRIGHT HARGREAVES MINES LTD (ON)
Each share Capital Stock $1 par exchanged for (2) shares Capital Stock no par 00/00/1927
Capital Stock no par changed to 40¢ par 06/26/1958
Capital Stock 40¢ par changed to no par 12/12/1968
Merged into LAC Minerals Ltd. (New) 07/29/1985
Each share Capital Stock no par exchanged for (0.498) share Common no par
LAC Minerals Ltd. (New) acquired by American Barrick Resources Corp. 10/17/1994 which name changed to Barrick Gold Corp. 01/18/1995

WRIGHT HOMES, INC. (NC)
Adjudicated bankrupt 8/23/66
No stockholders' equity

WRIGHT LABS INC (NY)
Name changed to Wolf Financial Group, Inc. 12/17/1985
(See Wolf Financial Group, Inc.)

WRIGHT LINE, INC. (MA)
Merged into Barry-Wright Corp. 8/31/60
Each share Class B Common $1 par exchanged for (1) share Common $1 par 8/31/60
(See Barry-Wright Corp.)

WRIGHT MACHY INC (NC)
Merged into Rexham Corp. 06/19/1978
Each share Capital Stock $1 par exchanged for $24 cash

WRIGHT MED GROUP INC (DE)
Merged into Wright Medical Group N.V. 10/02/2015
Each share Common 1¢ par exchanged for (1.0309) shares Ordinary EUR 0.03 par

WRIGHT WM E CO (DE)
Common $1 par changed to 50¢ par and (1) additional share issued 07/15/1971
Merged into Newell Co. 04/28/1987
Each share Common 50¢ par exchanged for $14.25 cash
Note: Holders of record 10/23/1985 received an additional $0.875 cash in settlement of certain legal claims

WRIGHTBAR MINES LTD (QC)
Merged into Corporation Lithos 10/26/94
Each share Common $1 par exchanged for (1) share Common no par
Corporation Lithos name changed to Limtech Lithium Metal Technologies Inc. 10/26/94 which recapitalized as Limtech Lithium Industries Inc. 12/16/2002
(See Limtech Lithium Industries Inc.)

WRIGHTSVILLE & TENNILLE RR CO (GA)
Merged into Southern Railway Co. 06/01/1971
Each share Common $25 par exchanged for $3.25 cash

WRIGLEY (WM.), JR., CO. (WV)
Reorganized as Wrigley (Wm.) Jr. Co. (DE) in 1927
(See Wrigley (Wm.) Jr., Co.)

WRIGLEY CDO LTD (CAYMAN ISLANDS)
Accredited Investors Preferred Shares called for redemption at $1,000 on 8/8/2006

WRIGLEY PHARMACEUTICAL CO. (DE)
No longer in existence having become inoperative and void for non-payment of taxes 4/1/41

WRIGLEY PROPERTIES, INC. (OK)
Liquidation completed 8/1/61

WRIGLEY TOOTH PASTE CO. LTD. (CANADA)
Declared dissolved for failure to file annual reports 12/16/80

WRIGLEY WM JR CO (DE)
Capital Stock no par split (2) for (1) by issuance of (1) additional share 04/02/1973
Capital Stock no par reclassified as Common no par and (1) additional share issued 04/02/1980
Common no par split (2) for (1) by issuance of (1) additional share 04/11/1986
Each share Common no par received distribution of (1) share Non-Transferable Conv. Class B Common no par 04/11/1986
Common no par split (2) for (1) by issuance of (1) additional share 04/04/1988
Non-Transferable Conv. Class B Common no par split (2) for (1) by issuance of (1) additional share 04/04/1988
Common no par split (3) for (1) by issuance of (2) additional shares 09/15/1992
Non-Transferable Conv. Class B Common no par split (3) for (1) by issuance of (2) additional shares 09/15/1992
Common no par split (2) for (1) by issuance of (1) additional share payable 02/28/2001 to holders of record 02/06/2001 Ex date - 03/01/2001
Non-Transferable Conv. Class B Common no par split (2) for (1) by issuance of (1) additional share payable 02/28/2001 to holders of record 02/06/2001 Ex date - 03/01/2001
Acquired by Mars, Inc. 10/06/2008
Each share Common no par exchanged for $80 cash
Each share Non-Transferable Conv. Class B no par exchanged for $80 cash

WRIKING FOOD BEVERAGE SYS INC (DE)
Placed in straight Chapter IV Bankruptcy 04/18/1972
Trustee opined there is no stockholders' equity

WRISLEY (ALLEN B.) CO. (IL)
100% acquired by Purex Corp. thru voluntary exchange offer in 1958

WRITER CORP (CO)
Common 10¢ par split (5) for (2) by issuance of (1.5) additional shares 03/31/1981
Stock Dividends - 25% 03/31/1982; 100% 12/31/1982
Merged into Standard Pacific Corp. (New) 08/25/2000
Each share Common 10¢ par exchanged for $3.35 cash

WRITERS GROUP FILM CORP (DE)
Each share old Common $0.00001 par exchanged for (0.001) share new Common $0.00001 par 01/28/2011
Recapitalized as WRIT Media Group, Inc. 02/04/2014
Each share new Common $0.00001 par exchanged for (0.001) share Common $0.00001 par

WROUGHT IRON CO.
Name changed to Lebanon Steel & Iron Co. in 1938 which was completely liquidated in 1948

WROUGHT IRON CO. OF AMERICA
Reorganized as Wrought Iron Co. in 1935 whose name was changed to Lebanon Steel & Iron Co. in 1938

which was completely liquidated in 1948

WRP CORP (MD)
Each share old Common 1¢ par exchanged for (1/3) share new Common 1¢ par 1/26/2004
Name changed to AHPC Holdings, Inc. 5/14/2004
Each share new Common 1¢ par exchanged for (1) share Common 1¢ par

WRT ENERGY CORP (TX)
Plan of reorganization under Chapter 11 Federal Bankruptcy Code effective 07/11/1997
Each share 9% Conv. Preferred 1¢ par exchanged for (0.183936759) Common Stock Purchase Warrant expiring 07/02/2002
Each share old Common 1¢ par exchanged for (0.024138915) Common Stock Purchase Warrant expiring 07/02/2002
Reincorporated under the laws of Delaware as Gulfport Energy Corp. 03/30/1998

WRVA-FM, INC. (VA)
Completely liquidated 12/16/69
(See WRVA Radio, Inc.)

WRVA RADIO, INC. (VA)
Completely liquidated 12/16/69
Each Unit (consisting of (1) share WRVA Radio, Inc. Common and (1) share WRVA-FM, Inc. Common) exchanged for first and final distribution of $21.09 cash

WS ATKINS PLC (ENGLAND & WALES)
ADR agreement terminated 07/28/2017
Each Sponsored ADR for Ordinary exchanged for $27.10648 cash

WSB BANCORP INC (MO)
Merged into Roosevelt Financial Group Inc. 10/20/1995
Each share Common 1¢ par exchanged for $22.75 cash

WSB FINL GROUP INC (WA)
Company's sole asset placed in receivership 05/08/2009
Stockholders' equity unlikely

WSB HLDGS INC (DE)
Merged into Old Line Bancshares, Inc. 05/10/2013
Each share Common $0.0001 par exchanged for $6.0743 cash

WSB HLDG CO (PA)
Merged into ESB Financial Corp. 10/01/2001
Each share Common 10¢ par exchanged for either (1.414) shares Common 1¢ par or $17.10 cash
Note: Option to receive cash expired 11/06/2001
ESB Financial Corp. merged into WesBanco, Inc. 02/10/2015

WSC GROUP INC (NY)
Charter cancelled and proclaimed dissolved for failure to pay taxes 06/23/1993

WSF CORP (DE)
SEC revoked common stock registration 5/8/2002
Stockholders' equity unlikely

WSFS FINL CORP (DE)
10% Conv. Exchangeable Preferred 1¢ par exchanged for (6.47) shares Common 1¢ par 06/27/1994
5% Preferred Ser. A 1¢ par called for redemption at $1,000 plus $1.527777 accrued dividends on 08/26/2013
(Additional Information in Active)

WSG GROUP SYS INC (AB)
Reorganized as GFI Oil & Gas Corp. 03/10/2006
Each share Common no par exchanged for (1) share Common no par
(See GFI Oil & Gas Corp.)

WSI ACQUISITION CORP (DE)
Reorganized 06/18/1998
Reorganized from WSI Acquisitions, Inc. (TX) to WSI Acquisition Corp. (DE) 06/18/1998
Each share Common no par exchanged for (0.025) share Common $0.001 par
Note: No shareholder will receive fewer than (100) shares
Name changed to iParty Corp. 07/02/1998
(See iParty Corp.)

WSI INTERACTIVE CORP (BC)
Recapitalized as iaNett International Systems Ltd. 05/07/2001
Each share Common no par exchanged for (0.1) share Common no par
iaNett International Systems Ltd. name changed to Data Fortress Systems Group Ltd. 09/03/2002
(See Data Fortress Systems Group Ltd.)

WSMP INC (NC)
Name changed to Fresh Foods Inc. 5/7/98
Fresh Foods Inc. name changed to Pierre Foods Inc. 7/27/2000
(See Pierre Foods Inc.)

WSN GROUP INC (NV)
Recapitalized as Niteagle Systems, Inc. 04/11/2006
Each share Common $0.001 par exchanged for (0.01) share Common $0.001 par
Niteagle Systems, Inc. recapitalized as Alternative Green Technologies Inc. 12/12/2008

WSP HLDGS LTD (CAYMAN ISLANDS)
Each old Sponsored ADR for Ordinary exchanged for (0.2) new Sponsored ADR for Ordinary 02/15/2012
Basis changed from (1:2) to (1:10) 02/15/2012
ADR agreement terminated 06/13/2016
Details not available

WSR ENERGY RES INC (DE)
Recapitalized as Biomass Resources Corp. 02/17/2006
Each share Common $0.001 par exchanged for (0.002) share Common $0.001 par
Biomass Resources Corp. recapitalized as Eagle Resource Holdings, Inc. 05/31/2007

WSR GOLD INC (ON)
Recapitalized as White Pine Resources Inc. 12/18/2004
Each share Common no par exchanged for (0.1) share Common no par
White Pine Resources Inc. name changed to SBD Capital Corp. 09/15/2017

WSS RES INC (NV)
Recapitalized as Trendsetter Industries Inc. 03/06/2006
Each share Common $0.001 par exchanged for (0.1) share Common $0.001 par
(See Trendsetter Industries Inc.)

WT HLDGS CORP (DE)
Recapitalized as Asiamart, Inc. 12/04/2006
Each share Common $0.0001 par exchanged for (0.25) share Common $0.0001 par
(See Asiamart, Inc.)

WTAA INTL INC (FL)
Each share old Common $0.001 par exchanged for (0.06666666) share new Common $0.001 par 02/22/2001
Name changed to Gravitas International, Inc. (FL) 12/06/2001
Gravitas International, Inc. (FL) reorganized in Nevada as Formcap Corp. 10/12/2007

WTC FINANCIAL (CA)
Charter suspended for failure to file reports and pay fees 7/15/97

WTC INDS INC (DE)
Each share old Common 1¢ par exchanged for (0.1) share new Common 1¢ par 01/06/1999
Merged into CUNO Inc. 08/02/2004
Each share new Common 1¢ par exchanged for $39.87 cash

WTC INTL N V (NETHERLANDS ANTILLES)
Acquired by Pittston Co. (VA) 7/1/87
Each share Common 1¢ par exchanged for (0.523) share Common $1 par
Pittston Co. (VA) name changed to Brink's Co. 5/5/2003

WTD INDS INC (OR)
Reorganized under Chapter 11 Federal Bankruptcy Code 11/23/92
Each share old Common no par received (0.4) share new Common no par
Note: Certificates were not required to be exchanged and are without value
Name changed to Treesource Industries, Inc. 10/27/98
(See Treesource Industries, Inc.)

WTE RES INC (ON)
Delisted from Alberta Stock Exchange 08/09/1990

W3 GROUP INC (DE)
Reincorporated 05/07/2003
State of incorporation changed from (CO) to (DE) 05/07/2003
Each share Conv. Preferred Ser. B $0.0001 par exchanged for (0.5) share old Common $0.0001 par 04/25/2005
Each share old Common $0.0001 par exchanged for (0.06666666) share new Common $0.0001 par 05/09/2005
Name changed to Aftersoft Group, Inc. 01/19/2006
Aftersoft Group, Inc. name changed to MAM Software Group, Inc. 05/27/2010

W3 SOLUTIONS INC (AB)
Name changed to WWI Resources Ltd. (AB) 11/09/2006
WWI Resources Ltd. (AB) reincorporated in British Columbia 07/11/2007 which name changed to Petromanas Energy Inc. 02/25/2010 which recapitalized as PMI Resources Ltd. 06/14/2016 which name changed to PentaNova Energy Corp. 06/05/2017 which recapitalized as CruzSur Energy Corp. 09/04/2018

WTS CAP CORP (CO)
Name changed to Scott Capital Resources, Inc. 04/21/1987
Scott Capital Resources, Inc. name changed to American Educational Products, Inc. 02/19/1990
(See American Educational Products, Inc.)

WTS III CAP CORP (CO)
Name changed to Bartel Financial Group, Inc. 12/07/1987
Bartel Financial Group, Inc. recapitalized as Desert Springs Acquisition Corp. (CO) 03/01/1996 which reincoporated in Nevada as iDial Networks, Inc. 01/14/2000 which name changed to GlobalNet Corp. 12/19/2003
(See GlobalNet Corp.)

WTS II CAP CORP (CO)
Name changed to Sold Corp. 06/30/1987

W2 ENERGY INC (NV)
Common no par changed to Common $0.001 par 09/15/2006
Each share old Common $0.001 par exchanged for (0.05) share new Common $0.001 par 01/25/2008
Each share new Common $0.001 par exchanged again for (0.01) share new Common $0.001 par 11/21/2011
Recapitalized as Converde Energy USA, Inc. (NV) 01/20/2015
Each share new Common $0.001 par exchanged for (0.002) share Common $0.001 par
Converde Energy USA, Inc. (NV) reorganized in Colorado as American Energy Partners, Inc. 08/17/2017

W270 INC (NV)
Name changed to Saleen Automotive, Inc. 07/05/2013

W2007 GRACE ACQUISITION I INC (TN)
Acquired by W2007 Grace Acquisition II, Inc. 01/15/2016
Each share 8.75% Preferred Ser. B 1¢ par exchanged for $26 cash
Each share 9% Preferred Ser. C 1¢ par exchanged for $26 cash

WUI INC (DE)
Common no par split (2) for (1) by issuance of (1) additional share 09/12/1978
Merged into Xerox Corp. 11/21/1979
Each share Common no par exchanged for (0.64864) share Common $1 par

WULF INTL LTD (CO)
Each share old Common 1¢ par exchanged for (0.1) share new Common 1¢ par 09/29/1991
SEC revoked common stock registration 10/15/2009

WULF OIL CORP (CO)
Name changed to Wulf International, Ltd. 09/30/1991
(See Wulf International, Ltd.)

WULPA PKG SYS INC (NY)
Charter cancelled and proclaimed dissolved for failure to pay taxes 12/15/1972

WUMART STORES INC (CHINA)
ADR agreement terminated 09/01/2016
No ADR's remain outstanding

WUNDIES INDS INC (DE)
Merged into Walfra Partners, L.P. 06/30/1999
Each share $11.25 Preferred $2.40 par exchanged for $2.40 cash
Each share Common 1¢ par exchanged for $8 cash

WUNMOR INC (DE)
Name changed to Whitehorse Oil & Gas Corp., Inc. 12/08/1987
(See Whitehorse Oil & Gas Corp., Inc.)

WURLITZER (RUDOLPH) CO. (OH)
Each share Common $100 par exchanged for (10) shares Common $10 par in 1937
Stock Dividend - 100% 12/20/44
Name changed to Wurlitzer Co. (OH) 6/4/57
Wurlitzer Co. (OH) reincorporated under the laws of Delaware 3/30/68 which name changed to Wurltech Industries, Inc. 2/23/88
(See Wurltech Industries, Inc.)

WURLTECH INDS INC (DE)
Reincorporated 3/29/68
Name changed 2/23/88
Stock Dividend - 33-1/3% 1/21/66
State of incorporation changed from (OH) to (DE) 3/29/68
Common $10 par split (3) for (2) by issuance of (0.5) additional share 3/25/77

WUL-WYM   **FINANCIAL INFORMATION, INC.**

Name changed from Wurlitzer Co. to Wurltech Industries, Inc. 2/23/88
Common $10 par changed to no par 8/8/85
Charter cancelled and declared inoperative and void for non-payment of taxes 3/1/92

WUXI PHARMATECH CAYMAN INC (CAYMAN ISLANDS)
Acquired by New WuXi Life Science Ltd. 12/10/2015
Each Sponsored ADR for Ordinary exchanged for $45.95 cash

WW OIL & GAS INC (NV)
Merged into Paco Oil & Gas Inc. 11/04/2008
Each share Common $0.001 par exchanged for (1) share Common $0.001 par
Note: Unexchanged certificates were cancelled and became without value 01/31/2009
Paco Oil & Gas Inc. recapitalized as Paco Integrated Energy, Inc. 05/04/2009
(See Paco Integrated Energy, Inc.)

WWA GROUP INC (NV)
Recapitalized as Genie Gateway 09/09/2015
Each share Common $0.001 par exchanged for (0.01) share Common $0.001 par

WWB OIL & GAS LTD (AB)
Recapitalized as Cigar Oil & Gas Ltd. 10/22/1997
Each share Common no par exchanged for (0.2) share Common no par
Cigar Oil & Gas Ltd. merged into Pivotal Energy Ltd. 01/10/2003 which merged into Fairborne Energy Ltd. (Old) 07/08/2003
(See Fairborne Energy Ltd. (Old))

WWBROADCAST NET INC (WY)
Reorganized 07/14/1999
Reorganized from under the laws of (BC) to (WY) 07/14/1999
Each share old Common no par exchanged for (0.5) share new Common no par
Each share new Common no par exchanged again for (0.2) share new Common no par 07/05/2002
Name changed to Luna Gold Corp. (WY) 08/12/2003
Luna Gold Corp. (WY) reincorporated in Canada 12/01/2005 which merged into Trek Mining Inc. 03/31/2017 which name changed to Equinox Gold Corp. 12/22/2017

WWI RES LTD (BC)
Reincorporated 07/11/2007
Place of incorporation changed from (AB) to (BC) 07/11/2007
Name changed to Petromanas Energy Inc. 02/25/2010
Petromanas Energy Inc. recapitalized as PMI Resources Ltd. 06/14/2016 which name changed to PentaNova Energy Corp. 06/05/2017 which recapitalized as CruzSur Energy Corp. 09/04/2018

WWS CAP INC (AB)
Name changed to VenPath Investments Inc. 04/01/2003
VenPath Investments Inc. name changed to OPE Holdings Ltd. 11/09/2007 which name changed to SSP Offshore Inc. 05/21/2009
(See SSP Offshore Inc.)

WWV DEV INC (DE)
Name changed to Lumenon Innovative Lightwave Technology, Inc. 07/27/1998
(See Lumenon Innovative Lightwave Technology, Inc.)

WWW EBIZNET COM INC (FL)
Name changed to Biznet Group Inc. 06/01/2000
Biznet Group Inc. recapitalized as ProMed Alliance International, Inc. 02/21/2006 which name changed to Biomedtex, Inc. 10/09/2007
(See Biomedtex, Inc.)

WYANDOT COPPER CO.
Dissolved in 1927

WYANDOTTE CHEMICALS CORP. (MI)
Stock Dividend - 100% 12/10/64
Merged into WYC Corp. 8/3/70
Each share Common $1 par exchanged for $33.50 cash

WYANDOTTE HOTEL INC (KS)
Voluntarily dissolved 7/24/80
No stockholders' equity

WYANDOTTE INDS CORP (ME)
Common $5 par split (3) for (2) by issuance of (0.5) additional share 07/31/1967
Common $5 par changed to $1 par 04/07/1971
Name changed to First Hartford Corp. 03/29/1972

WYANDOTTE SVGS BK (WYANDOTTE, MI)
Each share Common $50 par exchanged for (5) shares Common $10 par and 25% stock dividend paid 00/00/1954
Stock Dividends - 20% 00/00/1957; 11.1% 02/11/1960; 10% 01/31/1962; 10% 01/28/1966; 16-2/3% 02/10/1969; 10% 03/24/1971; 25% 04/15/1974; 10% 04/12/1977; 20% 04/16/1979; 20% 04/26/1984
Reorganized as Omnibank Corp. 07/01/1985
Each share Common $10 par exchanged for (2) shares Common $5 par
(See Omnibank Corp.)

WYANDOTTE WORSTED CO. (ME)
Each share Common $100 par exchanged for (20) shares Common $5 par 00/00/1944
Stock Dividend - 100% 06/03/1946
Name changed to Wyandotte Industries Corp. 03/28/1967
Wyandotte Industries Corp. name changed to First Hartford Corp. 03/29/1972

WYANT CORP (NY)
Common 1¢ par split (4) for (3) by issuance of (1/3) additional share payable 5/21/98 to holders of record 4/28/98
Merged into Perkins Papers Ltd. 11/17/2000
Each share Common 1¢ par exchanged for $4 cash

WYATT & CO LTD (NV)
Charter revoked for failure to file reports and pay fees 06/01/1987

WYATT INDUSTRIES, INC. (TX)
Common $20 par changed to $10 par and (1) additional share issued 8/18/65
Merged into U.S. Industries, Inc. 5/31/68
Each share Common $10 par exchanged for (1.7165) shares Common $1 par
(See U.S. Industries, Inc.)

WYATT JOB P & SONS CO (NC)
6% Preferred called for redemption at $102 plus $1.35 accrued dividends on 12/31/2012

WYATT METAL & BOILER WORKS (TX)
Each share Common $100 par exchanged for (5) shares old Common $20 par in 1938
Each share old Common $20 par exchanged for (2) shares new Common $20 par in 1948
Stock Dividend - 50% 3/14/52
Name changed to Wyatt Industries, Inc. 12/31/59

Wyatt Industries, Inc. merged into U.S. Industries, Inc. 5/31/68
(See U.S. Industries, Inc.)

WYCKOFF CHEM INC (MI)
Merged into Catalytica, Inc. 09/20/1999
Each share Common exchanged for (13.36386344) shares Common $0.001 par
Note: An additional initial distribution of approximately (0.6318999) share Common $0.001 par was paid from escrow 11/20/2000
A second and final distribution of approximately (0.025339) share Common $0.001 par and $1.604496 cash was paid from escrow 12/12/2002
(See Catalytica, Inc.)

WYCKOFF DRAWN STEEL CO.
Name changed to Wyckoff Steel Co. in 1944
Wyckoff Steel Co. name changed to W.S. Liquidating Corp. (Pa.) 12/29/64 which completed liquidation 12/17/65

WYCKOFF STEEL CO. (PA)
Each share Capital Stock no par exchanged for (2) shares Capital Stock $10 par and a 50% stock dividend 00/00/1946
Stock Dividend - 100% 12/10/1953
Name changed to W.S. Liquidating Corp. (PA) 12/29/1964
(See W.S. Liquidating Corp. (PA))

WYCLIFFE RES INC (ON)
Name changed to Renforth Resources Inc. 7/28/2006

WYCO DEVELOPMENT CORP. (DE)
Charter forfeited for failure to maintain a registered agent 12/20/73

WYCO URANIUM INC (UT)
Recapitalized as Creative Financial, Inc. 03/13/1972
Each share Common 1¢ par exchanged for (0.5) share Common 1¢ par
(See Creative Financial, Inc.)

WYCOTAH OIL & URANIUM, INC. (DE)
Each share Common 1¢ par exchanged for (1/3) share Common $1 par 1/18/57
Name changed to Distillers & Vintners Corp. of America and Common $1 par changed to 5¢ par 2/17/68
Distillers & Vintners Corp. of America name changed to U.S. Dynamics, Inc. 7/10/69
(See U.S. Dynamics, Inc.)

WYDMAR DEV CORP (BC)
Struck off register and declared dissolved for failure to file returns 8/20/93

WYETH (DE)
$2 Conv. Preferred $2.50 par called for redemption at $60.08 on 07/15/2009
Acquired by Pfizer Inc. 10/15/2009
Each share Common 33-1/3¢ par exchanged for (0.985) share Common 5¢ par and $33 cash

WYLAIN INC (DE)
Merged into Marley Co. 05/06/1980
Each share Common 25¢ par exchanged for (1) share Preferred Ser. A $30 par
(See Marley Co.)

WYLE ELECTRS (CA)
Name changed 1/26/95
Common no par split (2) for (1) by issuance of (1) additional share 3/14/69
$3.45 Conv. Preference Ser. A no par called for redemption 10/13/78
Common no par split (5) for (4) by issuance of (0.25) additional share 4/27/79
Common no par split (5) for (4) by issuance of (0.25) additional share 4/30/80
Common no par split (5) for (4) by issuance of (0.25) additional share 10/29/87
Name changed from Wyle Laboratories to Wyle Electronics 1/26/95
Merged into Raab Karcher AG 8/20/97
Each share Common no par exchanged for $50 cash

WYLY CORP (DE)
Each share old Common 10¢ par exchanged for (0.25) share new Common 10¢ par 02/24/1978
New Common 10¢ par reclassified as Capital Stock 10¢ par 06/27/1978
Name changed to Uccel Corp. 05/22/1984
Uccel Corp. merged into Computer Associates International, Inc. 08/19/1987 which name changed to CA, Inc. 02/01/2006

WYMAN GORDON CO (MA)
Common no par split (5) for (1) by issuance of (4) additional shares 05/01/1972
Common no par split (2) for (1) by issuance of (1) additional share 04/29/1974
Common no par split (2) for (1) by issuance of (1) additional share 07/12/1976
Common no par split (2) for (1) by issuance of (1) additional share 09/11/1978
Common no par changed to $1 par 04/18/1979
Stock Dividend - 100% 07/15/1981
Merged into Precision Castparts Corp. 01/12/2000
Each share Common $1 par exchanged for $20 cash

WYMAN PK BANCORPORATION INC (DE)
Merged into Bradford Bank (Baltimore, MD) 2/25/2003
Each share Common 1¢ par exchanged for $14.50 cash

WYN DEVS INC (BC)
Reorganized as Canada Gas Corp. 06/10/2008
Each share Common no par exchanged for (0.2) share Common no par and (0.09090909) share Wyn Metals Inc. Common no par
(See each company's listing)

WYN METALS INC (BC)
Recapitalized as Award Ventures Ltd. 07/15/2009
Each share Common no par exchanged for (0.33333333) share Common no par
Award Ventures Ltd. name changed to Auracle Resources Ltd. 05/28/2010 which recapitalized as Four River Ventures Ltd. 06/16/2015 which recapitalized as Canabo Medical Inc. 11/09/2016 which name changed to Aleafia Health Inc. 03/28/2018

WYNDHAM HOTEL CORP (DE)
Merged into Patriot American Hospitality, Inc. (DE) 1/5/98
Each share Common 1¢ par exchanged for (1.372) Paired Certificates
Patriot American Hospitality Inc. merged into Wyndham International, Inc. 6/29/99
(See Wyndham International, Inc.)

WYNDHAM INTL INC (DE)
Stock Dividends - In Conv. Ser. A Preferred to holders of Conv. Ser. A Preferred 1.7895% payable 6/30/2001 to holders of record 6/30/2001; 1.8009% payable 9/30/2001 to holders of record 9/30/2001; 1.8122% payable 12/31/2001 to holders of record

12/31/2001; 1.8233% payable 3/31/2002 to holders of record 3/31/2002 Ex date - 3/28/2002; 1.834% payable 6/30/2002 to holders of record 6/28/2002; 2.345% payable 9/30/2002 to holders of record 9/30/2002 Ex date - 9/26/2002; 2.3125% payable 12/31/2002 to holders of record 12/31/2002 Ex date - 1/9/2003; 2.31468% payable 3/31/2003 to holders of record 3/31/2003 Ex date - 4/1/2003; 2.31748% payable 6/30/2003 to holders of record 6/30/2003 Ex date - 6/26/2003; 2.3873% payable 9/30/2003 to holders of record 9/30/2003 Ex date - 9/26/2003; 2.3093% payable 12/31/2003 to holders of record 12/31/2003; 2.2439% payable 3/31/2004 to holders of record 3/31/2004 Ex date - 3/29/2004; 2.059% payable 6/30/2004 to holders of record 6/30/2004 Ex date - 6/30/2004; 2.3152% payable 9/30/2004 to holders of record 9/30/2004 Ex date - 9/30/2004; 2.32927% payable 12/31/2004 to holders of record 12/31/2004 Ex date - 12/29/2004; 2.6453% payable 3/31/2005 to holders of record 3/31/2005 Ex date - 4/11/2005; 2.32201% payable 6/30/2005 to holders of record 6/30/2005 Ex date - 6/28/2005; In Conv. Ser. B Preferred to holders of Conv. Ser. B Preferred 2.3873% payable 9/30/2003 to holders of record 9/30/2003 Ex date - 9/26/2003; 2.32927% payable 12/31/2004 to holders of record 12/31/2004 Ex date - 12/29/2004; 2.3312% payable 3/31/2005 to holders of record 3/31/2005 Ex date - 3/30/2005; 2.33312% payable 6/30/2005 to holders of record 6/30/2005 Ex date - 6/28/2005
Merged into Wind Hotels Holdings Inc. 8/16/2005
Each share new Conv. Preferred Ser. A 1¢ par exchanged for $72.17 cash
Each share new Conv. Preferred Ser. B exchanged for $72.17 cash
Each share Class A Common 1¢ par exchanged for $1.15 cash

WYNDHAM WORLDWIDE CORP (DE)
Each share Common 1¢ par received distribution of (1) share Wyndham Hotels & Resorts, Inc. Common 1¢ par payable 05/31/2018 to holders of record 05/18/2018 Ex date - 06/01/2018
Name changed to Wyndham Destinations, Inc. 06/01/2018

WYNDON CORP (CO)
Each share Common 10¢ par exchanged for (0.5) share Common 20¢ par 03/14/1974
Liquidation completed
Each share Common 20¢ par exchanged for initial distribution of $1.44 cash 01/06/1981
Each share Common 20¢ par received second and final distribution of $0.291 cash 07/10/1981

WYNDON HOTEL LIQUIDATION TRUST
Trust liquidated in 1944

WYNDSTORM CORP (NV)
Filed a petition under Chapter 7 Federal Bankruptcy Code 10/07/2011
Stockholders' equity unlikely

WYNN INDS INC (CO)
Voluntarily dissolved 04/06/1995
Undistributed funds were deposited with Colorado State Treasurer

WYNN OIL CO (CA)
Common $1 par split (3) for (2) by issuance of (0.5) additional share 06/01/1972
Reorganized under the laws of Delaware as Wynn's International, Inc. 07/31/1973
Each share Common $1 par exchanged for (1) share Common $1 par
(See Wynn's International, Inc.)

WYNN PHARMACEUTICALS, INC. (PA)
Merged into Cooper Laboratories, Inc. 2/29/68
Each share Common $1 par exchanged for (1) share Common 10¢ par
(See Cooper Laboratories, Inc.)

WYNN YELLOWKNIFE GOLD MINES, LTD. (ON)
Charter cancelled for failure to file reports and pay taxes 10/4/54

WYNNS INTL INC (DE)
Merged into Parker-Hannifin Corp. 07/21/2000
Each share Common $1 par exchanged for $23 cash

WYNTEX ML INC (DE)
Name changed to Wintex Mill Inc. 06/18/1999
(See Wintex Mill Inc.)

WYOGA GAS & OIL CORP. (DE)
Capital Stock $1 par changed to 25¢ par in 1937
No longer in existence having become inoperative and void for non-payment of taxes 4/1/44

WYOMING BANCORPORATION (WY)
Stock Dividends - 10% 02/29/1980; 10% 02/27/1981; 10% 02/26/1982
Name changed to First Wyoming Bancorporation 09/01/1982
First Wyoming Bancorporation merged into KeyCorp 12/30/1988 which merged into KeyCorp (New) (OH) 03/01/1994

WYOMING COAL CORP (WY)
Name changed to Wyoming Oil & Minerals Inc. 08/18/1981
Wyoming Oil & Minerals Inc. name changed to Sun Motor International, Inc. 09/02/2005
(See Sun Motor International, Inc.)

WYOMING GAS CO. (ME)
Merged out of existence 09/28/1984
Details not available

WYOMING-GULF SULPHUR CORP. (DE)
Common $1 par changed to 10¢ par in 1952
Charter revoked for non-payment of taxes 10/1/58

WYOMING HUB OIL CO. (WY)
Charter forfeited for failure to pay taxes 7/19/27

WYOMING INDUSTRIAL DEVELOPMENT CORP. (WY)
Merged out of existence 10/01/2009
Details not available

WYOMING MICA & METALS CORP. (WY)
Name changed to Swingers International, Inc. (WY) 07/16/1970
Swingers International, Inc. (WY) reincorporated under the laws of Delaware 08/30/1970
(See Swingers International, Inc. (DE))

WYOMING MINERALS CORP. (WY)
Charter revoked for failure to file reports and pay fees 3/25/63

WYOMING NATL BANCORPORATION (WY)
Acquired by Norwest Corp. 01/28/1991
Each share Common $1 par exchanged for $19 cash

WYOMING NATL BK (CASPER, WY)
97.69% held by Affiliated Bank Corp. of Wyoming as of 12/31/1984
Public interest eliminated

WYOMING NATL BK (WILKES BARRE, PA)
Each share Common $50 par exchanged for (5) shares Common $10 par 00/00/1953
Common $10 par changed to $5 par and (1) additional share issued 12/15/1972
Common $5 par changed to $2.50 par and (1) additional share issued 04/30/1981
Stock Dividend - 10% 06/26/1953
Merged into Merchants Bancorp, Inc. (PA) 06/01/1985
Each share Common $2.50 par exchanged for $74 cash

WYOMING NATL CORP (WY)
Name changed to Affiliated Bank Corp. of Wyoming 12/15/1981
Affiliated Bank Corp. of Wyoming name changed to Wyoming National Bancorp 06/28/1988
(See Wyoming National Bancorp)

WYOMING NUCLEAR CORP (NV)
Each share Common 3¢ par exchanged for (0.1) share Common 30¢ par 8/10/61
Recapitalized as NETEC 5/26/90
Each share Common 30¢ par exchanged for (0.01) share Common 30¢ par

WYOMING OIL & MINERALS INC (WY)
Each share old Common 1¢ par exchanged for (0.01) share new Common 1¢ par 02/18/2000
Each share new Common 1¢ par exchanged for (0.1) share Common $0.001 par 01/20/2004
Each share Common $0.001 par received distribution of (0.25) share New Frontier Energy, Inc. new Common $0.001 par payable 04/23/2004 to holders of record 06/30/2003
Name changed to Sun Motor International, Inc. 09/02/2005
(See Sun Motor International, Inc.)

WYOMING OIL CO. (CO)
Merged into Wyoming Oil Co. (DE) on a (0.1) for (1) basis 6/30/56
(See Wyoming Oil Co. (DE))

WYOMING OIL CO. (DE)
Declared bankrupt in 1962
No stockholders' equity

WYOMING-PEERLESS CO. (CO)
Declared defunct and inoperative for failure to pay taxes and file annual reports 10/22/25

WYOMING RES CORP (NV)
Reincorporated 06/09/1983
State of incorporation changed from (WY) to (NV) 06/09/1983
Recapitalized as USENCO Inc. 04/09/1984
Each share Common $0.001 par exchanged for (0.1) share Common 1¢ par
USENCO Inc. name changed to Arch Petroleum, Inc. (NV) 06/01/1988 which reincorporated in Delaware 12/31/1991 which merged into Pogo Producing Co. 08/14/1998 which merged into Plains Exploration & Production Co. 11/06/2007 which merged into Freeport-McMoRan Copper & Gold Inc. 05/31/2013

WYOMING SHOVEL WORKS, INC.
Merged into Ames Baldwin Wyoming Shovel Co. which name changed to Ames Baldwin Wyoming in 1931 which name changed to Ames (O.) Co. in 1951 which name changed to McDonough Co. 7/1/55
(See McDonough Co.)

WYOMING SOUTHERN OIL CORP. (UT)
Recapitalized as Delcor Inc. 08/04/1969
Each share Common 10¢ par exchanged for (0.2) share Common 10¢ par
(See Delcor Inc.)

WYOMING SOUTHN RES (UT)
Each share Capital Stock 1¢ par exchanged for (0.005) share Capital Stock no par 10/05/1972
Proclaimed dissolved for failure to pay taxes 12/31/1983

WYOMING URANIUM CORP. (UT)
Merged into Green Mountain Uranium Corp. share for share 11/15/57
(See Green Mountain Uranium Corp.)

WYOMING VALLEY VETERANS BUILDING, INC. (PA)
Charter withdrawn 09/24/1984

WYOMISSING CORP (PA)
Merged into Alcosub, Inc. 10/26/1976
Each share Common $3 par exchanged for $8.625 cash

WYOTT CORP. (WY)
Merged into AMF Inc. 8/18/77
Each share Capital Stock no par exchanged for (0.0914136) share Common $1.75 par
(See AMF Inc.)

WYSAK PETE INC (DE)
Name changed to Wild Brush Energy, Inc. 4/11/2006

WYSE TECHNOLOGY (DE)
Reincorporated 08/26/1988
State of incorporation changed from (CA) to (DE) 08/26/1988
Merged into Channel International Corp. 02/21/1990
Each share Common no par exchanged for $10 cash

WYSONG & MILES CO (NC)
Stock Dividend - 200% 08/15/1969
Plan of reorganization under Chapter 11 Federal Bankruptcy proceedings effective 12/20/2011
Stockholders' retained their interests in private company

WYTEX CORP (DE)
Each share Common $5 par received distribution of (1) share Harris Corp. (TX) Common no par 03/08/1974
Preference $25 par conversion privilege expired 05/01/1976
Preference $25 par called for redemption 12/03/1980
Liquidation completed
Each share Common $5 par received initial distribution of (0.8) Conwest Partnership Part. Unit of Conwest Associates Limited Partnership 07/20/1982
Each share Common $5 par received second distribution of (1) share Conroy, Inc. Common $1 par 02/05/1983
Note: Details on subsequent distributions, if any, are not available

WYTEX OIL CORP. (DE)
Stock Dividend - 100% 6/1/56
Under plan of merger name changed to South Texas Development Co. (Del.) and Class A Common $1 par and Class B Common $1 par changed to $20 par 8/1/60
South Texas Development Co. (Del.) merged into Sabine Royalty Corp. 8/31/72 which was reincorporated in Louisiana as Sabine Corp. 1/3/77
(See Sabine Corp.)

WYTEX OIL CORP. (NY)
Reincorporated under the laws of Delaware 12/31/53
Wytex Oil Corp. (Del.) name changed to South Texas Development Co. (Del.) 8/1/60 which merged into Sabine Royalty Corp. 8/31/72 which

was reincorporated in Louisiana as Sabine Corp. 1/3/77
(See Sabine Corp.)

WYTOMIC LTD (AUSTRALIA)
Name changed to Sultan Corp. Ltd. 12/06/2006
Sultan Corp. Ltd. name changed to Balamara Resources, Ltd. 02/07/2012

WYTON OIL & GAS CO. (DE)
Each share Common 10¢ par exchanged for (0.1) share Common no par 10/3/61
No longer in existence having become inoperative and void for non-payment of taxes 11/1/65

X CAL RES LTD (BC)
Merged into Paramount Gold & Silver Corp. 08/23/2010
Each share Common no par exchanged for (0.125) share Common $0.001 par
Note: Unexchanged certificates were cancelled and became without value 08/23/2016
Paramount Gold & Silver Corp. merged into Coeur Mining, Inc. 04/17/2015

X-CHANGE CORP (NV)
Each share old Common $0.001 par exchanged for (0.05) share new Common $0.001 par 08/09/2010
Name changed to Endocan Corp. 11/06/2013

X-CHEQUER RES INC (QC)
Recapitalized as International X-Chequer Resources Inc. (QC) 09/29/2004
Each (12) shares Common no par exchanged for (1) share Common no par
International X-Chequer Resources Inc. (QC) reorganized in British Columbia as Passport Metals Inc. 10/18/2007 which name changed to Passport Potash Inc. 11/10/2009

X CORP (AB)
Charter cancelled 10/00/2002

X HIV INC (NV)
Name changed to Avalon Group Inc. 4/1/97
Avalon Group Inc. merged into Appropriate Health Services.Com, Inc. 6/15/99 which name changed to Stayhealthy Inc. 4/14/2000

X L LABS INC (IA)
Company went private 00/00/1979
Details not available

X-L REFINERIES LTD. (CANADA)
Completely liquidated 05/12/1964
Each share 6% Preference $10 par exchanged for $7.878 cash
No equity for holders of Common no par

X MARK CORP (NV)
Charter revoked for failure to file reports and pay fees 4/1/88

X-NET SVCS CORP. (NV)
Name changed to Third Millennium Industries, Inc. 11/03/2003
Third Millennium Industries, Inc. recapitalized as Millennium Energy Corp. 03/11/2014

X O CORP (NV)
Each share old Common $0.001 par exchanged for (0.1) share new Common $0.001 par 7/7/95
Recapitalized as Calimont Corp. 10/16/97
Each share new Common $0.001 par exchanged for (0.1) share Common $0.001 par
(See Calimont Corp.)

X O EXPL INC (CO)
Each share Common 1¢ par exchanged for (10) shares Common $0.001 par 07/16/1979
Declared defunct and inoperative for failure to pay taxes and file annual reports 01/01/1990

X ONICS CORP (CA)
Each share old Common $1 par exchanged for (0.5) share new Common $1 par 11/22/68
Name changed to Consolidated Diversified Enterprises, Inc. 6/4/71
Consolidated Diversified Enterprises, Inc. reincorporated in Delaware as Walter Enterprises, Inc. 8/30/73
(See Walter Enterprises, Inc.)

X RAIL ENTMT INC (NV)
Reincorporated 03/29/2016
Name changed 05/17/2017
State of incorporation changed from (WY) to (NV) 03/29/2016
Name changed from X Rail Enterprises, Inc. to X Rail Entertainment, Inc. 05/17/2017
Recapitalized as Las Vegas Xpress, Inc. 09/17/2018
Each share Common $0.00001 par exchanged for (0.0002) share Common $0.00001 par

X-RAMP COM INC (NV)
SEC revoked common stock registration 05/18/2009

X-RAY GOLD MINING & SMELTING CO. (WA)
Charter revoked for failure to file reports and pay fees 7/1/23

X RAY MONITORING CORP (NY)
Charter cancelled and proclaimed dissolved for failure to file reports and pay fees 12/15/1972

X-RITE INC (MI)
Common 10¢ par split (2) for (1) by issuance of (1) additional share 08/12/1988
Common 10¢ par split (2) for (1) by issuance of (1) additional share 08/10/1992
Common 10¢ par split (2) for (1) by issuance of (1) additional share 12/27/1994
Acquired by Danaher Corp. 05/15/2012
Each share Common 10¢ par exchanged for $5.55 cash

X-STREAM NETWORK INC (DE)
Merged into Liberty Surf Group S.A. 3/14/2000
Each share Common $0.0001 par exchanged for $1.2644 cash

X T C RES LTD (BC)
Struck off register and declared dissolved for failure to file annual returns 06/24/1994

X-TAL MINERALS CORP (BC)
Under plan of merger name changed to Lion One Metals Ltd. 01/31/2011

X-TECH INNOVATIONS INC (MB)
Name changed to IDYIA Innovations Inc. 07/26/2002
(See IDYIA Innovations Inc.)

X-TERRA RES CORP (CANADA)
Reincorporated 09/04/2008
Place of incorporation changed from (BC) to (Canada) 09/04/2008
Each share Common no par received distribution of (0.25) share X-Terra Resources Inc. Common no par payable 06/04/2014 to holders of record 04/22/2014
Name changed to Norvista Capital Corp. 07/03/2014

X-TRA PETROLEUM (WY)
Recapitalized as Xtra Energy Corp. 11/05/2010
Each share Common $0.0001 par exchanged for (0.001) share Common $0.0001 par

X ZEL INC (DE)
Charter cancelled and declared inoperative and void for non-payment of taxes 03/01/1994

XA INC (NV)
Assets assigned for the benefit of creditors 02/24/2015
No stockholders' equity

XACORD CORP (DE)
Each share old Common $0.0001 par exchanged for (0.05) share new Common 0.0001 par 08/11/2006
Recapitalized as Empire Minerals, Corp. 01/22/2007
Each share new Common $0.0001 par exchanged for (0.05) share Common $0.0001 par
Empire Minerals, Corp. name changed to Dominion Minerals Corp. 02/14/2008

XACRON CORP (DE)
Charter cancelled and declared inoperative and void for non-payment of taxes 6/27/80

XACT AID INC (NV)
Name changed to China Premium Lifestyle Enterprise, Inc. 12/28/2006
(See China Premium Lifestyle Enterprise, Inc.)

XACTLY CORP (DE)
Acquired by Vista Equity Partners Management, LLC 07/31/2017
Each share Common $0.001 par exchanged for $15.65 cash

XAIBE INC (NV)
Recapitalized as Carbon Products Industries, Inc. 1/9/2006
Each share Common $0.001 par exchanged for (0.0125) share Common $0.001 par

XANADOO CO (DE)
Name changed to Pegasus Companies, Inc. 06/09/2015

XANARO TECHNOLOGIES INC (BC)
Name changed to Canadian Industrial Minerals Corp. (BC) 11/24/1986
Canadian Industrial Minerals Corp. (BC) reincorporated in Alberta 01/20/1995 which merged into Abacan Resource Corp. (New) 02/10/1995
(See Abacan Resource Corp. (New))

XANSER CORP (DE)
Name changed to Furmanite Corp. 05/17/2007
Furmanite Corp. merged into Team, Inc. 02/29/2016

XANTHIC ENTERPRISES INC (CO)
Recapitalized as International Wood Corp. 1/28/98
Each share Common $0.0001 par exchanged for (0.4) share Common $0.0001 par

XANTREX TECHNOLOGY INC (CANADA)
Acquired by Schneider Electric S.A. 09/29/2008
Each share Common no par exchanged for $15 cash

XATA CORP (MN)
Each share old Common 1¢ par exchanged for (0.33333333) share new Common 1¢ par 09/08/1995
Name changed to XRS Corp. 08/14/2012
(See XRS Corp.)

XAVIER CORP (DE)
SEC revoked common stock registration 08/05/2004

XAVIER MINES LTD (ON)
Common no par split (2) for (1) by issuance of (1) additional share 05/26/1993
Reorganized under the laws of Delaware as Xavier Corp. 07/24/1996
Each share Common no par exchanged for (0.25) share Common no par
(See Xavier Corp.)

XBOX TECHNOLOGIES INC (DE)
Name changed to Knowledge Mechanics Group, Inc. 10/16/2001
(See Knowledge Mechanics Group, Inc.)

XCARE NET INC (DE)
Issue Information - 5,000,000 shares COM offered at $18 per share on 02/10/2000
Name changed to Quovadx, Inc. 10/01/2001
(See Quovadx, Inc.)

XCEED INC (DE)
Name changed to Worldwide Xceed Group, Inc. 11/29/2000
(See Worldwide Xceed Group, Inc.)

XCEED MTG CORP (ON)
Merged into MCAN Mortgage Corp. 07/05/2013
Each share Common no par exchanged for (0.118) share Common no par
Note: Unexchanged certificates will be cancelled and become without value 07/05/2019

XCEL CAP CORP (AB)
Recapitalized as Xcel Consolidated Ltd. 01/18/2006
Each share Common no par exchanged for (0.1) share Common no par
(See Xcel Consolidated Ltd.)

XCEL CONS LTD (AB)
Cease trade order 08/04/2009

XCEL ENERGY INC (MN)
$3.60 Preferred $100 par called for redemption at $103.75 on 10/31/2011
$4.08 Preferred $100 par called for redemption at $102 on 10/31/2011
$4.10 Preferred $100 par called for redemption at $102.50 on 10/31/2011
$4.11 Preferred $100 par called for redemption at $103.732 on 10/31/2011
$4.16 Preferred $100 par called for redemption at $103.75 on 10/31/2011
$4.56 Preferred $100 par called for redemption at $102.47 on 10/31/2011
(Additional Information in Active)

XCEL MGMT INC (UT)
Each share old Common $0.001 par exchanged for (0.01) share new Common $0.001 par 10/05/1999
Reincorporated under the laws of Delaware as InsynQ, Inc. and (1) additional share issued 08/04/2000
InsynQ, Inc. (DE) reincorporated in Nevada 12/24/2002
(See InsynQ, Inc. (NV))

XCEL SECS INC (CO)
Name changed to Barton (William) Financial Inc. 05/03/1990

XCELARATOR INTERACTIVE INC (NV)
Name changed to Harley Street Clinics, Inc. 06/21/2004
Harley Street Clinics, Inc. name changed to Nutribrands, Inc. 10/05/2004 which name changed to St. James Capital Holdings, Inc. 04/25/2005
(See St. James Capital Holdings, Inc.)

XCELARATOR STUDIOS INC (OR)
Reincorporated 03/15/2004
Place of incorporation changed from (Canada) to (OR) 03/15/2004
Involuntarily dissolved for failure to file reports and pay fees 04/27/2007

XCELERA INC. (CAYMAN ISLANDS)
Name changed 12/06/2000
Common 1¢ par split (2) for (1) by issuance of (1) additional share payable 03/04/2000 to holders of

record 02/14/2000 Ex date - 03/03/2000
Common 1¢ par split (2) for (1) by issuance of (1) additional share payable 04/29/2000 to holders of record 04/10/2000 Ex date - 04/28/2000
Name changed from Xcelera.com, Inc. to Xcelera Inc. 12/06/2000
SEC revoked common stock registration 11/03/2006

XCELERON INC (AB)
Merged into Zaio Corp. 02/23/2004
Each share Common no par exchanged for (0.6) share Common no par
Zaio Corp. name changed to Claroicity Corp. 10/17/2016

XCELLENET INC (GA)
Issue Information - 2,000,000 shares COM offered at $11 per share on 04/14/1994
Merged into Sterling Commerce, Inc. 07/21/1998
Each share Common 1¢ par exchanged for (0.2885) share Common 1¢ par and $8.80 cash
(See Sterling Commerce, Inc.)

XCELLINK INTL INC (DE)
Recapitalized as Trxade Group, Inc. 02/06/2014
Each share Common $0.0001 par exchanged for (0.001) share Common $0.00001 par

XCELPLUS GLOBAL HLDGS INC (NV)
Name changed to Clean Energy Pathways, Inc. 02/04/2011

XCERRA CORP (MA)
Merged into Cohu, Inc. 10/01/2018
Each share Common 5¢ par exchanged for (0.2109) share Common $1 par and $9 cash

XCITE ENERGY LTD (BRITISH VIRGIN ISLANDS)
Shares transferred to British Virgin Island register 11/30/2015

XCL CORP (DE)
Name changed to Sunbelt Oil & Gas Inc. 11/10/1980
Sunbelt Oil & Gas Inc. name changed to Dallas Sunbelt Oil & Gas, Inc. 05/08/1981
(See Dallas Sunbelt Oil & Gas, Inc.)

XCL LTD NEW (DE)
Stock Dividends - In 144A to holders of 144A 4.75% payable 11/01/1999 to holders of record 10/15/1999
In Preferred to holders of Preferred 4.75% payable 05/03/1999 to holders of record 04/15/1999; 4.75% payable 11/01/1999 to holders of record 10/15/1999
SEC revoked common stock registration 10/24/2008

XCL LTD OLD (DE)
Recapitalized as XCL Ltd. (New) 12/17/1997
Each (15) shares Common 1¢ par exchanged for (1) share Common 1¢ par
(See XCL Ltd. (New))

XCOR INTL INC (DE)
Name changed to Biscayne Holdings, Inc. (DE) 06/30/1986
Biscayne Holdings, Inc. (DE) reorganized in Florida 07/01/1990 which name changed to Biscayne Apparel, Inc. 05/31/1994 which recapitalized as El Apparel, Inc. 08/29/2005 which recapitalized as NutriOne Corp. 07/27/2006
(See NutriOne Corp.)

XCYTE THERAPIES INC (DE)
Issue Information 4,200,000 shares COM offered at $8 per share on 03/16/2004
Recapitalized as Cyclacel Pharmaceuticals, Inc. 03/28/2006
Each share new Common $0.001 par exchanged for (0.1) share Common $0.001 par
Preferred not affected except for change of name

XDOGS COM INC (NV)
Recapitalized as Xdogs Inc. 08/22/2000
Each share Common 1¢ par exchanged for (0.2) share Common 1¢ par
Xdogs Inc. name changed to Avalon Oil & Gas, Inc. 07/22/2005 which name changed to Groove Botanicals, Inc. 05/14/2018

XDOGS INC (NV)
Name changed to Avalon Oil & Gas, Inc. and Common 1¢ par changed to $0.001 par 07/22/2005
Avalon Oil & Gas, Inc. name changed to Groove Botanicals, Inc. 05/14/2018

XEBEC (CA)
Charter cancelled for failure to file reports and pay taxes 7/2/90

XEBEC CORP. (MO)
Stock Dividend - 100% 04/06/1967
Merged into Susquehanna Corp. 03/06/1968
Each share Common no par exchanged for (0.9) share Common $1 par
(See Susquehanna Corp.)

XEBEC GALLEON INC (NV)
Name changed to Herzog International Holdings Inc. 07/03/1992
(See Herzog International Holdings Inc.)

XECHEM INTL INC (DE)
Each share old Common 1¢ par exchanged for (0.00033333) share new Common 1¢ par 05/28/2003
Chapter 7 bankruptcy proceedings terminated 12/17/2014
Stockholders' equity unlikely

XECOM CORP (NV)
Name changed to AirStar Technologies, Inc. 04/28/1998
(See AirStar Technologies, Inc.)

XEDAR CORP (CO)
Each share old Common no par exchanged for (0.11561087) share new Common no par 01/03/2007
Acquired by IHS Inc. 05/11/2012
Each share new Common no par exchanged for $0.7512 cash

XEIKON N V (BELGIUM)
Declared bankrupt 3/6/2002
No stockholders' equity

XELEX CORP (FL)
Recapitalized as Automax Group, Inc. 02/16/2001
Each share Common $0.001 par exchanged for (0.01) share Common $0.001 par
Automax Group, Inc. recapitalized as Heritage Capital Credit Corp. 04/01/2004 which recapitalized as Protective Capital Structures Corp. 12/11/2008

XELR8 HLDGS INC (NV)
Name changed to Bazi International, Inc. 10/01/2010
Bazi International, Inc. recapitalized as True Drinks Holdings, Inc. 01/22/2013

XEMAC RES INC (CANADA)
Reincorporated 04/07/1997
Place of incorporation changed from (BC) to (Canada) 04/07/1997
Recapitalized as Abitex Resources Inc. 03/26/2004
Each share Common no par exchanged for (0.1) share Common no par
Abitex Resources Inc. recapitalized as ABE Resources Inc. 04/16/2013 which name changed to Vision Lithium Inc. 03/27/2018

XENCET INVTS INC (CANADA)
Name changed to Games Trader Inc. 11/11/98
Games Trader Inc. name changed to GTR Group Inc. 6/29/99 which name changed to Mad Catz Interactive, Inc. 9/5/2001

XENDA CORP (TX)
Recapitalized as Latoka, Inc. 11/14/88
Each share Common $0.0001 par exchanged for (0.2) share Common $0.0005 par
Latoka, Inc. merged into Lomak Petroleum, Inc. 7/23/91 which name changed to Range Resources Corp. 8/25/98

XENEJENEX INC (DE)
Name changed to Health Management International, Inc. 12/11/1991
Health Management International, Inc. name changed to TDX Corp. 01/05/1993
(See TDX Corp.)

XENEREX CORP (DE)
Reincorporated 2/21/84
State of incorporation changed from (CO) to (DE) and Common no par changed to $0.001 par 2/21/84
Each share Common $0.001 par exchanged for (0.05) share Common 2¢ par 12/18/84
Name changed to DJN, Inc. 10/19/87
DJN, Inc. recapitalized as Allen Energy Co. 9/27/90
(See Allen Energy Co.)

XENEX INDS & RES LTD (BC)
Dissolved 9/22/89
Details not available

XENEX MINERALS LTD (BERMUDA)
Struck from register 02/00/2013

XENIC CAP CORP (UT)
Name changed to Dry Cleaning Depot, Inc. in June 1993
(See Dry Cleaning Depot, Inc.)

XENICENT INC (NC)
Each share old Common $0.001 par exchanged for (0.2) share new Common $0.001 par 4/20/2004
Name changed to Pingchuan Pharmaceutical, Inc. (NC) 8/3/2004
Pingchuan Pharmaceutical, Inc. (NC) reincorporated in Delaware as Shandong Zhouyuan Seed & Nursery Co., Ltd. 4/5/2007

XENITH BANKSHARES INC NEW (VA)
Each share old Common 1¢ par exchanged for (0.1) share new Common 1¢ par 12/13/2016
Merged into Union Bankshares Corp. 01/01/2018
Each share new Common 1¢ par exchanged for (0.9354) share Common $1.33 par

XENITH BANKSHARES INC OLD (VA)
Merged into Xenith Bankshares, Inc. (New) 08/01/2016
Each share Common $1 par exchanged for (4.4) shares Common 1¢ par
Xenith Bankshares, Inc. (New) merged into Union Bankshares Corp. 01/01/2018

XENIUM RES INC (BC)
Recapitalized as Zeal Capital Ltd. 11/29/1989
Each share Common no par exchanged for (0.5) share Common no par
Zeal Capital Ltd. recapitalized as First Quantum Ventures Ltd. (BC) 06/16/1993 which reincorporated in Yukon as First Quantum Minerals Ltd. 07/18/1996 which reincorporated in Canada 08/11/2003 which reincorporated in British Columbia 06/03/2005

XENOGEN CORP (DE)
Issue Information - 4,200,000 shares COM offered at $7 per share on 07/16/2004
Merged into Caliper Life Sciences, Inc. 08/09/2006
Each share Common $0.001 par exchanged for (0.5792) share Common $0.001 par and (0.2249) Common Stock Purchase Warrant expiring 08/09/2011
(See Caliper Life Sciences, Inc.)

XENOLIX TECHNOLOGIES INC (NV)
Name changed to Pershing Resources Co., Inc. 4/27/2004

XENOMETRIX INC (DE)
Merged into Discovery Partners International, Inc. 5/8/2001
Each share Common $0.001 par exchanged for $0.57 cash
Note: An additional $0.06 cash per share will be held in escrow to pay any indemnity obligations

XENOMICS INC (FL)
Reincorporated under the laws of Delaware as TrovaGene, Inc. and Common $0.0001 par changed to $0.001 par 03/01/2010

XENONICS HLDGS INC (NV)
Chapter 7 bankruptcy proceedings terminated 02/23/2017
No stockholders' equity

XENOPORT INC (DE)
Acquired by Arbor Pharmaceuticals, LLC 07/05/2016
Each share Common $0.001 par exchanged for $7.03 cash

XENOS GROUP INC (ON)
Acquired by Actuate Corp. 03/05/2010
Each share Common no par exchanged for $3.50 cash

XENOTECH INC (AB)
Recapitalized as Dynamic Digital Depth, Inc. 10/19/98
Each share Common no par exchanged for (0.2) share Common no par
(See Dynamic Digitial Depth, Inc.)

XENOVA GROUP PLC (ENGLAND & WALES)
Each old Sponsored ADR for Ordinary 10p par exchanged for (0.1) new Sponsored ADR for Ordinary 10p par 07/10/2001
ADR basis changed from (1:1) to (1:10) 07/10/2001
Acquired by Celtic Pharma Phinco B.V. 09/01/2005
Each new Sponsored ADR for Ordinary 10p par exchanged for $1.10 nominal value of Secured Loan Notes due 04/25/2007

XENTEL DM INC (AB)
Name changed to iMarketing Solutions Group Inc. 11/26/2010
(See iMarketing Solutions Group Inc.)

XENTEL INTERACTIVE INC (AB)
Recapitalized as Xentel DM Inc. 07/01/1998
Each (30.64) shares Common no par exchanged for (1) share Class A Common no par
Xentel DM Inc. name changed to iMarketing Solutions Group Inc. 11/26/2010
(See iMarketing Solutions Group Inc.)

XEON FINL CORP (NV)
Merged into First Security Corp. 6/14/99
Each share Common no par exchanged for (0.483) share Common $1.25 par
First Security Corp. merged into Wells Fargo & Co. (New) 10/26/2000

XERART CORP (ON)
Name changed to Artagraph

Reproduction Technology, Inc. 10/07/1987
Artagraph Reproduction Technology, Inc. recapitalized as A.R.T. International Inc. 09/14/1998 which recapitalized as ART International Corp. 06/16/2003 which name changed to Diamant Art Corp. 11/26/2004
(See Diamant Art Corp.)

XERION ECOSOLUTIONS GROUP INC (CO)
Reorganized under the laws of Nevada as SINO-American Development Corp. 06/19/2006
Each share Common $0.001 par exchanged for (0.125) share Common $0.001 par
SINO-American Development Corp. recapitalized as Harvest Bio-Organic International Co., Ltd. 12/07/2010
(See Harverst Bio-Organic International Co., Ltd.)

XERIUM TECHNOLOGIES INC (DE)
COM ($0.001) 98416J 11 8
Plan of reorganization under Chapter 11 Federal Bankruptcy proceedings effective 05/25/2010
Each share Common 1¢ par exchanged for (0.05) share Common $0.001 par and (0.0324) Common Stock Purchase Warrant expiring 05/25/2014
Acquired by Andritz AG 10/17/2018
Each share Common $0.001 par exchanged for $13.50 cash

XERO MOBILE INC (NV)
Old Common $0.001 par split (25) for (1) by issuance of (24) additional shares payable 04/11/2006 to holders of record 04/10/2006
Ex date - 04/12/2006
Each share old Common $0.001 par exchanged for (0.0025) share new Common $0.001 par 02/11/2011
Name changed to MYEZSMOKES, Inc. 05/06/2011
MYEZSMOKES, Inc. name changed to Icon Vapor, Inc. 02/06/2014

XEROGRAPHIC COPY SVC INC (NY)
Merged into Touchette Corp. 11/30/1979
Each share Common 5¢ par exchanged for $0.50 cash

XEROGRAPHIC LASER IMAGES CORP (DE)
Each share old Common 1¢ par exchanged for (1/6) share new Common 1¢ par 11/29/94
Merged into OTI Acquisition Corp. 8/11/98
Each share 9% Conv. Preferred Ser. A 1¢ par exchanged for $2.09296835 cash
Each share Common 1¢ par exchanged for $0.84109 cash

XEROX CDA INC (ON)
Common no par reclassified as Non-Vtg. Exchangeable Class B no par 02/14/1990
Each share Non-Vtg. Exchangeable Class B no par exchanged for (2.12) shares Xerox Corp. Common $1 par 12/22/2010

XEROX CAP TR II (DE)
144A Guaranteed Trust Conv. Preferred Securities called for redemption at $51.875 on 12/6/2004

XEROX CORP (NY)
$5.45 Preferred $1 par called for redemption 4/1/88
$4.125 20 Year Preferred $1 par called for redemption 5/26/94
$3.6875 10 Year Preferred $1 par called for redemption 4/1/95
Each share 6.25% Mandatory Conv. Preferred Ser. C $1 par exchanged for (8.1301) shares Common $1 par 7/1/2006
(Additional Information in Active)

XETA TECHNOLOGIES INC (OK)
Name changed 04/17/2000
Common 10¢ par changed to 5¢ par and (1) additional share issued payable 08/13/1999 to holders of record 07/30/1999
Name changed from XETA Corp. to XETA Technologies Inc. 04/17/2000
Common 5¢ par changed to $0.002 par 06/30/2000
Common $0.002 par changed to $0.001 par and (1) additional share issued payable 07/17/2000 to holders of record 06/30/2000
Acquired by PAETEC Holding Corp. 05/31/2011
Each share Common $0.001 par exchanged for $5.50 cash

XETAL INC (UT)
Each share old Common $0.001 par exchanged for (0.1) share new Common $0.001 par 08/22/1996
Name changed to Sick-Bay.Com Inc. 01/20/2000
Sick-Bay.Com Inc. name changed to Sickbay Health Media, Inc. 08/23/2000
(See Sickbay Health Media, Inc.)

XETEL CORP (DE)
Plan of reorganization under Chapter 11 Federal Bankruptcy Code effective 6/9/2003
No stockholders' equity

XETHANOL CORP (DE)
Name changed to Global Energy Holdings Group, Inc. 10/28/2008
(See Global Energy Holdings Group, Inc.)

XEXEX INDS INC (NY)
Dissolved by proclamation 09/28/1994

XFONE INC (NV)
Name changed to NTS, Inc. 02/02/2012
(See NTS, Inc.)

XFORMITY TECHNOLOGIES INC (CO)
Recapitalized as Gold Star North American Mining, Inc. 10/17/2014
Each share Common $0.0001 par exchanged for (0.00333333) share Common $0.0001 par
Gold Star North American Mining, Inc. name changed to Clearwave Telecommunications, Inc. 08/27/2015

XGA GOLF INTL INC (FL)
Name changed to Phon-Net Corp. 1/22/99
Phon-Net Corp. name changed to Phon-Net.com, Inc. 6/4/99 which name changed to Environmental Strategies & Technologies International, Inc. 4/14/2002 which recapitalized as Tango Inc. 2/10/2003 which recapitalized as AutoBidXL Inc. 10/24/2005 which name changed to Trophy Resources, Inc. 2/28/2006

XGEN VENTURES INC (ON)
Delisted from NEX 12/16/2011

XHIBIT CORP (NV)
Plan of reorganization under Chapter 11 Federal Bankruptcy proceedings effective 09/11/2015
Assets transferred to a liquidating trust for possible future distribution

XI PRODTNS INC (NV)
Acquired by Universal Coverage Corp. 04/02/1969
Each share Capital Stock 10¢ par exchanged for (1.5) shares Common 13-1/3¢ par
Universal Coverage Corp. recapitalized as Unico American Corp. 08/01/1973

XI TEC INC (DE)
Each share Common $0.001 par exchanged for (0.1) share Common 1¢ par 06/20/1996

Charter cancelled and declared inoperative and void for non-payment of taxes 03/01/2008

XIANBURG DATA SYS CDA CORP (AB)
Reincorporated under the laws of British Columbia 08/15/2013

XICOR INC (CA)
Merged into Intersil Corp. 07/29/2004
Each share Common no par exchanged for either (0.82236) share Class A Common 1¢ par or $13.50 cash
Note: Option to receive stock expired 07/29/2004
(See Intersil Corp.)

XIDEX CORP (DE)
Reincorporated 12/21/1984
Common 70¢ par changed to 35¢ par and (1) additional share issued 01/24/1980
Common 35¢ par changed to $0.175 par and (1) additional share issued 12/09/1982
Common $0.175 par changed to $0.0875 par and (1) additional share issued 08/08/1983
State of incorporation changed from (CA) to (DE) and Common $0.0875 par changed to 1¢ par 12/21/1984
Acquired by Anacomp Acquisition Corp. 08/26/1988
Each share Common 1¢ par exchanged for $9.25 cash

XIDEX MAGNETICS CORP (CA)
Merged into Xidex Corp. (DE) 03/15/1985
Each share Common no par exchanged for (1.24) shares Common $0.0875 par
(See Xidex Corp. (DE))

XILLIX TECHNOLOGIES CORP (BC)
Name changed to Biomerge Industries Ltd. (BC) 09/27/2007
Biomerge Industries Ltd. (BC) reincorporated in Alberta 04/15/2009 which merged into Total Energy Services Inc. 05/20/2009

XIN NET CORP (FL)
Recapitalized as China Mobility Solutions, Inc. 06/24/2004
Each share Common $0.001 par exchanged for (1/3) share Common $0.001 par
China Mobility Solutions, Inc. recapitalized as Global Peopleline Telecom Inc. 08/06/2008
(See Global Peopleline Telecom Inc.)

XINAO GAS HLDGS LTD (CAYMAN ISLANDS)
Name changed to ENN Energy Holdings Ltd. 12/01/2010

XINDE TECHNOLOGY CO (NV)
Old Common $0.001 par split (4) for (1) by issuance of (3) additional shares payable 04/14/2011 to holders of record 04/14/2011
Each share old Common $0.001 par exchanged for (0.01) share new Common $0.001 par 07/18/2012
SEC revoked common stock registration 11/24/2014

XINERGY LTD (ON)
Plan of reorganization under Chapter 11 Federal Bankruptcy proceedings effective 02/10/2016
No stockholders' equity

XINETIX INC (DE)
Merged into S&H greenpoints.com, Inc. 4/14/2000
Each share Common 1¢ par exchanged for $1.576 cash
Note: An additional $0.394 cash per share was paid in 2001

XING HAI RES LTD (BC)
Recapitalized as RSI Retail Solutions Inc. 07/23/1986
Each share Common no par exchanged for (2) shares Common no par
RSI Retail Solutions Inc. recapitalized as Consolidated Retail Solutions Inc. 01/30/1990 which name changed to Ventir Challenge Enterprises Ltd. 07/18/1994 which recapitalized as Whistler Gold Corp. 02/03/2006 which name changed to Svit Gold Corp. 08/11/2008 which name changed to Catalyst Copper Corp. 02/02/2010 which merged into NewCastle Gold Ltd. 05/27/2016 which merged into Equinox Gold Corp. 12/22/2017

XINHUA FIN LTD (CAYMAN ISLANDS)
Basis changed from (1:0.00333333) to (1:0.01) 09/22/2005
ADR agreement terminated 04/12/2011
Each Sponsored ADR for Ordinary exchanged for $0.140261 cash

XINHUA SPORTS & ENTMT LTD (CAYMAN ISLANDS)
Name changed 03/02/2009
Issue Information - 23,076,923 SPONSORED ADRS offered at $13 per ADR on 03/08/2007
Name changed from Xinhua Finance Media Ltd. to Xinhua Sports & Entertainment Ltd. 03/02/2009
Each old Sponsored ADR for Class A Common exchanged for (0.06666666) new Sponsored ADR for Class A Common 01/18/2011
ADR basis changed from (1:2) to (1:30) 01/18/2011
ADR agreement terminated 05/17/2013
No ADR holders' equity

XINJIANG XINXIN MNG IND CO LTD (CHINA)
ADR agreement terminated 12/26/2017
No ADR's remain outstanding

XINO CORP (DE)
Reorganized as AsherXino Corp. 08/19/2009
Each share Common 1¢ par exchanged for (1.5) shares Common 1¢ par
(See AsherXino Corp.)

XIOM CORP (DE)
Name changed to Environmental Infrastructure Holdings Corp. 01/27/2010

XIONICS DOCUMENT TECHNOLOGIES INC (DE)
Merged into Oak Technology, Inc. 01/11/2000
Each share Common 1¢ par exchanged for (0.8031) share Common $0.001 par and $2.94 cash
Oak Technology, Inc. merged into Zoran Corp. 08/11/2003 which merged into CSR PLC 08/31/2011
(See CSR PLC)

XIOX CORP (DE)
Name changed to @Comm Corp. 4/3/2000
(See @Comm Corp.)

XIOX INTL INC (FL)
Proclaimed dissolved for failure to file reports and pay fees 12/11/76

XIRCOM (CA)
Merged into Intel Corp. 3/13/2001
Each share Common $0.001 par exchanged for $25 cash

XISS CAP CORP (ON)
Recapitalized as IFuture Inc. 08/03/1999
Each share Common no par exchanged for (0.25) share Common no par and (0.125) Common Stock Purchase Warrant, Ser. A expiring 01/31/2000
iFuture Inc. name changed to iFuture.com Inc. 10/09/2000 which merged into Red Dragon Resources

Corp. (ON) 05/20/2005 which
reincorporated in British Columbia
08/23/2007 which name changed to
Brazilian Gold Corp. 01/06/2010
which merged into Brazil Resources
Inc. (BC) 11/22/2013 which
reincorporated in Canada as
GoldMining Inc. 12/07/2016

XL CAP LTD (CAYMAN ISLANDS)
Each 6.5% Equity Security Unit
automatically became (0.32727)
share Class A Ordinary 1¢ par
05/15/2007
8% Ser. A Ordinary Preference 1¢ par
called for redemption at $25 plus
$0.24 accrued dividends on
08/14/2007
7.625% Ser. B Ordinary Preference
1¢ par called for redemption at
$25.26 on 11/19/2007
Each 7% Equity Security Unit
automatically became (0.3846)
share Class A Ordinary 1¢ par
02/17/2009
Each 10.75% Equity Security Unit
automatically became (1) XL Co.
Switzerland GMBH 10.75% Equity
Security Unit 07/01/2010
Reorganized under the laws of Ireland
as XL Group PLC 07/01/2010
Each share Class A Ordinary 1¢ par
exchanged for (1) share Ordinary
XL Group PLC (Ireland)
reincorporated in Bermuda as XL
Group Ltd. 07/25/2016
(See XL Group Ltd.)

XL CO SWITZERLAND GMBH (SWITZERLAND)
Each 10.75% Equity Security Unit
automatically became (1.3242)
shares XL Group PLC (Ireland)
Ordinary 08/15/2011
XL Group PLC (Ireland)
reincorporated in Bermuda as XL
Group Ltd. 07/25/2016
(See XL Group Ltd.)

XL CORP (NV)
Common 5¢ par split (2) for (1) by
issuance of (1) additional share
03/01/1994
Recapitalized as Commercial Labor
Management, Inc. 03/20/1995
Each share Common 5¢ par
exchanged for (1/3) share Common
5¢ par
Commercial Labor Management, Inc.
name changed to Zeros & Ones,
Inc. 07/01/1999 which name
changed to Voyant International
Corp. 04/30/2007
(See Voyant International Corp.)

XL DATACOMP INC (DE)
Common 1¢ par split (3) for (2) by
issuance of (0.5) additional share
5/28/87
Common 1¢ par split (3) for (2) by
issuance of (0.5) additional share
3/24/89
Acquired by Storage Technology
Corp. 11/26/91
Each share Common 1¢ par
exchanged for (0.2675) share
Common 10¢ par
(See Storage Technology Corp.)

XL FOODS LTD (AB)
Name changed 06/15/1989
Name changed from XL Food
Systems Ltd. to XL Foods Ltd.
06/15/1989
Name changed to Sevenway Capital
Corp. 03/09/1999
Sevenway Capital Corp. merged into
Glacier Ventures International Corp.
(Canada) (New) 04/28/2000 which
name changed to Glacier Media Inc.
07/01/2008

XL GENERATION INTL INC (NV)
Name changed to Ecolocap Solutions
Inc. 11/13/2007

XL GROUP LTD (BERMUDA)
Acquired by AXA S.A. 09/12/2018

Each share Common 1¢ par
exchanged for $57.60 cash

XL GROUP PLC (IRELAND)
Reincorporated under the laws of
Bermuda as XL Group Ltd. and
Ordinary 1¢ par reclassified as
Common 1¢ par 07/25/2016
(See XL Group Ltd.)

XL-ID SOLUTIONS INC (CANADA)
Proposal under Bankruptcy &
Insolvency Act approved 02/13/2014
No stockholders' equity

XLCONNECT SOLUTIONS INC (PA)
Issue Information - 2,900,000 shares
Common offered at $15 per share
on 10/17/1996
Merged into Xerox Corp. 5/20/98
Each share Common 1¢ par
exchanged for $20 cash

XM SATELLITE RADIO HLDGS INC (DE)
Each share 8.25% Conv. Preferred
Ser. B received distribution of
(0.0311591) share Class A 1¢ par
payable 05/01/2000 to holders of
record 04/12/2000
Each share 8.25% Conv. Preferred
Ser. B received distribution of
(0.193) share Class A 1¢ par
payable 11/01/2001 to holders of
record 10/22/2001
8.25% Conv. Preferred Ser. B called
for redemption at $51.65 plus
$0.630208 accrued dividends on
06/26/2006
Merged into Sirius Satellite Radio Inc.
07/29/2008
Each share Class A Common 1¢ par
exchanged for (4.6) shares Common
$0.001 par
Sirius Satellite Radio Inc. name
changed to Sirius XM Radio Inc.
08/06/2008 which name changed to
Sirius XM Holdings Inc. 11/15/2013

XML GLOBAL TECHNOLOGIES INC (CO)
Recapitalized as Xformity
Technologies Inc. 09/28/2004
Each share Common $0.0001 par
exchanged for (0.25) share Common
$0.0001 par
Xformity Technologies Inc.
recapitalized as Gold Star North
American Mining, Inc. 10/17/2014
which name changed to Clearwave
Telecommunications, Inc.
08/27/2015

XMP MNG LTD (BERMUDA)
Reorganized under the laws of British
Columbia as Nu XMP Ventures Ltd.
06/05/2003
Each share Common 1¢ par
exchanged for (0.25) share Common
no par
Nu XMP Ventures Ltd. name changed
to New Pacific Metals Corp. (Old)
11/04/2004 which name changed to
New Pacific Holdings Corp.
07/04/2016 which name changed to
New Pacific Metals Corp. (New)
07/24/2017

XNE INC (NV)
Each share old Common $0.001 par
exchanged for (0.1) share new
Common $0.001 par 01/19/2010
SEC revoked common stock
registration 06/11/2014

XO COMMUNICATIONS INC (WA)
Stock Dividends - In 14% Sr.
Exchangeable Preferred to holders
of 14% Sr. Exchangeable Preferred
3.5% payable 02/01/2001 to holders
of record 01/15/2000; 3.5% payable
05/01/2001 to holders of record
04/15/2001; 3.5% payable
11/01/2001 to holders of record
10/15/2001 Ex date - 10/11/2001; In
13.50% Sr. Exchangeable Preferred
to holders of 13.50% Sr.
Exchangeable Preferred 3.375%
payable 03/01/2001 to holders of

record 02/15/2001; 3.375% payable
06/01/2001 to holders of record
05/15/2001 Ex date - 05/11/2001;
3.5% payable 08/01/2001 to holders
of record 07/15/2001 Ex date -
07/17/2001; 3.375% payable
09/01/2001 to holders of record
08/15/2001 Ex date - 08/13/2001;
3.375% payable 12/01/2001 to
holders of record 11/15/2001
Ex date - 11/13/2001
Plan of reorganization under Chapter
11 Federal Bankruptcy Code
effective 01/16/2003
No stockholders' equity
Name changed to XO Holdings, Inc.
03/02/2006
(See XO Holdings, Inc.)

XO HLDGS INC (DE)
Acquired by ACF Industries Holding
Corp. 08/18/2011
Each share Common 1¢ par
exchanged for $1.40 cash and (1)
Contractual Value Right

XO LOGIC INC (NV)
Reorganizied under the laws of
Washington as Doll Technolgy
Group, Inc. 06/30/2005
Each share Common 10¢ par
exchanged for (0.001) share
Common $0.0001 par

XODTEC LED INC (NV)
Name changed 04/16/2010
Name changed from Xodtec Group
USA, Inc. to Xodtec LED, Inc.
04/16/2010
Name changed to Cala Energy Corp.
10/21/2013
Cala Energy Corp. name changed to
Lingerie Fighting Championships,
Inc. 04/29/2015

XOIL ENERGY RES INC (DE)
Name changed to Parliament Hill
Corp. 2/27/85
(See Parliament Hill Corp.)

XOMA CORP OLD (DE)
Reincorporated under the laws of
Bermuda as Xoma Ltd. 12/31/1998
Xoma Ltd. (Bermuda) reincorporated
in Delaware as XOMA Corp. (New)
12/31/2011

XOMA LTD (BERMUDA)
Each (15) shares Common $0.0005
par exchanged for (1) share
Common $0.0075 par 08/18/2010
Reincorporated under the laws of
Delaware as XOMA Corp. (New)
12/31/2011

XOMED SURGICAL PRODS INC (DE)
Common 1¢ par split (3) for (2) by
issuance of (0.5) additional share
payable 11/30/1998 to holders of
record 11/16/1998
Merged into Medtronic, Inc. (MN)
11/05/1999
Each share Common 1¢ par
exchanged for (1.74723) shares
Common 1¢ par
Medtronic, Inc. (MN) reincorporated in
Ireland as Medtronic PLC
01/27/2015

XOMOX CORP (OH)
Common no par split (3) for (2) by
issuance of (0.5) additional share
7/8/76
Common no par split (3) for (2) by
issuance of (0.5) additional share
8/5/77
Merged into Emerson Electric Co.
7/1/80
Each share Common no par
exchanged for (0.838) share
Common $1 par

XONDI INC (NV)
Reincorporated under the laws of
California as Force Air Technology,
Inc. 06/19/1987
(See Force Air Technology, Inc.)

XONICS INC (DE)
Reincorporated 03/24/1980
Common 10¢ par split (3) for (2) by
issuance of (0.5) additional share
11/01/1973
State of incorporation changed from
(CA) to (DE) 03/24/1980
Plan of reorganization under Chapter
11 Federal Bankruptcy proceedings
confirmed 08/28/1985
No stockholders' equity

XOOM COM INC (DE)
Issue Information - 4,000,000 shares
COM offered at $14 per share on
12/09/1998
Merged into NBC Internet, Inc.
11/29/99
Each share Common $0.001 par
exchanged (1) share Class A
Common 1¢ par
(See NBC Internet, Inc.)

XOOM CORP (DE)
Acquired by PayPal, Inc. 11/12/2015
Each share Common $0.0001 par
exchanged for $25 cash

XOX CORP (DE)
Name changed to Teledigital, Inc.
04/15/2003
(See Teledigital, Inc.)

XOZ ENTMT S A (NV)
Name changed to SMSmobility, Inc.
01/04/2005
SMSmobility, Inc. name changed to
Star Petroleum Corp. 07/25/2005
which recapitalized as Exact Energy
Resources, Inc. 12/11/2007
(See Exact Energy Resources, Inc.)

XPEDIAN INC (FL)
Name changed to Gala Hospitality
Corp. 11/06/2001
Gala Hospitality Corp. name changed
to Gala Holding Corp. 09/04/2002
which recapitalized as Global
TransNet Corp. 10/14/2003 which
recapitalized as Legacy Brands
Holding, Inc. (FL) 11/19/2009 which
reincorporated in British Virgin
Islands as Revelation MIS, Inc.
10/22/2010 which reincorporated in
Florida as Jolen, Inc. 04/08/2015
which name changed to WOWI, Inc.
06/23/2016

XPEDIOR INC (DE)
Issue Information - 8,535,000 shares
COM offered at $19 per share on
12/15/1999
Plan of reorganization under Chapter
11 Federal Bankruptcy Code
effective 4/6/2002
No stockholders' equity

XPEDITE SYS INC (DE)
Merged into Premiere Technologies,
Inc. 02/27/1998
Each share Common 1¢ par
exchanged for (1.165) shares
Common 1¢ par
Premiere Technologies, Inc.
reorganized as PTEK Holdings, Inc.
02/17/2000 which name changed to
Premiere Global Services, Inc.
01/03/2005
(See Premiere Global Services, Inc.)

XPENTION GENETICS INC (NV)
Recapitalized as Cancer Detection
Corp. 10/14/2008
Each share Common $0.001 par
exchanged for (0.05) share Common
$0.001 par
Cancer Detection Corp. name
changed to Tremont Fair, Inc.
09/18/2009 which name changed to
Vican Resources, Inc. 06/10/2011

XPERIA CORP (ON)
Recapitalized as Xgen Ventures Inc.
11/26/2004
Each share Common no par
exchanged for (0.16666666) share
Common no par
(See Xgen Ventures Inc.)

XPF DEV INC (ON)
Recapitalized as GolfNorth Properties Inc. 1/12/98
Each share Common no par exchanged for (0.1) share Common no par
(See GolfNorth Properties Inc.)

XPLOR CORP (CO)
Name changed to Venus Exploration, Inc. 6/6/97

XPLOR ENERGY CORP (CO)
Recapitalized as Xplor Corp. 3/5/86
Each share Common 1¢ par exchanged for (1/30) share Common 1¢ par
Xplor Corp. name changed to Venus Exploration, Inc. 6/6/97

XPLORE TECHNOLOGIES CORP (DE)
Reincorporated 06/20/2007
Each share old Common no par exchanged for (0.25) share new Common no par 09/22/2000
Place of incorporation changed from (Canada) to (DE) and Preferred and Common no par changed to $0.001 par 06/20/2007
Each share old Common $0.001 par exchanged for (0.0025) share new Common $0.001 par 09/13/2012
Each share Preferred Ser. A $0.001 par automatically became (0.0327) share new Common $0.001 par 10/31/2012
Acquired by Zebra Technologies Corp. 08/14/2018
Each share new Common $0.001 par exchanged for $6 cash

XPLORER S A (NV)
Name changed to Netholdings.com Inc. 12/8/99
Netholdings.com Inc. name changed to Global Axcess Corp. 5/9/2001

XPONENTIAL INC (DE)
Liquidation completed
Each share Common 1¢ par received initial distribution of $1 cash payable 01/31/2014 to holders of record 01/24/2014 Ex date - 02/06/2014
Each share Common 1¢ par received second distribution of $0.50 cash payable 12/29/2014 to holders of record 12/19/2014 Ex date - 01/08/2015
Each share Common 1¢ par received third and final distribution of $1.45 cash payable 01/27/2016 to holders of record 01/17/2016 Ex date - 01/28/2016

XPRES COMMUNICATIONS INC (BC)
Recapitalized as Stratacom Technology Inc. 02/14/2000
Each share Common no par exchanged for (0.25) share Common no par
Stratacom Technology Inc. name changed to Strategic Oil & Gas Ltd. (BC) 03/31/2005 which reincorporated in Alberta 09/09/2010

XPRESS GROUP LTD (HONG KONG)
Name changed to Heng Fai Enterprises Ltd. 10/22/2013
(See Heng Fai Enterprises Ltd.)

XQUISITE ENTMT INC (DE)
Reorganized under the laws of Nevada as Alternative Energy Corp. 04/14/2008
Each share Common $0.001 par exchanged for (0.01) share Common $0.001 par

XRAYMEDIA COM INC (MN)
Name changed to Xraymedia, Inc. 12/04/2003
Xraymedia, Inc. recapitalized as T.W. Christian, Inc. 08/14/2007
(See T.W. Christian, Inc.)

XRAYMEDIA INC (MN)
Recapitalized as T.W. Christian, Inc. 08/14/2007
Each (2,605) shares Common $0.001 par exchanged for (1) share Common $0.001 par
(See T.W. Christian, Inc.)

XRF INC (UT)
Each (140) shares old Common $0.001 par exchanged for (1) share new Common $0.001 par 8/24/93
Name changed to NDS Software, Inc. 7/26/94
NDS Software, Inc. name changed to HomeSeekers.Com Inc. 7/1/98
(See HomeSeekers.Com Inc.)

XRG INC (DE)
Each share old Common $0.001 par exchanged for (0.05) share new Common $0.001 par 12/21/2004
Recapitalized as Metatron Inc. (Old) 06/03/2009
Each share Common $0.001 par exchanged for (0.025) share Common $0.001 par
Metatron Inc. (Old) reorganized as Metatron Inc. (New) 02/01/2017

XRG INC (TX)
Name changed to Doran Energy Corp. 01/20/1981
Doran Energy Corp. name changed to Wright Brothers Energy Inc. 10/30/1985

XRG INTL INC (NJ)
Each share old Capital Stock $0.001 par exchanged for (0.1) share new Capital Stock $0.001 par 9/30/86
Charter revoked for failure to file reports and pay fees 11/4/94

XRPRO SCIENCES INC (DE)
Name changed to Icagen, Inc. (New) 09/22/2015

XRS CORP (MN)
Acquired by Amundsen Holdings, LLC 10/31/2014
Each share Common 1¢ par exchanged for $5.60 cash

XS CARGO INCOME FD (AB)
Acquired by KarpReilly Capital Partners L.P. 06/15/2011
Each Trust Unit no par received $0.7263 cash

XSCRIBE CORP (CA)
Each share old Common no par exchanged for (1/3) share new Common no par 08/18/1994
Name changed to Photomatrix Inc. 02/14/1997
Photomatrix Inc. name changed to National Manufacturing Technologies Inc. 10/01/1999
(See National Manufacturing Technologies Inc.)

XSILENT SOLUTIONS INC (NV)
Name changed to Saxon Capital Group Inc. 06/05/2015

XSINVENTORY (NV)
Common $0.001 par split (5) for (1) by issuance of (4) additional shares payable 01/23/2007 to holders of record 1/22/2007 01/22/2007 Ex date - 01/24/2007
Name changed to Noble Innovations, Inc. 05/25/2007
(See Noble Innovations, Inc.)

XSIRIUS INC (DE)
Name changed 3/13/90
Name changed from Xsirius Scientific, Inc. to Xsirius, Inc. 3/13/90
Common 1¢ par split (3) for (1) by issuance of (2) additional shares 4/30/90
Name changed to Advanced Detectors, Inc. 1/1/96

XSIRIUS SUPERCONDUCTIVITY INC (DE)
Charter cancelled and declared inoperative and void for non-payment of taxes 3/1/94

XSPAND PRODS LAB INC (NV)
Name changed to Edison Nation, Inc. 09/13/2018

XSTELOS HLDGS INC (DE)
Each share old Common $0.001 par exchanged for (1) share new Common $0.001 par to reflect a (1) for (2,000) reverse split followed by a (2,000) for (1) forward split 12/24/2013
Note: Holders of (1,999) or fewer pre-split shares received $1.37 cash per share
Each share new Common $0.001 par exchanged again for (0.0000005) share new Common $0.001 par 09/23/2014
Note: In effect holders received $0.34 cash per share and public interest was eliminated

XSTRATA CDA CORP NEW (ON)
Preferred Ser. H no par called for redemption at $25 plus $0.040179 accrued dividends on 06/30/2008
Preferred Ser. 2 no par called for redemption at $25.50 plus $0.11875 accrued dividends on 07/10/2008
Preferred Ser. 3 no par called for redemption at $25 plus $0.2863 accrued dividends on 03/01/2009

XSTRATA CDA CORP OLD (ON)
Under plan of reorganization each share Ser. H Preferred no par, Ser. 2 Preferred no par and Ser. 3 Preferred no par automatically became (1) share Xstrata Canada Corp. (New) Ser. H Preferred no par, Ser. 2 Preferred no par or Ser. 3 Preferred no par respectively 06/01/2008

XSTRATA PLC (UNITED KINGDOM)
Acquired by Glencore International PLC 05/16/2013
Each ADR for Ordinary exchanged for approximately $3.177082 cash

XSTREAM BEVERAGE NETWORK INC (NV)
Name changed 10/06/2004
Each share old Common $0.001 par exchanged for (0.05) share new Common $0.001 par 07/19/2004
Name changed from XStream Beverage Group Ltd. to XStream Beverage Network, Inc. 10/06/2004
Each share new Common $0.001 par exchanged again for (0.0025) share new Common $0.001 par 08/07/2007
Name changed to Hull Energy, Inc. 05/12/2008
Hull Energy, Inc. name changed to Gemini Group Global Corp. 11/04/2013 which name changed to Gemini Group Global Corp. 11/04/2013

XTAL CORP (MN)
Name changed to Intercim Corp. 11/1/87
Intercim Corp. merged into Effective Management Systems, Inc. 2/17/95
(See Effective Management Systems, Inc.)

XTEK, INC. (OH)
Merged into Wesray Systems, Inc. 6/14/85
Each share Common $5 par exchanged for $33.33 cash

XTEN NETWORKS INC (NV)
Name changed to CounterPath Solutions, Inc. 09/16/2005
CounterPath Solutions, Inc. name changed to CounterPath Corp. 10/15/2007

XTEND MED CORP (DE)
Stock Dividend - 10% payable 03/07/2008 to holders of record 02/20/2008 Ex date - 02/15/2008
Name changed to MultiCorp International Inc. 08/28/2012

XTENT INC (DE)
Issue Information - 4,700,000 shares COM offered at $16 per share on 01/31/2007
Liquidation completed
Each share Common $0.001 par exchanged for initial distribution of $0.391469 cash 08/27/2009
Each share Common $0.001 par received second and final distribution of $0.029785 cash payable 12/29/2009 to holders of record 08/27/2009

XTERRA BLDG SYS INC (FL)
Each share old Common $0.00001 par exchanged for (0.01) share new Common $0.00001 par 06/04/2015
Name changed to North America Frac Sand, Inc. 08/14/2015

XTF MORNINGSTAR CDA DIVID TARGET 30 INDEX ETF (ON)
Name changed to First Asset Morningstar Canada Dividend Target 30 Index ETF 06/06/2012

XTF MORNINGSTAR CDA MOMENTUM INDEX ETF (ON)
Name changed to First Asset Morningstar Canada Momentum Index ETF 06/06/2012

XTF MORNINGSTAR CDA VALUE INDEX ETF (ON)
Name changed to First Asset Morningstar Canada Value Index ETF 06/06/2012

XTF MORNINGSTAR EMERGING MKTS COMPOSITE BD INDEX ETF (ON)
Name changed to First Asset Morningstar Emerging Markets Composite Bond Index ETF 06/05/2012
(See First Asset Morningstar Emerging Markets Composite Bond Index ETF)

XTF MORNINGSTAR NATL BK QUE INDEX ETF (ON)
Name changed to First Asset Morningstar National Bank Quebec Index ETF 06/06/2012

XTF MORNINGSTAR US DIVID TARGET 50 INDEX ETF (ON)
Name changed to First Asset Morningstar US Dividend Target 50 Index ETF 06/06/2012

XTO ENERGY INC (DE)
Common 1¢ par split (3) for (2) by issuance of (0.5) additional share payable 06/05/2001 to holders of record 05/23/2001 Ex date - 06/06/2001
Common 1¢ par split (4) for (3) by issuance of (1/3) additional share payable 03/18/2003 to holders of record 03/05/2003 Ex date - 03/19/2003
Common 1¢ par split (5) for (4) by issuance of (0.25) additional share payable 03/17/2004 to holders of record 03/03/2004 Ex date - 03/18/2004
Common 1¢ par split (4) for (3) by issuance of (1/3) additional share payable 03/15/2005 to holders of record 03/01/2005 Ex date - 03/16/2005
Each share Common 1¢ par received distribution of (0.0596) Hugoton Royalty Trust Unit of Ben. Int. payable 05/12/2006 to holders of record 04/26/2006 Ex date - 04/24/2006
Common 1¢ par split (5) for (4) by issuance of (0.25) additional share payable 12/13/2007 to holders of record 11/28/2007 Ex date - 12/14/2007
Merged into Exxon Mobil Corp. 06/25/2010
Each share Common 1¢ par exchanged for (0.7098) share Common no par

XTOL ENERGY INC (NV)
Old Common $0.0001 par split (2) for (1) by issuance of (1) additional

share payable 10/01/2007 to holders of record 10/01/2007
Name changed to LAUD Resources Inc. 10/23/2007
LAUD Resources Inc. name changed to MASS Petroleum Inc. 07/11/2008 which name changed to Cannamed Corp. 04/07/2014 which name changed to Chuma Holdings, Inc. 08/29/2014

XTRA CORP (DE)
Reincorporated 12/31/1976
Common $1 par split (3) for (2) by issuance of (0.5) additional share 09/01/1965
$1.40 Conv. Preferred $25 par called for redemption 09/09/1966
Common $1 par split (3) for (1) by issuance of (2) additional shares 03/14/1968
Name and state of incorporation changed from Xtra, Inc. (MA) to Xtra Corp. (DE) 12/31/1976
Common $1 par changed to 50¢ par and (1) additional share issued 02/28/1979
Preferred Stock Purchase Rights declared for Common stockholders of record 01/02/1987 were redeemed at $0.06 per right 05/31/1990 for holders of record 05/21/1990
$1.9375 Conv. Preferred Ser. B no par called for redemption 12/29/1992
Common 50¢ par split (2) for (1) by issuance of (1) additional share 05/18/1993
Stock Dividends - 10% 07/30/1973; 20% 09/30/1974
Merged into Berkshire Hathaway Inc. 09/20/2001
Each share Common 50¢ par exchanged for $55 cash

XTRA DEVS INC (ON)
Merged into Sumtra Diversifed Inc. 08/30/1978
Each share Capital Stock no par exchanged for (1/3) share Common no par

XTRA-GOLD RES CORP (NV)
Reincorporated under the laws of British Virgin Islands and Common $0.001 par changed to no par 12/24/2012

XTRACARD CORP (FL)
Each (2,400) shares old Common $0.001 par exchanged for (1) share new Common $0.001 par 02/07/2008
Reincorporated under the laws of Nevada as Hero International USA Holding Corp. 08/19/2008

XTRALIFE (CA)
Charter cancelled for failure to file reports and pay taxes 4/1/87

XTRAMEDICS INC (NV)
Recapitalized as Athena Medical Corp. 6/7/94
Each share Common 1¢ par exchanged for (0.1) share Common 1¢ par
Athena Medical Corp. name changed to A Fem Medical Corp. 7/10/94 which name changed to Quantrx Biomedical Corp. 12/23/2005

XTRANA INC (DE)
Recapitalized as Alpha Innotech Corp. 10/06/2005
Each share Common 1¢ par exchanged for (0.1) share Common 1¢ par
(See Alpha Innotech Corp.)

XTRANET SYS INC (NV)
Name changed to Great American Food Chain Inc. 4/2/2003

XTRASAFE INC (FL)
Reincorporated under the laws of Nevada as Titan Oil & Gas, Inc.

(Ctfs. dated after 06/30/2010) 06/30/2010

XTREME COIL DRILLING CORP (AB)
Name changed to Xtreme Drilling & Coil Services Corp. 04/24/2012
Xtreme Drilling & Coil Services Corp. name changed to Xtreme Drilling Corp. 07/13/2016 which merged into Akita Drilling Ltd. 09/14/2018

XTREME COS INC (NV)
Each share old Common $0.001 par exchanged for (0.01) share new Common $0.001 par 10/6/2003
Each share new Common $0.001 par exchanged again for (0.1) share new Common $0.001 par 1/30/2004
Name changed to Challenger Powerboats, Inc. 11/21/2006
(See Challenger Powerboats, Inc.)

XTREME DRILLING CORP (AB)
Name changed from Xtreme Drilling & Coil Services Corp. to Xtreme Drilling Corp. 07/13/2016
Merged into Akita Drilling Ltd. 09/14/2018
Each share Common no par exchanged for (0.3732394) share Non-Vtg. Class A no par
Note: Unexchanged certificates will be cancelled and become without value 09/14/2021

XTREME GREEN PRODS INC (NV)
Plan of reorganization under Chapter 11 Federal Bankruptcy proceedings effective
Each share Common $0.001 par received distribution of (0.21) share Xtreme Green Electric Vehicles Inc. Common $0.001 par 01/00/2015
Note: Certificates were not required to be surrendered and are without value

XTREME LINK INC (NV)
Name changed to Orient Petroleum & Energy, Inc. 10/14/2010
Orient Petroleum & Energy, Inc. recapitalized as Chun Can International Group 01/27/2017 which name changed to Yutudao Marine Biotechnology Inc. 03/27/2018

XTREME MOTORSPORTS CALIF INC (NV)
Each share old Common $0.001 par exchanged for (0.01) share new Common $0.001 par 08/08/2006
Name changed to Extreme Motorsports of California, Inc. 05/21/2007

XTREME MOTORSPORTS INTL INC (NV)
Charter revoked for failure to file reports and pay taxes 08/31/2011

XTREME OIL & GAS INC NEW (NV)
Name changed to Massive Interactive, Inc. 12/13/2013

XTREME OIL & GAS INC OLD (NV)
Reincorporated 12/00/2009
State of incorporation changed from (WA) to (NV) 12/00/2009
Reorganized as Xtreme Oil & Gas, Inc. (New) 08/15/2013
Each share Common $0.001 par exchanged for (0.01) share Common $0.001 par
Xtreme Oil & Gas, Inc. (New) name changed to Massive Interactive, Inc. 12/13/2013

XTREME TECHNOLOGIES INC (WA)
Reorganized as Xtreme Oil & Gas, Inc. (WA) 01/31/2007
Each share Common $0.001 par exchanged for (0.002) share Common $0.001 par
Xtreme Oil & Gas, Inc. (WA) reorganized in Nevada as Xtreme Oil & Gas, Inc. (Old) 12/00/2009 which reorganized as Xtreme Oil & Gas, Inc. (New) 08/15/2013 which

name changed to Massive Interactive, Inc. 12/13/2013

XTREME WEBWORKS (NV)
Recapitalized as Xtreme Companies, Inc. 05/10/2002
Each share Common $0.001 par exchanged for (0.2) share Common $0.001 par
Xtreme Companies, Inc. name changed to Challenger Powerboats, Inc. 11/21/2006
(See Challenger Powerboats, Inc.)

XTX ENERGY INC (NV)
Recapitalized as Atomic Guppy, Inc. 06/25/2007
Each share Common $0.001 par exchanged for (0.05) share Common $0.001 par
Atomic Guppy, Inc. recapitalized as Quamtel, Inc. 09/09/2009 which name changed to DataJack, Inc. 12/31/2012 which name changed to Unified Signal, Inc. 11/28/2014

XUEDA ED GROUP (CAYMAN ISLANDS)
Acquired by Xiamen Insight Investment Co., Ltd. 06/03/2016
Each Sponsored ADR for Ordinary exchanged for $5.45 cash

XUMA CORP (FL)
Name changed to Zanart Publishing Inc. 05/23/1990
Zanart Publishing Inc. recapitalized as Zanart Entertainment Inc. 12/30/1994 which name changed to Continucare Corp. 10/21/1996 which merged into Metropolitan Health Networks, Inc. 10/04/2011
(See Metropolitan Health Networks, Inc.)

XUMANII (NV)
Common $0.00001 par split (5.5) for (1) by issuance of (4.5) additional shares payable 11/08/2012 to holders of record 11/08/2012
Name changed to Xumanii International Holdings Corp. 07/30/2013
Xumanii International Holdings Corp. recapitalized as Imerjn Inc. 11/19/2014

XUMANII INTL HLDGS CORP (NV)
Recapitalized as Imerjn Inc. 11/19/2014
Each share Common $0.00001 par exchanged for (0.0001) share Common $0.00001 par

XURA INC (DE)
Acquired by Sierra Private Holdings II Ltd. 08/19/2016
Each share Common 1¢ par exchanged for $25 cash

XVARIANT INC (NV)
Name changed to Easy Groups, Ltd. 12/08/2006
Easy Groups, Ltd. name changed to China Bionanometer Industries Corp. 07/24/2007
(See China Bionanometer Industries Corp.)

XWEST ENERGY INC (NV)
Recapitalized as Transystem Services, Inc. 3/5/85
Each share Common 1¢ par exchanged for (0.1) share Common 10¢ par
(See Transystem Services, Inc.)

XXI CENTY INVTS PUB LTD (UKRAINE)
GDR agreement terminated 03/10/2016
No GDR's remain outstanding

XXIS CORP (FL)
Reincorporated 12/03/2007
State of incorporation changed from (DE) to (FL) 12/03/2007
Common $0.001 par split (50) for (1) by issuance of (49) additional shares payable 12/24/2007 to

holders of record 12/17/2007
Ex date - 12/26/2007
Name changed to 141 Capital, Inc. 01/21/2009

XXPERT RENT TOOL INC (ON)
Reorganized under the laws of Yukon as Kazakhstan Minerals Corp. 09/27/1995
Each share Common no par exchanged for (0.04) share Common no par
Kazakhstan Minerals Corp. name changed to European Minerals Corp. (Yukon) 08/14/2001 which reincorporated in British Virgin Islands 04/08/2005 which name changed to Orsu Metals Corp. 07/14/2008

XXSYS TECHNOLOGIES INC (CA)
Recapitalized as LeaseSmart, Inc. 10/13/2005
Each share Common no par exchanged for (0.001) share Common no par
(See LeaseSmart, Inc.)

XXX ACQUISITION CORP (NV)
Name changed to NightCulture, Inc. 09/20/2011
(See NightCulture, Inc.)

XYBERNAUT CORP (DE)
Plan of reorganization under Chapter 11 Federal Bankruptcy Code effective 12/31/2006
No stockholders' equity

XYLAN CORP (CA)
Merged into Alcatel 04/26/1999
Each share Common $0.001 par exchanged for $37 cash

XYLITOL CDA INC (ON)
Each share old Common no par exchanged for (0.2) share new Common no par 03/06/2017
Name changed to Sweet Natural Trading Co. 12/12/2017

XYLOGICS INC (DE)
Common 10¢ par split (2) for (1) by issuance of (1) additional share 12/02/1994
Merged into Bay Networks, Inc. 12/15/1995
Each share Common 10¢ par exchanged for (1.575) shares Common 1¢ par
Bay Networks, Inc. merged into Northern Telecom Ltd.-Northern Telecom Ltee. 08/31/1998 which name changed to Nortel Networks Corp. (Old) 04/30/1999 which reorganized as Nortel Networks Corp. (New) 05/01/2000
(See Nortel Networks Corp. (New))

XYNERGY CORP (NV)
Each share old Common $0.001 par exchanged for (0.01) share new Common $0.001 par 07/06/2006
Each share new Common $0.001 par exchanged again for (0.025) share new Common $0.001 par 10/15/2007
Name changed to Xynergy Holdings, Inc. 09/11/2008

XYNETICS, INC. (CA)
Acquired by General Signal Corp. 4/30/80
Each share Preferred $200 par exchanged for (11.16878) shares Common $1 par
Each share Common 10¢ par exchanged for (0.93073) share Common $1 par
General Signal Corp. merged into SPX Corp. 10/6/98

XYOVEST INC (OH)
Through purchase offer over 99.2% acquired by Third National Bank & Trust Co. (Dayton, OH) as of 03/31/1972
Public interest eliminated

XYN-YAL

XYPLEX (MA)
Merged into Raytheon Co. 2/28/95
Each share Common 1¢ par exchanged for $28 cash

XYQUEST VENTURE CORP (BC)
Name changed to Polar Bear Ventures Ltd. 11/25/1996
Polar Bear Ventures Ltd. recapitalized as Iciena Ventures Inc. 02/24/1999 which recapitalized as Barksdale Capital Corp. 02/08/2013

XYRATEX LTD (BERMUDA)
Issue Information - 6,956,522 shares COM offered at $14 per share on 06/23/2005
Acquired by Seagate Technology PLC 03/31/2014
Each share Common 1¢ par exchanged for $13.25 cash

XYTEC INTL INDS INC (WA)
Name changed 09/16/1983
Name changed from Xytec Inc. to Xytec International Industries, Inc. 09/16/1983
Each share Common 10¢ par exchanged for (1.5) shares Common no par 09/28/1983
Merged into Perstop Xytec, Inc. 07/02/1991
Each share Common no par exchanged for $0.40 cash

XYTRONYX INC (DE)
Name changed to Pacific Pharmaceuticals Inc. 08/08/1997
Pacific Pharmaceuticals Inc. merged into Procept, Inc. 03/17/1999 which name changed to HeavenlyDoor.com, Inc. 01/31/2000 which name changed to Paligent Inc. 12/31/2000 which recapitalized as International Fight League, Inc. 11/29/2006 which recapitalized as IFLI Acquisition Corp. 07/08/2010 which name changed to SimplePons, Inc. 12/27/2011 which recapitalized as Eco-Shift Power Corp. 11/26/2013

XYVISION INC (DE)
Each share old Common 3¢ par exchanged for (0.2) share new Common 3¢ par 10/21/1998
Name changed to Azul Holdings Inc. 09/28/1999
(See Azul Holdings Inc.)

XYZ LIQUIDATING CORP (DE)
In process of liquidation
Each share Common 10¢ par received initial distribution of $5.75 cash 7/2/81
Property transferred to PRF Liquidating Trust 9/8/81
(See PRF Liquidating Trust)

XZERES CORP (NV)
Name changed 05/17/2011
Name changed from XZERES Wind Corp. to XZERES Corp. 05/17/2011
Acquired by Xzeres Merger Sub, Inc. 01/06/2016
Each share Common $0.001 par exchanged for $0.072 cash

XZERON, INC. (UT)
Recapitalized as Teleware, Inc. 9/27/83
Each share Common $0.001 par exchanged for (2) shares Common $0.001 par

Y & O VENTURES CORP (BC)
Name changed to Hanwei Energy Services Corp. 12/12/2006

Y & R PPTYS LTD (ON)
Merged into Oxford Development Group Ltd. 9/29/78
Each share Common no par exchanged for (1) share $1.75 Class Y Preference $5 par
(See Oxford Development Group Ltd.)

Y & S CANDIES INC (NY)
Stock Dividends - 10% 12/17/75; 10% 2/10/76
Merged into Hershey Foods Corp. 11/30/77
Each share Common $3 par exchanged for (1.3841) shares Common no par
Hershey Foods Corp. name changed to Hershey Co. 4/19/2005

Y B MEATS INC (KS)
Charter forfeited 10/15/1990

Y.G. DEV CO (CA)
Name changed to Western Water Co. (CA) 9/11/92
Western Water Co. (CA) reincorporated in Delaware 3/23/94
(See Western Water Co. (DE))

Y O SYS LTD (NV)
Name changed to Metro Systems, Inc. 02/27/1987
Metro Systems, Inc. recapitalized as Adelaide Holdings, Inc. 07/30/1991 which name changed to Tasty Fries, Inc. 09/28/1993
(See Tasty Fries, Inc.)

Y-TEL INTL INC (DE)
Recapitalized as NexHorizon Communications, Inc. 02/01/2007
Each share Common $0.001 par exchanged for (0.11764705) share Common $0.001 par
NexHorizon Communications, Inc. name changed to NX Capital Co. 09/16/2013 which recapitalized as NX Uranium, Inc. 09/29/2014

Y&A GROUP INC (DE)
Common $0.0025 par split (2) for (1) by issuance of (1) additional share 06/29/1990
Company reported out of business 05/00/1991
Stockholders' equity unlikely

YAAK RIV RES INC (CO)
Recapitalized as Lifeline Therapeutics, Inc. 10/05/2004
Each share Common $0.0001 par exchanged for (0.01470588) share Common $0.0001 par
Lifeline Therapeutics, Inc. name changed to LifeVantage Corp. (CO) 02/02/2007 which reincorporated in Delaware 03/09/2018

YACHT HAVENS INTL CORP (NV)
Each share old Common 2¢ par exchanged for (0.04) share new Common 2¢ par 06/30/1995
Name changed to Promotel Inc. 07/10/1995
Promotel Inc. recapitalized as DigiTEC 2000, Inc. 10/18/1996
(See DigiTEC 2000, Inc.)

YADKIN FINL CORP (NC)
Merged into F.N.B. Corp. 03/11/2017
Each share Common $1 par exchanged for (2.16) shares Common 1¢ par

YADKIN VY BK & TR CO (ELKIN, NC)
Common $5 par split (3) for (2) by issuance of (0.5) additional share 01/26/1990
Common $5 par split (5) for (4) by issyance of (0.25) additional share 12/28/1994
Common $5 par split (2) for (1) by issuance (1) additional share payable 12/28/1998 to holders of record 12/07/1998
Stock Dividends - 10% 01/29/1993; 5% payable 12/31/1997 to holders of record 12/08/1997
Under plan of reorganization each share Common $5 par automatically became (1) share Yadkin Valley Financial Corp. Common $1 par 07/01/2006
Yadkin Valley Financial Corp. recapitalized as Yadkin Financial Corp. 05/28/2013 which merged into F.N.B. Corp. 03/11/2017

YADKIN VY CO (NC)
Each share Common $1 par exchanged for (0.02) share Common $50 par 4/24/2006
Note: Holders of (49) or fewer pre-split shares received $78 cash per share and public interest was eliminated

YADKIN VY FINL CORP (NC)
Recapitalized as Yadkin Financial Corp. 05/28/2013
Each share Common $1 par exchanged for (0.33333333) share Common $1 par
Yadkin Financial Corp. merged into F.N.B. Corp. 03/11/2017

YAFARM TECHNOLOGIES INC (DE)
Common $0.001 par split (5) for (1) by issuance of (4) additional shares payable 01/18/2013 to holders of record 01/18/2013 Ex date - 01/22/2013
Recapitalized as Profile Solutions, Inc. 07/31/2014
Each share Common $0.001 par exchanged for (0.1) share Common $0.001 par

YAHOO INC (DE)
Reincorporated 05/14/1999
Common $0.001 par split (3) for (2) by issuance of (0.5) additional share payable 8/29/97 to holders of record 08/11/1997
Common $0.001 par split (2) for (1) by issuance of (1) additional share payable 07/31/1998 to holders of record 07/17/1998 Ex date - 08/03/1998
Common $0.001 par split (2) for (1) by issuance of (1) additional share payable 02/05/1999 to holders of record 01/22/1999
State of incorporation changed from (CA) to (DE) 05/14/1999
Common $0.001 par split (2) for (1) by issuance of (1) additional share payable 02/11/2000 to holders of record 01/20/2000
Common $0.001 par split (2) for (1) by issuance of (1) additional share payable 05/11/2004 to holders of record 04/26/2004 Ex date - 05/12/2004
Name changed to Altaba Inc. 06/19/2017

YAK COMMUNICATIONS INC (FL)
Name changed 12/16/2003
Each share old Common no par exchanged for (0.2) share new Common no par 12/17/99
Name changed from Yak Communications USA Inc. to Yak Communications Inc. 12/16/2003
Common no par split (2) for (1) by issuance of (1) additional share payable 1/29/2004 to holders of record 1/15/2004 Ex date - 1/30/2004
Merged into Globalive Communications Corp. 11/7/2006
Each share new Common no par exchanged for $5.25 cash

YAKIMA HOLDING CORP.
Liquidation approved in 1936

YAKIMA SHOSHONE MNG CO (WA)
Completely liquidated 02/03/1969
Each share Capital Stock 10¢ par exchanged for first and final distribution of (0.23) share Consolidated Silver Corp. Common 10¢ par
Consolidated Silver Corp. name changed to ConSil Corp. (ID) 11/15/1995 which reorganized in Nevada as LumaLite Holdings, Inc. 03/22/2002 which name changed to MEMS USA, Inc. 01/19/2004 which name changed to Convergence Ethanol, Inc. 12/13/2006
(See Convergence Ethanol, Inc.)

YAKUN INTL INVT & HLDG GROUP (NV)
Name changed to QHY Group 09/26/2018

YALAKUM RESOURCES LTD. (BC)
Charter cancelled 10/25/85

YALE & TOWNE MANUFACTURING CO. (CT)
Capital Stock $25 par changed to $10 par and (1.5) additional shares issued 04/26/1956
Merged into Eaton Manufacturing Co. 10/31/1963
Each share Capital Stock $10 par exchanged for (0.25) share 3-3/4% Preferred $25 par and (0.75) share Common $1 par
Eaton Manufacturing Co. name changed to Eaton Yale & Towne Inc. 12/31/1965 which name changed to Eaton Corp. (OH) 04/21/1971 which reincorporated in Ireland as Eaton Corp. PLC 11/30/2012

YALE (MARTIN) BUSINESS MACHINES CORP. (IL)
See - Martin Yale Business Machines Corp.

YALE EXPRESS SYS INC (NY)
Each share Class A 25¢ par exchanged for (0.263157) share Common 1¢ par 12/1/72
Each share Class B 25¢ par exchanged for (0.263157) share Common 1¢ par 12/1/72
Note: Unexchanged certificates were cancelled and became without value in 1978
Filed a petition under Chapter XI Federal Bankruptcy Code 5/21/79
No stockholders' equity

YALE (MARTIN) INDUSTRIES, INC. (IL)
See - Martin Yale Industries Inc.

YALE LEAD & ZINC MINES LTD. (ON)
Merged into International Mogul Mines Ltd. 11/20/68
Each share Capital Stock $1 par exchanged for (0.011904) share Capital Stock no par
International Mogul Mines Ltd. merged into Conwest Exploration Co. Ltd. (Old) (ONT) 8/27/82 which merged into Conwest Exploration Co. Ltd. (New) (ALTA) 9/1/93 which merged into Alberta Energy Co. Ltd. 1/31/96 which merged into EnCana Corp. 1/3/2003

YALE RES LTD (BC)
Recapitalized as Alta Vista Ventures Ltd. 05/29/2013
Each share Common no par exchanged for (0.1) share Common no par
Alta Vista Ventures Ltd. name changed to Global UAV Technologies Ltd. 05/17/2017

YALETOWN ENTMT CORP (BC)
Delisted from NEX 07/23/2010

YALIAN STL CORP (BC)
Acquired by 0957703 B.C. Ltd. 05/07/2013
Each share Common no par exchanged for $0.40 cash

YALTA GOLD MINES, LTD. (ON)
Charter cancelled for failure to file reports and pay taxes 10/7/57

YAMA GOLD MINES LTD.
Acquired by Cathroy Larder Mines Ltd. 00/00/1943
Each share Capital Stock exchanged for (0.33333333) share Capital Stock $1 par
(See Cathroy Larder Mines Ltd.)

YAMAHA MTR CO LTD (JAPAN)
ADR agreement terminated 06/29/2009
Each ADR for Common no par exchanged for $25.84974 cash

YAMAHAMAS INC (NV)
Name changed to Accesspoint Corp. 03/19/1999
(See Accesspoint Corp.)

YAMANA RES INC (CANADA)
Recapitalized as Yamana Gold Inc. 08/21/2003
Each (27.86) shares Common no par exchanged for (1) share Common no par

YAMIRI GOLD & ENERGY INC (BC)
Name changed to Cannon Point Resources Ltd. 04/27/2010
Cannon Point Resources Ltd. merged into Northern Dynasty Minerals Ltd. 10/29/2015

YANCEY-HARRIS CO., INC. (DE)
Dissolved 1/1/56

YANDEL NORTHWEST PETES INC (DE)
Name changed to Allerton Resources Inc. 8/17/78
(See Allerton Resources Inc.)

YANEX GROUP INC (NV)
Name changed to Proto Script Pharmaceutical Corp. 10/13/2016

YANGARRA RES INC (AB)
Merged into Yangarra Resources Ltd. 11/9/2005
Each share Common no par exchanged for (0.95) share Common no par

YANGTZE RIV DEV LTD (NV)
Name changed to Yangtze River Port & Logistics Ltd. 02/14/2018

YANK YELLOWKNIFE GOLD MINES, LTD. (ON)
Charter cancelled for failure to file reports and pay taxes 5/26/58

YANKEE BANCORPORATION (MA)
Merged into Massachusetts Bay Bancorp, Inc. 3/31/76
Each share Common $1 par exchanged for (1) share Common $1 par
Massachusetts Bay Bancorp, Inc. merged into New England Merchants Co., Inc. 5/31/80 which name changed to Bank of New England Corp. 5/1/82
(See Bank of New England Corp.)

YANKEE BOWLING CENTERS, INC. (DE)
No longer in existence having become inoperative and void for non-payment of taxes 4/1/67

YANKEE CANADIAN MINING CO. LTD.
Acquired by Yankee Canuck Oil & Mining Corp. Ltd. share for share 00/00/1949
Yankee Canuck Oil & Mining Corp. Ltd. liquidated for Acroll Oil & Gas Ltd. 12/31/1966 which recapitalized as Acroll Petroleums Ltd. 12/30/1977 which merged into Trans-Canada Resources Ltd. (New) 11/01/1982 which recapitalized as Consolidated Trans-Canada Resources Ltd. 09/22/1988 which merged into Ranchmen's Resources Ltd. 09/30/1989 which merged into Crestar Energy Inc. 10/11/1995 which was acquired by Gulf Canada Resources Ltd. 11/13/2000
(See Gulf Canada Resources Ltd.)

YANKEE CANDLE INC (MA)
Merged into Madison Dearborn Partners, LLC 02/06/2007
Each share Common 1¢ par exchanged for $34.75 cash

YANKEE CANUCK OIL & MNG CORP (ON)
Capital Stock $1 par changed to 20¢ par 07/04/1955
Completely liquidated 12/31/1966
Each share Capital Stock 20¢ par exchanged for first and final distribution of (0.037037) Acroll Oil & Gas Ltd. Common no par
Acroll Oil & Gas Ltd. recapitalized as Acroll Petroleums Ltd. 12/30/1977 which merged into Trans-Canada Resources Ltd. (New) 11/01/1982 which recapitalized as Consolidated Trans-Canada Resources Ltd. 09/22/1988 which merged into Ranchmen's Resources Ltd. 09/30/1989 which merged into Crestar Energy Inc. 10/11/1995 which was acquired by Gulf Canada Resources Ltd. 11/13/2000
(See Gulf Canada Resources Ltd.)

YANKEE CONS MNG CO (UT)
Merged into North Lily Mining Co. 12/1/76
Each share Common 10¢ par exchanged for (0.0108) share Capital Stock 10¢ par
(See North Lily Mining Co.)

YANKEE COS INC (MD)
Under plan of reorganization name changed to National Environmental Group Inc. 10/11/1989
Each share $1.15 Preferred Stock 10¢ par exchanged for (1.2) shares Common 10¢ par and (1) Common Stock Purchase Warrant expiring 12/31/1993
National Environmental Group Inc. reorganized as Key Energy Group, Inc. 12/04/1992 which name changed to Key Energy Services Inc. (MD) 12/09/1998
(See Key Energy Services Inc. (MD))

YANKEE DOODLE ENTERPRISES INC (AL)
Reorganized under the laws of Delaware as Mexus, Inc. 11/18/1993
Each share Common 20¢ par exchanged for (0.05) share Common no par
Mexus, Inc. name changed to Wittcomm Inc. 04/29/1997
(See Wittcomm Inc.)

YANKEE DOODLE OIL CO. (AZ)
Charter expired by time limitation 3/21/25

YANKEE DUNDEE MINES LTD. (BC)
Recapitalized as Dundee Mines Ltd. 04/19/1963
Each share Capital Stock 50¢ par exchanged for (0.14285714) share Capital Stock no par
Dundee Mines Ltd. acquired by Palliser Petroleums Ltd. 05/03/1973 which name changed to Dundee-Palliser Resources Inc. 05/17/1973 which recapitalized as Scorpion Minerals Inc. 04/01/1996 which name changed to Nextair Inc. 03/05/2001 which recapatallized as NXA Inc. 02/23/2005 which recapitalized as Ellipsiz Communications Ltd. 11/26/2015

YANKEE ENERGY GROUP (NV)
Common 10¢ par changed to 1¢ par 12/13/1981
Each share old Common 1¢ par exchanged for (0.1) share new Common 1¢ par 10/15/1986
Company dissolved 09/09/1997
Details not available

YANKEE ENERGY SYS INC (CT)
Common $5 par split (3) for (2) by issuance of (0.5) additional share 06/28/1993
Merged into Northeast Utilities 03/01/2000
Each share Common $5 par exchanged for either (2.31) shares Common $5 par or $45 cash
Note: Option to make a definitive election expired 03/03/2000. Non-electing holders received (1.9173) shares and $7.65 cash per share
Northeast Utilities name changed to Eversource Energy 02/19/2015

YANKEE FIBER TILE MANUFACTURING CO. (MI)
Name changed to Color-Craft Products, Inc. in 1952
(See Color-Craft Products, Inc.)

YANKEE GIRL OIL CO. (AZ)
Charter expired in 1926
No known value

YANKEE HAT INDS CORP (AB)
Reincorporated under the laws of British Columbia as Yankee Hat Minerals Ltd. 02/09/2005

YANKEE OIL & GAS INC (MD)
Common 10¢ par split (3) for (2) by issuance of (0.5) additional share 11/17/1981
Common 10¢ par split (4) for (3) by issuance of (0.33333333) additional share 07/08/1983
Name changed to Yankee Companies, Inc. 11/28/1984
Yankee Companies, Inc. reorganized as National Environmental Group Inc. 10/11/1989 which reorganized as Key Energy Group, Inc. 12/04/1992 which name changed Key Energy Services Inc. (MD) 12/09/1998
(See Key Energy Services Inc. (MD))

YANKEE PETES LTD (BC)
Name changed to Yankee Power, Inc. 06/12/1987
(See Yankee Power, Inc.)

YANKEE PLASTICS INC (NY)
Name changed to Mr. Hanger, Inc. 3/16/71
(See Mr. Hanger, Inc.)

YANKEE PWR INC (BC)
Struck off register and declared dissolved for failure to file returns 07/09/1993

YANKEE PRINCESS OILS LTD. (AB)
Merged into Medallion Petroleums Ltd. 09/11/1956
Each share Capital Stock 10¢ par exchanged for (0.28571428) share Capital Stock $1.25 par
Medallion Petroleums Ltd. merged into Canadian Industrial Gas & Oil Ltd. 03/05/1965 which merged into Norcen Energy Resources Ltd. (AB) 10/28/1975 which reincorporated in Canada 04/15/1977
(See Norcen Energy Resources Ltd.)

YANKEE STORES INC (DE)
Name changed to Specialty Retail Ventures Inc. 8/15/90
(See Specialty Retail Ventures Inc.)

YANKEE URANIUM CO. (UT)
Merged into Consolidated Oil & Resources, Inc. on a (1) for (147.45) basis 05/24/1956
Consolidated Oil & Resources, Inc. merged into Randex Consolidated Oil Co. 00/00/1956 which recapitalized as American-Caribbean Oil Co. 03/21/1958 which merged into Elgin Gas & Oil Co. 06/30/1959
(See Elgin Gas & Oil Co.)

YANKEE YOGURT INC (NV)
Name changed to Cornerstone Capital Inc. (NV) 07/31/1991
Cornerstone Capital Inc. (NV) reorganized in Florida as Medhealth Service Corp. 08/16/1991
(See Medhealth Service Corp.)

YANKS PEAK RES LTD (BC)
Recapitalized as BHR Buffalo Head Resources Ltd. 06/01/1998
Each share Common no par exchanged for (0.1) share Common no par
BHR Buffalo Head Resources Ltd. recapitalized as White Tiger Mining Corp. 07/03/2008 which name changed to Copper Lake Resources Ltd. 09/24/2014

YANTAI DAHUA HLDGS CO LTD (BELIZE)
Common $0.001 par split (3) for (1) by issuance of (2) additional shares payable 04/23/2003 to holders of record 04/13/2003 Ex date - 04/24/2003
Name changed to China Agro-Technology Holdings, Ltd. 01/14/2008
(See China Agro-Technology Holdings, Ltd.)

YAP INTL INC (NV)
Common no par split (2) for (1) by issuance of (1) additional share payable 8/3/2004 to holders of record 7/30/2004 Ex date - 8/4/2004
Name changed to Nomad International, Inc. 5/13/2005
Nomad International, Inc. recapitalized as iPackets International, Inc. 11/22/2005

YARANDRY SILVER MINES LTD (ON)
Recapitalized as New Yarandry Ltd. 04/28/1972
Each share Capital Stock no par exchanged for (0.2) share Capital Stock no par
New Yarandry Ltd. name changed to Merbank Capital Corp. (ONT) 02/23/1988 which reincorporated in British Columbia 06/13/1995 which merged into Gran Colombia Resources Inc. 07/11/1995 which name changed to Wavve Telecommunications, Inc. 10/29/1999
(See Wavve Telecommunications, Inc.)

YARC SYS INC (CA)
Filed a petition under Chapter 7 Federal Bankruptcy Code 4/17/2001
Stockholders' equity unlikely

YARD MAN INC (MI)
Each share Common $10 par exchanged for (8) shares Common $2 par 11/00/1954
Acquired by Leisure Group, Inc. 04/29/1970
Each share Common $2 par exchanged for (1.2065) shares Common no par
(See Leisure Group, Inc.)

YARDLEY & CO LTD (ENGLAND)
Stock Dividend - ADR's for Ord. Reg. and A Ord. Reg. - 66-2/3% 07/29/1963
Acquired by British-American Tobacco Co. Ltd. 09/29/1967
Each ADR for Ordinary Reg. 4s par exchanged for $4.28 cash
Each ADR for A Ordinary Reg. 4s par exchanged for $3.79 cash

YARDLEY CAP INC (BC)
Recapitalized as Golden Patriot Mining Inc. 09/12/2003
Each share Common no par exchanged for (0.25) share Common no par
Golden Patriot Mining Inc. name changed to Hana Mining Ltd. (Old) 03/01/2007
(See Hana Mining Ltd. (Old))

YARDLEY VENTURES INC (DE)
Recapitalized as Magnavision Corp. 12/30/91
Each share old Common $0.00001 par exchanged for (0.0025) share new Common $0.00001 par 12/30/91
(See Magnavision Corp.)

YARDLEY WATER & POWER CO. (PA)
Name changed to Yardley Water Co. 4/16/58

YARDNEY CORP (NY)
Merged into Whittaker Corp. 06/28/1985
Each share Common 25¢ par exchanged for $5.50 cash

YARDNEY ELECTRIC CORP. (NY)
Common 50¢ par changed to 25¢ par and (1) additional share issued 8/4/61
Name changed to Yardney Corp. 5/5/83
(See Yardney Corp.)

YARDVILLE CAP TR (DE)
9.25% Trust Preferred Securities called for redemption at $10 on 3/31/2003

YARDVILLE NATL BANCORP (NJ)
Common no par split (2) for (1) by issuance of (1) additional share payable 01/20/1998 to holders of record 01/05/1998
Stock Dividend - 2.5% payable 04/21/1998 to holders of record 04/07/1998
Merged into PNC Financial Services Group, Inc. 10/26/2007
Each share Common no par exchanged for $34.17 cash

YARDVILLE NATL BK (YARDVILLE, NJ)
Under plan of reorganization each share Common $5 par automatically became (1) share Yardville National Bancorp Common no par 11/26/1985
(See Yardville National Bancorp)

YARG PRODUCING & REFINING CORP.
Dissolved in 1945

YARRAMAN WINERY INC (NV)
Name changed to Global Beverages, Inc. 03/25/2010
(See Global Beverages, Inc.)

YASHENG ECO-TRADE CORP (DE)
Recapitalized as Eco-Trade Corp. 12/09/2010
Each share Common $0.001 par exchanged for (0.01) share Common $0.001 par

YASUDA TR & BKG LTD (JAPAN)
Name changed to Mizuho Asset Trust & Banking Co., Ltd. 4/1/2002
(See Mizuho Asset Trust & Banking Co., Ltd.)

YATERRA VENTURES CORP (NV)
Name changed to Mining Global, Inc. 08/07/2014

YATES AMERN MACH CO (DE)
Each share Preferred no par exchanged for (0.5) share old Common $5 par in 1936
Each share old Common $5 par exchanged for (0.5833) share new Common $5 par and $10.008 cash 4/29/68
Stock Dividend - 50% 4/30/65
Merged into Y.A. Machine Co. 2/12/76
Each share new Common $5 par exchanged for $25 cash

YATES INDS INC (NJ)
Common 25¢ par split (2) for (1) by issuance of (1) additional share 07/28/1970
Common 25¢ par split (2) for (1) by issuance of (1) additional share 08/23/1979
Merged into Square D Co. 07/31/1980
Each share Common 25¢ par exchanged for $40 cash

YATES RANCH OIL & RTYS (TX)
Common no par changed to $1 par in 1937
Acquired by Triton Oil & Gas Corp. 11/20/68
Each share Common $1 par exchanged for (0.25) share Common Capital Stock $1 par
Triton Oil & Gas Corp. name changed to Triton Energy Corp. (TX) 12/1/81 which reincorporated in Delaware 5/12/95

YAVAPAI GOLD, INC. (NM)
Charter forfeited for failure to pay taxes 10/12/62

YAVAPAI HILLS INC (DE)
Name changed to J.P. Cabot Realty, Inc. 10/26/2004

YAWMAN & ERBE MANUFACTURING CO. (NY)
Merged into Sterling Precision Corp. 1/3/56
Each share 4-1/2% Preferred $25 par exchanged for (2.5) shares 5% Conv. Ser. A Preferred $10 par
Sterling Precision Corp. name changed to Steego Corp. 8/23/79
(See Steego Corp.)

YAYI INTL INC (DE)
SEC revoked common stock registration 04/06/2016

YAZICILAR OTOMOTIV VE GIDA YATIRIM VE PAZARLAMA SANAYI VE TICARET ANONIM SIRKETI (TURKEY)
Reg. S GDR's for Class A split (3) for (2) by issuance of (0.5) additional GDR payable 06/19/2001 to holders of record 05/31/2001 Ex date - 05/31/2001
144A GDR's for Class A split (3) for (2) by issuance of (0.5) additional GDR payable 06/19/2001 to holders of record 05/31/2001 Ex date - 05/31/2001
Reg. S GDR's for Class A split (4) for (1) by issuance of (3) additional GDR's payable 07/06/2007 to holders of record 02/12/2007
144A GDR's for Class A split (4) for (1) by issuance of (3) additional GDR's payable 07/06/2007 to holders of record 02/12/2007
Stock Dividends - 30% payable 06/25/2002 to holders of record 06/11/2002; 50% payable 07/23/2004 to holders of record 07/14/2004; 95.36001% payable 09/26/2005 to holders of record 07/01/2005
ADR agreement terminated 03/02/2010
Each Reg. S GDR for Class A exchanged for $1.043 cash
Each 144A GDR for Class A exchanged for $1.043 cash

YBM MAGNEX INTL INC (AB)
Placed in receivership in January 1999
No stockholders' equity

YDI WIRELESS INC (DE)
Name changed to Terabeam, Inc. 11/07/2005
Terabeam, Inc. named changed to Proxim Wireless Corp. 09/10/2007

YEAHRONIMO MEDIA VENTURES INC (CO)
Name changed to Commodore International Corp. 10/10/2005

YEARS FINL TR (ON)
Each Unit received distribution of (1) Warrant expiring 08/31/2006 payable 03/16/2006 to holders of record 03/15/2006
Merged into Dividend Growth Split Corp. 12/31/2008
Each Unit exchanged for (0.815986) Unit consisting of (1) share Preferred and (1) share Class A no par

YEARS TR (ON)
Merged into Years Financial Trust 12/16/2005
Each Unit no par exchanged for (1.0537) Units no par
Years Financial Trust merged into Dividend Growth Split Corp. 12/31/2008

YELL GROUP PLC (UNITED KINGDOM)
Name changed to Hibu PLC 08/02/2012
(See Hibu PLC)

YELLOHILL GOLD MINES, LTD. (ON)
Charter cancelled for failure to file reports and pay taxes in 1952

YELLOREX MINES LTD (ON)
Recapitalized as Bras-American Corp. 09/18/1990
Each share Common $1 par exchanged for (0.1) share Common $1 par
(See Bras-American Corp.)

YELLOW & CHECKER CAB CO.
Merged into Yellow Cab Co. of San Francisco in 1946
Each share Class A Common Series 1 and 2 exchanged for $25 principal amount of 10 year debentures and (2) shares 6% Preferred $25 par
Each share Class B Common exchanged for (7) shares Common $1 par

YELLOW BAND GOLD MINES, INC. (AK)
Charter cancelled for failure to pay corporate taxes 1/1/62

YELLOW BAND RES INC (BC)
Merged into Commonwealth Gold Corp. 03/01/1991
Each share Common no par exchanged for (0.5) share Common no par
Commonwealth Gold Corp. merged into Aber Resources Ltd. (New) 04/19/1994 which name changed to Aber Diamond Corp. 08/18/2000 which name changed to Harry Winston Diamond Corp. 11/19/2007 which name changed to Dominion Diamond Corp. 03/27/2013
(See Dominion Diamond Corp.)

YELLOW BKS CLAY PRODS INC (IN)
Proclaimed dissolved for failure to file reports 4/20/92

YELLOW CAB, INC.
Acquired by Public Service Coordinated Transport in 1930 which is a subsidiary of Public Service Electric & Gas Co.

YELLOW CAB CO PHILADELPHIA (PA)
Each share Common no par exchanged for (20) shares Common $3 par 00/00/1949
Reverted to private company 00/00/1966
Details not available

YELLOW CAP OIL, INC. (DE)
Declared inoperative and void for non- payment of taxes 4/1/52

YELLOW CAT URANIUM CO. (UT)
Recapitalized as Trans-Pacific Enterprises, Inc. 2/21/67
Each share Capital Stock 1¢ par exchanged for (0.01) share Common no par

YELLOW CORP (DE)
Each share Common $1 par received distribution of (0.5) share SCS Transportation Inc. Common $0.001 par payable 9/30/2002 to holders of record 9/3/2002 Ex date - 10/1/2002
Under plan of merger name changed to Yellow Roadway Corp. 12/12/2003
Yellow Roadway Corp. name changed to YRC Worldwide Inc. 1/4/2006

YELLOW FGHT SYS INC (IN)
Common $1 par split (5) for (2) by issuance of (1.5) additional shares 4/9/69
Stock Dividends - 100% 12/31/71; 100% 10/8/74
Under plan of reorganization each share Common $1 par automatically became (1) share Yellow Freight System, Inc. of Delaware Common $1 par 6/1/83
Yellow Freight System, Inc. of Delaware name changed to Yellow Corp. 4/22/93 which name changed to Yellow Roadway Corp. 12/12/2003 which name changed to YRC Worldwide Inc. 1/4/2006

YELLOW FGHT SYS INC DEL (DE)
Common $1 par split (2) for (1) by issuance of (1) additional share 8/26/85
Name changed to Yellow Corp. 4/22/93
Yellow Corp. name changed to Yellow Roadway Corp. 12/12/2003 which name changed to YRC Worldwide Inc. 1/4/2006

YELLOW GOLD CRIPPLE CREEK INC (CO)
Each share old Common $0.0025 par exchanged for (0.025) share new Common $0.0025 par 10/06/1997
Recapitalized as International Cavitation Technologies, Inc. 12/04/1998
Each share new Common $0.0025 par exchanged for (0.25) share Common $0.0025 par
(See International Cavitation Technologies, Inc.)

YELLOW HILL ENERGY INC (NV)
Name changed to American Eagle Energy Inc. 10/14/2009
American Eagle Energy Inc. merged into Eternal Energy Corp. 12/20/2011 which recapitalized as American Eagle Energy Corp. 12/20/2011
(See American Eagle Energy Corp.)

YELLOW JACKET CONSOLIDATED GOLD MINES, LTD. (NV)
Charter revoked for failure to file reports and pay fees 3/5/56

YELLOW JACKET CORP (UT)
Reorganized under the laws of Nevada as Waco Holding Co. 10/31/1993
Each share Common 1¢ par exchanged for (0.005) share Common $0.001 par
Waco Holding Co. name changed to Millenia Corp. 10/31/1994 which name changed to Internet Multi-Media Corp. 01/25/2000 which recapitalized as AmEurotech Corp. (NV) 12/18/2000 which reincorporated in Florida 04/18/2007 which recapitalized as Scott Contracting Holdings, Inc. 07/11/2007 which name changed to Liverpool Group, Inc. 04/29/2008

YELLOW MEDIA INC NEW (CANADA)
Recapitalized as Yellow Media Ltd. 12/20/2012
Each share 4.25% 1st Preferred Ser. 1 no par exchanged for (0.06252229) share Common no par and (0.03572702) Common Stock Purchase Warrant expiring 12/20/2022
Each share 5% 1st Preferred Ser. 2 no par exchanged for (0.06252229) share Common no par and (0.03572702) Common Stock Purchase Warrant expiring 12/20/2022
Each share Rate Reset 1st Preferred Ser. 3 no par exchanged for (0.06252229) share Common no par and (0.03572702) Common Stock Purchase Warrant expiring 12/20/2022
Each share Rate Reset 1st Preferred Ser. 5 no par exchanged for (0.06252229) share Common no par and (0.03572702) Common Stock Purchase Warrant expiring 12/20/2022
Each share Common no par exchanged for (0.00500178) share Common no par and (0.00285816) Common Stock Purchase Warrant expiring 12/20/2022
Yellow Media Ltd. name changed to Yellow Pages Ltd. 01/05/2015

YELLOW MEDIA INC OLD (CANADA)
Under plan of reorganization each share 4.25% 1st Preferred Ser. 1 no par, 5% 1st Preferred Ser. 2 no par, Rate Reset 1st Preferred Ser. 3 no par and Rate Reset 1st Preferred Ser. 5 no par automatically became (1) share Yellow Media Inc. (New) 4.25% 1st Preferred Ser. 1 no par, 5% 1st Preferred Ser. 2 no par, Rate Reset 1st Preferred Ser. 3 no par or Rate Reset 1st Preferred Ser. 5 no par respectively 11/01/2010
Yellow Media Inc. (New) recapitalized as Yellow Media Ltd. 12/20/2012 which name changed to Yellow Pages Ltd. 01/05/2015

YELLOW MEDIA LTD (CANADA)
Name changed to Yellow Pages Ltd. 01/05/2015

YELLOW PAGES INCOME FD (ON)
Each Instalment Receipt plus final payment of $4.50 cash received (1) Trust Unit prior to 06/10/2005
Under plan of reorganization each Unit automatically became (1) share Yellow Media Inc. (New) Common no par 11/01/2010
Yellow Media Inc. (New) recapitalized as Yellow Media Ltd. 12/20/2012 which name changed to Yellow Pages Ltd. 01/05/2015

YELLOW PAN GOLD MINES, LTD. (ON)
Charter cancelled for failure to file reports and pay taxes 12/10/62

YELLOW PINE MINING CO. (NV)
Foreclosed in 1935
No stockholders' equity

YELLOW POINT MNG CORP (BC)
Recapitalized as Desert Sun Mining Corp. (BC) 8/26/94
Each share Common no par exchanged for (0.2) share Common no par
Desert Sun Mining Corp. (BC) reincorporated in Canada 3/20/2003 which was acquired by Yamana Gold Inc. 4/5/2006

YELLOW ROADWAY CORP (DE)
Name changed to YRC Worldwide Inc. 1/4/2006

YELLOW TAXI CORP. (NY)
Charter forfeited for failure to file reports in 1939

YELLOW TRAN FGHT LINES INC (IN)
Under plan of merger name changed to Yellow Freight System, Inc. and Class A Common $1 par reclassified as Common $1 par 12/9/68
Yellow Freight System, Inc. reorganized as Yellow Freight System, Inc. of Delaware 6/1/83 which name changed to Yellow Corp. 4/22/93 which name changed to Yellow Roadway Corp. 12/12/2003 which name changed to YRC Worldwide Inc. 1/4/2006

YELLOW TRUCK & COACH MANUFACTURING CO.
Acquired by General Motors Corp. 00/00/1943
Each share 7% Preferred exchanged for (2.7) shares Common $10 par
Each (3) shares Common exchanged for (1) share Common $10 par
General Motors Corp. name changed to Motors Liquidation Co. 07/15/2009

YELLOW WING URANIUM CORP. (NV)
Recapitalized as Petroleum Development Corp. 07/20/1970
Each share Capital Stock 1¢ par exchanged for (0.01666666) share Common 1¢ par
Petroleum Development Corp. name changed to PDC Energy, Inc. (NV) 06/13/2012 which reincorporated in Delaware 06/11/2015

YELLOWAVE CORP (NV)
Reincorporated 06/07/2000
Common 10¢ par split (2) for (1) by issuance of (1) additional share payable 02/14/2000 to holders of record 02/01/2000
Common 10¢ par split (3) for (2) by issuance of (0.5) additional share payable 03/31/2000 to holders of record 03/24/2000
State of incorporation changed from (NY) to (NV) and Common 10¢ par changed to 3¢ par 06/07/2000
Name changed to Xologic Inc. (NV) 01/23/2001
Xologic Inc. (NV) reorganized in Washington as Doll Technology Group, Inc. 06/30/2005

YELLOWBUBBLE COM INC (NV)
Reorganized under the laws of Florida as Reality Racing, Inc. 08/02/2005
Each share Common $0.001 par exchanged for (0.001) share Common $0.001 par
(See Reality Racing, Inc.)

YELLOWCAKE MNG INC (NV)
Recapitalized as SKY Digital Stores Corp. 04/20/2011
Each share Common $0.001 par exchanged for (0.005) share Common $0.001 par
Note: No holder will receive fewer than (100) shares
SKY Digital Stores Corp. recapitalized as Qualis Innovations, Inc. 02/14/2018

YELLOWJACK RES LTD (BC)
Merged into Canoro Resources Ltd. (BC) 08/11/1995
Each share Common no par exchanged for (0.1) share Common no par
Canoro Resources Ltd. (BC) reincorporated in Alberta 09/21/2001 which reincorporated in British Columbia 03/22/2011

YELLOWJACKET RES LTD (AB)
Name changed to Athabasca Nuclear Corp. (AB) 06/06/2013
Athabasca Nuclear Corp. (AB) reincorporated in British Columbia 11/10/2015 which name changed to Clean Commodities Corp. 06/10/2016

YELLOWKNIFE BASE METALS LTD (MB)
Charter cancelled for failure to file returns 03/00/1973

YELLOWKNIFE BEAR MINES LTD (CANADA)
Reincorporated 10/12/1978
Capital Stock $1 par changed to no par 11/24/1971
Place of incorporation changed from (ON) to (Canada) 10/12/1978
Name changed to Yellowknife Bear Resources Inc. 03/06/1981
Yellowknife Bear Resources Inc. merged into Rayrock Yellowknife Resources Inc. 02/03/1986 which name changed to Rayrock Resources Inc. 11/27/1998
(See Rayrock Resources Inc.)

YELLOWKNIFE BEAR RES INC (CANADA)
Merged into Rayrock Yellowknife Resources Inc. 02/03/1986
Each share Capital Stock no par exchanged for (1) share Subordinate no par
Rayrock Yellowknife Resources Inc. name changed to Rayrock Resources Inc. 11/27/1998
(See Rayrock Resources Inc.)

YELLOWKNIFE GOLD MINES LTD.
Merged into Yellowknife Bear Mines Ltd. (ONT) in 1948
Each (1,000) shares Capital Stock $1 par exchanged for (2,063) shares new Capital Stock $1 par

Yellowknife Bear Mines Ltd. (ONT) reincorporated in Canada 10/12/78 which name changed to Yellowknife Bear Resources Inc. 3/6/81 which merged into Rayrock Yellowknife Resources Inc. 2/3/86 which name changed to Rayrock Resources Inc. 11/27/98
(See Rayrock Resources Inc.)

YELLOW7 INC (TX)
Common $0.0001 par split (5) for (1) by issuance of (4) additional shares payable 08/05/2011 to holders of record 07/22/2011 Ex date - 08/08/2011
Common $0.0001 par split (3) for (1) by issuance of (2) additional shares payable 04/03/2012 to holders of record 03/30/2012 Ex date - 04/04/2012
Recapitalized as Energy Today Inc. 04/18/2013
Each share Common $0.0001 par exchanged for (0.0002) share Common $0.0001 par

YELLOWSTONE ENVIRONMENTAL SVCS INC (CO)
Merged into Growth Environmental Inc. 11/22/1994
Each share Common no par exchanged for (0.021) share new Common no par
(See Growth Environmental Inc.)

YELLOWSTONE MINES LTD (BC)
Name changed to Glendora Resources Inc. 10/06/1981
Glendora Resources Inc. name changed to Romulus Resources Ltd. 09/26/1986 which merged into Misty Mountain Gold Ltd. 11/07/1995 which recapitalized as Misty Mountain Gold Ltd. 11/10/1995 which recapitalized as Continental Minerals Corp. (Incorporated 02/07/1962) 10/18/2001
(See Continental Minerals Corp. (Incorporated 02/07/1962))

YELLOWSTONE OIL & REFINING CO. (SD)
Charter cancelled for failure to file annual reports 7/1/70

YELLOWSTONE PERMANENT SAVINGS & LOAN ASSOCIATION, INC. (ID)
Name changed to Home Security Savings & Loan Association, Inc. 8/10/62
Home Security Savings & Loan Association, Inc. completely liquidated 12/31/73

YELLOWSTONE PETES LTD (AB)
Name changed to Kingbird Resources Inc. (ALTA) 8/18/87
Kingbird Resources Inc. (ALTA) reincorporated in Canada 8/29/88 which recapitalized as Gold Bar Resources Inc. 9/29/88
(See Gold Bar Resources Inc.)

YELLOWSTONE RES INC (CO)
Each share old Common no par exchanged for (0.04) share new Common no par 11/06/1989
Name changed to Yellowstone Environmental Services, Inc. 06/12/1991
Yellowstone Environmental Services, Inc. merged into Growth Environmental Inc. 11/22/1994
(See Growth Environmental Inc.)

YENISEI TERRITORIAL GENERATING CO OJSC (RUSSIA)
GDR agreement terminated 10/16/2014
Each Sponsored Reg. S GDR for Ordinary exchanged for $0.077201 cash
Each Sponsored 144A GDR for Ordinary exchanged for $0.077201 cash

YEOMAN GOLD MINES LTD. (ON)
Charter cancelled for failure to file reports and pay taxes in 1956

YES CAP CORP (BC)
Name changed to 222 Pizza Express Corp. 06/24/2002
222 Pizza Express Corp. name changed to Kadywood Capital Corp. 05/01/2008 which name changed to Gold Wheaton Gold Corp. 07/16/2008
(See Gold Wheaton Gold Corp.)

YES CLOTHING CO (NV)
Reorganized 10/27/2000
State of incorporation changed from (CA) to (NV) 10/27/2000
Each share Common no par exchanged for (0.01) share Common $0.001 par
Name changed to BioSecure Corp. 01/24/2002
(See BioSecure Corp.)

YES ENTMT CORP (DE)
Reincorporated 10/25/96
Issue Information - 2,500,000 shares COM offered at $4.75 per share on 06/07/1995
State of incorporation changed from (CA) to (DE) 10/25/96
Plan of reorganization under Chapter 11 Federal Bankruptcy Code effective 4/17/2002
No stockholders' equity

YES I C TECHNOLOGIES INC (AB)
Name changed to EarlyRain Inc. 10/26/2000
(See EarlyRain Inc.)

YESDTC HLDGS INC (NV)
Stock Dividend - 49.23413% payable 01/19/2010 to holders of record 12/18/2009 Ex date - 01/20/2010
Ceased operations 02/23/2012
Stockholders' equity unlikely

YESMAIL COM INC (DE)
Merged into CMGI Inc. 03/13/2000
Each share Common $0.001 par exchanged for (0.2504) share Common 1¢ par
CMGI Inc. name changed to ModusLink Global Solutions, Inc. 09/30/2008

YFMC HEALTHCARE INC (AB)
Acquired by Med-Emerg International Inc. 12/22/1999
Each share Common no par exchanged for (0.14545) share Common no par
Med-Emerg International Inc. acquired by AIM Health Group Inc. 01/30/2009
(See AIM Health Group Inc.)

YGAC CORP (DE)
Name changed to Hargrom Services Corp. 5/19/69
(See Hargrom Services Corp.)

YGC RES LTD (BC)
Each share old Common no par exchanged for (0.2) share new Common no par 01/07/2004
Under plan of merger name changed to Yukon-Nevada Gold Corp. 06/25/2007
Yukon-Nevada Gold Corp. recapitalized as Veris Gold Corp. 10/11/2012

YI WAN GROUP INC (FL)
Name changed to U.S. National Telecom, Inc. 10/30/2007

YIELD ADVANTAGE INCOME TR (ON)
Trust terminated 12/31/2015
Each Unit received $7.418687 cash

YIELD ADVANTAGED CONV DEBS FD (ON)
Name changed to Convertible Debentures Income Fund 03/05/2014
Convertible Debentures Income Fund

merged into Canoe 'GO CANADA!' Fund Corp. 04/22/2016

YIELD MGMT GROUP HIGH INCOME TR (ON)
Each Installment Receipt plus final payment of $12.50 cash received (1) Trust Unit prior to 11/12/1998
Name changed to Fiera High Income Trust 01/22/2008
(See Fiera High Income Trust)

YIELDPLUS INCOME FD (ON)
Each Trust Unit received distribution of (1) Warrant expiring 02/26/2010 payable 08/31/2009 to holders of record 08/28/2009 Ex date - 08/26/2009
Under plan of merger each Trust Unit automatically became (0.89235573) MINT Income Fund Trust Unit 03/21/2017

YIELDUP INTL CORP (DE)
Merged into FSI International, Inc. 10/21/1999
Each share Common $0.001 par exchanged for (0.1567) share Common no par and $0.7313 cash
(See FSI International, Inc.)

YIFAN COMMUNICATIONS INC (DE)
Each share Common $0.0002 par exchanged for (0.025) share old Common $0.008 par 09/25/2000
Each share old Common $0.008 par exchanged for (1/7) share new Common $0.008 par 05/16/2006
SEC revoked common stock registration 04/24/2009
Stockholders' equity unlikely

YIN 88 CORP (AB)
Name changed 05/24/1994
Name changed 12/05/1995
Name changed from YIN 88 Resources Ltd. to YIN 88 Gaming Corp. 05/24/1994
Name changed from YIN 88 Gaming Corp. to YIN 88 Corp. 12/05/1995
Recapitalized as Continental Cash Technologies Corp. (AB) 05/15/2003
Each share Common no par exchanged for (0.2) share Common no par
Continental Cash Technologies Corp. (AB) reincorporated in Ontario 07/06/2004 which name changed to Cenit Corp. 12/29/2004 which name changed to Superior Copper Corp. 01/24/2012 which merged into Nighthawk Gold Corp. 05/30/2016

YINGDE GASES GROUP CO LTD (CAYMAN ISLANDS)
ADR agreement terminated 10/18/2017
Each ADR for Ordinary issued by Bank of New York exchanged for $7.622687 cash

YINLIPS TECHNOLOGY INC (DE)
SEC revoked common stock registration 07/24/2013

YIU WING INTL HLDGS LTD (BERMUDA)
Name changed to King Pacific International Holdings Ltd. 03/31/1998
(See King Pacific International Holdings Ltd.)

YIZHONG BIOENGINEERING USA INC (NV)
Name changed to Tianxin Mining (USA), Inc. 07/12/2007
(See Tianxin Mining (USA), Inc.)

YKR INTL RES LTD (YT)
Recapitalized as Gtech International Resources Ltd. (YT) 01/10/2001
Each share Common no par exchanged for (0.5) share Common no par
Gtech International Resources Ltd. (Yukon) reorganized in British Columbia as Simavita Ltd. 12/06/2013

Note: Yukon Territory changed to Yukon 03/27/2002

YM BIOSCIENCES INC (NS)
Class B Preferred Ser. 1 no par reclassified as Common no par 06/12/2003
Acquired by Gilead Sciences, Inc. 02/08/2013
Each share Common no par exchanged for USD$2.95 cash
Note: Unexchanged certificates were cancelled and became without value 02/08/2015

YMG CAP MGMT INC (CANADA)
Merged into Fiera Capital Management Inc. 2/6/2006
Each share Common no par exchanged for $3.25 cash

YMG VENTURES INC (AB)
Under plan of reorganization each share Common no par exchanged for $0.011 cash 10/1/2004

YMIR YANKEE GIRL GOLD MINES LTD.
Acquired by Alana Mines Ltd. on a (1) for (4) basis in 1949
(See Alana Mines Ltd.)

YMIR YANKEE GIRL GOLD MINES LTD. (BC)
Struck off register and declared dissolved for failure to file returns 7/12/51

YMIR YANKEE GIRL MINES LTD.
Dissolved in 1948

YNOT ED INC NEW (NV)
Name changed to King Media Holdings Inc. 10/04/2007
King Media Holdings Inc. recapitalized as Extreme Fitness, Inc. 10/09/2007
(See Extreme Fitness, Inc.)

YNOT ED INC OLD (NV)
Name changed to Physiognomy Interface Technologies, Inc. 05/01/2006
Physiognomy Interface Technologies, Inc. name changed to Ynot Education, Inc. (New) 01/10/2007 which name changed to King Media Holdings Inc. 10/04/2007 which recapitalized as Extreme Fitness, Inc. 10/09/2007
(See Extreme Fitness, Inc.)

YOCAM BATTERIES, INC. (FL)
Stock Dividends - 10% 9/14/62; 10% 11/15/65
Merged into Graves (C.), Inc. 6/24/66
Each share Common $2.50 par exchanged for (1.00476) shares Common $5 par
Graves (C.), Inc. acquired by Connrex Corp. (DE) 8/29/69 which name changed to Chloride Connrex Corp. 8/27/73
(See Chloride Connrex Corp.)

YOCREAM INTL INC (OR)
Acquired by Danone 12/31/2010
Each share Common no par exchanged for $35.358914 cash
Note: An additional initial distribution of $0.945486 cash per share was paid from escrow 03/25/2011
A second additional distribution of $1.48633 cash per share was paid from escrow 12/31/2012
A third and final additional distribution of $1.58668 cash per share was paid from escrow 12/04/2014

YODLEE INC (DE)
Merged into Envestnet, Inc. 11/19/2015
Each share Common $0.001 par exchanged for (0.1889) share Common $0.005 par and $11.51 cash

YOGEN FRUZ WORLD-WIDE INC (NS)
Reorganized 03/18/1998
Reorganized from (AB) to under the laws of Nova Scotia 03/18/1998
Each share Common no par exchanged for either (1) Multiple share no par or (1.05) Subordinate shares no par
Note: Option to receive Multiple shares expired 02/27/1998
Name changed to CoolBrands International Inc. (NS) 10/06/2000
CoolBrands International Inc. (NS) reincorporated in Canada 03/27/2006 which reorganized in Delaware as Swisher Hygiene Inc. 11/04/2010

YOHO RES INC NEW (AB)
Acquired by One Stone Energy Partners L.P. 09/08/2016
Each share Common no par exchanged for $0.475 cash
Note: Unexchanged certificates will be cancelled and become without value 09/07/2019

YOHO RES INC OLD (AB)
Each share Non-Vtg. Class C Common no par exchanged for (1) share Common no par 02/10/2009
Reorganized as Yoho Resources Inc. (New) 03/21/2014
Each share Common no par exchanged for (1) share Common no par and (0.25910239) share Storm Resources Ltd. Common no par
(See Yoho Resources Inc. (New))

YOLANDE CORP. (NY)
Merged into Top Form-Yolande, Inc. on a share for share basis 12/31/62

YONDATA CORP (NY)
Name changed to Growers Express Inc. 10/5/92
Growers Express Inc. name changed to Nuko Information Systems Inc. (NY) 5/27/94 which reincorporated in Delaware 1/8/97
(See Nuko Information Systems Inc.)

YONGE STR CAP CORP (CANADA)
Name changed to Ecosse Energy Corp. 12/10/2009
(See Ecosse Energy Corp.)

YONGYE BIOTECHNOLOGY INTL INC (NV)
Name changed to Yongye International, Inc. 07/27/2009
(See Yongye International, Inc.)

YONGYE INTL INC (NV)
Acquired by Yongye International Ltd. 07/03/2014
Each share Common $0.001 par exchanged for $7.10 cash

YONKERS FINL CORP (DE)
Issue Information - 3,570,750 shares COM offered at $10 per share on 02/12/1996
Merged into Atlantic Bank of New York (New York, NY) 5/9/2002
Each share Common 1¢ par exchanged for $29 cash

YONKERS NATIONAL BANK & TRUST CO. (YONKERS, NY)
Merged into Bank of Westchester (Yonkers, NY) 12/20/1941
Each share Common $10 par exchanged for (0.925925) share Common $10 par
Bank of Westchester (Yonkers, NY) merged into County Trust Co. (White Plains, NY) 07/30/1947 which merged into Bank of New York Co., Inc. 05/29/1969 which merged into Bank of New York Mellon Corp. 07/01/2007

YONKERS RACEWAY INC (NY)
Recapitalized 12/16/1960
Each share Class A $1 par exchanged for (1) share 6%

Preferred $5 par and (1) share old Common $1 par
Each share Class B $1 par exchanged for (5) shares old Common $1 par Old Common $1 par changed to 25¢ par and (3) additional shares issued 10/05/1961
6% Preferred $5 par called for redemption 05/01/1967
Each share Common 25¢ par exchanged for (0.25) share new Common $1 par 09/16/1968
Stock Dividends - 10% 06/02/1956; 10% 11/21/1957; 10% 02/08/1961; 10% 04/10/1961; 10% 12/30/1961; 10% 12/31/1962
Completely liquidated 06/15/1972
Each share new Common $1 par exchanged for first and final distribution of $46 cash

YONKERS TROTTING ASSOCIATION, INC. (NY)
Merged into Yonkers Raceway, Inc. on a (4.75) for (1) basis in August 1954
Yonkers Raceway, Inc. liquidated 6/15/72

YOO HOO CHOCOLATE BEVERAGE CORP (DE)
Merged into Iroquois Brands, Ltd. 5/6/76
Each share Common 10¢ par exchanged for (0.25) share $1 Conv. Preferred no par
(See Iroquois Brands, Ltd.)

YOO HOO MIDWEST INC (DE)
Completely liquidated 2/26/71
Each share Common 10¢ par exchanged for first and final distribution of (0.5) share Yoo-Hoo Chocolate Beverage Corp. Common 10¢ par
Yoo-Hoo Chocolate Beverage Corp. merged into Iroquois Brands, Ltd. 5/6/76
(See Iroquois Brands, Ltd.)

YOO INC (DE)
Common $0.0001 par split (11) for (4) by issuance of (1.75) additional shares payable 01/26/2009 to holders of record 01/12/2009 Ex date - 01/27/2009
Name changed to IX Energy Holdings, Inc. 01/27/2009

YOOX NET A PORTER GROUP S P A (ITALY)
ADR agreement terminated 07/06/2018
Each ADR for Common exchanged for $43.954 cash

YOOX SPA (ITALY)
Name changed to YOOX NET-A-PORTER GROUP S.p.A 10/16/2015
(See YOOX NET-A-PORTER GROUP S.p.A)

YORBEAU MINES INC (QC)
Name changed to Yorbeau Resources Inc.-Les Ressources Yorbeau Inc. 02/29/1984

YORCAN EXPLORATION LTD. (ON)
Acquired by Campbell Chibougamau Mines Ltd. 12/16/1957
Each share Common exchanged for (0.25) share Common $1 par
Campbell Chibougamau Mines Ltd. name changed to Campbell Resources Inc. (Old) 09/22/1980 which merged into Campbell Resources Inc. (New) 06/08/1983
(See Campbell Resources Inc. (New))

YORK AXLE & FORGE CO.
Liquidation completed in 1952

YORK BANCORP (PA)
Merged into Continental Bancorp, Inc. 03/18/1983
Each share Capital Stock $2.50 par exchanged for (1.3) shares Common $5 par
Continental Bancorp, Inc. merged into

Midlantic Corp. 01/30/1987 which merged into PNC Bank Corp. 12/31/1995 which name changed to PNC Financial Services Group, Inc. 03/15/2000

YORK BANCSHARES, INC. (DE)
Common $5 par changed to $1.25 par and (3) additional shares issued 05/05/1987
Merged into First Colonial Bankshares Corp. 06/26/1990
Each share Common $1.25 par exchanged for (2.53876) shares Class A Common $1.25 par
First Colonial Bankshares Corp. merged into Firstar Corp. (Old) 01/31/1995 which merged into Firstar Corp. (New) 11/20/1998 which merged into U.S. Bancorp (DE) 02/27/2001

YORK BK & TR CO (YORK, PA)
Capital Stock $10 par changed to $5 par and (1) additional share issued 07/15/1970
Capital Stock $5 par changed to $2.50 par and (1) additional share issued 07/15/1974
Stock Dividend - 100% 05/17/1968
Under plan of reorganization each share Capital Stock automatically became (1) share York Bancorp Capital Stock $2.50 par 01/01/1982
York Bancorp merged into Continental Bancorp, Inc. 03/18/1983 which merged into Midlantic Corp. 01/30/1987 which merged into PNC Bank Corp. 12/31/1995 which name changed to PNC Financial Services Group, Inc. 03/15/2000

YORK BAY CAP CORP (ON)
Each Restricted Vtg. Share no par exchanged for (1/3) share Common no par 01/22/1997
Name changed to CDNet Canada Inc. 06/04/1999
(See CDNet Canada Inc.)

YORK BOUSQUET GOLD MINES LTD. (QC)
Charter cancelled in 1961

YORK CAP CORP (ON)
Name changed to SilverBirch Inc. 10/07/2005
(See SilverBirch Inc.)

YORK CENTRE CORP (ON)
Name changed to Georgian Bancorp Inc. 04/12/1995
(See Georgian Bancorp Inc.)

YORK CONS EXPL LTD (ON)
Name changed to Amco Industrial Holdings Ltd. 09/09/1983
Amco Industrial Holdings Ltd. recapitalized as International Amco Corp. (ONT) 11/04/1985 which reorganized in England & Wales as Amco Corp. PLC 11/10/1989 which name changed to Billington Holdings Plc 03/31/2009

YORK CORP (DE)
Merged into Borg-Warner Corp. (Ill.) on a (0.5) for (1) basis plus $2 cash 7/1/56
Borg-Warner Corp. (Ill.) reincorporated under the laws of Delaware 10/31/67
(See Borg-Warner Corp. (Del.))

YORK CNTY GAS CO (PA)
Recapitalized 00/00/1945
Each share 7% Preferred $100 par exchanged for (2) shares Common $20 par Old Common $10 par declared to be without value
Common $20 par changed to new Common $10 par and (1) additional share issued 08/15/1962
Stock Dividend - 100% 07/16/1951
Acquired by Columbia Gas System, Inc. 08/29/1968
Each share new Common $10 par exchanged for (2.85) shares Common $10 par Columbia Gas System, Inc. name changed to Columbia Energy Group 01/16/1998 which merged into NiSource Inc. 11/01/2000

YORK COUNTY NATIONAL BANK (YORK, PA)
Each share Capital Stock $20 par exchanged for (3-1/3) shares Capital Stock $10 par to effect a (2) for (1) split and a 66-2/3% stock dividend 06/16/1956
Stock Dividend - 100% 07/31/1943
Under plan of merger name changed to National Bank of York County (York, PA) 02/28/1959
National Bank of York County (York, PA) merged into National Bank & Trust Co. of Central Pennsylvania (York, PA) 10/13/1961 which merged into National Central Bank (Lancaster, PA) 12/07/1970 which reorganized as National Central Financial Corp. 12/31/1972 which merged into CoreStates Financial Corp 05/02/1983 which merged into First Union Corp. 04/28/1998 which name changed to Wachovia Corp. (Ctfs. dated after 09/01/2001) 09/01/2001 which merged into Wells Fargo & Co. (New) 12/31/2008

YORK EMPLOYMENT SERVICE, INC. (MN)
Name changed to York Enterprises Inc. 04/05/1966
York Enterprises Inc. name changed to Optimizer Industries Inc. 06/25/1970 which recapitalized as Metropane, Inc. 11/03/1994 which name changed to Intermountain Ventures Inc. 08/28/2007

YORK ENHANCED STRATEGIES FD LLC (DE)
144A Term Preferred called for redemption at $1,000 on 02/04/2011

YORK ENTERPRISES INC (MN)
Name changed 04/05/1966
Name changed from York Employment Service, Inc. to York Enterprises Inc. 04/05/1966
Name changed to Optimizer Industries Inc. 06/25/1970
Optimizer Industries Inc. recapitalized as Metropane, Inc. 11/03/1994 which name changed to Intermountain Ventures Inc. 08/28/2007 which name changed to Voice One Corp. 01/11/2011

YORK FED SVGS & LN ASSN PA (USA)
Common $1 par split (2) for (1) by issuance of (1) additional share 04/15/1986
Reorganized as York Financial Corp. 08/01/1986
Each share Common $1 par exchanged for (1) share Common $1 par
York Financial Corp. merged into Waypoint Financial Corp. 10/17/2000
(See Waypoint Financial Corp.)

YORK FINL CORP (PA)
Common $1 par split (5) for (4) by issuance of (0.25) additional share 5/5/87
Common $1 par split (5) for (4) by issuance of (0.25) additional share payable 11/17/97 to holders of record 11/3/97
Stock Dividends - 10% 8/15/88; 10% 11/15/91; 10% 11/16/92; 10% 11/15/93; 10% 11/15/94; 10% 11/15/95; 10% payable 11/15/96 to holders of record 11/4/96; 5% payable 11/17/98 to holders of record 11/6/98; 5% payable 11/15/99 to holders of record 11/5/99
Merged into Waypoint Financial Corp. 10/17/2000
Each share Common 1¢ par exchanged for (1.55) shares Common 1¢ par
(See Waypoint Financial Corp.)

YORK FOOD PRODUCTS INC. (NY)
Charter cancelled and proclaimed dissolved for failure to pay taxes and file reports 12/15/71

YORK GROUP INC (DE)
Merged into Matthews International Corp. 12/4/2001
Each share Common no par exchanged for $11 cash

YORK HEATING & VENTILATING CORP.
Merged into Carrier Corp. 10/31/30
Carrier Corp. acquired by United Technologies Corp. 7/6/79

YORK-HOOVER CORP. (PA)
Stock Dividend - 50% 1/8/53
Acquired by Simmons Co. 3/31/67
Each share Common $10 par exchanged for (0.7) share Common no par
(See Simmons Co.)

YORK ICE MACHINERY CORP. (DE)
Recapitalized as York Corp. in 1943
Each share Preferred $100 par exchanged for (15) shares Common $1 par
Each share Common no par exchanged for (1) share Common $1 par
York Corp. merged into Borg-Warner Corp. (Ill.) 7/1/56 which reincorporated under the laws of Delaware 10/31/67
(See Borg-Warner Corp. (Del.))

YORK INTL CORP NEW (DE)
Acquired by Johnson Controls, Inc. 12/09/2005
Each share Common $0.005 par exchanged for $56.50 cash

YORK INTL CORP OLD (DE)
Merged into Arctic Acquisition Corp. 12/19/1988
Each share Common $0.001 par exchanged for $97.96 principal amount of York Holdings Corp. 17.50% Subord. Deferred Interest Debentures due 12/15/2004 and $15.16 cash

YORK KNITTING MILLS, LTD. (ON)
Recapitalized 00/00/1948
Each share 1st Preference $100 par exchanged for (25) shares Class A no par and (2) shares Class B no par
Each share 2nd Preference $100 par exchanged for (21) shares Class A no par and (2) shares Class B no par
Each share Common no par exchanged for (1) share Class A no par and (1) share Class B no par
Name changed to Woods (Harvey) Ltd. 05/02/1966
(See Woods (Harvey) Ltd.)

YORK LAMBTON INC (CANADA)
Name changed 05/29/1979
Name changed from York Lambton Corp. to York Lambton Inc. and Class A no par and Class B no par reclassified as Common no par respectively 05/29/1979
Company declared bankrupt 09/21/1982
Stockholders' equity unlikely

YORK MANUFACTURING CO.
Acquired by Bates Manufacturing Co. in 1946
Details not available

YORK OIL & URANIUM CO. (WY)
Charter revoked for non-payment of corporate license taxes 2/26/57

YORK OILS LTD. (BC)
Recapitalized as New York Oils Ltd. (BC) 9/19/58
Each (10) shares Capital Stock no par exchanged for (1) share Capital Stock no par
New York Oils Ltd. (BC) reincorporated in Alberta 7/19/82 which was acquired by Sceptre Resources Ltd. 3/14/89 which merged into Canadian Natural Resources Ltd. 8/15/96

YORK PACKING CO. (ID)
Charter forfeited for failure to file reports 11/30/67

YORK PETE INC (BC)
Name changed to Winzen International Inc. 12/01/1986
Winzen International Inc. name changed to Winzen Properties Inc. 01/02/2003
(See Winzen Properties Inc.)

YORK RAILWAYS CO.
Liquidated in 1946
No Common stockholders' equity

YORK RESH CORP (DE)
Class A Common $1 par reclassified as Common $1 par 2/16/72
Plan of reorganization under Chapter 11 Federal Bankruptcy Code effective 11/14/2002
No stockholders' equity

YORK RES INC (NV)
Name changed to Revonergy Inc. 02/25/2010
(See Revonergy Inc.)

YORK RES LTD (AB)
Merged into Aviva Petroleum Canada Inc. 07/10/1990
Each share Common no par exchanged for (0.1) share Common no par
Aviva Petroleum Canada Inc. name changed to Pero Development Group Inc. 06/06/1994 which merged into Canadiana Genetics Inc. 04/30/1996
(See Canadiana Genetics Inc.)

YORK RIDGE LIFETECH INC (ON)
Recapitalized as Acadian Energy Inc. 03/16/2011
Each share Common no par exchanged for (0.25) share Common no par

YORK RUSSEL INC (CANADA)
Name changed to YRI-York Ltd. 3/30/84
(See YRI-York Ltd.)

YORK SHARE CORP.
Acquired by Broad Street Investing Co., Inc. in 1933
Broad Street Investing Co., Inc. name changed to Broad Street Investing Corp. in 1939 which name changed to Seligman Common Stock Fund, Inc. 5/11/82

YORK SPECULATIVE INVESTMENT FUND OF CANADA LTD. (CANADA)
Name changed to Select Financial Industries Ltd. 7/27/64
Select Financial Industries Ltd. name changed to Deltan Corp. Ltd. 8/18/71
(See Deltan Corp. Ltd.)

YORK TR & SVGS CORP (TORONTO, ONT)
Merged into Metropolitan Trust Co. (Toronto, Ont.) 6/27/68
Each share Capital Stock $10 par received (0.111111) share Common $10 par
Note: Certificates were not required to be surrendered and are without value
(See Metropolitan Trust Co. (Toronto, Ont.))

YORKRIDGE CALVERT SVGS & LN ASSN BALTIMORE MD (USA)
Placed in receivership 12/31/89
Stockholders' equity undetermined

YORKSHIRE CAP TR I (DE)
8.08% Trust Securities Preferred

YORKSHIRE ELECTRICITY GROUP PLC (UNITED KINGDOM)
called for redemption at $25 plus $0.381555 accrued dividends on 6/9/2003

YORKSHIRE ELECTRICITY GROUP PLC (UNITED KINGDOM)
Merged into Public Service Co. of Colorado 5/9/97
Each new Sponsored ADR for Ordinary 50p par exchanged for approximately $15.03 cash

YORKSHIRE FOOD GROUP PLC (UNITED KINGDOM)
Placed in receivership 12/00/1997
ADR holders' equity unlikely

YORKSHIRE LEVERAGED GROUP INC (CO)
Name changed to Freedom Funding Inc. 02/21/1989
Freedom Funding Inc. recapitalized as CBQ Inc. (CO) 12/02/1998 which reincorporated in Florida as China Direct Trading Corp. 05/17/2004 which name changed to CHDT Corp. 07/16/2007 which name changed to Capstone Companies, Inc. 07/06/2012

YORKSHIRE RES LTD (ON)
Each share old Common $1 par exchanged for (1) share Conv. Class A Special Stock no par 03/02/1979
Merged into Dolly Varden Minerals Inc. 12/21/1979
Each share Conv. Class A Special Stock no par exchanged for (1.5752) shares Conv. Class A Special Stock no par
Each share new Common no par exchanged for (1.5752) shares Conv. Class A Special Stock no par
Dolly Varden Minerals Inc. recapitalized as New Dolly Varden Minerals Inc. 11/16/1992 which recapitalized as Dolly Varden Resources Inc. 04/17/2000 which name changed to DV Resources Ltd. 01/31/2012 which name changed to DLV Resources Ltd. 11/27/2019

YORKTOWN PRODS CORP (NY)
Each share Common 10¢ par exchanged for (10) shares Common 1¢ par 00/00/1958
Charter cancelled and proclaimed dissolved for failure to pay taxes and file reports 12/15/1975

YOSEMITE BK (MARIPOSA, CA)
Stock Dividend - 5% payable 12/15/1997 to holders of record 12/01/1997
Acquired by Premier Valley Bank (Fresno, CA) 03/30/2005
Each share Common no par exchanged for $34.92 cash

YOSEMITE HOLDING CORP.
Dissolved in 1934

YOSEMITE PARK & CURRY CO (CA)
Stock Dividends - 50% 11/30/1953; 10% 08/30/1955; 10% 12/10/1958; 10% 02/09/1962; 10% 12/10/1964; 10% 02/23/1967
Merged into MCA Inc. 12/31/1974
Each share Common $5 par exchanged for $14 cash

YOSEMITE PORTLAND CEMENT CORP.
Liquidation completed in 1950

YOU BET INTL INC (DE)
Name changed to Youbet.com, Inc. 01/22/1999
Youbet.com, Inc. merged into Churchill Downs, Inc. 06/02/2010

YOU ON DEMAND HLDGS INC (NV)
Each share old Common $0.001 par exchanged for (0.01333333) share new Common $0.001 par 02/13/2012
Name changed to Wecast Network, Inc. 11/14/2016
Wecast Network, Inc. name changed to Seven Stars Cloud Group, Inc. 07/17/2017

YOUBET COM INC (DE)
Each share Conv. Preferred Ser. A $0.001 par automatically became (10) shares Common $0.001 par 06/15/1999
Merged into Churchill Downs, Inc. 06/02/2010
Each share Common $0.001 par exchanged for (0.0591) share Common no par and $0.99 cash

YOUBLAST GLOBAL INC (DE)
SEC revoked common stock registration 05/15/2014

YOUCHANGE HLDGS CORP (NV)
Recapitalized as Infinity Resources Holdings Corp. 11/13/2012
Each share Common $0.001 par exchanged for (0.2) share Common $0.001 par
Infinity Resources Holdings Corp. name changed to Quest Resource Holding Corp. 10/28/2013

YOUGHIOGENY & OHIO COAL CO (OH)
Each share Common no par exchanged for (4) shares Common $10 par in 1957
Merged into Panhandle Eastern Pipe Line Co. 8/16/76
Each share Common $10 par exchanged for (6.557958536) shares Common no par and $8.06 cash
Panhandle Eastern Pipeline Co. reorganized as Panhandle Eastern Corp. 5/22/81 which merged into Duke Energy Corp. (NC) 6/18/97 which merged into Duke Energy Corp. (DE) 4/3/2006

YOUKU TUDOU INC (CAYMAN ISLANDS)
Name changed 12/21/2011
Name changed 08/27/2012
Name changed from Youku.com Inc. to Youku Inc. 12/21/2011
Name changed from Youku Inc. to Youku Tudou Inc. 08/27/2012
Acquired by Ali YK Investment Holding Ltd. 04/05/2016
Each Sponsored ADR for Class A Ordinary exchanged for $27.55 cash

YOUMEE INC (CA)
Name changed to Liberty Presidental Investment Funds 02/23/2007
Liberty Presidental Investment Funds name changed to American Pacific Rim Commerce Group (CA) 03/28/2008 which reincorporated in Florida as American Pacific Rim Commerce Corp. 11/21/2012

YOUNG & RUBICAM INC (DE)
Issue Information - 16,600,000 shares COM offered at $25 per share on 05/11/1998
Merged into WPP Group PLC (United Kingdom) 10/03/2000
Each share Common 1¢ par exchanged for either (0.835) new Sponsored ADR for Ordinary or (4.175) shares Ordinary
Note: Option to receive Ordinary expired 12/05/2000
WPP Group PLC (United Kingdom) reorganized in Jerseys as WPP PLC (Old) 11/20/2008
WPP PLC (Old) reorganized as WPP PLC (New) 01/02/2013

YOUNG AMERICA, INC. (MN)
Statutorily dissolved 10/4/91

YOUNG BROADCASTING INC (DE)
Issue Information - 4,440,000 shares CL A offered at $19 per share on 11/07/1994
Plan of reorganization under Chapter 11 Federal Bankruptcy proceedings effective 06/24/2010
No stockholders' equity

YOUNG CLIFF RESTAURANTS INC (CO)
Recapitalized as Nikron Technologies Inc. 11/20/2000
Each share Common $0.00001 par exchanged for (0.01) share Common $0.00001 par

YOUNG DAVIDSON MINES LTD (ON)
Each share old Common no par exchanged for (3) shares new Common no par 06/21/2002
Merged into Northgate Minerals Corp. 11/02/2005
Each share new Common no par exchanged for (0.7212) share Common no par
Northgate Minerals Corp. merged into AuRico Gold Inc. 10/26/2011

YOUNG DESIGNS INC (DE)
Name changed to Young Industries, Inc. 5/15/69
Young Industries, Inc. name changed to National Hygienics, Inc. 2/5/70
(See National Hygienics, Inc.)

YOUNG DEV CORP (PA)
Declared out of existence for failure to meet Corporation Tax Bureau requirements 12/4/67

YOUNG F E CONSTR CO (CA)
Name changed to Young Properties, Inc. 4/20/65
(See Young Properties, Inc.)

YOUNG H G MINES INTL LTD (ON)
Name changed 12/31/79
Name changed from Young (H.G.) Mines Ltd. to Young (H.G.) Mines International Ltd. and each share Capital Stock $1 par exchanged for (0.05) share Capital Stock no par 12/13/79
Charter cancelled and proclaimed dissolved for failure to pay taxes and file returns 11/1/82

YOUNG INDUSTRIES, INC. (DE)
Ctfs. dated prior to 4/1/65
No longer in existence having become inoperative and void for non-payment of taxes 4/1/65

YOUNG INDS INC (DE)
Ctfs. dated after 5/14/69
Name changed to National Hygienics, Inc. 2/5/70
(See National Hygienics, Inc.)

YOUNG INNOVATIONS INC (MO)
Issue Information - 2,000,000 shares COM offered at $12 per share on 11/04/1997
Common 1¢ par split (3) for (2) by issuance of (0.5) additional share payable 03/28/2002 to holders of record 03/22/2002 Ex date - 04/01/2002
Acquired by Young Innovations Holdings LLC 01/31/2013
Each share Common 1¢ par exchanged for $39.50 cash

YOUNG MANUFACTURING CO. (WY)
Charter revoked for failure to file reports and pay fees 2/15/67

YOUNG (THOMAS) NURSERIES, INC.
Name changed to Young (Thomas) Orchids, Inc. 00/00/1944
(See Young (Thomas) Orchids, Inc.)

YOUNG (THOMAS) ORCHIDS, INC. (NJ)
Liquidation completed 05/20/1958
Details not available

YOUNG-PIERCE OIL CO. (DE)
Charter cancelled and declared inoperative and void for non-payment of taxes 3/22/22

YOUNG PROPERTIES, INC. (CA)
Liquidation completed
Each share Capital Stock no par exchanged for initial distribution of $1 cash 4/30/66
Each share Capital Stock no par received second and final distribution of $0.0803874 cash 10/8/73

YOUNG SHANNON GOLD MINES LTD (ON)
Name changed to Metallum Resources Inc. 07/11/2008
Metallum Resources Inc. recapitalized as Torrent Capital Ltd. 02/06/2017

YOUNG SPRING & WIRE CORP. (MI)
Under plan of merger name changed to Hardeman (Paul), Inc. (MI) Common $5 par changed to $2.50 par and (1) additional share issued 4/30/64
(See Hardeman (Paul), Inc. (MI))

YOUNG (L.A.) SPRING & WIRE CORP. (MI)
Common no par changed to $5 par 11/28/55
Name changed to Young Spring & Wire Corp. 11/29/57
Young Spring & Wire Corp. merged into Hardeman (Paul), Inc. (MI) 4/30/64
(See Hardeman (Paul), Inc. (MI))

YOUNG WORLD CORP (DE)
Completely liquidated 1/16/70
Each share Common 10¢ par exchanged for first and final distribution of (1/3) share Go Publishing Co., Inc. Common 2¢ par
(See Go Publishing Co., Inc.)

YOUNGMAN OIL & GAS LTD (BC)
Name changed 8/29/83
Name changed from Youngman Oil & Gas Corp. to Youngman Oil & Gas Ltd. 8/29/83
Merged into Aurex Resources Inc. 7/11/85
Each share Common no par exchanged for (0.5) share Common no par
Aurex Resources Inc. merged into Galveston Resources Ltd. 7/29/86 which merged into Corona Corp. 7/1/88 which recapitalized as International Corona Corp. 6/11/91
(See International Corona Corp.)

YOUNGS MKT CO (DE)
Reincorporated 08/20/1974
State of incorporation changed from (CA) to (DE) 08/20/1974
Merged into Young's Acquisition Corp. 01/31/1990
Each share Capital Stock $100 par exchanged for $3,500 cash

YOUNGSTOWN CLUB CORP.
Liquidated in 1952

YOUNGSTOWN DRY GOODS CO. (OH)
Common $100 par changed to $1 par in February 1954
Liquidation completed
Each share Preferred $100 par exchanged for initial distribution of $50 cash 12/22/72
Each share Preferred $100 par received second distribution of $125 cash 1/24/73
Each share Common $1 par exchanged for first and final distribution of $1 cash 1/24/73
Each share Preferred $100 par received third distribution of $6.92 cash 2/28/73
Each share Preferred $100 par received fourth and final distribution of $1.973 cash 4/6/73

YOUNGSTOWN FOUNDRY & MACHINE CO. (OH)
Stock Dividend - 100% 5/1/57
Merged into Wean Industries, Inc. 5/1/67
Each share Common $5 par exchanged for (1.7) shares 5-1/4% Conv. Preferred Ser. A $24 par
Wean Industries, Inc. name changed to Wean United, Inc. (OH) which reincorporated in Delaware as Wean Inc. 9/16/87

(See Wean Inc.)

YOUNGSTOWN RESH & DEV CO (OH)
Each share of Common $3.50 par exchanged for (0.0025) share Common $3.50 in 1989
Note: In effect holders received $3.50 cash per share and public interest was eliminated

YOUNGSTOWN SHEET & TUBE CO (OH)
Common no par split (3) for (1) by issuance of (2) additional shares 3/20/64
Stock Dividend - 100% 10/11/50
Merged into Lykes-Youngstown Corp. 5/28/69
Each share Common no par exchanged for (1) share $2.50 Conv. Preferred Ser. A $1 par
Lykes-Youngstown Corp. name changed to Lykes Corp. (DE) 5/11/76 which merged into LTV Corp. (Old) 12/5/78 which reorganized as LTV Corp. (New) 6/28/93
(See LTV Corp. (New))

YOUNGSTOWN STEEL CO.
In process of liquidation in 1940

YOUNGSTOWN STL DOOR CO (OH)
Each share old Common no par exchanged for (2) shares new Common no par 00/00/1937
New Common no par split (2) for (1) by issuance of (1) additional share 01/17/1966
Merged into Lamson & Sessions Co. 12/21/1976
Each share Common no par exchanged for $17 cash

YOUNGSTOWN TERMINAL BLDG. CO. (OH)
Liquidation completed 12/21/62

YOUNKER BROS INC (DE)
Each share 7% Class B Preferred $100 par exchanged for (10) shares 7% Non-Callable Preferred $10 par in 1949
5% Preferred $50 par called for redemption 7/1/62
Common no par split (3) for (2) by issuance of (0.5) additional share 3/16/64
Common no par split (4) for (3) by issuance of (1/3) additional share 3/31/65
Common no par split (4) for (3) by issuance of (1/3) additional share 9/30/66
Common no par split (4) for (3) by issuance of (1/3) additional share 7/10/71
Merged into Equitable of Iowa Companies 1/5/79
Each share 5% Preferred $100 par exchanged for $105 cash
Each share 5% 2nd Ser. Preferred $100 par exchanged for $105 cash
Each share 7% Non-Callable Preferred $10 par exchanged for $13 cash
Each share Common no par exchanged for $52 cash

YOUNKERS INC (DE)
Merged into Proffitt's, Inc. 02/03/1996
Each share Common 1¢ par exchanged for (0.98) share Common 10¢ par
Proffitt's, Inc. merged into Saks Inc. 09/17/1998
(See Saks Inc.)

YOUR BK ONLINE COM (CO)
Name changed to Secure Sign, Inc. 10/31/2000
Secure Sign, Inc. name changed to SVC Financial Services, Inc. 02/03/2004
(See SVC Financial Services, Inc.)

YOUR CMNTY BANKSHARES INC (IN)
Merged into WesBanco, Inc. 09/09/2016
Each share Common 10¢ par exchanged for (0.964) share Common $2.0833 par and $7.70 cash

YOUR DIGITAL MEMORIES INC (NV)
Reorganized as Waste to Energy Group, Inc. 09/04/2008
Each share Common $0.0001 par exchanged for (25) shares Common $0.0001 par
Waste to Energy Group, Inc. name changed to Abakan, Inc. 12/08/2009

YOUR HOST FOODS INC (BC)
Name changed to Diaz Resources Ltd. 06/01/1994
Diaz Resources Ltd. merged into Tuscany Energy Ltd. (Old) 07/18/2013 which reorganized as Tuscany Energy Ltd. (New) 07/19/2013
(See Tuscany Energy Ltd. (New))

YOUR INTERNET DEFENDER INC (NV)
Name changed to Corindus Vascular Robotics, Inc. (NV) 08/27/2014
Corindus Vascular Robotics, Inc. (NV) reincorporated in Delaware 06/28/2016

YOUR WAY HLDG CORP (CO)
Name changed to Industry Concept Holdings, Inc. 02/05/2010
(See Industry Concept Holdings, Inc.)

YOURNET INC (NV)
Reincorporated under the laws of Delaware as Global Path Inc. 8/14/2001
Global Path Inc. name changed to Swiss Medica, Inc. 6/27/2003

YOUTH DYNAMICS INC (NY)
Charter cancelled and proclaimed dissolved for failure to pay taxes 12/16/1974

YOUTH ENHANCEMENT SYS INC (DE)
Name changed to Dynamic Response Group, Inc. 03/30/2007
(See Dynamic Response Group, Inc.)

YOUTH SVCS INTL INC (MD)
Common 1¢ par split (3) for (2) by issuance of (0.5) additional share payable 05/24/1996 to holders of record 05/16/1996
Merged into Correctional Services Corp. 03/31/1999
Each share Common 1¢ par exchanged for (0.275) share Common 1¢ par
(See Correctional Services Corp.)

YOUTHCRAFT CREATIONS, INC. (NY)
Merged into Russ Togs, Inc. 1/31/68
Each share Class A $1 par exchanged for $15 cash

YOUTHLINE USA INC (DE)
SEC revoked common stock registration 07/30/2004
Stockholders' equity unlikely

YOUTHSTREAM MEDIA NETWORKS INC (DE)
Name changed to ALJ Regional Holdings, Inc. 12/8/2006

YOUTICKET COM INC (NV)
Each share old Common no par exchanged for (0.03333333) share new Common no par 06/05/2001
Name changed to Weight Loss Forever International, Inc. 04/03/2002
Weight Loss Forever International, Inc. name changed to Beverly Hills Weight Loss & Wellness, Inc. (NV) 07/08/2004 which reorganized in Delaware as Cardiovascular Sciences, Inc. 05/30/2006

YOW CAP CORP (ON)
Name changed to Caribou Copper Resources Ltd. (ON) 09/16/2006
Caribou Copper Resources Ltd. (ON) reincorporated in British Columbia as Caribou King Resources Ltd. 12/20/2011 which name changed to CKR Carbon Corp. (BC) 11/09/2015 which reincorporated in Ontario 01/01/2017 which name changed to Gratomic Inc. 12/22/2017

YP CORP (NV)
Name changed 07/28/2004
Name changed from YP.Net, Inc. to YP Corp. 07/28/2004
Recapitalized as LiveDeal, Inc. 08/27/2007
Each share Common $0.001 par exchanged for (0.1) share Common $0.001 par
Preferred not affected except for change of name
LiveDeal, Inc. name changed to Live Ventures Inc. 10/09/2015

YPG HLDGS INC (CANADA)
Name changed to Yellow Media Inc. (Old) 02/11/2010
Yellow Media Inc. (Old) reorganized as Yellow Media Inc. (New) 11/01/2010 which recapitalized as Yellow Media Ltd. 12/20/2012 which name changed to Yellow Pages Ltd. 01/05/2015

YPRES CADILLAC MINES LTD. (ON)
Dissolved 12/1/58

YPSILANTI SVGS BK (YPSILANTI, MI)
Stock Dividends - 25% 02/10/1971; 20% 07/01/1980
Merged into Trustcorp, Inc. 12/31/1987
Each share Common $10 par exchanged for (1.935) shares Common $20 par
Trustcorp, Inc. acquired by Society Corp. 01/05/1990 which merged into KeyCorp (New) 03/01/1994

YRC WORLDWIDE INC (DE)
Each share Conv. Class A Preferred $1 par exchanged for (220.28) shares Common 1¢ par 02/17/2010
(Additional Information in Active)

YREKA GOLD DREDGING CO. (CA)
Charter suspended for failure to file reports and pay fees 09/01/1960

YREKA MINES LTD. (ON)
Charter cancelled and proclaimed dissolved for failure to pay taxes and file reports 5/6/80

YREKA MINING CO. (ID)
Merged into Yreka United, Inc. (ID) 06/07/1957
Each share Class A Common exchanged for (0.5) share Common 50¢ par
Each share Class B Common exchanged for (0.5) share Common 50¢ par
Yreka United, Inc. (ID) reorganized in Nevada as Southern Home Medical Equipment, Inc. 10/23/2006 which name changed to Southern Home Medical, Inc. 07/27/2012

YREKA UTD INC (ID)
Common 50¢ par changed to 10¢ par 11/20/1973
Reorganized under the laws of Nevada as Southern Home Medical Equipment, Inc. 10/23/2006
Each share Common 10¢ par exchanged for (0.025) share Common $0.001 par
Southern Home Medical Equipment, Inc. name changed to Southern Home Medical, Inc. 07/27/2012

YRI YORK LTD (CANADA)
Cease trade order effective 2/25/93
Stockholders' equity unlikely

YSEEK INC (FL)
Name changed to Advanced 3-D Ultrasound Services, Inc. 05/12/2003
Advanced 3-D Ultrasound Services, Inc. name changed to World Energy Solutions, Inc. 11/18/2005 which name changed to EClips Energy Technologies, Inc. (FL) 03/26/2009 which reincorporated in Delaware as EClips Media Technologies, Inc. 05/13/2010 which name changed to Silver Horn Mining Ltd. (DE) 04/27/2011 which reorganized in Nevada as Great West Resources, Inc. 04/21/2014 which name changed to Orbital Tracking Corp. 02/20/2015

YTB INTL INC (DE)
Each share Common $0.001 par exchanged for (1) share Class A Common $0.001 par and (2) shares Class B Common $0.001 par 08/01/2007
Chapter 11 bankruptcy proceedings dismissed 10/14/2014
Stockholders' equity unlikely

Y3K SECURE ENTERPRISE SOFTWARE INC (NV)
Name changed to Ecuity, Inc. 06/01/2004
(See Ecuity, Inc.)

YTW WESLEA GROWTH CAP CORP (ON)
Name changed to Broadband Learning Corp. 12/20/2005
(See Broadband Learning Corp.)

YTXP CORP (NV)
Name changed to TXP Corp. 07/10/2006
(See TXP Corp.)

YUBA CONSOLIDATED GOLD FIELDS (ME)
Merged into Yuba Consolidated Industries, Inc. on a share for share basis 08/01/1957
Yuba Consolidated Industries, Inc. reorganized as Yuba Industries, Inc. (DE) 12/06/1965
(See Yuba Industries, Inc. (DE))

YUBA CONSOLIDATED INDUSTRIES, INC. (DE)
Reorganized as Yuba Industries, Inc. (DE) 12/06/1965
No stockholders' equity

YUBA GOLDFIELDS INC (DE)
Stock Dividend - 200% 6/19/81
Name changed to Yuba Natural Resources, Inc. 12/23/81
Yuba Natural Resources, Inc. name changed to Yuba WestGold, Inc. 8/9/90
(See Yuba Westgold, Inc.)

YUBA INDUSTRIES, INC. (CA)
Merged into Yuba Consolidated Industries, Inc. on a (6) for (1) basis 08/01/1957
Yuba Consolidated Industries, Inc. reorganized as Yuba Industries, Inc. (DE) 12/06/1965
(See Yuba Industries, Inc. (DE))

YUBA INDS INC (DE)
Merged into Standard Prudential Corp. (New) 02/28/1969
Each share 5% Part. Preferred $10 par exchanged for (0.4) share Conv. Preferred Ser. B $5 par
Each share Common no par exchanged for (1) share Conv. Preferred Ser. B $5 par
Standard Prudential Corp. (New) name changed to Sterling Bancorp 10/24/1978
(See Sterling Bancorp)

YUBA MANUFACTURING CO. (CA)
Name changed to Yuba Industries, Inc. (Calif.) in April 1957
Yuba Industries, Inc. (Calif.) merged into Yuba Consolidated Industries,

Inc. 8/1/57 which reorganized as Yuba Industries, Inc. (Del.) 12/6/65
(See listing for Yuba Industries, Inc. (Delaware))

YUBA WESTGOLD INC (DE)
Name changed 08/09/1990
Name changed from Yuba Natural Resources, Inc. to Yuba WestGold, Inc. and Class A Common 10¢ par reclassified as Common $0.001 par 08/09/1990
Plan of reorganization under Chapter 11 Federal Bankruptcy Code effective 06/02/1994
No stockholders' equity

YUCANA RES INC (BC)
Recapitalized as Shamrock Resources Inc. 03/09/1987
Each share Common no par exchanged for (0.4) share Common no par
Shamrock Resources Inc. name changed to Pacific Energy Resources Ltd. (BC) 08/22/2003 which reincorporated in Delaware 02/04/2005
(See Pacific Energy Resources Ltd. (DE))

YUCATAN PETROLEUM CORP.
Out of existence in 1932

YUCATAN RES LTD (BC)
Struck off register and declared dissolved for failure to file returns 05/27/1983

YUCCA MINING & PETROLEUM CO., INC. (CO)
Recapitalized as National Growth Corp. on a (1) for (25) basis 10/3/60
(See National Growth Corp.)

YUCCA URANIUM, INC. (NM)
Name changed to Yucca Mining & Petroleum Co., Inc. and Common 5¢ par changed to 25¢ par 2/23/57
Yucca Mining & Petroleum Co., Inc. recapitalized as National Growth Corp. 10/3/60
(See National Growth Corp.)

YUCHENG TECHNOLOGIES LTD (BRITISH VIRGIN ISLANDS)
Acquired by New Sihitech Ltd. 12/28/2012
Each share Common $0.0001 par exchanged for $3.90 cash

YUESHOU ENVIRONMENTAL HLDGS LTD (HONG KONG)
ADR agreement terminated 04/03/2009
No ADR's remain outstanding

YUEXIU PPTY CO LTD (HONG KONG)
ADR agreement terminated 01/19/2018
Each Sponsored ADR for Common exchanged for (20) shares Common
Note: Unexchanged ADR's will be sold and the proceeds, if any, held for claim after 01/24/2019

YUKENO LEAD & SILVER MINES LTD.
Merged into Consolidated Yukeno Mines Ltd. 00/00/1949
Each share Capital Stock $1 par exchanged for (0.33333333) share Capital Stock $1 par
Consolidated Yukeno Mines Ltd. recapitalized as Yukeno Mines Ltd. 00/00/1951 which recapitalized as Gradore Mines Ltd. 03/04/1966
(See Gradore Mines Ltd.)

YUKENO MINES LTD. (ON)
Recapitalized as Gradore Mines Ltd. 03/04/1966
Each share Capital Stock $1 par exchanged for (0.2) share Capital Stock $1 par
(See Gradore Mines Ltd.)

YUKON ALASKA TRUST
Succeeded by Pacific Tin Corp. in 1929

Details not available

YUKON ANTIMONY LTD (BC)
Merged into International Mariner Resources Ltd. 2/9/71
Each share Common 50¢ par exchanged for (0.066666) share Common no par and (0.033333) Ser. C Common Stock Purchase Warrant which expired 7/31/72
(See International Mariner Resources Ltd.)

YUKON CO-OPERATIVE OIL CO. (OK)
Charter revoked for failure to file reports and pay fees 11/25/25

YUKON CONS GOLD LTD (CANADA)
Common $1 par changed to no par 07/06/1977
Merged into Teck Corp. 02/08/1979
Each share Common no par exchanged for (1/3) share Class B Common no par
Teck Corp. name changed to Teck Cominco Ltd. 09/12/2001 which name changed to Teck Resources Ltd. 04/27/2009

YUKON ENERGY CORP (MN)
Company believed out of business 00/00/2007
Details not available

YUKON EXPLORATIONS LTD. (BC)
Liquidation completed in December, 1963
Bondholders received partial payment
Capital Stock is worthless

YUKON GALENA HILL MINES LTD.
Merged into Consolidated Yukeno Mines Ltd. 00/00/1949
Each share Capital Stock $1 par exchanged for (0.33333333) share Capital Stock $1 par
Consolidated Yukeno Mines Ltd. recapitalized as Yukeno Mines Ltd. 00/00/1951 which recapitalized as Gradore Mines Ltd. 03/04/1966
(See Gradore Mines Ltd.)

YUKON GOLD CO.
Name changed to Yukon-Pacific Mining Co. in 1938
Yukon-Pacific Mining Co. merged into Pacific Tin Consolidated Corp. (Me.) in 1939 which reincorporated in Delaware 4/23/86 which name changed to Zemex Corp. 6/13/86

YUKON GOLD CORP (NV)
Recapitalized as GlobalMin Ventures Inc. 07/17/2014
Each share Common $0.0001 par exchanged for (0.1) share Common $0.0001 par
GlobalMin Ventures Inc. recapitalized as VetaNova Inc. 06/27/2018

YUKON GOLD CORP (WA)
Reincorporated under the laws of Yukon as Alliance Pacific Gold Corp. 06/12/1997
Alliance Pacific Gold Corp. recapitalized as International Alliance Resources, Inc. 09/24/1998 which name changed to Bluenose Gold Corp. 07/25/2012

YUKON GOLD CORP INC (DE)
Reorganized under the laws of Nevada 05/18/2011
Each share Common $0.0001 par exchanged for (0.2) share Common $0.0001 par
Yukon Gold Corp., Inc. recapitalized as GlobalMin Ventures Inc. 07/17/2014 which recapitalized as VetaNova Inc. 06/27/2018

YUKON GOLD PLACERS LTD (CANADA)
Recapitalized as Carlin Resources Corp. 01/09/1986
Each share Capital Stock no par exchanged for (0.25) share Common no par
Carlin Resources Corp. recapitalized

as Consolidated Carlin Resources Corp. 06/03/1999 which recapitalized as Carlin Gold Corp. (Canada) 05/16/2000 which reincorporated in British Columbia 08/29/2007

YUKON MINERALS CORP (AB)
Recapitalized as Consolidated Yukon Minerals Corp. 05/30/1991
Each share Common no par exchanged for (0.2) share Common no par
(See Consolidated Yukon Minerals Corp.)

YUKON-NEVADA GOLD CORP (BC)
Recapitalized as Veris Gold Corp. 10/11/2012
Each share Common no par exchanged for (0.1) share Common no par

YUKON-PACIFIC MINING CO.
Merged into Pacific Tin Consolidated Corp. (ME) in 1939
Each (5) shares Capital Stock $5 par exchanged for (1) share Capital Stock $1 par
Pacific Tin Consolidated Corp. (ME) reincorporated in Delaware 4/23/86 which name changed to Zemex Corp. (DE) 6/13/86 reincorporated in Canada 1/12/99

YUKON RANGES EXPLORATION, LTD. (CANADA)
Charter surrendered 00/00/1959

YUKON RES CORP (NV)
Each share old Common $0.001 par exchanged for (3) shares new Common $0.001 par 09/26/2005
Reincorporated under the laws of Minnesota as Uranium Star Corp. 01/03/2007
Uranium Star Corp. name changed to Energizer Resources Inc. 04/29/2010 which name changed to NextSource Materials Inc. (MN) 04/24/2017 which reincorporated in Canada 12/27/2017

YUKON REV MINES LTD (YT)
Recapitalized as YKR International Resources, Ltd. 12/29/1997
Each share Common $1 par exchanged for (0.33333333) share Common $1 par
YKR International Resources, Ltd. recapitalized as Gtech International Resources Ltd. (YT) 01/10/2001 which reorganized in British Columbia as Simavita Ltd. 12/06/2013

YUKON SPIRIT MINES LTD (BC)
Recapitalized as Gainey Resources Ltd. 3/26/98
Each (7.4) shares Common no par exchanged for (1) share Common no par

YUKON ZINC CORP (BC)
Acquired by Jinduicheng Molybdenum Group, Ltd. 07/02/2008
Each share Common no par exchanged for $0.22 cash

YUKONADIAN MINERAL EXPLS LTD (BC)
Recapitalized as Yucatan Resources Ltd. 02/09/1977
Each share Capital Stock no par exchanged for (1/3) share Capital Stock no par
(See Yucatan Resources Ltd.)

YUKONG LTD (KOREA)
Name changed to SK Corp. 3/30/98
(See SK Corp.)

YUKONIC MINERALS CORP (NV)
Name changed to Georgetown Corp. 02/06/2012

YUKORE MINES LTD. (ON)
Merged into Continental Consolidated Mines & Oils Co. Ltd. on a (0.2) for (1) basis 10/4/57

(See Continental Consolidated Mines & Oils Co. Ltd.)

YUKOS CORP (RUSSIA)
Sponsored ADR's for Ordinary split (3.75) for (1) by issuance of (2.75) additional ADR's payable 05/22/2003 to holders of record 05/21/2003 Ex date - 05/23/2003
ADR agreement terminated 12/18/2007
No ADR holders' equity

YULETIDE ENTERPRISES, INC. OLD (NY)
Ctfs. dated prior to 12/31/68
Merged into American Technical Industries, Inc. 12/31/68
Each share Common 10¢ par exchanged for (0.8) share Common 6-2/3¢ par
(See American Technical Industries, Inc.)

YULETIDE ENTERPRISES INC NEW (NY)
Ctfs. dated after 1/28/71
Recapitalized as Y.E. Enterprises, Inc. 8/15/75
Each share Common 6-2/3¢ par exchanged for (0.2) share Common 33-33/100¢ par

YUM YUM INTL RESTAURANTS INC (DE)
Charter cancelled and declared inoperative and void for non-payment of taxes 04/15/1973

YUMA COPPER CORP (BC)
Name changed 12/1/96
Name changed from Yuma Gold Mines Ltd. to Yuma Copper Corp. 12/1/96
Cease trade order effective 2/2/98
Stockholders' equity unlikely

YUMA ENERGY INC (CA)
Each share 9.25% Preferred Ser. A no par automatically became (35) shares Common no par 10/27/2016
Reorganized under the laws of Delaware 10/27/2016
Each share Common no par exchanged for (0.05) share Common $0.001 par

YUME INC (DE)
Merged into RhythmOne PLC 02/02/2018
Each share Common $0.001 par exchanged for (0.7325) share Ordinary £0.10 par and $1.70 cash

YUMMY FLIES INC (CO)
Reorganized as Pura Naturals, Inc. 11/17/2016
Each share Common $0.001 par exchanged for (3.7) shares Common $0.001 par

YURIE SYS INC (DE)
Merged into Lucent Technologies Inc. 05/29/1998
Each share Common no par exchanged for $35 cash

YURIKO RES CORP (BC)
Recapitalized as Candy Express Stores Ltd. 1/23/92
Each share Common no par exchanged for (0.2) share Common no par
Candy Express Stores Ltd. recapitalized as Patriots Venture Group Ltd. 9/21/93 which recapitalized as Tearlach Resources Ltd. 5/22/97

YWL CORP (ON)
Merged into Icefloe Technologies Inc. 04/01/2004
Each share Common no par exchanged for (0.12067) share Common no par
(See Icefloe Technologies Inc.)

YZAPP INTL INC (NV)
Recapitalized as Shuaiyi International New Resources Development Inc. 05/28/2009

Each share Common $0.001 par exchanged for (0.00872676) share Common $0.001 par
Shuaiyi International New Resources Development Inc. name changed to Nutrastar International Inc. 01/20/2010

Z

Z & F ASSETS REALIZATION CORP.
Dissolved in 1944

Z & Z FASHIONS LTD (CA)
Stock Dividends - 50% 01/25/1977; 50% 04/15/1981
Acquired by Webster West, Inc. 11/30/1987
Each share Common 10¢ par exchanged for $2.75 cash

Z AXIS CORP (CO)
Recapitalized as Silicon Mountain Holdings, Inc. 09/07/2007
Each share Common $0.001 par exchanged for (0.11111111) share Common $0.001 par
(See Silicon Mountain Holdings, Inc.)

Z-COAT GROUP INC (DE)
Charter forfeited 10/29/1991

Z GOLD EXPL INC (AB)
Name changed to Brunswick Resources Inc. 05/22/2014

Z HLDGS GROUP INC (DE)
Name changed to Ariel Clean Energy, Inc. 08/20/2015

Z I P INC (NY)
Recapitalized as Triumph Management Group, Inc. 2/16/96
Each share new Common $0.001 par exchanged for (1/60) share Common $0.001 par
(See Triumph Management Group, Inc.)

Z K RES INC (UT)
Recapitalized as ABCO, Inc. (UT) 06/14/1989
Each share Common $0.001 par exchanged for (0.05) share Common $0.001 par
ABCO, Inc. (UT) name changed to Club Aquarius, Inc. 09/01/1989
(See Club Aquarius, Inc.)

Z-LANDERBANK BK AUSTRIA AKTIENGESELLSCHAFT (AUSTRIA)
Each old Sponsored ADR for Ordinary AS100 par exchanged for (1) new Sponsored ADR for Ordinary AS100 par 08/02/1993
Name changed to Bank Austria A.G. 01/30/1995
Bank Austria A.G. merged into Bayerische Hypo-Und Vereinsbank AG 02/08/2001
(See Bayerische Hypo-und Vereinsbank AG)

Z SEVEN FD INC (MD)
Common $1 par split (3) for (2) by issuance of (0.5) additional share 06/02/1986
Common $1 par split (2) for (1) by issuance of (1) additional share payable 12/30/1997 to holders of record 12/19/1997
Completely liquidated 12/29/2010
Each share Common $1 par received net asset value

Z-TEL TECHNOLOGIES INC (DE)
Issue Information - 6,000,000 shares COM offered at $17 per share on 12/15/1999
Each share old Common 1¢ par exchanged for (0.2) share new Common 1¢ par 12/02/2004
Name changed to Trinsic, Inc. 01/03/2005
Each share new Common 1¢ par exchanged for (1) new Common 1¢ par
(See Trinsic, Inc.)

Z-TREX CORP (DE)
Name changed to Old Tyme Soft Drinks, Inc. 7/12/89
(See Old Tyme Soft Drinks, Inc.)

Z TRIM HLDGS INC (IL)
Each share old Common $0.00005 par exchanged for (0.03333333) share new Common $0.00005 par 02/09/2009
Reincorporated under the laws of Nevada as Agritech Worldwide, Inc. and Common $0.00005 par changed to $0.0001 par 04/04/2016

Z YACHTS INC (NV)
Name changed to Boveran Diagnostics, Inc. 08/18/2008
Boveran Diagnostics, Inc. name changed to Thrive World Wide, Inc. 09/28/2009

ZA-MATIC PRODUCTS CORP. (OR)
Merged into Old Town Charge-A-Copy, Inc. 6/16/70
Each share Common no par exchanged for (0.21427) share Old Town Corp. Common $1 par
(See Old Town Corp.)

ZAB RES INC (BC)
Recapitalized as Kokomo Enterprises Inc. 04/15/2009
Each share Common no par exchanged for (0.04) share Common no par
Kokomo Enterprises Inc. recapitalized as High 5 Ventures Inc. 08/29/2012 which recapitalized as 37 Capital Inc. 07/07/2014

ZABA LEE ENTERPRISES INC (BC)
Name changed to Eurotech Building Products Inc. 08/12/1991
Eurotech Building Products Inc. recapitalized as Eurotech Technologies Inc. 09/16/1992 which recapitalized as Artemis Venture Inc. 04/29/1996 which recapitalized as Paradym Ventures Inc. 01/04/1999 which recapitalized as Pacific Paradym Energy Inc. 10/01/2007

ZABS BACKYARD HOTS INC (NY)
Chapter 11 Federal Bankruptcy Code converted to Chapter 7 on 5/15/90
Stockholders' equity unlikely

ZACHERRA HLDGS INC (ON)
Reincorporated 08/01/1997
Place of incorporation changed from (Canada) to (ON) 08/01/1997
Name changed to First Interactive Inc. 01/18/2000
(See First Interactive Inc.)

ZAG INDS LTD (ISRAEL)
Issue Information - 2,700,000 shares ORD offered at $10 per share on 11/01/1996
Acquired by Stanley Works 08/05/1998
Each share Ordinary ILS 0.01 par exchanged for $14.30 cash

ZAGABELT MINING CORP. LTD. (ON)
Dissolved 5/26/58

ZAGG INC (NV)
Reincorporated under the laws of Delaware 06/27/2016

ZAGREBACKA BANKA D.D. (CROATIA)
GDR agreement terminated 01/09/2003
Each 144A GDR for Ordinary exchanged for $15.5693 cash
Each Reg. S GDR for Ordinary exchanged for $15.5693 cash

ZAHAVY MINES LTD (ON)
Recapitalized as Xavier Mines Ltd. 02/10/1993
Each share Common no par exchanged for (0.2) share Common no par
Xavier Mines Ltd. reorganized in Delaware as Xavier Corp. 07/24/1996
(See Xavier Corp.)

ZAIO CORP (AB)
Each share old Common no par exchanged for (0.25) share new Common no par 06/25/2012
Name changed to Clarocity Corp. 10/17/2016

ZAIS FINL CORP (MD)
Name changed to Sutherland Asset Management Corp. 11/01/2016
Sutherland Asset Management Corp. name changed to Ready Capital Corp. 10/01/2018

ZAIS GROUP HLDGS INC (DE)
Acquired by Z Acquisition LLC 05/18/2018
Each share Class A Common $0.0001 par exchanged for $4.10 cash

ZAKOR GOLD MINES, LTD. (ON)
Charter cancelled for failure to file reports and pay taxes May 1958

ZALAKERAMIA RESZVENYTARSASAG (HUNGARY)
GDR agreement terminated 10/31/2005
Each 144A GDR for Ordinary exchanged for $0.94562 cash
Each Reg. S GDR for Ordinary exchanged for $0.94562 cash

ZALDIVA INC (NV)
Reorganized 01/09/2012
Reorganized from (FL) to under the laws of (NV) 01/09/2012
Each share Common $0.001 par exchanged for (0.5) share Common $0.001 par
Name changed to FONU2 Inc. 04/23/2012

ZALE CORP (TX)
Common $1 par and Conv. Class B Common $1 par split (3) for (2) by issuance of (0.5) additional share respectively 08/16/1965
Common $1 par and Conv. Class B Common $1 par split (3) for (2) by issuance of (0.5) additional share respectively 07/16/1968
80¢ Conv. Preferred Ser. A $1 par called for redemption 02/09/1987
Merged into PS Associates 06/08/1987
Each share Conv. Class B Common $1 par exchanged for $50 cash
Each share Common $1 par exchanged for $50 cash

ZALE CORP NEW (DE)
Common 1¢ par split (2) for (1) by issuance of (1) additional share payable 06/08/2004 to holders of record 05/28/2004 Ex date - 06/09/2004
Acquired by Signet Jewelers Ltd. 05/29/2014
Each share Common 1¢ par exchanged for $21 cash

ZALE JEWELRY CO., INC. (TX)
Common and Class B Common $1 par split (2) for (1) by issuance of (1) additional share 5/15/62
Name changed to Zale Corp. 7/30/65
(See Zale Corp.)

ZALICUS INC (DE)
Each share old Common $0.001 par exchanged for (0.16666666) share new Common $0.001 par 10/03/2013
Recapitalized as EPIRUS Biopharmaceuticals, Inc. 07/16/2014
Each share new Common $0.001 par exchanged for (0.1) share Common $0.001 par

ZAMAGE DIGITAL IMAGING INC (CO)
Reorganized under the laws of Nevada as Provectus Pharmaceuticals, Inc. 04/11/2002
Each share Common no par received (0.00333333) share Common $0.001 par
Holders of (100) or fewer pre-split shares received share for share
Holders of between (101) and (30,000) shares received (100) shares only
Provectus Pharmaceuticals, Inc. (NV) reincorporated in Delaware as Provectus Biopharmaceuticals, Inc. 01/23/2014

ZAMBA CORP (DE)
Merged into Technology Solutions Co. 1/3/2005
Each share Common 1¢ par exchanged for (0.15) share Common 1¢ par

ZAMBIA BROKEN HILL DEV LTD (ZAMBIA)
Completely liquidated 06/28/1971
Each ADR for Ordinary ZMK 0.50 par exchanged for (0.6) Zambia Copper Investments Ltd. ADR for Ordinary BMD 24¢ par
Zambia Copper Investments Ltd. name changed to ZCI Ltd. 05/24/2010

ZAMBIA CONS COPPER MINES LTD (ZAMBIA)
ADR agreement terminated 03/05/2001
Each American Share for Ordinary Kwacha-4 par exchanged for $0.0688 cash

ZAMBIA COPPER INVTS LTD (BERMUDA)
Name changed to ZCI Ltd. 05/24/2010

ZAMBIAN ANGLO AMERN LTD (BERMUDA)
Reincorporated 06/26/1970
Stock Dividend - 100% 11/22/1968
Place of incorporation changed from Zambia to Bermuda and ZMK 1 par changed to BMD $1.40 par 06/26/1970
Name changed to Minerals & Resources Corp., Ltd. (Bermuda) 08/05/1974
Minerals & Resources Corp., Ltd. (Bermuda) reincorporated in Luxembourg as Minorco 11/27/1987
(See Minorco)

ZAMS INC (MO)
Plan of reorganization under Chapter 11 Federal Bankruptcy proceedings confirmed 08/19/1996
No stockholders' equity

ZANART ENTMT INC (FL)
Recapitalized 12/30/1994
Each share old Common $0.0001 par exchanged for (0.1) share new Common $0.0001 par 02/08/1994
Recapitalized from Zanart Publishing Inc. to Zanart Entertainment Inc. 12/30/1994
Each share new Common $0.0001 par exchanged for (0.5) share Common $0.0001 par
Name changed to Continucare Corp. 10/21/1996
Continucare Corp. merged into Metropolitan Health Networks, Inc. 10/04/2011
(See Metropolitan Health Networks, Inc.)

ZANDARIA VENTURES INC (NV)
Name changed to Webtradex International Corp. 07/23/2010
Webtradex International Corp. name changed to ZD Ventures Corp. 09/11/2013 which name changed to Plyzer Technologies Inc. 05/01/2017

ZANDPAN GOLD MNG LTD (SOUTH AFRICA)
Each ADR for Ordinary Reg. Rand-1 par exchanged for (10) ADR's for Ordinary Reg. Rand-10 par 12/14/84
Depositary Agreement terminated 10/15/96
Each ADR for Ordinary Rand-10 par exchanged for $0.404 cash
(Additional Information in Active)

ZAM-ZAR

ZANETT INC (DE)
Each share old Common $0.001 par exchanged for (0.25) share new Common $0.001 par 06/30/2008
SEC revoked common stock registration 04/04/2014

ZANEX N L (AUSTRALIA)
Each ADR for Ordinary A$0.20 par exchanged for (0.1) ADR for Ordinary A$2 par 11/21/1991
Each new ADR for Ordinary A$2 par exchanged for (1) Sponsored ADR for Ordinary A$2 par 12/06/1993
ADR agreement terminated 05/24/1999
Details not available

ZANNWELL INC (NV)
Recapitalized as BlackHawk Fund 01/03/2005
Each share Common $0.001 par exchanged for (0.00125) share Common $0.001 par
BlackHawk Fund recapitalized as Vidable, Inc. 07/01/2011 which recapitalized as Vibe I, Inc. 08/03/2015 which name change to Coresource Strategies, Inc. (NV) 10/26/2015 which reincorporated in Oklahoma as NUGL, Inc. 12/11/2017

ZANY BRAINY INC (PA)
Assets sold for the benefit of creditors 9/6/2001
No stockholders' equity

ZAP (CA)
Name changed 7/13/2001
Name changed from Zapworld.Com to Zap 7/13/2001
Plan of reorganization under Chapter 11 Federal Bankruptcy Code effective 6/28/2002
Each share old Common no par exchanged for (1/6) share new Common no par 6/28/2002
(Additional Information in Active)

ZAP COM CORP (NV)
Name changed to NZCH Corp. 08/10/2016
(See NZCH Corp.)

ZAP PWR SYS (CA)
Name changed to Zapworld.com 6/2/99
Zapworld.com name changed to ZAP 7/13/2001

ZAPATA CORP (NV)
Reincorporated 04/30/1999
Common 25¢ par split (2) for (1) by issuance of (1) additional share 08/15/1975
$5.75 Conv. Preferred no par called for redemption 09/28/1979
Common 25¢ par split (2) for (1) by issuance of (1) additional share 01/15/1981
Each share old Common 25¢ par exchanged for (0.2) share new Common 25¢ par 05/02/1994
$2 Conv. Non-Cum. Preference $1 par called for redemption at $80 on 09/01/1997
State of incorporation changed from (DE) to (NV) and new Common 25¢ par changed to 1¢ par 04/30/1999
Each share old Common 1¢ par received distribution of (0.02) share Zap.com Corp. Common $0.001 par payable 11/12/1999 to holders of record 11/05/1999
Each share old Common 1¢ par exchanged for (0.1) share new Common 1¢ par 01/30/2001
New Common 1¢ par split (8) for (1) by issuance of (7) additional shares payable 04/06/2005 to holders of record 03/30/2005 Ex date - 04/07/2005
Reincorporated under the laws of Delaware as Harbinger Group Inc. 12/23/2009
Harbinger Group Inc. name changed to HRG Group, Inc. 03/11/2015 which recapitalized as Spectrum Brands Holdings, Inc. (New) 07/16/2018

ZAPATA ENERGY CORP (AB)
Name changed to Surge Energy Inc. 06/30/2010

ZAPATA EXPL CO (DE)
Merged into Zapata Corp. (DE) 04/01/1977
Each share Common $1 par exchanged for (0.37) share Common 25¢ par
Zapata Corp. (DE) reincorporated in Nevada 04/30/1999 which reincorporated in Delaware as Harbinger Group Inc. 12/23/2009 which name changed to HRG Group, Inc. 03/11/2015 which recapitalized as Spectrum Brands Holdings, Inc. (New) 07/16/2018

ZAPATA FOODS INC (MN)
Merged into Heublein, Inc. 7/17/74
Each share Common 10¢ par exchanged for (0.162792) share Common no par
Heublein, Inc. merged into Reynolds (R.J.) Industries, Inc. 10/13/82 which name changed to RJR Nabisco, Inc. 4/25/86
(See RJR Nabisco, Inc.)

ZAPATA GRANBY CORP (BC)
$0.40 Conv. Preference no par called for redemption 11/15/1979
Public interest eliminated

ZAPATA INTERNATIONAL INC. (MN)
Name changed to Zapata Foods Inc. 7/1/71
Zapata Foods Inc. merged into Heublein, Inc. 7/17/74 which merged into Reynolds (R.J.) Industries, Inc. 10/13/82 which name changed to RJR Nabisco, Inc. 4/25/86
(See RJR Nabisco, Inc.)

ZAPATA NORNESS INC (DE)
Name changed to Zapata Corp. (DE) 02/15/1972
Zapata Corp. (DE) reincorporated in Nevada 04/30/1999 which reincorporated in Delaware as Harbinger Group Inc. 12/23/2009 which name changed to HRG Group, Inc. 03/11/2015 which recapitalized as Spectrum Brands Holdings, Inc. (New) 07/16/2018

ZAPATA OFF SHORE CO (DE)
Capital Stock 50¢ par reclassified as Common 50¢ par 08/31/1966
Common 50¢ par changed to 25¢ par and (1) additional share issued 02/02/1968
Name changed to Zapata Norness Inc. 11/25/1968
Zapata Norness Inc. name changed to Zapata Corp. (DE) 02/15/1972 which reincorporated in Nevada 04/30/1999 which reincorporated in Delaware as Harbinger Group Inc. 12/23/2009 which name changed to HRG Group, Inc. 03/11/2015 which recapitalized as Spectrum Brands Holdings, Inc. (New) 07/16/2018

ZAPATA PETROLEUM CORP. (DE)
Merged into Pennzoil Co. (PA) (New) 7/3/63
Each share Common 10¢ par exchanged for (0.25) share Common $5 par
Pennzoil Co. (PA) (New) merged into Pennzoil United, Inc. 4/1/68 which name changed to Pennzoil Co. (DE) 6/1/72 which name changed to PennzEnergy Co. 12/30/98

ZAPATA PRODUCING & REFINING CO. (DE)
Charter cancelled and declared inoperative and void for non-payment of taxes 3/18/25

ZAPLINK INTL INC (UT)
Each share old Common $0.001 par exchanged for (0.2) share new Common $0.001 par 3/22/88
Brands Holdings, Inc. (New) 07/16/2018

ZAPME CORP (DE)
Issue Information - 9,000,000 shares COM offered at $11 per share on 10/19/1999
Name changed to rStar Corp. 3/21/2001
(See rStar Corp.)

ZAPNAPS INC (NV)
Name changed to FusionTech, Inc. 11/12/2010

ZAPORIZHZHYA FERROALLOY PLT JSC (UKRAINE)
GDR agreement terminated 05/17/2017
Each Reg. S Sponsored GDR for Ordinary exchanged for (100) shares Ordinary
Note: Unexchanged GDR's will be sold and the proceeds, if any, held for claim after 05/21/2018

ZAPOROZHSTAL IRON & STL WKS OPEN JT STK CO (UKRAINE)
Reg. S GDR's for Ordinary split (5) for (1) by issuance of (4) additional GDR's payable 03/28/2005 to holders of record 03/25/2005
Basis changed from (1:50) to (1:10) 03/28/2005
GDR agreement terminated 08/13/2018
Each Reg. S GDR exchanged for (10) shares Ordinary
Note: Unexchanged GDR's will be sold and the proceeds, if any, held for claim after 02/12/2019

ZAPOROZHTRANSFORMATOR OPEN JT STK CO (UKRAINE)
ADR agreement terminated 01/16/2009
No ADR's remain outstanding

ZAPPA RES LTD (BC)
Recapitalized as AKA Ventures Inc. 07/02/2008
Each share Common no par exchanged for (0.5) share Common no par
AKA Ventures Inc. name changed to Phoenix Copper Corp. 09/07/2012 which recapitalized as Phoenix Metals Corp. 12/04/2013 which name changed to Envirotek Remediation Inc. 04/27/2018

ZAQ INC (CANADA)
Name changed to Isacsoft Inc. 03/18/2004
(See Isacsoft Inc.)

ZARA RES INC (ON)
Reincorporated under the laws of British Columbia 07/03/2013

ZARA TRADING INC (WY)
Administratively dissolved 06/17/2009

ZARAHEMLA CORP (DE)
Name changed to Noetix Medical Technologies, Inc. 10/11/1988

ZARARA ENERGY LTD (SOUTH AFRICA)
Stock Dividend - 28% payable 06/28/2001 to holders of record 5/11/2001 Ex date - 05/14/2001
ADR basis changed from (1:1) to (1:01) 10/09/2001
ADR agreement terminated 06/27/2006
Each ADR for Ordinary Rand-2-1/2 par exchanged for $0.00317 cash

ZARARA OIL & GAS LTD (CHANNEL ISLANDS)
Reorganized under the laws of Wyoming as Zara Trading, Inc. 03/05/2007
Each share Common no par exchanged for (1) share Common no par
(See Zara Trading, Inc.)

ZARCAN INTL RES INC (BC)
Each share old Common no par exchanged for (0.1) share new Common no par 08/05/2004
Name changed to Bighorn Petroleum Ltd. 01/30/2006
Bighorn Petroleum Ltd. recapitalized as Sunset Pacific Petroleum Ltd. 05/07/2009

ZAREBA SYS INC (MN)
Acquired by Woodstream Corp. 04/01/2010
Each share Common 1¢ par exchanged for $9 cash

ZARGON ENERGY TR (AB)
Reorganized as Zargon Oil & Gas Ltd. (New) 01/07/2011
Each Trust Unit no par exchanged for (1) share Common no par
Note: Unexchanged certificates were cancelled and became without value 01/07/2014

ZARGON OIL & GAS LTD OLD (AB)
Reorganized as Zargon Energy Trust 07/21/2004
Each share Common no par exchanged for (1) Trust Unit no par
Each Exchangeable Share no par exchanged for (1.84716) shares Zargon Oil & Gas Ltd. (New) Common no par 01/07/2011
Note: Unexchanged certificates were cancelled and became without value 01/07/2014
Zargon Energy Trust reorganized as Zargon Oil & Gas Ltd. (New) 01/07/2011

ZARING HOMES INC (OH)
Under plan of reorganization each share Common 10¢ par automatically became (1) share Zaring National Corp. Common 10¢ par 05/08/1997
Zaring National Corp. name changed to First Cincinnati, Inc. 01/31/2001
(See First Cincinnati, Inc.)

ZARING NATL CORP (OH)
Name changed to First Cincinnati, Inc. 1/31/2001
(See First Cincinnati, Inc.)

ZARKON CORP (DE)
Name changed 10/7/85
Name changed from Zarkon Computer Inc. to Zarkon Corp. 10/7/85
Charter cancelled and declared inoperative and void for non-payment of taxes 3/1/87

ZARLINK SEMICONDUCTOR INC (CANADA)
$2 Conv. Preferred 1983 R&D Ser. no par called for redemption at $25 plus $0.4837 accured dividends on 06/27/2011
Acquired by Microsemi Corp. 10/28/2011
Each share Common no par exchanged for $3.98 cash

ZARON CAP INC (ON)
Recapitalized as PMR Corp. 11/03/1989
Each share Common $0.001 par exchanged for (0.1) share Common 1¢ par
PMR Corp. recapitalized as Psychiatric Solutions, Inc. 08/05/2002
(See Psychiatric Solutions, Inc.)

ZARUMA RES INC (YT)
Recapitalized as Red Tiger Mining Inc. 11/08/2011
Each share Common no par exchanged for (0.1) share Common no par

ZAURAK CAP CORP (ON)
Cease trade order effective 09/06/2002
Stockholders' equity unlikely

ZAUSNER FOODS CORP (PA)
Class A Common $1 par reclassified as Common $1 par 06/11/1971

Stock Dividend - 100% 12/06/1971
Merged into Bongrain Foods Corp. 08/05/1977
Each share Common $1 par exchanged for $15 cash

ZAVALA RISS PRODTNS INC (NY)
Name changed to Cine-Prime Corp. 11/24/1971
(See Cine-Prime Corp.)

ZAVITZ PETE INC (AB)
Recapitalized 08/31/1993
Recapitalized from Zavitz Technology Inc. to Zavitz Petroleum Inc. 08/31/1993
Each share Common no par exchanged for (0.2) share Common no par
Name changed to Jaguar Petroleum Corp. 11/21/1994 which merged into Probe Exploration Inc. 05/09/1997
(See Probe Exploration Inc.)

ZAXIS INTL INC (DE)
Common 1¢ par changed to $0.0001 par 11/30/2004
Each share old Common $0.0001 par exchanged for (0.01) share new Common $0.0001 par 08/04/2008
Each share new Common $0.0001 par exchanged again for (0.25) share new Common $0.0001 par 03/20/2015
Name changed to Emerald Medical Applications Corp. 10/06/2015
Emerald Medical Applications Corp. name changed to Virtual Crypto Technologies Inc. 03/07/2018

ZAYRE CORP (DE)
Conv. Preferred Ser. A $1 par called for redemption 1/13/69
Common $1 par split (3) for (2) by issuance of (0.5) additional share 5/16/69
Common $1 par split (2) for (1) by issuance of (1) additional share 6/29/83
Common $1 par split (4) for (3) by issuance of (1/3) additional share 5/29/85
Common $1 par split (2) for (1) by issuance of (1) additional share 6/25/86
Stock Dividends - 40% 10/15/65; 20% 6/10/82; 10% 5/31/84
Name changed to TJX Companies, Inc. 6/20/89

ZAZU METALS CORP (CANADA)
Merged into Solitario Zinc Corp. 07/18/2017
Each share Common no par exchanged for (0.3572) share Common no par
Note: Unexchanged certificates will be cancelled and become without value 07/18/2023

ZBB ENERGY CORP (WI)
Each share old Common 1¢ par exchanged for (0.2) share new Common 1¢ par 10/31/2013
Name changed to EnSync, Inc. 08/17/2015

ZCOM NETWORKS INC (NV)
Each share old Common $0.001 par exchanged for (0.005) share new Common $0.001 par 12/19/2008
Recapitalized as Global Gateway Media & Communications, Inc. 12/02/2009
Each (600) shares new Common $0.001 par exchanged for (1) share Common $0.001 par

ZCOMM INDS INC (BC)
Recapitalized as Labrador International Mining Ltd. 8/25/95
Each share Common no par exchanged for (0.5) share Common no par
Labrador International Mining Ltd. recapitalized as Royal International Venture Corp. 3/18/99 which recapitalized as RCOM Venture Corp. 7/28/2000 which name changed to Wellstar Energy Corp. 7/21/2005

ZCONNEXX CORP (ON)
Placed in receivership 06/00/2002
No stockholders' equity

ZD VENTURES CORP (NV)
Name changed to Plyzer Technologies Inc. 05/01/2017

ZDIGITAL COM INC (NV)
Name changed to Squaremoon Inc. 05/17/2001
Squaremoon Inc. name changed to KidSational Inc. 12/17/2002 which name changed to Stratton Holdings Inc. 02/09/2009 which recapitalized as Profitable Developments, Inc. 12/24/2012

ZEACAN PRODS INC (AB)
Recapitalized as Canadian Zeolite Ltd. 07/26/1993
Each share Common no par exchanged for (0.2) share Common no par
Canadian Zeolite Ltd. name changed to Canadian Mining Co. Ltd. 01/08/1997 which name changed to Zeo-Tech Enviro Corp. 05/19/2000 which name changed to Canadian Mining Co. Inc(AB) 02/08/2007 which reincorporated in British Columbia as Canadian Zeolite Corp. 02/08/2016 which name changed to International Zeolite Corp. 03/06/2018

ZEAL CAP LTD (BC)
Recapitalized as First Quantum Ventures Ltd. (BC) 06/16/1993
Each share Common no par exchanged for (0.25) share Common no par
First Quantum Ventures Ltd. (BC) reincorporated in Yukon as First Quantum Minerals Ltd. 07/18/1996 which reincorporated in Canada 08/11/2003 which reincorporated in British Columbia 06/03/2005

ZEALOUS INC (NV)
Name changed to CoreStream Energy Inc. 09/03/2010
(See CoreStream Energy Inc.)

ZEALOUS TRADING GROUP INC (NV)
Name changed to Adult Entertainment Capital, Inc. 08/25/2008
Adult Entertainment Capital, Inc. name changed to Zealous, Inc. 03/05/2009 which name changed to CoreStream Energy Inc. 09/03/2010
(See CoreStream Energy Inc.)

ZEBALLOS MNG CO (NV)
Common $0.001 par split (3.5) for (1) by issuance of (2.5) additional shares payable 04/11/2000 to holders of record 03/20/2000
Name changed to Y3K Secure Enterprise Software Inc. 11/06/2001
Y3K Secure Enterprise Software Inc. name changed to Ecuity, Inc. 06/01/2004
(See Ecuity, Inc.)

ZEBEC RES LTD (BC)
Delisted from Vancouver Stock Exchange 01/10/1990

ZEBEDEE OIL LTD. (CANADA)
Name changed to Osias Resources Canada Ltd. 04/19/1971
Osias Resources Canada Ltd. recapitalized as Troy Gold Industries Ltd. 06/12/1974
(See Troy Gold Industries Ltd.)

ZEBRA RES INC (NV)
Name changed to American Paramount Gold Corp. 04/12/2010
American Paramount Gold Corp. name changed to Indigenous Roots Corp. 02/09/2018

ZEBRAMART COM INC (NV)
Each share old Common $0.00001 par exchanged for (0.5) share new Common $0.00001 par 08/16/2000
Name changed to Cottage Investments, Inc. 11/15/2000
Cottage Investments, Inc. recapitalized as Paving Stone Corp. 12/19/2001
(See Paving Stone Corp.)

ZEBU INC (NV)
Name changed to Greenland Corp. 09/21/1994
(See Greenland Corp.)

ZECOTEK MED SYS INC (BC)
Name changed to Zecotek Photonics Inc. 11/26/2007

ZED I SOLUTIONS INC (AB)
Name changed to Zedi Inc. 06/20/2007
(See Zedi Inc.)

ZEDI INC (AB)
Acquired by 1779958 Alberta Ltd. 02/21/2014
Each share Common no par exchanged for $1.05 cash
Note: Unexchanged certificates were cancelled and became without value 02/21/2017

ZEEZOO SOFTWARE CORP (NV)
Common $0.001 par split (2) for (1) by issuance of (1) additional share payable 07/11/2008 to holders of record 07/11/2008 Ex date - 07/14/2008
Name changed to Enhance Skin Products Inc. 09/08/2008

ZEGARELLI GROUP INTL INC (CA)
Recapitalized as 2050 Motors, Inc. 05/05/2014
Each share Common no par exchanged for (0.25) share Common no par

ZEHNTEL INC (DE)
Merged into Teradyne, Inc. 12/01/1987
Each share Common 1¢ par exchanged for (0.2) share Common 12-1/2¢ par

ZEIGLER COAL & COKE CO. (IL)
Stock Dividends - 25% 1/8/46; 25% 2/11/71
Name changed to Zeigler Coal Co. 7/1/71
Zeigler Coal Co. merged into Houston Natural Gas Corp. (Tex.) 12/14/73
(See Houston Natural Gas Corp. (Tex.))

ZEIGLER COAL CO (IL)
Merged into Houston Natural Gas Corp. (TX) 12/14/1973
Each share Common $10 par exchanged for (2.862) shares Common $1 par
(See Houston Natural Gas Corp. (TX))

ZEIGLER COAL HLDG CO (DE)
Issue Information - 10,467,564 shares COM offered at $15 per share on 09/29/1994
Acquired by AEI Resources, Inc. 09/04/1998
Each share Common 1¢ par exchanged for $21.25 cash

ZEINITRON CORP (NY)
Charter cancelled and proclaimed dissolved for failure to pay taxes 12/15/1975

ZEITGEIST WERKS INC (CO)
Name changed to Mediax Corp. 8/15/96

ZELLERS LTD (CANADA)
Preferred $100 par changed to $25 par in 1937
Each share old Common no par exchanged for (5) shares new Common no par 6/5/64
New Common no par split (4) for (1) by issuance of (3) additional shares 6/5/64
New Common no par split (4) for (1) by issuance of (3) additional shares 5/23/68
4-1/2% Preferred $50 par called for redemption 10/31/80
Acquired by Hudson's Bay Co. 6/17/81
Each share Conv. Class A Common no par exchanged for $18 cash
Each share Conv. Class B Common no par exchanged for $18 cash

ZELTIQ AESTHETICS INC (DE)
Acquired by Allergan Holdco US, Inc. 04/28/2017
Each share Common $0.001 par exchanged for $56.50 cash

ZEMARC LTD (PA)
Liquidation completed
Each share Common 25¢ par exchanged for initial distribution of $2.40 cash 02/03/1977
Each share Common 25¢ par received second and final distribution of $0.529 cash 04/10/1979

ZEMCO INDS INC (DE)
Under plan of merger each share Common 60¢ par exchanged for $5 cash 09/30/1979

ZEMEX CDA CORP (CANADA)
Merged into Cementos Pacasmayo S.A.A. 5/8/2003
Each share Common no par exchanged for $8.80 cash

ZEMEX CORP (DE)
Stock Dividends - 2% payable 11/18/96 to holders of record 11/4/96; 2% payable 12/15/97 to holders of record 12/1/97; 2% payable 11/2/98 to holders of record 10/19/98
Reincorporated under the laws of Canada and Common $1 par changed to no par 1/21/99
(See Zemex Corp. (Canada))

ZEN HLDGS CORP (DE)
Old Common $0.0001 par split (7) for (1) by issuance of (6) additional shares payable 09/30/2008 to holders of record 09/12/2008 Ex date - 10/01/2008
Each share old Common $0.0001 par exchanged for (0.0625) share new Common $0.0001 par 01/20/2011
Name changed to Millennium Healthcare Inc. 07/26/2011

ZEN INTL RES LTD (YUKON)
Reorganized under the laws of Alberta as Orca Petroleum Inc. 4/1/2002
Each share Common no par exchanged for (0.1) share Common no par
Orca Petroleum Inc. (ALTA) reorganized in British Columbia as Nautilus Minerals Inc. 5/10/2006

ZEN POTTERY EQUIP INC (CO)
Reincorporated under the laws of Delaware as Xethanol Corp. 03/30/2005
Xethanol Corp. name changed to Global Energy Holdings Group, Inc. 10/28/2008
(See Global Energy Holdings Group, Inc.)

ZENA CAP CORP (BC)
Name changed to Zena Mining Corp. 06/30/2009

ZENAS ENERGY CORP (AB)
Merged into Tusk Energy Corp. 01/04/2007
Each share Common no par exchanged for (1.033) shares Common no par
Note: Unexchanged certificates were cancelled and became without value 01/04/2013
(See Tusk Energy Corp.)

ZENASCENT INC (DE)
Name changed to Cedric Kushner Promotions Inc. 01/16/2003
Cedric Kushner Promotions Inc. name changed to Ckrush, Inc. 12/27/2005
(See Ckrush, Inc.)

ZENCO RES INC (BC)
Recapitalized as Solidor Resources Inc. 03/08/1988
Each share Common no par exchanged for (0.2) share Common no par
Solidor Resources Inc. recapitalized as Sheffield Resources Inc. (BC) 03/12/1997 which reincorporated in Nova Scotia as Globalstore.com, Inc. 04/27/1999 which name changed to GSO Solutions, Inc. 03/24/2000
(See GSO Solutions, Inc.)

ZENDA CAP INC (ON)
Name changed 11/10/1999
Name changed from Zenda Gold Corp. to Zenda Capital Inc. 11/10/1999
Name changed to Terex Resources Inc. 03/07/2005
Terex Resources Inc. name changed to Trelawney Resources Inc. 11/07/2006 which recapitalized as Trelawney Mining & Exploration Inc. 04/17/2009
(See Trelawney Mining & Exploration Inc.)

ZENDA EXPLORATION CO., LTD. (BC)
Charter revoked for failure to file reports and pay fees 4/13/67

ZENDA GOLD MINING (CANADA) LTD. (BC)
Name changed to Zenda Exploration Co., Ltd. 1/8/53
Zenda Exploration Co., Ltd. charter revoked 4/13/67

ZENDA GOLD MINING CO. (DE)
Common $1 par changed to 25¢ par in 1937
Common 25¢ par changed to 10¢ par in 1949
No longer in existence having become inoperative and void for non-payment of taxes 4/1/59

ZENDEX HLDGS INC (NV)
Name changed to Kingsmen Capital Group Ltd. 09/20/2016

ZENDORA INC (UT)
Recapitalized as Inter*Act Communications Inc. 07/20/1994
Each share Common $0.001 par exchanged for (0.1) share Common $0.001 par
(See Inter*Act Communications Inc.)

ZENECA GROUP PLC (UNITED KINGDOM)
Sponsored ADR's for Ordinary split (3) for (1) by issuance of (2) additional ADR's payable 04/07/1998 to holders of record 03/30/1998 Ex date - 04/08/1998
Under plan of merger name changed to AstraZeneca PLC 04/06/1999

ZENEX INTL INC (CO)
Name changed 8/6/2002
Name changed from Zenex Telecom to Zenex International, Inc. 8/6/2002
Reincorporated under the laws of Oklahoma as Aduddell Industries, Inc. 6/19/2006

ZENEX SYNTHETIC LUBRICANTS INC (FL)
Recapitalized as Home Intensive Care, Inc. 2/25/85
Each share Common 1¢ par exchanged for (0.125) share Common 1¢ par
(See Home Intensive Care, Inc.)

ZENGINE INC (DE)
Issue Information - 4,290,000 shares COM offered at $13 per share on 09/20/2000
Merged into MCSi, Inc. 11/20/2001
Each share Common no par exchanged for (0.2259) share Common no par
(See MCSi, Inc.)

ZENITECH CORP (DE)
Recapitalized as China Tianfeihong Wine Inc. 08/12/2013
Each share Common $0.0001 par exchanged for (0.16666666) share Common $0.0006 par

ZENITH AMERN CORP (FL)
Adjudicated bankrupt 08/19/1976
Stockholders' equity unlikely

ZENITH CAP INC (FL)
Name changed to Heidi's Frogen Yozurt Shoppes, Inc. 3/13/87
(See Heidi's Frogen Yozurt Shoppes, Inc.)

ZENITH CAPITAL CORP. (UT)
Name changed to Players Club International, Inc. (UT) 4/23/85
Players Club International, Inc. (UT) reorganized in Nevada as Players International, Inc. 9/18/86
(See Players International, Inc.)

ZENITH COMPANIES, INC. (SD)
Charter expired by time limitations 11/20/41

ZENITH DEV CORP (UT)
Name changed to Alternative Energy Resources Inc. 4/17/80
Alternative Energy Resources Inc. name changed to Trafalgar Resources, Inc. 7/17/2006

ZENITH ELEC SUPPLY LTD (ON)
Acquired by Northern Telecom Ltd.-Northern Telecom Ltee. 00/00/1979
Each share Common no par exchanged for $3.25 cash

ZENITH ELECTRS CORP (DE)
Plan of reorganization under Chapter 11 Federal Bankruptcy Code effective 11/9/99
No stockholders' equity

ZENITH ENERGY CORP (BC)
Struck off register 11/29/85

ZENITH EPIGENETICS CORP (AB)
Name changed to Zenith Capital Corp. 08/01/2016

ZENITH FDG CORP (FL)
Name changed to Zenith American Corp. 05/30/1973
(See Zenith American Corp.)

ZENITH INCOME FD INC (MD)
Name changed to Zenix Income Fund Inc. 10/20/1989
Zenix Income Fund Inc. name changed to Western Asset Zenix Income Fund, Inc. 10/09/2006 which merged into Western Asset High Income Fund II Inc. 09/24/2008

ZENITH INDS CORP (CANADA)
Name changed to LGC Skyrota Wind Energy Corp. 08/21/2009
(See LGC Skyrota Wind Energy Corp.)

ZENITH INTERNATIONAL INC (LA)
Name changed to NexTech Solutions, Inc. 06/12/2006

ZENITH INV CORP (CO)
Reorganized under the laws of Delaware as Building Technologies Industries, Inc. 4/8/88
Each share Common $0.00001 par exchanged for (0.1) share Common $0.00001 par
(See Building Technologies Industries, Inc.)

ZENITH LABS INC (NJ)
Common 10¢ par split (3) for (2) by issuance of (0.5) additional share 2/14/69
Common 10¢ par reclassified as Class B Common 9¢ par 9/15/78 Class B Common 9¢ par reclassified as Common 9¢ par 7/19/82
Common 9¢ par split (3) for (2) by issuance of (0.5) additional share 3/12/85
Common 9¢ par split (2) for (1) by issuance of (1) additional share 6/18/85
Common 9¢ par split (2) for (1) by issuance of (1) additional share 6/18/86
Reorganized under Chapter 11 Federal Bankruptcy Code 12/20/89
Each (75) shares Common 9¢ par exchanged for (1) share Common no par
Common no par split (3) for (1) by issuance of (2) additional shares 12/9/93
Merged into IVAX Corp. 12/30/94
Each share new Common no par exchanged for (1.307) shares Common 10¢ par
(See IVAX Corp.)

ZENITH LIFE INS CO (IL)
Each share old Common $1 par exchanged for (0.5) share new Common $1 par 5/26/67
Reorganized under the laws of Nevada as Zenith United Corp. 7/3/69
Each share new Common $1 par exchanged for (1) share Common $1 par
Zenith United Corp. merged into First Continental Life Group, Inc. 10/28/79
(See First Continental Life Group, Inc.)

ZENITH METALS RECOVERY INC (BC)
Delisted from Vancouver Stock Exchange 09/02/1989

ZENITH MNG LTD (BC)
Name changed to Zenore Resources Inc. 06/20/1977
Zenore Resources Inc. recapitalized as Zenco Resources Inc. 01/27/1982 which recapitalized as Solidor Resources Inc. 03/08/1988 which recapitalized as Sheffield Resource Inc. 03/12/1997 which name changed to Globalstore.com, Inc. 04/27/1999 which name changed to GSO Solutions, Inc. 03/24/2000
(See GSO Solutions, Inc.)

ZENITH MOLYBDENITE CORP., LTD. (ON)
Charter revoked for failure to file reports and pay fees 1/2/56

ZENITH NATL INS CORP (DE)
Common $1 par split (2) for (1) by issuance of (1) additional share 07/31/1978
Common $1 par split (3) for (2) by issuance of (0.5) additional share 07/31/1979
Common $1 par split (5) for (4) by issuance of (0.25) additional share 01/30/1981
Common $1 par split (3) for (2) by issuance of (0.5) additional share 07/29/1983
Conv. Depositary Preferred Ser. A $1 par called for redemption 04/14/1986
Common $1 par split (3) for (2) by issuance of (0.5) additional share payable 10/11/2005 to holders of record 09/19/2005 Ex date - 10/12/2005
Stock Dividends - 10% 06/15/1978; 10% 01/31/1983; 10% 08/12/1988
Acquired by Fairfax Financial Holdings Ltd. 05/20/2010
Each share Common $1 par exchanged for $38 cash

ZENITH PACIFIC MINES, INC. (ID)
Completely liquidated 07/06/1973
Each share Capital Stock 10¢ par exchanged for first and final distribution of (0.01) share Selectors, Inc. Common no par
Selectors, Inc. reorganized as Source Capital Corp. 09/00/1991 which merged into Sterling Financial Corp. 09/28/2001 which merged into Umpqua Holdings Corp. 04/18/2014

ZENITH RADIO CORP (DE)
Reincorporated 3/3/58
State of incorporation changed from (IL) to (DE) and Common no par changed to $1 par and (1) additional share issued 3/3/58
Common $1 par split (3) for (1) by issuance of (2) additional shares 5/22/59
Common $1 par split (3) for (1) by issuance of (2) additional shares 11/20/61
Common $1 par split (2) for (1) by issuance of (1) additional share 6/6/66
Name changed to Zenith Electronics Corp. 4/24/84
(See Zenith Electronics Corp.)

ZENITH TECHNOLOGY INC (NV)
Name changed to Adsouth Partners, Inc. 01/13/2004

ZENITH TIRE & RUBBER CO. (DE)
No longer in existence having become inoperative and void for non-payment of taxes 3/19/24

ZENITH UTD CORP (NV)
Common $1 par changed to 80¢ par and (0.25) additional share issued 06/01/1972
Merged into First Continental Life Group, Inc. 10/28/1979
Each share Common 80¢ par exchanged for (0.385) share Participating Preferred Ser. A $1 par
(See First Continental Life Group, Inc.)

ZENIX INCOME FD INC (MD)
7% Preferred 1¢ par called for redemption at $1,000 on 04/14/2000
Name changed to Western Asset Zenix Income Fund, Inc. 10/09/2006
Western Asset Zenix Income Fund, Inc. merged into Western Asset High Income Fund II Inc. 09/24/2008

ZENMAC ZINC LTD (ON)
Recapitalized 5/17/79
Recapitalized 7/25/85
Recapitalized from Zenmac Metal Mines Ltd. to Zenmac Explorations Ltd. 5/17/79
Each share Capital Stock no par exchanged for (3) shares Common no par
Recapitalized from Zenmac Explorations Ltd. to Zenmac Zinc Ltd. 7/25/85
Each share Common no par exchanged for for (0.125) share Common no par
Charter cancelled 6/24/99

ZENN MOTOR CO INC (ON)
Name changed to EEStor Corp. 04/06/2015

ZENO INC (NV)
Reorganized as HS3 Technology, Inc. 10/11/2005
Each share Common $0.001 par exchanged for (13) shares Common $0.001 par

ZENON ENVIRONMENTAL INC (CANADA)
Non-Vtg. Class A no par split (2) for (1) by issuance of (1) additional share payable 6/9/99 to holders of record 6/8/99
Common no par split (2) for (1) by issuance of (1) additional share payable 6/9/99 to holders of record 6/8/99
Merged into General Electric Co. 6/1/2006

Each share Non-Vtg. Class A no par exchanged for $24 cash
Each share Common no par exchanged for $24 cash

ZENORE RES INC (BC)
Recapitalized as Zenco Resources Inc. 01/27/1982
Each share Common no par exchanged for (0.5) share Common no par
Zenco Resources Inc. recapitalized as Solidor Resources Inc. 03/08/1988 which recapitalized as Sheffield Resources Inc. (BC) 03/12/1997 which reincorporated in Nova Scotia as Globalstore.com, Inc. 04/27/1999 which name changed to GSO Solutions, Inc. 03/24/2000
(See GSO Solutions, Inc.)

ZENOX INC (DE)
Plan of reorganization under Chapter 11 Federal Bankruptcy Code confirmed 03/16/1995
Stockholders' equity unlikely

ZENTEC CORP (CA)
Charter cancelled for failure to file reports and pay taxes 3/1/93

ZENTEX CORP (DE)
Recapitalized as Brighton Technologies Corp. 11/11/96
Each share Common $0.001 par exchanged for (1/3) share Common $0.001 par
Brighton Technologies name changed to Seedling Technologies Corp. 2/28/2001

ZENTIVA N A (CZECH REPUBLIC)
GDR agreement terminated 06/30/2009
Each Reg. S GDR for Ordinary exchanged for $64.181457 cash
Each 144A GDR for Ordinary exchanged for $64.181457 cash

ZENTRAC TECHNOLOGIES INC (NV)
Each share old Common $0.001 par exchanged for (10) shares new Common $0.001 par 08/15/2005
Each share new Common $0.001 par exchanged again for (0.1) share new Common $0.001 par 08/22/2007
Charter revoked 11/01/2010

ZENXUS INC (NV)
Name changed to Stafford Ventures Inc. 10/08/2001
Stafford Ventures Inc. name changed to Stafford Energy Inc. 08/01/2002 which recapitalized as Nucon-RF, Inc. 05/23/2006 which changed to NNRF, Inc. 09/10/2007

ZENYTH THERAPEUTICS LTD (AUSTRALIA)
ADR agreement terminated 03/07/2007
No ADR's remain outstanding

ZEO-TECH ENVIRO CORP (AB)
Name changed to Canadian Mining Co. Inc. (AB) 02/08/2007
Canadian Mining Co. Inc. (AB) reincorporated in British Columbia as Canadian Zeolite Corp. 02/08/2016 which name changed to International Zeolite Corp. 03/06/2018

ZEOLITE EXPL CO (NV)
Each share old Common $0.00001 par exchanged for (0.5) share new Common $0.00001 par 02/14/2006
Name changed to ShengdaTech, Inc. 01/03/2007
(See ShengdaTech, Inc.)

ZEOLITE MNG CORP (NV)
Common $0.00001 par split (5) for (1) by issuance of (4) additional shares payable 10/27/2004 to holders of record 10/25/2004 Ex date - 10/28/2004
Name changed to Global National Communications Corp. (NV) 11/15/2004
Global National Communications Corp. (NV) reorganized in Delaware as GNCC Capital, Inc. 12/01/2008

ZEON CORP (CO)
Each share old Common 1¢ par exchanged for (0.002) share new Common 1¢ par 06/12/2002
Note: In effect holders received $4 cash per share and public interest was eliminated

ZEOS INTL LTD (MN)
Common 1¢ par split (3) for (2) by issuance of (0.5) additional share 05/26/1989
Common 1¢ par split (2) for (1) by issuance of (1) additional share 04/22/1991
Under plan of merger name changed to Micron Electronics, Inc. 04/07/1995
Micron Electronics, Inc. name changed to Interland, Inc. 08/06/2001 which name changed to Web.com, Inc. 03/20/2006 which merged into Website Pros, Inc. 10/01/2007 which name changed to Web.com Group, Inc. 10/27/2008
(See Web.com Group, Inc.)

ZEOX CORP (AB)
Cease trade order 11/01/2012

ZEP AERO (CA)
Name changed to 111 Penn Corp. 3/13/67
(See 111 Penn Corp.)

ZEP ENERGY CORP (BC)
Recapitalized as Achilles Resources Ltd. 07/19/1984
Each share Common no par exchanged for (0.33333333) share Common no par
Achilles Resources Ltd. merged into Aegis Resources Ltd. 08/01/1990 which recapitalized as New Aegis Resources Ltd. 03/17/1993 which was acquired by Norcan Resources Ltd. 08/19/1994 which recapitalized as Odyssey Exploration Inc. 06/07/2000 which recapitalized as Consolidated Odyssey Exploration Inc. 12/08/2000 which reorganized as Odyssey Petroleum Corp. 08/25/2005 which recapitalized as Petrichor Energy Inc. 03/03/2011

ZEP INC (DE)
Acquired by New Mountain Capital LLC 06/26/2015
Each share Common 1¢ par exchanged for $20.05 cash

ZEPHYR ASSOC INC (DE)
Reorganized under the laws of Nevada as Worldwide Financial Holdings Inc. 07/19/1999
Each share Common no par exchanged for (0.001) share Common no par
Worldwide Financial Holdings Inc. recapitalized as Integrated Software Development Inc. 03/31/2003 which name changed to BSK & Tech, Inc. 05/29/2008

ZEPHYR PRODS INC (FL)
Out of business 00/00/1966
Details not available

ZEPHYR RES LTD (CANADA)
Merged into Maynard Energy Inc. 09/09/1983
Each (4.25) shares Common no par exchanged for (1) share Common no par
(See Maynard Energy Inc.)

ZEPPELIN ENERGY INC (DE)
Name changed to Rocketinfo Inc. 8/25/2004

ZEPPELIN PRODTN CORP (NV)
Recapitalized as Power Technology Inc. 03/20/1998
Each Common $0.001 par exchanged for (0.2) share Common $0.001 par
Power Technology Inc. recapitalized as 1st Prestige Wealth Management 07/31/2014

ZEPPELIN SOFTWARE INC (DE)
Name changed to Zeppelin Energy Inc. 12/9/2002
Zeppelin Energy Inc. name changed to Rocketinfo Inc. 8/25/2004

ZEREZ HLDGS (OK)
Name changed to Smart Cannabis Corp. 09/06/2017

ZERMATT CAP INC (CANADA)
Name changed to Aptilon Corp. 12/12/2006
Aptilon Corp. name changed to DMD Digital Health Connections Group Inc. 08/07/2014
(See DMD Digital Health Connections Group Inc.)

ZERMATT LIMOUSINE INC (NY)
Charter cancelled and proclaimed dissolved for failure to pay taxes 12/30/81

ZERO CORP (DE)
Reincorporated 8/16/88
Common $1 par split (5) for (4) by issuance of (0.25) additional share 6/19/78
Common $1 par split (5) for (4) by issuance of (0.25) additional share 3/6/80
Common $1 par split (5) for (4) by issuance of (0.25) additional share 2/27/81
Common $1 par split (5) for (4) by issuance of (0.25) additional share 1/13/82
Common $1 par split (5) for (4) by issuance of (0.25) additional share 3/4/83
Common $1 par split (3) for (2) by issuance of (0.5) additional share 12/2/83
Common $1 par split (5) for (4) by issuance of (0.25) additional share 3/1/85
Common $1 par split (5) for (4) by issuance of (0.25) additional share 3/7/86
State of incorporation changed from (CA) to (DE) and Common $1 par changed to 1¢ par 8/16/88
Common 1¢ par split (5) for (4) by issuance of (0.25) additional share 9/1/89
Merged into Applied Power Inc. 7/31/98
Each share Common 1¢ par exchanged for (0.85) share Common 20¢ par
Applied Power Inc. name changed to Actuant Corp. 1/12/2001

ZERO MANUFACTURING CO. (CA)
Common $1 par split (3) for (2) by issuance of (0.5) additional share 12/13/68
Stock Dividend - 25% 8/13/76
Name changed to Zero Corp. (CA) 12/10/76
Zero Corp. (CA) reincorporated in Delaware 8/16/88 which merged into Applied Power Inc. 7/31/98 which name changed to Actuant Corp. 1/12/2001

0373849 B C LTD (BC)
Acquired by Procon Mining & Tunnelling Ltd. 06/24/2011
Each share Common no par exchanged for $0.00000311 cash

007 PRECIOUS METALS INC (BC)
Recapitalized as Cansib Energy Inc. 10/15/1993
Each share Common no par exchanged for (1/3) share Common no par
(See Cansib Energy Inc.)

ZERON ACQUISITION I INC (NV)
Name changed to Advanced Orthopedic Technologies Inc. 5/6/92
(See Advanced Orthopedic Technologies Inc.)

ZERON ACQUISITIONS II INC (NV)
Name changed to Deotexis Inc. 11/26/97

ZERON RES LTD (BC)
Merged into Deex Resources Corp. 05/05/1983
Each share Common no par exchanged for (0.2) share Common no par
Deex Resources Corp. recapitalized as Seam Resources Corp. 05/22/1987

0915988 B C LTD (BC)
Acquired by MFC Industrial Ltd. 04/19/2013
Each share Common no par exchanged for $0.02 cash
Note: Unexchanged certificates will be cancelled and become without value 04/19/2019

012 SMILE COMMUNICATIONS LTD (ISRAEL)
Issue Information - 6,675,000 shs. ORD offered at $12 per share on 10/30/2007
Name changed to B Communications Ltd. 03/17/2010

ZEROPLUS COM INC (DE)
Ceased operations 06/05/2001
Stockholders' equity unlikely

ZEROS & ONES INC (NV)
Each share old Common $0.001 par exchanged for (3) shares new Common $0.001 par 02/24/2000
Each share new Common $0.001 par received distribution of (0.05) share Zeros & Ones Technologies Inc. Common 1¢ par payable 10/15/2001 to holders of record 09/24/2001
Name changed to Voyant International Corp. 04/30/2007
(See Voyant International Corp.)

ZEROS & ONES TECHNOLOGIES INC (DE)
90% owned by Zeros & Ones, Inc. as of 03/31/2008
Public interest eliminated

ZEROS USA INC (TX)
SEC revoked common stock registration 12/01/2006
Stockholders' equity unlikely

ZEROTREE TECHNOLOGIES INC (UT)
Recapitalized as Global Equity Fund, Inc. 03/20/2006
Each share Common $0.001 par exchanged for (0.001) share Common $0.001 par
(See Global Equity Fund, Inc.)

ZEROZONE, INC. (DE)
Charter cancelled and declared inoperative and void for non-payment of taxes 4/1/35

ZESTEE FOODS INC (OK)
Acquired by Midland Oil Corp. 12/31/1968
Each share Common $1 par exchanged for (0.75) share Common 10¢ par
(See Midland Oil Corp.)

ZETA CORP (FL)
Common $0.001 par split (4) for (1) by issuance of (3) additional shares payable 07/31/2001 to holders of record 07/31/2001 Ex date - 08/01/2001
Name changed to HepaLife Technologies, Inc. 04/18/2003
HepaLife Technologies, Inc. name changed to Alliqua, Inc. (FL) 01/05/2011 which reincorporated in Delaware as Alliqua BioMedical, Inc. 06/06/2014

ZETA LABS INC (CA)
Merged into Whittaker Corp. 03/12/1986
Each share Common no par exchanged for $6.50 cash

ZETA MINING CORP.
Acquired by Cardiff Uranium Mines Ltd. 00/00/1953
Each share Common exchanged for (0.125) share Common $1 par
Cardiff Uranium Mines Ltd. merged into Insulblock Systems Inc. 09/01/1988
(See Insulblock Systems Inc.)

ZETEK INC (CO)
Company terminated common stock registration and is no longer public as of 12/15/2006

ZETKA TELEVISION TUBES, INC. (NY)
Involuntarily dissolved 12/16/57

ZEUS COMPONENTS INC (NY)
Name changed to Zing Technologies Inc. 7/2/93
(See Zing Technologies Inc.)

ZEUS ENERGY CORP (BC)
Merged into U.S. Oil & Gas Resources Inc. 11/13/1997
Each share Common no par exchanged for (1) share Common no par
U.S. Oil & Gas Resources Inc. reorganized as Odyssey Petroleum Corp. 08/25/2005 which recapitalized as Petrichor Energy Inc. 03/03/2011

ZEUS ENERGY INC (UT)
Reorganized under the laws of Nevada as Tamasek Corp. Ltd. 12/10/1996
Each share Common $0.002 par exchanged for (0.01) share Common $0.001 par
Tamasek Corp. Ltd. recapitalized as Demert & Dougherty, Inc. 01/26/1998
(See Demert & Dougherty, Inc.)

ZEUS ENTERPRISE INC (NV)
Name changed to Pacific Forest Corp. 05/31/1996
Pacific Forest Corp. name changed to Green Capital Group, Inc. 04/30/1998
(See Green Capital Group, Inc.)

ZEUS RED LAKE GOLD MINES LTD. (ON)
Name changed to Principle Strategic Minerals Ltd. in 1949

ZEV VENTURES INC (NV)
Common $0.0001 par split (10) for (1) by issuance of (9) additional shares payable 08/14/2018 to holders of record 08/13/2018
Name changed to Ondas Holdings Inc. 10/05/2018

ZEVEX INTL INC (DE)
Reincorporated 11/21/1997
Each share old Common $0.001 par exchanged for (0.025) new share Common 4¢ par 03/16/1993
Stock Dividend - 20% 04/03/1995
State of incorporation changed from (NV) to (DE) 11/21/1997
New Common 4¢ par split (3) for (2) by issuance of (0.5) additional share payable 05/19/2006 to holders of record 05/04/2006 Ex date - 05/22/2006
Merged into Moog Inc. 03/16/2007
Each share new Common 4¢ par exchanged for $13 cash

ZEWAR JEWELLERY INC (NV)
Name changed to Next Graphite, Inc. 12/16/2013

ZFAX IMAGE CORP (BC)
Name changed to Stelax Industries Ltd. 6/6/96

ZG ENERGY CORP (DE)
Reorganized under the laws of Oklahoma as Vantage Point Energy, Inc. 04/30/1990
Each share 5% Conv. Preferred Ser. B $1 par exchanged for (1) share 5% Conv. Preferred Ser. A $1 par
Each share Common 1¢ par exchanged for (0.66666666) share Common 15¢ par
(See Vantage Point Energy, Inc.)

ZHAIKMUNAI L P (KAZAKHSTAN)
Name changed to Nostrum Oil & Gas L.P. 12/18/2013
(See Nostrum Oil & Gas L.P.)

ZHAOHENG HYDROPOWER CO (NV)
Reincorporated under the laws of British Virgin Islands as Zhaoheng Hydropower Ltd. and Common $0.001 par changed to 1¢ par 09/30/2009

ZHAOPIN LTD (CAYMAN ISLANDS)
ADR agreement terminated 11/01/2017
Each Sponsored ADR for Ordinary exchanged for $16.27 cash

ZHEJIANG EXPWY CO LTD (CHINA)
Sponsored ADR's for Ordinary split (3) for (1) by issuance of (2) additional ADR's payable 06/29/2010 to holders of record 06/28/2010 Ex date - 06/30/2010
Basis changed from (1:30) to (1:10) 06/30/2010
ADR agreement terminated 11/28/2017
Each Sponsored ADR for Ordinary exchanged for (10) shares Ordinary
Note: Unexchanged ADR's will be sold and the proceeds, if any, held for claim after 12/03/2018

ZHEJIANG SOUTHEAST ELEC PWR LTD (CHINA)
ADR agreement terminated 02/21/2013
No ADR's remain outstanding

ZHIDALI RADIO & TELEVISION NETWORK INC (CO)
SEC revoked common stock registration 08/20/2014

ZHONE TECHNOLOGIES INC (DE)
Each share old Common $0.001 par exchanged for (0.2) share new Common $0.001 par 03/12/2010
Name changed to DASAN Zhone Solutions, Inc. 09/12/2016

ZHONG HUI DAO MING FINL GROUP LTD (NV)
Recapitalized as Zhong Hui Dao Ming Copper Holding Ltd. 12/02/2010
Each share Common $0.001 par exchanged for (0.5) share Common $0.001 par

ZHONG SEN INTL TEA CO (FL)
Each share old Common $0.001 par exchanged for (0.01666666) share new Common $0.001 par 06/23/2011
Name changed to Music of Your Life, Inc. 07/26/2013

ZHONGDE WASTE TECHNOLOGY AG (GERMANY)
ADR agreement terminated 08/25/2010
No ADR's remain outstanding
ADR agreement terminated 12/12/2016
No ADR's remain outstanding

ZHONGKE HLDGS CO (NV)
Recapitalized as Worry Free Holdings Co. 10/04/2018
Each share Common $0.0001 par exchanged for (0.30120481) share Common $0.0001 par

ZHONGPIN INC (DE)
Acquired by Golden Bridge Holdings Ltd. 06/27/2013
Each share Common $0.001 par exchanged for $13.50 cash

ZHOU LIN INTL INC (DE)
Name changed to Renu-U-International Inc. 12/24/1996
Renu-U-International Inc. name changed to Colormax Technologies, Inc. 09/07/1999
(See Colormax Technologies, Inc.)

ZHUZHOU CSR TIMES ELEC CO LTD (CHINA)
Name changed to Zhuzhou CRRC Times Electric Co., Ltd. 04/08/2016

ZHYTOMYRGAZ JT STK CO (UKRAINE)
GDR agreement terminated 01/16/2009
No GDR's remain outstanding

ZI CORP (AB)
Merged into Nuance Communications, Inc. (New) 04/09/2009
Each share Common no par exchanged for (0.037) share Common $0.001 par and $0.34 cash

ZIA CORP (CO)
Name changed to Biocorp Global, Inc. 12/09/1987
(See Biocorp Global, Inc.)

ZIASUN TECHNOLOGIES INC (NV)
Common $0.001 par split (2) for (1) by issuance of (1) additional share payable 05/21/1999 to holders of record 05/14/1999
Merged into INVESTools Inc. 12/06/2001
Each share Common $0.001 par exchanged for (1) share Common 1¢ par
INVESTools Inc. name changed to thinkorswim Group Inc. 06/06/2008 which merged into TD AMERITRADE Holding Corp. 06/11/2009

ZICCO CORP. (HI)
Involuntarily dissolved 2/24/71

ZICOR MNG INC (YT)
Reincorporated 00/00/1996
Place of incorporation changed from (BC) to (YT) 00/00/1996
Name changed to Mano River Resources Inc. (YT) 09/18/1998
Mano River Resources Inc. (YT) reincorporated in British Columbia 07/19/2004 which recapitalized as African Aura Mining Inc. 10/14/2009
(See African Aura Mining Inc.)

ZICTON GOLD LTD (BC)
Name changed to Saddle Mountain Mining Corp. (BC) 01/27/1994
Saddle Mountain Mining Corp. (BC) reincorporated in Alberta 08/26/1994 which name changed to Saddle Mountain Timber Corp. 02/09/1995 which name changed to Global Tree Technologies Inc. (AB) 02/25/1997 which reorganized in British Columbia as Acadia Resources Corp. 02/07/2011 which reincorporated in Jersey as Horizon Petroleum PLC 10/08/2013 which reincorporated in Alberta as Horizon Petroleum Ltd. 04/05/2016

ZIEBART CORP (QC)
Merged into Ziebart International Corp. 6/30/84
Each share Common no par exchanged for $0.32526 cash

ZIEGLER EXCHANGE TRADED TR (DE)
Completely liquidated
Each share NYSE Arca Tech 100 ETF received first and final distribution of $15.80501 cash payable 12/26/2008 to holders of record 12/15/2008

ZIEGLER EXPLORATION CO. (CO)
Liquidated in 1960
No stockholders' equity

ZIEGLER FD INC (MD)
Name changed to Newton Investors Fund, Inc. 01/30/1976
Newton Investors Fund, Inc. name changed to Newton Income Fund, Inc. 04/29/1977
(See Newton Income Fund, Inc.)

ZIEGLER INC (DE)
Reincorporated under the laws of Wisconsin as Ziegler Companies, Inc. 4/19/93

ZIEGLER SELECT FD INC (MD)
Name changed to Newton Select Fund, Inc. 01/30/1976
Newton Select Fund, Inc. reorganized as Newton Income Fund, Inc. 11/16/1977
(See Newton Income Fund, Inc.)

ZIELEY PROCESSES CORP.
Name changed to Petroleum Derivatives, Inc. of Maine in 1929
(See Petroleum Derivatives, Inc.)

ZIFF DAVIS HLDGS INC (DE)
Plan of reorganzation under Chapter 11 Federal Bankruptcy Code effective 07/01/2008
No stockholders' equity

ZIFF-DAVIS INC (DE)
Issue Information - 25,800,000 shares COM offered at $15.50 per share on 04/28/1998
Issue Information - 10,000,000 shares COM ZDNET offered at $19 per share on 03/30/1999
Each share Common 1¢ par received distribution of (0.5) share Key3Media Group, Inc. Common 1¢ par and $2.50 cash payable 08/18/2000 to holders of record 08/14/2000 Ex date - 08/22/2000
Merged into CNET Networks, Inc. 10/17/2000
Each share Common 1¢ par exchanged for (0.3397) share Common $0.0001 par
Each share Common ZDnet 1¢ par exchanged for (0.5932) share Common $0.0001 par
(See CNET Networks, Inc.)

ZIGGO N V (NETHERLANDS)
ADR agreement terminated 07/13/2015
Each ADR for Ordinary exchanged for $22.19523 cash

ZILA INC (DE)
Reorganized 10/28/1980
Reincorporated 09/01/1988
Reorganized from under the laws of (CA) to Nevada 10/28/1980
Each share Common 10¢ par exchanged for (5) shares Common $0.001 par
Each share old Common $0.001 par exchanged for (1/3) share new Common $0.001 par 05/14/1982
Reincorporated from Zila Pharmaceutical, Inc. (NV) to under the laws of Delaware as Zila, Inc. 09/01/1988
Each share old Common $0.001 par exchanged for (1/7) share new Common $0.001 par 09/17/2008
Acquired by TOLMAR Holding, Inc. 09/21/2009
Each share new Common $0.001 par exchanged for $0.45 cash

ZILLOW INC (WA)
Under plan of merger name changed to Zillow Group, Inc. 02/18/2015

ZILOG INC (DE)
Reincorporated 05/16/1997
Common no par split (3) for (2) by issuance of (0.5) additional share 02/15/1993
State of incorporation changed from (CA) to (DE) and Common no par changed to 1¢ par 05/16/1997
Merged into Texas Pacific Group 02/27/1998

Each share old Common 1¢ par exchanged for $20 cash
Note: Holders of 10% of shares elected to retain their interests
Plan of reorganization under Chapter 11 Federal Bankruptcy Code effective 05/13/2002
Each share old Common 1¢ par received $0.0012 cash 07/19/2002
Each share new Common 1¢ par exchanged for (0.5) share new Common 1¢ par 03/02/2004
Acquired by IXYS Corp. 02/18/2010
Each share new Common 1¢ par exchanged for $3.5858 cash

ZILOG-MOD III INC (DE)
Liquidation completed
Each Ser. A & B Preferred Unit 1¢ par received initial distribution of $258.05 cash payable 9/24/2004 to holders of record 9/13/2004
Each Ser. A & B Preferred Unit 1¢ par received second and final distribution of $175.59 cash payable 10/31/2006 to holders of record 10/24/2006 Ex date - 11/22/2006
Note: Certificates were not required to be surrendered and are without value

ZIM ENERGY CORP (DE)
Recapitalized as Mustang Resources Corp. (DE) 06/30/1987
Each share Common 10¢ par exchanged for (0.25) share Common 40¢ par
(See Mustang Resources Corp. (DE))

ZIM-GOLD RES LTD (BC)
Name changed to Noise Media Inc. 02/05/2001
Noise Media Inc. recapitalized as GFK Resources Inc. (BC) 01/17/2008 which reincorporated in Canada 07/13/2012 which name changed to Opus One Resources Inc. 07/31/2017

ZIMMER CORP (DE)
Name changed 05/10/1982
Common no par split (2) for (1) by issuance of (1) additional share 09/16/1968
Common no par split (9) for (5) by issuance of (0.8) additional share 01/06/1982
Name and state of incorporation changed from Zimmer Homes Corp. (OH) to Zimmer Corp. (DE) and Common no par changed to $1 par 05/10/1982
Common $1 par split (2) for (1) by issuance of (1) additional share 01/17/1983
Charter forfeited for failure to maintain a registered agent 07/20/1991

ZIMMER HLDGS INC (DE)
Name changed to Zimmer Biomet Holdings, Inc. 06/29/2015

ZIMMERKNIT CO., LTD.
Acquired by York Knitting Mills, Ltd. and each share Common exchanged for (1) share Common in 1937
York Knitting Mills, Ltd. name changed to Woods (Harvey) Ltd. 5/2/66
(See Woods (Harvey) Ltd.)

ZIMMERMAN SIGN CO (TX)
Merged into Zimmerman Holdings, Inc. 12/15/2003
Each share Common 1¢ par exchanged for $0.25 cash

ZIMMERMAN STOVE HEATER CORP. (DE)
Charter declared inoperative and void for non-payment of taxes 1/20/28

ZIMOCO PETE CORP (DE)
Completely liquidated 2/21/68
Each share Common 10¢ par exchanged for first and final distribution of (3) shares Alscope Consolidated Ltd. Common no par

Alscope Consolidated Ltd. recapitalized as Almarco Industries Ltd. 8/3/76
(See Almarco Industries Ltd.)

ZIMTU TECHNOLOGIES INC (BC)
Recapitalized as International Zimtu Technologies Inc. (BC) 04/04/2003
Each share Common no par exchanged for (0.03333333) share Common no par
International Zimtu Technologies Inc. (BC) reincorporated in Canada as Petrol One Corp. 09/26/2006

ZINAT MINES LTD (CANADA)
Name changed to Newport Mining & Land Development Ltd. 1/15/73
(See Newport Mining & Land Development Ltd.)

ZINC LAKE MINES LTD. (ON)
Charter cancelled for default in January 1962

ZINCCORP RES INC (BC)
Each share old Common no par exchanged for (0.16666666) share new Common no par 10/22/2010
Delisted from Toronto Venture Stock Exchange 05/14/2015

ZINDART LTD (HONG KONG)
Name changed to Corgi International Ltd. 10/26/2005
(See Corgi International Ltd.)

ZINETICS MED INC (UT)
Merged into Medtronic, Inc. 2/13/98
Each share Common $0.001 par exchanged for $0.04528 cash

ZING TECHNOLOGIES INC (NY)
Merged into Rectifier Corp. 3/17/2000
Each share Common 1¢ par exchanged for $15.36 cash

ZINGIT INC (DE)
Recapitalized as North Park Holdings, Inc. 3/23/2004
Each share Common $0.001 par exchanged for (0.1) share Common $0.001 par
North Park Holdings, Inc. name changed to Wyncrest Group, Inc. 2/22/2005

ZINGO INC (NV)
Name changed to Superlattice Power, Inc. 05/12/2008
Superlattice Power, Inc. recapitalized as Sky Power Solutions Corp. 04/25/2011 which recapitalized as Clean Enviro Tech Corp. 01/18/2013 which recapitalized as Cyber Apps World Inc. 04/30/2015

ZION FOODS CORP (NY)
Under plan of merger each share Common $1 par automatically became (1) share Halco Products Corp. (NY) Common $1 par 03/14/1974
Halco Products Corp. (NY) merged into Tobin Packing Co., Inc. 11/02/1979
(See Tobin Packing Co., Inc.)

ZION NEV CORP (NV)
Name changed to Royal Union Holding Corp. 10/12/2010
Royal Union Holding Corp. name changed to Allied American Steel Corp. 05/16/2011

ZIONS BANCORPORATION (UT)
Common no par split (2) for (1) by issuance of (1) additional share 01/26/1993
Common no par split (4) for (1) by issuance of (3) additional shares payable 05/14/1997 to holders of record 05/09/1997
11% Depositary Preferred Ser. E no par called for redemption at $25 plus $0.6875 accrued dividends on 06/15/2012
9.5% Depositary Preferred Ser. C called for redemption at $25 plus $0.606944 accrued dividends on 09/15/2013

7.9% Depositary Preferred Ser. F called for redemption at $25 plus $0.49375 accrued dividends on 06/15/2017
Under plan of merger each share Depositary Preferred Ser. A, 6.3% Depositary Preferred Ser. G, 6.75% Depositary Preferred Ser. H, 7.2% Preferred Ser. J or Common no par automatically became (1) share Zions Bancorporation, N.A. (Salt Lake City, UT) Depositary Preferred Ser. A, 6.3% Depositary Preferred Ser. G, 6.75% Depositary Preferred Ser. H, 7.2% Preferred Ser. J or Common $0.001 par respectively 10/01/2018

ZIONS CAP TR B (DE)
Issue Information - 6,000,000 CAP SEC 8% offered at $25 per share on 9/20/2002
8% Capital Securities called for redemption at $25 plus $0.344444 accrued dividends on 05/03/2013

ZIONS CO OPERATIVE MERCANTILE INSTN (UT)
Capital Stock $100 par changed to $50 par in 1932
Capital Stock $50 par changed to $20 par and (2) additional shares issued 5/25/65
Capital Stock $20 par split (2) for (1) by issuance of (1) additional share 6/23/78
Capital Stock $20 par changed to no par 5/20/81
Capital Stock no par split (3) for (1) by issuance of (2) additional shares 8/25/83
Capital Stock no par changed to $0.001 par 5/23/90
Stock Dividend - 100% 6/15/56
Merged into May Department Stores Co. 12/31/99
Each share Common $0.001 par exchanged for (0.7367387) share Common $0.001 par
May Department Stores Co. merged into Federated Department Stores, Inc. 8/30/2005 which name changed to Macy's, Inc. 6/1/2007

ZIONS FIRST NATL BK (SALT LAKE CITY, UT)
Capital Stock $10 par changed to $2 par and (4) additional shares issued plus a 2% stock dividend paid 01/15/1964
Capital Stock $2 par changed to $4 par 02/27/1970
Merged into Zions Utah Bancorporation (UT) 04/07/1972
Each share Capital Stock $4 par exchanged for (1.1) shares Common no par
Zions Utah Bancorporation (UT) name changed to Zions Bancorporation 04/30/1987 which merged into Zions Bancorporation, N.A. (Salt Lake City, UT) 10/01/2018

ZIONS UTAH BANCORPORATION (UT)
Reincorporated 06/08/1971
State of incorporation changed from (NV) to (UT) 06/08/1971
Each (1.5) shares Conv. Preferred Ser. A $25 par exchanged for (1) share Common no par 02/05/1982
$9.75 Preferred 1980 Ser. called for redemption 07/30/1986
Stock Dividends - 50% 10/20/1978; 50% 08/14/1981
Name changed to Zions Bancorporation 04/30/1987
Zions Bancorporation merged into Zions Bancorporation, N.A. (Salt Lake City, UT) 10/01/2018

ZIP TOP INC (CO)
Common $0.001 par split (14) for (1) by issuance of (13) additional shares payable 08/07/1998 to holders of record 08/07/1998
Name changed to Pangea Petroleum

Corp. and (2) additional shares issued 12/11/1998
Pangea Petroleum Corp. recapitalized as AvStar Aviation Group, Inc. 09/21/2009 which recapitalized as Spotlight Capital Holdings, Inc. 11/06/2014

ZIPCAR INC (DE)
Issue Information - 9,684,109 shares COM offered at $18 per share on 04/13/2011
Acquired by Avis Budget Group, Inc. 03/14/2013
Each share Common $0.001 par exchanged for $12.25 cash

ZIPLINK INC (DE)
Company terminated common stock registration and is no longer public as of 12/04/2000

ZIPLOCAL INC (ON)
Each share old Common no par exchanged for (0.1) share new Common no par 05/09/2017
Acquired by Intercap Inc. 08/19/2017
Each share new Common no par exchanged for $0.0035 cash

ZIPPI NETWORKS INC (NV)
Each share old Common $0.001 par exchanged for (0.1) share new Common $0.001 par 03/14/2008
Each share new Common $0.001 par exchanged again for (0.001) share new Common $0.001 par 02/17/2009
Each share new Common $0.001 par exchanged again for (0.0005) share new Common $0.001 par 09/18/2009
Each share new Common $0.001 par exchanged again for (0.0005) share new Common $0.001 par 10/04/2010
Recapitalized as Mobile Matchmaking Inc. 05/02/2013
Each share new Common $0.001 par exchanged for (0.0004) share Common $0.001 par 05/02/2013

ZIPPY BAGS INC (NV)
Each share old Common $0.001 par exchanged for (5) shares new Common $0.001 par 04/16/2012
New Common $0.001 par split (2) for (1) by issuance of (1) additional share payable 02/12/2013 to holders of record 02/12/2013
Each share new Common $0.001 par exchanged again for (0.001) share new Common $0.001 par 10/21/2013
Name changed to Glorywin Entertainment Group, Inc. 11/24/2014

ZIPREALTY INC (DE)
Acquired by Realogy Group LLC. 08/14/2014
Each share Common $0.001 par exchanged for $6.75 cash

ZIRC CO (MN)
Each share Common 10¢ par exchanged for (5) shares Common 2¢ par 8/1/69
Name changed to Marco Dental Products, Inc. (MN) 8/17/72 which reincorporated in Oregon 6/25/75
(See Marco Dental Products, Inc. OR))

ZIRCONIUM TECHNOLOGY CORP (OR)
Merged into Kawecki Berylco Industries, Inc. 12/31/1974
Each share Common no par exchanged for $1.50 cash

ZITEL CORP (CA)
Common no par split (2) for (1) by issuance of (1) additional share payable 11/27/1996 to holders of record 11/18/1996
Name changed to Fortel Inc. (CA) 05/08/2000
Fortel Inc. (CA) reorganized in

Delaware as Envit Capital Group, Inc. 08/22/2008
(See Envit Capital Group, Inc.)

ZIXIT CORP (TX)
Name changed to Zix Corp. 08/13/2002

ZIYAD INC (NJ)
Merged into Gradco Systems, Inc. (CA) 5/8/87
Each share Common no par exchanged for (0.5202) share Common no par
Gradco Systems, Inc. (CA) reincorporated in Nevada 4/3/92
(See Gradco Systems, Inc. (NV))

ZIYANG CERAMICS CORP (FL)
Administratively dissolved 09/27/2013

ZKID NETWORK CO (NV)
Each share Common $0.001 par received distribution of (0.1) share 144A Common payable 06/24/2004 to holders of record 06/11/2004
Recapitalized as EATware Corp. 04/12/2006
Each share Common $0.0001 par exchanged for (0.00025) share Common $0.0001 par
EATware Corp. name changed to Star Metro Corp. 11/27/2006 which name changed to BioPack Environmental Solutions Inc. 02/27/2007 which recapitalized as Tristar Wellness Solutions Inc. 01/18/2013

ZLATO INC (NV)
Name changed to Vilacto Bio Inc. 04/04/2017

ZLIN AEROSPACE INC (ON)
Each share Class A Subordinate no par exchanged for (0.1) share Common no par 12/23/1996
Delisted from NEX 09/30/2004

ZMAX CORP (DE)
Reincorporated 12/12/1997
Each share old Common $0.001 par exchanged for (0.0125) share new Common $0.001 par 07/23/1996
State of incorporation changed from (NV) to (DE) 12/12/1997
Name changed to WidePoint Corp. 06/26/2000

ZNEXTMINING CORP INC (DE)
Each share old Preferred $0.00000001 par exchanged for (0.001) share new Preferred $0.00000001 par 11/13/2008
Each share Common $0.001 par received distribution of (0.001) share new Preferred $0.00000001 par payable 11/13/2008 to holders of record 11/12/2008 Ex date - 11/14/2008
Note: Company filed certificate of dissolution 03/13/2009
Reorganized under the laws of Philippines as AU Marcge Minerals AG 06/24/2013
Each share new Preferred $0.00000001 par exchanged for (10,000) shares Restricted Common $0.001 par
Each (50) shares Common $0.001 par exchanged for (75) shares Restricted Common $0.001 par
Note: Unexchanged certificates were escheated to holders' last known state of domicile after 06/24/2014
Each share AU Marcge Minerals AG Restricted Common $0.001 par exchanged for (0.04) share Au Min Africa Pty Ltd. Common USD$0.10 par 08/27/2014
Note: Holders of (100,000) or fewer shares received (4,000) shares

ZNOMICS INC (NV)
Each share old Common $0.001 par exchanged for (0.00350877) share new Common $0.001 par 11/01/2013
Name changed to Williston Holding Co., Inc. 11/27/2013

ZOA PETE LTD (AB)
Merged into Newgate Resources Ltd. 7/22/92
Each share Common no par exchanged for (0.724637) share Common no par
Newgate Resources Ltd. recapitalized as Para-Tech Energy Inc. 12/16/96

ZODIAC AEROSPACE (FRANCE)
Name changed 11/23/2009
Name changed from Zodiac S.A. to Zodiac Aerospace 11/23/2009
ADR's for Common split (5) for (1) by issuance of (4) additional ADR's payable 03/11/2014 to holders of record 03/06/2014 Ex date - 03/12/2014
ADR agreement terminated 04/10/2018
Each ADR for Common issued by Bank of New York exchanged for $6.0965 cash

ZODIAC EXPL CORP (BC)
Recapitalized as Donnybrook Resources Inc. 12/21/1998
Each share Common no par exchanged for (0.14285714) share Common no par
Donnybrook Resources Inc. recapitalized as Rodinia Minerals Inc. (BC) 08/13/2003 which reincorporated in Ontario 11/03/2009 which name changed to Rodinia Lithium Inc. 06/30/2010 which recapitalized as Routemaster Capital Inc. 09/20/2016

ZODIAC EXPL INC (AB)
Recapitalized as Mobius Resources Inc. 05/01/2014
Each share Common no par exchanged for (0.06666666) share Common no par
Mobius Resources Inc. name changed to Sintana Energy Inc. 08/10/2015

ZODIAC HURRICANE MARINE CONS INC (BC)
Name changed 6/28/89
Name changed from Zodiac Hurricane Marine Ltd. to Zodiac Hurricane Marine (Consolidated) Inc. and each share Common no par exchanged for (0.1) share Common no par 6/28/89
Name changed to Zodiac Hurricane Technologies Inc. 4/5/90
(See Zodiac Hurricane Technologies Inc.)

ZODIAC HURRICANE TECHNOLOGIES INC (BC)
Conv. Preference no par called for redemption 5/14/90
Merged into Hurricane Investments Ltd. 1/1/99
Each share Common no par exchanged for $0.80 cash

ZODIAC LTD (QC)
Name changed 04/01/1964
Under plan of merger name changed from Zodiac Inc. to Zodiac Ltd. and each share Class A $20 par exchanged for (1) share Class A $20 par and each share Class B $5 par exchanged for (1) share Class B $5 par 04/01/1964
Class A $20 par changed to $4 par and (4) additional shares issued 03/12/1965
Class B $5 par changed to $1 par and (4) additional shares issued 03/12/1965
Class A $4 par changed to $1.25 par 02/00/1970
Class B $1 par changed to 35¢ par 02/00/1970
Name changed to Zodiac Supreme Inc. 10/28/1978
(See Zodiac Supreme Inc.)

ZODIAC OIL CO. LTD.
Merged into Calvan Consolidated Oil & Gas Co. Ltd. and each (3) shares Capital Stock no par exchanged for (1) share new Capital Stock $1 par in 1951
Calvan completed liquidation 11/30/61

ZODIAC RES LTD (AB)
Merged into Reigate Resources (Canada) Ltd. 1/31/83
Each share Capital Stock no par exchanged for (0.25) share Class A Stock no par
(See Reigate Resources (Canada) Ltd.)

ZODIAC SUPREME INC (QC)
Declared dissolved for failure to file reports and pay fees 07/11/1987

ZOE PRODS INC (NV)
Charter revoked for failure to file reports and pay fees 02/02/1987

ZOECON CORP (DE)
Common no par changed to $1 par 06/04/1974
Merged into Occidental Petroleum Corp. 08/10/1977
Each share Common $1 par exchanged for $18 cash

ZOLL MED CORP (MA)
Common 2¢ par changed to 1¢ par and (1) additional share issued payable 02/26/2007 to holders of record 02/12/2007 Ex date - 02/27/2007
Acquired by Asahi Kasei Corp. 04/30/2012
Each share Common 1¢ par exchanged for $93 cash

ZOLLER & DANNEBERG INC (CO)
Name changed to Premier Resources, Ltd. 08/12/1976
Premier Resources, Ltd. merged into Oxford Consolidated, Inc. 01/02/1991
(See Oxford Consolidated, Inc.)

ZOLLER BREWING CO.
Name changed to Blackhawk Brewing Co. in 1944
(See Blackhawk Brewing Co.)

ZOLLER (WM.) CO.
Property sold in 1936
No stockholders' equity

ZOLON CORP (FL)
Name changed to Quadrant 4 Systems Corp. (FL) 05/31/2011
Quadrant 4 Systems Corp. (FL) reincorporated in Illinois 04/25/2013
(See Quadrant 4 Systems Corp.)

ZOLOTA YELLOWKNIFE MINES LTD. (ON)
Charter revoked for failure to file reports and pay fees 10/22/65

ZOLTEK COS INC (MO)
Common 1¢ par split (3) for (2) by issuance of (0.5) additional share 09/29/1995
Common 1¢ par split (2) for (1) by issuance of (1) additional share payable 06/17/1996 to holders of record 06/03/1996
Acquired by Toray Industries, Inc. 02/28/2014
Each share Common 1¢ par exchanged for $16.75 cash

ZOMAX INC (MN)
Name changed 5/4/99
Name changed from Zomax Optical Media, Inc. to Zomax Inc. 5/4/99
Common no par split (2) for (1) by issuance of (1) additional share payable 8/11/99 to holders of record 7/30/99
Common no par split (2) for (1) by issuance of (1) additional share payable 5/8/2000 to holders of record 4/27/2000
Merged into Inomax, LLC 10/20/2006
Each share Common no par exchanged for $2.09 cash

ZOMAX INC (NV)
Charter revoked for failure to file reports and pay fees 6/1/97

ZON OPTIMUS SGPS SA (PORTUGAL)
Name changed 04/02/2014
Name changed from Zon Multimedia to Zon Optimus SGPS S.A. 04/02/2014
Name changed to NOS, SGPS, S.A. 12/30/2014
(See NOS, SGPS, S.A.)

ZONAGEN INC (DE)
Name changed to Repros Therapeutics, Inc. 05/02/2006
(See Repros Therapeutics, Inc.)

ZONDERVAN CORP (MI)
Reincorporated 5/15/78
State of incorporation changed from (DE) to (MI) 5/15/78
Common $1 par split (3) for (2) by issuance of (0.5) additional share 7/16/79
Common $1 par split (3) for (2) by issuance of (0.5) additional share 5/16/83
Merged into Harper & Row, Publishers, Inc. (DE) 9/1/88
Each share Common $1 par exchanged for $13.50 cash

ZONE 4 PLAY INC (NV)
Name changed to Win Gaming Media, Inc. 05/01/2008
Win Gaming Media, Inc. name changed to Win Global Markets, Inc. 11/09/2011 which name changed to EZTrader, Inc. (NV) 10/09/2014 which reincorporated in Delaware as EZTD Inc. 12/29/2015

ZONE PETE CORP (BC)
Struck off register and declared dissolved for failure to file returns 7/22/94

ZONES INC (WA)
Acquired by Zones Acquisition Corp. 12/31/2008
Each share Common no par exchanged for $7 cash

ZONEX PETE CORP (UT)
Name changed to Trans Global Industries, Inc. 02/15/1982

ZONGSHEN PEM PWR SYS INC (BC)
Acquired by Hong Kong VAS International Development Ltd. 12/21/2012
Each share Common no par exchanged for $0.60 cash
Note: Unexchanged certificates will be cancelled and become without value 12/21/2018

ZONIC CORP (OH)
Chapter 11 bankruptcy proceedings converted to Chapter 7 on 01/25/2002
No stockholders' equity

ZONITE PRODUCTS CORP. (DE)
Common no par changed to $1 par in 1931
Name changed to Chemway Corp. 2/29/56
Chemway Corp. completely liquidated for Cooper Laboratories, Inc. 4/30/71
(See Cooper Laboratories, Inc.)

ZONNE INVT CORP (AB)
Struck off register for failure to file annual returns 11/01/1994

ZONOLITE CO. (MT)
Merged into Grace (W.R.) & Co. (CT) 04/16/1963
Each share Common $1 par exchanged for (0.255) share Common $1 par
Grace (W.R.) & Co. (CT) reincorporated in New York 05/19/1988
(See Grace (W.R.) & Co.)

FINANCIAL INFORMATION, INC. ZON-ZUR

ZOO ENTMT INC (DE)
Each (600) shares old Common $0.001 par exchanged for (1) share new Common $0.001 par 05/11/2010
Name changed to indiePub Entertainment, Inc. 05/25/2012

ZOOLANDER CORP (ON)
Each share old Common no par exchanged for (0.5) share new Common no par 05/31/2011
Name changed to Mezzotin Minerals Inc. 09/19/2013

ZOOLINK CORP (NV)
Recapitalized as Action Energy Corp. 04/02/2009
Each share Common $0.001 par exchanged for (0.001) share Common $0.001 par
Action Energy Corp. name changed to SMC Recordings Inc. 09/03/2009 which recapitalized as SMC Entertainment, Inc. 05/06/2011

ZOOM TELEPHONICS INC (CANADA)
Reincorporated under the laws of Delaware as Zoom Technologies, Inc. and Common no par changed to 1¢ par 2/28/2002

ZOOTECH 2000 INC (CO)
Reorganized under the laws of Wyoming as Premium Petroleum Corp. 02/24/2005
Each share Common $0.0001 par exchanged for (0.00025) share Common $0.0001 par
Premium Petroleum Corp. recapitalized as Premium Energy Corp. 02/12/2013

ZORAH MEDIA CORP (BC)
Delisted from Vancouver Stock Exchange 03/01/1999

ZORAN CORP (DE)
Common $0.001 par split (3) for (2) by issuance of (0.5) additional share payable 05/22/2002 to holders of record 05/07/2002 Ex date - 05/23/2002
Merged into CSR PLC 08/31/2011
Each share Common $0.001 par exchanged for (0.14725) Sponsored ADR for Ordinary and $6.26 cash
(See CSR PLC)

ZORBAS PALACE INC (NY)
Each share old Common $0.0001 par exchanged for (0.1) share new Common $0.0001 par 08/17/1987
Charter cancelled and proclaimed dissolved for failure to pay taxes 03/25/1992

ZORIN EXPL LTD (AB)
Merged into Hawker Resources Inc. 03/17/2004
Each share Common no par exchanged for (0.07746383) share Common no par
Hawker Resources Inc. name changed to Iteration Energy Ltd. 07/11/2005 which merged into Chinook Energy Inc. (Old) 07/05/2010
(See Chinook Energy Inc. (Old))

ZORO MNG CORP (NV)
Each share old Common $0.00001 par exchanged for (0.05) share new Common $0.00001 par 04/22/2009
SEC revoked common stock registration 01/19/2016

ZORRO CAP INC (AB)
Completely liquidated
Each share Common no par received first and final distribution of (0.36) Avanti Energy Inc. Unit consisting of (1) share Common no par and (0.5) Common Stock Purchase Warrant expiring 03/11/2017 payable 03/23/2016 to holders of record 03/17/2016

ZORRO INTL INC (UT)
Recapitalized as Health & Wealth Inc. 07/12/1994
Each share Common $0.001 par exchanged for (0.2) share Common $0.001 par
Health & Wealth Inc. recapitalized as Twenty First Century Health Inc. 05/23/1995 which name changed to Bio-Tech Industries Inc. 05/21/1997
(See Bio-Tech Industries Inc.)

ZOSANO INC (DE)
Name changed to J.E.M. Capital Inc. 03/15/2017

ZOTEK INC (WA)
Name changed to American Health Products Inc. 11/29/1990
(See American Health Products Inc.)

ZOTOX PHARMACAL CO., INC. (CT)
Each share Common $1 par exchanged for (10) shares Common no par 11/10/1954
Name changed to New Medical Techniques, Inc. 08/31/1961
(See New Medical Techniques, Inc.)

ZOWCOM INC (NV)
Name changed to Procera Networks, Inc. (NV) 10/22/2003
Procera Networks, Inc. (NV) reincorporated in Delaware 06/18/2013
(See Procera Networks, Inc.)

ZR INTERIM CORP. (NY)
Completely liquidated 02/15/1979
Each share Common 10¢ par exchanged for first and final distribution of $27.46 cash

ZS PHARMA INC (DE)
Acquired by AstraZeneca PLC 12/17/2015
Each share Common $0.001 par exchanged for $90 cash

ZSA ZSA LTD. (DE)
Adjudicated bankrupt 02/03/1972
No stockholders' equity

ZSTAR ENTERPRISES INC (NV)
Name changed to Onvantage Inc. 07/17/2000
(See Onvantage Inc.)

Z3 ENTERPRISES INC (NV)
Name changed to HPEV, Inc. 04/23/2012
HPEV, Inc. name changed to Cool Technologies, Inc. 04/12/2016

Z28 CAP CORP (AB)
Recapitalized as illumiCell Corp. 02/12/2007
Each share Common no par exchanged for (0.47393364) share Common no par
illumiCell Corp. name changed to Multiplied Media Corp. 08/16/2007 which name changed to Poynt Corp. 10/27/2010
(See Poynt Corp.)

ZULAPA MNG LTD (ON)
Capital Stock $1 par changed to no par 12/16/1971
Placed in receivership 05/15/1975
No stockholders' equity

ZULILY INC (DE)
Merged into Liberty Interactive Corp. 10/01/2015
Each share Class A Common $0.0001 par exchanged for (0.3098) share QVC Group Common Ser. A 1¢ par and $9.375 cash
Liberty Interactive Corp. name changed to Qurate Retail, Inc. 04/10/2018

ZULU ENERGY CORP (CO)
Common $0.0001 par split (10) for (1) by issuance of (9) additional shares payable 02/09/2007 to holders of record 02/09/2007
Name changed to Vortex Brands Co. 07/03/2014

ZUMA MINING & MILLING CO. (UT)
Recapitalized as Zuma Uranium & Oil Corp. 6/25/55
Each share Capital Stock 50¢ par exchanged for (1) share Common 25¢ par
Zuma Uranium & Oil Corp. recapitalized as Baronet Products, Inc. 12/14/62 which name changed to Continental Properties, Inc. 6/10/63
(See Continental Properties, Inc.)

ZUMA MINING CORP. (NV)
Charter revoked for failure to file reports and pay fees 03/02/1959

ZUMA URANIUM & OIL CORP. (UT)
Recapitalized as Baronet Products, Inc. 12/14/1962
Each share Common 25¢ par exchanged for (0.1) share Common no par
Baronet Products, Inc. name changed to Continental Properties, Inc. 06/10/1963
(See Continental Properties, Inc.)

ZUNGUI HAIXI CORP (ON)
Ontario Securities Commission ceased trading 09/00/2011
Stockholders' equity unlikely

ZUNI ENERGY CORP (BC)
Recapitalized as Home Ventures Ltd. 05/24/1991
Each share Common no par exchanged for (0.2) share Common no par
Home Ventures Ltd. recapitalized as Buck Lake Ventures Ltd. 02/15/2000 which recapitalized as Ultra Uranium Corp. 05/11/2006 which recapitalized as Ultra Resources Corp. 11/14/2012 which recapitalized as Empire Rock Minerals Inc. 10/22/2015 name changed to Empire Metals Corp. 02/02/2017

ZUNI HLDGS INC (ON)
Reincorporated 11/22/1995
Place of incorporation changed from (AB) to (ON) 11/22/1995
Recapitalized as Magnifoam Technology International Inc. 12/05/1995
Each share Common no par exchanged for (0.5) share Common no par
Magnifoam Technology International Inc. name changed to MTI Global Inc. 05/12/2005 which name changed to Zuni Holdings Inc. (New) 07/15/2010 which merged into Pacific Safety Products Inc. 01/04/2011

ZUNI HLDGS INC NEW (ON)
Merged into Pacific Safety Products Inc. 01/04/2011
Each share Common no par exchanged for (1) share Common no par

ZUOAN FASHION LTD (CAYMAN ISLANDS)
Each old Sponsored ADR for Ordinary exchanged for (0.25) new Sponsored ADR for Ordinary 05/01/2015
Basis changed from (1:4) to (1:16) 05/01/2015
ADR agreement terminated 02/23/2017
Each new Sponsored ADR for Ordinary exchanged for (16) shares Ordinary
Note: Unexchanged ADR's will be sold and the proceeds, if any, held for claim after 08/23/2017
Due to the absence of a trading market it is possible shares will not be sold and value realized

ZUPINTRA CORP INC (FL)
SEC revoked common stock registration 03/21/2014

ZURFUND INTL LTD (BC)
Recapitalized as Atacama Resources Ltd. 02/02/1990
Each share Common no par exchanged for (0.2) share Common no par
Atacama Resources Ltd. merged into KAP Resources Ltd. 11/14/1990
(See KAP Resources Ltd.)

ZURI CAP CORP (BC)
Name changed to Phoenix Gold Resources Corp. 04/23/2014

ZURICH AMERN FINL GROUP S A (NV)
Name changed to Compound Natural Foods, Inc. 10/27/2004
(See Compound Natural Foods, Inc.)

ZURICH CAP MKTS INC
Accredited Investors Flexible Money Market Preferred Ser. B called for redemption at $100,000 on 09/07/2001
Accredited Investors Flexible Money Market Preferred Ser. P called for redemption at $100,000 on 09/10/2001
Accredited Investors Flexible Money Market Preferred Ser. Q called for redemption at $100,000 on 09/17/2001
Accredited Investors Flexible Money Market Preferred Ser. R called for redemption at $100,000 on 09/24/2001
Accredited Investors Flexible Money Market Preferred Ser. S called for redemption at $100,000 on 10/01/2001
Accredited Investors Flexible Money Market Preferred Ser. T called for redemption at $100,000 on 10/09/2001
Accredited Investors Flexible Money Market Preferred Ser. N called for redemption at $100,000 on 10/11/2001
Accredited Investors Flexible Money Market Preferred Ser. O called for redemption at $100,000 on 10/11/2001
Accredited Investors Flexible Money Market Preferred Ser. U called for redemption at $100,000 on 10/15/2001
Accredited Investors Flexible Money Market Preferred Ser. H called for redemption at $100,000 on 10/19/2001
Accredited Investors Flexible Money Market Preferred Ser. V called for redemption at $100,000 on 10/22/2001

ZURICH ENERGY CORP (BC)
Delisted from Vancouver Stock Exchange 01/13/1988

ZURICH FINL SVCS (SWITZERLAND)
Name changed to Zurich Insurance Group Ltd. 04/09/2012

ZURICH INS CO (SWITZERLAND)
ADR agreement terminated 07/15/1998
Details not available

ZURICH REGCAPS FDG TR I (DE)
144A Variable Rate Trust Capital Securities called for redemption at $1,000 on 03/30/2006

ZURICH REGCAPS FDG TR II (DE)
144A Variable Rate Trust Capital Securities called for redemption at $1,000 on 03/30/2011

ZURICH REGCAPS FDG TR III (DE)
144A Trust Capital Securities called for redemption at $1,000 on 04/11/2006

ZURICH REGCAPS FDG TR IV (DE)
144A Trust Capital Securities called for redemption at $1,000 on 04/18/2008

ZURICH REGCAPS FDG TR V (DE)
144A Trust Capital Securities called for redemption at $1,000 on 04/04/2011

ZURICH REGCAPS FDG TR VI (DE)
144A Trust Capital Securities called for redemption at $1,000 on 04/25/2011

ZURICKIRCH CORP (NV)
Name changed to DND Technologies, Inc. 09/24/2002

ZURN INDS INC (PA)
Common $1 par changed to 50¢ par and (1) additional share issued 08/10/1967
Common 50¢ par split (2) for (1) by issuance of (1) additional share 06/30/1987
$1 Conv. Preferred Ser. B $1 par called for redemption at $40 plus $0.25 accrued dividends on 04/06/1998
Merged into U.S. Industries, Inc. (Holding Co.) 06/11/1998
Each share Common 50¢ par exchanged for (1.6) shares Common 1¢ par

ZVUE CORP (DE)
SEC revoked common stock registration 08/07/2014

ZWEIG CASH FD INC (MD)
Under plan of reorganization each share Government Securities Portfolio $0.0001 par and Money Market Portfolio $0.0001 par automatically became Zweig Series Trust (MA) Cash Fund Class C on a net asset basis 05/01/1994
Zweig Series Trust (MA) reincorporated in Delaware 04/19/1996 which name changed to Phoenix-Zweig Trust 01/19/1999 which name changed to Phoenix Trust 09/30/2002
(See Phoenix Trust)

ZWEIG FD INC (MD)
Each share old Common 10¢ par exchanged for (0.25) share new Common 40¢ par 06/27/2012
Under plan of merger name changed to Virtus Total Return Fund Inc. 04/03/2017

ZWEIG SER TR (DE)
Reincorporated 04/19/1996
State of incorporation changed from (MA) to (DE) 04/19/1996
Cash Fund Class A reclassified as Government Cash Fund Class A 05/01/1998
Cash Fund Class B reclassified as Government Cash Fund Class B 05/01/1998
Cash Fund Class C reclassified as Government Cash Fund Class C 05/01/1998
Name changed to Phoenix-Zweig Trust 01/19/1999
Phoenix-Zweig Trust name changed to Phoenix Trust 09/30/2002
(See Phoenix Trust)

ZWEIG TAX FREE FD INC (MD)
Merged into Industrial Series Trust 4/1/91
Limited Term Portfolio Common $0.0001 par exchanged for Mackenzie Limited Term Municipal Fund Shares of Bene. Int. $0.001 par on a dollar for dollar basis
Long Term Portfolio Common $0.0001 par exchanged for Mackenzie National Municipal Fund Shares of Bene. Int. $0.001 par on a dollar for dollar basis
Money Market Portfolio Common $0.0001 par exchanged for Mackenzie Limited Term Municipal Fund Shares of Bene. Int. $0.001 par on a dollar for dollar basis

ZWEIG TOTAL RETURN FD INC (MD)
Each share old Common $0.001 par exchanged for (0.25) share new Common $0.001 par 06/27/2012
Name changed to Virtus Global Dividend & Income Fund Inc. 09/27/2016

ZWICKER ELEC INC (NY)
Each (251) shares Common 10¢ par exchanged for (1) share Common $25.10 par 10/30/1985
Merged out of existence 12/30/1988
Details not available

ZYCAD CORP (DE)
Name changed to GateField Corp. 10/10/97

ZYCOM CORP (AB)
Delisted from Alberta Stock Exchange 06/07/1999

ZYCOM INC (CO)
Each share old Common $0.001 par exchanged for (0.004) share new Common $0.00001 par 01/19/2000
Reincorporated under the laws of Delaware as Tutornet.com Group, Inc. and (6) additional shares issued 04/17/2000
Tutornet.com Group, Inc. recapitalized as Sunmark International Industries, Inc. (DE) 02/07/2005 which reorganized in Washington as Royal Sunmark Energy Corp. 08/22/2005 which name changed to Detex Security Systems, Inc. 10/19/2005 which name changed to Detection Security Systems, Inc. 05/15/2006 which recapitalized as Nexis International Industries, Inc. 08/30/2007
(See Nexis International Industries, Inc.)

ZYCON CORP (DE)
Merged into Hadco Corp. 01/16/1997
Each share Common $0.001 par exchanged for $18 cash

ZYDANT CORP (NV)
SEC revoked common stock registration 05/18/2009
Stockholders' equity unlikely

ZYDECO ENERGY INC (DE)
Under plan of merger name changed to DTVN Holdings Inc. 12/26/2000
(See DTVN Holdings Inc.)

ZYGO CORP (DE)
Common 10¢ par split (3) for (2) by issuance of (0.5) additional share 02/16/1993
Common 10¢ par split (3) for (2) by issuance of (0.5) additional share 08/21/1995
Common 10¢ par split (2) for (1) by issuance of (1) additional share payable 02/27/1997 to holders of record 02/03/1997
Acquired by AMETEK, Inc. (New) 06/20/2014
Each share Common 10¢ par exchanged for $19.25 cash

ZYGON CORP (NV)
Name changed to Essential Resources Inc. 01/17/1996
(See Essential Resources Inc.)

ZYGOTE RES LTD (BC)
Recapitalized as Consolidated Technologies Holdings Inc. 06/07/1993
Each share Common no par exchanged for (0.782985) share Common no par
Consolidated Technologies Holdings Inc. name changed to TigerTel Telecommunications Corp. (BC) 11/26/2001 which reincorporated in Canada as TigerTel Communications Inc. 05/01/2002
(See TigerTel Communications Inc.)

ZYMED INC
Merged into Algilent Technologies Inc. 6/9/2000
Each share Preferred Ser. C no par exchanged for $3.02 cash
Note: A portion of the merger consideration will be held in escrow for future payment

ZYMETX INC (DE)
SEC revoked common stock registration 10/24/2008

ZYMOGENETICS INC (WA)
Acquired by Bristol-Myers Squibb Co. 10/12/2010
Each share Common no par exchanged for $9.75 cash

ZYNAXIS INC (PA)
Merged into Vaxcel, Inc. 5/21/97
Each share Common 1¢ par exchanged for (0.0947) share Common $0.001 par
Vaxcel, Inc. name changed to Chattown.com Network Inc. 3/2/2000 which name changed to eLocity Networks Corp. 12/19/2000 which name changed to Diversified Financial Resources Corp. (DE) 8/23/2002 which name changed to China Fruits Corp. 9/8/2006

ZYNEX INTL CORP (ON)
Reincorporated under the laws of Nevada as Edgeworth Ventures Inc. 4/7/2006

ZYNEX MED HLDGS INC (NV)
Name changed to Zynex, Inc. 07/08/2008

ZYP CAP CORP (BC)
Name changed to Baikal Forest Corp. 04/27/2011
(See Baikal Forest Corp.)

ZYTEC CORP (MN)
Common no par split (2) for (1) by issuance of (1) additional share payable 6/3/96 to holders of record 5/20/96
Merged into Computer Products, Inc. 12/29/97
Each share Common no par exchanged for (1.33) shares Common 1¢ par
Computer Products, Inc. name changed to Artesyn Technologies Inc. 5/6/98
(See Artesyn Technologies Inc.)

ZYTEC SYS INC (BC)
Name changed 10/07/1987
Name changed from Zytec Computers Ltd. to Zytec Systems Inc. 10/07/1987
Cease trade order effective 05/04/1992
Stockholders' equity unlikely

ZYTECH INDS INC (CO)
Charter forfeited 09/06/1990

ZYTO CORP (DE)
Name changed to Global Unicorn Holdings, Inc. 05/02/2018

ZZAP NET INC (FL)
Name changed to High Speed Net Solutions, Inc. 12/10/1998
High Speed Net Solutions, Inc. name changed to Summus, Inc. (FL) 02/27/2002 which reorganized in Delaware 03/16/2005 which name changed to Oasys Mobile, Inc. 02/06/2006

ZZZZ BEST INC (NV)
Common $0.001 par changed to 1¢ par 01/00/1986
Each share old Common 1¢ par exchanged for (0.5) share new Common 1¢ par 10/30/1986
Charter permanently revoked 10/01/1993